SPECIMEN ENTR

The numbers preceding the page numbers refer to sectio

fingerbreadth

The main entry,
1, p. xvii. ——— **fin·ger·breadth** (fing′gər·bredth′, -bretth, of a finger, from ¾ inch to one inch.

fin·ger·ing (fing′gər·ing) *n.* **1.** The act of touching or feeling with the fingers. **2.** *Music* a The action or technique of using the fingers in playing an instrument. b The notation indicating what fingers are to be used. ——— **Definition numbers, 5, p. xviii.**

Word division, 1, p. xvii.

Pronunciation, 2, p. xvii.

fin·ick·y (fin′i·kē) *adj.* Excessively fastidious or precise; fussy; exacting: also spelled *finnicky*. [< FINE¹ + -ICAL] ——— **Definition dividers, 5, p. xviii.**

Part of speech,
3, p. xvii. ——— **fis·sile** (fis′əl) *adj.* **1.** Capable of being split or separated into layers. **2.** Tending to split. [< L *fissilis* < *findere* to split] — **fis·sil·i·ty** (fi·sil′ə·tē) *n.*

Run-in part of speech,
3, p. xvii. ——— **fis·si·ped** (fis′i·ped) *adj.* Having the toes separated: also **fis·si·pe·dal** (fi·sip′ə·dəl, fis′i·ped′l), **fis·si·pe′di·al** (-pē′dē·əl). — *n. Zool.* Any of a suborder (*Fissipedia*) of terrestrial carnivores with separate toes, as [matter omitted] ——— **Etymology, p. xxi.**

Scientific name

Homographs,
p. 642. ——— **fist¹** (fist) *n.* **1.** The hand closed tightly, as for striking; the clenched hand; also, grip; clutch. **2.** [matter omitted]
fist² (fist). *n.* A fice.

fla·vor (flā′vər) *n.* **1.** Taste; especially, a distinctive element in the overall taste of something. **2.** Something added, as to food, to increase taste or to impart a specific taste; flavoring. **3.** A special, subtle quality pervading something: a novel that has the *flavor* of Dickens. **4.** *Archaic* Odor. — *v.t.* To give flavor to. Also *Brit.* **fla′vour.** [< OF *flaor, fleur*, prob. ult. < L *flare* to blow; *v* added on analogy with *savor*] — **fla′vor·er** *n.* — **fla′vor·less** *adj.* ——— **Currency label, 6, p. xviii.** / **Illustrative phrase** / **Run-on derivatives, 11, p. xviii.**

Variant form, 8, p. xviii.

flea (flē) *n.* **1.** A small, wingless, parasitic insect (order *Siphonaptera*) that sucks the blood of mammals and birds and is capable of leaping for relatively great distances. For illustration see INSECTS (injurious). ◆ Collateral adjective: *pulicene.* **2.** One of several small beetles or crustaceans that jump like fleas, as a beach flea. — *a flea in one's ear* **1.** A pointed hint. **2.** An upsetting or stinging rebuke, refusal, or rejection. [OE *fléa, fléah.* Akin to FLEE.] ——— **Collateral adjective, 7, p. xviii.** / **Idiomatic phrase**

Cross-reference, 9, p. xviii.

Level label, p. xx. ——— **flite** (flīt) *Dial. v.i.* flit·ed, flit·ing To wrangle; quarrel. — *n.* Abusive quarreling. Also spelled *flyte.* ——— **Inflected forms, 4, p. xvii.**

flu (flōo) *n. Informal* Influenza.
fly·er (flī′ər) See FLIER. ——— **Variant form, 8, p. xviii.**

Cross-references,
9, p. xviii. ——— **fold·boat** (fōld′bōt′) *n.* A faltboat (which see).

forb (fôrb) *n. SW U.S.* A weed or other herb that is not grass. [Appar. < Gk. *phorbē* fodder]

Locality label, 6, p. xviii. ——— **force ma·jeure** (fôrs mà·zhœr′) *French* Superior and irresistible force. ——— **Foreign-language label, 6, p. xviii.**

Phrasal entry, 1, p. xvii. ——— **foreign office** The department of government in charge of foreign affairs. Abbr. *F.O.* ——— **Abbreviation**

fret·ful (fret′fəl) *adj.* Inclined to fret; peevish or restless. — **fret′ful·ly** *adv.* — **fret′ful·ness** *n.* — Syn. complaining, impatient, pettish, petulant, restive. — Ant. patient, calm, uncomplaining. ——— **Synonym and antonym list, 13, p. xix.**

friend·ship (frend′ship) *n.* **1.** The state or fact of being friends. **2.** Mutual liking and esteem. **3.** [matter omitted] — Syn. *Friendship, amity,* and *comity* characterize the relation between persons, nations, etc. In *friendship* there is an affectionate desire to give sympathy and aid. *Amity* refers to the absence of discord rather than to positive affection or regard. *Comity* is applied to nations or parties more often than to individuals and denotes a courteous respect for the wishes or rights of others. ——— **Discriminated synonyms, 13, p. xix.**

Style label, p. xx. ——— **friv·ol** (friv′əl) *v.* friv·oled or ·olled, friv·ol·ing or ·ol·ling *Informal v.i.* **1.** To behave frivolously [matter omitted]

Abbreviation ——— **gamp** (gamp) *n. Brit.* A large heavy umbrella: a humorous usage. [matter omitted] ——— **Usage note, 12, p. xix.**

got·ten (got′n) Past participle of GET. ◆ *Gotten,* obsolete in British, is current in American English along with *got.* In the informal senses of obligation and possession only *got* is used: *I've got to go, He's got a fine library.*

Combining form,
p. 269. ——— **GPM** or **gpm** or **g.p.m.** Gallons per minute.

-graph *combining form* **1.** That which writes or records: *seismograph.* **2.** [matter omitted] ——— **Biographical entry, 1, p. xvii.**

Geographical entry,
1, p. xvii. ——— **Hal·lam** (hal′əm), Henry, 1777–1859, English historian.
Hamilton River A river in southern Labrador, flowing 600 miles, generally east, to **Hamilton Inlet,** a bay of the Atlantic. ——— **Related phrase**

Prefix, p. 1063. ——— **-hood** *suffix of nouns* **1.** Condition or quality of; state of being: *babyhood, falsehood.* **2.** [matter omitted]

hyper- *prefix* **1.** Over; above; excessive: *hypercritical.* **2.** *Med.* Denoting an abnormal state of excess: *hypertension:* opposed to *hypo-.* [matter omitted] ——— **Suffix, p. 1338.**

Field label, 6, p. xviii.

FUNK & WAGNALLS®

Standard®
COLLEGE
DICTIONARY

FUNK & WAGNALLS
NEW YORK

"FUNK & WAGNALLS" AND "STANDARD"
ARE REGISTERED TRADEMARKS OF FUNK & WAGNALLS, INC.

FUNK & WAGNALLS STANDARD COLLEGE DICTIONARY

Copyright © 1977 by Harper & Row, Publishers, Inc.

Previous editions copyright © 1963, 1966, 1968, 1973, 1974
by Funk & Wagnalls Publishing Company, Inc.

LIBRARY OF CONGRESS CATALOGING IN PUBLICATION DATA

Main entry under title:

Funk & Wagnalls Standard college dictionary.
    1. English language—Dictionaries.   I. Title: Standard college dictionary.

PE1628.S586   1973   423   72-13007
ISBN 0-308-10309-2 (plain)
        0-308-10310-6 (indexed)

MANUFACTURED IN THE UNITED STATES OF AMERICA
13 14 15 16 17 18 19 20

TABLE OF CONTENTS

iv

ADVISORY BOARD

These linguistic authorities determined the policies and practices of the dictionary.

CHAIRMAN: Allen Walker Read, B.Litt. (Oxon.)
Professor of English, Columbia University

Albert C. Baugh, M.A., Ph.D., Litt.D., LL.D.
Felix E. Schelling Memorial Professor of English
University of Pennsylvania

Morton W. Bloomfield, M.A., Ph.D.
Professor of English
Harvard University

Donald C. Bryant, Ph.D.
Professor of Speech
University of Iowa

Margaret M. Bryant, A.M., Ph.D.
Professor of English
Brooklyn College

John Bissell Carroll, Ph.D., M.A. (hon.)
Professor of Education
Harvard University

Frederic G. Cassidy, Ph.D.
Professor of English
University of Wisconsin

Grover Cronin, Jr., M.A. (Oxon.), Ph.D.
Associate Professor of English
Chairman, Department of English
Fordham University

Alva L. Davis, Ph.D.
Professor of English and Linguistics
Illinois Institute of Technology

Richard Harter Fogle, Ph.D.
Professor of English
Chairman, Department of English
Tulane University

Robert A. Hall, Jr., Litt.D.
Professor of Linguistics
Cornell University

Frederick Hard, Ph.D., D.C.L., Litt.D., LL.D.
President
Scripps College

Atcheson L. Hench, Ph.D.
Professor of English
University of Virginia

George W. Hibbitt, Ph.D.
Professor of English
Columbia University

Charles F. Hockett, M.A., Ph.D.
Professor of Linguistics and Anthropology
Cornell University

Edgar Johnson
Professor of English
Chairman, Department of English
The City College of the
City University of New York

William N. Locke, Ph.D.
Professor of Modern Languages
Head of the Department of Modern Languages
Massachusetts Institute of Technology

Albert H. Marckwardt, A.M., Ph.D.
Professor of English and Linguistics
Princeton University

Herbert Dean Meritt, M.A., Ph.D.
Professor of English Philology
Stanford University

Marjorie Nicolson, Ph.D., Litt.D., L.H.D., LL.D.
Professor Emeritus of English
Columbia University

Harold Orton, M.A., B.Litt.
Professor of the English Language and
Medieval English Literature
The University of Leeds

Robert C. Pooley, Ph.D.
Professor of English
University of Wisconsin

Frederick A. Pottle, Ph.D., Litt.D., LL.D.
Sterling Professor of English
Yale University

Thomas Pyles, Ph.D.
Professor of English and Linguistics
Northwestern University

Esther K. Sheldon, Ph.D.
Professor of English
Queens College

Henry Lee Smith, Jr., A.M., Ph.D.
Professor of Linguistics and English
Chairman, Department of Anthropology and
Linguistics
State University of New York at Buffalo

Charles K. Thomas, Ph.D.
Professor of Speech
Director, English Language Institute for
Foreign Students
University of Florida

Lorenzo D. Turner, Ph.D.
Professor of English Language and Literature
Roosevelt University

Jean-Paul Vinay, m.s.r.c.
Directeur, Section de Linguistique
Université de Montréal

v

CONTRIBUTING SPECIALISTS

These authorities wrote, or made editorial revisions of, definitions in their fields.

Walter S. Avis, Ph.D.
Professor of English
Royal Military College (Canada)

Donald Baird, Ph.D.
Assistant Curator of Vertebrate Paleontology
Department of Geology
Princeton University

Marshall D. Berger, Ph.D.
Assistant Professor of Speech
The City College of the
City University of New York

William Bergsma, M.A.
Former Chairman, Composition Faculty
Juilliard School of Music

Abel Bomberault, Ph.D.
Mathematician, Math and Applications
Department
International Business Machines Corporation

William C. Boyd, Ph.D.
Professor of Immunochemistry
School of Medicine, Boston University

Gwilym S. Brown, A.B.
Staff Writer, *Sports Illustrated*

Anatole Chujoy
Editor, *Dance News*

Russell M. Church, Ph.D.
Associate Professor of Psychology
Brown University

Carey Croneis, Ph.D., Sc.D., LL.D., D.Eng.
Harry C. Weiss Professor of Geology
Rice University

Marshall B. Davidson
Former Editor of Publications
Metropolitan Museum of Art

Melvin Ferentz, Ph.D.
Associate Professor of Physics
St. John's University

Norman Charles Firth, B.S.
Research Director (retired)
Dun & Bradstreet, Inc.

Moses M. Frohlich, A.B., M.D.
Professor of Psychiatry
University of Michigan

Frances Fuller
President and Director
American Academy of Dramatic Arts

Wilfred Funk, Litt. D.
Publisher and Author

I. Leo Glasser, LL.B.
Professor of Law
Brooklyn Law School

Benjamin Harrow, Ph.D.
Professor Emeritus of Chemistry
The City College of the
City University of New York

Robert D. Hodgson, Ph.D.
Geographer
United States Department of State

Bernard Jaffe
Science Editor and Writer

Willy Ley
Research Engineer and Science Writer

Frederick B. Llewellyn, M.E., Ph.D.
Bell Telephone Laboratories

Leon A. Michaelis, Graduate, Army War College
Colonel, United States Army

Ernest Nagel, Ph.D.
John Dewey Professor of Philosophy
Columbia University

Peter Selz, Ph.D.
Curator, Department of Painting and Sculpture
Museum of Modern Art

Harry L. Shapiro, Ph.D.
Chairman, Department of Anthropology
American Museum of Natural History
Professor of Anthropology
Columbia University

Kenneth G. Wilson, Ph.D.
Professor of English
University of Connecticut

Henry Wright
Architectural Consultant

PREFACE

The making of a dictionary is both a science and an art. The painstaking accumulation of reliable data, consisting of thousands upon thousands of individual facts of the language; the proper classification of this data; and finally the formulation of sound conclusions from this mass of material — all illustrate the inductive process that is basic to every science. At the same time, the presentation of information about the language, the phrasing of definitions, and the ordering of word treatments demand of the lexicographer the ability to manipulate the language with economy and precision. The science without the art is likely to be ineffective; the art without the science is certain to be inaccurate. The editors of FUNK & WAGNALLS STANDARD COLLEGE DICTIONARY have conscientiously attempted to exercise both the scientific function and the artistic virtuosity of the lexicographer.

The dictionary also possesses a duality for the person who uses it, the same duality that is reflected in the receptive and the productive use of language. For comprehension, both of the spoken and of the written language, the dictionary offers its treatment of word meanings. Yet it is of primary importance to find the meaning which applies to the use of the word about which one is in doubt. The dictionary is not a tool to be used hastily or casually. Status or usage labels may throw light upon the way in which a total context should be interpreted, or upon the style of a writer. The etymology, though by no means an arbiter of current use, can be revealing about past use and suggestive as to the connotations of present use.

The dictionary has even more to offer to the person who consults it as a guide to his own use of the language, whether spoken or written. It is a guide to spelling and to the various combinations, both compound and derivative, into which a word may enter. Grammatical information is to be found in the part-of-speech labels, the treatment of tense and number forms, and many incidental observations. Use of the synonymy and antonymy will lend variety and precision to speech and writing. Pronunciation serves both reader and speaker, but again the use of the dictionary for pronunciation carries with it the responsibility of interpreting information in the way in which the editors intended. This applies particularly to the pronunciation symbols and the treatment of alternate forms.

In short, the dictionary has a wealth of information about the language to offer, but like any other form of wealth, it calls for wise and judicious use. The general attitude of the user is more important than any of the specific and concrete functions of the dictionary, since it can color his attitude toward the language. Let him view his dictionary not as a series of *ex cathedra* pronouncements. It is neither commandment nor holy writ, but a reference work, a body of data about the language, deriving its authority from the care and completeness with which the facts were collected and interpreted. It is in this spirit that my associates on the Supervisory Board, and the Funk & Wagnalls editorial staff, have worked, and it is in this light that we trust the product of our efforts will be used and judged.

ALBERT H. MARCKWARDT

A BRIEF HISTORY OF THE ENGLISH LANGUAGE

By Allen Walker Read

As SPEAKERS OF ENGLISH we take our language for granted most of the time, without inquiring into its origin or history. And yet a knowledge of the early stages of English gives us a background for making decisions when problems arise. Our horizons can be broadened when we see the vast sweep of change, as the English language has developed.

When did its history begin? Documents are known in the earliest form of English from about the year 700; but considerable reconstruction of prehistoric forms can be made, and earlier linguistic conditions and relations can be worked out.

The furthermost roots of English are to be found in a language called "Indo-Hittite," which was flourishing, probably, about 3500 B.C. in east central Europe — perhaps on the plains north of the Black Sea, or in the Danube valley, or in the region to the south of the Baltic Sea. The first known group to branch off were the Hittites, who migrated into Asia Minor; and then "Indo-European" was left, about 2500 B.C. Another migration, a few hundred years later, got as far as Persia and northern India, and this became known as the Indo-Iranian branch. Its sacred literature was early preserved in writing, and from Sanskrit we can gather our best notion of what Indo-European was like. It is not the ancestor language of English, but gives us forms close to those in the ancestor language. The modern descendants are Hindustani, Hindi, Urdu, etc.

The dispersion of Indo-European continued over the centuries. The Hellenic branch went south of the Balkans and adopted the advanced Minoan civilization that they had conquered. An Italic branch went to the southeast and out of their empire-building grew the great "Romance family" of languages. The Celtic speakers pushed all the way to the Atlantic Ocean, and remnants of their tongue are still found in modern Irish, Welsh, and the Gaelic of the Scottish Highlands. The great Balto-Slavic family did not move very far from its original homeland.

The closer roots of English are found in the Germanic branch of the Indo-European family. It is conjectured that a people living in the north of Europe, about 1000 B.C., speaking a language that is now lost, were conquered by a great trading people of the Danube valley, the Veneti, who spoke a form of Indo-European. The attempt to learn "Venetic," with the modifications caused by the substratum language, may be the cause of the peculiarities of the Germanic, which in many ways is the most isolated branch of the whole family. For instance, the sounds of "p," "t," and "k" become in Germanic "f," "th," and "h." Thus the form that appears in Latin as *cornu* is *horn* in English, and the *pecus* of Latin is *feoh* in Old English, later *fee*. The set of sound shifts here referred to are tabulated in what is called "Grimm's Law."

The earliest written record in the Germanic family was made in Gothic in a translation of the Bible by Bishop Wulfila (called Ulfilas in the Greek form), who died about A.D. 383. The Goths and related Vandals harried the Roman Empire but were ultimately absorbed and their language lost. The Northern Germanic, or Scandinavian, has survived in several national languages: Icelandic, Norwegian, Swedish, and Danish.

In the West Germanic group, we come to the languages that are immediately related to English. Their present-day representatives are Dutch and Flemish, Frisian, and the Plattdeutsch dialects of northern Germany. But for the origins of English we must go back to the beginning centuries of this era, before A.D. 449. A group of barbarous tribes that lived along the coast of the North Sea, from Jutland (now Denmark) to the mouth of the Rhine, spoke a set of mutually intelligible dialects. Attracted by the ease of living on the island west of them, where a vacuum of power had been created by the departure of the Romans, they began migrations about the middle of the fifth century, and in successive steps drove the Celtic inhabitants to the western fastnesses of the island.

From the linguistic situation of this early time we can discern a remarkable fact — from the very beginning "English" has consisted of a variety of dialects, each with its own individuality and historical background. The Jutes came from what is now Denmark and settled in the southeast area, the Thames valley, and the Isle of Wight, but their dialect after a while retreated to the county of Kent. Southwest of the Jutes lived the Angles, and they migrated to the part of Britain lying north of the Thames. Their "Anglian" had two forms, the Mercian, in the middle area, and Northumbrian, north of the Humber. The Saxons, from the shore along the North Sea, migrated to the southwest area, establishing the West Saxon dialect. Probably some Frisians migrated too, but most of them remained in a corner of what is now the Netherlands, and they now speak the language that is most closely related to English on the Continent. An old folk rhyme makes reference to the closeness:

> Bread, butter, and green cheese
> Is good English and good Friese.

The dialects of Old English had their ups and downs of prestige. The Kentish took the earliest leadership, then it passed to East Anglia, and then to Northumbria, where much literary activity went on. That area was continually devastated by Viking raids and was finally so overrun that the Danelaw was established. The ascendancy in dialects then passed to Wessex, where King Alfred the Great fostered a high degree of literary culture. Most of the remains that we have were rewritten in this dialect, and for a time a standard written form of the language prevailed.

The stock of words in Old English from A.D. 700 to 1100 was remarkably large for its time. Well over 40,000 words are recorded for it. It had a core of effective short words, such as *feld*, now "field"; *fugol*, now "fowl"; *heofon*, now "heaven"; *weorc*, now "work"; etc. But it also had important devices for forming new words. Besides using many prefixes and suffixes, it made compounds freely, such as *larhus* (lore-house) for school, *leorning-cniht* (learning-knight) for disciple, *fotadl* (foot-pain) for gout, *ban-cofa* (bone-chamber) for body, etc. Some of them had a strong poetic effect, such as *whale-path* or *swan's road* as names for the sea.

A clear distinction can be made between native words, such as the foregoing, and those that were borrowed from other languages, called loan-words. Even while the Anglo-Saxons were still on the Continent, before they got to England, they adopted some loan-words in the course of trade or warfare with surrounding peoples. Some early terms in the Christian religion, all ultimately Greek, found their way up the Danube valley, such as *deofol*, now "devil"; *cirice*, now "church"; and *bisceop*, now "bishop." More important were the borrowings from Latin, taken from the Roman traders along the Rhine. Modern words like the following go back to this source: *chalk, cheese, cup, dish, pillow, pitch, pound, street, toll, wine*, and many others.

One such word of special interest is *dicker*. The Romans who traded with the Germanic tribes for skins or hides would take them in a *decuria*, or bundle of ten, from *decem*, ten. The word was borrowed into the West Germanic tongues as *dicker*, and for about fifteen hundred years it meant a unit of ten articles. Then a similar situation arose on the American frontier, in the eighteenth century, when the English colonists traded for skins with the Indians. "Dicker? Dicker?" they would say. In this way, probably, the word took on a new meaning, referring to haggling and bargaining in trade. Thus two similar situations, fifteen hundred years apart, when a civilized people traded with a primitive people, resulted in leaps of meaning in the word *dicker*.

The speakers of English brought in another layer of borrowings from the Celtic peoples whom they dominated and displaced. One such word is *bin*, a compartment for storage; and others refer to topographical features, such as *crag*, a rock, *tor*, a steep hill, and *coomb*, a deep valley. The word *ambeht*, meaning servant, was taken from Celtic into Old English. It died out there, but was taken into Latin as *ambactus* and then later reborrowed into English from French and Italian as the modern word *ambassador*.

The Viking invasions of the North of England, from the end of the eighth century on, brought many Scandinavian words into English, especially after the invaders settled down and mixed with the English. These words can sometimes be recognized by the sharp *k* sound, as in *dank, keel, kid, skin, skirt, sky, kindle, cake*, or by the sharp *g* sound, as in *egg, girth, guess, leg, rugged, gasp, nag*. Such important verbs as *get, call, hit*, and *take* came from this source, as well as the pronouns *they, their*, and *them*. Such examples show that there was a very intimate intermingling of the native population and the Norse settlers.

The fortunes of English were profoundly changed by the Norman conquest. The high degree of culture achieved in Wessex was overthrown by a less cultivated race — the Northman adventurers that had taken on a veneer, thin and cracked, from their settlement in northern France. The Saxons were systematically plundered, and their speech fell to the status of a peasants' patois. This period is now known as "Middle English," commonly said to begin about 1050. Untrammeled by literary guidance, the language became more and more simplified. The arbitrary gender of words was shuffled into "natural" gender. The inflectional endings of Old English were obscured and then dropped. Between 1300 and 1400 a revolutionary change in grammatical structure took place: word order, selected form words, and intonation became the central devices by which the structural relationships in sentences were signaled.

In dialect prestige, London, together with the nearby area to the northeast, gradually took leadership. The commercial activity and governmental administration led to the development of a "koine" or common speech, in which clashing regional variations were regularized. Especially for writing, a "standard" form was gradually established. The fine old speech of King Alfred, once standard, was left behind to be the ancestor of the peasant talk in Dorset and Devonshire. Modern Scottish English is the descendant of the speech of the northern Angles.

In vocabulary, English took in many words from the French. The resources of another language were in effect poured into English, giving English a twofold verbal power. Probably the earliest French word to be taken into English was the adjective *proud*, at first meaning valiant, gallant, and brave. But the English quickly altered it to an unfavorable sense, since it was usually applied to the "proud barons" who seemed so arrogant and haughty to the lowly English peasants and townsmen. Among other early words taken from French, some even before the Norman conquest, were (here in modern form) *bacon, catch, chapel, chancellor, justice*, and *market*. Before the end of the Middle English period, by 1475, French words by the thousand had permeated all areas of the English vocabulary, especially those relating to social rank, finance, law, religion, clothing, food, the arts and sciences, moral qualities, etc. The poet Chaucer used 8072 words in his recorded English vocabulary, and forty-eight percent of them are derived from Old French and Anglo-French.

From one point of view, this freedom of borrowing has added greatly to the richness of the resources of English. Yet it curtailed the ability of English to create new words out of its native elements. The taking in of loan-words so freely has given the language, according to Kemp Malone, "a chronic case of linguistic indigestion." It is a moot point — do the great stores of words in English represent a treasure or merely indigestion?

The modern period of English may be said to begin in 1475, the year in which Caxton printed his first book in English. Already an important set of sound changes were under way — the "great vowel shift," it is called, which set English in a separate class from other languages of Europe in its vowel sounds. Chaucer now seems difficult, as he wrote before this shift took place, while Shakespeare wrote after it had been mostly completed. In actual speaking there continued to be considerable diversity. Even upper-class gentlemen prided themselves on their loyalties to the regions where they hunted foxes, supervised their estates, and administered the local laws, and they were not ashamed of a rural accent. A cultivated gentleman had considerable leeway in the forms of speech that he could use. Both the actor Garrick and Dr. Samuel Johnson were remarked on in the eighteenth century as having Midland accents.

But in the half century from 1800 to 1850 a great tightening took place, and in England for the last few generations cultivated people have been obliged to acquire the "standard" speech, gained mostly at the great boarding schools or the universities. Formerly there was a rather wide "area of negligible variation," as it has been called, in which varieties in speech are accepted without criticism; but this area has become narrower and narrower in England. It can be argued that a language is in a healthy state when it has an "area of negligible variation" that is as wide as possible.

The vocabulary continued to expand. Throughout the centuries of the early modern period, Latin was the language of scholarship, and it was used as a reservoir from which to draw newly made-up English words. Some writers prided themselves on using many of them, to give their work a learned, "aureate" quality. Sometimes a word that had come into the language through Old French was borrowed over again in its purely Latin form. Thus *count* had come in from French, but the Latin *compute* was added later to English; *ray* had come in but *radius* was added; and similarly *strait, strict; poor, pauper; frail, fragile*, etc. As science progressed in modern times, more and more Latin words were taken in. The following are samples: *antenna* in 1698, *axis* in 1549, *bacillus* in 1883, *cerebrum* in 1615, *cirrus* in 1708, *forceps* in 1634, *fulcrum* in 1674, *inertia* in 1713, *momentum* in 1699, *nebula* in 1661, *nucleus* in 1708, and *stamen* in 1668.

Furthermore, as the interests of English speakers spread over the world, many strange and exotic languages were drawn upon. From Hungarian came *coach, Hussar, goulash,* and *paprika.* From Basque came *jai alai* and perhaps *bizarre.* Trade with the Near East and Far East added many words. From India alone have come such useful words as *bandanna, jute, gunny, shampoo, cashmere, chutney, polo, pachisi, dungarees, bungalow, chintz.* Further afield we have some words from the Malay — *amuck, bamboo, gingham, gong, launch,* etc. Even the Australian aborigines have contributed by giving us *kangaroo, boomerang,* and *kookaburra.*

An important new factor entered the history of English when it became spread abroad as a world-wide language. The first colonists who went to the New World of course carried with them the language that they were accustomed to use in England, and it is difficult to determine how soon it began to be modified. Words were adopted from the Indians almost at once — *moccasin, moose, opossum, papoose, persimmon, squaw, tomahawk,* etc. In the area of pronunciation, intonation, grammar, etc., changes took place gradually, so that American English developed a character of its own.

The new environment caused the development of various Americanisms. When the settlers reached the wide-stretching, grass-covered areas of the Mississippi valley, they had only the traditional old word *meadow* to describe them, and it must have seemed inadequate. Thereupon they took over from the French voyageurs the word *prairie,* and it has become the habitual word in the Middle West and elsewhere. Furthermore, the blinding, furious snowstorms that blew down from the Rocky Mountains in wintertime were more intense than anything the speakers of English had encountered before. In this case the coinage of the French voyageurs (*poudrerie,* or "powdermill") was passed by. Shortly before 1870 the word *blizzard,* which had for forty years meant a sharp blow or volley of shot, was transferred to the snowstorm. This leap in meaning was created at a frontier village in northwest Iowa, Estherville, according to local folklore, by a droll old character named "Lightnin' Ellis" (so called because he was the slowest man in the community). So expressive was the word, with its buzzing *z* sound, that it spread quickly and within two decades had become commonplace even in England.

American political conditions have given rise to new words. When the American colonies in 1774 adopted the word *congress* rather than *parliament* as the name for their legislative body, they soon needed an adjective form for it, and within a year the word *congressional* was coined. Its form has been an annoyance to critics, for it is hard to explain where the syllable *-ion-* came from. One of the most colorful of political words is *buncombe.* This has been in print since 1828 and goes back, it is believed, to an incident in the Congress of 1819–21, when Felix Walker, a representative from Buncombe County, North Carolina, insisted on talking long and tediously, because he wished to "make a speech for Buncombe." First respelled *bunkum,* it is now cut down to *bunk.*

Other Americanisms have been taken from the languages brought in by various immigrant groups. From the Dutch of the Hudson River valley have come the words *boss, cole slaw, cooky* (reinforcing an old Scottish word, *cuckie*), *spook, stoop,* and others. The German influence spread from a strong center in Pennsylvania, giving us *loafer, sauerkraut, pretzel* (which the English call *bent biscuit*), *delicatessen, noodle,* etc. The French influence was felt from both Quebec and Louisiana. Some of these words are *levee, crevasse, portage, dalles, gopher, cariole* (often altered by folk etymology to *carryall*). The

word *charivari,* usually pronounced *shivaree* and often so spelled, worked its way up from New Orleans into regions that did their trading along the Mississippi. From the Spanish Southwest the borrowings have been many — *adobe, corral, hoosegow, lariat, rodeo, vamoose,* etc. It was long thought that the Negro had not brought many words from Africa, but investigation has extended the list considerably — *okra, goober, gumbo, voodoo, tote, yam, zombi,* and many more.

At one time it seemed probable that two separate languages would develop, and some patriots of the American Revolution hoped that this would be so. Noah Webster wrote in 1789, "As a nation, we have a very great interest in opposing the introduction of any plan of uniformity with the British language, even were the plan proposed perfectly unexceptionable." However, the constant communication and travel between England and America has effectively kept the divergences from going as far as they might.

The cultural differences between England and America are clearly revealed by the language differences. England has its own sets of terms in many fields, such as officers of the government (*prime minister, Lord High Chancellor, Remembrancer, beefeater*), occupational names (*grazier, hosier, fruiterer, ironmonger, greengrocer*), parts of an automobile (*accumulator, bonnet, wing, saloon*), railroad terms (*permanent way, platelayer, goods wagon*), parts of a house (*scullery, buttery, W. C.*), architectural features seldom found in America (*lady chapel, galilee, reredos*), etc. England has retained a number of ecclesiastical terms that never took root in America — *advowson, benefice, glebe, living.* As America has no established church, it can have no "dissenters." Certain place names are traditional with foods — *Aylesbury duck, Dover sole, Bakewell pudding, Bath bun, Bradenham ham, Devonshire cream,* etc. Sometimes Briticisms have only small telltale differences in form, such as *aluminium* where Americans have *aluminum; crematorium* instead of *crematory; devilry* instead of *deviltry;* or *diplomatist* instead of *diplomat.*

These Briticisms may occur on all levels, from formal writing down to informal conversation. Englishmen at a public meeting show their approval by calling out "Hear! Hear!" while Americans have no way except the clapping of hands. Even an English child, in his "pram" (not "baby carriage"), on his way to a "creche" (not "day nursery"), hears about a "puff-puff" (not a "choo-choo"). As the child grows up he will play with "conkers" (i.e., horse chestnuts) and "keep cave" (i.e., the Latin *cave,* beware, for keeping watch).

Many British terms were borrowed into America in the mid-nineteenth century, chiefly because the lack of copyright made it easy to reprint English books. The industrial revolution took place in England several decades before it did in America, and the new technical vocabulary for machinery was brought over to America in a body. From 1776 to about 1835 American travelers in England expressed surprise at a strange product called "coke," and in 1833 Henry Clay declared: "The successful introduction of the process of coking would have great effect." But after 1835 *coke* became a commonplace word in America.

The British origin of some words has been almost completely forgotten. *Brunch,* for instance, originated in Oxford slang, first recorded in 1897, but when it gained currency in America, in the 1920's, it was assumed by many to be an Americanism. The "weekend" was at first a British institution, and when the word was first used in America, about 1910, it was felt to be very British. The word *varsity* was sporting slang at the English universities in the 1880's, but it was adopted in America in the 1890's. Even high schools now have a "varsity team."

British English and American English are most easily distinguished in their spoken form. An American receives a jolt when he hears the Englishman give his own stress on *centénary* or *fináncier* or *labóratory.* The different lilt and speech tune can hardly be caught in a dictionary.

The term "American language," made popular by H. L. Mencken, served a useful propaganda purpose in emphasizing that Americans have a right to an independent enjoyment of their linguistic heritage, just as Englishmen have a right to their heritage. But the two branches have remained one language because of continuous cultural interchanges.

English has shown its vitality in special developments in other parts of the world. Canadian English presents fascinating patterns; and Bermuda, the West Indies, South Africa, Ghana, India, Malaya, the Philippines, Australia, New Zealand, etc., all have individual traits of speech that are worth treasuring. The branches of the language, though they sprang from a common center, have now become coordinate. One branch is no more important than another, except to those who speak it.

In all parts of the English-speaking world, normal semantic change has been going on continuously. A child in growing up is obliged to learn what the limits of meaning are. For instance, a seven-year-old boy happened to be a witness of a traffic accident and was taken to the police station to tell what he had seen. When he got home that afternoon he gave a lively account to his mother and concluded, "After I'd confessed, they took me back to school." No doubt he had heard the word *confess* many times, and he had taken it to mean "to tell what one knows." His mother would have to tell him, "You 'confess' only when you're guilty of something."

A word when used in any context has its effect as a whole — an "impact," as it could be called — and it is misleading to split this up into an "emotional" effect or an "intellectual" effect. The so-called "connotation" is an integral part of the use of a word. And yet semantic changes, in all their complexity, can be described according to a number of classifications. Many words have moved along a scale of generalization vs. specialization, melioration vs. deterioration, euphemism vs. pejoration, hyperbole vs. understatement, and so on.

Let us begin with the first of these pairs, the scale of generalization vs. specialization. Words have moved in both directions since the earliest times. The word *doom* shows specialization: in Old English it meant judgment in general, but it has narrowed to the meaning of a ruinous fate or even death — "He met his doom." Similarly *disease* originally was discomfort ("dis-ease"), but it became narrowed to illness of the body. *Corn* formerly referred to grain in general, but it has become specialized in America to maize, in Scotland to oats, and in England to wheat. In the other direction, a word of narrow meaning can become broadened. Thus the "Colossus of Rhodes" was a particular statue of Apollo in ancient Rhodes, but a "colossus" came to mean something strikingly large. A "symposium" was originally a drinking together, but it has developed to mean a collection of opinions on a subject. Likewise *person*, originally referring to an actor in a play (from speaking through a mask, *per + sonāre*), was generalized to mean a human individual. But one pronunciation variant of the very same word, namely, *parson*, shows specialization — it has come to mean a clergyman only.

Some words rise or decline in status, on a scale of melioration vs. deterioration. *Yankee* was originally a term of contempt, applied by the British soldiers to the colonial settlers of New England, but it was accepted and has risen in prestige, now often applied to Americans in general. An outstanding example of deterioration is the word *churl*. Before the Norman conquest it was a term of respect, meaning "a freeman," but the Norman contempt for the Anglo-Saxons turned it into a name for an uncouth boor. *Knave* took a similar course.

Other words move along the scale of euphemism vs. pejoration. A social taboo may intervene to blight the standing of some words, and a pleasanter word will have currency — *pass away* replaces *die*, *smell* replaces *stink*, *falsehood* replaces *lie*, etc. The danger here is that the new term may be a "genteelism" and consequently regarded as in bad taste. Some speakers enjoy following the pejorative tendency — calling their clothes *duds*, their father *the old man*, their food *eats* or *chow*.

Finally, the scale of hyperbole vs. understatement applies to some semantic change. There is typical American exaggeration in the term *skyscraper*, and hyperbole is especially common in the area of slang: "The heat drives me *crazy*" or "That's a *smashing* new dress you have on." Examples of understatement are *the big pond* for the Atlantic ocean or the ironical "That's a *pretty* story."

No matter how we may classify and organize sets of words, and the changes they have undergone, we must come back to the realization that words are conventional symbols, deriving their meaning from the way in which people use them in everyday life. The best linguistic procedure is to be constantly alert in observing how language affects people's actions.

Worldwide English presents a remarkable equilibrium of unity in diversity and of diversity in unity. It can be a source of pride to belong to such a far-flung speech community. We face a continuing challenge to enrich our lives by availing ourselves of the incomparable resources of English.

REGIONAL VARIATIONS IN AMERICAN PRONUNCIATION

By Charles K. Thomas

STANDARD SPEECH in England and France is relatively easy to determine. It is the speech used by educated persons in the political, commercial, and cultural capitals: London in England, Paris in France. Speakers in other parts of England and France who do not wish to be considered provincial adopt the speech which commands respect in the capital. The prestige of the capital sets up such strong pressures that only the ignorant and the strong-minded fail to conform.

In the United States, on the other hand, no single city combines the various sources of prestige that have developed in Paris and London. On the contrary, Boston, New York, Philadelphia, Pittsburgh, Richmond, New Orleans, Chicago, St. Louis, Salt Lake City, Seattle, and San Francisco have different traditions, including differences in speech based on the gradual settlement of the Atlantic seaboard in the seventeenth and eighteenth centuries and on the westward movements of population. Each of these cities is the center of an important regional complex. Each carries its own prestige. Nor is the story yet complete, as the growth of Los Angeles, Phoenix, and Miami attests, and as technical developments have facilitated distant communication and internal migration.

Variability must not, of course, be overemphasized. Most English words, including the unfamiliar and the technical terms for which the reader is most likely to consult a dictionary, have uniform American pronunciations, which the reader can ignore only at his own risk. But neither the reader nor the lexicographer can ignore the variations which spring from diverse backgrounds. The lexicographer must not prescribe; he must describe the regionally acceptable patterns.

At present we can recognize three main speech areas, with numerous subdivisions: the Northern, the Midland, and the Southern, each with differences in tradition and development. Because such references to points of the compass as northern, southern, eastern, and western may refer either to specific speech areas or mere geographical locations, they have been capitalized when used in this article as references to speech areas and left without capitals when used merely for geographical reference. Thus Western Pennsylvania refers to a speech area; northeastern New Jersey is purely a geographical reference.

On the Atlantic seaboard, the northernmost area is Eastern New England, with Boston as its focus. West of Eastern New England is the North Central area, which originated in the Housatonic valley of western New England and which has spread out to include the Champlain and Great Lakes basins and the northern plains as far west as the central Dakotas. Despite the size of this area, with Hartford, Syracuse, Cleveland, Detroit, Chicago, and Minneapolis serving as important regional

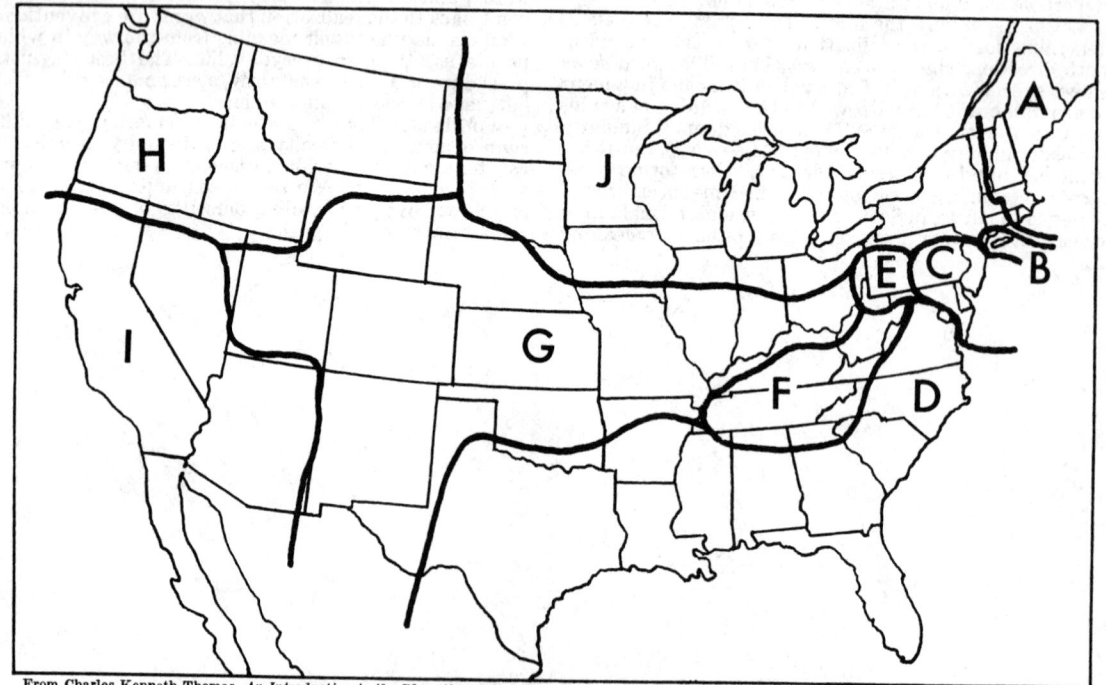

MAJOR REGIONAL SPEECH AREAS
A Eastern New England. *B* New York City. *C* Middle Atlantic. *D* Southern. *E* Western Pennsylvania.
F Southern Mountain. *G* Central Midland. *H* Northwest. *I* Southwest. *J* North Central.

foci, its speech is remarkably uniform. Eastern New England and the North Central area together represent the Northern type, though the speech of the Southwest Coastal area, comprising much of California, Arizona, and Nevada, is very similar.

Though geographically adjacent to both the Eastern New England and North Central areas, the New York City area does not speak the Northern type; it contains both Midland and Southern elements. Though small in extent — southern New York and parts of southwestern Connecticut and northeastern New Jersey — it is important because of its large population and the prestige of New York City. The Middle Atlantic area, extending from New Jersey to Maryland, and westward to the Pennsylvania mountains, is the easternmost of the Midland areas, with Philadelphia as its most important focus. West of the mountains the Midland areas fan out and the regional boundaries become less distinct. Western Pennsylvania, the Southern Mountain area, the Central Midland area, and the Northwest (see map) have similarities, but also subtle differences (see table of illustrative words). Pittsburgh, St. Louis, Salt Lake City, and Seattle serve as regional foci.

The Southern area is a complex of types extending from Virginia to Georgia and westward through the Gulf states, with fringe areas in parts of Maryland, Florida, and Texas. Its diversity is represented in the speech of such regional foci as Richmond, Charleston, Montgomery, New Orleans, and Houston. Though highly varied, the speech of the South has elements of vocabulary, pronunciation, and sentence melody that unify it and mark it off from the other regions.

Before considering the pronunciations of these main areas, the reader should consult the list of symbols of the International Phonetic Alphabet in the Table of English Spellings on p. xxvi. In their various combinations, these symbols can be used to represent all the pronunciations with which we shall have to deal. To avoid ambiguity in this article, phonetic symbols are enclosed in square brackets; references to words and spellings are italicized; thus, there is an *h*, but no [h], in *hour*. To indicate added vowel length without change of vowel quality we add a colon to the vowel symbol; thus, *calm* [ka:m] has a longer vowel than *comma* [kamǝ].

Omission of the various sounds [r, ɝ, ǝ] represented by r, whenever these sounds would otherwise precede a consonant or a pause, is a feature of Eastern New England, New York City, and the South. In all three areas, however, r is gradually reasserting itself, and more and more of the population is gradually falling in line with the other large areas. Radio, television, and motion-picture practices encourage this trend.

Vowels associated with r frequently indicate regional variations. In Eastern New England the traditional

REGIONAL PRONUNCIATIONS

The form listed first is the most frequent in the area indicated.

WORD	EASTERN NEW ENGLAND	NORTH CENTRAL	NEW YORK CITY	MIDDLE ATLANTIC	WESTERN PENNSYLVANIA
barn	[ba:n] [ba:n]	[barn] [barn]	[barn] [ba:n]	[barn] [bɔrn]	[barn] [bɔrn]
orange	[arɪndʒ]	[ɔrɪndʒ]	[arɪndʒ]	[arɪndʒ]	[ɔrɪndʒ]
cot	[kat] [kɒt]	[kat] [kat]	[kat]	[kat]	[kɒt]
caught	[kɔt] [kɒt]	[kɔt]	[kɔt]	[kɔt]	[kɒt]
barren	[bɛrǝn]	[bɛrǝn] [bærǝn]	[bærǝn]	[bærǝn]	[bærǝn]
various	[vɛriǝs]	[vɛriǝs]	[vɛriǝs] [væriǝs]	[vɛriǝs] [væriǝs]	[vɛriǝs]
ask	[æsk] [ask] [ask]	[æsk]	[æsk]	[æsk]	[æsk]
greasy	[grisi]	[grisi]	[grisi]	[grisi] [grizi]	[grisi] [grizi]
hurry	[hʌri]	[hɝi]	[hʌri]	[hʌri]	[hʌri]
due	[du] [dju]	[du]	[du]	[du]	[du]
horse	[hɔ:s] [hɒs]	[hɔrs]	[hɔ:s] [hɔrs]	[hɔrs]	[hɔrs]
hoarse	[hoǝs] [hɔ:s]	[hɔrs]	[hɔ:s] [hɔrs]	[hɔrs] [hɔrs]	[hɔrs] [hɔrs]
log	[lag]	[lɔg]	[lag]	[lɔg] [lag]	[lɔg]

WORD	SOUTHERN MOUNTAIN	SOUTHERN	CENTRAL MIDLAND	NORTH-WEST	SOUTH-WEST
barn	[barn]	[ba:n] [bɒ:n]	[barn] [bɔrn]	[barn] [bɔrn]	[barn]
orange	[ɔrɪndʒ]	[arɪndʒ]	[ɔrɪndʒ]	[ɔrɪndʒ]	[ɔrɪndʒ]
cot	[kat]	[kat]	[kat] [kɒt]	[kat] [kɒt]	[kat]
caught	[kɔt]	[kɔt]	[kɔt] [kɒt]	[kɔt] [kɒt]	[kɔt]
barren	[bærǝn] [bɛrǝn]	[bærǝn]	[bɛrǝn]	[bɛrǝn]	[bɛrǝn] [bærǝn]
various	[vɛriǝs] [vɛriǝs]	[vɛriǝs] [vɛriǝs]	[vɛriǝs]	[vɛriǝs] [vɛriǝs]	[vɛriǝs]
ask	[æsk]	[æsk]	[æsk]	[æsk]	[æsk]
greasy	[grizi] [grizi]	[grizi] [grizi]	[grisi] [grizi]	[grisi] [grizi]	[grisi]
hurry	[hʌri] [hʌri]	[hʌri] [hʌri]	[hɝi]	[hɝi]	[hɝi]
due	[du] [dju]	[dju] [du]	[du]	[du]	[du]
horse	[hɔrs]	[hɔ:s] [hɔrs]	[hɔrs]	[hɔrs]	[hɔrs]
hoarse	[hɔrs] [hɔrs]	[hoǝs]	[hɔrs] [hɔrs]	[hɔrs] [hɔrs]	[hɔrs]
log	[lɔg] [lɔg]	[lɔg]	[lɔg] [lɔg]	[lɔg] [lɒg]	[lɔg]

vowel of such words as *far, farm, hard* and *heart* is [a:], a lengthened vowel intermediate in sound between the [æ] of *hat* and the [ɑ] of *father*. Characteristically these words are pronounced: *far* [fa:], *farm* [fa:m], *hard* [ha:d], and *heart* [ha:t]; words like *calm* [ka:m] and *father* [faðə] follow the same pattern. In all such words, [ɑ:] occurs occasionally; [æ:] occurs sporadically along the northeast coast of Maine. In the North Central area [a] also occurs frequently; here *heart* may be [hart] or [hɑrt]; *far*, [far] or [fɑr]; *calm*, [ka:m] or [kɑ:m]; and even *hot*, [hat] or [hɑt]. The use of [a] is one of the most important criteria of the Northern type.

Elsewhere such words have either [ɑ] or [ɒ], the latter a sound intermediate between the [ɑ] of *farm* and the [ɔ] of *form*. In the New York City area *heart* may be [hɑ:t], [hɒ:t], [hart], or [hɒrt]; in the Middle Atlantic area, [hart] or [hɒrt]. In the South, pronunciations with [ɒ:] become more frequent in all such words.

In such words as *coral, foreign, forest, horrid, moral, orange, quarrel, quarry, torrent,* and *warrant,* the predominant vowel of the stressed syllable in Eastern New England, New York City, the Middle Atlantic area, and the South is [ɑ]; elsewhere it is [ɔ]. A line extending southward through western New England, westward across the lower Hudson valley, and southwestward from the Pennsylvania mountains to Texas marks the boundary line; *forest* has [ɑ] predominantly east of the line, [ɔ] predominantly west of the line and in the country as a whole.

To the east of the same Vermont–Texas line such words as *barren, carriage, carrot, carry, marry, narrow,* and *parrot* usually have [æ]; west of the line [ɛ] is frequent, in some areas predominant. East of the line *marry* [mæri] and *merry* [mɛri] are usually audibly distinct; west of the line they may both be [mɛri].

Words like *area, dairy, fairy, Mary,* and *various* introduce an additional complication. In the South they frequently have [e]; in the Middle Atlantic and New York City areas, sometimes [æ]; in the rest of the country usually, and in all parts of the country occasionally, they have [ɛ] or a slightly lengthened [ɛ:]. Thus in the South, *Mary* [meri], *merry* [mɛri], and *marry* [mæri] may all three be audibly distinct. In the Middle Atlantic and New York City areas, *Mary* and *marry* may both be [mæri], but *merry* [mɛri] remains distinct. In Eastern New England, *Mary* and *merry* may both be [mɛri], but *marry* [mæri] is usually distinct. West of the Vermont–Texas line all three are frequently, if not always, [mɛri].

The traditional distinction between such pairs as *horse* [hɔrs] and *hoarse* [hors] survives in some areas, not in others. In the New York City area the distinction has been lost, and either word may occur as [hɔrs], [hoəs], or [hɔ:s]. In the North Central and Southwest coastal areas both words usually occur as [hɔrs]. In the Midland areas most speakers maintain the distinction between [ɔr] and [or]; a few do not. In the South the usual pronunciations are *horse* [hɔ:s] and *hoarse* [hoəs], and much the same distinction holds in Eastern New England. Wherever the distinction survives it also survives in other pairs like *for* and *four, border* and *boarder,* and *morning* and *mourning*; and [o] survives in words like *more* and *glory*.

The most important variation not associated with a following *r* is the vowel of such words as *ask, dance, path, aunt,* and *rather*. Traditionally Eastern New England and eastern Virginia use either [a] or [ɑ] in such words, other varieties of American English use [æ], and London English uses [ɑ]. This use of [a] and [ɑ], however, seems to be rapidly declining, in both New England and Virginia, except for the two words *aunt* and *rather*, for which [a] and [ɑ] occur frequently in both areas, and occasionally in all parts of the country. Those New Englanders and Virginians who use [a] in the traditional pattern make a sharp contrast with the [æ] of *bad, land,* and *fancy*. Some speakers in other areas, especially in the New York City area, use [a], often as an acquired pronunciation, but frequently use [a] in such words as *bad, land,* and *fancy* too, thereby losing the distinction between the two categories.

Loss of the distinction between such pairs as *cot* [kɑt] and *caught* [kɔt] characterizes some of the Midland areas. In Pittsburgh, Salt Lake City, and parts of the Northwest, either word may be heard as [kɑt], [kɒt], or [kɔt], and the meaning must be determined from the context of the sentence. Such words as *loss, cough, cloth, lost, stop, hot, lock, on,* and *God* vary considerably, especially in the Midland areas west of the Pennsylvania mountains. Words of the type of *fog, frog, hog, log, gong,* and *prong* run the entire range from [ɑ] to [ɔ], but the regional patterns are too complex for inclusion in this article.

Variations between vowels and diphthongs are especially characteristic of the South, which changes some sounds heard as simple vowels elsewhere into diphthongs, and vice versa. Thus *dog* and *class*, which are usually [dɔg] and [klæs] elsewhere, are often [dɔug] and [klæɪs] in the South. *Time* and *oil*, which are usually [taɪm] and [ɔɪl] elsewhere, are often [ta:m] and [ɔ:l] in the South. The diphthong of such a word as *town* varies from North to South, more often [taʊn] in the North, [taʊn] in the Midland areas, and often [tæʊn] in the South. There is, of course, overlapping, and New York City, in particular, uses all three forms.

Except for *r*, consonantal variations are not very important. For the verb *grease* and the adjective *greasy*, but not for the noun *grease*, a line drawn westward from Philadelphia to the Ohio valley, where it joins the Vermont–Texas line, separates the territory to the north, where [s] predominates for both verb and adjective, from the territory to the south, where [z] predominates. The normal pronunciation of the noun *grease* is everywhere [gris].

Words with the so-called "long-*u*" after *t, d,* or *n*, as in *tune, due, dew, numerous,* and *new*, have retained the older [ju] of *unit* only to a limited extent, and only, in natural speech, in the South, where *due* and *dew* may be [dju] in contrast with *do* [du]. Elsewhere in the country, despite the preference of radio and television studios for the forms with [j], the normal pronunciations are *tune* [tun], *due* and *dew* [du], and *new* [nu].

Other variations occur, but are usually of minor importance and can be ignored. The purpose of this article has been to demonstrate not the lack of standards, but their diversity in a diversified country.

CANADIAN ENGLISH

By Walter S. Avis
Royal Military College of Canada and Consultant on Canadianisms

One Canadian had his eyes opened to the existence of Canadian English in a rather curious way. While shopping in a large Chicago department store, he asked where he might find chesterfields. Following directions to the letter, he was somewhat dismayed when he ended up at the cigar counter. He soon made other discoveries as well. Blinds were "shades" to his American neighbors; taps were "faucets," braces "suspenders," and serviettes "napkins."

Before long his American friends were pointing out differences between his speech and theirs. He said *been* to rhyme with "bean," whereas for them it rhymed with "bin"; and he said *shone* to rhyme with "gone," whereas for them it rhymed with "bone." In fact, their Canadian friend had quite a few curious ways of saying things: *ration* rhymed with "fashion" rather than with "nation"; *lever* with "beaver" rather than "sever"; *Z* with "bed" rather than "bee." Moreover, he pronounced certain vowels in a peculiar way, for *lout* seemed to have a different vowel sound from *loud*, and *rice* a different vowel from *rise*.

The Englishman is also quick to observe that Canadians talk differently from himself. For example, he doesn't say *dance, half, clerk, tomato, garage,* or *war* as Canadians do; and he always distinguishes *cot* from *caught,* a distinction that few Canadians make. He also finds that many of the words he used in England are not understood by people in Canada. Suppose he gets into a conversation about cars. Says he, "I think a car should have a roomy boot." No headway will be made till somebody rescues him by explaining that in Canada the boot is called a "trunk." Before the session is finished, he will probably learn that a bonnet is called a "hood" and the hood of a coupé is "the top of a convertible."

Canadian English, then, at this stage of its development, is a dialect which reflects both American and British patterns of speech and which includes a great deal that is distinctively Canadian. The explanation of this mixed character lies in the settlement of the country. As the several areas of Canada were opened up for settlement, before, during, and after the Revolutionary War, Americans were prominent among the settlers, in many, if not most, communities. American influence has been great ever since: Canadians often learn from American textbooks, listen to American radio, watch American TV and movies, read American periodicals and books. Moreover, Canadians in large numbers are constantly moving back and forth across the border, as immigrants, as tourists, as students, and as bargain hunters. Finally, as a North American country, Canada naturally shares with the United States a large vocabulary made up of words denoting all manner of things indigenous to this continent. There is nothing very surprising about the closeness of Canadian and American English.

On the other hand, Britain has also made an enormous contribution to the settlement of Canada. For more than a century, an almost steady stream of British immigrants, speaking various dialects, has come to this country. In most communities, especially those along the border (where most of Canada's population is still to be found), these newcomers came into contact with already established Canadians, and, as might be expected, their children adopted the speech habits of the communities they were brought up in. Generations of British immigrants are undoubtedly responsible for the British features observable in Canadian English. Also, it must be remembered that the prestige of British English has always exerted strong influence on Canadian speech habits, especially among the educated. There is, then, nothing very surprising about the British coloring in the speech of Canadians.

Most of the differences that Englishmen notice in our speech are common to both Canada and the Northern United States. On the other hand, most of the differences noticed by Americans are shared by Canadians and Englishmen. As a result, Canadian speech-patterns are neither British nor American. Their distinctiveness is strengthened by a great many Canadianisms, that is, words, pronunciations, and meanings which are typically, if not always exclusively, Canadian.

Prominent among Canadianisms are proper nouns — names of regions: *Barren Ground, French Shore, Eastern Townships, Lakehead*; names given to the natives of certain regions: *Newfies, Bluenoses, Spud Islanders, Hogtowners*; names of things associated with persons or places: *York boat, Winnipeg goldeye, Digby chicken*.

A great many Canadianisms are loan-words from languages other than English — from French: *lacrosse, aboideau, joual, prairie, portage, syne*; from Eskimo: *mukluk, igloo, komatik, kayak, pingo, oomiak*; from sundry Indian languages: *nitchie, pemmican, potlatch, wapiti, shaganappi, kokanee, wavey*.

Many Canadianisms are characteristic of certain regions — the Maritimes: *bogan, shiretown, togue, fiddlehead, longlinerman*; Ontario: *firereels, dew worm, concession road, police village, hydro*; the Prairie Provinces: *grid road, graduand, pothole, bluff* ("a stand of trees"); British Columbia: *salt chuck, skookum, steelhead, Siwash*; the Northland: *bush line, bombardier, rampike, cheechako, babiche*.

Hundreds of Canadian words fall into the category of animal and plant names: *carcajou, malemute, whistler; Arctic char, capelin, cisco, splake; whisky-jack, Canada goose, venison bird; hackmatack, Manitoba maple, Nootka fir; fameuse, menominee, bakeapple, snow apple*.

For many terms there are special Canadian significations: *reeve, warden, riding, Confederation, separate school, Mountie, height of land, NDPers, Grit, MLA*. From the sports field come a number of contributions, especially from hockey and a game we used to call *rugby,* a term now almost displaced by the American term *football: puck, boards, blueline, cushion; snap, flying wing, rouge*. And in the same area there are a number of slang terms that merit mention: *homebrew, import, rink rat*.

In pronunciation, as in vocabulary, Canadians are neither American nor British, though they have much in common with both. Although most Canadians pronounce *docile* and *textile* to rhyme with *mile,* as the British do, it is probable that most pronounce *fertile* and *missile* to rhyme with *hurtle* and *missal,* as the Americans do. And no doubt Canadians pronounce some words in a way that is typically Canadian. Most of us, for example, would describe the color of a soldier's uniform as *khaki,* pronounced [karki].* Yet dictionaries seldom recognize this Canadianism. Most Americans say [kæki], while the British say [kɑːkɪ]. In Canada, many people put flowers in a vase, pronounced [vez]; most Americans use a [ves] and the British a [vɑz]. To be sure, quite a number of Canadians say something like [vɑz], especially if the vase is Ming.

If we accept imported British and American dictionaries as our authority, such pronunciations as [karki] and [vez] are unacceptable. But surely the true test of correctness for Canadians should be the usage of the educated natives of Canada. In Canada, [karki] is certainly an acceptable variant; and what goes for this word almost certainly goes for many others. Here are some examples of pronunciations widely heard among educated Canadians; not all of them are recorded in our imported dictionaries: *absolve* [əbzɑlv], *arctic* [artɪk], *chassis* [tʃæsi], *culinary* [kʌləneri], *evil* [ivəl], *finale* [fənæli], *fungi* [fʌngi], *jackal* [dʒækəl], *longitude* [laŋgətud], *official* [ofɪʃəl], *opinion* [opɪnjən], *placate* [plæket], *plenary* [plenəri], *prestige* [prestidʒ], *resources* [rəzɔrsɪz], *senile* [senaɪl], *species* [spisiz].

All of these forms are used regularly by educated Canadians in large numbers. Who can deny that [rəzɔrsɪz] and [spisiz] are more often heard at all levels of Canadian society than [spiʃiz] and [risɔrsɪz], the pronunciations indicated in most dictionaries? Surely, when the evidence of usage justifies it, pronunciations such as these should be entered as variants in any dictionary intended to reflect Canadian speech.

Another of the functions of the dictionary is to record the spellings used by the educated people of the community. In spelling, as in vocabulary and pronunciation, Canadian usage is influenced by the practice of both Americans and British. It should, however, be pointed out that over the language as a whole, British, American, and Canadian practices differ little; all of us are saddled with a similar burden.

Nevertheless, in the areas where British and American habits do differ, Canadian usage is far from uniform. Until recent years, British forms have predominated in most instances, for example in *axe, centre,* and *colour,* in spite of the obvious practical advantages of the American forms: *ax, center,* and *color.* In some cases, however, American spellings have long since asserted themselves to the virtual exclusion of the corresponding British forms, as in *connection, curb, jail, peddler, recognize* for *connexion, kerb, gaol, pedlar, recognise.*

In recent years there have been indications that American spellings are becoming more commonly used in Canada. Many have, for example, been adopted by Canadian newspapers, especially those in the larger centres, and by Canadian magazine and book publishers. Young people seem to use such spellings as *honor, center,* and *program* more freely than was formerly the case, the implication being that at least some American forms are accepted as proper in many Canadian schools. For the most part, Canadians respond to these variants with equal ease.

—by permission of Gage Educational Publishing Ltd.

*For the symbols of the International Phonetic Alphabet, see the Table of English Spellings on p. xxvi.

THE PLAN OF THIS DICTIONARY

The following explanatory material deals with the different kinds of information given in this dictionary and with their arrangement within each entry. A careful reading of the thirteen items discussed below, and of the essays on **Pronunciations, Level and Style Labels, Etymologies,** and **Synonyms** that begin on page xix, will help the reader use this dictionary effectively. Items 1–13 are listed in roughly the same order in which the information they describe appears in most individual entries:

1. The Main Entry
2. Pronunciations
3. Parts of Speech
4. Inflected Forms
5. Definitions
6. Restrictive Labels
7. Collateral Adjectives
8. Variant Forms
9. Cross-references
10. Etymologies
11. Run-on Derivatives
12. Usage Notes
13. Synonyms and Antonyms
14. Geographical Entries

1. The Main Entry

The main entry word or words have been printed in large, boldface type, set slightly into the left-hand margin so as to be easily found. General vocabulary words and phrases, prefixes and suffixes, foreign terms, biographical and geographical entries, etc., are arranged in one alphabetic list. Thus, the entry for **Bridge of Sighs** follows **bridgehead** and precedes **Bridgeport.** When both capitalized and uncapitalized forms are entered, of a word otherwise spelled the same, the uncapitalized form or forms precede. Thus, the entry for **chesterfield** precedes that for **Chesterfield, Lord.** Words identical in spelling but different in meaning and origin are separately entered and differentiated by a superior figure, as **pink**^{1} (color), **pink**^{2} (stab), **pink**^{3} (sailing vessel), **pink**^{4} (fade).

A center period is used to indicate division in main entry words, as **ad·jec·ti·val.** In other boldface entries, such as run-on derivatives and variant forms, the center period is eliminated wherever the primary and secondary syllable stresses are marked, as **ad′jec·ti′·val·ly.** Phrasal entries, such as **high fashion,** are not divided when the elements are individually entered elsewhere.

2. Pronunciations

Pronunciations are shown in parentheses immediately following the boldface main entry, as **di·chot·o·my** (dī·kot′ə·mē). The pronunciation system used in this dictionary utilizes, with a few exceptions, the letters of the alphabet, combined with certain standard diacritical marks, such as the macron for the so-called "long vowels" (ā, ē, ī, ō, yoō). The "short vowels" have no diacritical marks. The breve is retained in the one symbol (oŏ), the vowel in *book*, to avoid confusion with the vowel in *pool*, for which the macron is used (ōō). The dieresis is used for one symbol (ä), and the circumflex for three (â, ô, û). The schwa (ə) is used for the unstressed neutral vowel, however spelled. This pronunciation key is based on phonemic principles to the extent that each symbol represents a single sound or closely associated cluster of sounds, and no sound is transcribed with more than one symbol.

The pronunciation key appears in full on p. xxiv and inside the front cover; an abbreviated key is given at the foot of every odd-numbered page in the main vocabulary section. For a fuller discussion of the treatment given pronunciation in this dictionary, see p. xix.

3. Parts of Speech

These are shown in italics following the pronunciation for main entries, and are abbreviated as follows: *n.* (noun), *v.* (verb), *pron.* (pronoun), *adj.* (adjective), *adv.* (adverb), *prep.* (preposition), *conj.* (conjunction), *interj.* (interjection). When more than one part of speech is entered under a main entry, the additional designations are run in and preceded by a boldface dash, as **cor·ner** (kôr′nər) *n.* . . . — *v.t.* . . . — *v.i.* . . . — *adj.* . . . .

Verbs used transitively are identified as *v.t.,* those intransitively as *v.i.*; those used both transitively and intransitively in all senses are designated *v.t. & v.i.*

4. Inflected Forms

These include the past tense, past participle, and present participle of verbs, the plural of nouns, and the comparative and superlative of adjectives and adverbs. Inflected forms are entered wherever there is some irregularity in spelling or form. They are shown in boldface type, with syllabication, immediately after the part-of-speech designation. Only the syllable affected is shown, unless ambiguity may occur, as **com·pute** (kəm·pyōōt′) *v.t. & v.i.* **·put·ed, ·put·ing.** An inflected form that requires pronunciation or is alphabetically distant from the main entry will also be separately entered and pronounced in its proper vocabulary place.

Principal parts of verbs The order in which the principal parts are shown is past tense, past participle, and present participle, as **come** (kum) *v.i.* **came, come, com·ing.** Where the past tense and past participle are identical, only two forms are entered, as **bake** (bāk) *v.* **baked, bak·ing.** When alternative forms are given, the first form indicated is usually the one preferred, as **grov·el** (gruv′əl, grov′-) *v.i.* **grov·eled** or **·elled, grov·el·ing** or **·el·ling.** Principal parts entirely regular in formation — those that add *-ed* and *-ing* directly to the infinitive without spelling modification — are not shown.

Plurals of nouns Irregular forms are here preceded by the designation *pl.,* as **a·lum·nus** (ə·lum′nəs) *n. pl.* **·ni** (-nī); **co·dex** (kō′deks) *n. pl.* **co·di·ces** (kō′də·sēz, kod′ə-); **deer** (dir) *n. pl.* **deer.** When alternative

xvii

plurals are given, the first shown is the preferred form, as **buf·fa·lo** (buf'ə·lō) *n. pl.* **·loes** or **·los; chrys·a·lis** (kris'ə·lis) *n. pl.* **chrys·a·lis·es** or **chry·sal·i·des** (kri·sal'ə·dēz).

Comparison of adjectives and adverbs The comparatives and superlatives of adjectives and adverbs are shown immediately after the part of speech when there is some spelling modification or a complete change of form, as **mer·ry** (mer'ē) *adj.* **·ri·er, ·ri·est; bad¹** (bad) *adj.* **worse, worst; well²** (wel) *adv.* **bet·ter, best.**

5. Definitions

In entries for words having several senses, the definition appearing first is the one most frequently used. Successive definitions are listed, wherever possible, in order of declining frequency of use rather than according to semantic evolution. Each such definition is distinguished by a boldface numeral, the numbering starting anew after each part-of-speech designation when more than one sense follows. Closely related meanings, especially those within a specific field or area of study, are defined under the same number and set apart by boldface letters.

6. Restrictive Labels

No restrictive label is required for those general-purpose words and meanings, usable in any context, which make up the bulk of the English language as it is spoken and written throughout the world. Words or particular senses of words, however, which have any restriction of use are labeled. A number of different types of labels are used in this dictionary to indicate where, by whom, or in what context a particular word or expression is most commonly used. For a full discussion of **Level and Style Labels,** including the labels *Informal, Dial.* (for *dialectal*), *Slang,* and *Illit.* (for *illiterate*), see p. xx. The following are other types of labels found in this dictionary:

Currency Labels Both standard and nonstandard words may be in less than general currency. If these are included they are labeled *Rare, Archaic,* or *Obs.* (obsolete). (See the definitions of these words in the body of the dictionary.)

Locality Labels These identify the geographical region of the English-speaking world in which a word or meaning, either standard or nonstandard, is used exclusively or more characteristically than it is in other regions. (For example, *elevator* is labeled *U.S.,* while the synonymous *lift* is labeled *Brit.*)

Field Labels These identify the field of learning or of activity in which a word or sense belongs. (Some common examples are *Bot., Chem., Mil., Photog.* — see the list of abbreviations.) Because of the frequent overlapping between fields, however, these labels can be applied only broadly.

Foreign-language Labels These identify the source of words or phrases not fully naturalized into English. Because these retain the foreign spelling and pronunciation, though used in English context, they should be italicized when written. (Examples are *joie de vivre* labeled *French, Weltschmerz* labeled *German.*)

7. Collateral Adjectives

Because of extensive borrowing in English from Norman French and Medieval Latin, we find a good many English nouns which have adjectives closely connected with them in meaning, but not in form, such as *arm* and *brachial, horse* and *equine, neck* and *cervical,*

winter and *hibernal, day* and *diurnal,* etc. These functionally related adjectives are defined in this dictionary in their alphabetic place, but as an added convenience many of them are also shown with their associated nouns. Collateral adjectives follow the sense or senses of the noun to which they apply, and are introduced with a diamond symbol:

arm (ärm)   *n.* **1.** *Anat.* **a** The upper limb of the human body.... ◆ Collateral adjective: *brachial.*

8. Variant Forms

Some words have more than one standard spelling or form, as *center, centre; algebraic, algebraical.* Sometimes, completely different forms have the same meaning, as *doom palm* and *gingerbread tree.* These variants are listed in two ways: (1) When the variant form is alphabetically close to the commoner form, it is entered with the main entry in boldface type, syllabicated, stressed, and, where necessary, pronounced; (2) When the variant is alphabetically distant, it is shown in italic print under the main entry, and is also listed in its proper alphabetic place with a cross-reference to the main entry.

bach·e·lor (bach'ə·lər, bach'lər)   *n.* .... **3.** A young knight serving under another's banner: also **bach'e·lor-at-arms'** .... **5.** A young male fur seal kept from the breeding grounds by the older males: also called *hollus-chick* ....

Forms that have some restricted usage are labeled accordingly, as **hon·or** .... Also *Brit.* **hon'our.**

9. Cross-references

Cross-references are directions to see another entry for additional information. The entry to be sought is generally indicated in small capital letters, as **car·a·cul** ... See KARAKUL; **cor·po·ra** ... Plural of CORPUS; **Old English** See under ENGLISH.

Some entries are defined by citing another form:

Paraguay tea Maté.
mat·zoon ... *n.* Yogurt.
sour gum The black gum (which see).

Complete information will be found under the word or term used in the definition.

Cross-references are also used to indicate where more information may be found, or when an important semantic distinction might otherwise be missed, as **aquaplane** ... Compare SURFBOARD; **atom** .... **2.** .... See ATOMIC STRUCTURE.

For information about the system of cross-referencing used in the etymologies, see pp. xxi–xxii.

10. Etymologies

Etymologies are given in brackets at the end of each entry. For a full discussion of the treatment given etymology in this dictionary, see p. xxi.

11. Run-on Derivatives

Words that are actually or apparently derived from other words by the addition or replacement of a suffix, and whose sense can be inferred from the meaning of the main word, are run on, in smaller boldface type, at the end of the appropriate main entries. The run-on entries are preceded by a heavy dash and followed by a part-of-speech designation. They are syllabicated and stressed, and, when necessary, a full or partial pronunciation is indicated:

in·sip·id (in·sip'id) *adj.* .... — **in·si·pid·i·ty** (in'si·pid'ə·tē), **in·sip'id·ness** *n.* — **in·sip'id·ly** *adv.*

12. Usage Notes

Special points of grammar and idiom, when essential to correct usage, are included, following a colon, after the particular sense of a word to which they apply, as **anx·ious** . . . **3.** Intent; eagerly desirous; solicitous: with *for* or the infinitive: *anxious* for success; *anxious* to succeed. . . . More extensive notes consisting of supplementary information on grammar, accepted usage, the relative status of variant forms, etc., are entered at the end of the relevant entries and prefaced with the symbol ◆. Examples may be found under the entries **Asiatic, gotten,** and **me.**

13. Synonyms and Antonyms

Extended discussions of the differentiation in shades of meaning within a group of related words are given at the end of relevant entries in paragraphed form. They are introduced by the abbreviation **Syn.** Since a word may have distinct synonyms for each of several senses, the discussions are numbered, where necessary, to accord with the numbering of relevant definitions in the preceding entry. In addition to the discussions, lists of synonyms and antonyms are entered in cases where the distinctions between the words in question are easily ascertained from the definitions. For a full discussion of the treatment given synonyms in this dictionary, see p. xxii.

14. Geographical Entries

Population figures for places in the United States are based on the 1970 census, and those for Canada on the 1971 census. Population figures for foreign places are dated to show the time of census or estimate.

Pronunciations by James B. McMillan

A pronunciation is correct when it is normally and unaffectedly used by cultivated people. Strictly, any pronunciation is correct when it serves the purposes of communication and does not call unfavorable attention to the speaker, but the user of a desk dictionary does not need or expect to find every pronunciation of every word that may be heard in the smallest, most isolated communities. He expects to find the pronunciations that he can use comfortably before educated audiences.

We do not have in the English-speaking world a standard of pronunciation like the standard specimens of meters, liters, feet, and gallons that national bureaus of standards keep to preserve and enforce uniformity. It would be technically simple to have a professional speaker record on magnetic tape his pronunciation of every word in a dictionary and to store the tapes in libraries where they could be heard, even in distant cities, by dialing the telephone number of a computer that would select and play back the pronunciation of any desired word. But choosing the model speaker would not be simple. Should he pronounce *forest* as it sounds in Boston? Or Chicago? Or Atlanta? Or Spokane? If he pronounced *dew* and *do* differently, would educated people who pronounce the two words alike change to conform? Or if he pronounced both (dōō), would educated people who distinguish the two words be willing to give up their distinction? Simple inanimate quart jars and foot rulers can easily be taken to a government bureau and compared with a standard measure, but pronunciations are articulations of sounds by individual human vocal organs, with all the diversity of human beings. One standard of correctness is impractical, unenforceable, impossible.

Correctness in pronunciation is so flexible and pronunciations are so varied that a desk dictionary cannot list nearly all the acceptable forms of even common words; for this reason the absence of a pronunciation, for example *said* as (sād), rhyming with *laid*, does not mean that the pronunciation is necessarily "incorrect," but simply that there is not space to record every minority practice. The editors do not include (bûr′ē) for *bury* (rhyming with *hurry*) because they have heard it very rarely, and not usually in cultivated speech. On the other hand, when a pronunciation is listed the dictionary user can be confident that the pronunciation is in actual use among educated people. Disagreements that arise because two people do not pronounce the key words alike cannot be settled; the fact that every user has to interpret the pronunciation symbols in terms of his own pronunciation of the key words makes each one, in a sense, his own standard.

Because words are listed in a dictionary as separate items, not as segments of a flow of speech, the pronunciations given are for words pronounced in isolation; for example the pronunciation (fāt) is what one would say in answering "How do you pronounce the word spelled *f-e-t-e*?" In the stream of speech, many words, particularly pronouns, articles, and auxiliaries, occur in shortened or changed form when they are weakly stressed. Thus the words (tel), (him), (hē), (haz), (tōō), (sē), (hûr) may appear in sentence form as (tel·im·ē·has·tə·sē·ər). The changed pronunciations that actual utterance produces are not normally listed.

Syllabication in pronunciation follows, in general, the breaks heard in speech, rather than the conventional division of the boldface entry, as **hid·ing** (hī′ding), **lat·er** (lā′tər), **of·fi·cial** (ə·fish′əl). Syllable boundaries are sometimes impossible to set with certainty and are sometimes variable. Thus words like **met·ric** (met′rik) and **cad·re** (kad′rē) are divided between the consonants, although many people pronounce both consonants in the second syllable (me′trik) and (ka′drē), as the contrast between *metric* and *met Rick* will show.

Three levels of stress are indicated in the pronunciations. Syllables with weakest stress are not marked; every word with two or more syllables has one primary stress marked, as *editor* (ed′it·ər); and words with three or more syllables frequently have a secondary stress marked by a light symbol, as *acceleration* (ak·sel′ə·rā′shən), or a secondary stress indicated simply by a vowel, as in the final syllable of *ameliorate* (ə·mēl′yə·rāt). These three levels correspond to the primary, tertiary (*not* secondary), and weak levels in the four-stress system commonly used by linguists. The secondary level of the four-stress system is not used here because it occurs only in phrases or other word groups, not in single words.

Because a dictionary records and reports the pronunciations of educated people, and all educated people do not pronounce identically, a dictionary must list variant forms of thousands of words. When two or more pronunciations are indicated for a word, the one that the editors believe most frequent in the northern and western sections of the United States is listed first, but other pronunciations are equally reputable. (The dictionary does not list socially substandard pronunciations, no matter how common they may be.)

Pronunciation differences are of seven principal kinds:

(1) Different consonants may be used in the same word; e.g. some people pronounce *exit* (ek′sit), others (eg′zit); some pronounce *blouse* (blous), others (blouz).

(2) Different vowels may be used in the same word; e.g. for some people the word *lever* rhymes with *clever* (klev′ər), for others it rhymes with *beaver* (bē′vər); the first syllable of *economics* may rhyme with *peck* (ek·ə·nom′iks) or with *peak* (ē·kə·nom′iks).

(3) A word may have different syllables stressed; e.g. *altimeter* (al·tim′ə·tər) or (al′tə·mē·tər), and *abdomen* (ab′də·mən) or (ab·dō′mən).

(4) The same consonant may be used in a word, but it may be articulated very differently; e.g. the /t/* in *metal*, or *writer*, or *winter*, or *veddy*, or the /r/ in *very* (sometimes humorously written *veddy*).

*The symbols printed between virgules represent phonemes.

(5) The same vowel may be used in a word, but it may be articulated very differently; e.g. the /ô/ in *raw*, the /ou/ in *house*, the /ī/ in *ice*, and the /ä/ in *park*, which have wide regional variations.

(6) Although all dialects of American English seem to have the same twenty-four consonants, some have fewer vowels than others; e.g., the contrasts made in some regions between *morning* and *mourning*, *cot* and *caught*, *burred* and *bird*, and *Cary*, *Kerry*, and *Carrie* are not made in other regions.

(7) The same vowel or consonant may not occur in the same positions in all varieties; e.g., some speakers pronounce /y/ before /o͞o/ in *cute* (kyo͞ot) but not in *new* (no͞o) or *due* (do͞o) or *tune* (to͞on), while others of equal education pronounce these words (nyo͞o), (dyo͞o), and (tyo͞on). Some speakers have /zh/ normally between vowels, as in *pleasure* (plezh'ər) and *vision* (vizh'ən) but not at the ends of words, so that *garage* is both (gə·räzh') and (gə·räj'), and *beige* is both (bāzh) and (bāj).

Some differences in pronunciation can be correlated with geography and others are purely personal in nature. No dictionary can pick one pronunciation of *dog*, or *room*, or *greasy*, or *aunt*, or *water* and ignore other pronunciations of equal repute. The principal variants must be acknowledged. For rare words, such as terms in the arts and sciences that are not learned vernacularly, analogy and the pattern of source languages provide the pronunciations listed.

Two methods of providing variants are used, (1) multiple pronunciations, as *fog* (fog, fôg), and (2) variable symbols keyed to common words, such as /â/ as in *dare, fair*; it is assumed that when a dictionary user looks up *parterre* and finds (pär·târ') he will pronounce the first syllable to rhyme with *bar* and the second syllable to rhyme with *dare, air*, since /ä/ is keyed to the word *father*, and /â/ is keyed to the words *dare, air*. The dictionary does not tell the user how to pronounce the key words, assuming that they represent stable basic patterns.

When a variant pronunciation differs only in part from the first pronunciation recorded, only the differing syllable or syllables are shown, provided there is no possibility of misinterpretation, as **eq·ua·bil·i·ty** (ek'·wə·bil'ə·tē, ē'kwə-).

Phrasal entries of two or more words are not pronounced if the individual elements are separately entered in proper alphabetic place.

Sometimes a word will differ in its pronunciation depending on its use as a noun, verb, etc., or in some particular sense. The differing pronunciations are shown immediately after the entry word, with the applications clearly indicated, as follows:

ad·dress (ə·dres'; *for n. defs. 2, 3, also* ad'res)
re·ject (*v.* ri·jekt'; *n.* rē'jekt)

A few foreign words occur with sufficient frequency in English to require dictionary entry; as their use increases they usually become adapted to English pronunciation patterns. For the dictionary user who speaks the language from which a word is imported, no pronunciation is necessary; he recognizes the word or can pronounce it from his knowledge of the spelling of the foreign language. However, the dictionary user who does not speak the foreign language may wish to pronounce a word in a recognizable approximation of its native form. Such words are respelled with the English vowels and consonants that are closest to the foreign phonemes, plus a handful of symbols for French and German sounds that have no counterparts in English. Thus the French word *feuilleton* is respelled (fœ·yə·tôn'), which warns that non-English vowels occur in the first and last syllables and that there is no consonant /n/ at the end. It is assumed that the /f/, /y/, and /t/ will be reasonably similar to the corresponding (but not identical) French consonants, and that the stress on the last syllable will be lighter than English primary stress.

Level and Style Labels by Frederic G. Cassidy

The language is often thought of as existing on two "levels of usage," the standard and the nonstandard. This distinction rests on the fact that, though there is nothing intrinsically higher or lower, better or worse in one word than in another *considered as words* (language signals), every speech community nevertheless responds more or less favorably toward individual words and senses on the basis of association, habit, imposed value judgments, and the like. The language of cultivation, being that normally used by the leading part of the community, and that most widely understood within the English-speaking world, has high prestige and is considered to be of the "upper" level. This is *Standard English*. In contrast, the language of limited, local, or uncultivated use is nonstandard and of "lower" level. The following scheme represents the relative positions of various types of discourse and the corresponding labels used in this dictionary.

	Throughout the English-speaking world (No label)
	Characteristic of a national division of English
Standard	Labels: *U.S., Brit., Scot., Austral.*, etc.
English	Characteristic of a broad region of a national division
	Labels: *Southern U.S., SW U.S.*, etc.
	Characteristic of general informal use
	Label: *Informal*
	Used within a small geographical area, and often rural and traditional
	Label: *Dial.*
	Used to express a humorous, racy, and irreverent attitude, often within a particular group
Nonstandard	Label: *Slang*
English	Used within a group in connection with a common activity, trade, or profession (No label or a field label)
	Used by the least educated, and considered incorrect by most users of Standard English
	Label: *Illit.*

The dictionary concentrates on standard words and meanings; only those nonstandard ones are included which have wide currency or which deserve notice for some other reason (e.g., their relationship to standard words). Lines of distinction cannot always be sharply drawn between the various types of nonstandard words or meanings. It is sometimes necessary also to combine the labels (e.g., *Brit. Dial., U.S. Slang*) for precise discriminations.

In addition, since the response to words depends in part upon the stylistic context in which they are used, the dictionary maker must take this response into consideration in applying labels. Two distinct styles are generally recognized: Formal and Informal.*

Formal style is that appropriate to all public and serious expression; to spoken use in legislative assemblies, in courts, in the pulpit; to "belles lettres" or artistic literature; to legal and scientific writing. Because its users belong to the cultivated and literate part of the public it tends to be more deliberate, precise, discriminating, and orderly than the casual usage normal to everyday discourse, even that carried on by this same cultivated group.

Informal style, that employed by most people a great part of the time in both speaking and writing, differs from the formal in being less consciously controlled, less precise, less complex and compact, less careful in diction — though quite acceptable within its sphere, and more appropriate to relaxed situations than formal style would be.

*The label *Colloq.* (colloquial — see its definition in the body of the dictionary) is now so widely misunderstood by the public as to be no longer serviceable and is therefore not used in this dictionary.

In pronunciation the formal style is more controlled, with conscious use of prosodic features (pitch, pause, stress) and with clear articulation and syllabication (though without restressing, spelling-pronunciation, or other distortions). In grammar it is conservative; in sentence form it has more variety and range than everyday discourse has. Its vocabulary is far broader and richer, demanding sharper distinctions and more sensitive choice. In overall structure it is orderly, consicously articulated, intellectually directed.

In pronunciation the informal style is easy, relaxed; it admits a degree of slurring and ellipsis, though not to the point of becoming unclear. It makes fuller use of voice qualifiers (indicating emotional attitudes) than does formal style; it is therefore far more personal. In grammar it is less conservative, reflecting contemporary tendencies in the development of the language. In sentence form it is less complex and varied, and in vocabulary less discriminating, than is formal style: it experiments with neologisms, slang, and the livelier words of current vogue. It is given to abbreviation and contraction. In overall structure it is likely to be casual, not closely knit, additive rather than integral.

New scientific and literary words are apt to enter the sphere of standard usage at once; new popular words, by contrast, tend to remain nonstandard for a time — perhaps always; but they may and sometimes do rapidly gain status and enter the standard sphere.

Since "formal" and "informal" properly describe *styles* of discourse, the application of one of these terms to an individual word or meaning indicates only that such an item is appropriate to the one style or the other. If a word of one style is employed in a context not its own, it will give some effect of its own style to that context. Further, since no meaning is irrevocably fixed, the connotation of a word repeatedly used in a stylistic context not its own may change.

A word or meaning labeled *Informal* is therefore one which, though as well known as any other standard one, is less acceptable (i.e., less accepted at any given time) for formal use than for informal. The actual usage of cultivated writers and speakers is the only valid test of such status. Words not labeled are appropriate to formal use.

The "levels" and "styles" do not coincide exactly. Their relationship may best be expressed by the following diagram, in which the sphere of Standard English is represented by a circle, the nonstandard lying outside it. The circle is broken to indicate that nonstandard usages sometimes enter and become standard, and that formerly standard words also drop out into nonstandard usage or disappear altogether. Elliptical lines to left and right, drawn through the circle of Standard English, set off those parts that are appropriate respectively to formal and informal style. The Common Core comprises those words and senses which are used in all types of English.

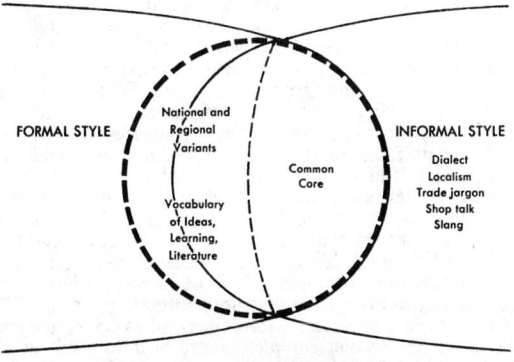

THE CIRCLE OF STANDARD ENGLISH

Distinctions within the levels of language can be made nowadays with a considerable degree of objectivity. Distinctions of style, on the other hand, are partly esthetic and subjective. In every case an accurate application of labels must rest on the investigation of the situations in which any word or sense is actually used, the kind of people who do or do not use it, and the kind of response (apart from that of its denotative meaning) which it is likely to elicit in any linguistic community. Ultimately, however, it must also depend to some extent upon the judgment of the lexicographer.

Etymologies by Albert H. Marckwardt

Etymology is the systematic study of word origins, or in a particular sense the facts relating to the derivation or formation of a word. To illustrate, *etymology* is a borrowing of French *étymologie*, which developed from Latin *etymologia*, itself a borrowing from the Greek. The Greek form may be divided into two parts, *etymon* a form of the adjective "true" and *logos* "word, study, account." Thus we have the elements which entered into the formation of this word and the languages through which it passed into English.

The etymology of a word is given after the definition. It appears in square brackets, and precedes the boldface listing of derivative forms. The following three symbols are used: < "derived from"; + "and" or "combined with"; ? "possible." Abbreviations used in the etymologies are given in the list on p. xxv and inside the back cover.

Native words that were present in the earliest period of the language (450–1050) are shown in their Old English form.

bed·rid·den ... [Earlier *bedrid* < OE *bedrida* < *bed* bed + *rida* rider]

For borrowed words, the immediate source is given first, followed by those intermediate forms and languages which show significant changes.

pi·ra·nha ... [< Pg. (Brazilian) < Tupi, toothed fish < *piro* fish + *sainha* tooth]

If the specific language of origin cannot be determined but the general provenance is known, a linguistic family or a geographical area is indicated as the source.

gar·den ... [< AF *gardin* < Gmc.]
ba·nan·a ... [< Sp. < native African name]

Words of unknown or uncertain origin are so marked. If there is a Middle English form for a word of obscure origin, it is cited. Even though the origin of a word cannot be determined, it is sometimes possible to give cognate forms from related languages. Be careful to note the difference between the mark < which means "derived from" and the abbreviation *cf.* which indicates a cognate relationship but not a derivation.

boy ... [ME *boi*; origin unknown]
gloat ... [Cf. ON *glotta* to grin]

English has many pairs or sets of words which have developed from the same ultimate source word either within English itself or in some other language. These are treated in two different ways in the etymologies.

1. When two or more words may be traced back to the same primitive root. This is the earliest type of divergence, often having occurred before there was a common recorded form for the words in question. Such cognates are indicated by the phrase "Akin to ..."

tongue ... [OE *tunge*. Akin to LANGUAGE.]
lan·guage ... [< OF *langage* < *langue* tongue < L *lingua* tongue, language. Akin to TONGUE.]

2. When two or more words have entered English through different intermediate languages or dialects but from an ultimate source word. The etymologies of such words will show a common form, indicating the point at which the divergence of form and/or meaning first occurred and the intermediate forms needed to show clearly the development of the modern words. Pairs or sets of words of this type are called "doublets."

ci·pher... [< OF *cyfre* < Arabic *sifr*. Doublet of ZERO.]
ze·ro... [< F *zéro* < Ital. *zero* < Arabic *sifr*. Doublet of CIPHER.]

In order to avoid repetition and to present as much information as possible within a limited space, cross-references are used liberally in the etymological treatment. They are indicated by small capital letters and direct attention to main entries where more detailed information may be found.

de·cep·tion... [< L *deceptio, -onis* < *decipere*. See DECEIVE.]
has·sle... [? < HAGGLE + TUSSLE]

The etymologies of words representing various types of combinations of free and bound forms (*wildcat, prejudge, goodness*) may be found under the main entries for *wild, cat; pre-, judge; good, -ness*. In other combined forms where the component parts are likely not to be easily recognized, the breakdown is made in the form of cross-references to the source of additional information.

mor·phol·o·gy... [< MORPHO- + -LOGY]
az·ine... [< AZ- + -INE²]

Etymologies of a somewhat unusual character, especially those connecting words with particular people, places, or events are recorded with additional notes explaining the historic background of the word. For examples of this see *buncombe, gerrymander, millinery, knickerbocker*. Acronyms and blends are shown by placing the portions of the source words which have survived in the new formation in distinctive type. Back formations and instances of folk etymology are so labeled. See *NATO, luscious, legislate, isinglass*.

A knowledge of etymology can be useful in many ways. If, for example, those words which have come into English from any one language are considered as a group, they often reveal much about the nature of the cultural impact of that language and the people who speak it upon English. The fact that so many of our mineralogical terms come from German suggests the preeminence of that nation in the development of the science and our indebtedness to its scientists. The same might be said with respect to the Italian origin of our musical terminology. The common and intimate character of many of the Scandinavian borrowings in English tells us something of the nature of the relationship between the Norse and the English during the tenth and eleventh centuries.

It may also be true that in certain instances a knowledge of the etymology of a word may give the individual speaker or writer a surer sense of its meaning and use. A word like *supercilious* would seem, at least, to be more vivid to someone who can connect it with raised eyebrows than to the person for whom it is merely a polysyllable with a general implication of superiority of attitude. The word *equinox* will be employed with a greater feeling of certainty by one who connects the component parts of the word with the simple facts behind them.

A note of warning is called for, however. Etymology, informative and interesting though it may be, is not a valid criterion of present meaning or determiner of use. Meaning is determined by present usage; the meanings assigned to the words included in this dictionary were determined by a careful and systematic examination of their use in actual context.

The fact that *dilapidated* contains a form of *lapis* "stone" does not signify that this word can be applied only to stone structures. The word *etymology* itself is an excellent illustration of this point. Despite the fact that its first element is the neuter form of *etymos* "true," the etymology of a word is not the sole determiner of a single "true" or correct meaning, however much light it may shed upon aspects of its significance.

Synonyms by S. I. Hayakawa

The English language is unusually rich in synonyms and near-synonyms. This richness is due to the fact that the vocabulary of English, a language especially hospitable to loan-words, is drawn from many sources. The vocabulary of Anglo-Saxon, already containing loan-words from Celtic, Latin, and Scandinavian, was just about doubled after the Norman Conquest by borrowings from French, to form the Middle English vocabulary. From the sixteenth century on, with the revival of classical learning, there was vast borrowing from Latin and Greek. Wherever English-speaking people have subsequently gone, in war, travel, or colonization, they have added new words to the language, and they continue to do so today. Thus, one may give a *speech* or *talk* (Anglo-Saxon words), a *lecture* or *address* or *harangue* (French words), an *oration* (Latin), or a *homily* (Greek). One may live on a wide and open *plain* (Old French), *steppe* (Russian), *prairie* (French), *tundra* (Lapp), *pampas* (South American Indian), or *savanna* (Spanish). A person may adhere to a *teaching* (Anglo-Saxon), a *doctrine* (French), a *tenet* (Latin), a *dogma* (Greek). Some words were borrowed more than once, at different times and in different forms, like *warden* and *warranty* (Norman French) as compared with *guardian* and *guarantee* (Central French); like *loyal* and *legal, royal* and *regal, fancy* and *fantasy, count* and *compute, gentle* and *genteel, priest* and *presbyter*. Some of these "doublets" are alike in meaning, some are quite different.

Often the borrowings were in a strict sense unnecessary; many that remain today are simply relics of the sixteenth-century fad of embellishing one's speech and writing with Latinisms. Certainly it is possible to talk about *kissing* without using the word *osculatory*, about *today* without *hodiernal*, about *walking* without *gressorial*. Nevertheless, the availability of foreign and learned vocabularies, even if they partly duplicate the native vocabulary, is a tremendous asset to any language. An advanced civilization needs, in addition to a language of everyday life (from which emerges the language of poetry), a language for law and social organization and the discussion of policy, and an even more abstract language for scientific and philosophical discourse. These many distinct needs are more easily met by a language that has had a long history of borrowing than by a language (like Gaelic) whose speakers insist on a fanatical "purity" of vocabulary, such as can only result in a poverty of things to talk about.

Are there any *exact* synonyms? The general semanticists, who assert that "no word ever has exactly the same meaning twice," would seem to assert that a word cannot even be synonymous with itself. What they mean is that the word *apple*, for example, cannot be applied twice to *exactly* the same referent, because every apple is different from every other apple, and because each apple is itself changing from moment to moment. However, in a dictionary we are concerned not so much with referents as with *verbal* equivalences: what word or phrase or circumlocution can serve as an equivalent for the word defined. Thus, *entire* means "having no part missing; whole; complete." Insofar as certain words can be substituted for others without affecting the meaning of a sentence, one can indeed speak of exact synonyms. "The *entire (whole, complete)* cast was invited to the party." The test for exact synonymy, then, is interchangeability. Despite Hilaire Belloc's haughty distinction, "what Anglo-Saxons call a *foreword*, but gentlemen a *preface*," these terms are also genuinely interchangeable in most contexts. But interchangeability in certain contexts does not mean interchangeability in all. "The cast is now *complete*" — not *whole*, or *entire*. A skirmish may be a *preface* to a battle, but not a *foreword*.

Hence interchangeability is by no means the whole story on synonyms. What are treated as synonyms in this dictionary are more often words that point to the same facts but convey different attitudes on the part of the speaker. An individual's regard for himself may be termed *egotism*, *conceit*, or *self-esteem*, depending on whether or not the speaker approves of it. Other synonyms point to similar actions or events, but in different contexts or applications: a *journey* is usually by land, a *voyage* by water; a short journey, whether by land or water, is a *trip*; an *excursion* is a short trip (usually for pleasure) from which one soon returns to a starting point; a military excursion is a *sortie*. We *accompany* our equals, *attend* those whom we serve, *conduct* those whom we guide, *escort* those whom we protect, except for merchant ships, which we *convoy*. It would be simpler if *go with* could be used in all these contexts. But the language would be infinitely poorer if these shades of meaning, expressive of innumerable nuances of human relationships, attitudes, and perceptions, were to be lost.

Occupational and regional differences also account for many synonyms. Is a *loch* a *lake*? Is an *arroyo* a *dry wash*? Is a *billabong* the same as an *oxbow*? What is the difference between the *headmaster* of a school and a *principal*, between a *dining room* and a *mess*, between being *cashiered*, *disbarred*, *unfrocked*, and *drummed out*? Words not only point to things and events and ideas; they also advertise our social affiliations and reinforce our self-concepts. It is as important for a sailor to refer to a privy as a *head* as it is for him to wear his uniform; indeed, his nautical vocabulary is part of his uniform. And a Honolulu host inviting you to have *pupus* is not only offering canapés; he is announcing his attachment to Hawaii. The richness of English synonymy attests to the variety of adventures of both body and mind encountered by speakers of English in many climes over many centuries.

PRONUNCIATION KEY

The primary stress mark (ʹ) is placed after the syllable bearing the heavier stress or accent; the secondary stress mark (ʹ) follows a syllable having a somewhat lighter stress, as in **com·men·da·tion** (kom′ən·dā′shən).

a	add, map	m	move, seem	u	up, done
ā	ace, rate	n	nice, tin	û(r)	urn, term
â(r)	care, air	ng	ring, song	yōō	use, few
ä	palm, father				
b	bat, rub	o	odd, hot	v	vain, eve
ch	check, catch	ō	open, so	w	win, away
d	dog, rod	ô	order, jaw	y	yet, yearn
		oi	oil, boy	z	zest, muse
e	end, pet	ou	out, now	zh	vision, pleasure
ē	even, tree	ōō	pool, food		
f	fit, half	ŏŏ	took, full	ə	the schwa, an un-
g	go, log				stressed vowel
h	hope, hate	p	pit, stop		representing the
		r	run, poor		sound spelled
i	it, give	s	see, pass		*a* in *above*
ī	ice, write	sh	sure, rush		*e* in *sicken*
		t	talk, sit		*i* in *clarity*
j	joy, ledge	th	thin, both		*o* in *melon*
k	cool, take	th	this, bathe		*u* in *focus*
l	look, rule				

The schwa (ə) varies widely in quality from a sound close to the (u) in *up* to a sound close to the (i) in *it* as heard in pronunciations of such words as *ballot, custom, landed, horses.*

The (r) in final position as in *star* (stär) and before a consonant as in *heart* (härt) is regularly indicated in the respellings, but pronunciations without (r) are unquestionably reputable. Standard British is much like the speech of Eastern New England and the Lower South in this feature.

In a few words, such as *button* (but′n) and *sudden* (sud′n), no vowel appears in the unstressed syllable because the (n) constitutes the whole syllable.

FOREIGN SOUNDS

à   as in French *ami, patte.* This is a vowel midway in quality between (a) and (ä).

œ   as in French *peu,* German *schön.* Round the lips for (ō) and pronounce (ā).

ü   as in French *vue,* German *grün.* Round the lips for (ōō) and pronounce (ē).

кh   as in German *ach,* Scottish *loch.* Pronounce a strongly aspirated (h) with the tongue in position for (k) as in *cool* or *keep.*

ṅ   This symbol indicates that the preceding vowel is nasal. The nasal vowels in French are œṅ (*brun*), aṅ (*main*), äṅ (*chambre*), ôṅ (*dont*).

ʼ   This symbol indicates that a preceding (l) or (r) is voiceless, as in French *fin-de-siècle* (faṅ·də·sye′kl′) or *fiacre* (fyà′kr′); that a preceding (y) is pronounced consonantly in a separate syllable followed by a slight schwa sound, as in French *fille* (fē′y′); or that a consonant preceding a (y) is palatalized, as in Russian *oblast* (ô′bləsty′).

NOTE ON THE ACCENTUATION OF FOREIGN WORDS

Many languages do not employ stress in the manner of English; only an approximation can be given of the actual situation in such languages. As it is not possible to reproduce the tones of Chinese in a work of this kind, Chinese names have been here recorded with primary stress on each syllable and may be so pronounced. Japanese and Korean have been shown without stress and may be pronounced with a level accent throughout. French words are shown conventionally with a primary stress on the last syllable; however, this stress tends to be evenly divided among the syllables (except for those that are completely unstressed), with slightly more force and higher pitch on the last syllable.

ABBREVIATIONS USED IN THIS BOOK

A.D.	year of our Lord	Hos.	Hosea
adj.	adjective	Hung.	Hungarian
adv.	adverb	Icel.	Icelandic
Aeron.	Aeronautics	Illit.	Illiterate
AF	Anglo-French	imit.	imitative
Agric.	Agriculture	infl.	influence, influenced
Alg.	Algebra	intens.	intensive
alter.	alteration	interj.	interjection
Am. Ind.	American Indian	Isa.	Isaiah
Anat.	Anatomy	Ital.	Italian
Ant.	Antonyms	Jas.	James
Anthropol.	Anthropology	Jer.	Jeremiah
appar.	apparently	Jon.	Jonah
Archeol.	Archeology	Josh.	Joshua
Archit.	Architecture	Judg.	Judges
assoc.	association	L, Lat.	Latin (Classical, 80 B.C.– A.D. 200)
Astron.	Astronomy		
aug.	augmentative		
Austral.	Australian	Lam.	Lamentations
Bacteriol.	Bacteriology	Lev.	Leviticus
B.C.	Before Christ	LG	Low German
Biochem.	Biochemistry	LGk.	Late Greek (200–600)
Biol.	Biology		
Bot.	Botany	Ling.	Linguistics
Brit.	British	lit.	literally
c.	century	LL	Late Latin (200–600)
cap.	capitalized		
cf.	compare	M	Middle
Chem.	Chemistry	Mal.	Malachi
Chron.	Chronicles	masc.	masculine
Col.	Colossians	Math.	Mathematics
compar.	comparative	Matt.	Matthew
conj.	conjunction	MDu.	Middle Dutch
contr.	contraction	ME	Middle English (1050–1475)
Cor.	Corinthians		
Crystall.	Crystallography	Mech.	Mechanics
Dan.	Daniel, Danish	Med.	Medicine, Medieval
def.	definition		
Dent.	Dentistry	Med. Gk.	Medieval Greek (600–1500)
Deut.	Deuteronomy		
Dial.	Dialect, Dialectal	Med. L	Medieval Latin (600–1500)
dim.	diminutive		
Du.	Dutch	Metall.	Metallurgy
E	English	Meteorol.	Meteorology
Eccl.	Ecclesiastical	MF	Middle French (1400–1600)
Eccles.	Ecclesiastes		
Ecclus.	Ecclesiasticus	MHG	Middle High German (1100–1450)
Ecol.	Ecology		
Econ.	Economics		
Electr.	Electricity	Mic.	Micah
Engin.	Engineering	Mil.	Military
Entomol.	Entomology	Mineral.	Mineralogy
Eph.	Ephesians	MLG	Middle Low German (1100–1450)
esp.	especially		
est.	estimate		
Esth.	Esther	n.	noun
Ex.	Exodus	Nah.	Nahum
Ezek.	Ezekiel	N. Am. Ind.	North American Indian
F, Fr.	French		
fem.	feminine	Naut.	Nautical
freq.	frequentative	NE	Northeast
G, Ger.	German	Neh.	Nehemiah
Gal.	Galatians	neut.	neuter
Gen.	Genesis	NL	New Latin (after 1500)
Geog.	Geography		
Geol.	Geology	Norw.	Norwegian
Geom.	Geometry	Num.	Numbers
Gk.	Greek (Homer — A.D. 200)	NW	Northwest
		O	Old
Gmc.	Germanic	Obad.	Obadiah
Govt.	Government	Obs.	Obsolete
Gram.	Grammar	OE	Old English (before 1050)
Hab.	Habakkuk		
Hag.	Haggai	OF	Old French (before 1400)
Heb.	Hebrews		
HG	High German		
Hind.	Hindustani		

OHG	Old High German (before 1100)	ppr.	present participle
		prep.	preposition
OIrish	Old Irish	prob.	probably
ON	Old Norse (before 1500)	pron.	pronoun
		pronun.	pronunciation
orig.	original, originally	Prov.	Proverbs
		Ps.	Psalms
Ornithol.	Ornithology	Psychoanal.	Psychoanalysis
OS	Old Saxon (before 1100)	Psychol.	Psychology
		pt.	preterit
Paleontol.	Paleontology	ref.	reference
Pathol.	Pathology	Rev.	Revelation
Pet.	Peter	Rom.	Romans
Pg.	Portuguese	Russ.	Russian
Phil.	Philippians	Sam.	Samuel
Philem.	Philemon	S. Am. Ind.	South American Indian
Philos.	Philosophy		
Phonet.	Phonetics	Scand.	Scandinavian
Photog.	Photography	Scot.	Scottish
Physiol.	Physiology	SE	Southeast
pl.	plural	sing.	singular
pop.	population	Skt.	Sanskrit
pp.	past participle, pages	Sociol.	Sociology
		S. of Sol.	Song of Solomon
		Sp.	Spanish
		Stat.	Statistics
		superl.	superlative
		Surg.	Surgery
		Sw.	Swedish
		SW	Southwest
		Syn.	Synonyms
		Telecom.	Telecommunication
		Theol.	Theology
		Thess.	Thessalonians
		Tim.	Timothy
		Tit.	Titus
		trans.	translation
		Trig.	Trigonometry
		ult.	ultimate, ultimately
		U.S.	American (adj.)
		v.	verb
		var.	variant
		Vet.	Veterinary medicine
		v.i.	intransitive verb
		v.t.	transitive verb
		WGmc.	West Germanic
		Zech.	Zechariah
		Zeph.	Zephaniah
		Zool.	Zoology

< from   + plus   ? possibly

TABLE OF ENGLISH SPELLINGS

FOLLOWING is a list of words exemplifying the possible spellings for the sounds of English. The sounds represented by these spellings are shown in the pronunciation symbols used in this dictionary, followed by their equivalents in the International Phonetic Alphabet.

DICTIONARY KEY	IPA SYMBOL	EXAMPLES
a	æ	cat, plaid, calf, laugh
ā	eɪ,e	mate, bait, gaol, gauge, pay, steak, skein, weigh, prey
â(r)	ɛ,er	dare, fair, prayer, where, bear, their
a	a	bar, ask, cot (a vowel midway in quality between [æ] and [ɑ], used in some regional American speech)
ä	ɑ	dart, ah, sergeant, heart
b	b	boy, rubber
ch	tʃ	chip, batch, righteous, bastion, structure
d	d	day, ladder, called
e	ɛ	many, aesthete, said, says, bet, steady, heifer, leopard, friend, foetid
ē	i	Caesar, quay, scene, meat, see, seize, people, key, ravine, grief, phoebe, city
f	f	fake, coffin, cough, half, phase
g	g	gate, beggar, ghoul, guard, vague
h	h	hot, whom
hw	hw,ʍ	whale
i	ɪ	pretty, been, tin, sieve, women, busy, guilt, lynch
ī	aɪ	aisle, aye, sleight, eye, dime, pie, sigh, guile, buy, try, lye
j	dʒ	edge, soldier, modulate, rage, exaggerate, joy
k	k	can, accost, saccharine, chord, tack, acquit, king, talk, liquor
l	l	let, gall
m	m	drachm, phlegm, palm, make, limb, grammar, condemn
n	n	gnome, know, mnemonic, note, banner, pneumatic
ng	ŋ	sink, ring, meringue
o	ɑ, ɒ	watch, pot
ō	ou,o	beau, yeoman, sew, over, soap, roe, oh, brooch, soul, though, grow
ô	ɔ	ball, balk, fault, dawn, cord, broad, ought
oi	ɔɪ	poison, toy
ou	aʊ	out, bough, cow
o͞o	u	rheum, drew, move, canoe, mood, group, through, fluke, sue, fruit
o͝o	ʊ	wolf, foot, could, pull
p	p	map, happen
r	r	rose, rhubarb, marry, diarrhea, wriggle
s	s	cite, dice, psyche, saw, scene, schism, mass
sh	ʃ	ocean, chivalry, vicious, pshaw, sure, schist, prescience, nauseous, shall, pension, tissue, fission, potion
t	t	walked, thought, phthisic, ptarmigan, tone, Thomas, butter
th	θ	thick
th	ð	this, bathe
u	ʌ	some, does, blood, young, sun
yo͞o	ju,ɪu	beauty, eulogy, queue, pew, ewe, adieu, view, fuse, cue, youth, yule
û(r)	ɜr, ɝ	yearn, fern, err, girl, worm, journal, burn, guerdon, myrtle
v	v	of, Stephen, vise, flivver
w	w	choir, quilt, will
y	j	onion, hallelujah, yet
z	z	was, scissors, xylophone, zoo, muzzle
zh	ʒ	rouge, pleasure, incision, seizure, glazier
ə	ə	above, fountain, darken, clarity, parliament, cannon, porpoise, vicious, locus
ər	ər, ɚ	mortar, brother, elixir, donor, glamour, augur, nature, zephyr

A

a, A (ā) *n.* *pl.* **a's** or **as, A's** or **As, aes** (āz) **1.** The first letter of the English alphabet. The shape of the Phoenician *aleph* was adopted by the Greeks as *alpha* and became Roman *A.* **2.** Any sound represented by the letter *a.* — *symbol* **1.** Primacy in class: grade *A* beef. **2.** A substitute for the numeral 1: section *A.* **3.** *Music* **a** One of a series of tones, the sixth in the natural diatonic scale of C, or the first note in the related minor scale. **b** The pitch of this tone, used as a reference point for tuning instruments, 440.0 cycles per second or this value multiplied by any power of 2, in standard pitch. **c** A written note representing this tone. **d** The scale built upon A. **4.** *U.S.* The highest grade for school work; also, a person or thing receiving such a grade.

a¹ (ə, *stressed* ā) *indefinite article* or *adj.* In each; to each; for each: twice *a* year; one dollar *a* bushel: equivalent to *per.* [OE *on, an* in, on, at; orig. a prep.]

a² (ə, *stressed* ā) *indefinite article* or *adj.* One; any; some; each: expressing singleness, unity, etc., more or less indefinitely. It is used: **1.** Before a noun expressing an individual object or idea: *a* bird; *a* hope. **2.** Before an abstract noun used concretely: to show *a* kindness. **3.** Before a collective noun: *a* crowd. **4.** Before a proper noun denoting a type: He is *a* Hercules in strength. **5.** Before plural nouns with *few, great many,* or *good many:* *a* few books. **6.** After *on, at,* or *of,* denoting oneness, sameness: birds of *a* feather. ◆ Before vowel sounds the form becomes an. See note under AN¹. [Reduced form of AN¹ used before consonant sounds]

a³ (ə, ä) *v.* *Brit. Dial.* Have.

a⁴ (ā, ô, ə) *pron.* *Brit. Dial.* He, she, it, they: an unstressed form.

a' (ô, ä) *adj.* *Scot.* All. Also **a.**

a-¹ *prefix* In; on; at: *aboard, asleep, agog, agoing.* [OE *on, an* in, on, at]

a-² *prefix* Up; on; away: *arise, abide.* [OE *ā-* up, on, away]

a-³ *prefix* Of; from: *athirst, akin, anew.* [OE *of* off, of]

a-⁴ *prefix* **1.** Without; not: *achromatic.* **2.** Apart from; unconcerned with: *amoral.* [Reduced form of AN-¹ used before consonant sounds]

a-⁵ Reduced var. of AB-¹.

a-⁶ Reduced var. of AD-.

a. **1.** About. **2.** Accepted. **3.** Acre(s). **4.** Acting. **5.** Active. **6.** Ad (L, at). **7.** Adjective. **8.** After. **9.** Afternoon. **10.** *Music* Alto. **11.** Amateur. **12.** *Electr.* Ampere. **13.** Anno (L, in the year). **14.** *Electr.* Anode. **15.** Anonymous. **16.** Ante (L, before). **17.** Approved. **18.** Are (measure). **19.** Area. **20.** *Heraldry* Argent. **21.** Assist(s) (baseball).

A or **Å** *Physics* Angstrom unit(s).

A. **1.** Absolute (temperature). **2.** Academy. **3.** Acre. **4.** America; American.

aa (ä'ä) *n.* Scoriaceous lava. [< Hawaiian]

AA or **A.A.** **1.** *Psychol.* Achievement age. **2.** Alcoholics Anonymous. **3.** *Mil.* Antiaircraft. **4.** *Printing* Author's alteration(s).

AAA **1.** Agricultural Adjustment Administration. **2.** *Mil.* Antiaircraft Artillery.

AAA or **A.A.A.** **1.** Amateur Athletic Association. **2.** American Automobile Association. **3.** Automobile Association of America.

AAAA or **A.A.A.A.** **1.** Amateur Athletic Association of America. **2.** Associated Actors and Artists of America.

A.A.A.L. American Academy of Arts and Letters.

AAAS or **A.A.A.S.** **1.** American Academy of Arts and Sciences. **2.** American Association for the Advancement of Science.

Aa·chen (ä'kən, *Ger.* ä'khən) A city in West Germany, in North Rhine–Westphalia, on the Belgian border; pop. 177,642 (est. 1970); capital of Charlemagne's empire: French *Aix-la-Chapelle.*

AACS Airways and Air Communications Service.

AAE or **A.A.E.** American Association of Engineers.

A.A.E.E. American Association of Electrical Engineers.

AAF or **A.A.F.** Formerly, Army Air Forces.

aal (äl) *n.* **1.** An East Indian shrub (*Morinda royoc*), the root of which yields a red dye: also called *Indian mulberry.* **2.** The dye. [< Hind.]

Aa·land Islands (ō'län) See ÅLAND ISLANDS.

Aal·borg (ôl'bôr) A county of northern Denmark; 1,125 sq. mi.; pop. 252,850 (1969); capital, **Aalborg,** pop. 82,871.

a·a·li·i (ä'ä·lē'ē) *n.* A small tropical tree (*Dodonaea viscosa*)

native in Australia, Hawaii, Jamaica, and Madagascar, valued for its dark, hard, and durable timber. [< Hawaiian]

Aalst (älst) The Flemish name for ALOST.

A. and M. Agricultural and Mechanical (College).

A.A.O.N.M.S. Ancient Arabic Order of Nobles of the Mystic Shrine.

Aar (är) The longest river in Switzerland, flowing 183 miles to the Rhine. Also **Aa·re** (ä'rə).

aard·vark (ärd'värk') *n.* A burrowing, ant-eating African mammal (genus *Orycteropus*), with long, sticky tongue and strong digging forefeet. [< Afrikaans < Du. *aarde* earth + *vark* pig]

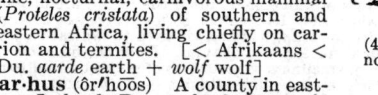

AARDVARK
(4 to 5½ feet from nose to tail; tail 2 to 2½ feet)

aard·wolf (ärd'woolf') *n.* A hyena-like, nocturnal, carnivorous mammal (*Proteles cristata*) of southern and eastern Africa, living chiefly on carrion and termites. [< Afrikaans < Du. *aarde* earth + *wolf* wolf]

Aar·hus (ôr'hoos) A county in eastern Jutland, Denmark; 310 sq. mi.; pop. 244,099 (1969); capital, **Aarhus,** pop. 111,266 (1965).

Aar·on (âr'ən, ar'ən) The first high priest of the Hebrews, older brother of Moses. *Ex.* xxviii 1–4.

Aa·ron·ic (â·ron'ik) *adj.* **1.** Of or pertaining to Aaron, the high priest, or his descendants. **2.** Of or denoting the lesser priesthood of the Mormon Church. Also **Aa·ron'i·cal.**

Aaron's rod **1.** The rod cast by Aaron before Pharaoh, which became a serpent (*Ex.* vii 9–15), and later blossomed (*Num.* xvii 8). **2.** *Archit.* A rod-shaped molding, ornamented with leaves or a twined serpent. **3.** A plant that flowers on long stems, as the mullein.

A.A.S.R. or **A. & A.S.R.** Ancient and Accepted Scottish Rite.

aas·vo·gel (äs'fō'gəl) *n.* *Afrikaans* A vulture. [< Afrikaans < Du. *aas* carrion + *vogel* bird]

A.A.U. Amateur Athletic Union.

A.A.U.P. American Association of University Professors.

A.A.U.W. American Association of University Women.

ab-¹ *prefix* Off; from; away: *absolve, abduct, abrogate.* Also: *a-* before *m, p, v,* as in *avocation; abs-* before *c, t,* as in *abscess, abstract.* [< L < *ab* from]

ab-² Var. of AD-.

ab. or **a.b.** In baseball, (times) at bat.

Ab (äb, äb) *n.* The eleventh month of the Hebrew year. See (Hebrew) CALENDAR.

Ab *Chem.* Alabamine.

A.B. Bachelor of Arts (L *Artium Baccalaureus*).

A.B. or **a.b.** Able-bodied seaman.

a·ba (ä'bə) *n.* A sleeveless garment of camel's- or goat's-hair cloth worn in Arabia, Syria, etc. [< Arabic]

ab·a·ca (ab'ə·kä, ä'bə·kä') *n.* **1.** A banana plant (*Musa textilis*) of the Philippines. **2.** The inner fiber of this plant, used for cordage. Also **ab'a·ka.** [< Tagalog]

a·back (ə·bak') *adv.* *Naut.* Back against the mast: said of sails so blown by the wind. — **taken aback** Disconcerted, as by a sudden check. [OE *on bæc* on or to the back]

ab·a·cus (ab'ə·kəs) *n.* *pl.* **·cus·es** or **·ci** (-sī) **1.** A calculating device with counters sliding in grooves, or on rods or wires. **2.** *Archit.* A slab forming the top of a capital. For illustration see CAPITAL. [< L < Gk. *abax* counting table]

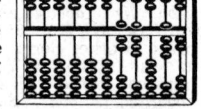

CHINESE ABACUS
The counters in the upper compartment have five times the value of those below.

A·bad·don (ə·bad'ən) In the Bible, the bottomless pit; realm of Apollyon. [< Hebrew *abaddon* destruction]

a·baft (ə·baft', ə·bäft') *Naut. adv.* Toward the stern; aft. — *prep.* Further aft than; astern of: *abaft* the mainmast. [OE *on be-æftan < on* on, at + *be* by + *æftan* behind, back]

ab·a·lo·ne (ab'ə·lō'nē) *n.* An edible shellfish (genus *Haliotis*), having a perforated ear-shaped shell lined with mother-of-pearl. Also called *ear shell.* [< Am. Sp.]

ab·am·pere (ab-am'pir) *n.* The cgs electromagnetic unit of electric current, equivalent to 10 amperes. [< AB(SOLUTE) + AMPERE]

a·ban·don (ə·ban'dən) *v.t.* **1.** To give up wholly; desert;

forsake, as an effort or attempt. **2.** To surrender or give over: with *to*. **3.** To yield (oneself) without restraint, as to an emotion or pastime. — *n.* Utter surrender to one's feelings or natural impulses: to dance with *abandon*. [< OF *abandoner* < *a bandon* under one's control < LL *bannum* proclamation] — **a·ban'don·er** *n.* — **a·ban'don·ment** *n.*
— **Syn.** (verb) **1.** *Abandon*, *desert*, and *forsake* all mean to leave someone or something completely. *Abandon* denotes a complete giving up, especially of what one has previously been interested in or responsible for; the scientist *abandons* unpromising projects, children are *abandoned*. *Desert* adds the idea that an obligation or trust is being violated; soldiers *desert* armies. *Forsake* implies previous close attachment; a man may *forsake* home or friends. **2.** See RELINQUISH. — **Ant.** adopt, retain.
a·ban·doned (ə-ban'dənd) *adj.* **1.** Deserted; left behind; forsaken. **2.** Unrestrained; without moderation. **3.** Given over to dissolute practices; profligate; shameless.
à bas (à bä') *French* Down with: opposed to *vive*.
a·base (ə-bās') *v.t.* **a·based, a·bas·ing 1.** To lower in position, rank, prestige, or estimation; cast down; humble. **2.** *Obs.* To reduce in value, as coin; debase. [< OF *abaissier* < *a-* to (< L *ad-*) + *baissier* to lower < LL *bassus* low] — **a·bas·ed·ly** (ə-bā'sid·lē) *adv.* — **a·bas'ed·ness** *n.* — **a·base'ment** *n.* — **a·bas'er** *n.*
— **Syn. 1.** *Abase*, *debase*, *degrade*, *demean*, *humble*, and *humiliate* all mean to lower greatly the prestige or dignity of a person or a group. *Abase* stresses outward conditions, whereas *debase* emphasizes the inner loss of value or quality; the proud are *abased*, coins are *debased* when they lose value. *Degrade* stresses corruption: a *degrading* vice; *demean*, however, is used to indicate a loss of standing through unseemly behavior. *Humble* indicates a personal realization of smallness without loss of respect and differs from *humiliate*, which implies public shame. — **Ant.** exalt.
a·bash (ə-bash') *v.t.* To deprive of self-possession; disconcert; make ashamed or confused. — **Syn.** See EMBARRASS. [< AF *abaïss-*, OF *esbaïss-*, stem of *esbaïr* to astonish] — **a·bash·ed·ly** (ə-bash'id·lē) *adv.* — **a·bash'ment** *n.*
a·bate (ə-bāt') *v.* **a·bat·ed, a·bat·ing** *v.t.* **1.** To make less; reduce in quantity, value, force, or intensity. **2.** To deduct, as part of a payment. **3.** *Law* To do away with (a nuisance); annul (a writ). — *v.i.* **4.** To become less, as in strength or degree: The wind *abated*. **5.** *Law* To fail; become void. — **Syn.** See ANNUL, DECREASE. [< OF *abatre* to beat down < *a-* to (< L *ad-*) + *batre* to beat < L *batuere*] — **a·bat·a·ble** (ə-bā'tə-bəl) *adj.* — **a·bat'er** *n.*
a·bate·ment (ə-bāt'mənt) *n.* **1.** The act of abating, or the state of being abated; diminution. **2.** The amount abated. **3.** *Law* A doing away with; annulment. [< OF]
ab·a·tis (ab'ə-tis, ab'ə-tē') *n.* *Mil.* An obstruction of felled trees or bent saplings, often interwoven with barbed wire, pointed in the direction of expected enemy attack. Also **ab'at·tis.** [< F *abatre* to fell, beat down. See ABATE.]
a·ba·tor (ə-bā'tər) *n.* *Law* **1.** The agent in effecting an abatement. **2.** One who unlawfully seizes an inheritance. [< AF < OF *abatre*. See ABATE.]
A battery *Electr.* A battery that supplies the power for the filaments of an electron tube or for transistors.
ab·at·toir (ab'ə-twär') *n.* A slaughterhouse. [< F]
ab·ax·i·al (ab-ak'sē-əl) *adj.* Situated off or away from the axis. Also **ab·ax·ile** (ab-ak'səl). [< AB-¹ + AXIAL]
Ab·ba (ab'ə) *n.* **1.** Father: a title used in the Syrian, Coptic, and Ethiopian churches. **2.** God: used in the New Testament. *Mark* xiv 36. [< Aramaic]
ab·ba·cy (ab'ə-sē) *n.* *pl.* **·cies** The office, term of office, dignity, or jurisdiction of an abbot. [< LL *abbatia* < *abbas.* See ABBOT.]
Ab·bas·side (ə-bas'īd, ab'ə-sīd) *n.* Any of the caliphs of the dynasty ruling at Baghdad, 749–1258, and claiming descent from **Abbas**, uncle of Mohammed. — *adj.* Of or pertaining to this dynasty. Also **Ab·bas·sid** (ə-bas'īd, ab'ə-sid).
ab·ba·tial (ə-bā'shəl) *adj.* Of or pertaining to an abbot or an abbey. Also **ab·bat·i·cal** (ə-bat'i-kəl). [< MF < LL *abbatialis* < *abbatia* abbacy]
ab·bé (ab'ā, *Fr.* a-bā') *n.* **1.** In France, a title given to a priest or other cleric. **2.** An abbot. [< F]
ab·bess (ab'is) *n.* The female superior of a community of nuns connected with an abbey. [ME < OF *abbesse* < LL *abbatissa* < *abbas.* See ABBOT.]
Ab·be·vil·li·an (ab'ə-vil'ē-ən) *adj. Anthropol.* Designating possibly the oldest culture stage of the Lower Paleolithic period of western Europe, represented by crude hand axes. [after *Abbeville*, France, where artifacts were found]
ab·bey (ab'ē) *n.* *pl.* **·beys 1.** A monastic establishment under the jurisdiction of an abbot or abbess; a monastery or convent. **2.** A church or building attached to a monastery or convent. — **Syn.** See CLOISTER. [ME < OF *abaïe* < LL *abbatia* < *abbas.* See ABBOT.]
Ab·bey (ab'ē), **Edwin Austin,** 1852–1911, U.S. artist.
Abbey Theatre A repertory theater in Dublin, associated since 1904 with the Irish literary revival.
ab·bot (ab'ət) *n.* The superior of a community of monks connected with an abbey. [OE *abbod* < LL *abbas, abbatis* < Gk. < Aramaic *abbā* father] — **ab'bot·cy, ab'bot·ship** *n.*
Ab·bot (ab'ət), **Charles Greeley,** born 1872, U.S. astrophysicist.

Ab·bots·ford (ab'əts-fərd) An estate on the Tweed in SE Scotland: residence of Sir Walter Scott.
Ab·bott (ab'ət), **Jacob,** 1803–79, U.S. clergyman and author of juvenile literature. — **Lyman,** 1835–1922, U.S. clergyman, editor, and author; son of Jacob.
abbr. or **abbrev.** Abbreviation.
ab·bre·vi·ate (ə-brē'vē-āt) *v.t.* **·at·ed, ·at·ing 1.** To condense or make briefer. **2.** To shorten, as a word or expression, especially by omission or contraction: Mister is *abbreviated* to Mr. [< L *abbreviatus*, pp. of *abbreviare* < *ad-* to + *breviare* to shorten < *brevis* short] — **ab·bre'vi·a'tor** *n.*
— **Syn.** shorten, curtail, abridge, contract. Compare DECREASE.
ab·bre·vi·a·tion (ə-brē'vē-ā'shən) *n.* **1.** A shortened form or contraction, as of a word or phrase, used to represent the full form. **2.** The act of abbreviating, or the state of being abbreviated; abridgment. **3.** *Music* A notation indicating repeated notes, or a series of them, by a single symbol.

ABBREVIATION (*def.* 3)

— **Syn. 1.** *Abbreviation* and *contraction* both denote a reduction in size or scope. An *abbreviation* is a shortening by any method; a *contraction* is a reduction by the drawing together of the parts. A *contraction* is made by omitting certain medial elements (whether sounds or letters) and bringing together the first and last elements. Thus, a *contraction* is a type of *abbreviation*. *Rec't* for *receipt* is a written *contraction* as well as *abbreviation*; *Am.* for *American* is a written *abbreviation*, but not a *contraction*. *Bus* for *omnibus* is a spoken *abbreviation* or clipped form. Such *contractions* as *I'll*, *don't*, and *he's* occur in both writing and speaking.
ABC (ā'bē'sē') *pl.* **ABC's 1.** *Usually pl.* The alphabet. **2.** The rudiments, elements, or basic facts (of a subject).
ABC 1. American Broadcasting Company. **2.** Australian Broadcasting Commission. **3.** Audit Bureau of Circulations.
ab·cou·lomb (ab'kōō-lom') *n.* The cgs electromagnetic unit of charge, equal to 10 coulombs. [< AB(SOLUTE) + COULOMB]
Ab·dal·lah-ibn-Ya·sin (äb'däl-lä'ib'ən-yä-sēn') , died 1058?, Arab scholar, founder of the Almoravides. Also **Ab·dul·lah-ibn-Ya·sin** (äb'dōōl-lä'-).
Abd-el-Ka·der (äb'del-kä'dir), 1807?–83, Algerian tribal leader. Also **Abd'-al-Ka'dir.**
Abd-el-Krim (äb'del-krim'), 1880?–1963, Moroccan chieftain, leader of the Berbers in the Rif region of North Africa.
Abd-er-Rah·man I (äb'dər-rä'män), 731–788, founder of the Ommiad dynasty in southern Spain in 756.
Ab·di·as (ab-dī'əs) The Douai Bible name for OBADIAH.
ab·di·cate (ab'də-kāt) *v.* **·cat·ed, ·cat·ing** *v.t.* **1.** To give up formally; renounce, as claims to or possession of a throne, power, or rights. — *v.i.* **2.** To relinquish power, sovereignty, or rights: The king was forced to *abdicate*. [< L *abdicatus*, pp. of *abdicare* to renounce < *ab-* away + *dicare* to proclaim] — **ab·di·ca·ble** (ab'di·kə-bəl) *adj.* — **ab'di·ca'tion** *n.* — **ab'di·ca'tive** *adj.* — **ab'di·ca'tor** *n.*
ab·do·men (ab'də-mən, ab-dō'mən) *n.* **1.** In mammals, the body cavity between the diaphragm and the pelvic floor containing the viscera; the belly. **2.** In vertebrates other than mammals, the region or cavity that contains the viscera. **3.** In insects and some other arthropods, the hindmost of the main body divisions. [< L]
ab·dom·i·nal (ab-dom'ə-nəl) *adj.* Of, pertaining to, or situated on or in the abdomen. — **ab·dom'i·nal·ly** *adv.*
ab·dom·i·nous (ab-dom'ə-nəs) *adj.* Big-bellied.
ab·du·cent (ab-dōō'sənt, -dyōō'-) *adj. Physiol.* Drawing away; abducting: said of muscles. [< L *abducens, -entis*, ppr. of *abducere.* See ABDUCT.]

ABDOMINAL REGIONS
1. Right hypochondriac.
2. Left hypochondriac.
3. Epigastric.
4. Umbilical.
5. Right lumbar.
6. Left lumbar.
7. Right iliac.
8. Left iliac.
9. Hypogastric.

ab·duct (ab-dukt') *v.t.* **1.** To carry away wrongfully, as by force or fraud; kidnap. **2.** *Physiol.* To draw away from the original position: opposed to *adduct*. [< L *abductus*, pp. of *abducere* < *ab-* away + *ducere* to lead] — **ab·duc'tor** *n.*
ab·duc·tion (ab-duk'shən) *n.* The act of abducting or the condition of being abducted.
Ab·dul-A·ziz (äb'dōōl-ä-zēz'), 1830–76, sultan of Turkey 1861–76.
Ab·dul Ba·ha (äb'dōōl bä-hä'), 1844–1921, Persian religious leader of Bahaism and son of its founder, Bahaullah. Also **Ab·bas Ef·fen·di** (äb-bäs' e-fen'dē).
Ab·dul-Ha·mid II (äb'dōōl-hä-mēd'), 1842–1918, sultan of Turkey 1876–1909; deposed.
Ab·dul Ka·rim Kas·sim (äb'dōōl kä-rēm' kä-sim') See KASSIM.
Ab·dul·la ibn-Hu·sein (äb-dul'ə ib'ən-hōō-sīn'), 1882–1951, emir and king of Jordan 1921–51; assassinated.

Ab·dul-Me·jid (äb'dŏŏl·me·jēd'), 1823–61, sultan of Turkey 1839–61. Also **Ab'dul-Me·djid'.**

Ab·dul-Wah·hab (äb'dŏŏl·wä·hôb'), 1691–1787, Moslem reformer; founder of Wahabiism.

a·beam (ə·bēm') *adv. Naut.* **1.** At right angles to the keel of a vessel. **2.** At or off the side of a vessel: with *of.*

a·be·ce·dar·i·an (ā'bē·sē·dâr'ē·ən) *adj.* **1.** Pertaining to the alphabet. **2.** Alphabetically arranged. **3.** Pertaining to a learner of the alphabet; rudimentary. — *n.* **1.** A teacher or learner of the alphabet. **2.** A novice; beginner. Also **a·be·ce·da·ry** (ā'bē·sē'dər·ē). [< Med.L *abecedarius*]

a·bed (ə·bed') *adv.* In bed; on a bed; to bed. [OE *on* in + *bedde* bed]

A·bed·ne·go (ə·bed'ni·gō) A Hebrew captive in Babylon. *Dan.* iii. See SHADRACH.

A·bel (ā'bəl) Second son of Adam. *Gen.* iv 2.

Ab·e·lard (ab'ə·lärd), **Pierre,** 1079–1142, French philosopher; lover of Héloïse. *French* **A·bé·lard** (à·bā·làr').

a·bele (ə·bēl', ā'bəl) *n.* The white poplar. [< Du. *abeel* < OF *abel* < LL *albellus,* dim. of L *albus* white]

Ab·er·deen (ab'ər·dēn' *for def. 1;* ab'ər·dēn *for def. 2*) **1.** A county in NE Scotland, 1,972 sq. mi.; pop. 317,803 (1969); county seat, **Aberdeen.** Also **Ab'er·deen'shire** (-shir, -shər). **2.** A town in NE Maryland near Chesapeake Bay; pop. 12,375; site of **Aberdeen Proving Ground,** a U.S. Army reservation.

Aberdeen An·gus (ang'gəs) A breed of hornless black cattle of Scottish origin.

ab·er·rance (ab·er'əns, ab'ər·əns) *n.* A wandering from the right way; deviation from rectitude. Also **ab·er'ran·cy.**

ab·er·rant (ab·er'ənt, ab'ər·ənt) *adj.* **1.** Straying from the right way or usual course; wandering. **2.** Varying from type; abnormal; exceptional. [< L *aberrans, -antis,* ppr. of *aberrare* < *ab-* from + *errare* to wander]

ab·er·ra·tion (ab'ə·rā'shən) *n.* **1.** Deviation from a right, customary, prescribed, or natural course or condition. **2.** Partial mental derangement. **3.** *Optics* The failure of a lens or mirror to bring all light rays to the same focus: called **chromatic aberration** when caused by different refrangibility of light of different colors, and **spherical aberration** when resulting from the form of lens or mirror. **4.** *Astron.* An apparent displacement of a heavenly body, caused by the effect of relative motion upon its light. — **Syn.** See DEVIATION. [< L *aberratio, -onis* < *aberrare.* See ABERRANT.]

a·bet (ə·bet') *v.t.* **a·bet·ted, a·bet·ting** To encourage and support; especially, to support wrongdoing or a wrongdoer. [< OF *abeter* to incite, arouse < *a-* to (< L *ad-*) + *beter* to tease, bait < ON *beita* to cause to bite] — **a·bet'ment, a·bet'tal** *n.*

a·bet·tor (ə·bet'ər) *n.* One who abets. Also **a·bet'ter.** — **Syn.** See ACCESSORY.

ab extra *Latin* From without. *Abbr.* **ab ex.**

a·bey·ance (ə·bā'əns) *n.* **1.** Suspension or temporary inaction. **2.** *Law* An undetermined condition, as of an estate not legally assigned. Also **a·bey'an·cy.** [< AF *abeiance,* OF *abeance* < *abair* < *a-* to, at (< L *ad-*) + *bair* to gape < LL *badare*] — **a·bey'ant** *adj.*

ab·far·ad (ab·far'əd, -ad) *n.* The cgs electromagnetic unit of capacitance, equal to 1 billion farads. [< AB(SOLUTE) + FARAD]

ab·hen·ry (ab·hen'rē) *n.* The cgs electromagnetic unit of conductance, equal to one millionth of a henry. [< AB(SOLUTE) + HENRY]

ab·hom·i·na·ble (ab·hom'ə·nə·bəl) *adj. Obs.* Abominable.

ab·hor (ab·hôr') *v.t.* **·horred, ·hor·ring** To regard with repugnance; detest; loathe. — **Syn.** See HATE. [< L *abhorrere* < *ab-* from + *horrere* to shudder] — **ab·hor'rer** *n.*

ab·hor·rence (ab·hôr'əns, -hor'-) *n.* **1.** A feeling of utter loathing. **2.** Something loathsome or repugnant.

— **Syn. 1.** *Abhorrence, aversion,* and *disgust* all indicate feelings of hatred or loathing. *Abhorrence* is the strongest, and implies fear as well as hatred or loathing, while *aversion* and *disgust* may merely mean an intense distaste or repugnance. *Disgust* carries the additional meaning of tending to produce nausea.

ab·hor·rent (ab·hôr'ənt, -hor'-) *adj.* **1.** Repugnant or detestable: *abhorrent* acts. **2.** Opposed: with *to:* This idea is *abhorrent* to reason. **3.** Feeling repulsion: with *of: abhorrent* of greed. [< L *abhorrens, -entis,* ppr. of *abhorrere.* See ABHOR.] — **ab·hor'rent·ly** *adv.*

A·bib (ä·bib', *Hebrew* ä·vēv') *n.* Nisan. See (Hebrew) CALENDAR.

a·bi·dance (ə·bīd'ns) *n.* **1.** The act of abiding. **2.** Adherence to or an abiding by (rules, methods, etc.): with *by.*

a·bide (ə·bīd') *v.* **a·bode** or **a·bid·ed, a·bid·ing** *v.i.* **1.** To continue in a place; remain. **2.** To have one's abode; dwell; reside. **3.** To continue in some condition or state; remain faithful or unchanging. — *v.t.* **4.** To look for; wait for: to *abide* the event. **5.** To await expectantly or defiantly. **6.** To endure; put up with; suffer. — **to abide by 1.** To behave in accordance with; adhere to, as a promise or rule. **2.** To accept the consequences of; submit to. [OE *ābīdan*] — **a·bid'er** *n.* — **a·bid'ing·ly** *adv.*

— **Syn. 1.** *Abide, stay, linger, tarry, wait,* and *remain* all mean to continue in one place. To *abide* is to *stay* or dwell patiently. *Linger* implies reluctance to leave; to *tarry* is to *stay* beyond the proper time for leaving. We *wait* for someone or something, but *remain* after others have left. **2.** See LIVE. — **Ant.** depart, leave.

Ab·i·djan (ab'i·jän') The capital of the Republic of the Ivory Coast, a port city on the Gulf of Guinea; pop. 285,000 (est. 1963).

ab·i·et·ic acid (ab'ē·et'ik) *Chem.* An acid, $C_{20}H_{30}O_2$, isolated from pine rosin in the form of a slightly yellow crystalline powder, and used in lacquers, varnishes, soaps, and driers. [< NL *abiet-* silver fir + -IC]

Ab·i·gail (ab'ə·gāl) *n.* A lady's maid. [after a character in Beaumont and Fletcher's *The Scornful Lady*]

Ab·i·gail (ab'ə·gāl) The wife of Nabal and afterward of David. I *Sam.* xxv 14.

A·bi·jah (ə·bī'jə) King of Judah. I *Kings* xiv 1.

Ab·i·lene (ab'ə·lēn) A city in north central Texas; pop. 89,653.

a·bil·i·ty (ə·bil'ə·tē) *n. pl.* **·ties 1.** The state or quality of being able; physical, mental, legal, or financial power to do; capacity; skill. **2.** *pl.* Talents. **3.** Competence or skill as determined by training and present development. [< OF *ablete, habilite* < L *habilitas, -tatis* < *habilis.* See ABLE.]

— **Syn.** *Ability, capability, capacity, talent, faculty, facility, competence,* and *skill* all refer to the quality of being able to accomplish some task or tasks. *Ability* is the power or authority to do something; *capability* adds a note of adequacy or sufficiency on the part of the agent; *capacity* is the power to receive. We speak of the musical *ability* of a pianist, the destructive *capability* of a bomb, the mental *capacity* of a student. A *talent* is a natural ability in a special field; a *faculty* may be inborn or acquired: a *talent* for writing, a *faculty* for public speaking. *Facility, competence,* and *skill* imply satisfactory or easy performance, based on past experience, training, or natural aptitude. — **Ant.** inability, incapacity, ineptitude.

A·bim·e·lech (ə·bim'ə·lek) Son of Gideon; king of Shechem. *Judg.* viii 31.

Ab·ing·ton (ab'ing·tən) An urban township in SE Pennsylvania; pop. 8,594.

ab in·i·ti·o (ab i·nish'ē·ō) *Latin* From the beginning.

ab in·tra (ab in'trə) *Latin* From within.

ab·i·o·gen·e·sis (ab'ē·ō·jen'ə·sis) *n.* The springing up of living from nonliving matter: also called *heterogenesis.* Compare BIOGENESIS. [< A-⁴ + BIO- + GENESIS] — **ab·i·o·ge·net·ic** (ab'ē·ō·jə·net'ik) or **·i·cal** *adj.* — **ab·i·og·e·nist** (ab'ē·oj'ə·nist) *n.*

ab·i·o·sis (ab'ē·ō'sis) *n.* Absence of life; a lifeless state. [< NL < Gk. *abios* lifeless] — **ab·i·ot·ic** (ab'ē·ot'ik) *adj.*

ab·ir·ri·tant (ab·ir'ə·tənt) *n.* A soothing agent; medicine that eases irritation. — *adj.* Relieving irritation; soothing.

ab·ir·ri·tate (ab·ir'ə·tāt) *v.t.* **·tat·ed, ·tat·ing** *Med.* To diminish sensibility or irritation in. — **ab·ir'ri·ta'tion** *n.*

ab·ject (ab'jekt, ab·jekt') *adj.* **1.** Sunk to a low condition; groveling; mean; despicable: an *abject* coward. **2.** Hopelessly low; disheartening: *abject* poverty. — **Syn.** See MEAN². [< L *abjectus,* pp. of *abjicere* to throw away < *ab-* away + *jacere* to throw] — **ab·jec'tive** *adj.* — **ab'ject·ly** *adv.* **ab'ject·ness, ab·jec'tion** *n.*

ab·ju·ra·tion (ab'jŏŏ·rā'shən) *n.* The act of abjuring, or the state of being abjured; repudiation.

ab·jure (ab·jŏŏr') *v.t.* **·jured, ·jur·ing 1.** To renounce under oath; forswear. **2.** To retract or recant, as an opinion; repudiate. — **Syn.** See RENOUNCE. [< L *abjurare* to deny on oath < *ab-* away + *jurare* to swear] — **ab·jur·a·to·ry** (ab·jŏŏr'ə·tôr'ē, -tō'rē) *adj.* — **ab·jur'er** *n.*

Ab·kha·zi·an A.S.S.R. (äb·kä'zhən) An administrative division of the NW Georgian S.S.R., between the Black Sea and Greater Caucasus; 3,320 sq. mi.; pop. 487,000 (1970); capital, Sukhumi. Also **Ab·kha·zia** or **Ab·kha·sia** (äb·kä'zhə, *Russ.* äb·khä'zyə). *Russian* **Ab·khaz·ska·ya A.S.S.R.** (əb·khäz'skä·yä).

abl. *Gram.* Ablative.

ab·la·tion (ab·lā'shən) *n.* **1.** *Surg.* The removal of growths, organs, or parts from the body. **2.** *Geol.* A wearing away, as of rocks. **3.** *Aerospace* The removal of excess heat from a vital part through its absorption by an expendable part, as by the planned vaporization of the outer surface of the nose cone of a rocket. [< L *ablatio, -onis* a carrying away < *ablatus,* pp. of *auferre* < *ab-* away + *ferre* to carry]

ab·la·tive (ab'lə·tiv) *adj. Gram.* In some inflected languages, as Latin and Sanskrit, pertaining to a case expressing separation, position, motion from, instrumentality, etc.: usually translated by the words *from, with, in,* and *by.* — *n.* **1.** The ablative case. **2.** A word in this case. [< L *ablativus < ablatus* carried away. See ABLATION.]

ablative absolute In Latin grammar, a construction in the ablative case constituting an adverbial phrase that stands apart in syntax from the rest of the sentence; as, *sole oriente,* nox fugit (*the sun rising,* night flees).

ab·laut (äb'lout, ab'-; *Ger.* äp'lout) *n. Ling.* A patterned alternation of root vowels characteristic of the Indo-European languages, indicating variations of tense, function, or meaning, as *sing, sang, sung*: also called *gradation*. Compare UMLAUT. [< G < *ab-* off + *laut* sound]

a·blaze (ə-blāz′) *adv.* On fire. — *adj.* **1.** Flaming. **2.** Zealous; ardent.

a·ble (ā′bəl) *adj.* **a·bler** (ā′blər), **a·blest** (ā′blist) **1.** Having adequate power: *able* to win. **2.** Having or exhibiting superior abilities; skillful: an *able* writer. [< OF *hable* able < L *habilis* manageable, suitable, fit < *habere* to have, hold] — **Syn. 1.** *Able, competent, capable,* and *qualified* mean having the power or authority to do something. *Able* indicates power adequate for a task; *competent* suggests skill, while *capable* implies satisfactory performance. *Qualified* assumes the existence of set standards: a *qualified* voter. — **Ant.** inept, unable.

-able *suffix* **1.** Given to; tending to; likely to: *peaceable, changeable.* **2.** Fit to; able to; capable of; worthy of: *eatable, salable, solvable.* Also spelled *-ble, -ible.* [< F < L *-abilis, -ibilis, -bilis*]

◆ **-able, -ible** The suffix *-ible* is used to form words from Latin verbs of the third and fourth conjugations (ending in *-ere, -ire*) as *edible* from *edere, audible* from *audire*. The *-able* ending, originally used to form adjectives from Latin verbs of the first conjugation, as *disputable, estimable,* etc., is now extended in English to form adjectives from native verbs, nouns, and phrases, as *answerable, plowable, get-at-able,* etc.

a·ble-bod·ied (ā′bəl·bod′ēd) *adj.* Having a sound, strong body; competent for physical service; robust.

able-bodied seaman An experienced and skilled seaman. Compare ORDINARY SEAMAN. Abbr. *a.b., A.B.*

ab·le·gate (ab′li·gāt) *n.* A special papal envoy who bears their insignia to newly appointed cardinals. [< L *ablegatus,* pp. of *ablegare* to dispatch < *ab-* away + *legare* to send]

able seaman *pl.* **·men** **1.** In the Royal Canadian Navy, the fourth lowest grade. See table at GRADE. **2.** One who holds this grade.

a·blins (ā′blinz) *adv. Scot.* Perhaps: also spelled *aiblins.*

a·bloom (ə·blōōm′) *adj. & adv.* Blooming; in blossom.

ab·lu·ent (ab′lōō·ənt) *adj.* Cleansing. — *n.* A cleansing agent; detergent. [< L *abluens, -entis,* ppr. of *abluere* < *ab-* away + *luere* to wash]

a·blush (ə·blush′) *adj.* Blushing.

ab·lu·tion (ab·lōō′shən) *n.* **1.** A washing or cleansing, especially of the body; a bath. **2.** *Eccl.* **a** A ceremonial washing, especially of the priest's hands or of the chalice and paten during the Eucharist. **b** The liquid used for this. **3.** Any liquid used in washing or cleansing. [< L *ablutio, -onis* < *abluere*. See ABLUENT.] — **ab·lu′tion·ar′y** *adj.*

a·bly (ā′blē) *adv.* With ability; capably.

-ably *suffix* Like; in the manner of: *peaceably*: used to form adverbs from adjectives ending in *-able.*

abn. Airborne.

ab·ne·gate (ab′nə·gāt) *v.t.* **·gat·ed, ·gat·ing** To deny to oneself; renounce. [< L *abnegatus,* pp. of *abnegare* < *ab-* away + *negare* to deny] — **ab′ne·ga′tor** *n.*

ab·ne·ga·tion (ab′nə·gā′shən) *n.* Renunciation; self-denial.

ab·nor·mal (ab·nôr′məl) *adj.* Not according to rule; different from the average; unusual; irregular. [Earlier *anormal* < F < Med.L *anormalus,* alter. of *anomalus* < Gk. *anōmalos* irregular; re-formed on L *abnormis* irregular < *ab-* from + *norma* rule] — **ab·nor′mal·ly** *adv.*

ab·nor·mal·i·ty (ab′nôr·mal′ə·tē) *n. pl.* **·ties** **1.** The state or condition of being abnormal; irregularity. **2.** An abnormal or unusual thing.

ab·nor·mi·ty (ab·nôr′mə·tē) *n. pl.* **·ties** **1.** An irregularity. **2.** A malformation; monstrosity. [< L *abnormitas, -tatis* < *abnormis* irregular < *ab-* from + *norma* rule]

A·bo (ō′bōō) Swedish name for TURKU.

a·board (ə·bôrd′, ə·bōrd′) *adv.* **1.** On board; into, in, or on a ship, train, etc. **2.** Alongside. — **all aboard!** Get on board! Get in!: a warning to passengers that their conveyance is about to start. — *prep.* **1.** On board of; upon or within: *aboard* the train. **2.** Alongside of.

a·bode¹ (ə·bōd′) Past tense and past participle of ABIDE. — *n.* **1.** A place of abiding; dwelling; home. **2.** The state or act of abiding; sojourn; stay. — **Syn.** See HOME. [OE *ābād*]

a·bode² (ə·bōd′) *Obs. v.t. & v.i.* **a·bod·ed, a·bod·ing** To forebode; be ominous. — *n.* An omen: also **a·bode′ment.** [ME *abeden* to announce < OE *ābēodan*]

ab·ohm (ab·ōm′) *n.* The cgs electromagnetic unit of resistance, equal to one millionth of an ohm. [< AB(SOLUTE) + OHM]

a·boi·deau (à·bwä·dō′) *n. pl.* **·deaus** (-dōz′) or **·deaux** (-dō′) *Canadian* A sluicegate in the dikes along the Bay of Fundy; also, a dike with sluicegates. Also **a·boi·teau′.** [< dial. F (Canadian)]

a·bol·ish (ə·bol′ish) *v.t.* To do away with; put an end to; annul; destroy. [< F *aboliss-,* stem of *abolir* < L *abolescere* to decay, vanish, inceptive of *abolere* to destroy] — **a·bol′ish·a·ble** *adj.* — **a·bol′ish·er** *n.* — **a·bol′ish·ment** *n.* — **Syn.** *Abolish, annihilate, exterminate, eradicate, extirpate, obliterate,* and *terminate* mean to bring to an end or do away with. *Abolish* is used only of institutions or conditions, not of people. *Annihilate* and *exterminate* signify total destruction of some material object. *Eradicate* and *extirpate* suggest the complete destruction of a thing pulled up by its roots. *Obliterate* means to wipe out utterly, while *terminate* is merely the formal verb for end.

ab·o·li·tion (ab′ə·lish′ən) *n.* **1.** The act of abolishing, or the state of being abolished; annulment; extinction. **2.** The abolishing of slavery in the United States. [< L *abolitio, -onis* < *abolere* to destroy] — **ab′o·li′tion·al** *adj.*

ab·o·li·tion·ar·y (ab′ə·lish′ən·er′ē) *adj.* Having to do with abolition; destructive.

ab·o·li·tion·ism (ab′ə·lish′ən·iz′əm) *n.* The principles of those who opposed slavery in the United States. — **ab′o·li′tion·ist** *n.*

a·bol·la (ə·bol′ə) *n. pl.* **·lae** (-lē) A Roman cloak. [< L]

a·bo·ma (ə·bō′mə) *n.* The ringed boa, or one of other large South American snakes of the family *Boidae.* [< Pg.; ult. prob. Bantu (Congo)]

ab·o·ma·sum (ab′ə·mā′səm) *n. pl.* **·sa** (-sə) The fourth or true digestive stomach of a ruminant: also called *reed.* Also **ab·o·ma·sus** (ab′ə·mā′səs). [< NL < L *ab-* away from + *omasum* bullock's tripe]

A–bomb (ā′bom′) *n.* An atomic bomb (which see).

ABOMA
(To 11 feet long)

a·bom·i·na·ble (ə·bom′in·ə·bəl) *adj.* **1.** Very hateful; loathsome; detestable. **2.** Extremely disagreeable; bad. [< OF < L *abominabilis* < *abominari.* See ABOMINATE.] — **a·bom′i·na·ble·ness** *n.* — **a·bom′i·na·bly** *adv.*

abominable snowman A legendary manlike monster said to inhabit snow-covered Himalayan peaks: also called *yeti.* [Trans. of Tibetan *metkokhangmi,* lit., evil-smelling man of the snows]

a·bom·i·nate (ə·bom′ə·nāt) *v.t.* **·nat·ed, ·nat·ing** **1.** To regard with loathing; abhor. **2.** To dislike strongly. — **Syn.** See HATE. [< L *abominatus,* pp. of *abominari* to abhor as an ill omen < *ab-* off + *omen* omen] — **a·bom′i·na′tor** *n.*

a·bom·i·na·tion (ə·bom′ə·nā′shən) *n.* **1.** Anything that excites disgust, hatred, or loathing; any detestable act or practice. **2.** Strong aversion or loathing.

à bon droit (à′ bôn′ drwà′) *French* With justice; rightfully.

à bon mar·ché (à′ bôn′ màr·shā′) *French* At a good bargain; inexpensively.

a·boon (ə·bōōn′) *adv. & prep. Scot. & Brit. Dial.* Above.

ab·o·ral (ab·ôr′əl, -ō′rəl) *adj. Zool.* Situated away from the mouth. — **ab·o′ral·ly** *adv.*

ab·o·rig·i·nal (ab′ə·rij′ə·nəl) *adj.* **1.** Of or pertaining to aborigines; primitive. **2.** Native; indigenous. — **Syn.** See NATIVE. — *n.* An aborigine. — **ab′o·rig′i·nal·ly** *adv.*

ab·o·rig·i·ne (ab′ə·rij′ə·nē) *n.* **1.** One of the original native inhabitants of a country. **2.** *pl.* Flora and fauna indigenous to a geographical area. [< L *aborigines* earliest inhabitants of a place < *ab origine* from the beginning]

ab o·rig·i·ne (ab ō·rij′ə·nē) *Latin* From the origin.

a·bort (ə·bôrt′) *v.i.* **1.** To bring forth young prematurely; miscarry. **2.** *Biol.* To fail of complete development. **3.** *Mil.* To fail to carry out a mission, especially for reasons other than enemy action. — *v.t.* **4.** To cause to have a miscarriage. **5.** To bring to a premature or unsuccessful conclusion. [< L *abortus,* pp. of *aboriri* to miscarry < *ab-* off, away + *oriri* to arise, be born]

a·bor·ti·cide (ə·bôr′tə·sid) *n.* **1.** The intentional destruction of the fetus in the womb. **2.** An agent for killing the fetus. [< L *abortus* (see ABORT) + -CIDE]

a·bor·ti·fa·cient (ə·bôr′tə·fā′shənt) *adj.* Causing abortion. — *n.* Anything used to cause abortion. [< L *abortus* (see ABORT) + -FACIENT]

a·bor·tion (ə·bôr′shən) *n.* **1.** *Law* A miscarriage produced artificially, especially as an illegal operation. **2.** The expulsion of a fetus prematurely; miscarriage. **3.** The defective result of a premature birth; a monstrosity. **4.** *Biol.* Partial or complete arrest of development, as of an embryo in its early stages. **5.** Failure in anything during progress and before maturity. [< L *abortio, -onis* < *aboriri.* See ABORT.] — **a·bor′tion·al** *adj.*

a·bor·tion·ist (ə·bôr′shən·ist) *n.* One who causes abortion.

a·bor·tive (ə·bôr′tiv) *adj.* **1.** Coming to naught; failing: an *abortive* revolt. **2.** Brought forth or born prematurely. **3.** Imperfectly developed; rudimentary, as an organ or stamen. **4.** *Med.* **a** Shortened in its course: an *abortive* fever. **b** Shortening the course of a disease. **c** Abortifacient. — **Syn.** See FUTILE. — **a·bor′tive·ly** *adv.* — **a·bor′tive·ness** *n.*

A·bou·kir (ā′bōō·kir′, ä·bōō′kir) See ABUKIR.

a·bou·li·a (ə·bōō′lē·ə), **a·bou·lic** (ə·bōō′lik) See ABULIA, etc.

a·bound (ə·bound′) *v.i.* **1.** To be in abundance; be plentiful. **2.** To have plenty; be rich: with *in*: The book *abounds* in anecdotes. **3.** To be full; teem: with *with*: The lakes *abound* with fish. [< OF *abunder* < L *abundare* to overflow < *ab-* from + *undare* to flow in waves < *unda* wave]

a·bout (ə·bout′) *adv.* **1.** Approximately; nearly: *about* five dollars; *about* right. **2.** *Informal* Almost; not quite: *about* finished. **3.** Nearby; in the vicinity: to stand idly *about.* **4.** To a reversed position; around: Turn your chair *about.* **5.** In rotation; around and around. **6.** In every direction; to all sides: to look *about.* **7.** Here and there, as without direction: to wander *about.* **8.** Astir; in motion; active: to be *about* early in the day; Influenza is *about.* **9.** On every side; around: Blessings compass thee *about.* — *prep.* **1.** On every side of; encircling; walls *about* a city. **2.** Near; within; on some side of: Stay *about* the house. **3.** Here and there in or upon: to walk *about* the town. **4.** Near; close to: *about* my size. **5.** Engaged in; concerned with: to be *about* one's business. **6.** Concerning; in reference to: a book *about* Italy. **7.** In one's possession; on hand: I have no money *about* me. **8.** Attached to (a person) as an attribute: She had a certain grace *about* her. **9.** On the point of; ready to: with the infinitive: *about* to speak. Abbr. *a*. [OE *onbūtan, abūtan < on, a* on + *būtan* outside]

a·bout-face (*n.* ə·bout′fās′; *v.* ə·bout′fās′) *n.* **1.** *Mil.* A pivoting turn to the rear executed when halted. **2.** Any turning around or reversal, as of opinion or point of view; volte-face. — *v.i.* -**faced**, -**fac·ing** To perform an about-face.

a·bout-ship (ə·bout′ship′) *v.i.* -**shipped**, -**ship·ping** *Naut.* To change a ship's course by going on the opposite tack.

a·bove (ə·buv′) *adv.* **1.** In or to a higher place; overhead; up: the stars *above*. **2.** Superior in rank or position: the court *above*. **3.** In an earlier section of something written: in the paragraph *above*. **4.** In heaven. — *adj.* The *above* men named, etc., in what is above; preceding: The *above* men were acquitted. — *n.* That which is higher up or just before: preceded by *the*. — *prep.* **1.** Directly over; on top of: *above* the mountains. **2.** Higher than; rising beyond: a voice heard *above* the din. **3. a** Farther north than: *above* Memphis. **b** *U.S.* Farther upstream than. **4.** More than, in number, quantity, degree, etc.; beyond: He ran *above* 500 yards. **5.** Superior to in authority or power. **6.** Beyond the influence or reach of: *above* suspicion. [ME *abofen < OE onbufan*] *Above* may appear as a combining form or as the first element in two-word phrases:

above-cited   aboveground   above-named
above deck   above-listed   above-quoted
above-found   above measure   above-said
above-given   above-mentioned   above-written

a·bove·board (ə·buv′bôrd′, -bōrd′) *adj. & adv.* In open sight; without concealment, fraud, or trickery.

ab o·vo (ab ō′vō) *Latin* From the beginning; literally, from the egg.

Abp. or **abp.** Archbishop.

abr. **1.** Abridged. **2.** Abridgment.

a·bra·ca·dab·ra (ab′rə·kə·dab′rə) *n.* **1.** A cabalistic word written in triangular form, anciently used as a preventive or curative charm. **2.** Any spell or incantation. **3.** A jargon of conjuring or nonsensical words; nonsense. [< L]

a·brade (ə·brād′) *v.t.* **a·brad·ed, a·brad·ing** To rub or wear off by friction; scrape away. [< L *abradere < ab-* away + *radere* to scrape] — **a·bra′dant** *adj. & n.* — **a·brad′er** *n.*

A·bra·ham (ā′brə·ham) The progenitor of the Hebrews; first called **A·bram** (ā′brəm). *Gen.* xvii 5.

a·bran·chi·al (ā·brang′kē·əl) *adj. Zool.* Without gills. Also **a·bran·chi·ate** (ā·brang′kē·it, -āt). [< A-⁴ without + Gk. *branchia* gills]

a·bra·sion (ə·brā′zhən) *n.* **1.** A wearing or rubbing away, as of rocks by glaciers. **2.** An abraded area, as on the skin. [< L *abrasio, -onis < abradere.* See ABRADE.]

a·bra·sive (ə·brā′siv, -ziv) *adj.* Abrading or tending to abrade. — *n.* An abrading substance, as emery or sand.

ab·re·act (ab′rē·akt′) *v.t. Psychoanal.* To relieve by abreaction. [< ABREACTION]

ab·re·ac·tion (ab′rē·ak′shən) *n. Psychoanal.* The releasing of repressed emotions by reliving, in words, feelings, or actions, the original traumatic situation. [< AB-¹ from + RE-ACTION, after G *abreagierung*]

a·breast (ə·brest′) *adv. & adj.* Side by side and equally advanced. — **abreast of** (or **with**) Side by side with; not behind or ahead of.

a·bri (ə·brē′, *Fr.* à·brē′) *n. pl.* **a·bris** (ə·brēz′, *Fr.* à·brē′) A refuge or shelter; especially, a bomb shelter. [< F]

a·bridge (ə·brij′) *v.t.* **a·bridged, a·bridg·ing 1.** To give the substance of in fewer words; condense; epitomize. **2.** To shorten, as in time. **3.** To curtail or lessen, as rights. **4.** To deprive. [< OF *abregier < L abbreviare.* See ABBREVIATE.] — **a·bridg′a·ble** or **a·bridge′a·ble** *adj.* — **a·bridg′er** *n.*

a·bridg·ment (ə·brij′mənt) *n.* **1.** The act of abridging, or the state of being abridged. **2.** A condensation, as of a book; epitome; abstract. Also **a·bridge′ment.** Abbr. *abr.*
— **Syn. 2.** *Abridgment, epitome, compendium, abstract, digest, précis, analysis, outline,* and *synopsis* all refer to giving the heart, gist, or basic sense of a printed work. An *abridgment* keeps the most important portions of a work substantially as they stand. An *epitome* or *compendium* is a condensed view of a subject, whether derived from a previous publication or not. An *abstract, digest,* or *précis* is an independent statement of what a book or an article contains, the *abstract* closely following the main heads, the *digest* or *précis* giving the substance with careful consideration of all the contents. An *analysis* draws out the chief thoughts or arguments, expressed or implied. An *outline* or *synopsis* is a kind of sketch closely following the plan. — **Ant.** amplification.

a·broach (ə·brōch′) *adj. & adv.* **1.** In a condition to let out the liquor; broached. **2.** Astir. [< A-¹ on + BROACH]

a·broad (ə·brôd′) *adv.* **1.** Out of one's home or abode; out-of-doors. **2.** Out of one's own country; in or into foreign

lands. **3.** At large; in circulation: Rumors are *abroad*. **4.** Broadly; widely. **5.** Wide of the mark; astray. [ME. See A-¹ and BROAD.]

ab·ro·gate (ab′rə·gāt) *v.t.* -**gat·ed**, -**gat·ing** To annul by authority, as a law; abolish; repeal. — **Syn.** See ANNUL. [< L *abrogatus*, pp. of *abrogare < ab-* away + *rogare* to propose a law] — **ab·ro·ga·ble** (ab′rə·gə·bəl) *adj.* — **ab′ro·ga′tion** *n.* — **ab′ro·ga′tive** *adj.* — **ab′ro·ga′tor** *n.*

a·brupt (ə·brupt′) *adj.* **1.** Beginning, ending, or changing suddenly; unexpected. **2.** Unceremonious; sudden, as a departure. **3.** Rude or curt, as in speech; brusque. **4.** Changing subject suddenly; unconnected, as literary style. **5.** Steep, as a cliff. **6.** *Biol.* Truncate. — **Syn.** See BLUNT, STEEP¹. [< L *abruptus*, pp. of *abrumpere < ab-* off + *rumpere* to break] — **a·brupt′ly** *adv.* — **a·brupt′ness** *n.*

a·brup·tion (ə·brup′shən) *n.* A sudden breaking off.

A·bruz·zi (ä·brōōt′sē), **Duke of the**, 1873–1933, Prince Luigi of Savoy-Aosta, Italian naval officer and explorer.

A·bruz·zi (ä·brōōt′sē) A Region of central Italy, on the Adriatic; 4,170 sq. mi.; pop. 1,206,266 (1961); capital, Aquila. Formerly, **Abruzzi e Molise** (ē mô′lē zā).

abs- Var. of AB-¹.

abs. 1. Absent. **2.** Absolute (temperature). **3.** Absolutely. **4.** Abstract.

Ab·sa·lom (ab′sə·ləm) The favorite and rebellious son of David. II *Sam.* xiii–xix.

ab·scess (ab′ses) *Pathol. n.* A collection of pus in any part of the body, formed by the disintegration of tissue. It may be caused by bacteria and is often accompanied by painful inflammation. — *v.i.* To form an abscess. [< L *abscessus < abscedere* to go away < *ab-* away + *cedere* to go; with ref. to the flowing of humors into the area] — **ab′scessed** *adj.*

ab·scis·sa (ab·sis′ə) *n. pl.* **ab·scis·sas** or **ab·scis·sae** (-sis′ē) *Math.* **1.** The distance of any point from the Y-axis of ordinates in a coordinate system, measured on a line parallel to the X-axis. **2.** The line or number indicating such distance. Abbr. *x* [< L (*linea*) *abscissa* (line) cut off, fem. pp. of *abscindere.* See ABSCISSION.]

ABSCISSA
AB: x axis.
AC: y axis.
Ae abscissa
of point *f*.

ab·scis·sion (ab·sizh′ən, -sish′ən) *n.* **1.** The act of cutting off or removing. **2.** *Bot.* **a** The shedding of parts of a plant by the action of certain cells in the branch or bark. **b** The freeing of a fungus spore through breakdown of a portion of its stalk. **3.** In rhetoric, an abrupt breaking off for effect, as in the middle of a sentence. Compare APOSIOPESIS. [< L *abscissio, -onis < abscindere < ab-* off + *scindere* to cut]

ab·scond (ab·skond′) *v.i.* To depart suddenly and secretly, especially to escape the law. — **Syn.** See ESCAPE. [< L *abscondere < ab-* away + *condere* to store away, conceal] — **ab·scond′er** *n.*

ab·sence (ab′səns) *n.* **1.** The state of being absent: *absence* from home. **2.** The period of being away: a week's *absence*. **3.** Lack: an *absence* of humility. — **absence of mind** Absentmindedness. [< F < L *absentia < absens.* See ABSENT.]

ab·sent (*adj.* ab′sənt; *v.* ab·sent′) *adj.* **1.** Not present; away. **2.** Lacking; nonexistent: In some fishes the ribs are *absent*. **3.** Inattentive; absent-minded. Abbr. *abs.* — **Syn.** See ABSTRACTED. — *v.t.* To take or keep (oneself) away. [< L *absens, -entis*, ppr. of *abesse < ab-* away + *esse* to be] — **ab·sent′er** *n.* — **ab′sent·ly** *adv.* — **ab′sent·ness** *n.*

ab·sen·tee (ab′sən·tē′) *n.* One who is absent, as from a job. — *adj.* **1.** Temporarily absent: an *absentee* voter. **2.** Non-resident: an *absentee* landlord.

ab·sen·tee·ism (ab′sən·tē′iz·əm) *n.* Habitual or frequent absence, especially from work.

ab·sen·te re·o (ab·sen′tē rē′ō) *Law* In the absence of the defendant. [< L]

ab·sent-mind·ed (ab′sənt·mīn′did) *adj.* Inattentive to one's immediate surroundings or business because of preoccupation of the mind; forgetful. — **Syn.** See ABSTRACTED. — **ab′sent-mind′ed·ly** *adv.* — **ab′sent-mind′ed·ness** *n.*

absent without leave Absent from a military duty or post without permission from the proper authority, but not intending to desert. Abbr. *awol, AWOL, a.w.o.l., A.W.O.L.*

ab·sinthe (ab′sinth) *n.* **1.** A green, bitter liqueur having the flavor of licorice, made from oils of wormwood, or some substitute, and other aromatics. **2.** Wormwood. Also **ab′sinth.** [< F < L *absinthium* wormwood < Gk. *apsinthion*] — **ab·sin′thi·al, ab·sin′thi·an** *adj.*

ab·sinth·ism (ab′sinth·iz′əm) *n.* A nervous and mental disorder induced by habitual or excessive use of absinthe.

ab·sin·thi·um (ab·sin′thē·əm) *n.* **1.** The common wormwood. **2.** The dried leaves and flowers of this herb. [< L. See ABSINTHE.]

ab·so·lute (ab′sə·lōōt) *adj.* **1.** Free from restriction; unlimited; unconditional: an *absolute* monarchy. **2.** Complete; perfect: *absolute* goodness. **3.** Unadulterated; pure. **4.** Not relative to anything else; independent. **5.** Positive; certain.

6. *Gram.* **a** Free from the usual relations of syntax or construction with other words in the sentence, as *It being late* in *It being late, we started home.* **b** Of a transitive verb, having no object expressed and, hence, functioning as intransitive, as *That professor inspires and stimulates.* **c** Of an adjective, standing without a noun, as *the brave and the fair.* **7.** *Physics* **a** Relating to the absolute-temperature scale: 15° *absolute.* Abbr. *A., abs.* **b** Determined or measured only by the fundamental notions of space, mass, and time: *absolute* measurement. — *n.* That which is absolute or perfect. — **the Absolute** *Philos.* The ultimate basis of all thought, reasoning, or being. [< L *absolutus*, pp. of *absolvere.* See ABSOLVE.] — **ab′so·lute′ness** *n.*
— **Syn.** (adj.) **1.** *Absolute, supreme, arbitrary, autocratic, despotic, tyrannical,* and *tyrannous* all apply to government, usually monarchy, that is all-encompassing and responsible only to itself. As used of human authority, all these words signify freedom from limitation by any higher authority. An *absolute* monarch is the *supreme* authority in his kingdom; he is *arbitrary* if he governs by his personal opinion or caprice; *autocratic* if he haughtily imposes his authority on others; *despotic* if his rule is masterful and severe; *tyrannical* or *tyrannous* if cruelty and injustice mark his reign.
absolute alcohol See under ALCOHOL.
ab·so·lute·ly (ab′sə·lōōt′lē, *emphatic* ab′sə·lōōt′lē) *adv.* **1.** Completely; unconditionally. **2.** Positively. **3.** *Gram.* So as not to take an object: to use a verb *absolutely.* Abbr. *abs.*
absolute magnitude *Astron.* A measure of the intrinsic as distinguished from the apparent brightness of a star, equal to the luminosity a star would have if located 10 parsecs from the earth.
absolute monarchy See under MONARCHY.
absolute music See under MUSIC.
absolute pitch *Music* **1.** The pitch of a musical tone as distinguished by the number of its vibrations per second. **2.** The ability to name the pitch of any note sounded without reference to the prior sound of an established pitch: also called *perfect pitch.*
absolute temperature Temperature reckoned from absolute zero. See illustration of THERMOMETER. Abbr. *T.*
absolute zero That temperature at which a body would be wholly deprived of heat, and at which a perfect gas would exert no pressure, equivalent to about − 273.16° C. or − 459.7° F.
ab·so·lu·tion (ab′sə·lōō′shən) *n.* **1.** The act of absolving, as from guilt, penalties, etc.; forgiveness. **2.** The state of being absolved. **3.** *Eccl.* **a** A remission of sin and its penalties pronounced by a priest. **b** A formula declaring the forgiveness of sin. **c** In some Protestant churches, the declaration or imploring of God's forgiveness by a priest or minister. **d** The act of releasing from an ecclesiastical sentence or censure. [< L *absolutio, -onis* < *absolvere.* See ABSOLVE.]
ab·so·lut·ism (ab′sə·lōō·tiz′əm) *n.* **1.** In government, the doctrine or practice of unlimited authority and control; despotism. **2.** Absoluteness; positiveness. **3.** *Philos.* Any doctrine about the Absolute. **4.** *Theol.* Predestination. — **ab′·so·lut′ist** *n.* — **ab′so·lu·tis′tic** *adj.*
ab·sol·u·to·ry (ab·sol′yə·tôr′ē, -tō′rē) *adj.* Having power to absolve; absolving. [< L *absolutorius* < *absolvere.* See ABSOLVE.]
ab·solve (ab·solv′, -zolv′, əb-) *v.t.* **·solved, ·solv·ing 1.** To free from the penalties or consequences of an action: His excuses do not *absolve* him. **2.** To acquit, as of guilt or complicity. **3.** To release, as from an obligation: with *from.* **4.** *Eccl.* To grant a remission of sin or its penalties; pardon. [< L *absolvere* < *ab-* from + *solvere* to loosen. Doublet of ASSOIL.] — **ab·solv′a·ble** *adj.* — **ab·sol′vent** *adj. & n.* — **ab·solv′er** *n.*
— **Syn.** *Absolve, acquit, exonerate, pardon, forgive,* and *vindicate* all mean to free a person from the consequences of a sin or alleged crime, either out of mercy or justice. To *absolve* is to set free from obligation or penalty. To *acquit* is to set free from accusation, usually for lack of evidence. The innocent are rightfully *acquitted*; the guilty may be mercifully *absolved. Exonerate* stresses freedom from future blame. *Pardon* and *forgive* denote release from punishment; *forgive* additionally implies complete giving up of resentment. To *vindicate* is to clear through evidence. — **Ant.** blame, incriminate.
ab·so·nant (ab′sə·nənt) *adj.* Discordant; unreasonable. [<AB-¹ + L *sonans* sounding; formed on analogy with *dissonant, consonant*]
ab·sorb (ab·sôrb′, -zôrb′) *v.t.* **1.** To drink in or suck up, as through or into pores. **2.** To engross completely; occupy wholly: Study *absorbs* him. **3.** To take up or in by chemical or molecular action, as gases, heat, liquid, light, etc.: distinguished from *adsorb.* **4.** To take in and incorporate: swallow up: The city *absorbs* the suburbs. **5.** To receive the force or action of; intercept: The walls *absorbed* his cries for help. [< L *absorbere* < *ab-* from + *sorbere* to suck in] — **ab·sorb′a·bil′i·ty** *n.* — **ab·sorb′a·ble** *adj.* — **ab·sorb′er** *n.* — **ab·sorb′ing·ly** *adj.* — **ab·sorb′ing·ly** *adv.*
ab·sorbed (ab·sôrbd′, -zôrbd′) *adj.* **1.** Engrossed; rapt. **2.** Sucked up or sunken in, as paint on a porous surface. — **Syn.** See ABSTRACTED. — **ab·sorb·ed·ly** (ab·sôr′bid·lē, -zôr′-) *adv.* — **ab·sorb′ed·ness** *n.*
ab·sor·be·fa·cient (ab·sôr′bə·fā′shənt, -zôr′-) *adj.* Causing absorption. — *n.* A substance causing or promoting absorption. [< L *absorbere* (see ABSORB) + -FACIENT]

ab·sor·bent (ab·sôr′bənt, -zôr′-) *adj.* Absorbing or tending to absorb. — *n.* A substance, duct, etc., that absorbs. [< L *absorbens, -entis,* ppr. of *absorbere.* See ABSORB.] — **ab·sor′ben·cy** *n.*
absorbent cotton Cotton from which all fatty matter has been removed, used as an absorbent in surgical dressings, sanitary preparations, etc.
ab·sorp·tance (ab·sôrp′təns, -zôrp′-) *n. Physics* The ratio of the radiant flux absorbed by a body to that which strikes it.
ab·sorp·tion (ab·sôrp′shən, -zôrp′-) *n.* **1.** The act of absorbing, or the condition of being absorbed. **2.** Assimilation, as by incorporation or by the digestive process. **3.** Preoccupation of the mind. **4.** *Physics* **a** The process by which a liquid or gas is taken into the interstices of a porous substance and held there. **b** The transformation of any form of radiant energy as it passes through a material substance. [< L *absorptio, -onis* < *absorbere.* See ABSORB.] — **ab·sorp′tive** *adj.* — **ab·sorp′tive·ness, ab·sorp·tiv′i·ty** *n.*
absorption spectrum *Physics* A spectrum that indicates, by characteristic dark lines, the presence of a substance absorbing certain wavelengths that would give bright lines in an emission spectrum.
ab·stain (ab·stān′) *v.i.* To keep oneself back; refrain voluntarily: with *from.* — **Syn.** See REFRAIN¹. [< OF *abstenir* < L *abstinere* < *ab-* from + *tenere* to hold]
ab·stain·er (ab·stā′nər) *n.* One who abstains, especially from using alcoholic beverages.
ab·ste·mi·ous (ab·stē′mē·əs) *adj.* Eating and drinking sparingly; abstinent; temperate. [< L *abstemius* temperate < *ab-* from + root of *temetum* intoxicating drink] — **ab·ste′mi·ous·ly** *adv.* — **ab·ste′mi·ous·ness** *n.*
ab·sten·tion (ab·sten′shən) *n.* A refraining or abstaining. [< L *abstentio, -onis* < *abstinere.* See ABSTAIN.] — **ab·sten′tious** *adj.*
ab·sterge (ab·stûrj′) *v.t.* **·sterged, ·sterg·ing** *Archaic* **1.** To wipe away; cleanse. **2.** To purge. [< L *abstergere* < *ab-* away + *tergere* to wipe] — **ab·ster·sion** (ab·stûr′shən, -zhən) *n.* — **ab·ster·sive** (ab·stûr′siv) *adj.*
ab·ster·gent (ab·stûr′jənt) *adj.* Cleansing. — *n.* A cleansing substance.
ab·sti·nence (ab′stə·nəns) *n.* **1.** The act or practice of abstaining, as from food, pleasure, etc. **2.** Abstention from alcoholic beverages: also called *total abstinence.* **3.** *Eccl.* Abstention from certain foods, as from meat during Lent. **4.** Self-denial; forbearance. [< F < L *abstinentia* < *abstinere.* See ABSTAIN.] — **ab′sti·nent** *adj.* — **ab′sti·nent·ly** *adv.*
— **Syn. 1.** *Abstinence, abstemiousness, self-denial, fasting, sobriety,* and *temperance* all imply voluntary restraint of one's appetites. *Abstinence* from food signifies going without; *abstemiousness,* partaking moderately; *abstinence* may be for a single occasion, *abstemiousness* is habitual moderation. *Self-denial* is giving up what one wishes; *abstinence* may be refraining from what one does not desire. *Fasting* is abstinence from food for a limited time, and generally for religious reasons. *Sobriety* and *temperance* signify moderate indulgence. — **Ant.** hedonism, self-indulgence.
ab·stract (*adj.* ab·strakt′, ab′strakt; *n.* ab′strakt; *v. defs. 1–4* ab·strakt′; *v. def. 5* ab′strakt) *adj.* **1.** Considered apart from matter or from specific examples; not concrete: *abstract* truth. **2.** Theoretical; ideal, as opposed to practical. **3.** Abstruse: *abstract* reasoning. **4.** Considered or expressed without reference to particular example, as numbers, attributes, or qualities: 8 is an *abstract* number; "Redness" and "valor" are *abstract* nouns. **5.** In art, generalized or universal, as opposed to concrete, specific, or representational; tending away from the realistic or literal. — *n.* **1.** A summary or epitome, as of a document. **2.** That which concentrates in itself the essential properties of some larger object or whole; essence. **3.** An abstract idea or term. **4.** *Med.* A special preparation of a drug in powder form, having twice the strength of the original drug. Abbr. *abs.* — **Syn.** See ABRIDGMENT. — **in the abstract** Apart from concrete relation or embodiment; in its general reference or meaning; abstractly. — *v.t.* **1.** To take away; remove. **2.** To take away secretly; purloin. **3.** To withdraw or disengage (the attention, interest, etc.). **4.** To consider apart from particular or material instances; form a general notion of: to *abstract* the idea of humanity from a crowd of men. **5.** To make an abstract of, as a book or treatise; summarize; abridge. [< L *abstractus,* pp. of *abstrahere* < *ab-* away + *trahere* to draw] — **ab·stract′er** *n.* — **ab·stract′ly** *adv.* — **ab·stract′ness** *n.*
ab·stract·ed (ab·strak′tid) *adj.* **1.** Lost in thought; absent-minded. **2.** Separated from all else; apart. — **ab·stract′·ed·ly** *adv.* — **ab·stract′ed·ness** *n.*
— **Syn. 1.** *Abstracted, absorbed, preoccupied, absent-minded, absent, inattentive,* and *oblivious* all mean partly or fully unaware of one's surroundings or actions. *Abstracted, absorbed,* and *preoccupied* refer to the cause of this unawareness; *absent-minded, absent,* and *inattentive,* to its effect. The man *absorbed* in one thing will appear *absent* in others. The *absent-minded* man is *oblivious* of ordinary matters, because his thoughts are elsewhere. One who is *preoccupied* is intensely busy in thought; one may be *absent-minded* simply through inattention, with fitful and aimless wandering of thought. *Inattentive* refers to an obvious lack of concern for that which properly demands one's attention. — **Ant.** attentive.
abstract expressionism A movement in painting, originating in New York City in the 1940's, in which the artist

concerns himself primarily with color, design, rhythm, manner of applying paint to the surface, etc., and does not in any way attempt to reproduce specific or recognizable objects.
ab·strac·tion (ab-strak′shən) *n.* **1.** The process of separating qualities or attributes from the individual objects to which they belong. **2.** A product of this process; a concept: Beauty is an *abstraction*. **3.** A visionary or impractical theory. **4.** The act of withdrawing; separation. **5.** Dishonest removal; theft. **6.** Absence of mind; preoccupation. **7.** An art form or work of art in which the qualities are either predominantly or totally abstract. [< L *abstractio, -onis* < *abstractus*. See ABSTRACT.]
ab·strac·tive (ab-strak′tiv) *adj.* **1.** Of, pertaining to, or tending to abstraction. **2.** Having the power of abstraction; epitomizing. **— ab·strac′tive·ly** *adv.* **— ab·strac′tive·ness** *n.*
abstract noun *Gram.* A noun that names a quality, idea, or anything having no actual physical existence, as *goodness, democracy, reputation*: distinguished from *concrete noun.*
abstract of title *Law* A document containing a brief and orderly statement of the original grant and subsequent conveyances and encumbrances relating to the title and ownership of real estate.
ab·stric·tion (ab-strik′shən) *n. Bot.* A process of spore formation in certain fungi, in which the sporophore becomes constricted by septa at the place of division. [< AB-¹ + L *strictio, -onis* a binding < *stringere* to bind]
ab·struse (ab-stroos′) *adj.* **1.** Hard to understand. **2.** *Obs.* Hidden; concealed. **— Syn.** See COMPLEX, MYSTERIOUS. [< L *abstrusus,* pp. of *abstrudere* to conceal < *ab-* away + *trudere* to thrust] **— ab·struse′ly** *adv.* **— ab·struse′ness** *n.*
ab·surd (ab-sûrd′, -zûrd′) *adj.* Opposed to manifest reason or truth; irrational; ridiculous. [< F *absurde* < L *absurdus* out of tune, incongruous, senseless < *ab-* completely + *surdus* deaf, dull] **— ab·surd′ly** *adv.* **— ab·surd′ness** *n.*
— Syn. *Absurd, ridiculous,* and *preposterous* refer to something beyond normal belief. That is *absurd* which is contrary to reason or good sense. *Absurd* implies obvious error, while *ridiculous* carries the added implication that the error is laughable. *Preposterous* refers to what is overwhelmingly *absurd.* **— Ant.** sensible.
ab·surd·i·ty (ab-sûr′də-tē, -zûr′-) *n. pl.* **·ties 1.** The quality of being absurd. **2.** Something absurd.
A·bu-Bek·r (ə-boo′bek′ər), 573–634, first Moslem caliph 632–634, Mohammed's successor.
A·bu·kir (ä′boo-kir′, ə-boo′kər) A village in northern Egypt on Abukir Bay on the Mediterranean; site of the Battle of the Nile, 1798, British victory over Napoleonic naval forces: also *Aboukir.*
a·bu·li·a (ə-boo′lē-ə, ə-byoo′-) *n. Psychiatry* Loss or impairment of will power: also spelled *aboulia.* [< NL < Gk. *aboulia* < *a-* without + *boulē* will] **— a·bu′lic** *adj.*
A·bul Ka·sim (ə-bool′ kä′sim), died 1013?, Arab surgeon and medical encyclopedist. Also *Albucasis.*
a·bun·dance (ə-bun′dəns) *n.* **1.** A plentiful or overflowing supply; great number or quantity. **2.** Fullness: *abundance* of the heart. **3.** Wealth; affluence.
a·bun·dant (ə-bun′dənt) *adj.* **1.** Existing in plentiful supply; ample. **2.** Abounding: with *in*: a land *abundant* in cattle. **— Syn.** See PLENTIFUL. [< OF < L *abundans, -antis,* ppr. of *abundare.* See ABOUND.] **— a·bun′dant·ly** *adv.*
ab ur·be con·di·ta (ab ûr′bē kon′di·tə) *Latin* From the founding of the city (of Rome, about 753 B.C.). Abbr. *A.U.C.*
a·buse (*v.* ə-byooz′; *n.* ə-byoos′) *v.t.* **a·bused, a·bus·ing 1.** To use improperly or injuriously; misuse. **2.** To hurt by treating wrongly; injure: to *abuse* friendship. **3.** To speak in coarse or bad terms of or to; revile; malign. **4.** *Archaic* To deceive. **— n. 1.** Improper or injurious use; misuse: *abuse* of power. **2.** Ill-treatment; injury. **3.** Vicious conduct, practice, or action. **4.** Abusive language; slander. **5.** *Archaic* Deception. [< F *abuser,* ult. < L *abusus,* pp. of *abuti* to misuse < *ab-* away + *uti* to use] **— a·bus′er** *n.*
— Syn. (verb) **1.** *Abuse, ill-treat, persecute,* and *oppress* mean to treat badly. *Abuse* covers all unreasonable or improper use or treatment by word or act, of a person or a thing. *Ill-treat* is commonly limited to injurious acts towards persons. To *persecute* one is to *ill-treat* him for opinion's sake, commonly for religious belief; to *oppress* is generally to *ill-treat* for political or pecuniary motives. Compare ASPERSE, POLLUTE, SCOLD.
a·bu·sive (ə-byoo′siv) *adj.* **1.** Of the nature of or characterized by abuse. **2.** Insulting; vituperative. **3.** Used wrongly; misapplied. **— a·bu′sive·ly** *adv.* **— a·bu′sive·ness** *n.*
a·but (ə-but′) *v.* **a·but·ted, a·but·ting** *v.i.* **1.** To touch, join, or adjoin at the end or side; border: with *on, upon,* or *against.* **— v.t. 2.** To border on; end at: This building *abuts* the park. [< OF *abouter* to border on (< *a-* to + *bout* end); infl. by OF *abuter* to touch with an end (< *a-* to + *but* end)] **— a·but′ter** *n.* **— a·but′ting** *adj.*
a·bu·ti·lon (ə-byoo′tə·lon) *n.* Any plant of a genus (*Abutilon*) of the mallow family having single, bell-shaped flowers. Some cultivated varieties are called *flowering maple.* [< NL < Arabic *aubūtilūn*]
a·but·ment (ə-but′mənt) *n.* **1.** The act of abutting. **2.**

Something that abuts, the thing abutted upon, or the point of junction. **3.** A supporting or buttressing structure, as at the end of a bridge or wall; also, the part of an arch that takes the thrust or strain. For illustration see ARCH¹.
a·but·tal (ə-but′l) *n.* **1.** An abutting or abutment. **2.** *Usually pl.* An abutting part; boundary.
ab·volt (ab-vōlt′) *n.* The cgs electromagnetic unit of electromotive force, equal to a hundred-millionth of a volt. [< AB(SOLUTE) + VOLT]
ab·watt (ab-wot′) *n.* A unit of power, equal to 1×10^7 ergs per second; 0.001 kilowatt. [< AB(SOLUTE) + WATT]
a·by (ə-bī′) *v.t.* **a·bought** *Archaic* **1.** To pay the penalty for. **2.** To endure; suffer, as a fate. Also **a·bye′.** [OE *ābycgan* to buy, pay for]
A·by·dos (ə-bī′dos) **1.** An ancient city of Asia Minor opposite Sestos at the narrowest point of the Hellespont. **2.** An ancient town in central Egypt, on the Nile; site of a group of ancient temples.
a·bysm (ə-biz′əm) *n.* An abyss. [< OF *abisme,* ult. < L *abyssus.* See ABYSS.]
a·bys·mal (ə-biz′məl) *adj.* Unfathomable; immeasurable; extreme: an *abysmal* ignorance. **— a·bys′mal·ly** *adv.*
a·byss (ə-bis′) *n.* **1.** A bottomless gulf; chasm. **2.** Any profound depth or void: an *abyss* of shame; the *abyss* of time. **3.** The lowest depths of the sea. **4.** The bottomless pit; hell. [< L *abyssus* < Gk. *abyssos* < *a-* without + *byssos* bottom]
a·bys·sal (ə-bis′əl) *adj.* **1.** Abysmal. **2.** Pertaining to the lowest depths of the ocean. **— Syn.** See OCEANIC.
Ab·ys·sin·i·a (ab′ə-sin′ē-ə) Ethiopia. **— Ab′ys·sin′i·an** *adj. & n.*
ac- Assimilated var. of AD-.
ac. 1. Account. **2.** Acre.
-ac *suffix* **1.** Having; affected by: *demoniac.* **2.** Pertaining to; of: *cardiac.* [< Gk. *-akos* or L *-acus* or F *-aque*]
a/c or **A/C** (*pl.* **a/cs** or **A/Cs**) Account; account current.
Ac 1. *Chem.* Actinium. **2.** *Meteorol.* Altocumulus.
AC or **A.C. 1.** Air Corps. **2.** Army Corps.
AC or **A.C.** or **a.c.** *Electr.* Alternating current.
A.C. 1. After Christ. **2.** Athletic Club.
a·ca·cia (ə-kā′shə) *n.* **1.** Any of a large genus (*Acacia*) of flowering, leguminous trees and shrubs of the tropics and warm temperate regions. **2.** The locust tree. **3.** Gum arabic. [< L < Gk. *akakia,* a thorny tree of Egypt < *akē* point]
acad. Academic; academy.
Ac·a·deme (ak′ə-dēm′, ak′ə-dēm) The garden or grove near ancient Athens where Plato taught. **— the groves of Academe** *Poetic* **1.** A school. **2.** The scholarly life. [< L *academia.* See ACADEMY.]
ac·a·dem·ic (ak′ə-dem′ik) *adj.* **1.** Pertaining to an academy, college, or university; scholarly. **2.** *U.S.* Offering or having to do with liberal or classical rather than vocational or technical studies: an *academic* high school. **3.** Theoretical, as opposed to practical; speculative: often used disparagingly. **4.** According to scholastic usage; traditional. Also **ac′a·dem′i·cal.** Abbr. *acad.* **— n.** A college or university student or faculty member. **— ac′a·dem′i·cal·ly** *adv.*
ac·a·dem·i·cals (ak′ə-dem′i·kəlz) *n.pl.* Academic dress; cap and gown.
academic freedom The liberty to pursue legitimate study or teaching.
a·cad·e·mi·cian (ə-kad′ə-mish′ən, ak′ə-də-) *n.* A member of an academy of art, science, or literature.
ac·a·dem·i·cism (ak′ə-dem′ə-siz′əm) *n.* **1.** The quality of being academic. **2.** Pedantic formalism, as in art or literature. Also **a·cad·e·mism** (ə-kad′ə-miz′əm).
a·cad·e·my (ə-kad′ə-mē) *n. pl.* **·mies 1.** A secondary school, usually a private one. **2.** A school giving instruction in some science or art. **3.** A learned society for the advancement of arts or sciences. Abbr. *A., acad.*
A·cad·e·my (ə-kad′ə-mē) *n.* **1.** Academe; hence, the pupils of Plato collectively or Plato's philosophy. **2.** The French Academy. **3.** The Royal Academy. [< F *académie* < L *academia* < Gk. *Akadēmeia* the grove of Akadēmos where Plato taught] **— Ac′a·dem′ic** *adj. & n.*
A·ca·di·a (ə-kā′dē-ə) **1.** A former name for a region in eastern Canada, including Nova Scotia and New Brunswick. **2.** A parish in southern Louisiana settled by deported Acadians; pop. 52,109.
A·ca·di·an (ə-kā′dē-ən) *adj.* Of or pertaining to Acadia or Nova Scotia. **— n.** One of the early French settlers of Acadia or their descendants. See CAJUN.
Acadia National Park A rocky, mountainous area mainly on Mount Desert island off southern Maine; 44 sq. mi.; established 1929.
ac·a·jou (ak′ə-zhoo) *n.* **1.** A tropical American wood (genus *Cedrela*), valued for fine furniture and interior trim. **2.** The cashew tree, its fruits, or gum. [< F < Pg. *acajú*]
ac·a·leph (ak′ə-lef) *n. pl.* **ac·a·le·phae** (ak′ə-lef′fē) A jellyfish. Also **ac·a·lephe** (ak′ə-lef). [< Gk. *akalēphē* nettle] **— ac·a·le·phan** (ak′ə-lef′fən) *adj. & n.* **— ac·a·le·phoid** (ak′ə-lef′foid) *adj.*

a·can·tha·ceous (ak′ən-thā′shəs) *adj. Bot.* **1.** Of, like, or belonging to the acanthus family. **2.** Prickly.

a·can·thine (ə-kan′thin) *adj.* **1.** Pertaining to or like an acanthus. **2.** Decorated with the acanthus leaf.

acantho- *combining form* Thorn or thorny; spine, point. Also, before vowels, **acanth-.** [< Gk. *akantha* thorn]

a·can·tho·ceph·a·lan (ə-kan′thō-sef′ə-lən) *n. Zool.* One of a phylum or class (*Acanthocephala*) of worms parasitic in the intestines of man and other vertebrates, and having a retractile proboscis covered with hooks. [< ACANTHO- + Gk. *kephalē* head]

a·can·thoid (ə-kan′thoid) *adj.* Spiny.

a·can·thop·ter·yg·i·an (ak′an-thop′tə-rij′ē-ən) *n. Zool.* One of an order or suborder of teleost fishes (*Acanthopterygii*), including all or most fishes with spines in the fins, as the mackerel, bass, etc. [< ACANTHO- + Gk. *pterygion* fin]

a·can·thous (ə-kan′thəs) *adj.* Spinous.

a·can·thus (ə-kan′thəs) *n. pl.* **·thus·es** or **·thi** (-thī) **1.** Any of a genus (*Acanthus*) of plants having large spiny leaves, common in the Mediterranean region. The acanthus is typical of a large family (*Acanthaceae*) of chiefly herbaceous tropical plants noted for their showy flowers and striking foliage. **2.** *Archit.* A conventionalized and decorative representation of its leaf, characteristic of the Corinthian capital: also **acanthus leaf.** [< L < Gk. *akanthos* < *akē* thorn]

ACANTHUS (def. 2)

a cap·pel·la (ä′ kə·pel′ə, *Ital.* ä′ käp·pel′lä) *Music* Sung without instrumental accompaniment. [< Ital., in chapel style]

a ca·pric·cio (ä′ kä·prēt′chō) *Music* At the performer's pleasure as to tempo and expression; capriciously. [< Ital.]

A·ca·pul·co (ä′kä·pool′kō) A port and resort city in SW Mexico; pop. 234,866 (1970).

ac·a·ri·a·sis (ak′ə·rī′ə·sis) *n.* An itch caused by mites.

ac·a·rid (ak′ə·rid) *Zool. n.* Any of an order (*Acarina*) of arachnids, including the mites and ticks. — *adj.* Of or pertaining to the acarids. [< Gk. *akari* mite]

ac·a·roid (ak′ə·roid) *adj.* Of or like the acarids; mitelike. [< Gk. *akari* mite + -OID]

acaroid gum A yellow, fragrant resin from the Australian grass tree, chiefly the Botany Bay resin, used in varnishes, paper sizings, etc. Also **acaroid resin.**

a·car·pel·ous (ā·kär′pəl·əs) *adj. Bot.* Having no carpels. Also **a·car′pel·lous.**

a·car·pous (ā·kär′pəs) *adj. Bot.* Not bearing fruit; sterile.

a·cat·a·lec·tic (ā·kat′ə·lek′tik) *adj.* In prosody, having the required number of feet or of syllables, especially in the last foot. — *n.* A full or metrically complete verse.

a·cau·dal (ā·kôd′l) *adj. Zool.* Having no tail; tailless. Also **a·cau·date** (ā·kô′dāt).

ac·au·les·cence (ak′ô·les′əns) *n. Bot.* Absence, real or apparent, of the stem. — **ac′au·les′cent, a·cau·line** (ā·kô′lin, -līn), **a·cau·lose** (ā·kô′lōs), **a·cau·lous** (ā·kô′ləs) *adj.*

acc. 1. Account. **2.** *Gram.* Accusative.

Acc *Meteorol.* Altocumulus castellatus.

Ac·cad (ak′ad, ä′käd), **Ac·ca·di·an** (ə·kā′dē·ən, ə·kä′-) See AKKAD, etc.

ac·cede (ak·sēd′) *v.i.* **·ced·ed, ·ced·ing 1.** To give one's consent or adherence; agree; assent: with *to.* **2.** To come into or enter upon an office or dignity: with *to.* — **Syn.** See ASSENT. [< L *accedere* < *ad-* to + *cedere* to yield, go]

accel. 1. *Music* Accelerando. **2.** Accelerate.

ac·cel·er·an·do (ak·sel′ə·ran′dō, *Ital.* ät·chä′lä·rän′dō) *Music adj.* Gradually quickening in time. — *adv.* In gradually quickening tempo. Abbr. *accel.* [< Ital.]

ac·cel·er·ant (ak·sel′ər·ənt) *adj.* Accelerating; hastening. — *n.* That which accelerates.

ac·cel·er·ate (ak·sel′ə·rāt) *v.* **·at·ed, ·at·ing** *v.t.* **1.** To cause to act or move faster; increase the speed of. **2.** To hasten the natural or usual course of: to *accelerate* combustion. **3.** To cause to happen ahead of time. **4.** *Physics* To increase the velocity of (a body). — *v.i.* **5.** To move or become faster; increase in speed. Abbr. *accel.* — **Syn.** See QUICKEN. [< L *acceleratus*, pp. of *accelerare* < *ad-* to + *celerare* to hasten < *celer* quick] — **ac·cel′er·a·ble** *adj.*

ac·cel·er·a·tion (ak·sel′ə·rā′shən) *n.* **1.** The act of accelerating, or the process of being accelerated; a quickening, as of progress, action, functional activity, etc. **2.** *Physics* The rate at which the velocity of a body increases per unit of time, usually given in centimeters or feet per second per second: distinguished from *deceleration.*

acceleration of gravity An increase in the velocity of a body caused by the force of gravity, amounting to about 32.17 feet per second per second at or near sea level.

ac·cel·er·a·tive (ak·sel′ər·ā′tiv) *adj.* Of, pertaining to, or causing acceleration; tending to accelerate. Also **ac·cel·er·a·to·ry** (ak·sel′ər·ə·tôr′ē, -tō′rē).

ac·cel·er·a·tor (ak·sel′ər·ā′tər) *n.* **1.** One who or that which accelerates. **2.** *Physics* Any of various devices for accelerating the velocity of electrons or nuclear particles by subjecting them to the force of a synchronized electromagnetic field, as a cyclotron or synchrotron: also called *atom smasher.* **3.** *Photog.* Any chemical or device for hastening development.

4. *Mech.* A device for increasing the speed of a machine; especially, the foot throttle of an automobile. **5.** *Chem.* A substance or agent that quickens the speed of a chemical reaction. Compare CATALYST. **6.** *Physiol.* A muscle or nerve that acts to increase the speed of a function.

ac·cel·er·om·e·ter (ak·sel′ə·rom′ə·tər) *n.* An instrument for measuring and recording the acceleration of an aircraft.

ac·cent (*n.* ak′sent; *v.* ak′sent, ak·sent′) *n.* **1.** The prominence given in speech to a particular sound, syllable, or word, by means of stress, pitch, or other articulatory device. **2.** A mark used to indicate the place of accent in a word. The **primary accent** notes the chief stress, and the **secondary accent** a somewhat weaker stress. In ə·brē′vē·ā′shən, the primary accent is on the fourth syllable, and the secondary accent is on the second syllable. **3.** A mark used in some languages to show the quality of a vowel. In French, the accents are acute (′), grave (`), and circumflex (ˆ); these are written over vowels to indicate pronunciation or, in some cases, to distinguish similarly spelled words. **4.** A modulation of the voice. **5.** Mode of utterance; pronunciation: a Southern *accent.* **6.** In prosody: **a** The stress determining the rhythm of poetry; ictus. **b** A mark showing this stress. **7.** *Music* The emphasis or predominance given to one tone over that given to those around it; also, a mark indicating this. **8.** *pl.* Speech; words. **9.** *Math.* A mark or marks to indicate the value or order of similar symbols: b′ (*b prime*), b″ (*b second*), b‴ (*b third*), etc.; also to denote minutes and seconds in geometry, trigonometry, etc.: ′ = minutes; ″ = seconds. **10.** In mensuration, a similar mark or marks to denote feet and inches: ′ = feet; ″ = inches. **11.** Distinctive character or quality, as of an artist or work of art. — *v.t.* **1.** To speak, pronounce, play, or sing with an accent; stress. **2.** To write or print with a mark indicating accent or stress. **3.** To call attention to; accentuate. [< L *accentus*, lit., song added to speech (a trans. of Gk. *prosōidia* prosody) < *ad-* to + *cantus* a singing < *canere* to sing]

ac·cen·tu·al (ak·sen′choo·əl) *adj.* **1.** Of or pertaining to accent. **2.** In prosody, having a stress accent; not quantitative. — **ac·cen′tu·al·ly** *adv.*

ac·cen·tu·ate (ak·sen′choo·āt) *v.t.* **·at·ed, ·at·ing 1.** To strengthen or heighten the effect of; emphasize. **2.** To mark or pronounce with an accent. [< Med.L. *accentuatus*, pp. of *accentuare* < L *accentus.* See ACCENT.] — **ac·cen′tu·a′tion** *n.*

ac·cept (ak·sept′) *v.t.* **1.** To receive with favor, willingness, or consent: to *accept* a gift, job, office, etc. **2.** To give an affirmative answer to: to *accept* an invitation. **3.** To receive as satisfactory or sufficient; admit: to *accept* an apology. **4.** To take with good grace; submit to: to *accept* the inevitable. **5.** In commerce, to agree to pay, as a draft. **6.** To believe in: to *accept* Christianity. **7.** *Law* To acknowledge as valid or received. — *v.i.* **8.** To accept an offer, position, etc. — **Syn.** See ASSENT, RECEIVE. [< L *acceptare*, freq. of *accipere* to take < *ad-* to + *capere* to take] — **ac·cept′er** *n.*

ac·cept·a·ble (ak·sep′tə·bəl) *adj.* Worthy or capable of acceptance; pleasing; welcome. — **ac·cept′a·ble·ness, ac·cept′a·bil′i·ty** *n.* — **ac·cept′a·bly** *adv.*

ac·cep·tance (ak·sep′təns) *n.* **1.** The act of accepting. **2.** The state of being accepted or acceptable. **3.** Favorable reception; approval. **4.** Assent; belief. **5.** In commerce, an agreement to pay a bill of exchange, draft, order, or the like, according to its terms; also, the paper itself when endorsed "accepted." **6.** *Law* Any form or act by which one acknowledges the validity of an act, contract, or the like. Also **ac·cep′tan·cy.** Abbr. (for def. 5) *acpt.*

ac·cep·tant (ak·sep′tənt) *adj.* Willing to accept; receptive.

ac·cep·ta·tion (ak′sep·tā′shən) *n.* **1.** The accepted meaning of a word or expression. **2.** Favorable reception; assent.

ac·cept·ed (ak·sep′tid) *adj.* Commonly recognized, believed, or approved; popular. Abbr. *a.*

ac·cep·tor (ak·sep′tər) *n.* In commerce, one who gives his acceptance on a check, draft, or the like. [< L]

ac·cess (ak′ses) *n.* **1.** The act or opportunity of coming to or near; admittance. **2.** A way of approach or entrance; passage; path. **3.** The state or quality of being approachable; accessibility: difficult of *access.* **4.** A sudden attack of a disease. **5.** An outburst of passion, emotion, etc. **6.** *Theol.* Approach to God through Jesus Christ: a prayer of *access.* **7.** *Rare* An addition; increase. **8.** *Obs.* The act of approaching; entrance. — **Syn.** See ENTRANCE[1]. [< L *accessus* an approach, pp. of *accedere.* See ACCEDE.]

ac·ces·sa·ry (ak·ses′ər·ē) See ACCESSORY.

ac·ces·si·ble (ak·ses′ə·bəl) *adj.* **1.** Easy of access; approachable. **2.** Attainable; obtainable. **3.** Open to the influence of: with *to: accessible* to bribery. — **ac·ces′si·bil′i·ty** *n.* — **ac·ces′si·bly** *adv.*

ac·ces·sion (ak·sesh′ən) *n.* **1.** The act of coming to or attaining an office, dignity, or right. **2.** An increase by something added; also, the addition. **3.** *Law* Addition to property by growth or improvement; also, the property owner's right to such addition. **4.** Assent; agreement: *accession* to a demand. **5.** Admittance; entrance. **6.** A coming on, increase, or paroxysm, as of rage. — *v.t.* To record, as additions to a library or museum. [< L *accessio, -onis* < *accedere.* See ACCEDE.] — **ac·ces′sion·al** *adj.*

ac·ces·so·ry (ak·ses'ər·ē) *n. pl.* **·ries** **1.** Something subordinate that contributes to a general effect; any item or appurtenance added for convenience, display, etc., as to an automobile or to one's attire. **2.** *Law* A person who, though absent during the perpetration of a felony, instigates, aids, or encourages another to commit the felony (**accessory before the fact**), or knowingly comforts, conceals, or assists the felon (**accessory after the fact**). — *adj.* **1.** Aiding the principal design, or assisting subordinately the chief agent, as in the commission of a crime. **2.** Contributory; supplemental; additional. Also spelled *accessary*. [< LL *accessorius* < *accessus*, pp. of *accedere*. See ACCEDE.] — **ac·ces·so·ri·al** *adj.* — **ac·ces·so·ri·ly** *adv.* — **ac·ces·so·ri·ness** *n.*

♦ **accessory, accessary** The earlier form is *accessary* (see -ARY¹). The adjective was later refashioned to *accessory* (on analogy with *promissory, amatory, illusory*, etc.), which also influenced the form of the noun. *Accessory* is now the commoner form, in both general and legal usage.

— **Syn.** (noun) **1.** See APPENDAGE. **2.** *Accessory, abettor, accomplice*, and *confederate* are almost always used in a bad sense, and usually refer to one who, in some way, aids another in the commission of a crime. In law, an *accessory* assists in planning or concealing a crime, though he is not present when it is committed. An *abettor* is actively or constructively present during the act itself: *accomplice* has much the same meaning as *abettor*, but is the more popular word. *Confederate* is a general term for one who assists another in any way. — (adj.) See AUXILIARY. — **Ant.** principal.

Ac·cho (ak'ō) The Old Testament name for ACRE.

ac·ciac·ca·tu·ra (ät·chäk'kä·tōō'rä) *n. Music* In old keyboard music, a grace in which the principal note is sustained while adjacent notes are struck for an instant or held as a sustained dissonance. [< Ital. < *acciaccare* to crush]

ac·ci·dence (ak'sə·dəns) *n.* **1.** *Gram.* The part of morphology that treats of inflection. **2.** The rudiments of any art or science. [< *accidents*, pl. of ACCIDENT (def. 5)]

ac·ci·dent (ak'sə·dənt) *n.* **1.** Anything occurring unexpectedly, or without known or assignable cause. **2.** Any unpleasant or unfortunate occurrence involving injury, loss, suffering, or death; a casualty; mishap. **3.** Chance; fortune: It happened by *accident*. **4.** Any nonessential circumstance or attribute. **5.** *Gram.* An inflection, as of case, gender, number, etc. **6.** *Logic* Any feature, element, or accompaniment of an object not essential to the conception of it. **7.** *Geol.* A nontypical or unexplained irregularity in a rock formation. — **Syn.** See CHANCE. [< L *accidens, -entis*, ppr. of *accidere* to happen < *ad-* upon + *cadere* to fall]

ac·ci·den·tal (ak'sə·den'təl) *adj.* **1.** Happening or coming by chance or without design; taking place unexpectedly. **2.** Not making part of the irreducible nature of a thing; nonessential; subordinate; incidental. **3.** *Music* Pertaining to or indicating a sharp, natural, flat, etc., elsewhere than in the signature. — *n.* **1.** A casual, incidental, or nonessential feature or circumstance. **2.** *Music* An accidental sign or note. — **ac·ci·den'tal·ly** *adv.* — **ac·ci·den'tal·ness** *n.*

— **Syn.** (adj.) **1.** *Accidental, casual, fortuitous*, and *unpremeditated* all refer to acts or events that are unexpected or unforeseen. *Accidental* stresses lack of intention or forethought; *casual* adds a note of carelessness or indifference: an *accidental* discovery, a *casual* remark. *Fortuitous* often implies that which is apparently without cause or design, and *unpremeditated* emphasizes a lack of planning. **2.** adventitious, contingent.

ac·ci·den·tal·ism (ak'sə·den'tal·iz'əm) *n.* **1.** An accidental condition or effect. **2.** *Med.* A theory that ignores the causes of disease and deals only with symptoms. **3.** *Philos.* The theory that events occur by accident or without cause. — **ac·ci·den'tal·ist** *n.*

accident insurance Insurance awarding payment in the event of personal injury or death accidentally incurred.

ac·cip·i·tral (ak·sip'ə·trəl) *adj.* Of, pertaining to, or of the nature of a bird of prey; hawklike.

ac·cip·i·trine (ak·sip'ə·trin, -trīn) *adj.* **1.** Of or pertaining to a family of hawks (*Accipitridae*). **2.** Raptorial. [< L *accipiter* hawk + -INE¹]

ac·claim (ə·klām') *v.t.* **1.** To proclaim by acclamation; hail: They *acclaimed* him victor. **2.** To shout approval of; show enthusiasm for. **3.** To shout; call out. — *v.i.* **4.** To applaud; shout approval. — *n.* A shout of applause; acclamation. — **Syn.** See PRAISE. [< L *acclamare* < *ad-* to + *clamare* to shout] — **ac·claim'a·ble** *adj.* — **ac·claim'er** *n.*

ac·cla·ma·tion (ak'lə·mā'shən) *n.* **1.** The act of acclaiming. **2.** A shout or other manifestation of applause, approval, or welcome. **3.** An oral vote; especially, a loud vote of approval, as in public assembly. **4.** *Canadian Election* without opposition. — **by acclamation** By unanimous consent without balloting. — **Syn.** See APPLAUSE. [< L *acclamatio, -onis* < *acclamare*. See ACCLAIM.] — **ac·clam·a·to·ry** (ə·klam'ə·tôr'ē, -tō'rē) *adj.*

ac·cli·mate (ə·klī'mit, ak'lə·māt) *v.t. & v.i.* **·mat·ed, ·mat·ing** *Chiefly U.S.* To adapt or become adapted to a foreign climate or new environment: said of persons, plants, or animals. [< F *acclimater* < *à* to (< L *ad-*) + *climat.* See CLIMATE.] — **ac·cli·ma·ta·ble** (ə·klī'mə·tə·bəl) *adj.* — **ac-**

cli·ma·tion (ak'lə·mā'shən), **ac·cli·ma·ta·tion** (ə·klī'mə·tā'shən) *n.*

ac·cli·ma·tize (ə·klī'mə·tīz) *v.t. & v.i.* **·tized ·tiz·ing** To acclimate. — **ac·cli·ma·tiz'a·ble** *adj.* — **ac·cli·ma·ti·za'tion** *n.* — **ac·cli·ma·tiz'er** *n.*

ac·cliv·i·ty (ə·kliv'ə·tē) *n. pl.* **·ties** An upward slope: opposed to *declivity*. [< L *acclivitas, -tatis* steepness < *acclivis* steep < *ad-* to + *clivus* hill] — **ac·cliv'i·tous, ac·cli·vous** (ə·klī'vəs) *adj.*

ac·co·lade (ak'ə·lād', -läd') *n.* **1.** The salutation (at first an embrace, later a light blow with a sword) in conferring knighthood. **2.** An honor; award. **3.** *Music* A vertical brace or heavy bar. **4.** *Archit.* A curved ornamental molding. [< F < Ital. *accollata* < *accollare* to embrace about the neck < L *ad* to + *collum* neck]

ACCOLADE
(*def.* 4)

ac·com·mo·date (ə·kom'ə·dāt) *v.* **·dat·ed, ·dat·ing** *v.t.* **1.** To do a favor for; oblige; help. **2.** To provide for; give lodging to. **3.** To be suitable for; contain comfortably. **4.** To adapt or modify; adjust or conform, as to new conditions. **5.** To reconcile or settle, as conflicting opinions. — *v.i.* **6.** To be or become adjusted, as the eye to distance. [< L *accommodatus*, pp. of *accommodare* < *ad-* to + *commodare* to make fit, suit < *com-* with + *modus* measure] — **ac·com'mo·da'tive** *adj.* — **ac·com'mo·da'tive·ness** *n.*

— **Syn.** **2.** receive, take in, entertain, lodge. **4.** See ADAPT.

ac·com·mo·dat·ing (ə·kom'ə·dā'ting) *adj.* Disposed to make adjustment; pliable to the will or wish of others; obliging. — **ac·com'mo·dat'ing·ly** *adv.*

ac·com·mo·da·tion (ə·kom'ə·dā'shən) *n.* **1.** The act of accommodating, or the state of being accommodated; adjustment; adaptation. **2.** Reconciliation; compromise. **3.** Anything that supplies a need; convenience. **4.** *Usually pl. U.S.* Lodging, board, etc. **5.** Willingness to please or help; obligingness. **6.** A loan or other help or favor; especially, an accommodation bill. **7.** An accommodation train. **8.** *Physiol.* The adjustment of the eye to vision at different distances.

accommodation bill or **note** A note given, or bill of exchange accepted, not for value received but as an accommodation or favor in the course of business.

accommodation ladder A ladder or stairway hung over the side of a ship.

accommodation train *U.S.* A local (*n.* def. 2); also, a train having both passenger and freight cars.

ac·com·pa·ni·ment (ə·kum'pə·ni·mənt, ə·kump'ni-) *n.* **1.** Anything that accompanies; something added for completeness or symmetry. **2.** *Music* A subordinate part, vocal or instrumental, accompanying, enriching, or supporting a leading part. — **Syn.** See CIRCUMSTANCE.

ac·com·pa·nist (ə·kum'pə·nist, ə·kump'nist) *n.* One who plays or sings the accompaniment. Also **ac·com·pa·ny·ist.**

ac·com·pa·ny (ə·kum'pə·nē) *v.t.* **·nied, ·ny·ing** **1.** To go with; attend; escort. **2.** To be or occur with; coexist with: Weakness often *accompanies* disease. **3.** To supplement: He *accompanied* his insults with blows. **4.** To play a musical accompaniment to or for. [< F *accompagner* < *à* to + *compagne*. See COMPANION.] — **ac·com'pa·ni·er** *n.*

— **Syn.** **1.** *Accompany, attend, follow, escort, conduct*, and *convoy* all mean to go with, but each suggests a different relationship between persons. We *accompany* our equals, but *attend* those to whom we would show courtesy, or to whom we are subordinate. *Follow* implies even greater respect or subordination than *attend*; a servant *follows* his master, mourners *follow* a hearse. Persons requiring protection are usually *escorted*; those needing guidance are *conducted*. Things are *convoyed*, and *convoy* is also commonly used for journeys by sea: to *convoy* merchant ships in wartime.

ac·com·plice (ə·kom'plis) *n.* An associate in wrongdoing; partner in crime, whether as principal or accessory. — **Syn.** See ACCESSORY. [< *a*, indefinite article + F *complice* accomplice < LL *complex* accomplice. See COMPLEX.]

ac·com·plish (ə·kom'plish) *v.t.* **1.** To bring to pass; perform; effect. **2.** To bring to completion; finish. **3.** *Archaic* To make complete. [< OF *acompliss-* stem of *acomplir* < LL *accomplere* < L *ad-* to + *complere* to fill up, complete] — **ac·com'plish·a·ble** *adj.* — **ac·com'plish·er** *n.*

— **Syn.** **1.** *Accomplish* and *perform* both imply working toward the end; but *perform* always allows a possibility of not attaining, while *accomplish* carries the thought of full completion. Compare EFFECT. **2.** do, finish, complete, execute, fulfill.

ac·com·plished (ə·kom'plisht) *adj.* **1.** Completed; done: an *accomplished* fact. **2.** Proficient; skilled: an *accomplished* dancer. **3.** Trained in the social graces; polished.

ac·com·plish·ment (ə·kom'plish·mənt) *n.* **1.** The act of accomplishing; fulfillment. **2.** Something done or accomplished; achievement. **3.** An acquirement or attainment that tends to perfect or equip in character, manners, or person. — **Syn.** See ATTAINMENT.

ac·cord (ə·kôrd') *v.t.* **1.** To render as due; grant; concede: to *accord* merited honor. **2.** To bring into agreement; make harmonize or correspond, as opinions. **3.** *Obs.* To reconcile, as former enemies. — *v.i.* **4.** To agree; harmonize: Our opinions *accord* with theirs. — **Syn.** See GRANT. — *n.* **1.** Harmony, as of sentiment, colors, sounds, etc.; agreement. **2.** A settlement of any difference; reconciliation; especially, an agreement between governments. — **Syn.** See HARMONY. — **of one's own accord** By one's own choice; voluntarily. [< OF *acorder* < LL *accordare* to be of one mind, agree < L *ad-* to + *cor* heart] — **ac·cord'a·ble** *adj.* — **ac·cord'er** *n.*

ac·cord·ance (ə-kôr'dəns) *n.* Agreement; conformity.

ac·cord·ant (ə-kôr'dənt) *adj.* Consonant; agreeing; corresponding. — **ac·cord'ant·ly** *adv.*

ac·cord·ing (ə-kôr'ding) *adj.* Being in accordance or agreement; harmonizing. — *adv.* Accordingly. — **according as 1.** In proportion as; just as. **2.** Depending on whether. — **according to 1.** In accordance with. **2.** As stated by; on the authority of. **3.** In proportion to.

ac·cord·ing·ly (ə-kôr'ding-lē) *adv.* **1.** In accord; correspondingly. **2.** Consequently; so. — **Syn.** See THEREFORE.

ac·cor·di·on (ə-kôr'dē-ən) *n.* A portable musical wind instrument with metallic reeds and often a keyboard, the air for which is furnished by a bellows operated by the performer. [< Ital. *accordare* to harmonize] — **ac·cor'di·on·ist** *n.*

accordion pleating Pleating that resembles the folds of the bellows part of an accordion.

ac·cost (ə-kôst', ə-kost') *v.t.* **1.** To speak to first; address; greet. **2.** To approach for sexual purposes; solicit. — *n.* Salutation; greeting. — **Syn.** See GREET. [< F *accoster* < LL *accostare* to be side to side < L *ad-* to + *costa* rib]

ac·couche·ment (ə-kōōsh'mənt, Fr. à-kōōsh-män') *n.* Confinement; childbirth. [< F *accoucher* to put to bed, give birth < *à* to (< L *ad-*) + *coucher* to put to bed. See COUCH.]

ac·cou·cheur (à-kōō-shœr') *n.* French An obstetrician.

ac·cou·cheuse (à-kōō-shœz') *n.* French A midwife.

ac·count (ə-kount') *v.t.* **1.** To hold to be; consider; estimate. — *v.i.* **2.** To provide a reckoning, as of funds paid or received: with *to* or *with* (someone), *for* (something). **3.** To give a rational explanation; refer to some cause or natural law: with *for*. **4.** To be responsible; answer: with *for*. **5.** To cause death, capture, or incapacitation: with *for*. — *n.* **1.** A record of events; narrative; description. **2.** A statement of causes; explanation. **3.** A record of debits and credits, or of any monetary transactions; any methodical enumeration, score, or reckoning. Abbr. *ac.*, *a/c*, *A/C* (pl. *a/cs*, *A/Cs*), *acc.*, *acct.* **4.** Worth; importance: a man of no *account*. **5.** Judgment; estimation: to take a warning into *account*. **6.** Profit; advantage: to turn something to *account*. — **on account of 1.** Because of; for the sake of. **2.** *Southern U.S.* Because: He's shivering *on account of* he's cold. — **on no account** Under no circumstances. [< OF *aconter* < LL *accomptare* < L *ad-* to + *computare*. See COMPUTE.]
— **Syn.** (verb) See CONSIDER. — (noun) **1.** *Account, chronicle, report, version,* and *story* all refer to a history or statement of actual or purported events. An *account* is a factual statement of events or conditions, usually given by an eyewitness. A *chronicle* is a detailed historical account of events in their order of occurrence. A *report* is an official statement, usually made by a subordinate to his superior: a patrolman's *report* of a burglary. *Version* and *story* purport to be statements of fact. A *version* is one-sided, although not always deliberately so; a *story* may be fanciful, but can also be a legitimate *account*.

ac·count·a·ble (ə-koun'tə-bəl) *adj.* **1.** Liable to be called to account; responsible. **2.** Capable of being explained. — **ac·count'a·bil'i·ty** *n.* — **ac·count'a·bly** *adv.*

ac·count·an·cy (ə-koun'tən-sē) *n.* The work or art of an accountant.

ac·count·ant (ə-koun'tənt) *n.* One whose business is to keep or examine books, as of a mercantile or banking house or in a public office. Abbr. *acct.* — **certified public accountant** In the United States, a public accountant who has been granted a certificate of proficiency by a State examining body, and is allowed to use the designation CPA or C.P.A. — **public accountant** An accountant whose services, for a compensation, are available to the public.

account executive An executive, usually in an advertising agency, who manages the business carried on in behalf of certain clients.

ac·count·ing (ə-koun'ting) *n.* The art or system of recording, classifying, and summarizing commercial transactions in monetary terms. Compare BOOKKEEPING.

account rendered An account or bill presented by the creditor for examination by the debtor, to be paid if correct.

account stated An account presented by the creditor and assented to as correct by the debtor.

ac·cou·ter (ə-kōō'tər) *v.t.* To furnish with dress or trappings; equip, as for military service. Also *Brit.* **ac·cou'tre**. [< F *accoutrer*; ult. origin uncertain]

ac·cou·ter·ment (ə-kōō'tər-mənt) *n.* **1.** *pl.* Equipment; trappings; especially, the equipment of a soldier other than arms and dress. **2.** The act of accoutering. Also **ac·cou'tre·ment**. — **Syn.** See CAPARISON.

Ac·cra (ə-krä', ak'rə) The capital of Ghana, a port city on the Gulf of Guinea, pop. 337,828 (est. 1968). Also *Akkra*.

ac·cred·it (ə-kred'it) *v.t.* **1.** To give credit to as the owner, author, or creator of; attribute to: with *with*: He is *accredited* with a quick mind. **2.** To accept as true; believe: to *ac-*

credit a story. **3.** To bring into credit; vouch for: His actions do not *accredit* his words. **4.** To furnish or send with credentials, as an ambassador; authorize. **5.** To certify as fulfilling official requirements, as a school. **6.** To enter on the credit side of the ledger; give credit for. [< F *accréditer* < *à* to (< L *ad-*) + *crédit*. See CREDIT.]

ac·cred·i·ta·tion (ə-kred/ə·tā'shən) *n. U.S.* The granting of approved status to an academic institution by an accrediting body after examination of its courses, standards, etc.

ac·cres·cence (ə-kres'əns) *n.* **1.** Gradual growth. **2.** An accretion.

ac·cres·cent (ə-kres'ənt) *adj.* **1.** *Bot.* Continuing to grow after flowering: said of a calyx or other part of the flower. **2.** Growing continuously; expanding with age. [< L *accrescens, -entis,* ppr. of *accrescere*. See ACCRETE.]

ac·crete (ə-krēt') *v.* **·cret·ed, ·cret·ing** *v.i.* **1.** To grow together or be united by adhesion: with *to*. **2.** To increase by a series of additions. — *v.t.* **3.** To cause to be added: with *to*: One should *accrete* discretion to his other qualities. — *adj.* **1.** Formed or marked by accretions. **2.** *Bot.* Grown together: said of parts normally separate. [< L *accretus,* pp. of *accrescere* to increase < *ad-* to + *crescere* to grow]

ac·cre·tion (ə-krē'shən) *n.* **1.** Growth or increase by external additions or by adhesion or inclusion. **2.** An external addition; something added. **3.** Increase by natural growth. **4.** *Pathol.* Abnormal growing together. **5.** *Law* Increase, as of land along the seashore or a river, by deposit of alluvium. **6.** *Geol.* The enlargement of rock masses and inorganic bodies by the addition of new material. — **ac·cre'tive** *adj.*

ac·cru·al (ə-krōō'əl) *n.* **1.** The act of accruing; increase. **2.** The amount of increase. Also **ac·crue'ment**.

accrual basis The keeping of accounts so as to show accrued earned income and accrued expense without regard to actual received income and disbursements: opposed to *cash basis*.

ac·crue (ə-krōō') *v.i.* **·crued, ·cru·ing 1.** To come as a natural result or increment, as by growth: with *to*. **2.** To arise as an addition, accession, or advantage; accumulate, as the interest on money: with *from*. **3.** *Law* To become a permanent right. [< obs. *accrue* increment, growth < F *accrû,* pp. of *accroître* to increase < L *accrescere*. See ACCRETE.]

acct. 1. Account. **2.** Accountant.

ac·cul·tur·a·tion (ə-kul'chə·rā'shən) *n. Sociol.* The process by which one culture may be affected by another.

ac·cum·bent (ə-kum'bənt) *adj.* **1.** Lying down. **2.** *Bot.* Lying against something, as a cotyledon against a radicle. [< L *accumbens, -entis,* ppr. of *accumbere* to lie down < *ad-* to + *cubare* to lie down] — **ac·cum'ben·cy** *n.*

ac·cu·mu·late (ə-kyōōm/yə·lāt) *v.* **·lat·ed, ·lat·ing** *v.t.* **1.** To heap or pile up; amass; collect. — *v.i.* **2.** To become greater in quantity or number; increase. — **Syn.** See AMASS. [< L *accumulatus,* pp. of *accumulare* < *ad-* to + *cumulare* to heap < *cumulus* a heap] — **ac·cu'mu·la·ble** (-lə-bəl) *adj.*

ac·cu·mu·la·tion (ə-kyōōm/yə·lā'shən) *n.* **1.** The act or process of accumulating; an amassing. **2.** That which is accumulated; a mass. **3.** The addition of earnings or profits to capital. **4.** *Geol.* The underground movement of oil and gas into porous rock formations.

ac·cu·mu·la·tive (ə-kyōōm/yə·lā'tiv, -lə·tiv) *adj.* Tending to accumulate; characterized by accumulation; cumulative. — **ac·cu'mu·la·tive·ly** *adv.* — **ac·cu'mu·la·tive·ness** *n.*

ac·cu·mu·la·tor (ə-kyōōm/yə·lā'tər) *n.* **1.** A power-storing hydraulic apparatus. **2.** *Brit.* A storage battery.

ac·cu·ra·cy (ak'yər·ə·sē) *n.* The condition or quality of being accurate; exactness; precision; correctness.

ac·cu·rate (ak'yər·it) *adj.* Conforming exactly to truth or to a standard; without error; precise; exact; correct. — **Syn.** See CORRECT. [< L *accuratus* done with care, pp. of *accurare* to take care of < *ad-* to + *cura* care] — **ac'cu·rate·ly** *adv.*

ac·curs·ed (ə-kûr'sid, ə-kûrst') *adj.* **1.** Lying under a curse; doomed. **2.** Deserving a curse; detestable. Also **ac·curst'**. — **ac·curs'ed·ly** *adv.* — **ac·curs'ed·ness** *n.*

accus. *Gram.* Accusative.

ac·cu·sa·tion (ak'yŏŏ·zā'shən) *n.* **1.** A charge of crime or misconduct; an indictment. **2.** The act of accusing; arraignment. **3.** The crime or act charged. Also **ac·cu·sal** (ə-kyōō'zəl). [< L *accusatio, -onis* < *accusare*. See ACCUSE.]

ac·cu·sa·to·ry (ə-kyōō'zə·tôr'ē, -tō'rē) *adj.*

ac·cu·sa·tive (ə-kyōō'zə·tiv) *Gram. adj.* Denoting, in inflected languages, the case or relation of the direct object of a verb or preposition, or the goal toward which an action is directed; objective. Also **ac·cu·sa·ti·val** (ə-kyōō'zə·tī'vəl). — *n.* **1.** The case of Latin and Greek nouns corresponding to the English objective. **2.** A word in this case. Abbr. *acc., accus.* [< L *accusativus,* trans. of Gk. *(ptōsis) aitiatikē* (the case) of the effect < *aitiatos* effected, produced by a cause] — **ac·cu'sa·tive·ly** *adv.*

ac·cu·sa·to·ri·al (ə-kyōō'zə·tôr'ē·əl, -tō'rē·əl) *adj.* Pertaining to an accuser.

ac·cuse (ə-kyōōz') *v.* **·cused, ·cus·ing** *v.t.* **1.** To charge with fault or error; blame; censure. **2.** To bring charges against: with *of*: They have *accused* him of theft. — *v.i.* **3.** To make accusation; utter charges. [< OF *acuser* < L *accusare* to call to account < *ad-* to + *causa* cause, lawsuit] — **ac·cus'er** *n.* — **ac·cus'ing·ly** *adv.*

—Syn. 2. *Accuse, charge, arraign, indict, impeach,* and *incriminate* all refer to a public statement that a person is guilty or probably guilty of an offense or crime. *Accuse* is a general word for declaring a person guilty of a fault; *charge* is more formal and stresses the serious or criminal nature of an act: to *accuse* a man of lying, to *charge* him with perjury. *Arraign, indict,* and *impeach* are all legal terms. An *accused* man is *indicted* by a grand jury, and *arraigned* before a court to answer the indictment. *Impeach* is used specifically of public officials charged with malfeasance in office. *Incriminate* implies involvement in a serious crime.

ac·cused (ə-kyōōzd′) *n. Law* The defendant or defendants in a criminal case: preceded by *the.*

ac·cus·tom (ə-kus′təm) *v.t.* To familiarize by custom or use; habituate or inure: with *to*: to *accustom* oneself to noise. [< OF *acostumer* < *a-* to (< L *ad-*) + *costume.* See CUSTOM.]

ac·cus·tomed (ə-kus′təmd) *adj.* **1.** Habitual; usual. **2.** In the habit; wont; used: with the infinitive or *to*: *accustomed* to hard work. **—Syn.** See ADDICTED.

ac·cus·tom·ize (ə-kus′təm-īz) *v.t. & v.i.* **·ized, ·iz·ing** To adapt or become adapted to the conditions and requirements of a new environment. **— ac·cus′tom·i·za′tion** *n.*

AC/DC or **A.C./D.C.** or **a.c.–d.c.** *adj.* **1.** *Electr.* Alternating current or direct current. **2.** *Informal* Erotically attracted to both sexes; bisexual.

ace (ās) *n.* **1.** A single spot, as on a playing card or die; also, a card or side of a die so marked. **2.** A very small amount, distance, or degree; a jot; particle: within an *ace* of death. **3.** One who excels in any field. **4.** A military aviator who has destroyed five or more enemy aircraft. **5.** In tennis and similar games, a point won by a single stroke, as upon the service. **— ace in the hole** *U.S. Slang* A hidden advantage or winning stroke. **— within an ace of** Very close to; to the brink of. **— v.t. aced** (āst), **ac·ing** **1.** To score a point against in a single stroke, as upon the service in tennis. **2.** *Slang* To get the better of, as by a timely move or act. [< OF *as* < L *as* unity, unit]

-acea *suffix Zool.* Used in forming names of classes and orders of animals: *Crustacea* (class), *Cetacea* (order). [< L, neut. pl. of *-aceus*]

-aceae *suffix Bot.* Used in forming names of families of plants: *Vitaceae,* the vine family; *Rosaceae,* a family of polypetalous plants, including roses. [< L, fem. pl. of *-aceus*]

-acean *suffix* **1.** Forming adjectives equivalent to those in *-aceous.* **2.** Forming singular nouns to collective plurals in *-acea*: *crustacean.* [< L *-aceus* + -AN]

a·ce·di·a (ə-sē′dē-ə) *n.* **1.** A pathological mental or spiritual torpor. **2.** Sloth regarded as one of the seven deadly sins. [< LL *akēdia* < *a-* without + *kēdos* care]

A·cel·da·ma (ə-sel′də-mə) *n.* **1.** The potter's field near Jerusalem, bought with the money Judas received for betraying Jesus. *Matt.* xxvii 8 and *Acts* i 18–19. **2.** Any place of bloody or murderous associations. [< L < Gk. *Akeldama* < Aramaic *hakal damā* the field of blood]

a·cen·tric (ā-sen′trik) *adj.* Without a center.

-aceous *suffix* Of the nature of; belonging or pertaining to; like: used in botany and zoology to form adjectives corresponding to nouns in *-acea, -aceae,* as *cretaceous, herbaceous.* [< L *-aceus* of the nature of]

a·ceph·a·lous (ā-sef′ə-ləs) *adj.* **1.** Headless. **2.** Having no leader. **3.** *Zool.* Without a clearly defined head, as certain mollusks. **4.** Lacking proper beginning. [< LL *acephalus* < Gk. *akephalos* headless < *a-* without + *kephalē* head]

a·ce·qui·a (ä-sā′kē-ə) *n. SW U.S.* A canal for irrigation. [< Sp.]

a·cer·ate (as′ə-rāt) *adj. Bot.* Acerose. Also **ac′e·rat·ed.**

a·cerb (ə-sûrb′) *adj.* Sour and astringent; harsh; sharp. [< L *acerbus* < *acer* sharp] Also **a·cer·bic** (ə-sûr′bik).

a·cer·bate (as′ər-bāt) *v.t.* **·bat·ed, ·bat·ing** **1.** To make sour; embitter. **2.** To irritate; exasperate.

a·cer·bi·ty (ə-sûr′bə-tē) *n. pl.* **·ties** **1.** Sourness, bitterness, or astringency of flavor, as that of unripe fruit. **2.** Severity, as of temper, etc.; harshness; sharpness. Also **a·cer·bi·tude** (ə-sûr′bə-tōōd, -tyōōd). **—Syn.** See ACRIMONY. [< F *acerbité* < L *acerbitas* < *acerbus* sharp]

ac·e·rose¹ (as′ə-rōs) *adj. Bot.* Needle-shaped, like pine leaves. [< L *acerosus* (see ACEROSE²); later erroneously derived from L *acus* needle]

ac·e·rose² (as′ə-rōs) *adj.* Like chaff. [< L *acerosus* < *acus* chaff]

a·cer·vate (ə-sûr′vit, -vāt) *adj. Bot.* Massed or heaped together; growing compactly in clusters. [< L *acervatus,* pp. of *acervare* to heap up < *acervus* heap] **— a·cer′vate·ly** *adv.*

a·ces·cent (ə-ses′ənt) *adj.* Becoming sour; slightly sour. **— n.** That which is slightly sour. [< L *acescens, -entis,* ppr. of *acescere* to become sour] **— a·ces′cence** *n.*

acet- Var. of ACETO-.

ac·e·tab·u·lum (as′ə-tab′yə-ləm) *n. pl.* **·la** (-lə) **1.** *Anat.* The socket in the hip in which the head of the femur rests and revolves. **2.** *Zool.* A sucker, as on the arms of cuttlefish and other cephalopods. **3.** In ancient Rome, a small cup for condiments. [< L, a small vinegar cup < *acetum* vinegar]

ac·e·tal (as′ə-tal) *n.* **1.** *Med.* A volatile, colorless liquid compound of acetaldehyde and alcohol, $C_6H_{14}O_2$, having hypnotic and sedative properties. **2.** *Chem.* Any of a class of such compounds used as solvents and in cosmetics.

ac·et·al·de·hyde (as′ə-tal′də-hīd) *n. Chem.* A flammable, colorless, fuming liquid, C_2H_4O, with a characteristic pungent odor, used chiefly in organic synthesis, in photography, and for the silvering of mirrors.

ac·et·al·dol (as′ə-tal′dôl, -dol) *n. Chem.* Aldol (which see).

ac·et·am·ide (as′ə-tam′īd, -id; ə·set′ə-mid, -mid) *n. Chem.* The amide of acetic acid, a white crystalline compound, C_2H_5NO, formed by heating acetic ether with ammonia.

ac·et·an·i·lide (as′ə-tan′ə-līd, -lid) *n. Chem.* An acetyl derivative of aniline, C_8H_9ON, consisting of white, shining, crystalline scales, used as a sedative and antipyretic.

ac·e·tate (as′ə-tāt) *n. Chem.* A salt or ester of acetic acid.

acetate rayon Any of a class of synthetic textile fibers and filaments made from cellulose acetate.

a·ce·tic (ə-sē′tik, ə-set′ik) *adj.* Pertaining to or like vinegar; sour. [< L *acetum* vinegar + -IC]

acetic acid *Chem.* A colorless, pungent, mobile liquid, $C_2H_4O_2$, usually obtained by the destructive distillation of wood or by the oxidation of alcohol with ferments. Vinegar is a dilute and impure acetic acid produced by fermentation.

acetic anhydride *Chem.* The anhydride of acetic acid, $(CH_3CO)_2O$, a pungent, colorless liquid, used in the manufacture of acetyl compounds, cellulose acetate, and as a reagent in chemical analysis.

a·cet·i·fy (ə-set′ə-fī) *v.t. & v.i.* **·fied, ·fy·ing** To convert into or become acid or vinegar. **— a·cet′i·fi·ca′tion** *n.*

aceto- *combining form* Of, pertaining to, or from acetic acid or acetyl. Also, before vowels, *acet-.* [< L *acetum* vinegar]

ac·e·tom·e·ter (as′ə-tom′ə-tər) *n.* A device for measuring the amount or strength of acetic acid in any solution.

ac·e·tone (as′ə-tōn) *n. Chem.* A clear, flammable liquid, C_3H_6O, with a bitter taste and characteristic wood-smoke odor, obtained by the destructive distillation of wood spirit and various organic compounds, used in making chloroform, and as a solvent for fats, camphor, and resins. [< ACET- + -ONE] **— ac·e·ton·ic** (as′ə-ton′ik) *adj.*

ac·e·to·phe·net·i·din (as′ə-tō-fə-net′ə-din) *n. Chem.* A white, crystalline, coal-tar compound, $C_{10}H_{13}NO_2$, used in medicine as an antipyretic: also called *phenacetin.*

ac·e·tous (as′ə-təs, ə-sē′təs) *adj.* **1.** Of, pertaining to, or producing vinegar or acetic acid. **2.** Tasting like vinegar; sour. Also **ac·e·tose** (as′ə-tōs).

ac·e·tox·yl (as′ə-tok′səl) *n. Chem.* The univalent radical, $C_2H_3O_2.$

a·ce·tum (ə-sē′təm) *n.* Vinegar. [< L]

·ac·e·tyl (as′ə-til) *n. Chem.* The univalent radical, CH_3CO, of acetic acid. [< ACET- + -YL] **— ac′e·tyl′ic** *adj.*

a·cet·y·late (ə-set′ə-lāt) *v.t.* **·lat·ed, ·lat·ing** *Chem.* To introduce an acetyl group into (the molecule of an organic compound), as by treatment with acetic anhydride. **— a·cet′y·la′tion** *n.*

ac·e·tyl·cho·line (as′ə-til-kō′lēn, -kol′in) *n. Chem.* An alkaloid, $C_7H_{17}O_3N$, obtained from ergot and present in many tissues of the body, used in medicine to decrease blood pressure and increase peristalsis.

ac·et·y·lene (ə-set′ə-lēn) *n. Chem.* A colorless hydrocarbon gas, C_2H_2, produced by the action of water upon calcium carbide, used as an illuminant, for welding, and for cutting metals. [< ACETYL + -ENE]

ac·e·tyl·sal·i·cyl·ic acid (as′ə-til-sal′ə-sil′ik, ə-sē′təl-) Aspirin.

ace·y–deuc·y (ā′sē-dōō′sē, -dyōō′sē) *n.* A variety of backgammon.

A·chae·a (ə-kē′ə) A district of the northern Peloponnesus, comprising a Department of modern Greece; 1,164 sq. mi.; pop. about 240,000; capital, Patras. Also **A·cha·ia** (ə-kā′ə, ə-kī′ə). See map of ATTICA.

A·chae·an (ə-kē′ən) *adj.* Pertaining to Achaea, its people, or their culture. **— n.** **1.** A member of one of the four major tribes of ancient Greece. **2.** A Greek. Also **A·cha·ian** (ə-kā′ən, -kī-).

A·cha·tes (ə-kā′tēz) In Vergil's *Aeneid,* the faithful friend of Aeneas. **— n.** Any loyal companion.

ache (āk) *v.i.* **ached** (ākt), **ach·ing** **1.** To suffer dull, continued pain; be in pain or distress. **2.** *Informal* To yearn; be eager; with *for* or the infinitive. **— n.** A local, dull, and protracted pain. **—Syn.** See PAIN. [OE *acan*] **— ach′ing·ly** *adv.*

a·chene (ā-kēn′) *n. Bot.* A small, dry, indehiscent pericarp containing one seed, as in the dandelion, buttercup, etc.: also spelled *akene.* [< NL *achenium* < A-⁴ not + Gk. *chainein* to gape] **— a·che′ni·al** *adj.*

A·cher·nar (ā′kər-när) *n.* One of the 20 brightest stars, 0.51 magnitude; Alpha in the constellation Eridanus. See STAR. [< Arabic *ākhir al-nahr* end of the river]

Ach·e·ron (ak′ə-ron) **1.** In Greek and Roman mythology,

ACHENES
(Dandelion:
actual
size)

the river of woe, one of the rivers surrounding Hades. **2.** Hades. [< L < Gk. *Acherōn*]

Ach·e·son (ach/ə·sən), **Dean** (**Gooderham**), 1893–1971, U.S. lawyer and statesman, secretary of state 1949–53.

A·cheu·le·an (ə·shōō/lē·ən) *adj. Anthropol.* Describing a Lower Paleolithic culture stage distinguished by the characteristic features of its stone hand axes. Also **A·cheu/li·an.** [after *St. Acheul*, France, where artifacts were found]

à che·val (á shə·vál/) *French* On horseback; astraddle.

a·chieve (ə·chēv/) *v.* **a·chieved, a·chiev·ing** *v.t.* **1.** To accomplish; do successfully. **2.** To win or attain, as by effort, skill, or perseverance: He *achieved* wide renown. — *v.i.* **3.** To accomplish something; attain an object. [< OF *achever* < *a chief* (*venir*) (to come) to a head, finish < LL *ad caput* (*venire*)] — **a·chiev/a·ble** *adj.* — **a·chiev/er** *n.*

a·chieve·ment (ə·chēv/mənt) *n.* **1.** Something accomplished, especially by valor, skill, or exertion; a feat; exploit. **2.** The act of achieving. — **Syn.** See ACT.

achievement age See under AGE.

achievement quotient *Psychol.* The ratio of achievement age to chronological age. Abbr. *AQ, A.Q.*

achievement test *Psychol.* A test for measuring an individual's progress in the mastery of a subject to be learned. Compare INTELLIGENCE TEST.

A·chil·les (ə·kil/ēz) In the *Iliad*, the son of Peleus and Thetis; foremost Greek hero of the Trojan War, he killed Hector and was killed by an arrow Paris shot into his right heel, his only vulnerable spot. — **Ach·il·le·an** (ak/ə·lē/ən) *adj.*

Achilles' heel A vulnerable point.

Achilles' tendon *Anat.* The large tendon for the superficial muscles of the calf of the leg, attached to the heel bone: also called *tendon of Achilles.*

A·chit·o·phel (ə·kit/ə·fel) A counselor of King David who joined Absalom in rebelling against him. II *Sam.* xv–xvii.

ach·la·myd·e·ous (ak/lə·mid/ē·əs) *adj. Bot.* Having no protecting envelope, as a flower without a perianth. [< A-⁴ without + Gk. *chlamys, chlamydos* cloak]

a·chon·dro·pla·si·a (ə·kon/drō·plā/zhē·ə) *n. Pathol.* A disease characterized by inadequate formation of cartilage at ends of the long bones, resulting in a form of dwarfism: also called *fetal rickets.* [< NL < A-⁴ not + Gk. *chondros* cartilage + -PLASIA]

ach·ro·mat·ic (ak/rə·mat/ik) *adj.* **1.** *Optics* Free from color or iridescence; transmitting light without showing or separating it into its constituent colors, as a lens. **2.** *Biol.* a Resisting the usual staining agents. b Containing achromatin. **3.** *Music* Diatonic; without accidentals. [< Gk. *achrōmatos* < *a-* without + *chrōma* color] — **ach/ro·mat/i·cal·ly** *adv.* — **a·chro·ma·tism** (ā·krō/mə·tiz/əm), **a·chro·ma·tic·i·ty** (ā·krō/mə·tis/ə·tē) *n.*

achromatic color See under COLOR.

a·chro·ma·tin (ā·krō/mə·tin) *n. Biol.* The substance in the cell nucleus that does not readily take color from stains.

a·chro·ma·tize (ā·krō/mə·tīz) *v.t.* **·tized, ·tiz·ing** To make achromatic.

a·chro·ma·top·si·a (ā·krō/mə·top/sē·ə) *n. Pathol.* Color blindness. [< Gk. *achrōmatos* without color + *opsis* sight]

a·chro·ma·tous (ā·krō/mə·təs) *adj.* Having less than the normal color; colorless.

a·chro·mic (ā·krō/mik) *adj.* Colorless. Also **a·chro/mous.**

a·cic·u·la (ə·sik/yə·lə) *n.* *pl.* **·lae** (-lē) **1.** *Biol.* A slender, needlelike process; a bristle or prickle, as on a plant or animal. **2.** *Mineral.* A needle-shaped body, as some crystals. [< L, dim. of *acus* needle] — **a·cic/u·lar, a·cic/u·late** (-lit, -lāt), **a·cic/u·lat/ed** *adj.*

ac·id (as/id) *adj.* **1.** Sharp and biting to the taste, as vinegar; sour. **2.** *Chem.* Pertaining to, yielding, like, or reacting like, an acid. **3.** *Geol.* Acidic. **4.** Sharp-tempered; biting. — *n.* **1.** Any sour substance. **2.** *Chem.* a A compound containing hydrogen in which all or a part of the hydrogen may be exchanged for a metal or a basic radical, forming a salt. b A compound that yields hydrogen ions when dissolved in an ionizing solvent. Aqueous solutions of acids are sour, and redden vegetable substances. **3.** *slang* LSD. — **Syn.** See SOUR. [< L *acidus*] — **ac/id·ly** *adv.* — **ac/id·ness** *n.*

ac·id-fast (as/id·fast/, -fäst/) *adj.* Not readily decolorized by acids when stained: said of bacteria, epithelial tissue, etc.

ac·id-form·ing (as/id·fôr/ming) *adj.* **1.** *Chem.* Denoting an element whose oxides yield acids in water solution; acidic. **2.** *Biochem.* Pertaining to or designating foods that in metabolism yield a large acid residue.

a·cid·ic (ə·sid/ik) *adj.* **1.** *Geol.* Containing a high percentage of silica: said of rocks. **2.** *Chem.* Acid.

a·cid·i·fy (ə·sid/ə·fī) *v.t. & v.i.* **·fied, ·fy·ing** To make or become acid; change into an acid. — **a·cid/i·fi/a·ble** *adj.* — **a·cid/i·fi·ca/tion** *n.* — **a·cid/i·fi/er** *n.*

ac·i·dim·e·ter (as/i·dim/ə·tər) *n.* A hydrometer for determining the amount or strength of acids. — **ac·i·di·met·ric** (as/i·di·met/rik) or **·ri·cal** *adj.* — **ac/i·dim/e·try** *n.*

a·cid·i·ty (ə·sid/ə·tē) *n.* **1.** The state or quality of being acid. **2.** Degree of acid strength. **3.** *Chem.* The combining power of a base with reference to an acid. **4.** Hyperacidity.

ac·i·doph·i·lus (as/ə·dof/ə·ləs) *adj.* Staining easily with acid. [< ACID + Gk. *philos* loving]

acidophilus milk Milk fermented by the bacteria *Lactobacillus acidophilus,* used as an intestinal tonic.

ac·i·do·sis (as/ə·dō/sis) *n. Pathol.* Acid intoxication due to faulty metabolism. — **ac·i·dot·ic** (as/ə·dot/ik) *adj.*

acid test A final, decisive test, as of worth or integrity: from the testing of the composition of metals with acids.

a·cid·u·late (ə·sij/ŏŏ·lāt) *v.t.* **·lat·ed, ·lat·ing** To make somewhat acid or sour. — **a·cid/u·la/tion** *n.*

a·cid·u·lous (ə·sij/ŏŏ·ləs) *adj.* Slightly acid; sour. Also **a·cid/u·lent.** [< L *acidulus* slightly sour, dim. of *acidus* sour]

ac·i·er·ate (as/ē·ə·rāt) *v.t.* **·at·ed, ·at·ing** To turn into steel. [< F *acier* steel] — **ac/i·er·a/tion** *n.*

ac·i·form (as/ə·fôrm) *adj.* Needle-shaped. [< L *acus* needle + -FORM]

ac·i·nac·i·form (as/ə·nas/ə·fôrm, ə·sin/ə·sə-) *adj. Bot.* Scimitar-shaped; having one edge thick and slightly concave, the other thin and convex: said of a leaf. [< L *acinaces* scimitar (< Gk. *akinakēs*) + -FORM]

a·cin·i·form (ə·sin/ə·fôrm) *adj. Bot.* **1.** Shaped like a grape cluster. **2.** Grapelike. [< L *acinus* grape + -FORM]

ac·i·nous (as/ə·nəs) *adj. Bot.* Composed of small racemose lobules or acini.

ac·i·nus (as/ə·nəs) *n.* *pl.* **·ni** (-nī) **1.** *Bot.* One of the drupelets of an aggregate baccate fruit, as a raspberry; also, a grape seed. **2.** A berry, as a grape, growing in bunches; a bunch of such berries. **3.** *Anat.* The terminal division of the secreting portion of a racemose gland. [< L, grape]

-acious *suffix of adjectives* Abounding in; characterized by; given to: *pugnacious, vivacious.* [< L *-ax, -acis* + -OUS]

-acity *suffix* Quality or state of: *tenacity, pugnacity:* used to form abstract nouns corresponding to adjectives in *-acious.* [< L *-acitas, -acitatem*]

ack. Acknowledge; acknowledgment.

ack-ack (ak/ak/) *n.* Antiaircraft fire. [British radio operator's code for *A.A.* (antiaircraft)]

ac·knowl·edge (ak·nol/ij) *v.t.* **·edged, ·edg·ing** **1.** To admit the truth or fact of; confess: He *acknowledged* his ignorance. **2.** To recognize as or avow to be: The people *acknowledged* him as king. **3.** To admit the validity of, as a claim or right. **4.** To show appreciation of or admit obligation for; express thanks for: to *acknowledge* a favor. **5.** To report receipt or arrival of: to *acknowledge* a letter. **6.** *Law* To admit as genuine; certify. Abbr. *ack.* — **Syn.** See CONFESS. [Earlier *aknowledge* < obs. *aknow* to admit, confess (OE *oncnāwan*) + *knowledge,* v., to admit] — **ac·knowl/edge·a·ble** *adj.* — **ac·knowl/edg·er** *n.*

ac·knowl·edg·ment (ak·nol/ij·mənt) *n.* **1.** The act of admitting; confession. **2.** Recognition of the existence or truth of something. **3.** Something done or given in return. **4.** *Law* A formal declaration of an act before competent authority, or the official certificate of such declaration. Also **ac·knowl/edge·ment.** — **Syn.** See APOLOGY.

a·clin·ic (ā·klin/ik) *adj.* Having no inclination or dip, as the compass needle near the magnetic equator. [< Gk. *aklinēs* < *a-* not + *klinein* to bend]

aclinic line The magnetic equator.

ACLS or **A.C.L.S.** American Council of Learned Societies.

ac·me (ak/mē) *n.* The highest point, or summit. [< Gk. *akmē* point]

ac·ne (ak/nē) *n. Pathol.* An eruptive skin disease, caused by inflammation of the sebaceous glands, chiefly about the face, chest, and back. [? Alter of Gk. *akmē* point]

ac·node (ak/nōd) *n. Math.* A point outside a curve whose coordinates satisfy the equation of the curve; a conjugate point. [< L *acus* needle + NODE]

a·cock (ə·kok/) *adj.* **1.** In cocked fashion or position. **2.** Alert; vigilant. — *adv.* In a cocked manner or position.

ac·o·lyte (ak/ə·līt) *n.* **1.** An attendant or assistant. **2.** *Eccl.* An attendant on the ministers officiating at a sacred rite, who performs subordinate duties; an altar boy; in the Roman Catholic Church, a member of the highest minor order. [< Med.L *acolitus* < Gk. *akolouthos* follower, attendant]

à compte (á kônt/) *French* On account; in part payment.

A·con·ca·gua (ä/kôn·kä/gwä) An extinct volcano in west central Argentina; 22,834 ft.; highest peak in the Western Hemisphere.

ac·o·nite (ak/ə·nīt) *n.* **1.** The monkshood, or any plant of the genus *Aconitum.* **2.** An extract from the root and leaves of this plant, used as a sedative. Also **ac·o·ni·tum** (ak/ə·nī/təm). [< F *aconit* < L *aconitum* < Gk. *akoniton*]

a·corn (ā/kôrn, ā/kərn) *n.* **1.** The fruit of the oak, a one-seeded nut, fixed in a woody cup. **2.** *Aeron.* A special type of fitting used to prevent abrasion of intersecting wires in the cross-bracing of an aircraft. [OE *æcern*]

acorn tube *Electronics* A small electron tube for use at high frequencies. Also *Brit.* **acorn valve.**

ACORNS

a Red oak. *b* Scarlet oak. *c* Pin oak. *d* Black oak. *e* White oak.

à corps per·du (á kôr per·dü/) *French* Headlong; impetuously; literally, with lost body.

a·cot·y·le·don (ā/kŏt·ə·lēd/n) *n. Bot.* A plant without cotyledons or seed lobes. [< A-⁴ without + COTYLEDON] — **a/cot·y·le/don·ous** *adj.*

acouo- *combining form* Hearing; of or related to hearing. Also **acou-.** [< Gk. *akouein* to hear]

a·cous·tic (ə·kōōs/tĭk) *adj.* **1.** Pertaining to the act or sense of hearing, heard sound, or the science of sound. **2.** Adapted for conveying sound or aiding hearing. Also **a·cous/ti·cal.** — *n.* Any medicine or appliance to aid hearing. [< F *acoustique* < Gk. *akoustikos* pertaining to hearing < *akouein* to hear] — **a·cous/ti·cal·ly** *adv.*

a·cous·ti·cian (ak/ōōs·tĭsh/ən) *n.* A specialist in the theory and practical applications of acoustics.

acoustic phonetics See under PHONETICS.

a·cous·tics (ə·kōōs/tĭks) *n.pl. (construed as sing. in def. 1)* **1.** The branch of physics that treats of the phenomena and laws of sound. **2.** The sound-producing qualities of an auditorium, room, etc.

à cou·vert (á kōō·vâr/) *French* Under cover; sheltered.

A.C.P. American College of Physicians.

acpt. Acceptance (in banking).

ac·quaint (ə·kwānt/) *v.t.* **1.** To make familiar or conversant: with *with*: *Acquaint* yourself with your duties. **2.** To cause to know; inform: with *with*: He *acquainted* me with his suspicions. [< OF *acointer* < LL *adcognitare* to make known < L *ad-* to + *cognitus*, pp. of *cognoscere* to know < *com-* together + *gnoscere* to come to know]

ac·quain·tance (ə·kwān/təns) *n.* **1.** Knowledge of any person or thing. **2.** A person or persons with whom one is acquainted. — **Syn.** See FRIEND. — **ac·quain/tance·ship** *n.*

ac·quaint·ed (ə·kwān/tĭd) *adj.* Having acquaintance; having personal knowledge: with *with*.

ac·quest (ə·kwest/) *n.* **1.** Something acquired. **2.** *Law* Property acquired by means other than inheritance. [< MF < LL *acquistum*, var. of L *acquisitum* < *acquirere*. See ACQUIRE.]

ac·qui·esce (ak/wē·es/) *v.i.* **·esced** (-est/), **·esc·ing** To consent or concur tacitly; assent; comply: with *in* (formerly with *to*): The candidate *acquiesced* in all his party's plans. — **Syn.** See ASSENT. [< MF *acquiescer* < L *acquiescere* < *ad-* to + *quiescere* to rest] — **ac/qui·esc/ing·ly** *adv.*

ac·qui·es·cence (ak/wē·es/əns) *n.* Quiet submission; passive consent: with *in* (formerly with *to*).

ac·qui·es·cent (ak/wē·es/ənt) *adj.* Disposed to yield or assent; compliant. [< L *acquiescens, -entis,* ppr. of *acquiescere.* See ACQUIESCE.] — **ac/qui·es/cent·ly** *adv.*

ac·quire (ə·kwīr/) *v.t.* **·quired, ·quir·ing** **1.** To obtain by one's own endeavor or action. **2.** To come to possess; receive. — **Syn.** See GET, RECEIVE. [< L *acquirere* < *ad-* to + *quaerere* to seek] — **ac·quir/a·ble** *adj.* — **ac·quir/er** *n.*

acquired character *Biol.* A structural or functional modification of an organism resulting from the postnatal influences of environment.

ac·quire·ment (ə·kwīr/mənt) *n.* **1.** The act of acquiring. **2.** Something acquired, as a skill; an attainment. — **Syn.** See ATTAINMENT.

ac·qui·si·tion (ak/wə·zĭsh/ən) *n.* **1.** The act of acquiring. **2.** Anything gained or acquired, as a possession or skill. — **Syn.** See ATTAINMENT. [< L *acquisitio, -onis* < *acquirere.* See ACQUIRE.]

ac·quis·i·tive (ə·kwĭz/ə·tĭv) *adj.* Able or inclined to acquire (money, property, etc.); grasping. — **ac·quis/i·tive·ly** *adv.* — **ac·quis/i·tive·ness** *n.*

ac·quit (ə·kwĭt/) *v.t.* **·quit·ted, ·quit·ting** **1.** To free or clear, as from an accusation; declare innocent; exonerate: He was *acquitted* of the crime. **2.** To relieve, as of an obligation; absolve. **3.** To repay or return, as a favor; discharge, as a debt. **4.** To conduct (oneself); behave: He *acquitted* himself like a man. — **Syn.** See ABSOLVE. [< OF *aquiter,* ult. < L *ad-* to + *quietare* to settle, quiet] — **ac·quit/ter** *n.*

ac·quit·tal (ə·kwĭt/l) *n.* **1.** The act of acquitting; discharge; release. **2.** *Law* A setting free from a criminal charge by judicial action. Also **ac·quit/ment.**

ac·quit·tance (ə·kwĭt/ns) *n.* **1.** A release or discharge, as from indebtedness. **2.** Satisfaction of indebtedness or obligation. **3.** A receipt.

a·cre (ā/kər) *n.* **1.** In the United States and Great Britain, a measure of land, equal to 43,560 square feet or 0.404 hectare. Abbr. *a., A., ac.* See table inside back cover. **2.** *pl.* Lands; estate. **3.** *pl. Informal* A large amount; lots: *acres* of books. — **God's acre** A churchyard or burial ground. [OE *æcer* field]

A·cre (ā/kər, ä/kər *for def. 1*; ä/kri *for def. 2*) **1.** A port city of NE Israel, on the **Bay of Acre** of the eastern Mediterranean; pop. 28,100 (est. 1963): Old Testament *Accho*; New Testament *Ptolemais*; called **Saint Jean d'A·cre** (saṅ zhäṅ dä/kr) during the Crusades. **2.** A Federal Territory in western Brazil; 58,915 sq. mi.; pop. 196,000 (1960); capital, Rio Branco.

a·cre·age (ā/kər·ĭj, -krĭj) *n.* Area in acres; acres collectively.

a·cred (ā/kərd) *adj.* Comprising or owning acres of land.

a·cre-foot (ā/kər·fŏŏt/) *n.* The amount of water required to cover one level acre to a depth of 1 foot; 43,560 cubic feet.

a·cre-inch (ā/kər·inch/) *n.* One twelfth of an acre-foot.

ac·rid (ak/rĭd) *adj.* **1.** Of a cutting, burning taste; pungent; bitter. **2.** Of a sharp, satirical nature, speech, etc.; acrimonious. — **Syn.** See SOUR. [< L *acer, acris*; infl. by *acid*] — **a·crid·i·ty** (ə·krĭd/ə·tē), **ac/rid·ness** *n.* — **ac/rid·ly** *adv.*

ac·ri·dine (ak/rə·dēn, -dĭn) *n. Chem.* A hydrocarbon compound, $C_{13}H_9N$, of very pungent odor, obtained from the anthracene fraction of coal tar and used in the synthesis of an important series of dyes. [< ACRID + -INE²]

ac·ri·fla·vine (ak/rə·flā/vēn, -vĭn) *n. Chem.* An odorless, brownish red, granular compound, $C_{14}H_{14}N_3Cl$, derived from acridine, and used as an antiseptic and disinfectant.

ac·ri·mo·ni·ous (ak/rə·mō/nē·əs) *adj.* Full of bitterness; sarcastic; caustic; sharp: an *acrimonious* debate. — **ac/ri·mo/ni·ous·ly** *adv.* — **ac/ri·mo/ni·ous·ness** *n.*

ac·ri·mo·ny (ak/rə·mō/nē) *n. pl.* **·nies** Sharpness or bitterness of speech or temper; acridity. [< L *acrimonia* < *acer* sharp]

— **Syn.** *Acrimony, asperity,* and *acerbity* refer to words, or possibly actions, that are sharp, bitter, or hostile. *Acrimony* expresses deep resentment or great dislike. *Asperity* involves keen irritation, but not necessarily bitterness, and is often expressed by tone of voice rather than by words. *Acerbity* includes bitterness and sharpness, which may arise from momentary annoyance or habitual irritation. Compare ANGER, ENMITY. — **Ant.** gentleness, suavity, sweetness.

acro- *combining form* **1.** At the top; highest; topped with; at the tip or end of: *acrogen.* **2.** *Med.* Pertaining to the extremities: *acromegaly.* [< Gk. *akros* at the top or end]

ac·ro·bat (ak/rə·bat) *n.* One skilled in feats requiring muscular coordination, as in tightrope walking, tumbling, trapeze performing, etc.; a gymnast. [< F *acrobate* < Gk. *akrobatos* walking on tiptoe < *akros* at the tip + *bainein* to walk, go] — **ac/ro·bat/ic** or **·i·cal** *adj.* — **ac/ro·bat/i·cal·ly** *adv.*

ac·ro·bat·ics (ak/rə·bat/ĭks) *n.pl.* The skills or activities of an acrobat, as in gymnastics or aerobatics.

ac·ro·car·pous (ak/rō·kär/pəs) *adj. Bot.* Bearing fruit at the end of a stem, as some mosses.

ac·ro·dont (ak/rə·dont) *Zool. adj.* Having rootless teeth firmly ankylosed at the base with the bony edge of the jaw, as certain lizards. — *n.* An acrodont creature.

ac·ro·drome (ak/rə·drōm) *adj. Bot.* Running to the point: said of leaves in which the nerves all point to or reach the apex. Also **a·crod·ro·mous** (ə·krod/rə·məs).

ac·ro·gen (ak/rə·jən) *n. Bot.* An organism growing at the apex only, as ferns, mosses, etc. — **ac·ro·gen·ic** (ak/rə·jen/ik), **a·crog·e·nous** (ə·kroj/ə·nəs) *adj.* — **a·crog/e·nous·ly** *adv.*

ac·ro·le·in (ə·krō/lē·ĭn) *n. Chem.* A volatile, colorless liquid, C_3H_4O, intensely irritating to the nose and eyes, obtained variously, as by destructively distilling fats, and used as a tear gas. [< ACR(ID) + L *olere* to smell + -IN]

ac·ro·lith (ak/rə·lĭth) *n.* A statue with stone head and extremities, the trunk being usually of wood and draped. [< L *acrolithus* < Gk. *akrolithos* < *akros* at the end + *lithos* stone] — **a·crol·i·than** (ə·krol/ə·thən), **ac/ro·lith/ic** *adj.*

ac·ro·meg·a·ly (ak/rō·meg/ə·lē) *n. Pathol.* A glandular disorder characterized by an enlargement of the extremities, thorax, and face, including both soft and bony parts. [< F *acromégalie* < Gk. *akros* at the tip + *megas, megalou* big] — **ac·ro·me·gal·ic** (ak/rō·mi·gal/ĭk) *adj. & n.*

a·cro·mi·on (ə·krō/mē·ən) *n. pl.* **·mi·a** (-mē·ə) *Anat.* The projecting extension of the scapula or shoulder blade forming the point of the shoulder. Also **acromial process.** [< NL < Gk. *akrōmion* < *akros* at the tip + *ōmos* shoulder] — **a·cro/mi·al** *adj.*

a·cron·i·cal (ə·kron/i·kəl) *adj.* Occurring at sunset: said of the rising or setting of a star. Also **a·cron/ic, a·cron/y·cal, a·cron/y·chal** (-i·kəl). [< Gk. *akronychos* at nightfall < *akros* on the edge + *nyx* night]

ac·ro·nym (ak/rə·nĭm) *n.* A word formed by combining initial letters (*Eniac, UNESCO*) or syllables and letters (*radar, sonar*) of a series of words or a compound term. [< ACRO- + -nym name, as in *homonym*]

a·crop·e·tal (ə·krop/ə·təl) *adj. Bot.* Developing from the base upward toward the apex, as certain forms of inflorescence. [< ACRO- + L *petere* to seek, go toward] — **a·crop/e·tal·ly** *adv.*

a·crop·o·lis (ə·krop/ə·lĭs) *n.* The citadel of an ancient Greek city. — **the Acropolis** The citadel of Athens. [< Gk. *akropolis* < *akros* at the top + *polis* city]

ac·ro·spire (ak/rə·spīr) *n. Bot.* The first sprout from germinating or malted grain; the first leaf above ground. [< ACRO- + Gk. *speira* anything twisted]

a·cross (ə·krôs/, ə·kros/) *adv.* **1.** From one side to the other: The ocean was calm when we came *across.* **2.** On or at the other side: We shall soon be *across.* **3.** Crosswise; crossed, as arms. — *prep.* **1.** On or from the other side of; beyond; over: the music from *across* the street. **2.** Through or over the surface of: riding *across* the field. **3.** From side to side of: A tree fell *across* the ditch. [< A-¹ on, in + CROSS]

PRONUNCIATION KEY: add, āce, câre, pälm; end, ēven; it, īce; odd, ōpen, ôrder; tŏŏk, pōōl; up, bûrn; ə = a in *above,* e in *sicken,* i in *flexible,* o in *melon,* u in *focus;* yōō = u in *fuse;* oil; pout; check; go; ring; thin; this; zh, vision. For à, œ, ü, kh, ṅ, see inside front cover.

a·cros·tic (ə·krôs′tik, ə·kros′-) *n.* A poem or other composition in which initial or other letters, taken in order, form a word or phrase. — *adj.* Of or resembling an acrostic. [< L *acrostichis* < Gk. *akrostichis* < *akros* at the end + *stichos* line of verse] — **a·cros′ti·cal·ly** *adv.*

ac·ro·tism (ak′rə·tiz′əm) *n. Pathol.* Absence or weakness of the pulse beat. [< A-⁴ without + Gk. *krotos* a beat] — **a·crot·ic** (ə·krot′ik) *adj.*

A·crux (ā′kruks) *n.* One of the 20 brightest stars, 0.9 magnitude; Alpha in the constellation Crux. See STAR.

a·cryl·ic acid (ə·kril′ik) *Chem.* Any of a series of unsaturated aliphatic acids of the general formula $C_nH_{2n-2}O_2$, having a sharp, acrid odor, prepared from alkenes, and used in organic synthesis and in the making of plastics: also called *propenoic acid.* [< ACR(OLEIN) + -YL + -IC]

acrylic resin Any of a class of transparent thermosetting plastics or resins made from acrylic acid. Also **ac·ry·late resin** (ak′ri·lāt).

ACS or **A.C.S.** American Chemical Society.

A/Cs Pay. Accounts payable.

A/Cs Rec. Accounts receivable.

act (akt) *v.t.* **1.** To play the part of; impersonate, as in a drama: to *act* Juliet. **2.** To perform on the stage, as a play. **3.** To perform as if on a stage; feign the character of: Don't *act* the martyr. **4.** To behave as suitable to: *Act* your age. **5.** *Obs.* To actuate. — *v.i.* **6.** To behave or conduct oneself: He knows how to *act* in society. **7.** To carry out a purpose or function; perform: The police *acted* promptly. **8.** To carry out a purpose or function in a particular way: with *as:* The test *acted* as a check. **9.** To produce an effect: often with *on:* The sedative *acted* on her swiftly. **10.** To serve temporarily or as a substitute, as in some office or capacity: with *for:* The corporal *acted* for his commanding officer. **11.** To perform on the stage; be an actor. **12.** To pretend; play a part so as to appear: She concealed her feelings and *acted* friendly. **13.** To serve for theatrical performance or use: This scene *acts* well. — **to act on** (or **upon**) To order one's conduct in accordance with; obey: to *act on* someone's advice. — **to act up** *Informal* To behave mischievously; appear troublesome. — *n.* **1.** The exertion of mental or physical power; the performance of a function or process; a doing: taken in the very *act.* **2.** Something done; a deed; action: an *act* of charity. **3.** An enactment or edict, as of a legislative body. **4.** *Often pl.* A formal written record or statement of a transaction, action taken, etc. **5.** A section of a drama; one of the main divisions of a play or opera. **6.** A short theatrical performance, often part of a longer program: a song-and-dance *act.* **7.** *Informal* Something feigned; a pose. [< L *actus* a doing, and *actum* a thing done, pp. of *agere* to do]

— **Syn.** (noun) 2. *Act, deed, action, feat, achievement,* and *exploit* all mean something accomplished. *Act* and *deed* are both used for something done, while *action* refers more to the doing of it. *Acts* and *deeds* may be good or bad, but a *deed* is commonly great or notable. A *feat* requires daring and skill, and usually involves physical *action. Achievement* is usually distinguished, and accomplished despite difficulties. An *exploit* is a conspicuous or glorious *deed,* involving valor and heroism.

Act *Chem.* Actinium.

A.C.T. Australian Capital Territory.

ac·ta (ak′tə) *n.pl.* Acts; especially, proceedings or minutes of proceedings in a court. [< L, pl. of *actum* a thing done]

act·a·ble (ak′tə·bəl) *adj.* That can be acted, as a role in a play. — **act′a·bil′i·ty** *n.*

Ac·tae·on (ak·tē′ən) In Greek mythology, a hunter who surprised Artemis bathing and was turned by her into a stag and killed by his own dogs.

actg. Acting.

ACTH A hormone extracted from the pituitary gland of hogs and other animals, and stimulating the action of the cortical area of the human adrenal glands, with the release of cortisone. [< A(DRENO)-C(ORTICO)-T(ROPIC) H(ORMONE)]

ac·ti·nal (ak′tə·nəl, ak·tī′-) *adj. Zool.* **1.** Bearing tentacles or rays. **2.** Of or pertaining to the oral region of a radiate. — **ac′ti·nal·ly** *adv.*

act·ing (ak′ting) *adj.* **1.** Operating or officiating, especially in place of another: *acting* secretary. Abbr. *a., actg.* **2.** Functioning; working. **3.** Containing directions for actors: the *acting* script. — *n.* **1.** Performance, as of a part in a play; the occupation of an actor. **2.** Pretense or simulation.

acting sub·lieu·ten·ant (sub′lə·ten′ənt) In the Royal, Royal Canadian, and other Commonwealth navies, an officer ranking next below sublieutenant. See table at GRADE.

ac·tin·i·a (ak·tin′ē·ə) *n.* A sea anemone. Also **ac·tin′i·an**. [< NL < Gk. *aktis, aktinos* ray]

ac·tin·ic (ak·tin′ik) *adj.* Of, pertaining to, or having actinism. Also **ac·tin′i·cal.** — **ac·tin′i·cal·ly** *adv.*

actinic rays Those wavelengths in the violet and ultraviolet part of the spectrum capable of effecting chemical changes.

ac·ti·nide series (ak′ti·nīd) *Physics* A transition series of radioactive elements arranged within the periodic table on the analogy of the lanthanide or rare-earth series, which it resembles in certain properties. It begins with actinium, atomic number 89, and continues to the position represented by lawrencium, atomic number 103.

ac·tin·i·form (ak·tin′ə·fôrm) *adj. Zool.* Having a radiated form, as actiniae.

ac·tin·ism (ak′tin·iz′əm) *n.* **1.** The property of radiant energy that effects chemical changes. **2.** The production of such change. [< ACTIN(O)- + -ISM]

ac·tin·i·um (ak·tin′ē·əm) *n.* A radioactive element (symbol Ac), isolated from pitchblende, and having a half life of about 13 years. See ELEMENT. Abbr. *Act*

actinium series *Physics* The group of radioactive elements beginning with actinouranium and continuing through successive disintegration products to actinium D, the stable isotope of lead of mass 207.

actino- *combining form* **1.** *Zool.* Pertaining to a radiate structure or to the presence of tentacles: *actinozoan.* **2.** *Chem.* Relating to light rays as promoting chemical action: *actinograph.* Also **actin-, actini-.** [< Gk. *aktis, aktinos* ray]

ac·tin·o·graph (ak·tin′ə·graf, -gräf) *n.* A recording actinometer.

ac·ti·noid (ak′ti·noid) *adj.* Having the form of rays; radiate, as a starfish. [< ACTIN(O)- + -OID]

ac·tin·o·lite (ak·tin′ə·līt) *n. Mineral.* A type of amphibole.

ac·tin·o·mere (ak·tin′ə·mir) See ANTIMERE.

ac·ti·nom·e·ter (ak′ti·nom′ə·tər) *n.* **1.** An instrument for measuring the heat intensity of the sun's rays and for determining the actinic effect of the light rays. **2.** An instrument for determining the power of radiation by its chemical effect on gases, acids, etc. — **ac·ti·no·met·ric** (ak′ti·nō·met′rik) or **·ri·cal** *adj.* — **ac′ti·nom′e·try** *n.*

ac·ti·no·mor·phic (ak′ti·nō·môr′fik) *adj. Bot.* Designating flowers that may be divided into similar halves in two or more vertical planes. Also **ac′ti·no·mor′phous.**

ac·ti·no·my·cete (ak′ti·nō·mī·sēt′) *n. Bacteriol.* One of a class or genus (*Actinomycetes*) of filamentous, often pathogenic microorganisms intermediate between molds and the true bacteria.

ac·ti·no·my·co·sis (ak′ti·nō·mī·kō′sis) *n.* A chronic infectious disease of cattle, hogs, and people, caused by the ray fungus (genus *Actinomyces*) and characterized by the formation of lesions and tumors about the jaws: also called *lumpy jaw.* — **ac′ti·no·my·cot′ic** (-kot′ik) *adj.*

ac·ti·non (ak′ti·non) *n. Chem.* A radioactive isotope of radon, occurring as an emanation of actinium, with a half life of nearly four seconds. [< NL]

ac·ti·no·ther·a·py (ak′ti·nō·ther′ə·pē) *n. Med.* The treatment of disease by means of violet and ultraviolet rays.

ac·ti·no·u·ra·ni·um (ak′ti·nō·yŏŏ·rā′nē·əm) *n. Chem.* The isotope of uranium of mass 238, the initial member of the actinium series.

ac·ti·no·zo·an (ak′ti·nə·zō′ən) *n. Zool.* An anthozoan (which see). [< ACTINO- + Gk. *zōion* animal + -AN] — **ac′ti·no·zo′al** *adj.*

ac·tion (ak′shən) *n.* **1.** The process of acting, doing, or working; operation. **2.** The result of putting forth power; a deed; act: a manly *action.* **3.** *pl.* Habitual behavior; conduct. **4.** Activity; energy: a man of *action.* **5.** The exertion of power; influence: the *action* of water on rock. **6.** *Physiol.* The performance by an organ of its proper function. **7.** *Mech.* **a** The mechanism by which a machine operates: the *action* of a gun. **b** The movement of the parts of a machine: the *action* of a typewriter. **8.** *Mil.* A battle; combat. **9.** *Law* The lawful demand of one's right through judicial proceedings; a lawsuit. **10.** The posture and gestures of an actor or orator. **11.** In literature, the series of connected events that form the plot in a story or play. **12.** In sculpture or painting, gesture or attitude intended to express passion or sentiment. **13.** *Physics* A magnitude describing the condition of any dynamic system, expressible as twice the mean kinetic energy of the system during a given interval, multiplied by the duration of the interval. — **Syn.** See ACT, BATTLE. [< F < L *actio, -onis* < *agere* to do]

ac·tion·a·ble (ak′shən·ə·bəl) *adj.* Affording ground for prosecution, as a trespass or a libel. — **ac′tion·a·bly** *adv.*

Ac·ti·um (ak′tē·əm, ak′shē·əm) An ancient Greek town and promontory in NW Acarnania; site of the naval victory by Octavian's forces over Mark Antony, 31 B.C.

ac·ti·vate (ak′tə·vāt) *v.t.* **·vat·ed, ·vat·ing** **1.** To make active. **2.** To put into or make capable of action. **3.** *Mil.* To order (a previously constituted and designated unit, post, etc.) into official existence so that it can be organized for its assigned function. **4.** *Physics* To make radioactive. **5.** *Chem.* To promote or hasten a reaction in, as by heat. **6.** To purify by aeration, as sewage.

activated carbon Charcoal obtained by the destructive distillation of vegetable matter and important as an adsorbent of gases and vapors and in medicine.

activated sludge A mixture of aerobic bacteria and mineral substances found in aerated sewage, having the effect of purifying other sewage brought into contact with it.

ac·ti·va·tion (ak′tə·vā′shən) *n.* The art or process of activating; as: **a** The process of mixing sewage with air and bacteria to purify it. **b** *Chem.* Any process, such as heating, whereby a metallic catalyst is restored to activity. **c** *Biochem.* The transforming, by a kinase, of an inert enzyme into one that is active. **d** Excitation (def. 2a).

ac·ti·va·tor (ak′tə-vā′tər) *n.* One who or that which activates; as: **a** *Biochem.* A substance that renders active an enzyme that is secreted in an inactive form. **b** *Chem.* A catalyst.

ac·tive (ak′tiv) *adj.* **1.** Abounding in or exhibiting action; busy: an *active* man. **2.** Being in or pertaining to a state of action, not extinct or quiescent: an *active* volcano. **3.** Agile; quick; nimble. **4.** Characterized by much activity; brisk; lively: *active* trading. **5.** Causing or promoting action or change; not contemplative: an *active* life. **6.** Bearing interest: *active* investments. **7.** In business, busy; productive: *active* accounts. **8.** *Gram.* **a** Designating a voice of the verb that indicates that the subject of the sentence is performing the action, as *fires* is in the active voice in *The soldier fires the gun*: distinguished from *passive*. **b** Describing verbs expressing action as distinguished from being and state, as *run, hit, jump*. **9.** *Med.* Immediately effective; working quickly: an *active* remedy. — *n. Gram.* The active voice. Abbr. *a.* [< F *actif*, fem. *active* < L *activus* < *agere* to do] — **ac′tive·ly** *adv.* — **ac′tive·ness** *n.*
— **Syn.** vigorous, strenuous, lively, energetic, bustling. Compare BUSY.

active duty Full-time duty in the active military service of the United States. Also **active service**. Abbr. *AD*.

ac·ti·vist (ak′tə-vist) *n.* One who believes in and practices direct and decisive action, especially in politics.

ac·tiv·i·ty (ak-tiv′ə-tē) *n. pl.* **·ties 1.** The state of being active; action: the *activity* of the heart. **2.** Brisk or vigorous movement or action; liveliness; energy: *activity* in the stock market; a man of *activity* **3.** A particular action or sphere of action: weekend *activities*. **4.** *Physics* The degree of emission from a radioactive substance in unit time. **5.** *Chem.* The ion concentration of a given element or substance.

activity series Electromotive series (which see).

act of God *Law* An inevitable event occurring by reason of the operations of nature unmixed with human agency or human negligence.

Ac·ton (ak′tən), **Lord**, 1834–1902, John Emerich Edward Dalberg-Acton, English historian.

ac·tor (ak′tər) *n.* **1.** A player on the stage, in motion pictures, etc. **2.** One who acts or is active; a doer. — **Syn.** See DOER. [< L, a doer < *agere* to do]

ac·tress (ak′tris) *n* A woman or girl who acts, as on the stage.

Acts of the Apostles The fifth book of the New Testament. Also **Acts**.

ac·tu·al (ak′chōō-əl) *adj.* **1.** Existing in fact; real. **2.** Being in existence or action now; existent; present. [< F *actuel* < LL *actualis* < L *actus* a doing. See ACT.] — **ac′tu·al·ness** *n.*

ac·tu·al·i·ty (ak′chōō-al′ə-tē) *n. pl.* **·ties 1.** The state or quality of being actual; reality; realism. **2.** *pl.* Actual circumstances or conditions.

ac·tu·al·ize (ak′chōō-əl-īz′) *v.t.* **·ized, ·iz·ing 1.** To make real; realize in action, as a possibility. **2.** To make seem real; represent realistically. — **ac′tu·al·i·za′tion** *n.*

ac·tu·al·ly (ak′chōō-əl-ē) *adv.* As a matter of fact; really.

ac·tu·ar·y (ak′chōō-er′ē) *n. pl.* **·ar·ies** A statistician who calculates and states risks, premiums, etc., for insurance purposes. [< L *actuarius* clerk < *actus*. See ACT.] — **ac·tu·ar·i·al** (ak′chōō-âr′ē-əl) *adj.* — **ac′tu·ar′i·al·ly** *adv.*

ac·tu·ate (ak′chōō-āt) *v.t.* **·at·ed, ·at·ing 1.** To set into action or motion, as a mechanism. **2.** To incite or influence to action: *actuated* by motives of kindness. [< Med.L *actuatus*, pp. of *actuare* < L *actus* a doing. See ACT.] — **ac′tu·a′tion** *n.* — **ac′tu·a′tor** *n.*
— **Syn. 2.** *Actuate, impel*, and *urge* all mean to prompt a person to act. *Actuate* and *impel* both imply mental or moral reasons for acting, while *urge* more often involves persuasion or reasons as given by others. One is *urged* from without, *actuated* or *impelled* from within. Compare INFLUENCE. — **Ant.** deter.

acu- *combining form* Needle; point: *acupuncture*. [< L *acus*]

ac·u·ate (ak′yōō-it, -āt) *adj.* Sharpened; sharp. [< Med.L *acuatus*, pp. of *acuare* to sharpen to a point < L *acus* needle]

a·cu·i·ty (ə-kyōō′ə-tē) *n.* Acuteness; sharpness. [< MF *acuité* < Med.L *acuitas, -tatis* < L *acus* needle]

a·cu·le·ate (ə-kyōō′lē-it, -āt) *adj.* **1.** *Zool.* Armed with a sting. **2.** *Bot.* Provided with prickles; prickly. Also **a·cu′le·at′ed**. [< L *aculeatus* < *aculeus*, dim. of *acus* needle]

a·cu·men (ə-kyōō′mən, ak′yōō-mən) *n.* **1.** Quickness of insight or discernment; keenness of intellect. **2.** *Bot.* A sharply tapering point. [< L, point, sharpness (of the mind) < *acuere* to sharpen]
— **Syn.** *Acumen, sharpness, acuteness, insight, perception, cleverness*, and *perspicacity* all refer to sharp, outstanding, intellectual ability. *Sharpness, acuteness*, and *insight*, however keen, and *perception*, however deep, fall short of the meaning of *acumen*, which belongs to an astute and discriminating mind. *Cleverness* is a practical aptitude for study or learning. *Perspicacity* is the power to see clearly and quickly through that which is difficult or involved.

a·cu·mi·nate (ə-kyōō′mə-nāt; *for adj., also* ə-kyōō′mə-nit) *v.t.* **·nat·ed, ·nat·ing** To sharpen; make pointed. — *adj.*

Ending in a long, tapering point, as a leaf, feather, fin, etc.: also **a·cu′mi·nat′ed**. See illustration of LEAF. [< L *acuminatus*, pp. of *acuminare* point < *acumen*. See ACUMEN.] — **a·cu′mi·na′tion** *n.*

ac·u·punc·ture (ak′yōō-pungk′chər) *n. Med.* A pricking of body tissues with a needle or needles, as for diagnostic or remedial purposes. Also **ac′u·punc·ta′tion**.

a·cute (ə-kyōōt′) *adj.* **1.** Coming to a crisis quickly; violent: said of a disease: opposed to *chronic*: *acute* appendicitis. **2.** Of the greatest importance; crucial. **3.** Affecting keenly; poignant; intense: *acute* pain. **4.** Keenly discerning or sensitive: an *acute* mind. **5.** *Bot.* Having a sharp point, as a leaf: opposed to *obtuse*. **6.** *Music* High in pitch; shrill. [< L *acutus*, pp. of *acuere* to sharpen] — **a·cute′ly** *adv.* — **a·cute′ness** *n.*
— **Syn. 2.** *Acute, critical*, and *crucial* are used to describe circumstances of great tension and possible danger. *Acute* implies an extreme degree of stress, while *critical* suggests that a decisive change is about to occur. *Crucial* adds the idea of a trial or test that will determine the course of events. **4.** See ASTUTE.

acute accent See ACCENT (def. 3).

acute angle *Geom.* An angle less than a right angle.

A.C.W.A. Amalgamated Clothing Workers of America.

-acy *suffix of nouns* Forming nouns of quality, state, or condition from adjectives in *-acious*, and nouns and adjectives in *-ate*: *fallacy, celibacy, curacy*. [< F *-atie* < L *-acia*, *-atia* < Gk. *-ateia*; or directly < L or < Gk.]

a·cy·clic (ā-sī′klik,ā-sik′lik) *adj.* **1.** *Bot.* Not whorled; not cyclic. **2.** *Chem.* Pertaining to organic compounds of the aliphatic, open-chain series, as methane.

ad (ad) *n. Informal* An advertisement.

ad- *prefix* To; toward; near: *adhere, advert, adrenal*: also, often without perceptible force. Also: *a-* before *sc, sp, st*, as in *ascribe*; *ab-* before *b*, as in *abbreviate*; *ac-* before *c, q*, as in *acquire*; *af-* before *f*, as in *afferent*; *ag-* before *g*, as in *agglutinate*; *al-* before *l*, as in *allude*; *an-* before *n*, as in *annex*; *ap-* before *p*, as in *append*; *ar-* before *r*, as in *arrive*; *as-* before *s*, as in *associate*; *at-* before *t*, as in *attract*. [< L *ad-* < *ad* to]

ad. **1.** Adapted; adaptor. **2.** Add. **3.** Advertisement.

a.d. After date.

-ad[1] *suffix of nouns* Of or pertaining to; used to form: **a** Collective numerals: *triad*. **b** Names of poems: *Iliad, Dunciad*. **c** *Bot.* Names of some plants: *cycad*. [< Gk. *-as, -ados*]

-ad[2] *suffix of adverbs* *Anat. & Zool.* To; toward; in the direction of: *dorsad*, toward the back. [< L *ad* to, toward]

AD *Mil.* Active duty.

A.D. In the year of our Lord (L *anno domini*).

A.D.A. **1.** American Dental Association. **2.** Americans for Democratic Action.

a·dac·ty·lous (ā-dak′tə-ləs) *adj. Zool.* Without fingers or toes. [< Gk. *a-* without + *daktylos* finger]

ad·age (ad′ij) *n.* A saying that has obtained credit or force by long use; a proverb. — **Syn.** See PROVERB. [< F < L *adagium* < *ad-* to + root of *aio* I say]

a·da·gio (ə-dä′jō, -zhē-ō, -zhō) *Music adj.* Slow; faster than largo but slower than andante. — *adv.* Slowly. — *n.* A composition, movement, etc., in adagio time. [< Ital., lit., at ease]

adagio dance A ballet dance in slow tempo.

Ad·am (ad′əm) *adj.* Of or pertaining to a neoclassic style of architecture, furniture, etc., originated in England by the **Adam** brothers, **Robert**, 1728–92, and **James**, 1730–94.

Ad·am (ad′əm) In the Bible, the first man, progenitor of the human race. *Gen.* ii 7. — *n.* Mankind collectively. — **the old Adam** Unregenerate human nature. — **A·dam·ic** (ə-dam′ik) *adj.*

Ad·am-and-Eve (ad′əm-ənd-ēv′) *n.* The puttyroot.

ad·a·mant (ad′ə-mant, -mənt) *n.* **1.** A very hard legendary mineral, later identified with the diamond or lodestone. **2.** *Archaic* Exceeding hardness; impenetrability. — *adj.* **1.** Immovable; unyielding. **2.** Adamantine. [< OF *adamaunt* < L *adamas, -antis* the hardest metal (hence, unyielding) < Gk. *adamas* < *a-* not + *damaein* to conquer. Doublet of DIAMOND.]

ad·a·man·tine (ad′ə-man′tin, -tēn, -tīn) *adj.* **1.** Made of or like adamant; of impenetrable hardness. **2.** Unyielding; resolute. **3.** Having a diamondlike luster. Also **ad·a·man·te·an** (ad′ə-man-tē′ən).

Ad·am·ic (ad′əm-ik), **Louis**, 1899–1951, U.S. author.

Ad·am·ite (ad′əm-īt) *adj.* Descended from Adam. — *n.* **1.** A descendant of Adam; a human being. **2.** A nudist. — **Ad·am·it·ic** (ad′əm-it′ik) or **·i·cal** *adj.*

Ad·ams (ad′əmz) A prominent Massachusetts family, including **John**, 1735–1826, second president of the United States 1797–1801, signer of Declaration of Independence; his wife **Abigail**, *née* Smith, 1744–1818; their son **John Quincy**, 1767–1848, sixth president of the United States 1825–29; his son **Charles Francis**, 1807–86, diplomat; his sons **Brooks**, 1848–1927, lawyer and historian, **Charles Francis**, 1835–1915, railroad authority and historian, and

Henry, 1838–1918, historian and author; **Samuel,** 1722–1803, patriot, signer of Declaration of Independence, cousin of John.
— **Franklin Pierce,** 1881–1960, U.S. journalist: also called *F.P.A.*
— **James Truslow,** 1878–1949, U.S. historian.
— **John Couch,** 1819–92, English astronomer.
— **Maude,** 1872–1953, U.S. actress: original name **Maude Kis·kad·den** (kis·kad'ən).
Ad·ams (ad'əmz), **Mount 1.** A peak of the White Mountains in New Hampshire; 5,798 ft. **2.** A peak of the Cascade Range in Washington; 12,307 ft.
Adam's apple The prominence made by the thyroid cartilage at the front of the human throat, conspicuous in males.
ad·ams·ite (ad'əmz·ĭt) *n. Chem.* An odorless, chemically stable, yellow crystalline compound, $(C_6H_4)_2NHAsCl$, used in the form of vapor as a lung-irritant war gas: also called *diphenylaminechlorarsine.* (Symbol DM). [after Major Roger *Adams,* born 1889, U.S. army officer, who invented it]
Ad·am's-nee·dle (ad'əmz·nēd'l) *n.* A species of yucca (*Yucca filamentosa*) with leaves bearing threadlike fibers on the margin.
Ad·ams-Stokes disease (ad'əmz·stōks') Heartblock. [after Robert *Adams,* 1791–1875, and William *Stokes,* 1804–1878, Irish physicians]
A·da·na (ä'dä·nä) A Province of southern Turkey; 7,896 sq. mi.; pop. 763,222 (1960); capital, **Adana,** pop. 230,024.
a·dapt (ə·dapt') *v.t.* **1.** To fit for a new use; make suitable: with *for:* to *adapt* Shakespeare for children. **2.** To adjust (oneself or itself) to a new situation or environment. — *v.i.* **3.** To become adjusted to a circumstance or environment: with *to:* Some plants *adapt* well to high altitudes. [< F *adapter* < L *adaptare* < *ad-* to + *aptare* to fit]
— **Syn.** *Adapt, adjust, accommodate, reconcile, fit,* and *conform* all mean to make harmonious in structure, function, etc. *Adapt* involves considerable change to meet new requirements, while *adjust* implies a minor change, as in the alignment of parts. We *adapt* a novel for the stage, *adjust* a motor, or the differences between two parties. *Accommodate* and *reconcile* suggest a greater degree of yielding or concession to secure harmony: to *accommodate* oneself to circumstances, to *reconcile* enemies. *Fit* and *conform* connote agreement with a pattern, but *conform* often means superficial agreement only: to *fit* covers to a chair, to *conform* to social customs. Compare CHANGE.
a·dapt·a·ble (ə·dap'tə·bəl) *adj.* **1.** Capable of being adapted. **2.** Able to change easily to meet new circumstances. — **a·dapt'a·bil'i·ty, a·dapt'a·ble·ness** *n.*
ad·ap·ta·tion (ad'əp·tā'shən) *n.* **1.** The act of suiting or fitting one thing to another. **2.** The state of being suited or fitted. **3.** The process of adjusting to fit new conditions. **4.** Anything produced by adapting; a modification to new uses. **5.** *Biol.* An advantageous conformation of an organism to changes in its environment. **6.** *Physiol.* The change in the response of an organ of sense due to prolonged or repeated stimulation. **7.** *Sociol.* A slow modification of individual or group behavior in adjusting to a general cultural environment: also **a·dap·tion** (ə·dap'shən). — **ad'ap·ta'tion·al** *adj.* — **ad'ap·ta'tion·al·ly** *adv.*
a·dapt·er (ə·dap'tər) *n.* **1.** A person or thing that adapts. **2.** *Mech.* **a** A device that permits the use or connection of parts not designed to fit together. **b** A device that extends or alters the function of an apparatus. Also **a·dap'tor.** *Abbr. ad.*
a·dap·tive (ə·dap'tiv) *adj.* Capable of, fit for, or manifesting adaptation. — **a·dap'tive·ly** *adv.* — **a·dap'tive·ness** *n.*
adaptive radiation *Zool.* An evolutionary process by which a type or line of animals develops forms adapted to survival under a wide variety of environmental conditions.
a·dap·to·me·ter (ə·dap'tə·mē'tər) *n. Physiol.* An instrument for measuring individual adaptation to various sensory, motor, and physiological stimuli.
A·dar (ə·där', ä'där) *n.* The sixth month of the Hebrew year. See (Hebrew) CALENDAR.
A.D.C. or **ADC** or **A.D.C.** Aide-de-camp.
add (ad) *v.t.* **1.** To join or unite, so as to increase the importance, size, quantity, or scope: with *to:* He has *added* insult to injury. **2.** To find the sum of, as a column of figures; unite in a total. **3.** To say or write further. — *v.i.* **4.** To make or be an addition: with *to:* His new duties *added* to his worries. **5.** To perform the arithmetical process of addition. *Abbr. ad.* — **to add up 1.** To accumulate to a total. **2.** *Informal* To make sense. [< L *adders* < *ad-* to + *dare* to give, put] — **add'a·ble** or **add'i·ble** *adj.*
— **Syn. 1.** *Add, append,* and *annex* agree in meaning to join something to something else. *Add* is the most general of these words and denotes the joining of one thing to another to increase it. To *append* is to add something supplemental; *annex* indicates that the addition is subordinate, and often remains distinct. Compare INCREASE.
add. 1. Addenda; addendum. **2.** Addition; additional. **3.** Address.
Ad·dams (ad'əmz), **Jane,** 1860–1935, U.S. social worker.
ad·dax (ad'aks) *n.* A North African and Arabian antelope (*Addax nasomaculata*) with long and twisted horns and a light-colored body. [< L < native African word]

ad·dend (ad'end, ə·dend') *n. Math.* A quantity or number that is to be united in one sum with another (the *augend*). [See ADDENDUM]
ad·den·dum (ə·den'dəm) *n.* pl. **·da** (-də) **1.** A thing added, or to be added. **2.** A supplement, as to a book; appendix. **3.** *Mech.* The radial distance between the pitch circle and the outer ends of the teeth on a geared wheel; also, the part of a tooth outside the pitch circle. *Abbr. add.* [< L, neut. gerundive of *addere* to add]
— **Syn. 1.** addition, annex.
ad·der (ad'ər) *n.* **1.** A viper, especially the common European viper (*Vipera berus*), about two feet long, of a brownish color variegated with black. **2.** One of various other snakes, as the harmless puff adder of the United States. [OE *nædre* (*a nadder* in ME becoming an *adder*)]
ad·der's-mouth (ad'ərz·mouth') *n.* A delicate North American tree orchid (genus *Malaxis*) having small greenish flowers: also called *bog orchid.*
ad·der's-tongue (ad'ərz·tung') *n.* **1.** A cosmopolitan fern (genus *Ophioglossum*), so named from the form of its spike of fruit. **2.** Any of various flowering plants, as the dog-tooth violet.
ad·dict (*v.* ə·dikt'; *n.* ad'ikt) *v.t.* To apply or devote (oneself) persistently or habitually: with *to.* — *n.* One who is given to some habit, especially to the use of narcotic drugs. [< L *addictus,* pp. of *addicere* to assign, devote < *ad-* to + *dicere* to say]
ad·dict·ed (ə·dik'tid) *adj.* Given over to a pursuit, practice, or habit: with *to: addicted* to drugs.
— **Syn.** *Addicted, given, devoted, habituated,* and *accustomed* mean giving oneself frequently or persistently to an indulgence, practice, etc. *Addicted* suggests a pathological weakness; *given,* a tendency or usual practice. Both words may apply to good or bad things, but usually to bad: *addicted* to alcohol, *given* to lying. *Devoted* implies fondness and is usually applied only in good senses: *devoted* to children. *Habituated* and *accustomed* suggest less of compulsion than of merely getting used to something. *Habituated* is the stronger word, as habit is stronger than custom: *habituated* to early rising, *accustomed* to reading the morning paper.
ad·dic·tion (ə·dik'shən) *n.* The state of being addicted or given over, as to narcotics. Also **ad·dict'ed·ness.**
ad·dic·tive (ə·dik'tiv) *adj.* Of, pertaining to, or causing addiction; habit-forming. — *n.* A habit-forming drug.
adding machine (ad'ing) A keyboard machine that automatically adds a series of numbers recorded by the user.
Ad·dis A·ba·ba (ä'dis ä'bə·bä, ad'is ab'ə·bə) The capital and largest city of Ethiopia, in the central part; pop. about 400,000. Also *Adis Ababa.*
Ad·di·son (ad'ə·sən), **Joseph,** 1672–1719, English essayist, poet, and statesman.
Ad·di·so·ni·an (ad'ə·sō'nē·ən) *adj.* Of or pertaining to Joseph Addison, especially with reference to the clarity and urbanity of his literary style.
Addison's disease *Pathol.* A disease of the adrenal glands manifesting itself in brownish pigmentation of the skin, progressive anemia, and prostration. [after Thomas *Addison,* 1793–1860, English physician]
ad·dit·a·ment (ə·dit'ə·mənt) *n.* A thing added; addition. Also **ad·dit'i·ment.** [< L *additamentum*]
ad·di·tion (ə·dish'ən) *n.* **1.** The act of adding. **2.** That which is added; an increase; annex; accession. **3.** *Math.* The uniting of two or more quantities in one sum, indicated by the plus sign (+). **4.** *Law* A title or mark of designation attached to a man's name. *Abbr. add.* — **Syn.** See APPENDAGE. [< F < L *additio, -onis* < *addere.* See ADD.]
ad·di·tion·al (ə·dish'ən·əl) *adj.* Being in addition; supplementary. *Abbr. add.* — **ad·di'tion·al·ly** *adv.*
ad·di·tive (ad'ə·tiv) *n.* **1.** Something added or to be added to a product or device. **2.** Any of various substances that are supposed to improve the performance or quality of a fuel, battery, etc. — *adj.* That is to be added; serving or tending to increase. [< L *additivus* < *addere.* See ADD.] — **ad'di·tive·ly** *adv.*
ad·dle (ad'l) *v.t. & v.i.* **·dled, ·dling 1.** To become or cause to become confused or muddled. **2.** To spoil, as eggs. — *adj.* **1.** Confused; mixed up, as discourse: now generally in compounds: *addlepated.* **2.** Spoiled, as eggs; rotten. [OE *adela* liquid filth]
ad·dle-brained (ad'l·brānd') *adj.* Confused; mixed up. Also **ad'dle-head'ed, ad'dle-pat'ed, ad'dle-wit'ted.**
ad·dress (ə·dres'; *for n. defs.* 2, 3, *also* ad'res) *v.t.* **·dressed, ·dress·ing 1.** To speak to: I *addressed* him humbly. **2.** To deliver a set discourse to: The president *addressed* the council. **3.** To direct, as spoken or written words, to the attention of: with *to:* to *address* prayers to God. **4.** To devote the energy or force of (oneself): with *to:* to *address* oneself to a task. **5.** To superscribe or mark with a destination, as a letter. **6.** To consign, as a cargo to a merchant. **7.** To aim or direct. **8.** To pay court to, as a lover; woo. **9.** To assume a preparatory stance toward (a golf ball, etc.). **10.** *Obs.* To prepare; arrange. — *n.* **1.** A prepared statement

ADDAX
(3 to 4 feet high at shoulder; horns 3 to 4 feet)

or speech, especially one presented formally: the president's inaugural *address*. **2.** The writing on an envelope, package, etc., directing it to a particular person or place. **3.** The name, place, residence, etc., of a person or organization. **4.** The manner of a person, especially in speaking to another; one's bearing or manner of delivery. **5.** Skillful conduct or action; adroitness; tact. **6.** *Chiefly pl.* Any courteous or devoted attention, especially in courtship. **7.** *Electronics* A particular location in the storage element of a computer, as indicated by a number or other symbol. **8.** *Obs.* Preparation, or that which is prepared. Abbr. (for *n.* defs. 2 & 3) *add.* [< OF *adresser*, ult. < L *ad-* to + *directus* straight]
— **Syn.** (verb) See GREET. — (noun) **1.** See SPEECH. **6.** *Address, adroitness, tact,* and *discretion* here refer to suave dealings with persons. *Address* refers to smooth approach and readiness to deal with whatever comes. *Adroitness* is skillful management, especially in achieving one's own purposes. *Tact* is courteous adroitness that avoids arousing hostility or resentment. *Discretion* is care or caution to avoid mistakes.

ad·dress·ee (ad′res-ē′, ə-dres′ē′) *n.* One who is addressed.
ad·dress·er (ə-dres′ər) *n.* **1.** One who presents or signs an address or petition or a formal document. **2.** Anything that addresses. Also **ad·dres′sor.**
Ad·dres·so·graph (ə-dres′ə-graf, -gräf) *n.* A machine for printing postal addresses from stencils: a trade name.
ad·duce (ə-dōōs′, ə-dyōōs′) *v.t.* **·duced, ·duc·ing** To bring forward for proof or consideration, as an example; cite; allege. [< L *adducere* < *ad-* to + *ducere* to lead] — **ad·duce′· a·ble** or **ad·duc′i·ble** *adj.*
ad·du·cent (ə-dōō′sənt, ə-dyōō′-) *adj. Physiol.* Drawing or binding together. [< L *adducens, -entis,* ppr. of *adducere.* See ADDUCE.]
ad·duct (ə-dukt′) *v.t. Physiol.* To draw toward the axis: said of muscles: opposed to *abduct.* [< L *adductus,* pp. of *adducere.* See ADDUCE.] — **ad·duc′tion** *n.* — **ad·duc′tive** *adj.*
ad·duc·tor (ə-duk′tər) *n.* An adducting muscle.
-ade¹ *suffix of nouns* **1.** Act or action: *cannonade.* **2.** A person or group concerned in an action or process: *cavalcade.* **3.** That which is produced by an action or process, or from a raw material, basic form, etc.: *colonnade, masquerade, pomade.* **4.** A beverage made with or containing a fruit juice: *lemonade.* [< F *-ade* < Provençal, Pg., or Sp. *-ada* or Ital. *-ata* < L *-ata,* fem. pp. ending]
-ade² *suffix of nouns* Relating to; pertaining to: *decade.* See -AD¹. [< F *-ade* < Gk. *-as, -ados*]
Ade (ād), **George,** 1866–1944, U.S. humorist.
a·deem (ə-dēm′) *v.t.* **1.** To take away. **2.** *Law* To revoke, as the bequest of a legacy. [< L *adimere* < *ad-* to (oneself) + *emere* to take]
Ad·e·laide (ad′ə-lād) The capital of South Australia, in the SE part; pop. 727,916 (est. 1970).
A·dé·lie Coast (ad′ə-lē, *Fr.* ȧ·dȧ·lē′) A region on the coast of Wilkes Land, Antarctica, under French sovereignty; 150,000 sq. mi.
a·demp·tion (ə-demp′shən) *n. Law* Disposal by a testator in his lifetime of specific property bequeathed in his will so that the bequest is invalidated. [< L *ademptio, -onis* < *adimere* to deprive < *ad-* to (oneself) + *emere* to take]
A·den (äd′n, ād′n) A former British colony at the sw tip of the Arabian peninsula, now a part of South Yemen; principal city **Aden,** pop. about 100,000.
Aden, Gulf of A western inlet of the Arabian Sea, between South Yemen and Somalia.
ad·e·nal·gi·a (ad′ə-nal′jē-ə) *n. Med.* Pain in a gland. [< ADEN(O)- + -ALGIA]
Ad·en·au·er (ad′n-ou′ər, *Ger.* ä′dən-ou′ər), **Konrad,** 1876–1967, German statesman; chancellor of the Federal Republic of Germany, 1949–63.
ad·en·ec·to·my (ad′ən-ek′tə-me) *n. pl.* **·mies** *Surg.* The removal of a gland or of adenoid growths.
A·den·i (ä′dən-ē) *n. pl.* **A·den·is** A native or inhabitant of Aden. — *adj.* Of or pertaining to Aden. Also **A·den·ese** (äd′n-ēz′, -ēs′, äd′n-).
ad·e·nine (ad′ə-nin, -nēn, -nīn) *n. Biochem.* An alkaloid of the purine series, $C_5H_5N_5$, found as a product of nucleic acids in the pancreas and other glands: formerly called *vitamin* B_4. [< ADEN(O)- + -INE²]
adeno- *combining form* Gland: *adenology.* Also, before vowels, **aden-.** [< Gk. *adēn* gland]
ad·e·noid (ad′ə-noid) *adj.* Of or like a gland; glandular. Also **ad′e·noi′dal.** — *n. Usually pl.* An enlarged lymphoid growth behind the pharynx. [< ADEN(O)- + -OID]
ad·e·nol·o·gy (ad′ə-nol′ə-jē) *n.* The branch of anatomy that treats of glands. — **ad·e·no· log′i·cal** (ad′ə-nə-loj′i·kəl) *adj.*
ad·e·no·ma (ad′ə-nō′mə) *n. Pathol.* A tumor of glandular origin or structure. [< ADEN(O)- + -OMA] — **ad·e·nom·a·tous** (ad′ə-nom′ə-təs) *adj.*
ad·e·no·sine (ad′ə-nō′sin) *n. Biochem.* An

organic compound, $C_{10}H_{13}N_5O_4$, obtained from the nucleic acid of yeast. One of its phosphoric esters, **adenosine triphosphate** (ATP), plays an important part in the energy processes of muscle contraction.
Aden Protectorate Formerly, a group of Arab tribal districts on the southern coast of the Arabian Peninsula comprising a British protectorate, now a part of South Yemen.
a·dept (ə-dept′; *for n., also* ad′ept) *adj.* Highly skilled; proficient: *adept* in tennis. — **Syn.** See SKILLFUL. — *n.* **1.** One fully skilled in any art; an expert. **2.** *Archaic* An alchemist who professed ability to convert base metals into gold. [< L *adeptus* having attained, pp. of *adipisci* to attain < *ad-* to + *apisci* to get] — **a·dept′ly** *adv.* — **a·dept′ness** *n.*
ad·e·qua·cy (ad′ə-kwə·sē) *n.* The state or quality of being adequate.
ad·e·quate (ad′ə-kwit) *adj.* **1.** Equal to what is required; suitable to the case or occasion; fully sufficient: *adequate* fuel for the winter. **2.** Barely sufficient. [< L *adaequatus,* pp. of *adaequare* < *ad-* to + *aequus* equal] — **ad′e·quate·ness** *n.* — **ad′e·quate·ly** *adv.*
— **Syn. 1.** *Adequate, sufficient, satisfactory,* and *equal* characterize something regarded as enough for a given situation. *Adequate* is applied to ability or power; *sufficient,* to quantity or number. A man is *adequate* to a situation; a supply is *sufficient* for a need. A thing is *satisfactory* if it measures up, more or less; it is *equal* if it is exactly commensurate. The connotation of these terms varies widely in different fields and contexts. An actor called *adequate* is usually regarded as mediocre. A *sufficient* reason may range from the flimsiest pretext to the surest demonstration. *Satisfactory* is a term in many grading systems, varying from barely passing to superlatively good. *Equal* is often used to denote, by understatement, not mere adequacy but great superiority.
à deux (à dœ′) *French* Of or for two; intimate.
ad ex·tre·mum (ad eks·trē′məm) *Latin* To the extreme; finally.
ad fin. At, to, or toward the end (L *ad finem*).
ad·here (ad·hir′) *v.i.* **·hered, ·her·ing** **1.** To stick fast or together: crude oil *adhering* to beach sand. **2.** To be attached or devoted to a party or faith: with *to.* **3.** To follow closely or without deviation: with *to:* He *adhered* to the plan. **4.** *Obs.* To be consistent. [< L *adhaerere* < *ad-* to + *haerere* to stick] — **ad·her′er** *n.*
ad·her·ence (ad·hir′əns) *n.* The act or state of adhering; attachment; adhesion.
ad·her·ent (ad·hir′ənt) *adj.* **1.** Clinging or sticking fast. **2.** *Bot.* Adnate. — *n.* One who is devoted or attached, as to a cause or leader; a follower: an *adherent* of nonviolence [< L *adhaerens, -entis,* ppr. of *adhaerere.* See ADHERE.] — **ad· her′ent·ly** *adv.*
— **Syn.** (noun) *Adherent, follower, disciple, supporter,* and *partisan* mean one who gives allegiance to a leader or a cause. *Adherent* is the weakest term, denoting one who attaches himself, for whatever reason. A *follower* is more fervid in his attachment. A *disciple* has a pupil-teacher relationship with the one he follows. A *supporter* is one who aids in any way, whether by intellectual agreement or material contribution, while a *partisan* is militant in his support of a person, party, or cause.
ad·he·sion (ad·hē′zhən) *n.* **1.** The act of adhering, or the state of being joined. **2.** Firm attachment, as to a cause; fidelity. **3.** Assent; concurrence. **4.** *Physics* The binding force exerted by molecules of unlike substances in contact: distinguished from *cohesion.* **5.** *Med.* **a** The joining of fractured or severed parts of the body. **b** Abnormal surface union of dissimilar tissues as a result of inflammation, etc. [< F *adhésion* < L *adhaesio, -onis* < *adhaerere.* See ADHERE.]
ad·he·sive (ad·hē′siv) *adj.* **1.** Tending to adhere; sticky; clinging: labels treated to be *adhesive.* **2.** Prepared to adhere; gummed: *adhesive* tape. — *n.* A substance that causes adhesion; glue; paste. — **ad·he′sive·ly** *adv.* — **ad·he′sive· ness** *n.*
— **Syn. 1.** glutinous, gummy, sticky, viscid, viscous.
adhesive tape A piece or strip of fabric coated with adhesive material, used for bandages, dressings, etc.
ad·hib·it (ad·hib′it) *v.t.* **1.** To let in; admit, as to a court of law. **2.** To apply; administer. **3.** To affix; attach. [< L *adhibitus,* pp. of *adhibere* to hold toward, apply to < *ad-* to + *habere* to have, hold] — **ad·hi·bi·tion** (ad′hi·bish′ən) *n.*
ad hoc (ad hok′) *Latin* With respect to this (particular thing); up to this time.
ad hoc committee A committee formed for a specific purpose in a specific situation.
ad hom·i·nem (ad hom′ə-nəm) *Latin* Literally, to the man; appealing to one's individual passions and prejudices: an argument *ad hominem.*
ad·i·a·bat·ic (ad′ē·ə·bat′ik, ā′dē·ə-) *adj. Physics* Pertaining to a closed thermodynamic system in which changes are effected without gain or loss of heat, as in the insulated cylinder of an engine. [< Gk. *adiabatos* impassable < *a-* not + *dia-* through + *bainein* to go + -IC]
ad·i·aph·o·rous (ad′ē·af′ər·əs) *adj.* **1.** Not involving morality; morally neutral. **2.** *Med.* Incapable of doing either harm or good, as a drug. [< Gk. *adiaphoros* < *a-* not + *dia- phoros* different < *dia-* through + *pherein* to carry]

ADENOIDS
(a)

ad·i·a·ther·man·cy (ad'ē·ə·thûr'mən·sē) *n. Physics* The quality of being impervious to radiant heat. [< Gk. *a-* not + *dia* through + *thermē* heat]

a·dieu (ə·dōō', ə·dyōō'; *Fr.* à·dyœ') *n. pl.* **a·dieus,** *Fr.* **a·dieux** (à·dyœ') A farewell. — *interj.* Good-by; farewell: literally, to God (I commend you). [< F]

A·di·ge (ä'dē·jā) A river of northern Italy, flowing about 220 miles to the Adriatic.

ad in·fi·ni·tum (ad in·fə·nī'təm) *Latin* To infinity; hence, limitlessly. Abbr. *ad inf.*

ad i·ni·ti·um (ad i·nish'ē·əm) *Latin* At or to the beginning.

ad in·ter·im (ad in'tə·rim) *Latin* In the meantime.

a·di·os (ä'dē·ōs', ad'ē·ōs'; *Sp.* ä·thyōs') *interj.* Farewell; good-by: literally, to God (I commend you). [< Sp.]

a·dip·ic (ə·dip'ik) *adj.* Pertaining to or derived from fat. [< L *adeps, adipis* fat + -IC]

ad·i·po·cere (ad'ə·pō·sir') *n. Physiol.* A fatty substance formed by decomposition of animal tissues under the influence of moisture and deprivation of air: also called *corpse fat.* [< F *adipocire* < L *adeps, adipis* fat + *cera* wax] — **ad·i·poc·er·ous** (ad'ə·pos'ər·əs) *adj.*

ad·i·pose (ad'ə·pōs) *adj.* Of or pertaining to fat; fatty: also **ad·i·pous** (ad'ə·pəs). — *n.* Fat. [< NL *adiposus* < L *adeps, adipis* fat] — **ad'i·pose'ness, ad·i·pos·i·ty** (ad'ə·pos'ə·tē) *n.*

adipose fin A fatty, rayless dorsal fin in certain fishes, as the salmon. For illustration see FISH.

Ad·i·ron·dack Mountains (ad'ə·ron'dak) A mountain range in NE New York; highest peak, Mount Marcy, 5,344 ft. Also **Ad'i·ron'dacks.**

A·dis A·ba·ba (ä'dis ä'bə·bä; ad'is ab'ə·bə) See ADDIS ABABA.

ad·it (ad'it) *n.* **1.** An approach; entrance. **2.** A nearly horizontal entrance to a mine. **3.** Access; admission. [< L *aditus,* pp. of *adire* to approach < *ad-* to + *ire* to go]

adj. 1. Adjacent. **2.** Adjective. **3.** Adjourned. **4.** Adjunct. **5.** Adjustment (in banking). **6.** Adjutant.

ad·ja·cen·cy (ə·jā'sən·sē) *n. pl.* **·cies 1.** The state of being adjacent; contiguity. **2.** That which is adjacent.

ad·ja·cent (ə·jā'sənt) *adj.* Lying near or close at hand; adjoining; contiguous. Abbr. *adj.* [< L *adjacens, -entis,* ppr. of *adjacere* < *ad-* near + *jacere* to lie] — **ad·ja'cent·ly** *adv.*
— **Syn.** *Adjacent, adjoining, neighboring, abutting, contiguous,* and *conterminous* mean lying side by side or in contact. *Adjacent* includes both the sense of *adjoining,* in actual contact with, and *neighboring,* nearby: *adjacent* or *adjoining* desks, *adjacent* or *neighboring* islands. *Abutting* implies contact, even though slight. *Contiguous* suggests extensive, though not always complete, contact, while *conterminous* suggests contact at a boundary.

adjacent angle *Geom.* An angle having a common side with another angle and the same vertex.

ad·jec·ti·val (aj'ik·tī'vəl, aj'ik·ti·vəl) *adj.* Pertaining to or like an adjective. — **ad'jec·ti'val·ly** *adv.*

ad·jec·tive (aj'ik·tiv) *n.* **1.** *Gram.* Any of a class of words used to limit or qualify a noun: one of the eight traditional parts of speech. **2.** *Ling.* One of a form class, the members of which are marked by certain suffixes, as, in English, *-ful, -able,* and *-ous,* as well as the comparative *-er* and superlative *-est,* or identified by their ability to occupy certain syntactic positions in sentences and phrases, as, in English, in *the good man, good* is an adjective by virtue of its position between *the* and *man,* or by a combination of both morphologic and syntactic criteria. **3.** A dependent or corollary. — *adj.* **1.** *Gram.* Functioning as an adjective; depending upon or standing in adjunct relation to a noun. **2.** Of the nature of an adjunct; dependent. **3.** Procedural: *adjective* law. **4.** *Chem.* Requiring the use of a mordant, as in dyeing. Abbr. *a., adj.* [< L *adjectivus* that is added < *adjicere* to add to < *ad-* to + *jacere* to throw] — **ad'jec·tive·ly** *adv.*

adjective clause *Gram.* A dependent clause usually introduced by a relative pronoun and qualifying its antecedent, as *who painted my house* in *the man who painted my house:* also called *relative clause.* Also **adjectival clause.**

adjective pronoun *Gram.* Any pronoun that functions as an adjective, as *that* and *which* in *that boy, which house.*

ad·join (ə·join') *v.t.* **1.** To be next to; border upon. **2.** To join to; append; unite: with *to.* — *v.i.* **3.** To lie close together; be in contact. [< OF *ajoindre* < L *adjungere* < *ad-* to + *jungere* to join]

ad·join·ing (ə·joi'ning) *adj.* Lying next; contiguous. — **Syn.** See ADJACENT.

ad·journ (ə·jûrn') *v.t.* **1.** To put off to another day or place, as a meeting or session; postpone. **2.** To put off to the next session, as the decision of a council. — *v.i.* **3.** To postpone or suspend proceedings for a specified time: The court *adjourned* for three days. **4.** *Informal* To move or go to another place: Let's *adjourn* to the porch. — **Syn.** See POSTPONE. [< OF *ajorner, ajurner* < LL *adjurnare* to set a day < L *ad-* to + *diurnus* daily < *dies* day]

ad·journ·ment (ə·jûrn'mənt) *n.* **1.** The act of adjourning. **2.** The period or state of being adjourned.

ad·judge (ə·juj') *v.t.* **·judged, ·judg·ing 1.** To determine or decide judicially, as a case. **2.** To pronounce or order by law: His testimony was *adjudged* perjury. **3.** To condemn or sentence: with *to:* He was *adjudged* to imprisonment. **4.** To

award by law, as damages. **5.** *Obs.* To regard or consider. [< OF *ajugier* < L *adjudicare* < *ad-* to + *judicare* to judge]

ad·ju·di·cate (ə·jōō'də·kāt) *v.* **·cat·ed, ·cat·ing** *v.t.* **1.** To determine judicially, as a case; adjudge. — *v.i.* **2.** To act as a judge. [< L *adjudicatus,* pp. of *adjudicare.* See ADJUDGE.] — **ad·ju'di·ca'tor** *n.*

ad·ju·di·ca·tion (ə·jōō'də·kā'shən) *n.* **1.** The act or process of adjudicating or adjudging. **2.** A judicial decision.

ad·junct (aj'ungkt) *n.* **1.** Something joined to something else, but in an auxiliary or subordinate position. **2.** A person associated with another person in an auxiliary or subordinate relation; a helper; assistant. Abbr. *adj.* **3.** *Gram.* A word or words added to define, limit, qualify, or modify other words. **4.** *Logic* Any nonessential quality of a thing. — **Syn.** See APPENDAGE. — *adj.* Joined subordinately; auxiliary. [< L *adjunctus,* pp. of *adjungere.* See ADJOIN.]

ad·junc·tive (ə·jungk'tiv) *adj.* Constituting or forming an adjunct. — **ad·junc'tive·ly** *adv.*

ad·ju·ra·tion (aj'ōō·rā'shən) *n.* The act of adjuring; a solemn oath. — **ad·jur·a·to·ry** (ə·jōōr'ə·tôr'ē, -tō'rē) *adj.*

ad·jure (ə·jōōr') *v.t.* **·jured, ·jur·ing 1.** To charge or entreat solemnly, as under oath or penalty. **2.** To appeal to earnestly. [< L *adjurare* < *ad-* to + *jurare* to swear < *jus, juris* oath] — **ad·jur'er** or **ad·ju'ror** *n.*

ad·just (ə·just') *v.t.* **1.** To arrange so as to fit or match; make correspond, as to a standard. **2.** To harmonize or compose, as differences. **3.** To regulate or make accurate. **4.** To determine the amount to be paid in settlement of (an insurance claim). **5.** To arrange in order; systematize. **6.** *Mil.* To allow for the elevation and deflection of (a gun) in firing. — *v.i.* **7.** To adapt oneself; conform, as to a new environment. — **Syn.** See ADAPT. [< OF *ajouster* < L *ad-* to + *juxta* near; refashioned on F *juste* right < L *justus*] — **ad·just'a·ble** *adj.* — **ad·just'er** or **ad·jus'tor** *n.* — **ad·jus'tive** *adj.*

ad·just·ment (ə·just'mənt) *n.* **1.** The act or process of adjusting; regulation; arrangement. **2.** The state of being adjusted, or the result of adjusting; settlement; adaptation. **3.** An instrument or means of adjusting. **4.** The determination of the amount to be paid in settling a claim, as in insurance; also, the amount paid. Abbr. (for def. 4) *adj.*

ad·ju·tant (aj'ōō·tənt) *n.* **1.** *Mil.* A staff officer who assists a commanding officer in administrative duties. Abbr. *adj.* **2.** A carrion-eating East Indian stork (*Leptophilus dubius*): also called *marabou:* also **adjutant crane, adjutant stork.** [< L *adjutans, -antis,* ppr. of *adjutare* to assist, freq. of *adjuvare.* See AID.] — **ad'ju·tan·cy, ad'ju·tant·ship** *n.*

adjutant general *pl.* **adjutants general** The adjutant of a military unit having a general staff. Abbr. *AG.* — **The Adjutant General** The major general in charge of the administrative branch of the United States Army. Abbr. *TAG*

ad·ju·vant (aj'ōō·vənt) *adj.* Assisting; helpful. — **Syn.** See AUXILIARY. — *n.* **1.** A helper. **2.** *Med.* Any substance added to a drug or remedy to assist or heighten its action. [< L *adjuvans, -antis,* ppr. of *adjuvare.* See AID.]

Ad·ler (äd'lər), **Alfred,** 1870–1937, Austrian psychiatrist.

Ad·ler (ad'lər), **Felix,** 1851–1933, U.S. educator; founder of the Ethical Culture Society.

ad-lib (ad'lib') *Informal* *v.t. & v.i.* **·libbed, ·lib·bing** To improvise, as words, gestures, or music. — *n.* An instance of this. [< AD LIBITUM]

ad lib·i·tum (ad lib'ə·təm) **1.** *Latin* At will; as one pleases. **2.** *Music* Freely: a direction indicating that a section or passage may be omitted or varied as the performer wishes. Abbr. *ad lib.* or *ad libit.*

ad loc. At or to the place (L *ad locum*).

adm. 1. Administrative; administrator. **2.** Admitted.

ADM or **Adm.** Admiral.

ad·man (ad'man') *n. pl.* **·men** (-men') A copywriter, artist, or salesman employed in the advertising business.

ad·meas·ure (ad·mezh'ər) *v.t.* **·ured, ·ur·ing** To assign a share of or to; apportion. [< OF *amesurer* < LL *admensurare* < *ad-* to + *mensurare.* See MEASURE.] — **ad·meas'ur·er** *n.*

ad·meas·ure·ment (ad·mezh'ər·mənt) *n.* **1.** The act of admeasuring. **2.** Measure; size; dimensions. Also **ad·men·su·ra·tion** (ad·men'shə·rā'shən).

Ad·me·tus (ad·mē'təs) In Greek mythology, a king of Thessaly, husband of Alcestis.

admin. Administration; administrator.

ad·min·i·cle (ad·min'i·kəl) *n.* **1.** A help or support; an auxiliary. **2.** *Law* Corroborative or explanatory evidence. [< L *adminiculum* a prop, orig., a support < *ad-* to + *manus* hand] — **ad·mi·nic·u·lar** (ad'mə·nik'yə·lər) *adj.*

ad·min·is·ter (ad·min'is·tər) *v.t.* **1.** To have the charge or direction of; manage: to *administer* the government. **2.** To supply or provide with; apply, as medicine or treatment. **3.** To inflict; mete out; dispense: to *administer* the death penalty. **4.** *Law* To settle by testamentary or official appointment; act as executor or trustee of: to *administer* an estate. **5.** To tender, as an oath. — *v.i.* **6.** To contribute toward an end; minister: with *to.* **7.** To carry out the functions of an administrator. [< OF *aministrer* < L *administrare* < *minister* to < *ad-* to + *ministrare* to serve] — **ad·min·is·te·ri·al** (ad·min'is·tir'ē·əl) *adj.* — **ad·min'is·tra·ble** *adj.*

ad·min·is·trant (ad·min'is·trənt) *adj.* Managing affairs; executive. — *n.* One who administers.

ad·min·is·trate (ad·min'is·trāt) *v.t.* **·trat·ed, ·trat·ing** To administer.

ad·min·is·tra·tion (ad·min'is·trā'shən) *n.* **1.** The act of administering, or the state of being administered; management or direction of affairs. **2.** The persons collectively who compose a government, especially its executive department. **3.** The official tenure of such a government. **4.** *U.S.* The persons collectively who manage or supervise, especially in schools. **5.** *Law* The legal management of an estate. *Abbr.* **admin.** [< L *administratio, -onis* < *administrare.* See ADMINISTER.]

ad·min·is·tra·tive (ad·min'is·trā'tiv) *adj.* Pertaining to administration; executive. *Abbr.* **adm.** — **ad·min·is·tra'tive·ly** *adv.*

ad·min·is·tra·tor (ad·min'is·trā'tər) *n.* **1.** One who administers something; especially, one skilled in administration. **2.** *Law* One commissioned by a competent court to administer the personal property of a deceased or incompetent person. *Abbr.* **adm., admin.** [< L] — **ad·min'is·tra'tor·ship** *n.*

ad·min·is·tra·trix (ad·min'is·trā'triks) *n.* *pl.* **·tra·trix·es** or **·tra·tri·ces** (-trā'trə·sēz, -tra·trī'sēz) A woman administrator. *Abbr.* **admrx., admx.** Also **ad·min'is·tra'tress.**

ad·mi·ra·ble (ad'mər·ə·bəl) *adj.* Worthy of admiration; excellent. [< F < L *admirabilis* < *admirari.* See ADMIRE.] — **ad'mi·ra·ble·ness, ad'mi·ra·bil'i·ty** *n.* — **ad'mi·ra·bly** *adv.*

ad·mi·ral (ad'mər·əl) *n.* **1.** The supreme commander of a navy or fleet. **2.** In the U.S. Navy and Royal Canadian Navy, an officer of the next to highest rank, equivalent to a general in the respective armies; also, loosely, a rear admiral or a vice admiral. See tables at GRADE. **3.** An equivalent officer in other navies or maritime services. **4.** *Canadian* In the Maritimes, the leader of a fishing fleet. **5.** Either of two European butterflies, the **red admiral** (*Vanessa atalanta*), and the **white admiral** (*Limenitis sybilla*). *Abbr.* (for defs. 1–4) *ADM, Adm.* [< OF *amiral, admiral* < Arabic *amīr-al* (as *amīr-al-bahr* commander of the sea); infl. by L *admirabilis* admirable]

ADMIRALS' INSIGNIA
(Shoulder and sleeve)
a Rear admiral. *b* Vice admiral. *c* Admiral. *d* Admiral of the Fleet.

Admiral of the Fleet The highest rank in the U.S. and Royal Canadian Navies, corresponding to General of the Army or Field Marshal. See tables at GRADE. Also, as a form of address, *Fleet Admiral.*

ad·mi·ral·ship (ad'mər·əl·ship') *n.* The office or rank of an admiral.

ad·mi·ral·ty (ad'mər·əl·tē) *n.* *pl.* **·ties 1.** The office or functions of an admiral. **2.** *Law* **a** The branch of jurisprudence that takes cognizance of maritime affairs; maritime law. **b** A court that administers this.

Ad·mi·ral·ty (ad'mər·əl·tē) *n.* **1.** A department of the British government (the **Board of Admiralty**) having supreme charge of naval affairs. **2.** The building in London that houses this department.

Admiralty Islands An island group of the western Pacific, in the Bismarck Archipelago; 800 sq. mi.; pop. about 14,000; capital, Lorengau, on Manus. Also **Admiralties.**

Admiralty Range A mountain range on the north coast of Victoria Land, Antarctica.

ad·mi·ra·tion (ad'mə·rā'shən) *n.* **1.** A feeling of wonder and approbation, as at the sight of anything rare, excellent, or sublime. **2.** Pleased and gratified contemplation or observation. **3.** That which is admired. **4.** *Archaic* Wonder. [< L *admiratio, -onis* < *admirari.* See ADMIRE.]

ad·mire (ad·mīr') *v.* **·mired, ·mir·ing** *v.t.* **1.** To regard with wonder, pleasure, and approbation. **2.** To have respect or esteem for. **3.** *Archaic* To wonder or marvel at. — *v.i.* **4.** To feel or express admiration. **5.** *U.S. Dial.* To like or desire: with an infinitive: I would *admire* to go to your party. [< F *admirer* < L *admirari* < *ad-* at + *mirari* to wonder] — **ad·mir'er** *n.* — **ad·mir'ing** *adj.* — **ad·mir'ing·ly** *adv.*

— **Syn. 2.** *Admire, esteem, respect,* and *regard* mean to look upon as worthy. *Admire* is the strongest term, as it implies liking or affection as well as approval. *Esteem* suggests active, enthusiastic approval, while *respect* is more passive: to *esteem* a writer's work, to *respect* an opponent's opinions. *Regard* is the weakest of these words, often needing an attached phrase to give it meaning: to *regard* a plan with approval. Compare VENERATE. — **Ant.** abhor, despise, disapprove, dislike.

ad·mis·si·ble (ad·mis'ə·bəl) *adj.* **1.** Worthy of being considered; allowable. **2.** Such as may be admitted. — **ad·mis'si·bil'i·ty, ad·mis'si·ble·ness** *n.* — **ad·mis'si·bly** *adv.*

ad·mis·sion (ad·mish'ən) *n.* **1.** The act of admitting, or the state of being admitted; entrance. **2.** Permission or authority to enter; access. **3.** A price charged or paid to be admitted;

entrance fee. **4.** The act or condition of acceptance into an office or position; appointment. **5.** A confession, as to a crime. **6.** An acknowledgment of the validity of a statement, fact, etc. **7.** Anything admitted or conceded. — **Syn.** See ENTRANCE¹. [< L *admissio, -onis* < *admittere.* See ADMIT.]

Admission Day *U.S.* A legal holiday to commemorate the admission of a State into the Union.

ad·mis·sive (ad·mis'iv) *adj.* Characterized by, implying, or granting admission. Also **ad·mis·so·ry** (ad·mis'ər·ē).

ad·mit (ad·mit') *v.* **·mit·ted, ·mit·ting** *v.t.* **1.** To allow to enter; grant entrance to: to *admit* visitors to a house. **2.** To be the means or channel of admission to; let in: This key will *admit* you. **3.** To allow to join; consider as entitled to exercise the functions or privileges of: to *admit* a person to the bar. **4.** To have room for; contain: The port *admits* only two ships at once. **5.** To leave room for; permit: His impatience *admits* no delay. **6.** To concede or grant as valid. **7.** To acknowledge or avow: He *admitted* his part in the conspiracy. — *v.i.* **8.** To afford possibility or opportunity: with *of:* This problem *admits* of several solutions. **9.** To afford entrance; open on: with *to:* This gate *admits* to the garden. — **Syn.** See CONFESS, RECEIVE. [< OF *amettre* < L *admittere* < *ad-* to + *mittere* to send, let go]

ad·mit·tance (ad·mit'ns) *n.* **1.** The act of admitting, or the state or fact of being admitted; entrance. **2.** Right or permission to enter. **3.** Actual entrance; admission. **4.** *Electr.* The ability of a circuit to carry an alternating current, combining the effects of conductance and susceptance; the reciprocal of *impedance:* expressed in mhos. — **Syn.** See ENTRANCE¹.

ad·mit·ted·ly (ad·mit'id·lē) *adv.* By admission; confessedly.

ad·mix (ad·miks') *v.t. & v.i.* **·mixed** or **·mixt, ·mix·ing** To mingle or mix with something else. [Back formation from ME *admixt* mixed with < L *admixtus,* pp. of *admiscere* < *ad-* to + *miscere* to mix]

ad·mix·ture (ad·miks'chər) *n.* **1.** The act of mixing, or the state of being mixed; mixture. **2.** Anything added in forming a mixture; alloy. [< L *admixtus,* pp. of *admiscere* to mix with. See ADMIX.]

ad·mon·ish (ad·mon'ish) *v.t.* **1.** To advise of a fault; administer mild reproof to: to *admonish* an inattentive student. **2.** To caution against danger or error; warn. **3.** To charge authoritatively; exhort; urge. [< OF *amonester* < LL *admonestare* < L *admonere* < *ad-* to + *monere* to warn] — **ad·mon'ish·er** *n.*

ad·mo·ni·tion (ad'mə·nish'ən) *n.* **1.** The act of admonishing. **2.** A gentle reproof. Also **ad·mon'ish·ment.** — **Syn.** See REPROOF. [< OF *amonition* < L *admonitio, -onis* < *admonere.* See ADMONISH.]

ad·mon·i·tor (ad·mon'ə·tər) *n.* One who admonishes. [< L]

ad·mon·i·to·ry (ad·mon'ə·tôr'ē, -tō'rē) *adj.* Giving admonition; cautionary. Also **ad·mon'i·tive.**

admrx. or **admx.** Administratrix.

ad·nate (ad'nāt) *adj.* *Bot.* Congenitally united; grown together: said of the union or cohesion of parts not normally joined. [< L *adnatus,* pp. of *adnasci* to grow upon < *ad-* to + *nasci* to be born] — **ad·na'tion** *n.*

ad nau·se·am (ad nô'zē·əm, -sē-; -zhē-, -shē-; äd) *Latin* To the point of nausea or disgust.

ad·noun (ad'noun) *n.* *Gram.* An adjective, especially when used as a noun, as in *the brave.* [< AD- + NOUN; modeled on *adverb*] — **ad·nom'i·nal** (ad·nom'ə·nəl) *adj.*

a·do (ə·doo') *n.* Activity; bustle; fuss. [ME *at do,* northern dial. form for the infinitive *to do*]

a·do·be (ə·dō'bē) *n.* **1.** An unburnt, sun-dried brick. **2.** The mixed earth or sandy, calcareous clay of which such bricks are made. **3.** A structure made of such bricks. [< Sp.]

adobe flat *Geol.* A smooth, gently sloping, and usually narrow plain of clay deposited by an ephemeral stream.

ad·o·les·cence (ad'ə·les'əns) *n.* **1.** The period of growth from the onset of puberty to the stage of adult development. **2.** The quality or condition of being adolescent. Also **ad'o·les·cen·cy.**

ad·o·les·cent (ad'ə·les'ənt) *adj.* **1.** Approaching manhood or maturity. **2.** Characteristic of or pertaining to youth. — *n.* A person in the period of adolescence — **Syn.** See YOUTHFUL. [< L *adolescens, -entis,* ppr. of *adolescere* to grow up. See ADULT.]

Ad·o·na·i (ad'ə·nā'ī, -nī') Lord: in Judaism, also used as a substitute to avoid pronouncing the sacred name of God. See TETRAGRAMMATON. [< Hebrew, my Lord]

A·don·ic (ə·don'ik) *adj.* **1.** In classical prosody, designating a verse consisting of a dactyl and a spondee or a trochee, supposedly first used in laments for Adonis. **2.** Pertaining to Adonis. — *n.* An Adonic verse.

A·don·is (ə·don'is, ə·dō'nis) In Greek mythology, a youth beloved by Aphrodite for his beauty and killed by a wild boar. — *n.* Any man of rare beauty.

a·dopt (ə·dopt') *v.t.* **1.** To take into some new relationship, as that of son, heir, etc. **2.** To take into one's family or as one's child by legal measures. **3.** To take and follow as one's own, as a course of action. **4.** To take up from someone else and use as one's own, as a phrase, practice, or creed. **5.** To vote to accept, as a motion or committee report. [< MF *adopter* < L *adoptare* < *ad-* to + *optare* to choose] — **a·dopt'a·ble** *adj.* — **a·dopt'er** *n.*

a·dop·tion (ə-dop'shən) *n.* **1.** The act of adopting, or the state of being adopted. **2.** The legal act of taking a minor as one's child. **3.** The acceptance of a word from one language into another without change in form.

a·dop·tive (ə-dop'tiv) *adj.* **1.** Of, tending to, or characterized by adoption: an *adoptive* language. **2.** Related by adoption: an *adoptive* father. — **a·dop'tive·ly** *adv.*

a·dor·a·ble (ə-dôr'ə-bəl, ə-dōr'-) *adj.* **1.** Worthy of adoration. **2.** Causing affection or attachment. **3.** *Informal* Delightful; lovable. — **a·dor'a·ble·ness, a·dor·a·bil'i·ty** *n.* — **a·dor'a·bly** *adv.*

ad·o·ra·tion (ad'ə-rā'shən) *n.* **1.** The act of adoring, as in worship or reverence of a deity. **2.** A feeling of profound admiration, utmost love, and devotion. **3.** An act of homage to a person or object. [< F < L *adoratio, -onis* < *adorare*. See ADORE.]

a·dore (ə-dôr', ə-dōr') *v.* **a·dored, a·dor·ing** *v.t.* **1.** To render divine honors to; worship as divine. **2.** To love or honor with intense devotion. **3.** *Informal* To like especially. — *v.i.* **4.** To worship. — **Syn.** See VENERATE. [< OF *adorer* < L *adorare* < *ad-* to + *orare* to speak, pray] — **a·dor'er** *n.* — **a·dor·ing** *adj.*

a·dorn (ə-dôrn') *v.t.* **1.** To be an ornament to; increase the beauty of; enhance. **2.** To furnish or decorate with or as with ornaments. [< OF *adorner* < L *adornare* < *ad-* to + *ornare* to furnish, deck out] — **a·dorn'er** *n.*
— **Syn.** *Adorn, decorate, ornament, embellish, garnish, deck,* and *bedeck* mean to beautify, usually by the addition of something. That which *adorns* satisfies a refined esthetic taste. We *decorate* that which would otherwise be plain, bare, or insipid. *Ornament* and *embellish* most clearly indicate the addition of something beautiful in itself; *embellish* suggests the greater ostentation and is sometimes used ironically of meretricious decoration. *Garnish* is applied almost exclusively to foods, *deck* and *bedeck* to persons, places, or things, with *bedeck* connoting excessive ornamentation: fish *garnished* with parsley, halls *decked* with holly, a robe *bedecked* with jewels.

a·dorn·ment (ə-dôrn'mənt) *n.* **1.** The act of adorning. **2.** That which adorns; ornament.

a·down (ə-doun') *adv. & prep. Archaic & Poetic* Downward; down. [OE *of dūne* off the hill]

ad pa·tres (ad pā'trēz) *Latin* Dead; literally, to the fathers.

ad quem (ad kwem') *Latin* At or to which.

A·dras·tus (ə-dras'təs) An ancient Greek hero. See SEVEN AGAINST THEBES.

ad rem (ad rem') *Latin* To the point; direct; pertinent.

ad·re·nal (ə-drē'nəl) *Physiol. n.* An adrenal gland. — *adj.* **1.** Near or upon the kidneys. **2.** Of or from the adrenal glands. [< AD- + L *renes* kidneys + -AL³]

adrenal gland One of a pair of small ductless glands situated on the kidneys of most vertebrates, in man secreting epinephrine and cortin: also called *renal capsule, renal gland, suprarenal gland.*

Ad·ren·a·lin (ə-dren'ə-lin) *n.* Proprietary name for a brand of epinephrine. Also **ad·ren·a·lin** (ə-dren'ə-lin).

ad·re·no·cor·ti·co·tro·pic hormone (ə-drē'nō-kôr'ti-kō-trō'pik) *Physiol.* ACTH.

A·dri·an (ā'drē-ən) See HADRIAN.

Adrian, Edgar Douglas, born 1889, English physiologist.

Adrian IV, 1100?–59, pope 1154–59; the only English pope: original name *Nicholas Breakspear.*

A·dri·a·no·ple (ā'drē-ə-nō'pəl) A city in northern European Turkey; pop. 33,591 (1955); ancient *Uskudama* and *Hadrianopolis*: also *Edirne.*

A·dri·at·ic (ā'drē-at'ik) *adj.* Of or pertaining to the Adriatic Sea or to the inhabitants of its coastal regions.

Adriatic Sea An inlet of the Mediterranean Sea, east of Italy; 500 mi. long.

a·drift (ə-drift') *adv. & adj.* In a drifting state; drifting.

a·droit (ə-droit') *adj.* Skillful or ready in the use of bodily or mental powers; dexterous; expert: *adroit* in arithmetic. [< F < *à* to (< L *ad-*) + *droit* right < L *directus*] — **a·droit'ly** *adv.* — **a·droit'ness** *n.*
— **Syn.** clever, deft, handy. Compare SKILLFUL.

à droite (à drwàt') *French* To, toward, or on the right.

ads or **A.D.S.** Autograph document signed.

A.D.S. American Dialect Society.

ad·sci·ti·tious (ad'sə-tish'əs) *adj.* Added from without; not essential; supplemental. [< L *adscitus,* pp. of *adsciscere* to admit, accept < *ad-* to + *sciscere* to acknowledge]

ad·script (ad'skript) *adj.* Written after: distinguished from *subscript.* [< L *adscriptus,* pp. of *adscribere, ascribere.* See ASCRIBE.] — **ad·scrip'tion** *n.*

ad·sorb (ad-sôrb', -zôrb') *v.t. Chem.* To condense and hold by adsorption: distinguished from *absorb.* [< AD- + L *sorbere* to suck in] — **ad·sor'bent** *n. & adj.*

ad·sor·bate (ad-sôr'bāt, -zôr'-) *n.* A substance that has been or is being adsorbed.

ad·sorp·tion (ad-sôrp'shən, -zôrp'-) *n. Chem.* The action of a body, as charcoal, in condensing and holding a gas or soluble substance upon its surface. [< ADSORB; modeled on *absorption*] — **ad·sorp'tive** *adj.*

ad·su·ki bean (ad-soo'kē, -zoo'-) A kidney bean (*Phaseolus angularis*) cultivated in northern China and Japan: also *adzuki bean.* [< Japanese *azuki*]

ad sum (ad'sum) *Latin* I am present: an answer to a roll call.

ad sum·mum (ad sum'əm) *Latin* To the highest point or amount.

ad·u·lar·i·a (aj'ōō-lâr'ē-ə) *n. Mineral.* Moonstone. [after *Adula,* a mountain group in Switzerland]

ad·u·late (aj'ōō-lāt) *v.t.* **·lat·ed, ·lat·ing** To flatter servilely; praise extravagantly. [< L *adulatus,* pp. of *adulari* to fawn] — **ad'u·la·tor** *n.* — **ad·u·la·to·ry** (aj'ōō-lə-tôr'ē, -tō'rē) *adj.*

ad·u·la·tion (aj'ōō-lā'shən) *n.* Extravagant and hypocritical praise; servile flattery.

a·dult (ə-dult', ad'ult) *n.* **1.** A person who has attained the age of maturity or legal majority. **2.** *Biol.* A fully developed animal or plant. — *adj.* **1.** Pertaining to mature life; full-grown. **2.** Of or intended for mature people: an *adult* novel. [< L *adultus,* pp. of *adolescere* to grow up < *ad-* to + *alescere* to grow. Related to ADOLESCENT.] — **a·dult'ness** *n.*

a·dul·ter·ant (ə-dul'tər·ənt) *n.* An adulterating substance. — *adj.* Adulterating.

a·dul·ter·ate (ə-dul'tə-rāt; *for adj.,* -rit) *v.t.* **·at·ed, ·at·ing** To make impure or inferior by admixture of other ingredients; corrupt. — *adj.* **1.** Adulterated; corrupted; debased. **2.** Adulterous. [< L *adulteratus,* pp. of *adulterare* to corrupt < *ad-* to + *alter* other, different] — **a·dul'ter·a'·tor** *n.*

a·dul·ter·a·tion (ə-dul'tə-rā'shən) *n.* **1.** The act of adulterating; corruption. **2.** The result of being adulterated; a debased or impure substance or condition.

a·dul·ter·er (ə-dul'tər-ər) *n.* One who commits adultery. [< obs. *adulter* to commit adultery, a refashioning after L *ad-,* < ME *avoutre* < OF *avoutrer* < L *adulterare* + -ER¹. See ADULTERATE.]

a·dul·ter·ess (ə-dul'tər-is, ə-dul'tris) *n.* A woman who commits adultery.

a·dul·ter·ine (ə-dul'tər-in, -īn) *adj.* **1.** Originating in, or pertaining to, adultery: *adulterine* children. **2.** Unauthorized; spurious. [< L *adulterinus*]

a·dul·ter·ous (ə-dul'tər-əs) *adj.* Of, pertaining to, or given to adultery; illicit. — **a·dul'ter·ous·ly** *adv.*

a·dul·ter·y (ə-dul'tər-ē) *n. pl.* **·ter·ies 1.** The voluntary sexual intercourse of a married person with someone not the spouse; unfaithfulness. **2.** In the Bible: **a** Idolatry. *Jer.* iii 8–9. **b** Any lewd or unchaste act or thought. *Matt.* v 27–28. [< L *adulterium*]

a·dult·hood (ə-dult'hōōd) *n.* The state of being an adult.

ad·um·bral (ad-um'brəl, ə-dum'-) *adj.* Overshadowing; shady.

ad·um·brate (ad-um'brāt, ə-dum'-) *v.t.* **·brat·ed, ·brat·ing** **1.** To represent the mere shadow of; outline sketchily. **2.** To foreshadow; prefigure. **3.** To shade or overshadow; darken. [< L *adumbratus,* pp. of *adumbrare* < *ad-* to + *umbrare* to shade < *umbra* shade]

ad·um·bra·tion (ad'əm-brā'shən) *n.* **1.** A slight sketch. **2.** A foreshadowing. **3.** An overshadowing; obscuration.

ad·um·bra·tive (ad-um'brə-tiv) *adj.* Faintly indicative.

a·dunc (ə-dungk') *adj.* Hooked; bent inward. Also **a·dun·cous** (ə-dung'kəs), **a·dunc·ate** (ə-dung'kāt). [< L *aduncus* < *ad-* to + *uncus* hooked]

a·dust (ə-dust') *adj.* **1.** Burning; hot; seared. **2.** Browned; sunburnt. **3.** Parched. **4.** Melancholy; gloomy. [< L *adustus,* pp. of *adurere* to burn up < *ad-* to + *urere* to burn]

A·du·wa (ä'dōō-wä) A town in NE Ethiopia; scene of victory of Emperor Menelik II over the Italians, 1896; pop. about 5,000. *Italian* **A·du·a** (ä'dōō·ä).

adv. 1. Ad valorem (L). **2.** Advance. **3.** *Gram.* Adverb; adverbial. **4.** Advertisement. **5.** Advise. **6.** Advocate. **7.** Against (L *adversus*)

ad va·lo·rem (ad və-lôr'əm, -lō'rəm) *Latin* According or in proportion to the value. Abbr. *adv., ad val.*

ad·vance (ad-vans', -väns') *v.* **·vanced, ·vanc·ing** *v.t.* **1.** To move or cause to go forward or upward. **2.** To offer; propose: to *advance* a suggestion. **3.** To further; promote: to *advance* the progress of science. **4.** To put in a better or more advantageous rank, position, or situation. **5.** To make occur earlier; accelerate. **6.** To raise (a rate, price, etc.). **7.** To pay, as money or interest, before legally due. **8.** To lend: Can you *advance* me some money? **9.** *Law* To provide an advancement for. — *v.i.* **10.** To move or go forward: The armies *advance* on all fronts. **11.** To make progress; rise or improve: The stock market *advanced.* — *adj.* **1.** Being before in time; early: an *advance* payment. **2.** Being or going before; in front: the *advance* guard. — *n.* **1.** The act of going forward; progress. **2.** Improvement; promotion. **3.** An increase or rise, as of prices. **4.** *pl.* Personal approaches; overtures: His *advances* were rejected. **5.** The supplying of goods, money, etc., on credit. **6.** The goods or money so supplied; a loan. **7.** The payment of money before it is legally due: He requested an *advance* on his salary. **8.** *U.S.* The front or foremost part. Abbr. *adv.* **— Syn.** See PROGRESS. **— in advance 1.** In front. **2.** Before due; beforehand: to prepare for lunch *in advance*. [ME *avauncen* < OF *avancier* < L *ab ante* from before < *ab-* away + *ante* before; the initial *a-* was later altered to *ad-* as if from L *ad-* to, toward] **— ad·vanc′er** *n.*

ad·vanced (ad-vanst′, -vänst′) *adj.* **1.** In advance of others, as in progress or thought: *advanced* ideas. **2.** In front; moved forward. **3.** At a late or forward stage, as of life, time, etc.: an *advanced* age.

advanced standing Status granted by a college to a student entering with credits from elsewhere.

advance guard A detachment of troops moving ahead of the main body to insure its security and to reconnoiter.

ad·vance·ment (ad-vans′mənt, -väns′-) *n.* **1.** The act of advancing, or the state of being advanced. **2.** Progression; promotion; preferment. **3.** *Law* A gift of property made to a child or heir and charged against a future bequest.

advance poll *Canadian* A preelection poll for those required to be absent on election day.

ad·van·tage (ad-van′tij, -vän′-) *n.* **1.** Any circumstance, state, or condition favoring success: the *advantage* of a good mind. **2.** Benefit or gain; profit: It's to your *advantage* to be there. **3.** A better state or position; superiority: often with *over* or *of.* **4.** In tennis, the first point scored after deuce; also, the score for it: also called *ad, vantage.* **— to advantage** To good effect; favorably. **— to take advantage of 1.** To avail oneself of. **2.** To impose upon; use selfishly. **— v.t.** **·taged, ·tag·ing** To give advantage or profit to; be of benefit or service to. [< OF *avantage* < *avant* before < L *ab ante* from before. See ADVANCE.]

— Syn. *Advantage, benefit, gain, profit,* and *avail* refer to anything that favors a person's success, advancement, welfare, or the like. *Advantage* is a general term applied to any circumstance that makes one person superior to others in a given undertaking: the *advantage* of an early start. *Benefits* and *gains* promote a person's welfare in some way; *benefit* often suggests the addition of some new good, and *gain,* the increase of a good already possessed: the *benefits* of a summer vacation, the *gain* in prestige accompanying a promotion. *Profit* is any useful or valuable *gain*; it is often, though not always, material. *Avail,* almost always used with a negative in the sense here compared, refers to an *advantage* that is useful or helpful for a particular purpose: All his persuasive powers were of no *avail* in altering her refusal.

ad·van·ta·geous (ad′vən·tā′jəs) *adj.* Affording advantage; profitable; favorable; beneficial. **— Syn.** See EXPEDIENT. **— ad′van·ta′geous·ly** *adv.* **— ad′van·ta′geous·ness** *n.*

ad·vec·tion (ad·vek′shən) *n.* *Meteorol.* Heat transfer by the horizontal motion of air. [< L *advectio, -onis* < *advehere* to convey < *ad-* to + *vehere* to carry] **— ad·vec′tive** *adj.*

ad·vent (ad′vent) *n.* A coming or arrival, as of any important event or person. [< L *adventus,* pp. of *advenire* < *ad-* to + *venire* to come]

Ad·vent (ad′vent) *n.* **1.** The birth of Christ. **2.** The Second Advent (which see). **3.** The season from Advent Sunday to Christmas.

Ad·vent·ist (ad′ven·tist, ad·ven′-) *n.* A member of a denomination that believes the Second Advent, the Last Judgment, and the end of the world are imminent. The largest U.S. Adventist bodies are the **Advent Christian Church** and the **Seventh-Day Adventists.** See MILLERITE. **— Ad′·vent·ism** *n.*

ad·ven·ti·ti·a (ad′ven·tish′ē-ə) *n.* *Anat.* The outer coat of an organ, especially of a blood vessel. [< L *adventicia*]

ad·ven·ti·tious (ad′ven·tish′əs) *adj.* **1.** Not inherent; accidentally acquired; extrinsic. **2.** *Biol.* Formed without order or in unusual places; sporadic. **3.** Adventive. [< L *adventicius* coming from abroad, foreign < *adventus.* See ADVENT.] **— ad′ven·ti′tious·ly** *adv.* **— ad′ven·ti′tious·ness** *n.*

ad·ven·tive (ad·ven′tiv) *adj.* *Ecol.* Occurring away from the natural habitat: partly naturalized; exotic.

Advent Sunday The Sunday nearest to St. Andrew's Day, the last day of November.

ad·ven·ture (ad·ven′chər) *n.* **1.** A hazardous or perilous undertaking. **2.** A stirring or thrilling experience. **3.** Risky or exciting activity, or participation in such activity: to relish *adventure.* **4.** A commercial venture; speculation. **5.** *Obs.* Danger; hazard; chance. **— v. ·tured, ·tur·ing** *v.t.* **1.** To venture upon; take the chance of. **2.** To risk the loss of; imperil. **— v.i. 3.** To run risks. **4.** To venture upon daring or dangerous undertakings. [< OF *aventure* < L *adventura* (*res*) (a thing) about to happen < *advenire.* See ADVENT.]

ad·ven·tur·er (ad·ven′chər·ər) *n.* **1.** One who seeks after or takes part in adventures. **2.** One who seeks his fortune in war; a soldier of fortune. **3.** A speculator in commerce. **4.** A person who seeks advancement by questionable means.

ad·ven·tur·ess (ad·ven′chər·is) *n.* **1.** A woman adventurer. **2.** A woman who attempts to gain wealth or social position by unscrupulous or equivocal means.

ad·ven·tur·ous (ad·ven′chər·əs) *adj.* **1.** Disposed to seek

adventures or take risks; venturesome. Also **ad·ven′ture·some** (-səm). **2.** Attended with risk; hazardous. **— ad·ven′tur·ous·ly** *adv.* **— ad·ven′tur·ous·ness** *n.*

ad·verb (ad′vûrb) *n.* **1.** *Gram.* Any of a class of words used to modify the meaning of a verb, adjective, or other adverb, in regard to time, place, manner, means, cause, degree, etc.: one of the eight traditional parts of speech. **2.** *Ling.* One of a form class, the members of which are marked by certain suffixes, as, in English, *-ly,* or identified by their ability to occupy certain syntactic positions in sentences and phrases, as, in English, in *very good, very* is an adverb by virtue of its position before *good,* or by a combination of both morphologic and syntactic criteria. Abbr. *adv.* [< L *adverbium* < *ad-* to + *verbum* verb]

adverb clause *Gram.* A dependent clause that functions as an adverb in a sentence, as *when the guests arrive* in We *will eat when the guests arrive*: also **adverbial clause.**

ad·ver·bi·al (ad·vûr′bē-əl) *adj.* **1.** Of or pertaining to adverbs. **2.** Containing or used like an adverb. Abbr. *adv.* **— ad·ver′bi·al·ly** *adv.*

ad·ver·sar·y (ad′vər·ser′ē) *n. pl.* **·sar·ies** One actively hostile to another; an opponent; enemy. **— Syn.** See ENEMY. **— the Adversary** Satan. [< OF *adversarie* < L *adversarius,* lit., one turned toward < *adversus.* See ADVERSE.]

ad·ver·sa·tive (ad·vûr′sə·tiv) *adj.* Expressing opposition or antithesis. *However* is an adversative conjunction. **— n.** An antithetic word or proposition. [< LL *adversativus* < L *adversatus* opposite] **— ad·ver′sa·tive·ly** *adv.*

ad·verse (ad·vûrs′, ad′vûrs) *adj.* **1.** Opposing or opposed; antagonistic. **2.** Unpropitious; detrimental: *adverse* fortune. **3.** *Bot.* Turned toward the stem or main axis. **4.** Opposite. [< L *adversus* turned against, pp. of *advertere* < *ad-* to + *vertere* to turn] **— ad·verse′ly** *adv.* **— ad·verse′ness** *n.*

ad·ver·si·ty (ad·vûr′sə·tē) *n. pl.* **·ties 1.** A condition of hardship or affliction; severe trial. **2.** *Often pl.* An adverse or calamitous circumstance or occurrence; a misfortune. [< OF *aversite* < L *adversitas, -tatis* < *adversus.* See ADVERSE.]

ad·vert (ad·vûrt′) *v.i.* To call attention; refer: with *to.* [< L *advertere* < *ad-* to + *vertere* to turn]

ad·ver·tent (ad·vûr′tənt) *adj.* Giving attention; heedful. [< L *advertens, -entis,* ppr. of *advertere.* See ADVERT.] **— ad·ver′tence, ad·ver′ten·cy** *n.* **— ad·ver′tent·ly** *adv.*

ad·ver·tise (ad′vər·tīz, ad′vər·tīz′) *v.* **·tised, ·tis·ing** *v.t.* **1.** To make known by public notice; proclaim the qualities of, as by publication or broadcasting, generally in order to sell. **2.** *Obs.* To notify or warn. **— v.i. 3.** To inquire by public notice, as in a newspaper: with *for*: to *advertise* for a house. **4.** To distribute or publish advertisements: The company *advertised* widely in national magazines. Also **ad′ver·tize.** [< MF *advertiss-,* stem of *advertir* to warn, give notice to < L *advertere.* See ADVERT.] **— ad′ver·tis′er** *n.*

— Syn. 1. publish, proclaim, broadcast, announce, declare.

ad·ver·tise·ment (ad′vər·tīz′mənt, ad·vûr′tis·mənt, -tiz-) *n.* **1.** A public notice, as in a newspaper or on a radio program. **2.** A giving notice; notification; information. Also **ad′ver·tize′ment.** Abbr. *ad., adv., advt.*

ad·ver·tis·ing (ad′vər·tī′zing) *n.* **1.** The act or practice of attracting public notice so as to create interest or induce purchase; also, any system or method used for such purposes. **2.** Advertisements collectively. **3.** The business of writing and publicizing advertisements; promoting. Also **ad′ver·tiz′ing.**

ad·vice (ad·vīs′) *n.* **1.** Counsel given to encourage or dissuade; suggestion. **2.** *Often pl.* Information; notification: *advices* from a foreign correspondent. [< OF *avis* view, opinion < LL *advisum* < L *ad-* to + *visum,* pp. of *videre* to see]

ad·vis·a·ble (ad·vī′zə·bəl) *adj.* Proper to be advised or recommended; expedient. **— Syn.** See EXPEDIENT. **— ad·vis′·a·bil′i·ty, ad·vis′a·ble·ness** *n.* **— ad·vis′a·bly** *adv.*

ad·vise (ad·vīz′) *v.* **·vised, ·vis·ing** *v.t.* **1.** To give advice to; counsel. **2.** To recommend. **3.** To notify; inform, as of a transaction: with *of.* **— v.i. 4.** To take counsel: with *with*: He advised with his lawyer. **5.** To give advice. Abbr. *adv.* [< OF *aviser* < LL *advisare* < *advisum.* See ADVICE.]

ad·vised (ad·vīzd′) *adj.* **1.** Done with counsel or forethought; deliberate: chiefly in *ill-advised, well-advised.* **2.** Informed: Keep me *advised.* **— ad·vis·ed·ness** (ad·vī′zid·nis) *n.*

ad·vis·ed·ly (ad·vī′zid·lē) *adv.* With forethought or advice.

ad·vise·ment (ad·vīz′mənt) *n.* Consultation; deliberation.

ad·vis·er (ad·vī′zər) *n.* **1.** One who advises. **2.** A teacher in a school or college who counsels students about their studies, careers, etc. Also **ad·vi′sor.**

ad·vi·so·ry (ad·vī′zər·ē) *adj.* **1.** Having power to advise. **2.** Containing or given as advice; not mandatory.

ad·vo·ca·cy (ad′və·kə·sē) *n.* The act of advocating or pleading a cause; vindication; defense. [< OF *advocacie* < Med.L *advocatia* < L *advocatus.* See ADVOCATE.]

ad·vo·cate (*v.* ad′və·kāt; *n.* ad′və·kit, -kāt) *v.t.* **·cat·ed, ·cat·ing** To speak or write in favor of; defend; recommend. **— n. 1.** One who pleads the cause of another; an intercessor. **2.** One who espouses or defends a cause by argument: an *ad-*

---

vocate of slavery. **3.** In Scottish law, a counselor. *Abbr.* (for *n.* defs. 1, 3) *adv.* **— Syn.** See LAWYER. [< OF *avocat* < L *advocatus* one summoned to assist another < *advocare* < *ad-* to + *vocare* to call] **— ad·vo·ca'tor** *n.* **— ad·voc·a·to·ry** (ad·vok'ə·tôr'ē, -tō'rē) *adj.*

ad·vo·ca·tion (ad'və·kā'shən) *n.* **1.** In Scottish and papal law, a process whereby a superior court calls to itself an action still pending in a lower court. **2.** *Obs.* Advocacy.

ad·vo·ca·tus di·ab·o·li (ad'və·kā'təs dī·ab'ə·lī) *Latin* The devil's advocate; one who deliberately takes the unfavorable side in a dispute.

ad·vow·son (ad·vou'zən) *n.* In English law, the right of presentation to a vacant benefice; patronage. [< AF *avoeson* < L *advocatio, -onis* < *advocare.* See ADVOCATE.]

advt. Advertisement.

ad·y·na·mi·a (ad'ə·nā'mē·ə) *n. Pathol.* Lack of physical strength, resulting from disease. [< NL < Gk. *a-* without + *dynamis* strength] **— ad·y·nam·ic** (ad'ə·nam'ik) *adj.*

ad·y·tum (ad'ə·təm) *n.* *pl.* **·ta** (-tə) **1.** In ancient temples, an inner or secret shrine. **2.** Any secret place. [< L < Gk. *adyton*, neut. of *adytos* not to be entered < *a-* not + *dyein* to enter]

adz (adz) *n.* *pl.* **adz·es** A hand cutting tool with its blade at right angles to its handle and usually curved inward, used for dressing timber, etc. Also **adze**. [OE *adesa*]

A·dzhar A.S.S.R. (ə·jär', ä'jär) An administrative division of the SW Georgian S.S.R.; 1,150 sq. mi.; pop. 310,000 (est. 1970); capital, Batum. Also **A·dzha·ri·stan** (ə·jär'i·stan). *Russian* **A·dzhar·ska·ya A.S.S.R.** (ə·jär'skä·yä).

ad·zu·ki bean (ad·zōō'kē) See ADSUKI BEAN.

ae (ā) *adj. Scot.* One.

ae- For those words not entered below, see under E-.

æ 1. A ligature of Latin origin, equivalent to Greek *ai:* usually printed *ae.* It is sometimes retained in the spelling of Greek and Latin proper names and in certain scientific terms, but, in modern use, is generally reduced to *e.* **2.** A character in Old English, representing the sound of *a* in modern *hat.*

ae. At the age of; aged (L *aetatis*).

-ae The plural ending of Latin feminine nouns in *-a* and of Latinized Greek plurals in *-ai:* used in many botanical and zoological proper names, as *Canidae, Leptidae,* etc., and in various adopted words, as *alumnae, larvae, formulae,* etc.

Æ See (George William) RUSSELL.

A.E.A. Actors' Equity Association.

Ae·a·cus (ē'ə·kəs) In Greek mythology, a son of Zeus and king of Aegina who ruled so justly that after his death he was made a judge in Hades.

A.E. and P. Ambassador Extraordinary and Plenipotentiary.

AEC Atomic Energy Commission.

A.E.C. American Engineering Council.

ae·cid·i·um (ē·sid'ē·əm) *n.* *pl.* **·cid·i·a** (-sid'ē·ə) *Bot.* An aecium. [< NL, dim. of Gk. *aikia* injury]

ae·ci·o·stage (ē'sē·ō·stāj') *n. Bot.* The first stage in the life cycle of certain parasitic fungi of the order *Uredinales,* during which spores are produced. [< AECIUM + STAGE]

ae·ci·um (ē'sē·əm, ē'shē-) *n.* *pl.* **·ci·a** (-sē·ə, -shē·ə) *Bot.* The sorus developed from the haploid mycelium of certain rust fungi (*Uredinales*) and usually bearing spores in a chainlike formation. [< NL < Gk. *aikia* injury] **— ae'ci·al** *adj.*

a·e·des (ā·ē'dēz) *n.* One of a genus (*Aëdes*) of mosquitoes (family *Culicidae*); especially, *A. aegypti,* that carries yellow fever and dengue: formerly called *stegomyia.* [< NL < Gk. *aēdēs* unpleasant < *a-* not + *hēdys* sweet]

ae·dile (ē'dīl) *n.* A magistrate of ancient Rome who had charge of public lands, buildings, public spectacles, etc.: also spelled *edile.* [< L *aedilis* < *aedes* building] **— ae'dile·ship** *n.*

Ae·e·tes (ē·ē'tēz) In Greek mythology, king of Colchis; father of Medea and possessor of the Golden Fleece.

AEF or **A.E.F.** American Expeditionary Force(s).

Ae·ge·an (i·jē'ən) *adj.* **1.** Of or pertaining to the Aegean Islands or the Aegean Sea. **2.** Of or pertaining to the Bronze Age civilization of this region. Also spelled *Egean.*

Aegean Islands The islands of the Aegean Sea, comprising an administrative division of Greece; 3,564 sq. mi.; pop. 477,476 (1961).

Aegean Sea An inlet of the Mediterranean Sea between Greece and Asia Minor.

Ae·geus (ē'jōōs, ē'jē·əs) In Greek mythology, a king of Athens, father of Theseus.

Ae·gi·na (ē·jī'nə) **1.** A SE coastal island of Greece, in the Saronic Gulf (also **Gulf of Aegina**), an inlet of the Aegean Sea; 32 sq. mi. **2.** The chief town of this island; pop. about 6,500. **— Ae·gi·ne·tan** (ē'jə·nē'tən) *adj. & n.*

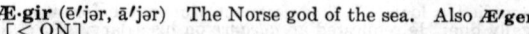

Æ·gir (ē'jər, ā'jər) The Norse god of the sea. Also **Æ'ger**. [< ON]

ae·gis (ē'jis) *n.* **1.** In Greek mythology, the breastplate of Zeus, used by several other gods, especially Athena. See GORGONEION. **2.** Any shield or armor. **3.** A protecting influence or power; sponsorship. Also spelled *egis.* [< Gk. *aigis* goatskin]

Ae·gis·thus (ē·jis'thəs) In Greek legend, the son of Thyestes and lover of Clytemnestra. See ORESTES.

Ae·gos·pot·a·mi (ē'gəs·pot'ə·mī) **1.** A river in ancient Thrace flowing into the Hellespont; site of Lysander's victory over the Athenian fleet (405 B.C.) that ended the Peloponnesian War. **2.** An ancient town on this river. Also **Ae'gos·pot'a·mos.**

Ae·gyp·tus (ē·jip'təs) In Greek mythology, king of Egypt; brother of Danaus, whose daughters his sons married. See DANAIDES.

Æl·fric (al'frik), 955?–1020?, English monk and writer: called **Gram·ma·ti·cus** (gra·mat'i·kəs).

-aemia See -EMIA.

Ae·ne·as (i·nē'əs) In classical legend, a Trojan, son of Anchises and Venus, and hero of the *Aeneid.* After the sack of Troy he wandered for seven years before reaching Latium where he founded the city of Lavinium. See ASCANIUS, DIDO.

Ae·ne·as Sil·vi·us (i·nē'əs sil'vē·əs) See PIUS II. Also **Ae·ne'as Syl'vi·us.**

Ae·ne·id (i·nē'id) A Latin epic poem by Vergil, narrating the adventures of Aeneas.

a·e·ne·ous (ā·ē'nē·əs) *adj.* Having a golden green or brassy color, as certain insects. [< L *aeneus* < *aes* copper, bronze]

ae·o·li·an (ē·ō'lē·ən) *adj.* Pertaining to or caused by the winds; wind-borne: also spelled *eolian.*

Ae·o·li·an (ē·ō'lē·ən) *adj.* **1.** Of or pertaining to ancient Aeolis, its people, or their language. **2.** Pertaining to Aeolus, Greek god of the winds. **— n. 1.** A member of one of the four major tribes of ancient Greece. They settled in central Greece, Lesbos, and Aeolis. **2.** Aeolic. Also spelled *Eolian.*

Aeolian harp A stringed instrument so constructed as to produce musical sounds when exposed to a current of air.

Ae·ol·ic (ē·ol'ik) A dialect of ancient Greek spoken in Aeolis, Lesbos, Thessaly, and Boeotia, used by Sappho and Alcaeus. **— adj.** Aeolian. Also spelled *Eolic.*

ae·o·li·pile (ē·ol'ə·pīl) See EOLIPILE.

Ae·o·lis (ē'ə·lis) A country in ancient Greece and NW Asia Minor. Also **Ae·o·li·a** (ē·ō'lē·ə).

ae·o·lo·trop·ic (ē'ə·lō·trop'ik) See EOLOTROPIC.

Ae·o·lus (ē'ə·ləs) **1.** In Greek mythology, the god of the winds. **2.** In Greek legend, a Thessalian king; son of Hellen and ancestor of the Aeolians.

ae·on (ē'ən, ē'on), **ae·o·ni·an** (ē·ō'nē·ən) See EON, etc.

Ae·qui·an (ē'kwē·ən) *n.* The Indo-European language of an early Italic people inhabiting Latium.

aer- Var. of AERO-.

aer·ate (âr'āt, ā'ə·rāt) *v.t.* **at·ed, ·at·ing 1.** To supply or charge with air or gas. **2.** To purify by exposure to air. **3.** *Physiol.* To oxygenate, as blood. [< AER- + -ATE¹] **— aer·a'tion** *n.*

aer·a·tor (âr'ā·tər, ā'ə·rā'tər) *n.* **1.** An apparatus for charging liquids with gas under pressure. **2.** A device for supplying a stream of gas or air, as for fumigating, etc.

aeri- Var. of AERO-.

aer·i·al (âr'ē·əl, ā·ir'ē·əl) *adj.* **1.** Of or in the air: an *aerial* disturbance. **2.** Living or moving in the air. **3.** Extending into the air; lofty. **4.** Light as air; airy: *aerial* beings. **5.** Unsubstantial; intangible; imaginary: *aerial* fears. **6.** Of, by, or pertaining to aircraft, or to flying: an *aerial* attack. **7.** *Bot.* Growing in the air, as the roots of certain plants. **— Syn.** See AIRY. **— n.** An antenna, as in television and radio. [< L *aerius* airy < *aer* air] **— aer'i·al·ly** *adv.*

aerial bomb Any bomb dropped from an aircraft.

aer·i·al·ist (âr'ē·əl·ist, ā·ir'ē·əl-) *n.* One who performs on a tightrope, trapeze, etc.

aer·i·al·i·ty (âr'ē·al'ə·tē, ā·ir'ē-) *n.* Lack of substance.

aerial ladder A free-standing extension ladder, commonly mounted on a truck and used by firemen.

aerial perspective In painting, drawing, etc., the means of indicating the relative distances of objects by gradations of tone and color.

aerial sickness Airsickness (which see).

aer·ie (âr'ē, ir'ē) *n.* **1.** The nest of a predatory bird, as the eagle, on a crag. **2.** The brood or young of such a bird. **3.** A house or stronghold situated on a height. Also spelled *aery, eyrie, eyry.* [< Med.L *aeria* < OF *aire, ?* < L *area* open space] **— aer'ied** *adj.*

aer·if·er·ous (âr·if'ər·əs, ā'ə·rif'-) *adj.* Conveying air. [< AERI- + -FEROUS]

aer·i·fi·ca·tion (âr'ə·fi·kā'shən, ā'ər·ə-) *n.* **1.** The act or process of converting into air, gas, or vapor. **2.** Purification by exposure to air; aeration. Also **aer'i'fac'tion**.

aer·i·form (âr'ə·fôrm, ā'ər·ə·fôrm') *adj.* **1.** Like air; gaseous. **2.** Unsubstantial.

aer·i·fy (âr'ə·fī, ā'ər·ə·fī) *v.t.* **·fied, ·fy·ing 1.** To aerate. **2.** To change into a gaseous form. [< AERI- + -FY]

ADZES

a Sculptor's.
b Cooper's.
c Carpenter's.

aero- *combining form* **1.** Air; of the air: *aerobiology.* **2.** Of aircraft or flying: *aeromarine.* **3.** Gas; of gases: *aerogenic.* Also *aer-, aeri-.* [< Gk. *aēr* air]

aer·o·bal·lis·tics (âr′ō·bə·lis′tiks, ā′ər·ō-) *n.pl.* (construed as *sing.*) The ballistics of missiles dropped, launched, or fired from aircraft in flight.

aer·o·bat·ics (âr′ə·bat′iks, ā′ər·ə-) *n.pl.* (construed as *sing.* in def. 2) **1.** Feats of skill, as rolls, loops, etc., performed with an aircraft. **2.** The art or act of performing such aerial feats. [< AERO- + (ACRO)BATICS]

aer·obe (âr′ōb, ā′ər·ōb) *n.* A microorganism that can live only in air or free oxygen: distinguished from *anaerobe.* Also **aer·o·bi·um** (âr·ō′bē·əm, ā/ə·rō′-). [< AERO- + Gk. *bios* life] — **aer·o′bic** *adj.*

aer·o·bi·ol·o·gy (âr′ō·bī·ol′ə·jē, ā′ər·ō-) *n.* The study of the transportation of microorganisms, as bacteria, viruses, and pollens, through the air.

aer·o·car·to·graph (âr′ō·kär′tə·graf, -gräf, ā′ər·ō-) *n.* A map-making device that utilizes air photographs.

aer·o·do·net·ics (âr′ō·də·net′iks, ā′ər·ō-) *n.pl.* (construed as *sing.*) The branch of dynamics that treats of gliding and soaring flight. [< AERO- + Gk. *donētos* shaken < *doneein* to shake]

aer·o·drome (âr′ə·drōm, ā′ər·ə-) *n.* An airdrome.

aer·o·duct (âr′ə·duct, ā′ər·ə-) *n.* *Aerospace* A proposed type of ramjet engine in which ions and electrons scooped up in space generate the propulsive force for continued flight.

aer·o·dy·nam·ics (âr′ō·dī·nam′iks, ā′ər·ō-) *n.pl.* (construed as *sing.*) The branch of physics that treats of the laws of motion of gases, especially atmospheric, under the influence of gravity and other mechanical forces, and of the mechanical effects of such motion. — **aer′o·dy·nam′ic** *adj.*

aer·o·dyne (âr′ə·dīn, ā′ər·ə-) *n.* Any aircraft that is heavier than air. [< AERO- + Gk. *dynamis* power]

aer·o·em·bo·lism (âr′ō·em′bə·liz′əm, ā′ər·ō-) *n.* *Pathol.* An acute condition characterized by the formation of nitrogen bubbles in the blood and tissues, as a result of rapid decrease in atmospheric pressure. Compare CAISSON DISEASE.

aer·o·em·phy·se·ma (âr′ō·em′fə·sē′mə, ā′ər·ō-) *n.* *Pathol.* A form of emphysema caused by flying at high altitudes without the corrective of pressurized cabins.

aer·o·foil (âr′ə·foil, ā′ər·ə-) *n.* Airfoil (which see).

aer·o·gel (âr′ə·jel, ā′ər·ə-) *n.* *Chem.* A gel in which the liquid has been replaced by a gas to reduce shrinkage and increase absorptive power.

aer·o·gen·ic (âr′ə·jen′ik, ā′ər·ə-) *adj.* Gas-producing.

aer·o·gram (âr′ə·gram, ā′ər·ə-] *n.* **1.** A wireless message; radiogram. **2.** The record traced by a meteorograph.

aér·o·gramme (âr′ə·gram, ā′ər·ə-) *n.* An international airmail letter consisting of a single sheet folded together and sealed without enclosures. [< Fr.]

aer·og·ra·phy (âr·og′rə·fē, ā′ə·rog′-) *n.* *pl.* **·phies** A description of or treatise on the atmosphere and its phenomena. — **aer·og′ra·pher** *n.* — **aer·o·graph′ic** (-ə·graf′ik) or **·i·cal** *adj.* — **aer·o·graph′i·cal·ly** *adv.*

aer·o·lite (âr′ə·līt, ā′ər·ə-) *n.* A meteorite composed more stone than iron. Also **aer·o·lith** (-lith). [< AERO- + Gk. *lithos* stone] — **aer′o·lit′ic** (-lit′ik) *adj.*

aer·ol·o·gy (âr·ol′ə·jē, ā′ə·rol′-) *n.* *pl.* **·gies** **1.** *Physics* The science of the atmosphere. **2.** *Meteorol.* The study of the atmosphere. — **aer·o·log·ic** (âr′ə·loj′ik, ā′ər·ə-) or **·i·cal** *adj.* — **aer·ol′o·gist** *n.*

aer·o·ma·rine (âr′ō·mə·rēn′, ā′ər·ō-) *adj.* Pertaining to the navigation of aircraft over the ocean.

aer·o·me·chan·ics (âr′ō·mə·kan′iks, ā′ər·ō-) *n.pl.* (construed as *sing.*) **1.** The science that treats of equilibrium and motion of air and gases, including aerostatics and aerodynamics. **2.** Pneumatics. — **aer′o·me·chan′ic** *adj.* & *n.*

aer·o·med·i·cine (âr′ō·med′ə·sin, ā′ər·ō-) *n.* Aerospace medicine, especially with reference to flight within the earth's atmosphere. Also called *aviation medicine.* — **aer′·o·med′i·cal** *adj.*

aer·o·me·te·or·o·graph (âr′ō·mē′tē·ôr′ə·graf, -gräf, ā′ər·ō-) *n.* A device for recording atmospheric conditions, as temperature, pressure and moisture, wind velocities, etc.

aer·om·e·ter (âr·om′ə·tər, ā′ə·rom′ə·tər) *n.* An apparatus for weighing and estimating the density of air or other gases.

aer·om·e·try (âr·om′ə·trē, ā′ə·rom′-) *n.* The science of weighing and measuring air and other gases. — **aer·o·met·ric** (âr′ə·met′rik, ā′ər·ə-) *adj.*

aer·on. Aeronautic; aeronautics.

aer·o·naut (âr′ə·nôt, ā′ər·ə-) *n.* One who navigates the air, especially in a balloon or other lighter-than-air craft. [< F *aéronaute* < Gk. *aēr* air + *nautēs* sailor]

aer·o·nau·tic (âr′ə·nô′tik, ā′ər·ə-) *adj.* **1.** Pertaining to, floating in, or navigating the air. **2.** Pertaining to aeronautics. Also **aer·o·nau′ti·cal.** *Abbr.* **aeron.**

aer·o·nau·tics (âr′ə·nô′tiks, ā′ər·ə-) *n.pl.* (construed as *sing.*) **1.** The science or art of navigating aircraft. **2.** That branch of engineering that deals with the design, construction, operation, and performance of aircraft. *Abbr.* **aeron.**

aer·o·neu·ro·sis (âr′ō·nŏŏ·rō′sis, -nyŏŏ-, ā′ər·ō-) *n. Pathol.* A nervous disorder sometimes affecting airplane pilots, usually associated with prolonged anoxia and characterized by emotional tension, irritability, gastric distress, and insomnia: also called *flying fatigue.*

aer·o·pause (âr′ə·pôz, ā′ər·ə-) *n. Meteorol.* The region of the atmosphere where the conditions of outer space are gradually approached.

aer·o·pha·gi·a (âr′ə·fā′jē·ə, ā′ər·ə-) *n. Med.* The swallowing of air, a symptom in certain neurotic conditions affecting the gastric functions.

aer·o·phore (âr′ə·fôr, ā′ər·ə-) *n.* A breathing apparatus for inflating the lungs of a newborn child or for supplying air to firemen, aviators, etc., under abnormal conditions.

aer·o·pho·tog·ra·phy (âr′ō·fə·tog′rə·fē, ā′ər·ō-) *n.* Photography from aircraft.

aer·o·phys·ics (âr′ō·fiz′iks, ā′ər·ō-) *n.pl.* (construed as *sing.*) Physical science considered with reference to aeronautics.

aer·o·phyte (âr′ə·fīt, ā′ər·ə-) *n.* An epiphyte (which see).

aer·o·plane (âr′ə·plān, ā′ər·ə-) *n. Brit.* Airplane (which see).

aer·o·scope (âr′ə·skōp, ā′ər·ə-) *n.* An instrument by which microscopic objects and bacteria may be gathered from the atmosphere. — **aer′o·scop′ic** (-skop′ik) *adj.*

aer·o·sid·er·ite (âr′ō·sid′ə·rīt, ā′ər·ō-) *n.* A meteorite composed chiefly of iron.

aer·o·sid·er·o·lite (âr′ō·sid′ər·ə·līt′, ā′ər·ō-) *n.* A meteorite that is both metallic and stony.

aer·o·sol (âr′ə·sōl, -sol, ā′ər·ə-) *n.* **1.** A colloid system of solid or liquid particles dispersed in a gas: fog or smoke *aerosol.* **2.** *Chem.* Any of a class of such colloid dispersions prepared for use as wetting agents, emulsifiers, detergents, and insecticides. [< AERO- + SOL(UTION)]

aerosol bomb A small spraying can holding a liquid, as an insecticide, etc., under gas pressure.

aer·o·space (âr′ō·spās, ā′ər·ō-) *n.* **1.** The earth's atmosphere and outer space, considered as a single region in the operation of rockets, guided missiles, and spacecraft. **2.** The study and investigation of this region, especially with reference to space travel.

aerospace medicine The branch of medicine that deals with conditions and disorders associated with flight through or beyond the earth's atmosphere.

aer·o·sphere (âr′ə·sfir, ā′ər·ə-) *n.* The entire atmosphere considered as a single gaseous shell surrounding the earth.

aer·o·stat (âr′ə·stat, ā′ər·ə-) *n.* Any aircraft, as a balloon or dirigible, that derives its lift from one or more chambers containing a gas lighter than air. [< F *aérostat* < Gk. *aēr* air + *statos* standing] — **aer·o·stat′ic** or **·i·cal** *adj.*

aer·o·stat·ics (âr′ə·stat′iks, ā′ər·ə-) *n.pl.* (construed as *sing.*) The branch of physics that treats of the mechanical properties of air and gases in equilibrium.

aer·o·sta·tion (âr′ə·stā′shən, ā′ər·ə-) *n.* **1.** The art and science of operating lighter-than-air aircraft, as balloons and dirigibles: distinguished from *aviation.* **2.** Aerostatics.

aer·o·ther·a·peu·tics (âr′ō·ther′ə·pyŏŏ′tiks, ā′ər·ō-) *n.pl.* (construed as *sing.*) *Med.* A system of treating disease by varying the atmospheric pressure upon the patient or by changing the composition of the air. Also **aer′o·ther′a·py.**

aer·ot·ro·pism (âr·ot′rə·piz′əm, ā′ə·rot′-) *n. Biol.* The response of plant or animal organisms to the influence of air or gases. — **aer·o·trop·ic** (âr′ə·trop′ik, ā′ər·ə-) *adj.*

ae·ru·go (i·rōō′gō) *n.* Copper rust, especially green copper rust of old bronzes; verdigris. [< L < *aer-, aes* brass, copper]

aer·y¹ (âr′ē, ā′ər·ē) *adj.* Airy; aerial.

aer·y² (âr′ē, ir′ē) See AERIE.

Aes·chi·nes (es′kə·nēz), 389–314 B.C., Athenian orator; political opponent of Demosthenes.

Aes·chy·lus (es′kə·ləs), 525–456 B.C., Greek tragic dramatist. — **Aes′chy·le′an** (-lē′ən) *adj.*

Aes·cu·la·pi·an (es′kyə·lā′pē·ən) *adj.* Relating to Aesculapius or the art of healing; medicinal. — *n.* **1.** A disciple of Aesculapius. **2.** Any physician or healer. Also spelled *Esculapian.*

Aes·cu·la·pi·us (es′kyə·lā′pē·əs) In Roman mythology, the god of medicine: identified with the Greek *Asclepius.*

Æ·sir (ā′sir, ē′-) *n.* *pl. of* **As** (äs) The gods of the Norse pantheon collectively. See VANIR.

Ae·sop (ē′səp, ē′sop) Sixth-century B.C. Greek compiler of fables. — **Ae·so·pi·an** (ē·sō′pē·ən) *adj.*

aes·the·sia (es′tə·vəl, es′thē′zhə, -zhē-ə), etc. See ESTHESIA, etc.

aes·thete (es′thēt), **aes·thet·ic** (es·thet′ik), etc. See ESTHETE, etc.

aes·ti·val (es′tə·vəl, es·tī′-), **aes·ti·vate** (es′tə·vāt), etc. See ESTIVAL, etc.

aet. or **aetat.** At the age of; aged (L *aetatis*).

ae·ta·tis su·ae (ē·tā′tis sōō′ē) *Latin* Of his (or her) age; at a specified age.

Æth·el·bert (ath′əl·bûrt) See ETHELBERT.

Æth·el·red (ath′əl·red) See ETHELRED II.

ae·ther (ē′thər) See ETHER (defs. 3 and 4).

ae·ti·ol·o·gy (ē′tē·ol′ə·jē) See ETIOLOGY.

Aet·na (et′nə) See ETNA.

Ae·to·li·a (ē·tō′lē·ə) A country of ancient Greece on the Ionian Sea. *Greek* Ai·to·li·a (ā′tô·lē′ä). — **Ae·to′li·an** *adj.* & *n.*

Ae·to·li·a-Ac·ar·na·ni·a (ē·tō′lē·ə·ak′ər·nā′nē·ə) A Department of western Greece; 2,205 sq. mi.; pop. 220,138 (1951); capital, Missolonghi.

af- Assimilated var. of AD-.

Af. Africa; African.

AF 1. Air Force. 2. Anglo-French: also **A.F.**

AF or **A.F.**, **a.f.**, or **a-f** Audio frequency.

A.F.A.M. or **A.F. & A.M.** Ancient Free and Accepted Masons.

a·far (ə·fär′) *adv.* At, from, or to a distance; remotely. [< A-¹ on + FAR]

A·fars and Is·sas (ä′färz; ē′säz), **French Territory of the** A French Overseas Territory in E Africa, on the Gulf of Aden; formerly *French Somaliland*; 8,498 sq. mi.; pop. 125,000 (est. 1968); cap. Djibouti.

AFB Air Force Base.

af·fa·ble (af′ə·bəl) *adj.* 1. Easy to approach and speak to; friendly; courteous. 2. Benign; mild. [< F < L *affabilis*, lit., able to be spoken to < *affari* < *ad-* to + *fari* to speak] — **af′fa·bil′i·ty, af′fa·ble·ness** *n.* — **af′fa·bly** *adv.* — **Syn.** 1. cordial, genial. Compare AMIABLE, GRACIOUS.

af·fair (ə·fâr′) *n.* 1. Anything done or to be done; business; concern. 2. *pl.* Matters of business or concern. 3. A thing; matter or occurrence (of a specified quality): The raft was a crude *affair*. 4. A love affair. [< OF *afaire* < *à faire* to do < L *ad-* to + *facere* to do]

af·faire (à·fâr′) *n.* *French* Short for **affaire d'a·mour** (dä·mōōr′), a love affair, or **affaire de cœur** (də kœr′), affair of the heart.

af·faire d'hon·neur (à·fâr′ dô·nœr′) *French* A duel.

af·fect¹ (*v.* ə·fekt′; *n.* af′ekt) *v.t.* 1. To act upon or have an effect upon; influence: Fear *affects* the mind. 2. To touch or move emotionally: The audience was deeply *affected*. 3. To attack or attaint, as a part of the body. — **Syn.** See INFLUENCE. — *n.* *Psychol.* **a** That which tends to arouse emotion rather than to stimulate thought or perception. **b** The fundamental controlling element in an emotional state. ◆ See note under EFFECT. [< L *affectus*, pp. of *afficere* to influence, attack < *ad-* to + *facere* to do; noun < G *affekt*]

af·fect² (ə·fekt′) *v.t.* 1. To show a preference for by wearing, using, etc.; fancy: to *affect* large hats. 2. To imitate or counterfeit for effect; assume: to *affect* a British accent. 3. To tend toward naturally; frequent: said of animals and plants. 4. *Obs.* To aim at. [< F *affecter* < L *affectare* to aim at, freq. of *afficere*. See AFFECT¹.] — **af·fect′er** *n.*

af·fec·ta·tion (af′ek·tā′shən) *n.* 1. A studied pretense; display: with *of*: an *affectation* of wealth. 2. Artificiality of manner or behavior; affectedness. [< L *affectatio, -onis* < *affectare*. See AFFECT².]

af·fect·ed¹ (ə·fek′tid) *adj.* 1. Acted upon, as by a drug. 2. Moved emotionally; influenced. 3. Attacked, as by disease; diseased. [pp. of AFFECT¹]

af·fect·ed² (ə·fek′tid) *adj.* 1. Assumed falsely or in outward semblance only; feigned. 2. Showing affectation. 3. Having a liking or inclination; inclined. [pp. of AFFECT²] — **af·fect′ed·ly** *adv.* — **af·fect′ed·ness** *n.*

af·fect·ing¹ (ə·fek′ting) *adj.* Having power to move the feelings; touching; pathetic. — **af·fect′ing·ly** *adv.*

af·fect·ing² (ə·fek′ting) *adj.* *Obs.* 1. Showing love. 2. Pretending; falsely displaying.

af·fec·tion (ə·fek′shən) *n.* 1. Good disposition, as toward another; fond attachment or kind feeling: usually distinguished from *love*. 2. *Often pl.* A mental state brought about by any influence; an emotion or feeling: to play on someone's *affections*. 3. An abnormal state of the body; disease. 4. The act of affecting or influencing. 5. The state of being affected. 6. A property or attribute: Time and place are *affections* of matter. 7. *Psychol.* Conscious perception of feeling or emotion. 8. *Obs.* Inclination of mind; tendency. — **Syn.** See DISEASE, LOVE.

af·fec·tion·al (ə·fek′shən·əl) *adj.* Of or pertaining to affections. — **af·fec′tion·al·ly** *adv.*

af·fec·tion·ate (ə·fek′shən·it) *adj.* 1. Having or expressing affection; loving; fond. 2. *Obs.* Favorably inclined. — **af·fec′tion·ate·ly** *adv.* — **af·fec′tion·ate·ness** *n.*

af·fec·tive (ə·fek′tiv) *adj.* 1. Pertaining to or exciting affection; emotional. 2. *Psychol.* Pertaining to or arising from feeling or emotional reactions rather than from thought.

af·fer·ent (af′ər·ənt) *adj.* *Physiol.* Conducting inward, or toward the center: said of those nerve processes that transmit sensory stimuli from receptor organs to the central nervous system: opposed to *efferent*. [< L *afferens, -entis*, ppr. of *afferre* < *ad-* to + *ferre* to bear]

af·fet·tu·o·so (äf·fet′tōō·ō′zō) *Music adj.* Tender; soft; pathetic: designating a passage or piece to be rendered with feeling. — *adv.* Tenderly; softly. [< Ital.]

af·fi·ance (ə·fī′əns) *v.t.* **·anced, ·anc·ing** 1. To promise in marriage; betroth. 2. *Archaic* To pledge. — *n.* 1. A betrothal; pledge of faith. 2. *Obs.* Confidence. [< OF *afiancer* < *afiance* trust, confidence < *afier* to trust < Med.L *affidare* < L *ad-* to + *fidus* faithful]

af·fi·ant (ə·fī′ənt) *n.* *Law* One who makes an affidavit.

af·fi·da·vit (af′ə·dā′vit) *n.* *Law* A sworn, written declaration, made before competent authority. — **Syn.** See TESTIMONY. [< Med.L, he has stated on oath, perfect tense of *affidare*. See AFFIANCE.]

af·fil·i·ate (*v.* ə·fil′ē·āt; *n.* ə·fil′ē·it) *v.* **·at·ed, ·at·ing** *v.t.* 1. To associate or unite, as a member or branch to a larger or principal body: with *to* or *with*. 2. To join or associate (oneself): with *with*. 3. To receive as a child; adopt. 4. *Law* To fix the paternity of: with *upon*. 5. To determine relations of, as the sources or branches of a field of study. — *v.i.* 6. To associate or ally oneself: with *with*. — *n.* An affiliated person, company, etc.; associate. [< L *affiliatus*, pp. of *affiliare* to adopt < *ad-* to + *filius* son]

af·fil·i·a·tion (ə·fil′ē·ā′shən) *n.* The act of affiliating, or the state of being affiliated; association; connection.

af·fi·na·tion (af′ə·nā′shən) *n.* In sugar refining, the removal by centrifugal filtration methods of syrup or molasses from the first concentration of sugar liquors.

af·fined (ə·fīnd′) *adj.* 1. Joined by artificial ties; allied; related. 2. *Zool.* Having similar structural characters. 3. *Obs.* Under obligation because of some close relation. [< F *affiné* related < *affin* < L *affinis* + *-ED*. See AFFINITY.]

af·fin·i·ty (ə·fin′ə·tē) *n.* *pl.* **·ties** 1. A natural attraction or inclination: an *affinity* for tweed sports coats. 2. Any close relation or agreement; kinship in general; similarity: an *affinity* of colors. 3. Relationship by marriage: opposed to *consanguinity*. 4. A spiritual attraction thought to exist between certain persons, especially of opposite sexes; also, the person exerting such attraction. 5. *Biol.* Structural or physiological likeness in organisms. 6. *Chem.* The property or attraction by which differing chemical elements or groups of elements, when brought into contact, unite to form a new compound; chemical attraction. [< L *affinitas, -tatis* < *affinis* adjacent, related < *ad-* to + *finis* end] — **Syn.** 2. similarity, correspondence. See RELATIONSHIP. 4. sympathy, liking. — **Ant.** antipathy, dissimilarity.

af·firm (ə·fûrm′) *v.t.* 1. To declare or state positively; assert and maintain to be true. 2. To confirm or ratify, as a judgment or law. — *v.i.* 3. *Law* To make a formal judicial declaration, but not under oath. — **Syn.** See ASSERT. [< OF *afermer* < L *affirmare* < *ad-* to + *firmare* to make firm < *firmus* strong] — **af·firm′a·ble** *adj.* — **af·firm′a·bly** *adv.* — **af·firm′ance** *n.* — **af·firm′ant** *adj.* & *n.* — **af·firm′er** *n.*

af·fir·ma·tion (af′ər·mā′shən) *n.* 1. The act of affirming; assertion. 2. That which is affirmed or asserted. 3. A solemn declaration made before a competent officer, in place of a judicial oath. 4. Confirmation; ratification, as of laws. — **Syn.** See OATH.

af·firm·a·tive (ə·fûr′mə·tiv) *adj.* 1. Characterized by affirmation; asserting that the fact is so. 2. Positive: an *affirmative* quantity. 3. *Logic* Affirming that all or part of one class of things is included within another class: an *affirmative* proposition. Also **af·firm·a·to·ry** (ə·fûr′mə·tôr′ē, -tō′rē). — *adv.* Yes; that is so: a military usage. — *n.* 1. A word or expression of affirmation or assent; that which affirms or asserts: to answer in the *affirmative*. 2. The side in a debate that affirms the proposition debated. — **af·firm′a·tive·ly** *adv.*

af·fix (*v.* ə·fiks′; *n.* af′iks) *v.t.* 1. To fix or attach; fasten; append: to *affix* a seal to a document. 2. To connect with or lay upon, as blame, responsibility, etc. — *n.* 1. That which is attached, appended, or added. 2. *Ling.* An element that always appears with a base, stem, or root; a prefix, suffix, or infix. [< L *affixus*, pp. of *affigere* < *ad-* to + *figere* to fasten]

af·fix·ture (ə·fiks′chər) *n.* The act of affixing, or the state of being affixed; attachment.

af·fla·tus (ə·flā′təs) *n.* 1. The communication of supernatural knowledge, as in a state of exaltation: the divine *afflatus*. 2. Any creative inspiration or impulse. 3. *Obs.* A breathing or hissing. [< L, a breathing upon < *afflare* to blow on < *ad-* to + *flare* to blow]

af·flict (ə·flikt′) *v.t.* 1. To distress with continued suffering; trouble greatly. 2. *Obs.* To cast down; overthrow. [< Obs. *afflict*, adj., afflicted < L *afflictus*, pp. of *affligere* to dash against, strike down < *ad-* to + *fligere* to dash, strike] — **af·flict′er** *n.* — **af·flic′tive** *adj.* — **af·flic′tive·ly** *adv.*

af·flic·tion (ə·flik′shən) *n.* 1. The state of being afflicted; sore distress of body or mind. 2. A cause of great suffering or distress; misfortune; calamity.

af·flu·ence (af′lōō·əns) *n.* 1. A profuse or abundant supply, as of riches; wealth; abundance; opulence. 2. A flowing toward. [< F < L *affluentia* < *affluere*. See AFFLUENT.]

af·flu·ent (af′lōō·ənt) *adj.* 1. Abounding; abundant. 2. Wealthy; opulent. 3. Flowing freely; fluent. — *n.* A stream that flows into another; a tributary. [< L *affluens, -entis*, ppr. of *affluere* < *ad-* to + *fluere* to flow] — **af′flu·ent·ly** *adv.*

affluent society A group of people, often a nation, considered as a social unit that possesses or controls great wealth.

af·flux (af′luks) *n.* A flowing toward a point, as of blood to the head; also, that which flows thus; a gathering; collection. [< Med.L *affluxus*, pp. of L *affluere*. See AFFLUENT.]

af·ford (ə·fôrd′, ə·fōrd′) *v.t.* 1. To have sufficient means for; be able to meet the expense of: Can you *afford* the trip? 2. To incur without detriment; endure with advantage or triumph: He can *afford* to be merciful. **3.** To spare: I can't *afford* the time. **4.** To provide, yield, or furnish. [OE *geforthian* to further, promote] — **af·ford'a·ble** *adj.*

af·for·est (ə-fôr'ist, ə-for'ist) *v.t.* To convert (land) into forest. [< Med.L *afforestare* < *ad-* to + *foresta* forest] — **af·for·es·ta·tion** (ə-fôr'is-tā'shən, ə-for'-) *n.*

af·fran·chise (ə-fran'chīz) *v.t.* **·chised, ·chis·ing** To free from bondage, obligation, etc.; liberate. [< F *affranchiss-*, stem of *affranchir* < *à* to + *franchir* to free. See FRANCHISE.]

af·fray (ə-frā') *n.* **1.** A public brawl or fight; a disturbance of the peace. **2.** *Law* The fighting in public of two or more persons to the terror of others. — *v.t. Archaic* To frighten. [< OF *effrei, esfrei*, ult. < L *ex-* out + a Gmc. word for "peace" (cf. OHG *fridu*)]

af·fri·cate (af'ri-kit) *n. Phonet.* A sound consisting of a stop followed by the fricative release of breath at the point of contact, as *ch* in *church*. [< L *affricatus*, pp. of *affricare* < *ad-* against + *fricare* to rub]

af·fric·a·tive (ə-frik'ə-tiv) *Phonet. n.* An affricate. — *adj.* Of or pertaining to an affricate.

af·fright (ə-frīt') *Archaic v.t.* To frighten. — *n.* **1.** Sudden fear; fright. **2.** A cause of terror. [OE *āfyrhtan*]

af·front (ə-frunt') *v.t.* **1.** To insult openly; treat with insolence; offend by word or act. **2.** To confront in defiance; accost. **3.** *Archaic* To face toward. — *n.* **1.** An open insult or indignity. **2.** *Obs.* A meeting. [< OF *afronter* to strike on the forehead < LL *affrontare* to strike against < L *ad-* to + *frons* forehead] — **af·front'er** *n.* — **af·fron'tive** *adj.*
— **Syn.** See OFFEND. — **Ant.** conciliate, gratify.

af·fu·sion (ə-fyōō'zhən) *n.* A pouring on or into; a sprinkling, as in baptism. [< L *affusus*, pp. of *affundere* to pour on or into < *ad-* to + *fundere* to pour]

Afg. or **Afgh.** Afghanistan.

af·ghan (af'gən, -gan) *n.* A soft wool coverlet, knitted or crocheted, often in many-colored geometrical patterns.

Af·ghan (af'gən, -gan) *n.* **1.** A native of Afghanistan. **2.** The Pashto language. **3.** A hound originally from Afghanistan, having long, silky, thick hair, a long, narrow head with pendulous ears, and high, widely set hipbones. — *adj.* Of or pertaining to Afghanistan, its inhabitants, or their language.

af·gha·ni (af-gan'ē) *n. pl.* **·ghan·is** The monetary unit of Afghanistan, equivalent to 100 puls.

Af·ghan·i·stan (af-gan'ə-stan) An independent Kingdom of central Asia; 250,000 sq. mi.; pop. 18,293,000 (est. 1973): capital. Kabul.

a·fi·cio·na·do (ə-fē'syō-nä'dō, ə-fish'-yō-; *Sp.* ä-fē'thyō-nä'thō) *n. pl.* **·dos** (-dōz, *Sp.* -thōs) An enthusiast; devotee. [< Sp.]

a·field (ə-fēld') *adv.* **1.** In or to the field; abroad. **2.** Off the track; astray.

a·fire (ə-fīr') *adv. & adj.* On fire. [ME]

AFL or **A.F.L.** or **A.F. of L.** American Federation of Labor.

a·flame (ə-flām') *adv. & adj.* Flaming; glowing.

AFL-CIO or **A.F.L.–C.I.O.** A United States labor organization created in 1955 by merging *American Federation of Labor* and the *Congress of Industrial Organizations.*

a·float (ə-flōt') *adv. & adj.* **1.** Floating on the surface of a liquid or a body of water. **2.** Not aground or ashore; at sea. **3.** In motion or circulation: Rumors were *afloat.* **4.** Overflowed; flooded, as the deck of a ship. **5.** Adrift; unfixed.

a·flut·ter (ə-flut'ər) *adj. & adv.* In a flutter.

A.F.M. American Federation of Musicians.

a·foot (ə-fŏŏt') *adv.* **1.** On foot. **2.** In motion or progress; on the move; astir: There's dirty work *afoot.* [ME *on fot*]

a·fore (ə-fôr', ə-fōr') *adv., prep., & conj. Archaic & Dial.* Before. [OE *onforan*, blended with *æt-foran* before. See ON, AT, and FORE.]

a·fore·men·tioned (ə-fôr'men'shənd, ə-fōr'-) *adj.* Mentioned previously.

a·fore·said (ə-fôr'sed', ə-fōr'-) *adj.* Mentioned before.

a·fore·thought (ə-fôr'thôt', ə-fōr'-) *adj.* Intended beforehand; premeditated: now chiefly in the phrase *malice aforethought.* — *n. Rare* Premeditation.

a·fore·time (ə-fôr'tīm', ə-fōr'-) *adv.* At a previous time.

a for·ti·o·ri (ā fôr'shē-ôr'ī, ā fôr'shē-ō'rī) *Latin* By a stronger reason; all the more.

a·foul (ə-foul') *adv. & adj.* In entanglement or collision; entangled. — **to run** (or **fall**) **afoul of** To become entangled with; get into difficulties with.

Afr. Africa; African.

a·fraid (ə-frād') *adj.* Filled with fear or apprehension; apprehensive; fearful: often used to soften an unpleasant statement: I'm *afraid* you're wrong. [Orig. pp. of AFFRAY]

A-frame (ā'frām') *n.* A structural framework in the form of a triangle or an A. — *adj.* Of or pertaining to such a framework.

a·fresh (ə-fresh') *adv.* Once more; anew; again.

Af·ri·ca (af'ri-kə) The second largest continent, located in the Eastern Hemisphere south of Europe and joined to Asia by the Sinai peninsula; 11,710,000 sq. mi.; pop. 345 million (UN est. 1969).

Af·ri·can (af'ri-kən) *adj.* Of or pertaining to Africa, or its inhabitants. — *n.* **1.** A native or naturalized inhabitant of Africa. **2.** A member of one of the African peoples; Negro.

Af·ri·can·i·za·tion (af'ri-kən-i-zā'shən) *n.* The process of becoming African in character, or of coming under the influence or domination of Africans, especially black Africans. Also *Brit.* **Af'ri·can·i·sa'tion.**

African lily A greenhouse potted plant (*Agapanthus africanus*) from Africa, with blue flowers.

African violet Any of a genus (*Saintpaulia*) of tropical African perennial herbs with purple, pink, or white flowers.

Af·ri·kaans (af'ri-käns', -känz') *n.* A South African language that developed from the speech of the 17th-century Dutch settlers in this region: also called *Cape Dutch, South African Dutch, Taal.*

Af·ri·ka·ner (af'ri-kä'nər) *n.* An Afrikaans-speaking South African of Dutch ancestry. Also **Af'ri·kan'der** (-kan'dər).

Af·ro (af'rō) *n. pl.* **·ros** A hairdo in which the hair is frizzed or teased to make it stick out stiffly in all directions and then trimmed to resemble a sphere.

Afro- *combining form* Africa; African.

Af·ro-A·mer·i·can (af'rō-ə-mer'ə-kən) *adj.* Of or pertaining to Americans of black African descent. — *n.* An Afro-American person.

AFROTC Air Force Reserve Officers Training Corps.

aft (aft, äft) *Naut. adj.* Of or near the rear or stern of a vessel. — *adv.* At, toward, or near the rear; astern. [OE *æftan* behind]

A.F.T. American Federation of Teachers.

af·ter (af'tər, äf'-) *prep.* **1.** In the rear of; farther back than; following: He came *after* me. **2.** In search or pursuit of: Strive *after* wisdom. **3.** In relation to; concerning: to inquire *after* one's health. **4.** Subsequent to; at a later period than: His will was read *after* his death. **5.** In succession to; following repeatedly: day *after* day. **6.** As a result of; subsequently and because of: *After* their quarrel they separated. **7.** Notwithstanding; subsequently and in spite of: *After* the best endeavors, one may fail. **8.** Next below in order or importance: *after* the king in power. **9.** According to the nature, wishes, or customs of; in conformity with: a man *after* my own heart. **10.** In imitation of; in the manner of: a painting *after* Vermeer. **11.** In honor, remembrance, or observance of: named *after* Lincoln. **12.** *U.S.* Of time by the clock, past. — *adv.* **1.** In the rear; behind: His attendants followed *after.* **2.** At a later time; subsequently: three months *after.* — *adj.* **1.** Following in time or place; later; subsequent: In *after* years they lived as friends. **2.** *Naut.* Toward the stern; farther aft. — *conj.* Following the time that: *After* I went home, I went to bed. Abbr. *a.* [OE *æfter* behind]
After may appear as a combining form meaning:
1. Following in place, order, or time:

after-acquired	after-designed	after-specified
afterages	after-dinner	after-supper
afterdays	after-mentioned	after-written
after-described	after-named	afteryears

2. Secondary; following the main occurrence:

afterattack	aftercrop	aftermass	afterstorm
afterclause	aftergrowth	aftershock	aftertreatment

3. Following not at once; eventual; after delay:

afterfame	afterglory	afterpenitence	afterreckoning

after all 1. When everything is taken into consideration; on the whole. **2.** In the long run.

af·ter·birth (af'tər-bûrth', äf'-) *n.* The placenta and fetal membranes expelled from the mammalian uterus after parturition: also called *secundines.*

af·ter·bod·y (af'tər-bod'ē, äf'-) *n. Aerospace* A section of a rocket or missile that continues to trail the nose cone or satellite from which it was separated in flight.

af·ter·brain (af'tər-brān', äf'-) *n. Anat.* The metencephalon.

af·ter·burn·er (af'tər-bûr'nər, äf'-) *n. Aeron.* **1.** A device located on a tail pipe using hot exhaust gases to inject extra fuel into the exhaust system of a jet engine as a means of increasing the thrust: also called *augmenter.* **2.** An auxiliary device used in internal-combustion engines and incinerators for burning undesirable exhaust gases produced during the original combustion.

af·ter·care (af'tər-kâr', äf'-) *n.* Care or treatment of convalescents, especially after a surgical operation.

af·ter·cool·er (af'tər-kōō'lər, äf'-) *n. Aeron.* A radiator designed to cool the fuel mixture in the supercharging system of a jet airplane flying at extreme altitudes.

af·ter·damp (af'tər-damp', äf'-) *n. Mining* A mixture of gases, chiefly nitrogen and carbon dioxide, with traces of free hydrogen and carbon monoxide, resulting from a fire or explosion in a mine and dangerous to breathe.

af·ter·deck (af'tər-dek', äf'-) *n. Naut.* That part of a deck aft of amidships.

---

af·ter·ef·fect (af'tər-ə-fekt', äf'-) *n.* **1.** An effect succeeding its cause after an interval. **2.** *Med.* A result following the initial effects of a drug, X-rays, etc.

af·ter·glow (af'tər-glō', äf'-) *n.* **1.** A glow after a light has disappeared, as in metals cooling after being heated to incandescence or in the western sky after sunset. **2.** The luminosity of a rarefied gas after the passage of an electric charge through it. **3.** An agreeable feeling occurring after a pleasant or profitable experience.

af·ter·im·age (af'tər-im'ij, äf'-) *n. Physiol.* **1.** The persistence or renewal of the i nage of an object appearing after the direct stimulation has been withdrawn from the retina: also called *photogene*. **2.** A similar effect of other senses.

af·ter·life (af'tər-lif', äf'-) *n.* **1.** Life after death. **2.** The period of life following a particular time or event.

af·ter·math (af'tər-math, äf'-) *n.* **1.** Results; consequences, especially ill consequences. **2.** *Agric.* The second grass crop of the season; a second mowing. [< AFTER + MATH¹]

af·ter·most (af'tər-mōst, äf'-) *adj.* **1.** *Naut.* Nearest the stern: also **aft'most. 2.** Last.

af·ter·noon (af'tər-nōon', äf'-) *n.* **1.** The part of the day between noon and sunset. **2.** The closing part: the *afternoon* of life. — *adj.* Of, for, or occurring in the afternoon: *afternoon* tea. *Abbr. a.*

af·ter·pains (af'tər-pānz', äf'-) *n.pl.* The pains succeeding childbirth, caused by contraction of the womb.

af·ter·peak (af'tər-pēk', äf'-) *n. Naut.* The extreme after part of a vessel's hold, toward the sternpost.

af·ter·piece (af'tər-pēs', äf'-) *n.* **1.** A farce or other short piece after a play. **2.** *Naut.* The heel of a rudder.

af·ter·sen·sa·tion (af'tər-sen-sā'shən, äf'-) *n. Physiol.* An afterimage.

af·ter·shaft (af'tər-shaft', äf'tər-shäft') *n. Ornithol.* A secondary shaft of the feather in many birds, springing from near the junction of the quill with the rachis. For illustration see FEATHER.

af·ter·taste (af'tər-tāst', äf'-) *n.* A taste persisting in the mouth, as after a meal.

af·ter·thought (af'tər-thôt', äf'-) *n.* **1.** An expedient, explanation, etc., that occurs to one after decision or action. **2.** A subsequent or second thought.

af·ter·time (af'tər-tīm', äf'-) *n.* Time following the present; the future.

af·ter·ward (af'tər-wərd, äf'-) *adv.* In time following; subsequently. Also **af'ter·wards.** [OE æfterweard]

af·ter·world (af'tər-wûrld', äf'-) *n.* A future world, thought of as existing after death.

af·to·sa (af-tō'sə) *n. SW U.S.* Foot-and-mouth disease. [< Sp., fem., aphthous]

AFTRA or **A.F.T.R.A.** American Federation of Television and Radio Artists.

ag- Assimilated var. of AD-.

Ag *Chem.* Silver (L *argentum*).

Ag. August.

AG Adjutant General.

A.G. 1. Attorney General. **2.** Joint-stock company (G *Aktiengesellschaft*).

a·ga (ä'gə) *n.* An officer of high military or civil rank in Moslem countries: also spelled *agha*. [< Turkish]

A·ga·dir (ä'gə-dir', ag'ə-) A port city in SW Morocco; pop. 16,695 (1960).

a·gain (ə-gen', *esp. Brit.* ə-gān') *adv.* **1.** Another time; once more; anew: to bring to life *again*. **2.** Once repeated: half as much *again*. **3.** To the same place or over the same course; back, as in a previous condition: Here we are *again!* **4.** Further; moreover: *Again*, it is not at all certain. **5.** On the other hand: I might, and *again* I might not. **6.** *Archaic* In reply; in return; back: The walls rang *again.* — **again and again** Repeatedly. [OE *ongegn, ongēan*]

a·gainst (ə-genst', *esp. Brit.* ə-gänst') *prep.* **1.** In the opposite direction to; counter to: to walk *against* the wind. **2.** In contact or collision with; upon: dashed *against* the rocks. **3.** In contact with and pressing upon: to lean *against* a wall. **4.** In opposition to; contrary to: *against* the law. **5.** In contrast or comparison with: *against* the background of the sky. **6.** In preparation for: to hoard wealth *against* old age. **7.** In hostility to: to legislate *against* minorities. **8.** In resistance to: *against* aggression. **9.** To the debit of: Charge it *against* my account. **10.** Directly opposite; facing: now usually *over against*: Stand over *against* me. [OE *ongegn* + *-es*, adverbial genitive suffix + inorganic *-t*]

A·ga Khan (ä'gə kän') A hereditary Moslem title passing to the heads of families descended from Ali.
— **Aga Khan III**, 1877–1957, leader of Ismailian Moslems 1885–1957.

a·gal·loch (ə-gal'ək, ag'ə-lok) *n.* The fragrant wood of a tree (*Aquilaria agallocha*) of Indochina and neighboring regions, the aloes of the Scriptures: also called *aloes, eaglewood, lignaloes.* Also **a·gal·wood** (ä'gəl-wŏŏd', ag'əl-). [< NL *agallochum* < Gk. *agallochon* bitter aloe]

ag·a·ma (ag'ə-mə) *n.* A terrestrial lizard (family *Agamidae*) of the tropical regions of the Old World.

Ag·a·mem·non (ag'ə-mem'non, -nən) In Greek legend, king of Mycenae; brother of Menelaus and father of Orestes, Elec-

tra, and Iphigenia; chief of the Greek army in the Trojan War. See ORESTES.

a·gam·ic (ə-gam'ik) *adj.* **1.** *Biol.* **a** Without the union of the two sexes, as reproduction in certain insects, etc. **b** Capable of development without impregnation. **2.** *Bot.* Cryptogamic. Also **ag·a·mous** (ag'ə-məs). [< Gk. *agamos* unmarried < *a-* without + *gamos* marriage] — **a·gam'i·cal·ly** *adv.*

ag·a·mo·gen·e·sis (ag'ə-mō-jen'ə-sis) *n. Biol.* Reproduction without the union of opposite sexual elements, as by buds or by cell division. [< NL < Gk. *agamos* unmarried + GENESIS] — **ag'a·mo·ge·net'ic** (-jə-net'ik) *adj.*

A·ga·ña (ä-gä'nyä) The capital of Guam, on the western coast; pop. 2,131 (est. 1970).

ag·a·pan·thus (ag'ə-pan'thəs) *n.* Any of a genus (*Agapanthus*) of South African plants of the lily family bearing umbels of blue or white flowers. [< NL < Gk. *agapē* love + *anthos* flower]

a·gape¹ (ə-gāp', ə-gap') *adv. & adj.* In a gaping state; gaping.

ag·a·pe² (ä-gä'pā) *n. pl.* **·pae** (-pē) **1.** The social meal or love feast of the primitive Christians that usually accompanied the Eucharist. **2.** Love (def. 7). [< Gk. *agapē* love]

a·gar-a·gar (ä'gär-ä'gär, ä'gər-, ä'gär-, ag'ər-) *n.* A gelatinous substance obtained from certain seaweeds, used as a laxative and as a food medium in the artificial cultivation of bacteria. Also **a/gar.** [< Malay]

ag·a·ric (ag'ə-rik, ə-gar'ik) *n.* **1.** A fungus of the mushroom group (order *Agaricales*), especially the common edible variety, *Agaricus campestris.* **2.** The dried fruit body of certain mushrooms. [< L *agaricum* < Gk. *agarikon* < *Agaria*, a town in Sarmatia] — **a·gar·i·ca·ceous** (ə-gar'i-kā'shəs) *adj.*

Ag·as·siz (ag'ə-sē, *Fr.* ä·gà·sē'), **Alexander**, 1835–1910, U.S. zoologist born in Switzerland; son of (**Jean**) **Louis** (**Rodolphe**), 1807–73, U.S. naturalist born in Switzerland.

ag·ate (ag'it) *n.* **1.** A variegated waxy quartz or chalcedony, in which the colors are usually in bands. **2.** A child's playing marble. **3.** *Printing* A size of type, 5½ points, between pearl and nonpareil. **4.** *Obs.* A tiny person. [< F < L *achates* < Gk. *achatēs*, < *Achátēs*, a river in Sicily]

agate line *U.S.* A measure of printed space 1 column wide and 1/14 of an inch high, by which advertising space in newspapers and magazines is sold.

ag·ate·ware (ag'it-wâr') *n.* **1.** Pottery veined and mottled to resemble agate. **2.** Steel or iron kitchenware enameled to resemble agate.

ag·a·tho·de·mon (ag'ə-thō-dē'mən) *n.* A benevolent spirit; a good genius: opposed to *cacodemon.* [< Gk. *agathodaimōn* < *agathos* good + *daimōn* spirit]

ag·a·tize (ag'ə-tīz) *v.t.* **·tized, ·tiz·ing** To make into or cause to resemble agate or agateware.

à gauche (à gōsh') *French* To or on the left.

a·ga·ve (ə-gä'vē) *n.* Any plant of a large genus (*Agave*) of the amaryllis family, of the southern United States, Mexico, etc., including the century plant. [< NL < Gk. *Agauē*, a personal name, orig. fem. of *agauōs* illustrious, noble]

a·gaze (ə-gāz') *adv.* Gazing.

agcy. Agency.

age (āj) *n.* **1.** The period of existence of a person, thing, nation, etc., particularly as measured by the time past: children of any *age.* **2.** The entire span of life of any being or thing: The traditional *age* of man is 70 years. **3.** The time of life marked by maturity and discretion; adulthood; especially, that age when full civil rights or certain personal rights can be legally exercised, usually 18 or 21 years: chiefly in the phrases *of age, under age*: also called *legal age.* **4.** Any period of life which, by reason of natural development or custom, fits or unfits for anything: the *age* of reason. **5.** Any distinct stage of life: It would not be wise at his *age.* **6.** The closing period of life; the state of being old: the wisdom of *age.* **7.** Any great period of time in the history of man, of the earth, etc., marked off by certain distinctive features or characters: the Elizabethan *age*; the *age* of mammals. **8.** The people alive at a given time; a generation: *ages* yet unborn. **9.** *Informal* A long time: He has been gone an *age.* — **achievement age** *Psychol.* A measure of performance on an achievement test, expressed as an empirically determined average age for the same performance. *Abbr. AA, A.A.* — **chronological age** *Psychol.* The actual age of an individual, measured from birth. *Abbr. CA, C.A.* — **mental age** *Psychol.* The level of mental development as measured against the chronological age at which this level is reached by the average child. *Abbr. MA, M.A.* — *v.* **aged, ag·ing** or **age·ing** *v.t.* **1.** To make or cause to grow mature or old. — *v.i.* **2.** To assume or show some characteristics of age; ripen: Tobacco *ages* in storing. [< OF *aage* < L *aetas* age, a span of life]

-age *suffix of nouns* **1.** Collection or aggregate of: *leafage.* **2.** Condition, office, service, or other relation or connection of: *haulage.* [< OF < L *-aticum*, neut. adj. suffix]

a·ged (ä'jid *for defs. 1, 2, 4*; äjd *for def. 3*) *adj.* **1.** Advanced in years; old. **2.** Of, like, or characteristic of old age. **3.** Of or at the age of: a child, *aged* six. **4.** *Geol.* Nearing reduction to base level. — **Syn.** See OLD. — **the aged** Those who are old. — **a'ged·ly** *adv.* — **a'ged·ness** *n.*

a·gee (ə-jē') See AJEE.

age·ing (ā′jing) See AGING.

age·less (āj′lis) *adj.* 1. Not seeming to grow old. 2. Having no limits of duration; eternal.

age·long (āj′lông′, -long′) *adj.* Lasting for a long time.

a·gen·cy (ā′jən-sē) *n. pl.* ·cies 1. Active power or operation; activity: human *agency.* 2. Means; instrumentality: by the *agency* of mediators. 3. A firm or establishment where business is done for others: an employment *agency.* 4. The office or function of an agent. [< L *agentia* < *agere* to do]

a·gen·da (ə-jen′də) *n. pl. of* **a·gen·dum** (ə-jen′dəm) 1. (*usually construed as sing.*) A list of things to be done; especially, a program of business to be transacted or papers to be read at a meeting. 2. *Eccl.* Matters of ethical or liturgical practice, as distinguished from *credenda*, matters of faith. [< L, neut. pl. gerundive of *agere* to do]
♦ *Agenda*, originally the plural of the Latin *agendum*, now has a regular English plural *agendas*, as, the *agendas* of both meetings.

a·gen·e·sis (ə-jen′ə-sis) *n.* 1. The absence or imperfect development of any part of the body. 2. Sexual sterility or impotence. Also **ag·e·ne·sia** (aj′ə-nē′zhə, -zhē-ə). [< A-⁴ without + GENESIS]

age norm *Psychol.* The average score made on a standard set of tests by a random group of children of given age; the score typical for a child of stated age.

a·gent (ā′jənt) *n.* 1. One who or that which acts or has power to act; an efficient cause of anything; actor; doer. 2. One who acts for or by the authority of a government, company, person, etc.; a representative; factor. 3. Any force, substance, or organism that causes a material change: a chemical *agent.* 4. A means by which something is done; instrument. 5. *Informal* A traveling salesman or canvasser. — Syn. See DOER. — *adj. Obs.* Acting. [< L *agens, agentis*, ppr. of *agere* to do]

a·gen·tial (ā-jen′shəl) *adj.* Of or pertaining to an agent or agency.

a·gent pro·vo·ca·teur (à-zhän′ prô-vô-kà-tœr′) *pl.* **a·gents pro·vo·ca·teurs** (à-zhän′ prô-vô-kà-tœr′) *French* A secret agent planted in a trade union, political party, etc., to incite actions or declarations that will incur punishment.

age of consent *Law* The age at which a girl may legally consent to sexual relations. See STATUTORY RAPE.

age of mammals See CENOZOIC.

ag·e·ra·tum (aj′ə-rā′təm, ə-jer′ə-təm) *n.* 1. One of a large genus (*Ageratum*) of tropical American herbs of the composite family with blue or white flowers in small heads. 2. Any of several plants having similar heads of blue flowers. [< NL < Gk. *agēraton*, a kind of plant < *agēratos* ageless < *a-* not + *gēras* old age]

A·ges·i·la·us (ə-jes′ə-lā′əs), 444?–360 B.C., Spartan king.

ag·ger (aj′ər) *n.* A mound or earthwork; especially, in ancient Rome, the rampart of a fortified camp. [< L]

Ag·ge·us (ə-gē′us) The Douai Bible name for HAGGAI.

ag·glom·er·ate (ə-glom′ə-rāt; *for adj. & n., also* -ər-it) *v.t. & v.i.* ·at·ed, ·at·ing To gather, form, or grow into a ball or rounded mass. — *adj.* Gathered into a mass or heap; clustered densely. — Syn. See AGGREGATE. — *n.* 1. A heap or mass of things thrown together indiscriminately. 2. *Geol.* An unstratified mass of compacted volcanic debris with fragments of all sizes. [< L *agglomeratus*, pp. of *agglomerare* < *ad-* to + *glomerare* to gather into a ball < *glomus* ball] — **ag·glom′er·a·tive** *adj.*

ag·glom·er·a·tion (ə-glom′ə-rā′shən) *n.* 1. The process of agglomerating. 2. The state or condition of being agglomerated. 3. A jumbled heap or mass.

ag·glu·ti·nant (ə-glōō′tə-nənt) *adj.* Tending to cause adhesion; uniting. — *n.* Any sticky substance that causes bodies to adhere together.

ag·glu·ti·nate (ə-glōō′tə-nāt; *for adj., also* -nit) *v.t. & v.i.* ·nat·ed, ·nat·ing 1. To unite, as with glue; join by adhesion. 2. *Ling.* To form (words) by agglutination. 3. *Physiol.* To mass together, as living cells or bacteria, by agglutination. — *adj.* Joined by adhesion. [< L *agglutinatus*, pp. of *agglutinare* to glue to < *ad-* to + *glutinare* < *gluten* glue]

ag·glu·ti·na·tion (ə-glōō′tə-nā′shən) *n.* 1. Adhesion of distinct parts; also, a mass formed by adhesion. 2. *Ling.* A process of word formation in which the constituent meaningful elements (morphemes) retain their characteristic forms, rather than coalescing or blending with surrounding elements. 3. *Physiol.* The clumping together of living cells or bacteria, caused by an antibody.

ag·glu·ti·na·tive (ə-glōō′tə-nā′tiv) *adj.* 1. Tending toward, pertaining to, or characterized by agglutination. 2. *Ling.* Denoting a language in which words are formed predominantly by agglutination.

ag·glu·ti·nin (ə-glōō′tə-nin) *n. Biochem.* An antibody arising in blood serum and causing the red corpuscles or any bacteria it touches to coalesce into floccules.

ag·glu·tin·o·gen (ag′lōō-tin′ə-jən) *n. Med.* A bacterial antigen whose injection into an animal body causes the formation of agglutinins.

ag·grade (ə-grād′) *v.t.* ·grad·ed, ·grad·ing *Geol.* To add to or raise, as the bed of a river by the deposition of silt. [< AD- + GRADE] — **ag·gra·da·tion** (ag′rə-dā′shən) *n.*

ag·gran·dize (ə-gran′dīz, ag′rən-dīz) *v.t.* ·dized, ·diz·ing 1. To make great or greater; enlarge or intensify. 2. To increase the power, rank, or wealth of: to *aggrandize* oneself. 3. To make appear greater; exalt. [< F *agrandiss-*, stem of *agrandir* < L *ad-* to + *grandire* to make great] — **ag·gran·dize·ment** (ə-gran′diz-mənt) *n.* — **ag·gran′diz·er** *n.*

ag·gra·vate (ag′rə-vāt) *v.t.* ·vat·ed, ·vat·ing 1. To make worse; intensify, as an illness. 2. To make heavier or more burdensome, as a duty. 3. *Informal* To provoke or exasperate; arouse to anger. [< L *aggravatus*, pp. of *aggravare* to make heavy or burdensome < *ad-* to + *gravare* to make heavy < *gravis* heavy] — **ag′gra·vat′ing** *adj.* — **ag′gra·vat′ing·ly** *adv.* — **ag′gra·va′tive** *adj.*
— Syn. 1. heighten, magnify. 3. See IRRITATE. — Ant. alleviate, assuage, reduce, lessen.

ag·gra·va·tion (ag′rə-vā′shən) *n.* 1. A making, or the fact of being made, heavier or worse. 2. Some extrinsic circumstance considered as increasing the atrocity of a crime. 3. *Informal* Exasperation; irritation.

ag·gre·gate (*v.* ag′rə-gāt; *adj. & n.* -git) *v.t.* ·gat·ed, ·gat·ing 1. To bring or gather together, as into a mass, sum, or body; collect; mass. 2. To amount to; form a total of. — *adj.* 1. Collected into a sum or mass; gathered into a whole; total; collective. 2. *Bot.* Clustered or collected together, as flowers gathered into a head. 3. *Geol.* Composed of distinct minerals separable by mechanical means, as granite. — *n.* 1. The entire number, mass, or quantity of anything; amount; total. 2. Material for making concrete. — **in the aggregate** Collectively; as a whole. [< L *aggregatus*, pp. of *aggregare*, lit., to bring to the flock < *ad-* to + *gregare* to collect < *grex* flock] — **ag′gre·ga′tive** *adj.* — **ag′gre·ga′tor** *n.*
— Syn. (adj.) 1. *Aggregate, agglomerate*, and *conglomerate* mean gathered together in a mass. *Aggregate* is applied to a mass that is closely compacted (or thought of as a whole) without losing the identity of its parts. *Agglomerate* suggests that the parts are heterogeneous, loosely compacted, or brought together by chance. *Conglomerate* implies that the parts are widely disparate, even incongruous, or that they are brought together from widely scattered regions.

ag·gre·ga·tion (ag′rə-gā′shən) *n.* 1. The act of aggregating, or the state of being aggregated. 2. A collection into a whole; aggregate.

ag·gress (ə-gres′) *v.i.* To undertake an attack; begin a quarrel. [< L *aggressus*, pp. of *aggredi* to approach, attack < *ad-* to + *gradi* to step, go < *gradus* a step]

ag·gres·sion (ə-gresh′ən) *n.* 1. An unprovoked attack; encroachment, as by one nation upon the territory of another. 2. Habitual aggressive action or practices. 3. *Psychoanal.* A tendency toward hostile action, generally associated with emotional states.
— Syn. 1. assault, intrusion, invasion, trespass. — Ant. defense, resistance.

ag·gres·sive (ə-gres′iv) *adj.* 1. Of or characterized by aggression or attack. 2. Disposed to vigorous activity; assertive. — **ag·gres′sive·ly** *adv.* — **ag·gres′sive·ness** *n.*

ag·gres·sor (ə-gres′ər) *n.* One who commits an aggression or begins a quarrel.

ag·grieve (ə-grēv′) *v.t.* ·grieved, ·griev·ing 1. To cause sorrow to; distress or afflict. 2. To give cause for just complaint, as by injustice. [< OF *agrever* < L *aggravare*]
— Syn. wrong, injure, oppress, ill-treat. Compare AFFLICT.

ag·grieved (ə-grēvd′) *adj.* 1. Feeling sorrow or distress. 2. Subjected to ill-treatment; wronged. 3. *Law* Injured by legal decision infringing upon one's rights.

a·gha (ä′gə) See AGA.

a·ghast (ə-gast′, ə-gäst′) *adj.* Struck dumb with horror. [Pp. of ME *agasten* to frighten < OE *ā* + *gǣstan* to terrify; spelling infl. by *ghost*]

ag·ile (aj′əl, aj′īl) *adj.* Able to move or act quickly and easily; active; nimble. — Syn. See NIMBLE. [< F < L *agilis* < *agere* to do, move] — **ag′ile·ly** *adv.*

a·gil·i·ty (ə-jil′ə-tē) *n.* Quickness and readiness in movement; nimbleness. [< F *agilité* < L *agilitas* < *agilis.* See AGILE.]

Ag·in·court (aj′in-kôrt, -kōrt) A village in northern France; site of an English victory over the French, 1415.

ag·ing (ā′jing) *n.* 1. The process of growing mature or old. 2. The effect of age or time on the appearance or properties of a thing. 3. Any artificial process for producing the effects or changes of age. Also, *Brit.*, *ageing.*

ag·i·o (aj′ē-ō) *n. pl.* **ag·i·os** 1. The premium payable for the exchange of one kind or quality of money into another; exchange premium. 2. An allowance for depreciation of coin by wear. [< Ital. *aggio* exchange]

ag·i·o·tage (aj′ē-ə-tij) *n.* 1. Brokerage; speculation in stocks. 2. Exchange business.

a·gist (ə-jist′) *v.t. Law* 1. To feed and care for, as horses or cattle, at a fixed rate. 2. To assess, as land or its owner, for a public purpose. [< OF *agister* < *a-* to (< L *ad-*) + *gister* to lodge, ult. < L *jacere* to lie] — **a·gist′ment** *n.*

ag·i·tate (aj'ə·tāt) v. **·tat·ed, ·tat·ing** v.t. **1.** To disturb or shake irregularly: The wind *agitates* the sea. **2.** To set or keep moving. **3.** To excite or stir up; perturb: Sorrow *agitates* the heart. **4.** To keep alive interest in; keep before the public, as a controversial issue. **5.** *Archaic* To revolve in the mind; plan. — v.i. **6.** To excite, or endeavor to excite, public interest and action: to *agitate* for reform. [< L *agitatus*, pp. of *agitare* to set in motion, freq. of *agere* to move]

ag·i·ta·tion (aj'ə·tā'shən) n. **1.** Violent motion; commotion. **2.** Strong emotional disturbance; extreme nervousness. **3.** The exciting of public interest and feeling on a controversial matter.

a·gi·ta·to (ä'jē·tä'tō) *Music adj.* Stirring; restless; agitated. — adv. Restlessly; agitatedly. [< Ital.]

ag·i·ta·tor (aj'ə·tā'tər) n. One who or that which agitates; especially, one who persists in political or social agitation.

A·gla·ia (ə·glā'ə) One of the three Graces.

a·gleam (ə·glēm') adv. & adj. Bright; gleaming.

ag·let (ag'lit) n. **1.** A metal sheath at the end of a lace or ribbon to facilitate threading. **2.** Any ornamental pendant resembling this. Also spelled *aiglet*. [< F *aiguillette*, dim. of *aiguille* needle, ult. < L *acus*]

a·gley (ə·glē', ə·gli') adv. *Scot.* Awry. Also **a·glee** (ə·glē').

a·glit·ter (ə·glit'ər) adv. & adj. Glittering.

a·glow (ə·glō') adv. & adj. In a glow; glowing.

A.G.M.A. American Guild of Musical Artists.

ag·mi·nate (ag'mə·nit, -nāt) adj. Grouped in clusters. Also **ag'mi·nat'ed.** [< L *agmen, agminis* troop, crowd + -ATE¹]

ag·nail (ag'nāl) n. A hangnail (which see). [OE *angnægl* < *ange* painful + *nægl* nail]

ag·nate (ag'nāt) adj. **1.** Related on the male or the father's side. **2.** Akin; similar. — n. A relative in the male line only. Compare COGNATE, ENATE. [< F *agnat* < L *agnatus* a relation (on the father's side), orig. pp. of *agnasci* < *ad-* in addition to + *nasci* to be born] — **ag·nat·ic** (ag·nat'ik) adj. — **ag·nat'i·cal·ly** adv. — *Scot.* **ag·na'tion** (ag·nā'shən) n.

Ag·ni (ug'nē, ag'nē) In Hindu mythology, the god of fire in the Vedas. Also **Ag'nis.** [< Skt.]

ag·nize (ag·nīz') v.t. **·nized, ·niz·ing** *Archaic* To acknowledge; recognize. [< L *agnoscere* to acknowledge < *ad-* to + *gnoscere* to get to know; on analogy with *recognize*]

ag·no·men (ag·nō'mən) n. pl. **ag·nom·i·na** (ag·nom'ə·nə) **1.** In ancient Rome, an additional name, usually given in honor of some special achievement. **2.** A nickname. — **Syn.** See NICKNAME. [< L < *ad-* to + (g)*nomen* name] — **ag·nom'i·nal** adj.

ag·nos·tic (ag·nos'tik) adj. Of or pertaining to agnostics or their theory; professing ignorance of anything beyond material phenomena. — n. One who holds the theory of agnosticism. — **Syn.** See SKEPTIC. [< Gk. *agnōstos* unknowing, unknown < *a-* not + *gignōskein* to know]

ag·nos·ti·cism (ag·nos'tə·siz'əm) n. **1.** The doctrine of nescience; especially, the philosophical theory that man cannot know first truths, ultimate causes, or anything beyond material phenomena. **2.** *Theol.* The doctrine that God is unknown and unknowable: distinguished from *atheism.*

Ag·nus De·i (ag'nəs dē'ī, dä'ē) **1.** *Eccl.* A figure of a lamb, as an emblem of Christ, often bearing a cross and banner. **2.** In the Roman Catholic Church, a medallion or cake of wax stamped with this emblem and blessed by the Pope. **3.** *Eccl.* **a** A Eucharistic prayer beginning with the words *Agnus Dei*. **b** A translation of this prayer, beginning "O Lamb of God." **c** A musical setting for this prayer. [< LL, Lamb of God. See *John* i 29.]

a·go (ə·gō') adv. In the past; since: long *ago*. — adj. Gone by; past: a year *ago*. [OE *āgān* past, gone away]

a·gog (ə·gog') adv. & adj. In a state of eager curiosity; excited; expectant. [< MF *en gogues* in a merry mood]

-agogue *combining form* Leading, promoting, or inciting: *demagogue, pedagogue.* Also **-agog.** [< Gk. *agōgos* leading < *agein* to lead]

ag·on (ag'on, -on) n. pl. **a·go·nes** (ə·gō'nēz) **1.** One of the great national game festivals of ancient Greece. **2.** In ancient Greek drama, the conflict between the principal characters. [< Gk. *agōn* assembly, contest]

a·gone (ə·gôn', ə·gon') adj. & adv. *Archaic* Ago.

a·gon·ic (ə·gon'ik) adj. Having or forming no angle. [< Gk. *agōnos* < *a-* without + *gōnia* angle]

agonic line *Geog.* One of several lines on the earth's surface on which the direction of the magnetic needle is truly north and south; a line of no magnetic declination.

ag·o·nis·tic (ag'ə·nis'tik) adj. **1.** Striving to defeat in argument; polemic. **2.** Aiming at effect; strained. **3.** Pertaining to an agon. Also **ag'o·nis'ti·cal.** — **ag'o·nis'ti·cal·ly** adv.

ag·o·nize (ag'ə·nīz) v. **·nized, ·niz·ing** v.i. **1.** To be in or suffer extreme pain or anguish. **2.** To make convulsive efforts, as in wrestling; strive. — v.t. **3.** To subject to agony; torture. [< F *agoniser* < Med.L *agonizare* < Gk. *agōnizesthai* to contend, strive < *agōn* contest]

ag·o·ny (ag'ə·nē) n. pl. **·nies 1.** Intense suffering of body or mind; anguish. **2.** Any intense or sudden emotion. **3.** The suffering or struggle that precedes death. **4.** Violent or earnest striving. [< L *agonia* < Gk. *agōnia* < *agōn* contest] — **Syn. 1.** pain, torture, torment, passion, misery.

ag·o·ra (ag'ər·ə) n. pl. **ag·o·rae** (-ər·ē) or **ag·o·ras 1.** In ancient Greece, a popular assembly for political or other purposes. **2.** A place of popular assembly, especially the market place. [< Gk.]

a·gou·ti (ə·gōō'tē) n. pl. **·tis** or **·ties 1.** A slender-limbed, tropical American rodent (genus *Dasyprocta*) of grizzly color, with three hind toes. **2.** An animal having fur like that of the agouti. **3.** The grizzly color common to many rodents. Also **a·gou'ty.** [< F < Sp. *aguti* < Tupi]

AGOUTI (*def.* 1)
(About 20 inches long)

agr. Agricultural; agriculture; agriculturist.

A·gra (ä'grä, ä'grə) **1.** A division of western Uttar Pradesh, India; 8,646 sq. mi.; pop. about 5,330,000. **2.** A district of Agra division; 1,861 sq. mi.; pop. about 1,300,000. **3.** A city, capital of the division and the district, on the Jumna river; site of the Taj Mahal; pop. 509,108 (1961).

a·graffe (ə·graf') n. **1.** A hook or clasp; especially, an ornamental clasp used on armor or for fastening rich clothing. **2.** A builder's cramp iron. Also **a·grafe'.** [< F]

A·gram (ä'gräm) The German name for ZAGREB.

a·gran·u·lo·cy·to·sis (ə·gran'yōō·lō'sī·tō'sis) n. *Pathol.* A disease characterized by the loss, or nearly complete absence, of granular leucocytes from the blood or bone marrow.

a·gra·pha (ag'rə·fə) n.pl. *Often cap.* The sayings attributed to Jesus, but not found in the Bible. [< Gk., neut. pl. of *agraphos* unwritten]

a·graph·i·a (ā·graf'ē·ə) n. *Pathol.* Partial or complete inability to understand or express ideas in writing, caused by disorder of the brain. [< NL < Gk. *a-* without + *graphein* to write] — **a·graph'ic** adj.

a·grar·i·an (ə·grâr'ē·ən) adj. **1.** Pertaining to land or its tenure or to a general distribution of lands: *agrarian* reform. **2.** Organizing or furthering agricultural interests and aid to farmers: an *agrarian* investment. **3.** *Bot.* Growing wild in cultivated fields. — n. One who advocates agrarianism. [< L *agrarius* < *ager* field]

a·grar·i·an·ism (ə·grâr'ē·ən·iz'əm) n. **1.** The theory or practice of equal or equitable distribution of lands. **2.** Agitation for the redistribution of lands or the equalizing of farm income, especially by government control.

a·gree (ə·grē') v. **a·greed, a·gree·ing** v.i. **1.** To give consent; accede: with *to* or the infinitive. **2.** To come into or be in harmony: The sources do not *agree.* **3.** To be of one mind; concur: often with *with*: Do you *agree* with me? **4.** To come to terms, as in the details of a transaction: with *about* or *on.* **5.** To be acceptable or favorable; suit: with *with*: Cold weather does not *agree* with him. **6.** *Gram.* To correspond in person, number, case, or gender. — v.t. **7.** To grant as a concession: with a noun clause: I *agree* that the choice is difficult. [< OF *agreer* < *a gre* to one's liking < L *ad* to + *gratus* pleasing] — **Syn. 1.** See ASSENT. **2.** correspond, tally, jibe, match, coincide. — **Ant.** disagree, clash, conflict.

a·gree·a·ble (ə·grē'ə·bəl) adj. **1.** Pleasant to the mind or senses; giving pleasure by manner, bearing, or conversation: an *agreeable* companion. **2.** Being in accordance or conformity: a truth *agreeable* to reason. **3.** Ready or willing to agree; favorably inclined; giving assent. — **a·gree'a·bil'i·ty, a·gree'a·ble·ness** n. — **a·gree'a·bly** adv. — **Syn. 1.** pleasing, pleasant, gratifying, comfortable, amiable, delightful. — **Ant.** disagreeable, displeasing, unpleasant, uncomfortable, obnoxious, offensive.

a·greed (ə·grēd') adj. **1.** In agreement: Both men were *agreed.* **2.** Settled by consent, bargain, or contract: the *agreed* rate. **3.** Granted: used as a rejoinder.

a·gree·ment (ə·grē'mənt) n. **1.** The act of coming into accord. **2.** The state of being in accord; conformity. **3.** An arrangement or understanding between two or more parties as to a course of action; a covenant or treaty. **4.** *Law* A contract. **5.** *Gram.* Correspondence in person, number, case, or gender between words in a phrase or sentence.

a·gres·tal (ə·gres'təl) adj. *Bot.* Pertaining to uncultivated plants that flourish on cultivated ground, as weeds; indigenous to the fields; wild. Also **a·gres·tial** (ə·gres'chəl).

a·gres·tic (ə·gres'tik) adj. Rural; unpolished. Also **a·gres'ti·cal.** [< L *agrestis* < *ager* field]

agric. Agricultural; agriculture; agriculturist.

A·gric·o·la (ə·grik'ə·lə), **Georgius** Latin name of Georg Bauer, 1490?–1555, German alchemist and metallurgist. — **Gnaeus Julius,** 37–93, Roman governor of Britain.

ag·ri·cul·ture (ag'rə·kul'chər) n. **1.** The cultivation of the soil; the raising of food crops, breeding and raising of livestock, etc.; tillage; farming. **2.** The science that treats of the cultivation of the soil. Abbr. *agr., agric.* — **Department of Agriculture** An executive department of the U.S. government (established 1862), headed by the Secretary of Agriculture, that administers loans and grants-in-aid to farmers and assists in production, irrigation, etc. [< F < L *agricultura* < *ager* field + *cultura* cultivation] — **ag'ri·cul'tur·al** adj. — **ag'ri·cul'tur·al·ly** adv.

— **Syn.** *Agriculture, farming, agronomy,* and *gardening* refer to the cultivation of useful crops. *Agriculture* includes not only tillage of soil but also raising of livestock, not only the arts but also the sciences involved. The practice of *agriculture* as a business is *farming. Agronomy* relates to the scientific aspects of crop production. *Gardening* is the raising of flowers, or of food crops on a small scale.

ag·ri·cul·tur·ist (ag′rə·kul′chər·ist) *n.* **1.** An expert in agriculture. **2.** A farmer: also **ag′ri·cul′tur·al·ist.** Abbr. *agr., agric.*

Ag·ri Da·ği (ä·ri′ dä·i′) The Turkish name for (Mount) ARARAT.

A·gri·gen·to (ä′grē·jen′tō) A town in SW Sicily; site of Greek temples; pop. 47,094 (1961): formerly *Girgenti.* Ancient **Ag·ri·gen·tum** (ag′ri·jen′təm).

ag·ri·mo·ny (ag′rə·mō′nē) *n.* **1.** An erect perennial herb (genus *Agrimonia*) of the rose family with small, yellow flowers and bristly fruit covered with hooked hairs. **2.** Any of several similar plants, as the hemp agrimony, the bur marigold, Spanish needles, etc. [< L *agrimonia,* var. of *argemonia* < Gk. *argemōnē*]

A·grip·pa (ə·grip′ə), **Herod** See HEROD AGRIPPA.

Agrippa, Marcus Vipsanius, 63–12 B.C., Roman statesman, geographer, and general.

Ag·rip·pi·na (ag′ri·pī′nə), 13? B.C.–A.D. 33, wife of Germanicus and mother of Caligula: called **the Elder.**

Agrippina, A.D. 15–59, daughter of the preceding; mother of Nero: called **the Younger.**

agro- *combining form* Of or pertaining to fields or agriculture: *agronomy.* [< Gk. < *agros* field]

ag·ro·bi·ol·o·gy (ag′rō·bī·ol′ə·jē) *n.* The quantitative study of plant life, especially in relation to factors that determine the yields of cultivated plants. — **ag·ro·bi·o·log·ic** (ag′rō·bī′ə·loj′ik) or **·i·cal** *adj.* — **ag′ro·bi′o·log′i·cal·ly** *adv.* — **ag′ro·bi·ol′o·gist** *n.*

a·grol·o·gy (ə·grol′ə·jē) *n.* The science of soils, especially in its practical applications. — **ag·ro·log·ic** (ag′rə·loj′ik) or **·i·cal** *adj.* — **ag′ro·log′i·cal·ly** *adv.*

ag·ro·nom·ic (ag′rə·nom′ik) *adj.* Of or pertaining to agronomy or agronomics. Also **ag′ro·nom′i·cal.**

ag·ro·nom·ics (ag′rə·nom′iks) *n.pl.* (*construed as sing.*) **1.** In political economy, the science that treats of the distribution and management of land, especially as a source of the wealth of a nation. **2.** Agronomy.

a·gron·o·my (ə·gron′ə·mē) *n.* The application of scientific principles to the cultivation of land; scientific husbandry, especially in production of field crops. — **Syn.** See AGRICULTURE. [< Gk. *agronomos* an overseer of lands < *agros* field + *nemein* to distribute, manage] — **a·gron′o·mist** *n.*

ag·ros·tol·o·gy (ag′rə·stol′ə·jē) *n.* The branch of botany that treats of grasses. [< Gk. *agrōstis,* a kind of grass + -LOGY] — **a·gros·to·log·ic** (ə·gros′tə·loj′ik) or **·i·cal** *adj.*

a·ground (ə·ground′) *adv. & adj.* **1.** With the bottom stuck or dragging on the shore or ground. **2.** On the ground.

ag·ryp·not·ic (ag′rip·not′ik) *adj.* Preventing sleep. — *n.* A substance or drug that prevents sleep. [< F *agrypnotique* < Gk. *agrypnos* sleepless < *agrein* to chase + *hypnos* sleep]

a·guar·dien·te (ä′gwär·dyen′tā) *n.* **1.** An inferior brandy of Spain and Portugal. **2.** Any common distilled liquor, as whisky or pulque. [< Sp. < *agua ardiente* burning water]

A·guas·ca·lien·tes (ä′gwäs·kä·lyen′tās) A State in central Mexico; 2,499 sq. mi.; pop. 334,936 (1970); capital, **Aguascalientes;** pop. 222,105 (1970).

a·gue (ā′gyōo) *n.* **1.** *Pathol.* A periodic malarial fever marked by intermittent chills and sweating. **2.** A chill or paroxysm. [< OF < L (*febris*) *acuta* acute (fever)]

a·gue-cake (ā′gyōo·kāk′) *n. Pathol.* An enlargement and hardening of the spleen, resulting from malarial disease.

a·gue·weed (ā′gyōo·wēd′) *n.* **1.** Boneset. **2.** The stiff gentian (*Gentiana quinquefolia*), a tall, slender plant with clusters of blue or bluish purple, tubular flowers.

a·gu·ish (ā′gyōo·ish) *adj.* **1.** Like, producing, or tending to produce ague. **2.** Chilly; subject to ague. — **a′gu·ish·ly** *adv.* — **a′gu·ish·ness** *n.*

A·gul·has (ə·gul′əs, Pg. ə·gōol′yəs), **Cape** The southernmost point of Africa, in the Republic of South Africa, on the dividing line between the Indian and Atlantic oceans.

AGVA or **A.G.V.A.** American Guild of Variety Artists.

ah (ä) *interj.* An exclamation expressive of various emotions, as surprise, triumph, satisfaction, contempt, etc. [ME]

a.h. *Electr.* Ampere-hour.

A.H. In the year of the Hegira (L *anno Hegirae*).

a·ha (ä·hä′) *interj.* An exclamation expressing surprise, triumph, or mockery. [ME]

A·hab (ā′hab) Ninth-century B.C. king of Israel. I *Kings* xvi 29–xxii 40.

A·has·u·e·rus (ə·haz′yōo·ir′əs, ə·has′-) **1.** One of several Medean and Persian kings mentioned in the Old Testament, especially in the Book of Esther, generally identified with Xerxes. **2.** The Wandering Jew.

a·head (ə·hed′) *adv.* **1.** At the head or front. **2.** In advance.

3. Onward; forward: He pressed *ahead.* **4.** Without restraint; headlong. — **ahead of** In advance of, as in time, rank, achievement, etc. — **to be ahead** *U.S. Informal* To have as profit or advantage; be winning. — **to get ahead** To make one's way socially, financially, etc. [< A⁻¹ + HEAD]

a·hem (ə·hem′) *interj.* An exclamation similar to the sound of clearing the throat, made to attract attention.

a·him·sa (ə·him′sä) *n.* The doctrine that all life is sacred, exemplified in Brahmanism, Buddhism, and Jainism by strict nonviolence. [< Skt. *ahimsā* noninjury]

Ah·mad·nag·ar (ä′məd·nug′ər) Formerly, a district of Bombay State India; since 1960 part of Maharashtra State; 6,646 sq. mi.; pop. 1,200,000; capital, **Ahmadnagar;** pop. 118,226 (1961). Also **Ah′med·nag′ar.**

Ah·med·a·bad (ä′məd·ä·bäd′) **1.** Formerly, a northern district of Bombay State, India; since 1960 a part of Gujarat State; 3,879 sq. mi.; pop. about 1,400,000. **2.** A city in western India; temporary capital of Gujarat, 1960; pop. 1,746,111 (est. 1971). Also **Ah′mad·a·bad′.**

a·hoy (ə·hoi′) *interj.* Ho there!: a call used in hailing: Ship ahoy! [Var. of HOY]

Ah·ri·man (ä′ri·mən) In Zoroastrian religion, the spirit of evil and darkness, source of death, disease, and disorder. See ORMUZD.

A·hu·ra Maz·da (ä′hōo·rä mäz′dä) See ORMUZD.

a·i (ä′ē) *n.* A three-toed sloth (*Bradypus tridactylus*) of South and Central America. [< Pg. or Sp. < Tupi *ai hai*]

A.I.A. American Institute of Architects.

ai·blins (ā′blinz) See ABLINS.

A.I.C. American Institute of Chemists.

A.I.Ch.E. American Institute of Chemical Engineers.

aid (ād) *v.t. & v.i.* To render assistance (to); help; succor. — *n.* **1.** The act or result of helping or succoring, or the means employed; cooperation; assistance. **2.** A person or thing that affords assistance; a helper; assistant. **3.** *U.S.* An aide-de-camp. **4.** In English history, a special grant or subsidy made to the king. — **in aid of** *Brit. Informal* For; for the purpose of. [< OF *aidier* < L *adjutare,* freq. of *adjuvare* to give help to < *ad-* to + *juvare* to help] — **aid′er** *n.* — **Syn.** (verb) assist, support, abet, foster, serve, encourage. — **Ant.** hinder, oppose, obstruct, thwart, discourage. See HELP.

A.I.D. American Institute of Decorators.

A·i·da (ä·ē′dä) The heroine and title of an opera (1871) by Giuseppe Verdi.

aide (ād) *n.* **1.** An aide-de-camp. **2.** An assistant: nurse's *aide.* [< F, assistant]

aide-de-camp (ād′də·kamp′) *n. pl.* **aides-de-camp** A military or naval officer on the personal staff of a superior officer in a high command as his confidential assistant and secretary: also *aide.* Also *U.S.* **aid′-de-camp′.** Abbr. *ADC, a.d.c., A.D.C.* [< F *aide de camp,* lit., field assistant]

aide-mé·moire (ed·mā·mwär′) *n. French* A memorandum of a discussion, proposal, etc.; literally, aid to memory.

Ai·din (ī·din′) See AYDIN.

aid·man (ād′man′, -mən) *n. pl.* **·men** (-men′, -mən) A corpsman (def. 2).

aid station A dressing station (which see).

A.I.E.E. American Institute of Electrical Engineers.

AIF or **A.I.F.** Australian Imperial Force.

ai·glet (ā′glit) See AGLET.

ai·grette (ā′gret, ā·gret′) *n.* **1.** The tail plume of the egret. **2.** A tuft of feathers or gems, worn on a helmet, headdress, etc. Also **ai′gret.** [< F, a heron]

ai·guille (ā·gwēl′, ā′gwēl) *n.* **1.** *Geol.* A sharp, rocky mountain peak, as those of the Alps near Mont Blanc. **2.** A slender, rock-perforating drill. [< F, needle]

ai·guil·lette (ā′gwi·let′) *n.* An ornamental shoulder tag; aglet; especially, such a decoration on a uniform, consisting of loops, knots, and tassels. [< F, dim. of *aiguille* needle]

Ai·ken (ā′kin), **Conrad,** born 1889, U.S. poet.

ail (āl) *v.t.* **1.** To cause uneasiness or pain to; trouble; make ill. — *v.i.* **2.** To be somewhat ill; feel pain. [OE *eglan*]

ai·lan·thus (ā·lan′thəs) *n.* Any of a genus (*Ailanthus*) of large, deciduous trees of the quassia family, native to China and Japan, now naturalized in the United States: also called *tree of heaven.* [< NL < Amboina name *ailanto* tree of heaven] — **ai·lan′thic** *adj.*

ai·le·ron (ā′lə·ron) *n. Aeron.* Any of several types of movable auxiliary surfaces, usually located near the trailing edge of an airplane wing and used to bank the airplane. [< F, dim. of *aile* wing]

ail·ing (ā′ling) *adj.* Slightly ill. — **Syn.** See SICK.

ail·ment (āl′mənt) *n.* Indisposition of body or mind; slight illness. — **Syn.** See DISEASE.

aim (ām) *v.t.* **1.** To direct, as a weapon, remark, or act, toward or against some object or person; point; level. — *v.i.* **2.** To have a purpose; try: with the infinitive: to *aim* to please. **3.** To direct a missile, weapon, etc. — *n.* **1.** The act of aiming or pointing a weapon, missile, remark, etc., at anything. **2.** The line of direction of anything aimed. **3.** The object or point aimed at or to be aimed at; a mark or

target. **4.** Design; purpose. **5.** *Obs.* Conjecture; guess. [< OF *aesmer* < *a-* to (< L *ad-*) + *esmer* < L *aestimare* to estimate]
— **Syn.** (noun) 3, 4. goal, objective, end. See PURPOSE.
A.I.M.E. American Institute of Mining Engineers.
aim·less (ām'lis) *adj.* Wanting in aim or purpose. — **aim'·less·ly** *adv.* — **aim'less·ness** *n.*
ain[1] (ān) *adj. Scot.* Own.
a·in[2] (ä'yēn) See AYIN.
Ain (aṅ) A river in eastern France, flowing south 118 miles to the Rhône.
ain't (ānt) *Illit. & Dial.* Am not: also used for *are not, is not, has not,* and *have not.*
♦ **ain't, aren't I?** *Ain't* is now nonstandard, although users of standard English sometimes say or write it for amusing effect when they are sure it will not be taken as their normal usage. *Aren't I?* is an ungrammatical locution used to avoid *Ain't I?* when one means *Am I not?*
Ain·tab (īn·täb') A former name for GAZIANTEP.
Ai·nu (ī'nōō) *n.* **1.** One of a primitive, aboriginal people of Japan, now found only in the northern parts. **2.** The unclassified, unrelated language of the Ainu. Also **Ai·no** (ī'nō).
air[1] (âr) *n.* **1.** The mixture of gases that forms the atmosphere of the earth, consisting chiefly of the gases oxygen and nitrogen very nearly in the proportions one to four. **2.** The open space around and above the earth; sky. **3.** An atmospheric movement or current; wind; breeze. **4.** Utterance abroad; publicity: to give *air* to one's predilections. **5.** The atmosphere thought of as having some special character or effect on the senses: to breathe free *air* again. **6.** Peculiar or characteristic appearance; mien; manner: an *air* of extravagance; an honest *air.* **7.** *pl.* Assumed manner; affectation: to put on *airs.* **8.** *Music* A melody; tune; especially, one for a solo instrument or voice, with or without accompaniment. **9.** The atmosphere as the medium through which radio signals are sent. — **in the air 1.** Prevalent; abroad, as gossip; in the making, as plans. **2.** Without foundation in fact; unformed: The project is still *in the air.* **3.** *Informal* Excited; mentally upset: often preceded by *up.* — **on the air** Now broadcasting or transmitting, as by radio; being broadcast. — **up in the air** *Informal* Undecided. — *v.t.* **1.** To expose to the air; admit air into so as to purify or dry; ventilate. **2.** To make public; exhibit. [< OF < L *aer* < Gk. *āēr* air]
Air may appear as a combining form or as the first element in two-word phrases, with the following meanings:
1. By means of air or the air:

air-blasted	air-cooling	air-driven	air-insulated
air-blown	air-cured	air-filled	air-slaked
air-bred	air-dried	air-formed	air-spun

2. Of or pertaining to the atmospheric air:

air-breathing	air-defiling	airlike	airward
air-conveying	air-heating	air-swallowing	airwise

3. Conducting, confining, or regulating air:

air compressor	air duct	air filter	air regulator

4. Operating or operated by air, especially by the power of heated or compressed air:

air condenser	air drill	air hammer	air motor

5. Performed by or suitable for aircraft:

air action	air group	air show
air armament	air landing	air squadron
air attack	air meet	air strike
air echelon	air navigation	air terminal
air express	air race	air unit
air evacuation	air refueling	air war
air freight	air rescue	

— **Syn.** (noun) 6. *Air, appearance, look, demeanor, mien,* and *bearing* are here compared as they apply to what one sees in looking at a person. *Air* is the broadest of these words; a person's *air* includes his *appearance* (or dress), his *look* (or facial expression), and his *demeanor* (or manner of behaving). *Mien* is closely synonymous with *air,* but refers more specifically to facial expression and *bearing,* the manner of carrying and moving the limbs and body. **7.** pose, affectation, mannerism. **8.** See MELODY.
air[2] (âr) *adv. & adj. Scot.* Early.
Air (īr) A mountainous region of the Sahara in the northern Republic of Niger; a former kingdom: also *Asben, Azbine.*
air alert A signal warning of the expected or imminent approach of enemy aircraft.
air-a·tom·ic (âr'ə·tom'ik) *adj.* Of or pertaining to the use of aircraft and guided missiles in atomic warfare.
air·bag (âr'bag') *n.* A strong plastic bag that automatically inflates in front of car drivers and passengers to protect them in collisions.
air base A base for operations by aircraft.
air bladder 1. *Zool.* In fishes, a sac filled with air, generally situated under the anterior part of the spinal column, aiding them to maintain an equilibrium in the water: also called *sound, swimming bladder.* **2.** Any vesicle filled with air, as in the alveoli of the lungs, seaweed, etc. Also **air cell.**
air·boat (âr'bōt') *n.* A swamp boat (which see).
air·borne (âr'bôrn', -bōrn') *adj.* **1.** Carried through the air, as bacteria, pollen, etc. **2.** Transported in aircraft; especially, designating specialized troop units so carried: *airborne* infantry. **3.** In flight; flying. Abbr. *abn.*
air·bound (âr'bound') *adj.* Impeded or stopped up by air.
air brake A brake operated by compressed air.

air·brush (âr'brush') *n.* A kind of atomizer for spraying paint or other liquids by compressed air. Also **air brush.**
air·burst (âr'bûrst') *n.* An explosion in the air, as of a bomb.
air castle A visionary project; a daydream.
air chamber An enclosed space holding or designed to hold air, especially in a hydraulic device. Also **air cavity.**
air chief marshal In the Royal, Royal Canadian, and other Commonwealth air forces, an officer of the next to highest rank. See table at GRADE.
air coach *U.S.* The second-best and cheaper class of accommodations in commercial aircraft. Also **air-coach** (âr'cōch').
air cock *Mech.* A valve designed to control air flow.
air commodore In the Royal, Royal Canadian, and other Commonwealth air forces, an officer ranking next above group captain. See table at GRADE.
air-con·di·tion (âr'kən-dish'ən) *v.t.* To equip with or ventilate by air conditioning. — **air'-con·di'tioned** *adj.*
air conditioner Any of various installations or devices for maintaining cool and comfortable atmospheric conditions in an enclosed room, building, or other structure.
air conditioning A system for treating air in buildings, etc., so as to maintain a desired temperature.
air conduction 1. The transmission of the waves of sound through air. **2.** Hearing in the normal manner, through the auditory canal: distinguished from *bone conduction.*
air-cool (âr'kōōl') *v.t.* To cool, as the cylinders of an engine, with a flow of air instead of liquid. — **air'-cooled** *adj.*
air corridor An air route, especially one established by international agreement.
air cover *Mil.* **1.** Protection given by aircraft in military operations. **2.** The aircraft giving this protection.
air·craft (âr'kraft', -kräft') *n. pl.* **·craft** Any form of craft designed for flight through or navigation in the air, as airplanes, dirigibles, balloons, helicopters, and gliders.
aircraft carrier *Naval* A large ship designed to carry aircraft, having a level flight deck usually extending beyond the bow and stern, and serving as a mobile air base at sea.
air·craft·man (âr'kraft/mən, -kräft/-) *n. pl.* **·men** *Brit.* **1.** Any of the four lower grades in the Royal or Royal Canadian Air Force. See table at GRADE. **2.** One holding this rank.
air·crew (âr'krōō') *n.* The full complement of personnel serving on a commercial or military aircraft in flight.
air cushion 1. A bag inflated with air, especially one used as a pillow. **2.** An air spring.
air cylinder 1. A nearly airtight cylinder having a piston playing in it: used to check the recoil of a gun. **2.** A cylinder that holds compressed air for operating air brakes.
air defense The measures taken to counteract aerial attack.
air·drome (âr'drōm') *n. Chiefly Brit.* An airport.
air·drop (âr'drop') *n.* Aerial delivery of supplies and equipment in which unloading is accomplished from the aircraft in flight. — *v.t. & v.i.* **·dropped, ·drop·ping** To drop (supplies, etc.) from an aircraft.
air-dry (âr'drī') *adj.* Yielding no further moisture on exposure to the atmosphere. — *v.t.* **-dried, -dry·ing** To dry by exposing to air.
Aire·dale (âr'dāl) *n.* A large terrier with a wiry tan coat and black markings. [after *Airedale,* the Aire river valley, England]
air·field (âr'fēld') *n.* An airport; especially, the field of an airport.
air·flow (âr'flō') *n.* **1.** A flow of air. **2.** The air currents developed by the motion of an automobile, aircraft, etc.
air·foil (âr'foil') *n. Aeron.* A surface, as a wing, aileron, etc., designed to provide lift or control for an airplane in flight.

AIREDALE
(About 23 inches high at shoulder)

air force The air arm of a country's defense forces. Abbr. *AF.* — **United States Air Force** The air force of the United States, established in 1947. Before then it was part of the Army, and from 1942 to 1947 had the title of the Army Air Forces. Abbr. *USAF*
air force academy A school where young men are trained for service in the air force; especially, the **U.S. Air Force Academy,** Colorado Springs, Colo.
air·frame (âr'frām') *n.* An airplane complete except for the engine and its controls.
air freight *n.* **1.** A system of transporting cargo by air. **2.** The cargo so transported. **3.** The charge for such transportation.
air gas Producer gas (which see).
air gun A gun impelling a charge by compressed air.
air hole 1. A hole containing, or made by or for, gas or air. **2.** A flaw in a casting. **3.** An opening in the ice over a body of water. **4.** *Aeron.* An air pocket.
air·i·ly (âr'ə·lē) *adv.* **1.** In a light or airy manner; delicately. **2.** In light spirits; jauntily; gaily.
air·ing (âr'ing) *n.* **1.** An exposure to air, as for drying. **2.** Public exposure or discussion. **3.** Exercise in the open air.
air jacket *Mech.* An air-filled compartment around some part of a machine, usually designed to control temperature.

air lane A lane for air traffic, especially one characterized by steady winds; airway.

air·less (âr′lis) *adj.* Destitute of air or of fresh air.

air·lift (âr′lift′) *n.* The transporting of passengers and cargo by aircraft; especially, the **Berlin airlift**, carried out during the land blockade of Berlin imposed by the Soviet Union in 1948. — *v.t. & v.i.* To transport (food and supplies) by airplane, especially during a land blockade.

air·line (âr′līn′) *n.* **1.** A system for the transportation of passengers and freight by air; also, the business organization operating such a system. **2.** Any route traveled by an air transport system. **3.** The shortest distance between two points on the earth's surface; the great-circle course.

air·lin·er (âr′lī′nər) *n.* A large passenger aircraft operated by an airline.

air lock An airtight antechamber, as of a caisson, for maintaining the air pressure. For illustration see CAISSON.

air mail **1.** Mail carried by airplane. **2.** A system of carrying mail by airplane. — **air′-mail′, air′mail′** *adj.*

air·man (âr′mən) *n. pl.* **·men** (-mən) **1.** *Mil.* In the U.S. Air Force, an enlisted person, especially one below the grade of staff sergeant. See table at GRADE. **2.** One occupied with the navigation of an aircraft; an aviator.

air marshal In the Royal, Royal Canadian, and other Commonwealth air forces, an officer ranking next below air chief marshal. See table at GRADE.

air mass *Meteorol.* Any broad portion of the earth's atmosphere characterized by essentially uniform conditions of temperature, pressure, moisture, etc.

Air Medal A decoration awarded by the U.S. Air Force or Army for meritorious achievement while participating in an aerial flight: instituted September, 1939. See DECORATION.

air meter A gauge showing the rate of flow of air or gas.

air mile See under MILE.

air-mind·ed (âr′mīn′did) *adj.* Having an inclination for or interest in aircraft. — **air′-mind′ed·ness** *n.*

airn (ârn) *n. Scot.* Iron; also, an iron tool.

air·plane (âr′plān′) *n.* A heavier-than-air flying craft supported by aerodynamic forces acting upon fixed wings and kept in flight by engine power: also called *plane.* Also, *Brit.*, *aeroplane.*

airplane cloth A cotton fabric of plain weave in varying weights, used for sportswear, etc.: originally unbleached linen used for the outer covering of airplanes.

air plant An epiphyte.

air pocket *Aeron.* A sudden downward air current caused by the sinking of a mass of heavy cooled air.

air·port (âr′pôrt′, -pōrt′) *n.* A field laid out as a base for aircraft, including all structures and appurtenances necessary for operation, housing, storage, and maintenance.

air post Air mail.

air power The strength of a nation in terms of its command of the air in peace and war.

air·proof (âr′prōof′) *adj.* Impenetrable by air. — *v.t.* To make airproof.

air raid An attack by military aircraft, especially by bombers in mass formation.

air-raid shelter A place set aside and equipped for the protection of people during an air raid.

air-raid warden A person officially designated to exercise police authority during an air raid.

air rifle A rifle utilizing compressed air to propel a lead pellet or other missile: also called *BB gun.*

air sac **1.** *Ornithol.* One of the membranous sacs filled with air in different parts of the body in birds, often extending through the bones and communicating with the lungs. **2.** *Zool.* Any of the terminations of the air passages of the lungs in mammals.

air scoop A device for using the airstream to maintain pressure and furnish ventilation within an aircraft.

air·screw (âr′skrōo′) *n. Brit.* The propeller of an aircraft.

air shaft An open shaft intended to provide proper ventilation of a building or other structure.

air·ship (âr′ship′) *n.* Any lighter-than-air, mechanically propelled craft depending upon buoyant gases for flotation, as a balloon or dirigible.

air·sick·ness (âr′sik′nis) *n.* A sickness to which travelers by air are liable, caused by constant variations in altitude combined with rapidity of motion. — **air′sick′** *adj.*

air·space (âr′spās′) *n.* **1.** The atmosphere. **2.** That portion of the atmosphere overlying a designated area, considered as subject to territorial jurisdiction or international law, or as available for building, as the space over a railroad.

air speed The speed of an airplane with relation to the air: distinguished from *ground speed.*

air spray **1.** A compressed-air device for spraying liquids. **2.** The liquid used in such a device. — **air′-sprayed′** *adj.*

air spring A device for resisting sudden pressure by the elasticity of compressed air: also *air cushion.*

air station *Brit. & Canadian* An air base.

air·stream (âr′strēm′) *n.* A current or flow of air, especially one set up by the propeller or propellers of an aircraft.

air·strip (âr′strip′) *n.* A flat land, snow, or ice surface used with little or no improvement as an airfield: when used by fighter planes, called *fighter strip.*

airt (ârt) *Scot. v.t.* To guide. — *n.* A cardinal point of the compass; a direction.

air thermometer A thermometer in which temperature differences are measured by the expansion and contraction of enclosed air or other gas.

air·tight (âr′tīt′) *adj.* **1.** Not allowing air to escape or enter. **2.** Having no weak places; flawless: an *airtight* case.

air turbine A turbine operated by air currents fed to the vanes under pressure.

air umbrella A heavy concentration of military aircraft sent out to protect and support ground forces.

air valve *Mech.* A valve, usually automatic, for the control of the flow of air; an air cock.

air vesicle *Bot.* A large air chamber serving as a float in many water plants, especially in certain seaweeds.

air vice-marshal (vīs′mär′shəl) In the Royal, Royal Canadian, and other Commonwealth air forces, an officer ranking next below air marshal. See table at GRADE.

air·way (âr′wā′) *n.* **1.** Any passageway for air, as the ventilating passage of a mine. **2.** *Aeron.* A specific route of travel selected for aircraft. **3.** *Med.* A device inserted through the mouth into the trachea to allow a clear passage for air, as in mouth-to-mouth resuscitation.

air·wom·an (âr′wŏŏm′ən) *n. pl.* **·wom·en** A woman aviator.

air·wor·thy (âr′wûr′thē) *adj.* Being in fit condition to fly: said of aircraft. — **air′wor′thi·ness** *n.*

air·y (âr′ē) *adj.* **air·i·er, air·i·est** **1.** Of or pertaining to the air. **2.** Like or resembling air; immaterial: *airy* spirits. **3.** Thin or light as air; delicate: an *airy* evening dress. **4.** Light or buoyant in manner; lively; gay: *airy* music. **5.** Unsubstantial as air; unreal; empty: *airy* nothings. **6.** Dealing with fancies; visionary; speculative. **7.** Open to the air; breezy: an *airy* retreat. **8.** Performed in the air; aerial: an *airy* flight. **9.** *Informal* Giving oneself airs; affected. **10.** *Poetic* High in the air; lofty; ethereal. — **air′i·ness** *n.*

— **Syn.** *Airy, aerial,* and *ethereal* make some comparison with air: *airy* and *aerial* with the earthly air we know, and *ethereal* with the supposed air of heaven. *Airy* suggests lightness and insubstantiality: a veil *airy* as gossamer. In extended use, *airy* is often ambiguous; *airy* ideas may be vague, unreal, or affected. *Aerial* sometimes means simply of the air: *aerial* plants; but more often it is a poetical word suggesting extreme delicacy or tenuousness: the *aerial* tints of the calla lily. *Ethereal* suggests otherworldliness; *ethereal* beauty seems too transcendent to be of this world.

A·i·sha (ä′i-shä), 611?–678; Mohammed's favorite wife; daughter of Abu-Bekr. Also *Ayesha.*

aisle (īl) *n.* **1.** A passageway, as in a church, auditorium, supermarket, between the rows, sections, or counters. **2.** A lateral division or wing of a church, flanking the main structure or nave, and usually divided from it by a range of columns or piers. **3.** Any similar wing or passage, as in a forest. [< MF *aile* wing (of a building) < L *ala* wing; spelling infl. by *isle*]

aisled (īld) *adj.* Provided with or placed in an aisle.

Aisne (ān, *Fr.* en) A river in northern France, flowing about 175 miles west to the Oise.

ait (āt) *n. Brit. Dial.* A little island. [OE *īggath, īgeoth*]

aitch (āch) *n.* The letter *H.*

aitch·bone (āch′bōn′) *n.* **1.** The rump bone in cattle. **2.** The cut of beef with this bone. [< OF *nache* buttock + BONE; in ME a *nache bone* became an *ache bone*]

ai·ver (ā′vər) *n. Scot.* A draft horse.

Aix-en-Pro·vence (eks′äṅ-prô-väṅs′) A city in SE France; pop. 74,948 (1968). Also **Aix.**

Aix-la-Cha·pelle (āks′lä-shä-pel′, *Fr.* eks′là-shà-pel′) The French name for AACHEN.

A.J.A. Americans of Japanese Ancestry.

A·jac·cio (ä-yät′chō) The capital of Corsica, a port in the western part; birthplace of Napoleon; pop. 38,776 (1968).

a·jar[1] (ə-jär′) *adv. & adj.* Partly open, as a door. [ME *a-on* + *char,* OE *cerr* turn]

a·jar[2] (ə-jär′) *adv. & adj.* In a jarring or discordant condition; not in harmony. [< A-[1] + JAR[2]]

A·jax (ā′jaks) In the *Iliad,* the son of Telamon, second in bravery only to Achilles of the Greeks who besieged Troy.

Ajax the Lesser In the *Iliad,* son of the king of Locris, and one of Helen's suitors.

a·jee (ə-jē′) *adv. & adj. Scot.* Awry; askew; also, ajar: also spelled *agee.*

Aj·mer-Mer·wa·ra (uj·mir′, -mer′; mer·wä′rə) Formerly, a State of NW India, since 1956 a province of Rajasthan State; 2,400 sq. mi.; pop. about 600,000; capital, **Ajmer,** pop. 230,999 (1961).

aj·o·wan (aj′ō-wən) *n.* The ripe fruit of a plant (*Trachyspermum ammi*) cultivated in Egypt, India, and Persia as a source of thymol and cymene. [Origin uncertain]

a.k.a. Also known as.

PRONUNCIATION KEY: add, āce, câre, pälm; end, ēven; it, īce; odd, ōpen, ôrder; tŏŏk, pōōl; up, bûrn; ə = a in *above,* e in *sicken,* i in *flexible,* o in *melon,* u in *focus;* yōō = u in *fuse;* oil; pout; check; go; ring; thin; **this;** zh, vision. For à, œ, ü, kh, ṅ, see inside front cover.

Ak·bar (ak′bär), 1542–1605, Mogul emperor of Hindustan. Also **Ak·ber** (ak′bər).

AKC or **A.K.C.** American Kennel Club.

a·kene (ā·kēn′) See ACHENE.

A·khe·na·ten (ä′kə·nä′tən) See IKHNATON.

a·kim·bo (ə·kim′bō) *adv. & adj.* With hands on hips and elbows outward. [ME *in kenebowe* in a sharp bow]

a·kin (ə·kin′) *adj. & adv.* **1.** Of the same kin; related by blood. **2.** Of similar nature or qualities. [< A-³ + KIN]

A·ki·ta (ä·kē·tä) A port city in northern Japan, on Honshu island; pop. 190,202 (1955).

Ak·kad (ak′ad, ä′käd) **1.** A region of Mesopotamia occupying the northern part of Babylonia. **2.** In the Bible, a city of Nimrod's kingdom. *Gen.* x 10. Also *Accad.*

Ak·ka·di·an (ə·kā′dē·ən, ə·kä′-) *n.* **1.** One of the inhabitants of ancient Akkad. **2.** The extinct group of East Semitic languages of Akkad, Assyria, and Babylonia, or any language of this group. — *adj.* **1.** Of Akkad or its inhabitants. **2.** Of the extinct Semitic languages of the Assyrians and Babylonians. Also spelled *Accadian.*

Ak·ker·man (ä·kir·män′) The former Russian and Turkish name for BYELGOROD–DNIESTROVSKI.

Ak·kra (ə·krä′, ak′rə) See ACCRA.

Ak·ron (ak′rən) A city in NE Ohio; world's largest rubber-manufacturing center; pop. 275,425.

Ak·sum (äk·sŏŏm′) A town in northern Abyssinia; site of the ancient capital of Ethiopia; pop. about 5,000: also *Axum.*

ak·va·vit (äk′vä·vēt) *n.* Aquavit, a liquor.

al-¹ *prefix* The Arabic definite article, seen in words of Arabic origin, as *Alkoran, algebra.*

al-² Assimilated var. of AD-.

al. **1.** Other things (L *alia*) **2.** Other persons (L *alii*).

-al¹ *suffix of adjectives and nouns* Of or pertaining to; characterized by; connected with: *personal, musical;* also in some nouns that were originally adjectives: *animal.* [< L *-alis*]

-al² *suffix of nouns* The act of doing or the state of suffering that which is expressed by the verb stem: *betrayal, refusal.* [< OF *-aille* < L *-alia,* neut. pl. of *-alis*]

-al³ *suffix Chem.* Denoting a compound having the properties of or derived from an aldehyde: *chloral.* [< AL(DEHYDE)]

Al *Chem.* Aluminum.

AL. or **AL.** or **A.L.** Anglo-Latin.

a·la (ā′lə) *n. pl.* **a·lae** (ā′lē) **1.** A wing or a winglike part, as one of the lateral projections of the nose. **2.** *Bot.* One of the two side petals in a papilionaceous flower, or the little winglike process found on some seeds. [< L, wing]

à la (ä′ lä, ä′ lə; *Fr.* à lä) **1.** After the manner of: hair dressed *à la* Pompadour. **2.** In cooking, as done in, by, or for: lobster *à la* Newburg. Also **a la.** [< F]

Ala. Alabama.

ALA or **A.L.A.** American Library Association.

Al·a·bam·a (al′ə·bam′ə) A State in the SE United States, bordering on the Gulf of Mexico; 51,609 sq. mi.; pop. 3,444,-165; capital, Montgomery; entered the Union Dec. 14, 1819: nickname, *Cotton State.* — **Al·a·bam·i·an** (al′ə·bam′ē·ən), **Al′a·bam′an** *adj. & n.*

Alabama River A river in Alabama, flowing 315 miles SW to the Mobile River.

al·a·bam·ine (al′ə·bam′ēn, -in) *n.* A hypothetical element of atomic number 85: replaced by astatine. Abbr. *Ab* [after *Alabama*]

al·a·bas·ter (al′ə·bas′tər, -bäs′-) *n.* **1.** A white or tinted fine-grained gypsum. **2.** A banded variety of calcite: also called *Oriental alabaster.* — *adj.* Made of or like alabaster; smooth and white: also **al′a·bas′trine** (-trin). [< L < Gk. *alabast(r)os* alabaster box; ult. origin uncertain]

al·a·bas·ter·stone (al′ə·bas′tər·stōn′, -bäs′-) *n.* A hotspring or cave deposit of aragonite.

à la bonne heure (ä lä bôn œr′) *French* Good; well done; literally, at a good hour.

à la carte (ä′ lə kärt′) In accordance with the bill of fare; each item having a separate price; literally, by the menu. Compare PRIX FIXE, TABLE D′HOTE. [< F]

a·lack (ə·lak′) *interj. Archaic* An exclamation of regret or sorrow. Also **a·lack·a·day** (ə·lak′ə·dā′). [< *ah* oh + *lack* failure, disgrace]

a·lac·ri·ty (ə·lak′rə·tē) *n.* Cheerful willingness and promptitude; liveliness. [< L *alacritas, -tatis* < *alacer* lively] — **a·lac′ri·tous** *adj.*

A·la Dag (ä′lä däkh′) Name of several mountains and mountain ranges in Turkey; highest point, 12,251 ft., in Kaldi Dağ. Also **A·la Dagh** (ä′lä däkh′).

A·lad·din (ə·lad′n) In the *Arabian Nights,* a boy who can summon one jinni to do his bidding by rubbing a magic lamp, and another by rubbing a magic ring.

à la fin (ä lä faṅ′) *French* In the end; at last; finally.

à la fran·çaise (ä lä frän·sez′) *French* In the French style.

A·la·gez (ä′lə·gez′) An extinct volcano of Erivan, Armenian S.S.R.; 13,435 ft.: also *Aragats.* Also **A·la·göz** (ä′lä·gœz′).

A·la·go·as (ä′lə·gō′əs) A State in eastern Brazil; 10,731 sq. mi.: pop. 1,381,000 (est. 1967); capital, Maceió.

Al Ah·sa (al ä·sä′) See EL HASA.

A·lai (ä·lī′) A mountain range of Kirghiz S.S.R., in the Tien Shan system; highest peak, 19,554 ft.

A·lain-Four·nier (ä·laṅ′fŏŏr·nyā′) Pseudonym of Henri Fournier, 1886–1914, French novelist.

à la king (ä′ lə king′) Cooked in a cream sauce, with pimento or green pepper, mushrooms, etc.

Al·a·man·ni (al′ə·man′ī), etc. See ALEMANNI, etc.

al·a·me·da (al′ə·mē′də, -mä′-) *n. SW U.S.* A shaded walk: so called because generally planted with alamos or poplar trees. [< Sp. < *álamo* poplar]

Al·a·me·da (al′ə·mē′də, -mä′-) A city in western California, on an island near the eastern shore of San Francisco Bay; pop. 70,698.

A·la·mein (ä′lə·mān′, al′ə-), **El** A village of northern Egypt; site of a decisive British recovery and victory against Axis forces (1942) in World War II. Also **A′la·mein′.**

al·a·mo (al′ə·mō, ä′lə·mō) *n. pl. ·mos* **1.** The cottonwood, a tree. **2.** The poplar tree. [< Sp. *álamo*]

Al·a·mo (al′ə·mō) A Franciscan mission building, San Antonio, Texas; besieged and taken by Mexicans, 1836.

à la mode (ä′ lə mōd′, al′ə mŏd′) **1.** In style; fashionable; literally, according to the mode. **2.** In cookery: **a** Served with ice cream: said of pie. **b** Braised with vegetables and served in a rich gravy. [< F]

Al·a·mo·gor·do (al′ə·mə·gôr′dō) A town in southern New Mexico near the site of the first atomic bomb trial explosion, July 16, 1945; pop. 23,038.

à la mort (ä lä môr′) *French* Mortally ill in mind or body; mortally; literally, to the death.

al·an (al′ən) *n.* **1.** *Heraldry* A short-eared mastiff. **2.** *Obs.* A wolfhound. Also **al·and** (al′ənd), **al·ant** (al′ənt). [< OF]

Å·land Islands (ō′län) An archipelago of Finland at the entrance of the Gulf of Bothnia; 572 sq. mi.; pop. 22,000 (est. 1959); chief town, Mariehamn: also *Aaland Islands.*

a·lane (ə·lān′) *adv. & adj. Scot.* Alone.

à la New·burg (ä′ lə nŏŏ′bûrg, nyŏŏ′bûrg) Cooked with a sauce made of egg yolks, cream, sherry, and butter.

a·lang (ə·lang′) *adv. & prep. Scot.* Along.

à l'an·glaise (ä läṅ·glez′) *French* In the English style.

al·a·nine (al′ə·nēn, -nin) *n. Biochem.* An amino acid, $C_3H_7O_2N$, one of the constituents of protein molecules, produced biosynthetically from pyruvic acid and artificially from a mixture of ammonia and hydrocarbons. Also **al·a·nin** (al′·ə·nin). [< AL(DEHYDE) + infix *-an-* + *-INE²*]

a·lar (ā′lər) *adj.* **1.** Having or pertaining to an ala or wing; wing-shaped. **2.** *Bot.* Axillary. **3.** *Anat.* Pertaining to the shoulder or armpit. [< L *alaris* < *ala* wing]

A·lar·cón (ä′lär·kōn′), **Pedro Antonio de,** 1833–91, Spanish writer and statesman.

Al·a·ric (al′ə·rik), 370?–410, Visigoth king; sacked Rome.

Alaric II, died 507, Visigoth king; issued legal code.

a·larm (ə·lärm′) *n.* **1.** Sudden fear or apprehension caused by awareness of danger. **2.** Any sound or signal intended to awaken or apprise of danger; a warning. **3.** Any device, as a bell, for giving such a signal. **4.** A call to arms, to meet danger or attack. **5.** In fencing, a stamp on the ground made with the advancing foot. **6.** *Obs.* A loud noise or din. **7.** *Obs.* A sudden attack. — *v.t.* **1.** To strike with sudden fear. **2.** To arouse to a sense of danger; give warning to. [< OF *alarme* < Ital. *all' arme* to arms] — **a·larm′a·ble** *adj.* — **Syn.** (noun) **1.** *Alarm, apprehension, disquiet, dread, dismay,* and *consternation* are emotions caused by imminent danger. *Alarm* is the sudden arousal to meet and repel danger and may be quite consistent with courage and confidence. *Apprehension, disquiet,* and *dread* are in anticipation of danger. *Apprehension* suggests worry or anxiety over what may happen; *disquiet* refers to a feeling of uneasiness, and may be without definite cause; *dread* is a strong word, describing a feeling of fear or terror. *Dismay* may also be anticipatory, but often implies confusion and failure of initiative in the actual presence of danger. *Consternation* describes great *dismay* and inability to act in a perilous situation.

alarm clock A clock fitted with a device to sound a bell or buzzer when the hands reach a predetermined hour.

a·larm·ing (ə·lär′ming) *adj.* Exciting alarm; causing fear and apprehension; disturbing. — **a·larm′ing·ly** *adv.*

a·larm·ist (ə·lär′mist) *n.* **1.** One who needlessly excites or tries to excite alarm. **2.** One who is easily alarmed.

a·lar·um (ə·lär′əm) *n. Obs.* An alarm.

a·la·ry (ā′lər·ē, al′ər·ē) *adj.* Pertaining to alae or wings; wing-shaped. [< L *alarius* < *ala* wing]

a·las (ə·las′, ə·läs′) *interj.* An exclamation of disappointment, regret, sorrow, etc. [< OF *a ah!* + *las* wretched < L *lassus* weary]

Alas. Alaska (unofficial).

A·las·ka (ə·las′kə) A State of the United States in NW North America, including the Aleutian Islands and the Alexander Archipelago; 586,400 sq. mi.; pop. 302,173; capital, Juneau; entered the Union January 3, 1959. — **A·las′kan** *adj. & n.*

Alaska, Gulf of A broad northern inlet of the Pacific on the south coast of Alaska between Alaska Peninsula and the Alexander Archipelago.

Alaska Highway A road from Dawson Creek, British Columbia, through the Yukon to Fairbanks, Alaska, built in 1942 as a United States military supply route; 1,527 mi.: unofficially *Alcan Highway.*

Alaska Peninsula A long, narrow promontory of SW Alaska, extending about 400 miles between the Bering Sea and the Pacific. See map of BERING SEA.

Alaska Range A mountain range in south central Alaska; highest peak, Mount McKinley, 20,270 ft.

a·late (ā'lāt) *adj. Bot.* Winged, as a stem, petiole, or fruit, with membranous expansions. Also **a'lat·ed.** [< L *alatus* < *ala* wing]

a·la·tion (ā-lā'shən) *n.* **1.** The condition of being winged. **2.** *Entomol.* The way in which an insect's wings are arranged.

alb (alb) *n. Eccl.* A white linen eucharistic vestment reaching to the ankles, close-sleeved and girded at the waist. [OE *albe* < L *alba (vestis)* white garment]

Alb. **1.** Albania; Albanian. **2.** Albany. **3.** Alberta, Canada.

al·ba¹ (al'bə) *n. Physiol.* The white substance of the brain. [< NL < L, white]

al·ba² (al'bə, al'bä) *n.* In Provençal troubadour literature, a short, formal lyric, originally describing the separation of lovers at dawn; aubade. [< Provençal, dawn]

Al·ba (äl'bä), **Duke of,** 1508–82, Fernando Álvarez de Toledo, Spanish general and statesman. Also *Alva.*

Alba. Alberta, Canada (unofficial).

Al·ba·ce·te (äl'vä·thā'tā) A Province of SE central Spain; 5,738 sq. mi.; pop. 358,290 (est. 1965); capital, **Albacete;** pop. 61,635 (1960).

al·ba·core (al'bə·kôr, -kōr) *n.* One of various tunas or large scombroid fishes, especially *Thunnus alulunga* of the Atlantic. Also spelled *albicore.* [< Pg. *albacor* < Arabic *al* the + *bukr* young camel]

Al·ba Lon·ga (al'bə lông'gə, long'gə) A city of ancient Latium, SE of Rome; birthplace of Romulus and Remus.

Al·ba·ni·a (al·bā'nē·ə, -bān'yə) **1.** A Balkan Republic south of Yugoslavia; 10,629 sq. mi.; pop. 1,964,800 (est. 1967); capital, Tirana. Officially **People's Republic of Albania.** See map of ADRIATIC SEA. **2.** *Obs.* Scotland; the Highlands.

Al·ba·ni·an (al·bā'nē·ən, -bān'yən) *adj.* Of or pertaining to Albania, its people, or their language. — *n.* **1.** A native or inhabitant of Albania. **2.** The language of Albania, comprising the Albanian subfamily of Indo-European languages.

Al·ba·ny (ôl'bə·nē) **1.** The capital of New York, in the eastern part, on the Hudson River; pop. 115,781. **2.** A city in SW Georgia; pop. 72,623.

Albany River A river in north central Ontario, Canada, flowing about 600 miles eastward to James Bay.

al·ba·ta (al·bä'tə) *n.* German silver. [< NL, fem. pp. of L *albare* to make white < *albus* white]

al·ba·tross (al'bə·trôs, -tros) *n. pl.* **·tross·es** or **·tross** Any of various large, web-footed sea birds (family *Diomedeidae*), with long, narrow wings and a hooked beak. — **an albatross around one's neck** A heavy and persistent burden. [Orig. *alcatras* frigate bird < Sp., Pg. *alcatraz* < Pg. *alcatruz* bucket on a water wheel < Arabic *alquādūs* the bucket < Gk. *kados* vessel, jar, ? < Phoenician: prob. infl. in form by L *albus* white]

al·be·do (al·bē'dō) *n. Astron.* The percentage of the total illumination of a planet or satellite that is reflected from its surface. [< L, whiteness < *albus* white]

Al·bee (ôl'bē), **Edward,** born 1928, U.S. playwright.

al·be·it (ôl·bē'it) *conj.* Even though; although. [ME *al be it* although it be]

Al·be·marle (al'bə·märl), **Duke of** See MONK.

Albemarle Sound An inlet of the Atlantic in NE North Carolina.

Al·bé·niz (äl·vā'nēth), **Isaac,** 1860–1909, Spanish composer and pianist.

Al·ber·ich (äl'bər·ikh) **1.** In Germanic mythology, the king of the dwarfs. **2.** In the *Nibelungenlied,* the dwarf who guards the treasure of the Nibelungs.

Al·bert (al'bərt), **Lake** A lake in central Africa surrounded by Kenya, the Republic of the Congo (Leopoldville), and Uganda; 2,064 sq. mi. Also **Albert Ny·an·za** (nī·an'zə).

Al·bert (al'bərt), **Prince,** 1819–61, Prince of Saxe-Coburg-Gotha, consort of Victoria of England.

Albert I, 1875–1934, King of the Belgians 1909–34.

Al·ber·ta (al·bûr'tə) A Province in western Canada; 255,285 sq. mi.; pop. 1,634,000; capital, Edmonton. Abbr. *Alta.* —

Al·ber'tan *n. & adj.*

al·bert·ite (al'bərt·tīt) *n.* A jet-black, bituminous hydrocarbon, used as fuel. [after *Albert* County, New Brunswick + -ITE¹]

Albert Memorial A monument to Prince Albert in Kensington Gardens, London.

Al·ber·tus Mag·nus (al·bûr'təs mag'nəs), **Saint,** 1193?–1280, German scholastic philosopher and theologian; teacher of Thomas Aquinas.

al·bes·cent (al·bes'ənt) *adj.* Growing white or moderately white; becoming whitish. [< L *albescens, -entis,* ppr. of *albescere* to become white < *albus* white] — **al·bes'cence** *n.*

al·bi·core (al'bə·kôr, -kōr) See ALBACORE.

Al·bi·gen·ses (al'bə·jen'sēz) *n.pl.* A sect of religious reformers during the 11th to 13th centuries in the south of France, suppressed as heretics. [< Med.L, after *Albi,* a town in southern France] — **Al·bi·gen'si·an** (-sē·ən, -shən) *adj. & n.*

al·bin·ism (al'bə·niz'əm) *n.* **1.** An abnormal condition in human beings, characterized by a genetically determined lack of pigment in certain cells of the skin, hair, and eyes, and giving a very white or pale appearance. **2.** Deficient pigmentation in an animal or plant. **3.** The state or condition of being an albino. — **al·bin·ic** (al·bin'ik) *adj.*

al·bi·no (al·bī'nō) *n. pl.* **·nos** Any organism lacking normal pigmentation. [< Pg. < *albo* < L *albus* white]

Al·bi·on (al'bē·ən) *Poetic* England. [< L]

al·bite (al'bīt) *n.* A triclinic, white feldspar, NaAlSi₃O₈, common in granite and other rocks. See FELDSPAR. [< L *albus* white + -ITE¹] — **al·bit·i·cal** (al·bit'i·kəl) *adj.*

Al·boin (al'boin, -bō·in) died 573?, founder and king of the Lombard dominion in Italy.

Al·bo·rak (al'bə·rak) In Moslem legend, the white mule on which Mohammed is said to have visited the seven heavens. [< Arabic *al-burāq*]

Al·borz (äl·bōrz') See ELBURZ.

Al·bu·ca·sis (al'byoo·kā'sis) Latinized name of ABUL KASIM.

al·bum (al'bəm) *n.* **1.** A book or booklike container for storing or preserving stamps, pictures, autographs, phonograph records, etc. **2.** A set of phonograph records stored in such a container. [< L, blank tablet]

al·bu·men (al·byoo'mən) *n.* **1.** The white of an egg. **2.** *Bot.* The nutritive material that fills the space in a seed between the embryo and the seed coats; endosperm or perisperm. **3.** Albumin. [< L, white of an egg < *albus* white]

al·bu·men·ize (al·byoo'mən·īz), etc. See ALBUMINIZE, etc.

al·bu·min (al·byoo'mən) *n. Biochem.* Any of a class of protein substances found in many animal and vegetable juices and solids. They contain carbon, oxygen, nitrogen, hydrogen, and sulfur, and are soluble in water. [< F *albumine* < L *albumen, -minis.* See ALBUMEN.]

al·bu·mi·nate (al·byoo'mə·nāt) *n. Biochem.* A compound formed by the union of albumin with another substance, particularly a base or an acid. [< ALBUMIN + -ATE³]

al·bu·min·ize (al·byoo'mən·īz) *v.t.* **·ized, ·iz·ing** *Biochem.* **1.** To convert into albumin. **2.** To coat or saturate with albumin. Also spelled *albumenize.* — **al·bu'min·i·za'tion** *n.* — **al·bu'min·iz'er** *n.*

al·bu·mi·noid (al·byoo'mə·noid) *adj.* Of or like albumen or albumin. Also **al·bu'mi·noi'dal.** — *n. Biochem.* One of a subclass of the simple proteins derived mainly from supporting and connective animal tissues. Also **al·bu'me·noid.**

al·bu·mi·nous (al·byoo'mə·nəs) *adj.* Of or pertaining to albumen or albumin. Also **al·bu'mi·nose** (-nōs).

al·bu·mi·nu·ri·a (al·byoo'mə·nŏŏr'ē·ə, -nyŏŏr'-) *n. Pathol.* The presence of albumin in the urine. [< NL < ALBUMIN + Gk. *ouron* urine] — **al·bu'mi·nu'ric** *adj.*

al·bu·mose (al·byoo'mōs, al'byoo·mōs) *n. Biochem.* A substance formed from the proteins during digestion; also, any of the proteoses. [< ALBUM(IN) + -OSE²]

Al·bu·quer·que (al'bə·kûr'kē) A resort city in NW New Mexico on the Rio Grande; pop. 243,751.

Al·bu·quer·que (äl'bŏŏ·ker'kə), **Affonso de,** 1453–1515, Portuguese seafarer and explorer.

al·bur·num (al·bûr'nəm) *n. Bot.* Sapwood. [< L < *albus* white]

Al·cae·us (al·sē'əs) Seventh-century B.C. Greek poet of Mitylene. See ALCAIC.

Alcaeus In Greek mythology, father of Amphitryon.

Al·ca·ic (al·kā'ik) *adj.* **1.** Of or in the manner of the poet Alcaeus. **2.** Denoting a meter or verse form used by Alcaeus, consisting of a strophe of four verses having four feet apiece. — *n.* Verse written in Alcaic strophes.

al·caide (al·kād', *Sp.* äl·kä'ē·thä) *n.* **1.** The governor of a Spanish, Portuguese, or Moorish castle or fortress. **2.** The warden of a prison; a jailer. Also **al·cayde'.** [< Sp. < Arabic *al-qādē* the leader]

al·cal·de (al·kal'dē, *Sp.* äl·käl'thä) *n.* A mayor or chief magistrate in a Spanish or Spanish-American pueblo or town. [< Sp. < Arabic *al-qādī* the judge]

Al·can Highway (al'kan) See ALASKA HIGHWAY.

Al·ca·traz (al'kə·traz) A small island in San Francisco Bay, California; former site of a Federal prison.

al·caz·ar (al′kə·zär; *Sp.* äl·kä′thär) *n.* A Moorish castle in Spain. — **the Alcazar** A Moorish palace in Seville, later used by the Spanish kings. [< Sp. < Arabic *al-qasr* the castle]

Al·ces·tis (al·ses′tis) In Greek mythology, the heroic wife of Admetus; she volunteered to die to save her husband's life but was rescued from Hades by Hercules.

al·che·mist (al′kə·mist) *n.* One skilled in or practicing alchemy. — **al′che·mis′tic** or **·ti·cal** *adj.*

al·che·mize (al′kə·mīz) *v.t.* **·mized, ·miz·ing** To transmute by or as by alchemy.

al·che·my (al′kə·mē) *n.* **1.** The empirical and speculative chemistry of the Middle Ages, concerned primarily with the transmutation of base metals into gold and the search for the alkahest and the panacea. **2.** Any preternatural power or process of transmutation. Also **al′chy·my.** [< OF *alkemie* < Med.L *alchimia* < Arabic *al-kīmīa* < LGk. *chēmeia* transmutation of metals, later prob. confused with *chymeia* pouring, infusion < *cheein* to pour] — **al·chem·ic** (al·kem′ik) *adj.* — **al·chem′i·cal·ly** *adv.*

Al·ci·bi·a·des (al′sə·bī′ə·dēz), 450–404 B.C., Athenian general and statesman.

Al·ci·des (al·sī′dēz) See HERCULES.

al·ci·dine (al′sə·dīn) *adj.* Pertaining to or belonging to a family (*Alcidae*) of three-toed, web-footed sea birds of the northern hemisphere, including the auks, puffins, and guillemots. [< LL *alca* auk + ·IDAE]

Al·cin·o·us (al·sin′ō·əs) In Homer's *Odyssey*, the king of Phaeacia and father of Nausicaa.

Alc·man (alk′man) Seventh-century B.C. Spartan poet.

Alc·me·ne (alk·mē′nē) In Greek mythology, the mother of Hercules by Zeus, who seduced her in the guise of her husband Amphitryon.

al·co·hol (al′kə·hôl, -hol) *n.* **1.** A volatile, flammable, colorless liquid of a penetrating odor and burning taste, one of the products of the distillation of fermented grains, fruit juices, and starches. The two principal forms are ethyl alcohol (ethanol, C₂H₅OH), and methyl alcohol (methanol, CH₃OH). **2.** The intoxicating principle of wines and liquors; ethyl alcohol. **3.** Any liquor containing alcohol; spirits. **4.** *Chem.* One of a group of organic compounds derived from the alkanes by the substitution of one hydroxyl radical for one hydrogen atom. They have the general formula C$_n$H$_{2n+1}$OH. — **absolute alcohol** Dehydrated alcohol, in the United States alcohol containing 92.3% by weight or 94.9% by volume pure ethanol. [< Med. L, orig., fine powder < Arabic *al-kohl* fine powder (of antimony), kohl]

al·co·hol·ic (al′kə·hôl′ik, -hol′-) *adj.* **1.** Of, pertaining to, or having the qualities of alcohol. **2.** Containing or using alcohol: an *alcoholic* thermometer. **3.** Caused by alcohol or alcoholism: *alcoholic* insanity. **4.** Suffering from alcoholism. **5.** Preserved in alcohol. — *n.* One who uses alcoholic liquors habitually to excess; a dipsomaniac.

al·co·hol·ic·i·ty (al′kə·hôl·is′ə·tē, -hol-) *n.* The quality of being alcoholic; alcoholic strength: the *alcoholicity* of a wine.

al·co·hol·ism (al′kə·hôl′iz·əm, -hol′-) *n. Pathol.* A diseased condition resulting from the excessive or persistent use of alcoholic beverages; dipsomania.

al·co·hol·ize (al′kə·hôl·īz′, -hol-) *v.t.* **·ized, ·iz·ing 1.** To change into alcohol. **2.** To mix or saturate with alcohol.

al·co·hol·om·e·ter (al′kə·hôl·om′ə·tər, -hol-) *n.* An instrument or apparatus, as a hydrometer, for ascertaining the strength of alcohol or the percentage of absolute alcohol in liquors. — **al′co·hol·om′e·try** *n.*

Al·co·ran (al′kō·rän′, -ran′) *n.* The Koran. — **Al′co·ran′ic** (-ran′ik) *adj.* [< Arabic *al-qurān* the reading]

Al·cott (ôl′kət, -kot), Amos Bronson, 1799–1888, U.S. educator. — **Louisa May,** 1832–88, U.S. novelist; daughter of the preceding.

al·cove (al′kōv) *n.* **1.** A recess connected with or at the side of a larger room, as to contain a bed. **2.** Any embowered or secluded spot. [< F *alcôve* < Sp. *alcoba* < Arabic *al-qobbah* the vaulted chamber]

Al·cuin (al′kwin), 735–804, English scholar and ecclesiastical reformer; friend and adviser of Charlemagne. Also **Al′cwin.**

Al·cy·o·ne (al·sī′ə·nē) *n.* In Greek mythology: **a** The daughter of Aeolus who, mourning her husband Ceyx, cast herself into the sea and was changed into a kingfisher: also *Halcyone.* **b** One of the Pleiades. — *n. Astron.* The brightest of the six visible stars in the Pleiades cluster.

Ald. or, as title, **Aldm.** Alderman.

Al·dan (äl·dän′) A river of the Soviet Union, in the Yakut A.S.S.R., flowing north 1,767 miles to the Lena.

Al·deb·a·ran (al·deb′ə·rən) *n.* A red star, one of the 20 brightest, 0.86 magnitude, Alpha in the constellation Taurus. See STAR. [< Arabic *al-dabarān* the follower (i.e., of the Pleiades)]

al·de·hyde (al′də·hīd) *n.* **1.** *Chem.* Any one of a group of aliphatic compounds derived from the alcohols and intermediate between the alcohols and the acids. They have the general formula R–CHO. **2.** Acetaldehyde (which see). [< AL(COHOL) + DEHYD(ROGENIZED)]

Al·den (ôl′dən), John, 1599?–1687, Pilgrim settler in Plymouth Colony (1620); a character in Longfellow's poem *The Courtship of Miles Standish.*

al·der (ôl′dər) *n.* **1.** Any of various shrubs or small trees (genus *Alnus*) of the birch family, growing in wet ground and bearing small catkins. **2.** One of various other shrubs or small trees resembling it, as the dwarf alder. [OE *alor*]

al·der·man (ôl′dər·mən) *n. pl.* **·men 1.** *U.S.* In many municipalities, a member of the governing body, ranking below the mayor or other chief magistrate. **2.** In England and Ireland a member of the higher branch of a municipal or borough council, in Scotland a baillie. [OE *ealdorman* < *eald* old, senior + *man*] — **al′der·man·cy** (-mən·sē), **al′der·man·ship′** *n.* — **al′der·man′ic** (-man′ik) *adj.*

Al·der·ney (ôl′dər·nē) *n.* Any of the breeds of cattle found on the Channel Islands, as the Jersey or Guernsey.

Al·der·ney (ôl′dər·nē) The northernmost of the Channel Islands; 3 sq. mi.

Al·der·shot (ôl′dər·shot) A municipal borough in Hampshire, southern England; site of a permanent military camp; pop. 31,260 (1961).

Al·dine (ôl′dīn, al′-, -dēn) *adj.* Pertaining to or printed by the press of Aldus Manutius (see MANUTIUS) or his family: applied also to a modern series of books, and a style of display type. — *n.* A book printed by the Aldine press.

al·dol (al′dôl, -dol) *n. Chem.* A colorless, viscous compound, C₄H₈O₂, prepared from an acetaldehyde condensate, used in organic synthesis, ore flotation, and in the manufacture of perfumes: also called *acetaldol.* [< ALD(EHYDE) + -OL¹]

al·dose (al′dōs) *n. Chem.* A sugar or a class of sugars having the same chemical constitution as an aldehyde alcohol.

Al·drich (ôl′drich), Thomas Bailey, 1836–1907, U.S. poet and novelist.

Al·drin (ôl′drin), Edward Eugene, Jr., born 1930, U.S. astronaut and second man to walk on the moon: called **Buzz Aldrin.**

ale (āl) *n.* **1.** A fermented malt flavored with hops, resembling beer but generally having more body. **2.** *Brit.* A rural ale-drinking festival. [OE *ealu*]

a·le·a·to·ry (ā′lē·ə·tôr′ē, -tō′rē) *adj.* **1.** Dependent on contingency. **2.** Of or pertaining to gambling or luck. [< L *aleatorius* < *aleator* gambler < *alea* a die, chance]

A·lec·to (ə·lek′tō) One of the three Furies.

a·lee (ə·lē′) *adv. Naut.* At, on, or to the lee side. [< ON]

a·le·gar (al′ə·gər, ā′lə-) *n.* Sour ale; malt vinegar. [< ALE + (VINE)GAR]

ale·house (āl′hous′) *n.* A place where ale is sold to the public.

A·leich·em (ə·lā′khəm), Sho·lem (shō′ləm) Pseudonym of Solomon Ra·bin·o·witz (rä′bi·nô′vits, ra·bin′ə·vits) 1859–1916, Russian writer in Yiddish. Also **Shalom Aleichem.**

A·lek·san·drovsk (ä·lyik·sän′drəfsk) **1.** A port city in the Soviet Union, on western Sakhalin island; pop. 30,000. **2.** The former name for ZAPOROZHE.

A·le·mán (ä′lä·män′), Mateo, 1547–1610?, Spanish novelist. — **Miguel,** born 1902, Mexican lawyer; president 1946–52.

Al·e·man·ni (al′ə·man′ī) *n.pl.* A group of South Germanic tribes that fought against Rome in the third to fifth centuries: also spelled *Alamanni, Allemanni.*

Al·e·man·nic (al′ə·man′ik) *adj.* Of or pertaining to the Alemanni or their language. Also **Al′e·man′ni·an.** — *n.* The language of the Alemanni, a dialect of Old High German. Also spelled *Alamannic, Allemannic.*

A·lem·bert (dä·län·bâr′), Jean le Rond d', 1717–83, French mathematician and philosopher.

a·lem·bic (ə·lem′bik) *n.* **1.** An apparatus of glass or metal formerly used in distilling. **2.** Anything that tests, purifies, or transforms. [< OF *alambic,* ult. < Arabic *al-anbīq* the still < Gk. *ambix* a cup]

A·len·çon (à·län·sôn′) A town in NW France; pop. 21,893.

A·len·çon lace (ə·len′sən, *Fr.* à·län·sôn′) A fine needlepoint lace originally made in Alençon.

a·leph (ä′lif) *n.* The first letter in the Hebrew alphabet. Also **a′lef.** See ALPHABET.

A·lep·po (ə·lep′ō) A city in NE Syria; pop. 451,435 (1958). **Aleppo gall** Nutgall (which see).

a·lert (ə·lûrt′) *adj.* **1.** Keenly watchful; ready for sudden action; vigilant. **2.** Lively; nimble. **3.** Intelligent; bright. — *n.* **1.** A warning against attack; especially, a signal to prepare for an air raid. **2.** The time during which such a warning is in effect. — **on the alert** On the lookout; vigilant. — *v.t.* To prepare (someone) for action; warn, as of a threatened attack or raid. [< Ital. *all'erta* on the watch] — **a·lert′ly** *adv.* — **a·lert′ness** *n.*
— **Syn.** (adj.) **1.** wide-awake, active, alive, prompt. See VIGILANT. **2.** brisk, agile, bustling. — **Ant.** sluggish, slow, supine, inactive.

-ales *suffix Bot.* A feminine plural used to form the scientific names of plant orders. [< L, pl. of *-alis*]

A·les·san·dri·a (ä′läs·sän′drē·ä) A Province in Piedmont, northern Italy; 1,386 sq. mi.; pop. 474,925 (1961); capital, **Alessandria,** pop. 92,921.

a·leu·rone (ə·lŏŏr′ōn) *n. Bot.* An albuminoid substance found in minute solid granules in the seeds of some plants. In seeds of wheat and other cereals they form the outermost or **aleurone layer** of the endosperm. [< Gk. *aleuron* flour] — **al·eu·ron·ic** (al′yŏŏ·ron′ik) *adj.*

Al·e·ut (al′ē-ōōt) *n. pl.* **Al·e·uts** or **Al·e·ut 1.** A native of the Aleutian Islands belonging to either of two Eskimoan tribes called *Unungun*. **2.** A subfamily of the Eskimo–Aleut family of languages, comprising the dialects of the Aleutian Islands. — **A·leu·tian** (ə-lōō′shən), **A·leu′tic** *adj.*

A·leu·tian Islands (ə-lōō′shən) A chain of volcanic islands, extending some 1,100 miles from the tip of the Alaska Peninsula between the North Pacific and the Bering Sea. Also **A·leu′tians.**

Aleutian Range A mountain range of SW Alaska, extending along the Alaska Peninsula and continued by the Aleutian Islands.

ale·wife[1] (āl′wīf′) *n. pl.* **·wives** A small North American fish of the herring family (*Alosa pseudoharengus*): also called *hardhead, oldwife, skipjack*. [Origin unknown]

ale·wife[2] (āl′wīf′) *n. pl.* **·wives** A woman who keeps an alehouse.

Al·ex·an·der II (al′ig-zan′dər, -zän′-), 1818–81, czar of Russia 1855–81.

Alexander III, died 1181, pope 1159–81: original name **Orlando Ban·di·nel·li** (ban′də-nel′lē).

Alexander VI See (Rodrigo) BORGIA.

Alexander Archipelago A group of more than 1,000 islands, SE Alaska. Also **Alexander Islands.**

Alexander Nev·ski (nev′skē, nef′-), 1220?–63, Russian hero.

Alexander Se·ve·rus (sə-vir′əs), 208?–235; Roman emperor 222–235.

Alexander the Great, 356–323 B.C., king of Macedon 336–323; conqueror of the Persian Empire.

Al·ex·an·dret·ta (al′-ig-zan-dret′ə, -zän-) A former name for İSKENDERUN.

Al·ex·an·dri·a (al′-ig-zan′drē-ə, -zän′-) **1.** A city in the United Arab Republic, of which it is the chief port; ancient capital of Egypt; pop. 1,801,056 (1966): Arabic *Al Iskandariyah*. **2.** A city in northern Virginia, on the Potomac River; pop. 110,938. **3.** A city in central Louisiana; pop. 41,557.

Al·ex·an·dri·an (al′ig-zan′drē-ən, -zän′-) *adj.* **1.** Of Alexandria in Egypt. **2.** Of or pertaining to the Alexandrian school or its influence. **3.** Of Alexander the Great, his reign, or his conquests. **4.** In prosody, Alexandrine. — *n.* **1.** A native or inhabitant of Alexandria. **2.** In prosody, an Alexandrine verse.

Alexandrian school 1. A Hellenistic school of literature, science, and philosophy, at Alexandria, Egypt, during the last three centuries B.C. **2.** The school of Christian philosophers and theologians at Alexandria during the first five centuries A.D., that sought to combine Christianity and Greek philosophy.

Al·ex·an·drine (al′ig-zan′drin, -drēn, -zän′-) *n.* In prosody, a line of verse having six iambic feet with the caesura generally after the third. — *adj.* Of, composed of, or characterized by Alexandrines. Also **Alexandrian.**

al·ex·an·drite (al′ig-zan′drīt, -zän′-) *n.* A green variety of chrysoberyl, red by artificial light. [after *Alexander* II, czar of Russia]

A·lex·an·drou·po·lis (ä′lek-sän-drōō′pô-lēs) A port city in NE Greece, on the Aegean; pop. about 18,500: formerly *Dedeagach.*

a·lex·i·a (ə-lek′sē-ə) *n. Pathol.* Inability to read correctly, caused by a cerebral lesion in a person who previously could read and has not become blind: also called *word blindness.* [< NL < Gk. *a-* without + *lexis* speech < *legein* to speak]

a·lex·in (ə-lek′sin) *n. Bacteriol.* Complement (def. 7). [< Gk. *alexein* to ward off]

a·lex·i·phar·mic (ə-lek′si-fär′mik) *Med. adj.* Serving to ward off or resist poison; antidotal. — *n.* An antidote, or poison preventive. [< Gk. *alexipharmakos* < *alexein* to ward off + *pharmakon* poison]

A·lex·is Mi·khai·lo·vich (ə-lek′sis mē-khī′lə-vich), 1629–1676, czar of Russia 1645–76; father of Peter the Great.

al·fal·fa (al-fal′fə) *n.* A cloverlike plant (*Medicago sativa*) of the bean family, used as forage in the United States and Europe: also called *purple medic.* Also, *Brit., lucerne.* [< Sp. < Arabic *al-faṣfaṣah*, the best kind of fodder]

al·fa·qui (al′fə-kē′) *n.* A teacher of Moslem law or of the Koran; a priest of Islam. Also **al′fa·ki** or **al′fa·quin′** (-kēn′). [< Sp. < Arabic *al-faqīh*]

Al·fie·ri (äl-fyâ′rē), **Vittorio,** 1749–1803, Italian dramatist.

al·fil·e·ri·a (al-fil′ə-rē′ə) *n.* A European weed (*Erodium cicutarium*) of the geranium family, now used as forage in the United States: also called *pingrass.* Also **al·fil′a·ri′a.** [< Amer. Sp. < Sp. *alfiler* pin < Arabic *al-khilāl* thorn]

Al·fon·so I (al-fon′sō, -zō), 1110?–85, first king of Portugal.

Al·fon·so XIII (al-fon′sō, -zō; *Sp.* äl-fōn′sō), 1886–1941, king of Spain 1886–1931; deposed.

al·for·ja (al-fôr′jə, *Sp.* äl-fôr′hä) *n.* **1.** A leather pouch; saddlebag. **2.** A cheek pouch, as of a prairie dog. [< Sp. < Arabic *al-khorj*]

Al·fred (al′frid), 849–899, king of Wessex and overlord of England 871–899; defeated the Danish invaders; built the first English navy; considered the father of English prose literature: called **the Great.**

al·fres·co (al-fres′kō) *adv.* In the open air. — *adj.* Occurring outdoors, as a meal. Also **al fresco.** [< Ital.]

alg. *Math.* Algebra.

Alg. 1. Algeria; Algerian. **2.** Algiers.

al·ga (al′gə) *n. pl.* **·gae** (-jē) Any plant of a subdivision (*Algae*) of thallophytes, consisting of primitive, chlorophyllbearing plants widely distributed in fresh and salt water and moist lands, including the seaweeds, kelps, diatoms, pond scums, and stoneworts. [< L, seaweed] — **al·gal** (al′gəl) *adj.*

al·gar·ro·ba (al′gə-rō′bə) *n.* **1.** The carob or its pods or beans. **2.** The mesquite (def. 1). Also **al′ga·ro′ba.** [< Sp. < Arabic *al-kharrūbah* the carob]

al·ge·bra (al′jə-brə) *n.* The branch of mathematics that treats of quantity and the relations of numbers in the abstract, and in which calculations are performed by means of letters and symbols. It includes the solution of equations of any degree. [< Ital. < Arabic *al-jebr* the reunion of broken parts, bonesetting]

al·ge·bra·ic (al′jə-brā′ik) *adj.* **1.** Of or pertaining to algebra. **2.** Used in or involving algebra. Also **al′ge·bra′i·cal.** — **al′ge·bra′i·cal·ly** *adv.*

al·ge·bra·ist (al′jə-brā′ist) *n.* One skilled in algebra.

Al·ge·cir·as (al′jə-sir′əs, *Sp.* äl′hä-thē′räs) A port city in SW Spain, on the Strait of Gibraltar; pop. 62,592 (est. 1958).

al·ge·don·ic (al′jə-don′ik) *adj.* Characterized by or relating to pleasure and pain. [< Gk. *algos* pain + *hēdonikos* pleasurable]

Al·ger (al′jər), **Horatio,** 1834–99, U.S. writer of boys' stories.

Al·ge·ri·a (al-jir′ē-ə) A Republic in NW Africa, formerly a dependency of France; 919,352 sq. mi.; pop. 12,101,994 (1966); administrative capital, Algiers. *French* **Al·gé·rie** (äl-zhā-rē′). — **Al·ge′ri·an** *adj. & n.*

al·ge·rine (al′jə-rēn′) *n.* A soft woolen fabric or shawl with bright stripes. [after *Algeria*, where formerly made]

Al·ge·rine (al′jə-rēn′) *n.* **1.** An Algerian. **2.** A pirate.

Algerine War The war between the United States and the pirates of the Algerian coast, 1815.

-algia *suffix* Pain or disease of: *neuralgia.* [< Gk. *algos* pain]

al·gid (al′jid) *adj.* Cold; chilly. [< F *algide* < L *algidus* cold < *algere* to be cold] — **al·gid′i·ty** *n.*

Al·giers (al-jirz′) The capital and chief port of Algeria, on the Mediterranean; pop. 943,142 (est. 1966). *French* **Al·ger** (äl-zhā′).

al·gin (al′jin) *n.* The dried, gelatinous form of various seaweeds, especially the giant kelp, used as an emulsifier, thickening and ripening agent, and demulcent. [< ALGA]

al·gi·nate (al′jə-nāt) *n. Chem.* Any metal salt of algin. — *adj.* Denoting any of various synthetic yarns or textile fibers made from algin or alginates.

al·goid (al′goid) *adj.* Of or like algae.

Al·gol (al′gol) *n.* The variable star Beta in Perseus: also called *Demon Star.* [< Arabic *al-ghūl* the ghoul, the demon]

al·go·lag·ni·a (al′gə-lag′nē-ə) *n. Psychiatry* Sexual pleasure resulting from the infliction or the experiencing of pain. See MASOCHISM, SADISM. [< NL < Gk. *algos* pain + *lagneia* lust] — **al·go·lag′nic** *adj.* — **al′go·lag′nist** *n.*

al·gol·o·gy (al-gol′ə-jē) *n.* The branch of botany that treats of algae. [< L *alga* seaweed + -(O)LOGY] — **al·go·log·i·cal** (al′gə-loj′i-kəl) *adj.* — **al·gol′o·gist** *n.*

al·gom·e·ter (al-gom′ə-tər) *n.* An instrument for measuring sensitivity to pain caused by pressure. [< Gk. *algos* pain + -METER] — **al·go·met·ric** (al′gə-met′rik) or **·ri·cal** *adj.* — **al·gom′e·try** *n.*

Al·gon·ki·an (al-gong′kē-ən) *adj. & n.* **1.** *Geol.* Proterozoic. **2.** Algonquian.

Al·gon·kin (al-gong′kin) *n. pl.* **·kin** or **·kins** Algonquin.

Al·gon·qui·an (al-gong′kē-ən, -kwē-ən) *n. pl.* **·qui·an** or **·qui·ans 1.** A family of North American Indian languages formerly spoken in the area from Hudson Bay south to North Carolina and Tennessee, and from the North Atlantic seaboard to the northern plains, including Arapaho, Blackfoot, Cheyenne, Cree, Ojibwa, Micmac, Delaware, and Massachusett. **2.** A member of an Algonquian-speaking tribe. — *adj.* Of or pertaining to the Algonquian family of languages.

Al·gon·quin (al-gong′kin, -kwin) *n. pl.* **·quin** or **·quins 1.** A member of certain Algonquian tribes formerly inhabiting territory near the mouth of the Ottawa River and a region north of the St. Lawrence River. **2.** The Algonquian language spoken by these tribes.

al·gor (al′gôr) *n. Pathol.* Cold; chilliness; especially, an abnormal coldness, as in the early stages of a fever. [< L]

al·go·rism (al′gə·riz′əm) *n.* **1.** The Arabic or decimal system of numeration. **2.** Any method of computation using Arabic notation. **3.** Arithmetic. Also **al·go·rithm** (al′gə·rith′əm). [< OF *algorisme* < Med.L *algorismus* < Arabic *al-Khowārazmī,* lit., the native of Khwārazm (Khiva), surname of a 9th c. Arab mathematician]

al·gum (al′gum) *n.* Almug, a kind of wood.

Al·ham·bra (al·ham′brə) **1.** The palace of the Moorish kings at Granada, Spain, built in the 13th and 14th centuries. **2.** A city in SW California, near Los Angeles; pop. 62,125. [< Sp. < Arabic *al-hamrā'* the red (house)]

Al·ham·bresque (al′ham·bresk′) *adj.* Like the Alhambra or its peculiar and delicate type of Moorish architecture.

A·li (ä′lē), 600?–661, fourth Moslem caliph; husband of Fatima and adopted son of Mohammed.

a·li·as (ā′lē·əs) *n. pl.* **a·li·as·es** An assumed name. — *Syn.* See PSEUDONYM. — *adv.* Otherwise called: Miller, *alias* Brown. [< L, at another time]

A·li Ba·ba (ä′lē bä′bä) In the *Arabian Nights,* a poor woodcutter who gains entrance to the cave of the forty thieves by crying out the magic words "Open sesame."

al·i·bi (al′ə·bī) *n. pl.* **·bis** **1.** *Law* A form of defense by which an accused person attempts to show that he was elsewhere when the crime was committed. **2.** *U.S. Informal* An excuse. — *v.i.* **·bied, ·bi·ing** *U.S. Informal* To make excuses for oneself. [< L, elsewhere]

al·i·ble (al′ə·bəl) *adj.* Nourishing; nutritive. [< L *alibilis* < *alere* to nourish] — **al′i·bil′i·ty** *n.*

A·li·can·te (ä′lē·kän′tä) A Province of eastern Spain; 2,264 sq. mi.; pop. 696,165 (1959); capital, Alicante, pop. 177,204.

al·i·cy·clic (al′i·sī′klik, -sik′lik) *adj. Chem.* Denoting any of a class of organic compounds that exhibit aliphatic characteristics but whose carbon atoms are of the cyclic rather than open-chain form. [< ALI(PHATIC) + CYCLIC]

al·i·dade (al′i·dād) *n.* **1.** A circle, frame, or movable arm carrying microscopes or verniers, for reading the divisions of a graduated circle or arc. **2.** A theodolite having such an arm. Also **al·i·dad** (al′i·dad). [< F < Med.L *alhidada* < Arabic *al-'idādah* the revolving radius of a graduated circle]

al·ien (āl′yən, ā′lē·ən) *adj.* **1.** Owing allegiance to another country; unnaturalized; foreign. **2.** Of or related to others: *alien* property. **3.** Not one's own; strange: *alien* customs. **4.** Not consistent with; incongruous; opposed: with *to: alien* to his tastes. — *n.* **1.** An unnaturalized foreign resident. **2.** A member of a foreign nation, tribe, people, etc. **3.** One estranged or excluded. **4.** *Bot.* A plant native to one region maintaining itself under conditions prevailing in another. — *v.t.* **1.** To transfer to another, as property. **2.** To estrange. [< L *alienus* belonging to another < *alius* another] — *Syn.* (adj.) **4.** extrinsic, extraneous, irrelevant. — (noun) **1.** *Alien, foreigner,* and *stranger* denote one set apart from the persons among whom he lives. An *alien* is not a citizen of the country in which he resides. A *foreigner* is not a native of the country where he lives, but he may become a naturalized citizen. A *stranger* is one previously unknown to his neighbors; he may be an *alien* or a citizen from another part of the same country. — **Ant.** citizen, countryman, native.

al·ien·a·ble (āl′yən·ə·bəl, ā′lē·ən-) *adj. Law* Capable of being made over or transferred, as property to the ownership of another. — **al′ien·a·bil′i·ty** *n.*

al·ien·age (āl′yən·ij, ā′lē·ən-) *n.* The state of being alien.

al·ien·ate (āl′yən·āt, ā′lē·ən-) *v.t.* **·at·ed, ·at·ing** **1.** To make indifferent or unfriendly; estrange: to *alienate* a friend. **2.** To cause to feel estranged or withdrawn from society. **3.** To turn away; to *alienate* the affections. **4.** *Law* To make over; transfer, as property. [< L *alienatus,* pp. of *alienare* to estrange < *alienus* of another] — **al′ien·a′tor** *n.*

al·ien·a·tion (āl′yən·ā′shən, ā′lē·ən-) *n.* **1.** Estrangement or withdrawal, as from the affections of another. **2.** A feeling of not belonging to or having a fit place in society, often accompanied by anxiety and sometimes by resentment or hostility: the growing *alienation* of students from the adult world. **3.** *Psychiatry* A Deprivation, entire or partial, of mental power. **b** Insanity. **4.** *Law* The transfer of property, or title, to another.

al·ien·ee (āl′yən·ē′, ā′lē·ən·ē′) *n. Law* One who takes over transferred property.

al·ien·ism (āl′yən·iz′əm, ā′lē·ən-) *n.* **1.** Alienage. **2.** The study and treatment of mental derangement.

al·ien·ist (āl′yən·ist, ā′lē·ən-) *n.* One skilled in the study or treatment of mental disorders: used chiefly in medical jurisprudence. [< F *aliéniste,* ult. < L *alienus,* strange, insane]

al·ien·or (āl′yən·ər, ā′lē·ən·ôr′) *n. Law* One who alienates property to another; a vendor. Also **al′ien·er.** [< AF]

a·lif (ä′lif) *n.* The first letter in the Arabic alphabet.

al·i·form (al′ə·fôrm, ā′lə·fôrm) *adj.* Wing-shaped; alar. [< L *ala* wing + -FORM]

Al·i·garh (al′i·gûr′) A city in western Uttar Pradesh, India; pop. 232,278 (est. 1969).

a·light¹ (ə·līt′) *v.i.* **a·light·ed** or **a·lit, a·light·ing** **1.** To descend and come to rest; settle, as after flight. **2.** To dismount. **3.** To come by accident: with *on* or *upon.* [OE

ālihtan < *ā-* out, off + *lihtan* to alight, orig., to make light] — *Syn.* land, settle, light. Compare DESCEND.

a·light² (ə·līt′) *adj. & adv.* Lighted; burning. [ME *aliht,* pp. of *alihten* to light up]

a·lign (ə·līn′) *v.t.* **1.** To arrange or place in a line; bring into line. **2.** To put (oneself, one's party, etc.) on one side of an issue, controversy, etc. — *v.i.* **3.** To fall into line. Also spelled *aline.* [< F *aligner* < *a-* to (< L *ad-*) + *ligner* to place in line < L *lineare* < *linea* line]

a·lign·ment (ə·līn′mənt) *n.* **1.** Position or place in line; arrangement in line. **2.** A line or lines so made. **3.** *Engin.* A ground plan, as of a railroad. **4.** The state of being on one side of an issue, controversy, etc. Also spelled *alinement.*

a·like (ə·līk′) *adj.* Having resemblance; like one another; resembling, wholly or in part: used predicatively of plural and collective subjects: The family are all *alike.* — *adv.* In the same or like manner; equally. [Fusion of ON *ālīkr* and OE *gelīc, anlīc*] — **a·like′ness** *n.*

al·i·ment (al′ə·mənt) *n.* **1.** Food for body or mind; nutriment. **2.** That which sustains or supports. — *v.t.* To furnish with food; nourish. [< L *alimentum* < *alere* to nourish] — **al·i·men·tal** (al′ə·men′təl) *adj.* — **al′i·men′tal·ly** *adv.*

al·i·men·ta·ry (al′ə·men′trē, -tə·rē) *adj.* **1.** Supplying nourishment. **2.** Connected with food or the function of nutrition. **3.** Providing support; sustaining.

alimentary canal The food canal between the mouth and the anus, including esophagus, stomach, and intestines.

al·i·men·ta·tion (al′ə·men·tā′shən) *n.* **1.** The act or process of supplying or receiving nourishment. **2.** Maintenance; support. — **al·i·men·ta·tive** (al′ə·men′tə·tiv) *adj.*

A·li Mo·ham·med (ä′lē mō·ham′id) See under BABISM.

al·i·mo·ny (al′ə·mō′nē) *n.* **1.** *Law* The allowance made to a woman by order of court, from her husband's estate or income, for her maintenance after a divorce or legal separation, or during a suit therefor. **2.** Maintenance; sustenance. [< L *alimonia* food, support < *alere* to nourish]

a·line (ə·līn′), **a·line·ment** (ə·līn′mənt) See ALIGN, etc.

A·li Pa·sha (ä′lē pä·shä′), 1741–1822, Albanian warrior and leader: called the **Lion of Janina.**

al·i·ped (al′ə·ped) *Zool. n.* A wing-footed animal, as a bat. — *adj.* Wing-footed; having a membrane connecting the digits. [< L *alipes, -pedis* wing-footed < *ala* wing + *pes* foot]

al·i·phat·ic (al′ə·fat′ik) *adj. Chem.* Designating a large class of saturated or unsaturated hydrocarbon compounds of the open-chain formation, including the alkanes, alkenes, and alkynes. [< Gk. *aleinhar, aleiphatos* fat, oil]

al·i·quant (al′ə·kwənt) *adj. Math.* Not dividing evenly into another number: 4 is an *aliquant* part of 11. [< L *aliquantus* some < *alius* other + *quantus* how large, how much]

Al·i·quip·pa (al′ə·kwip′ə) A borough in western Pennsylvania, on the Ohio River; pop. 22,277.

al·i·quot (al′ə·kwət) *adj. Math.* Dividing evenly into another number: 4 is an *aliquot* part of 12. [< L *aliquot* < *alius* other + *quot* how many]

Al Is·kan·da·ri·yah (al is·kan·da·rē′yə) The Arabic name for ALEXANDRIA.

a·lit (ə·lit′) Alternative past tense and past participle of ALIGHT¹.

a·li·un·de (ā′lē·un′dē) *adv. Law* From a source extrinsic to the matter; from elsewhere: evidence *aliunde.* [< L]

a·live (ə·līv′) *adj.* **1.** In a living or functioning state; having life: said of organisms. **2.** In existence or operation; in full vigor; active: to keep hope *alive.* **3.** In lively action; in an animated state; sprightly: *alive* with enthusiasm. **4.** Open or susceptible; sensitive: with *to: alive* to the needs of others. **5.** Abounding in life or living things, or in evidences of life: *alive* with bees. [OE *on līfe* in life] — *Syn.* **1.** living, existent, existing, animate. **2.** active, alert. **3.** animated, brisk, quick, vivacious. **4.** sentient. **5.** teeming. — *Ant.* dead, deceased, defunct, lifeless, inanimate.

a·liz·a·rin (ə·liz′ə·rin) *n. Chem.* A basic, orange-red, crystalline coloring compound, $C_{14}H_8O_4$, formerly prepared from madder, now manufactured from anthraquinone and used as a dye. — *adj.* Designating any dyestuff derived from anthraquinone. Also **a·liz·a·rine** (ə·liz′ə·rin, -rēn). [< F *alizarine* < *alizari* madder, prob. < Arabic *al-asārah* juice]

al·ka·hest (al′kə·hest) *n.* The hypothetical universal solvent sought by the ancient alchemists. [A pseudo-Arabic word coined by Paracelsus]

al·ka·les·cent (al′kə·les′ənt) *adj.* Becoming or tending to become alkaline. — *n.* An alkalescent compound. — **al′ka·les′cence, al′ka·les′cen·cy** *n.*

al·ka·li (al′kə·lī) *n. pl.* **·lis** or **·lies** **1.** *Chem.* **a** A hydroxide of any of the alkali metals, or of the ammonium radical, characterized by great solubility in water and capable of neutralizing acids and of turning red litmus paper blue. **b** Any compound that will neutralize an acid, as lime, magnesia, etc. **c** Any of several other compounds, as sodium carbonate. **2.** Mineral matter, not including sodium chloride, found in natural waters and in soils. [< MF *alcali* < Arabic *al-qaliy* the ashes of saltwort]

al·kal·ic (al·kal′ik) *adj.* **1.** Containing or characterized by a considerable amount of the alkaline bases, especially soda and potash. **2.** Alkaline.

al·ka·li flat *Geol.* An arid plain, permeated or incrusted with alkaline salts; the bed of an evaporated lake.

al·ka·li·fy (al'kə-lə-fī', al·kal'ə-fī) *v.t. & v.i.* **-fied, -fy·ing** To change into or become alkaline or an alkali.

alkali metals *Chem.* Elements in the first group of the periodic table, including lithium, sodium, potassium, rubidium, cesium, and francium. Also **alkaline metals.**

al·ka·lim·e·ter (al'kə-lim'ə-tər) *n.* An instrument for determining the quantity of carbon dioxide in solids. — **al'ka·lim'e·try** *n.*

al·ka·line (al'kə-līn, -lin) *adj.* **1.** Of, pertaining to, or like an alkali. **2.** Containing or produced by an alkali. Also **al'ka·lin** (-lin).

alkaline earths *Chem.* The oxides of calcium, strontium, barium, and sometimes magnesium.

alkaline soil A soil containing an unusual amount of soluble mineral salts, principally chlorides, sulfates, carbonates, and bicarbonates of sodium, potassium, magnesium, and calcium, and sometimes borates and nitrates.

al·ka·lin·i·ty (al'kə-lin'ə-tē) *n.* The state or quality of being alkaline.

al·ka·lize (al'kə-līz) *v.t. & v.i.* **-lized, -liz·ing** To convert into or become alkali or alkaline. — **al'ka·li·za'tion** *n.*

al·ka·loid (al'kə-loid) *n. Chem.* Any of a class of nitrogenous organic bases, especially one of vegetable origin, having a physiological effect on animals and man, as strychnine or morphine. — **al'ka·loi'dal** *adj.*

al·ka·lo·sis (al'kə-lō'sis) *n. Pathol.* Excessive alkali in the blood and tissues of the body.

al·kane (al'kān) *n. Chem.* Any of a group of saturated aliphatic hydrocarbon compounds having the general formula C_nH_{2n+2}, as those of the methane series. [< ALK(YL) + (METH)ANE]

alkane series *Chem.* The methane series (which see).

al·ka·net (al'kə-net) *n.* **1.** The root of a plant (*Alkanna tinctoria*) yielding a red dye. **2.** The plant. **3.** Anchusin, the red dye. **4.** One of several similar dye-producing plants of other genera, as **European alkanet** (*Anchusa officinalis*), and **evergreen alkanet** (*Anchusa sempervirens*): also called *bugloss.* **5.** The puccoon (def. 1). [< Sp. *alcaneta,* dim. of *alcana* henna < Arabic *al-hinnā'* the henna]

al·kene (al'kēn) *n. Chem.* Any of a group of unsaturated aliphatic hydrocarbon compounds having a double bond and the general formula C_nH_{2n}, as ethylene: also called *olefin.* [< ALK(YL) + -ENE]

Alk·maar (älk'mär) A commune in the NW Netherlands; pop. 42,507 (est. 1959).

Al·ko·ran (al'kō-rän', -ran') *n.* The Koran. — **Al'ko·ran'ic** (-ran'ik) *adj.* [< Arabic *al-qurān* the reading]

al·kyd resin (al'kid) *Chem.* A synthetic resin made from phthalic anhydride and glycerol and used as a bonding agent in paints, lacquers, etc.

al·kyl (al'kil) *n. Chem.* A univalent radical obtained by removing one hydrogen atom from an aliphatic compound. [< ALK(ALI) + -YL]

al·kyl·a·tion (al'kə-lā'shən) *n. Chem.* The introduction, by replacement or addition, of an alkyl group into an organic compound.

al·kyne (al'kīn) *n. Chem.* Any of a group of unsaturated aliphatic hydrocarbon compounds having a triple bond and the general formula C_nH_{2n-2}, as acetylene. [< ALKY(L) + -INE²]

all (ôl) *adj.* **1.** The entire substance or extent of: *all* Europe; *all* wisdom. **2.** The entire number of; the individual components of, without exception: known to *all* men. **3.** The greatest possible: in *all* haste. **4.** Any whatever: beyond *all* doubt. **5.** Every: used in phrases with *manner, sorts,* and *kinds: all* manner of men. **6.** Nothing except: He was *all* skin and bones. — *n.* **1.** Everything that one has; entire interest or possession: to give one's *all.* **2.** Whole being; totality. — *pron.* **1.** Everyone: *All* are condemned. **2.** Each one: When he questioned his students, *all* were ready. **3.** Everything: *All* is lost. **4.** Every part, as of a whole: *All* of it is gone. — **above all** Primarily; of the first importance. — **after all** Everything else being considered; nevertheless. — **all in all** All things considered; taken as a whole. — **at all 1.** In any way: I can't come *at all.* **2.** To any degree or extent: no luck *at all.* — **for all** To the degree that: *For all* I care, you can go alone. — **for all of** As for: You can leave now, *for all of* me. — **in all** Including everything; all told: ten books *in all.* — *adv.* **1.** Wholly; entirely: fallen *all* to bits; *all* at once; *all* too dear. **2.** Exclusively; only: This desk is *all* for me. **3.** For each; on each side: a score of three *all.* — **all but 1.** Almost; on the verge of: I was *all but* exhausted. **2.** Every one except: He took *all but* six. — **all in** *Informal* Wearied, as from exertion. — **all of** No less than; quite: It's *all of* ten miles. — **all out** Making every effort: They went *all out* for victory. — **all over 1.** Finished; past and gone. **2.** Everywhere; in all parts: He's been *all over.* **3.** *Informal* Typically; in every way: That's George *all over.* — **all the** (better, more, etc.) So much the (better, more, etc.). [OE]

al·la bre·ve (ä'lä brev'ā, *Ital.* äl'lä brā'vā) *Music* A measure of duple time in which the beat is represented by the half note, performed twice as quickly as common time. Symbol ₵. [< Ital., lit., according to the breve]

Al·lah (al'ə, ä'lə) In Islam, the one supreme being; God. [< Arabic]

Al·la·ha·bad (al'ə-hə-bad', ä'lə-hä-bäd') A city in northern India, at the confluence of the Ganges and Jumna rivers; former capital of Uttar Pradesh; pop. 431,007 (1961).

all-A·mer·i·can (ôl'ə-mer'ə-kən) *adj.* **1.** Representative of America or of the United States. **2.** Composed of the best in the United States: an *all-American* football team. **3.** Of or composed of Americans exclusively. **4.** Of all the Americas. **5.** Within or confined to America or the United States. — *n.* A player selected for an all-American team; also, the status of such a player.

Al·lan-a-Dale (al'ən-ə-dāl') In English legend, an outlaw of Robin Hood's band.

al·lan·toid (ə-lan'toid) *adj.* **1.** Of or pertaining to the allantois. **2.** Sausage-shaped. Also **al·lan·toi·dal** (al'ən-toid'l). [< Gk. *allantoeidēs < allas, -antos* sausage + *eidos* form]

al·lan·to·is (ə-lan'tō·is) *n. Zool.* A membranous saclike appendage developed from the hinder part of the alimentary tract in the embryos of mammals, birds, and reptiles. It plays an important part in embryonic blood supply and nutrition. [< NL < *allantoīdes* < Gk. *allantoeidēs.* See ALLANTOID.] — **al·lan·to·ic** (al'ən-tō'ik) *adj.*

al·lar·gan·do (äl'lär-gän'dō) *Music adj.* Becoming slower and broader in style. — *adv.* More slowly and more broadly. [< Ital.]

all-a·round (ôl'ə-round') *adj.* All-round (which see).

al·lay (ə-lā') *v.t.* **-layed, -lay·ing 1.** To lessen the violence or reduce the intensity of. **2.** To lay to rest, as fears; pacify; calm. [OE *ālecgan < ā-* away + *lecgan* to lay] — **al·lay'er** *n.* — **Syn. 1.** abate, lighten, moderate. Compare ALLEVIATE. **2.** soothe, mollify.

all clear The signal indicating that an air raid is over.

al·le·ga·tion (al'ə-gā'shən) *n.* **1.** The act of alleging. **2.** That which is alleged. **3.** Something alleged without proof. **4.** *Law* The assertion that a party to a suit undertakes to prove. [< L *allegatio, -onis* < *allegare* to send a message < *ad-* to + *legare* to commission]

al·lege (ə-lej') *v.t.* **-leged, -leg·ing 1.** To assert to be true without proving; affirm. **2.** To plead as an excuse, in support of or in opposition to a claim or accusation. **3.** *Archaic* To cite or quote. — **Syn.** See ASSERT. [< AF *alegier,* OF *esligier* < L *ex-* out + *litigare* to sue; infl. by L *allegare* (see ALLEGATION) and *lex* law] — **al·lege'a·ble** *adj.* — **al·leged'** (ə-lejd', ə-lej'id) *adj.* — **al·leg'er** *n.*

al·leg·ed·ly (ə-lej'id-lē) *adv.* According to allegation.

Al·le·ghe·ny (al'ə-gā'nē) *adj.* Of or pertaining to the Allegheny Mountains or River. Also **Al'le·gha'ny.**

Allegheny Mountains A mountain range of the Appalachian system, extending from Pennsylvania to Virginia.

Allegheny River A river in western New York and Pennsylvania, flowing SW 325 miles to join with the Monongahela, forming the Ohio River.

Allegheny Series *Geol.* The middle Coal Measures of the eastern United States.

al·le·giance (ə-lē'jəns) *n.* **1.** Fidelity, or an obligation of fidelity, to a government or sovereign. **2.** The recognition or observance of fidelity in general, as to a principle; faithful adherence. **3.** *Archaic* The duty and obligation of a vassal holding lands by fealty to the superior lord. [ME *alegeaunce* < *a-* to (< L *ad-*) + OF *ligeance < liege.* See LIEGE.] — **Syn. 1.** loyalty, fealty. Compare FIDELITY.

al·le·giant (ə-lē'jənt) *adj. Obs.* Loyal; faithful.

al·le·gor·ic (al'ə-gôr'ik, -gor'-) *adj.* Pertaining to, appearing in, or containing allegory; figurative. Also **al'le·gor'i·cal.** [< L *allegoricus* < Gk. *allēgorikos < allēgoria.* See ALLEGORY.] — **al'le·gor'i·cal·ly** *adv.*

al·le·go·rist (al'ə-gôr'ist, -gō'rist, al'ə-gər·ist) *n.* One who composes or uses allegories.

al·le·go·ris·tic (al'ə-gə·ris'tik) *adj.* Allegorizing.

al·le·go·rize (al'ə-gə-rīz') *v.* **-rized, -riz·ing** *v.t.* **1.** To turn into an allegory; relate in the manner of an allegory. **2.** To explain or interpret as an allegory. — *v.i.* **3.** To make or use allegory. — **al·le·go·ri·za·tion** (al'ə-gôr'ə-zā'shən, -gor'-) *n.* — **al'le·go·riz'er** *n.*

al·le·go·ry (al'ə-gôr'ē, -gō'rē) *n. pl.* **-ries 1.** A story or narrative, as a fable, in which a moral principle or abstract truth is presented by means of fictional characters, events, etc. **2.** The presentation of a truth or moral by such stories. **3.** Loosely, any symbolic representation in literature or art; an emblem. [< L *allegoria* < Gk. *allēgoria,* lit., a speaking otherwise < *allos* other + *agoreuein* to speak in public assembly < *agora* forum] — **Syn. 2.** *Allegory, parable, fable,* and *apologue* denote a story told about fictional persons and events to teach or illustrate a moral principle. In *allegory* and *parable* the moral is not stated, but is left to the hearer to discover. An *allegory* is usually long and elaborate, with many characters and incidents; a *parable* is brief, and typically shows the application of a moral precept to a familiar situation. A *fable* or *apologue* usually states the moral at the end, and is told in terms of animals and inanimate things that speak, and reflect the nature of human beings. Compare FICTION.

al·le·gret·to (al/ə-gret/ō, *Ital.* äl/lā-gret/tō)　*Music adj. & adv.* Rather fast; faster than andante but slower than allegro. — *n. pl.* ·tos A composition, movement, etc., in such tempo. [< Ital., dim. of *allegro* lively]

al·le·gro (ə-lā/grō, ə-leg/rō; *Ital.* äl-lā/grō)　*Music adj. & adv.* Lively; faster than allegretto but slower than presto. — *n. pl.* ·gros A composition, movement, etc., in such tempo. [< Ital.]

allegro non tan·to (nōn tän/tō)　*Music* Moderately lively. [< Ital.]

al·lele (ə-lēl/)　*n. Genetics* One of a series of hereditary characters alternative to each other. A fertilized gamete will normally contain two of any series. Also **al·le·lo·morph** (ə-lē/lə-môrf, ə-lel/ə-). [< Gk. *allēlōn* of one another + *morphē* form] — **al·le/lo·mor/phic** *adj.* — **al·le/lo·mor/· phism** *n.*

al·le·lu·ia (al/ə-lōō/yə)　*i. & interj.* Hallelujah: the Latin spelling and more common liturgic form. Also **al/le·lu/iah.**

al·le·mande (al/ə-mand/, *Fr.* äl-mänd/)　*n.* **1.** A processional dance originating in Germany. **2.** Music for or in the manner of this dance, in duple meter. [< F, lit., German]

Al·le·man·ni (al/ə-man/ī), etc. See ALEMANNI, etc.

Al·len (al/ən), **Ethan,** 1737–89, American soldier; leader of the Green Mountain Boys. — **Ira,** 1751–1814, American soldier and legislator; brother of preceding.

Al·len Park (al/ən)　A village in SE Michigan, near Detroit; pop. 40,747.

Al·len·town (al/ən-toun/)　A city in eastern Pennsylvania; pop. 109,527.

al·ler·gen (al/ər-jən)　*n.* Any substance capable of producing allergy. Also **al/ler·gin.**

al·ler·gen·ic (al/ər-jen/ik)　*adj.* Producing allergy.

al·ler·gic (ə-lûr/jik)　*adj.* **1.** Characteristic of or pertaining to allergy. **2.** Having an allergy. **3.** *Informal* Having an aversion: *allergic* to work.

al·ler·gist (al/ər-jist)　*n.* A specialist in the diagnosis and treatment of allergies.

al·ler·gy (al/ər-jē)　*n. pl.* ·gies *Med.* **1.** A condition of heightened sensitivity in an individual to a substance that in similar amounts is harmless to a majority of the group. **2.** A reaction to a second injection that differs from the reaction to a first of the same agent. Compare ANAPHYLAXIS. [< NL *allergia* < Gk. *allos* other + *ergon* work]

al·le·vi·ate (ə-lē/vē-āt)　*v.t.* ·at·ed, ·at·ing To make lighter or easier to bear; relieve, as pain; mitigate. [< L *alleviatus,* pp. of *alleviare* < *ad-* to + *levis* light, not heavy] — **al·le· vi·a·tion** (ə-lē/vē-ā/shən) *n.*

— **Syn.** *Alleviate, relieve, mitigate,* and *assuage* mean to make less painful or distressing. *Alleviate* suggests a temporary, *relieve* a more lasting, lessening of pain. We *alleviate* what we cannot cure, but *relieve* by providing a satisfactory remedy. We *mitigate* pain by reducing its intensity, and *assuage* it with something pleasant, literally something sweet, that offsets it. Compare ALLAY. —**Ant.** aggravate, intensify, augment, magnify, embitter.

al·le·vi·a·tive (ə-lē/vē-ā/tiv, ə-lē/vē-ə-tiv)　*adj.* Tending to alleviate. Also **al·le·vi·a·to·ry** (ə-lē/vē-ə-tôr/ē, -tō/rē). — *n.* Anything that alleviates.

al·ley¹ (al/ē)　*n.* **1.** A narrow passageway; especially, a narrow way between or behind city buildings. **2.** A bowling alley (which see). **3.** A walk bordered with trees or shrubbery, as in a park or garden. [< OF *alee* a going, passage < *aler* to go, ? < L *ambulare*]

al·ley² (al/ē)　*n.* A large playing marble. [< ALABASTER]

alley cat　A mongrel cat that forages for food in alleys, etc.

al·ley·way (al/ē-wā/)　*n.* A short or narrow passageway between buildings.

all-fired (ôl/fīrd/)　*U.S. Slang adj.* Excessive: an *all-fired* shame. — *adv.* Extremely: He walked *all-fired* slow. [Alter. of *hell-fired*]

All Fools' Day　The first of April, a day on which jokes and tricks are commonly practiced: also *April Fools' Day.*

all fours　**1.** The four legs of a quadruped, or the arms and legs of a person. **2.** Seven-up, a card game. — **to go (or be) on all fours 1.** To rest or crawl on all four limbs. **2.** To run smoothly, as a machine. — **to be on all fours with** *Brit.* To present an exact comparison or analogy with.

all hail　*Archaic* All health! a friendly salutation.

All·hal·low·mas (ôl/hal/ō-məs)　*n.* All Saints' Day. Also **All·hal·lows** (ôl·hal/ōz).

All·hal·low·tide (ôl·hal/ō-tīd)　*n.* The season near Nov. 1.

all·heal (ôl/hēl/)　*n.* Any one of several healing herbs, as the common valerian.

al·li·a·ceous (al/ē-ā/shəs)　*adj.* **1.** *Bot.* Of or pertaining to a large genus (*Allium*) of bulbous herbs of the lily family, including the onion, leek, and garlic. **2.** Having the taste or smell of the onion or garlic. [< ALLI(UM) + -ACEOUS]

al·li·ance (ə-lī/əns)　*n.* **1.** The state or condition of being allied; federation; connection. **2.** The relationship or union brought about by marriage; kinship; also, a marriage itself. **3.** Any union, coalition, or formal agreement between par-

ties, sovereigns, nations, etc., in their common interest. **4.** Relationship in qualities or characteristics; affinity. [< OF *aliance* < L *alligantia* < *alligare.* See ALLY.]

— **Syn. 3.** *Alliance, league, federation, union, confederation, confederacy, coalition,* and *fusion* denote a group of nations, states, parties, etc., that have agreed to combine for joint action. *Alliance,* applied to families or nations, stresses common interest and the pooling of resources. A *league* is a more formal compact with a more limited area of interest: a mercantile *league,* a baseball *league.* A *federation* is formed by independent states or clubs, who delegate a part of their sovereignty to a central authority. A closely knit *federation* is a *union;* political *federations* whose central direction is largely confined to foreign affairs are *confederations* or *confederacies. Coalition* and *fusion* refer to the temporary *unions* of rival groups, such as political parties or factions. —**Ant.** disunion, separation, secession.

Al·li·ance (ə-lī/əns)　A city in NE Ohio; pop. 26,547.

al·lied (ə-līd/, al/īd)　*adj.* **1.** United, confederated, or leagued. **2.** Closely related: *allied* interests.

Al·lier (à-lyā/)　**1.** A river in central France, flowing NW 250 miles to the Loire. **2.** A Department of central France; 2,850 sq. mi.; pop. 386,533 (1968); capital, Moulins.

Al·lies (al/īz, ə-līz/)　*n.pl.* **1.** The twenty-seven nations allied against the Central Powers in World War I; specifically, Russia, France, Great Britain, Italy, and Japan, adhering to the Declaration of London; the **Allied and Associated Powers** included twenty-two other nations, cobelligerent but not adhering to the Declaration. **2.** The nations and governments-in-exile known as the United Nations in World War II. — **Al·lied** (al/īd, al/īd) *adj.*

al·li·ga·tor (al/ə-gā/tər)　*n.* **1.** A large crocodilian reptile found only in the southern United States and in the Yangtze river, China having a shorter, blunter snout than the crocodile and two of the lower teeth clamping into pits in the upper jaw. **2.** Loosely, any crocodile. **3.** Leather made from the skin of the alligator. **4.** Any of various machines or devices with strong, movable jaws like those of the alligator. [Earlier *alligarta* < Sp. *el lagarto* the lizard < L *lacertus*]

ALLIGATOR
(To 16 feet long)

alligator pear　The fruit of the avocado.

all-im·por·tant (ôl/im-pôr/tənt)　*adj.* Very important; crucial; necessary.

all-in·clu·sive (ôl/in-klōō/siv)　*adj.* Including everything.

al·lit·er·ate (ə-lit/ə-rāt)　*v.* ·at·ed, ·at·ing *v.i.* **1.** To speak alliteratively; use alliteration, as in writing verse. **2.** To contain alliteration. — *v.t.* **3.** To make alliterative. [< AL-² to + L *littera* a letter (of the alphabet)]

al·lit·er·a·tion (ə-lit/ə-rā/shən)　*n.* The occurrence, in a phrase or line, of two or more words having the same initial sound or sound cluster, as in "A fair field full of folk."

al·lit·er·a·tive (ə-lit/ə-rā/tiv, -ər-ə-tiv)　*adj.* Of or characterized by alliteration. — **al·lit/er·a/tive·ly** *adv.* — **al·lit/er·a/· tive·ness** *n.*

al·li·um (al/ē-əm)　*n.* Any plant of a widely distributed genus (*Allium*) of the lily family, with a tunicate bulb, leafless scapes, flowers in a terminal umbel, and a pungent taste, including the onion, garlic, leek, and chive. [< L, garlic]

allo-　*combining form* **1.** Other; alien: *allobar.* **2.** *Chem.* The more stable form of isomer: *allomaleic.* **3.** *Biol. & Med.* Extraneousness; difference from or opposition to the normal: *allopathy.* [< Gk. *allos* other]

al·lo·bar (al/ə-bär)　*n. Meteorol.* An area above which the barometric pressure has changed during a specified interval. [< ALLO- + Gk. *baros* weight, pressure] — **al·lo·bar·ic** (al/· ə-bar/ik) *adj.*

al·lo·cate (al/ə-kāt)　*v.t.* ·cat·ed, ·cat·ing **1.** To set apart for a special purpose, as funds. **2.** To apportion; assign as a share or in shares. **3.** To locate or localize, as a person or event. — **Syn.** See ALLOT. [< Med.L *allocatus,* pp. of *allocare* < L *ad-* to + *locare* to place < *locus* a place] — **al·lo·ca·ble** (al/ə-kə-bəl) *adj.*

al·lo·ca·tion (al/ə-kā/shən)　*n.* **1.** The act of allocating, or the state of being allocated; apportionment. **2.** That which is allocated; a share.

al·lo·ca·tur (al/ə-kā/tər)　*n. Law* The judicial endorsement of a writ or order. [< Med.L, lit., it is allowed]

al·lo·cu·tion (al/ə-kyōō/shən)　*n.* A formal or authoritative exhortation or address. [< L *allocutio, -onis* < *alloqui* < *ad-* to + *loqui* to speak]

al·lo·di·al (ə-lō/dē-əl)　*adj.* Pertaining to the absolute ownership of land, free from rent or service: opposed to *feudal.* Also spelled *alodial.*

al·lo·di·um (ə-lō/dē-əm)　*n. pl.* ·di·a (-dē-ə) Land held in absolute ownership, without obligations to any superior: also spelled *alodium.* [< Med.L *allodium, alodium* < OHG *alōd, allōd* entire property < *all* all + *ōt* property]

al·log·a·my (ə-log/ə-mē)　*n. Bot.* Fertilization of a flower by pollen from another flower of the same species; cross-fertilization: opposed to *autogamy.* [< ALLO- + -GAMY] — **al·log/a·mous** *adj.*

al·lom·er·ism (ə-lom/ər-iz/əm)　*n. Crystall.* Constancy of crystalline form with variation in chemical constitution. [< ALLO- + Gk. *meros* a part] **— al·lom′er·ous** *adj.*

al·lo·morph (al′ə·môrf) *n.* **1.** *Mineral.* **a** A pseudomorph formed without change of chemical composition, as calcite after aragonite. **b** A variety of pseudomorph the constituents of which have been partially or totally changed, or one which has assumed a substitute constituent. **2.** *Ling.* Any of the variant forms of a morpheme, occurring in a specific environment. [< ALLO- + Gk. *morphē* form] **— al′lo·mor′phic** *adj.* **— al′lo·mor′phism** *n.*

al·lo·nym (al′ə·nim) *n.* **1.** The name of one person taken by another, especially by an author. **2.** A book under such a name. **— Syn.** See PSEUDONYM. [< ALLO- + Gk. *onyma* name] **— al·lon·y·mous** (ə·lon′ə·məs) *adj.*

al·lo·path (al′ə·path) *n.* One who practices or favors allopathy. Also **al·lop·a·thist** (ə·lop′ə·thist).

al·lop·a·thy (ə·lop′ə·thē) *n.* A system of treatment that seeks to cure a disease by producing a condition different from or incompatible with the effects of the disease: opposed to *homeopathy.* [< ALLO- + -PATHY] **— al·lo·path·ic** (al′ə·path′ik) *adj.* **— al·lo·path′i·cal·ly** *adv.*

al·lo·phane (al′ə·fān) *n.* *Mineral.* An amorphous, usually sky-blue, hydrous aluminum silicate. [< Gk. *allophanēs* appearing otherwise < *allos* other + *phainesthai* to appear; with ref. to its change of appearance under the blowpipe]

al·lo·phone (al′ə·fōn) *n.* *Ling.* Any of the nondistinctive variants of a phoneme, occurring in a specific environment. The velar (k) of *coop* and the palatal (k) of *keep* are *allophones* of the phoneme /k/. Also called *positional variant.* [< ALLO- + Gk. *phōnē* a sound, voice] **— al′lo·phon′ic** (-fon′ik) *adj.*

al·lo·phyl·i·an (al′ə·fil′ē·ən) *adj.* *Ling.* Designating the non-Indo-European and non-Semitic languages of Europe and Asia, such as Ural-Altaic, Basque, etc., or the peoples speaking these languages. [< L *allophylus* foreign < Gk. *allophylos* < *allos* other + *phylē* tribe]

al·lo·plasm (al′ə·plaz′əm) *n.* *Biol.* The substance of the living cell that is specially differentiated for the performance of particular functions, as in cilia. [< ALLO- + PLASM] **— al·lo·plas·mic** (al′ə·plaz′mik) *adj.*

al·lot (ə·lot′) *v.t.* **·lot·ted, ·lot·ting 1.** To assign by lot; distribute so that the recipients have no choice: to *allot* duties. **2.** To apportion or assign, as to a special function, person, or place: with *to*: to *allot* ten days to a task. [< OF *aloter* < *a-* to (< L *ad-*) + *loter* to apportion < *lot* lot < Gmc.] **— Syn.** Allot, *assign*, and *allocate* mean to give as a portion. *Allot* suggests an arbitrary or chance distribution; we *allot* money, time, duties, etc. *Assign* suggests an act of authority: to *assign* a task to a pupil, to *assign* a soldier to a post. *Allocate* means to set aside for a fixed purpose: to *allocate* funds for maintenance. Compare APPORTION, DISTRIBUTE.

al·lot·ment (ə·lot′mənt) *n.* **1.** The act of allotting, or that which is allotted. **2.** *U.S. Mil.* A portion of a serviceman's pay regularly assigned, as to a member of his family or for insurance. **3.** *Brit.* A plot of land for gardening.

al·lo·trope (al′ə·trōp) *n.* *Chem.* One of the forms assumed by an allotropic substance.

al·lo·trop·ic (al′ə·trop′ik) *adj.* *Chem.* Of, pertaining to, or having the property of allotropy. Also **al′lo·trop′i·cal.** **— al′lo·trop′i·cal·ly** *adv.*

al·lot·ro·py (ə·lot′rə·pē) *n.* *Chem.* The variation in properties shown by elements or their compounds without change of chemical composition. Also **al·lot·ro·pism** (ə·lot′rə·piz′əm). [< Gk. *allotropia* variation < *allos* other + *tropos* turn, manner]

all′ ot·ta·va (äl ōt·tä′vä) *Music* A symbol (*8va, 8*) placed above or below the staff or clef to indicate that the music is to be performed an octave higher or lower than written. [< Ital., lit., at the octave]

al·lot·tee (al′ot·tē′) *n.* One to whom anything is allotted.

all-out (ôl′out′) *adj.* Complete and entire; total.

all-o·ver (*adj.* ôl′ō′vər; *n.* ôl′ō′vər) *adj.* Extending over the whole or surface of anything: the *allover* effect. **— n.** A fabric or other substance having an allover pattern.

al·low (ə·lou′) *v.t.* **1.** To put no obstacle in the way of; permit to occur or do: to *allow* access to the sea; to *allow* flowers to wither. **2.** To concede; admit: to *allow* a point in an argument. **3.** To make allowance or provision for: to *allow* an hour for lunch. **4.** To make concession of: to *allow* a month to pay. **5.** To grant; allot. **6.** *U.S. Dial.* To maintain; declare. **7.** *Archaic* To approve; sanction. **— v.i. 8.** To permit or admit: with *of*: Your remark *allows* of several interpretations. **9.** To make concession or due allowance: with *for*: to *allow* for discrepancies. [< OF *alouer* to place, use, assign < Med.L *allocare* (< L *ad-* to + *locare* to place) and OF *alouer, aloer* to approve < L *allaudare* to extol < *ad-* + *laudare* to praise] **— Syn. 1.** *Allow, let, suffer, permit, sanction,* and *authorize* refer to the act of not preventing. *Allow* implies definite forbearance, whereas we may *let* things happen through mere indifference or inattention. To *suffer,* implying mild concession, is obsolescent. *Permit* suggests authority that could prevent, if it so chose: to

permit someone to speak. In contrast with the foregoing words, *sanction* and *authorize* imply positive approval of a proposed course of action: to *sanction* the use of military force, to *authorize* the construction of a new road.

al·low·a·ble (ə·lou′ə·bəl) *adj.* Permissible; admissible. **— al·low′a·ble·ness** *n.* **— al·low′a·bly** *adv.*

al·low·ance (ə·lou′əns) *n.* **1.** That which is allowed; a portion or share allotted; especially, a definite sum of money given at regular intervals. **2.** An amount granted in exchange for a used article, for a purchase in volume, etc.; discount; deduction. **3.** A taking into account of modifying circumstances; also, a deduction or addition made because of this: *allowance* for wastage. **4.** The act of allowing; toleration; sanction. **5.** Admission; acceptance: the *allowance* of a claim. **6.** *Obs.* Acknowledgment. **— v.t. ·anced, ·anc·ing 1.** To put on an allowance; limit to a regular amount. **2.** To supply in limited or meager quantities. [< OF *alouance* < *alouer.* See ALLOW.]

Al·lo·way (al′ə·wā) A village near Ayr, Scotland; birthplace of Robert Burns.

al·low·ed·ly (ə·lou′id·lē) *adv.* By general allowance or admission; admittedly.

al·loy (*n.* al′oi, ə·loi′; *v.* ə·loi′) *n.* **1.** *Metall.* **a** A mixture or combination formed by the fusion of two or more metals: Brass is an *alloy* of copper and zinc. **b** A substance obtained by the mixture or combination of a metal and a nonmetal. **c** A baser metal mixed or combined with a finer one. **2.** Anything that reduces purity. **— v.t. 1.** To reduce the purity of, as a metal, by mixing with an alloy. **2.** To mix (metals) so as to form into an alloy. **3.** To modify or debase, as by mixture with something inferior. [< F *aloi* < OF *alei* < *aleier* to combine < L *alligare* < *ad-* to + *ligare* to bind]

all-pur·pose (ôl′pûr′pəs) *adj.* Generally useful; answering every purpose.

all-right (ôl′rīt′) *adj. Slang* **1.** Dependable; honest; loyal: an *all-right* guy. **2.** Good; excellent: an *all-right* book.

all right 1. Satisfactory: His work is *all right.* **2.** Correct, as a sum in addition. **3.** Uninjured. **4.** Certainly; without a doubt: I'll be there *all right!* **5.** Yes: usually in answer to a question: May I leave now? *All right.* See ALRIGHT.

all-round (ôl′round′) *adj.* **1.** *U.S.* Of comprehensive range or scope; complete in action or effect: an *all-round* education. **2.** Excelling in all or many aspects; many-sided; versatile: an *all-round* athlete. Also *all-around.*

All Saints' Day *Eccl.* November 1, a festival commemorative of all saints and martyrs: also called *Allhallowmas, Allhallows.* Also **All Saints.**

all·seed (ôl′sēd′) *n.* Any of various small, many-seeded plants, as knotgrass, goosefoot, flaxwort, etc.

All-Soul (ôl′sōl′) *n.* The world soul (which see).

All Souls' Day In the Roman Catholic Church, November 2, a day of commemoration on which intercession is made for the souls of all the faithful departed. Also **All Souls.**

all·spice (ôl′spīs′) *n.* **1.** The aromatic dried berry of the pimento. **2.** The sharply flavored, fragrant spice made from it. Also called *pimento.* [So called because thought to combine the flavors of several spices]

all-star (ôl′stär′) *adj.* Consisting wholly of star performers.

All·ston (ôl′stən), **Washington,** 1779–1843, U.S. painter.

all the same Without difference; notwithstanding.

all told When all are counted; in all.

al·lude (ə·lōōd′) *v.i.* **·lud·ed, ·lud·ing** To refer without express mention; make indirect or casual reference: with *to.* [< L *alludere* to play with, joke < *ad-* to + *ludere* to play]

al·lure (ə·lōōr′) *v.t. & v.i.* **·lured, ·lur·ing** To draw with or as with a lure; attract or exercise attraction; entice. **— n.** That which allures; allurement. [< OF *alurer, aleurrer* < *a-* to (< L *ad-*) + *leurre* lure. See LURE.] **— al·lur′er** *n.* **— Syn.** attract, entice, lure, draw, tempt. Compare CHARM[1].

al·lure·ment (ə·lōōr′mənt) *n.* **1.** Attractive quality; enticement; fascination. **2.** A charm or bait. **3.** The act of alluring, as by some charm or bait.

al·lur·ing (ə·lōōr′ing) *adj.* That draws as with a lure; attractive; fascinating. **— al·lur′ing·ly** *adv.* **— al·lur′ing·ness** *n.*

al·lu·sion (ə·lōō′zhən) *n.* **1.** The act of alluding; indirect reference; suggestion. **2.** A casual but significant reference: They made *allusions* to his personal life. [< L *allusio, -onis* < *allusus,* pp. of *alludere.* See ALLUDE.]

al·lu·sive (ə·lōō′siv) *adj.* Making allusion; suggestive. **— al·lu′sive·ly** *adv.* **— al·lu′sive·ness** *n.*

al·lu·vi·al (ə·lōō′vē·əl) *adj.* Pertaining to or composed of earth deposited by water. **— n. 1.** Alluvial soil. **2.** *Austral.* Alluvial soil bearing gold.

alluvial cone *Geol.* The fan-shaped accumulation of detritus deposited where a river issues from a steep course upon flat land: also called *fan delta.* Also **alluvial fan.**

al·lu·vi·on (ə·lōō′vē·ən) *n.* **1.** Alluvium. **2.** Inundation; flood. **3.** The wash or flow of waves against the shore or banks. **4.** *Law* The gradual increase of land by the action of flowing water. **5.** *Geol.* A downpour of volcanic cinder mud. [< F < L *alluvio, -onis* a washing against, a flooding < *alluere* < *ad-* to + *luere* to wash]

al·lu·vi·um (ə·lōō′vē·əm) *n. pl.* **·vi·a** (-vē·ə) or **·vi·ums** *Geol.* A deposit, as of sand or mud, transported and laid down by flowing water in river beds, flood plains, etc. [< L]

al·ly (ə·lī′, al′ī) *v.* **·lied, ·ly·ing** *v.t.* **1.** To connect by some relationship or bond: with *to* or *with*: England *allies* herself with France. — *v.i.* **2.** To enter into alliance; become allied. — *n. pl.* **·lies 1.** A person or thing connected with another, usually in some relation of helpfulness or kinship; a state, sovereign, or chief leagued with another, as by treaty or common action. **2.** Any friendly associate or helper. **3.** An organism or substance associated with another by similarity of structure or properties. — **Syn.** See ASSOCIATE. [< OF *alier* < L *alligare* < *ad-* to + *ligare* to bind]

al·lyl (al′il) *n. Chem.* A univalent aliphatic radical, C_3H_5, known through its compounds. [< L *allium* garlic + -YL] — **al·lyl·ic** (ə·lil′ik) *adj.*

allyl alcohol *Chem.* A pungent liquid, $CH_2{:}CHCH_2OH$, obtained by distilling glycerol with crystallized oxalic acid.

allyl sulfide *Chem.* An essential oil, $(C_3H_5)_2S$, contained in garlic, onions, and other vegetables, giving them their characteristic taste and odor.

Al·ma A·ta (äl′mä ä′tä) The capital of the Kazakh S.S.R., in the Asian part of the Soviet Union; pop. 455,000 (1959); formerly *Vernyi, Vernyy.*

Al·ma·dén (äl′mä·thän′) A city in south central Spain; site of several rich mercury mines; pop. about 13,000.

Al·ma·gest (al′mə·jest) *n.* **1.** Ptolemy's work on astronomy, explaining the celestial motions on the geocentric system, and named from the title of the Arabic translation of this work made in 827. **2.** In medieval science, any authoritative treatise, as upon astrology or alchemy. Also **al′ma·gest.** [< OF *almageste* < Arabic *al-majistī* < al the + Gk. *megistē* (*syntaxis*) the greatest (work)]

al·mah (al′mə) *n.* An Egyptian dancing and singing girl. Also **al′ma, al·me** (al′me), **al′meh.** [< Arabic *'almah* one who knows]

al·ma ma·ter (al′mə mä′tər, al′mə mä′tər, äl′mə mä′tər) The institution of learning that one has attended. [< L, fostering mother]

al·ma·nac (ôl′mə·nak) *n.* A yearly calendar giving the days, weeks, and months of the year, weather forecasts, astronomical information, times of high and low tides, and other tabulated data. [< Med.L < Sp. < Arabic *al-manākh*]

al·man·dine (al′mən·dēn, -din) *n.* A deep red or violet garnet. Also **al′man·dite** (-dīt). [Alter. of earlier *alabandine,* from *Alabanda,* city in Asia Minor]

Al·ma-Tad·e·ma (al′mə·tad′ə·mə), **Sir Lawrence,** 1836–1912, English painter born in the Netherlands.

Al·me·rí·a (äl′mä·rē′ä) A Province of southern Spain; 3,426 sq. mi.; pop. 367,833 (1959); capital, **Almería,** a port on the Gulf of Almería, an inlet of the Mediterranean. pop. 86,808 (1960).

al·might·y (ôl·mīt′ē) *adj.* **1.** Able to do all things; omnipotent. **2.** *U.S. Informal* Great; extreme: an *almighty* noise. — *adv. U.S. Informal* Exceedingly: *almighty* mad. — **the Almighty** God; the Supreme Being. [OE *ealmihtig < eal* all + *mihtig* mighty] — **al·might′i·ly** *adv.* — **al·might′i·ness** *n.*

almighty dollar *Informal* Money conceived of as having or imparting great power.

Al·mo·hades (al′mə·hädz, -hadz) *n.pl.* **1.** Followers of a monotheistic reform among Moslems of North Africa, founded in the twelfth century. **2.** The Moslem dynasty in North Africa and Spain founded by them, which lasted from 1145 to 1269. [< Arabic *al-muwahhid* the one who professes monotheism] — **Al′mo·hade** *adj.*

al·mond (ä′mənd, am′ənd) *n.* **1.** A small tree (*Prunus amygdalus*) of the rose family, originally a native of NW Africa, now widely cultivated in the warmer temperate regions. **2.** The kernel of the fruit of the almond tree. **3.** Anything having the pointed, oval shape of an almond. **4.** A pale brown, the color of an almond shell. [< OF *almande, amande* < LL *amandola* < L *amygdala* < Gk. *amygdalē*]

al·mon·er (al′mən·ər, ä′mən-) *n.* An official dispenser of alms; formerly, a household chaplain, as of a prince. Also **alm·ner** (alm′nər, äm′nər). [< OF *almosnier,* ult. < LL *eleemosynarius* pertaining to alms < L *eleemosyna.* See ALMS.]

al·mon·ry (al′mən·rē, ä′mən-) *n. pl.* **·ries** The residence of an almoner; a place where alms are dispensed.

Al·mo·ra·vides (al·môr′ə·vĭdz, -mō′rə-) *n.pl.* A Moslem dynasty in Africa and Spain that began as a religious revival under Abdallah ibn-Yasin and lasted from 1056 to 1145. [< Arabic *al-murābit*] — **Al·mo′ra·vide** *adj.*

al·most (ôl′mōst, ôl·mōst′) *adv.* Approximately; very nearly; all but: almost complete. [OE *ealmæst.* See ALL, MOST.]

alms (ämz) *n. sing. & pl.* A gift or gifts for the poor; charity. ◆ Collateral adjective: *eleemosynary.* Some self-explanatory compounds have *alms* as their first element: **almsgiver, almsgiving, almsmoney,** etc. [OE *ælmesse* < LL *eleemosyna* < Gk. *eleēmosynē* < *eleos* pity]

alms·house (ämz′hous′) *n.* A house where paupers are supported; a poorhouse.

alms·man (ämz′mən) *n. pl.* **·men** (-mən) **1.** One supported by charity. **2.** *Obs.* A giver of alms. — **alms′wom′an** *n.fem.*

al·muce (al′myōōs) *n.* A hood or hooded cape lined with fur, formerly worn by clergymen and monks: also called *amice.* [< OF *aumuce* < Med.L *almutia*; ult. origin uncertain]

al·mud (al·mōōd′) *n.* A liquid and dry measure of Turkey, Spain, and some other countries, varying from about 2 to 32 quarts. Also **al·mude′.** [< Sp. < Arabic *al-mudd*]

al·mug (al′mug) *n.* In the Bible, a precious wood used for harps, psalteries, etc.; also called *algum.* [< Hebrew]

a·lo·di·al (ə·lō′dē·əl), **a·lo·di·um** (-əm) See ALLODIAL, etc.

al·oe (al′ō) *n. pl.* **·oes 1.** Any member of a genus (*Aloe*) of Old World plants of the lily family some species of which furnish a drug, and others valuable fiber. **2.** *pl.* (*construed as sing.*) A cathartic made from the juice of certain species of aloe. **3.** *pl.* (*construed as sing.*) Agalloch, a wood. [OE *aluwe* < L *aloe* < Gk. *aloē*] — **al·o·et·ic** (al′ō·et′ik) or **·i·cal** *adj.*

a·loft (ə·lôft′, ə·loft′) *adv.* **1.** In or to a high or higher place; on high; high up. **2.** *Naut.* At or to the higher parts of a ship's rigging: opposed to *alow.* [< ON *ā lopt* in (the) air]

a·lo·ha (ə·lō′ə, ä·lō′hä) *n. Hawaiian* Love: used as a salutation and a farewell.

Aloha State Nickname of HAWAII.

al·o·in (al′ō·in) *n. Chem.* A bitter, crystalline substance of varying composition, obtained from aloes and forming its purgative principle. [< ALO(E) + -IN]

a·lone (ə·lōn′) *adv. & adj.* **1.** Without company; solitary: to live *alone.* **2.** Excluding all others; solely: only: He alone survived. **3.** Without equal; unique; unparalleled: As an artist, he stands *alone.* ◆ When functioning as an adjective, *alone* appears in predicate position or following the word it modifies. [ME *al one* solitary]

a·long (ə·lông′, ə·long′) *adv.* **1.** Following the length or course of; lengthwise: usually with *by*: a brook running *along* by the hedge. **2.** Progressively onward in a course; forward: The years roll *along* quickly. **3.** In company or association; together: usually with *with*: to take one truth *along* with another. **4.** *U.S.* As a companion: Bring a friend *along.* **5.** *U.S. Informal* Advanced in its natural course: The afternoon is well *along.* **6.** *U.S. Informal* Approaching a time, age, number, etc.: usually with *about*: *along* about sundown. — **all along** From the outset; throughout; continuously: I suspected her all *along.* — **to be along** *U.S. Informal* To arrive at a place; come: The train will *be along* soon. — **right along** *U.S. Informal* Without interruption: This project is moving *right along.* — *prep.* Throughout or over the length or course of: to plant trees *along* the road. [OE *andlang* continuous, extended]

along of *Brit. Dial.* Because of.

a·long·shore (ə·lông′shôr′, ə·long′-, -shōr′) *adv.* Along the shore, either on the water or on the land.

a·long·side (ə·lông′sīd′, ə·long′-) *adv.* Close to or along the side. — *prep.* Side by side with; at the side of.

a·loof (ə·lōōf′) *adj.* Distant, especially in manner or interest; unsympathetic. — *adv.* At a distance; apart: to stand aloof. [< A-1 + *loof* < Du. *loef* windward] — **a·loof′ly** *adv.* — **a·loof′ness** *n.*

al·o·pe·ci·a (al′ə·pē′shē·ə, -sē·ə) *n. Med.* Baldness, partial or complete, congenital or acquired. [< L, baldness, fox mange < Gk. *alōpekia < alōpex* fox]

A·lost (ä·lôst′) A commune in central Belgium near Brussels; pop. 44,478 (est. 1958). Flemish *Aalst.*

a·loud (ə·loud′) *adv.* Loudly or audibly.

a·low (ə·lō′) *adv. Naut.* In or to a lower position; below: opposed to *aloft.*

alp (alp) *n.* **1.** A lofty mountain. **2.** Any peak of the Alps. [Back formation < L *Alpes* the Alps]

ALP or **A.L.P.** American Labor Party.

al·pac·a (al·pak′ə) *n.* **1.** A domesticated ruminant (genus *Lama*) of South America, related to the llama and vicuña. **2.** Its long silky wool. **3.** A thin cloth made of or containing this wool. **4.** A glossy black fabric of cotton and wool. [< Sp. < Arabic *al* the + Peruvian *paco,* name of the animal]

ALPACA
(About 3½ feet high at shoulder)

al·pen·glow (al′pən·glō′) *n.* A rosy light or glow seen on mountain summits just before sunrise or just after sunset. [Trans. of G *alpenglühen*]

al·pen·horn (al′pən·hôrn′) *n.* A slightly curved, very sonorous horn, made of wood and from three to seven feet long, used by herdsmen in the Alps. Also *alphorn.* [< G]

al·pen·stock (al′pən·stok′) *n.* A long, iron-pointed staff used by mountain climbers. [< G]

al·pes·trine (al·pes′trin) *adj.* **1.** Of or pertaining to the Alps, or any lofty mountains; alpine. **2.** Subalpine (def. 2). [< L *alpestris* < *Alpes* Alps]

al·pha (al′fə) *n.* **1.** The first letter in the Greek alphabet (A, α), corresponding to English *a.* See table for ALPHABET. **2.** The beginning or first of anything. **3.** *Astron.* Often *cap.* The principal or brightest star in a constellation. — **the**

alpha and omega Both the first and the last; beginning and end; the sum total: used of Christ. *Rev.* i 8. — *adj.* **1.** Designating the first in order of importance or discovery: *alpha* test. **2.** *Chem.* **a** Denoting the first of two or more isomeric compounds. **b** Designating a compound containing an atom or radical in a special position. **3.** *Physics* Designating the first of a series of radiations or emissions arranged in order of increasing frequency: *alpha* rays. [< Gk. < Hebrew *āleph* ox]

al·pha·bet (al′fə-bet) *n.* **1.** The letters that form the elements of written language, in an order fixed by usage. See tables on pp. 42 and 43. **2.** Any system of characters or symbols representing the sounds of speech. **3.** The simplest elements or rudiments of anything. — *v.t.* To alphabetize. [< L *alphabetum* < Gk. *alpha* a + *bēta* b < Hebrew *āleph* ox + *beth* house]

al·pha·bet·i·cal (al′fə-bet′i-kəl) *adj.* **1.** Arranged in the order of the alphabet. **2.** Pertaining to or expressed by an alphabet. Also **al′pha·bet′ic.** — **al′pha·bet′i·cal·ly** *adv.*

al·pha·bet·ize (al′fə-bə-tīz′) *v.t.* **·ized, ·iz·ing** **1.** To put in alphabetical order. **2.** To express by or furnish with an alphabet or alphabetic symbols. — **al·pha·bet·i·za·tion** (al′fə-bet′ə-zā′shən) *n.* — **al′pha·bet·iz′er** *n.*

Alpha Cen·tau·ri (sen-tôr′ē) The star nearest to the solar system, in the constellation Centaurus.

alpha particle *Physics* The positively charged nucleus of the helium atom, consisting of two protons and two neutrons, emitted from certain radioactive substances.

alpha privative In Greek grammar, a prefix having negative or privative force, as in *atheos* godless. See A-[4], AN-[1].

alpha ray *Physics* A stream of alpha particles.

alpha rhythm *Physiol.* The recurring cycles of electrical change in the brain, as shown in the record of an encephalogram, each cycle being known as an **alpha wave.**

alpha test *Psychol.* A series of tests used by the U.S. Army in World War I to determine the intelligence of recruits.

Al·phe·ratz (al′fə-rats′) *n.* A star, 2.15 magnitude; Alpha in the constellation Andromeda. See STAR. [< Arabic *al-faras* the mare]

Al·phe·us (al-fē′əs) In Greek mythology, a river god who fell in love with the nymph Arethusa and changed into a river to mingle with her when she had become a fountain.

Al·phon·sus de Li·guo·ri (al-fon′səs dā lē-gwô′rē), Saint, 1696–1787, Italian theologian; founder of the Redemptorists: original name **Alfonso Maria de′ Liguori.**

alp·horn (alp′hôrn′) An alpenhorn (which see).

al·pho·sis (al-fō′sis) *n. Pathol.* Lack of skin pigmentation; albinism. [< NL < Gk. *alphos* leprosy]

al·phyl (al′fil) *n. Chem.* A radical indicating both aromatic and aliphatic structure in an organic compound. [< AL-(KYL) + PH(EN)YL]

al·pine (al′pīn, -pin) *adj.* **1.** Like an alp; lofty and towering. **2.** *Biol.* Inhabiting or growing in mountain regions above the limits of forest growth.

Al·pine (al′pīn, -pin) *adj.* **1.** Pertaining to or characteristic of the Alps. **2.** Designating a European ethnic stock found in the Alps and adjacent districts, and marked by medium height, broad, short skull and face, and brunet coloring. [< L *Alpinus* < *Alpes* the Alps]

alpine garden A garden for alpine plants, especially a rock garden.

al·pi·nist (al′pə-nist) *n.* A climber of alps; a mountaineer. Also **Al′pi·nist.** — **al′pi·nism, Al′pi·nism** *n.*

Alps (alps) A mountain system of southern Europe, extending 680 miles from the Mediterranean coast of southern France to the Adriatic coast of Yugoslavia, separating the Po valley of northern Italy from the lowlands of France, Germany, and the Danubian plain; highest peak, Mont Blanc, 15,781 ft.

Al-Qâ·hi·rah (al-kä′hi-rä) The Arabic name for CAIRO.

al·read·y (ôl-red′ē) *adv.* Before or by this time or the time mentioned. [< ALL + READY]

al·right (ôl-rīt′) *adv.* All right: a spelling not yet considered acceptable.

als or **A.L.S.** Autograph letter signed.

Al·sace (al-sās′, al′sas; *Fr.* ȧl·zȧs′) A region and former province of France along the Rhine border of Germany: ancient **Al·sa·tia** (al-sā′shə): Latin *Elsass.*

Al·sace-Lor·raine (al′sās-lə-rān′, al′sas-; *Fr.* ȧl·zȧs′lô·ren′) A disputed border region between NE France and SW Germany; ceded to Germany in 1871, regained by France in 1919, annexed by Germany in 1940, regained by France in 1945: German *Elsass-Lothringen.*

Al·sa·tia (al-sā′shə) A section of London, formerly a sanctuary for insolvent debtors and criminals: also *Whitefriars.* [< Med.L < G *Elsass,* lit., foreign settlement]

Al·sa·tian (al-sā′shən) *adj.* **1.** Of

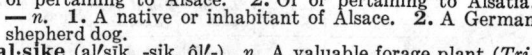

or pertaining to Alsace. **2.** Of or pertaining to Alsatia. — *n.* **1.** A native or inhabitant of Alsace. **2.** A German shepherd dog.

al·sike (al′sīk, -sik, ôl′-) *n.* A valuable forage plant (*Trifolium hybridum*) with pinkish or white flowers: also called *Swedish clover.* Also **Alsike clover.** [after *Alsike,* Swedish town]

Al·si·rat (al′sē-rät′) *n.* In Islam: **a** The correct way of religion. **b** The bridge, sharper than a razor's edge, leading to paradise over the abyss of hell. [< Arabic *al-ṣirāṭ* the road]

al·so (ôl′sō) *adv.* In addition; besides; likewise. [OE *alswā, ealswā* all (wholly) so]

al·so-ran (ôl′sō-ran′) *n. U.S. Informal* **1.** A horse that fails to win, place, or show in a race. **2.** Any unsuccessful competitor.

alt (alt) *Music adj.* Alto; high-pitched in the musical scale. — *n.* The octave next above the treble staff. — **in alt** In this octave. [< Ital. *alto* < L *altus* high]

alt. **1.** Alternate; alternating; alternation(s); alternative. **2.** Altitude. **3.** *Music* Alto.

Alta. Alberta, Canada.

Al·ta·de·na (al′tə-dē′nə) An unincorporated place in SW California, near Los Angeles; pop. 42,380.

Al·ta·ic (al-tā′ik) *n.* A family of languages of Europe and Asia, generally considered to be composed of the Turkic, Mongolian, and Manchu-Tungusic subfamilies, and sometimes classified with Uralic in a Ural-Altaic family. — *adj.* **1.** Of the Altai Mountains. **2.** Pertaining to the Altaic languages, or to the peoples speaking any of these languages; Turanian. Also **Al·tai·an** (al-tā′ən, -tī′-) *adj.*

Al·tai Mountains (al-tī′, äl-) A mountain system of central Asia at the juncture of China, Mongolia, and the Soviet Union; highest peak, Belukha, 15,157 ft. Also **Al′tay′.**

Al·ta·ir (al-tā′ir, al-târ′) *n.* One of the 20 brightest stars, 0.77 magnitude; Alpha in the constellation Aquila. See STAR. [< Arabic *al-ṭā′ir* the bird]

Altai Territory A Territory of the R.S.F.S.R., in the southern Siberian part; 101,000 sq. mi.; pop. 2,683,265 (1959); capital, Barnaul. Also **Al·tay′.** *Russian* **Al·tai·skiy kray** (al-tī′skyĕ krī).

Al·ta·mi·ra (äl′tä-mē′rä) A cave near Santander, in Spain, noted for the early Stone Age paintings on its walls.

al·tar (ôl′tər) *n.* **1.** Any raised place or structure on which sacrifices may be offered or incense burned as an act of worship. **2.** *Eccl.* The structure of wood or stone on which the elements are consecrated in the Eucharist; the communion table. — **to lead to the altar** To marry. [OE < L *altare* high altar < *altus* high]

Al·tar (ôl′tər) *n.* The constellation Ara.

altar boy An attendant at the altar; acolyte.

altar bread *Eccl.* Bread used in the Eucharist, especially the unleavened wafer used in some churches.

al·tar·piece (ôl′tər-pēs′) *n.* A painting, mosaic, or bas-relief over and behind the altar; a reredos (def. 1).

alt·az·i·muth (alt-az′ə-məth) *n. Astron.* An instrument with two graduated circles, one vertical and one horizontal, for measuring the altitude and azimuth of celestial bodies. [< ALT(ITUDE) + AZIMUTH]

Alt·dorf (ält′dôrf) The capital of Uri Canton in central Switzerland; scene of traditional exploits of William Tell; pop. about 6,600.

al·ter (ôl′tər) *v.t.* **1.** To cause to be different; change; modify; transform. **2.** *U.S.* To castrate or spay. — *v.i.* **3.** To become different; change. — **Syn.** See CHANGE. [< MF *altérer* < Med.L *alterare* < L *alter* other]

alter. Alteration.

al·ter·a·ble (ôl′tər-ə-bəl) *adj.* Capable of alteration. — **al′ter·a·bil′i·ty, al′ter·a·ble·ness** *n.* — **al′ter·a·bly** *adv.*

al·ter·a·tion (ôl′tə-rā′shən) *n.* **1.** The act or process of altering: the *alteration* of a house. **2.** A change or modification. **3.** *Geol.* Any change in the composition or texture of a rock occurring subsequent to its formation but not due to a cementing or induration of its original constituents. [< MF < Med.L *alteratio, -onis* < *alterare.* See ALTER.]

al·ter·a·tive (ôl′tə-rā′tiv) *adj.* **1.** Tending to produce change. **2.** *Med.* Tending to change gradually the bodily condition to a normal state. — *n. Med.* An alterative medicine or treatment; especially, one that changes the nutrition processes of the body. Also **al·ter·ant** (ôl′tər-ənt).

al·ter·cate (ôl′tər-kāt, al′-) *v.i.* **·cat·ed, ·cat·ing** To dispute vehemently; wrangle. [< L *altercatus,* pp. of *altercari* < *alter* other]

al·ter·ca·tion (ôl′tər-kā′shən, al′-) *n.* A heated dispute; angry controversy; wrangling.

al·ter e·go (ôl′tər ē′gō, al′tər eg′ō) **1.** Another self; a double. **2.** An intimate friend. [< L, lit., other I]

al·ter i·dem (al′tər ī′dem) *Latin* Another self; a duplicate.

al·ter·nant (ôl-tûr′nənt, ôl′tər-nənt, al-) *adj.* Alternating. [< Med.L *alternans, -antis,* ppr. of *alterare.* See ALTER.]

al·ter·nate (*v.* ôl′tər-nāt, al′-; *adj. & n.* ôl′tər-nit, al′-) *v.* **·nat·ed, ·nat·ing** *v.i.* **1.** To follow one another by turns:

THE INTERNATIONAL PHONETIC ALPHABET
(Revised to 1951.)

		Bi-labial	Labio-dental	Dental and Alveolar	Retroflex	Palato-alveolar	Alveolo-palatal	Palatal	Velar	Uvular	Pharyngal	Glottal
CONSONANTS	Plosive . .	p b		t d	ʈ ɖ			c ɟ	k g	q ɢ		ʔ
	Nasal . .	m	ɱ	n	ɳ			ɲ	ŋ	N		
	Lateral Fricative .			ɬ ɮ								
	Lateral Non-fricative .			l	ɭ			ʎ				
	Rolled . .			r						R		
	Flapped . .			ɾ	ɽ					ʀ		
	Fricative . .	ɸ β	f v	θ ð ǀ s z ɹ	ʂ ʐ	ʃ ʒ	ʑ ʐ	ç j	x ɣ	χ ʁ	ħ ʕ	h ɦ
	Frictionless Continuants and Semi-vowels	w ɥ	ʋ	ɹ				j (ɥ)	(w)	ʁ		

		Front	Central	Back
VOWELS	Close . . . (y ʉ u)	i y	ɨ ʉ	ɯ u
	Half-close . . (ø o)	e ø	ə	ɤ o
	Half-open . . (œ ɔ)	ɛ œ ɜ	ɐ	ʌ ɔ
		æ		
	Open . . . (ɒ)	a	ɑ ɒ	

(Secondary articulations are shown by symbols in brackets.)

OTHER SOUNDS.—Palatalized consonants: ṭ, ḍ, etc.; palatalized ʃ, ʒ : ʆ, ʓ. Velarized or pharyngalized consonants: ɫ, ɑ̵, z̵, etc. Ejective consonants (with simultaneous glottal stop): p', t', etc. Implosive voiced consonants: ɓ, ɗ, etc. ɼ fricative trill. σ, ʒ (labialized θ, ð, or s, z). ʆ, ʓ (labialized ʃ, ʒ). ʇ, ʗ, ʘ (clicks, Zulu c, q, x). ɺ (a sound between r and l). ŋ̩ Japanese syllabic nasal. ʓ (combination of x and ʃ). ʍ (voiceless w). ɪ, ʏ, ɷ (lowered varieties of i, y, u). ɜ (a variety of ə). ɵ (a vowel between ø and o).

Affricates are normally represented by groups of two consonants (ts, tʃ, dʒ, etc.), but, when necessary, ligatures are used (ʦ, ʧ, ʤ, etc.), or the marks ͡ or ͜ (t͡s or t͜s, etc.). ͡ ͜ also denote synchronic articulation (m͡ŋ = simultaneous m and ŋ). c, ɟ may occasionally be used in place of tʃ, dʒ, and ʦ, ʣ for ts, dz. Aspirated plosives: ph, th, etc. r-coloured vowels: eɹ, aɹ, ɔɹ, etc., or eʳ, aʳ, ɔʳ, etc., or e̢, a̢, ɔ̢, etc.; r-coloured ə : əɹ or əʳ or ɹ or ə̢ or ɚ.

LENGTH, STRESS, PITCH.— : (full length). ˑ (half length). ˈ (stress, placed at beginning of the stressed syllable). ˌ (secondary stress). ˉ (high level pitch) ; ˍ (low level) ; ˊ (high rising) ; ˏ (low rising) ; ˋ (high falling) ; ˎ (low falling) ; ˆ (rise-fall) ; ˇ (fall-rise).

MODIFIERS.— ˜ nasality. ˳ breath (l̥ = breathed l). ˬ voice (s̬ = z). ʻ slight aspiration following p, t, etc. ˷ labialization (n̫ = labialized n). ˌ dental articulation (t̪ = dental t). ˙ palatalization (ż = z̧). ˌ specially close vowel (ẹ = a very close e). ˴ specially open vowel (e̦ = a rather open e). ˔ tongue raised (e̝ or e̩ = ẹ). ˕ tongue lowered (e̞ or e̦ = ę). + tongue advanced (u+ or u̟ = an advanced u, t̟ = t̪). - or ˗ tongue retracted (i- or i̠ = ɨ, t̠ = alveolar t). ˒ lips more rounded. ˓ lips more spread. Central vowels: ɪ̈(= ɨ), ü(= ʉ), ë(= ə̈), ö(= ɵ), ë, ö. ˌ (e.g. n̩) syllabic consonant. ˘ consonantal vowel. ʃ̯ variety of ʃ resembling s, etc.

Courtesy, Association Phonétique Internationale

THE INITIAL TEACHING ALPHABET

æ face	b bed	c cat	d dog	ee key	f feet	g leg
h hat	ie fly	j jug	k key	l letter	m man	n nest
œ over	p pen	r red	s spoon	t tree	ue use	v voice
w window	y yes	z zebra	ʒ daisy	wh when	ch chair	th three
th the	ſh shop	ʒ vision	ŋ drink	a father	au ball	a cap
e egg	i milk	o box	u up	ꞷ book	ꞷ spoon	ou out	oi oil

THE SEMAPHORE ALPHABET

A-1 B-2 C-3 D-4 E-5 F-6 G-7 H-8
I-9 J-0 K L M N O P
Q R S T U V W
X Y Z Attention Interval Numeral

42

INTERNATIONAL FLAG CODE + INTERNATIONAL MORSE CODE + PHONETIC ALPHABET

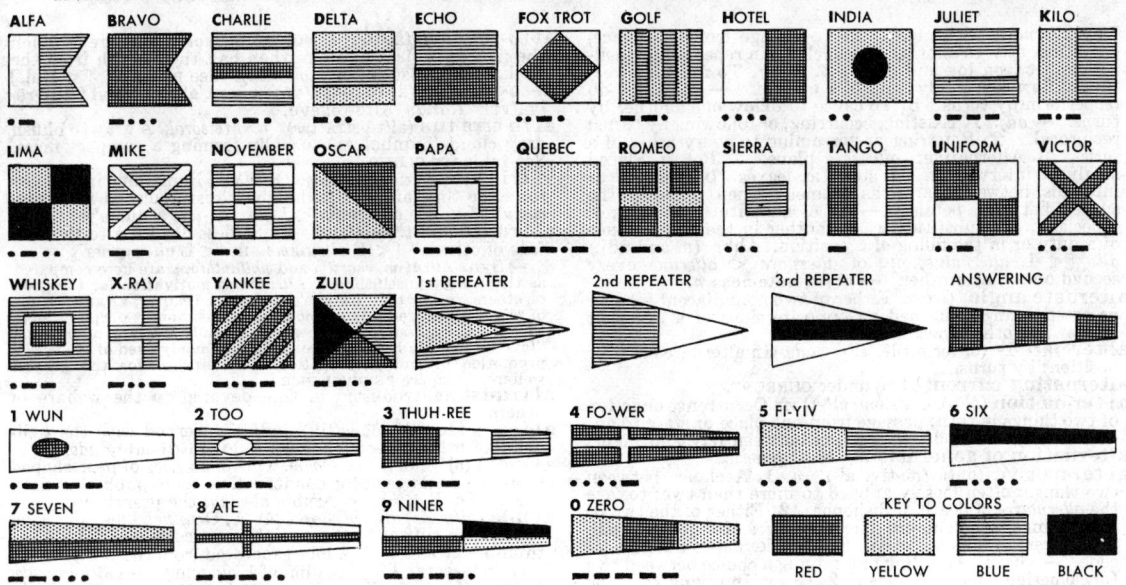

ALFA · BRAVO · CHARLIE · DELTA · ECHO · FOX TROT · GOLF · HOTEL · INDIA · JULIET · KILO
LIMA · MIKE · NOVEMBER · OSCAR · PAPA · QUEBEC · ROMEO · SIERRA · TANGO · UNIFORM · VICTOR
WHISKEY · X-RAY · YANKEE · ZULU · 1st REPEATER · 2nd REPEATER · 3rd REPEATER · ANSWERING
1 WUN · 2 TOO · 3 THUH-REE · 4 FO-WER · 5 FI-YIV · 6 SIX
7 SEVEN · 8 ATE · 9 NINER · 0 ZERO · KEY TO COLORS
RED · YELLOW · BLUE · BLACK

TABLE OF FOREIGN ALPHABETS

(1) ARABIC

Character	Name	Sound
ا	alif	—[1]
ب	ba	b
ت	ta	t
ث	sa	th
ج	jim	j
ح	ha	h
خ	kha	kh
د	dal	d
ذ	zal	th
ر	ra	r
ز	za	z
س	sin	s
ش	shin	sh
ص	sad	s
ض	dad	d
ط	ta	t
ظ	za	z
ع	ain	—[2]
غ	ghain	gh[3]
ف	fa	f
ق	qaf	k[4]
ك	kaf	k[5]
ل	lam	l
م	mim	m
ن	nun	n
ه	ha	h
و	waw	w
ي	ya	y

(2) HEBREW

Character	Name	Sound
א	aleph	—[6]
ב ,ב	beth	b, v
ג ,ג	gimel	g, gh[3]
ד ,ד	daleth	d, th
ה	he	h
ו	vav	v
ז	zayin	z
ח	heth	kh
ט	teth	t
י	yod	y
כ ,ך ,כ[8]	kaph	k[5], kh
ל	lamed	l
מ ,ם[8]	mem	m
נ ,ן[8]	nun	n
ס	samek	s
ע	ayin	—[7]
פ ,פ ,ף[8]	pe	p, f
צ ,ץ[8]	sade	s
ק	koph	k[4]
ר	resh	r
ש, ש	sin, shin	s, sh
ת ,ת	tav	t, th

(3) GREEK

Upper	Lower	Name	Sound
A	α	alpha	ä
B	β	beta	b
Γ	γ	gamma	g
Δ	δ	delta	d
E	ε	epsilon	e
Z	ζ	zeta	z
H	η	eta	ā
Θ	θ	theta	th[9]
I	ι	iota	ē
K	κ	kappa	k
Λ	λ	lambda	l
M	μ	mu	m
N	ν	nu	n
Ξ	ξ	xi	ks
O	o	omicron	o
Π	π	pi	p
P	ρ	rho	r
Σ	σ, ς[8]	sigma	s
T	τ	tau	t
Υ	υ	upsilon	ü, ōō
Φ	φ	phi	f[10]
X	χ	chi	kh[11]
Ψ	ψ	psi	ps
Ω	ω	omega	ō

(4) RUSSIAN

Upper	Lower	Name	Sound
А	а	ä	ä
Б	б	be	ä[21]
В	в	ve	v
Г	г	ge	g
Д	д	de	d
Е	е	ye	ye, e[12]
Ё	ё	yô	yô, ô[12,13]
Ж	ж	zhe	zh[14]
З	з	ze	z
И	и	ē	ē[15]
Й	й	ē krät'. kə·yə	ē[16]
К	к	kä	k
Л	л	el	l
М	м	em	m
Н	н	en	n
О	о	ô	ô
П	п	pe	p
Р	р	er	r
С	с	es	s
Т	т	te	t
У	у	ōō	ōō
Ф	ф	ef	f
Х	х	khä	kh
Ц	ц	tse	ts[17]
Ч	ч	che	ch[17]
Ш	ш	shä	sh[14]
Щ	щ	shchä	shch[17]
Ъ	ъ	tvyôr'dē znäk	—[18]
Ы	ы	i[19]	i[19]
Ь	ь	myäkh'. kyē znäk	—[20]
Э	э	e	e
Ю	ю	yōō	yōō, ōō[12]
Я	я	yä	yä, ä[12]

(5) GERMAN

Fraktur		Name	Latin	
𝔄	a	ä	A	a
𝔄̈	ä	ä[21]	Ä	ä
𝔅	b	bä	B	b
ℭ	c	tsä	C	c
𝔇	d	dä	D	d
𝔈	e	ä[22]	E	e
𝔉	f	ef	F	f
𝔊	g	gä	G	g
𝔥	h	hä	H	h
𝔍	i	ē	I	i
𝔍	j	yôt	J	j
𝔎	k	kä	K	k
𝔏	l	el	L	l
𝔐	m	em	M	m
𝔑	n	en	N	n
𝔒	o	ō[22]	O	o
𝔒̈	ö	œ[21]	Ö	ö
𝔓	p	pä	P	p
𝔔	q	kōō	Q	q
𝔯	r	er	R	r
𝔖	f, ß	es	S	s
	ß	es'set	β[23], ss	
𝔗	t	tä	T	t
𝔘	u	ōō	U	u
𝔘̈	ü	ü[21]	Ü	ü
𝔙	v	fou	V	v
𝔚	w	vä	W	w
𝔵	x	iks	X	x
𝔜	y	üp'si·lŏn	Y	y
𝔷	z	tset	Z	z

In each column the characters of the alphabet are given first, followed by their names. In columns 4 (Russian) and 5 (German) the names are printed in the phonetic system used in this dictionary. The last rows of columns 1 through 4 show the approximate sound represented by each character. Columns 3 through 5 show the upper- and lower-case forms.

The Arabic characters are given in their final, unconnected forms. The German style letter, called *fraktur*, has been gradually replaced by the Latin letter. The last row of column 5 gives the Latin equivalents.

[1] Functions as the bearer of *hamza* (the glottal stop), or as a lengthener of short *a*. [2] A voiced pharyngeal fricative. [3] A voiced velar fricative. [4] A uvular stop. [5] A voiceless velar stop. [6] A glottal stop, now usually silent, or pronounced according to the accompanying vowel points. [7] A pharyngeal fricative, now usually silent, or pronounced according to the accompanying vowel points. [8] The alternate form is restricted to the ends of words. [9, 10, 11] In classical Greek these were pronounced as aspirated stops similar to the sounds in foot*h*ill, hap*h*azard, and bloc*kh*ouse. [12] Preceded by a *y* glide when initial, following a vowel, or following a previously palatalized consonant. The glide is otherwise omitted and the preceding consonant palatalized. [13] The diacritical mark is most often omitted. [14] Never palatalized. [15] Palatalizes the consonant preceding it. [16] A short vowel, as *y* in *boy*, used only as the second element of diphthongs. [17] Always palatalized. [18] No phonetic value, used to separate parts of compounds and indicate that the consonant preceding it is not palatalized; a hard sign. [19] No English equivalent, similar to *i* as in *kick* with the tongue drawn back. [20] Indicates that the preceding consonant is to be palatalized. [21] See UMLAUT in vocabulary section. [22] In German this vowel is not a diphthong. [23] Restricted to the ends of words.

43

Day *alternates* with night. **2.** To change from one place, condition, etc., to another and back again repeatedly: to *alternate* between joy and grief. **3.** *Electr.* To reverse direction of flow repeatedly: said of a current. — *v.t.* **4.** To do or perform by turns. **5.** To cause to follow one another by turns. — *adj.* **1.** Existing, occurring, or following by turns; reciprocal. **2.** Referring or pertaining to every other of a series. **3.** Alternative: *alternate* plans. **4.** *Bot.* **a** Placed singly at intervals on the stem, as leaves. **b** Disposed at intervals between parts, as stamens when opposite the spaces between petals. — *n.* A substitute or second; especially, one substituting for another in the performance of a duty or in the filling of a position. Abbr. (n. and adj.) *alt.* [< L *alternatus*, pp. of *alternare* < *alternus* every second one < *alter* other] — **al'ter·nate·ness** *n.*

alternate angle *Geom.* Either of two nonadjacent interior or exterior angles formed on opposite sides of a line that crosses two other lines.

al·ter·nate·ly (ôl'tər·nit·lē, al'-) *adv.* In alternate order or position; by turns.

alternating current See under CURRENT.

al·ter·na·tion (ôl'tər·nā'shən, al'-) *n.* Occurrence or action of two things in turn; passage from one place or state to another and back again: *alternation* between day and night.

alternation of generations Metagenesis.

al·ter·na·tive (ôl·tûr'nə·tiv, al-) *n.* **1.** A choice between two things: often loosely applied to more than two: to face the *alternative* of death or dishonor. **2.** Either of the two or more things to be chosen: The *alternative* of a fine was jail. **3.** The remaining choice: We had no *alternative* but to concede. — *adj.* **1.** Affording or implying a choice between two (or sometimes more) things. **2.** *Gram.* Implying that the terms it connects are to be taken as alternatives: "Or" is an *alternative* conjunction. Abbr. *alt.* — **al·ter'na·tive·ly** *adv.* — **al·ter'na·tive·ness** *n.* [< Med.L *alternativus*] — **Syn.** (noun) *Alternative, choice, option, selection, election,* and *preference* agree in denoting one of several things that may be chosen. *Alternative* implies that the things to be chosen are mutually exclusive. *Choice* and *option* emphasize the right or opportunity to choose; in addition, *option* suggests the existence of a few possibilities. *Selection* is used when there are many possibilities and the choice between them is a matter of taste. *Election* is the result of purposeful judgment, *choice* is an act of will; *preference* is based on sentiment or personal liking.

al·ter·na·tor (ôl'tər·nā'tər, al'-) *n.* **1.** One who or that which alternates. **2.** *Electr.* A generator giving an alternating current. Also **al'ter·nat'er.**

Alt·geld (ält'geld, ôlt'-), **John Peter,** 1847–1902, U.S. political administrator; governor of Illinois 1892–96.

al·the·a (al·thē'ə) *n.* Any plant of a small but widely distributed genus (*Althaea*) of herbs of the mallow family, including the common hollyhock and the rose of Sharon. Also **al·thae'a.** [< L < Gk. *althaia* wild mallow, lit., healer < *althainein* to heal]

Al·the·a (al·thē'ə) In Greek mythology, the wife of Oeneus and mother of Meleager.

alt·horn (alt'hôrn') *n.* An alto flügelhorn or saxhorn. [< ALT + HORN]

al·though (ôl·thō') *conj.* Notwithstanding the fact that; supposing that; though. Also **al·tho'.** [< ALL + THOUGH]

alti- *combining form* High: *altimeter.* Also **alto-.** [< L *altus* high]

al·tim·e·ter (al·tim'ə·tər, al'tə·mē'tər) *n.* **1.** An aneroid barometer calibrated to permit accurate determination of altitudes above sea level, used especially in aircraft. **2.** Any instrument for determining altitude, as one operating by radio waves or sound echoes. — **al·tim·e·try** (al·tim'ə·trē) *n.*

al·ti·tude (al'tə·tood, -tyood) *n.* **1.** Vertical elevation above any given point, especially above mean sea level; height. **2.** *Astron.* Angular elevation above the horizon. **3.** *Geom.* The vertical distance from the base of a figure to its highest point. **4.** A high place or rank. Abbr. *alt.* [< L *altitudo, -inis* < *altus* high] — **al'ti·tu'di·nal** *adj.*

al·to (al'tō) *Music* *n.* *pl.* **·tos** **1.** The lowest female voice; contralto. **2.** The highest male voice; countertenor. **3.** A singer who has an alto voice. **4.** A musical part for this voice. — *adj.* Sounding or ranging between tenor and treble. Abbr. *a., alt.* [< Ital. < L *altus* high]

alto- Var. of ALTI-.

alto clef See under CLEF.

al·to·cu·mu·lus (al'tō·kyoo'myə·ləs) *n. Meteorol.* A fleecy cloud (Symbol Ac), usually a rounded mass: also called *cumulocirrus.* See table for CLOUD.

altocumulus cas·tel·la·tus (kas'tə·lā'təs) *Meteorol.* A cloud formation (symbol Acc) resembling altocumulus but having turretlike formations on a horizontal base.

al·to·geth·er (ôl'tə·geth'ər, ôl'tə·geth'ər) *adv.* **1.** Completely; wholly; entirely. **2.** With everything included; in all; all told. — *n.* A whole. — **in the altogether** *Informal* Nude. [< ALL + TOGETHER]

Al·ton (ôl'tən) A city in SW Illinois, on the Mississippi River; pop. 39,700.

Al·too·na (al·too'nə) A city in south central Pennsylvania; pop. 63,115.

al·to·re·lie·vo (al'tō·ri·lē'vō) *n. pl.* **·vos** Sculpture in which the figures project by more than half their depth from the background: also called *high relief.* See RELIEF. [< Ital.]

al·to·ri·lie·vo (äl'tō·rē·lyä'vō) *n. pl.* **al·ti·ri·lie·vi** (äl'tē·rē·lyä've) *Italian* Alto-relievo.

al·to·stra·tus (al'tō·strā'təs) *n. Meteorol.* A gray to bluish gray cloud (Symbol As), usually forming a compact mass. See table for CLOUD.

al·tri·cial (al·trish'əl) *adj. Ornithol.* Remaining in the nest for some time after being hatched: distinguished from *precocial.* [< NL *altricialis* < L *altrix, -icis* a nurse]

al·tru·ism (al'trŏo·iz'əm) *n.* Selfless devotion to the welfare of others. [< F *altruisme,* ult. < L *alter* other] — **Syn.** *Altruism, charity,* and *philanthropy* are here compared as they imply unselfishness. *Altruism* is motivation for the good of others, rather than for one's own gain. *Charity,* as an attitude of mind, is the crediting of good intentions, honest purposes, etc., to others. *Philanthropy* was also originally a state of mind, a "love for mankind," but is now most commonly used of the active promotion of and participation in enterprises for the general welfare. Compare BENEVOLENCE.

al·tru·ist (al'trŏo·ist) *n.* One devoted to the welfare of others.

al·tru·is·tic (al'trŏo·is'tik) *adj.* Concerned with the well-being of others; benevolent. — **al'tru·is'ti·cal·ly** *adv.*

a·lu·del (al'yə·del) *n. Chem.* One of a series of pear-shaped nesting vessels used for condensation, as in subliming mercury. [< F < Sp. < Arabic *al-uthāl* the utensil]

a·lu·la (al'yə·lə) *n. pl.* **·lae** (-lē) **1.** *Ornithol.* The false wing of a bird; a tuft of feathers on the part corresponding to the thumb. **2.** *Entomol.* A lobe separated from the wing base in certain insects. [< NL, dim. of L *ala* wing] — **al'u·lar** *adj.*

al·um (al'əm) *n. Chem.* **1.** An astringent, crystalline, double sulfate of aluminum and potassium, $K_2SO_4Al_2(SO_4)_3$·$24H_2O$, widely used in medicine, manufacturing, and the arts. **2.** Any of a class of double sulfates formed from an alkali metal and a trivalent metal. [< OF < L *alumen* alum]

alum. Aluminum.

a·lu·mi·na (ə·loo'mə·nə) *n.* **1.** *Chem.* Aluminum oxide, Al_2O_3, occurring abundantly in the silicate minerals and as corundum in the sapphire and ruby. **2.** *Obs.* Aluminum. Also **al·u·min** (al'yə·min), and **al·u·mine** (al'yə·mēn, -min). [< NL < L *alumen, -minis* alum]

a·lu·min·ate (ə·loo'mə·nāt) *n. Chem.* Any of several aluminum compounds having the formula $MAlO_2$ or M_3AlO_3, where M indicates a monovalent metal.

a·lu·mi·nif·er·ous (ə·loo'mə·nif'ər·əs) *adj.* Containing or yielding alum, alumina, or aluminum. [< *alumini-* (< ALUMINUM) + -FEROUS]

a·lu·mi·nize (ə·loo'mə·nīz) *v.t.* **·nized, ·niz·ing** To cover or treat with aluminum. Also **a·lu·me·tize** (ə·loo'mə·tīz).

a·lu·mi·no·ther·my (ə·loo'mə·nō·thûr'mē) *n. Metall.* The process of generating heat by the chemical combination of aluminum with oxygen from a metallic oxide. [< *alumino-* (< ALUMINUM) + Gk. *thermē* heat]

a·lu·mi·num (ə·loo'mə·nəm) *n.* A light, bluish white, malleable and ductile metallic element (symbol Al) found only in combination. It is widely used in alloys. Also *Brit.* **al·u·min·i·um** (al'yə·min'ē·əm). See ELEMENT. [< NL < L *alumen, -minis* alum] — **a·lu'mi·nous** *adj.*

a·lum·na (ə·lum'nə) *n. pl.* **·nae** (-nē) *U.S.* A female graduate or former student of a college or school. [< L, fem. of *alumnus*]

a·lum·nus (ə·lum'nəs) *n. pl.* **·ni** (-nī) **1.** *Chiefly U.S.* A male graduate or former student of a college or school. **2.** Originally, any pupil. [< L, foster son, pupil < *alere* to nourish]

al·um·root (al'əm·root', -root') *n.* **1.** One of several low herbs (genus *Heuchera*) of the saxifrage family; especially, *H. americana,* or its astringent root. **2.** The spotted cranebill. See under CRANEBILL.

A·lun·dum (ə·lun'dəm) *n.* A fused crystalline bauxite used as an abrasive, for refractories, etc.: a trade name.

a·lu·nite (al'yə·nīt) *n. Chem.* A white, hydrous, potassium-aluminum sulfate, $KAl_2(SO)_4(OH)_6$, crystallizing in the hexagonal system. Also **al'um·stone'.** [< F < *alun* alum < L *alumen*]

Al·va (al'və, *Sp.* äl'vä), **Duke of** See ALBA.

Al·va·ra·do (äl'vä·rä'thō), **Pedro de,** 1495?–1541, Spanish officer; companion of Cortés in Mexico.

Al·va·rez (al'və·rez), **Luis Walter,** born 1911, U.S. physicist.

Ál·va·rez Quin·te·ro (äl'vä·räth kēn·tā'rō), **Joaquín,** 1873–1944, and **Serafín,** 1871–1938, brothers, Spanish dramatists.

al·ve·o·lar (al·vē'ə·lər) *adj.* **1.** *Anat.* Denoting that part of the jaws in which the teeth are set. **2.** *Phonet.* Formed with the tongue tip touching or near the alveolar ridge, as (t), (d), and (s) in English. — *n. Phonet.* A sound so produced.

alveolar arch *Anat.* The arch of the upper jawbone in vertebrates.

alveolar point In craniometry, the point situated between the two middle incisors of the upper jaw.

alveolar ridge *Anat.* The inwardly projecting bony ridge of the upper jawbone, between the front teeth and the hard palate.

al·ve·o·late (al·vē′ə·lit, al′vē·ə-) *adj.* Having alveoli arranged like the cells of a honeycomb; deeply pitted. Also **al·ve·o·lat·ed** (al·vē′ə·lā′tid). [< L *alveolatus*] — **al·ve′·o·la′tion** *n.*

al·ve·o·lus (al·vē′ə·ləs) *n. pl.* **·li** (-lī) *Anat.* **1.** A small cavity or pit, resembling a honeycomb cell. **2.** The socket in which a tooth is set. **3.** *pl.* The alveolar ridge. **4.** An air cell of the lungs formed by the terminal dilations of the bronchioles. **5.** An acinus. [< L, dim. of *alveus* a hollow]

al·vine (al′vin, -vīn) *adj. Physiol.* Pertaining to or proceeding from the abdomen and lower intestines. [< L *alvinus* < *alvus* belly]

al·ways (ôl′wāz, -wiz) *adv.* **1.** Perpetually; for all time; ceaselessly. **2.** At every time; on all occasions. Also *Archaic* or *Poetic* **al·way** (ôl′wā). [ME *alles weyes* < OE *aelne weg*]

a·lys·sum (ə·lis′əm) *n.* **1.** Any of a large genus (*Alyssum*) of plants of the mustard family, bearing white or yellow flowers. **2.** One of various other plants of the same family, as the white or purple sweet alyssum. Also called *madwort.* [< NL < Gk. *alysson,* name of a plant, ? < *alyssos* curing madness < *a-* not + *lyssa* madness]

am (am, *unstressed* əm) Present indicative, first person singular, of BE. [OE *eom, am*]

am. Ammeter.

Am *Chem.* Americium.

Am. America; American.

AM or **A.M., a.m.,** or **a-m** Amplitude modulation.

A.M. 1. Annus mirabilis. **2.** Anno mundi. **3.** Master of Arts (L *Artium Magister*). **4.** Associate member.

A.M. or **a.m.** Ante meridiem; before noon.

AMA or **A.M.A. 1.** American Management Association. **2.** American Medical Association. **3.** American Missionary Association. **4.** American Municipal Association. **5.** Automobile Manufacturers' Association.

am·a·da·vat (am′ə·də·vat′) *n.* A small singing bird of India (*Estrilda amandava*), having red and black plumage flecked with white, and a red beak. [< an East Indian name]

Am·a·dis of Gaul (am′ə·dis) The hero in a medieval Spanish romance of this title.

am·a·dou (am′ə·dōō) *n.* A soft, spongy, combustible substance, prepared from several species of fungus (as *Boletus, Polyporus,* or *Hernandia*), found on old trees, used as tinder and as a styptic: also called *touchwood.* [< F < Provençal]

A·ma·ga·sa·ki (ä·mä·gä·sä·kē) A city on southern Honshu island, Japan, on Osaka Bay; pop. 335,513 (1955).

a·mah (ä′mə, am′ə) *n.* In India and the Orient, a female attendant for children; especially, a wet nurse. Also **a′ma.** [< Anglo-Indian < Pg. *ama* nurse]

a·main (ə·mān′) *adv. Archaic & Poetic.* **1.** Vehemently. **2.** Exceedingly. **3.** Without delay. [< A-¹ + MAIN¹]

Am·a·lek·ite (am′ə·lek·īt, ə·mal′ə·kīt) *n.* In the Bible, a member of a marauding, nomadic tribe descended from Esau and hostile to the Israelites. *Gen.* xxxvi 12; *Ex.* xvii 8–13.

a·mal·gam (ə·mal′gəm) *n.* **1.** An alloy or union of mercury with another metal. **2.** A silver-white, brittle compound of mercury and silver, crystallizing in the isometric system. **3.** Any combination of two or more bodies, substances, or things. [< MF *amalgame* < Med.L *amalgama,* ult. < Gk. *malagma* an emollient < *malassein* to soften]

a·mal·ga·mate (ə·mal′gə·māt) *v.t. & v.i.* **·mat·ed, ·mat·ing 1.** To form an amalgam; unite in an alloy with mercury, as a metal. **2.** To unite or combine. — **a·mal·ga·ma·ble** (ə·mal′gə·mə·bəl) *adj.* — **a·mal·ga·ma·tive** (ə·mal′gə·mā′tiv) *adj.* — **a·mal′ga·ma′tor** or **a·mal′ga·mat′er** *n.*

a·mal·ga·ma·tion (ə·mal′gə·mā′shən) *n.* **1.** The forming of an amalgam, or the substance formed. **2.** A merger, as of two corporations. **3.** A mingling of racial or ethnic stocks. **4.** *Metall.* The removal of metals from their ores by treatment with mercury.

Am·al·the·a (am′əl·thē′ə) In Greek mythology, the goat who suckled Zeus. One of her horns (**horn of Amalthea**) became the cornucopia, or horn of plenty.

am·a·ni·ta (am′ə·nī′tə) *n.* Any of a genus (*Amanita*) of highly poisonous fungi of the agaric order. [< Gk. *amanitai,* a kind of fungus]

a·man·u·en·sis (ə·man′yōō·en′sis) *n. pl.* **·ses** (-sēz) One who copies manuscript or takes dictation; a secretary. [< L < (*servus*) *a manu* hand (servant), secretary + -*ensis* belonging or relating to]

am·a·ranth (am′ə·ranth) *n.* **1.** Any of various allied plants (family *Amaranthaceae*) having flowers that do not readily fade when gathered, as the love-lies-bleeding. **2.** *Poetic* An imaginary nonfading flower. **3.** *Chem.* A deep-red azo dye used to color food products. [< L *amarantus* < Gk. *amarantos,* lit., unfading < *a-* not + *marainein* to wither]

am·a·ran·thine (am′ə·ran′thin) *adj.* **1.** Pertaining to, like, or containing amaranth. **2.** Unfading; everlasting. **3.** Of purplish hue.

Am·a·ril·lo (am′ə·ril′ō) A city in NW Texas; pop. 127,010.

am·a·ryl·li·da·ceous (am′ə·ril′ə·dā′shəs) *adj. Bot.* Of or

pertaining to the amaryllis family, including the amaryllis, narcissus, and agave. [< NL < AMARYLLIS]

am·a·ryl·lis (am′ə·ril′is) *n.* **1.** Any one of a genus (*Amaryllis,* family *Amaryllidaceae*) of bulbous South African plants, frequent in cultivation, as the belladonna lily. **2.** The flower of one of these plants. [< L < Gk. *Amaryllis,* fem. personal name]

Am·a·ryl·lis (am′ə·ril′is) In pastoral poetry, a country girl or shepherdess.

a·mass (ə·mas′) *v.t.* To heap up; accumulate, especially as wealth or possessions for oneself. [< OF *amasser* < *a-* to (< L *ad-*) + *masser* to pile up < L *massa* mass] — **a·mass′·a·ble** *adj.* — **a·mass′er** *n.* — **a·mass′ment** *n.*

— **Syn.** *Amass, accumulate, collect,* and *gather* mean to bring together. *Amass* suggests large quantity and great value: to *amass* riches. To *accumulate* is to increase by regular additions: Interest *accumulates* on a bank deposit. We *amass* or *accumulate* similar things to make a homogeneous bulk; we may *collect* or *gather* diverse things. *Collect* suggests discriminating selection, and *gather* emphasizes the act of bringing widely scattered things to one place: to *collect* stamps, to *gather* wildflowers.

am·a·teur (am′ə·choor, -tōōr, -tyōōr, am′ə·tûr′) *n.* **1.** One who practices an art or science for his own pleasure, rather than as a profession. **2.** An athlete who has not engaged in contests for money, or used any athletic art as a means of livelihood. **3.** One who does something without professional skill or ease. — *adj.* **1.** Pertaining to or done by an amateur. **2.** Composed of amateurs: an *amateur* cast. **3.** Not expert or professional. *Abbr. a.* [< F < L *amator, -oris* lover < *amare* to love] — **am′a·teur·ism** *n.*

— **Syn.** (noun) **1.** *Amateur, connoisseur, dilettante,* and *dabbler* are compared in the sense of one who has some knowledge or proficiency in a certain area, but who is not an expert or professional. Etymologically, an *amateur* is one who loves a subject, and a *connoisseur* one who knows it; in present usage, *amateur* is often used to indicate lack of skill, while *connoisseur* implies the ability to make discriminating judgments. A *dilettante* loves the arts, and often possesses great esthetic sensitivity, but lacks technical mastery. Superficiality is characteristic of the *dabbler,* who dips into a subject without reaching its depths.

am·a·teur·ish (am′ə·choor′ish, -tōōr′-, -tyōōr′-, -tûr′-) *adj.* Lacking the skill or perfection of an expert or professional. — **am′a·teur′ish·ly** *adv.* — **am′a·teur′ish·ness** *n.*

A·ma·ti (ä·mä′tē) *n.* A violin made by any of the Amati, a family of violinmakers at Cremona, Italy, in the 16th and 17th centuries, notably **Nicolò** (or **Nicola**) **Amati,** 1596–1684.

am·a·tive (am′ə·tiv) *adj.* Disposed to love; amorous. — **Syn.** See AMOROUS. [< L *amatus,* pp. of *amare* to love] — **am′a·tive·ly** *adv.* — **am′a·tive·ness** *n.*

am·a·tol (am′ə·tol, -tōl) *n.* A mixture of TNT and ammonium nitrate used as a high explosive. [< AM(MONIUM) + TOL(UENE)]

am·a·to·ry (am′ə·tôr′ē, -tō′rē) *adj.* Pertaining to, expressing, or exciting love, especially sexual love; erotic, as a poem. Also **am′a·to′ri·al.** — **Syn.** See AMOROUS. [< L *amatorius* < *amator.* See AMATEUR.]

am·au·ro·sis (am′ô·rō′sis) *n. Pathol.* Loss of sight without apparent organic defect. [< NL < Gk. *amaurōsis* < *amauros* dark] — **am·au·rot·ic** (am′ô·rot′ik) *adj.*

a·maze (ə·māz′) *v.t.* **a·mazed, a·maz·ing 1.** To overwhelm, as by wonder or surprise; astonish greatly. **2.** *Obs.* To bewilder. — *n. Poetic* Wonder. [OE *āmasian*] — **a·maz·ed·ly** (ə·māz′zid·lē) *adv.* — **a·maz′ed·ness** *n.*

— **Syn.** (verb) **1.** *Amaze, surprise, astonish, astound,* and *flabbergast* mean to fill with wonder or incredulity by confronting with something unexpected. We are *amazed* at what seems impossible, highly improbable, extremely difficult, or otherwise beyond normal experience. That which is merely unexpected *surprises* us; we are *astonished* when the surprise is great enough to silence or daze us. Paralyzing shock is implied by *astound,* and its informal equivalent, *flabbergast.*

a·maze·ment (ə·māz′mənt) *n.* **1.** Extreme wonder or surprise; astonishment. **2.** *Obs.* Bewilderment; distraction.

a·maz·ing (ə·mā′zing) *adj.* Causing amazement; astonishing; wonderful. — **a·maz′ing·ly** *adv.*

Am·a·zon (am′ə·zon, -zən) *n.* **1.** In Greek mythology, one of a race of female warriors said to have lived in Scythia, near the Black Sea. **2.** A female warrior. **3.** Any large, strong or athletic woman or girl: also **am′a·zon.** [< L < Gk. *Amazōn;* derived by the Greeks as < *a-* without + *mazos* breast, because of the fable that they cut off the right breast to facilitate the use of the bow]

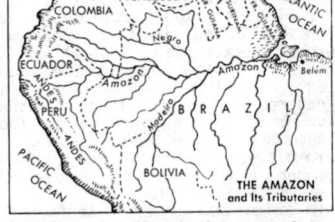

THE AMAZON and Its Tributaries

Am·a·zon (am′ə·zon, -zən) A river in South America, carrying the largest volume of water of any in the world and flowing about 3,300 miles from the Andes through northern Brazil to the Atlantic.

Amazon ant An ant (*Polyergus rufescens*) that enslaves the young of other species.

A·ma·zo·nas (*Sp.* ä'mä·sō'näs, *Pg.* ä·mə·zō'nəs) **1.** A State in NW Brazil; 614,913 sq. mi.; pop. 875,000 (1967); capital, Manaus. **2.** A Commissary of SE Colombia; 48,008 sq. mi.; pop. 8,230 (est. 1957); capital, Letica. **3.** A Department of northern Peru; 13,948 sq. mi.; pop. 16,000 (1970); chief city, Chachapoyas. **4.** A Territory of southern Venezuela; 67,857 sq. mi.; pop. 12,831 (1961); capital, Puerto Ayacucho.

Am·a·zo·ni·an (am'ə·zō'nē·ən) *adj.* **1.** Like or characteristic of an Amazon; warlike; masculine: said of women. **2.** Pertaining to the Amazon river.

am·a·zon·ite (am'ə·zən·īt') *n.* Green orthoclase, used as a gemstone. Also **Amazon stone.** [after the *Amazon* river]

Amb. Ambassador.

am·bage (am'bij) *n. pl.* **am·bag·es** (am'bij·iz, *Lat.* am·bä'·jēz) **1.** A winding or circuitous path. **2.** *Usually pl.* An indirect method of proceeding. [< OF *ambages* < L < *ambi-* around + *agere* to go]

am·ba·gious (am·bā'jəs) *adj.* Roundabout; devious. — **am·ba'gious·ly** *adv.* — **am·ba'gious·ness** *n.*

Am·ba·la (um·bä'lə) A city in eastern Punjab, India; pop. 105,507 (1961).

am·ba·ry (am·bā'rē) *n.* **1.** An important commercial malvaceous plant (*Hibiscus cannabinus*) cultivated in the East Indies. **2.** Its fibers, used for making cordage, sacking, and canvas. Also **am·ba'ri.** [< Hind. *ambārī*]

am·bas·sa·dor (am·bas'ə·dər, -dôr) *n.* **1.** An accredited diplomatic agent of the highest rank, appointed as the representative of one government to another: in full **ambassador extraordinary and plenipotentiary.** *Abbr.* **A.E.** *and* **P.** **2.** Any personal representative or messenger. Also, *Archaic,* **embassador.** — **ambassador-at-large** An ambassador accredited to no specific government. [< F *ambassadeur,* ult. < LL *ambactus* servant, goer about, prob. < Celtic] — **am·bas·sa·do·ri·al** (am·bas'ə·dôr'ē·əl, -dō'rē-) *adj.* — **am·bas'sa·dor·ship** *n.*

— **Syn. 1.** *Ambassador, minister, envoy, nuncio,* and *legate* are here compared in their technical usage. A diplomatic representative of highest rank is an *ambassador;* one of lower rank is a *minister.* Most *ambassadors* and *ministers* reside in the countries to which they are accredited. A *minister* sent on a special mission is called an *envoy.* A *nuncio* is a papal *ambassador;* a papal *envoy* is a *legate.*

am·bas·sa·dress (am·bas'ə·dris) *n.* **1.** A woman ambassador. **2.** The wife of an ambassador.

am·ber (am'bər) *n.* **1.** A yellow, reddish-yellow, or brownish-yellow fossilized vegetable resin, hard, brittle, and translucent, and easily electrified by friction, used in jewelry and in pharmacy. **2.** The color of amber. **3.** An amber-colored light used to produce the effect of sunlight, as on a stage. — *adj.* Pertaining to, like, or of the color of amber. [< OF *ambre* < Arabic *anbar* ambergris]

am·ber·gris (am'bər·grēs, -gris) *n.* An opaque, grayish, waxy secretion from the intestines of the sperm whale, sometimes found floating on the ocean or lying on the shore, used in perfumery. [< F *ambre gris* gray amber]

am·ber·oid (am'bər·oid) See AMBROID.

ambi- *combining form* Both: *ambidextrous.* [< L *ambo* both]

am·bi·dex·ter (am'bə·dek'stər) *adj.* Ambidextrous. — *n.* **1.** One who uses both hands equally well. **2.** A double-dealer; hypocrite. [< L *ambo* both + *dexter* right (hand)] — **am'bi·dex'tral** (-dek'strəl) *adj.*

am·bi·dex·ter·i·ty (am'bə·dek·ster'ə·tē) *n.* **1.** The state or quality of being ambidextrous. **2.** Duplicity; trickery.

am·bi·dex·trous (am'bə·dek'strəs) *adj.* **1.** Able to use both hands equally well. **2.** Very dexterous or skillful. **3.** Dissembling; double-dealing. — **am'bi·dex'trous·ly** *adv.* — **am'bi·dex'trous·ness** *n.*

am·bi·ence (am'bē·əns) *n.* The environment or pervading atmosphere of a place, situation, etc. Also *French* **am·bi·ance** (äN·bē·äN'). [< L *ambiens.* See AMBIENT.]

am·bi·ent (am'bē·ənt) *adj.* **1.** Surrounding; encircling; encompassing. **2.** Circulating. [< L *ambiens, -entis,* ppr. of *ambire* < *ambi-* around + *ire* to go]

am·bi·gu·i·ty (am'bə·gyoo'ə·tē) *n. pl.* **·ties 1.** The quality of being ambiguous; doubtfulness. **2.** An expression, statement, situation, etc., that can be variously interpreted.

am·big·u·ous (am·big'yoo·əs) *adj.* **1.** Capable of being understood in more senses than one; having a double meaning; equivocal. **2.** Doubtful or uncertain: a liquid of *ambiguous* nature. **3.** Obscure; indistinct: *ambiguous* shadows. [< L *ambiguus* < *ambigere* to wander about < *ambi-* around + *agere* to go] — **am·big'u·ous·ly** *adv.* — **am·big'u·ous·ness** *n.*

am·bit (am'bit) *n.* **1.** Circumference; circuit. **2.** Extent or sphere, as of actions or words; scope. [< L *ambitus* circuit < *ambire.* See AMBIENT.]

am·bi·ten·den·cy (am'bə·ten'dən·sē) *n. Psychol.* The state of having conflicting tendencies.

am·bi·tion (am·bish'ən) *n.* **1.** Eager desire to succeed, to achieve power, wealth, fame, etc. **2.** A strong desire or steadfast purpose to achieve something commendable. **3.**

The object of aspiration or desire: His *ambition* was the presidency. — *v.t.* To desire and seek eagerly. [< L *ambitio, -onis* a going about (to solicit votes) < *ambire.* See AMBIENT.] — **am·bi'tion·less** *adj.*

am·bi·tious (am·bish'əs) *adj.* **1.** Actuated or characterized by ambition. **2.** Greatly desiring; eager for: with *of* or the infinitive. **3.** Aspiring, as to a high or imposing position; pretentious. **4.** Challenging; difficult: an *ambitious* project. — **am·bi'tious·ly** *adv.* — **am·bi'tious·ness** *n.*

— **Syn. 3.** *Ambitious, aspiring,* and *emulous* mean desirous of increasing one's personal possessions or attainments. The *ambitious* man seeks wealth, power, honors, or the like, and actively tries to obtain them. An *aspiring* man seeks something above himself, as excellence for its own sake, and the word usually implies lofty ideals. Those who are *emulous* seek to equal or surpass others.

am·biv·a·lent (am·biv'ə·lənt) *adj.* **1.** Uncertain or changeful, especially because composed of or influenced by contradictory emotions: an *ambivalent* attitude toward his ex-wife. **2.** *Psychol.* Experiencing or expressing contradictory thoughts or emotions, as love and hate, toward the same object at the same time. [< AMBI- + L *valens, -entis,* ppr. of *valere* to be strong, be worth] — **am·biv'a·lence** *n.*

am·bi·ver·sion (am'bə·vûr'zhən, -shən) *n. Psychol.* A condition between introversion and extroversion. [< AMBI- + -*version,* as in *introversion*] — **am'bi·vert** *n.*

am·ble (am'bəl) *v.i.* **·bled** (-bəld), **·bling 1.** To move, as a horse, by lifting the two feet on one side together, alternately with the two feet on the other. **2.** To move with an easy, swaying motion resembling this gait; proceed leisurely. — *n.* **1.** The gait of a horse when ambling. **2.** Any movement resembling this. [< OF *ambler* < L *ambulare* to walk] — **am'bler** *n.* — **am'bling** *adj.* — **am'bling·ly** *adv.*

am·blyg·o·nite (am·blig'ə·nīt) *n.* A lithium-aluminum fluophosphate, Li(AlF)PO₄, crystallizing in the triclinic system. [< G *amblygonit* < Gk. *amblygōnios* having obtuse angles]

am·bly·o·pi·a (am'blē·ō'pē·ə) *n. Pathol.* Dimness of vision without discoverable change in the eye. Also **am·bly·o·py** (am'blē·ə·pē). [< NL < Gk *amblyōpia* < *amblys* dull + *ōps* eye] — **am·bly·op·ic** (am'blē·op'ik) *adj.*

am·bo (am'bō) *n. pl.* **am·bos** (am'bōz) *or* **am·bo·nes** (am-bō'nēz) In early Christian churches, a raised, pulpitlike stand or desk, where parts of the service were read or chanted. [< Gk. *ambōn* a rising ground]

am·bo·cep·tor (am'bə·sep'tər) *n. Biochem.* A cytolysin. [< L *ambo* both + (RE)CEPTOR]

Am·boi·na pimple (am·boi'nə) *Pathol.* Yaws.

Amboina wood The mottled wood of an Indonesian tree (genus *Pterocarpus*), used in furniture as veneer and inlay; also called *Padauk wood, Padouk wood.*

Am·boise (äN·bwäz') A commune in west central France, on the Loire; residence of the Valois kings from Charles VIII to Francis II; pop. about 6,000.

Am·bon (äm'bôn) An Indonesian island SW of Ceram; 314 sq. mi.; pop. about 67,000; chief town, Amboina: also **Amboi·na, Am·boy·na** (am·boi'nə).

am·broid (am'broid) *n.* A synthetic amber made by heating and pressing amber fragments: also spelled *amberoid.*

Am·brose (am'brōz), **Saint,** 340?–397, bishop of Milan; one of the Latin church fathers.

Ambrose Channel An entrance to New York Harbor.

am·bro·sia (am·brō'zhə, -zhē·ə) *n.* **1.** In classical mythology, the food of the gods, giving immortality. **2.** Any very delicious food or drink. **3.** Beebread. **4.** *Bot.* Any of a genus (*Ambrosia*) of herbs, as ragweed. [< L < Gk. *ambrosia* < *ambrotos* immortal < *a-* not + *brotos* mortal]

am·bro·si·a·ceous (am·brō'zē·ā'shəs) *adj.* Belonging to the genus *Ambrosia,* comprising weedy herbs of the composite family, as the ragweeds.

am·bro·sial (am·brō'zhəl, -zhē·əl) *adj.* **1.** Of or like ambrosia; fragrant; delicious. **2.** Worthy of the gods; heavenly. Also **am·bro·sian** (am·brō'zhən, -zhē·ən) — **am·bro'sial·ly** *adv.*

Am·bro·sian (am·brō'zhən, -zhē·ən) *adj.* Of, in the style of, or attributed to St. Ambrose.

Ambrosian chant The mode of singing or chanting divine service introduced by St. Ambrose in the cathedral at Milan and superseded by Gregorian chant.

Ambrosian hymn A metrical hymn written by St. Ambrose or in his style.

am·bro·type (am'brō·tīp') *n.* A thin photographic glass negative made to serve as a positive picture. [after (James) *Ambro(se* Cutting), 1814–67, inventor + -TYPE]

am·bry (am'brē) *n. pl.* **·bries 1.** A depository for goods or money; pantry; cupboard. **2.** *Eccl.* A closet near the altar for the sacred vessels. Also **am·ber·y** (am'bər·ē). [ME *almarie, ambrie* < L *armarium* a chest, orig., a place for storing arms < *arma* arms, weapons]

ambs·ace (āmz'ās' amz'-) *n.* **1.** Both aces, the lowest throw at dice. **2.** Bad luck; misfortune. **3.** That which is next to nothing; the least amount possible. Also spelled *amesace.* [< OF *ambes as* < L *ambas as* double ace]

AMBROSIA (*def.* 4)
Common ragweed (3 to 6 feet high)

am·bu·la·crum (am/byə·lā/krəm) *n. pl* **·cra** (-krə) *Zool.* One of the perforated areas through which are protruded the pedicels or tube feet, as in the starfishes. [< L, a covered walk < *ambulare* to walk] **—am/bu·la/cral** *adj.*

am·bu·lance (am/byə·ləns) *n.* **1.** A special vehicle, as a truck, boat, or aircraft, equipped for conveying the sick and wounded. **2.** A moving or field hospital. [< F < (*hôpital*) *ambulant* walking (hospital) < L *ambulare* to walk]

ambulance chaser *U.S. Slang* A lawyer or his agent who seeks to persuade an injured person to sue for damages.

am·bu·lant (am/byə·lənt) *adj.* Walking or moving about from place to place; shifting. [< L *ambulans, -antis,* ppr. of *ambulare* to walk]

am·bu·late (am/byə·lāt) *v.i.* **·lat·ed, ·lat·ing** To walk about; move from place to place. [< L *ambulatus,* pp. of *ambulare* to walk] **—am/bu·la/tion** *n.*

am·bu·la·to·ry (am/byə·lə·tôr/ē, -tō/rē) *adj.* **1.** Of or for walking. **2.** Able to walk, as an invalid. **3.** Shifting; not fixed or stationary. **4.** *Law* Alterable, as a writ or pleading until filed, or a will at any time during the testator's life. — *n.pl.* **·ries** A sheltered place for walking, as a cloister.

am·bus·cade (am/bəs·kād/) *n.* An ambush. Also *Archaic* **am·bus·ca·do** (am/bəs·kā/dō). —*v.t.* **·cad·ed, ·cad·ing** To ambush. [< F *embuscade* < Ital. *imboscata* an ambush < *imboscare.* See AMBUSH.] **—am/bus·cad/er** *n.*

am·bush (am/bŏŏsh) *n.* **1.** A lying in wait to attack unawares. **2.** A surprise attack launched from hiding. **3.** Any unseen peril or snare. **4.** A secret position for surprise attack; also, the attackers. Also **am/bush·ment.** —*v.t.* To attack from a hidden place; waylay. [< OF *embusche* < *embuscher* < Ital. *imboscare* to place in a bush, set an ambush < L *in-* in + *boscus* a wood] **—am/bush·er** *n.*

AMC Air Materiel Command.

AMDG or **A.M.D.G.** To the greater glory of God (L *ad majorem Dei gloriam*).

A.M.E. African Methodist Episcopal.

a·me·ba (ə·mē/bə) *n. pl.* **·bas** or **·bae** (-bē) Any of a genus (*Amoeba*) of unicellular, naked protozoans (class *Sarcodina*), found in stagnant water or as a parasite on other animals, of indefinite shape, moving and feeding by the action of pseudopodia, and reproducing by simple division of one individual into two separate organisms: also spelled *amoeba.* [< NL < Gk. *amoibē* change] **—a·me·bic** (ə·mē/bik) *adj.*

am·e·be·an (am/ə·bē/ən) *adj.* Alternately or reciprocally responsive, as lines of dialogue: also spelled *amoebaean, amoebean.* [< L *amoebaeum* (*carmen*) < Gk. (*aisma*) *amoibaion* responsive (song) < *amoibē* change]

amebic dysentery *Pathol.* A form of dysentery caused by infection of the colon with a protozoan parasite (*Endamoeba histolytica*): also **amebic colitis, am·e·bi·a·sis** (am/ə·bī/ə·sis).

a·me·boid (ə·mē/boid) *adj.* Resembling an ameba, as in its change of form: also spelled *amoeboid.*

a·meer (ə·mir/) See AMIR.

am·el·corn (am/əl·kôrn/) *n.* An inferior kind of wheat (*Triticum sativum dicoccum*) cultivated in Europe mainly for the manufacture of starch: also called *emmer.* [< G *amelkorn* starch corn]

a·mel·io·rate (ə·mēl/yə·rāt) *v.t. & v.i.* **·rat·ed, ·rat·ing** To make or become better; meliorate; improve. [< F *améliorer* < L *ad-* to + *meliorare* to better < *melior* better] **—a·mel·io·ra·ble** (ə·mēl/yər·ə·bəl) *adj.* **—a·mel/io·rant** (-rənt) *n.* **—a·mel·io·ra·tive** (ə·mēl/yə·rā/tiv, -rə·tiv) *adj.* **—a·mel/io·ra/tor** *n.*

a·mel·io·ra·tion (ə·mēl/yə·rā/shən) *n.* The act of ameliorating, or the state of being ameliorated; improvement.

a·men (ā/men/, ä/-) *interj.* So it is; so be it: used at the end of a prayer or statement to express agreement. — *n.* **1.** The word *amen* or any use of it. **2.** Any expression of hearty assent or conviction. — *adv.* Verily; truly. [< L < Gk. < Hebrew *āmēn* verily]

A·men (ä/mən) In Egyptian mythology, the god of life and procreation, represented as having a ram's head, later identified with the sun god as the supreme deity, and called **Amen-Ra** (-rä/). Also spelled *Ammon, Amon.*

a·me·na·ble (ə·mē/nə·bəl, ə·men/ə-) *adj.* **1.** Capable of being persuaded; submissive; tractable. **2.** Liable to be called to account; responsible to authority. **3.** Capable of being tested or judged by rule or law. — **Syn.** See DOCILE. [< AF < *amener* to bring to < *a-* to (< L *ad-*) + *mener* to lead < L *minare* to drive (with threats) < *minari* to threaten] **—a·me/na·bil/i·ty, —a·me/na·ble·ness** *n.* **—a·me/na·bly** *adv.*

amen corner *U.S.* In some churches, the corner laterally facing the pulpit, where those who lead the responsive amens usually sit.

a·mend (ə·mend/) *v.t.* **1.** To change for the better; improve. **2.** To free from faults; correct; reform. **3.** To change or alter by authority: to *amend* a bill. —*v.i.* **4.** To become better in conduct. [< OF *amender* < L *emendare* to free from faults < *ex-* from + *mendum* fault] **—a·mend/a·ble** *adj.* **—a·mend/a·ble·ness** *n.* **—a·mend/er** *n.*

— Syn. 1. *Amend, emend, correct, rectify,* and *revise* mean to change so as to make better. We *amend* by altering or adding; we *emend* by removing that which is faulty. To *correct* or *rectify* is to make conform to some standard of truth, accuracy, or excellence. To *revise* is to examine and change in any way, though a change for the better is implied. **—Ant.** debase, impair, mar.

a·mend·a·to·ry (ə·men/də·tôr/ē, -tō/rē) *adj.* Tending to amend; corrective.

a·mend·ment (ə·mend/mənt) *n.* **1.** Change for the better. **2.** A removal of faults; correction. **3.** The changing, as of a law, bill, or motion. **4.** The statement of such a change, as in a clause or paragraph.

a·mends (ə·mendz/) *n.pl.* Reparation, as in satisfaction or compensation for loss, damage, or injury. [< OF *amendes,* pl. of *amende* a fine < *amender.* See AMEND.]

A·men·ho·tep III (ä/mən·hō/tep), died 1375 B.C., king of Egypt 1411–1375 B.C.; conqueror; builder of monuments.

Amenhotep IV See IKHNATON.

a·men·i·ty (ə·men/ə·tē) *n. pl* **·ties 1.** Agreeableness; pleasantness. **2.** *pl.* Acts or expressions of courtesy; civilities. [< L *amoenitas, -tatis* < *amoenus* pleasant]

a·men·or·rhe·a (ā·men/ə·rē/ə) *n. Pathol.* An abnormal suppression or nonoccurrence of menstruation. [< NL < Gk. *a-* not + *mēn* month + *rheein* to flow]

A·men-Ra (ä/mən·rä/) See AMEN.

a men·sa et tho·ro (ā men/sə et thō/rō) *Law* From table and bed: used to designate a judicial marriage separation. Also **a men/sa et to/ro** (tō/rō). [< L]

am·ent[1] (am/ənt, ā/mənt) *n. Bot.* A catkin. [< L *amentum* a thong]

a·ment[3] (ā/mənt, ā/ment) *n. Psychiatry* A mentally deficient person; an idiot. [< L *amens, amentis* mad < *a-, ab-* away + *mens* mind]

am·en·ta·ceous (am/ən·tā/shəs) *adj. Bot.* Like, pertaining to, or bearing catkins.

a·men·tia (ā·men/shə, -shē·ə) *n. Psychiatry* **1.** Lack of intellectual development; idiocy. **2.** Temporary mental confusion. [< L < *a-, ab-* away + *mens* mind]

am·en·tif·er·ous (am/ən·tif/ər·əs) *adj. Bot.* Bearing aments.

Amer. America; American.

a·merce (ə·mûrs/) *v.t.* **a·merced, a·merc·ing 1.** To punish by an assessment or arbitrary fine. **2.** To punish, as by deprivation. [< AF *amercier* to fine < *a merci* at the mercy of] **—a·merce/a·ble** *adj.* **—a·merce/ment** *n.* **—a·merc/er** *n.*

A·mer·i·ca (ə·mer/ə·kə) **1.** The United States of America. **2.** The lands in the Western Hemisphere; especially, either of the two continents, North America or South America. Also **the Americas.** Abbr. *A., Am., Amer.*

A·mer·i·can (ə·mer/ə·kən) *adj.* **1.** Pertaining to the United States of America, its history, government, people, etc. **2.** Pertaining to the continent or people of North or South America, or of the Western Hemisphere. — *n.* **1.** A citizen of the United States. **2.** American English. **3.** An inhabitant of America. Abbr. *A., Am., Amer.*

A·mer·i·ca·na (ə·mer/ə·kä/nə, -kan/ə, -kā/nə) *n.pl.* Things American, collectively; any collection of American literary papers, sayings, or other data, especially relating to American history and traditions.

American aloe The century plant.

American Beauty A rose flowering in the summer and autumn, noted for its large, pink to deep red blossoms.

American cheese Any of several white to yellow, fairly hard cheeses popular in the United States; especially, a mild kind of Cheddar.

American crawl See under CRAWL (*n.* def. 2).

American eagle The bald eagle. See under EAGLE.

American English The English language as spoken in the United States, with especial reference to pronunciation and vocabulary: also called *American.*

American Expeditionary Forces United States troops sent to Europe in World War I. Abbr. *AEF, A.E.F.*

American Federation of Labor A federation of trade unions, founded in 1886, in 1955 merged with the Congress of Industrial Organizations. Abbr. *AFL, A.F.L., A.F. of L.*

American Indian An Indian (def. 3). Abbr. *Am. Ind.*

A·mer·i·can·ism (ə·mer/ə·kən·iz/əm) *n.* **1.** A trait, custom, or tradition especially characteristic of the people of the United States or of some of them. **2.** A word, phrase, or usage especially characteristic of American English. **3.** Devotion to the United States, its institutions, etc.

A·mer·i·can·ist (ə·mer/ə·kən·ist) *n.* One who makes a special study of subjects pertaining to America, as its history, geography, or resources.

American ivy The Virginia creeper.

A·mer·i·can·ize (ə·mer/ə·kən·iz/) *v.t. & v.i.* **·ized, ·iz·ing** To make or become American in spirit or methods; assimilate to the institutions, speech, etc., of the United States. **—A·mer/i·can·i·za/tion** *n.*

American League See under MAJOR LEAGUE.

American Legion An organization, founded in 1919, of veterans of United States armed forces of World War I, World War II, and the Korean War.

American Library Association An organization of librarians and libraries, founded in 1876. Abbr. *ALA, A.L.A.*

American plan At a hotel, the system of paying for room, meals, and other services at a fixed, inclusive rate. Compare EUROPEAN PLAN.

American Revolution See under REVOLUTION.

American Samoa See SAMOA.

American Standard Version or **American Revised Version** See under KING JAMES BIBLE.

American Veterans Committee An organization of veterans of United States armed forces of World War I, World War II, and the Korean War. Abbr. *AVC, A.V.C.*

American Veterans of World War II and Korea An organization of veterans of United States armed forces of World War II and the Korean War: also called *Amvets.* Abbr. *AMVETS.*

Americas, the See AMERICA (def. 1).

America's Cup A trophy first won in England in 1851 by the schooner-yacht *America* in a race with British yachts, now the chief trophy of international yacht racing.

am·er·ic·i·um (am'ə·rish'ē·əm) *n.* An unstable radioactive element (symbol Am), resulting from the bombardment of uranium and plutonium by high-energy helium ions. See ELEMENT. [< NL, after *America*]

Amerigo Vespucci See VESPUCCI.

Am·er·in·di·an (am'ə·rin'dē·ən) *adj.* Of or pertaining to the American Indians or the Eskimos. Also **Am'er·in'dic.** — *n.* An American Indian or Eskimo. Also **Am·er·ind** (am'-ə·rind). [< AMER(ICAN) + INDIAN]

Ames (āmz) A city in central Iowa; pop. 39,505.

ames·ace (āmz'ās') See AMBSACE.

am·e·thyst (am'ə·thist) *n.* **1.** Quartz with clear purple or violet color, a semiprecious stone. **2.** A purple variety of sapphire or corundum used as a gem: amethystine sapphire: also called *Oriental amethyst.* **3.** A purplish violet. [< OF *ametiste* < L *amethystus* < Gk. *amethystos* not drunken < *a-* not + *methystos* drunken < *methy* wine; from the ancient belief that a wearer of the stone would be unaffected by wine]

am·e·thys·tine (am'ə·this'tin, -tīn) *adj.* Of the color of amethyst; violet; purple.

am·e·tro·pi·a (am'ə·trō'pē·ə) *n. Pathol.* Any abnormal condition of the refracting parts of the eye, causing confused or imperfect vision, as astigmatism. [< NL < Gk. *ametros* irregular + *ōps* eye] — **am·e·trop·ic** (am'ə·trop'ik) *adj.*

Am·for·tas (äm·fôr'täs) In Wagner's *Parsifal*, chief knight of the Holy Grail.

AMG Allied (or American) Military Government.

Am·ha·ra (äm·hä'rä) A former province of Ethiopia; divided in 1942 into two.

Am·har·ic (am·har'ik, äm·hä'rik) *n.* A Southwest Semitic language spoken officially in Ethiopia. — *adj.* Of or pertaining to Amharic.

Am·herst (am'ərst), **Jeffrey, Baron,** 1717–97, English general.

a·mi (á·mē') *n.masc. pl.* **a·mis** (á·mē') *French* A friend. — **a·mie** (á·mē') *n.fem.*

am·i·a (am'ē·ə) *n.* The bowfin, a fish. [< NL < Gk. *amia,* a kind of tuna]

a·mi·a·ble (ā'mē·ə·bəl) *adj.* **1.** Pleasing in disposition; kindly. **2.** Free from irritation; friendly: an *amiable* rivalry. [< OF < L *amicabilis* friendly < *amicus* friend; infl. in OF by *amable* lovable < L *amare* to love. Doublet of AMICABLE.] — **a'mi·a·bil'i·ty, a'mi·a·ble·ness** *n.* — **a'mi·a·bly** *adv.*

— **Syn. 1.** good-natured, agreeable, obliging, complaisant. — **Ant.** unamiable, ill-natured, surly, churlish.

am·i·an·thus (am'ē·an'thəs) *n.* **1.** A fine and silky variety of asbestos: also called *earth flax.* **2.** A fabric made from this mineral. [< L *amiantus* < Gk. *amiantos* (*lithos*), lit., unsoiled (stone), a stone like asbestos]

am·i·ca·ble (am'i·kə·bəl) *adj.* Showing or promoting good will; friendly; peaceable: an *amicable* separation. [< L *amicabilis.* Doublet of AMIABLE.] — **am·i·ca·bil·i·ty** (am'i·kə·bil'ə·tē), **am'i·ca·ble·ness** *n.* — **am'i·ca·bly** *adv.*

— **Syn.** *Amicable, peaceable, neighborly,* and *friendly* refer to the manifestation of good will toward others. *Amicable* suggests formal politeness, but also stronger sentiment than *peaceable,* which refers merely to a disposition to avoid dispute. The *neighborly* person wants to live on good terms with his associates; *friendly* is the same, with an added note of greater warmth and personal regard. — **Ant.** unfriendly, hostile, antagonistic.

am·ice[1] (am'is) *n. Eccl.* A vestment consisting of a rectangular piece of fine white linen worn around the neck and shoulders under an alb. [< OF *amit* < L *amictus* cloak]

am·ice[2] (am'is) *n.* An almuce.

a·mi·cro·bic (ā'mī·krō'bik) *adj. Pathol.* Not caused by microbes: said of a disease. [< A-⁴ not + MICROBIC]

a·mi·cus cu·ri·ae (ə·mē'kəs kyōōr'ē·ī) *Law* One who advises or is asked to advise a court upon a pending cause to which he is not a party. [< L, friend of the court]

a·mid (ə·mid') *prep.* In the midst of; among. Also *amidst, midst.* [ME *amidden* < OE *on middan* in the middle]

— **Syn.** *Amid, amidst, among, amongst,* and *between* refer to a position that is surrounded. *Amid* or *amidst* denotes surrounded by; *among* or *amongst,* mingled with. *Between* is said of two persons or objects, or of two groups of persons or objects. *Amid* denotes

mere position; *among,* some active relation. as of companionship, hostility, etc. We say *among* (never *amid*) friends, or *among* (sometimes *amid*) enemies. — **Ant.** beyond, outside, without.

am·ide (am'id, -id) *n. Chem.* **1.** Any compound of the type formula RCONH₂. **2.** A derivative of ammonia in which a metal replaces a hydrogen atom. Also **am·id** (am'id). [< AM(MONIA) + -IDE] — **a·mid·ic** (ə·mid'ik) *adj.*

am·i·din (am'ə·din) *n.* A transparent gelatinous solution of starch in hot water. [< F *amidon* starch]

amido- *combining form Chem* **1.** Pertaining to or containing both the NH₂ radical and an acid radical. **2.** Less frequently, amino-. [< AMIDE]

a·mi·do·gen (ə·mē'də·jən, ə·mid'ə-) *n. Chem.* The univalent radical NH₂, known from its existence in various organic compounds. [< AMIDO- + -GEN]

am·i·dol (am'ə·dol, -dōl) *n.* A white crystalline powder, C₆H₈N₂O·2HCl, used in photography as a developer for bromide plates. [< AMIDO- + (PHEN)OL]

a·mid·ships (ə·mid'ships') *adv. Naut.* Halfway between bow and stern; toward the middle of a ship: also *midships.*

a·midst (ə·midst') *prep.* Amid. [ME *amidde* + -s³ + inorganic *t*]

A·miel (á·myel'), **Henri Frédéric,** 1821–81, Swiss poet and philosopher.

Am·i·ens (am'ē·ənz, *Fr.* à·myaN') A city of northern France, on the Somme; pop. 117,888 (1968). — **Treaty of Amiens** An agreement between England, Holland, France, and Spain (1802), marking a period of peace in the Napoleonic Wars.

a·mi·go (ə·mē'gō) *n. pl.* **·gos** A friend; comrade. [< Sp.]

Am. Ind. American Indian.

a·mine (ə·mēn', am'in) *n. Chem.* One of a class of organic compounds derived from ammonia by replacement of one or more of its hydrogen atoms by an alkyl radical. Also **am·in** (am'in). [< AM(MONIA) + -INE²]

-amine *combining form Chem.* An amine: *methylamine.*

a·mi·no (ə·mē'nō, am'ə·nō) *adj. Chem.* Of or pertaining to the NH₂ group combined with a nonacid radical. [< AMINE]

amino- *combining form Chem.* Pertaining to or containing the NH₂ group combined with a nonacid radical.

amino acid *Biochem.* Any of a group of organic compounds containing the amino group combined with the carboxyl radical and forming an essential part of the protein molecule.

a·mir (ə·mir') *n.* **1.** A sovereign of Afghanistan. **2.** A Moslem prince or governor. Also spelled *ameer.* [< Arabic *amīr* ruler, commander]

Am·ish (am'ish, ä'mish) *adj.* Relating to or designating the adherents of Jacob Ammann, a 17th-century Mennonite. — *n.pl.* A sect of Mennonites, founded by Jacob Ammann.

a·miss (ə·mis') *adj.* Out of order or relation; wrong; improper: used predicatively: Something is *amiss.* — *adv.* In a wrong or defective way; improperly; erroneously: to judge a person *amiss.* — **to take amiss** To take offense at; feel resentment toward. [ME *amis* < *a-* at + *mis* failure]

a·mi·to·sis (am'ə·tō'sis) *n. Biol.* Cell division without the formation and splitting of chromosomes; direct division. [< NL < A-⁴ without + MITOSIS] — **am·i·tot·ic** (am'ə·tot'ik) *adj.* — **am'i·tot'i·cal·ly** *adv.*

am·i·ty (am'ə·tē) *n. pl.* **·ties** Peaceful relations, as between nations; mutual good will; friendship. — **Syn.** See FRIENDSHIP. [< MF *amitié,* ult. < L *amicus* friend]

Am·man (äm'män) The capital of Jordan, in the north central part; pop. 333,400 (est. 1967): Old Testament *Rabbath Ammon.*

Am·mann (äm'män), **Jacob,** 17th-century Swiss Mennonite bishop; founder of the Amish sect.

am·me·ter (am'mē'tər) *n. Electr.* An instrument for measuring amperage. Abbr. *am.* [<AM(PERE) + -METER]

Am·mi·a·nus Mar·cel·li·nus (am'ē·ā'nəs mär'sə·lī'nəs) Fourth-century Roman historian.

am·mine (am'ēn) *n. Chem.* **1.** The ammonia molecule NH₃ in combination. **2.** Any of various complex compounds containing the ammonia molecule. [< AMM(ONIA) + -INE²]

am·mo (am'ō) *n. Mil. Slang* Ammunition.

am·mo·cete (am'ə·sēt) *n. Zool.* The larva of various lampreys, used as bait. [< Gk. *ammos* sand + *koitē* bed]

Am·mon (am'ən) *n.pl.* In the Bible, a people descended from Ben Ammi, the son of Lot: chiefly in the phrase **children of Ammon.** *Deut.* ii 19. Also **Am·mon·ites** (am'ən·īts).

Am·mon (am'ən) The Greek and the Roman name for the Egyptian god Amen: also *Zeus-Ammon, Jupiter-Ammon.*

am·mo·nal (am'ə·nəl) *n.* An explosive mixture containing TNT, ammonium nitrate, and aluminum powder, used as a bursting charge in shells. [< AMMON(IUM) + AL(UMINUM)]

am·mo·nia (ə·mōn'yə, ə·mō'nē·ə) *n.* **1.** A colorless, pungent, suffocating gas, NH₃, obtained chiefly by the catalytic synthesis of nitrogen and hydrogen. **2.** Spirits of hartshorn. [< NL < SAL AMMONIAC]

am·mo·ni·ac[1] (ə·mō'nē·ak) *adj.* Of, pertaining to, or like ammonia. Also **am·mo·ni·a·cal** (am'ə·nī'ə·kəl).

am·mo·ni·ac[2] (ə·mō'nē·ak) *n.* The resinous gum of a tree (*Dorema ammoniacum*) found in Persia and Western India: also called *gum ammoniac.* [< F < L *ammoniacum* < Gk. *ammoniakon,* a resinous gum said to come from a plant growing near the temple of *Ammon* in Libya]

am·mo·ni·ate (v. ə·mō′nē·āt; n. ə·mō′nē·it) v.t. ·at·ed, ·at·ing To treat or combine with ammonia. — n. A compound containing ammonia.

am·mon·i·fi·ca·tion (ə·mon′ə·fə·kā′shən) n. 1. The act or process of saturating with ammonia or an ammonium salt. 2. The state of being so saturated. 3. The formation of ammonia, as in the soil, by the action of microorganisms upon nitrogenous organic substances. Also **am·mon·i·za·tion** (ə·mon′ə·zā′shən).

am·mon·ite[1] (am′ən·īt) n. Paleontol. A curved or spiral fossil cephalopod shell, commonly found in Mesozoic rocks. [< NL ammonites < L (cornu) Ammonis (horn) of Ammon; so called from its shape]

am·mon·ite[2] (am′ən·īt) n. 1. A fertilizer composed of animal wastes. 2. An explosive containing ammonium nitrate as the principal component. [< AMMON(IA) + -ITE[1]]

am·mo·ni·um (ə·mō′nē·əm) n. Chem. The univalent radical NH4, that in compounds formed from ammonia acts as an alkali metal. [< NL < AMMONIA]

ammonium carbonate Chem. A colorless, crystalline compound, $(NH_4)_2CO_3$, used as a reagent.

ammonium chloride Chem. A white, crystalline, soluble compound, NH_4Cl, used in medicine and industry: also called sal ammoniac.

ammonium hydroxide Chem. A compound, NH_4OH, formed in ordinary aqueous or caustic ammonia.

ammonium nitrate Chem. A colorless, crystalline, soluble salt, NH_4NO_3, used as an ingredient of explosives and in freezing mixtures.

am·mu·ni·tion (am′yə·nish′ən) n. 1. Any one of various articles used in the discharge of firearms and ordnance, as cartridges, shells, rockets, etc. 2. Any resources for attack or defense. [< F amunition, for munition (la munition taken as l'amunition) < munitio < munire to fortify]

am·ne·sia (am·nē′zhə, -zhē·ə) n. Psychiatry Partial or total loss or impairment of memory, involving restricted or extensive areas of experience. [< NL < Gk. amnēsia forgetfulness < a- not + mnasthai to remember] — **am·ne·sic** (am·nē′sik, -zik), **am·nes·tic** (am·nes′tik) adj.

am·nes·ty (am′nəs·tē) n. pl. ·ties 1. A general pardon by which a government absolves offenders. 2. Intentional overlooking, especially of wrongdoing; forgetfulness. — v.t. ·tied, ·ty·ing To pardon; grant amnesty to. [< F amnestie < L amnestia < Gk. amnēstia < a- not + mnasthai to remember]

am·ni·on (am′nē·ən) n. pl. ·ni·ons or ·ni·a (-nē·ə) Biol. A membranous sac enclosing the embryo and fetus in mammals, birds, and reptiles. [< Gk. amnion the fetal envelope, dim. of amnos lamb] — **am·ni·ot·ic** (am′nē·ot′ik), **am·ni·on·ic** (am′nē·on′ik) adj.

a·moe·ba (ə·mē′bə), **a·moe·bic** (ə·mē′bik), **a·moe·boid** (ə·mē′boid), etc. See AMEBA, etc.

am·oe·bae·an, am·oe·be·an (am′ə·bē′ən) See AMEBEAN.

a·mok (ə·muk′, ə·mok′) See AMUCK.

a·mo·le (ə·mō′lā) n. 1. The roots or parts of certain plants, employed in Mexico and the SW United States as a substitute for soap. 2. Any plant that produces such roots, as the century plant and the soap plant. [< Am. Sp. < Nahuatl]

A·mon (ä′mən) See AMEN.

a·mong (ə·mung′) prep. 1. In the midst of: a house among the trees. 2. In the class or number of: He was among the dead. 3. Within or by the group of: a practice among the French. 4. By the joint or concerted action of: Among us, we can build the wall. 5. In portions for each of: to distribute money among the poor. 6. Reciprocally between: disputes among friends. Also **a·mongst′**. ◆ See note under BETWEEN. — Syn. See AMID. [OE on gemonge in the crowd]

a·mon·til·la·do (ə·mon′tə·lä′dō, Sp. ä·mōn′tē·lyä′ᵗħō) n. A pale dry sherry. [< Sp., from Montilla, a town in southern Spain]

a·mor·al (ā·môr′əl, ā·mor′əl) adj. 1. Not subject to or concerned with moral or ethical judgment or distinctions. 2. Lacking a sense of right and wrong; lacking moral responsibility. — Syn. See IMMORAL. [< A-[4] not + MORAL] — **a·mor·al·i·ty** (ā′mə·ral′ə·tē) n. — **a·mor′al·ly** adv.

am·o·ret·to (am′ə·ret′ō) n. pl. ·ret·ti (-ret′ē) A cupid. [< Ital., dim. of amore love < L amor]

a·mo·ri·no (ä′mō·rē′nō) n. pl. ·ni (-nē) An amoretto. [< Ital.]

am·o·rist (am′ə·rist) n. A lover; one given to amours.

Am·o·rites (am′ə·rīts) n.pl. In the Bible, a powerful people in Canaan before the Israelite conquest. Num. xxi 21.

a·mo·ro·so (ä′mō·rō′sō) Music adj. Tender; loving. — adv. Tenderly; lovingly. [< Ital., amorous]

am·o·rous (am′ər·əs) adj. 1. Tending to fall in love; affectionate; loving: an amorous nature. 2. Of or related to love: an amorous song. 3. Showing or arising from love or sexual desire; ardent: an amorous glance. 4. In love; enamored: often with of: amorous of the truth. [< OF < LL amorosus < L amor love] — **am′o·rous·ly** adv. — **am′o·rous·ness** n. — Syn. 1, 2. Amorous, amative, and amatory refer to sexual love but differ in application. Amorous is applied to persons and

emotions; amative is used to describe dispositions or temperaments; and amatory refers to literature and other things that deal with love. — Ant. frigid.

a·mor pa·tri·ae (ā′môr pā′tri·ē) Latin Love of country.

a·mor·phism (ə·môr′fiz·əm) n. 1. The state or quality of being amorphous. 2. Mineral. Absence of crystals.

a·mor·phous (ə·môr′fəs) adj. 1. Without definite form or shape: amorphous slag. 2. Of no fixed character; anomalous; unorganized. 3. Geol. Found or occurring in masses lacking definite stratification or crystalline structure. 4. Chem. Uncrystallized. [< Gk. amorphos < a- without + morphē form] — **a·mor′phous·ly** adv. — **a·mor′phous·ness** n.

a·mort (ə·môrt′) adj. & adv. Archaic Without life; dejected. [See À LA MORT]

am·or·ti·za·tion (am′ər·tə·zā′shən, ə·môr′tə·zā′shən) n. 1. The act of a nortizing. 2. The money set aside or devoted to amortizing. Also **a·mor·tize·ment** (ə·môr′tiz·mənt).

am·or·tize (am′ər·tīz, ə·môr′tīz) v.t. ·tized, ·tiz·ing 1. To extinguish gradually, as a debt or liability, by installment payments or by a sinking fund. 2. Law To sell and convey (lands) in mortmain. Also Brit. **am′or·tise**. [< OF amortiss-, stem of amortir to extinguish, sell in mortmain, ult. < L ad- to + mors, mortis death] — **am·or·tiz·a·ble** (am′ər·tīz′ə·bəl, ə·môr′tiz·ə·bəl) adj.

A·mos (ā′məs) Eighth-century B.C. Hebrew minor prophet. — n. A book of the Old Testament containing his prophecies.

a·mo·tion (ə·mō′shən) n. Law 1. The removal from office of an official of a corporation before expiration of his term, but without expulsion from the corporation. 2. Illegal deprivation of property. [< L amotio, -onis < amotus, pp. of amovere to remove < ab- from + movere to move]

a·mount (ə·mount′) n. 1. A sum total of two or more quantities; aggregate. 2. The value of the principal with the interest upon it, as in a loan. 3. The entire significance, value, or effect. 4. Quantity: a considerable amount of discussion. Abbr. amt. — v.i. 1. To reach in number or quantity: with to: This bill amounts to ten dollars. 2. To be equivalent in effect or importance: with to: His actions amount to treason. [< OF amonter < amont upward < a mont to the mountain < L ad to + mons, montis mountain]

a·mour (ə·mŏŏr′) n. A love affair, especially an illicit one; intrigue. [< F]

a·mour-pro·pre (à·mŏŏr′prôpr′) n. French Self-respect.

A·moy (ə·moi′) 1. An island in Formosa Strait, Fukien Province, SE China. 2. A port city and industrial center on Amoy island; pop. 400,000 (est. 1958). Formerly Szeming.

amp. Electr. Amperage; ampere(s).

am·pe·lop·sis (am′pə·lop′sis) n. Any of a genus (Ampelopsis) of vitaceous climbing shrubs having small greenish flowers and alternate simple or compound leaves. [< NL < Gk. ampelos vine + opsis appearance]

am·per·age (am′pir·ij, am′pər·ij) n. Electr. The strength of a current in amperes. Abbr. amp.

am·pere (am′pir, am·pir′) n. Electr. The practical unit of current strength; such a current as would be given with an electromotive force of one volt through a wire having a resistance of one ohm. Abbr. a., amp. — **international ampere** The current which on passing through a silver-nitrate solution will deposit silver at the rate of 0.001118 gram a second. [after A. M. Ampère]

Am·père (än·pâr′), André Marie, 1775–1836, French physicist.

am·pere-hour (am′pir·our′) n. Electr. A quantity of electricity sufficient to furnish a current of one ampere for one hour: equivalent to 3,600 coulombs. Abbr. a.h., amp.-hr.

am·pere-turn (am′pir·tûrn′) n. Electr. One ampere flowing through one turn of a coil, considered with reference to electromagnetic effect.

am·per·sand (am′pər·sand, am′pər·sand′) n. The character & or & or ℰ meaning and. [< and per se and, lit., & by itself = and]

am·phet·a·mine (am·fet′ə·mēn, -min) n. An acrid and colorless liquid compound, $C_9H_{13}N$, used as a spray or inhalant for the relief of colds, asthma, etc., or internally as a stimulant for the central nervous system. [< a(lpha)-m(ethyl)-ph(enyl)-et(hyl)-amine]

amphi- prefix 1. On both or all sides; at both ends: amphicoelous. 2. Around: amphitheater. 3. Of both kinds; in two ways: amphibious. [< Gk. < amphi around]

Am·phi·a·ra·us (am′fē·ə·rā′əs) An ancient Greek hero. See SEVEN AGAINST THEBES.

am·phi·ar·thro·sis (am′fē·är·thrō′sis) n. pl. ·ses (-sēz) Anat. A joint in which bony surfaces are united by intervening fibrous or cartilaginous substance so as to permit of slight movement, as in the vertebrae.

am·phi·as·ter (am′fē·as′tər) n. 1. Biol. a That stage of cell division in which the chromatin filaments assume a radiate appearance at each end of the nuclear spindle. b The figure so formed. 2. Zool. A spicule with two whorls of spines connected by a vertical axis, as in certain sponges. [< NL < AMPHI- + Gk. astēr star]

am·phib·i·an (am·fib′ē·ən) *adj.* **1.** *Zool.* Of or pertaining to a class (*Amphibia,* formerly *Batrachia*) of cold-blooded, chiefly egg-laying vertebrates adapted for life both on land and in water. The young have gills and develop through a larval or tadpole stage into the typically lung-breathing forms represented by frogs, newts, salamanders, etc. **2.** Amphibious. — *n.* **1.** An amphibian organism. **2.** An amphibious plant. **3.** An airplane constructed to rise from and alight on either land or water: also **am·phib·i·on** (am·fib′ē·ən). **4.** A vehicle capable of self-propulsion upon land and upon water.

am·phib·i·ot·ic (am·fib′ē·ot′ik, am′fə·bī·ot′ik) *adj. Zool.* Living in water in the larval stage, on land as adults: said of certain insects, as dragonflies and May flies.

am·phib·i·ous (am·fib′ē·əs) *adj.* **1.** Living or adapted to life on land or in water. **2.** Capable of operating or landing on land or water. **3.** Of a mixed nature; connected with two ranks, classes, etc. [< Gk. *amphibios* having a double life < *amphi-* of two kinds + *bios* life] — **am·phib′i·ous·ly** *adv.* — **am·phib′i·ous·ness** *n.*

am·phi·bole (am′fə·bōl) *n. Mineral.* Any of a class of variously colored hydrous silicates, consisting chiefly of calcium, magnesium, iron, aluminum, and sodium, as actinolite, asbestos, and hornblende. [< F < L *amphibolus* ambiguous < Gk. *amphibolos* < *amphiballein* to throw around, cast about, doubt < *amphi-* around + *ballein* to throw]

am·phi·bol·ic (am′fə·bol′ik) *adj.* Ambiguous; equivocal. Also **am·phib·o·lous** (am·fib′ə·ləs).

am·phib·o·lite (am·fib′ə·līt) *n.* A rock consisting chiefly of amphibole and plagioclase, often with inclusions of garnet and quartz.

am·phi·bol·o·gy (am′fə·bol′ə·jē) *n. pl.* **·gies 1.** Doubtful meaning; ambiguity arising from uncertain grammatical construction. **2.** An ambiguous phrase or sentence. Also **am·phib′o·ly.** [< OF *amphibologie* < LL *amphibologia,* for L *amphibolia* < Gk. *amphibolia* ambiguity < *amphiballein.* See AMPHIBOLE.] — **am·phib·o·log·i·cal** (am·fib′ə·loj′i·kəl) *adj.*

am·phi·brach (am′fə·brak) *n.* In prosody, a metrical foot consisting of a long or accented syllable between two short or unaccented ones (◡–◡), as in the word *uneven.* [< L *amphibrachys* < Gk. < *amphi-* at both ends + *brachys* short]

am·phi·chro·ic (am′fə·krō′ik) *adj. Chem.* Exhibiting either of two colors, as certain substances when subjected to tests with acids or alkalis. Also **am·phi·chro·mat·ic** (am′fə·krō·mat′ik). [< AMPHI- + Gk. *chroa* color]

am·phi·coe·lous (am′fə·sē′ləs) *adj. Zool.* Concave at both ends; biconcave, as the vertebrae of fishes and of certain extinct reptiles and birds. [< AMPHI- + Gk. *koilos* hollow]

am·phic·ty·on (am·fik′tē·on) *n.* A delegate to one of the ancient Greek amphictyonic councils. [< L *amphictyones* < Gk. *amphiktyones* neighbors]

am·phic·ty·on·ic (am·fik′tē·on′ik) *adj.* Of or pertaining to an amphictyony or an amphictyon.

am·phic·ty·o·ny (am·fik′tē·ə·nē) *n. pl.* **·nies** A league of ancient Greek states allied in the worship of a common deity, as around a religious center or shrine like Delphi.

am·phi·dip·loid (am′fə·dip′loid) *n. Genetics* A plant variety, originating in a hybrid of two species or genera, in which the chromosome number is twice the sum of the diploid numbers of the parent forms.

am·phi·go·ry (am′fə·gôr′ē, -gō′rē) *n. pl.* **·ries** A meaningless rigmarole with a semblance of sense; a burlesque, as one written in nonsensical verse. Also **am·phi·gou·ri** (am′fə·gŏŏ′rē) *pl.* **·ris** (-rēz). [< F *amphigouri;* ult. origin unknown] — **am·phi·gor·ic** (am′fə·gôr′ik, -gor′-) *adj.*

am·phim·a·cer (am·fim′ə·sər) *n.* In prosody, a foot consisting of one short or unaccented syllable between two long or accented ones (–◡–), as in the word *evensong:* opposed to *amphibrach.* Also called *cretic.* [< L *amphimacrus* < Gk. *amphimakros < amphi-* on both sides + *makros* long]

am·phi·mix·is (am′fə·mik′sis) *n. Biol.* The mingling of the germ plasm or hereditary substance of two individuals in sexual reproduction. [< NL < AMPHI- + Gk. *mixis* a mingling]

Am·phi·on (am·fī′ən) In Greek mythology, a son of Zeus and Antiope and husband of Niobe, who with his twin brother Zethus walled Thebes by the music of a magical lyre given him by Hermes.

am·phi·ox·us (am′fē·ok′səs) *n. Zool.* The most primitive of the chordates, a lancelet. [< AMPHI- + Gk. *oxys* sharp]

am·phi·pod (am′fə·pod) *Zool. n.* Any of an order (*Amphipoda*) of crustaceans having usually seven pairs of legs, including the beach fleas, etc. — *adj.* Of or pertaining to the *Amphipoda:* also **am·phip·o·dan** (am·fip′ə·dən), **am·phip′o·dous** (-dəs). [< AMPHI- + Gk. *pous, podos* foot]

am·phi·pro·style (am·fip′rə·stīl, am′fə·prō′stīl) *Archit. n.* A building having a columned portico at each end but no columns at the sides. — *adj.* Built like such a building: also **am·phi·pro·sty·lar** (am·fip′rə·stī′lər, am′fə·prō·stī′lər). [< L *amphiprostylus* < Gk. *amphiprostylos* < *amphi-* on both sides + *prostylos.* See PROSTYLE.]

am·phis·bae·na (am′fis·bē′nə) *n.* **1.** A mythical serpent having a head at each end. **2.** *Zool.* A tropical, legless lizard

(family *Amphisbaenidae*) having head and tail much alike. [< L < Gk. *amphisbaina < amphis-, amphi-* at both ends + *bainein* to go] — **am′phis·bae′nic** *adj.*

am·phis·cians (am·fish′ənz) *n.pl.* The inhabitants of the Torrid Zone, whose shadows fall at one season to the north, at the other to the south. Also **am·phis·ci·i** (am·fish′ē·ī). [< Med.L *amphiscii* < Gk. *amphiskios* throwing a shadow both ways < *amphi-* on both sides + *skia* shadow]

am·phi·sty·lar (am′fə·stī′lər) *adj. Archit.* With columns at each end or on each side. [< AMPHI- + Gk. *stylos* pillar]

am·phi·the·a·ter (am′fə·thē′ə·tər) *n.* **1.** An oval structure having tiers of seats built around an open space or arena. **2.** A level area surrounded by slopes. **3.** The upper gallery in a theater. **4.** A place of contest; arena. Also *Brit.* **am′phi·the·a·tre.** [< L *amphitheatrum* < Gk. *amphitheatron* < *amphi-* around + *theatron* theater] — **am·phi·the·at·ric** (am′fə·thē·at′rik) or **·ri·cal** *adj.* — **am′phi·the·at′ri·cal·ly** *adv.*

am·phi·the·ci·um (am′fə·thē′shē·əm, -sē·əm) *n. pl.* **·ci·a** (-shē·ə, -sē·ə) *Bot.* The outer layer of cells surrounding the endothecium in the spore case of mosses. [< NL < AMPHI- + Gk. *thēkion,* dim. of *thēkē* case, container]

am·phit·ri·cha (am·fit′ri·kə) *n.pl.* Bacteria having flagella at both ends. [< AMPHI- + Gk. *thrix, trichos* hair] — **am·phit′ri·chous** *adj.*

Am·phi·tri·te (am′fə·trī′tē) In Greek mythology, one of the Nereids, wife of Poseidon and goddess of the sea.

Am·phit·ry·on (am·fit′rē·ən) In Greek mythology, the husband of Alcmene.

am·pho·ra (am′fə·rə) *n. pl.* **·rae** (-rē) In ancient Greece and Rome, a tall, two-handled earthenware jar for wine or oil, narrow at the neck and the base. [< L < Gk. *amphoreus,* var. of *amphiphoreus* < *amphi-* on both sides + *phoreus* bearer < *pherein* to bear] — **am′pho·ral** *adj.*

am·pho·ter·ic (am′fə·ter′ik) *adj. Chem.* Exhibiting the characteristics of both an acid and a base. [< Gk. *amphoteros* both]

amp.-hr. *Electr.* Ampere-hour.

am·ple (am′pəl) *adj.* **1.** Of great dimension, capacity, amount, degree, etc,; large: an *ample* house. **2.** More than enough; abundant; liberal. **3.** Fully sufficient to meet all needs or requirements; adequate: an *ample* income. [< F < L *amplus* large, abundant] — **am′ple·ness** *n.*
— **Syn. 2.** liberal. See PLENTIFUL. **3.** sufficient, enough. — **Ant.** insufficient, inadequate, deficient, scant.

am·plec·tant (am·plek′tənt) *adj. Bot.* Twining about; clasping; embracing. [< L *amplecti* to embrace < *ambi-* around + *plectere* to twine]

am·plex·i·caul (am·plek′si·kôl) *adj. Bot.* Clasping a stem, as the base of some leaves. See illustration of LEAF. [< NL *amplexicaulis* < L *amplexus* embracing + *caulis* stem]

am·pli·a·tion (am′plē·ā′shən) *n.* Amplification; enlargement; extension. [< L *ampliatio, -onis* < *ampliare* to widen] — **am·pli·a·tive** (am′plē·ā′tiv) *adj.*

am·pli·fi·ca·tion (am′plə·fi·kā′shən) *n.* **1.** The act of extending or enlarging; augmentation; addition. **2.** An extended statement, phrase, report, etc. **3.** The matter added to amplify a subject; details. **4.** *Electronics* An increase in the voltage or power of an electromagnetic signal, as in radio.

am·pli·fi·er (am′plə·fī′ər) *n.* **1.** One who or that which amplifies or increases. **2.** A megaphonelike device for increasing the volume of sound. **3.** *Electronics* Any of a class of devices for reinforcing a signal by means of power supplied to the output from a source other than the input.

am·pli·fy (am′plə·fī) *v.* **·fied, ·fy·ing** *v.t.* **1.** To enlarge or increase in scope, significance, or power. **2.** To add to so as to make more complete, as by illustrations. **3.** To exaggerate; magnify. **4.** *Electronics* To increase the strength or amplitude of, as electromagnetic impulses. — *v.i.* **5.** To make additional remarks; expatiate. [< F *amplifier* < L *amplificare* < *amplus* large + *facere* to make] — **am·pli·fi·ca·tive** (am′plə·fi·kā′tiv, am·plif′i·kə·tiv), **am·plif·i·ca·to·ry** (am·plif′i·kə·tôr′ē, -tō′rē) *adj.*
— **Syn. 1.** expand, enlarge, extend, augment, dilate, develop. — **Ant.** reduce, abridge, curtail, condense.

am·pli·tude (am′plə·tōōd, -tyōōd) *n.* **1.** Greatness of extent; largeness; breadth. **2.** Fullness; abundance. **3.** Scope or range, as of mind. **4.** *Astron.* The arc of the horizon between true east and west and the center of the sun, moon, or any star at its rising or setting. **5.** *Physics* **a** The extent of the swing of a vibrating body on each side of the mean position. **b** The peak value attained by a wave or an alternating current during one complete cycle. [< L *amplitudo, -inis* < *amplus* large]

amplitude modulation *Telecom.* That form of radio transmission in which the carrier wave is modulated by varying the amplitude above and below a standard value in accordance with the signals to be transmitted. Compare FREQUENCY MODULATION. Abbr. *AM, a-m, a.m., A.M.*

am·ply (am′plē) *adv.* In an ample manner; largely; liberally; sufficiently.

am·pule (am′pyōōl) *n. Med.* A sealed glass vial used as a

AMPHORAE

container for one dose of a hypodermic solution. Also **am·poule** (am′pōōl), **am·pul** (am′pul, am′pōōl). [< F *ampoule* < L *ampulla* ampulla (def. 1)]
am·pul·la (am·pul′ə) *n. pl.* **·pul·lae** (-pul′ē) **1.** An ancient Roman bottle or vase with slender neck and flattened mouth, used for oil, wine, or perfume. **2.** *Eccl.* **a** A cruet for wine or water at the Eucharist. **b** A small flask for chrism. **3.** *Anat.* A small sac or dilation, as in the semicircular canals of the ear. [< L, dim. of *amphora* jar] — **am·pul′lar** *adj.*
am·pul·la·ceous (am′pə·lā′shəs) *adj.* Of, pertaining to, or like an ampulla; bladder-shaped; inflated.
am·pu·tate (am′pyōō·tāt) *v.t. & v.i.* **·tat·ed**, **·tat·ing** To cut off (a limb, etc.) by surgical means. [< L *amputatus*, pp. of *amputare* < *ambi-* around + *putare* to trim, prune] — **am′·pu·ta′tion** *n.* — **am′pu·ta′tor** *n.*
am·pu·tee (am′pyōō·tē′) *n.* One who has had a limb or limbs removed by amputation.
am·ri·ta (um·rē′tə) *n.* In Hindu mythology: **1.** The ambrosia of immortality, sometimes represented as the fruit of a tree or the cream of the ocean churned by the gods. **2.** Immortality. Also **am·ree′ta.** [< Skt. *amṛta*]
Am·rit·sar (um·rit′sər) A city in western Punjab, India; pop. 424,961 (est. 1969).
Am·ster·dam (am′stər·dam) **1.** The constitutional capital of the Netherlands, a port in the western part; pop. 820,406 (est. 1971). **2.** A city in east central New York; pop. 25,524.
amt. Amount.
Am·trak (am′trak′) A U.S. government corporation that provides rail passenger service between cities.
am·u (am′yōō) *n. Physics* **1.** A unit of mass, equal to ¹⁄₁₆ of the mass of an oxygen atom, or 1.657×10^{-24} gram. **2.** A unit of energy equal to 931,000,000 electron volts. [< A(TOMIC) M(ASS) U(NIT)]
a·muck (ə·muk′) *adv.* In a murderous or frenzied manner: only in the phrase **to run amuck.** Also **amok.** [< Malay *amoq* engaging furiously in battle]
A·mu Dar·ya (ä·mōō′ där′yä) A principal river of Central Asia, flowing 872 miles to the Aral Sea from the Soviet Union–Afghanistan border: ancient *Oxus*: Arabic *Jaihun.*
am·u·let (am′yə·lit) *n.* Anything worn about the person as protection against accident, evil, etc.; a charm. — **Syn.** See TALISMAN. [< L *armuletum* charm; ult. origin unknown]
A·mund·sen (ä′mŏŏn·sən), **Roald,** 1872–1928, Norwegian explorer; discovered the South Pole 1911.
A·mur (ä·mōōr′) A river in eastern Asia, flowing 2,700 miles to the Sea of Okhotsk and forming the boundary between NE China and the Soviet Union.
a·muse (ə·myōōz′) *v.t.* **a·mused, a·mus·ing 1.** To occupy pleasingly; entertain; divert. **2.** To cause to laugh or smile, as with pleasure. **3.** *Archaic* To beguile; delude. — **Syn.** See ENTERTAIN. [< MF *amuser* < *à* at (< L *ad-*) + OF *muser* to stare] — **a·mus′a·ble** *adj.* — **a·mus′er** *n.*
a·muse·ment (ə·myōōz′mənt) *n.* **1.** The state of being amused; the feeling of delight or joy, as in some diversion. **2.** That which diverts or entertains, as a spectacle or game.
amusement park A commercially operated park having various devices for entertainment, as roller coasters, etc.
amusement tax A tax on certain forms of entertainment, such as the theater, paid in the admission price.
a·mus·ing (ə·myōō′zing) *adj.* **1.** Entertaining or diverting. **2.** Arousing laughter or mirth. — **a·mus′ing·ly** *adv.* — **a·mus′ing·ness** *n.*
a·mu·sive (ə·myōō′ziv, -siv) *adj.* Having power to amuse.
Am·vets (am′vets′) American Veterans of World War II and Korea.
a·myg·da·la (ə·mig′də·lə) *n. pl.* **·lae** (-lē) **1.** *Anat.* **a** Any almond-shaped structure or part. **b** A tonsil. **c** A small lobe projecting from the underside of the cerebellum. **d** A collection of gray matter at the lower portion of the temporal lobe of the brain. **2.** An almond. [< L < Gk. *amygdalē* almond]
a·myg·da·late (ə·mig′də·lit, -lāt) *adj.* Pertaining to or like almonds.
a·myg·da·lin (ə·mig′də·lin) *n.* A crystalline glycoside, $C_{20}H_{27}O_{11}N \cdot 3H_2O$, found in almonds, laurel leaves, peach kernels, etc. On being decomposed it yields glucose, hydrocyanic acid, and oil of bitter almonds.
a·myg·da·line (ə·mig′də·lin, -līn) *adj.* **1.** Pertaining to or like almonds. **2.** Pertaining to an amygdala.
a·myg·da·loid (ə·mig′də·loid) *adj.* **1.** Almond-shaped. **2.** *Geol.* Containing amygdules or resembling an amygdaloid. Also **a·myg′da·loi′dal.** — *n. Geol.* An igneous rock, usually basaltic, containing almond-shaped cavities filled with mineral secretions.
a·myg·dule (ə·mig′dyōōl) *n. Geol.* One of the mineral nodules in an amygdaloid.
am·yl (am′il) *n. Chem.* The univalent alcohol radical, C_5H_{11}, derived from pentane and entering into many organic compounds. [< Gk. *amylon* starch + -YL] — **a·myl′ic** (ə·mil′ik) *adj.*
am·y·la·ceous (am′ə·lā′shəs) *adj.* Pertaining to or like starch; starchy.

amyl alcohol *Chem.* An oily, colorless liquid, $C_5H_{11}OH$, present in fusel oil.
am·y·lase (am′ə·lās) *n. Biochem.* **1.** An enzyme, found in plant and animal tissue, that promotes the conversion of starch and glycogen into maltose. **2.** One of several digestive enzymes, as ptyalin and amylopsin. [< AMYL + -ASE]
am·y·lene (am′ə·lēn) *n. Chem.* Any of the isomeric hydrocarbons, C_5H_{10}, of the ethylene series. [< AMYL + -ENE]
amyl nitrite A yellowish, aromatic liquid, $C_5H_{11}NO_2$, having a fruity odor, used by inhalation to diminish arterial pressure in spasmodic diseases.
amylo- *combining form* **1.** Of starch: *amylolysis.* **2.** Of amyl. Also **amyl-.** [def. 1 < AMYLUM; def. 2 < AMYL]
am·y·loid (am′ə·loid) *n.* **1.** *Bot.* A gummy or starchlike substance formed in woody tissues in the process of lignification. **2.** *Pathol.* Waxy matter, not chemically related to starch, formed in certain diseased tissues of the body. — *adj.* Like or containing starch: also **am′y·loi′dal.**
am·y·lol·y·sis (am′ə·lol′ə·sis) *n.* The conversion of starch into sugar. — **am·y·lo·lyt·ic** (am′ə·lō·lit′ik) *adj.* [< AMYLO- (def. 1) + -LYSIS]
am·y·lo·pec·tin (am′ə·lō·pek′tin) *n. Biochem.* A water-insoluble component of starch that turns red in iodine.
am·y·lop·sin (am′ə·lop′sin) *n. Biochem.* An enzyme contained in pancreatin that changes starch into glucose. Also **am′y·lop′sase** (-sās). [< AMYLO- + (TRY)PSIN]
am·y·lose (am′ə·lōs) *n. Biochem.* A water-soluble component of starch that turns blue in iodine. [< AMYL(O)- (def. 1) + -OSE²]
am·y·lum (am′ə·ləm) *n.* Starch (def. 1) [< L < Gk. *amylon* starch]
Am·y·tal (am′ə·tal, -tôl) *n.* Proprietary name for a white or colorless, crystalline, slightly bitter compound, $C_{11}H_{18}N_2O_3$, used in medicine as a sedative.
an¹ (an, *unstressed* ən) *indefinite article or adj.* Equivalent to the article *a*, but used before words beginning with a vowel sound, as *an* eagle, *an* honor, *an* X-ray. [OE *ān* one] ◆ Some writers and speakers still use *an*, rather than *a*, before words beginning with *h* in an unstressed syllable, as *an* hotel —a holdover from the period when the *h* was unpronounced. In British usage *an* sometimes appears before words beginning with the sound (yōō), as *an* union, *an* eulogy.
an² (an, *unstressed* ən) *conj. Archaic* And, especially in the sense *and if*, or *if*: often written **an′.** [Var. of AND]
an-¹ *prefix* Without; not: *anarchy.* Also, before consonants (except *h*) *a-.* [< Gk.]
an-² Var. of ANA-.
an-³ Assimilated var. of AD-.
an. Anno (L, in the year).
-an *suffix* Used to form adjectives and nouns denoting connection with a country, person, group, doctrine, etc., as follows: **1.** Pertaining to; belonging to: *human, sylvan.* **2.** Originating in; living in: *Italian.* **3.** Adhering to; following: *Lutheran.* **4.** *Zool.* Belonging to a class or order: used to form singulars for collective plurals in *-a:* *amphibian.* See -IAN. [< L *-anus*]
AN or **A.N.** or **A.-N.** Anglo-Norman.
a·na¹ (ā′nə, ä′nə) *n.* **1.** A collection of notes, sketches, or scraps of literature bearing on some particular subject. **2.** The information in such a collection. See -ANA.
an·a² (an′ə) *adv. Med.* Of each: used in prescriptions to signify the amount to be taken of two or more substances prescribed: often abbr. *ā* or *āā.* [< Gk. *ana* throughout]
ana- *prefix* **1.** Up; upward: *anadromous.* **2.** Back; backward: *anapest.* **3.** Anew: sometimes capable of being rendered *re-*, as *anabaptism*, rebaptism. **4.** Throughout; thoroughly: *analysis.* Also, before vowels or *h*, **an-.** [< Gk. < *ana* up, back]
-ana *suffix* Pertaining to: added to the names of notable persons, places, etc., to indicate a collection of materials, such as writings or anecdotes, about the subject: *Americana.* Also **-iana.** [< L, neut. pl. of *-anus.* See -AN.]
an·a·bae·na (an′ə·bē′nə) *n. pl.* **·nas** *Bot.* Any plant of a genus (*Anabaena*) of fresh-water, bluish-green algae whose decay sometimes causes foul odor and hurtful properties in drinking water. [< NL < Gk. *anabainein.* See ANABASIS.]
An·a·bap·tist (an′ə·bap′tist) *n.* One of a Zwinglian sect that arose in Switzerland about 1520, who rejected the practice of infant baptism, limited church membership to adults baptized after a confession of faith, and advocated various social reforms. [< NL *anabaptista* < LL *anabaptismus* < Gk. *anabaptismos* rebaptism < *anabaptizein* to rebaptize < *ana-* anew + *baptizein* to baptize] — **An′a·bap′tism** *n.*
an·a·bas (an′ə·bas) *n.* Any member of a genus (*Anabas*) of fresh-water perchlike fishes of Africa and southern Asia, one species of which (*Anabas scandens*) can travel on land for long distances. Also called *climbing fish.* [< NL < Gk. *anabas* < *anabainein.* See ANABASIS.]
a·nab·a·sis (ə·nab′ə·sis) *n. pl.* **·ses** (-sēz) **1.** A military advance or incursion, as that of Cyrus the Younger, with 10,000 Greek auxiliaries, against Artaxerxes II in 401 B.C.,

described in Xenophon's *Anabasis*. **2.** *Med.* The increase of a disease or fever to a climax: opposed to *catabasis*. [< Gk. < *anabainein* to go up, invade < *ana-* up + *bainein* to go]

an·a·bat·ic (an'ə·bat'ik) *adj.* **1.** Of or pertaining to an anabasis. **2.** *Meteorol.* Rising upward, as air currents. **3.** *Med.* Increasing to a crisis, as a fever. [< Gk. *anabatikos* < *anabatēs* one who goes up < *anabainein*. See ANABASIS.]

an·a·bi·o·sis (an'ə·bī·ō'sis) *n.* A return to life; resuscitation. [< NL < ANA- + Gk. *bios* life]

an·a·bi·ot·ic (an'ə·bī·ot'ik) *adj.* Apparently lifeless, but capable of resuscitation. — *n.* *Med.* Any resuscitating agent. [< Gk. *ana-* again + *biōtikos* of life, living < *bios* life]

an·a·bleps (an'ə·bleps) *n.* A fresh-water cyprinodont fish of tropical America having each eye divided into two segments, the upper portion adapted for vision in air, the lower for vision in water: also called *four-eyed fish*. [< NL < Gk. *anablepein* to look up]

a·nab·o·lism (ə·nab'ə·liz'əm) *n.* *Biol.* The process by which food is built up into protoplasm; constructive metabolism: opposed to *catabolism*. [< Gk. *anabolē* a heaping up < *ana-* up + *bolē* a stroke] — **an·a·bol·ic** (an'ə·bol'ik) *adj.*

an·a·branch (an'ə·branch, -bränch) *n.* *Geog.* An effluent of a stream that rejoins the main stream, forming an island between the two watercourses. [< *ana(stomosing) branch*]

an·a·car·di·a·ceous (an'ə·kär'dē·ā'shəs) *adj.* *Bot.* Pertaining or belonging to the cashew family (*Anacardiaceae*) of trees or shrubs with resinous, milky, acrid juice, alternate leaves, and small flowers. [< NL < ANA- similar to + Gk. *kardia* heart; with ref. to the shape of the fruit]

a·nach·o·rism (ə·nak'ə·riz'əm) *n.* Something foreign to a country or unsuited to local conditions; a geographical error. Compare ANACHRONISM. [< ANA- backward, against + Gk. *chōrion* country, place]

a·nach·ro·nism (ə·nak'rə·niz'əm) *n.* **1.** The assigning of an event, person, etc., to a wrong time, especially an earlier, date. **2.** Something out of its proper time. [< F *anachronisme* < L *anachronismus* < Gk. *anachronismos* < *anachronizein* to refer to a wrong time < *ana-* against + *chronos* time] — **a·nach'ro·nis'tic, a·nach'ro·nis'ti·cal, a·nach'ro·nous** *adj.*

an·a·clas·tic (an'ə·klas'tik) *adj.* *Optics* Pertaining to, caused by, or causing refraction. [< NL < Gk. *anaklastos* < *anaklaein* to bend back < *ana-* back + *klaein* to break]

an·a·cli·nal (an'ə·klī'nəl) *adj.* *Geol.* Transverse to the course of underlying rocks and against the dip, as a valley: distinguished from *cataclinal*. [< ANA- on + Gk. *klinein* to lean]

an·a·cli·sis (an'ə·klī'sis, ə·nak'lə·sis) *n.* *Psychoanal.* A strong emotional dependence upon others, typified by an infant's need of his mother for nourishment, protection, and support. [< NL < Gk. *anaklisis* < *anaklinein* to lean upon < *ana-* upon + *klinein* to lean]

an·a·clit·ic (an'ə·klit'ik) *adj.* *Psychoanal.* Pertaining to or exhibiting anaclisis. [< Gk. *anaklitos* < *anaklinein*. See ANACLISIS.]

an·a·co·lu·thon (an'ə·kə·loo'thon) *n.* *pl.* **·thons** or **·tha** (-thə) A changing from one grammatical sequence in a sentence to another. [< L < Gk., orig. neut. sing. of *anakolouthos* lacking sequence < *an-* not + *akolouthos* following] — **an'a·co·lu'thic** *adj.*

an·a·con·da (an'ə·kon'də) *n.* **1.** A very large, nonvenomous tropical serpent (*Eunectes murinus*), that crushes its prey in its coils. **2.** Any boa constrictor or python. [? < Singhalese]

An·a·con·da (an'ə·kon'də) A copper-mining city in SW Montana; site of the world's largest copper smelter; pop. 9,771.

an·a·cous·tic (an'ə·koos'tik, -kous'-) *adj.* **1.** Without sound; soundproof. **2.** *Aerospace* Of or pertaining to the region beyond the earth's atmosphere where sound waves are not propagated, because of a deficiency of air or other fluid medium.

A·nac·re·on (ə·nak'rē·ən, -on), 563?–478? B.C., Greek poet.

A·nac·re·on·tic (ə·nak'rē·on'tik) *adj.* **1.** Pertaining to or like the lyrics of Anacreon. **2.** Praising love and wine; convivial; amatory. — *n.* A poem in the manner of Anacreon.

an·a·cru·sis (an'ə·kroo'sis) *n.* In prosody, one or more unemphatic introductory syllables in a line of verse that would properly begin with a stressed syllable. [< NL < Gk. *anakrousis* < *anakrouein* to push back < *ana-* back + *krouein* to strike] — **an·a·crus·tic** (an'ə·krus'tik) *adj.*

an·a·dem (an'ə·dem) *n.* *Poetic* A wreath for the head; garland; fillet. [< L *anadema* < Gk. *anadēma* < *anadeein* to wreathe < *ana-* up + *deein* to bind]

an·a·di·plo·sis (an'ə·di·plō'sis) *n.* Rhetorical repetition, in which the ending of a sentence, line, or clause is repeated and emphasized at the beginning of the next. [< L < Gk. *anadiplōsis* < *ana-* again + *diploein* to double < *diploos* double]

a·nad·ro·mous (ə·nad'rə·məs) *adj.* *Zool.* Of fishes, as the salmon, going from the sea up rivers to spawn: opposed to *catadromous*. [< Gk. *anadromos* < *ana-* up + *dromos* a running, course < *dramein* to run]

a·nae·mi·a (ə·nē'mē·ə), **a·nae·mic** (ə·nē'mik), etc. See ANEMIA, etc.

an·aer·obe (an·âr'ōb, an·ā'ə·rōb) *n.* A microorganism that

flourishes without free oxygen: distinguished from *aerobe*. [See ANAEROBIUM] — **an·aer·o·bic** (an'âr·ō'bik, -ob'ik, an·ā'ə·rō'bik, -rob'ik] *adj.*

an·aer·o·bi·um (an'âr·ō'bē·əm, an'ā·ə·rō'-) *n.* *pl.* **·bi·a** (-bē·ə) An anaerobe. [< NL < AN-¹ without + AERO- < Gk. *bios* life]

an·aes·the·sia (an'is·thē'zhə, -zhē·ə), **an·aes·thet·ic** (an'·is·thet'ik), etc. See ANESTHESIA, etc.

an·a·glyph (an'ə·glif) *n.* An ornament in low relief, as a cameo. [< Gk. *anaglyphē* < *ana-* up + *glyphein* to carve] — **an'a·glyph'ic** or **·i·cal, an·a·glyp·tic** (an'ə·glip'tik) *adj.*

an·a·go·ge (an'ə·gō'jē) *n.* The spiritual or mystical interpretation of words, especially of the types and allegories of the Old Testament. Also **an'a·go·gy**. [< NL < Gk. *anagōgē* elevation, lit., a leading up < *ana-* up + *agein* to lead]

an·a·gog·ic (an'ə·goj'ik) *adj.* **1.** Pertaining to or using anagoge; mystical: also **an'a·gog'i·cal**. **2.** *Psychoanal.* Pertaining to the transformation of drives from the unconscious into constructive ideals. — **an'a·gog'i·cal·ly** *adv.*

an·a·gram (an'ə·gram) *n.* **1.** A word or phrase formed by transposing the letters of another word or phrase. **2.** *pl.* (*construed as sing.*) A game in which the players make words by transposing or adding letters. [< MF *anagramme* < LGk. *anagramma* < Gk. *ana-* backwards + *gramma* letter (of the alphabet)] — **an·a·gram·mat·ic** (an'ə·grə·mat'ik) or **·i·cal** *adj.* — **an·a·gram·mat'i·cal·ly** *adv.*

an·a·gram·ma·tize (an'ə·gram'ə·tīz) *v.t.* **·tized, ·tiz·ing** To arrange as an anagram.

An·a·heim (an'ə·hīm) A city in SW California; pop. 166,701.

a·nal (ā'nəl) *adj.* *Anat.* Of, pertaining to, or situated in the region of the anus. [< L *anus* + -AL²]

anal. **1.** Analogous; analogy. **2.** Analysis; analytic(al).

a·nal·cite (a·nal'sit, -sīt) *n.* *Mineral.* An isometric, usually white, sodium-aluminum silicate; zeolite: formerly called **a·nal'cime** (-sīm, -sim). [< AN-¹ not + Gk. *alkimos* strong]

an·a·lects (an'ə·lekts) *n.pl.* Selections or fragments from a literary work or group of works. Also **an·a·lec·ta** (an'ə·lek'-tə). [< L *analecta*, *pl* < Gk. *analekta* < *analegein* to collect < *ana-* up + *legein* to gather] — **an'a·lec'tic** *adj.*

an·a·lep·tic (an'ə·lep'tik) *Med. adj.* Restorative to strength; reinvigorating. — *n.* A restoring medicine. [< NL < Gk. *analēptikos* restorative < *analambanein* to recover < *ana-* up + *lambanein* to take]

anal fin *Zool.* The unpaired median ventral fin just behind the anus in fishes. For illustration see FISH.

an·al·ge·si·a (an'əl·jē'zē·ə, -sē·ə) *n.* *Pathol.* Inability to feel pain. Also **an·al·gi·a** (an·al'jē·ə). [< NL < Gk. *analgēsia* < *an-* without + *algos* pain]

an·al·ge·sic (an'əl·jē'zik, -sik) *Med. n.* A drug for the alleviation or diminishing of pain. — *adj.* Pertaining to or promoting analgesia.
— **Syn.** (noun) anodyne, opiate, narcotic, anesthetic.

analog computer A computer that processes continuous quantities, as voltage, resistance, etc., that are analogous with the values of the problem presented. Compare DIGITAL COMPUTER.

an·a·log·i·cal (an'ə·loj'i·kəl) *adj.* Pertaining to, containing, or based on analogy. Also **an'a·log'ic**. — **an'a·log'i·cal·ly** *adv.*

a·nal·o·gist (ə·nal'ə·jist) *n.* One who seeks, uses, or reasons from analogy.

a·nal·o·gize (ə·nal'ə·jīz) *v.* **·gized, ·giz·ing** *v.i.* **1.** To use or reason by analogy. — *v.t.* **2.** To show to be analogous.

a·nal·o·gous (ə·nal'ə·gəs) *adj.* **1.** Resembling or comparable in certain respects. **2.** *Biol.* Having a similar function but differing in origin and structure, as the wings of birds and insects: distinguished from *homologous*. Abbr. *anal.* — **a·nal'o·gous·ly** *adv.* — **a·nal'o·gous·ness** *n.*

an·a·logue (an'ə·lôg, -log) *n.* **1.** Anything analogous to something else. **2.** *Ling.* A word or term in one language corresponding in use or function to one in another. **3.** *Biol.* An organ analogous to one in another species or group. Also **an'a·log**. [< F < Gk. *analogon*, orig. neut. sing. of *analogos*. See ANALOGY.]

a·nal·o·gy (ə·nal'ə·jē) *n.* *pl.* **·gies 1.** Agreement or resemblance in certain aspects, as form or function, between otherwise dissimilar things; similarity without identity. **2.** Any similarity or agreement. **3.** *Biol.* A similarity in function and superficial appearance, but not in origin. **4.** *Logic* Reasoning in which relations or resemblances are inferred from others that are known or observed; reasoning that proceeds from the individual or particular to a coordinate individual or particular. **5.** *Ling.* A process whereby words take on inflections or constructions imitative of more familiar words and existing patterns without having undergone the same linguistic development: The past tense of *climb* changed from the strong form *clomb* to the weak form *climbed* on analogy with the weak verbs. Abbr. *anal.* [< L *analogia* < Gk. < *analogos* proportionate, conformable < *ana-* according to + *logos* proportion]
— **Syn. 1, 2.** *Analogy, resemblance, similarity,* and *similitude* refer to likeness between things. In careful usage, an *analogy* is drawn only between things clearly unlike in kind, form, or appearance, and refers to their similar properties, relations, behavior,

etc. A *resemblance* is almost always a likeness in appearance, while *similarity* is usually a likeness in some external or superficial aspect or characteristic. A boy bears a *resemblance* to his father; there may be a *similarity* in their gait, or in their dress. *Similitude* is sometimes used for *similarity*, but more often denotes the drawing of a rhetorical comparison. See SIMILE. — **Ant.** dissimilarity, unlikeness.

an·al·pha·bet·ic (an-al′fə-bet′ik) *adj. & n.* Illiterate.

a·nal·y·sand (ə-nal′ə-zand, -sand) *n. Psychoanal.* One who is being psychoanalyzed.   [< ANALYZE, on analogy with *multiplicand, confirmand,* etc.]

a·nal·y·sis (ə-nal′ə-sis) *n. pl.* **·ses** (-sēz) **1.** The separation of a whole into its parts or elements: opposed to *synthesis.* **2.** A statement of the results of this; logical synopsis. **3.** A method of determining or describing the nature of a thing by separating it into its parts. **4.** *Math.* The investigation of the relations of variable or indeterminate quantities by means of symbols, including those of algebra and of differential and integral calculus. **5.** *Chem.* **a** The determination of the kind, quantity, and proportions of constituents forming a compound or substance by the separation of the ingredients. **b** The determination of the presence and nature of impurities or special ingredients in a compound, whether or not by actual separation. **6.** Psychoanalysis. Compare SYNTHESIS. Abbr. *anal.* — **Syn.** See ABRIDGMENT.   [< Med.L < Gk. < *analyein* to dissolve < *ana-* throughout, completely + *lyein* to loosen]

analysis si·tus (sī′təs) *Math.* Topology.   [< NL, analysis of region]

an·a·lyst (an′ə-list) *n.* **1.** One who analyzes or is skilled in analysis. **2.** A psychoanalyst (which see).

an·a·lyt·ic (an′ə-lit′ik) *adj.* **1.** Pertaining to or proceeding by analysis. **2.** Separating into constituent parts or first principles. **3.** *Ling.* Denoting a language that uses words or free forms to express grammatical relationships, either entirely, as Chinese, or predominantly, as English and French: opposed to *synthetic* or *inflectional.* Also **an′a·lyt′i·cal.** Abbr. *anal.*   [< Med.L *analyticus* < Gk. *analytikos,* ult. < *analyein.* See ANALYSIS.] — **an′a·lyt′i·cal·ly** *adv.*

analytical psychology 1. The analysis of psychological phenomena by systematic introspection. **2.** The systematic psychology and analytic methods originated by and associated with C. G. Jung.

analytic geometry Geometry in which position is represented analytically by a system of coordinates and the procedure by which solutions are obtained is largely algebraic.

an·a·lyt·ics (an′ə-lit′iks) *n.pl.* (*construed as sing.*) **1.** The science or use of analysis. **2.** The part of logic concerned with analysis.

an·a·lyze (an′ə-līz) *v.t.* **·lyzed, ·lyz·ing 1.** To separate into constituent parts or elements, especially so as to determine the nature, form, etc., of the whole by examination of the parts. **2.** To examine critically or minutely. **3.** To make a chemical or mathematical analysis of. **4.** *Gram.* To separate (a sentence) into its grammatical elements. **5.** To psychoanalyze. Also *Brit.* **an′a·lyse.**   [< F *analyser* < *analyse* analysis < Med.L *analysis.* See ANALYSIS.] — **an′a·lyz′a·ble** *adj.* — **an′a·ly·za′tion** *n.* — **an′a·lyz′er** *n.*

A·nam (ə-nam′, an′əm) See ANNAM.

An·a·mese (an′ə-mēz′, -mēs′) See ANNAMESE.

an·am·ne·sis (an′am·nē′sis) *n.* **1.** *Psychol.* A reproducing in memory; recollection. **2.** *Med.* The past history of a disease: distinguished from *catamnesis.*   [< Gk. *anamnēsis* < *ana-* back + *mimnēskein* to call to mind]

an·a·mor·phism (an′ə-môr′fiz·əm) *n.* **1.** Distortion of shape. **2.** *Biol.* Evolution from a lower to a higher type.   [< ANA- up + Gk. *morphē* form]

an·a·mor·pho·scope (an′ə-môr′fə-skōp) *n. Optics* A vertical cylindrical mirror for viewing an anamorphosis.

an·a·mor·pho·sis (an′ə-môr′fə-sis, -môr·fō′sis) *n. pl.* **·ses** (-sēz) *Optics* A distorted representation of an object, unrecognizable except when viewed from a particular point, reflected in an anamorphoscope, etc.   [< NL < Gk. *anamorphōsis* < Gk. *anamorphoein* < *ana-* again + *morphoein* to form]

an·an·drous (an-an′drəs) *adj. Bot.* Destitute of stamens, as a female flower.   [< Gk. *anandros* without a husband < *an-* without + *anēr, andros* man]

An·a·ni·as (an′ə-nī′əs) In the Bible, a man who fell dead after Peter rebuked him for lying. *Acts* v 1–6. — *n.* A liar.

a·nan·ke (ə-nan′kē) *n. Often cap.* In ancient Greek religion, absolute necessity, prevailing even over the gods.

an·an·thous (an-an′thəs) *adj. Bot.* Flowerless.   [< AN-¹ without + Gk. *anthos* flower]

an·a·pest (an′ə-pest) *n.* **1.** In prosody, a metrical foot consisting of two short or unaccented syllables followed by one long or accented syllable (◡◡ —). **2.** A line of verse made up of or characterized by such feet: Thĕn thĕ rāin | ănd thĕ trēe | wĕre ălōne. Also **an′a·paest.**   [< L *anapaestus* < Gk. *anapaistos,* lit., reversed < *ana-* back + *paiein* to strike; so called because it is a reversed dactyl] — **an′a·pes′tic** *adj.*

an·a·phase (an′ə·fāz) *n. Biol.* A stage of mitosis in which the divided chromosomes move toward each pole of the nuclear spindle.   [< ANA- up + PHASE]

a·naph·o·ra (ə-naf′ə-rə) *n.* In rhetoric, the repetition of a word or phrase at the beginning of several successive verses, clauses, etc.   [< L < Gk. < *ana-* back + *pherein* to carry]

an·aph·ro·dis·i·a (an-af′rə-diz′ē-ə) *n.* Absence or impairment of sexual desire.   [< NL < AN-¹ without + Gk. *aphrodisia* sexual pleasure < *Aphroditē,* the goddess of love]

an·aph·ro·dis·i·ac (an-af′rə-diz′ē-ak) *adj.* Of, pertaining to, or tending to produce anaphrodisia. — *n.* An anaphrodisiac agent or treatment.

an·a·phy·lax·is (an′ə-fə-lak′sis) *n. Pathol.* Increased susceptibility to an agent, especially a protein, after a first injection into the blood. Compare ALLERGY.   [< NL < ANA- + (PRO)PHYLAXIS] — **an′a·phy·lac′tic** (-lak′tik) *adj.*

an·a·pla·sia (an′ə-plā′zhə, -zhē-ə) *n. Biol.* A reversion of cells to an undifferentiated or more primitive form, destroying their capacity for full development and functioning.   [< NL < ANA- + -PLASIA]

an·a·plas·mo·sis (an′ə-plaz-mō′sis) *n. Vet.* An infectious disease of cattle caused by a bloodsucking protozoan (*Anaplasma marginale*) transmitted by ticks, flies, mosquitoes, etc.   [< NL < *Anaplasma,* generic name + -OSIS]

an·a·plas·tic (an′ə-plas′tik) *adj.* **1.** *Surg.* Restoring lost or absent parts, as by transplanting tissue. **2.** *Biol.* Of or pertaining to anaplasia.

an·a·plas·ty (an′ə-plas′tē) *n.* Plastic surgery.   [< NL < Gk. *anaplastos* < *ana-* anew + *plassein* to form]

an·ap·tyx·is (an′ap-tik′sis) *n. Ling.* The evolution of a vowel out of a consonant group containing, usually, *m, n, l,* or *r,* as in (fil′əm) for *film*; epenthesis of vowels.   [< Gk. *anaptyseein* to unfold] — **an′ap·tyc′tic** (-tik′tik) *adj.*

an·ar·chic (an-är′kik) *adj.* **1.** Pertaining to or like anarchy. **2.** Advocating anarchy. **3.** Inducing anarchy; lawless. Also **an·ar′chi·cal.** — **an·ar′chi·cal·ly** *adv.*

an·ar·chism (an′ər-kiz′əm) *n.* **1.** The theory that all forms of government are incompatible with individual and social liberty and should be abolished. **2.** The methods, especially terroristic ones, of anarchists. — **philosophic anarchism** The advocacy of voluntary cooperation and mutual aid as a substitute for the coercive power of the state. — **an·ar·chis·tic** (an′ər-kis′tik) *adj.*

an·ar·chist (an′ər-kist) *n.* **1.** One who believes in and advocates anarchism. **2.** One who encourages or furthers anarchy. Also **an·arch** (an′ärk).

an·ar·chy (an′ər-kē) *n.* **1.** Absence of government. **2.** Lawless confusion and political disorder. **3.** General disorder.   [< Gk. *anarchia* < *anarchos* without a leader < *an-* without + *archos* leader, chief]

an·ar·throus (an-är′thrəs) *adj.* **1.** *Gram.* Used without the article. **2.** *Zool.* Lacking distinct joints.   [< Gk. *anarthros* unjointed < *an-* without + *arthron* joint]

an·a·sar·ca (an′ə-sär′kə) *n. Pathol.* A general dropsy in the cellular tissues of the body.   [< NL < Gk. *ana-* throughout + *sarx, sarkos* flesh] — **an′a·sar′cous** *adj.*

An·as·ta·si·us I (an′ə-stā′shē-əs), 430?–518, Byzantine emperor 491–518.

Anastasius II, died 721?, Byzantine emperor 713–716.

an·as·tig·mat·ic (an·as′tig-mat′ik) *adj. Optics* **1.** Not astigmatic; especially, corrected for astigmatism, as a lens. **2.** Pertaining to a compound photographic lens, each element of which is adapted to correct the astigmatism of the other.   [< AN-¹ + ASTIGMATIC]

a·nas·to·mose (ə-nas′tə-mōz) *v.i.* **·mosed, ·mos·ing** To connect by anastomosis.

a·nas·to·mo·sis (ə-nas′tə-mō′sis) *n. pl.* **·ses** (-sēz) **1.** *Physiol.* A union, interlacing, or running together, as of veins, nerves, or canals of animal bodies. **2.** Any intercommunication, as of two or more lines, branches, or rivers.   [< NL < Gk. *anastomōsis* opening < *ana-* again + *stoma* mouth] — **a·nas′to·mot′ic** (-mot′ik) *adj.*

a·nas·tro·phe (ə-nas′trə-fē) *n.* In rhetoric, the inversion of the natural or usual order of words, as "Homeward directly he went." Also **a·nas′tro·phy.**   [< Gk. *anastrophē* < *ana-* back + *strephein* to turn]

anat. Anatomical; anatomist; anatomy.

an·a·tase (an′ə-tās, -tāz) *n. Mineral.* An adamantine, brown, indigo-blue, or black titanium dioxide, TiO₂, that crystallizes in the tetragonal system, commonly in pyramidal form: formerly called *octahedrite.*   [< F < Gk. *anatasis* extension; so called from its long crystals]

a·nath·e·ma (ə-nath′ə·mə) *n. pl.* **·mas** or **·ma·ta** (-mə·tə) **1.** A formal ecclesiastical ban or curse, excommunicating a person or damning something, as a book or doctrine. **2.** Any curse or imprecation. **3.** One who or that which is excommunicated or damned. **4.** One who or that which is greatly disliked or detested. — **Syn.** See CURSE.   [< L < Gk. *anathema* a thing devoted to (evil) < *anatithenai* to dedicate < *ana-* up + *tithenai* to set, place]

a·nath·e·ma·tize (ə-nath′ə-mə-tīz′) *v.* **·tized, ·tiz·ing** *v.t.* **1.**

To pronounce an anathema against. — *v.i.* **2.** To utter or express anathemas. — **a·nath'e·ma·ti·za'tion** *n.*

An·a·to·li·a (an'ə·tō'lē·ə) A mountainous peninsula comprising the westernmost part of Asia and almost all of Turkey; 287 117 sq. mi ; Asia Minor. — **An'a·to'lic** *adj.*

An·a·to·li·an (an'ə·tō'lē·ən) *adj.* Pertaining to Anatolia or its people. — *n.* A family of languages of which Cuneiform Hittite is the best known. See HITTITE, INDO-HITTITE.

an·a·tom·i·cal (an'ə·tom'i·kəl) *adj.* **1.** Pertaining to anatomy or dissection; produced by dissection. **2.** Structural, especially as distinguished from functional. Also **an/a·tom'ic.** Abbr *anat.* — **an'a·tom'i·cal·ly** *adv.*

a·nat·o·mist (ə·nat'ə·mist) *n.* One skilled in anatomy. Abbr. *anat.*

a·nat·o·mize (ə·nat'ə·mīz) *v.t.* **·mized, ·miz·ing 1.** To dissect (an animal or plant) for the purpose of investigating the structure, position, and interrelationships of its parts. **2.** To examine minutely; analyze. — **a·nat'o·mi·za'tion** *n.*

a·nat·o·my (ə·nat'ə·mē) *n. pl.* **·mies 1.** The structure of an organism, or of any of its parts. **2.** The science of the structure of organisms, as of the human body, and of the interrelations of their parts. **3.** The art or practice of anatomizing. **4.** A skeleton. **5.** An anatomical model or cast. Abbr. *anat.* [< F *anatomie* < L *anatomia* < Gk. *anatomia*, earlier *anatomē* dissection < *anatemnein* to cut up < *ana-* up + *temnein* to cut]

a·nat·ro·pous (ə·nat'rə·pəs) *adj. Bot.* Inverted: said of an ovule with the micropyle or orifice beside the hilum at one end and with the chalaza at the other. See OVULE. Also **a·nat'ro·pal** (-pəl). [< NL < ANA- + -TROPOUS]

a·nat·to (ə·nä'tō) *n.* A yellowish red dye obtained from the pulp enclosing the seeds of the arnotto tree of Central America, used in coloring butter, cheese, and varnish, and as a dyestuff for textiles: also spelled *annatto.* See ARNOTTO. [< Carib]

An·ax·ag·o·ras (an'ak·sag'ə·rəs), 500?–428 B.C., Greek philosopher.

An·ax·i·man·der (an·ak'sə·man'dər), 610–546? B.C., Greek philosopher and astronomer.

anc. Ancient; anciently.

ANC or **A.N.C.** Army Nurse Corps.

-ance *suffix of nouns* Used to form nouns of action, quality, state, or condition from adjectives in *-ant,* and also directly from verbs, as in *abundance, resistance, forbearance.* Compare -ANCY. [< F *-ance* < L *-antia, -entia,* a suffix used to form nouns from present participles; or directly from Latin]

◆ **-ance, -ence** The modern spelling of words in this group is unpredictable. The confusion arose originally in borrowings from Old French (*resistance, assistance*) where *-ance* had come to represent Latin *-entia,* as well as *-antia.* Since 1500, however, some have been altered back to *-ence* for the Latin model, as in the case of *dependence,* earlier *dependance.* Later Latin borrowings in French and in English (through French or directly from Latin) discriminate between *-ance* and *-ence* according to the vowel of the Latin original.

an·ces·tor (an'ses·tər) *n.* **1.** One from whom a person is descended, especially when more remote than a grandfather; forefather; progenitor; forebear. **2.** *Law* One who precedes another in the line of legal inheritance, whether or not a direct progenitor: correlative of *heir.* **3.** *Biol.* An organism of an earlier type from which later organisms have been derived; a progenitor. [< OF *ancestre* < L *antecessor* forerunner, predecessor < *antecedere* < *ante-* before + *cedere* to go] — **an·ces·tress** (an'ses·tris) *n.fem.*

— **Syn. 1.** *Ancestor, progenitor, forefather,* and *forebear* denote a person from whom one is descended. *Ancestor,* denoting one from whom a person is directly descended, is the commonest term. *Progenitor* is used in the discussion of heredity, as in biology, while *forefather* and *forebear* are chiefly poetical. All these words when used in the plural usually denote previous generations without regard to direct descent.

an·ces·tral (an·ses'trəl) *adj.* **1.** Of, pertaining to, or descending from an ancestor. **2.** *Biol.* Pertaining to an earlier and usually simpler type or species. Also **an·ces·to·ri·al** (an'ses·tôr'ē·əl, -tō'rē·). — **an·ces·tral·ly** *adv.*

an·ces·try (an'ses·trē) *n. pl.* **·tries 1.** A line or body of ancestors; ancestors collectively. **2.** Ancestral lineage. **3.** Noble or gentle lineage.

An·chi·ses (an·kī'sēz) In classical legend, the father of Aeneas, rescued from burning Troy on his son's shoulders.

an·chor (ang'kər) *n.* **1.** A heavy implement, usually of iron or steel, with hooks or flukes to grip the bottom, attached to a cable and dropped from a ship or boat to hold it in place. **2.** Any object used for a similar purpose. **3.** Anything that makes stable or secure; anything depended on for support or security. — **at anchor** Anchored, as a ship. — **to drop** (or **cast**) **anchor** To put down the anchor in order to hold fast a vessel. — **to ride at anchor** To be anchored, as a ship. — **to weigh anchor** To take up the anchor so as to sail away. — *v.t.* **1.** To secure or make secure by an anchor. **2.** To fix firmly. — *v.i.* **3.** To come to anchor; lie at anchor, as a ship. **4.** To become fixed; hold oneself fast, as to a place. [OE *ancor* < L *ancora* < Gk. *ankyra*]

an·chor·age (ang'kər·ij) *n.* **1.** A place for anchoring. **2.** A

coming to or lying at anchor. **3.** A source or place of stability or security. **4.** A fee charged for anchoring.

An·chor·age (ang'kər·ij) A port city in southern Alaska, on Cook Inlet; the largest city in the State; pop. 48,081.

an·cho·ress (ang'kə·ris) *n.* A female anchorite.

an·cho·rite (ang'kə·rīt) *n.* One who has withdrawn from the world for religious reasons; hermit: distinguished from *cenobite.* Also **an'cho·ret** (-rit, -ret). [< L *anachoreta* < Gk. *anachō-rētēs* < *anachōreein* to retire, retreat < *ana-* back + *chōrein* to withdraw] — **an'cho·rit'ic** (-rit'ik) *adj.*

anchor man The key man or main support of a team, as the man who runs the last stage of a relay race.

an·cho·vy (an'chō·vē, -chə·vē, an·chō'vē) *n. pl.* **·vies** or **·vy 1.** Any of several very small, herringlike fishes (family *Engraulidae*) inhabiting warm seas, valued as a delicacy and used industrially to make fishmeal. **2.** *U S.* Smelt. [< Sp., Pg. *anchova*]

anchovy pear 1. A West Indian fruit tasting like the mango. **2.** The tall unbranched tree (*Grias cauliflora*) of the myrtle family that bears this fruit.

an·chu·sa (ang·kyōō'sə, an·chōō'zə) *n.* Any member of a genus (*Anchusa*) of hairy-stemmed plants, including the alkanet and bugloss. [< NL < L < Gk. *anchousa*]

an·chu·sin (ang·kyōō'sin, an·chōō'zin) *n.* A red resinous compound extracted from alkanet for use in dyeing.

an·chy·lose (ang'kə·lōs), **an·chy·lo·sis** (ang'kə·lō'sis) See ANKYLOSE, etc.

an·cienne no·blesse (äṅ·syen' nô·bles') *French* The old nobility; especially, that prior to the French Revolution.

an·cien ré·gime (äṅ·syaṅ' rā·zhēm') *French* A former political and social system; especially the system in France before the revolution of 1789. Also **Ancient Regime.**

an·cient[1] (ān'shənt) *adj.* **1.** Existing or occurring in times long past, especially before the fall of the Western Roman Empire, in A.D. 476. **2.** Having existed from remote antiquity; of great age: *ancient* relics. **3.** Very old: said of persons. **4.** *Archaic* Venerable; sage. Abbr. *anc.* — *n.* **1.** One who lived in ancient times. **2.** An aged or venerable person. — **the ancients 1.** The ancient Greeks, Romans, Hebrews, or other civilized nations of antiquity. **2.** The ancient authors of Greece and Rome. [< OF *ancien* < LL *antianum,* ult. < L *ante* before] — **an'cient·ness** *n.* — **an'cient·ly** *adv.*

— **Syn.** (adj.) **1.** *Ancient, old, archaic,* and *antique* refer to a long time ago. Something *ancient* existed at such a time and does not exist now: the *ancient* peoples of Asia. *Old* must often be qualified to avoid ambiguity, as it sometimes means *ancient:* cowrie shells and other *old* forms of currency; and sometimes aged: Oxford is an *old* university. The *archaic* flourished in the past, but may still have a limited existence: *archaic* words and phrases. That which is *antique* is in the style of a former period, and may be greatly valued for its age: *antique* pottery. — **Ant.** modern, recent.

an·cient[2] (ān'shənt) *n. Archaic* **1.** An ensign or flag. **2.** One who bears an ensign or a flag. [Alter. of ENSIGN]

Ancient of Days God. *Dan.* vii 9.

an·cil·lar·y (an'sə·ler'ē) *adj.* Serving as an aid or subsidiary; auxiliary. — **Syn.** See AUXILIARY. [< L *ancillaris* < *ancilla* maid]

an·cip·i·tal (an·sip'ə·təl) *adj. Bot.* Two-edged, as the stems of certain plants. Also **an·cip'i·tous.** [< L *anceps, ancipitis* two-headed < *an-* (*ambi-*) on both sides + *caput* head]

an·con (ang'kon) *n. pl.* **an·co·nes** (ang·kō'nēz) **1.** *Anat.* The enlarged upper end of the ulna, forming the salient point of the elbow. **2.** *Archit.* An elbow-shaped projection; a console, as for an ornament on a keystone. Also **an·cone** (ang'·kōn). [< Gk. *ankōn* a bend, the elbow] — **an·co·nal** (ang'kə·nəl), **an·co·ne·al** (ang·kō'nē·əl) *adj.*

An·co·na (äng·kō'nä) A Province of central Italy; 748 sq. mi.; pop. 404,922 (1961); capital **Ancona,** pop. 99,678.

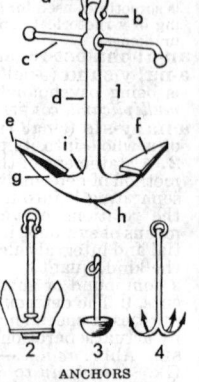

ANCHORS
1. Fluke. 2. Patent.
3. Mushroom. 4. Grapnel. *a* Ring. *b* Eye.
c Stock. *d* Shank.
e Bill. *f* Fluke or palm.
g Arm. *h* Crown.
i Throat.

ANCON
(def. 2)

-ancy *suffix of nouns* A modern variant of -ANCE: used to form new words expressing quality, state, or condition (*infancy, vacancy*), or to refashion older nouns of quality in *-ance* (*constancy*). [< L *-antia*]

an·cy·los·to·mi·a·sis (an'sə·lōs'tə·mī'ə·sis) *n. Pathol.* A progressive anemia common in tropical countries, caused by parasitic nematode worms (especially *Ancylostoma duodenale*) that suck the blood from the small intestine. Also spelled *ankylostomiasis.* Also called *hookworm disease, uncinariasis.* [< NL < *Ancylostoma,* generic name (< Gk. *ankylos* crooked + *stoma* mouth) + -IASIS]

and (and, *unstressed* ənd, ən, 'n) *conj.* **1.** Also; added to; as well as: a particle denoting addition, emphasis, or union, used as a connective between words, phrases, clauses, and sentences: shoes *and* ships *and* sealing wax. **2.** As a result or consequence: Make one move *and* you are dead! **3.** To: in idiomatic use with *come, go, try,* etc.: Try *and* stop me; Go *and* find the answer. **4.** *Archaic* Then: *And* she answered unto him. **5.** *Archaic* If: *and* it please you. [OE *ond, and*]

and. Andante.

And. Andorra.

An·da·lu·sia (an/də-lōō/zhə, -shə) A region of southern Spain bordering on the Atlantic, the Strait of Gibraltar, and the Mediterranean. *Spanish* **An·da·lu·ci·a** (än/dä·lōō·thē/ä). **— An/da·lu/sian** *adj. & n.*

an·da·lu·site (an/də·lōō/sīt) *n.* An orthorhombic aluminum silicate, Al$_2$SiO$_5$, found in gem form in Ceylon and Brazil. [after *Andalusia*, where it was discovered]

An·da·man and Nic·o·bar Islands (an/də·mən; nik/ə·bär/) A Territory of India in the east Bay of Bengal; 3,143 sq. mi.; pop. 63,438 (1961); capital, Port Blair on South Andaman: comprising the northerly **Andaman Islands**; 2,508 sq. mi.; and the southerly **Nicobar Islands**; 635 sq. mi.

Andaman Sea A part of the Bay of Bengal between the Malay Peninsula, the Andaman and Nicobar islands, and Sumatra.

an·dan·te (an·dan/tē, än·dän/tā) *Music adj. & adv.* Moderately slow; slower than allegretto but faster than larghetto. **— n.** An andante movement or passage. [< Ital., walking]

an·dan·ti·no (an/dan·tē/nō, än/dän-) *Music adj. & adv.* Slightly quicker than andante; originally, slower than andante. **— n.** An andantino movement or passage. [< Ital., dim. of *andante*]

An·de·an (an·dē/ən, an/dē·ən) *adj.* Of or pertaining to the Andes.

An·der·lecht (än/dər·lekht) A commune in central Belgium, near Brussels; pop. 103,832 (est. 1969).

An·ders (än/ders), **Wladyslaw**, 1892–1970, Polish general.

An·der·sen (an/dər·sən), **Hans Christian**, 1805–75, Danish writer of fairy tales.

Andersen Nexö, **Martin** See NEXÖ.

An·der·son (an/dər·sən) **1.** A city in east central Indiana; pop. 70,787. **2.** A city in NW South Carolina; pop. 27,556.

An·der·son (an/dər·sən), **Carl David**, born 1905, U.S. physicist. **— Marian**, born 1902, U.S. contralto. **— Maxwell**, 1888–1959, U.S. playwright. **— Sherwood**, 1876–1941, U.S. author.

An·der·son·ville (an/dər·sən·vil/) A village in SW central Georgia; site of a Confederate prison for Union soldiers during the Civil War.

An·des (an/dēz) A mountain range in western South America, connected with the Rockies, and extending over 4,000 miles from Venezuela southward to Tierra del Fuego; highest peak, Aconcagua, 23,081 ft.

an·de·site (an/də·zīt) *n.* A volcanic rock, containing essentially plagioclase with biotite, hornblende, or augite. Also **an/de·syte.** [from the *Andes*]

An·dhra Pra·desh (än/drä prə·dāsh/) A State in SE India; 105,963 sq. mi.; pop. 43,394,951 (est. 1971); cap., Hyderabad.

and·i·ron (and/ī/ərn) *n.* One of two metal supports for holding wood in an open fireplace: also called *firedog.* [< OF *andier;* infl. by *iron*]

and/or Either *and* or *or,* according to the meaning intended: Place bills *and/or* coins in this container.

An·dor·ra (an·dôr/ə, -dor/ə) A Republic between France and Spain, subject to the joint suzerainty of the president of France and the Bishop of Urgel, Spain; 179 sq. mi.; pop. 26,500 (1976); capital, **Andorra la Vel·la** (lä ve/yä), pop. about 8,000. Officially **The Valleys of Andorra.**

an·dra·dite (an/drə·dīt) *n.* One of the common calcium-iron garnets, varying in color from green to black. Compare GARNET. [after J. B. de *Andrada* e Silva, 1763?–1838, Brazilian geologist]

An·drás·sy (än/drä·shē), **Count Gyula**, father 1823–90, son 1860–1929, Hungarian statesmen.

An·dré (än/drā, an/drē), **John**, 1751–80, British major; hanged as a spy during the American Revolution.

An·dre·a del Sar·to (än·drā/ä del sär/tō) See SARTO.

An·dre·a·nof Islands (än/drā·ä/nôf) An island group in the central Aleutians between Rat and Fox islands.

An·dre·ev (än·drā/yef), **Leonid Nikolaievich**, 1871–1919, Russian writer.

An·drew (an/drōō) One of the apostles; brother of Peter: also **Saint Andrew.**

An·drews (an/drōōz), **Roy Chapman**, 1884–1960, U.S. naturalist, explorer, and author.

andro- *combining form* **1.** Man in general: *androcephalous.* **2.** The male sex: *androgen.* **3.** *Bot.* Stamen: anther: *androecium.* [< Gk. *anēr, andros* man]

an·dro·ceph·a·lous (an/drə·sef/ə·ləs) *adj.* Having a human head, especially when joined to the body of an animal, as the Egyptian sphinx. [<ANDRO- + Gk. *kephalē* head]

An·dro·cles (an/drə·klēz) In Roman legend, a slave spared in the arena by a lion because he had once drawn a thorn from its paw. Also **An/dro·clus** (-kləs).

an·dro·clin·i·um (an/drə·klin/ē·əm) *n.* *Bot.* The clinandrium. [< NL < ANDRO- + Gk. *klinē* a bed]

an·droe·ci·um (an·drē/shē·əm, -sē·əm) *n. pl.* **·ci·a** (-shē·ə, -sē·ə) *Bot.* The stamens of a flower collectively. [< NL < ANDRO- + Gk. *oikos* house] **— an·droe/cial** (-shəl) *adj.*

an·dro·gen (an/drə·jən) *n.* *Biochem.* Any of various hormones that control the appearance and development of masculine characteristics, as androsterone, testosterone, etc. Compare ESTROGEN. **— an·dro·gen·ic** (an/drə·jen/ik) *adj.*

an·drog·e·nous (an·droj/ə·nəs) *adj.* *Biol.* Pertaining to or characterized by the production of male offspring.

an·drog·y·nous (an·droj/ə·nəs) *adj.* **1.** Uniting the characteristics of both sexes; hermaphrodite. **2.** *Bot.* Having the male and female flowers in the same cluster. Also **an·drog·y·nal** (an·droj/ə·nəl), **an·drog·gyn·ic** (an/drə·jin/ik). [< L *androgynus* < Gk. *androgynos* hermaphrodite < *anēr, andros* man + *gynē* woman]

an·drog·y·ny (an·droj/ə·nē) *n.* Hermaphroditism.

an·droid (an/droid) *adj.* Having human shape. **— n.** An android robot: also **an·droi·des** (an·droi/dēz). [< NL < *androides* < Gk. *anēr, andros* man + *-eidēs* -like, -shaped] **— an·droi/dal** *adj.*

An·drom·a·che (an·drom/ə·kē) In Greek legend, the wife of Hector and mother of Astyanax, taken captive to Greece after the fall of Troy.

An·drom·e·da (an·drom/ə·də) In Greek mythology, the daughter of Cepheus and Cassiopeia, rescued from a sea monster by Perseus, who then married her. **— n.** A constellation containing the bright star Alpheratz. See CONSTELLATION.

An·dros (an/drəs), **Sir Edmund**, 1637–1714, English colonial governor in America.

An·dros·cog·gin River (an/drə·skog/in) A river in New Hampshire and Maine, flowing SE about 175 miles to the Kennebec River.

an·dro·sphinx (an/drə·sfingks/) *n.* A sphinx with a man's head and a lion's body.

an·dros·ter·one (an·dros/tə·rōn) *n.* *Biochem.* A male sex hormone, C$_{19}$H$_{30}$O$_2$, typically present in the urine of men. [< ANDRO- + STER(OL) + -ONE]

-androus *suffix* **1.** *Bot.* Having a (specified) number or kind of stamens: *diandrous.* **2.** Having a (given) number of husbands: *polyandrous.* [< Gk. *anēr, andros* man]

and so forth Together with more of the same kind, or along the same line; et cetera.

An·dva·ri (än/dwä·rē) In Norse mythology, the dwarf from whom Loki stole the Nibelung treasure and the ring that carried the curse. Also **An/dwa·ri.**

ane (ān) *adj. & n. Scot.* One. [OE *ān*]

-ane[1] *suffix* Used primarily to differentiate words that have a corresponding form in -AN, as *human, humane.* [< L -*anus*]

-ane[2] *suffix Chem.* Denoting an open-chain saturated hydrocarbon compound of the methane series: *pentane.* [An arbitrary formation]

a·near (ə·nir/) *adv. & prep. Poetic* or *Archaic* Near.

an·ec·dot·age (an/ik·dō/tij) *n.* **1.** Anecdotes collectively. **2.** *Informal* Old Age: a pun on *dotage.*

an·ec·do·tal (an/ik·dōt/l) *adj.* Pertaining to, characterized by, or consisting of anecdotes.

an·ec·dote (an/ik·dōt) *n.* A brief account of some incident; a short narrative of an interesting or entertaining nature. [< Med.L *anecdota* < Gk. *anekdota,* neut. pl. of *anekdotos* unpublished < *an-* not + *ekdotos* published < *ekdidonai* to give out, publish < *ek-* out + *didonai* to give]

an·ec·dot·ic (an/ik·dot/ik) *adj.* **1.** Anecdotal. **2.** Habitually telling or given to anecdotes. Also **an/ec·dot/i·cal.**

an·ec·dot·ist (an/ik·dō/tist) *n.* One who collects, publishes, or is given to telling anecdotes.

an·e·cho·ic (an/e·kō/ik) *adj. Physics* Having sound-wave reverberations reduced to a minimum, as a soundproof room. [< AN-[1] + ECHO + -IC]

a·nele (ə·nēl/) *v.t.* **a·neled, a·nel·ing** *Archaic* To anoint, especially as in administering extreme unction. [ME *anelien* < *an-* on + *elien* to oil < OE *ele* oil < L *oleum*]

an·e·lec·tric (an/ə·lek/trik) *adj.* That cannot be electrified by friction.

a·ne·mi·a (ə·nē/mē·ə) *n. Pathol.* A general or local deficiency in the amount of hemoglobin or the number of red corpuscles in the blood, variously caused, and characterized by pallor, loss of energy, and other symptoms: also spelled *anaemia.* [< NL < Gk. *anaimia* < *an-* without + *haima* blood]

a·ne·mic (ə·nē/mik) *adj.* **1.** Of, having, or characterized by anemia. **2.** Pale; without strength or vigor. Also spelled *anaemic.*

anemo- *combining form* Wind: *anemometer.* [< Gk. *anemos*]

a·nem·o·chore (ə·nem/ə·kôr, -kōr) *n. Bot.* A plant distributed by wind.

a·nem·o·graph (ə·nem′ə·graf, -gräf) *n. Meteorol.* An instrument that makes an automatic record of the velocity or force, and sometimes the direction, of the wind. **—a·nem′o·graph′ic** *adj.*

an·e·mog·ra·phy (an′ə·mog′rə·fē) *n. pl.* **·phies** *Meteorol.* The technique of recording automatically the velocity and direction of the wind.

an·e·mol·o·gy (an′ə·mol′ə·jē) *n.* The branch of meteorological science that deals with the wind and related phenomena. **—an·e·mo·log·ic** (an′ə·mə·loj′ik) or **·i·cal** *adj.* [< ANEMO- + LOGY]

an·e·mom·e·ter (an′ə·mom′ə·tər) *n. Meteorol.* An instrument for measuring the velocity of the wind. [< ANEMO- + -METER] **—an·e·mo·met·ric** (an′ə·mō·met′rik) or **·ri·cal** *adj.*

an·e·mo·met·ro·graph (an′ə·mō·met′rə·graf -gräf) *n. Meteorol.* An anemograph, especially one that records both velocity and direction.

an·e·mom·e·try (an′ə·mom′ə·trē) *n. Meteorol.* The technique of determining the velocity and direction of the wind.

ANEMOMETER

a·nem·o·ne (ə·nem′ə·nē) *n.* **1.** Any member of a genus (*Anemone*) of plants of the crowfoot family, having flowers with no petals but showy, multicolored sepals: also called *windflower.* **2.** *Zool.* The sea anemone (which see). [< Gk. *anemōnē* < *anemos* wind]

an·e·moph·i·lous (an′ə·mof′ə·ləs) *adj. Bot.* Fertilized by wind-borne pollen. [< ANEMO- + Gk. *philos* loving]

a·nem·o·scope (ə·nem′ə·skōp) *n. Meteorol.* An instrument for determining the presence and direction of the wind.

an·e·mot·ro·pism (an′ə·mot′rə·piz′əm) *n. Biol.* The tropism of a plant or animal with respect to the velocity and direction of the wind. [< ANEMO- + TROPISM] **—an·e·mo·trop·ic** (an′ə·mō·trop′ik) *adj.*

an·en·ceph·a·lous (an′en·sef′ə·ləs) *adj.* Lacking a brain. [< NL < Gk. *an-* without + *enkephalos* brain]

a·nent (ə·nent′) *prep.* **1.** *Archaic & Scot.* Concerning; in regard to. **2.** *Obs.* or *Dial.* In a line with; on a level with. [OE *onefen, onemn* near to + inorganic *-t*]

an·er·gy (an′ər·jē) *n.* **1.** *Pathol.* Lack of energy. **2.** *Bacteriol.* A diminished sensitivity to specific antigens. Also **an·er·gi·a** (an·ûr′jē·ə). [< NL *anergia* < Gk. *an-* without + *ergon* work] **—an·er·gic** (an·ûr′jik) *adj.*

an·er·oid (an′ə·roid) *adj.* Not containing or using a fluid. **—n.** An aneroid barometer. [< F < Gk. *a-* not + *nēros* wet + -OID]

aneroid barometer An instrument for measuring atmospheric pressure through its effect upon the flexible top of a partially evacuated chamber.

an·es·the·sia (an′is·thē′zhə, -zhē·ə) *n.* **1.** *Pathol.* Partial or total loss of physical sensation, particularly of touch, due to disease or psychic disturbances. **2.** *Med.* Local or general insensibility to pain induced by an anesthetic. Also spelled *anaesthesia:* also **an·es·the·sis** (an′is·thē′sis). [< NL < Gk. *anaisthēsia* insensibility < *an-* without + *aisthēsis* sensation]

an·es·the·si·ol·o·gist (an′is·thē′zē·ol′ə·jist) *n.* A physician specializing in anesthesiology.

an·es·the·si·ol·o·gy (an′is·thē′zē·ol′ə·jē) *n.* The branch of medicine that deals with the study and administration of anesthetics.

an·es·thet·ic (an′is·thet′ik) *n.* A drug, gas, etc., that causes unconsciousness or deadens sensation, as procaine, ether, laughing gas, etc. **— adj. 1.** Pertaining to or like anesthesia. **2.** Producing anesthesia; making insensible to pain. Also spelled *anaesthetic.* [< Gk. *anaisthētos* insensible]

an·es·the·tist (ə·nes′thə·tist) *n.* A person trained to administer anesthetics: also spelled *anaesthetist.*

an·es·the·tize (ə·nes′thə·tīz) *v.t.* **·tized, ·tiz·ing** To render insensible, especially to pain by means of an anesthetic: also spelled *anaesthetize.* **—an·es′the·ti·za′tion** *n.*

an·e·thole (an′ə·thōl) *n.* A colorless crystalline compound, $C_{10}H_{12}O$, obtained from anise and fennel oils, used in perfumery and in medicine as an aromatic carminative. Also **an′e·thol** (-thôl, -thol) [< L *anethum* anise + -OL¹]

A·ne·to (ä·nā′tō), Pi·co de See PICO DE ANETO.

an·eu·rysm (an′yə·riz′əm) *n. Pathol.* A dilatation of the wall of an artery, forming a pulsating sac and usually accompanied by pain due to abnormal pressure, caused principally by syphilis and arteriosclerosis. Also **an′eu·rism.** [< Gk. *aneurysma < aneurynein* to dilate < *ana-* up + *eurys* wide] **— an·eu·rys·mal** (an′yə·riz′məl) or **·ris′mal** *adj.*

a·new (ə·nōō′, ə·nyōō′) *adv.* **1.** Again. **2.** Over again in a different way. [OE *of nīwe*]

an·frac·tu·os·i·ty (an·frak′chōō·os′ə·tē) *n. pl.* **·ties 1.** The state or quality of being anfractuous. **2.** A sinuous channel.

an·frac·tu·ous (an·frak′chōō·əs) *adj.* Having many windings and turnings; tortuous; sinuous. Also **an·frac′tu·ose** (-ōs). [< L *anfractuosus < anfractus* a winding < *an- (ambi-)* around + *frangere* to break]

An·ga·ra (ən·gə·rä′) A river of the Soviet Union, in southern Siberia, flowing 1,151 miles NW from southern Lake Baikal to the Yenisei: also *Upper Tunguska.*

an·ga·ry (ang′gə·rē) *n.* In international law, the right of a belligerent, in case of need, to seize, use, or destroy neutral property, especially ships, subject to claim for full compensation. Also **an·gar·i·a** (ang·gâr′ē·ə). [< F *angarie* < LL *angaria* forced service to a lord < Gk. *angaros* courier]

an·gel (ān′jəl) *n.* **1.** *Theol.* **a** A spiritual being endowed with immortality, attendant upon the Deity; a heavenly guardian, ministering spirit, or messenger. **b** In traditional angelology, one of nine orders of spiritual beings: seraphim, cherubim, thrones, dominations or dominions, virtues, powers, principalities, archangels, and angels. **c** A fallen spiritual being, also immortal. **2.** A conventional representation of an angel, usually a youthful winged human figure in white robes and with a halo. **3.** A guardian spirit; genius. **4.** A person of real or fancied angelic qualities, as of character or beauty. **5.** *Informal* The financial backer of a play, or of any enterprise. **6.** In Christian Science, a message from Truth and Love. **7.** A former English gold coin with the archangel Michael shown on it. [OE *engel* < L *angelus* < Gk. *angelos* messenger; trans. of Hebrew *mal'āk* (*YHWH*) messenger (of Yahweh)]

An·ge·la Me·ri·ci (än′jä·lä mä·rē′chē), **Saint,** 1474-1540, Italian religious; founder of Ursuline order 1535.

An·ge·le·no (an′jə·lē′nō) *n.* A native or inhabitant of Los Angeles.

An·gel Falls (ān′jəl) The world's highest uninterrupted waterfall, in SE Venezuela; 3,212 ft.

an·gel·fish (ān′jəl·fish′) *n. pl.* **·fish** or **·fish·es 1.** A ray-like shark of temperate seas (genus *Squatina*), having very large, winglike pectoral fins. **2.** A fish of warm seas having brilliant coloration, as the porgy. **3.** A butterfly fish (def. 1). **4.** The scalare.

angel food cake A delicate, spongy cake made without shortening or egg yolks. Also **angel cake.**

an·gel·ic (an·jel′ik) *adj.* **1.** Pertaining to of, or consisting of angels; celestial. **2.** Like an angel; pure; beautiful; saintly. Also **an·gel′i·cal.** [< L *angelicus* < Gk. *angelikos* < *angelos.* See ANGEL.] **—an·gel′i·cal·ly** *adv.*

an·gel·i·ca (an·jel′i·kə) *n.* **1.** A fragrant, aromatic plant of a widely distributed genus (*Angelica*) of stout perennial herbs of the parsley family. **2.** The stalks of one species of this plant (*A. archangelica*), often candied and used as a flavoring and an aromatic. **3.** A sweet white or pale-yellow fortified wine. [< Med.L (*herba*) *angelica* the angelic (herb); so called from its use against poisons]

angelica tree Hercules'-club (def. 2).

Angelic Doctor See AQUINAS.

An·gel·i·co (än·jel′i·kō), **Fra,** 1387-1455, Giovanni da Fiesole, Florentine painter and monk: original name **Guido di Pi·e·tro** (dē pē·ā′trō).

An·gell (ān′jəl), **James Burrill,** 1829-1916, U.S. educator. **— James Rowland,** 1869-1949, U.S. psychologist and educator; son of preceding. **— Sir Norman,** 1874-1967, Ralph Norman Angell Lane, English author and pacifist.

an·gel·ol·o·gy (ān′jəl·ol′ə·jē) *n.* The branch of theology that treats of angels. [< *angelo-* (< ANGEL) + -LOGY] **—an·gel·o·log·ic** (ān′jəl·ə·loj′ik) or **·log′i·cal** *adj.*

an·ge·lus (an′jə·ləs) *n. Eccl.* **1.** A devotional prayer used to commemorate the Annunciation. **2.** A bell rung at morning, noon, and night as a call to recite this prayer: also called **angelus bell.** Also **An′ge·lus.** [< L]

an·ger (ang′gər) *n.* **1.** A feeling of sudden and strong displeasure and antagonism directed against the cause of an assumed wrong or injury; wrath; ire. **2.** *Obs.* Affliction; trouble. **3.** *Dial.* Inflammation. **—v.t. 1.** To make angry; enrage. **2.** *Dial.* To inflame; make painful. [< ON *angr* grief]

— Syn. (noun) *Anger, rage, fury, resentment, wrath, indignation,* and *choler* all refer to a feeling of extreme displeasure. *Anger* is a general term and provides no clue as to the direction of this feeling or its means of expression. *Rage* and *fury* refer to the violent expression of *anger,* and often imply a loss of self-control; *fury* is the more extreme, sometimes verging on madness. *Resentment* is directed at the cause of displeasure and describes a sense of grievance; it is more internal and suggests a brooding over injuries rather than an outburst of passion. *Wrath* is angry, often vengeful *resentment,* while *indignation* is justifiable *resentment* felt over wrong done to another or for any other reason. *Ire* was originally a strong word, denoting great *wrath,* but is now more often applied to mere vexation or slight *anger. Choler* is the disposition to be easily angered. Compare ACRIMONY, ENMITY. — (verb) **1.** incense, infuriate. Compare IRRITATE, PIQUE. — **Ant.** forbearance, gentleness, patience, peaceableness, self-control.

an·ger·ly (ang′gər·lē) *adv. Obs.* Angrily.

An·gers (an′jərz, ang′gərz; *Fr.* än·zhā′) A city in western France, on the Maine; pop. 128,533 (1968).

An·ge·vin (an′jə·vin) *adj.* **1.** Of or from Anjou. **2.** Of or pertaining to the Plantagenet kings of England or to the period of their rule, particularly from 1154 to 1204. **— n. 1.** A native or inhabitant of Anjou. **2.** A member of the royal house of Anjou. Also **An′ge·vine** (-vin, -vīn). [< F]

an·gi·na (an·ji′nə, an′jə·nə) *n. Pathol.* **1.** Any disease characterized by spasmodic suffocation, as quinsy, croup, etc. **2.** Angina pectoris. [< L, quinsy < *angere* to choke]

angina pec·to·ris (pek′tə·ris) *Pathol.* A syndrome of insufficient coronary circulation, characterized by paroxysmal pain below the sternum and usually associated with changes in the arterial system. [< NL, angina of the chest]

angio- *combining form* **1.** *Bot.* Seed vessel: *angiosperm.* **2.** *Med.* Blood vessel; lymph vessel: *angiology.* Also, before vowels, **angi-.** [< Gk. *angeion* case, vessel, capsule]

an·gi·ol·o·gy (an'jē·ol'ə·jē) *n.* That part of anatomy that relates to blood and lymph vessels. [< ANGIO- + -LOGY]

an·gi·o·ma (an'jē·ō'mə) *n.* *pl.* **-mas** or **·ma·ta** (-mə·tə) *Pathol.* A tumor or abnormal formation resulting from dilated blood or lymph vessels. [< NL < ANGI(O)- + -OMA] **— an·gi·om·a·tous** (an'jē·om'ə·təs) *adj.*

an·gi·o·sperm (an'jē·ə·spûrm') *n.* Any of a class (*Angiospermae*) of vascular plants having the seeds contained in a closed seed vessel, as the apple, rose, oak, maple, etc.: distinguished from *gymnosperm.* **— an'gi·o·sper'mal, an'gi·o·sper'ma·tous** (-spûr'mə·təs), **an'gi·o·sper'mous** *adj.*

Ang·kor (ang'kôr) An assemblage of ruins in NW Cambodia; site of **Angkor Thom** (tôm), an ancient Khmer capital, and **Angkor Wat** or **Angkor Vat** (wät), the best-preserved Khmer temple.

Angl. **1.** Anglian. **2.** Anglican. **3.** Anglicized.

an·gle¹ (ang'gəl) *v.i.* **·gled, ·gling** **1.** To fish with a hook and line. **2.** To try to get something, gain an end, etc., slyly or artfully: with *for.* **—** *n.* *Obs.* A fishhook; fishing tackle. [< OE *angel* fishhook]

an·gle² (ang'gəl) *n.* **1.** *Geom.* **a** The figure formed by the divergence of two straight lines from a common point or of two or more planes from a common straight line: also called *plane angle.* **b** The space between these lines or surfaces. **c** The amount of divergence of these lines or surfaces, measured in degrees.

ANGLES
1. Acute: *aeb, bec*; Right: *aec, ced*; Obtuse: *bed.* 2. Dihedral.

2. A projecting corner, as of a building. **3.** A secluded place; nook. **4.** The point of view or aspect from which something is regarded. **5.** *U.S. Slang* Special selfish motive or interest. **— critical angle** **1.** *Optics* The least angle of incidence at which a ray is totally reflected. **2.** *Aeron.* The angle of attack at which the airflow striking the undersurface of an airplane changes abruptly, causing similar changes in lift and drag. **— gliding angle** *Aeron.* The angle formed with the horizontal by the path of an airplane gliding in still air. **—** *v.* **an·gled, an·gling** *v.t.* **1.** To move or turn at an angle or by angles: to *angle* a ball to avoid a hazard. **2.** *Informal* To impart a particular bias or interpretation to, as a story or report. **—** *v.i.* **3.** To proceed or turn itself at an angle or by angles: The road *angled* up the hill. [< F < L *angulus* a corner, angle]

An·gle (ang'gəl) *n.* **1.** A member of a Germanic tribe that migrated from southern Denmark to Britain in the fifth and sixth centuries and founded the kingdoms of East Anglia, Mercia, and Northumbria. From their descendants the country came to be called England (Angle-land). **2.** A national of any of the kingdoms in the parts of Britain settled by this tribe. [< L *Anglus,* sing. of *Angli* < Gmc.]

an·gled (ang'gəld) *adj.* **1.** Having angles. **2.** Set or placed at an angle.

angle iron A piece of iron in the form of an angle, especially a right angle, for joining or strengthening beams, girders, and corners, or as part of an iron structure. Also **an'gle-i'ron** (ang'gəl·ī'ərn).

an·gle·me·ter (ang'gəl·mē'tər) *n.* A clinometer (which see).

angle of attack *Aeron.* The acute angle between the chord of an airfoil and the line of the undisturbed relative airflow.

angle of incidence **1.** *Physics* The angle relative to the perpendicular drawn from the point of impact at which an object, beam of light, or any form of radiant energy strikes a surface. **2.** *Aeron.* The angle of attack.

angle of view *Optics* The angle formed by two lines drawn from the edges of an object or scene to the center of a lens.

angle of yaw *Aeron.* The angle between the longitudinal axis and the line of flight of an aircraft, viewed from above.

angle plate *Mech.* One of two metal plates that may be securely bolted at right angles to each other as a support for tools or in machine-working.

an·gle·pod (ang'gəl·pod') *n.* A vine (genus *Vincetoxicum*) of the milkweed family, especially *V. gonocarpos* of the southern United States, bearing angular pods.

an·gler (ang'glər) *n.* **1.** One who fishes with rod, hook, and line. **2.** One of a family (*Lophiidae*) of fishes having a wide, froglike mouth and antennalike filaments attached to the head with which it angles for its prey: also called *frogfish.*

An·gle·sey (ang'gəl·sē) An island and former county of NW Wales; 275 sq. mi.; pop. 58,210 (est. 1971) chief town, Llangefni. Also **An'gle·sea.**

an·gle·site (ang'glə·sīt) *n.* A lustrous white orthorhombic lead sulfate, PbSO₄. [after *Anglesey,* where first found]

an·gle·worm (ang'gəl·wûrm') *n.* An earthworm, commonly used as bait on fishhooks.

An·gli·a (ang'glē·ə) The Latin name for ENGLAND.

An·gli·an (ang'glē·ən) *adj.* Pertaining to the Angles or their country. **—** *n.* The Northumbrian and Mercian dialects of Old English. Abbr. *Angl.*

An·glic (ang'glik) *n.* A simplified form of English evolved for use as an auxiliary international language by R. E. Zachrisson, 1880–1937, Swedish linguist. **—** *adj.* Anglian.

An·gli·can (ang'glə·kən) *adj.* Pertaining to or characteristic of the Church of England, or of the churches that agree with it in faith and order. **—** *n.* **1.** A member of the Church of England, or of any church derived from it. **2.** A High Churchman. Abbr. *Angl.* [< Med.L *Anglicanus* < *Anglicus* English < L *Angli* the Angles, the English]

Anglican Church **1.** The Church of England. **2.** A body of churches, including the Protestant Episcopal Church, mostly derived from the Church of England and in communion with it: also **Anglican Communion.**

An·gli·can·ism (ang'glə·kən·iz'əm) *n.* The doctrine, discipline, and practice of the Anglican Church.

An·gli·ce (ang'glə·sē) *adv.* In English; according to the usage of the English language: Napoli, *Anglice* Naples. [< Med.L]

An·gli·cism (ang'glə·siz'əm) *n.* **1.** An idiom or turn of phrase peculiar to the English language. **2.** A Briticism. **3.** The state or quality of being English.

An·gli·cist (ang'glə·sist) *n.* An authority on or student of English language and literature.

An·gli·cize (ang'glə·sīz) *v.* **·cized, ·ciz·ing** *v.t.* **1.** To give an English form, style, or idiom to. **—** *v.i.* **2.** To acquire some English trait or peculiarity; become like the English. Also *Brit.* **An'gli·cise.** **— An'gli·ci·za'tion** *n.*

An·gli·fy (ang'glə·fī) *v.t. & v.i.* **·fied, ·fy·ing** To Anglicize.

an·gling (ang'gling) *n.* The act or art of fishing with a hook, line, and rod.

An·glist (ang'glist) *n.* An authority on England.

Anglo- *combining form* English; English and: used in various adjectives and nouns indicating relations between the countries concerned or natives of them: *Anglo-Indian.* [< L *Anglus* an Angle, an Englishman]

An·glo-A·mer·i·can (ang'glō·ə·mer'ə·kən) *adj.* **1.** Of or pertaining to England and America or the relations of the peoples of both: *Anglo-American* trade. **2.** Of or pertaining to the English people who have settled in America. **—** *n.* A native of England or a descendant of a native of England who has settled in the United States or in America.

An·glo-Boer War (ang'glō·bōr', -bôr', -bōōr') The Boer War. See table for WAR.

An·glo-Ca·na·di·an (ang'glō·kə·nā'dē·ən) *n.* An English-speaking Canadian. **—** *adj.* Of or pertaining to Anglo-Canadians.

An·glo-Cath·o·lic (ang'glō·kath'ə·lik, -kath'lik) *n.* **1.** A member of the Anglican Church who stresses its Catholic character and traditions. **2.** A High Churchman. **—** *adj.* **1.** Of or pertaining to Anglo-Catholics, their principles, or their practices. **2.** High-Church. **— An·glo-Cath'o·li·cism** (ang'glō·kə·thol'ə·siz'əm) *n.*

An·glo-E·gyp·tian Sudan (ang'glō·i·jip'shən) A former condominium coextensive with the (Republic of the) SUDAN.

An·glo-French (ang'glō·french') *adj.* **1.** Pertaining jointly to the English and French, or to their countries. **2.** Relating to Anglo-French. **—** *n.* The dialect of Old French used in England from the Norman Conquest through the 14th century, especially that used in the later part of this period. Compare ANGLO-NORMAN. Abbr. *AF, A.F.*

An·glo-In·di·an (ang'glō·in'dē·ən) *adj.* **1.** Pertaining to or between England and India. **2.** Of the Anglo-Indians or their speech. **—** *n.* **1.** An Englishman living in India. **2.** A person of mixed English and Indian parentage. **3.** The vocabulary, consisting of Anglicized Hindi or other Indian words, developed by British subjects in civil and military service in India: also called *Hobson-Jobson.*

An·glo·ma·ni·a (ang'glō·mā'nē·ə) *n.* Overfondness for or imitation of English manners, speech, institutions, or customs. **— An'glo·ma'ni·ac** (-ak) *n.*

An·glo-Nor·man (ang'glō·nôr'mən) *adj.* Pertaining to the Normans who settled in England after the Norman Conquest, their descendants, or their language. **—** *n.* **1.** One of the Norman settlers in England after the Norman Conquest. **2.** The dialect of Old French used in England from the Norman Conquest through the 14th century, especially that used in the earlier part of this period. Compare ANGLO-FRENCH. Abbr. *AN, A.N., A.-N.*

An·glo·phile (ang'glə·fīl, -fil) *n.* A lover of England or its people, customs, institutions, or manners. **—** *adj.* Of or like Anglophiles. Also **An'glo·phil** (-fil).

An·glo·phobe (ang'glə·fōb) *n.* One who has Anglophobia. **—** *adj.* Of or like Anglophobes.

An·glo·pho·bi·a (ang'glə·fō'bē·ə) *n.* Hatred or dread of England or English customs, people, manners, or institutions. — **An′glo·pho′bic** (-fō′bik, -fob′ik) *adj.*

An·glo·phone (ang′glə-fōn′) *n. Often l.c. Canadian.* A native speaker of English. Compare FRANCOPHONE.

An·glo-Sax·on (ang′glō-sak′sən) *n.* **1.** A member of one of the Germanic tribes (Angles, Saxons, and Jutes) that conquered Britain in the fifth and sixth centuries. **2.** A member of the nation descended from these peoples that dominated England until the Norman Conquest. **3.** Their West Germanic language; Old English. **4.** A person of English nationality or descent. **5.** *Informal* Simple, unadorned English. **6.** *Informal* The short, vulgar words of the language. **7.** Loosely, the modern English language. — *adj.* Of or pertaining to the Anglo-Saxons, their language, customs, or descendants. Abbr. (n. defs. 1, 2, 3, and adj.) *AS, AS., A.S.*

Anglo-Saxon Chronicle A chronological prose history of England in Old English from early Christian times to 1154, especially those recensions to 892 usually accredited to Alfred the Great. Also **Anglo-Saxon Annals.**

An·go·la (ang-gō′lə) A Republic in western Africa; 481,351 sq. mi.; pop. 5,900,000 (est. 1972); capital, Luanda: formerly *Portuguese West Africa.* See map of (Republic of) SOUTH AFRICA.

An·go·ra (ang-gôr′ə, -gō′rə) *n.* **1.** An Angora goat. **2.** The long, silky hair of this goat or the cloth woven from it. **3.** An imitation of Angora cloth made of rabbit hair. **4.** A shawl, cloth, etc., made of Angora wool or its imitations. **5.** An Angora cat.

An·go·ra (ang-gôr′ə, -gō′rə, ang′gə-rə) See ANKARA.

Angora cat A variety of cat, originally from Angora (Ankara), with long, silky hair.

Angora goat A goat, originally from Angora (Ankara), reared for its long, silky hair.

Angora wool The hair of the Angora goat.

an·gos·tu·ra bark (ang′gəs-tŏor′ə, -tyŏor′ə) A bark from a South American tree (*Galipea officinalis*), used in the preparation of a tonic and flavoring. Also **an′gos·tu′ra.** [after *Angostura*, former name of Ciudad Bolivar, Venezuela]

Angostura Bitters A bitter aromatic tonic and flavoring prepared from angostura bark and other roots, herbs, etc.: a trade name. Also **angostura bitters.**

an·gry (ang′grē) *adj.* **an·gri·er, an·gri·est 1.** Feeling, showing, or excited by anger; indignant: *angry* with (or at) his brother; *angry* at (or about) an insult. **2.** Showing signs of anger; wrathful: an *angry* tone. **3.** Seeming to be in anger: *angry* skies. **4.** Badly inflamed: an *angry* sore. — **an·gri·ly** (ang′grə-lē) *adv.* — **an′gri·ness** *n.*
— Syn. 1, 2. irate, enraged, infuriated, incensed, mad, sore.

angst (ängst) *n.* A feeling of dread or anxiety. [< G]

ang·strom (ang′strəm) *n.* A linear unit equal to 10⁻⁸ centimeter or 3.937 × 10⁻⁹ inch, used for minute measurements, as of wavelengths of light. Also **angstrom unit.** Abbr. *A, Å., a.u., å.u., A.U., Å.U.* [after A. J. *Ångström*]

Ång·ström (ang′strəm, Sw. ŏng′strœm), **Anders Jonas,** 1814-74, Swedish physicist.

an·gui·form (ang′gwə-fôrm) *adj.* Shaped like a snake. [< L *anguis* snake + -FORM]

An·guil·la (ang-gwil′ə) See ST. CHRISTOPHER NEVIS, AND ANGUILLA.

an·guil·li·form (ang-gwil′ə-fôrm) *adj.* Having the form of an eel. [< L *anguilla* eel + -FORM]

an·guine (ang′gwin) *adj.* Of, pertaining to, or like a snake. [< L *anguinus* < *anguis* snake]

an·guish (ang′gwish) *n.* Excruciating mental or bodily pain; agony; torture. — *v.t. & v.i.* To affect or suffer with anguish. [< OF *anguisse* < L *angustia* tightness, difficulty < *angustus* narrow, tight]
— Syn. See SORROW. — Ant. See synonyms under PLEASURE.

an·gu·lar (ang′gyə-lər) *adj.* **1.** Having, forming, or constituting an angle or angles; sharp-cornered. **2.** Measured by an angle: *angular* distance. **3.** Pertaining to angles. **4.** Bony; gaunt. **5.** Awkward or ungraceful. **6.** Of a crabbed or unaccommodating disposition. [< L *angularis* < *angulus* corner, angle] — **an′gu·lar·ly** *adv.*
— Syn. 4. raw-boned, thin. Compare LEAN².

an·gu·lar·i·ty (ang′gyə-lar′ə-tē) *n. pl.* **·ties 1.** The state or condition of being angular: also **an′gu·lar·ness. 2.** *pl.* Angular outlines or corners.

an·gu·late (ang′gyə-lit, -lāt) *adj.* Having angles; angular: used chiefly in botany: *angulate* leaves. Also **an′gu·lat′ed.** — *v.t. & v.i.* **·lat·ed, ·lat·ing** To make or become angular. [< L *angulatus*, pp. of *angulare* to make angular < *angulus* corner, angle] — **an′gu·late·ly** *adv.*

an·gu·la·tion (ang′gyə-lā′shən) *n.* **1.** The making of angles. **2.** An angular formation or position.

An·gus (ang′gəs) A county in eastern Scotland; 874 sq. mi.; pop. 277,279 (1969); county seat, Forfar: formerly *Forfar.*

ANGUS Air National Guard of the United States.

Angus Og (ōg) In Irish mythology, Angus the Young, god of love and beauty; son of Dagda. Also **Angus mac án Og.**

an·gus·tate (ang-gus′tāt) *adj.* Compressed; narrowed. [< L *angustatus*, pp. of *angustare* to narrow < *angustus* narrow]

an·ha·lo·nine (an′hə-lō′nēn, -nin) *n.* A crystalline alkaloid, $C_{12}H_{15}O_3N$, obtained from mescal, sometimes used in medicine as a cardiac stimulant. Also **an′ha·lo′nin** (-nin). [< NL *Anhalonium*, former name of a genus of cacti]

an·hi·dro·sis (an′hi-drō′sis) *n. Pathol.* Partial or complete lack of perspiration. Also **an·i·dro·sis** (an′i-drō′sis). [< NL < Gk. *an-* without + *hidrōs* perspiration] — **an′hi·drot′ic** (-drot′ik) *adj.*

an·hin·ga (an-hing′gə) *n.* The snakebird. [< Tupi]

An·hwei (än′hwā′) A Province in eastern China; 56,371 sq. mi.; pop. 33,560,000 (est. 1957); capital, Hofei. Also **An′hui′.**

an·hy·drate (an-hī′drāt) *v.t.* **·drat·ed, ·drat·ing** To dehydrate (which see).

an·hy·dride (an-hī′drīd, -drid) *n. Chem.* **1.** Any organic or inorganic compound that has been dehydrated. **2.** A compound formed from another compound, especially an acid or base, by the removal of one or more molecules of water, the process being generally reversible. [See ANHYDROUS]

an·hy·drite (an-hī′drīt) *n.* An orthorhombic calcium sulfate, $CaSO_4$, found as a whitish or light-colored mineral.

an·hy·drous (an-hī′drəs) *adj. Chem.* Pertaining to or designating a compound that has no water in its composition, especially one having no water of crystallization. [< Gk. *anydros* waterless < *an-* without + *hydōr* water]

a·ni (ä′nē) *n.* A bird of the cuckoo family (*Crotophaga ani*), generally black with metallic reflections, ranging from Florida southward. [< Tupi]

an·il (an′il) *n.* **1.** A West Indian leguminous shrub (*Indigofera suffruticosa*). **2.** The indigo dye made from this plant. [< F < Pg. < Arabic *al-nīl* the blue < Skt.]

an·ile (an′īl, ā′nīl, an′il) *adj.* Like an old woman; weak or feeble-minded. [< L *anilis* < *anus* old woman] — **a·nil·i·ty** (ə-nil′ə-tē) *n.*

an·i·line (an′ə-lin, -līn) *n. Chem.* A colorless oily compound, $C_6H_5NH_2$, the base of many coal-tar dyes, resins, and varnishes, originally distilled from indigo, but now chiefly made from nitrobenzene. Also called *phenylamine.* — *adj.* Made of, derived from, or pertaining to aniline. Also **an·i·lin** (an′ə-lin). [< ANIL + -INE²]

anim. Animato.

an·i·ma (an′ə-mə) *n.* **1.** The vital principle; source of energy and creative action; soul; life. **2.** In Jung's psychology, the unconscious apprehension of woman in man. [< L]

an·i·mad·ver·sion (an′ə-mad-vûr′zhən, -shən) *n.* Criticism or censure; a censorious comment or reflection: with *on* or *upon.* [< L *animadversio, -onis* < *animadvertere.* See ANIMADVERT.] — **an′i·mad·ver′sive** (-siv) *adj.* — **an′i·mad·ver′sive·ness** *n.*
— Syn. blame, reprehension, reflection, disapproval. Compare REPROOF. — Ant. praise, approbation, commendation, approval.

an·i·mad·vert (an′ə-mad·vûrt′) *v.i.* **1.** To comment critically, usually in an adverse sense: with *on* or *upon.* **2.** *Obs.* To take note. [< L *animadvertere* to take notice of < *animus* mind + *advertere* to turn to < *ad-* to, toward + *vertere* to turn]

an·i·mal (an′ə-məl) *n.* **1.** A sentient living organism typically capable of voluntary motion and sensation: distinguished from *plant.* **2.** Any such creature as distinguished from man; a beast or brute. **3.** A bestial human being. **4.** *pl.* Domestic quadrupeds. **5.** Any creature but a bird, fish, or insect. — *adj.* **1.** Of, characteristic of, derived from, or resembling animals. **2.** Pertaining to the physical rather than the spiritual nature of man; carnal; sensual: *animal* appetites. [< L, a living being < *anima* breath, soul, life]
— Syn. (noun) **2.** *Animal, brute,* and *beast* are all applied to sentient organic beings other than man. *Animal* merely makes the distinction. *Brute* stresses the inferiority of the lower *animals* to man, while *beast* suggests the complete subservience of the lower *animals* to their appetites. — (adj.) See BRUTE.

animal charcoal Boneblack.

animal crackers Small, sweetened cookies made in the shape of various animals.

an·i·mal·cu·la (an′ə-mal′kyə-lə) Plural of ANIMALCULUM.

an·i·mal·cu·lae (an′ə-mal′kyə-lē) Erroneous plural of *animalcula,* thought of as a feminine singular noun.

an·i·mal·cule (an′ə-mal′kyōol) *n.* **1.** An animal of microscopic smallness, usually found in ponds or stagnant water, as an ameba. **2.** *Obs.* Any small animal, as a gnat. Also **an′i·mal′cu·lum** (-kyə-ləm). [< L *animalculum,* dim. of *animal* animal] — **an′i·mal′cu·lar** (-kyə-lər) *adj.*

animal glue Glue (def. 1).

animal husbandry The branch of agriculture specializing in the breeding, raising, and care of farm animals.

an·i·mal·ism (an′ə-məl-iz′əm) *n.* **1.** The state or condition of a mere animal, actuated by sensual appetites only. **2.** Animal activity. **3.** The belief or doctrine that man is entirely animal, having no soul or spirit.

an·i·mal·ist (an′ə-məl-ist) *n.* An adherent to the doctrine of animalism.

an·i·mal·is·tic (an′ə-məl-is′tik) *adj.* **1.** Pertaining to animalism. **2.** Resembling an animal.

an·i·mal·i·ty (an′ə-mal′ə-tē) *n.* **1.** The nature or qualities of an animal. **2.** Animal life; the animal kingdom. **3.** The merely animal nature of man, as distinguished from the moral and spiritual.

an·i·mal·ize (an′ə-məl-īz′) *v.t.* **·ized, ·iz·ing 1.** To render brutal; sensualize. **2.** To change into animal matter, especially by digestive assimilation. **3.** *Obs.* To give animal form to. — **an·i·mal·i·za·tion** (an′ə-məl-ə-zā′shən, -ī-zā′-) *n.*

animal kingdom One of the three great divisions of nature, embracing all animal organisms. Compare MINERAL KINGDOM, VEGETABLE KINGDOM.

an·i·mal·ly (an′ə-məl-ē) *adv.* Physically, as distinguished from spiritually or mentally.

animal magnetism 1. Mesmerism. **2.** Magnetic personal qualities. **3.** Sensualism.

animal spirits The buoyancy of good health; joyous energy.

animal starch Glycogen.

an·i·mate (*v.* an′ə-māt; *adj.* an′ə-mit) *v.t.* **·mat·ed, ·mat·ing 1.** To impart life to; make alive. **2.** To move to action; incite; inspire: He was *animated* by love. **3.** To produce activity or energy in: The wind *animated* the flags. — *adj.* **1.** Possessing animal life; living. **2.** Full of life; vivacious; lively: also **an′i·mat′ed** (-mā′tid). [< L *animatus*, pp. of *animare* to fill with breath, make alive < *anima* breath, soul] — **an′i·mat′ed·ly** *adv.*

animated cartoon See CARTOON (def. 3).

an·i·ma·tion (an′ə-mā′shən) *n.* **1.** The act of imparting life, or the state of possessing life. **2.** The quality of being lively or quick; vivacity. **3.** The process and technique of preparing animated cartoons.

an·i·ma·tive (an′ə-mā′tiv) *adj.* Enlivening; inspiring.

a·ni·ma·to (ä′nē-mä′tō) *Music adj.* Lively; animated. — *adv.* In an animated manner. Abbr. *anim.* [< Ital.]

an·i·ma·tor (an′ə-mā′tər) *n.* **1.** One who or that which animates. **2.** An artist who prepares animated cartoons. Also **an′i·ma·ter.**

an·i·mé (an′ə-mā, -mē) *n.* A hard, fossilized resin obtained from the stem of an East African tree (*Hymenaea courbaril*), used in making flavorings, varnishes, and lacquers. [< F < Sp., prob. < native name]

an·i·mism (an′ə-niz′əm) *n.* **1.** The belief in the existence of spirit or soul, as distinct from matter. **2.** The doctrine that inanimate objects and natural phenomena possess a soul. [< L *anima* soul] — **an′i·mist** *n.* — **an′i·mis′tic** *adj.*

an·i·mos·i·ty (an′ə-mos′ə-tē) *n. pl.* **·ties** Active and vehement enmity; hatred. — **Syn.** See ENMITY. [< L *animositas, -tatis* high spirit, boldness < *animus* soul, mind, spirit]

an·i·mus (an′ə-məs) *n.* **1.** Hostile feeling; animosity. **2.** The animating thought or purpose; intention. [< L]

an·i·on (an′ī′ən) *n. Chem.* The electronegative ion of an electrolyte, which moves toward the anode in electrolysis: opposed to *cation.* [< Gk. *anion,* ppr. neut. of *anienai* < *ana-* up + *ienai* to go] — **an′i·on′ic** (-on′ik) *adj.*

an·ise (an′is) *n.* A small South European and North African plant (*Pimpinella anisum*) that furnishes aniseed. **2.** Aniseed. [< OF *anis* < L *anisum* < Gk. *anison*]

an·i·seed (an′i·sēd′) *n.* The fragrant seed of the anise plant, used in cookery and medicine.

an·i·sei·ko·ni·a (an·ī′sī-kō′nē-ə, an·is′ī-) *n. Pathol.* A disorder of vision in which the images perceived by the eyes differ in size. [< NL < Gk. *anisos* unequal + *eikōn* image] — **an′i·sei·kon′ic** (-kon′ik) *adj.*

an·i·sette (an′ə-zet′, -set′) *n.* A cordial made from or flavored with aniseed. [< F]

aniso- *combining form* Unequal; dissimilar: *anisogamy.* See ISO-. [< Gk. *anisos* unequal]

an·i·sog·a·my (an′ī·sog′ə-mē) *n. Biol.* A union of gametes similar in general type but unequal in size: opposed to *isogamy.* [< ANISO- + -GAMY] — **an′i·sog′a·mous** *adj.*

an·i·sole (an′ə-sōl) *n. Chem.* A colorless liquid compound, C_7H_8O, used as an insecticide and in the manufacture of perfumes. [< L *anisum* anise + -OLE¹]

an·i·so·mer·ic (an·ī′sə-mer′ik) *adj. Chem.* Composed of the same elements but in differing proportions: opposed to *isomeric.*

an·i·som·er·ous (an′ī-som′ər-əs) *adj. Bot.* Having an unequal number of parts in different floral whorls; unsymmetrical. [< ANISO- + -MEROUS]

an·i·so·met·ric (an·ī′sə-met′rik) *adj.* **1.** Not isometric. **2.** *Mineral.* Dissimilar in the direction of the different axes, as some crystals.

an·i·so·me·tro·pi·a (an·ī′sə-mə-trō′pē-ə) *n. Pathol.* Inequality in the refracting power of the eyes.

an·i·so·phyl·ly (an·ī′sə-fil′ē) *n. Bot.* The property of having leaves of different size and character on different sides of plagiotropic shoots. — **an·i′so·phyl′lous** *adj.*

an·i·so·trop·ic (an·ī′sə-trop′ik) *adj.* **1.** *Physics* Having different properties in different directions. Also *aelotropic, eolotropic.* **2.** *Bot.* Responding unequally to external influences, as plant organs. Compare ISOTROPIC. — **an·i·sot·ro·py** (an′ī·sot′rə-pē), **an′i·sot′ro·pism** *n.*

An·jou (an′jōō, *Fr.* äṅ-zhōō′) A family of French nobles, originally ruling the duchy of Anjou, who succeeded to the English throne in 1154 upon the accession of Henry II, son of Geoffrey IV of Anjou. See PLANTAGENET.

Anjou A former province of western France; divided in 1790 into several departments.

An·ka·ra (äng′kə-rə, ang′-) The capital of Turkey since 1923, located in central Anatolia; pop. 905,660 (1965): formerly *Angora.*

an·ker·ite (ang′kər-īt) *n.* A mineral resembling dolomite, composed of a white, red, or grayish calcium-magnesium-iron carbonate crystallizing in the hexagonal system. [after M. J. *Anker,* Austrian mineralogist]

ankh (angk) *n.* In Egyptian art and mythology, a tau cross having a looped top; the ansate cross: an emblem of generation. For illustration see CROSS. [< Egyptian *ānkh* life, soul]

An·king (än′king′) A city on the Yangtze; former capital of Anhwei Province, China; pop. about 120,000: formerly *Hwaining.*

an·kle (ang′kəl) *n.* **1.** The joint connecting the foot and the leg. **2.** The part of the leg between the foot and the calf near the ankle joint. [ME *ankel* < OE *anclēow*]

an·kle·bone (ang′kəl-bōn′) *n.* The talus. Also **ankle bone.**

an·klet (ang′klit) *n.* **1.** An ornament or fetter for the ankle. **2.** A short sock reaching just above the ankle.

an·kus (ang′kəs, -kash) *n.* An elephant goad consisting of a sharp spike and hook set on a short staff. Also **an·kush** (ang′kŭsh). [< Hind. < Skt. *ankusa*]

ankylo- *combining form* Bent; crooked: in anatomy, referring to adhesion of bones: *ankylosis.* [< Gk. *ankylos* crooked]

an·ky·lose (ang′kə-lōs) *v.t. & v.i.* **·losed, ·los·ing** To unite or join by ankylosis: also spelled *anchylose.*

an·ky·lo·sis (ang′kə-lō′sis) *n.* **1.** *Anat.* The fusing of bones or parts of bones. **2.** *Pathol.* The abnormal adhesion of bones, especially those forming a joint; stiffening of a joint. Also spelled *anchylosis.* [< NL < Gk. *ankylōsis < ankyloein* to bend < *ankylos* crooked] — **an′ky·lot′ic** (-lot′ik) *adj.*

an·ky·los·to·mi·a·sis (ang′kə-los′tə-mī′ə-sis) See ANCYLOSTOMIASIS.

an·lace (an′lis) *n.* A broad, two-edged dagger or short sword. Also **an′las.** [< OF *alenas, alenaz* dagger < *alesne* awl < Gmc.]

an·la·ge (än′lä-gə) *n. pl.* **·gen 1.** Basis; foundation; rudiment. **2.** *Biol.* The first recognizable traces of an organ or part seen as an accumulation of cells in a developing embryo. Also **An′la·ge.** [< G]

ann. 1. Annals. **2.** Anni (L, years). **3.** Annual. **4.** Annuity.

an·na (an′ə) *n.* A former coin of India and Pakistan equal to one sixteenth of a rupee. [< Hind. *ānā*]

an·na·berg·ite (an′ə-bûr′gīt) *n.* A green, hydrous nickel arsenate crystallizing in the monoclinic system: also called *nickelbloom.* [after *Annaberg,* town in eastern Germany]

an·nal (an′əl) *n.* The record of a single year; an item or entry in a book of annals.

an·nal·ist (an′əl-ist) *n.* A writer of annals; a historian. — **an′nal·is′tic** *adj.*

an·nals (an′əlz) *n.pl.* **1.** A record of events in their chronological order, year by year. **2.** History or records in general. **3.** A periodical publication of discoveries, transactions, etc. Abbr. *ann.* — **Syn.** See HISTORY. [< L *annales* (*libri*) yearly (records), chronicles < *annus* year]

An·nam (ə-nam′, an′am) A former empire and French protectorate of Indochina; now divided between North and South Vietnam: also *Anam.*

An·na·mese (an′ə-mēz′, -mēs′) *n. pl.* **An·na·mese 1.** A native or inhabitant of Annam. **2.** Formerly, the Vietnamese language. Also spelled *Anamese.* — *adj.* Of or pertaining to Annam, its inhabitants, or their language.

An·na·mite (an′ə-mīt) *n. & adj.* Annamese.

An·nap·o·lis (ə-nap′ə-lis) The capital of Maryland, on the Severn River, near Chesapeake Bay; seat of the United States Naval Academy; pop. 29,592.

Annapolis Royal A port town on an arm of the Bay of Fundy, Nova Scotia; pop. 765: formerly *Port Royal.*

An·na·pur·na (ä′nə-pŏŏr′nə) A mountain of the Himalayas, in north central Nepal; 26,502 ft.

Ann Ar·bor (an′ är′bər) A city in SE Michigan; pop. 99,797.

an·nates (an′āts, -its) *n.pl.* Formerly, in the Roman Catholic Church, the first year's revenue of bishops and certain other ecclesiastics, paid to the Pope. [< MF *annate* < Med.L *annata* a year's work < L *annus* year]

an·nat·to (ä-nä′tō) See ANATTO.

Anne (an), 1665–1714, queen of Great Britain and Ireland 1702–14.

Anne, Saint Traditionally, the mother of the Virgin Mary.

an·neal (ə-nēl′) v.t. **1.** To reduce the brittleness and increase the toughness of, as glass and various metals, by heating and then slowly cooling. **2.** To toughen; render enduring, as the will. **3.** *Archaic* To fix in place by heating and then cooling, as colors or enamel. [OE *onælan* to burn]

Anne Boleyn See BOLEYN.

an·ne·lid (an′ə-lid) *Zool. adj.* Of or belonging to a phylum (*Annelida*) of segmented invertebrates, including the earthworm, leeches, marine worms, etc. — *n.* An annelid invertebrate. Also **an·nel·i·dan** (ə-nel′ə-dən). [< NL < F *annélide* < *anneler* to arrange in rings < OF *annel* a ring < L *annellus* for *anellus*, dim. of *anulus* a ring]

Anne of Austria, 1601–66, consort of Louis XIII of France; regent 1643–61 for her son, Louis XIV.

Anne of Bohemia, 1366–94, wife of Richard II of England.

Anne of Cleves (klēvz), 1515–57, fourth wife of Henry VIII.

an·nex (v. ə-neks′; n. an′eks) v.t. **1.** To add or append, as an additional or minor part, to existing possessions; affix. **2.** To attach, as an attribute, condition, or consequence. — **Syn.** See ADD. — *n.* **1.** An addition to a building; also, a nearby building used in addition to the main building. **2.** An addition to a document; addendum. **3.** *Mil.* An appendix to a combat order specifying the details prescribed in a given field or subject: an artillery *annex*. Also *Brit.* **an′nexe**. [< F *annexer* < L *annexus*, pp. of *annectere* to tie together < *ad-* to + *nectere* to tie] — **an·nex′a·ble** *adj.*

an·nex·a·tion (an′ek·sā′shən) n. **1.** The act of annexing. **2.** That which is added or attached. Also **an·nex′ment**.

an·ni·hi·la·ble (ə-nī′ə-lə·bəl) *adj.* That can be annihilated.

an·ni·hi·late (ə-nī′ə-lāt) v.t. **·lat·ed, ·lat·ing** **1.** To destroy utterly. **2.** To annul; abolish; make void. — **Syn.** See ABOLISH. [< L *annihilatus*, pp. of *annihilare* < *ad-* to + *nihil* nothing] — **an·ni′hi·la·tive** *adj.* — **an·ni′hi·la·tor** *n.*

an·ni·hi·la·tion (ə-nī′ə·lā′shən) n. **1.** The act of annihilating. **2.** Utter extinction.

An·nis·ton (an′is·tən) A city in NE Alabama; pop. 31,533.

an·ni·ver·sa·ry (an′ə·vûr′sər·ē) n. pl. **·ries** **1.** A day in the year on the date of which an event occurred in some preceding year; especially, *U.S.*, the day on whose date one's wedding took place. **2.** A commemorative observance or celebration on such occasion. — *adj.* **1.** Recurring annually or at the same date every year. **2.** Pertaining to or occurring on an anniversary. [< L *anniversarius* < *annus* year + *versus*, pp. of *vertere* to turn]

Anniversary Day Australia Day (which see).

an·no Dom·i·ni (an′ō dom′ə·nī) *Latin* In the year of our Lord or of the Christian era. Abbr. *A.D.*

an·no mun·di (an′ō mun′dī) *Latin* In the year of the world: used in chronology, with the supposed date of creation set at 4004 B.C. Abbr. *A.M.*

an·no·tate (an′ō·tāt) v.t. & v.i. **·tat·ed, ·tat·ing** To provide (a text, etc.) with explanatory or critical notes. [< L *annotatus*, pp. of *annotare* < *ad-* to + *notare* to note, mark < *nota* mark] — **an′no·ta·tive** *adj.* — **an′no·ta·tor** *n.*

an·no·ta·tion (an′ō·tā′shən) n. **1.** The act of annotating. **2.** A critical or explanatory note; a comment.

an·nounce (ə-nouns′) v.t. **·nounced, ·nounc·ing** **1.** To make known publicly or officially; proclaim. **2.** To give notice of the approach or appearance of: to *announce* guests. **3.** To make known to the senses. **4.** To serve as the announcer for, as a radio program. [< OF *anoncer, anoncier* < L *annuntiare* < *ad-* to + *nuntiare* to report < *nuntius* messenger] — **Syn.** **1.** declare, promulgate, broadcast. See ASSERT.

an·nounce·ment (ə-nouns′mənt) n. **1.** The act of announcing. **2.** That which is announced. **3.** A printed declaration or publication.

an·nounc·er (ə-noun′sər) n. **1.** One who announces. **2.** A person who identifies the station from which a radio or television program is broadcast, introduces the performers, etc.

an·noy (ə-noi′) v.t. **1.** To be troublesome to; bother; irritate. **2.** To do harm to or injure continuously or by repeated acts. — *n. Obs.* An annoyance. [< OF *anuier, anoier*, ult. < L *in odio* in hatred] — **an·noy′er** *n.*

an·noy·ance (ə-noi′əns) n. **1.** That which annoys; a nuisance. **2.** The act of annoying. **3.** The feeling incident to being annoyed; vexation: to show one's *annoyance*.

an·noy·ing (ə-noi′ing) *adj.* Vexatious; troublesome. — **an·noy′ing·ly** *adv.* — **an·noy′ing·ness** *n.*

an·nu·al (an′yōō·əl) *adj.* **1.** Returning, performed, or occurring every year. **2.** Pertaining to the year; reckoned by the year. **3.** *Bot.* Lasting or living only one year. — *n.* **1.** A book or pamphlet issued once a year. **2.** *Bot.* A plant living for a single year or season. Abbr. *ann.* [< OF *annuel* < L *annualis* yearly < *annus* year] — **an′nu·al·ly** *adv.*

annual parallax See under PARALLAX.

annual ring A layer of wood produced by a tree during a single season's growth, visible in cross section.

an·nu·i·tant (ə-nōō′ə·tənt, ə·nyōō′-) n. One receiving or entitled to receive, an annuity.

an·nu·i·ty (ə-nōō′ə·tē, ə·nyōō′-) n. pl. **·ties** **1.** An allowance or income paid yearly or at specified periods. **2.** The right to receive such an allowance, or the duty of paying it. **3.** The return from an investment of capital, with interest, in a series of yearly payments. Abbr. *ann.* [< OF *annuite* < Med.L *annuitas, -latis* < L *annus* year]

an·nul (ə-nul′) v.t. **·nulled, ·nul·ling** **1.** To render null or declare invalid, as a law or a marriage. **2.** To reduce to nothing; put an end to. [< OF *anuller* < LL *annullare* < L *ad-* to + *nullus* none] — **an·nul′la·ble** *adj.*

— **Syn. 1.** *Annul, nullify, cancel, abate, void, vacate, quash, abrogate, repeal, rescind,* and *revoke* mean to make or declare to be invalid, and usually refer to the action of some competent legal authority. *Annul* and *nullify* are general terms; *nullify* may also be used in an extralegal sense. A marriage is *annulled*; a law may be *nullified* by a new law, or by the effects of popular defiance. The other synonyms listed differ chiefly in technical usage, rather than in meaning. Typically, we *cancel* a lease, *abate* or *void* a writ, *vacate* an injunction, *quash* an indictment, *abrogate* a treaty, *repeal* a law, *rescind* a ruling, and *revoke* a will. Compare ABOLISH. — **Ant.** confirm, enact, establish, maintain, sustain, uphold.

an·nu·lar (an′yə·lər) *adj.* Formed like a ring; ring-shaped. [< L *annularis* < *annulus, anulus* ring] — **an′nu·lar·ly** *adv.*

annular eclipse *Astron.* A solar eclipse in which a narrow ring of the sun is visible beyond the dark mass of the moon.

annular ligament *Anat.* A ligament encircling the wrist or ankle.

an·nu·late (an′yə·lit, -lāt) *adj.* Furnished with rings; ringed, as an annelid. Also **an′nu·lat′ed**. [< L *annulatus* < *annulus* a ring]

an·nu·la·tion (an′yə·lā′shən) n. **1.** The act of forming rings. **2.** A ringlike formation or segment.

an·nu·let (an′yə·lit) n. **1.** A small ring. **2.** *Archit.* A small, projecting molding encircling the capital of a pillar. [< L *annulus* a ring + -ET]

an·nul·ment (ə-nul′mənt) n. **1.** The act of annulling. **2.** An invalidation, as of a marriage.

an·nu·lose (an′yə·lōs) *adj.* Composed of or furnished with rings. [< L *annulus* a ring + -OSE¹]

an·nu·lus (an′yə·ləs) n. pl. **·li** (-lī) or **·lus·es** A ringlike part, body, or space. [< L, a ring]

an·nun·ci·ate (ə-nun′shē·āt, -sē-) v.t. **·at·ed, ·at·ing** To announce. [< L *annuntiatus*, pp. of *annuntiare*. See ANNOUNCE.]

an·nun·ci·a·tion (ə-nun′sē·ā′shən, -shē-) n. The act of announcing, or that which is announced; proclamation.

An·nun·ci·a·tion (ə-nun′sē·ā′shən, -shē-) n. *Eccl.* **1.** The announcement of the Incarnation to the Virgin Mary by an angel. *Luke* i 28–38. **2.** The festival (March 25) commemorating this event. **3.** A work of art portraying this event.

an·nun·ci·a·tor (ə-nun′shē·ā′tər, -sē-) n. **1.** An announcer. **2.** An electrical indicator used in hotels, etc., that shows a number or name when a bell is rung.

An·nun·zio (dän·nōōn′tsyō), **Gabriele D′** See D'ANNUNZIO.

an·nus mi·rab·i·lis (an′əs mə·rab′ə·lis) *Latin* Wonderful year. Abbr. *A.M.*

An·nus Sanc·tus (an′əs sangk′təs) Jubilee (def. 2). [< L, holy year]

an·ode (an′ōd) n. *Electr.* **1.** The positive electrode toward which anions migrate in an electrolytic cell. **2.** The plate of an electron tube toward which electrons are attracted. Abbr. *a.* [< Gk. *anodos* a way up < *ana-* up + *hodos* road, way]

an·od·ic (an·od′ik) *adj.* **1.** Pertaining to an anode. **2.** Proceeding upward.

an·o·dize (an′ə·dīz) v.t. **·dized, ·diz·ing** To oxidize or coat the surface of (a metal) by making it the anode of an electrolytic bath.

an·o·dyne (an′ə·dīn) *adj.* Having power to allay pain; soothing. — *n. Med.* Anything that relieves pain or soothes. [< L *anodynus* < Gk. *anōdynos* < *an-* without + *odynē* pain]

a·noint (ə-noint′) v.t. **1.** To smear with oil or any soft substance; apply oil or ointment to. **2.** To put oil on as a sign of consecration, as in a religious ceremony. [< OF *enoint*, pp. of *enoindre* < L *inungere* < *in-* on + *ungere* to smear] — **a·noint′er** *n.* — **a·noint′ment** *n.*

an·o·lyte (an′ə·līt) n. In electrolysis, that portion of the electrolyte nearest the anode. [< ANO(DE) + (ELECTRO)LYTE]

a·nom·a·lous (ə-nom′ə·ləs) *adj.* Deviating from the common rule; irregular; exceptional; abnormal. [< L *anomalus* < Gk. *anōmalos* < *an-* not + *homalos* even < *homos* same] — **a·nom′a·lous·ly** *adv.* — **a·nom′a·lous·ness** *n.*

a·nom·a·ly (ə-nom′ə·lē) n. pl. **·lies** **1.** Deviation from rule, type, or form; irregularity. **2.** Anything anomalous. **3.** *Astron.* **a** The angular distance of a planet from its perihelion, as seen from the sun. **b** The angle measuring apparent irregularities in the movement of a planet. [< L *anomalia* < Gk. *anōmalia* < *anōmalos*. See ANOMALOUS.] — **a·nom·a·lis·tic** (ə-nom′ə·lis′tik) or **·ti·cal** *adj.*

an·o·mie (an′ə·mē) n. An anxious awareness that the prevailing values of society have little or no personal relevance to one's condition; also, a condition of society characterized by the relative absence of norms or moral standards. [< F < Gk. *anomia* lawlessness < *a-* without (See A-⁴) + *nomos* law] — **a·nom·ic** (ə-nom′ik) *adj.*

a·non (ə-non′) *adv.* **1.** In a little while; soon. **2.** At another time; again. **3.** *Archaic* Immediately. [OE *on ān* in one]

anon. Anonymous.

an·o·nym (an′ə·nim) n. **1.** An anonymous person or writer. **2.** A pseudonym.

a·non·y·mous (ə-non′ə-məs) *adj.* **1.** Having no acknowledged name; bearing no name. **2.** Of unknown authorship or agency. *Abbr. a., anon.* [< Gk. *anōnymos* < *an-* without + *onoma, onyma* name] **— a·non′y·mi·ty** (an′ə-nim′-ə-tē), **a·non′y·mous·ness** *n.* **— a·non′y·mous·ly** *adv.*

a·noph·e·les (ə-nof′ə-lēz) *n.* Any of a genus (*Anopheles*) of mosquitoes carrying the malaria parasite, especially *A. gambiae.* [< NL < Gk. *anōphelēs* harmful] **— a·noph·e·line** (ə-nof′ə-lĭn, -lĭn) *adj.*

a·no·rak (ä′nə-räk) *n.* A warm, hooded jacket, worn in arctic climates. [< Eskimo *anoraq*]

an·o·rex·i·a (an′ə-rek′sē-ə) *n. Med.* Loss of appetite. Also **an′o·rex′y.** [< NL < Gk. *anorexia* < *an-* without + *orexis* appetite] **— an·o·rec·tic** (an′ə-rek′tĭk), **an′o·rec′tous** *adj.*

an·or·thic (an-ôr′thĭk) *adj.* Triclinic. [< Gk. *an-* not + *orthos* straight]

an·or·thite (an-ôr′thīt) *n. Mineral.* A triclinic feldspar, $CaAl_2Si_2O_8$, found in igneous rocks. [< AN-¹ + Gk. *orthos* straight + -ITE¹] **— an·or·thit·ic** (an′ôr-thit′ĭk) *adj.*

an·or·tho·site (an-ôr′thə-sīt) *n. Geol.* A granular igneous rock composed essentially or wholly of plagioclase, which in the typical anorthosite is labradorite. [< AN-¹ + Gk. *orthos* straight + -ITE¹]

an·os·mi·a (an-oz′mē-ə, -os′-) *n. Pathol.* Loss of the sense of smell. [< NL < Gk. *an-* without + *osmē* smell] **— an·os′mic** *adj.*

an·oth·er (ə-nuth′ər) *adj.* **1.** A further; an additional; one more. **2.** Not the same; distinct; different: *another* man. **3.** Different in substance while of the same or similar character. **— pron. 1.** An additional one; one more: Take *another.* **2.** A different one. **3.** A similar or identical one. ♦ *Another* was originally written as two words, *an other.* As a pronoun its plural is *others.* [< *an other*]

an·ox·i·a (an-ok′sē-ə) *n. Pathol.* A condition characterized by a defective or insufficient oxygen supply to the body tissues. [< AN-¹ + OX(YGEN) + -IA] **— an·ox′ic** *adj.*

ans. Answer; answered.

an·sa (an′sə) *n. pl.* **·sae** (-sē) *Astron. pl.* The handlelike extremities of the rings of Saturn. [< L, a handle]

an·sate (an′sāt) *adj.* Having a handle. Also **an′sat·ed.** [< L *ansatus < ansa* a handle]

ansate cross A cross in the form of a T with a loop at the top; ankh: also called *crux ansata.* For illustration see CROSS.

An·schluss (än′shlŏos) *n.* German Political union.

An·selm (an′selm), **Saint**, 1033–1109, theologian and archbishop of Canterbury born in Italy.

an·ser·ine (an′sə-rīn, -sər·in) *adj.* **1.** Pertaining or belonging to a subfamily (*Anserinae*) of web-footed birds, the geese. **2.** Resembling a goose; gooselike, as the human skin when chilled. **3.** Silly; stupid. Also **an′ser·ous.** **— n.** An organic substance, $C_{10}H_{16}O_3N_4$, obtained from the muscles of birds, fishes, and reptiles. [< L *anserinus < anser* a goose]

an·swer (an′sər, än′-) *v.i.* **1.** To reply or respond, as by words or actions. **2.** To be responsible or accountable: with *for:* I will *answer* for his honesty. **3.** To serve the purpose; prove sufficient. **4.** To correspond or match, as in appearance: with *to:* This man *answers* to your description. **— v.t. 5.** To speak, write, or act in response or reply to. **6.** To be sufficient for; fulfill. **7.** To pay for; discharge, as a debt or liability: to *answer* damages. **8.** To conform or correspond to; match: to *answer* a description. **9.** *Law* To reply favorably to, as a petition or petitioner. **— to answer back** To reply emphatically or rudely; talk back, as in contradiction. **— n. 1.** A reply, especially one that is definite and final. **2.** Any action in return or in kind; retaliation. **3.** The result of a calculation or solution, as of a problem in mathematics. **4.** *Law* The defense of a defendant in an action to charges filed against him. **5.** *Music* The restatement of a musical theme or phrase by a different voice or instrument. [OE *andswarian*] **— an′swer·er** *n.*

— Syn. (noun) **1.** *Answer, reply, response, rejoinder,* and *retort* refer primarily to words said in return to a question, call, charge, etc. When a question is asked, any words or actions in return may be called an *answer*: a prompt *answer* to a letter, his *answer* was an uppercut to the jaw. An *answer* in the form of a statement appropriate to the question asked is a *reply*. A *response* is the reaction to a stimulus; hence, an *answer* to an urgent question or appeal, or to a set question: a *response* to a cry for help, the *responses* of a litany. A *reply* to a *reply* is a *rejoinder*, while a *retort* is a sharp *answer*, as to an accusation or criticism.

an·swer·a·ble (an′sər-ə-bəl, än′-) *adj.* **1.** Liable to be called to account (*for* anything or *to* someone); responsible. **2.** That may be answered. **3.** Corresponding; suitable: with *to.* **— an′swer·a·ble·ness** *n.* **— an′swer·a·bly** *adv.*

ant (ant) *n.* A small, social, hymenopterous insect (family *Formicidae*), widely distributed in communities consisting typically of winged males, females winged till after pairing, and wingless neuters or workers. For illustration see INSECTS. (injurious) [OE *æmete.* Doublet of EMMET.]

an′t (ant, änt, änt) *Archaic* **1.** Are not. **2.** *Brit.* Am not. **3.** *Illit. & Dial.* Is not; has not; have not.

ant- Var. of ANTI-.

ant. 1. Antenna. **2.** Antiquarian. **3.** Antiquity. **4.** Antonym(s).

-ant *suffix* **1.** In the act or process of doing (what is denoted by the stem): used to form adjectives with nearly the meaning of the present participle: *militant, litigant,* etc. **2.** One who or that which does (what is indicated by the stem): forming nouns of participial origin: *servant,* one who serves. [< F *-ant* < L *-ans* (*-antis*), *-ens* (*-entis*), present participial suffixes]

an·ta (an′tə) *n. pl.* **·tae** (-tē) *Archit.* A pilaster formed at the termination of a wall. [< L *antae* (pl.) < *ante* before]

ANTA American National Theatre and Academy.

ant·ac·id (ant-as′id) *adj.* Correcting acidity. **— n.** An alkaline remedy for stomach acidity. [< ANT- + ACID]

An·tae·us (an-tē′əs) In Greek legend, a wrestler, invincible while in contact with the earth; crushed by Hercules, who lifted him into the air. **— An·tae′an** *adj.*

an·tag·o·nism (an-tag′ə-niz′əm) *n.* **1.** Mutual opposition or resistance; hostility. **2.** An opposing principle or force. **— Syn.** See ENMITY. [< Gk. *antagōnisma < antagōnizesthai.* See ANTAGONIZE.]

an·tag·o·nist (an-tag′ə-nist) *n.* **1.** An adversary; opponent. **2.** *Anat.* A muscle that acts counter to another muscle. **— Syn.** See ENEMY.

an·tag·o·nis·tic (an-tag′ə-nis′tik) *adj.* Opposed; hostile. **— an·tag′o·nis′ti·cal·ly** *adv.*

an·tag·o·nize (an-tag′ə-nīz) *v.* **·nized, ·niz·ing** *v.t.* **1.** To make unfriendly; make an enemy of. **2.** To struggle against; oppose. **3.** To counteract; neutralize. **— v.i. 4.** To act antagonistically. [< Gk. *antagōnizesthai* to struggle against < *anti-* against + *agōnizesthai* to struggle, strive]

An·ta·ki·ya (än′tä-kē′yä) The Arabic name for ANTIOCH. Also *Turkish* **An·ta·kya** (än′tä-kyä′).

ant·al·gic (ant-al′jik) *adj.* Tending to alleviate pain. **— n.** An anodyne. [< ANT- + Gk. *algos* pain]

ant·al·ka·li (ant-al′kə-lī) *n. pl.* **·lis** or **·lies** Any substance able to neutralize alkalis, or counteract an alkaline tendency in the system. [< ANT- + ALKALI] **— ant·al·ka·line** (-lĭn, -lin) *adj. & n.*

ant·aph·ro·dis·i·ac (ant′af′rə-diz′ē-ak) *adj.* Counteracting or reducing sexual desire or potency. **— n.** An antaphrodisiac drug, food, etc. [< ANT- + APHRODISIAC]

Ant·arc·tic (ant-ärk′tik, -är′tik) *adj.* Of or relating to the South Pole, or the regions within the Antarctic Circle. **— the Antarctic** The regions around the South Pole. [< L *antarcticus* < Gk. *antarktikos* southern < *anti-* opposite + *arktos* the Bear (a northern constellation), the north]

Ant·arc·ti·ca (ant-ärk′tə-kə, -är′-) A continent surrounding the South Pole, extending at certain points north of the Antarctic Circle and almost entirely covered by a vast ice sheet; over 5,000,000 sq. mi. Also **Antarctic Continent.**

Antarctic Archipelago See PALMER ARCHIPELAGO.

Antarctic Circle The parallel at 66°33′ south latitude; the boundary of the South Frigid Zone.

Antarctic Ocean Loosely, the ocean within the Antarctic Circle and bordering Antarctica.

Antarctic Zone The region, including most of Antarctica, enclosed by the Antarctic Circle.

An·tar·es (an-târ′ēz) *n.* A giant red star, one of the 20 brightest, 0.92 magnitude; Alpha in the constellation Scorpio. See STAR. [< Gk. *Antarēs < anti-* similar to + *Arēs* Mars; with ref. to its color]

ant bear A large edentate mammal (*Myrmecophaga jubata*), of tropical America feeding chiefly on ants. It has a long snout, protrusible tongue, powerful digging claws, and a shaggy, black-banded coat.

ANT BEAR
(8 feet long;
2 feet high)

ant bird Any of numerous small birds (family *Formicariidae*), of South America, that feed upon ants. Also called **ant catcher.**

ant cow An aphid insect that yields a honeylike fluid on being stroked on the abdomen by the antennae of ants.

an·te (an′tē) *v.t. & v.i.* **·ted** or **·teed, ·te·ing 1.** In poker, to put up (one's stake) before the cards are dealt. **2.** *Slang* To pay (one's share). **— n. 1.** In poker, the stake put up before receiving the hand, or before drawing new cards. **2.** *Slang* The amount required as a share. [< L, before]

ante- *prefix* **1.** Before in time or order: *antenatal.* **2.** Before in position; in front of: *antechamber.* [< L *ante* before]

ant·eat·er (ant′ē′tər) *n.* **1.** The ant bear. **2.** One of several other mammals that feed partly on ants, as the tamandua, echidna, or aardvark. **3.** An ant bird.

an·te·bel·lum (an′tē-bel′əm) *adj.* Before the war; especially, before the Civil War in the United States. [< L *ante bellum* before the war]

an·te·cede (an′tə-sēd′) *v.t. & v.i.* **·ced·ed, ·ced·ing** To go or come before, as in rank, place, or time; precede. [< L *antecedere < ante-* before + *cedere* to go]

an·te·ce·dence (an'tə-sēd'ns) n. 1. A going before; precedence; priority. 2. Astron. The apparent retrograde motion of a planet. Also **an'te·ce'den·cy. — Syn.** See PRECEDENCE.
an·te·ce·dent (an'tə-sēd'nt) adj. 1. Going or being before; preceding; anterior: often with to. 2. Geol. Having a course across a fold or fault of the earth's surface: contrasted with consequent. — n. 1. One who or that which precedes or goes before. 2. Gram. The word, phrase, or clause to which a pronoun, especially a relative pronoun, refers. 3. pl. The past events, circumstances, etc., of a person's life; also, ancestry. 4. Math. The first term of a ratio; in a proportion, the first and third terms. 5. Logic The condition on which a hypothetical proposition depends. [< L antecedens, -entis, ppr. of antecedere. See ANTECEDE.] — **an'te·ce'dent·ly** adv. — **Syn.** (adj.) 1. previous, earlier, preceding. — (noun) See CAUSE. — **Ant.** consequent, subsequent, later.
an·te·ces·sor (an'tə-ses'ər) n. Rare A predecessor (which see). [< L < antecedere. See ANTECEDE.]
an·te·cham·ber (an'ti-chām'bər) n. A room serving as an entranceway to another room.
an·te·choir (an'ti-kwīr') n. An enclosed, or partially enclosed, portion of a chapel in front of the choir.
an·te·date (an'ti-dāt') v.t. **·dat·ed, ·dat·ing** 1. To be or occur earlier than; precede in time. 2. To assign to a date earlier than the actual one, as a document; date back. 3. To cause to happen at an earlier date; accelerate.
an·te·di·lu·vi·an (an'ti-di-lōō'vē-ən) adj. 1. Pertaining to the times, events, etc., before the Flood. 2. Antiquated; primitive. — n. 1. A person, animal, or plant that lived before the Flood. 2. An old or old-fashioned person. [< ANTE- + L diluvium deluge]
an·te·fix (an'ti-fiks) n. pl. **·fix·es** or **·fix·a** (-fik'sə) Archit. An upright ornament at the eaves of a tiled roof, to hide the joints between two rows of tiles. [< L antefixum, orig. neut. sing. of antefixus, pp. of antefigere < ante- before + figere to fix, place] — **an'te·fix'al** adj.
an·te·lope (an'tə-lōp) n. pl. **·lope** or **·lopes** 1. Any of various Old World hollow-horned ruminants (family Bovidae), including the gazelle, chamois, gnu, etc. 2. Leather made from the hide of such an animal. 3. U.S. The pronghorn. [< OF antelop < Med.L antalopus < LGk. antholops]
an·te me·rid·i·em (an'tē mə-rid'ē-em) Latin Before the sun reaches the meridian, counted from the preceding midnight; before noon. Abbr. a.m., A.M. — **an'te·me·rid'i·an** adj.
an·te mor·tem (an'tē môr'təm) Latin Before death.
an·te·mun·dane (an'ti-mun'dān) adj. Existing or occurring before the creation of the world: also premundane. [< ANTE- + L mundus world]
an·te·na·tal (an'ti-nāt'l) adj. Prenatal (which see).
an·ten·na (an-ten'ə) n. pl. **·ten·nae** (-ten'ē) for def. 1, **·ten·nas** for def. 2 1. Entomol. One of the paired, lateral, movable, jointed appendages on the head of an insect or other arthropod. 2. Telecom. A system of wires, a rod or rods, reflecting disk, etc., for transmitting or receiving electromagnetic waves. Abbr. ant. [< NL < L, a yard for a sail]
an·ten·nule (an-ten'yōōl) n. Zool. A small antenna or antennalike appendage. Also **an·ten·nu·la** (an-ten'yə-lə).
an·te·past (an'ti-past, -päst) n. 1. Foretaste. 2. Obs. An appetizer. [< ANTE- + L pastus food]
an·te·pen·di·um (an'ti-pen'dē-əm) n. pl. **·di·a** (-dē-ə) Eccl. A covering for the front of an altar; frontal. [< Med.L < L ante before + pendere to hang]
an·te·pe·nult (an'ti-pē'nult, -pi'nult') n. The last syllable but two in a word. Also **an·te·pe·nul·ti·ma** (an'ti-pi-nul'tə-mə). [< L (syllaba) antepaenultima]
an·te·pe·nul·ti·mate (an'ti-pi-nul'tə-mit) adj. Pertaining to the last but two of any series. — n. The antepenult.
an·te·ri·or (an-tir'ē-ər) adj. 1. Antecedent in time; prior; earlier: ages anterior to the Flood. 2. Farther front or forward in space. 3. Anat. a In the lower animals, situated relatively near the head. b In man, situated on the ventral side of the body. 4. Bot. Turned away from the main axis or stem, as the side of a leaf or flower; lower. [< L, compar. of ante before] — **an·te'ri·or·ly** adv. — **Syn.** 1. previous, preceding. Compare ANTECEDENT. — **Ant.** subsequent, later; posterior, hind.
antero- combining form Anterior; placed in front. [< L anterus (assumed form)]
an·te·room (an'ti-rōōm', -rŏŏm') n. A waiting room; antechamber.
an·te·type (an'ti-tīp') n. A preceding type; prototype.
an·te·ver·sion (an'ti-vûr'zhən, -shən) n. Pathol. A turning or tipping forward, as of the uterus. [< L anteversio, -onis < antevertere. See ANTEVERT.]
an·te·vert (an'ti-vûrt') v.t. Pathol. To displace by turning or tipping forward, as the uterus. [< L antevertere < ante- before + vertere to turn]
anth- Var. of ANTI-.
ant·he·li·on (ant-hē'lē-ən, an-thē'-) n. pl. **·li·a** (-lē-ə) Astron. A faint halo or series of diffraction rings about the shadow of an object cast by a low sun upon a cloud or fog bank. Compare PARHELION. [< NL < Gk. anthēlion < anti- against + hēlios sun]
ant·he·lix (ant-hē'liks, an-thē'-) n. pl. **ant·hel·i·ces** (ant-

hel'ə-sēz, an-thel'-) Anat. The inner curved ridge on the cartilage of the external ear: also antihelix. [< ANT- + HELIX]
ant·hel·min·tic (ant'hel-min'tik) adj. Med. Tending to expel intestinal worms. — n. A vermifuge. Also **ant'hel·min'thic** (-thik). [< ANT- + Gk. helmins, -inthos worm]
an·them (an'thəm) n. 1. A song or hymn of gladness or praise: a national anthem. 2. A musical composition, usually set to words from the Bible. — v.t. To celebrate with an anthem. [OE antefn < LL antiphona < Gk. antiphōna, lit., things sounding in response < anti- against + phōnē voice. Doublet of ANTIPHON.]
an·the·mi·on (an-thē'mē-ən) n. pl. **·mi·a** (-mē-ə) A honeysuckle or palm-leaf pattern in decorative designs, common in Greek art: also called honeysuckle ornament. [< Gk., flower]
an·ther (an'thər) n. Bot. The pollen-bearing part of a stamen. For illustration see FLOWER. [< F anthère < L anthera, medicine obtained from flowers < Gk. anthēra, fem. of anthēros flowery < anthos flower]

ANTHEMION

an·ther·id·i·um (an'thə-rid'ē-əm) n. pl. **·ther·id·i·a** (-thə-rid'ē-ə) Bot. The male sexual organ in cryptogams. Also **an·ther·id** (an'thər-id). [< NL, dim. of Gk. anthēros flowery] — **an'ther·id'i·al** adj.
an·ther·o·zo·id (an'thər-ə-zō'id, an'thər-ə-zoid') n. Bot. The male cell in cryptogams, provided with vibratory cilia, and produced in an antheridium. Also **an'ther·o·zo'oid** (-zō'oid). [< anthero- (< ANTHER) + ZOOID] — **an'ther·o·zo'i·dal** (zō'ə-dəl-), **an'ther·o·zo·oi'dal** (-zō-oid'l) adj.
an·the·sis (an-thē'sis) n. Bot. The time or process of expansion in a flower; full bloom of a flower. [< NL < Gk. anthēsis full bloom < antheein to bloom]
ant·hill (ant'hil') n. A mound of earth, leaves, etc., which ants heap up around the entrance to their nests. Also **ant hill.**
antho- combining form Flower: anthophore. [< Gk. anthos a flower]
an·tho·cy·a·nin (an'thō-sī'ə-nin) n. The water-soluble coloring matter of flowers, leaves, and other parts of plants that imparts red, violet, or blue, colors: also called cyanin, erythrophyll. [< ANTHO- + Gk. kyanos blue]
an·tho·di·um (an-thō'dē-əm) n. pl. **·di·a** (-dē-ə) Bot. The flowering head of plants of the composite family. [< NL < Gk. anthōdēs flowerlike < anthos a flower]
an·thoid (an'thoid) adj. Like a flower.
an·thol·o·gize (an-thol'ə-jīz) v. **·gized, ·giz·ing** v.i. 1. To make an anthology or anthologies. — v.t. 2. To put into an anthology or make an anthology of.
an·thol·o·gy (an-thol'ə-jē) n. pl. **·gies** A collection of choice or representative literary extracts. [< L anthologia < Gk. anthologia a garland, collection of poems < anthos flower + legein to gather] — **an·tho·log·i·cal** (an'thə-loj'i-kəl) adj. — **an·thol'o·gist** n. — **Syn.** chrestomathy, treasury, garland.
An·tho·ny (an'thə-nē, -tə-), **Saint**, 250?–356?, Egyptian hermit and monk; founder of monastic life.
An·tho·ny (an'thə-nē), **Susan Brownell**, 1820–1906, U.S. suffragist.
Anthony of Padua, Saint, 1195–1231, Franciscan friar, theologian, and preacher.
an·tho·phore (an'thə-fôr, -fōr) n. Bot. A stipe formed by the prolongation of an internode between the calyx and the corolla.
an·thoph·o·rous (an-thof'ər-əs) adj. Flower-bearing. [< Gk. anthophoros < anthos flower + pherein to bear]
an·tho·zo·an (an'thə-zō'ən) Zool. adj. Of or belonging to a class (Anthozoa) of sessile marine coelenterates, growing singly or in colonies, including the sea anemones and corals. — n. An anthozoan coelenterate. Also **an'tho·zo'on**. [< NL < ANTHO- + Gk. zōion animal] — **an'tho·zo'ic** adj.
an·tho·zo·oid (an'thə-zō'oid) n. An individual polyp in a compound colony.
an·thra·cene (an'thrə-sēn) n. Chem. A blue, fluorescent crystalline compound, $C_{14}H_{10}$, obtained in coal-tar distillation and used in manufacturing alizarin dyes. [< Gk. anthrax, -akos coal + -ENE]
an·thra·cite (an'thrə-sīt) n. Mineral coal of nearly pure carbon that burns slowly and with little flame: also called hard coal. [< L anthracites < Gk. anthrakitēs coallike < anthrax coal] — **an·thra·cit·ic** (an'thrə-sit'ik) adj.
an·thrac·nose (an-thrak'nōs) n. A destructive disease of plants usually manifested by sharply defined discolored spots and caused by various fungi. [< Gk. anthrax, -akos coal, carbuncle + nosos disease]
an·thra·coid (an'thrə-koid) adj. Resembling anthrax.
an·thra·qui·none (an'thrə-kwi-nōn') n. Chem. A yellow crystalline compound, $C_{14}H_8O_2$, made from anthracene by oxidation with chromic and sulfuric acid, used in the manufacture of alizarin dyes and certain laxatives. [< Gk. anthrax, -akos coal + QUINONE]
an·thrax (an'thraks) n. pl. **·thra·ces** (-thrə-sēz) 1. Pathol. An infectious, malignant disease of man and some animals, caused by Bacillus anthracis, often with carbuncles. 2. A carbuncle caused by this bacillus. [< Gk., coal, carbuncle]

anthropo- *combining form* Man; human: *anthropometry.* Also, before vowels, **anthrop-.** [< Gk. *anthrōpos* man]
an·thro·po·cen·tric (an′thrə·pō·sen′trik) *adj.* **1.** Regarding man as the central fact or final aim of the universe, or of any system. **2.** Based on comparison with man.
an·thro·pog·e·ny (an′thrə·poj′ə·nē) *n.* The branch of anthropology that treats of the origin and development of man, either individually (ontogeny) or ethnically (phylogeny). Also **an·thro·po·gen·e·sis** (an′thrə·pō·jen′ə·sis). [< ANTHROPO- + -GENY]
an·thro·poid (an′thrə·poid) *adj.* **1.** Like a human being in form or other characteristics; manlike: said of apes, as the gorilla, chimpanzee, and orang-utan. **2.** *Zool.* Of or pertaining to a suborder (*Anthropoidea*) of primate mammals, including man, apes, and monkeys. Also **an′thro·poi′dal.** — *n.* An ape.
anthropol. or **anthrop.** Anthropological; anthropology.
an·thro·pol·o·gy (an′thrə·pol′ə·jē) *n.* **1.** The science treating of the physical, social, material, and cultural development of man, his origin, evolution, geographic distribution, ethnology, and communal forms. **2.** The detailed study of the customs, beliefs, folkways, etc., of an ethnic group, especially on a comparative basis. [< ANTHROPO- + -LOGY] — **an·thro·po·log·i·cal** (an′thrə·pə·loj′i·kəl) or **·log′ic** *adj.* — **an′thro·po·log′i·cal·ly** *adv.* — **an′thro·pol′o·gist** *n.*
an·thro·pom·e·try (an′thrə·pom′ə·trē) *n.* The science and technique of human measurements, especially of anatomical and physiological features. [< ANTHROPO- + -METRY] — **an·thro·po·met·ric** (an′thrə·pō·met′rik) or **·ri·cal** *adj.*
an·thro·po·mor·phic (an′thrə·pō·môr′fik) *adj.* Of or characterized by anthropomorphism.
an·thro·po·mor·phism (an′thrə·pō·môr′fiz·əm) *n.* The ascription of human form or characteristics to a deity, or to any being or thing not human. Compare ZOOMORPHISM. — **an′thro·po·mor′phist** *n.*
an·thro·po·mor·phize (an′thrə·pō·môr′fīz) *v.t. & v.i.* **·phized, ·phiz·ing** To ascribe human traits or qualities (to).
an·thro·po·mor·pho·sis (an′thrə·pō·môr′fə·sis) *n.* Transformation into human shape.
an·thro·po·mor·phous (an′thrə·pō·môr′fəs) *adj.* Having or resembling human form. [< Gk. *anthrōpomorphos* < *anthrōpos* man + *morphē* form, shape]
an·thro·pon·o·my (an′thrə·pon′ə·mē) *n.* The science of the laws that regulate the development of man in relation to environment and to other organisms. Also **an·thro·po·nom·ics** (an′thrə·pō·nom′iks). [< ANTHROPO- + Gk. *nomos* law] — **an′thro·po·nom′i·cal** *adj.*
an·thro·pop·a·thy (an′thrə·pop′ə·thē) *n.* The attributing of human emotions or passions to gods or to natural objects. Also **an′thro·pop′a·thism.** [< Med.L *anthropopathia* < Gk. *anthrōpopatheia* humanity < *anthrōpos* man + *pathos* feeling]
an·thro·poph·a·gi (an′thrə·pof′ə·jī) *n.pl.* of **an·thro·poph·a·gus** (-pof′ə·gəs) Eaters of human flesh; cannibals. [< L, pl. of *anthropophagus* < Gk. *anthrōpophagos* < *anthrōpos* man + *phagein* to eat]
an·thro·poph·a·gite (an′thrə·pof′ə·jīt) *n.* A cannibal. Also **an′thro·poph′a·gist.**
an·thro·poph·a·gy (an′thrə·pof′ə·jē) *n.* Cannibalism. [< Gk. *anthrōpophagia*] — **an′thro·po·phag′ic** (-pō·faj′ik) or **·i·cal, an′thro·poph′a·gous** (-pof′ə·gəs) *adj.*
an·thro·po·zo·ic (an′thrə·pō·zō′ik) *adj. Geol.* Characterized by the existence of man: applied to the Quaternary period. [< ANTHROPO- + Gk. *zōē* life + -IC]
an·thu·ri·um (an·thoor′ē·əm) *n.* Any of a genus (*Anthurium*) of tropical American perennials of the arum family, with heart-shaped or lobed leaves and densely flowered spathes. [< NL < Gk. *anthos* flower + *oura* tail]
an·ti (an′tī, an′tē) *n.* *pl.* **·tis** *Informal* One opposed to some policy, group, etc.
anti- *prefix*
1. Against; opposed to:

antiabrasion	anticontagion	antifeminism
antiagglutinating	anticontagious	antifeminist
antiaggression	anticorrosive	antiferment
antialien	anti-Darwinian	antifeudalism
anti-Americanism	antidemocratic	antiforeign
antianarchic	antidogmatic	antigambling
anti-Aristotelian	antidraft	antigrowth
antiascetic	antidynamic	antihierarchist
antibigotry	antidynastic	antihuman
anticaste	antiempirical	antihypnotic
anticensorship	antiepiscopal	anti-imperialism
antichurch	antierosion	anti-imperialist
anticivic	antievangelical	anti-imperialistic
anticlogging	antievolutionist	anti-intellectual
anticoagulating	antiexpansionist	antilabor
anticombination	antifaction	anti-Lamarckian
anticommercial	antifanatic	antileveling
anticommunist	anti-Fascism	antiliturgical
anticonductor	anti-Fascist	antilottery
anticonscription	antifat	antilynching

antimachine	antioxygenating	antiskid
anti-Malthusian	antiparasitic	antismoking
antimaterialist	anti-Platonic	antistalling
antimerger	antiplethoric	antistatism
antimiasmatic	antipolitical	antisubmarine
antimilitarism	antipollution	antisuffragist
antimilitarist	antipuritan	antitarnish
antimiscegenation	antiradiation	antitax
antimonarchic	antiradical	antitobacco
antimonarchist	antirationalism	antitorpedo
antimonopolist	antireformist	antiunion
antimoral	antireligious	antivaccinationist
antimusical	antirevolutionary	antivibratory
antinational	antiromantic	antivivisection
antinepotism	antiroyalist	antivivisectionist
antinicotine	antirust	antiwar
antinoise	antischolastic	antiwaste
antioxidase	antiscientific	antizealot
antioxidizer	antisensitizer	anti-Zionism

2. Opposite to; reverse:

anticyclic	antilogic	antipole

3. Rivaling; spurious:

anti-Caesar	antiemperor	anti-Messiah
anticritic	antiking	antiprophet

4. *Med.* Counteracting; curative; neutralizing:

antianemic	antidysenteric	antipathogen
antiapoplectic	antiemetic	antipneumococcic
antiarithritic	antiepileptic	antipruritic
antiasthmatic	antihemolytic	antirheumatic
antibacterial	antihemorrhagic	antiscrofulous
antibacteriolytic	antihemorrhoidal	antisoporific
antibilious	antihydrophobic	antispirochetic
antibubonic	antiluetic	antistaphylococcic
anticachetic	antimalarial	antistreptococcal
anticarious	antimephitic	antisudorific
anticatarrhal	antimicrobic	antitetanic
antichlorotic	antimycotic	antithrombin
anticolic	antinarcotic	antityphoid
anticonvulsive	antineuritic	antivirus

Anti- usually changes to *ant-* before words beginning with a vowel, as in *antacid*, and occasionally to *anth-* before the aspirate in words of Greek formation or analogy. [< Gk. < *anti* against]
an·ti·air·craft (an′tē·âr′kraft′, -âr′kräft′, an′tī-) *adj.* Used for defense against enemy aircraft. Abbr. *AA, A.A.*
antiaircraft artillery Weapons and equipment for actively combating aerial targets from the ground. Abbr. *AAA*
an·ti·ar (an′tē·är) *n.* **1.** The upas tree. **2.** The acrid, virulent poison found in the gum of this tree, the glycoside **anti·arin**, $C_{27}H_{42}O_{10}·4H_2O$, used as an arrow poison. [< Javanese *antjar*]
an·ti·bar·y·on (an′tī·bar′ē·on) *n. Physics* The antiparticle of a baryon. [< ANTI- + BARYON]
an·ti·bi·o·sis (an′ti·bī·ō′sis) *n. Biol.* The condition of associated organisms in which one is detrimental to the other.
an·ti·bi·ot·ic (an′ti·bī·ot′ik, an′tī-, an′ti·bē·ot′ik) *n.* **1.** That which is antagonistic toward or destructive of life. **2.** *Biochem.* Any of a large class of substances produced by various microorganisms and fungi and having the power of arresting the growth of other microorganisms or of destroying them, as penicillin, streptomycin, etc., used in treating certain infectious diseases. [< ANTI- + Gk. *biōtikos* of life, living < *bios* life]
an·ti·bod·y (an′ti·bod′ē) *n.* *pl.* **·bod·ies** *Biochem.* Any of a class of proteins related to globulin serum and serving to immunize the body against specific antigens. [< ANTI- + -BODY]
an·tic (an′tik) *n.* **1.** *Usually pl.* A prank; caper. **2.** A clown; buffoon. — *adj.* Odd; fantastic; ludicrous. — *v.i.* **an·ticked, an·tick·ing** To play the clown; perform antics. Also *Obs.* **an′tick.** [< Ital. *antico* old, grotesque < L *antiquus.* Doublet of ANTIQUE.] — **an′tic·ly** *adv.*
an·ti·cat·a·lyst (an′ti·kat′ə·list) *n. Chem.* A substance that stops or retards a chemical reaction; an inhibitor.
an·ti·cath·ode (an′ti·kath′ōd) *n.* The electrode in an electron or X-ray tube that receives and reflects the rays emitted from the cathode.
an·ti·chlor (an′ti·klôr, -klōr) *n.* *Chem.* Any substance, as sodium hyposulfite, used to neutralize the chlorine left in fabrics or the like after bleaching with hypochlorites. [< ANTI- + CHLOR(INE)] — **an′ti·chlo·ris′tic** *adj.*
an·ti·christ (an′ti·krīst′) *n.* **1.** A false claimant of the attributes and characteristics of Christ. **2.** *Often cap.* A denier or opponent of Christ or Christianity. — **an·ti·chris·tian** (an′ti·kris′chən) *adj.*
An·ti·christ (an′ti·krīst′) *n.* The great and blasphemous antagonist of Christ, thought of by early Christians as appearing before Christ's second coming. *I John* ii 18.
an·tic·i·pant (an·tis′ə·pənt) *adj.* Coming or acting in advance; anticipating; expectant. — *n.* One who anticipates. [< L *anticipans, -antis,* ppr. of *anticipare.* See ANTICIPATE.]
an·tic·i·pate (an·tis′ə·pāt) *v.t.* **·pat·ed, ·pat·ing 1.** To experience or realize beforehand; foresee. **2.** To look forward to;

expect. **3.** To act or arrive sooner than, especially so as to forestall: to *anticipate* an opponent's tactics. **4.** To foresee and fulfill beforehand, as desires. **5.** To u ake use of beforehand, as income not yet available. **6.** To discharge, as a debt, before it is due. **7.** To cause to happen earlier; accelerate. [< L *anticipatus*, pp. of *anticipare* < *ante-* before + *capere* to take] **— an·tic′i·pa′tor** *n.*

an·tic·i·pa·tion (an-tis′ə-pā′shən) *n.* **1.** The act of anticipating. **2.** A foreseeing or foretaste; expectation. **3.** An intuitive prevision; preconception. **4.** *Music* A tone or chord initiated before the point where musical context leads one to expect it.

an·tic·i·pa·tive (an-tis′ə-pā′tiv) *adj.* Anticipating, or characterized by anticipation. **— an·tic′i·pa′tive·ly** *adv.*

an·tic·i·pa·to·ry (an-tis′ə-pə-tôr′ē, -tō′rē) *adj.* Of, showing, or embodying anticipation. **— an·tic′i·pa·to′ri·ly** *adv.*

an·ti·clas·tic (an′ti-klas′tik) *adj. Math.* Having opposite curvature in different directions; convex in one direction and concave in another. Compare SYNCLASTIC. [< ANTI- + Gk. *klastos* broken *klaein* to break]

an·ti·cler·i·cal (an′ti-kler′i-kəl) *adj.* Opposed to clerical influence in political and civic affairs. **— an′ti·cler′i·cal·ism** *n.*

an·ti·cli·mac·tic (an′ti-klī-mak′tik) *adj.* Of, pertaining to, or like an anticlimax. **— an′ti·cli·mac′ti·cal·ly** *adv.*

an·ti·cli·max (an′ti-klī′maks) *n.* **1.** In speaking or writing, a sudden and often ludicrous change from an important and impressive idea or thought to one that is trivial or commonplace. Compare CLIMAX. **2.** An event or incident that is disappointingly less interesting or important than the events or incidents that preceded it.

an·ti·cli·nal (an′ti-klī′nəl) *adj.* **1.** Inclining in opposite directions. **2.** *Geol.* Of, pertaining to, or forming an anticline.

an·ti·cline (an′ti-klīn) *n. Geol.* A system of roughly parallel folds in stratified rock in which the folds slope downward from a crest in opposite directions. Compare SYNCLINE. [< ANTI- + Gk. *klinein* to slope]

an·ti·cli·no·ri·um (an′ti-klī-nôr′ē-əm, -nō′rē-əm) *n. pl.* **·no·ri·a** (-nôr′ē-ə, -nō′- rē-ə) *Geol.* A system of roughly parallel folds in stratified rocks, having on the whole an anticlinal structure and forming a great compound arch. [< NL < ANTI- + Gk. *klinein* to slope + *oros* mountain]

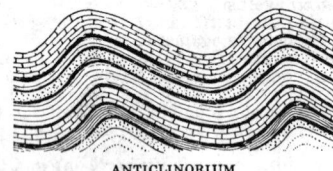

ANTICLINORIUM

antic masque See ANTIMASQUE.

An·ti·cos·ti (an′ti-kôs′tē, -kos′-) An island in the Gulf of St. Lawrence, Quebec, Canada; about 3,040 sq. mi.

an·ti·cy·clone (an′ti-sī′klōn) *n. Meteorol.* An atmospheric condition of high central pressure relative to the surrounding area, with horizontal spiral currents flowing clockwise in the northern hemisphere, counterclockwise in the southern. **— Syn.** See WHIRLWIND. **— an′ti·cy·clon′ic** (-klon′ik) *adj.*

an·ti·dote (an′ti-dōt) *n.* Anything that will counteract or remove the effects of poison, disease, or any evil. [< L *antidotum* < Gk. *antidoton*, orig. neut. sing. of *antidotos* given against < *anti-* against + *didonai* to give] **— an′ti·do′tal** *adj.* **— an′ti·do′tal·ly** *adv.*

an·ti·drom·ic (an′ti-drom′ik) *adj. Physiol.* Denoting a movement or course opposed to the normal, as of a nerve impulse. [< ANTI- + Gk. *dromos* running + -IC]

an·ti·en·er·gis·tic (an′tē-en′ər-jis′tik) *adj.* Resisting applied energy: distinguished from *synergistic.* [< ANTI- + (SYN)ERGISTIC]

An·tie·tam (an-tē′təm) A village near Sharpsburg in western Maryland; site of the fiercest day's battle of the Civil War, September 17, 1862.

an·ti·fe·brile (an′ti-fē′brəl, -feb′rəl) *adj.* Having the power to allay fever; antipyretic. **— n.** An antifebrile agent.

an·ti·fed·er·al·ist (an′ti-fed′ər-əl-ist, -fed′rəl-) *n.* One who opposes federalism. **— an′ti·fed′er·al** *adj.* **— an′ti·fed′er·al·ism** *n.*

An·ti·fed·er·al·ist (an′ti-fed′ər-əl-ist, -fed′rəl-) *n.* A member of the political party that opposed the ratification of the U.S. Constitution. After it was ratified, the Antifederalists, led by Jefferson, opposed any extension of the powers of the Federal government. **— An′ti·fed′er·al** *adj.* **— An′ti·fed′er·al·ism** *n.*

an·ti·freeze (an′ti-frēz′) *n.* A liquid of low freezing point, added to or substituted for the cooling agent in combustion-engine radiators, to prevent freezing.

an·ti·fric·tion (an′ti-frik′shən) *adj.* Lessening or tending to lessen friction, as by lubricants or rollers. **— n. 1.** A lubricant. **2.** A roller or other device for lessening friction.

an·ti·gen (an′tə-jən) *n. Biochem.* Any of several substances, such as toxins, enzymes, or foreign proteins, that cause the development of antibodies. Also **an′ti·gene** (-jēn). [< ANTI(BODY) + -GEN] **— an·ti·gen·ic** (an′tə-jen′ik) *adj.*

An·tig·o·ne (an-tig′ə-nē) In Greek legend, a daughter of Oedipus and Jocasta who accompanied her blinded father into exile; later, sentenced to death by her uncle Creon for illegally burying her brother Polynices, she hanged herself. Compare OEDIPUS, SEVEN AGAINST THEBES.

An·tig·o·nus I (an-tig′ə-nəs), 382–301 B.C., general of Alexander the Great and king of Macedon 306–301 B.C.: called **Cyclops.**

an·ti·grav·i·ty (an′ti-grav′ə-tē) *n.* **1.** *Physics* The gravitational repulsion that would occur between any normal object and an object with hypothetical mass. **2.** Any effect that can counteract the effect of gravity.

An·ti·gua (an-tē′gwə, -gə) One of the Leeward Islands; formerly a British colony; since 1967 a self-governing member of the West Indies Associated States; 108 sq. mi.; pop. 63,000 (1969); capital, St. Johns.

an·ti·he·lix (an′ti-hē′liks) See ANTHELIX.

an·ti·he·ro (an′ti-hir′ō, -hē′rō) *n. pl.* **·roes** The principal male character in a drama, fictional work, etc., who lacks the traditional virtues of a hero.

an·ti·his·ta·mine (an′ti-his′tə-mēn, -min) *n. Med.* Any of certain drugs that neutralize the vasoconstrictor action of histamine in the body, used especially in the treatment of allergic conditions, as hay fever, asthma, etc., and of the common cold. **— an′ti·his′ta·min′ic** (-min′ik) *adj.*

an·ti·ic·er (an′tē-ī′sər) *n. Aeron.* A device for preventing the formation of ice on airplanes. Compare DEICER.

an·ti·ke·to·gen·e·sis (an′ti-kē′tə-jen′ə-sis) *n. Biochem.* The reduction or prevention of ketosis by the oxidation of sugar or allied substances in the body. [< ANTI- + KETO-(SIS) + GENESIS]

an·ti·knock (an′ti-nok′) *n.* An agent, as tetraethyl lead, that prevents knock or premature combustion when added to the fuel of an internal-combustion engine.

An·ti-Leb·a·non (an′ti-leb′ə-nən) A mountain range on the Syria-Lebanon border; highest point, Mt. Hermon, 9,232 ft. *French* **An·ti-Li·ban** (äṅ·tē·lē·bäṅ′).

An·til·les (an-til′ēz) The islands of the West Indies, except the Bahamas; divided into the **Greater Antilles:** Cuba, Hispaniola, Jamaica, and Puerto Rico; and the **Lesser Antilles:** Trinidad, the Leeward and Windward Islands, Barbados, and other islands: also *Caribbees.*

an·ti·log·a·rithm (an′ti-lôg′ə-rith′əm, -log′-) *n. Math.* The number corresponding to a given logarithm. Also, in shortened form, **an·ti·log** (an′ti-lôg, -log).

an·ti·ma·cas·sar (an′ti-mə-kas′ər) *n.* A covering for the backs and arms of chairs and sofas to prevent soiling; a tidy. [< ANTI- + MACASSAR (OIL)]

an·ti·masque (an′ti-mask′, -mäsk′) *n.* An interlude between the acts of a mask, often burlesquing it: also called *antic masque.* Also **an′ti·mask′.** [< ANTI- opposed + MASQUE]

an·ti·mat·ter (an′ti-mat′ər) *n. Physics* A form of matter composed of antiparticles.

an·ti·mere (an′tə-mir) *n. Biol.* A part symmetrical with, or corresponding to, a part on the opposite side of the main axis, as an arm of a starfish, or the right or left half of a bilaterally symmetrical animal: also called *actinomere.* [< ANTI- opposite + Gk. *meros* part] **— an′ti·mer′ic** (an′tə-mer′ik) *adj.* **— an·tim·er·ism** (an-tim′ə-riz′əm) *n.*

an·ti·mo·ni·al (an′tə-mō′nē-əl) *adj.* Of or containing antimony. **— n.** A medicine containing antimony.

an·ti·mon·ic (an′tə-mō′nik, -mon′ik) *adj.* Of, pertaining to, or containing antimony, especially when combined in its higher valence: *antimonic sulfide,* Sb₂S₅.

an·ti·mo·nous (an′tə-mō′nəs) *adj.* Of, pertaining to, or containing antimony, especially in its lower valence: *antimonous oxide,* Sb₂O₃. Also **an′ti·mo′ni·ous.**

an·ti·mon·soon (an′ti-mon-sōōn′) *n. Meteorol.* An atmospheric current that, moving over a monsoon, travels in an opposite direction to it.

an·ti·mo·ny (an′tə-mō′nē) *n.* A silver-white, hard, crystalline, metallic element (symbol Sb) related to arsenic and tin, used largely in chemistry and medicine, and, in alloys, in the arts: also called *stibium.* See ELEMENT. ◆ Collateral adjective: *stibial.* [< Med.L *antimonium,* ? < Arabic]

antimony glance Stibnite.

an·ti·mo·nyl (an′tə-mə-nil′, an-tim′ə-nil) *n. Chem.* The univalent radical SbO, forming the base of several salts.

an·ti·neu·tri·no (an′ti-nōō-trē′nō) *n. Physics* An antiparticle corresponding to a neutrino.

an·ti·neu·tron (an′ti-nōō′tron, -nyōō′-) *n. Physics* An antiparticle corresponding to a neutron.

an·ti·node (an′ti-nōd′) *n. Physics* The point or section between the nodes of a vibrating system where some characteristic is at a maximum; a loop.

an·ti·no·mi·an (an′ti-nō′mē-ən) *n. Theol.* One holding that faith frees the Christian from the obligations of the moral law. **— adj.** Of or pertaining to this doctrine. **— an′ti·no′mi·an·ism** *n.*

an·tin·o·my (an-tin′ə-mē) *n. pl.* **·mies 1.** Self-contradiction in a law; opposition of one law or rule to another. **2.** In Kantian philosophy, irreconcilability of seemingly necessary inferences or conclusions; paradox. [< L *antinomia* < Gk. < *anti-* against + *nomos* law]

An·tin·o·us (an-tin′ō-əs) In the *Odyssey*, the most insistent of Penelope's suitors and the first to be slain by Odysseus.

An·ti·och (an′tē-ok) A city in southern Turkey, on the Orontes; pop. 37,484 (1955); capital of ancient Syria: Arabic *Antakiya*, Turkish *Antakya*.

An·ti·o·chi·an (an′tē-ō′kē-ən) *adj.* Of or pertaining to **Antiochus of Ascalon**, died 68 B.C.?, the founder of an eclectic school of philosophy uniting Platonic, Aristotelian, and Stoic doctrines.

An·ti·o·chus III (an-tī′ə-kəs), 242–187 B.C., king of Syria 223–187, conquered Egypt and much of the Near East; defeated by the Romans at Magnesia, 190 B.C.: called **the Great**.

Antiochus IV, died 163 B.C., king of Syria 175–163; attempted to suppress Judaism and brought on the Maccabean revolt: called **Antiochus E·piph·a·nes** (ə-pif′ə-nēz).

An·ti·o·pe (an-tī′ə-pē) In Greek mythology: **a** A maiden loved by Zeus, who changed himself into the form of a satyr, and to whom she bore two sons, Amphion and Zethus. **b** Hippolyta, queen of the Amazons.

an·ti·par·ti·cle (an′ti-pär′ti-kəl) *n. Physics* Any of a group of elementary particles, as positrons, antiprotons, antineutrons, etc., having masses equal to the electron, proton, neutron, etc., but with opposite charges and reversed magnetic moments. Contact between any contrasting pair of particles results in immediate mutual annihilation with the release of energy.

an·ti·pas·to (än′tē-päs′tō) *n.* A course of smoked or salted meat, fish, vegetables, etc., served as an appetizer. [< Ital. < *anti-* before (< L *ante*) + *pasto* food < L *pastus*]

An·tip·a·ter (an-tip′ə-tər), 398?–319 B.C., regent of Macedon.

Antipater, died 43 B.C., procurator of Judea; father of Herod the Great.

an·ti·pa·thet·ic (an-tip′ə-thet′ik, an′ti-pə-) *adj.* Having a natural aversion; constitutionally repugnant or opposed: often with *to*. Also **an·tip′a·thet′i·cal.** — **an·tip′a·thet′i·cal·ly** *adv.*

an·tip·a·thy (an-tip′ə-thē) *n. pl.* **·thies** **1.** An instinctive feeling of aversion or dislike. **2.** The object of such a feeling. [< L *antipathia* < Gk. *antipatheia* < *anti-* against + *pathein* to feel, suffer]
— **Syn. 1.** antagonism, repugnance, hostility, abhorrence. Compare ENMITY, HATRED. — **Ant.** affinity, sympathy, liking, congeniality, regard.

an·ti·pe·ri·od·ic (an′ti-pir′ē-od′ik) *Med. adj.* Remedial of periodic diseases, as quinine for malaria. — *n.* An antiperiodic agent.

an·ti·per·son·nel (an′ti-pûr′sə-nel′, an′tī-) *adj. Mil.* Designating weapons, such as bombs, mines, etc., that are employed against troops rather than against defenses or mechanized equipment.

an·ti·per·spi·rant (an′ti-pûr′spə-rənt, an′tī-) *n.* An astringent applied to the skin that acts to diminish or prevent perspiration. [< ANTI- + PERSPIR(E) + -ANT]

an·ti·phlo·gis·tic (an′ti-flō-jis′tik) *Med. adj.* Capable of reducing inflammation. — *n.* A remedy for inflammation. [< ANTI- + Gk. *phlogiston* burnt < *phlogizein* to burn < *phloga* flame]

an·ti·phon (an′tə-fon) *n.* **1.** A verse of a psalm or hymn said or chanted in response to another. **2.** *Eccl.* **a** A composition consisting of passages for responsive singing or chanting. **b** A versicle chanted before, and often after, a psalm or canticle, and varying with the season or feast. [< LL *antiphona* < Gk. *antiphōna*. Doublet of ANTHEM.]

an·tiph·o·nal (an-tif′ə-nəl) *adj.* Of or like an antiphon; sung responsively. Also **an·tiph·on·ic** (an′tə-fon′ik). — *n.* An antiphonary. — **an·tiph′o·nal·ly** *adv.*

an·tiph·o·nar·y (an-tif′ə-ner′ē) *n. pl.* **·nar·ies** A book of antiphons. — *adj.* Of or pertaining to a book of antiphons.

an·tiph·o·ny (an-tif′ə-nē) *n. pl.* **·nies** **1.** Opposition of sound, or the harmony resulting from this. **2.** Antiphonal singing. **3.** A musical response. **4.** An anthem or other composition to be sung antiphonally.

an·ti·ra·sis (an-tif′rə-sis) *n. pl.* **·ses** (-sēz) In rhetoric, the use of a term in a sense opposite to its meaning; irony. [< L < Gk. *antiphrazein* to express by antithesis < *anti-* against + *phrazein* to speak]

an·tip·o·dal (an-tip′ə-dəl) *adj.* **1.** Pertaining to or situated on the opposite side of the earth. **2.** Diametrically opposed. Also **an·tip·o·de·an** (an-tip′ə-dē′ən).

an·ti·pode (an′ti-pōd) *n.* An exact opposite.

an·tip·o·des (an-tip′ə-dēz) *n.* (*construed as sing. or pl.*) A place or region on the opposite side of the earth, or its inhabitants. [< L < Gk. *antipodes*, pl. of *antipous* having the feet opposite < *anti-* opposite + *pous* foot]

An·tip·o·des (an-tip′ə-dēz) A group of uninhabited islands SE of and belonging to New Zealand; 24 sq. mi.: so called from their almost antipodal position to Greenwich, England.

an·ti·pope (an′ti-pōp′) *n.* A usurping pope or one considered not canonically elected.

an·ti·pro·ton (an′ti-prō′ton) *n. Physics* An antiparticle corresponding to a proton.

an·ti·py·ic (an′ti-pī′ik) *Med. adj.* Preventive of suppuration. — *n.* A remedy against suppuration. [< ANTI- + Gk. *pyon* pus]

an·ti·py·ret·ic (an′ti-pī-ret′ik) *Med. adj.* Preventive or alleviative of fever. — *n.* A medicine to allay fever. [< ANTI- + Gk. *pyretos* fever]

an·ti·py·rine (an′ti-pī′rin, -rēn) *n.* A white crystalline compound, $C_{11}H_{12}N_2O$, used in medicine as an antipyretic. Also **an′ti·py′rin** (-rin).

antiq. 1. Antiquarian. **2.** Antiquities.

an·ti·quar·i·an (an′ti-kwâr′ē-ən) *adj.* Pertaining to the study of antiquities. — *n.* An antiquary. Abbr. *ant., antiq.* — **an′ti·quar′i·an·ism** *n.*

an·ti·quar·y (an′ti-kwer′ē) *n. pl.* **·quar·ies** One who collects, deals in, or studies antiques or antiquities. [< L *antiquarius < antiquus* ancient]

an·ti·quate (an′ti-kwāt) *v.t.* **·quat·ed, ·quat·ing 1.** To make old or out-of-date; make obsolete. **2.** To cause to look antique. [< L *antiquatus,* pp. of *antiquare* to make old < *antiquus* old] — **an′ti·qua′tion** *n.*

an·ti·quat·ed (an′ti-kwā′tid) *adj.* **1.** Out-of-date; old-fashioned; obsolete. **2.** Ancient; very old. — **Syn.** See ANTIQUE.

an·tique (an-tēk′) *adj.* **1.** Of or pertaining to ancient times. **2.** Of an earlier period: an *antique* chair. **3.** Old-fashioned; out-of-date. **4.** Of or in the style of ancient Greece or Rome. **5.** *Archaic* Old; venerable. — *n.* **1.** The style of ancient art, or a specimen of it. **2.** Any old object, as a piece of furniture, glass, etc.; especially, an old object prized for its rarity, excellence of style or craft, etc. **3.** *Printing* A style of type with all the lines of nearly equal thickness. — *v.t.* **an·tiqued, an·tiquing** To make seemingly old; give the appearance of antiquity to. [< F < L *antiquus* ancient < *ante* before. Doublet of ANTIC.] — **an·tique′ly** *adv.* — **an·tique′· ness** *n.*
— **Syn.** (adj.) **1.** See ANCIENT. **2, 3.** *Antique, antiquated, old-fashioned,* and *quaint* mean the style of a past era, but the words differ markedly in connotation. Something *antique* is interesting today because it is a relic of ancient times; the *antiquated* is no longer of use or interest: an *antique* table, *antiquated* weapons. An *old-fashioned* thing is less ancient than an *antique* one, and less worthless than an *antiquated* one, and may be restored to favor by future changes in fashion. *Quaint* originally meant both antique and fanciful, but now refers to anything that is interestingly odd, regardless of its age: a *quaint* way of speaking, a *quaint* costume. — **Ant.** modern, recent, fashionable, modish, stylish.

an·tiq·ui·ty (an-tik′wə-tē) *n. pl.* **·ties 1.** The quality of being ancient. **2.** Ancient times, especially before the Middle Ages. **3.** The people of ancient times collectively; the ancients. **4.** *Usually pl.* Anything belonging to or surviving from times long past; ancient relics. Abbr. *ant., antiq.*

an·ti·ra·chit·ic (an′ti-rə-kit′ik) *Med. adj.* Acting to prevent or cure rickets. — *n.* A remedy for rickets.

an·ti·re·mon·strant (an′ti-ri-mon′strənt) *n.* An opponent of remonstrance. — *adj.* Opposed to remonstrance.

An·ti·re·mon·strant (an′ti-ri-mon′strənt) *n.* A foe of the Remonstrance. — *adj.* Pertaining to such opposition.

an·tir·rhi·num (an′tə-rī′nəm) *n.* Any of a genus (*Antirrhinum*) of chiefly Old World herbs of the figwort family, including the common American snapdragon. [< NL < Gk. *antirrhinon < anti-* resembling + *rhis* nose]

An·ti·sa·na (än′tē-sä′nä) A volcano in the Andes, north central Ecuador; 18,885 ft.

an·ti·scor·bu·tic (an′ti-skôr-byoo′tik) *Med. adj.* Relieving or preventing scurvy. — *n.* A remedy for scurvy.

an·ti·Sem·i·tism (an′ti-sem′ə-tiz′əm, an′tī-) *n.* Opposition to, prejudice or discrimination against, or intolerance of Jews, Jewish culture, etc. — **an′ti-Sem′ite** *n.* — **an′ti-Se·mit′ic** (-sə-mit′ik) *adj.* — **an′ti-Se·mit′i·cal·ly** *adv.*

an·ti·sep·sis (an′tə-sep′sis) *n.* The condition in which or method by which a substance, or organism, is kept sterile against the growth of pathogenic or putrefactive bacteria. [< NL < ANTI- + Gk. *sēpsis* putrefaction]

an·ti·sep·tic (an′tə-sep′tik) *adj.* **1.** Of, pertaining to, or used in antisepsis. **2.** Preventing or counteracting putrefaction, etc. Also **an′ti·sep′ti·cal.** — *n.* Any substance having antiseptic qualities. — **an′ti·sep′ti·cal·ly** *adv.*

an·ti·sep·ti·cize (an′tə-sep′tə-sīz) *v.t.* **·cized, ·ciz·ing** To render antiseptic; treat with antiseptics.

an·ti·se·rum (an′ti-sir′əm) *n.* A serum that contains antibodies, the injection of which into the blood stream provides immunity from specific diseases.

an·ti·slav·er·y (an′ti-slā′vər-ē, -slāv′rē, an′tī-) *adj.* Opposed to human slavery.

an·ti·so·cial (an′ti-sō′shəl, an′tī-) *adj.* **1.** Averse to the society of others; unsociable. **2.** Opposed to or disruptive of society or the general good.

an·ti·spas·mod·ic (an′ti-spaz-mod′ik) *Med. adj.* Relieving or checking spasms. — *n.* An antispasmodic agent.

An·tis·the·nes (an-tis′thə-nēz), 444?–371? B.C., Greek philosopher; founder of the Cynic School.

an·tis·tro·phe (an·tis′trə·fē) *n.* **1.** In ancient Greek poetry, the verses sung by the chorus in a play while returning from left to right, in answer to the previous strophe. **2.** In classical prosody, the lines of an ode comprising a stanza and alternating with the strophe. **3.** The second of two alternating metrical systems in a poem. [< L < Gk. *antistrophē* < *antistrephein* to turn against < *anti-* against, opposite + *strephein* to turn] **— an·ti·stroph·ic** (an′ti-strof′ik) *adj.*

an·ti·tank (an′ti·tangk′) *adj. Mil.* Designed to combat tanks and other armored vehicles: *antitank* guns. Abbr. *AT*

an·tith·e·sis (an·tith′ə·sis) *n. pl.* **·ses** (-sēz) **1.** In rhetoric: **a** The balancing of two contrasted words, ideas, or phrases against each other. Example: *My prayers go up; my thoughts remain below.* **b** One part, especially the second, of such an expression. **2.** Opposition; contrast: the *antithesis* of peace and war. **3.** The direct opposite; a strong contrast: Love is the *antithesis* of hate. **4.** One of the three categories found in the dialectic systems of Hegel, Marx, etc. See DIALECTICAL MATERIALISM. [< L < Gk. < *antitithenai* to oppose < *anti-* against + *tithenai* to place]

an·ti·thet·i·cal (an′tə·thet′i·kəl) *adj.* **1.** Of or involving antithesis. **2.** Directly opposed; strongly contrasted. Also **an′·ti·thet′ic.** [< Gk. *antithetikos* < *antitithenai.* See ANTITHESIS.] **— an′ti·thet′i·cal·ly** *adv.*

an·ti·tox·ic (an′ti·tok′sik) *adj.* Counteracting toxin.

an·ti·tox·in (an′ti·tok′sin) *n. Biochem.* An antibody formed in the living tissues of an animal, that neutralizes a specific bacterial poison; also, serum containing this antibody. Also **an′ti·tox′ine** (-tok′sin, -sēn).

an·ti·trade (an′ti·trād′) *n.* One of the upper air currents in the tropics, moving parallel to the trade winds. **—** *adj.* Designating such an air current.

an·tit·ra·gus (an·tit′rə·gəs) *n. pl.* **·gi** (-jī) *Anat.* The conical eminence behind the opening of the external ear. [< ANTI- + TRAGUS]

an·ti·trust (an′ti·trust′) *adj.* Pertaining to the regulation of or opposition to trusts, cartels, pools, monopolies, and other organizations and practices in restraint of trade.

an·ti·type (an′ti·tīp′) *n.* **1.** That which a type or symbol represents. **2.** Something in the New Testament prefigured in the Old. **3.** An opposite type. [< Gk. *antitypos* < *anti-* corresponding to, against + *typos* stamp, type] **— an·ti·ty·pal** (an′ti·tī′pəl), **an·ti·typ·ic** (an′ti·tip′ik) or **·i·cal** *adj.*

an·ti·ven·in (an′ti·ven′in) *n.* **1.** The active principle of a serum that protects animals against venom. **2.** A serum used to counteract venom. Also **an·ti·ven·ene, an·ti·ven·ine** (an′ti·ven′ēn, -və·nēn′). [< ANTI- + L *venenum* poison]

an·ti·vi·ral (an′ti·vī′rəl) *adj.* **1.** Injurious to or destructive of viruses. **2.** Counteracting a virus, as certain drugs.

an·ti·vi·rot·ic (an′ti·vī·rot′ik) *n.* A substance that destroys viruses or inhibits their development. **—** *adj.* Antiviral. [< ANTI- + VIRUS, on analogy with *antibiotic*]

an·ti·world (an′ti·wûrld′) *n. Physics* A supposed world or universe made of antimatter.

ant·ler (ant′lər) *n. Usually pl.* A deciduous bony outgrowth or horn, usually branched, on the head of various members of the deer family. [< OF *antoillier,* ult. < L *ante-* before + *oculus* eye] **— ant′lered** *adj.*

Ant·li·a (ant′lē·ə) *n.* A constellation, the Water Pump. See CONSTELLATION.

ant lion An insect (family *Myrmeleontidae*) resembling a dragonfly; especially, its long-jawed, louselike larva, usually called *doodlebug,* that preys on ants and other insects. For illustration see INSECTS (beneficial).

An·to·fa·gas·ta (än′tō·fä·gäs′tä) A Province of northern Chile; 47,515 sq. mi.; pop. 214,090 (1960); capital, Antofagasta, pop. 89,111.

An·to·nes·cu (än′tō·nes′koo), **Ion** (yon), 1882–1946, Rumanian general; prime minister 1940–44; executed.

An·to·ni·nus (an′tə·nī′nəs) See AURELIUS.

Antoninus Pi·us (pī′əs), A.D. 86–161, emperor of Rome 131–161.

An·to·ni·o (an·tō′nē·ō, -tōn′yō) In Shakespeare's *Merchant of Venice,* the merchant; in *The Tempest,* Prospero's brother, who has usurped his dukedom.

an·to·no·ma·sia (an′tə·nō·mā′zhə, -zhē·ə) *n.* **1.** The substitution of a title or epithet for a proper name, as *his Honor,* for a judge. **2.** The use of the name of an individual for a class, as a *Cicero,* for an orator. [< L < Gk. < *antonomazein* to name instead < *anti-* instead of + *onoma* name]

An·to·ny (an′tə·nē), **Mark** Anglicized name of **Marcus An·to·ni·us** (an·tō′nē·əs), 83–30 B.C., Roman general and triumvir.

an·to·nym (an′tə·nim) *n.* A word that is the opposite of another in meaning: opposed to *synonym.* Abbr. *ant.* [< Gk. *antōnymia* < *anti-* opposite + *onoma, onyma* name]

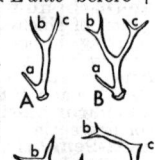
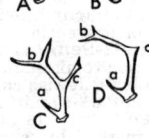
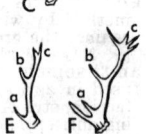
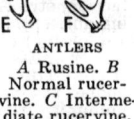

ANTLERS
A Rusine. *B* Normal rucervine. *C* Intermediate rucervine. *D* Extreme rucervine. *F* Subelaphine. *F* Elaphine.
a Brow tine. *b* Bez tine. *c* Royal tine.

An·trim (an′trim) A county of Ulster province in NE Northern Ireland; 1,098 sq. mi.; pop. 333,800 (est. 1969, excluding Belfast); county seat, Belfast.

an·trorse (an·trôrs′) *adj. Biol.* Directed forward or upward. [< NL *antrorsus* < ANTERO- + L *versus,* pp. of *vertere* to turn] **— an·trorse′ly** *adv.*

an·trum (an′trəm) *n. pl.* **·tra** (-trə) *Anat.* A cavity, usually in a bone; especially, the cavity in the upper jaw opening into the nose. [< L < Gk. *antron* cave]

An·tung (än′toong′, *Chinese* än′doong′) A port city in southern Manchuria, China, on the Yalu; pop. 450,000 (1970).

Ant·werp (ant′wûrp) A Province of northern Belgium·1,104 sq. mi.; pop. 1,529,826 (est. 1970); capital, Antwerp, pop. 234,099 (est. 1969): French *Anvers. Flemish* Ant·wer·pen (änt′ver·pən).

A·nu (ä′noo) In Babylonian mythology, the sky god.

A·nu·bis (ə·noo′bis, ə·nyoo′-) In Egyptian mythology, the jackal-headed conductor of the dead to judgment: identified with the Greek *Hermes.*

a·nu·ran (ə·noor′ən, ə·nyoor′-) *adj. & n. Zool.* Salientian. [< AN-¹ without + Gk. *oura* tail] **— a·nu′rous** *adj.*

a·nus (ā′nəs) *n. Anat.* The excretory opening at the lower extremity of the alimentary canal. [< L, orig., a ring]

An·ver (än·vâr′) The French name for ANT·WERP.

an·vil (an′vil, -vəl) *n.* **1.** A heavy block of iron or steel on which metal may be forged. **2.** Anything similar in function to an anvil, as the lower contact of a telegraph key, etc. **3.** *Anat.* The incus of the inner ear. **4.** *Mech.* The fixed element of a measuring device, as in calipers. For illustration see MICROMETER. **—** *v.t. & v.i.* **an·viled** or **·villed, an·vil·ing** or **·vil·ling** To work at or shape on an anvil. [OE *anfilt*]

ANUBIS

DOUBLE-BEAK ANVIL
a Rounded beak. *b* Flat beak. *c* Hardy hole, cutter, or chisel hole.

an·vil·top (an′vil·top′, -vəl-) *n.* A large, dense, anvil-shaped mass of cloud formed at the top of a cumulonimbus cloud preceding heavy showers or thunderstorms: also called *incus.*

anx·i·e·ty (ang·zī′ə·tē) *n. pl.* **·ties** **1.** Disturbance of mind regarding some uncertain event; misgiving; worry. **2.** Strained or solicitous desire; eagerness. **3.** *Psychiatry* A tense emotional state characterized by fear and apprehension regarding the future. [< L *anxietas, -tatis* < *anxius.* See ANXIOUS.] **— Syn. 1.** *Anxiety, worry, fretfulness, misgiving, apprehension,* and *foreboding* denote a disturbed state of mind. *Anxiety* may vary from mild concern to paralyzing dread. *Worry* and *fretfulness* refer to nagging doubts or fears, and suggest excessive or needless brooding. *Misgiving* is doubt about the outcome of an event, while *apprehension* and *foreboding* are fear or uneasiness directed at future events which one expects to be unfavorable. **2.** solicitude, concern. Compare CARE. **— Ant.** confidence, assurance, calmness, nonchalance.

anx·ious (angk′shəs, ang′-) *adj.* **1.** Troubled in mind respecting some uncertain matter; having anxiety: *anxious* at the delay. **2.** Fraught with or causing anxiety; worrying; distressing: an *anxious* matter. **3.** Intent; eagerly desirous; solicitous: with *for* or the infinitive: *anxious* for success; *anxious* to succeed. [< L *anxius* < *angere* to choke, distress] **— anx′ious·ly** *adv.* **— anx′ious·ness** *n.* **— Syn. 1.** worried, concerned, apprehensive, fearful, uneasy.

anxious seat *U.S.* The mourner's bench. **— to sit in the anxious seat** *Informal* To be worried and apprehensive.

an·y (en′ē) *adj.* **1.** One, no matter which; a or an, or (plural) some; of whatever kind or quality: Has *any* man helped us? Have we *any* choice? **2.** Some, however much or little: Did he eat *any* supper? **3.** Every: *Any* fool knows that. **—** *pron.* Any person or persons; one or more persons or things of a number: Have *any* of the guests arrived? **—** *adv.* At all; to any extent: Are they *any* nearer? ✦ *Any* meaning "at all" is sometimes used informally in negative and interrogative sentences: Did you hurt yourself *any*? [OE *ǣnig* < *ān* one]

an·y·bod·y (en′i·bod′ē, -bud′ē) *pron.* Any person whatever; anyone. **—** *n. pl.* **·bod·ies** **1.** Any common or ordinary person. **2.** A person of importance: He isn't *anybody.*

an·y·how (en′i·hou′) *adv.* **1.** In any way whatever; by any means. **2.** Notwithstanding; in any case. **3.** Carelessly.

any more **1.** Anything added: Do not give me *any more.* **2.** Now; from now on: He's not welcome *any more.* ✦ *Any more* meaning "now, nowadays" is used in affirmative contexts, especially in the Midland and Middle Atlantic areas: We go twice a day *any more.*

any more than With more reason or likelihood than: I couldn't do that *any more than* I could fly.

an·y·one (en′i·wun′, -wən) *pron.* Any person. ✦ **any one, anyone** *Any one* is used to distinguish one person from others in the same group or class: *Any one* of these men may be guilty. *Anyone* (indefinite pronoun) means any person at all: Can *anyone* identify the culprit?

an·y·place (en'i·plās') *adv. U.S. Informal* Anywhere.

an·y·thing (en'i·thing') *pron.* Any thing, event, or matter whatever. — *n.* A thing of any kind. — *adv.* To any degree; in any way: now only in the expression *anything like.*

anything but By no means; far from: *anything but* safe.

an·y·way (en'i·wā') *adv.* **1.** In any manner. **2.** Nevertheless; anyhow. **3.** Carelessly; haphazardly.

an·y·ways (en'i·wāz') *adv. Dial.* Anyway.

an·y·where (en'i·hwâr') *adv.* In, at, or to any place.

an·y·wise (en'i·wīz') *adv.* In any manner.

An·zac (an'zak) *adj.* Pertaining to the Australian and New Zealand Army Corps during World War I. — *n.* **1.** A member of this army corps. **2.** Any soldier from Australia or New Zealand.

ANZAC or **A.N.Z.A.C.** Australian and New Zealand Army Corps.

An·zi·o (an'zē·ō, *Ital.* än'tsyō) A town on the west coast of Italy south of Rome; site of Allied beachhead in the invasion of Italy in World War II, January, 1944; pop. about 10,000.

A/O or **a/o** Account of.

AOL or **A.O.L.** or **a.o.l.** *Mil.* Absent over leave.

A–one (ā'wun') *adj.* **1.** First or highest class: said of a vessel to denote the condition of its hull and equipment. **2.** *Informal* Excellent; first-rate. Also **A–1.**

A·o·ran·gi (ä'ō·räng'gē) See (Mount) COOK.

a·o·rist (ā'ə·rist) *Gram. n.* A tense of Greek verbs expressing past action without reference to completion, continuance, etc. — *adj.* Pertaining to or in the aorist. [< Gk. *aoristos* indefinite < *a-* without + *horizein* to limit]

a·o·ris·tic (ā'ə·ris'tik) *adj.* **1.** *Gram.* Relating to the aorist tense. **2.** Indefinite; undefined.

a·or·ta (ā·ôr'tə) *n. pl.* **·tas** or **·tae** (-tē) *Anat.* The great artery springing from the left ventricle of the heart and forming the main arterial trunk that distributes blood to all of the body except the lungs. [< NL < Gk. *aortē* < *aeirein* to raise, heave] — **a·or'tal, a·or'tic** *adj.*

a·ou·dad (ä'ōō·dad) *n.* The bearded argali (genus *Ammotragus*), a wild sheep of North Africa: also spelled *audad.* [< F < Berber *audad*]

ap-[1] Assimilated var. of AD-.

ap-[2] Var. of APO-.

ap. Apothecaries' (weight or measure).

Ap. **1.** Apostle. **2.** April.

AP *Mil.* **1.** Air Police. **2.** Armor-piercing.

AP or **A.P.** Associated Press.

a·pace (ə·pās') *adv.* Rapidly; quickly. [< A-[1] on + PACE]

a·pache (ə·päsh', ə·pash'; *Fr.* à·pàsh') *n.* A ruffian or gangster of Paris. [< F < APACHE]

A·pach·e (ə·pach'ē) *n. pl.* **A·pach·es** or **A·pach·e** One of a group of North American Indians of Athapascan stock, inhabiting the southern and SW United States.

Apache State Nickname of ARIZONA.

ap·a·go·ge (ap'ə·gō'jē) *n. Logic* Establishment of a thesis by showing its contrary to be absurd. [< Gk. *apagōgē* a leading away < *apagein* < *apo-* away + *agein* to lead] — **ap'a·gog'ic** (-goj'ik) or **·i·cal** *adj.*

Ap·a·lach·ee Bay (ap'ə·lach'ē) An inlet of the Gulf of Mexico in NW Florida.

Ap·a·lach·i·co·la River (ap'ə·lach'i·kō'lə) A river in NW Florida, flowing south 112 miles to the Gulf of Mexico.

ap·a·nage (ap'ə·nij) See APPANAGE.

a·pa·re·jo (ä'pä·rā'hō) *n. pl.* **·jos** (-hōz) *SW U.S.* A type of packsaddle with stuffed leather cushions. [< Sp.]

A·par·ri (ä·pä'rē) A port city in northern Luzon, Philippines, on Babuyan Channel; pop. 26,409 (est. 1955).

a·part (ə·pärt') *adv.* **1.** Separated; not together: Keep them *apart.* **2.** One from another: No one can tell the twins *apart.* **3.** Separately for some use or purpose: to set *apart* an allowance. **4.** Independently in logic or thought: Let us view this matter *apart.* **5.** Aside; to one side: She stood *apart.* **6.** In pieces or to pieces; part from part: The ship broke *apart.* — *adj.* Separate; distinct: a breed *apart.* [< MF *à part* < L *ad* to + *pars, partis* part]

a·part·heid (ə·pärt'hīt, -hāt) *n.* Racial segregation and discrimination against nonwhites in the Republic of South Africa, especially as supported by law as an instrument of government policy. [< Afrikaans, apartness]

a·part·ment (ə·pärt'mənt) *n.* **1.** One of several suites of rooms in a building, each equipped for housekeeping; a flat. **2.** A room. Abbr. *apt.* (*pl. apts.*). [< F *appartement* < Ital. *appartamento*, ult. < L *ad* to + *pars, partis* part]

apartment house *U.S.* A multiple-dwelling building divided into a number of apartments. Also *Canadian* **apartment block.**

ap·a·tet·ic (ap'ə·tet'ik) *adj. Zool.* Having natural camouflage of imitative coloration or form. [< Gk. *apatētikos* deceiving < *apatē* deceit]

ap·a·thet·ic (ap'ə·thet'ik) *adj.* **1.** Lacking emotion. **2.** Indifferent; unconcerned. Also **ap'a·thet'i·cal.** [< APATHY, on analogy with *sympathetic*] — **ap'a·thet'i·cal·ly** *adv.*

ap·a·thy (ap'ə·thē) *n. pl.* **·thies** **1.** Lack of emotion. **2.** Indifference; lack of interest. [< L *apathia* < Gk. *apatheia* < *a-* without + *pathos* feeling < *pathein* to feel]

— **Syn. 1, 2.** *Apathy, indifference, insensibility,* and *unconcern* denote a lack of emotion or interest. *Apathy* may refer to a habitual lack of feeling, or it may be used in the sense of *indifference* to describe a temporary lack of interest caused by depression, sorrow, ignorance, despair, etc. *Insensibility* is a lack of feeling or sympathy for other persons or things, and may imply either great absorption in one's own affairs, or mere callousness. *Unconcern* is almost always blameworthy, and suggests a lack of an appropriate emotional response or an unwillingness to become personally involved. — **Ant.** feeling, sensibility, sensitiveness, interest, sympathy.

ap·a·tite (ap'ə·tīt) *n. Mineral.* A hexagonal, usually brown or green calcium phosphate of chlorine or fluorine. [< Gk. *apatē* deceit + -ITE[1]; because mistaken for other minerals]

ape (āp) *n.* **1.** A large, tailless, Old World primate, as a gorilla or chimpanzee. **2.** Loosely, any monkey. **3.** A mimic. — *v.t.* **aped, ap·ing** To imitate; mimic. [OE *apa*]

a·peak (ə·pēk') *adv. Naut.* In or nearly in a vertical position, as an anchor.

A·pel·doorn (ä'pəl·dōrn) A commune in east central Netherlands; pop. 103,126 (est. 1960).

A·pel·les (ə·pel'ēz) Fourth-century B.C. Greek painter.

ape man Any primate resembling man, as Pithecanthropus.

Ap·en·nines (ap'ə·nīnz) A mountain range constituting most of the Italian peninsula south of the Po valley; highest peak, Mt. Corno, 9,585 ft.

a·per·çu (a·per·sü') *n. pl.* **a·per·çus** (-sü') *French* **1.** A glance. **2.** An insight; perception. **3.** An outline; conspectus.

a·per·i·ent (ə·pir'ē·ənt) *Med. adj.* Tending mildly to stimulate the bowels; laxative. — *n.* A gentle purgative. Also **a·per·i·tive** (ə·per'ə·tiv). [< L *aperiens, -entis,* ppr. of *aperire* to open]

a·pe·ri·od·ic (ā'pir·ē·od'ik) *adj.* **1.** *Pathol.* Not manifesting periodicity, as some diseases. **2.** Deadbeat.

a·pé·ri·tif (a·pā·rē·tēf') *n. French* A drink of alcoholic liquor or wine taken as an appetizer.

ap·er·ture (ap'er·chŏŏr, -chər) *n.* **1.** An opening; orifice; hole; cleft. **2.** *Optics* An opening, often adjustable in diameter, through which light enters the lens of a camera or other optical instrument. [< L *apertura* < *apertus,* pp. of *aperire* to open] — **ap'er·tur·al** *adj.* — **ap'er·tured** *adj.*

ap·er·y (ā'pər·ē) *n. pl.* **·er·ies** The act of aping; mimicry.

a·pet·al·ous (ā·pet'l·əs) *adj. Bot.* Without petals.

a·pex (ā'peks) *n. pl.* **a·pex·es** or **ap·i·ces** (ap'ə·sēz, ā'pə-) **1.** The highest point; tip; top. **2.** *Geom.* The vertex of an angle. **3.** Climax. **4.** *Phonet.* The tip of the tongue. [< L]

aph- Var. of APO-.

aph. Aphetic.

a·pha·gi·a (ə·fā'jē·ə) *n. Pathol.* Loss of the power to swallow. [< NL < Gk. *a-* not + *phagein* to eat]

a·phan·i·sis (ə·fan'ə·sis) *n. Psychoanal.* The fear of losing sexual potency. [< NL < Gk., obliteration < *aphanizein* to make unseen, destroy < *a-* not + *phainein* to show]

aph·a·nite (af'ə·nīt) *n. Mineral.* A dense, fine-grained diabase with a compact texture. [< Gk. *aphanēs* unseen + -ITE[1]; so called because its grains are invisible to the naked eye] — **aph'a·nit'ic** (-nit'ik) *adj.*

a·pha·sia (ə·fā'zhə, -zhē·ə) *n. Pathol.* Any partial or total loss of the power of articulate speech not due to defects in the peripheral organs, but to disorder in some of the cerebral centers. [< NL < Gk. *aphasia* < *aphatos* speechless < *a-* not + *phanai* to speak] — **a·pha·sic** (ə·fā'zik, -sik), **a·pha·si·ac** (ə·fā'zē·ak) *adj. & n.*

a·phe·li·on (ə·fē'lē·ən) *n. pl.* **·li·a** (-lē·ə) *Astron.* The point in an orbit, as of a planet, farthest from the sun: opposed to *perihelion.* [< APH (APO-) away from + Gk. *hēlios* sun] — **a·phe'li·an** (-ən) *adj.*

a·phe·li·o·trop·ic (ə·fē'lē·ə·trop'ik) *adj.* Turning away from the source of light; having negative heliotropism. [< APH- (APO-) + HELIOTROPIC] — **a·phe'li·o·trop'i·cal·ly** *adv.* — **a·phe·li·ot·ro·pism** (ə·fē'lē·ot'rə·piz'əm) *n.*

a·pher·e·sis (ə·fer'ə·sis) *n.* The dropping of an unaccented syllable or sound from the beginning of a word, as in *'neath* for *beneath.* Also **a·phaer'e·sis.** [< L *aphaeresis* < Gk. *aphairesis* < *aphairein* to take away < *apo-* away + *hairein* to take] — **aph·e·ret·ic** (af'ə·ret'ik) *adj.*

aph·e·sis (af'ə·sis) *n.* The gradual, developmental loss of a short or unaccented vowel from the beginning of a word, as in *mend* for *amend:* a form of apheresis. [< NL < Gk., a letting go < *aphienai* < *apo-* from + *hienai* to send] — **a·phet·ic** (ə·fet'ik) *adj.*

a·phid (ā'fid, af'id) *n.* Any of a family (*Aphididae*) of numerous, small, juice-sucking insects, injurious to plants: also called *plant louse.* [< APHIS] — **a·phid·i·an** (ə·fid'ē·ən) *adj.*

a·phis (ā'fis, af'is) *n. pl.* **aph·i·des** (af'ə·dēz) An aphid. [< NL; origin uncertain]

APHELION
P Perihelion.
S Sun. *A* Aphelion.

a·pho·ni·a (ə-fō/nē-ə, ā-) *n. Pathol.* Loss of voice, especially when due to organic or structural causes. [< NL < Gk. *aphōnia* < *a-* without + *phōnē* voice]

a·phon·ic (ə-fŏn/ĭk, ā-) *adj.* **1.** *Pathol.* Affected with or characterized by aphonia. **2.** *Phonet.* **a** Not representing a sound: said of a letter. **b** Voiceless.

aph·o·rism (ăf/ə-rĭz/əm) *n.* **1.** A brief statement of a truth or principle. **2.** A proverb; maxim. — **Syn.** See PROVERB. [< MF *aphorisme* < Med.L *aphorismus* < Gk. *aphorismos* definition < *aphorizein* to mark off, define < *apo-* from + *horizein* to divide < *horos* boundary]

aph·o·ris·mic (ăf/ə-rĭz/mĭk) *adj.* Aphoristic. Also **aph·o·ris·mat·ic** (ăf/ə-rĭz-măt/ĭk).

aph·o·rist (ăf/ə-rĭst) *n.* A maker or user of aphorisms.

aph·o·ris·tic (ăf/ə-rĭs/tĭk) *adj.* **1.** Of, like, or characterized by aphorisms. **2.** Given to aphorisms. Also **aph/o·ris/ti·cal.** — **aph/o·ris/ti·cal·ly** *adv.*

aph·o·rize (ăf/ə-rīz) *v.i.* **·rized, ·riz·ing** To use aphorisms.

a·pho·tic (ā-fō/tĭk) *adj.* Without light; dark. [< Gk. *aphōs, aphōtos* < *a-* without + *phōs, photos* light]

aph·ro·dis·i·a (ăf/rə-dĭz/ē-ə) *n. Pathol.* Excessive sexual desire. [< NL < Gk. *aphrodisios* of Aphrodite]

aph·ro·dis·i·ac (ăf/rə-dĭz/ē-ăk) *adj.* Arousing or increasing sexual desire or potency. — *n.* An aphrodisiac drug, food, etc. [< Gk. *aphrodisiakos* < *Aphroditē*, goddess of love]

aph·ro·di·te (ăf/rə-dī/tē) *n.* A brilliantly colored butterfly (*Argynnis aphrodite*) of the United States.

Aph·ro·di·te (ăf/rə-dī/tē) In Greek mythology, the goddess of love and beauty; the daughter of Zeus and Dione, also said to have been born from the foam of the sea: identified with the Phoenician *Astarte* and the Roman *Venus.* [< Gk. *Aphroditē* the foam-born]

aph·tha (ăf/thə) *n. pl.* **·thae** (-thē) *Pathol.* A small vesicle or speck in the mouth or stomach, caused by a fungous parasite. [< L < Gk.] — **aph/thous** *adj.*

a·phyl·lous (ə-fĭl/əs, ā-) *adj. Bot.* Leafless. Also **a·phyl·lose** (-ōs, ā-). [< Gk. *aphyllos* < *a-* without + *phyllon* leaf]

a·phyl·ly (ə-fĭl/ē, ā-) *n. Bot.* Leaflessness.

A·pi·a (ä-pē/ä, ä/pē-ä) The capital of Western Samoa, a port city on Upolu island; pop. 27,000 (est. 1968).

a·pi·an (ā/pē-ən) *adj.* Of or pertaining to bees. [< L *apianus* < *apis* bee]

a·pi·ar·i·an (ā/pē-âr/ē-ən) *adj.* Of or relating to bees or the keeping of bees. — *n.* An apiarist.

a·pi·a·rist (ā/pē-ə-rĭst) *n.* A beekeeper.

a·pi·ar·y (ā/pē-er/ē) *n. pl.* **·ar·ies** A place where bees are kept; a set of hives, bees, etc. [< L *apiarium* < *apis* bee]

ap·i·cal (ăp/ĭ-kəl, ā/pĭ-) *adj.* **1.** Situated at or belonging to the apex or top, as of a conical figure. **2.** *Phonet.* Describing those consonants produced with the tip of the tongue, as (t), (d), and (s). [< L *apex, apicis* tip]

ap·i·ces (ăp/ə-sēz, ā/pə-) Alternative plural of APEX.

a·pi·cul·ture (ā/pĭ-kŭl/chər) *n.* The raising and care of bees. [< L *apis* bee + CULTURE] — **a/pi·cul/tur·ist** *n.*

a·pic·u·lus (ə-pĭk/yə-ləs) *n. pl.* **·li** (-lī) *Bot.* The point terminating a leaf. [< NL, dim. of L *apex* tip] — **a·pic/u·late** (-lĭt, -lāt) *adj.*

a·piece (ə-pēs/) *adv.* For or to each one; each.

à pied (à pyā/) *French* On foot.

a·pi·ol·o·gy (ā/pē-ŏl/ə-jē) *n.* The study of bees. [< L *apis* bee + -(O)LOGY] — **a/pi·ol/o·gist** *n.*

A·pis (ā/pĭs) A sacred bull worshiped by the ancient Egyptians. See SERAPIS.

ap·ish (ā/pĭsh) *adj.* Like an ape; servilely imitative; foolish and tricky. — **ap/ish·ly** *adv.* — **ap/ish·ness** *n.*

a·piv·o·rous (ā-pĭv/ər-əs) *adj. Zool.* Bee-eating. [< L *apis* bee + -VOROUS]

a·pla·cen·tal (ā/plə-sen/təl, ăp/lə-) *adj. Zool.* Having no placenta, as the monotremes and marsupials.

ap·la·nat·ic (ăp/lə-năt/ĭk) *adj. Optics* Free from aberration. [< A-⁴ not + Gk. *planatikos* wandering]

a·pla·sia (ə-plā/zhə, -zhē-ə) *n. Pathol.* Arrested development of parts of the body; congenital atrophy. [< NL < Gk. *a-* without + *plasis* a molding]

a·plas·tic (ā-plăs/tĭk) *adj. Pathol.* Lacking the power of normal growth. [< Gk. *aplastos* unformed]

ap·lite (ăp/līt) *n.* A fine-grained, acidic granite, composed mostly of quartz and feldspar, and sometimes muscovite, and occurring in dikes: also spelled *haplite.* [< Gk. *haploos* simple + -ITE¹] — **ap·lit·ic** (ăp-lĭt/ĭk) *adj.*

a·plomb (ə-plŏm/, *Fr.* à·plôn/) *n.* Assurance; self-confidence. [< F < *à* according to + *plomb* plumb bob]

apmt. Appointment.

ap·ne·a (ăp-nē/ə) *n. Pathol.* Suspension of respiration, partial or entire; suffocation. Also **ap·noe/a.** [< NL < Gk. *apnoia* < *a-* without + *pnoē* breath] — **ap·ne/al, ap·ne/ic** *adj.*

A·po (ä/pō), **Mount** A volcano in SE Mindanao; highest peak in the Philippines; 9,690 ft.

apo- *prefix* **1.** Off; from; away: *apostasy.* **2.** *Chem.* Used to indicate a derived compound: *apomorphine.* Also **ap-** before vowels, as in *apagoge;* **aph-** before an aspirate, as in *aphelion.* [< Gk. < *apo* from, off]

APO Army Post Office.

Apoc. **1.** Apocalypse. **2.** Apocrypha; Apocryphal.

a·poc·a·lypse (ə-pŏk/ə-lĭps) *n.* A prophecy or disclosure; any remarkable revelation. [< L *apocalypsis* < Gk. *apokalypsis* < *apokalyptein* to disclose < *apo-* from + *kalyptein* to cover]

A·poc·a·lypse (ə-pŏk/ə-lĭps) The book of Revelation, the last book of the New Testament. Abbr. *Apoc.*

a·poc·a·lyp·tic (ə-pŏk/ə-lĭp/tĭk) *adj.* **1.** Of or of the nature of a revelation. **2.** Pertaining to the Apocalypse. Also **a·poc/a·lyp/ti·cal.** — **a·poc/a·lyp/ti·cal·ly** *adv.*

ap·o·carp (ăp/ə-kärp) *n. Bot.* A gynoecium having separate carpels, as the distinct ovaries of the crowfoot family. [< APO- distinct + Gk. *karpos* fruit] — **ap/o·car/pous** *adj.*

ap·o·chro·mat·ic (ăp/ə-krō-măt/ĭk) *adj. Optics* More exactly achromatic than an ordinary achromatic lens. — **ap/o·chro/ma·tism** (-krō/mə-tiz/əm) *n.*

a·poc·o·pate (*v.* ə-pŏk/ə-pāt; *adj.* ə-pŏk/ə-pĭt) *v.t.* **·pat·ed, ·pat·ing** To shorten by apocope. — *adj.* Shortened by apocope: also **a·poc/o·pat/ed** (-pā/tĭd). — **a·poc/o·pa/tion** *n.*

a·poc·o·pe (ə-pŏk/ə-pē) *n.* A cutting off or elision of the last sound or syllable of a word. [< Gk. *apokopē* < *apokoptein* to cut off < *apo-* off + *koptein* to cut]

A·poc·ry·pha (ə-pŏk/rə-fə) *n.pl.* (*often construed as sing.*) **1.** Those books of the Septuagint included in the Vulgate but rejected by Protestants as uncanonical because not in the Hebrew Scriptures. The Apocrypha consists of the following books (names in the Douai Bible, when different, are given in parentheses): I Esdras (III Esdras), II Esdras (IV Esdras), Tobit (Tobias), Judith, Additions to Esther, Additions to Daniel, Wisdom of Solomon, Ecclesiasticus, Baruch, I Maccabees (I Machabees), II Maccabees (II Machabees). **2.** A collection of unauthenticated early Christian writings, proposed as additions to the New Testament, but not admitted. Compare PSEUDEPIGRAPHA. Abbr. *Apoc.* [< LL, neut. pl. of *apocryphus* < Gk. *apokryphos* hidden < *apokryptein* < *apo-* away + *kryptein* to hide] — **A·poc/ry·phal** *adj.*

a·poc·ry·phal (ə-pŏk/rə-fəl) *adj.* Having little or no authenticity. — **a·poc/ry·phal·ly** *adv.* — **a·poc/ry·phal·ness** *n.*

a·poc·y·na·ceous (ə-pos/ə-nā/shəs) *adj. Bot.* Belonging to the dogbane family (*Apocynaceae*) of herbaceous or woody plants, mainly tropical, with milky, acrid juice and simple leaves, as Indian hemp, and periwinkle. [< NL *Apocynaceae* < Gk. *apokynon* dogbane < *apo-* away + *kyōn* dog]

ap·o·dal (ăp/ə-dəl) *adj. Zool.* **1.** Of or relating to an animal lacking distinct footlike appendages. **2.** Of or relating to an order (*Apoda*) which includes the holothurians. [< Gk. *apous, apodos* < *a-* without + *pous* foot]

ap·o·dic·tic (ăp/ə-dĭk/tĭk) *adj.* Clearly demonstrable; indisputable. Also **ap/o·deic/tic** (-dīk/tĭk), **ap/o·dic/ti·cal.** [< L *apodicticus* < Gk. *apodeiktikos* < *apodeiknynai* to show by argument < *apo-* from + *deiknynai* to show] — **ap/o·dic/ti·cal·ly** *adv.*

ap·o·do·sis (ə-pŏd/ə-sĭs) *n. pl.* **·ses** (-sēz) The conclusion in a conditional sentence; also, the clause expressing result in a sentence not conditional. [< L < Gk., a giving back < *apo-* back + *didonai* to give]

a·pog·a·my (ə-pŏg/ə-mē) *n. Bot.* The development of the mature plant from the prothallium without intervention of sexual organs. [< APO- + Gk. *gamos* marriage] — **ap·o·gam·ic** (ăp/ə-găm/ĭk), **a·pog/a·mous** *adj.*

ap·o·gee (ăp/ə-jē) *n.* **1.** *Astron.* That point in the orbit of a celestial body, such as the moon or an artificial satellite, which is farthest from the earth: opposed to *perigee.* **2.** The highest point; climax. [< MF *apogée* < L *apogaeum* < Gk. *apogaion* < *apo-* away from + *gē, gaia* earth] — **ap·o·ge·al** (ăp/ə-jē/əl), **ap/o·ge/an** *adj.*

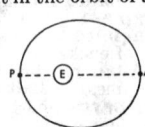

ap·o·ge·ot·ro·pism (ăp/ə-jē-ŏt/rə-piz/əm) *n. Bot.* The tendency to grow away from the earth, in opposition to gravitation; negative geotropism. [< APO- + GEOTROPISM] — **ap·o·ge·o·trop·ic** (ăp/ə-jē/ə-trop/ĭk) *adj.*

APOGEE
P Moon at perigee. E Earth.
A Moon at apogee.

A·pol·li·naire (à·pô·lē·nâr/), **Guillaume,** 1880–1918, French poet born in Rome: original name **de Kos·tro·wit·sky** (də kos/trō-vĭt/skē).

A·pol·lo (ə-pŏl/ō) In Greek and Roman mythology, the god of music, poetry, prophecy, and medicine: later identified with *Helios.* — *n.* **1.** Any handsome young man. **2.** The U.S. space-flight project that landed men on the moon in 1969. **3.** The spacecraft used in this project.

Ap·ol·lo·ni·us Rho·di·us (ăp/ə-lō/nē-əs rō/dē-əs) Third century B.C. Greek poet and grammarian.

A·pol·lyon (ə-pŏl/yən) The angel of the bottomless pit. *Rev.* ix 11. See ABADDON. [< Gk. *apollyōn* destroying < *apollyein* to destroy completely]

ap·o·log·et·ic (ə-pŏl/ə-jet/ĭk) *adj.* **1.** Of the nature of an apology; excusing. **2.** Defending or explaining. Also **a·pol/o·get/i·cal.** — *n.* An apology or defense. [< F *apologétique* < L *apologeticus* < Gk. *apologētikos* < *apologia* a speech in defense. See APOLOGY.] — **a·pol/o·get/i·cal·ly** *adv.*

a·pol·o·get·ics (ə-pŏl/ə-jet/ĭks) *n.pl.* (*construed as sing.*) The branch of theology that deals with the defensive facts and proofs of Christianity.

a·po·lo·gi·a (ap'ə-lō'jē-ə) *n.* A justification or defense. [< L < Gk.]

a·pol·o·gist (ə-pol'ə-jist) *n.* One who argues in defense of any person or cause.

a·pol·o·gize (ə-pol'ə-jīz) *v.i.* **·gized** **·giz·ing 1.** To offer or make excuse; acknowledge, with regret, any fault or offense. **2.** To make a justification or formal defense in speech or writing. **— a·pol'o·giz'er** *n.*

ap·o·logue (ap'ə-lôg, -log) *n.* A fable or tale having a moral. Also **ap'o·log. — Syn.** See ALLEGORY. [< L *apologus* < Gk. *apologos* < *apo-* from + *logos* speech]

a·pol·o·gy (ə-pol'ə-jē) *n. pl.* **·gies 1.** A statement or explanation expressing regret for some error or offense. **2.** Originally, a justification or defense. [< L *apologia* < Gk. *apologia* a speech in defense < *apo-* from, off + *logos* speech]
— Syn. 1. *Apology, excuse, acknowledgment,* and *confession* concern the admission of fault or error. In present usage, the man who makes an *apology* admits himself to be in the wrong. An *excuse* is also an implicit admission of wrong, but it is offered as a full or partial justification of one's actions. *Acknowledgment* is neutral, and when used with reference to an alleged fault, it is merely an admission of responsibility, not of guilt. A *confession* is a full *acknowledgment* of grave wrongdoing or crime, with or without *apology* or *excuse.*

ap·o·lune (ap'ə-lōōn) That point in the lunar orbit of an artificial satellite or other celestial body which is farthest from the moon. [< APO- away from + Fr. *lune* moon]

ap·o·mix·is (ap'ə-mik'sis) *n.* **1.** *Biol.* Parthenogenesis. **2.** *Bot.* Reproduction from cells other than ovules. [< NL < APO- from + Gk. *mixis* a mingling] **— ap'o·mic'tic** (-mik'-tik) *adj.*

ap·o·mor·phine (ap'ə-môr'fēn, -fin) *n.* A crystalline alkaloid, $C_{17}H_{17}O_2N$, obtained from morphine by removing one molecule of water, used as an emetic and expectorant.

ap·o·neu·ro·sis (ap'ə-nŏŏ-rō'sis, -nyŏŏ-) *n. pl.* **·ses** (-sēz) *Anat.* The white fibrous tissue at the end or attachment of certain muscles. [< NL < Gk. *aponeurōsis* < *apo-* from + *neuron* a nerve] **— ap'o·neu·rot'ic** (-rot'ik) *adj.*

ap·o·pemp·tic (ap'ə-pemp'tik) *Archaic adj.* Valedictory. **—** *n.* A farewell hymn or ode. [< Gk. *apopemptikos* < *apopempein* to send away < *apo-* away + *pempein* to send]

a·poph·a·sis (ə-pof'ə-sis) *n.* A mentioning of something by denying that it will be mentioned. Example: *I will not remind you of his heroism.* [< NL < Gk. *apophasis* denial < *apophanai* deny < *apo-* away + *phanai* to speak]

ap·o·phthegm (ap'ə-them) See APOTHEGM.

a·poph·y·ge (ə-pof'ə-jē) *n. Archit.* **1.** A concave curve in a column where the shaft rises from the base or joins the capital. For illustration see TUSCAN ORDER. **2.** A hollow molding immediately below the echinus of some Doric capitals. Also called *scape.* [< Gk. *apophygē* escape < *apopheugein* to flee away < *apo-* away + *pheugein* to flee]

a·poph·yl·lite (ə-pof'ə-līt, ap'ə-fil'īt) *n. Chem.* A white, crystalline silicate of calcium and hydrogen, often with potassium and fluorine. [< APO- + Gk. *phyllon* leaf + -ITE¹]

a·poph·y·sis (ə-pof'ə-sis) *n. pl.* **·ses** (-sēz) **1.** *Anat.* A bony protuberance, as of a vertebra. **2.** *Zool.* In arthropods, any hardened process of the body wall. **3.** *Geol.* A branching offshoot from an intrusion of igneous rock. [< NL < Gk., branch, offshoot < *apo-* from + *phyein* to grow]

ap·o·plec·tic (ap'ə-plek'tik) *adj.* Pertaining to, affected with, or tending toward apoplexy. Also **ap'o·plec'ti·cal. —** *n.* A person subject to apoplexy.

ap·o·plex·y (ap'ə-plek'sē) *n. Pathol.* **1.** Sudden loss or diminution of sensation and of the power of voluntary motion, caused by an acute vascular lesion of the brain, as from hemorrhage; a stroke of paralysis. **2.** A sudden discharge of blood within an organ. [< OF *apoplexie* < L *apoplexia* < Gk. *apoplēxia* < *apoplēssein* to disable by a stroke < *apo-* from, off + *plēssein* to strike]

a·port (ə-pōrt', ə-pôrt') *adj. Naut.* On or toward the port side.

ap·o·si·o·pe·sis (ap'ə-sī'ə-pē'sis) *n.* In rhetoric, a sudden interruption of a thought in the middle of a sentence, as if the speaker were unable or unwilling to continue. [< L < Gk. *aposiōpēsis* < *aposiōpaein* < *apo-* from + *siōpaein* to be silent] **— ap'o·si'o·pet'ic** (-pet'ik) *adj.*

a·pos·ta·sy (ə-pos'tə-sē) *n. pl.* **·sies** Desertion of one's faith, religion, party, or principles. Also **a·pos'ta·cy.** [< L *apostasia* < Gk., var. of *apostasis* a standing off, desertion < *apo-* away + *stasis* a standing]

a·pos·tate (ə-pos'tāt, -tit) *adj.* Guilty of apostasy; false. **—** *n.* One who apostatizes.

a·pos·ta·tize (ə-pos'tə-tīz) *v.i.* **·tized, ·tiz·ing** To forsake one's faith or principles; become an apostate.

a pos·te·ri·o·ri (ā' pos·tir'ē·ôr'ī, -ō'rī) **1.** *Logic* Reasoning from facts to principles or from effect to cause: opposed to *a priori.* **2.** Inductive; empirical. [< L, from the later]

a·pos·til (ə-pos'til) *n.* A marginal note; annotation. Also **a·pos'tille.** [< F *apostille*; ult. origin unknown]

a·pos·tle (ə-pos'əl) *n.* **1.** One of the twelve disciples originally commissioned by Christ to preach the gospel (*Matt.*

x 2–4); later also denoting Matthias, who replaced Judas Iscariot (*Acts* i 26), and Paul (*Rom.* i 1). **2.** One of a class of missionaries or preachers in the early church (I *Cor.* xii 28). **3.** A Christian missonary who first evangelizes a nation or place. **4.** The earliest or foremost advocate of a cause. **5.** In the Mormon Church, one of the twelve members of the church's administrative council. Abbr. (for defs. 1, 5) *Ap.* [OE *apostol* < L *apostolus* < Gk. *apostolos* one sent forth, a messenger < *apostellein* < *apo-* from + *stellein* to send]

Apostles' Creed A traditional and still widely accepted Christian confession of faith, beginning "I believe in God the Father Almighty": originally attributed to the twelve apostles, but now assigned to the fourth or fifth century.

a·pos·to·late (ə-pos'tə·lit, -lāt) *n.* The dignity or office of an apostle. Also **a·pos'tle·ship.**

ap·os·tol·ic (ap'ə-stol'ik) *adj.* **1.** Of or pertaining to an apostle, the apostles, or their times. **2.** According to the doctrine or practice of the apostles. **3.** *Often cap.* Papal. Also **ap'os·tol'i·cal. — ap'os·tol'i·cism** *n.*

apostolic delegate A delegate or diplomatic agent sent to represent the Holy See in countries where no formal diplomatic relations with Rome exist.

Apostolic Fathers 1. A group of early Christian writers, including Clement of Rome, Ignatius, Polycarp, and others who were younger contemporaries of the apostles. **2.** An ancient collection of writings attributed to them.

apostolic see A church or diocese founded by an apostle, especially one in Rome, Jerusalem, or Antioch.

Apostolic See 1. The Church of Rome, regarded as having been founded by St. Peter. **2.** The papacy.

apostolic succession The regular and uninterrupted transmission of spiritual authority from the apostles, claimed for their bishops by the Anglican, Eastern Orthodox, Roman Catholic, and some other churches.

a·pos·tro·phe¹ (ə-pos'trə-fē) *n.* A symbol (') written above the line to mark the omission of a letter or letters from a word, to indicate the possessive case, and to denote certain plurals, as *5's,* cross your *t's.* [< F < L *apostrophus* < Gk. *apostrophos* (*prosōidia*) (the accent) of elision < *apostrephein* to elide, turn away < *apo-* away + *strephein* to turn] **— ap·os·troph·ic** (ap'ə-strof'ik) *adj.*

a·pos·tro·phe² (ə-pos'trə-fē) *n.* **1.** A digression from a discourse; especially, a turning aside, as from an audience, to speak to an imaginary or absent person. **2.** *Bot.* The arrangement of chlorophyll granules, as on the lateral walls of leaf cells, when exposed to strong light: opposed to *epistrophe.* [< L < Gk. *apostrophē* < *apostrephein.* See APOSTRO-PHE¹.] **— ap·os·troph·ic** (ap'ə-strof'ik) *adj.*

a·pos·tro·phize¹ (ə-pos'trə-fīz) *v.t. & v.i.* **·phized, ·phiz·ing** To shorten (a word) by the omission of a letter or letters.

a·pos·tro·phize² (ə-pos'trə-fīz) *v.t. & v.i.* **·phized, ·phiz·ing** To speak or write an apostrophe (to).

apothecaries' measure A system of liquid measure used in pharmacy. See table inside back cover. Abbr. *ap.*

apothecaries' weight A system of weights used in pharmacy. See table inside back cover. Abbr. *ap.*

a·poth·e·car·y (ə-poth'ə-ker'ē) *n. pl.* **·car·ies** One who keeps drugs for sale and puts up prescriptions; a druggist; pharmacist. [< OF *apotecaire* < LL *apothecarius* storekeeper < L *apotheca* storehouse < Gk. *apothēkē* < *apoti-thenai* to put away < *apo-* away + *tithenai* to put]

ap·o·the·ci·um (ap'ə-thē'shē·əm, -sē·əm) *n. pl.* **·ci·a** (-shē·ə, -sē·ə) *Bot.* An open, cup-shaped fruit body in lichens in which the asci-bearing layer lies exposed as the asci mature. Also **ap·o·the·ce** (ap'ə-thē'sē, ap'ə-thēs). [< NL, dim. of Gk. *apothēkē* storehouse] **— ap/o·the'cial** (-shəl) *adj.*

ap·o·thegm (ap'ə-them) *n.* A terse, instructive, practical saying; maxim: also spelled *apophthegm.* **— Syn.** See PROVERB. [< Gk. *apophthegma* a thing uttered, terse saying < *apophthengesthai* < *apo-* from + *phthengesthai* to utter] **— ap·o·theg·mat·ic** (ap'ə-theg·mat'ik) or **·i·cal** *adj.*

ap·o·them (ap'ə-them) *n. Geom.* The perpendicular from the center to any side of a regular polygon. [< APO- + Gk. *thema* that which is placed < *tithenai* to place]

a·poth·e·o·sis (ə-poth'ē·ō'sis, ap'ə·thē'ə·sis) *n. pl.* **·ses** (-sēz) **1.** Exaltation of a human to divine rank; deification. **2.** Supreme exaltation of any person, principle, etc. **3.** The essence or perfect example of something. [< L < Gk. *apotheosis* < *apo-* from + *theos* a god]

a·poth·e·o·size (ə-poth'ē·ə·sīz', ap'ə·thē·ə·sīz) *v.t.* **·sized, ·siz·ing 1.** To deify. **2.** To glorify; exalt.

ap·o·tro·pa·ic (ap'ə-trō·pā'ik) *adj.* Warding off evil. [< Gk. *apotropaios* < *apo-* away + *trepein* to turn]

app. 1. Apparent(ly): also **appar. 2.** Appended. **3.** Appendix. **4.** Appointed. **5.** Apprentice.

ap·pal (ə-pôl') *v.t.* **·palled, ·pal·ling** *Brit.* Appall.

Ap·pa·la·chi·a (ap'ə-lā'chē·ə, -lā'chə) The area surrounding the central and southern parts of the Appalachian Mountains, including parts of Alabama, Georgia, Kentucky, North Carolina, South Carolina, Tennessee, Virginia, West Virginia, and Pennsylvania.

Ap·pa·la·chi·an (ap'ə·lā'chē·ən, -chən, -lāch'ən) *adj.* Of, pertaining to, in, or near the Appalachian Mountains.

Appalachian Mountains A mountain system of eastern North America extending from the Gaspé Peninsula to Alabama; highest peak, Mt. Mitchell, 6,684 ft.

Appalachian tea 1. The leaves of either of two shrubs, the inkberry or the withe rod, used for tea in some localities of the United States. 2. Either of these two plants.

ap·pall (ə·pôl') *v.t.* To fill with dismay or horror; terrify; shock: also, *Brit.*, *appal.* [< OF *apallir* to pale < *a-* to (< L *ad-*) + *pale* pale < L *pallidus.* See PALLID.]

ap·pall·ing (ə·pô'ling) *adj.* Causing dismay or terror; frightful. — **ap·pall'ing·ly** *adv.*

ap·pa·nage (ap'ə·nij) *n.* 1. Provision made by a king for the support of his younger sons. 2. A territory or property so given; dependency. 3. A natural accompaniment, attribute, or endowment. Also spelled *apanage.* [< F *apanage* < OF *apaner* to nourish, ult. < L *ad-* to + *panis* bread]

ap·pa·ra·tus (ap'ə·rā'təs, -rat'əs) *n.*, *pl.* ·tus or (rarely) ·tus·es 1. A device or machine for a particular purpose: an X-ray *apparatus.* 2. An integrated assembly of tools, appliances, instruments, etc., used for a specific purpose. 3. *Physiol.* Those organs and parts of the body by means of which natural processes are carried on: digestive *apparatus.* 4. Apparatus criticus. — **Syn.** See MACHINE. [< L, preparation < *apparare* to make ready < *ad-* to + *parare* to prepare]

apparatus cri·ti·cus (krit'i·kəs) *Latin* 1. Books, materials, etc., used in literary work. 2. The body of notes, glossaries, etc., in an edition of a text.

ap·par·el (ə·par'əl) *n.* 1. Outer clothing; raiment. 2. *Eccl.* Any oblong piece of embroidery ornamenting the alb and amice. 3. Equipment or furnishings, especially for a ship. — **Syn.** See DRESS. — *v.t.* ·eled or ·elled, ·el·ing or ·el·ling. To clothe; dress. [< OF *apareil* preparation, provision < *apareiller* to prepare, ult. < L *ad-* to + *par* equal]

ap·par·ent (ə·par'ənt, ə·pâr'-) *adj.* 1. Readily perceived by the mind; evident; obvious. 2. Easily seen; visible. 3. Seeming, in distinction from real or true. Abbr. *app.*, *appar.* [< OF *aparant*, ppr. of *aparoir* to appear < L *apparere.* See APPEAR.] — **ap·par'ent·ness** *n.*
— **Syn.** 1. See EVIDENT. 3. *Apparent*, *seeming*, and *probable* all indicate a semblance of truth or reality. *Apparent* conveys more assurance than *seeming*, but less than *probable*: the *apparent* motion of the earth around the sun, the *seeming* honesty of his intentions, the *probable* cause of the fire.

ap·par·ent·ly (ə·par'ənt·lē, ə·pâr'-) *adv.* 1. Obviously; plainly. 2. Seemingly. Abbr. *app.*, *appar.*

ap·pa·ri·tion (ap'ə·rish'ən) *n.* 1. A visual appearance of a disembodied spirit; specter; phantom; ghost. 2. Anything that appears, especially if remarkable or startling; a phenomenon. 3. The act of appearing or being visible. 4. *Astron.* The period most favorable for observation of a heavenly body. — **Syn.** See GHOST. [< MF < L *apparitio*, *-onis* < *apparere.* See APPEAR.] — **ap'pa·ri'tion·al** *adj.*

ap·par·i·tor (ə·par'ə·tər, ə·pâr'-) *n.* 1. Formerly, an official of a civil court. 2. An official who serves summonses, etc., for an ecclesiastical court. [< L < *apparere* to appear]

ap·peal (ə·pēl') *n.* 1. An earnest entreaty for aid, sympathy, or the like; prayer; supplication. 2. The quality of being attractive. 3. A resort to some higher power or final means, for sanction, proof, or aid. 4. *Law* **a** The carrying of a case from a lower to a higher tribunal for a rehearing. **b** The right to do this. **c** A request to do this. **d** A case so carried. 5. In old English law, an accusation. — *v.t.* 1. *Law* To refer or remove, as a case, to a higher court. 2. *Archaic* To challenge. — *v.i.* 3. To make an earnest supplication or request, as for sympathy, corroboration, or aid. 4. To awaken a favorable response; be interesting: Does it *appeal* to you? 5. *Law* To remove a case, or request that a case be moved, to a higher court. 6. To resort or have recourse: with *to*: to *appeal* to reason. [< OF *apeler* < L *appellare* to accost, call upon, var. of *appellere* < *ad-* to + *pellere* to drive] — **ap·peal'a·ble** *adj.* — **ap·peal'er** *n.* — **ap·peal'ing·ly** *adv.*
— **Syn.** (noun) 1. plea, request, petition, suit.

ap·pear (ə·pir') *v.i.* 1. To come into view; become visible. 2. To seem, or seem likely. 3. To be clear to the mind; be obvious. 4. To come before the public; also, to be published, as a book. 5. *Law* To come formally into court as defendant or plaintiff, or as counsel. [< OF *aparoir* < L *apparere* < *ad-* to + *parere* to come forth, appear]

ap·pear·ance (ə·pir'əns) *n.* 1. The act of appearing or coming into view. 2. A coming into public view, as in the publication of a book. 3. External or physical aspect; presence: a commanding *appearance.* 4. *pl.* Circumstances or indications: *Appearances* are against him. 5. Outward show; pretense: an *appearance* of wealth. 6. An apparition; phenomenon. — **Syn.** See AIR.

ap·pease (ə·pēz') *v.t.* ·peased, ·peas·ing 1. To reduce or bring to peace; placate; soothe, as by making concessions or yielding to demands. 2. To satisfy or allay: *Appease* your hunger with this bread. [< OF *apaisier* < *a-* to (< L *ad-*) + *pais* peace < L *pax*] — **ap·peas'a·ble** *adj.* — **ap·peas'-a·bly** *adv.* — **ap·peas'er** *n.* — **ap·peas'ing·ly** *adv.*
— **Syn.** 1. calm, mollify, pacify.

ap·pease·ment (ə·pēz'mənt) *n.* 1. The act of placating or pacifying. 2. The policy of making territorial or other concessions to potential aggressors in order to maintain peace. — **Syn.** See PROPITIATION.

ap·pel (à·pel') *n.* In fencing, a feint, often accompanied by a stamp of the foot, to procure an opening. [< F, lit., a call]

ap·pel·lant (ə·pel'ənt) *adj.* *Law* Of or pertaining to an appeal; appellate. — *n.* One who appeals, in any sense. [< L *appellans*, *-antis*, ppr. of *appellare.* See APPEAL.]

ap·pel·late (ə·pel'it) *adj.* *Law* Pertaining to or having jurisdiction of appeals: an *appellate* court. [< L *appellatus*, pp. of *appellare.* See APPEAL.]

ap·pel·la·tion (ap'ə·lā'shən) *n.* 1. A name or title. 2. The act of calling or naming. — **Syn.** See NAME.

ap·pel·la·tive (ə·pel'ə·tiv) *adj.* 1. Serving to designate or name. 2. *Gram.* Denoting a class: said of common nouns. — *n.* 1. A title; appellation. 2. A common noun. — **ap·pel'la·tive·ly** *adv.* — **ap·pel'la·tive·ness** *n.*

ap·pel·lee (ap'ə·lē') *n.* *Law* One against whom an appeal is taken; the defendant in an appeal. [< F *appelé*, pp. of *appeler* to appeal]

ap·pel·lor (ə·pel'ôr, ap'ə·lôr') *n.* In old English law, a confessed criminal who accused an accomplice. [< AF *apelour*, OF *apeleor* < L *appellator* one who appeals < *appellare.* See APPEAL.]

ap·pend (ə·pend') *v.t.* 1. To add, as something subordinate or supplemental. 2. To hang or attach: to *append* a seal. — **Syn.** See ADD. [< L *appendere* < *ad-* to + *pendere* to hang]

ap·pend·age (ə·pen'dij) *n.* 1. Anything appended; a subordinate addition or adjunct. 2. *Zool.* Any part joined to or diverging from the axial trunk or from any adjunct of it. 3. *Bot.* A subordinate or subsidiary part, as a leaf.
— **Syn.** 1. *Appendage*, *adjunct*, *appurtenance*, *addition*, *attachment*, *accessory*, *appendix*, and *supplement* denote an added and usually subordinate part. An *appendage* is usually an organic part of the whole; an *adjunct* is joined to something else without becoming a part of it. We speak of a tree's leafy *appendages* (its limbs), but the suburban *adjuncts* of a city. *Appurtenance* is chiefly a legal term, denoting a right or privilege that goes with a property. *Addition* has a wide application, but usually denotes more of the same added to what already exists: an *addition* to a house; while an *attachment* is an optional *addition*, usually of a part, which increases the efficiency or usefulness of an object: an *attachment* for a sewing machine. *Accessories* contribute to the convenience, comfort, ease of operation, or good appearance of a thing, without being essential to it: automobile *accessories*, *accessories* for a blue dress. *Appendix* and *supplement* are used chiefly of parts added to a book or document for further explanation or detail.

ap·pen·dant (ə·pen'dənt) *adj.* 1. Attached or associated in a subordinate capacity; adjunct. 2. Hanging attached: *appendant* by a gold chain. 3. Attendant; consequent: a fee *appendant* to the work. 4. *Law* Belonging to a land grant or tenure as an added but lesser right. — *n.* 1. Something appended or attached. 2. *Law* A subsidiary right attached to one more important. Also **ap·pen'dent.**

ap·pen·dec·to·my (ap'ən·dek'tə·mē) *n.*, *pl.* ·mies *Surg.* The removal of the vermiform appendix. [< APPENDIX + -ECTOMY]

ap·pen·di·ceal (ap'ən·dish'əl, ə·pen'də·sē'əl) *adj.* *Anat.* Of or relating to the vermiform appendix.

ap·pen·di·ces (ə·pen'də·sēz) Alternative plural of APPENDIX.

ap·pen·di·ci·tis (ə·pen'də·sī'tis) *n.* *Pathol.* Inflammation of the vermiform appendix.

ap·pen·di·cle (ə·pen'di·kəl) *n.* A small appendage. [< L *appendicula*, dim. of *appendix*]

ap·pen·dic·u·lar (ap'ən·dik'yə·lər) *adj.* 1. Of, pertaining to, or being an appendage or appendicle. 2. *Anat.* Of or pertaining to the limbs or appendages.

ap·pen·dix (ə·pen'diks) *n.*, *pl.* ·dix·es or ·di·ces (-də·sēz) 1. An addition or appendage, as of supplementary matter at the end of a book. 2. *Anat.* **a** The vermiform appendix (which see). **b** A process or projection; an outgrowth or prolongation. — **Syn.** See APPENDAGE. [< L, an appendage < *appendere.* See APPEND.]

ap·per·ceive (ap'ər·sēv') *v.t.* ·ceived, ·ceiv·ing *Psychol.* To perceive with conscious attention, integrating new experiences, concepts, ideas, etc., with the old. [< OF *aperceveir*, ult. < L *ad-* to + *percipere.* See PERCEIVE.]

ap·per·cep·tion (ap'ər·sep'shən) *n.* 1. *Psychol.* Conscious perception. 2. The act of apperceiving, or the state of being apperceived. [< F *aperception* < *apercevoir* to see, recognize] — **ap'per·cep'tive** *adj.*

ap·per·son·a·tion (ə·pûr'sə·nā'shən) *n.* *Psychiatry* The compulsive identification with or impersonation of another person, noted in many mental disorders, especially schizophrenia. [< AD- + (IM)PERSONATION]

ap·per·tain (ap'ər·tān') *v.i.* To pertain or belong as by custom, function, nature, right, or fitness; relate: with *to.* [< OF *apertenir* < LL *appertinere* < L *ad-* to + *pertinere.* See PERTAIN.]

ap·pe·tence (ap'ə·təns) *n.* 1. Strong craving or propensity. 2. Instinct or tendency: the *appetence* of ducks for water. 3. *Chem.* Affinity. Also **ap'pe·ten·cy.** — **Syn.** See DESIRE. [< L *appetentia* < *appetere.* See APPETITE.] — **ap'pe·tent** *adj.*

ap·pe·tite (ap'ə·tīt) *n.* 1. A desire for food or drink. 2. An

physical craving or natural desire. **3.** A strong liking; inclination. [< OF *appetit* < L *appetitus* < *appetere* to strive for < *ad-* to + *petere* to seek] — **ap·pe·ti/tive** *adj.*
— **Syn. 2.** yearning, longing, appetence, propensity. See DESIRE. — **Ant.** aversion, antipathy, dislike, distaste, repugnance.

ap·pe·tiz·er (ap/ə·tī/zər) *n.* Anything that excites appetite or gives relish; especially, food or drink served before a meal to stimulate the appetite. Also *Brit.* **ap/pe·tis/er.**

ap·pe·tiz·ing (ap/ə·tī/zing) *adj.* Stimulating or tempting to the appetite. Also *Brit.* **ap/pe·tis/ing.** [Orig. ppr. of rare *appetize*] — **ap/pe·tiz/ing·ly** *adv.*

Ap·pi·an Way (ap/ē·ən) A paved road extending from Rome to Brundisium, begun in 312 B.C. and still existing in part. [after *Appius* Claudius Caecus, Roman consul]

ap·plaud (ə·plôd/) *v.t. & v.i.* **1.** To express approval (of) by clapping the hands. **2.** To commend; praise. — **Syn.** See PRAISE. [< L *applaudere* < *ad-* to + *plaudere* to clap hands, strike] — **ap·plaud/er** *n.* — **ap·plaud/ing·ly** *adv.*

ap·plause (ə·plôz/) *n.* Approval or commendation, especially as shown by clapping the hands, shouting, etc. [< L *applausus,* pp. of *applaudere.* See APPLAUD.] — **ap·plau·sive** (ə·plô/siv) *adj.* — **ap·plau/sive·ly** *adv.*
— **Syn.** *Applause, plaudit,* and *acclamation* refer to simultaneous expressions of approval or praise by a number of persons. *Applause* may be given by voice or by clapping the hands. A *plaudit* is a burst of *applause,* and is therefore chiefly used in the plural. *Acclamation* is vocal, referring to cries or shouts of praise.

ap·ple (ap/əl) *n.* **1.** The fleshy, edible fruit or pome of any variety of a widely distributed tree (*Malus malus*) of the rose family, usually of a roundish or conical shape with a depression at each end. **2.** The similar fruit of several allied species, as the crab apple. **3.** A tree of any one of the species bearing apples as its natural fruit; also, the wood of such a tree. **4.** One of several fruits or plants with little or no resemblance to the apple: May *apple,* love *apple,* etc. [OE *æppel*]

apple blossom The flower of any species of the genus *Malus:* State flower of Arkansas and Michigan.

apple butter A thick, brown, spiced applesauce used as a spread for bread.

apple cart A handcart used for peddling apples, etc. — **to upset the apple cart** To ruin someone's plans.

apple green A clear, light, yellowish green.

ap·ple·jack (ap/əl·jak/) *n.* Brandy made from fermented cider.

apple of discord In Greek mythology, the golden apple inscribed "for the fairest," thrown among the gods by Eris. Claimed by Hera, Aphrodite, and Athena, it was awarded by Paris to Aphrodite after she promised him Helen.

apple of Peru An annual herb (*Nicandra physalodes*) of the nightshade family.

apple of the eye 1. The pupil of the eye. **2.** Something precious.

apple polisher *U.S. Slang* One who seeks favor by obsequious behavior, flattery, etc.

ap·ple·sauce (ap/əl·sôs/) *n.* **1.** Apples stewed to a pulp. **2.** *U.S. Slang* Nonsense; bunk.

Ap·ple·seed (ap/əl·sēd/), **Johnny** See (John) CHAPMAN.

Ap·ple·ton (ap/əl·tən) A city in eastern Wisconsin; pop. 57,143.

Ap·ple·ton (ap/əl·tən), **Sir Edward** (**Victor**), 1892–1965, English physicist.

Appleton layer A region of the ionosphere about 150 miles above sea level that acts as a reflector of certain frequencies of radio waves: also called *F layer.* [after Sir E. V. *Appleton*]

ap·pli·ance (ə·plī/əns) *n.* **1.** A device or instrument; especially, an electrically powered device for household work, as a washer, vacuum cleaner, etc. **2.** The act of applying; application. **3.** *Obs.* Compliance. — **Syn.** See MACHINE.

ap·pli·ca·ble (ap/li·kə·bəl, ə·plik/ə-) *adj.* Capable of or suitable for application; relevant; fitting. [< L *applicare* to apply + -ABLE] — **ap/pli·ca·bil/i·ty, ap/pli·ca·ble·ness** *n.* — **ap/pli·ca·bly** *adv.*

ap·pli·cant (ap/li·kənt) *n.* One who applies, as for a position; a candidate. [< L *applicans, -antis,* ppr. of *applicare.* See APPLY.]

ap·pli·ca·tion (ap/li·kā/shən) *n.* **1.** The act of applying. **2.** That which is applied, especially as a remedial agent. **3.** Employment for a special purpose or use: the *application* of child psychology to education. **4.** Capacity of being used; relevance, as of a theory. **5.** Close attention: *application* to one's books. **6.** A request; especially, a formal, written request, as for a position. [< L *applicatio, -onis* a joining to < *applicare.* See APPLY.]

ap·pli·ca·tive (ap/li·kā/tiv) *adj.* Applying or capable of being applied; applicatory; practical.

ap·pli·ca·tor (ap/li·kā/tər) *n.* An instrument or utensil for applying medication, etc.

ap·pli·ca·to·ry (ap/li·kə·tôr/ē, -tō/rē) *adj.* Fit for application; practical.

ap·plied (ə·plīd/) *adj.* Put in practice; utilized: opposed to *abstract, theoretical,* or *pure: applied* science.

ap·pli·qué (ap/li·kā/) *adj.* Applied: said of ornaments, as in needlework, wood, metal, etc., cut from one piece of material and fastened to the surface of another. — *n.* Decoration or ornaments so applied. — *v.t.* **·quéd** (-kād/), **·qué·ing** (-kā/ing) To sew or decorate by appliqué work. [< F]

ap·ply (ə·plī/) *v.* **·plied, ·ply·ing** *v.t.* **1.** To bring into contact with something; put on or to. **2.** To devote or put to a particular use: to *apply* steam to navigation. **3.** To connect, as an epithet, with a particular person or thing. **4.** To give (oneself) wholly to; devote: to *apply* oneself to study. — *v.i.* **5.** To make a request or petition; ask: with *for:* to *apply* for a position. **6.** To have reference or appropriate relation; be relevant: This order *applies* to all. [< OF *aplier* < L *applicare* to join to < *ad-* to + *plicare* to fold]

ap·pog·gia·tu·ra (ə·poj/ə·tŏŏr/ə, -tyŏŏr/ə) *Ital.* äp·pôd/jä·tŏŏ/rä) *n. pl.* **·ras,** *Ital.* **·re** (-rā) *Music* A metrically accented tone of more complex relation to the prevailing harmony than the following tone, one step above or below it. [< Ital. < *appoggiare* to lean upon, rest]

ap·point (ə·point/) *v.t.* **1.** To name or select, as a person for a position, a time and place for an act, etc. **2.** To ordain, as by decree; command; prescribe: laws *appointed* by God. **3.** To fit out; equip: used chiefly in combination in the past participle: a *well-appointed* yacht. **4.** *Law* To establish as a trustee or guardian. [< OF *apointer* to arrange, settle < LL *appunctare* < L *ad-* to + *punctum* a point]

ap·point·ee (ə·poin/tē/) *n.* One appointed to an office or position.

ap·poin·tive (ə·poin/tiv) *adj.* Filled by appointment: an *appointive* office.

ap·point·ment (ə·point/mənt) *n.* **1.** The act of appointing or placing in office: the *appointment* of a judge. **2.** A position held by someone appointed. **3.** An agreement to meet someone or to be somewhere at a specified time; engagement. **4.** *Usually pl.* Equipment; furnishings. **5.** *Law* A power or right to control or designate the disposition of property.

Ap·po·mat·tox (ap/ə·mat/əks) A village in central Virginia; pop. 1,400. At **Appomattox Court House,** established in 1940 as a national monument, Lee surrendered to Grant, April 9, 1865, virtually ending the Civil War.

Appomattox River A river of central Virginia, flowing east about 150 miles to the James River.

ap·por·tion (ə·pôr/shən, ə·pōr/-) *v.t.* To divide and assign proportionally; allot. [< OF *apportionner* < *a-* to (< L *ad-*) + *portionner* to divide < L *portio, -onis* share]
— **Syn.** *Apportion, prorate,* and *ration* mean to divide up and distribute a quantity of something. We *apportion,* usually not in equal shares, but according to some just rule that fixes the size of each share. To *apportion* in accordance with some variable quantity, as population, income, need, etc., is to *prorate. Ration* refers to the distribution of a scarce commodity, usually in equal parts, so that no one is deprived of a share. Compare ALLOT.

ap·por·tion·ment (ə·pôr/shən·mənt, ə·pōr/-) *n.* **1.** The act of apportioning; allotment. **2.** *U.S.* The assignment of the number of representatives that a State may have in the Federal House of Representatives, or that a county or other political subdivision may have in a State legislature.

ap·pos·a·ble (ə·pō/zə·bəl) *adj.* Capable of being apposed; especially, of the human thumb, capable of being touched to the tip of each of the fingers.

ap·pose (ə·pōz/) *v.t.* **·posed, ·pos·ing 1.** To apply or put, as one thing to another: with *to:* to *appose* a seal to a document. **2.** To arrange side by side. [< OF *apposer* < *a-* to (< L *ad-*) + *poser* to put. See POSE[1].]

ap·po·site (ap/ə·zit) *adj.* Fit for or well adapted to the purpose; appropriate; relevant: an *apposite* simile. [< L *appositus,* pp. of *apponere* to put near to < *ad-* to + *ponere* to put] — **ap/po·site·ly** *adv.* — **ap/po·site·ness** *n.*

ap·po·si·tion (ap/ə·zish/ən) *n.* **1.** *Gram.* **a** The placing of one word beside another so that the second adds to or explains the first, and both have the same grammatical form or function, as *John, president* of the class. **b** The syntactical relationship between such words. **2.** A placing or being in immediate connection; application; addition. **3.** *Biol.* Growth or increase by juxtaposition, as of tissue. — **ap/po·si/tion·al** *adj.* — **ap/po·si/tion·al·ly** *adv.*

ap·pos·i·tive (ə·poz/ə·tiv) *adj.* In or pertaining to apposition. — *n.* A word or phrase in apposition.

ap·prais·al (ə·prā/zəl) *n.* **1.** An appraising. **2.** An official valuation, as for sale, taxation, etc. Also **ap·praise/ment.**

ap·praise (ə·prāz/) *v.t.* **·praised, ·prais·ing 1.** To make an official valuation of; set a price or value on. **2.** To estimate the amount, quality, or worth of; judge. [< AD- + PRAISE] — **ap·prais/a·ble** *adj.* — **ap·prais/er** *n.*
— **Syn. 1.** evaluate, value, assess, assay.

ap·pre·ci·a·ble (ə·prē/shē·ə·bəl, -shə·bəl) *adj.* Capable of being valued or estimated. — **ap·pre/ci·a·bly** *adv.*

ap·pre·ci·ate (ə·prē/shē·āt) *v.* **·at·ed, ·at·ing** *v.t.* **1.** To be fully aware of the value, importance, magnitude, etc., of. **2.** To esteem adequately or highly: to *appreciate* Homer. **3.** To be keenly sensible of or sensitive to: to *appreciate* shades

of meaning. **4.** To show gratitude for. **5.** To increase the price or value of. **6.** To estimate the worth of. — *v.i.* **7.** To rise in value. [< LL *appretiatus*, pp. of *appretiare* to appraise < *ad-* to + *pretium* price] — **ap·pre'ci·a'tor** *n.*
— **Syn. 2.** esteem, prize, value. — **Ant.** depreciate, undervalue.

ap·pre·ci·a·tion (ə·prē'shē·ā'shən) *n.* **1.** The act of placing an estimate on persons or things; judgment. **2.** Perception or awareness, as of qualities, values, etc.; sympathetic recognition of excellence. **3.** Gratitude. **4.** Formerly, expressed criticism. **5.** Increase in value.

ap·pre·ci·a·tive (ə·prē'shē·ā'tiv, -shə·tiv) *adj.* Capable of showing appreciation; manifesting appreciation. — **ap·pre'·ci·a'tive·ly** *adv.* — **ap·pre'ci·a'tive·ness** *n.*

ap·pre·ci·a·to·ry (ə·prē'shē·ə·tôr'ē, -tō'rē, -shə-) *adj.* Appreciative. — **ap·pre'ci·a·to'ri·ly** *adv.*

ap·pre·hend (ap'ri·hend') *v.t.* **1.** To lay hold of or grasp mentally; understand; perceive. **2.** To expect with anxious foreboding; dread. **3.** To arrest; take into custody. **4.** *Obs.* To take hold of. — *v.i.* **5.** To understand; grasp. [< L *apprehendere* < *ad-* to + *prehendere* to seize] — **ap'pre·hend'er** *n.*
— **Syn. 1.** *Apprehend*, *comprehend*, and *understand* agree in meaning to seize with the mind, but to *apprehend* is merely to perceive, while to *comprehend* something is to grasp its meaning in its entirety: to *apprehend* the difference between right and wrong, to try to *comprehend* the meaning of love. *Understand* is close in meaning to *comprehend*, but can also mean to have insight into or sympathy with: My wife doesn't *understand* me. **2.** See CATCH. — **Ant.** misapprehend, misunderstand, miss, overlook.

ap·pre·hen·si·ble (ap'ri·hen'sə·bəl) *adj.* Capable of being apprehended. — **ap'pre·hen'si·bil'i·ty** *n.*

ap·pre·hen·sion (ap'ri·hen'shən) *n.* **1.** Distrust or fear concerning the future; foreboding; misgiving. **2.** The power of apprehending; understanding. **3.** An estimate; opinion. **4.** Arrest; capture. — **Syn.** See ALARM, KNOWLEDGE.

ap·pre·hen·sive (ap'ri·hen'siv) *adj.* **1.** Fearful concerning the future; anxious; uneasy. **2.** Quick to apprehend or capable of understanding; perceptive. — **ap'pre·hen'sive·ly** *adv.* — **ap'pre·hen'sive·ness** *n.*

ap·pren·tice (ə·pren'tis) *n.* **1.** One who is bound by a legal agreement to serve another for a fixed period of time in order to learn a trade or business. **2.** Any learner or beginner. Also *prentice*. Abbr. *app.* — *v.t.* **·ticed**, **·tic·ing** To bind or take on as an apprentice. [< OF *aprentis* < *aprendre* to teach, learn < L *apprehendere* to comprehend. See APPREHEND.] — **ap·pren'tice·ship** *n.*

ap·pressed (ə·prest') *adj. Bot.* Pressed or applied closely against something, as leaves against a stem. [< L *appressus*, pp. of *apprimere* < *ad-* to + *premere* to press]

ap·pres·sor (ə·pres'ər) *n. Bot.* The expansion on the hyphae of certain parasitic fungi, with which they fasten onto the host. Also **ap·pres·so·ri·um** (ap'rə·sôr'ē·əm, -sō'rē-).

ap·prise (ə·prīz') *v.t.* **·prised**, **·pris·ing** To notify, as of an event; inform. Also **ap·prize'**. [< F *appris*, pp. of *apprendre* to teach, inform < L *apprehendere*. See APPREHEND.] — **ap·prise'ment** *n.* — **ap·pris'er** *n.*

ap·prize (ə·prīz') *v.t.* **·prized**, **·priz·ing** To appraise. Also **ap·prise'**. [Prob. < OF *apriser*, *aprisier* < *a-* on, to + *prisier* to value, appraise]

ap·proach (ə·prōch') *v.i.* **1.** To come near or nearer in time or space. — *v.t.* **2.** To come near or nearer to. **3.** To come close to, as in character or condition; approximate. **4.** To make advances to; offer a solicitation, proposal, or bribe to. **5.** To cause to move nearer. **6.** To start to deal with: to *approach* a problem. — **Syn.** See APPROXIMATE. — *n.* **1.** The act of approaching; a coming near. **2.** An approximation; nearness: an *approach* to the truth. **3.** A way or means of approaching; access. **4.** A method of beginning or accomplishing something. **5.** *Often pl.* An overture of friendship, etc.; advance. **6.** In golf, a stroke made after the tee shot, intended to land the ball on the putting green. **7.** *pl. Mil.* Constructed works, trenches, etc., by which besiegers attack a fortified position. [< OF *aprochier* < LL *appropiare* < L *ad-* to + *prope* near]

ap·proach·a·ble (ə·prō'chə·bəl) *adj.* **1.** Capable of being approached; accessible. **2.** Receptive to advances; easily approached. — **ap·proach'a·bil'i·ty, ap·proach'a·ble·ness** *n.*

ap·pro·bate (ap'rə·bāt) *v.t.* **·bat·ed**, **·bat·ing** *Rare* To approve. [< L *approbatus*, pp. of *approbare*. See APPROVE.]

ap·pro·ba·tion (ap'rə·bā'shən) *n.* **1.** The act of approving; approval. **2.** Sanction. **3.** *Obs.* Proof.

ap·pro·ba·tive (ap'rə·bā'tiv) *adj.* Expressing or implying approbation. Also **ap·pro·ba·to·ry** (ə·prō'bə·tôr'ē, -tō'rē). — **ap'pro·ba'tive·ness** *n.*

ap·pro·pri·a·ble (ə·prō'prē·ə·bəl) *adj.* Capable of being appropriated.

ap·pro·pri·ate (*adj.* ə·prō'prē·it; *v.* ə·prō'prē·āt) *adj.* Suitable for or belonging to the person, circumstance, or place; fit; proper; relevant. — *v.t.* **·at·ed**, **·at·ing** **1.** To set apart for a particular use: Congress *appropriated* the funds. **2.** To take for one's own use. [< L *appropriatus*, pp. of *appropriare* < *ad-* to + *proprius* one's own] — **ap·pro'pri·ate·ly** *adv.* — **ap·pro'pri·ate·ness** *n.* — **ap·pro'pri·a·tive** *adj.* — **ap·pro'pri·a'tor** *n.*

— **Syn.** (adj.) *Appropriate*, *proper*, *fit*, *suitable*, *fitting*, *meet*, *apt*, *relevant*, and *pertinent* mean in close accord with a purpose, need, circumstance, etc. *Appropriate* and *proper* things belong by their very nature to that with which they are associated. Something *fit* is adapted to the end in view, while *suitable* or *fitting* things conform to an occasion or to circumstances. Something particularly *suitable*, especially in the moral sense of right, fair, or deserved, is *meet*. *Apt* suggests clever contrivance to meet a need or serve a purpose. *Relevant* and *pertinent* are the weakest of these words, denoting merely actual connection between what is so described and some other matter. — **Ant.** inappropriate, unfair, unsuitable, irrelevant.

ap·pro·pri·a·tion (ə·prō'prē·ā'shən) *n.* **1.** The act of appropriating or setting apart; also, a taking or using as one's own. **2.** Anything, especially money, set apart for a special use, as by a legislature.

ap·prov·al (ə·prōo'vəl) *n.* **1.** The act of approving; approbation. **2.** Official consent; sanction. **3.** Favorable opinion; praise; commendation. — **on approval** For (a customer's) examination without obligation to purchase.

ap·prove[1] (ə·prōov') *v.* **·proved**, **·prov·ing** *v.t.* **1.** To regard as worthy, proper, or right; be favorably disposed toward. **2.** To confirm formally or authoritatively; sanction; ratify. **3.** *Archaic* To show or prove: often reflexive. **4.** *Obs.* To prove by trial; test. — *v.i.* **5.** To show or state approval: often with *of.* [< OF *aprover* < L *approbare* < *ad-* to + *probare* to approve, prove < *probus* good] — **ap·prov'a·ble** *adj.* — **ap·prov'er** *n.* — **ap·prov'ing·ly** *adv.*

ap·prove[2] (ə·prōov') *v.t. Law* To turn to one's profit; appropriate, as waste or common land. [< OF *approuer* profit < *a* to + *pro* profit]

approx. Approximate(ly).

ap·prox·i·mal (ə·prok'sə·məl) *adj. Anat.* Close together: said of the surfaces of teeth.

ap·prox·i·mate (*adj.* ə·prok'sə·mit; *v.* ə·prok'sə·māt) *adj.* **1.** Nearly exact, accurate, or complete. **2.** Like; resembling. **3.** Near; close together. — *v.* **·mat·ed**, **·mat·ing** *v.t.* **1.** To come close to, as in quality, degree, or quantity; approach. **2.** To cause to come near. **3.** *Math.* To calculate a value progressively closer to exactitude: to *approximate* the square root of 6. — *v.i.* **4.** To come near in quality, degree, etc. [< L *approximatus*, pp. of *approximare* to come near < *ad-* to + *proximus*, superl. of *prope* near] — **ap·prox'i·mate·ly** *adv.*

— **Syn.** (verb) **1.** *Approximate*, *near*, and *approach* mean to draw close to. *Approximate* is chiefly used in the estimate of measurement or conformance to a standard: to *approximate* the value of pi, to *approximate* the style of Tacitus. *Near* is rarely used in any other than a spatial sense: Hannibal *neared* the Alps; while *approach* may be used in a wide variety of senses: to *approach* a place, a person, a subject, a specified age or condition, etc.

ap·prox·i·ma·tion (ə·prok'sə·mā'shən) *n.* **1.** The act or result of approximating. **2.** *Math.* A result sufficiently exact for a specified purpose.

ap·pulse (ə·puls') *n.* **1.** *Physics* An approach or impact of one moving body toward or upon another. **2.** *Astron.* The approach of a heavenly body toward another or toward the meridian. [< L *appulsus*, pp. of *appellere* to drive to < *ad-* to + *pellere* to drive]

ap·pur·te·nance (ə·pûr'tə·nəns) *n.* **1.** Something attached to another, more important thing; an accessory; adjunct. **2.** *pl.* Apparatus. **3.** *Law* A thing annexed to another thing more worthy, as principal, and that passes as an incident to it. — **Syn.** See APPENDAGE. [< AF *apurtenance*, OF *apertenance* < LL *appertinere*. See APPERTAIN.]

ap·pur·te·nant (ə·pûr'tə·nənt) *adj.* Appertaining or belonging, as by right; accessory. — *n.* An appurtenance.

Apr or **Apr.** April.

a·prax·i·a (ə·prak'sē·ə, ā-) *n. Pathol.* The inability to use or to understand the uses of objects or to make purposeful movements, owing to lesions in the cortex of the brain. [< NL < Gk. *apraxia* inaction < *a-* not + *prassein* to do]

a·près moi le dé·luge (à·pre mwà' lə dā·lüzh') *French* After me the deluge: attributed to Louis XV.

a·pri·cot (ā'pri·kot, ap'ri·kot) *n.* **1.** A yellow, juicy fruit of a tree (*Prunus armeniaca*) of the rose family, similar to a small peach. **2.** The tree bearing this fruit. **3.** A pinkish yellow color. [Earlier *apricock* (prob. directly < Pg.), *abricot* < F *abricot* < Pg. *albricoque* or Sp. *albaricoque* < Arabic *al-barqūq* < Med.Gk. *praikokion* < L *praecoquus* early ripe < *prae-* before + *coquere* to cook]

A·pril (ā'prəl) *n.* The fourth month of the year, containing 30 days. Abbr. *Ap.*, *Apr*, *Apr.* [< L *Aprilis*]

April fool The victim of a practical joke on April 1, known as **April** (or **All**) **Fools' Day.**

a pri·o·ri (ā' prī·ô'rī, ā' prī·ō'rē) **1.** *Logic* Proceeding, as an argument, from cause to effect, or from an assumption to its logical conclusion: opposed to *a posteriori*. **2.** Prior to, and thus independent of, experience; innate. **3.** Previous to examination, or with insufficient examination. [< L, from what is before] — **a·pri·or·i·ty** (ā'prī·ôr'ə·tē, -or'-) *n.*

a·pron (ā'prən, ā'pərn) *n.* **1.** A garment of cloth, leather, etc., worn to protect or adorn the front of a person's clothes. **2.** *Mech.* Any of various overlapping pieces protecting parts of machines. **3.** A belt conveyer. **4.** *Engin.* **a** The platform or sill at the entrance to a dock. **b** The platform below a dam or in a sluiceway. **5.** *Geol.* A sheet of sand or gravel lying for some distance in front of the terminal moraines of a glacier. **6.** *Aeron.* A hard-surfaced area in front of and around a hangar or aircraft shelter. **7.** The part of a theater stage in front of the curtain. **8.** *Mil.* **a** A movable screen of camouflage material, used to conceal artillery. **b** A network of barbed wire surrounding a post or stake in an entanglement. — *v.t.* To cover or furnish with an apron. [< OF *naperon*, dim. of *nape* cloth < L *mappa* cloth, napkin; in ME *a napron* became *an apron*] — **a′pron·like′** *adj.*

ap·ro·pos (ap′rə-pō′) *adj.* Suited to the time, place, or occasion; pertinent; opportune: an *apropos* remark. — *adv.* **1.** With reference or regard; in respect: with *of*: *apropos* of spring. **2.** To the purpose; pertinently: He spoke quite *apropos*. **3.** By the way; incidentally: used to introduce a remark. [< F *à propos* < *à* to + *propos* purpose]

apse (aps) *n.* **1.** *Archit.* An extending portion of an edifice, usually semicircular with a half dome; especially, the eastern or altar end of a church. **2.** *Astron.* Apsis. [< L *apsis* arch < Gk. *hapsis* a fastening, loop, wheel < *haptein* to fasten] — **ap·si·dal** (ap′sə-dəl) *adj.*

ap·sis (ap′sis) *n.* *pl.* **ap·si·des** (ap′sə-dēz) **1.** *Astron.* **a** A point of an eccentric orbit that is nearest to or farthest from the center of attraction, as the aphelion or perihelion of a planet. **b** The line joining these points to form the major axis of such an orbit. **2.** *Archit.* An apse. **3.** A reliquary. [< L. See APSE.]

apt (apt) *adj.* **1.** Inclined; liable; likely. **2.** Quick to learn; intelligent. **3.** Pertinent; relevant. [< L *aptus* fitted, suited] — **apt′ly** *adv.* — **apt′ness** *n.*
— **Syn. 2.** quick, bright, clever, smart, alert. **3.** See APPROPRIATE.

apt. (*pl.* **apts.**) Apartment.

ap·ter·al (ap′tər·əl) *adj.* **1.** *Entomol.* Apterous. **2.** *Archit.* Having no lateral ranges of columns, as a temple. [< Gk. *apteros* wingless < *a-* without + *pteron* wing]

ap·ter·ous (ap′tər·əs) *adj.* **1.** *Entomol.* Lacking wings, as the silverfish and other thysanurans. **2.** *Bot.* Having no winglike expansions, as a petiole or stem. [See APTERAL.]

ap·ter·yx (ap′tər·iks) *n.* The kiwi, a bird. [< NL < Gk. *a-* without + *pteryx* wing]

ap·ti·tude (ap′tə-tood, -tyood) *n.* **1.** Natural or acquired ability or bent. **2.** Quickness of understanding; intelligence. **3.** The state or quality of being apt or fitting. — **Syn.** See GENIUS. [< F < LL *aptitudo* < L *aptus* fitted, suited. Doublet of ATTITUDE.]

aptitude test A test designed to indicate the ability or fitness of an individual to engage successfully in any of a number of specialized activities.

Ap·u·le·ius (ap′yə-lē′əs), **Lucius** Second-century Roman satirist and philosopher.

A·pu·lia (ə-pyōo′lyə) A Region of SE Italy; 7,469 sq. mi.; pop. 3,409,687 (1961); capital, Bari. Italian *Puglia.* — **A·pu′lian** *adj. & n.*

A·pu·re (ä-pōō′rä) A river in west central Venezuela, flowing east about 350 miles to the Orinoco.

A·pu·rí·mac (ä′pōō-rē′mäk) A river in southern Peru, flowing generally NW about 550 miles to the Ucayali.

A·pus (ā′pəs) *n.* A constellation, the Bird of Paradise. See CONSTELLATION. [< NL < Gk. *apous* footless]

a·py·ret·ic (ā′pī-ret′ik, ap/ī-) *adj. Med.* Without fever. [< Gk. *apyretos* < *a-* without + *pyretos* fever]

aq. or **Aq.** Aqua.

AQ or **A.Q.** *Psychol.* Achievement quotient.

A·qa·ba (ä′kä·bä) A port town in southern Jordan on the Gulf of Aqaba, the NE arm of the Red Sea; pop. 8,908 (1961).

aq·ua (ak′wə, ä′kwə) *n.* *pl.* **aq·uae** (ak′wē, ä′kwē) or **aq·uas** **1.** Water. **2.** A light bluish green color; aquamarine. — *adj.* Light bluish green. [< L]

aqua am·mo·ni·ae (ə-mō′ni-ē) Ammonium hydroxide. [< NL, ammonia water]

aq·ua·cade (ak′wə·kād) *n.* A spectacle of swimming and diving, often set to music. [< L *aqua* water + (CAVAL)CADE]

aqua for·tis (fôr′tis) Commercial nitric acid. Also **aq′ua·for′tis.** [< L, strong water]

Aq·ua-Lung (ak′wə·lung′) *n.* A scuba: a trade name. Also **aq′ua·lung′.**

aq·ua·ma·rine (ak′wə-mə-rēn′) *n.* **1.** A sea-green variety of precious beryl. **2.** A light bluish green color. — *adj.* Light bluish green. [< L *aqua marina* sea water]

aq·ua·naut (ak′wə-nôt) *n.* One who explores or performs tasks underwater and is trained and equipped to live underwater over a period of time. [< L *aqua* water + *-naut* (< Gk. *nautēs* sailor), on analogy with *aeronaut, astronaut*]

aq·ua·plane (ak′wə-plān) *n.* A board on which one stands while being towed over water by a motorboat. Compare SURFBOARD. — *v.i.* **planed, ·plan·ing** To ride an aquaplane. [< L *aqua* water + PLANE⁴]

aqua re·gi·a (rē′jē-ə) A mixture of nitric and hydrochloric acid, a chemical solvent for gold and platinum: also called *nitrohydrochloric acid.* [< L, royal water]

aq·ua·relle (ak′wə·rel′) *n.* A painting done in transparent water colors. [< F < Ital. *acquerella* water color, dim. of *acqua* water < L *aqua*] — **aq′ua·rel′list** *n.*

a·quar·i·um (ə-kwâr′ē·əm) *n.* *pl.* **a·quar·i·ums** or **a·quar·i·a** (ə-kwâr′ē·ə) **1.** A tank, pond, or the like for the exhibition or study of aquatic animals or plants. **2.** A public building containing such an exhibition. [< L, neut. sing. of *aquarius* pertaining to water < *aqua* water]

A·quar·i·us (ə-kwâr′ē·əs) *n.* A constellation, the Water Bearer; also, the eleventh sign of the zodiac. See CONSTELLATION, ZODIAC. [< L]

a·quat·ic (ə-kwat′ik, ə-kwot′-) *adj.* **1.** Living or growing in or near water: *aquatic* plants or birds. **2.** Performed on or in water: *aquatic* sports. — *n.* **1.** An aquatic animal or plant. **2.** *pl.* Aquatic sports, as boating, etc. [< L *aquaticus* < *aqua* water]

aq·ua·tint (ak′wə·tint′) *n.* **1.** A technique of producing tones in an engraving by treating the surface of a copper plate with an acid to give the effect of washes or tints in monochrome. **2.** An engraving printed from a plate so prepared. — *v.t.* To etch by aquatint. [< F *aquatinte* < Ital. *aqua tinta* dyed water < L *aqua tincta*]

a·qua·vit (ä′kwə-vēt) *n.* A Scandinavian liquor distilled from a grain or potato mash and flavored with caraway seed: also *akvavit.* [See AQUA VITAE.]

aqua vi·tae (vī′tē) **1.** Alcohol. **2.** Distilled spirits; whisky; brandy. [< L, water of life]

aq·ue·duct (ak′wə-dukt) *n.* **1.** A water conduit, especially one for supplying water to a community from a distance. **2.** A structure supporting a canal carried across a river or over low ground. **3.** *Anat.* Any of several canals through which body fluids are conducted: the Fallopian *aqueduct.* [< L *aquaeductus* < *aqua* water + *ductus*, pp. of *ducere* to lead]

a·que·ous (ā′kwē·əs, ak′wē-) *adj.* **1.** Pertaining to, like, or containing water; watery. **2.** Composed of matter deposited by water. [< L *aqua* water + *-ous*]

aqueous humor *Physiol.* A clear fluid filling the space in the eye between the cornea and the lens.

aqui- *combining form* Water: *aquiferous.* [< L *aqua*]

aq·ui·cul·ture (ak′wi·kul′chər, ā′kwi-) *n.* Hydroponics.

A·quid·neck (ə·kwid′nek) Rhode Island: the Indian and early colonial name.

a·quif·er·ous (ə·kwif′ər·əs) *adj.* Conveying or supplying water or watery fluid.

Aq·ui·la (ak′wə-lə) *n.* A constellation, the Eagle, containing the bright star Altair. See CONSTELLATION. [< L]

aq·ui·le·gi·a (ak′wə-lē′jē-ə) *n.* A plant, the columbine. [< NL < Med.L]

A·qui·le·ia (ä′kwē·lā′yä) A town in NE Italy; one of the chief cities of the Roman Empire; pop. about 1,400.

aq·ui·line (ak′wə-līn, -lin) *adj.* **1.** Of or like an eagle. **2.** Curving or hooked, like an eagle's beak: an *aquiline* nose. [< L *aquilinus* < *aquila* eagle]

A·qui·nas (ə-kwī′nəs), **Saint Thomas,** 1225?–74, Italian Dominican monk and theologian: called *the Angelic Doctor.*

Aq·ui·taine (ak′wə-tān′) A region of SW France; formerly a duchy, an independent kingdom, and the province of Guienne. Ancient

Aq·ui·ta·ni·a (ak′wə·tā′nē-ə).

a quo (ā′ kwō′) *Latin* From which.

ar¹ (är) See ARE².

ar² (är) *n.* The letter R.

ar- Assimilated var. of AD-.

ar. 1. *Heraldry* Argent. **2.** Aromatic. **3.** Arrival; arrive.

a.r. In the year of the reign (L *anno regni*).

-ar¹ *suffix* **1.** Pertaining to; like: *regular, singular.* **2.** The person or thing pertaining to: *scholar.* [< OF *-er, -ier* < L *-aris* (in nouns *-are*), var. of *-alis,* suffix of adjectives; or directly < L]

-ar² *suffix* A form of -ARY, -ER², refashioned in imitation of -AR¹: *vicar,* in ME *vicary, viker.*

-ar³ *suffix* A form of -ER¹, refashioned in imitation of -AR²: *pedlar.*

Ar *Chem.* Argon.

Ar. 1. Arabia; Arabic. **2.** Aramaic. **3.** Silver (L *argentum*).

A·ra (ā′rə) *n.* A constellation, the Altar. See CONSTELLATION. [< L]

A.R.A. 1. Air Reserve Association. **2.** American Railway Association. **3.** Associate of the Royal Academy.

Ar·ab (ar′əb) *n.* **1.** A native or inhabitant of Arabia. **2.** One of a Semitic-speaking people inhabiting Arabia from ancient times, commonly the nomadic Bedouins, now scattered and admixed with various other peoples. **3.** A horse of a graceful, intelligent breed originally native to Arabia. **4.** A street Arab (which see). — *adj.* Arabian.

Arab. Arabian; Arabic.

ar·a·besque (ar′ə·besk′) *n.* **1.** An ornament or design, as those used in Arabian or Moorish architecture, employing patterns of intertwined scrollwork, conventionalized leaves or flowers, etc. **2.** In ballet, a position in which the dancer extends one leg straight backward, one arm forward, and the other arm backward. **3.** *Music* **a** A short piano piece somewhat like a rondo. **b** An elaborate figuration or ornamentation of a melody or melodic passage. — *adj.* Relating to, executed in, or resembling arabesque; fanciful; ornamental. Also **ar′a·besk′**. [< F < Ital. *arabesco* < *Arabo* Arab]

ARABESQUE (*def.* 1)

A·ra·bi·a (ə·rā′bē·ə) A peninsula of SW Asia, between the Red Sea and the Persian Gulf; 1 million sq. mi.; anciently divided into **Arabia De·ser·ta** (di·zûr′tə), northern Arabia, **Arabia Fe·lix** (fē′liks), generally restricted to Yemen, and **Arabia Pe·trae·a** (pe·trē′ä), NW Arabia.

A·ra·bi·an (ə·rā′bē·ən) *adj.* Of or pertaining to Arabia or the Arabs. — *n.* An Arab (defs. 1 and 3).
Arabian camel See under CAMEL.
Arabian Desert 1. The desert in eastern Egypt between the Nile and the Gulf of Suez. **2.** Popularly, the desert in northern Arabia.
Arabian Nights A collection of stories from Arabia, India, Persia, etc., dating from the tenth century: also called *The Thousand and One Nights.*
Arabian Sea The part of the Indian Ocean between Arabia and India.
Ar·a·bic (ar′ə·bik) *adj.* Of or pertaining to Arabia, the Arabs, their language, culture, etc. — *n.* The Southwest Semitic language of the Arabs, now widely spread among Moslem nations.
ar·a·bic acid (ar′ə·bik) *Chem.* A white amorphous powder, $C_5H_{10}O \cdot H_2O$, contained in gum arabic and other gums.
Arabic numerals The symbols 1, 2, 3, 4, 5, 6, 7, 8, 9, and 0, in general use in Europe since about the tenth century.
a·rab·i·nose (ə·rab′ə·nōs, ar′ə·bə-) *n. Biochem.* A colorless crystalline sugar, $C_5H_{10}O_5$, of the pentose class, obtained from the gums of certain plants or by synthesis from glucose. [< (GUM) ARAB(IC) + -IN + -OSE²]
Ar·a·bist (ar′ə·bist) *n.* A student of or one versed in Arabic, Arabic literature, science, medicine, etc.
ar·a·ble (ar′ə·bəl) *adj.* Capable of being plowed or cultivated. — *n.* Arable land. [< L *arabilis* < *arare* to plow] — **ar′a·bil′i·ty** *n.*
Arab League A confederation, established 1945, of the states of Iraq, Jordan (then Trans-Jordan), Lebanon, Saudi Arabia, the United Arab Republic (Egypt), Syria, and Yemen, joined by 1959 by Libya, Morocco, Sudan, and Tunisia, and in 1961 by Kuwait.
Ar·a·by (ar′ə·bē) *Archaic or Poetic* Arabia.
a·ra·ceous (ə·rā′shəs) *adj. Bot.* Belonging to the arum family (*Araceae*) of plants, mainly tropical, and bearing flowers on a spadix that is usually surrounded by a spathe. [< NL *Araceae*, generic name < Gk. *aron* the cuckoopint]
A·rach·ne (ə·rak′nē) In Greek mythology, a Lydian girl who challenged Athena to a weaving contest and was changed by the goddess into a spider.
a·rach·nid (ə·rak′nid) *n.* Any of a class (*Arachnida*) of arthropods, including the spiders, scorpions, harvestmen, mites, etc. [< NL *Arachnida* < Gk. *arachnē* spider] — **a·rach·ni·dan** (ə·rak′nə·dən) *adj. & n.*
a·rach·noid (ə·rak′noid) *adj.* **1.** Like a spider's web; thin and fine. **2.** Of or pertaining to the arachnids. **3.** Of or pertaining to the arachnoid membrane. **4.** *Bot.* Composed of slender, entangled hairs; cobwebby. — *n.* **1.** An arachnid. **2.** *Anat.* The arachnoid membrane. [< Gk. *arachnē* spider + -OID]
arachnoid membrane *Anat.* The serous membrane enveloping the brain and the spinal cord between the dura mater and the pia mater. Also **arachnoid tissue.**
A·rad (ä·räd′) A city in western Rumania, on the Mureş; pop. 106,460 (1956).
A·ra·fu·ra Sea (ä′rä·fōō′rä) The part of the Pacific Ocean between northern Australia and New Guinea.
A·ra·gats (ä′rä·gäts′) See ALAGEZ.
Ar·a·gon (ar′ə·gon) A region of NE Spain comprising several modern provinces; 18,382 sq. mi.; formerly an independent kingdom. *Spanish.* **A·ra·gón** (ä′rä·gōn′).
A·ra·gon (à·rá·gôn′), Louis, born 1897, French poet, novelist, and journalist.
Ar·a·go·nese (ar′ə·gə·nēz′, -nēs′) *adj.* Of or pertaining to Aragon, its people, or their language. — *n.* **1.** *pl.* **·nese** A native or inhabitant of Aragon. **2.** The dialect of Spanish spoken in Aragon.
a·rag·o·nite (ə·rag′ə·nīt, ar′ə·gə-) *n.* A form of calcite crystallizing in the orthorhombic system. [after *Aragon*, Spain]

A·ra·guai·a (ä′rə·gwī′ə) A river in central Brazil flowing generally north 1,100 to 1,500 miles (est.) to the Tocantins. Also **A′ra·guay′a.**
a·ra·li·a·ceous (ə·rā′lē·ā′shəs) *adj. Bot.* Belonging to a family (*Araliaceae*) of plants having more than two carpels and a drupaceous fruit, as the English ivy and ginseng. [< NL *Aralia*, genus of plants + -ACEOUS]
Ar·al Sea (ar′əl) A salt inland sea in the SW Asiatic Soviet Union; 24,635 sq. mi. Also **Lake of Aral.** *Russian* **A·ral·sko·ye Mo·re** (ə·räl′y′skə·yə mô′ryə). See map of UNION OF SOVIET SOCIALIST REPUBLICS.
Ar·am (âr′əm) The Biblical name of an ancient country of SW Asia, roughly equivalent to modern Syria. Also **Ar·a·me·a** (ar′ə·mē′ə).
Ar·am (âr′əm), **Eugene,** 1704–59, English philologist; executed for murder.
Aram. Aramaic.
Ar·a·ma·ic (ar′ə·mā′ik) *n.* Any of a group of Northwest Semitic languages, including Syriac and the language spoken by Christ. *Abbr.* Ar., Aram. — **Biblical Aramaic** The language of the non-Hebrew portions of the Old Testament: erroneously called *Chaldee.* — *adj.* Aramean.
Ar·a·me·an (ar′ə·mē′ən) *adj.* Of or pertaining to ancient Aram or Aramea, or its peoples, languages, etc. — *n.* **1.** An inhabitant of Aram. **2.** Aramaic. Also **Ar′a·mae′an.**
A·ran·ta (ə·ran′tə) See ARUNTA.
Ar·an·y (ôr′ôn·y′), **Janos,** 1817–82, Hungarian poet.
A·rap·a·ho (ə·rap′ə·hō) *n. pl.* **·ho** or **·hoes** A member of a nomadic Algonquian tribe, now dwelling primarily in Oklahoma and Wyoming. Also **A·rap′a·hoe.**
ar·a·pai·ma (ar′ə·pī′mə) *n.* A large South American fresh-water food fish (*Arapaima gigas*), sometimes over 400 pounds in weight and 15 feet long. [< Pg. < Tupi]
Ar·a·rat (ar′ə·rat), **Mount** The highest peak in Turkey, in the eastern part; 16,945 ft.; traditional resting place of Noah's ark. *Gen.* viii 4. Turkish *Ağrı Dağı.*
A·ras (ä·räs′) A river forming the border between the Soviet Union and Turkey and Iran, flowing generally east 666 miles to the Kara River. Ancient **A·rax·es** (ə·rak′sēz). *Russian* **A·raks** (ä·räks′).
Ar·au·ca·ni·an (ar′ô·kā′nē·ən) *n.* **1.** A family of South American Indian languages spoken in Chile and northern Argentina. **2.** A member of a tribe speaking Araucanian. Also **A·rau·can** (ə·rô′kən). — *adj.* Of or pertaining to the Araucanians, their culture, or their language.
ar·au·ca·ri·a (ar′ô·kā′rē·ə) *n.* Any of a genus (*Araucaria*) of usually South American or Australian evergreen trees. [< NL < Sp. *araucano* Araucanian]
A·ra·wak (ä′rä·wäk) *n.* **1.** A family of South American Indian languages spoken in a wide area north of southern Bolivia and, at one time, also throughout the Antilles. **2.** A member of an Arawak-speaking tribe. — **A′ra·wa′kan** *adj.*
ar·ba·lest (är′bə·list) *n.* A medieval crossbow requiring a mechanical appliance to bend it. Also **ar′ba·list.** [< OF *arbaleste* < L *arcuballista* < *arcus* a bow + *ballista.* See BALLISTA.] — **ar′ba·lest′er** *n.*
Ar·be·la (är·bē′lə) A city in ancient Assyria on the site of modern Erbil, near which, at Gaugamela, Alexander the Great defeated Darius III in 331 B.C.
Ar·ber (är′bər), **Edward,** 1836–1912, English scholar and editor.
ar·bi·ter (är′bə·tər) *n.* **1.** A chosen or appointed judge or umpire, as between parties in a dispute. **2.** One who has matters under his sole control; an absolute and final judge. — **Syn.** See JUDGE. [< L, one who goes to see, a witness, judge < *ad-* to + *bitere, betere* to go] — **ar′bitress** *n.fem.*
ar·bi·tra·ble (är′bə·trə·bəl) *adj.* Subject to, capable of, or suitable for arbitration.
ar·bi·trage (är′bə·trij; *for def. 1, also* är′bə·träzh′) *n.* **1.** The simultaneous buying and selling of the same stocks, bonds, etc., in different markets, to profit from unequal prices. **2.** *Archaic* Arbitration. [< F < *arbitrer* to arbitrate] — **ar·bi·trag·ist** (är′bə·trə·jist) *n.*
ar·bi·tral (är′bə·trəl) *adj.* Pertaining to an arbitrator or arbitration; subject to arbitration.
ar·bit·ra·ment (är·bit′rə·mənt) *n.* **1.** Arbitration. **2.** The decision of an arbitrator; an award. **3.** The power or right to make such decision. Also **ar·bit′re·ment.** [< OF *arbitrement* < *arbitrer* to decide < L *arbitrari* < *arbiter.* See ARBITER.]
ar·bi·trar·y (är′bə·trer′ē) *adj.* **1.** Based on or subject to one's opinion, judgment, prejudice, etc. **2.** Absolute; despotic. **3.** *Law* Not determined by statute; discretionary.

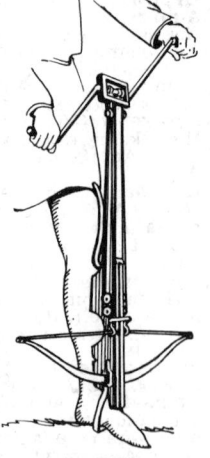

ARBALEST

[< L *arbitrarius* < *arbiter*. See ARBITER.] **— ar′bi·trar′i·ly** *adv.* **— ar′bi·trar′i·ness** *n.*
— Syn. 1. dogmatic, dictatorial. 2. See ABSOLUTE. **— Ant.** rational, reasonable, constitutional, restricted.

ar·bi·trate (är′bə·trāt) *v.* **·trat·ed, ·trat·ing** *v.t.* 1. To decide as arbitrator. 2. To submit to or settle by arbitration. **— v.i.** 3. To act as arbitrator 4. To submit a dispute to arbitration. [< L *arbitratus*, pp. of *arbitrari* < *arbiter*. See ARBITER.] **— ar′bi·tra′tive** *adj.*

ar·bi·tra·tion (är′bə·trā′shən) *n.* The hearing and settlement of a dispute between two parties by the decision of a third party or court to which the matter is referred by the contestants as a means of avoiding war, a strike, a lawsuit, etc. **— Syn.** See MEDIATION.

ar·bi·tra·tor (är′bə·trā′tər) *n.* 1. A person chosen by agreement of parties to decide a dispute between them. 2. One empowered to decide a matter; an arbiter. **— Syn.** See JUDGE. [< L]

Ar·blay (där′blā), **Madame d'** See BURNEY.

ar·bor¹ (är′bər) *n.* 1. A bower, as of latticework, supporting vines or trees. 2. *Obs.* An orchard. Also *Brit.* **ar′bour.** [Earlier *erber, herber* < AF, var. of OF *erbier, herbier* < L *herbarium* a collection of herbs < *herba* grass, herb]

ar·bor² (är′bər) *n.* *pl.* **ar·bo·res** (är′bər·ēz) *for def. 1*; **ar·bors** *for def. 2* 1. A tree: used chiefly in botanical names. 2. *Mech.* **a** A shaft, mandrel, spindle, or axle. **b** A principal support of a machine. [< L, tree]

Arbor Day A U.S. spring holiday observed in some States by planting trees.

ar·bo·re·al (är·bôr′ē·əl, -bō′rē-) *adj.* 1. Of or like a tree; arborescent. 2. Inhabiting trees, or adapted to life in trees. [< L *arboreus* < *arbor* tree]

ar·bo·re·ous (är·bôr′ē·əs, -bō′rē-) *adj.* 1. Arboreal. 2. Wooded.

ar·bo·res·cent (är′bə·res′ənt) *adj.* Treelike in character or shape; branching. [< L *arborescens, -entis,* ppr. of *arborescere* to grow into a tree < *arbor* tree] **— ar·bo·res′cence** *n.*

ar·bo·re·tum (är′bə·rē′təm) *n.* *pl.* **·tums** or **·ta** (-tə) A botanical garden exhibiting trees for their scientific interest and educational value. [< L < *arbor* tree]

arbori- *combining form* Tree: arboriculture. [< L *arbor* tree]

ar·bo·ri·cul·ture (är′bə·ri·kul′chər) *n.* The cultivation of trees and shrubs. **— ar′bo·ri·cul′tur·ist** *n.*

ar·bor·i·za·tion (är′bər·ə·zā′shən, -ī·zā′-) *n.* A treelike arrangement or figure, as in some minerals and fossils.

ar·bor·ous (är′bər·əs) *adj.* Of, pertaining to, or formed by trees.

ar·bor·vi·tae (är′bər·vī′tē) *n.* 1. An evergreen shrub or tree (genus *Thuya* or *Thuja*) of the pine family, especially *T. occidentalis*: also called *white cedar, tree of life.* 2. *Anat.* The branching appearance of the white matter shown in a section of the cerebellum. Also **arbor vitae.** [< L *arbor vitae* tree of life]

ar·bus·cle (är′bus·əl) *n.* 1. A dwarf tree. 2. An arbuscule. [< L *arbuscula,* dim. of *arbor* tree]

ar·bus·cule (är·bus′kyōōl) *n.* *Zool.* A tuft, as of cilia, etc. [See ARBUSCLE.]

ar·bute (är′byōōt) *n.* 1. The European strawberry tree. 2. The arbutus. [< L *arbutus* strawberry tree] **— ar·bu·te·an** (är·byōō′tē·ən) *adj.*

Ar·buth·not (är′bəth·not, är·buth′nət), **John,** 1667–1735, Scottish satirist and physician.

ar·bu·tus (är·byōō′təs) *n.* 1. Any member of a small genus (*Arbutus*) of evergreen trees or shrubs of the heath family, whose bark, leaves, and fruit are used in drugs. 2. The trailing arbutus (which see). [< L, strawberry tree]

arc (ärk) *n.* 1. Anything in the shape of an arch, a curve, or a part of a circle; a bow; arch. 2. *Geom.* A part of any curve, especially of a circle. 3. *Electr.* The bow of flame formed by the passage of an electric current across the gap between two conductors. 4. *Astron.* A part of the apparent path of a heavenly body. **— v.i. arced** (ärkt) or **arcked, arc·ing** (är′king) or **arck·ing** *Electr.* To form an arc. [< L *arcus* bow, arch. Doublet of ARCH¹.]

Arc (därk), **Jeanne d'** See JOAN OF ARC.

ARC or **A.R.C.** American Red Cross.

ar·cade (är·kād′) *n.* 1. *Archit.* **a** A series of arches with supporting columns or piers, standing against the face of a wall (**blind arcade**) or free, as a support of a ceiling, roof, etc. **b** *Rare* A single arch. 2. A roofed passageway or street, especially one having shops, etc., opening from it. **— v.t. ·cad·ed, ·cad·ing** To furnish with or form into an arcade or arcades. [< F < Med.L *arcata* < L *arcus* bow, arch]

Ar·ca·di·a (är·kā′dē·ə) 1. A Department of Greece, in the central Peloponnesus: 1,681 sq. mi.; pop. 154,361 (1951): capital, Tripolis; traditionally associated with the pastoral pursuits of its ancient inhabitants. See map of ATTICA. *Modern Greek* **Ar·ka·dhi·a** (är′kä·thē′ä). 2. Any region of ideal rustic simplicity and contentment. 3. A city in SW California, near Los Angeles; pop. 42,868.

Ar·ca·di·an (är·kā′dē·ən) *adj.* 1. Of or pertaining to Arcadia. 2. Rural or simple; pastoral. **— n.** 1. A native of or dweller in Arcadia. 2. One with simple, pastoral tastes.

Ar·ca·dy (är′kə·dē) *Archaic & Poetic* Arcadia.

ar·cane (är·kān′) *adj.* Secret; hidden. **— Syn.** See MYSTERIOUS. [< L *arcanus.* See ARCANUM.]

ar·ca·num (är·kā′nəm) *n.* *pl.* **·na** (-nə) 1. An inner secret or mystery. 2. One of the great secrets of nature which the alchemists sought to discover. 3. A secret remedy; elixir. [< L, neut. of *arcanus* hidden < *arca* chest]

ar·ca·ture (är′kə·chōōr) *n.* *Archit.* 1. A small arcade. 2. A blind arcade, used for ornament.

arc-bou·tant (är·bōō·tän′) *n.* *pl.* **arcs-bou·tants** (är·bōō·tän′) *French* An arched buttress.

arch¹ (ärch) *n.* 1. A curved structure spanning an opening, formed of wedge-shaped parts resting on supports at the two extremities. 2. Any similar structure or object. 3. A bowlike curve. 4. *Anat.* A curved or archlike part: the dental *arch.* **— v.t.** 1. To cause to form an arch or arches. 2. To furnish with an arch or arches. 3. To span; extend over, as an arch. **— v.i.** 4. To form an arch or arches. [< OF *arche* < Med.L *arca* < L *arcus* bow, arch. Doublet of ARC.]

ARCHES

A Rounded arch. B Segmental arch. C Elliptical arch. D Equilateral pointed arch with trefoil arches above. E Arch of discharge. F Rampant arch. G Extrados (*ex*) and intrados (*in*) of an arch. *a* Abutment or skewback. *c* Crown. *i* Impost. *k* Keystone. *p* Pier. *s* Springer. *sp* Spandrel. *t* Trefoil arch. *v* Voussoir.

arch² (ärch) *adj.* 1. Cunning; roguish; sly. 2. Most eminent; chief. [< ARCH-] **— arch′ly** *adv.* **— arch′ness** *n.*

arch- *prefix* 1. Chief; principal: *archbishop.* 2. Very great; extreme: *archenemy.* Also **archi-,** as in *archidiaconal.* [OE *arce-, erce-* < L *arch-, arche-, archi-* < Gk. *archos* ruler]

arch. 1. Archaic; archaism. 2. Archery. 3. Archipelago. 4. Architect; architectural; architecture.

Arch. Archbishop.

Ar·chae·an (är·kē′ən) See ARCHEAN.

archaeo- See ARCHEO-.

ar·chae·ol·o·gy (är′kē·ol′ə·jē), etc. See ARCHEOLOGY, etc.

ar·chae·op·ter·yx (är′kē·op′tər·iks) *n.* *Paleontol.* A fossil bird of the Upper Jurassic period, combining reptilian and avian characteristics: also spelled *archeopteryx.* [< NL < ARCHAEO- + Gk. *pteryx* wing]

Ar·chae·o·zo·ic (är′kē·ə·zō′ik) See ARCHEOZOIC.

ar·cha·ic (är·kā′ik) *adj.* 1. Belonging to a former period; no longer in use; antiquated. 2. Characterizing a word, an inflectional form, or a phrase used in an earlier period and having the flavor of the period, but no longer in current use. Also **ar·cha′i·cal.** *Abbr. arch.* **— Syn.** See ANCIENT, OBSOLETE. [< Gk. *archaikos* < *archaios* ancient]

ar·cha·ism (är′kē·iz′əm, -kā-) *n.* 1. An archaic word, idiom, or expression. 2. Archaic style or usage. *Abbr. arch.* **— ar′cha·ist** *n.* **— ar′cha·is′tic** *adj.*

ar·cha·ize (är′kē·īz, -kā-) *v.* **·ized, ·iz·ing** *v.t.* 1. To make archaic or archaistic. **— v.i.** 2. To use archaisms. Also *Brit.* **ar′cha·ise.** **— ar′cha·iz′er** *n.*

arch·an·gel (ärk′ān′jəl) *n.* 1. An angel of highest rank; in Christian legend one of seven, in the Koran one of four, chief angels. 2. *pl. Theol.* The eighth of the nine orders of angels. See ANGEL. 3. **the angelica.** **— the Archangel** In Christian legend, usually Michael. [< LL *archangelus* < Gk. *archangelos* < *arch-* chief + *angelos* angel] **— arch·an·gel·ic** (ärk′an·jel′ik) or **·i·cal** *adj.*

Arch·an·gel (ärk′ān′jəl) See ARKHANGELSK.

Archangel Bay See DVINA BAY.

arch·bish·op (ärch′bish′əp) *n.* *Eccl.* The chief bishop of a province. *Abbr. abp., Abp., Arch., Archbp.*

arch·bish·op·ric (ärch′bish′əp·rik) *n.* 1. The office, rank, term of office, or jurisdiction of an archbishop. 2. The province over which an archbishop has jurisdiction.

Archbp. Archbishop.

Archd. 1. Archdeacon. 2. Archduke.

arch·dea·con (ärch′dē′kən) *n.* *Eccl.* An official who administers the property, temporal affairs, missionary work, etc., of a diocese under powers delegated from the bishop: chiefly an Anglican usage. *Abbr. Archd.*

arch·dea·con·ry (ärch′dē′kən·rē) *n.* *pl.* **·ries** 1. The jurisdiction or office of an archdeacon. Also **arch′dea′con·ate** (-it), **arch′dea′con·ship.** 2. An archdeacon's residence.

---

arch·di·o·cese (ärch/dī/ə·sēs, -sis) *n.* The diocese or jurisdiction of an archbishop.

arch·du·cal (ärch/dōō/kəl, -dyōō/-) *adj.* Of or pertaining to an archduke or an archduchy.

arch·duch·ess (ärch/duch/is) *n.* **1.** The wife or widow of an archduke. **2.** A princess of the former royal family of Austria.

arch·duch·y (ärch/duch/ē) *n. pl.* **·duch·ies** The territory ruled by an archduke. Also **arch/duke/dom.** [< OF *archeduc*]

arch·duke (ärch/dōōk/, -dyōōk/) *n.* A chief duke, especially a prince of the former royal family of Austria. Abbr. *Archd.*

Ar·che·an (är·kē/ən) *adj. Geol.* Pertaining to a rock group associated with the Archeozoic era, consisting of the oldest stratified rocks, predominantly igneous and without fossil remains: also spelled *Archaean.* [< Gk. *archaios* ancient < *archē* beginning]

arched (ärcht) *adj.* **1.** Having the form of an arch. **2.** Covered or furnished with arches.

ar·che·go·ni·ate (är/kə·gō/nē·it, -āt) *adj.* Having archegonia.

ar·che·go·ni·um (är/kə·gō/nē·əm) *n. pl.* **·ni·a** (-nē·ə) *Bot.* The female sexual organ of the higher cryptogams, the analogue of the pistil of flowering plants. Also **ar·che·gone** (är/kə·gōn). [< NL < Gk. *archegonos* primitive parent < *archos* chief, first + *gonos* race, offspring] — **ar/che·go/ni·al** *adj.*

Ar·che·la·us (är/kə·lā/əs) Ruler of Judea 4 B.C.–A.D 6; son and successor of Herod I. *Matt.* ii 22.

arch·en·e·my (ärch/en/ə·mē) *n. pl.* **·mies** A principal enemy; especially, Satan.

ar·chen·ter·on (är·ken/tə·ron) *n. Biol.* The primitive enteron or alimentary cavity of embryos. [< ARCH(I)- + Gk. *enteron* intestine] — **ar·chen·ter·ic** (är/ken·ter/ik) *adj.*

archeo- *combining form* Ancient: *Archeozoic.* Also *archaeo-.* [< Gk. *archaios* ancient]

archeol. Archeology.

ar·che·ol·o·gy (är/kē·ol/ə·jē) *n.* The science or study of history from the remains of early human cultures as discovered chiefly by systematic excavations: also, *esp. Brit., archaeology.* [< ARCHEO- + -LOGY] — **ar·che·o·log·i·cal** (är/kē·ə·loj/i·kəl) or **·log/ic** *adj.* — **ar/che·ol/o·gist** *n.*

ar·che·op·ter·yx (är/kē·op/tər·iks) See ARCHAEOPTERYX.

Ar·che·o·zo·ic (är/kē·ə·zō/ik) *adj. Geol.* Of or pertaining to the oldest of the eras making up the geological record. See chart for GEOLOGY. Also spelled *Archaeozoic.* [< ARCHEO- + Gk. *zōion* animal]

arch·er (är/chər) *n.* One who shoots with a bow and arrow. [< AF *archer,* OF *archier* < L *arcarius* bowman < *arcus* bow]

Arch·er (är/chər) *n.* The constellation and sign of the zodiac Sagittarius.

Ar·cher (är/chər), **William,** 1856–1924, Scottish critic and dramatist.

arch·er·fish (är/chər·fish/) *n. pl.* **·fish** or **·fish·es** A percoid fish (*Toxotes jaculator*) of India and Polynesia, able to shoot drops of water to bring down its insect prey.

arch·er·y (är/chər·ē) *n.* **1.** The art or sport of shooting with bow and arrows. **2.** The weapons and outfit of an archer. **3.** Archers collectively. Abbr. *arch.*

ar·che·spore (är/kə·spôr, -spōr) *n. Bot.* The cell, or group of cells, from which the pollen mother cells are formed within a pollen sac, or the spore mother cells within a sporangium. Also **ar/che·spo/ri·um** (-spôr/ē·əm, -spō/rē·əm). [< NL *archesporium* < ARCHI- + Gk. *sporos* seed] — **ar/che·spo/·ri·al** *adj.*

ar·che·type (är/kə·tīp) *n.* An original or standard pattern or model; a prototype. — **Syn.** See IDEAL. [< L *archetypum* < Gk. *archetypon* pattern, model < *arche-* first + *typos* stamp, pattern] — **ar/che·typ/al** (-tī/pəl), **ar/che·typ/ic** (-tip/ik) or **·i·cal** *adj.*

arch·fiend (ärch/fēnd/) *n.* A chief fiend; especially, Satan.

archi- *prefix* **1.** Var. of ARCH-. **2.** *Biol.* Original; primitive: *archicarp.* [See ARCH-]

ar·chi·carp (är/kə·kärp) *n. Bot.* A female sex organ of certain fungi; an ascogonium. [< ARCHI- + Gk. *karpos* fruit]

ar·chi·di·ac·o·nal (är/ki·dī·ak/ə·nəl) *adj.* Pertaining to an archdeacon or an archdeaconry. [< L *archidiaconus* archdeacon]

ar·chi·di·ac·o·nate (är/ki·dī·ak/ə·nit, -nāt) *n.* The office of an archdeacon.

ar·chi·e·pis·co·pate (är/kē·i·pis/kə·pit, -pāt) *n.* The office or tenure of an archbishop. — **ar/chi·e·pis/co·pal** *adj.*

ar·chil (är/kil) *n.* A lichen (*Roccella tinctoria*) of the Cape Verde and Canary islands, yielding the dyestuff orchil: also spelled *orchil.* [Earlier *orchil* < OF *orchel, orcheil* < Ital. *orcello:* ult. origin uncertain]

Ar·chi·lo·chi·an (är/kə·lō/kē·ən) *adj.* Characteristic of or pertaining to **Ar·chil·o·chus** (är·kil/ə·kəs), Greek satiric poet of the early seventh century B.C., or to the verse form named after him. — *n.* The iambic trimeter or trochaic tetrameter as used by Archilochus.

ar·chi·mage (är/kə·māj) *n.* A chief magician; great wizard. Also **ar·chi·ma·gus** (är/kə·mā/gəs). [< ARCHI- + Gk. *magos* magician]

ar·chi·man·drite (är/kə·man/drīt) *n.* In the Eastern Orthodox Church: **a** The head of a monastery or of several monasteries. **b** A title of honor granted to distinguished celibate priests. [< Med.L *archimandrita* < LGk. *archimandrītēs* < *archi-* chief + *mandra* enclosure, monastery]

Ar·chi·me·de·an (är/kə·mē/dē·ən, -mə·dē/ən) *adj.* Of, discovered by, or pertaining to Archimedes.

Archimedean screw *Mech.* A spiral conduit about an inclined axis, for raising liquid. Also **Archimedes' screw.**

Ar·chi·me·des (är/kə·mē/dēz), 287?–212 B.C., Greek mathematician born in Sicily.

Archimedes' principle *Physics* The law that a body immersed in a fluid is buoyed up by a force equal to the weight of the displaced fluid.

ar·chine (är·shēn/) *n.* A Russian unit of linear measure, about 28 inches. [< Russ. *arshin* < Turkish *arsin*]

arch·ing (är/ching) *n.* **1.** An arch or series of arches. **2.** Any arch or curve.

ar·chi·pel·a·go (är/kə·pel/ə·gō) *n. pl.* **·goes** or **·gos** **1.** A sea with many islands. **2.** The islands in such a sea. Abbr. *arch.* — **the Archipelago** The Aegean Sea. [< Ital. *arcipelago,* ult. < Gk. *archi-* chief + *pelagos* sea; orig., with ref. to the Aegean Sea] — **ar·chi·pe·lag·ic** (är/kə·pə·laj/ik) *adj.*

Ar·chi·pen·ko (är/ki·peng/kō), **Alexander,** 1887–1964, Russian sculptor active in the United States.

ar·chi·pho·neme (är/ki·fō/nēm) *n.* The total of relevant features common to two phonemes after neutralization.

ar·chi·plasm (är/kə·plaz/əm) *n. Biol.* The permanent substance of the spindle fibers and astral rays of the cell, dispersed in the form of granules: originally spelled *archoplasm.*

ar·chi·tect (är/kə·tekt) *n.* **1.** One whose profession is to design and draw up the plans for buildings, etc., and supervise their construction. **2.** One who devises, plans, or creates anything. Abbr. *arch., archt.* [< F < L *architectus* < Gk. *architektōn* < *archi-* chief + *tektōn* worker]

ar·chi·tec·ton·ic (är/kə·tek·ton/ik) *adj.* **1.** Pertaining to an architect or architecture; constructive. **2.** Having architectural qualities of design and structure. **3.** *Philos.* Relating to the scientific classification of knowledge. Also **ar/chi·tec·ton/i·cal.** [< L *architectonicus* < Gk. *architektonikos* < *architektōn.* See ARCHITECT.]

ar·chi·tec·ton·ics (är/kə·tek·ton/iks) *n.pl.* (construed as *sing.*) **1.** The science of architecture. **2.** *Philos.* The scientific arrangement and construction of systems of knowledge. **3.** Structural design, as in works of music or art.

ar·chi·tec·ture (är/kə·tek/chər) *n.* **1.** The science, art, or profession of designing and constructing buildings or other structures. **2.** A style or system of building: Gothic *architecture.* **3.** Construction or structure generally; any ordered arrangement of the parts of a system: the *architecture* of the universe. **4.** A building, or buildings collectively. Abbr. *arch., archit.* [< F < L *architectura* < *architectus.* See ARCHITECT.]—**ar/chi·tec/tur·al** *adj.*—**ar/chi·tec/tur·al·ly** *adv.*

ar·chi·trave (är/kə·trāv) *n. Archit.* **1.** The part of an entablature that rests upon the column heads and supports the frieze: also called *epistyle.* For illustration see ENTABLATURE, COLUMN. **2.** A molded ornament skirting the head and sides of a door or window. [< F < Ital. < *archi-* chief (< Gk.) + *trave* beam < L *trabs*]

ar·chives (är/kīvz) *n.pl.* **1.** A place where public records and historical documents are kept. **2.** Public records, documents, etc., as kept in such a depository. [< F *archives,* pl. of *archif* < LL *archivum* < Gk. *archeion* a public office < *archē* government] — **ar·chi·val** (-kī/vəl) *adj.*

ar·chi·vist (är/kə·vist) *n.* A keeper of archives.

ar·chi·volt (är/kə·vōlt) *n. Archit.* **1.** An ornamental molding following the outer curve of an arch. **2.** An arch considered as supporting superincumbent weight. Also **ar/chi·vault** (-vôlt). [< Ital. *archivolto* an arched vault]

ar·chon (är/kon) *n.* **1.** One of the nine chief magistrates of ancient Athens. **2.** One of various officials in the Byzantine Empire and modern Greece. **3.** Any ruler or supreme commander. [< Gk. *archōn,* orig. ppr. of *archein* to rule]

ar·cho·plasm (är/kə·plaz/əm) See ARCHIPLASM.

arch·priest (ärch/prēst/) *n.* **1.** Formerly, the chief or senior priest of a cathedral chapter, serving as assistant to a bishop: later called *dean.* **2.** A rural dean. **3.** A papal delegate appointed in 1598 as superior of Roman Catholic secular clergy in England, succeeded in 1623 by a vicar apostolic. — **arch/priest/hood, arch/priest/ship** *n.*

arch·way (ärch/wā/) *n.* An entrance or passage under an arch.

-archy *combining form* Rule; government: *heptarchy.* [< Gk. *-archia* < *archos* ruler]

arc-jet engine (ärk/jet/) A jet engine in which the propellant gas is heated by passing through an electric arc.

arc light A lamp in which light of high intensity is produced between two adjacent electrodes connected with a powerful source of electricity. Also **arc lamp.**

ar·co·graph (är/kə·graf, -gräf) *n.* An instrument for drawing curves without striking them from a center point: also called *cyclograph.* [< L *arcus* arc + -GRAPH]

A.R.C.S. Associate of the Royal College of Science (Surgeons).

arc·tic (ärk′tik, är′tik) *adj.* **1.** Characteristic of the Arctic; extremely cold; frigid. **2.** *Biol.* Native to or inhabiting the Arctic or the regions near it: an *arctic* plant. — *n.* *Usually pl.* A warm, waterproof overshoe. [Earlier *artik* < OF *artique* < L *articus, arcticus* < Gk. *arktikos* of the Bear (the northern constellation *Ursa Major*), northern < *arktos* bear]

Arc·tic (ärk′tik, är′tik) *adj.* Of or relating to the region within the Arctic Circle. — **the Arctic** The region within the Arctic Circle.

Arctic char See under CHAR.

Arctic Circle The parallel at 66°33′ north latitude; the boundary of the North Frigid Zone.

Arctic Ocean An almost landlocked sea north of the Arctic Circle and surrounding the North Pole; 5,440,000 sq. mi.

Arc·tu·rus (ärk-tŏor′əs, ·tyŏor′-) *n.* An orange-red star, one of the 20 brightest, −0.06 magnitude; Alpha in the constellation Boötes. See STAR. [< L < Gk. *Arktouros* guardian of the bear < *arktos* a bear + *ouros* a guard]

ar·cu·ate (är′kyōo-it, -āt) *adj.* Bent or curved like a bow; arched. Also **ar′cu·at·ed.** [< L *arcuatus,* pp. of *arcuare* to curve like a bow < *arcus* a bow]

ar·cu·a·tion (är′kyōo-ā′shən) *n.* **1.** The act of curving or bending, or the state of being bent. **2.** *Archit.* The use of arches in building; arched work.

ar·cus (är′kəs) *n.* *Meteorol.* A cloud resembling an arch, seen usually in cumulonimbus clouds. [< L, arch]

-ard *suffix of nouns* One who does something to excess or who is to be disparaged: *drunkard, coward;* sometimes changed to *-art: braggart.* [< OF *-ard, -art* < G *-hard, -hart* hardy]

ar·deb (är′deb) *n.* A unit of capacity for dry measure, officially equivalent to 5.6 U.S. bushels, but varying from 4 quarts to 8 bushels as used in Egypt and neighboring countries. [< Arabic]

Ar·den (är′dən), **Forest of** Formerly, a large wooded tract in Warwickshire, England.

Ar·den Ar·cade (är′dən är·kād′) An unincorporated place in central California; pop. 82,492.

ar·den·cy (är′dən-sē) *n.* Intensity of emotion; ardor.

Ar·dennes (är-den′) A wooded plateau, mostly in SW Belgium, extending into NE France. Also **Ardennes Forest.**

ar·dent (är′dənt) *adj.* **1.** Passionate; zealous; intense. **2.** Glowing; flashing. **3.** Hot; burning. [< L *ardens, -entis,* ppr. of *ardere* to burn] — **ar′dent·ly** *adv.* — **ar′dent·ness** *n.* — **Syn.** 1. fervent, fervid, passionate, impassioned, vehement. Compare EAGER. — **Ant.** cool, cold, dispassionate, apathetic, indifferent.

ardent spirits Alcoholic distilled liquors.

ar·dor (är′dər) *n.* **1.** Warmth or intensity of passion or affection; eagerness; vehemence; zeal. **2.** Great heat, as of fire. Also *Brit.* **ar′dour.** [< L, a flame, fire > *ardere* to burn]

ar·du·ous (är′jōo-əs) *adj.* **1.** Involving great labor or hardship; difficult. **2.** Toiling strenuously; energetic. **3.** Steep; hard to climb or surmount. — **Syn.** See DIFFICULT. [< L *arduus* steep] — **ar′du·ous·ly** *adv.* — **ar′du·ous·ness** *n.*

are[1] (är, *unstressed* ər, r, ə) *v.* First, second, and third person plural, present indicative, of BE: also used as second person singular. [OE (Northumbrian) *aron*]

are[2] (âr, är) *n.* In the metric system, a surface measure equal to one hundred square meters: also spelled **ar.** See table inside back cover. Abbr. *a.* [< F < L *area.* Doublet of AREA.]

ar·e·a (âr′ē-ə) *n.* *pl.* **ar·e·as;** *for def. 6, often* **ar·e·ae** (âr′i-ē) **1.** A particular portion of the earth's surface; region. **2.** The surface included within a bounding line. **3.** The extent or scope of anything. **4.** The yard of a building. **5.** Any flat, open space. **6.** *Anat.* A section of the cerebral cortex with a specific function. Abbr. *a.* [< L, an open space or level ground. Doublet of ARE[2].] — **ar′e·al** *adj.*

ar·e·a·way (âr′ē-ə-wā′) *n.* **1.** A small sunken court before basement windows or a passageway to a basement door. **2.** A passageway.

ar·e·ca (âr′i-kə, ə-rē′kə) *n.* **1.** The fruit of any tree of a genus (*Areca*) of tropical palms, as the betel palm. **2.** Any tree of this genus. [< Pg. < Malayalam *ādekka*]

A·re·ci·bo (ä′rā-sē′bō) A port town in NW Puerto Rico; pop. 35,420 (est. 1970).

ar·e·ic (ar′ē-ik) *adj.* *Geog.* Pertaining to a region of the earth contributing little or no surface drainage, as the Sahara. [< L *arere* to be dry]

a·re·na (ə-rē′nə) *n.* **1.** The oval space in a Roman amphitheater, where contests and shows were held. **2.** Any place of this nature: a football *arena.* **3.** A scene or sphere of action or contest: the political *arena.* [< L, sand, sandy place]

ar·e·na·ceous (ar′ə-nā′shəs) *adj.* **1.** Growing in sandy places. **2.** Sandy. [< L *arenaceus* < *arena* sand]

arena theater A stage in the center of a room or auditorium, surrounded by seats and without proscenium: also called *theater-in-the-round.*

ar·e·nic·o·lous (ar′ə-nik′ə-ləs) *adj.* Living in sand. [< L *arena* sand + -COLOUS]

aren't (ärnt) Are not.

aren't I ◆ See note under AIN'T.

areo- *combining form* Mars: *areography.* [< Gk. *Arēs*]

ar·e·o·cen·tric (âr′ē-ō-sen′trik) *adj.* *Astron.* Having the planet Mars as center or origin.

ar·e·og·ra·phy (âr′ē-og′rə-fē) *n.* *Astron.* A description of the physical features of the planet Mars.

a·re·o·la (ə-rē′ə-lə) *n.* *pl.* **·lae** (-lē) or **·las** **1.** *Bot.* An interstice in a network of leaf veins. **2.** *Anat.* The colored circle about a nipple or about a vesicle. Also **ar·e·ole** (âr′ē-ōl) [< L, dim. of *area* open space] — **a·re′o·lar, a·re·o·late** (ə-rē′ə-lit, -lāt) *adj.* — **ar·e·o·la·tion** (âr′ē-ə-lā′shən) *n.*

Ar·e·op·a·gite (ar′ē-op′ə-jīt, -gīt) *n.* A member of the court of the Areopagus.

Ar·e·op·a·gus (ar′ē-op′ə-gəs) **1.** A hill NW of the Acropolis on which the highest court of ancient Athens held its sessions; also, the court itself. **2.** Any court whose judgments are final or authoritative. [< L < Gk. *Areiopagos* < *Areios* of Ares + *pagos* hill]

A·re·qui·pa (ä′rā-kē′pä) A Department of southern Peru; 24,528 sq. mi.; pop. 518,300 (est. 1970); capital, **Arequipa,** pop. 194,700.

Ar·es (âr′ēz) In Greek mythology, the god of war: identified with the Roman *Mars.*

a·rête (ə-rāt′) *n.* *Geog.* A sharp mountain spur or ridge. [< F < L *arista* awn of wheat, fishbone]

ar·e·thu·sa (ar′ə-thōo′zə, -sə) *n.* Any plant of a bulbous genus (*Arethusa*) of North American orchids, having a leafless or one-leaved scape and rose-colored flowers. [< NL, after *Arethusa*]

A·re·thu·sa (ar′ə-thōo′zə, -sə) In Greek mythology, a nymph who was changed into a fountain to escape her pursuer Alpheus.

A·re·ti·no (ä′rā-tē′nō), **Pietro,** 1492–1556, Italian poet and satirist.

A·rez·zo (ä-ret′tsō) A Province of Tuscany, central Italy; 1,247 sq. mi.; pop. 306,702 (1961); capital, **Arezzo,** pop. 74,245.

arg. **1.** *Heraldry* Argent. **2.** Silver (L *argentum*).

Arg. **1.** Argentina. **2.** Argyll.

ar·gal[1] (är′gəl) See ARGOL.

ar·gal[2] (är′gəl) *n.* The argali.

ar·ga·li (är′gə-lē) *n.* *pl.* **·lis** or **·li** **1.** An Asian wild sheep (*Ovis ammon*) with large horns curved spirally outward. **2.** Any of several other wild sheep, as the **bearded argali** or aoudad, or the **American argali** or bighorn. Also *argal.* [< Mongolian]

Ar·gand (är-gän′), **Aimé,** 1755–1803, Swiss physician and chemist.

ar·gent (är′jənt) *n.* **1.** *Heraldry* The silver or white color in armorial bearings. Abbr. *a., ar., arg.* **2.** *Archaic & Poetic* Silver. — *adj.* Like or made of silver; white; silvery: also **ar·gen·tal** (är-jen′təl). [< F < L *argentum* silver]

ARGALI
(4 feet high at shoulder)

Ar·gen·teuil (ár′zhän-tœ′y′) A city in north central France on the Seine; a suburb of Paris; pop. 90,480 (1968).

ar·gen·tic (är-jen′tik) *adj.* *Chem.* Containing or pertaining to silver, especially in its higher valence or ordinary proportion: *argentic* oxide, AgO.

ar·gen·tif·er·ous (är′jən-tif′ər-əs) *adj.* Containing or producing silver: *argentiferous* ore. [< L *argentum* silver + -FEROUS]

Ar·gen·ti·na (är′jən-tē′nə, *Sp.* är′hen-tē′nä) A Republic of southern South America between the Andes and the Atlantic; 1,084,362 sq. mi.; pop. 23,983,000 (est. 1969); capital, Buenos Aires. Officially **Argentine Republic.**

ar·gen·tine (är′jən-tin, -tīn) *n.* **1.** A metal resembling silver. **2.** A silvery substance obtained from fish scales and used in making artificial pearls. **3.** Silver. — *adj.* Silvery. [< F *argentin* < L *argentinus* < *argentum* silver]

Ar·gen·tine (är′jən-tēn, -tīn) *adj.* Of or pertaining to Argentina. — *n.* A native or citizen of Argentina: also **Ar·gen·tin·e·an** (är′jən-tin′ē-ən). — **the Argentine** Argentina.

ar·gen·tite (är′jən-tīt) *n.* An isometric, lead-gray, sectile silver sulfide, Ag₂S. [< L *argentum* silver + -ITE[1]]

ar·gen·tous (är-jen′təs) *adj.* *Chem.* Of or pertaining to a compound containing univalent silver.

ar·gen·tum (är-jen′təm) *n.* *Chem.* Silver. [< L]

ar·gil (är′jil) *n.* Potters' clay; white clay. [< MF *argille* < L *argilla* white clay < Gk. *argilla* < *argos* white]

ar·gil·la·ceous (är′jə-lā′shəs) *adj.* Containing, consisting of, or like clay; clayey.

ar·gil·lif·er·ous (är′jə-lif′ər-əs) *adj.* Containing or yielding clay. [< L *argilla* white clay + -FEROUS]

ar·gil·lite (är′jə-līt) *n.* An argillaceous sedimentary rock, with or without slaty cleavage: also called *mudrock, pelite.* [< L *argilla* white clay + -ITE[1]]

ar·gi·nine (är′jə-nēn, -nin, -nīn) *n.* *Biochem.* One of the amino acids essential to nutrition, C₆H₁₄O₂N₄, obtained from animal and vegetable proteins by hydrolysis or bacterial action. [< NL *argin*- (? < Gk. *arginoes* bright, white) + -INE²]

Ar·give (är′jīv, -gīv) *adj.* **1.** Of or pertaining to Argos or Argolis. **2.** Greek. — *n.* **1.** An inhabitant of Argos or Argolis. **2.** A Greek.

ar·gle (är′gəl) *v.i. Scot.* To argue.

Ar·go (är′gō) *n.* **1.** In Greek legend, the ship in which Jason and the Argonauts sailed for the Golden Fleece. **2.** Argo Navis.

ar·gol (är′gəl) *n.* Crude potassium bitartrate, the base of tartaric acid: also spelled *argal*. [ME *argoile* < AF *argoil*]

Ar·go·lis (är′gə·lis) A Department of Greece, in the NE Peloponnesus; 873 sq. mi.; pop. 85,389 (1951); capital, Nauplia. The Department borders on the **Gulf of Argolis**, an inlet of the Aegean.

ar·gon (är′gon) *n.* A colorless, gaseous element (symbol Ar) present in the atmosphere, used in electric display signs and as a filter for incandescent electric lamps. See ELEMENT. [< NL < Gk. neut. of *argos* idle, inert + -ON]

ar·go·naut (är′gə·nôt) *n. Zool.* The paper nautilus. Also **ar·go·nau′tid** (-nô′tid). [< NL *Argonauta*, generic name, after the Argonauts]

Ar·go·naut (är′gə·nôt) *n.* **1.** In Greek legend, one who sailed with Jason in the ship Argo to find the Golden Fleece. **2.** One who went to California in 1849 to hunt gold. [< L *Argonauta* < Gk. *Argonautēs* < *Argō*, the ship + *nautēs* sailor] — **ar′go·nau′tic** *adj.*

Argo Na·vis (nā′vis) Formerly, a large constellation, the Ship, now distinguished as four smaller constellations. See CONSTELLATION.

Ar·gonne (är′gon, *Fr.* år·gôn′) A wooded ridge in northern France; site of several major battles of World War I and World War II. Also **Argonne Forest.**

Ar·gos (är′gos, -gəs) A city in southern Greece; principal city of ancient Argolis; pop. 15,000.

ar·go·sy (är′gə·sē) *n. pl.* ·sies **1.** A large merchant ship. **2.** A fleet of merchant vessels. [Earlier *ragusy* < Ital. (*nave*) *Ragusea* (ship) from Ragusa, after *Ragusa*, Italian name of Dubrovnik, Yugoslav port]

ar·got (är′gō, -gət) *n.* The specialized vocabulary or jargon of any class or group, as that of the underworld. — **Syn.** See DIALECT. [< F] — **ar·got·ic** (är·got′ik) *adj.*

ar·gue (är′gyōō) *v.* ·gued, ·gu·ing *v.i.* **1.** To present reasons to support or contest a measure or opinion. **2.** To contend in argument; quarrel. — *v.t.* **3.** To present reasons for or against; discuss, as a proposal. **4.** To contend or maintain, by reasoning. **5.** To prove or indicate, as from evidence. **6.** To influence or convince, as by argument: *to argue someone into buying a house.* [< OF *arguer* < L *argutare*, freq. of *arguere* to make clear, prove] — **ar′gu·a·ble** *adj.* — **ar′·gu·er** *n.*
— **Syn. 1, 3.** *Argue, debate, discuss, dispute,* and *contend* refer to a verbal interchange among a number of persons, most usually to settle a question of fact or opinion. One *argues* by stating reasons for his views; a group *argues* by an interchange of views. To *debate* is to *argue* formally in accordance with a set of rules or an agreed procedure. Unlike *argue* and *debate, discuss* does not necessarily imply a difference of opinion: to *discuss* the details of a plan. To *dispute* is to offer opposing statements: to *dispute* the opinions of another; to *contend* is to offer statements favorable to one's own, or another's, point of view.

ar·gu·fy (är′gyə·fī) *v.t. & v.i.* ·fied, ·fy·ing *Informal* or *Dial.* To argue, especially obstinately. [< ARGUE + -FY]

ar·gu·ment (är′gyə·mənt) *n.* **1.** An angry discussion or quarrel; debate; disputation. **2.** A reason or reasons offered for or against something. **3.** Discourse intended to persuade or to convince. **4.** Something offered as evidence; proof. **5.** The plot or gist of a literary work; also, a short summary of its main points. **6.** *Logic* A Reasoning designed to prove or disprove a proposition. **b** The minor premise of a syllogism. **7.** *Stat.* A number given on the margin of a table to facilitate finding any of the included values. **8.** *Math.* An independent variable from which another quantity can be deduced or on which its calculation depends. **9.** *Obs.* Subject matter; theme. [< OF < L *argumentum* < *arguere* to make clear, prove]
— **Syn. 1.** dispute, fight, controversy. Compare QUARREL¹, ROW³. **2.** See REASON.

ar·gu·men·ta·tion (är′gyə·men·tā′shən) *n.* **1.** The methodical setting forth of premises and the drawing of conclusions therefrom. **2.** Interchange of argument; discussion; debate. **3.** A sequence of arguments; process of reasoning.

ar·gu·men·ta·tive (är′gyə·men′tə·tiv) *adj.* **1.** Characterized by argument; controversial. **2.** Given to argumentation; disputatious. — **ar′gu·men′ta·tive·ly** *adv.* — **ar′gu·men′ta·tive·ness** *n.*

ar·gu·men·tum ad ho·mi·nem (är′gyə·men′təm ad hom′·ə·nem) *Latin* An argument addressed to feelings and prejudices rather than to reason; literally, an argument to the man.

ar·gus (är′gəs) *n.* An East Indian pheasant (genus *Argusianus*). [after *Argus*]

Ar·gus (är′gəs) In Greek mythology, a giant with a hundred eyes, killed by Hermes, after which his eyes were put into the peacock's tail.

Ar·gus-eyed (är′gəs-īd′) *adj.* Sharp-sighted; vigilant.

Ar·gyle plaid (är′gīl) Plaid design of solid blocks or diamonds overlaid by a contrasting plaid. [after the tartan of the clan Campbell of *Argyll*]

Ar·gyll (är·gīl′) A county of western Scotland; 3,110 sq. mi.; pop. 59,345 (1961); county seat, Inverary. Also **Ar·gyll·shire** (är·gil′shir).

Ar·gy·rol (är′jə·rōl, -rol) *n.* Proprietary name of a compound of silver oxide and a protein, used as a local antiseptic in membranous infections: also **ar′gy·rol.**

a·ri·a (ä′rē·ə, âr′ē·ə) *n.* **1.** An air; melody. **2.** An elaborate melody for single voice, as in an opera or oratorio, often with instrumental accompaniment. [< Ital. < L *aer* air]

-aria *suffix* Used in forming new Latin names, especially in zoological and botanical classifications. [< NL < L -*arius*]

Ar·i·ad·ne (ar′ē·ad′nē) In Greek mythology, the daughter of Minos and Pasiphae, who gave Theseus the thread by which he found his way out of the Labyrinth.

-arian *suffix* Used in forming adjectives and adjectival nouns denoting occupation, age, sect, beliefs, etc.: *nonagenarian, predestinarian.* [< L -*arius* -ary + -AN]

Ar·i·an (âr′ē·ən) *adj.* Of or pertaining to Arius or Arianism. — *n.* A believer in Arianism.

Ar·i·an (âr′ē·ən, ar′-, är′yən) See ARYAN.

Ar·i·an·ism (âr′ē·ən·iz′əm) *n. Theol.* The doctrines of Arius and his followers, denying that Christ is of one substance with God the Father.

A·ri·ca (ä·rē′kä) A port city in northern Chile; pop. 46,542 (1960).

ar·id (ar′id) *adj.* **1.** Parched with heat; dry. **2.** Without interest or feeling; dull. [< L *aridus* < *arere* to be dry] — **a·rid·i·ty** (ə·rid′ə·tē), **ar′id·ness** *n.* — **ar′id·ly** *adv.*

ar·i·el (âr′ē·əl) *n.* **1.** An African gazelle (*Gazella dama*). Also **ariel gazelle.** [< Arabic *aryil*]

Ar·i·el (âr′ē·əl) *n.* The inner satellite of Uranus.

Ar·i·el (âr′ē·əl) In Shakespeare's *Tempest*, an airy spirit employed by Prospero.

Ar·ies (âr′ēz, âr′i·ēz) *n.* A constellation, the Ram; also, the first sign of the zodiac. See CONSTELLATION, ZODIAC. [< L]

ar·i·et·ta (ar′ē·et′ə) *n.* A short aria. Also **ar·i·ette** (ar′ē·et′) [< Ital.]

a·right (ə·rīt′) *adv.* In a right way; correctly; rightly.

A·ri·ka·ra (ə·rē′kə·rə) *n.* A member of a North American Indian tribe of Caddoan linguistic stock, formerly inhabiting the Dakotas.

ar·il (ar′il) *n. Bot.* An accessory covering of a seed, originating at or around the funiculus. [< NL *arillus* < Med.L *arilli* dried grapes] — **ar·il·late** (ar′ə·lāt), **ar′il·lat′ed** *adj.*

ar·il·lode (ar′ə·lōd) *n. Bot.* A false aril; an outgrowth originating at or around the micropyle. [< NL *arillus* (see ARIL) + -ODE²]

Ar·i·ma·the·a (ar′ə·mə·thē′ə) A town in ancient Palestine. Also **Ar′i·ma·thae′a.**

A·rim·i·num (ə·rim′ə·nəm) The ancient name for RIMINI.

A·ri·on (ə·rī′on) Seventh-century B.C. Greek poet and musician, reputed originator of the classical dithyramb.

ar·i·ose (ar′ē·ōs, ar′ē·ōs′) *adj. Music* Characterized by melody; songlike. [< Ital. *arioso* < *aria* air]

a·ri·o·so (ä·ryō′sō) *adj. Music* Characteristic of an aria. — *adv.* In the manner of an aria. — *n.* A passage, composition, etc., resembling an aria. [< Ital.]

A·ri·os·to (ä′rē·ôs′tō), Lodovico, 1474–1533, Italian poet.

-arious *suffix of adjectives* Connected with; pertaining to: *gregarious.* [< L -*arius* -ary + -OUS]

a·rise (ə·rīz′) *v.i.* **a·rose** (ə·rōz′), **a·ris·en** (ə·riz′ən), **a·ris·ing** **1.** To get up, as from a prone position. **2.** To rise; ascend. **3.** To come into being; originate; issue. **4.** To result; proceed. [OE *ārīsan* < *ā*- up + *rīsan* to rise]

a·ris·ta (ə·ris′tə) *n. pl.* **-tae** (-tē) *Biol.* An awn or any bristlelike appendage. [< L. Doublet of ARRIS.]

Ar·is·tae·us (ar′is·tē′əs) In Greek mythology, a son of Apollo, the tutelary deity of herdsmen and beekeepers.

Ar·is·tar·chus of Samos (ar′is·tär′kəs) Third-century B.C. Greek astronomer at Alexandria.

Aristarchus of Samothrace Second-century B.C. Greek grammarian and critic at Alexandria.

a·ris·tate (ə·ris′tāt) *adj. Biol.* Having a beardlike appendage; awned.

Ar·is·ti·des (ar′is·tī′dēz), 530?–468? B.C., Athenian general and statesman: called **the Just.**

Ar·is·tip·pus (ar′is·tip′əs), 435–366? B.C., Greek philosopher at Cyrene.

aristo- *combining form* Best; finest: *aristotype.* [< Gk. *aristos*]

a·ris·toc·ra·cy (ar′is·tok′rə·sē) *n. pl.* ·cies **1.** A hereditary nobility or privileged class. **2.** A state ruled by a privileged upper class, or by the nobility; also, its governing body; an oligarchy. **3.** Government by an upper class or the nobility. **4.** Originally, government by the best citizens, or a state governed by its best citizens. **5.** Any preeminent group: the *aristocracy* of talent. [< L *aristocratia* < Gk. *aristokratia* < *aristos* best + *krateein* to rule]

a·ris·to·crat (ə·ris′tə·krat, ar′is·tə·krat′) *n.* **1.** A member of an aristocracy. **2.** A proud and exclusive person. **3.** One who prefers an aristocratic form of government. **— a·ris'to·crat'ic** or **·i·cal** *adj.* **— a·ris'to·crat'i·cal·ly** *adv.*

Ar·is·toph·a·nes (ar'is·tof'ə·nēz), 450?–380?B.C., Greek comic dramatist.

Aristophanes of Byzantium, 257?–180? B.C., Greek grammarian and critic at Alexandria.

Ar·is·to·te·li·an (ar'is·tə·tē'lē·ən, -tēl'yən, ə·ris'tə-) *adj.* Pertaining to or characteristic of Aristotle or his philosophy. *— n.* An adherent of Aristotle's teachings; one who tends to be empirical or scientific in his method, rather than speculative or metaphysical. Also **Ar'is·to·te'le·an.** **— Ar'is·to·te'li·an·ism** *n.*

Aristotelian logic 1. The deductive logic of Aristotle, especially the theory of the syllogism. **2.** Logic dealing with relations between propositions in virtue of their form rather than their content.

Ar·is·tot·le (ar'is·tot'l), 384–322 B.C., Greek philosopher; pupil of Plato and teacher of Alexander the Great: called *the Stagirite.*

a·ris·to·type (ə·ris'tə·tīp) *n. Photog.* A print made on paper treated with mixed collodion and gelatin. [< ARISTO- + -TYPE]

arith. Arithmetic(al).

a·rith·me·tic (*n.* ə·rith'mə·tik; *adj.* ar'ith·met'ik) *n.* The art and technique of computing with numbers under the four operations of addition, subtraction, multiplication, and division. *— adj.* Of or pertaining to arithmetic: also **ar'ith·met'i·cal.** [< L *arithmetica* < Gk. (*hē*) *arithmetikē* (*technē*) (the) counting (art) < *arithmein* to count, number < *arithmos* number] **— ar'ith·met'i·cal·ly** *adv.*

a·rith·me·ti·cian (ə·rith'mə·tish'ən, ar'ith-) *n.* One who uses or is skilled in arithmetic.

arithmetic mean (ar'ith·met'ik) *Math.* The sum of a set of numbers, divided by the number of terms in the set. Compare GEOMETRIC MEAN.

arithmetic progression (ar'ith·met'ik) *Math.* A sequence of terms in which each, except the first, differs from the preceding one by a constant quantity, either plus or minus, as 2, 4, 6, 8. Compare GEOMETRIC PROGRESSION. Also **arithmetic series, arithmetic sequence.**

-arium *suffix of nouns* **1.** A place for: *herbarium.* **2.** Connected with: *honorarium.* [< L *-arius.* See -ARY[1].]

A·ri·us (ə·rī'əs, âr'ē·əs), 250?–336, Greek theologian of Alexandria. See ARIANISM.

a ri·ve·der·ci (ä rē'vā·der'chē) *Italian* Until we meet again.

Ariz. Arizona.

Ar·i·zo·na (ar'ə·zō'nə) A State of the SW United States, bordering on Mexico; 113,909 sq. mi.; pop. 1,772,482; capital, Phoenix; entered the Union Feb. 14, 1912: nicknames *Apache State, Grand Canyon State.* **— Ar'i·zo'nan** or **Ar'i·zo'ni·an** (-nē·ən) *adj. & n.*

ark (ärk) *n.* **1.** In the Bible: **a** The ship of Noah. *Gen.* vi–viii. **b** The chest containing the stone tablets bearing the Ten Commandments: also called **ark of the covenant.** *Ex.* xxv 10. **2.** In a synagogue, the chest or closet in which the scrolls of the Torah are kept. **3.** A large, flat-bottomed or awkward boat; scow. **4.** *Dial.* A chest or a bin. [OE *arc* < L *arca* chest]

Ark. Arkansas.

Ar·kan·san (är·kan'zən) *n.* A native or inhabitant of Arkansas.

Ar·kan·sas (är'kən·sô) A State of the south central United States, just west of the Mississippi River; 53,104 sq. mi.; pop. 1,923,295; capital, Little Rock; entered the Union June 15, 1836: nicknames *Land of Opportunity, Wonder State.* *— n.* A Quapaw.

Ar·kan·sas River (är'kən·sô, är·kan'zəs) A river rising in the Rocky Mountains of central Colorado and flowing 1,450 miles SE to the Mississippi in Arkansas.

Ar·khan·gelsk (är·khän'gelsk) A port city in the NW R.S.F.S.R., on the Dvina river; pop. 343,000 (1970): also *Archangel.*

Ark·wright (ärk'rīt), **Sir Richard,** 1732–92, English cotton manufacturer; invented the spinning jenny.

Arl·berg (ärl'berkh) An Alpine peak in western Austria; 5,910 ft.; winter sports center and site of the **Arlberg Tunnel,** 6.38 mi.

Ar·len (är'lən), **Michael,** 1895–1956, English novelist born in Bulgaria: original name **Dikran Kou·youm·djian** (kōō·yōōm·jän').

arles (ärlz) *n. Brit. Dial.* Money given in confirmation of a bargain. Also **arles'-pen'ny.**

Arles (ärlz, *Fr.* årl) A city in SE France, on the Rhône; site of Roman ruins: pop. 33,576 (1968).

Ar·ling·ton (är'ling·tən) **1.** An urban county of NE Virginia on the Potomac River opposite Washington, D.C.; site of a national cemetery containing the tomb of the Unknown Soldier; pop. 174,284. **2.** A town in NE Massachusetts, a residential suburb of Boston; pop. 53,524. **3.** A city in northern Texas, near Fort Worth; pop. 84,723.

Arlington Heights A village in NE Illinois; pop. 64,884.

arm[1] (ärm) *n.* **1.** *Anat.* **a** An upper limb of the human body, from the shoulder to the hand or wrist. **b** The part from the shoulder joint to the elbow joint. ◆ Collateral adjective: *brachial.* **2.** The forelimb of certain other vertebrates. **3.** An armlike part or appendage. **4.** Something intended to support or cover the human arm: *arm* of a chair. **5.** Anything branching out like an arm from a main body, or considered as a distinct part: an *arm* of the sea. **6.** *Naut.* **a** One of the projecting members of an anchor, ending in a fluke. **b** An end of a spar. **7.** Strength; power: the *arm* of the law. **— at arm's length** At a distance, so as to keep from being friendly or intimate. **— with open arms** Cordially; warmly. [OE *earm, arm*]

arm[2] (ärm) *n.* **1.** A weapon. **2.** A distinct branch of the military service: the air *arm.* *— v.t.* **1.** To supply with weapons; equip, as with tools. **2.** To make secure, as with a protective covering. **3.** *Mil.* To make (a bomb, torpedo, mine, etc.) ready for detonation, as by removing the safety pin. *— v.i.* **4.** To supply or equip oneself with weapons. **5.** To supply oneself with the means necessary for an undertaking. [< OF *armes.* See ARMS.] **— arm'er** *n.*

Arm. 1. Armenian. **2.** Armoric.

Ar.M. Master of Architecture (L *Architecturae Magister*).

ar·ma·da (är·mä'də, -mä'-) *n.* A fleet of war vessels. **— the Armada** The fleet sent against England by Spain in 1588, defeated by the English navy and almost entirely destroyed by storms: also **Invincible Armada, Spanish Armada.** [< Sp. < L *armata,* pp. of *armare* to arm. Doublet of ARMY.]

ar·ma·dil·lo (är'mə·dil'ō) *n. pl.* **·los** An American burrowing nocturnal mammal (family *Dasypodidae*) of the edentate order, having an armorlike covering of jointed plates; especially, the **Texas armadillo** (*Dasypus novemcinctus*) of Mexico and Texas. [< Sp., dim. of *armado* armed < L *armatus,* pp. of *armare* to arm]

ARMADILLO
(30 inches long; tail 12 inches)

Ar·ma·ged·don (är'mə·ged'n) *n.* **1.** In Biblical prophecy, the scene of a great battle between the forces of good and evil, to occur at the end of the world. *Rev.* xvi 16. **2.** Any great or decisive conflict. [< LL *Armagedon* < Gk. *Armageddon,* prob. < Hebrew *har* mountain + *Megiddo* (the plain of) Mount Megiddo, a perennial battlefield]

Ar·magh (är·mä') A county of Ulster province, Northern Ireland; 489 sq. mi.; pop. 128,200 (est. 1969); county seat, **Armagh,** pop. 11,920 (1961).

ar·ma·ment (är'mə·mənt) *n.* **1.** Often *pl.* The guns and other military equipment of a fortification, military unit, warship, etc. **2.** Any land, naval, or air force equipped for war. **3.** The act of arming or equipping for war. [< L *armamenta,* pl. < *armare* to arm < *arma* weapons]

ar·ma·men·tar·i·um (är'mə·mən·târ'ē·əm) *n. pl.* **·i·ums** or **·i·a** *Med.* The whole set or array of available methods, skills, drugs, equipment, etc.

ar·ma·ture (är'mə·chŏŏr) *n.* **1.** A piece of soft iron joining the poles of a magnet to prevent the loss of magnetic power. **2.** *Electr.* **a** In a dynamo or motor, the cylindrical, laminated iron core carrying the coils of insulated wire to be revolved through the magnetic field. **b** The part of a relay, as a buzzer or bell, that vibrates when activated by a magnetic field. **3.** *Biol.* **a** Protective covering for defense or offense, as the shells of animals. **b** A set of organs: the gastric *armature.* **4.** In sculpture, a framework to support the clay or other substance in modeling. **5.** Arms; armor. *— v.t.* **·tured, ·tur·ing** To furnish or provide with an armature. [< MF < L *armatura* armor < *armare* to arm. Doublet of ARMOR.]

arm·band (ärm'band') *n.* A brassard. Also **arm band.**

arm·chair (ärm'châr') *n.* A chair with side supports for the arms or elbows. *— adj.* **1.** Disposed to take a passive or inactive role: an *armchair* general. **2.** Lacking direct experience or knowledge: an *armchair* strategist.

armed (ärmd) *adj.* **1.** Provided with, supported by, or bearing arms or weapons. **2.** Having or characterized by a (specified kind of) arm or (a specified number of) arms: used in combination: *strong-armed; four-armed.* **3.** Prepared.

armed forces The combined military and naval forces of a nation; in the United States, the Army, Navy, Air Force, Marine Corps, and Coast Guard. Also **armed services.**

Armen. Armenian.

Ar·me·ni·a (är·mē'nē·ə, -mēn'yə) **1.** A former kingdom of NE Asia Minor; generally understood to include eastern Turkey and the Armenian S.S.R. **2.** A constituent republic of the Transcaucasian Soviet Union; 11,500 sq. mi.; pop. 2,493,000 (1970); capital, Yerevan. Officially **Armenian S.S.R.** Russian *Armyanskaya S.S.R.*

Ar·me·ni·an (är·mē'nē·ən, -mēn'yən) *adj.* Of or pertaining to the country, people, or language of Armenia. *— n.* **1.** A native of Armenia. **2.** The language of the Armenians, belonging to the Indo-European family of languages. Abbr. *Arm., Armen.*

Ar·men·tières (âr·män·tyâr') A commune in northern

France, near Lille; scene of heavy fighting in World War I, 1918; pop. about 25,000.

ar·met (är′met) *n.* A light helmet with visor and neck-guard. [< F < OF *armette,* dim. of *arme* weapon]

arm·ful (ärm′fo͝ol′) *n.* *pl.* **·fuls** That which is held, or as much as can be held, in the arm or arms.

arm·hole (ärm′hōl′) *n.* An opening for the arm in a garment.

ar·mi·ger (är′mə·jər) *n.* **1.** A knight's armorbearer; squire. **2.** One entitled to bear heraldic arms. Also **ar·mig·e·ro** (är·mij′ə·rō). [< L < *arma* weapons + *gerere* to bear]

ar·mil·la (är·mil′ə) *n. Bot.* A frill. [< NL < L, bracelet]

ar·mil·lar·y (är′mə·ler′ē, är·mil′ə·rē) *adj.* Of or consisting of a ring or rings. [< L *armilla* arm ring, bracelet]

armillary sphere *Astron.* An arrangement of concentric rings in the form of a skeleton sphere, representing the relative positions of the ecliptic and other celestial circles.

arm·ing (är′ming) *n.* **1.** The act or function of one who or that which arms. **2.** That with which anything is armed. **3.** *Naut.* Tallow on a sounding lead to bring up matter from sea bottom. **4.** *Heraldry* A coat of arms.

Ar·min·i·an·ism (är·min′ē·ən·iz′əm) *n. Theol.* The doctrines of Jacobus Arminius and his followers, opposed to Calvinism chiefly as holding a less rigorous view of predestination. **— Ar·min′i·an** *adj. & n.*

Ar·min·i·us (är·min′ē·əs), 17? B.C.–A.D. 21, Germanic chieftain; defeated Roman army at Teutoburger Wald A.D. 9: sometimes called *Hermann.*

Arminius, Jacobus, 1560–1609, Dutch Protestant theologian; originator of Arminianism.

ar·mip·o·tent (är·mip′ə·tənt) *adj. Archaic & Rare* Mighty in arms. [< L *armipotens, -entis* < *arma* arms + *potens.* See POTENT.] **— ar·mip′o·tence** *n.*

ar·mi·stice (är′mə·stis) *n.* A temporary cessation of hostilities by mutual agreement; a truce. [< F < L *armistitium* < *arma* arms + *sistere* to stop, stand still]

Armistice Day See VETERANS DAY.

arm·let (ärm′lit) *n.* **1.** A little arm, as of the sea. **2.** A band worn around the arm. **3.** A small, short sleeve.

ar·moire (är·mwär′) *n.* A large, movable, often ornate cabinet or cupboard. [< F < OF *aumoire* < L *armarium* a chest, orig., a place for storing arms]

ar·mon·i·ca (är·mon′i·kə) *n.* Harmonica (def. 2).

ar·mor (är′mər) *n.* **1.** A defensive covering, as of mail for a warrior, or of metallic plates for a war vessel, a tank, etc. **2.** The aggregate of armored assault vehicles available to a military command. **3.** Any protective covering, as the shell of a turtle, a diver's suit, etc. **—** *v.t. & v.i.* To furnish with or put on armor. Also *Brit.* **ar′mour.** [< OF *armeüre* < L *armatura.* Doublet of ARMATURE.]

ar·mor·bear·er (är′mər·bâr′ər) *n.* One bearing the arms of a warrior; a squire; armiger.

ar·mored (är′mərd) *adj.* **1.** Protected by armor. **2.** Equipped with armored vehicles. Also *Brit.* **ar′moured.**

armored cable *Electr.* Cable encased in a flexible metal protective sheathing.

armored car 1. *Mil.* A wheeled motor vehicle provided with light armor and a machine gun or other ordnance, used especially for reconnaissance. **2.** A small truck or other vehicle with light armor plate, used to carry money, etc.

armored force A combination of tanks, armored cars, and other armored vehicles functioning as an offensive unit.

ar·mor·er (är′mər·ər) *n.* **1.** A maker, repairer, or custodian of arms or armor. **2.** A manufacturer of arms. **3.** *Mil.* An enlisted man in charge of the repair, maintenance, and supply of small arms. Also *Brit.* **ar′mour·er.**

ar·mo·ri·al (är·môr′ē·əl, -mō′rē-) *adj.* Pertaining to heraldry or heraldic arms. **—** *n.* A treatise on heraldry.

Ar·mor·i·ca (är·môr′ə·kə, -mor′-) An ancient name for the NW part of France, later identified with Brittany.

Ar·mor·i·can (är·môr′ə·kən, -mor′-) *adj.* Of Armorica, its people, or their language. **—** *n.* **1.** A native or inhabitant of Armorica. **2.** The Breton language. Also **Ar·mor′ic.** *Abbr. Arm.*

ar·mor·pierc·ing (är′mər·pir′sing) *adj.* Designating a type of projectile designed to penetrate heavy armor. *Abbr. AP*

armor plate A plate or covering of special high-carbon steel alloy containing variable proportions of nickel, chrome, and manganese, forged under great pressure and given a hard surface. **— ar′mor-plat′ed** (är′mər·plā′tid) *adj.*

ar·mor·y¹ (är′mər·ē) *n. pl.* **·mor·ies 1.** A place where arms are kept; arsenal. **2.** *U.S.* A building for the use of a body of militia, including storage for arms and equipment, drill rooms, etc. **3.** *U.S.* A factory for making firearms. **4.** *Archaic* Arms collectively; armor. **5.** *Archaic* The craft of the armorer. Also *Brit.* **ar′moury.** [Prob. < ARMOR]

ar·mor·y² (är′mər·ē) *n. Archaic* **1.** Armorial bearings; heraldic arms. **2.** Heraldry. [< OF *armoirie* < *armoier* blazoner < *armoier* to blazon, publish a coat of arms]

ar·mour (är′mər), etc. See ARMOR, etc.

Ar·mour (är′mər), **Philip Danforth,** 1832–1901, U.S. meat packer.

arm·pit (ärm′pit′) *n.* The cavity under the arm at the shoulder; axilla.

arms (ärmz) *n.pl.* **1.** Weapons collectively. **2.** Warfare. **3.** The official insignia or device of a state, person, or family. **4.** Heraldic symbols. **— to arms!** Arm yourselves! Make ready for battle! **— to bear arms 1.** To carry weapons. **2.** To serve as a member of the armed forces. **— under arms** Provided with weapons; ready for war. **— up in arms** Aroused and ready to fight. [< F *armes* < L *arma* weapons]

arms race A competitive increase in the quantity or efficiency of military weapons and operations by two or more nations.

Arm·strong (ärm′strông, -strong), **(Daniel) Louis,** 1900–71, U.S. jazz trumpeter. **— Neil,** born 1930, U.S. astronaut; first man to walk on the moon.

ar·mure (är′myo͝or) *n.* A twilled fabric woven in ridges to resemble chain mail. [< F < OF *armeüre.* See ARMOR.]

ar·my (är′mē) *n. pl.* **·mies 1.** A large organized body of men armed for military service on land. **2.** The total military land forces of a country, in some countries exclusive of the air forces. **3.** The largest administrative and tactical unit of the U.S. land forces, consisting of a headquarters, a variable number of corps, and supporting troops and trains: also called *field army.* **4.** Any large body of people, animals, etc.; host; multitude. **— United States Army 1.** The U.S. military land forces administered by the Department of the Army under the Department of Defense, and including the Regular Army, the Army Reserve, and the National Guard of the United States. **2.** Loosely, the Regular Army. *Abbr. USA* [< OF *armee* < L *armata.* Doublet of ARMADA.]
— Syn. 4. *Army, host, multitude,* and *legion* denote a large number of persons or things. *Army* suggests orderliness and common purpose: an *army* of ants advancing across the plain. *Host* and *multitude* both suggest great numbers, but a *host* also impresses the beholder by its striking array: a *host* of golden daffodils, *multitudes* of stars. *Legion,* usually in the plural, is a poetic substitute for *army.*

Army Air Forces The air arm of the U.S. Army before establishment of the separate U.S. Air Force in 1947. *Abbr. AAF, A.A.F.*

army ant A driver ant (which see).

army of occupation An army maintained in a defeated country to keep the peace and enforce the terms of surrender.

Army of the United States Formerly, the total body of personnel on active service with the United States Army, as differentiated from the Regular Army. See UNITED STATES ARMY under ARMY. *Abbr. AUS, A.U.S.*

army worm The larva of a noctuid moth (genera *Leucania* and *Persectania*) moving at times in vast destructive hosts.

Arne (ärn), **Thomas Augustine,** 1710–78, English composer.

Arn·hem (ärn′hem) The capital of Gelderland province, eastern Netherlands; a port on the Rhine; pop. 132,531 (est. 1970). *German* **Arn·heim** (ärn′hīm).

Arn·hem Land (ärn′hem) An area in northern Australia designated an aboriginal reserve in 1931; about 31,200 sq. mi.

ar·ni·ca (är′ni·kə) *n.* **1.** Any of a genus (*Arnica*) of widely distributed herbaceous perennials of the composite family. **2.** A tincture prepared from this herb, used for sprains and bruises. [< NL; ult. origin unknown]

Ar·no (är′nō) A river of central Italy, flowing 150 miles, generally west, to the Ligurian Sea.

Ar·nold (är′nəld), **Benedict,** 1741–1801, American Revolutionary general who became a traitor. **— Sir Edwin,** 1832–1904, English poet and Orientalist. **— Matthew,** 1822–88, English poet and critic. **— Thomas,** 1795–1842, English educator; father of Matthew.

Ar·nold von Win·kel·ried (är′nōlt fôn ving′kəl·rēt), died 1386, Swiss hero; victor over the Austrians at Sempach.

ar·not·to (är·not′ō) *n.* **1.** A small tropical American tree (*Bixa orellana*) that produces anatto. **2.** Anatto. [< Carib]

ar·oid (ar′oid) *Bot. adj.* Araceous. Also **a·roi·de·ous** (ə·roi′-dē·əs). **—** *n.* Any araceous plant. [< AR(UM) + -OID]

a·roint (ə·roint′) *v.i. Archaic* Avaunt! Begone!: used with reflexive *thee* or *ye.* Also **a·roynt′.** [Origin unknown]

a·ro·ma (ə·rō′mə) *n.* **1.** Fragrance, as from appetizing food, spices, etc.; agreeable odor. **2.** Characteristic quality or style. **— Syn.** See SMELL. [< L < Gk. *arōma, -atos* spice] **— a·ro·ma·tous** (ə·rō′mə·təs) *adj.*

ar·o·mat·ic (ar′ə·mat′ik) *adj.* **1.** Having an aroma; fragrant; spicy. Also **ar′o·mat′i·cal. 2.** *Chem.* Pertaining to a group of unsaturated hydrocarbon compounds of the closed-ring structure, including benzene. **—** *n.* Any vegetable or drug of agreeable odor. *Abbr. ar.* **— ar′o·mat′i·cal·ly** *adv.*

a·ro·ma·tic·i·ty (ə·rō′mə·tis′ə·tē) *n. Chem.* The aromatic character of certain hydrocarbons as determined by their molecular structure rather than by their smell.

a·ro·ma·tize (ə·rō′mə·tīz) *v.t.* **·tized, ·tiz·ing 1.** To make fragrant or aromatic. **2.** *Chem.* To convert (an aliphatic hydrocarbon) into one of the aromatic group.

A·roos·took River (ə·rōōs′to͝ok) A river in northern Maine, flowing generally east about 140 miles to the St. John River in New Brunswick, Canada.

a·rose (ə·rōz′) Past tense of ARISE.

A·rou·et (à·rwe′), **François Marie** See VOLTAIRE.

a·round (ə·round′) *adv.* **1.** On all sides; in various directions: It is raining all *around.* **2.** In the opposite direction to turn *around*. **3.** *U.S.* From place to place; here and there: to walk *around*. **4.** *U.S. Informal* Nearby; in the vicinity: Wait *around* until I call. **5.** In or to a particular place: Come *around* to see us again. **— to get around** *U.S. Informal* **1.** To be experienced and up to date. **2.** To overcome or cope with (someone or something). **— to get around to** *U.S. Informal* To give attention to or accomplish: He'll *get around to* it in time. **— to have been around** *U.S. Informal* To be experienced in the ways of the world. **—** *prep.* **1.** About the circumference or circuit of: *around* the world. **2.** On all sides of; surrounding or enveloping. **3.** *U.S. Informal* Here and there in: He wandered *around* the city. **4.** *U.S. Informal* Somewhere near or within: You'll find me *around* the house. **5.** *U.S. Informal* Somewhere near in time, amount, etc.; about: *around* midnight. [< A-¹ + ROUND]

a·rouse (ə·rouz′) *v.* **a·roused, a·rous·ing** *v.t.* **1.** To stir up, as from sleep; awaken. **2.** To excite, as to a state of high emotion; animate. **—** *v.i.* **3.** To arouse oneself. [< A-² + ROUSE] **— a·rous′al** (-zəl) *n.*

Arp (ärp), **Hans**, 1887–1966, French painter and sculptor born in Strasbourg (then Germany). Also **Jean Arp.**

ARP or **A.R.P.** Air raid precautions.

Ár·pád (är′päd), died 907, Magyar leader; founded Árpád dynasty; national hero of Hungary.

ar·peg·gi·o (är·pej′ē·ō, -pej′ō) *n. pl.* **·gi·os** *Music* **1.** The sounding or playing of the notes of a chord in rapid succession instead of simultaneously. **2.** A chord so played. [< Ital. < *arpeggiare* to play on a harp < *arpa* a harp]

ar·pent (är′pənt, *Fr.* àr·pän′) *n.* An old French measure of land, equivalent to about an acre. Also **ar′pen.** [< F]

ARPEGGIO
a and *b* express the same harmony.

ar·que·bus (är′kwə·bəs) *n.* A harquebus (which see).

arr. **1.** Arrange; arranged; arrangement(s). **2.** Arrival; arrive; arrived.

ar·rack (ar′ək) *n.* A strong Oriental liquor distilled from rice, molasses, etc. [< Arabic *'araq* juice]

ar·raign (ə·rān′) *v.t.* **1.** *Law* To call into court and cause to answer to an indictment. **2.** To call upon for an answer; accuse. **— Syn.** See ACCUSE. **—** *n.* Arraignment. [< AF *arainer*, OF *araisnier* < LL *arrationare* to call to account < L *ad-* to + *ratio, -onis* reason] **— ar·raign′er** *n.*

ar·raign·ment (ə·rān′mənt) *n.* **1.** *Law* The act of arraigning, or the state of being arraigned. **2.** An accusation.

Ar·ran (ar′ən) An island in the Firth of Clyde, Bute, Scotland; 166 sq. mi.

ar·range (ə·rānj′) *v.* **·ranged, ·rang·ing** *v.t.* **1.** To put in definite or proper order. **2.** To plan the details of; prepare for. **3.** To adjust, as a conflict or dispute; settle. **4.** *Music* To change or adapt for other instruments or voices. **—** *v.i.* **5.** To come to an agreement or understanding: with *with*. **6.** To see about the details; make plans: to *arrange* for a trip. Abbr. *arr.* [< OF *arangier* < *a-* to (< L *ad-*) + *rangier* to put in order < *rang* rank. See RANK¹.] **— ar·rang′er** *n.*

ar·range·ment (ə·rānj′mənt) *n.* **1.** The act of arranging, or the state of being arranged; disposition. **2.** That which is arranged; the result of arranging. **3.** The style in which something is arranged; order: the *arrangement* of a library. **4.** A settlement, as of a dispute; adjustment. **5.** *Usually pl.* The plans or preparations made, or measures taken, for a particular purpose: the *arrangements* for a wedding. **6.** *Music* **a** The adaptation of a composition to other voices or instruments. **b** The composition so adapted. Abbr. *arr.*

ar·rant (ar′ənt) *adj.* **1.** Notoriously bad; unmitigated. **2.** *Obs.* Wandering. [Var. of ERRANT] **— ar′rant·ly** *adv.*

ar·ras (ar′əs) *n.* **1.** A tapestry. **2.** A wall hanging, especially one made of tapestry. [after *Arras*, France]

ar·ray (ə·rā′) *n.* **1.** Regular or proper order; arrangement, as for a battle, display, etc. **2.** The persons or things arrayed. **3.** An orderly or impressive arrangement, as of gems. **4.** *Poetic* Clothing; fine dress. **—** *v.t.* **1.** To draw up in order of battle; set in order. **2.** To adorn; dress, as for display. [< AF *arai*, OF *arei* < *a-* to (< L *ad-*) + *rei* order < Gmc.] **— Syn.** (verb) **1.** order, marshal. **2.** deck, clothe, attire. **—** (noun) See DRESS.

ar·ray·al (ə·rā′əl) *n.* **1.** The act or process of arraying. **2.** Anything arrayed; an array.

ar·rear (ə·rir′) *n.* **1.** The state of being behind or behindhand, as with obligations, business, etc. **2.** *Usually pl.* That which is behindhand; a part, as of a debt, overdue and unpaid. **— in arrears** (or **arrear**) Behind in meeting payment, fulfilling an obligation, etc. [< OF *arere* backward < L *ad-* to + *retro* backward]

ar·rear·age (ə·rir′ij) *n.* **1.** The state of being in arrears. **2.** The amount in arrears. **3.** A thing kept in reserve.

ar·rest (ə·rest′) *v.t.* **1.** To stop suddenly; check, as the course, movement, or growth of. **2.** To take into custody by legal authority. **3.** To attract and fix, as the attention; engage. **—** *n.* **1.** The act of arresting, or the state of being ar-

rested. **2.** Seizure by legal authority. Also **ar·rest′ment. 3.** A device for arresting motion. **— under arrest** In custody; arrested. [< OF *arester* < LL *arrestare* < L *ad-* to + *restare* to stop, remain] **— ar·rest′er** *n.*

Ar·rhe·ni·us (är·rā′nē·ŏos), **Svante August**, 1859–1927, Swedish chemist.

ar·rhi·zal (ə·rī′zəl) *adj. Bot.* Rootless. Also **ar·rhi′zous** (-zəs). [< Gk. *arrhizos* < *a-* without + *rhiza* a root]

ar·rhyth·mi·a (ə·rith′mē·ə, ə·rith′-) *n. Pathol.* Irregularity of the heart or pulse. [< NL < Gk. *arrhythmia* lack of rhythm < *a-* without + *rhythmos* measure] **— ar·rhyth·mic** (ə·rith′mik, ə·rith′-) *adj.*

ar·ri·ère-ban (ar′ē·âr·ban′, *Fr.* à·ryâr·bän′) *n.* **1.** In medieval France, a royal edict summoning vassals to military service. **2.** The vassals summoned. [< F, ult. < OHG *hari, heri* army + *ban* edict]

ar·rière-pen·sée (à·ryâr·pän·sā′) *n. French* A mental reservation; concealed motive; literally, backward thought.

Ar Ri·mal (är rē·mäl′) See RUB AL KHALI.

ar·ris (ar′is) *n. Archit.* The ridge formed by the meeting of two surfaces, as two channels of a Doric column. [< OF *areste* < L *arista* awn, fishbone. Doublet of ARISTA.]

ar·ri·val (ə·rī′vəl) *n.* **1.** The act of arriving: the *arrival* of a train. **2.** A coming to anything as a result of effort, action or natural process: *arrival* at the truth. **3.** One who or that which arrives or has arrived. Abbr. *ar., arr.*

ar·rive (ə·rīv′) *v.i.* **·rived, ·riv·ing 1.** To reach a destination or place. **2.** To come to a desired object, state, etc., by any process or course: often with *at*: to *arrive* at an idea. **3.** To attain success or fame. **4.** To come at length: The hour has arrived. Abbr. *ar., arr.* [< OF *ariver* < LL *arripare* to come to shore < L *ad-* to + *ripa* shore]

ar·ro·ba (ä·rō′bä) *n.* **1.** A liquid measure used in Spain, Mexico, etc., varying from 3.32 to 4.26 U.S. gallons. **2.** A Spanish weight equivalent to 25.37 pounds avoirdupois. **3.** A Brazilian weight equivalent to 32.38 pounds avoirdupois. [< Sp. < Arabic *al-rub′* the quarter (part)]

ar·ro·gance (ar′ə·gəns) *n.* The quality or state of being arrogant or haughty; overbearing pride. Also **ar′ro·gan·cy, ar′ro·gant·ness.** [< OF < L *arrogantia* < *arrogans*, ppr. of *arrogare*. See ARROGATE.]

ar·ro·gant (ar′ə·gənt) *adj.* **1.** Unduly or excessively proud; overbearing; haughty. **2.** Characterized by or due to arrogance: *arrogant* proposals. [< OF < L *arrogans, -antis*, ppr. of *arrogare*. See ARROGATE.] **— ar′ro·gant·ly** *adv.*
— Syn. 1. *Arrogant, haughty, insolent, disdainful, supercilious,* and *presumptuous* mean unduly proud of one's own station or achievements and scornful of others. The *arrogant* person is domineering and assumes more power or authority than are rightly his. The *haughty* man is unduly proud of his high station and treats others as inferior; the *insolent* man holds the rights and feelings of others in contempt and is rude and boorish. One who is *disdainful* is quick to show scornful dislike, and *supercilious* describes a man who is both *haughty* and *disdainful*, though sometimes masking his feelings under formal politeness. *Presumptuous* is a close synonym of *arrogant*, with an added note of insolence or impertinence. Compare IMPERIOUS. **— Ant.** humble, modest, unassuming, meek.

ar·ro·gate (ar′ə·gāt) *v.t.* **·gat·ed, ·gat·ing 1.** To claim or take presumptuously or without right; assume; usurp. **2.** To attribute or ascribe to another without just reason. [< L *arrogatus*, pp. of *arrogare* to claim for oneself < *ad-* to + *rogare* to ask] **— ar·ro·ga′tion** *n.* **— ar′ro·ga′tive** *adj.*

ar·ron·disse·ment (à·rôṅ·dēs·mäṅ′) *n. pl.* **·ments** (-mäṅ′) *French* **1.** The chief subdivision of a French department. **2.** A municipal district, as in Paris.

ar·row (ar′ō, -ə) *n.* **1.** A straight, slender shaft, generally feathered at one end and with a pointed head at the other, to be shot from a bow. ◆ Collateral adjective: *sagittal.* **2.** Anything resembling an arrow in shape, function, speed, etc. **3.** A sign or figure in the shape of an arrow, used to indicate directions. [OE *earh, arwe*] **— Syn. 1.** bolt, barb, dart.

Ar·row (ar′ō, -ə) *n.* The Constellation Sagitta.

ar·row·head (ar′ō·hed′, -ə-) *n.* **1.** The sharp-pointed head of an arrow. **2.** Something resembling an arrowhead, as a mark used to point direction, etc. **3.** *Archit.* The dart or anchor of an egg-and-dart molding. **4.** *Bot.* Any aquatic plant of the genus *Sagittaria*, of the water plantain family with arrow-shaped leaves.

ar·row·root (ar′ō·rŏot′, -ə-, -rŏŏt′) *n.* **1.** A nutritious starch obtained from the rhizomes of a tropical American plant (*Maranta arundinacea*). **2.** The plant itself. **3.** A similar starchy product from other tropical plants. [Plant so called because used to treat arrow wounds]

ar·row·wood (ar′ō·wŏŏd′, -ə-) *n.* One of various North American shrubs or small trees with many straight shoots or branches, used by the Indians for making arrows, as certain species of viburnum.

ar·row·worm (ar′ō·wûrm′, -ə-) *n. Zool.* A chaetognath, especially a pelagic species (*Sagitta bipunctata*) with a transparent body, capable of descent to great depths: also called *glassworm*. [So called from its long, arrowlike body]

PRONUNCIATION KEY: add, āce, câre, pälm; end, ēven; it, īce; odd, ōpen, ôrder; tŏŏk, pōōl; up, bûrn; ə = a in *above*, e in *sicken*, i in *flexible*, o in *melon*, u in *focus*; yōō = u in *fuse*; oil; pout; check; go; ring; thin; this; zh, vision. For à, œ, ü, kh, ṅ, see inside front cover.

ar·roy·o (ə·roi′ō) *n. pl.* **·os** (-ōz) *SW U.S.* **1.** The channel of an intermittent stream; a deep, dry gully. **2.** A brook or creek. [< Sp., ult. < L *arrugia* pit, shaft]

ARS Agricultural Research Service.

ar·se·nal (är′sə·nəl) *n.* **1.** A government facility for manufacturing and storing arms and munitions. **2.** A store of arms. [< Ital. *arsenale* < Arabic *dār aṣ-ṣin′ah* workshop]

ar·se·nate (är′sə·nāt, -nit) *n. Chem.* A salt of arsenic acid containing the trivalent radical AsO₄. Also **ar·se·ni·ate** (är·sē′nē·āt, -it).

ar·se·nic (är′sə·nik) *n.* **1.** A grayish white, brittle, crystalline, metallic element (symbol As), forming many poisonous compounds and used in medicine, industry, and the arts. See ELEMENT. **2.** White arsenic or arsenic trioxide, As₂O₃, a tasteless, poisonous compound. [< OF < L *arsenicum* < Gk. *arsenikon* yellow orpiment, ult. < Persian]

ar·sen·ic acid (är·sen′ik) *Chem.* A crystalline compound, H₃AsO₄, from which arsenates are derived.

ar·sen·i·cal (är·sen′i·kəl) *adj.* Of, pertaining to, or containing arsenic. Also **ar·sen′ic.** — *n.* Any arsenical insecticide.

ar·se·nide (är′sə·nīd, -nid) *n. Chem.* A compound of arsenic, in which arsenic is the electronegative constituent.

ar·se·nite (är′sə·nīt) *n. Chem.* A salt of arsenous acid.

ar·se·niu·ret·ed (är·sen′yə·ret′id, -sen′-) *adj.* Chemically combined with arsenic to form an arsenide: *arseniureted* hydrogen. Also **ar·se′niu·ret·ted.**

ar·se·no·py·rite (är′sə·nō·pī′rīt, är·sen′ə-) *n. Mineral.* A silver-white, orthorhombic, iron sulfarsenide, FeAsS: also called *mispickel.* [< ARSENIC + PYRITE]

ar·se·nous (är′sə·nəs) *adj. Chem.* Of, pertaining to, or containing arsenic, especially in its triad valence: *arsenous* acid, H₃AsO₃. Also **ar·se·ni·ous** (är·sē′nē·əs).

ars gra·ti·a ar·tis (ärz grā′shē·ə är′tis) *Latin* Art for art's sake.

ar·sine (är·sēn′, är′sēn, är′sin) *n. Chem.* **1.** A poisonous, flammable, gaseous compound, AsH₃, with a nauseating odor, used in chemical warfare. **2.** Any of various derivatives of this compound in which an organic radical replaces one or more hydrogen atoms. [< ARS(ENIC) + -INE²]

ar·sis (är′sis) *n. pl.* **·ses** (-sēz) **1.** In prosody: **a** The syllable that receives the ictus or stress of voice. **b** The stress itself. **c** In the original Greek usage, the metrically unaccented part of the foot: the reverse of modern usage. **2.** *Music* The unaccented part of a measure. [< L < Gk. *arsis* a lifting, raising < *airein* to raise]

ars lon·ga, vi·ta bre·vis (ärz lông′gə vī′tə brev′is) *Latin* Art (is) long, life short.

ar·son (är′sən) *n. Law* The malicious burning of a dwelling or other structure belonging to another; also, the similar burning of other property, including one's own, when insured, with the intent to defraud the insurers. [< OF < LL *arsio, -onis* a burning < L *arsus,* pp. of *ardere* to burn]

ars·phen·a·mine (ärs·fen′ə·mēn, -min) *n.* A brownish, yellow, crystalline arsenic compound, C₁₂H₁₄O₂N₂Cl₂As₂ · 2H₂O, first prepared by Paul Ehrlich as a treatment for syphilis, relapsing fever, frambesia, etc.: also called *Salvarsan.* [< ARS(ENIC) + PHEN(YL) + AMINE]

ars po·et·i·ca (ärz pō·et′i·kə) *Latin* The art of poetry.

art¹ (ärt) *n.* **1.** An esthetically pleasing and meaningful arrangement of elements, as words, sounds, colors, shapes, etc.; also, the productions embodying such arrangements. **2.** Forms of human activity whose chief character is determined by such arrangement, as literature or music, and especially painting, sculpture, drawing, etc. **3.** Any system of rules and principles that facilitates skilled human accomplishment; also, the application of these rules and principles: the *art* of navigation, the *art* of cooking, the *art* of public speaking, etc. **4.** A pursuit or occupation that depends upon the skilled application of such a system of rules and principles: the mariner's *art.* **5.** Practical skill; dexterity: the *art* of a craftsman. **6.** Human work or endeavor: contrasted with *nature.* **7.** *pl.* The liberal arts (which see); as distinguished from sciences. **8.** In journalism, an illustration. **9.** Studied or crafty conduct; cunning. **10.** *Usually pl.* Wily actions or devices; tricks. [< OF < L *ars, artis* skill]

art² (ärt) *Archaic* or *Poetic* Second person singular present tense of BE: used with *thou.* [OE *eart*]

art. 1. Article. **2.** Artificial. **3.** Artist.

-art *suffix* Var. of -ARD.

Ar·ta·xerx·es II (är′tə·zûrk′sēz) King of Persia 404–359 B.C.

ARTC Air Route Traffic Control.

art dec·o (dek′ō) *Fine Arts* An influential style of design of the 1930's characterized by conventionalized geometric forms and decorations and the use of plastics, aluminum, steel, and other modern materials. Also called **art de·co·ra·tif** (dek′ə·rə·tēf′), or *Brit.* **art de·cor** (dā′kôr). [Shortened form of F **art decoratif** decorative art]

ar·tel (är·tel′) *n.* In the Soviet Union, a cooperative organization of producers. [< Russian]

Ar·te·mis (är′tə·mis) In Greek mythology, the virgin goddess of the chase and of the moon, twin sister of Apollo: identified with the Roman *Diana.*

ar·te·mis·i·a (är′tə·miz′ē·ə, -mish′ē·ə) *n.* **1.** Any of a large

genus (*Artemisia*) of bitter, aromatic herbs of the composite family. **2.** The sagebrush. [< L, mugwort < Gk.]

ar·te·ri·al (är·tir′ē·əl) *adj.* **1.** Of, pertaining to, or contained or carried in the arteries or an artery. **2.** *Physiol.* Pertaining to the blood that has undergone aeration in the lungs, distinguished by its bright red color. **3.** Resembling an artery: an *arterial* highway.

ar·te·ri·al·ize (är·tir′ē·əl·īz′) *v.t.* **·ized, ·iz·ing** *Physiol.* To convert (venous blood) into arterial blood by oxygenation during passage through the lungs in respiration. Also *Brit.* **ar·te′ri·al·i·za′tion** *n.*

arterio- *combining form* Artery. Also, before vowels, **arter-.** [< Gk. *artēria*]

ar·te·ri·o·scle·ro·sis (är·tir′ē·ō·sklə·rō′sis) *n. Pathol.* The thickening and hardening of the inner walls of an artery, with impairment of circulation, as in old age. [< NL < ARTERIO- + SCLEROSIS] — **ar·te′ri·o·scle·rot′ic** (-rot′ik) *adj.*

ar·ter·y (är′tər·ē) *n. pl.* **·ter·ies 1.** *Anat.* Any of a large number of muscular vessels conveying blood away from the heart to every part of the body. **2.** Any main channel or route. [< L *arteria,* windpipe < Gk. *artēria*]

ar·te·sian well (är·tē′zhən) A well that penetrates to a water-bearing stratum between impermeable strata, from a surface lower than the source of the water supply, so that the water pressure forces a flow of water out at the surface. [< F *artésien,* after *Artois,* town in France]

ARTESIAN WELL (*d*)
a Precipitation. *b* Seepage.
c Water table.

Ar·te·vel·de (är′tə·vel′də), **Jacob van,** 1290?–1345. Flemish leader. — **Philip van,** 1340?–82, Flemish leader; son of Jacob. Also **Ar·te·veld** (är′tə·veld).

art·ful (ärt′fəl) *adj.* **1.** Crafty; cunning. **2.** Skillful; ingenious. **3.** Artificial. — **art′ful·ly** *adv.* — **art′ful·ness** *n.*

ar·thral·gia (är·thral′jə) *n. Pathol.* Neuralgic pain in a joint. [< ARTHR(O)- + -ALGIA] — **ar·thral′gic** (-jik) *adj.*

ar·thri·tis (är·thrī′tis) *n. Pathol.* Inflammation of a joint or joints. [< L Gk. *arthritis* < *arthron* joint] — **ar·thrit·ic** (är·thrit′ik) *adj. & n.*

arthro- *combining form* Joint: *arthropod.* Also, before vowels, **arthr-,** as in *arthralgia.* [< Gk. *arthron*]

ar·thro·mere (är′thrə·mir) *n. Zool.* Any typical segment in the body of a jointed invertebrate. [< ARTHRO- + -MERE]

ar·thro·plas·ty (är′thrə·plas′tē) *n. Surg.* A plastic operation on a joint, or the formation of an artificial joint. — **ar′thro·plas′tic** *adj.*

ar·thro·pod (är′thrə·pod) *Zool. n.* Any of a large phylum (*Arthropoda*) of invertebrate animals having jointed legs, chitinous exoskeletons, and segmented body parts, including insects, spiders, and crabs. — *adj.* Of or pertaining to the *Arthropoda.* [< ARTHRO- + Gk. *pous, podos* foot] — **ar·throp·o·dous** (är·throp′ə·dəs), **ar·throp′o·dal** *adj.*

ar·thro·sis (är·thrō′sis) *n. pl.* **·ses** (-sēz) **1.** Connection of parts by joints; articulation. **2.** *Pathol.* A degenerative condition of the joints. [< L < Gk. *arthrōsis* < *arthron* joint]

ar·thro·spore (är′thrə·spôr, -spōr) *n.* **1.** *Bot.* One of a series of spores in some algae and fungi, formed by fission and resembling a string of beads. **2.** *Bacteriol.* An isolated vegetative cell in a resting state. — **ar·thro·spor′ic** (-spôr′ik, -spōr′ik), **ar·thros·po·rous** (är·thros′pər·əs) *adj.*

ar·throt·o·my (är·throt′ə·mē) *n. pl.* **·mies** *Surg.* Incision into a joint. [< ARTHRO- + -TOMY]

Ar·thur (är′thər) Legendary sixth-century British king; hero of the Round Table and of many romances. [? < Celtic, high, admirable] — **Ar·thu′ri·an** (-thôor′ē·ən) *adj.*

Ar·thur (är′thər), **Chester Alan,** 1830–86, 21st president of the United States 1881–85.

ar·ti·choke (är′tə·chōk) *n.* **1.** A thistlelike garden plant (*Cynara scolymus*). **2.** Its succulent flower head, used as a vegetable. **3.** The Jerusalem artichoke (which see). [< Ital. *articiocco,* ult. < Arabic *al-kharshāf*]

ar·ti·cle (är′ti·kəl) *n.* **1.** A particular object or substance; a thing. **2.** An individual item in a class: an *article* of food. **3.** A literary composition forming an independent part of a newspaper, magazine, etc. **4.** A separate division, heading, or paragraph of a series in a document, as in a constitution, treaty, contract, statute, etc. **5.** *Gram.* One of a class of auxiliary words inserted before a noun or a word used as a noun, or, in some languages, prefixed or suffixed to it, to limit or modify it in some way, as English *a, an* (**indefinite article**) and *the* (**definite article**). **6.** A definite part, as of a system; item; point. Abbr. *art.* — *v.* **cled, cling** *v.t.* **1.** To bind to service by a written contract: to *article* a seaman for a voyage. **2.** To set forth in articles; specify. **3.** To charge specifically; accuse by formal articles. — *v.i.* **4.** To make accusations: with *against.* [< F < L *articulus*, dim. of *artus* a joint]

Articles of Confederation The constitution of the 13 original American colonies, adopted in 1781 and replaced in 1788 by the Constitution.

Articles of War, Articles for the Government of the Navy See under UNIFORM CODE OF MILITARY JUSTICE.

ar·tic·u·lar (är·tik′yə-lər) *adj.* Pertaining to a joint or the joints. [< L *articularis*]

ar·tic·u·late (*adj.* är·tik′yə-lit; *v.* är·tik′yə-lāt) *adj.* **1.** Having the power of speech. **2.** Able to speak well or expressively. **3.** Divided into distinct words and syllables; clearly enunciated. **4.** Arranged with coherence; interrelated: an *articulate* thesis. **5.** Jointed; segmented, as limbs. Also **ar·tic′u·lat′ed.** — *v.* ·lat·ed, ·lat·ing *v.t.* **1.** To utter distinctly; enunciate. **2.** To give utterance to; express in words. **3.** *Phonet.* To produce, as a speech sound, by the movement of the organs of speech. **4.** To joint together; unite by joints. — *v.i.* **5.** To speak distinctly. **6.** *Phonet.* To produce a speech sound. [< L *articulatus*, pp. of *articulare* to divide into joints, utter distinctly < *articulus*. See ARTICLE.] — **ar·tic′u·late·ly** *adv.* — **ar·tic′u·late·ness** *n.*

ar·tic·u·la·tion (är·tik′yə-lā′shən) *n.* **1.** A jointing or being jointed together. **2.** The manner or method of jointing. **3.** *Anat.* The union forming a joint, as of bones. **4.** The utterance of speech sounds; enunciation. **5.** *Phonet.* **a** A speech sound, especially a consonant. **b** The movements of the organs of speech in producing a speech sound. **6.** *Bot.* **a** A joint between two parts, as a leaf and a stem. **b** A node or the space between two nodes. — **ar·tic·u·la·tive** (är·tik′yə-lā′tiv, -lə·tiv), **ar·tic·u·la·to·ry** (är·tik′yə-lə·tôr′ē, -tō′rē) *adj.*

ar·tic·u·la·tor (är·tik′yə-lā′tər) *n.* **1.** One who or that which articulates. **2.** *Phonet.* A movable organ of speech, as the tongue.

articulatory phonetics See under PHONETICS.

ar·ti·fact (är′tə-fakt) *n.* **1.** Anything made by human work or art. **2.** *Biol.* A structure or appearance that is not normally present in a cell or tissue but is produced by artificial means. Also **ar′te·fact.** [< L *ars, artis* art, skill + *factus*, pp. of *facere* to make]

ar·ti·fice (är′tə-fis) *n.* **1.** An ingenious expedient; stratagem; maneuver. **2.** Subtle or deceptive craft; trickery. **3.** Skill; ingenuity. [< F < L *artificium* handicraft, skill < *ars, artis* art + *facere* to make]

— **Syn. 1.** *Artifice, trick, dodge, ruse, blind, stratagem, maneuver,* and *wile* all agree in meaning any expedient used to gain an end. An *artifice* is specially manufactured or contrived for the purpose, though it need not be mechanical. *Trick* and *dodge,* originally denoting a sly or underhand act, are freely applied to any clever move. A *ruse* or *blind* deceives by a false appearance, while *stratagems* and *maneuvers,* once military terms, now denote any grand or complex *trick* or *dodge.* A *wile* entraps the victim by his own credulity or susceptibility.

ar·tif·i·cer (är·tif′ə·sər) *n.* **1.** One who constructs with skill; a craftsman. **2.** *Mil.* A skilled mechanic. **3.** A skillful designer; an inventor. — **Syn.** See ARTIST.

ar·ti·fi·cial (är′tə·fish′əl) *adj.* **1.** Produced by human art rather than by nature. **2.** Made in imitation of something natural: *artificial* flowers. **3.** Feigned; fictitious: an *artificial* joy. **4.** Not genuine or natural; affected: *artificial* manners. Abbr. *art.* [< L *artificialis* < *artificium.* See ARTIFICE.] — **ar′ti·fi′cial·ly** *adv.* — **ar′ti·fi′cial·ness** *n.*

— **Syn. 2.** manufactured, fabricated, synthetic. **3.** pretended, sham, simulated, assumed, factitious.

artificial horizon 1. *Aeron.* An instrument incorporating a gyroscope to indicate the deviations of an aircraft from level flight: also called *gyrohorizon.* **2.** *Astron.* A level reflector, as a surface of mercury, used to determine the altitude of celestial bodies.

artificial insemination Impregnation of the female without direct sexual contact: also called *eutelegenesis.*

ar·ti·fi·ci·al·i·ty (är′tə·fish′ē·al′ə·tē) *n.* *pl.* ·ties **1.** The quality or state of being artificial. **2.** Something artificial.

artificial language An arbitrary, auxiliary language devised for use in international communication.

ar·til·ler·y (är·til′ə·rē) *n.* **1.** Guns of larger caliber than machine guns, usually classified according to caliber as *light, medium,* and *heavy.* **2.** Military units armed with such guns. **3.** A branch of the U.S. Army, combining the former Field Artillery, Coast Artillery, and Antiaircraft Artillery Corps. **4.** The science of gunnery. **5.** *U.S. Slang* A firearm. **6.** *Obs.* Implements of war. Abbr. *Arty.* [< OF *artillerie* < *artiller* to fortify]

ar·til·ler·y·man (är·til′ə·rē·mən) *n.* *pl.* ·men (-mən) A soldier in the artillery. Also **ar·til′ler·ist.**

ar·ti·o·dac·tyl (är′tē·ō·dak′təl) *Zool.* *n.* A member of a mammalian order or suborder (*Artiodactyla*) of ungulate quadrupeds with two or four digits to each foot, including the ruminants, hogs, etc. — *adj.* Of or pertaining to the *Artiodactyla.* [< NL < Gk. *artios* even + *daktylos* finger, toe] — **ar′ti·o·dac′ty·lous** (-ləs) *adj.*

ar·ti·san (är′tə·zən) *n.* **1.** A trained or skilled workman. **2.** *Obs.* An artist. — **Syn.** See ARTIST. [< F < Ital. *artigiano,* ult. < L *ars, artis* art]

ar·tist (är′tist) *n.* **1.** One who is skilled in or makes a profession of any of the fine arts. **2.** One whose work exhibits artistic qualities and skill; a craftsman. **3.** An artiste. Abbr. *art.* [< F *artiste* < Ital. *artista* < L *ars, artis* art]

— **Syn. 1.** *Artist, artisan,* and *artificer* are here compared as they mean one associated with art. The work of an *artist* is creative; that of an *artisan,* mechanical. The *artificer* is between the two, having less scope for the embodiment of his own ideas than the *artist,* but more than the *artisan,* who usually has none.

ar·tiste (är·tēst′) *n.* **1.** An entertainer, as a dancer or singer. **2.** An artist: often used ironically. [< F. See ARTIST.]

ar·tis·tic (är·tis′tik) *adj.* **1.** Of or pertaining to art or artists. **2.** Conforming or conformable to the principles of art; tastefully executed. **3.** Fond of or sensitive to art. Also **ar·tis′ti·cal.** — **ar·tis′ti·cal·ly** *adv.*

art·ist·ry (är′tis·trē) *n.* **1.** Artistic workmanship or ability. **2.** The pursuits or occupation of an artist.

art·less (ärt′lis) *adj.* **1.** Lacking craft or deceit; guileless; naive. **2.** Natural; simple. **3.** Devoid of art or skill; clumsy. **4.** Uncultured; ignorant. — **Syn.** See INGENUOUS. — **art′less·ly** *adv.* — **art′less·ness** *n.*

art nou·veau (är nōō·vo′, ärt) A style of art, architecture, and decoration current in the late 19th and early 20th century and marked by the use of curvilinear forms derived from nature. [< F, new art]

Ar·tois (är·twä′) A region of northern France.

art·y (är′tē) *adj.* *Informal* Ostentatiously claiming artistic worth or interest. — **art′i·ness** *n.*

Arty. Artillery.

A·ru·ba (ä·rü′bə) An island in the western group of the Netherlands Antilles; 73 sq. mi.; pop. 53,199 (1960).

ar·um (âr′əm) *n.* **1.** Any of a genus (*Arum*) of Old World herbs of a family (*Araceae*) that includes the philodendron. **2.** One of various related plants. [< L < Gk. *aron*]

Ar·un·del (ar′ən·dəl) A municipal borough in southern Sussex, England; site of a famous castle; pop. 2,614 (1961).

a·run·di·na·ceous (ə·run′də·nā′shəs) *adj.* *Bot.* Pertaining to a reed; reedlike. [< L *arundinaceus* < *arundo, -inis* reed]

A·run·ta (ə·run′tə) *n.* **1.** One of a primitive, aboriginal people of central Australia. **2.** The language of this people. Also spelled *Aranta.*

a·rus·pex (ə·rus′peks) See HARUSPEX.

A·ru·wi·mi (ä′rōō·wē′mē) A river in the NE Republic of Zaire, flowing generally west about 620 miles to the Congo river.

A.R.V. American (Standard) Revised Version (of the Bible).

ar·val (är′vəl) *adj.* Of or pertaining to plowed land. [< L *arvalis* < *arvum* field < *arare* to plow]

-ary[1] *suffix of adjectives and nouns* **1.** Connected with or pertaining to what is expressed in the root word: *elementary, honorary.* **2.** A person employed as or engaged in: *apothecary, secretary.* **3.** A thing connected with or a place dedicated to: *dictionary, diary, sanctuary.* [< L *-arius, -arium*]

-ary[2] *suffix of adjectives* Of or pertaining to; belonging to: *military, salutary.* See -AR[1]. [< L *-aris*]

Ar·y·an (âr′ē·ən, ar′-, är′yən) *n.* **1.** A member or descendant of a prehistoric people who spoke Indo-European. **2.** In Nazi ideology, a Caucasian gentile, especially one of Nordic stock. **3.** *Ling.* **a** The Indo-Iranian subfamily of Indo-European. **b** Formerly, the parent language of the Indo-European family. — *adj.* **1.** Of or pertaining to the Aryans or their languages. **2.** In Nazi ideology, of or pertaining to Caucasian gentiles. Also spelled *Arian.* [< Skt. *ārya* noble]

Ar·y·an·ize (âr′ē·ən·īz′, ar′-, är′yən-) *v.t.* ·ized, ·iz·ing In Nazi ideology, to make characteristically Aryan. Also **Ar′i·an·ize′.**

ar·yl (ar′il) *adj. Chem.* Pertaining to any of a group of monovalent radicals derived from the aromatic hydrocarbon compounds, as phenyl. [< AR(OMATIC) + -YL]

ar·y·te·noid (ar′ə·tē′noid) *Anat. adj.* Of, connected with, or pertaining to two small cartilages in the larynx mounted on the cricoid cartilage and attached posteriorly to the vocal cords, for the action of which they are largely responsible. Also **ar·yt′e·noi′dal.** — *n.* An arytenoid cartilage. [< Gk. *arytainoeidēs* pitcher-shaped < *arytaina* pitcher + *eidos* form]

as[1] (az, *unstressed* əz) *adv.* To the same degree; equally: Can you see *as* well from here? — *conj.* **1.** To the same degree or extent that: often used in correlative constructions with *as* or *so* to denote equality or identity: *as* fair *as* the sun; *As* we live, so we die. **2.** In the way that; in the same manner that: Do *as* I do. **3.** In proportion that; to the degree in which: He became gentler *as* he grew older. **4.** At the same time that; while: They waved *as* we sailed away. **5.** Because; since. ◆ This sense, though standard, often involves an ambiguity in meaning, and should be used with care. In the sentence *As it was raining, we stayed at home, as* may mean *while, when,* or *because.* **6.** With the result or purpose that: Be so good *as* to come; Speak louder, so *as* to make yourself heard. **7.** For instance: used to introduce examples or illustrations: Some animals are cunning, *as* the fox. **8.** Though; however: Bad *as* it was, it might have been worse. **9.** *Dial.* That: I can't say *as* I will. **— as for** (or **as to**) In the matter of; concerning. **— as if** (or **as though**) The same, or in the same manner, that it would be if. **— as is** *Informal* Just as it is; in its present condition. **—** *pron.* **1.** That; who; which: after *same* and *such*: He lived in the same city *as* I did; such people *as* like sports. **2.** A fact which: He is dead, *as* everyone knows. **3.** *Dial.* Who; which: Those *as* lived here knew him well. **—** *prep.* In the role or character of: to act *as* umpire. [ME *as, als, alse,* OE *ealswā* entirely so, just as. See ALSO.]

as² (as) *n. pl.* **as·ses** (as'iz) **1.** An early Roman coin of copper or copper alloy, originally weighing about a pound. **2.** An ancient Roman unit of weight of about one pound. [< L]

as- Assimilated var. of AD-.

As (äs) Singular of ÆSIR.

As 1. *Meteorol.* Altostratus. **2.** *Chem.* Arsenic.

AS *Mil.* Antisubmarine.

AS or **AS., A.S.,** or **A.-S.** Anglo-Saxon.

ASA or **A.S.A.** American Standards Association.

as·a·fet·i·da (as'ə-fet'ə-də) *n.* A fetid substance prepared from the juice of certain plants of the parsley family, formerly used in medicine as an antispasmodic: also spelled *assafoetida.* Also **as'a·foet'i·da.** [< Med. L *asa* gum (< Persian *azā*) + L *foetida,* fem., ill-smelling]

A·sa·ma (ä-sä-mä) The highest and most violent of Japan's active volcanoes, on central Honshu island; 8,340 ft.

as·a·rum (as'e-rəm) *n.* **1.** The dried rootstock of a North American perennial herb (*Asarum canadense*) of the birthwort family, used as an aromatic and carminative. **2.** The herb itself. [< L, hazelwort, wild spikenard < Gk. *asaron*]

asb. Asbestos.

As·ben (az-ben') See AÏR.

as·bes·tos (as-bes'təs, az-) *n.* **1.** A white or light gray mineral, obtained chiefly from actinolite and amphibole, occurring in long slender needles or fibrous masses that may be woven or shaped into acid-resisting, nonconducting, and fireproof articles: also called *earth flax, mountain cork.* **2.** A fireproof curtain, as in a theater. **—** *adj.* Pertaining to, containing, or made of asbestos. Also **as·bes'tus.** [< L < Gk. unquenchable < *a-* not + *sbennynai* to quench; orig. applied to quicklime] **— as·bes·tine** (as-bes'tin, az-), **as·bes'tic** *adj.*

as·bes·to·sis (as'bes-tō'sis, az'-) *n. Pathol.* Pneumoconiosis caused by inhaling particles of asbestos.

As·bur·y (az'ber'ē, -bər-ē) Francis, 1745-1816, English clergyman; first American Methodist bishop.

As·bur·y Park (az'ber'ē, -bər-ē) A resort city in eastern New Jersey, on the Atlantic Ocean; pop. 17,336.

As·ca·ni·us (as-kā'nē-əs) In Roman legend, son of Aeneas and Creusa and ancestor of the Caesars: also called *Iulus.*

ASCAP or **A.S.C.A.P.** American Society of Composers, Authors and Publishers.

as·ca·rid (as'kə-rid) *n. Zool.* A nematode worm (family *Ascaridae*), as a roundworm or pinworm. [< Gk. *askaris, -idos* worm in the intestines]

ASCE or **A.S.C.E.** American Society of Civil Engineers.

as·cend (ə-send') *v.i.* **1.** To ascend or move upward; rise. **2.** To rise by degrees, as from particulars to generals, from the lower to the higher notes of a musical scale, etc. **3.** To lie along an ascending slope. **—** *v.t.* **4.** To move upward on; mount; climb. [< L *ascendere* < *ad-* to + *scandere* to climb] **— as·cend'a·ble** or **as·cend'i·ble** *adj.* **— as·cen'sive** *adj.*

as·cen·dan·cy (ə-sen'dən-sē) *n.* The quality, fact, or state of being in the ascendant; domination; sway. Also **as·cen'dance, as·cen'dence, as·cen'den·cy.**

as·cen·dant (ə-sen'dənt) *adj.* **1.** Ascending; rising. **2.** Superior; dominant. **3.** *Astron.* Coming to or above the horizon. **—** *n.* **1.** A position of preeminence; domination. **2.** In astrology: **a** The point of the ecliptic that is rising above the eastern horizon at any instant. **b** Horoscope. **3.** *Rare* An ancestor: opposed to *descendant.* Also **as·cen'dent. — to be in the ascendant** To approach or occupy a predominating position; have controlling power, influence, etc. [< OF < L *ascendens, -entis,* ppr. of *ascendere.* See ASCEND.]

as·cend·er (ə-sen'dər) *n.* **1.** One who or that which ascends. **2.** *Printing* **a** The part of a letter that reaches into the top of the body of the type. **b** Any of such letters, as *b, d, h,* etc.

as·cend·ing (ə-sen'ding) *adj.* **1.** Rising or directed upward. **2.** *Bot.* Slanting or curving upward.

as·cen·sion (ə-sen'shən) *n.* **1.** The act of ascending. **2.** *Astron.* The elevating or rising of a star above the horizon in the celestial sphere. **— the Ascension** *Theol.* The bodily ascent of Christ into heaven after the Resurrection, commemorated on **Ascension Day** (also *Holy Thursday*), the fortieth day after Easter. [< L *ascensio, -onis* < *ascendere.* See ASCEND.] **— as·cen'sion·al** *adj.*

As·cen·sion (ə-sen'shən) A British island in the South Atlantic, administered with St. Helena; 34 sq. mi.; pop. 1,486 (est. 1967).

as·cent (ə-sent') *n.* **1.** The act of ascending in space; a rising, soaring, or climbing: the *ascent* of a mountain. **2.** A rise in state, rank, or station; advancement. **3.** A way or means of ascending; upward slope; acclivity. **4.** The degree of ac-

clivity: an *ascent* of 30°. **5.** *Rare* A going back in time or genealogical succession. [< ASCEND, on analogy with *descent*]

as·cer·tain (as'ər-tān') *v.t.* **1.** To learn with certainty; find out by experiment or investigation. **2.** *Obs.* To make certain; determine; define. **— Syn.** See DISCOVER. [< OF *acertener* < *a-* to (< L *ad-*) + *certain.* See CERTAIN.] **— as'cer·tain'a·ble** *adj.* **— as'cer·tain'a·ble·ness** *n.* **— as'cer·tain'a·bly** *adv.* **— as'cer·tain'ment** *n.*

as·cet·ic (ə-set'ik) *n.* **1.** In the early church, one who renounced social life and comfort for solitude, self-mortification, and religious devotion; a hermit; recluse. **2.** One who leads a very austere and self-denying life. **—** *adj.* **1.** Pertaining to ascetics or asceticism. **2.** Rigidly abstinent; austere. Also **as·cet'i·cal** *adj.* [< Gk. *askētikos* exercised, industrious, athletic < *askētēs* one who practices (self-denial), a monk < *askeein* to exercise] **— as·cet'i·cal·ly** *adv.*

as·cet·i·cism (ə-set'ə-siz'əm) *n.* Ascetic doctrine, belief, or conduct.

Asch (äsh), **Sholem,** 1880-1957, U.S. novelist and playwright in Yiddish and English; born in Poland.

As·cham (as'kəm), **Roger,** 1515-68, English classical scholar; tutor of Queen Elizabeth I.

as·ci (as'ī) Plural of ASCUS.

as·cid·i·an (ə-sid'ē-ən) *Zool. n.* One of a class (*Ascidia*) of marine animals having a leathery sac; a sea squirt or tunicate. **—** *adj.* Of or pertaining to this class of animals: also **as·cid·i·oid** (ə-sid'ē-oid). [< NL < ASCIDIUM]

as·cid·i·um (ə-sid'ē-əm) *n. pl.* **·cid·i·a** (-sid'ē-ə) *Bot.* A flask-shaped plant appendage: also called *vasculum.* [< NL < Gk. *askidion,* dim. of *askos* bag, wineskin]

as·ci·tes (ə-sī'tēz) *n. Pathol.* Abdominal dropsy. [< L < Gk. *askitēs < askos* bag] **— as·cit·ic** (ə-sit'ik) or **·i·cal** *adj.*

as·cle·pi·a·da·ceous (as-klē'pē-ə-dā'shəs) *adj. Bot.* Belonging to a large family (*Asclepiadaceae*) of erect or twining plants, the milkweed family, having milky juice. [< NL *Asclepiadaceae < L asclepias, -adis* milkweed < Gk. *asklēpias;* named after *Asclepius*]

As·cle·pi·a·de·an (as-klē'pē-ə-dē'ən) *adj.* Denoting a type of classical verse consisting of a spondee, two or three choriambs, and an iambus. **—** *n.* An Asclepiadean verse. [after *Asclepiades* of Samos, 3rd-century B.C. Greek lyric poet]

As·cle·pi·us (as-klē'pē-əs) In Greek mythology, the son of Apollo and god of medicine: identified with the Roman *Aesculapius.*

as·co·carp (as'kə-kärp) *n. Bot.* The sporocarp or fruit of ascomycetous fungi. [< *asco-* (< ASCUS) + -CARP]

as·cog·e·nous (as-koj'ə-nəs) *adj. Bot.* Producing asci.

as·co·go·ni·um (as'kə-gō'nē-əm) *n. pl.* **·ni·a** (-nē-ə) *Bot.* **1.** The female reproductive organ before fertilization in certain of the lower cryptogams. **2.** An archicarp. [< ASCUS + Gk. *gonos* offspring]

as·co·my·ce·tous (as'kə-mī-sē'təs) *adj. Bot.* Belonging to a large class (*Ascomycetes*) of fungi having the spores formed in asci, including mildews and yeasts. Many of the species cause destructive diseases of plants. [< NL *Ascomycetes* < ASCUS + -MYCETES]

a·scor·bic (ə-skôr'bik) *adj.* Antiscorbutic (which see).

ascorbic acid *Biochem.* The scurvy-preventing vitamin C, a white, odorless, crystalline compound, $C_6H_8O_6$, present in citrus and other fresh fruits, tomatoes, potatoes, and green leafy vegetables, and also made synthetically.

as·co·spore (as'kə-spôr, -spōr) *n. Bot.* A spore developed in an ascus. [< *asco-* (< ASCUS) + SPORE] **— as·cos·po·rous** (as-kos'pə-rəs), **as·co·spor·ic** (as'kə-spôr'ik, -spor'-) *adj.*

as·cot (as'kət, -kot) *n.* A kind of necktie knotted so that the broad ends are laid one across the other. [after *Ascot*]

As·cot (as'kət, -kot) A village in Berkshire, England, near Windsor; site of annual horse races instituted in 1711.

as·cribe (ə-skrīb') *v.t.* **·cribed, ·crib·ing 1.** To attribute or impute, as to a cause or source: I *ascribe* his conduct to insanity. **2.** To consider or declare as belonging (to); assign as a quality or attribute. **— Syn.** See ATTRIBUTE. [< L *ascribere < ad-* to + *scribere* to write] **— as·crib'a·ble** *adj.*

as·crip·tion (ə-skrip'shən) *n.* **1.** The act of ascribing. **2.** An expression that ascribes; especially, a text or sentence of praise to God. **3.** That which is ascribed. [< L *ascriptio, -onis < ascribere.* See ASCRIBE.]

as·cus (as'kəs) *n. pl.* **as·ci** (as'ī) *Bot.* A large cell or spore case in ascomycetous fungi and lichens. [< NL < Gk. *askos* bag, wineskin]

-ase *suffix Chem.* Used in naming enzymes: *amylase, casease.* [< (DIAST)ASE]

a·sea (ə-sē') *adv.* To or toward the sea; at sea.

a·sep·sis (ə-sep'sis, ā-) *n. Med.* **1.** Absence of or freedom from putrefactive infection. **2.** The prevention of septic infection by the use of sterilized instruments, dressings, etc. [< A-⁴ + SEPSIS]

a·sep·tic (ə-sep'tik, ā-) *adj.* Exempt from septic or blood-poisoning conditions and from pathogenic microorganisms. **— a·sep'ti·cal·ly** *adv.*

a·sex·u·al (ā-sek'shoō-əl) *adj. Biol.* **1.** Having no distinct sexual organs; without sex. **2.** Occurring or performed without commerce of the sexes; agamic. **— a·sex·u·al·i·ty** (ā-sek'shoō-al'ə-tē) *n.* **— a·sex'u·al·ly** *adv.*

a·sex·u·al·ize (ā-sek′shoō-əl-īz) *v.t.* ·ized, ·iz·ing To unsex. — **a·sex′u·al·i·za′tion** *n.*

As·gard (as′gärd, äs′-) In Norse mythology, the home of the Æsir; the residence of heroes slain in battle. See BIFROST. Also **As·garth** (äs′gärth), **As·gar·dhr** (äs′gär′thr). [< ON *āsgardhr* < *āss* god + *gardhr* yard, dwelling]

asgd. Assigned.

ash[1] (ash) *n.* 1. The powdery, whitish gray residue of a substance that has been burned. See also ASHES. 2. *Geol.* Pulverized lava as ejected by a volcano. [OE *æsce, asce*]

ash[2] (ash) *n.* 1. Any of a widely distributed genus (*Fraxinus*) of oleaceous trees, as the American white ash (*F. alba*) and the European ash (*F. excelsior*). 2. The light, tough, elastic wood of these trees. — *adj.* Made of ash wood. [OE *æsc*]

a·shamed (ə-shāmd′) *adj.* 1. Feeling shame; abashed by consciousness of fault or impropriety. 2. Deterred by fear of shame; reluctant. [OE *āscamod*, pp. of *āscamian*] — **a·sham·ed·ly** (ə-shā′mid-lē) *adv.* — **a·sham′ed·ness** *n.* — **Syn.** 1. humiliated, mortified. Compare EMBARRASS.

A·shan·ti (ə-shan′tē, ə-shän′-) *n. pl.* ·tis or ·ties 1. A native of Ashanti. 2. The Sudanic language of the Ashantis: also called *Tshi, Twi.* Also **A·shan′tee.**

A·shan·ti (ə-shan′tē, ə-shän′-) A former native kingdom and British protectorate in western Africa, included since 1957 in Ghana.

Ash·bur·ton (ash′bûr′tən) A river in NW Australia, flowing 220 miles NW to Exmouth Gulf.

Ash·bur·ton (ash′bûr′tən), **Lord**, 1774–1848, Alexander Baring, English statesman and banker.

ash can 1. A large can or metal receptacle for cinders and ashes. 2. *U.S. Slang* A depth bomb.

ash·en[1] (ash′ən) *adj.* 1. Of, pertaining to, or like ashes. 2. Pale in color; gray.

ash·en[2] (ash′ən) *adj.* Pertaining to or made of ash wood.

Ash·er (ash′ər) In the Old Testament, a son of Jacob and Zilpah; *Gen.* xxx 13. — *n.* The tribe of Israel descended from him.

ash·es (ash′iz) *n.pl.* 1. The grayish white, powdery particles, often intermixed with charred fragments, remaining after something has been burned. See also ASH[1]. 2. The remains of the human body after cremation. 3. Mortal remains: the *ashes* of our fathers. 4. Remains or ruins, as after destruction. 5. A symbol of victory in international cricket matches between Australia and England. [pl. of ASH[1]]

Ashe·ville (ash′vil) A resort city in western North Carolina; pop. 57,681.

Ash·ke·naz·im (ash′kə-naz′im, äsh′kə-nä′zim) *n.pl.* The Jews settled in northern and central Europe: distinguished from the *Sephardim.* [< Hebrew; used by the Rabbis for Germans, because Ashkenaz was a son of Gomer (*Gen.* x 3), the letters of whose name are identical with Germania] — **Ash′ke·naz′ic** *adj.*

Ash·kha·bad (äsh′khä-bäd′, *Russ.* əsh·khə·bät′) The capital and largest city of the Turkmen S.S.R., near the Iranian border; pop. 253,000 (1970).

Ash·land (ash′lənd) A city in NE Kentucky, on the Ohio River; pop. 29,245.

ash·lar (ash′lər) *n.* 1. In masonry, a roughhewn block of stone. 2. A thin, dressed, squared stone, used for facing a wall. 3. Masonry made of such stones. Also **ash′ler.** [< OF *aiseler*, ult. < L *axilla*, dim. of *axis* board, plank]

ash·man (ash′man′) *n. pl.* ·men (-men′) A man who collects and removes ashes.

a·shore (ə-shôr′, ə-shōr′) *adv. & adj.* 1. To or on the shore. 2. On land; aground.

Ash·ton-un·der-Lyne (ash′tən-un′dər-līn′) A municipal borough in SE Lancashire, England; pop. 50,165 (1951).

Ash·to·reth (ash′tə-reth) An ancient Phoenician and Syrian goddess of love and fertility: identified with *Astarte* and the Babylonian and Assyrian *Ishtar.*

ash tray A receptacle for tobacco ashes.

A·shur (ä′shoōr, ash′ər) In Assyrian mythology, the chief deity; god of war and empire: also spelled *Asshur.*

A·shur·ba·ni·pal (ä′shoōr-bä′ni-päl) Assyrian king 668–626? B.C.: also called *Sardanapalus.*

Ash Wednesday The first day of Lent: from the sprinkling of ashes on the heads of penitents.

ash·y (ash′ē) *adj.* ash·i·er, ash·i·est 1. Of, pertaining to, or like ashes; ash-covered. 2. Ash-colored; ashen.

A·sia (ā′zhə, ā′shə) The eastern part of the Eurasian land mass, and the islands adjacent, bounded by the Ural Mountains, the Ural river, the Greater Caucasus, the Black, Mediterranean, and Red seas, and the Indian, Pacific, and Arctic oceans; the largest of the earth's continents: 16.9 million sq. mi.; pop. 1.988 billion (est. 1969, excluding USSR).

Asia Minor The peninsula of extreme western Asia between the Black and Mediterranean seas, comprising most of Turkey in Asia: also *Anatolia.*

A·sian (ā′zhən, ā′shən) *adj.* Of, pertaining to, or characteristic of Asia or its peoples. — *n.* A native or inhabitant of Asia.

A·sian·ism (ā′zhən-iz′əm, ā′shən-) *n.* A florid rhetorical style practiced in Hellenistic Asia. Compare ATTICISM.

A·si·at·ic (ā′zhē-at′ik, ā′shē-) *adj. & n.* Asian. ◆ In most cases, especially in the ethnic sense, *Asian* is now preferred to *Asiatic.*

Asiatic beetle A scarabaeid beetle (*Anomala orientalis*) destructive of sugar cane and grass roots, introduced from Japan into Hawaii and the NE United States.

Asiatic cholera See under CHOLERA.

a·side (ə-sīd′) *adv.* 1. On or to one side; apart; away: Stand *aside!* 2. Out of thought or use: to put grief *aside.* 3. Away from the general company; in seclusion: He drew me *aside.* 4. Away from one's person; down: He cast his weapon *aside.* 5. In reserve: Keep some *aside* for me. — **aside from** *U.S.* 1. Apart from. 2. Excepting. — *n.* Lines spoken privately by an actor and supposed to be heard by the audience but not by the other actors. [< A-[1] on + SIDE]

as·i·nine (as′ə-nīn) *adj.* Pertaining to or like an ass, considered a stupid, obstinate animal. [< L *asinus* < *asinus* ass] — **as′i·nine′ly** *adv.* — **as·i·nin·i·ty** (as′ə-nin′ə-tē) *n.*

A·sir (ä-sir′) A mountainous region in western Arabia on the Red Sea between the Hejaz and Yemen.

ask (ask, äsk) *v.t.* 1. To put a question to: Don't *ask* me. 2. To put a question about; inquire after: to *ask* the time. 3. To say aloud: to *ask* a question. 4. To make a request of or for; solicit: *Ask* him for help; to *ask* advice. 5. To need or require: This job *asks* too much time. 6. To state the price of; demand: They are *asking* three dollars a plate. 7. To invite: Did you *ask* your aunt? 8. *Archaic* To publish or proclaim, as the banns of marriage. — *v.i.* 9. To make inquiries: with *for, after,* or *about.* 10. To make a request: often with *for:* He *asked* for aid. ◆ *Ask for* plus an infinitive (We *asked for* them to come) is not generally considered standard. [OE *āscian*] — **ask′er** *n.* — **ask′ing** *n.* — **Syn.** 1. Ask, *query, question, interrogate, catechize, quiz,* and *inquire* are compared in the sense of putting a question to a person. *Ask* is the most direct and inclusive term. *Query* suggests the effort to settle a doubt. To *question* is to put a series of questions; to *interrogate* is to *question* formally or by right of authority. We *catechize* to elicit prescribed answers, usually as a test of memory, and *quiz* as a test of knowledge. *Inquire* suggests the effort to ascertain facts or the truth. 3. *Ask, request,* and *solicit* mean to urge that something desired be granted or handed over. *Ask* suggests the expectation of compliance; *request* is more formal, and allows for the possibility of refusal. *Solicit* originally implied earnest entreaty, but now is applied chiefly to requests for patronage in fair exchange for services: a salesman *solicits* orders. Compare DEMAND, ENTREAT.

Ask (äsk) In Norse mythology, the first man, made from a tree.

a·skance (ə-skans′) *adv.* 1. With a side glance; sidewise. 2. Disdainfully; distrustfully. Also **a·skant′.** [Origin unknown]

a·skew (ə-skyoō′) *adj.* Oblique. — *adv.* In an oblique position or manner; to one side; awry. [< A-[1] on + SKEW]

Ask·ja (äsk′yä) An inactive volcano in east central Iceland; 3,376 ft.

a·slant (ə-slant′, ə-slänt′) *adj.* Slanting; oblique. — *adv.* At a slant; obliquely. — *prep.* Slantingly across or over.

a·sleep (ə-slēp′) *adj.* 1. In a state of sleep; sleeping. 2. Dormant; inactive. 3. Benumbed, as an arm or leg. 4. Dead. — *adv.* Into a sleeping condition: to fall *asleep.*

a·slope (ə-slōp′) *adj.* Sloping. — *adv.* At a slope.

As·ma·ra (äs-mä′rə) The capital of Eritrea Province, Ethiopia; pop. 145,600 (est. 1966).

ASME or A.S.M.E. American Society of Mechanical Engineers.

As·mo·de·us (az′mə-dē′əs, as′-) In Jewish demonology, an evil, destructive spirit.

ASN *Mil.* Army Service Number.

As·nières (ä-nyâr′) A commune in northern France; a suburb of Paris; pop. 79,942 (1968). Also **As·nières–sur–Seine** (-sür-sen′).

a·so·cial (ā-sō′shəl) *adj.* 1. Avoiding society; not gregarious. 2. Heedless of one's fellow beings; self-centered.

A·so·ka (ə-sō′kə), Indian emperor, reigned 273–232 B.C.; supporter of Buddhism.

a·so·ma·tous (ā-sō′mə-təs, ə-) *adj.* Without bodily form. [< L *asomatus* < Gk. *asōmatos* < *a-* without + *sōma, -atos* body]

A·so·san (ä-sō-sän) A group of five extinct volcanic cones on central Kyushu island, Japan; highest cone, Taka-dake 5,223 ft.; largest crater, Naka-dake, 10 by 15 mi. Also **Mount A·so** (ä-sō).

asp[1] (asp) *n.* 1. The common European viper. 2. The uraeus. [< L *aspis* < Gk.]

asp[2] (asp) *n.* The aspen.

as·par·a·gus (ə-spar′ə-gəs) *n.* 1. The succulent, edible shoots of a cultivated variety of a perennial herb (*Asparagus officinalis*) of the lily family. 2. Any plant of this genus. [< L < Gk. *asparagos, aspharagos*; ult. origin uncertain]

asparagus beetle A beetle (*Crioceris asparagi*) harmful to asparagus shoots. For illustration see INSECTS (injurious).

as·par·tic acid (as·pär′tik) *Biochem.* An amino acid, C_4-H_7O_4N, obtained from beet root and related substances in the form of white prisms or leaflets, used in organic synthesis. Also **as·pa·rag·ic acid** (as′pə·raj′ik), **as·par·a·gin·ic acid** (as·par′ə·jin′ik). [< ASPARAGUS]

As·pa·sia (as·pā′zhə, -shə), 470?–410 B.C., Athenian hetaera; mistress of Pericles.

A.S.P.C.A. American Society for the Prevention of Cruelty to Animals.

as·pect (as′pekt) *n.* **1.** The look of a person; facial expression. **2.** Appearance to the eye; look: the pleasant *aspect* of a lake. **3.** Appearance presented to the mind by circumstances, etc.; interpretation: all *aspects* of a problem. **4.** A looking or facing in a given direction: the southern *aspect* of a house. **5.** The side or surface facing in a certain direction: ventral *aspect*. **6.** In astrology: **a** Any configuration of the planets. **b** The supposed influence of this for good or evil. **7.** *Gram.* A category of the verb indicating, primarily, the nature of the action performed in regard to the passage of time, as in English *he ran* (perfective), *he was running* (imperfective or durative), and, in certain languages, the manner in which the action is performed, the intent of the subject, etc., as in Hebrew *'ākhal* he eats, *'ikkēl* he eats greedily. Aspect is shown in various languages by means of auxiliaries, affixes, root changes, etc. Compare MOOD. **8.** *Obs.* A look; glance. — **Syn.** See PHASE. [< L *aspectus* glance, view < *aspicere* to look at < *ad-* at + *specere* to look]

aspect ratio *Aeron.* The ratio of the square of the maximum span of an airfoil to the total wing area.

asp·en (as′pən) *n.* Any of several species of poplar of North America or Europe with leaves that tremble in the slightest breeze, especially the **quaking aspen** (*Populus tremuloides*) of North America: also *asp.* — *adj.* **1.** Of or pertaining to the aspen. **2.** Shaking, like aspen leaves. [OE *æspe*]

As·pen (as′pən) A resort town and cultural center in west central Colorado; pop. 2,404.

as·per[1] (as′pər) *n.* A Turkish money of account, equal to 1/120 of a piaster. [< F *aspre* < Med.Gk. *aspron*]

as·per[2] (as′pər) *n.* Rough breathing. [< L *asper* (*spiritus*) rough (breathing)]

as·per·ges (ə·spûr′jēz) *n.* **1.** *Often cap.* In the Roman Catholic Church, a short rite before the High Mass on Sundays, during which the celebrant sprinkles the altar and congregation with holy water. **2.** An anthem, beginning "Asperges me" sung during this service. [< L, thou shalt sprinkle (me)]

as·per·gill (as′pər·jil) *n.* In the Roman Catholic Church, a brush or other instrument used for sprinkling holy water: also called *aspersorium*. Also **as·per·gil·lum** (as′pər·jil′əm). [< LL *aspergillum* < L *aspergere*. See ASPERSE.]

ASPERGILL

as·per·gil·lic acid (as′pər·jil′ik) *Biochem.* A yellow crystalline antibiotic, $C_{12}H_{20}N_2O_2$, extracted from aspergillus.

as·per·gil·lo·sis (as·pûr′jə·lō′sis) *n.* An infectious disease of animals and man, caused by certain pathogenic fungi of the genus *Aspergillus*. [< NL < *Aspergillus* + -OSIS]

as·per·gil·lus (as′pər·jil′əs) *n.* *pl.* ·gil·li (-jil′ī) *Bot.* Any of a genus (*Aspergillus*) of fungi belonging to the Ascomycetes, including the common mold found on decaying vegetables, jellies, etc., and several used in preparing food products and antibiotics. [< NL; from its resemblance to an aspergill]

as·per·i·ty (as·per′ə·tē) *n.* *pl.* ·ties **1.** Roughness or harshness, as of surface, sound, style, weather, etc. **2.** Hardship; difficulty. **3.** Bitterness or sharpness of temper; acrimony. — **Syn.** See ACRIMONY. [< OF *asprete* < L *asperitas, -tatis* roughness < *asper* rough]

a·sper·mous (ā·spûr′məs) *adj. Bot.* Without seeds. Also **a·sper·ma·tous** (ā·spûr′mə·təs). [< Gk. *aspermos* < *a-* without + *sperma* seed]

as·perse (ə·spûrs′) *v.t.* **as·persed** (ə·spûrst′), **as·pers·ing 1.** To spread false charges against; slander. **2.** To besprinkle; bespatter. [< L *aspersus*, pp. of *aspergere* to sprinkle on < *ad-* to + *spargere* to sprinkle] — **as·pers′er** or **as·per′sor** *n.* — **as·per′sive** (-siv) *adj.*
— **Syn.** *Asperse, defame, calumniate, traduce, vilify, slander,* and *libel* all mean to make false charges against for the purpose of injuring. To *asperse* is to bespatter with injurious charges. *Defame* and *calumniate* mean to assail a person's good name, but *calumniate* means to do so maliciously and falsely. To *traduce* a person is to bring him into undeserved disrepute, and to *vilify* is to *asperse* by open abuse. In law, *slander* is oral defamation, and *libel* is written; in popular usage, both terms are applied to false accusations by any means. Compare ABUSE, DISPARAGE.

as·per·sion (ə·spûr′zhən, -shən) *n.* **1.** A slandering; defamation. **2.** A slanderous or damaging report; calumny. **3.** A sprinkling; specifically, baptism by sprinkling.

as·per·so·ri·um (as′pər·sôr′ē·əm, -sō′rē-ə) *n.* *pl.* ·so·ri·a (-sôr′ē-ə, -sō′rē-ə) or ·so·ri·ums **1.** A font for holy water. **2.** An aspergill. [< LL < L *aspersus*. See ASPERSE.]

as·phalt (as′fôlt, -falt) *n.* **1.** A solid, brownish black, combustible mixture of bituminous hydrocarbons, found native in various parts of the world and also obtained as a residue in the refining of petroleum: also called *mineral pitch*. **2.** A

mixture of this with sand or gravel, used for paving, etc. Also **as·phal·tum** (as·fal′təm), **as·phal′tus**. — *v.t.* To pave or cover with asphalt. [< LL *asphaltum* < Gk. *asphalton*] — **as·phal·tic** (as·fôl′tik, -fal′-) *adj.*

as·pho·del (as′fə·del) *n.* **1.** A plant (genus *Asphodelus*) of the lily family, bearing white, pink, or yellow flowers. **2.** Any one of certain somewhat similar plants, as the daffodil. [< L *asphodelus* < Gk. *asphodelos*. Doublet of DAFFODIL.]

as·phyx·i·a (as·fik′sē-ə) *n. Pathol.* Unconsciousness caused by too little oxygen and too much carbon dioxide in the blood, generally as a result of suffocation. Also **as·phyx·y** (as·fik′sē). [< NL < Gk. *asphyxia* lack of pulse < *a-* not + *sphyzein* to beat] — **as·phyx′i·al** *adj.*

as·phyx·i·ant (as·fik′sē-ənt) *adj.* Producing or tending to produce asphyxia. — *n.* An asphyxiant agent or condition.

as·phyx·i·ate (as·fik′sē-āt) *v.* ·at·ed, ·at·ing *v.t.* **1.** To cause asphyxia in; suffocate. — *v.i.* **2.** To undergo asphyxia. — **as·phyx′i·a′tion** *n.* — **as·phyx′i·a′tor** *n.*

as·pic[1] (as′pik) *n. Poetic* The asp, a viper. Also **as′pis**. [< MF < L *aspis*]

as·pic[2] (as′pik) *n.* Formerly, the spike lavender. See under LAVENDER. [< F < OF *espic* < L *spica* spike, ear of corn]

as·pic[3] (as′pik) *n.* A savory jelly of meat or vegetable juices, served as a relish or as a mold for meat, vegetables, etc. [< F; ult. origin uncertain]

as·pi·dis·tra (as′pə·dis′trə) *n.* Any of a small genus (*Aspidistra*) of smooth, stemless, Asian herbs of the lily family, with large, glossy, evergreen leaves, cultivated as a house plant. [< NL < Gk. *aspis, aspidos* shield + *astron* star]

as·pir·ant (ə·spīr′ənt, as′pər·ənt) *n.* One who aspires, as after honors or place; a candidate. — *adj.* Aspiring. [< L *aspirans, -antis,* ppr. of *aspirare*. See ASPIRE.]

as·pi·rate (*v.* as′pə·rāt; *n. & adj.* as′pər·it) *v.t.* ·rat·ed, ·rat·ing **1.** *Phonet.* **a** To utter with a puff of breath or as if preceded by an *h* sound. **b** In the articulation of a stop consonant, to follow with a puff of breath, as (p), (t), and (k) when before a vowel. **2.** *Med.* To draw out with an aspirator. — *n.* **1.** *Phonet.* **a** The glottal fricative represented in English and many other languages by the letter *h.* **b** The sudden expulsion of breath in the release of a stop consonant before a vowel, as after the (p) in *pat.* **2.** The rough breathing in Greek or the symbol (ʻ) indicating it. **3.** Any consonant pronounced with a puff of breath. — *adj. Phonet.* Uttered with an aspirate or strong *h* sound: also **as′pi·rat′ed** (-rā′tid). [< L *aspiratus,* pp. of *aspirare*. See ASPIRE.]

as·pi·ra·tion (as′pə·rā′shən) *n.* **1.** The act of aspiring; exalted desire; high ambition. **2.** The act or effect of aspirating; a breath. **3.** *Med.* The use of an aspirator for remedial purposes. **4.** *Phonet.* **a** The articulation of a consonant with an aspirate. **b** An aspirate.

as·pi·ra·tor (as′pə·rā′tər) *n.* **1.** An appliance for producing a suction current of air or other gas. **2.** *Med.* A device for drawing off fluid matter or gases from the body by suction.

as·pi·ra·to·ry (ə·spīr′ə·tôr′ē, -tō′rē) *adj.* Of, pertaining to, or adapted for breathing or suction.

as·pire (ə·spīr′) *v.i.* ·pired, ·pir·ing **1.** To have an earnest desire or ambition, as for something high and good: to *aspire* to (or after) fame; to *aspire* to be king. **2.** *Obs.* To rise or reach upward. [< L *aspirare* to breathe on, attempt to reach < *ad-* to + *spirare* to breathe] — **as·pir′er** *n.*

as·pi·rin (as′pər·in, -prin) *n.* A white crystalline compound, the acetyl derivative of salicylic acid, $C_9H_8O_4$, having antipyretic and antirheumatic properties. [< A(CETYL) + SPIR(AEIC ACID), former name of salicylic acid, + -IN]

as·pir·ing (ə·spīr′ing) *adj.* Characterized by aspiration; ambitious. — **Syn.** See AMBITIOUS. — **as·pir′ing·ly** *adv.*

a·squint (ə·skwint′) *adj. & adv.* With sidelong glance.

As·quith (as′kwith), **Herbert Henry**, 1852–1928, British statesman; prime minister 1908–16.

ass[1] (as, äs) *n.* *pl.* **ass·es 1.** A long-eared equine quadruped (*Equus asinus*) smaller than the ordinary horse, used as a beast of burden; the donkey. **2.** The onager. **3.** A stupid person; fool. [OE *assa* ? < OIrish *assan* < L *asinus*]

ass[2] (as, äs) *n. Slang* The buttocks. [older standard English *arse* < OE *ears*; cf. OHG *ars*]

ass. **1.** Assistant. **2.** Association.

as·sa·fet·i·da (as′ə·fet′ə·də), **as·sa·foet·i·da** See ASAFETIDA.

as·sa·gai (as′ə·gī) *n.* **1.** A light spear, used by Zulus, Kaffirs, etc. **2.** The assagai tree. — *v.t.* ·gaied, ·gai·ing To pierce with an assagai. Also spelled *assegai*. [< Sp. *azagaya* or Pg. *azagaia* < Arabic *az-zaghāyah* < *al* the + *zaghāyah* spear < native Berber word]

assagai tree A South African tree (*Curtisia faginea*) of the dogwood family, used for making spears.

as·sai[1] (ä·sä′ē) *n.* **1.** A palm of the genus *Euterpe*, especially *E. edulis,* bearing a purple, fleshy fruit. **2.** A drink made from this fruit. [< Pg. *assahy* < Tupi]

as·sai[2] (äs·sä′ē) *adv. Music* Very: Adagio *assai* means very slowly. [< Ital.]

as·sail (ə·sāl′) *v.t.* **1.** To attack violently, as by force, argument, or censure; assault. **2.** To approach, as a difficulty, with the intention of mastering. — **Syn.** See ATTACK. [< OF *asalir, asaillir* < LL *adsalire* to leap upon < L *ad-* to +

salire to leap] — **as·sail'a·ble** *adj.* — **as·sail'a·ble·ness** *n.*
— **as·sail'er** *n.*
as·sail·ant (ə-sā'lənt) *n.* One who assails. — *adj.* Attacking; hostile.
As·sam (a-sam') A State in NE India; 85,062 sq. mi.; pop. 15,851,338 (est. 1971); capital, Shillong.
As·sa·mese (as'ə-mēz', -mēs') *adj.* Of or pertaining to Assam. — *n.* 1. A native or inhabitant of Assam. 2. The Indo-European, Indic language of the Assamese.
as·sas·sin (ə-sas'in) *n.* One who kills; especially, one who murders a political figure from fanaticism or for a price.
As·sas·sin (ə-sas'in) *n.* One of a secret order of hashisheating Moslem fanatics who terrorized and murdered their opponents, especially Christians, in the time of the Crusades. [< Med.L *assassinus* < Arabic *hashshāshīn* hashisheaters < *hashīsh* hashish]
as·sas·si·nate (ə-sas'ə-nāt) *v.t.* **·nat·ed, ·nat·ing** 1. To kill by secret or surprise assault, especially a public figure. 2. To destroy or injure by treachery, as a reputation. — **Syn.** See KILL. — **as·sas'si·na'tion** *n.* — **as·sas'si·na'tor** *n.*
assassin bug Any of a large family (*Reduviidae*) of hempterous insects that prey upon harmful insects. Some also suck the blood of warm-blooded animals: also called *conenose*. For illustration see INSECTS (beneficial).
assassin fly A hairy, predatory fly (family *Asilidae*) of the United States: also called *robber fly*. For illustration see INSECTS (beneficial).
as·sault (ə-sôlt') *n.* 1. Any violent attack, as an act, speech, or writing assailing a person or institution. 2. *Law* An unlawful attempt or offer to do bodily injury to another: distinguished from *battery*. 3. A rape. 4. *Mil.* **a** An attack upon a fortified place. **b** A closing with the enemy. — *v.t.* & *v.i.* To attack with violence. — **Syn.** See ATTACK. [< OF *asaut*, ult. < L *ad-* + *salire* to leap]
assault and battery *Law* The carrying out of an assault with force and violence; a beating.
assault boat *Mil.* A small craft used to transport attacking soldiers and their equipment.
as·say (n. ə-sā', as'ā; v. ə-sā') *n.* 1. The chemical analysis or testing of an alloy or ore, especially of gold or silver, to ascertain the ingredients and their proportions. 2. The substance to be so examined. 3. The result of such a test. 4. Any examination or testing. 5. *Obs.* Attempt; trial. — *v.t.* 1. To subject to chemical analysis; make an assay of. 2. To prove; test. 3. *Obs.* To attempt. — *v.i.* 4. *U.S.* To show by analysis a certain value or proportion, as of a precious metal: to *assay* low in platinum. [< OF *assai*, var. of *essai* trial < L *exagium* a weighing < *exigere* to prove < *ex-* out + *agere* to drive, do. Doublet of ESSAY.] — **as·say'er** *n.*
as·se·gai (as'ə-gī) See ASSAGAI.
as·sem·blage (ə-sem'blij, *for def. 4, also Fr.* à-sän-bläzh') *n.* 1. The act of assembling, or the state of being assembled. 2. Any gathering of persons or things; collection; assembly. 3. A fitting together, as of the parts of a machine. 4. A work of art created by assembling materials and objects, often including manufactured articles such as nails, utensils, machine parts, etc.; also, the technique of making such works of art: compare COLLAGE. — **Syn.** See COMPANY. [< F]
as·sem·ble (ə-sem'bəl) *v.t.* & *v.i.* **·bled, ·bling** 1. To come or bring together; collect or congregate: to *assemble* a fortune. 2. To fit or join together, as the parts of a mechanism: to *assemble* a record player. — **Syn.** See CONVOKE. [< OF *as(s)embler* < L *assimulare* < *ad-* to + *simul* together] — **as·sem'bler** *n.*
as·sem·bly (ə-sem'blē) *n. pl.* **·blies** 1. The act of assembling, or the state of being assembled. 2. A number of persons met together for a common purpose. 3. The act or process of fitting together the parts of a machine, etc., especially from standard, interchangeable parts. 4. A unit made up of such parts; also, the parts themselves. 5. *Mil.* The signal calling troops to form ranks. — **Syn.** See COMPANY. [< OF *as(s)emblee* < *as(s)embler*. See ASSEMBLE.]
As·sem·bly (ə-sem'blē) *n.* In some States of the United States, the lower house of the legislature.
assembly line An arrangement of industrial equipment and workers in which the product passes from one specialized operation to another until completed.
as·sem·bly·man (ə-sem'blē-mən) *n. pl.* **·men** (-men', -mən) *U.S. & Canadian* A member of a legislative assembly, especially of a State or Provincial legislature.
as·sent (ə-sent') *v.i.* To express agreement, as with an abstract proposition; acquiesce; concur: usually with *to*. — *n.* 1. Mental concurrence or agreement. 2. Consent; sanction. [< OF *as(s)enter* < L *assentare*, freq. of *assentire* < *ad-* to + *sentire* to feel] — **as·sent'er** *n.*
— **Syn.** (verb) *Assent, agree, concur, accept, accede, consent,* and *acquiesce* mean to go along with another's proposals or views. *Assent* and *agree* are general terms, but *assent* is more formal and impersonal: to *assent* to an opinion, to *agree* with a speaker. *Concur* suggests some degree of hidden reservation, while *accept* implies the making of a concession. *Accede* often involves a yielding

to persuasion, demands, etc. To *consent* is to make a complete emotional or personal commitment, but one may *acquiesce* in what does not fully accord with one's views, because unwilling to raise objections. — **Ant.** dissent, disagree, demur, dispute, oppose, protest, refuse, deny, contradict.
as·sen·ta·tion (as'en-tā'shən) *n.* Obsequious assent.
as·sen·tor (ə-sen'tər) *n.* One who assents; especially, in Great Britain, one who, as required by law, endorses the nomination of a candidate for Parliament.
as·sert (ə-sûrt') *v.t.* 1. To state positively; affirm; declare. 2. To maintain as a right or claim, as by words or force. — **to assert oneself** To put forward and defend one's own rights or claims. [< L *assertus*, pp. of *asserere* to lay claim < *ad-* + *serere* to bind] — **as·sert'a·ble** or **as·sert'i·ble** *adj.* — **as·sert'er** or **as·ser'tor** *n.*
— **Syn.** 1. *Assert, asseverate, allege, avow, declare, state, affirm,* and *announce* mean to say with various degrees of emphasis. One *asserts,* or more positively, *asseverates,* that which one will defend against dispute. One *alleges* a controversial fact without offering proof. *Avow* implies an admission or confession. Merely to speak positively is to *declare,* while to say with very little or no emphasis is to *state* or *affirm. Announce* refers to the disclosure of something that was previously secret or unknown. — **Ant.** deny, gainsay.
as·ser·tion (ə-sûr'shən) *n.* 1. The act of asserting. 2. A positive declaration without attempt at proof.
as·ser·tive (ə-sûr'tiv) *adj.* Asserting or inclined to assert; confident; positive; dogmatic. — **as·ser'tive·ly** *adv.* — **as·ser'tive·ness** *n.*
as·ser·to·ry (ə-sûr'tər-ē) *adj.* Tending to assert.
as·sess (ə-ses') *v.t.* 1. To charge with a tax, fine, or other payment, as a person or property. 2. To determine the amount of, as a tax or other fine on a person or property. 3. To value, as property, for taxation. [< OF *assesser* < LL *assessare* to fix a tax < L *assidere* to sit by (as a judge in court) < *ad-* to + *sedere* to sit] — **as·sess'a·ble** *adj.*
as·sess·ment (ə-ses'mənt) *n.* 1. The act of assessing. 2. An amount assessed. 3. A valuation of taxable property.
as·ses·sor (ə-ses'ər) *n.* 1. One who makes assessments, as for taxation. 2. A specialist assisting a judge. 3. Any adviser or assistant. [< L, lit., one who sits beside, an assistant judge (in LL, an assessor of taxes) < *assidere.* See ASSESS.] — **as·ses·so·ri·al** (as'ə-sôr'ē-əl, -sō'rē-) *adj.*
as·set (as'et) *n.* 1. An item of property. 2. A useful or valuable thing or quality.
as·sets (as'ets) *n.pl.* 1. In accounting, a balance sheet showing all the property or resources of a person or business, and money owed: opposed to *liabilities.* 2. *Law* **a** The property of a deceased person that may be converted into money and used for the payment of debts or legacies. **b** All the property, real and personal, of a person, corporation, or partnership, that is or may be chargeable with their debts or legacies. — **liquid assets** Such securities and assets as can be realized immediately. — **working assets** Nonpermanent, convertible, invested funds. [< AF *asetz,* OF *asez* enough < LL *ad-* to + *satis* enough]
as·sev·er·ate (ə-sev'ə-rāt) *v.t.* **·at·ed, ·at·ing** To affirm or declare emphatically or solemnly. — **Syn.** See ASSERT. [< L *asseveratus,* pp. of *asseverare* < *ad-* to + *severus* serious] — **as·sev'er·a'tion** *n.*
As·shur (ä'shoor, ash'ər) See ASHUR.
as·sib·i·late (ə-sib'ə-lāt) *v.t.* **·lat·ed, ·lat·ing** To utter with a sibilant or hissing sound. [< L *assibilatus,* pp. of *assibilare* < *ad-* to + *sibilare* to hiss] — **as·sib'i·la'tion** *n.*
as·si·du·i·ty (as'ə-dyōo'ə-tē, -dyōo'-) *n. pl.* **·ties** 1. Close and continuous application or effort; diligence. 2. Usually *pl.* Faithful personal attentions.
as·sid·u·ous (ə-sij'ōo-əs) *adj.* 1. Devoted; attentive. 2. Unremitting; persistent: *assiduous* study. — **Syn.** See BUSY. [< L *assiduus* < *assidere* to sit by < *ad-* to + *sedere* to sit] — **as·sid'u·ous·ly** *adv.* — **as·sid'u·ous·ness** *n.*
as·sign (ə-sīn') *v.t.* 1. To set apart, as for a particular function; designate: to *assign* a day for trial. 2. To appoint, as to or for a post or duty. 3. To allot as a task: to *assign* a lesson. 4. To ascribe or attribute; refer: to *assign* a monument to Roman times. 5. *Law* To transfer, as personal property, rights, or interests. 6. *Mil.* To place with a military unit as an integral part: distinguished from *attach.* — *v.i.* 7. To transfer property, especially for the benefit of creditors. — **Syn.** See ATTRIBUTE. — *n. Law* Usually *pl.* Assignee. [< OF *as(s)igner* < L *assignare* < *ad-* to + *signare* to sign < *signum* sign] — **as·sign'a·bil'i·ty** *n.* — **as·sign'a·ble** *adj.* — **as·sign'a·bly** *adv.* — **as·sign'er,** *Law* **as·sign·or** (ə-sī'nôr', as'ə-nôr') *n.*
as·sig·nat (as'ig-nat, *Fr.* à-sē-nyà') *n.* A promissory note of the French revolutionary government circulated as currency (1789–96) against the security of confiscated lands. [< F < L *assignatus,* pp. of *assignare.* See ASSIGN.]
as·sig·na·tion (as'ig-nā'shən) *n.* 1. An appointment for meeting, especially a secret or illicit one as made by lovers. 2. An assignment. [< OF *assignacion* < L *assignatio, -onis* < *assignare.* See ASSIGN.]

as·sign·ee (ə·sī'nē', as'ə·nē') *n.* *Law* A person to whom property, rights, or powers are transferred.

as·sign·ment (ə·sīn'mənt) *n.* **1.** The act of assigning. **2.** Anything assigned, as a lesson or task. **3.** *Law* **a** The transfer of a clai n, right, or property, or the instrument or writing of transfer. **b** The clai n, right, or property transferred.

as·sim·i·la·ble (ə·sim'ə·lə·bəl) *adj.* Capable of being assimilated. **— as·sim'i·la·bil'i·ty** *n.*

as·sim·i·late (ə·sim'ə·lāt) *v.* **·lat·ed, ·lat·ing** *v.t.* **1.** *Physiol.* To take up and incorporate into the body, as food. **2.** To make into a homogeneous part, as of a substance or system. **3.** To make alike or similar; cause to resemble: to *assimilate* British law to the laws of Scotland. **4.** *Phonet.* To cause (a sound) to undergo assimilation. **—** *v.i.* **5.** To become alike or similar. **6.** To become absorbed or assimilated. **7.** *Phonet.* To become modified by assimilation. [< L *assimilatus*, pp. of *assimilare* < *ad-* to + *similare* to make like < *similis* like]

as·sim·i·la·tion (ə·sim'ə·lā'shən) *n.* **1.** The act or process of assimilating. **2.** *Physiol.* The transformation of digested nutriment into an integral and homogeneous part of the solids or fluids of the organism. **3.** *Bot.* The nutritive processes in plants, including photosynthesis. **4.** *Phonet.* The process whereby a sound is replaced by one more closely resembling a neighboring sound, as when *horseshoe* is pronounced (hôrsh'shōō'). **5.** *Psychol.* The process by which all new experience, when received into consciousness, is modified so as to be incorporated with the results of previous conscious processes. **6.** *Sociol.* The acceptance by one social group or community of cultural traits normally associated with another.

as·sim·i·la·tive (ə·sim'ə·lā'tiv) *adj.* Characterized by or tending to assimilation. Also **as·sim·i·la·to·ry** (ə·sim'ə·lə·tôr'ē, -tō'rē).

As·sin·i·boin (ə·sin'ə·boin) *n.* An Indian of a Siouan tribe.

As·sin·i·boine (ə·sin'ə·boin) A river in eastern Saskatchewan, Canada, flowing generally SE about 600 miles to the Red River at Winnipeg.

As·si·si (ə·sē'zē, *Ital.* äs·sē'zē) A commune in Umbria, central Italy; birthplace of St. Francis; pop. 5,302 (1967).

as·sist (ə·sist') *v.t.* **1.** To give or render help to; relieve; succor. **2.** To act as subordinate or deputy to. **—** *v.i.* **3.** To give help or support. **4.** In baseball, to aid a teammate in a put-out. **— Syn.** See HELP. **— to assist at** To be present at (a ceremony, entertainment, etc.). **—** *n.* **1.** An act of helping. **2.** In baseball, a play that helps to put out a runner. Abbr. (for n. def. 2) *a.* [< MF *assister* < L *assistere* < *ad-* to + *sistere* to cause to stand] **— as·sist'er,** *Law* **as·sis'tor** *n.*

as·sis·tance (ə·sis'təns) *n.* The act of helping, or the help given; aid; support. [< MF < *assister*. See ASSIST.]

as·sis·tant (ə·sis'tənt) *n.* One who assists; a subordinate or helper. **—** *adj.* **1.** Holding a subordinate or auxiliary place, office, or rank. **2.** Affording aid; assisting. Abbr. *ass., asst'* [< MF, ppr. of *assister*. See ASSIST.]

assistant professor *U.S.* A college teacher ranking immediately below an associate professor.

As·siut (ä·syōōt') See ASYUT.

as·size (ə·sīz') *n.* **1.** Originally, a session of a legislative or judicial body. **2.** *pl.* In England, one of the regular court sessions held in each county for the trial of civil and criminal cases by jury; also, the time and place of such sessions. **3.** An inquest, the writ by which it is instituted, or the verdict. **4.** *Obs.* A statute, edict, or rule of law, as for the regulation of weights, measures, prices, etc.; also, the standards set up by such an edict or ruling. [< OF *as(s)ise* < *aseeir* to sit at, settle < L *assidere*. See ASSESS.]

assn. Association.

assoc. **1.** Associate. **2.** Association.

as·so·ci·a·ble (ə·sō'shē·ə·bəl, -shə·bəl) *adj.* Capable of being associated, connected, or joined. **— as·so'ci·a·bil'i·ty** *n.*

as·so·ci·ate (*n.* *& adj.* ə·sō'shē·it, -āt, -sē-; *v.* ə·sō'shē·āt, -sē-) *n.* **1.** One who is frequently in the company of another; a companion. **2.** One who is connected with another, as in some business, interest, or position; a partner; colleague. **3.** Anything that habitually accompanies something else; a concomitant. **4.** One admitted to partial membership in an association, society, or institution. **5.** In some schools, one who has finished a course shorter than that set for a degree: an *associate* in arts. **—** *adj.* **1.** Joined with another or others in a common pursuit or office: an *associate* professor. **3.** Existing or occurring together; concomitant. **—** *v.* **·at·ed, ·at·ing** *v.t.* **1.** To bring into company with another or others, as in friendship or partnership; ally; unite. **2.** To combine; join together. **3.** To connect mentally: to *associate* poetry with madness. **—** *v.i.* **4.** To unite for a common purpose; form a league. **5.** To keep or be in company: to *associate* with thieves. [< L *associatus*, pp. of *associare* to join to < *ad-* to + *sociare* to join < *socius* ally]

— Syn. (noun) **1.** *Associate, companion, comrade, partner, mate, colleague,* and *ally* denote a person with whom one is closely connected. *Associates* may have common interests or may be merely thrown into each other's company by chance; when they seek each other's company, they become *companions,* or, if they share the same pleasures and adventures, *comrades. Partners* are bound together by some close tie, as in business or marriage. A *mate* is a person who is regarded as a necessary supplement, as a lieutenant or helper. A *colleague* is another person engaged in the same profession. *Allies* are *associates* who have agreed to work together for a common purpose. **— Ant.** opponent, rival.

Associated Press An organization for collecting news and distributing it to member newspapers. Abbr. *AP, A.P.*

associate professor *U.S.* A college teacher ranking immediately above an assistant professor and below a full professor.

as·so·ci·a·tion (ə·sō'sē·ā'shən, -shē-) *n.* **1.** The act of associating. **2.** The state of being associated; fellowship; companionship. **3.** A body of persons associated for some common purpose; society; league. Abbr. *ass., assn., assoc.* **4.** *Chem.* An aggregate, as of molecules. **5.** *Ecol.* A grouping of many plant species over a wide area, sharing a common habitat and similar geographic conditions. **6.** The connection or relation of ideas, feelings, etc. **7.** *Brit.* Association football. **— as·so'ci·a'tion·al** *adj.*

— Syn. **3.** club, fraternity, union, order, league, federation.

association football Soccer.

as·so·ci·a·tive (ə·sō'shē·ā'tiv, -shē·ə-) *adj.* **1.** Of or characterized by association. **2.** Causing association. **3.** *Math.* Designating an operation that may be applied to a group of quantities in any order, as addition, $a + (b + c) = (a + b) + c$, or multiplication, $a(bc) = (ab)c$. **— as·so'ci·a·tive·ly** *adv.*

associative memory *Electronics* A computer memory system in which storage locations are identified by contents rather than addresses.

as·soil (ə·soil') *v.t.* *Archaic* **1.** To absolve; acquit. **2.** To atone for; remove. [< OF *assoil,* present indicative of *assoldre* < L *absolvere*. Doublet of ABSOLVE.]

as·so·nance (as'ə·nəns) *n.* **1.** Resemblance in sound; especially, in prosody, correspondence of accented vowels, but not of consonants, as in *main, came.* **2.** Rough likeness; approximation. [< F, ult. < L *assonare* to sound to, respond to < *ad-* to + *sonare* to sound] **— as'so·nant** *adj. & n.*

as·sort (ə·sôrt') *v.t.* **1.** To distribute into groups or classes according to kinds; classify. **2.** To furnish, as a warehouse, with a variety of goods, etc. **—** *v.i.* **3.** To fall into groups or classes of the same kind. **4.** To associate; consort: with *with.* [< OF *assorter* < *a-* to (< L *ad-*) + *sorte* sort < L *sors* lot] **— as·sort·a·tive** (ə·sôr'tə·tiv) *adj.* **— as·sort'er** *n.*

as·sort·ed (ə·sôr'tid) *adj.* **1.** Containing or arranged in various sorts or kinds; miscellaneous. **2.** Sorted out; classified. **3.** Matched; suited.

as·sort·ment (ə·sôrt'mənt) *n.* **1.** The act of assorting; classification. **2.** A collection or group of various things; miscellany.

As·sou·an, As·su·an (äs·wän') See ASWAN.

A.S.S.R. or ASSR Autonomous Soviet Socialist Republic (Russian *Avtonomnaya Sovetskaya Sotsialisticheskaya Respublika*).

asst. Assistant.

as·suage (ə·swāj') *v.t.* **·suaged, ·suag·ing** **1.** To make less harsh or severe; alleviate; mitigate. **2.** To appease or satisfy, as thirst. **3.** To calm; pacify. Also *Obs.* **as·swage'.** **— Syn.** See ALLEVIATE. [< OF *as(s)ouagier,* ult. < L *ad-* to + *suavis* sweet] **— as·suage'ment** *n.*

as·sua·sive (ə·swā'siv) *adj.* Soothing; alleviating.

as·sume (ə·sōōm') *v.t.* **·sumed, ·sum·ing** **1.** To take on or adopt, as a style of dress, aspect, or character. **2.** To undertake, as an office or duty. **3.** To arrogate to oneself; usurp, as powers of state. **4.** To take for granted; suppose to be a fact. **5.** To affect; pretend to have: to *assume* a pious air. **6.** *Archaic* To take or receive, as into partnership or association. [< L *assumere* to take up, adopt < *ad-* to + *sumere* to take] **— as·sum·a·ble** (ə·sōō'mə·bəl) *adj.*

— Syn. **2.** accept. **3.** take, claim, appropriate. **4.** presuppose, presume, postulate, posit. **5.** feign, simulate, sham.

as·sumed (ə·sōōmd') *adj.* **1.** Taken for granted. **2.** Pretended; fictitious. **3.** Usurped.

as·sum·ing (ə·sōō'ming) *adj.* Presumptuous; arrogant.

as·sump·sit (ə·sump'sit) *n.* *Law* **1.** A promise or contract not under seal. **2.** An action to enforce this, or to recover damages for a breach of this. [< L, he has undertaken]

as·sump·tion (ə·sump'shən) *n.* **1.** The act of assuming, or that which is assumed. **2.** That which is taken for granted; a supposition. **3.** Presumption; arrogance. **4.** *Logic* A minor premise. **— Syn.** See HYPOTHESIS. **— the Assumption 1.** *Theol.* The doctrine that the Virgin Mary was bodily taken up into heaven at her death. **2.** A church feast, observed on August 15, commemorating this event. [< L *assumptio, -onis* < *assumere*. See ASSUME.] **— as·sump·tive** (ə·sump'tiv) *adj.*

as·sur·ance (ə·shōōr'əns) *n.* **1.** The act of assuring, or the state of being assured. **2.** A positive statement, intended to give confidence, encouragement, etc. **3.** Firmness of mind; confidence in self or in others; certainty. **4.** Boldness; effrontery. **5.** *Chiefly Brit.* Insurance, especially life insurance. [< OF *asseurance* < *aseürer*. See ASSURE.]

— Syn. See CERTAINTY. **— Ant.** doubt, distrust, misgiving, hesitancy, timidity.

as·sure (ə·shŏŏr′) *v.t.* **·sured, ·sur·ing 1.** To make sure or secure; establish firmly. **2.** To make (something) certain; guarantee: This edict *assures* a revolution. **3.** To cause to feel certain; convince. **4.** To promise; make positive declaration to: He *assured* us of his return. **5.** To give confidence to; encourage; reassure. **6.** To insure, as against loss. [< OF *aseurer* < LL *assecurare* < L *ad-* to + *securus* safe] — **as·sur′a·ble** *adj.* — **as·sur′er** *n.*

as·sured (ə·shŏŏr′) *adj.* **1.** Made certain; undoubted; sure: His defeat is *assured.* **2.** Self-possessed; confident. **3.** Insured. — *n.* An insured person. — **as·sur·ed·ly** (ə·shŏŏr′id·lē) *adv.* — **as·sur′ed·ness** *n.*

as·sur·gent (ə·sûr′jənt) *adj.* **1.** Rising or tending to rise. **2.** *Bot.* Curving upward. [< L *assurgens, -entis,* ppr. of *assurgere* < *ad-* to + *surgere* to rise] — **as·sur′gen·cy** *n.*

Assyr. Assyrian.

As·syr·i·a (ə·sir′ē·ə) An ancient empire of western Asia; capital, Nineveh.

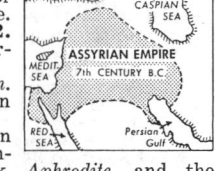

As·syr·i·an (ə·sir′ē·ən) *adj.* Of or pertaining to Assyria or its people. — *n.* **1.** A native of Assyria. **2.** The Semitic language of the Assyrians.

As·syr·i·ol·o·gy (ə·sir′ē·ol′ə·jē) *n.* The study of the ancient Assyrian civilization. — **As·syr′i·ol′o·gist** *n.*

As·tar·te (as·tär′tē) In Phoenician mythology, the goddess of love: identified with *Ashtoreth,* the Greek *Aphrodite,* and the Babylonian and Assyrian *Ishtar.*

a·stat·ic (ā·stat′ik) *adj.* **1.** *Physics* Being in neutral equilibrium; having no tendency toward any change of position. **2.** Unsteady. [< Gk. *astatos* < *a-* not + *statos* stable] — **a·stat′i·cal·ly** *adv.* — **a·stat·i·cism** (ā·stat′ə·siz′əm) *n.*

as·ta·tine (as′tə·tēn, -tin) *n.* An unstable chemical element (symbol At) of atomic number 85, related to the halogens and occupying the place formerly assigned to alabamine. See ELEMENT. [< Gk. *astatos* unstable + -INE²]

as·ter (as′tər) *n.* **1.** Any of a large genus (*Aster*) of plants of the composite family, having alternate leaves, and flowers with white, purple, or blue rays and yellow disc. **2.** One of various allied plants, as the China aster. **3.** *Biol.* The star-shaped figure appearing in the cytoplasm of a cell during mitosis and associated with the centrosome and spindle fibers. [< L < Gk. *astēr* star]

aster- Var. of ASTERO-.

-aster *suffix* Little; inferior: *poetaster, criticaster.* [< L *-aster,* dim. suffix]

as·ter·a·ceous (as′tə·rā′shəs) *adj.* Of or pertaining to a group of plants (*Asteraceae*) included in the composite family.

as·te·ri·at·ed (as·tir′ē·ā′tid) *adj.* **1.** Grouped like stars. **2.** Radiating, as the rays of a star. **3.** *Mineral.* Exhibiting asterism. [< Gk *asterios* starry < *astēr* star]

as·ter·isk (as′tər·isk) *n.* **1.** *Printing* A starlike figure (*) used to indicate omissions, footnotes, references, etc. **2.** Anything shaped like a star. [< L *asteriscus* < Gk. *asteriskos,* dim. of *astēr* star]

as·ter·ism (as′tə·riz′əm) *n.* **1.** *Printing* A group of three asterisks in triangular form set in front of a passage to call attention to it. **2.** *Astron.* **a** A cluster of stars. **b** A constellation. **3.** *Mineral.* The property of some crystals of showing a starlike figure by reflected or transmitted light. [< Gk. *asterismos* constellation < *astēr* star]

a·stern (ə·stûrn′) *adv. & adj. Naut.* **1.** In the rear; at any point behind a vessel. **2.** To the rear; backward.

a·ster·nal (ā·stûr′nəl) *adj. Anat.* **1.** Not attached to the sternum. **2.** Not having a sternum.

astero- *combining form* Of or related to a star. Also *aster-* (before vowels): also **asteri-.** [< Gk. *astēr* a star]

as·ter·oid (as′tə·roid) *adj.* **1.** Star-shaped. **2.** *Bot.* Pertaining to or like an aster. — *n.* **1.** *Astron.* Any of several hundred small planets between Mars and Jupiter: also called *planetoid.* **2.** *Zool.* A starfish. [< Gk. *asteroeidēs* starlike < *astēr* a star] — **as·ter·oi′dal** *adj.*

as·ter·oi·de·an (as′tə·roi′dē·ən) *Zool. adj.* Of or belonging to a class (*Asteroidea*) of echinoderms comprising the true starfishes. — *n.* An asteroidean echinoderm. [< ASTEROID]

As·ter·o·pe (as·ter′ə·pē) See STEROPE.

as·the·ni·a (as·thē′nē·ə, as′thə·nī′ə) *n. Pathol.* Lack of bodily strength; general debility. Also **as·the·ny** (as′thə·nē). [< NL < Gk. *astheneia* < *a-* without + *sthenos* strength]

as·then·ic (as·then′ik) *n.* One who is characterized by a lean, generally tall figure, and light muscular development. — *adj.* Of or characterized by asthenia. Also **as·then′i·cal** *adj.*

asth·ma (az′mə, as′-) *n. Pathol.* A chronic respiratory disorder characterized by recurrent paroxysmal coughing and a sense of constriction of the chest. [< Gk. *asthma, -atos* < *azein* to breathe hard]

asth·mat·ic (az·mat′ik, as-) *adj.* Of, pertaining to, or af-

fected with asthma. Also **asth·mat·i·cal.** — *n.* A person suffering from asthma. — **asth·mat′i·cal·ly** *adv.*

As·ti (äs′tē) A Province of Piedmont, NW Italy; 584 sq. mi.; pop. 213,195 (1961); capital, Asti, pop. 60,217.

as·tig·mat·ic (as′tig·mat′ik) *adj.* Of, characterized by, or correcting astigmatism.

a·stig·ma·tism (ə·stig′mə·tiz′əm) *n.* A defect of the eye or of a lens such that the rays of light from an object converge to more than one focus, thus causing imperfect vision or images. [< A-⁴ without + Gk. *stigma, -atos* mark, spot + -ISM]

a·stir (ə·stûr′) *adv. & adj.* Stirring; moving about.

As·to·lat (as′tə·lät, -lat) An English town in Arthurian legend, thought by some scholars to have been in Surrey.

a·stom·a·tous (ā·stom′ə·təs, ā·stō′mə-) *adj. Biol.* Without a mouth or breathing pores. Also **as·to·mous** (as′tə·məs). [< A-⁴ without + Gk. *stoma, stomatos* mouth]

As·ton (as′tən), **Francis William,** 1877–1945, English physicist.

a·ston·ish (ə·ston′ish) *v.t.* To affect with wonder and surprise; amaze; confound. — **Syn.** See AMAZE. [Prob. alter. of ASTONY] — **a·ston′ish·er** *n.* — **a·ston′ish·ing** *adj.* — **a·ston′ish·ing·ly** *adv.*

a·ston·ish·ment (ə·ston′ish·mənt) *n.* **1.** The state of being astonished; surprise; amazement. **2.** An object or cause of such emotion.

a·ston·y (ə·ston′ē) *v.t.* **a·ston·ied, a·ston·y·ing** *Obs.* **1.** To astound; astonish. **2.** To stun. [Var. of obs. *astone* shock, stun, prob. < OF *estoner,* ult. < L *ex-* out + *tonare* to thunder]

As·tor (as′tər), **John Jacob,** 1763–1848, U.S. fur merchant and capitalist. — **Lady,** 1879–1964, Viscountess Astor, *née* Nancy Langhorne, first woman member of the British House of Commons; born in the United States.

As·to·ri·a (as·tôr′ē·ə, -tō′rē·ə) A port city in NW Oregon, at the mouth of the Columbia River; pop. 10,244.

a·stound (ə·stound′) *v.t.* To overwhelm with wonder; confound. — **Syn.** See AMAZE. — *adj. Archaic* Astonished. [ME *astoned* stunned, pp. of *astonien* < OF *estoner.* See ASTONY.] — **a·stound′ing** *adj.* — **a·stound′ing·ly** *adv.*

astr. Astronomer; astronomical; astronomy.

As·tra·chan (as′trə·kan, -kən) *n.* A variety of apple of Russian origin. [after *Astrakhan*]

a·strad·dle (ə·strad′l) *adv. & adj.* Astride.

As·trae·a (as·trē′ə) In Greek mythology, the goddess of justice.

as·tra·gal (as′trə·gəl) *n.* **1.** *Archit.* **a** A small convex molding in the form of a string of beads. **b** A plain, narrow, convex molding. For illustration see MOLDING. **2.** *pl.* Dice: originally made from anklebones. [< L *astragalus.* See ASTRAGALUS.]

as·trag·a·lus (as·trag′ə·ləs) *n. pl.* **·li** (-lī) *Anat.* The talus. [< L < Gk. *astragalos*] — **as·trag′a·lar** (-lər) *adj.*

as·tra·khan (as′trə·kan, -kən) *n.* **1.** The black or gray, loosely curled fur made from the pelt of lambs raised in the region near Astrakhan. **2.** A fabric with a curled pile imitative of this. Also **as′tra·chan.**

As·tra·khan (as′trə·kan, -kən; *Russ.* äs′trə·khəny′) A city in the SE Russian S.F.S.R., on the Volga; pop. 411,000 (est. 1970).

as·tral (as′trəl) *adj.* **1.** Of, pertaining to, coming from, or like the stars; starry. **2.** *Biol.* Of, pertaining to, or resembling an aster; star-shaped. **3.** In alchemy, susceptible to influences from the stars: *astral* gold. **4.** In theosophy, pertaining to or consisting of a substance supposed to pervade all space and to be refined beyond the tangible world. — *n.* **1.** An astral body. **2.** An astral lamp. [< LL *astralis* < L *astrum* star < Gk. *astron*] — **as′tral·ly** *adv.*

astral lamp An oil lamp with a ring-shaped reservoir so placed that its shadow is not cast directly below the flame.

a·stray (ə·strā′) *adv. & adj.* Away from the right path; wandering in or into error or evil. [< OF *estraie,* pp. of *estraier* < L *extra-* beyond + *vagare* to wander]

as·trict (ə·strikt′) *v.t. Rare* **1.** To bind; restrict; limit. **2.** To bind by moral or legal obligation. [< L *astrictus,* pp. of *astringere.* See ASTRINGE.] — **as·tric′tion** *n.*

as·tric·tive (ə·strik′tiv) *adj.* Astringent; styptic. — *n.* An astringent. — **as·tric′tive·ly** *adv.* — **as·tric′tive·ness** *n.*

a·stride (ə·strīd′) *adv. & adj.* **1.** With one leg on each side. **2.** With the legs far apart. — *prep.* With one leg on each side of: *astride* a horse.

as·tringe (ə·strinj′) *v.t.* **·tringed, ·tring·ing** To bind or draw together; compress; constrict. [< L *astringere* < *ad-* to + *stringere* to bind fast]

as·trin·gent (ə·strin′jənt) *adj.* **1.** *Med.* Tending to contract or draw together organic tissues; binding; styptic. **2.** Harsh; stern; austere. — *n.* An astringent substance, as alum, tannin, etc. [< L *astringens, -entis,* ppr. of *astringere.* See ASTRINGE.] — **as·trin′gen·cy** *n.* — **as·trin′gent·ly** *adv.*

astro- *combining form* **1.** Star: *astrometry.* **2.** Of, pertaining to, occurring in, or characteristic of outer space: *astronautics.* [< Gk. *astron* star]

as·tro·bi·ol·o·gy (as'trō·bī·ol'ə·jē) *n.* The study of the forms and phenomena of life on celestial bodies.

as·tro·bot·a·ny (as'trō·bot'ə·nē) *n.* The investigation of plant life on other planets. **— as'tro·bot'a·nist** *n.*

as·tro·dome (as'trə·dōm) *n.* A transparent domelike structure in some aircraft for observation of celestial bodies.

as·tro·dy·nam·ics (as'trō·dī·nam'iks) *n.pl.* (*construed as sing.*) The branch of dynamics concerned with the motions of celestial bodies.

as·tro·gate (as'trə·gāt) *v.i.* **·gat·ed, ·gat·ing** *Aerospace* To direct the course and movements of a spacecraft from within.

astrol. Astrologer; astrological; astrology.

as·tro·labe (as'trə·lāb) *n.* An instrument formerly used for obtaining the altitudes of planets and stars. [< OF *astrelabe* < Med.L *astrolabium* < Gk. *astrolabon*, orig., star-taking < *astron* star + *lambanein* to take]

as·trol·o·gy (ə·strol'ə·jē) *n.* **1.** The study professing to foretell the future and interpret the influence of the heavenly bodies upon the destinies of men. **2.** Originally, the practical application of astronomy to human uses. [< L *astrologia* < Gk. *astrologia* < *astron* star + *logos* discourse < *legein* to speak] **— as·trol'o·ger** *n.* **— as·tro·log·ic** (as'trə·loj'ik) or **·i·cal, as·trol'o·gous** (-gəs) *adj.* **— as'tro·log'i·cal·ly** *adv.*

as·trom·e·try (ə·strom'ə·trē) *n.* The branch of astronomy that determines the apparent positions, motions, and magnitudes of the heavenly bodies.

astron. Astronomer; astronomical; astronomy.

as·tro·naut (as'trə·nôt) *n.* One who travels in space: also called *cosmonaut*. [< ASTRO- + (*aero*)*naut*]

as·tro·nau·tics (as'trə·nô'tiks) *n.pl.* (*construed as sing.*) The science and art of space travel. **— as'tro·nau'tic** or **·ti·cal** *adj.* **— as'tro·nau'ti·cal·ly** *adv.*

as·tro·nav·i·ga·tion (as'trō·nav'ə·gā'shən) *n.* Celestial navigation (which see). **— as'tro·nav'i·ga'tor** *n.*

as·tron·o·mer (ə·stron'ə·mər) *n.* One learned or expert in astronomy. Abbr. *astr.*, *astron.*

as·tro·nom·i·cal (as'trə·nom'i·kəl) *adj.* **1.** Of or pertaining to astronomy. Abbr. *astr.*, *astron.* **2.** Enormously or inconceivably large, like the quantities used in astronomy. Also **as'tro·nom'ic. — as'tro·nom'i·cal·ly** *adv.*

astronomical time Mean time (which see).

astronomical unit A space unit for expressing the distances of the stars, equal to the mean distance of the earth from the sun. Compare PARSEC.

astronomical year The period between two passages of the sun through the same equinox, equal to about 365 days, 5 hours, 48 minutes, and 46 seconds: also called *equinoctial*, *natural*, *solar*, or *tropical year*.

as·tron·o·my (ə·stron'ə·mē) *n.* The science that treats of the heavenly bodies, their motions, magnitudes, distances, and physical constitution. For symbols used in astronomy see Special Signs and Symbols section. Abbr. *astr.*, *astron.* [< OF *astronomie* < L *astronomia* < Gk. *astron* star + *nomos* law < *nemein* to distribute, arrange]

as·tro·pho·tog·ra·phy (as'trō·fə·tog'rə·fē) *n.* The art or practice of photographing heavenly bodies. **— as·tro·pho·to·graph·ic** (as'trō·fō'tə·graf'ik) *adj.*

as·tro·pho·tom·e·ter (as'trō·fō·tom'ə·tər) *n.* An instrument for determining the brightness of stars. **— as'tro·pho·tom'e·try** *n.* **— as·tro·pho·to·met·ri·cal** (as'trō·fō'tə·met'ri·kəl) *adj.*

as·tro·phys·ics (as'trō·fiz'iks) *n.pl.* (*construed as sing.*) The branch of astronomy that treats of the physical constitution and properties of the heavenly bodies, especially as revealed by spectrum analysis. **— as'tro·phys'i·cal** *adj.* **— as·tro·phys·i·cist** (as'trō·fiz'ə·sist) *n.*

as·tro·sphere (as'trə·sfir) *n.* *Biol.* **1.** The part of the aster that does not include the rays; the attraction sphere or centrosphere. **2.** The whole aster excluding the centrosome.

As·tro·turf (as'trō·tûrf') *n.* An artificial grass used to cover sports grounds: a trade name.

As·tu·ri·as (as·tŏŏr'ē·əs, *Sp.* äs·tōō'ryäs) A region and former kingdom of NW Spain.

as·tute (ə·stōōt', ə·styōōt') *adj.* Keen in discernment; acute; shrewd; sagacious; cunning. Also **as·tu·cious** (ə·stōō'shəs, ə·styōō'-), **as·tu'tious.** [< L *astutus* < *astus* cunning] **— as·tute'ly** *adv.* **— as·tute'ness** *n.*

— Syn. *Astute*, *shrewd*, *cunning*, *sagacious*, *perspicacious*, *sharp*, *keen*, and *acute* mean having good insight and judgment, particularly in practical matters. The *astute* person is worldly-wise and not easily misled; the *shrewd* man has native acumen and drives a hard bargain; and *cunning* is usually applied to those who are adept in deception and guile, though it sometimes means skillful in a good sense. *Sagacious* implies wisdom on a lofty plane and the ability to anticipate future events. *Perspicacious* refers to the strong power of insight, as do the homelier terms *sharp*, *keen*, and *acute*. **— Ant.** undiscerning, short-sighted, stupid, dull.

As·ty·a·nax (as·tī'ə·naks) In Greek legend, the young son of Hector and Andromache, killed by the Greeks.

a·sty·lar (ā·stī'lər) *adj.* *Archit.* Without columns or pilasters. [< A-⁴ + Gk. *stylos* pillar]

A·sun·ción (ä·sōōn·syôn') The capital of Paraguay, in the SW part; a major port on the Paraguay river; pop. 350,000 (est. 1965).

a·sun·der (ə·sun'dər) *adv.* **1.** Apart; into pieces. **2.** In or into a different place or direction. **— adj.** Separated; apart. [OE *on sundran*. See SUNDER.]

As·wan (äs·wän') A city on the Nile river in southern Egypt; site of the **Aswan Dam** (1¼ miles long; 176½ feet high); a new dam (2.6 miles long, 436 feet high) was completed in 1968; pop. 127,594 (est. 1966): also *Assouan*, *Assuan*: ancient *Syene*.

a·syl·lab·ic (ā'si·lab'ik) *adj.* Not syllabic.

a·sy·lum (ə·sī'ləm) *n.* *pl.* **·lums** or **·la** (-lə) **1.** An institution for the care of the mentally ill, the aged, the destitute, etc. **2.** A place of refuge; retreat; shelter. **3.** An inviolable shelter from arrest or punishment, as a temple or church in ancient times. **4.** The protection afforded by a sanctuary or refuge. [< L < Gk. *asylon* < *a-* without + *sylon* right of seizure]

a·sym·met·ric (ā'si·met'rik, as/i-) *adj.* **1.** Not symmetrical. **2.** *Chem.* Designating an unbalanced spatial arrangement of atoms and radicals within a molecule. Also **a'sym·met'ri·cal. — a'sym·met'ri·cal·ly** *adv.*

a·sym·me·try (ā·sim'ə·trē) *n.* Lack of symmetry or proportion.

as·ymp·tote (as'im·tōt) *n.* *Math.* A straight line that an indefinitely extended curve continually approaches as a tangent. [< Gk. *asymptōtos* not falling together < *a-* not + *syn-* together + *piptein* to fall] **— as'ymp·tot'ic** (-tot'ik) or **·i·cal** *adj.* **— as'ymp·tot'i·cal·ly** *adv.*

a·syn·chro·nism (ā·sing'krə·niz'əm) *n.* Lack of synchronism, or coincidence in time. **— a·syn'chro·nous** (-nəs) *adj.*

a·syn·de·ton (ə·sin'də·ton) *n.* In rhetoric, the omission of conjunctions between parts of a sentence, as "On your mark, get set, go!" Compare POLYSYNDETON. [< L < Gk. *asyndeton* < *a-* not + *syn-* together + *deein* to bind] **— as·yn·det·ic** (as'in·det'ik) *adj.* **— as'yn·det'i·cal·ly** *adv.*

as you were A drill command directing soldiers to assume the position or resume the movement preceding the last command, or canceling an earlier command that has not yet been executed.

As·yut (äs·yōōt') A city in east central Egypt, on the Nile; pop. 121,000 (est. 1959): also *Assiut*.

at (at, *unstressed* ət) *prep.* **1.** In or on the position of: *at* the center of the circle. **2.** Of time, on or upon the point or stroke of: *at* noon. **3.** During the course or lapse of: *at* night. **4.** In contact with; on; upon: *at* sea. **5.** To or toward: Look *at* that sunset! **6.** Through; by way of: Smoke came out *at* the windows. **7.** Within the limits of; present in: *at* home. **8.** Engaged or occupied in: *at* work. **9.** Attending: *at* a party. **10.** In the state or condition of: *at* war. **11.** In the region or vicinity of: *at* the door. **12.** Viewed from; with an interval of: *at* sixty paces. **13.** Having reference to; in connection with: He winced *at* the thought. **14.** In the manner of: *at* a trot. **15.** In pursuit or quest of; in the direction of; against: to catch *at* straws. **16.** Dependent upon: *at* an enemy's mercy. **17.** According to: Proceed *at* your discretion. **18.** To the extent of; amounting to: interest *at* two percent. **19.** From; out of: to draw water *at* a well. **20.** On the occasion of: She fainted *at* the news. [OE *æt*]

— Syn. 2. *At*, *in*, and *on* may be used with reference to time. An event occurs *at* an hour of the day, *in* a month or year, *on* a day of the week, a date, or a precise division of time: to arrive *on* the hour. **7.** *At*, *in*, and *on* may be used of spatial location. Something is *at* a place regarded as a point: *at* a city, displayed *at* the museum. It is *in* a place regarded as embracing it: *in* a country, *in* a suburb. A building is said to be *on* a street.

at- Assimilated var. of AD-.

at. *Physics* Atomic.

At *Chem.* Astatine.

AT *Mil.* Antitank.

at·a·bal (at'ə·bəl) *n.* A Moorish tabor or kettledrum. [< Sp. < Arabic *at-tabl* the drum]

At·a·brine (at'ə·brin, -brēn) *n.* Proprietary name for a brand of quinacrine. Also **at·a·brine.**

A·ta·ca·ma Desert (ä'tä·kä'mä) An arid region of northern Chile, rich in natural nitrate deposits, extending about 600 miles south from the border of Peru.

at·a·ghan (at'ə·gan) See YATAGHAN.

A·ta·hual·pa (ä'tä·wäl'pä), died 1533, last Inca emperor of Peru 1525–33.

At·a·lan·ta (at'ə·lan'tə) In Greek mythology, a maiden who agreed to marry any suitor who could outrun her, the losers being put to death. Hippomenes contrived to beat her by dropping three golden apples which she paused to pick up.

a·ta·la·ya (ä'tä·lä'yä) *n.* A watchtower. [< Sp.]

at·a·man (at'ə·man) *n.* A Cossack chief; hetman. [< Russian *atamanu* < Polish *hetman*. See HETMAN.]

at·a·mas·co (at'ə·mas'kō) *n.* A low North American plant (genus *Zephyranthes*) of the amaryllis family, bearing a large white and pink flower. [< Algonquian (Virginian)]

atamasco lily The atamasco or an allied plant.

at·a·rac·tic (at'ə·rak'tik) *adj.* **1.** Conducive to peace of mind. **2.** *Med.* Having the power to tranquilize and to lessen nervous tension: said of certain drugs, as reserpine. Also **at'a·rax'ic** (-rak'sik). [< NL < Gk. *ataraktos* untroubled < *atarakteein* to be calm. See ATARAXIA.]

at·a·rax·i·a (at/ə-rak/sē-ə) *n.* Freedom from anxiety; peace of mind. Also **at·a·rax·y** (at/ə-rak/sē). [< NL < Gk. *ataraxia* < *atarakteein* to be calm < *a-* not + *tarattein* to disturb, trouble]

A·ta·türk (ä·tä·türk/) See KEMAL ATATÜRK.

a·tav·ic (ə-tav/ik) *adj.* Pertaining to remote ancestors.

at·a·vism (at/ə-viz/əm) *n.* **1.** Reversion to an earlier or primitive type. **2.** *Biol.* Reversion. [< F *atavisme* < L *atavus* ancestor < *at-* beyond + *avus* grandfather] **— at/a·vist** *n.* **— at/a·vis/tic** *adj.*

a·tax·i·a (ə-tak/sē-ə) *n. Pathol.* **1.** Loss or failure of muscular coordination. **2.** Locomotor ataxia (which see). Also **a·tax·y** (ə-tak/sē). [< NL < Gk. *ataxia* lack of order < *a-* not + *tattein* to arrange] **— a·tax/ic** *adj. & n.*

At·ba·ra (at/bä-rä) A river flowing generally NW about 500 miles from NW Ethiopia to the Nile in NE Sudan.

ATC Air Traffic Control.

ate[1] (āt, *chiefly Brit.* et) Past tense of EAT.

a·te[2] (ä/tē) *n.* In ancient Greek thought, the fatal and reckless blindness inciting men to crime. [< Gk. *atē*]

-ate[1] *suffix* Forming: **1.** Participial adjectives equivalent to those in *-ated: desolate, separate.* **2.** Adjectives from nouns with the meaning "possessing or characterized by": *caudate, foliate.* **3.** Verbs, originally from stems of Latin verbs of the first conjugation, and, by analogy, extended to other stems: *fascinate, assassinate.* **4.** *Chem.* Verbs with the meaning "combine or treat with": *chlorinate.* [< L *-atus*, pp. ending of 1st conjugation verbs]

-ate[2] *suffix* Forming: **1.** Nouns denoting office, function, or agent: *magistrate.* **2.** Nouns denoting the object or result of an action: *mandate.* [< L *-atus*, suffix of nouns]

-ate[3] *suffix Chem.* Used to form the names of salts and esters derived from acids whose names end in *-ic: carbonate, nitrate.* [< L *-atum*, neut. of *-atus.* See -ATE[1].]

A·te (ä/tē) In Greek mythology, a goddess personifying men's blind impulse, associated with the punishment of crime.

at ease A drill command authorizing soldiers to relax but not to talk or leave their places.

a·tech·nic (ä-tek/nik) *adj.* Without technical knowledge. [< Gk. *atechnos* unskilled < *a-* without + *technē* skill]

at·el·ier (at/əl-yā, *Fr.* ȧ·tə·lyā/) *n.* A workshop, especially of an artist; studio. [< F, orig., pile of chips < OF *astele* chip < LL *astella* < L *astula* chip, splinter]

a tem·po (ä tem/pō) *Music* In the regular time; resuming the rate of speed originally indicated. [< Ital.]

a·tem·po·ral (ä-tem/pər-əl) *adj.* Timeless; apart from time.

Ath·a·bas·can (ath/ə-bas/kən) See ATHAPASCAN.

Ath·a·bas·ka River (ath/ə-bas/kə) A river in Alberta, Canada, flowing generally north 765 miles to Lake Athabaska (3,058 sq. mi.) in northern Alberta and Saskatchewan.

Ath·a·mas (ath/ə-mas) In Greek legend, king of Thessaly, husband of Nephele, who, seized with madness, killed his own son.

ath·a·na·sia (ath/ə-nā/zhə, -zhē-ə) *n.* Deathlessness; immortality. Also **a·than·a·sy** (ə-than/ə-sē). [< Gk. < *a-* without + *thanatos* death]

Ath·a·na·sian (ath/ə-nā/zhən) *adj.* Of Athanasius. **—** *n.* An adherent of Athanasius or of his teachings.

Athanasian creed A formulary of Christian belief formerly ascribed to Athanasius, but now assigned to a later date.

Ath·a·na·sius (ath/ə-nā/shəs, -shē-əs), **Saint,** 298?-373, bishop of Alexandria; theologian; opposed Arianism: called **Father of Orthodoxy.**

Ath·a·pas·can (ath/ə-pas/kən) *n.* **1.** A family of North American Indian languages, including languages of Alaska and NW Canada, of the Pacific coast, and the Apache and Navaho languages of the SW United States. **2.** A member of a tribe speaking Athapascan. Also spelled *Athabascan.*

A·thar·va-Ve·da (ə-tär/və-vā/də) See under VEDA.

a·the·ism (ā/thē-iz/əm) *n.* **1.** The belief that there is no God. **2.** Godlessness in life or conduct. [< MF *athéisme* < Gk. *atheos* < *a-* without + *theos* god]

a·the·ist (ā/thē-ist) *n.* One who denies or disbelieves in the existence of God. **— Syn.** See SKEPTIC.

a·the·is·tic (ā/thē-is/tik) *adj.* **1.** Of or pertaining to atheism or atheists. **2.** Given to atheism; godless. Also **a/the·is/ti·cal. — a/the·is/ti·cal·ly** *adv.*

ath·e·ling (ath/ə-ling) *n. Archaic* **1.** In early English history, a crown prince. **2.** Any member of a noble family. [OE *ætheling* < *æthelu* noble ancestry]

Ath·el·stan (ath/əl-stan), 895-940, king of England 924-940; grandson of Alfred.

a·the·mat·ic (ā/thē-mat/ik) *adj. Ling.* Not attached to or not constituting a stem.

A·the·na (ə-thē/nə) In Greek mythology, the virgin goddess of wisdom, war, and arts and crafts: identified with the Roman Minerva. *Also* **Athena Parthenos, A·the·ne** (ə-thē/nē). [< Gk. *Athēnē*]

ath·e·ne·um (ath/ə-nē/əm) *n.* **1.** A literary club, academy, or other institution for the promotion of learning. **2.** A reading room, library, etc. Also **ath/e·nae/um.**

Ath·e·ne·um (ath/ə-nē/əm) **1.** A temple of Athena at Athens. **2.** An academy founded by Hadrian at Rome. Also **Ath/e·nae/um.** [< L < Gk. *Athēnaion*]

A·the·ni·an (ə-thē/nē-ən) *adj.* Of or pertaining to Athens, or to its art or culture. **—** *n.* A native or citizen of Athens.

Ath·ens (ath/ənz) **1.** The capital of Greece, in the SE part; the center of ancient Greek culture; pop. with suburbs, 2,347,000 (1967). *Greek* **A·the·nai, A·thi·nai** (ä·thē/ne). **2.** A city in north central Georgia; pop. 44,342.

a·ther·ma·nous (ä·thûr/mə-nəs) *adj.* Impervious to radiant heat. [< A-[4] without + Gk. *thermainein* to heat < *thermos* hot] **— a·ther/man·cy** *n.*

ath·er·o·ma (ath/ə-rō/mə) *n. Pathol.* **1.** A sebaceous cyst. **2.** Arteriosclerosis accompanied by pronounced degenerative changes. [< L < Gk. *atherōma* < *athērē* gruel; with ref. to the encysted matter]

ath·er·o·scle·ro·sis (ath/ər-ō-sklə-rō/sis) *n. Pathol.* Hardening of the arteries, accompanied by the deposit of fat in the inner arterial walls. [< NL < Gk. *athērē* gruel + *sklēros* hard]

Ath·er·ton (ath/ər-tən), **Gertrude Franklin,** 1857-1948, *née* Horn, U.S. novelist.

a·thirst (ə·thûrst/) *adj.* **1.** Keenly desirous; longing; eager: with *for.* **2.** *Archaic* Thirsty. [OE *ofthyrsted*, pp. of *ofthyrstan* < *of-,* intensive + *thyrstan* to thirst]

athl. Athlete; athletic; athletics.

ath·lete (ath/lēt) *n.* **1.** One trained in acts or feats of physical strength and agility, as in sports. **2.** In classical antiquity, a contestant in the public games. [< L *athleta* < Gk. *athlētēs* a contestant in the games < *athleein* to contend for a prize < *athlos* a contest < *athlon* a prize]

athlete's foot Ringworm of the foot, caused by a parasitic fungus: also called *dermatophytosis.*

ath·let·ic (ath-let/ik) *adj.* **1.** Of, pertaining to, or befitting an athlete or athletics. **2.** Strong; vigorous; muscular. **— ath·let/i·cal·ly** *adv.* **— ath·let·i·cism** (ath-let/ə-siz/əm) *n.* **— Syn. 2.** brawny, husky, sinewy.

ath·let·ics (ath-let/iks) *n.pl. (construed as sing. in def. 2)* **1.** Athletic games and exercises, as rowing, wrestling, etc. **2.** A system of athletic training.

athletic supporter An elastic belt with a supporting pouch for the male genitals, worn for protection in sports: also called *jockstrap.*

ath·o·dyd (ath/ō-did) *n.* A simple jet engine consisting of a nozzlelike pipe to which air is admitted, heated by fuel combustion, and expelled from the rear at high velocity. [< A(ERO)- + TH(ERM)ODY(NAMIC) D(UCT)]

at-home (ət-hōm/) *n.* An informal party or reception given at one's home.

Ath·os (ath/os, ā/thos), **Mount 1.** The highest point on Chalcidice peninsula in Greek Macedonia, coextensive with the Akte prong; 6,670 ft. **2.** See MOUNT ATHOS.

a·thwart (ə-thwôrt/) *adv.* **1.** From side to side; across. **2.** So as to thwart; perversely. **—** *prep.* **1.** From side to side of. **2.** Contrary to; in opposition to. **3.** *Naut.* Across the course of. [< A-[1] on + THWART]

-atic *suffix* Of; of the kind of: used in adjectives of Latin or Greek origin: *erratic.* [< F *-atique* < L *-aticus* < Gk. *-atikos*]

a·tilt (ə-tilt/) *adv. & adj.* **1.** In a tilted manner; tilted up. **2.** Like one tilting with a lance.

-ation *suffix of nouns* **1.** Action or process of: *creation.* **2.** Condition or quality of: *affectation.* **3.** Result of: *reformation.* Also *-ion, -tion.* ◆ Originally found in English nouns borrowed from Latin, and now used by analogy to form nouns on any stem, as in *starvation, thunderation.* [< F *-ation* or L *-atio, -ationis* < *-atus* + *-io.* See -ATE[1], -ION.]

-ative *suffix* Denoting relation, tendency, or characteristic: *tentative, remunerative, laxative.* [< F *-atif*, masc., *-ative*, fem. or < L *-ativus*]

At·kins (at/kinz), **Tommy.** See TOMMY ATKINS.

At·lan·ta (at-lan/tə) The capital of Georgia, a city in the NW central part; pop. 497,421.

At·lan·te·an (at/lan-tē/ən) *adj.* **1.** Pertaining to Atlas. **2.** Pertaining to Atlantis. Also **At·lan·ti·an** (at-lan/tē-ən).

at·lan·tes (at-lan/tēz) *n. pl. of* **atlas** (at/ləs) *Archit.* Male human figures, used as columns or pilasters. [< L < Gk. *Atlantes*, pl. of *Atlas*]

At·lan·tic (at-lan/tik) *adj.* **1.** Of, near, in, or pertaining to the Atlantic Ocean. **2.** Pertaining to or derived from Mount Atlas or the Atlas Mountains in NW Africa. **—** *n.* The Atlantic Ocean. [< L *Atlanticus* < Gk. *Atlantikos* pertaining to Atlas]

Atlantic Charter A statement resulting from a meeting at sea and issued in August, 1941, by Churchill and Roosevelt, setting forth the basic aims of the Allied Nations for the peace after World War II.

Atlantic City A resort city in SE New Jersey, on the Atlantic; pop. 47,859.

Atlantic Ocean The world's second largest ocean, extending from the Arctic to the Antarctic between the Americas and Europe and Africa; 31.5 million sq. mi.; divided by the equator into the **North Atlantic Ocean** and the **South Atlantic Ocean.**

Atlantic Provinces The Canadian Provinces of Newfoundland, Prince Edward Island, Nova Scotia, and New Brunswick.

Atlantic Standard Time See under STANDARD TIME.

At·lan·tis (at-lan'tis) A mythical island west of Gibraltar, said by Plato to have been engulfed by the sea.

at·las (at'ləs) n. 1. A volume of maps usually bound together. 2. Any book of tables or illustrations showing systematically the development of a subject. 3. A large size of paper, 26 by 33 (or 34) inches. 4. *Anat.* The first cervical vertebra, supporting the head. 5. *Archit.* Any of the atlantes. [def. 1 < ATLAS; from a picture of Atlas supporting the heavens shown in some early volumes of maps]

At·las (at'ləs) n. 1. In Greek mythology, a Titan who supported the heavens on his shoulders. 2. Anyone bearing a great burden. 3. An intercontinental ballistic missile of the U.S. Air Force. [< L < Gk. *Atlas* < *tlēnai* to bear, carry]

Atlas Mountains A range in NW Africa; highest peak, Djebel Toubkal, 13,665 ft.

At·li (ät'lē) In the *Volsunga Saga*, a king who wed Gudrun and later murdered her brothers: identified with *Attila*.

atm. *Physics* Atmosphere; atmospheric.

at·man (ät'mən) n. In Hinduism, the soul; the divine life principle in man. **— Atman** The supreme soul, the source and goal of all individual souls. [< Skt.]

atmo- *combining form* Vapor: *almometer*. [< Gk. *atmos*]

at·mol·y·sis (at-mol'ə-sis) n. The act or process of partially separating mixtures of gases into their ingredients by virtue of their different diffusibility through porous substances. [< ATMO- + Gk. *lysis* a loosing]

at·mom·e·ter (at-mom'ə-tər) n. An instrument for measuring rate of evaporation: also called *evaporimeter*. **— at·mo·met·ric** (at/mə-met'rik) *adj.* **— at·mom'e·try** n.

at·mos·phere (at'məs-fir) n. 1. The body of gases surrounding the earth or a celestial body. 2. The particular climatic condition of any place or region. 3. Any surrounding or pervasive element or influence: an *atmosphere* of gloom. 4. The prevailing tone of a poem, novel, painting, etc. 5. *Informal* A quality regarded as especially characteristic or interesting: This café has *atmosphere*. 6. *Physics* A conventional unit of pressure per unit of area, equivalent to the pressure of air at sea level and at a temperature of 0°C., or 14.69 pounds per square inch. Abbr. (for def. 6) *at., atm.* [< NL *atmosphaera* < Gk. *atmos* vapor + *sphaira* sphere]

at·mos·pher·ic (at'məs-fir'ik, -fer'-) *adj.* 1. Of, pertaining to, or belonging to the atmosphere. 2. Dependent on, caused by, or resulting from the atmosphere. 3. Occurring in the atmosphere: *atmospheric* testing. Also **at'mos·pher'i·cal.** Abbr. *atm.* **— at'mos·pher'i·cal·ly** *adv.*

at·mos·pher·ics (at'məs-fer'iks) *n.pl.* (construed as sing.) Atmospheric conditions due to electromagnetic disturbances, especially as they affect radio transmission: also called *sferics, spherics.*

at. no. Atomic number.

at·oll (at'ôl, -ol, ə-tol') n. A ring-shaped coral island and its associated reef, nearly or completely enclosing a lagoon. [? < Malayalam *adal* closing, uniting]

at·om (at'əm) n. 1. *Chem.* The smallest part of an element capable of existing alone or in combination, and that cannot be changed or destroyed in any chemical reaction: distinguished from *molecule.* 2. *Physics* One of the elementary components of matter in all its forms, regarded as an aggregate of nucleons and electrons variously organized within and around a central nucleus, and exhibiting complex mass-energy characteristics. See ATOMIC STRUCTURE. 3. A hypothetical entity admitting of no division into smaller parts. 4. The smallest quantity or particle; iota. [< L *atomus* < Gk. *atomos* indivisible < *a-* not + *temnein* to cut]

a·tom·ic (ə-tom'ik) *adj.* 1. Of or pertaining to an atom or atoms. Also **a·tom'i·cal.** Abbr. *at.* 2. Very minute; infinitesimal. 3. Of, characterized by, or employing atomic energy: an *atomic* power plant. **— a·tom'i·cal·ly** *adv.*

atomic age The era characterized by the use and growing importance of atomic energy as a factor in human social development. Also **Atomic Age.**

atomic bomb A bomb of formidable destructive power using the energy released by the fission of atomic nuclei, especially those of radioactive elements, as uranium: also called *A-bomb.* Also **atom bomb.**

atomic clock A high-precision instrument for the measurement of time by a constant frequency associated with a selected line in the spectrum of ammonia gas or other suitable vibrator.

atomic energy The energy contained within the nucleus of the atom, especially when made available for human use by controlled nuclear fission or thermonuclear reactions.

Atomic Energy Commission A U.S. board formed in 1946 for the domestic control of atomic energy. Abbr. *AEC*

at·o·mic·i·ty (at'ə-mis'ə-tē) n. *Chem.* 1. The number of atoms in a molecule. 2. Valence. 3. In the molecule of a compound, the number of replaceable atoms or groups.

atomic number *Physics* A number that represents the unit positive charges (protons) in the atomic nucleus of each element and corresponds to the number of extranuclear electrons. Hydrogen is assigned an atomic number of 1.

atomic power Atomic energy as a source of power.

atomic reactor Reactor (def. 4).

a·tom·ics (ə-tom'iks) *n.pl.* (construed as sing.) Nuclear physics, especially in its practical applications.

atomic structure *Physics* 1. The configuration of the atom. 2. The conception of the atom as a system of particles made up of a central nucleus having a net positive charge neutralized by a cluster of negatively charged electrons, the number and arrangement of the component particles determining the intricate energy relations within and between atoms, as well as in all forms of matter.

atomic theory 1. *Chem.* The doctrine that elements unite with one another, atom by atom, and in definite simple proportions by weight. 2. *Physics* The modern concept of atomic structure as a complex of mass-energy relationships.

atomic weight *Chem.* **a** Since 1961, the weight of an atom of an element relative to that of an atom of carbon, taken as 12.01115. **b** Formerly, the weight of an atom of an element relative to that of an atom of oxygen, taken as 16. Abbr. *at. wt.*

at·om·ism (at'əm-iz'əm) n. 1. The atomic theory. 2. The philosophy that holds that the entire universe is composed of simple, indivisible atoms. **— at'om·ist** n. **— at'om·is'tic** or **-ti·cal** *adj.*

at·om·ize (at'əm-īz) *v.t.* **·ized, ·iz·ing** 1. To reduce to atoms. 2. To spray or reduce to a spray, as by an atomizer. Also *Brit.* **at'om·ise.** **— at'om·i·za'tion** n.

at·om·iz·er (at'əm-ī'zər) n. An apparatus for reducing a liquid, especially medicine or perfume, to a spray.

atom smasher *Physics* An accelerator.

at·o·my[1] (at'ə-mē) n. *pl.* **·mies** *Archaic* 1. An atom. 2. A pygmy. [< L *atomi*, pl. of *atomus* atom]

at·o·my[2] (at'ə-mē) n. *pl.* **·mies** *Obs.* A skeleton or an emaciated person. [< ANATOMY (misunderstood as *an atomy*)]

a·to·nal (ā-tō'nəl) *adj. Music* Without tonality; lacking key or tonal center. **— a·to'nal·ly** *adv.*

a·to·nal·i·ty (ā'tō-nal'ə-tē) n. *Music* The use of a system of tones, especially the chromatic scale, so that each tone is equal in its relation to the others and no one tone holds a central or primary position; absence of key or tonal center.

a·tone (ə-tōn') *v.* **a·toned, a·ton·ing** *v.i.* 1. To make expiation, as for sin or a sinner. 2. *Obs.* To agree. **— v.t.** 3. *Rare* To expiate. 4. *Obs.* To propitiate; reconcile. [< earlier adverbial phrase *at one* in accord, short for *to set at one*, i.e., reconcile] **— a·ton'a·ble** or **a·tone'a·ble** *adj.* **— a·ton'er** n.

a·tone·ment (ə-tōn'mənt) n. 1. Satisfaction, reparation, or expiation made for wrong or injury; amends. 2. *Usually cap. Theol.* **a** The redemptive work of Christ. **b** The reconciliation between God and man effected by Christ. 3. In Christian Science, the exemplification of man's unity with God, whereby man reflects divine Truth, Life, and Love. 4. *Obs.* Reconciliation; agreement. **— Syn.** See PROPITIATION.

a·ton·ic (ə-ton'ik, ā-) *adj.* 1. Not accented, as a word or syllable. 2. Lacking tone or vigor. **—** n. An unaccented syllable or word. [< Med.L *atonicus* < Gk. *atonos* slack, relaxed < *a-* not + *teinein* to stretch]

at·o·ny (at'ə-nē) n. 1. *Pathol.* Want of tone or power, especially of a muscle. 2. Lack of stress, as in a syllable. [< Med.L *atonia* slackness < Gk. < *a-* not + *teinein* to stretch]

a·top (ə-top') *adv. & adj.* On or at the top. **— prep.** *Chiefly U.S.* On the top of.

-ator *suffix of nouns* An agent; doer; actor; one who or that which: *arbitrator, mediator*. [< L]

-atory *suffix of adjectives* Pertaining to or of the nature of; producing or produced by: *conciliatory*. [< L *-atorius*, adj. suffix]

ATP *Biochem.* Adenosinetriphosphate. See under ADENOSINE.

at·ra·bi·lar·i·an (at'rə-bi-lâr'ē-ən) n. A hypochondriac. **—** *adj.* Atrabilious.

at·ra·bil·ious (at'rə-bil'yəs) *adj.* Disposed to hypochondria; melancholy; splenetic. Also **at'ra·bil'i·ar** (-bil'ē-ər). [< L *atra bilis* black bile, a trans. of Gk. *melancholia*. See MELANCHOLY.] **— at'ra·bil'ious·ness** n.

A·treus (ā'troos, ā'trē-əs) In Greek legend, a king of Mycenae, son of Pelops and father of Agamemnon and Menelaus, who, to avenge the treachery of his brother Thyestes, served Thyestes' sons to their father at a banquet.

a·trip (ə-trip') *adv. & adj. Naut.* Just clear of the bottom, as an anchor; aweigh. [< A-[1] on + TRIP]

a·tri·um (ā'trē-əm) n. *pl.* **-tri·a** (ā'trē-ə) 1. The entrance hall or central open court of an ancient Roman house. 2. A court or hall. 3. *Anat.* One of the upper chambers of the heart through which venous blood is transmitted to the ventricles: also called *auricle*. [< L, a hall] **— a'tri·al** *adj.*

ATOLL
a Islets. b
Barrier reef. c
Fringing reef.
d Lagoon. e
Passage.

a·tro·cious (ə·trō′shəs) *adj.* **1.** Outrageously wicked, criminal, vile, or cruel; heinous. **2.** *Informal* Very bad, or in bad taste: an *atrocious* book. [< L *atrox, atrocis* harsh, cruel < *ater* black] **— a·tro′cious·ly** *adv.* **— a·tro′cious·ness** *n.*

a·troc·i·ty (ə·tros′ə·tē) *n. pl.* **·ties 1.** The state or quality of being atrocious. **2.** An atrocious deed or act. **3.** *Informal* A bad piece of work; something in very bad taste. [< L *atrocitas, -tatis* cruelty < *atrox*. See ATROCIOUS.]

à trois (à trwä′) *French* Involving or limited to three persons: a little supper *à trois.*

at·ro·phied (at′rə·fēd) *adj.* Wasted away; withered.

at·ro·phy (at′rə·fē) *n. pl.* **·phies** *Pathol.* **1.** A wasting or withering of the body or any of its parts. **2.** A stoppage of growth or development, as of a part. **—** *v.* **·phied, ·phy·ing** *v.t.* **1.** To cause to waste away or wither; affect with atrophy. **—** *v.i.* **2.** To waste away; wither. [< F *atrophie* < L *atrophia* < Gk. < *a-* not + *trephein* to nourish] **— a·troph·ic** (ə·trof′ik), *and* **at·ro·phous** (at′rə·fəs) *adj.*

at·ro·pine (at′rə·pēn, -pin) *n.* A crystalline, bitter, poisonous alkaloid, $C_{17}H_{23}O_3N$, found in the deadly nightshade and in the seeds of the thorn apple or jimson weed, used in medicine as an antispasmodic and to enlarge the pupil of the eye. Also **at′ro·pin** (-pin). [< NL *Atropa*, the genus of belladonna < Gk. *Atropos*. See ATROPOS.]

at·ro·pism (at′rə·piz′əm) *n. Pathol.* A diseased state produced by overdoses of atropine.

At·ro·pos (at′rə·pos) One of the three Fates or Moirai. [< Gk., inflexible < *a-* not + *trepein* to turn]

att. 1. Attention. **2.** Attorney.

at·tach (ə·tach′) *v.t.* **1.** To make fast to something; fasten on; affix. **2.** To connect or join on as a part or adjunct. **3.** To add or append, as a signature. **4.** To connect by personal ties, as of affection. **5.** To ascribe; attribute: to *attach* great importance to an event. **6.** To appoint officially; assign. **7.** *Law* To secure for legal jurisdiction; seize or arrest by legal process: to *attach* an employee's salary. **8.** *Mil.* To allocate, as personnel, units, or materiel, temporarily or as a noninte-gral part. **9.** *Obs.* To seize. **—** *v.i.* **10.** To be attached; connect. [< OF *atachier* < *a-* to (< L *ad-*) + *tache* nail < Gmc. Related to ATTACK.] **— at·tach′a·ble** *adj.*

at·ta·ché (at′ə·shā′, *esp. Brit.* ə·tash′ā) *n.* A person officially attached to a diplomatic mission or staff in a specified capacity: military *attaché.* [< F, pp. of *attacher* to attach]

attaché case A boxlike hinged briefcase.

at·tach·ment (ə·tach′mənt) *n.* **1.** The act of attaching, or the state of being attached. **2.** That by which anything is attached; a bond; band; tie. **3.** Affection; devoted regard. **4.** An appendage or adjunct. **5.** *Law* a Seizure of a person or property. **b** The writ commanding this.

at·tack (ə·tak′) *v.t.* **1.** To set upon violently; begin battle or conflict with. **2.** To assail with hostile words; criticize; censure. **3.** To begin work on; set about, as an undertaking, with the intention of completing. **4.** To begin to affect seriously or injuriously; seize: Acid *attacks* metal. **—** *v.i.* **5.** To make an attack; begin battle: The enemy *attacked* at dawn. **—** *n.* **1.** The act of attacking; assault; onset. **2.** The first movement toward any undertaking. **3.** A seizure, as by disease. **4.** *Music* The manner of beginning a phrase or passage. [< F *attaquer* < Ital. *attaccare*, ult. < same source as ATTACH] **— Syn.** (verb) **1.** *Attack, assault,* and *assail* mean to set upon in physical battle, or with words. *Attack* is applied loosely to any offensive action, but strictly means to begin hostilities. *Assault* always suggests close physical contact and extreme violence. To *assail* is to belabor with repeated words or blows. **—** (noun) **1.** assault, onslaught, onset, invasion, incursion, raid.

at·tain (ə·tān′) *v.t.* **1.** To gain or arrive at by exertion of body or mind; achieve, as a desired purpose or state. **2.** To come to, as in time; arrive at: He *attained* old age. **— to attain to** To arrive at with effort; succeed in reaching: Few have *attained* to such power. [< OF *ataindre* < L *attingere* to reach < *ad-* to + *tangere* to touch]

at·tain·a·ble (ə·tā′nə·bəl) *adj.* That can be attained. **— at·tain′a·bil′i·ty, at·tain′a·ble·ness** *n.*

at·tain·der (ə·tān′dər) *n.* **1.** The loss of all civil rights consequent to a sentence of death or of outlawry for a capital offense. **2.** *Obs.* Dishonor. **— bill of attainder** Formerly, a legislative act inflicting attainder upon a person guilty of a capital offense. [< OF *ataindre* to attain, strike, accuse; infl. in meaning by F *taindre* to stain]

at·tain·ment (ə·tān′mənt) *n.* **1.** The act of attaining. **2.** That which is attained; an acquisition, as of skill. **— Syn. 2.** *Attainment, acquirement, accomplishment,* and *acquisition* denote things gained by effort. All are used chiefly in the plural. *Attainment* is the loftiest term, being applied to eminence in art or science. An *acquirement* is a skill gained by study or practice rather than through natural talent. An *accomplishment* is usually a social grace, designed to please or entertain. *Acquisition* stresses the utilitarian or self-serving nature of an *acquirement* and usually refers to something material.

at·taint (ə·tānt′) *v.t.* **1.** To inflict attainder upon; condemn. **2.** To touch or affect injuriously; disgrace; taint. **3.** *Obs.* To accuse: with *of.* **4.** *Obs.* To touch; hit, as in tilting. **—** *n.*

1. Imputation; stigma. **2.** Attainder. [< OF *ataint*, pp. of *ataindre*. See ATTAIN.]

at·tain·ture (ə·tān′chər) *n. Obs.* **1.** Imputation of dishonor. **2.** Attainder.

at·tar (at′ər) *n.* The fragrant essential oil extracted from the petals of flowers, especially roses: also called *ottar.* [< Persian '*aṭar* < Arabic '*iṭr* perfume]

at·tem·per (ə·tem′pər) *v.t.* **1.** To reduce or modify by or as by mixture. **2.** To modify the temperature of. **3.** To moderate or appease. **4.** To adapt (oneself) so as to harmonize. **5.** *Obs.* To control; regulate. [< OF *atemprer* < L *attemperare* to adjust < *ad-* to + *temperare* to regulate]

at·tempt (ə·tempt′) *v.t.* **1.** To make an effort to do or accomplish; try. **2.** To make an effort against; try to take by force; attack; assault: to *attempt* the life of someone. **3.** *Archaic* To tempt. **—** *n.* **1.** A putting forth of effort; a trial; endeavor. **2.** An attack; assault. [< OF *attenter, attempter* < L *attentare, attemptare* to try < *ad-* toward + *tentare, temptare,* freq. of *tendere* to stretch] **— at·tempt′a·bil′i·ty** *n.* **— at·tempt′a·ble** *adj.* **— at·tempt′er** *n.*

atten. Attention.

at·tend (ə·tend′) *v.t.* **1.** To be present at, as a meeting. **2.** To wait upon or go with as an attendant; escort. **3.** To visit or minister to (a sick person). **4.** To accompany as a result or circumstance. **5.** To give heed to; listen to. **6.** *Archaic* To await; expect. **—** *v.i.* **7.** To be present. **8.** To give heed; listen. **9.** *Obs.* To wait; delay. **— Syn.** See ACCOMPANY. **— to attend to 1.** To apply oneself to. **2.** To take care of; tend to. [< OF *atendre* to wait, expect < L *attendere* to give heed to, consider < *ad-* toward + *tendere* to stretch]

at·ten·dance (ə·ten′dəns) *n.* **1.** The act of attending. **2.** Those who attend; an audience or retinue. [< OF *atendance* < *atendre*. See ATTEND.]

at·ten·dant (ə·ten′dənt) *n.* **1.** One who attends, especially as a servant. **2.** One who is present. **3.** A concomitant; consequence. **—** *adj.* Following or accompanying.

at·tent (ə·tent′) *adj. Archaic* Attentive. [< L *attentus,* pp. of *attendere.* See ATTEND.]

at·ten·tion (ə·ten′shən) *n.* **1.** The concentrated direction of the mental powers; close or earnest attending. **2.** The power or faculty of mental concentration. **3.** Practical consideration; care: *attention* to one's appearance. **4.** *Usually pl.* Acts of courtesy or gallantry, especially on the part of a lover. **5.** *Mil.* The prescribed position of readiness: to stand at *attention*; also, the order to take this position. Abbr. *att., atten., attn.* [< L *attentio, -onis,* < *attendere.* See ATTEND.]

attention span *Psychol.* **1.** The time during which a person can concentrate on one thing without his attention weakening. **2.** The number of discrete objects that a person can perceive during a very brief display or exposure.

at·ten·tive (ə·ten′tiv) *adj.* **1.** Giving or showing attention; observant; thoughtful. **2.** Courteous or gallant; considerate; polite. **— at·ten′tive·ly** *adv.* **— at·ten′tive·ness** *n.*

at·ten·u·ant (ə·ten′yŏō·ənt) *adj.* Making thin; diluting. **—** *n. Med.* An attenuant substance. [< L *attenuans, -antis,* ppr. of *attenuare.* See ATTENUATE.]

at·ten·u·ate (*v.* ə·ten′yŏō·āt; *adj.* ə·ten′yŏō·it) *v.* **·at·ed, ·at·ing** *v.t.* **1.** To make thin, small, or fine; draw out, as a wire. **2.** To reduce in value, quantity, size, or strength; weaken; impair. **3.** To reduce in density; rarefy, as a liquid or gas. **4.** *Bacteriol.* To weaken the virulence of (a microorganism). **—** *v.i.* **5.** To become thin, weak, rarefied, etc. **—** *adj.* **1.** Made thin; slender; rarefied; diluted. **2.** *Bot.* Slender and tapering; narrow. [< L *attenuatus,* pp. of *attenuare* to weaken < *ad-* (intensive) + *tenuare* to make thin < *tenuis* thin] **— at·ten′u·a·ble** *adj.*

at·ten·u·a·tion (ə·ten′yŏō·ā′shən) *n.* **1.** The act or process of attenuating, or the state of being attenuated. **2.** *Bacteriol.* Reduction of the virulence of microorganisms by repeated cultivation in artificial media, exposure to light, etc.

at·test (ə·test′) *v.t.* **1.** To confirm as accurate, true, or genuine; vouch for. **2.** To certify, as by signature or oath. **3.** To be proof of: His many works *attest* his industry. **4.** To put upon oath. **—** *v.i.* **5.** To bear witness; testify: with *to.* **—** *n.* Attestation. [< MF *attester* < L *attestari* to confirm < *ad-* to + *testari* to bear witness] **— Syn.** (verb) **3.** shout, indicate, argue, bespeak. Compare CONFIRM. **— Ant.** belie, disprove.

at·tes·ta·tion (at′es·tā′shən) *n.* **1.** The act of attesting. **2.** Testimony.

at·tic (at′ik) *n.* **1.** A low story beneath the roof of a building; a garret. **2.** *Archit.* A low, decorative wall or structure, in classical style, above a cornice or entablature. [< F *attique* < L *Atticus,* architectural term]

At·tic (at′ik) *adj.* **1.** Of or pertaining to Attica. **2.** Of or characteristic of Athens, the Athenians, or their culture, art, etc. **3.** Simple and graceful; delicate; refined: also **at′tic. —** *n.* The dialect of Attica, closely related to Ionic, representing ancient Greek in its most refined form as used by Aeschylus, Sophocles, Euripides, etc. [< L *Atticus* < Gk. *Attikos* < *Attikē* Attica]

At·ti·ca (at/i·kə) **1.** A Department of east central Greece; 1,469 sq. mi.; pop. 1,556,029 (1951); capital, Athens. **2.** In ancient times, the region of Greece surrounding Athens.

At·ti·cism (at/ə·siz/əm) *n.* **1.** An Attic idiom or characteristic. **2.** A clear, concise, elegant expression. **3.** A simple rhetorical style. Compare ASIANISM.

At·ti·cize (at/ə·sīz) *v.* **-cized**, **·ciz·ing** *v.i.* **1.** To affect Attic literary style, customs, etc.; conform to Attic usage. **2.** To side with or favor the Athenians. — *v.t.* **3.** To cause to conform to Attic usage, style, etc. Also *Brit.* **At/ti·cise.**

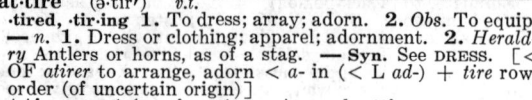

Attic salt Delicate, refined, graceful wit. Also **Attic wit.**

At·ti·la (at/ə·lə, ə·til/ə), 406?–453, king of the Huns: called *the Scourge of God.*

at·tire (ə·tīr/) *v.t.* **-tired**, **·tir·ing** **1.** To dress; array; adorn. **2.** *Obs.* To equip. — *n.* **1.** Dress or clothing; apparel; adornment. **2.** *Heraldry* Antlers or horns, as of a stag. — **Syn.** See DRESS. [< OF *atirer* to arrange, adorn < *a-* in (< L *ad-*) + *tire* row, order (of uncertain origin)]

at·tire·ment (ə·tīr/mənt) *n.* Apparel; attire.

At·tis (at/is) In classical mythology, a vegetation god worshiped with Cybele.

at·ti·tude (at/ə·tood, -tyood) *n.* **1.** Position of the body, as suggesting some thought, feeling, or action. **2.** State of mind, behavior, or conduct regarding some matter, as indicating opinion or purpose. **3.** *Aeron. & Aerospace* The position of a vehicle with reference to some plane, as the earth or the horizon; tilt or tip. **4.** *Med.* The position of the fetus in the womb. [< F < Ital. *attitudine* < LL *aptitudo, -inis* fitness < L *aptus* fitted, suited. Doublet of APTITUDE.] — **at·ti·tu·di·nal** (at/ə·tood/də·nəl, -tyood/-) *adj.*

— **Syn. 1, 2.** *Attitude, position, posture,* and *pose* refer to the physical aspect of a body, and, by extension, to mental outlook. *Attitude* is a *position* of body assumed consciously or unconsciously, expressing a feeling of mind; hence, it may refer to the feeling itself. *Position* is location or orientation in space, or arrangement of parts; in extension, it also means a chosen point of view or opinion. *Posture* is a habitual way of carrying the body, while *pose* is a *position* assumed temporarily for pictorial effect; hence, *pose* may also imply affectation.

at·ti·tu·di·nize (at/ə·tood/də·nīz, -tyood/-) *v.i.* **-nized**, **·niz·ing** To strike an attitude; pose. Also *Brit.* **at/ti·tu/di·nise.**

At·tle·bor·o (at/l·bûr/ō) A city in SE Massachusetts; pop. 32,907.

Att·lee (at/lē), **Clement Richard**, 1883–1967, Earl Attlee, British statesman; prime minister 1945–51.

attn. Attention.

atto- *combining form* One quintillionth (10^{-18}) of a specific quantity or dimension.

at·torn (ə·tûrn/) *Law v.i.* **1.** To agree to recognize a new owner as one's landlord. **2.** In feudal law, to accord homage to a new lord. — *v.t.* **3.** To make over to another; transfer. [< OF *atorner* to turn to, assign, appoint < *a-* to (< L *ad-*) + *torner* to turn. See TURN.] — **at·torn/ment** *n.*

at·tor·ney (ə·tûr/nē) *n.* **1.** A person empowered by another to act in his stead; especially, an attorney at law. Abbr. *att., atty.* **2.** *Obs.* An agent. — **Syn.** See LAWYER. — **by attorney** By proxy. [< OF *atorne*, pp. of *atorner.* See ATTORN.] — **at·tor/ney·ship** *n.*

attorney at law An attorney who is qualified to prosecute and defend actions in a court of law; lawyer.

attorney general *pl.* **attorneys general, attorney generals** The chief law officer of a government. Abbr. *A.G., Atty. Gen.*

at·tract (ə·trakt/) *v.t.* **1.** To draw to or cause to come near by some physical force, as magnetism, and without apparent mechanical connection. **2.** To draw, as the admiration or attention of, by some winning influence; allure; entice. — *v.i.* **3.** To exert attractive influence. [< L *attractus*, pp. of *attrahere* < *ad-* toward + *trahere* to draw, drag] — **at·tract/a·ble** *adj.* — **at·tract/a·ble·ness, at·tract/a·bil/i·ty** *n.* — **at·trac/tile** *adj.* — **at·trac/tor** or **at·tract/er** *n.*

at·trac·tion (ə·trak/shən) *n.* **1.** The act or power of attracting. **2.** Attractive quality or characteristic; enticement; charm. **3.** Something that attracts. **4.** *Physics* A physical force that, exerted between or among bodies, tends to make them approach each other or prevents their separating.

attraction sphere *Biol.* A minute spherical mass observed near the nucleus of many cells that appears to control the phenomena of indirect division; centrosphere.

at·trac·tive (ə·trak/tiv) *adj.* **1.** Having the quality of attracting interest or affection; pleasing; winning. **2.** Having the power or property of exerting physical attraction. — **at·trac/tive·ly** *adv.* — **at·trac/tive·ness** *n.*

— **Syn.** charming, enticing, lovely, fair. Compare ALLURE, BEAUTIFUL.

attrib. **1.** Attribute. **2.** Attributive.

at·trib·ute (ə·trib/yoot) *v.t.* **·ut·ed**, **·ut·ing** To consider or ascribe as belonging to, resulting from, owing to, or caused by; assign; refer: to *attribute* wisdom to old age.
— **at·tri·bute** (at/rə·byoot) *n.* **1.** A quality or characteristic of a person or thing. **2.** *Gram.* An adjective or its equivalent. **3.** In art and mythology, a distinctive mark or symbol. Abbr. *attrib.* [< L *attributus*, pp. of *attribuere* to bestow, assign < *ad-* to + *tribuere* to allot, give over] — **at·trib/ut·a·ble** *adj.* — **at·trib/ut·er** or **at·trib/u·tor** *n.*

— **Syn.** (verb) *Attribute, impute, ascribe, credit, charge, assign,* and *refer* are compared as they mean to consider a quality, character, type of behavior, etc., as belonging to a person or thing. The first three terms are largely interchangeable, but usually we *attribute* good things, *impute* bad, and *ascribe* either. *Credit* and *charge* are more emphatic; here, *credit* is used of good things, and *charge* of bad. We usually *assign* or *refer* a thing to a category, as time, place, cause, etc., rather than to a person. — (noun). **1.** *Attribute, quality,* and *property* denote an aspect or feature that distinguishes one person or thing from another. An *attribute* is what we conceive the object to be in some respect; a *quality* is what it really is. So we speak of the *attributes* of God, but the *qualities* of a man. A *property* is a *quality* which belongs so peculiarly to an object as to be part of its constitution. The word is applied only to things, never to persons: the *properties* of carbon, the *properties* of a dye.

at·tri·bu·tion (at/rə·byoo/shən) *n.* **1.** The act of attributing. **2.** An ascribed characteristic or quality; attribute.

at·trib·u·tive (ə·trib/yə·tiv) *adj.* **1.** Pertaining to or of the nature of an attribute or attribution. **2.** Ascribed, as a work of art: an *attributive* Vermeer. **3.** *Gram.* Expressing an attribute; in English, designating an adjective or its equivalent that stands before the noun it modifies, as opposed to a predicate adjective that follows a linking verb; as, in the expression "a silver watch," silver is an *attributive* adjective. — *n.* *Gram.* An attributive word or phrase. Abbr. *attrib.* — **at·trib/u·tive·ly** *adj.* — **at·trib/u·tive·ness** *n.*

at·trit·ed (ə·trī/tid) *adj.* Worn down by rubbing or friction. Also *Archaic* **at·trite/.** [< L *attritus*, pp. of *atterere.* See ATTRITION.]

at·tri·tion (ə·trish/ən) *n.* **1.** A rubbing out or grinding down, as by friction. **2.** A gradual wearing down or weakening: a war of *attrition.* **3.** *Theol.* Imperfect contrition. See under CONTRITION. — **Syn.** See REPENTANCE. [< L *attritio, -onis*, rubbing, friction < *atterere* to rub away < *ad-* to, against + *terere* to rub]

At·tu (at/too) The westernmost island of the Aleutians, largest of the Near Islands; recaptured from the Japanese by U.S. forces, 1943.

at·tune (ə·toon/, ə·tyoon/) *v.t.* **·tuned**, **·tun·ing** **1.** To bring into accord; harmonize. **2.** To tune. [< AD- + TUNE]

atty. Attorney.

Atty. Gen. Attorney General.

a·twain (ə·twān/) *adv. Archaic* In two; asunder. [< A-[1] + TWAIN]

a·twit·ter (ə·twit/ər) *adj. & adv.* Twittering.

at. wt. Atomic weight.

a·typ·i·cal (ā·tip/i·kəl) *adj.* Not typical; without typical character; differing from the type; irregular. Also **a·typ/ic.** [< A-[4] + TYPICAL] — **a·typ/i·cal·ly** *adv.*

a.u. or **å.u., A.U.** or **Å.U.** *Physics* Angstrom unit(s).

Au *Chem.* Gold (L *aurum*).

au·bade (ō·bäd/) *n. French* Morning music or song, as to greet or regret the dawn. Compare SERENADE.

Aube (ōb) A river of north central France, flowing 140 miles NW to the Seine.

Au·ber (ō·bâr/), **Daniel**, 1782–1871, French composer.

au·berge (ō·berzh/) *n. French* An inn.

au·ber·gine (ō/ber·zhēn, ō/bər·jin) *n.* Eggplant. [< F]

Au·ber·vil·liers (ō·ber·vē·lyā/) A commune of northern France, on the Seine; a suburb of Paris; pop. 73,559 (1968).

au·brey (ō/brē), **John**, 1626–97, English antiquary.

au·burn (ō/bûrn) *adj.* Reddish brown. — *n.* A reddish brown color. [< OF *auborne, alborne* < LL *alburnus* whitish < L *albus* white; infl. in meaning by ME *brun* brown]

Au·burn (ō/bûrn) A city in central New York; pop. 34,599.

A.U.C. Ab urbe condita.

Auck·land (ôk/lənd) The former capital of New Zealand, a port city on northern North Island; pop. 152,200 (est. 1968).

Auckland Islands A group of uninhabited islands south of and belonging to New Zealand; 234 sq. mi.

au con·traire (ō kôn·trâr/) *French* On the contrary.

au cou·rant (ō koo·rän/) *French* Up to date; well informed.

auc·tion (ôk/shən) *n.* **1.** A public sale in which the price is increased by bids until the highest bidder becomes the purchaser. **2.** The bidding in bridge. **3.** Auction bridge. — *v.t.* To sell by or at auction: usually with *off.* [< L *auctio, -onis* an increase, a public sale (with increasing bids) < *augere* to increase]

auction bridge A variety of the game of bridge in which tricks made by the declarer in excess of the contract count toward game. Compare CONTRACT BRIDGE.

auc·tion·eer (ôk/shən·ir/) *n.* One who conducts an auction, usually as a business. — *v.t.* To sell at auction.

aud. Auditor.

au·da·cious (ô·dā′shəs) *adj.* 1. Showing no fear; daring; bold. 2. Defiant of restraint, as of law or decorum; presumptuous; shameless. [< L *audax, -acis* (< *audere* to dare) + -OUS] — **au·da′cious·ly** *adv.* — **au·da′cious·ness** *n.*

au·dac·i·ty (ô·das′ə·tē) *n.* 1. Boldness; daring. 2. Disregard of law or decency; impudence; shamelessness. — **Syn.** See TEMERITY. [< L *audax, -acis* (< *audere* to dare) + -ITY]

a·u·dad (ä′ŏŏ·dad) See AOUDAD.

Au·den (ô′dən), **W(ystan) H(ugh)**, born 1907, U.S. poet born in England.

au·di·bil·i·ty (ô′də·bil′ə·tē) *n.* 1. Ability to be heard. 2. *Telecom.* The ratio of the strength of a transmitted signal to that of a barely audible signal, usually expressed in decibels.

au·di·ble (ô′də·bəl) *adj.* Perceptible by the ear; loud enough to be heard. [< Med.L *audibilis* < L *audire* to hear] — **au′·di·ble·ness** *n.* — **au′di·bly** *adv.*

au·di·ence (ô′dē·əns) *n.* 1. An assembly of listeners or spectators, as at a concert. 2. Those who are reached by a book, television program, etc. 3. A formal hearing, interview, or conference. 4. Opportunity to be heard. 5. The act of hearing; attention. [< OF < L *audientia* a hearing < *audire* to hear]

au·di·ent (ô′dē·ənt) *adj.* Listening; hearing. [< L *audiens, -entis,* ppr. of *audire* to hear]

au·dile (ô′dil, ô′dīl) *n. Psychol.* An individual having a tendency to derive mental images from auditory sensations. — *adj.* Auditory. [< L *audire* to hear + -ILE]

au·di·o (ô′dē·ō) *adj.* 1. Of or pertaining to characteristics associated with sound waves. 2. *Electronics* Designating devices used in transmission or reception of sound waves: in television, distinguished from *video*. [< L *audire* to hear]

audio- *combining form* Pertaining to hearing: *audiogram*. Also **audi-**. [< L *audire* to hear]

audio frequency *Physics* A frequency of electrical, sound, or other wave vibrations within the range of normal human hearing, or from about 20 to 20,000 cycles a second. *Abbr.* AF, a-f, a.f., A.F.

au·di·o·gram (ô′dē·ō·gram′) *n.* A graph showing variations in the hearing acuteness of an individual.

au·di·ol·o·gy (ô′dē·ol′ə·jē) *n.* The study of hearing, including treatment of the hard of hearing. [< AUDIO- + -LOGY] — **au·di·o·log·i·cal** (ô′dē·ə·loj′i·kəl) *adj.* — **au′di·ol′o·gist** *n.*

au·di·om·e·ter (ô′dē·om′ə·tər) *n.* An instrument to gauge and record the acuteness of hearing. — **au·di·o·met·ric** (ô′·dē·ə·met′rik) *adj.* — **au′di·om′e·try** *n.*

au·di·o·phile (ô′dē·ə·fīl′) *n.* An enthusiast of high-fidelity sound reproduction on radio, recordings, etc.

au·di·o·vis·u·al (ô′dē·ō·vizh′ŏŏ·əl) *adj.* Pertaining to forms of instruction and entertainment other than books, as radio, television, motion pictures, photographs, recordings, etc.

au·di·phone (ô′də·fōn) *n.* A device for directing sound through the bones of the head to the auditory nerve.

au·dit (ô′dit) *v.t.* 1. To examine, adjust, and certify, as accounts. 2. *U.S.* To attend (a college course) as a listener and without earning credit. — *v.i.* 2. To make an audit. — *n.* 1. An examination of an accounting document and of the evidence in support of its correctness. 2. An account examined and adjusted by auditors; a final statement of account. 3. An adjustment and settling of accounts. 4. *Obs.* A hearing. [< L *auditus* a hearing < *audire* to hear]

au·di·tion (ô·dish′ən) *n.* 1. The act or sense of hearing. 2. A trial test or hearing, as of an actor or singer. — *v.t.* 1. To judge (someone) in an audition. — *v.i.* 2. To take part in an audition; try out. [< L *auditio, -onis* a hearing < *audire* to hear]

au·di·tive (ô′də·tiv) *adj. & n.* Auditory.

au·di·tor (ô′də·tər) *n.* 1. One who audits accounts. *Abbr. aud.* 2. One who listens; a hearer. 3. *U.S.* One who audits classes. [< L] — **au′di·tress** *n.fem.*

au·di·to·ri·um (ô′də·tôr′ē·əm, -tō′rē·əm) *n. pl.* **·to·ri·ums** or **·to·ri·a** (-tôr′ē·ə, -tō′rē·ə) 1. The room or part of a school, church, theater, etc., occupied by the audience. 2. A building for concerts, public meetings, etc. [< L, lecture room, courtroom, orig. neut. of *auditorius*. See AUDITORY.]

au·di·to·ry (ô′də·tôr′ē, -tō′rē) *adj.* Of or pertaining to hearing or the organs or sense of hearing. — *n. pl.* **·ries** 1. An assembly of hearers; audience. 2. The nave of a church. [< L *auditorius* < *audire* to hear]

auditory canal *Anat.* The passage leading from the auricle to the tympanic membrane. For illustration see EAR.

Au·du·bon (ô′də·bon), **John James,** 1785–1851, U.S. ornithologist and painter born in Haiti.

Au·er·städt (ou′ər·shtet) A village in southern East Germany; scene of a French victory over the Prussians, 1806.

au fait (ō fe′) *French* Skilled; versed; literally, to the fact.

Auf·klä·rung (ouf′klä′rŏŏng) *n. German* The Enlightenment.

au fond (ō fôn′) *French* At bottom; essentially.

auf Wie·der·seh·en (ouf vē′dər·zā′ən) *German* Till we meet again; good-by for now.

aug. Augmentative.

Aug. or **Aug** 1. August. 2. Augustan; Augustus.

Au·ge·an (ô·jē′ən) *adj.* Exceedingly filthy; corrupt.

Augean stables In Greek mythology, the stables in which **Au·ge·as** (ô′jē·əs, ô·jē′əs), a king of Elis, kept 3,000 oxen and which, uncleaned for 30 years, were cleaned in a day when Hercules turned the river Alpheus through them.

au·gend (ô′jend) *n. Math.* A quantity or number to which another is to be added. See ADDEND. [< L *augendum,* neut. gerundive of *augere* to increase]

au·ger (ô′gər) *n.* 1. Any of various low-speed tools for boring wood. 2. An earth-boring tool. [OE *nafugār,* n., naveborer < *nafu* nave of a wheel + *gār* borer, spear (*a nauger* in ME becoming *an auger*)]

AUGERS
a Twisted.
b Post-hole.
c Ship.
d Chuck-shanked.
e Gimlet.
f Expanding.

aught¹ (ôt) *n.* Anything; any part or item. — *adv.* By any chance; at all; in any respect. Also spelled *ought.* [OE *āwiht, ōwiht* < *ā, ō* ever + *wiht* thing]

aught² (ôt) *n.* The figure 0; cipher; a naught; nothing: also spelled *ought.* [a *naught* taken as *an aught*]

Au·gier (ō·zhyā′), **Guillaume Victor Émile,** 1820–89, French dramatist.

au·gite (ô′jīt) *n. Mineral.* A dark-colored variety of aluminous pyroxene, occurring in igneous rocks. [< L *augites,* a precious stone < Gk. *augitēs* < *augē* brightness, gleam (of a gem)] — **au·git·ic** (ô·jit′ik) *adj.*

aug·ment (*v.* ôg·ment′; *n.* ô′g′ment) *v.t.* 1. To make greater, as in size, number, or amount; enlarge; intensify. 2. In Greek and Sanskrit grammar, to add the augment to. — *v.i.* 3. To become greater, as in size. — **Syn.** See INCREASE. — *n.* 1. Increase; enlargement. 2. In Greek and Sanskrit grammar, a vowel prefixed to a verb, or a lengthening of the initial vowel, to indicate past time. [< F *augmenter* < L *augmentare* < *augmentum* an increase < *augere* to increase] — **aug·ment′a·ble** *adj.*

aug·men·ta·tion (ôg′men·tā′shən) *n.* 1. The act of augmenting, or the state of being augmented. 2. That by which something is increased; an addition. 3. *Music* The repetition of a theme in notes of greater time value than those first used: opposed to *diminution.*

aug·men·ta·tive (ôg·men′tə·tiv) *adj.* 1. Having the quality or power of augmenting. 2. *Gram.* Denoting greater size or intensity, as the suffix *-agne* in French *montagne* a mountain (from *mont* a hill). — *n. Gram.* An augmentative form. Also **aug·men′tive.** *Abbr. aug.*

aug·ment·ed (ôg·men′tid) *adj. Music* 1. One semitone larger than the corresponding major or perfect interval. 2. Designating a theme or motif subjected to augmentation.

Augmented Roman Initial Teaching Alphabet (which see).

aug·ment·er (ôg·men′tər) *n.* 1. One who or that which augments. 2. *Aeron.* Afterburner.

au gra·tin (ō grät′n, grat′n; *Fr.* ō grà·tan′) Sprinkled with bread crumbs or grated cheese and baked until brown. [< F]

Augs·burg (ôgz′bûrg, *Ger.* ouks′bŏŏrkh) A city in Bavaria, southern West Germany; pop. 204,990 (est. 1959). Ancient **Au·gus·ta Vin·de·li·co·rum** (ô·gus′tə vin·del′i·kō′rəm).

au·gur (ô′gər, -gyər) *n.* 1. A religious official of ancient Rome whose duty it was to foretell and advise on future events by interpreting omens. 2. Any prophet; soothsayer. Also *Obs.* **au′gur·er.** — *v.t.* 1. To prognosticate from omens; prophesy. 2. To betoken; foreshadow; be an omen of. — *v.i.* 3. To conjecture from signs and omens. 4. To foreshadow an outcome. [< L *augere* to increase] — **au′gu·ral** *adj.*

— **Syn.** (verb) 1. *Augur, bode, forebode, presage, prognosticate, foretell, forecast, predict, divine, portend, betoken,* and *foretoken* mean to tell the nature of future events. Either persons or things may *augur, bode, forbode, presage,* or *prognosticate;* only persons *foretell, forecast, predict,* or *divine;* only things *portend, betoken,* or *foretoken.* One may *augur* or *divine* from indications too slight to be explained, and, like *foretell,* these words suggest the use of a mysterious or occult power. *Forecast* always, *predict* and *prognosticate* generally, imply careful study and calculation. *Bode, forebode,* and *portend* indicate evil or misfortune; *portend* also, with *presage, betoken,* and *foretoken,* refers to a present circumstance caused by or closely related to a coming event.

au·gu·ry (ô′gyə·rē) *n. pl.* **·ries** 1. The art or practice of foretelling by omens; divination. 2. A portent or omen; presage. 3. The rite or ceremony conducted by an augur.

au·gust (ô·gust′) *adj.* 1. Inspiring awe, admiration, or reverence; majestic; imposing. 2. Of high birth or rank; venerable; eminent. [< L *augustus* < *augere* to increase, exalt] — **au·gust′ly** *adv.* — **au·gust′ness** *n.*

— **Syn.** 1. imposing, awesome, stately. Compare AWFUL.

Au·gust (ô′gəst) *n.* The eighth month of the year, containing 31 days. *Abbr. Ag., Aug, Aug.* [< L *Augustus,* named after *Augustus Caesar*]

Au·gus·ta (ô·gus′tə, ə-) 1. The capital of Maine, a city in the southern part; pop. 21,945. 2. A city in eastern Georgia, on the Savannah River; pop. 59,864.

Au·gus·tan (ô·gus′tən) *adj.* **1.** Of or pertaining to Augustus Caesar or to his times. Abbr. *Aug, Aug.* **2.** Pertaining to any era that resembles that of Augustus Caesar in standards and taste. **3.** Classical; refined. **4.** Pertaining to Augsburg. — *n.* A writer or artist of an Augustan age.

Augustan age 1. The period of the reign of Augustus Caesar, the golden age of Roman literature. **2.** A corresponding period in other literatures, as in England during the reign of Queen Anne.

Au·gus·tine (ô′gəs·tēn, ô·gus′tin), **Saint,** 354–430, bishop of Hippo; one of the Latin church fathers.

Au·gus·tine (ô′gəs·tēn, ô·gus′tin), **Saint,** died 604, Roman missionary to England and first archbishop of Canterbury: called **Apostle of the English.**

Au·gus·tin·i·an (ô′gəs·tin′ē·ən) *adj.* **1.** Of or pertaining to St. Augustine of Hippo or his doctrines. **2.** Belonging to a monastic order named after him or following his rule. — *n.* **1.** A disciple of St. Augustine of Hippo. **2.** A member of a mendicant monastic order named after him: also **Au·gus·tin** (ô·gus′tin). — **Au·gus·tin′i·an·ism, Au·gus′tin·ism** *n.*

Au·gus·tus Cae·sar (ô·gus′təs sē′zər), 63 B.C.–A.D. 14, Gaius Julius Caesar Octavianus, the first Roman emperor 27 B.C.–A.D. 14: before 27 B.C. called *Octavian.*

au jus (ō zhü′) *French* Served with its natural juice or gravy.

auk (ôk) *n.* A short-winged, web-footed diving bird (family *Alcidae*) of northern seas; especially, the **razor-billed auk** (*Alca torda*) of the North Atlantic, having a compressed and deeply furrowed bill, and the now extinct **great auk** (*Pinguinus impennis*). [< ON *álka*]

auk·let (ôk′lit) *n.* One of the smaller auks; especially, the crested auklet.

au lait (ō le′) *French* With milk.

auld (ôld) *adj. Scot.* Old.

Auld Kloot·ie (klōōt′ē, klōō′tē) *Scot.* The devil. Also **Auld Hornie.**

auld lang syne (ôld′ lang sīn′, zīn′) *Scot.* Literally, old long since; long ago.

au·lic (ô′lik) *adj.* Pertaining to a royal court. [< F *aulique* < L *aulicus* < Gk. *aulikos* < *aulē* a court]

Aulic Council In the Holy Roman Empire, the emperor's privy council; also, later, the Austrian council of state.

Au·lis (ô′lis) An ancient town in Boeotia, on the Gulf of Euboea.

au na·tu·rel (ō nà·tü·rel′) *French* **1.** Plainly cooked; ungarnished. **2.** In the natural condition; nude.

aunt (ant, änt) *n.* **1.** A sister of one's father or mother, or the wife of one's uncle. **2.** An elderly woman: a familiar use. [< OF *aunte, ante* < L *amita* paternal aunt]

aunt·ie (an′tē, än′-) *n.* A familiar, diminutive form of AUNT. Also **aunt·y.**

au pair (ō pâr′) **1.** A girl, usually a foreigner, who does housework, acts as a nursemaid, etc., in return for a small payment and room and board. **2.** Denoting or pertaining to such a girl. **3.** Of or pertaining to such an arrangement. [< F, on mutual terms]

au·ra (ôr′ə) *n. pl.* **au·ras** or **au·rae** (ôr′ē) **1.** An invisible emanation or exhalation. **2.** A distinctive air or quality enveloping or characterizing a person or thing: an *aura* of wealth. **3.** A gentle breeze. **4.** *Electr.* **a** *Obs.* A subtile fluid supposed to surround an electrified body. **b** The current of air caused by a convective discharge from a sharp point. **5.** *Pathol.* The sensory, motor, or psychic manifestations preceding an epileptic attack or other paroxysm. **6.** In psychic research, the hypothetical emanations from living organisms. [< L, breeze < Gk. *aurē* breath]

au·ral[1] (ôr′əl) *adj.* Pertaining to the ear or the sense of hearing; auricular. [< L *auris* ear + -AL]

au·ral[2] (ôr′əl) *adj.* Pertaining to an aura.

Au·rang·zeb (ôr′əng·zeb), 1618–1707, sixth Mogul emperor of Hindustan 1658–1707. Also **Au·rang·zebe.**

au·rate (ôr′āt) *adj.* Having ears or earlike expansions. Also **au′rat·ed.** [< L *auris* ear + -ATE[1]]

au·re·ate (ôr′ē·it) *adj.* **1.** Golden. **2.** Splendid: *aureate* diction. [< LL *aureatus* < L *aureus* < *aurum* gold]

Au·re·li·an (ô·rē′lē·ən, ô·rēl′yən) Anglicized name of Lucius Domitius **Au·re·li·a·nus** (ô·rē′lē·ā′nəs), 212?–275, Roman emperor 270–275.

Au·re·li·us (ô·rē′lē·əs, ô·rēl′yəs), **Marcus,** 121–180, Roman emperor 161–180, and Stoic philosopher: full name **Marcus Aurelius An·to·ni·nus** (an′tə·nī′nəs).

au·re·ole (ôr′ē·ōl) *n.* **1.** In art, a radiance enveloping the whole figure or head of a sanctified being; a glory; halo. **2.** Any radiance or halo around a body. Also **au·re·o·la** (ô·rē′·ə·lə). [< L *aureola* (*corona*) golden (crown), orig. fem. sing. of *aureolus* golden, dim. of *aureus* < *aurum* gold]

Au·re·o·my·cin (ôr′ē·ō·mī′sin) *n.* Proprietary name for a brand of chlortetracycline, used as an antibiotic. Also **au·re·o·my·cin.** [< L *aureus* golden (from its color) + Gk. *mykēs* fungus + -IN]

au·re·us (ôr′ē·əs) *n. pl.* **au·re·i** (ôr′ē·ī) A gold coin of the

Roman Empire, weighing, during the reign of Augustus, ¹⁄₄₂ libra. [< L]

au re·voir (ō rə·vwàr′) *French* Good-by; till we meet again.

au·ric (ôr′ik) *adj.* Of, pertaining to, or containing gold, especially when combined in its highest or triad valence: *auric* chloride, $AuCl_3$. [< L *aurum* gold]

au·ri·cle (ôr′i·kəl) *n.* **1.** *Anat.* **a** An atrium of the heart. **b** The external ear; pinna. **2.** An ear or ear-shaped appendage or part. **3.** An ear trumpet. [< L *auricula*, dim. of *auris* ear] — **au′ri·cled** *adj.*

au·ric·u·la (ô·rik′yə·lə) *n. pl.* **·lae** (-lē) or **·las 1.** A primrose (*Primula auricula*) native to the Alps: also called *bear's-ear.* **2.** Auricle (def. 2). [< L, dim. of *auris* ear]

au·ric·u·lar (ô·rik′yə·lər) *adj.* **1.** Of or pertaining to the ear or the sense of hearing. **2.** Intended for or received by the ear: *auricular* confession. **3.** Ear-shaped. **4.** Of or pertaining to an auricle. — *n. Usually pl. Ornithol.* The feathers overlying the ear in birds.

au·ric·u·late (ô·rik′yə·lit, -lāt) *adj.* **1.** Having ear-shaped appendages or projections. **2.** *Bot.* Having rounded projections at the base, as a leaf. **3.** Like an ear. Also **au·ric′u·lat·ed.** — **au·ric′u·late·ly** *adv.*

au·rif·er·ous (ô·rif′ər·əs) *adj.* Containing gold. [< L *aurifer* < *aurum* gold + *ferre* to bear]

au·ri·flamme (ôr′ə·flam) See ORIFLAMME.

au·ri·form (ôr′ə·fôrm) *adj.* Ear-shaped. [< L *auris* ear + -FORM]

Au·ri·ga (ô·rī′gə) *n.* A constellation, the Charioteer or Wagoner, containing the bright star Capella. See table for CONSTELLATION. [< L]

Au·rig·na·cian (ôr′ig·nā′shən) *adj. Anthropol.* Of or pertaining to an Upper Paleolithic culture appearing toward the end of the Pleistocene and associated with the appearance of Cro-Magnon and other types of *Homo sapiens.* [after *Aurignac,* town in Haute-Garonne, France, where relics were discovered]

Au·ri·gny (ō·rē·nyē′) The French name for ALDERNEY.

au·ris (ôr′is) *n. pl.* **au·res** (ôr′ēz) *Latin* The ear.

au·rist (ôr′ist) *n.* A specialist in diseases of the ear.

au·rochs (ôr′oks) *n.* An extinct European ox, the urus. [< G *auerochs* < OHG *ūrohso* < *ūr* the urus + *ohso* ox]

au·ro·ra (ô·rôr′ə, ô·rō′rə) *n.* **1.** *Meteorol.* A luminous, sometimes richly colored display of arcs, bands, streamers, etc., occasionally seen in the skies of polar latitudes, caused by electrical disturbances in the atmosphere: also **au·ro′ra po·lar·is** (pō·lâr′is, -lar′-). **2.** The dawn. **3.** *Rare* The early stage of something. [< L, dawn]

Au·ro·ra (ô·rôr′ə, ô·rō′rə) **1.** A city in NE Illinois; pop. 74,182. **2.** A city in north central Colorado, near Denver; pop. 74,974.

Au·ro·ra (ô·rôr′ə, ô·rō′rə) In Roman mythology, the goddess of the dawn: identified with the Greek *Eos.*

aurora aus·tra·lis (ôs·trā′lis) *Meteorol.* The aurora seen in far southern latitudes: also called *southern lights.* [< NL, southern aurora < L *auster* south wind]

aurora bo·re·al·is (bôr′ē·al′is, -ä′lis, bō′rē-) *Meteorol.* The aurora seen in high northern latitudes: also called *northern lights.* [< NL, northern aurora < Gk. *boreas* north wind]

au·ro·ral (ô·rôr′əl, ô·rō′rəl) *adj.* **1.** Of, like, or pertaining to the dawn; dawning; roseate. Also *Poetic* **au·ro′re·an. 2.** *Meteorol.* Of, like, or caused by an aurora. — **au·ro′ral·ly** *adv.*

au·rous (ôr′əs) *adj.* Of, pertaining to, or containing gold, especially in its monad valence: *aurous* chloride, AuCl. See AURIC. [< L *aurum* gold]

au·rum (ôr′əm) *n.* Gold. [< L]

Aus. 1. Australasia. **2.** Australia. **3.** Austria.

AUS or **A.U.S.** Army of the United States.

Au·sa·ble River (ô·sā′bəl) A river 20 miles long in NE New York, flowing through **Ausable Chasm,** a gorge 1½ miles long, to Lake Champlain.

Au·schwitz (ou′shvits) A city in SW Poland; site of a Nazi extermination camp in World War II; pop. 14,400. Polish *Oświęcim.*

aus·cul·tate (ôs′kəl·tāt) *v.t. & v.i.* **·tat·ed, ·tat·ing** *Med.* To examine by auscultation. [< L *auscultatus,* pp. of *auscultare* to listen, give ear to] — **aus′cul·ta′tor** *n.*

aus·cul·ta·tion (ôs′kəl·tā′shən) *n.* **1.** *Med.* The act of listening, as with a stethoscope, for sounds produced in the chest, etc. **2.** A listening. — **aus·cul·ta·tive** (ôs′kəl·tā′tiv, ôs·kul′tə·tiv), **aus·cul·ta·to·ry** (ôs·kul′tə·tôr′ē, -tō′rē) *adj.*

Aus·gleich (ous′glīkh) *n. German* Adjustment; agreement; compromise; especially, the treaty of 1867 between Austria and Hungary, which formulated their organization into a dual monarchy.

aus·pex (ôs′peks) *n. pl.* **aus·pi·ces** (ôs′pə·sēz) An augur or soothsayer of ancient Rome; especially, one who observed and interpreted the omens connected with the actions of birds. [< L *auspex* < *avis* bird + *specere* to look at]

aus·pi·cate (ôs′pi·kāt) *v.t.* **·cat·ed, ·cat·ing** *Obs.* To initiate with a ceremony to ensure good luck. [< L *auspicatus,* pp. of *auspicari* to take omens, begin < *auspex.* See AUSPEX.]

aus·pice (ôs′pis) *n. pl.* **aus·pi·ces** (ôs′pə·sēz) **1.** *Usually pl.* Favoring influence or guidance; patronage. **2.** An augury, omen, or sign, especially when taken from the movements of birds, etc. **3.** The observation of such omens. [< F < L *auspicium* < *auspex*. See AUSPEX.]

aus·pi·cial (ôs-pish′əl) *adj.* **1.** Pertaining to augury. **2.** Auspicious.

aus·pi·cious (ôs-pish′əs) *adj.* **1.** Of good omen; propitious. **2.** Prosperous; fortunate. — **Syn.** See PROPITIOUS. — **aus·pi′cious·ly** *adv.* — **aus·pi′cious·ness** *n.*

Aust. Austria; Austrian.

Aus·ten (ôs′tən), **Jane**, 1775–1817, English novelist.

Aus·ter (ôs′tər) *n. Poetic* **1.** The south wind. **2.** The south. [< L]

aus·tere (ô-stir′) *adj.* **1.** Severe, grave, or stern, as in aspect or conduct. **2.** Morally strict; abstemious; ascetic. **3.** Sour and astringent. **4.** Severely simple; unadorned. [< OF < L *austerus* < Gk. *austēros* harsh, bitter < *auein* to dry, wither] — **aus·tere′ly** *adv.*

aus·ter·i·ty (ô-ster′ə-tē) *n. pl.* **·ties 1.** The quality of being austere; severity of demeanor, way of life, etc.: also **aus·tere′ness.** **2.** *Usually pl.* Severe or ascetic acts.

Aus·ter·litz (ôs′tər-lits, *Ger.* ous′tər-lits) A town in Moravia, Czechoslovakia; site of Napoleon's victory over the Russian and Austrian armies, 1805.

Aus·tin (ôs′tən) **1.** The capital of Texas, a city in the central part, on the Colorado River; pop. 251,808. **2.** A city in southern Minnesota; pop. 25,074.

Aus·tin (ôs′tən), **Alfred**, 1835–1913, English poet laureate 1896–1913. — **John**, 1790–1859, English jurist. — **Stephen Fuller**, 1793–1836, U.S. colonizer in Texas. — **Warren Robinson**, 1877–1963, U.S. statesman.

Austl. **1.** Australasia. **2.** Australia.

aus·tral (ôs′trəl) *adj.* Southern; torrid. [< L *australis* southern < *auster* south wind]

Austral. Australian.

Aus·tral·a·sia (ôs′trəl-ā′zhə, -ā′shə) The islands of the South Pacific, including Australia, New Zealand, New Guinea, and adjacent islands; sometimes applied to all of Oceania. — **Aus·tral·a′·sian** *adj. & n.*

Aus·tral·ia (ô-strāl′yə) An island continent SE of Asia, comprising the Commonwealth of Australia, a self-governing member of the Commonwealth of Nations, consisting of six states and two territories together with its dependencies; 2,971,081 sq. mi.; pop. 12,630,000 (1970, excluding aborigines); capital, Canberra.

Australia Day An Australian holiday, January 26th, commemorating the landing of the British in 1788. Also called *Anniversary Day.*

Aus·tral·ian (ô-strāl′yən) *n.* **1.** A native or naturalized inhabitant of Australia. **2.** An Australian aborigine. **3.** Any of the aboriginal languages of Australia. — *adj.* Designating a zoogeographic realm including Australia, New Guinea and adjacent islands, New Zealand, and Polynesia.

Australian Alps A mountain range in SE New South Wales and eastern Victoria, Australia; highest peak, Mt. Kosciusko, 7,316 ft.

Australian ballot A ballot bearing the names of all candidates of all parties, voted on in strict secrecy.

Australian Capital Territory A region within New South Wales containing Canberra, capital of Australia; 939 sq. mi.; pop. 136,300 (1970): formerly *Federal Capital Territory.*

Australian crawl See under CRAWL (*n.* def. 2).

Australian English The English language as spoken and written in Australia. Also **Aus·tral′ English** (ôs′trəl).

Aus·tral·ia·nism (ô-strāl′yə-niz′əm) *n.* **1.** A trait, custom, or tradition characteristic of the people of Australia. **2.** A word, phrase, or usage especially characteristic of Australian English

Austral Islands (ôs′trəl) See TUBUAI ISLANDS.

Aus·tra·loid (ôs′trə-loid) *adj.* Designating or belonging to the ethnic group composed of the aborigines of Australia.

Aus·tra·lo·pi·the·cus (ô-strāl′ō-pi-thē′kəs) *n.* A genus of small-brained hominoid primates of the early Pleistocene, first identified from a fossil juvenile skull found at Taungs, South Africa. [< NL < L *australis* southern + Gk. *pithēkos* ape] — **Aus·tra′lo·pi·the′cine** (-sīn, -sin) *adj.*

Aus·tra·sia (ô-strā′zhə, -shə) The eastern territory of the Franks, comprising parts of eastern France, western Germany, and the Netherlands. — **Aus·tra′sian** *adj. & n.*

Aus·tri·a (ôs′trē-ə) A federal Republic of central Europe; 32,375 sq. mi.; pop. 7,419,341 (1970); capital, Vienna; formerly an empire 1806–67: German *Österreich.* Officially **Republic of Austria.** — **Aus′tri·an** *adj. & n.*

Aus·tri·a-Hun·ga·ry (ôs′trē-ə-hung′gə-rē) A former dual monarchy of central Europe, 1867–1918, comprising the Austrian Empire, Hungary, and other crown lands.

Austro- *combining form* **1.** Austrian. **2.** Australian.

Aus·tro-A·si·at·ic (ôs′trō-ā′zhē-at′ik, -ā′shē-) *n.* A family of languages of SE Asia, including the Mon-Khmer and Munda subfamilies. — *adj.* Of or pertaining to this linguistic family.

Aus·tro-Hun·gar·i·an (ôs′trō-hung-gâr′ē-ən) *adj.* Of or pertaining to Austria-Hungary.

Aus·tro·ne·sia (ôs′trō-nē′zhə, -shə) The islands of Indonesia, Melanesia, Micronesia, and Polynesia.

Aus·tro·ne·sian (ôs′trō-nē′zhən, -shən) *adj.* Of or pertaining to Austronesia, its inhabitants, or their languages. — *n.* A family of languages of the Pacific comprising the Indonesian, Oceanic (including Melanesian and Micronesian), and Polynesian subfamilies. Also *Malayo-Polynesian.*

aut- Var. of AUTO-[1].

au·ta·coid (ô′tə-koid) *n.* A hormone. [< AUT- + Gk. *akos* remedy + -OID]

au·tar·chy (ô′tär-kē) *n. pl.* **·chies 1.** Absolute rule or sovereignty, or a country under such rule; unrestricted power; autocracy. **2.** Self-government. **3.** Autarky. [< Gk. *autarchos* absolute ruler < *autos* self + *archein* to rule] — **au·tar·chic** (ô-tär′kik) or **·chi·cal** *adj.*

au·tar·ky (ô′tär-kē) *n.* National economic self-sufficiency; a policy of establishing independence of imports. [< Gk. *autarkeia* self-sufficiency < *autos* self + *arkeein* to suffice] — **au·tar·kik** (ô-tär′kik) or **·ki·kal** *adj.*

au·te·col·o·gy (ô′tē-kol′ə-jē) *n.* The ecology of individual organisms: distinguished from *synecology.*

auth. **1.** Author. **2.** Authority. **3.** Authorized.

au·then·tic (ô-then′tik) *adj.* **1.** Entitled to belief; trustworthy; reliable. **2.** Of undisputed origin; genuine. **3.** *Law* Duly executed before the proper officer. **4.** *Music* Designating a type of medieval mode having its lowest tone as its final. Also **au·then′ti·cal.** [< OF *autentique* < L *authenti-cus* < Gk. *authentikos* < *authentēs* the doer of a deed] — **au·then′ti·cal·ly** *adv.* — **Syn.** 1. true, veritable. 2. real, legitimate, authorized, accredited. — **Ant.** spurious, counterfeit, fictitious, false.

au·then·ti·cate (ô-then′ti-kāt) *v.t.* **·cat·ed, ·cat·ing 1.** To make authentic or authoritative. **2.** To give legal validity to. **3.** To establish the authenticity of. — **au·then′ti·ca′·tion** *n.* — **au·then′ti·ca′tor** *n.*

authentic cadence *Music* A cadence in which the dominant chord immediately precedes the tonic chord.

au·then·tic·i·ty (ô′then-tis′ə-tē) *n.* The state or quality of being authentic, authoritative, or genuine.

au·thor (ô′thər) *n.* **1.** The original writer of a book, treatise, etc.; also, one who makes literary composition his profession. **2.** One who begins or originates; creator. **3.** An author's writings collectively: to read the Greek *authors.* — *v.t. Informal* To be the author of; write. *Abbr.* **auth.** [< AF *autour*, OF *autor* < L *auctor* originator, producer < *augere* to increase] — **au′thor·ess** *n.fem.* — **au·tho·ri·al** (ô-thôr′ē-əl, ô-thō′rē-) *adj.*

au·thor·i·tar·i·an (ə-thôr′ə-târ′ē-ən, ə-thor′-) *adj.* Favoring subjection to authority as opposed to individual freedom. — *n.* One who favors the principle of authority. — **au·thor′i·tar′i·an·ism** *n.*

au·thor·i·ta·tive (ə-thôr′ə-tā′tiv, ə-thor′-) *adj.* **1.** Possessing or proceeding from proper authority; duly sanctioned. **2.** Exercising authority; commanding; dictatorial. — **au·thor′i·ta′tive·ly** *adv.* — **au·thor′i·ta′tive·ness** *n.*

au·thor·i·ty (ə-thôr′ə-tē, ə-thor′-) *n. pl.* **·ties 1.** The right to command and to enforce obedience; the right to act, decide, etc. **2.** Delegated right or power; authorization: He has my *authority* to act. **3.** *pl.* Those having the power to govern or command; especially, police and judicial officers. **4.** Title to respect, confidence, etc.; personal influence, as from character or experience: He speaks with *authority.* **5.** A person, volume, etc., appealed to in support of action or belief. **6.** One who has special knowledge; an expert. **7.** An official or group having administrative control in a specified area: the Port *Authority.* **8.** An authoritative opinion, decision, or precedent. *Abbr.* **auth.** [< OF *autorité* < L *auctoritas*, *-tatis* power, authority < *augere* to increase]

au·thor·i·za·tion (ô′thər-ə-zā′shən) *n.* **1.** The act of authorizing. **2.** Formal legal power; sanction.

au·thor·ize (ô′thə-rīz) *v.t.* **·ized, ·iz·ing 1.** To confer authority upon; empower; commission. **2.** To warrant; justify. **3.** To sanction; approve. **4.** *Obs.* To vouch for. — **Syn.** See ALLOW. [< OF *autoriser* < Med.L *auctorizare* < L *auctor* originator] — **au'thor·iz'er** *n.*

au·thor·ized (ô'thə·rīzd) *adj.* **1.** Endowed with authority; accepted as authoritative. **2.** Formally or legally sanctioned. Abbr. *auth.*

Authorized Version See under KING JAMES BIBLE.

au·thor·ship (ô'thər·ship) *n.* **1.** The profession or occupation of an author. **2.** Origin or source.

Auth. Ver. Authorized Version (of the Bible).

au·tism (ô'tiz·əm) *n. Psychol.* The tendency toward day-dreaming or introspection in which external reality is unduly modified by wishful thinking. [< AUT- + -ISM] — **au·tis·tic** (ô·tis'tik) *adj.*

au·to (ô'tō) *U.S. Informal n.* An automobile. —*v.i.* **au·toed, au·to·ing** To ride in or travel by an automobile.

auto-[1] *combining form* **1.** Arising from some process or action within the object; not induced by any stimulus from without; as in:

autoagglutination autoelectrolysis autoinduction
autocombustion autoexcitation autoluminescence
autoconduction autofecundation autoretardation
autodiffusion autohybridization autosepticemia

2. Acting, acted, or directed upon the self; as in:

autoanalysis autodiagnosis autolavage

Also, before vowels, *aut-*, as in *autism*. [< Gk. *autos* self]

auto-[2] *combining form* Self-propelled: *autobus*. [< AUTOMOBILE]

auto. **1.** Automatic. **2.** Automotive.

au·to·bahn (ou'tō·bän) *n. pl.* **·bahns** or *German* **·bahn·en** In Germany, a superhighway.

au·to·bi·og·ra·phy (ô'tə·bī·og'rə·fē, -bē·og'-) *n. pl.* **·phies** The story of a person's life written by that person. — **au'to·bi·og'ra·pher** *n.* — **au·to·bi·o·graph·ic** (ô'tə·bī'ə·graf'ik) or **·i·cal** *adj.* — **au'to·bi'o·graph'i·cal·ly** *adv.*

au·to·bus (ô'tō·bus) *n.* A bus (which see).

au·to·ceph·a·lous (ô'tō·sef'ə·ləs) *adj. Eccl.* In the Eastern Orthodox Church: **a** Independent of patriarchal or archiepiscopal jurisdiction. **b** Having independent jurisdiction, as a bishop. Also **au·to·ce·phal·ic** (ô'tō·sə·fal'ik). [< Gk. *autokephalos* < *autos* self + *kephalē* head]

au·to·chrome (ô'tə·krōm) *n.* A single plate for three-color photography.

au·toch·thon (ô·tok'thən) *n. pl.* **·thons** or **·tho·nes** (-thə·nēz) **1.** Originally, one sprung from the earth itself. **2.** *pl.* The aboriginal inhabitants of a place. **3.** *Ecol.* An indigenous animal or plant. [< Gk. *autochthōn* indigenous < *autos* self + *chthōn* earth, land]

au·toch·thon·ism (ô·tok'thən·iz'əm) *n.* Origination in or primitive occupying of a region. Also **au·toch·tho·ny** (ô·tok'thə·nē).

au·toch·tho·nous (ô·tok'thə·nəs) *adj.* **1.** Native to a place; indigenous; aboriginal. **2.** *Geol.* Of or pertaining to rocks that have been formed *in situ*, as rock salt, stalactites, etc. Also **au·toch'tho·nal**, **au·toch·ton·ic** (ô'tok·thon'ik). — **Syn.** See NATIVE. — **au·toch'tho·nous·ly** *adv.*

au·to·clave (ô'tə·klāv) *n.* **1.** A strong, gastight vessel in which chemical reactions can be effected under pressure. **2.** An enclosed chamber for the sterilization of drugs, vaccines, instruments, etc., under specified pressure. **3.** A pressure cooker. [< F *auto-* self + L *clavis* a key]

au·toc·ra·cy (ô·tok'rə·sē) *n. pl.* **·cies** **1.** Absolute government by an individual; rule or authority of an autocrat. **2.** A state ruled by an autocrat. [< Gk. *autokrateia* < *autokratēs*. See AUTOCRAT.]

au·to·crat (ô'tə·krat) *n.* **1.** A supreme ruler of unrestricted power. **2.** An arrogant, dictatorial person. [< F *autocrate* < Gk. *autokratēs* self-ruling < *autos* self + *kratos* power] — **au'to·crat'ic** or **·i·cal** *adj.* — **au'to·crat'i·cal·ly** *adv.* — **Syn.** **1.** dictator, tyrant, despot. Compare ABSOLUTE.

au·to·da·fé (ô'tō·də·fā', ou'-) *n. pl.* **au·tos·da·fé** (ô'tōz-, ou'tōz-) The public announcement and execution of a sentence of the Inquisition; especially, the execution itself, as the burning of heretics at the stake, etc. Also *Spanish* **au·to de fe** (ou'tō dā fā'). [< Pg., lit., act of the faith]

au·toe·cious (ô·tē'shəs) *adj. Bot.* **1.** Having male and female reproductive organs on the same plant, as certain mosses. **2.** Completing the whole development on a single host, as seen in certain rust fungi and other parasites. [< AUTO-[1] + Gk. *oikos* dwelling] — **au·toe'cism** *n.*

au·to·e·rot·i·cism (ô'tō·i·rot'ə·siz'əm) *n. Psychoanal.* The arousal or satisfaction of sexual feeling through one's own acts or thoughts, as in masturbation. Also **au·to·er·o·tism** (ô'tō·er'ə·tiz'əm). [< AUTO-[1] + Gk. *erōs, erotos* love] — **au·to·e·rot·ic** (ô'tō·i·rot'ik) *adj.*

au·tog·a·mous (ô·tog'ə·məs) *adj. Bot.* Self-fertilized; capable of self-fertilization: said of certain flowers.

au·tog·a·my (ô·tog'ə·mē) *n.* **1.** *Bot.* Fertilization of a flower by its own pollen; self-fertilization: opposed to *allogamy*. **2.** *Biol.* The union of closely related cells or of nuclei within a cell. [< AUTO-[1] + -GAMY]

au·to·gen·e·sis (ô'tō·jen'ə·sis) *n. Biol.* Spontaneous formation of a tissue or organism. Also **au·tog·e·ny** (ô·toj'ə·nē).

au·to·ge·net·ic (ô'tō·jə·net'ik) *adj.* **1.** Of or resulting from autogenesis. **2.** *Geol.* Pertaining to a conformation resulting from the action of water. — **au'to·ge·net'i·cal·ly** *adv.*

au·tog·e·nous (ô·toj'ə·nəs) *adj.* **1.** Self-produced or self-generated. **2.** *Physiol.* Developed within the body, as new tissue or skeletal parts. **3.** *Mech.* Designating a process of welding without the use of solder. Also **au·to·gen·ic** (ô'tō·jen'ik). [< Gk. *autogenēs* self-produced]

au·to·gi·ro (ô'tō·jī'rō) *n. pl.* **·ros** An airplane that is supported in the air chiefly by nonpowered, freely-turning rotors but is drawn forward by a conventional propeller. Also **au'·to·gy'ro.** [< AUTO-[1] + Gk. *gyros* a circle]

au·to·graph (ô'tə·graf, -gräf) *n.* **1.** One's own signature or handwriting. **2.** A manuscript in the author's handwriting. —*v.t.* **1.** To write one's name in or affix one's signature to. **2.** To write in one's own handwriting. —*adj.* Written by one's own hand, as a will. [< L *autographum*, orig. neut. of *autographus* < Gk. *autographos* written with one's own hand < *autos* self + *graphein* to write] — **au'to·graph'ic** or **·i·cal** *adj.* — **au'to·graph'i·cal·ly** *adv.*

au·tog·ra·phy (ô·tog'rə·fē) *n.* **1.** The writing of a document in one's own handwriting. **2.** Autographs collectively.

au·to·harp (ô'tō·härp) *n.* A musical instrument resembling a zither, but having an arrangement of dampers enabling the player to produce the correct chords easily.

au·to·hyp·no·sis (ô'tō·hip·nō'sis) *n.* Self-induced hypnotism.

au·to·in·fec·tion (ô'tō·in·fek'shən) *n. Pathol.* Infection due to agents or toxins generated in the body.

au·to·in·oc·u·la·tion (ô'tō·in·ok'yə·lā'shən) *n.* **1.** Inoculation with a virus or other harmful matter already present in one's own body. **2.** The spreading of infection from a center to other portions of the same body.

au·to·in·tox·i·cant (ô'tō·in·tok'sə·kənt) *n.* Toxic matter produced within the body.

au·to·in·tox·i·ca·tion (ô'tō·in·tok'sə·kā'shən) *n.* Autotoxemia.

au·to·ki·net·ic (ô'tō·ki·net'ik, -kī-) *adj.* Self-moving. [< Gk. *autokinētos* self-moved < *autos* self + *kineein* to move]

au·to·load·ing (ô'tō·lō'ding) *adj.* Self-loading (which see).

Au·tol·y·cus (ô·tol'i·kəs) Fourth-century B.C. Greek astronomer and mathematician.

Au·tol·y·cus (ô·tol'i·kəs) In Greek mythology, a son of Hermes, famous for his thievery.

au·to·ly·sin (ô'tə·lī'sin) *n. Biochem.* A substance that initiates or promotes autolysis.

au·tol·y·sis (ô·tol'ə·sis) *n. Biochem.* The disintegration of cells and tissues by the action of enzymes already present: opposed to *heterolysis*. [< AUTO-[1] + -LYSIS] — **au·to·lyt·ic** (ô'tə·lit'ik) *adj.*

au·to·mat (ô'tə·mat) *n. U.S.* A restaurant in which food is automatically made available from a receptacle when coins are deposited in a slot alongside. [See AUTOMATIC]

au·to·mate (ô'tə·māt) *v.* **·mat·ed, ·mat·ing** *v.t.* **1.** To adapt, as a machine, factory, or process, for automation. —*v.i.* **2.** To install or convert to automation equipment. [Back formation < AUTOMATION]

au·to·mat·ic (ô'tə·mat'ik) *adj.* **1.** Acting from forces inherent in itself; self-moving. **2.** Self-acting and self-regulating, as machinery; mechanical. **3.** *Psychol.* Done from force of habit or without volition. **4.** *Physiol.* Independent of the will, as a reflex action. **5.** Of firearms, extracting and ejecting the empty case and chambering the next round, using the force of recoil or of part of the exploding gas, and firing continuously until the trigger is released: also *full-automatic*: compare SEMIAUTOMATIC (def. 2). Also (*except for def. 5*) **au'·to·mat'i·cal, au·tom·a·tous** (ô·tom'ə·təs). Abbr. *auto.* — **Syn.** See SPONTANEOUS. —*n.* **1.** An automatic device or machine. **2.** An automatic pistol. [< Gk. *automatos* acting of oneself] — **au'to·mat'i·cal·ly** *adv.*

automatic pilot *Aeron.* An automatic-control mechanism designed to keep an aircraft in level flight and on an even course: also called *gyro pilot, robot pilot.*

automatic pistol A pistol using the force of recoil to extract and eject used shells and chamber the next round.

automatic rifle A rifle capable of automatic or semiautomatic fire.

au·to·ma·tion (ô'tə·mā'shən) *n.* **1.** The automatic transfer of one unit of a complex industrial assembly to a succession of machines, each of which completes another stage in manufacture. **2.** The application of fully automatic procedures in the efficient performance and control of a sequence of standardized and repetitive processes. **3.** The theory, art, and technique of converting a mechanical process to maximum automatic operation, especially by the use of electronic control mechanisms. [< AUTOM(ATIC) + (OPER)ATION] — **au·to·ma·tive** (ô'tə·mā'tiv) *adj.*

au·tom·a·tism (ô·tom'ə·tiz'əm) *n.* **1.** The state or quality of being automatic or of having no voluntary action; automatic action. **2.** *Philos.* The theory that consciousness does not control one's actions but is only a by-product of physiological changes. **3.** *Physiol.* The functioning or power of functioning of muscular or other processes in response to external stimuli but independent of conscious control. **4.** *Biol.* Spontaneous activity of cells and tissues, as the beating of a heart freed from its nervous connections. **5.** *Psychol.* **a** A condition in which actions are performed without the conscious knowledge or will of the subject. **b** Any such action. **6.** Suspension of the conscious mind in order to release for expression the ideas and images of the subconscious, as practiced by surrealist artists and writers. **— au·tom′a·tist** *n.*

au·tom·a·ton (ô·tom′ə·ton, -tən) *n. pl.* **·tons** or **·ta** (-tə) **1.** An apparatus that appears to function of itself by the action of a concealed mechanism. **2.** Any living being whose actions are or appear to be involuntary or mechanical. **3.** Anything capable of spontaneous movement or action. [< Gk. *automaton*, neut. of *automatos* acting of oneself, independent]

au·to·mo·bile (*n. & v.* ô′tə·mə·bēl′, ô′tə·mə·bēl′, ô′tə·mō′·bēl; *adj.* ô′tə·mō′bil) *n.* A self-propelled vehicle; especially, a four-wheeled passenger vehicle that carries its own source of power and travels on roads or streets; motorcar. **—** *v.i.* **·biled, ·bil·ing** To ride in or drive an automobile. **—** *adj.* Automotive. [< F < *auto-* self (< Gk. *auto-*) + *mobile* moving < L *mobilis*] **— au·to·mo·bil·ist** (ô′tə·mə·bēl′ist, -mō′·bil·ist) *n.*

au·to·mo·tive (ô′tə·mō′tiv) *adj.* **1.** Self-propelling. **2.** Of or for automobiles; *automotive* parts. Abbr. *auto.*

au·to·nom·ic (ô′tə·nom′ik) *adj.* **1.** Autonomous. **2.** *Physiol.* Pertaining to the autonomic nervous system. **3.** *Bot.* Produced by inherent causes, as certain movements. Also **au′to·nom′i·cal.** [See AUTONOMOUS.] **— au′to·nom′i·cal·ly** *adv.*

autonomic nervous system A plexus of nerve ganglia and fibers originating in the spinal column and acting to innervate and control the efferent functions of all body tissues and organs not subject to voluntary control, as the heart, blood vessels, smooth muscle, glands, stomach, and intestines.

au·ton·o·mous (ô·ton′ə·məs) *adj.* **1.** Independent; self-governing. **2.** *Biol.* Independent; not influenced by another organism. **3.** *Bot.* Autonomic. [< Gk. *autonomos* independent < *autos* self + *nomos* law, rule] **— au·ton′o·mous·ly** *adv.*

au·ton·o·my (ô·ton′ə·mē) *n. pl.* **·mies 1.** The condition or quality of being autonomous; especially, the power or right of self-government. **2.** A self-governing community or group. **3.** Self-determination. [< Gk. *autonomia* independence < *autonomos*. See AUTONOMOUS.] **— au·ton′o·mist** *n.*

au·to·plas·ty (ô′tə·plas′tē) *n. pl.* **·ties** *Surg.* The operation of repairing wounds or diseased parts by grafts from other parts of the same body. **— au′to·plas′tic** *adj.*

au·top·sy (ô′top·sē, ô′təp-) *n. pl.* **·sies** Post-mortem examination of a human body, especially when ordered by a coroner. Compare BIOPSY. [< NL *autopsia* < Gk. *autopsia* a seeing for oneself < *autos* self + *opsis* a seeing]

au·to·ra·di·o·graph (ô′tō·rā′dē·ə·graf′, -gräf′) *n. Med.* A photograph taken by autoradiography: also called *radioautograph, radioautogram.*

au·to·ra·di·og·ra·phy (ô′tō·rā′dē·og′rə·fē) *n. Med.* Radiography that utilizes emanations of radioactive elements or isotopes incorporated for study and analysis in test material, as of a tissue: also called *radioautography.*

au·to·some (ô′tə·sōm) *n. Biol.* Any chromosome other than those that determine the sex of an organism. [< AUTO-¹ + (CHROMO)SOME] **— au′to·so′mal** *adj.*

au·to·sta·bil·i·ty (ô′tō·stə·bil′ə·tē) *n.* Stability owing to innate qualities, or to automatic machinery.

au·to·sug·gest·i·bil·i·ty (ô′tō·səg·jes′tə·bil′ə·tē) *n.* **1.** The state or quality of being autosuggestive. **2.** Ability to hypnotize oneself.

au·to·sug·ges·tion (ô′tō·səg·jes′chən) *n. Psychol.* Suggestion emanating from one's self only. **— au′to·sug·ges′tive** *adj.*

au·tot·o·my (ô·tot′ə·mē) *n. Zool.* The spontaneous shedding of a part from the whole, as in starfish, salamanders, and crabs. [< AUTO-¹ + Gk. *tomē* a cutting < *temnein* to cut]

au·to·tox·e·mi·a (ô′tō·tok·sē′mē·ə) *n.* Poisoning from noxious secretions of one's own body; autointoxication. Also **au′·to·tox·ae′mi·a, au·to·tox·i·co·sis** (ô′tō·tok′si·kō′sis).

au·to·tox·in (ô′tō·tok′sin) *n. Pathol.* Any toxin produced by changes of tissue within an organism. **— au′to·tox′ic** *adj.*

au·to·troph·ic (ô′tə·trof′ik) *adj. Biol.* Self-nourishing: said of plants that make their own food by photosynthesis, and of bacteria that can grow without organic carbon and nitrogen compounds: distinguished from *heterotrophic.* Also *holophytic.* [< AUTO-¹ + Gk. *trophē* food < *trephein* to nourish]

au·tot·ro·pism (ô·tot′rə·piz′əm) *n. Bot.* The tendency of the organs of a plant, uninfluenced from without, to grow in straight lines. [< AUTO-¹ + Gk. *tropē* a turning < *trepein* to turn] **— au·to·trop·ic** (ô′tə·trop′ik) *adj.*

au·to·truck (ô′tō·truk) *n.* A motor-propelled truck.

au·to·type (ô′tə·tīp) *n.* **1.** A photographic process by which pictures are produced in monochrome in a carbon pigment. **2.** The print so produced. **3.** A facsimile. **— au·to·typ·ic** (ô′tə·tip′ik) *adj.* **— au·to·typ·y** (ô′tə·tī′pē) *n.*

au·tox·i·da·tion (ô·tok′sə·dā′shən) *n. Chem.* **1.** Oxidation of a substance or compound on exposure to air. **2.** Oxidation occurring only in the presence of a second substance which serves to complete the reaction.

au·tumn (ô′təm) *n.* **1.** The season of the year occurring between summer and winter and in the northern hemisphere popularly regarded as including September, October, and November. Astronomically it extends from the autumnal equinox to the winter solstice. Often called *fall.* **2.** A time of maturity and incipient decline. [Earlier *autumpne* < OF *autompne* < L *autumnus*; ult. origin uncertain]

au·tum·nal (ô·tum′nəl) *adj.* **1.** Of, pertaining to, or like autumn. **2.** Ripening or harvested in autumn. **3.** Past maturity; declining. **— au·tum′nal·ly** *adv.*

autumnal equinox See under EQUINOX.

au·tun·ite (ô′tən·īt) *n. Mineral.* A pearly, light yellow, hydrous calcium-uranium phosphate, crystallizing in the orthorhombic system. [after *Autun*, a city in France]

Au·vergne (ō·vârn′, ō·vûrn′; *Fr.* ō·vern′y′) A region and former province of south central France.

aux (ō; *before vowel sounds* ōz) *French* To the; at the; according to: used before plurals.

aux. or **auxil.** Auxiliary.

aux armes (ō zärm′) *French* To arms!

Aux Cayes (ō kā′) See LES CAYES.

aux·il·ia·ry (ôg·zil′yər·ē, -zil′ər-) *adj.* **1.** Giving or furnishing aid. **2.** Subsidiary; accessory. **3.** Supplementary; reserve. **4.** *Naut.* Equipped with an engine and propeller in addition to sails: an *auxiliary* sloop. **—** *n. pl.* **·ries 1.** One who or that which aids or helps; assistant; associate. **2.** A ladies' auxiliary (which see). **3.** *Gram.* **a** A verb that helps to express the tense, mood, voice, or aspect of another verb, as *have* in "We *have* gone," *may* in "I *may* leave tomorrow": also called *helping verb:* also **auxiliary verb. b** A word that functions as a subordinate element in a sentence and is fully meaningful only in association with the main words, as a preposition or conjunction. **4.** *pl.* Foreign troops associated with those of a nation at war. **5.** *Naut.* A sailing vessel equipped with an engine and propeller. **6.** *Naval* A vessel not designed for or assigned to combat service. [< L *auxiliarius* < *auxilium* help < *augere* to increase]
— Syn. (adj.) **1, 2.** *Auxiliary, contributory, ancillary, adjuvant, subsidiary,* and *accessory* mean serving to aid or support. *Auxiliary* is applied to things that are supplementary but not necessarily subordinate: *auxiliary* ships in a fleet. *Contributory* is chiefly applied to an influence, means, etc., that promotes a result: High taxes were *contributory* to the popular discontent. *Ancillary* stresses service; the study of organic chemistry is *ancillary* to physiology. *Adjuvant* is applied to that which modifies for the better; an *adjuvant* ingredient makes a medicine more effective. *Subsidiary* and *accessory* imply subordination: a *subsidiary* business enterprise, an *accessory* device for a machine. Compare SUBORDINATE.

aux·in (ôk′sin) *n. Bot.* Any of a group of substances that in minute quantities act to promote or modify the growth of plants, as in root and bud formation, fruit drop, and the shedding of leaves. [< Gk. *auxein* to increase + -IN]

aux·o·chrome (ôk′sə·krōm) *n. Chem.* Any of certain radicals that will convert a chromophore into an acidic or basic textile dye. [< Gk. *auxein* to increase + -CHROME]

av. **1.** Average. **2.** Avoirdupois: also **avdp.**

av. or **Av.** Avenue.

A.V. Authorized Version (of the Bible).

a·va (ə·vä′) *adv. Scot.* At all; of all.

a·vail (ə·vāl′) *v.t.* **1.** To assist or aid; profit. **—** *v.i.* **2.** To be of value or advantage; suffice. **— to avail oneself of** To take advantage of; utilize. **—** *n.* **1.** Utility for a purpose; benefit; good: His efforts were of no *avail.* **2.** *pl.* Proceeds. **— Syn.** See ADVANTAGE. [< OF *a-* to (< L *ad-*) + *valoir* < L *valere* to be strong] **— a·vail′ing·ly** *adv.*

a·vail·a·ble (ə·vāl′bəl) *adj.* **1.** Capable of being used; at hand; usable. **2.** *Law* Valid. **3.** *Obs.* Effectual. **— a·vail′·a·bil·i·ty, a·vail′a·ble·ness** *n.* **— a·vail′a·bly** *adv.*

av·a·lanche (av′ə·lanch, -länch) *n.* **1.** The fall of a mass of snow or ice down a slope. **2.** The mass so falling. **3.** Something like an avalanche, as in power, destructiveness, etc. **—** *v.* **·lanched, ·lanch·ing** *v.i.* **1.** To fall or slide like an avalanche. **—** *v.t.* **2.** To fall or come down upon like an avalanche. [< F < dial. F (Swiss) *lavenche* (of uncertain origin); infl. by OF *avaler* to descend < *a val* to the valley < L *ad vallem*]

Av·a·lon (av′ə·lon) The legendary island tomb of King Arthur: generally identified with Glastonbury.

a·vant-garde (ə·vänt′gärd′, *Fr.* à·vän·gàrd′) *n.* The vanguard; especially, in art, the group regarded as most advanced or daring in technique and ideas. **—** *adj.* Of or pertaining to this group. [< F, lit., advance guard]

av·a·rice (av′ə·ris) *n.* Passion for acquiring and hoarding riches; covetousness; greed. [< OF < L *avaritia* < *avarus* greedy < *avere* to desire, crave]

av·a·ri·cious (av′ə·rish′əs) *adj.* Greedy of gain; grasping; miserly. **— av′a·ri′cious·ly** *adv.* **— av′a·ri′cious·ness** *n.* **— Syn.** greedy, acquisitive, covetous, rapacious. Compare STINGY. **— Ant.** generous, liberal.

A·vars (ä·värz′) *n.pl.* **1.** A people related to the Huns, who settled in Dacia in the sixth century, later invaded the Balkan Peninsula, Germany, and northern Italy, and were subdued by Charlemagne. **2.** A modern people of the Caucasus, probably related to the Lesghians. [< L *Avari*]

a·vast (ə·vast′, ə·väst′) *interj. Naut.* Stop! hold! cease! [< Du. *hou′ vast, houd vast* hold fast]

av·a·tar (av′ə·tär′) *n.* **1.** In Hindu mythology, the incarnation of a god. **2.** Any incarnation or visible manifestation. [< Skt. *avatāra* descent]

a·vaunt (ə·vônt′, ə·vänt′) *interj. Archaic* Go away! [< OF *avant* forward < LL *abante* < L *ab* from + *ante* before]

a·ve (ä′vē, ä′vā) *interj.* **1.** Farewell! — *n.* The salutation *ave.* [< L, hail, farewell]

ave. or **Ave.** Avenue.

A·ve (ä′vē, ä′vā) *n.* **1.** The Ave Maria. **2.** The time when the Ave Maria is to be said, marked by the ringing of a bell. Compare ANGELUS. **3.** One of the small beads on a rosary, used to number the Aves repeated.

a·vec plai·sir (ȧ·vek′ plā·zēr′) *French* With pleasure.

A·vel·la·ne·da (ä′vā·yä·nä′thä) A city in eastern Argentina; a suburb of Buenos Aires; pop. 346,600 (est. 1956).

A·ve Ma·ri·a (ä′vā mə·rē′ə, ä′vē) A Roman Catholic prayer to the Virgin Mary, consisting of Biblical salutations (*Luke* i 28, 42) and a plea for her intercession: also called *Hail Mary.* Also **A·ve Mar·y** (ä′vē mâr′ē). [< L, Hail, Mary]

av·e·na·ceous (av′ə·nā′shəs) *adj. Bot.* Of, pertaining to, or like oats or kindred grasses. [< L *avenaceus* < *avena* oats]

a·venge (ə·venj′) *v.* **a·venged, a·veng·ing** *v.t.* **1.** To take vengeance or exact exemplary punishment for or in behalf of: They *avenged* his murder. — *v.i.* **2.** To take vengeance. [< OF *avengier* < *a-* to (< L *ad-*) + *vengier* to punish < L *vindicare* to avenge] — **a·veng′er** *n.* — **a·veng′ing·ly** *adv.*
— **Syn. 1.** *Avenge* and *revenge* mean to inflict punishment in retaliation for an injury. One may *avenge* or *revenge* a wrong or a person (the one injured), but usually one *avenges* another and *revenges* himself. Compare REVENGE (noun). — **Ant.** forbear, remit, pardon, forgive.

av·ens (av′inz) *n.* **1.** Any plant of the genus *Geum*, of the rose family, as the herb bennet or **yellow avens** (*G. urbanum*), or the **purple avens** (*G. rivale*). **2.** A similar plant of some other genus, as the mountain avens. [< OF *avence*]

Av·en·tine (av′ən·tīn, -tin) *n.* One of the Seven Hills of Rome.

a·ven·tu·rine (ə·ven′chər·in) *n.* **1.** An opaque or semitranslucent typically brown glass, flecked with fine metal particles. **2.** A variety of quartz or feldspar containing shining particles, usually of mica or hematite: also called *sunstone.* Also **a·ven′tu·rin.** [< F < Ital. *avventurina* < *avventura* chance; def. 1 so called from its accidental discovery]

av·e·nue (av′ə·nōō, -nyōō) *n.* **1.** A broad street. **2.** A way of approach, as to a building, often bordered with trees. **3.** A mode of access or attainment. Abbr. *av., Av., ave., Ave.* [< F *avenue*, orig. fem. pp. of *avenir* to approach < L *advenire* < *ad-* toward + *venire* to come]

a·ver (ə·vûr′) *v.t.* **a·verred, a·ver·ring 1.** To declare confidently as fact; affirm. **2.** *Law* To assert formally; prove or justify (a plea). [< OF *averer* to confirm, ult. < L *ad-* to + *verus* true] — **a·ver′ment** *n.* — **a·ver′ra·ble** *adj.*

av·er·age (av′rij, av′ər·ij) *n.* **1.** *Math.* **a** An arithmetic mean. **b** A number representing a set of numbers of which it is a function. **2.** A mean, ratio, etc., showing a specific standing or accomplishment: batting *average*; B *average.* **3.** The ordinary rank, degree, or amount; general type. **4.** In marine law: **a** The loss arising by damage to a ship or cargo. **b** The proportion of such loss falling to a single person in an equitable distribution among those interested. **5.** Any small charge paid by the master of a ship, as pilotage. — *adj.* **1.** Obtained by calculating the mean of several. **2.** Medium; ordinary. **3.** In marine law, assessed according to the laws of average. — *v.* **·aged, ·ag·ing** *v.t.* **1.** To fix or calculate as the mean. **2.** To amount to or obtain an average of: He *averages* three dollars an hour. **3.** To apportion on the average. — *v.i.* **4.** To be or amount to an average. **5.** To buy or sell more goods, shares, etc., in order to get a better average price. Abbr. (n. and adj.) *av., avg.* [< F *avarie* damage to a ship or its cargo (see n. def. 3) < Ital. *avaria*; ult. origin uncertain] — **av′er·age·ly** *adv.*

A·ver·no (ä·ver′nō) A crater lake near Naples, Italy; anciently regarded as the entrance to Hades. Ancient **A·ver·nus** (ə·vûr′nəs). [< L *Avernus* < Gk. *aornos* without birds; because its volcanic vapors were said to kill birds] — **A·ver·ni·an** (ə·vûr′nē·ən), **A·ver·nal** (ə·vûr′nəl) *adj.*

A·ver·rho·ës (ə·ver′ō·ēz, av′ə·rō′ēz), 1126–98, Arab philosopher born in Spain. Also **A·ver′ro·ës.**

Av·er·rho·ism (av′ə·rō′iz·əm) *n.* The doctrines of Averrhoës and his disciples, chiefly consisting of a form of pantheism based on an interpretation of Aristotle. Also **Av′er·ro′·ism.** — **Av′er·rho′ist** *n.* — **Av′er·rho·is′tic** *adj.*

a·verse (ə·vûrs′) *adj.* **1.** Opposed; unfavorable; reluctant: with *to.* **2.** *Bot.* Turned away from the main axis: opposed to *adverse.* [< L *aversus*, pp. of *avertere* to turn aside. See AVERT.] — **a·verse′ly** *adv.* — **a·verse′ness** *n.*

a·ver·sion (ə·vûr′zhən, -shən) *n.* **1.** Extreme dislike; opposition; antipathy. **2.** A cause of repugnance or dislike. **3.** A turning away; averting. — **Syn.** See ABHORRENCE.

a·vert (ə·vûrt′) *v.t.* **1.** To turn or direct away or aside, as one's regard. **2.** To prevent or ward off, as a danger. — **Syn.** See PREVENT. [< OF *avertir* < L *avertere* to turn aside < *ab-* away + *vertere* to turn] — **a·vert′ed·ly** *adv.* — **a·vert′i·ble** or **a·vert′a·ble** *adj.*

A·ves·ta (ə·ves′tə) The sacred writings of Zoroastrianism. See ZEND–AVESTA.

A·ves·tan (ə·ves′tən) *n.* The ancient Iranian language in which the Avesta was written. — *adj.* Of or pertaining to the Avesta or its language.

avg. Average.

avi- *combining form* Bird; of or related to birds: *aviculture.* [< L *avis* bird]

a·vi·an (ā′vē·ən) *adj.* Pertaining to the class (*Aves*) of vertebrates that comprises the birds. Also **a·vic·u·lar** (ə·vik′yə·lər). — *n.* A bird. [< L *avis* bird]

a·vi·ar·y (ā′vē·er′ē) *n. pl.* **·ar·ies** An enclosure or large cage for live birds. [< L *aviarium* < *avis* bird] — **a·vi·ar·ist** (ā′vē·er′ist, -ə·rist) *n.*

a·vi·ate (ā′vē·āt, av′ē-) *v.i.* **·at·ed, ·at·ing** To fly an aircraft. [Back formation < AVIATION]

a·vi·a·tion (ā′vē·ā′shən, av′ē-) *n.* The act, science, or art of flying heavier-than-air aircraft: distinguished from *aerostation.* Abbr. *avn.* [< F < L *avis* bird]

aviation medicine Aeromedicine (which see).

a·vi·a·tor (ā′vē·ā′tər, av′ē-) *n.* One who flies airplanes and other heavier-than-air aircraft; a pilot. — **a′vi·a′tress** (-tris) or **a·vi·a·trix** (ā′vē·ā′triks, av′ē-) *n.fem.*

Av·i·cen·na (av′ə·sen′ə), 980–1037, Arab physician and philosopher. *Arabic* **ibn-Si·na** (ib′ən·sē′nä).

a·vi·cul·ture (ā′vi·kul′chər, av′i-) *n.* The rearing of birds.

av·id (av′id) *adj.* Very desirous; eager; greedy. [< L *avidus* < *avere* to crave] — **av′id·ly** *adv.*

av·i·din (av′ə·din) *n. Biochem.* A protein found in egg white that inhibits the action of biotin. [< AVID(ITY) + -IN; so called from its affinity for biotin]

a·vid·i·ty (ə·vid′ə·tē) *n.* **1.** Extreme eagerness; greediness. **2.** *Chem.* Affinity.

a·vi·fau·na (ā′və·fô′nə) *n. Ecol.* The birds of a given region: also called *ornis.* [< AVI- + FAUNA] — **a′vi·fau′nal** *adj.*

av·i·ga·tion (av′ə·gā′shən) *n.* The handling and guidance of aircraft in the air. [< AVI(ATION) + (NAVI)GATION]

A·vi·gnon (à·vē·nyôn′) A city in SE France, on the Rhône; papal seat, 1309–77; pop. 78,871 (1968).

a·vion (à·vyôn′) *n. French* Airplane.

a·vi·on·ics (ā′vē·on′iks, av′ē-) *n.pl.* (*construed as sing.*) The applications of electronics to aviation, astronautics, rockets, etc.

a·vi·so (ə·vī′zō) *n. pl.* **·sos 1.** Advice; information. **2.** A dispatch boat. [< Sp., information, advice]

a·vi·ta·min·o·sis (ā·vī′tə·min·ō′sis) *n. Pathol.* A condition caused by vitamin deficiency. [< A-⁴ without + VITAMIN + -OSIS]

Av·lo·na (äv·lō′nä) A former name for VALONA.

avn. Aviation.

av·o·ca·do (av′ə·kä′dō, ä′və-) *n. pl.* **·dos 1.** The pear-shaped, pulpy fruit of a West Indian lauraceous tree (*Persea americana*): also called *alligator pear.* **2.** The tree bearing this fruit. [< Sp., alter. of *aguacate* < Nahuatl *ahuacatl*]

av·o·ca·tion (av′ə·kā′shən) *n.* **1.** A casual or occasional occupation; diversion; hobby. **2.** *Rare* One's business or vocation. **3.** *Obs.* A calling away. — **Syn.** See OCCUPATION. [< L *avocatio, -onis* a calling away, diversion < *ab-* away + *vocare* to call]

a·voc·a·to·ry (ə·vok′ə·tôr′ē, -tō′rē) *adj.* Recalling; calling away or back.

av·o·cet (av′ə·set) *n.* A long-legged shore bird (genus *Recurvirostra*) having webbed feet and slender upcurved bill. Also **av′o·set.** [< F *avocette* < Ital. *avocetta*]

A·vo·ga·dro (ä′vō·gä′drō), Amedeo, 1776–1856, Conte di Quaregna, Italian physicist.

Avogadro number The actual number of molecules in one gram-molecule or of atoms in one gram-atom of an element or any pure substance. This number is 6.023×10^{23}. Also **Avogadro's constant.**

Avogadro's law *Chem.* The law stating that equal volumes of all gases, at the same temperature and pressure, contain the same number of molecules.

a·void (ə·void′) *v.t.* **1.** To keep away or at a distance from; shun; evade. **2.** *Law* To make void. **3.** *Obs.* To void; empty. — **Syn.** See ESCAPE. [< AF *avoider*, OF *esvuidier* to empty < *es-* out (< L *ex-*) + *vuidier* < L *viduare* to empty, deprive] — **a·void′a·ble** *adj.* — **a·void′a·bly** *adv.* — **a·void′er** *n.*

a·void·ance (ə·void′ns) *n.* **1.** The act of avoiding someone or something, especially someone or something unpleasant. **2.** *Law* Annulment; a making void.

avoir. Avoirdupois.

av·oir·du·pois (av′ər·də·poiz′) *n.* **1.** The ordinary system of weights of the United States and Great Britain in which 16 ounces avoirdupois make a pound. Abbr. *av., avdp., avoir.* See table inside back cover. **2.** *Informal* Weight; corpulence. [< OF *avoir de pois* goods of (i.e., sold by) weight < L *habere* to have, own + *de* of + *pensum* weight]

A·von (ā′vən, av′ən) **1.** A river in England, flowing SW 96 miles from Northampton past Stratford to the Severn at Tewkesbury. **2.** Any of several other rivers in England, Scotland, and Wales. **3.** A county in western England; 519 sq. mi.; pop. 915,300 (1976); county seat, Bristol.

à vo·tre san·té (à vô′tr′ sän·tā′) *French* To your health.

a·vouch (ə·vouch′) *v.t.* **1.** To vouch for; guarantee. **2.** To affirm positively; proclaim. **3.** To acknowledge; avow. [< OF *avochier* to affirm < L *advocare* to summon < *ad-* to + *vocare* to call. Doublet of AVOW.]

a·vow (ə·vou′) *v.t.* To declare openly, as facts; own; acknowledge: to *avow* oneself guilty. [< OF *avouer* < L *advocare* to summon. Doublet of AVOUCH.] **— a·vow′a·ble** *adj.* **— a·vow′a·ble·ness** *n.* **— a·vow′a·bly** *adv.* **— a·vow′er** *n.* **— Syn.** acknowledge, admit, avouch, own, testify, witness. See ASSERT. Compare CONFESS. **— Ant.** disavow, disown, deny.

a·vow·al (ə·vou′əl) *n.* Open declaration; frank admission or acknowledgment.

a·vowed (ə·voud′) *adj.* Openly acknowledged; plainly declared. **— a·vow·ed·ly** (ə·vou′id·lē) *adv.* **— a·vow′ed·ness** *n.*

a·vul·sion (ə·vul′shən) *n.* **1.** A pulling off or tearing away; forcible separation. **2.** That which is torn away. **3.** *Law* The removal of soil or a piece of land, by a flood or change in the course of a stream, from the estate of one owner to that of another. Compare ALLUVION. [< L *avulsio, -onis < avellere < ab- away + vellere to pull*]

a·vun·cu·lar (ə·vung′kyə·lər) *adj.* Of or pertaining to an uncle. [< L *avunculus* uncle, dim. of *avus* grandfather]

A/W 1. Actual weight. **2.** All water.

a·wa (ə·wô′, ə·wä′) *adv. Scot.* Away.

a·wait (ə·wāt′) *v.t.* **1.** To wait for; expect. **2.** To be ready or in store for. [< OF *awaitier* to watch for < *a-* to (< L *ad-*) + *waitier* to watch < OHG *wahtēn* to watch]

a·wake (ə·wāk′) *adj.* Not asleep; alert; vigilant. **— v.** *v. a·woke* (*Rare* **a·waked**), **a·waked** (*Rare* **a·woke**), **a·wak·ing** *v.t.* **1.** To arouse from sleep. **2.** To stir up; excite. **— v.i. 3.** To cease to sleep; become awake. **4.** To become alert or aroused. ◆ In practice the past participle *awaked* is sometimes felt to be awkward and is replaced by the form *awakened*, particularly in the passive: I was *awakened* early this morning. See usage note under WAKE[1]. [OE *onwæcnan* rise from sleep < *on-* + *wæcnan* to rise and *āwacian* to arise < *ā-* + *wacian* to watch]

a·wak·en (ə·wā′kən) *v.t. & v.i.* To awake. See note under WAKE[1]. [OE *onwæcnan* to arise < *on-* + *wæcnan* to rise] **— a·wak′en·er** *n.*

a·wak·en·ing (ə·wā′kən·ing) *adj.* Stirring; exciting. **—** *n.* **1.** The act of waking. **2.** An arousing of attention or interest; revival.

a·ward (ə·wôrd′) *v.t.* **1.** To adjudge as due, as by legal decision. **2.** To bestow as the result of a contest or examination, as a prize. **— Syn.** See GRANT. **—** *n.* **1.** A decision, as by a judge, umpire, or arbitrator. **2.** The document containing it. **3.** That which is awarded, as a badge, medal, citation, etc. [< AF *awarder*, OF *esguarder* to observe, examine < *es-* out (< L *ex-*) + *guarder* to watch < Gmc.] **— a·ward′a·ble** *adj.* **— a·ward′er** *n.*

a·ware (ə·wâr′) *adj.* Conscious; cognizant: often with *of.* [OE *gewær* watchful] **— a·ware′ness** *n.*

a·wash (ə·wosh′, ə·wôsh′) *adv. & adj.* **1.** Level with or just above the surface of the water. **2.** Tossed or washed about by waves. **3.** Covered or overflowed by water.

a·way (ə·wā′) *adv.* **1.** From a given place; off. **2.** Far; at or to a distance. **3.** In another direction; aside: to turn *away.* **4.** Out of existence; at or to an end: to waste *away.* **5.** On and on; continuously: to peg *away* at a task. **6.** From one's keeping, attention, or possession: to give food *away.* **7.** At once, without hesitation: Fire *away!* **— to do away with 1.** To get rid of. **2.** To kill. **— adj. 1.** Absent. **2.** At a distance. **— interj.** Begone! [OE *on weg* on (one's) way]

awe (ô) *n.* **1.** Reverential fear; dread mingled with veneration. **2.** *Archaic* Overawing influence. **3.** *Obs.* Dread; terror. **— v.t.** *awed, aw·ing* or **awe·ing** To impress with reverential fear. [< ON *agi* fear]

a·wea·ry (ə·wir′ē) *adj.* Wearied; weary.

a·weath·er (ə·weth′ər) *adv. & adj. Naut.* At, to, or toward the windward side.

a·wee (ə·wē′) *adv. Scot.* Awhile.

a·weigh (ə·wā′) *adv. Naut.* Hanging with the flukes just clear of the bottom: said of an anchor.

awe·less (ô′lis) *adj.* Devoid of fear; fearless. Also **aw′less.**

awe·some (ô′səm) *adj.* **1.** Inspiring awe. **2.** Characterized by or expressing awe; reverential. **— awe′some·ly** *adv.* **— awe′some·ness** *n.*

aw·ful (ô′fəl) *adj.* **1.** *Informal* Exceedingly bad or unpleasant; ugly. **2.** Inspiring awe; majestically or solemnly impressive. **3.** Causing fear or dread: the *awful* destruction of a tornado. **4.** *Informal* Very great. **5.** Filled with awe; reverential. **— aw′ful·ness** *n.* **— Syn. 1.** appalling, shocking. **2.** exalted, august, grand. **3.** dreadful, frightful, horrible, terrible.

aw·ful·ly (ô′fəl·ē *for def.* 1; ô′flē *for def.* 2) *adv.* **1.** In an awful manner. **2.** *Informal* Excessively; very: *awfully* rich.

a·while (ə·hwīl′) *adv.* For a brief time. [OE *āne hwīle* a while]

a·whirl (ə·hwûrl′) *adj. & adv.* In a whirl; whirling.

awk·ward (ôk′wərd) *adj.* **1.** Ungraceful in bearing. **2.** Unskillful in action; bungling. **3.** Embarrassing or perplexing: an *awkward* situation. **4.** Difficult or dangerous to deal with, as an opponent. **5.** Inconvenient for use; uncomfortable. **6.** *Obs.* Perverse; untoward. [< ON *ōfugr* turned the wrong way + *-WARD*] **— awk′ward·ly** *adv.* **— awk′ward·ness** *n.* **— Syn. 2.** *Awkward, clumsy, maladroit, gauche,* and *bungling* are compared as they refer to lack of grace in movement or action. *Awkward* originally meant turned the wrong way; *clumsy,* stiffened with cold. Thus *awkward* primarily refers to action, and *clumsy* to condition: an *awkward* gait, *clumsy* fingers. A *maladroit* person lacks tact or skill; one who is *gauche* (originally, left-handed) is more positively inept, or even boorish from ignorance. *Bungling* describes the person who makes a botch of what he tries to do.

awl (ôl) *n.* A pointed instrument for making small holes, as in wood or leather. [OE *awel* < OE *æl*]

awl·wort (ôl′wûrt′) *n.* A small, stemless aquatic plant (*Subularia aquatica*) having awl-shaped leaves.

awn (ôn) *n. Bot.* A bristlelike appendage of certain grasses; beard, as of wheat or rye. [ME < ON *ögn* chaff] **— awned** (ônd) *adj.* **— awn′less** *adj.* **— awn′y** *adj.*

awn·ing (ô′ning) *n.* **1.** A rooflike cover, as of canvas, for protection from sun or rain. **2.** A shelter resembling this. [Origin unknown]

a·woke (ə·wōk′) Past tense of AWAKE.

AWOL (*as an acronym pronounced* ā′wôl) *Mil.* Absent or absence without leave. Also **awol, A.W.O.L., a.w.o.l.**

a·wry (ə·rī′) *adj. & adv.* **1.** Toward one side; askew. **2.** Out of the right course; amiss; wrong. [< A[-1] on + WRY]

ax (aks) *n. pl.* **ax·es 1.** A tool with a bladed head mounted on a handle, used for chopping, hewing, etc. **2.** An ax-hammer. **— to have an ax to grind** *Informal* To have a private purpose or interest to pursue. **— v.t. 1.** To cut or trim with an ax. **2.** To dispose of as with an ax. Also *Brit.* **axe.** [OE *æx*] **— ax′like** *adj.*

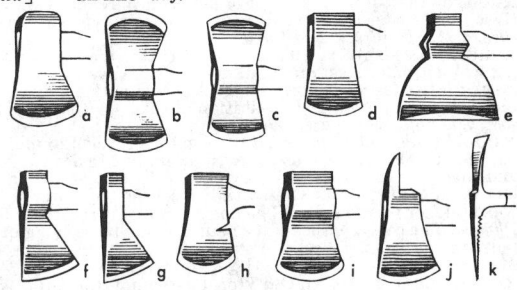

AXES
a Single-bit, Michigan pattern. *b* Double-bit, Michigan pattern. *c* Cruiser's. *d* Utility. *e* Broadax. *f* Hudson Bay. *g* Camp. *h* All-steel camp. *i* Half. *j* Fireman's. *k* Swiss ice.

ax. 1. Axiom. **2.** Axis.

ax·es[1] (ak′sēz) Plural of AXIS[1].

ax·es[2] (ak′siz) Plural of AX.

ax·ham·mer (aks′ham′ər) *n.* A stonecutter's tool with cutting edges at either end of the head, or one cutting edge and one hammer face. **— ax′-ham′mered** *adj.*

ax·i·al (ak′sē·əl) *adj.* **1.** Of, pertaining to, or forming an axis. **2.** Situated on or along an axis. Also **ax·ile** (ak′sil, -sīl).

ax·il (ak′sil) *n.* **1.** *Bot.* The cavity or angle formed by the junction of the upper side of a leafstalk, branch, etc., with a stem or branch. **2.** *Anat.* The axilla. [< L *axilla* armpit]

ax·il·la (ak·sil′ə) *n. pl.* **ax·il·lae** (-sil′ē) **1.** *Anat.* The armpit. **2.** An axil. [< L]

ax·il·lar (ak′sə·lər) *adj.* Axillary. **—** *n. Usually pl. Ornithol.* The relatively long, stiff feathers on the undersurface of the wing of a bird. [< F *axillaire,* ult. < L *axilla* armpit]

ax·il·lar·y (ak′sə·ler′ē) *adj.* **1.** *Bot.* Of, pertaining to, or situated in an axil: *axillary* buds. **2.** *Anat.* Pertaining to the axilla. **—** *n. pl.* **·lar·ies** *Ornithol.* An axillar.

ax·i·ol·o·gy (ak′sē·ol′ə·jē) *n. Philos.* The theory or study of values or of the nature of value, as in ethics.

ax·i·om (ak′sē·əm) *n.* **1.** A self-evident or universally recognized truth. **2.** An established principle or rule. **3.** *Logic & Math.* A self-evident proposition accepted as true without proof. Abbr. (def. 3) *ax.* [< L *axioma, -atos* < Gk. *axiōma* a thing thought worthy, a self-evident truth < *axioein* to think worthy < *axios* worthy] **— Syn. 1, 2.** *Axiom, theorem, law,* and *principle* are compared as they denote a proposition universal in form and widely accepted as true. An *axiom* is self-evident; a *theorem* is a proposition deduced from *axioms,* or, in general, any proposition susceptible of proof.

A scientific *law* is an assertion about cause and effect, or the regularity of phenomena, or the like, formulated by induction from data. A *principle* is a generalization useful as a guide to understanding or study. See TRUISM.

ax·i·o·mat·ic (ak/sē·ə·mat/ik) *adj.* **1.** Of, pertaining to, or resembling an axiom; self-evident. **2.** Aphoristic. Also **ax/·i·o·mat/i·cal.** — **ax/i·o·mat/i·cal·ly** *adv.*

ax·is[1] (ak/sis) *n.* *pl.* **ax·es** (ak/sēz) **1.** A line around which a turning body rotates or may be supposed to rotate. **2.** *Geom.* **a** A straight line through the center of a plane or solid figure, especially the line in relation to which the figure is symmetrical. **b** A fixed line, as in a graph, along which distances are measured or to which positions are referred. **3.** The central line about which the parts of a body or thing are regularly arranged. **4.** In art, an imaginary line through the center of a drawing or sculpture for purposes of measurement or reference. **5.** *Bot.* The central body, part, line, or longitudinal support on, along, or above which plant organs or other parts are arranged. **6.** *Anat.* **a** A short arterial trunk from which several nearly equal branches radiate. **b** The second cervical vertebra, or the odontoid process that surmounts it. **7.** *Crystall.* One of the lines of reference meeting at the center of a crystal, and determining to which system it belongs. **8.** *Geol.* The dominant central section of a mountain chain, or the line tracing the crest throughout its length. **9.** An affiliation of two or more nations to promote and ensure mutual interest, cooperation, and solidarity in their relations with foreign powers. Abbr. *ax.* [< L, axis, axle]

ax·is[2] (ak/sis) *n.* A small deer (genus *Axis*) of southern Asia, having the body spotted with white. Also **axis deer.** [< L]

Ax·is (ak/sis) *n.* A coalition that developed from the Rome-Berlin Axis of 1936 and ultimately included Germany, Italy, Japan, and others: opposed to the Allies and associated powers in World War II. Also **Axis Powers.**

ax·le (ak/səl) *n.* **1.** A crossbar supporting a vehicle, and on or with which its wheel or wheels turn. **2.** A shaft on which a wheel, as of a windlass, is mounted and on or with which it turns. [ME *axel* in *axeltre*. See AXLETREE.] — **ax/led** *adj.*

ax·le·tree (ak/səl·trē/) *n.* A bar or beam on the ends of which the opposite wheels of a carriage or wagon revolve. [ME *axeltre* < ON *öxultrē* < *öxull* axle + *trē* tree, bar]

ax·man (aks/mən) *n.* *pl.* **·men** (-mən) One who wields an ax; a woodsman. Also **axe/man.**

Ax·min·ster (aks/min·stər) *n.* **1.** A carpet with a long, soft pile. **2.** A carpet made in imitation of this. [after *Axminster*, England, where first made]

ax·o·lotl (ak/sə·lot/l) *n.* A North American tailed amphibian (genus *Ambystoma*), as *A. mexicanum* of Mexican lakes and marshes, that retains its external gills and breeds in a larval state. [< Sp. < Nahuatl, lit., servant of water]

ax·on (ak/son) *n.* **1.** *Zool.* The body axis of a vertebrate. **2.** *Physiol.* The central process of a neuron, usually carrying impulses away from the cells. Also **ax·one** (ak/sōn). See DENDRITE, NEURON. [< NL < Gk. *axōn* axis]

ax·seed (aks/sēd/) *n.* An Old World perennial (*Coronilla varia*) with odd-pinnate leaves and pink or white flowers, cultivated in the United States: also called *crown vetch.* [< AX + SEED; from the shape of the pods]

Ax·um (äk·sōōm/) See AKSUM.

ay[1] (ā) *adv.* *Poetic* Ever; always. Also spelled *aye.* [ME < ON *ei* always]

ay[2] (ī) See AYE[1].

ay[3] (ā) *interj.* *Archaic* O! oh! ah!: an expression of sorrow, surprise, etc. [ME *ey, ei*]

A·ya·cu·cho (ä/yä·kōō/chō) A Department of south central Peru; 17,569 sq. mi.; pop. 474,100 (est. 1970); capital, **Aya·cucho,** pop. 28,500 (est. 1970).

a·yah (ä/yə) *n.* *Anglo-Indian* A native nurse or lady's maid. [< Hind. *āyā* < Pg. *aia* nurse]

a·ya·huas·ca (ä/yä·wäs/kä) *n.* A Brazilian plant (*Banisteriopsis caapi*) whose alkaloid principle has powerful hallucinatory effects. See BANISTERINE. [< Quechua name]

Ay·de·lotte (ā/də·lot), **Frank,** 1880–1956, U.S. educator.

Ay·din (ī·din/) A Province of western Turkey; 2,953 sq. mi.; pop. 469,700 (1960); capital, **Aydin,** pop. 110,887. Also *Aidin.*

aye[1] (ī) *n.* An affirmative vote or voter. — *adv.* Yes; yea. Also spelled *ay.* [Origin unknown]

aye[2] (ā) See AY[1].

aye-aye (ī/ī/) *n.* A nocturnal lemur (genus *Daubentonia*) of Madagascar, about the size of a cat and having rodentlike teeth. [< F < Malagasy *aiay*; so called from its cry]

A·ye·sha (ä/i·shä) See AISHA.

AYH American Youth Hostels.

a·yin (ä/yēn) *n.* The sixteenth letter in the Hebrew alphabet: also spelled *'ain.* See table for ALPHABET.

Ay·ma·ra (ī/mä·rä/) *n.* **1.** A family of South American Indian languages, formerly spoken throughout most of what is now Bolivia and Peru, and later superseded by Quechua. **2.** A member of a tribe speaking an Aymara language. — **Ay/·ma·ran/** *adj.*

Ay·mé (e·mā/), **Marcel,** 1902–67, French novelist, dramatist, and short-story writer.

Ayr (âr) **1.** A county in SW Scotland; 1,132 sq. mi.; pop. 354,005 (1969): also **Ayr·shire** (âr/shir, -shər). **2.** Its county

seat; pop. 47,635 (est. 1969); a port on the **Ayr** river, that flows 38 miles west to the Firth of Clyde.

Ayr·shire (âr/shir, -shər) *n.* One of a breed of dairy cattle originating in Ayr.

a·yun·ta·mien·to (ä·yōōn/tä·myen/tō) *n.* *pl.* **·tos** (-tōz, *Sp.* -tōs) *SW U.S.* **1.** A municipal council or legislative body; town council. **2.** A city hall; municipal building. [< Sp.]

A·yur·ve·da (ä/yŏŏr·vä/də, -vē/də) An ancient Hindu medical treatise sometimes regarded as a fifth Veda. [< Skt. *ayus* span of life + *vid* know]

A·yut·tha·ya (ä·yōō/tä·yä) A former capital city in SE Thailand; site of early Thai ruins; destroyed, 1767; pop. 30,947 (est. 1957). Also **A·yu·thi·a** (ä·yōō/thē·ä).

az- Var. of AZO-.

az. 1. Azimuth. **2.** *Heraldry* Azure.

a·zal·ea (ə·zāl/yə) *n.* A flowering shrub of the heath family (genus *Rhododendron*, formerly *Azalea*), especially the **flame azalea** (*R. calendulaceum*), with showy scarlet or orange flowers. [< NL < Gk. *azalea*, fem. of *azaleos* dry < *azein* to parch, dry up; from its preference for dry soil]

a·zan (ä·zän/) *n.* In Moslem countries, the muezzin's call to prayer, usually given from the minaret of a mosque five times a day. [< Arabic *aḍān*]

A·za·ña (ä·thä/nyä), **Manuel,** 1880–1940, president of the Spanish Republic 1936–39.

A·za·zel (ə·zā/zəl, az/ə-zel) **1.** In the Bible, a spirit to whom a goat was sacrificed on the Day of Atonement (*Lev.* xvi), called in the Apocrypha the leader of the rebellious angels, identified with the sons of God who married the daughters of men (*Gen.* vi 1–4). **2.** In Milton's *Paradise Lost*, the standard-bearer of Satan. [< Hebrew *'azāzēl* complete removal]

Az·bine (az·bēn/) See AïR.

a·zed·a·rach (ə·zed/ə·rak) *n.* **1.** A large ornamental tree (*Melia azedarach*) of Asia and tropical America, with panicles of lilac-colored flowers: also called *chinaberry, hagbush, pride of China.* **2.** The bark from the roots of this tree, used as a cathartic, emetic, or vermifuge. [< F *azédarac*, ult. < Persian *āzād dirakht* noble tree]

a·ze·o·trope (ə·zē/ə·trōp) *n.* *Chem.* Any mixture which has a constant boiling point at a specified concentration. [< Gk. *a-* not + *zeein* to boil + *tropē* a turning] — **az·e·o·trop·ic** (az/ē·ō·trop/ik) *adj.* — **az·e·ot·ro·pism** (az/ē·ot/rə·piz/əm), **az/e·ot/ro·py** *n.*

A·zer·bai·jan (ä/zər·bī·jän/, az/ər-, *Russ.* ä/zyir·bī·jän/) **1.** A constituent Republic of the Soviet Union, west of the Caspian Sea; 33,590 sq. mi.; pop. 5,111,000 (est. 1970); capital, Baku: officially **Azerbaijan S.S.R.** Also **A/zer·bai·dzhan/.** *Russian* **A·zer·bai·dzhan/ska·ya S.S.R.** (ä/zər·bī·jän/ska·ya) **2.** Two Provinces of NW Iran, **Eastern Azerbaijan**: 28,448 sq. mi.; pop. 2,596,439 (1966); capital, Tabriz and **Western Azerbaijan**; 13,664 sq. mi.; pop. 1,087,182; capital, Rizaiyeh.

A·zer·bai·ja·ni (ä/zər·bī·jä/nē, az/ər-) *n.* *pl.* **·ni** or **·nis** (-nēz) **1.** A native or inhabitant of Azerbaijan. **2.** The Turkic language of these people.

A·zil·ian (ə·zil/yən) *adj.* *Anthropol.* Designating a subdivision of Mesolithic culture: named from the **Mas d'A·zil** (mäs dä·zēl/), a village of southern France.

az·i·muth (az/ə·məth) *n.* **1.** The angular distance in a horizontal plane measured clockwise from true or grid north to a given course or celestial object. When measured from grid north or magnetic north, it is described respectively as **grid azimuth** and **magnetic azimuth.** **2.** In celestial navigation, the angle measured at the zenith, clockwise, from true north to a vertical plane passing through a heavenly body; in astronomy, measured clockwise from the south point. **3.** *Mil.* The direction of a target with respect to an observer, measured clockwise as an angle from a reference line. Abbr. *az.* [< OF *azimut* < Arabic *as-sumūt* the ways, pl. of *samt* way] — **az·i·muth·al** (az/ə·muth/əl) *adj.* — **az/i·muth/al·ly** *adv.*

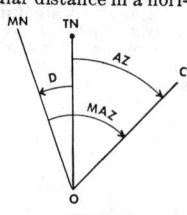

AZIMUTH

O Observation point. *TN* True north. *MN* Magnetic north. *C* Course line or celestial object. *D* Declination. *AZ* Grid azimuth. *MAZ* Magnetic azimuth.

az·ine (az/ēn, -in) *n.* *Chem.* One of a class of nitrogenous heterocyclic compounds arranged in a six-membered ring, identified by the number of nitrogen atoms, as diazine, triazine, etc. [< AZ- + -INE[2]]

az·o (az/ō, ā/zō) *adj.* *Chem.* Containing nitrogen: an *azo* compound; *azo* dye. [< AZOTE]

azo- *combining form Chem.* Indicating the presence of nitrogen, especially in organic compounds in which two atoms of nitrogen are connected with two similar radicals of the benzene series: *azobenzene*, $C_6H_5N : NC_6H_5$. Also, before vowels, *az-*. [< AZOTE]

azo dye Any of an important class of coal-tar dyes containing the azo radical N : N.

a·zo·ic (ə·zō/ik) *adj.* *Geol.* Of or pertaining to those periods on earth before life appeared; without organic remains. [< Gk. *azōos* lifeless < *a-* without + *zōē* life]

az·ole (az′ōl, ə·zōl′) *n. Chem.* **1.** Pyrrole. **2.** Any of a group of five-membered hydrocarbon compounds including the diazoles. [< AZ(O)- + -OLE[1]]

az·on (az′on) *n.* A type of bomb equipped with control surfaces in the tail to permit radio guidance in azimuth only. [< *az(imuth) on(ly)*]

a·zon·ic (ā·zon′ik) *adj.* Not peculiar to any zone or region; not local.

A·zores (ə·zôrz′, ā′zôrz) Three island groups west of the Portuguese mainland and comprising three administrative districts of Portugal; 922 sq. mi.; pop. 334,300 (est. 1968).

az·ote (az′ōt, ə·zōt′) *n.* Nitrogen: a former name. [< F < Gk. *a-* not + *zōein* live; so called by Lavoisier from its inability to support life]

az·oth (az′oth) *n.* **1.** Mercury: the name given by the alchemists. **2.** The universal remedy of Paracelsus. [< Arabic *az-zāūq* quicksilver]

a·zot·ic (ə·zot′ik) *adj.* Of, pertaining to, or containing azote or nitrogen.

az·o·tize (az′ə·tīz) *v.t.* **·tized, ·tiz·ing** To nitrogenize.

a·zo·to·bac·ter (ə·zō′tō·bak′tər) *n.* A type of bacteria, chiefly *Clostridium pasteurianum*, that live in soil and have the power of fixing nitrogen, thus contributing to soil fertility.

A·zov (ä·zôf′), **Sea of** A northern inlet of the Black Sea in the southern Soviet Union; 14,000 sq. mi. Also **A·zof′.**

Az·ra·el (az′rē·əl) In Moslem and ancient Jewish mythology, the angel who separates the soul from the body at death. [< Hebrew, help of God]

Az·tec (az′tek) *n.* **1.** One of a nation of Indians of Nahuatlan stock, founders of an empire that was at its height when Cortés invaded Mexico in 1519. **2.** Nahuatl. *— adj.* Of or pertaining to the Aztec Indians, their language, culture, or empire: also **Az·tec·an** (az′tek·ən).

az·ure (azh′ər, ā′zhər) *adj.* Sky blue. *— n.* **1.** A clear, sky-blue color or pigment. **2.** *Poetic* The sky. **3.** *Heraldry* Blue, represented in engraving by parallel horizontal lines. Abbr. (for def. 3) az. [< OF *azur* < Arabic *al-lāzward* < Persian *lāzhward* lapis lazuli]

az·u·rite (azh′ə·rīt) *n.* A vitreous, monoclinic, azure-blue, basic copper carbonate, often used as a gemstone.

az·y·gous (az′i·gəs) *adj. Biol.* Occurring singly; not paired. [< Gk. *azygos* unpaired < *a-* without + *zygon* a yoke]

B

b, B (bē) *n. pl.* **b's** or **bs, B's** or **Bs, bees** (bēz) **1.** The second letter of the English alphabet. The shape of the Phoenician *beth* was adopted by the Greeks as *beta* and became Roman *B.* Also *bee.* **2.** The sound represented by the letter *b*, usually a voiced bilabial stop. *— symbol* **1.** *Music* **a** One of a series of tones, the seventh in the natural diatonic scale of C. **b** The pitch of this tone, 493.9 cycles per second or this value multiplied by any power of 2, in standard pitch. **c** A written note representing it. **d** A scale built upon B. **2.** *Chem.* Boron (symbol B). **3.** The second in sequence or class. **4.** *U.S.* The second highest grade for school work.

b Base; baseman.

B Bishop (chess).

B- Bomber.

B. 1. Bacillus. **2.** Baumé. **3.** Bible. **4.** Boston. **5.** British. **6.** Brotherhood.

B. or b. 1. Bachelor. **2.** Balboa (coin). **3.** Base; baseman. **4.** *Music* Bass; basso. **5.** Bat. **6.** Bay. **7.** Belga. **8.** Bench. **9.** *Dent.* Bicuspid. **10.** Bolivar (coin). **11.** Boliviano. **12.** Book. **13.** Born. **14.** Brass. **15.** Breadth. **16.** Brother.

B/- 1. Bag. **2.** Bale.

ba (bä) *n.* In Egyptian mythology, the soul, believed to return to and reanimate the preserved body. [< Egyptian]

Ba *Chem.* Barium.

B.A. 1. Bachelor of Arts (L *Baccalaureus Artium*). **2.** British Academy. **3.** British Association (for the Advancement of Science). **4.** Buenos Aires.

baa (bä, ba) *v.i.* **baaed, baa·ing** To bleat, as a sheep. *— n.* A bleat, as of a sheep. [Imit.]

Ba·al (bā′əl, bāl) *n. pl.* **Ba·al·im** (bā′əl·im) **1.** Any of several ancient Semitic gods of fertility and flocks; especially, the sun god of the Phoenicians. **2.** An idol or false god. [< Hebrew *ba'al* lord] *— Ba′al·ish adj.*

Baal·bek (bäl′bek) A tourist center in central Lebanon; site of ancient Roman temples; pop. about 3,000: ancient Greek *Heliopolis.*

Ba·al·ist (bā′əl·ist) *n.* **1.** A worshiper of Baal. **2.** A worshiper of idols. Also **Ba′al·ite** (-īt). *— Ba′al·ism n.*

ba·ba (bä′bä) *n.* A cake made with yeast and steeped in rum. Also *French* **ba·ba au rhum** (bä·bä′ ō rôm′). [< F, prob. < Polish *baba* grandmother]

ba·bas·su (bä′bə·sōō′) *n.* **1.** The oil yielded by the nuts of a Brazilian palm tree (*Orbignya martiana*), used in making soap. Also **babassu oil.** **2.** The tree yielding this oil. [< native Brazilian name]

bab·bitt (bab′it) *v.t.* To line, bush, fill, or face with Babbitt metal. *— n.* Babbitt metal.

Bab·bitt (bab′it) *n.* A type of conventional American businessman, ambitious in his business, but otherwise provincial, mediocre, and smug. [after the title character in Sinclair Lewis's novel *Babbitt* (1922)] *— Bab′bitt·ry n.*

Bab·bitt (bab′it), **Irving,** 1865–1933, U.S. scholar and critic.

Babbitt metal 1. A soft, white, antifriction alloy of tin, copper, and antimony. **2.** Any of a group of similar alloys. [after Isaac Babbitt 1799–1862, U.S. metallurgist]

bab·ble (bab′əl) *v.* **·bled, ·bling** *v.i.* **1.** To utter inarticulate or meaningless sounds. **2.** To make a murmuring or rippling sound, as a stream. **3.** To talk unwisely or foolishly. *— v.t.* **4.** To utter unintelligibly. **5.** To blurt out thoughtlessly. *— n.* **1.** Inarticulate or confused speech. **2.** Prattle, as of an infant. **3.** A murmuring or rippling sound. [ME *babelen*; ult. origin unknown] *— bab′bler n.*

— Syn. (noun) *Babble, prattle, chatter, gabble, gibber,* and *jabber* denote a flow of confused sounds or incoherent speech. Most of these words are onomatopoeic. We speak of the *babble* of an infant or a brook, the *prattle* of a child learning to talk, the *chatter* of a magpie, the *gabble* of a goose, the *gibber* of an imbecile, the *jabber* of an alien tongue.

babe[1] (bāb) *n.* **1.** An infant; baby. **2.** *U.S. Informal* An artless or inexperienced person. **3.** *U.S. Slang* A girl. [ME; of uncertain origin]

babe[2] (bāb) *n. Physics* A unit of energy equal to 20,000 electron volts: used in nuclear physics research.

ba·bel (bā′bəl, bab′əl) *n.* A confusion of many voices or languages; tumult. Also **Ba′bel.** [from (*Tower of*) *Babel*]

Ba·bel (bā′bəl, bab′əl) In the Bible, an ancient city in Shinar, now identified with Babylon. *— Tower of Babel* **1.** A tower begun in Babel by the descendants of Noah and intended to reach heaven, but abandoned when God confused the language of the builders. *Gen.* xi 9. **2.** Any impractical scheme or structure; a visionary project.

Ba·bel (bä′bil), **Isaak Emanuilovich,** 1894–1941, Soviet writer.

Bab-el-Man·deb (bäb′el·män′deb) A strait between the Red Sea and the Gulf of Aden; 17 mi. wide.

Ba·ber (bä′bər), 1483–1530, Zahir ud-Din Mohammed, founder of the Mogul dynasty. Also **Ba′bar, Ba′bur.**

Ba·beuf (bà·bœf′), **François Noël,** 1760–97, French socialist.

Ba·bi (bä′bē) *n.* A disciple of the Bab. See BABISM.

ba·biche (bä·bēsh′) *n. Canadian* Rawhide thongs or lacings. [< dial. F (Canadian)]

ba·bies'-breath (bā′bēz·breth′) See BABY'S-BREATH.

bab·i·ru·sa (bab′ə·rōō′sə, bä′bə-) *n.* A wild hog (*Babirussa babirussa*) of SE Asia and the East Indies. The canines of the male are long and curve upward through the lips. Also **bab′i·rous′sa, bab′i·rus′sa.** [< Malay *bābi* hog + *rūsa* deer]

Ba·bism (bä′biz·əm) *n.* The pantheistic religious system founded in 1844 by **the Bab,** Ali Mohammed, 1819–50. Its teachings include the equality of the sexes, monogamy, asceticism, total abstinence, and a high personal morality. See BAHAISM. [< Persian *Bab* (*el-Dih*) gate (of faith)] *— Ba·bite* (bä′bīt), **Ba′bist** *adj. & n.*

ba·boo (bä′bōō) *n.* **1.** A Hindu gentleman: a form of address, equivalent to *sir* or *Mr.* **2.** In India, a native merchant or clerk who can write English. **3.** A native of India with a smattering of English education: a derogatory term. Also **ba′bu.** [< Hind. *bābū*, a term of respect] *— ba′boo·ism n.*

ba·boon (ba·bōōn′) *n.* A large, terrestrial monkey (*Papio* and related genera) of Africa and Asia, having front and back legs of nearly equal length, doglike muzzle, large bare callosities on the buttocks, and usually a short tail. [< OF *babuin*; ult. origin unknown] *— ba·boon′ish adj.*

---

ba·boon·er·y (ba-bōō'nər-ē) *n.* Behavior befitting a baboon.
ba·bul (bä-bōōl') *n.* **1.** A gum or hard wood yielded by an acacia (*Acacia arabica*) of India. **2.** The tree yielding this gum or wood. Also **ba·bool'.** [< Hind., the acacia tree]
Ba·bur (bä'bər) See BABER.
ba·bush·ka (bə-bōōsh'kə) *n.* A woman's scarf, often made or folded in a triangular shape, worn over the head. [< Russian, grandmother]
ba·by (bā'bē) *n. pl.* **·bies** **1.** A very young child of either sex; an infant. **2.** The youngest or smallest member of a family or group. **3.** One who looks or acts like a child. **4.** Any young animal. **5.** *Slang* A girl. **6.** *U.S. Slang* Any object of special affection or personal responsibility. — *adj.* **1.** For a baby: *baby* shoes. **2.** Childish; infantile: *baby* ways. **3.** Small; diminutive; miniature. — *v.t.* **·bied, ·by·ing** To treat as a baby; play tenderly with; pamper. [ME *baby*, dim. of *babe*] — **ba'by·hood** *n.* — **ba'by·like'** *adj.*
ba·by-blue-eyes (bā'bē-blōō'īz') *n.* Any of several annual plants (genus *Nemophila*) with alternate leaves and showy, sky-blue flowers. Also **baby blue-eyes.**
baby bonus *Canadian Slang* The Family Allowance.
baby carriage *Chiefly U.S.* A small carriage for a baby, pushed from behind: also *perambulator.* Also **baby buggy.**
baby farm A place where babies may be boarded.
ba·by·ish (bā'bē·ish) *adj.* Childish; infantile. — **ba'by·ish·ly** *adv.* — **ba'by·ish·ness** *n.*
Bab·y·lon (bab'ə-lən, -lon) **1.** An ancient city of Mesopotamia on the Euphrates, capital of Babylonia from about 2100 B.C.; celebrated as a seat of wealth, luxury, and vice. **2.** Any city or place of great wealth, luxury, or vice. **3.** Any place of captivity: in allusion to the Babylonian captivity. — **Bab'y·lon'ic** (-lon'ik), **Bab'y·lo'nish** (-lō'nish) *adj.*
Bab·y·lo·ni·a (bab'ə-lō'nē-ə) An ancient empire of Mesopotamia; capital, Babylon; conquered by Persia, 538 B.C.
Bab·y·lo·ni·an (bab'ə-lō'nē-ən) *adj.* **1.** Of, like, or pertaining to ancient Babylon or Babylonia. **2.** Wicked; luxurious. — *n.* **1.** A native or inhabitant of Babylonia. **2.** The Semitic language of ancient Babylonia, belonging to the Akkadian group.
Babylonian captivity **1.** The exile of the Jews deported by Nebuchadnezzar into Babylonia, 597 B.C. **2.** The interval of forced residence of the popes at Avignon, 1309–77. Also **Babylonian exile.**
ba·by's-breath (bā'bēz-breth') *n.* **1.** An Old World perennial (*Gypsophila paniculata*) with numerous clusters of small, white or pink, fragrant flowers. **2.** Any of certain other fragrant herbs, as the naturalized wild madder of the eastern United States. Also spelled *babies'-breath.*
baby-sit (bā'bē-sit') *v.i.* **·sat, ·sit·ting** *U.S.* To act as a baby sitter.
baby sitter *U.S.* A person employed to take care of young children while the parents are absent: also called *sitter.*
bac·ca·lau·re·ate (bak'ə-lôr'ē-it) *n.* **1.** The degree of bachelor of arts, bachelor of science, etc. **2.** A sermon or address to a graduating class at commencement: also **baccalaureate sermon.** [< Med.L *baccalaureatus* < *baccalaureus*, var. of *baccalaris*, (possibly) a young farmer, ? < LL *bacca* cow; infl. in form by L *bacca lauri* laurel berry]
bac·ca·rat (bak'ə-rä', bak'ə-rä) *n.* A gambling game in which winnings are decided by comparing cards held by the banker with those held by the players. Also **bac·ca·ra** (bak'ə-rä', bak'ə-rä). [< F *baccara*, a game of cards]
bac·cate (bak'āt) *adj. Bot.* **1.** Like a berry. **2.** Bearing berries. Also **bac'cat·ed.** [< L *baccatus* < *bacca* berry]
Bac·chae (bak'ē) *n.pl.* **1.** In Greek mythology, the female companions of Bacchus or Dionysus. **2.** Women taking part in the Dionysian celebrations.
bac·cha·nal (bak'ə-nəl) *n.* **1.** A votary of Bacchus. **2.** A drunken reveler. **3.** *pl.* Bacchanalia; drunken revelries. — *adj.* Bacchanalian. [< L *bacchanalis* of Bacchus]
bac·cha·na·li·a (bak'ə-nā'lē-ə, -nāl'yə) *n.pl.* Drunken revelries; orgies.
Bac·cha·na·li·a (bak'ə-nā'lē-ə, -nāl'yə) *n.pl.* An ancient Roman festival in honor of Bacchus. [< L, neut. pl. of *bacchanalis* of Bacchus]
bac·cha·na·li·an (bak'ə-nā'lē-ən, -nāl'yən) *adj.* Of, pertaining to, or indulging in orgies; carousing; uproariously drunk. — *n.* A bacchanal. — **bac'cha·na'li·an·ism** *n.*
bac·chant (bak'ənt) *n. pl.* **bac·chants** or **bac·chan·tes** (bə-kan'tēz) **1.** A votary of Bacchus. **2.** A carouser; reveler. — *adj.* Given to drunkenness. [< L *bacchans, -antis*, ppr. of *bacchari* to celebrate the festival of Bacchus, carouse < Gk *bacchaein*]
bac·chan·te (bə-kan'tē, bə-kant', bak'ənt) *n.* A female votary of Bacchus. [< F < L *bacchans, -antis*. See BACCHANT.]
bac·chic (bak'ik) *adj.* Riotous; orgiastic; drunken.
Bac·chic (bak'ik) *adj.* Of, pertaining to, or like Bacchus or his rites.

Bac·chus (bak'əs) In classical mythology, the god of wine and revelry: identified with *Dionysus.*
bacci- *combining form* Berry or berries: *bacciform.* [< L *bacca* berry]
bac·cif·er·ous (bak-sif'ər-əs) *adj. Bot.* Bearing or yielding berries. [< L *baccifer* < *bacca* berry + *ferre* to bear]
bac·ci·form (bak'sə-fôrm) *adj.* Berry-shaped.
bac·civ·o·rous (bak-siv'ər-əs) *adj. Zool.* Feeding on berries. [< BACCI- + -VOROUS]
bach (bach) *v.i. Informal* To live as a bachelor; keep house for oneself: usually in the expression **to bach it.**
bach. Bachelor.
Bach (bäkh) A family of German musicians and composers, of whom the best known are **Johann Sebastian,** 1685–1750, and his sons, **Karl Philipp Emanuel,** 1714–88, and **Johann Christian,** 1735–82.
bach·e·lor (bach'ə-lər, bach'lər) *n.* **1.** An unmarried man. **2.** One who has taken his first university or college degree. **3.** A young knight serving under another's banner: also **bach'e·lor-at-arms'. 4.** The crappie. **5.** A young male fur seal kept from the breeding grounds by the older males: also called *holluschick.* Abbr. *b., B.,* **bach.** [< OF *bacheler* < Med.L. *baccalaris.* See BACCALAUREATE.] — **bach'e·lor·hood', bach'e·lor·ship'** *n.*
Bachelor of Arts **1.** A degree usually given by a college or university to a person who has completed a four-year course, or its equivalent, in the humanities. **2.** One who has received this degree. Abbr. *B.A., A.B.*
Bachelor of Science **1.** A degree usually given by a college or university to a person who has completed a four-year course, or its equivalent, in the sciences. **2.** One who has received this degree. Abbr. *B.S., B.Sc., S.B., Sc.B.*
bach·e·lor's-but·ton (bach'ə-lərz-but'n, bach'lərz-) *n.* **1.** Any of several plants with button-shaped flowers or flower heads. **2.** The cornflower (def. 1).
bac·il·lar·y (bas'ə-ler'ē) *adj.* **1.** Rod-shaped: also **ba·cil·li·form** (bə-sil'ə-fôrm). **2.** Pertaining to, characterized by, or caused by bacilli. Also **ba·cil·lar** (bə-sil'ər, bas'ə-lər). [< NL *bacillarius* < *bacillum* rod]
ba·cil·lus (bə-sil'əs) *n. pl.* **·cil·li** (-sil'ī) **1.** *Bacteriol.* Any of a large and numerous class of straight, rod-shaped bacteria including both beneficial and pathogenic species: distinguished from *coccus* and *spirillum* types. **2.** Any of a family (*Bacillaceae*) of straight, rod-shaped, aerobic, spore-forming bacteria, occurring singly or in chains. **3.** A bacterium. For illustration see BACTERIUM. Abbr. *B.* — **Syn.** See MICROBE. [< NL < L *bacillum*, dim. of *baculus* stick]
back¹ (bak) *n.* **1.** The part of the body nearest the spine; in man the hinder, in quadrupeds the upper part, extending from the neck to the base of the spine. ◆ Collateral adjective: *dorsal.* **2.** The backbone. **3.** The rear or posterior part: the *back* of the car. **4.** The farther or other side; the reverse: the *back* of the door. **5.** The part behind or opposite to the part used: the *back* of a knife. **6.** Anything to cover, support, etc., the back: the *back* of a bench. **7.** The part of the body that is clothed: the shirt on his *back.* **8.** Physical strength: Put your *back* into it. **9.** The part of the leaves of a book sewed together into the binding; also, the part of the binding around this part. **10.** The lining attached to the unexposed side of a thing, as for reinforcement. **11.** In football, a member of the offensive or defensive backfield. **12.** *Phonet.* The part of the tongue directly behind the front and below the velum. — **at one's back** Following closely — **behind one's back 1.** Secretly. **2.** Treacherously. — **in back of** Behind; at or to the rear of. — **to be (flat) on one's back** To be helplessly ill. — **to get (or put) one's back up** To become (or make) angry or obstinate. — **to turn one's back on 1.** To show contempt or ill feeling toward by ignoring. **2.** To renounce. — **with one's back to the wall** Cornered; having no alternative but to fight. — *v.t.* **1.** To cause to move backward; reverse the action of: often with *up.* **2.** To furnish with a back; strengthen at the back. **3.** To support; uphold by money or influence: often with *up.* **4.** To bet on; have faith in. **5.** To form a background for. **6.** To mount, as a horse. **7.** To write on the back of; endorse, as a check. — *v.i.* **8.** To move backward: often with *up.* **9.** To shift counterclockwise: said of the wind: opposed to *veer.* — **to back and fill 1.** *Naut.* To stay in mid-channel by alternately filling and spilling the sails, so as to be advanced by the current alone. **2.** *U.S.* To be irresolute; vacillate. — **to back down** To withdraw from a position, abandon a claim, etc. — **to back off** To retreat, as from contact. — **to back out (of)** To withdraw from or refuse to carry out a promise, contest, etc. — **to back water 1.** To retard the progress or reverse the motion of a vessel by reversing the action of the oars or of the propelling machinery. **2.** To withdraw from a position; retract a claim, etc. — *adj.* **1.** In the rear; behind: a *back* room. **2.** Distant; remote: the *back* country. **3.** Of or for a date earlier than the present: a *back* issue. **4.** In arrears; overdue: *back* taxes. **5.** In a backward direction: a *back* thrust. **6.** *Phonet.* Describing those vowels produced with the tongue pulled back in the mouth, as (ōō) in *food.* [OE *bæc*]
back² (bak) *adv.* **1.** At, to, or toward the rear: to move

back. **2.** In, to, or toward a former place: to go *back* home. **3.** In, to, or toward a former condition: My cold has come *back.* **4.** Into time past: to look *back* to happier days. **5.** In return or retort: to talk *back.* **6.** In reserve or concealment: to keep something *back.* **7.** In check or hindrance: Sickness held him *back.* **8.** In withdrawal or repudiation: to take *back* an insult. **— back and forth** First in one direction and then in the opposite. **— back of** *U.S.* Behind. **— to go back on** *Informal* **1.** To fail to keep (an engagement, promise, etc.). **2.** To desert or betray. [< ABACK]
back³ (bak) *n.* A brewer's tub or vat. [< Du. *bak* trough < F *bac* tub, basin]
back·ache (bak′āk′) *n.* An ache or pain in one's back.
Back Bay A residential district of Boston.
back·bench·er (bak′ben′chər) *n. Brit. & Canadian* A junior or unimportant member of a party in parliament.
back·bite (bak′bīt′) *v.t. & v.i.* **·bit, ·bit·ten** (*Informal* ·bit), **·bit·ing** To revile or traduce behind one's back; slander. [< BACK² + BITE] **— back′bit′er** *n.*
back·blocks (bak′bloks′) *n.pl. Austral.* Inland farming areas.
back·board (bak′bôrd′, -bōrd′) *n.* **1.** A board forming or supporting the back of something. **2.** In basketball, the vertical board behind the basket.
back·bone (bak′bōn′) *n.* **1.** The spine or vertebral column. **2.** Something likened to a backbone in function or appearance. **3.** Strength of character. **— back′boned′** *adj.*
back·break·ing (bak′brā′king) *adj.* Physically exhausting.
back country Unpopulated or undeveloped areas.
back·cross (bak′krôs′, -kros′) *Genetics v.t. & v.i.* To cross (a hybrid offspring) with one of its parents. **— *n.*** The offspring of a hybrid and either of the parents.
back·door (bak′dôr′, -dōr′) *adj.* Clandestine; underhand.
back·drop (bak′drop′) *n.* The curtain hung at the rear of a stage, often representing a scene. Also **back cloth.**
backed (bakt) *adj.* **1.** Having a back or backing. **2.** Having or characterized by a (specified kind of) back or backing: used in combination: *low-backed; cardboard-backed.*
back·er (bak′ər) *n.* **1.** One who supports with money; a patron. **2.** One who bets on a contestant.
back·field (bak′fēld′) *n.* **1.** In football, the offensive players stationed behind the linemen or the defensive players behind the linebackers. **2.** The area where these are stationed.
back·fill (bak′fil′) *n.* Soil and other material used to refill an excavation. **— *v.t.*** To refill (an excavation.)
back·fire (bak′fīr′) *n.* **1.** A fire built to check an advancing forest or prairie fire by creating a barren area in its path. **2.** Premature explosion in the cylinder of an internal-combustion engine. **3.** An explosion of unburned fuel in the muffler of an internal-combustion engine. **4.** An explosion in the back part of a gun. **— *v.i.* ·fired, ·fir·ing 1.** To set or use a backfire. **2.** To explode in a backfire. **3.** To react in an unexpected and untoward manner: His scheme *backfired.*
back formation *Ling.* **1.** The creation by analogy of a new word from an existing word, where the existing word is mistakenly assumed to be a derivative of the new word. **2.** A word so formed, as *enthuse* from *enthusiasm.*
back·gam·mon (bak′gam′ən, bak/gam′ən) *n.* **1.** A game played by two persons, on a special board, the moves of the pieces being determined by dice throws. **2.** A victory in this game before the defeated player advances all his men beyond the first six points. **— *v.t.*** To win a backgammon from. [ME *back gamen* back game; because sometimes the pieces must go back to the start]
back·ground (bak′ground′) *n.* **1.** That part in a picture against which the principal elements, motifs, or subjects are represented. **2.** Ground in the rear or distance. **3.** A subordinate position; obscurity; retirement. **4.** The aggregate of one's experiences, education, etc. **5.** The events leading up to or causing a situation, event, etc. **6.** Music or sound effects employed in accompaniment to a dialogue, recital, etc.
back·hand (bak′hand′) *n.* **1.** Handwriting that slopes toward the left. **2.** The hand turned backward in making a stroke, as with a racket. **3.** A stroke made with the back of the hand turned forward, as in tennis. **— *adj.*** Backhanded. **— *adv.*** With a backhand stroke.
back·hand·ed (bak′han′did) *adj.* **1.** Delivered or made with the back of the hand, or with the back of the hand turned forward, as a stroke in tennis. **2.** Halfhearted, devious, and often insincere: a *backhanded* compliment. **3.** Sloping to the left, as handwriting. **4.** Turned or twisted in a direction opposite to the usual, as a cable. **— back′hand′ed·ly** *adv.* **— back′hand′ed·ness** *n.*
back·house (bak′hous′) *n. U.S.* A privy.
back·ing (bak′ing) *n.* **1.** Support or assistance. **2.** Supporters or promoters collectively. **3.** Endorsement. **4.** Motion backward. **5.** The back of anything; especially, anything added at the back for support or strength.
back·lash (bak′lash′) *n.* **1.** *Mech.* **a** A reaction or jarring recoil, as of the parts of a machine when poorly fitted or subjected to sudden strain. **b** The amount of loose play in the

parts subject to such reaction or recoil. **2.** In angling, a snarl or tangle of line on a reel, caused by a faulty cast. **3.** A sudden, violent recoil or reaction, as of popular opinion.
back·log (bak′lôg′, -log′) *n. U.S.* **1.** A large log at the back of an open fireplace to maintain and concentrate the heat. **2.** Any reserve supply, as of funds, business orders, etc.
back·most (bak′mōst) *adj.* Farthest to the rear; hindmost.
back number **1.** An out-of-date issue of a magazine or newspaper. **2.** *U.S. Informal* An old-fashioned, out-of-date person or thing.
back·out (bak′out′) *n. Aerospace* A progressive undoing of steps taken during a countdown that has been halted.
back·pack (bak′pak′) *n.* A bag worn on the back and having a lightweight frame to hold rations, a sleeping bag, mess kit, etc., for camping out, mountain climbing, etc.
back·rest (bak′rest′) *n.* A support for or at the back.
back seat **1.** A seat in the rear, as of a vehicle, hall, etc. **2.** An inconspicuous or subordinate position.
back-seat driver (bak′sēt′) A passenger in an automobile who persists in directing and advising the driver.
back·set (bak′set′) *n.* **1.** A reverse; setback. **2.** An eddy.
back·sheesh, back·shish (bak′shēsh) See BAKSHEESH.
back·side (bak′sīd′) *n.* **1.** The hind part. **2.** The rump.
back·sight (bak′sīt′) *n.* In surveying: **a** A sight laid on a known point in order to determine the position or elevation of an instrument. **b** A sight laid on a previously taken instrument station from a newly located point.
back·slide (bak′slīd′) *v.i.* **·slid, ·slid** or **·slid·den, ·slid·ing** To return to wrong or sinful ways. **— back′slid′er** *n.*
back·spin (bak′spin′) *n.* Reverse rotation of a round object that is moving forward, as a golf ball, baseball, etc.
back·stage (*n., adv.* bak′stāj′; *adj.* bak′stāj′) *adv.* **1.** In or toward the portion of a theater behind the stage, including the wings, dressing rooms, etc. **2.** To or toward the back portion of the stage. **— *n.*** The back portion of the stage. **— *adj.*** Situated or occurring backstage.
back·stairs (bak′stârz′) *n.* Stairs in back. **— *adj.*** Indirect; underhand. Also **back′stair′.**
back·stay (bak′stā′) *n.* **1.** *Naut.* A stay supporting a mast on the aft side. For illustration see SHROUD². **2.** A support for various mechanical purposes. **3.** The leather band at the back and sides of a shoe. For illustration see SHOE.
back·stitch (bak′stich′) *n.* A stitch made by carrying the thread back half the length of the preceding stitch. **— *v.t. & v.i.*** To sew with backstitches.
back·stop (bak′stop′) *n. U.S.* A fence, wire screen, or net to stop the ball from going too far, as in baseball, tennis, etc.
back·strap (bak′strap′) *n.* The harness band from crupper to hames or saddle. For illustration see HARNESS.
back·stretch (bak′strech′) *n.* That part of a racecourse farthest from the spectators, usually a straightaway.
back·stroke (bak′strōk′) *n.* **1.** A return blow or stroke. **2.** A backhanded stroke. **3.** In swimming, a stroke executed while on one's back. **— *v.* ·stroked, ·strok·ing 1.** To strike, as a ball, with a backstroke. **— *v.i.* 2.** To swim with a backstroke.
back·swept (bak′swept′) *adj. Aeron.* Sweptback.
back·sword (bak′sôrd′, -sōrd′) *n.* **1.** A sword with one sharp edge; a broadsword. **2.** A stick with a basket hilt, used in fencing practice, or in singlestick. **3.** One who uses a backsword: also **back′sword′man** (-mən), **back′swords′man.**
back talk Impudent retort; insolent answering back.
back·track (bak′trak′) *v.i. U.S.* **1.** To retrace one's steps. **2.** To withdraw from a position, undertaking, etc.
back·ward (bak′wərd) *adv.* **1.** Toward the back; to the rear. **2.** With the back foremost. **3.** In reverse order. **4.** From better to worse. **5.** To or into time past: to look *backward.* Also **back′wards.** **— *adj.* 1.** Turned to the back or rear; reversed. **2.** Done the reverse or wrong way. **3.** Behind in growth or development; retarded; slow. **4.** Hesitant; bashful. **— back′ward·ly** *adv.* **— back′ward·ness** *n.*
back·wash (bak′wosh′, -wôsh′) *n.* **1.** The water moved backward, as by a boat, oars, etc. **2.** The backward current of air set up by aircraft propellers, etc. **3.** Any condition resulting from some previous act, remark, etc.
back·wa·ter (bak′wô′tər, -wot′ər) *n.* **1.** Water turned or held back, as by a dam, a current, etc. **2.** Any place or condition regarded as stagnant, backward, etc.
back·woods (bak′wo͝odz′) *U.S. n.pl.* **1.** Wild, heavily wooded, or sparsely settled districts. **2.** An area considered backward or rude. **— *adj.*** In, from, or like the backwoods: also **back′wood′.** **— back′woods′man** (-mən) *n.*
ba·con (bā′kən) *n.* The salted and dried or smoked back and sides of the hog. **— to bring home the bacon** *U.S. Informal* **1.** To provide food, etc. **2.** To succeed. [< OF < OHG *bacho, bahho* ham, side of bacon]
Ba·con (bā′kən), **Francis,** 1561–1626, first Baron Verulam, Viscount St. Albans, English philosopher, essayist, and statesman. **— Nathaniel,** 1647–76, American colonial leader of a rebellion (1676) demanding governmental reforms in Virginia. **— Roger,** 1214?–94, English scientist and philosopher.

Ba·co·ni·an (bā-kō′nē-ən) *adj.* Of or pertaining to Francis Bacon, his philosophy, or his literary style. — *n.* **1.** An adherent of the philosophy of Francis Bacon. **2.** A believer in the Baconian theory.

Baconian theory The theory that Francis Bacon wrote the plays attributed to Shakespeare.

bac·te·re·mi·a (bak′tə-rē′mē-ə) *n. Pathol.* The presence of bacteria in the blood. [< BACTER(IO)- + -EMIA]

bac·te·ri·a (bak-tir′ē-ə) Plural of BACTERIUM.

bac·te·ri·cide (bak-tir′ə-sīd) *n.* An agent destructive of bacteria. — **bac·te·ri·ci′dal** *adj.*

bac·te·rin (bak′tə-rin) *n.* A vaccine prepared from dead pathogenic bacteria. Also **bac′te·rine** (-rēn).

bacterio- *combining form* Of or pertaining to bacteria: *bacterioscopy.* Also, before vowels, **bacter-.** Also **bacteri-, bactero-.** [< Gk. *bakterion,* dim. of *baktron* rod, staff]

bacteriol. or **bact.** Bacteriological; bacteriologist; bacteriology.

bac·te·ri·ol·o·gy (bak-tir′ē-ol′ə-jē) *n.* The branch of biology and medicine that deals with bacteria. — **bac·te·ri·o·log′i·cal** (bak-tir′ē-ə-loj′i-kəl) *adj.* — **bac·te·ri·o·log′i·cal·ly** *adv.* — **bac·te·ri·ol′o·gist** *n.*

bac·te·ri·ol·y·sis (bak-tir′ē-ol′ə-sis) *n.* The destruction of bacteria within or outside of the body. — **bac·te·ri·o·lyt′ic** (bak-tir′ē-ə-lit′ik) *adj.*

bac·te·ri·o·phage (bak-tir′ē-ə-fāj′) *n. Bacteriol.* An ultramicroscopic filter-passing agent that has the power of destroying bacteria and of inducing bacterial mutation.

bac·te·ri·os·co·py (bak-tir′ē-os′kə-pē) *n.* Microscopic study or investigation of bacteria. — **bac·te·ri·o·scop·ic** (bak-tir′ē-ə-skop′ik) or **·i·cal** *adj.* — **bac·te′ri·o·scop′i·cal·ly** *adv.*

bac·te·ri·o·stat·ic (bak-tir′ē-ə-stat′ik) *adj. Bacteriol.* Arresting the growth or development of bacteria.

bac·te·ri·um (bak-tir′ē-əm) *n. pl.* **·te·ri·a** (-tir′ē-ə) Any of numerous widely distributed unicellular microorganisms (class *Schizomycetes*), exhibiting both plant and animal characteristics, and in their three varieties of *bacillus, coccus,* and *spirillum* ranging from the harmless and beneficial to the intensely virulent and lethal. — **Syn.** See MICROBE. ◆ *Bacteria* normally takes a plural verb, but when used to designate a class, it may take a singular, as *This bacteria is new.* [< NL < Gk. *baktērion,* dim. of *baktron* staff, stick] — **bac·te′ri·al** *adj.* — **bac·te′ri·al·ly** *adv.*

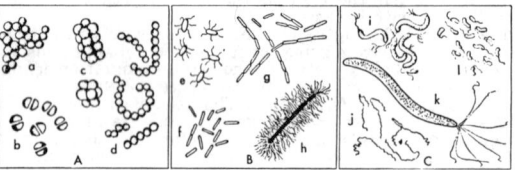

TYPES OF BACTERIA

A Cocci: a, Staphylococcus; b, Diplococcus; c, Sarcina; d, Streptococcus. B Bacilli: e, Salmonella typhi; f, Clostridium sporogenes; g, Bacillus subtilis; h, Bacillus proteus. C Spirilla: i, Spirillum undulum; j, Spirochetes; k, Thiospirillum; l, Vibrio comma.

bac·ter·ize (bak′tə-rīz) *v.t.* **·ized, ·iz·ing** To change by the action of bacteria. — **bac′ter·i·za′tion** *n.*

bac·ter·oid (bak′tə-roid) *adj.* Resembling the forms of bacteria. Also **bac′ter·oi′dal, bac·te·ri·oid** (bak-tir′ē-oid). — *n.* A bacterium found in tubercles on the roots of legumes.

Bac·tri·a (bak′trē-ə) A satrapy of the ancient Persian Empire, lying partly in NE Afghanistan and partly in the southern Soviet Union. — **Bac′tri·an** *adj. & n.*

Bactrian camel See under CAMEL.

ba·cu·li·form (bə-kyōō′li-fôrm) *adj.* Shaped like a rod; straight. [< L *baculum* rod + -FORM]

bac·u·line (bak′yə-lin, -līn) *adj.* Of or pertaining to a rod or to a beating with a rod. [< L *baculum* rod]

bad¹ (bad) *adj.* **worse, worst 1.** Not good in any manner or degree. **2.** Evil; wicked; immoral. **3.** Defective; worthless: *bad* wiring. **4.** Faulty or incorrect: *bad* grammar. **5.** Not valid or sound. **6.** Not sufficient; inadequate. **7.** Lacking skill or proficiency: a *bad* poet. **8.** Distressing; unfavorable: *bad* news. **9.** Offensive; disagreeable: a *bad* taste. **10.** Harmful; noxious: *bad* for the eyes. **11.** Rotted; spoiled. **12.** Severe: a *bad* storm. **13.** Sick; in ill health. **14.** Sorry; regretful: He felt *bad* about it. — **in bad** *Informal* **1.** In difficulty. **2.** In disfavor. — **not bad** Rather good: also **not half bad, not so bad.** — *n.* **1.** That which is bad. **2.** Those who are bad: with *the.* **3.** A bad state or condition; wickedness. — **to go bad** or **to the bad** *Informal* To degenerate; become bad. — *adv. Informal* Badly. [ME *bad, baddle,* ? < OE *bæddel* effeminate man] — **bad′ness** *n.*

— **Syn.** (adj.) **2.** evil, immoral, sinful, depraved, corrupt, vile, villainous, rascally, mischievous, naughty, base, false, fraudulent. **4.** wrong. **6.** defective, inferior, imperfect, inadequate. **7.** incompetent. **8.** unfortunate, unlucky. **9.** noxious, foul. **10.** hurtful, baneful, unwholesome, deleterious, detrimental. **11.** decayed, putrid. **12.** serious, grave.

◆ **bad, badly** Either form is standard in the sense of "ill" or "regretful," as *He felt bad, He felt badly,* but *bad* is usually preferred for more formal contexts.

bad² (bad) Archaic past tense of BID.

Ba·da·joz (bä′thä-hōth′) A Province of western Spain, constituting Lower Estremadura; 8,342 sq. mi.; pop. 834,370 (1960); capital, Badajoz; pop. 98,088.

bad blood Hostility; long-standing enmity; strife.

bad·der·locks (bad′ər-loks′) *n.* An edible European seaweed (*Alaria esculenta*). [Origin uncertain]

bade (bad) Past tense of BID.

Ba·den (bäd′n) A former state of SW Germany; currently part of Baden-Württemberg.

Ba·den-Ba·den (bäd′n-bäd′n) A resort city of southern Baden-Württemberg, West Germany; site of famous mineral springs; pop. 38,852 (est. 1970).

Ba·den-Pow·ell (bäd′n-pō′əl), Lord, 1857–1941, Robert Stephenson Smyth, British soldier; founder of the Boy Scouts in 1908.

Ba·den-Würt·tem·berg (bäd′n-wûr′təm-bûrg, *Ger.* bä′dən-vür′təm-berkh) A State in SW West Germany; 13,803 sq. mi.; pop. 8,909,700 (est. 1970); capital, Stuttgart.

badge (baj) *n.* **1.** Any device worn to indicate rank, office, membership in an organization, an award or prize, etc. **2.** Any distinguishing mark, token, or insignia. — *v.t.* **badged, badg·ing** To decorate or provide with a badge. [ME *bage, bagge*; ult. origin unknown]

badg·er (baj′ər) *n.* **1.** A small, burrowing, nocturnal, carnivorous mammal, with a broad body, short legs, and long-clawed toes. There are several species, including the American badger (*Taxidea americana*), the European badger (*Meles meles*), and the balisaur and the ratel of Asia. **2.** In Australia, the bandicoot or the wombat. **3.** The fur of a badger, or a brush made of its hair. — *v.t.* To harass; nag at. [? BADGE, with ref. to mark on head]

AMERICAN BADGER

(About 30 inches long; tail 6 inches)

Badger State Nickname of WISCONSIN.

bad·i·nage (bad′ə-näzh′, bad′ə-nij) *n.* Playful raillery; banter. — **Syn.** See BANTER. — *v.t.* **naged, nag·ing** To subject to or tease with badinage. [< F < *badiner* jest < *badin* silly, jesting < Provençal *bader* < LL *badare* to gape]

bad·lands (bad′landz′) *n.pl.* A barren area characterized by numerous ridges, peaks, and mesas cut by erosion.

Bad Lands An arid, eroded plateau in South Dakota and Nebraska. Also **Bad′lands.**

bad·ly (bad′lē) *adv.* **1.** In a bad manner; improperly, imperfectly, or grievously. ◆ See note under BAD. **2.** *Informal* Very much; greatly: I need to see you *badly.*

bad·man (bad′man′) *n. pl.* **·men** (-men′) A desperado.

bad·min·ton (bad′min·tən) *n.* **1.** A game played by batting a shuttlecock back and forth over a high, narrow net with a light racket. **2.** A drink made with claret. [after *Badminton* in England, the estate of the Duke of Beaufort]

Ba·do·glio (bä-dō′lyō), **Pietro,** 1871–1956, Italian military and political leader; premier 1943–44.

bad-tem·pered (bad′tem′pərd) *adj.* Having a bad temper; cross; irritable.

B.A.E. 1. Bachelor of Aeronautical Engineering. **2.** Bachelor of Arts in Education

Bae·da (bē′də) See BEDE.

Bae·de·ker (bā′di-kər) *n.* **1.** Any of a series of travelers' guidebooks issued by Karl Baedeker, 1801–59, German publisher, or his firm. **2.** Loosely, any guidebook.

Bae·yer (bā′yər), **Johann Friedrich Wilhelm Adolf von,** 1835–1917, German chemist.

baff (baf) *v.t. & v.i.* In golf, to strike under the ball so as to send it too high in the air. — *n.* **1.** *Scot.* A blow. **2.** In golf, a baffed stroke. [cf. OF *baffe* blow]

Baf·fin (baf′in), **William,** 1584–1622, English seafarer and explorer.

Baffin Bay A part of the North Atlantic between Greenland and the Northwest Territories, Canada. See map of GREENLAND.

Baffin Island The largest and most easterly island in the Arctic Archipelago, Northwest Territories, Canada; 197,754 sq. mi. Also **Baffin Land.** See map of GREENLAND.

baf·fle (baf′əl) *v.* **·fled, ·fling** *v.t.* **1.** To confuse mentally; perplex: The problem *baffled* him. **2.** To foil or frustrate; hinder. **3.** *Naut.* To beat back or impede: The ship was *baffled* by the storm. — *v.i.* **4.** To struggle to no avail. — *n.* **1.** *Electronics* A partition used to prevent transmission of sound waves between the front and rear of a loudspeaker and so to improve the fidelity of sound reproduction. **2.** Any movable surface, as a board, used to control and direct sound effects in filming motion pictures. **3.** A partition, as in a furnace or muffler, to alter the flow of gases. **4.** A grating in a pipe or channel to control eddies and secure a uniform flow. **5.** A baffling, or the state of one who is bewildered or confused. [Origin uncertain] — **baf′fle·ment** *n.* — **baf′fler** *n.* — **baf′fling** *adj.* — **baf′fling·ly** *adv.*

— **Syn.** (verb) **2.** *Baffle, balk, thwart, foil,* and *frustrate* mean to prevent the carrying out of a plan or intention. *Baffle* refers to the feeling of perplexity or confusion that arises when plans are blocked. *Balk* suggests that an obstacle has been put into our path; *thwart*, that we have been turned aside from our course. To be *foiled* is to be made to miss one's aim, while *frustrate* may be applied to any means or circumstances that defeat a purpose in any way. Compare HINDER. — **Ant.** help, aid, assist, promote, advance.

baf·fle·plate (baf'əl-plāt') *n.* A baffle (defs. 3 and 4).

baf·fy (baf'ē) *n. pl.* **·fies** A wooden golf club with a short shaft and deeply pitched face, for lofting the ball. [< BAFF]

bag (bag) *n.* **1.** A sack or pouch, usually of paper, cloth, or leather, used as a receptacle. **2.** The amount a bag will hold. **3.** A woman's purse. **4.** A suitcase or satchel. **5.** The quantity of game caught or·killed in hunting. **6.** A bulging or baggy part, as of a sail. **7.** A sac or similar part in various animals, as the udder of a cow. **8.** In baseball slang, a base. *Abbr. bg.* **9.** *U.S. Slang* An unattractive, slovenly woman. **10.** *Slang* One's special interest, talent, hobby, pastime, etc. *Abbr.* (for defs. 1, 2) *B/-*, (pl. *B/s*). **— in the bag** *U.S. Slang* Like game already caught; assured; certain. **— to be left holding the bag** *U.S. Informal* To be left to assume full responsibility or blame. **— v. bagged, bag·ging** *v.t.* **1.** To put into a bag. **2.** To cause to fill out or bulge like a bag. **3.** To capture or kill, as game. **— v.i. 4.** To bulge or swell like a bag. **5.** To hang loosely. [? < ON *baggi* pack, bundle]
— Syn. (noun) **1.** purse, poke², sack, pouch. **—** (verb) See CATCH.

bag and baggage *Informal* **1.** With all one's possessions; He cleared out *bag and baggage*. **2.** Entirely; completely.

ba·gasse (bə·gas') *n.* The dry refuse of sugar cane after the juice has been expressed, used in making paper and fiberboard: also called *megass, megasse.* Also **ba·gass'**. [< F < Sp. *bagazo* refuse of grapes, olives, etc., after pressing]

bag·a·telle (bag'ə·tel') *n.* **1.** A trifle. **2.** A game similar to billiards. **3.** A pinball. **4.** *Music* A short composition, usually for piano. [< F < Ital. *bagatella,* dim. of *baga* sack]

Bage·hot (baj'ət), **Walter,** 1826–77, English economist and political writer.

ba·gel (bā'gəl) *n.* A doughnut-shaped roll of yeast dough simmered in water and baked. [< Yiddish < *beigen* to twist]

bag·gage (bag'ij) *n.* **1.** *Chiefly U.S.* The trunks, packages, etc., of a traveler. **2.** An army's movable equipment. **3.** A lively, pert, or impudent young woman. **4.** *Archaic* A prostitute. [< MF *bagage* < *bague* bundle < Med.L *baga* sack]

bag·gage·mas·ter (bag'ij·mas'tər, -mäs'-) *n.* One in charge of receiving and sending baggage, as at a railway station.

bag·gie (bäg'ē, beg'ē) *n. Scot.* The stomach.

bag·ging (bag'ing) *n.* A coarse cloth for making bags.

bag·gy (bag'ē) *adj.* **bag·gi·er, bag·gi·est** Like a bag; loose; bulging. **— bag'gi·ly** *adv.* **— bag'gi·ness** *n.*

Bagh·dad (bag'dad, bäg·däd') The capital of Iraq, in the central part on the Tigris; pop. 502,503 (1965). Also **Bag'·dad.**

bag·man (bag'mən) *n. pl.* **·men** (-men', -mən) *U.S. Slang* A collector of money for racketeers.

bagn·io (ban'yō, bän'-) *n.* **1.** A brothel. **2.** A Turkish or Italian bathhouse. **3.** In the Orient, a prison. [< Ital. *bagno* < L *balneum* < Gk. *balaneion* bath]

bag·pipe (bag'pīp') *n. Often pl.* A reed musical instrument having a chanter for playing melodies, and several drone pipes, the air being forced through them from a leather bag inflated by the player. **— bag'pip'er** *n.*

B.Agr. or **B.Ag.** Bachelor of Agriculture (L *Baccalaureus Agriculturae*).

B.Ag.Sc. Bachelor of Agricultural Science.

ba·guette (ba·get') *n.* **1.** A gem or crystal cut in long, narrow, rectangular form. **2.** This form. **3.** *Archit.* A small, bead-shaped molding. Also **ba·guet'.** [< F < Ital. *bacchetta,* dim. of *bacchio* < L *baculum* staff]

Ba·gui·o (bag'ē-ō, bä'gē-ō) A city in northern Luzon; the summer capital of the Philippines; pop. 56,900 (1964).

bag·worm (bag'wûrm') *n.* The larva of any of certain moths (family *Psychidae*), characterized by its baglike cocoon. For illustration see COCOON.

bah (bä, ba) *interj.* An exclamation of contempt or dismissal.

ba·ha·dur (bə·hô'dŏor, -hä'-) *n.* A Hindu title of respect generally given to European officers in state documents or ceremonies. [< Hind. *bahādur* hero]

Ba·ha·i (bə·hä'ē) *n. pl.* **Ba·ha·is** A teacher or follower of Bahaism.

Ba·ha·ism (bə·hä'iz·əm) *n.* A religious system based on Babism founded in 1863 by Hussein Ali. It teaches the essential unity of all religions. **— Ba·ha'ist** *n. & adj.*

Ba·ha·ma Islands (bə·hä'mə, -hā'-) An island group in the

North Atlantic between Florida and Hispaniola; former British Colony, independent 1973; 5,386 sq. mi.; pop. 202,400 (est. 1973); capital, Nassau. Also **Ba·ha'mas.**

Ba·ha·sa Indonesia (bä·hä'sə) The official name for the language of Indonesia, based on Malay.

Ba·ha·ul·lah (bä·hä·ŏol·lä') The title assumed by Hussein Ali, 1817–92, Persian religious leader and founder of Bahaism. Also **Ba·ha' Ul·lah'.** [< Persian, splendor of God]

Ba·ha·wal·pur (bə·hä'wəl·pŏor) **1.** A city in Pakistan; pop. 84,377 (est. 1961). **2.** A former state of NW India, included in Pakistan, 1947; later a division of the Province of Punjab.

Ba·hi·a (bə·ē'ə) **1.** A coastal State of eastern Brazil; 217,456 sq. mi.; pop. 5,987,000 (est. 1960); capital, Salvador. Also **Ba·i'a. 2.** The former name for SALVADOR, Brazil.

Ba·hí·a Blan·ca (bä·ē'ä vläng'kä) A port city in eastern Argentina; pop. 135,800 (est. 1956).

Bah·rein (bä·rān') An archipelago in the Persian Gulf near the coast of Saudi Arabia, since 1971 an independent emirate; 213 sq. mi.; pop. 260,000 (est. 1974); capital, Manama. Also **Bah·rain', Bah·rayn'.**

baht (bät) *n. pl.* **bahts** or **baht 1.** The silver monetary unit of Thailand, equivalent to 100 stangs: formerly called *tical.* **2.** A tical, a Thai unit of weight. Also spelled *bat.* [< Siamese]

Ba·ia (bä'yä) A village in Campania, southern Italy; site of ancient **Bai·ae** (bä'ē), a Roman bathing resort.

Bai·kal (bī·käl') The world's deepest freshwater lake, in the southern part of the Soviet Union; 12,150 sq. mi.; greatest depth, 5,712 ft.

bail¹ (bāl) *n.* A scoop or bucket for dipping out fluids, as from a boat. **— v.t. & v.i. 1.** To dip (water) from a boat with a bail. **2.** To clear (a boat) of water by dipping out. **— to bail out** To jump with parachute from an aircraft. [< OF *baille,* ? < LL *bacula,* dim. of *baca, bacca* shallow trough, tub] **— bail'er** *n.*

bail² (bāl) *n.* **1.** A partition between stalls of a stable. **2.** In cricket, one of the crosspieces of the wicket. **3.** *pl. Obs.* Palisades. [< OF *baile* barrier, ? < *bailler* to enclose]

bail³ (bāl) *Law n.* **1.** One who becomes surety for the debt or default of another, especially of a person under arrest. **2.** The security or guaranty given or agreed upon. **3.** Release, or the privilege of release, on bail. **— to go bail** *U.S. Slang* To provide bail (n. def. 2). **— Syn.** See SECURITY. **— v.t. 1.** To release or obtain the release of (an arrested person) on bail for appearance at a stipulated time: often with *out.* **2.** To deliver, as goods, to another's disposition or care without transference of ownership. [< OF, power, custody < *baillier* to guard, control < L *bajulare* to carry, manage]

bail⁴ (bāl) *n.* **1.** The semicircular handle of a pail, kettle, etc. **2.** An arch-shaped support, as for a canopy. **— v.t.** To provide with a bail or handle. [< ON *beygla* hook, ring]

bail·a·ble (bā'lə·bəl) *adj. Law* Capable of being bailed.

Bai·le Á·tha Cli·ath (bä'lyä ä clē'ä) The Irish name for DUBLIN.

bail·ee (bā·lē') *n. Law* One to whom property is bailed.

bai·ley (bā'lē) *n. pl.* **·leys** The outer court of a castle, or the wall around it: chiefly in proper names, as in *Old Bailey.* Also **bai'lie.** [ME *baili, bailie,* var. of *bayle* castle wall]

Bai·ley (bā'lē), **Liberty Hyde,** 1858–1954, U.S. horticulturist and writer. **— Nathan** or **Nathaniel,** died 1742, English lexicographer.

bai·lie (bā'lē) *n.* **1.** *Scot.* A municipal officer corresponding to an alderman in England. **2.** *Obs.* A bailiff. [< OF *bailli* bailiff]

bai·liff (bā'lif) *n.* **1.** A court officer having custody of prisoners under arraignment. **2.** A sheriff's deputy for serving processes and warrants of arrest. **3.** One who oversees an estate for the owner; a steward. **4.** *Brit.* A subordinate magistrate with jurisdiction limited to a certain district or to certain functions, as keeping the peace. [< OF *baillif* < L *bajalus* porter, manager]

bai·li·wick (bā'lə·wik) *n.* **1.** The office, jurisdiction, or district of a bailiff. **2.** *U.S.* A person's own area of authority or competence. [< BAILI(E) + OE *wīc* village]

bail·ment (bāl'mənt) *n.* The act of bailing an accused person, goods, etc.

bail·or (bā'lər, bā'lôr') *n. Law* One who delivers goods, etc., to another in bailment.

bails·man (bālz'mən) *n. pl.* **·men** (-mən) One who provides bail for another.

Bai·ly's beads (bā'lēz) *Astron.* A series of luminous points appearing along the advancing edge of the moon's disk just before totality in a solar eclipse. [after Francis *Baily,* 1774–1844, English astronomer]

Bain (bān), **Alexander,** 1818–1903, Scottish psychologist.

bain-ma·rie (bań·mȧ·rē') *n. pl.* **bains-ma·rie** (bań-) *French* A double boiler.

Bai·ram (bī'räm) *n.* Either of two Moslem festivals, one (**lesser Bairam**) following immediately after Ramadan, and the other (**greater Bairam**) seventy days later. [< Turkish]

BAGPIPE

b Bag. *c* Chanter. *d* Bass drone. *p* Tenor drones.

Baird (bârd), **John Logie**, 1888–1946, Scottish inventor.

Baird Mountains (bârd) A range in NW Alaska.

bairn (bârn) *n. Scot.* A young child; a son or daughter.

bait[1] (bāt) *n.* **1.** Food or other enticement placed as a lure in a trap, on a hook, etc. **2.** Any allurement or enticement. **3.** A halt for food or refreshment during a journey. — *v.t.* **1.** To put food or some other lure on or in: to *bait* a trap. **2.** To set dogs upon for sport: to *bait* a bear. **3.** To harass; torment. **4.** To lure; entice. **5.** *Obs.* To feed (a horse, etc.) while resting. — *v.i.* **6.** *Obs.* To stop for rest and refreshment. [< ON *beita* food] — **bait′er** *n.* — **Syn.** (verb) **3.** badger, heckle, ride, hound[1], tease.

bait[2] (bāt) See BATE[3].

baith (bāth) *adj., pron., & conj. Scot.* Both.

baize (bāz) *n.* **1.** A plain, loosely woven cotton or woolen fabric, usually dyed green and napped to imitate felt, used for table covers, etc. **2.** An article made of this fabric. [< OF *baies*, fem. pl. of *bai* chestnut brown < L *badius*]

Ba·ja Ca·li·for·nia (bä′hä kä′lē·fôr′nyä), **Baja California Sur** (sŏŏr′). See LOWER CALIFORNIA.

bake (bāk) *v.* **baked, bak·ing** *v.t.* **1.** To cook (bread, pastry, etc.) by dry and continuous heat, as in an oven. **2.** To harden or vitrify by heat, as bricks or pottery. — *v.i.* **3.** To bake bread, pastry, etc. **4.** To become baked or hardened by heat, as soil. — *n.* **1.** A baking, or the amount baked. **2.** *U.S.* A social gathering at which certain of the foods are baked: a *clambake*. **3.** *Scot.* A cracker. [OE *bacan*]

bake·ap·ple (bāk′ap′əl) *n. Canadian* The cloudberry. Also **bake′-ap′ple, bake′ ap′ple, baked′-ap′ple berry**.

bake·house (bāk′hous′) *n.* A bakery.

Ba·ke·lite (bā′kə·līt) *n.* Any of a group of thermosetting plastics formed by the chemical reaction of phenol, formaldehyde, and their derivatives, having a wide range of properties and uses: a trade name. Also **ba′ke·lite**. [after Leo Hendrik *Baekeland*, 1863–1944, U.S. chemist]

bak·er (bā′kər) *n.* **1.** One who bakes and sells bread, cake, etc. **2.** A portable oven.

Ba·ker (bā′kər), **George Pierce**, 1866–1935, U.S. educator and editor. — **Newton Diehl**, 1871–1937, U.S. statesman and jurist; secretary of war 1916–21. — **Ray Stannard**, 1870–1946, U.S. author: pseudonym *David Grayson*. — **Sir Samuel White**, 1821–93, English explorer in Africa.

Baker, Mount A peak in the Cascade Range, northern Washington; 10,750 ft.

baker's dozen Thirteen: from a former custom of giving an excess to avoid penalties exacted for short weight or measure.

Ba·kers·field (bā′kərz·fēld) A city in southern California; pop. 56,848.

bak·er·y (bā′kər·ē, bāk′rē) *n. pl.* **·er·ies** **1.** A place for baking bread, cake, etc. **2.** A shop where bread, cake, etc., are sold: also **bake′shop′**.

bak·ing (bā′king) *n.* **1.** The act of one who or that which bakes. **2.** The quantity baked.

baking powder A finely powdered mixture of baking soda and an acid salt, giving off carbon dioxide when moist, used as a leavening agent in baking.

baking soda Sodium bicarbonate.

bak·la·va (bä′klə·vä′, bä′klə·vä′) *n.* An eastern Mediterranean pastry made of thin layers of dough filled with honey and chopped nuts. [< Turkish *baklawa*]

bak·sheesh (bak′shēsh) *n.* In India, Turkey, etc., a gratuity or a gift of alms. — *v.t. & v.i.* To give a tip or alms (to). Also spelled *backsheesh, bakshish*: also **bak′shish**. [< Persian *bakhshīsh* < *bakhshīdan* to give]

Ba·ku (bä·kŏŏ′) The fourth largest city in the Soviet Union, capital of the Azerbaijan S.S.R., an oil center and port on the Caspian Sea; pop. 847,000 (1970).

Ba·ku·nin (bä·kŏŏ′nyin), **Mikhail**, 1814–76, Russian anarchist writer.

bal. Balance; balancing.

Bal. Baluchistan.

Ba·laam (bā′ləm) In the Bible, a prophet hired to curse the Israelites but who blessed them by God's command after his donkey spoke to him. *Num.* xxii.

Ba·la·ki·rev (bä·lä′ki·ryif), **Mili**, 1837–1910, Russian composer.

Bal·a·kla·va (bal′ə·klä′və) A port village in the SE Soviet Union, in the Crimea on the Black Sea.

bal·a·lai·ka (bal′ə·lī′kə) *n.* A Russian musical stringed instrument having a triangular body. [< Russian]

bal·ance (bal′əns) *n.* **1.** *Sometimes pl.* An instrument for weighing; especially, a bar with two matched pans suspended from each end, that pivots on a central point as weights are placed in the pans. **2.** Figuratively, the scale by which deeds and principles are weighed and destinies determined. **3.** The power or authority to decide and determine. **4.** A state of equilibrium or equal relationship; equipoise: the *balance* of the solar system. **5.** Bodily poise: to lose one's *balance* and fall. **6.** Mental or emotional stability. **7.** Harmonious proportion, as in the design or arrangement of parts in a whole. **8.** Something used to produce an equilibrium; counterpoise. **9.** The act of balancing or weighing. **10.** In bookkeeping: **a** Equality between the debit and credit totals of an account. **b** A difference between such totals; the excess on either side. **11.** *U.S.* Whatever is left over; remainder. **12.** A balance wheel. **13.** A movement in dancing. Abbr. *bal.* — **to strike a balance** To find or take an intermediate position; compromise. — *v.* **·anced, ·anc·ing** *v.t.* **1.** To bring into or keep in equilibrium; poise. **2.** To weigh in a balance. **3.** To compare or weigh in the mind, as alternative courses of action. **4.** To offset or counteract. **5.** To place or keep in proportion. **6.** To be equal or in proportion to. **7.** In bookkeeping: **a** To compute the difference between the debit and credit sides of (an account). **b** To reconcile, as by making certain entries, the debit and credit sides of (an account). **c** To adjust (an account) by paying what is owed. **8.** In dancing, to move toward and then away from: to *balance* one's partner. — *v.i.* **9.** To be or come into equilibrium. **10.** To be equal: The accounts *balance*. **11.** To hesitate; tilt. **12.** In dancing, to balance one's partner. [< F < L *bilanx, -ancis* having two plates < *bis* two + *lanx, lancis* dish, plate] — **bal′ance·a·ble** *adj.*

Bal·ance (bal′əns) *n.* The constellation and sign of the zodiac Libra.

balance of power 1. A distribution of forces among nations such that none may acquire a degree of power dangerous to the others. **2.** The power of a minority to create a majority by joining with a larger group, as in a legislative body.

balance of trade The difference in value between exports and imports of a country.

bal·anc·er (bal′ən·sər) *n.* **1.** One who or that which balances. **2.** A tightrope walker; an acrobat. **3.** *Entomol.* A halter[2]. **4.** *Telecom.* An apparatus used to increase the precision of a radio direction finder.

balance sheet A statement in tabular form to show assets and liabilities, profit and loss, etc., of a business at a specified date. Abbr. *b.s.*

balance wheel The oscillating wheel of a watch or chronometer, that determines its rate of motion.

bal·as (bal′əs) *n. Mineral.* A rose-red variety of ruby spinel. Also **balas ruby**. [< OF *balais* < Arabic *balakhsh* < Persian *Badakhshan*, a Persian district where it is found]

bal·a·ta (bal′ə·tə) *n.* **1.** The juice of the bully tree, used as an elastic gum for making golf balls, insulating wires, etc. **2.** The bully tree. [< Sp. < Tupian]

Ba·la·ton (bä′lä·tŏn), **Lake** A lake in western Hungary; 231 sq. mi.: German *Plattensee*.

ba·laus·tine (bə·lôs′tin) *n.* The pomegranate, or its dried, astringent flowers, bark, or rind. [< L *balaustium* pomegranate flower < Gk. *balaustion*]

Bal·bo (bäl′bō), **Italo**, 1896–1940, Italian statesman and aviator.

bal·bo·a (bal·bō′ə) *n.* The monetary unit of Panama, equivalent to 100 centesimos. Abbr. *b., B.* [after Vasco de *Balboa*]

Bal·bo·a (bal·bō′ə) A port town at the Pacific end of the Panama Canal; pop. 2,568 (est. 1970).

Bal·bo·a (bal·bō′ə, *Sp.* bäl·vō′ä), **Vasco Núñez de**, 1475–1517, Spanish explorer; discovered the Pacific Ocean, 1513.

Balboa Heights The administrative center of the Canal Zone, adjacent to Balboa; pop. 118 (1960).

bal·brig·gan (bal·brig′ən) *n.* **1.** A fine, unbleached, knitted cotton hosiery fabric. **2.** *pl.* Clothes, especially underwear and hose, made of this fabric. — *adj.* Made of balbriggan. [after *Balbriggan*, a town in Ireland where first made]

bal·bu·ti·es (bal·byŏŏ′shi·ēz) *n. Psychiatry* A speech defect characterized by stuttering; stammering. [< NL < L *balbutire* to stammer]

bal·co·ny (bal′kə·nē) *n. pl.* **·nies** **1.** A balustraded platform projecting from a wall of a building. **2.** A projecting gallery in a theater or public building. [< Ital. *balcone* < *balco* scaffold < OHG *balcho* beam] — **bal′co·nied** *adj.*

BALCONY
(With balusters and balustrade)

bald (bôld) *adj.* **1.** Without hair on the head. **2.** Without natural covering or growth, as a mountain. **3.** Unadorned; without embellishments: *bald* prose. **4.** Without disguise; forthright: *bald* blasphemy. **5.** *Zool.* Having white feathers or fur on the head: the *bald* eagle. [? < Welsh *bāl* white] — **bald′ly** *adv.* — **bald′ness** *n.*

bal·da·chin (bôl′də·kin, bôl′-) *n.* **1.** A heavy brocade made of silk and gold: also called *baudekin*. **2.** A canopy of such fabric, as one carried in religious processions. **3.** *Archit.* A canopy of stone or metal, as over an altar or throne. Also **bal′da·quin**. [< F *baldaquin* < Ital *baldacchino* < *Baldacco* Baghdad, where the cloth was first made]

bald cypress A timber tree (genus *Taxodium*) of the swampy regions of the southern United States.

bald eagle See under EAGLE.

Bal·der (bôl′dər) In Norse mythology, god of sunlight, spring, and joy; son of Odin and Frigga; killed by the treachery of Loki. Also **Bal′dr**.

bal·der·dash (bôl′dər·dash) *n.* A meaningless flow of words; nonsense. [Origin uncertain]

bald·faced (bôld′fāst′) *adj.* **1.** Having a white face or white markings on the face: said of animals. **2.** Brash; undisguised: a *baldfaced* lie.

bald·head (bôld′hed′) *n.* **1.** One whose head is bald. **2.** A breed of pigeons.

bald·head·ed (bôld′hed′id) *adj.* Having a bald head.

bald·ing (bôl′ding) *adj. U.S. Informal* Beginning to grow bald.

bald·pate (bôld′pāt′) *n.* **1.** A baldheaded person. **2.** See under WIDGEON. **— bald′pat′ed** *adj.*

bald prairie *Canadian* A treeless prairie.

bal·dric (bôl′drik) *n.* A belt worn over one shoulder and across the breast, to support a sword, bugle, etc.: also *baw·dric.* Also **bal′drick.** [Cf. OF *baldrei*, ult. < L *balteus* belt]

bald rush An American sedge (genus *Psilocarya*).

Bald·win (bôld′win) *n.* A red variety of winter apple. [after Loammi *Baldwin*, 1740–1807, U.S. engineer, who developed it]

Bald·win (bôld′win) An unincorporated place in SE New York on Long Island; pop. 34,525.

Bald·win (bôld′win), **James Mark**, 1861–1934, U.S. psychologist. **— Roger Sherman**, 1793–1863, U.S. lawyer and abolitionist. **— Stanley**, 1867–1947, first Earl Baldwin of Bewdly, British statesman, prime minister 1923–24, 1924–29, 1935–37.

Bald·win I (bôld′win), 1058–1118, king of Jerusalem 1100–1118.

Baldwin Park A city in SW California, near Los Angeles; pop. 47,285.

bale[1] (bāl) *n.* A large package of bulky goods corded or otherwise prepared for transportation. Abbr. *B/-* (pl. *B/s*), *bl.* **—** *v.t.* **baled, bal·ing** To make into a bale or bales. [< OF *bale* round package, ? < OHG *balla* ball] **— bal′er** *n.*

bale[2] (bāl) *n. Archaic* **1.** That which causes ruin or sorrow; evil. **2.** Pain; woe. [OE *bealu* evil, wickedness]

bale[3] (bāl) *n.* A balefire. [OE *bæl* fire, funeral pile]

Bâle (bäl) French name for BASEL.

Bal·e·ar·ic Islands (bal′ē·ar′ik, bə·lir′ik) A group of islands in the western Mediterranean, a Province of Spain; 1,935 sq. mi.; pop. 451,343 (est. 1965); capital, Palma.

ba·leen (bə·lēn′) *n.* Whalebone. [< F *baleine* < L *balaena* < Gk. *phalaina* whale]

bale·fire (bāl′fīr′) *n.* **1.** A large outdoor fire; bonfire. **2.** A signal fire; beacon. **3.** *Obs.* A funeral pyre. [OE *bælfÿr* < *bæl* funeral pyre + *fÿr* fire]

bale·ful (bāl′fəl) *adj.* **1.** Hurtful; malignant. **2.** *Archaic* Sorrowful; miserable. **— bale′ful·ly** *adv.* **— bale′ful·ness** *n.*

bale hook A box hook.

Balfe (balf), **Michael William**, 1808–70, Irish composer.

Bal·four (bal′fŏŏr), **Arthur James**, 1848–1930, first Earl of Balfour, British statesman, prime minister 1902–05, foreign secretary 1916–19.

Balfour Declaration A declaration issued by the British government, November, 1917, favoring establishment of a Jewish "National Home" in Palestine.

Ba·li (bä′lē) An island of Indonesia, just east of Java; 2,243 sq. mi.; pop. 2,196,000 (1970). See map of INDONESIA.

Ba·li·nese (bä′lə·nēz′, -nēs′) *adj.* Of or pertaining to Bali, its people, or their language. **—** *n. pl.* **·nese 1.** A native or inhabitant of Bali. **2.** The Indonesian language of Bali.

Bal·iol (bāl′yəl, bā′lē·əl), **Edward de**, died 1363, king of Scotland 1332–41. **— John de**, 1249–1315, king of Scotland 1292–96; father of the preceding. Also *Balliol.*

bal·i·saur (bal′ə·sôr) *n.* A long-tailed badger (*Arctonyx collaris*) of Asia. [< Hind. *bālusūr* < *bālu* sand + *sūr* hog]

balk (bôk) *v.i.* **1.** To stop short and refuse to proceed or take action. **—** *v.t.* **2.** To render unsuccessful; thwart; frustrate. **3.** *Obs.* To heap up in ridges or balks; also, to make a balk in (land). **— Syn.** See BAFFLE. **—** *n.* **1.** A hindrance or check; defeat; disappointment; a *balk* to one's plans. **2.** An error or slip; blunder. **3.** In baseball, an illegal motion made by the pitcher when one or more runners are on base. **4.** A ridge between furrows; a strip of land not plowed. **5.** A squared beam or timber; a tie beam. **6.** One of the stringers placed from boat to boat in a pontoon bridge. **7.** In billiards, one of the spaces between the balk lines and the cushions. Also spelled *baulk.* [OE *balca* bank, ridge]

Bal·kan (bôl′kən) *adj.* **1.** Of or pertaining to the Balkan Peninsula, its people, or their customs. **2.** Of or pertaining to the Balkan Mountains.

Balkan frame *Med.* A frame supported on four posts, with pulleys and slats for holding up the legs.

bal·kan·ize (bôl′kən·īz) *v.t.* **·ized, ·iz·ing** *Sometimes cap.* To separate into small, dissenting political units or states. **— bal′kan·i·za′tion** *n.*

Balkan Mountains A mountain range in Bulgaria, extending 350 miles westward from the Black Sea to the Yugoslav border; highest point, Botev Peak, 7,793 ft.

Balkan Peninsula The large peninsula of SE Europe, bounded by the lower Danube River and the Black, Aegean, Mediterranean, Ionian, and Adriatic seas.

Balkan States The countries of the Balkan Peninsula: Albania, Bulgaria, Greece, Rumania, Yugoslavia, and the European part of Turkey. Also **the Balkans.**

Balkan Wars See table for WAR.

Balkh (bälkh) A town in northern Afghanistan, capital of ancient Bactria; pop. about 12,500.

Bal·khash (bäl·khäsh′) A salt lake in the SE Kazakh S.S.R.; 6,680 sq. mi.

Bal·kis (bal′kis) In the Koran, the Queen of Sheba.

balk line (bôk) **1.** In billiards, a line partitioning off a space in the corner, along the sides, or around the entire edge of the table. **2.** In sports, especially track events, a line, progress beyond which counts as a trial.

balk·y (bô′kē) *adj.* **balk·i·er, balk·i·est** Given to balking: also spelled *baulky.*

ball[1] (bôl) *n.* **1.** A spherical or nearly spherical body. **2.** Such a body, of any size and made of various substances, used in a number of games. **3.** A game played with a ball, especially baseball. **4.** In sports, a ball moving, thrown, or struck in a specified manner: a fast *ball*; a bouncing *ball.* **5.** In baseball, a pitch in which the ball fails to pass over the home plate between the batter's armpits and knees and is not struck at by him. **6.** *Mil.* **a** Any spherical or conoid projectile, larger than a small shot. **b** Such projectiles collectively: to load with *ball.* **7.** A roundish protuberance or part of something. **8.** *Usually pl. Slang* A testicle. **9.** A planet or star, especially the earth. **— to be on the ball** *U.S. Slang* To be alert or competent. **— to carry the ball** *U.S.* To be the ballcarrier. **2.** *Informal* To be the spokesman or play the leading role, as in negotiation, conference, etc. **— to have something on the ball** *U.S. Slang* To have ability. **— to play ball 1.** To begin or resume playing a ball game or some other activity. **2.** *U.S. Informal* To cooperate. **—** *v.t. & v.i.* To form, gather, or wind into a ball. **— to ball up** *Slang* To confuse. [< ON *böllr*]

ball[2] (bôl) *n.* A formal social assembly for dancing. **— to have a ball** *U.S. Slang* To enjoy oneself thoroughly. [< F *bal* a dance < *baler* to dance < LL *ballare*]

Ball (bôl), **John**, died 1381, English priest, a leader in Wat Tyler's peasants' revolt; executed.

bal·lad (bal′əd) *n.* **1.** A narrative poem or song of popular origin in short stanzas, often with a refrain. **2.** A sentimental song of several stanzas, in which the melody is usually repeated for each stanza. [Var. of BALLADE]

bal·lade (bə·läd′, ba-) *n.* **1.** A verse form having three stanzas of eight or ten lines each and an envoy of four or five lines. The last line of each stanza and of the envoy is the same. **2.** A musical composition of romantic or dramatic nature, usually for piano or orchestra. [< OF *balade* dancing song]

bal·lad·eer (bal′ə·dir′) *n.* A singer of ballads.

bal·lad·mon·ger (bal′əd·mung′gər, -mong′-) *n.* **1.** A seller of popular ballads. **2.** A poetaster.

bal·la·drom·ic (bal′ə·drom′ik) *adj. Aerospace* Pursuing a course heading for the target: said of rockets and guided missiles. [< Gk. *ballein* to hurl, throw + *dromos* course]

bal·lad·ry (bal′əd·rē) *n.* **1.** Ballad poetry. **2.** The art of making or singing ballads.

ballad stanza A four-line stanza often used in ballads, generally rhyming the second and fourth lines.

ball and chain 1. A heavy metal ball fastened by a chain to a prisoner's leg. **2.** Anything that restricts or impedes one's actions. **3.** *Slang* A wife.

ball-and-sock·et joint (bôl′ən·sok′it) **1.** *Mech.* A joint composed of a sphere in a bearing, permitting a degree of free turning in any direction. **2.** *Anat.* An enarthrosis.

Bal·la·rat (bal′ə·rat) A city in south central Victoria, Australia; pop. 53,680 (est. 1969, including suburbs).

bal·last (bal′əst) *n.* **1.** Any heavy substance, as sand, stone, etc., laid in the hold of a vessel or in the car of a balloon to steady it. **2.** Gravel or broken stone laid down as a stabilizer for a rail bed. **3.** That which gives stability to character, morality, etc. **—** *v.t.* **1.** To provide or fill with ballast. **2.** To steady with ballast; stabilize. [< ODan. *barlast* < *bar* bare, mere + *last* load]

ball bearing *Mech.* **1.** A bearing in which a shaft bears on small metal balls that turn freely as it revolves. **2.** A metal ball in such a bearing. For illustration see MACHINE.

ball·car·ri·er (bôl′kar′ē·ər) *n. U.S.* The player who carries the ball, as in football.

ball cock *Mech.* A stopcock for regulating the supply of water, as in toilets, tanks, etc., in which the valve is closed or opened by the rising or falling of a hollow, floating ball.

bal·le·ri·na (bal′ə·rē′nə) *n.* A female ballet dancer. [< Ital., fem. of *ballerino* dancer]

bal·let (bal′ā, ba·lā′) *n.* **1.** An elaborate dramatic group dance using conventionalized movements, often for narrative effects. **2.** This style of dancing. **3.** The performers or troupe of such dancing. **4.** A musical composition for a ballet performance. [< F, dim. of *bal* dance. See BALL[2].]

bal·let·o·mane (ba·let′ə·mān) *n.* A ballet enthusiast. [< F < *ballet* + -(o)*mane* < Gk. *mania* enthusiasm]

ball·flow·er (bôl′flou′ər) *n. Archit.* An ornament resembling a ball placed in a flower.

Bal·liol (bal′yəl, bā′lē·əl) See BALIOL.

bal·lis·ta (bə-lis′tə) *n.* *pl.* **·tae** (-tē) An engine used in ancient and medieval warfare for hurling missiles. [< L, ult. < Gk. *ballein* to throw]

bal·lis·tic (bə-lis′tik) *adj.* Of or pertaining to projectiles or to ballistics.

ballistic curve The actual path of a projectile, as affected by wind, etc.

ballistic missile A missile controlled to the apex of its trajectory, falling free thereafter. Compare GUIDED MISSILE.

ROMAN BALLISTA

bal·lis·tics (bə-lis′tiks) *n.pl.* (*construed as sing.*) 1. The science that deals with the motion of projectiles, either while they are still in the bore (**interior ballistics**) or after they leave the muzzle (**exterior ballistics**). 2. The study of the motion and flight behavior of all missiles, however discharged and propelled. — **bal·lis·ti·cian** (bal′ə-stish′ən) *n.*

ballistic table A table showing the character and values of the factors affecting the flight of a projectile, as range to summit, angle of fall, time of flight, etc.

bal·lo·net (bal′ə-net′) *n.* 1. A small balloon. 2. A gasbag in the interior of a nonrigid airship for maintaining shape and buoyancy. [< F *ballonnet*, dim. of *ballon* balloon]

bal·loon (bə-loon′) *n.* 1. A large, impermeable bag, inflated with gas lighter than air, and designed to rise and float in the atmosphere; especially, such a bag having a car or basket attached, for carrying passengers, instruments, etc. 2. A small, inflatable rubber bag, used as a toy. 3. *Chem.* A spherical glass vessel. 4. In comic strips, etc., a balloon-shaped outline connected with the mouth of a person, containing the words he is represented as speaking. — **barrage balloon** A captive balloon designed to act as protection against hostile aircraft. — **captive balloon** A balloon prevented from rising beyond a certain height by a cable attached to the ground. — **kite balloon** A captive balloon, fitted with a tail appendage to keep it headed into the wind. — **observation balloon** A captive balloon used as an observation post. — **sounding balloon** A balloon which carries the instruments of a radiosonde. — *v.i.* 1. To ascend or travel in a balloon. 2. To swell out like a balloon, as a sail. — *v.t.* 3. To inflate or distend with air. — *adj.* Like a balloon in shape; puffed out. [< Ital. *ballone* large ball < *balla* ball, sphere < Gmc.] — **bal·loon′ist** *n.*

balloon cloth A closely woven cotton fabric vulcanized with thin sheets of rubber so as to be gastight.

balloon foresail *Naut.* A light foresail set between the foretopmast head and the jib-boom end, used mostly by yachts in light winds. Also **balloon jib.**

balloon sail A spinnaker or a balloon foresail (which see).

balloon tire A pneumatic tire filled with air at low pressure.

balloon vine A tropical American climbing herb (*Cardiospermum halicacabum*) bearing inflated, membranaceous, three-celled pods: also called *heartseed.*

bal·lot (bal′ət) *n.* 1. A written or printed slip or ticket used in casting a secret vote. 2. The total number of votes cast in an election. 3. The act or system of voting secretly by ballots or by voting machines. 4. A list of candidates for office; ticket. 5. Originally, a little ball used in voting. — *v.* **·lot·ed, ·lot·ing** *v.i.* 1. To cast a ballot in voting. 2. To draw lots. — *v.t.* 3. To vote for or decide on by ballot. [< Ital. *ballotta*, dim. of *balla* ball. See BALLOON.]

bal·lotte·ment (bə-lot′mənt) *n.* *Med.* A method of diagnosing pregnancy, floating kidney, etc., by palpating, causing the part to rise on impact and return again. [< F *balloter* to toss < *ballotte* small ball]

ball peen A hemispherical peen on a hammerhead, used especially for riveting. For illustration see HAMMER.

ball·play·er (bôl′plā′ər) *n.* *U.S.* A baseball player.

ball-point pen (bôl′point′) A fountain pen having for a point a ball bearing that rolls to ink itself from a cartridge and deposits a line on the writing surface.

ball·room (bôl′room′, -room′) *n.* A large room for dancing.

ballroom dancing A kind of social dancing in which two people dance as partners.

ball valve *Mech.* A valve controlled by a ball that rests in a socket and is free to rise when the upward pressure exceeds the pull of gravity.

bal·ly (bal′ē) *adj. & adv. Brit. Slang* Bloody: a euphemism.

bal·ly·hoo (bal′ē-hoo′) *n.* *U.S. Informal* 1. Blatant or sensational advertising; noisy propaganda. 2. Clamor; uproar. — *v.t. & v.i.* **·hooed, ·hoo·ing** To advocate or promote by ballyhoo. [Origin unknown]

balm (bäm) *n.* 1. An aromatic, resinous exudation from various trees or shrubs, used medicinally; balsam. 2. Any oily, fragrant, resinous substance. 3. A tree or shrub yielding such a substance; especially, any tree of the genus *Commiphora*. 4. Any of various aromatic plants of the genus *Melissa*, especially *M. officinalis*. 5. A pleasing fragrance.

6. Anything that soothes or heals. [< OF *basme* < L *balsamum* < Gk. *balsamon*, ? < Semitic. Doublet of BALSAM.]

bal·ma·caan (bal′mə-kän′) *n.* A loose overcoat with raglan sleeves, made of rough woolen cloth. [after *Balmacaan*, an estate in Scotland]

balm of Gilead 1. The resinous, fragrant juice obtained from a small evergreen tree (*Commiphora opobalsamum*) growing on the shores of the Red Sea. 2. The balsam fir, or the balm obtained from it. 3. A North American shade tree (*Populus candicans*).

Bal·mor·al (bal-môr′əl, -mor′-) *n.* 1. A petticoat made of a striped, heavy woolen cloth. 2. The cloth itself. 3. A brimless, flat Scottish cap. 4. A laced walking shoe: also **bal·mo′ral.** [after *Balmoral* Castle, Scotland]

Bal·mung (bäl′moong) In the *Nibelungenlied*, the sword that Siegfried took from the Nibelungs.

balm·y (bä′mē) *adj.* **balm·i·er, balm·i·est** 1. Mild and soothing; soft. 2. Having the fragrance of balm; aromatic. 3. *Brit. Slang* Crazy. — **balm′i·ly** *adv.* — **balm′i·ness** *n.*

bal·ne·al (bal′nē-əl) *adj.* Of or pertaining to baths and bathing. [< L *balneum* bath]

bal·ne·ol·o·gy (bal′nē-ol′ə-jē) *n.* The science of treating disease by baths and the waters of mineral springs. [< L *balneum* bath + -LOGY]

ba·lo·ney (bə-lō′nē) *n.* 1. *Slang* Nonsense. 2. Bologna sausage. Also spelled *boloney.* [def. 1 < BOLOGNA SAUSAGE]

bal·sa (bôl′sə, bäl′-) *n.* 1. A tree (*Ochroma pyramidale*) of tropical America and the West Indies. 2. The very light wood of this tree: also called *corkwood.* 3. A raft made of light logs fastened together by a platform. [< Sp. *balza*]

bal·sam (bôl′səm) *n.* 1. Any of a group of fragrant oleoresins obtained chiefly from the exudations of various trees; especially, **balsam of Peru,** obtained from a tropical American tree (*Myroxylon pereirae*), and **balsam of Tolu** (tə-loo′), obtained from a South American evergreen (*Myroxylon balsamum*), containing the volatile oil toluene, and used as a basis for many cough mixtures. 2. Any tree yielding such a resinous substance, as the balsam fir. 3. Any fragrant ointment, especially one used medicinally. 4. An aromatic resin containing cinnamic or benzoic acid; also, a tree yielding such a resin. 5. Any of various flowering plants (genus *Impatiens*); especially, the **garden balsam.** 6. Any soothing or healing agent. 7. Canada balsam (which see). — *v.t.* To anoint with or as with balsam; salve. [< L *balsamum* < Gk. *balsamon* balsam tree, ? < Semitic. Doublet of BALM.] — **bal·sam·ic** (bôl-sam′ik) *adj.*

balsam fir A tree (*Abies balsamea*) of the pine family, growing in the northern United States and Canada and yielding Canada balsam: also called *balm of Gilead.*

bal·sam·if·er·ous (bôl′sə-mif′ər-əs, bal′-) *adj.* Yielding balsam or balm.

bal·sa·mi·na·ceous (bôl′sə-mə-nā′shəs, bal′-) *adj.* Belonging to a family (*Balsaminaceae*) of plants including plants of the genus *Impatiens*, as the touch-me-not and the garden balsam. [< Gk. *balsaminē* balsam plant + -ACEOUS]

balsam poplar The tacamahac (def. 3).

Balt (bôlt) *n.* A native or inhabitant of the Baltic States.

Balt. Baltic.

Bal·tha·zar (bal-thä′zər, -thaz′ər, bôl′thə-zär′, bal′-) Traditionally, one of the three Magi. Also **Bal·tha·sar.**

Bal·tic (bôl′tik) *adj.* Of or pertaining to the Baltic Sea or the Baltic States. — *n.* A branch of the Balto-Slavic languages, including Lithuanian, Lettish (or Latvian), and the now extinct Old Prussian.

Baltic Sea An inlet of the Atlantic enclosed by Sweden, Denmark, East Germany, West Germany, Poland, the Soviet Union, and Finland; 163,000 sq. mi.

Baltic States The Republics of Estonia, Latvia, and Lithuania, annexed in 1940 as constituents of the Soviet Union.

Bal·ti·more (bôl′tə-môr, -mōr) A port city in northern Maryland, at the upper end of Chesapeake Bay; pop. 905,759.

Baltimore, Lord See (Sir George) CALVERT.

Baltimore oriole An American oriole (*Icterus galbula*) of which the male has orange and black plumage: also called *golden robin, hangbird.* [after the colors of the coat of arms of Lord *Baltimore*]

Bal·to-Sla·vic (bôl′tō-slä′vik, -slav′ik) *n.* A subfamily of the Indo-European languages, consisting of Baltic and Slavic branches. — *adj.* Of the Balto-Slavic languages or the people who speak them.

Ba·lu·chi (bə-loo′chē) *n.* The Iranian language of Baluchistan.

Ba·lu·chi·stan (bə·lōō′chə·stän′, bə·lōō′chə·stan) A mountainous region and former province of West Pakistan; 134,-139 sq. mi.

bal·us·ter (bal′əs·tər) *n.* One of a set of small pillars supporting a handrail. For illustration see BALCONY. [< MF *baluStre* < Ital. *balaustro* baluster < *balaustra* pomegranate flower; so called from the resemblance in form]

bal·us·trade (bal′ə·strād′, bal′ə·strād) *n.* A handrail supported by balusters. For illustration see BALCONY. [< F < Ital. *balustrata* < *balaustro*. See BALUSTER.]

Bal·zac (bal′zak, bôl′-; *Fr.* bȧl·zȧk′), **Honoré de,** 1799–1850, French novelist.

Ba·ma·ko (bä·mä·kō′) The capital of the Republic of Mali, in the south central part on the Niger; pop. 88,500 (1968).

Bam·berg (bäm′berkh) A city in northern Bavaria, West Germany; pop. 73,600 (1960).

bam·bi·no (bam·bē′nō) *n.* *pl.* **·ni** (-nē) or **·nos** 1. A little child; a baby. 2. A figure of the child Jesus. [< Ital., dim. of *bambo* simple, childish]

bam·boo (bam·bōō′) *n.* 1. A tall, treelike or shrubby grass (genus *Bambusa* or related genera) of tropical and semitropical regions. 2. The tough, hollow, jointed stem of this plant, used for building, furniture, utensils, etc. [< Malay *bambu*]

bam·boo·zle (bam·bōō′zəl) *v.* **·zled,** **·zling** *Informal v.t.* 1. To mislead; cheat. 2. To perplex. — *v.i.* 3. To practice trickery or deception. [Origin unknown] — **bam·boo′zle·ment** *n.* — **bam·boo′zler** *n.*

ban¹ (ban) *v.t.* **banned, ban·ning** 1. To proscribe or prohibit; forbid. 2. To place under a ban; anathematize; interdict. 3. *Archaic* To curse; execrate. — **Syn.** See PROHIBIT. — *n.* 1. An official proclamation, especially of prohibition. 2. Condemnation, ostracism, or prohibition, as by public opinion. 3. *Eccl.* An edict of excommunication or interdiction. 4. A sentence of outlawry or banishment. 5. *Archaic* A curse; malediction. 6. *pl.* Banns. 7. Formerly, the summoning of vassals to arms; also, the force so assembled. [< OE *bannan* to proclaim and ON *banna* to curse, prohibit]

ban² (ban) *n.* *Archaic* A governor or ruler, as: **a** A military governor of the southern marches of Hungary. **b** A governor of Croatia and Slavonia. [< Serbo-Croatian *bān* lord, ruler, ult. < Persian]

ban³ (bän) *n.* *pl.* **ba·ni** (bä′nē) A Rumanian copper coin, worth one hundredth of a leu.

ba·nal (bā′nəl, bə·nal′, ban′əl) *adj.* Meaningless from overuse; hackneyed; trivial. [< BAN¹ def. 7; hence, ordinary, common] — **ba·nal·i·ty** (bə·nal′ə·tē) *n.* — **ba′nal·ly** *adv.*

ba·nan·a (bə·nan′ə) *n.* 1. The elongated, edible, pulpy fruit of a herbaceous plant (*Musa paradisiaca sapientum*) of tropical regions, having an easily removed rind and growing in drooping clusters. 2. The plant bearing this fruit. [< Sp. < native African name]

banana oil 1. Isoamyl acetate. 2. *U.S. Slang* Fulsome flattery; cajolery.

Pa·na·ras (bə·nä′rəs) A sacred city of the Hindus, on the Ganges River in SE Uttar Pradesh, India; pop. 619,822 (1969); formerly Benares.

Pa·nat (bä·nät′) A region of SE Hungary formerly governed by a ban; divided (1920) into the **Rumanian Banat;** 6,975 sq. mi.; the **Yugoslav Banat,** a small region of northern Serbia; and the **Hungarian Banat,** a small region near Szeged.

Ban·bur·y (ban′ber′ē, bam′bər·ē) A municipal borough in northern Oxfordshire, England; pop. 20,996 (1961).

Ban·croft (ban′krôft, -kroft), **George,** 1800–91, U.S. historian.

band¹ (band) *n.* 1. A flat, flexible strip of any material, often used for binding or securing. 2. A strip of fabric used to finish, strengthen, or trim an article of dress: often in combination: *hatband.* 3. Any broad stripe of contrasting color, material, or surface. 4. *pl.* Geneva bands (which see). 5. A high collar worn in the 16th and 17th centuries. 6. *Mech.* A belt or chain for communicating power. 7. *Telecom.* A range of frequencies or wavelengths between two stated limits. 8. *Physics* Any of the broad stripes found in typical molecular spectra, resolving into lines upon high magnification. — *v.t.* 1. To unite or tie with a band; encircle. 2. To mark or identify by attaching a band to, as a bird. [< F *bande* < OF *bende,* ult. < Gmc. Akin to BIND.]

band² (band) *n.* 1. A company of persons associated for a common purpose; a group, troop, or gang. 2. A company of persons organized to play musical instruments, especially wind and percussion instruments. 3. *Canadian* A group of reservation Indians having elective chiefs. — *v.t. & v.i.* To unite in a band; confederate. [< MF *bande.* Akin to BIND.]

band³ (band) *n.* That which binds, ties, or unites; a bond. [< ON. Akin to BIND.]

band·age (ban′dij) *n.* A strip of soft cloth or other material used in dressing wounds, etc. — *v.t.* **·aged, ·ag·ing** To bind or cover with a bandage. [< F < *bande* band]

Band-Aid (band′ād′) *n.* A gauze patch attached to an adhesive strip, used to cover minor wounds: a trade name. Also **band′-aid′.**

ban·dan·na (ban·dan′ə) *n.* A large, brightly colored handkerchief decorated with spots or figures. Also **ban·dan′a.** [< Hind. *bāndhnū,* a method of dyeing]

Ban·dar Shah·pur (bän·där′ shä·pōōr′) A port town of SW Iran, at the head of the Persian Gulf; pop. about 10,000.

Ban·da Sea (bän′də, ban′-) A section of the Pacific Ocean bounded by the southern Molucca Islands. See map of INDONESIA.

band·box (band′boks′) *n.* A light round or oval box, originally used to hold collars, and now used for carrying hats, etc. [< BAND¹, collar + BOX¹]

ban·deau (ban·dō′, ban′dō) *n.* *pl.* **·deaux** (-dōz′, -dōz) 1. A narrow band, especially one worn about the hair; fillet. 2. A short brassiere made without a wide band at the bottom. [< F < OF *bandel,* dim. of *bande* band]

ban·de·ril·la (bän′dā·rē′lyä) *n.* *Spanish* In bullfighting, a dart with streamers attached, stuck into the neck and shoulders of a bull by the banderillero.

ban·de·ril·le·ro (bän′dā·rē·lyä′rō) *n.* *Spanish* In bullfighting, one who places the banderillas.

ban·de·role (ban′də·rōl) *n.* 1. A small flag, pennant, or streamer. 2. In art, a ribbon or scroll bearing an inscription. 3. A banner placed over a tomb or carried at a funeral. Also spelled *bannerole:* also **ban′de·rol.** [< MF < Ital. *banderuola,* dim. of *bandiera* banner]

ban·di·coot (ban′di·kōōt) *n.* 1. A large rat (*Mus* or *Nesokia bandicota*) of India and Ceylon, often over a foot in length. 2. A small marsupial (genus *Perameles*) of Australia, Tasmania, etc. [Alter. of Telugu *pandikokku* pig-rat]

ban·dit (ban′dit) *n.* *pl.* **ban·dits** or **ban·dit·ti** (ban·dit′ē) 1. A robber. 2. An outlaw; brigand. [< Ital. *bandito,* pp. of *bandire* to proscribe, outlaw] — **ban′dit·ry** *n.*

Ban·djer·ma·sin (bän′jər·mä′sin) See BANJERMASIN.

band·mas·ter (band′mas′tər, -mäs′tər) *n.* The conductor of a musical band.

ban·do·leer (ban′də·lir′) *n.* A broad belt fitted with loops or cases for holding cartridges, and worn over the shoulder. Also **ban′do·lier′.** [< MF *bandouillere* < Ital. *bandoliera* shoulder belt, ult. < *banda* band]

ban·do·line (ban′də·lēn, -lin) *n.* A gummy hairdressing made from tragacanth and quince seeds. [Origin uncertain]

ban·dore (ban·dôr′, -dōr′) *n.* An ancient, lutelike musical instrument: also called *pandore.* [< Sp. *bandurria* < L *pandura* < Gk. *pandoura* lute]

band saw *Mech.* A saw consisting of a toothed endless belt mounted on wheels.

band shell A bandstand having a concave hemispherical rear wall.

bands·man (bandz′mən) *n.* *pl.* **·men** (-mən) A member of a musical band.

band·stand (band′stand′) *n.* A platform for a band of musicians, often roofed when outdoors.

Ban·dung (bän′dŏŏng) A city in Indonesia, on western Java; pop. 966,359 (1961). *Dutch* **Ban′doeng.**

band·wag·on (band′wag′ən) *n.* A high, decorated wagon used to carry a band in a parade. — **to climb** (hop, get, etc.) **on the bandwagon** *U.S. Informal* To give one's support to a principle or candidate apparently assured of success.

ban·dy (ban′dē) *v.t.* **·died, ·dy·ing** 1. To give and take; exchange, as blows or words. 2. To pass along; circulate: to *bandy* stories. 3. To pass, throw, or knock back and forth, as a ball. — *adj.* Crooked outward; bowed: said of legs. — *n. pl.* **·dies** 1. A game resembling hockey; also, a crooked stick used in this game. 2. An ancient form of tennis. [Origin uncertain]

ban·dy-leg·ged (ban′dē·leg′id, -legd′) *adj.* Bowlegged.

bane (bān) *n.* 1. Anything destructive or ruinous. 2. Poison: now only in combination: *henbane.* 3. *Poetic* Ruin; death. [OE *bana* killer]

bane·ber·ry (bān′ber′ē, -bər·ē) *n.* *pl.* **·ries** 1. The poisonous berry of a plant (genus *Actaea*). 2. The plant itself.

bane·ful (bān′fəl) *adj.* Poisonous; destructive. — **Syn.** See PERNICIOUS. — **bane′ful·ly** *adv.* — **bane′ful·ness** *n.*

Banff (bamf) 1. A county of NE Scotland; 630 sq. mi.; pop. 43,753 (1969); county seat, **Banff.** Also **Banffshire** (bamf′shir). 2. A resort town (pop. 2,518) in Banff National Park, SW Alberta, Canada, 2,564 sq. mi., established 1885.

bang¹ (bang) *n.* 1. A heavy, noisy blow or thump. 2. A sudden, loud noise or explosion. 3. *Informal* A sudden spurt of activity: To start with a *bang.* 4. *U.S. Slang* Thrill; enjoyment: He gets a *bang* out of flying. — *v.t.* 1. To beat or strike heavily and noisily; drub; slam. — *v.i.* 2. To make a loud sound. 3. To strike noisily; crash. — *adv.* With a bang; abruptly and loudly. [< ON *banga* to hammer]

BANANA PLANT
(10 to 20 feet high)

bang² (bang) *n. Usually pl.* A fringe of hair cut straight across the forehead. — *v.t.* To cut short and straight across. [< BANG¹, adv.; from the hair being cut off abruptly]

bang³ (bang) See BHANG.

Ban·ga·lore (bang′gə·lôr′, -lōr′) The capital of Mysore State, India, in the eastern part; pop. 1,027,327 (est. 1971).

ban·ga·lore torpedo (bang′gə·lôr, -lōr) *Mil.* A length of metal piping filled with high explosive and used chiefly to clear a safe path through a minefield.

Bang·ka (bäng′kä, bang′kə) An island of Indonesia, in the Java Sea SE of Sumatra; an important tin center; 4,611 sq. mi.; pop. 250,452 (1961). Also **Ban·ka.**

bang·kok (bang′kok) *n.* **1.** A finely textured straw used for hats. **2.** A hat made of this straw. [after *Bangkok*]

Bang·kok (bang′kok) The capital of Thailand, in the SW part on the Chao Phraya river; the nation's chief port; pop. 1,299,528 (est. 1968).

Ban·gla·desh (bang′glä·desh′) An independent Republic in SE Asia; 54,501 sq. mi.; pop. 50,844,000 (1961); capital, Dacca. Also **Bangla Desh.**

ban·gle (bang′gəl) *n.* A decorative bracelet or anklet. [< Hind. *bangrī* glass bracelet]

Ban·gor (bang′gôr, -gər) A city in south central Maine on the Penobscot River; pop. 33,168.

Bang's disease (bangz) *Vet.* An infectious brucellosis in cattle, caused by a bacterium (*Brucella abortus*), often resulting in abortion. Compare UNDULANT FEVER. [after B. L.F. Bang, 1848–1932, Danish veterinarian]

bang·tail (bang′tāl′) **1.** A horse's tail cut horizontally across. **2.** *U.S. Slang* A horse, especially a race horse. [< BANG² + TAIL] — **bang′tailed′** *adj.*

Ban·gui (bäng′gē) The capital of the Central African Republic, in the SW part; pop. 111,266 (est. 1964).

bang-up (bang′up′) *adj. Slang* Excellent.

Bang·we·u·lu (bäng′wä·ōō′lōō, bang′wē-) A lake in Zambia, in the northern part; about 3,800 sq. mi. (including swamps, varying with rainfall).

ba·ni (bä′nē) Plural of BAN³.

ban·ian (ban′yən) *n.* **1.** A Hindu merchant or trader of a caste that abstains from meat. **2.** A loose shirt, jacket, or gown. **3.** See BANYAN. [< Pg. < Arabic *banyān*, ult. < Skt. *vaṇij* merchant]

ban·ish (ban′ish) *v.t.* **1.** To compel to leave a country by political decree; exile. **2.** To expel, as from any customary or desired place; drive away; dismiss. [< OF *baniss-*, stem of *banir* < LL *bannire* to banish < *bannum* proclamation < Gmc.] — **ban′ish·er** *n.* — **ban′ish·ment** *n.*
— **Syn. 1.** *Banish, exile, expatriate, deport,* and *transport* all mean to send away from a place, and often imply compulsion. A person is *banished* only by another, but may *exile* or *expatriate* himself. A man may be *banished* from his own or another country; he is *expatriated* from his native land. *Exile* may refer to a country, home, friends, etc. Only aliens are *deported,* usually to their native land, while convicted criminals are *transported* to a penal colony. Compare EXPEL.

ban·is·ter (ban′is·tər) *n.* **1.** *Often pl.* A handrail or balustrade along a staircase or stairwell. **2.** Loosely, a baluster. Also spelled *bannister.* [Alter. of BALUSTER]

ban·is·ter·ine (ban·is′tər·ēn, -in) *n.* A hallucinating drug, C₁₃H₁₂ON₂, derived from a South American plant (*Banisteriopsis caapi*), and used for the treatment of encephalitis lethargica: also called *harmine.* [after John Banister, 1650–1692, American botanist]

Ban·jer·ma·sin (bän′jər·mä′sin) A port town of SW Borneo, Indonesia, on the Barito river; pop. 212,683 (1961): also *Bandjermasin.*

ban·jo (ban′jō) *n. pl.* **·jos** or **·joes** A long-necked, four- or five-stringed musical instrument having a hoop-shaped body covered on top with stretched skin and played by plucking the strings with the finger or a plectrum. [< a West African language; cf. Mandingo *bania*] — **ban′jo·ist** *n.*

bank¹ (bangk) *n.* **1.** Any moundlike formation or mass; ridge: a cloud *bank.* **2.** A steep slope; rising ground. **3.** *Often pl.* The slope of land at the edge of a watercourse or of any cut or channel. **4.** A raised portion of the ocean floor, a river bed, etc.; a shoal; shallow: the Newfoundland *banks.* **5.** The cushion of a billiard table. **6.** *Aeron.* The controlled sidewise tilt of an airplane in a turn, used to prevent skidding. **7.** *Mining* The ground at the top of a shaft. — *v.t.* **1.** To enclose, cover, or protect by a bank, dike, or border; embank. **2.** To heap up into a bank or mound. **3.** To give an upward lateral slope to, as the curve of a road. **4.** To tilt (an airplane) laterally in flight. **5.** In billiards and pool: **a** To cause (a ball) to rebound at an angle from a cushion. **b** To pocket (a ball) in this manner. — *v.i.* **6.** To form or lie in banks. **7.** To tilt an airplane laterally in flight. — **to bank (up) a fire** To cover a fire with ashes so as to keep it alive but burning low. [ME *banke,* prob. < Scand. Akin to BENCH.]
— **Syn.** (noun) **1.** *Bank, ridge,* and *mound* mean a pile of earthy or rocky material. A *bank* is a heap of any shape, such as a sand *bank.* A

BANJO

ridge is a long, narrow elevation, while a *mound* is usually earthy and roughly rounded or pyramidal in shape. **3.** See SHORE. **4.** *Bank, shoal, sandbar,* and *reef* all mean an elevation of the ground under water. A *bank* is an extensive plateau that may lie far below the surface, while the water above a *shoal* is shallow. A *sandbar* may come to or above the surface. A *reef* is a ridge, usually of coral or rock, near or above the surface.

bank² (bangk) *n.* **1.** An institution for lending, borrowing, exchanging, issuing, or safeguarding money. **2.** An office or building used for such purposes. **3.** The funds of a gambling house or the fund held by the dealer or banker in some gambling games. **4.** In some games, reserve pieces from which the players are permitted to draw, as in dominoes. **5.** A store or reserve supply of anything needed for future use or emergency: a blood *bank.* **6.** Any place of storage. **7.** *Obs.* A moneychanger's table. Abbr. *bk.* — *v.t.* **1.** To deposit in a bank. — *v.i.* **2.** To do business as or with a bank or banker. **3.** In gambling, to keep the bank in a game. — **to bank on** *Informal* To rely on; be sure about. [< F *banque* < Ital. *banca* money-changer's table, ult. < Gmc.]

bank³ (bangk) *n.* **1.** A set of like articles arranged in a line: a *bank* of spotlights. **2.** *Naut.* **a** A rowers' bench in a galley; thwart **b** A tier of oars in a galley. **3.** A horizontal rank of keys in a piano or organ. **4.** In journalism, lines under a head-line; deck. **5.** *Printing* A table or rack for holding type galleys, sheets, etc. — *v.t.* To arrange in a bank. [< OF *banc* < LL *bancus* bench, ult. < Gmc. Akin to BENCH.]

bank·a·ble (bangk′ə·bəl) *adj.* Receivable by a bank.

bank acceptance A draft endorsed or acknowledged by a bank on which it is drawn. Also **banker's acceptance.**

bank account Money deposited in a bank to the credit of, and subject to withdrawal by, the depositor.

bank and turn indicator *Aeron.* A flight instrument that shows the degree of bank and the change in direction about the vertical axis. Also **turn and bank indicator.**

bank annuities *Brit.* Consols.

bank barn *U.S. & Canadian* A barn built into a hillside, with entry to an upper floor from one side and a lower floor from the other.

bank bill 1. A bank note. **2.** A draft drawn on one bank by another: also **banker's bill.**

bank·book (bangk′bŏŏk′) *n.* A book kept by a depositor in which his accounts are entered: also called *passbook.*

bank discount A deduction beforehand of interest reckoned on the face of a bill or note.

bank·er¹ (bangk′ər) *n.* **1.** An employee or officer of a bank. **2.** One who keeps the bank in certain gambling games.

bank·er² (bangk′ər) *n. U.S. & Canadian* A vessel or person engaged in cod fishing on the Newfoundland banks.

bank·er³ (bangk′ər) *n.* A stonemason's or sculptor's workbench.

bank holiday 1. A legal holiday (which see). **2.** *Brit.* Any of six holidays on which banks are legally closed.

bank·ing (bangk′ing) *n.* The business of a bank or banker. Abbr. *bkg.*

bank note A promissory note issued by a bank, payable on demand and serving as currency. Abbr. *B.N.*

bank paper 1. Bank notes. **2.** Commercial paper, as securities, bills of exchange, etc., of such quality that a bank will buy or discount it.

bank rate The rate of discount determined by banks, or by a central bank.

bank·rupt [bangk′rupt] *n.* **1.** *Law* One who is judicially declared insolvent, his property being administered for and distributed among his creditors, under a bankruptcy law. **2.** Any person unable to pay his debts, or without resources. **3.** One ruined and unproductive in some way: a spiritual *bankrupt.* — *adj.* **1.** Subject to the conditions of a bankruptcy law; insolvent. **2.** Destitute; lacking: with *in.* — *v.t.* To make bankrupt. [< F *banqueroute* < Ital. *bancarotta* bankruptcy < *banca* bench + *rotta* broken < L *ruptus,* pp. of *rumpere* to break]

bank·rupt·cy (bangk′rupt·sē, -rəp·sē) *n. pl.* **·cies 1.** The state of being bankrupt; financial ruin. **2.** Any complete ruin or failure.

Banks (bangks), **Sir Joseph,** 1743–1820. English explorer and naturalist. — **Nathaniel Prentiss,** 1816–94, U.S. political leader and Union general in the Civil War.

bank·si·a (bangk′sē·ə) *n.* Any plant of a genus (*Banksia*) of Australian evergreens with leathery leaves and long, dense heads of yellow flowers. [after Sir Joseph *Banks*]

Bank·side (bangk′sīd) A district on the south bank of the Thames in London, site of Shakespeare's Globe Theater.

ban·ner (ban′ər) *n.* **1.** A flag or standard, as of a nation, sovereign, or army. **2.** A piece of cloth, often attached to a pole, bearing a motto or device, as of a religious organization. **3.** Anything symbolizing a person's beliefs or principles. **4.** *Bot.* The large upper petal of a papilionaceous blossom. **5.** In journalism, a headline extending across a newspaper page. — *adj.* Leading; foremost; outstanding. [< OF *banere* < LL *bandum* banner, ult. < Gmc.]

ban·ner·et¹ (ban′ə·ret′) *n.* A small banner. Also **ban′ner·ette′.** [< OF *banerette,* dim. of *banere* a banner]

ban·ner·et[2] (ban′ər·it, -et) *n.* **1.** A knight, next below a baron, entitled to lead vassals under his own banner. **2.** The title and rank of such a knight. Also called *knight banneret.* [< OF *baneret* having a banner < *banere* banner]

ban·ner·ole (ban′ə·rōl) See BANDEROLE.

ban·net (ban′it) *n. Scot.* A bonnet.

ban·nis·ter (ban′is·tər) See BANISTER.

ban·nock (ban′ək) *n. Scot. & Brit. Dial.* A thin cake of meal baked on a griddle: also *bonnock.* [OE *bannuc* bit]

Ban·nock·burn (ban′ək·bûrn) A village in NE Stirling, Scotland; site of a battle, 1314, in which Robert Bruce defeated the English; pop. 3,887 (1969).

banns (banz) *n.pl. Eccl.* A public announcement in church of a proposed marriage, usually made on three successive Sundays. Also **bans.** [< BAN[1]]

ban·quet (bang′kwit) *n.* **1.** A sumptuous feast. **2.** A formal or ceremonial dinner, often followed by speeches. — *v.t. & v.i.* To entertain at a banquet; feast sumptuously or formally. [< MF, dim. of *banc* table] — **ban′quet·er** *n.*

ban·quette (bang·ket′) *n.* **1.** *Mil.* A platform or bank behind a parapet, on which soldiers may stand and fire. For illustration see BASTION. **2.** An upholstered bench, as along a wall. **3.** Any bank, ledge, etc., as a shelf on a sideboard. **4.** A sidewalk. [< F < Ital. *banchetta,* dim. of *banca* bench]

Ban·quo (bang′kwō, -kō) In Shakespeare's *Macbeth,* a thane whose ghost appears only to Macbeth, who had ordered his murder.

ban·shee (ban′shē, ban·shē′) *n.* In Gaelic folklore, a supernatural being whose wailing was supposed to foretell a death. Also **ban′shie.** [< Irish *bean sidhe* < *bean* woman + *sidhe* fairy]

ban·tam (ban′təm) *n.* **1.** *Often cap.* Any of various breeds of very small domestic fowl, characterized by combativeness, as the **Cochin bantam** and the **Japanese bantam. 2.** A small, pugnacious person. — *adj.* Like a bantam; small and combative. [from *Bantam,* Java]

Ban·tam (bän·täm′, ban′təm) A ruined town in NW Java, Indonesia; site of the first Dutch East Indian settlement.

ban·tam·weight (ban′təm·wāt′) *n.* A boxer or wrestler who weighs between 113 and 118 pounds.

ban·ter (ban′tər) *n.* Good-humored ridicule; raillery; repartee. — *v.t.* **1.** To tease or ridicule good-naturedly. — *v.i.* **2.** To exchange good-natured repartee. [Origin unknown] — **ban′ter·er** *n.* — **ban′ter·ing·ly** *adv.*

— **Syn.** (noun) *Banter, badinage,* and *raillery* mean jesting ridicule without intention to offend. *Banter* is playful, with humor that may be very broad. *Badinage* is more restrained or subtle, with emphasis on verbal elegance, while *raillery* is more overtly critical, and may be sardonic or sarcastic, though still good-humored.

Ban·ting (ban′ting), **Sir Frederick Grant,** 1891–1941, Canadian physician; discovered insulin treatment for diabetes.

bant·ling (bant′ling) *n.* **1.** A young child; brat. **2.** *Obs.* A bastard. [< G *bänkling* bastard]

Ban·tu (ban′tōō) *n. pl.* **·tu** or **·tus** (-tōōz) **1.** A member of any of numerous Negro tribes of central and southern Africa, including the Kaffirs, Zulus, Bechuanas, and Damaras. **2.** A family of languages spoken by these tribes, including Xhosa, Zulu, Bechuana, Swahili, and Kikuyu. — *adj.* Of or pertaining to the Bantu tribes or their languages.

Ban·ville (bän·vēl′), **Théodore de,** 1823–91, French poet and dramatist.

ban·yan (ban′yən) *n.* An East Indian fig-bearing tree (*Ficus benghalensis*), whose branches send down roots that develop into new trunks, producing a thick and shady grove: also spelled *banian.* [< BANIAN, from the use of the ground under the tree as a market place]

ban·zai (bän·zī) *Japanese* (May you live) ten thousand years: used as a cheer, battle cry, etc.

banzai attack A suicidal attempt to carry a position by infantry charge, used by the Japanese in World War II. Also **banzai charge.**

ba·o·bab (bā′ō·bab, bä′ō-) *n.* An African tree (*Adansonia digitata*) with a thick trunk, bearing edible, gourdlike fruit: also called *monkey bread.* [< native African name]

bap. or **bapt.** Baptized.

Bapt. or **Bap.** Baptist.

bap·tism (bap′tiz·əm) *n.* **1.** The act of baptizing or of being baptized; especially, the Christian sacrament of initiation, symbolizing rebirth and purification, commitment to Christ, etc. **2.** Any initiatory or purifying experience. **3.** Any religious ablution signifying a purification or consecration. **4.** In Christian Science, purification by Spirit; submergence in Spirit. [< OF *baptesme* < LL *baptismus* < Gk. *baptismos* immersion] — **bap·tis·mal** (bap·tiz′məl) *adj.* — **bap·tis′mal·ly** *adv.*

baptismal name A name given a person at baptism; a Christian's given name: also called *Christian name.*

baptism of fire **1.** A soldier's first experience of actual combat. **2.** Any crucial ordeal or purifying experience.

Bap·tist (bap′tist) *n.* **1.** A member of any of various Pro-

testant denominations holding that baptism (generally by immersion) should be given only to professed believers. **2.** One who baptizes. — **the Baptist** John the Baptist.

bap·tis·ter·y (bap′tis·tər·ē, -tis·trē) *n. pl.* **·ter·ies 1.** A part of a church or building set apart for baptism. **2.** A font used for baptizing. **3.** In Baptist churches, a tank for baptizing by total immersion. Also **bap′tis·try** (-trē).

bap·tize (bap·tīz′, bap′tīz) *v.* **·tized, ·tiz·ing** *v.t.* **1.** To immerse in water or pour or sprinkle water on in Christian baptism. **2.** To christen or name. **3.** To cleanse, sanctify, or initiate. — *v.i.* **4.** To administer baptism. Also *Brit.* **bap·tise′.** [< OF *baptiser* < LL *baptizare* < Gk. *baptizein* to immerse, wash] — **bap·tiz′er** *n.*

bar[1] (bär) *n.* **1.** A piece of wood, metal, etc., evenly shaped and long in proportion to its width and thickness, used as a fastening, lever, etc. **2.** An oblong block of a solid material, as of soap or a precious metal. **3.** A unit of quantity based on such a block. **4.** Any barrier or obstruction; obstacle: a *bar* to success. **5.** A bank, as of sand, at the entrance to a river or harbor. **6.** The railing about the place in a court occupied by the judge, lawyers, etc., where prisoners stand to plead or to hear sentence. **7.** A place of justice; a court. **8.** Lawyers collectively; the legal profession. **9.** Any tribunal or place of judgment: the *bar* of conscience. **10.** *Music*

BAR (*def.* 10)
a and *b* are separated by a single bar; *b* is terminated by a double bar.

a The vertical line that divides a staff into measures. **b** A double bar (which see). **c** The unit of music between two bars; measure. **11.** A counter where drinks or food are served; also, a room or commercial establishment having such a counter. **12.** A stripe or band, as of color. **13.** The metal mouthpiece of a horse's bridle. **14.** The portion of a horse's foot that bends toward the frog. **15.** In needlepoint, a thread or group of threads passed across an opening. **16.** *Law* The preventing or stopping of an action by showing that the plaintiff has no right of action. **17.** *Heraldry* An ordinary formed by two horizontal parallel lines covering one fifth of the field. — **Syn.** See BARRIER. — *v.t.* **barred, bar·ring 1.** To fasten or secure with a bar. **2.** To confine or shut out with or as with bars. **3.** To obstruct or hinder: to *bar* the way. **4.** To exclude or except. **5.** To mark with bars. **6.** *Music* To provide with bars; divide into measures. — *prep.* Barring; excepting: *bar* none. [< OF *barre* < LL *barra* bar; ult. origin unknown]

bar[2] (bär) *n.* The cgs international unit of pressure, equal to 1,000,000 dynes a square centimeter or a pressure of 29.531 inches of mercury at 32° F. [< Gk. *baros* weight]

bar. 1. Barometer; barometric. **2.** Barrel. **3.** Barrister.

B.Ar. Bachelor of Architecture.

BAR *Mil.* Browning automatic rifle.

Ba·rab·bas (bə·rab′əs) A thief released in place of Jesus at the demand of the multitude. *Matt.* xxvii 16–21.

Bar·ak (bâr·ak′) A warrior who, with Deborah, overcame Sisera and the Canaanites. *Judg.* iv. 6.

Ba·ra·ny (bä′rä·ny′), **Robert,** 1876–1936, Austrian physician.

bar·a·the·a (bar′ə·thē′ə) *n.* A soft fabric of silk combined with cotton or wool. [Origin uncertain]

barb[1] (bärb) *n.* **1.** A point projecting backward on a sharp weapon, as on an arrow, fishhook, or spear, intended to prevent easy extraction. **2.** Any similar sharp point, as on barbed wire. **3.** Pointedness; sting, as of wit; also, a stinging remark. **4.** *Bot.* A beard, as in certain grains and grasses; awn. **5.** *Ornithol.* One of the lateral processes of a bird's feather. For illustration see FEATHER. **6.** A piece of cloth or scarf for covering a woman's neck and breast, now worn by certain nuns. **7.** *pl. Vet.* **a** Paps or folds of the mucous membrane under the tongue of cattle and horses. **b** A disease characterized by their inflammation. **8.** *Zool.* A beardlike growth near the mouth of some animals. **9.** *Obs.* A beard. — *v.t.* To provide with a barb or barbs: to *barb* an arrow. [< F *barbe* < L *barba* beard]

barb[2] (bärb) *n.* **1.** A horse of the breed introduced by the Moors from Barbary into Spain. **2.** A blackish or dun pigeon with a short, stout beak. [< F *barbe* < *Barbarie* Barbary, ult. < Arabic *Barbar* natives of North Africa]

Bar·ba·dos (bär·bā′dōz) The easternmost of the Caribbean islands, former British Colony, independent since 1966; 166 sq. mi.; pop. 253,620 (est. 1970); capital, Bridgetown.

Barbados pride Flowerfence.

bar·bal (bär′bəl) *adj. Obs.* Of or pertaining to the beard. [< L *barba* beard]

bar·bar·i·an (bär·bâr′ē·ən) *n.* **1.** One who belongs to a people, group, or tribe characterized by a primitive civilization. **2.** A rude, coarse, or brutal person. **3.** One who lacks or is indifferent to culture; a philistine, **4.** A foreigner; especially, in ancient Greece, one who was non-Hellenic. — *adj.* **1.** Of or resembling a barbarian; uncivilized. **2.** Foreign. — **Syn.** See BARBAROUS. — **bar·bar′i·an·ism** *n.*

bar·bar·ic (bär·bar′ik) *adj.* **1.** Of or befitting barbarians; uncivilized. **2.** Coarse: *barbaric* manners. **3.** Crudely ornate; unrestrained. — **Syn.** See BARBAROUS. [OF *barbarique* < L *barbaricus* < *barbarus* barbarian. See BARBAROUS.]

bar·ba·rism (bär′bə·riz′əm) *n.* **1.** The use of words or forms not approved or standard in a language. **2.** Such a word or form. **3.** A primitive stage of civilization. **4.** A trait, condition, act, etc., characteristic of such a stage.

bar·bar·i·ty (bär·bar′ə·tē) *n. pl.* **·ties** **1.** Barbaric conduct. **2.** A barbaric act. **3.** Crudity in style or taste.

bar·ba·rize (bär′bə·rīz) *v.t. & v.i.* **·rized, ·riz·ing** To make or become barbarous or corrupt, as a language.

Bar·ba·ros·sa (bär′bə·ros′ə) **1.** The name of two brothers, Barbary corsairs: **Horuk**, died 1518, and **Khair-ed-Din**, died 1546, rulers of Algiers. **2.** Nickname of FREDERICK I.

bar·ba·rous (bär′bər·əs) *adj.* **1.** Uncivilized; primitive. **2.** Lacking in refinement; coarse. **3.** Cruel; brutal. **4.** Rude or harsh in sound: *barbarous* music. **5.** Of language, abounding in barbarisms; also, not classical. **6.** Foreign; especially, in ancient Greece, non-Hellenic. [< L *barbarus* foreign, barbarian < Gk. *barbaros* non-Hellenic, foreign, rude] — **bar′ba·rous·ly** *adv.* — **bar′ba·rous·ness** *n.*

— **Syn. 1.** *Barbarous, barbarian,* and *barbaric* all refer to uncivilized or primitive peoples, things, or actions. *Barbarous* and *barbarian* are both used in simple description, though *barbarous* often has a pejorative note: *barbarian* tribes, a rude and *barbarous* age. *Barbaric* is used of persons and things resembling or appropriate to barbarians: the *barbaric* art of Assyria, *barbaric* laws and customs. **3.** *Barbarous, savage, brutal,* and *cruel* all refer to the harsher aspects of human behavior. *Barbarous* suggests the roughness of uncivilized peoples; *savage* is more extreme and adds a note of ferocity. *Brutal* emphasizes domination or abuse by physical force, and often an animallike unconcern for the object of brutality, whereas *cruel* implies a deliberate intention to hurt or injure: a *brutal* robbery, a *cruel* remark.

Bar·ba·ry (bär′bər·ē) North Africa west of Egypt, including the former Barbary States.

Barbary ape An easily trained, tailless ape (*Macaca sylvana*) of North Africa and southern Spain: also called *magot.*

Barbary Coast 1. The coastal region of Barbary. **2.** A waterfront region of San Francisco before the earthquake of 1906, infamous for its saloons, gambling houses, and brothels.

Barbary States Formerly, part of the northern coast of Africa, including Tripolitania, Algeria, Tunisia, and usually Morocco; centers of piracy until occupied by the European powers in the early 19th century.

bar·bate (bär′bāt) *adj.* **1.** Bearded. **2.** *Bot.* Tufted with long hairs. [< L *barbatus* bearded < *barba* beard]

bar·be·cue (bär′bə·kyōō) *n.* **1.** *U.S.* A social gathering, usually outdoors, at which animals are roasted whole over an open fire. **2.** A whole animal carcass or other meat roasted over an open fire. **3.** A grill, framework, or pit for roasting meat in this fashion. **4.** Formerly, a wooden framework for smoking or drying meat. — *v.t.* **·cued, ·cu·ing 1.** To roast (usually beef or pork) in large pieces or whole over an open fire or in a trench, often using a highly seasoned sauce. **2.** To cook (meat) with a highly seasoned sauce. [< Sp. *barbacoa* < Taino *barbacoa* framework of sticks]

barbed (bärbd) *adj.* **1.** Having a barb or barbs. **2.** Pointed, piercing, or wounding: a *barbed* remark.

barbed wire Fence wire having barbs at short intervals.

bar·bel (bär′bəl) *n.* **1.** One of the soft threadlike appendages to the jaws, chin, or nostrils of certain fishes, functioning as an organ of touch. **2.** A carplike, Old World cyprinoid fish (genus *Barbus*). [< OF < LL *barbellus*, dim. of *barbus* barbel (def. 2) < L *barba* beard]

bar·bell (bär′bel) *n.* A bar with one or more detachable weighted disks at both ends, used in weight lifting.

bar·bel·late (bär′bə·lāt, bär·bel′it) *adj. Bot.* Having or studded with short, stiff hairs or bristles. [< NL *barbella*, double dim. of L *barba* beard]

bar·ber (bär′bər) *n.* One who cuts hair, shaves beards, etc., as a business. ◆ Collateral adjective: *tonsorial.* — *v.t.* To cut or dress the hair of; shave or trim the beard of. [< AF *barbour,* OF *barbeor,* ult. < L *barba* beard]

Bar·ber (bär′bər), **Samuel,** born 1910, U.S. composer.

bar·ber·ry (bär′ber′ē, -bər·ē) *n. pl.* **·ries 1.** A shrub (genus *Berberis*) bearing yellow flowers and bright red, oblong berries, typical of a small family (*Berberidaceae*). **2.** Its acid berry. [< Med.L *berberis, barbaris*]

bar·ber·shop (bär′bər·shop′) *n.* The place of business of a barber. — *adj. Informal* Characterized by close harmony and usually by sentimentality of theme: said of a male singing group: *barbershop* quartet.

Bar·ber·ton (bär′bər·tən) A city in NE Ohio; pop. 33,052.

bar·bet (bär′bit) *n.* **1.** A tropical bird (family *Capitonidae*) having a broad bill surrounded by bristles at the base, related to the toucans. **2.** A variety of small poodle. [< F < OF, orig., bearded < L *barbatus*]

bar·bette (bär·bet′) *n.* **1.** *Naval* An armored cylinder protecting a revolving turret on a warship. **2.** *Mil.* A platform behind a parapet enabling guns to fire over the top. [< F *barbette,* dim. of *barbe* beard]

bar·bi·can (bär′bi·kən) *n.* An outer fortification; outwork. [< OF *barbaquenne;* ult. origin uncertain]

bar·bi·cel (bär′bə·sel) *n. Ornithol.* One of the very small, simple processes fringing the lower edges of the barbule of a feather. [< NL *barbicella,* dim. of L *barba* beard]

bar·bi·tal (bär′bə·tôl, -tal) *n. Chem.* A white, odorless, crystalline powder, $C_8H_{12}O_3N_2$, with a faintly bitter taste, derived from barbituric acid and used as a sedative and hypnotic. Also *Brit.* **bar′bi·tone** (-tōn).

bar·bit·u·rate (bär·bich′ər·it, bär′bə·tōōr′it, -tyōōr′it) *n.* **1.** *Chem.* A salt or ester of barbituric acid. **2.** A sedative or sleeping pill, as those derived from barbituric acid.

bar·bi·tu·ric acid (bär′bə·tōōr′ik, -tyōōr′-) *Chem.* A crystalline powder, $C_4H_4O_3N_2$, slightly soluble in water or alcohol, and the base from which several sedative and hypnotic drugs are derived: also called *malonylurea.* [< NL (*Usnea*) *barbata* bearded (lichen) + -URIC]

Bar·bi·zon school (bär′bə·zon, *Fr.* bár·bē·zôn′) A group of French landscape painters of the 19th century, including Corot, Daubigny, Millet, and Théodore Rousseau. [after *Barbizon,* a village near Paris where they worked]

Bar·bu·da (bär·bōō′də) One of the Leeward Islands in the West Indies, a dependency of Antigua; 62 sq. mi.

bar·bule (bär′byōōl) *n.* **1.** A small barb or beard. **2.** *Ornithol.* A process fringing the barb of a feather. For illustration see FEATHER. [< L *barbula,* dim. of *barba* beard]

Bar·busse (bär·büs′), **Henri,** 1873–1935, French novelist.

Bar·ca (bär′kə) An influential Carthaginian family to which Hamilcar, Hannibal, and Hasdrubal belonged.

bar·ca·role (bär′kə·rōl) *n.* **1.** A Venetian gondolier's song. **2.** A melody in imitation of such a song. Also **bar′ca·rolle.** [< F *barcarolle* < Ital. *barcaruola* boatman's song < *barca* boat]

Bar·ce·lo·na (bär′sə·lō′nə, *Sp.* bär′thä·lō′nä) A Province of NE Spain, in Catalonia; 2,985 sq. mi.; pop. 3,213,212 (1965); capital, **Barcelona,** a port city on the Mediterranean, pop. 1,655,603 (1965).

B.Arch. Bachelor of Architecture.

Bar·clay (bär′klē), **Robert,** 1648–90, Scottish Quaker author.

Bar·clay de Tol·ly (bär·klī′ də tô′lyi), **Prince Mikhail,** 1761–1818, Russian field marshal.

bard[1] (bärd) *n.* **1.** A Celtic poet and minstrel. **2.** A poet. [< Celtic] — **bard′ic** *adj.*

— **Syn. 1.** *Bard, skald, scop,* and *trouvère* denote poets who, at different times and in different lands, wrote and sang of historical and legendary events. The *bards* were ancient Welsh and Irish poets, but the word has now been extended to include all who write verses to be recited or sung. The *skalds* were ancient Scandinavians, the *scops* Anglo-Saxons, and the *trouvères* roamed northern France from the 11th to the 14th century. Compare MINSTREL, TROUBADOUR, POET.

bard[2] (bärd) *n.* Any piece of armor worn by horses. — *v.t.* To arm with bards. Also **barde.** [< F *barde,* ult. < Arabic *al-barda′ah* packsaddle]

Bard of Avon William Shakespeare.

bare[1] (bâr) *adj.* **1.** Without clothing or covering; naked. **2.** Open to view; exposed. **3.** Without the usual furnishings or equipment; empty: a *bare* room. **4.** Unadorned; plain; bald: the *bare* truth. **5.** Just sufficient; mere: the *bare* necessities. **6.** Threadbare. — *v.t.* **bared, bar·ing** To make or lay bare; reveal; expose. [OE *bær*]

bare[2] (bâr) Archaic past tense of BEAR[1].

bare·back (bâr′bak′) *adj.* Riding a horse without a saddle. — *adv.* Without a saddle. — **bare′backed′** *adj.*

bare·faced (bâr′fāst′) *adj.* **1.** Having the face bare. **2.** Unconcealed; open. **3.** Impudent; audacious. — **bare·fac·ed·ly** (bâr′fā′sid·lē, -fāst′lē) *adv.* — **bare′fac′ed·ness** *n.*

bare·fit (bâr′fit) *adj. Scot.* Barefoot.

bare·foot (bâr′fōōt′) *adj. & adv.* With the feet bare.

bare·foot·ed (bâr′fōōt′id) *adj.* Having the feet bare.

ba·rege (bə·rezh′) *n.* A sheer fabric of silk and wool or cotton and wool, used for veils, etc. [after *Barèges,* a French village]

bare·hand·ed (bâr′han′did) *adj. & adv.* **1.** With the hands uncovered. **2.** Without a weapon, tool, etc.

bare·head·ed (bâr′hed′id) *adj. & adv.* With the head bare. Also **bare′head′.**

Ba·reil·ly (bə·rā′li, bu–, -lē) A city in north central Uttar Pradesh, India; pop. 325,560 (est. 1969). Also **Ba·re′li.**

bare·leg·ged (bâr′leg′id, -legd′) *adj. & adv.* With the legs bare.

bare·ly (bâr′lē) *adv.* **1.** Only just; scarcely. ◆ See note under HARDLY. **2.** Openly; boldly; plainly. **3.** Nakedly. **4.** *Archaic* Simply; only.

Ba·rents (bä′rənts), **Willem,** died 1597, Dutch explorer.

Bar·ents Sea (bar′ənts, bä′rənts) A part of the Arctic Ocean north of Norway and the NW Soviet Union.

bare·sark (bâr′särk) *n.* A berserker (def. 1). — *adv.* Without armor. [Alter. of BERSERK]

Ba·ret·ti (bä·rāt′tē), **Giuseppe Marc Antonio,** 1719–89, Italian critic.
bar·fly (bär′flī′) *n. pl.* **·flies** *Slang* A frequenter of barrooms.
bar·gain (bär′gən) *n.* **1.** A mutual agreement between persons, especially an agreement to buy or sell goods. **2.** That which is agreed upon or the terms of the agreement. **3.** The agreement as it affects one of the parties: He made a bad *bargain*. **4.** An article bought or offered at a low price. **— into the bargain** In addition to what was agreed; besides. **— to strike a bargain** To come to an agreement. *— v.i.* **1.** To discuss terms for selling or buying. **2.** To make a bargain; reach an agreement. **3.** To negotiate. *— v.t.* **4.** To trade or arrange by bargaining. **— to bargain for** To expect; count on: more than I *bargained for*. [< OF *bargaine*; ult. origin uncertain] **— bar′gain·er, *Law* bar′gain·or** *n.*
barge (bärj) *n.* **1.** A flat-bottomed, often unpowered freight boat or lighter for harbors and inland waters. **2.** A large boat, for pleasure, pageants, or for state occasions. **3.** *Naval* A ship's boat for the use of a flag officer. *— v.* **barged, barg·ing** *v.t.* **1.** To transport by barge. *— v.i.* **2.** To move clumsily and slowly. **3.** *Informal* To collide: with *into*. **4.** *Informal* To enter or intrude rudely or awkwardly: to *barge* into a room. [< OF < LL *barga*. Akin to BARK³.]
barge·board (bärj′bôrd′, -bōrd′) *n. Archit.* A board, often ornate, attached along the barge couples and following the outline of a gable end.
barge couple One of a pair of outside rafters (**barge couples**) that support the projecting end of a gable roof.
barge course 1. The part of a gable roof projecting beyond the bargeboards or end wall. **2.** A course of bricks laid edgewise to form the coping of a wall.
barge·man (bärj′mən) *n. pl.* **·men** (-mən) One in charge of or employed on a barge. Also *Brit.* **bar·gee** (bär·jē′).

BARGEBOARD
a Barge course.
b Bargeboard. *c* Rafter. *d* Barge couple.

Bar Harbor An unincorporated resort and port on Mount Desert Island in south central Maine; pop. 3,716.
Ba·ri (bä′rē) A Province of Apulia, Italy; 1,980 sq. mi.; pop. 1,259,757 (1961); capital, **Bari** (formerly also **Bari delle Puglie**), also capital of the Region, pop. 311,268.
bar·ic¹ (bar′ik) *adj.* Of or pertaining to weight, especially the weight of air; barometric. [< Gk. *barys* heavy]
bar·ic² (bar′ik) *adj.* Of, pertaining to, derived from, or containing barium. [< BAR(IUM) + -IC]
ba·ril·la (bə·ril′ə) *n.* **1.** An impure sodium carbonate and sulfate obtained by burning certain land or marine plants. **2.** Any plant used in making soda ash, especially the saltwort. [< Sp. *barrilla* impure soda]
Bar·ing (bâr′ing), **Alexander** See (Lord) ASHBURTON. **— Evelyn,** 1841–1917, first earl of Cromer, English diplomat. **— Maurice,** 1874–1945, English novelist.
Bar·ing-Gould (bâr′ing·gōōld′), **Sabine,** 1834–1924, English clergyman and writer.
barit. *Music* Baritone.
bar·ite (bâr′īt) *n.* A heavy, vitreous, usually white, orthorhombic barium sulfate, BaSO₄: also called *heavy spar*. [< BAR(IUM) + -ITE¹]
bar·i·tone (bar′ə·tōn) *n.* **1.** A male voice of a register higher than bass and lower than tenor. **2.** One having such a voice. **3.** A brass instrument, used chiefly in military bands, having a similar range. *— adj.* **1.** Of or pertaining to a baritone. **2.** Having the range of a baritone. Also spelled *barytone.* [< Ital. *baritono* < Gk. *barytonos* deep-sounding < *barys* deep + *tonos* tone]
bar·i·um (bâr′ē·əm) *n.* A silver white to yellow, malleable, metallic element (symbol Ba) of the alkaline earth group, occurring in combination in nature and forming salts, of which the soluble ones and the carbonate are poisonous. See ELEMENT. [< NL < Gk. *barys* heavy]
barium oxide *Chem.* A yellowish white, poisonous alkaline compound, BaO, used in glassmaking and as a reagent: also called *baryta*.
barium sulfate An insoluble compound, BaSO₄, produced synthetically as a white precipitate, used to facilitate X-ray pictures of the stomach and intestines.
bark¹ (bärk) *n.* **1.** The short, abrupt, explosive cry of a dog. **2.** Any sound like this. *— v.i.* **1.** To utter a bark, as a dog, or to make a sound like a bark. **2.** *Informal* To cough. **3.** To speak loudly and sharply. **4.** *U.S. Slang* To solicit customers at the entrance to a show by proclaiming its attractions. *— v.t.* **5.** To say roughly and curtly: He *barked* an order. **— to bark up the wrong tree** *U.S. Informal* To be mistaken as to one's object or as to the means of attaining it. [OE *beorcan*]
bark² (bärk) *n.* **1.** The rind or covering of the stems, branches, and roots of a tree or other plant, as distinguished from the wood. For illustration see EXOGEN. **2.** Some variety of this substance, having special medicinal, tannic, or other qualities, as cinchona, sassafras, etc. *— v.t.* **1.** To remove the bark from; scrape; girdle. **2.** To rub off the skin of. **3.**

To cover with or as with bark. **4.** To tan or treat with an infusion of bark. [< Scand. Cf. ON *börkr*.]
bark³ (bärk) *n.* **1.** A sailing vessel of three or more masts, square-rigged on all but the mizzenmast, that is fore-and-aft-rigged. **2.** *Poetic* Any vessel or boat. Also spelled *barque.* [< MF *barque* < LL *barca* bark]

BARK

bark beetle One of several small burrowing beetles (family *Scolytidae*) that destroy the bark and wood of trees. For illustration see INSECTS (injurious).
bar·keep·er (bär′kē?pər) *n.* **1.** One who owns or manages a bar where alcoholic liquors are served. **2.** A bartender. Also **bar′keep′.**
bar·ken·tine (bär′kən·tēn) *n.* A sailing vessel of three or more masts, square-rigged on the foremast and fore-and-aft-rigged on the other masts: also spelled *barquentine.* [< BARK³, on analogy with *brigantine*]
bark·er¹ (bär′kər) *n.* **1.** One who or that which barks. **2.** *U.S. Informal* One who advertises a show, etc , at its entrance.
bark·er² (bär′kər) *n.* One who or that which removes bark from trees or works with bark.
Bark·la (bär′klə), **Charles Glover,** 1877–1944, English physicist.
Bark·ley (bärk′lē), **Alben William,** 1877–1956, U.S. statesman; vice president 1949–53: called **the Veep** (vēp).
bark·y (bär′kē) *adj.* **bark·i·er, bark·i·est** Covered with, resembling, or containing bark.
bar·ley¹ (bär′lē) *n.* **1.** A hardy, bearded cereal grass (*Hordeum vulgare*) of temperate regions, with long leaves, stout awns, and triple spikelets at the joints. **2.** The grain borne by this grass. [OE *bærlīc*]
bar·ley·corn (bär′lē·kôrn) *n.* **1.** A grain of barley. **2.** A unit of measure, originally the breadth of a barley grain, equal to one third of an inch.
Bar·ley·corn (bär′lē·kôrn), **John** A humorous personification of malt liquor, or of intoxicating liquors in general.
barley sugar A clear, brittle confection made by boiling sugar with a barley extract.
Bar·low (bär′lō), **Jane,** 1860–1917, Irish novelist. **— Joel,** 1754–1812, U.S. poet and diplomat.
Barlow's disease Infantile scurvy. [after Sir Thomas *Barlow,* 1845–1945, English physician]
barm (bärm) *n.* The froth or foam rising on fermented malt liquors. [OE *beorma*]
bar·maid (bär′mād) *n.* A woman who serves drinks at or in a bar.
bar·man (bär′mən) *n. pl.* **·men** (mən) A bartender (which see).
Bar·me·cide (bär′mə·sīd) In the *Arabian Nights*, a prince of Baghdad who serves an imaginary feast to a beggar in empty dishes.
Barmecide feast Any illusory hospitality or abundance.
bar mitz·vah (bär mits′və) In Judaism, a boy who has reached the age of thirteen, the age of religious duty and responsibility; also, the ceremony celebrating this. [< Hebrew, son of the commandment]
barm·y (bär′mē) *adj.* **barm·i·er, barm·i·est 1.** Full of barm; frothy. **2.** *Brit. Slang* Silly; flighty. Also *Scot.* **barm′ie.**
barn¹ (bärn) *n.* **1.** A building for storing hay, stabling livestock, etc. **2.** *Brit.* A building for storing grain. [OE *bern*]
barn² (bärn) *n. Physics* A unit of area used in measuring the cross sections of atomic nuclei, equal to 10⁻²⁴ square centimeter. [So called in allusion to the phrase "He can't hit the side of a barn door."]
Bar·na·bas (bär′nə·bəs) First-century Christian missionary and reputed author of an apocryphal gospel and epistle: also, called *Saint Barnabas*: original name **Jo·ses** (jō′sēz). *Acts* xiii 1.
bar·na·cle¹ (bär′nə·kəl) *n.* **1.** A marine shellfish (order *Cirripedia*) that attaches itself to rocks, ship bottoms, etc.; especially, the **rock barnacle** (*Balanus balanoides*) and the **goose barnacle** (*Lepas fascicularis*). **2.** A European wild goose of northern seas (*Branta leucopsis*): also called *bernicle*: also **barnacle goose. 3.** One who or that which clings tenaciously. [< ME *bernacle*; origin uncertain]
bar·na·cle² (bär′nə·kəl) *n. Usually pl.* An instrument for pinching the nose of an unruly horse. [< OF *bernacle*, dim. of *bernac* a bit]
bar·na·cled (bär′nə·kəld) *adj.* Covered with barnacles.
Bar·nard (bär′nərd), **George Grey,** 1863–1938, U.S. sculptor. **— Henry,** 1811–1900, U.S. educator.
Bar·na·ul (bär′nä·ōōl′) The capital of the Altai Territory of the Soviet Union, on the Ob in SW Siberia; pop. 439,000 (est. 1970).
barn dance 1. A social dance usually consisting of square dances with appropriate music and calls. **2.** A country dance resembling the schottische.

Barnes (bärnz), **Harry Elmer,** 1889–1968, U.S. sociologist and educator.

Bar·ne·veldt (bär′nə·velt), **Jan van Olden,** 1547–1619, Dutch patriot. Also **Bar′ne·veld.**

barn owl An owl (*Tyto alba*) of nearly world-wide distribution, often found in barns, where it preys on mice.

Barns·ley (bärnz′lē) A county borough in South Yorkshire, northern England, on the Dearne river; pop. 224,100 (1976).

barn·storm (bärn′stôrm′) *v.i. U.S. Informal* **1.** To tour rural districts, giving shows, political speeches, etc. **2.** To tour rural districts, giving exhibitions of stunt flying, short airplane rides, etc. [< BARN[1] + STORM, v.] — **barn′storm′·er** *n.*

barn·storm·ing (bärn′stôrm′ing) *n.* The act of one who barnstorms. — *adj.* Of or pertaining to barnstorming.

barn swallow See under SWALLOW[2].

Bar·num (bär′nəm), **P(hineas) T(aylor),** 1810–91. U.S. showman.

barn·yard (bärn′yärd′) *n.* A yard adjoining a barn. — *adj.* **1.** Of or pertaining to a barnyard. **2.** Fit for a barnyard; earthy; broad: said of speech, humor, etc.

baro- *combining form* Weight; atmospheric pressure: as *barometer.* [< Gk. *baros* weight]

Ba·roc·chio (bä·rôk′kyō), **Giacomo** See VIGNOLA.

Ba·ro·da (bə·rō′də) A former princely state of northern India, divided into several districts of Bombay State, 1948.

bar·o·gram (bar′ə·gram) *n.* The record of a barograph.

bar·o·graph (bar′ə·graf, -gräf) *n.* An automatically recording barometer. — **bar′o·graph′ic** *adj.*

Ba·ro·ja (bä·rō′hä), **Pío,** 1872–1956, Spanish novelist.

ba·rom·e·ter (bə·rom′ə·tər) *n.* **1.** An instrument for measuring atmospheric pressure, used in forecasting weather, measuring elevations, etc. Abbr. *bar.* **2.** Anything that indicates changes. — **bar·o·met·ric** (bar′ə·met′rik) or **·ri·cal** *adj.* — **bar·o·met′ri·cal·ly** *adv.* — **ba·rom′e·try** *n.*

bar·on (bar′ən) *n.* **1.** A member of the lowest order of hereditary nobility in several European countries; also, the dignity or rank itself. **2.** *U.S.* One who has great power in a commercial field: a coal *baron.* **3.** In English history, a feudal tenant of the king; a noble. **4.** A cut of beef consisting of two sirloins. [< OF < LL *baro, -onis* man < Gmc.]

bar·on·age (bar′ən·ij) *n.* **1.** Barons collectively. **2.** The dignity or rank of a baron.

bar·on·ess (bar′ən·is) *n.* **1.** The wife or widow of a baron. **2.** A woman holding a barony in her own right.

bar·on·et (bar′ən·it, -ə·net) *n.* **1.** An inheritable English title, below that of baron and not part of the nobility. **2.** The bearer of the title, designated by "Sir" before the name and "Baronet" or the abbreviation "Bart." or "Bt." after.

bar·on·et·age (bar′ən·it·ij, -ə·net′-) *n.* **1.** Baronets collectively. **2.** The dignity or rank of a baronet.

bar·on·et·cy (bar′ən·it·sē, -ə·net′-) *n. pl.* **·cies 1.** The title or rank of a baronet. **2.** The patent giving such rank.

ba·rong (bä·rông′, -rong′) *n.* In the Philippines, a cleaver-like knife used by the Moros.

ba·ro·ni·al (bə·rō′nē·əl) *adj.* Pertaining to or befitting a baron, a barony, or the order of barons.

ba·ronne (bà·rôn′) *n. French* A baroness.

bar·o·ny (bar′ə·nē) *n. pl.* **·nies** The rank, dignity, or domain of a baron.

ba·roque (bə·rōk′) *adj.* **1.** Of or characteristic of a style of art and architecture developed in Europe in the late 16th and 17th centuries, characterized by extravagantly contorted classical forms, dynamic curvilinear ornament, and theatrical effects. **2.** *Music* Of or resembling a style of composition dominant in the 17th and early 18th centuries, characterized by breadth of concept, rich harmonies, ornamentation, and brilliant effects. **3.** Fantastic in style; grotesque. **4.** Loosely, rococo. **5.** Irregular in shape: said of pearls. — *n.* **1.** The baroque style in music or art. **2.** An object, ornament, design, or composition in this style. [< F < Pg. *barroco* rough or imperfect pearl]

bar·o·scope (bar′ə·skōp) *n.* An instrument for approximately indicating atmospheric pressure; a weatherglass. — **bar′o·scop′ic** (-skop′ik) or **·i·cal** *adj.*

Ba·rot·se·land Protectorate (bə·rot′sē·land) A Province of western Northern Rhodesia; 44,920 sq. mi.; pop. about 298,000; capital, Mongu Lealui. Also **Ba·rot′se·land, Ba·rot′se.**

ba·rouche (bə·rōōsh′) *n.* A four-wheeled carriage with folding top, four inside seats, and an outside seat for the driver. [< G *barutsche* < Ital. *baroccio* < L *bis* twice + *rota* wheel]

Ba·roz·zi (bä·rôt′tsē), **Giacomo** See VIGNOLA.

barque (bärk), **bar·quen·tine** (bär′kən·tēn) See BARK[3], BARKENTINE.

BAROQUE ARCHITECTURE
(Church of Santa Maria della Salute, Venice, 1631–56)

bar·rack[1] (bar′ək) *v.t. & v.i.* To house in barracks.

bar·rack[2] (bar′ək) *v.t. & v.i. Austral. & Brit. Slang* To shout for or against (a group, team, etc.). [Origin unknown]

bar·racks (bar′əks) *n.pl.* (*construed as sing. or pl.*) **1.** A building or group of buildings for the housing of soldiers. Abbr. *bks.* **2.** Any large, plain building used for temporary housing. Also **bar′rack.** [< F *baraque* < Ital. *baracca* soldier's tent; ult. origin uncertain]

barracks bag A soldier's cloth bag with a draw cord, for holding clothing and equipment. Also **barrack bag.**

bar·ra·cu·da (bar′ə·kōō′də) *n. pl.* **·da** or **·das** A voracious pikelike fish (genus *Sphyraena*) of tropical seas. The **great barracuda** (*S. barracuda*), found off the Florida coast, is often 8 feet long. [< Sp.]

bar·rage[1] (bär′ij) *n.* **1.** The act of barring. **2.** An artificial bar placed in a watercourse, to increase its depth for irrigating, etc. [< F < *barre* bar]

bar·rage[2] (bə·räzh′) *n.* **1.** *Mil.* **a** A curtain of fire designed to protect troops by impeding enemy movements across defensive lines or areas. **b** Fire so placed that initial shots are ahead of rapidly moving targets. **c** Jamming of a wide range of radio or radar frequencies: also **barrage jamming. 2.** Any overwhelming attack, as of words or blows. — *v.t. & v.i.* **·raged, ·rag·ing** To lay down or subject to a barrage. [< F (*tir de*) *barrage* barrage (fire)]

barrage balloon See under BALLOON.

bar·ra·mun·da (bar′ə·mun′də) *n. pl.* **·da** or **·das** A large, edible, dipnoan mudfish (*Neoceratodus forsteri*) of Australia: also called *ceratodus.* Also **bar′ra·mun′di** (-dē). [< native Australian name]

bar·ran·ca (bä·räng′kə) *n. SW U.S.* A deep ravine or gorge. [< Sp.]

Bar·ran·quil·la (bär′räng·kē′yä) A port city in northern Colombia, on the Magdalena; pop. 452,140 (est. 1961).

bar·ra·tor (bar′ə·tər) *n. Law* One guilty of barratry. Also **bar′ra·ter.**

bar·ra·try (bar′ə·trē) *n. pl.* **·tries** *Law* **1.** Any willful and unlawful act by the master or crew of a ship, whereby the owners sustain injury. **2.** In Scottish law, the acceptance of a bribe by a judge. **3.** The buying or selling of ecclesiastical positions. **4.** The offense of exciting lawsuits, stirring up quarrels, etc. Also spelled *barretry.* [< OF *baraterie* misuse of office < *barat* fraud] — **bar′ra·trous** *adj.*

barred (bärd) *adj.* **1.** Secured with or obstructed by bars. **2.** Prohibited. **3.** Having or marked with bars or stripes.

barred owl A North American owl (*Strix varia*) having streaked plumage and a hooting cry.

bar·rel (bar′əl) *n.* **1.** A large, approximately cylindrical vessel, usually of wood, flat at the base and top and bulging slightly in the middle. **2.** As much as a barrel will hold, as the standard U.S. barrel containing 3.28 bushels dry measure, or 31.5 gallons liquid measure. See table inside back cover. **3.** *Brit.* The standard barrel for liquid measure containing 36 imperial gallons. **4.** Something resembling or having the form of a barrel. **5.** In firearms, the tube through which the projectile is discharged. For illustration see REVOLVER. **6.** *Naut.* The rotating drum of a windlass, capstan, etc., around which the rope winds. **7.** The cylindrical box containing the mainspring of a watch, around which the chain is wound. **8.** *Ornithol.* The quill of a feather. **9.** The piston chamber of a pump. **10.** The trunk or body of a quadruped. Abbr. (for defs. 1, 2) *bar., bbl.* (pl. *bbls.*), *bl.* (pl. *bls.*). — *v.* **bar·reled** or **·relled, bar·rel·ing** or **·rel·ling** *v.t.* **1.** To put or pack in a barrel. — *v.i.* **2.** *U.S. Slang* To move fast. [< OF *baril;* ult. origin unknown]

barrel chair An upholstered chair having a high, rounded back shaped like part of a barrel.

bar·rel·ful (bar′əl·fōōl) *n. pl.* **·fuls** As much as a barrel will hold.

bar·rel·house (bar′əl·hous′) *n. U.S. Slang* **1.** A cheap drinking house. **2.** *Music* An early style of jazz, originally played in barrelhouses.

barrel organ A hand organ (which see).

barrel roll *Aeron.* A maneuver in which an airplane rolls once on its own axis as it simultaneously spirals once about its original path.

bar·ren (bar′ən) *adj.* **1.** Not producing or incapable of producing offspring; sterile. **2.** Not productive; unfruitful: *barren land;* a *barren mind.* **3.** Unprofitable, as an enterprise. **4.** Lacking in interest or attractiveness; dull. **5.** Empty; devoid: *barren of good sense.* — *n.* **1.** A tract of barren land. **2.** *Usually pl.* A tract of level land, having a sandy soil without trees and producing only scrubby growth. [< OF *baraigne*] — **bar′ren·ly** *adv.* — **bar′ren·ness** *n.*

Barren Ground An Arctic prairie region of northern Canada, extending west from Hudson Bay. Also **Barren Lands, Barrens.**

Bar·rès (bà·res′), **Maurice,** 1862–1923, French novelist, essayist, and politician.

bar·ret (bar′it) *n.* A flat cap, especially a biretta. [< F *barrette* < LL *birettum* cap < *birrus* red cloak]

bar·re·try (bar′ə·trē) See BARRATRY.

bar·rette (bə·ret′) *n.* A small bar with a clasp used for keeping a woman's hair in place. [< F, dim. of *barre* bar]

bar·ri·cade (bar'ə·kād', bar'ə·kād) *n.* **1.** A barrier hastily built for obstruction or defense. **2.** Any barrier or obstruction blocking passage. — **Syn.** See BARRIER. — *v.t.* **·cad·ed, ·cad·ing** To enclose, obstruct, or defend with a barricade or barricades. [< F < Sp. *barricada* barrier < *barrica* barrel; the first barricades were barrels filled with earth, stones, etc.] — **bar'ri·cad'er** *n.*

Bar·rie (bar'ē), **Sir James Matthew,** 1860–1937, Scottish novelist and playwright.

bar·ri·er (bar'ē·ər) *n.* **1.** A fence, wall, gate, etc., erected to bar passage. **2.** Any obstacle or obstruction, natural or otherwise. **3.** Something that separates or keeps apart: a *barrier* of suspicion; a language *barrier*. **4.** In horse racing, the movable gate from which the horses start. **5.** *pl.* Formerly, the palisades enclosing the ground for a tournament; the lists. **6.** *Sometimes cap. Geog.* The part of the Antarctic icecap extending over the sea. [< OF *barriere* < *barre* bar]
— **Syn. 2.** *Barrier, bar,* and *barricade* all mean an obstacle or obstruction. A *barrier* checks or impedes progress, but is not necessarily impassable, while a *bar* prevents entry or passage. *Barriers* and *bars* may be physical objects or circumstances; a *barricade* is always a physical *barrier* hastily erected against advancing soldiers, rioters, crowds, etc.

barrier beach A low sandy strip between ocean and bay.

barrier reef A long, narrow ridge of rock or coral parallel to the coast and close to or above the surface of the sea.

Barrier Reef See GREAT BARRIER REEF.

bar·ring (bar'ing) *prep.* Excepting; apart from.

bar·ri·o (bar'rē·ō) *n. pl.* **·os** In Spanish-speaking countries, especially in the Philippines, one of the districts or wards into which a large town or city is divided; suburb. [< Sp.]

bar·ris·ter (bar'is·tər) *n.* In England, a member of the legal profession who argues cases in the courts: distinguished from *solicitor.* *Abbr. bar.* — **Syn.** See LAWYER. [< BAR[1]]

bar·room (bär'rōōm', -rōōm') *n.* A room where alcoholic liquors are served across a counter or bar.

Bar·ros (bär'rōōsh), **João de,** 1496–1570, Portuguese historian.

bar·row[1] (bar'ō) *n.* **1.** A frame or tray with handles at either end by which it is carried, used for transporting loads. **2.** A wheelbarrow. **3.** The load carried on a barrow. **4.** *Brit.* A pushcart. [OE *bearwe* < *beran* to bear]

bar·row[2] (bar'ō) *n.* **1.** *Anthropol.* A mound of earth or stones built over a grave. **2.** A hill: now only in place names. [OE *beorg*]

bar·row[3] (bar'ō) *n.* A castrated pig. [OE *bearg* pig]

Bar·row (bar'ō), **Point** The northernmost part of Alaska, on the Arctic Ocean.

Bar·row-in-Fur·ness (bar'ō·in·fûr'nes) A borough in Cumbria, England; pop. 75,490 (1976). Also **Bar'·row.**

Bar·ry (bar'ē, *Fr.* bä·rē'), **Comtesse Du** See DU BARRY.

Bar·ry (bar'ē), **Philip,** 1896–1949, U.S. dramatist.

Bar·ry·more (bar'ə·môr, -mōr) A family of U.S. actors: **Maurice** (original name, Herbert Blythe), 1847–1905, father of **Ethel,** 1879–1959, **John,** 1882–1942, and **Lionel,** 1878–1954.

bar sinister See BATON (def. 3).

Bart. Baronet.

bar·tend·er (bär'ten'dər) *n.* A man who mixes and serves alcoholic drinks over a bar.

bar·ter (bär'tər) *v.i.* **1.** To trade by exchange of goods or services without use of money. — *v.t.* **2.** To trade (goods or services) for something of equal value. — *n.* **1.** The act of bartering; exchange of goods. **2.** Anything bartered. [< OF *barater* to exchange] — **bar'ter·er** *n.*

Barth (bärt), **Heinrich,** 1821–65, German explorer. — **Karl,** 1886–1968, Swiss theologian.

Bar·thol·di (bär·thol'dē, *Fr.* bär·tôl·dē'), **Fré·déric Auguste,** 1834–1904, French sculptor; noted for the Statue of Liberty.

Bar·thol·o·mew (bär·thol'ə·myōō) **Saint** One of the twelve apostles. *Mark* iii 18. On his festival day, August 24, in 1572 there took place the slaughter of the Huguenots known as the **Massacre of St. Bartholomew.**

Bar·ti·mae·us (bär'tə·mē'əs) A beggar cured of blindness. *Mark* x 46–52. Also **Bar'ti·me'us.**

bar·ti·zan (bär'tə·zən, bär'tə·zan') *n. Archit.* A small turret jutting from a wall, tower, etc. [Alter. of *bratticing* < BRATTICE] — **bar·ti·zaned** (bär'tə·zənd, bär'tə·zand') *adj.*

Bar·tles·ville (bär'təlz·vil) A city in NE Oklahoma; pop. 29,683.

Bart·lett (bärt'lit) *n.* A variety of pear developed in England about 1770 and introduced into America by Enoch Bartlett of Dorchester, Massachusetts. Also **Bartlett pear.**

Bart·lett (bärt'lit), **John,** 1820–1905, U.S. publisher and editor. — **Josiah,** 1729–95, American patriot; signer of the Declaration of Independence. — **Robert Abram,** 1875–1946, Canadian Arctic explorer.

BARTIZAN

Bar·tók (bär'tôk), **Béla** (bā'lä), 1881–1945, Hungarian composer.

Bar·to·lom·me·o (bär'tō·lōm·mä'ō), **Fra,** 1475–1517, Florentine painter. Also **Baccio del·la Por·ta** (del·la pôr'tä).

Bar·ton (bär'tən), **Clara,** 1821–1912, U.S. founder of the American Red Cross.

Bar·uch (bär'ək) *n.* **1.** The amanuensis of Jeremiah. *Jer.* xxxii–xxxvi. **2.** A book in the Old Testament Apocrypha attributed to Baruch. [< Hebrew, blessed]

Ba·ruch (bə·rōōk'), **Bernard Mannes,** 1870–1965, U.S. financier and statesman.

bar·ye (bar'ē) *n.* In the cgs system, a unit expressing a pressure of one dyne per square centimeter. [< Gk. *barys* heavy]

bar·y·on (bar'ē·on) *n. Physics* Any strongly interacting particle whose spin is half an odd integer; a nucleon or a hyperon. [< Gk. *baryos* heavy + -ON]

baryon number *Physics* The number of baryons minus the number of antibaryons in a system, rigorously conserved in all known interactions.

ba·ry·ta (bə·rī'tə) *n. Chem.* Barium oxide: also called *heavy earth.* [< Gk. *barytēs* weight < *barys* heavy]

bar·y·tes (bə·rī'tēz) *n.* Barite.

bar·y·tone[1] (bar'ə·tōn) *adj.* In Greek grammar, not having the acute accent on the last syllable. Compare OXYTONE. — *n.* A barytone word. [< Gk. *barytonos* unaccented]

bar·y·tone[2] (bar'ə·tōn) See BARITONE.

B.A.S. or **B.A.Sc. 1.** Bachelor of Agricultural Science. **2.** Bachelor of Applied Science.

ba·sal (bā'səl) *adj.* **1.** Of, at, or forming the base. **2.** Basic; fundamental. **3.** *Surg.* Serving to prepare for deeper levels of anesthesia preliminary to surgical operations. — **Syn.** See FUNDAMENTAL. — **ba'sal·ly** *adv.*

basal metabolism *Physiol.* The minimum energy required by the body at rest in maintaining essential vital activities, measured by the rate (**basal metabolic rate.** *Abbr. BMR*) of oxygen intake and heat discharge.

ba·salt (bə·sôlt', bas'ôlt) *n.* **1.** A dense, dark volcanic rock, composed chiefly of plagioclase and pyroxene, usually exhibiting a columnar structure. **2.** A black, unglazed pottery developed by Josiah Wedgwood: also **ba·salt'ware'.** [< L *basaltes* dark marble] — **ba·sal'tic** *adj.*

bas bleu (bä blœ') *French* A bluestocking.

bas·cule (bas'kyōōl) *n.* A mechanical apparatus of which each end counterbalances the other, used in a kind of drawbridge (**bascule bridge**) operated by a counterpoise. [< F, seesaw]

BASCULE BRIDGE
(Tower Bridge, London)

base[1] (bās) *n.* **1.** The lowest or supporting part of anything; bottom. **2.** An underlying principle or datum; basis; foundation: the *base* of a theory. **3.** The essential or preponderant element; chief or fundamental ingredient: the *base* of a perfume. **4.** Any point, line, or quantity from which an inference, measurement, or reckoning is made. **5.** *Archit.* The lowest member of a structure, as the basement of a building, the plinth of a column, the lowest course of a wall, etc. **6.** *Geom.* The side of a polygon, or the face of a solid figure, on which it appears to rest. **7.** *Math.* **a** A number on which a numerical system depends: The *base* of the decimal system is 10. **b** Any collection of mathematical entities that are combined to form greater entities. **8.** In surveying, an accurately measured line on the earth's surface, from which other lines are determined. **9.** *Mil.* A locality or installation from which operations are projected or supported. **10.** *Chem.* A compound that is capable of so uniting with an acid as to neutralize it and form a salt, as sodium hydroxide. **b** A compound that yields hydroxyl ions in solution. **11.** *Biol.* **a** The part of an organ nearest its point of attachment. **b** The point of attachment of an organ. **12.** In baseball, any of the four points of the diamond, or the bag or plate marking one of these. *Abbr. b, b., B.* **13.** In a race, the starting point. **14.** In certain games, as hockey, the goal. **15.** *Ling.* A form to which prefixes, suffixes, or infixes are added; root or stem. **16.** *Electronics* The element of a transistor that, like the grid of a vacuum tube, controls the flow of current. **17.** *Heraldry* The lower part of a shield. — **off base 1.** In baseball, not in contact with the base occupied: said of base runners. **2.** *U.S. Slang* Thinking, speaking, etc., erroneously. — *v.t.* **based, bas·ing 1.** To found on a foundation or basis; ground; establish: with *on* or *upon.* **2.** To form a base for. — *adj.* **1.** Serving as a base: a *base* line. **2.** Situated at or near the base: a *base* angle. [< OF < L *basis* < Gk. *basis,* step, pedestal < *bainein* to go]

base² (bās) *adj.* **1.** Morally low; mean; vile; contemptible: *a base* fellow. **2.** Like or befitting an inferior person or thing; menial; degrading: *base* flattery **3.** Comparatively low in value: said of metals. **4.** Alloyed or debased, as money; counterfeit: *base* coin. **5.** Not classical; corrupted: said of languages. **6.** *Music Obs.* Bass. **7.** In old English law, held by villeinage; not free: said of a tenure of an estate. **8.** *Archaic* Of illegitimate birth; bastard. **9.** *Archaic* Of humble birth or position. **10.** *Archaic* Of small stature; short. [< OF *bas* < LL *bassus* low] — **base′ly** *adv.* — **base′ness** *n.*

base·ball (bās′bôl′) *n.* **1.** A game played with a wooden bat and a hard ball by two teams, properly of nine players each, one team being at bat and the other in the field, alternately. The object of the game is to make more runs than the opponents make in a specified number of innings, usually nine, or in extra innings in case of a tie, by advancing base runners around a square course having a base at each corner. **2.** The ball used in this game.

BASEBALL FIELD

A, B, C First, second, and third bases (detail *a*). *D* Home base (detail *b*). *E, F* Batters' boxes. *G* Catcher's box. *H* Pitcher's plate. *I* Next batter's box. *J* First baseman. *K* Second baseman. *L* Third baseman. *M* Shortstop. *N, O, P* Outfielders. *Q* Space to which runner must confine himself. *R, R* Coaches' boxes. *S* Backstop. *T* Grandstand or fence limits. *U, U* Foul lines.

base·board (bās′bôrd′, -bōrd′) *n.* **1.** A board skirting the interior wall of a room, next to the floor: also called *mopboard.* **2.** Any board forming a base.

base·born (bās′bôrn′) *adj.* **1.** Of humble birth; plebeian. **2.** Born out of wedlock. **3.** Mean; vile.

base·burn·er (bās′bûr′nər) *n.* A coal stove or furnace in which the fuel is fed from above into a central fuel chamber.

base command *Mil.* An area containing a base or group of bases organized under one command.

Ba·se·dow's disease (bä′zə-dōz) *Pathol.* Exophthalmic goiter. [after Carl A. von *Basedow,* 1799–1854, German physician]

base hit In baseball, a batted ball that enables the batter to reach a base unaided by a defensive error, an attempt to put out a preceding base runner, or a force play: also called *hit, safe hit.*

Ba·sel (bä′zəl) A city in northern Switzerland, on the Rhine at the French and German borders; pop. 206,200 (est. 1959): French *Bâle.* Also *Basle.*

base·less (bās′lis) *adj.* Without foundation in fact; unfounded; groundless.

base level *Geol.* The lowest level to which a watercourse can erode its bed.

base line 1. In baseball, a path of definite width connecting successive bases. **2.** A line marking the end of a tennis or other court. **3.** A line, value, etc., taken as a base for measurement or comparison.

base·ment (bās′mənt) *n.* **1.** The lowest story of a building, usually wholly or partly underground and just beneath the main floor. **2.** The substructure or the basal portion of any building or other structure. [< BASE¹ + -MENT]

ba·sen·ji (bə-sen′jē) *n.* A small, barkless dog, similar to a fox terrier, with a smooth, reddish coat. [< Bantu]

base runner In baseball, a member of the team at bat who has reached a base or is attempting to reach a base.

bas·es¹ (bā′siz) Plural of BASE¹.

bas·es² (bā′sēz) Plural of BASIS.

bash (bash) *Informal v.t.* To strike heavily; smash in. — *n.* A smashing blow. [? Akin to Dan. *baske* thwack]

Ba·shan (bā′shən) A region east of the Jordan in ancient Palestine.

ba·shaw (bə-shô′) *n.* **1.** Pasha. **2.** An important or pompous person. [< Turkish *bāshā,* var. of *pāshā,* ? < *bāsh* head]

bash·ful (bash′fəl) *adj.* **1.** Shrinking from notice; shy; timid; diffident. **2.** Characterized by or indicating sensitiveness and timid modesty: a *bashful* glance. [< *bash,* var. of ABASH + -FUL] — **bash′ful·ly** *adv.* — **bash′ful·ness** *n.*

bash·i·ba·zouk (bash′ē-bə-zōōk′) *n.* One belonging to a class of mounted Turkish irregular soldiers, noted for their brutality. [< Turkish *bāshī* headdress + *bōzuq* disorderly]

Bash·kir A.S.S.R. (bäsh-kir′) A division of the R.S.F.S.R.; 52,000 sq. mi.; pop. 3,819,000 (est. 1970); capital, Ufa. *Russian* **Bash·kir·ska·ya A.S.S.R.** (bəsh-kyēr′skä-yä).

ba·sic (bā′sik) *adj.* **1.** Pertaining to, forming, or like a base or basis; essential; fundamental. **2.** *Chem.* Of, pertaining to, or producing a base. **3.** *Geol.* Containing comparatively little silica: said of igneous rocks, as basalt. **4.** *Metall.* Designating, pertaining to, or made by the basic process (which see). — **Syn.** See FUNDAMENTAL. — *n.* In the U.S. Army or Air Force, an enlisted man who has completed or is pursuing the minimum course of military training.

ba·si·cal·ly (bā′sik·lē) *adv.* Essentially; fundamentally.

Basic English A highly simplified form of English, devised by C. K. Ogden for use as an international auxiliary language and in the teaching of English. It contains 850 words of general vocabulary, supplemented by an additional 150 for scientific purposes. Also called **Basic.** [< *Basic,* considered an acronym for British, American, Scientific, International, Commercial]

ba·sic·i·ty (bā-sis′ə-tē) *n. Chem.* **1.** The state or quality of being a base. **2.** The ability of an acid to unite with one or more equivalents of a base, depending on the number of replaceable hydrogen atoms contained in a molecule of the acid.

basic process *Metall.* A method of steelmaking that uses a furnace lined with a basic refractory material, as dolomite or magnesite. It yields a **basic slag** rich in lime and phosphorus.

ba·sid·i·o·my·ce·tous (bə-sid′ē-ō-mī-sē′təs) *adj. Bot.* Belonging to a class (*Basidiomycetes*) of fungi having the spores borne on basidia, including mushrooms, smuts, rusts, etc. [< BASIDIUM + Gk. *mykēs, -ētos* fungus]

ba·sid·i·um (bə-sid′ē-əm) *n. pl.* **·sid·i·a** (-sid′ē-ə) *Bot.* A mother cell in basidiomycetous fungi, on which spores (usually four) are borne at the extremity of slender stalks. [< NL < Gk. *baseidion,* dim. of *basis* base]

ba·si·fy (bā′sə-fī) *v.t.* **·fied, ·fy·ing** To change into a base by chemical means. — **ba·si·fi·ca′tion** *n.* — **ba·si·fi′er** *n.*

bas·il (baz′əl) *n.* Any of certain aromatic plants of the mint family (genus *Ocimum*), especially the European **sweet basil** (*O. basilicum*) and the **bush basil** (*O. suave*) used in cooking. [< OF *basile* < L *basilicum* < Gk. *basilikon* (*phyton*) royal (plant), basil < *basileus* king]

Bas·il (baz′əl), **Saint,** 329–379, bishop of Caesarea; a Greek church father: called **the Great.**

Bas·il I (baz′əl), 813?–886, Byzantine emperor 867–886, founded the Macedonian dynasty: called **the Macedonian.**

Basil II, 958?–1025, Byzantine emperor 976–1025, subjected and annexed Bulgaria 1018: called **the Bulgar-slayer.**

bas·i·lar (bas′ə-lər) *adj.* Pertaining to or situated at the base, especially that of the skull; basal. Also **bas·i·lar·y** (bas′ə-ler′ē).

basilar membrane *Anat.* The membrane separating the two vestibules of the cochlea of the ear and acting as a receptor of the sound waves transmitted by the auditory nerve.

ba·sil·ic (bə-sil′ik) *adj.* **1.** Pertaining to a basilica. **2.** *Anat.* Denoting the basilic vein. **3.** *Obs.* Kingly. Also **ba·sil′i·cah.** [< Gk. *basilikos* kingly]

ba·sil·i·ca (bə-sil′i-kə) *n.* **1.** In ancient Rome, a rectangular building divided by columns into a nave and two side aisles, with a rounded apse at one end and a clerestory, used as a court or place of assembly. **2.** A building of this type used as a Christian church. **3.** In the Roman Catholic Church: **a** Any one of thirteen ancient churches in Rome. **b** A church accorded certain liturgical privileges by the pope. [< L < Gk. *basilikē* (*stoa*) royal (hall) fem. of *basilikos* < *basileus* king] — **ba·sil′i·can** *adj.*

basilic vein *Anat.* A large vein on the inner side of the arm.

bas·i·lisk (bas′ə-lisk) *n.* **1.** A fabled reptile of the African desert whose breath and look were said to be fatal. Compare COCKATRICE. **2.** A tropical American lizard (genus *Basiliscus,* family *Iguanidae*) having an erectile crest and a dilatable pouch on the head. [< L *basiliscus* < Gk. *basiliskos,* dim. of *basileus* king]

ba·sin (bā′sən) *n.* **1.** A round, wide, shallow vessel, often with sloping sides, used for holding liquids. **2.** A vessel re-

BASILISK
(2½ to 3½ feet long)

sembling this, as the scale or pan of a balance. **3.** The amount that a basin will hold. **4.** A sink or washbowl. **5.** *Geog.* **a** Any large depression in the earth's surface, as a valley, or the bed of a lake or ocean. **b** The region drained by a river. **6.** An enclosed place or hollow containing water, as a cistern, pond, dock, inlet, etc. **7.** *Geol.* A tract in which the strata dip from all sides to a common center. [< OF *bacin* < LL *bachinus* < *bacca* bowl] — **ba′sined** *adj.*

bas·i·net (bas′ə·nit, -net) *n.* A close-fitting helmet worn in the Middle Ages. [< OF *bacinet*, dim. of *bacin* basin]

ba·si·on (bā′sē·ən) *n. Anat.* The point where the anterior border of the foramen magnum of the skull cuts the median plane. [< NL < Gk. *basis* base]

ba·sip·e·tal (bā·sip′ə·təl) *adj. Bot.* Growing in the direction of the base [< *basi-* (< BASE[1]) + -PETAL]

ba·sis (bā′sis) *n. pl.* **ba·ses** (bā′sēz) **1.** That on which anything rests; base. **2.** Fundamental principle. **3.** The chief component or ingredient. [< L < Gk., base, pedestal]

bask (bask, bäsk) *v.i.* **1.** To lie in and enjoy a pleasant warmth, as of the sun or a fire. **2.** To enjoy or benefit from a similar warmth, as of regard: to *bask* in royal favor. — *v.t.* **3.** To expose to warmth. [< ON *badhask* to bathe oneself]

Bas·ker·ville (bas′kər·vil) *n.* A style of type face created by the English printer **John Baskerville,** 1706–75.

bas·ket (bas′kit, bäs′-) *n.* **1.** A container made of interwoven splints, rushes, strips of wood, etc. **2.** Something like a basket in form or use. **3.** The amount a basket will hold. **4.** A basket hilt (which see). **5.** In basketball: **a** One of the goals, consisting of a metal ring with a cord net suspended from it. **b** The point or points made by throwing the ball through the basket. Abbr. (for defs. 1, 3) *bkt.* [ME; ?]

bas·ket·ball (bas′kit·bôl′, bäs′-) *n.* **1.** A game played by two teams of five men each, in which the object is to throw the ball through an elevated goal (basket) at the opponent's end of a zoned, oblong court. **2.** The round, inflated ball used in this game.

BASKETBALL COURT

AA, BB End lines. *AB, AB* Side lines *CC* Division line. *D* Center circle: radius 2 feet. *E* Restraining circle: radius 6 feet. *F* Free throw line: 12 feet. *G* Free throw lane. *H* Free throw circle. *J* Basket: upper edge 10 feet above floor. *K* Backboard (fan): 54 inches wide. *L* Backboard (rectangular): 72 inches wide. *M* Right guard. *N* Right forward. *O* Left forward. *P* Left guard.

basket fish A starfish (*Gorgonocephalus arctica*) having a network of branched or interlacing arms, common off the New England coast. Also **basket starfish.**

basket hilt A sword hilt with an openwork guard for the hand. — **bas·ket-hilt·ed** (bas′kit·hil′tid, bäs-) *adj.*

Basket Maker One of a class of prehistoric cave-dwelling people of SW North America, of a culture more ancient than the cliff dwellers or Pueblos.

bas·ket·ry (bas′kit·rē, bäs′-) *n.* **1.** Baskets collectively; basketwork. **2.** The art or craft of making baskets.

basket weave A weave with two or more warp and filling threads woven side by side to resemble a plaited basket.

bas·ket·work (bas′kit·wûrk′, bäs′-) *n.* Work made of or resembling interlaced osiers, twigs, etc.; wickerwork.

basking shark A large shark (*Cetorhinus maximus*) of the North Atlantic, that basks on the surface of the water.

Basle (bäl) See BASEL.

bas mitz·vah (bäs mits′və) In Judaism, a girl who has reached an age between twelve and fourteen, the age of religious duty and responsibility; also, the ceremony celebrating this. Also **bat mitz′vah, bath-matz′vah.** [< Hebrew, daughter of the commandment]

ba·so·phile (bā′sə·fil, -fil) *n. Biol.* A tissue or cell having a special affinity for basic staining dyes. Also **ba′si·phile.** [< *baso-* (< BASIC) + -PHILE] — **ba·so·phil·ic** (bā′sə·fil′ik), **ba·soph·i·lous** (bā·sof′ə·ləs) *adj.*

basque (bask) *n.* A woman's closely fitting bodice.

Basque (bask) *n.* **1.** One of a people of unknown origin living in the western Pyrenees in Spain and France. **2.** The language of the Basque people, unrelated to any other known language. — *adj.* Of or pertaining to the Basques or to their language, or to the Basque Provinces.

Basque Provinces Three provinces of northern Spain on the Bay of Biscay; inhabited by Basques; 2,803 sq. mi.

Bas·ra (bus′rə) A Province of SE Iraq; 4,747 sq. mi.; pop. 673,623 (1965); capital, **Basra,** pop. 313,327 (1965): also *Busra, Busrah.* Also **Bas′rah.**

bas-re·lief (bä′ri·lēf′, bas′-) *n.* That type of sculpture in which the figures project only slightly from the background:

also called *basso-relievo, low relief.* See RELIEF. [< F < Ital. *basso* low + *rilievo* relief]

Bas-Rhin (bä·raṅ′) A Department of NE France; 1,851 sq. mi.; pop. 827,367 (1968); capital, Strasbourg.

bass[1] (bas) *n. pl.* **bass** or **bass·es** **1.** One of various spiny-finned, marine and fresh-water food fishes, especially the European sea bass (*Labrax lupus*), the American **striped bass** or rockfish (*Roccus saxatilis*), and the black basses (genus *Micropterus*). **2.** The European perch (*Perca fluviatilis*). [OE *bærs*]

bass[2] (bās) *n. Music* **1.** The lowest-pitched male singing voice. **2.** A deep, low sound, as of this voice or of certain low-pitched instruments. **3.** The notes in the lowest register of the piano, pipe organ, etc. **4.** The lowest part in vocal or instrumental music; also, these parts collectively. **5.** One who sings or an instrument that plays such a part; especially, a bass viol. — *adj.* **1.** Low in pitch; having a low musical range. **2.** Pertaining to, for, or able to play bass. Abbr. *b., B.* [< OF *bas* low; infl. in spelling by Ital. *basso*]

bass[3] (bas) *n.* **1.** The basswood or linden. **2.** Bast. [Alter. of BAST]

bass clef (bās) See under CLEF.

bass drum (bās) The largest of the drums, beaten on both heads and having a deep sound: also called *double drum.* For illustration see DRUM[1].

bas·set[1] (bas′it) *n.* A hound characterized by a long, low body, long head and nose, and short, heavy, crooked forelegs. Also **basset hound.** [< OF *basset,* dim. of *bas* low]

bas·set[2] (bas′it) *Geol. n.* An outcropping. — *v.i.* **·set·ed, ·set·ing** To appear at the surface, as coal. [Origin uncertain.]

Basse·terre (bäs·târ′) The capital of St. Christopher, Nevis and Anguilla; a port on the island of St. Christopher; pop. 16,000 (est. 1971).

Basse-Terre (bäs·târ′) **1.** The capital of the French Overseas Department of Guadeloupe, a port on Basse-Terre island; pop. 16,000 (est. 1969). **2.** The westernmost of the two islands comprising Guadeloupe Department; 364 sq. mi.: also *Guadeloupe proper.*

basset horn A tenor clarinet having a compass of three and a half octaves, with four more low keys than the ordinary clarinet. [< Ital. *corno di bassetto* < *bassetto,* dim. of *basso* low + *corno* horn]

bas·si·net (bas′ə·net′) *n.* A basket used as a baby's cradle, usually with a hood over one end; also, a type of perambulator. [< F, dim. of *bassin* basin]

bas·so (bas′ō, bäs′ō; *Ital.* bäs′sō) *n. pl.* **bas·sos** (bas′ōz, bäs′ōz), *Ital.* **bas·si** (bäs′sē) **1.** A bass singer. **2.** The bass part. Abbr. *b., B.* [< Ital. bass]

basso con·tin·u·o (kən·tin′yōō·ō, *Ital.,* cōn·tē′nōō·ō) *Music* A figured bass.

bas·soon (ba·sōōn′, bə-) *n. Music* **1.** A large, low-pitched, double-reed woodwind instrument. **2.** An organ stop like a bassoon in tone. [< F *basson,* aug. of *bas* low]

basso pro·fun·do (prə·fun′dō, *Ital.* prō·fōōn′dō) **1.** A singer who sings the deepest bass. **2.** The lowest bass voice. [< Ital. *basso profondo* deep bass]

bas·so-re·lie·vo (bas′ō·ri·lē′vō) *n. pl.* **-vos** (-vōz) Bas-relief. [< Ital., *basso-rilievo*]

bas·so-ri·lie·vo (bäs′sō·ri·lyä′vō) *n. pl.* **-ri·lie·vi** (-ri·lyä′vē) *Italian* Bas-relief.

Bass Strait (bas) The passage between the coasts of the Australian mainland and Tasmania, extending from the Indian Ocean to the Tasman Sea.

bass viol (bās) *Music* **1.** The double bass. **2.** The viola da gamba.

bass·wood (bas′wŏŏd′) *n.* The American linden. See under LINDEN. Also called *bass.*

bast (bast) *n. Bot.* **1.** The fibrous inner bark of trees, originally of the linden, used in making cordage: also called *bass.* **2.** Phloem. [OE *bæst*]

bas·tard (bas′tərd) *n.* **1.** An illegitimate child. **2.** Any irregular, inferior, or counterfeit thing. **3.** A hybrid. **4.** *U.S. Slang* A worthless or cruel man. **5.** *Brit. Informal* A fellow; chap: a somewhat disparaging term. — *adj.* **1.** Born out of wedlock. **2.** False; spurious. **3.** Resembling but not typical of the genuine thing: *bastard* mahogany. **4.** Abnormal or irregular in size, shape, or proportion. [< OF < *fils de bast* packsaddle child; with ref. to the use of the saddle as a bed by muleteers]

bas·tard·ize (bas′tər·dīz) *v.* **·ized, ·iz·ing** *v.t.* **1.** To prove to be or proclaim to be a bastard. **2.** To make degenerate; debase. — *v.i.* **3.** To become debased. — **bas′tard·i·za′tion** *n.*

bas·tard·ly (bas′tərd·lē) *adj.* **1.** Of illegitimate birth. **2.** Counterfeit; false.

bastard wing *Ornithol.* An alula.

bas·tard·y (bas′tər·dē) *n.* **1.** The state of being a bastard; illegitimacy. **2.** The act of begetting a bastard.

baste[1] (bāst) *v.t.* **bast·ed, bast·ing** To sew loosely together, as with long, temporary stitches. [< OF *bastir* < OHG *bestan* to sew with bast.]

---

baste² (bāst) *v.t.* **bast·ed, bast·ing** To moisten (meat or fish) with drippings, butter, etc., while cooking. [? < OF *basser* to soak, moisten]

baste³ (bāst) *v.t.* **bast·ed, bast·ing** *Informal* **1.** To beat; thrash. **2.** To attack verbally; abuse. [Prob. < Scand. Cf. ON *beysta* to beat.]

bas·tille (bas-tēl´) *n.* **1.** A prison, especially one operated tyrannically. **2.** In ancient warfare, a tower or small fortress. Also **bas·tile´**. [< OF, building < LL *bastilia*, pl. < *bastire* to build]

Bas·tille (bas-tēl´, *Fr.* bàs-tē´y´) A fortress in Paris, built in 1369 and stormed and destroyed in the French Revolution on July 14, 1789.

Bastille Day The national holiday of republican France, July 14, commemorating the fall of the Bastille.

bas·ti·na·do (bas´tə-nā´dō) *n. pl.* **·does 1.** A beating with a stick, usually on the soles of the feet. **2.** A stick or cudgel. — *v.t.* **·doed, ·do·ing** To beat with a stick, usually on the soles of the feet. Also **bas´ti·nade´** (-nād´). [< Sp. *bastonada* < *baston* cudgel]

bast·ing (bās´ting) *n.* **1.** The act of sewing loosely together. **2.** The thread used for this purpose. **3.** *pl.* Long, loose, temporary stitches. [< BASTE¹]

bas·tion (bas´chən, -tē-ən) *n.* **1.** In fortifications, a projecting part of a rampart. **2.** Any fortified or strongly defended place or position: a *bastion* of democracy. — **Syn.** see BULWARK. [< MF < Ital. *bastione* < *bastire* to build] — **bas´tioned** *adj.*

Bas·togne (bas-tôn´, *Fr.* bàs-tôn´y´) A town in SE Belgium; besieged and nearly destroyed during the German counter-offensive of World War II in December, 1944; pop. 5,927 (est. 1959). Flemish **Bas·te·na·ken** (bäs´tə-nä´kən).

BASTION

a Boulevard. *b* Ramps. *c* Flank of rampart. *d* Banquette. *e* Salient. *f* Moat. *g* Face of rampart. *h* Glacis. *i* Scarp. *j* Embrasure in parapet.

Ba·su·to (bə-sōō´tō) *n. pl.* **·tos** or **·to** A native or inhabitant of Basutoland.

Ba·su·to·land (bə-sōō´tō-land´) A former British territory in southern Africa. See LESOTHO.

bat¹ (bat) *n.* **1.** In baseball, cricket, and similar games: **a** A stick or club for striking the ball, usually heavier and wider at one end than at the other. **b** The act of batting. **c** A turn at bat, or the right to such turn. Abbr. (in baseball) *b., B.* **2.** In cricket, the batsman. **3.** In tennis, badminton, etc., a racket. **4.** Any heavy cudgel or club. **5.** A piece of a brick or a lump of clay. **6.** *Informal* A blow, as with a stick. **7.** *Informal* Speed: at a lively *bat.* **8.** *Slang* A drunken spree. **9.** Batting (def. 1). — **at bat** In the act or position of batting. — **to go to bat for** *Informal* To defend or advocate the cause of. — *v.* **bat·ted, bat·ting** *v.i.* **1.** In baseball, cricket, and other games: **a** To use a bat. **b** To take a turn at bat. — *v.t.* **2.** To strike with or as with a bat. **3.** To have a batting average of: to bat .400. — **to bat around** *Slang* **1.** To travel about. **2.** To discuss. **3.** In baseball, to have the whole team bat in one inning. [OE *batt* cudgel]

bat² (bat) *n.* Any of numerous nocturnal flying mammals (order *Chiroptera*), having greatly elongated forelimbs and digits that support a thin wing membrane connecting the hind limbs and sometimes to the tail. — **blind as a bat** Altogether blind. — **to have bats in the belfry** *U.S. Slang* To be crazy. [ME *bakke*, ? < Scand.] — **bat´like** *adj.*

bat³ (bat) *v.t.* **bat·ted, bat·ting** *Informal* To wink; flutter. — **not bat an eye** or **eyelash** *Informal* Not show surprise or other reaction. [Var. of BATE³]

bat⁴ (bāt) See BAHT.

Ba·taan (bə-tan´, -tän´) A Province of the Philippines, on southern Luzon; 517 sq. mi.; pop. 115,980 (est. 1960); capital, Balanga; occupies **Bataan Peninsula**, scene of World War II surrender of U.S. and Philippine forces to the Japanese, April 1942.

Ba·tan·gas (bä-täng´gäs) A Province of the Philippines, on southern Luzon; 1,192 sq. mi.; pop. 636,960 (est. 1960); capital, **Batangas**.

Ba·tan Islands (bä-tän´) An island group of the northern Philippines, forming the Province of **Ba·ta·nes** (bä-tä´näs); 76 sq. mi.; pop. 13,360 (est. 1960); capital, Basco.

Ba·ta·vi (bə-tä´vī) *n.pl.* An ancient Germanic people who inhabited the region about the mouths of the Rhine. [L]

Ba·ta·vi·a (bə-tä´vē-ə, *Du.* bä-tä´vē-ä) A former name for JAKARTA. — **Ba·ta´vi·an** *adj. & n.*

batch (bach) *n.* **1.** A quantity or number taken together: a *batch* of friends. **2.** The amount of bread produced at one time. **3.** The quantity of material, as of dough, for one operation. **4.** Any set of things made, done, dispatched, etc., at one time. [ME *bacche.* Akin to BAKE.]

bate¹ (bāt) *v.* **bat·ed, bat·ing** *v.t.* **1.** To lessen the force or intensity of; moderate: He watched with *bated* breath. **2.** To deduct; decrease. — *v.i.* **3.** To diminish; become reduced. [Var. of ABATE]

bate² (bāt) *n.* A solution of chemicals or manure containing

natural or synthetic enzymes, used to soften skins or hides. — *v.t.* **bat·ed, bat·ing** To soften by soaking in bate. [? < ON *beita* to cause to bite. Akin to BAIT and BITE.]

bate³ (bāt) *v.i.* **bat·ed, bat·ing** To flap the wings, as an impatient hawk or falcon: also spelled *bait.* [< OF *batre* to beat, ult. < L *battuere* to strike, beat]

ba·teau (ba-tō´) *n. pl.* **·teaux** (-tōz´) **1.** *U.S. & Canadian* A light, flat-bottomed boat. **2.** A pontoon for a floating bridge. [< F < OF *batel,* ult. < Gmc.]

bateau bridge A pontoon bridge (which see).

Bates (bāts), **Katharine Lee,** 1859–1929, U.S. poet and educator.

bat·fish (bat´fish´) *n.* **1.** Any of a family (*Ogcocephalidae*) of North American marine fishes, having a batlike appearance, as the **longnose batfish** (*Ogcocephalus vespertilio*) of the Atlantic coast. **2.** A sting ray (*Myliobatis californicus*) found in California waters.

bat·fowl (bat´foul´) *v.i.* To catch birds at night by dazzling them with a light. [< BAT¹ + FOWL] — **bat´fowl´er** *n.*

bath¹ (bath, bäth) *n. pl.* **baths** (baṯHz, bäṯHz; baths, bäths) **1.** A washing or immersing of something, especially the body, in water or other liquid. ◆ Collateral adjective: *balneal.* **2.** The liquid used for this. **3.** The container for such a liquid; a bathtub. **4.** *Chiefly U.S.* A bathroom. **5.** *Often pl.* A set of rooms or a building equipped for bathing. **6.** *Often pl.* An establishment or resort where bathing is part of a medical treatment. **7.** A Turkish bath (which see). **8.** *Chem.* An apparatus for applying steady heat or heat of a given degree. **9.** *Photog.* Any solution, or the vessel containing it, in which photographic plates, etc., are immersed for treatment. **10.** *Metall.* The molten material in a reverberatory furnace. **11.** The condition of being soaked or covered with a liquid. — *v.t. Brit.* To place or wash in a bath; immerse. [OE *bæth*]

bath² (bath) *n.* An ancient Hebrew liquid measure, equivalent to about 10 gallons. [< Hebrew]

Bath (bath, bäth) A borough and city in Avon, England, famous since Roman times for its hot springs; pop. 84,700 (1976).

Bath brick A fine calcareous and siliceous material, usually pressed into brick shape, used for polishing and cleansing metal objects. [after *Bath,* England, where originally found]

Bath chair A hooded wheelchair for invalids. Also **bath chair.** [after *Bath,* England, where originally used]

bathe (bāṯH) *v.* **bathed, bath·ing** *v.t.* **1.** To place in liquid; immerse. **2.** To wash; wet. **3.** To apply liquid to for comfort or healing; lave. **4.** To cover or suffuse as with liquid: The hill was *bathed* in light. — *v.i.* **5.** To wash oneself; take a bath. **6.** To go into or remain in water so as to swim or cool off. **7.** To be covered or suffused as if with liquid: to *bathe* in sunshine. — *n. Brit.* The act of bathing, as in the sea. [OE *bathian*] — **bathe´a·ble** *adj.* — **bath´er** *n.*

bath·house (bath´hous´, bäth´-) *n.* **1.** A building with facilities for bathing. **2.** A small structure at a bathing resort used as a dressing room.

bathing suit A swimsuit (which see).

batho- *combining form* Depth: *bathometer.* [< Gk. *bathos* depth]

bath·o·lith (bath´ə-lith) *n. Geol.* A large, irregular mass of igneous rock that has melted or forced its way into surrounding strata, usually at great depths where it often forms the core of mountain ranges. Also **batho·lite** (-līt). [< BATHO- +-LITH] — **bath´o·lith´ic** or **bath´o·lit´ic** (-lit´ik) *adj.*

ba·thom·e·ter (bə-thom´ə-tər) *n.* An apparatus for determining the depth of water. [< BATHO- + -METER]

ba·thos (bā´thos) *n.* **1.** A descent from the lofty to the commonplace in discourse; anticlimax. **2.** Insincere pathos; sentimentality. [< Gk. *bathos* depth < *bathys* deep] **ba·thet·ic** (bə-thet´ik) *adj.*

bath·robe (bath´rōb´, bäth´-) *n.* A long, loose garment for wear before and after bathing: also called *robe.*

bath·room (bath´rōōm´, -rŏŏm´, bäth´-) *n.* **1.** A room in which to bathe. **2.** A toilet.

bath salts Perfumed crystal salts used to soften bath water.

Bath·she·ba (bath-shē´bə, bath´shi-bə) In the Bible, the wife of Uriah and later of David; mother of Solomon. II *Sam.* xi–xii.

bath·tub (bath´tub´, bäth´-) *n.* A vessel in which to bathe, especially one installed as a permanent fixture in a bathroom.

Bath·urst (bath´ərst, bäth´-) **1.** The capital of Gambia, a port on the Atlantic at the mouth of the Gambia River; pop. 31,800 (est. 1967). **2.** A city in east central New South Wales, Australia; pop. 17,222 (1966).

bathy- *combining form* Deep: of the sea or ocean depths: *bathysphere.* [< Gk. *bathys* deep]

ba·thym·e·try (bə-thim´ə-trē) *n.* The science or art of deep-sea sounding. — **bath·y·met·ric** (bath´ə-met´rik) *adj.*

bath·y·scaph (bath´ə-skaf) *n.* A free bathysphere with ballast and a gasoline-filled float to control depth, capable of ocean depths over 35,000 feet. Also **bath´y·scaphe** (-skāf). [< BATHY- + Gk. *skaphē* bowl]

bath·y·sphere (bath´ə-sfir) *n.* A spherical diving bell equipped with fused quartz windows for deep-sea observations. [< BATHY- + SPHERE]

ba·tik (bə·tēk′, bat′ik) *n.* **1.** A process for coloring fabrics, in which the parts not to be dyed are covered with wax. **2.** The fabric so colored. Also spelled *battik.* [< Malay]

Ba·tis·ta (bä·tēs′tä), **Fulgencio,** 1901–73, Cuban soldier and politician; president of Cuba 1940–44, 1952–54, 1955–59: full name **Fulgencio Batista Zal·di·var** (säl·dē′bär).

ba·tiste (bə·tēst′) *n.* **1.** A fine cotton fabric in plain weave, originally made of linen. **2.** Any of various similar fabrics made of silk, rayon, wool, etc. [< F; after Jean *Baptiste* of Cambrai, 13th c. French linen weaver]

bat·man (bat′mən, bä′mən) *n. pl.* **·men** (-mən) In the British army, an officer's servant. [< F *bat* < OF *bast* pack-saddle + MAN]

ba·ton (ba·ton′, bat′n; *Fr.* bà·tôn′) *n.* **1.** A short staff or truncheon borne as an emblem of authority or privilege. **2.** *Music* A slender stick or rod used by a conductor. **3.** *Heraldry* A bend borne sinisterwise across the shield as a mark of bastardy: also **baton sinister,** erroneously *bar sinister.* **4.** A staff with a knot at one end, used for twirling by drum majors, etc. **5.** A hollow stick passed by a runner to a teammate in a relay race. [< F *bâton* < OF *baston* < LL *bastum* stick]

Bat·on Rouge (bat′n roozh′) The capital of Louisiana, a city in the SE central part, on the Mississippi; pop. 165,963.

ba·tra·chi·an (bə·trā′kē·ən) *adj.* Of or pertaining to a former class (*Batrachia*) of amphibians, especially to frogs and toads; amphibian. — *n.* A frog or toad. [< NL < Gk. *batrachos* frog]

bat·ra·chite (bat′rə·kīt) *n.* **1.** A stone that is froglike in color. **2.** A fossil batrachian. [< L *batrochites,* ult. < Gk. *batrachos* frog]

bat·ra·choid (bat′rə·koid) *adj.* Froglike.

bats (bats) *adj. Slang* Batty.

bats·man (bats′mən) *n. pl.* **·men** (-mən) In baseball or cricket, the batter.

batt (bat) *n.* Batting (def. 1).

bat·ta·lia (bə·tāl′yə, -tāl′-) *n.* **1.** *Archaic* Order of battle. **2.** *Obs.* An armed force; army. [< Ital. *battaglia*]

bat·tal·ion (bə·tal′yən) *n.* **1.** *Mil.* **a** A unit consisting of a headquarters and two or more companies, batteries, or comparable units. **b** A body of troops. **2.** *Usually pl.* A large group or number. MF *battaillon* < Ital. *battaglione* < *battaglia* battle]

bat·ten[1] (bat′n) *v.i.* **1.** To grow fat; thrive. **2.** To prosper; live well, especially at another's expense. — *v.t.* **3.** To make fat, as cattle. [< ON *batna* to grow better, improve]

bat·ten[2] (bat′n) *n.* **1.** A light strip of wood, as for covering a joint between boards. **2.** A piece of sawed timber, used for flooring, scantling, etc. **3.** *Naut.* **a** A thin strip of wood placed in a sail to keep it flat. **b** A similar strip for fastening a tarpaulin over a hatch. — *v.t.* **1.** To make, furnish, or strengthen with battens. **2.** To fasten with battens. — **to batten down the hatches** *Naut.* To secure tarpaulins over a hatch by means of battens. [Var. of BATON] — **bat′ten·er** *n.*

bat·ter[1] (bat′ər) *v.t.* **1.** To strike with repeated, violent blows. **2.** To damage or injure with such blows or with hard usage. — *v.i.* **3.** To pound or beat with blow after blow; hammer. — **Syn.** See BEAT. — *n. Printing* Damage to a printing face; also, the resulting defect in print. [Partly < OF *batre* < L *battuere* to beat; partly freq. of BAT[1], v.]

bat·ter[2] (bat′ər) *n.* In baseball and cricket, the player whose turn it is to bat.

bat·ter[3] (bat′ər) *n.* A thick liquid mixture, as of eggs, flour, and milk, beaten for use in cookery. [? < OF *bature* beating < *battre* to beat]

bat·ter[4] (bat′ər) *v.t. & v.i.* To slope inward, as the outer face of a wall. — *n.* An inward slope of a wall. [Origin uncertain]

batter bread Spoonbread (which see).

battered child syndrome *Med.* Severe bruises and other injuries in a child of four years or less, usually caused by a parent or other family member. Also **battered baby syndrome.**

bat·ter·ing-ram (bat′ər·ing·ram′) *n.* A long, stout beam, used in ancient warfare for battering down walls.

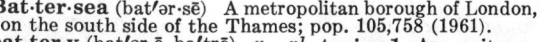

BATHYSCAPH

A A A Flotation hull. *a* Conning tower. *b* Snorkels. *c* Propellers. *dd* Search lights. *ee* Ballast tubes. *f* Gondola. *g* Stabilizer.

Bat·ter·sea (bat′ər·sē) A metropolitan borough of London, on the south side of the Thames; pop. 105,758 (1961).

bat·ter·y (bat′ər·ē, ba′trē) *n. pl.* **·ter·ies 1.** Any unit, apparatus, or grouping in which a series or set of parts or components is assembled to serve a common end. **2.** *Electr.* One or more primary or secondary cells operating together as a single source of direct current. **3.** *Mil.* **a** A tactical and administrative artillery unit equivalent to an infantry company. **b** A group of guns, rockets, or related equipment forming a tactical artillery unit. **c** An earthwork or parapet for one or more pieces of artillery. Abbr. *btry.* **4.** *Naval* The guns of a warship, or a specific group of them: the starboard *battery.* **5.** In baseball, the pitcher and catcher together. **6.** *Law* The illegal beating or touching of another person. See ASSAULT AND BATTERY. **7.** *Music* The percussion instruments of an orchestra. **8.** *Optics* The group of prisms in a spectroscope. — **in battery** *Mil.* In firing position, after recovery from recoil: said of an artillery gun or tube. [< OF *batterie* < *battre* to beat]

Battery, the A park at the southern extremity of Manhattan: so named from the guns mounted there in colonial and Revolutionary times. Also **Battery Park.**

bat·tik (bə·tēk′, bat′ik) See BATIK.

bat·ting (bat′ing) *n.* **1.** Wadded cotton or wool prepared in sheets or rolls, used for interlining, stuffing mattresses, etc.: also *bat, batt.* **2.** The act of one who bats. [< BAT[1], v.]

bat·tle (bat′l) *n.* **1.** A combat between hostile armies or fleets; a military or naval engagement. **2.** Any fighting, conflict, or struggle. **3.** *Obs.* A battalion. — *v.* **·tled, ·tling** *v.i.* **1.** To contend in or as in battle; struggle; strive. — *v.t.* **2.** *U.S.* To fight. [< OF *bataille* < LL *battalia* gladiators' exercises < L *battuere* to beat] — **bat′tler** *n.*

— **Syn.** (noun) **1.** *Battle, skirmish, action,* and *engagement* are all events in warfare. A *battle* is a more or less continuous fight and may last for many days, while a *skirmish* is brief and involves small groups of combatants. An *action* is one of the events in a *battle,* as by a part of the forces engaged. *Engagement* refers to a period of active combat, but may also be a complete *battle* or war.

bat·tle-ax (bat′l·aks′) *n.* **1.** A large ax formerly used in battle; a broadax. **2.** *U.S. Slang* A formidable, disagreeable woman. Also **bat′tle·axe.**

Battle Creek A city in southern Michigan, on the Kalamazoo River; pop. 38,931.

battle cruiser *Naval* A war vessel having cruiser speed, but less heavily armored than a battleship.

battle cry 1. A shout uttered by troops in battle. **2.** A slogan or distinctive phrase used in any conflict or contest.

bat·tle·dore (bat′l·dôr, -dōr) *n.* **1.** A flat paddle or bat used to strike a shuttlecock. **2.** A game in which a shuttlecock is battered back and forth: also **battledore and shuttlecock.** — *v.t. & v.i.* **·dored, ·dor·ing** To volley or hurl back and forth. [? < Provençal *batedor,* an implement for beating laundry]

battle fatigue *Psychiatry* Combat fatigue (which see).

bat·tle·field (bat′l·fēld′) *n.* The terrain on which a battle is fought. Also **bat′tle·ground′.**

bat·tle·ment (bat′l·mənt) *n.* A parapet indented along its upper line. [< OF *batillement* < *ba(s)tillier* to fortify] — **bat·tle·ment·ed** (bat′l·men′tid) *adj.*

battle plane A warplane (which see).

battle royal 1. A fight involving numerous combatants. **2.** A protracted, vehement altercation.

bat·tle-scarred (bat′l·skärd′) *adj.* Having scars, marks, etc., received in combat.

bat·tle·ship (bat′l·ship′) *n. Naval* A warship of great size, belonging to the class with heaviest armor and armament.

bat·tle-wag·on (bat′l·wag′ən) *n. Slang* A battleship.

bat·tue (ba·too′, -tyoo′) *n. Chiefly Brit.* **1.** The driving of game from cover toward sportsmen previously posted. **2.** A hunt so conducted. **3.** Any wanton slaughter, especially of unresisting persons. [< F, fem. pp. of *battre* to beat]

bat·ty (bat′ē) *adj.* **·ti·er, ·ti·est 1.** Characteristic of or resembling a bat. **2.** *Slang* Crazy; foolish; odd.

Ba·tu Khan (bä′too kän′) died 1255, Mongol ruler; grandson of Genghis Khan. See GOLDEN HORDE.

Ba·tum (bə·toom′) A port city of the Soviet Union, in the SW Georgian S.S.R. on the Black Sea; pop. 101,000 (est. 1970). *Georgian* **Ba·tu·mi** (bä·too′mē).

bau·ble (bô′bəl) *n.* **1.** A worthless, showy trinket; gewgaw; toy. **2.** *Archaic* A jester's wand. [< OF *baubel* toy, ? < L *bellus* pretty]

Bau·cis (bô′sis) In Greek mythology, a poor peasant woman who with her husband Philemon sheltered Zeus and Hermes disguised as travelers.

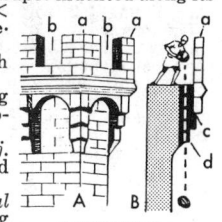

BATTLEMENT

A Outer view: *a* Merlons. *b* Embrasures. *B* Section, showing use of corbel (*c*) for machicolation (*d*).

bau·de·kin (bô′də·kin) *n.* Baldachin (def. 1).

Baude·laire (bōd·lâr′), **Charles Pierre**, 1821–67, French poet.

Bau·douin (bō·dwaṅ′), born 1930, king of Belgium 1951–.

baud·rons (bôd′rənz) *n. Scot.* A cat.

Bau·er (bou′ər), **Harold**, 1873–1951, English pianist.

Bau·haus (bou′hous′) *n. German* An institute of art study, design, and research, established by Walter Gropius in Weimar, Germany, in 1919.

baulk (bôk), **baulk·y** (bô′kē) See BALK, BALKY.

Baum (bôm), **L(yman) Frank**, 1856–1919, U.S. writer of children's story books.

Bau·mé (bō·mā′) *adj.* Designating or measured according to a scale used to gauge the density of liquids. Abbr. *B., Bé, Bé.* [after Antoine *Baumé*, 1728–1804, French pharmacist]

baum marten (boum) Marten (def. 2). [< G *baum* tree + MARTEN]

bau·sond (bô′sənd) *adj. Scot.* Marked with white, as the face of a horse. Also **baw/sunt** (-sənt).

baux·ite (bôk′sīt, bō′zīt) *n.* A white to red claylike substance containing aluminum oxide or hydroxide, the principal ore of aluminum. [after Les *Baux*, France]

Bav. Bavaria; Bavarian.

Ba·var·i·a (bə·vâr′ē·ə) A State of SE West Germany; 27,-235 sq. mi.; pop. 10,568,900 (est. 1970); capital, Munich; formerly a duchy, kingdom, and republic. German *Bayern.*

Ba·var·i·an (bə·vâr′ē·ən) *adj.* Of or pertaining to Bavaria, its people, or their dialect. —*n.* **1.** A native or inhabitant of Bavaria. **2.** The High German dialect spoken in Bavaria.

baw·bee (bô·bē′, bô′bē) *n. Scot.* A halfpenny.

baw·cock (bô′kok) *n. Archaic* A fine fellow. [< F *beau* fine + *coq* cock]

bawd (bôd) *n.* The keeper of a brothel; a procuress. [ME *bawde*; origin uncertain]

baw·dric (bô′drik) See BALDRIC.

bawd·ry (bô′drē) *n.* **1.** Obscene language or behavior. **2.** *Archaic* The occupation of a bawd.

bawd·y (bô′dē) *adj.* **bawd·i·er, bawd·i·est** Obscene; indecent. —**bawd′i·ly** *adv.* —**bawd′i·ness** *n.*

bawd·y·house (bô′dē·hous′) *n.* A brothel.

bawl (bôl) *v.t.* **1.** To call out noisily; bellow. **2.** To cry for sale. —*v.i.* **3.** To cry or sob noisily. —**to bawl out** *U.S. Slang* To berate; scold. —*n.* A loud shout or outcry. [Cf. Med.L *baulare* to bark and ON *baula* to low, moo] —**bawl′·er** *n.*

baw·tie (bô′tē) *n. Scot.* A dog. Also **baw′ty.**

Bax·ter (bak′stər), **Richard**, 1615–91, English Puritan minister and author.

bay¹ (bā) *n.* **1.** A body of water partly enclosed by land; an inlet of the sea. Abbr. *b., B.* **2.** A recess of low land between hills. **3.** *U.S.* Land partly surrounded by woods. [< OF *baie* < LL *baia*]

bay² (bā) *n.* **1.** *Archit.* **a** A bay window. **b** A division of a window between two mullions. **c** A principal part or division of a structure, as that between two piers or columns of a wall, between two piers of a bridge, etc. **d** An extension or wing of a building. **2.** Any opening or recess in a wall. **3.** *Naut.* The forward part of a ship between decks on each side, formerly uesd as a hospital. Compare SICKBAY. **4.** *Aeron.* **a** A compartment in the body of an aircraft: a bomb *bay*. **b** A portion of the fuselage between adjoining struts, bulkheads, or frame positions. [< OF *baee* < *baer* to stand open, ult. < LL *badare* to gape]

bay³ (bā) *adj.* Reddish brown: said especially of horses. —*n.* **1.** A reddish brown color. **2.** A horse (or other animal) of this color. [< F *bai* < L *badius*]

bay⁴ (bā) *n.* **1.** A deep bark or cry, as of dogs in hunting. **2.** The position of a hunted animal forced to turn and fight, or of a person compelled to face an opponent or difficulty: to stand at *bay.* **3.** The condition of being kept off by or as by one's quarry: to hold one's attackers at *bay.* —*v.i.* **1.** To utter a deep-throated, prolonged bark, as a hound. —*v.t.* **2.** To utter with or as with such a bark: to *bay* defiance. **3.** To pursue or beset with barking. **4.** To bring to bay. [Var. of *abay* < OF *abai* a barking; ult. origin uncertain; in sense "at bay" appar. < OF *tenir a bay* to hold in suspense < LL *badare* to gape]

bay⁵ (bā) *n.* **1.** Laurel (def. 1). **2.** A laurel wreath, bestowed as a garland of honor, especially on a poet. **3.** *pl.* Fame; renown. **4.** The bayberry. **5.** Any of several plants resembling the laurels. [< F *baie* < L *bacca* berry]

ba·ya·de·re (bä′yə·dir′, ə·dâr′) *n.* **1.** A dancing girl, especially one serving in a temple in India. **2.** A fabric or pattern with stripes crosswise. —*adj.* Striped crosswise. Also **ba′ya·deer′** (-dir′). [< F *bayadère* < Pg. *bailadeira* female dancer]

ba·ya·mo (bä·yä′mō) *n. Meteorol.* A violent wind blowing on the south coast of Cuba. [after *Bayamo*, Cuba]

bay·ard (bā′ərd) *n.* **1.** A bay horse. **2.** Any horse: a humorous use. —*adj.* Bay in color. [< BAYARD]

Bay·ard (bā′ərd) A magical bay steed mentioned in certain medieval romances.

Bay·ard (bā′ərd, *Fr.* bà·yàr′), **Chevalier de**, 1473?–1524, Pierre du Terrail, heroic French knight: called **the knight** without fear and without reproach. —*n.* A man of heroic courage and chivalry.

bay·ber·ry (bā′ber′ē, -bər·ē) *n. pl.* **·ries 1.** Any of various trees or shrubs having aromatic berries, as the wax myrtle or laurel. **2.** The fruit of such a plant. **3.** A tropical American tree (*Pimenta racemosa*) whose leaves are used in making bay rum. [< BAY⁵ + BERRY]

Bay City A city in east central Michigan, on Saginaw Bay; pop. 49,449.

Bay·ern (bī′ərn) The German name for BAVARIA.

Ba·yeux tapestry (bä·yöö′, bä-; *Fr.* bà·yœ′) An embroidered linen roll, 231 feet long and 20 inches wide, depicting over 70 scenes in the life of William the Conqueror, and traditionally ascribed to his queen, Matilda. It is preserved at Bayeux, a town in NW France.

Bayle (bel), **Pierre**, 1647–1706, French philosopher.

bay leaf The leaf of the laurel (def. 1), used as a cooking herb.

bay lynx See under LYNX.

Bay of, etc. See specific name, as (Bay of) BENGAL, (Bay of) BISCAY, etc.

bay·o·net (bā′ə·nit, -net, bā′ə·net′) *n.* A daggerlike weapon attachable to the muzzle of a firearm, used in close fighting. —*v.t.* **·net·ed, ·net·ing** To stab or pierce with a bayonet. [< F *bayonette,* after *Bayonne,* France, where first made]

BAYONETS

A Needle. B 18-19th century. C Sword. D U.S. Army. a Blade. b Guard. c Bayonet spring. d Scabbard catch. e Tang. f Pommel. g Bayonet catch. h Undercut groove.

Ba·yonne (bā·yōn′ for def. 1; bà·yōn′ for def. 2) **1.** A city in NE New Jersey; pop. 72,743. **2.** A port city in SW France, on the Adour river near the Bay of Biscay; pop. 39,761 (1968).

bay·ou (bī′ōō) *n. U.S.* A marshy inlet or outlet of a lake, river, etc. [< dial. F (Louisiana) < Choctaw *bayuk* small stream]

Bayou State Nickname of MISSISSIPPI.

Bay·reuth (bī·roit′) A city in NE Bavaria, West Germany; pop. 63,387 (est. 1970); known for its annual Wagner music festivals.

bay rum An aromatic liquid used in medicines and cosmetics, originally distilled from the leaves of the bayberry, but now also made from alcohol, water, and essential oils.

Bay State Nickname of MASSACHUSETTS.

Bay·town (bā′toun′) A city in SE Texas, on Galveston Bay; pop. 43,980.

bay tree Laurel (def. 1).

bay window 1. A window structure projecting from the wall of a building and forming a recess within. **2.** *Slang* A protruding belly, as of a fat person.

bay·wood (bā′wŏŏd′) *n.* A coarse mahogany from Honduras or the region around the Gulf of Campeche.

ba·zaar (bə·zär′) *n.* **1.** An Oriental market or street of shops. **2.** A shop or store for the sale of miscellaneous wares. **3.** A sale of miscellaneous articles, as for charity. Also **ba·zar′.** —**Syn.** See SHOP. [Ult. < Persian *bāzār* market]

Ba·zaine (bà·zen′), **François Achille**, 1811–88, French marshal.

Ba·zin (bà·zaṅ′), **René**, 1853–1932, French novelist.

ba·zoo·ka (bə·zōō′kə) *n. Mil.* A long, tubular, portable weapon that fires an explosive rocket, and is used for short-range action against tanks and fortifications. [from fancied resemblance to the bazooka, a musical instrument invented and named by Bob Burns, U.S. comedian]

b.b. or **bb** Base(s) on balls.

BB (bē′bē′) *n.* A standard size of shot, 0.18 in. in diameter.

B.B.A. or **B.Bus.Ad.** Bachelor of Business Administration.

B battery *Electr.* The battery that supplies direct-current voltage to the plate and grid of a vacuum tube.

BBC or **B.B.C.** British Broadcasting Corporation.

BB gun An air rifle.

bbl. (*pl.* **bbls.**) Barrel.

B.C. 1. Bachelor of Chemistry. **2.** Bachelor of Commerce. **3.** Before Christ. **4.** British Columbia.

B.C. or **b.c. 1.** *Music* Bass clarinet. **2.** Bicycle club. **3.** Boat club.

B.C.E. 1. Bachelor of Chemical Engineering. **2.** Bachelor of Civil Engineering.

BCG *Med.* Bacillus Calmette-Guérin (TB vaccine).

bch. (*pl.* **bchs.**) Bunch.

B.Ch.E. Bachelor of Chemical Engineering.

B.C.L. Bachelor of Civil Law.

B.C.P. Book of Common Prayer.

B.C.S. Bachelor of Chemical Science.

bd (*pl.* **bds.**) **1.** Board. **2.** Bond. **3.** Bound. **4.** Bundle.

B/D or **b.d. 1.** Bank draft. **2.** Bills discounted. **3.** Brought down.

B.D. 1. Bachelor of Divinity. **2.** Bills discounted.

bdel·li·um (del′ē·əm) *n.* **1.** A gum resin resembling myrrh, yielded by various trees (genus *Commiphora*) of India and Africa; also, any of such trees. **2.** A substance mentioned in the Old Testament, variously interpreted as crystal, carbuncle, pearl, or amber. [< L < Gk. *bdellion* < Semitic]

bd.ft. Board feet.

bdg. Binding.

bdl. or **bdle.** Bundle.

bds. 1. Bundles. **2.** (Bound in) boards.

B.D.S. Bachelor of Dental Surgery.

be (bē, *unstressed* bi) *v.i.* **been, be·ing** Present indicative: I am, he, she, it is, we, you, they **are**; past indicative: I, he, she, it **was**, we, you, they **were**; present subjunctive: **be**; past subjunctive: **were**; archaic forms: thou **art** (present), thou **wast** or **wert** (past) **1.** As the substantive verb, *be* is used to mean: **a** To have existence, truth, or actuality: God *is*; There *are* bears in the zoo. **b** To take place; happen: The party *is* today. **c** To stay or continue: She *was* here for one week. **d** To belong; befall: a subjunctive use, often with *to* or *unto*: Joy *be* unto you. **2.** As a copulative verb *be* forms a link between the subject and predicate nominative or qualifying word or phrase in declarative, interrogative, and imperative sentences, and also forms infinitive and participial phrases: George *is* my friend; He *is* sick; the pleasure of *being* here. **3.** As an auxiliary verb *be* is used: **a** With the present participle of other verbs to express continuous or progressive action: I *am* working. **b** With the past participle of transitive verbs to form the passive voice: He *was* injured. **c** With the past participle of intransitive verbs to form the perfect tense: Christ *is* come; I *am* finished. **d** With the infinitive or present participle to express purpose, duty, possibility, futurity, etc.: We *are* to start on Monday; We *are* leaving Monday. The verb is defective, and its conjugation is made up of fragments of three original verbs, furnishing be, am (are, is), was (were), respectively. [OE *bēon*]

be- *prefix* Used to form transitive verbs and participial adjectives from nouns, adjectives, and verbs. [OE *be-, bi-,* var. of *bī* near, by]

Be- appears as a prefix forming words with the following meanings:

1. (*from verbs*) Around; all over; throughout; as in:

beclasp	bedimple	bemingle	beshroud
beclog	bedrape	bemix	beslobber
beclothe	befinger	berake	besmother
becompass	befleck	bescour	besmudge
becrust	befreckle	bescreen	bespeckle
bedabble	begirdle	bescribble	betatter
bedarken	bejumble	beshackle	bewrap
bediaper	bekiss	beshadow	bewreathe

2. (*from verbs*) Completely; thoroughly; as in:

beclamor	bedrench	bemuddle	besoothe
becrowd	bedrug	bemuzzle	bethank
becudgel	beflatter	besanctify	bethump
becurse	befluster	bescorch	betrample
bedamn	begall	bescourge	beweary
bedeafen	beknot	beshame	bewelcome
bedrabble	bemadden	beshiver	beworry

3. (*from verbs*) Off; away from: *behead, bereave.*

4. (*from intransitive verbs*) About; at; on; over; against; for; as in:

bechatter	befret	beleap	beswarm
becrawl	begaze	bemurmur	bethunder
bedrivel	begroan	beshout	bevomit
bedrizzle	behowl	besmile	beweep

5. (*from adjectives and nouns*) To make; cause to be; as in:

beclown	bedirty	bedwarf	beknight
becoward	bedumb	beglad	besmooth
becripple	bedunce	begrim	bespouse

6. (*from nouns*) To provide with; affect by; cover with; as in:

beblister	becrime	begulf	besmoke
beblood	bedrape	bejewel	besmut
becap	beflea	beliquor	besnow
becarpet	beflower	bemist	bethorn
bechalk	befringe	bepimple	bewhisker
becharm	beglitter	beslime	bewig
becloak	begloom	beslipper	beworm

7. (*from nouns*) Archaic To call; name; as in:

bebrother	belady	bemonster	bescoundrel
becoward	bemadam	berascal	bevillain

8. (*from nouns*, in the form of participial adjectives) Furnished with, excessively or conspicuously; as in:

bealtared	beflowered	bepilgrimed	besteepled
bebuttoned	befrilled	beribboned	bestrapped
becapped	begarlanded	beringed	besworded
becarpeted	begartered	beringleted	betaxed
bechained	behusbanded	berobed	betinseled
becupided	bejeweled	berouged	beturbaned
becurtained	belaced	beruffled	beuncled
becushioned	bemedaled	besainted	beuniformed
bedotted	bemitered	beslaved	bewinged
befeathered	bemottoed	bestarred	bewreathed

Be *Chem.* Beryllium.

Bé or **Bé.** Baumé.

B.E. 1. Bachelor of Education. **2.** Bachelor of Engineering. **3.** Bank of England. **4.** Board of Education.

B.E. or **B/E** or **b.e.** Bill of exchange.

B.E.A. British East Africa.

beach (bēch) *n.* **1.** The sloping shore of a body of water; strand; especially, a sandy shore used for swimming. **2.** The sand or loose pebbles on the shore. **— Syn.** See SHORE¹. **— on the beach** *Naut.* Ashore; not employed at sea. *— v.t. & v.i.* To drive or haul up (a boat or ship) on a beach; strand. [Origin unknown]

beach buggy *U.S.* A car or truck with large balloon tires for driving on sand.

beach·comb·er (bēch′kō′mər) *n.* **1.** A vagrant living on what he can find or beg around the wharves and beaches of ports, especially in the South Sea Islands. **2.** A long wave rolling upon the beach. **3.** *Canadian* The owner or a crew member of a small tug that recovers, for a commission, logs that have strayed from log booms.

beach flea A small amphipod crustacean (family *Talitridae*) that hops like a flea and is found on sea beaches: also called *sand hopper.*

beach·head (bēch′hed′) *n. Mil.* An area on a hostile shore established by an advance force for the landing of troops and supplies and the launching of subsequent operations.

beach-la-mar (bēch′lə·mär′) *n.* Bêche-de-mer (which see).

beach·y (bē′chē) *adj.* Sandy or pebbly.

bea·con (bē′kən) *n.* **1.** A signal, especially a signal fire or light on a hill, building, etc., intended as a warning or guide. **2.** A light, buoy, etc., set on a shore, shoal, or similar place to guide or warn mariners. **3.** A lighthouse. **4.** Any hill, building, etc., from which signals are or may be given. **5.** Anything that warns or signals. **6.** *Aeron.* A mark, light, or radio transmitter used to plot flight courses. See RADIO BEACON. *— v.t.* **1.** To furnish with a beacon. **2.** To guide by a beacon. *— v.i.* **3.** To shine as a beacon. [OE *bēacn* sign, signal. Akin to BECKON.]

bead (bēd) *n.* **1.** A small, usually round, piece of glass, wood, stone, etc., pierced for stringing on thread or attaching to fabric as decoration. **2.** *pl.* A string of beads; necklace. **3.** *pl.* A rosary. **4.** Any small body resembling a bead. **5.** A bubble of gas in a liquid, or such bubbles collectively; froth; foam. **6.** A drop of liquid, as of sweat. **7.** A small knob used as the front sight of a gun. **8.** *Chem.* A small mass of flux placed on a platinum wire to receive a substance for blowpipe testing. **9.** *Metall.* The spherical piece of refined metal resulting from cupellation. **10.** *Archit.* **a** A molding composed of a row of half-oval ornaments resembling a string of beads. **b** A small convex molding. **11.** The part of a pneumatic tire that grips the rim of a wheel. **— to draw a bead on** To take careful aim at. **— to tell (count, or say) one's beads** To recite prayers with a rosary. *— v.t.* **1.** To decorate with beads or beading. *— v.i.* **2.** To collect in beads or drops. [OE *gebed* prayer; later, a rosary bead]

bead·house (bēd′hous′) *n.* An almshouse or hospital in which the inmates were required to pray for the founders: also spelled *bedehouse.*

bead·ing (bē′ding) *n.* **1.** Ornamentation with beads. **2.** Material consisting of or ornamented with beads. **3.** A narrow openwork lace through which a ribbon may be run. **4.** *Archit.* A bead, or beads collectively.

bea·dle (bēd′l) *n.* **1.** In the Church of England, a lay officer who ushers or keeps order during services. **2.** A shammes (def. 1). **3.** *Brit.* An official who leads university processions. **4.** A court messenger. Also, *Archaic, bedel, bedell.* [< OF *bedel* messenger, ult. < Gmc.]

bea·dle·dom (bēd′l·dəm) *n.* Petty officiousness.

bead·roll (bēd′rōl′) *n.* **1.** A list; catalogue. **2.** Formerly, in the Roman Catholic Church, a list of those to be prayed for.

beads·man (bēdz′mən) *n. pl.* **·men** (-mən) **1.** One who prays for another, especially when hired to do so. **2.** *Brit.* An inmate of an almshouse. **3.** *Scot.* A licensed beggar. Also spelled *bedeman*: also **bead′man.** **— beads′wom′an** *n.fem.*

bead·work (bēd′wûrk′) *n.* **1.** Decorative work made with or of beads. **2.** *Archit.* A bead.

bead·y (bē′dē) *adj.* **bead·i·er, bead·i·est 1.** Small and glittering: *beady* eyes. **2.** Covered with beads. **3.** Foamy.

bea·gle (bē′gəl) *n.* A small, short-coated hound with short legs and drooping ears. [ME *begle*; origin uncertain]

beak¹ (bēk) *n.* **1.** The horny, projecting mouth parts of birds; the bill or neb. **2.** A beaklike part or organ, as the horny jaws of cephalopods and turtles, the elongated snout of various fishes, etc. **3.** Something resembling a bird's beak, as the point of an anvil. **4.** *Slang* A person's nose. **5.** *Naut.* A pointed projection at the prow of old warships, used to ram and pierce enemy vessels. **6.** *Archit.* A downward-projecting molding on the under edge of a cornice, used to shed water and keep it from running down the wall. **7.** The part of a retort or

BEAGLE
(About 15 inches high at shoulder)

still that conducts the vapor to the worm or condenser. [< F *bec* < LL *beccus*, ult. < Celtic] — **beaked** *adj.* — **beak/less** *adj.* — **beak/like/** *adj.*

beak² (bēk) *n. Brit. Slang* **1.** A policeman. **2.** A magistrate. **3.** At Eton, a master.

beak·er (bē/kər) *n.* **1.** A large, wide-mouthed drinking cup or goblet. **2.** A cylindrical, flat-bottomed vessel of glass, aluminum, etc., with a lip for pouring, used in chemical analysis, etc. **3.** The contents or capacity of a beaker. [< ON *bikarr;* spelling infl. by *beak¹*]

beam (bēm) *n.* **1.** A long, heavy piece of wood, metal, or, sometimes, stone, shaped for use. **2.** A horizontal piece forming part of the frame of a building or other structure. **3.** *Naut.* **a** One of the heavy pieces of timber or iron set across a vessel to support the decks and stay the sides. **b** The greatest width of a vessel. **c** The side of a vessel, or the direction forming a right angle with the keel. **4.** The bar of a balance; also, the balance. **5.** A horizontal cylindrical bar, in a loom, upon which warp or woven goods are wound. **6.** The pole of a carriage. **7.** *Mech.* A walking beam (which see). **8.** A ray of light, or a group of nearly parallel rays. **9.** A gleam or ray; suggestion: a *beam* of truth. **10.** *Aeron.* A continuous radio signal along an airway to guide aircraft: also *radio beam.* **11.** The main stem of a deer's antler. **12.** The area of maximum sound clarity in front of a microphone. **13.** The horizontal piece in a plow to which the share and the handles are attached. **14.** The widest part of anything. **15.** *Slang* The hips: broad in the *beam.* — **off the beam 1.** *Aeron.* Not following the radio beam. **2.** *Informal* On the wrong track; wrong. — **on the beam 1.** *Naut.* In a direction at right angles with the keel; abeam. **2.** *Aeron.* Following the radio beam. **3.** *Informal* In the right direction; just right; correct. — *v.t.* **1.** To send out in beams or rays. **2.** *Telecom.* To aim or transmit (a signal) in a specific direction. **3.** *Aeron.* To guide (an airplane) by radio beams. — *v.i.* **4.** To emit light. **5.** To smile or grin radiantly. [OE *bēam* tree] — **beam/less** *adj.* — **beam/like/** *adj.*

beam-ends (bēm/endz/) *n.pl. Naut.* The ends of a ship's beams. — **on her beam-ends** Of a ship, tipped over so far as to be in danger of capsizing.

beam·ing (bē/ming) *adj.* Radiant; bright; smiling; cheerful. — **beam/ing·ly** *adv.*

beam·ish (bē/mish) *adj.* Beaming. [< BEAM + -ISH; coined by Lewis Carroll in *Through the Looking-Glass*]

beam·y (bē/mē) *adj.* **beam·i·er, beam·i·est 1.** Sending out beams of light; radiant. **2.** Like a beam; massive. **3.** *Naut.* Having much breadth of beam. **4.** Having antlers, as a stag.

bean (bēn) *n.* **1.** The oval, edible seed of any of various leguminous plants, usually of the genus *Phaseolus.* **2.** A plant that bears beans. **3.** Any of several beanlike seeds or plants: a vanilla *bean.* **4.** *Slang* The head. **5.** *Brit. Slang* Person; chap. — *v.t. U.S. Slang* To hit on the head, especially with a thrown object, as a baseball. [OE *bēan*]

bean·bag (bēn/bag/) *n.* A small cloth bag filled with beans, used as a toy.

bean ball In baseball, a pitch aimed at the batter's head.

bean beetle The Mexican bean beetle (which see).

bean caper A small tree or shrub (*Zygophyllum fabogo*) of the caltrop family, native to eastern Mediterranean regions, having flower buds that are used as capers.

bean·ie (bē/nē) *n.* A small, brimless cap.

bean·o (bē/nō) *n.* A form of bingo, usually using beans as counters. Compare BINGO, KENO, LOTTO. [< BEAN]

bean·pole (bēn/pōl/) *n.* **1.** A tall pole for a bean plant to climb on. **2.** *Slang* A tall, thin person.

bean·stalk (bēn/stôk/) *n.* The main stem of a bean plant.

bean tree Any of various trees or shrubs bearing beanlike pods, as the catalpa and the carob.

bear¹ (bâr) *v.* **bore** (*Archaic* **bare**), **borne, bear·ing** *v.t.* **1.** To support; hold up. **2.** To carry; convey: to *bear* gifts. **3.** To show visibly; carry: to *bear* a scar. **4.** To conduct or guide. **5.** To spread; disseminate: to *bear* tales. **6.** To hold in the mind; maintain or entertain: to *bear* a grudge. **7.** To suffer or endure; undergo: to *bear* pain. **8.** To accept or acknowledge; assume, as responsibility or expense. **9.** To produce; give birth to. ◆ In this sense, the participial form in the passive is **born**, except when followed by *by.* **10.** To conduct or comport (oneself). **11.** To manage or carry (oneself or a part of oneself): She *bears* her head high. **12.** To move by pressing against; drive: The wind *bore* the ship backward. **13.** To render; give: to *bear* witness. **14.** To be able to withstand; allow: His story will not *bear* investigation. **15.** To have or stand in (comparison or relation): with *to:* What relation does his story *bear* to yours? **16.** To possess as a right or power: to *bear* title. — *v.i.* **17.** To rest heavily; lean; press: His duties *bear* heavily upon him. **18.** To endure patiently; suffer: often with *with:* Bear with me. **19.** To produce fruit or young. **20.** To carry burdens. **21.** To move or lie in a certain direction; be pointed or aimed: to *bear* west. **22.** To be relevant; have reference: with *on* or *upon.* — **Syn.** See CARRY, ENDURE. — **to bear down 1.** To force down; overpower or overcome. **2.** To exert oneself; make an effort. — **to bear down on** (or **upon**) **1.** To put pressure on; press hard on. **2.** To make a great effort. **3.**

To approach, especially another vessel from windward. — **to bear out** To support; confirm; justify. — **to bear up** To keep up strength and spirits when under a strain. [OE *beran* to carry, wear, bear, suffer]

bear² (bâr) *n.* **1.** Any of various large, plantigrade mammals (family *Ursidae*) with massive, thickly furred body and a very short tail, as the grizzly bear, polar bear, etc. ◆ Collateral adjective: *ursine.* **2.** Any of various other animals resembling or believed to be the bear: ant *bear.* **3.** A gruff, ill-mannered, or clumsy person. **4.** A speculator, especially one in the stock exchange, who seeks to depress prices or who sells in the belief that a decline in prices is likely: opposed to *bull.* **5.** *Mech.* A portable device for punching holes. — **the Bear** Russia. — *adj.* Of, pertaining to, or caused by stock-market bears, or a decline in prices: a *bear* market. — *v.t.* To endeavor to depress the price of (stocks etc.) by selling or offering to sell. [OE *bera*]

bear³ (bir) *n. Scot.* Barley.

bear·a·ble (bâr/ə-bəl) *adj.* Capable of being borne; endurable. — **bear/a·ble·ness** *n.* — **bear/a·bly** *adv.*

bear·bait·ing (bâr/bā/ting) *n.* The sport of inciting dogs to attack a captive bear. — **bear/bait/er** *n.*

bear·ber·ry (bâr/ber/ē, -bər-ē) *n. pl.* **·ries 1.** A trailing, thick-leaved evergreen plant (*Arctostaphylos uva-ursi*) of the heath family, having small red berries and astringent leaves: also called *crowberry, dogberry.* **2.** The deciduous holly (*Ilex decidua*): also called *possumhaw.*

bear·cat (bâr/kat/) *n.* **1.** The panda (def. 1). **2.** A very fierce or energetic person or animal.

beard (bird) *n.* **1.** The hair on a man's face, especially on the chin, usually excluding the mustache. **2.** Any similar growth or appendage. **3.** *Zool.* **a** The long hair on the chin of some animals, as the goat. **b** The feathers near the mouth of certain birds, as the turkey. **4.** *Bot.* A tuft of hairlike processes; an awn, as of grass. For illustration see WHEAT. **5.** A barb, as of an arrow. **6.** *Ornithol.* The vane or barbs of a feather. **7.** *Printing* That part of a type between the face and the shoulder: also called *neck.* — *v.t.* **1.** To take by the beard; pull the beard of. **2.** To defy courageously. **3.** To furnish with a beard. [OE] — **beard/ed** *adj.* — **beard/less** *adj.* — **beard/less·ness** *n.* — **beard/like/** *adj.*

Beard (bird), **Charles Austin,** 1874–1948, and his wife, **Mary,** 1876–1958, *née* Ritter, U.S. historians. — **Daniel Carter,** 1850–1941, founder of the Boy Scouts of America.

bearded vulture The lammergeier.

Beards·ley (birdz/lē), **Aubrey Vincent,** 1872–98, English artist and illustrator.

beard·tongue (bird/tung/) *n.* The penstemon, a plant.

bear·er (bâr/ər) *n.* **1.** One who or that which bears, carries, or upholds. **2.** A person who bears or presents for payment a check, money order, etc. **3.** A tree or vine producing fruit. **4.** A carrier or porter. **5.** A pallbearer.

bear garden 1. A place where bears are exhibited or kept, especially for bearbaiting. **2.** Any place or scene of tumult.

bear grass 1. Any of various species of *Yucca.* **2.** The camass (*Camassia scilloides*) of Oregon. **3.** A yuccalike plant (*Dasylirion texanum*) of the SW United States.

bear·ing (bâr/ing) *n.* **1.** Manner of conducting or carrying oneself; deportment. **2.** The act, capacity, or period of producing. **3.** That which is produced; crops; yield. **4.** The act or capacity of enduring; endurance. **5.** *Mech.* A part on which something rests, or in which a pin, journal, etc., turns; also, the part supported. **6.** *Archit.* The part of an arch or beam that rests upon a support. **7.** The position or direction of an object or point, ordinarily expressed in degrees or points of the compass relative to a line between the observer and north. **8.** *Often pl.* The situation of an object relative to that of another, or of other points or places: to lose one's *bearings.* **9.** Reference or relation; connection: This evidence has no *bearing* on the case. **10.** *Heraldry* A device or charge on a field. — **Syn.** See AIR.

bearing rein A checkrein (def. 1).

bear·ish (bâr/ish) *adj.* **1.** Like a bear; rough; surly. **2.** Tending toward, counting on, or causing a depression in the price of stocks. — **bear/ish·ly** *adv.* — **bear/ish·ness** *n.*

bé·ar·naise sauce (bā·år·nâz/) A variation of hollandaise sauce made with chopped parsley and vinegar.

bear paw *Canadian* An almost circular snowshoe of simple construction and varying diameter.

Bear River A river in Utah, Wyoming, and SE Idaho, flowing 350 miles from NE Utah to Great Salt Lake.

bear's-breech (bârz/brēch/) *n.* Any species of acanthus.

bear's-ear (bârz/ir/) *n.* The auricula (def. 1).

bear·skin (bâr/skin/) *n.* **1.** The skin of a bear, or a coat or robe made of it. **2.** A tall, black fur military headdress. **3.** A coarse, shaggy, woolen cloth.

bear·wood (bâr/wōod/) *n.* Cascara (def. 1).

beast (bēst) *n.* **1.** Any animal except man; especially, any large quadruped. **2.** A domesticated animal: a *beast* of burden. **3.** A cruel, rude, or filthy person. [< OF *beste* < LL *besta* < L *bestia* beast] — **beast/like/** *adj.*

beast·ly (bēst/lē) *adj.* **·li·er, ·li·est 1.** Resembling a beast; bestial. **2.** *Informal* Disagreeable or unpleasant; nasty. — *adv. Brit. Slang* Very. — **beast/li·ness** *n.*

beast of burden An animal used for carrying loads.
beat (bēt) *v.* **beat, beat·en** or **beat, beat·ing** *v.t.* **1.** To strike repeatedly; pound. **2.** To punish by repeated blows; thrash; whip. **3.** To dash or strike against. **4.** To shape or break by blows. **5.** To make flat by tramping or treading. **6.** To make, as one's way, by or as by blows. **7.** To flap; flutter, as wings. **8.** To stir or mix rapidly so as to make lighter or frothier: to *beat* eggs. **9.** To mark or measure as with a baton: to *beat* time. **10.** To sound (a signal), as on a drum. **11.** To hunt over; search: to *beat* the countryside. **12.** To subdue or defeat; master. **13.** To surpass; be superior to. **14.** *Informal* To baffle; perplex: It *beats* me. **15.** *U.S. Slang* To defraud; swindle. — *v.i.* **16.** To strike repeated blows. **17.** To strike or smite as if with blows: The sound *beat* on my ears. **18.** To throb; pulsate. **19.** To give forth sound, as when tapped or struck. **20.** To sound a signal, as on a drum. **21.** *Physics* To alternate in intensity so as to pulsate. **22.** To be adaptable to beating. **23.** To hunt through underbrush, etc., as for game. **24.** To win a victory or contest. **25.** *Naut.* To work against contrary winds or currents by tacking. **— to beat about** To search by one means and then another. **— to beat about the bush** To approach a subject in a roundabout way. **— to beat a retreat 1.** To give a signal for retreat, as by the beat of drums. **2.** To turn back; flee. **— to beat down** To force or persuade (a seller) to accept a lower price. **— to beat it** *Slang* To depart hastily. **— to beat off** To repel; drive away. **— to beat the air** To make futile exertions. **— to beat up** *Informal* To thrash thoroughly. — *n.* **1.** A stroke or blow, especially one producing sound or serving as a signal. **2.** A regular stroke, or its sound; pulsation; throb. **3.** *Physics* **a** A regularly recurring pulsation or throb heard when two tones not quite in unison are sounded together, and caused by the interference of sound waves. **b** A similar property belonging to light waves and other waves. **4.** *Music* **a** A regular pulsation; the basic unit of musical time. **b** The gesture or symbol designating this. **5.** The measured sound of verse; rhythm. **6.** A round, line, or district regularly traversed, as by a sentry, policeman, or reporter. **7.** *Naut.* A tack to windward. **8.** *U.S.* A subdivision of a county, especially in the South. **9.** In newspaper slang, a scoop. **10.** *U.S. Slang* A deadbeat. **11.** A beatnik. **— on the beat** *Music* In tempo. — *adj.* **1.** *U.S. Informal* Fatigued; worn out. **2.** *Informal* Of or pertaining to beatniks or the Beat Generation. [OE *bēatan*]
— Syn. (verb) **1.** *Beat, pound, pommel, buffet,* and *batter* all mean to deliver repeated blows, but suggest different agents or instruments. *Beat* is the most general of these words and may refer to fists, clubs, waves, etc. *Pound* suggests the use of a heavy instrument, as a hammer, while *pommel* and *buffet* describe rapid, hostile blows given with the fists or open hand. *Buffet* may also refer to the beating of a storm against a house or other object. *Batter* emphasizes the result of a beating by which a person or thing is deformed, defaced, or broken. **2.** flog, scourge. Compare STRIKE.
be·a·tae me·mo·ri·ae (bē·ā′tē me·mō′rī·ē) *Latin* Of blessed memory.
beat·en (bēt′n) Past participle of BEAT. — *adj.* **1.** Shaped or made thin by beating: *beaten* gold. **2.** Mixed by beating. **3.** Worn by use; customary: the *beaten* path. **4.** Defeated; baffled. **5.** Exhausted.
beat·er (bē′tər) *n.* **1.** One who or that which beats. **2.** An implement or device for beating. **3.** In hunting, one who drives game from cover.
Beat Generation A group of post-World War II artists, intellectuals, and others, who seek spiritual fulfillment through sensual experience, disclaiming social responsibility.
be·a·tif·ic (bē′ə·tif′ik) *adj.* Imparting or expressing bliss or blessedness. [< L *beatificus* < *beatus* happy + *-ficus* < *facere* to make] **— be·a·tif′i·cal·ly** *adv.*
be·at·i·fi·ca·tion (bē·at′ə·fi·kā′shən) *n.* **1.** The act of beatifying, or the state of being beatified. **2.** In the Roman Catholic Church, an act of the pope declaring a deceased person beatified, usually the last step toward canonization.
be·at·i·fy (bē·at′ə·fī) *v.t.* **·fied, ·fy·ing 1.** To make supremely happy. **2.** In the Roman Catholic Church, to declare as blessed and worthy of public honor, by an act of the pope. **3.** To exalt above others. [< F *béatifier* < LL *beatificare* to bless < L *beatus* happy + *facere* to make]
beat·ing (bē′ting) *n.* **1.** The act of one who or that which beats. **2.** Punishment by blows; flogging. **3.** Pulsation; throbbing, as of the heart. **4.** A defeat.
be·at·i·tude (bē·at′ə·tōōd, -tyōōd) *n.* Supreme blessedness or felicity. **— the Beatitudes** Eight declarations of blessedness made by Jesus in the Sermon on the Mount. *Matt.* v 3-12. [< MF *béatitude* < L *beatitudo* blessedness < *beatus* happy]
beat·nik (bēt′nik) *n. Informal* One who acts and dresses in a manner calculated to show indifference to or contempt for accepted conventions. [< BEAT (GENERATION) + Yiddish *-nik,* suffix of nouns denoting a person connected with or engaged in something specified]

beat note A frequency caused by the interaction of two different frequencies and equal to the difference between them.
Be·a·trice (bē′ə·tris, *Ital.* bā′ä·trē′chä) **1.** The heroine of Shakespeare's *Much Ado About Nothing.* **2.** The idealized and symbolic heroine of Dante's *Divine Comedy:* identified with **Beatrice Por·ti·na·ri** (pōr′tē·nä′rē), 1266–90.
Beat·ty (bē′tē), **Lord David,** 1871–1936, first Earl of the North Sea and Brooksby, British admiral of the fleet in World War I.
beau (bō) *n. pl.* **beaus** or **beaux** (bōz) **1.** A sweetheart or lover of a girl or woman. **2.** A man very careful of his appearance and of social etiquette; a dandy. [< OF, var. of *bel* < L *bellus* fine, pretty] **— beau′ish** *adj.*
Beau Brum·mell (brum′əl) A dandy or fop. [after George "Beau" Brummell, 1778–1840, English dandy]
Beau·clerc (bō′klär) See HENRY I.
Beau·fort scale (bō′fərt) *Meteorol.* A scale of wind velocities, ranging from 0 (calm) to 12 (hurricane): also called *wind scale.* See table below for scale as used by the U.S. Weather Bureau. [after Sir Francis *Beaufort,* 1774–1857, British admiral]

BEAUFORT SCALE			
Code No.	Description	Pressure: lbs. per sq. ft.	Speed: miles per hour
0	Calm	0.	Less than 1
1	Light air	0.01	1–3
2	Light breeze	0.08	4–7
3	Gentle breeze	0.28	8–12
4	Moderate breeze	0.67	13–18
5	Fresh breeze	1.31	19–24
6	Strong breeze	2.3	25–31
7	*Moderate gale	3.6	32–38
8	Fresh gale	5.4	39–46
9	Strong gale	7.7	47–54
10	Whole gale	10.5	55–63
11	Storm	14.	64–75
12	Hurricane	Above 17	Above 75

*Intermediate between breeze and gale.
Beaufort Sea That part of the Arctic Ocean between northern Alaska and the Arctic Archipelago.
beau geste (bō zhest′) *pl.* **beaux gestes** (bō zhest′) *French* **1.** A fine or gracious gesture. **2.** Such an act or gesture made only for diplomatic or selfish reasons.
Beau·har·nais (bō·är·ne′), **Eugénie Hortense de,** 1783–1837, queen of Holland; daughter of Josephine and mother of Napoleon III. **— Josephine de** See JOSEPHINE.
beau i·de·al (bō ī·dē′əl) **1.** The highest concept of beauty or excellence. **2.** A model of perfection or excellence. [< F *beau idéal* (the) ideal beautiful]
Beau·mar·chais (bō·mär·she′), **Pierre Augustin Caron de,** 1732–1799, French dramatist.
beau monde (bō mônd′) *French* The fashionable world.
Beau·mont (bō′mont) A city in SE Texas; pop. 119,175.
Beau·mont (bō′mont), **Francis,** 1584–1616, English dramatist who collaborated with John Fletcher. **— William,** 1785–1853, U.S. surgeon.
Beau·re·gard (bō′rə·gärd), **Pierre Gustave Toutant de,** 1818–93, Confederate general in the Civil War.
beaut (byōōt) *n. U.S. Slang* Something beautiful or outstanding: often used ironically.
beau·te·ous (byōō′tē·əs) *adj.* Beautiful. **— beau′te·ous·ly** *adv.* **— beau′te·ous·ness** *n.*
beau·ti·cian (byōō·tish′ən) *n.* One who works in or operates a beauty parlor.
beau·ti·ful (byōō′tə·fəl) *adj.* Possessing the qualities or presenting an appearance of beauty, as in form or grace; arousing esthetic pleasure. **— beau′ti·ful·ly** *adv.* **— beau′·ti·ful·ness** *n.*
— Syn. *Beautiful, handsome, pretty,* and *comely* denote that which is pleasing in appearance. A *beautiful* object excites the highest degree of esthetic appreciation, whether it be a face, form, work of art, or idea. *Handsome,* the only one of these words commonly used of men as well as women, implies conformity to some objective esthetic standard. *Pretty* means pleasing of face, but is far short of *beautiful* and more superficial; *comely* describes that which is *pretty* with a suggestion of neatness or freedom from blemish. **— Ant.** ugly, unsightly, homely.
beau·ti·fy (byōō′tə·fī) *v.t. & v.i.* **·fied, ·fy·ing** To make or grow beautiful. **— beau′ti·fi·ca′tion** *n.* **— beau′ti·fi′er** *n.*
beau·ty (byōō′tē) *n. pl.* **·ties 1.** The quality of objects, sounds, ideas, attitudes, etc., that pleases and gratifies, as by their harmony, pattern, excellence, or truth. **2.** One who or that which is beautiful, especially a woman. **3.** A special grace or charm. [< OF *beaute,* ult. < L *bellus* handsome, fine, pretty]
beauty parlor An establishment where women may go for hairdressing, complexion care, or other cosmetic treatment. Also **beauty salon, beauty shop.**
beauty spot 1. A small patch or mark put on the face to set off the whiteness of the skin. **2.** A mole or other natural

mark resembling this. Also **beauty mark.** 3. Any place or feature regarded as beautiful.

Beau·voir (bō·vwär′), **Simone de,** born 1908, French writer.

beaux (bōz) Plural of BEAU.

beaux-arts (bō·zär′) *n.pl. French* The fine arts.

beaux-es·prits (bō·zes·prē′) Plural of BEL-ESPRIT.

bea·ver[1] (bē′vər) *n.* 1. An amphibious rodent (family *Castoridae*), with a scaly, flat, oval tail and webbed hind feet, valued for its fur, and noted for its skill in damming shallow streams. 2. The fur of the beaver. 3. A high silk hat, originally made of this fur. 4. A heavy woolen cloth with a napped finish, used for outer garments. 5. *Canadian* A coin formerly issued by the Hudson's Bay Company. [OE *beofor*]

bea·ver[2] (bē′vər) *n.* 1. A movable piece of medieval armor covering the lower face. 2. The visor of a helmet. 3. *Slang* A beard. [< OF *baviere* child's bib < *bave* saliva]

bea·ver·board (bē′vər·bôrd′, -bōrd′) *n.* A light, stiff building material made of compressed or laminated wood pulp, used chiefly for walls and partitions.

BEAVER
(About 2½–4 feet long, including tail)

Bea·ver·brook (bē′vər·brŏŏk′), **Baron,** 1879–1964, William Maxwell Aitken, English publisher and statesman born in Canada.

Beaver State Nickname of OREGON.

be·bee·rine (bi·bē′rēn, -rin) *n.* An amorphous alkaloid, $C_{36}H_{38}N_2O_6$, contained in the bark of the greenheart, used in medicine. [< BEBEERU + -INE[2]]

be·bee·ru (bi·bē′rŏŏ) *n.* The greenheart (def. 1). [< Sp. *bibiru* < Carib]

Be·bel (bā′bəl), **(Ferdinand) August,** 1840–1913, German socialist.

be·bop (bē′bop′) *n.* Bop[2]. [Imit. of the short phrasing characteristic of the music]

be·calm (bi·käm′) *v.t.* 1. *Naut.* To make motionless for lack of wind: usually in the past participle: We were *becalmed* off Africa. 2. To make calm; quiet.

be·came (bi·kām′) Past tense of BECOME.

be·cause (bi·kôz′) *conj.* For the reason that; on account of the fact that; since. — **because of** By reason of; on account of. [ME *bi cause* by cause]

— **Syn.** *Because, since, as, for,* and *inasmuch as* are used to introduce the reason for a foregoing or following statement. *Because* is the most direct and unequivocal of these words, and asserts a positive causal relationship. *Since* strictly refers to a previous step in a chain of reasoning or sequence of events, but may also introduce a merely attendant circumstance. *As* closely resembles *since,* but is less definite. *For* suggests an added thought or argument, while *inasmuch as* introduces a reason or justification for a statement, without which it might seem invalid.

bec·ca·fi·co (bek′ə·fē′kō) *n.* *pl.* **·cos** Any of various small European birds, mostly warblers, supposed to eat figs; especially, the garden warbler (*Sylvia hortensis*), much esteemed as food. [< Ital. < *beccare* to peck + *fico* < L *ficus* fig]

bé·cha·mel sauce (bā·shà·mel′) A white sauce flavored with onion and seasonings. [after its inventor, Louis de *Béchamel,* steward to Louis XIV]

be·chance (bi·chans′, -chäns′) *v.t. & v.i.* **·chanced, ·chancing** To befall; happen by chance.

bêche-de-mer (bâsh·də·mâr′) *n.* 1. The trepang. 2. A lingua franca of largely English vocabulary used in the SW Pacific, originally developed through commerce with trepang fishermen: also called *beach-la-mar.* [< F, sea spade]

Bech·u·a·na (bech′ŏŏ·ä′nə, bek′yŏŏ-) *n.* 1. An important Bantu tribe inhabiting the region between the Orange and Zambesi rivers in southwestern Africa. 2. The Bantu language of this tribe.

Bech·u·a·na·land Protectorate (bech′ŏŏ·ä′nə·land, bek′yŏŏ-) A former British territory in southern Africa. See BOTSWANA.

beck[1] (bek) *n.* A nod or other gesture of summons. — **at one's beck and call** Subject to one's slightest wish. — *v.t. & v.i.* To beckon. [Short for BECKON]

beck[2] (bek) *n.* *Brit. Dial.* A small brook. [< ON *bekkr* stream, brook]

beck·et (bek′it) *n.* *Naut.* A device for holding spars, ropes, etc., in position, as a cleat, a strap, loop, or rope, or a small grommet. [Origin unknown]

Beck·et (bek′it), **Saint Thomas à** See THOMAS À BECKET.

Beck·ett (bek′it), **Samuel,** born 1906, Irish poet, novelist, and playwright.

Beck·ford (bek′fərd), **William,** 1759–1844, English writer.

beck·on (bek′ən) *v.t. & v.i.* 1. To signal, direct, or summon by sign or gesture: to *beckon* a porter. 2. To entice or lure: Fame and fortune *beckoned* him. — *n.* A summoning gesture; beck. [OE *bīecnan, bēacnian* to make signs to. Akin to BEACON.]

be·cloud (bi·kloud′) *v.t.* 1. To obscure with clouds; darken. 2. To confuse, as an issue: to *becloud* his senses.

be·come (bi·kum′) *v.* **came, come, coming** *v.i.* 1. To come to be; grow to be: The land *became* dry. — *v.t.* 2. To be appropriate to; befit: Your words do not *become* you. 3. To be suitable to; show to advantage: The hat *becomes* you. — **to become of** To be the condition or fate of: What *became* of him? [OE *becuman* to happen, come about]

be·com·ing (bi·kum′ing) *adj.* 1. Appropriate; suitable. 2. Pleasing; attractive. — *n.* A coming to be. — **be·com′ing·ly** *adv.* — **be·com′ing·ness** *n.*

— **Syn.** (adj.) 1. proper, seemly, congruous, decorous. Compare APPROPRIATE.

Becque·rel (bek·rel′) Family of French physicists, including **Antoine César,** 1788–1878, **Alexandre Edmond,** 1820–1891, son of the preceding, and **Antoine Henri,** 1852–1908, son of Alexandre Edmond.

Becquerel rays A former term for the emissions of radioactive substances. [after A. H. *Becquerel*]

bed (bed) *n.* 1. An article of furniture to rest or sleep on, consisting of the mattress, on which the body rests, the mattress and bedclothes, the bedstead, or all combined. 2. Any place or thing used for resting or sleeping. 3. A place to sleep for the night; lodging. 4. A grave. 5. Conjugal union; also, matrimonial rights and duties. 6. A heap or mass resembling a bed. 7. A plot of ground prepared for planting; also, the plants growing in such a plot. 8. The ground at the bottom of a body of water. 9. A part or surface that serves as a foundation or support. 10. A foundation of rock, gravel, etc., for a pavement or track; roadbed. 11. A layer of mortar in which stones or bricks are to be laid. 12. The underside of a slate, tile, or brick in place. 13. The part of a printing press in which the form of type is placed. 14. *Geol.* Any layer in a mass of stratified rock; a seam. — **to be brought to bed (of)** *Archaic* To give birth (to). — **to get up on the wrong side of the bed** To be irritable, grouchy, or cross. — **to put (or go) to bed** *U.S. Slang* To go to press; be printed. — *v.* **bed·ded, bed·ding** *v.t.* 1. To furnish with a bed. 2. To put to bed. 3. To make a bed for; provide with litter: often with *down:* to *bed* down cattle. 4. To set out or plant in a bed of earth. 5. To lay flat or arrange in layers: to *bed* oysters. 6. To place firmly; embed. 7. *Archaic* To cohabit with. — *v.i.* 8. To go to bed. 9. To form a closely packed layer; stratify. [OE] — **bed′der** *n.*

Bed may appear as a combining form in or as the first element in two-word phrases, which name things used for, in, or about a bed; as in:

bedchair	bedgown	bed light	bed sock
bedcover	bed jacket	bed pad	bedstand
bedframe	bed lamp	bedquilt	bedwarmer

bed and board Lodging and meals.

be·daub (bi·dôb′) *v.t.* 1. To smear or daub; besmirch; soil. 2. To ornament vulgarly or excessively.

be·daz·zle (bi·daz′əl) *v.t.* **·zled, ·zling** 1. To confuse or blind by dazzling, as with a strong light. 2. To impress greatly; charm; overwhelm: He was *bedazzled* by the wealth of the people around him.

bed·bug (bed′bug′) *n.* A bloodsucking, hemipterous insect (*Cimex lectularius*) of reddish brown color, infesting houses and especially beds; cimex: also called *chinch.* For illustration see INSECTS (injurious).

bed·cham·ber (bed′chām′bər) *n.* A bedroom.

bed chesterfield *Canadian* A sofa bed.

bed·clothes (bed′klōz′, -klōthz′) *n.pl.* Covering for a bed, as sheets, blankets, quilts, etc.

bed·ding (bed′ing) *n.* 1. Mattress, blankets, etc., for a bed. 2. Straw or other litter for animals to sleep on. 3. A putting to bed. 4. That which forms a bed or foundation. 5. *Geol.* Stratification of rocks.

Bed·does (bed′ōz), **Thomas Lovell,** 1803–49, English poet and dramatist.

Bede (bēd), **Saint,** 673?–735, English theologian and historian: called **the Venerable Bede.** Also **Be·da** (bē′də).

be·deck (bi·dek′) *v.t.* To adorn. — **Syn.** See ADORN.

bede·house (bēd′hous′) See BEADHOUSE.

be·del (bēd′l) *n.* *Archaic* A beadle. Also **be′dell.**

bede·man (bēd′mən) See BEADSMAN.

be·dev·il (bi·dev′əl) *v.t.* **·iled or ·illed, ·il·ing or ·il·ling** 1. To treat diabolically; harass or torment. 2. To worry or confuse; bewilder. 3. To possess with or as with a devil; bewitch. 4. To spoil; corrupt. — **be·dev′il·ment** *n.*

be·dew (bi·dōō′, -dyōō′) *v.t.* To moisten with dew.

bed·fel·low (bed′fel′ō) *n.* 1. One who shares a bed with another. 2. A companion; associate.

Bed·ford (bed′fərd) 1. A municipal borough in south central England, county seat of Bedfordshire; pop. 68,650 (est. 1969). 2. Bedfordshire.

Bed·ford (bed′fərd), **Duke of,** 1389–1435, John of Lancaster, regent of England and France.

Bedford cord A strong rib-weave fabric having raised, lengthwise cords.

Bed·ford·shire (bed′fərd·shir, -shər) A county in south central England; 473 sq. mi.; pop. 501,500 (1976); county seat, Bedford. Shortened form **Beds** (bedz).

be·dight (bi·dīt′) *v.t.* **·dight, ·dight or ·dight·ed, ·dight·ing** *Archaic* To dress; adorn.

be·dim (bi-dim′) *v.t.* ·dimmed, ·dim·ming To make dim.

Bed·i·vere (bed′ə-vir) In Arthurian legend, a Knight of the Round Table who attended Arthur at his death.

be·diz·en (bi-diz′ən, -dī′zən) *v.t. Archaic* To dress or adorn with tawdry splendor. — **be·diz′en·ment** *n.*

bed·lam (bed′ləm) *n.* **1.** A place or scene of noisy confusion. **2.** An incoherent uproar. **3.** A lunatic asylum; madhouse. [< BEDLAM]

Bed·lam (bed′ləm) The hospital of St. Mary of Bethlehem in London for the insane. [Alter. of BETHLEHEM]

bed·lam·ite (bed′ləm-īt) *n.* A lunatic.

bed linen Sheets, pillowcases, etc., for beds.

Bed·ling·ton terrier (bed′ling-tən) A terrier with a thick coat, used for hunting.

Bed·loe's Island (bed′lōz) A former name for LIBERTY ISLAND.

bed molding *Archit.* **1.** A molding, or one of a series of moldings, under the corona in a cornice. **2.** Any molding below a projection.

Bed·ou·in (bed′ōō-in) *n.* **1.** One of the nomadic Arabs of Syria, Arabia, etc. **2.** Any nomad or vagabond. — *adj.* **1.** Of or pertaining to the Bedouins. **2.** Roving; nomadic. Also spelled *Beduin.* [< F < Arabic *badāwīn* desert dweller < *badw* desert]

BEDLINGTON
TERRIER

(About 16
inches high
at shoulder)

bed·pan (bed′pan′) *n.* **1.** A shallow vessel to be used as a toilet by one confined to bed. **2.** A warming pan (which see).

bed·plate (bed′plāt′) *n. Mech.* A plate or frame serving as a support, as one to which parts of a machine are bolted.

bed·post (bed′pōst′) *n.* One of the posts supporting a bed.

be·drag·gle (bi-drag′əl) *v.t.* ·gled, ·gling To make wet, soiled, or untidy, as by dragging through mire.

bed·rid·den (bed′rid′n) *adj.* Confined to bed. Also **bed′·rid′.** [Earlier *bedrid* < OE *bedrida* < *bed* bed + *rida* rider]

bed·rock (bed′rok′) *n.* **1.** *Geol.* The solid rock underlying the looser materials of the earth's surface. **2.** The lowest level; bottom: Prices dropped to *bedrock.* **3.** Fundamental principles; foundation: the *bedrock* of democracy.

bed·roll (bed′rōl′) *n.* Bedding rolled to facilitate carrying.

bed·room (bed′rōōm′, -rōōm′) *n.* A room for sleeping.

Beds (bedz) The shortened form of BEDFORDSHIRE.

bed·side (bed′sīd′) *n.* The space beside a bed, especially of a sick person; the side of a bed. — *adj.* Placed beside a bed.

— **bedside manner** A doctor's attitude or manner aimed at soothing, or inspiring confidence in, his patient.

bed·sore (bed′sôr′, -sōr′) *n.* A sore caused by prolonged pressure against a bed, occurring among bedridden persons.

bed·spread (bed′spred′) *n.* A cloth covering for a bed, usually for ornament.

bed·spring (bed′spring′) *n.* The framework of springs supporting the mattress of a bed: also, any of such springs.

bed·stead (bed′sted′) *n.* A framework for supporting the springs and mattress of a bed.

bed·straw (bed′strô′) *n.* Any of a genus (*Galium*) of woody herbs of the madder family with whorled, sessile leaves and small flowers, formerly used as stuffing in beds.

bed·time (bed′tīm′) *n.* The time for retiring to bed.

Bed·u·in (bed′ōō-in) See BEDOUIN.

bed·ward (bed′wərd) *adv.* To bed. Also **bed′wards.**

bee¹ (bē) *n.* **1.** Any of a large number of hymenopterous insects (superfamily *Apoidea*), solitary or social in habit, and feeding largely upon nectar and pollen; especially, the common hive bee or honeybee (*Apis mellifera*). **2.** *U.S.* A social gathering for work, competition, entertainment, etc.: a quilting *bee.* — **to have a bee in one's bonnet** To be excessively concerned about or obsessed with one idea. [OE *bēo*]

bee² (bē) *n. Naut.* A strip of timber or iron on each side of the bowsprit, through which to reeve stays. Also **bee block.** [OE *hēag* ring]

bee³ (bē) *n.* The letter B.

B.E.E. Bachelor of Electrical Engineering.

bee balm Any of various aromatic North American herbs (genus *Monarda*) of the mint family, especially Oswego tea.

Bee·be (bē′bē), (**Charles**) **William**, 1877–1962, U.S. naturalist and explorer.

bee beetle A European clerid beetle (*Trichodes apiarius*), parasitic in beehives.

bee·bread (bē′bred′) *n.* A mixture of pollen and certain proteins stored by bees for food: also called *ambrosia.*

beech (bēch) *n.* **1.** Any of a genus (*Fagus*) of trees of temperate regions with smooth, ash-gray bark, and bearing an edible nut; especially, the widely cultivated European beech (*F. sylvatica*) and the American beech (*F. grandifolia*). The beech is typical of a family (*Fagaceae*) of widely distributed woody plants that includes the oak and the chestnut. **2.** The wood of the beech. **3.** One of various trees similar to the beech, as the hornbeam. [OE *bēce*] — **beech′en** *adj.*

Bee·cham (bē′chəm), **Sir Thomas**, 1879–1961, English orchestral conductor.

beech·drops (bēch′drops′) *n.* **1.** A low-growing plant (genus *Epifagus*) of the broomrape family, parasitic on the roots of beech trees: also called *pinedrops.* **2.** The blue cohosh.

Beech·er (bē′chər), **Henry Ward**, 1813–87, U.S. clergyman and writer. — **Lyman**, 1775–1863, U.S. theologian; father of the preceding and of Harriet Beecher Stowe.

beech mast Beechnuts.

beech·nut (bēch′nut′) *n.* The edible nut of the beech.

bee eater Any of certain insectivorous European birds (family *Meropidae*) having slim beaks and bright plumage.

beef (bēf) *n. pl.* **beeves** (bēvz) or **beefs** for def. 2; **beefs** for def. 4 **1.** The flesh of a slaughtered adult bovine animal. **2.** Any adult bovine animal, as an ox, cow, steer, bull, etc., fattened for the table. **3.** *Informal* Human flesh; muscle; brawn. **4.** *U.S. Slang* A complaint. — *v.i. U.S. Slang* To complain. — **to beef up** *Informal* To strengthen or reinforce. [< OF *boef* < L *bos, bovis* ox]

beef·eat·er (bēf′ē′tər) *n.* **1.** A yeoman of the guard, or one of the similarly uniformed warders of the Tower of London. **2.** One who eats beef. **3.** *Slang* An Englishman.

bee fly A hairy fly (family *Bombyliidae*) somewhat resembling a bee, whose larvae destroy the young of wasps and other insects. For illustration see INSECTS (beneficial).

beef·steak (bēf′stāk′) *n.* A slice of beef suitable for broiling or frying.

beef tea A bouillon made from beef.

beef·y (bē′fē) *adj.* **beef·i·er, beef·i·est** **1.** Muscular and heavy. **2.** Beeflike. **3.** Stolid. — **beef′i·ness** *n.*

bee gum **1.** A hollow gum tree in which bees nest. **2.** A beehive, especially one made from a hollow tree.

bee·hive (bē′hīv′) *n.* **1.** A hive for a colony of honeybees. **2.** A place full of activity.

Beehive State Nickname of UTAH.

bee·keep·er (bē′kē′pər) *n.* One who keeps bees; an apiarist.

bee killer One of several species of large flies (family *Asilidae*) that prey on bees.

bee·line (bē′līn′) *n.* The shortest course from one place to another, as of a bee to its hive: chiefly in the phrase **to make a beeline for,** to go directly to.

Be·el·ze·bub (bē-el′zə-bub) **1.** The prince of the demons; the devil. **2.** In Milton's *Paradise Lost,* a chief of the fallen angels ranking next to Satan. **3.** An ancient Philistine deity, worshiped as the lord of flies. [< Hebrew *ba'alzebūb* lord of flies]

bee martin The Eastern Kingbird. See under KINGBIRD.

bee moth The honeycomb moth (which see).

been (bin, *Brit.* bēn) Past participle of BE.

beep (bēp) *n.* A short, high-pitched sound, as of a horn on a bicycle. — *v.i.* To make a beep. — *v.t.* To cause (a horn, etc.) to beep [Imit.]

bee plant Any plant valuable for its nectar; especially, *Cleome serrulata* of the western United States.

beer (bir) *n.* **1.** An alcoholic fermented beverage made from malt and hops. **2.** An unfermented or slightly fermented beverage made from the roots, etc., of various plants: ginger *beer.* [OE *bēor*]

beer and skittles See under SKITTLE.

Beer·bohm (bir′bōm), **Sir Max,** 1872–1956, English critic and caricaturist.

beer parlor *Canadian* A public room where beer is sold: also *beverage room.* Also **beer parlour.**

Beer-she·ba (bir-shē′bə, bir′shi-bə) A town in southern Israel. In Biblical history it marked the southern limit of Palestine; pop. 21,000.

beer·y (bir′ē) *adj.* **beer·i·er, beer·i·est** **1.** Of or like beer. **2.** Influenced by or suggestive of beer; tipsy.

beest·ings (bēs′tingz) *n.pl. & sing.* The first milk from a cow after calving; the colostrum: also spelled *biestings.* [OE *bÿstring* < *bēost* beestings]

bees·wax (bēz′waks′) *n.* A yellow fatty solid secreted by honeybees for honeycombs, and widely used in medicine and the arts. It becomes plastic in the heat of the hand, is insoluble in water, but dissolves in boiling alcohol.

bees·wing (bēz′wing′) *n.* **1.** A crust of tartar scales on some old wines, as port. **2.** The wine so crusted.

beet (bēt) *n.* **1.** The fleshy succulent root of a biennial herb of the crowfoot family (genus *Beta*), especially the common or red beet (*B. vulgaris*), used as a vegetable, and the sugar beet (*B. saccharifera*). **2.** The edible leaves of this plant. Also **beet greens. 3.** The plant itself. [OE *bēte* < L *beta*]

Bee·tho·ven (bā′tō-vən), **Ludwig van,** 1770–1827, German composer.

bee·tle¹ (bēt′l) *n.* **1.** Any coleopterous insect having biting mouth parts and hard, horny elytra that serve as a cover for the membranous posterior pair of wings when at rest. For illustrations see INSECTS. **2.** Loosely, any insect resembling a beetle. — *adj.* Jutting; overhanging: a *beetle* brow: also **bee′tling.** — *v.i.* ·tled, ·tling To jut out; overhang. [OE *bitula* < *bītan* to bite; adj. & v. prob. < BEETLE-BROWED]

bee·tle² (bēt′l) *n.* **1.** A heavy instrument, usually with a wooden head, used for ramming paving stones, driving wedges, etc. **2.** A pestle or mallet for pounding, mashing, etc. **3.** A machine for stamping and finishing a roll of cloth as it revolves under a row of wooden hammers. — *v.t.* **·tled, ·tling** **1.** To beat or stamp with a beetle. **2.** To finish with a beetle. [OE *bīetel* mallet. Akin to BEAT.]

bee·tle-browed (bēt′l-broud′) *adj.* **1.** Having prominent, overhanging eyebrows. **2.** Scowling; frowning.

bee tree **1.** A hollow tree inhabited by bees; a bee gum. **2.** The American linden (*Tilia americana*), or other tree with nectar-bearing flowers.

beet sugar Sucrose obtained from the sugar beet.

beeves (bēvz) Alternative plural of BEEF.

bee wolf The larva of the bee beetle.

bef. Before.

B.E.F. British Expeditionary Force(s).

be·fall (bi-fôl′) *v.* **·fell, ·fall·en, ·fall·ing** *v.i.* **1.** To come about; happen; occur. **2.** *Archaic* To fall as one's share; be fitting. — *v.t.* **3.** To happen to. — **Syn.** See HAPPEN. [OE *bef(e)allan* to fall]

be·fit (bi-fit′) *v.t.* **·fit·ted, ·fit·ting** To be suited to; be appropriate for.

be·fit·ting (bi-fit′ing) *adj.* Becoming; proper; suitable. — **be·fit′ting·ly** *adv.*

be·fog (bi-fôg′, -fog′) *v.t.* **·fogged, ·fog·ging** **1.** To envelop in fog. **2.** To confuse; obscure.

be·fool (bi-fōōl′) *v.t.* **1.** To make a dupe or fool of; hoodwink; delude. **2.** To call or treat as a fool.

be·fore (bi-fôr′, -fōr′) *adv.* **1.** In front; ahead: to ride *before*. **2.** Preceding in time; previously. **3.** Earlier; sooner: the day *before*. — *prep.* **1.** In front of; ahead of. **2.** Prior to in time; earlier or sooner than. **3.** In advance of in development, rank, etc. **4.** In preference to; rather than: They will die *before* surrendering. **5.** In the presence of; face to face with. **6.** Under the consideration or cognizance of: the issue *before* you. **7.** Ahead of; awaiting: Life is *before* you. — *conj.* **1.** Previous to the time when: *before* he left. **2.** Rather than; sooner than: I will starve *before* I steal. [OE *beforan* in front of] Abbr. *bef.*

be·fore·hand (bi-fôr′hand′, -fōr′-) *adv. & adj.* In anticipation or advance; ahead of time.

before the mast Forward of the foremast: said of common sailors in sailing ships, whose quarters were forward.

be·fore·time (bi-fôr′tim′, -fōr′-) *adv.* Formerly.

be·foul (bi-foul′) *v.t.* To make foul or dirty; sully.

be·friend (bi-frend′) *v.t.* To act as a friend to; help.

be·fud·dle (bi-fud′l) *v.t.* **·dled, ·dling** To confuse, as with liquor or glib arguments. — **be·fud′dle·ment** *n.*

beg[1] (beg) *v.* **begged, beg·ging** *v.t.* **1.** To ask for in charity: to *beg* alms. **2.** To ask for or of earnestly; beseech: to *beg* forgiveness. — *v.i.* **3.** To ask alms or charity; be a beggar. **4.** To ask humbly or earnestly. — **Syn.** See ENTREAT. — **to beg off** To ask to be excused or released (from an engagement, obligation, etc.). — **to beg the question** **1.** To take for granted the very matter in dispute. **2.** Loosely, to avoid answering directly. — **to go begging** To fail of acceptance, adoption, or use. [? < AF *begger* to beg < OF *begard* mendicant friar. Akin to BEGHARD.]

beg[2] (beg) *n.* A bey.

be·gan (bi-gan′) Past tense of BEGIN.

be·get (bi-get′) *v.t.* **·got** (*Archaic* **·gat**), **·got·ten** or **·got, ·get·ting** **1.** To procreate; be the father of. **2.** To cause to be; occasion. [OE *begitan*] — **be·get′ter** *n.* — **Syn.** **1.** sire, father, engender, breed, propagate.

beg·gar (beg′ər) *n.* **1.** One who asks alms, or lives by begging. **2.** A poor person; pauper. **3.** A rogue; rascal: often used humorously: a smart little *beggar*. — *v.t.* **1.** To reduce to want; impoverish. **2.** To exhaust the resources of: It *beggars* analysis. [< OF *begard* mendicant friar] — **beg′gar·dom, beg′gar·hood** *n.*

beg·gar·ly (beg′ər-lē) *adj.* Appropriate for a beggar; miserably poor; mean; sordid. — **beg′gar·li·ness** *n.*

beg·gar's-lice (beg′ərz-lis′) *n.* Any of various plants bearing prickly fruit that adheres readily to clothes, as bedstraws and stickseeds. Also **beg′gar-lice′.**

beg·gar-ticks (beg′ər-tiks′) *n.* **1.** The bur marigold or its seed vessels. **2.** Beggar's-lice. Also **beg′gar's-ticks′.**

beg·gar·weed (beg′ər-wēd′) *n.* **1.** Any of several species of plants used for forage and a cover crop in the southern United States, especially the Florida beggarweed or clover (*Desmodium tortuosum*). **2.** A low annual plant (*Spergula arvensis*), cultivated in some regions for forage and fertilizing.

beg·gar·y (beg′ər-ē) *n.* **1.** Extreme poverty; beggarhood. **2.** Beggars collectively. — **Syn.** See POVERTY.

Beg·hard (beg′ərd, bi-gärd′) *n.* A member of one of several lay fraternities that arose in Flanders in the 13th century in imitation of the Beguines: in France called *Beguin*. [< Med.L. *beghardus*, after Lambert *Bègue*, 12th c., founder of the order of Beguines]

be·gin (bi-gin′) *v.* **·gan, ·gun, ·gin·ning** *v.i.* **1.** To start to do something; take the first step; commence. **2.** To come into being; arise. — *v.t.* **3.** To do the first act or part of; start to do. **4.** To give origin to; start; originate. [OE *beginnan*] — **Syn.** **1.** commence, initiate, inaugurate. Compare BEGIN-NING.

be·gin·ner (bi-gin′ər) *n.* **1.** One beginning to learn a trade, study a subject, etc.; a novice; tyro. — **Syn.** See NOVICE. **2.** One who begins or originates; a founder.

be·gin·ning (bi-gin′ing) *n.* **1.** The act of starting; commencement. **2.** The point in time at which a thing begins. **3.** Source or first cause; origin. **4.** The first part: the *beginning* of a chapter. **5.** *Usually pl.* The first or rudimentary stage: the *beginnings* of Christian thought.
— **Syn.** **2.** *Beginning, commencement, opening, initiation,* and *inauguration* refer to the earliest period of a thing's existence. *Beginning* is the broadest term, and is applied freely to human and nonhuman activities; *commencement* is more formal, and is generally restricted to human actions: the *beginning* of winter, the *commencement* of a political campaign. An *opening* is the first putting on display or into activity: the *opening* of an art exhibit, or of a new shop. *Initiation,* besides the particular sense of the *beginning* of membership in an organization, refers to the *beginning* of things created by human effort or ingenuity: the *initiation* of air service between two cities. An *inauguration* is a formal *beginning* marked by a ceremony. **3.** *Beginning, origin,* and *source* refer to that which brings into existence. *Beginning* is applied to events or circumstances regarded either as causal or concomitant. *Origin* is a specific cause, or the point of time or space when something comes into existence, while a *source* furnishes that which is necessary for the existence or continuance of a thing: the *origin* of a fire, the *source* of a river.

be·gird (bi-gûrd′) *v.t.* **·girt** or **·gird·ed, ·gird·ing** To gird; encircle. [OE *begyrdan*]

be·gone (bi-gôn′, -gon′) *v.i. Archaic* Go away; depart: used only in the infinitive and imperative.

be·gon·ia (bi-gōn′yə) *n.* A plant of a large and widely distributed semitropical genus (*Begonia*) with succulent, brilliantly colored leaves and showy, irregular flowers. [after Michel *Bégon,* 1638–1710, French colonial administrator]

be·got (bi-got′) Past tense and past participle of BEGET.

be·got·ten (bi-got′n) Alternative past participle of BEGET.

be·grime (bi-grim′) *v.t.* **·grimed, ·grim·ing** To soil; make dirty with grime.

be·grudge (bi-gruj′) *v.t.* **·grudged, ·grudg·ing** **1.** To envy one the possession or enjoyment of (something): They *begrudge* his wealth. **2.** To give or grant reluctantly. — **be·grudg′ing·ly** *adv.*

be·guile (bi-gil′) *v.t.* **·guiled, ·guil·ing** **1.** To deceive; mislead by guile. **2.** To cheat; defraud: with *of* or *out of.* **3.** To while away pleasantly, as time. **4.** To charm; divert. — **Syn.** See ENTERTAIN. — **be·guile′ment** *n.* — **be·guil′er** *n.*

Beg·uin (beg′in, *Fr.* bā·gaň′) *n.* A Beghard.

be·guine (bə-gēn′) *n.* **1.** A popular dance of Saint Lucia and Martinique. **2.** A social dance based on this. **3.** The music for either dance. [? after *Beguine*]

Bé·guine (beg′ēn) *n.* One of a lay Roman Catholic sisterhood, originating in the Netherlands (12th century), devoted to a religious life, but not bound by irrevocable vows. Also **Bé·guine** (bā-gēn′). [< OF. Akin to BEGHARD.]

be·gum (bē′gəm) *n.* A Moslem princess, or woman of rank in India. [< Hind. *begam* < Turkish *bigim* princess]

be·gun (bi-gun′) Past participle of BEGIN.

be·half (bi-haf′, -häf′) *n.* The interest, part, or defense: usually preceded by *in* or *on* and followed by *of.* — **Syn.** See SAKE. ◆ Formerly, *on behalf of* meant in support or favor of, and *in behalf of* meant in the place or interest of, but in modern usage this distinction tends to disappear. [OE *be healfe* by the side (of)]

be·have (bi-hāv′) *v.* **·haved, ·hav·ing** *v.i.* **1.** To act; conduct oneself or itself: The car *behaves* well. **2.** To comport oneself properly. **3.** To react to stimuli or environment. — *v.t.* **4.** To conduct (oneself), especially in a proper or suitable manner. [ME *be-* thoroughly + *have* to hold oneself, act]

be·hav·ior (bi-hāv′yər) *n.* **1.** Manner of conducting oneself; demeanor; deportment. **2.** The way a person, substance, machine, etc., acts under given circumstances. **3.** *Psychol.* The form of glandular and muscular activity characteristic of an individual in relation to internal or external stimuli, with special reference to emotional, linguistic, and other responses. Also *Brit.* **be·hav′iour.** — **be·hav′ior·al** *adj.*
— **Syn.** **1.** *Behavior, conduct, deportment,* and *demeanor* refer to a person's manner of acting. *Behavior* usually refers to some commonly accepted standard of politeness; *conduct,* to an ethical standard: courteous *behavior,* honorable *conduct. Deportment* implies an arbitrary standard, such as that set for school children, while *demeanor* refers to the facial or bodily expression of feelings or moral outlook: a carefree *demeanor.*

be·hav·ior·ism (bi-hāv′yər·iz′əm) *n. Psychol.* The theory that the behavior of animals and man is determined by measurable external and internal stimuli acting independently. — **be·hav′ior·ist** *n.* — **be·hav′ior·is′tic** *adj.*

be·head (bi-hed′) *v.t.* To decapitate. [OE *behēafdian*]

be·held (bi-held′) Past tense and past participle of BEHOLD.

be·he·moth (bi-hē′məth, bē′ə-) *n.* **1.** In the Bible, a colossal beast, probably a hippopotamus. **2.** Any large beast or thing. [< Hebrew *behēmōth,* pl. of *behēmāh* beast, ? < Egyptian *p-ehe-mah* water ox]

be·hest (bi-hest′) *n.* An authoritative request; command. [OE *behǣs* promise, vow]

be·hind (bi-hīnd′) *adv.* **1.** In, at, or toward the rear: to walk *behind*. **2.** In a place, condition, or time previously passed or departed from: He left his keys *behind*. **3.** In arrears; late: to fall *behind* in one's rent. **4.** Slow, as a watch. **5.** In reserve; to be made known: There is no evidence *behind*. — *prep.* **1.** At the back or rear of: to sit *behind* someone. **2.** Toward the rear of; backward from: Look *behind* you. **3.** On the farther side of; beyond: *behind* the curtain. **4.** In a place, condition, or time left by (one): Leave your problems *behind* you. **5.** After (a set time): The train arrived *behind* time. **6.** Not so well advanced as; inferior to: *behind* his class. **7.** Hidden by; not revealed about: What is *behind* your actions? **8.** Backing up; supporting: His money is *behind* this venture. — *adj.* **1.** Following: the man *behind*. **2.** In arrears: He is *behind* in his payments. — *n. Informal* The buttocks. [OE *behindan*]

be·hind·hand (bi·hīnd′hand′) *adv. & adj.* **1.** Behind time; late. **2.** In arrears. **3.** Behind in development; backward.

behind the times Old-fashioned; antiquated; out-of-date.

Be·hi·stun (bā′hi·stōōn′) A village in western Iran; site of a rock with inscriptions in Old Persian, Elamite, and Babylonian that aided in the decipherment of cuneiform script: also *Bisutun, Bisitun*.

be·hold (bi·hōld′) *v.t.* **·held, ·hold·ing** To look at or upon; observe. — **Syn.** See SEE¹. — *interj.* Look! See! [OE *beh(e)aldan* to hold] — **be·hold′er** *n.*

be·hold·en (bi·hōl′dən) *adj.* Indebted; obligated.

be·hoof (bi·hōōf′) *n.* That which benefits; advantage; use. [OE *behōf* advantage]

be·hoove (bi·hōōv′) *v.* **·hooved, ·hoov·ing** *v.t.* **1.** To be incumbent upon; be needful or right for: used impersonally: It *behooves* me to leave. — *v.i.* **2.** *Archaic* To be needful, essential, or fit: used impersonally. Also *Brit.* **be·hove** (bi·hōv′). [OE *behōfian*]

Beh·ring (bā′ring), **Emil Adolf von,** 1854–1917, German physician; discoverer of diphtheria antitoxin.

Behr·man (bâr′mən), **S(amuel) N(athaniel),** born 1893, U.S. playwright.

beige (bāzh, bāj) *n.* The color of natural, undyed, unbleached wool; grayish tan. — *adj.* Of the color beige. [< F]

be·ing (bē′ing) Present participle of BE. — *n.* **1.** Existence, as opposed to nonexistence. **2.** Essential nature; substance: His whole *being* is musical. **3.** A living thing. **4.** A human individual; person. **5.** *Philos.* **a** Perfect or unqualified subsistence; essence. **b** That which has reality in time, space, or idea; anything that exists actually or potentially.

Be·ing (bē′ing) *n.* The Supreme Being; God.

Bei·ra (bā′rə) **1.** A former province of north central Portugal. **2.** A port city in eastern Mozambique; pop. 58,235 (1960).

Bei·rut (bā′rōōt, bā·rōōt′) The capital of Lebanon, a port city in the western part, on the Mediterranean; pop. 700,000 (1964): also *Beyrouth*.

Beith (bēth), **John Hay,** 1876–1952, English author: pseudonym *Ian Hay.*

bel (bel) *n. Physics* A unit expressing the ratio of the values of two amounts of power, being the logarithm to the base 10 of their ratio: a measure of sound intensity. [after A. G. *Bell*]

Bel (bāl) In Babylonian mythology, the god of heaven and earth. [< Babylonian, lord. Cf. BAAL.]

Bel. Belgian; Belgium.

be·la·bor (bi·lā′bər) *v.t.* **1.** To beat soundly; assail with blows; drub. **2.** To assail verbally. **3.** *Obs.* To toil over. Also *Brit.* **be·la·bour**.

Be·las·co (bə·las′kō), **David,** 1854–1931, U.S. playwright and producer.

be·lat·ed (bi·lā′tid) *adj.* **1.** Late or too late. **2.** *Archaic* Overtaken by night. — **be·lat′ed·ly** *adv.* — **be·lat′ed·ness** *n.*

be·lay (bi·lā′) *v.t. & v.i.* **·layed ·lay·ing 1.** *Naut.* To make fast (a rope) by winding on a cleat or pin. **2.** *Informal* To stop or hold: *Belay* there! [OE *belecgan*]

belaying pin *Naut.* A removable wooden or metal pin fitting in a hole, to which running gear may be made fast.

bel can·to (bel kän′tō) A method of singing that accents tonal lyricism and technical facility, first developed in 18th-century Italian opera. [< Ital., beautiful song]

belch (belch) *v.i.* **1.** To eject wind noisily from the stomach through the mouth; eructate. **2.** To issue spasmodically from within; gush. **3.** To expel its contents violently, as a volcano. — *v.t.* **4.** To eject or throw forth violently; give vent to. — *n.* A belching; eructation. [OE *bealcian*] — **belch′er** *n.*

bel·dam (bel′dəm) *n.* **1.** An old woman, especially one who is ugly or malicious; hag. **2.** *Obs.* Grandmother. Also **bel·dame** (bel′dəm, ·dām′). [ME, grandmother < *bel* grand (< OF *bel* fine) + *dam* mother < OF *dame* lady]

be·lea·guer (bi·lē′gər) *v.t.* **1.** To surround or shut in with an armed force. **2.** To surround; beset. [< Du. *belegeren* < *be-* about + *leger* camp] — **be·lea′guered** *adj.*

Be·lém (be·leñ′) A port city in northern Brazil, capital of Pará State; pop. 563,996 (est. 1968): also *Pará*.

bel·em·nite (bel′əm·nīt) *n. Paleontol.* The pointed cylindrical fossil shell of a cephalopod related to the cuttlefish. [< NL *belemnites* < Gk. *belemnon* dart]

bel·es·prit (bel·es·prē′) *n. pl.* **beaux-es·prits** (bō·zes·prē′) *French* A person of culture or wit.

Bel·fast (bel′fast, ·fäst) The capital of Northern Ireland, a county borough and port; pop. 385,900 (est. 1969); on **Belfast Lough** (lôkh), an inlet of the North Channel; width 12 mi.

Bel·fort (bel·fôr′) A fortress town in eastern France; pop. about 43,000; on **Belfort Gap,** a pass from the Rhine valley to the Paris Basin.

bel·fry (bel′frē) *n. pl.* **·fries 1.** A tower in which a bell is hung. **2.** The part of a tower or steeple containing the bell. [< OF *berfrei* tower, infl. by BELL¹; ult. < Gmc.] — **bel′fried** *adj.*

Belg. Belgian; Belgium.

bel·ga (bel′gə) *n.* The unit of Belgian currency in foreign exchange, equal to five Belgian francs. Abbr. *b., B.*

Bel·gae (bel′jē) *n.pl.* An ancient people formerly occupying what is now Belgium and northern France.

Bel·gian (bel′jən, ·jē·ən) *adj.* Of or pertaining to Belgium. — *n.* A native or citizen of Belgium. Abbr. *Bel., Belg.*

Belgian Congo A former Belgian colony in central Africa: formerly *Congo Free State, Democratic Republic of the Congo.* See *Zaire, Republic of.*

Belgian griffon A wire-haired toy dog, a type of Brussels griffon with a black, or black and brown or tan, coat.

Belgian hare One of a strain of dark red domestic rabbits, originally developed in England from Belgian stock.

Belgian marble Rance.

Bel·gic (bel′jik) *adj.* Of or pertaining to the ancient Belgae, to Belgium, or to the Netherlands.

Bel·gium (bel′jəm, ·jē·əm) A Kingdom of NW Europe; 11,775 sq. mi.; pop. 9,660,154 (est. 1970); capital, Brussels. Officially **Kingdom of Belgium.** *Flemish* **Bel·gi·ë** (bel′gē·ə); *French* **Bel·gique** (bel·zhēk′).

Bel·go·rod-Dnes·trov·sky (byel′gə·rət·dnyes·trôf′skē) See BYELGOROD-DNIESTROVSKI.

Bel·grade (bel′grād, bel·grād′) The capital of Yugoslavia, a port city in the eastern part, on the Danube; pop. 745,000 (est. 1970): Serbo-Croatian *Beograd*.

Bel·gra·vi·a (bel·grā′vē·ə) A formerly fashionable residential district of London surrounding Belgrave Square. — **Bel·gra′vi·an** *adj. & n.*

Be·li·al (bē′lē·əl, bēl′yəl) **1.** In the Bible, the personification of wickedness; the devil. **2.** In Milton's *Paradise Lost*, one of the fallen angels. [< Hebrew *beli-ya'al* without benefit, worthless]

be·lie (bi·lī′) *v.t.* **·lied, ·ly·ing 1.** To misrepresent; disguise: His clothes *belie* his station. **2.** To prove false; contradict: Her actions *belied* her words. **3.** To fail to fulfill: to *belie* hopes. **4.** To slander. [OE *belēogan*] — **be·li′er** *n.*

be·lief (bi·lēf′) *n.* **1.** Acceptance of the truth or actuality of anything without certain proof; mental conviction. **2.** That which is believed; something held to be true or actual. **3.** Trust in another person; confidence. **4.** A tenet or body of tenets; doctrine; creed. [ME *bileafe* < *bi-* complete + *leafe* < OE *lēafa, geleafa* belief]
— **Syn. 1.** *Belief, faith,* and *conviction* all mean the acceptance of something as true or valid. *Belief* denotes acceptance with or without proof or strong emotional feelings: *belief* in a news report, or in a friend's innocence. *Faith* is always the acceptance of something not susceptible of proof, while *conviction* is strong *belief* arising from a deep feeling of certainty. **2.** hypothesis, opinion, theory. **3.** credence. **4.** See DOCTRINE.

be·lieve (bi·lēv′) *v.* **·lieved, ·liev·ing** *v.t.* **1.** To accept as true or real: I don't *believe* a word of it. **2.** To credit (a person) with veracity. **3.** To think; assume: with a clause as object. — *v.i.* **4.** To accept the truth, existence, worth, etc., of something: with *in*: to *believe* in freedom. **5.** To have confidence; place one's trust: with *in*: His colleagues *believe* in him. **6.** To have religious faith. **7.** To think: I cannot *believe* badly of you. [ME *beleven* < *be-* completely + *leven* < OE *gelēfan* to believe] — **be·liev′a·ble** *adj.* — **be·liev′er** *n.*

be·like (bi·līk′) *adv. Archaic* Perhaps; probably.

Bel·i·sar·i·us (bel′ə·sâr′ē·əs), 505?–565, Byzantine general.

Be·li·toeng, Be·li·tung (be·lē′tōŏng) The Dutch name for BILLITON.

be·lit·tle (bi·lit′l) *v.t.* **·tled, ·tling** To cause to seem small or less; disparage; minimize. — **Syn.** See DISPARAGE.

be·live (bi·līv′) *adv. Scot.* Soon; before long.

Be·lize (bə·lēz′) The capital of British Honduras, a port city in the eastern part, on the Caribbean at the mouth of the **Belize river,** that flows 180 miles NE; pop. 37,000 (1968).

bell¹ (bel) *n.* **1.** A hollow metallic instrument, usually cup-shaped, which gives forth a ringing sound when struck. **2.** Anything in the shape of or suggesting a bell. **3.** The lower termination of a tubular musical instrument. **4.** A bell-shaped flower or corolla. **5.** *Naut.* **a** A stroke on a bell to mark the time. **b** With a numeral prefixed, the time so marked, in half-hours, in each period of four hours beginning at midnight. — *v.t.* **1.** To put a bell on. **2.** To shape like a bell. — *v.i.* **3.** To take the shape of a bell. **4.** To blossom; be in bell, as hops. [OE *belle*]

bell[2] (bel) *v.i.* To cry, as a hound, rutting stag, etc. — *n.* The cry of a deer, bittern, etc. [OE *bellan* to bellow]

Bell (bel), **Acton, Currer, Ellis** See BRONTË. — **Alexander Graham,** 1847–1922, U.S. scientist born in Scotland; inventor of the telephone. — **John,** 1745–1831, British type founder and publisher.

bel·la·don·na (bel′ə·don′ə) *n.* **1.** A perennial herb (*Atropa belladonna*) with purple-red flowers and black berries: also called *deadly nightshade.* **2.** A poisonous alkaloid, as atropine, obtained from this plant and used in medicine. **3.** The belladonna lily. [< Ital. *bella donna,* lit., beautiful lady]

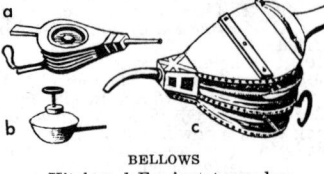

BELLOWS

a Kitchen. *b* For insect powders. *c* Blacksmith's.

belladonna lily An ornamental South African plant (*Amaryllis belladonna*), with large, showy, funnel-shaped flowers of pale rose streaked with red.

Bel·la·my (bel′ə·mē), **Edward,** 1850–98, U.S. author.

bell·bird (bel′bûrd′) *n.* **1.** Any of various birds having a bell-like note. **2.** The honey eater of Australia.

bell·boy (bel′boi′) *n.* *U.S.* A boy or man employed by a hotel to answer calls for service, carry suitcases, etc.

bell buoy See under BUOY.

belle (bel) *n.* A beautiful and attractive woman or girl; a reigning social beauty. [< F, fem. of *beau* beautiful]

Bel·leau Wood (bel′ō) A region in northern France, site of a notable American engagement in World War I, June, 1918. *French* **Bois de Bel·leau** (bwä də be·lō′).

bel·leek (bə·lēk′) *n.* A thin, delicate pottery resembling porcelain, having an iridescent or pearly glaze. Also **belleek ware.** [after *Belleek,* Northern Ireland, where it was first made]

Belle Isle An island (20 sq. mi.) at the entrance to the **Strait of Belle Isle,** the northern entrance to the Gulf of Saint Lawrence, lying between Labrador and Newfoundland; width 10–15 mi.

Bel·ler·o·phon (bə·ler′ə·fon) In Greek mythology, a hero who, on the winged horse, Pegasus, slew the Chimera.

belles-let·tres (bel′let′rə) *n.pl.* Literature having esthetic appeal, rather than didactic or informational value; poetry, drama, fiction, etc. [< F, fine letters] — **bel·let·rist** (bel′let′rist) *n.* — **bel·le·tris·tic** (bel′le·tris′tik) *adj.*

Belle·ville (bel′vil) **1.** A city in SW Illinois; pop. 41,699. **2.** A town in NE New Jersey, on the Passaic River near Newark; pop. 37,629.

bell·flow·er (bel′flou′ər) *n.* The campanula.

Bell·flow·er (bel′flou′ər) A city in SW California, near Los Angeles; pop. 51,454.

Bell Gardens An unincorporated place in SW California, a suburb of Los Angeles; pop. 29,308.

bell·hop (bel′hop′) *n.* *U.S. Informal* A bellboy.

bel·li·cose (bel′ə·kōs) *adj.* Pugnacious; warlike. [< L *bellicosus* warlike < *bellum* war] — **bel·li·cose′ly** *adv.* — **bel·li·cos′i·ty** (-kos′ə·tē) *n.*

bel·lig·er·ence (bə·lij′ər·əns) *n.* **1.** The state or quality of being warlike. **2.** Belligerency.

bel·lig·er·en·cy (bə·lij′ər·ən·sē) *n.* The status of a belligerent: condition of being at war.

bel·lig·er·ent (bə·lij′ər·ənt) *adj.* **1.** Warlike; bellicose. **2.** Engaged in or pertaining to warfare. — *n.* A person or nation engaged in warfare or fighting. [Earlier *belligerant* < F *belligérant* < L *belligerans, -antis,* ppr. of *belligerare* to wage war] — **bel·lig′er·ent·ly** *adv.*

Bel·ling·ham (bel′ing·ham) A city in NW Washington on Bellingham Bay, an inlet of the Pacific north of Seattle; pop. 39,375.

Bel·li·ni (bel·lē′nē) Name of three Venetian painters, **Jacopo,** 1400?–70?, and his two sons, **Gentile,** 1429?–1507, and **Giovanni,** 1430?–1516. — **Vincenzo,** 1801–35, Italian composer.

bell jar A bell-shaped glass vessel used as a cover for fragile articles, or in scientific experiments with gases and vacuums. Also **bell glass.**

bell·man (bel′mən) *n. pl.* **·men** (-mən) A town crier.

bell metal An alloy of copper and tin, used for the manufacture of bells.

bell-mouthed (bel′mouthed′, -moutht′) *adj.* Having a bell-shaped mouth, as a flask.

Bel·loc (bel′ok), **Hilaire,** 1870–1953, English writer born in France.

Bel·lo Ho·ri·zon·te (be′lô·rē·zôn′ti) See BELO HORIZONTE.

Bel·lo·na (bə·lō′nə) In Roman mythology, the goddess of war, sister or wife of Mars.

bel·low (bel′ō) *v.i.* **1.** To utter a loud, hollow cry, as a bull. **2.** To roar; shout: to *bellow* with anger. — *v.t.* **3.** To utter with a loud, roaring voice. — *n.* A loud, hollow cry or roar. [ME *belwen,* ? < OE *bylgian*] — **bel′low·er** *n.*

bel·lows (bel′ōz, earlier bel′əs) *n.pl. (construed as sing. or pl.)* **1.** An instrument with an air chamber and flexible sides, for drawing in air and expelling it under strong pressure through a nozzle or tube, used for blowing fires, filling the pipes of an organ, etc. **2.** The expansible portion of a camera. **3.** The lungs. [OE *belg, belig* bag; a later plural from the same source as BELLY]

Bel·lows (bel′ōz), **George Wesley,** 1882–1925, U.S. painter.

bell·weth·er (bel′weth′ər) *n.* **1.** A wether, or ram, with a bell about its neck, that leads a flock of sheep. **2.** One who leads a group, especially a thoughtless, sheeplike group.

bell·wort (bel′wûrt′) *n.* **1.** A plant of the lily family (genus *Uvularia*) having drooping flowers of a yellowish color with bell-shaped perianth. **2.** A campanula (def. 1).

bel·ly (bel′ē) *n. pl.* **·lies 1.** The abdomen in vertebrates, or the underpart of other animals, as of a snake. **2.** The stomach, especially as the source of appetite: a slave to one's *belly.* **3.** The protuberance of a bulging muscle. **4.** Any curved or protrusive line or surface: the *belly* of a flask or of a sail. **5.** The front or underpart of anything. **6.** A deep, interior cavity: the *belly* of a ship. **7.** The curved front piece, containing the sound holes, of a violin, viola, etc. **8.** *Obs.* The womb. — *v.t. & v.i.* **·lied, ·ly·ing** To swell out or fill, as a sail. [OE *belg, belig* bag]

bel·ly·ache (bel′ē·āk′) *n.* A pain in the stomach or bowels. — *v.i.* **·ached, ·ach·ing** *Slang* To complain sullenly.

bel·ly·band (bel′ē·band′) *n.* A strap passing around the belly, as of a draft animal, to hold the shafts. For illustration see HARNESS.

bel·ly·but·ton (bel′ē·but′n) *n. Informal* The navel.

bel·ly·ful (bel′ē·fool′) *n.* **1.** All that the stomach will hold. **2.** *Slang* All that one wants, or can endure.

belly laugh A hearty laugh; also, anything that causes such a laugh.

Bel·mont (bel′mont) A town in NE Massachusetts, a residential suburb of Boston; pop. 28,285.

Be·lo Ho·ri·zon·te (be′lô·rē·zôn′ti) A city in eastern Brazil, capital of Minas Gerais State: formerly *Bello Horizonte;* pop. 527,720 (est. 1958).

Bel·oit (bə·loit′) A city in southern Wisconsin, on the Rock River at the Illinois border; pop. 35,729.

be·long (bi·lông′, -long′) *v.i.* **1.** To be the property of someone: with *to.* **2.** To be a part of or an appurtenance to something: with *to.* **3.** To have a proper place; be suitable: That lamp *belongs* in this room. **4.** To have relation or be a member: with *to:* He *belongs* to the club. [ME *belongen* < *be-* completely + *longen* < OE *langian* to go along with]

be·long·ing (bi·lông′ing, -long′-) *n.* **1.** That which or one who belongs to a person or thing. **2.** *pl.* Possessions; effects, as clothes, furniture, etc.

Be·lo·rus·sian S.S.R. (bye′lə·rush′ən) See BYELORUSSIAN S.S.R., etc. Also **Be·lo·rus·sia** (bye′lə·rush′ə).

Be·lo·stok (bye′lə·stôk′) The Russian name for BIALYSTOK: also *Byelostok.*

be·lov·ed (bi·luv′id, -luvd′) *adj.* Greatly loved. — *n.* One greatly loved. [Orig. pp. of obs. *belove* love dearly]

be·low (bi·lō′) *adv.* **1.** In or to a lower place. **2.** On or to a lower floor or deck. **3.** Farther down on a page or farther on in a list, book, etc. **4.** On earth, as distinguished from heaven. **5.** In or to hell or Hades. **6.** In a lower rank or authority: the court *below.* — *prep.* **1.** Lower than in place, grade, degree, etc. **2.** Unworthy of. — **Syn.** See UNDER. [ME *biloogh* < *bi-* near + *loogh* low]

Bel·sen (bel′zən) A village in Lower Saxony, West Germany. See BERGEN.

Bel·shaz·zar (bel·shaz′ər) In the Old Testament, the son of Nebuchadnezzar and last ruler of Babylon, defeated by the Persians after being warned of his downfall by the handwriting on the wall. *Dan.* v.

belt (belt) *n.* **1.** A strap or band of leather or other flexible material worn about the waist to support clothing, tools, weapons, etc., or as ornamentation. **2.** Any band or strip resembling a belt. **3.** *Mech.* **a** An endless band of leather or other flexible material for transmitting power from one wheel or shaft to another. **b** A conveyor belt (which see). **4.** A region or zone exhibiting some specific quality or condition: a storm *belt.* **5.** *Ecol.* A region or zone suitable to the growth of a certain type of animal or plant: the corn *belt.* **6.** *Naval* A girdle of armor plates along the water line of a warship. **7.** *Slang* A blow, as with the fist. — **below the belt 1.** In boxing, below the waistband. **2.** In violation of the rules; unfair. — **to tighten one's belt** To practice thrift; consume less food. — *v.t.* **1.** To gird with or as with a belt. **2.** To fasten with a belt: to *belt* on a sword. **3.** To mark with belts or bands. **4.** To strike with a belt. **5.** *Informal* To give a blow to; strike. [OE *belt* < L *balteus* girdle]

Bel·tane (bel′tān) *n.* **1.** The Scottish name for May Day (Old Style). **2.** The ancient Celtic festival celebrating May Day. [< Scottish Gaelic *bealltainn*]

belt conveyor A conveyor belt (which see).

belt·ed (bel′tid) *adj.* **1.** Wearing or encircled by a belt. **2.** Having a mark like a belt: the *belted* kingfisher.

belt·ing (bel′ting) *n.* **1.** Belts collectively, or the material for belts. **2.** *Informal* The act of beating or striking.

belt line A transportation route encircling a city or district.

Belts·ville (belts′vil) A village in western Maryland; site of the principal experimental station of the U.S. Department of Agriculture.

be·lu·ga (bə·lōō′gə) *n.* **1.** A dolphin (*Delphinapterus leucas*) of Arctic and sub-Arctic seas, the adults being white and from 10 to 20 ft. long: also called *white whale.* **2.** The great white sturgeon (*Acipenser huso*), found in the Caspian and Black seas. [< Russian *byelukha* < *byelo* white]

bel·ve·dere (bel′və·dir′) *n. Archit.* A building, or an upper story of a building, that commands a view. **— the Belve-dere** A part of the Vatican containing many famous works of art. [< Ital., beautiful view] **— bel′ve·dered′** *adj.*

be·ma (bē′mə) *n. pl.* **·ma·ta** (-mə·tə) In Orthodox churches, the enclosure about the altar; sanctuary. [< Gk. *bēma* a step, a platform < *bainein* to go, walk]

be·mean (bi·mēn′) *v.t.* To make mean; abase; debase.

be·mire (bi·mīr′) *v.t.* **·mired, ·mir·ing 1.** To soil with mud or mire. **2.** To sink or stall in mud.

be·moan (bi·mōn′) *v.t.* **1.** To lament, as a loss. **2.** To express sympathy or pity for. **— v.i. 3.** To mourn or lament. [OE *bemǣnan*] **— be·moan′a·ble** *adj.*

be·muse (bi·myōōz′) *v.t.* **·mused, ·mus·ing** To stupefy.

be·mused (bi·myōōzd′) *adj.* **1.** Stupefied; dazed. **2.** Engrossed; deep in thought.

ben[1] (ben) *Scot. n.* The inner room of a house. **— adv. & adj.** Within; in; inner.

ben[2] (ben) *n.* **1.** A deciduous tree (genus *Moringa*) of Egypt, Arabia, and India, having an edible root and bearing winged seeds. **2.** The oil (**ben oil**) extracted from the seeds of this tree, used in cosmetics and as a lubricant for fine instruments, etc. [< Arabic *bān* tree]

Ben·a·dryl (ben′ə·dril) *n.* Proprietary name for a drug used to relieve bronchial spasm, hay fever, and certain skin ailments. Also **ben′a·dryl.**

be·name (bi·nām′) *v.t.* **·named, ·named** or **·nempt** or **·nempt-ed, ·nam·ing** *Archaic* To name; call. [OE *benemnan*]

Be·na·res (bə·nä′riz) See BANARAS.

Be·na·ven·te y Mar·ti·nez (bā′nä·vän′tā ē mär·tē′näth), Jacinto, 1866–1954, Spanish dramatist.

Ben·bow (ben′bō), **John,** 1653–1702, British admiral.

bench (bench) *n.* **1.** A long seat of wood, marble, etc., with or without a back. **2.** A stout table for mechanical work. **3.** A seat or thwart in a boat. **4.** The seat for judges in a court. **5.** The judge, or the judges collectively. **6.** The office or dignity of a judge. **7.** A seat for persons sitting in an official capacity; also, the officials or their office: the Treasury *bench.* **8.** A platform where animals, especially dogs, are exhibited. **9.** Level, elevated ground along a shore or coast, or on a slope. **10.** *Mining* A shelf or ledge formed in a mine. **11.** The substitutes on an athletic team. *Abbr. b., B.* **— on the bench** In sports, not participating. **— v.t. 1.** To furnish with benches. **2.** To seat on a bench. **3.** To exhibit, as dogs at a dog show. **4.** In sports, to remove (a player) from a game by sending him to a bench on the sidelines. [OE *benc.* Akin to BANK[1], BANK[3].]

bench dog A dog exhibited at a show.

bench·er (ben′chər) *n. Brit.* **1.** A senior member of the bar; a governor of one of the Inns of Court. **2.** One who sits on a bench, as a magistrate, a member of Parliament, etc.

bench hook A clamp, usually of wood, for holding work upon a carpenter's bench.

Bench·ley (bench′lē), **Robert (Charles),** 1889–1945, U.S. humorist.

bench mark A mark made in some durable object, as a wall or other landmark, of known position and elevation, for use as a reference point in surveys or tidal observations.

bench show An indoor exhibition of animals, especially dogs.

bench warrant *Law* A warrant issued by the judge presiding at a session, directing that an offender be brought into court.

bend[1] (bend) *v.* **bent** (*Archaic* **bend·ed**), **bend·ing** *v.t.* **1.** To cause to take the form of a curve; crook; bow. **2.** To direct or turn, as one's course, in a certain direction; deflect. **3.** To subdue or cause to yield, as to one's will. **4.** To apply closely; concentrate, as the mind. **5.** *Naut.* To tie; make fast, as a rope; place in position, as a sail. **6.** *Archaic* To strain; make tense: with *up.* **— v.i. 7.** To assume the form of a curve. **8.** To take a certain direction. **9.** To bow in submission or respect; yield; conform. **10.** To apply one's energies: with *to.* **— n. 1.** An act of bending, or the state of being bent. **2.** Something curved or bent; a curve or crook. **3.** *Naut.* **a** A knot by which a rope is fastened to something else. **b** A wale. [OE *bendan*] **— Syn.** (verb) **1.** *Bend, bow, crook, turn,* and *twist* mean to change the form or direction of a thing. *Bend* and *bow* suggest a smooth curve, but *bend* may also be used for angular or irregular turns: to *bend* a strip of metal. *Crook* means to *bend* into a hooklike shape. *Turn* refers to a change in direction rather than a change in shape, while *twist* suggests a deformity or distortion caused by a great or violent force: to *turn* the course of a stream, to *twist* a person's arm. **3.** coerce, influence, mold, persuade. **7.** *Bend, bow,* and *stoop* refer to bodily positions. *Bend* is used of any departure from an upright stance: to *bend* over a table. *Bow* is usually formal, and describes a forward and downward inclination of the head or upper body. *Stoop* denotes the lowering of the body by bending the knees. **8.** incline, tend.

bend[2] (bend) *n. Heraldry* A band drawn diagonally across a shield from dexter chief to sinister base. [OE *bend* strap; infl. in meaning by OF *bende* strip, band]

BENDS[2]

a A bend. *b* A bend cottised. *c* A bend sinister.

Ben·da (bän·dä′), **Julien,** 1867–1956, French philosopher.

Ben Da·vis (ben dā′vis) A variety of large, red, winter apple, used chiefly in cooking.

Ben Day (ben′ dā′) *Printing* A photoengraving method that produces a pattern of shaded areas of dots, lines, or other markings in an illustration. Also **ben′day′.** [after Ben(*jamin*) *Day,* 1838–1916, U.S. printer]

bend·er (ben′dər) *n.* **1.** One who or that which bends. **2.** *U.S. Slang* A drinking spree. **3.** *Brit. Slang* A sixpence.

Ben·di·go (ben′di·gō) A city in central Victoria, Australia; pop. 41,140 (est. 1959).

Ben·dix (ben′diks), **Vincent,** 1882–1945, U.S. inventor and industrialist.

bends (bendz) *n.pl. Informal* Caisson disease: preceded by *the.*

bend sinister *Heraldry* A band drawn diagonally from sinister chief to dexter base, used to indicate bastardy. Compare BATON SINISTER under BATON.

ben·dy (ben′dē) *n. Anglo-Indian* Okra. Also **ben′dee.**

ben·e (ben′ē) See BENNE.

be·neath (bi·nēth′) *adv.* **1.** In a lower place; below. **2.** underneath; directly below. **— prep. 1.** Under; underneath; below: *beneath* the stars. **2.** On the underside of; covered by: *beneath* a blanket. **3.** Under the power or sway of; subdued by. **4.** Lower in rank or station: A major is *beneath* a colonel. **5.** Unworthy of; unbefitting: She married *beneath* her station. **— Syn.** See UNDER. [OE *beneothan*]

ben·e·dic·i·te (ben′ə·dis′ə·tē) *n.* A blessing; grace or thanksgiving, especially at table. **— interj.** Bless you!

Ben·e·dic·i·te (ben′ə·dis′ə·tē) *n. Eccl.* **1.** A canticle beginning "O all ye works of the Lord, bless ye the Lord": so called from its first word in Latin. **2.** A musical setting for this canticle. [< LL, bless ye]

Ben·e·dick (ben′ə·dik) In Shakespeare's *Much Ado About Nothing,* the hero, a bachelor, who eventually marries Beatrice. **— n.** A married man.

ben·e·dict (ben′ə·dikt) *n.* A newly married man, especially one who has long been a bachelor. Also **ben′e·dick.** [< BENEDICK]

Ben·e·dict (ben′ə·dikt), **Ruth Fulton,** 1887–1948, U.S. anthropologist.

Benedict, Saint, 480?–543, Italian monk; founder of the Benedictine order: also **Benedict of Nur·sia** (nûr′shē·ə, -shə).

Ben·e·dict XIV (ben′ə·dikt), 1675–1758, pope 1740–58: original name **Prospero Lam·ber·ti·ni** (läm′ber·tē′nē).

Benedict XV, 1854–1922, pope 1914–22: original name **Giacomo del·la Chie·sa** (del′lä kyä′sä)

Ben·e·dic·tine (ben′ə·dik′tin, -tēn; *for n. def. 3,* -tēn) *adj.* Pertaining to St. Benedict or his order. **— n. 1.** A monk of the order established by St. Benedict at Subiaco, in Italy, about 530. **2.** A nun following the Benedictine rule. **3.** A trade name for a brandy liqueur formerly made at the Benedictine monastery at Fécamp, France.

ben·e·dic·tion (ben′ə·dik′shən) *n.* **1.** The act of blessing, as at the close of worship. **2.** The invocation of divine favor upon a person. **3.** Any of various formal ecclesiastical ceremonies of blessing; a dedication or consecration. **4.** The state of blessedness or grace. [< LL *benedictio, -onis < benedicere* to bless] **— ben′e·dic′tive, ben·e·dic·to·ry** (ben′ə·dik′tər·ē) *adj.*

Ben·e·dic·tus (ben′ə·dik′təs) *n.* **1.** Either of two canticles, *Luke* i 68–71, and *Matt.* xxi 9: so called from their first word in Latin. **2.** A musical setting of either canticle. [< LL, blessed]

ben·e·fac·tion (ben′ə·fak′shən) *n.* **1.** The act of giving help or conferring a benefit. **2.** A charitable deed; generous act. [< LL *benefactio, -onis < benefacere* to do well]

ben·e·fac·tor (ben′ə·fak′tər, ben′ə·fak′-) *n.* One who gives help or confers a benefit; a patron. [< L] **— ben′e·fac′-tress** *n. fem.*

be·nef·ic (bə·nef′ik) *adj.* Beneficent; kindly. [< L *benef-icus* generous]

ben·e·fice (ben′ə·fis) *n. Brit.* **1.** *Eccl.* **a** A church office, especially a rectory, vicarage, or curacy, endowed with funds or property; a living. **b** The revenue of such an office. **2.** A feudal fee or life interest in land; later, a fief. — *v.t.* **·ficed, ·fic·ing** To invest with a benefice. [< OF < L *beneficium* favor] — **ben'e·ficed** *adj.*

be·nef·i·cence (bə-nef'ə-səns) *n.* **1.** The quality of being beneficent; active goodness. **2.** A beneficent act or gift. — **Syn.** See BENEVOLENCE. [< F *bénéficence* < L *beneficentia* < *beneficus* generous]

be·nef·i·cent (bə-nef'ə-sənt) *adj.* **1.** Bringing about or doing good. **2.** Resulting in benefit. — **be·nef'i·cent·ly** *adv.*

ben·e·fi·cial (ben'ə-fish'əl) *adj.* **1.** Benefiting or tending to benefit; advantageous; helpful. **2.** *Law* Receiving or entitled to receive proceeds or advantages: a *beneficial* interest in land. [< F *bénéficial* < LL *beneficialis* < L *beneficium* favor] — **ben·e·fi'cial·ly** *adv.* — **ben·e·fi'cial·ness** *n.*

ben·e·fi·ci·ar·y (ben'ə-fish'ē-er'ē, -fish'ər-ē) *n. pl.* **·ar·ies** **1.** One who receives benefits or advantages. **2.** *Eccl.* The holder of a benefice. **3.** *Law* **a** One entitled to the proceeds of property held in trust. **b** The person to whom an insurance policy or annuity is payable. — *adj.* Pertaining to or holding a feudal benefice. [< L *beneficiarius* < *beneficium* favor]

ben·e·fit (ben'ə-fit) *n.* **1.** That which is helpful; advantage; profit. **2.** An act of kindness; charitable deed. **3.** A theatrical or musical performance given to raise funds for a worthy cause. **4.** Pecuniary aid extended by a benefit society, insurance company, etc. — **Syn.** See ADVANTAGE. — *v.* **·fit·ed, ·fit·ing** *v.t.* **1.** To be helpful or useful to. — *v.i.* **2.** To profit; gain advantage. [< AF *benfet*, OF *bienfait* < L *benefactum* good deed < *benefacere* to do well]

benefit of clergy **1.** Churchly approval or sanction. **2.** Formerly, the privilege accorded to the clergy of demanding trial by an ecclesiastical rather than a secular court.

benefit society An association of persons who, by the payment of dues, become entitled to pecuniary aid in time of sickness, need, etc. Also **benefit association.**

Ben·e·lux (ben'ə-luks) *n.* The economic union of Belgium, the Netherlands, and Luxembourg. [< BE(LGIUM) + NE-(THERLANDS) + LUX(EMBOURG)]

be·nempt (bi-nempt'), **be·nempt·ed** (bi-nemp'tid) Alternative past participles of BENAME.

Be·neš (be'nesh), **Eduard,** 1884–1948, Czechoslovak statesman; president 1935–38, 1946–48.

Be·nét (bi-nā'), **Stephen Vincent,** 1898–1943, U.S. poet and writer. — **William Rose,** 1886–1950, U.S. poet, writer, and critic; brother of the preceding.

be·nev·o·lence (bə-nev'ə-ləns) *n.* **1.** Disposition to do good; kindliness; charitableness. **2.** Any act of kindness; a gift of charity. **3.** In English history, a forced loan sometimes exacted by a sovereign.

— **Syn.** *Benevolence, beneficence, kindness, philanthropy,* and *charity* imply sympathy or generosity in a person's dealings with his fellow men. *Benevolence* is a subjective disposition of mind that results in *beneficence* or the doing of good deeds. *Kindness* is like *benevolence,* but has more of sympathy and consideration for others, and is manifested in particular actions. *Philanthropy* and *charity* refer to the giving of time and money for the care of the poor, needy, or destitute, but *charity* is often individual or small-scale almsgiving, while *philanthropy* is large-scale, organized, and purposeful. — **Ant.** malevolence, unkindness.

be·nev·o·lent (bə-nev'ə-lənt) *adj.* **1.** Disposed to do good; kindly. **2.** Marked by good will: a *benevolent* act. [< OF *benivolent* < L *benevolens, -entis* < *bene* well + *volens,* ppr. of *velle* to wish] — **be·nev'o·lent·ly** *adv.*

Beng. Bengali.

Ben·gal (ben-gôl', beng-, ben'gəl) A former province of NE British India, divided (1947) into **East Bengal,** coextensive with Bangladesh, and **West Bengal,** a State of India; 33,928 sq. mi.; pop. 44,440,095 (est. 1971); capital, Calcutta. — **Ben·ga·lese** (ben'gə-lēz', -lēs', beng-/-) *adj. & n.*

Bengal, Bay of The part of the Indian Ocean between the east coast of India and the west coast of Burma.

Ben·ga·li (ben-gô'lē, beng-) *adj.* Of or pertaining to Bengal. — *n.* **1.** A native of Bengal. **2.** The modern vernacular Indic language of Bengal.

ben·ga·line (beng'gə-lēn, beng'gə-lēn') *n.* A corded silk, wool, or rayon fabric of fine weave. [< BENGAL]

Bengal light A firework that burns with a blue flame, used in signaling, etc. Also **Bengal fire.**

Ben·ga·si (ben-gä'zē, beng-) One of the two capitals of Libya, a port city in the northern part, on the Gulf of Sidra; pop. 278,826 (1964). Also **Ben·gha'zi, Ben·ga'zi.**

Ben-Gur·i·on (ben-gŏŏr'ē-ən), **David,** 1886–1973, Israeli statesman born in Poland; prime minister 1948–53, 1955–57, 1958–63.

Be·ni (bā'nē) A river in NW Bolivia, flowing about 600 miles, generally NE, to the Mamoré.

be·night·ed (bi-nī'tid) *adj.* **1.** Involved in darkness, intellectual or moral; ignorant; unenlightened. **2.** Overtaken by night. — **be·night'ed·ness** *n.*

be·nign (bi-nīn') *adj.* **1.** Of a kind disposition; kindly. **2.** Gentle; mild. **3.** Favorable. **4.** *Pathol.* Of tumors, not liable to recur after removal; opposed to *malignant.* **b** Favorable for recovery; not permanently damaging. [< OF *benigne* < L *benignus* kindly] — **be·nign'ly** *adv.*

be·nig·nant (bi-nig'nənt) *adj.* **1.** Kind; gracious, especially to inferiors. **2.** Favorable; benign. [< BENIGN, on analogy with *malignant*] — **be·nig'nant·ly** *adv.*

be·nig·ni·ty (bi-nig'nə-tē) *n. pl.* **·ties** **1.** The quality of being benign. Also **be·nig·nan·cy** (bi-nig'nən-sē). **2.** A gracious action or influence.

Be·nin (be-nēn') **1.** A river in southern Nigeria, flowing west 60 miles into the **Bight of Benin,** a bay of the Gulf of Guinea. **2.** A Republic in west central Africa, independent since 1960; 8,482 sq. mi.; pop. 3,110,000 (est. 1975); capitals, Porto-Novo and Cotonou.

ben·i·son (ben'ə-zən, -sən) *n.* A benediction; blessing. [< OF *beneison* < LL *benedictio, -onis* benediction]

ben·ja·min (ben'jə-mən) *n.* Benzoin (def. 1). [alter. of BENZOIN]

Ben·ja·min (ben'jə-mən) In the Old Testament, the youngest son of Jacob and Rachel. *Gen.* xxxv 18. — *n.* The tribe of Israel descended from him.

Ben·ja·min (ben'jə-mən), **Judah Philip,** 1811–84, U.S. lawyer and Confederate statesman.

benjamin bush The spicebush (which see).

Ben Lo·mond (ben lō'mənd) **1.** A mountain in NW Stirling, Scotland; 3,192 ft. **2.** The highest mountain range in Tasmania; highest peak, Legge Tor, 5,160 ft.

ben·ne (ben'ē) *n.* An East Indian plant, the sesame, widely cultivated for its seeds, that yield **benne oil:** also spelled *bene.* [< Malay *bijen* seed]

ben·net (ben'it) *n.* **1.** Either of two American species (*Geum canadense* and *G. strictum*) of avens. **2.** Herb bennet. See under AVENS. [< OF (*herbe*) *beneite* blessed (herb) < L *benedicta*]

Ben·nett (ben'it), **(Enoch) Arnold,** 1867–1931, English novelist and playwright. — **James Gordon,** 1795–1872, U.S. journalist born in Scotland; founded New York *Herald* 1835. — **James Gordon,** 1841–1918, U.S. newspaper proprietor and editor; son of the preceding. — **Viscount Richard Bedford,** 1870–1947, Canadian prime minister 1930–35.

Ben Ne·vis (nē'vis, nev'is) A mountain in western Scotland; highest peak in Great Britain; 4,406 ft.

Ben·ning·ton (ben'ing-tən) A town in SW Vermont; near site of battle, 1777, in which American colonial forces defeated the British; pop. 7,950.

Be·no·ni (bə-nō'nī) A city in Transvaal, Republic of South Africa; a gold-mining center; pop. 149,052 (1966).

bent¹ (bent) Past tense and past participle of BEND¹. — *adj.* **1.** Not straight; crooked. **2.** Set in a course; resolved: on pleasure *bent.* — *n.* **1.** State of being bent or turned. **2.** A personal inclination or penchant; leaning: a *bent* for teaching. **3.** Limit of endurance or capacity: usually in the phrase **to the top of (one's) bent. 4.** *Engin.* A transverse section of a framed structure, designed to carry vertical and horizontal loads.

bent² (bent) *n.* **1.** Any of various stiff, wiry grasses (genus *Agrostis*). Also **bent grass. 2.** The stiff flower stalk of various grasses. **3.** *Archaic* A heath; moor. [OE *beonet*]

Ben·tham (ben'thəm, -təm), **Jeremy,** 1748–1832, English jurist and philosopher.

Ben·tham·ism (ben'thəm-iz'əm, -təm-) *n.* The political and ethical philosophy of Jeremy Bentham, maintaining that mankind is under the governance of two sovereign masters, pain and pleasure, and that pleasure is the supreme end of life. — **Ben'tham·ite** (-īt) *n.*

ben·thos (ben'thos) *n. Ecol.* The whole assemblage of plants or animals living on the sea bottom: distinguished from *plankton.* [< Gk., depth of the sea] — **ben·thic** (ben'thik), **ben·thon·ic** (ben-thon'ik) *adj.*

Ben·tinck (ben'tingk), **Lord William Cavendish,** 1774–1839, first governor general of India 1833. — **William Henry Cavendish,** 1738–1809, third duke of Portland; British prime minister 1783, 1807–09; father of the preceding.

Bent·ley (bent'lē), **Richard,** 1662–1742, English classical scholar.

Ben·ton (ben'tən), **Thomas Hart,** 1782–1858, U.S. politician; senator 1821–51. — **Thomas Hart,** 1889–1975, painter; grandnephew of the preceding.

bent wood Designating a style of furniture made of wood curved and bent into the desired shapes.

Be·nue (bā'nwā) A river in Nigeria, flowing about 800 miles, generally SW, to the Niger river.

be·numb (bi-num') *v.t.* **1.** To make numb; deaden. **2.** To render insensible; stupefy. [OE *benumen,* pp. of *beniman* to deprive. See NUMB.] — **be·numbed** (bi-numd') *adj.* — **be·numb'ment** *n.*

ben·zal·de·hyde (ben-zal'də-hīd) *n. Chem.* A colorless, highly refractive liquid, C_7H_6O, having the characteristic odor of essence of almonds, used in the dye and perfume industries. [< BENZ(OIN) + ALDEHYDE]

Ben·ze·drine (ben'zə-drēn, -drin) *n.* Proprietary name of a brand of amphetamine. Also **ben'ze·drine.**

ben·zene (ben'zēn, ben-zēn') *n. Chem.* A colorless, volatile, flammable, liquid hydrocarbon, C_6H_6, of the aromatic group, obtained chiefly from coal tar by fractional distillation, used as a solvent and in the synthesis of many organic compounds. Abbr. *Bz.* [< BENZ(OIN) + -ENE]

benzene ring *Chem.* The nucleus of benzene, consisting of six carbon atoms arranged in a ring, each joined to a hydrogen atom that may be replaced by other elements or radicals; also, the structural representation of this nucleus. Also **benzene nucleus.**

ben·zi·dine (ben′zə-dēn, -din)   *n. Chem.* A crystalline hydrocarbon, $C_{12}H_{12}N_2$, synthesized from benzene derivatives, used in the preparation of dyes and as a test for blood. Also **ben′zi·din** (-din).   [< BENZ(ENE) + ID(E) + -INE²]

BENZENE RING

ben·zine (ben′zēn, ben-zēn′)   *n.* A colorless, flammable liquid derived from crude petroleum by fractional distillation and consisting of various hydrocarbons, used as a solvent, cleaner, and motor fuel: also called *petroleum spirit.* Also **ben′zin** (-zin), **ben·zo·line** (ben′zə-lēn).

ben·zo·ate (ben′zō·it, -āt)   *n. Chem.* A salt of benzoic acid.

benzoate of soda   Sodium benzoate.

ben·zo·ic (ben·zō′ik)   *adj.* **1.** Pertaining to or derived from benzoin.   **2.** Pertaining to benzoic acid.

benzoic acid   *Chem.* An aromatic compound, $C_7H_6O_2$, contained in resins, as benzoin, in coal-tar oil, etc., and obtained by synthesis, used as a food preservative and in medicine.

ben·zo·in (ben′zō·in, -zoin)   *n.* **1.** A gum resin from various East Indian plants (genus *Styrax*), used in medicine and as a perfume: also called *benjamin, gum benzoin.*   **2.** *Chem.* A crystalline aromatic compound, $C_{14}H_{12}O_2$, obtained variously, as from benzaldehyde: also called *flowers of benzoin.*   **3.** Any plant of a small genus (*Lindera*) of North American and Asian shrubs or trees of the laurel family, including the spicebush.   [< F *benjoin* < Pg. *beijoim* or Ital. *benzoi* < Arabic *lubān jāwī* incense of Java]

ben·zol (ben′zōl, -zol)   *n.* A grade of crude benzene.

ben·zo·phe·none (ben′zō·fē′nōn)   *n. Chem.* An aromatic crystalline ketone compound, $C_{13}H_{10}O$, obtained variously, as from calcium benzoate by dry distillation, used in organic synthesis.   [< BENZO- (< BENZENE) + PHENOL + -ONE]

ben·zo·yl (ben′zō·il)   *n. Chem.* The univalent organic radical, C_6H_5CO, derived from benzoic acid.

ben·zyl (ben′zil)   *n. Chem.* The univalent radical, $C_6H_5CH_2$, derived from toluene.

Be·o·grad (be·ô′gräd)   The Serbo-Croatian name for BELGRADE.

Be·o·thuk (bē·oth′ək, -ot′ək) *n.* An extinct tribe of Algonkian-speaking Indians of Newfoundland; called "Red Indians" because of their custom of daubing their bodies with red ocher.

Be·o·wulf (bā′ə·wŏŏlf)   The hero of an Old English epic poem of the eighth century, a warrior prince who kills the monster Grendel and Grendel's mother and dies in old age of a wound received in battle with a dragon; also, the poem.

be·queath (bi·kwēth′, -kwēth′)   *v.t.* **1.** *Law* To give (personal property) by will. Compare DEVISE.   **2.** To hand down; transmit.   **3.** *Obs.* To devote; entrust.   [OE *becwethan*]

be·quest (bi·kwest′)   *n.* The act of bequeathing, or that which is bequeathed.   [ME *biqueste*]

Bé·ran·ger (bā·rän·zhā′), **Pierre Jean de**, 1780–1857, French poet.

be·rate (bi·rāt′)   *v.t.* **·rat·ed, ·rat·ing** To scold severely.

Ber·ber (bûr′bər)   *n.* **1.** One who belongs to a group of Moslem tribes, especially the Kabyles, inhabiting northern Africa.   **2.** One of a group of Hamitic languages of the Berbers, comprising the dialects spoken in Algeria, Tunisia, Morocco, and the Sahara, including Kabyle, Tuareg, etc.   — *adj.* Of or pertaining to the Berbers or their language.

Ber·be·ra (bûr′bər·ə)   A port city in northern Somalia, on the Gulf of Aden; pop. 12,200 (est. 1966).

ber·ber·i·da·ceous (bûr′bər·i·dā′shəs)   *adj.* Pertaining or belonging to the barberry family of herbs and shrubs (*Berberidaceae*), as the blue cohosh and May apple.

ber·ber·ine (bûr′bər·ēn, -in)   *n. Chem.* A yellow, crystalline, bitter alkaloid, $C_{20}H_{19}O_5N$, contained in the bark of the barberry and some other plants, used in medicine. Also **ber′ber·in** (-in).   [< Med.L *berberis* barberry + -INE²]

ber·ceuse (ber·sœz′)   *n. pl.* **·ceuses** (-sœz′) A lullaby [< F]

Berch·tes·ga·den (berkh′tes·gä′dən)   A resort village in SE Bavaria; site of the private retreat of Adolf Hitler; pop. 5,736.

be·reave (bi·rēv′)   *v.t.* **·reaved** or **·reft** (-reft′), **·reav·ing** **1.** To deprive, as of hope or happiness: *bereft* of joy.   **2.** To leave desolate or saddened through loss: *bereaved* of one's father.   **3.** *Obs.* To rob.   [OE *berēafian*]   — **be·reave′ment** *n.*

be·reft (bi·reft′)   Past tense and past participle of BEREAVE.   — *adj.* Deprived or dispossessed.

Berenice's Locks   The constellation Coma Berenices. Also **Berenice's Hair.**

Ber·en·son (ber′ən·sən), **Bernard**, 1865–1959, U.S. art critic and writer born in Russia.

be·ret (bə·rā′, ber′ā)   *n.* A soft, flat cap, usually of wool, originating in the Basque Provinces.   [< F, ult. < LL *birretum* cap]

Ber·e·zi·na (ber′ə·zē′nə)   A river in the Byelorussian S.S.R. flowing south 350 miles to the Dnieper; crossed by Napoleon (1812) at the battle of Borisov.

berg (bûrg)   *n.* An iceberg (which see).

Berg (berkh), **Alban**, 1885–1935, Austrian composer.

Ber·ga·ma (ber′gä·mä′)   A town in western Turkey, on the site of ancient Pergamum; pop. 24,121 (1965).

Ber·ga·mo (ber′gä·mō)   A Province of Lombardy, northern Italy; 1,065 sq. mi.; pop. 746,117 (1961); capital, **Bergamo,** pop. 113,512.

ber·ga·mot¹ (bûr′gə·mot)   *n.* **1.** A small, spiny rutaceous tree (*Citrus bergamia*) whose fruit furnishes a fragrant essential oil (**essence of bergamot**).   **2.** The oil itself.   **3.** Any of several plants of the mint family, as the horsemint in the United States.   [? after *Bergamo,* Italy]

ber·ga·mot² (bûr′gə·mot)   *n.* A minor variety of pear.   [< F *bergamote* < Ital. *bergamotta* < Turkish *beg-armūdi* prince's pear; spelling infl. by BERGAMOT¹]

Ber·gen (bûr′gən, *Norw. & Ger.* ber′gən)   **1.** A port city in SW Norway; pop. 115,845 (1960).   **2.** A village in Lower Saxony, West Germany; with Belsen the former site of **Bergen-Belsen,** a Nazi extermination camp.

Ber·gen·field (bûr′gən·fēld)   A borough in NE New Jersey; pop. 33,131.

Ber·ge·rac (ber′zhə·rak, *Fr.* ber·zhə·räk′), **Cyrano de** See CYRANO DE BERGERAC.

Ber·gi·us (ber′gē·ōōs), **Friedrich,** 1884–1949, German chemist.

berg·schrund (bûrg′shrund, *Ger.* berkh′shrŏŏnt)   *n. Geol.* A crevasse or series of crevasses at the head of a glacier, near the base of the cliff against which the snow field lies.   [< G]

Berg·son (berg′sən, *Fr.* berg·sôn′), **Henri Louis,** 1859–1941, French philosopher.   — **Berg·so·ni·an** (berg·sō′nē·ən) *adj. & n.*

Berg·son·ism (berg′sən·iz′əm)   *n.* The philosophy of Henri Bergson, for whom ultimate reality is a process of creative evolution capable of being grasped intuitively but not understood scientifically, and evolution is itself the expression of a life force in nature (*élan vital*). Compare VITALISM.

be·rhyme (bi·rīm′)   *v.t.* **·rhymed, ·rhym·ing** **1.** To mention or celebrate in rhyme.   **2.** To compose in rhyme. Also **be·rime′.**

Be·ri·a (be′rē·ə), **La·vren·ti** (lə·vren′tē) **Pavlovich,** 1899–1953, Soviet politician; executed. Also **Be′ri·ya.**

ber·i·ber·i (ber′ē·ber′ē)   *n. Pathol.* A disease of the peripheral nerves characterized by partial paralysis, swelling of the legs, and general dropsy, and resulting from the absence of thiamine (vitamin B_1).   [< Singhalese *beri* weakness]   — **ber′i·ber′ic** *adj.*

Ber·ing (bâr′ing, bir′-; *Dan.* bā′ring), **Vi·tus** (vē′tōōs), 1680–1741, Danish explorer.

Bering Sea   A part of the North Pacific Ocean between Alaska and Siberia, north of the Aleutian Islands, connected by **Bering Strait** to the Arctic Ocean.

Berke·le·ian·ism (bûrk·lē′ən·iz′əm, *Brit.* bärk-)   *n.* The philosophy of George Berkeley, who taught that reality consists only of minds and their ideas, and denied the existence of material objects except as ideas or perceptions in some human or divine mind.   — **Berk·le′ian** *adj. & n.*

Berke·ley (bûrk′lē)   A city in western California, on San Francisco Bay; pop. 116,716.

Berke·ley (bûrk′lē, *Brit.* bärk′-), **George,** 1685–1753, Irish Anglican prelate and philosopher.   — **Sir William,** 1606?–1677, British governor of Virginia.

berke·li·um (bûrk′lē·əm)   *n.* The unstable radioactive element of atomic number 97 (symbol Bk), obtained by bombarding americium with alpha particles.   [after *Berkeley,* California, location of the University of California]

Berks or **Berks.**   Berkshire, England.

Berk·shire (bûrk′shir, -shər; *Brit.* bärk′-)   A county of southern England; 725 sq. mi.; pop. 653,400 (1976); county seat, Reading.

Berk·shire (bûrk′shir, -shər)   *n.* One of a breed of black and white swine originating in Berkshire, England.

Berk·shire Hills (bûrk′shir, -shər)   A wooded region of western Massachusetts; highest peak, Mount Greylock, 3,505 ft. Also **Berk′shires.**

Ber·le (bûr′lē), **Adolf Augustus,** 1895–1971, U.S. lawyer and diplomat.

Ber·lich·ing·en (ber′likh·ing′ən), **Götz** (or **Gottfried**) **von** (gœts fôn), 1480–1562, German knight; the hero of Goethe's drama of the same name: called **Götz of the Iron Hand.**

ber·lin (bər·lin′, bûr′lin)   *n.* **1.** A four-wheeled covered carriage with the body suspended on springs.   **2.** See BERLINE.   **3.** Zephyr or worsted for knitting: also **Berlin wool.**   [after *Berlin,* Germany]

Ber·lin (bər·lin′, *Ger.* ber·lēn′) A city in east central Germany, the capital of Germany prior to 1945, when it was divided into the British, French, Soviet, and U.S. sectors of occupation. In 1949 the Soviet sector, **East Berlin,** was designated capital of East Germany; pop. 1,084,000 (est. 1970); the remaining sectors formed **West Berlin,** associated with West Germany; pop. 2,134,256 (est. 1970).

Ber·lin (bər·lin′), **Irving,** born 1888, U.S. song writer born in Russia: original name **Israel Ba·line** (bə·lēn′).

Berlin blue Prussian blue (which see).

ber·line (bər·lin′, *Fr.* ber·lēn′) *n.* A limousine automobile with the driver's seat enclosed: also spelled *berlin.*

Ber·li·oz (ber′lē·ōz, *Fr.* ber·lyôz′), **Hector,** 1803–69, French composer.

berm (bûrm) *n.* **1.** A narrow ledge, shelf, or shoulder, as on a slope or at the side of a road. **2.** In fortifications, a ledge between the base of a parapet and the moat: also **berme.** [< F *berme*]

Ber·me·jo (ber·me′hō) A river in northern Argentina, flowing about 650 miles SE to the Paraguay river.

Ber·mu·da (bər·myōō′də) An island group in the western Atlantic, a British Colony; 21 sq. mi.; pop. 52,000 (est. 1969); capital, Hamilton. Also **Ber·mu′das** (-dəz). — **Ber·mu·di·an** (bər·myōō′dē·ən) *adj. & n.*

Ber·mu·dan rig (bər·myōō′dən) *Brit.* Marconi rig (which see). Also **Bermudian rig.**

Bermuda shorts Shorts that extend to just above the knees.

Bern (bûrn, bern) The capital of Switzerland, in the west central part on the Aar river; pop. 166,800 (est. 1969). Also **Berne.** — **Ber·nese** (bûr·nēz′, -nēs′) *n. & adj.*

Ber·na·dotte (bûr′nə·dot, *Fr.* ber·nä·dôt′) The royal house of Sweden, founded by **Jean Baptiste Jules Bernadotte,** 1763–1844, French marshal, who became king of Sweden and Norway as Charles XIV John, in 1818.

Ber·nard (ber·när′), **Claude,** 1813–78, French physiologist.

Ber·nard of Clair·vaux (bûr′nərd, bər·närd′, *Fr.* ber·når′; klâr·vō′), **Saint,** 1090–1153, French Cistercian monastic reformer.

Bernard of Cluny, Saint Twelfth-century French Benedictine monk and poet.

Ber·nar·din de Saint-Pierre (ber·när·daṅ′ də saṅ·pyâr′), **Jacques Henri,** 1737–1814, French author.

Ber·nar·dine (bûr′nər·din, -dēn) *adj.* Of or pertaining to St. Bernard of Clairvaux, or to the Cistercian order. — *n.* A member of a Cistercian order.

Ber·nese Alps (bûr·nēz′, -nēs′) The northern division of the Swiss Alps; highest peak, Finsteraarhorn, 14,026 ft.: also **Bernese Oberland.**

Bern·hardt (bûrn′härt, *Fr.* ber·når′), **Sarah,** 1844–1923, French actress: original name **Rosine Bernard** (ber·når′).

ber·ni·cle (bûr′ni·kəl, bär′-) *n.* The barnacle goose. See under BARNACLE[1].

Ber·ni·na (ber·nē′nä), **Piz** (pēts) Highest peak (13,304 ft.) of the **Bernina Alps,** the southern part of the Rhaetian Alps, Switzerland; traversed by **Bernina Pass;** elevation, 7,645 ft.

Ber·ni·ni (ber·nē′nē), **Giovanni Lorenzo,** 1598–1680, Italian sculptor and architect.

Ber·noul·li (bûr·nōō′lē, *Fr.* ber·nōō·yē′), **Daniel,** 1700–82, Swiss mathematician. — **Jacob** (or **Jacques**), 1654–1705, Swiss mathematician; uncle of the preceding. Also **Ber·nouli′li′.**

Bernoulli's principle *Physics* The statement that in any horizontally moving fluid the pressure increases as the velocity of flow decreases. [after Daniel *Bernoulli*]

Bern·stein (bûrn′stīn), **Leonard,** born 1918, U.S. conductor and composer.

ber·ret·ta (bə·ret′ə) *n.* A biretta.

ber·ry (ber′ē) *n. pl.* **·ries 1.** Any small, succulent fruit: often used in combination: *blackberry, strawberry, gooseberry.* **2.** *Bot.* A simple fruit with the seeds in a juicy pulp, as the tomato, grape, and currant. ◆ Collateral adjective: *baccate.* **3.** The dry kernel of various grains, or the fruit of certain plants, as a coffee bean, etc. **4.** Something likened to a berry, as an egg of a crustacean. **5.** *U.S. Slang* A dollar. — *v.i.* **·ried, ·ry·ing 1.** To form or bear berries. **2.** To gather berries. [OE *berie*]

Ber·ry (be·rē′) A region and former province of central France. Also **Ber·ri′.**

Ber·sa·glie·re (ber′sä·lye′rā) *n. pl.* **·ri** (-rē) *Italian* A member of a corps of sharpshooters in the Italian army.

ber·seem (bər·sēm′) *n.* A clover (*Trifolium alexandrinum*) grown as forage in Egypt and the United States. [< Arabic *birshīm* clover]

ber·serk (bûr′sûrk, bər·sûrk′) *adj.* Violently or frenetically destructive. — **to go** (or **run**) **berserk** To have a fit of destructive rage; run wild. — *n.* A berserker. [< BERSERKER]

ber·serk·er (bûr′sûrk′ər) *n.* **1.** In Norse legend, a warrior who fought with frenzied fury, and whom fire and iron could not harm: also called *baresark.* **2.** A violent and furious person. [< ON *berserkr*]

berth (bûrth) *n.* **1.** A bunk or bed in a vessel, sleeping car, etc. **2.** *Naut.* **a** Any place in which a vessel may lie at anchor or at a dock. **b** Space in which a vessel may maneuver;

sea room. **3.** Situation or employment on a vessel. **4.** Office or employment in general. — **to give a wide berth to** To avoid; keep out of the way of. — *v.t.* **1.** *Naut.* To bring to a berth. **2.** To provide with a berth. — *v.i.* **3.** *Naut.* To come to a berth. [Origin uncertain. ? Akin to BEAR[1].]

ber·tha (bûr′thə) *n.* A deep collar worn by women, falling over the shoulders from a low neckline. [< F *berthe*, after *Berthe*, mother of Charlemagne]

Ber·the·lot (ber·tə·lō′), **Pierre Eugène Marcelin,** 1827–1907, French chemist and statesman.

Ber·til·lon system (bûr′tə·lon, *Fr.* ber·tē·yôn′) A system of coded physical measurements, later extended to include characteristics such as color of the eyes, scars, etc., used as a means of identification, especially of criminals. [after Alphonse *Bertillon*, 1853–1914, French anthropologist]

Ber·wick (ber′ik) A county in SE Scotland; 485 sq. mi.; pop. 20,499 (1969); county seat, Duns. Also **Ber′wick·shire** (-shir, -shər).

Ber·wyn (bûr′win) A city in NE Illinois; pop. 52,502.

ber·yl (ber′əl) *n.* A vitreous, green, light blue, yellow, pink, or white silicate of aluminum and beryllium crystallizing in the hexagonal system. The aquamarine and emerald are varieties used as gems. [< OF < L *beryllus* < Gk. *bēryllos* beryl]

be·ryl·li·um (bə·ril′ē·əm) *n.* A hard, grayish black, noncorrosive metallic element (symbol Be) of the magnesium group, used in copper and aluminum alloys and for windows of X-ray tubes: formerly called *glucinum.* See ELEMENT. [< NL < L *beryllus* beryl]

Ber·ze·li·us (bər·zē′lē·əs, *Sw.* ber·sä′lē·ŏŏs), **Baron Jöns Jacob,** 1779–1848, Swedish chemist.

Bes (bes) In Egyptian mythology, a god of art, the dance, and music, having power to avert witchcraft.

Be·san·çon (bə·zän·sôn′) A city in eastern France, on the Doubs; pop. 107,939 (1968).

Bes·ant (bez′ənt), **Annie,** 1847–1933, *née* Wood, English theosophist.

Be·sant (bi·zant′), **Sir Walter,** 1836–1901, English novelist and historian.

be·seech (bi·sēch′) *v.t.* **·sought** or **·seeched, ·seech·ing 1.** To entreat earnestly; implore. **2.** To beg for earnestly; crave. — **Syn.** See ENTREAT. [ME *bisechen* < *bi-* greatly + *sechen* < OE *sēcan* to seek] — **be·seech′er** *n.*

be·seem (bi·sēm′) *v.i.* To be fitting or appropriate: used impersonally: It ill *beseems* you to speak thus. — **be·seem′ing** *adj.*

be·set (bi·set′) *v.t.* **·set, ·set·ting 1.** To attack on all sides; harass. **2.** To hem in; encircle. **3.** To set or stud, as with gems. [OE *besettan*] — **be·set′ment** *n.* — **Syn. 1.** besiege. Compare ATTACK. **2.** surround.

be·set·ting (bi·set′ing) *adj.* Constantly attacking or troubling.

be·shrew (bi·shrōō′) *v.t. Archaic* To wish ill to; curse.

be·side (bi·sīd′) *prep.* **1.** At the side of; in proximity to. **2.** In comparison with: My merit is little *beside* yours. **3.** Away or apart from: This discussion is *beside* the point. **4.** Other than; over and above: I have no treasure *beside* this. — **beside oneself** Out of one's senses, as from anger, fear, etc. — *adv.* In addition; besides. [OE *be sīdan* by the side (of)]

be·sides (bi·sīdz′) *adv.* **1.** In addition; as well. **2.** Moreover; furthermore. **3.** Apart from that mentioned; otherwise; else. — *prep.* **1.** In addition to; other than. **2.** Beyond; apart from: I care for nothing *besides* this.

be·siege (bi·sēj′) *v.t.* **·sieged, ·sieg·ing 1.** To beset or surround; lay siege to, as a castle. **2.** To crowd around. **3.** To harass or overwhelm, as with invitations. — **be·siege′ment** *n.* — **be·sieg′er** *n.*

B. ès L. Bachelor of Letters (Fr. *Bachelier ès Lettres*).

be·smear (bi·smir′) *v.t.* To smear over; sully. [OE *bismierwan*]

be·smirch (bi·smûrch′) *v.t.* **1.** To soil; stain. **2.** To sully; dim the luster of. — **be·smirch′er** *n.* — **be·smirch′ment** *n.*

be·som (bē′zəm) *n.* **1.** A bundle of twigs used as a broom. **2.** Anything that cleans. **3.** Broom (def. 2). [OE *besma* broom]

be·sot (bi·sot′) *v.t.* **·sot·ted, ·sot·ting 1.** To stupefy, as with drink. **2.** To make foolish or stupid. **3.** To infatuate.

be·sought (bi·sôt′) Past tense and past participle of BESEECH.

be·span·gle (bi·spang′gəl) *v.t.* **·gled, ·gling** To decorate with or as with spangles.

be·spat·ter (bi·spat′ər) *v.t.* **1.** To cover or soil by spattering, as with mud. **2.** To sully; slander.

be·speak (bi·spēk′) *v.t.* **·spoke** (*Archaic* **·spake**), **·spo·ken** or **·spoke, ·speak·ing 1.** To ask or arrange for in advance; reserve. **2.** To give evidence of; indicate: His face *bespeaks* good news. **3.** To foretell; foreshadow: The present *bespeaks* a sad future. **4.** *Archaic* To speak to. [OE *bisprecan*]

be·spec·ta·cled (bi·spek′tə·kəld) *adj.* Wearing spectacles.

be·spoke (bi·spōk′) Past tense and alternative past participle of BESPEAK. — *adj. Brit.* Made to order, as a suit; custom-made: also **be·spo′ken.**

be·spread (bi·spred′) *v.t.* **·spread, ·spread·ing** To cover or spread over thickly.

be·sprent (bi·sprent′) *adj. Poetic* Besprinkled; strewed. [OE, pp. of *besprengan* to sprinkle]

be·sprin·kle (bi·spring′kəl) *v.t.* **·kled, ·kling** To scatter or spread over by sprinkling.

Bes·sa·ra·bi·a (bes′ə·rā′bē·ə) A region of the SW Soviet Union; 17,147 sq. mi.; formerly a Rumanian province. — **Bes·sa·ra′bi·an** *adj. & n.*

Bes·se·mer (bes′ə·mər) A city in central Alabama; pop. 33,428.

Bes·se·mer (bes′ə·mər), **Sir Henry,** 1813–98, English engineer.

Bessemer converter *Metall.* A large, pear-shaped vessel for containing the molten iron to be converted into steel by the Bessemer process.

Bessemer process *Metall.* **1.** A process for eliminating impurities from pig iron by forcing a blast of air through the molten metal before its conversion into steel or ingot iron. **2.** A similar process for eliminating sulfur from copper matte.

BESSEMER CONVERTER

a, b Exhaust gases. *c* Silica refractory lining. *d* Flames. *e* Steel shell. *f* Compressed air. *g* Molten iron.

best (best) Superlative of GOOD, WELL². — *adj.* **1.** Excelling all others; of the highest quality. **2.** Most advantageous, desirable, or serviceable. **3.** Most; largest: the *best* part of an hour. — *adv.* **1.** In the most excellent way; most advantageously. **2.** To the utmost degree; most thoroughly. — *n.* **1.** The best thing, part, etc. **2.** Best condition or quality; utmost: Be at your *best*; Do your *best*. **3.** One's best clothes. — **at best** Under the most favorable circumstances. — **to get** (or **have**) **the best of** To defeat or outwit. — **to make the best of** To adapt oneself to the disadvantages of. — *v.t.* To defeat; surpass. [OE *betst*]

be·stead (bi·sted′) *v.t.* To be of service to; help; avail.

bes·tial (bes′chəl, best′yəl) *adj.* **1.** Of or pertaining to beasts; animal. **2.** Having the ignoble qualities or instincts of an animal; brutish; depraved. **3.** Like a beast in want of intelligence; irrational; rude; savage. [< OF < L *bestialis* < *bestia* beast]

bes·ti·al·i·ty (bes′chē·al′ə·tē, -tē·al′-) *n. pl.* **·ties 1.** Bestial quality or nature. **2.** Character or conduct befitting a beast. **3.** Human sexual relations with an animal; sodomy.

bes·tial·ize (bes′chəl·īz, best′yəl-) *v.t.* **·ized, ·iz·ing** To brutalize.

bes·ti·ar·y (bes′tē·er′ē) *n. pl.* **·ar·ies** A medieval treatise on animals giving a symbolic moral and religious interpretation of their traits and habits. [< Med.L *bestiarium,* orig. neut. of L *bestiarius* of beasts]

be·stir (bi·stûr′) *v.t.* **·stirred, ·stir·ring** To rouse to activity. [OE *bestyrian*]

best man The chief attendant of a bridegroom at a wedding.

be·stow (bi·stō′) *v.t.* **1.** To present as a gift; with *on* or *upon.* **2.** To apply; expend, as time. **3.** *Archaic* To place; deposit; also, to house. **4.** To give in marriage. — **Syn.** See GIVE. [ME *bistowen* < *bi-* to, upon + *stowen* to place] — **be·stow′a·ble** *adj.* — **be·stow′al, be·stow′ment** *n.*

be·strad·dle (bi·strad′l) *v.t.* **·dled, ·dling** To bestride.

be·strew (bi·strōō′) *v.t.* **·strewed, ·strewed** or **·strewn, ·strew·ing 1.** To cover or strew (a surface). **2.** To scatter about. **3.** To lie scattered over. Also **be·strow** (bi·strō′). [OE *bestrēowian*]

be·stride (bi·strīd′) *v.t.* **·strode, ·strid·den, ·strid·ing 1.** To mount; sit or stand astride of; straddle. **2.** To stride over or across. [OE *bestrīdan*]

best seller A book, phonograph record, etc., that sells or has sold in large numbers.

bet (bet) *n.* **1.** An agreement to risk something of one's own in return for the chance of winning something belonging to another or others, the outcome usually depending on the result of an uncertain event. **2.** That which is risked in a bet, as a sum of money; a stake. **3.** The subject or event about which a bet is made; also, the conditions agreed upon in a bet. Also called *wager.* **4.** That on which something is staked, as a horse in a race. **5.** *Informal* Course of action: usually in the phrase **best bet.** — *v.* bet or (less commonly) **bet·ted, bet·ting** *v.t.* **1.** To stake or pledge (money, etc.) in a bet. **2.** To declare as in a bet: I *bet* he doesn't come. — *v.i.* **3.** To place a bet. Also *wager.* — **you bet** *U.S. Slang* Certainly. [Origin uncertain]

bet. Between.

be·ta (bā′tə, bē′-) *n.* **1.** The second letter of the Greek alphabet (B, β), corresponding to English *b.* See ALPHABET. **2.** The second object in any order of arrangement or classification, as, in astronomy the second brightest star in a constellation, in chemistry the second of a group of isomeric compounds, in botany the second subspecies, etc. [< Gk.]

be·ta·ine (bē′tə·ēn, -in) *n. Chem.* A crystalline alkaloid compound, $C_5H_{11}O_2N \cdot H_2O$, related to glycine, found in the beet and various other plants. [< L *beta* beet + -INE²]

be·take (bi·tāk′) *v.t.* **·took, ·tak·en, ·tak·ing 1.** To resort to; undertake: used reflexively: She *betook* herself to prayer. **2.** To go; take (oneself): He *betook* himself to an inn. [ME *bitaken*]

be·ta·naph·thol (bā′tə·naf′thōl, -thol, -nap′-) *n. Chem.* An isomer of naphthol, used in medicine and in the manufacture of dyes.

beta particle An electron.

beta rays *Physics* A stream of electrons projected by some radioactive substances. They are identical with cathode rays, and are easily deflected by an electric or magnetic field.

beta test *Psychol.* A series of tests used by the U.S. Army in World War I to determine the mental capacity of illiterate recruits.

be·ta·tron (bā′tə·tron) *n. Physics* An accelerator that uses a rapidly-changing magnetic field to increase the velocity of electrons. [< BETA (RAY) + (ELEC)TRON]

beta wave *Physiol.* A secondary wave of electrical charge in the brain. See ALPHA RHYTHM.

be·tel (bēt′l) *n.* A climbing plant (*Piper betle*) of Asia, the leaves of which are chewed by the natives of Malaya and other Asian countries. [< Pg. *betel* < Malayalam *vettila*]

Be·tel·geuse (bēt′l·jōōz, bet′l·joez) *n.* A giant red star, one of the 20 brightest, variable magnitude; Alpha in the constellation Orion. Also **Be′tel·geux.** See STAR. [< F *Bételgeuse* < Arabic *bat al-jauza,* ? shoulder of the giant]

be·tel·nut (bēt′l·nut′) *n.* The astringent seed of an East Indian palm, the **betel palm** (*Areca catechu*), used for chewing with betel leaves and lime.

bête noire (bāt′ nwär′, *Fr.* bet nwàr′) Anything that is an object of hate or dread; a bugaboo. [< F, black beast]

beth (beth) *n.* The second letter of the Hebrew alphabet. See ALPHABET.

Beth·a·ny (beth′ə·nē) In the New Testament, a village near Jerusalem: the home of Lazarus, Martha, and Mary.

beth·el (beth′əl) *n.* **1.** A hallowed place. *Gen.* xxviii 19. **2.** A seamen's church or chapel. **3.** *Brit.* A dissenters' chapel. [< Hebrew *bēth-ēl* house of God]

Beth·el (beth′əl) An ancient town of Palestine, near Jerusalem.

Be·thes·da (bə·thez′də) *n.* **1.** In the Bible, a pool in Jerusalem with healing properties. *John* v 2. **2.** A village and district in western Maryland; pop. 71,621. **3.** A chapel.

be·think (bi·thingk′) *v.* **·thought, ·think·ing** *v.t.* **1.** To remember; bear in mind; consider: generally used reflexively. — *v.i.* **2.** *Archaic* To meditate. [OE *bethencan*]

Beth·le·hem (beth′lē·əm, -lə·hem) **1.** An ancient town in Jordan, SW of Jerusalem; pop. 23,240 (1967); birthplace of Jesus. *Matt.* ii 1. **2.** A manufacturing city on the Lehigh River in eastern Pennsylvania; pop. 72,686. [< Hebrew *bēth lehem* place of food] — **Beth′le·hem·ite′** *n.*

Beth-mann-Holl·weg (bāt′män·hôl′vākh), **Theobald von,** 1856–1921, German statesman; chancellor 1909–17.

Beth·nal Green (beth′nəl) A metropolitan borough of London, north of the Thames; pop. 47,018 (1961).

be·thought (bi·thôt′) Past tense and past participle of BETHINK.

Beth·sa·i·da (beth·sā′ə·də) A ruined town on the northern shore of the Sea of Galilee, Palestine. *John* i 44. Also **Beth·saida** of Galilee.

be·tide (be·tīd′) *v.t. & v.i.* **·tid·ed, ·tid·ing** To happen (to) or befall. — **Syn.** See HAPPEN. [ME *bitiden*]

be·times (bi·tīmz′) *adv.* In good time; early; also, soon. Also *Obs.* **be·time′.** [ME *betymes* in time, seasonably]

bê·tise (be·tēz′) *n.* **1.** A stupid thing or act; an absurdity. **2.** Stupidity; nonsense. [< F < *bête* beast]

be·to·ken (bi·tō′kən) *v.t.* **1.** To be a sign of; presage. **2.** To give evidence of; indicate. — **Syn.** See AUGUR. [ME *bitacnien*] — **be·to′ken·er** *n.*

bé·ton (bā·tôn′) *n. French* A concrete of gravel, sand, and cement, and sometimes lime.

bet·o·ny (bet′ə·nē) *n. pl.* **·nies 1.** A European herb (genus *Stachys,* formerly *Betonica*) of the mint family. **2.** Any of various similar plants. [< F *bétoine* < L *betonica,* var. of *vettonica* < *Vettones,* a people of Portugal]

be·took (bi·tŏŏk′) Past tense of BETAKE.

be·tray (bi·trā′) *v.t.* **1.** To aid an enemy of; be a traitor to. **2.** To prove faithless to; disappoint: to *betray* a trust. **3.** To disclose, as secret information. **4.** To reveal unwittingly: to *betray* ignorance. **5.** To deceive; seduce and desert. **6.** To indicate; show: The smoke *betrays* a fire. [ME *bitraien* < *bi-* over, to + OF *trair* < L *tradere* to deliver, give up] — **be·tray′al, be·tray′ment** *n.* — **be·tray′er** *n.* — **Syn. 3.** divulge, reveal, expose, tell.

be·troth (bi·trōth′, -trôth′) *v.t.* **1.** To engage to marry; affiance. **2.** To contract to give in marriage. [ME *bitreuthien* < *bi-* to + *treuthe* truth]

be·troth·al (bi·trō′thəl, -trôth′əl) *n.* The act of betrothing; engagement or contract to marry. Also **be·troth′ment.**

be·trothed (bi·trōthd′, -trôtht′) *adj.* Engaged to be married; affianced. — *n.* A person engaged to be married.

bet·ter[1] (bet'ər) Comparative of GOOD, WELL[2]. — *adj.* **1.** Superior in excellence; of higher quality. **2.** More advantageous, desirable, or serviceable. **3.** Larger; greater: the *better* part of the cake. **4.** Improved in health; convalescent. — *adv.* **1.** In a more excellent manner; more advantageously. **2.** To a larger degree; more thoroughly. **3.** More: *better* than a week. — **better off** In a better condition or improved circumstances. — **had better** See note under HAVE. — *v.t.* **1.** To make better; improve. **2.** To surpass; excel. — *v.i.* **3.** To become better. — *n.* **1.** That which is better. **2.** *Usually pl.* One's superiors, as in ability, rank, etc. **3.** Advantage: to get the *better* of one's enemies. [OE *betera*]

bet·ter[2] (bet'ər) *n.* One who lays bets. Also **bet'tor.**

bet·ter·ment (bet'ər-mənt) *n.* **1.** Improvement. **2.** *Law* An improvement adding to the value of real property.

Bet·ter·ton (bet'ər-tən), **Thomas,** 1635?–1710, English actor and producer.

bet·u·la·ceous (bech'ŏŏ-lā'shəs) *adj.* Belonging to a family (*Betulaceae*) of trees and shrubs including the birch, the alder, and the hazel. [< NL *Betulaceae* < L *betula* birch]

betw. Between.

be·tween (bi-twēn') *prep.* **1.** In the space that separates (two places or objects). **2.** Intermediate in relation to, as times, qualities, etc.: *between* sweet and sour. **3.** From one to another of; connecting: the plane *between* New York and Paris. **4.** Involving reciprocal action among: an agreement *between* nations. **5.** By the joint action of: *Between* them, they killed three deer. **6.** In the joint possession of: not a cent *between* them. **7.** The decisive virtue or value of one alternative over another: to judge *between* right and wrong. *Abbr. bet., betw.* — **Syn.** See AMID. — **between you and me** Confidentially. — *adv.* In intervening time, space, position, or relation; at or during intervals: few and far *between*. — **in between** In an intermediate position or state; undecided. [Fusion of OE *bitwēonum* and *bitwēon* < *bi-* by + *-tweonum* and *-tweon*, both < *twā* two]

◆ **among, between** Although *between* is usually limited to two things and *among* to more than two, *between* is often extended to more than two objects or persons when they are considered individually: All the candidates were so similar that it was difficult to choose *between* them. *Among* is related to *mingle* and suggests a group and a less precise relationship: He lived *among* the Indians. See AMID.

be·twixt (bi-twikst') *adv. & prep.* Archaic Between. — **betwixt and between** In an intermediate or indecisive state. [OE *betweons* twofold < *be-* by + *-tweons* < *twā* two]

Beu·lah (byōō'lə) The land of Israel. *Isa.* lxii 4. — **Land of Beulah** In Bunyan's *Pilgrim's Progress*, the land of rest where pilgrims abide till death. [<Hebrew *be'ūlāh* married]

Beu·then (boi'tən) The German name for Bytom.

BeV or **BEV** or **bev** Billion electron volts.

bev·a·tron (bev'ə-tron) *n.* *Physics* A large accelerator using several principles of operation and yielding particle velocities equivalent to 6 billion electron volts. [< B(ILLION) E(LECTRON) V(OLTS) + (ELEC)TRON]

bev·el (bev'əl) *n.* **1.** Any inclination of two surfaces other than 90°, as at the edge of a timber, etc. **2.** An adjustable instrument for measuring angles: also **bevel square.** — *adj.* Oblique; slanting. — *v.* **bev·eled** or **·elled, bev·el·ing** or **·el·ling** *v.t.* **1.** To cut or bring to a bevel. — *v.i.* **2.** To slant. [? < OF. Cf. F *beveau* bevel (n. def. 2).]

bevel gear *Mech.* A gear having beveled teeth, as for transmitting rotary motion at an angle. For illustration see GEAR.

bev·er·age (bev'rij, bev'ər-ij) *n.* That which is drunk; any drink. [< OF *bevrage* < *beivre* drinking < L *bibere* to drink]

beverage room *Canadian* A beer parlor.

Bev·er·idge (bev'ər-ij), **Albert Jeremiah,** 1862–1927, U.S. politician and historian. — **Sir William (Henry),** 1879–1963, English economist.

Bev·er·ly (bev'ər-lē) A city in NE Massachusetts, on the Atlantic Ocean; pop. 38,348.

Beverly Hills A residential city in California, on the western boundary of Los Angeles; pop. 33,416.

Bev·in (bev'in), **Ernest,** 1884–1951, British statesman; foreign secretary 1945–51.

bev·y (bev'ē) *n. pl.* **bev·ies** **1.** A group, especially of girls or women. **2.** A flock, especially of quail, grouse, or larks. — **Syn.** See FLOCK. [ME *bevey*; origin uncertain]

be·wail (bi-wāl') *v.t. & v.i.* To lament. — **Syn.** See MOURN.

be·ware (bi-wâr') *v.t. & v.i.* **wared, war·ing** To look out (for); be cautious or wary (of). [OE *wær* cautious; orig. imperative *be ware* be on guard, be cautious]

be·wil·der (bi-wil'dər) *v.t.* **1.** To confuse utterly; perplex. **2.** *Archaic* To cause to lose the way or course. — **Syn. 1.** mystify, dumbfound, confound, nonplus, puzzle.

be·wil·dered (bi-wil'dərd) *adj.* In a state of confusion or perplexity; puzzled. — **be·wil'dered·ly** *adv.*

be·wil·der·ment (bi-wil'dər-mənt) *n.* **1.** A state of being bewildered. **2.** A confusion; tangle.

be·witch (bi-wich') *v.t.* **1.** To gain power over by charms or incantations. **2.** To attract irresistibly; charm; fascinate. [ME *biwicchen* < *bi-* completely + *wicchen* to enchant < OE *wiccian* < *wicce* witch] — **be·witch'er** *n.* — **be·witch'ment, be·witch'er·y** *n.*

be·witch·ing (bi-wich'ing) *adj.* Charming; captivating. — **be·witch'ing·ly** *adv.*

be·wray (bi-rā') *v.t. Obs.* To disclose; betray. [ME *bewreien* < *be-* + *wreien,* OE *wrēgan* to accuse]

bey (bā) *n.* **1.** The governor of a minor Turkish province or district. **2.** A native ruler of Tunis. **3.** A Turkish title of respect. Also called *beg.* [< Turkish *beg* lord]

Beyle (bāl), **Marie Henri** See STENDHAL.

be·yond (bi-yond') *prep.* **1.** On or to the far side of; farther on than. **2.** Later than; past: staying *beyond* the hour. **3.** Outside the reach or scope of: *beyond* help. **4.** Surpassing; superior to: lovely *beyond* description. **5.** More than; over and above. — *adv.* Farther on or away; at a distance. — **the (great) beyond** Whatever comes after death. [OE *begeondan* < *be-* near + *geondan* yonder]

Bey·routh (bā'rōōt, bā-rōōt') See BEIRUT.

bez·ant (bez'ənt, bə-zant') *n.* **1.** The Byzantine solidus, a coin. **2.** *Archit.* A flat ornamental disk. Also spelled *byzant.* [< OF *besan* < L *Byzantius* Byzantine]

bez·el (bez'əl) *n.* **1.** A bevel on the edge of a cutting tool. **2.** That part of a cut gem above the girdle, including the table and surrounding facets. **3.** A groove and flange made to receive a beveled edge. [? < OF. Cf. F *biseau* a bias.]

Bé·ziers (bā-zyā') A city in SW France; pop. 74,517 (1968).

be·zique (bə-zēk') *n.* A game of cards resembling pinochle. [Alter. of F *bésigue*; ult. origin unknown]

be·zoar (bē'zôr, -zōr) *n.* **1.** A concretion found in the stomach and intestines of ruminants and some other animals, formerly supposed to have medicinal value. **2.** *Obs.* An antidote or panacea. [< NL ult. < Persian *pādzahr* < *pād* expelling + *zahr* poison]

bez·tine (bez, bāz) The second branch of a deer's antler, the one above the brow antler. Also **bez antler.** For illustration see ANTLER. [< OF *bes-* < L *bis* twice]

bf or **b.f.** *Printing* Boldface.

B/F Brought forward.

B.F. **1.** Bachelor of Finance. **2.** Bachelor of Forestry.

B.F.A. Bachelor of Fine Arts.

bg. (*pl.* **bgs.**) Bag.

B.G. **1.** Birmingham gauge. **2.** Brigadier General.

Bha·ga·vad-Gi·ta (bug'ə-vəd-gē'tä) A sacred Hindu text consisting of philosophical dialogue in the *Mahabharata,* expounding the duties of caste and the yoga doctrines of devotion to the Supreme Spirit. [< Skt., Song of the Blessed One (i.e. Krishna)]

bhang (bang) *n.* **1.** Hemp (def. 1). **2.** Hashish. Also spelled *bang.* [< Hind. < Skt. *bhangā* hemp]

Bha·rat (bu'rut) The Hindi name for INDIA.

Bhau·nag·ar (bou-nug'ər) **1.** A former princely state of western India, on the Kathiawar peninsula. **2.** A port city on the Gulf of Cambay; former capital of the state; pop. 217,533 (est. 1971). Also **Bhav·nag'ar** (bou-).

bhees·ty (bēs'tē) *n.* In India, a water carrier. Also **bhees'·tie, bhis'tie.** [< Hind. *bhīstī* < Persian *bihishtī,* lit., one from heaven]

Bho·pal (bō-päl') A former state of central India; 6,921 sq. mi.; since 1956 part of Madhya Pradesh; capital, **Bhopal,** in the east central part, pop. 310,732 (est. 1971).

Bhu·tan (bōō-tän') A semi-independent State (whose foreign affairs are guided by India) between NE India and Tibet; about 18,000 sq. mi.; pop. 770,000 (est. 1969); capital, Thimbu. Officially **Kingdom of Bhutan.** See map of TIBET.

Bhu·tan·ese (bōō'tən-ēz', -ēs') *n. pl.* **·ese** **1.** A native of Bhutan. **2.** The Sino-Tibetan language of Bhutan. — *adj.* Of or pertaining to Bhutan, its people, or their language.

bi- *prefix* **1.** Twice; doubly; two; especially, occurring twice or having two: *bi*angular. **2.** *Chem.* **a** Indicating the doubling of a radical, etc., in an organic compound. **b** In former usage, having double the proportion of the substance named: *bi*carbonate. Also: *bin-* before a vowel, as in *bin*aural; *bis-* before *c, s,* as in *bis*sextile. [< L *bi-* < *bis* twice]

Bi *Chem.* Bismuth.

B.I. British India.

bi·a·cu·mi·nate (bī'ə-kyōō'mə-nāt) *adj. Bot.* Two-pointed.

bi·a·ly (bē-äl'ē) *n. pl.* **·lys** A flat roll made with gluten flour and topped with chopped onions. [< Yiddish *Bialy-(stoker) (kuchen)* roll from Bialystok]

Bia·lys·tok (bya'li-stok, *Polish* byä'wi-stôk) A city in NE Poland; pop. 166,600 (est. 1959). Russian *Belostok, Byelostok.*

bi·an·gu·lar (bī-ang'gyə-lər) *adj.* Having two angles. Also **bi·an'gu·late** (-lit, -lāt).

bi·an·nu·al (bī-an'yōō-əl) *adj.* Occurring twice a year; semiannual. ◆ *Biannual* should not be used in place of *biennial* to mean once every two years. — **bi·an'nu·al·ly** *adv.*

bi·an·nu·late (bī-an'yōō-lit, -lāt) *adj. Zool.* Having two rings or bands, as of color.

Bi·ar·ritz (bē'ə-rits, *Fr.* byà-rēts') A resort town in SW France, on the Bay of Biscay; pop. about 23,000.

bi·as (bī'əs) *n. pl.* **bi·as·es** **1.** A line running obliquely across a fabric: to cut on the *bias.* **2.** A mental tendency, preference, or prejudice. **3.** *Engin.* A steady force, voltage, magnetic field, etc., applied to a device to establish a reference level or determine the range of operation. **4.** In bowling, lopsidedness in a ball, causing it to swerve; also, the swerving course of such a ball. — **Syn.** See PREJUDICE. — *adj.* Cut, running, set, or folded diagonally; slanting. — *adv.* Slantingly; diagonally. — *v.t.* **bi·ased** or **·assed, bi·as·ing** or **·as·sing 1.** To influence or affect unduly or unfairly. **2.** *Engin.* To apply a bias to. [< MF *biais* oblique]

bi·au·ric·u·lar (bī/ô·rik/yə·lər) *adj.* Of, pertaining to, or having two auricles. Also **bi/au·ric/u·late** (-lāt, -lit).

bi·ax·i·al (bī·ak/sē·əl) *adj.* Having two axes, as a crystal. Also **bi·ax·al** (bī·ak/səl). — **bi·ax/i·al·ly** *adv.*

bib (bib) *n.* **1.** A cloth worn under a child's chin at meals to protect the clothing. **2.** The upper front part of an apron or of overalls. — *v.t. & v.i.* **bibbed, bib·bing** *Obs.* To drink; tipple. [? < L *bibere* to drink]

Bib. Bible; Biblical.

bib and tucker *Informal* Clothes.

bi·ba·sic (bī·bā/sik) *adj. Chem.* Dibasic (which see).

bibb (bib) *n.* **1.** *Naut.* One of a pair of wooden brackets on a mast to support the trestletrees. **2.** A bibcock. [< BIB; because of the resemblance of the bracket to a child's bib]

bib·ber (bib/ər) *n.* A habitual drinker; tippler.

bib·cock (bib/kok/) *n.* A faucet having the nozzle bent downward.

bibe·lot (bib/lō, *Fr.* bēb·lō/) *n.* A small, decorative and often rare object or trinket. [< F]

bi·bi·va·lent (bī/bī·vā/lənt, bī·biv/ə-) *adj. Chem.* Designating an electrolyte that breaks down into two bivalent ions.

bibl. Bibliographical.

Bibl. Biblical.

bi·ble (bī/bəl) *n.* Any authoritative book, record, etc.

Bi·ble (bī/bəl) *n.* **1.** In Christianity, the collection of ancient writings held by most Christians to be divinely inspired. See OLD TESTAMENT, NEW TESTAMENT, APOCRYPHA. **2.** In Judaism, the Old Testament. **3.** The sacred book or writings of any religion. [< OF < L *biblia* < Gk., pl. of *biblion* book]

Bible paper A thin, tough, and opaque paper, used for Bibles, etc.: also called *India paper.*

Bib·li·cal (bib/li·kəl) *adj.* **1.** Of or in the Bible. **2.** In harmony with the Bible. Also **bib/li·cal.** — **Bib/li·cal·ly** *adv.*

Bib·li·cist (bib/lə·sist) *n.* **1.** One versed in the Bible. **2.** One who adheres to the letter of the Bible. Also *Biblist.*

biblio- *combining form* Pertaining to books, or to the Bible: *bibliophile, bibliomancy.* [< Gk. *biblion* book]

bib·li·o·film (bib/lē·ə·film/) *n.* A kind of microfilm used especially to reproduce books.

bibliog. Bibliographer; bibliography.

bib·li·og·ra·pher (bib/lē·og/rə·fər) *n.* One skilled in bibliography. Also **bib·li·o·graph** (bib/lē·ə·graf/, -gräf/).

bib·li·og·ra·phy (bib/lē·og/rə·fē) *n.* pl. **·phies 1.** A list of the works of an author, or of the literature bearing on a subject. **2.** The description and history of books including details of authorship, editions, dates, typography, etc.; also, a book containing such descriptions. [< BIBLIO- + -GRAPHY] — **bib·li·o·graph·ic** (bib/lē·ə·graf/ik) or **·i·cal** *adj.*

bib·li·o·la·try (bib/lē·ol/ə·trē) *n.* **1.** Extravagant adherence to the letter of the Bible. **2.** Excessive reverence for books. [< BIBLIO- + -LATRY] — **bib/li·ol/a·ter** *n.* — **bib/li·ol/a·trous** *adj.*

bib·li·o·man·cy (bib/lē·ō·man/sē) *n.* Divination by reference to a passage taken at random from a book, usually the Bible. [< BIBLIO- + -MANCY]

bib·li·o·ma·ni·a (bib/lē·ō·mā/nē·ə) *n.* A passion for collecting books. — **bib/li·o·ma/ni·ac** (-ak) *n. & adj.* — **bib·li·o·ma·ni·a·cal** (bib/lē·ō·mə·nī/ə·kəl) *adj.*

bib·li·op·e·gy (bib/lē·op/ə·jē) *n.* The art or practice of bookbinding. [< BIBLIO- + Gk. *pēgnynai* to fasten, join]

bib·li·o·phile (bib/lē·ə·fil/, -fil/) *n.* One who loves books. [< BIBLIO- + -PHILE] Also **bib/li·o·phil/** (-fil/), **bib·li·oph·i·list** (bib/lē·of/ə·list). — **bib/li·oph/i·lism** *n.*

bib·li·o·pole (bib/lē·ə·pōl/) *n.* A dealer in rare books. Also **bib·li·op·o·list** (bib/lē·op/ə·list). [< L *bibliopola* < Gk. *bibliopōlēs* bookseller < *biblion* book + *pōlein* to sell] — **bib/li·o·pol/ic** (-pol/ik) or **·i·cal** *adj.* — **bib·li·op·o·lism** (bib/op/ə·liz/əm), **bib/li·op/o·ly** *n.*

bib·li·o·the·ca (bib/lē·ə·thē/kə) *n.* **1.** A library. **2.** The catalogue of a bookseller. [< L < Gk. *bibliothēkē* library < *biblion* book + *thēkē* chest, storage place]

Bib·list (bib/list, bib/blist) *n.* A Biblicist.

bib·u·lous (bib/yə·ləs) *adj.* **1.** Given to drink; fond of drinking. **2.** Absorbent. [< L *bibulus* drinking readily < *bibere* to drink] — **bib/u·lous·ly** *adv.* — **bib/u·lous·ness** *n.*

bi·cam·er·al (bī·kam/ər·əl) *adj.* Consisting of two chambers, houses, or branches. [< BI- + L *camera* chamber]

bi·cap·su·lar (bī·kap/sə·lər, -syə-) *adj. Bot.* **1.** Having two capsules. **2.** Having a two-celled capsule.

bicarb. Sodium bicarbonate.

bi·car·bo·nate (bī·kär/bə·nit, -nāt) *n. Chem.* A salt of carbonic acid in which one of the hydrogen atoms of the acid is replaced by a metal: sodium *bicarbonate.*

bicarbonate of soda Sodium bicarbonate (which see). *Abbr. bicarb.*

bice (bīs) *n.* **1.** Any of several blue or green pigments made from varieties of basic copper carbonate ore. **2.** The color of any of these pigments. [< OF *bis* dark-colored]

bi·cen·ten·ni·al (bī/sen·ten/ē·əl) *adj.* **1.** Occurring once in 200 years. **2.** Lasting or consisting of 200 years. — *n.* A 200th anniversary. Also **bi·cen·te·nar·y** (bī·sen/tə·ner/ē, bī/sen·ten/ər·ē).

bi·ceph·a·lous (bī·sef/ə·ləs) *adj. Biol.* Having two heads. Also **bi·ce·phal·ic** (bī/sə·fal/ik). [< BI- + -CEPHALOUS]

bi·ceps (bī/seps) *n.* pl. **bi·ceps 1.** *Anat.* **a** The large front muscle, or flexor, of the upper arm: also **biceps bra·chi·i** (brā/kē·ī). **b** The large flexor muscle at the back of the thigh: also **biceps fe·mor·is** (fē/mər·is) **2.** Loosely, muscular strength. [< L, two-headed < *bis* twofold + *caput* head]

Bi·chat (bē·shä/), **Marie François Xavier,** 1771–1802, French anatomist; founder of histology.

bi·chlo·ride (bī·klôr/īd, -id, -klō/rīd, -rid) *n. Chem.* **1.** A salt having two atoms of chlorine. **2.** Bichloride of mercury.

bichloride of mercury *Chem.* Mercuric chloride.

bi·chro·mate (bī·krō/māt, -mit) *n. Chem.* Dichromate (which see).

bi·cip·i·tal (bī·sip/ə·təl) *adj. Anat.* **1.** Having two heads, or points of attachment, as a muscle. **2.** Of or pertaining to the biceps. [< L *biceps, bicipitis.* See BICEPS.]

bick·er (bik/ər) *v.i.* **1.** To dispute petulantly; wrangle. **2.** To flow noisily, as a brook; gurgle. **3.** To flicker, as a flame; twinkle. — *n.* A petulant or angry dispute; petty altercation. — **Syn.** See QUARREL[1]. [ME *bikeren*; origin uncertain] — **bick/er·er** *n.*

Bi·col (bē·kōl/) *n.* See BIKOL.

bi·col·or (bī/kul/ər) *adj.* Two-colored. Also **bi/col/ored.**

bi·con·cave (bī·kon/kāv, -kong/-, bī/kon·kāv/) *adj.* Concave on both sides, as a lens: also *concavo-concave, double concave.* For illustration see FOCUS, LENS.

bi·con·vex (bī·kon/veks, bī/kon·veks/) *adj.* Convex on both sides, as a lens: also *convexo-convex, double convex.* For illustration see FOCUS, LENS.

bi·corn (bī/kôrn) *adj.* Having two horns or two hornlike projections. Also **bi·cor·nu·ate** (bī·kôr/nyŏŏ-āt). [< L *bicornis* < *bis* twofold + *cornu* horn]

bi·cor·po·ral (bī·kôr/pər·əl) *adj.* Having two bodies or main parts. Also **bi·cor·po·re·al** (bī/kôr·pôr/ē·əl, -pō/rē-).

bi·cul·tur·al (bī·kul/chər·əl) *adj.* Having two prominent cultures in one country, as the English and French in Canada. — **bi·cul/tur·al·ism** *n.*

bi·cus·pid (bī·kus/pid) *adj.* Having two cusps or points. Also **bi·cus/pi·dal** (-dəl), **bi·cus/pi·date** (-dāt). — *n.* A premolar tooth. *Abbr.* **b., B.** For illustration see TOOTH. [< BI- + L *cuspis, -idis* point]

bi·cy·cle (bī/sik·əl) *n.* A vehicle consisting of a metal frame mounted on two large wheels, one in back of the other, having a saddle for the rider, handlebars for steering, and pedals or a small motor by which it is propelled. — *v.i.* **·cled, ·cling** To ride a bicycle. [< F < *bi-* two + Gk. *kyklos* wheel] — **bi/cy·cler, bi/cy·clist** *n.*

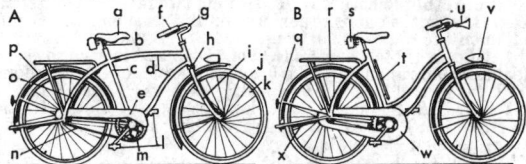

BICYCLES

A Man's bicycle, showing mechanical and structural parts: *a* Saddle, *b* Saddle post, *c* Saddle pillar, *d* Frame tubes, *e* Chain guard, *f* Handlebar grip, *g* Handlebar, *h* Crown, *i* Front (steering) fork, *j* Pneumatic tire, *k* Valve, *l* Pedals, *m* Chain wheel, *n* Chain, *o* Rear fork, *p* Mudguard. B Lady's bicycle, showing accessories: *q* Rear reflector, *r* Luggage carrier, *s* Tool bag, *t* Tire pump, *u* Horn, *v* Headlight, *w* Skirt and chain guard, *x* Stand.

bi·cy·clic (bī·sī/klik, -sik/lik) *adj. Bot.* Disposed in two cycles or whorls, as the stamens of a flower. Also **bi·cy/cli·cal.**

bid (bid) *n.* **1.** An offer to pay or accept a price, as at an auction or in competition for a contract. **2.** The amount offered. **3.** In card games, the number of tricks or points that a player engages to make; also, a player's turn to bid. **4.** An effort to acquire, win, or attain: a *bid* for the governorship. **5.** *Informal* An invitation. — **Syn.** See PROPOSAL. — *v.* **bade** (*Archaic* bad) *for ds.* 3, 4, 6, or **bid** *for defs.* 1, 2, 5, 7, **bid·den** or **bid, bid·ding** *v.t.* **1.** To make an offer of (a price). **2.** In card games, to declare (the number of tricks or points one will engage to make). **3.** To command; order. **4.** To invite. **5.** *U.S. Informal* To invite to join: The fraternity will *bid* you. **6.** To utter, as a greeting or farewell: I *bid* you good day. — *v.i.* **7.** To make a bid. — **to bid fair** To seem probable. **—to bid in** At an auction, to outbid a prospective purchaser on behalf of the owner, when the price offered is too low. **— to bid up** To increase the price by offering higher bids. [Fusion of OE *biddan* to ask, demand and *bēodan* to proclaim, command] **— bid′der** *n.*

b.i.d. *Med.* Twice a day (L *bis in die*).

bi·dar·ka (bĭ-där′kə) *n.* A skin-covered canoe used by Alaskan Eskimos. Also **bi·dar′kee** (-kē). [< Russian *baidarka*, dim. of *baidara* canoe]

bid·da·ble (bid′ə-bəl) *adj.* **1.** Of sufficient value to bid on. **2.** Inclined to do as bidden; obedient; docile.

bid·ding (bid′ing) *n.* **1.** A command; order. **2.** An invitation or summons. **3.** The making of a bid or bids; also, the bids collectively.

Bid·dle (bid′l) A prominent Philadelphia family, including **Francis**, 1886–1968, U.S. attorney general 1941–45; **George**, 1885–1973, brother of Francis, painter and sculptor; **Nicholas**, 1786–1844, financier. **— John**, 1615–62, founder of Unitarianism in England.

bid·dy¹ (bid′ē) *n.* *pl.* **·dies** A hen. [Origin uncertain]

bid·dy² (bid′ē) *n.* *pl.* **·dies** *Slang* A gossipy, usually elderly woman. [< *Bridget*, fem. personal name; orig., an Irish servant girl]

bide (bīd) *v.* **bid·ed** or **bode, bid·ed, bid·ing** *v.t.* **1.** To endure; withstand. **2.** *Archaic* To tolerate; submit to. **—** *v.i.* **3.** To dwell; abide; stay. **— to bide one's time** To await the best opportunity. [OE *bīdan*]

bi·den·tate (bī-den′tāt) *adj.* *Biol.* Having two teeth or toothlike processes. Also **bi·den′tal**. [< BI- + DENTATE]

bi·det (bē-dā′) *n.* A stoollike fixture with facilities for running water, straddled for washing the genitals. [< F]

Bie·der·mei·er (bē′dər-mī′ər) *adj.* Of or pertaining to a style of German furniture of the first half of the 19th century, based on French Empire forms. [after Gottlieb *Biedermeier*, character invented by the poet L. Eichrodt, 1827–92]

Bie·la (bē′lä), **Baron Wilhelm von**, 1782–1856, German astronomer.

Bie·le·feld (bē′lə-felt) A city in central West Germany; pop. 174,752 (est. 1959).

bien en·ten·du (byăn näñ·täñ·dü′) *French* Of course; literally, well understood.

bi·en·ni·al (bī-en′ē-əl) *adj.* **1.** Occurring every second year. **2.** Lasting or living for two years. **—** *n.* **1.** *Bot.* A plant that produces flowers and fruit in its second year, then dies. **2.** An event occurring once in two years. [< L *biennis* < *bis* twofold + *annus* year] **— bi·en′ni·al·ly** *adv.*

bien·ve·nue (byăn·və·nü′) *n.* *French* A welcome.

Bien·ville (byăn·vēl′), **Jean Baptiste Le Moyne, Sieur de**, 1680–1768?, French governor of Louisiana and founder of New Orleans.

bier (bir) *n.* A framework for carrying a corpse to the grave; also, a coffin. [OE *bǣr*]

Bierce (birs), **Ambrose (Gwinnett)**, 1842–1914?, U.S. journalist and author.

Bie·rut (bye′rŏŏt), **Bo·le·slaw** (bô·le′släf), 1892–1956, president of Poland 1947–52; premier 1952–54.

biest·ings (bēs′tingz) See BEESTINGS.

bi·fa·cial (bī-fā′shəl) *adj.* **1.** Having two faces or fronts. **2.** *Bot.* Having the opposite surfaces unlike, as a leaf. **3.** Being alike on the opposite surfaces. [< BI- + FACIAL]

bi·far·i·ous (bī-fâr′ē·əs) *adj.* *Bot.* Disposed in two rows, as leaves on a branch. [< LL *bifarius* double, of two opinions < L *bis* twofold + *fari* to speak] **— bi·far′i·ous·ly** *adv.*

biff (bif) *U.S. Slang v.t.* To strike; hit. **—** *n.* A blow. [Imit.]

bif·fin (bif′in) *n.* *Brit.* A red cooking apple. [< BEEF, from its color + -ING³]

bif·fy (bif′ē) *n.* *Slang* A toilet or bathroom.

bi·fid (bī′fid) *adj.* Cleft; forked. [< L *bifidus* < *bis* twofold + *findere* to split] **— bi·fid′i·ty** *n.* **— bi′fid·ly** *adv.*

bi·fi·lar (bī-fī′lər) *adj.* Formed of, having, or supported by two threads. [< BI- + FILAR] **— bi·fi′lar·ly** *adv.*

bi·flag·el·late (bī-flaj′ə-lāt, -lit) *adj.* *Zool.* Having two flagella or whiplike processes.

bi·flex (bī′fleks) *adj.* Bent in two places; alternately convex and concave. [< BI- + L *flexus*, pp. of *flectere* to bend]

bi·fo·cal (bī-fō′kəl) *adj.* *Optics* Having two foci: said of a lens ground for both near and far vision. [< BI- + FOCAL]

bi·fo·cals (bī-fō′kəlz, bī′fō-kəlz) *n.pl.* Eyeglasses with bifocal lenses.

bi·fold (bī′fōld′) *adj.* Twofold; double.

bi·fo·li·ate (bī-fō′lē-it) *adj.* *Bot.* Having two leaves. [< NL *bifolius* < BI- + L *folium* leaf]

bi·fo·li·o·late (bī-fō′lē·ə-lāt′, -lit′) *adj.* *Bot.* Having two leaflets. [< BI- + NL *foliolum* leaflet]

bi·fo·rate (bī-fôr′āt, -it, -fō′rāt, -rit) *adj.* *Biol.* Having two perforations. [< BI- + L *foratus*, pp. of *forare* to bore]

bi·forked (bī′fôrkt′) *adj.* Bifurcate.

bi·form (bī′fôrm′) *adj.* Having or combining two distinct forms, as the Minotaur. Also **bi′formed′**.

Bif·rost (bēf′rost) In Norse mythology, the bridge of the rainbow between Asgard and Midgard.

bi·fur·cate (bī′fər-kāt, bī-fûr′kāt; *adj. also* bī-fûr′kit) *v.t. & v.i.* **·cat·ed, ·cat·ing** To divide into two branches or stems; fork. **—** *adj.* Forked: also **bi′fur·cat′ed** (-kā′tid), **bi·fur·**

cous (bī-fûr′kəs). [< Med.L *bifurcatus* < L *bi-* two + *furca* fork] **— bi·fur·cate·ly** (bī′fər-kit·lē, bī-fûr′kit·lē) *adv.* **— bi·fur·ca′tion** *n.*

big (big) *adj.* **big·ger, big·gest** **1.** Of great size, extent, etc.; large; bulky. **2.** Pregnant: usually with *with*. **3.** Full to overflowing; teeming. **4.** Pompous; pretentious. **5.** Important; prominent: a *big* day. **6.** Loud. **7.** Generous; magnanimous. **—** *adv.* *Informal* Pompously; extravagantly: to talk *big*. [ME; origin uncertain] **— big′gish** *adj.* **— big′ly** *adv.* **— big′ness** *n.*

big·a·mist (big′ə·mist) *n.* One guilty of bigamy.

big·a·mous (big′ə-məs) *adj.* **1.** Guilty of or living in bigamy. **2.** Characterized by bigamy. [< LL *bigamus*. See BIGAMY.] **— big′a·mous·ly** *adv.*

big·a·my (big′ə-mē) *n.* *Law* The criminal offense of marrying any other person while having a legal spouse living. [< OF *bigamie* < *bigame* bigamous < LL *bigamus* < L *bis* twice + Gk. *gamos* wedding]

big·ar·reau (big′ə-rō, big′ə-rō′) *n.* A type of sweet, firm-fleshed, heart-shaped cherry. Also **big·a·roon** (big′ə-rōōn′). [< F *bigarré*, pp. of *bigarrer* to variegate]

big-bang theory *Astron.* A cosmological theory that the universe began with an explosion and will eventually contract again. Compare STEADY-STATE THEORY.

Big Ben **1.** A bell that strikes the hour in the Westminster clock in the tower of the House of Parliament, London. **2.** The clock itself.

Big Bend National Park A government reservation in westernmost Texas, in the bend of the Rio Grande forming the Mexican border; 1,082 sq. mi.; established 1944.

Big Dipper The constellation Ursa Major.

big game **1.** Large animals hunted or fished for in sport. **2.** *Informal* The objective of an important or risky venture.

big·gin¹ (big′in) *n.* **1.** A cap or hood, especially that of a child. **2.** *Brit.* The coif of a sergeant at law. **3.** *Brit. Dial.* A nightcap. [< F *béguin* cap, orig. worn by the Beguines]

big·gin² (big′in) *n.* *Scot.* A house; building. Also **big′ging**.

big·gi·ty (big′ə-tē) *adj.* *U.S. Dial.* Assertive; conceited.

big·head (big′hed′) *n.* **1.** *Vet.* **a** A bulging of the skull of an animal, caused by osteomalacia. **b** A contagious inflammation of the lungs and intestines of young turkeys. **2.** *Informal* Conceit: also **big head**. **— big′-head′ed** *adj.*

big-head·ed fly A fly (family *Pipunculidae*) with a large hemispherical head almost completely covered by two large compound eyes. The larvae destroy leafhoppers. For illustration see INSECTS (beneficial).

big-heart·ed (big′här′tid) *adj.* Generous; charitable.

big·horn (big′hôrn) *n.* *pl.* **·horns** or **·horn** The Rocky Mountain sheep (*Ovis canadensis*), remarkable for its large horns: also called *mountain sheep*.

Bighorn Mountains A range of the Rockies in southern Montana and northern Wyoming; highest peak, Cloud Peak, 13,165 ft.

Big Horn Mountains A range of mountains in western Arizona, rising to about 3,000 ft.

Bighorn River A river in northern Wyoming and southern Montana, flowing north 461 miles to the Yellowstone River.

big house *U.S. Slang* A penitentiary.

bight (bīt) *n.* **1.** The loop, or middle part, of a rope. **2.** A bend or curve in a shoreline, a river, etc. **3.** A bay bounded by such a bend. **—** *v.t.* To secure with a bight. [OE *byht*]

Big Inch A 24-inch oil pipeline, reaching 1,400 miles from Longview, Texas, to the Atlantic seaboard.

big·no·ni·a (big-nō′nē-ə) *n.* Any of a genus (*Bignonia*) of climbing plants, mostly of tropical America, with clusters of large, trumpet-shaped flowers. [after Abbé *Bignon*, 1711–1772, librarian to Louis XV]

big·no·ni·a·ceous (big-nō′nē·ā′shəs) *adj.* Of or belonging to the Bignoniaceae, or bignonia family.

big·ot (big′ət) *n.* **1.** One whose attitude or behavior expresses intolerance, as because of race, religion, politics, etc. **2.** A narrow-minded, intolerant adherent of a particular religion. **— Syn.** See ENTHUSIAST. [< F; ult origin unknown]

big·ot·ed (big′ət·id) *adj.* Of or characteristic of a bigot; expressing bigotry. **— big′ot·ed·ly** *adv.*

big·ot·ry (big′ə-trē) *n.* *pl.* **·ries** **1.** Attitudes, beliefs, or actions characteristic of a bigot; intolerance. **2.** The manner of thinking of a bigot.

big shot *Slang* Someone of importance. Also **big wheel**.

Big Spring A city in western Texas; pop. 28,735.

big top *U.S. Informal* The main tent of a circus.

big tree A sequoia (def. 2).

big·wig (big′wig′) *n.* *Informal* Someone of importance.

Bi·har (bi-här′) A State of NE India; 67,198 sq. mi.; pop. 56,387,296 (1971); capital, Patna; formerly **Bihar and Oris-sa**, a province of British India.

Bi·ha·ri (bi-hä′rē) *n.* **1.** A native of Bihar. **2.** The Indic language spoken in NE India.

bi·hour·ly (bī-our′lē) *adj.* Occurring once every two hours.

bi·jou (bē′zhōō, bē-zhōō′) *n. pl.* **bi·joux** (bē′zhōōz, bē-zhōōz′) A jewel, or a finely wrought trinket. [< MF]

bi·jou·te·rie (bē-zhōō′tər-ē) *n.* Jewelry. [< F]

bi·ju·gate (bī′jōō-gāt, bī-jōō′git) *adj.* *Bot.* Two-paired. Also **bi·ju·gous** (bī′jōō-gəs). [< BI- + JUGATE]

Bi·ka·ner (bē′kə· nir′) A city in northern Rajasthan State, India; former capital of Bikaner, a former princely state now included in Rajasthan; pop. 150,494 (1961).

bike (bīk) *n. Informal* A bicycle. [Alter. of BICYCLE]

bi·ki·ni (bi·kē′nē) *n.* A type of very scanty bathing suit. [< BIKINI]

Bi·ki·ni (bi·kē′nē) An atoll in the Marshall Islands; 2 sq. mi.; site of U.S. atomic bomb tests, July 1946.

Bi·kol (bi·kōl′) *n.* **1.** One of a Malayan people, inhabiting SE Luzon and converted to Christianity before the completion of the Spanish conquest. **2.** The Indonesian language of these people. Also spelled *Bicol.*

bi·la·bi·al (bī·lā′bē·əl) *adj.* **1.** *Phonet.* Articulated with both lips, as certain consonants. **2.** Having two lips. — *n. Phonet.* A bilabial speech sound, as (b), (p), (m), and (w). [< BI- + LABIAL]

bi·la·bi·ate (bī·lā′bē·āt, -it) *adj. Bot.* Two-lipped: said of a corolla. [< BI- + LABIATE]

bil·an·der (bil′ən·dər, bī′lən-) *n.* A small, two-masted vessel used on canals in the Low Countries. [< Du. *bijlander*]

bi·lat·er·al (bī·lat′ər·əl) *adj.* **1.** Pertaining to or having two sides; two-sided. **2.** Arranged equivalently or symmetrically on both sides, as of an axis. **3.** Mutually binding on both parties: a *bilateral* treaty. [< BI- + LATERAL] — **bi·lat′er·al·ly** *adv.* — **bi·lat′er·al·ness** *n.*

Bil·ba·o (bil·bä′ō) A port city in northern Spain, on **Bilbao Bay,** an inlet of the Bay of Biscay; pop. 297,947 (1960).

bil·ber·ry (bil′ber′ē, -bər·ē) *n. pl.* **·ries** The whortleberry. [< Scand. Cf. Dan. *böllebær.*]

bil·bo (bil′bō) *n. pl.* **·boes** *pl.* A fetter consisting of two sliding shackles attached to an iron bar. [after *Bilbao*]

bile (bil) *n.* **1.** *Physiol.* A bitter yellow or greenish liquid secreted by the liver and serving to promote digestion. **2.** Anger; peevishness. [< F < L *bilis* bile, anger]

bi·lec·tion (bī·lek′shən) *n. Archit.* Bolection (which see).

bile ducts *Physiol.* The excretory ducts of the gall bladder.

bile·stone (bīl′stōn′) *n. Pathol.* A gallstone (which see).

bilge (bilj) *n.* **1.** *Naut.* The rounded part of a ship's bottom; especially, that part extending from the keel to the point from which the sides rise vertically. **2.** The bulge of a barrel. **3.** Bilge water. **4.** *Slang* Stupid or trivial talk or writing. — *v.t. & v.i.* **bilged, bilg·ing 1.** To break open in the bilge; spring or cause to spring a leak: said of a ship. **2.**To bulge. [Var. of BULGE] — **bilg′y** *adj.*

bilge keel *Naut.* An outside keel set lengthwise on each side of the bilge of a vessel to lessen rolling. Also **bilge piece.**

bilge water Foul water that collects in the bilge of a ship.

bil·har·zi·a·sis (bil′här·zī′ə·sis) *n.* Schistosomiasis. [after Theodore M. *Bilharz,* 1825–62, German parasitologist]

bil·i·ar·y (bil′ē·er′ē) *adj.* Pertaining to or conveying bile. [< F *biliaire*]

bi·lin·e·ar (bī·lin′ē·ər) *adj.* Of or related to two lines. [< BI- + LINEAR]

bi·lin·gual (bī·ling′gwəl) *adj.* **1.** Written or expressed in or using two languages. **2.** Able to speak two languages, often with equal skill. — *n.* A bilingual person. [< L *bilinguis* able to speak two languages] — **bi·lin′gual·ism** *n.* — **bi·lin′gual·ly** *adv.*

bil·ious (bil′yəs) *adj.* **1.** Affected or caused by an excess of bile. **2.** Of or containing bile: a *bilious* discharge. **3.** Ill-tempered; peevish. **4.** Of a sickly color. [< F *bilieux* < L *biliosus*] — **bil′ious·ly** *adv.* — **bil′ious·ness** *n.*

bi·lit·er·al (bī·lit′ər·əl) *adj.* Composed of two letters. [< BI- + LITERAL] — **bi·lit′er·al·ism** *n.*

-bility *suffix* Forming nouns from adjectives ending in *-ble: probability* from *probable.* [< F *-bilité* < L *-bilitas, -tatis*]

bilk (bilk) *v.t.* **1.** To cheat; deceive. **2.** To evade payment of. **3.** To balk. — *n.* **1.** A swindler; cheat. **2.** A hoax. [Origin unknown] — **bilk′er** *n.*

bill[1] (bil) *n.* **1.** A statement listing charges for goods delivered or services rendered. **2.** A statement of particulars; itemized list. **3.** *U.S.* A piece of paper money; a bank note. **4.** A bill of exchange (which see); also, loosely, a promissory note. **5.** A draft of a proposed law. **6.** A printed advertisement or notice; a handbill or poster. **7.** The program of a theatrical performance; also, the performance or entertainment itself. **8.** *Law* A document filed in a court containing a formal statement of a case, a complaint, a petition for relief, etc. **9.** *Obs.* A written document. — *v.t.* **1.** To enter in a bill. **2.** To present a bill to. **3.** To announce by advertising; promote. [< LL *billa,* var. of L *butta.* See BULL².]

bill[2] (bil) *n.* A beak, as of a bird. — *v.i.* To join bills, as doves; caress. — **to bill and coo** To caress lovingly and speak in soft, murmuring tones. [OE *bile*]

bill[3] (bil) *n.* **1.** A hook-shaped instrument used in pruning, etc.: also **bill′hook′. 2.** An ancient weapon with a hook-shaped blade; a halberd. **3.** The point of an anchor's fluke. For illustration see ANCHOR. [OE]

bill[4] (bil) *n. Rare* The cry of the bittern. [Var. of BELL²]

bill·a·ble (bil′ə·bəl) *adj.* **1.** Capable of being billed. **2.** Indictable.

bil·la·bong (bil′ə·bong) *n. Austral.* **1.** A blind branch of a river. **2.** A stagnant backwater. [< native Australian *billa* water + *bong* dead]

bill·board[1] (bil′bôrd′, -bōrd′) *n.* A panel, usually outdoors, for notices or advertisements. [< BILL¹ + BOARD]

bill·board[2] (bil′bôrd′, -bōrd′) *n. Naut.* A ledge on the bow of a ship for the bill of the anchor. [< BILL³ + BOARD]

bil·let[1] (bil′it) *n.* **1.** Lodging for troops in private or non-military buildings. **2.** An order for such lodging. **3.** A place assigned, as for a sailor to sling his hammock; quarters. **4.** A job; berth. **5.** *Archaic* A brief note. — *v.t.* **1.** To lodge (soldiers) in a private house. **2.** To serve with a billet. **3.** To lodge; quarter. [< OF *billete,* dim. of *bille* a writing < L *bulla* seal, document] — **bil′let·er** *n.*

bil·let[2] (bil′it) *n.* **1.** A short, thick stick, as of firewood. **2.** *Archit.* One of a series of square or cylindrical ornaments, forming part of a molding. For illustration see MOLDING. **3.** A harness strap that passes through a buckle; also, the loop or pocket for holding the loose end of the strap. **4.** *Metall.* A bloom of iron or steel drawn into a small bar. [< OF *billete,* dim. of *bille* log]

bil·let-doux (bil′ē-dōō′, *Fr.* bē·ye-dōō′) *n. pl.* **bil·lets-doux** (bil′ē-dōōz′, *Fr.* bē·ye-dōō′) A love letter; lover's note. [< F, lit., sweet note]

bill·fish (bil′fish′) *n. pl.* **·fish** or **·fish·es** One of various fishes having elongated jaws, as the marlin or the spearfish.

bill·fold (bil′fōld′) *n.* A wallet.

bil·liard (bil′yərd) *n. U.S. Informal* A carom (def. 1). — *adj.* Of or pertaining to billiards: *billiard* player.

bil·liards (bil′yərdz) *n.pl.* (construed as sing.) Any of various games played with hard balls (**billiard balls**) of ivory or similar material hit by cues on an oblong, cloth-covered table (**billiard table**) having cushioned edges; especially, one of these games played with three balls on a table without pockets. [< F *billard* < OF *billart* cue, *bille* log] — **bil′liard·ist** *n.*

bill·ing (bil′ing) *n.* The relative eminence given to an actor or an act on a theater marquee, playbill, etc.

Bil·lings (bil′ingz) A city in south central Montana, on the Yellowstone River; pop. 61,581.

Bil·lings (bil′ingz) **Josh** See (Henry Wheeler) SHAW.

bil·lings·gate (bil′ingz·gāt) *n.* Vulgar or abusive language. [after *Billingsgate* fish market, London]

bil·lion (bil′yən) *n.* **1.** *U.S.* A thousand millions, written as 1,000,000,000: a cardinal number: called a *milliard* in Great Britain. **2.** *Brit.* A million millions, written as 1,000,000-000,000: a cardinal number: called a *trillion* in the United States. [< F < *bi-* two + (*mi*)*llion* million]

bil·lionth (bil′yənth) *adj.* **1.** Having the number one billion: the ordinal of billion. **2.** Being one of a billion equal parts. — *n.* **1.** One of a billion equal parts. **2.** That which is numbered one billion.

bil·lion·aire (bil′yən·âr′) *n.* One who owns a billion of money. [< BILLION, on analogy with *millionaire*]

Bil·li·ton (bi·lē′ton) An island of Indonesia, near the SE coast of Sumatra; 1,866 sq. mi.; pop. 102,050 (1961); site of important tin mines. Dutch *Belitoeng, Belitung.*

bill of attainder See under ATTAINDER.

bill of exchange A written order for the payment of a given sum to a designated person. Abbr. *b.e., B/E, B.E.*

bill of fare A list of the dishes provided at a meal; menu.

bill of health An official certificate of the crew's health issued to a ship's master on departure from a port. — **a clean bill of health** *Informal* A good record; favorable report.

bill of lading A written acknowledgment of goods received for transportation. Abbr. *b.l., B/L* (pl. *Bs/L*).

bill of rights 1. A formal summary and declaration of the fundamental principles and rights of individuals. **2.** *Often cap.* The first ten amendments to the U.S. Constitution. **3.** *Often cap.* The declaration of rights enacted by the British Parliament in 1689. Abbr. *B/R, B.R.*

bill of sale An instrument attesting the transfer of personal property. Abbr. *b.s., B/S*

bil·lon (bil′ən) *n.* **1.** An alloy of gold or silver with some baser metal, generally copper or tin, used in coinage. **2.** A low alloy of silver with a large proportion of copper, used in making tokens and medals. [< F < OF *bille* log]

bil·low (bil′ō) *n.* **1.** A great wave or swell of the sea. **2.** Any wave or surge, as of sound. — **Syn.** See WAVE. — *v.t.* To rise or roll in billows; surge; swell. [< ON *bylgja*]

bil·low·y (bil′ō-ē) *adj.* **·low·i·er, ·low·i·est** Of, full of, or resembling billows; surging; swelling. — **bil′low·i·ness** *n.*

bill·post·er (bil′pōs′tər) *n.* A person who posts bills, notices, or advertisements on walls, fences, etc. Also **bill′·stick′er.** — **bill′post′ing** *n.*

bil·ly[1] (bil′ē) *n. pl.* **·lies** A short bludgeon, as a policeman's club. [< *Billy,* a nickname for William]

bil·ly[2] (bil′ē) *n. Scot.* A comrade. Also **bil′lie.**

bil·ly[3] (bil′ē) *n. Austral.* A tin pot for heating water. [< native Australian *billa* water]

bil·ly·cock (bil′ē-kok′) *n. Brit.* A low-crowned felt hat; also, a bowler or derby. Also **billycock hat.** [Appar. var. of

18th c. *bully-cocked* (*hat*) (a hat) worn or cocked like a bully's hat]

billy goat   *Informal* A male goat.

Billy the Kid   Nickname of **William H. Bon·ney** (bon′ē), 1859–81, U.S. outlaw active in the Southwest.

bi·lo·bate (bī·lō′bāt) *adj.* Divided into or having two lobes. Also **bi·lo′bat·ed.**

bi·loc·u·lar (bī·lok′yə·lər) *adj. Biol.* Two-celled; divided into two cells. Also **bi·loc·u·late** (-lāt, -lit). [< BI- + LOCULAR. See LOCULUS.]

Bi·lox·i (bi·lok′sē) *n.* One of a tribe of North American Indians of Siouan stock.

Bi·lox·i (bi·lok′sē) A city in SE Mississippi, on a peninsula in Biloxi Bay, an inlet of Mississippi Sound; pop. 48,486.

bil·sted (bil′sted) *n. U.S.* The sweet gum.

bil·tong (bil′tong) *n.* In South Africa, dried and cured meat cut into strips. [< Afrikaans < *bil* rump + *tong* tongue; because it resembles smoked tongue]

bim·a·nous (bim′ə·nəs, bī·mā′-) *adj.* Two-handed. [< NL *bimanus* < L *bis* twofold + *manus* hand]

bi·man·u·al (bī·man′yōō·əl) *adj.* Employing or involving both hands. — **bi·man′u·al·ly** *adv.*

bi·men·sal (bī·men′səl) *adj.* Bimonthly. [< BI- + MENSAL²]

bi·mes·tri·al (bī·mes′trē·əl) *adj.* 1. Lasting two months. 2. Occurring once in two months. [< L *bimestris*]

bi·met·al·ism (bī·met′l·iz′əm) *n.* 1. The concurrent use of both gold and silver as the standard of currency and value. 2. The doctrine of such use. Also **bi·met·al·lism.** — **bi·met′al·ist** or **bi·met′al·list** *n.*

bi·me·tal·lic (bī′mə·tal′ik) *adj.* 1. Consisting of or relating to two metals. 2. Having a double metallic coin standard. 3. Of or pertaining to bimetalism. [< F *bimétallique*]

bi·mo·lec·u·lar (bī′mə·lek′yə·lər) *adj. Chem.* Relating to or formed by two molecules: a *bimolecular* reaction.

bi·month·ly (bī·munth′lē) *adj.* 1. Occurring once every two months. 2. Occurring twice a month; semimonthly. — *n.* A bimonthly publication. — *adv.* 1. Once in two months. 2. Twice a month. ◆ **bimonthly, biweekly** These words are ambiguous, since they can mean either once every two months (or weeks), or twice a month (or week). The ambiguity can be avoided by using *semimonthly* (or *semiweekly*) when the latter meaning is intended.

bi·mo·tored (bī·mō′tərd) *adj.* Having two motors.

bin (bin) *n.* An enclosed place or large receptacle for holding meal, coal, etc. — *v.t.* **binned, bin·ning** To store or deposit in a bin. [OE *binn* basket, crib < Celtic]

bin- Var. of BI-.

bi·nal (bī′nəl) *adj.* Double; twofold. [< NL *binalis* < L *bini* two]

bi·na·ry (bī′nər·ē) *adj.* 1. Pertaining to, characterized by, or made up of two; double; paired. 2. *Chem.* Composed of two elements: a *binary* compound. — *n. pl.* **·ries** 1. A combination of two things. 2. *Astron.* A binary star. [< L *binarius* < *bini* two, double]

binary star *Astron.* A pair of stars revolving about a common center of gravity.

binary system *Math.* A system of enumeration with base 2 such that any number can be expressed by 0 or 1 or a combination of these digits: used especially in digital computers.

bi·nate (bī′nāt) *adj. Bot.* Being or growing in couples or pairs. See illustration of LEAF. [< NL *binatus* paired < L *bini* double, two] — **bi′nate·ly** *adv.*

bin·au·ral (bin·ôr′əl) *adj.* 1. Hearing with both ears. 2. Communicating faint or distant sounds simultaneously to both ears: a *binaural* stethoscope. 3. Two-eared. 4. *Electronics* Stereophonic. [< BIN- + AURAL¹]

bind (bīnd) *v.* **bound, bind·ing** *v.t.* 1. To tie or fasten with a band, cord, etc. 2. To fasten around; encircle; gird. 3. To bandage; swathe: often with *up*. 4. To constrain or obligate, as by moral authority. 5. *Law* To subject to a definite legal obligation. 6. To stitch or fasten together and enclose between covers, as a book. 7. To provide with a border for reinforcement or decoration. 8. To cause to cohere; cement. 9. To constipate. 10. To make irrevocable; seal, as a bargain. 11. To apprentice or indenture: often with *out* or *over*. — *v.i.* 12. To tie up anything. 13. To cohere; stick together. 14. To have binding force; be obligatory. 15. To become stiff or hard, as cement; jam, as gears. — **to bind over** *Law* 1. To hold on bail or under bond for future appearance in court. 2. To put under bond to keep the peace. — *n.* 1. That which binds. 2. *Music* A tie. — **in a bind** *U.S. Informal* In a tight situation. [OE *bindan*] — **Syn.** (verb) 1. fasten, secure, fetter, shackle. 4. engage, restrict, compel. — **Ant.** 1. unbind, unfasten, untie.

bind·er (bīn′dər) *n.* 1. One who binds; especially, a bookbinder. 2. Anything used to bind or tie, as a cord or band, or to cause cohesion of separate particles, as tar or cement. 3. In painting, a material for causing pigments to adhere to a surface, as solutions of gum, glue, or casein. 4. A cover in which sheets of paper may be fastened. 5. *Law* A written statement binding parties to an agreement pending preparation of a formal contract. 6. *Agric.* **a** A device on a reaping machine for tying grain. **b** A machine that cuts and ties

grain. 7. *Metall.* A substance for promoting the cohesion of ore particles or metallic dust before or during sintering.

bind·er·y (bīn′dər·ē) *n. pl.* **·er·ies** A place where books are bound.

bind·ing (bīn′ding) *n.* 1. The act of tying or joining. 2. Anything that binds; binder. 3. The cover holding together and enclosing the leaves of a book. Abbr. *bdg.* 4. A strip sewed over an edge for protection. — *adj.* 1. Tying; restraining. 2. Having the force of necessity; obligatory. — **bind′ing·ly** *adv.* — **bind′ing·ness** *n.*

binding energy *Physics* The energy with which the constituent particles of a system are bound together.

bind·weed (bīnd′wēd′) *n.* 1. A convolvulus. 2. Any similar plant of strong twining habit.

bine (bīn) *n.* 1. A flexible shoot or climbing stem, as of the hop. 2. The bindweed. 3. The woodbine. [Var. of BIND]

Bi·net-Si·mon scale (bi·nā′si′mən, *Fr.* bē·ne′sē·môn′) *Psychol.* A system of rating the intelligence and mental development of children according to their performance in selected and graded tests. Also **Bi·net′-Si′mon test, Bi·net′ scale, Bi·net′ test.** [after Alfred *Binet*, 1857–1911, and Théodore *Simon*, 1873–1961, French psychologists]

binge (binj) *n. Slang* A drunken carousal; spree. [? < dial. E *binge* to soak]

Bing·en (bing′ən) A town on the Rhine in central West Germany; pop. about 19,000.

Bing·ham·ton (bing′əm·tən) A city in south central New York, at the confluence of the Chenango and Susquehanna rivers; pop. 64,123.

bin·go (bing′gō) *n.* A gambling game resembling lotto, usually played in large groups. Compare LOTTO, KENO, BEANO. [Origin unknown]

Binh-dinh (bin′din′) A city in South Vietnam; pop. 147,200 (est. 1955). Also **Binh Dinh.**

bin·it (bin′it) *n.* A bit⁴. [< *bin*(*ary*) (*dig*)*it*]

bin·na·cle (bin′ə·kəl) *n. Naut.* A stand or case for a ship's compass, usually placed before the steering wheel. [Earlier *bittacle* < Pg. *bitacola* < L *habitaculum* little house]

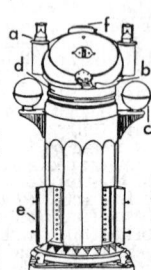

BINNACLE

a Lamp. *b* Hood. *c* Quadrantal sphere. *d* Compass chamber. *e* Magnet chamber. *f* Window to admit light to compass chamber.

bin·oc·u·lar (bə·nok′yə·lər, bī-) *adj.* Pertaining to, using, or intended for both eyes at once. — *n.* Often *pl.* A telescope, opera glass, etc., adapted for use by both eyes at once: also **bin·o·cle** (bin′ə·kəl). [< L *bini* two, double + *ocularis* of the eyes < *oculus* eye] — **bin·oc′u·lar′i·ty** (-lar′ə·tē) *n.* — **bin·oc′u·lar·ly** *adv.*

bi·no·mi·al (bī·nō′mē·əl) *adj.* Consisting of two names or terms. — *n.* 1. *Math.* An algebraic expression consisting of two terms joined by a plus or minus sign. 2. *Biol.* A name consisting of two Latinized words, one indicating the genus, the other the species of a plant or animal, as *Hippopotamus amphibius*, the hippopotamus. [< LL *binominus* having two names] — **bi·no′mi·al·ly** *adv.*

binomial theorem *Math.* The theorem stating the general form of any power of an algebraic binomial.

bi·nu·cle·ate (bī·nōō′klē·āt, -nyōō′-) *adj. Biol.* Having two nuclei, as a cell. Also **bi·nu′cle·ar, bi·nu′cle·at′ed.**

Bin·ue (bin′wā) See BENUE.

bio- *combining form* Life: *biology.* [< Gk. *bios* life]

bi·o·as·say (bī′ō·as′ā) *n.* The determination of the properties and effects of a drug by testing it under controlled conditions in the bodies of laboratory animals. [< BIO- + ASSAY]

bi·o·as·tro·nau·tics (bī′ō·as′trə·nô′tiks) *n.pl.* (construed as *sing.*) The branch of astronautics concerned with the effects of space travel upon plant and animal life.

Bí·o-Bí·o (bē′ō·bē′ō) A river in south central Chile, flowing generally NW about 240 miles to the Pacific.

bi·o·cat·a·lyst (bī′ō·kat′ə·list) *n.* A substance that acts to promote or modify some physiological process; especially, an enzyme, vitamin, or hormone.

bi·o·cel·late (bī·ō·sel′āt, bī′ō·sel′it) *adj. Biol.* Having two eyelike marks or ocelli. [< BI- + OCELLATE]

biochem. Biochemistry.

bi·o·chem·is·try (bī′ō·kem′is·trē) *n.* The branch of chemistry relating to the processes and physical properties of living organisms. — **bi·o·chem′i·cal** or **bi·o·chem′ic** *adj.* — **bi′o·chem′i·cal·ly** *adv.* — **bi·o·chem′ist** *n.*

bi·o·coe·no·sis (bī′ō·sē·nō′sis) *n. Ecol.* An association of plants and animals in a given habitat and under similar environmental conditions. Also **bi·o·ce·no′sis, bi·o·coe·nose** (bī′ō·sē·nōs). [< BIO- + Gk. *koinōsis* sharing] — **bi·o·coe·not′ic** (-not′ik) *adj.*

bi·o·cy·cle (bī′ō·sī′kəl) *n. Ecol.* One of the three major regions (terrestrial, oceanic, and fresh-water) of the biosphere capable of supporting life. [< BIO- + CYCLE]

bi·o·de·grad·a·ble (bī′ō·di·grā′də·bəl) *adj. Ecol.* Capable of being biologically decomposed, as some detergents in sewage. [< BIO- + DEGRAD(E) + -ABLE]

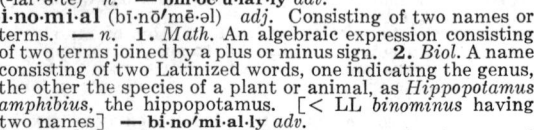

bi·o·dy·nam·ics (bī′ō·dī·nam′iks) *n.pl.* (*construed as sing.*) The branch of biology that treats of the activities of living organisms: distinguished from *biostatics.* — **bi′o·dy·nam′ic** or **·i·cal** *adj.*

bi·o·en·er·get·ics (bī′ō·en·ər·jet′iks) *n.pl.* (*construed as sing.*) The study of energy in living matter.

bi·o·eth·ics (bī′ō·eth′iks) *n.pl.* (*construed as sing.*) The study of ethical and legal problems related to biological research and its medical application, especially in eugenics, euthanasia, and organ transplants.

bi·o·feed·back (bī′ō·fēd′bak) *n.* A process of bringing unconscious functions, such as brain waves, under conscious control for healing, tranquility, increased energy, and the like.

bi·o·fla·vo·noid (bī′ō·flā′və·noid) *n.* Any of several compounds forming a part of the Vitamin P complex.

biog. Biographer; biographical; biography.

bi·o·gen (bī′ə·jən) *n. Biochem.* The hypothetical large protein molecular unit assumed to be active in the functioning of body tissues. [< BIO- + -GEN]

bi·o·gen·e·sis (bī′ō·jen′ə·sis) *n.* 1. The doctrine that life is generated from living organisms only. 2. Such generation itself. Also **bi·og·e·ny** (bī·oj′ə·nē). — **bi·o·ge·net·ic** (bī′ō·jə·net′ik) or **·i·cal** *adj.* — **bi′o·ge·net′i·cal·ly** *adv.*

bi·o·ge·og·ra·phy (bī′ō·jē·og′rə·fē) *n.* The science of geographical distribution of living organisms. — **bi′o·ge′o·graph′ic** (-jē′ə·graf′ik) or **·i·cal** *adj.* — **bi′o·ge′o·graph′i·cal·ly** *adv.*

bi·og·ra·pher (bī·og′rə·fər, bē-) *n.* A writer of biography.

bi·o·graph·i·cal (bī′ə·graf′i·kəl) *adj.* 1. Of or concerning a person's life. 2. Pertaining to biography. Also **bi′o·graph′ic.** — **bi′o·graph′i·cal·ly** *adv.*

bi·og·ra·phy (bī·og′rə·fē, bē-) *n. pl.* **·phies** An account of a person's life; also, such accounts as a form of literature. [< LGk. *biographia* < Gk. *bios* life + *graphein* to write]

bi·o·herm (bī′ō·hûrm) *n. Geol.* A rocky unstratified mass of fragmented marine fossils, often found surrounded by other types of rock, and believed to have been collected by waves and currents. Compare BIOSTROME. [< BIO- + Gk. *herma* sunken rock]

biol. Biological; biologist; biology.

bi·o·lin·guis·tics (bī′ō·ling·gwis′tiks) *n.pl.* (*construed as sing.*) The study of language as a biological activity of the human organism, with emphasis on the neurophysiological factors involved in communication.

bi·o·log·i·cal (bī′ə·loj′i·kəl) *adj.* 1. Of or pertaining to biology. 2. Used for or produced by biological research or practice. — *n. Often pl.* A drug or medicinal preparation obtained from animal tissue or some other organic source. Also **bi′o·log′ic.** — **bi′o·log′i·cal·ly** *adv.*

biological clock A hypothetical, natural timing mechanism in organisms that seems to control certain instinctive functions and routines, such as the migration, nesting, and mating of birds.

biological warfare Warfare that employs bacteria, viruses, and other biological agents noxious to or destructive of life.

bi·ol·o·gy (bī·ol′ə·jē) *n.* The science of life in all its manifestations, and of the origin, structure, reproduction, growth, and development of living organisms collectively. Its two main divisions are botany and zoology. [< BIO- + -LOGY] — **bi·ol′o·gist** *n.*

bi·o·lu·mi·nes·cence (bī′ō·lōō′mə·nes′əns) *n.* The emission of light by living organisms, as fireflies and certain fungi or deep-sea fishes. — **bi′o·lu′mi·nes′cent** *adj.*

bi·ol·y·sis (bī·ol′ə·sis) *n.* 1. The disintegration of organic matter, especially by the action of microorganisms. 2. The destruction or cessation of life. [< BIO- + -LYSIS] — **bi·o·lyt·ic** (bī′ə·lit′ik) *adj.*

bi·om·e·try (bī·om′ə·trē) *n.* 1. A measuring or calculating of the probable duration of human life. 2. Biology from a statistical point of view, especially with reference to variation: also **bi·o·met·rics** (bī′ə·met′riks). [< BIO- + -METRY] — **bi′o·met′ric** or **·ri·cal** *adj.* — **bi′o·met′ri·cal·ly** *adv.*

Bi·on (bī′ən) Second-century B.C. Greek pastoral poet.

bi·on·ics (bī·on′iks) *n.pl.* (*construed as sing.*) The branch of electronics that investigates the behavior of animals applied to the field of computers and other electronic devices.

bi·o·nom·ics (bī′ə·nom′iks) *n.pl.* (*construed as sing.*) Ecology (def. 1). [< BIO- + (ECO)NOMICS] — **bi′o·nom′ic** or **·i·cal** *adj.* — **bi·on·o·mist** (bī·on′ə·mist) *n.*

bi·o·phys·ics (bī′ō·fiz′iks) *n.pl.* (*construed as sing.*) The study of biological function, structure, and organization in relation to and using the methods of physics. — **bi′o·phys′i·cal** *adj.* — **bi′o·phys′i·cist** *n.*

bi·o·plasm (bī′ō·plaz′əm) *n.* Formative living matter; protoplasm. [<BIO- + -PLASM]

bi·o·po·e·sis (bī′ō·pō·ē′sis) *n.* The formation of living matter from nonliving material, especially in evolution. Compare ABIOGENESIS. [< BIO- + Gk. *poiesis* making, creation]

bi·op·sy (bī′op·sē) *n. pl.* **·sies** *Med.* The clinical and diagnostic examination of tissue and other material excised from the living subject. Compare AUTOPSY. [< BI(O)- + -OPSY] — **bi·op·sic** (bī·op′sik) *adj.*

bi·o·psy·chol·o·gy (bī′ō·sī·kol′ə·jē) *n.* Psychobiology.

bi·o·scope (bī′ə·skōp) *n.* An early motion-picture projector.

bi·os·co·py (bī·os′kə·pē) *n. Med.* An examination to ascertain whether life exists or has ceased. [< BIO- + -SCOPY] — **bi′o·scop·ic** (bī′ə·skop′ik) *adj.*

-biosis *combining form* Manner of living: *symbiosis.* [< Gk. *biosis* < *bios* life]

bi·o·sphere (bī′ə·sfir) *n.* That portion of the earth and its environment within which life in any of its forms is manifested. [< BIO- + SPHERE]

bi·o·stat·ics (bī′ō·stat′iks) *n.pl.* (*construed as sing.*) The branch of biology that treats of structure as related to function: distinguished from *biodynamics.* [< BIO- + STATICS] — **bi′o·stat′ic** or **·i·cal** *adj.*

bi·o·strome (bī′ō·strōm) *n. Geol.* A rocky layer, bed, or stratum of marine fossils. Compare BIOHERM. [< BIO- + LL *stroma* bed covering < Gk. *strōma* bed]

bi·o·syn·the·sis (bī′ō·sin′thə·sis) *n.* The chemical synthesis of organic materials from elementary living units or cells. — **bi·o·syn·thet·ic** (bī′ō·sin·thet′ik) *adj.*

bi·o·ta (bī·ō′tə) *n. Ecol.* The combined fauna and flora of any geographical area or geological period. [< Gk. *biotē* life, living < *bios* life]

bi·ot·ic (bī·ot′ik) *adj.* Pertaining to life. Also **bi·ot′i·cal.** [< Gk. *biōtikos* < *bios* life]

bi·ot·ics (bī·ot′iks) *n.pl.* (*construed as sing.*) The science of the functions of living organisms.

bi·o·tin (bī′ə·tin) *n. Biochem.* A crystalline acid, $C_{10}H_{16}O_3$-N_2S, forming part of the vitamin B complex, and essential in preventing the death of animals from an excess of egg white in the diet: also called *vitamin H.* [< Gk. *biotos* life + -IN]

bi·o·tite (bī′ə·tīt) *n.* A common, brown or dark green mica containing magnesium and iron. [after J. B. *Biot,* 1774–1862, French physicist] — **bi′o·tit′ic** (-tit′ik) *adj.*

bi·o·tope (bī′ə·tōp) *n. Ecol.* An area, usually small and of uniform environmental conditions, characterized by relatively stable biotypes. [< BIO- + Gk. *topos* region]

bi·o·type (bī′ō·tīp) *n. Biol.* A group of individuals all of which have the same genotype. — **bi·o·typ′ic** (-tip′ik) *adj.*

bi·pa·ri·e·tal (bī′pə·rī′ə·təl) *adj. Anat.* Of or pertaining to the two parietal bones.

bip·a·rous (bip′ə·rəs) *adj.* 1. *Bot.* Having two lateral axes. 2. *Zool.* Bringing forth two at a birth. [< BI- + -PAROUS]

bi·par·ti·san (bī·pär′tə·zən) *adj.* Advocated by or consisting of members of two parties, especially the Democratic and Republican parties. — **bi·par′ti·san·ship′** *n.*

bi·par·tite (bī·pär′tīt) *adj.* 1. Consisting of two parts, especially two corresponding parts. 2. *Bot.* Divided into two parts almost to the base, as certain leaves. Also **bi·part′ed.** [< L *bipartitus,* pp. of *bipartire* to divide] — **bi·par′tite·ly** *adv.* — **bi·par·ti·tion** (bī′pär·tish′ən) *n.*

bi·ped (bī′ped) *n.* An animal having two feet. — *adj.* Two-footed: also **bi·pe·dal** (bī′pə·dəl, bip′ə-). [< L *bipes, bipedis* two-footed]

bi·pet·al·ous (bī·pet′l·əs) *adj. Bot.* Dipetalous (which see).

bi·phen·yl (bī·fen′əl, -fē′nəl) *n. Chem.* A colorless crystalline hydrocarbon, $C_6H_5·C_6H_5$, found in coal tar, and used in lacquers and as a preservative of citrus fruit: also called *diphenyl.* [< BI- + PHENYL]

bi·pin·nate (bī·pin′āt) *adj. Bot.* Twice or doubly pinnate, as a leaf. Also **bi·pin′nat·ed.** — **bi·pin′nate·ly** *adv.*

bi·plane (bī′plān′) *n.* A type of airplane having two wings, one above the other: distinguished from *monoplane.*

bi·pod (bī′pod) *n.* A two-legged stand. [< BI- +-POD]

bi·po·lar (bī·pō′lər) *adj.* 1. Relating to or possessing two poles: *bipolar* nerve cells. 2. Denoting or belonging to both polar regions. 3. Containing two contradictory qualities, opinions, etc. — **bi·po·lar·i·ty** (bī′pō·lar′ə·tē) *n.*

bi·pro·pel·lant (bī′prə·pel′ənt) *n. Aerospace* A rocket propellant consisting of two chemicals.

bi·quad·rate (bī·kwod′rāt) *n. Math.* A fourth power.

bi·quad·rat·ic (bī′kwod·rat′ik) *Math. adj.* Containing or referring to a fourth power. — *n.* 1. A biquadrate. 2. An equation of the fourth power.

bi·quar·ter·ly (bī·kwôr′tər·lē) *adj.* Occurring or appearing twice every quarter.

bi·ra·di·al (bī·rā′dē·əl) *adj. Biol.* Having symmetry both bilaterally and radially, as certain sea anemones.

bi·ra·di·ate (bī·rā′dē·it) *adj.* Having two rays.

birch (bûrch) *n.* 1. A tree or shrub (genus *Betula*) typical of a small family that includes the alder and hazel, with the outer bark separable in thin layers; especially, the canoe or paper birch (*B. papyrifera*) of North America: also called *white birch.* 2. A rod from this tree, used as a whip. 3. The tough, close-grained hardwood of the birch. — *v.t.* To whip with a birch rod. [OE *birce*] — **birch·en** (bûr′chən) *adj.*

Birch·er (bûr′chər) *n.* A member or supporter of the John Birch Society (which see). Also **John Bircher.** — **Birch′ite, Birch′ist** *n. & adj.*

bird (bûrd) *n.* **1.** A warm-blooded, feathered, egg-laying vertebrate (class *Aves*), having the forelimbs modified as wings. ◆ Collateral adjective: *avian*. **2.** A game bird; in England, a partridge. **3.** A shuttlecock. **4.** A clay pigeon. **5.** *Slang* A person, especially one who is peculiar or remarkable. **6.** *Slang* A hiss or jeer: usually in the phrases **to give (someone) the bird, to get the bird. 7.** *Brit. Slang* A girl or girlfriend. **8.** *Obs.* The young of a fowl; nestling. — *v.i.* **1.** To observe or identify wild birds in their natural habitats: also **bird-watch. 2.** To trap or shoot birds. [OE *bridd*]

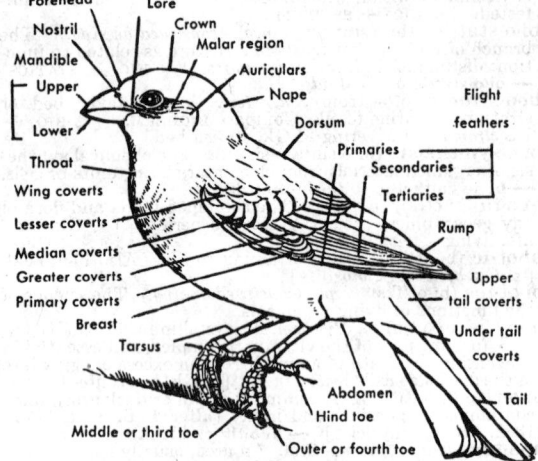

Forehead
Lore
Nostril
Crown
Malar region
Mandible
Auriculars
Upper
Nape
Flight
Lower
Dorsum
feathers
Throat
Primaries
Wing coverts
Secondaries
Lesser coverts
Tertiaries
Median coverts
Rump
Greater coverts
Upper
Primary coverts
tail coverts
Breast
Under tail
Tarsus
coverts
Abdomen
Tail
Hind toe
Middle or third toe
Outer or fourth toe

BIRD (Anatomical nomenclature)

bird-bath (bûrd′bath′, -bäth′) *n.* A bowl, often on a pedestal, used to ornament a lawn or for birds to bathe in.
bird-call (bûrd′kôl′) *n.* **1.** A bird's note in calling. **2.** A sound in imitation of this, or an instrument for producing such a sound.
bird dog A dog used in hunting game birds.
bird grass A North American grass (*Poa trivialis*), much cultivated for lawns.
bird-house (bûrd′hous′) *n.* **1.** A small house or enclosure for birds; an aviary. **2.** A small house, placed in trees, etc., in which birds may nest. Also **bird house.**
bird-ie (bûr′dē) *n.* **1.** *Informal* A small bird. **2.** In golf, one stroke less than par on a given hole.
bird-lime (bûrd′līm′) *n.* A sticky substance made from holly or mistletoe and smeared on twigs to catch small birds. — *v.t.* **-limed, -lim·ing** To smear or snare with birdlime; trap.
bird-man (bûrd′man′, -mən) *n.* *pl.* **-men** (-men′, -mən) **1.** *Informal* An aviator. **2.** A fowler. **3.** An ornithologist.
bird of paradise Any of a family (*Paradiseidae*) of chiefly tropical birds noted for the form and beauty of the plumage in the male; especially, *Paradisea apoda* of New Guinea.
Bird of Paradise The constellation Apus.
bird of passage A migratory bird.
bird of prey Any of various predatory birds, as an eagle, hawk, vulture, falcon, etc.
bird pepper Capsicum (def. 2).
bird's-eye (bûrdz′ī′) *adj.* **1.** Marked with spots resembling birds' eyes: *bird's-eye* maple. **2.** Seen from above or from afar: a *bird's-eye* view. — *n.* **1.** A plant (*Primula farinosa*) with small, bright-colored flowers: also **bird's-eye primrose. 2.** The germander speedwell. See under SPEEDWELL. **3.** A pattern woven with small, eyelike indentations. **4.** Any of various fabrics having such a pattern. Also **birds'eye′.**
bird's-foot (bûrdz′foot′) *n.* **1.** Any plant of the genus *Ornithopus*, of the bean family, bearing curving pods. **2.** Any of various other plants, as a euphorbia of South Africa.
bird's-foot fern A fern (*Pellaea mucronata*) of California, with tufted, deltoid fronds, 4 to 6 inches long.
bird's-foot trefoil A leguminous plant (genus *Lotus*); especially, *L. corniculatus* of the Old World, a hardy perennial trailer: also called *five-fingers.*
bird's-foot violet A violet (*Viola pedata*) with pedate leaves and large, pale blue or purple flowers: also called *johnny-jump-up, wood violet.*
bird's-nest (bûrdz′nest′) *n.* **1.** The mucus secreted in the salivary glands of certain Asian swifts, used for building nests, and highly esteemed for making soup. **2.** One of various plants resembling a bird's nest, as the wild carrot. **3.** *Naut.* A crow's-nest (which see). Also **birds′nest′.**
bird's nest A nest built by birds.
bird-watch (bûrd′wach′) *v.i.* To bird (def. 1). [Back formation < BIRD WATCHER]
bird watcher One who observes or identifies wild birds in their natural habitats as a pastime. — **bird watching**

bi·reme (bī′rēm) *n.* An ancient galley having two banks of oars on each side. [< L *biremis* < *bis* twofold + *remus* oar]
bi·ret·ta (bi·ret′ə) *n.* A stiff, square, clerical cap with three or four upright projections on the crown: also called *barret, berretta.* [< Ital. *berretta* or Sp. *birreta* < LL *birretum* cap, dim. of *birrus* cape, cloak]
Bir·ken·head (bûr′kən-hed) A county borough and port in NW Cheshire, England, on the Mersey river opposite Liverpool; pop. 143,550 (est. 1967).
birl¹ (bûrl) *v.t. & v.i.* **1.** To rotate (a floating log). **2.** To whirl. — *n.* A droning noise. [Blend of BIRR and WHIRL]
birl² (bûrl, birl) *v.t. & v.i. Dial* To ply with drink; carouse: also *byrl.* Also **birle.** [OE *byrelian < byrele* cupbearer]
birl·ing (bûr′ling) *n.* A sport in which two contestants balance on a floating log and try to dislodge one another: also called *logrolling.*
Bir·ming·ham (bûr′ming-əm *for def. 1;* bûr′ming-ham *for defs.* 2, 3) **1.** A borough and city of West Midlands, England; pop. 1,084,000 (1976). **2.** A manufacturing city in north central Alabama; pop. 300,910. **3.** A city in SE Michigan, near Pontiac; pop. 26,170.
birr (bûr) *Archaic & Dial. n.* **1.** Force or momentum; also, vigor. **2.** A whirring sound. — *v.i.* To make a whirring noise. [< ON *byrr* favorable wind]
birse (bûrs, *Scot.* birs) *n. Scot.* **1.** A bristle or bristles. **2.** Short hair of the head or beard. **3.** Temper; rage.
birth (bûrth) *n.* **1.** The fact or act of being born. **2.** The bringing forth of offspring; parturition. **3.** Beginning; origin. **4.** Ancestry or descent: of humble *birth.* **5.** Noble lineage; good family: a woman of *birth.* **6.** Natural or inherited tendency: an artist by *birth.* **7.** The fact of being born under certain circumstances of location, parentage, etc., as an element of nationality: a Turk by *birth.* **8.** That which is born; issue. [ME *byrth,* prob. < Scand. Cf. ON *byrth,* Dan. *byrd.* Related to BEAR¹.]
birth canal *Anat.* The passage through which a baby is delivered, extending from the cervix uteri to the vulva.
birth control The regulation of conception by preventive methods or devices.
birth·day (bûrth′dā′) *n.* The day of one's birth or its anniversary.
birth·mark (bûrth′märk′) *n.* A mark or stain existing on the body from birth; nevus.
birth·place (bûrth′plās′) *n.* **1.** Place of birth. Abbr. *bp.* **2.** Place where something originates.
birth rate The number of births per a given number of individuals (usually 1,000), in a specified district and in a specified period of time.
birth·right (bûrth′rīt′) *n.* A privilege or possession into which one is born.
birth·root (bûrth′root′, -root′) *n.* Any of a genus (*Trillium*) of typically North American perennial herbs of the lily family; especially, *T. erectum,* that has astringent roots formerly used to hasten birth: also called *birthwort.*
birth·stone (bûrth′stōn′) *n.* A jewel identified with a particular month of the year and thought to bring good luck when worn by a person whose birthday falls in that month.
birth·wort (bûrth′wûrt′) *n.* **1.** Any plant of the genus *Aristolochia;* especially, *A. clematitis* of Europe, with stimulant tonic roots used as aromatic bitters. **2.** Birthroot.
bis (bis) *adv.* Twice: used to denote repetition. [< L]
bis- Var. of BI-.
Bi·sa·yan (bē-sä′yən) *adj. & n.* Visayan.
Bisayan Islands The Visayan Islands. Also **Bi·sa·yas** (bē-sä′yəz).
Bis·cay (bis′kā, -kē) See VIZCAYA.
Biscay, Bay of A wide inlet of the Atlantic between the west and SW coast of France and the north and NW coast of Spain.
Bis·cayne Bay (bis′kān, bis-kān′) A shallow inlet of the Atlantic south of Miami, Florida.
bis·cuit (bis′kit) *n.* **1.** *U.S.* A kind of shortened bread baked in small cakes, raised with baking powder or soda. **2.** *Brit.* A thin, crisp wafer. **3.** A light brown color. **4.** In ceramics, pottery baked once but not glazed. [< OF *bescoit, bescuit,* ult. < L *bis* twice + *coctus,* pp. of *coquere* to cook]
bise (bēz) *n.* A cold northerly wind in Switzerland, parts of France, and nearby regions. [< F]
bi·sect (bī·sekt′) *v.t.* **1.** To cut into two parts; halve. **2.** *Geom.* To divide into two parts of equal size. — *v.i.* **3.** To fork, as a road. [< BI- + L *sectus,* pp. of *secare* to cut] — **bi·sec′tion** *n.* — **bi·sec′tion·al** *adj.* — **bi·sec′tion·al·ly** *adv.*
bi·sec·tor (bī·sek′tər) *n.* **1.** That which bisects. **2.** *Geom.* A line or plane that bisects an angle or another line.
bi·sec·trix (bī·sek′triks) *n. pl.* **bi·sec·tri·ces** (bī′sek-trī′sēz) **1.** The line bisecting the angle formed by the optic axes of a crystal. **2.** *Geom.* A bisector.
bi·ser·rate (bī·ser′āt, -it) *adj.* **1.** *Bot.* Doubly serrate, as a leaf. **2.** *Entomol.* Notched on both sides, as an antenna.
bi·sex·u·al (bī·sek′shoo-əl) *adj.* **1.** Of both sexes. **2.** Having the organs of both sexes; hermaphrodite. **3.** Erotically attracted by both sexes. — *n.* **1.** A hermaphrodite. **2.** A bisexual person. — **bi·sex′u·al·ism, bi·sex·u·al·i·ty** (bī-sek′shoo-al′ə-tē) *n.* — **bi·sex′u·al·ly** *adv.*

bish·op (bish′əp) *n.* **1.** A prelate in the Christian church; especially, the head of a diocese. Abbr. *bp.* **2.** A miter-shaped chess piece that may be moved diagonally any number of unoccupied squares of the same color. Abbr. *B.* **3.** A hot drink made with mulled wine, sugar, oranges, etc. [OE *biscop* < LL *episcopus* bishop < Gk. *episkopos* overseer]

bish·op·ric (bish′əp·rik) *n.* The office or the diocese of a bishop.

bish·op's-cap (bish′əps·kap′) *n.* Any species of miterwort; especially, *Mitella diphylla.* Also **bish′ops·cap′.**

Bi·si·tun (bē′sə·tōōn′) See BEHISTUN.

Bis·kra (bis′krä) A town and oasis in NE Algeria; pop. about 53,000.

Bis·marck (biz′märk) The capital of North Dakota, a city in the south central part, on the Missouri River; pop. 34,703.

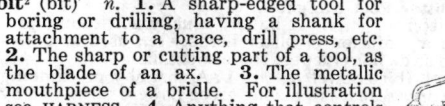

BISHOP (def. 2)

Bis·marck (biz′märk, *Ger.* bis′-), **Prince Otto Eduard Leopold von,** 1815–98, German statesman; founder of the German Empire: called **the Iron Chancellor.**

Bismarck Archipelago An island group in the UN Trust Territory of New Guinea, comprising New Britain, New Ireland, Lavongai, and the Admiralty Islands; about 19,200 sq. mi.

bis·muth (biz′məth) *n.* A lustrous, reddish white metallic element (symbol Bi) occurring native as well as in combination, used in medicine, in the manufacture of cosmetics, etc. See ELEMENT. [< G] — **bis·muth·al** (biz′məth·əl) *adj.*

bis·mu·thic (biz·myoo′thik, -muth′ik) *adj. Chem.* Containing bismuth in its highest valence.

bis·muth·ous (biz′məth·əs) *adj. Chem.* Containing bismuth in its lowest valence.

bi·son (bī′sən, -zən) *n. pl.* **bi·son** A bovine ruminant, closely related to the true ox; especially, the North American buffalo (*Bos* or *Bison bison*). [< L *bison* wild ox, ult. < Gmc.]

NORTH AMERICAN BISON (5 to 6 feet high at shoulder)

bisque[1] (bisk) *n.* **1.** A thick, rich soup made from meat or fish, especially shellfish. **2.** Any thickened, creamy soup. **3.** A kind of ice cream containing crushed macaroons or nuts. [< F]

bisque[2] (bisk) *n.* **1.** In ceramics, biscuit. **2.** Any of several shades of pinkish beige. [< BISCUIT]

bisque[3] (bisk) *n.* An advantage of a point, turn, etc., given to an opponent in various games, as lawn tennis. [< F]

Bis·sau (bi·sou′) The capital of Portuguese Guinea, a port city in the western part on the Atlantic; pop. 20,000 (1964).

bis·sex·tile (bi·seks′təl, -tīl) *adj.* **1.** Pertaining to the extra day occurring in leap year. **2.** Pertaining to a leap year. — *n.* A leap year. [< L *bisextilis* intercalary < *bis* twice + *sextilis* sixth; so called because the sixth day before March 1 was doubled in leap year in the Julian calendar]

bis·ter (bis′tər) *n.* **1.** A nonpermanent, yellowish brown pigment made from beechwood soot, used chiefly as a watercolor wash. **2.** A dark brown color. Also **bis′tre.** [< F *bistre* dark brown] — **bis′tered** *adj.*

bis·tort (bis′tôrt) *n.* **1.** A perennial herb (*Polygonum bistorta*) of Europe and Asia, with creeping rootstocks having astringent properties: also called *snakeweed.* **2.** An allied herb, the **Virginia bistort** (*Tovara virginiana*). [< F < L *bis* twice + *tortus*, pp. of *torquere* to twist]

bis·tou·ry (bis′tŏŏ·rē) *n. pl.* **·ries** *Surg.* A narrow-bladed knife for minor incisions. [< OF *bistorie* dagger]

bis·tro (bis′tro, *Fr.* bē·strō′) *n. Informal* A small bar, tavern or night club. [< F]

bi·sul·cate (bī·sul′kāt) *adj.* **1.** Cleft in two; cloven-hoofed. **2.** Having two grooves. Also **bi·sul′cat·ed.** [< L *bisulcus* < *bis* twofold + *sulcus* furrow]

bi·sul·fate (bī·sul′fāt) *n. Chem.* An acid sulfate containing the radical HSO4: also called *disulfate.* Also **bi·sul′phate.**

bi·sul·fide (bī·sul′fīd) *n. Chem.* A disulfide (which see). Also **bi·sul′phide.**

bi·sul·fite (bī·sul′fīt) *n. Chem.* A salt of sulfurous acid in which the metal has replaced half the hydrogen in the acid. Also **bi·sul′phite.**

Bi·su·tun (bē′sə·tōōn′) See BEHISTUN.

bi·sym·met·ri·cal (bī′si·met′ri·kəl) *adj.* Bilaterally symmetrical. Also **bi′sym·met′ric.** — **bi′sym·met′ri·cal·ly** *adv.* — **bi·sym·met·ry** (bī·sim′ə·trē) *n.*

bit[1] (bit) *n.* **1.** A small piece, portion, or quantity; a little. **2.** A short time: Wait a *bit.* **3.** A small part, as in a play or movie; also, *U.S. Slang,* an instance or episode of behavior, activity, etc.: the crying *bit.* **4.** *Brit.* A small coin: a threepenny *bit.* **5.** *U.S.* The Spanish real, worth 12½ cents, formerly used as currency in the SW United States: now used chiefly in the expression *two bits* (which see). — **a bit (of)** To a certain extent; somewhat: *a bit* tired; *a bit of* a shop. — **to do one's bit** To make one's contribution; do one's share. — *adj.* Small; insignificant; minor: a *bit* player. [OE *bita* < *bītan* to bite]

— **Syn. 1.** particle, scrap; iota, mite, speck; drop, driblet, grain.

bit[2] (bit) *n.* **1.** A sharp-edged tool for boring or drilling, having a shank for attachment to a brace, drill press, etc. **2.** The sharp or cutting part of a tool, as the blade of an ax. **3.** The metallic mouthpiece of a bridle. For illustration see HARNESS. **4.** Anything that controls or restrains. **5.** The part of a key that engages the bolt or tumblers of a lock. — *v.t.* **bit·ted, bit·ting 1.** To put a bit in the mouth of; train (a horse) to the bit. **2.** To curb; restrain. **3.** To make a bit on (a key). [OE *bite* a biting < *bītan* to bite]

bit[3] (bit) Past tense and alternative past participle of BITE.

bit[4] (bit) *n.* In information theory, a unit equal to the information content inherent in a choice between two equally probable alternative messages or symbols, as between a "yes" and a "no" or a dot and a dash: also called *binit.* Compare BINARY SYSTEM. [< *b(inary) (dig)it*]

BITS AND BRACE *a* Brace (or bit-stock). Bits: *b* Screwdriver, *c* Drill, *d* Ship auger, *e* Auger, *f* Expanding. *g* Chuck (cross-section).

bi·tar·trate (bī·tär′trāt) *n. Chem.* A salt containing the univalent tartaric acid radical; acid tartrate. [< BI- + TARTRATE]

bitch (bich) *n.* **1.** The female of the dog or other canine animal. **2.** *Slang* A malicious or promiscuous woman: an abusive term. — *v.i. Slang* To complain. — **to bitch up** *Slang* To botch. [< OE *bicce*]

bitch·y (bich′ē) *adj.* **bitch·i·er, bitch·i·est** *Slang* Bitchlike.

bite (bīt) *v.* **bit, bit·ten** or **bit, bit·ing** *v.t.* **1.** To seize, tear, or wound with the teeth. **2.** To cut or tear off with or as with the teeth: usually with *off:* He *bit* off his words. **3.** To puncture the skin of with a sting or fangs. **4.** To cut or pierce: The sword *bit* the bone. **5.** To cause to sting or smart. **6.** To eat into; corrode, as acid. **7.** To grip; take hold of: The anchor *bit* the ground. **8.** To cheat; deceive: usually passive. — *v.i.* **9.** To seize or cut into something with the teeth. **10.** To have the effect of biting, as mustard; sting. **11.** To take firm hold; grip. **12.** To take a bait, as fish. **13.** To be tricked. — **to bite off more than one can chew** To attempt something beyond one's capabilities. — *n.* **1.** The act of biting. **2.** A wound inflicted by biting. **3.** A painful sensation; smart; sting: a *bite* to his remarks. **4.** A morsel of food; mouthful. **5.** *Informal* A light meal; snack. **6.** The grip or hold taken by a tool or a piece of mechanism. [OE *bītan*] — **bit′a·ble** or **bite′a·ble** *adj.* — **bit′er** *n.*

Bi·thyn·i·a (bi·thin′ē·ə) An ancient country in NW Asia Minor.

bit·ing (bī′ting) *adj.* **1.** Sharp; stinging. **2.** Sarcastic; caustic. — **bit′ing·ly** *adv.* — **bit′ing·ness** *n.*

Bi·tolj (bē′tôly′) A city in southern Yugoslavia; pop. 52,000 (est. 1963). Also **Bi·tol** (bē′tôl). Turkish *Monastir.*

bit·stock (bit′stok′) *n.* A brace for a bit. For illustration see BIT[2].

bitt (bit) *Naut. n.* A post or vertical timber on a ship's deck, to which cables, etc., are made fast, usually in pairs. — *v.t.* To take a turn of (a cable) around a bitt or bitts. [? < ON *biti* beam]

bit·ten (bit′n) Past participle of BITE.

bit·ter (bit′ər) *adj.* **1.** Having an acrid, disagreeable taste, as quinine. **2.** Unpleasant to accept; distasteful: the *bitter* truth. **3.** Painful to body or mind; harsh; severe: *bitter* cold; a *bitter* loss. **4.** Feeling or showing intense animosity: a *bitter* enemy. **5.** Stinging; sharp: *bitter* words. — **Syn.** See SOUR. — **bitter pill to swallow** A consequence that is especially humiliating or hateful. — *n.* That which is bitter. — *v.t. & v.i.* To make or become bitter. [OE *biter* < *bītan* to bite] — **bit′ter·ly** *adv.* — **bit′ter·ness** *n.*

bitter apple The colocynth.

bitter end 1. *Naut.* The extreme end of a cable or rope, attached to the bitt. **2.** The last extremity, as defeat or death.

Bitter Lakes Two lakes in NE Egypt, joined and traversed by the Suez Canal.

bit·tern[1] (bit′ərn) *n.* Any of various wading birds related to the heron; especially, the **American bittern** (*Botaurus lentiginosus*), having brown and buff plumage, and the smaller **least bittern** (*Ixobrychus exilis*). [< OF *butor, ?* < L *butio, -onis* a bittern]

bit·tern[2] (bit′ərn) *n.* **1.** In salt manufacture, the bitter liquor remaining after crystallization from brine. **2.** A bitter mixture of quassia. [< BITTER]

bitter principle Any of numerous bitter substances found in plants and not yet chemically classified.

bit·ter·root (bit′ər·rōōt′, -rŏŏt′) *n.* **1.** An herb (*Lewisia rediviva*) with nutritious roots and pink or white flowers: the State flower of Montana. **2.** Any one of certain other North American plants, as the dogbane.

Bitterroot Range A range of the Rockies along the Idaho-

Montana border; highest peak, Garfield Mountain, 10,961 ft. Also **Bitter Root Range.**

bit·ters (bit'ərz) *n.pl.* A liquor, usually spirituous, prepared with an infusion of bitter herbs, etc., used as a stomachic and as an ingredient in some cocktails.

bitter·sweet (bit'ər·swēt') *n.* **1.** A shrubby or climbing plant (*Celastrus scandens*), having green flowers succeeded by orange pods that display a red aril. **2.** The bittersweet nightshade. — *adj.* **1.** Bitter and sweet. **2.** Pleasant and unpleasant.

bittersweet nightshade See under NIGHTSHADE.

bit·ter·weed (bit'ər·wēd') *n.* Any of various plants yielding a bitter principle, as the ragweed and sneezeweed.

bi·tu·men (bi·tōō'mən, -tyōō'-, bich'ŏŏ-mən) *n.* **1.** Any natural mixture of solid and semisolid hydrocarbons, as naphtha or asphalt: also called *jew's-pitch.* **2.** A brown paint made by mixing asphalt with a drying oil. [< L] — **bi·tu·mi·noid** (bi·tōō'mə·noid, -tyōō'-) *adj.*

bi·tu·mi·nize (bi·tōō'mə·nīz, -tyōō'-) *v.t.* **·nized, ·niz·ing** To render bituminous; treat with bitumen. — **bi·tu'mi·ni·za'tion** *n.*

bi·tu·mi·nous (bi·tōō'mə·nəs, -tyōō'-, bī-) *adj.* **1.** Of, pertaining to, or containing bitumen. **2.** Containing many volatile hydrocarbons, as shale. [< F *bitumineux*]

bituminous coal A mineral coal low in carbon content, yielding many volatile hydrocarbons and burning with a yellow, smoky flame: also called *soft coal.*

bi·va·lent (bī·vā'lənt, biv'ə-) *adj.* **1.** *Chem.* **a** Having a valence of two. **b** Having two valences. Also *divalent.* **2.** *Biol.* Composed of two chromosomes joined end to end. — *n. Biol.* A single group of paired, homologous chromosomes. [< BI- + L *valens, -entis,* ppr. of *valere* to have power] — **bi·va·lence** (bī·vā'ləns, biv'ə-), **bi·va'len·cy** (-vā'lən·sē) *n.*

bi·valve (bī'valv') *n.* **1.** *Zool.* A mollusk having a shell of two lateral valves hinged together, as the oyster or clam. **2.** *Bot.* A seed vessel that splits into two parts, as a pea pod. — *adj.* Having two valves or parts: also **bi'valved'**, **bi·val'vous** (bī·val'vəs), **bi·val·vu·lar** (bī·val'vyə·lər).

biv·ou·ac (biv'ŏŏ·ak, biv'wak) *n.* A temporary encampment, especially for soldiers in the field, usually without shelter. — *v.i.* **·acked, ·ack·ing** To encamp in a bivouac. [< F < G *beiwacht* guard]

bi·week·ly (bī·wēk'lē) *adj.* **1.** Occurring once every two weeks. **2.** Occurring twice a week; semiweekly. — *n.* A biweekly publication. — *adv.* **1.** Once in two weeks. **2.** Twice a week. ◆ See note under BIMONTHLY.

bi·year·ly (bī·yir'lē) *adj. & adv.* **1.** Occurring twice yearly. **2.** Biennial. — *adv.* Twice a year.

bi·zarre (bi·zär') *adj.* Singular or eccentric in style, manner, etc.; odd; fantastic; grotesque. [< F, ? ult. < Basque] — **bi·zarre'ly** *adv.* — **bi·zarre'ness** *n.*

Bi·zer·te (bi·zûr'tə, Fr. bē·zert') A port city in northern Tunisia, the northernmost city in Africa; pop. 46,681 (1956). Also **Bi·zer'ta.**

Bi·zet (bē·zā'), **Georges,** 1838–75, French composer: original name **Alexandre César Léopold Bizet.**

B.J. Bachelor of Journalism.

Björn·son (byœrn'sən), **Björn·stjer·ne,** 1832–1910, Norwegian poet, novelist, and dramatist.

bk. **1.** Bank. **2.** Block. **3.** Book.

Bk *Chem.* Berkelium.

bkg. Banking.

bkkpg. Bookkeeping.

bklr. *Printing* Black letter.

bks. **1.** Barracks. **2.** Books.

bkt. **1.** Basket(s). **2.** Bracket.

bl. **1.** Bale(s). **2.** Barrel(s). **3.** Black. **4.** Blue.

b.l. or **B/L** Bill of Lading.

B.L. Bachelor of Laws.

B.L.A. Bachelor of Liberal Arts.

blab (blab) *v.t. & v.i.* **blabbed, blab·bing** **1.** To reveal or disclose indiscreetly. **2.** To prattle. [< n.] — *n.* **1.** One who blabs. **2.** Idle chatter. [ME *blabbe* idle talker] — **blab'ber** *n.*

blab·ber·mouth (blab'ər·mouth') *n.* One who talks too much and can't be trusted to keep secrets.

black (blak) *adj.* **1.** Having no brightness or color; reflecting no light: opposed to *white.* **2.** Destitute of light; in total darkness. **3.** Gloomy; dismal; forbidding: a *black* future. **4.** Belonging to a racial group characterized by dark skin; especially, Negroid. **5.** Of, pertaining to, or controlled by black men: *black* power. **6.** Soiled; stained. **7.** Indicating disgrace or censure: a *black* mark. **8.** Angry; threatening: *black* looks. **9.** Evil; wicked; malignant: a *black* heart. **10.** Wearing black garments. **11.** *Informal* Confirmed; unchangeable, as in political views. **12.** Of coffee, without cream. — **Syn.** See DARK. — *n.* **1.** The absence or complete absorption of light; the darkest of all colors: opposed to *white.* **2.** Something black, as soot. **3.** A member of the so-called black race; a Negro. — **in the black** In the credit column of an account; prosperous; thriving: distinguished from *in the red.* — *v.t.* **1.** To make black; blacken. **2.** To put blacking on and polish (shoes). — *v.i.* **3.** To become black. — **to black out** **1.** To delete by scoring through.

2. To suffer a temporary loss of vision or consciousness. **3.** To extinguish or screen all lights, especially as a precaution in air raids. Abbr. (for adj. and n.) *bl., blk.* [OE *blæc* dark] — **black'ness** *n.*

Black (blak), **Hugo La Fayette,** 1886–1971, U.S. politician and jurist; associate justice of the Supreme Court 1937–71.

black Africa Those states or parts of Africa whose inhabitants mainly belong to the Negroid ethnic division of mankind; central Africa. — **black African**

black-and-blue (blak'ən·blōō') *adj.* Discolored: said of skin that has been bruised.

Black and Tan *Informal* A member of the Royal Irish Constabulary recruited to combat the Sinn Fein rebellion, so called from the color of the uniform.

Black-and-Tan terrier (blak'ən·tan') A Manchester terrier (which see).

black and white **1.** Writing or print. **2.** A sketch or picture in various shades of black and white.

black art Necromancy; magic.

black·ball (blak'bôl') *n.* **1.** A negative vote. **2.** Formerly, a black ball placed in a ballot box to indicate such a vote. — *v.t.* **1.** To vote against. **2.** To ostracize; exclude, as from a club. — **black'ball'er** *n.*

black bass Any of various related species of fresh-water game fishes (genus *Micropterus*) of the eastern United States and Canada, as the **large-mouthed bass** (*M. salmoides*), the **small-mouthed bass** (*M. dolomieui*), and the **spotted bass** (*M. punctulatus*).

black bear The common North American bear (*Euarctos americanus*) having fur that varies from glossy black to cinnamon brown: also called *brown bear.*

black belt **1.** A black sash worn by a judo or karate expert indicating he is of the highest rank in skill. **2.** *U.S.* Part of a State or area where the Negro population outnumbers the white. **3.** *U.S.* A section of certain States, especially of Alabama and Mississippi, characterized by rich black soil.

black·ber·ry (blak'ber'ē, -bər·ē) *n.* *pl.* **·ries** **1.** The black, edible fruit of certain shrubs (genus *Rubus*) of the rose family. **2.** Any of the plants producing it.

black bindweed **1.** A twining, perennial vine (*Tamus communis*) having long angular stems and a small red fruit. **2.** A herbaceous twining plant (*Polygonum convolvulus*) growing as a weed in the United States.

black·bird (blak'bûrd') *n.* **1.** A common European thrush (*Turdus merula*), the male of which is black with a yellow bill. **2.** One of various black or blackish North American birds (family *Icteridae*), as the **crow blackbird** (*Quiscalus quiscula*), **red-winged blackbird** (*Agelaius phoeniceus*), etc.

black·board (blak'bôrd', -bōrd') *n.* A large panel with a black or dark-colored surface for drawing and writing upon with chalk, usually as a visual aid in teaching.

black body *Physics* An ideal body that completely absorbs all radiant energy incident upon it.

black book A record of those who have been blacklisted. — **to be in one's black book** To be in disfavor.

black·boy (blak'boi') *n.* The grass tree (def. 1).

black buck The common Indian antelope (*Antilope cervicapra*), of a blackish brown color: also called *sasin.*

Black·burn (blak'bərn) A county borough in central Lancashire, England; pop. 106,114 (1961).

Blackburn, Mount A peak in the Wrangell Mountains, southern Alaska; 16,140 ft.

Black Canyon **1.** A gorge of the Colorado River, between Arizona and Nevada; site of Hoover Dam. **2.** A gorge of the Gunnison River in SW Colorado, a section of which is included in **Black Canyon of the Gunnison National Monument,** 21 sq. mi., established 1933.

black·cap (blak'kap') *n.* **1.** Any of several birds having a black crown, as the European warbler, chickadee, etc. **2.** The black raspberry, or its fruit: see under RASPBERRY.

black cherry See under CHERRY.

black·cock (blak'kok') *n.* The male of the heath grouse.

Black Country A highly industrialized region of England in Staffordshire, Warwickshire, and Worcestershire.

black·damp (blak'damp') *n. Mining* Carbon dioxide mixed with nitrogen, produced by mine fires and the explosion of firedamp: also called *chokedamp.*

Black Death An exceptionally virulent plague, epidemic in Asia and Europe during the 14th century: also called *plague.*

black diamond **1.** *pl.* Mineral coal. **2.** Carbonado or bort.

black disease *Vet.* An acute, infectious, generally fatal hepatic disease of sheep, caused by an anaerobic bacterium (*Clostridium novyi*) transmitted by liver flukes.

black·en (blak'ən) *v.* **·ened, ·en·ing** *v.t.* **1.** To make black or dark. **2.** To slander; defame. — *v.i.* **3.** To become black; darken. [ME *blaknen* < *blak* black] — **black'en·er** *n.*

Black·ett (blak'it), **P(atrick) M(aynard) S(tuart),** 1897–1974, English physicist.

black eye **1.** An eye with a black iris. **2.** An eye having the adjacent surface discolored by a blow or bruise. **3.** *Informal* A cause of discredit; blot. — **black'-eyed'** *adj.*

black-eyed pea The edible seed of the cowpea.

black-eyed Susan **1.** One of the coneflowers (*Rudbeckia* *hirta*), with black-centered yellow flowers: the State flower of Maryland: also called *yellow daisy.*   **2.** An acanthaceous vine (*Thunbergia alata*) with dark-centered white or yellow flowers: also called *bladder ketmia.*

black·face (blak′fās′) *n.* **1.** An entertainer with exaggerated Negro make-up, especially a minstrel comedian. **2.** The make-up worn by such an entertainer. **3.** *Printing* Boldface. — *adj.* **1.** Wearing or acted in blackface: a *blackface* show.   **2.** *Printing Boldface.*

black·fel·low (blak′fel′ō) *n.* An Australian aborigine.

black·fish (blak′fish′) *n.* *pl.* **·fish** or **·fish·es 1.** Any of various small, dark-colored, toothed whales (genus *Globicephala*). **2.** Any of various other dark-colored fishes, as the tautog. **3.** A food fish (*Dallia pectoralis*) of the Bering Sea. **4.** The black sea bass: see under SEA BASS.

black flag The pirate flag, having a white skull and crossbones on a black field; the Jolly Roger.

black·fly (blak′flī′) *n.* Any of certain small, dark, thick-bodied biting flies (family *Simuliidae*) having aquatic larvae, common in forested mountainous regions, as the buffalo gnat.

Black·foot (blak′foŏt′) *n.* *pl.* **·feet** (-fēt′) A member of any of the tribes of Algonquian North American Indians living in Alberta and Montana.

Black Forest A mountainous wooded region in SW West Germany; highest peak, Feldberg, 4,898 ft: German *Schwarzwald.*

Black Friar A Dominican friar, named for his black cloak.

black frost A frost severe enough to turn vegetation black.

black grouse The heath grouse (genus *Lyrurus*) of Europe and northern Asia.

black·guard (blag′ərd, -ärd) *n.* An unprincipled scoundrel; a rogue. — *v.t.* **1.** To revile; vilify. — *v.i.* **2.** To act like a blackguard. — *adj.* Of or like a blackguard; base; vile: also **black′guard·ly.** [< *black guard*, orig., the scullions and low menials of a great house or army; later applied to any base person] — **black′guard·ism** *n.*

black guillemot See under GUILLEMOT.

black·gum (blak′gum′) *n.* A species of tupelo (*Nyssa sylvatica*), with an ovoid, blue-black drupe and close-grained wood hard to split: also called *pepperidge, sour gum.*

Black Hand **1.** A society of anarchists in Spain, repressed in 1883. **2.** A secret organization in the United States, especially of Italians, for the purpose of vengeance or blackmail. Compare MAFIA.

black haw **1.** The black, oval drupe of certain species of *Viburnum.* **2.** The sheepberry.

Black Hawk, 1767–1838, American Indian chief; led the Fox and Sauk Indians against the United States, 1831–1832.

black·head (blak′hed′) *n.* **1.** Any of various birds having a black head, as the American scaup duck. **2.** *Vet.* An infectious, often fatal protozoan disease of turkeys and certain wildfowl, chiefly attacking the liver and intestines. **3.** A blackish plug of dried, fatty matter excreted by a skin follicle, especially on the face: also called *comedo.*

black·heart (blak′härt′) *n.* **1.** A variety of early black cherry. **2.** A plant disease in which the internal tissues of various trees and of the potato turn black.

black·heart·ed (blak′här′tid) *adj.* Evil; wicked.

Black Hills A mountainous region in SW South Dakota and NE Wyoming; highest point, Harney Peak, 7,242 ft.

black hole **1.** A prison cell, or a military punishment cell. **2.** *Astron.* A theoretical shrinking star so dense that light cannot escape its gravitational field.

Black Hole of Calcutta A small cell in which, allegedly, 146 British subjects were confined on June 20, 1756, of whom 123 died of asphyxia.

black horehound A fetid herb (*Ballota nigra*) of the mint family.

black·ing (blak′ing) *n.* A preparation used to give blackness or luster to shoes, stoves, etc.

black·ish (blak′ish) *adj.* Somewhat black.

black·jack (blak′jak′) *n.* **1.** A small bludgeon with a flexible handle. **2.** A pirate's black flag. **3.** A small oak (*Quercus marilandica*) of the SE United States having black bark. **4.** Twenty-one, a card game. **5.** A large drinking cup, formerly of leather tarred or waxed. **6.** Sphalerite or zinc blende. **7.** Caramel used to color soups, wines, etc. — *v.t.* **1.** To strike with a blackjack. **2.** To coerce by threat.

black knot A disease of plum and cherry trees, producing black knotlike excrescences on the branches, caused by a fungus (*Sphaeria morbosa*). **2.** The fungus.

black lead Graphite.

black·leg (blak′leg′) *n.* **1.** *Vet.* An acute, infectious, often fatal disease of cattle, caused by an anaerobic bacterium (*Clostridium chauvoei*) and characterized by swellings under the skin. **2.** A disease of cabbage and other cruciferous plants; also, a bacterial rot of potatoes. **3.** One who cheats in gambling; a sharper. **4.** *Brit. Informal* A strikebreaker.

black letter *Printing* A type face characterized by heavy black letters resembling those of early 𝕿𝖍𝖎𝖘 𝖑𝖎𝖓𝖊 𝖎𝖘 𝖎𝖓 𝖇𝖑𝖆𝖈𝖐 𝖑𝖊𝖙𝖙𝖊𝖗.

printed works: also called *gothic, Old English.* Abbr. *bklr.*

black·list (blak′list′) *n.* A list of persons or organizations under suspicion or censure, or refused approval or employment for any cause. — *v.t.* To place on a blacklist.

black·ly (blak′lē) *adv.* Darkly, gloomily, or threateningly.

black magic Witchcraft.

black·mail (blak′māl′) *n.* Extortion by threats of public exposure; also, that which is so extorted. — *v.t.* **1.** To levy blackmail upon. **2.** To force (to do something), as by threats: with *into.* [< BLACK + MAIL³] — **black′mail′er** *n.*

black man A person belonging to a racial group characterized by dark skin; especially, in the U.S., an Afro-American. **2.** A male member of the so-called black race.

Black Ma·ri·a (mə-rī′ə) *Informal* **1.** A prison van or police patrol wagon. **2.** A hearse.

black mark A mark of censure, failure, etc.

black market A market where goods are sold in violation of official prices, quotas, etc.

black mass See under MASS.

black match A fuse (def. 1).

black measles *Pathol.* A severe form of measles.

black medic An annual herb (*Medicago lupulina*) of the bean family, with yellow flowers and curved pods: also called *hop clover, nonesuch.*

Black Mountains The highest range of the Appalachians and a spur of the Blue Ridge Mountains in western North Carolina; highest point, Mt. Mitchell, 6,684 ft.

Black·mun (blak′mən). **Harry Andrew,** born 1908, U.S. jurist; associate justice of the Supreme Court 1970–.

Black Muslim A member of a sect (the **Nation of Islam**) of Negroes in the U.S. and some other countries, which follows the religious and ethical practices of Islam and rejects integration with the white race.

black nightshade See under NIGHTSHADE.

black·out (blak′out′) *n.* **1.** The extinguishing or screening of all lights, especially as a precaution against air raids. **2.** A momentary impairment or loss of vision and sometimes of consciousness, as that caused by being subjected to rapid changes in velocity. **3.** In the theater, the extinguishing of the stage lights. **4.** A loss of memory. **5.** A ban, as on news.

Black Panthers *U.S.* A faction of militant Negroes whose object is to secure by force rights and opportunities equal to those of whites — **Black Panther**

black pepper See under PEPPER.

black·poll (blak′pōl′) *n.* A North American wood warbler (*Dendroica striata*), the male of which has glossy black plumage on the top of the head.

Black·pool (blak′poōl′) A county borough, port, and resort in western Lancashire, England, on the Irish Sea; pop. 152,133 (1961).

black powder Gunpowder (which see).

Black Power *U.S.* A Negro movement whose purpose is to secure rights equal to those of whites through the influence of united Negro organizations and institutions.

Black Prince See EDWARD (Prince of Wales).

black race The Negroid ethnic division of mankind.

Black Rod **1.** *Brit.* An official of the House of Lords and the Order of the Garter, the **gentleman usher of the Black Rod,** who, carrying a black rod, attends the sovereign in the Upper House and summons the Commons to hear speeches from the throne. **2.** A similar functionary in British colonies and dominions.

black rot Leaf spot, a plant disease.

Black Sea A large inland sea between Europe and Asia, connected with the Aegean Sea by the Bosporus, the Sea of Marmara, and the Dardanelles; 159,000 sq. mi.: also *Euxine Sea.* Ancient *Pontus Euxinus.*

black sheep One regarded as a disgrace by his family or group.

Black Shirt **1.** A member of the Italian Fascist party: from the black shirts that were part of the uniform of its members. **2.** A member of the Nazi Schutzstaffel.

black·smith (blak′smith′) *n.* **1.** One who shoes horses. **2.** One who works iron on an anvil and using a forge, hammer, tongs, etc. [< *black* (metal) + SMITH]

black·snake (blak′snāk′) *n.* **1.** Any of various agile, non-venomous snakes of the eastern United States, having smooth, black scales; especially, the **black racer** (*Coluber constrictor*). **2.** A venomous Australian snake (*Pseudechis porphyriacus*) with blue-black scales. **3.** *U.S.* A heavy, pliant whip of braided leather or rawhide. Also **black snake.**

black spruce See under SPRUCE.

Black·stone (blak′stōn′, -stən), **Sir William,** 1723–80, English jurist.

black·tail (blak′tāl′) *n.* The mule deer.

black tea Tea produced from tea leaves that have been fermented before undergoing a heating process.

black·thorn (blak′thôrn′) *n.* **1.** A thorny European shrub (*Prunus spinosa*) of the rose family. **2.** The small, plumlike

astringent fruit of this plant. Also called *sloe*. **3.** A cane made from its wood. **4.** A hawthorn (*Crataegus calpodendron*) of North America.
black tie 1. A black bow tie. **2.** A tuxedo and its correct accessories.
black·top (blak′top′) *n.* **1.** Asphalt or a bituminous asphaltlike material, used to pave roads, etc. **2.** Any surface so paved.
black vomit 1. The dark, bloody matter vomited in the later stages of yellow fever: also *vomito*. **2.** Yellow fever.
black vulture A large vulture (*Coragyps atratus*) of North America, having black plumage and white wing tips.
black walnut See under WALNUT.
Black Watch A famous Highland regiment of the British Army, officially known as the Royal Highlanders: so called because of their somber tartan.
black·wa·ter fever (blak′wô′tər, -wot′ər) *Pathol.* A dangerous form of malaria characterized by the excretion of black or dark-red urine; malarial hematuria.
black·weed (blak′wēd′) *n.* The ragweed (which see).
Black·wells Island (blak′welz, -wəlz) Former name for WELFARE ISLAND.
black widow The venomous female of a North American spider (*Latrodectus mactans*): so called from its color and its practice of eating its mate.
black·wood (blak′wŏŏd′) *n.* The mangrove (def. 2).
blad·der (blad′ər) *n.* **1.** *Anat.* **a** A distensible membranous sac in the anterior part of the pelvic cavity, for the temporary retention of urine. **b** Some part or organ of analogous structure. ◆ Collateral adjective: *vesical*. **2.** *Bot.* An air vessel or an air cell in some seaweeds. **3.** A blister or pustule. **4.** Anything puffed out, empty, or unsubstantial. **5.** An inflatable object resembling a bladder: the *bladder* of a basketball. [OE *blædre*]
bladder campion A perennial herb (*Silene latifolia*) belonging to the pink family, and having the calyx much inflated: also called *cowbell, rattlebox*.
bladder ket·mi·a (ket′mē-ə) **1.** A European annual (*Hibiscus trionum*) of the mallow family, naturalized in America, with ephemeral, pale yellow flowers and a purple-veined, bladderlike calyx: also called *flower-of-an-hour*. **2.** The black-eyed Susan (def. 2). Also **bladder ket·mie** (ket′mē).
blad·der·nose (blad′ər-nōz′) *n.* The hooded seal.
blad·der·nut (blad′ər-nut′) *n.* **1.** Any plant of the genus *Staphylea* of the soapberry family, with large, inflated, three-lobed pods. **2.** A seed pod of one of these plants.
bladder worm *Zool.* The encysted larval stage of a tapeworm, as a cysticercus or hydatid.
blad·der·wort (blad′ər-wûrt′) *n.* Any aquatic herb of the genus *Utricularia*, usually having little bladders on the leaves, in which minute organisms are trapped for nutriment.
blad·der·wrack (blad′ər-rak′) *n.* Any rockweed of the genus *Fucus.* See FUCUS.
blad·der·y (blad′ər-ē) *adj.* **1.** Like a bladder. **2.** Covered with or having bladders or vesicles.
blade (blād) *n.* **1.** The flat, cutting part of any edged tool or weapon. **2.** The thin, flat part of an oar, plow, etc. **3.** The leaf of grasses or certain other plants. **4.** A sword. **5.** A dashing or reckless young man. **6.** *Phonet.* The upper surface of the tongue behind the tip and below the alveolar ridge. **7.** *Bot.* The broad, flat part of a leaf, petal, etc.; the lamina. **8.** *Anat.* The shoulder blade or scapula. [OE *blæd*]
blade·bone (blād′bōn′) *n.* The scapula.
blad·ed (blā′did) *adj.* Shaped like or having a blade.
blae (blā, blā) *adj. Scot.* Blackish blue; also, bleak.
Bla·go·vesh·chensk (blä′gə-vyesh′chensk) A city in the SE R.S.F.S.R., on the Amur river; pop. 94,000 (1959).
blah (blä) *n. U.S. Slang* Nonsense.
blain (blān) *n. Pathol.* A pustule; blister. [OE *blegen*]
Blaine (blān), **James Gillespie**, 1830–93, U.S. statesman.
Blake (blāk), **Robert**, 1599–1657, British admiral. — **William**, 1757–1827, English poet, artist, and mystic.
blam·a·ble (blā′mə-bəl) *adj.* Deserving blame; culpable. Also **blame·a·ble.** — **blam′a·ble·ness** *n.* — **blam′a·bly** *adv.*
blame (blām) *v.t.* **blamed, blam·ing 1.** To hold responsible; accuse: I *blame* you for the error. **2.** To find fault with; reproach. **3.** To place the responsibility for (an action or error) on a person: They *blamed* the crash on the pilot. — **to be to blame** To be at fault. — *n.* **1.** Expression of censure; reproof. **2.** Responsibility for something wrong; culpability. [< OF *blasmer* < LL *blasphemare* to revile, reproach < Gk. *blasphēmeein*. Doublet of BLASPHEME.]
— **Syn.** (verb) **2.** *Blame, criticize, censure, reprove, rebuke,* and *chide* all mean to find fault with a person's actions. *Blame* and *criticize* are the most general of these words, with *blame* emphasizing the feeling of disapproval and *criticize* stressing the actual finding of fault or passing of judgment on another. *Censure* is a strong word, and implies openly expressed, and sometimes formal, criticism: to *censure* a public official for misconduct. *Reprove* implies concern for another, and a desire to correct his faults, while *rebuke* is to *reprove* harshly, abruptly, or angrily. *Chide* suggests a scolding or impatient manner of reproving. — **Ant. 2.** praise.
blamed (blāmd) *adj. & adv. U.S. Dial.* Damned: a *blamed* fool; *blamed* hot: a euphemism.

blame·ful (blām′fəl) *adj.* **1.** Deserving of blame. **2.** Imputing blame. — **blame′ful·ly** *adv.* — **blame′ful·ness** *n.*
blame·less (blām′lis) *adj.* Innocent; guiltless. — **blame′less·ly** *adv.* — **blame′less·ness** *n.*
blame·wor·thy (blām′wûr′thē) *adj.* Deserving of blame. — **blame′wor′thi·ness** *n.*
Blanc (blängk, blängk), **Cape** A cape in Tunisia, the northernmost point of Africa.
Blanc (bläṅ), **Louis**, 1811–82, French socialist and historian: full name **Jean Joseph Charles Louis Blanc.**
Blanc, Mont See MONT BLANC.
Blan·ca Peak (blang′kə) Highest peak in the Sangre de Cristo Mountains, southern Colorado; 14,363 ft.
blanc fixe (bläṅ fēks′) Fine-grained barium sulfate, used as a base in certain pigments, and in water colors, where it retains its white color. [< F]
blanch (blanch, blänch) *v.t.* **1.** To remove the color from; bleach. **2.** To cause to turn pale, as from fear. **3.** To remove the skin of (almonds, etc.) by scalding. **4.** To whiten, as meat, by scalding. **5.** In horticulture, to bleach by removing from light, as celery. **6.** *Metall.* To whiten or brighten (metals), as with acids or by coating with tin. — *v.i.* **7.** To turn or become white or pale. — **Syn.** See WHITEN. [< F *blanchir* < *blanc* white] — **blanch′er** *n.*
blanc·mange (blə·mänzh′) *n.* A whitish, jellylike preparation of milk, eggs, sugar, cornstarch, flavoring, etc., used chiefly for desserts. [< OF *blanc-manger*, lit., white food]
bland (bland) *adj.* **1.** Gentle and soothing in manner; suave: a *bland* smile. **2.** Not stimulating or irritating; mild: a *bland* diet. **3.** Of a soft and balmy quality: *bland* weather. **4.** Lacking individual character; flavorless; dull. [< L *blandus* mild] — **bland′ly** *adv.* — **bland′ness** *n.*
blan·dish (blan′dish) *v.t.* To wheedle; flatter; cajole. [< OF *blandiss*-, stem of *blandir* to flatter < L *blandiri* < *blandus* mild, gentle] — **blan′dish·er** *n.*
blan·dish·ment (blan′dish-mənt) *n.* **1.** Flattering speech or action. **2.** Something that attracts; allurement.
blank (blangk) *adj.* **1.** Free from writing or print. **2.** Not completed or filled out, as a check. **3.** Showing no expression or interest; vacant: a *blank* stare. **4.** Lacking variety or interest: a *blank* prospect. **5.** Disconcerted; bewildered. **6.** Utter; complete: *blank* dismay. **7.** Empty or void; also, fruitless. **8.** Having no opening; filled in: a *blank* arch. **9.** Having no finishing cuts, grooves, teeth, or the like: a *blank* file. — *n.* **1.** An empty space; void. **2.** A blank space in a printed document, to be filled in. **3.** A paper or document with such spaces. **4.** A lottery ticket that has drawn no prize. **5.** A blank cartridge. **6.** A partially prepared piece, as of metal, ready for forming into a finished object, as a key. **7.** A dash used in place of an omission, usually of a profane or obscene word. **8.** The central white spot of a target; bull's-eye. **9.** Something aimed at; target. — *v.t.* **1.** To delete; invalidate: often with *out*. **2.** In games, to prevent (an opponent) from scoring. **3.** To punch or stamp from flat stock, as with a die: often with *out*. [< OF *blanc* white, ult. < Gmc.] — **blank′ly** *adv.* — **blank′ness** *n.*
blank·book (blangk′bŏŏk′) *n.* A book with blank leaves, for accounts, memoranda, etc.
blank cartridge A cartridge loaded only with powder.
blank check *Informal* **1.** A check bearing a signature but no specified amount. **2.** Unlimited authority or freedom; carte blanche.
blank endorsement An endorsement on a negotiable instrument that names no payee, making it payable to the bearer: also called *endorsement in blank.*
blan·ket (blang′kit) *n.* **1.** A large piece of woolen or other soft, warm fabric, used as a covering in bed, as a robe, etc. **2.** Anything that covers, conceals, or protects: a *blanket* of fog. — *adj.* Covering a wide range of conditions, items, or the like: a *blanket* indictment. — *v.t.* **1.** To cover with or as with a blanket. **2.** To cover or apply to uniformly: The new law *blankets* the nation. **3.** To obscure or suppress; interfere with. **4.** *Naut.* To deprive (a sailboat) of wind by passing close on the windward side. **5.** To toss in a blanket as sport or punishment. [< OF *blankete*, dim. of *blanc* white; orig. a white or undyed woolen cloth]
blan·ket flow·er (blang′kit-flou′ər) *n.* The gaillardia.
blank verse Verse without rhyme; especially, iambic pentameter verse, used in English epic and dramatic poetry.
blare (blâr) *v.t. & v.i.* **blared, blar·ing 1.** To sound loudly, as a trumpet. **2.** To exclaim noisily. — *n.* **1.** A loud brazen sound. **2.** Brightness or glare, as of color. [Prob. imit.]
blar·ney (blär′nē) *n.* Wheedling flattery; cajolery. — *v.t. & v.i.* To flatter, cajole, or wheedle. [< BLARNEY STONE]
Blarney Stone A stone in a 15th-century castle in Blarney, Ireland, that reputedly endows one who kisses it with skill in flattery.
Blas·co-I·bá·ñez- (bläs′kō-ē-vä′nyäth), **Vicente**, 1867–1928, Spanish novelist.
bla·sé (blä-zā′, blä′zā) *adj.* Wearied or bored, as from over-indulgence in pleasure. [< F, pp. of *blaser* to satiate]
blas·pheme (blas-fēm′) *v.* **-phemed, -phem·ing** *v.t.* **1.** To speak in an impious manner of (God or sacred things). **2.** To speak ill of; malign. — *v.i.* **3.** To utter blasphemy. [<

OF *blasfemer* < LL *blasphemare* < Gk. *blasphēmeein* to revile < *blasphēmos* evil-speaking. Doublet of BLAME.] — **blas·phem′er** *n.*

blas·phe·mous (blas′fə·məs) *adj.* Expressing blasphemy; irreverent; profane. — **blas′phe·mous·ly** *adv.* — **blas′phe·mous·ness** *n.*

blas·phe·my (blas′fə·mē) *n. pl.* **·mies** **1.** Impious or profane speaking of God, or of sacred persons or things. **2.** *Theol.* The act of claiming the attributes of God. **3.** In early Judaism, any irreverent act toward God, as cursing his name; later, the saying of the ineffable name of God. **4.** Any irreverent act or utterance. — **Syn.** See PROFANITY. [< OF *blasfemie* < LL *blasphemia* < Gk. *blasphēmia*]

blast (blast, bläst) *v.t.* **1.** To rend in pieces by or as by explosion. **2.** To cause to wither or shrivel; destroy. — *v.i.* **3.** *Telecom.* To distort sound as the result of overloading: said of a microphone or loudspeaker. — **to blast off** *Aerospace* To begin an ascent by means of rocket or jet propulsion. — *n.* **1.** A strong wind; gust. **2.** A loud, sudden sound, as of a trumpet. **3.** A rush of air, as from the mouth. **4.** A strong, artificial current of air, steam, etc., especially one to help combustion, as in a blast furnace. **5.** An explosion of dynamite, etc., or its effect; also, the charge set off. **6.** A blight. — **at full blast** At capacity operation or maximum speed. [OE *blǣst.* Akin to BLOW[1].] — **blast′er** *n.*

-blast *combining form Biol.* Growth; sprout: *hypoblast.* [< Gk. *blastos* sprout]

blast·ed (blas′tid, bläs′-) *adj.* **1.** Blighted; withered or destroyed; blighted. **2.** Damned: a euphemism.

blas·te·ma (blas·tē′mə) *n. pl.* **·ma·ta** (-mə·tə) *Biol.* Embryonic protoplasm; the formative material of an ovum. [< Gk. *blastēma* offspring]

blast furnace *Metall.* A smelting furnace in which the fire is intensified by an air blast.

blas·tie (blas′tē, bläs′-) *n. Scot.* A dwarf.

blasto- *combining form Biol.* Growth; sprout: *blastoderm.* Also, before vowels, **blast-**. [< Gk. *blastos* sprout]

blas·to·cele (blas′tə·sēl) *n. Biol.* The cavity of a blastula: also called *segmentation cavity.* Also **blas′to·coele.** [< BLASTO- + -CELE[2]]

blas·to·cyst (blas′tə·sist) *n. Biol.* The germinal vesicle (def. 1). [< BLASTO- + CYST]

blas·to·derm (blas′tə·dûrm) *n. Biol.* The delicate membrane formed by segmentation of the blastomeres, especially around the eggs of most vertebrates. [< BLASTO- + -DERM] — **blas·to·der′mic** *adj.*

blas·to·disc (blas′tə·disk) *n. Biol.* A germinal disc (def. 2).

blast·off (blast′ôf′, -of′, bläst′-) *n. Aerospace* The series of events immediately before and after a rocket leaves its launching pad; also the moment of leaving.

blas·to·gen·e·sis (blas′tə·jen′ə·sis) *n. Biol.* **1.** The theory that inherited characters are transmitted by germ plasm. Compare PANGENESIS. **2.** Reproduction by budding. [< BLASTO- + GENESIS] — **blas′to·gen′ic** *adj.*

blas·to·mere (blas′tə·mir) *n. Biol.* Any cell formed during the cleavage of the fertilized ovum. [< BLASTO- + -MERE] — **blas′to·mer′ic** (-mer′ik) *adj.*

blas·to·pore (blas′tə·pôr, -pōr) *n. Biol.* The exterior opening of the primitive intestine. [< BLASTO- + PORE[2] opening] — **blas′to·por′ic** (-pôr′ik, -por′ik) *adj.*

blas·to·sphere (blas′tə·sfir) *n. Biol.* **1.** The small vesicle appearing on the blastoderm of the mammalian egg. **2.** A blastula. [< BLASTO- + SPHERE]

blas·tu·la (blas′chōō·lə) *n. pl.* **·lae** (-lē) *Biol* The stage of the embryo just preceding the formation of the gastrula; a hollow sphere of one layer of blastomeres enclosing a blastocele or segmentation cavity: also called *blastosphere.* [< NL < Gk. *blastos* sprout] — **blas′tu·lar** *adj.*

blat (blat) *v.* **blat·ted, blat·ting** *v.t.* **1.** *Informal* To blurt out. — *v.i.* **2.** To bleat, as a sheep. [Var. of BLEAT]

bla·tant (blā′tənt) *adj.* **1.** Offensively loud or noisy; clamorous. **2.** Obvious; obtrusive: *blatant* stupidity. **3.** Bellowing or bleating: said of animals. [Coined by Edmund Spenser. Cf. L *blatire* to babble; ME *blait* to bleat.] — **bla′tan·cy** *n.* — **bla′tant·ly** *adv.*

blath·er (blath′ər) *v.t. & v.i.* To speak or utter foolishly; babble. — *n.* Foolish talk; nonsense. Also spelled *blether.* [< ON *blathra* to talk stupidly < *blathr* nonsense]

blath·er·skite (blath′ər·skīt) *n.* **1.** A blustering, talkative person. **2.** Foolish talk. **3.** The ruddy duck. [< BLATHER + SKATE[3]]

blau·bok (blou′bok) *n. pl.* **·bok** or **·boks** An extinct South African antelope (*Hippotragus leucophaeus*) with bluish hair. [< Afrikaans *blauwbok,* lit., blue buck]

Bla·vat·sky (blə·vät′skē), **Helena Petrovna,** 1831–91, Russian theosophist: called **Madame Blavatsky.**

blaw (blô) *v.t. & v.i. Scot. & Brit. Dial.* To blow.

blaze[1] (blāz) *v.* **blazed, blaz·ing** *v.i.* **1.** To burn brightly. **2.** To burn as with emotion: to *blaze* with anger. **3.** To shine; be resplendent. — *v.t.* **4.** *Rare* To cause to flame or shine brightly. — **to blaze away** **1.** To keep on shooting.

2. To proceed vigorously with anything. — *n.* **1.** A vivid glowing flame; fire. **2.** Brightness or brilliance; effulgence; glow. **3.** Sudden activity; outburst, as of anger. **4.** *pl. Slang* Hell. — **Syn.** See FIRE. [OE *blæse*]

blaze[2] (blāz) *v.t.* **blazed, blaz·ing** **1.** To mark (a tree) by chipping off a piece of bark. **2.** To indicate (a trail) by marking trees in this way. — *n.* **1.** A white spot on the face of a horse, etc. **2.** A mark chipped on a tree to indicate a trail. [Akin to ON *blesi* white spot on a horse's face]

blaz·er (blā′zər) *n.* **1.** A lightweight, often striped, jacket for informal wear. **2.** A dish with a small heating apparatus under it. [< BLAZE[1]]

blazing star **1.** A smooth herb (*Chamaelirium luteum*) of the lily family, with wandlike racemes of white flowers: also called *fairy wand.* **2.** One of various perennial herbs (genus *Liatris*) of the composite family, especially *L. squarrosa.*

bla·zon (blā′zən) *v.t.* **1.** To inscribe or adorn, as with names or symbols. **2.** To describe or depict (coats of arms) in technical detail. **3.** To proclaim; publish. — *n.* **1.** A coat of arms; armorial bearing. **2.** A technical description of armorial bearings. **3.** Ostentatious display. [< OF *blason* coat of arms, shield] — **bla′zon·er** *n.* — **bla′zon·ment** *n.*

bla·zon·ry (blā′zən·rē) *n.* **1.** The description or depiction of armorial bearings. **2.** A heraldic device; coat of arms. **3.** A brilliant display; show.

bld. *Printing* Boldface.

bldg. Building.

-ble See -ABLE.

B.L.E. Brotherhood of Locomotive Engineers.

bleach (blēch) *v.t. & v.i.* To make or become colorless or white; whiten. — **Syn.** See WHITEN. — *n.* **1.** The act of bleaching. **2.** The degree of bleaching obtained. **3.** A fluid or powder used as a bleaching agent. [OE *blǣcean*]

bleach·er (blē′chər) *n.* **1.** One who or that which bleaches. **2.** *Usually pl. U.S.* An unroofed outdoor seat or grandstand for spectators.

bleach·er·y (blē′chər·ē) *n. pl.* **·er·ies** A place where bleaching is done.

bleaching powder A powder used for bleaching, as chloride of lime.

bleak[1] (blēk) *adj.* **1.** Exposed to wind and weather; bare; barren. **2.** Cold; cutting. **3.** Cheerless; dreary. [? < ON *bleikr* pale] — **bleak′ly** *adv.* — **bleak′ness** *n.*

bleak[2] (blēk) *n. pl.* **bleak** or **bleaks** A small European cyprinoid fish (genus *Alburnus*), having scales lined with a silvery pigment used in making artificial pearls. [< ON *bleikja*]

blear (blir) *v.t.* **1.** To dim (the eyes) with or as with tears. **2.** To blur or make dim, as an image. — *adj.* Bleary. — *n. Rare* That which blears, or the condition of being bleared. [ME *blere.* Akin to LG *bleer-oged* blear-eyed.]

blear-eyed (blir′īd′) *adj.* **1.** Having eyes bleared by tears, old age, etc. **2.** Dull of perception. Also **bleary-eyed.**

blear·y (blir′ē) *adj.* **·i·er, ·i·est** **1.** Made dim by or as by tears, as the eyes. **2.** Blurred; dim; indistinct. — **blear′i·ly** *adv.* — **blear′i·ness** *n.*

bleat (blēt) *v.i.* **1.** To utter the characteristic cry of a sheep, goat, or calf. **2.** To speak or complain with a similar sound. — *v.t.* **3.** To utter with a bleat. **4.** To babble; prate. — *n.* The cry of a sheep, goat, or calf; also, any similar sound. [OE *blǣtan*] — **bleat′er** *n.*

bleb (bleb) *n.* **1.** *Pathol.* A bulla. **2.** An air bubble. [ME] — **bleb′by** *adj.*

bleed (blēd) *v.* **bled, bleed·ing** *v.i.* **1.** To lose or shed blood. **2.** To suffer wounds or die: to *bleed* for one's country. **3.** To feel grief, sympathy, or anguish. **4.** To exude sap or other fluid. **5.** To run, as dyes in wet cloth. **6.** *Printing* To extend to or beyond the edge of a page, as an illustration. — *v.t.* **7.** To draw blood from; leech. **8.** To exude, as sap, blood, etc. **9.** To empty of liquid or gaseous matter. **10.** *Informal* To obtain large amounts of money from, as by extortion. **11.** *Printing* **a** To print (an illustration, etc.) so that it will bleed. **b** To trim (a page or plate) so as to cut into the printed or engraved matter. — *n. Printing* An illustration or part of a page that bleeds. — *adj. Printing* Printed or trimmed so as to bleed: a *bleed* page. [OE *blēdan*]

bleed·er (blē′dər) *n.* **1.** One who draws blood for remedial purposes. **2.** A hemophiliac.

bleeding heart Any of various plants (genus *Dicentra*) having racemes of pink, drooping, heart-shaped flowers; especially, an ornamental garden herb (*D. spectabilis*) native to China.

blel·lum (blel′əm) *n. Scot.* A noisy talker.

blem·ish (blem′ish) *v.t.* To mar the perfection of; sully. — *n.* **1.** A disfiguring defect, especially of the skin. **2.** A moral fault or stain. [< OF *blemiss-,* stem of *blemir* to make livid < *blesme* pale, wan] — **blem′ish·er** *n.*

— **Syn.** (noun) **Blemish,** *blot, stain, flaw,* and *defect* are all imperfections. *Blemish, blot,* and *stain* are superficial, but a *blemish* may be structural, while

BLEEDING HEART (1 to 3 feet high)

blot or *stain* suggests a mere surface discoloration. A *flaw* is a structural fault within a body, especially one arising from lack of cohesion of the parts or material. A *defect* is an error or a lack of something needed for completion.

blench[1] (blench) *v.i.* **1.** To shrink back; flinch. **2.** *Obs.* To turn aside. [OE *blencan* to deceive] — **blench'er** *n*.

blench[2] (blench) *v.t. & v.i.* To make or become pale; blanch. [Var. of BLANCH[1]]

blend (blend) *v.* **blend·ed** or *less commonly,* **blent, blend·ing** *v.t.* **1.** To mingle and combine so as to obscure or harmonize the varying components: to *blend* modern and medieval architecture. **2.** To mix so as to obtain a uniform product of a desired quality, taste, color, or consistency: to *blend* paints, whiskies, etc. — *v.i.* **3.** To mix; intermingle. **4.** To pass or shade imperceptibly into each other, as colors. **5.** To harmonize; suit one another. — *n.* **1.** The act or result of mixing; mixture. **2.** *Ling.* A word formed by combining parts of two distinct words of generally similar meaning, as *brunch* from *breakfast* and *lunch:* also called *portmanteau word, telescope word.* [Prob. < ON *blanda* to mix]

blende (blend) *n. Mineral.* **1.** Sphalerite. **2.** One of a number of rather bright minerals combining sulfur with a metallic element. [< G *blendendes erz* deceptive ore]

blended whisky *U.S.* Whisky of at least 80 proof that contains at least 20 per cent by volume of 100 proof straight whisky, in combination with other whisky or neutral spirits.

blend·er (blen'dər) *n.* **1.** One who or that which blends. **2.** A mechanical device used to produce a uniform consistency or homogeneous mixture.

Blen·heim (blen'əm) A village in western Bavaria, West Germany; scene of Marlborough's and Eugene of Savoy's victory (1704) in the War of the Spanish Succession: German *Blindheim.*

Blenheim spaniel A variety of spaniel with white and reddish markings, developed at Blenheim Park, Oxfordshire, England.

blen·ny (blen'ē) *n. pl.* **·nies** Any of various small marine fish typical of a family (*Blenniidae*) having an elongated body and the pelvic fins placed close together near the throat. [< L *blennius* < Gk. *blennos* slime]

bleph·a·ri·tis (blef'ə·rī'tis) *n. Pathol.* Inflammation of the eyelids.

blepharo- *combining form Anat. & Pathol.* Eyelid. Also, before vowels, **blephar-**. [< Gk. *blepharon* eyelid]

Blé·riot (blā·ryō'), Louis, 1872–1936, French aviator and inventor.

bles·bok (bles'bok) *n. pl.* **·bok** or **·boks** A large antelope (*Damaliscus albifrons*) of South Africa, having a white blaze on its face, related to the bontebok. Also **bles'buck** (-buk). [< Afrikaans]

bless (bles) *v.t.* **blessed** or **blest, bless·ing** **1.** To consecrate; make holy by religious rite. **2.** To honor and exalt; glorify. **3.** To make the sign of the cross over, as for sanctification or protection. **4.** To invoke God's favor upon (a person or thing). **5.** To bestow happiness or prosperity upon; make happy. **6.** To endow, as with a gift: She was *blessed* with a beautiful face. **7.** To guard; protect: used as an exclamation: *Bless* me! [OE *blēdsian* to consecrate (with blood) < *blōd* blood] — **bless'er** *n*

bless·ed (bles'id, blest) *adj.* **1.** Made holy by a religious rite; consecrated: *blessed* oils. **2.** Worthy of worship or adoration. **3.** Enjoying the happiness of heaven; beatified: a *blessed* martyr. **4.** Blissful; happy. **5.** Causing happiness or bliss: a *blessed* vision. **6.** Cursed; damned: a euphemistic or intensive use: not a *blessed* cent. Also spelled *blest.* — **Syn.** See HOLY. — **the Blessed** In the Roman Catholic Church, the title and designation granted to a deceased person beatified by an act of the Pope. — **bless'ed·ly** *adv.*

blessed event (bles'id) *Informal* The birth of a baby.

bless·ed·ness (bles'id·nis) *n.* The state of being blessed; felicity. — **Syn.** See HAPPINESS. — **single blessedness** *Informal* The unmarried state.

Bless·ed Sacrament (bles'id) In the Roman Catholic Church, the consecrated elements in the Mass, especially the Host.

Blessed Virgin The Virgin Mary.

bless·ing (bles'ing) *n.* **1.** An invocation or declaration of divine favor; benediction; grace. **2.** The form of words used for this. **3.** The bestowal of divine favor. **4.** That which makes happy or prosperous; boon; gift. **5.** Grateful adoration; worship. **6.** A cursing or scolding: a euphemism.

blest (blest) Alternative past participle of BLESS. — *adj.* Blessed.

blet (blet) *n.* Internal decay in overripe fruit. [< F *blet* overripe]

bleth·er (bleth'ər) *n. & v.* Blather.

blew (bloō) Past tense of BLOW.

B.L.F.E. Brotherhood of Locomotive Firemen and Enginemen.

Bligh (blī), **William,** 1754–1817, British admiral.

blight (blīt) *n.* **1.** Any of a number of destructive plant diseases, as mildew, rust, smut, etc. **2.** Anything causing such a disease. **3.** Anything that withers hopes, destroys prospects, or impairs growth. **4.** The state of being blighted.

— *v.t.* **1.** To cause to decay; blast. **2.** To ruin; frustrate. — *v.i.* **3.** To suffer blight. [Origin unknown]

bligh·ty (blī'tē) *n. Often cap. Brit. Slang* **1.** England; home. **2.** A wound causing one's being sent home. [Alter. of Hindustani *Bilāyati* foreign country]

blimp (blimp) *n. Informal* A nonrigid dirigible. [< Type *B-Limp,* a kind of British dirigible]

blind (blīnd) *adj.* **1.** Unable to see. **2.** Lacking in perception or judgment. **3.** Acting or done without intelligent control; random. **4.** Unreasoning; heedless: *blind* prejudice. **5.** Hidden; concealed: a *blind* ditch. **6.** Closed at one end: a *blind* alley. **7.** Having no opening or outlet: a *blind* wall. **8.** Insensible. **9.** *Informal* Drunk. **10.** Difficult to understand; unintelligible; also, illegible: *blind* writing. **11.** Performed without the aid of visual reference: *blind* flying. **12.** Of or for blind persons. **13.** Not producing buds or fruit, as a shoot. — *n.* **1.** Something that obstructs vision or shuts off light; especially, a window shade. **2.** A hiding place, as for a hunter; ambush. **3.** Something intended to deceive; subterfuge; decoy. — **Syn.** See ARTIFICE. — *adv.* **1.** Blindly. **2.** Without the aid of visual reference: to fly *blind.* — *v.t.* **1.** To make blind. **2.** To dazzle. **3.** To deprive of judgment or discernment. **4.** To darken; obscure. **5.** To outshine; eclipse. [OE] — **blind'ly** *adv.* — **blind'ness** *n.*

blind·age (blīn'dij) *n. Mil.* A screen or other structure for protection from enemy fire.

blind alley **1.** An alley, road, etc., open at one end only. **2.** Any search, occupation, or the like, in which progress is blocked.

blind date *Informal* A date with a person of the opposite sex whom one has not previously met, usually arranged by a third person.

blind·er (blīn'dər) *n.* **1.** One who or that which blinds. **2.** *U.S.* A flap on the side of a horse's bridle, serving to obstruct sideways vision, also called *blinker.* For illustration see HARNESS.

blind·fish (blīnd'fish') *n.* Any of various fish lacking functional eyes and living in subterranean streams; especially, a sightless fish (*Amblyopsis spelaeus*) found in the Mammoth Cave of Kentucky: also called *cavefish.*

blind·fold (blīnd'fōld') *v.t.* **1.** To cover or bandage the eyes of. **2.** To hoodwink; mislead. — *n.* A bandage over the eyes. — *adj.* **1.** Having the eyes bandaged. **2.** Reckless; rash. [ME *blindfellen* < *blind* blind + *fellen* to strike; infl. in spelling by *fold* (to crease)]

blind gut The cecum.

Blind·heim (blint'hīm) The German name for BLENHEIM.

blind hinge A hinge for a shutter, etc., constructed so that the piece hinged thereby closes by its own weight when not held open. For illustration see HINGE.

blind·ing (blīn'ding) *adj.* **1.** Causing blindness. **2.** Dazzling. — **blind'ing·ly** *adv.*

blindman's buff A game in which one player is blindfolded and must catch and identify another player.

blind pig *U.S. Slang* A place where intoxicants are illegally sold. Also **blind tiger.**

blind spot **1.** *Anat.* A small area on the retina of the eye that is insensible to light because of the entrance of the fibers of the optic nerve. **2.** A subject or a phase of thought in which one is ignorant, or incapable of objective thought. **3.** An area where radio reception is poor.

blind staggers Staggers (def. 1).

blind·sto·ry (blīnd'stôr'ē, -stō'rē) *n. pl.* **·ries** *Archit.* A story without windows.

blind·worm (blīnd'wurm') *n.* A small, limbless, snakelike lizard (*Anguis fragilis*) of Europe and Africa, having small but keen eyes: also called *slowworm.*

blink (blingk) *v.i.* **1.** To wink rapidly. **2.** To look with half-closed eyes, as in sunlight; squint. **3.** To twinkle; glimmer; also, to flash on and off. **4.** To look indifferently or evasively: with *at.* — *v.t.* **5.** To cause to wink. **6.** To shut the eyes to; evade: to *blink* matters. **7.** To send (a message) by blinker light. — *n.* **1.** A blinking; wink. **2.** A gleam; sparkle. **3.** Iceblink (which see). **4.** A glance or glimpse. [< Du. *blinken;* ult. origin uncertain]

blink·ard (blingk'ərd) *n.* **1.** One who habitually blinks, as from poor vision. **2.** A slow-witted person; dullard.

blink·er (blingk'ər) *n.* **1.** A light that blinks, as in warning or for sending messages: also **blinker light.** **2.** *Slang* An eye. **3.** *pl.* Goggles. **4.** A blinder for a horse.

blint·ze (blint'sə) *n.* A thin pancake folded about a filling of cottage cheese, potato, fruit, etc., and usually eaten with sour cream or jam. Also **blintz.** [< Yiddish]

blip (blip) *n. Telecom.* One of the luminous signals recorded on a radarscope. [? Var. of *flip*]

bliss (blis) *n.* **1.** Gladness; joy. **2.** Heavenly joy; supreme happiness. **3.** A cause of delight or happiness. — **Syn.** See HAPPINESS. [OE *blīths* < *blīthe* joyous] — **bliss'ful** *adj.* — **bliss'ful·ly** *adv.* — **bliss'ful·ness** *n.*

Bliss (blis), **Tasker Howard,** 1853–1930, U.S. general.

blis·ter (blis'tər) *n.* **1.** A thin vesicle, especially on the skin, containing watery matter, as from rubbing, a burn, etc. **2.** A similar vesicle on a plant, on steel, or on a painted surface. **3.** Any substance used for blistering. **4.** *Naval* A bulge below the waterline of a warship to protect it from torpedoes. **5.** *Aeron.* A domelike, often transparent projection on certain aircraft, used for observation or to mount a gun. — *v.t.* **1.** To produce a blister or blisters upon. **2.** To rebuke severely. — *v.i.* **3.** To become blistered. [< OF *blestre* < ON *blāstr* swelling] — **blis'ter·y** *adj.*

blister beetle **1.** A beetle (family *Meloidae*), yielding a blistering substance; especially, the Spanish fly. **2.** A long, slender beetle (genus *Epicauta*), widely distributed in the United States, especially *E. pennsylvanicus*, very destructive to the potato. For illustration see INSECTS (injurious).

blister gas *Mil.* A gaseous vesicant used in warfare.

blister rust A serious disease of pine trees, especially the white-pine blister rust, caused by a fungus (genus *Cronartium*) that raises blisters on the bark.

B.Lit. or **B.Litt.** Bachelor of Letters (Literature) (L *Baccalaureus Litterarum*).

blithe (blīth, blĭth) *adj.* **1.** Characterized by cheerfulness or mirth; joyous; gay. **2.** Casual or indifferent in manner; airy. [OE] — **blithe'ly** *adv.* — **blithe'ness** *n.*

blith·er·ing (blĭth'ər·ĭng) *adj.* Blathering; jabbering: a *blithering* idiot. [< *blither*, dial. var. of BLATHER]

blithe·some (blīth'səm, blĭth'-) *adj.* Showing or imparting gladness. — **blithe'some·ly** *adv.* — **blithe'some·ness** *n.*

blitz (blĭts) *Informal n.* A sudden attack; blitzkrieg. — *v.t.* **1.** To subject to a blitzkrieg. **2.** In football, to red-dog.

blitz·krieg (blĭts'krēg) *n.* **1.** *Mil.* A swift, sudden attack by tanks, aircraft, etc.; also, warfare so waged. **2.** Any sudden attack or assault. [< G *blitz* lightning + *krieg* war]

Blix·en (blĭk'sən), **Baroness Karen** See DINESEN.

bliz·zard (blĭz'ərd) *n.* **1.** A severe and heavy snowstorm. **2.** A high, cold wind accompanied by blinding snow. [< dial. E *blizzer* sudden blow, flash of lightning]

blk. **1.** Black. **2.** Block. **3.** Bulk.

B.LL. Bachelor of Laws (L *Baccalaureus Legum*).

bloat¹ (blōt) *v.t.* **1.** To cause to swell, as with fluid or gas. **2.** To puff up; make proud or vain. — *v.i.* **3.** To swell; become puffed up. — *n. Vet.* An accumulation of gas in the rumen or intestinal tract of an animal brought on by the fermentation of green forage. [ME *blout*, ? < ON *blautr* soft, soaked]

bloat² (blōt) *v.t.* To cure, as herring, by half-drying in smoke. — *adj.* Smoke-cured: a *bloat* herring. [ME *blote*, ? < ON *blautr* soft, soaked]

bloat·er (blō'tər) *n.* **1.** A smoked herring. **2.** A whitefish (*Coregonus hoyi*) of the Great Lakes of North America.

blob (blŏb) *n.* **1.** A soft, globular mass; a drop, as of viscous liquid. **2.** A daub or spot, as of color. — *v.t.* **blobbed, blob·bing** To mark with ink or color; blot. [Origin unknown]

bloc (blŏk) *n.* A group, as of politicians, nations, etc., combined to foster special interests. — **Syn.** See FACTION. [< F]

Bloch (blŏk, *Ger.* blôkh), **Ernest,** 1880–1959, U.S. composer born in Switzerland.

block¹ (blŏk) *n.* **1.** A solid piece of wood, metal, etc., usually with one or more flat surfaces. **2.** Such a piece on which cutting or chopping is done. **3.** A wooden stand or platform on which persons are beheaded. **4.** A support or form on which something is shaped or displayed: a hat *block*. **5.** A stand from which articles are sold at auction. **6.** A piece of wood, metal, etc., used as a support. **7.** A cubelike piece of wood, plastic, etc., used by children for building. **8.** A set or section, as of tickets, shares of stock, etc., handled as a unit. **9.** A section of railroad, often of several miles, controlled by signals. See BLOCK SYSTEM. **10.** *U.S.* An area or group of buildings bounded, usually on four sides, by streets; also, one side of such an area. **11.** *U.S. & Canadian* An office building. **12.** *Canadian* A group of townships in the midst of unsurveyed land. **13.** A pulley, or set of pulleys, in a frame or shell with a hook or the like at one end. **14.** A woodblock. **15.** *Austral.* An area of farming land. **16.** In philately, a group of four or more attached stamps not in a strip. *Abbr. bk, blk.* — *v.t.* **1.** To shape into blocks. **2.** To shape, mold, or stamp with a block, as a hat. **3.** To secure or strengthen with blocks. — **to block out** To plan broadly without details. — **to block up** To raise and secure on blocks. [< F *bloc,* ult. < Gmc.] — **block'er** *n.*

block² (blŏk) *n.* **1.** An obstacle or hindrance. **2.** The act of blocking or obstructing, or the state or condition of being obstructed. **3.** In sports, interference with an opponent's actions. **4.** *Med. & Pathol.* **a** An obstruction, as of a nerve or blood vessel. **b** Anesthesia of a specific region: saddle *block.* **5.** *Psychol.* The involuntary prevention of thought or action

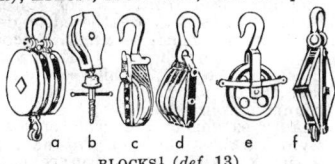

BLOCKS¹ *(def. 13)*
a Tackle. b Dock, with attaching screw. c Snatch. d Triple-sheave steel. e Gin. f Square-cheeked.

in an existing objective situation, traceable neither to physical sources nor to forgetfulness. — *v.t.* **1.** To stop the progress of or prevent passage through; obstruct. **2.** In sports, to hinder the movements of (an opposing player); also, to stop (a ball), as with the body. **3.** *Med. & Pathol.* To stop (a nerve) from functioning, as with an anesthetic. — *v.i.* **4.** To obstruct an opponent's actions. — **to block out** To obscure from view. — **to block up** To fill (an area or space) so as to prevent movement into or through. [< MF *bloquer* to obstruct < *bloc* block, ult. < Gmc.] — **block'er** *n.* — **Syn.** (verb) **1.** impede, stop, thwart. Compare HINDER, OBSTRUCT. — **Ant.** promote, further.

block·ade (blo·kād') *n.* **1.** The closing by hostile ships or forces of a coast, city, etc., to traffic or communication. **2.** The ships or forces used for this. **3.** An obstruction to action or passage. — **to run the blockade** To elude a blockade. — *v.t.* **·ad·ed, ·ad·ing** To subject to a blockade; obstruct. [< BLOCK²] — **block·ad'er** *n.*

blockade runner A vessel or person engaged in passing through a blockade.

block·age (blŏk'ij) *n.* **1.** The act of blocking or stopping. **2.** An obstruction: a *blockage* in traffic.

block and tackle A set of pulley blocks and ropes for pulling or hoisting.

block·bust·er (blŏk'bus'tər) *n. Informal* **1.** An aerial bomb of two or more tons, capable of demolishing a large area. **2.** Someone or something impressive or of devastating effect. **3.** One who engages in block-busting.

block·bust·ing (blŏk'bust'ĭng) *n. U.S.* The practice of inducing home owners to sell hurriedly by arousing their fear that a member of a racial minority is to be their neighbor and thus lower the value of their houses.

block·head (blŏk'hed') *n.* A stupid person; dolt.

block·house (blŏk'hous') *n.* **1.** A fortification, formerly of logs and heavy timbers, now of concrete or other very resistant material, having loopholes from which to fire. **2.** *U.S.* A house made of hewn logs set square.

block·ish (blŏk'ĭsh) *adj.* Like a block; stupid; dull. Also **block'like'.** — **block'ish·ly** *adv.* — **block'ish·ness** *n.*

Block Island An island off the south coast of Rhode Island, a part of the State.

BLOCKHOUSE

block lava Lava in the form of angular blocks.

block letter **1.** Printing type cut from wood. **2.** A style of letters without serifs, resembling letters cut from wood. — **block-let·ter** (blŏk'let'ər) *adj.*

block·line (blŏk'līn') *n.* A line passing through one or more pulleys.

block plane A small carpenter's plane for trimming wood across the grain.

block printing Printing from engraved wooden blocks or from linoleum backed with wood.

block system A system for safety and control in which a railroad track is divided into sections or blocks of suitable length, the movement of trains through each block being controlled by an automatic signal (**block signal**).

block tin **1.** Tin cast in ingots. **2.** Pure tin.

block·y (blŏk'ē) *adj.* **block·i·er, block·i·est** **1.** Unequally shaded, as if printed in blocks. **2.** Short and stout; stocky.

Bloem·fon·tein (blōōm'fon·tān) A city in the central Republic of South Africa, capital of the Orange Free State; pop. 146,200 (est. 1967).

Blois (blwä) A city in north central France, on the Loire; pop. about 28,000.

bloke (blōk) *n. Brit. Slang* A fellow; guy.

blond (blŏnd) *adj.* **1.** Having fair hair with light eyes and skin. **2.** Flaxen or golden, as hair. — *n.* **1.** A blond person. **2.** Blonde (def. 2). [< F, yellow-haired < Med.L *blondus*, prob. < Gmc.]

blonde (blŏnd) *adj.* Blond: feminine form. — *n.* **1.** A blonde woman or girl. **2.** A variety of silk lace, originally the color of blond hair, now usually white or black.

blood (blŭd) *n.* **1.** *Physiol.* The fluid circulating through the vascular system of animals, consisting essentially of semisolid, usually red, corpuscles suspended in plasma, that delivers oxygen and nutrients to the cells and tissues, distributes internal secretions, guards against infection, and helps to maintain homeostasis of the organism. ◆ Collateral adjective: *hemal.* **2.** A liquid or juice resembling this in some way, as the sap of plants. **3.** The shedding of blood; slaughter; murder: Only *blood* will avenge this deed. **4.** Disposition of mind; temperament; mood: hot *blood.* **5.** The principle of life; vitality; lifeblood. **6.** Descent from a common ancestor; kinship: joined by *blood.* **7.** Family; descent; especially, noble or royal family. **8.** Racial or national extraction: of French *blood.* **9.** A dashing young man; gallant; also, a rake. **10.** Descent from purebred stock; also, a purebred animal. **11.** *U.S. Slang* Everything that one can obtain: Do you want *blood?* **12.** Personnel: chiefly in the phrase **young blood.** — **in cold blood** **1.** Deliberately;

without passion. **2.** Cruelly; without mercy. **— to make one's blood boil** (or **run cold**) To make one angry (or frightened). **—** *v.t.* To give a first sight or experience of blood to, as hunting dogs or troops. **—** *adj.* Of superior breed; purebred: a *blood* mare. [OE *blōd*]

blood bank A place where blood is stored, either in liquid form or as dried plasma, for use in transfusion; also, a reserve of such blood.

blood bath Wanton killing; a massacre.

blood count *Med.* A measure of the number and proportion of red and white cells in a given sample of blood.

blood·cur·dling (blud'kûrd'ling) *adj.* Terrifying or horrifying.

blood·ed (blud'id) *adj.* **1.** Having blood or temper of a specified character: *cold-blooded*. **2.** Bred from pure stock; thoroughbred.

blood group *Physiol.* One of the classes into which members of a species may be divided on the basis of specific differences in the composition of the blood: also called *blood type*. **—**

blood·guilt·y (blud'gil'tē) *adj.* Guilty of bloodshed. **— blood'guilt', blood'guilt·i·ness** *n.*

blood heat *Physiol.* The normal temperature of human blood, about 98.6° F. or 37° C.

blood·hound (blud'hound') *n.* **1.** A large, smooth-coated hound remarkable for its keen sense of smell, and often used to track fugitives: also called *sleuthhound*. **2.** *Informal* Any persistent pursuer; a sleuth.

blood·less (blud'lis) *adj.* **1.** Devoid of blood; pale. **2.** Without bloodshed. **3.** Lacking vigor; listless. **4.** Coldhearted. **— blood'less·ly** *adv.* **— blood'less·ness** *n.* **— Syn. 1.** anemic, wan, pallid, ashen.

blood·let·ting (blud'let'ing) *n.* **1.** Bleeding for a therapeutic purpose. **2.** Bloodshed.

blood·line (blud'līn') *n.* Strain or pedigree, as of livestock.

blood·mo·bile (blud'mə·bēl') *n.* A motor vehicle equipped for obtaining and carrying donations of blood.

blood money **1.** *Informal* Money obtained at the cost of another's life, welfare, etc. **2.** Money paid to a hired murderer. **3.** Compensation paid to the kin of a murdered man: see WERGELD.

blood plasma *Physiol.* The liquid part of the blood, without its cellular components.

blood platelet *Physiol.* One of the minute circular or oval bodies found in the blood of higher vertebrates, essential to the coagulating process; a thrombocyte.

blood poisoning *Pathol.* Deterioration of the blood caused by the introduction of pathogenic substances, usually bacterial, into the blood stream; septicemia: also called *toxemia*.

blood pressure *Physiol.* The pressure of the blood on the walls of the arteries, varying with the force of the heart action, resilience of the arteries and blood vessels, amount and viscosity of blood, etc.

blood pudding An article of food composed of swine's blood, coagulated by cooking, intermingled with particles of fat and usually stuffed into skins. Also **blood sausage.**

blood-red (blud'red') *adj.* Of the red color of blood.

blood relation One who is related by birth; kinsman. Also **blood relative. — blood relationship**

blood·root (blud'rōōt', -rŏŏt') *n.* **1.** A perennial North American herb (*Sanguinaria canadensis*), having a fleshy rootstalk with deep red sap: also called *puccoon*. **2.** Tormentil.

blood·shed (blud'shed') *n.* The shedding of blood; slaughter; carnage. Also **blood'shed'ding. — blood'shed'der** *n.*

blood·shot (blud'shot') *adj.* Suffused or shot with blood; red and inflamed or irritated: said of the eye.

blood·stain (blud'stān') *n.* A spot produced by blood. **—** *v.t.* To stain with blood. **— blood'stained'** *adj.*

blood·stone (blud'stōn') *n.* A stone of green chalcedony flecked with particles of red jasper, often cut as a gem: also called *heliotrope*.

blood stream The stream of blood coursing through a living body.

blood·suck·er (blud'suk'ər) *n.* **1.** An animal that sucks blood, as a leech. **2.** *Informal* One who extorts or sponges. **— blood'suck'ing** *adj.*

blood test *Med.* Any of various procedures for determining the blood group, condition of blood, etc.

blood·thirst·y (blud'thûrs'tē) *adj.* Thirsting for blood; murderous; cruel. **— blood'thirst'i·ly** *adv.* **— blood'thirst'-i·ness** *n.*

blood transfusion *Med.* The transfer of blood from one person or animal into the vascular system of another.

blood type Blood group.

blood vessel Any tubular canal, as an artery, vein, or capillary, through which the blood circulates.

blood·wood (blud'wŏŏd') *n.* **1.** Haematoxylon. **2.** Any of various other woods characterized by a red or reddish heartwood, especially the **Jamaica ironwood** (*Laplacea haematoxylon*), valued as timber, and the **bloodwood cacique** (*Brosimum caloxylon*), used by the Panama Indians as a medicine.

blood·worm (blud'wûrm') *n.* Any of various annelid worms (genera *Polycirrus* and *Enoplobranchus*), having bright red blood, found in mud and shallow water.

blood·wort (blud'wûrt') *n.* **1.** Any of various plants

(family *Haemodoraceae*) characterized by red roots. **2.** A species of the burnet (*Sanguisorba minor*).

blood·y (blud'ē) *adj.* **blood·i·er, blood·i·est** **1.** Stained with blood. **2.** Of, like, containing, or consisting of blood. **3.** Involving bloodshed. **4.** Delighting in bloodshed; bloodthirsty. **5.** Of the color of blood; deep red. **6.** *Brit. Slang.* Damned: a vulgarism. **—** *v.t.* **blood·ied, blood·y·ing** To stain or color with blood. **—** *adv. Brit. Slang* Very: a vulgarism. [OE *blōdig*] **— blood'i·ly** *adv.* **— blood'i·ness** *n.* **— Syn.** (adj.) *Bloody, gory,* and *sanguinary* refer to an excess of blood. *Bloody* suggests fresh blood; *gory,* clotted blood: a *blot* riot, a *gory* ax. *Sanguinary* is a more literary word, and is often used figuratively: a *sanguinary* temper, *sanguinary* laws.

Bloody Mary **1.** See MARY I. **2.** *U.S.* A drink made of vodka and tomato juice: also **bloody Mary.**

bloom¹ (blōōm) *n.* **1.** The flower of a plant; blossom. **2.** The state of being in flower: lilacs in *bloom.* **3.** A growing or flourishing condition; freshness: the *bloom* of youth. **4.** The rosy tint of the cheeks or skin; glow. **5.** *Bot.* The powdery, waxy substance on certain fruits, as the plum or grape, and on certain leaves, as of the cabbage. **6.** Any of various earthy minerals found as a powdery incrustation on certain ores. **—** *v.i.* **1.** To bear flowers; blossom. **2.** To glow with health and beauty; flourish. **3.** To glow with a warm color. **—** *v.t.* **4.** To bring into bloom; cause to flourish. **5.** To give a bloom to. [< ON *blōm* flower, blossom. Akin to BLOSSOM.] **— bloom'y** *adj.*

bloom² (blōōm) *n.* **1.** *Metall.* A mass of malleable iron from which the slag has been forced by a hammer or roller. **2.** A lump of melted glass. [OE *blōma* lump of metal]

bloom·er (blōō'mər) *n.* A costume consisting of loose trousers drawn close at the ankles, worn under a short skirt. [after Mrs. Amelia *Bloomer*, 1818–94, U.S. feminist]

bloom·ers (blōō'mərz) *n.pl.* **1.** Loose, wide trousers gathered at the knee, worn by women as a gymnasium costume. **2.** A woman's undergarment resembling these.

bloom·er·y (blōō'mər·ē) *n.* *pl.* **·er·ies** *Metall.* A forge or furnace for making malleable iron directly from the ore.

Bloom·field (blōōm'fēld) A city in NE New Jersey; pop. 52,029.

Bloom·field (blōōm'fēld), **Leonard,** 1887–1949, U.S. linguist.

bloom·ing (blōō'ming) *adj.* **1.** In flower; blossoming. **2.** Thriving; flourishing. **3.** *Slang* Thorough; utter: a *blooming* fool. **— bloom'ing·ly** *adv.* **— bloom'ing·ness** *n.*

Bloom·ing·ton (blōō'ming·tən) **1.** A city in central Illinois; pop. 39,992. **2.** A city in south central Indiana; pop. 42,890. **3.** A city in eastern Minnesota, near Minneapolis; pop. 81,970.

bloop·er (blōō'pər) *n.* **1.** In baseball slang: **a** A weakly hit ball. **b** A shallow, looping curve ball. **2.** *U.S. Slang* A blunder; boner. [Imit.]

blos·som (blos'əm) *n.* **1.** A flower, especially one of a plant yielding edible fruit. **2.** The state or period of flowering; bloom. **3.** *Geol.* A weathered or decomposed outcrop of a coal or mineral bed. **—** *v.i.* **1.** To come into blossom; bloom. **2.** To prosper; thrive. [OE *blōstm.* Akin to BLOOM.] **— blos'som·less** *adj.* **— blos'som·y** *adj.*

blot¹ (blot) *n.* **1.** A spot or stain, as of ink. **2.** A stain on reputation or character; blemish. **3.** A detraction from beauty, excellence, etc.: a *blot* on the city. **4.** An erasure. **— Syn.** See BLEMISH. **—** *v.* **blot·ted, blot·ting** *v.t.* **1.** To spot, as with ink; stain. **2.** To disgrace; sully. **3.** To mark over or obliterate; as writing: often with *out.* **4.** To obscure; darken: usually with *out.* **5.** To dry, as with blotting paper. **6.** To paint roughly; daub. **—** *v.i.* **7.** To spread in a blot or blots, as ink. **8.** To become blotted; stain. **9.** To absorb: This paper *blots* well. [ME *blotte*; origin uncertain]

blot² (blot) *n.* **1.** In backgammon, an exposed man liable to be forfeited. **2.** A weak spot. [Origin uncertain]

blotch (bloch) *n.* **1.** A spot or blot. **2.** An eruption on the skin. **—** *v.t.* **1.** To mark or cover with blotches. **—** *v.i.* **2.** To become blotched. [Blend of BLOT¹ and BOTCH²] **— blotch'i·ness** *n.* **— blotch'y** *adj.*

blot·ter (blot'ər) *n.* **1.** A sheet or pad of blotting paper. **2.** The daily record of arrests in a police station.

blotting paper Unsized paper for absorbing excess ink.

blouse (blous, blouz) *n.* **1.** A woman's loose garment extending from the neck to the waist or just below, and worn tucked into the skirt or outside. **2.** A loose, knee-length shirt or frock, usually belted at the waist, worn chiefly by European workmen. **3.** The service coat of the U.S. Army uniform. **—** *v.t. & v.i.* **bloused** (bloust, blouzd), **blous·ing** To drape or hang loosely or fully. [< F; ult. origin uncertain] **— blouse'like'** *adj.*

blow¹ (blō) *v.* **blew, blown, blow·ing** *v.i.* **1.** To be in motion: said of wind or air. **2.** To move in a current of air; be carried by the wind. **3.** To emit a current or jet of air, steam, etc., as from the mouth. **4.** To produce sound by blowing or being blown, as a trumpet. **5.** To pant; gasp for breath. **6.** To spout air and water preparatory to taking breath, as a whale. **7.** To fail or become useless, as a fuse, tire, etc.: often with *out.* **8.** *Informal* To talk boastfully; brag. **9.** *U.S. Slang* To depart; go. **—** *v.t.* **10.** To drive or impel by a current of air. **11.** To direct a current of air upon, as from the mouth. **12.** To sound by blowing into, as a bugle. **13.** To sound (a signal): to *blow* taps. **14.** To emit, as air or smoke, from the mouth. **15.** To clear by forcing air into or through. **16.** To put out of breath, as a horse. **17.** To form by inflating a material: to *blow* bubbles. **18.** To break, shatter, or destroy by explosion: usually with an adverb, as *up, down,* etc. **19.** *Informal* To melt (a fuse). **20.** To lay eggs in (meat): said of flies. **21.** *Rare* To spread abroad by report. **22.** *Slang* To damn: a euphemism: *Blow* me if I don't! ◆ In this sense the nonstandard *blowed* is commonly employed as the past participle, as in the phrase *I'll be blowed.* **23.** *U.S. Slang* To spend (money) lavishly; also, to treat or entertain. **24.** *U.S. Slang* To depart from; leave. **— to blow a fuse** *Informal* To lose self-control; become enraged. **— to blow hot and cold** *Informal* To vacillate; be uncertain. **— to blow off 1.** To let off, as steam from a boiler. **2.** *Slang* To speak in anger. **— to blow out 1.** To extinguish by blowing. **2.** To burst, as a tire. **3.** To become less intense; subside. **4.** To melt, as a fuse. **5.** To clean or clear by blowing: We *blow out* the dirt with air. **— to blow over 1.** To pass, as a storm; subside. **2.** To pass without bad result. **— to blow up 1.** To inflate. **2.** To make an enlargement of (a photograph). **3.** To explode. **4.** *Informal* To lose one's temper. **5.** To arise; become intense, as a storm. **— n. 1.** A blowing, as of wind or of a wind instrument; blast. **2.** A storm or gale. **3.** *Slang* Boasting; a boast. **4.** *Metall.* A single blast of the Bessemer converter, or the quantity of metal acted on at one time. **5.** *Mining* The violent inrush of gas from or into a coal seam; also, the collapse of a mine roof. [OE *blāwan.* Akin to BLAST.]

blow² (blō) *n.* **1.** A sudden stroke dealt with the fist, a weapon, etc. **2.** A sudden, disastrous, shocking occurrence; calamity. **3.** A sudden or hostile act; assault. **— at a** (or **one**) **blow** By a single stroke or action. **— to come to blows** To start fighting. [ME *blaw*]
— Syn. 1. *Blow, slap, punch, cuff,* and *thump* all describe the forceful impact of one object against another. A *blow* may be with the hand or a weapon. A *slap* is delivered with the open hand; a *punch,* with the fist. A *cuff* is a sidelong *blow* with the hand. A *thump* is a heavy, resounding *blow.* Compare BEAT. **2.** See MISFORTUNE.

blow³ (blō) *Archaic & Poetic v.* **blew, blown, blow·ing** *v.i.* **1.** To bloom; blossom. **— v.t. 2.** To cause to bloom. **3.** To produce, as flowers. **— n. 1.** The state of flowering. **2.** A display, as of blossoms. [OE *blōwan* to blossom]

blow·back (blō′bak′) *n.* The escape to the rear of a gun of gases formed by discharge of the projectile.

blow·by (blō′bī′) *n. pl.* **·bys** (-bīz′) **1.** The exhaust fumes from the crankcase of a car, truck, etc. **2.** A device on the car, etc., to reduce such fumes.

blow·er (blō′ər) *n.* **1.** One who or that which blows. **2.** A device for forcing a draft of air through a building, furnace, machinery, etc. **3.** *Slang* A boaster.

blow·fish (blō′fish′) *n.* A globefish (which see).

blow·fly (blō′flī′) *n. pl.* **·flies** Any of several blue or green flies (family *Calliphoridae*), whose larvae live in carrion or in living flesh: also called *bluebottle.*

blow·gun (blō′gun′) *n.* A long tube through which a missile, as a dart, may be blown by the breath.

blow·hard (blō′härd′) *n. U.S. Slang* A braggart.

blow·hole (blō′hōl′) *n.* **1.** *Zool.* The nasal openings in the heads of certain whales or other cetaceans. **2.** A vent for gas and bad air, as in mines. **3.** *Metall.* A defect in a metal casting due to an air bubble caught during solidification. **4.** A hole in the ice to which seals, etc., come to breathe.

blown¹ (blōn) Past participle of BLOW¹. **— adj. 1.** Out of breath, as from overexertion. **2.** Inflated; swollen, especially with gas. **3.** Made with a blowtube, blowpipe, etc.: *blown* glass. **4.** Flyblown (which see).

blown² (blōn) Past participle of BLOW³. **— adj.** In full bloom.

blow·off (blō′ôf′, -of′) *n.* **1.** The expelling of water, vapor, etc. **2.** An apparatus for this. **3.** *Slang* A boaster.

blow·out (blō′out′) *n.* **1.** A bursting, as of a pneumatic tire, or the hole so made. **2.** The explosive melting of a fuse. **3.** *Slang* An elaborate meal or party; also, a rowdy party. **4.** A flameout (which see).

blow·pipe (blō′pīp′) *n.* **1.** A tube for blowing air or gas through a flame to direct and intensify its heat. **2.** *Med.* A tubelike instrument for cleaning or examining a body cavity. **3.** A blowtube (def. 1). **4.** A blowgun.

blow·torch (blō′tôrch′) *n.* An apparatus for vaporizing a combustible fluid under pressure and expelling it from a nozzle as a long, intensely hot flame, used for soldering, etc.

BLOWTORCH

blow·tube (blō′tōōb′, -tyōōb′) *n.* **1.** A tube used for blowing molten glass into the desired shape. **2.** A blowgun. **3.** A blowpipe (def. 1).

blow·up (blō′up′) *n.* **1.** An explosion. **2.** *Informal* A loss of self-control; outburst; also, a fight; quarrel. **3.** An enlargement, as of a photograph.

blow·y (blō′ē) *adj.* **blow·i·er, blow·i·est** Windy.

blowz·y (blou′zē) *adj.* **blowz·i·er, blowz·i·est 1.** Disheveled; slovenly. **2.** Fat and red-faced. Also **blowzed** (blouzd). [< earlier *blowse* a fat, ruddy woman; origin uncertain]

bls. 1. Bales. **2.** Barrels.

BLS Bureau of Labor Statistics.

B.L.S. Bachelor of Library Science.

blub·ber (blub′ər) *v.i.* **1.** To weep and sob noisily. **— v.t. 2.** To utter with sobs. **3.** To wet or disfigure with weeping. **— n. 1.** *Zool.* The layer of fat beneath the skin of a whale or other cetacean, used as a source of oil. **2.** The act of blubbering; weeping. **— adj.** Swollen; protruding: *blubber* lips. [ME *blubren;* imit.] **— blub′ber·er** *n.* **— blub′ber·ing·ly** *adv.* **— blub′ber·y** *adj.*

blu·cher (blōō′chər, -kər) *n.* **1.** A half boot; high shoe. **2.** A shoe in which there is no front seam, the upper meeting above in two projecting flaps. [after G. L. von *Blücher*]

Blü·cher (blōō′chər, -kər; *Ger.* blü′khər), **Gebhard Leberecht von,** 1742–1819, Prussian field marshal commanding the Prussian army at Waterloo.

bludg·eon (bluj′ən) *n.* A short club, commonly loaded at one end, used as a weapon. **— v.t. 1.** To strike with or as with a bludgeon. **2.** To coerce; bully. [Origin unknown]

blue (blōō) *adj.* **blu·er, blu·est 1.** Having the color of the clear sky. **2.** Of a gray or purplish color; livid, as the skin from contusion or cold. **3.** Depressed in spirits; melancholy. **4.** Dismal; dreary: a *blue* day. **5.** Puritanical; strict: *blue* laws. **6.** Learned; pedantic: said of women. Compare BLUESTOCKING. **7.** Suggestive of demons and the fires of hell: The air was *blue* with curses. **8.** Denoting venous blood that shows through the skin. **9.** *Slang* Obscene. **— once in a blue moon** Very seldom; only rarely. **— n. 1.** The color of the clear sky, between green and violet in the spectrum; azure. **2.** Any pigment or dye used to impart a blue color. **3.** Bluing. **4.** *Sometimes cap.* One who wears a blue uniform, as a soldier in the Union army in the American Civil War; also, such soldiers collectively. **5.** A small butterfly of the family *Lycaenidae.* **6.** A bluestocking. **— out of the blue** At an unexpected time and from an unsuspected source. **— the blue 1.** The sky. **2.** The sea. **— v.t. blued, blu·ing 1.** To make blue. **2.** To treat with bluing. Abbr. (for adj. and n.) *bl.* [< OF *bleu,* ult. < Gmc.] **— blue′ly** *adv.* **— blue′ness** *n.*

blue baby An infant born with cyanosis resulting from a congenital heart lesion or from defective lungs.

blue·ball (blōō′bôl′) *n.* A European herb (*Succisa pratensis*), allied to the scabious, whose roots were formerly used in medicine.

Blue·beard (blōō′bird′) In folklore, a man who married and then murdered six women in succession. **— n.** A wife-slayer: also **blue′beard′.**

blue·bell (blōō′bel′) *n.* Any one of various plants that bear blue, bell-shaped flowers, as the grape hyacinth, the Virginia cowslip, the wood hyacinth, or the harebell.

blue·ber·ry (blōō′ber′ē, -bər-ē) *n. pl.* **·ries 1.** A many-seeded, edible, blue or black American berry of the genus *Vaccinium.* **2.** The plant that bears it.

blue·bill (blōō′bil′) *n.* A duck, the scaup.

blue·bird (blōō′bûrd′) *n.* A small American passerine bird (genus *Sialia*), with predominantly blue plumage, especially the **eastern bluebird** (*S. sialis*) common in North America.

blue blindness Tritanopia.

blue blood 1. Aristocratic blood or descent. **2.** One of aristocratic family: also **blue-blood** (blōō′blud′). **— blue′-blood′ed** *adj.* **— blue′blood′ed·ness** *n.*

blue-bon·net (blōō′bon′it) *n.* **1.** The cornflower. **2.** An annual leguminous herb (*Lupinus subcarnosus*) with blue flowers: the State flower of Texas. **3.** A blue, woolen cap worn by the Scots; also, a Scot.

blue book 1. *U.S.* **a** A register of persons employed by the U.S. government. **b** *Informal* A register of socially prominent people. **c** A booklet with blue paper covers, used for college examinations; also, an examination. **2.** *Brit.* A governmental publication bound in blue covers. Also **blue-book** (blōō′bŏŏk′).

blue-bot·tle (blōō′bot′l) *n.* **1.** A blowfly. **2.** Any of various flowers, wild or cultivated, with tubular, usually blue florets. **3.** The cornflower.

blue bream See under BREAM¹.

blue cheese A type of cheese resembling Roquefort, usually made from cow's milk.

blue chip In finance, the stock of a well-known company with a good sustained record of dividends, earnings, etc. Also **blue-chip stock** (blōō′chip′). **2.** A gambling chip of the highest value.

blue·coat (blōō′kōt′) *n.* A person wearing a blue uniform, as a policeman. **— blue′-coat′ed** *adj.*

blue cohosh See under COHOSH.

blue-col·lar (blōō′kol′ər) *adj.* Designating workers, jobs, attitudes, etc., associated with skilled and unskilled manual labor: distinguished from *white-collar*.

blue·curls (bloo′kûrlz′) *n.* **1.** Any herb of the genus *Trichostema*, of the mint family, resembling pennyroyal. **2.** The selfheal (def. 1). Also **blue curls**.

blue devils **1.** Despondency. **2.** Delirium tremens.

blue-eyed grass (bloo′īd′) Any of a genus (*Sisyrinchium*) of delicate grasslike plants of the iris family, with blue flowers.

Blue·field (bloo′fēld′) A city in southern West Virginia; pop. 19,256.

Blue·fields (bloo′fēldz′) A port city in SE Nicaragua; pop. 18,844 (est. 1958).

blue·fish (bloo′fish′) *n. pl.* **·fish** or **·fish·es** **1.** A voracious food fish (*Pomatomus saltatrix*) common along the Atlantic coast of the United States. **2.** One of various other fishes of a bluish color, as the weakfish and cunner.

blue flag See under FLAG².

blue fox A small fox (*Alopex lagopus*) of arctic regions whose pelt acquires a bluish color in summer; also, its fur.

blue·gill (bloo′gil′) *n.* An edible American fresh-water sunfish (*Lepomis macrochirus*).

blue·grass (bloo′gras′, -gräs′) *n.* **1.** One of various grasses (genus *Poa*); especially, the **Kentucky bluegrass** (*P. pratensis*). **2.** *U.S. Informal* Hillbilly music.

Bluegrass Country A region of central Kentucky. Also **Bluegrass Region, the Bluegrass**.

Bluegrass State Nickname of KENTUCKY.

blue-green algae (bloo′grēn′) Primitive unicellular and unspecialized algae (phylum *Mixophyta*) in many of which the chlorophyll is mixed with a blue pigment.

blue ground Kimberlite.

blue grouse Any of several grouse of western North America (genus *Dendrogapus*), with dusky gray plumage: also called *sooty grouse*.

blue·gum (bloo′gum′) *n.* Any of several eucalyptus trees with aromatic, bitter, astringent leaves.

blue·hearts (bloo′härts′) *n.* A figwort (*Buchnera americana*) with a terminal spike of dark blue flowers.

blue·ing (bloo′ing), **blue·ish** (bloo′ish) See BLUING, BLUISH.

blue·jack (bloo′jak′) *n.* **1.** Blue vitriol. **2.** A small oak (*Quercus cinerea*) of the southern United States.

blue·jack·et (bloo′jak′it) *n.* An enlisted man in the United States or British navy. — **Syn.** See SAILOR.

blue jay A crested, corvine bird (*Cyanocitta cristata*) of North America. Also **blue·jay** (bloo′jā′).

blue jeans Blue denim trousers.

blue law *Often pl. U.S.* **1.** A puritanical law regulating private behavior. **2.** Any law prohibiting entertainment or recreation on Sunday: also *Sabbath* or *Sunday law*.

blue·line (bloo′līn′) *n.* Either of two blue lines between the center of a hockey rink and each goal.

blue mass A medicine prepared by rubbing mercury with glycerin, honey, confection of rose, etc., until it forms a pill-shaped mass. Also **blue pill**.

blue mold **1.** A destructive rotting disease of apples and citrus fruits, caused respectively by the fungi *Penicillium expansum* and *P. digitatum*. **2.** The typical blue-green mold of bread, cheese, etc., caused by other species of *Penicillium*: also called *green mold*.

Blue Mountains **1.** A wooded range in NE Oregon extending into SE Washington; highest point, Rock Creek Butte, 9,097 ft. **2.** An extensive plateau west of Sydney, Australia; highest point, Bird's Rock, 3871 ft.

Blue Nile See under NILE.

blue·nose (bloo′nōz′) *n. Informal* **1.** A puritanical person. **2.** *Usually cap.* A Nova Scotian person or ship.

blue-pen·cil (bloo′pen′səl) *v.t.* **·ciled** or **·cilled**, **·cil·ing** or **·cil·ling** To edit or cancel with or as with a blue pencil.

blue peter *Naut.* A blue flag with a white square in the center, raised to signal immediate sailing, etc. [< *blue* (re)*peater*]

blue point An oyster found off the shore of Blue Point, Great South Bay, Long Island, New York.

blue·print (bloo′print′) *n.* **1.** A plan or drawing made by printing on paper sensitized with a ferricyanide of potassium, the drawing showing in white lines on a blue ground. **2.** Any detailed plan. — *v.t.* To make a blueprint of.

blue racer A variety of the American blacksnake.

blue ribbon **1.** The highest award or distinction; first prize. **2.** The badge of the Order of the Garter. **3.** The badge of certain temperance societies.

blue-rib·bon jury (bloo′rib′ən) A jury selected for special qualifications. Also **blue-ribbon panel**.

Blue Ridge The SW portion of the Appalachian Mountains extending from Virginia into northern Georgia. Also **Blue Ridge Mountains**.

blues (blooz) *n.pl.* **1.** Depression of spirits; melancholy: often preceded by *the*. **2.** *Music* A style having a characteristic melodic and harmonic flavor and using deliberately mistuned scale degrees (**blue notes**), often in 4/4 meter with 12-measure phrases; also, the often mournful songs sung to this music. [Short for BLUE DEVILS]

blue-sky law (bloo′skī′) *Informal* A statute enacted to protect inexperienced purchasers of securities from fraud.

blue-stock·ing (bloo′stok′ing) *n.* A learned, pedantic, or literary woman. — *adj.* Of or characteristic of a bluestocking. [from the informal blue stockings worn by a leading literary figure in 18th-century London]

blue·stone (bloo′stōn′) *n.* **1.** Blue vitriol. **2.** A bluish, fine-grained, argillaceous sandstone, used for paving and building. **3.** Any blue-gray stone.

blue streak *Informal* Anything lightninglike in speed.

blu·et (bloo′it) *n.* **1.** One of various plants having blue flowers. **2.** A delicate meadow flower (*Houstonia caerulea*) of the madder family: also called *innocence, innocents, quaker-ladies*. [< F *bleut*, dim. of *bleu* blue]

blue vitriol *Chem.* A deep blue, crystalline copper sulfate, CuSO₄·5H₂O, used in electric batteries, calico printing, etc.: also called *bluejack, bluestone*.

blue·weed (bloo′wēd′) *n.* A rough, bristly herb (*Echium vulgare*) of the borage family, with showy blue flowers, naturalized in the United States: also called *viper's bugloss*.

blue whale The sulfur-bottom.

blue-winged teal See under TEAL.

blue·wood (bloo′wood′) *n.* A shrub or small tree (*Condalia obovata*) of the buckthorn family, of the SW United States.

bluff¹ (bluf) *v.t.* **1.** To deceive by putting on a bold front. **2.** To frighten with empty threats. **3.** In poker, to attempt to deceive (an opponent) by betting heavily on a poor hand. — *v.i.* **4.** To deceive or mislead someone; make empty threats or statements. — **to bluff one's way** To obtain an object by bluffing. — *n.* **1.** The act of bluffing. **2.** One who bluffs. [? < Du. *bluffen* to deceive, mislead] — **bluff′er** *n.*

bluff² (bluf) *n.* **1.** A bold, steep headland or bank. **2.** *Canadian* A clump of trees on a prairie; copse. — *adj.* **1.** Rough and hearty in manner; blunt but kindly. **2.** Having a broad, steep appearance. **3.** *Naut.* Broad and full: said of a ship's bows. [? < Du. *blaf* flat] — **bluff′ly** *adv.* — **bluff′ness** *n.*

blu·ing (bloo′ing) *n.* A blue coloring matter used in laundry work to counteract yellowing in linen: also spelled *blueing*.

blu·ish (bloo′ish) *adj.* Somewhat blue: also spelled *blueish*. — **blu′ish·ness** *n.*

Blum (bloom, blum), **Léon**, 1872–1950, French statesman and socialist; premier 1936–37, 1938, 1946–47.

blume (blüm) *v.i.* **blumed**, **blum·ing** *Scot.* To blossom.

blun·der (blun′dər) *n.* A stupid mistake; error. — *v.i.* **1.** To act or move blindly, awkwardly, or stupidly; stumble; bungle. **2.** To make a stupid and awkward mistake. — *v.t.* **3.** To utter stupidly or confusedly: often with *out*. **4.** To do badly; bungle. [ME *blondren* to mix up, confuse] — **blun′der·er** *n.* — **blun′der·ing·ly** *adv.*

blun·der·buss (blun′dər·bus) *n.* **1.** An old-fashioned, short gun with large bore and flaring mouth, used for scattering shot at close range. **2.** A stupid, blustering person. [BLUNDER and Du. *donderbus* thunder box]

BLUNDERBUSS (def. 1)

blunge (blunj) *v.t.* **blunged**, **blung·ing** In ceramics, to mix (clay) with water in a pug. [? Blend of BLEND and PLUNGE]

blung·er (blun′jər) *n.* One who or that which blunges.

blunt (blunt) *adj.* **1.** Having a thick end or edge; not sharp or piercing. **2.** Abrupt in manner; brusque. **3.** Slow of wit; dull. — *v.t.* **1.** To make blunt or dull. **2.** To make less keen or hurtful. — *v.i.* **3.** To become blunt or dull. [ME; origin unknown] — **blunt′ly** *adv.* — **blunt′ness** *n.* — **Syn.** *adj.* **1.** dull, round, smooth. **2.** *Blunt, abrupt, brusque*, and *curt* mean frank, direct, or harsh in speech and manner. *Blunt* suggests an unpleasant frankness and *abrupt* a disconcerting directness: a *blunt* opinion, an *abrupt* departure. *Brusque* implies ungraciousness, while *curt* connotes undue brevity, and often intentional rudeness: a *brusque* handshake, a *curt* rejoinder. Compare CANDID. — **Ant.** **1.** sharp, pointed, acute, keen.

blur (blûr) *v.* **blurred**, **blur·ring** *v.t.* **1.** To make vague or indistinct in outline; as by smearing. **2.** To stain; blemish. **3.** To impair the perceptiveness of; dim. — *v.i.* **4.** To become indistinct. **5.** To make blurs; smear. — *n.* **1.** A smear, as of ink; smudge. **2.** Something indistinct; a blurred appearance. [? Akin to BLEAR] — **blur′ry** *adj.*

blurb (blûrb) *n.* A brief and highly commendatory description or advertisement, especially one appearing on a book jacket. [Coined by Gelett Burgess]

blurt (blûrt) *v.t.* To utter abruptly or impulsively: often with *out*. — *n.* A sudden utterance. [? Blend of BLOW and SPURT]

blush (blush) *v.i.* **1.** To become red in the face from sudden suffusion of blood, as from modesty or confusion; flush. **2.** To become red or rosy, as flowers. **3.** To feel shame or regret: usually with *at* or *for*. — *v.t.* **4.** To make red. **5.** To reveal by blushing. — *n.* **1.** A reddening of the face from modesty, shame, or confusion. **2.** A red or rosy tint. **3.** A glance; glimpse: now only in the phrase **at** or **on first blush** — *adj.* Of the color of a blush. [OE *blyscan* to redden] — **blush′er** *n.* — **blush′ful** *adj.* — **blush′ing·ly** *adv.*

blus·ter (blus′tər) *v.i.* **1.** To blow gustily and with violence and noise, as the wind. **2.** To utter threats; swagger. — *v.t.* **3.** To utter noisily and boisterously. **4.** To force or bully by blustering. — *n.* **1.** Boisterous talk or swagger. **2.** Fitful and noisy blowing of the wind; blast. [Cf. ON *blāstr* blast, blowing] — **blus/ter·er** *n.* — **blus/ter·ing·ly** *adv.* — **blus/ter·y, blus/ter·ous** *adj.*

blvd. Boulevard.

blype (blīp) *n. Scot.* A shred; piece.

b.m. Board measure.

BM Bureau of Mines.

B.M. 1. Bachelor of Medicine (L *Baccalaureus Medicinae*). **2.** Bachelor of Music (L *Baccalaureus Musicae*). **3.** British Museum.

B.M.E. 1. Bachelor of Mechanical Engineering. **2.** Bachelor of Mining Engineering.

B.Mech.E. Bachelor of Mechanical Engineering.

BMEWS *Mil.* Ballistic Missile Early Warning System.

BMR *Physiol.* Basal metabolic rate.

B.Mus. Bachelor of Music.

bn. or **Bn.** Battalion.

B.N. Bank note.

B.N.A. 1. Basle Anatomical Nomenclature (L *Basel Nomina Anatomica*). **2.** British North America.

B'nai B'rith (bə·nā/ brith/) A Jewish fraternal organization. [< Hebrew, sons of the covenant]

b.o. 1. Back order. **2.** Bad order. **3.** Box office. **4.** Branch office. **5.** Broker's order. **6.** Buyer's option. **7.** Body odor.

B/O Brought over (bookkeeping).

bo·a (bō/ə) *n. pl.* **bo·as 1.** Any of several nonvenomous serpents (family *Boidae*) having vestigial hind legs and notable for the crushing power of their coils, as the anaconda and python; especially, the **boa constrictor** (*Constrictor constrictor* or *Boa constrictor*) of South and Central America. **2.** A long feather or fur scarf for women. [< L]

Bo·ab·dil (bō/əb·dēl/), died 1533?, last Moorish ruler of Granada.

Bo·ad·i·ce·a (bō/ad·ə·sē/ə), died A.D. 62, British queen; suffered defeat by the Romans and poisoned herself.

Bo·a·ner·ges (bō/ə·nûr/jēz) The name given by Jesus to the two sons of Zebedee; literally, sons of thunder. *Mark* iii 17. — *n.pl.* (construed as *sing.*) A vehement preacher.

boar (bôr, bōr) *n. pl.* **boars** or **boar 1.** An uncastrated male swine. **2.** The wild boar (which see). [OE *bār*]

board (bôrd, bōrd) *n.* **1.** A flat, thin slab of sawed wood much longer than it is wide. **2.** A thin slab of wood or the like for a specific purpose: an ironing *board*. **3.** One of the pasteboard covers of a book. **4.** A table set for serving food. **5.** Food or meals; especially, meals furnished for pay, and sometimes including lodging. **6.** An organized official body: chairman of the *board*. **7.** A table at which meetings are held. **8.** A border or edge: used in combination: *seaboard*. **9.** A wood or cardboard square used for games, as chess, go, etc. **10.** *pl.* The wooden enclosure of a hockey rink. **11.** *Electr.* A panel bearing switches, jacks, meters, or the like: a control *board*. **12.** *Naut.* **a** The side of a ship. **b** The course followed by a vessel on one tack. Abbr. *bd.* (pl. *bds*). — **across the board** *Informal* **1.** Designating a racing bet whereby equal sums are wagered on a single horse, etc., to win, place, and show. **2.** Affecting all members or categories in the same degree: said of changes in salary, taxes, etc. — **by the board** Overboard. — **on board 1.** On or in a vessel or other conveyance. **2.** *Naut.* Alongside. — **the boards** The stage. — **to go by the board** To fall into ruin, disuse, etc. — **to tread the boards** To appear as an actor. — *v.t.* **1.** To cover or enclose with boards: often with *up.* **2.** To furnish with meals, or meals and lodging, for pay. **3.** To place (someone) where meals are provided, as in a boarding school. **4.** To enter, as a ship or train. **5.** *Naut.* To come alongside or go on board of (a ship), as to attack. **6.** *Obs.* To approach; accost. — *v.i.* **7.** To take meals, or meals and lodging. **8.** In hockey, to bodycheck an opponent against the boards with excessive violence. **9.** *Naut.* To tack. [OE *bord* board, side of a ship, table]

board·er (bôr/dər, bōr/-) *n.* **1.** One who receives regular meals, or meals and lodging, for pay. **2.** One who is detailed to board an enemy's ship.

board foot *pl.* **board feet** The contents of a board 1 foot square and 1 inch thick; the common unit of measure for logs and lumber in the United States, equal to 144 cubic inches or 2359.8 cubic centimeters. Abbr. *bd. ft.*

boarding house A house where meals, or meals and lodging, can be had regularly for pay. Also **board·ing·house** (bôr/ding·hous/, bōr/-).

boarding school A school in which pupils are boarded: distinguished from *day school.*

board measure A cubic measure applied to boards, the unit of which is the board foot. Abbr. *b.m.*

board of education *U.S. & Canadian* A local group, usually elective, that supervises the school system.

board of trade An association of merchants, bankers, etc., to promote business interests.

Board of Trade *Brit.* A special governmental committee dealing with matters of trade and commerce. Abbr. *B.O.T.*

board rule A graduated stick for determining the number of board feet in boards of given dimensions.

board·walk (bôrd/wôk/, bōrd/-) *n.* **1.** A promenade along a beach, usually of boards. **2.** A walk made of planks.

boar·fish (bôr/fish/, bōr/-) *n. pl.* **·fish** or **·fish·es** Any of several marine fishes (order *Zeomorphi*) related to the john dory, having a hoglike snout.

boar·hound (bôr/hound/, bōr/-) *n.* A dog used for hunting boars, usually the Great Dane.

boar·ish (bôr/ish, bōr/-) *adj.* Swinish; lecherous; brutal. — **boar/ish·ly** *adv.* — **boar/ish·ness** *n.*

Bo·as (bō/az), Franz, 1858–1942, U.S. anthropologist born in Germany.

boast[1] (bōst) *v.i.* **1.** To talk in a vain or bragging manner, especially about one's deeds, abilities, or possessions; brag. **2.** To speak or possess with pride: used with *of.* — *v.t.* **3.** To brag about; extol. **4.** To be proud to possess; take pride in: The school *boasts* a new laboratory. — *n.* **1.** A boastful speech; bragging. **2.** That which is boasted about. [ME *bosten*; origin unknown] — **boast/er** *n.* — **boast/ing·ly** *adv.*

boast[2] (bōst) *v.t.* To shape roughly with a broad chisel.

boast·ful (bōst/fəl) *adj.* Characterized by or addicted to boasting. — **boast/ful·ly** *adv.* — **boast/ful·ness** *n.*

boat (bōt) *n.* **1.** A small, open watercraft propelled by oars, sails, or an engine. **2.** *Informal* Any watercraft of any size, from a rowboat to an ocean liner. **3.** An article, as a dish, resembling a small watercraft. — **in the same boat** In the same situation or condition; equally involved. — *v.i.* **1.** To travel by boat. **2.** To go boating for pleasure. — *v.t.* **3.** To transport or place in a boat: to *boat* oars. [OE *bāt*]

boat·bill (bōt/bil/) *n.* A tropical American wading bird (*Cochlearius cochlearius*) related to the night herons, with a greatly depressed bill widened laterally.

boat hook A pole having a point and hook at one end, for holding or pushing a boat. For illustration see HOOK.

boat·house (bōt/hous/) *n.* A building along the water used for storing boats.

boat·ing (bō/ting) *n.* The act or sport of one who boats.

boat·load (bōt/lōd/) *n.* **1.** The amount that a boat can hold. **2.** The load carried by a boat.

boat·man (bōt/mən) *n. pl.* **·men** (-mən) **1.** A man who deals in or works on boats. **2.** An aquatic insect (family *Corixidae*) of which one pair of legs is long and oarlike. Also **boat bug. 3.** An aquatic insect (family *Notonectidae*) that swims on its back.

boat·swain (bō/sən, *rarely* bōt/swān/) *n.* A warrant officer of a naval ship, or a subordinate officer of a merchantman who is in charge of the rigging, anchors, etc., and calls the crew to duty with his whistle, which is his badge. Also spelled *bo·sun, bo's'n.* [OE *bātswegen*]

boatswain's chair A short board slung by ropes, used as a seat while working aloft, over a ship's side, etc.

boat-tailed grackle (bōt/tāld/) See under GRACKLE.

Bo·az (bō/az) In the Old Testament, the man who married Ruth. *Ruth* ii–iv.

bob[1] (bob) *v.* **bobbed, bob·bing** *v.i.* **1.** To move up and down with an irregular motion. **2.** To snatch at hanging or floating objects with the teeth: usually with *for:* to *bob* for apples. **3.** To curtsy. — *v.t.* **4.** To move up and down: to *bob* the head. **5.** To offer by moving up and down: to *bob* a curtsy. — **to bob up** To appear or emerge suddenly. — *n.* **1.** A short, jerky movement: a *bob* of the head. **2.** A quick bow or curtsy. **3.** In fishing, a float or cork. [ME; origin uncertain. ? Akin to BOB², n. (def. 3)] — **bob/ber** *n.*

bob[2] (bob) *n.* **1.** A short haircut for a woman or child. **2.** The docked tail of a horse. **3.** A small, pendant object, as the weight on a plumb line. For illustration see PENDULUM, PLUMB BOB. **4.** In fishing, a large, ball-shaped bait made of worms, rags, etc. **5.** *Dial.* A bunch; cluster. — *v.* **bobbed, bob·bing** *v.t.* **1.** To cut short, as hair. — *v.i.* **2.** To fish with a bob. [ME *bobbe*; origin unknown] — **bob/ber** *n.*

bob[3] (bob) *n. pl.* **bob** *Brit. Informal* A shilling. [< *Bob*, a nickname for *Robert*, a personal name]

bob[4] (bob) *n.* **1.** A bobsled. **2.** A bob skate.

bob[5] (bob) *v.t.* **bobbed, bob·bing** To strike lightly and quickly; tap. — *n.* A tap or blow. [ME *bobben*; origin unknown]

bob[6] (bob) *Obs. v.t.* **1.** To mock. **2.** To delude; cheat. — *n.* A trick; also, a jeer or taunt. [< OF *bober*]

Bo·ba·dil·la (bō/və·thē/lyä), Francisco de, died 1502, Spanish viceroy of the West Indies; arrested Columbus.

bob·ber·y (bob/ər·ē) *n. pl.* **·ber·ies** *Informal* A disturbance; tumult. [< Anglo-Indian < Hind. *bāp re* O father!]

bob·bin (bob/in) *n.* **1.** A spool or reel holding thread for spinning, weaving, or machine sewing. **2.** A small pin or spool used in making bobbin lace. **3.** A cord or braid used as trimming or binding. [< F *bobine*]

bob·bi·net (bob/ə·net/) *n.* A machine-made net having hexagonal meshes. [< BOBBIN + NET¹]

bobbin lace A handmade lace worked on a pillowlike pad

in which several bobbins are used to form a pattern: also called *pillow lace.*

bob·ble (bob′əl) *U.S. Informal n.* A fumble or miss. — *v.t.* **·bled, ·bling** To handle ineptly; fumble. [Freq. of BOB[1]]

bob·by (bob′ē) *n. pl.* **·bies** *Brit. Informal* A policeman. [after Sir Robert (*Bobby*) Peel]

bobby pin A metal hairpin shaped so as to clasp and hold the hair tightly. Also **bob′bie pin.**

bobby socks *Informal* Short socks worn by girls.

bob·by·sox·er (bob′ē·sok′sər) *U.S. Informal* A young girl who follows fads and fashions current among adolescents.

bob·cat (bob′kat′) *n.* A lynx; especially, the bay lynx of North America.

bob·o·link (bob′ə·lingk) *n.* A thrushlike singing bird (*Dolichonyx oryzivorus*) of the New World: also called *reedbird, ricebird.* [Imit.; from its call]

bob skate A skate having two parallel runners.

bob·sled (bob′sled′) *n.* **1.** A racing sled steered by a steering wheel controlling the front runners. **2.** Either of two short sleds connected in tandem; also, the vehicle so formed. — *v.i.* **·sled·ded, ·sled·ding** To go coasting on a bobsled. Also **bob′sleigh′** (-slā′). [Origin unknown]

bob·stay (bob′stā′) *n. Naut.* A chain or rope from the bowsprit end to the stem of a vessel, serving to counteract the strain of the forestays.

bob·tail (bob′tāl′) *n.* **1.** A short tail or a tail cut short. **2.** An animal with such a tail. — *adj.* **1.** Having the tail docked. **2.** Cut short; incomplete. — *v.t.* **1.** To cut the tail of; dock. **2.** To cut short. — **bob′tailed′** *adj.*

bob·white (bob′hwīt′) *n.* A quail (*Colinus virginianus*) of North America having brownish, mottled plumage: also called *partridge.* [Imit.; from its call]

bo·cac·ci·o (bə·kä′chō) *n.* A rockfish (*Sebastodes paucispinis*) of the California coast. [< Ital. *boccaccio* < *boccaccia* ugly mouth]

Boc·cac·ci·o (bō·kä′chē·ō, *Ital.* bōk·kät′chō), **Giovanni,** 1313–75, Italian writer and poet; author of the *Decameron.*

Boc·che·ri·ni (bōk′kā·rē′nē), **Luigi,** 1743–1805, Italian composer.

boc·cie (boch′e) *n.* A game of bowls played on a narrow outdoor court. [< Ital.]

Boche (bosh, *Fr.* bôsh) *n. Slang* A German: a derogatory term. Also **boche.** [< F < slang *alboche* ? < *al(lemand)* German + (*ca*)*boche* thickhead, hardhead]

Bo·chum (bō′kHŏŏm) A city in central North Rhine–Westphalia, West Germany; pop. 361,357 (est. 1959).

bock beer (bok) A dark, strong beer brewed in the winter and served in early spring. Also **bock.** [< G *bockbier* < dial. *Eimbockbier* beer from *Einbeck,* a German town]

bode[1] (bōd) Alternative past tense of BIDE.

bode[2] (bōd) *v.* **bod·ed, bod·ing** *v.t.* **1.** To be a foretoken of; presage. **2.** *Obs.* To predict; foretell. — *v.i.* **3.** To presage good or ill. — **Syn.** See AUGUR. [OE *bodian* to announce] — **bode′ment** *n.*

bo·de·ga (bō·dē′gə, *Sp.* bō·тнā′gä) *n.* **1.** A wine shop or warehouse. **2.** A grocery. [< Sp.]

Bo·den·see (bō′dən·zā) The German name for (Lake of) CONSTANCE. Also **Bo′den-See.**

bo·dhi·satt·va (bō′di·sat′wə) *n.* In Buddhism, one who has attained the degree of enlightenment to become a Buddha but who declines out of compassion for the suffering of others; a future Buddha. Also **bod′dhi·satt′va.** [< Skt. < *bodhi* knowledge + *sattva* essence]

bod·ice (bod′is) *n.* **1.** The upper portion of a woman's dress. **2.** A woman's ornamental waist, laced in front. **3.** *Obs.* A corset laced in front. [Var. of *bodies,* pl. of BODY]

bod·ied (bod′ēd) *adj.* **1.** Having a body. **2.** Having a (specified kind of) body: used in combination: *full-bodied.*

bod·i·less (bod′i·lis) *adj.* Having no body; lacking material form; incorporeal.

bod·i·ly (bod′ə·lē) *adj.* **1.** Of or pertaining to the body. **2.** Physical, as opposed to mental: *bodily* illness. — **Syn.** See PHYSICAL. — *adv.* **1.** In the flesh; in person. **2.** All together; as a single entity; completely.

bod·ing (bō′ding) *adj.* Portending evil; ominous. — *n.* An omen; presage, especially of evil. — **bod′ing·ly** *adv.*

bod·kin (bod′kin) *n.* **1.** A pointed instrument for piercing holes in cloth, etc. **2.** A blunt needle for drawing tape through a hem. **3.** A long pin for fastening the hair. **4.** *Printing* A pick for extracting type from a form. **5.** *Archaic* A stiletto. [ME *boydekin* dagger; origin unknown]

Bod·lei·an (bod·lē′ən, bod′lē·ən) *adj.* Of or designating the library of Oxford University, England, restored by **Sir Thomas Bodley,** 1545–1613. Also **Bod·ley′an.**

Bo·do·ni (bō·dō′nē) *n.* A modern style of type face created by the Italian printer **Giambattista Bodoni,** 1740–1813.

bod·y (bod′ē) *n. pl.* **bod·ies** **1.** The entire physical part of a human being, animal, or plant. **2.** A corpse; carcass. **3.** The main portion of a human being or animal, excluding the head and limbs; the trunk. **4.** The principal part or mass of anything, as of a building. **5.** The main part of a document, excluding the introduction, appendix, etc. **6.** The part of a vehicle in which the load is carried. **7.** A collection of persons or things taken as a whole; also, the ma-

jority of such a group. **8.** A distinct mass or portion of matter: a *body* of clear water. **9.** Matter, as opposed to spirit; physical substance. **10.** Density or consistency; substance: a wine with *body.* **11.** That part of a garment that covers the body or the upper body. **12.** *Informal* A person. **13.** *Physics* An object having mass. **14.** *Geom.* A solid. **15.** *Naut.* The hull of a ship. **16.** *Printing* The part of a piece of type that carries the impression surface. **17.** *Aeron.* The fuselage of an aircraft. — *v.t.* **bod·ied, bod·y·ing** **1.** To furnish with or as with a body. **2.** To exhibit in bodily form; represent: usually with *forth.* [OE *bodig*] — **Syn.** (noun) **1.** *Body, frame,* and *form* refer to the material of a living or dead animal. *Body* is a general term for the entire physical structure. *Frame* suggests the supporting internal bony structure, and *form* the outer shape. **2.** *Corpse, carcass,* and *cadaver* mean dead *bodies.* A *corpse* is a human *body,* while *carcass* usually refers to animal *bodies,* and is used of humans only contemptuously or humorously. *Cadaver* is generally restricted to medical usage. **7.** See COMPANY.

bod·y·check (bod′ē·chek) *n.* In hockey, a defensive bumping of the puck-carrier. — *v.i.* To apply a bodycheck.

body corporate *Law* An association of persons duly incorporated for a specific purpose or enterprise; a corporation.

bod·y·guard (bod′ē·gärd′) *n.* **1.** A guard responsible for the physical safety of an individual. **2.** A retinue; escort.

body politic The state or nation as an organized political entity; the people collectively.

bod·y·shirt (bod′ē·shûrt′) *n.* A man's shirt made to fit closely around the chest and waist.

body snatcher One who steals bodies from graves.

Boe·o·tia (bē·ō′shə, -shē·ə) A department of east central Greece; 1,210 sq. mi.; pop. 106,838 (1951); capital, Levadia; a state of ancient Greece. See map of ATTICA.

Boe·o·tian (bē·ō′shən) *adj.* **1.** Of or pertaining to Boeotia. **2.** Dull; clownish. — *n.* **1.** A native of Boeotia. **2.** A stupid, doltish person.

Boer (bōr, bôr, bŏŏr) *n.* A Dutch colonist, or person of Dutch descent, in South Africa. — *adj.* Of or pertaining to the Boers. [< Du., farmer]

Boer War A war, 1899–1902, between England and the Orange Free State and Transvaal Republic. Also called *South African War.* See table for WAR.

Bo·e·thi·us (bō·ē′thē·əs), **Anicius Manlius Severinus,** 480?–524?, Roman philosopher. Also **Bo·e·ti·us** (bō·ē′shē·əs).

bog (bog, bôg) *n.* Wet and spongy ground; marsh; morass. — *v.t. & v.i.* **bogged, bog·ging** To sink or be impeded in or as in a bog: often with *down.* [< Irish *bogach* < *bog* soft] — **bog′gish** *adj.* — **bog′gish·ness** *n.*

bo·gan (bō′gən) *n. Canadian* A backwater or tributary.

bog asphodel Any of various plants (genus *Narthecium*) of the lily family; especially, *N. americanum* and *N. californicum,* of North America.

bog·bean (bog′bēn′, bôg′-) *n.* The buck bean (which see).

bo·gey (bō′gē) *n. pl.* **·geys** In golf: **a** An estimated standard score. **b** One stroke over par on a hole. Also **bo′gie.** [after Col. *Bogey,* an imaginary faultless golfer]

bo·gey[2] (bō′gē) See BOGY[1].

bog·gle[1] (bog′əl) *v.* **·gled, ·gling** *v.i.* **1.** To hesitate, as from doubt or scruples; shrink back: often with *at.* **2.** To start with fright, as a horse. **3.** To equivocate; dissemble. **4.** To work clumsily; fumble. — *v.t.* **5.** To make a botch of; bungle. — *n.* **1.** The act of boggling. **2.** A scruple; objection. **3.** *Informal* A botch. [< BOGLE] — **bog′gler** *n.*

bog·gle[2] (bog′əl) A bogle.

bog·gy (bog′ē, bôg′ē) *adj.* **·gi·er, ·gi·est** Swampy; miry. — **bog′gi·ness** *n.*

bo·gie[1] (bō′gē) *n.* **1.** A railway truck mounted on one axle and two wheels or two axles and four wheels. **2.** One of the small rollers or wheels that distribute the weight of a tractor or tank along the track: also **bogie wheel.** Also spelled *bogy.* [< dial.E (Northern), a kind of truck or cart]

bo·gie[2] (bō′gē) See BOGY[1].

bo·gle (bō′gəl) *n.* A hobgoblin or bogy; bugbear: also *boggle.*

bog oak Bogwood, especially of oak.

Bo·gor (bō′gôr) A city in western Java; pop. 146,907 (1961). Dutch *Buitenzorg.*

bog orchid **1.** The adder's-mouth. **2.** An orchid (*Malaxis paludosa*) having small green flowers. Also **bog orchis.**

Bo·go·tá (bō′gə·tä′) The capital of Colombia, in the east central part; pop. 2,037,904 (est. 1969).

bog·trot·ter (bog′trot′ər, bôg′-) *n.* **1.** One who frequents or inhabits bogs. **2.** An Irish peasant: a contemptuous term.

bo·gus (bō′gəs) *adj. U.S.* Counterfeit; spurious; fake. [Origin unknown; first applied to a counterfeiting device]

bog·wood (bog′wŏŏd′, bôg′-) *n.* Wood of trees buried and preserved in peat bogs.

bo·gy[1] (bō′gē) *n. pl.* **·gies** **1.** A goblin; bugbear. **2.** An aircraft that cannot be identified. Also spelled *bogey, bogie.* [? Akin to BUG[2]] — **bo′gy·ism** *n.*

bo·gy[2] (bō′gē) See BOGIE[1].

Boh. or **Bohem.** Bohemia; Bohemian.

bo·hea (bō·hē′) *n.* A black tea: once applied to the choicest, now to the poorest grade. [from the *Wu-i* Hills (pronounced bōō′ē) of China]

Bo·he·mi·a (bō·hē′mē·ə) A former province of western Czechoslovakia abolished in 1949; with Moravia and Silesia it comprised the Czech region of the country.

Bo·he·mi·an (bō·hē′mē·ən) *adj.* **1.** Of or pertaining to Bohemia. **2.** Leading the life of a Bohemian; unconventional. — *n.* **1.** An inhabitant of Bohemia. **2.** A gypsy. **3.** A person, usually of artistic or literary tastes, who lives in an unconventional manner. Also (for *adj.* def. 2, *n.* def. 3) **bo·he′mi·an.** **4.** A former name for the Czech dialect of Czechoslovakian. — **Bo·he′mi·an·ism** *n.*

Bohemian Brethren A religious association formed by Hussites in the 15th century. See MORAVIAN CHURCH.

Bohemian Forest A wooded mountain range along the Czechoslovak-German border. *German* **Böh·mer-Wald** (bœ′mər-wält′).

Böh·me (bœ′mə), **Jakob,** 1575–1624, German mystic. Also **Böhm** (bœm).

Bo·hol (bō·hôl′) One of the Visayan Islands of the south central Philippines; 1,492 sq. mi.

Bohr (bōr), **Niels,** 1885–1962, Danish physicist.

bo·hunk (bō′hungk) *n. U.S. Slang* A foreign-born laborer, especially one from central Europe: also called *hunky*: an offensive term. [< BO(HEMIAN) + HUNG(ARIAN)]

Bo·iar·do (bō·yär′dō), **Matteo Maria,** 1434?–94, Count of Scandiano, Italian poet. Also *Bojardo.*

boil¹ (boil) *v.i.* **1.** To be agitated by escaping gaseous bubbles, usually from the effect of heat: said of liquids. **2.** To reach the boiling point: Water *boils* at 212° F. **3.** To undergo the action of a boiling liquid: The potatoes are *boiling.* **4.** To contain a boiling liquid: The kettle is *boiling.* **5.** To be agitated like boiling water; seethe: The water *boiled* with sharks. **6.** To be stirred by rage or passion. — *v.t.* **7.** To bring to the boiling point. **8.** To cook or cleanse by boiling: to *boil* rice; to *boil* shirts. **9.** To separate by means of evaporation caused by boiling: to *boil* sugar. — **to boil away** To evaporate in boiling. — **to boil down 1.** To reduce in bulk by boiling. **2.** To condense; summarize. — **to boil over 1.** To overflow while boiling. **2.** To give vent to one's rage or passion. — *n.* The act or state of boiling. [< OF *boillir* < L *bullire* to boil]

boil² (boil) *n. Pathol.* A painful purulent nodule of bacterial origin beneath the skin: also called *furuncle.* [OE *byl*]

Boi·leau-Des·pré·aux (bwä·lō′dā·prä·ō′), **Nicolas,** 1636–1711, French poet and critic: called *Boileau.*

boiled shirt *U.S. Informal* A man's dress shirt.

boil·er (boi′lər) *n.* **1.** A closed vessel, usually cylindrical and containing a system of tubes, used for generating steam, as for heating or power. **2.** A container in which something is boiled. **3.** A tank for hot water.

boil·er·mak·er (boi′lər·mā′kər) *n.* **1.** One who makes or repairs boilers. **2.** *U.S.* A drink of whiskey followed by beer as a chaser.

boiling point The temperature at which the vapor pressure in a liquid equals the external pressure. At normal atmospheric pressure the boiling point of water is 212° F. or 100° C.

bois brû·lé (bwä brü·lā′) *Canadian* A half-breed Indian. [< dial. F (Canadian)]

Bois de Bou·logne (bwä′də bōō·lôn′, *Fr.* bwäd·bōō·lôn′y′) A park in Paris, France. Also **the Bois.**

Boi·se (boi′zē, -sē) The capital of Idaho, in the SW part of the State; pop. 74,990.

Bois-le-Duc (bwä·lə·dük′) The French name for 's HERTO-GENBOSCH.

bois·ter·ous (bois′tər·əs, -trəs) *adj.* **1.** Noisy and unrestrained: uproarious. **2.** Stormy; violent, as the weather. **3.** *Obs.* Coarse; big; rank. [ME *boistous*; origin unknown] — **bois′ter·ous·ly** *adv.* — **bois′ter·ous·ness** *n.*

Ro·i·to (bō′ē·tō), **Arrigo,** 1842–1918, Italian composer.

Bo·jar·do (bō·yär′dō) See BOIARDO.

Bøj·er (boi′ər), **Johan,** 1872–1959, Norwegian author.

Bok (bok), **Edward William,** 1863–1930, U.S. editor.

Bo·kha·ra (bō·kä′rə) See BUKHARA.

Bol. Bolivia; Bolivian.

bo·la (bō′lə) *n.* A throwing weapon, consisting of balls fastened to cords, used in South America for catching cattle and large game. Also **bo·las** (bō′ləs). [< Sp., a ball]

bold (bōld) *adj.* **1.** Having courage; fearless. **2.** Showing or requiring courage; daring: a *bold* plan. **3.** Presuming unduly; brazen; forward. **4.** Vigorous in conception or expression; unconventional. **5.** Standing out prominently; distinct. **6.** Abrupt; steep, as a cliff. **7.** *Obs.* Confident; assured. — **Syn.** See BRAVE. — **to make bold** To take the liberty; venture. [OE *bald*] — **bold′ly** *adv.* — **bold′ness** *n.*

bold·face (bōld′fās′) *n. Printing* A type in which the lines have been thickened to give a very black impression, often used for emphasis. Abbr. *bf, b.f., bld.*

bole¹ (bōl) *n.* The trunk of a tree. [< ON *bolr*]

bole² (bōl) *n.* A fine, compact, soft clay. [< Med.L *bolus,* ult. < Gk. *bōlos* clod of earth] — **bo′lar** (-lər) *adj.*

bo·lec·tion (bō·lek′shən) *n. Archit.* A molding along the edge of a panel, projecting above the surface of the frame: also called *bilection.* [Origin unknown]

bo·le·ro (bō·lâr′ō) *n. pl.* **·ros 1.** A short jacket open at the front. **2.** A Spanish dance, usually accompanied by castanets. **3.** The music for this dance. [< Sp.]

bo·le·tus (bō·lē′təs) *n.* One of a genus (*Boletus*) of umbrella-shaped fungi of the family *Polyporaceae,* widely distributed in the United States. [< L *boletus* < Gk. *bōlītēs* mushroom]

Bol·eyn (bōōl′in, bō·lin′), **Anne,** 1507–36, second wife of Henry VIII of England; mother of Elizabeth I; beheaded.

bo·lide (bō′līd, -lid) *n. Astron.* An exploding meteor. [< F < L *bolis, -idis* meteor < Gk. *bolis* missile < *ballein* to hurl]

Bol·ing·broke (bol′ing·brŏŏk, bŏŏl′-) See HENRY IV (of England).

Bolingbroke, Viscount, 1678–1751, Henry St. John, British statesman.

bol·i·var (bol′ə·vər, -vär; *Sp.* bō·lē′vär) *n. pl.* **bol·i·vars,** *Sp.* **bo·li·va·res** (bō′lē·vä′räs) The monetary unit of Venezuela, equivalent to 100 centimos. Abbr. *b., B.* [after Simón *Bolívar*]

Bol·í·var (bol′ə·vər, -vär; *Sp.* bō·lē′vär), **Simón,** 1783–1830, Venezuelan general and statesman; liberated South America.

bo·liv·i·a (bə·liv′ē·ə) *n.* A soft woolen or worsted pile fabric, with a finish resembling velvet or plush. [< BOLIVIA]

Bo·liv·i·a (bə·liv′ē·ə) A Republic in west central South America; 424,162 sq. mi.; pop. 5,330,000 (est.1973); capitals, Sucre (constitutional), La Paz (de facto). Officially **Republic of Bolivia.** — **Bo·liv′i·an** *adj. & n.*

bo·li·vi·a·no (bō·lē′vyä′nō) *n. pl.* **·nos** (-nōs) A monetary unit of Bolivia, worth one thousandth of a peso. Abbr. *b., B.*

boll (bōl) *n.* A round pod or seed capsule, as of flax or cotton. — *v.i.* To form pods. [Var. of BOWL¹]

Bol·land·ist (bol′ən·dist) *n.* One of the editors of the **Acta Sanctorum** (Lives of the Saints), begun in 1643. [after John van *Bolland,* 1596–1665, Flemish Jesuit and first editor]

bol·lard (bol′ərd) *n. Naut.* A vertical post, as on a wharf, for securing ropes. [? < BOLE¹ + -ARD]

bol·lix (bol′iks) *v.t.* **·lixed, ·lix·ing** *Slang* To bungle; botch: often with *up.* [Alter. of *bollocks* testicles, dim. pl. of BALL¹]

boll weevil A grayish long-snouted beetle (*Anthonomus grandis*) that infests and destroys cotton bolls. For illustration see INSECTS (injurious).

boll·worm (bōl′wûrm′) *n.* **1.** The very destructive larva of a pale brown moth (*Pectinophora gossypiella*) that feeds on cotton bolls: also called *pink bollworm.* **2.** The corn earworm (which see).

bo·lo (bō′lō) *n. pl.* **·los** (-lōz) A large, single-edged knife used by natives of the Philippines. [< Sp. < Visayan]

Bo·lo·gna (bō·lō′nyä) A Province of Emilia-Romagna Region, north central Italy; 1,429 sq. mi.; pop. 836,971 (1961); capital, Bologna, also capital of the Region, pop. 481,740. — **Bo·lo·gnese** (bō·lə·nēz′, -nēs′) *adj. & n.*

Bo·lo·gna sausage (bə·lō′nə, -lōn′yə, -lō′nē) A highly seasoned sausage of mixed meats: also *baloney, boloney.* Also **bo·lo′gna.**

bo·lo·graph (bō′lə·graf, -gräf) *n. Physics* A record of the findings of a bolometer. [< Gk. *bolē* ray of light + -GRAPH] — **bo·lo·graph′ic** *adj.* — **bo·lo·graph′i·cal·ly** *adv.* — **bo·log·ra·phy** (bō·log′rə·fē) *n.*

bo·lom·e·ter (bō·lom′ə·tər) *n. Physics* An instrument for measuring minute differences of radiant energy by changes in the electric resistance of a blackened conductor exposed to it. [< Gk. *bolē* ray of light + -METER] — **bo·lo·met·ric** (bō′lə·met′rik) *adj.*

bo·lo·ney (bə·lō′nē) See BALONEY.

Bol·she·vik (bōl′shə·vik, bol′-) *n. pl.* **Bol·she·viks** or **Bol·she·vi·ki** (bōl′shə·vē′kē, bol′-) **1.** A member of the radical and dominant branch of the Russian Social Democratic Party or, since 1918, of the Russian Communist Party. Compare MENSHEVIK. **2.** A member of any Communist party. **3.** Loosely, any radical. Also **bol′she·vik.** Also *Slang* **Bol′shie.** [< Russian *bolshe* greater; because orig. the majority group in the party]

Bol·she·vism (bōl′shə·viz′əm, bol′-) *n.* The Marxian doctrines and policies of the Bolsheviks; also, any practice, government, etc., based on them. Also **bol′she·vism.**

Bol·she·vist (bōl′shə·vist, bol′-) *n.* A Bolshevik. Also **bol′she·vist.** — **Bol′she·vis′tic** *adj.*

bol·son (bōl′sən) *n. SW U.S.* A low, enclosed basin of ground surrounded by hills. [< Sp. *bolsón,* aug. of *bolso* purse]

bol·ster (bōl′stər) *n.* **1.** A narrow pillow as long as a bed's width. **2.** A pad used as a support or for protection. **3.** Anything shaped like a bolster or used as a support. **4.** *Archit.* The lateral part of the volute of an Ionic capital. — *v.t.* **1.** To support with a pillow. **2.** To prop or reinforce, as something ready to fall: with *up.* **3.** To furnish with padding. [OE] — **bol′ster·er** *n.*

bolt¹ (bōlt) *n.* **1.** A sliding bar or piece for fastening a door, etc. **2.** A pin or rod for holding something in place, usually having a head at one end, and threaded at the other. **3.** The part of a lock that is shot or withdrawn by turning the key.

4. A sliding mechanism that closes the breech of some small arms. **5.** An arrow, especially a quarrel for a crossbow. **6.** A stroke of lightning; thunderbolt. **7.** Anything that comes suddenly or unexpectedly: a *bolt* of bad luck. **8.** A sudden start or spring: He made a *bolt* for the door. **9.** *U.S.* A desertion of or refusal to support one's party, its candidate, etc. **10.** A roll of cloth, wallpaper, etc., of varying length. **11.** A large jet or spurt of water, oil, etc. **12.** *Obs.* A fetter. **— a bolt from the blue 1.** A thunderbolt on a clear day. **2.** A sudden and wholly unexpected event. **— to shoot one's bolt** To do one's utmost; perform to the point of exhaustion. **—** *v.i.* **1.** To move, go, or spring suddenly: usually with *out* or *from:* He *bolted* from the room. **2.** To start suddenly; break from control and run away. **3.** *U.S.* To break away, as from a political party; refuse to support party policy. **—** *v.t.* **4.** To fasten or lock with or as with a bolt or bolts. **5.** *U.S.* To break away from, as a political party. **6.** To chew and swallow hurriedly; gulp, as food. **7.** To arrange or roll into bolts, as cloth. **8.** To blurt out; say impulsively or hastily. **—** *adv.* Like an arrow; suddenly. **— bolt upright** Stiffly erect. [OE, arrow for a crossbow] **— bolt'er** *n.*

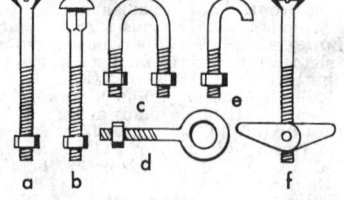

BOLTS
a Stove. *b* Carriage. *c* U-bolt.
d Eye. *e* Hook. *f* Toggle.

bolt² (bōlt) *v.i.* **1.** To pass through a sieve; sift. **2.** To examine as by sifting. [< OF *bulter, buleter* to sift < *burete*, dim. of *bure* coarse cloth] **— bolt'er** *n.*
bolt·head (bōlt'hed') *n.* **1.** The head of a bolt. **2.** A mattrass.
Bol·ton (bōl'tən) A county borough in Greater Manchester, England; pop. 261,800 (1976). Also **Bolton-le-Moors** (-lə-mŏŏrz').
bol·to·ni·a (bōl·tō'nē-ə) *n.* Any of a genus (*Boltonia*) of tall, erect perennials bearing white to purplish asterlike flowers. [< NL, after James Bolton, 18th c. English botanist]
bolt·rope (bōlt'rōp') *n. Naut.* A rope at the border of a sail.
bo·lus (bō'ləs) *n. pl.* **·lus·es 1.** A large pill. **2.** Any rounded lump or mass. [< Med.L. See BOLE².]
bomb (bom) *n.* **1.** *Mil.* A hollow projectile containing explosive, incendiary, or chemical material to be discharged by concussion or by a time fuse. **2.** Any similar receptacle, of any shape, containing an explosive: a dynamite *bomb.* **3.** *Geol.* A roughly spherical mass of lava hurled from a volcano during an explosive eruption. **4.** An aerosol bomb (which see). **5.** *Informal* A total failure; a flop. **—** *v.t. & v.i.* To attack or destroy with or as with bombs. **—** *v.i. Informal* To fail utterly; flop. [< F *bombe* < Sp. *bomba* < L *bombus* loud sound < Gk. *bombos* hollow noise]
bom·ba·ca·ceous (bom'bə-kā'shəs) *adj. Bot.* Of or pertaining to the silk-cotton family (*Bombacaceae*) of tropical American trees, with dry or fleshy fruit, some yielding a cottony fiber. [< LL *bombax, -acis* cotton. See BOMBAST.]
bom·bard (*v.* bom·bärd'; *n.* bom'bärd) *v.t.* **1.** To attack with bombs or shells. **2.** To attack as with missiles: to *bombard* someone with questions. **3.** *Physics* To expose (substances) to radiation or the impact of high-energy particles. **—** *n.* The earliest form of cannon, originally hurling stones. [< MF *bombarder* < OF *bombarde* a cannon, ult. < L *bombus.* See BOMB.] **— bom·bard'er** *n.* **— bom·bard'ment** *n.*
bom·bar·dier (bom'bər-dir') *n.* **1.** *Mil.* The member of the crew of a bomber who operates the bombsight and releases bombs. **2.** A ground beetle (*Brachinus tscherniki*) that, on irritation, ejects an acrid liquid. **3.** *Brit. & Canadian* An artillery corporal. **4.** *Canadian* A vehicle having caterpillar treads at the rear and skis at the front. [< F]
bom·bar·don (bom'bər-dən, bom-bär'dən) *n.* **1.** A valved brass instrument resembling a tuba, but lower in pitch; a bass tuba. **2.** A 16-foot pedal reed stop on the organ. **3.** An early wind instrument of the oboe family, predecessor of the bassoon. [< Ital. *bombardone*]
bom·bast (bom'bast) *n.* **1.** Grandiloquent or pompous language. **2.** *Obs.* Stuffing or padding, as of cotton, wool, etc. [< OF *bombace* padding < LL *bombax, -acis* cotton, ult. < Persian *pambak*; infl. in LL by L *bombyx* silk < Gk.]
bom·bas·tic (bom-bas'tik) *adj.* High-flown; grandiloquent. Also **bom·bas'ti·cal. — Syn.** See RHETORICAL. **— bom·bas'ti·cal·ly** *adv.*
Bom·bay (bom-bā') **1.** The capital of Maharashtra State, western India, a port and industrial city on the Arabian Sea; pop. 5,931,989 (1971). **2.** A former state of India, divided (1960) into the Gujarat and Maharashtra states.
Bombay hemp Sunn.
bom·ba·zine (bom'bə-zēn', bom'bə-zēn) *n.* A fine twilled fabric usually with silk or artificial silk warp and worsted filling. Also **bom'ba·sine'.** [< F *bombasin* < LL *bombasinum* < *bombax* cotton. See BOMBAST.]

bomb bay A compartment in military aircraft in which bombs are carried and from which they are dropped.
bomb calorimeter See under CALORIMETER.
bombe (bônb) *n.* A confection in the form of a ball; especially, a mold containing different kinds of ice cream. [< F, *bomb*; so called from its shape]
bomb·er (bom'ər) *n.* **1.** An airplane designed to carry and drop bombs. Abbr. B-. **2.** One who bombs.
bomb·proof (bom'prōōf') *adj.* So constructed as to resist damage from bombs. **—** *n.* A bombproof shelter.
bomb run Run (*n.* def. 33). Also **bomb'ing run.**
bomb·shell (bom'shel') *n.* **1.** A bomb (def. 1). **2.** A complete surprise: His sudden appearance was a *bombshell.*
bomb·sight (bom'sīt') *n. Mil.* An instrument on an aircraft that enables the bombardier to aim accurately.
bomb thrower *Mil.* A gun of the howitzer type formerly used in firing heavy shells.
bom·by·cid (bom'bə-sid) *n.* A moth belonging to the family *Bombycidae*, that includes the silkworm moths. [< NL *Bombycidae* < L *bombyx* silkworm < Gk.]
bom·byx (bom'biks) *n.* A silkworm (genus *Bombyx*). [< L. See BOMBYCID.]
Bon (bōn) *n.* A Japanese festival celebrated in July, honoring the ancestral household spirits: sometimes called *Feast of Lanterns.*
Bon (bon, *Fr.* bôn), **Cape** A promontory of NE Tunisia; 50 mi. long.
Bo·na (bō'nə) A former name for BÔNE.
bo·na·ci (bō'nä-sē') *n.* One of various important food fishes of the grouper type found in Floridian and West Indian waters, especially the **bonaci cardinal** (*Mycteroperca venenosa apua*). [< Am. Sp. *bonasí* < native name]
bo·na fide (bō'nə-fīd', -fī'dē) *adj.* Being, acting, or carried out in good faith; authentic; genuine: *bona fide* transactions. [< L *bona fide* in good faith]
bon a·mi (bôn nà-mē') *French* Good friend; sweetheart. **— bonne a·mie** (bôn à-mē') *fem.*
bo·nan·za (bə-nan'zə) *n. U.S.* **1.** A rich mine, vein, or find of ore. **2.** A source of great wealth; lucky strike. [< Sp., success, prosperity < L *bonus* good]
Bo·na·parte (bō'nə-pärt) A prominent Corsican French family, including: **Napoleon,** 1769–1821, French military leader and conqueror; emperor of France 1804–15 as Napoleon I; his brothers, **Jerome,** 1784–1860, king of Westphalia 1807–13, **Joseph,** 1768–1844, king of Naples 1806–08, of Spain 1808–13, **Louis,** 1778–1846, king of Holland 1806–10, and **Lucien,** 1775–1840; **François Charles Joseph,** 1811–32, titular emperor of France as Napoleon II; son of Napoleon: called *L'Aiglon* (the Eaglet); **Louis Napoleon,** 1808–73, emperor of France 1852–70 as Napoleon III; son of Louis. Also *Buonaparte.*
Bo·na·part·ist (bō'nə-pär'tist) *n.* An adherent of Napoleon Bonaparte, his policies, or the Bonaparte dynasty. **— Bo'na·part'ism** *n.*
Bon·ar Law (bon'ər lô) See (Andrew Bonar) LAW.
Bon·a·ven·tu·ra (bon'ə-ven-tōōr'ə, -tyōōr'ə), **Saint,** 1221–74, Giovanni di Fidanza, Italian Franciscan monk and theologian: called the *Seraphic Doctor.* Also **Bon·a·ven·ture** (bon'ə-ven'chər).
bon·bon (bon'bon', *Fr.* bôn·bôn') *n.* A sugared candy. [< F < *bon* good]
bon·bon·nière (bôn·bô·nyâr') *n. French* A decorated box or dish for confections.
bond (bond) *n.* **1.** That which binds or holds together; a band; tie. **2.** A uniting force or influence: *bonds* of friendship. **3.** A voluntary obligation, with or without forfeit, or the binding force of such an obligation: My word is my *bond.* **4.** A substance that cements or unites; also, the union itself. **5.** *Law* An obligation in writing under seal, the simple form being that in which a person or corporation agrees to pay a certain sum at a specified time. **6.** In finance, an interest-bearing certificate of debt, usually issued by a government, municipality, or corporation, obligating the issuer to pay the principal at a specified time. **7.** In insurance, a policy covering losses suffered through the acts of an employee. **8.** In commerce, the condition of imported goods stored in a bonded warehouse until duties are paid: such goods are said to be *in bond.* **9.** One who provides bail; bondsman; also, bail; surety. **10.** In building, the connection formed by overlapping bricks or other parts of a structure. **11.** Bond paper. **12.** *Chem.* A unit of combining power between the atoms of a molecule, associated with the energy of electrons. Abbr. **bd.** (pl. **bds.**). **— Syn.** See SECURITY. **— bottled in bond** *U.S.* Bottled under government supervision before payment of duties and stored in a bonded warehouse for a stated period, as certain whiskies. **—** *v.t.* **1.** To put a certified debt upon; mortgage. **2.** To furnish bond for; be surety for (someone). **3.** To place, as goods or an employee, under bond; guarantee. **4.** To unite, as with glue, cement, etc. **5.** To lay (bricks, etc.) in interlocking patterns for strength. **—** *v.i.* **6.** To interlock or cohere. **—** *adj.* In bondage; enslaved. [Var. of BAND¹] **— bond'er** *n.*
bond·age (bon'dij) *n.* **1.** Involuntary servitude; slavery; serfdom. **2.** Subjection to any influence or domination.

3. In old English law, villeinage. [< Med.L *bondagium* < OE *bonda* serf < ON *bônde* peasant; infl. in sense by *bonds* fetters, chains]

bond·ed (bon′did) *adj.* **1.** Secured or pledged by a bond or bonds. **2.** Stored in a bonded warehouse; placed in bond.

bonded warehouse A warehouse for storing goods for which duties have not been paid, pending their sale or re-export.

bond·hold·er (bond′hōl′dər) *n.* One owning or holding bonds. **— bond′hold′ing** *adj. & n.*

bond·maid (bond′mād′) *n.* A female bondservant.

bond·man (bond′mən) *n. pl.* **·men** (-mən) **1.** A male slave or serf. **2.** A man bound to serve without wages. **— Syn.** See SLAVE. [< obs. *bond* serf + MAN] **— bond′wom′·an, bonds′wom′an** *n. fem.*

bond paper A strong grade of paper made wholly or in part from rag pulp and treated to resist penetration of ink or moisture: also called *bond*.

bond·ser·vant (bond′sûr′vənt) *n.* **1.** A person bound to serve without wages. **2.** A slave; serf: also **bond′slave′.**

bonds·man (bondz′mən) *n. pl.* **·men** (-mən) **1.** One who provides bond for another. **2.** A bondman. [< BOND (surety) + MAN]

bon·duc·nut (bon′duk·nut′) *n.* The prickly seed of various trees of the genus *Caesalpina*. Also **bon′duc.** [< F *bonduc* < Arabic *bunduq* hazelnut + NUT]

bone (bōn) *n.* **1.** *Anat.* **a** A hard, dense porous material developed from connective tissue and forming the skeleton of vertebrate animals. **b** A separate piece of the skeleton of a vertebrate animal. ◆ Collateral adjectives: *osseous, osteal.* **2.** *pl.* The skeleton as a whole; also, the body. **3.** An animal substance resembling bone, as ivory. **4.** Something made of bone or similar material. **5.** *pl. Informal* Dice. **6.** A strip of whalebone in a waist or corset. **7.** *pl. U.S.* **a** Clappers of bone or wood used in minstrel shows. **b** (*construed as sing.*) The end man in a minstrel show, who plays the bones. **— to feel in (one's) bones** To be sure of; have an intuition of. **— to have a bone to pick** To have grounds for complaint or dispute. **— to make no bones about** To have no scruples about; be direct or straightforward with: He *makes no bones about* his difficulties in studying. **— v. boned, bon·ing** *v.t.* **1.** To remove the bones from. **2.** To stiffen (a garment) with whalebone, etc. **— v.i. 3.** *Slang* To study intensely and quickly: often with *up*. [OE *bān*]

Bône (bôn) A port city in NE Algeria; pop. 150,000 (est. 1960): formerly *Bona.*

bone ash A white, friable substance, the ash of bones, composed mainly of calcium phosphate. Also **bone earth.**

bone·black (bōn′blak′) *n.* A black pigment made by calcining finely ground bones in airtight containers; animal charcoal. Also **bone black.**

bone china Porcelain in which bone ash is used.

bone conduction The transmission of sounds to the inner ear by means of the bones of the skull rather than through the auditory canal: distinguished from *air conduction.*

bone-dry (bōn′drī′) *adj.* Very dry.

bone·head (bōn′hed′) *n. Informal* A stupid person; dolt. Also **bone dust.**

bone meal Pulverized bone, used as feed and fertilizer. Also **bone dust.**

bone of contention A cause or subject of disagreement.

bone oil A viscid, oily substance obtained from bones by dry distillation, used in disinfectants and insecticides.

bon·er (bō′nər) *n. Slang* An error; blunder.

Bon·er (bon′ər), Edmund See BONNER.

bone·set (bōn′set′) *n.* A composite herb (*Eupatorium perfoliatum*), formerly used in medicine as a diaphoretic: also called *agueweed, feverwort, thoroughwort.*

bon·fire (bon′fīr′) *n.* **1.** A large fire built in the open air. **2.** Formerly, a fire for burning corpses. [< BONE + FIRE]

bong (bông, bong) *v.t. & v.i.* To make or cause to make a deep, resounding sound like that of a bell. **— n.** A deep, resounding sound. [Imit.]

bon·go (bong′gō) *n. pl.* **·gos** A large, reddish, white-striped, forest antelope (genus *Taurotragus*) of equatorial Africa, related to the eland, and having heavy, lyrate horns in both sexes. [< native African name]

bongo drums A pair of connected drums, held between the knees and played with the hands, originally from Africa. Also **bon′gos.** For illustration see DRUM[1].

Bon·heur (bôn·nœr′), Rosa, 1822–99, French painter: full name Marie Rosalie Bonheur.

bon·ho·mie (bon′ə·mē′, *Fr.* bô·nô·mē′) *n.* Good nature; genial disposition. Also **bon′hom·mie′.** [< F]

bon·i·face (bon′ə·fās′) *n.* An innkeeper. [after *Boniface,* innkeeper in Farquhar's *Beaux' Stratagem*]

Bon·i·face (bon′ə·fās′), Saint, died 755, English monk: original name Wynfrith: called the Apostle of Germany.

Boniface VIII, 1235?–1303, pope 1294–1303: original name Benedetto Ga·e·ta·ni (gä·ē·tä′nē).

Bo·nin Islands (bō′nin) A Pacific island group SE of Japan, administered by the United States; 40 sq. mi.: held by Japan, 1880–1945, as *Ogasawara Jima.*

bo·ni·to (bə·nē′tō) *n. pl.* **·to** or **·toes** Any of various large, mackerellike marine fishes (genus *Sarda*), as the **Pacific bonito** (*S. chiliensis*): also called *skipjack.* [< Sp.]

bon jour (bôn zhŏŏr′) *French* Good day; good morning.

BONITO
(To 30 inches long)

bon mot (bôn mō) *pl.* **bons mots** (bôn mōz′, *Fr.* mō′) A clever saying; terse witticism. [< F]

Bonn (bon) The capital of the German Federal Republic, in the western part, on the Rhine; pop. 299,376 (est. 1970).

Bon·nard (bô·nàr′), Pierre, 1867–1947, French painter.

bonne (bôn) *n. French* A housemaid or nursemaid.

Bon·ner (bon′ər), Edmund, 1500?–69, English bishop. Also *Boner.*

bon·net (bon′it) *n.* **1.** An outdoor headdress for women or children, typically covering most of the hair and held in place by ribbons tied under the chin. **2.** *Chiefly Scot.* A cap for men and boys. **3.** An American Indian headdress of feathers. **4.** Something analogous to a bonnet in form or use, such as a metal hood or covering. **5.** A cover or plate that can be removed to inspect a valve or other part of machinery in a chamber. **6.** *Brit.* The hood of an automobile. **7.** *Naut.* A supplementary strip of canvas laced to the foot of a fore-and-aft sail, as a jib in light winds. **— v.t.** To cover with a bonnet. [< OF (*chapel de*) *bonet* (cap of) bonet (a fabric) < Med.L *bonetus*]

Bon·net (bô·ne′), Georges, born 1889, French statesman; foreign minister 1938–39.

bon·net rouge (bô·ne rōōzh′) *pl.* **bon·nets rouges** (bô·ne rōōzh′) *French* **1.** The red cap of the French revolutionists of 1793. **2.** An extremist or revolutionist.

bon·nock (bon′ək) *n. Scot.* A bannock (which see).

bon·ny (bon′ē) *adj.* **·ni·er, ·ni·est** *Scot. & Brit. Dial.* **1.** Having beauty; comely. **2.** Merry; cheerful. **3.** Fine; good. **4.** Robust; healthy. Also **bon′nie.** [< F *bon* good] **— bon′ni·ly** *adv.* **— bon′ni·ness** *n.*

bon·ny·clab·ber (bon′ē·klab′ər) *n. Dial.* Milk curdled by natural souring. [< Irish *bainne clabair* < *bainne* milk + *clabair* clabber < *claba* thick]

bon·sai (bon′sī′, bôn′-) *n. pl.* **·sai 1.** A dwarfed tree or shrub grown in a pot or tray and trained, by pruning and other techniques, into an esthetically pleasing design. **2.** The art of creating such miniature trees or shrubs. [< Japanese]

bon soir (bôn swàr′) *French* Good evening; good night.

bon·spiel (bon′spēl, -spəl) *n. Scot. & Canadian* A tournament or match, especially at curling. Also **bon′spell** (-spəl).

bon·te·bok (bon′tə·bok) *n. pl.* **·bok** or **·boks** A nearly extinct South African antelope (*Damaliscus pygargus*) related to the blesbok. [< Afrikaans < *bont* pied + *bok* buck, deer]

bon ton (bôn tôn′) **1.** The fashionable world. **2.** Good style or breeding. [< F, lit., good style]

bo·nus (bō′nəs) *n. pl.* **bo·nus·es 1.** Something paid or given in addition to what is usual or stipulated, as a sum of money paid to a salesman over his regular wages. **2.** A grant, as of money or insurance, made by a government to citizens who have rendered military service. **3.** A premium paid for the obtaining of a charter, a loan, etc. [< L, good]

bon vi·vant (bôn vē·vän′) *pl.* **bons vi·vants** (bôn vē·vän′) *French* One who enjoys luxurious living; an epicure.

bon vo·yage (bôn vwà·yàzh′) *French* Pleasant trip.

bon·y (bō′nē) *adj.* **bon·i·er, bon·i·est 1.** Of, like, pertaining to, or consisting of bone or bones. **2.** Having prominent bones; thin; gaunt. **— bon′i·ness** *n.*

bonze (bonz) *n.* A Buddhist monk. [< F < Pg. *bonzo* < Japanese < Chinese *fan seng* religious person]

bon·zer (bon′zər) *adj. Austral. Slang* Very good.

boo (bōō) *n. & interj.* A vocal sound made to indicate contempt or to frighten. **— v. booed, boo·ing** *v.i.* **1.** To utter "boo." **— v.t. 2.** To shout "boo" at. [Imit.]

boob (bōōb) *n. Slang* A simpleton; booby.

boo·boo (bōō′bōō′) *n. pl.* **·boos** *Slang* An embarrassing error; blunder. Also **boo′-boo′.** [Origin uncertain]

boo·by (bōō′bē) *n. pl.* **·bies 1.** A stupid person; dunce. **2.** In some games, the person who makes the poorest score. **3.** Any of several gannets (genus *Sula*) of the coasts of tropical and subtropical America: also **booby gannet.** [< Sp. *bobo* fool, ? < L *balbus* stupid, dull]

booby hatch 1. *Naut.* A raised hood over a small hatchway. **2.** *U.S. Slang* A hospital for the mentally ill.

booby prize A mock award for the worst score or performance in a contest, game, etc.

booby trap 1. A concealed bomb, mine, etc., placed so as to be detonated by casual or careless movements of the unwary victim. **2.** Any device for taking someone unawares.

boo·dle (bōōd′l) *n. U.S. Slang* **1.** Money. **2.** Bribery money; graft. **3.** Loot; swag. **4.** Caboodle. **— v.i. ·dled, ·dling** To receive money corruptly. [Cf. Du. *boedel* property] **— boo′dler** *n.*

boog·ie-woog·ie (bŏŏg′ē·wŏŏg′ē) *n.* **1.** A style of jazz piano playing characterized by repetition of bass rhythms in 8/8 time accompanying melodic and harmonic treble variations. **2.** A piece of music in this style. — *adj.* Of, in, or pertaining to this style. [Origin uncertain]

boo·hoo (bōō/hōō′) *v.i.* **·hooed**, **·hoo·ing** To weep loudly. — *n. pl.* **·hoos** Noisy sobbing. [Imit.]

book (bŏŏk) *n.* **1.** A bound set of printed sheets of paper, usually between covers, forming a volume of some bulk. **2.** A literary composition or treatise of some length, written or printed. **3.** A volume of blank or ruled pages for written entries; a ledger, register, etc. **4.** A main division of a literary composition or treatise: a *book* of the Bible. **5.** A libretto. **6.** The script of a play. **7.** A booklike packet, as of stamps or matches. **8.** Something regarded as a source of instruction: the *book* of experience. **9.** A record of bets, especially on a horse race. **10.** A number of tricks or cards won by a side, as the first six tricks won by the declarer in bridge. *Abbr. b., B., bk.,* (pl. *bks*). — **by the book** According to rule; authoritatively. — **like a book** Thoroughly: He knows the town *like a book.* — **one for the book** (or **books**) Something noteworthy. — **on the books 1.** Recorded. **2.** Enrolled. — **to bring to book** To demand an account from. — **to make book** *U.S. Slang* To bet or accept bets. — **without book 1.** By memory. **2.** Without authority. — *v.t.* **1.** To enter or list in a book. **2.** To arrange for beforehand, as accommodations or seats. **3.** To engage, as actors or a play, for performance. **4.** To make a record of charges against (someone) on a police blotter. [OE]

book·bind·er (bŏŏk/bīn′dər) *n.* One whose trade is the binding of books.

book·bind·er·y (bŏŏk/bīn′dər·ē) *n. pl.* **·er·ies** A place where books are bound.

book·bind·ing (bŏŏk/bīn′ding) *n.* **1.** The art or trade of binding books. **2.** The binding of a book.

book·case (bŏŏk/kās′) *n.* A case having shelves for books.

book club 1. An organization that sells books at reduced rates to members who have agreed to purchase a certain number each year. **2.** A club given over to the reading and discussion of books.

book end A support or prop used to hold books upright.

book·ie (bŏŏk/ē) *n. Informal* A bookmaker (def. 2).

book·ing (bŏŏk/ing) *n.* An engagement to perform, etc.

book·ish (bŏŏk/ish) *adj.* **1.** Fond of books; studious. **2.** Knowing only what has been read in books; unpractical. **3.** Stiltedly literary; pedantic. **4.** Of or pertaining to books; literary. — **book/ish·ly** *adv.* — **book/ish·ness** *n.*

book jacket A dust jacket (which see).

book·keep·er (bŏŏk/kē′pər) *n.* One whose work is bookkeeping.

book·keep·ing (bŏŏk/kē′ping) *n.* The art or practice of recording business transactions systematically. *Abbr. bkkpg.*

book learning Knowledge obtained from books, as opposed to that derived from experience. Also **book knowledge**, **book/lore/.** — **book-learn·ed** (bŏŏk/lûr′nid) *adj.*

book·let (bŏŏk/lit) *n.* A small book or pamphlet.

book louse Any of various small, fragile, winged or wingless insects (order *Corrodentia*) that damage books by eating away the glue of the bindings.

book·mak·er (bŏŏk/mā′kər) *n.* **1.** One who compiles, prints or binds books. **2.** One who makes a business of accepting bets, as in horse racing.

book·man (bŏŏk/mən) *n. pl.* **·men** (-mən) **1.** One versed in books; a scholar. **2.** One who publishes or sells books.

book·mark (bŏŏk/märk′) *n.* **1.** Any object, as a ribbon, inserted in a book to mark a place. **2.** A bookplate.

book·mo·bile (bŏŏk/mə·bēl) *n.* A motor truck equipped to serve as a traveling library. [< BOOK + (AUTO)MOBILE]

book of account 1. A book in which accounts are kept. **2.** *pl.* The original records of the transactions of a business, needed when accounts are audited.

Book of Common Prayer The book of ritual used in the Church of England, and, with certain modifications, in the other Anglican churches. *Abbr. B.C.P.*

Book of Mormon See under MORMON.

book·plate (bŏŏk/plāt′) *n.* A printed label, often having a design, pasted in a book to indicate ownership.

book·rack (bŏŏk/rak′) *n.* **1.** A frame to hold an open book. Also **book/rest/.** **2.** A rack to hold books.

book review An article or essay discussing or critically examining a book, especially a recently published book.

book scorpion Any of various small, flattened, tailless arachnids (order *Chelonethida*), especially the common house scorpion (*Chelifer cancroides*), found in old books, etc.

book·sell·er (bŏŏk/sel′ər) *n.* One whose business is selling books.

book·shelf (bŏŏk/shelf′) *n. pl.* **·shelves** A shelf where books may be kept for ready use.

book·stack (bŏŏk/stak′) *n.* A tall rack containing shelves for books, as in a library.

book·stall (bŏŏk/stôl′) *n.* **1.** A stall or stand where books are sold. **2.** *Brit.* A newsstand.

book·stand (bŏŏk/stand′) *n.* A bookrack or bookstall.

book·store (bŏŏk/stôr′, -stōr′) *n.* A store where books are sold. Also **book/shop/.**

book value 1. The net worth of a business as reflected in its records. **2.** The value of stock as determined by dividing the net worth of a business by its outstanding shares: distinguished from *face value, market value, par value.*

book·worm (bŏŏk/wûrm′) *n.* **1.** One who is excessively devoted to books and study. **2.** Any of various insects destructive to books, especially one of the order *Corrodentia*.

Bool·e·an algebra (bōōl/ē·ən) A form of algebra originally applied to mathematical analysis of logic, but having other applications, notably in the design of digital computers. [after George *Boole*, 1815–64, English mathematician]

boom¹ (bōōm) *v.i.* **1.** To emit a deep, resonant sound, as cannon or drums. **2.** To hum loudly, as bees. **3.** To rush swiftly or in tumult. **4.** *U.S.* To grow rapidly; flourish. — *v.t.* **5.** To utter or sound in a deep resonant tone: often with *out*: to *boom* out the hour. **6.** *U.S.* To praise or advertise vigorously. **7.** *U.S.* To cause to flourish: Prosperous times *boomed* his business. — *n.* **1.** A deep, reverberating sound, as of a cannon, waves, etc. **2.** *U.S.* A sudden increase, as in growth, prosperity, activity, etc.; spurt. — *adj. U.S.* Caused or maintained by a boom: a *boom* town. [Imit. Cf. G *bummen* to hum, Gk. *bombos* hollow noise.]

boom² (bōōm) *n.* **1.** *Naut.* A long spar or pole used to hold or extend the bottom of certain sails. **2.** A long pole or beam extending upward at an angle from the foot of the mast of a derrick, and from which are suspended the objects to be lifted. **3.** A long pole used to suspend or move about a microphone, as during the shooting of films. **4.** *U.S.* A floating chain of connected logs used to enclose other floating logs; also, the area so enclosed. **5.** *U.S.* A barrier, as of floating logs or a cable, used to intercept or retard the advance of a vessel, etc. — *v.t.* **1.** To extend (a sail) by means of a boom: with *out*. **2.** To shove off or away, as a vessel from a wharf: with *off*. **3.** *U.S.* To obstruct (a river, lake, etc.) with a boom. [< Du. *boom* tree, beam. Akin to BEAM.]

BOOM² (def. 2)

boom-and-bust (bōōm/ən·bust′) *n. U.S.* A period of great economic prosperity followed by a severe depression.

boom·e·rang (bōō/mə·rang) *n.* **1.** A curved, wooden missile originated in Australia, one form of which will return to the thrower. **2.** A plan, statement, etc., that recoils upon the originator. — *v.i.* To react harmfully on the originator. [< native Australian name]

BOOMERANGS

boon¹ (bōōn) *n.* **1.** A good thing bestowed; blessing. **2.** *Archaic* A request. [< ON *bōn* petition]

boon² (bōōn) *adj.* **1.** Convivial; merry: now only in the phrase **boon companion**. **2.** *Poetic* Bounteous; benign. [< F *bon* < L *bonus* good]

boon·docks (bōōn/doks′) *n.pl. U.S. Slang* An uncivilized, out-of-the-way, or backwoods area: used with *the*. [< Tagalog *bundok* mountain]

boon·dog·gle (bōōn/dog′əl, -dog/əl) *U.S. Informal v.i.* **·gled**, **·gling** To work on wasteful or unnecessary projects. — *n.* Useless work. [Origin uncertain] — **boon/dog′gler** *n.*

Boone (bōōn), **Daniel**, 1735?–1820, American frontiersman in Kentucky and Missouri.

boor (bŏŏr) *n.* **1.** An awkward, ill-mannered person. **2.** A clownish rustic. **3.** A peasant, especially a Dutch peasant. [< Du. *boer* farmer, rustic]

boor·ish (bŏŏr/ish) *adj.* Rude or ill-mannered; rustic. — **boor/ish·ly** *adv.* — **boor/ish·ness** *n.* — *Syn.* churlish, loutish, unmannerly, clownish, uncouth.

boost (bōōst) *U.S. v.t.* **1.** To raise by pushing from beneath or behind. **2.** To increase: to *boost* prices. **3.** To advance by speaking well of; promote or extol vigorously. — *n.* **1.** A lift; help. **2.** An increase. [Origin uncertain]

boost·er (bōōs/tər) *U.S. n.* **1.** Any device or substance for increasing power, effectiveness, etc. **2.** *Electr.* A device for increasing the electromotive force in an alternating-current circuit. **3.** *Informal* One who gives enthusiastic support.

booster shot *Informal* A supplementary injection, as of a vaccine, to increase immunity.

boot¹ (bōōt) *n.* **1.** A covering, usually of leather, for the foot and part or most of the leg. **2.** *Brit.* A shoe that reaches above the ankle. **3.** An instrument of torture for compressing the foot and leg. **4.** *Brit.* A receptacle for baggage at either end of a vehicle. **5.** A sheath on a saddle or vehicle to hold a rifle or carbine. **6.** A flap on an open vehicle for shielding the driver against rain or mud. **7.** A thick patch for the inside of a tire casing. **8.** A protective covering for the leg of a horse. **9.** The part of the reed pipe of an organ that contains the reed. **10.** A kick. **11.** *U.S.* The lowest leaf-bearing segment of a stalk of wheat. **12.** *Ornithol.* A tarsal covering in certain birds, as thrushes. **13.** In U.S. Navy and Marine Corps slang, a recent recruit. — **too big for one's boots** *U.S.* Proud; conceited. — **the boot** *Slang* Dismissal; discharge. — **to die with one's boots on** To die fighting or working. — *v.t.* **1.** To put boots on. **2.** To torture with the boot. **3.** To kick; also, in football, to punt.

4. *Slang* To dismiss; fire; also, to eject forcibly: often with *out.* [< OF *bote*; ult. origin uncertain]
boot² (boŏt) *v.t.* **1.** *Archaic* To benefit. — *v.i.* **2.** *Obs.* To be of avail. — *n.* **1.** *Dial.* Something given in addition. **2.** *Obs.* Advantage; also, remedy. — **to boot** In addition; over and above. [ME *boten* < OE *bōt* profit]
boot·black (boŏt′blak′) *n.* One whose business is shining boots and shoes.
boot·ed (boŏt′id) *adj.* **1.** Wearing boots. **2.** *Ornithol.* Not divided into scutella except at the extreme lower portion; covered with feathers, as the tarsi of some birds.
boo·tee (boŏ-tē′, boŏ′tē) *n.* **1.** A baby's knitted woolen boot. **2.** A light half boot for women. Also **boo·tie** (boŏ′tē).
Bo·ö·tes (bō-ō′tēz) *n.* A constellation, the Bear Keeper: also called *Herdsman*. See CONSTELLATION. [< L < Gk. *boōtēs* plowman]
booth (boŏth, boŏth) *n.* **1.** A small compartment or cubicle for privacy or keeping out sound, etc.: a voting *booth;* telephone *booth.* **2.** A seating compartment, as in a restaurant, usually consisting of a table and benches whose backs serve as partitions. **3.** A small, temporary enclosure or stall for the display or sale of goods, as at an exhibition or fair. **4.** A temporary, slightly built shelter or shed. [ME *bothe* < Scand. Cf. Dan. *bad* booth and ON *buth* dwelling.]
Booth (boŏth) A family of English reformers and religious leaders, including **William**, 1829–1912, founder of the Salvation Army: called **General Booth; Ballington**, 1859–1940, son of William; founder of the Volunteers of America; **Evangeline Cory**, 1865–1950, daughter of William; **William Bramwell**, 1856–1929, son of William.
— **Junius Brutus**, 1796–1852, U.S. actor born in England; father of **Edwin Thomas**, 1833–93, U.S. actor, and **John Wilkes**, 1838–65, U.S. actor; assassinated Abraham Lincoln.
Boo·thi·a, Gulf of (boŏ′thē-ə) An inlet of the Arctic 250 miles long in the Northwest Territories, Canada, between Baffin Island and **Boothia Peninsula**, formerly **Boothia Felix** (fē′liks), extending 190 miles and containing the northernmost point of the North American continent.
boot·jack (boŏt′jak′) *n.* A forked device for holding a boot while the foot is withdrawn.
Boo·tle (boŏt′l) A county borough and port adjoining Liverpool, England; pop. 82,829 (1961).
boot·leg (boŏt′leg′) *U.S. v.t. & v.i.* **·legged, ·leg·ging** To make, sell, or carry for sale (liquor, etc.) illegally; smuggle. — *adj.* Unlawful: *bootleg* whisky. — *n.* **1.** The part of a boot above the instep. **2.** Liquor, or other merchandise, unlawfully carried, produced, sold, or offered for sale. [With ref. to the smuggling of liquor in bootlegs] — **boot′leg′ger** *n.* — **boot′leg′ging** *n.*
boot·less (boŏt′lis) *adj.* Profitless; useless; unavailing. — **Syn.** See FUTILE. [< BOOT² + -LESS] — **boot′less·ly** *adv.* — **boot′less·ness** *n.*
boot·lick (boŏt′lik′) *U.S. Slang v.t. & v.i.* To flatter servilely; toady. — **boot′lick′er** *n.* — **boot′lick′ing** *n. & adj.*
boots (boŏts) *n. pl.* **boots** *Brit.* A servant at an inn or hotel who shines shoes or boots.
boot tree An apparatus for stretching boots or shoes, or for keeping them in shape.
boo·ty (boŏ′tē) *n. pl.* **·ties** **1.** The spoil of war; plunder. **2.** Goods taken by violence or robbery. **3.** Any prize or gain. [< F *butin* < MLG; infl. by obs. *boot* advantage, profit]
booze (boŏz) *Informal n.* **1.** Alcoholic drink. **2.** A drunken spree. — *v.i.* **boozed, booz·ing** To drink to excess; tipple. Also, *Brit.,* **bouse.** [< MDu. *busen* to drink, tipple] — **booz′er** *n.*
booz·y (boŏ′zē) *adj. Informal* Drunken; alcoholic: also, *Brit.,* **bousy.** — **booz′i·ly** *adv.* — **booz′i·ness** *n.*
bop¹ (bop) *v.t.* **bopped, bop·ping** *Slang* To hit or strike. [Imit.]
bop² (bop) *n.* A variety of jazz characterized by deliberate departures from key and extreme variation of rhythmic pattern, sometimes sung with meaningless sounds: also called *bebop.* [Short for BEBOP]
bor. Borough.
bo·ra (bō′rä) *n.* A cold, stormy wind from the Alps, blowing over the Adriatic in winter. [< dial. Ital., var. of Ital. *borea* < L *Boreas* the north wind]
bo·rac·ic (bə-ras′ik) *adj. Chem.* Boric.
bo·ra·cite (bôr′ə-sīt, bō′rä-) *n.* A vitreous, white, translucent chloride and borate of magnesium that crystallizes in the isometric system. [< BORAX + -ITE¹]
bor·age (bûr′ij, bôr′-, bor′-) *n.* An erect European herb (*Borago officinalis*) typical of a family (*Boraginaceae*), having blue flowers and hairy leaves, used medicinally and in salads. [< Med.L *borrago* < *borra*, burra rough hair]
bo·rag·i·na·ceous (bə-raj′ə-nā′shəs) *adj. Bot.* Pertaining or belonging to the borage family. [< NL *Boraginaceae* < *borrago.* See BORAGE.]
Bor·ah (bôr′ə, bō′rä), **William Edgar**, 1865–1940, U.S. lawyer; senator from Idaho.

bo·rane (bôr′ān, bō′rān) *n. Chem.* Boron hydride, BH_3, forming part of many boron compounds and their organic derivatives. [< BOR(ON) + -ANE²]
bo·rate (bôr′āt, bō′rāt) *n. Chem.* A salt of boric acid. — **bo′rat·ed** *adj.*
bo·rax (bôr′aks, bō′raks) *n.* A white crystalline compound, $Na_2B_4O_7 \cdot 10H_2O$, found native as tincal, and used as a cleansing agent, in medicine, as a flux, in manufacturing glass, etc. [< OF *boras* < Med.L *borax* < Arabic *būraq* < Persian *būrah*]
bo·ra·zon (bôr′ə-zon, bō′rə-) *n. Chem.* A crystalline compound of boron and nitrogen, BN, equaling the diamond in hardness but with a much higher melting point. [< BOR(ON) + AZO- + -n]
Bor·deaux (bôr·dō′) *n.* A white or red wine produced in the vicinity of Bordeaux, France. See CLARET (def. 1).
Bor·deaux (bôr·dō′) A port city in SW France, on the Garonne; pop. 263,808 (1968).
Bordeaux mixture A fungicide and insecticide for trees and plants, prepared by mixing solutions of copper sulfate and lime, or of copper arsenate and phenols.
bor·del·lo (bôr·del′ō) *n.* A brothel. Also **bor·del** (bôr′dəl) [< Ital. < Med.L *bordellus,* dim. of *borda* cottage]
bor·der (bôr′dər) *n.* **1.** A margin or edge. **2.** The frontier line or district of a country or state; boundary. **3.** A design or stripe in the margins of a page of a book, an illustration, etc. **4.** A decorative edging or margin, as of lace on a cap. **5.** A bordering strip of ground, commonly planted with flowers, as along the edge of a walk. — **the Border** (or **Borders**) The boundary and nearby land between England and Scotland. — *adj.* Of, on, or forming the border. — *v.t.* **1.** To put a border or edging on. **2.** To lie along the border of; bound. — **to border on** (or **upon**) **1.** To be adjacent to; bound. **2.** To approach in character; verge on: That act *borders on* piracy. [< OF *bordure* < *bord* edge, ult. < Gmc.] — **bor′dered** *adj.* — **bor′der·er** *n.* — **bor′der·ing** *adj.*
bor·de·reau (bôr′də-rō, bôr′də-rō′) *n. pl.* **·reaux** (-rō′, -rōz′) **1.** A digest of insurance transactions, chiefly those between companies engaged in reinsurance. **2.** A memorandum, note, or invoice, especially one that details accompanying documents. [< F]
bor·der·land (bôr′dər-land′) *n.* **1.** Land on or near the border of two adjoining countries. **2.** Debatable or indeterminate ground: the *borderland* between love and hate.
bor·der·line (bôr′dər-līn′) *n.* A line of demarcation. Also **border line.** — *adj.* Difficult to classify; doubtful.
Border States Five of the former slave States of the United States, Delaware, Kentucky, Maryland, Missouri, and Virginia, that bordered on the free States of the North.
Bor·det (bôr-de′), **Jules**, 1870–1961, Belgian bacteriologist.
bor·dure (bôr′jər) *n. Heraldry* A border around a shield.
bore¹ (bôr, bōr) *v.* **bored, bor·ing** *v.t.* **1.** To make a hole in or through, as with a drill. **2.** To make (a tunnel, etc.) by or as by drilling. **3.** To force (one's way). **4.** To weary by being dull, tedious, long-winded, etc.; tire. — *v.i.* **5.** To make a hole, etc., by or as by drilling. **6.** To admit of being drilled: This wood *bores* easily. **7.** To force one's way; advance by persistent motion. — *n.* **1.** A hole made by or as if by boring. **2.** The interior diameter of a firearm or cylinder; caliber. **3.** One who or that which is tiresome. [v., OE *borian* < *bor* auger; n. < v. + ON *bora* hole]
bore² (bôr, bōr) *n.* A high, crested wave caused by the rush of a flood tide, as in the Amazon. Compare EAGRE. [< ON *bāra* billow]
bore³ (bôr, bōr) Past tense of BEAR¹.
bo·re·al (bôr′ē-əl, bō′rē-) *adj.* Pertaining to the north or the north wind. [< LL *borealis* < L *Boreas,* the north wind]
Bo·re·al (bôr′ē-əl, bō′rē-) *adj. Geog.* Describing a subdivision of the Holarctic region, including the great belt of coniferous forests extending from New England to Alaska.
Bo·re·as (bôr′ē-əs, bō′rē-) In Greek mythology, the north wind. [< L < Gk.]
bore·dom (bôr′dəm, bōr′-) *n.* The condition of being bored; ennui.
bor·er (bôr′ər, bō′rər) *n.* **1.** A tool used for boring. **2.** A beetle, moth, or worm that burrows in plants, wood, etc.; especially, the **metallic wood borer** (family *Buprestidae*), the **palm borer** (family *Bostrichidae*), and the **maple borer** (family *Cerambycidae*). For illustration see INSECTS (injurious). **3.** The shipworm.
Bor·gia (bôr′jä) An aristocratic Spanish family, a branch of which emigrated to Italy, including **Alfonso**, 1378–1458, pope 1455–58 as *Calixtus III;* his nephew **Rodrigo**, 1431?–1503, pope 1492–1503 as *Alexander VI;* the children of Rodrigo, notably **Cesare**, 1475?–1507, soldier and statesman, and **Lucrezia**, 1480–1519, duchess of Ferrara; **Francisco**, 1510–1572, Spanish Jesuit; canonized 1670; great-grandson of Rodrigo.
Bor·glum (bôr′gləm), **Gutzon**, 1867–1941, U.S. sculptor: full name **John Gutzon de la Mothe Borglum.**

---

bo·ric (bôr′ik, bō′rik) *adj. Chem.* Of, pertaining to, or derived from boron: also *boracic.*

boric acid *Chem.* A white crystalline compound, H_3BO_3, found native and obtained by treating borax with sulfuric acid, used as a preservative, and as a mild antiseptic.

bo·ride (bôr′īd, bō′rīd) *n.* A binary compound of boron and another element. [< BOR(ON) + -IDE]

bor·ing (bôr′ing, bō′ring) *n.* **1.** The act of one who or that which bores. **2.** A hole so made; a bore. **3.** *pl.* Material removed by boring. — *adj.* Tedious; wearisome. [OE *boren,* pp. of *beran* to bear]

Bo·ris III (bôr′is, bō′ris), 1894–1943, king of Bulgaria 1918–1943.

born (bôrn) *adj.* **1.** Brought forth or into being, as offspring. Abbr. *b., B.* **2.** Natural; by birth: a *born* musician. [OE *boren,* pp. of *beran* to bear]

borne (bôrn, bōrn) Past participle of BEAR[1].

Bor·ne·o (bôr′nē·ō, bôr′-) The third largest island of the world, between the Java and South China seas; 286,969 sq. mi.; divided into: **North Borneo,** Malay *Sabah,* 29,338 sq. mi.; pop. 633,000 (est. 1969); capital, Jesselton; Sarawak (which see), with North Borneo comprising a part of Malaysia; Brunei (which see); and **Indonesian Borneo,** formerly **Dutch Borneo,** Indonesian *Kalimantan,* 208,285 sq. mi. See map of INDONESIA.

bor·ne·ol (bôr′nē·ōl, -ol, bôr′-) *n. Chem.* A translucent crystalline solid, $C_{10}H_{18}O$, found in cavities in the trunk of a large tree (*Dryobalanops aromatica*) of Borneo and Sumatra: also called *camphol.* [< BORNE(O) + -OL[1]]

Born·holm (bôrn′hōlm) An island in the Baltic Sea, constituting a county of Denmark; 227 sq. mi.; pop. 48,373 (1960); capital, Rønne.

born·ite (bôr′nīt) *n.* A metallic, reddish brown, copper-iron sulfide showing purple tarnish, an important ore of copper. Also called *peacock ore.* [after Ignaz von *Born,* 1742–91, Austrian metallurgist]

Bor·nu (bôr·nōō′) A province of NE Nigeria; 45,900 sq. mi.; pop. about 1,331,000; capital, Maiduguri; formerly a Moslem native kingdom.

Bor·o·din (bôr′ə·dēn, *Russian* bə·rə·dyēn′), **Aleksandr Porfirevich,** 1834–87, Russian composer.

Bor·o·di·no (bôr′ə·dē′nō, *Russian* bə·rə·dyi·nô′) A village near Moscow; site of a victory by Napoleon over the Russians, 1812.

bo·ron (bôr′on, bō′ron) *n.* A nonmetallic element (symbol B) obtained amorphous, or in crystalline form by reduction of its compounds. See ELEMENT. [< BOR(AX) + (CARB)ON]

boron carbide *Chem.* An extremely hard compound of carbon and boron, B_4C, often used in cutting tools.

bo·ro·sil·i·cate (bôr′ə·sil′ə·kit, -kāt, bō′rə-) *n. Chem.* A salt in which boric and silicic acids are united with a base.

bor·ough (bûr′ō, -ə) *n.* **1.** An incorporated village or town. **2.** One of the five administrative divisions of New York, N.Y. **3.** *Brit.* **a** A town with a municipal corporation and certain privileges granted by royal charter: also **municipal borough. b** A town entitled to representation in Parliament: also **parliamentary borough. 4.** *Obs.* Any town. Abbr. *bor.* [OE *burg, burh* fort, town, ult. < Gmc. Akin to BOURG, BURG.]

bor·ough-Eng·lish (bûr′ō·ing′glish) *n.* An old custom in certain parts of England by which the youngest son, or, in default of issue, the youngest brother, inherits the estate.

bor·row (bôr′ō, bor′ō) *v.t.* **1.** To take or obtain (something) with the promise or understanding that one will return it or its equivalent. **2.** To adopt for one's own use, as words or ideas. **3.** In arithmetical subtraction, to withdraw (a unit of ten) from any figure of the minuend in order to add it to the next lower denomination. — *v.i.* **4.** To borrow something. — *n. Obs.* **1.** A pledge; surety. **2.** The act of borrowing, or something borrowed. [OE *borgian* to give a pledge, borrow < *borg* pledge] — **bor′row·er** *n.*

Bor·row (bôr′ō, bor′ō), **George Henry,** 1803–81, English writer and authority on Romany language and customs.

borscht (bôrsht) *n.* A Russian beet soup, eaten hot or cold. Also **borsch** (bôrsh). [< Russian *borshch*]

borscht circuit *U.S. Slang* A series of summer resorts, chiefly in the Catskill Mountains, where professional entertainment is provided. [after a characteristic item of the cuisine]

bort (bôrt) *n.* An impure diamond, used only for cutting and polishing: sometimes called *carbonado.* Also **bortz** (bôrts). [? < OF *bort* bastard] — **bort′y** *adj.*

Bo·rus·sian (bō·rush′ən) *n.* Prussian (*n.* def 2).

bor·zoi (bôr′zoi) *n.* A breed of Russian hounds, resembling the greyhound but larger, and having a long, silky coat: also called *Russian wolfhound.* [< Russian, swift]

Bo·san·quet (bō′zən·ket), **Bernard,** 1848–1923, English philosopher.

bos·cage (bos′kij) *n.* A mass of shrubbery; thicket; clump. Also **bos′kage.** [< OF, ult. < Gmc. Akin to BUSH.]

Bosch (bos), **Hieronymus,** 1450?–1516, Dutch painter. Also **Jerom Bos.**

Bosch (bôsh), **Karl,** 1874–1940, German chemist.

bosch·bok (bosh′bok) *n.* The bushbuck (which see). Also **bosh′bok.**

bosch·vark (bosh′värk) *n.* A wild hog (*Potamochoerus choeropotamus*) of South Africa: also called *bush pig.* Also **bosh′vark.** [< Afrikaans < Du. *bosch* wood + *vark* pig]

Bose (bōs), **Sir Jagadis Chandra,** 1858–1937, Indian physicist and plant physiologist.

bosh[1] (bosh) *n. Informal* Empty words; nonsense. [< Turkish, empty, worthless]

bosh[2] (bosh) *n.* **1.** The part of one of the sloping sides of a blast furnace extending from the belly to the hearth. **2.** A trough for cooling ingots, etc. [Cf. G *böschung* slope]

bosk (bosk) *n.* A thicket of bushes; a small wood. [ME, var. of *busk* bush]

bos·ket (bos′kit) *n.* A clump of trees; thicket. Also **bos′quet.** [< F *bosquet* < Ital. *boschetto,* dim. of *bosco* wood, ult. < Gmc.]

bosk·y (bos′kē) *adj.* **1.** Wooded; bushy. **2.** Shaded by or as by trees. — **bosk′i·ness** *n.*

bo's'n (bō′sən) See BOATSWAIN.

Bos·ni·a and Her·ze·go·vi·na (boz′nē·ə; hûr′tsə·gō·vē′nə) A constituent Republic of central Yugoslavia; 19,745 sq. mi.; pop. 3,594,000 (est. 1965); capital, Sarajevo: divided into two regions, **Bosnia** in the north and **Herzegovina** in the south.

Bos·ni·an (boz′nē·ən) *adj.* Of or pertaining to Bosnia. Also **Bos·ni·ac** (boz′nē·ak). — *n.* **1.** A native or inhabitant of Bosnia. **2.** The Serbo-Croatian language of the Bosnians.

bos·om (bŏoz′əm, bōō′zəm) *n.* **1.** The breast of a human being, especially of a woman. **2.** The breast with the arms, considered as an enclosure in embracing. **3.** The portion of a garment covering the breast. **4.** The breast as the seat of thought and emotion. **5.** Something suggesting the human breast: the *bosom* of the earth. **6.** Inner circle; midst: in the *bosom* of the church. — *adj.* **1.** Close; intimate: a *bosom* friend. **2.** Of or pertaining to the bosom. — *v.t.* **1.** To have or cherish in the bosom; embrace. **2.** To hide in the bosom; conceal. [OE *bōsm*]

Bos·po·rus (bos′pə·rəs) A strait between the Black Sea and the Sea of Marmara, separating European from Asian Turkey; length, 17 mi. Also **Bos·pho·rus** (bos′fə·rəs). Turkish *Karadeniz Boğazi.*

boss[1] (bôs, bos) *U.S. Informal n.* **1.** A superintendent or employer of workmen; manager; foreman. **2.** A professional politician who controls a political organization. — *v.t.* **1.** To supervise; direct. **2.** To order or command in a peremptory or highhanded manner. — *v.i.* **3.** To act as boss. — *adj.* Head; chief. [< Du. *baas* master]

boss[2] (bôs, bos) *n.* **1.** A circular prominence; a knob; stud. **2.** *Archit.* A projecting ornament, as at the intersection of the ribs of a groined arch. **3.** *Mech.* An enlarged part of a shaft, coupling with a wheel or another shaft. **4.** *Geol.* A domelike mass of igneous rock. — *v.t.* **1.** To ornament with bosses. **2.** To emboss. [< OF *boce* bump, knob]

boss[3] (bos, bôs) *n. U.S. Informal* A calf or a cow. [Cf. L *bos* cow]

Bos·sier City (bō′zhər) A city in NW Louisiana, near Shreveport; pop. 41,595.

boss·ism (bôs′iz·əm, bos′-) *n. U.S.* Control by political bosses.

Bos·suet (bô·swe′), **Jacques Bénigne,** 1627–1704, French bishop and writer.

boss·y[1] (bôs′ē, bos′ē) *adj.* **boss·i·er, boss·i·est** *U.S. Informal* Tending to boss; domineering.

boss·y[2] (bôs′ē, bos′ē) *adj.* Decorated with bosses.

boss·y[3] (bôs′ē, bos′ē) *n. U.S. Informal* A cow or a calf.

bos·ton (bôs′tən, bos′-) *n.* **1.** A game of cards, somewhat resembling whist; also, a bid in this game. **2.** A form of waltz. [after *Boston,* Mass.]

Bos·ton (bôs′tən, bos′-) The capital of Massachusetts; a port in the eastern part, on Boston Bay; pop. 641,071. Abbr. *B.* — **Bos·to·ni·an** (bôs·tō′nē·ən, bos·-) *n. & adj.*

Boston bag A small handbag or satchel opening at the top and having a handle at each side of the opening.

Boston Bay The inner portion of Massachusetts Bay, containing **Boston Harbor,** its NE inlet.

Boston brown bread A dark steamed bread containing corn meal, rye flour, and molasses: also called *brown bread.*

Boston cream pie A rich, two-layer cake with a cream filling.

Boston Massacre A riot in Boston in 1770 against British troops, in which three colonials were killed.

Boston rocker An American 19th-century rocking chair having an upcurved wooden seat and a high back with spindles held at the top by a wide rail.

Boston Tea Party An uprising in Boston, Massachusetts, December 16, 1773, against the British customs officials, during which colonists, disguised as Indians, boarded British ships in the harbor and dumped chests of tea overboard.

Boston terrier A small terrier having a short, smooth, brindled coat with white markings, originally crossbred from a bulldog and a white terrier. Also **Boston bull.**

bo·sun (bō′sən) See BOATSWAIN.

Bos·well (boz′wel, -wəl), **James**, 1740–95, Scottish lawyer and writer; biographer of Samuel Johnson.

Bos·worth Field (boz′wûrth) A region near Leicestershire, England; scene of the final battle (1485) in the Wars of the Roses.

bot (bot) *n.* The larva of a botfly: also spelled *bott.* [Origin unknown]

bot. 1. Botanical; botanist; botany. 2. Bottle.

B.O.T. Board of Trade.

bo·tan·i·cal (bə·tan′i·kəl) *adj.* 1. Of or pertaining to botany. 2. Of or pertaining to plants. Also **bo·tan′ic.** — *n.* A drug derived from the leaves, roots, stems, etc., of a plant. [< F *botanique* < Gk. *botanikos* < *botanē* plant, pasture < *boskein* to feed, graze] — **bo·tan′i·cal·ly** *adv.*

bot·a·nist (bot′ə·nist) *n.* One versed in botany.

bot·a·nize (bot′ə·nīz) *v.* **·nized, ·niz·ing** *v.i.* 1. To study botanical specimens. 2. To gather plants for study. — *v.t.* 3. To search for botanical specimens. — **bot′a·niz′er** *n.*

bot·a·ny (bot′ə·nē) *n.* 1. The division of biology that treats of plants with reference to their structure, functions, classification, etc. 2. The total plant life of a country, region, zone, etc.: the *botany* of Oceania. 3. The characteristics of a group of plants treated collectively: the *botany* of orchids. 4. A text or treatise on botany. Sometimes called *phytology.* [Back formation < BOTANICAL]

Botany Bay An inlet of the Pacific south of Sydney, Australia, near the former site of a British penal colony.

botch[1] (boch) *v.t.* 1. To put together, do, or present ineptly; bungle. 2. To patch or mend clumsily. — *n.* 1. A bungled piece of work; a bad job. 2. A clumsy patch. [ME *bocchen*; origin unknown] — **botch′er** *n.* — **botch′er·y** *n.*

botch[2] (boch) *n. Brit. Dial.* A superficial swelling or ulcer; a boil. [< OF *boche*, var. of *boce* knob, lump]

botch·y (boch′ē) *adj.* **botch·i·er, botch·i·est** Imperfect; poorly done. — **botch′i·ly** *adv.*

bot·fly (bot′flī′) *n.* A fly (family *Gasterophilidae* or *Oestridae*) of which the larvae are parasitic in vertebrates; especially, the **horse botfly** (*Gasterophilus intestinalis*). For illustration see INSECTS (injurious). [< BOT + FLY[2]]

both (bōth) *adj. & pron.* The two together; one and the other: *Both* girls laughed; *Both* were there. — *conj. & adv.* Equally; alike; as well: with *and*: The bill passed *both* the House and the Senate. [< ON *bādhar*]

Bo·tha (bō′tə), **Louis**, 1862–1919, South African statesman; premier 1910–19.

both·er (both′ər) *v.t.* 1. To pester; give trouble to. 2. To confuse; fluster. — *v.i.* 3. To trouble or concern oneself. — *n.* 1. A state of annoyance; vexation. 2. One who or that which bothers. [? dial. E (Irish) var. of POTHER] — **Syn.** (verb) 1. annoy, vex, harass, trouble, pester, worry. Compare IRRITATE, PIQUE.

both·er·a·tion (both′ə·rā′shən) *n. Informal* Annoyance; vexation. — *interj.* An exclamation of annoyance.

both·er·some (both′ər·səm) *adj.* Causing bother; annoying.

Both·ni·a (both′nē·ə), **Gulf of** A northern inlet of the Baltic Sea between Sweden and Finland; length about 400 mi.

bo tree (bō) The sacred Buddhist pipal under which Gautama received enlightenment and became the Buddha. [Trans. of Singhalese *bogaha*, alter. of Pali *bodhi-taru*, lit., tree of perfect knowledge]

bot·ry·oi·dal (bot′rē·oid′l) *adj.* Like a cluster of grapes. Also **bot′ry·oid.** [< Gk. *botryoeidēs* < *botrys* cluster of grapes + *eidos* form, shape] — **bot′ry·oi′dal·ly** *adv.*

bot·ry·ose (bot′rē·ōs) *adj.* 1. *Bot.* Racemose. 2. Botryoidal.

bots (bots) *n.pl.* (*construed as sing.*) *Vet.* A disease of horses, sheep, etc., caused by botfly larvae.

Bot·swa·na (bot·swä′nä) *n.* An independent member of the Commonwealth of Nations in southern Africa; 222,000 sq. mi.; pop. 629,000 (est. 1969); capital, Gaberones: formerly *Bechuanaland Protectorate.* Officially **Republic of Botswana.** See map of (Republic of) SOUTH AFRICA.

bott (bot) See BOT.

Bot·ti·cel·li (bot′ə·chel′ē, *Ital.* bôt′tē·chel′lē), **Sandro**,1447?–1515, Florentine painter: original name **Alessandro di Mariano dei Fi·li·pe·pi** (fē·lē·pā′pē).

bot·tle (bot′l) *n.* 1. A vessel, usually of glass, for holding liquids, having a neck and a narrow mouth that can be stopped. 2. As much as a bottle will hold: also **bot′tle·ful′.** *Abbr. bot.* — **the bottle** 1. Alcoholic drink. 2. Milk from a bottle for babies. — **to hit the bottle** *U.S. Slang* To drink liquor to excess. — *v.t.* **·tled, ·tling** 1. To put into a bottle or bottles. 2. To restrain; shut in, as if in a bottle: often with *up* or *in.* [< OF *bouteille, botel* < LL *buticula* flask, dim. of *butis* vat, vessel] — **bot′tler** *n.*

bottled in bond See under BOND.

bottle green A dark, dull green.

bot·tle·neck (bot′l·nek′) *n.* 1. A narrow or congested passageway. 2. Anything that retards progress; hindrance.

bot·tle·nose (bot′l·nōz′) *n.* One of various dolphins, especially *Tursiops truncatus* of the North Atlantic.

bot·tle·stone (bot′l·stōn′) *n.* A mineral, as chrysolite or

moldavite, having the characteristics of ordinary bottle glass, sometimes used as a gemstone.

bottle tree A Queensland tree (*Brachychiton rupestrie*) the trunk of which is swollen out like a bottle, or a related species (*B. populneum*) of Victoria.

bot·tom (bot′əm) *n.* 1. The lowest part of anything. 2. The underside or undersurface. 3. The ground beneath a body of water. 4. Source or foundation; fundamental quality: to get to the *bottom* of an affair. 5. *Often pl.* Lowland along a river: also *bottom* land. 6. *Naut.* The part of a vessel below the water line. 7. *Informal* The buttocks. 8. The seat of a chair. 9. Staying power; stamina. — **at bottom** Fundamentally. — **bottoms up!** *Informal* Empty your glass! — *adj.* Lowest; fundamental; basal. — *v.t.* 1. To provide with a bottom. 2. To base or found: with *on* or *upon.* 3. To fathom; comprehend. — *v.i.* 4. To be founded; rest. 5. To touch or rest on the bottom. [OE]

bottom dollar *U.S. Slang* One's last dollar.

bottom land Bottom (def. 5).

bot·tom·less (bot′əm·lis) *adj.* 1. Having no bottom. 2. Unfathomable; limitless; endless. — **the bottomless pit** Hell.

bot·tom·ry (bot′əm·rē) *n.* A maritime contract whereby the owner or master of a vessel borrows money, pledging the vessel as security.

bot·u·lin (boch′ŏŏ·lin) *n.* A highly active nerve poison formed by an anaerobic bacterium (*Clostridium botulinum*) and sometimes present in spoiled or badly prepared food.

bot·u·lism (boch′ŏŏ·liz′əm) *n.* Poisoning caused by botulin and characterized by acute gastrointestinal and nervous disorders. [< G *botulismus* < L *botulus* sausage; so called because the bacteria were first isolated from spoiled sausage]

Bou·cher (bŏŏ·shā′), **François**, 1703–70, French painter.

Bou·ci·cault (bŏŏ′si·kō), **Dion**, 1822?–90, U.S. dramatist and actor born in Ireland: original name **Dionysius Lardner Bour·si·quot** (bŏŏr′si·kō).

bou·clé (bŏŏ·klā′) *n.* A woven or knitted fabric with a looped or knotted surface; also, the yarn from which this is made. [< F, pp. of *boucler* to buckle, curl]

bou·doir (bŏŏ′dwär, bŏŏ·dwär′) *n.* A lady's private sitting room or bedroom. [< F, lit., pouting room < *bouder* to pout, sulk] — **bou·doir·esque** (bŏŏ′dwär·esk′) *adj.*

bouf·fant (bŏŏ·fänt′) *adj.* Puffed-out; flaring, as a skirt. [< F, ppr. of *bouffer* to swell]

bouffe (bŏŏf) *n.* Opéra bouffe (which see). [< F (*opéra*) *bouffe* comic (opera) < Ital. *buffa* joke, jest]

Bou·gain·ville (bŏŏ′gən·vil) The largest of the Solomon Islands, a part of the UN Trust Territory of New Guinea; 3,880 sq. mi.; pop. 53,130 (est. 1959).

Bou·gain·ville (bŏŏ·gañ·vēl′), **Louis Antoine de**, 1729–1811, French navigator.

bou·gain·vil·le·a (bŏŏ′gən·vil′ē·ə) *n.* Any of a genus (*Bougainvillea*) of small climbing shrubs of the four-o'clock family: also spelled *Buginvillea.* Also **bou′gain·vil′lae·a.** [< NL, after L. A. de *Bougainville*]

bough (bou) *n.* 1. A large branch of a tree. 2. *Archaic* The gallows. [OE *bōg* shoulder, bough. Akin to BOW[1].]

bought (bôt) Past tense and past participle of BUY. — *adj. Dial.* Boughten.

bought·en (bôt′n) *adj. Dial.* Bought at a store or shop: opposed to *homemade.*

bou·gie (bŏŏ′jē, -zhē) *n.* 1. *Med.* **a** A smooth, slender, flexible instrument to be introduced into a canal of the body, for removing obstructions, etc. **b** A suppository. 2. A wax candle. [< F, a candle, after *Bougie*, a town in Algeria, where candles were made]

Bou·gue·reau (bŏŏ·grō′), **Adolphe William**, 1825–1905, French painter.

bouil·la·baisse (bŏŏl′yə·bās′, *Fr.* bŏŏ·yà·bes′) *n.* A chowder made of several varieties of fish and crustaceans, flavored with wine and saffron. [< F < Provençal *bouiabaisso* < *boui* boil + *abaisso* to settle, go down]

bouil·lon (bŏŏl′yon, -yən; *Fr.* bŏŏ·yôn′) *n.* 1. Clear soup from beef, chicken, or other meats. 2. *Bacteriol.* A special type of culture medium. [< F < *bouillir* to boil]

Bou·lan·ger (bŏŏ·läñ·zhā′), **Georges Ernest**, 1837–91, French general and politician: called **the Man on Horseback.** — **Nadia (Juliette)**, born 1887, French musician and teacher.

boul·der (bōl′dər) *n.* A large stone or rock that has been moved from its original bed: also spelled *bowlder.* [ME *bulderston* < Scand.]

Boul·der (bōl′dər) A city in north central Colorado, pop. about 66,870 (1969).

Boulder Canyon A gorge of the Colorado River above Hoover Dam, now covered by Lake Mead.

Boulder Dam The former name for HOOVER DAM.

bou·le[1] (bŏŏ′lē) *n. Greek* An ancient Greek legislative council.

boule[2] (bŏŏl) *n.* A small mass of fused alumina, usually pear-shaped, and tinted to resemble the natural ruby, sapphire, etc. [< F, ball]

PRONUNCIATION KEY: add, āce, câre, pälm; end, ēven; it, īce; odd, ōpen, ôrder; tŏŏk, pŏŏl; up, bûrn; ə = a in *above*, e in *sicken*, i in *flexible*, o in *melon*, u in *focus*; yŏŏ = u in *fuse*; oil; pout; check; go; ring; thin; this; zh, vision. For à, œ, ü, kh, ñ, see inside front cover.

Bou·le (bōō′lē) *n.* The modern Greek legislative assembly, especially the lower house.

boul·e·vard (bŏŏl′ə·värd, bōō′lə-) *n.* **1.** A broad city avenue or main road, often lined with trees. **2.** *Chiefly Canadian* The grass between sidewalk and street; also, the center strip of a divided highway or street. *Abbr. blvd.* [< F < G *bollwerk* fortification. Akin to BULWARK.]

bou·le·var·dier (bōōl·vär·dyā′) *n.* **1.** A frequenter of the (Parisian) boulevards. **2.** A man about town. [< F]

bou·le·ver·se·ment (bōōl·vers·män′) *n.* *French* An overthrow; confusion; convulsion.

Bou·logne (bōō·lôn′, *Fr.* bōō·lôn′y′) A port city of northern France, on the English Channel; pop. about 42,000. Also **Boulogne-sur-Mer** (-sür·mâr′).

Bou·logne-Bil·lan·court (bōō·lôn′y′·bē·yän·kōōr′) A city in north central France, near Paris, on the Seine; pop. 108,846 (1968).

bounce (bouns) *v.* **bounced, bounc·ing** *v.i.* **1.** To move with a bound or bounds, as a ball; rebound. **2.** To move suddenly and violently; spring: He *bounced* from his chair. **3.** *U.S. Slang* To be returned by a bank as worthless: said of a check. — *v.t.* **4.** To cause to bounce. **5.** *Slang* To eject forcibly; also, to discharge from employment. — *n.* **1.** A bound or rebound. **2.** A sudden spring or leap. **3.** Ability or capacity to bounce or spring; spring. **4.** *Informal* Vivacity; verve; spirit. **5.** *U.S. Slang* Expulsion; also, dismissal. **6.** *Brit. Informal* An audacious lie; impudence; bluster. [ME *bunsen* to thump < MLG. Cf. Du. *bonzen* to thump, strike.]

bounc·er (boun′sər) *n.* **1.** One who or that which bounces. **2.** *U.S. Slang* One employed in a bar, night club, etc., to eject disorderly persons. **3.** Something large. **4.** *Brit. Informal* An audacious lie; also, a braggart.

bounc·ing (boun′sing) *adj.* Strong and active; strapping.

bouncing Bet (bet) The soapwort. Also **bouncing Bess** (bes).

bounc·y (boun′sē) *adj.* **bounc·i·er, bounc·i·est** **1.** Having a resilient vigor; lively; animated; active. **2.** Inclined to bounce readily, as a tennis ball or baseball.

bound¹ (bound) *v.i.* **1.** To strike and spring back from a surface, as a ball. **2.** To leap; move by a series of leaps. — *v.t.* **3.** To cause to bound. — *n.* A leap or spring; also, a rebound. [< MF *bondir* to resound, rebound]

bound² (bound) *n.* **1.** *Usually pl.* A boundary; limit: out of *bounds*; the *bounds* of reason. **2.** *pl.* The area near or within a boundary. — *Syn.* See BOUNDARY. — *v.t.* **1.** To set limits to; restrict. **2.** To form the boundary of. **3.** To name the boundaries of. — *v.i.* **4.** To adjoin; abut. [< OF *bonne, bonde* < LL *bodina* limit. Akin to BOURN¹.]

bound³ (bound) Past tense and past participle of BIND. — *adj.* **1.** Made fast; tied with bonds. **2.** Having a cover or binding. *Abbr. bd.* **3.** Morally or legally obligated. **4.** Certain; sure: It's *bound* to rain. **5.** *U.S. Informal* Determined; resolved. **6.** Constipated. — **bound up in** (or **with**) **1.** Inseparably connected with. **2.** Devotedly attached to.

bound⁴ (bound) *adj.* Having one's course directed; on the way; destined: often with *for* or *to*: *bound* for home. [< ON *búinn* < *búa* to prepare]

bound·a·ry (boun′də·rē, -drē) *n.* *pl.* **·ries** **1.** A limiting or dividing line or mark. **2.** Anything indicating a limit or confine. [< BOUND², n., + -ARY¹]
— **Syn. 1.** *Boundary, bounds, bourn, edge,* and *limit* denote a line that marks the outermost extent of an area, or a division between areas. *Boundary* is used chiefly of territory, and suggests a definite demarcation; *bounds* are less definite, and may be used figuratively of behavior: His impudence exceeds all *bounds*. *Bourn* is an archaic and poetic word for a *boundary*. An *edge* is a sharp terminal line, as where river or ocean meets the land. *Limit* is now used almost wholly in a figurative sense: the *limit* of discussion, of time, or of jurisdiction.

boundary layer *Aeron.* An extremely thin layer of air in contact with the surface of an airfoil.

bound·en (boun′dən) *adj.* **1.** Obligatory: our *bounden* duty. **2.** Under obligations; obliged. [Var. of BOUND³]

bound·er (boun′dər) *n.* *Chiefly Brit. Informal* An offensive, ill-mannered person; a cad. [< BOUND¹]

bound form *Ling.* A morpheme that occurs only as part of a larger form, as the *-s* in *cats* and the *-ing* in *looking*: opposed to *free form.*

bound·less (bound′lis) *adj.* Having no limit; vast; measureless; infinite. — **Syn.** See INFINITE. — **bound′less·ly** *adv.* — **bound′less·ness** *n.*

boun·te·ous (boun′tē·əs) *adj.* **1.** Generous; beneficent: a *bounteous* king. **2.** Marked by abundance; plentiful: a *bounteous* repast. [ME *bountevous* < OF *bontif* < *bonté* goodness; infl. in form by BOUNTY] — **boun′te·ous·ly** *adv.* — **boun′te·ous·ness** *n.*

boun·ti·ful (boun′tə·fəl) *adj.* **1.** Free and generous in bestowing gifts; liberal. **2.** Showing abundance; plentiful: a *bountiful* harvest. — **Syn.** See GENEROUS. — **boun′ti·ful·ly** *adv.* — **boun′ti·ful·ness** *n.*

boun·ty (boun′tē) *n.* *pl.* **·ties** **1.** Liberality in giving. **2.** Gifts or favors generously bestowed. **3.** A reward from a government, as for the killing of predatory animals, etc. — **Syn.** See SUBSIDY. [< OF *bonte* < L *bonitas, -tatis* goodness]

bou·quet (bō·kā′, bōō·kā′ *for def.* 1; bōō·kā′ *for def.* 2) *n.* **1.** A bunch of flowers; a nosegay. **2.** Delicate odor; especially, the distinctive aroma of a wine. — **Syn.** See SMELL. [< F < OF *boschet,* dim. of *bosc* wood, ult. < Gmc.]

bour·bon (bûr′bən) *n.* A whisky distilled from a fermented mash containing at least 51 percent corn. Also **bourbon whisky.** [after *Bourbon* County, Ky., where first made]

Bour·bon (bōōr′bən) *n.* **1.** A dynasty that reigned over France, 1589–1792, 1815–48, or a related branch that ruled Spain, 1700–1931. **2.** One who is stubbornly conservative in politics. — **Bour′bon·ism** *n.* — **Bour′bon·ist** *n.*

Bour·bon (bōōr′bən, *Fr.* bōōr·bôn′), **Charles,** 1490–1527, French military commander: called **Connétable de Bourbon.**

Bour·bon Island (bōōr′bən) The former name for RÉUNION.

bour·don (bōōr′dən) *n.* **1.** An organ stop, commonly of 16-foot tone. **2.** The drone of a bagpipe. [< OF, drone. Doublet of BURDEN².]

bourg (bōōrg) *n.* **1.** A medieval town, especially when near a castle. **2.** A French market town. [< F < LL *burgus,* ult. < Gmc. Akin to BOROUGH.]

bour·geois¹ (bōōr′zhwä, bōōr·zhwä′) *n.* *pl.* **·geois** **1.** A member of the middle class; a tradesman. **2.** *pl.* The middle class. **3.** In Marxism, a member of the class in conflict with the working class. — *adj.* Of or characteristic of the middle class or bourgeoisie: often used disparagingly. [< F < OF *burgeis* < LL *burgensis* < *burgus* town < Gmc. Doublet of BURGESS.] — **bour·geoise** (bōōr·zhwäz′) *n. & adj. fem.*

bour·geois² (bər·jois′) *n.* A size of type, about 9-point. [? after a French printer]

Bour·geois (bōōr·zhwä′), **Léon Victor,** 1851–1925, French statesman.

bour·geoi·sie (bōōr′zhwä·zē′) *n.* **1.** The middle class of society, especially in France. **2.** In Marxism, that social class opposed in the class struggle to the proletariat or working class. [< F. See BOURGEOIS¹.]

bour·geon (bûr′jən) See BURGEON.

Bourges (bōōrzh) A city in central France; pop. 67,137 (1968).

Bour·get (bōōr·zhe′), **Paul,** 1852–1935, French author.

Bour·gogne (bōōr·gôn′y′) The French name for BURGUNDY.

bourn¹ (bôrn, bōrn, bōōrn) *n.* *Archaic* **1.** Goal; destination. **2.** Boundary; limit. **3.** Realm; domain. Also **bourne.** — **Syn.** See BOUNDARY. [< F *borne* < OF *bodne* < LL *bodina* limit. Akin to BOUND².]

bourn² (bôrn, bōrn, bōōrn) *n.* A brook or rivulet: used also in combination: *Eastbourne.* Compare BURN². Also **bourne.** [Var. of BURN²]

Bourne·mouth (bôrn′məth, bōrn′-) A county borough and seaside resort in SW Hampshire, England; pop. 149,820 (est. 1969).

bour·rée (bōō·rā′) *n.* An old French dance similar to the gavotte; also, the music for it. [< F]

bour·re·let (bōōr·lā′) *n.* *Mil.* A ridgelike band around a shell. For illustration see PROJECTILE. [< F]

Bourse (bōōrs) *n.* An exchange or money market; especially, the Paris stock exchange. [< F, purse < LL *bursa* bag]

bour·tree (bōōr′trē) *n.* *Brit.* The elder (*Sambucus nigra*) of Europe and Asia.

bouse¹ (bōōz, bouz), **bous·y** (bōō′zē, bou′-) See BOOZE, BOOZY.

bouse² (bous, bouz) *v.t. & v.i.* **boused, bous·ing** *Naut.* To lift or haul with blocks and tackle: also spelled *bowse.* [Origin unknown]

bou·stro·phe·don (bōō′strə·fēd′n, bou′-) *n.* An ancient method of writing in which the rows alternate in direction from right to left and from left to right. [< Gk. *boustrophēdon* turning like oxen (in plowing) < *bous* ox + *strephein* to turn] — **bou·stroph·e·don·ic** (bōō·strof′ə·don′ik, bou-), **bou·stroph·ic** (bōō·strof′ik, bou-) or **·i·cal** *adj.*

bout (bout) *n.* **1.** A contest; trial: a boxing *bout.* **2.** A fit or spell, as of drinking or illness. **3.** A going and coming back; a round, as in plowing. [Var. of ME *bought* bending, turn. Cf. LG *bucht* a bend, turn.]

bou·tique (bōō·tēk′) *n.* *French* A small retail shop.

bou·ton·niere (bōō′tən·yâr′) *n.* A bouquet or flower worn in the buttonhole. Also **bou′ton·nière′.** [< F]

bovi- *combining form* Ox or cattle; of or related to cattle. [< L *bos, bovis* ox]

bo·vid (bō′vid) *Zool.* Of or pertaining to a family of ruminants (*Bovidae*) including cattle, sheep, goats, etc.

bo·vine (bō′vīn, -vin) *adj.* **1.** Pertaining or belonging to the genus *Bos,* as an ox, cow, etc. **2.** Stolid; dull. — *n.* A bovine animal. [< LL *bovinus* < L *bos, bovis* ox]

bow¹ (bou) *n.* **1.** The forward part of a ship, boat, etc. **2.** The forward oarsman of a boat. — *adj.* Of or at the bow. [< LG or Scand. Cf. Du. *boeg,* Dan. *bov* bow of a ship. Akin to BOUGH.]

bow² (bou) *v.* **bowed, bow·ing** *v.i.* **1.** To bend the body or head, as in salutation, worship, or assent. **2.** To bend or incline downward. **3.** To submit; yield. — *v.t.* **4.** To bend (the body, head, etc.) in reverence, courtesy, or submission. **5.** To express by bowing. **6.** To escort with bows: He *bowed* us into the room. **7.** To cause to yield; subdue: He *bowed* her to his will. **8.** To cause to bend or stoop; bend down. **— Syn.** See BEND[1]. **— to bow out** To withdraw; resign. — *n.* An inclination of the body or head, as in salutation or worship. [OE *būgan* to bow, bend, flee]

bow[3] (bō) *n.* **1.** A weapon made from a strip of elastic wood or other pliable material, bent by a string and used to project an arrow. **2.** An archer. **3.** Something bent or curved; a bend. **4.** A rainbow. **5.** A knot with a loop or loops, as of ribbon, etc. **6.** *Music* **a** A rod with hairs stretched between raised ends, used for playing a violin or related stringed instrument. **b** A stroke with a bow. **7.** One of the rims of a pair of spectacles; also, one of the curved supports passing over the ears. **8.** An oxbow (which see). — *adj.* Bent; curved; bowed. — *v.t.* & *v.i.* **bowed, bow·ing 1.** To bend into the shape of a bow. **2.** *Music* To play (a stringed instrument) with a bow. **— Syn.** See BEND[1]. [OE *boga*]

Bow bells (bō) The bells of St. Mary-le-Bow, in Cheapside, London. See COCKNEY.

Bow china (bō) A delicate ware made at Stratford-le-Bow, near London, in the 18th century.

bow compass (bō) *Geom.* A pair of small compasses having no joint but a curved metal strip between the legs, for drawing small circles or arcs of small radius.

Bow·ditch (bou′dich), **Nathaniel**, 1773–1838, U.S. mathematician and navigator.

bowd·ler·ize (boud′lər-īz) *v.t.* **·ized, ·iz·ing** To expurgate or edit prudishly. [after Dr. Thomas *Bowdler's* "family" edition of Shakespeare (1818)] **— bowd′ler·ism** *n.* **bowd′ler·i·za′tion** *n.*

bow·el (bou′əl, boul) *n.* **1.** An intestine. **2.** *pl.* The intestines or entrails. **3.** *pl.* The inner part of anything: the *bowels* of the earth. **4.** *pl. Archaic* Pity; compassion. — *v.t.* **bow·eled** or **·elled, bow·el·ing** or **·el·ling** To disembowel. [< OF *boel* < L *botellus*, dim. of *botulus* sausage]

bow·er[1] (bou′ər) *n.* **1.** A shaded recess; arbor. **2.** *Poetic* A private room; boudoir. **3.** *Poetic* A rustic cottage; retreat. — *v.t.* To enclose in or as in a bower; embower. [OE *būr* chamber] **— bow′er·y** *adj.*

bow·er[2] (bou′ər) *n.* In euchre and other card games, either of the two highest cards, the knave of trumps (**right bower**) and the other knave of the same color (**left bower**), unless the joker (**best bower**) is used. [< G *bauer* peasant, knave in a deck of cards]

bow·er[3] (bou′ər) *n. Naut.* A large anchor carried on the bow of a vessel. Also **bower anchor.**

bow·er·bird (bou′ər·bûrd′) *n.* Any of several Australian birds that build a bower or playhouse to attract the female; especially, the **great bowerbird** (*Chlamydera nuchalis*).

bow·er·y (bou′ər·ē, -rē) *n. pl.* **·er·ies** A farm or plantation of the Dutch settlers of New York. [< Du. *bouwerij* farm < *bouwer, boer* farmer]

Bow·er·y (bou′ər·ē) A street in New York City noted for its hoboes, saloons, shabby hotels, etc.: often preceded by *the*.

bow·fin (bō′fin′) *n.* A small, voracious, dark-colored, ganoid fish (*Amia calva*) found in many of the fresh waters of the United States and not highly regarded as food; a mudfish.

bow·head (bō′hed′) *n.* The right whale.

bow·ie knife (bō′ē, bōō′ē) A strong, single-edged hunting knife with a hilt, crosspiece, and sheath. [after James *Bowie*, 1799–1836, U.S. soldier, its reputed inventor]

BOWIE KNIFE

bow·knot (bō′not′) *n.* An ornamental slipknot made with one or more loops. For illustration see KNOT.

bowl[1] (bōl) *n.* **1.** A concave vessel, nearly hemispherical and larger than a cup. **2.** The amount a bowl will hold. **3.** A large drinking vessel; goblet. **4.** Drink, or convivial drinking. **5.** An amphitheater or stadium. **6.** Something shaped like a bowl: the *bowl* of a pipe. [OE *bolla*]

bowl[2] (bōl) *n.* **1.** A large ball for bowls or tenpins; especially, the slightly flattened ball used in bowls. **2.** A throw of the ball in bowling. **3.** A roller or wheel in a machine to reduce friction. — *v.i.* **1.** To play at bowls, tenpins, etc. **2.** To roll a ball or rounded object. **3.** To move smoothly and swiftly: usually with *along*. **4.** In cricket, to deliver the ball to the batsman. — *v.t.* **5.** To roll or throw, as a ball. **6.** To carry or transport on or as on wheels. **7.** In cricket, to retire (the batsman): with *out*. **— to bowl over** To cause to be confused or helpless; knock down or out. [< F *boule* ball < L *bulla* bubble] **— bowl′er** *n.*

bowl·der (bōl′dər) See BOULDER.

bow·leg (bō′leg′) *n.* **1.** An outward curvature of the legs at or below the knee. **2.** *pl.* Legs so curved.

bow·leg·ged (bō′leg′id, -legd′) *adj.* Having bowlegs.

bowl·er (bō′lər) *n. Brit.* A derby. [< BOWL[1], *n.* + -ER[2]; from its shape]

bow·line (bō′lin, -līn′) *n.* **1.** A knot tied so as to form a loop. Also **bowline knot. 2.** *Naut.* A rope to keep the weather edge of a vessel's square sail forward when sailing close-hauled. **— on a bowline** *Naut.* Sailing close-hauled.

bowl·ing (bō′ling) *n.* **1.** The game of bowls or of tenpins. **2.** In cricket, the act of delivering the ball.

bowling alley A long, narrow space for bowling, or the building containing it.

bowling green A smooth lawn for playing at bowls.

Bowling Green 1. A small park at the foot of Broadway, New York City. **2.** A city in southern Kentucky; pop. 36,253.

bowls (bōlz) *n.pl.* **1.** *Brit.* An outdoor game played by rolling slightly flattened or weighted balls at a stationary ball. **2.** Tenpins, ninepins, or skittles.

BOWLINE (a)
AND RUNNING
BOWLINE (b)

bow·man[1] (bō′mən) *n. pl.* **·men** (-mən) An archer.

bow·man[2] (bou′mən) *n. pl.* **·men** (-mən) The oarsman nearest the bow.

bow pen (bō) *Geom.* A bow compass carrying a pen or pencil on one leg.

bowse (bous, bouz) See BOUSE[2].

bow·shot (bō′shot′) *n.* The distance which an arrow may be sent from the bow.

bow·sprit (bou′sprit′, bō′-) *n. Naut.* A spar projecting forward from the bow of a vessel. [? < M.Du. *boegspriet* < *boeg* bow of a ship + *spriet* spear]

bow·string (bō′string′) *n.* **1.** The string of a bow. **2.** A string for strangling criminals. **3.** Execution by strangling. — *v.t.* **·strung, ·string·ing** To execute by strangling with a bowstring; garrote.

bowstring hemp A perennial, erect herb of the lily family (genus *Sansevieria*) with narrow, white or yellowish white flowers and hemplike fiber.

bow tie A necktie worn in a bowknot.

bow window (bō) A projecting, usually curved window built up from the ground level. Compare BAY WINDOW.

bow-wow (bou′wou′) *n.* **1.** The bark of a dog, or an imitation of it. **2.** A dog: a child's word. — *v.i.* To bark.

bow·yer (bō′yər) *n.* A maker or seller of bows.

box[1] (boks) *n.* **1.** A receptacle or case of wood, metal, etc., usually rectangular and having a lid. **2.** The quantity contained in a box. **3.** A gift packed in a box: a Christmas *box*. **4.** Something resembling a box in form or use. **5.** A small booth for a sentry, watchman, etc. **6.** A small country house: a hunting *box*. **7.** A box stall. **8.** The raised driver's seat of a coach, or the compartment under it. **9.** The part of a vehicle in which the load is carried. **10.** A space partitioned off for seating, as in a theater, courtroom, stadium, etc.: the jury *box*. **11.** In baseball, any of several designated spaces, as for the pitcher, batter, coach, etc. **12.** *Mech.* An axle bearing, casing, or other enclosed cavity. **13.** A cavity made in the trunk of a tree to collect its sap. **14.** A predicament; difficulty. **15.** An enclosed space on a page of a newspaper, magazine, etc. Abbr. *bx* (pl. *bxs.*). **16.** *U.S. Informal & Dial.* Guitar. — *v.t.* **1.** To place in a box. **2.** To surround or confine as in a box: with *in* or *up*. **3.** To furnish with a bushing or box. **4.** To make box-shaped. **5.** To boxhaul. **— to box in 1.** In racing, to block (another contestant) so that he is unable to get ahead. **2.** To box up. **— to box the compass 1.** To recite in order the 32 points of the compass. **2.** To make a complete revolution or turn. **— to box up** To confine in, or as in, a small space. [OE < Med.L *buxis*, blend of *buxus* boxwood and *pyxis* box (both < Gk. *pyxos* boxwood). Doublet of PYX.] **— box′er** *n.*

box[2] (boks) *v.t.* **1.** To strike or buffet with the hand; cuff. **2.** To fight (another) in a boxing match. — *v.i.* **3.** To fight with one's fists; be a boxer. — *n.* A blow on the ear or cheek; cuff. [ME; origin uncertain]
— Syn. 1. slap, clout, hit, swat.

box[3] (boks) *n.* **1.** Any of a small family (*Buxaceae*) of evergreen herbs, shrubs, and trees, many of which are cultivated as borders and hedges, especially *Buxus sempervirens*, yielding a hard wood. **2.** The wood itself. [OE < L *buxus* < Gk. *pyxos* boxwood]

Box The constellation Pyxis.

box·ber·ry (boks′ber′ē, -bər·ē) *n. pl.* **·ries** The wintergreen (def. 1).

box calf Tanned calfskin with square markings on the grain produced by lengthwise and crosswise rolling.

box camera A simple, boxlike camera with a fixed focus.

box·car (boks′kär′) *n.* **1.** A roofed, enclosed freight car. **2.** *pl.* In craps, two sixes on the first throw.

box coat 1. A coachman's heavy overcoat. **2.** A greatcoat. **3.** A loosely fitting overcoat, snug only at the shoulders.

box elder A North American tree (*Acer negundo*) of the maple family, having leaves with 3 or 5 compound leaflets: also called *Manitoba maple*.

box·er[1] (bok′sər) *n.* One who fights with his fists; pugilist.

box·er[2] (bok′sər) *n.* A breed of medium-sized working dog, related to the bulldog, having a sturdy body, smooth fawn or brindle coat, and a black mask. [Alter. of G *-beisser* in *Bullenbeisser* bulldog]

Box·er (bok'sər) *n.* A member of a Chinese secret society, active in 1900, that aimed to rid China of foreigners by force. [So called from their practice of traditional posture boxing, which they believed would make them immune to bullets]

box·haul (boks'hôl') *v.t. Naut.* To veer (a square-rigged vessel) round instead of tacking, when tacking is impracticable.

box hook A hook with a wooden handle, used in handling heavy boxes or bales: also called *bale hook.*

box·ing[1] (bok'sing) *n.* The art or practice of fighting with the fists, especially when gloved; pugilism.

box·ing[2] (bok'sing) *n.* **1.** The act of enclosing in a box. **2.** Material for making boxes. **3.** A casing or niche, as for window shutters.

Boxing Day In England, the first weekday after Christmas, a holiday on which presents are given to employees, etc.

boxing glove A padded mitten used for prizefighting.

boxing match A prize fight or sparring contest.

box kite A kite consisting of a rectangular, box-shaped frame covered with fabric or paper except at the ends and in a space at the middle.

box office **1.** The ticket office of a theater, stadium, etc. Abbr. *b.o.* **2.** *Informal* Receipts at the box office, as a measure of success.

box pleat A double pleat, with the edges folded so as to meet underneath. Also **box plait.**

box seat A seat in a box of a theater, stadium, etc.

box spring A mattress foundation consisting of an upholstered frame set with coil springs to provide resiliency.

box stall A large, enclosed stall for a horse, cow, etc.

box·thorn (boks'thôrn') *n.* Any of various evergreen or deciduous ornamental plants (genus *Lycium*) of the nightshade family, with long, drooping, flowering branches and usually scarlet berries, especially *L. halimifolium*: also called *matrimony vine.*

box·wood (boks'wŏŏd') *n.* **1.** The hard, close-grained, durable wood of box (genus *Buxus*). **2.** The shrub.

boy (boi) *n.* **1.** A male child; lad; youth. **2.** A man; fellow; a familiar use. **3.** A male servant. [ME *boi*; origin unknown]

bo·yar (bō-yär', boi'ər) *n.* **1.** Formerly, a member of a class of Russian aristocracy, abolished in the time of Peter the Great. **2.** Formerly, in Rumania, one of a privileged class. Also **bo·yard** (bō-yärd', boi'ərd). [< Russian *boyarin* noble]

boy·cott (boi'kot) *v.t.* **1.** To combine together in refusing to deal or associate with, so as to punish or coerce. **2.** To refuse to use or buy. — *n.* The act or practice of boycotting, or an instance of it. [after Capt. C. *Boycott*, 1832–97, landlord's agent in Ireland, who was the first victim, 1880]

Boy·den (boid'n), **Seth**, 1788–1870, U.S. inventor.

boy friend **1.** *Informal* A preferred male companion or intimate friend of a girl or woman. **2.** A male friend.

boy·hood (boi'hŏŏd) *n.* **1.** The state or period of being a boy. **2.** Boys collectively.

boy·ish (boi'ish) *adj.* Of or characteristic of or befitting boys or boyhood. — **Syn.** See YOUTHFUL. — **boy'ish·ly** *adv.* — **boy'ish·ness** *n.*

Boyle (boil), **Robert**, 1627–91, English chemist and physicist born in Ireland.

Boyle's law *Physics* The statement that the volume of a gas kept at constant temperature varies inversely with the pressure. [after Robert *Boyle*]

Boyne (boin) A river in NE Ireland, flowing 70 miles NE to the Irish Sea; scene of a battle (1690) in which William III defeated James II. See OLDBRIDGE.

boy scout **1.** A member of the **Boy Scouts**, an organization for training boys between the ages of 11 and 17 in self-reliance and good citizenship, initiated in England in 1908 by Lieut. Gen. Sir Robert Baden-Powell. Abbr. *B.S.A.* **2.** A member of the **Boy Scouts of America**, incorporated in 1910.

boy·sen·ber·ry (boi'zən-ber'ē) *n. pl.* **·ries** The edible fruit of a hybrid plant obtained by crossing the blackberry, raspberry, and loganberry. [after Rudolph *Boysen*, 20th c. U.S. horticulturist, the originator]

Boz (boz) See DICKENS.

Boz·ca·a·da (bôz-jä'ä-dä') The Turkish name for TENEDOS.

bo·zo (bō'zō) *n. U.S. Slang* A fellow; guy. [? < dial. Sp. *boso* you (pl.), mistaken as a name or epithet]

Boz·za·ris (bot'sä-rēs, bō-zar'is), **Marco**, 1788?–1823, Greek patriot.

bp. **1.** Birthplace. **2.** Bishop.

b.p. or **bp.** **1.** Below proof. **2.** Boiling point.

B.P. Bachelor of Pharmacy (L *Baccalaureus Pharmaciae*).

B.P. or **B.Ph.** or **B.Phil.** Bachelor of Philosophy (L *Baccalaureus Philosophiae*).

B/P or **b.p.** **1.** Bill of parcels. **2.** Bills payable.

B.Pd. or **B.Pe.** Bachelor of Pedagogy.

B.P.E. Bachelor of Physical Education.

B.P.H. Bachelor of Public Health.

B.P.O.E. Benevolent and Protective Order of Elks.

br. **1.** Branch. **2.** Brand. **3.** Bronze. **4.** Brother.

Br *Chem.* Bromine.

Br. **1.** Breton. **2.** Britain; British.

B/R or **b.r.** Bills receivable.

B/R or **B.R.** Bill of Rights.

bra (brä) *n. U.S. Informal* A brassiere.

Bra·bant (brə·bant', brä'bənt) **1.** A former duchy, now divided into North Brabant, Netherlands, and Antwerp and Brabant provinces in Belgium. **2.** A Province in central Belgium; 1,268 sq. mi.; pop. 1,973,729 (est. 1960); capital, Brussels.

brab·ble (brab'l) *v.i.* **·bled**, **·bling** To quarrel noisily. — *n.* A petty squabble. [? < Du. *brabbelen* to jabber] — **brab'ble·ment** *n.*

brace (brās) *v.* **braced**, **brac·ing** *v.t.* **1.** To make firm or steady; strengthen by or as by braces. **2.** To make ready to withstand pressure, impact, assault, etc. **3.** To increase the tension of; strain. **4.** To tie or fasten firmly, as with straps. **5.** To stimulate; enliven. **6.** *Naut.* To turn (the yards) by means of the braces. **7.** *Slang* To ask a loan or favor from. — *v.i.* **8.** To strain against pressure. — **to brace up** *Informal* To rouse one's courage or resolution. — *n.* **1.** A support, as of wood or metal, used to strengthen something or hold it in place. **2.** A clasp or clamp for fastening, connecting, etc. **3.** A cranklike handle for holding and turning a bit or other boring tool. **4.** A device for producing or maintaining tension in a drumhead. **5.** A pair; couple: a *brace* of pheasants. **6.** *Printing* A doubly curved line, { or }, used to connect words, lines, staves of music, etc. **7.** *Naut.* A rope fastened to a yardarm for swinging it about. **8.** *pl. Brit.* Suspenders. **9.** *Often pl. Dent.* A wire or wires fastened on irregular teeth and gradually tightened to align them. **10.** *Med.* Any of various devices for supporting a joint, limb, or other part. [< OF *bracier* to embrace < *brace, brache* two arms < L *brachia*, pl. of *brachium* arm]

brace·let (brās'lit) *n.* **1.** An ornamental band worn around the wrist or arm. **2.** *Informal* A handcuff. [< OF, dim. of *bracel* < L *brachiale* bracelet < *brachium* arm]

brac·er[1] (brā'sər) *n.* **1.** One who or that which braces or steadies; a support; brace. **2.** *U.S. Informal* A stimulating drink. [< BRACE, v. + -ER[1]]

brac·er[2] (brā'sər) *n.* In archery and fencing, a protective covering for the forearm. [< OF *brasseure*]

bra·ce·ro (brə-sâr'ō) *n. pl.* **·ros** A Mexican laborer brought into the United States under contract for seasonal farm work. [< Sp., day laborer]

brach (brach, brak) *n. Archaic* A hound bitch. Also **brach·et** (brach'it). [< OF *brachet* hunting dog, ult. < OHG]

bra·chi·al (brā'kē·əl, brak'ē-) *adj.* **1.** Of or pertaining to the arm, especially the upper arm. **2.** *Zool.* Of, pertaining to, or designating the armlike appendages of various animals. **3.** Armlike. [< L *brachialis* < *brachium* arm]

bra·chi·ate (*adj.* brā'kē-it, -āt, brak'ē-; *v.* brā'kē-āt, brak'ē-) *adj. Bot.* Having widely diverging branches in alternate pairs. — *v.i.* **·at·ed**, **·at·ing** *Zool.* To move by a swinging motion of the arms, as certain arboreal apes. [< L *brachiatus* having arms < *brachium* arm] — **bra'chi·a'tion** *n.*

brachio- *combining form* Arm; of the arm: *brachiopod.* Also, before vowels, **brachi-**. [< Gk. *brachiōn* arm]

bra·chi·o·pod (brā'kē-ə-pod', brak'ē-) *n. Zool.* One of a phylum or class (*Brachiopoda*) of nearly extinct molluscoid marine animals having a bivalve shell and a pair of brachial appendages rising from the sides of the mouth: also called *lamp shell.* [< NL < BRACHIO- + -PODA] — **bra·chi·op·o·dous** (brā'kē·op'ə-dəs, brak'ē-) *adj.*

bra·chi·um (brā'kē-əm, brak'ē-) *n. pl.* **bra·chi·a** (brā'kē-ə, brak'ē-) **1.** *Anat.* **a** The arm, especially that part above the elbow. **b** An analogous part in any animal. **2.** Any armlike process or appendage. [< L]

brachy- *combining form* Short: *brachycephalic.* [< Gk. *brachys* short]

brach·y·ce·phal·ic (brak'i-sə-fal'ik) *adj.* Having a short, broad skull, the cephalic index being at least 80; shortheaded. Also **brach·y·ceph·a·lous** (brak'i-sef'ə-ləs). [< NL *brachycephalicus* < Gk. *brachykephalos* < *brachys* short + *kephalē* head] — **brach'y·ceph'a·lism, brach'y·ceph'a·ly** *n.*

brach·y·cra·nic (brak'i-krā'nik) *adj.* Brachycephalic. [< BRACHY- + Gk. *kranion* head]

brach·y·dac·tyl·ic (brak'i-dak-til'ik) *adj.* Having abnormally short fingers or toes. [< Gk. *brachydaktylos* < *brachys* short + *daktylos* finger] — **brach'y·dac·tyl'i·a, brach'y·dac'tyl·ism** (-dak'təl·iz/əm) *n.*

bra·chyl·o·gy (brə-kil'ə-jē) *n.* **1.** Brevity and conciseness of speech. **2.** An abridged form of expression. [< Gk. *brachylogia* < *brachys* short + *-logia* speech]

bra·chyp·ter·ous (brə-kip'tər-əs) *adj. Ornithol.* Having short wings. [< Gk. *brachypteros* < *brachys* short + *pteron* wing] — **bra·chyp'ter·ism** *n.*

brach·y·u·ran (brak'i-yŏŏr'ən) *Zool. adj.* Of or relating to a suborder (*Brachyura*) of decapods, comprising the crabs. Also **brach'y·u'rous** (-yŏŏr'əs). — *n.* A crab or similar crustacean. [< NL *brachyura* < Gk. *brachys* short + *oura* tail]

brac·ing (brā'sing) *adj.* Strengthening; invigorating. — *n.* A brace or system of braces, as in bridge building.

brack·en (brak'ən) *n.* **1.** A coarse, hardy fern (*Pteridium aquilinum*) with fronds up to four feet long and three feet wide, some varieties of which are common in North America: also called *brake.* **2.** A clump of such ferns. [ME *braken* < Scand. Cf. Sw. *bräken* fern.]

brack·et (brak'it) *n.* **1.** A piece of wood, metal, stone, etc., projecting from a wall, used to support a shelf or other weight. **2.** A brace used to strengthen an angle. **3.** A small shelf or set of shelves supported by brackets. **4.** A projecting wall fixture for a gaslight, electric lamp, etc. **5.** A classification according to income for tax purposes: the high-income *brack-et.* **6.** *Printing* One of two marks [] used to enclose any part of a text: also called *square bracket.* **7.** *Brit.* Any of various marks, as (), [], or { }. **8.** *Math.* A vinculum. **9.** *Mil.* The space between two rounds of artillery fired beyond and short of a target, used in determining range. — *v.t.* **1.** To provide or support with a bracket or brackets. **2.** To enclose within brackets. **3.** To group or categorize together. **4.** *Mil.* To fire both over and short of (a target). [< Sp. *bragueta,* dim. of *braga* < L *bracae,* pl., breeches]

brack·et·ing (brak'it·ing) *n. Archit.* A wooden framework for the construction or support of a cornice or other molding.

brack·ish (brak'ish) *adj.* **1.** Somewhat saline; briny. **2.** Distasteful. [< Du. *brak* salty] — **brack'ish·ness** *n.*

bract (brakt) *n. Bot.* A modified leaf in a flower cluster or subtending a flower. [< L *bractea* thin metal plate] — **brac·te·al** (brak'tē·əl) *adj.*

brac·te·ate (brak'tē·it, -āt) *adj. Bot.* Having bracts.

brac·te·o·late (brak'tē·ə·lāt') *adj. Bot.* Having bracteoles.

brac·te·ole (brak'tē·ōl) *n. Bot.* A diminutive bract. Also **bract·let** (brakt'lit).

BRACTS
(Around a flower cluster)

brad (brad) *n.* A small, slender nail with a small head, or a lip on one side in place of a head. [< ON *broddr* spike]

brad·awl (brad'ôl') *n.* A short awl for making holes in wood, as for brads or screws.

Brad·dock (brad'ək), **Edward,** 1695–1755, British general in French and Indian War.

Brad·ford (brad'fərd) A county borough in West Yorkshire, England; pop. 461,000 (1976).

Brad·ford (brad'fərd), **Ga·ma·li·el** (gə·mā'lē·əl), 1863–1932, U.S. biographer. — **William,** 1590?–1657, Pilgrim governor of Plymouth Colony.

Brad·ley (brad'lē), **Henry,** 1845–1923, English lexicographer. — **Omar Nelson,** born 1893, U.S. general.

Brad·street (brad'strēt), **Anne,** 1612–72, *née* Dudley, American poet. — **Simon,** 1603–97, colonial governor of Massachusetts; husband of Anne.

brady- *combining form* Slow: *bradycardia.* [< Gk. *bradys* slow]

Bra·dy (brā'dē), **Mathew B.,** 1823?–96, U.S. photographer.

brad·y·car·di·a (brad'i·kär'dē·ə) *n. Pathol.* Slowness of the heartbeat, indicated by a pulse rate of 60 or less. [< NL < BRADY- + Gk. *kardia* heart] — **brad'y·car'dic** *adj.*

brae (brā) *n. Scot.* A bank; hillside; slope.

brag (brag) *v.* **bragged, brag·ging** *v.i.* **1.** To boast about oneself or one's deeds or abilities. — *v.t.* **2.** To declare or assert boastfully; boast of. — *n.* **1.** Boastful language; boasting. **2.** A thing bragged of; boast. **3.** One who brags. **4.** A game of cards resembling poker. — *adj.* **1.** *Archaic* Worthy of being bragged about; fine. **2.** *Obs.* Spirited. **3.** *Obs.* Boastful. [Origin uncertain] — **brag'ger** *n.*

Bragg (brag), **Braxton,** 1817–76, Confederate general in the Civil War. — **Sir William Henry,** 1862–1942, English physicist and chemist. — **Sir William Lawrence,** 1890–1971, English physicist; son of Sir William Henry.

brag·ga·do·ci·o (brag'ə·dō'shē·ō) *n. pl.* **·ci·os** **1.** Pretentious boasting. **2.** One who boasts; a swaggerer. [after *Braggadochio,* a boastful character in Spenser's *Faerie Queene*]

brag·gart (brag'ərt) *n.* A bragger. — *adj.* Boastful. [< MF *bragard* < *braguer* to brag] — **brag'gart·ism** *n.*

Bra·gi (brä'gē) In Norse mythology, the god of poetry, son of Odin and husband of Ithunn. Also **Bra·ge** (brä'gə).

Bra·he (brä'ə), **Ty·cho** (tü'kō), 1546–1601, Danish astronomer.

brah·ma (brä'mə, brā'-) *n. Often cap.* A large breed of domestic fowl developed in Asia. [after *Brahmaputra*]

Brah·ma (brä'mə) *n.* **1.** In Hindu religion, the absolute primordial essence; the supreme soul of the universe, self-existent and eternal, from which all things emanate and to which all return. **2.** God, comprising the Hindu trinity Brahma, Vishnu, and Siva; especially, the personification of the first of the trinity as supreme creator. [< Skt. *Brahmā*]

Brah·man (brä'mən) *n. pl.* **·mans** **1.** A member of the first of the four Hindu castes of India, the sacerdotal caste: also spelled *Brahmin.* **2.** A breed of cattle originally imported from India and bred in the southern United States. [< Skt. *brāhmana* < *brahman* praise, worship] — **Brah·man·i** (brä'mən·ē) *n.fem.* — **Brah·man·ic** (brä·man'ik) or **·i·cal** *adj.*

Brah·man·ism (brä'mən·iz'əm) *n.* The religious and social system of the Brahmans: also spelled *Brahminism.* — **Brah'man·ist** *n.*

Brah·ma·pu·tra (brä'mə·pōō'trə) A river of southern Asia, flowing about 1,800 miles across Tibet, SW China, Assam, and East Pakistan to the Bay of Bengal.

Brah·min (brä'min) *n.* **1.** See BRAHMAN. **2.** A highly cultured or aristocratic person, especially an ultraconservative or snobbish one. [Var. of BRAHMAN]

Brah·min·ism (brä'min·iz'əm) *n.* **1.** See BRAHMANISM. **2.** The attitude, mannerisms, etc., of Brahmins.

Brahms (brämz, *Ger.* bräms), **Johannes,** 1833–97, German composer.

braid[1] (brād) *v.t.* **1.** To weave together or intertwine several strands of; plait. **2.** To bind or ornament (the hair) with ribbons, etc. **3.** To form by braiding: to *braid* a mat. **4.** To ornament (garments) with braid. — *n.* **1.** A narrow, flat tape or strip for binding or ornamenting fabrics. **2.** Anything braided or plaited: a *braid* of hair. **3.** A string or band used in arranging the hair. [OE *bregdan* to brandish, weave, braid] — **braid'er** *n.*

braid[2] (brād) *adj. Scot.* Broad.

braid·ing (brā'ding) *n.* **1.** Braids collectively. **2.** Embroidery done with braid.

brail (brāl) *Naut. n.* One of the ropes for gathering up and furling the foot and leeches of a fore-and-aft sail. — *v.t.* To haul in (a sail) by means of brails: usually with *up.* [< OF *braiel* < L *bracale* a belt for breeches < *bracae* breeches]

Bră·i·la (bra·ē'lä) A port city in eastern Rumania, on the Danube; pop. 147,495 (1968).

Braille (brāl) *n.* A system of printing or writing for the blind in which the characters consist of raised dots to be read by the fingers; also, the characters themselves. Also **braille.** [after Louis *Braille,* 1809–52, French educator, the inventor]

brain (brān) *n.* **1.** *Anat.* The enlarged and greatly modified part of the central nervous system contained in the cranium of vertebrates. **2.** *Often pl.* Mind; intellect. **3.** *Zool.* The principle ganglion of invertebrates. **4.** *U.S. Slang* A very intelligent person. — *Syn.* See INTELLECT. — **to have on the brain** To be obsessed by. — *v.t.* **1.** To dash out the brains of. **2.** *Slang* To hit on the head. [OE *brægen*]

brain child *Informal* That which one has created or originated, as an idea, technique, device, etc.

brain death The comatose condition in which no activity of the central nervous system, including brain waves, is detectable for at least five hours.

brain fever Inflammation of the meninges.

brain-in·jured (brān'in'jərd) *adj. U.S.* Suffering from a brain injury, especially such an injury from birth.

brain·less (brān'lis) *adj.* Lacking intelligence; senseless; stupid. — **brain'less·ly** *adv.* — **brain'less·ness** *n.*

brain·pan (brān'pan') *n.* The cranium; skull.

brain·sick (brān'sik') *adj.* Exhibiting mental disorder; crazy. — **brain'sick'ly** *adv.* — **brain'·sick'ness** *n.*

brain·stem (brān'stem') *n.* All the brain except the cerebellum and the cerebral cortex.

brain·storm (brān'stôrm') *n.* **1.** Sudden and violent cerebral disturbance. **2.** *Informal* A sudden inspiration. Also **brain storm.**

Brain·tree (brān'trē) A town in eastern Massachusetts; pop. 35,050.

brain trust A group of experts who act as consultants on matters of policy, etc. — **brain truster**

brain·wash (brān'wosh', -wôsh') *v.t.* To alter the convictions, beliefs, etc., of by means of brainwashing.

brain·wash·ing (brān'wosh'ing, -wôsh'ing) *n.* The systematic alteration of personal convictions, beliefs, habits, and attitudes by means of intensive, coercive indoctrination.

brain wave **1.** *Physiol.* A rhythmical fluctuation of electrical potential in the brain as shown on an electroencephalogram. **2.** *Informal* A sudden inspiration.

brain·y (brā'nē) *adj.* **brain·i·er, brain·i·est** *Informal* Intelligent; smart. — **brain'i·ly** *adv.* — **brain'i·ness** *n.*

braise (brāz) *v.t.* **braised, brais·ing** To cook (meat) by searing till brown and then simmering in a covered pan. [< F *braiser* < *braise* charcoal]

brake[1] (brāk) *n.* **1.** A device for slowing or stopping a vehicle or wheel, especially by friction. **2.** An instrument for separating the fiber of flax, hemp, etc., by bruising or crushing. **3.** A harrow for breaking clods. **4.** A lever for operating a pump or other machine. — *v.* **braked, brak·ing** *v.t.* **1.** To apply a brake to; reduce the speed of. **2.** To bruise and crush, as flax. **3.** To pulverize (clods) with a harrow. **4.** To knead (dough). — *v.i.* **5.** To operate a brake or brakes. [< M Du. *braeke* brake for flax; infl. in meaning by OF *brac,* var. of *bras* arm, and by BREAK] — **brake'age** *n.* — **brake'less** *adj.*

brake[2] (brāk) See BREAK (*n.* def. 21).

brake[3] (brāk) *n.* Bracken, a kind of fern. [ME, back formation < *braken* (mistaken as a plural). See BRACKEN.]

brake[4] (brāk) *n.* An area covered with brushwood, briers, cane, etc.; thicket. [Cf. MLG *brake* stumps]

brake[5] (brāk) Archaic past tense of BREAK.

brake band *Mech.* A flexible band or strap that encircles a brake drum and slows or stops it when tightened.

brake drum *Mech.* A metal drum attached to the wheel, axle, or transmission shaft of a vehicle and connecting with the brake mechanism.

brake fluid The liquid used in hydraulic brakes.

brake horsepower The useful or effective horsepower of an engine, as measured by a brake or dynamometer attached to the drive shaft.

brake lining *Mech.* The material, usually of woven asbestos, cotton, or wire, used to cover a brake band or shoe.

brake·man (brāk'mən) *n. pl.* **·men** (-mən) One who tends brakes on a railroad car or assists in operating a train. Also *Brit.* **brakes'man.**

brake shoe A rigid metal casting shaped to press against a wheel or brake drum when braking action is applied.

bra·ky (brā'kē) *adj.* Overgrown with bracken or brush.

Bra·man·te (brä·män'tā), **Donato d'Agnolo,** 1444–1514, Italian architect and painter.

bram·ble (bram'bəl) *n.* **1.** Any of a genus (*Rubus*) of plants of the rose family, especially the blackberry of Europe. **2.** Any prickly plant or shrub: also **bram'ble·bush** (-boosh'). [OE *bræmble.* Akin to BROOM.] — **bram'bly** *adj.*

bram·bling (bram'bling) *n.* The European mountain finch (*Fringilla montifringilla*). [Cf. G *brämling*]

bran (bran) *n.* **1.** The coarse, outer coat of cereals, as separated from the flour by sifting or bolting. **2.** Grain by-products used as feed. [< OF *bran, bren*] — **bran'ny** *adj.*

Bran (bran) **1.** A mythical king of Britain. **2.** In Celtic mythology, a god of the underworld.

branch (branch, bränch) *n.* **1.** A secondary stem of a tree or other large plant; limb. **2.** A part analogous to a branch; an offshoot: the *branches* of a deer's antlers. **3.** Any separate part or division of a system, subject, etc.; department: Geometry is a *branch* of mathematics. **4.** A subordinate or local store, office, agency, etc. **5.** A division of a family, tribe, nation, etc., having or thought to have a common ancestor. **6.** *Ling.* A subdivision of a linguistic family, larger than a group. **7.** A tributary stream of a river. **8.** *U.S.* Any small stream or brook. *Abbr* br. — *v.i.* **1.** To put forth branches; spread in branches. **2.** To separate into branches or subdivisions; go off from the main part. — *v.t.* **3.** To embroider with a pattern of flowers or foliage. **4.** To divide into branches. — **to branch off 1.** To separate into branches; fork, as a road. **2.** To diverge; go off on a tangent. — **to branch out** To extend or expand, as one's business or interests. [< OF *branche* < LL *branca* paw]

-branch *combining form Zool.* Having a specified type of branchiae: *nudibranch.* [< Gk. *branchia* gills]

bran·chi·ae (brang'ki·ē) *n. pl. of* **bran·chi·a** (brang'kē-ə) *Zool.* Gills or gill-like appendages; the respiratory organs of fish, modified for breathing the air contained in water. [< L < Gk. *branchia,* pl., gills] — **bran'chi·al** *adj.*

bran·chi·ate (brang'kē·it, -āt) *adj.* Having gills.

branchio- *combining form Zool.* Gills: *branchiopod.* Also, before vowels, **branchi-.** [< Gk. *branchia,* pl., gills]

bran·chi·o·pod (brang'kē·ə·pod') *n.* One of a group (*Branchiopoda*) of aquatic crustaceans having a typically elongated body and many pairs of leaflike thoracic appendages with a respiratory function. [< NL < BRANCHIO- + -PODA]

Bran·cuși (brong'koosh), **Constantin,** 1876–1957, Rumanian sculptor active in France.

brand (brand) *n.* **1.** A distinctive name or trademark identifying the product of a manufacturer. **2.** The kind or make of a product: a good *brand* of coffee. **3.** A mark made with a hot iron, as on cattle, to indicate ownership. **4.** Formerly, a mark burned on criminals with a hot iron. **5.** Any mark of disgrace or infamy; stigma. **6.** A branding iron. **7.** A burning piece of wood; also, a torch. **8.** *Archaic* A sword. **9.** *Bot.* A disease of plants caused by a parasitic fungus, giving a pustular, burnt appearance. *Abbr. br.* — *v.t.* **1.** To mark with a brand. **2.** To mark as infamous; stigmatize. [OE, torch, sword. Akin to BURN¹.] — **brand'er** *n.*

Bran·deis (bran'dīs), **Louis Dembitz,** 1856–1941, U.S. jurist; associate justice of the Supreme Court 1916–39.

Bran·den·burg (bran'dən·bûrg, *Ger.* brän'dən·boorkh) A former state in East Germany; 10,416 sq. mi.; capital, Potsdam; formerly a province of Prussia.

Bran·des (brän'dēs), **Georg** (**Morris Cohen**), 1842–1927, Danish literary critic.

bran·died (bran'dēd) *adj.* Mixed, flavored with, or preserved in brandy: *brandied* cherries.

branding iron An iron for burning in a brand. Also **brand iron.**

bran·dish (bran'dish) *v.t.* To wave, shake, or flourish triumphantly, menacingly, or defiantly. — *n.* A flourish, as with a weapon. [< OF *brandiss-,* stem of *brandir* < *brand* sword] — **bran'dish·er** *n.*

brand·ling (brand'ling) *n. Brit.* A small red earthworm (*Eisenia foetida*), used as bait. [< BRAND]

brand-new (brand'noo', -nyoo', bran'-) *adj.* Very new; fresh and bright. Also **bran'-new'** (bran'-).

bran·dy (bran'dē) *n. pl.* **·dies** An alcoholic liquor distilled from wine or from other fermented fruit juices. — *v.t.* **·died,** **·dy·ing** To mix, flavor, strengthen, or preserve with brandy. [< Du. *brandewijn,* lit., distilled (burned) wine]

Bran·dy·wine (bran'di·wīn') A creek in SE Pennsylvania and northern Delaware; site of Washington's defeat by the British, 1777.

Brang·wyn (brang'win), **Sir Frank,** 1867–1956, English painter, etcher, and illustrator.

brant (brant) *n. pl.* **brants** or **brant** A small, black-necked wild goose (*Branta bernicla*) of the coasts of Europe and eastern North America, breeding in the arctic: also called *brent.* Also **brant goose.** [Cf. ON *brandgås* sheldrake]

Brant (brant), **Joseph,** 1742–1807, Mohawk chief; fought for the British in the American Revolution: Indian name **Tha·yen·da·ne·ge·a** (thə·yen·də·nā'gē·ə).

bran·tail (bran'tāl') *n.* The redstart (def. 1).

Braque (bräk), **Georges,** 1882–1963, French painter.

brash¹ (brash) *adj. U.S.* **1.** Acting hastily; rash; impetuous. **2.** Impudent in manner; saucy; pert. **3.** *Dial.* Active; quick. [Cf. G *barsch* harsh and Sw. *barsk* impetuous] — **brash'ly** *adv.* — **brash'ness** *n.*

brash² (brash) *adj. U.S.* Brittle: said of timber. [Cf. dial. E (northern) *brassish* brittle]

brash³ (brash) *n. Dial.* **1.** A transient attack of sickness. **2.** *Brit.* A shower of rain. [? Blend of *break* and *crash, dash, splash,* etc.] — **brash'i·ness** *n.* — **brash'y** *adj.*

brash⁴ (brash) *n.* A heap of fragments or rubble, as of stones, ice, etc. [Prob. < F. *brèche* rubble]

bra·sier (brā'zhər) See BRAZIER.

Bra·sil (brä·zēl') The Portuguese name for BRAZIL: officially **Es·ta·dos U·ni·dos do Brasil** (ēsh·tä'thooz oo·nē'thooz thoo).

Bra·sí·lia (brə·zē'lyə) The capital of Brazil since 1960, in a Federal District (2,257 sq. mi.) in the SE Goiás State; pop. 348,000 (1968, including Federal District).

bras·i·lin (braz'ə·lin) See BRAZILIN.

Bra·șov (brä·shôv') A city of central Rumania; capital of Brașov District; pop. 172,343 (1968); from 1950–61 *Stalin.* Also **Bra·shov'.**

brass (bras, bräs) *n.* **1.** An alloy essentially of copper and zinc, harder than copper, and both ductile and malleable. **2.** Formerly, any alloy of copper, especially one with tin. **3.** *Usually pl.* Ornaments or utensils of brass. **4.** *Sometimes pl. Music* The brass instruments of an orchestra or band collectively: also *Rare* **brass winds. 5.** A bearing or bushing made of a copper alloy. **6.** *Brit.* A memorial tablet of brass, often with an effigy of the deceased. **7.** *Informal* Effrontery. **8.** *U.S. Informal* High-ranking military officers; any high officials. **9.** *Slang* Money. *Abbr. b., B* — *adj.* **1.** Made of brass; brazen. **2.** *Music* Of or pertaining to a group of wind instruments in which a column of air is set into vibration directly by a buzzing movement of the player's lips, as trumpets, horns, tubas, etc. [OE *bræs*]

bras·sage (bras'ij, bräs'-) *n.* The mintage fee for coining. Compare SEIGNIORAGE. [< F < *brasser* to stir]

bras·sard (bras'ärd, brə·särd') *n.* **1.** A band worn on the upper arm as a badge or insignia. **2.** A piece of armor for the arm. Also **bras·sart** (bras'ərt). [< F < *bras* arm]

brass band *Music* A band using mostly brass instruments.

brass hat *Slang* **1.** A high-ranking military officer. **2.** Any high official.

bras·si·ca·ceous (bras'i·kā'shəs) *adj. Bot.* Of, pertaining to, or belonging to a genus (*Brassica*) of erect, tall, branched herbs of the mustard family, yielding many edible plants, as cabbages, turnips, and radishes. [< L *brassica* cabbage]

brass·ie (bras'ē, bräs'ē) *n.* A wooden golf club with a brass plate on the sole: also spelled *brassy.* For illustration see GOLF CLUB.

bras·siere (brə·zir') *n.* A woman's undergarment to support or shape the breasts. Also **bras·siè're'.** [< F, arm protector < *bras* arm]

brass knuckles A metal device that fits over the knuckles of a closed fist, used in rough fighting: also called *knuckledusters.* Also **brass knucks** (nuks).

brass tacks *Informal* Basic facts; essentials: usually in the phrase **to get** (or **come**) **down to brass tacks.**

brass·y¹ (bras'ē, bräs'ē) *adj.* **brass·i·er, brass·i·est 1.** Of or ornamented with brass. **2.** Like brass, as in sound or color. **3.** Cheap and showy. **4.** *Informal* Insolent; brazen. — **brass'i·ly** *adv.* — **brass'i·ness** *n.*

brass·y² (bras'ē, bräs'ē) See BRASSIE.

brat¹ (brat) *n.* A nasty child. [? < BRAT² (def. 1)]

brat² (brat) *n. Scot.* **1.** A coarse apron or bib; rag. **2.** The scum on boiled milk, etc. [OE *bratt,* ult. < Celtic]

Bra·ti·sla·va (brä'ti·slä'və) A city in southern Czechoslovakia, on the Danube; pop. 252,046 (est. 1958): Hungarian *Pozsony,* German *Pressburg.*

brat·tice (brat'is) *n.* A partition; especially, a partition in a mine to control ventilation [< OF *bretesche,* ult. < Gmc.]

brat·tle (brat'l) *v.i.* **·tled, ·tling** To make a clattering noise; rush noisily. — *n.* A rattling or clattering noise. [Imit.]

brat·wurst (brät'wûrst, -vürst, brat'-) *n.* A small pork sausage. [< G < *brat* fried + *wurst* sausage]

Braun (broun), **Karl Ferdinand,** 1850–1918, German physicist and inventor in wireless telegraphy.

Braun·schweig (broun'shvīkh) The German name for BRUNSWICK.

bra·va (brä′vä) *interj.* Bravo: used in applauding a woman.
bra·va·do (brə·vä′dō) *n. pl.* **·does** or **·dos** Boastful defiance or menace; affectation of bravery. [< Sp. *bravada* < *bravo* brave]
brave (brāv) *adj.* **brav·er, brav·est** **1.** Having or showing courage; intrepid; courageous. **2.** Making a fine display; elegant; showy. **3.** *Obs.* Excellent. — *v.* **braved, brav·ing** *v.t.* **1.** To meet or face with courage and fortitude: to *brave* danger. **2.** To defy; challenge: to *brave* the heavens. **3.** *Obs.* To make splendid. —*v.i.* **4.** *Obs.* To boast. — *n.* **1.** A man of courage. **2.** A North American Indian warrior. **3.** *Obs.* A bully; bravo. **4.** *Obs.* A boast or defiance. [< F < Ital. *bravo*, ? < L *barbarus* wild, fierce] — **brave′ly** *adv.* — **brave′ness** *n.*
— **Syn.** (adj.) **1.** *Brave, courageous, bold, fearless, intrepid, valiant,* and *gallant* mean confident and undismayed in the face of danger. *Brave* is the most general, implying confidence, self-possession, and resolution. *Courageous* refers to firmness arising from strong moral convictions. The *bold* man is undeterred by fear of consequences, while the *fearless* or *intrepid* man is cool and self-possessed. *Valiant* suggests bravery in a worthy cause, or with commendable consequences, while *gallant* implies chivalrous actions or display. — **Ant.** cowardly, craven, timid, timorous, fearful, fainthearted.
brav·er·y (brā′vər·ē) *n. pl.* **·er·ies** **1.** The quality of being brave; valor; heroism. **2.** Elegance of attire; show; splendor.
bra·vis·si·mo (brä·vēs′sē·mō) *interj.* Italian Excellent!
bra·vo[1] (brä′vō) *interj.* Good! well done! — *n. pl.* **·vos** A shout of "bravo!" [< Ital. See BRAVE.]
bra·vo[2] (brä′vō, brä′-) *n. pl.* **·voes** or **·vos** A lawless ruffian; hired killer; desperado. [< Ital. See BRAVE.]
bra·vu·ra (brə·vyŏŏr′ə, *Ital.* brä·vōō′rä) *n.* **1.** *Music* A passage requiring dashing and brilliant execution; also, a brilliant style of execution. **2.** Any brilliant or daring performance. [< Ital., dash, daring < *bravo*. See BRAVE.]
braw (brô, brä) *adj. Scot.* Splendid; handsome; fine.
brawl[1] (brôl) *n.* **1.** A noisy quarrel; fight. **2.** *U.S. Slang* An uproarious party. — **Syn.** See ROW[3]. — *v.i.* **1.** To quarrel noisily; fight. **2.** To move noisily, as water. [ME *braulen,* ? < LG. Cf. Du. *brallen.*] — **brawl′er** *n.* — **brawl′ing·ly** *adv.*
brawl[2] (brôl) *n.* An old French folk dance; also, the music for it. [< F *branle* < *branler* to shake, sway]
brawn (brôn) *n.* **1.** Firm or well-developed muscles. **2.** Muscular power; strength. **3.** Pork or boar's flesh, especially when boiled, pickled, and pressed. [< OF *braon* slice of flesh, ult. < Gmc.]
brawn·y (brô′nē) *adj.* **brawn·i·er, brawn·i·est** Muscular; strong. — **brawn′i·ness** *n.*
braws (brôz, bräz) *n.pl. Scot.* Finery; best clothes.
Brax·ton (braks′tən), **Charles,** 1736–97, American patriot; signer of the Declaration of Independence.
brax·y (brak′sē) *Vet. n.* A carbuncular fever of sheep, caused by a bacterium (*Clostridium septicum*). — *adj.* Affected with braxy. [Cf. OE *bræc* sickness, rheum]
bray[1] (brā) *v.i.* **1.** To utter a loud, harsh cry, as an ass. **2.** To sound harshly, as a trumpet. — *v.t.* **3.** To utter loudly and harshly. — *n.* **1.** The cry of an ass, mule, etc. **2.** Any loud, harsh sound. [< OF *braire* to cry out] — **bray′er** *n.*
bray[2] (brā) *v.t.* To bruise, pound, or mix, as in a mortar. [< OF *breier,* ult. < Gmc.]
bray·er (brā′ər) *n.* A roller mounted for use by hand, to spread ink evenly over a printing surface. [See BRAY[2]]
Braz. Brazil; Brazilian.
bra·za (brä′thä, -sä) *n.* A Spanish measure of length equivalent to 5.48 feet; in Argentina, 5.68 feet. [< Sp.]
braze[1] (brāz) *v.t.* **brazed, braz·ing** **1.** To make of brass. **2.** To make like brass in hardness or appearance. **3.** To ornament with or as with brass. [OE *brasian* < *bræs* brass]
braze[2] (brāz) *v.t.* **brazed, braz·ing** *Metall.* To join the surfaces of (similar or dissimilar metals) by partial fusion with a layer of a soldering alloy applied under very high temperature. [< F *braser* solder < OF, burn, ult. < Gmc.; infl. in meaning by BRAZE[1]] — **braz′er** *n.*
bra·zen (brā′zən) *adj.* **1.** Made of brass. **2.** Resembling brass in hardness, color, sound, etc. **3.** Impudent; shameless. — *v.t.* **1.** To face with effrontery or impudence: with *out.* **2.** To make bold or reckless. [OE *bræsen* < *bræs* brass] — **bra′zen·ly** *adv.* — **bra′zen·ness** *n.*
brazen age See BRONZE AGE.
bra·zen·face (brā′zən·fās′) *n.* An impudent, shameless person. — **bra′zen·faced′** *adj.*
bra·zier[1] (brā′zhər) *n.* A worker in brass: also spelled *brasier.* [ME *brasiere*]
bra·zier[2] (brā′zhər) *n.* An open pan for holding live coals: also spelled *brasier.* [< F *brasier* < *braise* hot coals]
bra·zil (brə·zil′) *n.* **1.** The red wood of several Brazilian trees of the genus *Caesalpinia,* used as a dyestuff. **2.** A dyewood from closely allied genera. **3.** The dye obtained from the wood. **4.** Sapanwood. Also **bra·zil′wood′** (-wŏŏd′). [< Sp. *brasil,* or Ital. *brasile,* an Oriental dyewood]

Bra·zil (brə·zil′) A Republic, the largest of South America; 3,287,951 sq. mi.; pop. 90,840,000 (est. 1969); capital, Brasília: officially **Federated Republic of Brazil.** Portuguese *Brasil.* — **Bra·zil·ian** (brə·zil′yən) *adj. & n.*
braz·i·lin (braz′ə·lin) *n. Chem.* A crystalline compound, $C_{16}H_{14}O_5$, the red coloring principle contained in brazil: also spelled *brasilin.*
Brazil nut The triangular edible seed of a South American tree (*Bertholletia excelsa*).
Bra·zos River (brä′zəs, bra′-, brä′-) A river in central Texas, flowing SE about 800 miles to the Gulf of Mexico.
Braz·za·ville (braz′ə·vil, *Fr.* brå·zà·vēl′) The capital of the Republic of the Congo (Brazzaville), in the SE part, on the Congo river; pop. 94,000 (UN est. 1969).
B.R.C.A. Brotherhood of Railroad Carmen of America.
B.R.C.S. British Red Cross Society.
breach (brēch) *n.* **1.** The act of breaking, or the state of being broken; infraction; infringement. **2.** Violation of a right, legal obligation, promise, etc.: *breach* of contract. **3.** A gap or break in a dike, wall, fortification, etc.: to leap into the *breach.* **4.** A breaking up of friendly relations; quarrel; estrangement. **5.** The leaping of a whale from the water. **6.** The breaking of waves, as over the side of a vessel or on a shore; billows; surf. **7.** *Obs.* A wound or injury. — *v.t.* To make a breach in; break through. [OE *bryce*; infl. in form by F *brèche* fragment, piece. Akin to BREAK.]
— **Syn. 3.** opening, crack, fissure, chink, cleft, crevice. Compare BREAK, GAP, HOLE. **4.** rupture, disagreement.
breach of promise Failure to fulfill a promise, especially a promise to marry.
bread (bred) *n.* **1.** An article of food made with moistened flour or meal, commonly leavened with yeast, kneaded, and baked. **2.** Food in general. **3.** The necessities of life; subsistence. — *v.t.* To dress with bread crumbs before cooking. [OE *brēad* bit, crumb] — **bread′ed** *adj.*
bread-and-but·ter (bred′n·but′ər) *adj.* **1.** Actuated by personal need; mercenary: *bread-and-butter* candidates. **2.** Youthful; immature or unformed: a *bread-and-butter* miss. **3.** Prosaic; commonplace. **4.** Expressing gratitude for hospitality: a *bread-and-butter* letter.
bread and butter. 1. Bread spread with butter. **2.** *Informal* Subsistence; maintenance; livelihood.
bread·bas·ket (bred′bas′kit, -bäs′-) *n.* **1.** A basket for carrying bread. **2.** A region that is a principal source of grain. **3.** *Slang* The stomach.
bread·fruit (bred′frōōt′) *n.* **1.** The fruit of a moraceous tree (*Artocarpus altilis*) native to the South Sea Islands, that when roasted resembles bread. **2.** The tree.
bread line A line of persons waiting to be given bread or other food as charity.
bread mold A mold developed on bread by a black fungus (*Rhizopus nigricans*).
bread·nut (bred′nut′) *n.* The edible fruit of a West Indian tree (*Brosimum alicastrum*) of the mulberry family.
bread·root (bred′rōōt′, -rŏŏt′) *n.* **1.** A leguminous plant (*Psoralea esculenta*) of the plains of the United States. **2.** Its starchy, edible root.
bread·stuff (bred′stuf′) *n.* **1.** Material for bread; grain, meal, or flour. **2.** Bread.
breadth (bredth, bretth) *n.* **1.** Measure or distance from side to side, as distinguished from length and thickness; width. *Abbr. b., B.* **2.** Freedom from narrowness; liberality. **3.** That which is measured by its width, or which has a definite width: a *breadth* of cloth. **4.** In art, the impression of largeness and comprehensiveness. [OE *brēdu* < *brād* broad; *-th* added on analogy with *length*]
breadth·wise (bredth′wīz′, bretth′-) *adv.* In the direction of the breadth. Also **breadth′ways′** (-wāz′).
bread·win·ner (bred′win′ər) *n.* One who supports himself and others by his earnings.

break (brāk) *v.* **broke** (*Archaic* **brake**), **bro·ken** (*Archaic* **broke**), **break·ing** *v.t.* **1.** To separate into pieces or fragments, as by a blow; shatter. **2.** To crack without separating. **3.** To part the surface of; pierce or wound: to *break* ground. **4.** To burst or cause to discharge, as an abscess. **5.** To disable by shattering or crushing; render useless or inoperative. **6.** To destroy the order, continuity, or completeness of: to *break* ranks; to *break* stride. **7.** To diminish the force or effect of; moderate: to *break* a fall. **8.** To overcome by opposing; put an end to: to *break* a strike. **9.** To interrupt the course of, as a journey. **10.** To violate: to *break* one's promise. **11.** To reduce in spirit or health, as by toil. **12.** To reduce to discipline; tame, as a horse. **13.** To demote. **14.** To give or obtain smaller units for: to *break* a dollar. **15.** To make bankrupt or short of money. **16.** To force (a way), as through a barrier. **17.** To escape from: to *break* jail. **18.** To surpass; excel: to *break* a record. **19.** To make known; tell, as news. **20.** To cause to discontinue a habit. **21.** *Law* To invalidate (a will) by court action. —

v.i. **22.** To become separated into pieces or fragments. **23.** To give way; become unusable or inoperative: *His pencil broke.* **24.** To dissolve and disperse: *The clouds broke.* **25.** To come into being or evidence: *The storm broke* suddenly. **26.** To appear above the surface. **27.** To start or move suddenly: *He broke* from the crowd. **28.** To become overwhelmed with grief: *His heart broke.* **29.** To change direction suddenly: *The horse broke* from the track. **30.** To fall off abruptly: *The fever broke.* **31.** To change tone, as a boy's voice. **32.** *Music* To change from one quality of tone to another. **33.** In baseball, to curve at or near the plate: said of a pitch. **— to break bread** To take or share a meal. **— to break down 1.** To undergo mechanical failure. **2.** To suffer physical or mental collapse. **3.** To yield, especially to grief or strong feelings. **4.** To cause to yield. **5.** To analyze or be analyzed. **6.** To decompose. **— to break in** To cause to obey; train; adapt. **— to break into** (or **in**) **1.** To interrupt or intervene. **2.** To enter by force. **— to break in on** (or **upon**) To interrupt. **— to break off 1.** To stop or cease, as from speaking. **2.** To sever (relations); discontinue. **3.** To become separate or detached. **— to break out 1.** To start unexpectedly or suddenly, as a fire or plague. **2.** To have an eruption or rash, as the skin. **3.** To make an escape, as from prison. **— to break out into** (or **forth in**, etc.) To begin to do or perform: *The birds broke out into* song. **— to break up 1.** To disperse; scatter: *The meeting broke up.* **2.** To dismantle; take apart. **3.** To put an end to; stop. **4.** *Informal* To distress: *The loss broke up* the old man. **5.** *Informal* To sever relations: *They broke up.* **— to break with** To sever relations with. **—** *n.* **1.** The act or result of breaking; fracture; breach; rupture. **2.** A starting or opening: the *break* of day. **3.** *U.S.* A dash or run; especially, an attempt to escape: to make a *break* for the door. **4.** A breach of continuity; sudden interruption or change: a *break* in a fever. **5.** A pause, as from work. **6.** *U.S. Informal* A chance or opportunity: a lucky *break*. **7.** *Electr.* The opening of a circuit; interruption of current. **8.** A rupture in friendship; falling out; quarrel. **9.** An interruption in a text or discourse caused by an omission, digression, etc. **10.** *Printing* **a** The place where one paragraph ends and another begins. **b** A series of three dots (. . .) used to mark an omission in a text. **11.** In prosody, a caesura. **12.** A sudden decline in prices, as in the stock market. **13.** *Music* **a** The point where one register or quality of a voice changes to another in singing; also, a similar point in the tones of a musical instrument. **b** In jazz, a syncopated cadenza bridging two phrases or choruses of a jazz melody. **14.** In baseball or cricket, the swerving of a ball from a straight course when thrown. **15.** *U.S.* A sudden or abrupt change in the gait of a horse, especially of a race horse. **16.** *U.S. Informal* An unfortunate or ill-considered remark or action; blunder. **17.** In pool, the first play; the shot that scatters the balls. **18.** In bowling, the completion of a frame without making a strike or spare. **19.** In billiards, pool, and croquet, an uninterrupted series of successful shots; run. **20.** *U.S.* An agitation on the surface of water caused by the rising of a fish. **21.** A high, four-wheeled carriage or wagonette: also spelled *brake*. [OE *brecan*. Akin to BREACH.]
— Syn. (verb) **1.** *Break, burst, crush, shatter, shiver,* and *smash* mean to fracture or deform forcibly. *Break* suggests the separation of a rigid body into pieces. *Burst* refers to a breaking from internal pressure; *crush,* to the effect of great external pressure. Brittle objects are *shattered* or *shivered,* but *shatter* connotes many small pieces, while *shiver* suggests fine, needlelike ones. *Smash* describes the complete deformation resulting from a heavy, noisy blow. **—** (noun) **6.** See OPPORTUNITY.
break·a·ble (brā′kə·bəl) *adj.* Capable of being broken. **— break′a·ble·ness** *n.*
break·age (brā′kij) *n.* **1.** A breaking, or its result; a break. **2.** Articles broken. **3.** Loss, or compensation for loss, due to articles broken.
break·bone (brāk′bōn′) *n. Pathol.* Dengue.
break·down (brāk′doun′) *n.* **1.** A collapse or failure, as of a machine, one's health, etc. **2.** An analysis or summary, as of facts or statistics. **3.** *Chem.* Decomposition or analysis of a compound. **4.** *U.S.* A shuffling, stamping dance.
break·er¹ (brā′kər) *n.* **1.** One who or that which breaks. **2.** A wave of the sea that breaks on rocks, a reef, etc. **3.** A structure in which large masses of anthracite coal are broken up, sorted, and cleaned. **— Syn.** See WAVE.
break·er² (brā′kər) *n. Naut.* A small cask of water for use in a lifeboat. [Alter. of Sp. *barrica* cask?]
break·fast (brek′fəst) *n.* The morning meal. **—** *v.t.* **1.** To furnish with a breakfast. **—** *v.i.* **2.** To eat breakfast. [< BREAK, *v.,* + FAST²] **— break′fast·er** *n.*
break·front (brāk′frunt′) *n.* A large cabinet, the front of which is divided into two surfaces, the middle part having the greater depth.
break·ing (brā′king) *n. Ling.* In prehistoric Old English, the dipthongization of *æ* and of *e, i* to *eo, io,* under the influence of a following preconsonantal *r, l,* and *h,* and *h* final, as in *feallan* fall, *weorc* work. [Trans. of G *brechung*]
breaking and entering *Law* The removal or putting aside of some tangible part of a dwelling house and gaining access with intent to commit a crime. See BURGLARY.

break·neck (brāk′nek′) *adj.* Likely to break the neck; dangerous: *breakneck* speed.
Break·spear (brāk′spir), **Nicholas** See ADRIAN IV.
break·through (brāk′thrōō′) *n.* **1.** *Mil.* An attack that penetrates through an enemy's defenses into the rear area. **2.** Any sudden, important success, as in scientific research.
break·up (brāk′up′) *n.* **1.** A breaking up or separation; dissolution; disruption. **2.** *Canadian* The time when the ice breaks up in the northern streams; spring.
break·wa·ter (brāk′wô′tər, -wot′ər) *n.* A barrier for protecting a harbor or beach from the force of waves.
bream¹ (brēm) *n. pl.* **breams** or **bream 1.** Any of several fresh-water cyprinoid fishes (genus *Abramis*) with deep, compressed bodies, especially the common European species (*A. brama*). **2.** Any of various fresh-water sunfishes; especially, the **blue bream** (*Lepomis pallidus*). The sea bream (which see). [< F *brème* < OF *bresme* < Gmc.]
bream² (brēm) *v.t. Naut.* To clean (a ship's bottom) by heating the pitch and scraping. [< Du. *brem* furze]
breast (brest) *n.* **1.** *Anat.* The front of the chest from the neck to the abdomen. **2.** One of the mammary glands. **3.** That part of a garment that covers the breast. **4.** The breast as the seat of the affections or emotions; bosom; heart. **5.** Anything likened to the human or animal breast. **6.** The working face of a mine, from which material is removed. **— to make a clean breast of** To make a complete confession of. **—** *v.t.* **1.** To encounter or oppose with the breast: to *breast* the waves. **2.** To meet or oppose boldly; advance against: to *breast* one's problems. [OE *brēost*]
breast·bone (brest′bōn′) *n. Anat.* The sternum.
Breast·ed (bres′tid), **James Henry**, 1865–1935, U.S. Egyptologist.
breast-feed (brest′fēd′) *v.t. & v.i.* **-fed, -feed·ing** To suckle.
breast·pin (brest′pin′) *n.* A pin worn at the breast to close a garment; brooch.
breast·plate (brest′plāt′) *n.* **1.** A piece of plate armor for the breast. **2.** A strap crossing a horse's breast. **3.** A square piece of linen cloth adorned with twelve precious stones symbolizing the twelve tribes of Israel, worn by the Jewish high priest. **4.** The plastron of a turtle.

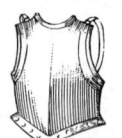

BREAST-
PLATE

breast stroke In swimming, a stroke made while lying face down, the arms being thrust forward from the breast under or on the surface, then brought laterally back to the sides, the legs at the same time being moved in a frog kick.
breast·work (brest′wûrk′) *n.* A low, temporary defensive work, usually breast-high: also called *parapet*. **— Syn.** See BULWARK.
breath (breth) *n.* **1.** Air inhaled and exhaled in respiration. **2.** Power or ability to breathe, especially to breathe freely: to lose one's *breath*. **3.** The act of breathing; respiration; also, life; existence: to hope while *breath* remains. **4.** A single respiration: to draw a long *breath*. **5.** The time of a single respiration; instant. **6.** A slight delay or respite. **7.** A slight movement of air. **8.** Anything slight or inconsequential; trifle. **9.** An articulate utterance; murmur; whisper. **10.** Moisture from exhaled air, when condensed on cold objects or visible in cold air. **11.** *Phonet.* An exhalation of air without vibration of the vocal cords, as in the production of (p) and (f). Compare VOICE. **— in the same breath** At the same moment; without a pause or break. **— out of breath** Breathless; gasping, as from exertion. **— to take one's breath away** To awe or produce sudden emotion in. **— under one's breath** In a whisper or mutter. [OE *brǣth* vapor, odor]
breathe (brēth) *v.* **breathed** (brēthd), **breath·ing** *v.i.* **1.** To inhale and exhale air; respire. **2.** To be alive; live. **3.** To pause for breath; rest. **4.** To murmur; whisper. **5.** To move gently, as breezes. **6.** To be exhaled, as fragrance. **—** *v.t.* **7.** To inhale and expel from the lungs, as air; respire. **8.** To inject or infuse as if by breathing: to *breathe* life into a statue. **9.** To utter, especially softly; whisper. **10.** To express; manifest: *His appearance breathes* confidence. **11.** To exhale: to *breathe* fire. **12.** To allow a rest to, as for breath: to *breathe* one's horse. **13.** *Obs.* To put out of breath; exhaust. **14.** *Obs.* To exercise. **15.** *Phonet.* To utter with the breath only, without vibration of the vocal cords. [ME *brethen* < *breth* breath] **— breath′a·ble** *adj.*
breath·er (brē′thər) *n.* **1.** One who breathes, especially in a specified manner: a heavy *breather*. **2.** *Informal* That which increases breathing or exhausts the breath, as exercise. **3.** *Informal* A brief rest period.
breath·ing (brē′thing) *adj.* Respiring; living. **—** *n.* **1.** The act of respiration; also, a single breath. **2.** A gentle breeze. **3.** Words spoken; utterance. **4.** Aspiration; longing. **5.** Time to breathe. **6.** *Phonet.* An aspiration; aspirate.
breathing space 1. A space or area in which one can breathe or move about freely. **2.** A pause, as for rest or thought: also **breathing spell.**
breath·less (breth′lis) *adj.* **1.** Out of breath. **2.** Holding the breath from fear, excitement, etc. **3.** That takes the breath away: *breathless* speed. **4.** Devoid of breath; dead. **5.** Motionless. **— breath′less·ly** *adv.* **— breath′less·ness** *n.*

breath·tak·ing (breth′tā′king) *adj.* Thrilling; overawing.
breath·y (breth′ē) *adj.* Characterized by audible breathing.
B.Rec. or **b.rec.** Bills receivable.
brec·ci·a (brech′ē-ə, bresh′-) *n. Geol.* A rock made up of angular fragments embedded in a matrix of the same or different nature or origin. [< Ital., gravel] — **brec·ci·at·ed** (brech′ē-ā′tid, bresh′-) *adj.*
brech·am (brekh′əm) *n. Scot.* A collar for a draft horse. Also **brech·an** (brekh′ən).
Brecht (brekht), **Bertolt**, 1898–1956, German playwright and poet.
Breck·in·ridge (brek′in-rij), **John Cabell**, 1821–75, vice president of the United States 1857–61; Confederate general in the Civil War.
Breck·nock (brek′nok) **1.** Formerly, the county seat of Brecknockshire: also **Brec·on** (brek′ən). **2.** Brecknockshire.
Breck·nock·shire (brek′nək-shir) A former county in SE central Wales; 733 sq. mi.; pop. 53,234 (1971). Also **Brec·on·shire** (brek′ən-).
bred (bred) Past tense and past participle of BREED.
Bre·da (brā-dä′) A commune in the SW Netherlands; pop. 107,127 (est. 1960).
brede (brēd) *n. Archaic* A braid; a piece of braiding or embroidery. [Var. of BRAID¹, n.]
bree (brē) *n. Scot.* Broth; liquid: also **brie, broo.**
breech (brēch; *for v. def. 1, also* brich) *n.* **1.** The posterior and lower part of the body; the buttocks. **2.** The part of a gun, cannon, etc., that is behind the bore or barrel. **3.** The lower part of something, as of a pulley. — *v.t.* **1.** To clothe with breeches. **2.** To provide with a breech, as a gun. [OE *brēc*]
breech·block (brēch′blok′) *n.* The movable piece which closes the breech of a breechloading firearm, withdrawn to insert the cartridge, and replaced before firing.
breech·cloth (brēch′klôth′, -kloth′) *n.* A loincloth (which see). Also **breech′clout** (-klout′).
breech·es (brich′iz) *n.pl.* **1.** A man's garment covering the hips and thighs. **2.** Trousers. [OE *brēc*]
breeches buoy *Naut.* An apparatus, used chiefly in lifesaving, consisting of canvas breeches attached at the waist to a life buoy and run on a rope from one vessel to another or to the shore.
breech·ing (brich′ing, brē′ching) *n.*
1. A harness strap passing behind a horse's haunches. For illustration see HARNESS. **2.** The parts composing the breech of a gun. **3.** Formerly, a heavy rope attached to the breech of a ship's cannon for checking recoil.
breech·load·er (brēch′lō′dər) *n.* A firearm loaded at the breech. — **breech′load′ing** *adj.*
breech presentation *Med.* The presentation of the buttocks of the fetus during labor.

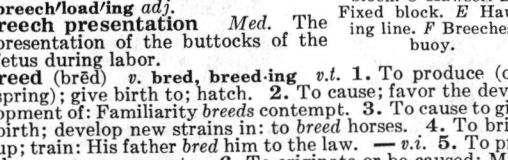

BREECHES BUOY
A Mast. *B* Traveling block. *C* Hawser. *D* Fixed block. *E* Hauling line. *F* Breeches buoy.

breed (brēd) *v.* **bred, breed·ing** *v.t.* **1.** To produce (offspring); give birth to; hatch. **2.** To cause; favor the development of: Familiarity *breeds* contempt. **3.** To cause to give birth; develop new strains in: to *breed* horses. **4.** To bring up; train: His father *bred* him to the law. — *v.i.* **5.** To produce young; procreate. **6.** To originate or be caused: Militarism *breeds* in armies. — *n.* **1.** The progeny of one stock; a race or strain of animals deliberately cultivated by man. **2.** A sort or kind; species: a warlike *breed* of men. [OE *brēdan* < *brōd* brood. Akin to BROOD.]
breed·er (brē′dər) *n.* **1.** One who breeds animals. **2.** An animal suitable or primarily used for producing offspring. **3.** One who or that which breeds; a producer; source.
breeder reactor *Physics* An apparatus for the generation of atomic energy in which the fuel is converted into more fissionable material than is consumed.
breed·ing (brē′ding) *n.* **1.** The act of bearing young; generation. **2.** The nurture and training of the young; rearing. **3.** The training or development of character or behavior; manners, especially good manners. **4.** The scientific production of new, improved varieties of plants, animals, etc. — Syn. See REFINEMENT.
Breed's Hill (brēdz) A hill near Bunker Hill. See BUNKER HILL.
breeks (brēks) *n.pl. Scot.* Breeches.
breeze¹ (brēz) *n.* **1.** *Meteorol.* A moderate current of air; a gentle wind. See BEAUFORT SCALE. **2.** *Brit. Informal* A flutter of excitement; agitation; disturbance. — **in a breeze** *Slang* Without difficulty; easily. — *v.i.* **breezed, breez·ing** *Slang* To go quickly and blithely: She *breezed* through the room. — **to breeze up** To spring up, as a wind; also, to blow more strongly. [< Sp. and Pg. *brisa, briza* northeast wind]
breeze² (brēz) *n.* A gadfly or a botfly. [OE *breosa* gadfly]
breeze³ (brēz) *n. Brit.* Refuse cinders, small coke, or fine coal used in brickmaking. [? < F *braise* hot embers]

breeze·way (brēz′wā′) *n.* A roofed, open passageway between two structures, as a house and garage.
breez·y (brē′zē) *adj.* **breez·i·er, breez·i·est** **1.** Having breezes; windy. **2.** Brisk or carefree; sprightly. — **breez′·i·ly** *adv.* — **breez′i·ness** *n.*
Bre·genz (brā′gents) A city in western Austria, on Lake Constance; capital of Vorarlberg Province; pop. 78,729 (1961): Roman *Brigantium.*
breg·ma (breg′mə) *n. pl.* **·ma·ta** (-mə-tə) *n. Anat.* That point on the vault of the skull where the coronal and sagittal sutures meet. [< Gk., front of the head] — **breg·mat·ic** (breg-mat′ik) *adj.*
Breiz (brez) The Breton name for BRITTANY.
Brem·en (brem′ən, *Ger.* brā′mən) A State of NW West Germany; 156 sq. mi.; consisting of the noncontiguous port cities of **Bremen**, on the Weser; pop. 601,884 (est. 1966); and **Brem·er·hav·en** (brem′ər-hä′vən, *Ger.* brā′mər-hä′fən), at the mouth of the Weser; pop. 147,765 (est. 1966).
Brem·er·ton (brem′ər-tən) A city in western Washington, on Puget Sound; site of Puget Sound Navy Yard; pop. 35,307.
Bren gun (bren) *Mil.* A fast, accurate machine gun, introduced into the British Army in World War II. [< *Br(no),* Czechoslovakia, where first made + *En(field),* England]
Bren·nan (bren′ən), **William J(oseph)**, born 1906, U.S. jurist; associate justice of the Supreme Court 1956–.
Bren·ner Pass (bren′ər) Lowest of the main Alpine passes, on the Austrian-Italian border; elevation 4,495 ft. Italian *Passo Brennero.*
brenn·schluss (bren′shlŏŏs) *n. Aerospace* Burnout, especially of a rocket engine or motor. [< G, end of burning]
brent¹ (brent) *adj. Scot.* Smooth; unwrinkled; also, high; prominent: said of the forehead.
brent² (brent) *n.* The brant, a bird.
br'er (brûr, brer) *n. Southern U.S.* Brother.
Bre·scia (brā′shä) A Province of Lombardy, northern Italy, 1,834 sq. mi.; pop. 881,576 (1961); capital, **Brescia,** pop. 174,116.
Bres·lau (bres′lou, brez′-) The German name for WROCŁAW.
Brest (brest) **1.** A fortified port commune in NW France, on the Atlantic; chief French naval station; 159,857 (1968). **2.** A fortified city in the SW Byelorussian S.S.R., on the Bug river; Russo-German peace treaty signed here, 1918; pop. 150,696 (1968). Prior to 1921 **Brest-Li·tovsk′** (-li-tôfsk′). Polish *Brześć nad Bugiem.*
Bre·tagne (brə-tän′y′) The French name for BRITTANY.
breth·ren (breth′rən) Alternative plural of BROTHER. ◆ See note at BROTHER. [ME]
Bret·on (bret′n) *adj.* Of or pertaining to Brittany, its inhabitants, or their language. — *n.* **1.** A native of Brittany. **2.** The language of the Bretons, one of the Brythonic branch of the Celtic languages: also called *Armorican.* Abbr. *Br.*
Bre·ton (brə-tôn′), **André,** 1896–1966, French surrealist poet and critic. — **Jules Adolphe,** 1827–1906, French painter.
Bret·ton Woods (bret′n) A resort in north central New Hampshire; site of an international monetary conference, September, 1944.
Breu·ghel (brœ′gəl) See BRUEGHEL.
brev. Brevet; brevetted.
breve (brev, brēv) *n.* **1.** A mark (˘) placed over a vowel to indicate that it has a short sound, as *a* in *hat, e* in *set, i* in *pit,* etc. Compare MACRON. **2.** In prosody, a similar mark (˘) indicating a short or unstressed syllable. **3.** *Law* A judicial writ or brief. **4.** *Music* A note equivalent to two whole notes, or the symbol for it. [< Ital. < L *brevis* short]
bre·vet (brə-vet′, *esp. Brit.* brev′it) *n. Mil.* **1.** A commission advancing an officer in honorary rank without advance in pay or in command. **2.** A commission or promotion awarded for achievement, usually on the field of battle. — *v.t.* **bre·vet·ted** (brə-vet′id) or **brev·et·ed** (brev′it·id), **bre·vet·ting** (brə-vet′ing) or **brev·et·ing** (brev′it·ing) To raise in rank by brevet. — *adj.* Held or conferred by brevet. [< OF *brevet,* dim. of *bref* letter, document]
bre·vet·cy (brə-vet′sē) *n. pl.* **·cies** Honorary rank conferred by brevet; brevet rank.
brevi- *combining form* Short; brevirostrate. [< L *brevis* short]
bre·vi·ar·y (brē′vē-er′ē, brev′ē-) *n. pl.* **·ar·ies** *Eccl.* In the Roman Catholic Church and Eastern Orthodox churches, a book of daily offices and prayers for the canonical hours. [< L *breviarium* abridgment < *brevis* short]
bre·vier (brə-vir′) *n. Printing* A size of type, about 8-point. [? < G, breviary; because once used in breviaries]
brev·i·ros·trate (brev′i-ros′trāt) *adj. Ornithol.* Having a short bill or beak. Also **brev′i·ros′tral.** [< BREVI- + L *rostrum* beak]
brev·i·ty (brev′ə-tē) *n.* **1.** Shortness of duration; brief time. **2.** Condensation of language; conciseness. [< L *brevitas, -tatis* < *brevis* short]
brew (brōō) *v.t.* **1.** To make, as beer or ale, by steeping, boiling, and fermenting malt, hops, etc. **2.** To prepare (any beverage) as by boiling or mixing: to *brew* tea. **3.** To con-

coct; devise: to *brew* mischief. — *v.i.* **4.** To make ale, beer, or the like. — **to be brewing** To be imminent; gather, as a storm, trouble, etc. — *n.* **1.** Something brewed, as beer or ale. **2.** The amount brewed at one time. [OE *brēowan.* Akin to BROTH.] — **brew′er** *n.*

brew·age (brōō′ij) *n.* **1.** A beverage prepared by brewing or mixing. **2.** The process of brewing.

brew·er·y (brōō′ər·ē) *n. pl.* **·er·ies** An establishment for brewing; also, the apparatus used in brewing.

brew·ing (brōō′ing) *n.* **1.** The process of making fermented undistilled liquids, as beer or ale. **2.** The amount brewed at one time; a brew.

brew·is (brōō′is) *n.* **1.** Bread soaked in pot liquor, gravy, or the like. **2.** Thickened broth or pot liquor. [ME *browes* < OF *brouet,* dim. of *breu, bro* broth; infl. by BREW]

Brew·ster (brōō′stər), **William,** 1567?–1644, one of the Pilgrim Fathers.

Brezh·nev (brezh·nyôf′), **Leonid Ilich,** born 1906, Soviet statesman; first secretary of the Communist party 1964–.

Br. Gu. British Guiana.

Br. Hond. British Honduras.

Bri·an Bo·ru (brī′ən bô·rōō′, bô·rōō′), 926–1014, king of Ireland; killed at battle of Clontarf. Also **Brian Bo·roimhe′.**

Bri·and (brē·äN′), **Aristide,** 1862–1932, French statesman.

Briansk (bryansk) See BRYANSK.

bri·ar (brī′ər) *n.* **1.** A pipe made of brierroot. **2.** See BRIER² (def. 1).

bri·ar·root (brī′ər·rōōt′, -rŏŏt′) See BRIERROOT.

bri·ar·wood (brī′ər·wŏŏd′) *n.* Brierroot.

bribe (brīb) *n.* **1.** Any gift or emolument used corruptly to influence public or official action. **2.** Anything that seduces or allures; an allurement. — *v.* **bribed, brib·ing** *v.t.* **1.** To offer or give a bribe to. **2.** To gain or influence by means of bribery. — *v.i.* **3.** To give bribes. [< OF, piece of bread given a beggar] — **brib′a·ble** *adj.* — **brib′er** *n.*

brib·er·y (brī′bər·ē) *n. pl.* **·er·ies** The giving, offering, or accepting of a bribe.

bric-a-brac (brik′ə·brak) *n.* Objects of curiosity or decoration; rarities; antiques; knickknacks. [< F]

brick (brik) *n.* **1.** A molded block of clay, sun-baked or kiln-burned in various shapes and sizes, used for building, paving, etc. **2.** Bricks collectively. **3.** Any object shaped like a brick. **4.** A unit out of which something is built. **5.** *Informal* An admirable fellow. — *v.t.* **1.** To build or line with bricks. **2.** To cover or wall with bricks: with *up* or *in.* — *adj.* **1.** Of brick. **2.** Brick-red. [< MF *brique* fragment, bit, ult. < Gmc. Akin to BREAK.]

brick·bat (brik′bat′) *n.* **1.** A piece of a brick, especially when used as a missile. **2.** *Informal* An insulting remark.

brick·kiln (brik′kil′, -kiln′) *n.* A structure in which bricks are burned or baked.

brick·lay·er (brik′lā′ər) *n.* One who builds with bricks. — **brick′lay′ing** *n.*

brick·le (brik′əl) *adj. Brit. Dial.* Brittle; fragile.

brick red Any of several shades of dull yellowish or brownish red, like the color of the common red clay brick.

brick·work (brik′wûrk′) *n.* Construction of or with bricks.

brick·yard (brik′yärd′) *n.* A place where bricks are made.

bri·cole (bri·kōl′, brik′əl) *n.* **1.** In billiards, a shot in which the cue ball first strikes the cushion. **2.** An indirect, unexpected stroke. **3.** A medieval catapult. **4.** A harness worn by men for dragging guns. [< F; ult. origin uncertain]

bri·dal (brīd′l) *adj.* Pertaining to a bride or a wedding; nuptial. — *n.* A wedding. [OE *brȳdealo* wedding feast]

Bridal Veil A cataract in Yosemite National Park, California; 620 ft. Also **Bri·dal·veil** (brīd′l·väl).

bridal wreath A flowering shrub (*Spiraea prunifolia*) of the rose family, blooming in the spring.

bride¹ (brīd) *n.* A newly married woman, or a woman about to be married. [OE *brȳd*]

bride² (brīd) *n.* **1.** A loop, tie, etc., in lace or needlework. **2.** A bonnet string. [< F, bridle, string, ult. < Gmc.]

Bride (brīd), **Saint** See BRIGID, SAINT.

bride·groom (brīd′grōōm′, -grŏŏm′) *n.* A man newly married or about to be married. [OE *brȳdguma* < *brȳd* bride + *guma* man; infl. in ME by *grome* lad, groom]

brides·maid (brīdz′mād′) *n.* A young, usually unmarried woman who attends a bride at her wedding.

bride·well (brīd′wel, -wəl) *n.* A house of correction; jail. [after St. *Bride's Well,* in London, near a prison]

bridge¹ (brij) *n.* **1.** A structure erected across a waterway, ravine, road, etc., to afford passage. For illustrations of specific types see BASCULE, CANTILEVER BRIDGE, DRAWBRIDGE, PONTOON BRIDGE, SUSPENSION BRIDGE. **2.** A partial deck or observation platform built athwart the forward part of a ship for the officers, pilot, etc. **3.** *Anat.* The upper bony ridge of the nose. **4.** The curved central part of a pair of spectacles that rests on the bridge of the nose. **5.** In some string instruments, a thin piece of wood that raises the strings above the soundboard. For illustration see VIOLIN. **6.** *Music* A transitional passage connecting two sections of a composition. **7.** *Dent.* A mounting for false teeth, attached on each side to a natural tooth. **8.** *Electr.* One of a variety of circuits used in measuring resistance, capacitance, inductance, and

frequency. **9.** A means of access or communication: a *bridge* between past and present. **10.** In pool and billiards, a position of the hand, or a notched piece of wood, used to support the cue in striking a ball. **11.** A low, vertical, crosswise wall, as in a metallurgic furnace. — **to burn one's bridges (behind one)** To cut off all means of retreat. — *v.t.* **bridged, bridg·ing** **1.** To construct a bridge or bridges over. **2.** To make a passage over or across by a bridge; get over. [OE *brycg*] — **bridge′a·ble** *adj.*

bridge² (brij) *n.* A card game, derived from whist, in which the trump suit (or the fact that there will be no trumps) is determined by the side proposing to take the higher number of tricks. The person who first names the trump suit then plays his partner's hand (the dummy), which is exposed on the table, as well as his own. See AUCTION BRIDGE, CONTRACT BRIDGE. [Origin uncertain]

bridge·board (brij′bôrd′, -bōrd′) *n.* A notched board to which stair treads and risers are fastened.

bridge·head (brij′hed′) *n. Mil.* A position on the hostile side of a river or defile, established by advance troops of an attacking force to protect the crossing of the main body.

Bridge of Sighs A covered bridge in Venice over which prisoners to be tried were formerly led from the prisons to the palace of the doge.

Bridge·port (brij′pôrt, -pōrt) A city in SW Connecticut, on Long Island Sound; pop. 156,542.

Bridg·es (brij′iz), **Calvin Blackman,** 1889–1938, U.S. geneticist. — **Robert,** 1844–1930, English poet; poet laureate 1913–30.

Bridges Creek See WAKEFIELD.

Bridg·et (brij′it), **Saint** (of Ireland) See BRIGID.

Bridget, Saint (of Sweden), 1303?–73, Roman Catholic nun; founder of the order of St. Saviour, or the Brigittines.

Bridge·town (brij′toun) The capital of Barbados, a port town on the SW coast; pop. 12,430 (1970).

bridge·work (brij′wûrk′) *n.* **1.** *Dent.* **a** A partial denture, variously attached to the natural teeth. **b** Such dentures collectively. **2.** The construction of bridges.

bridg·ing (brij′ing) *n.* Wooden struts or braces between joists or other beams to keep them in place.

Bridg·man (brij′mən), **Percy Williams,** 1882–1961, U.S. physicist.

bri·dle (brīd′l) *n.* **1.** The head harness, including bit and reins, used to guide or restrain a horse. **2.** Anything that restrains, limits, or guides movement; a check; curb. **3.** *Naut.* **a** A sling of cordage or wire fixed at both ends so that the pull of a single line attached to its middle is distributed to two points. **b** A mooring cable or hawser. **4.** A bridling, as in resentment. — *v.* **·dled, ·dling** *v.t.* **1.** To put a bridle on. **2.** To check or control with or as with a bridle. — *v.i.* **3.** To raise the head and draw in the chin through resentment, pride, etc. [OE *brīdel*] — **bri′dler** *n.*

bridle hand The left hand, in which the reins are usually held.

bridle path A path for saddle horses or pack animals only.

bri·dle-wise (brīd′l·wīz′) *adj.* Answering the pressure of the bridle rein on the neck, instead of on the bit.

brie (brē) See BREE.

Brie (brē) *n.* A soft, creamy cheese, ripened by mold or by bacteria. [after *Brie-Comte-Robert,* town in central France, where first made]

brief (brēf) *adj.* **1.** Short in time or extent; quickly ending. **2.** Of few words; concise. **3.** Curt or abrupt. — *n.* **1.** A short or abridged statement; summary. **2.** *Law* A memorandum of the material facts, points of law, precedents, etc., in a case, prepared for the guidance of counsel in arguing a case in court. **b** An abstract of all the documents affecting the title of a piece of real property: also **brief of title.** **3.** *pl.* Short underpants. **4.** In the Roman Catholic Church, a papal letter regarding disciplinary matters. **5.** A briefing. — **in brief** In short; briefly. — **to hold a brief for** To be on the side of; champion; aid. — *v.t.* **1.** To make a summary of; epitomize. **2.** To prepare in advance by instructing or advising; give a briefing to: to *brief* salesmen. **3.** *Brit.* To inform by a legal brief. **4.** *Brit.* To retain as counsel. [< OF *bref* < L *brevis* short] — **brief′ly** *adv.* — **brief′ness** *n.*

brief·case (brēf′kās′) *n.* A flexible, rectangular case, usually of leather, for carrying documents, papers, books, etc.

brief·ing (brē′fing) *n.* **1.** A short lecture setting forth the details of a flight, given to the crews of combat aircraft prior to their taking off. **2.** Any similar discussion of procedure.

Bri·enz (brē·ents′) A village in central Switzerland, on the **Lake of Brienz** (11 sq. mi.).

bri·er¹ (brī′ər) *n.* **1.** A prickly bush or shrub, especially one of the rose family, as the sweetbrier. **2.** A growth of such prickly bushes. **3.** A thorny or prickly twig. Also spelled *briar.* [OE *brēr, brēr*] — **bri′er·y** *adj.*

bri·er² (brī′ər) *n.* **1.** The tree heath (*Erica arborea*) of southern Europe: also spelled *briar.* **2.** See BRIAR (def. 1). [< F *bruyère* heath]

bri·er·root (brī′ər·rōōt′, -rŏŏt′) *n.* **1.** The root wood of the brier or tree heath, used in making tobacco pipes. **2.** A pipe made from this wood. Also called *briarwood:* also spelled *briarroot.* Also **bri·er·wood** (brī′ər·wŏŏd′).

Bri·eux (brē·œ′), **Eugène,** 1858–1932, French dramatist.

brig[1] (brig) *n. Naut.* A two-masted ship, square-rigged on both masts, and sometimes carrying a spanker. [Short for BRIGANTINE]

brig[2] (brig) *n. Scot.* A bridge.

brig[3] (brig) *n.* 1. A place of confinement on shipboard. 2. Humorously, a guardhouse. [Origin unknown]

Brig. *Mil.* 1. Brigade. 2. Brigadier.

bri·gade (bri·gād′) *n.* 1. *Mil.* A tactical or tactical and administrative unit consisting of a headquarters and two or more groups or regiments, usually commanded by a brigadier general. 2. Any considerable body of persons more or less organized: a fire brigade. — *v.t.* **·gad·ed, ·gad·ing** 1. To form into a brigade. 2. To classify or combine. [< MF < Ital. *brigata* company, crew < *brigare* to brawl, fight]

BRIG

brig·a·dier (brig′ə·dir′) *n.* 1. *Mil.* A brigadier general. 2. *Obs.* In the British, Canadian, and other Commonwealth armies, an office ranking next below a major general. See table at GRADE. 3. In the Napoleonic armies, a cavalry corporal. [< F]

brigadier general *Mil.* An officer ranking next above a colonel and next below a major general. Abbr. *B.G., Brig. Gen.* See table at GRADE.

brig·and (brig′ənd) *n.* A robber or bandit; especially, one of a band of outlaws. [< MF < Ital. *brigante* fighter < *brigare* to brawl, fight] — **brig′and·ish** *adj.*

brig·and·age (brig′ən·dij) *n.* The practices of brigands; robbery; plundering. Also **brig′and·ism.**

brig·an·dine (brig′ən·dēn, -dīn) *n.* A medieval coat of mail made of metal plates, sewn upon linen, leather, etc. [< MF, armor for a fighter < *brigand.* See BRIGAND.]

brig·an·tine (brig′ən·tēn, -tīn) *n. Naut.* A two-masted vessel, square-rigged on the foremast, and fore-and-aft rigged on the mainmast: also called *hermaphrodite brig, jackass brig.* [< MF *brigandin* a fighting vessel < Ital. *brigantino* < *brigare* to fight]

Bri·gan·ti·um (bri·gan′shē·əm) The Roman name for BREGENZ.

Brig. Gen. Brigadier General.

bright (brīt) *adj.* 1. Emitting or reflecting much light; full of light; shining. 2. Of brilliant color; vivid. 3. Splendid or glorious; illustrious: *bright* fame. 4. Having or showing high intelligence; quick-witted. 5. Marked by wit; lively; vivacious. 6. Full of gladness or hope; cheerful; auspicious: a *bright* future. 7. Clear or translucent: said of liquids. 8. Clear and distinct: said of a voice. — *adv.* In a bright manner; brightly. — *n. Poetic* Brightness; splendor. [OE *beorht, bryht*] — **bright′ly** *adv.*

— Syn. (adj.) 1. luminous, lustrous, glowing, shining, gleaming, sparkling, radiant, effulgent, refulgent. 4. clever, smart, intelligent. Compare INTELLIGENT. 6. beaming, happy, promising.

Bright (brīt), **John,** 1811–89, English statesman.

bright·en (brīt′n) *v.t. & v.i.* To make or become bright or brighter. — **bright′en·er** *n.*

bright·ness (brīt′nis) *n.* 1. The quality or condition of being bright. 2. *Physics* Luminance. 3. The attribute of a color that identifies it as equivalent to some member of the achromatic color series, ranging from black or very dim to white or very bright.

Brigh·ton (brīt′n) A borough and seaside resort in East Sussex, England; pop. 160,290 (1976).

Bright's disease *Pathol.* A disease characterized by degeneration of the kidneys and imperfect elimination of uric acid from the system. [after Richard *Bright,* 1789–1858, English physician]

bright·work (brīt′wûrk′) *n.* Metal parts or articles, as aboard ship, made bright by planing, turning, or polishing.

Brig·id (brij′id, brē′id), **Saint,** 451?–525, patroness of Ireland; identified with **Brigid,** ancient Irish goddess of fire, fertility, and the manual arts: also *Bride, Bridget.*

brill (bril) *n. pl.* **brill** or **brills** A flatfish of Europe (*Bothus* or *Scophthalmus rhombus*) related to the turbot. [Cf. Cornish *brilli* mackerel]

Bril·lat-Sa·va·rin (brē·yà′sà·và·raṅ′), **Anthelme,** 1755–1826, French writer and epicure.

bril·liance (bril′yəns) *n.* 1. Intense brightness or luster; splendor. 2. Great talent or intellect. 3. Excellence; preeminence. 4. *Music* Clarity of sound; vivid tone. 5. Brightness (def. 3). Also **bril′lian·cy.**

bril·liant (bril′yənt) *adj.* 1. Sparkling or glowing with light; very bright. 2. Splendid; illustrious: a *brilliant* achievement. 3. Having great intellect or talent. 4. *Music* Sounding in the most sensitive range of the human ear; clear; vivid; intense. — *n.* 1. A diamond of the finest cut, having a single large face surrounded by a bezel of 33 facets and, below the girdle, a pavilion of 25 facets; also, this method of cutting a gem. For illustration see DIAMOND. 2. *Printing* A

very small size of type, about 3½-point. [< F *brillant,* ppr. of *briller* to sparkle, ? ult. < L *beryllus* beryl] — **bril′liant·ly** *adv.* — **bril′liant·ness** *n.*

bril·lian·tine (bril′yən·tēn) *n.* 1. A perfumed oil used to dress the hair. 2. A smooth, fine, wiry fabric made of cotton and worsted or mohair. [< F]

brim (brim) *n.* 1. The rim or upper edge of a cup, bowl, etc. 2. A projecting rim, as of a hat. 3. An edge or margin. — *v.t. & v.i.* **brimmed, brim·ming** To fill or be full to the brim. — **to brim over** To overflow. [OE *brim* seashore]

brim·ful (brim′fool′, brim′fool′) *adj.* Full to the brim.

brim·mer (brim′ər) *n.* A cup, bowl, etc., full to the brim.

brim·stone (brim′stōn) *n.* 1. Sulfur. 2. A spitfire; scold. [OE *brynstān* < *bryn-* burning (< *brinnen* to burn) + *stān* stone] — **brim′ston/y** *adj.*

brind·ed (brin′did) *adj. Archaic* Irregularly streaked; brindled. [Akin to BRAND]

Brin·di·si (brēn′dē·zē) A Province of Apulia, southern Italy; 710 sq. mi.; pop. 343,382 (1961); capital **Brindisi** (ancient *Brundisium*), pop. 70,084.

brin·dle (brin′dəl) *adj.* Brindled. — *n.* A brindled color, or a brindled animal. [Back formation < BRINDLED]

brin·dled (brin′dəld) *adj.* Tawny or grayish with irregular streaks or spots; barred; streaked. [Var. of BRINDLED]

brine (brīn) *n.* 1. Water saturated or strongly impregnated with salt. 2. Saline water for pickling or preserving food. 3. The water of the sea; the ocean. — *v.t.* **brined, brin·ing** To treat with or steep in brine. [OE *brӯne*] — **brin′ish** *adj.*

Bri·nell machine (bri·nel′) *Metall.* An apparatus for measuring the hardness (**Brinell hardness**) of steel and other metals by determining the diameter of the indentation (**Brinell number**) made by a steel ball pressed at a given force into the metal tested. [after J. A. *Brinell,* 1849–1925, Swedish engineer]

bring (bring) *v.t.* **brought, bring·ing** 1. To convey or cause (a person or thing) to come with oneself or toward a place. 2. To cause to come about; involve as a consequence: War *brings* destruction. 3. To introduce into the mind; cause to appear. 4. To cause (a person or oneself) to adopt or admit, as a persuasion, course of action, etc. 5. To sell for: The house *brought* a good price. 6. *Law* **a** To prefer, as a charge. **b** To institute: to *bring* suit. **c** To set forth, as evidence or an argument. — **to bring about** 1. To accomplish; cause to happen. 2. *Naut.* To reverse; turn, as a ship. — **to bring around** (or **round**) 1. To cause to adopt or admit, as an opinion or persuasion. 2. To revive; restore to consciousness. — **to bring down** 1. To cause to fall. 2. To fell by wounding or killing. — **to bring down the house** To evoke wild applause or acclaim. — **to bring forth** 1. To give birth or produce. 2. To give rise to. — **to bring forward** 1. To adduce, as an argument. 2. In bookkeeping, to carry, as a sum, from one page or column to another. — **to bring in** 1. To import. 2. To render or submit (a verdict). 3. To yield or produce, as profits. — **to bring off** To do successfully. — **to bring on** 1. To cause; lead to. 2. To produce; cause to appear: *Bring on* the actors. — **to bring out** 1. To reveal; cause to be evident, as the truth. 2. To publish or produce, as a book or play. 3. To introduce, as a young girl to society. — **to bring to** 1. To revive; restore to consciousness. 2. *Naut.* To cause (a ship) to come up into the wind and lie to. — **to bring to bear** To cause to have reference, application, or influence. — **to bring up** 1. To rear; educate. 2. To suggest or call attention to, as a subject. 3. To cough or vomit up. [OE *bringan*] — **bring′er** *n.*

bring·ing-up (bring′ing·up′) *n.* Care, training, and education of a person in childhood; upbringing.

brink (bringk) *n.* 1. The edge or verge of a steep place; also, the shore of a river, etc. 2. The very edge or extreme limits. [ME < Scand. Cf. Sw. *brink* declivity.]

brink·man·ship (bringk′mən·ship) *n.* A willingness to expose oneself to major risk to achieve some end; especially, a national policy embodying such a position. [< BRINK + -*manship,* on analogy with *showmanship,* etc.]

brin·y (brī′nē) *adj.* **brin·i·er, brin·i·est** Of the nature of or like brine. — **the briny** *Slang* The sea. — **brin′i·ness** *n.*

bri·o (brē′ō) *n.* Liveliness; spirit; animation. [< Ital.]

bri·oche (brē′ōsh, -osh; *Fr.* brē·ôsh′) *n.* A soft roll made of butter, eggs, flour, and yeast. [< F]

bri·o·lette (brē′ə·let′) *n.* A gemstone, generally pear- or drop-shaped, cut with triangular or long facets. For illustration see DIAMOND. [< F < *brillant* diamond]

bri·quette (bri·ket′) *n.* A block of compressed coal dust for fuel. Also **bri·quet′.** [< F *briquette,* dim. of *brique* brick]

bri·sance (brē·zäns′) *n.* The shattering effect of an explosive. [< F *brisant,* ppr. of *briser* to crush]

Bris·bane (briz′bān, -bən) The capital of Queensland, Australia, in the SE part on Moreton Bay; a prominent port; pop. 656,222 (1966).

Bri·se·is (brī·sē′is) In the *Iliad,* a maiden captured by Achilles whose seizure by Agamemnon leads to a quarrel between the two men.

brisk (brisk) *adj.* **1.** Moving, acting, or taking place quickly; lively; energetic: *brisk* trade; a *brisk* run. **2.** Sharp or stimulating: *brisk* air. **3.** Sparkling; effervescent: said of liquors. — **Syn.** See NIMBLE. — *v.t.* & *v.i.* To make or become brisk; animate: with *up.* [Cf. F *brusque* abrupt, sudden] — **brisk′ly** *adv.* — **brisk′ness** *n.*

bris·ket (bris′kit) *n.* The breast of an animal, especially of one whose flesh is used as food. For illustration see SHEEP. [< OF *bruschet*, ult. < Gmc.]

bris·ling (bris′ling) *n.* The sprat. [< Norw.]

bris·tle (bris′əl) *n.* **1.** One of the coarse, stiff hairs of swine, used in making brushes. **2.** Any similar hair, or a hairlike part. **3.** *Bot.* A slender, stiff hair of a plant; a trichome. — *v.* **·tled**, **·tling** *v.i.* **1.** To erect the bristles in anger or excitement, as a hog. **2.** To show anger or irritation: often with *up.* **3.** To stand or become erect, like bristles. **4.** To be thickly set as if with bristles: The plain *bristled* with bayonets. — *v.t.* **5.** To erect as or like bristles: often with *up.* **6.** To furnish with bristles. **7.** To ruffle or agitate. [ME *bristel* < OE *byrst*] — **bris′tly** *adj.*

bris·tle·tail (bris′əl·tāl′) *n.* The silverfish, an insect.

Bris·tol (bris′təl) **1.** A county borough and port in Avon, England; pop. 418,600 (1976). **2.** A city in west central Connecticut; pop. 55,487. **3.** An urban township in SE Pennsylvania, on the Delaware River; pop. 67,498.

Bristol board A fine quality of calendered cardboard. Also **Bristol paper.** [after *Bristol,* England]

Bristol Channel An inlet of the Atlantic between Wales and SW England; 85 mi. long.

brit (brit) *n. pl.* **brit 1.** A young herring. **2.** Small, free-swimming marine copepods (genus *Calanus*) eaten by whalebone whales, herring, and mackerel. [Origin unknown]

Brit (brit) *n. Canadian Slang* Britisher.

Brit. **1.** Britain; British. **2.** Britannia. **3.** Britannica.

Brit·ain (brit′n) See GREAT BRITAIN. Abbr. *Br., Brit.*

bri·tan·ni·a (bri·tan′ē·ə, -tan′yə) *n.* An alloy of tin, copper, and antimony, and often also bismuth and zinc, used for tableware. Also **britannia metal, Britannia metal.** [after *Britannia*]

Bri·tan·ni·a (bri·tan′ē·ə, -tan′yə) **1.** The ancient Roman name for Great Britain. **2.** *Poetic* Great Britain and Ireland. **3.** The British Empire. **4.** A female figure, as on coins, representing Great Britain or the British Empire.

Bri·tan·nic (bri·tan′ik) *adj.* Of or pertaining to Great Britain; British. [< L *Britannicus*]

Brit·i·cism (brit′ə·siz′əm) *n.* An idiom or turn of phrase peculiar to the British, such as "petrol" for "gasoline" or "underground" for "subway." Also **Britishism.**

Brit·ish (brit′ish) *adj.* **1.** Pertaining to Great Britain, the United Kingdom, or the British Empire. **2.** Of or pertaining to the ancient Britons. — *n.* **1.** The people of Great Britain or of the British Empire: preceded by *the.* **2.** British English. **3.** The language of the ancient Britons; Brythonic. Abbr. *B., Br., Brit.* [OE *Bretisc* < *Bret* a Briton] — **Brit′ish·ly** *adv.* — **Brit′ish·ness** *n.*

British America 1. Canada. **2.** British possessions in or adjacent to North America. Also **British North America.**

British Antarctic Territory A British Colony in the South Atlantic, comprising the South Orkney Islands, the South Shetland Islands, and Graham Land; 1,450 sq. mi.; uninhabited: formerly *Falkland Island Dependencies.*

British Borneo See under BORNEO.

British Cam·e·roons (kam′ə·roonz′) A former UN Trust Territory on the border of Nigeria and Cameroun, administered by Great Britain, and comprising the two noncontiguous areas of **Northern Cameroons,** part of Nigeria since June 1961, and **Southern Cameroons,** part of Cameroun since October 1961.

British Columbia The westernmost Province of Canada; 366,255 sq. mi.; pop. 2,196,000; capital, Victoria. Abbr. *B.C.* — **British Columbian**

British Commonwealth of Nations A political association of independent nations, including their colonies and dependent territories, united by common consent to the British Crown. The association was formed in 1931 by the former British Empire. In 1972 there were 31 independent member nations. Officially the *Commonwealth of Nations.* Also *The Commonwealth.*

British East Africa A former association of territories including Kenya, Tanganyika, Uganda, and Zanzibar. Abbr. *B.E.A.*

British Empire Formerly, the sovereign states under the British Crown, comprising those in the British Commonwealth of Nations with their dependencies, colonies, territories, and condominiums.

British English The English language as spoken and written in England.

Brit·ish·er (brit′ish·ər) *n.* A native or subject of Great Britain, especially an Englishman.

British Guiana A former British Colony on the NE coast of South America. See GUYANA.

British Honduras A British Crown Colony on the NE coast of Central America that changed its name to Belize in 1973. See BELIZE.

British India Formerly, the territories in India subject to British law.

British Isles Great Britain, Ireland, the Isle of Man, and the Channel Islands.

Brit·ish·ism (brit′ish·iz′əm) See BRITICISM.

British Malaya Formerly, the British possessions and dependencies in Malaya; now substantially the same as the Federation of Malaya.

British North America Act The act of Parliament that in 1867 created the Government of Canada for the federation of Ontario, Quebec, Nova Scotia, and New Brunswick. Manitoba joined in 1870, British Columbia in 1871, Prince Edward Island in 1873, Alberta and Saskatchewan in 1905, and Newfoundland in 1949.

British Solomon Islands See under SOLOMON ISLANDS.

British Somaliland (sō·mä′lē·land) A former British protectorate in eastern Africa, on the Gulf of Aden; 68,000 sq. mi.; since 1960 part of Somalia.

British thermal unit *Physics* The quantity of heat required to raise the temperature of one pound of water one degree Fahrenheit.

British Togoland From 1946, a British-administered UN Trust Territory in western Africa; after 1957, a part of Ghana. See TOGOLAND.

British Virgin Islands A British Colony at the eastern end of the Greater Antilles, comprising 36 islands of which 11 are inhabited; 59 sq. mi.; pop. 10,484 (est. 1970); capital, Road Town.

British West Africa A former association of territories including British Cameroons, Gambia, Nigeria, and Sierra Leone. Abbr. *B.W.A.*

British West Indies The former name for islands of the West Indies that were British colonies.

Brit. Mus. British Museum.

Brit·on (brit′n) *n.* **1.** A member of a Celtic people inhabiting ancient Britain, conquered by the Romans, and later dispossessed by the Anglo-Saxon invaders. **2.** A Britisher. [< OF *Breton* < L *Britto, -onis* < Celtic]

Brit·ta·ny (brit′ə·nē) A region and former province of western France, occupying the peninsula between the English Channel and the Bay of Biscay: French *Bretagne,* Breton *Breiz.*

Brit·ten (brit′n), **(Edward) Benjamin,** 1913–76, English composer.

brit·tle (brit′l) *adj.* Liable to break or snap; fragile. — **Syn.** See FRAGILE. [ME *britil.* Akin to OE *brēotan* to break.] — **brit′tle·ness** *n.*

Brit·ton (brit′n), **Nathaniel Lord,** 1859–1934, U.S. botanist.

britz·ska (brits′kə) *n.* A light, four-wheeled carriage with calash top. Also **brits′ka, britz′ka.** [< Polish *bryczka,* dim. of *bryka* freight wagon]

Brno (bûr′nô) A city in central Czechoslovakia, the second largest in the country; former capital of Moravia; pop. 333, 831 (est. 1967); German *Brünn.*

bro. (*pl.* **bros.**) Brother.

broach¹ (brōch) *v.t.* **1.** To mention or suggest for the first time; introduce: to *broach* a subject. **2.** To pierce so as to withdraw a liquid: to *broach* a cask. **3.** To draw off; let out: to *broach* wine. **4.** To dress or enlarge with a broach. — *n.* **1.** *Mech.* A pointed, tapering tool for boring or reaming; a reamer. For illustration see REAMER. **2.** A spit for roasting. [< OF *broche* < Med.L *brocca* spike, spit, ult. < Celtic] — **broach′er** *n.*

broach² (brōch) *v.t.* & *v.i.* To veer. — **to broach to** *Naut.* To fall off with the wind, especially broadside to the wind and waves, and thus risk capsizing. [? < BROACH¹, v.]

broad (brôd) *adj.* **1.** Extended in measurement from side to side; wide. **2.** Of great extent; vast or spacious: a *broad* plain. **3.** Fully diffused; open and clear: *broad* daylight. **4.** Of wide scope or application; extensive: a *broad* rule. **5.** Liberal in spirit; tolerant. **6.** Setting forth the chief features; not detailed; general. **7.** Obvious; clear: a *broad* hint. **8.** Vulgar and indelicate; ribald. **9.** Outspoken or unrestrained. **10.** Rude and vigorous; unrefined: said of speech. **11.** Strongly dialectal: a *broad* pronunciation. **12.** *Phonet.* Formed with the oral passage open wide and the tongue low and flat, as the *a* in *calm;* low. — *n.* **1.** The broad part of anything. **2.** *Brit. Dial.* A spreading of a river over flat land. **3.** *Slang* A woman or girl. — *adv.* Completely; fully. [OE *brād*] — **broad′ly** *adv.* — **broad′ness** *n.*

broad arrow 1. A broad-headed arrow. **2.** A mark shaped like a barbed arrow, placed on British government property, as convicts' uniforms, ordnance stores, etc.

broad·ax (brôd′aks′) *n.* An ax with a broad edge and a short handle. Also **broad′axe′.** For illustration see AX.

broad bean The large, usually flat seed of a strong, erect annual vine (*Vicia faba*) of the Old World.

broad·bill (brôd′bil′) *n.* **1.** Any of several ducks having a broad bill, as the scaup and the shoveler. **2.** The spoonbill (which see). **3.** The swordfish.

Broad·brim (brôd′brim′) *n. Informal* A Friend; Quaker.

broad·cast (brôd′kast′, -käst′) *v.* **·cast** or (*esp. for defs.* 1, 4) **·cast·ed, ·cast·ing** *v.t.* **1.** To send or transmit (music, newscasts, etc.) by radio or television. **2.** To scatter, as seed, over a wide area. **3.** To disseminate; make public. — *v.i.* **4.** To make a radio or television broadcast. — *n.* **1.** The transmission of news, music, etc., by radio or television. **2.** A radio or television program, or its time period. **3.** A scattering or sowing over a wide area, as of seed. — *adj.* **1.** By or for radio or television transmission. **2.** Scattered far and wide. — *adv.* So as to be scattered over a wide area: to sow wheat *broadcast*. — **broad′cast′er** *n.*

Broad-Church (brôd′chûrch′) *adj.* Of or pertaining to a liberal group (**Broad Church**) in the Anglican Church that advocates comprehensiveness and toleration in matters of doctrine, ceremony, church fellowship, etc. Compare HIGH-CHURCH, LOW-CHURCH. — **Broad′-Church′man** *n.* — **Broad′-Church′man·ship** *n.*

broad·cloth (brôd′klôth′, -kloth′) *n.* **1.** A fine woolen cloth in plain or twill weave, used for suits, skirts, etc. **2.** A closely woven fabric of silk, cotton, etc., with a light crosswise rib, used for shirts, dresses, etc.

broad·en (brôd′n) *v.t. & v.i.* To make or become broad or broader.

broad-gauge (brôd′gāj′) *adj.* **1.** Having a width of railroad track greater than the standard gauge of 56½ inches. **2.** *U.S.* Having a wide range: a *broad-gauge* mind. Also **broad′-gage′, broad′-gaged′, broad-gauged′.**

broad hatchet A hatchet with a broad blade. For illustration see HATCHET.

broad jump In athletics, a jump or jumping contest for distance: distinguished from *high jump.*

broad·leaf (brôd′lēf′) *n.* **1.** A tree (*Terminalia catappa*) native to Jamaica, with almondlike fruit. **2.** Any variety of tobacco plant suitable for cigar making, having especially broad leaves.

broad·loom (brôd′lōōm′) *n.* Carpet woven in widths of from 6 to 18 feet. Also **broadloom carpet.**

broad-mind·ed (brôd′mīn′did) *adj.* Liberal and tolerant; free from bigotry and prejudice. — **broad′-mind′ed·ly** *adv.* — **broad′-mind′ed·ness** *n.*

Broads (brôdz), **The** A region of marshy lakes in Norfolk (**the Norfolk Broads**) and Suffolk (**the Suffolk Broads**), England.

broad seal The official seal of a government.

broad·side (brôd′sīd′) *n.* **1.** All the guns on one side of a man-of-war, or their simultaneous discharge. **2.** A volley of abuse or denunciation. **3.** *Naut.* A vessel's side above the water line. **4.** Formerly, a large sheet of paper, printed on one side: also **broad′sheet′. 5.** The broad, unbroken surface of anything. — *adv.* With the broadside turned or exposed.

broadside ballad In the 16th and 17th centuries, a song or verse usually on some current topic printed on a broadside and sold in the streets.

broad·sword (brôd′sôrd′, -sōrd′) *n.* A sword with a broad cutting blade.

broad·tail (brôd′tāl′) *n.* The lustrous black fur obtained from prematurely born lambs of the karakul sheep, having a wavy pattern resembling moiré silk rather than the curl characteristic of older lambs and sheep. Compare PERSIAN LAMB.

Broad·way (brôd′wā) A street in New York City, noted for its theatres and entertainment district. — *n.* The principal theatre industry of New York City.

Brob·ding·nag (brob′ding·nag) In Swift's *Gulliver's Travels*, the country of the giants. — **Brob′ding·nag′i·an** (-nag′-ē-ən) *adj. & n.*

bro·cade (brō·kād′) *n.* A rich fabric interwoven with a raised design, as in silken or gold or silver threads. — *v.t.* **·cad·ed, ·cad·ing** To weave (a cloth) with a raised design or figure. [Earlier *brocado* < Sp. < Med.L *broccata*, fem. pp. of *broccare* to embroider]

broc·a·tel (brok′ə·tel′) *n.* A fabric like brocade, but with a more highly raised pattern. Also **broc′a·telle′.** [< F *brocatelle* < Ital. *broccatello*, dim. of *broccato* brocade]

broc·co·li (brok′ə·lē) *n.* A variety of cauliflower that does not produce a head, of which the sprouts and tender stalks are eaten. [< Ital., pl. of *broccolo* cabbage sprout]

bro·ché (brō·shā′) *adj.* Woven with a raised design; brocaded. [< F *broché*, pp. of *brocher* to stitch, brocade]

bro·chette (brō·shet′) *n.* A small spit used in roasting; a skewer. [< F, dim. of *broche* skewer, spit]

bro·chure (brō·shōōr′) *n.* A pamphlet or similar publication. [< F, lit., a stitched book < *brocher* to stitch]

brock (brok) *n. Brit. Dial.* **1.** A badger. **2.** A foul, dirty fellow. [OE *broc* < Celtic]

Brock·en (brok′ən) The highest peak of the Harz Mountains in central Germany; 3,747 ft.; famous in German folklore.

brock·et (brok′it) *n.* **1.** A stag in its second year with its first horns as simple spikes. **2.** A small deer of tropical America (genus *Mazama*). [< F *brocart* < *broche* tine of antlers]

Brock·ton (brok′tən) A city in eastern Massachusetts; pop. 89,040.

bro·gan (brō′gən) *n.* A coarse, heavy shoe. [< Irish *brógan*, dim. of *brog* shoe]

Bro·glie (brō·glē′, *Fr.* brô′y′), **de** A distinguished French family, especially **Duc Achille Charles Léonce Victor,** 1785–1870, statesman; **Louis Victor,** born 1892, and his brother **Maurice,** 1875–1960, physicists.

brogue¹ (brōg) *n.* An Irish accent in the pronunciation of English. [< Irish *barróg* defect of speech]

brogue² (brōg) *n.* **1.** A heavy oxford shoe, decorated with stitchings, pinkings, and perforations. **2.** A rude shoe of untanned hide worn formerly in Ireland and the Scottish Highlands. [< Irish *brog* a shoe]

brogue³ (brōg) *n. Scot.* A fraud; cheating trick.

broi·der (broi′dər) *v.t.* Obs. To embroider. [< MF *broder* to stitch; infl. by ME *broid*, var. of *braid*] — **broi′der·y** *n.*

broil¹ (broil) *v.t.* **1.** To cook, as meat, by subjecting to direct heat. **2.** To expose to great heat; scorch. — *v.i.* **3.** To be exposed to great heat; cook. **4.** To become impatient; burn with anger. — *n.* **1.** Something broiled. **2.** A broiling heat. [< OF *bruller, bruillir* to burn]

broil² (broil) *n.* A turmoil; noisy quarrel; brawl. — *v.i.* To engage in a broil; brawl. [< F *brouiller* to confuse]

broil·er (broi′lər) *n.* **1.** A device for broiling. **2.** A young, tender chicken suitable for broiling.

broke (brōk) Past tense and archaic past participle of BREAK. — *adj. Informal* Having no money; bankrupt.

bro·ken (brō′kən) Past participle of BREAK. — *adj.* **1.** Forcibly separated into pieces; shattered; fractured. **2.** Violated; transgressed: *broken* vows. **3.** Interrupted; disturbed: *broken* sleep. **4.** Incomplete; fragmentary: in *broken* lots. **5.** Rough; uneven, as terrain. **6.** Veering abruptly: a *broken* line. **7.** In disorder; routed; scattered, as troops. **8.** Humbled; crushed. **9.** Weakened or infirm; exhausted. **10.** Bankrupt; ruined. **11.** Trained in procedure; disciplined; adapted: often with *in*: *broken* in on a new job. **12.** Imperfectly spoken; disjointed: *broken* English. — **bro′ken·ly** *adv.* — **bro′ken·ness** *n.*

bro·ken-down (brō′kən·doun′) *adj.* **1.** Incapable of functioning; out of repair. **2.** Ruined; decayed.

bro·ken-heart·ed (brō′kən·här′tid) *adj.* Overwhelmed or crushed in spirit, as by grief.

Broken Hill A city in western New South Wales, Australia; an important mining center; pop. 30,036 (est. 1966).

broken wind The heaves. — **bro′ken-wind′ed** *adj.*

bro·ker (brō′kər) *n.* One who buys and sells for another on commission or who arranges for the negotiation of contracts of various types; especially, a stockbroker. [< AF *brocour* < OF *brochier* to tap, broach (a wine cask)]

bro·ker·age (brō′kər·ij) *n.* The business or commission of a broker. Also **bro·kage.**

brom- Var. of BROMO-.

bro·mal (brō′məl) *n. Chem.* A colorless liquid, C₂HBr₃O, with a pungent taste and penetrating odor, used in medicine as a hypnotic and anodyne. [< BROM- + al(COHOL)]

bro·mate (brō′māt) *n. Chem.* A salt of bromic acid containing the univalent BrO₃ radical. — *v.t.* **·mat·ed, ·mat·ing** To combine, saturate, or impregnate with bromine.

Brom·berg (brôm′berkh) The German name for BYDGOSZCZ.

brome-grass (brōm′gras′, -gräs′) *n.* Any grass of the genus *Bromus*, widely cultivated for hay and pasturage. Also **brome.** [< NL *bromus* oats < L < Gk. *bromos* oats]

bro·me·li·a·ceous (brō·mē′lē·ā′shəs) *adj. Bot.* Belonging to a family (*Bromeliaceae*) of tropical or subtropical American monocotyledonous plants, including the Spanish moss and the pineapple. [< NL *Bromeliaceae*, after Olaf *Bromel*, 1639–1705, Swedish botanist]

Brom·field (brom′fēld), **Louis,** 1896–1956, U.S. novelist.

bro·mic (brō′mik) *adj. Chem.* Containing bromine, especially in its higher valence. [< BROM- + -IC]

bromic acid *Chem.* A compound of bromine with hydrogen and oxygen, HBrO₃, known only in aqueous solution.

bro·mide¹ (brō′mīd, -mid) *n.* **1.** *Chem.* A compound of bromine with an element or an organic radical. **2.** A photograph printed on paper, etc., that has been subjected to the effects of bromide of silver. Also **bro′mid** (-mid). [< BROM- + -IDE]

bro·mide² (brō′mīd, -mid) *n. Informal* **1.** One who utters platitudes; a bore. **2.** A platitude; dull remark. — **Syn.** See TRUISM. [< BROMIDE¹; with ref. to the sedative effect of some bromides]

bro·mid·ic (brō·mid′ik) *adj. Informal* Commonplace; trite.

bro·mi·nate (brō′mə·nāt) *v.t.* **·nat·ed, ·nat·ing** To bromate.

bro·mine (brō′mēn, -min) *n.* A dark reddish brown, nonmetallic, fuming liquid element (symbol Br) of the halogen group, with a suffocating odor. Also **bro′min** (-min). See ELEMENT. [< F *brome* (< Gk. *brōmos* stench) + -INE².]

bro·mism (brō′miz·əm) *n. Pathol.* A diseased condition, usually of the skin, caused by the overuse of bromides.

bromo- *combining form* Used to indicate the presence of bromine as a principal element in chemical compounds. Also, before vowels, **brom-**. [< BROMINE]

bron·chi (brong′kī) Plural of BRONCHUS.

bron·chi·a (brong′kē·ə) *n.pl. Anat.* The bronchial tubes. [< LL < Gk. *bronchia* bronchial tubes]

bron·chi·al (brong′kē·əl) *adj. Anat.* Of or pertaining to the chief air passages of the lungs.

bronchial tube *Anat.* Any of the subdivisions of the trachea conveying air into the lungs.

bron·chi·tis (brong·kī′tis) *n. Pathol.* Inflammation of the bronchial tubes, or, loosely, of the bronchi or trachea. [< BRONCH(O)- + -ITIS] — **bron·chit·ic** (brong·kit′ik) *adj.*

broncho- *combining form* Windpipe: *bronchoscope.* Also, before vowels, **bronch-**. [< Gk. *bronchos*]

bron·cho·pneu·mon·ia (brong′kō·nŏŏ·mōn′yə, -nyŏŏ-) *n. Pathol.* Bronchitis complicated with inflammation of the surrounding substance of the lungs; catarrhal pneumonia.

bron·cho·scope (brong′kə·skōp) *n. Med.* An instrument for inspecting or treating the interior of the bronchi. [< BRONCHO- + -SCOPE] — **bron·chos·co·py** (brong·kos′kə·pē) *n.*

bron·chus (brong′kəs) *n. pl. ·chi* (-kī) *Anat.* One of the two forked branches of the trachea. For illustration see LUNG. [< NL < Gk. *bronchos* windpipe]

bron·co (brong′kō) *n. pl. ·cos* **1.** *U.S.* A small, wild or partly broken horse of the West. **2.** *Canadian* An Englishman. Also **bronc, bron′cho.** [< Sp. *bronco* rough]

bron·co·bust·er (brong′kō·bus′tər) *n. U.S. Informal* One who breaks a bronco to the saddle. Also **bron′cho·bust′er.**

Bron·të (bron′të) Name of three English novelists, sisters: **Anne,** 1820–49; **Charlotte,** 1816–55; **Emily Jane,** 1818–48. Pseudonyms, respectively, *Acton, Currer,* and *Ellis Bell.*

bron·tides (bron′tīdz) *n.pl. Meteorol.* Brief, thunderlike noises accompanying the activity of faint earthquakes. [< Gk. *brontē* thunder + -*eidēs* like, similar to]

bron·to·sau·rus (bron′tə·sôr′əs) *n. pl. ·rus·es* *Paleontol.* A huge, herbivorous dinosaur (suborder *Sauropoda*) of the Jurassic period. Also **bron′to·saur.** [< Gk. *brontē* thunder + *sauros* lizard]

BRONTOSAURUS
(To 70 feet long; about 20 tons)

Bronx (brongks) A mainland borough of New York City; pop. 1,471,701: often preceded by *the.*

Bronx cheer *U.S. Slang* A noisy expulsion of the breath through nearly closed lips with tongue protruded: an expression of contempt or derision: also called *raspberry, razzberry.*

bronze (bronz) *n.* **1.** *Metall.* **a** A reddish brown alloy essentially of copper and tin, used in making bells and statues. **b** A similar alloy of copper and some other metal, as aluminum or manganese. **2.** A pigment of the color of bronze. **3.** A reddish brown color similar to bronze. **4.** A statue, bust, etc., done in bronze. Abbr. *br.* — *v.* **bronzed, bronz′ing** *v.t.* **1.** To color like bronze; make brown. — *v.i.* **2.** To become brown or tan. [< MF < Ital. *bronzo, bronzino,* ? < L (*aes*) *Brundisinum* (alloy) of Brundisium] — **bronz′y** *adj.*

bronze age In classical mythology, a period of time characterized by violence and war, following the golden and silver ages: often called *brazen age.*

Bronze Age *Archeol.* A stage of prehistory following the Stone Age and preceding the Iron Age, during which weapons and implements were made of bronze.

Bronze Star A U.S. military decoration in the form of a bronze star, awarded for heroism, meritorious service or achievement, or meritorious or exemplary conduct in ground combat. See DECORATION.

broo (brŏŏ) *n.* Bree.

brooch (brōch, brŏŏch) *n.* An ornamental pin with a clasp for wearing on the breast or shoulder. For illustration see KILT. [Var. of BROACH[1], n.]

brood (brŏŏd) *n.* **1.** The young of animals, especially of birds, produced at one time. **2.** All the young of the same mother. **3.** Kind or species; type. — **Syn.** See FLOCK. — *v.i.* **1.** To meditate or ponder moodily and deeply: usually with *on* or *over.* **2.** To sit on eggs; incubate. — *v.t.* **3.** To sit upon or incubate (eggs). **4.** To protect (young) by covering with the wings. — *adj.* Kept for breeding: a *brood* mare. [OE *brōd.* Akin to BREED.]

brood·er (brŏŏd′dər) *n.* **1.** A covered and warmed structure for artificially rearing young fowl. **2.** One who or that which broods.

brood·y (brŏŏd′dē) *adj.* **brood·i·er, brood·i·est 1.** Meditative; moody. **2.** Inclined to sit on eggs: said of hens.

brook[1] (brŏŏk) *n.* A natural stream, smaller than a river or creek; a rivulet. [OE *brōc*]

brook[2] (brŏŏk) *v.t.* To put up with; tolerate: usually with the negative: I cannot *brook* such conduct. — **Syn.** See ENDURE. [OE *brūcan* to use, enjoy]

Brooke (brŏŏk), **Rupert,** 1887–1915, English poet.

Brook Farm A farm near West Roxbury, Massachusetts, where a group of American scholars and writers attempted to set up a communistic community, 1841–47.

brook·let (brŏŏk′lit) *n.* A little brook.

Brook·line (brŏŏk′līn) A town in eastern Massachusetts; pop. 58,689.

Brook·lyn (brŏŏk′lin) A borough of New York City, on the western end of Long Island; pop. 2,602,012.

Brooks (brŏŏks), **Phillips,** 1835–93, U.S. divine and writer. **— Van Wyck,** 1886–1963, U.S. biographer and critic.

Brooks Range The northernmost part of the Rocky Mountains, in northern Alaska; highest point, Mt. Michelson, 9,239 ft.

brook trout 1. The speckled trout (*Salvelinus fontinalis*) of eastern North America. **2.** The brown trout (*Salmo trutta*) of Europe.

brook·weed (brŏŏk′wēd′) *n.* Either of two perennial herbs (genus *Samolus*) bearing small, white flowers: also called *water pimpernel.*

broom (brŏŏm, brŏŏm) *n.* **1.** A brush attached to a long handle for sweeping, formerly made from twigs of broom. **2.** Any of various leguminous shrubs (genus *Cytisus*), especially the **Scotch broom** (*C. scoparius*), with yellow flowers and stiff green branches: also called *besom.* — *v.t.* To sweep. [OE *brōm* broom. Akin to BRAMBLE.] — **broom′y** *adj.*

broom·corn (brŏŏm′kôrn′, brŏŏm′-) *n.* A canelike grass (genus *Sorghum*) of which brooms are made.

broom·rape (brŏŏm′rāp′, brŏŏm′-) *n.* Any of various fleshy herbs (genus *Orobanche*) typical of the family *Orobanchaceae,* destitute of green foliage and parasitic on the roots of other plants. [Partial trans. of Med. *rapum genistae* broom tuber]

broom·stick (brŏŏm′stik′, brŏŏm′-) *n.* The handle of a broom.

brose (brōz) *n. Scot.* Porridge hastily made by pouring boiling liquid on meal, and stirring together.

broth (brôth, broth) *n.* A soup made by boiling meat, vegetables, etc., in water; a thin or strained soup. [OE. Akin to BREW.]

broth·el (broth′əl, brŏth′-, brôth′əl, brôth′-) *n.* A house of prostitution. [ME, a worthless person < OE *brothen,* pp. of *brēothan* to ruin, decay; infl. by *bordel*]

broth·er (bruth′ər) *n. pl.* **broth·ers** or **breth·ren** (breth′rən) **1.** A male individual having the same parents as another or others of either sex. Sons of the same two parents are **full** or **whole brothers,** while those having only one parent in common are **half brothers. 2.** A kinsman, or one of the same tribe, country, etc.; also, a fellow human being. **3.** A fellow member, as of a church or a fraternal order. **4.** A comrade. **5.** One of a male religious order who is not a priest; a monk. ◆ The plural form *brethren* is archaic in the sense of def. 1, but is still common in other senses. Abbr. *b., B., br., bro.* (pl. *bros.*). — *v.t.* To treat or address as a brother. [OE *brōthor*]

broth·er·ger·man (bruth′ər·jûr′mən) *n. pl.* **broth·ers·ger·man** A full brother.

broth·er·hood (bruth′ər·hŏŏd) *n.* **1.** The relationship of or state of being brothers, especially by blood. **2.** A society, fraternity, guild, etc. **3.** All the persons engaged in an enterprise, profession, etc. Abbr. *B.*

broth·er·in·law (bruth′ər·in·lô′) *n. pl.* **broth·ers·in·law 1.** A brother of one's husband or wife. **2.** The husband of one's sister. **3.** The husband of one's wife's or husband's sister.

Brother Jonathan *Archaic* The people or government of the United States: originally a derisive nickname applied by the British to any American patriot.

broth·er·ly (bruth′ər·lē) *adj.* Pertaining to or characteristic of a brother; fraternal; affectionate. — *adv.* As a brother; kindly. — **broth′er·li·ness** *n.*

broug·ham (brŏŏm, brŏŏm′əm, brō′əm) *n.* **1.** A closed, four-wheeled carriage seating two or more persons, and having a high, uncovered driver's seat. **2.** An automobile with a limousine body and the driver's seat outside. **3.** Formerly, an automobile resembling a coupé, driven by electricity. [after Lord Henry *Brougham,* 1778–1868, British statesman]

BROUGHAM (def. 1)

brought (brôt) Past tense and past participle of BRING.

brou·ha·ha (brŏŏ′hä·hä) *n.* Hubbub; uproar. [< F]

Broun (brŏŏn), **Heywood Campbell,** 1888–1939, U.S. newspaper columnist and critic.

brow (brou) *n.* **1.** The front upper part of the head; forehead. **2.** The eyebrow. **3.** The countenance in general. **4.** The upper edge of a steep place: the *brow* of a hill. [OE *brū*]

brow·beat (brou′bēt′) *v.t.* **·beat, ·beat·en, ·beat·ing** To intimidate by a stern, overbearing manner; bully. — **Syn.** See INTIMIDATE.

brown (broun) *adj.* **1.** Of a dark color combining red, yellow, and black. **2.** Dark-complexioned; tanned. **— to do up brown** *Informal* To do thoroughly. — *n.* **1.** A dark color combining red, yellow, and black. **2.** A pigment or dye used to produce this color. — *v.t. & v.i.* To make or become brown. [OE *brūn*] — **brown′ish** *adj.* — **brown′ness** *n.*

Brown (broun), **Charles Brockden,** 1771–1810, U.S. novelist. **— John,** 1800–59, U.S. abolitionist; planned slave rebellion; led raid on arsenal at Harpers Ferry; hanged for treason.

brown algae Any of various algae (class *Phaeophyceae*), including the giant kelps and the rockweeds, containing a brown pigment in addition to chlorophyll.

brown bear **1.** The black bear (which see). **2.** One of several very large bears (genus *Ursus*) of North America and Europe, related to the grizzly, with fur varying from yellowish to dark brown.

brown Betty Baked pudding made of bread crumbs, apples, sugar, and spices. Also **brown bet′ty.**

brown bread **1.** Any bread made of a dark-colored flour, as graham or whole-wheat bread. **2.** Boston brown bread (which see).

brown coal Lignite.

brown creeper A bird (*Certhia familiaris*) of Canada and the United States that obtains its food by creeping along trees.

Browne (broun), **Charles Far·rar** (far′ər) See (Artemus) WARD. **— Sir Thomas,** 1605–82, English physician and writer.

Brown·i·an movement (brou′nē·ən) *Physics* The rapid random movement of small particles when suspended in fluids. Also **Brownian motion.** [after Robert *Brown,* 1773–1858, Scottish botanist, who discovered it]

brown·ie (brou′nē) *n.* **1.** In folklore, a goblin or sprite, supposed to do useful work at night. **2.** *U.S.* A small, flat chocolate cake with nuts. [< BROWN; from its color]

Brown·ie (brou′nē) *n.* A junior girl scout of the age group seven through nine.

Brown·ing (brou′ning), **Elizabeth Barrett,** 1806–61, English poet; wife of Robert. **— Robert,** 1812–89, English poet.

Browning automatic rifle An air-cooled, gas-operated, automatic or semiautomatic magazine-fed shoulder weapon with bipod. Abbr. *BAR.* [after John Moses *Browning* 1855–1926, U.S. inventor]

Browning machine gun A machine gun used by the U.S. Army, firing .30 or .50 caliber ammunition.

brown·out (broun′out′) *n.* A partial diminishing of lights either as a defensive measure or to save fuel.

brown rice Unpolished rice grains, with the bran layers and most of the grains intact.

brown rot *Bot.* A disease of stone fruits caused by certain fungi (genus *Sclerotinia*).

Brown Shirt **1.** A storm trooper. **2.** A Nazi.

brown·stone (broun′stōn′) *n.* A brownish red sandstone used for building; also, a house with a front of brownstone. **— adj.** Made of brownstone.

brown study A state of absent-mindedness, as in deep thought; reverie.

brown sugar Sugar that is unrefined or partly refined.

Browns·ville (brounz′vil) **1.** A port city in southern Texas, on the Rio Grande; pop. 52,522. **2.** A village in NW Florida, near Pensacola; pop 20,924.

Brown Swiss A type of hardy dairy cattle.

brown·tail (broun′tāl′) *n.* A white European moth (*Euproctis chrysorrhoea*), reddish brown at the posterior end, whose larvae harm shade trees. Also **brown′-tailed′ moth.**

brown thrasher See under THRASHER.

brown trout See under TROUT.

browse (brouz) *v.* **browsed, brows·ing** *v.i.* **1.** To feed on leaves, shoots, etc. **2.** To glance through a book, or the books of a library, for casual reading. **— v.t. 3.** To nibble at; crop; also, to graze on. **— n.** Growing shoots or twigs used as fodder. [< MF *broust* bud, sprout] **— brows′er** *n.*

brow tine The branch of an antler nearest the brow. For illustration see ANTLER. Also **brow antler.**

Broz (brōz), **Josip** See TITO.

B.R.T. Brotherhood of Railroad Trainmen.

Bruce (brōōs), **Sir David,** 1855–1931, English physician and bacteriologist. **— Robert′the,** 1274–1329, king of Scotland 1306–29; defeated Edward II at Bannockburn, 1314: also called **Robert I, Robert Bruce. — Stanley Melbourne,** born 1883, Viscount Bruce of Melbourne, Australian statesman; prime minister 1923–29.

bru·cel·lo·sis (brōō′sə·lō′sis) *n. Pathol.* Any of several infectious diseases caused by a parasitic, Gram-negative bacterium (genus *Brucella*) as Bang's disease in cattle and undulant fever in man. [after Sir David *Bruce*]

bru·cine (brōō′sēn, -sin) *n. Chem.* A bitter, poisonous, crystalline alkaloid, $C_{23}H_{26}O_4N_2$, found, with strychnine, in the seed and bark of the nux vomica, and in other species of the same genus (*Strychnos*). Also **bru′cin** (-sin) [after James *Bruce,* 1730–94, Scottish explorer in Africa]

Bruck·ner (brōōk′nər), **Anton,** 1824–96, Austrian composer.

Brue·ghel (broe′gəl) Family of Flemish painters, especially, **Pieter,** 1520?–69, known as **the Elder,** and his sons, **Pieter,** 1564?–1638?, known as **the Younger,** and **Jan,** 1568–1625. Also spelled *Breughel.* also **Brue′gel.**

Bruges (brōōzh, brōō′jiz) A commune in NW Belgium, capital of West Flanders province; pop. 52,249 (est. 1967). *Flemish* **Brug·ge** (brōōkh′ə).

brugh (brōōkh) *n. Scot.* A borough.

bru·in (brōō′in) *n.* A bear; especially, a brown bear. [< MDu., lit., brown; name of the bear in medieval folklore]

bruise (brōōz) *v.* **bruised, bruis·ing** *v.t.* **1.** To injure, as by a blow, without breaking the surface of the skin; contuse. **2.** To dent or mar the surface of. **3.** To hurt or offend slightly, as feelings. **4.** To crush; pound small, as in a mortar. **— v.i. 5.** To become discolored as from a blow. **— n.** An injury caused by bruising; contusion. [Fusion of OE *brȳsan* to crush and OF *bruisier* to break, shatter]

bruis·er (brōō′zər) *n.* **1.** A professional boxer. **2.** *Informal* A bully.

bruit (brōōt) *v.t.* To noise abroad; talk about: usually in the passive. [< *n.*] **— n. 1.** *Obs.* A rumor. **2.** *Archaic* A din; clamor. **3.** *Med.* A sound, generally abnormal, heard in auscultation. [< F *bruit* noise < *bruire* to roar, make a noise, ? < L *rugire* to roar, bellow] **— bruit′er** *n.*

bru·lot (brū·lō, brōō′lō) *n. Canadian* The buffalo gnat.

brul·yie (brūl′yē) *n. Scot.* A broil; fray. Also **brul′zie** (-yē).

Bru·maire (brü·mâr′) *n.* The second month of the Republican calendar. See (Republican) CALENDAR. [< F < *brume* fog, mist]

bru·mal (brōō′məl) *adj.* Wintry. [< L *brumalis* wintry]

brume (brōōm) *n.* Fog; mist. [< F < L *bruma* winter] **— bru·mous** (brōō′məs) *adj.*

brum·ma·gem (brum′ə·jəm) *adj.* Cheap and showy. **— n.** A cheap imitation. [Alter. of *Birmingham,* England, where cheap jewelry was made]

Brum·mell (brum′əl), **George Bryan.** See BEAU BRUMMELL.

brunch (brunch) *n. U.S. Informal* A late morning meal combining breakfast and lunch. [Blend of BREAKFAST and LUNCH]

Brun·dis·i·um (brun·diz′ē·əm) An ancient name for BRINDISI.

Bru·nei (brōō·nī′) A sultanate under British protection in NW Borneo; 2,226 sq. mi.; pop. 116,000 (est. 1969); capital, **Brunei.** See map of INDONESIA.

Bru·nel (brōō·nel′), **Isambard Kingdom,** 1806–59, English engineer.

Bru·nel·les·chi (brōō′nāl·les′kē), **Filippo,** 1377–1446, Florentine architect and sculptor. Also **Bru′nel·les′co** (-les′kō).

bru·net (brōō·net′) *adj.* Dark-hued; having dark complexion, hair, and eyes. **— n.** A brunet man or boy. [< F, dim. of *brun* brown]

Bru·ne·tière (brü·nə·tyâr′), **Ferdinand,** 1849–1906, French critic.

bru·nette (brōō·net′) *adj.* Brunet: feminine form. **— n.** A brunette woman or girl. [< F]

Brun·hild (brōōn′hild, *Ger.* brōōn′hilt) In the *Nibelungenlied,* a queen of Iceland, married to Gunther, for whom she is won by Siegfried. Compare BRÜNNHILDE, BRYNHILD.

Brü·ning (brü′ning), **Heinrich,** 1885–1970, German statesman; chancellor of Germany 1930–32. Also **Brue′ning.**

Brünn (brün) The German name for BRNO.

Brünn·hil·de (brün·hil′də) In Wagner's *Ring of the Nibelung,* a Valkyrie who incurs the anger of Wotan for assisting Siegmund and is put in a trance and encircled by flames, but is eventually released by Siegfried. Compare BRUNHILD, BRYNHILD.

Bru·no (brōō′nō), **Giordano,** 1548?–1600, Italian philosopher; burned as a heretic. **— Bru·nis·tic** (brōō·nis′tik) *adj.*

Bru·no (brōō′nō), **Saint,** 1030?–1101, German monk; founder of the Carthusian Order.

Bruns·wick (brunz′wik) **1.** A former duchy and state in north central Germany. **2.** A city in Lower Saxony, West Germany, on the Oker; capital of the former state of Brunswick; pop. 225,168 (est. 1970). *German* **Braunschweig.**

brunt (brunt) *n.* **1.** The main force, shock, or strain of a blow, attack, etc. **2.** *Obs.* A blow; assault. [? < ON *bruna* to advance quickly, as a fire]

Bru·sa (brōō′sä) See BURSA.

brush¹ (brush) *n.* **1.** An implement having bristles, hairs, wires, or other flexible fibrous material, fixed in a handle or a back, and used for sweeping, scrubbing, painting, smoothing the hair, etc. **2.** The act of brushing. **3.** A light, grazing touch. **4.** A brief encounter, especially a skirmish. **5.** Brushwork (which see). **6.** Any object resembling a brush. **7.** *Electr.* **a** A conductor, resting on the commutator cylinder of a dynamo, for carrying off the current or for an external current through a motor. **b** A brush discharge. **— v.t. 1.** To use a brush on; sweep, polish, smooth, paint, etc. with a brush. **2.** To remove with or as with a brush. **3.** To touch lightly in passing; touch upon briefly. **— v.i. 4.** To move lightly and quickly, often with a touch. **— to brush aside** To deny consideration to. **— to brush off** *U.S. Slang* To dismiss or refuse abruptly. **— to brush up 1.** To refresh one's knowledge of. **2.** To renovate; refurbish. [< OF *brosse* butcher's-broom, brush, ? < Gmc.] **— brush′y** *adj.*

brush² (brush) *n.* **1.** A growth of small trees and shrubs. **2.** Wooded country sparsely settled; backwoods. **3.** Lopped-off bushes or branches; brushwood. [< OF *broche, brosse,* ? < Gmc.] — **brush′y** *adj.*

brush discharge *Electr.* The form of corona that appears between the terminals of a high-frequency electrical generator. Compare CORONA (def. 8).

brush-off (brush′ôf′, -of′) *n. U.S. Slang* An abrupt refusal or dismissal.

brush turkey A jungle fowl (*Alectura Lathami*) of Australia, about the size of a turkey, but having a bright yellow wattle.

brush-wood (brush′wŏŏd′) *n.* **1.** Bushes or branches cut or broken off. **2.** A thicket of small trees or shrubs.

brush-work (brush′wûrk′) *n.* A painter's characteristic style of applying paint with a brush.

Bru-si-lov (brōō-sē′lôf), Aleksei Alekseevich, 1853–1926, Russian general in World War I.

brusque (brusk, *esp. Brit.* brŏŏsk) *adj.* Rude or curt; blunt. Also **brusk.** — **Syn.** See BLUNT. [< MF < Ital. *brusco* rude, rough] — **brusque′ly** *adv.* — **brusque′ness** *n.*

brus-que-rie (brüs-kə-rē′) *n. French* Brusqueness; bluntness.

Brus-sels (brus′əlz) The capital of Belgium, in the central part on the Senne river; also capital of Brabant Province; pop. 1,073,111 (est. 1970, including suburbs): French *Bruxelles.* Flemish **Brus-sel** (brœs′əl).

Brussels carpet A machine-made carpet of variously colored woolen yarns, the loops of which form a heavy, patterned pile.

Brussels lace Net lace with designs appliquéd upon it, formerly made by hand but now by machine.

Brussels sprouts 1. A cultivated variety of wild cabbage (*Brassica oleracea gemmifera*), with blistered leaves and stems covered with heads like little cabbages. **2.** The small, edible heads or sprouts of this plant.

brut (brüt, brŏŏt) *adj.* Dry: said of wines, especially champagne. [< F, lit., rough < L *brutus*]

bru-tal (brōōt′l) *adj.* **1.** Characteristic of or like a brute; cruel; savage. **2.** Unfeeling; rude; coarse. — **Syn.** See BRUTE. [< L *brutus* stupid, rough] — **bru′tal-ly** *adv.*

bru-tal-i-ty (brōō-tal′ə-tē) *n. pl.* **-ties 1.** The state or quality of being brutal; cruelty. **2.** A brutal act.

bru-tal-ize (brōōt′l-īz) *v.t. & v.i.* **-ized, -iz-ing** To make or become brutal. — **bru′tal-i-za′tion** *n.*

brute (brōōt) *n.* **1.** Any animal other than man. **2.** A brutal person. **3.** The animal qualities in man. — *adj.* **1.** Incapable of reasoning; merely animal. **2.** Like a brute or animal; unintelligent. **3.** Dominated or controlled by appetite or desire; gross; sensual. [< F *brut* < L *brutus* stupid]

— **Syn.** (adj.) *Brute, brutish, brutal,* and *animal* suggest degraded character or behavior. *Brute* means simply like or in the manner of a lower animal and is often without pejorative sense: *brute* strength. *Brutish* adds a note of stupidity or sensuality; *brutal,* one of cruelty or violence: *brutish* intellects, a *brutal* crime. *Animal* is close to *brute,* but often implies sensuality or sexual desire: *animal* passions.

bru-ti-fy (brōō′tə-fī) *v.t. & v.i.* **-fied, -fy-ing** To brutalize.

brut-ish (brōō′tish) *adj.* Of, relating to, or characteristic of a brute or brutes; stupid; gross; sensual. — **Syn.** See BRUTE. — **brut′ish-ly** *adv.* — **brut′ish-ness, brut′ism** *n.*

Brut-ti-um (brut′ē-əm) The ancient Roman name for CALABRIA.

Bru-tus (brōō′təs), Marcus Junius, 85?–42 B.C., Roman politican and general; one of Caesar's assassins.

Brux-elles (brü-sel′, brük-sel′) The French name for BRUSSELS.

brux-ism (bruk′siz-əm) *n.* A nervous grinding of the teeth, especially during sleep. [< Gk. *bruchē* gnashing (of teeth) < *bruchein* to gnash]

Bry-an (brī′ən) A city in east central Texas; pop. 33,719.

Bry-an (brī′ən), William Jennings, 1860–1925, U.S. statesman and orator.

Bry-ansk (brē-änsk′; *Russ.* bryänsk) A port city in the western Russian S.F.S.R., on the Desna; pop. 318,000 (est. 1970): also *Briansk.*

Bry-ant (brī′ənt), William Cullen, 1794–1878, U.S. poet.

Bryce (brīs), James, 1838–1922, Viscount Bryce of Dechmont, British diplomat and writer.

Bryce Canyon National Park A region of canyons and eroded pinnacles in SW Utah; 56 sq. mi.; established 1928.

Bryn-hild (brün′hilt) In the *Volsunga Saga,* a Valkyrie who is thrown into an enchanted sleep by Odin, from which she is awakened by Sigurd. Compare BRUNHILD, BRÜNNHILDE.

bry-ol-o-gy (brī-ol′ə-jē) *n.* The branch of botany that treats of mosses. [< Gk. *bryon* moss + -LOGY] — **bry-o-log-i-cal** (brī′ə-loj′i-kəl) *adj.* — **bry-ol′o-gist** *n.*

bry-o-ny (brī′ə-nē) *n.* A common English herb (genus *Bryonia*) of the gourd family, with white or yellowish flowers and black or red berries. [< L *bryonia* < Gk. *bryōnia*]

bry-o-phyte (brī′ə-fīt) *n. Bot.* Any moss or liverwort of the phylum *Bryophyta.* [< Gk. *bryon* moss + -PHYTE] — **bry′o-phyt′ic** (-fit′ik) *adj.*

bry-o-zo-an (brī-ə-zō′ən) *n. Zool.* One of a phylum or class (*Bryozoa*) of small, aquatic animals that generate by budding, usually found in permanent colonies of delicately branched or mosslike formation, or else of flat, crustlike growth. — *adj.* Of or pertaining to the *Bryozoa.* Also *polyzoan.* [< Gk. *bryon* moss + *zōion* animal]

Bryth-on (brith′ən) *n.* A Celt speaking a language of the Brythonic branch; a Briton. [< Welsh]

Bry-thon-ic (bri-thon′ik) *adj.* Of or pertaining to the Brythons or their languages. — *n.* The branch of the Celtic languages that includes Welsh, Breton, and the extinct Cornish; Cymric: distinguished from *Goidelic.*

Brześć nad Bu-giem (bzheshch näd bōō′gyem) The Polish name for BREST (def. 2).

b.s. 1. Balance sheet. **2.** Bill of sale.

B/s 1. Bags. **2.** Bales.

B.S. or B.Sc. Bachelor of Science (L *Baccalaureus Scientiae*).

B.S.A. 1. Bachelor of Scientific Agriculture. **2.** Bibliographical Society of America. **3.** Boy Scouts of America. **4.** British South Africa.

B.S.C.P. Brotherhood of Sleeping Car Porters.

B.S.Ed. Bachelor of Science in Education.

bsh. Bushel(s).

Bs/L Bills of lading.

BSM Bronze Star Medal.

B.S.S. or B.S.Sc. or B.S. in S.S. Bachelor of (Science in) Social Sciences.

Bt. Baronet.

B.T. or B.Th. Bachelor of Theology (L *Baccalaureus Theologiae*).

btry. *Mil.* Battery.

BTU or B.T.U., B.Th.U., b.t.u., or btu British thermal unit.

bu. or bu 1. Bureau. **2.** Bushel(s).

bub (bub) *n. Informal* Brother; youngster; young man: used in direct address. [Alter. of BROTHER]

bu-bal (byōō′bəl) *n.* A large antelope (genus *Alcelaphus*), especially the North African **bubal hartebeest** (*A. bosélaphus*). Also **bu-bale** (byōō′bəl), **bu-ba-lis** (byōō′bə-lis). [< L *bubalus* < Gk. *boubalos,* an African antelope. Related to BUFFALO.]

bu-ba-line (byōō′bə-līn, -lin) *adj.* **1.** Resembling the bubal. **2.** Of, pertaining to, or like a buffalo.

bub-ble (bub′əl) *n.* **1.** A film of liquid in the form of a globule, filled with air or other gas. **2.** A globule of air or other gas in any confined space, as in a liquid or solid substance. **3.** Anything unsubstantial; a delusion; fraud. **4.** The process or sound of bubbling. **5.** A glass or plastic dome. — *v.* **-bled, -bling** *v.i.* **1.** To form or emit bubbles; rise in bubbles. **2.** To move or flow with a gurgling sound. **3.** To express joy, delight, exultation, etc., in an irrepressible manner: He *bubbled* with glee. — *v.t.* **4.** To cause to bubble; form bubbles in, as a liquid. **5.** *Archaic* To cheat; swindle. [ME *buble;* prob. imit.] — **bub′bly** *adj.*

bubble chamber *Physics* An apparatus for the study of the reactions of high-energy atomic particles, consisting of a superheated liquid under pressure, in which the paths of ions are shown by a trail of vapor bubbles large enough to be photographed.

bubble gum A heavy-fibered chewing gum that can be blown into large bubbles.

bub-bler (bub′lər) *n.* A drinking fountain fitted with a vertical nozzle from which water flows in a small stream.

Bu-ber (bōō′bər), Martin, 1878–1965, Austrian Jewish religious philosopher and scholar.

bu-bo (byōō′bō) *n. pl.* **bu-boes** *Pathol.* An inflammatory swelling of a lymph gland in the groin or armpit. [< LL < Gk. *boubōn* groin] — **bu-bon-ic** (byōō-bon′ik) *adj.*

bubonic plague *Pathol.* A malignant, contagious, epidemic disease, characterized by fever, vomiting, diarrhea, and buboes. It is caused by a bacterium of the genus *Pasteurella* and transmitted to man by fleas from infected rats.

bu-bon-o-cele (byōō-bon′ə-sēl) *n. Pathol.* A hernia in the groin. [< Gk. *boubōnokēlē* < *boubōn* groin + *kēlē* abscess]

Bu-ca-ra-man-ga (bōō′kä-rä-mäng′gä) A city in north central Colombia; a tobacco and coffee center; pop. 208,640 (1961).

buc-cal (buk′əl) *adj. Anat.* **1.** Of or pertaining to the cheek: the *buccal* artery. **2.** Pertaining to the mouth; oral. [< L *bucca* cheek]

buc-ca-neer (buk′ə-nir′) *n.* **1.** A pirate or freebooter. **2.** One of the piratical rovers of the 17th and 18th centuries who preyed along the Spanish coasts of America. [< F *boucanier,* orig. one of the hunters of wild oxen in Haiti, who later turned to piracy < Tupi *boucan* a frame for smoking and curing meat]

buc-ci-na-tor (buk′sə-nā′tər) *n. Anat.* A muscle of the middle cheek, used in blowing. [< L, trumpeter < *buccina* trumpet]

bu-cen-taur (byōō-sen′tôr) *n.* **1.** The state barge of Venice, used by the doge. **2.** A mythical monster, half bull and half man. [< Ital. *bucentoro,* ? < Med. Gk. *boukentauros* bucentaur < Gk. *bous* bull + *kentauros* centaur; def. 1 with ref. to the vessel's figurehead]

Bu-ceph-a-lus (byōō-sef′ə-ləs) The war horse of Alexander the Great. [< L < Gk. *boukephalos* bull-headed]

Buch·an (buk/ən), **Sir John,** 1875–1940, first Baron Tweedsmuir, Scottish writer and statesman.

Bu·chan·an (byōō-kan/ən), **James,** 1791–1868, 15th president of the United States 1857–61.

Bu·cha·rest (bōō/kə-rest, byōō/-) The capital of Rumania, in the southern part; pop. 1,518,725 (est. 1968); also the capital of **Bucharest Province** (7,220 sq. mi., pop. 1,431,993): Rumanian *Bucuresti.*

Buch·en·wald (bōōk/ən-wôld, *Ger.* bōōkh/ən-vält) A Nazi concentration and extermination camp in central Germany.

Buch·man·ism (bōōk/mən-iz/əm) *n.* A religious movement emphasizing absolute virtue: also called *Moral Rearmament, Oxford Group movement.* [after Frank *Buchman,* 1878–1961, U.S. evangelist, who founded it] **— Buch/man·ite** (-īt) *n.*

Buch·ner (bōōkh/nər), **Eduard,** 1860–1917, German chemist.

buck¹ (buk) *n.* **1.** The male of certain animals, as of antelopes, deer, goats, rabbits, and rats. **2.** A dandy; fop. **3.** *Informal* A young man, especially one of carefree spirit. **4.** *U.S. Informal* An adult male Negro or Indian: an offensive term. **5.** The act of bucking. **— v.i. 1.** To leap upward suddenly and come down with the legs stiff, as a horse or pack animal, in an attempt to dislodge rider or burden. **2.** *U.S. Informal* To resist stubbornly; object. **3.** *U.S. Informal* To move with jerks and jolts: said of vehicles. **— v.t. 4.** To throw by bucking. **5.** *U.S. Dial.* To butt with the head. **6.** *U.S. Informal* To resist stubbornly; oppose. **7.** In football, to charge into (the opponent's line) with the ball. **— to buck for** *U.S. Slang* To try hard to obtain (a promotion, raise, etc.). **— to buck up** *Informal* To encourage or take courage. [Fusion of OE *bucca* he-goat and *buc* male deer]

buck² (buk) *n.* **1.** A sawhorse. **2.** A padded frame in the shape of a sawhorse, used for vaulting, etc. [< Du. *zaagbok* sawbuck]

buck³ (buk) *n. U.S. Slang* A dollar. [Short for BUCKSKIN, formerly taken as a standard of value by North American Indians]

buck⁴ (buk) *n.* In poker, a marker occasionally put into a jackpot, indicating that he who receives it must order another jackpot when it is his deal. **— to pass the buck** *U.S. Informal* To shift responsibility, blame, etc., to someone else. [Origin uncertain]

buck. Buckram.

Buck (buk), **Pearl,** 1892–1973, *nee* Sydenstricker, U.S. novelist.

buck and wing An intricate, fast tap dance.

buck·a·roo (buk/ə-rōō, buk/ə-rōō/) *n. U.S.* A cowboy. Also **buck·ay·ro** (buk-ā/rō). [Alter of Sp. *vaquero* cowboy]

buck bean A plant (*Menyanthes trifoliata*) found in damp places, having white or reddish flowers: also called *bogbean.*

buck·ber·ry (buk/ber/ē, -bər-ē) *n.* A small, wild, black huckleberry (*Gaylussacia ursina*) native in SE United States.

buck·board (buk/bôrd/, -bōrd/) *n.* A light, four-wheeled, open carriage having a long, flexible board in place of body and springs. [< BUCK¹, v. (def. 3) + BOARD]

buck·een (buk-ēn/) *n.* In Ireland, formerly, a young man who aped the wealthy. [< BUCK¹ (n. def. 2)]

BUCKBOARD

buck·er (buk/ər) *n.* A horse that bucks.

buck·et (buk/it) *n.* **1.** A deep cylindrical vessel, with a rounded handle, used for carrying water, coal, etc.; a pail. **2.** As much as a bucket will hold: also **buck/et·ful.** **3.** A bucketlike compartment, as on a water wheel or a conveyor. **4.** A piston, as in a lifting pump, with a valve opening upward. **— v.t. & v.i. 1.** To draw or carry in a bucket. **2.** *Informal* To ride (a horse) hard. **3.** To move along rapidly. [? < OF *buket* kind of tub; infl. by OE *būc* pitcher]

bucket seat A single seat, usually with a rounded back, used in racing and sports cars, airplanes, etc.

bucket shop An office ostensibly acting as an agent in buying and selling stocks, grain, etc., but actually not executing its customers' orders while gambling that prices will decline.

buck·eye (buk/ī/) *n. Chiefly U.S.* **1.** The horse chestnut. **2.** The glossy brown seed or nut of this tree. [< BUCK¹ + EYE]

Buck·eye (buk/ī/) *n.* A native or inhabitant of Ohio.

Buckeye State Nickname of OHIO.

buck fever *U.S. Informal* The nervous excitement felt by an inexperienced hunter when first sighting game.

buck·hound (buk/hound/) *n.* A hound used for hunting deer.

Buck·ing·ham (buk/ing-əm), **Duke of,** 1592–1628, George Villiers, English courtier. **— Duke of,** 1628–87, George Villiers, English statesman, son of the preceding.

Buckingham Palace The official London residence of the British sovereign.

Buck·ing·ham·shire (buk/ing-əm-shir/) A county in southern England; 749 sq. mi.; pop. 497,800 (1976); county seat, Aylesbury. Also **Buck/ing·ham;** shortened form **Bucks.**

buck·ish (buk/ish) *adj.* Dandified; foppish. **— buck/ish·ly** *adv.*

buck·le¹ (buk/əl) *n.* **1.** A device for fastening together two loose ends, as of a strap, usually consisting of a metal frame with a movable tongue. **2.** An ornament for shoes, etc., resembling a buckle. **— v. ·led, ·ling** *v.t.* **1.** To fasten or attach with or as with a buckle. **— v.i. 2.** To be fastened or joined by a buckle. **3.** To fight; grapple. **— to buckle down** To apply oneself vigorously. [< F *boucle* cheekstrap, boss of a shield < L *buccula,* dim. of *bucca* cheek]

buck·le² (buk/əl) *v.t. & v.i.* ·**led,** ·**ling** To bend under pressure; warp, curl, or crumple. **— n.** A bend, bulge, kink, or twist. [< F *boucler* to bulge]

Buck·le (buk/əl), **Henry Thomas,** 1821–62, English historian.

buck·ler (buk/lər) *n.* **1.** A small, round shield. **2.** A means of defense. **— v.t.** To shield, as with a buckler; defend; protect. [< OF *boucler* having a boss. See BUCKLE¹.]

Buck·ner (buk/nər), **Simon Bolivar,** 1823–1914, Confederate general in the Civil War.

buck·o (buk/ō) *n. pl.* **buck·oes** A bully. [< BUCK¹]

buck private *U.S. Slang* An enlisted man of the grade of private in the U.S. Army.

buck·ra (buk/rə) *n.* A white man: often a contemptuous term among Negroes. [< Efik *mbàkara*]

buck·ram (buk/rəm) *n.* **1.** A coarse cotton fabric sized with glue, used for stiffening garments, in bookbinding, etc. **2.** Stiffness of manner; formality. **— v.t.** To stiffen with or as with buckram. [OF *boquerant* coarse cloth < *Bokhara,* Persia, where first made]

Bucks or **Bucks.** Buckinghamshire.

buck·saw (buk/sô/) *n.* A wood-cutting saw set in an adjustable H-shaped frame. For illustration see SAWBUCK.

buck·shee (buk/shē) *adj. Brit. & Canadian Slang* Free; gratis.

buck·shot (buk/shot/) *n.* Shot of a large size, used in hunting deer and other large game.

buck·skin (buk/skin/) *n.* **1.** The skin of a buck. **2.** A soft, strong, grayish yellow leather, formerly made from deerskins, now chiefly from sheepskins. **3.** *pl.* Breeches or clothing made of such skin. **4.** *Usually cap. U.S.* A person clad in buckskin, especially a backwoodsman. **5.** *U.S.* A horse having the characteristic color of buckskin.

buck·thorn (buk/thôrn/) *n.* A shrub or small tree (genus *Rhamnus*), typical of the family *Rhamnaceae,* having alternate pinnately veined leaves and axillary flowers; especially, *R. frangula,* having bark formerly used as a laxative. **— southern buckthorn** A tree (*Bumelia lycioides*) of the southern United States. [< BUCK¹ + THORN]

buck·tooth (buk/tōōth/) *n. pl.* ·**teeth** A projecting tooth. [< BUCK¹ + TOOTH]

buck·toothed (buk/tōōtht/, -tōōthd/) *adj.* Having protruding upper front teeth.

buck·wheat (buk/hwēt/) *n.* **1.** A plant (genus *Fagopyrum*), yielding triangular seeds used as fodder and for flour. **2.** Its seeds. **3.** The flour. [OE *bōc* beech + WHEAT; from resemblance of seeds to beech seeds]

bu·col·ic (byōō-kol/ik) *adj.* Pertaining to or characteristic of shepherds or herdsmen; pastoral; rustic. **— Syn.** See RURAL. **— n. 1.** A pastoral poem. **2.** A rustic; farmer. [< L *bucolicus* < Gk. *boukolikos* < *boukolos* herdsman < *bous* ox] **— bu·col/i·cal·ly** *adv.*

Bu·co·vi·na (bōō/kə-vē/nə) See BUKOVINA.

Bu·cu·reşti (bōō-kōō-resht/) The Rumanian name for BUCHAREST.

bud¹ (bud) *n.* **1.** *Bot.* **a** An undeveloped stem, branch, or shoot of a plant, with rudimentary leaves or unexpanded flowers. **b** The act or stage of budding. **2.** *Zool.* **a** A budlike projection, as in some lower animals, developing into a new individual. **b** A budlike part. **3.** Any immature person or thing. **— to nip in the bud** To stop in the initial stage. **— v. bud·ded, bud·ding** *v.i.* **1.** To put forth buds. **2.** To begin to grow or develop. **— v.t. 3.** To put forth as buds. **4.** To cause to bud. **5.** To graft to another type of tree or plant. [ME *budde;* origin uncertain] **— bud/der** *n.*

bud² (bud) *n. U.S. Informal* A man or boy: used in direct address. [Alter. of BROTHER]

Bu·da·pest (bōō/də·pest) The capital of Hungary, a county borough in the central part, on the Danube; pop. 2,023,000 (est. 1971).

Bud·dha (bōōd/ə, bōō/də) *n.* An incarnation of selflessness, virtue, and wisdom embodied in the person of Gautama or Gotama Siddhartha, 563?–483? B.C., the founder of Buddhism, regarded by his followers as the last of a series of deified religious teachers of central and eastern Asia. [< Skt., the Enlightened]

Bud·dhism (bōōd/iz·əm, bōō/diz-) *n.* A mystical and ascetic religious faith of eastern Asia, founded in northern India by Buddha in the sixth century B.C., and teaching that the ideal state of nirvana is reached by right living and believing, and peace of mind through meditation. **— Bud/dhist** *adj. & n.* **— Bud·dhis/tic** or ·ti·cal *adj.*

bud·ding (bud′ing) *adj.* Just beginning; incipient.

bud·dle (bud′l) *n. Mining* An inclined, shallow trough, used for separating ores in running water. [Origin unknown]

bud·dle·ia (bud·lē′ə, bud′lē-ə) *n.* Any plant of a large genus (*Buddleia*) of chiefly tropical shrubs or herbs, with lanceolate, opposite leaves and small yellow or purplish flowers: also called *butterfly bush.* [after Adam *Buddle*, died 1715, English botanist]

bud·dy (bud′ē) *n. pl.* **·dies** *U.S. Informal* Pal; chum; companion. [See BUD²]

Bu·dën·ny (bōō-den′ē, *Russian* bŏō-dyôn′ĭ), **Semën Mikhailovich,** 1883–1973, Soviet marshal.

budge¹ (buj) *v.t. & v.i.* **budged, budg·ing** To move or stir slightly. [< F *bouger* to stir, move]

budge² (buj) *Archaic n.* Lambskin, formerly used on scholars' gowns, etc. — *adj.* **1.** Trimmed with or wearing budge. **2.** Pompous; solemn. [Origin uncertain]

budg·er·i·gar (buj′ə·rē·gär′) *n.* A small parrot (*Melopsittacus undulatus*) of Australia, popular as a pet. Also **budg′er·i·gah**(-gä), **budg′ie** (buj′ē).

budg·et (buj′it) *n.* **1.** A summary of probable income and expenditures for a given period; also, a plan for adjusting expenditures to income. **2.** A collection or stock. **3.** *Obs.* A sack or pouch, or its contents. — *v.t.* **1.** To determine in advance the expenditure of (time, money, etc.). **2.** To provide for in a budget; plan according to a budget: to *budget* a trip. [< F *bougette*, dim. of *bouge* < L *bulga* leather bag] — **budg·et·ar·y** (buj′ə-ter′ē) *adj.* — **budg′et·er** *n.*

Bud·weis (bōŏt′vīs) The German name for ČESKÉ BUDĚJOVICE.

Bu·ell (byōō′əl), **Don Carlos,** 1818–98, Union general in the Civil War.

Bue·na Park (bwā′nə) A city in SW California, near Los Angeles; pop. 63,646.

Bue·na Vis·ta (bwā′nə vis′tə) A village in SE Coahuila, Mexico; scene of U.S. victory (1847) in the Mexican War.

Bue·nos Ai·res (bwā′nəs ī′riz, ā′nəs âr′ēz) **1.** The capital of Argentina, comprising a Federal District in the eastern part; a port at the mouth of the Rio de la Plata; 74 sq. mi.; pop. 3,549,000 (1969). **2.** A Province in eastern Argentina; 118,752 sq. mi.; pop. 6,734,548 (1960); capital, La Plata.

buff¹ (buf) *n.* **1.** A thick, soft, flexible leather, undyed and unglazed, made from the skins of buffalo, elk, oxen, etc. **2.** Its color, a light brownish yellow. **3.** A military coat made of buff leather. **4.** *Informal* The bare skin; the nude: in the *buff.* **5.** A stick covered with leather, velvet, etc., and used for polishing. **6.** A buffing wheel. — *adj.* **1.** Made of buff. **2.** Light, brownish yellow. — *v.t.* **1.** To clean or polish with or as with a buff. **2.** To make buff in color. **3.** In leather-making, to shave until very thin, producing an imitation of calf leather. [< F *buffle* buffalo] — **buff′y** *adj.*

buff² (buf) *v.t.* To deaden the shock of. — *n.* A blow; buffet: now only in *blindman's buff.* [< OF *buffe* blow]

buff³ (buf) *n.* An enthusiast or devotee. [Origin uncertain]

buf·fa·lo (buf′ə·lō) *n. pl.* **·loes** or **·los 1.** Any of various large Old World oxen, as the **Cape buffalo** (*Syncerus caffer*), of Africa, having horns that broaden at the base. **2.** The water buffalo (which see). **3.** The North American bison. **4.** A buffalo robe. **5.** A buffalo fish. — *v.t.* **·loed, ·lo·ing** *U.S. Slang* To overawe; intimidate; hoodwink. [< Ital. < LL *bufalus*, var. of L *bubalus* < Gk. *boubalos* buffalo. Related to BUBAL.]

Buf·fa·lo (buf′ə·lō) A city in western New York, at the eastern end of Lake Erie; pop. 462,768.

CAPE BUFFALO
(About 5 feet high at shoulder)

buffalo berry 1. The edible crimson berry of either of two American shrubs, *Shepherdia argentea* or *S. canadensis.* **2.** Either of these shrubs.

Buffalo Bill See CODY.

Buffalo Bill Dam A dam on the Shoshone River in NW Wyoming; 325 ft. high; formerly *Shoshone Dam.*

buffalo bug The carpet beetle. Also **buffalo moth.**

buffalo fish Any of various large carplike North American fresh-water fishes (genus *Ictiobus*) of the sucker family.

buffalo gnat A small, black, dipterous insect (*Simulium* and related genera) that attacks all warm-blooded animals, usually in swarms: also called *brulot, black fly.*

buffalo grass A low, creeping grass (*Buchloë dactyloides*) covering prairies east of the Rocky Mountains, highly esteemed for winter forage.

Buffalo Indian A Plains Indian (which see).

buffalo robe The skin of the North American bison, dressed with the hair on for use as a lap robe.

buff·er¹ (buf′ər) *n.* One who or that which buffs or polishes. [< BUFF¹, v.]

buff·er² (buf′ər) *n.* **1.** A device for lessening the shock of concussion; shock absorber. **2.** One who or that which serves to diminish or neutralize shock of any kind by bearing the main force, stress, or effect. **3.** *Chem.* A substance that tends to stabilize a chemical system, as by causing resistance to changes in pH. [< BUFF², v.]

buffer state A small country situated between two larger rival powers and regarded as lessening the danger of conflict between them.

buf·fet¹ (bŏŏ-fā′, *Brit.* buf′it) *n.* **1.** A sideboard for china, glassware, etc. **2.** A counter for serving meals or refreshments, or a restaurant with such a counter. **3.** A light meal at which the guests serve themselves. [< F]

buf·fet² (buf′it) *v.t.* **1.** To strike or cuff, as with the hand. **2.** To strike repeatedly; knock about. **3.** To force (a way) by pushing or striking, as through a crowd. — *v.i.* **4.** To fight; struggle. **5.** To force a way. — **Syn.** See BEAT. — *n.* **1.** A blow or cuff, as with the hand. **2.** Something like a blow or slap. [< OF *buffet*, dim. of *buffe* a blow, slap] — **buf′fet·er** *n.*

buff·ing wheel (buf′ing) A wheel covered with leather, velvet, etc., for polishing metal.

buf·fle·head (buf′əl-hed′) *n.* A North American duck (*Bucephala albeola*) having the feathers of the head elongated, and with plumage black above and white below: also called *butterball.* [< F *buffle* buffalo + HEAD]

buf·fo (bōō′fō, *Ital.* bŏŏf′fō) *n. pl.* **·fi** (-fē) A male singer of comic opera roles, usually a bass. [< Ital., foolish, comic]

Buf·fon (bü-fôn′), **Comte de,** 1707–88, Georges Louis Leclerc, French naturalist.

buf·foon (bu-fōōn′) *n.* **1.** A clown. **2.** One given to jokes, coarse pranks, etc. [< F *buffon* < Ital. *buffone* clown < *buffa* jest] — **buf·foon′er·y** *n.* — **buf·foon′ish** *adj.*

bug¹ (bug) *n.* **1.** Any of an order (*Hemiptera*) or suborder (*Heteroptera*) of terrestrial or aquatic insects with piercing, sucking mouth parts, wingless or with two pairs of wings, the anterior pair typically horny with an apical membranous part, as the stinkbug, squashbug, or bedbug. **2.** Loosely, any insect or small arthropod. **3.** *Brit.* A bedbug. **4.** *Informal* A microorganism, especially one causing disease; germ. **5.** *Slang* An enthusiast; monomaniac. **6.** *U.S. Slang* A minor defect, as in a machine. **7.** *U.S. Slang* A miniature electronic microphone, used in wiretapping, etc. — *v.* **bugged, bug·ging** *v.i.* **1.** To stare; stick out: said of eyes. — *v.t. U.S. Slang* **2.** To annoy; pester; irritate; bewilder. **3.** To fit (a room, telephone circuit, etc.) with a concealed listening device. [Prob. < BUG²]

bug² (bug) *n. Obs.* A specter; bugbear. [ME *bugge* scarecrow. Cf. Welsh *bwg* ghost.]

Bug (bōōg) **1.** A river in the southern Ukrainian S.S.R., flowing 532 miles SE to the Black Sea. Also **Southern Bug.** Russian *Yuzhnyy Bug.* **2.** A river rising in the western Ukrainian S.S.R., flowing about 500 miles, generally NW, to the Narew in Poland; forms part of the boundary between Poland and the Soviet Union. Also **Western Bug.** Russian *Zapadnyy Bug.*

bug·a·boo (bug′ə·bōō) *n. pl.* **·boos** A bugbear. [< BUG² + BOO]

Bu·gan·da (byōō-gan′də) A kingdom comprising a Province of southern Uganda; 25,631 sq. mi.; pop. about 1,300,000; capital, Kampala.

bug·bane (bug′bān′) *n.* A perennial herb (genus *Cimicifuga*) of the crowfoot family, as the **European bugbane** (*C. foetida*), the flowers of which are supposedly repellent to insects, or the **American bugbane** (*C. americana*).

bug·bear (bug′bâr′) *n.* **1.** A real or imaginary object of dread. **2.** *Obs.* A hobgoblin believed to devour naughty children. [< BUG² + BEAR²]

bug-eyed (bug′īd′) *adj. Slang* With the eyes bulging.

bug·ger (bug′ər, bŏŏg′-) *n.* **1.** One guilty of sodomy. **2.** A contemptible person. **3.** *U.S. Slang* A person; child: a humorous use. — *v.i.* **1.** To commit sodomy. **2.** *Slang* To be clumsy. — *v.t.* **3.** To commit sodomy with. **4.** *Slang* To botch: with *up.* — **to bugger off** *Chiefly Canadian Slang* To clear out; scram: usually in the imperative. [< OF *boulgre* < Med.L *Bulgarus* a Bulgarian; with ref. to a Bulgarian sect of heretics (11th c.) to whom sodomy was imputed]

bug·ger·y (bug′ər-ē, bŏŏg′-) *n.* Sodomy.

bug·gy¹ (bug′ē) *n. pl.* **·gies 1.** A light, four-wheeled carriage. **2.** A baby carriage. [Origin uncertain]

bug·gy² (bug′ē) *adj.* **·gi·er, ·gi·est 1.** Infested with bugs. **2.** *U.S. Slang* Crazy. — **bug′gi·ness** *n.*

bug·house (bug′hous′) *U.S. Slang n.* An asylum for the insane. — *adj.* Crazy; insane.

Bu·gin·vil·lae·a (bōō′gən·vil′ē·ə) *n.* See BOUGAINVILLEA.

bu·gle¹ (byōō′gəl) *n.* **1.** A brass wind instrument resembling a trumpet, usually without keys or valves. **2.** A huntsman's horn. — *v.* **·gled, ·gling** *v.t.* **1.** To summon with a bugle. — *v.i.* **2.** To sound a bugle. [< OF < L *buculus,* dim. of *bos* ox; because first made from the horns of oxen] — **bu′gler** *n.*

BUGLE¹ (def. 1)

bu·gle² (byōō′gəl) *n.* A tube-shaped glass bead used for ornamenting garments. — *adj.* Of, resembling, or adorned with bugles. [Origin uncertain] — **bu′gled** *adj.*

bu·gle³ (byōō′gəl) *n.* A plant of the mint family (genus *Ajuga*), especially the **carpet bugle** (*A. reptans*). [< F < LL *bugula*]

bu·gle·weed (byōō′gəl·wēd′) *n.* Any of several herbs (genus

Lycopus); especially, **sweet** or **Virginia bugleweed** (*L. vir-ginicus*) used medicinally, and **bitter** or **American bugle-weed** (*L. americanus*).

bu·gloss (byōō′glos, -glôs) *n.* Any of a genus (*Anchusa*) of plants of the borage family, especially a species (*A. offi-cinalis*) having stiff, hairy stems. [< F *buglosse* < L *buglossa* < Gk. *bouglōssos* < *bous* bull, ox + *glōssa* tongue]

bug·seed (bug′sēd′) *n.* A low, branching annual herb (*Cori-spermum hyssopifolium*) of the goosefoot family, the flat seeds of which resemble bugs.

buhl (bōōl) *n.* Elaborate ornamentation of furniture con-sisting of inlaid metal, tortoise shell, ivory, etc.; also, a piece so decorated. Also **buhl′work′.** [after A. C. *Boulle,* 1642–1732, French cabinetmaker]

buhr·stone (bûr′stōn′) See BURRSTONE.

build (bild) *v.* **built** (*Archaic* **build·ed**), **build·ing** *v.t.* **1.** To construct, erect, or make by assembling separate parts or materials. **2.** To establish and increase: to *build* a business. **3.** To found; make a basis for: We *build* our hopes on peace. **4.** In card games, to form sequences or combinations of (cards), as by suit or number. — *v.i.* **5.** To construct or erect a house, etc. **6.** To be a builder. **7.** To base or develop an idea, theory, etc.: with *on* or *upon.* **8.** To increase in in-tensity, excitement, etc. — **to build in** To incorporate or add permanently. — **to build up 1.** To create or build by degrees. **2.** To renew or strengthen; also, to increase. **3.** To construct buildings in (an area). — *n.* The manner or style in which anything is constructed; form; figure. [OE *byldan* < *bold* house]

build·er (bil′dər) *n.* **1.** One who or that which builds. **2.** One who contracts for and directs the work of building. **3.** An abrasive or other substance added to soap.

build·ing (bil′ding) *n.* **1.** That which is built; a structure; edifice, as a house or barn. Abbr. *bldg.* **2.** The occupation, act, or art of constructing.

building block 1. One of a set of children's blocks used for building. **2.** A basic or supporting unit; element: Atoms are the *building blocks* of matter.

building and loan association An organization that aids its members in building or purchasing homes by loans from a fund accumulated by periodic payments of the members.

build·up (bild′up′) *n.* **1.** The act of increasing or strength-ening; accumulation, as of troops. **2.** *Informal* Extravagant publicity or praise designed to arouse interest, gain favor, etc.

built-in (bilt′in′) *adj.* **1.** Built as a permanent part; not removable. **2.** Of its very nature.

buird·ly (bûrd′lē) *adj. Scot.* Sturdy; stout; burly.

Bui·ten·zorg (boi′tən-zôrkh) The Dutch name for BOGOR.

Bu·kha·ra (bōō-kä′rə, *Russ.* bōō-khä′rə) An Oblast in the central Uzbek S.S.R.; 49,600 sq. mi.; pop. 573,000 (1959); center, Bukhara; pop. 112,000 (est. 1970): also *Bokhara.*

Bu·kha·rin (bōō-khä′rin), **Nikolai Ivanovich,** 1888–1938, Soviet revolutionist and editor; executed.

Bu·ko·vi·na (bōō′kə-vē′nə) A region of eastern Europe in NE Rumania and the western Ukrainian S.S.R.; formerly an Austrian duchy: Rumanian *Bucovina.* German **Bu·ko·wi·na** (bōō′kō-vē′nä).

bul. Bulletin.

Bul (bōōl) *n.* Heshwan. See (Hebrew) CALENDAR.

Bu·la·wa·yo (bōō′lə-wä′yō) A city in SW Rhodesia; pop. 117,871 (est. 1969).

bulb (bulb) *n.* **1.** *Bot.* **a** A leaf bud comprising a cluster of thickened, scalelike leaves, growing usually underground and sending forth roots from the lower face, as the onion or lily. **b** Any of several underground stems resembling bulbs, as the corm of a crocus or a dahlia tuber. **2.** Any plant growing from a bulb. **3.** A rounded protuberance, as at the end of a tube: the *bulb* of a syringe. **4.** An incandescent lamp, or its glass globe. **5.** An electron tube. **6.** *Anat.* **a** A rounded enlargement at the end of some tissues or organs. **b** The medulla oblongata. [< L *bulbus* < Gk. *bolbos* bulbous root]

bul·bar (bul′bər) *adj.* Of or pertaining to a bulb, especially the bulb of the medulla oblongata: *bulbar* paralysis.

bul·bif·er·ous (bul-bif′ər-əs) *adj.* Producing bulbs.

bulb·i·form (bul′bə-fôrm) *adj.* Having the form of a bulb.

bul·bil (bul′bil) *n.* **1.** A small bulb. **2.** *Bot.* An aerial, de-ciduous, fleshy leaf bud, capable of developing into a new in-dividual, as in the tiger lily: also **bul′bel** (-bel). [< NL *bul-billus,* dim. of L *bulbus* bulb]

bul·bous (bul′bəs) *adj.* **1.** Of, producing, or growing from bulbs. Also **bul·ba·ceous** (bul-bā′shəs). **2.** Shaped like a bulb; swollen: a *bulbous* nose.

bul·bul (bōōl′bōōl) *n.* **1.** Any of various thrushlike birds (family *Pycnonotidae*) of the tropics of the Old World, with short legs, rounded wings, and typically dull coloration. **2.** A nightingale (*Luscinia golzii*) of Persia, often mentioned in Persian poetry. [< Persian < Arabic]

Bul·finch (bōōl′finch), **Charles,** 1763–1844, U.S. architect. — **Thomas,** 1796–1867, U.S. author; compiler of myths; son of the preceding.

Bulg. Bulgaria; Bulgarian.

Bul·ga·nin (bōōl-gä′nyin), **Nikolai Aleksandrovich,** 1895–1975, Soviet marshal and statesman; premier 1955–58.

Bul·gar (bul′gär, bōōl′-) *n.* Bulgarian.

Bul·gar·i·a (bul-gâr′ē-ə, bōōl-) A Republic in SE Europe; 42,796 sq. mi.; pop. 8,501,000 (est. 1970); capital, Sofia. Officially **People's Republic of Bulgaria.** See map of BLACK SEA.

Bul·gar·i·an (bul-gâr′ē-ən, bōōl-) *adj.* Of or pertaining to Bulgaria, the Bulgarians, or their language. — *n.* **1.** A na-tive or citizen of Bulgaria. **2.** The Slavic language of the Bulgarians.

bulge (bulj, bōōlj) *n.* **1.** A protuberant, rounded part; a hump. **2.** *U.S. Slang* Advantage. — **to get the bulge on** *U.S. Slang* To gain the advantage over. — *v.t. & v.i.* **bulged, bulg·ing** To swell out. [< OF *boulge* a bag, swelling < L *bulga,* ult. < Celtic] — **bulg′i·ness** *n.* — **bulg′y** *adj.*

Bulge (bulj), **Battle of the** The last major German counter-offensive of World War II, repulsed in January, 1945, during which the line of combat formed a deep bulge in Belgium.

bulg·er (bul′jər) *n.* In golf, a driver or a brassie having a convex face. Also **bulger driver.**

bu·lim·i·a (byōō-lim′ē-ə) *n. Pathol.* Insatiable appetite, or the disease causing it. [< Gk. *boulimia* great hunger < *bou-* oxlike, great + *limos* hunger] — **bu·lim′ic** *adj.*

bulk¹ (bulk, bōōlk) *n.* **1.** Magnitude, volume, or size; espe-cially, great size. **2.** The greater or principal part; main body: the *bulk* of the population. **3.** A large body or mass. **4.** A ship's cargo, or its space for stowing cargo. Abbr. *blk.* — **in bulk 1.** Not packaged; loose. **2.** In large quantities. — *v.i.* **1.** To be of bulk; appear large or important; loom. **2.** To increase in magnitude; grow: with *up.* — *v.t.* **3.** To cause to expand or grow large: with *out.* [Cf. ON *bulki* heap, cargo, and Dan. *bulk* lump]

bulk² (bulk) *n.* A light structure, as a stall, at the front of a building. [? < ON *bōlkr* beam]

bulk·head (bulk′hed′) *n.* **1.** *Naut.* An upright partition in a vessel, separating compartments. **2.** A partition or wall to keep back earth, gas, etc., as in a mine. **3.** A horizontal or sloping door outside a house, leading to the cellar. **4.** A small structure built on a roof to cover an elevator shaft.

bulk·y (bul′kē, bōōl′kē) *adj.* **bulk·i·er, bulk·i·est** Of great size; massive; also, large and unwieldy. — **bulk′i·ly** *adv.* — **bulk′i·ness** *n.*

bull¹ (bōōl) *n.* **1.** The uncastrated male of an animal of the genus *Bos,* especially of the domesticated ox (*Bos taurus*). ◆ Collateral adjective: *taurine.* **2.** The male of some other animals, as of the elephant, whale, etc. **3.** One likened to a bull, as in strength or manner. **4.** A speculator who buys so as to profit from a rise in prices he anticipates or hopes to cause: opposed to *bear².* **5.** *U.S. Slang* A policeman or de-tective. **6.** *U.S. Slang* Empty talk; nonsense. — *v.t.* **1.** To speculate for a rise in price of or in. **2.** To push or force (a way). — *v.i.* **3.** To go up in price. **4.** To go or push ahead. — *adj.* **1.** Male; masculine. **2.** Like a bull; large. **3.** Marked by rising prices: a *bull* market. [ME *bule.* Related to OE *bulluc* bullock]

bull² (bōōl) *n.* **1.** An official and authoritative document is-sued by the Pope, usually an edict, decree, or other procla-mation, sealed with a bulla. **2.** A bulla (def. 1). [< L *bulla* edict, seal]

bull³ (bōōl) *n.* A funny blunder in speech. [? < F *boule* lie]

Bull (bōōl) *n.* The constellation and sign of the zodiac Taurus.

Bull (bōōl), **Ole Bornemann,** 1810–80, Norwegian violinist.

bull. Bulletin.

bul·la (bōōl′ə, bul′ə) *n. pl.* **bul·lae** (bōōl′ē, bul′ē) **1.** An official seal attached to a document, as to a papal bull. **2.** *Pathol.* A large blister: also called *bleb.*

bul·late (bōōl′āt, -it, bul′-) *adj.* **1.** *Biol.* Having blisterlike prominences, as a leaf or surface. **2.** *Anat.* Inflated. [< L *bullatus* < *bulla* bubble]

bull·bait·ing (bōōl′bā′ting) *n.* The setting of dogs upon bulls: a former English sport.

bull·bat (bōōl′bat′) *n.* The nighthawk.

bull·dog (bōōl′dôg′, -dog′) *n.* **1.** A medium-sized, short-haired, powerful dog, originally bred in England for use in bullbaiting: also called *English bulldog.* **2.** A pistol; especially, a short-barreled revolver of large caliber; also, formerly, a can-non. **3.** *Brit.* An assistant to the proctor at Oxford and Cambridge. — *adj.* Resembling a bulldog; coura-geous; tenacious. — *v.t.* **dogged, ·dog·ging** *U.S. Informal* To throw (a steer) by gripping its horns and twisting its neck.

BULLDOG
(About 14 inches high at shoulder)

bulldog edition *U.S.* The early edi-tion of a daily newspaper.

bull·doze (bōōl′dōz′) *v.t.* **·dozed, ·doz·ing 1.** *U.S. Slang* To intimidate; bully. **2.** To clear, dig, scrape, etc., with a bulldozer. — **Syn.** See INTIMIDATE. [? < BULL[1], adj. + DOSE, with ref. to the violent or excessive treatment given to the victim]

bull·doz·er (bŏŏl'dō'zər) *n.* **1.** A tractor of the caterpillar type equipped with a heavy steel blade, used for moving earth, clearing wooded areas, etc. **2.** *U.S. Slang* One who intimidates.

bul·let (bŏŏl'it) *n.* **1.** A small projectile for a firearm. **2.** Any small ball. [< F *boulette*, dim. of *boule* ball]

bul·le·tin (bŏŏl'ə-tən, -tin) *n.* **1.** A brief official public statement. **2.** A brief account of news, as in a newspaper or on radio. **3.** A periodical publication, as of the proceedings of a society. — *v.t.* To make public by bulletin. [< F < Ital. *bulletino*, double dim. of *bulla* < L, edict]

bulletin board A board for posting announcements, etc.

bul·let·proof (bŏŏl'it-prŏŏf') *adj.* Not penetrable by bullets.

bull·fight (bŏŏl'fīt') *n.* A combat in an arena between men and a bull or bulls, popular among the Spanish and Spanish Americans. — **bull'fight'er** *n.* — **bull'fight'ing** *n.*

bull·finch[1] (bŏŏl'finch') *n.* **1.** A European songbird (genus *Pyrrhula*) having a short bill and red breast. **2.** Any of certain American grosbeaks. [< BULL[1], adj. + FINCH]

bull·finch[2] (bŏŏl'finch') *n. Brit.* A high hedge that cannot be cleared by horse and rider.

bull·frog (bŏŏl'frog', -frôg') *n.* A large frog with a deep bass croak; especially, *Rana catesbiana* of North America. [< BULL[1], adj. + FROG]

bull·head (bŏŏl'hed') *n.* **1.** *U.S.* Any of several fresh-water catfishes (genus *Ictalurus*). Also **bull'pout'** (-pout'). **2.** A stubborn or stupid person. **3.** The miller's-thumb, a fish.

bull·head·ed (bŏŏl'hed'id) *adj.* Stubborn; headstrong.

bull·horn (bŏŏl'hôrn') *n.* A portable electrical voice amplifier resembling a megaphone. Also **bull horn.**

bul·lion[1] (bŏŏl'yən) *n.* Gold or silver uncoined or in mass, as in bars, plates, etc. [< AF *bullion*, OF *bouillon* boiling, melting < *bouillir* to boil; ? infl. by OF *billon* base metal]

bul·lion[2] (bŏŏl'yən) *n.* A heavy, twisted, cord fringe, especially one made with fine gold or silver wire. [< OF *bouillon* < L *bulla* bubble; infl. by BULLION[1]]

bull·ish (bŏŏl'ish) *adj.* **1.** Bull-like. **2.** Tending to cause prices to rise; also, marked by rising prices: a *bullish* market. **3.** Bullheaded. — **bull'ish·ly** *adv.* — **bull'ish·ness** *n.*

Bull Moose Party Progressive Party (def. 1).

bull·neck (bŏŏl'nek') *n.* **1.** A short, thick neck like a bull's. **2.** *U.S.* Any of several wild ducks. — **bull'necked'** *adj.*

bull nose *Vet.* A form of rhinitis occurring in swine, caused by a microorganism (*Actinomyces necrophorus*) and characterized by enlargement and necrosis of the nasal tissues.

bul·lock (bŏŏl'ək) *n.* **1.** A gelded bull; a steer or ox. **2.** Formerly, a bull calf. [OE *bulluc*]

bull·pen (bŏŏl'pen') *n. U.S.* **1.** An enclosure for bulls. **2.** *Informal* A place for temporary detention of prisoners; prison; jail. **3.** *Informal* The living quarters in a lumber camp. **4.** In baseball, a place where pitchers practice during a game.

bull·ring (bŏŏl'ring') *n.* A circular enclosure for bullfights.

bull·roar·er (bŏŏl'rôr'ər, -rōr'-) *n.* A wood slat on a string that is whirled in the air to produce a roaring sound.

Bull Run A creek in NE Virginia; scene of Civil War battles, 1861 and 1862, in which Union forces were defeated. See MANASSAS.

bull session *U.S. Informal* An informal discussion of broad topics, usually among men.

bull's-eye (bŏŏlz'ī) *n.* **1.** The central colored disk on a target; also, a shot that hits this disk. **2.** A circular opening or window. **3.** A thick disk of glass set in a pavement, deck, etc., to admit light. **4.** A plano-convex lens. **5.** A lantern with such a lens: also **bull's-eye lantern. 6.** A thick, round lump of candy. **7.** *Naut.* A small, round, sheaveless block. **8.** *Meteorol.* **a** The eye of a cyclonic storm. **b** A small cloud, reddish at the center, supposed to indicate the approach of a cyclonic storm (**bull's-eye squall**) off South Africa.

bull snake A gopher snake (which see).

bull terrier A white terrier having a long head and stiff coat, originally bred from a bulldog and a white terrier.

bull tongue In cotton farming, a heavy plow with a nearly vertical moldboard.

bull·weed (bŏŏl'wēd') *n.* Knapweed (which see).

bull·whip (bŏŏl'hwip') *n.* A long, heavy whip. — *v.t.* **·whipped, ·whip·ping** To strike with a bullwhip.

bul·ly[1] (bŏŏl'ē) *n. pl.* **·lies 1.** A swaggering, quarrelsome, usually cowardly person who terrorizes weaker people. **2.** *Archaic* A hired ruffian. **3.** *Obs.* A pimp. **4.** *Obs.* Sweetheart; darling. — *v.* **·lied, ·ly·ing** *v.t.* **1.** To intimidate or coerce by threats. — *v.i.* **2.** To act the bully. — **Syn.** See INTIMIDATE. — *adj.* **1.** *U.S. Informal* Excellent; admirable. **2.** Jolly; dashing; gallant. — *interj. U.S. Informal* Well done! [Cf. Du. *boel* friend, lover; infl. in meaning by BULL[1]]

bul·ly[2] (bŏŏl'ē) *n.* Canned or pickled beef. Also **bully beef.** [Prob. < F *bouilli*, pp. of *bouillir* to boil]

bul·ly·rag (bŏŏl'ē-rag') *v.t.* **·ragged, ·rag·ging** To bully; intimidate. [? < BULLY, v. + RAG[1]]

bully tree One of several tropical American trees yielding balata, especially *Manilkara bidentata*.

Bü·low (bü'lō), **Prince Bernhard von,** 1849–1929, German chancellor 1900–09.

bul·rush (bŏŏl'rush') *n.* **1.** Any of various tall, rushlike plants (genus *Scirpus*) growing in water or damp ground. **2.** In the Bible, papyrus. *Ex.* ii 3. [< BULL[1], adj. + RUSH[2]]

bul·wark (bŏŏl'wərk) *n.* **1.** A defensive wall or rampart; fortification. **2.** Any safeguard or defense. **3.** *Usually pl. Naut.* The raised side of a ship, above the upper deck. — *v.t.* To surround and fortify with a bulwark. [< MHG *bolwerc.* Akin to BOULEVARD.]

— **Syn.** (noun) **1.** *Bulwark, rampart, parapet, breastwork,* and *bastion* denote a protecting barricade in a military fortification. *Bulwark* is the most general term, being applicable to temporary or permanent structures, or to anything that protects or shelters. The other words have narrower, more technical senses. A *rampart* is a permanent, high, and strong outer wall of a fort. A *parapet* is also permanent, but is usually lower so that soldiers may fire or throw missiles over it; often a *parapet* is erected on a *rampart.* A *breastwork* is a low *parapet* hastily thrown up, and is generally temporary, while a *bastion* is a projecting angle in a *rampart,* from which defenders may fire upon those who come close to the wall on either side.

Bul·wer (bŏŏl'wər), **William Henry Lytton Earle,** 1801–72, Baron Dalling and Bulwer, British diplomat.

Bul·wer-Lyt·ton (bŏŏl'wər-lit'n) See LYTTON.

bum[1] (bum) *U.S. Slang n.* A worthless or dissolute loafer; tramp. — **on the bum 1.** Out of order; broken. **2.** Living as a vagrant. — **the bum's rush** Forcible ejection. — *adj.* Bad; inferior. — *v.* **bummed, bum·ming** *v.i.* **1.** To live by sponging on others. **2.** To live idly and in dissipation. — *v.t.* **3.** To get by begging: to *bum* a ride. [Short for *bummer,* alter. of G *bummler* loafer, dawdler] — **bum'mer** *n.*

bum[2] (bum) *n. Brit. Slang* The buttocks. [ME *bom*; origin uncertain]

bum·bai·liff (bum'bā'lif) *n. Brit.* A sheriff's deputy or county-court bailiff: a contemptuous term. Also **bum'bail'ey** (-bā'lē). [< BUM[2] + BAILIFF; because he follows closely behind a person]

bum·ber·shoot (bum'bər-shŏŏt') *n. U.S. Slang* An umbrella. [Var. of UMBR(ELLA) + (PARA)CHUTE]

bum·ble (bum'bəl) *v.t. & v.i.* **·bled, ·bling** To bungle, especially in an officious manner. [?Imit.] — **bum'bling** *adj. & n.*

bum·ble·bee (bum'bəl-bē') *n.* Any of various large, hairy, bees (family *Bombidae*). [< dial. E *bumble* to hum + BEE[1]]

bum·ble·foot (bum'bəl-fŏŏt') *n. Vet.* A suppurative bacterial swelling of the foot in domestic fowls.

bum·boat (bum'bōt') *n.* A boat used in peddling provisions and small wares to vessels in port or offshore. [? < LG *bumboot* broad-beamed boat] — **bum'boat'man** (-mən) *n.*

bum·kin (bum'kin) *n. Naut.* A short boom, especially one at a ship's bows to extend the foresail, or at the stern to extend the mizzen sail: also *bumpkin.* [< Du. *boomkin,* dim. of *boom* tree, beam]

bump (bump) *v.t.* **1.** To come into contact with; knock into. **2.** To cause to knock into or against: to *bump* one's head against a post. **3.** *U.S. Slang* To displace, as from a position or seat. — *v.i.* **4.** To strike heavily or with force; come together with a bump: often with *into* or *against.* **5.** To move with jerks and jolts. **6.** *U.S. Slang* To thrust the pelvic region forward in performing a dance, etc. — **to bump off** *Slang* To kill, especially with a gun. — *n.* **1.** An impact or collision; a blow; jolt. **2.** A protuberance or uneven place. **3.** One of the protuberances of the human head said to denote a particular faculty. **4.** *Aeron.* An upward gust of wind striking an aircraft with the effect of a blow. **5.** *U.S. Slang* A forward thrusting of the pelvic region as performed by a striptease er, etc. [Imit.]

bump·er[1] (bum'pər) *n.* Something designed to absorb the shock of collision, as the horizontal bar at the front or rear of an automobile.

bump·er[2] (bum'pər) *n.* A cup or glass filled to the brim. — *adj.* Unusually full or large: a *bumper* crop. — *v.t.* **1.** To fill to the brim. **2.** To drink toasts to. — *v.i.* **3.** To drink from bumpers. [? Alter. of F *bombarde* large cup; infl. in form by *bump*]

bump·kin (bump'kin) *n.* **1.** An awkward rustic; a lout. **2.** *Naut.* A bumkin. [? < Du. *boomkin* little tree, block. Cf. BLOCKHEAD.]

bump·tious (bump'shəs) *adj.* Aggressively self-assertive. [Appar. < BUMP, on analogy with FRACTIOUS, CONTENTIOUS, etc.] — **bump'tious·ly** *adv.* — **bump'tious·ness** *n.*

bump·y (bum'pē) *adj.* **bump·i·er, bump·i·est 1.** Having bumps. **2.** Jolting. — **bump'i·ly** *adv.* — **bump'i·ness** *n.*

bun (bun) *n.* **1.** A small bread roll, sometimes sweetened and containing currants, citron, etc. **2.** *Brit.* A small sweet cake. **3.** A roll of hair shaped like a bun. Also spelled *bunn.* [ME *bunne*; origin uncertain]

bu·na (bŏŏ'na, byŏŏ'-) *n. Chem.* A synthetic rubber made by the polymerization of butadiene with certain other substances, as styrene. [< BU(TADIENE) + NA(TRIUM)]

bunch (bunch) *n.* **1.** A number of things of the same kind growing, occurring, or fastened together; a cluster: a *bunch* of bananas: a *bunch* of newspapers. Abbr. *bch.* (*bchs.*). **2.** *Informal* A group: a *bunch* of boys. **3.** *Rare* A hump; protuberance. — *v.t. & v.i.* **1.** To make into or form bunches or groups. **2.** To gather, as in pleats or folds. [ME *bonche, bunche*; origin unknown] **— bunch'y** *adj.*

bunch·ber·ry (bunch'ber'ē, -bər·ē) *n. pl.* **·ries** A species of dwarf cornel (*Cornus canadensis*), with bright red berries.

Bunche (bunch), **Ralph Johnson,** 1904–71, U.S. educator and United Nations official.

bunch·flow·er (bunch'flou'ər) *n.* A plant (*Melanthium virginicum*) of the lily family of the United States, having linear leaves and a pyramidal panicle of greenish flowers.

bunch grass Any of various grasses growing in tufts.

bun·co (bung'kō) *U.S. Informal n.* A swindle in which confederates join to cheat or victimize a stranger; confidence game. **—** *v.t.* **·coed, ·co·ing** To swindle or rob. Also spelled *bunko.* [Prob. < Sp. *banco*, a card game]

bun·combe (bung'kəm) *n. U.S. Informal* **1.** Empty speechmaking for political effect or to please constituents. **2.** Empty talk; humbug. Also spelled *bunkum.* [from *Buncombe* County, N.C., whose congressman (1819–21) often insisted on making empty, unimportant speeches "for Buncombe"]

bunco steerer *U.S. Slang* A swindler.

bund¹ (bund) *n.* **1.** An embankment or dike. **2.** A street along a waterfront. **— the Bund** An esplanade in Shanghai, China. [< Hind. *band*]

bund² (boond, *Ger.* boont) *n.* A confederation; league; society. [< G]

Bund (boond, *Ger.* boont) *n. pl.* **Bun·de** (bün'də) A confederation of German states established in 1867.

Bun·del·khand (boon'dəl·khund) A region in central India, a subdivision, **Bundelkhand Agency,** of the former Central India Agency, including about 30 native states.

Bun·des·rat (boon'dəs·rät') *n.* A federal council, as in Germany, Austria, or Switzerland. Also **Bun'des·rath'.** [< G, lit., council of the league]

bun·dle (bun'dəl) *n.* **1.** A number of things or a quantity of anything bound together. **2.** Anything folded or wrapped and tied up; a package. **3.** A group; collection. **4.** *Bot.* A cluster of large parenchymatous cells forming part of the vascular system of a plant: also called *vascular bundle.* Abbr. (for defs. 1, 2) *bd., bdl., bdle.* ◆ Collateral adjective: *fascicular.* **—** *v.* **·dled, ·dling** *v.t.* **1.** To tie, roll, or otherwise secure in a bundle. **2.** To send or put hastily and unceremoniously: with *away, off, out,* or *into.* **—** *v.i.* **3.** To go hastily; hustle. **4.** To lie or sleep in the same bed without undressing, formerly a courting custom in Wales and New England. **— to bundle up** To dress warmly. [< MDu. *bondel,* dim. of *bond* group. Akin to BIND.] **— bun'dler** *n.*

bung (bung) *n.* **1.** A stopper for the hole through which a cask is filled. **2.** Bunghole. **—** *v.t.* **1.** To close with or as with a bung: often with *up* or *down.* **2.** *Slang* To damage; maul: usually with *up.* [< MDu. *bonghe*]

bun·ga·low (bung'gə·lō) *n.* **1.** A small house or cottage, usually with one or one and a half stories. **2.** In India, a one-storied house with wide verandas. [< Hind. *banglā,* lit., Bengalese (house) < *Banga* Bengal]

bung·hole (bung'hōl') *n.* A hole in a keg or barrel from which liquid is tapped. [BUNG + HOLE]

bun·gle (bung'gəl) *v.t. & v.i.* **·gled, ·gling** To work, make, or do (something) clumsily; botch. **—** *n.* An awkward and imperfect job or performance; botch. [Cf. Sw. *bangla* to work ineffectually] **— bun'gler** *n.* **— bun'gling·ly** *adv.*

Bu·nin (boo'nyin), **Ivan Alekseevich,** 1870–1953, Russian novelist and poet.

bun·ion (bun'yən) *n. Pathol.* A painful swelling of the foot, usually at the bursa of the great toe. [Akin to OF *bugne* swelling]

bunk¹ (bungk) *n.* **1.** A narrow, built-in bed or shelf for sleeping; a berth. **2.** *Informal* A bed. **—** *v.i. Informal* **1.** To sleep in a bunk. **2.** To go to bed; sleep: to *bunk* on the floor. [Cf. MDu. *banc* bench, shelf and BANK³ rowers' bench]

bunk² (bungk) *n. U.S. Slang* Empty talk; nonsense. [Short for BUNCOMBE]

bun·ker (bung'kər) *n.* **1.** A large bin, as for coal on a ship. **2.** In golf, a sandy hollow or a mound of earth serving as an obstacle. **3.** *Mil.* **a** A steel and concrete fortification, usually underground. **b** A bulwark of earth to protect a gun emplacement. **—** *v.t.* In golf, to drive (a ball) into a bunker. [Cf. OSw. *bunke* hold of a ship and BANK³ rowers' bench]

Bunker Hill (bung'kər) A hill in Charlestown, Massachusetts, near which (on Breed's Hill) occurred the first organized engagement of the American Revolution, June 17, 1775.

bunk·house (bungk'hous') *n.* A building having bunks or cots for miners, workers, etc.

bunk·mate (bungk'māt') *n.* One who shares a bunk.

bun·ko (bung'kō) See BUNCO.

bun·kum (bung'kəm) See BUNCOMBE.

bunn (bun) See BUN.

bun·ny (bun'ē) *n. pl.* **·nies** A rabbit: a pet name. [Dim. of dial. E *bun* a rabbit; ult. origin unknown]

bunny hop *U.S.* In skiing, a dip or rut in a ski trail. Compare MOGUL.

bunny hug *U.S.* A dance of about 1910 in ragtime rhythm.

Bun·sen (bun'sən, *Ger.* boon'zən), **Robert Wilhelm,** 1811–99, German chemist and inventor.

Bun·sen burner (bun'sən) A type of gas burner in which a mixture of gas and air is burned at the top of a short metal tube, producing a very hot flame. [after R. W. *Bunsen*]

bunt¹ (bunt) *v.t. & v.i.* **1.** To strike or push as with horns; butt. **2.** In baseball, to bat (the ball) lightly into the infield, without swinging the bat. **—** *n.* **1.** A push or shove; a butt. **2.** In baseball: **a** The act of bunting. **b** A ball that has been bunted. [Nasalized var. of BUTT¹]

bunt² (bunt) *n.* **1.** *Naut.* The bellying part of a square sail. **2.** The sagging part of a fishnet. [Origin unknown]

bunt³ (bunt) *n.* **1.** A parasitic fungus (*Tilletia foetens*), a species of smut that converts grains of wheat into a fetid black powder. **2.** The disease caused by this fungus: also called *stinking smut.* [Origin unknown]

bunt·ing¹ (bun'ting) *n.* **1.** A light woolen stuff or cotton fabric used for flags, etc. **2.** Flags, banners, etc., collectively. **3.** A type of sleeping bag for infants. [? ME *bonten* to sift]

bunt·ing² (bun'ting) *n.* One of various birds related to the finches and sparrows, as the indigo bunting, reed bunting, and snow bunting. [ME *bountyng*; origin unknown]

bunt·line (bunt'lin, -lin') *n. Naut.* A rope used in hauling a square sail up to the yard for furling.

bun·ya-bun·ya (bun'ya-bun'ya) *n.* An evergreen tree of Australia (*Araucaria bidwillii*), of the pine family, having edible seeds. Also **bun'ya, bun'ya pine.** [< native name]

Bun·yan (bun'yən), **John,** 1628–88, English preacher and author of *Pilgrim's Progress.* **— Paul** See PAUL BUNYAN.

Buo·na·par·te (bwô'nä·pär'tä) See BONAPARTE.

Buo·nar·ro·ti (bwô'när·rô'tē) See MICHELANGELO.

buoy (boi, boo'ē) *n.* **1.** *Naut.* A warning float moored on a dangerous rock or shoal or at the edge of a channel. Many are named according to shape or function: **can buoy** (cylindrical); **nun buoy** (conical); **spar buoy** (a spar anchored at one end); or from the way in which their presence is indicated: **bell buoy, light buoy, whistling buoy. 2.** A device for keeping a person afloat; a life buoy. Compare BREECHES BUOY. **—** *v.t.* **1.** To keep from sinking in a liquid; keep afloat. **2.** To sustain the courage or heart of; encourage: usually with *up.* **3.** *Naut.* To mark with buoys. [< MDu. *boeie* or OF *boye* < L *boia* fetter; because it is chained to one spot]

BUOYS (*def.* 1)
a Nun. *b* Can. *c* Spar. *d* Bell.
e Whistling. *f* Gas-lighted

buoy·age (boi'ij, boo'ē·ij) *n. Naut.* **1.** Buoys collectively. **2.** A system of buoys.

buoy·an·cy (boi'ən·sē, boo'yən·sē) *n.* **1.** The tendency or ability to keep afloat. **2.** The power of a fluid to keep an object afloat. **3.** The upward pressure of fluid on an immersed or floating body. **4.** Elasticity of spirits; cheerfulness. Also **buoy'ance.**

buoy·ant (boi'ənt, boo'yənt) *adj.* Having or exhibiting buoyancy in any sense: a *buoyant* boat; *buoyant* spirits. [Prob. < Sp. *boyante* < *boyar* to float] **— buoy'ant·ly** *adv.*

bu·pres·tid (byoo·pres'tid) *n.* Any of a family (*Buprestidae*) of brilliantly colored beetles whose larvae are destructive woodborers. [< L *buprestis* < Gk. *bouprēstis* < *bous* ox + *prēthein* to swell]

bur¹ (bûr) *n.* **1.** *Bot.* A rough or prickly flower head or seedcase, as of the chestnut and burdock. **2.** A plant that bears burs. **3.** A person or thing that clings like a bur. **—** *v.t.* **burred, bur·ring** To remove burs from, as wool. Also spelled *burr.* [< Scand. Cf. Dan. *borre* bur.]

bur² (bûr) See BURR².

bu·ran (boo·rän') *n.* A violent windstorm of Siberia and the Russian steppes, a hot duststorm in summer and a snowstorm in winter. Also **bu·ra** (boo·rä'). [< Russian *buranu*]

Bur·bage (bûr'bij), **Richard,** 1567?–1619, English actor; associate of Shakespeare.

Bur·bank (bûr'bangk) A city in SW California; pop. 88,871.

Bur·bank (bûr'bangk), **Luther,** 1849–1926, U.S. horticulturist.

Bur·ber·ry (bûr'bər·ē, -ber'ē) *n. pl.* **·ries** An outer coat, especially a raincoat: a trade name.

bur·ble (bûr'bəl) *v.i.* **·bled, ·bling 1.** To bubble; gurgle. **2.** To talk excitedly and confusedly. **—** *n. Aeron.* A turbulence in the boundary layer of an airfoil. [ME; imit.]

bur·bot (bûr'bət) *n. pl.* **·bot** A fresh-water fish (*Lota lota*) of the northern hemisphere, with barbels on the nose and chin: also called *cusk, eelpout, lawyer, ling.* [< F *bourbotte,* blend of *bourbe* mud and *barbote,* ult. < L *barbata* bearded]

burd (bûrd) *n. Poetic* A maiden. Also **burd·ie** (bûr'dē). [ME *burde*; origin uncertain]

bur·den[1] (bûr′dən) *n.* **1.** Something carried; a load. **2.** Something that weighs heavily, as responsibility or anxiety. **3.** *Naut.* **a** The carrying capacity of a vessel. **b** The weight of the cargo. **4.** The carrying of loads: beasts of *burden.* — *v.t.* To load or overload; oppress, as with care. Also, *Archaic,* *burthen.* [OE *byrthen* load]

bur·den[2] (bûr′dən) *n.* **1.** Something often repeated or dwelt upon; the prevailing idea: the *burden* of a speech. **2.** A refrain of a song. **3.** The drone of a bagpipe. [< F *bourdon* bass < LL *burdo* drone. Doublet of BOURDON.]

burden of proof The obligation to prove a controversial or contested point, as in an argument or an action at law.

bur·den·some (bûr′dən·səm) *adj.* Hard or heavy to bear; oppressive. — **bur′den·some·ly** *adv.* — **bur′den·some·ness** *n.* — **Syn.** heavy, onerous, cumbersome, troublesome.

bur·dock (bûr′dok) *n.* A coarse, biennial weed (*Arctium lappa*) of the composite family, with a globular bur and large roundish leaves: also called *cocklebur.* [< BUR[1] + DOCK[4]]

bu·reau (byŏŏr′ō) *n.* *pl.* **bu·reaus** or **bu·reaux** (byŏŏr′ōz) **1.** *U.S.* A chest of drawers for clothing, etc., usually with a mirror. **2.** A government department. **3.** An office for transacting business: a travel *bureau.* **4.** *Brit.* A writing desk or table with drawers. *Abbr.* bu, by. [< F, a desk, formerly cloth-covered < OF *burel* coarse woolen cloth]

bu·reauc·ra·cy (byŏŏ·rok′rə·sē) *n.* *pl.* **·cies** **1.** Government by bureaus; also, the group of officials so governing. **2.** The undue extension of bureaus in the departments of a government, or the use by them of undue influence and authority. **3.** Rigid adherence to administrative routine; government red tape. [< F *bureaucratie* < *bureau* office, bureau + Gk. *kratia* power, rule]

bu·reau·crat (byŏŏr′ə·krat) *n.* **1.** A member of a bureaucracy. **2.** An official who narrowly and arbitrarily adheres to a rigid routine. — **bu·reau·crat′ic** or **·i·cal** *adj.*

bu·rette (byŏŏ·ret′) *n.* *Chem.* A finely graduated glass tube with a stopcock at the bottom. Also **bu·ret′.** [< F, dim. of *buire* a vase, vial]

burg (bûrg) *n.* **1.** *U.S. Informal* A town; city; especially, a small, quiet rural town. **2.** *Archaic* A fortified town. [OE *burg.* Akin to BOROUGH.]

bur·gage (bûr′gij) *n.* **1.** In feudal law, a tenure by which houses and lands in a borough were held of the lord at a yearly rent. **2.** *Scot.* A tenure by which property in royal burgs is held of the king for the nominal service of watching and warding. [< Med.L *burgagium* < *burgus* town < Gmc.]

Bur·gas (bŏŏr′gäs′) A port city in SE Bulgaria, on the **Gulf of Burgas,** an inlet of the Black Sea; pop. 122,212 (1968).

bur·gee (bûr′jē) *n. Naut.* A triangular or swallow-tailed pennant flown for identification. [Origin unknown]

Bur·gen·land (bŏŏr′gən·länt) A Province of eastern Austria; 1,531 sq. mi.; pop. 270,895 (1961); capital, Eisenstadt.

bur·geon (bûr′jən) *v.i.* **1.** To flourish; grow. **2.** To bud; sprout. — *v.t.* **3.** To put forth (buds, etc.). [< n.] — *n.* A bud; sprout. Also spelled *bourgeon.* [< OF *burjon*]

burg·er (bûr′gər) *n.* A hamburger (def. 2): often used in combination: *cheeseburger.* [Shortened from HAMBURGER]

Bur·ger (bûr′gər) **Warren Earl,** born 1907, U.S. jurist; chief justice of the Supreme Court 1969–.

bur·gess (bûr′jis) *n.* **1.** A freeman, citizen, or officer of a borough or burg. **2.** In colonial times, a member of the lower house (**House of Burgesses**) of the legislature of Virginia: now called *delegate.* **3.** *Brit.* Formerly, a member of Parliament for a borough or university. [< OF *burgeis.* Doublet of BOURGEOIS[1].] — **bur′gess-ship** *n.*

Bur·gess (bûr′jis), **(Frank) Gelett,** 1866–1951, U.S. humorist and illustrator.

burgh (bûrg, *Scot.* bûr′ō, -ə) *n.* **1.** In Scottish law, a chartered town; borough. **2.** *Archaic* A castle or fortified place. [Var. of BOROUGH] — **burgh·al** (bûr′gəl) *adj.*

burgh·er (bûr′gər) *n.* A citizen of a burgh, town, or city. [< Du. *burger* < *burg* town. Akin to BURGESS.]

Burgh·ley (bûr′lē), **Lord** See (William) CECIL. Also **Bur·leigh.**

bur·glar (bûr′glər) *n.* One who commits burglary. [< Med.L *burglator,* ? < OF *bourg* dwelling (< Gmc.) + *laire* robbery < L *latro* robber]

bur·glar·i·ous (bər·glâr′ē·əs) *adj.* Relating to, involving, or given to burglary. — **bur·glar′i·ous·ly** *adv.*

bur·glar·ize (bûr′glə·rīz) *v.t.* **·ized, ·iz·ing** To commit burglary upon.

bur·gla·ry (bûr′glər·ē) *n.* *pl.* **·ries** *Law* The breaking and entering of a dwelling by another, at night, with intent to commit a crime therein, extended by statute in some States to the breaking and entering of any building at any time with intent to commit a crime therein. — **Syn.** See THEFT.

bur·gle (bûr′gəl) *v.t. & v.i.* **·gled, ·gling** *Informal* To commit burglary (upon). [Back formation < BURGLAR]

bur·go·mas·ter (bûr′gə·mas′tər, -mäs′-) *n.* **1.** A Dutch, Flemish, German, or Austrian municipal magistrate; a mayor. **2.** A large arctic gull (*Larus hyperboreus*): also called *glaucous gull.* [< Du. *burgemeester*]

bur·go·net (bûr′gə·net) *n.* A light, open helmet of the 16th century. [< OF *bourguignotte* Burgundian < *Bourgogne* Burgundy, where first used]

bur·goo (bûr′gŏō, bər·gŏō′) *n.* *pl.* **·goos** **1.** Oatmeal porridge or mush formerly served at sea. **2.** *U.S. Dial.* A thick, highly seasoned meat and vegetable soup; also, an outdoor feast at which this is served. Also **bur′gout** (-gŏō). [Cf. Turkish *burghul* porridge]

Bur·gos (bŏŏr′gōs) A Province of northern Spain; 5,532 sq. mi.; pop. 380,791 (1960); capital, **Burgos,** pop. 82,177.

Bur·goyne (bər·goin′), **John,** 1722–92, British general in the American Revolution.

bur·grave (bûr′grāv) *n.* In German history, the governor of a town, or, later, the hereditary lord of a town and its domain. [< G *burg* town + *graf* count]

Bur·gun·dy (bûr′gən·dē) *n.* *pl.* **·dies** A kind of red or white wine originally made in Burgundy.

Bur·gun·dy (bûr′gən·dē) A region of east central France; formerly a kingdom, duchy, and province: French *Bourgogne.* — **Bur·gun·di·an** (bər·gun′dē·ən) *adj. & n.*

Burgundy, Free County of See FRANCHE-COMTÉ.

bur·i·al (ber′ē·əl) *n.* The burying of a dead body; interment; sepulture. — *adj.* Of or pertaining to burial. [ME *buryel, biriel* < *biriels* (mistaken as plural) < OE *brygels* tomb]

bu·rin (byŏŏr′in) *n.* **1.** A steel tool with a lozenge-shaped point for engraving or carving. **2.** The style or manner of execution of an engraver. [< F]

BURINS
For: *a* wood, *b* copper or stone, *c* steel, *d* use by mechanics.

burke (bûrk) *v.t.* **burked, burk·ing** **1.** To murder by suffocating. **2.** To suppress quietly. [after William Burke, 1792–1829, Irish murderer who sold his bodies for dissection]

Burke (bûrk), **Edmund,** 1729–97, British statesman, writer, and orator born in Ireland.

burl (bûrl) *n.* **1.** A knot or lump in wool or cloth. **2.** A large, wartlike excrescence formed on the trunks of trees. **3.** A veneer made from such excrescences: also **burl/wood veneer** (bûrl′wŏŏd′). — *v.t.* To dress (cloth) by removing burls, loose thread, etc. [< OF *bourle* tuft of wool < LL *burra* shaggy hair] — **burled** *adj.* — **burl′er** *n.*

bur·lap (bûr′lap) *n.* A coarse fabric made of jute, flax, hemp, or cotton, used for wrapping, bagging, etc. [Origin uncertain]

bur·lesque (bər·lesk′) *n.* **1.** A literary or dramatic composition that provokes laughter by grotesque satire or ludicrous imitation, usually of a serious, dignified subject. **2.** Any ludicrous imitation or caricature; travesty. **3.** *U.S.* A theatrical entertainment marked by low comedy, striptease, etc. — **Syn.** See CARICATURE. — *adj.* **1.** Marked by ridiculous incongruity or broad caricature. **2.** *U.S.* Of or pertaining to theatrical burlesque. — *v.* **·lesqued, ·les·quing** *v.t.* **1.** To represent laughably; travesty: to *burlesque* the rhetorical excesses of some politicians. — *v.i.* **2.** To use broad caricature. [< F < Ital. *burlesco* < *burla* joke] — **bur·les′quer** *n.*

bur·ley (bûr′lē) *n.* A fine, light tobacco grown principally in Kentucky. Also **Bur′ley.** [? after *Burley,* a grower]

Bur·ling·ton (bûr′ling·tən) **1.** A city in NW Vermont, on Lake Champlain; the largest city in the state; pop. 38,633. **2.** A city in north central North Carolina; pop. 35,930. **3.** A city in SE Iowa, on the Mississippi River; pop. 32,366.

bur·ly[1] (bûr′lē) *adj.* **·li·er, ·li·est** Large of body; bulky; stout; lusty. [ME *borlich;* origin unknown] — **bur′li·ly** *adv.*

bur·ly[2] (bûr′lē) *adj.* Having burls or knots, as a tree.

Bur·ma (bûr′mə) An independent State in SE Asia, between Bangladesh and Thailand; 261,789 sq. mi.; pop. 27,000,000 (est. 1969); capital, Rangoon; often divided into **Lower Burma,** the coastal districts, and **Upper Burma,** the inland districts. Officially **Union of Burma.**

bur marigold An herb of the composite family (genus *Bidens*) having barbed, clinging awns: also called *agrimony, beggar-ticks, sticktight.*

Burma Road The road from northern Burma to Yünnan Province, China, completed in 1938 and vital as a supply route during World War II.

Bur·mese (bər·mēz′, -mēs′) *adj.* Of or pertaining to Burma, its inhabitants, or their language. Also **Bur′man** (-mən). — *n.* *pl.* **·mese** **1.** A native or inhabitant of Burma. **2.** The Sino-Tibetan language of Burma.

burn[1] (bûrn) *v.* **burned** or **burnt, burn·ing** *v.t.* **1.** To destroy or consume by fire. **2.** To set afire; ignite. **3.** To injure or kill by fire; execute by fire. **4.** To injure or damage by friction, heat, steam, etc.; scald; wither. **5.** To produce by fire: to *burn* a hole in a suit. **6.** To brand; also, to cauterize. **7.** To finish or harden by intense heat; fire. **8.** To use or employ, so as to give off light, heat, etc.: to *burn* a candle. **9.** To cause a feeling of heat in: The pepper *burned* his tongue. **10.** To sunburn. **11.** *Chem.* To cause to undergo combustion. **12.** *U.S. Slang* To electrocute. **13.** *U.S. Slang* To cheat. — *v.i.* **14.** To be on fire; blaze. **15.** To be destroyed or scorched by fire; undergo change by fire. **16.** To give off light, heat, etc.; shine. **17.** To die by fire. **18.** To appear or feel hot: He *burns* with fever. **19.** To be eager, excited, or inflamed: to *burn* with love. **20.** *Chem.* To oxidize; undergo combustion. **21.** *U.S. Slang* To be electrocuted. **— to burn down** To raze or be razed by fire. **— to burn out 1.** To become extinguished through lack of fuel. **2.** To destroy or wear out by heat, friction, etc. **3.** To burn up the house, store, or property of. **4.** To drive out by heat. **— to burn the candle at both ends** To exhaust one's strength by overwork or dissipation. **— to burn up 1.** To consume by fire. **2.** *Slang* To make or become irritated or enraged. **— n. 1.** An effect or injury from burning; a burned place. **2.** *Pathol.* A lesion caused by heat, extreme cold, corrosive chemicals, gases, electricity, radiation, etc. In the order of increasing severity, a **first-degree burn** produces redness; a **second-degree burn**, blistering; a **third-degree burn**, destruction of the entire skin with charring of the tissue. **3.** The process or result of burning: a good *burn* of bricks. [Fusion of OE *beornan* to be on fire, and OE *bærnan* to set afire] **— Syn.** (verb) **1.** incinerate, cremate. **4.** *Burn, scorch, singe, char,* and *scald* mean to injure by heat. *Burn* is of the widest sense, and may refer to flame, steam, radiant heat, friction, acid, etc., and the injury may be superficial or deep. *Scorch* and *singe* refer to superficial injuries, usually by an open flame or hot metal. *Char* means to reduce to carbon in whole or part, by flame or heat. *Scald* means to *burn* by a very hot liquid or steam.

burn² (bûrn) *n. Scot.* A brook or rivulet: also spelled *bourn, bourne.*

Burne-Jones (bûrn′jōnz′), **Sir Edward Coley,** 1833–98, English painter.

burn·er (bûr′nər) *n.* **1.** One who or that which burns. **2.** That part of a stove, lamp, etc., from which the flame comes.

burn·et (bûr′nit) *n.* Any of several perennial herbs (genus *Sanguisorba*) of the rose family, with alternate, pinnate leaves and small flowers in a spike. [Var. of BRUNETTE]

Bur·nett (bər·net′), **Frances Hodgson,** 1849–1924, U.S. novelist.

Bur·ney (bûr′nē), **Fanny,** 1752–1840, Madame d'Arblay, English novelist: original name **Frances Burney.**

bur·nie (bûr′nē) *n. Scot.* A little burn; brooklet.

burn·ing (bûr′ning) *adj.* **1.** Consuming or being consumed by or as if by fire. **2.** Causing intense feeling; exciting; urgent: a *burning* question.

burning bush Any of various plants, as the wahoo or fraxinella.

burning glass A convex lens for concentrating the sun's rays upon an object so as to heat or ignite it: also called *sunglass.*

bur·nish (bûr′nish) *v.t. & v.i.* To polish by friction; make or become shiny. **— n.** Polish; luster. [< OF *burniss-,* stem of *burnir* to polish] **— bur′nish·ment** *n.*

bur·nish·er (bûr′nish·ər) *n.* **1.** One who burnishes. **2.** A tool for burnishing or smoothing, usually having a smooth, rounded head.

Burn·ley (bûrn′lē) A county borough in eastern Lancashire, England; pop. 76,610 (est. 1969).

bur·noose (bər·nōōs′, bûr′nōōs) *n.* An Arab hooded cloak. Also **bur·nous′.** [< F *burnous* < Arabic *burnus*]

burn·out (bûrn′out′) *n.* **1.** A destruction or failure due to burning or to excessive heat. **2.** *Aerospace* The cessation of burning in a jet or rocket engine, especially when caused by stoppage or exhaustion of fuel; also, the time at which the cessation occurs. Compare BRENNSCHLUSS, FLAMEOUT.

Burns (bûrnz), **Robert,** 1759–96, Scottish poet.

burn·sides (bûrn′sīdz) *n.pl.* Side whiskers and mustache: also called *sideburns.* [after A. E. *Burnside,* 1824–81, Union general in the Civil War]

burnt (bûrnt) Alternative past tense and past participle of BURN¹. **— adj. 1.** Affected or consumed by fire; charred. **2.** Diseased, as grain.

burnt ocher A permanent, brick red pigment.

burnt offering An animal, food, etc., burned upon an altar as a sacrifice or offering to a god.

burnt orange A shade of light orange, with a brownish cast.

burnt sienna A dark brown pigment made by calcining raw sienna.

burnt umber A reddish brown pigment made by calcining raw umber.

burp (bûrp) *U.S. Informal n.* A belch. **— v.i.** To belch. **— v.t.** To cause to belch: to *burp* a baby. [Imit.]

burr¹ (bûr) *n.* **1.** A roughness or rough edge, especially one left on metal in casting or cutting. **2.** Any of several tools for cutting, reaming, etc. **3.** A dentist's drill with a rough head: also **burr drill. 4.** A protuberant knot or excrescence on a tree. **5.** A halo around the moon or a star. **6.** A washer slipped upon the end of a rivet before swaging. **7.** A blank punched out of a sheet of metal. **8.** A hard lump of rock embedded in a vein of softer material. **— v.t. 1.** To form a rough edge on. **2.** To remove a rough edge from. Also spelled *bur.* [Var. of BUR¹] **— bur′ry** *adj.*

burr² (bûr) *n.* **1.** A rough guttural sound of *r* produced by vibration of the uvula against the back of the tongue, common in the north of England and Scotland. **2.** Any rough, dialectal pronunciation: the Scottish *burr.* **3.** A whirring sound; a buzz. **— v.i. 1.** To pronounce with a rough or gut-

tural articulation. **— v.i. 2.** To speak with a burr. **3.** To whir. Also spelled *bur.* [Imit.]

Burr (bûr), **Aaron,** 1756–1836, American lawyer and statesman; vice president of the United States 1801–05.

bur reed An herb (genus *Sparganium*), with ribbon-shaped leaves and spherical, burlike fruit.

bur·ro (bûr′ō, bōōr′ō) *n. pl.* **·ros** A small donkey. [< Sp.]

Bur·roughs (bûr′ōz), **John,** 1837–1921, U.S. naturalist.

bur·row (bûr′ō) *n.* **1.** A hole made in the ground, as by a rabbit, for habitation and refuge. **2.** Any similar place of refuge or retreat. **— v.i. 1.** To live or hide in a burrow. **2.** To dig a burrow or burrows. **3.** To dig into, under, or through something. **— v.t. 4.** To dig a burrow or burrows in. **5.** To make by burrowing. **6.** To hide (oneself) in a burrow. [ME *borow.* Akin to BOROUGH.] **— bur′row·er** *n.*

burrowing owl A small, chiefly terrestrial owl (*Speotyto cunicularia*) of southern and western North America, nesting in holes or burrows in open country: also called *ground owl.*

burr·stone (bûr′stōn′) *n.* A cellular, compact siliceous rock used for millstones: also spelled *buhrstone, burstone.*

bur·sa (bûr′sə) *n. pl.* **·sae** (-sē) or **·sas 1.** *Anat.* A pouch or saclike cavity; especially, one containing synovia and located at points of friction in the bodies of vertebrates. **2.** *Pathol.* A cyst or abnormal sac. [< Med.L, sac, pouch]

Bur·sa (bōōr′sä) A Province of NW Turkey, in Asia; 3,845 sq. mi.; pop. 659,099 (1960); capital, **Bursa,** pop. 153,574; ancient *Prusa.* Also *Brusa.*

bur·sal (bûr′səl) *adj.* Of or pertaining to a bursa.

bur·sar (bûr′sər, -sär) *n.* A business officer in the administration of a college, university, etc.; treasurer. [< Med.L *bursarius* treasurer < *bursa* bag, purse]

bur·sar·i·al (bər·sâr′ē·əl) *adj.* Relating to a bursar or bursary.

bur·sa·ry (bûr′sər·ē) *n. pl.* **·ries 1.** The treasury of a public institution or a religious order. **2.** *Scot.* An endowment for a student or pupil.

Bur·schen·schaft (bōōr′shən·shäft′) *n. pl.* **·schaf·ten** (-shäf′tən) *German* A students' association, especially one operated as a social organization; a fraternity.

burse (bûrs) *n.* **1.** A purse. **2.** *Eccl.* A lined case used to hold the corporal. **3.** *Scot.* A bursary. **4.** *Obs.* A bourse. [< F *bourse* < Med.L *bursa* wallet < Gk. *byrsa* hide. Doublet of PURSE.]

bur·seed (bûr′sēd′) *n.* An Old World stickseed (*Lappula echinata*), naturalized in northern North America.

bur·ser·a·ceous (bûr′sə·rā′shəs) *adj. Bot.* Designating or belonging to a small family (*Burseraceae*) of tropical balsamiferous trees or shrubs with alternate compound leaves. [< NL *Burseraceae,* after J. *Burser,* 1603–89, German botanist]

bur·si·form (bûr′sə·fôrm) *adj.* Pouch-shaped; saclike. [< NL *bursiformis* < Med.L *bursa* bag + *forma* shape]

bur·si·tis (bər·sī′tis) *n. Pathol.* Inflammation of a bursa. [< NL]

burst (bûrst) *v.* **burst, burst·ing** *v.i.* **1.** To break open or apart suddenly and violently; explode, as from internal force. **2.** To be full to the point of breaking open; bulge. **3.** To appear, issue forth or enter suddenly or violently. **4.** To become audible or evident: A sound *burst* upon their ears. **5.** To give sudden expression to passion, grief, etc.: to *burst* into tears; also, to be filled with violent emotion: to *burst* with rage. **— v.t. 6.** To cause to break open suddenly or violently; force open; puncture. **7.** To fill or cause to swell to the point of breaking open. **— Syn.** See BREAK. **— n. 1.** A sudden exploding or breaking forth. **2.** A sudden effort or spurt; rush: a *burst* of speed. **3.** The result of bursting; a crack or break. **4.** *Mil.* **a** The explosion of a bomb or shell on impact or in the air. **b** The number of bullets fired by one pressure on the trigger of an automatic weapon. [OE *berstan*] **— burst′er** *n.*

bur·stone (bûr′stōn′) See BURRSTONE.

bur·then (bûr′thən) See BURDEN¹.

bur·ton (bûr′tən) *n. Naut.* A light hoisting tackle, usually having a single and a double block. [Origin uncertain]

Bur·ton (bûr′tən), **Harold Hitz,** 1888–1964, U.S. jurist; associate justice of the Supreme Court 1945–58. **— Sir Richard Francis,** 1821–1890, English traveler and writer. **— Robert,** 1577–1640, English scholar, author, and clergyman.

Bur·ton-up·on-Trent (bûr′tən·ə·pon′trent′) A county borough in eastern Staffordshire, England; pop. 50,766 (1961). Also **Bur′ton-on′-Trent′.**

Bu·run·di (bōō·rōōn′dē) A Republic in central Africa; formerly the southern part of the UN Trust Territory of Ruanda-Urundi; 10,747 sq. mi.; pop. 3,475,000 (1969); capital, Bujumbura. See **Rwanda.**

bur·weed (bûr′wēd′) *n.* Any of various weeds bearing burlike fruits, as the burdock.

bur·y (ber′ē) *v.t.* **bur·ied, bur·y·ing 1.** To put (a dead body) in a grave, tomb, or the sea; perform burial rites for; inter. **2.** To cover over and thereby conceal. **3.** To deluge or swamp, as by a wave: *buried* under a flood of offers. **4.** To embed; sink: to *bury* a nail in a wall. **5.** To put out of mind;

forget: to *bury* a grudge. **6.** To occupy deeply; engross: He *buried* himself in study. [OE *byrgan*]

burying beetle The sexton (def. 2).

burying ground A cemetery.

bus (bus) *n. pl.* **bus·es** or **bus·ses 1.** A large passenger vehicle sometimes with two decks: also, *Archaic, omnibus.* **2.** *Informal* An automobile. — *v.t.* **bused** or **bussed, bus·ing** or **bus·sing 1.** To transport by bus. — *v.i.* **2.** To go by bus. **3.** *Informal* To do the work of a bus boy. [Short form of OMNIBUS]

bus bar *Electr.* A bar of copper or aluminum forming a connection between circuits: also called *omnibus bar.*

bus boy An employee in a restaurant who clears tables of soiled dishes, assists the waiters, etc.

bus·by (buz′bē) *n. pl.* **·bies** A tall fur cap worn as part of the full-dress uniform of British hussars, artillerymen, and engineers. [Origin uncertain]

BUSBY

bush[1] (boŏsh) *n.* **1.** A low, treelike or thickly branching shrub. **2.** A clump of shrubs; thicket; undergrowth. **3.** Wild, uncleared land covered with scrub; also, any rural or unsettled area: usually preceded by *the.* **4.** A fox's tail. **5.** *Canadian* Wood lot. **6.** Formerly, a bough used as a sign for a tavern; also, the tavern. — *v.i.* **1.** To grow or branch like a bush. **2.** To be or become bushy. — *v.t.* **3.** To protect (plants) with bushes set round about; support with bushes. [< ON *buskr*]

bush[2] (boŏsh) *v.t.* To line with a bushing, as a bearing, pivot hole, etc. — *n.* A bushing. [< MDu. *busse* box]

Bush (boŏsh), **Vannevar,** born 1890, U.S. electrical engineer.

bush·buck (boŏsh′buk′) *n.* A small South African forest antelope (*Tragelaphus sylvaticus*): also *boschbok, boshbok, harnessed antelope.* Also **bush′goat′.** [Trans. of Du. *boschbok*]

bush clover A North American plant (*Lespedeza capitata*) with an erect, simple, woolly stem.

bush cranberry The guelder-rose.

bushed (boŏsht) *adj. Informal* **1.** *U.S. & Canadian* Exhausted. **2.** *Austral.* Lost; confused. [< BUSH[1]]

bush·el[1] (boŏsh′əl) *n.* **1.** A unit of dry measure containing 2150.42 cubic inches (four pecks or 32 quarts). **2.** A container holding this amount. **3.** A weight considered as equal to the weight of a bushel. Abbr. *bsh., bu, bu.* See table inside back cover. [< OF *boissiel*, dim. of *boisse* box]

bush·el[2] (boŏsh′əl) *v.t. & v.i.* **bush·eled** or **·elled, bush·el·ing** or **·el·ling** *U.S.* To repair and restore (a garment). [Cf. G *bosseln* to do small jobs] — **bush′el·er** or **bush′el·ler, bush′·el·man** (-mən) *n.*

bush honeysuckle Any of various shrubs (genus *Diervilla*) having opposite leaves and reddish yellow flowers.

bu·shi·do (boŏ′shē-dō) *n.* The code of the Samurai, prescribing rigorous military training and practice, severe self-discipline, personal honor, and loyalty to superiors and country. Also **Bu′shi·do.** [< Japanese, way of the warrior]

bush·ing (boŏsh′ing) *n.* **1.** *Mech.* **a** A metallic lining for a hole, as in the hub of a wheel, designed to insulate or to prevent abrasion between parts. **b** A tube for insertion in a pump barrel or a pulley bore to reduce the diameter. Also *ferrule.* **2.** *Electr.* A lining inserted in a socket to insulate an electric current. [< BUSH[2]]

bush·land (boŏsh′land′) *n. Canadian* Unsettled northern forest land; bush (def. 3).

bush league In baseball slang, an obscure minor league.

bush leaguer 1. In baseball slang, a player in a bush league. **2.** *U.S. Slang* A mediocre person.

bush line *Canadian* An airline in the bushland.

bush lot *Canadian* Wood lot (which see).

Bush·man (boŏsh′mən) *n. pl.* **·men** (-mən) **1.** One of a nomadic people of South Africa, considered to be related to the Pygmies. **2.** The language of the Bushmen, forming with Hottentot the Khoisan family of African languages. [Trans. of Du. *boschjesman*]

bush·mas·ter (boŏsh′mas′tər, -mäs′) *n.* A very venomous pit viper (*Lachesis mutus*) of Central and tropical South America, sometimes attaining a length of 12 feet.

bush partridge *Canadian* The spruce grouse. See under GROUSE[1].

bush pig The boschvark.

bush·rang·er (boŏsh′rān′jər) *n.* **1.** One living in the bush. **2.** *Austral.* A robber; originally, one living in the bush.

bush·whack (boŏsh′hwak′) *U.S. v.t.* **1.** To attack or fire upon from hiding; ambush. — *v.i.* **2.** To range through the bush; fight as a guerrilla. [< Du. *boschwachter* forest keeper; infl. by *whack*] — **bush′whack′ing** *n.*

bush·whack·er (boŏsh′hwak′ər) *n.* **1.** *U.S.* **a** One who ranges through the bush. **b** A Confederate guerrilla. **c** Any guerrilla. **2.** *Austral.* A dweller or worker in the bush.

bush·y (boŏsh′ē) *adj.* **bush·i·er, bush·i·est 1.** Covered with or full of bushes. **2.** Like a bush; shaggy. — **bush′i·ly** *adv.* — **bush′i·ness** *n.*

bus·ied (biz′ēd) Past tense and past participle of BUSY.

bus·i·ly (biz′ə·lē) *adv.* In a busy manner; industriously.

busi·ness (biz′nis; biz′ē·nis *for def. 10*) *n.* **1.** An occupation, trade, or profession. **2.** Any of the various operations or details of trade or industry. **3.** A commercial enterprise or establishment engaged in such operations; a firm, factory, store, etc. **4.** The amount or volume of trade: *Business* is good. **5.** Commercial procedure or policy: Courtesy is good *business.* **6.** A proper interest or concern; responsibility; duty: It is his *business* to examine us. **7.** Work; employment; serious pursuits: *Business* before pleasure. **8.** A matter or affair: a strange *business.* **9.** In the theater, the movements, facial expressions, etc., apart from dialogue, by which actors interpret a part. **10.** *Obs.* Busyness. — **Syn.** See OCCUPATION. — **to give (someone) the business** *Slang* **1.** To deal with harshly or summarily. **2.** To beat severely or kill. **3.** To cheat or defraud. — **to have no business** To have no right (to do something). — **to mean business** *Informal* To have a serious intention. [OE *bysignis*]

business card A card printed with one's name, business, telephone number, and business address.

business college A school that gives training in clerical and secretarial skills: also called *commercial college.*

busi·ness·like (biz′nis·līk′) *adj.* Methodical or systematic, as in matters of business; practical.

busi·ness·man (biz′nis·man′) *n. pl.* **·men** (-men′) One engaged in commercial or industrial activity. — **busi′ness·wom′an** (-woŏm′an) *n.fem.*

bus·ing (bus′ing) *n. U.S.* The practice of transporting children to attend schools away from their home neighborhoods, now commonly associated with establishing a balanced ratio among the races in a community. Also **bus′sing.**

busk[1] (busk) *n.* **1.** A thin, elastic strip of wood, whalebone, etc., placed in a corset or the front. **2.** *Dial.* A corset. [< F *busc,* ? < LL *boscum* bush, wood]

busk[2] (busk) *v.t. Scot.* or *Obs.* **1.** To dress. **2.** To prepare· [< ON *būask* to get ready] — **busk′er** *n.*

bus·kin (bus′kin) *n.* **1.** A high shoe or half boot reaching halfway to the knee, and strapped or laced to the ankle. **2.** A laced half boot, worn by Greek and Roman tragic actors; also called *cothurnus.* **3.** Tragedy. Compare SOCK[1]. [Origin uncertain]

bus·kined (bus′kind) *adj.* **1.** Wearing buskins. **2.** Of or pertaining to tragedy; tragic; lofty.

bus·man (bus′mən) *n. pl.* **men** (-mən) One who operates a bus.

BUSKIN
(def. 2)

busman's holiday A holiday spent by choice in activity similar to one's regular work.

Bus·ra (bus′rə), **Bus·rah** See BASRA.

buss[1] (bus) *Archaic & Dial. n.* A kiss; smack. — *v.t. & v.i.* To kiss heartily. [Imit. Cf. dial. G *bussen.*]

buss[2] (boŏs, boŏs) *n. Scot.* A bush.

bus·ses (bus′iz) Alternative plural of BUS.

bust[1] (bust) *n.* **1.** The human chest or breast, especially the bosom of a woman. **2.** A piece of statuary representing the human head, shoulders, and breast. [< F *buste* < Ital. *busto* trunk of the body]

bust[2] (bust) *Slang v.t.* **1.** To burst: also an illiterate usage. **2.** To tame; train, as a horse. **3.** To make bankrupt or short of funds. **4.** To reduce in rank; demote. **5.** To hit; strike. **6.** *Slang* To arrest or take into custody. — *v.i.* **7.** To burst: also an illiterate usage. **8.** To become bankrupt or short of funds. — *n.* **1.** Failure; bankruptcy. **2.** A spree. **3.** A blow. **4.** *Slang* An arrest. [Alter. of BURST]

bus·tard (bus′tərd) *n.* Any member of a family (*Otididae*) of large Old World game birds related to the plovers and cranes, especially the European **great bustard** (*Otis tarda*). [< OF *bistarde, oustarde* < L *avis tarda,* lit., slow bird]

bust·er (bus′tər) *n.* **1.** *U.S. Slang* One who breaks or breaks up: *broncobuster;* trust *buster.* **2.** *Slang* **a** Something great or remarkable. **b** A spree. **3.** *U.S. Informal* Little boy: used in direct address. — **southerly buster** *Austral.* A powerful southerly wind.

bus·tic (bus′tik) *n.* A tree (*Dipholis salicifolia*) of southern Florida, with very hard wood. [Origin unknown]

bus·tle[1] (bus′əl) *n.* Excited activity; noisy stir; fuss. — *v.* **·tled, ·tling** *v.i.* **1.** To move noisily or energetically; hurry. — *v.t.* **2.** To cause to hurry. [? Akin to BUSK[2]]

bus·tle[2] (bus′əl) *n.* **1.** A large bow, peplum, or gathering of material, worn over the back of a skirt below the waist. **2.** A frame or pad formerly worn by women on the back of the body below the waist to distend the skirt. [? < BUSTLE[1]]

bus·tling (bus′ling) *adj.* Active; busy. — **bus′tling·ly** *adv.*

bus·y (biz′ē) *adj.* **bus·i·er, bus·i·est 1.** Actively engaged in something; occupied. **2.** Filled with activity; never still: a *busy* day; *busy* hands. **3.** Officiously active; meddling; prying. **4.** Temporarily engaged, as a telephone line. — *v.t.* **bus·ied, bus·y·ing** To make busy; occupy (oneself). [OE *bysig* active] — **Syn.** (adj.) **1.** *Busy, industrious, diligent,* and *assiduous* mean active in work. *Busy* refers to sustained activity, which may be temporary; the other terms describe habits. The *industrious* man is disposed to work regularly and steadily; the *diligent* man applies himself thoroughly to a particular task. *Assiduous* describes the man who is patient and unremitting in his work.

bus·y·bod·y (biz′ē·bod′ē) *n. pl.* **·bod·ies** One who officiously meddles in the affairs of others.

busy signal In a dial telephone, a recurrent buzzing tone indicating that the number called is already connected.

but¹ (but, *unstressed* bət) *conj.* **1.** On the other hand; yet: He was poor *but* honest. **2.** Without the result that: It never rains *but* it pours. **3.** Other than; otherwise than: I have no choice *but* to listen. **4.** Except: anything *but* that. **5.** With the exception that: often with *that*: Nothing will do *but* I must leave. **6.** That: We don't doubt *but* he is there. **7.** That . . . not: He is not so ill *but* exercise will benefit him. **8.** Who . . . not; which . . . not: Few sought his advice *but* were helped by it. — *prep.* With the exception of; save: owning nothing *but* his clothes. — *adv.* Only; just: She is *but* a child. — **all but** Almost; nearly. — **but for** Were it not for. — *n.* An objection or condition; exception: no ifs or *buts*. [OE *būtan* on the outside, without < *be* by + *ūtan* outside] — **Syn.** (conj.) **1.** *But, however, nevertheless,* and *yet* introduce a statement or idea in opposition to what has gone before. *But* is the widest term, ranging from faintest contrast to absolute negation. *However* suggests a moderate concession or a second point to be considered. *Nevertheless* emphasizes direct opposition, and *yet* serves to introduce a mildly inconsequential outcome or inference.

but² (but) *n. pl.* **but** or **buts** *Brit.* Any of various kinds of flatfish, especially the halibut and flounder: also spelled *butt*. [? < Gmc. Cf. Du. *bot* flounder, Sw. *butta* turbot.]

but³ (but) *n. Scot.* The kitchen of a two-roomed house. — **but and ben with** In close intimacy with.

bu·ta·di·ene (byōō′tə·dī′ēn, -dī·ēn′) *n. Chem.* A hydrocarbon, C_4H_6, similar to isoprene, used in the manufacture of synthetic rubber. [< BUTA(NE) + DI-² (def. 2) + -ENE]

bu·tane (byōō′tān, byōō·tān′) *n. Chem.* A colorless, flammable, gaseous hydrocarbon, C_4H_{10}, of the methane series, contained in petroleum and formed synthetically. [< L *but(yrum)* butter + -ANE²]

bu·ta·none (byōō′tə·nōn) *n. Chem.* A colorless, flammable ketone, C_4H_8O, used in making plastics and as a solvent. [< BUTAN(E) + -ONE]

butch·er (booch′ər) *n.* **1.** One who slaughters or dresses animals for market; also, a dealer in meats. **2.** One guilty of cruel or needless bloodshed. **3.** *U.S.* A vendor of candy, etc., on trains. **4.** A bungler; botcher. — *v.t.* **1.** To slaughter or dress for market. **2.** To kill cruelly or indiscriminately. **3.** To ruin by bungling; botch. [< OF *bouchier* slaughterer of bucks < *boc* buck, he-goat] — **butch′er·er** *n.*

butch·er·bird (booch′ər·bûrd′) *n.* A shrike, named from its habit of impaling its prey upon thorns.

butch·er's-broom (booch′ərz·broom′, -broom′) *n.* A low, evergreen shrub (*Ruscus aculeatus*), with leathery, leaflike branches bearing scarlet berries. Also **butch′er·broom′**.

butch·er·y (booch′ər·ē) *n. pl.* **·er·ies** **1.** Wanton or wholesale slaughter; carnage. **2.** A slaughterhouse. **3.** The butcher's trade. — **Syn.** See MASSACRE.

Bute (byōōt) **1.** A county in SW Scotland; 218 sq. mi.; pop. 12,465 (1969); capital, Rothesay: also **Bute′shire** (-shir). **2.** An island in the Firth of Clyde, Scotland; 47 sq. mi.

Bu·te·nandt (boo′tə·nänt), **Adolph**, born 1903, German chemist.

but·ler (but′lər) *n.* A manservant in charge of the dining room, wine, plate, etc., usually the head servant in a household. [< AF *butuiller*, OF *bouteillier* cupbearer < Med. L *buticularius* < *buticula* bottle] — **but′ler·ship** *n.*

But·ler (but′lər), **Benjamin Franklin**, 1818–93, U.S. general. — **Nicholas Murray**, 1862–1947, U.S. educator; president of Columbia University, New York, 1902–45. — **Pierce**, 1866–1939, U.S. jurist; associate justice of the Supreme Court 1923–39. — **Samuel**, 1612–80, English satirical poet. — **Samuel**, 1835–1902, English novelist.

butler's pantry A room between the kitchen and the dining room, suitable for storage, serving, etc.

but·ler·y (but′lər·ē) *n. pl.* **·ler·ies** The butler's pantry.

butt¹ (but) *v.t.* **1.** To strike with the head or horns; ram. **2.** To drive, push, or bump as with the head. — *v.i.* **3.** To strike or attempt to strike something with the head or horns. **4.** To move or drive head foremost. **5.** To project; jut. — **to butt in** *Informal* To interrupt; intrude. — *n.* **1.** A blow or push with the head. **2.** A thrust in fencing. [< OF *buter* to strike, push, project; infl. by BUTT² to abut]

butt² (but) *v.t.* **1.** To abut; especially, to join at the ends; attach (one thing) to another. — *v.i.* **2.** To touch or be joined at the ends. [Aphetic var. of ABUT; infl. by BUTT³ goal, target, end]

butt³ (but) *n.* **1.** A person or thing subjected to jokes, ridicule, criticism, etc. **2.** A target, as on a rifle range. **3.** *pl.* A target range. **4.** An embankment or wall behind a target to stop the shot. **5.** *Obs.* A goal; limit. [< OF *but* end, goal, ult. < Gmc.]

butt⁴ (but) *n.* **1.** The larger or thicker end of anything, as the rear end of the stock of a rifle. **2.** An end or extremity, as of a plank. **3.** A butt hinge. **4.** An unused end, as of a cigar or cigarette; stub; stump. **5.** The thick part of a tanned hide. **6.** *U.S. Informal* The buttocks. [Akin to Dan. *but* blunt, Du. *bot* short, stumpy]

butt⁵ (but) *n.* **1.** A large cask. **2.** A measure of wine, 126 U.S. gallons. [< OF *boute*]

butt⁶ (but) See BUTT².

butte (byōōt) *n. U.S. & Canadian* A conspicuous hill, especially one with steep sides and a flattened top. [< F]

Butte (byōōt) A city in SW Montana; pop. 23,368.

but·ter¹ (but′ər) *n.* **1.** The fatty constituent of milk, separated as a soft, whitish yellow solid, usually by churning, and prepared for cooking and table use. **2.** A substance having the consistency or some of the qualities of butter; especially: **a** The chlorides of some metals: *butter* of bismuth. **b** Vegetable butter (which see). **c** Any of several food preparations of semisolid consistency: apple *butter*. **3.** *Informal* Flattery. — **to look as if butter wouldn't melt in one's mouth** To look innocent. — *v.t.* **1.** To put butter on. **2.** *Informal* To flatter: usually with *up*. — **to know which side one's bread is buttered on** To be aware of the true sources of one's fortune or security. [OE *butere* < L *butyrum* < Gk. *boutyron* < *bous* cow + *tyros* cheese]

but·ter² (but′ər) *n.* One who or that which butts.

but·ter-and-eggs (but′ər·ən·egz′) *n.* Any of various plants having two shades of yellow in the flower, as the toadflax in the United States, and a species of narcissus in England.

but·ter·ball (but′ər·bôl′) *n.* **1.** The bufflehead, a duck. **2.** *Informal* A very fat person.

butter bean **1.** The wax bean (which see). **2.** In the southern United States, the lima bean.

but·ter·bough (but′ər·bou′) *n.* The inkwood.

but·ter·burr (but′ər·bûr′) *n.* An Old World herb (genus *Petasites*), with round or roundish leaves, often a foot wide. Also **but′ter·bur′**.

but·ter·cup (but′ər·kup′) *n.* Any of various plants (genus *Ranunculus*) of the crowfoot family, with yellow, cup-shaped flowers, as the **tall** or **meadow buttercup** (*R. acris*). Also **but′ter·flow′er** (-flou′ər).

but·ter·fat (but′ər·fat′) *n.* The fatty substance of milk, from which butter is made, consisting of the glycerides of various fatty acids.

but·ter·fin·gers (but′ər·fing′gərz) *n.* One who drops things easily or often, as if his fingers were slippery. — **but′ter·fin′gered** *adj.*

but·ter·fish (but′ər·fish′) *n. pl.* **·fish** or **·fishes** A silvery, laterally compressed fish (genus *Poronotus*) common along the Atlantic coast of the United States: also called *dollarfish*.

but·ter·fly (but′ər·flī′) *n. pl.* **·flies** **1.** A diurnal lepidopterous insect (division *Rhopalocera*) with large, often brightly colored wings, club-shaped antennae, and slender body. **2.** In swimming, a breaststroke in which the arms are brought forward out of the water. **3.** A frivolous idler or trifler. [OE *buttorflēoge*]

butterfly bush Buddleia.

butterfly fish 1. One of various tropical marine fishes (family *Chaetodontidae*) having brightly colored bodies: sometimes called *angelfish.* **2.** A brilliantly colored Chinese fish (*Macropodus viridiauratus*).

butterfly table A small drop-leaf table, the leaves having brackets resembling a butterfly's wings.

butterfly valve *Mech.* **1.** A pump valve composed of two semicircular pieces hinged to a cross-rib in the pump bucket. **2.** A disk turning on a diametrical axis, used as a damper in a pipe.

butterfly weed 1. A milkweed (*Asclepias tuberosa*) of North America, having bright reddish orange flowers: also called *pleurisy root.* **2.** A North American plant (*Gaura coccinea*) having pink or red flowers.

but·ter·ine (but′ər·ēn, -in) *n.* Artificial butter; oleomargarine. [< BUTTER¹ + -INE²]

butter knife A small, blunt-edged knife for cutting or spreading butter.

BUTTERFLY WEED (*def.* 1)

but·ter·milk (but′ər·milk′) *n.* The sour liquid left after the butterfat has been separated from milk.

but·ter·nut (but′ər·nut′) *n.* **1.** The oily, edible nut of a walnut (*Juglans cinerea*) of North America. **2.** The tree, or its cathartic inner bark. **3.** A yellowish brown, as of cloth dyed with butternuts. **4.** *U.S.* A Confederate soldier, so called from the color of their homespun clothes; also, a Confederate sympathizer. **5.** The nut of the souari tree.

but·ter·scotch (but′ər·skoch′) *n.* **1.** Hard, sticky candy made with brown sugar, butter, and flavoring. **2.** A syrup or flavoring consisting of similar ingredients. — *adj.* Made of or flavored with butterscotch.

but·ter·weed (but′ər·wēd′) *n.* **1.** The horseweed. **2.** A species of groundsel (*Senecio glabellus*) of the southern United States. **3.** The Indian mallow.

but·ter·wort (but′ər·wûrt′) *n.* Any of several small, stemless herbs (genus *Pinguicula*) with broad, fleshy leaves that secrete a greasy substance in which insects are captured.

but·ter·y¹ (but′ər·ē) *adj.* **1.** Containing, like, or smeared with butter. **2.** *Informal* Grossly flattering; adulatory.

but·ter·y[2] (but′ər·ē, but′rē) *n. pl.* **·ter·ies** *Chiefly Brit.* **1.** A pantry or wine cellar. **2.** In English universities, a place in a college from which students may obtain bread, butter, ale, etc. [< OF *boterie* < LL *botaria* < *butta* bottle]

butt hinge A hinge composed of two plates screwed to the abutting surfaces of the door and the jamb. For illustration see HINGE.

butt joint A joint formed by placing two pieces squarely together without fitting one into the other.

but·tock (but′ək) *n.* **1.** *Anat.* **a** Either of the two fleshy prominences that form the rump. **b** *pl.* The rump. ◆ Collateral adjective: *gluteal.* **2.** *Naut.* The rounded, overhanging part of a ship's stern. [Dim. of BUTT[4]]

but·ton (but′n) *n.* **1.** A knob or disk sewn to a garment, etc., serving as a fastening when passed through a narrow opening or buttonhole, or used merely for ornamentation. **2.** Anything resembling a button, as the knob for operating an electric bell. **3.** *Bot.* **a** A bud, or a similar protuberance. **b** The head of an immature mushroom. **4.** *Metall.* A small globular mass found in a crucible after fusion. **5.** *U.S.* The small knob at the end of a rattlesnake's rattles. **6.** *U.S.* An old guessing game. **7.** *Slang* The point of the chin. **8.** In fencing, a guard on the tip of a foil. — **on the button** *Informal* Exactly; precisely. — *v.t.* **1.** To fasten or provide with a button or buttons. — *v.i.* **2.** To be capable of being fastened with or as with buttons. [< OF *boton* button, bud] — **but′ton·er** *n.* — **but′ton·like′** *adj.*

but·ton·bush (but′n·boŏsh′) *n.* A North American shrub (*Cephalanthus occidentalis*) having spherical white flower heads.

but·ton·hole (but′n·hōl′) *n.* A slit or loop to receive and hold a button. — *v.t.* **·holed, ·hol·ing 1.** To work buttonholes in. **2.** To sew with a buttonhole stitch. **3.** To seize as by the buttonhole so as to detain in conversation. — **but′ton·hol′er** *n.*

buttonhole stitch A stitch with a loop at the top, used to edge buttonholes, etc.: also called *close stitch.*

but·ton·hook (but′n·hoŏk′) *n.* A hook for buttoning gloves or shoes.

but·ton·mold (but′n·mōld′) *n.* A disk of wood or other material, covered with fabric, leather, etc., to make a button.

but·tons (but′nz) *n.pl.* (construed as *sing.*) *Brit. Informal* A bellboy; page.

BUTTONHOLE STITCH

button snakeroot 1. Any of several plants (genus *Liatris*), so called from the small round flower heads. **2.** A stout-stemmed plant (*Eryngium aquaticum*), with linear leaves and globose heads of flowers: also called *rattlesnake weed.*

button tree A tree or shrub (*Conocarpus erecta*) of tropical America and Africa, with heavy, close-grained wood: also called *buttonwood.*

but·ton·wood (but′n·woŏd′) *n.* **1.** A plane tree (*Platanus occidentalis*) of North America, yielding a wood used for furniture and interior trim of houses. Also **but·ton·ball** (-bôl′). **2.** The wood of this tree. **3.** The button tree.

but·ton·y (but′n·ē) *adj.* **1.** Of or like a button. **2.** Having many buttons.

butt plate A plate, usually corrugated to prevent slipping on the shoulder, attached to the end of a gunstock.

but·tress (but′tris) *n.* **1.** *Archit.* A structure built against a wall to strengthen it. **2.** Any support or prop: *buttresses* to faith. **3.** Something suggesting a buttress, as a projecting rock or hillside. **4.** A horny growth on a horse's hoof. — *v.t.* **1.** *Archit.* To support with a buttress. **2.** To prop up; sustain. [< OF *bouterez* < *bouter, buter* to push, thrust]

butt shaft An arrow with a blunt head and no barbs.

butt weld A weld made between two abutting ends or edges without overlapping.

bu·tyl (byoō′til) *n. Chem.* A univalent hydrocarbon radical, C_4H_9, from butane. [< BUT(YRIC) + -YL]

butyl alcohols *Chem.* A group of three isomeric alcohols derived from butane, and having the formula C_4H_9OH.

bu·ty·lene (byoō′tə·lēn) *n. Chem.* A gaseous hydrocarbon, C_4H_8, of the alkene series, existing in three isomeric modifications, an ingredient of synthetic rubber.

bu·ty·ra·ceous (byoō′tə·rā′shəs) *adj.* Having the nature or appearance of, or yielding, butter; buttery. Also **bu·ty·rous** (byoō′tər·əs). [< L *butyrum* (see BUTTER[1]) + -ACEOUS]

bu·ty·rate (byoō′tə·rāt) *n. Chem.* A salt or ester of butyric acid.

FLYING BUTTRESS

bu·tyr·ic (byoō·tir′ik) *adj.* Of, pertaining to, or derived from butter. [< L *butyrum* (see BUTTER[1]) + -IC]

butyric acid *Chem.* Either of two isomeric acids, C_3H_7COOH, especially one found as an ester in butter and certain oils, and free in rancid butter, perspiration, etc.

bu·ty·rin (byoō′tər·in) *n. Chem.* Any one of three analogous compounds formed by treating glycerol with butyric acid at a high temperature.

bux·om (buk′səm) *adj.* **1.** Characterized by health and vigor; plump; comely: said of women. **2.** *Archaic* Lively; blithe. **3.** *Archaic* Pliant; yielding; unresisting. [ME *buhsum* pliant. Akin to OE *būgan* to bend, bow.] — **bux′om·ly** *adv.* — **bux′om·ness** *n.*

buy (bī) *v.* **bought, buy·ing** *v.t.* **1.** To acquire the ownership of, for money or other equivalent; purchase. **2.** To be a means of purchasing; be a price for: A dollar *buys* little nowadays. **3.** To obtain by some exchange or sacrifice: to *buy* wisdom with experience. **4.** To bribe; corrupt: He was *bought* cheap. **5.** *Theol.* To redeem; ransom. — *v.i.* **6.** To make purchases; be a purchaser. — **to buy in 1.** To buy back for the owner, as at an auction when the bids are too low. **2.** To buy stock or an interest, as in a company. **3.** *Slang* To pay money as a price for joining. — **to buy off** To get rid of the interference or opposition of a person or group, or obtain exemption from something, by payment; bribe. — **to buy out** To purchase the stock, interests, etc., of. — **to buy over** To win over to one's interest by a bribe or other inducement. — **to buy up** To purchase the entire available supply of. — *n. Informal* **1.** Anything bought or about to be bought. **2.** A bargain. [OE *bycgan*] — **buy′a·ble** *adj.*

buy·er (bī′ər) *n.* **1.** One who makes purchases. **2.** A purchasing agent, as for a department store.

buzz[1] (buz) *v.i.* **1.** To make the humming, vibrating sound of the bee. **2.** To talk or gossip excitedly: The town *buzzed* with excitement. **3.** To go busily or hastily; bustle. — *v.t.* **4.** To cause to buzz. **5.** To spread or express by buzzing; whisper. **6.** To signal with a buzz. **7.** *Informal* To fly an airplane low over: to *buzz* a ship. **8.** *Informal* To call by telephone. — *n.* **1.** A vibrating hum. **2.** A low murmur, as of many voices. **3.** *Informal* A phone call. [Imit.]

buzz[2] (buz) *v.t. Brit.* To drain dry. [Origin unknown]

buz·zard[1] (buz′ərd) *n.* **1.** One of several large, slow-flying hawks, as the **red-tailed buzzard** (*Buteo borealis*), an American species. **2.** A turkey buzzard (which see). [< OF *busart*, prob. < L *buteo* hawk]

buz·zard[2] (buz′ərd) *n. Brit. Dial.* A noisy insect, as a cockchafer. [< BUZZ[1] + -ARD]

Buz·zards Bay (buz′ərdz) An inlet of the Atlantic in southern Massachusetts.

buzz bomb A robot bomb (which see).

buzz·er (buz′ər) *n.* An electric signal making a buzzing sound, as on a telephone switchboard.

buzz saw A circular saw, so called from the sound it emits.

buzz·wig (buz′wig′) *n. Archaic* **1.** A large, thick wig. **2.** A person who wears such a wig. **3.** A person of importance.

B.V. 1. Blessed Virgin (L *Beata Virgo*). **2.** Farewell (L *bene vale*).

B.V.M. Blessed Virgin Mary (L *Beata Virgo Maria*).

bvt. Brevet; brevetted.

Bwa·na (bwä′nä) *n.* Master; sir. [< Swahili < Arabic *abuna* our father]

bx. (pl. **bxs.**) Box.

by (bī) *prep.* **1.** Next to; near: the house *by* the river. **2.** Past and beyond; The train roared *by* us. **3.** Through the agency of or by means of; as a result of the action of: to hang *by* a rope; to travel *by* plane; to die *by* poison. **4.** By way of; over; through: Come *by* the nearest road. **5.** On the part of: a loss felt *by* all. **6.** According to; on the authority of: *by* law. **7.** In the course of; during: to travel *by* night. **8.** Not later than: Be here *by* noon. **9.** After; in succession to: day *by* day; step *by* step. **10.** According to as a standard: to work *by* the day. **11.** To the extent or amount of: insects *by* the thousands. **12.** In multiplication or measurement with: a room 10 *by* 12; Multiply 6 *by* 8. **13.** With reference to; regarding: to do well *by* one's friends. **14.** In the name of: *by* all that's holy. — **by the way** (or **by the by, bye the bye**) Incidentally. — *adv.* **1.** At hand; near. **2.** Up to and beyond something; past: The years go *by.* **3.** Apart; aside: to lay something *by.* — **by and by** After a time; before long. — **by and large** On the whole; generally. — *adj. & n.* See BYE. [OE *bī* near, about]

— **Syn.** (prep.) **3, 6.** *By, through,* and *with* point to an agent or an agency. *By* introduces the agent himself: appointed *by* the chairman. *Through* refers to the means or cause: to govern *through* a council; *with* is usually used before the instrument: to write *with* a pen.

by- *combining form* **1.** Secondary; inferior; incidental: *by*-*product.* **2.** Near; close: *bystander.* **3.** Aside; out of the way: *byway.*

by-and-by (bī′ən·bī′) *n.* Future time; hereafter.

by-bid·der (bī′bid′ər) *n.* A person who runs up prices at an auction for the seller or owner. — **by′-bid′ding** *n.*

by-blow (bī′blō′) *n.* **1.** A side or chance blow. **2.** An illegitimate child.

Byd·goszcz (bid′gôshch) A city in north central Poland; pop. 264,400 (est. 1968): German *Bromberg*.
bye (bī) *n.* **1.** Something of minor or secondary importance; a side issue. **2.** In cricket, a run made on a ball missed by both batsman and wicketkeeper. **3.** The position of one who, assigned no opponent, automatically advances to the next round, as in a tennis tournament **4.** In golf, any hole or holes remaining unplayed when the match ends. — *adj.* Not principal or main; secondary. Also spelled *by.* [Var. of BY]
bye-bye (bī′bī′) *interj.* A child's word for good-by.
by·e·lec·tion (bī′i·lek′shən) *n. Brit.* A parliamentary election between general elections, held to fill a vacancy.
Byel·go·rod-Dnies·trov·ski (byel′gə·rət·dnyes·trôf′skē) A port city in the Ukrainian S.S.R., on the Dniester estuary; pop. 151,000 (1970): former Russian and Turkish *Akkerman.* Rumanian *Cetatea Albă.* Also *Belgorod-Dnestrovski.*
Bye·lo·rus·sian (bye′lə·rush′ən) *adj.* Of or pertaining to the Byelorussian S.S.R., its people, or their language. — *n.* **1.** A native or inhabitant of the Byelorussian S.S.R. **2.** The East Slavic language of the Byelorussians. Also *White Russian.*
Byelorussian S.S.R. A constituent Republic of the Soviet Union, in the western European part; 80,154 sq. mi.; pop. 9,003,000 (1970); capital, Minsk: also *White Russia, Belorussian S.S.R.* Also **Bye·lo·rus·sia** (bye′lə·rush′ə). *Russian* **Bye·lo·russ·ka·ya S.S.R.** (bye·lo·rōōs′kä·yä).
Bye·lo·stok (bye·lə·stôk′) Russian name for Bialystok: also *Belostok.*
bye-low (bī′lō′) *adv. & interj.* Hush!: used in lullabies.
by·gone (bī′gôn′, -gon′) *adj.* Gone by; former; past; out-of-date. — *n. Often pl.* Something past; that which has gone by. — **to let bygones be bygones** To let disagreements and difficulties in the past be overlooked.
by-lane (bī′lān′) *n.* A byway.
by·law (bī′lô′) *n.* **1.** A rule or law adopted by an association, a corporation, or the like, and subordinate to a constitution or charter. **2.** A secondary or accessory law. [ME *bilawe < by, bi* village (*< ON bȳr*) + *lawe* law; infl. by BY]
by-line (bī′līn′) *n.* The line at the head of an article in a newspaper, etc., giving the name of the writer.
by-name (bī′nām′) *n.* **1.** A secondary name; surname. **2.** A nickname; epithet.
Byng (bing) **Julian Hedworth George,** 1862–1935, Viscount Byng of Vimy, British field marshal.
by-pass (bī′pas′, -päs′) *n.* **1.** Any road, path, or route connecting two points in a course other than that normally used; a detour. **2.** A device to lead a flow of gas or liquid around a pipe, fixed connection, or obstacle. **3.** *Electr.* A shunt. — *v.t.* **1.** To go around or avoid (an obstacle). **2.** To provide with a by-pass.
by·past (bī′past′, -päst′) *adj.* Bygone.
by-path (bī′path′, -päth′) *n.* A secluded or indirect path.
by-play (bī′plā′) *n.* Action or speech apart from the main action, especially in a play.
by-prod·uct (bī′prod′əkt) *n.* A secondary product or result.
Byrd (bûrd) **Harry Flood,** 1887–1966, U.S. politician. — **Richard Evelyn,** 1888–1957, U.S. rear admiral, aviator, polar explorer, and writer; brother of the preceding.
byre (bīr) *n.* A cow stable. [OE *bȳre* stall, shed]
byrl (bûrl, birl) See BIRL[2].
Byrnes (bûrnz) **James Francis,** 1879–1972, U.S. statesman; secretary of state 1945–47.

byr·nie (bûr′nē) *n. Archaic* A coat of mail. [Var. of ME *brynie < ON brynja*]
by·road (bī′rōd′) *n.* A back or side road.
By·ron (bī′rən) **Lord,** 1788–1824, George Gordon Noel, sixth Baron Byron, English poet.
By·ron·ic (bī·ron′ik) *adj.* **1.** Of or pertaining to Lord Byron. **2.** Like or characteristic of Byron or his style; melancholy, romantic, passionate, etc. Also **By·ro·ni·an** (bī·rō′nē·ən), **By·ron′i·cal.**
bys·sus (bis′əs) *n. pl.* **bys·sus·es** or **bys·si** (bis′ī) **1.** *Zool.* A bunch of silky threads secreted by the foot of certain stationary bivalve mollusks, as mussels, and serving as a means of attachment to an object, as a rock. **2.** In classical times, a variety of flax, or a fine, white cloth made from it; later, any fine, white cloth of cotton, silk, or linen. [< L < Gk. *byssos* fine linen < Hebrew *būts,* a fine white fabric]
by·stand·er (bī′stan′dər) *n.* One present but not taking part; an onlooker.
by·street (bī′strēt′) *n.* A side street; a byway.
by-talk (bī′tôk′) *n.* Incidental talk; small talk.
By·tom (bī′tôm) A city in SW Poland; pop. 191,000 (est. 1968): German *Beuthen.*
by·way (bī′wā′) *n.* A branch or side road.
by·word (bī′wûrd′) *n.* **1.** A proverbial saying; also, a pet phrase. **2.** A person, institution, etc., that proverbially represents a type. **3.** An object of scorn or mockery. **4.** A nickname, especially a derogatory one. [OE *bīword* proverb]
by·work (bī′wûrk′) *n.* Work done during leisure time.
byz·ant (biz′ənt) See BEZANT.
Byz·an·tine (biz′ən·tēn, -tīn, bi·zan′tin) *adj.* **1.** Of or pertaining to Byzantium or its civilization. **2.** In the arts: **a** Pertaining to the style of architecture developed in Byzantium during the fifth and sixth centuries, using rounded arches, centralized plans surmounted by large domes, and lavishness of mosaic and other decoration. **b** Pertaining to the style of painting, design, etc., developed in By-

BYZANTINE ARCHITECTURE
(Santa Sophia, Constantinople, A.D. 538)

zantium during the sixth century, characterized by precision, formality, and very rich color. **c** Pertaining to the encyclopedic, complex, and exhaustive quality of the literature and scholarship produced in Byzantium from the sixth century. **3.** Complicated and clandestine; full of intrigues. — *n.* A native or inhabitant of Byzantium. Also **By·zan·ti·an** (bi·zan′shē·ən, -shən). [< L *Byzantinus < Byzantium*]
Byzantine Empire The eastern part of the later Roman Empire (395–1453); capital, Constantinople: Arabic *Rum:* also *Byzantium, Eastern Empire, Eastern Roman Empire.*
Byzantine rite Religious ceremonies as performed by the Orthodox Church.
By·zan·ti·um (bi·zan′shē·əm, -tē·əm) **1.** An ancient city on the Bosporus, later Constantinople. See ISTANBUL. **2.** The Byzantine Empire.
Bz. *Chem.* Benzene.

C

c, C (sē) *n. pl.* **c's** or **cs, C's** or **Cs, cees** (sēz) **1.** The third letter of the English alphabet. The shape of the Phoenician *gimel* was adopted by the Greeks as *gamma* and became Roman *C* or *G.* Also *cee.* **2.** Any sound represented by the letter *c.* — *symbol* **1.** The Roman numeral for 100. **2.** *Chem.* Carbon (symbol C). **3.** *Music* **a** The tonic note of the natural musical scale; do. **b** The pitch of this tone, 261.6 cycles per second or this value multiplied by any power of 2, in standard pitch. **c** A written note representing it. **d** The scale built upon C. **e** Common or 4/4 time: originally a symbol in the shape of a half-circle. **4.** The third in sequence or class. **5.** *U.S.* The third highest grade in school work.
c. or **C.** **1.** About (L *circa*). **2.** Calends. **3.** Candle. **4.** *Electr.* Capacity. **5.** Cape. **6.** Carbon. **7.** Carton. **8.** Case. **9.** Catcher (baseball). **10.** Cathode. **11.** Cent(s). **12.** Center. **13.** Centigrade. **14.** Centime(s). **15.** Cen-

timeter(s). **16.** Century. **17.** Chancery. **18.** Chapter. **19.** Chief. **20.** Child. **21.** Church. **22.** City. **23.** Cloudy. **24.** Consul. **25.** Copper. **26.** Copy. **27.** Copyright. **28.** Corps. **29.** Cost. **30.** Cubic. **31.** *Electr.* Current. **32.** Gallon (L *congius*). **33.** Hundredweight.
C *Math.* Constant.
C. **1.** Catholic. **2.** Celsius. **3.** Celtic. **4.** Chancellor. **5.** Companion (title). **6.** Congress. **7.** Conservative. **8.** Court.
ca' (kä, kô) *v.t. Scot.* **1.** To call. **2.** To drive, as cattle, sheep, etc.
ca. **1.** About (L *circa*). **2.** Cathode. **3.** Centare(s).
Ca *Chem.* Calcium.
CA or **CA.** *Psychol.* Chronological age.
C.A. **1.** Catholic Action. **2.** Central America. **3.** Confederate Army. **4.** Court of Appeal.
C.A. or **c.a.** **1.** Chartered accountant. **2.** Chartered agent.

3. Chief accountant. **4.** Claim agent. **5.** Commercial agent. **6.** Consular agent. **7.** Controller of accounts. **C/A 1.** Capital account. **2.** Credit account. **3.** Current account.

Caa·ba (käʹbə, käʹə·bə) See KAABA.

cab[1] (kab) *n.* **1.** A taxicab (which see). **2.** A one-horse carriage for public hire. **3.** A covered compartment of a locomotive, motor truck, etc., for the operator. [Short form of CABRIOLET]

cab[2] (kab) *n.* A Hebrew measure equivalent to about two quarts: also spelled *kab.*

CAB or **C.A.B. 1.** Civil Aeronautics Board. **2.** Consumers Advisory Board.

ca·bal (kə·balʹ) *n.* **1.** A number of persons secretly united for some private purpose. **2.** An intrigue; plot. — *v.i.* **·balled, ·bal·ling** To form a cabal; plot. [< MF *cabale* < Med.L *cabbala* < Hebrew *qabbālāh.* See CABALA.]
— **Syn. 1.** *Cabal, junta, gang,* and *crew* denote a group working together for some sinister or underhand purpose. *Cabal* and *junta* are used for a group of political leaders. *Gang* suggests criminal intent; *crew,* the blind obedience of underlings to a leader: a *gang* of hoodlums, the mayor and his *crew.* Compare FACTION.

cab·a·la (kabʹə·lə, kə·bäʹlə) *n.* **1.** *Often cap.* An occult system of theosophy, originating in a mystical interpretation of the Scriptures among certain Jewish rabbis. **2.** Any secret, occult, or mystic system. Also spelled *cabbala, kabala, kabbala.* [< Hebrew *qabbālāh* tradition < *qābal* to receive] — **cab′a·lism** *n.* — **cab′a·list** *n. & adj.*

cab·a·lis·tic (kab′ə·lisʹtik) *adj.* **1.** Pertaining to the cabala. **2.** Having a mystic meaning; mysterious. Also **ca·bal·ic** (kə·balʹik), **cab′a·lis′ti·cal.** — **cab′a·lis′ti·cal·ly** *adv.*

cab·al·le·ro (kab′əl·yârʹō) *n. pl.* **·ros 1.** A Spanish gentleman; cavalier. **2.** *SW U.S.* A horseman. **b** A lady's escort. [< Sp. < L *caballarius* horseman < *caballus* horse]

ca·ban·a (kə·banʹə, -bäʹnə) *n.* **1.** A small cabin. **2.** A beach bathhouse. Also **ca·ba·ña** (kə·bänʹyə, -banʹ-). [< Sp.]

cab·a·ret (kab′ə·rāʹ) *n.* **1.** A restaurant or café that provides singing, dancing, etc., for its patrons. **2.** Entertainment of this type. **3.** A tavern. [< F]

cab·bage[1] (kabʹij) *n.* **1.** The close-leaved edible head formed by cultivated varieties of a plant (*Brassica oleracea*) of the mustard family. **2.** The leaf bud of the cabbage palm used as a vegetable. — *v.i.* **·baged, ·bag·ing** To form a head, as cabbage. [< OF *caboche,* ult. < L *caput* head]

cab·bage[2] (kabʹij) *Brit. v.t. & v.i.* **·baged, ·bag·ing** To steal; purloin. — *n.* Cloth appropriated by a tailor in cutting out garments; anything purloined. [Origin uncertain]

cabbage bug The harlequin bug (which see).

cabbage butterfly Any of several white butterflies (genus *Pieris*) whose larvae feed on plants of the mustard family; especially, *P. rapae,* the green larvae of which destroy cabbage. For illustration see INSECTS (injurious).

cabbage palm A palm with a terminal leaf bud used as a vegetable, as *Sabal palmetto* of Florida.

cab·ba·la (kabʹə·lə, kə·bäʹlə) See CABALA.

cab·by (kabʹē) *n. pl.* **·bies** *Informal* The driver of a cab.

Cab·ell (kabʹəl), **James Branch,** 1879–1958, U.S. novelist.

ca·ber (käʹbər) *n. Scot.* A heavy pole, used in the athletic game tossing the caber: also spelled *kabar, kebar.* [< Scottish Gaelic, pole]

ca·bes·tro (kä·besʹtrō) *n. SW U.S.* A hair rope used as a lariat or lasso: also *cabresta, cabresto.* [< Sp., halter]

Ca·be·za de Va·ca (kä·väʹthä thä väʹkä), **Alvar Núñez,** 1490?–1559?, Spanish explorer of North and South America.

cab·e·zon (kab′ə·zon, *Sp.* käʹbä·sōn′) *n.* A sculpin (*Scorpaenichthys marmoratus*) of the Pacific coast of North America. Also **cab′e·zone** (-zōn). [< Sp., aug. of *cabeza* head]

cab·in (kabʹin) *n.* **1.** A small, rude house; a hut. **2.** In the U.S. Navy, the quarters of the captain. **3.** *Naut.* **a** On passenger vessels, the living quarters for passengers and officers. **b** On small vessels, a compartment below deck fitted for a living area or as a shelter. **4.** *Aeron.* The enclosed space in an aircraft for the crew, passengers, or cargo: compare COCKPIT. — **Syn.** See HUT. — *v.t. & v.i.* To confine or dwell in or as in a cabin. [< F *cabane* < LL *capanna* cabin]

cabin boy A boy who waits on the officers and passengers of a ship.

cabin class A class of accommodations for steamship passengers, higher than tourist class, lower than first class.

cabin cruiser A cruiser (def. 3).

Ca·bin·da (kə·binʹdə) An enclave, administratively part of Angola, on the west coast of Africa between the Republic of Congo and the Republic of Zaire; 2,807 sq. mi.; pop. 55,919 (1960).

cab·i·net (kabʹə·nit) *n.* **1.** A piece of furniture fitted with shelves and drawers; a cupboard. **2.** A council, or the chamber in which it meets. **3.** *Often cap.* The body of official advisers and executive chiefs serving a head of state. **4.** A small, private room. — *adj.* **1.** Of or suitable for a cabinet. **2.** Secret; confidential. [< F < Ital. *gabinetto* closet, chest of drawers]

cab·i·net·mak·er (kabʹə·nit·mā′kər) *n.* One who does fine woodworking, as for cabinets, furniture, etc.

cab·i·net·work (kabʹə·nit·wûrk′) *n.* Expert woodwork.

ca·ble (käʹbəl) *n.* **1.** A heavy rope, now usually of steel wire. **2.** *Naut.* **a** A heavy rope or chain for mooring vessels. **b** A cable's length. **3.** *Electr.* **a** An insulated electrical conductor or group of conductors. **b** An underwater telegraph line. **4.** A cablegram. — *v.* **·bled, ·bling** *v.t.* **1.** To make fast by a cable. **2.** To furnish with cable. **3.** To signal by underwater telegraph. — *v.i.* **4.** To send a message by underwater telegraph. [Akin to F *câble,* Sp. *cable* < LL *capulum, caplum* rope < L *capere* to take, grasp]

Ca·ble (käʹbəl), **George Washington,** 1844–1925, U.S. writer.

cable car A car or cage traveling along an overhead cable or pulled along tracks by an underground cable.

ca·ble·gram (käʹbəl·gram) *n.* A telegraphic message sent by underwater cable.

ca·ble·laid (käʹbəl·lād′) *adj.* Made up of three three-stranded ropes twisted together counterclockwise.

cable railroad A railroad in which the cars are pulled by an endless moving cable.

cable's length A unit of nautical measure, in the United States 720 feet, in England 608 feet.

ca·blet (käʹblit) *n.* A cable-laid rope less than 10 inches in circumference; a hawser. [Dim. of CABLE]

cab·man (kabʹmən) *n. pl.* **·men** (-mən) A cab driver.

ca·bob (kə·bobʹ) *n.* Shish kebob (which see).

ca·boched (kə·boshtʹ) *adj. Heraldry* Full-faced: said of the head of a beast. Also **ca·boshed′.** [< OF *caboche,* pp. of *cabocher* to cut off the head < L *caput* head]

cab·o·chon (kabʹə·shon, *Fr.* kȧ·bô·shôn′) *n.* A precious stone, cut convex and highly polished but not faceted. — **en cabochon** Cut and polished but not faceted. [< F, aug. of *caboche* head]

ca·boo·dle (kə·bōōdʹl) *n. Informal* Collection; lot: usually in the phrases **the whole caboodle, the whole kit and caboodle.** [Prob. intens. form of BOODLE]

ca·boose (kə·bōōsʹ) *n.* **1.** *U.S.* A car, usually at the rear of a freight or work train, for use by the train crew. **2.** *Canadian* A mobile bunkhouse; also, a small cabin on a sleigh. **3.** *Brit.* The galley of a ship. [< MDu. *cabuse* galley]

Cab·ot (kabʹət), **John** Anglicized name of **Giovanni Ca·bo·to** (kä·bōʹtō), 1451?–98, Venetian seafarer and explorer in English service; discovered North America (Labrador) 1497. — **Sebastian,** 1474?–1557, English seafarer and explorer; son of preceding.

Ca·bral (kə·vrälʹ), **Pedro Alvarez,** 1460?–1526?, Portuguese seafarer and explorer; claimed Brazil for Portugal.

ca·bres·ta (kä·bresʹtä), **ca·bres·to** (-tō) See CABESTRO.

ca·bril·la (kə·brilʹə, *Sp.* kä·vrēʹyä) *n.* One of various sea basses; especially, *Epinephelus analogus* of Lower California and western South America. [< Sp., prawn, orig. dim. of *cabra* goat]

Ca·bri·ni (kä·brēʹnē), **Saint Frances Xavier,** 1850–1917, first U.S. citizen canonized, 1946: called **Mother Cabrini.**

cab·ri·ole (kabʹrē·ōl) *n.* A curved, tapering leg, often with a decorative foot, characteristic of Chippendale and Queen Anne furniture. [< MF (see CABRIOLET); from its resemblance to the leg of a leaping animal]

cab·ri·o·let (kab′rē·ə·lāʹ, -letʹ) *n.* **1.** A light, one-horse carriage with two seats and a folding top. **2.** An automobile of the coupé type, having a collapsible top. [< F, dim. of MF *cabriole* leap, caper < Ital. *capriola* < L *capreolus* wild goat]

ca' can·ny (kä kanʹē, kô) **1.** *Brit.* A deliberate slowing down of production on the part of workers. **2.** *Scot.* Go warily.

ca·ca·o (kə·käʹō, -käʹō) *n. pl.* **·ca·os 1.** A small, evergreen tree (*Theobroma cacao*) of tropical America. **2.** The large, nutritive seeds of this tree, used in making cocoa and chocolate. [< Sp. < Nahuatl *cacauatl* cacao seed]

cacao butter Cocoa butter (which see).

cach·a·lot (kashʹə·lot, -lō) *n.* The sperm whale. [< F, prob. < dial. F *cachalut* toothed]

cache (kash) *v.t.* **cached, cach·ing** To conceal or store, as in the earth; hide in a secret place. — *n.* A place for hiding or storing provisions, equipment, etc.; also, the things stored or hidden. [< F < *cacher* to hide]

cache·pot (kashʹpot, *Fr.* kȧsh·pōʹ) *n.* An ornamental container used to conceal an ordinary flower pot. [< F]

ca·chet (ka·shāʹ, kashʹā) *n.* **1.** A seal, as for a letter, document, etc. **2.** A distinctive mark; stamp of individuality. **3.** A hollow wafer for enclosing nauseous medicine. **4.** A mark, slogan, etc., printed or stamped on mail. [< F < *cacher* to hide]

ca·chex·i·a (kə·kekʹsē·ə) *n. Pathol.* Malnutrition and general bad health, characterized by a waxy or sallow complexion. Also **ca·chex·y** (kə·kekʹsē). [< L *cachexia* < Gk. *kachexia* poor condition or state < *kakos* bad + *-hexia* < *echein* to hold oneself, be] — **ca·chec·tic** (kə·kekʹtik) or **·ti·cal** *adj.*

cach·in·nate (kakʹə·nāt) *v.i.* **·nat·ed, ·nat·ing** To laugh immoderately or noisily. [< L *cachinnatus,* pp. of *cachinnare* to laugh loudly] — **cach′in·na′tion** *n.*

ca·chou (kə·shōōʹ, ka-) *n.* **1.** An aromatic pill or pastille to perfume the breath. **2.** Catechu, a wood extract. [< F < Malay *kachu* catechu]

ca·chu·cha (kä·chōōʹchä) *n. Spanish* An Andalusian dance or dance tune in 3/4 time, resembling the bolero.

ca·cique (kə·sēkʹ) *n.* **1.** A chief among the Indians of the

West Indies, Mexico, etc. **2.** An oriole of tropical America. Also spelled *cazique.* [< Sp. < native Haitian word for "chief"]

cack·le (kak′əl) *v.* **·led, ·ling** *v.i.* **1.** To make a shrill, broken cry, as a hen that has laid an egg. **2.** To laugh or talk with a similar sound. — *v.t.* **3.** To utter in a cackling manner. — *n.* **1.** The shrill, broken cry of a hen or goose. **2.** Idle talk; chatter. **3.** A short, shrill laugh. [Imit.] — **cack′ler** *n.*

caco- *combining form* Bad; vile: *cacography.* [< Gk. *kakos* bad, evil]

cac·o·de·mon (kak′ə·dē′mən) *n.* A devil or evil spirit: opposed to *agathodemon.* Also **cac′o·dae′mon.** [< Gk. *kakodaimōn* evil genius]

cac·o·dyl (kak′ə·dil, -dēl) *n. Chem.* The univalent arsenic radical, C_2H_6As, that unites with oxygen, sulfur, chlorine, etc., to form stinking compounds. [< Gk. *kakōdēs* (< *kakos* bad + *ozein* to smell) + -YL] — **cac′o·dyl′ic** (-dil′ik) *adj.*

cac·o·e·thes (kak′ō·ē′thēz) *n.* An addiction or mania. [< L < Gk. *kakoēthes* < *kakos* bad + *ēthos* habit, disposition]

cac·o·gen·ics (kak′ə·jen′iks) *n.pl.* (*construed as sing.*) Dysgenics (which see). [< CACO- + (EU)GENICS] — **cac′o·gen′ic** *adj.*

ca·cog·ra·phy (kə·kog′rə·fē) *n.* Bad handwriting or spelling. [< CACO- + -GRAPHY] — **ca·cog′ra·pher** *n.* — **cac·o·graph·ic** (kak′ə·graf′ik) or **·i·cal** *adj.*

cac·o·mis·tle (kak′ə·mis′əl) *n.* A long-tailed, raccoonlike carnivore (*Bassariscus astutus*), of Mexico and adjacent parts of the United States. Also **cac′o·mix′l** (-mik′səl), **cac′o·mix′le.** [< Sp. < Nahuatl *tlacomiztli*]

ca·coph·o·nous (kə·kof′ə·nəs) *adj.* Having a harsh, disagreeable sound; discordant: a *cacophonous* din. Also **cac·o·phon·ic** (kak′ə·fon′ik) or **·i·cal.** — **ca·coph′o·nous·ly, cac′o·phon′i·cal·ly** *adv.*

ca·coph·o·ny (kə·kof′ə·nē) *n.* **1.** Disagreeable or discordant sound; dissonance. **2.** *Music* The frequent use of dissonance. [< F *cacophonie,* ult. < Gk. *kakophōnia* < *kakos* bad + *phōneein* to sound]

cac·ta·ceous (kak·tā′shəs) *adj. Bot.* Of or belonging to the cactus family (*Cactaceae*).

cac·tus (kak′təs) *n. pl.* **·tus·es** or **·ti** (-tī) Any of various green, fleshy, mostly leafless and spiny plants (family *Cactaceae*), often having showy flowers, and native in arid regions of America. [< L < Gk. *kaktos,* prickly plant]

ca·cu·mi·nal (kə·kyōō′mə·nəl) *Phonet. adj.* Pronounced with the tip of the tongue turned back toward the hard palate, as *t* and *d* in the Indic languages: also *cerebral, retroflex.* — *n.* A cacuminal consonant. [< L *cacumen, -inis* apex]

cad (kad) *n.* **1.** An ungentlemanly or despicable fellow; one violating the code of gentlemanly behavior. **2.** *Brit.* At Oxford University, a townsman. — **Syn.** See SCOUNDREL. [Short form of CADET] — **cad′dish** *adj.* — **cad′dish·ly** *adv.* — **cad′dish·ness** *n.*

ca·das·ter (kə·das′tər) *n.* A register, survey, or map of the extent, ownership, value, etc., of lands as a basis of taxation. Also **ca·das′tre.** [< F *cadastre* < LL *capitastrum* tax register < L *caput* head] — **ca·das′tral** *adj.*

ca·dav·er (kə·dav′ər, -dā′vər) *n.* A dead body; especially, a human body for dissection; a corpse. [< L]

ca·dav·er·ine (kə·dav′ər·in, -ēn) *n. Biochem.* A thick, colorless, liquid ptomaine, $C_5H_{14}N_2$, of noxious odor, formed by putrefying animal tissue.

ca·dav·er·ous (kə·dav′ər·əs) *adj.* Resembling or characteristic of a corpse; pale; ghastly; gaunt. Also **ca·dav′er·ic.** — **ca·dav′er·ous·ly** *adv.* — **ca·dav′er·ous·ness** *n.*

cad·die (kad′ē) *n.* **1.** One paid to carry clubs for golf players. **2.** *Scot.* A messenger or errand boy. — *v.i.* **·died, ·dy·ing** To act as a caddie. Also spelled *caddy.* [< CADET]

cad·dis (kad′is) *n.* **1.** A coarse, sergelike fabric. **2.** A narrow worsted fabric for bindings, etc. **3.** Worsted yarn. Also **cad′dice.** [< MF *cadis,* a woolen fabric]

cad·dis fly (kad′is) Any of certain four-winged insects (order *Trichoptera*) whose aquatic larvae (**caddis worms** or **straw worms**) construct cylindrical, silk-lined cases covered with sand, gravel, etc.: also, *Brit., May fly.* [Origin uncertain]

Cad·do (kad′ō) *n. pl.* **·does** or **·do** A member of a North American Indian confederacy belonging to the southern group of the Caddoan linguistic stock: also called *Texas.*

Cad·do·an (kad′ō·ən) *n.* A North American Indian linguistic stock including the languages spoken by the Arikaras of the Dakotas, the Pawnees of Nebraska and Kansas, the Caddoes of Oklahoma, Arkansas, Louisiana, and Texas, and the Wichitas of Oklahoma and Texas.

cad·dy[1] (kad′ē) *n. pl.* **·dies** A small box or case, as for tea. [Alter. of earlier *catty* < Malay *kātī,* a measure of weight]

cad·dy[2] (kad′ē) *n. pl.* **·dies** A caddie.

cade[1] (kād) *adj.* Left by the mother and brought up by hand: a *cade* colt. [Origin unknown]

cade[2] (kād) *n.* A large, bushy shrub (*Juniperus oxycedrus*) of Mediterranean regions, of which the wood yields a brown, thick liquid (**cade oil**) used in soaps and medicinally. [< F]

ca·delle (kə·del′) *n.* A small, black beetle (*Tenebrioides mauritanicus*) that in both larval and adult stages feeds upon stored grain. [< F]

ca·dence (kād′ns) *n.* **1.** Rhythmic or measured flow, as of poetry or oratory. **2.** The measure or beat of music, marching, etc., in marching usually expressed in steps per minute. **3.** Modulation, as of the voice; intonation. **4.** A fall of the voice, as at a period. **5.** *Music* A melodic, harmonic, or rhythmic formula ending a phrase, movement, or other division of a piece of music. **b** A cadenza. — **Syn.** See RHYTHM. [< F < Ital. *cadenza* < LL *cadentia* a falling < L *cadere* to fall. Doublet of CADENZA, CHANCE.] — **ca′denced** *adj.*

ca·den·cy (kād′n·sē) *n. pl.* **·cies** **1.** Cadence; rhythm. **2.** *Heraldry* The relative position of the younger members or branches of the same family.

ca·dent (kād′nt) *adj.* **1.** Having cadence or rhythm. **2.** *Archaic* Falling.

ca·den·za (kə·den′zə, *Ital.* kä·dent′sä) *n. Music* A flourish or thematic ornamentation, often improvised, for displaying the virtuosity of a solo performer, usually introduced just before the end of a composition or near the close of a movement in a concerto. [< Ital. Doublet of CADENCE, CHANCE.]

ca·det (kə·det′) *n.* **1.** A student at a military or naval school. **2.** A student in training at the United States Military or Coast Guard Academy for commissioning as an officer, and at the United States Air Force Academy officially designated **Air Force cadet. 3.** A younger son or brother. **4.** *Archaic* A gentleman who entered the army to gain military experience and thus earn a commission. **5.** *Obs. Slang* A pander. [< F, ult. < dim. of L *caput* head, chief] — **ca·det′ship** *n.*

Ca·det (kə·det′) *n.* A member of the Constitutional Democratic party of Russia, formed about 1905. [< Russ. *Kadet* < K(onstitutsionalnyie) + D(emokrati)]

cadge (kaj) *v.* **cadged, cadg·ing** *v.t.* **1.** *Informal* To get by begging. — *v.i.* **2.** *Dial.* To go about peddling or begging. [? Var. of CATCH] — **cadg′er** *n.*

cadg·y (kaj′ē) *adj. Scot. & Brit. Dial.* **1.** Cheerful; frolicsome. **2.** Wanton; amorous. [Origin uncertain]

ca·di (kä′dē, kä′-) *n. pl.* **·dis** In Moslem communities, a judge or magistrate: also spelled *kadi.* [< Arabic *qādī*]

Cad·il·lac (kad′ə·lak, *Fr.* kà·dē·yàk′), **Antoine de la Mothe,** 1657?–1730, French explorer; founded Detroit.

Cá·diz (kə·diz′, kā′diz; *Sp.* kä′thēth) A Province of SW Spain; 2,851 sq. mi.; pop. 874,837 (est. 1965); capital, **Cádiz,** on the Gulf of Cádiz, an inlet of the Atlantic, pop. 117,871 (1960).

Cad·man (kad′mən), **Charles Wakefield,** 1884–1946, U.S. composer.

Cad·me·an (kad·mē′ən) *adj.* Pertaining to Cadmus.

Cadmean victory A victory ruinous to the victor.

cad·mi·um (kad′mē·əm) *n.* A bluish white metallic element (symbol Cd), occurring in small quantities in zinc ores, and used in the manufacture of fusible alloys, in electroplating, and in the control of atomic fission. See ELEMENT. [< NL < L *cadmia* zinc ore < Gk. *kadmeia* (gē) calamine]

cadmium sulfide A pigment, CdS, varying in hue from lemon to orange: also **cadmium yellow** or **cadmium orange.**

Cad·mus (kad′məs) In Greek mythology, a Phoenician prince who killed a dragon and sowed its teeth, from which sprang armed men who fought one another until all but five were slain. With these he founded Thebes. He was supposed to have introduced the Phoenician alphabet into Greece.

cad·re (kad′rē, *Fr.* kä′dr′) *n.* **1.** *Mil.* The nucleus of officers and men necessary to the organization and training of a new military unit. **2.** A framework; nucleus; core. [< F, frame of a picture < Ital. *quadro* < L *quadrum* square]

ca·du·ce·us (kə·dōō′sē·əs, -dyōō′-) *n. pl.* **·ce·i** (-sē·ī) **1.** In ancient Greece and Rome, a herald's wand or staff; especially, the staff of Hermes or Mercury. **2.** A similar wand used as the emblem of a medical corps or of the medical profession. [< L < Gk. (Doric) *karykion* herald's staff] — **ca·du′ce·an** *adj.*

CADUCEUS

ca·du·ci·ty (kə·dōō′sə·tē, -dyōō′-) *n.* **1.** Transitoriness; perishableness. **2.** The weakness of old age; senility.

ca·du·cous (kə·dōō′kəs, -dyōō′-) *adj.* **1.** *Biol.* Dropping or falling off, especially at an early stage of development, as the sepals of a poppy or the gills of salamanders, etc. **2.** Transitory; perishable. [< L *caducus* falling < *cadere* to fall]

cae- For those words not entered below, see under CE-.

cae·cil·i·an (si·sil′ē·ən) *n.* One of a family (*Caeciliidae*) of tropical, burrowing, legless amphibians, resembling worms or small snakes. [< L *caecilia,* a kind of lizard]

cae·cum (sē′kəm) See CECUM.

Cæd·mon (kad′mən) Seventh-century English poet.

Cae·li·an (sē′lē·ən) *n.* One of the Seven Hills of Rome. Also *Latin* **Cae·li·us Mons** (sē′lē·əs monz).

Cae·lum (sē′ləm) *n.* A constellation, the Chisel. See CON-STELLATION. [< L]

Caen (kän) A port city in NW France, on the Orne; pop. 106,790 (1968).

Cae·no·zo·ic (sē′nə·zō′ik, sen′ə-) See CENOZOIC.

cae·o·ma (sē·ō′mə) *n. Bot.* An aecium of a fungus (genus *Caeoma*) in which the spores are formed in chains lacking an outer protective coat. [< NL < Gk. *kaiein* to burn; with ref. to its color]

caer·i·mo·ni·a·ri·us (ser′i·mō′nē·ā′rē·əs) *n. pl.* ·ri·i (-rē·ī) *Eccl.* A master of ceremonies. [< L *caerimonia* ceremony]

Caer·le·on (kär·lē′ən) An urban district in Monmouthshire, England, on the Usk; pop. 6,030 (est. 1969): identified with Camelot.

Caer·mar·then (kär·mär′thən), **Caer·mar·then·shire.** See CARMARTHENSHIRE.

Caern. Caernarvonshire.

Caer·nar·von·shire (kär·när′vən·shir) A former county of NW Wales; 569 sq. mi.; pop. 122,852 (1971); county seat, Caernarvon: also *Carnarvonshire.* Also **Caer·nar·von.**

caes·al·pin·i·a·ceous (sez′al·pin′ē·ā′shəs, ses′-) *adj. Bot.* Belonging to a genus (*Caesalpinia*) of tropical trees, shrubs, or herbs of the bean family, as brazil and sapanwood. [after A. *Caesalpinus*, 1519–1603, Italian botanist]

Cae·sar (sē′zər) *n.* 1. The title of any one of the Roman emperors from Augustus to Hadrian. 2. Any despot.

Caesar, Gaius Julius, 100–44 B.C., Roman general, statesman, and historian.

Caes·a·re·a (ses′ə·rē′ə, sez′-) An ancient port in Palestine, site of the Sdot Yam settlement. Also **Caesarea Palestine, Caesarea Maritime.**

Caesarea Maz·a·ca (maz′ə·kə) The ancient name for KAYSERI.

cae·sar·e·an (si·zâr′ē·ən), **cae·sar·i·an,** etc. See CESAREAN, etc.

Cae·sar·e·an (si·zâr′ē·ən) *adj.* Pertaining to Caesar. — *n.* Loosely, a cesarean section. Also spelled *Cesarean, Cesarian:* also **Cae·sar′i·an.**

Cae·sar·ism (sē′zə·riz′əm) *n.* Imperialism or military despotism, as the governments of the Caesars. — **Cae′sar·ist** *n.* — **Cae′sar·is′tic** *adj.*

cae·si·um (sē′zē·əm) See CESIUM.

caes·pi·tose (ses′pə·tōs) See CESPITOSE.

caes·tus (ses′təs) See CESTUS.

cae·su·ra (si·zhŏŏr′ə, -zyōōr′ə) *n. pl.* ·su·ras or ·su·rae (-zhŏŏr′ē, -zyōōr′ē) 1. In Greek and Latin prosody, a break occurring when a word ends within a foot, usually in the third or fourth foot. 2. In modern prosody, a pause, especially a sense pause, in a line, usually near the middle. Caesura is indicated by two vertical lines (‖). 3. *Music* A pause indicating a rhythmic division point. Also spelled *cesura.* [< L, cutting, caesura < *caedere* to cut] — **cae·su′ral** *adj.*

C.A.F. or **c.a.f.** 1. Cost and freight. 2. Cost, assurance, and freight.

ca·fé (ka·fā′, kə-) *n.* 1. A coffee house; restaurant. 2. A barroom. 3. Coffee. Also **ca·fe′.** [< F]

ca·fé au lait (kà·fā′ ō lā′) *French* 1. Coffee with scalded milk. 2. A light brown.

café curtain A curtain suspended from a rod by movable rings and covering only the lower half of a window.

ca·fé noir (kà·fā′ nwàr′) *French* Black coffee.

café society The social set customarily frequenting cafés or night clubs, especially in New York City.

caf·e·te·ri·a (kaf′ə·tir′ē·ə) *n.* A restaurant where the patrons wait upon themselves. [< Am. Sp., coffee store]

caf·feine (kaf′ēn, *in technical usage* kaf′ē·in) *n. Chem.* A crystallizable, slightly bitter alkaloid, $C_8H_{10}O_2N_4$, obtained from the leaves and berries of coffee, and chemically identical with theine, used as a stimulant and diuretic. Also **caf′-fein.** [< F *caféine* < *café* coffee]

caf·tan (kaf′tən, käf·tän′) *n.* An undercoat having long sleeves and a sash, worn in eastern Mediterranean countries: also spelled *kaftan.* [< F *cafetan* < Turkish *qaftän*]

cage (kāj) *n.* 1. A boxlike structure with openwork of wires or bars, for confining birds or beasts. 2. A place for confining prisoners; also, anything that confines. 3. Any cagelike structure or framework, as the car of some elevators or the skeleton of a tall building. 4. In baseball, a movable backstop for batting practice. 5. In hockey, the frame and net used as the goal. 6. In basketball, the basket. — *v.t.* **caged,** **cag·ing** To shut up in a cage; confine; imprison. [< OF, ult. < L *cavea* cavity, cell < *cavus* empty, hollow]

cage·ling (kāj′ling) *n.* A caged bird.

cage·y (kā′jē) *adj.* **cag·i·er, cag·i·est** *Informal* Wary of being duped; shrewd and careful. Also **cag′y.** [Origin uncertain] — **cag′i·ly** *adv.* — **cag′i·ness** *n.*

Ca·glia·ri (kä′lyä·rē) A Province of Southern Sardinia, Italy; 3,590 sq. mi.; pop. 750,410 (1961); capital, **Cagliari,** also the capital of Sardinia, on the **Gulf of Cagliari,** an inlet of the Mediterranean, pop. 181,499.

Ca·glia·ri (kä′lyä·rē), **Paolo** See VERONESE.

Ca·glio·stro (kä·lyō′strō), **Count Alessandro di,** 1743–95, Sicilian adventurer: original name **Giuseppe Bal·sa·mo** (bäl′sä′mō).

Ca·gou·lard (kà·gōō·làr′) *n.* A member of a secret French organization whose conspiracy to restore the monarchy was exposed in 1937. [< F < *cagoule* monk's hood]

ca·hier (kä·yā′) *n.* 1. A number of sheets, as of printed matter, loosely bound together. 2. A report, as of proceedings, etc. [< F < OF *quaier.* See QUIRE[1].]

ca·hoots (kə·hōōts′) *n.pl. U.S. Slang* Affiliation; partnership; collusion: usually in the phrase **in cahoots.** — **to go (in) cahoots (with)** To affiliate or associate (with); share equally. [? < F *cahute* cabin]

Cai·a·phas (kā′ə·fəs, kī′-) The Jewish high priest who presided at the council that condemned Jesus. *Matt.* xxvi 57–68.

Cai·cos (kī′kōs) See TURKS AND CAICOS ISLANDS.

cai·man (kā′mən) See CAYMAN.

cain (kān) See KAIN.

Cain (kān) The eldest son of Adam, who slew his brother Abel. *Gen.* iv. — 1. A fratricide or murderer. — **to raise Cain** *U.S. Slang* To cause a disturbance.

ca·in·ca root (kə·ing′kə) The root of the tropical American snowberry, yielding a glycoside used as a purgative. Also **ca·hin·ca root** (kə·hing′kə).

Caine (kān), **(Sir Thomas Henry) Hall,** 1853–1931, English novelist.

Cai·no·zo·ic (kī′nə·zō′ik) See CENOZOIC.

ca·ique (kä·ēk′) *n.* 1. A long, narrow skiff with from two to ten oars, used on the Bosporus. 2. A small Levantine sailing vessel. [< F < Ital. *caicco* < Turkish *kāyik*]

ça i·ra (sà′ ē·rà′) *French* Literally, it will go; it will succeed: the refrain of a popular song of the French Revolution.

caird (kârd) *n. Scot.* A wandering tinker; gypsy.

Caird (kârd), **Edward,** 1835–1908, Scottish philosopher.

Caird Coast (kârd) The part of Antarctica on the SE coast of the Weddell Sea.

cairn (kârn) *n.* A mound or heap of stones set up as a memorial or a marker. [< Scottish Gaelic *carn* heap of stones] — **cairned** (kârnd) *adj.*

cairn·gorm (kârn′gôrm) *n.* A smoky, yellow to brown variety of quartz: also called *smoky quartz.* [after *Cairngorm* Mountains, Scotland]

Cairn terrier (kârn) A small, short-legged terrier having a broad head and rough outer coat.

Cai·ro (kī′rō; *for def.* 2, *also* kâr′ō) 1. The capital of the United Arab Republic, in the NE part, on the Nile; pop. 4,219,853 (1966): Arabic *Al-Qâhirah.* 2. A city in SW Illinois at the confluence of the Mississippi and Ohio rivers; pop. 6,277.

cais·son (kā′sən, -son) *n.* 1. A large watertight chamber within which work is done under water, as on a bridge pier. 2. *Naut.* A watertight device used to raise sunken ships; camel. 3. A gate for closing the entrance to a dry dock. 4. A two-wheeled vehicle carrying a chest of ammunition to serve a gun. 5. A chest of ammunition. 6. A box of explosives used as a mine. [< F, aug. of *caisse* box, chest]

CAISSON (*def.* 1)

A Airlock. B Entry shaft. C Work chamber. D Water level. E River bottom. F Bedrock.

caisson disease *Pathol.* A painful, paralyzing, sometimes fatal disease caused by too rapid a transition from the compressed air of caissons, diving bells, etc., while the system still contains an excess of nitrogen: also called *decompression sickness, the bends, tunnel disease.*

Caith. Caithness.

Caith·ness (käth′nes, käth·nes′) A county of NE Scotland; 686 sq. mi.; pop. 28,202 (1969); capital, Wick. Also **Caith′ness·shire** (-shir).

cai·tiff (kā′tif) *n.* A base scoundrel. — *adj.* Base. [< AF *caitif* weak, wretched < L *captivus.* Doublet of CAPTIVE.]

Cai·us (kā′əs, kī′-) See GAIUS.

caj·e·put (kaj′ə·pət) *n.* 1. The California laurel. See CAJUPUT. [< Malay *kāyupūtih* < *kāyu* tree + *pūtih* white]

ca·jole (kə·jōl′) *v.t. & v.i.* ·**joled,** ·**jol·ing** To coax with flattery or false promises; wheedle. [< F *cajoler*] — **ca·jole′-ment** *n.* — **ca·jol′er** *n.* — **ca·jol′ing·ly** *adv.*

ca·jol·er·y (kə·jō′lər·ē) *n. pl.* ·**er·ies** The act or practice of cajoling or wheedling; artful persuasion; coaxing.

ca·jon (kä·hōn′) *n. pl.* **ca·jo·nes** (kä·hō′nās) *SW U.S.* A canyon or narrow gorge with steep sides. [< Sp.]

Ca·jun (kā′jən) *n.* A reputed descendant of the Acadian French in Louisiana. [Alter. of ACADIAN]

caj·u·put (kaj′ə·pət) *n.* 1. A small tree (*Melaleuca leucadendron*) of the myrtle family, native in the Moluccas. 2. An odorous, greenish yellow oil distilled from the leaves and twigs of this tree, used in the treatment of skin diseases. Also spelled *cajeput, kajeput:* also **caj′a·put.** [See CAJEPUT]

cake (kāk) *n.* 1. A mixture of flour, milk, sugar, etc., baked in various forms and generally sweeter and richer than bread. 2. A small, usually thin mass of dough or other food, baked or fried: fish *cake.* 3. A mass of matter compressed or hardened into a compact form: a *cake* of soap, ice, etc.

— to take the cake *Informal* To take or deserve a prize; excel: often used sarcastically. — *v.t. & v.i.* **caked, cak·ing** To form into a hardened mass. [< ON *kaka*]

cakes and ale Pleasures of life; easy living.

cake·walk (kāk′wôk′) *n.* **1.** Formerly, an entertainment in which American Negroes performed a promenade or march and a cake was awarded for the most original steps; also, the promenade itself. **2.** A dance based on the promenade, or the music for such a dance. — *v.i.* To do a cakewalk; strut. — **cake′walk′er** *n.*

cal. 1. Calendar; calends. **2.** Caliber. **3.** Calorie(s) (small).

Cal. 1. California (unofficial). **2.** Large calorie(s).

Cal·a·bar bean (kal′ə-bär′) The poisonous seed of an African twining climber (*Physostigma venenosum*) of the bean family, the source of physostigmine: also called *ordeal bean*.

cal·a·bash (kal′ə-bash) *n.* **1.** The calabash tree. **2.** A calabash gourd, or a utensil made from this. [< F *calabasse* < Sp. *calabaza* pumpkin, ? < Persian *kharbuz* melon]

calabash gourd The common gourd from the calabash tree, used for making pipes, etc.

calabash tree A tropical American tree (*Lagenaria siceraria*) of the gourd family, bearing a hard-shelled fruit. **2.** A tropical American tree (*Crescentia cujete*) of the bignonia family, with a hard-shelled, gourdlike fruit.

cal·a·boose (kal′ə-bōōs) *n. U.S. Informal* A jail; lockup. [< Sp. *calaboozo*]

Ca·la·bri·a (kə-lä′brē-ə, *Ital.* kä-lä′bryä) A Region of extreme SW Italy; 5,828 sq. mi.; pop. 2,045,215 (1961); capital, Reggio di Calabria: ancient *Bruttium*.

ca·la·di·um (kə-lā′dē-əm) *n.* One of a genus (*Caladium*) of tuberous tropical American herbs of the arum family with large, variegated sagittate leaves. [< NL < Malay *kelādy*]

Cal·ais (kal′ā, ka·lā′, kal′is; *Fr.* kà·le′) A port city in northern France, on the Strait of Dover; pop. 70,153 (1968).

cal·a·man·co (kal′ə-mang′kō) *n. pl.* **·cos** or **·coes** A glossy woolen fabric in satin weave: also spelled *calimanco*. [Cf. Sp. *calamaco*, Med.L *calamancus* a type of fabric]

cal·a·man·der (kal′ə-man′dər) *n.* The wood of various trees of the ebony family, especially the rare *Diospyros quaesita* of Ceylon, finely veined, hard, and valued for cabinetnetwork. [Alter. of *Coromandel* (Coast)]

cal·a·mar·y (kal′ə-mâr′ē) *n. pl.* **·mar·ies** A squid. [< L *calamarius* < *calamus* pen < Gk. *kalamos* reed]

cal·a·mine (kal′ə-mīn, -min) *n.* **1.** A hydrous zinc silicate; hemimorphite. **2.** *Brit.* A vitreous zinc carbonate; smithsonite. **3.** A pink powder made from smithsonite, much used in the form of a zinc and ferric oxide as a lotion or ointment for the treatment of skin ailments. — *v.t.* **·mined, ·min·ing** To apply calamine to. [< F < LL *calamina, calmia,* alter. of L *cadmia.* See CADMIUM.]

cal·a·mint (kal′ə-mint) *n.* A menthaceous plant (genus *Satureia*) of the North Temperate Zone, especially *S. calamintha.* Also **calamint balm.** [< MF *calament* < Med.L *calamentum* < L *calaminthe* < Gk. *kalaminthē*]

cal·a·mite (kal′ə-mīt) *n.* A fossil plant (genus *Calamites,* division *Pteridophyta*) of the later Paleozoic era, resembling the modern horsetail but growing to a height of 100 feet and more. [< NL *Calamites* < L *calamus* reed]

ca·lam·i·tous (kə-lam′ə-təs) *adj.* Causing or resulting in a calamity; disastrous. — **ca·lam′i·tous·ly** *adv.*

ca·lam·i·ty (kə-lam′ə-tē) *n. pl.* **·ties 1.** A grievous misfortune; a disaster. **2.** A state of affliction or adversity; great distress. — **Syn.** See DISASTER. [< F *calamité* < L *calamitas, -tatis*]

Cal·am·i·ty Jane (kə-lam′ə-tē jān′), 1852?–1903, U.S. frontier sharpshooter: full name **Martha Jane Burke,** *née* Canary.

cal·a·mon·din (kal′ə-mon′din) *n.* A very small orange (*Citrus mitis*) resembling the tangerine in shape and color, with a deep orange flesh and a juice much esteemed for beverages. [< Tagalog *kalamunding*]

cal·a·mus (kal′ə-məs) *n. pl.* **·mi** (-mī) **1.** The sweet flag, a plant. **2.** The quill of a feather. **3.** Any of a genus (*Calamus*) of Oriental climbing palms; the rattan. [< L < Gk. *kalamos* reed]

ca·lash (kə-lash′) *n.* **1.** A low-wheeled light carriage with folding top. **2.** A folding carriage top: also **calash top. 3.** A woman's folding bonnet or hood, fashionable in the 18th century. Also spelled *calèche.* [< F *calèche,* ult. < Slavic]

cal·a·thus (kal′ə-thəs) *n. pl.* **·thi** (-thī) In ancient Greece, a vase-shaped basket for fruit, a symbol of fruitfulness. [< L < Gk. *kalathos* basket]

CALASH (*def.* 3)

cal·a·ver·ite (kal′ə-vâr′īt) *n.* A telluride of gold and silver, usually granular in structure, with a silvery white metallic luster. It is an ore of gold. [after *Calaveras* County, Calif.]

cal·ca·ne·us (kal-kā′nē-əs) *n. pl.* **·ne·i** (-nē-ī) *Anat.* **1.** The large quadrangular bone at the back of the foot: also called *heel bone.* **2.** A similar bone in other vertebrates. Also **cal·ca′ne·um.** [< L (*os*) *calcaneum* heel bone < *calx* heel]

cal·car (kal′kär) *n. pl.* **cal·car·i·a** (kal-kâr′ē-ə) *Biol.* A spur, or spurlike projection, as at the base of a petal or on the leg or wing of a bird. [< L, spur < *calx, calcis* heel]

cal·ca·rate (kal′kə-rāt, -rit) *adj. Biol.* Having a calcar, or spur; spurred. Also **cal′ca·rat′ed.**

cal·car·e·ous (kal-kâr′ē-əs) *adj.* **1.** Composed of, containing, or like limestone or calcium carbonate. **2.** Containing calcium. [< L *calcarius* of lime < *calx, calcis* lime]

cal·ca·rif·er·ous (kal′kə-rif′ər-əs) *adj. Biol.* Bearing spurs. [< L *calcar, -is* spur + -FEROUS]

cal·ce·ate (kal′sē-āt, -it) *adj.* Wearing shoes: said of certain religious orders. [< L *calceatus,* pp. of *calceare* to shoe]

cal·ced·o·ny (kal-sed′ə-nē) See CHALCEDONY.

cal·ce·i·form (kal′sē-ə-fôrm′) *adj. Bot.* Calceolate.

cal·ce·o·lar·i·a (kal′sē-ə-lâr′ē-ə) *n.* One of a large genus (*Calceolaria*) of herbs and shrub of the figwort family, with small flowers resembling slippers: also called *slipperwort.* [< NL < L *calceolus,* dim. of *calceus* shoe]

cal·ce·o·late (kal′sē-ə-lāt) *adj. Bot.* Slipper-shaped: also *calceiform.* [< L *calceolus* slipper + -ATE¹]

cal·ces (kal′sēz) Alternative plural of CALX.

Cal·chas (kal′kəs) In Homer's *Iliad,* a priest of Apollo who accompanied the Greeks to Troy.

calci- *combining form* Lime: *calciferous.* [< L *calx, calcis* lime]

cal·cic (kal′sik) *adj.* Of, pertaining to, or containing calcium or lime. [< L *calx, calcis* lime]

cal·cif·er·ol (kal-sif′ər-ōl, -ol) *n. Biochem.* The antirachitic vitamin D₂, a white, crystalline, fat-soluble, accessory food factor, $C_{28}H_{44}O$, formed by ultraviolet irradiation of ergosterol, found in fish oils, milk, eggs, etc. [< CALCIFER-(OUS) + (ERGOSTER)OL]

cal·cif·er·ous (kal-sif′ər-əs) *adj.* Yielding or containing calcium carbonate, as rocks. Also **cal·cif·ic** (kal-sif′ik). [< CALCI- + -FEROUS]

cal·ci·fi·ca·tion (kal′sə-fi·kā′shən) *n.* **1.** Conversion into chalk, or into stony or bony substance, by the deposition of lime salts, as in petrifaction and ossification. **2.** Such a lime formation. **3.** *Pathol.* The hardening of tissues through the deposition of calcium salts. **4.** The accumulation by a surface soil of sufficient calcium to bring soil colloids close to saturation.

cal·ci·form (kal′sə-fôrm) *adj.* Having a projection like a heel. [< L *calx, calcis* heel + -FORM]

cal·ci·fy (kal′sə-fī) *v.t. & v.i.* **·fied, ·fy·ing** To make or become stony by the deposit of lime salts. [< CALCI- + -FY]

cal·ci·mine (kal′sə-mīn, -min) *n.* A white or tinted wash consisting of whiting, or zinc white, with glue and water, for ceilings, walls, etc. — *v.t.* **·mined, ·min·ing** To apply calcimine to. Also, *Brit.,* distemper: also spelled *kalsomine.* [< L *calx, calcis* lime; orig. a trade name]

cal·cin·a·to·ry (kal-sin′ə-tôr′ē, -tō′rē) *adj.* For calcining. — *n. pl.* **·ries** An apparatus for calcining, as a furnace.

cal·cine (kal′sīn, -sin) *v.* **·cined, ·cin·ing** *v.t.* **1.** To render (a substance) friable by the expulsion of its volatile content through heat. **2.** To reduce to a calx, as copper ore, by subjecting to heat; roast. — *v.i.* **3.** To become changed by the action of dry heat into a friable powder. Also **cal′cin·ize.** [< F *calciner* < Med.L *calcinare* < L *calx* lime] — **cal·ci·na·tion** (kal′sə-nā′shən) *n.*

cal·cite (kal′sīt) *n.* A widely distributed calcium carbonate mineral, white or variously tinted, occurring in hexagonal crystals, and including chalk, limestone, marble, and Iceland spar as massive varieties. — **cal·cit·ic** (kal-sit′ik) *adj.* [< CALC(I) + -ITE¹]

cal·ci·um (kal′sē-əm) *n.* A silver-white, malleable, metallic element (symbol Ca), never occurring free, but widely distributed in combination, as in chalk, gypsum, and limestone. See ELEMENT. [< NL < L *calx, calcis* lime]

calcium carbide *Chem.* A compound, CaC_2, made from quicklime and carbon in an electric furnace and yielding acetylene when mixed with water. Also **calcium acetylide.**

calcium carbonate *Chem.* A compound, $CaCO_3$, forming the principal constituent of certain rocks and minerals, as limestone, aragonite, and calcite, and used in the preparation of lime and as the basis of dentifrices.

calcium chloride *Chem.* A white, very deliquescent, hygroscopic salt, $CaCl_2$, used as a drying agent, preservative, refrigerant, and dust preventer.

calcium cyanamide *Chem.* A compound, $CaCN_2$, produced in an electric furnace from the nitrogen of the air, used as an artificial fertilizer.

calcium hydroxide *Chem.* Slaked lime, $Ca(OH)_2$: when used in solution called *limewater.*

calcium light A powerful light produced by the incandescence of lime in an oxyhydrogen flame; limelight: also called *Drummond light.*

calcium phosphate *Chem.* Any of a class of earthy phosphates formed in various animal tissues and rocks, and used as an antacid, polishing agent, etc.

cal·cog·ra·phy (kal-kog′rə-fē) *n.* The art of drawing with

chalks or pastels. [< L *calx, calcis* chalk, lime + -GRAPHY]
— **cal·co·graph·ic** (kal/kə·graf/ik) *adj.*

calc·sin·ter (kalk/sin/tər) *n.* Travertine. [< G *kalksinter* < *kalk* chalk (< L *calx* lime) + *sinter* slag]

calc·spar (kalk/spär/) *n.* Crystallized carbonate of lime. [< CALC(AREOUS) + SPAR³]

calc·tuff (kalk/tuf/) *n. Geol.* A porous deposit of carbonate of lime found in calcareous springs. Also **calc·tu·fa** (kalk/-tōō/fə, -tyōō/-). [< CALC(AREOUS) + TUFA]

cal·cu·la·ble (kal/kyə·lə·bəl) *adj.* 1. Capable of being calculated. 2. Reliable; dependable. — **cal/cu·la·bly** *adv.*

cal·cu·late (kal/kyə·lāt) *v.* **·lat·ed, ·lat·ing** *v.t.* 1. To determine by computation; arrive at by arithmetical means. 2. To ascertain beforehand; form an estimate of: to *calculate* the depth. 3. To plan or design: used chiefly in the passive: *calculated* to carry two tons. 4. *U.S. Dial.* To think; expect. — *v.i.* 5. To perform a mathematical process; compute. — **to calculate on** To depend or rely on. [< L *calculatus,* pp. of *calculare* to reckon < *calculus* pebble < *calx, calcis* lime; with ref. to the use of pebbles in counting]
— **Syn.** 1. *Calculate, compute,* and *reckon* mean to determine mathematically. *Calculate* is used of all mathematical operations, from the simplest to the most complex, but usually implies complexity. *Compute* is used for simpler operations, such as arithmetic, while *reckon* suggests the simplest type of counting, or mental arithmetic. Compare ESTIMATE.

cal·cu·lat·ing (kal/kyə·lā/ting) *adj.* 1. Inclined to reckon or estimate, especially for one's own interests; cautious; shrewd; scheming. 2. That calculates or computes.

calculating machine A keyboard machine that automatically adds, subtracts, multiplies, and divides.

cal·cu·la·tion (kal/kyə·lā/shən) *n.* 1. The act or process of computing; also, the result of computing. 2. An estimate of probability; forecast. 3. Shrewd forethought; prudence.
— **cal/cu·la·tive** *adj.*

cal·cu·la·tor (kal/kyə·lā/tər) *n.* 1. One who calculates. 2. A calculating machine or a set of tables for computing.

cal·cu·lous (kal/kyə·ləs) *adj. Pathol.* Pertaining to or affected with a calculus or calculi. [< L *calculosus* pebbly]

cal·cu·lus (kal/kyə·ləs) *n. pl.* **·li** (-lī) *or* **·lus·es** 1. *Pathol.* A stonelike mass, as in the bladder. 2. *Math.* A method of calculating by the use of a highly specialized system of algebraic symbols. — **differential calculus** The branch of analysis that investigates the infinitesimal changes of constantly varying quantities when the relations between the quantities are given. — **integral calculus** The branch of analysis that, from the relations among the infinitesimal changes or variations of quantities, deduces relations among the quantities themselves, as in finding the area enclosed by a given curve. [< L, a pebble (used in counting)]

Cal·cut·ta (kal·kut/ə) The capital of West Bengal State, India; a port city in NE India, on the Hooghly; pop. 7,040,345 (est. 1970).

cal·dar·i·um (kal·dâr/ē·əm) *n. pl.* **·dar·i·a** (-dâr/ē·ə) In ancient Rome, a room for a hot bath. [< L < *calidus* hot]

cal·de·ra (kal·dē/rə, *Sp.* käl·dā/rä) *n. Geol.* A large depression formed by explosive disruption of a volcanic cone or collapse of a crater floor. [< Sp. < L *caldaria.* See CAULDRON.]

Cal·de·rón de la Bar·ca (käl/dā·rōn/ dä lä vär/kä), **Pedro,** 1600–81, Spanish dramatist.

cal·dron (kôl/drən) See CAULDRON.

Cald·well (kôld/wel, -wəl), **Erskine,** born 1903, U.S. writer.

Ca·leb (kā/ləb) In the Old Testament, a Hebrew leader who was permitted to enter Canaan with Joshua. *Num.* xxvi 65.

ca·lèche (kà·lesh/) See CALASH.

Cal·e·do·ni·a (kal/ə·dō/nē·ə, -dōn/yə) *Poetic* Scotland. [< L] — **Cal/e·do/ni·an** *adj. & n.*

Caledonian Canal A waterway from Moray Firth to Loch Linnhe, Argyll, Scotland; 60.5 mi.

cal·e·fa·cient (kal/ə·fā/shənt) *adj.* Causing heat or warmth. — *n. Med.* Something that produces heat or warmth, as a mustard plaster. [< L *calefaciens, -entis,* ppr. of *calefacere* < *calere* to be warm + *facere* to make, cause]

cal·e·fac·tion (kal/ə·fak/shən) *n.* The act of warming or the state of being warmed. — **cal/e·fac/tive** *adj.*

cal·e·fac·to·ry (kal/ə·fak/tər·ē) *adj.* Giving heat or warmth. — *n.* An artificially warmed room in a monastery.

cal·en·dar (kal/ən·dər) *n.* 1. A system of fixing the order, length, and subdivisions of the years and months: Julian *calendar.* 2. A table showing the days, weeks, and months of a year. 3. A schedule or list, especially one arranged in chronological order: a court *calendar* of cases; a *calendar* of saints. 4. *Obs.* A guide; example. *Abbr. cal.* — *v.t.* To place in a calendar; list. [< L *calendarium* account book < *calendae* calends]
— **Chinese calendar** An ancient calendar, no longer in official use, with days and years reckoned in cycles of sixty. Each year consists of twelve lunar months, with adjustment to the solar year by periodic intercalation.
— **ecclesiastical calendar** A lunisolar calendar reckoning the year from Advent Sunday, used for regulating the dates of church feasts.
— **Gregorian calendar** The calendar now in general use in most parts of the world; first prescribed in 1582 by Pope

Gregory XIII to correct the Julian year to the astronomical year; adopted in England Sept. 3/14, 1752, the first being the **Old Style** (*O.S.*) date and the second being the **New Style** (*N.S.*).
— **Hebrew (or Jewish) calendar** A calendar used by the Jews, based on the lunar month and adjusted to the solar year. It reckons the year of creation as 3761 B.C. (thus, Tishri 1, 5725 would, in the Gregorian calendar, be September 7 A.D. 1964). Its principal periods are the *cycle,* of 19 years; the *year,* containing 12 or (in leap years) 13 lunar months, or 353–355 and 383–385 days; the *month,* of 29 or 30 days. In a leap year an intercalary month (Veadar) of 29 days is added and 1 day is added to Adar. Each cycle contains seven leap years, the 3rd, 6th, 8th, 11th, 14th, 17th, and 19th years. Since the Hebrew months are mostly shorter, they do not coincide in any systematic manner with those of the Gregorian calendar except by approximation, as shown below:

Months	Number of days	Approximate month in Gregorian calendar
1 Tishri	30	October
2 Heshwan	29 or 30	November
3 Kislew	29 or 30	December
4 Tebet	29	January
5 Shebat	30	February
6 Adar	29 or 30	March
– Veadar[1]	29	–
7 Nisan	30	April
8 Iyyar	29	May
9 Sivan	30	June
10 Tammuz	29	July
11 Ab	30	August
12 Elul	29	September

[1]The **additional** intercalary month.

The civil year now begins on Tishri 1, though anciently it began in Nisan; the ecclesiastical year still begins in Nisan.
— **Hindu calendar** A solar calendar, reckoned in 12 months, each beginning when the sun enters a new sign of the zodiac.
— **Julian calendar** The calendar prescribed by Julius Caesar, which, though using the bissextile year, was in error one day in 128 years (it is now 13 days behind the Gregorian calendar). The months, after some changes by Augustus, had the length now in use in Europe and America.
— **Moslem (or Mohammedan) calendar** The calendar generally used in all Moslem countries, reckoning time from July 16 A.D. 622, the day following Mohammed's flight from Mecca to Medina (the Hegira). The year consists of 12 lunar months of a mean duration of 29 days, 12 hours, 44 minutes. A cycle consists of 30 years, of which 19 are ordinary years of 354 days each, and 11 are leap years, with 355 days. The calendar has no provision for adjustment to the solar year; hence, the months retrogress through the seasons, making a complete cycle every 32½ years. The following list gives the names and duration of the months:

Months	Number of days	Months	Number of days
1 Muharram	30	7 Rajab	30
2 Saphar	29	8 Shaaban	29
3 Rabia 1	30	9 Ramadan	30
4 Rabia 2	29	10 Shawwal	29
5 Jomada 1	30	11 Dulkaada	30
6 Jomada 2	29	12 Dulheggia	29[1]

[1]In leap years, 30.

— **Republican (or Revolutionary) calendar** The calendar instituted on Oct. 5, 1793, by the first French republic, and abolished Dec. 31, 1805. It divided the year into 12 months of 30 days each, with five (in leap years six) supplementary days (*sansculottides*) at the end of the last month. The months were divided into three decades, every tenth day being a day of rest, Sundays being ignored. Provision was made for leap years by adding a sixth day to the supplementary days whenever necessary to make the year terminate at the equinox, which was generally every fourth year. The calendar was retrospective in action, and its first year (Year 1) began Sept. 22, 1792. The months and their approximately corresponding periods in the Gregorian calendar are as follows:

Vendémiaire, Sept. 22 to Oct. 21.
Brumaire, Oct. 22 to Nov. 20.
Frimaire, Nov. 21 to Dec. 20.
Nivôse, Dec. 21 to Jan. 19.
Pluviôse, Jan. 20 to Feb. 18.
Ventôse, Feb. 19 to Mar. 20.
Germinal, Mar. 21 to April 19.
Floréal, April 20 to May 19.
Prairial, May 20 to June 18.
Messidor, June 19 to July 18.
Thermidor (or Fervidor), July 19 to Aug. 17.
Fructidor, Aug. 18 to Sept. 16.
sansculottides, Sept. 17 to Sept. 21.
— **Roman calendar** A lunar calendar, attributed to Numa. The day of the new moon was the *calends,* and the day of the full moon the *ides* (the 13th or 15th of the month). Days were reckoned backward from these dates and from the *nones,* ninth day before the ides by inclusive reckoning.

calendar year The 365, or, in leap year, 366 days from midnight of December 31 to the same hour twelve months thereafter: also called *civil* or *legal year.*

cal·en·der[1] (kal′ən-dər) *n.* A machine for giving a gloss to cloth, paper, etc., by pressing between rollers. — *v.t.* To press in a calender. [< F *calendre*, ult. < L *cylindrus* < Gk. *kylindros* roller] — **cal′en·der·er** *n.*

cal·en·der[2] (kal′ən-dər) *n.* A mendicant dervish of Persia or Turkey. [< Persian *qalandar*]

cal·ends (kal′əndz) *n.pl.* The first day of the Roman month: also spelled *kalends.* Abbr. *c., C., cal., k., K., kal.* [< L *calendae*] — **ca·len·dal** (kə-len′dəl) *adj.*

ca·len·du·la (kə-len′jōō-lə) *n.* Any of a small genus (*Calendula*) of annual or perennial herbs of the composite family, having bright orange or yellow flowers: sometimes called *pot marigold.* [< NL, dim. of L *calendae* calends; because it blooms almost every month]

cal·en·ture (kal′ən-chŏŏr) *n.* *Pathol.* A tropical fever caused by extreme heat and accompanied by delirium and hallucinations: also **cal′en·tu′ra** (kal′ən-tŏŏr′ə). [< F Sp. *calentura* fever, ult. < L *calere* to be warm]

ca·le·sa (kä-lä′sä) *n. Spanish* A calash or cab used in the Philippines.

ca·les·cence (kə-les′əns) *n.* The condition of growing warm; increasing warmth. [< L *calescens, -entis,* ppr. of *calescere,* inceptive of *calere* to be warm] — **ca·les′cent** *adj.*

calf[1] (kaf, käf) *n. pl.* **calves** (kavz, kävz) **1.** The young of the cow or various other bovine animals. **2.** The young of various mammals, as the elephant, whale, etc. **3.** Calfskin. Abbr. *cf.* **4.** *Informal* A gawky, witless young man. **5.** A floating fragment of an iceberg, glacier, etc. [OE *cealf*]

calf[2] (kaf, käf) *n. pl.* **calves** (kavz, kävz) The muscular rear part of the human leg below the knee. [< ON *kālfi*]

calf love *Informal* Adolescent infatuation; puppy love.

calf's-foot jelly (kafs′fŏŏt′, käfs′-) A gelatinous preparation made by boiling calves' feet: also *calvesfoot jelly.*

calf·skin (kaf′skin′, käf′-) *n.* **1.** The skin or hide of a calf. **2.** Leather made from this.

Cal·ga·ry (kal′gər-ē) A city in southern Alberta, Canada; pop. 400,154.

Calgary redeye *Canadian Slang* Beer and tomato juice.

Cal·houn (kal-hōōn′), **John Caldwell,** 1782–1850, U.S. statesman; vice president 1825–32.

Ca·li (kä′lē) A city in SW Colombia; pop. 639,900 (1961).

Cal·i·ban (kal′ə-ban) In Shakespeare's *Tempest,* a deformed, savage slave of Prospero.

cal·i·ber (kal′ə-bər) *n.* **1.** The internal diameter of a tube. **2.** *Mil.* **a** The internal diameter of the barrel of a gun, cannon, etc., expressed in decimals of an inch for small arms and millimeters for rifles or cannon. **b** The diameter of a bullet, shell, etc. **c** A unit of length equivalent to the ratio of the length of a gun's bore to its diameter. Abbr. *cal.* **3.** Degree of personal excellence: a man of high *caliber.* Also *Brit.* **cal′i·bre.** [< F *calibre,* ? < Arabic *qālib* mold, form]

cal·i·brate (kal′ə-brāt) *v.t.* **·brat·ed, ·brat·ing 1.** To graduate, correct, or adjust the scale of (a measuring instrument) into appropriate units. **2.** To determine the reading of (such an instrument). **3.** To ascertain the caliber of. [Cf. F *calibrer*] — **cal′i·bra′tion** *n.* — **cal′i·bra′tor** *n.*

cal·i·ces (kal′ə-sēz) Plural of CALIX.

cal·i·che (kä-lē′chä) *n.* **1.** A native, impure sodium nitrate, NaNO₃, found in Chile: also called *Chile saltpeter.* **2.** A calcareous sediment typical of soils in warm, semiarid, or desert regions. [< Am. Sp.]

cal·i·cle (kal′i·kəl) *n. Zool.* A small, cup-shaped part, as a polyp cell in corals. [< L *caliculus,* dim. of *calix* cup]

cal·i·co (kal′i·kō) *n. pl.* **·coes** or **·cos 1.** Cheap cotton cloth printed in a figured pattern of bright colors. **2.** *Brit.* White cotton cloth. — *adj.* **1.** Made of calico. **2.** Resembling printed calico; dappled or streaked: a *calico* cat. [after *Calicut,* where first obtained]

cal·i·co·back (kal′i·kō-bak′) *n.* The harlequin bug.

calico bass A varicolored food fish (*Pomoxys sparoides*) of the Mississippi Valley, etc.: also called *strawberry bass.*

calico bush The mountain laurel. Also **calico tree.**

Cal·i·cut (kal′ə-kut) See KOZHIKODE.

ca·lif (kā′lif, kal′if), **cal·i·fate** (kal′ə-fāt, -fit) See CALIPH, CALIPHATE.

Calif. California.

Cal·i·for·nia (kal′ə-fôrn′yə, -fôr′nē-ə) A Pacific State of the United States; 158,693 sq. mi.; pop. 19,953,534; capital, Sacramento; entered the Union Sept. 9, 1850: nickname *Golden State.* Abbr. *Calif., Cal,* — **Cal′i·for′nian** *adj & n.*

California, Gulf of An inlet of the Pacific in western Mexico, separating Lower California from the rest of the country: Spanish *Golfo de California.*

California, Lower See LOWER CALIFORNIA.

California condor A very large, almost extinct bird (*Gymnogyps californianus*) of the southern California mountains.

California fuchsia A perennial herbaceous shrub (*Zauschneria californica*), with large scarlet flowers.

California holly Toyon.

California laurel A tall evergreen tree (*Umbellularia cali-*

fornica) of the laurel family, native in California and Oregon: also called *cajeput, myrtle.*

California poppy 1. A plant (*Eschscholtzia californica*) of the poppy family having showy yellow flowers: the State flower of California. **2.** Any of several related plants, as the creamcups.

cal·i·for·ni·um (kal′ə-fôr′nē-əm) *n.* An unstable radioactive element (symbol Cf), artificially produced by bombardment of curium with alpha particles. See ELEMENT. [after the University of *California,* where first produced]

ca·lig·i·nous (kə-lij′ə-nəs) *adj.* Obscure; dark; dim. [< L *caliginosus* misty, dark < *caligo, caliginis* fog, darkness] — **ca·lig′i·nous·ly** *adv.* — **ca·lig′i·nous·ness, ca·lig′i·nos′i·ty** (-nos′ə·tē) *n.*

ca·lig·ra·phy (kə·lig′rə·fē) See CALLIGRAPHY.

Ca·lig·u·la (kə·lig′yə·lə), A.D. 12–41, Roman emperor 37–41; assassinated: original name **Gaius Caesar.**

cal·i·man·co (kal′ə·mang′kō) See CALAMANCO.

cal·i·pash (kal′ə·pash, kal′ə·pash′) *n.* The part of a turtle next to the upper shell, a greenish, gelatinous, edible substance: also spelled *callipash.* [? < Sp. *carapacho* carapace]

cal·i·pee (kal′ə·pē, kal′ə·pē′) *n.* The part of a turtle next to the lower shell, a yellowish, gelatinous, edible substance: also spelled *callipee.* [See CALIPASH]

cal·i·per (kal′ə·pər) *n.* **1.** *Usually pl.* An instrument resembling a pair of compasses, usually with curved legs, used for measuring diameters: also **caliper compass. 2.** A caliper rule. — *v.t. & v.i.* To measure by using calipers. Also spelled *calliper.* [Var. of CALIBER]

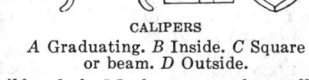

caliper rule A graduated rule having one sliding jaw and one stationary jaw.

CALIPERS

A Graduating. *B* Inside. *C* Square or beam. *D* Outside.

ca·liph (kā′lif, kal′if) *n.* The spiritual and civil head of a Moslem state: also spelled *calif, kalif, kaliph, khalif.* [< F *caliphe* < Arabic *khalīfah* successor (to Mohammed)]

cal·i·phate (kal′ə·fāt, -fit) *n.* The office, dominion, or reign of a caliph.

cal·i·sa·ya (kal′ə·sā′ə) *n.* The bark of the cinchona, especially that species (*Cinchona calisaya*) rich in quinine: also called *yellowbark.* [< Sp. < Quechua]

cal·is·then·ics (kal′is·then′iks) *n.pl.* (*construed as sing. def.* 2) **1.** Light gymnastics to promote grace and health. **2.** The science of such exercises. Also spelled *callisthenics.* [< Gk. *kalli-* (< *kalos* beautiful) + *sthenos* strength] — **cal′is·then′ic** or **·i·cal** *adj.*

ca·lix (kā′liks, kal′iks) *n. pl.* **cal·i·ces** (kal′ə·sēz) **1.** A cup; also, any cup-shaped organ or part. **2.** *Eccl.* A chalice. Compare CALYX. [< L, cup]

Ca·lix·tus III (kə·lik′stəs) See (Alfonso) BORGIA.

calk[1] (kôk) See CAULK.

calk[2] (kôk) *n.* **1.** A spur on a horse's shoe to prevent slipping. **2.** *U.S.* A plate with sharp points worn on the sole of a boot or shoe to prevent slipping. Also **calk′er.** — *v.t.* **1.** To furnish with calks. **2.** To wound with a calk. [Prob. < L *calx* heel]

calk·er (kô′kər) See CAULKER.

call (kôl) *v.t.* **1.** To say in a loud voice; utter or read aloud; announce; proclaim. **2.** To convoke; convene: to *call* a meeting. **4.** To invoke solemnly: to *call* God to witness. **5.** To summon to a specific work: to *call* someone to the ministry. **6.** To arouse, as from sleep. **7.** To communicate with by telephone. **8.** To summon or lure (birds or animals) by imitating their cry. **9.** To name; style: They *called* him "Shorty." **10.** To designate or characterize in any way. **11.** To estimate loosely; consider: I *call* it 10 pounds. **12.** To bring to action or consideration: to *call* a case to court. **13.** To insist upon payment of, as by written notice. **14.** In baseball: **a** To stop or suspend (a game). **b** To designate a pitch as (a ball or strike). **c** To declare (a player) out, safe, etc. **15.** In poker, to demand a show of hands by a bet equal to that of (another). **16.** In pool, etc., to predict (a shot) before making the play. — *v.i.* **17.** To raise one's voice; speak loudly. **18.** To make a brief visit, stop, or stay: with *at, on,* or *upon.* **19.** To communicate by telephone. **20.** In poker, to demand a show of hands. **21.** In some card games, to make a demand or signal, as for trumps. — **Syn.** See CONVOKE. — **to call back 1.** To summon back; recall. **2.** To call in return, as by telephone. — **to call down 1.** To invoke from heaven. **2.** *Informal* To rebuke; reprimand. — **to call for 1.** To stop so as to obtain. **2.** To require; need. — **to call forth** To summon into action; draw out. — **to call in 1.** To collect, as debts. **2.** To retire, as currency, from circulation. **3.** To invite or summon, as for consultation. **— to call off 1.** To summon away; divert. **2.** To say or read aloud. **3.** To cancel. **— to call out 1.** To say in a loud voice. **2.** To order into service or action; summon. **— to call up 1.** To remember; recollect. **2.** To bring up for action or discussion. **3.** To summon. **4.** To communicate with by telephone. — *n.* **1.** A shout or cry; loud utterance. **2.** A summons or invitation. **3.** A signal, as on a bell or a horn. **4.** A demand; claim: the *call* of duty. **5.** A communication by telephone. **6.** A roll call. **7.** An inward urge to some specific work, often regarded as divinely inspired; vocation. **8.** A blast on a hunting horn to encourage the hounds. **9.** A brief, often formal, visit: to make (or pay) a *call* on someone. **10.** The cry of an animal, especially of a bird. **11.** A whistle, etc., with which to imitate such a cry and lure the animal. **12.** A need; occasion: You've no *call* to do that. **13.** In the theater, a notice of rehearsals. **14.** A request that redeemable bonds be presented for payment. **15.** An assessment, as on stockholders, for payment of additional cash to meet losses, etc. **16.** In the securities trade, an option that for a consideration paid entitles the holder to buy a stock or other commodity at a certain time for a stipulated price. Compare PUT, STRADDLE. **17.** In poker, a demand for a show of hands. **18.** In square dancing, a direction to begin a new step or figure. **19.** In baseball, an umpire's decision. **— on call 1.** Payable on demand. **2.** Available by calling. **— within call** Readily called; accessible. [< ON *kalla*]

cal·la (kal′ə) *n.* **1.** A plant (*Zantedeschia aethiopica*) of the arum family, native in South Africa but widely cultivated in the United States, and having a large milk-white spathe that resembles a flower. Also **calla lily. 2.** A marsh plant (*Calla palustris*) of North America and Europe, bearing red berries in dense clusters. [< L *calla*, a plant name]

Cal·lag·han (kal′ə-han′); **(Leonard) James,** born 1912, British public official; prime minister, 1976–.

Cal·la·o (kä·yä′ō) A port city in western Peru, near Lima, on **Callao Bay,** a small inlet of the Pacific; pop. 131,705.

call·board (kôl′bôrd′, -bōrd′) *n.* A theater bulletin board for posting notices of rehearsals, instructions, etc.

call·boy (kôl′boi′) *n.* **1.** A boy who calls actors to go on stage. **2.** A bellboy.

call·er[1] (kô′lər) *n.* **1.** One who or that which calls. **2.** One making a brief visit. **3.** One who calls out the steps in a square dance.

cal·ler[2] (kal′ər, kä′lər) *adj. Scot.* **1.** Cool or refreshing. **2.** Fresh: said of food.

Cal·les (kä′yäs), **Plutarco Elías,** 1877–1945, Mexican general; president 1924–28.

cal·let (kal′it) *n. Brit. Dial.* **1.** A strumpet; prostitute. **2.** A scolding or gossiping woman. [Origin uncertain]

call girl *Informal* A prostitute who goes to assignations in response to telephone calls.

calli- For words not found here, see under CALI-.

cal·lig·ra·phy (kə·lig′rə·fē) *n.* **1.** Beautiful penmanship. **2.** Handwriting in general. Also spelled *caligraphy.* [< Gk. *kalligraphia* < *kalos* beautiful + *graphein* to write] — **cal·lig′ra·pher, cal·lig′ra·phist** *n.* — **cal·li·graph′ic** *adj.*

Cal·lim·a·chus (kə·lim′ə·kəs) Fifth-century B.C. Greek sculptor.

call·ing (kô′ling) *n.* **1.** A speaking or crying aloud. **2.** A convocation or summons. **3.** A vocation or profession.

calling card A small card, printed or engraved with one's name, used to announce a visit or call: also *visiting card.*

cal·li·o·pe (kə·lī′ə·pē, kal′ē·ōp) *n.* A musical instrument consisting of a series of steam whistles played by means of a keyboard: also called *steam organ.* [after *Calliope*]

Cal·li·o·pe (kə·lī′ə·pē) The Muse of eloquence and epic poetry. [< L < Gk. *Kalliopē* the beautiful-voiced < *kalos* beautiful + *ops* voice]

cal·li·op·sis (kal′ē·op′sis) *n.* Coreopsis, a plant.

cal·li·pash (kal′ə·pash, kal′ə·pash′) See CALIPASH.

cal·li·pee (kal′ə·pē, kal′ə·pē′) See CALIPEE.

cal·li·per (kal′ə·pər) See CALIPER.

cal·li·pyg·i·an (kal′ə·pij′ē·ən) *adj.* Having beautiful buttocks. Also **cal′li·py′gous** (-pī′gəs). [< Gk. *kallipygos* < *kalos* beautiful + *pygē* buttocks]

Cal·lis·the·nes (kə·lis′thə·nēz), 360?–328? B.C., Greek philosopher and historian.

cal·lis·then·ics (kal′is·then′iks) See CALISTHENICS.

Cal·lis·to (kə·lis′tō) *n.* **1.** In classical mythology, a nymph loved by Zeus, transformed into a bear, and set as Ursa Major among the stars by Zeus. **2.** *Astron.* The fourth and second largest satellite of Jupiter.

Cal·lis·tra·tus (kə·lis′trə·təs), died 355 B.C., Athenian orator and general.

call letters The code letters identifying a radio or television transmitting station. Also **call sign.**

call loan A loan of money to be repaid on demand, or call, at any time: also called *demand loan.*

call money Money loaned on security, or deposited in a bank, subject to repayment on demand of the lender.

call number A classifying number employed by libraries to indicate the subject of a book and its place on the shelves.

cal·los·i·ty (kə·los′ə·tē) *n. pl.* **·ties 1.** *Physiol.* A callus **2.** *Bot.* A hard or thickened part on or in a plant. **3.** Callousness of feelings; insensibility.

cal·lous (kal′əs) *adj.* **1.** Thickened and hardened, as a callus. **2.** Hardened in feelings; insensible. — *v.t. & v.i.* To make or become callous. [< L *callosus* < *callus* hard skin] — **cal′lous·ly** *adv.* — **cal′lous·ness** *n.*

cal·low (kal′ō) *adj.* **1.** Inexperienced; immature: a *callow* youth. **2.** Unfledged, as a bird. [OE *calu* bare, bald]

call rate The interest rate on call loans.

call slip A printed form on which a library patron writes the title, author, and call number of a desired book.

cal·lus (kal′əs) *n. pl.* **·lus·es 1.** *Physiol.* A thickened, hardened part of the skin: also called *callosity.* **2.** *Anat.* The new bony tissue between and around the fractured ends of a broken bone in the process of reuniting. **3.** *Bot.* The tissue that forms over a cut on a stem and protects the exposed wood. — *v.i.* To form a callus. [< L, hard skin]

calm (käm) *adj.* **1.** Free from agitation; still or nearly still. **2.** Not excited by passion or emotion; peaceful. — *n.* **1.** Lack of wind or motion; stillness. **2.** *Meteorol.* A state in which there is little or no wind. See BEAUFORT SCALE. **3.** Serenity. — *v.t. & v.i.* To make or become quiet or calm: often with *down.* [< MF *calme,* orig., quiet, stillness < Ital. *calma* < LL *cauma* heat of the day < Gk. *kauma* heat; with ref. to the midday siesta] — **calm′ly** *adv.* — **calm′ness** *n.* — **Syn.** (adj.) *Calm, tranquil, placid, serene, quiet,* and *still* denote freedom from violent movement or emotion. *Calm* describes a present state that may be transient; *tranquil* suggests a more enduring condition: a *calm* sea, a *tranquil* life. A *placid* person is regarded as temperamentally stolid; a *placid* lake is always peaceful and untroubled. Things elevated above earthly turmoil are *serene*: a *serene* sky, a *serene* smile. *Quiet* and *still* imply absence of noise as well as of bustle; of the two, *quiet* is more relative, while *still* verges on the absolute: a *quiet* meeting, *still* waters.

calm·a·tive (kal′mə·tiv, kä′mə-) *adj.* Having a soothing effect; sedative. — *n.* A sedative or tranquilizer.

cal·o·mel (kal′ə·mel, -məl) *n. Med.* Mercurous chloride, $HgCl$, a heavy, white, tasteless compound, used as a purgative, etc. [< F < Gk. *kalos* beautiful + *melas* black]

cal·o·res·cence (kal′ə·res′əns) *n. Physics* Incandescence produced in a body, as a platinum sheet, by infrared radiation. [< L *calor* heat + -ESCENCE] — **cal′o·res′cent** *adj.*

ca·lor·ic (kə·lôr′ik, -lor′-) *adj.* Of or pertaining to heat or to calories. — *n.* **1.** Heat. **2.** Formerly, the fluid supposed to produce heat. [< F *calorique* < L *calor* heat]

cal·o·ric·i·ty (kal′ə·ris′ə·tē) *n.* The power of developing heat, possessed by animals.

cal·o·rie (kal′ə·rē) *n.* **1.** One of two recognized units of heat, used especially to express the heat- or energy-producing content of foods. The **large, great, greater,** or **kilogram calorie** (Abbr. *Cal.*) is the amount of heat required to raise the temperature of one kilogram of water 1° C. The **small, lesser,** or **gram calorie** (Abbr. *cal.*) is the amount of heat required to raise one gram of water 1° C. **2.** *Physiol.* The large calorie, a measure of the energy value of foods or the heat output of organisms. Also **cal′o·ry.** [< F *calorie* < L *calor* heat]

cal·o·rif·ic (kal′ə·rif′ik) *adj.* Pertaining to or producing heat. [< F *calorifique* < L *calorificus*]

ca·lor·i·fi·ca·tion (kə·lôr′ə·fi·kā′shən, -lor′-) *n.* The production of heat.

cal·o·rim·e·ter (kal′ə·rim′ə·tər) *n.* Any apparatus for measuring the quantity of heat generated by friction, combustion, or chemical change. — **bomb calorimeter** *Physiol.* A steel-walled container in which measured quantities of foods may be tested to determine their calorific value. [< L *calor* heat + -METER]

cal·o·rim·e·try (kal′ə·rim′ə·trē) *n.* The measurement of heat. — **cal·o·ri·met·ric** (kə·lôr′ə·met′rik, -lor′-) or **·met·ri·cal** *adj.*

ca·lotte (kə·lot′) *n.* A skullcap, especially that worn by the Roman Catholic clergy. [< F, appar. dim. of *cale* cap, caul]

cal·o·yer (kal′ə·yər, kə·loi′ər) *n.* An Eastern Orthodox monk. [< F < Ital. *caloiero* venerable < LGk. *kalogéros* < Gk. *kalos* fair + *gēras* old age]

cal·pac (kal′pak) *n.* A black sheepskin or felt cap worn by Armenians, Turks, etc.: also spelled *kalpak.* Also **cal′pack.** [< Turkish *kälpäk*]

Cal·pe (kal′pē) Ancient name for the ROCK OF GIBRALTAR.

cal·trop (kal′trəp) *n.* **1.** *Mil.* A small iron ball with four sharp-pointed spikes so mounted that one is always upright, formerly used to impede cavalry or infantry: also called *crowfoot.* **2.** One of various plants constituting a family (*Zygophyllaceae*), with spiny heads or fruit that entangle the feet, as the **hairy caltrop** (*Kallstroemia hirsutissima*) and the puncturevine: also called *crowfoot.* Also **cal′trap** (-trəp). [OE *coltetræppe* < L *calx* heel + LL *trappa* trap]

cal·u·met (kal′yə·met, kal′yə·met′) *n.* A tobacco pipe with a long, ornamented stem, used by American Indians in ceremonies, to ratify treaties, etc.: also called *peace pipe, pipe of peace.* See illustration on next page. [< dial. F, pipe stem < L *calamellus,* dim. of *calamus* reed]

Cal·u·met City (kal′yə·met) A city in NE Illinois; pop. 33,107.

ca·lum·ni·ate (kə·lum′nē·āt) *v.t.* & *v.i.* ·at·ed, ·at·ing To accuse falsely; defame; slander. — **Syn.** See ASPERSE. [< L *calumniatus,* pp. of *calumniari* to slander < *calumnia* slander] — **ca·lum′ni·a′tion** *n.* — **ca·lum′ni·a′tor** *n.*

ca·lum·ni·ous (kə·lum′nē·əs) *adj.* Slanderous; defamatory. Also **ca·lum′ni·a·to·ry** (-tôr′ē, -tō′rē). — **ca·lum′ni·ous·ly** *adv.*

cal·um·ny (kal′əm·nē) *n. pl.* ·nies 1. A false and malicious accusation or report, made to injure another. 2. Defamation; slander. [< MF *calomnie* < L *calumnia* slander. Doublet of CHALLENGE.]

cal·u·tron (kal′yə·tron) *n. Physics* A mass spectrograph used for separating isotopes. [< *Cal(ifornia) U(niversity) (cyclo)tron*]

Cal·va·dos (kȧl·vȧ·dōs′) *n.* A brandy made from cider. Also **cal′va·dos.** [after *Calvados,* department in NW France]

cal·var·i·a (kal·vâr′ē·ə) *n. Anat.* The vaulted upper portion of the cranium. Also **cal·var′i·um** (-ē·əm). [< L, skull]

cal·va·ry (kal′vər·ē) *n. pl.* ·ries A sculptured representation of the Crucifixion, usually erected in the open air.

Cal·va·ry (kal′vər·ē) The place, near the site of ancient Jerusalem, where Christ was crucified; Golgotha. *Luke* xxiii 33. [< L *calvaria* skull, trans. of Aramaic *gogolthā*]

Calvary cross *Heraldry* A Latin cross set on three graduated steps. For illustration see CROSS.

calve (kav, käv) *v.t.* & *v.i.* **calved, calv·ing** 1. To bring forth (a calf). 2. To throw off (a berg), as a glacier. [OE *cealfian* < *cealf* calf]

Cal·vert (kal′vərt), **Sir George,** 1580?–1632, first Baron Baltimore, English statesman; founder of Maryland. — **Leonard,** 1606?–47, English statesman; first governor of Maryland; son of the preceding.

calves (kavz, kävz) Plural of CALF.

calves·foot jelly (kavz′fŏŏt′, kävz′-) Calf's-foot jelly (which see).

Cal·vin (kal′vin), **John,** 1509–64, French Protestant reformer.

Cal·vin·ism (kal′vin·iz′əm) *n.* 1. *Theol.* **a** The system or doctrines of John Calvin, emphasizing the depravity and helplessness of man, the sovereignty of God, and predestination, and characterized by an austere moral code. **b** Any later system based upon the teachings of Calvin. 2. Belief in or support for such a system. — **Cal′vin·ist** *n.* — **Cal′vin·is′tic** or ·ti·cal *adj.* — **Cal′vin·is′ti·cal·ly** *adv.*

cal·vi·ties (kal·vish′i·ēz) *n.* Baldness, especially on the top or back of the head. [< L < *calvus* bald]

calx (kalks) *n. pl.* **calx·es** or **cal·ces** (kal′sēz) 1. The residue from the calcination of minerals. 2. Lime or chalk. [< L]

cal·y·ces (kal′ə·sēz, kā′lə-) Alternative plural of CALYX.

cal·y·cine (kal′ə·sin, -sīn) *adj.* Of, pertaining to, or like a calyx. Also **ca·lyc·i·nal** (kə·lis′ə·nəl).

cal·y·cle (kal′i·kəl) *n. Bot.* A secondary calyx. [< L *calyculus,* dim. of *calyx.* See CALYX.] — **ca·lyc·u·lar** (kə·lik′yə·lər), **ca·lyc′u·late** (-lāt, -lit) *adj.*

Cal·y·don (kal′ə·don) A city in ancient Greece, in Aetolia. — **Cal·y·do·ni·an** (kal′ə·dō′nē·ən, -dōn′yən) *adj.* & *n.*

Calydon, Gulf of See (Gulf of) PATRAS.

Calydonian boar In Greek mythology, a great boar sent by Artemis to ravage Calydon. See MELEAGER.

ca·lyp·so[1] (kə·lip′sō) *n.* An orchid (*Calypso bulbosa*), growing in boggy regions of northern Europe and North America. [after *Calypso*]

ca·lyp·so[2] (kə·lip′sō) *n.* An improvised song, originally Trinidadian, dealing with news, love, etc. [Origin uncertain]

Ca·lyp·so (kə·lip′sō) In the *Odyssey,* a nymph who kept Odysseus for seven years on the island of Ogygia where he had been shipwrecked.

ca·lyp·tra (kə·lip′trə) *n. Bot.* 1. In mosses, the hood or covering of the capsule. 2. In flowering plants, any similar hood-shaped organ. Also **ca·lyp′ter.** [< NL < Gk. *kalyptra* veil < *kalyptein* to cover] — **ca·lyp′trate** (-trāt) *adj.*

ca·lyx (kā′liks, kal′iks) *n. pl.* **ca·lyx·es** or **cal·y·ces** (kal′ə·sēz, kā′lə-) 1. *Bot.* The outermost series of leaflike parts of a flower, usually green; the sepals. 2. *Zool.* A cup-shaped part or organ. [< L < Gk. *kalyx* husk, pod]

cam[1] (kam) *n. Mech.* An irregularly shaped piece or projection, as on a wheel or rotating shaft, that imparts reciprocating or variable motion to another piece bearing on it. For illustration see MACHINE. [< Du. tooth, cog of a wheel. Akin to COMB[1].]

cam[2] (kam) *Scot.* Came.

Ca·ma·cho (kä·mä′chō), **(Manuel) Ávila,** 1897–1955, president of Mexico 1940–46.

Ca·ma·güey (kä′mä·gwā′) A Province of eastern Cuba; 10,169 sq. mi.; pop. 889,600 (1970); capital **Camagüey,** pop. 178,600 (1970).

ca·ma·ra·de·rie (kä′mə·rä′dər·ē) *n.* Comradeship; fellowship. [< F]

---

cam·a·ril·la (kam′ə·ril′ə, *Sp.* kä′mä·rē′lyä) *n.* 1. A group of secret, unofficial advisers, especially to a Spanish king; clique; cabal. 2. A small room, as for a king's audiences. [< Sp., dim. of *camara* chamber]

cam·ass (kam′əs) *n.* Any of several North American bulbous herbs of the lily family (genus *Camassia*); especially, the **common camass** (*C. quamash*), having an edible bulb, and the **Eastern camass** (*C. Scilloides*), or wild hyacinth. Also called *quamash:* also **cam′as.** [< Chinook jargon]

Camb. or **Cam.** Cambridge.

cam·ber (kam′bər) *v.t.* 1. To cut or bend to a slight upward convex form. — *v.i.* 2. To have or assume a slight upward curve, as a ship's deck. — *n.* 1. A slight upward bend, as of a timber or an airfoil. 2. An outward inclination of the front wheels of an automobile so that they are farther apart at the top than at the bottom. [< ME *cambrer* to arch < L *camerare* < *camera* curved roof, vault]

Cam·ber·well (kam′bər·wel) A metropolitan borough in SE London; pop. 174,697 (1961).

Camberwell beauty The mourning cloak, a butterfly.

cam·bist (kam′bist) *n. Archaic* 1. A manual of equivalent moneys, weights, and measures. 2. One who deals in bills of exchange, or is versed in exchange values. [< F *cambiste* < Ital. *cambista* < LL *cambiare* to exchange] — **cam′bism, cam′bis·try** *n.*

cam·bi·um (kam′bē·əm) *n. Bot.* A layer of tissue in exogenous plants, from which new wood and bark are formed. For illustration see EXOGEN. [< LL, exchange]

Cam·bo·di·a (kam·bō′dē·ə) A Republic in SE Asia; 69,884 sq. mi.; pop. 7,290,000 (est. 1973); officially *Khmer Republic;* capital, Pnom-Penh. *French* **Cam·bodge** (kän·bôj′). See map of Thailand. — **Cam·bo′di·an** *adj.* & *n.*

cam·bo·gi·a (kam·bō′jē·ə) *n.* Gamboge, a resin.

Cam·brai (kän·brā′) A city in northern France, on the Schelde; pop. about 30,000; formerly **Cam·bray′.**

Cam·bri·a (kam′brē·ə) The Medieval Latin name for WALES.

Cam·bri·an (kam′brē·ən) *adj.* 1. Of or pertaining to Cambria; Welsh. 2. *Geol.* Denoting or of the earliest of the periods of the Paleozoic era. See chart under GEOLOGY. — *n.* 1. The Cambrian strata or period. 2. A Welshman.

cam·bric (kām′brik) *n.* A fine white linen, or a similar fabric of cotton. [< Flemish *Kameryk* Cambrai]

cambric tea A drink made of sweetened hot water and milk, sometimes flavored with a little tea.

Cam·bridge (kām′brij) 1. The county seat of Cambridgeshire, England, in the southern part of the county; site of Cambridge University; pop. 100,250 (1976): Medieval Latin *Cantabrigia.* See CANTABRIGIAN. 2. A city in eastern Massachusetts; pop. 100,361. 3. Cambridgeshire.

Cam·bridge·shire (kām′brij·shir) A county in SE England; 492 sq. mi.; pop. 540,300 (1976, with Isle of Ely); county seat, Cambridge.

Cam·by·ses (kam·bī′sēz), died 521? B.C., king of Persia 529?–522 B.C.; son of Cyrus the Great.

Cam·den (kam′dən) 1. A port city on the Delaware River in SW New Jersey; pop. 102,551. 2. A town in central South Carolina; scene of Revolutionary War battles, 1780, 1781; pop. 8,532.

came[1] (kām) Past tense of COME.

came[2] (kām) *n. Brit.* A grooved leaden strip for fastening panes in latticed or stained-glass windows. [Prob. var. of obs. *calm* a mold]

cam·el (kam′əl) *n.* 1. A large Asian or African ruminant (genus *Camelus*) with a humped back, capable of subsisting for extended periods of time without water, used as a beast of burden. There are two species, the **Arabian camel** or dromedary, having one hump, and the **Bactrian camel** (*C. bastrianus*), having two. 2. *Naut.* A watertight device attached to a vessel and filled with air to increase its buoyancy. [OE < L *camelus* < Gk. *kamēlos* < Semitic]

CAMELS
A Arabian (to 7 feet high at shoulder) B Bactrian (about 6 feet)

cam·el·eer (kam′əl·ir′) *n.* A camel driver.

cam·el·hair (kam′əl·hâr′) *n.* Camel's hair (which see). — *adj.* Camel's-hair.

ca·mel·lia (kə·mēl′yə, -mel′ē·ə) *n.* A tropical Asian tree or shrub (*Camellia* or *Thea japonica*) with glossy leaves and white, pink, red, or variegated flowers: also called *japonica.* [< NL, after G. J. *Kamel,* 1661–1706, Jesuit traveler]

ca·mel·o·pard (kə·mel′ə·pärd) *n. Archaic* The giraffe. [< L *cameleopardus* < Gk. *kamēlopardalis* < *kamēlos* camel + *pardalis* leopard]

Ca·mel·o·par·da·lis (kə·mel′ə·pär′də·lis) *n.* A constellation, the Giraffe. See CONSTELLATION. Also **Ca·mel′o·pard, Ca·mel′o·par′dus** (-dəs).

Cam·e·lot (kam′ə·lot) In Arthurian legend, the seat of King Arthur's court, variously identified with Caerleon, Camelford, Winchester, and a hill in Somerset.

camel's hair **1.** The hair of the camel. **2.** A soft, warm, usually tan cloth made of camel's hair, sometimes mixed with wool or other fibers. — **cam·el′s-hair** (kam′əlz-hâr′) *adj.*

camel's-hair brush A painter's small brush made of the hairs from a squirrel's tail.

Cam·em·bert (kam′əm·bâr, *Fr.* kà·mäⁿ·bâr′) *n.* A rich, creamy, soft cheese. [after *Camembert*, town in NW France]

cam·e·o (kam′ē·ō) *n.* *pl.* **·os** **1.** A gem of differently colored layers, having a design carved in relief on one with the other layer or layers serving as background. **2.** Carving done in this manner. [< Ital. *cammeo*; ult. origin unknown]

cam·er·a (kam′ər·ə, kam′rə) *n.* *pl.* **·er·as** *for defs. 1 and 2,* **·er·ae** (-ə·rē) *for defs. 3 and 4.* **1.** A lightproof chamber or box in which the image of an exterior object is projected upon a sensitized plate or film through a shuttered opening usually equipped with a lens or lenses. **2.** *Telecom.* An enclosed unit containing the light-sensitive electron tube that converts optical images into electrical impulses for television transmission. **3.** A camera obscura. **4.** A chamber; especially, a judge's private room. — **in camera** *Law* Not in public court; privately. [< L, vaulted room < Gk. *kamara*. Doublet of CHAMBER.]

cam·er·al (kam′ər·əl) *adj.* Pertaining to a judge's chamber, public office, or treasury.

camera lu·ci·da (lōō′si·də) A device by which the image of a body appears as if projected on a sheet of paper or other surface, where it may be traced.

cam·er·a·man (kam′ər·ə·man′, kam′rə-) *n.pl.* **·men** (-men′) The operator of a camera, especially a motion-picture camera.

camera ob·scu·ra (ob·skyŏōr′ə) A darkened box in which the real image of an object, received through a small aperture, usually with a lens, is projected in its natural colors upon a plane surface for viewing, tracing, or photographing.

CAMERA LUCIDA
a Eyepiece.
b Mirror. *c* Glass slide.
d Image plane.

cam·er·lin·go (kam′ər·ling′gō) *n.* In the Roman Catholic Church, the cardinal who administers the finances and secular interests of the Pope. Also **cam′er·len′go** (-leng′gō). [< Ital. *camerlingo* chamberlain < L *camera* chamber]

Cam·e·roon (kam′ə·rōōn′) **1.** A Republic in Africa, on the Gulf of Guinea; 183,376 sq. mi. (including part of the former British Cameroons); pop. 6,000,000 (est. 1970); capital, Yaoundé: formerly *French Cameroons.* French **Ca·me·roun** (kàm·rōōn′). **2.** A volcanic mountain in western Cameroun; highest point 13,350 ft.

Cam·e·roons (kam′ə·rōōnz′) A former German colony in western equatorial Africa; divided in 1946 into the UN Trust Territories of British Cameroons (which see) and French Cameroons (which see): German *Kamerun.*

cam·i·on (kam′ē·ən, *Fr.* kà·myôⁿ′) *n.* **1.** A military truck. **2.** A low, heavy wagon; dray. [< F]

cam·i·sa·do (kam′i·sā′dō) *n.* *Archaic* A night attack by soldiers wearing shirts over their armor for identification. Also **cam′i·sade′** (-sād′) [< Sp. *camisada* < *camisa* shirt]

ca·mise (kə·mēs′) *n.* A loose shirt, smock, or gown. Also **ca·mis·i·a** (kə·mis′ē·ə). [< Arabic *qamīs* < LL *camisia* shirt]

cam·i·sole (kam′ə·sōl) *n.* **1.** A woman's fancy underwaist, worn with a sheer bodice. **2.** A brief negligee. **3.** A type of straitjacket. **4.** Formerly, a man's jacket or jersey with sleeves. [< F < Sp. *camisola,* dim. of *camisa* shirt]

Cam·lan (kam′lən) In Arthurian legend, the battlefield where King Arthur was mortally wounded.

cam·let (kam′lit) *n.* **1.** A stiff, closely woven fabric of camel's hair, or an imitation of it. **2.** A garment made from this fabric. [< MF *camelot* < OF *chamelot,* ? < Arabic *khamlat* nap, pile on cloth]

Cam·maerts (käm′ärts), **Émile,** 1878–1953, Belgian poet.

Cam·o·ëns (kam′ō·ens), **Luis de,** 1524–80, Portuguese poet. Portuguese **Ca·mões** (kə·moiñsh′).

cam·o·mile (kam′ə·mīl) *n.* **1.** A strongly scented, bitter herb of the genus *Anthemis;* especially, a European perennial (*A. nobilis*) whose bitter, aromatic flowers and leaves are used in medicine. **2.** Any plant of a genus (*Matricaria*) of widely distributed herbs of the composite family. Also spelled *chamomile.* [< F *camomille* < L *chamomilla,* alter. of Gk. *chamaimēlon* < *chamai* on the ground + *mēlon* apple]

Ca·mor·ra (kə·môr′ə, -mor′ə, *Ital.* kä·môr′rä) *n.* A secret society of Naples, Italy, formed about 1820, practicing violence and extortion. Compare MAFIA. — **Ca·mor′rism** *n.* — **Ca·mor′rist** *n.*

cam·ou·flage (kam′ə·fläzh, -fläj) *n.* **1.** *Mil.* Measures or material used to conceal or misrepresent the identity of installations, ships, etc. **2.** Any disguise or pretense. — *v.t.* & *v.i.* **·flaged, ·flag·ing** To hide or obscure, as with disguises. [< F < *camoufler* to disguise] — **cam′ou·flag′er** *n.*

camp¹ (kamp) *n.* **1.** A group of tents or other temporary shelters, as for soldiers or hunters; also, the ground or area so employed. **2.** The persons occupying a group of tents, etc.

3. A tent, cabin, etc., or a group of such structures, usually in the country, for vacations or outings: a fishing *camp;* summer *camp.* **4.** *U.S.* A town hastily constructed near a mine: so called because originally consisting of tents. **5.** Military life. **6.** A body of persons supporting a policy, theory, or doctrine; also, the position so upheld. — *v.i.* **1.** To set up or live in a camp; encamp. **2.** To hold stubbornly to a position: Strikers *camped* in front of the factory. — *v.t.* **3.** To shelter or station in a camp. — **to camp out** To sleep in a tent; live in the open. [< MF < Ital. *campo* field < L *campus* level plain]

camp² (kamp) *n.* **1.** A comical style or quality typically perceived in banal, flamboyant, or patently artificial gestures, appearances, literary works, etc., that intentionally or unwittingly seem to parody themselves. **2.** A person, thing, aspect, etc., marked by this style or quality. — *adj.* Of or characterized by camp, or by a ready appreciation of camp: the *camp* sensibility; in the *camp* tradition of Hollywood's gangster films. — *v.i. Slang* **1.** To behave, dress, etc., in a theatrical or bizarre way to get attention. — *v.t. Slang* **2.** To invest with a camp quality. [? < dial. E *camp* or *kemp* bold, impetuous fellow]

Cam·pa·gna (käm·pä′nyə) A lowland surrounding Rome; about 800 sq. mi. Also **Campagna di Ro·ma** (dē rō′mä).

cam·paign (kam·pān′) *n.* **1.** A series of connected military operations conducted for a common objective, in a particular area, etc. **2.** An organized series of activities designed to obtain a definite result. — *v.i.* To serve in, conduct, or go on a campaign. [< F *campagne,* lit., open country, field < Ital. *campagna,* orig. < L *campus*] — **cam·paign′er** *n.*

Cam·pa·ni·a (kam·pā′nē·ə, *Ital.* käm·pä′nyä) A Region of southern Italy; 5,249 sq. mi.; pop. 4,756,094 (1961); capital, Naples. — **Cam·pa′ni·an** *adj.* & *n.*

cam·pa·ni·le (kam′pə·nē′lē, *Ital.* käm′pä·nē′lä) *n.* *pl.* **·les** or **·li** (-lē) A bell tower, especially one that is not part of a building. [< Ital. < LL *campana* bell]

cam·pa·nol·o·gy (kam′pə·nol′ə·jē) *n.* **1.** The study of bells. **2.** The art of casting and ringing bells. [< LL *campana* bell + -LOGY] — **cam′pa·nol′o·gist** *n.*

cam·pan·u·la (kam·pan′yə·lə) *n.* **1.** A member of a large genus of plants (*Campanula*), the bellflowers, as the harebell, Canterbury bell, etc.: also called *bellwort.* **2.** *Zool.* A bell-shaped structure or part. [< NL, dim. of LL *campana* bell]

cam·pan·u·la·ceous (kam·pan′yə·lā′shəs) *adj. Bot.* Belonging to the bellflower family (*Campanulaceae*) of plants.

cam·pan·u·late (kam·pan′yə·lit, -lāt) *adj.* Bell-shaped, as a corolla. Also **cam·pan′i·form.**

Camp·bell (kam′bəl, kam′əl), **Alexander,** 1788–1866, U.S. theologian born in Ireland; founder of the Disciples of Christ. — **Thomas,** 1777–1844, Scottish poet. — **Thomas,** 1763–1854, U.S. theologian born in Ireland; founder, with his son Alexander, of the Disciples of Christ.

Camp·bell-Ban·ner·man (kam′bəl·ban′ər·mən, kam′əl-), **Sir Henry,** 1836–1908, British statesman; prime minister 1905–1908.

Camp·bel·lite (kam′bə·līt, kam′ə-) A member of the Disciples of Christ, founded by Thomas and Alexander Campbell. The name is rejected by the denomination.

camp chair A light, folding chair.

camp·craft (kamp′kraft′, -kräft) *n.* The art or practice of camping out.

Cam·pe·che (kam·pē′chē, *Sp.* käm·pā′chä) A State in SE Mexico; 19,673 sq. mi.; pop. 250,391 (1970); capital, **Campeche;** pop. 81,147 (1970).

Campeche, Gulf of The SW part of the Gulf of Mexico. Also **Bay of Campeche.**

camp·er (kamp′ər) *n.* **1.** One who camps out or lives in a camp. **2.** A member of a camp, as a summer camp for children. **3.** A vehicle affording shelter and usually sleeping accommodations for travelers and campers: also **camper wagon.**

cam·pes·tral (kam·pes′trəl) *adj.* Growing in or pertaining to fields or open country. [< L *campestris* < *campus* field]

camp·fire (kamp′fīr′) *n.* **1.** A fire in an outdoor camp, for cooking, warmth, etc. **2.** A meeting or gathering, as around a campfire; especially, a reunion. Also **camp fire.**

campfire girl A girl between seven and eighteen years of age, belonging to the **Camp Fire Girls of America,** an organization incorporated in 1914 for promoting the health and welfare of young women by encouraging outdoor life, etc.

camp follower **1.** A civilian who follows an army about, usually a merchant or prostitute. **2.** One who supports a movement, etc., without formally belonging to it; hanger-on.

camp·ground (kamp′ground′) *n.* An area used for a camp.

cam·phene (kam′fēn, kam·fēn′) *n. Chem.* A hydrocarbon, $C_{10}H_{16}$, found in certain essential oils. [< CAMPHOR]

cam·phol (kam′fōl, -fol) *n. Chem.* Borneol.

cam·phor (kam′fər) *n.* A white, volatile, translucent crystalline compound, $C_{10}H_{16}O$, with a penetrating, fragrant odor and pungent taste, distilled from the wood and bark of the camphor tree and also obtained by organic synthesis, used in medicine and in the chemical and plastics industries. [< F *camphre* < Arabic *kāfūr* < Malay *kāpūr*] — **cam·phor·ic** (kam·fôr′ik, -for′-) *adj.*

cam·phor·ate (kam′fə·rāt) *v.t.* **·at·ed, ·at·ing** To treat or saturate with camphor.

camphor ball A moth ball (which see).

camphor ice A mixture of camphor, white wax, spermaceti, and castor oil, used for chapped skin, etc.

camphor tree 1. A large evergreen tree (*Cinnamomum camphora*) of eastern Asia yielding the camphor of commerce. **2.** A tree (*Dryobalanops aromatica*) of Borneo, Sumatra, and Malaya yielding borneol.

Cam·pi·nas (kaṅm·pē′nəs) A city in SE Brazil; pop. 252,-145 (est. 1968, with suburbs).

camp·ing (kamp′ing) *n.* The act or practice of living outdoors, as in tents or without any shelter, especially for recreation.

cam·pi·on (kam′pē·ən) *n.* One of various herbs of the pink family (genera *Lychnis* and *Silene*), as the rose campion.

Cam·pi·on (kam′pē·ən), **Thomas,** 1567–1620, English poet and song writer.

camp meeting A series of religious meetings held in a grove or field, usually in a tent; also, one such meeting.

cam·po[1] (kam′pō, käm′-) *n. pl.* **·pi** (-pē) In Italy, an open space in a town. [< Ital.]

cam·po[2] (kam′pō, käm′-) *n. pl.* **·pos** (-pōz) In South American countries, an open, level plain, with scattered shrubbery and trees. [< Sp.]

Cam·po·bel·lo (kam′pō·bel′ō) An island in SW New Brunswick, eastern Canada, in the Bay of Fundy.

Cam·po·for·mi·do (käm′pō·fôr′mē·dō) A town in NE Italy; site of the signing of a treaty between Austria and France (1797); pop. about 1,000; formerly **Cam′po·for′mio** (-fôr′-myō), **Cam′po For′mio.**

cam·po san·to (käm′pō sän′tō) *Italian* A cemetery; literally, holy field.

camp robber *Canadian* The Canada jay.

camp·site (kamp′sīt′) *n. U.S. & Canadian* A small plot in an area designated for camping, usually with a table and fireplace, available toilets and water, and often having facilities for sports, games, etc.

camp·stool (kamp′stōol′) *n.* A light, folding stool.

cam·pus (kam′pəs) *n. U.S.* The grounds of a school or college, or the court enclosed by the buildings. [< L, field]

camp·y (kam′pē) *adj.* **camp·i·er, camp·i·est** Being or characteristic of camp[2]; comically exaggerated, theatrical, or bizarre: a *campy* style. [< CAMP[2] + -Y[1]]

cam·shaft (kam′shaft′, -shäft′) *n.* A shaft having one or more cams on it.

Ca·mus (kȧ·mü′), **Albert,** 1913–60, French writer.

can[1] (kan, *unstressed* kən) *v.* Present *3rd person sing.* **can;** *past* **could** A defective verb now used only in the present and past tenses as an auxiliary followed by the infinitive without *to,* or elliptically with the infinitive unexpressed, in the following senses: **1.** To be able to. **2.** To know how to. **3.** To have the right to. **4.** *Informal* To be permitted to; may. [OE *cunnan*]

♦ **can, may** In informal speech and writing, *can* is now acceptable in the sense of *may,* to express permission, especially in questions or negative statements: *Can* I leave now? You *cannot.* At the formal level, the distinction between *can* and *may* is still observed: *can,* to express ability to perform, either mentally or physically; *may,* to denote permission.

can[2] (kan) *n.* **1.** A vessel, usually of tinned iron, for holding or carrying liquids, garbage, etc. **2.** *U.S.* A container of tin plate in which fruits, tobacco, etc., are hermetically sealed; a tin. **3.** *U.S.* The contents of a sealed tin container. **4.** A drinking cup; tankard. **5.** *U.S. Slang* **a** Jail. **b** A toilet. **c** The buttocks. — *v.t.* **canned, can·ning 1.** To put up in cans, jars, etc.; preserve. **2.** *Slang* To record for sound or film reproduction. **3.** *U.S. Slang* **a** To dismiss; discharge. **b** To cease; stop: *Can* it! [OE *canne* cup] — **can′ner** *n.*

can. 1. Canon. **2.** Canto.

Can. 1. Canada. **2.** Canadian.

Ca·na (kā′nə) A Biblical locality in northern Palestine; scene of Christ's first miracle. *John* ii 1. Also **Cana of Galilee.**

Ca·naan (kā′nən) **1.** The fourth son of Ham. **2.** The name given by the Israelites to the part of Palestine between the Jordan and the Mediterranean; the Promised Land.

Ca·naan·ite (kā′nən·īt) *n.* **1.** A dweller in Canaan prior to the Israelite conquest. **2.** A descendant of Canaan, the son of Ham. — **Ca′naan·it′ish** (-ī′tish), **Ca′naan·it′ic** (-it′ik) *adj.*

Canad. Canadian.

Can·a·da (kan′ə·də) A self-governing member of the British Commonwealth of Nations, in northern North America, comprising ten Provinces and two Territories; 3,851,809 sq. mi.; pop. 21,681,000 (est. 1969); capital, Ottawa. — **Ca·na·di·an** (kə·nā′dē·ən) *adj. & n.*

Canada balsam A yellowish turpentine derived from the balsam fir, used as a mounting cement in microscopy.

Canada bluegrass Wiregrass (which see).

Canada goose The common wild goose of North America (*Branta canadensis*), brownish gray with black neck and head.

Canada hemp Indian hemp (def. 2).

Canada jay A nonmigratory, sooty gray bird (*Perisoreus canadensis*) of the crow family, native in Canada and the NE United States: also called *camp robber, lumber-jack, moosebird, venison bird, whisky-jack.*

CANADA GOOSE
(To 43 inches long)

Canada lily An American lily (*Lilium canadense*) with drooping orange or yellow flowers: also called *meadow lily.*

Canada sparrow A tree sparrow (which see).

Canada thistle See under THISTLE.

Canadian English The English language as characteristically spoken and written by Canadians.

Canadian French The French language as characteristically spoken and written by French-Canadians.

Ca·na·di·an·ism (kə·nā′dē·ən·iz′əm) *n.* **1.** A trait, custom, or tradition characteristic of the people of Canada or some of them. **2.** A word, phrase, or usage especially characteristic of Canadian English or French. **3.** Devotion to Canada, its institutions, etc.

Canadian River A river in the SW United States, flowing 906 miles east to the Arkansas River.

Canadian Shield See LAURENTIAN PLATEAU.

Ca·na·dien (kȧ·nȧ·dyaṅ′) *n.* A French Canadian. — **Ca·na·dienne** (-dyen′) *n. fem.*

ca·naille (kə·nāl′, *Fr.* kȧ·nä′y′) *n.* The rabble; mob. [< F < Ital. *canaglia* pack of dogs < L *canis* dog]

Ça·nak·ka·le Bo·ğa·zi (chä′nä·kä·le′ bō′ä·zi′) The Turkish name for the DARDANELLES.

ca·nal (kə·nal′) *n.* **1.** An artificial waterway for inland navigation, irrigation, etc. **2.** *Anat. & Zool.* A passage or duct; tube: the auditory *canal.* **3.** *Astron.* One of the faint, linear markings visible on Mars. — **central canal** *Anat.* The ventricle of the spinal cord. — *v.t.* **ca·nalled** or **·naled, ca·nal·ling** or **·nal·ing** To dig a canal through, or provide with canals. [< MF < L *canalis* groove. Doublet of CHANNEL.]

canal boat A long barge, used on canals.

can·a·lic·u·late (kan′ə·lik′yə·lit, -lāt) *adj.* Channeled or grooved. Also **can′a·lic′u·lar** (-lər), **can′a·lic′u·lat′ed.**

can·a·lic·u·lus (kan′ə·lik′yə·ləs) *n. pl.* **·li** (-lī) *Anat.* A small tube or canal, as in a bone. [< L *canaliculus,* dim. of *canalis* pipe, groove]

ca·nal·i·za·tion (kə·nal′ə·zā′shən, kan′əl·ə-) *n.* **1.** The act of making canals. **2.** A system of canals. **3.** *Surg.* A method of draining wounds through the formation of canals, but without the use of tubes.

ca·nal·ize (kə·nal′īz, kan′əl·īz) *v.t.* **·ized, ·iz·ing 1.** To convert into a canal, as a stream or chain of lakes. **2.** To furnish with a canal, or a system of canals. **3.** To direct into set channels; furnish with an outlet: to *canalize* emotions.

canal rays *Physics* A stream of positively charged ions emitted from the anode of an electron tube and emerging through openings in the cathode: also called *positive rays.*

Canal Zone A strip of territory leased in perpetuity to the United States by the Republic of Panama, extending five miles on each side of the Panama Canal, across the Isthmus of Panama; 648 sq. mi.; pop. 44,650 (est. 1970); administrative headquarters, Balboa Heights. Abbr. *C.Z.*

Can·an·dai·gua Lake (kan′ən·dā′gwə) One of the Finger Lakes in western New York.

can·a·pé (kan′ə·pē, -pā, *Fr.* kȧ·nȧ·pā′) *n.* A thin piece of toasted or fried bread spread with cheese, caviar, etc. [< F. See CANOPY.]

Ca·na·ra (kä′nə·rə, kə·nä′rə) See KANARA.

ca·nard (kə·närd′, *Fr.* kȧ·när′) *n.* A false or absurd story or rumor; a hoax. [< F, duck]

Ca·na·rese (kä′nə·rēz′, -rēs′) See KANARESE.

ca·nar·y (kə·nâr′ē) *n. pl.* **·nar·ies 1.** A small finch (*Serinus canarius*) originally native in the Canary Islands, having generally yellow plumage, popular as a cage bird for its song. **2.** A bright yellow color. Also **canary yellow. 3.** A sweet, white wine from the Canary Islands. **4.** An old French dance in rapid time. [< F *canarie* < Sp. *canario* < L *Canaria* (*Insula*) Dog (Island) < *canis* dog]

canary grass A grass (*Phalaris canariensis*) native in the Canary Islands and cultivated for its seeds (**canary seed**), used as food for cage birds.

Canary Islands An island group near the NW coast of Africa, comprising two Provinces of Spain; 2,808 sq. mi.; pop. 1,017,361 (est. 1965). Also **Canaries.** Spanish *Islas Canarias.*

ca·nas·ta (kə·nas′tə) *n.* A card game for two to six players, based on rummy. [< Sp., basket]

Ca·nav·er·al (kə·nav′ər·əl), **Cape** See (Cape) KENNEDY.

Map showing MEDITERRANEAN SEA, Damascus, Sea of Galilee, Jordan, Jerusalem, DEAD SEA

Can·ber·ra (kan′bər-ə) The capital of Australia, in Australian Capital Territory; pop. 92,308 (1966).

can buoy See under BUOY.

Can·by (kan′bē), **Henry Seidel**, 1878–1961, U.S. editor and writer.

canc. Cancel; cancellation; canceled.

can·can (kan′kan′, *Fr.* kän·kän′) *n.* A dance, introduced in Paris about 1830, in which the figures of the quadrille were diversified by high kicking and exaggerated movements. [< MF, noise, disturbance]

can·cel (kan′səl) *v.* **can·celed** or **·celled, can·cel·ing** or **·cel·ling** *v.t.* **1.** To mark out or off, as by drawing lines through; strike out; obliterate. **2.** To render null and void; annul. **3.** To delete or withdraw, as from a schedule or program; call off. **4.** To mark or otherwise deface, as a postage stamp, to show that it has been used. **5.** To make up for; compensate or neutralize. **6.** *Math.* To eliminate (a common factor, as a figure or quantity) from the numerator and denominator of a fraction, or from both sides of an equation. **7.** *Printing* To omit; delete. — *v.i.* **8.** To cancel one another: with *out.* — *n. Printing* **1.** The striking out or omission of printed matter. **2.** The matter omitted, or the replacement for it. Abbr. *canc.* [< MF *canceller* < L *cancellare* to cross out < *cancelli,* dim. pl. of *cancer* lattice] — **can′cel·er** or **can′cel·ler** *n.*
   — **Syn.** (verb) **1.** *Cancel, efface, erase, expunge, obliterate,* and *delete* mean to remove written or engraved characters from paper, wax, stone, etc. To *cancel* is to cross out by drawing lines through. Incised characters are *effaced* by smoothing away the surface until they disappear; written characters are *erased* by rubbing away the ink. *Expunge* originally meant to punch or scratch out with a sharp instrument; it now suggests the wiping away of what has been written. To *obliterate* is to cover over or remove completely. Something *canceled* can still be read; that which is *erased* may still appear faintly; but that which is *obliterated* is gone forever. *Delete* is used of material that is marked for removal or omission by a printer. **2.** See ANNUL. **6.** *Cancel* and *eliminate* mean to remove terms in mathematical expressions. Terms are *canceled* in multiplication and division, but *eliminated* in addition and subtraction.

can·cel·a·ble (kan′səl-ə-bəl) *adj.* That can be canceled. Also **can′cel·la·ble.**

can·cel·late (kan′sə-lāt, -lit) *adj. Anat.* Having a lattice-like structure. Also **can′cel·lat′ed, can′cel·lous** (-ləs).

can·cel·la·tion (kan′sə-lā′shən) *n.* **1.** The act of canceling or rendering void. **2.** The marks used in canceling. **3.** That which is canceled. Also **can·ce·la′tion.** Abbr. *canc.*

can·cer (kan′sər) *n.* **1.** Any of a group of often fatal diseases characterized by abnormal cellular growth and by malignancy. See CARCINOMA, LEUKEMIA, SARCOMA. **2.** A malignant tumor. **3.** Any dangerous and spreading evil. [< L, crab] — **can′cer·ous** *adj.* — **can′cer·ous·ly** *adv.*

Can·cer (kan′sər) *n.* A constellation, the Crab; also, the fourth sign of the zodiac. See CONSTELLATION, ZODIAC.

can·cer·ate (kan′sə-rāt) *v.i.* **·at·ed, ·at·ing** *Pathol.* To become cancerous; develop into a cancer. — **can′cer·a′tion** *n.*

can·croid (kang′kroid) *adj.* **1.** Like a crab. **2.** Resembling a cancer. — *n. Pathol.* A mild epithelioma.

can·de·la·brum (kan′də-lä′brəm, -lā′-) *n. pl.* **·bra** (-brə) or **·brums** A large, branched candlestick. Also **can′de·la′bra** (-brə) *pl.* **·bras.** [< L *candela* candle]

can·dent (kan′dənt) *adj. Archaic* Incandescent. [< L *candens, -entis,* ppr. of *candere* to gleam]

can·des·cence (kan-des′əns) *n. Rare* Incandescence. [< L *incandescens, -entis,* ult. < *candere* to gleam] — **can·des′cent** *adj.* — **can·des′cent·ly** *adv.*

Can·di·a (kan′dē-ə) **1.** A port city in northern Crete; pop. 63,458 (1961): Greek *Iraklion, Herakleion.* **2.** See CRETE.

can·did (kan′did) *adj.* **1.** Honest and open; sincere; frank. **2.** Impartial; fair. **3.** *Archaic* Pure. **4.** *Obs.* White. [< MF *candide* pure, honest < L *candidus* < *candere* to gleam] — **can′did·ly** *adv.* — **can′did·ness** *n.*
   — **Syn. 1.** *Candid, frank,* and *open* imply truthfulness in speech or action. A *candid* statement is intended to be accurate and complete. A *frank* person speaks his mind freely sometimes to an embarrassing degree, while the *open* man is one who does not conceal motives, reasons, or facts. Compare BLUNT, HONEST. — **Ant.** deceitful, insincere, reserved.

can·di·da·cy (kan′də-də-sē) *n. pl.* **·cies** The state or position of being a candidate. Also **can·di·da·ture** (kan′də-də-chŏŏr, -dā′chər), **can·di·date·ship′** (-dit-ship′).

can·di·date (kan′də-dāt, -dit) *n.* One who seeks, or is nominated for, an office, honor, or privilege. [< L *candidatus* wearing white < *candidus* white; because office seekers in Rome wore white togas]

candid camera A small camera with a fast lens, used for taking informal, unposed pictures.

Can·dide (kän-dēd′) Hero of Voltaire's satire *Candide* (1759), that ironically illustrates the optimistic doctrine that this is "the best of all possible worlds."

can·died (kan′dēd) *adj.* **1.** Saturated or incrusted with sugar or the like. **2.** Crystallized or granulated. **3.** Flattering; honeyed; sugared.

Can·di·ot (kan′dē-ot) *adj.* Of or pertaining to Candia; Cretan. — *n.* A Cretan. Also **Can′di·ote** (-ōt).

can·dle (kan′dəl) *n.* **1.** A cylinder of tallow, wax, or other solid fat, containing a wick, that gives light when burning. **2.** Anything like a candle in shape or purpose: a fumigating *candle.* **3.** *Mil.* A cylindrical container that, when ignited, emits a cloud of smoke or gas. **4.** *Physics* A unit of luminous intensity now equal to that of ⅟₆₀ square centimeter of a black body operating at the temperature of solidification of platinum: also called *standard candle.* **5.** An international candle (which see). Abbr. (def. 4) *c., C.* — **to hold a candle to** To compare with favorably: usually used in the negative. — *v.t.* **·dled, ·dling** To test, as eggs, by holding between the eye and a light. [OE *candel* < L *candela* < *candere* to gleam] — **can′dler** *n.*

can·dle·ber·ry (kan′dəl-ber′ē) *n. pl.* **·ries** **1.** The wax myrtle. **2.** Its fruit. **3.** An East Indian and Polynesian tree (*Aleurites moluccana*): also called *candlenut.*

can·dle·fish (kan′dəl-fish′) *n.* An edible, oily, smeltlike fish (*Thaleichthys pacificus*) of the northern Pacific that may be burned as a candle when dried: also called *eulachon.*

can·dle·foot (kan′dəl-fŏŏt′) *n.* A foot-candle (which see).

can·dle·hold·er (kan′dəl-hōl′dər) *n.* A candlestick.

candle ice *Canadian* Candle-shaped crystals of rotten ice, as on a river or a lake.

can·dle·light (kan′dəl-līt′) *n.* **1.** Light given by a candle; artificial light. **2.** Twilight, when candles are first needed: also **can′dle·light′ing.** Also **candle light.**

Can·dle·mas (kan′dəl-məs) *n.* February 2, the feast of the Purification, or of the Presentation of Christ in the temple. [OE *candelmæsse* < *candel* candle + *mæsse* mass]

can·dle·nut (kan′dəl-nut′) *n.* **1.** The candleberry (def. 3). **2.** The fruit of this tree, burned as candles by Polynesians.

can·dle·pin (kan′dəl-pin′) *n.* A slender, nearly cylindrical pin used in a bowling game called **candlepins.**

can·dle·pow·er (kan′dəl-pou′ər) *n.* The illuminating power of a standard candle, used as a measure. Abbr. *cp, c.p.*

can·dle·stick (kan′dəl-stik′). *n.* A holder with sockets or spikes for a candle or candles. [OE *candelsticca* < *candel* candle + *sticca* stick]

can·dle·wick (kan′dəl-wik′) *n.* The wick of a candle. — *adj.* Made with, using, or for candlewicking: *candlewick* embroidery. [OE *candelweoca* < *candel* candle + *weoca* wick]

can·dle·wick·ing (kan′dəl·wik′ing) *n.* Thick, soft cotton thread like that used to make candlewicks; also, tufts of such thread worked into a fabric to form a design.

can·dle·wood (kan′dəl-wŏŏd′) *n.* **1.** Any resinous wood finely split so as to give light when burned on the hearth. **2.** Any tree or shrub having such wood, as the ocotillo.

can·dor (kan′dər) *n.* **1.** Openness; frankness. **2.** Impartiality; fairness. **3.** *Obs.* Brightness; purity. Also *Brit.* **can′dour.** [< L, sincerity, purity < *candere* to gleam]

can·dy (kan′dē) *n. pl.* **·dies** Any of numerous confections consisting chiefly of sugar or syrup, usually with chocolate, nuts, fruits, etc., added; also, such confections collectively: usually called *sweets* in Great Britain. — *v.* **·died, ·dy·ing** *v.t.* **1.** To cause to form into crystals of sugar. **2.** To preserve by boiling or coating with sugar. **3.** To render pleasant; sweeten. **4.** To overlay with any crystalline substance, as ice or sugar. — *v.i.* **5.** To become crystallized into or covered with sugar. [Short for *sugar candy* < F (*sucre*) *candi* < Arabic *qandī* made of sugar < *qand* sugar, ult. < Skt.]

Can·dy (kan′dē) See KANDY.

can·dy·tuft (kan′dē-tuft′). *n.* A plant of the mustard family (*Iberis amara*) with white, pink, or purple flowers.

cane (kān) *n.* **1.** A walking stick. **2.** The jointed, woody stem of the bamboo, rattan, cane grass, and certain palm trees, used as a weaving material in chairs, etc. **3.** Either of two large shrubby grasses of the southern U.S., the **giant cane** (*Arundaria gigantia*) and the **switch cane** (*A. tecta*). **4.** Sugar cane (which see). **5.** The stem of a raspberry or allied plant. **6.** Any rod, especially one used for flogging. — *v.t.* **caned, can·ing 1.** To strike or beat with a cane. **2.** To make or repair with cane, as a chair. [< OF < L *canna* < Gk. *kanna* reed < Semitic] — **can′er** *n.*

Ca·ne·a (kä-nē′ä) The capital of Crete, a port city in the NW part, on the **Gulf of Canea,** an inlet of the Aegean; pop. 38,467 (1961): ancient *Cydonia.* Greek *Khania.*

cane·brake (kān′brāk′) *n.* A thick growth of cane.

cane grass Any of various plants with slender, flexible stems, usually jointed, as the rattan or sugar cane.

ca·nel·la (kə-nel′ə) *n.* The pale, orange-yellow, aromatic inner bark of a tropical American tree (*Canella winterana*), used as a tonic and condiment. Also **canella bark.** [< Med.L, dim. of *canna* reed]

ca·neph·o·rus (kə-nef′ə-rəs) *n. pl.* **·ri** (-rī) In ancient Greece, the basket bearer, a maiden selected to carry on her head a basket of sacred utensils in religious processions. Also **ca·neph′o·ros** (-ros), **ca·neph′o·ra** (-rə). [< L *canephora* < Gk. *kanēphoros* < *kaneon* basket + *pherein* to carry]

cane sugar Sucrose obtained from the sugar cane.

Ca·nes Ve·nat·i·ci (kā′nēz vi·nat′ə-sī) A constellation, the Hunting Dogs. See CONSTELLATION. [< L]

can·field (kan′fēld) *n.* A gambling game resembling solitaire.

Can·field (kan′fēld), **Dorothy** See (Dorothy Canfield) FISHER.

cangue (kang) *n.* A heavy wooden collar or yoke, formerly used in China for punishment. [< F < Pg. *cango*]

Ca·nic·u·la (kə·nik′yə·lə) *n.* The star Sirius; the Dog Star.

ca·nic·u·lar (kə·nik′yə·lər) *adj.* Relating to the Dog Star or to the dog days. [< L *canicularis* < *canis* dog]

can·i·kin (kan′ə·kin) See CANNIKIN.

ca·nine (kā′nīn) *adj.* 1. Of or like a dog. 2. *Zool.* Of the dog family (*Canidae*). 3. Of or pertaining to a canine tooth. — *n.* 1. A dog or other canine animal. 2. *Anat.* One of the four pointed teeth situated one on either side of the upper and lower incisors; a cuspid: also **canine tooth**. For illustration see TOOTH. [< L *caninus* < *canis* dog]

Ca·nis Ma·jor (kā′nis mā′jər) A constellation, the Greater Dog. See CONSTELLATION. [< L]

Canis Mi·nor (mī′nər) A constellation, the Lesser Dog; also called *Little Dog*. See CONSTELLATION. [< L]

can·is·ter (kan′is·tər) *n.* 1. A container, usually metal, for tea, spices, etc. 2. Formerly, fragments packed in a metallic cylinder, to be fired from a cannon: also **canister shot**. [< L *canistrum* basket < Gk. *kanastron* < *kanna* reed]

ca·ni·ties (kə·nish′i·ēz) *n.* The turning gray of the hair. [< L < *canus* white]

can·ker (kang′kər) *n.* 1. *Pathol.* An ulceration, chiefly of the mouth and lips. 2. Anything that causes corruption, evil, decay, etc. 3. A disease of trees, causing decay of the bark and wood. 4. *Vet.* a A disease of the feet of horses. b An inflammation of the external ear in cats and dogs. 5. The cankerworm. — *v.t.* 1. To affect with canker. 2. To eat away like a canker; corrode; corrupt. — *v.i.* 3. To become infected with or as with canker; rot. [< AF *cancre* < L *cancer* crab, ulcer. Doublet of CHANCRE.]

can·ker·ous (kang′kər·əs) *adj.* 1. Of the nature of a canker. 2. Causing canker. 3. Corroding; corrupting.

can·ker·worm (kang′kər·wûrm′) *n.* Any of several insect larvae that destroy fruit and shade trees.

can·na[1] (kan′ə) *n.* Any of a genus (*Canna*) of erect, mostly tropical American plants with red or yellow irregular flowers. [< L < Gk. *kanna* reed] — **can·na·ceous** (kə·nā′shəs) *adj.*

can·na[2] (kan′ə) *Scot.* Cannot.

can·na·bin (kan′ə·bin) *n.* A greenish black, poisonous crystalline resin extracted from Indian hemp.

can·na·bis (kan′ə·bis) *n.* Hemp (def. 1). [< L < Gk. *kannabis* hemp]

Can·nae (kan′ē) An ancient town of southern Italy; scene of Hannibal's victory over the Romans, 216 B.C.

canned (kand) *adj.* 1. Preserved in a can or jar. 2. *Slang* Recorded: *canned music.*

can·nel (kan′əl) *n.* A bituminous coal with low heating power. Also **cannel coal**. [Alter. of *candle* (*coal*)]

can·nel·lo·ni (kan′ə·lō′nē) *n. pl.* Large macaroni filled with a mixture of meat or cheese, baked, and served with a tomato or cream sauce. [< Ital., pl. of *cannellone* tubular noodle < *cannello* small tube, dim. of *canna* reed]

can·ner (kan′ər) *n.* One who cans foods.

can·ner·y (kan′ər·ē) *n. pl.* **·ner·ies** A place where foods are canned.

Cannes (kan, kanz; *Fr.* kän) A port and resort city in SE France, on the Riviera; pop. 66,590 (1968).

can·ni·bal (kan′ə·bəl) *n.* 1. A human being who eats human flesh. 2. An animal that devours members of its own species. — *adj.* Of or characteristic of cannibals; given to cannibalism. [< Sp. *Canibales*, var. of *Caribes* Caribs]

can·ni·bal·ism (kan′ə·bəl·iz′əm) *n.* 1. The act or practice of eating the flesh of one's own kind. 2. Inhuman cruelty. — **can·ni·bal·is·tic** *adj.* — **can·ni·bal·is·ti·cal·ly** *adv.*

can·ni·bal·ize (kan′ə·bəl·īz′) *v.t.* **·ized, ·iz·ing** 1. To take parts from (damaged tanks, airplanes, etc.) in order to repair others. 2. To take anything from in order to strengthen or enlarge something else. — **can′ni·bal·i·za′tion** *n.*

can·ni·kin (kan′ə·kin) *n.* 1. A small can or cup. 2. A wooden pail. Also spelled *canikin*. [Dim. of CAN[2]]

can·ning (kan′ing) *n.* The act, process, or business of preserving foods in hermetically sealed tin cans, glass jars, etc.

Can·ning (kan′ing), **Charles John**, 1812–62, British statesman; first viceroy of India. — **George**, 1770–1827, British statesman; father of the preceding.

can·non (kan′ən) *n. pl.* **·nons** or **·non** 1. *Mil.* A large tubular weapon, usually mounted on a fixed or mobile carriage, that discharges a projectile by the use of an explosive, as a gun, howitzer, or breechloading mortar. 2. *Mech.* A loose, independently revolving metal sleeve that fits over a shaft. 3. The part of a bell by which it is hung. 4. A smooth, round bit for a horse. Also **cannon bit**. 5. The large bone between the fetlock and knee or hock of the horse and allied animals. Also **cannon bone**. For illustration see HORSE. 6. *Brit.* A carom. — *v.i.* 1. To fire cannon. 2. *Brit.* To carom. — *v.t.* 3. To attack with cannon shot. 4. *Brit.* To cause to carom. [< OF *canon* < Ital. *cannone*, aug. of *canna* tube, pipe]

Can·non (kan′ən), **Annie Jump**, 1863–1941, U.S. astronomer. — **Joseph Gurney**, 1836–1926, U.S. politician; member of the House of Representatives 1873–91, 1893–1913, 1915–23.

can·non·ade (kan′ən·ād′) *v.* **·ad·ed, ·ad·ing** *v.t.* 1. To attack with cannon shot. — *v.i.* 2. To fire cannon repeatedly. — *n.* A continued discharge of or attack with cannon.

cannon ball A spherical solid shot formerly fired from a cannon.

can·non·eer (kan′ən·ir′) *n.* An artilleryman who serves as gunner. Also **can′non·ier′**.

cannon fodder Soldiers considered as that which is consumed by war.

cannon shot 1. A shot fired by cannon; also, collectively, projectiles so fired. 2. The range of a cannon.

can·not (kan′ot, ka·not′) The negative of the auxiliary verb CAN: written *can not* for emphasis. — **cannot but** Have no alternative except to: objected to by some as a double negative, but long established in formal literary usage.

can·nu·la (kan′yə·lə) *n. Med.* A tube inserted into a cavity, through which pus, etc., may escape or medicine be introduced: also spelled *canula*. [< L, dim. of *canna* reed, tube]

can·nu·late (kan′yə·lāt; *for adj.*, also kan′yə·lit) *v.t.* **·lat·ed, ·lat·ing** To make hollow or tubular. — *adj.* Tubular: also **can′nu·lar**. Also spelled *canulate*.

can·ny (kan′ē) *adj.* *Originally Scot.* **·ni·er, ·ni·est** 1. Cautiously shrewd; prudent; wary. 2. Frugal; thrifty. 3. Skillful; clever. 4. Gentle or quiet. 5. Pleasant; good; attractive. 6. Safe to deal with; lucky: usually with a negative. — *adv.* In a canny manner. Also, *Scot.*, **can′nie**. [< CAN[1] (defs. 1 and 2)] — **can′ni·ly** *adv.* — **can′ni·ness** *n.*

Ca·no (kä′nō), **Alonso**, 1601–67, Spanish painter, sculptor, and architect.

ca·noe (kə·nōō′) *n.* A small, long, narrow boat, pointed at both ends, and propelled by paddles. Compare illustration under CATAMARAN. — *v.* **·noed, ·noe·ing** *v.t.* 1. To convey by canoe. — *v.i.* 2. To paddle, sail, or travel in a canoe. [< Sp. *canoa* < Taino] — **ca·noe′ist** *n.*

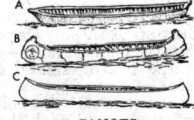

CANOES

A Dugout. *B* Birchbark. *C* Modern.

ca·noe·wood (kə·nōō′wŏŏd′) *n.* The tulip tree.

can·on[1] (kan′ən) *n.* 1. A rule or law; especially, a rule of faith and practice enacted by a church council and, in the Roman Catholic Church, ratified by the Pope; also, a body of such rules or laws. 2. An established rule; principle. 3. A standard for judgment; criterion. 4. The books of the Bible recognized as the divinely inspired rule of faith and practice. 5. The sacred books of any sect or religion. 6. A list, as of the recognized works of an author. 7. The list of canonized saints. 8. *Often cap. Eccl.* The portion of the Mass between the Sanctus and the Lord's Prayer. 9. *Music* a A composition or passage in which one or more voices follow and imitate the melody of the first voice, the various parts overlapping in time. Compare FUGUE, ROUND. b Any of various similar devices. 10. *Printing* A size of type, 48-point. Abbr. *can.* — **Syn.** See LAW. — **the canon** Canon law. [OE < L < Gk. *kanōn* rule, straight rod]

can·on[2] (kan′ən) *n.* A member of the chapter of a cathedral or collegiate church. [OE *canonic* < LL *canonicus* cleric < L *canon* rule. See CANON[1].]

ca·ñon (kan′yən, *Sp.* kä·nyōn′) See CANYON.

can·on·ess (kan′ən·is) *n.* A member of a religious community of women who live under a canon or rule, but not under vows.

ca·non·i·cal (kə·non′i·kəl) *adj.* 1. Relating or conforming to, or prescribed by, a canon or canons. 2. Of or contained in the canon of Scripture. 3. Authoritative; recognized. Also **ca·non′ic**. [< Med.L *canonicalis* < LL *canonicus* < L *canon*. See CANON[1].] — **ca·non′i·cal·ly** *adv.*

canonical age The age required by canon law for ordination or for the performance of any particular act.

canonical hours 1. *Eccl.* The seven stated daily periods, fixed by canon, for prayer and devotion: matins with lauds, prime, tierce, sext, nones, vespers, and complin: also called *Divine Office*. 2. The hours from 8 A.M. to 3 P.M., during which marriage may be legally performed in parish churches.

ca·non·i·cals (kə·non′i·kəlz) *n.pl.* The habits or robes prescribed by canon to be worn by the clergy when officiating.

ca·non·i·cate (kə·non′i·kāt, -kit) *n.* The office of a canon; canonry.

can·on·ic·i·ty (kan′ən·is′ə·tē) *n.* 1. The quality of being canonical. 2. Conformity to the canon; orthodoxy.

can·on·ist (kan′ən·ist) *n.* One skilled in canon law. — **can′on·is′tic** or **·ti·cal** *adj.*

can·on·ize (kan′ən·īz) *v.t.* **·ized, ·iz·ing** 1. To place (a deceased person) in the canon of saints; declare to be a saint. 2. To recognize as part of the canon of Scripture. 3. To sanction as being conformable to the canons of the church. 4. To give or ascribe glory to; glorify. — **can′on·i·za′tion** *n.*

canon law The body of ecclesiastical law of a Christian church or denomination.

can·on·ry (kan′ən·rē) *n. pl.* **·ries** **1.** The office, dignity, or benefice of a canon. **2.** Canons collectively. Also **can′on·ship.**

can opener A device for opening cans.

Ca·no·pic (kə·nō′pik) *adj.* Of or pertaining to Canopus, Egypt.

Canopic jar A vase with a top in the form of a human or animal head, used in ancient Egypt to hold the viscera of embalmed bodies. Also **Canopic urn, Canopic vase.**

Ca·no·pus (kə·nō′pəs) *n.* One of the 20 brightest stars, − 0.72 magnitude; Alpha in the constellation Carina. See STAR. [< L]

Ca·no·pus (kə·nō′pəs) A port city in ancient Egypt, NE of Alexandria.

can·o·py (kan′ə·pē) *n. pl.* **·pies** **1.** A covering suspended over a throne, bed, shrine, etc., or held over a person. **2.** Any covering overhead, as the sky. **3.** *Archit.* An ornamental covering over a niche, altar, or tomb. **4.** *Aeron.* **a** The main lifting surface of a parachute. **b** The transparent, sliding cover of a cockpit — *v.t.* **·pied, ·py·ing** To cover with or as with a canopy. [< MF *canapé* sofa < L *canopeum* mosquito net < Gk. *kōnōpeion* bed with mosquito net < *kōnōps* mosquito]

ca·no·rous (kə·nôr′əs, -nō′rəs) *adj.* Melodious; musical. [< L *canorus* < *canor* song < *canere* to sing] — **ca·no′rous·ly** *adv.*

Ca·nos·sa (kə·nos′ə, *Ital.* kä·nôs′sä) An ancient town in north central Italy; site of a ruined castle where Henry IV, Holy Roman Emperor, did penance before Gregory VII in 1077. — **to go to Canossa** To do penance; be humbled.

Ca·no·va (kä·nō′vä), **Antonio,** 1757–1822, Italian sculptor.

can·so (kan·sō′) *n. pl.* **·sos** (-sōz′) A Provençal love lyric. [< Provençal < L *cantio* < *canere* to sing]

Can·so (kan′sō), **Cape** The eastern extremity of the Nova Scotia peninsula. — **Strait of Canso** The strait between Cape Breton Island and the Nova Scotian mainland: also **Gut of Canso.**

canst (kanst) Archaic second person singular, present tense of CAN[1]: used with *thou.*

cant[1] (kant) *n.* **1.** An inclination from the vertical or horizontal; a slope or tilt. **2.** A sudden motion that tilts or overturns. **3.** An outer corner or angle. **4.** A slant surface, as one produced by cutting off a corner or edge. — *v.t.* **1.** To set slantingly; tilt. **2.** To give a bevel to. **3.** To throw out or off; jerk; toss. — *v.i.* **4.** To tilt; slant. — **Syn.** See TIP[1]. — *adj.* **1.** Oblique; slanting. **2.** Having canted sides or corners. [Prob. < OF < Med.L *cantus* corner, side]

cant[2] (kant) *n.* **1.** The hypocritical expression of pious sentiments; insincere religious or moralistic talk. **2.** Phraseology used merely for effect; stock phrases. **3.** Words or phraseology peculiar to a sect, class, or calling: legal *cant.* **4.** The secret jargon of thieves, gypsies, etc.; argot. **5.** Whining speech, especially of beggars. — *v.i.* **1.** To use cant; especially, to speak with affected piety. **2.** To whine, as a beggar. — *v.t.* **3.** To say in an affectedly pious way. — *adj.* Having the character of cant; hypocritical. [< AF, singing < L *cantus* song < *canere* to sing] — **cant′er** *n.* — **Syn.** **1.** See HYPOCRISY. **4.** See DIALECT.

cant[3] (känt) *adj. Scot. & Brit. Dial.* Bold; brisk; lively.

can't (kant, känt) Cannot.

Cant. **1.** Canterbury. **2.** Canticles. **3.** Cantonese.

Cantab. Of Cambridge (L *Cantabrigiensis*).

can·ta·bi·le (kän·tä′bē·lā) *Music adj.* Melodious; flowing. — *n.* Music characterized by flowing melody. [< Ital.]

Can·ta·brig·i·a (kan′tə·brij′i·ə) The Medieval Latin name for CAMBRIDGE.

Can·ta·brig·i·an (kan′tə·brij′ē·ən) *adj.* Of or pertaining to Cambridge, England, or Cambridge University. — *n.* A resident of Cambridge, England; also, a student or graduate of Cambridge University. [< LL *Cantabrigia* Cambridge]

can·ta·lev·er (kan′tə·lev′ər, -lē′vər) See CANTILEVER.

can·ta·loupe (kan′tə·lōp) *n.* A variety of muskmelon (*Cucumis melo cantalupensis*), having a ribbed, warty rind and sweet, orange flesh. Also **can′ta·loup.** [< F, after *Cantalupo*, Italian castle where first grown in Europe]

can·tank·er·ous (kan·tang′kər·əs) *adj.* Quarrelsome; ill-natured; perverse. [Prob. akin to ME *contak* strife] — **can·tank′er·ous·ly** *adv.* — **can·tank′er·ous·ness** *n.*

can·ta·ta (kən·tä′tə) *n. Music* A vocal composition in the style of a short oratorio or drama, with arias, choruses, recitatives, etc., to be sung but not acted. [< Ital.]

can·ta·tri·ce (*Ital.* kän′tä·trē′chä; *Fr.* kän′tà·trēs′) *n. pl. Ital.* **·tri·ci** (-trē′chē) or *Fr.* **·trices** (-trēs′) A female professional singer. [< F < Ital.]

can·teen (kan·tēn′) *n.* **1.** A small, usually metal flask for carrying water or other liquids. **2.** A shop at a military camp where soldiers can buy provisions, refreshments, etc. See POST EXCHANGE. **3.** A place of entertainment operated by civilians for enlisted personnel. **4.** A place for refreshments, as in a factory. **5.** A box for cooking and table utensils, as of an officer. [< F *cantine* < Ital. *cantina* cellar]

can·ter (kan′tər) *n.* A moderate, easy gallop. — *v.t. & v.i.* To ride or go at a canter. [Short for *Canterbury gallop*; with ref. to the pace of pilgrims riding to Canterbury]

Can·ter·bur·y (kan′tər·ber′ē; *Brit.* -bər·ē, -brē) A county

borough in eastern Kent, England; the seat of the highest prelate of the Church of England; pop. 33,140 (est. 1969). Medieval Latin *Cantuaria.*

Canterbury bell One of the various cultivated bellflowers, especially *Campanula medium.*

Canterbury Tales An uncompleted work (1387–1400) by Chaucer, consisting of a series of tales, largely in verse, told by a group of pilgrims on their way to Canterbury.

can·tha·ris (kan′thə·ris) *n. pl.* **can·thar·i·des** (kan·thar′ə·dēz) **1.** *pl.* (*sometimes construed as sing.*) The dried powder obtained by crushing the blister beetle, especially the Spanish fly, used in medicine as a rubefacient and as a diuretic. **2.** The beetle itself. Abbr. *Cant.* [< L < Gk. *kantharis*]

cant hook A lever equipped with an adjustable hook for handling logs. Also **cant-dog** (kant′dôg′, -dog′).

can·thus (kan′thəs) *n. pl.* **·thi** (-thī) *Anat.* The angle at the outer or inner junction of the eyelids. [< L < Gk. *kanthos*]

can·ti·cle (kan′ti·kəl) *n.* A nonmetrical hymn, such as one taken directly from the Bible, said or chanted in church. [< L *canticulum,* dim. of *canticum* song]

Canticle of Can·ti·cles (kan′ti·kəlz) In the Bible, the Song of Solomon. Abbr. *Cant.*

Can·ti·gny (kän·tē·nyē′) A village in northern France; site of first engagement of U.S. troops in World War I, May, 1918.

can·ti·lev·er (kan′tə·lev′ər, -lē′vər) *n.* **1.** *Engin.* A long structural member, as a truss, beam, or slab, lying across a support with the two projecting arms in balance. **2.** *Archit.* **a** Any structural part projecting horizontally and anchored at one end only. **b** A heavy bracket supporting a balcony or the like. **3.** *Aeron.* A form of wing without external bracing. — *v.t. & v.i.* To project (a building member) outward and in balance beyond the base. Sometimes spelled *cantalever:* also **can′ti·liv·er** (-liv′ər). [Origin uncertain]

CANTILEVER BRIDGE
(Section of Queensboro Bridge, New York City)

cantilever bridge A bridge formed by the meeting of two freely projecting beams, trusses, etc., each supported near its center and anchored at the opposite ends.

can·til·late (kan′tə·lāt) *v.t. & v.i.* **·lat·ed, ·lat·ing** To recite by intoning or chanting, as in Jewish or other rituals. [< L *cantillatus,* pp. of *cantillare* to sing low, hum < *cantare* to sing] — **can′til·la′tion** *n.*

can·ti·na (kan·tē′nə) *n. SW U.S.* A place where liquor is sold; a bar or saloon. [< Sp.]

can·tle (kan′təl) *n.* **1.** A piece cut or broken off; a segment; corner. **2.** The hind part of a saddle, projecting upward. For illustration see SADDLE. [< AF *cantel* < Med.L *cantellus,* dim. of *cantus* corner]

can·to (kan′tō) *n. pl.* **·tos** **1.** A division of an extended poem. **2.** *Archaic* The part of a musical score having the melody; the air. Abbr. *can.* [< Ital. < L *cantus* song]

can·ton (kan′tən, -ton, kan·ton′; *for v. def. 2* kan·ton′, -tōn′, -tōon′) *n.* **1.** A district; especially, one of the states of Switzerland, or a subdivision of an arrondissement in France. **2.** A rectangular division of a flag, usually in the upper corner next to the staff. **3.** *Heraldry* A division of the quarter, usually on the dexter side of the shield. — *v.t.* **1.** To divide; especially, to divide into cantons or districts. **2.** To assign quarters to, as troops. [< OF. Cf. Ital. *cantone,* aug. of *canto* corner < Med.L *cantus*] — **can·ton·al** (kan′tən·əl) *adj.*

Can·ton (kan·ton′ *for defs. 1 & 3*; kan′tən *for def. 2*) **1.** The capital of Kwangtung Province, southern China, a port city on the Canton river; pop. 2,300,000 (est. 1970): Chinese *Kwangchow.* **2.** A city in NE Ohio; pop. 110,053. **3.** A river in southern Kwangtung Province flowing 110 miles to the South China Sea: also *Pearl.* Chinese *Chu-Kiang.*

Canton crepe (kan′tən) A soft silk crepe, having more body than crepe de Chine. [after *Canton,* China]

Can·ton·ese (kan′tən·ēz′, -ēs′) *n. pl.* **·ese** **1.** A native of Canton, China. **2.** The Chinese language spoken in Kwangtung province and adjacent parts of southern China. Abbr. *Cant.*

Canton flannel (kan′tən) A heavy cotton fabric having a long nap, usually on one side only, used for undergarments, infants′ nightwear, etc.: also called *swan's-down.* [after *Canton,* China]

can·ton·ment (kan·ton′mənt, -tōn′-, -tōon′-, kan′tən·mənt) *n.* **1.** A group of temporary buildings for housing troops. **2.** The assignment of troops to such quarters. [< F *cantonnement* < *cantonner* to quarter]

can·tor (kan′tər, -tôr) *n.* **1.** The chief liturgical singer in a synagogue. **2.** A precentor, or chief singer. [< L]

can·trip (kan′trip) *n. Scot.* **1.** A charm; spell. **2.** A trick.

Can·tu·ar·i·a (kan′tōō·âr′i·ə) The Medieval Latin name for CANTERBURY.

can·tus (kan′təs) *n. pl.* **can·tus** **1.** A style of church song.

2. A melody or song; also, the principal voice of a polyphonic work. [< L, song, singing]

cantus fir·mus (fûr′məs) *Music* A basic melody to which other parts of a polyphonic work are added.

can·ty (kän′tē) *adj. Scot. & Brit. Dial.* Cheerful; lively.

Ca·nuck (kə-nuk′) *n. U.S. Slang* A Canadian, especially a French Canadian: sometimes derogatory.

can·u·la (kan′yə-lə) See CANNULA.

can·u·late (kan′yə-lāt) See CANNULATE.

Ca·nute (kə-nōōt′, -nyōōt′), 995?–1035, king of England 1016?–35, of Denmark 1018–35, and of Norway 1028–35: also *Cnut, Knut.*

can·vas (kan′vəs) *n.* **1.** A heavy, closely woven cloth of hemp, flax, or cotton, used for sails, tents, etc. **2.** A piece of such material on which to paint, especially in oils. **3.** A painting on canvas. **4.** Sailcloth. **5.** Sails collectively. **6.** A tent, especially a circus tent. **7.** A square-meshed fabric of linen, silk, or the like, on which to work embroidery or tapestry. **— under canvas 1.** With sails set. **2.** In tents. [< AF *canevas*, ult. < L *cannabis* hemp]

can·vas·back (kan′vəs-bak′) *n.* A sea duck (*Aythya valisineria*) of North America, having a grayish white back.

can·vass (kan′vəs) *v.t.* **1.** To go about (a region) or among (persons) to solicit votes, opinions, orders for goods, etc. **2.** To examine searchingly; scrutinize; sift; discuss. **3.** *Obs.* To criticize unsparingly. **— v.i. 4.** To go about seeking votes, opinions, etc. **— n. 1.** A solicitation of votes, opinions, orders, etc., often to determine the public's attitude toward a candidate, a commercial product, etc. **2.** A detailed examination or discussion. [< CANVAS; with ref. to the early use of canvas for sifting] **— can′vass·er** *n.*

can·yon (kan′yən) *n.* A deep valley with steep, clifflike walls, often having a stream flowing through it; gorge: also spelled *cañon.* [< Sp. *cañón*]

can·zo·ne (kän-tsō′nā) *n. pl.* **·ni** (-nē) or **·ne** (-ne) A Provençal or Italian lyric resembling a madrigal. Also **can·zo′na** (-nä). [< Ital. < L *cantio* song]

can·zo·net (kan′zə-net′) *n.* A short song; light air. [< Ital. *canzonetta*, dim. of *canzone* song]

caout·chouc (kōō′chōōk, kou-chōōk′) *n.* Rubber; especially, crude rubber. [< F < Tupi *cahuchu*]

cap¹ (kap) *n.* **1.** A covering for the head, usually snug, brimless, and of soft material; especially, such a headpiece for men and boys, often with a visor, or one of lace, etc., for women and infants. **2.** Any headgear especially designed to denote rank, function, membership, etc.: an academic *cap*; policeman's *cap.* **3.** Something suggesting a cap in form, function, or position: a bottle *cap.* **4.** A primer, as of a cartridge. **5.** A small quantity of explosive in a piece of paper, used in toy guns. **6.** *Bot.* The pileus of a mushroom. **7.** Any of various sizes of writing paper. See FOOLSCAP (defs. 1, 2), LEGAL CAP. **8.** *Archit.* A capital. **— blasting cap** A detonator for an explosive charge. **— test cap** A protective covering for the exposed end of a cable. **— to set one's cap for** To try to win as a suitor or husband. **— v.t.** *capped,* **cap·ping 1.** To put a cap on; cover. **2.** To serve as a cap or cover to; lie on top of. **3.** To add the final touch to; complete. **4.** To excel; top. **— to cap the climax** To surpass the climax; exceed the limit. [OE *cæppe* < LL *cappa* hooded cloak, cap, prob. < L *caput* head]

cap² (kap) *n. Printing* A capital letter.

cap. 1. Capacity. **2.** (*pl.* caps.) Capital. **3.** Capitalize. **4.** Capitulum. **5.** Chapter (L *caput*).

CAP or **C.A.P.** Civil Air Patrol.

ca·pa·bil·i·ty (kā′pə-bil′ə-tē) *n. pl.* **·ties 1.** The quality of being capable; capacity or ability. **2.** Susceptibility to use or treatment. **3.** *Usually pl.* Qualities that may be used or developed; potentialities. **— Syn.** See ABILITY.

ca·pa·ble (kā′pə-bəl) *adj.* **1.** Having ability; efficient; able; competent. **2.** *Obs.* Capacious. **— Syn.** See ABLE. **— capable of 1.** Having the capacity or qualities needed for: *capable of* good judgment. **2.** Of such nature as to allow; susceptible to. [< F < LL *capabilis* < L *capere* to take, receive] **— ca′pa·ble·ness** *n.* **— ca′pa·bly** *adv.*

ca·pa·cious (kə-pā′shəs) *adj.* Able to contain much; large; roomy. [< L *capax, -acis* able to hold, roomy < *capere* to take] **— ca·pa′cious·ly** *adv.* **— ca·pa′cious·ness** *n.*

ca·pac·i·tance (kə-pas′ə-təns) *n. Electr.* **1.** The property of a circuit or body that permits it to store an electrical charge, measured by the accumulated charge divided by the voltage: expressed in farads. **2.** Capacitive reactance. [< CAPACIT(Y) + -ANCE]

ca·pac·i·tate (kə-pas′ə-tāt) *v.t.* **·tat·ed, ·tat·ing 1.** To render capable. **2.** To qualify according to law.

ca·pac·i·tive (kə-pas′ə-tiv) *adj. Electr.* Relating to capacitance.

capacitive reactance *Electr.* That element of reactance in a circuit caused by capacitance, equal to the reciprocal of $2\pi fc$, where f is the frequency of the current and c is the capacitance, and expressed in ohms. See IMPEDANCE.

ca·pac·i·tor (kə-pas′ə-tər) *n. Electr.* A device consisting of conductors isolated in a dielectric medium, with each of them attached to only one side of a circuit, used to increase the capacitance to a desired value: also called *condenser.*

ca·pac·i·ty (kə-pas′ə-tē) *n. pl.* **·ties 1.** Ability to receive, contain, or absorb; cubic extent or space. **2.** Maximum ability to hold, contain, etc.: filled to *capacity.* **3.** Adequate mental power to receive, understand, etc.; mental ability; capability. **4.** The ability or aptitude to do something; talent; faculty: with *for, of,* or the infinitive: a *capacity* for research. **5.** Specific position, character, or office: in the *capacity* of tutor. **6.** Legal qualification. **7.** Maximum output or production: to operate below *capacity.* **8.** *Electr.* **a** Capacitance. **b** The output of an electric generator. Abbr. *c., C., cap., cap′y,* (for def. 8) *k.* **— Syn.** See ABILITY. [< MF *capacité* < L *capacitas, -tatis* < *capax.* See CAPACIOUS.]

cap and bells A cap ornamented with little bells, worn by a fool or court jester.

cap and gown Academic garb consisting of a cap or mortarboard and a characteristic robe or gown, worn at certain college or university ceremonies.

Cap·a·neus (kap′ə-nōōs, -nyōōs, kə-pā′nē-əs) An ancient Greek hero. See SEVEN AGAINST THEBES.

cap-a-pie (kap′ə-pē′) *adv.* From head to foot. Also **cap′-à-pie′.** [< OF]

ca·par·i·son (kə-par′ə-sən) *n.* **1.** An ornamental covering for a horse. **2.** Rich or sumptuous apparel or trappings. **— v.t.** To put a caparison on; clothe richly. [< OF *caparasson* < Sp. *caparazón*, ult. < LL *cappa* cape]

— Syn. (noun) *Caparison, trappings, harness,* and *accouterments* denote showy or elaborate apparel. *Caparison* and *trappings* originally referred only to horses; both are now used humorously of human garb, *caparison* to imply showiness, *trappings* to suggest elaboration. *Harness* was formerly used of the armor of a knight as well as of a horse, and this sense survives in isolated instances: the *harness* of a test pilot; but the word is now chiefly used for the gear of a horse when attached to a vehicle. *Accouterments* is used chiefly for the equipment of a soldier; it suggests utility rather than display. Compare DRESS.

cap case *Printing* Upper case (which see).

cape¹ (kāp) *n.* A point of land extending into the sea or a lake. Abbr. *c., C.* **— the Cape 1.** The Cape of Good Hope. **2.** *U.S.* Cape Cod. [< F *cap,* ult. < L *caput* head]

cape² (kāp) *n.* A sleeveless garment fastened at the neck and hanging loosely from the shoulders. [< F < LL *cappa*]

Cape, Cape of, etc. See specific name, as (Cape) COD, (Cape of) GOOD HOPE, etc.

Cape Bret·on Island (brit′n, bret′n) An island of Nova Scotia, just NE of the mainland; 3,975 sq. mi.

Cape Cod Canal A canal, 13 miles long, across Cape Cod from Buzzards Bay to **Cape Cod Bay,** the southern end of Massachusetts Bay.

Cape Dutch Afrikaans, a language.

Ča·pek (chä′pek), **Karel,** 1890–1938, Czech playwright and novelist.

cap·e·lin (kap′ə-lin) *n. pl.* **·lin** or **·lins** *U.S. & Canadian* A small, edible fish (*Mallotus villosus*) of northern seas, much used as bait: also spelled *caplin.* Also **cap′e·lan.** [< dial. F (Canadian) *capelan* < F]

Ca·pel·la (kə-pel′ə) *n.* One of the 20 brightest stars, 0.05 magnitude; Alpha in the constellation Auriga. See table for STAR. [< L, she-goat]

Cape of Good Hope Province A Province of the southern Republic of South Africa; 278,465 sq. mi.; pop. 3,936,306 (1960); capital, Cape Town: Afrikaans *Kaapland.* Also **Cape Province.** Formerly **Cape Colony.**

ca·per¹ (kā′pər) *n.* **1.** A playful leap; a skip or jump. **2.** A wild prank; antic; escapade. **3.** *Slang* A crime or robbery. **— to cut a caper** (or **capers**) To caper; frolic. **— v.i.** To leap playfully; frisk. [Short for CAPRIOLE] **— ca′per·er** *n.*

ca·per² (kā′pər) *n.* **1.** The flower bud of a low shrub (*Capparis spinosa*) of Mediterranean countries, pickled and used as a condiment. **2.** The shrub itself. [< L *capparis* < Gk. *kapparis*]

ca·per³ (kā′pər) *n. Archaic* A privateer. [< Du. *kaper*]

cap·er·cail·lie (kap′ər-kāl′yē) *n.* A large, black European grouse (*Tetrao urogallus*): also called *wood grouse.* Also **cap′er·cail′zie** (-yē, -zē). [Alter. of Scottish Gaelic *capull-coille,* lit., horse of the wood]

Ca·per·na·um (kə-pûr′nē-əm) A Biblical locality in NE Palestine on the Sea of Galilee. *Matt.* iv 13.

cape·skin (kāp′skin′) *n.* A leather made from lamb or sheep skins and used especially for gloves. [after Cape of Good Hope, where originally made]

Ca·pet (kā′pit, kap′it; *Fr.* kà·pe′) See HUGH CAPET.

Ca·pe·tian (kə-pē′shən) *adj.* Of or belonging to the dynasty (987–1328) founded in France by Hugh Capet. **— n.** A descendant, direct or indirect, of Hugh Capet.

Cape Town The legislative capital of the Republic of South Africa and the capital of Cape of Good Hope Province, a port city in the SW part of the Province, on Table Bay; pop. 625,000 (1967). Also **Cape·town** (kāp′toun′).

Cape Verde Islands A group of volcanic islands in the Atlantic west of Cape Verde, comprising a Portuguese Overseas Province; 1,552 sq. mi.; pop. 250,000 (est. 1969); capital, Praia.

Cape York Peninsula A peninsula of NE Australia, part of Queensland; length about 450 mi.

Cap Ha·i·tien (káp à·ē·syañ′) A port city in northern Haiti; pop. 30,000 (est. 1968): also *Le Cap*.

ca·pi·as (kā′pē·əs, kap′ē·əs) *n. pl.* **·as·es** *Law* A judicial writ commanding an officer to take and hold in custody the person named therein. [< L, you may take]

cap·il·la·ceous (kap′ə·lā′shəs) *adj.* Hairlike; capillary. [< L *capillaceus* < *capillus* hair]

cap·il·lar·i·ty (kap′ə·lar′ə·tē) *n. pl.* **·ties** **1.** The state of being capillary. **2.** *Physics* A form of surface tension between the molecules of a liquid and those of a solid. When the adhesive force is stronger (**capillary attraction**) the liquid will tend to rise above mean level at the points of contact with the solid, as water in clean glass; when cohesion dominates (**capillary repulsion**), the liquid will tend to fall below this level, as mercury. [< F *capillarité*]

cap·il·lar·y (kap′ə·ler′ē) *adj.* **1.** Of, pertaining to, or like hair; fine; slender. **2.** Having a hairlike bore, as a tube or vessel. — *n. pl.* **·lar·ies 1.** *Anat.* A minute vessel, as those connecting the arteries and veins. **2.** Any tube with a fine bore. [< L *capillaris* < *capillus* hair]

cap·i·ta (kap′ə·tə) Plural of CAPUT.

cap·i·tal[1] (kap′ə·təl) *n.* **1.** The capital city or town of a country, state, etc.; seat of government. Abbr. *cap.* **2.** A capital letter (which see). **3.** The total amount of money or property owned or used by an individual or corporation. **4.** Wealth in any form employed in or available for the production of more wealth. **5.** In accounting, the net worth of a business after the deduction of all liabilities. **6.** Possessors of wealth as a class: *capital* and labor. — **to make capital of** To turn to advantage. — *adj.* **1.** Chief, as comprising the seat of government: the *capital* city. **2.** Standing at the head; first; principal. **3.** Of or pertaining to funds or capital: *capital* stock. **4.** Of the first quality; excellent. **5.** Punishable by or involving the death penalty, formerly by decapitation: a *capital* crime. **6.** Very injurious; grave: a *capital* error. [< OF < L *capitalis* < *caput* head]

cap·i·tal[2] (kap′ə·təl) *n. Archit.* The upper member of a column or pillar. [< L *capitellum*, double dim. of *caput* head]

capital account **1.** A statement of the value of a business at a given time, representing assets minus liabilities. **2.** An account of an owner's or stockholder's interest in a business. Abbr. *C/A.*

capital expenditure Expenditure for permanent additions or improvements to property.

capital gain Profit from the sale of capital investments, such as stocks, real estate, etc.

capital goods Equipment, machinery, etc., used in the production of consumers' goods.

cap·i·tal·ism (kap′ə·təl·iz′əm) *n.* **1.** An economic system in which the means of production and distribution are for the most part privately owned and operated for private profit. **2.** The possession and concentration of private capital and its resulting power and wealth.

cap·i·tal·ist (kap′ə·təl·ist) *n.* **1.** An owner of capital; especially, one who has large means employed in productive enterprise. **2.** Loosely, any person of apparent wealth. **3.** A supporter of capitalism. — **cap′i·tal·is′tic** *adj.* — **cap′i·tal·is′ti·cal·ly** *adv.*

cap·i·tal·i·za·tion (kap′ə·təl·ə·zā′shən, -ī·zā′-) *n.* **1.** The act or process of capitalizing. **2.** A sum arrived at by capitalizing. **3.** The total capital employed in a business, consisting of ownership capital (in corporations, stock, surplus, and undivided profits; in other cases, net worth); or ownership capital and long-term borrowed funds (bonds, etc.).

cap·i·tal·ize (kap′ə·təl·īz′) *v.* **·ized, ·iz·ing** *v.t.* **1.** To begin with capital letters, or print or write in capital letters. **2.** To convert into capital. **3.** To provide capital for; organize on a basis of capital. **4.** To estimate the worth of (a business or stock) from earnings or potential earnings; to compute the present value of (future income or periodical payment), as of annuities. **5.** In accounting, to record (expenses) as assets. — *v.i.* **6.** To acquire an advantage; profit: with *on* or *by.* **7.** To accumulate capital. Abbr. *cap.*

capital letter The form of a letter used at the beginning of a sentence, with proper names, etc., as the A in Africa. Abbr. *cap.* (pl. *caps.*). Compare SMALL CAPITAL, SMALL LETTER.

capital levy A tax on capital; a property tax: distinguished from *income tax.*

cap·i·tal·ly (kap′ə·təl·ē) *adv.* In a capital or excellent way.

capital punishment The death penalty for a crime.

capital ship A warship of large size, as a battleship or aircraft carrier, carrying guns of over 8-inch caliber.

capital stock **1.** The amount of stock a corporation is authorized to issue. **2.** The total face value of such stock. Abbr. *c.s., C.S.*

cap·i·tate (kap′ə·tāt) *adj.* **1.** *Bot.* Head-shaped; capitular: a *capitate* flower. **2.** *Zool.* Enlarged or knobbed at the end, as tentacles. [< L *capitatus* having a head < *caput* head]

cap·i·ta·tion (kap′ə·tā′shən) *n.* **1.** An assessment on each person (or head); poll tax. **2.** A counting or assessing of individuals. [< LL *capitatio, -onis* poll tax < L *caput* head]

cap·i·tol (kap′ə·təl) *n.* The building in which a State legislature convenes; a statehouse.

Cap·i·tol (kap′ə·təl) **1.** The official building of the U.S. Congress in Washington, D.C. **2.** The temple of Jupiter Capitolinus in ancient Rome, or the Capitoline Hill on which it stood. [< L *Capitolium* the Capitoline < *caput* head]

Cap·i·to·line (kap′ə·tə·līn′) *adj.* Pertaining to the Roman Capitol, to its presiding god, Jupiter Capitolinus, or to the Capitoline Hill. — *n.* The highest of the Seven Hills of Rome; site of the temple of Jupiter and of the Tarpeian rock.

ca·pit·u·lar (kə·pich′oō·lər) *adj.* **1.** Of or pertaining to an ecclesiastical chapter; capitulary. **2.** *Bot.* Capitate. — *n.* **1.** A member of a cathedral chapter. **2.** *Usually pl.* Capitularies. [< Med.L *capitularis* < *capitulum* chapter, dim. of *caput* head]

ca·pit·u·lar·y (kə·pich′oō·ler′ē) *adj.* Of or pertaining to a chapter, especially to an ecclesiastical chapter; capitular. — *n. pl.* **·lar·ies** *Usually pl.* Ordinances, or a collection of them; especially, those decreed by Charlemagne and his successors. [< Med.L *capitularius*]

ca·pit·u·late (kə·pich′oō·lāt) *v.i.* **·lat·ed, ·lat·ing** **1.** To surrender on stipulated terms; come to terms. **2.** To surrender; give up. [< L *capitulatus,* pp. of *capitulare* to draw up in chapters, arrange terms] — **ca·pit′u·la′tor** *n.*

ca·pit·u·la·tion (kə·pich′oō·lā′shən) *n.* **1.** The act of surrendering conditionally; also, the instrument containing the terms of surrender. **2.** A surrender or giving up; yielding. **3.** A statement of the heads of a subject; summary. **4.** A treaty or declaration; especially, one by which a sultan of Turkey gave immunities to resident foreign citizens. — **ca·pit′u·la·to·ry** (kə·pich′oō·lə·tôr′ē, -tō′rē) *adj.*

ca·pit·u·lum (kə·pich′oō·ləm) *n. pl.* **·la** (-lə) **1.** *Bot.* A close, head-shaped cluster of sessile flowers, as in the daisy. **2.** *Anat.* A small rounded body, as at the head of a rib. **3.** *Zool.* The headlike part of ticks and mites. **4.** *Entomol.* The enlarged tip of the antenna or mouth of certain insects. Abbr. *cap.* [< L, dim. of *caput* head]

cap·lin (kap′lin) See CAPELIN.

ca·po das·tro (kä′pō däs′trō) A clamp or nut attached to the fingerboard of a guitar to raise uniformly the pitch of the strings. [< Ital. *capo di tastro* cap for the keys]

ca·pon (kā′pon, -pən) *n.* A rooster gelded to improve the flesh for eating. [OE *capun* < L *capo, -onis*]

cap·o·niere (kap′ə·nir′) *n. Mil.* A defensive work across the ditch of a fortification, to provide enfilading fire. Also **cap′o·nier′, cap′on·niere′.** [< F *caponnière* < Sp. *caponera,* orig., capon coop]

cap·o·ral (kap′ə·ral′) *n.* A form of cut tobacco. [< F (*tabac du*) *caporal* corporal's (tobacco)]

Cap·o·ret·to (kap′ə·ret′ō, *Ital.* kä′pō·ret′tō) A town in NW Slovenia, Yugoslavia; in Italy until 1947; scene of Italian defeat (1917) in World War I. Serbo-Croatian *Kobarid.*

ca·pote (kə·pōt′) *n.* **1.** A hooded cloak or overcoat. **2.** A bonnet worn by women and children. **3.** The adjustable top of a vehicle. [< F, dim. of *cape* cape, hood]

ca·pouch (kə·pōosh′, -pōoch′) See CAPUCHE.

Cap·pa·do·ci·a (kap′ə·dō′shē·ə, -shə) An ancient region of Asia Minor; annexed by Rome (A.D. 17). — **Cap′pa·do′ci·an** *adj. & n.*

cap·pa·ri·da·ceous (kap′ə·ri·dā′shəs) *adj. Bot.* Belonging to the caper family (*Capparidaceae*) of herbs and shrubs. [< NL *capparis* caper]

cap·per (kap′ər) *n.* **1.** One who or that which caps; especially, a machine that caps or makes caps. **2.** *U.S. Slang* A decoy for a gambling house, etc.

cap·re·o·late (kap′rē·ə·lāt, -rē·ə·-) *adj.* **1.** *Bot.* Bearing a tendril. **2.** *Anat.* Tendril-shaped. [< L *capreolus* tendril]

Ca·pri (kä′prē) A rocky island at the SE entrance of the Bay of Naples; famed for its Blue Grotto; 4 sq. mi.

cap·ric (kap′rik) *adj.* Of, pertaining to, derived from, or like a goat. [< L *caper, capri* goat]

ca·pric·ci·o (kə·prē′chē·ō, *Ital.* kä·prēt′chō) *n. pl.* **·ci·os** or *Ital.* **ca·pric·ci** (kä·prēt′chē) **1.** *Music* A composition of lively and spirited mood, fancifully irregular in form. **2.** A prank; also, a caprice. [< Ital., whim < *capro* goat < L *caper*]

ca·pric·ci·o·so (kə·prē′chē·ō′sō, *Ital.* kä′prēt·chō′sō) *adj. Music* Fanciful; lively; irregular; fantastic. [< Ital.]

ca·price (kə·prēs′) *n.* **1.** A sudden change of mind or action without adequate motive; a whim. **2.** A tendency to make such changes; capriciousness. **3.** *Music* A capriccio. [< F < Ital. *capriccio.* See CAPRICCIO.]

ca·pri·cious (kə·prish′əs) *adj.* **1.** Characterized by or resulting from caprice; fickle; whimsical. **2.** *Obs.* Fanciful; witty. [< F *capricieux*] — **ca·pri′cious·ly** *adv.* — **ca·pri′cious·ness** *n.*

Cap·ri·corn (kap′rə·kôrn) *n.* A constellation, the Goat; also, the tenth sign of the zodiac. See CONSTELLATION, ZODIAC. Also **Cap′ri·cor′nus** (-kôr′nəs). [< L *capricornus* < *caper* goat + *cornu* horn]

cap·ri·fi·ca·tion (kap′rə·fi·kā′shən) *n.* Artificial fertilization of the cultivated fig by piercing the growing fruit, especially by the agency of a chalcid insect that infests the wild fig. [< L *caprificatio, -onis* < *caprificare* to ripen figs < *caprificus* wild fig]

cap·ri·fo·li·a·ceous (kap′ri·fō′lē·ā′shəs) *adj. Bot.* Belonging to the honeysuckle family (*Caprifoliaceae*) of herbs, woody shrubs, and vines. [< NL < Med.L *caprifolium* honeysuckle < L *caper* goat + *folium* leaf]

cap·ri·ole (kap′rē·ōl) *n.* **1.** An upward leap made by a trained horse, with all feet off the ground and no forward motion. **2.** A leap or spring. — *v.i.* ·oled, ·ol·ing To perform a capriole. [< F, leap, caper < Ital. *capriola*, dim. of *capra* she-goat < L *capra*]

ca·pro·ic acid (kə·prō′ik) *Chem.* A colorless, flammable fatty acid, $C_6H_{12}O_2$, derived from butter and other sources, used in organic synthesis. [< *capro-* (< L *caper* goat) + -IC; from its odor]

caps or **caps.** *Printing* Capital letters.

cap·sa·i·cin (kap·sā′ə·sin) *n. Chem.* A white crystalline compound, $C_{18}H_{27}O_3N$, extracted from cayenne pepper, used as a rubefacient. [< NL *capsicum*]

cap screw A screw bolt with a long thread and, generally, a square head, used to secure cylinder covers, etc.

Cap·si·an (kap′sē·ən) *adj. Anthropol.* Denoting an Upper Paleolithic culture, centered in North Africa, roughly contemporaneous with the Magdalenian, characterized by silhouette rock paintings of animals and persons. [after *Capsa* (now Gafsa), where cultural remains were found]

cap·si·cum (kap′si·kəm) *n.* **1.** An herb or shrub of the nightshade family (genus *Capsicum*), including the common red pepper, producing pods prepared as condiments or gastric stimulants. **2.** The fruit of these plants: also called *bird pepper.* [< L *capsa* box (from the shape of the fruit)]

cap·size (kap·sīz′, kap′sīz) *v.t. & v.i.* ·sized, ·siz·ing To upset or overturn. [? < Sp. *capuzar* to sink a ship by the head < *cabo* head]

cap·stan (kap′stən) *n. Naut.* A drumlike apparatus, formerly turned by bars or levers but now driven by a motor or engine, for hoisting anchors or other weights. [< F *cabestan*, ult. < L *capistrum* halter < *capere* to hold]

CAPSTAN
a Drumhead. *b* Bar hole. *c* Capstan bar. *d* Barrel. *e* Pawls. *f* Pawl rim. *g* Whelp.

capstan bar A lever used in turning a capstan.

cap·stone (kap′stōn′) *n.* Copestone (which see).

cap·su·lar (kap′sə·lər, -syŏŏ-) *adj.* Of, in, or of the nature of a capsule.

cap·su·late (kap′sə·lāt, -syŏŏ-) *adj.* In or formed into a capsule. Also **cap′su·lat′ed.** — **cap′su·la′tion** *n.*

cap·sule (kap′səl, -syŏŏl) *n.* **1.** A small container made of gelatin or other soluble material for enclosing a dose of medicine. **2.** A detachable part of an airplane, rocket, etc., containing the pilot, or instruments, specimens, etc. **3.** A thin cap, covering, or seal, as over the cork of a bottle. **4.** Any of various specialized containers, usually free or detachable: a protective *capsule.* **5.** *Bot.* **a** A dry dehiscent seed vessel made up of more than one carpel, as of a pink or lily. **b** The spore case of a moss or other cryptogam. **6.** *Anat.* **a** A fibrous or membranous structure that envelops some organ or part of the body. **b** Either of two laminae of cerebral white matter. **7.** *Chem.* A small container for evaporating liquids. — *adj.* In concise form; condensed: a *capsule* description. [< F < L *capsula*, dim. of *capsa* box]

CAPT or **Capt.** *Mil.* Captain.

cap·tain (kap′tən, -tin) *n.* **1.** One at the head or in command; a chief; leader. **2.** The master or commander of a vessel. **3.** *Mil.* A commissioned officer ranking above a lieutenant or first lieutenant and below a major. See tables at GRADE. **4.** *Naval* A commissioned officer ranking above a commander and below a commodore or rear admiral. See tables at GRADE. **5.** A member of a team and designated as its leader. **6.** An able leader, strategist, etc. — *v.t.* To act as captain to; command; lead. [< OF *capitaine* < LL *capitaneus* < L *caput* head. Doublet of CHIEFTAIN.] — **cap′tain·cy, cap′tain·ship** *n.*

captain's walk A widow's walk (which see).

cap·tion (kap′shən) *n.* **1.** A heading, as of a chapter, document, or newspaper article. **2.** The title and descriptive legend of an illustration. **3.** A subtitle in a motion picture.

4. *Law* The heading of a legal document, showing time, place, and authority of execution. — *v.t.* To provide a caption for. [< L *captio, -onis* seizure, deception, sophism < *capere* to take; infl. in meaning by L *caput* head]

cap·tious (kap′shəs) *adj.* **1.** Apt to find fault; disposed to criticize; caviling; carping. **2.** Designed to ensnare or perplex; sophistical; subtle: a *captious* question. [< L *captiosus* fallacious < *captio, -onis* sophism < *capere* to take] — **cap′tious·ly** *adv.* — **cap′tious·ness** *n.*

cap·ti·vate (kap′tə·vāt) *v.t.* ·vat·ed, ·vat·ing **1.** To enthrall by excellence or beauty; fascinate; charm. **2.** *Obs.* To capture; subdue. [< LL *captivatus*, pp. of *captivare* to capture < L *captivus.* See CAPTIVE.] — **cap′ti·va′tion** *n.* — **cap′ti·va′tor** *n.*

cap·tive (kap′tiv) *n.* **1.** One who or that which is captured and held in confinement or restraint; a prisoner. **2.** One enthralled by beauty, passion, etc. — *adj.* **1.** Taken or held prisoner, as in war. **2.** Held in restraint; confined: a *captive* balloon. **3.** Enslaved or rendered helpless by strong emotion, desire, etc.; captivated. **4.** Of or pertaining to a captive or captivity: *captive* chains. [< F *captif* < L *captivus* < *capere* to take. Doublet of CAITIFF.]

captive audience *U.S.* A group of people forced by circumstances to listen to something.

captive balloon See under BALLOON.

cap·tiv·i·ty (kap·tiv′ə·tē) *n. pl.* ·ties The state of being held captive; thralldom.

cap·tor (kap′tər) *n.* One who takes or holds captive. [< L]

cap·ture (kap′chər) *v.t.* ·tured, ·tur·ing **1.** To take by force, stratagem, etc., as in war; take captive. **2.** To gain or win, as in competition. — **Syn.** See CATCH. — *n.* **1.** The act of capturing; seizure. **2.** The person or thing captured. **3.** *Physics* A process or event in which an atom or nucleus acquires an additional particle. [< MF < L *captura* < *capere* to take]

Cap·u·a (kap′yŏŏ·ə, *Ital.* kä′pwä) A town in southern Italy; pop. about 13,200.

ca·puche (kə·pōōsh′, -pōōch′) *n.* A hood or cowl, especially that worn by a Capuchin: also spelled *capouch.* [< F < Ital. *cappuccio*, aug. of *cappa* hood]

cap·u·chin (kap′yŏŏ·chin, -shin) *n.* **1.** A woman's hooded cloak. **2.** A long-tailed South American monkey (genus *Cebus*) whose head is covered with a cowlike growth of hair: also called *sapajou, sajou.* [< MF < Ital. *cappuccino* < *cappuccio.* See CAPUCHE.]

Cap·u·chin (kap′yŏŏ·chin, -shin) *n.* A member of a branch of the Franciscan order, wearing a habit with a distinctive, pointed capuche.

Cap·u·let (kap′yə·let, -lit) The family name of Juliet in Shakespeare's *Romeo and Juliet.*

ca·put (kā′pət, kap′ət) *n. pl.* **cap·i·ta** (kap′ə·tə) *Anat.* A head or headlike part. [< L]

cap′y Capacity.

cap·y·ba·ra (kap′i·bä′rə) *n.* A South American rodent (*Hydrochoerus capybara*) about 4 feet long, having a stubby tail and frequenting the borders of lakes and rivers. [< Sp. *capibara* < Tupi *kapigwara*]

car (kär) *n.* **1.** An automobile. **2.** A vehicle for use on rails: freight *car; streetcar.* **3.** *Brit.* Any of various wheeled vehicles: a jaunting *car.* **4.** *Poetic* A chariot. **5.** *U.S.* The enclosed platform on which passengers are carried in an elevator. **6.** The part of a balloon or airship for carrying the crew, passengers, etc. **7.** A perforated floating box for storing live fish. [< AF *carre* < LL *carra*, var. of L *carrus* wagon, ult. < Celtic]

CAR or **C.A.R.** Civil Air Regulations.

Car. Carat(s).

ca·ra·ba·o (kä′rə·bä′ō) *n. pl.* ·ba·os or ·ba·o In the Philippines. the water buffalo. [< Sp. < Malay *karbau*]

car·a·bid (kar′ə·bid) *n.* Any of an extensive family (*Carabidae*) of predatory ground beetles, variously colored and usually nocturnal, including the caterpillar hunters. [< NL < L *carabus* small crab < Gk. *karabos* crayfish]

car·a·bin (kar′ə·bin), **car·a·bine** (-bīn) See CARBINE.

car·a·bin·eer (kar′ə·bin·ir′), **car·a·bin·ier** See CARBINEER.

ca·ra·bi·nie·re (kä′rä·bē·nyä′rā) *n. pl.* ·nie·ri (-nyä′rē) An Italian policeman. [< Ital.]

car·a·cal (kar′ə·kal) *n.* **1.** A lynx (*Felis* or *Lynx caracal*) of SW Asia and most of Africa, having reddish brown fur and black-tipped ears. **2.** Its pelt or fur. [< F < Turkish *qarah qulaq* < *qarah* black + *qulaq* ear]

Car·a·cal·la (kar′ə·kal′ə), 188–217, Roman emperor, 211–217: also known as **Marcus Aurelius An·to·ni·nus** (an′tō·nī′nəs). Compare AURELIUS.

ca·ra·ca·ra (kä′rä·kä′rə) A large, vulturelike hawk (genus *Caracara*) found chiefly in South America; especially, **Audubon's caracara** (*C. cheriway audubonii*), ranging into the southern United States. [< Sp. *caracará* < Tupi]

Ca·ra·cas (kə·rä′kəs, -rak′əs; *Sp.* kä·rä′käs) The capital of Venezuela, in a Federal District in the northern part; pop. 786,710 (est. 1970).

car·ack (kar'ək) See CARRACK.

car·a·cole (kar'ə·kōl) *n.* A half turn to the right or left made by a horseman's mount in riding. — *v.i.* **·coled, ·col· ing** To perform caracoles; wheel. Also **car·a·col** (-kol). [< F < Ital. *caracollo* < Sp. *caracol* snail shell]

Ca·rac·ta·cus (kə·rak'tə·kəs) First-century British chieftain; defeated by the Romans. Also **Ca·rad·oc** (kə·rad'ək).

car·a·cul (kar'ə·kəl) See KARAKUL.

ca·rafe (kə·raf', -räf') *n.* A glass water bottle; decanter. [< F, ? < Arabic *gharafa* to draw water]

car·a·geen (kar'ə·gēn), **car·a·gheen,** etc. See CARRAGEEN, etc.

car·a·mel (kar'ə·məl, -mel, kär'məl) *n.* **1.** A chewy confection composed of sugar, butter, milk, etc. **2.** Burnt sugar, used to color and flavor foods. [< F, alter. of OF *calemele* < Med.L *calamellus,* alter. of *canna mellis* sugar cane, under the infl. of L *calamus* reed]

car·a·mel·ize (kar'ə·məl·īz', kär'məl-) *v.t. & v.i.* **·ized, ·iz· ing** To convert into caramel. — **car'a·mel·i·za'tion** *n.*

ca·ran·goid (kə·rang'goid) *adj.* Of, pertaining to, or belonging to a family (*Carangidae*) of fishes having soft dorsal and anal fins, as the pompano. — *n.* A member of this family. [< NL *caranx, -angis* < Sp. *carangue* flatfish]

car·a·pace (kar'ə·pās) *n. Zool.* A hard, bony, or chitinous outer case or covering, as of a turtle or lobster. Also **car'a· pax** (-paks). [< F < Sp. *carapacho*]

ca·ras·sow (kə·ras'ō) See CURASSOW.

car·at (kar'ət) *n.* **1.** A unit of weight for gems, one metric carat being 200 milligrams, or 3.086 grains. Abbr. *car.* **2.** Loosely, a karat. [< F < Ital. *carato* < Arabic *qīrāt* weight of 4 grains < Gk. *keration* seed, small weight]

ca·ra·te (kä·rä'tā) *n. Pathol.* Pinta. [< Sp.]

Ca·ra·vag·gio (kä·rä·väd'jō), **Michelangelo Amerighi da,** 1569–1609, Italian painter.

car·a·van (kar'ə·van) *n.* **1.** A company of traders, pilgrims, or the like, traveling together, especially across deserts. **2.** A number of vehicles traveling together. **3.** A large, covered vehicle; a van. **4.** *Chiefly Brit.* A covered wagon or house on wheels. [< F *caravane* < Persian *kārwān* caravan]

car·a·van·sa·ry (kar'ə·van'sə·rē) *n. pl.* **·ries 1.** In Oriental countries, an inn enclosing a court for sheltering caravans. **2.** Any hostelry or inn. Also **car'a·van'se·rai** (-rī, -rä). [< F *caravansérai* < Persian *kārwānsarāī* < *kārwān* caravan + *sarāī* inn]

car·a·vel (kar'ə·vel) *n.* A small ship of the 15th and 16th centuries, used especially by the Portuguese and Spanish: also called *carvel.* Also **car'a·velle.** [< MF *caravelle* < Sp. *cara-bela,* dim. of *caraba* boat < LL *carabus* < Gk. *karabos*]

car·a·way (kar'ə·wā) *n.* An herb (*Carum carvi*) of the parsley family having small, spicy seeds (**caraway seeds**), used for flavoring. [< Sp. *al-carahueya* < Arabic *al* the + *karawiyā, karwiyā* caraway < Gk. *karon*]

CARAVEL
(The *Santa Maria* of Columbus)

car·ba·mate (kär'bə·māt, kär·bam'āt) *n. Chem.* A salt or ester of carbamic acid containing the univalent NH₂COO radical. [< CARB- + AM(IDE) + -ATE³]

car·bam·ic acid (kär·bam'ik) *Chem.* A compound, NH₂-COOH, known only by its salts and esters.

car barn A shed for railroad cars, streetcars, or buses.

car·ba·zole (kär'bə·zōl) *n. Chem.* A white crystalline compound, C₁₂H₉N, derived from coal tar and used in dyes. [< CARB- + AZOLE]

car·bide (kär'bīd, -bid) *n. Chem.* A compound of carbon with a more electropositive element.

car·bine (kär'bīn, -bēn) *n.* **1.** A light, short-barreled rifle originally devised for mounted troops: also *carabin, carabine.* **2.** *U.S. Mil.* A semi-automatic and now automatic, gas-operated, .30-caliber rifle, adopted by the United States in World War II for troops previously armed with pistols. [Earlier *carabine* < F]

car·bi·neer (kär'bə·nir') *n.* A soldier armed with a carbine: also *carabineer, carabinier.*

car·bi·nol (kär'bə·nōl, -nol) *n. Chem.* Methanol, or any alcohol derived from it. [< G; name given to wood alcohol by Adolf Kolbe, 1818–84, German chemist]

carbo- *combining form* Carbon; carbohydrate. Also, before vowels, **carb-.** [< L *carbo* coal]

car·bo·hy·drate (kär'bō·hī'drāt) *n. Biochem.* Any one of a group of compounds containing carbon combined with hydrogen and oxygen, taking part in the metabolism of plants and animals, and including sugars, starches, and cellulose. [< CARBO- + HYDRATE]

car·bo·lat·ed (kär'bə·lā'tid) *adj.* Containing carbolic acid.

car·bol·ic acid (kär·bol'ik) *Chem.* Phenol (def. 2). [< CARB- + -OL² + -IC]

car·bo·lize (kär'bə·līz) *v.t.* **·lized, ·liz·ing** *Chem.* To treat or impregnate with carbolic acid.

car·bon (kär'bən) *n.* **1.** A nonmetallic element (symbol C) found in all organic substances and in some inorganic substances, as diamonds, graphite, coal, charcoal, lampblack, etc. See ELEMENT. **2.** *Electr.* **a** A rod of carbon, used as an electrode in an arc light. **b** The negative electrode of a primary cell. **3.** A piece of carbon paper. **4.** A carbon copy. Abbr. *c., C.* — *adj.* **1.** Of, pertaining to, or like carbon. **2.** Treated with carbon: *carbon* paper. [< F *carbone* < L *carbo, -onis* coal]

carbon 13 *Physics* A carbon isotope of mass 13, used as a tracer element in the study of physiological processes.

carbon 14 *Physics* Radiocarbon.

car·bo·na·ceous (kär'bə·nā'shəs) *adj.* Of, pertaining to, or yielding carbon.

car·bo·na·do¹ (kär'bə·nā'dō) *n. pl.* **·does** or **·dos** A bird, fish, or piece of meat scored and broiled. — *v.t.* **·doed, ·do· ing 1.** To score and broil. **2.** To hack or slash. [< Sp. *carbonada* < *carbón* coal < L *carbo, -onis*]

car·bo·na·do² (kär'bə·nä'dō) *n. pl.* **·does** A variety of impure diamond; bort. [< Pg.]

Car·bo·na·ri (kär'bō·nä'rē) *n. pl.* of **Car·bo·na·ro** (-rō) A 19th-century secret society, organized in Italy to establish a republic. [< Ital. < L *carbonarius* charcoal burner < *carbo, -onis* coal] — **Car'bo·na'rism** *n.*

car·bon·ate (kär'bə·nāt; *for n., also* kär'bə·nit) *Chem. v.t.* **·at·ed, ·at·ing 1.** To impregnate or charge with carbon dioxide. **2.** To carbonize. — *n.* A salt or ester of carbonic acid. [< F]

car·bon·a·tion (kär'bə·nā'shən) *n. Chem.* **1.** The operation of precipitating lime by mixing with carbon dioxide. **2.** Saturation with carbon dioxide, as in manufacturing soda water: also **car·bon·a·ta·tion** (kär'bən·ə·tā'shən).

carbon black Lampblack (which see).

carbon copy 1. A copy of a letter, etc., made by means of carbon paper. Abbr. *c.c., C.C.* **2.** An exact or close replica; duplicate.

carbon cycle *Physics* A thermonuclear process taking place in the interior of stars, by which hydrogen is transformed into helium through the catalytic action of carbon and nitrogen. Compare PROTON–PROTON REACTION.

carbon dioxide *Chem.* A heavy, odorless, incombustible gas, CO₂, widely used as a fire extinguisher, in carbonated beverages, and, in solid forms, as a refrigerant. It is taken from the atmosphere in the photosynthesis of plants and returned to it by the respiration of both plants and animals.

carbon dioxide snow *Chem.* Dry Ice.

carbon disulfide *Chem.* A colorless, limpid, volatile, and highly flammable liquid, CS₂, with a disagreeable odor, used as a solvent for oils, resins, etc., and for exterminating vermin. Also **carbon bisulfide.**

carboni- *combining form* Carbon; coal. [< L *carbo, -onis* coal]

car·bon·ic (kär·bon'ik) *adj.* Of, pertaining to, or obtained from carbon.

carbonic acid *Chem.* A weak, unstable dibasic acid, H₂CO₃, existing only in solution and readily dissociating into water and carbon dioxide.

car·bon·ic-ac·id gas (kär·bon'ik·as'id) Formerly, carbon dioxide.

car·bon·if·er·ous (kär'bə·nif'ər·əs) *adj.* Of, pertaining to, containing, or yielding carbon or coal.

Car·bon·if·er·ous (kär'bə·nif'ər·əs) *adj. Geol.* Of or pertaining to a period of the Upper Paleozoic era succeeding the Devonian, characterized by the formation of extensive coal beds. In North America the Carboniferous system of strata is divided into the Mississippian and Pennsylvanian series. — *n.* The Carboniferous period or system of rocks. See chart under GEOLOGY.

car·bon·i·za·tion (kär'bən·ə·zā'shən, -ī·zā'-) *n.* The conversion of organic matter, as wood, into coal or charcoal.

car·bon·ize (kär'bən·īz) *v.t.* **·ized, ·iz·ing 1.** To reduce to carbon; char. **2.** To coat with carbon, as paper. **3.** To charge with carbon. — **car'bon·iz'er** *n.*

carbon monoxide *Chem.* A colorless, odorless gas, CO, formed by the incomplete oxidation of carbon, burning with a blue flame and highly poisonous when inhaled.

carbon paper 1. Thin paper coated with carbon or the like, placed between two sheets of paper to reproduce on the bottom sheet what is written or typed on the upper sheet. **2.** Paper used in the carbon process.

carbon process A photographic printing process employing a tissue or film of gelatin colored with a permanent and insoluble pigment. Also **carbon printing.**

carbon tetrachloride *Chem.* A colorless, nonflammable liquid, CCl₄, used as a solvent, cleaning fluid, etc.

car·bon·yl (kär'bən·il) *n. Chem.* **1.** A bivalent organic radical, CO, known only in combination. **2.** A compound of a metal and carbon monoxide: nickel *carbonyl.* [< CARBON + -YL] — **car'bon·yl'ic** *adj.*

arbonyl chloride *Chem.* Phosgene.

ar·bo·ra (kär·bôr′ə, -bō′rə) *n.* An Australian worm that bores into timbers, as those of piers, exposed at low tide. [< native Australian name]

Car·bo·run·dum (kär′bə·run′dəm) *n.* An abrasive af silicon carbide: a trade name. Also **car′bo·run′dum.**

ar·box·yl (kär·bok′sil) *n. Chem.* A univalent acid radical, COOH, the characteristic group of most organic acids. [< CARB- + OX(Y)- +-YL] — **car·box·yl·ic** (kär′bok·sil′ik) *adj.*

:ar·box·y·lase (kär·bok′sə·lās) *n. Biochem.* An enzyme found in yeast that splits carbon dioxide from pyruvic acid.

:ar·boy (kär′boi) *n.* A large glass bottle enclosed in a box or in wickerwork, used as a container for corrosive acids, etc. [Alter. of Persian *qarābah* demijohn]

:ar·bun·cle (kär′bung·kəl) *n.* **1.** *Pathol.* An inflammation of the subcutaneous tissue, resembling a boil but larger. **2.** A red garnet cut without facets and concave below, to show the color. [< AF < L *carbunculus,* dim. of *carbo, -onis* coal] — **car·bun·cu·lar** (kär·bung′kyə·lər) *adj.*

car·bu·ret (kär′bə·rāt, -byə·ret) *v.t.* **·ret·ed** or **·ret·ted, ·ret·ing** or **·ret·ting** To combine chemically with carbon; especially, to charge (air or gas) with carbon compounds to impart illuminative or explosive power. [< CARB- + -URET] — **car·bu·re·tion** (kär′bə·rā′shən, -byə·resh′ən) *n.*

:ar·bu·re·tor (kär′bə·rā′tər, -byə·ret′ər) *n.* An apparatus used to charge air or gas with volatile hydrocarbons to give it illuminative or explosive power. Also *Brit.* **car·bu·ret·tor** (kär′byə·ret′ər) or **car′bu·ret′ter.**

car·bu·rize (kär′bə·rīz, -byə-) *v.t.* **·rized, ·riz·ing** **1.** To carburet. **2.** *Metall.* To impregnate the surface layer of (low-carbon steel) with carbon, a stage in casehardening. Also *Brit.* **car′bu·rise.** [< *carbure* carbide + -IZE] — **car·bu·ri·za·tion** (kär′bə·ri·zā′shən). — **car′bu·riz′er** *n.*

car·byl·a·mine (kär′bil·ə·mēn′, -am′in) *n. Chem.* An organic compound containing the radical NC. [< CARB- + -YL + -AMINE]

car·ca·jou (kär′ka·jōō, -zhōō) *n. Canadian* The wolverine. [< dial. F (Canadian) < native Algonquian name]

car·ca·net (kär′kə·net) *n.* **1.** *Archaic* An ornamental collar or necklace, usually of gold with jewels. **2.** *Obs.* A jeweled band for the head. [< MF, dim. of *carcan* iron collar worn by prisoners < Med.L *carcanum* < Gmc.]

car·cass (kär′kəs) *n.* **1.** The dead body of an animal. **2.** The human body, living or dead: a contemptuous or humorous use. **3.** Something from which the life or essence is gone; shell. **4.** A framework or skeleton, as of a structure. Also **car′case.** [< AF *carcas* < Med.L *carcasium;* infl. in form by MF *carcasse* a corpse < Ital. *carcassa*]

Car·cas·sonne (kár·kà·sôn′) A city in southern France; pop. 40,580 (1968).

car·cel (kär′səl) *n.* A former French unit of illumination, equal to 9.6 international candles. [after B. G. *Carcel,* 1750–1812, French inventor]

car·cin·o·gen (kär·sin′ə·jən) *n. Pathol.* A substance that causes cancer. [< CARCINO(MA) + -GEN] — **car·ci·no·gen·ic** (kär·sə·nō·jen′ik) *adj.*

car·ci·no·ma (kär′sə·nō′mə) *n. pl.* **·mas** or **·ma·ta** (-mə·tə) *Pathol.* A malignant epithelial tumor that invades adjacent tissue and spreads by metastasis; cancer. Also **car·ci·nus** (kär′sə·nəs). [< L < Gk. *karkinōma* < *karkinos* cancer] — **car·ci·nom·a·tous** (kär′sə·nom′ə·təs, -nō′mə-) *adj.*

card[1] (kärd) *n.* **1.** A small, usually rectangular piece of thin pasteboard or stiff paper, used for a variety of purposes: postal *card;* business *card.* **2.** One of a pack of such pieces with figures, numbers, or other symbols, used for various games. **3.** *pl.* Games played with playing cards. **4.** A greeting card (which see). **5.** A card certifying the identity of its owner or bearer: library *card.* **6.** A program or form of events, as at the races, etc. **7.** *Naut.* The dial of a compass. **8.** A piece of pasteboard containing small articles of merchandise: a *card* of buttons. **9.** An advertisement or public announcement printed on a card: a window *card.* **10.** *Informal* A person manifesting some specified peculiarity: a queer *card.* **11.** *Informal* A witty person. — **in the cards** Likely to happen; possible. — **to put one's cards on the table** To reveal one's intentions or resources with complete frankness. — *v.t.* **1.** To fasten or write upon a card or cards. **2.** To provide with a card. [< MF *carte* < Ital. *carta* card, sheet of paper < L *charta* paper < Gk. *chartēs.* Doublet of CHART.]

card[2] (kärd) *n.* **1.** A wire-toothed brush for combing and cleansing wool and other fiber. **2.** A similar instrument for raising a nap on cloth. — *v.t. & v.i.* To comb, dress, or cleanse with a card. [< MF *carde* < Ital. *carda* card < Med.L *cardus* < L *carduus* thistle] — **card′er** *n.*

Card. **1.** Cardiganshire. **2.** (title) Cardinal.

car·da·mom (kär′də·məm) *n.* **1.** The aromatic seeds of either of two Asian plants (genera *Elettaria* and *Amomum*) of the ginger family, used as a condiment and a mild carminative. **2.** One of the plants yielding these seeds. Also **car′da·mon** (-mən), **car′da·mum.** [< L *cardamomum* < Gk. *kardamōmon* < *kardamon* cress + *amōmon* spice]

card·board (kärd′bôrd′, -bōrd′) *n.* A thin, stiff pasteboard used for making cards, boxes, etc.

card·case (kärd′kās′) *n.* A case to hold cards; especially, a pocket case for calling cards.

card catalogue A catalogue made out on cards, especially one showing the books, etc., in a library.

Cár·de·nas (kär′thā·näs) A port city in western Cuba; pop. about 43,800.

Cár·de·nas (kär′thā·näs), **La·za·ro,** 1895–1970, president of Mexico 1934–40.

card file A systematic arrangement of cards containing records or other data: also called *card index.*

cardi- Var. of CARDIO-.

car·di·ac (kär′dē·ak) *Med. adj.* **1.** Pertaining to, situated near, or affecting the heart. **2.** Of or pertaining to the upper esophageal orifice of the stomach. Also **car·di·a·cal** (kär·dī′ə·kəl). — *n.* **1.** One suffering from a heart disease. **2.** A cardiac remedy or stimulant. [< F *cardiaque* < L *cardiacus* < Gk. *kardiakos* < *kardia* heart]

car·di·al·gi·a (kär′dē·al′jē·ə) *n. Pathol.* Heartburn. Also **car′di·al′gy.** [< NL < Gk. *kardialgia* < *kardia* heart + *algos* pain] — **car′di·al′gic** *adj.*

Car·diff (kär′dif) The county seat of Mid Glamorgan, a county borough and port in SE Wales; pop. 284,700 (1976).

car·di·gan (kär′də·gən) *n.* A jacket or sweater opening down the front. Also **cardigan jacket, cardigan sweater.** [after the seventh Earl of *Cardigan,* 1797–1868]

Cardigan Bay An inlet of the Irish Sea in western Wales.

Car·di·gan·shire (kär′də·gən·shir′) A former county in western Wales; 692 sq. mi.; pop. 54,844 (1971); county seat, **Cardigan.** Also **Car′di·gan.**

car·di·nal (kär′də·nəl, kärd′nəl) *adj.* **1.** Of prime importance; chief; principal. **2.** Of a deep scarlet color. **3.** Of or relating to a cardinal or cardinals. — *n.* **1.** In the Roman Catholic Church, a member of the College of Cardinals, or Sacred College. *Abbr. Card.* **2.** A bright red, crested finch (*Richmondina cardinalis*) of the eastern United States: also called *redbird.* Also **cardinal bird, cardinal grosbeak.** **3.** A short, hooded woman's cloak of the 18th century. **4.** A deep scarlet, the color of a cardinal's cassock. **5.** A cardinal number. [< F < L *cardinalis* important < *cardo, cardinis* hinge, that on which something turns or depends] — **car′di·nal·ly** *adv.*

car·di·nal·ate (kär′də·nəl·āt, kärd′nəl·āt) *n.* The rank, dignity, or term of office of a cardinal. Also **car′di·nal·ship′.** [< F *cardinalat* < Med.L *cardinalatus*]

cardinal flower An herb (*Lobelia cardinalis*) of North America having large red flowers: also called *red lobelia.*

car·di·nal·i·ty (kär′də·nal′ə·tē) *n. Math.* The property of being expressible by a cardinal number, as any finite or restricted series of numbers.

cardinal number *Math.* Any number that expresses the number of objects or units under consideration, as 1, 2, 3, etc.: distinguished from *ordinal number.*

cardinal point One of the four principal compass points.

cardinal sins The seven deadly sins (which see).

cardinal virtues Justice, prudence, temperance, and fortitude, classified by Plato as the four primary types of moral excellence, and sometimes called the **natural virtues.** See THEOLOGICAL VIRTUES.

card index A card file (which see).

card·ing (kär′ding) *n.* **1.** The cleansing and combing of natural fibers before spinning. **2.** Carded fibers.

carding machine A machine for carding cotton, wool, flax, etc., by the action of wire-toothed cylinders. Also **carding engine.**

cardio- *combining form* Heart: *cardiogram.* Also, before vowels, **cardi-.** [< Gk. *kardia* heart]

car·di·o·gram (kär′dē·ə·gram′) *n.* The graphic record of heart movements produced by the cardiograph.

car·di·o·graph (kär′dē·ə·graf′, -gräf′) *n.* An instrument for tracing and recording the force and character of the heart movements. [< CARDIO- + -GRAPH] — **car′di·o·graph′ic** *adj.* — **car·di·og·ra·phy** (kär′dē·og′rə·fē) *n.*

car·di·oid (kär′dē·oid) *n. Math.* A heart-shaped curve generated by a point on the circumference of a circle that rolls around another fixed circle of the same size. [< Gk. *kardioides* heart-shaped]

car·di·ol·o·gy (kär′dē·ol′ə·jē) *n.* The study of the heart, its physiology and pathology. — **car′di·ol′o·gist** *n.* [< CARDIO- + -LOGY]

car·di·o·scope (kär′dē·ə·skōp′) *n.* An instrument for examining the inside of the heart. [< CARDIO- + -SCOPE]

car·di·tis (kär·dī′tis) *n. Pathol.* Inflammation of the heart. [< CARDIO- + -ITIS]

car·doon (kär·dōōn′) *n.* A perennial plant (*Cynara cardunculus*) of the Mediterranean region, allied to the artichoke and eaten as a vegetable. [< MF *cardon* < Ital. *cardone,* aug. of *cardo* thistle < L *carduus*]

Car·do·zo (kär·dō′zō), **Benjamin Nathan,** 1870–1938, U.S. jurist; associate justice of the Supreme Court 1932–38.

card·play·er (kärd′plā′ər) *n.* One who plays cards. — **card′play′ing** *n.*
cards (kärdz) *n.pl.* (*construed as sing.*) **1.** Any game played with playing cards. **2.** The playing of card games.
Cards. Cardiganshire.
card·sharp (kärd′shärp′) *n.* One who cheats at cards, especially as a livelihood. Also **card′sharp′er.** — **card′· sharp′ing** *n.*
car·du·a·ceous (kär′jōō·ā′shəs) *adj. Bot.* Of or belonging to the thistle group (formerly the *Carduaceae*) of the composite family, having heavy-headed radiate flowers. [< NL *Carduaceae* < L *carduus* thistle]
Car·duc·ci (kär-dōot′chē), **Gio·suè**, 1835–1907, Italian poet.
care (kâr) *n.* **1.** A feeling of anxiety or concern; worry. **2.** A cause of worry or anxiety: not a *care* in the world. **3.** Watchful regard or attention; heed. **4.** Charge or guardianship; custody; supervision. **5.** An object of solicitude or attention. **6.** *Obs.* Grief; affliction. — *v.i.* **cared, car·ing 1.** To have or show regard, interest, or concern. **2.** To be inclined; desire: with *to*: Do you *care* to read the book? **3.** To mind or be concerned; have an objection: used chiefly in negative or conditional expressions: I don't *care* if it rains. — **to care for 1.** To look after or provide for. **2.** To feel interest concerning; also, to have a fondness for; like. **3.** To want; desire. [OE *caru*, *cearu*] — **car′er** *n.*
— **Syn.** (noun) **1.** *Care, concern, solicitude,* and *worry* denote a troubled state of mind. *Care* arises from responsibility or affection for others, and may vary from mild *concern* to profound *worry*: care for one's children. *Concern* is the absence of indifference, and hence implies voluntary involvement: *concern* for the nation's welfare. *Solicitude* is deep *concern* arising from kindliness: *solicitude* for a sick friend. *Worry* implies an oppressive and fretful anxiety, and is often needless or excessive. Compare ANXIETY. — **Ant.** disregard, indifference.
CARE Cooperative for American Remittances Everywhere.
ca·reen (kə·rēn′) *v.i.* **1.** *U.S.* To lurch or twist from side to side while moving, as if scarcely under control. **2.** To lean or heel, as a ship in the wind. **3.** To clean, repair, or caulk a ship when it is turned on one side. — *v.t.* **4.** To turn (a ship) on one side so as to clean, repair, or caulk. **5.** To clean, repair, or caulk (a careened ship). — **Syn.** See TIP[1]. — *n.* **1.** The act of careening a vessel. **2.** The position of a ship careened or heeled over. [< F *cariner, caréner* < *carène* keel of a ship < L *carina*] — **ca·reen′er** *n.*
ca·reer (kə·rir′) *n.* **1.** The course or progress of a person's life, or some portion of it, especially as related to some noteworthy activity or pursuit: His was a remarkable *career*. **2.** One's lifework; occupation; profession: to make medicine one's *career*. **3.** Successful pursuit of an occupation: Make a *career* for yourself. **4.** A free and swift course, run, or charge. **5.** Speed; full speed. **6.** *Obs.* A racecourse. — *adj. U.S.* Making his or her profession a lifework; professional: *career* diplomat. — *v.i.* To move with a swift, free, and headlong motion. [< F *carrière* racecourse < LL *carraria* (*via*) road for carriages < L *carrus* wagon] — **ca·reer′er** *n.*
— **Syn.** (noun) **2.** business, profession, pursuit, vocation. Compare OCCUPATION. **4.** charge, flight, race, rush.
ca·reer·ist (kə·rir′ist) *n.* A person chiefly concerned with advancing himself professionally. — **ca·reer′ism** *n.*
career woman A woman devoted to a business or professional career. Also **career girl.**
care·free (kâr′frē′) *adj.* Free of troubles or anxiety.
care·ful (kâr′fəl) *adj.* **1.** Exercising care in one's work; thorough; painstaking. **2.** Done with care: a *careful* job. **3.** Watchful of one's thoughts or actions; cautious. **4.** *Obs.* Overanxious. — **care′ful·ly** *adv.* — **care′ful·ness** *n.*
care·less (kâr′lis) *adj.* **1.** Not attentive enough to what one is doing: a *careless* worker. **2.** Not done with care; neglectful. **3.** Without regard or concern; indifferent: with *about, in,* or *of: careless* of one's appearance. **4.** Artless; unstudied: *careless* elegance. **5.** Carefree: a *careless* life. — **care′less·ly** *adv.* — **care′less·ness** *n.*
ca·ress (kə·res′) *n.* A gentle, affectionate touch or gesture, as an embrace, pat, etc. — *v.t.* To touch or treat lovingly; fondle; embrace; pet. [< MF *caresse* < Ital. *carezza*, ult. < L *carus* dear] — **ca·ress′er** *n.* — **ca·ress′ing·ly** *adv.* — **ca·res′sive** *adj.* — **ca·res′sive·ly** *adv.*
— **Syn.** (verb) *Caress, fondle, pet,* and *neck* mean to treat affectionately. *Caressing* may be done with the hands, the voice, or with words and tender attentions; *fondling* is always done with the hands. *Pet* originally meant to treat in any favored way. It is now used with its close synonym, *neck,* in a slang sense to refer to amorous play by embracing and kissing. Compare PAMPER.
car·et (kar′ət) *n.* A sign (∧) placed below a line to indicate where something should be inserted. [< L, it is missing]
care·tak·er (kâr′tā′kər) *n.* One who takes care of a place, thing, or person; a custodian.
Ca·rew (kə·rōō′, kâr′ōō, kâr′ē), **Thomas**, 1595?–1645, English poet.
care·worn (kâr′wôrn′, -wōrn′) *adj.* Showing the effects of care and anxiety.
car·fare (kär′fâr′) *n.* The fare for a ride on a bus, etc.
car·go (kär′gō) *n.* *pl.* **·goes** or **·gos** Goods and merchandise carried by a vessel, aircraft, etc.; freight; load. [< Sp. < LL *carricum* load < *carricare* to load < L *carrus* wagon]

car·hop (kär′hop′) *n.* *U.S. Informal* A waiter or waitress at a drive-in restaurant.
Car·ib (kar′ib) *n.* **1.** One of a Cariban tribe of Indians formerly found in Brazil, Guiana, Venezuela, and the Lesser Antilles, now surviving on the coasts of Guiana, Venezuela, Dominica, Honduras, Guatemala, and Nicaragua. **2.** The family of languages spoken by the Cariban Indians. [< Sp. *Caribe* Carib, cannibal < *Carib/ caribe* brave]
Car·ib·an (kar′ə·bən) *n.* **1.** A stock of South American and Caribbean coastal Indians. **2.** Carib (def. 2). — *adj.* Of or pertaining to this ethnic stock or linguistic family.
Car·ib·be·an (kar′ə·bē′ən, kə·rib′ē·ən) *n.* A Carib. — **the Caribbean** The Caribbean Sea and lands in and around it. — *adj.* **1.** Of or pertaining to the Caribbean Sea. **2.** Of or pertaining to the Caribs, their language, or their culture.
Caribbean Sea A part of the Atlantic between the West Indies and Central and South America.
car·i·be (kar′ə·be, *Sp.* kä·rē′bā) *n.* The piranha, a fish. [< Sp., cannibal]
Car·i·bees (kar′ə·bēz) The Lesser Antilles.
car·i·bou (kar′ə·bōō) *n. pl.* **·bou** or **·bous** A deer of North America related to the reindeer; especially, the **woodland cari·bou** (*Rangifer tarandis caribou*), found from Maine to Lake Superior and northward, and the smaller and lighter colored **Barren Grounds caribou** (*R. t. arcticus*) of the treeless arctic regions. [< dial. F (Canadian) < Algonquian *khalibu* pawer, scratcher]

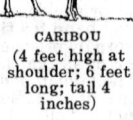

CARIBOU
(4 feet high at shoulder; 6 feet long; tail 4 inches)

car·i·ca·ture (kar′i·kə·chŏŏr, -chər) *n.* **1.** A picture or description in which features are exaggerated or distorted so as to produce an absurd effect. **2.** The act or art of caricaturing. **3.** A poor, inept, or badly distorted likeness or imitation. — *v.t.* **·tured, ·tur·ing** To represent so as to make ridiculous; travesty; burlesque. [< F < Ital. *caricatura,* lit., an overloading < *caricare* to load, exaggerate] — **car′i·ca·tur′al** *adj.* — **car′i·ca·tur′ist** *n.*
— **Syn.** (noun) **1.** *Caricature, burlesque, takeoff, parody,* and *travesty* are imitations for the purpose of ridicule or banter. A *caricature* (most commonly pictorial) exaggerates the prominent features of the original. A *burlesque* (most commonly dramatic) mimics behavior or action in a comical way. A *takeoff,* usually goodnatured, is a mild *caricature* or *burlesque.* A *parody* (usually written) follows the style of the original, but alters the subject ludicrously, while a *travesty* follows the subject of the original, but exaggerates the peculiarities of its style. Compare LAMPOON.
car·ies (kâr′ēz, -i·ēz) *n. Pathol.* Decay of a bone or of a tooth. [< L]
car·il·lon (kar′ə·lon, kə·ril′yən) *n.* **1.** A set of stationary bells rung by hammers operated from a keyboard or by a mechanism. **2.** A melody rung on a carillon. **3.** An organ stop imitating bells. — *v.i.* **·lonned, ·lon·ning** To play a carillon. [< F < Med.L *quadrilio, -onis* set of four bells]
car·il·lon·neur (kar′ə·lə·nûr′) *n.* One who plays a carillon. [< F]
ca·ri·na (kə·rī′nə) *n. pl.* **·nae** (-nē) *Biol.* A longitudinal ridge or keel-shaped formation in certain plants and animals. [< L, keel] — **ca·ri′nal** *adj.*
Ca·ri·na (kə·rī′nə) *n.* A constellation, the Keel. See CONSTELLATION.
car·i·nate (kar′ə·nāt, -nit) *adj.* **1.** *Biol.* Having a carina. **2.** Ridged in profile; keel-shaped. Also **car′i·nat′ed.** [< L *carinatus,* pp. of *carinare* to supply with a keel]
Ca·rin·thi·a (kə·rin′thē·ə) A Province of southern Austria; formerly a duchy; 3,681 sq. mi.; pop. 493,972 (1961); capital Klagenfurt: German *Kärnten.*
car·i·o·ca (kar′ē·ō′kə) *n.* A type of South American dance, or the music for it. See [CARIOCAN]
Car·i·o·can (kar′ē·ō′kən) *n.* A resident of Rio de Janeiro, Brazil. Also **Car′i·o·ca.** [after Serra de *Carioca,* a mountain range near the city]
car·i·ole (kar′ē·ōl) *n.* **1.** A small, open carriage. **2.** A light cart. **3.** *Canadian* A dog sled, often ornate, designed to carry one person lying down. Also spelled *carriole.* [< F *carriole* < Ital. *carriuola,* dim. of *carra* cart, wagon]
car·i·op·sis (kar′ē·op′sis) See CARYOPSIS.
car·i·ous (kâr′ē·əs) *adj.* Affected with caries; decayed. Also **car·ied** (kâr′ēd). — **car′i·os′i·ty** (-os′ə·tē), **car′i·ous·ness** *n.*
cark (kärk) *Archaic* *n.* Worry; anxiety. — *v.t. & v.i.* To fill or be filled with anxiety. [< AF *karke,* var. of OF *carche* < *carchier,* ult. < LL *carricare.* See CHARGE.]
cark·ing (kär′king) *adj.* Archaic Worrisome; vexing.
carl (kärl) *n.* **1.** *Archaic* A countryman; peasant. **2.** *Scot.*

A churl; also, a robust man. **3.** *Obs.* A bondman; villein. Also **carle.** [< ON *karl* man, freeman. Akin to CHURL.]

carl hemp *Bot.* The seed-bearing or female hemp plant: so named because formerly thought to be the male.

car·lin (kär′lin) *n. Scot.* A hag; witch.

car·line¹ (kär′lin) *adj.* Relating to a genus (*Carlina*) of thistles. — *n.* A plant of the genus *Carlina.* [? after *Charlemagne*, whose soldiers it supposedly cured of a plague]

car·line² (kär′lin) *n.* Carling.

car·ling (kär′ling) *n. Naut.* One of the short fore-and-aft timbers connecting the beams on which the deck of a vessel is laid: also called *carline.* [Cf. F *carlingue*]

Car·lisle (kär·līl′) The county seat of Cumbria, in northern England; pop. 99,600 (1976).

Carl·ist (kär′list) *n.* **1.** In France, a supporter of Charles X and his line. **2.** In Spain, a supporter of the pretender, Don Carlos, and of his representatives. — **Carl′ism** *n.*

car·load (kär′lōd′) *n.* **1.** The load carried in a car, especially in a railroad freight car. **2.** The minimum load required to ship at the **carload rate,** a rate lower than that for smaller loads. Abbr. *c.l.*

carload lot A freight shipment meeting the official minimum weight for a carload rate. Abbr. *c.l.*

Car·los (kär′lōs), **Don,** 1788–1855, pretender to the Spanish throne: full name **Carlos María Isidro de Bourbon.**

Car·lo·ta (kär·lō′tä), 1840–1927, Marie Charlotte Amélie, wife of Maximilian, Archduke of Austria; empress of Mexico 1864–67.

Car·lo·vin·gi·an (kär′lə·vin′jē·ən) *adj.* Carolingian.

Carls·bad (kärlz′bad, *Ger.* kärls′bät) See KARLOVY VARY.

Carls·bad (kärlz′bad) A city in SE New Mexico; pop. 21,297.

Carlsbad Caverns National Park (kärlz′bad) An area in SE New Mexico that includes the **Carlsbad Caverns,** a series of limestone caves; 71 sq. mi.; established 1930.

Carls·ruh·e (kärls′rōō′ə) See KARLSRUHE.

Car·lyle (kär·līl′), **Thomas,** 1795–1881, Scottish essayist and historian.

car·ma·gnole (kär′mən·yōl′, *Fr.* kȧr·mȧ·nyôl′) *n.* **1.** A wild dance and song of the French revolutionists of 1789. **2.** The costume of the French revolutionists, consisting of a jacket with metal buttons and wide lapels, a tricolored waistcoat, black pantaloons, and a red cap. **3.** A soldier of the French Revolution. [< F, after *Carmagnola,* a town in Piedmont occupied by the revolutionists]

car·man (kär′mən) *n. pl.* **·men** (-mən) **1.** The driver, or one of the crew, of a streetcar, etc. **2.** One who drives a cart.

Car·man (kär′mən), **(William) Bliss,** 1861–1929, Canadian poet.

Car·mar·then·shire (kär·mär′thən·shir) A former county in southern Wales; 919 sq. mi.; pop. 162,313 (1971); county seat, **Carmarthen,** pop. 50,100 (1976): also *Caermarthen, Caermarthenshire.* Also **Car·mar′then.**

Carmarths. or Carm. Carmarthenshire.

Car·mel (kär′məl), **Mount** A ridge in NW Israel; length 13 mi.; height 1,791 ft.

Car·mel·ite (kär′məl·īt) *n.* **1.** A monk or friar of the mendicant order of Our Lady of Mt. Carmel, the White Friars, founded in Syria in 1156. **2.** A nun of this order. — *adj.* Of or relating to the Carmelites.

car·min·a·tive (kär·min′ə·tiv, kär′mə·nā′tiv) *Med. adj.* Tending to, or used to, relieve flatulence. — *n.* A remedy for flatulence. [< L *carminatus,* pp. of *carminare* to cleanse]

car·mine (kär′min, -mīn) *n.* **1.** A deep red or purplish red color. **2.** A crimson pigment obtained from cochineal; rouge. — *adj.* Deep red or purplish red. [< F *carmin* < Med.L *carminus,* contraction of *carmesinus* < O Sp. *carmesin.* Doublet of CRIMSON.]

Car·mo·na (kär·mō′nə), **Antonio Oscar,** 1869–1951, Portuguese general; president of Portugal 1926–51.

car·nage (kär′nij) *n.* **1.** Extensive and bloody slaughter, as in war; massacre. **2.** *Obs.* Bodies of the slain. — **Syn.** See MASSACRE. [< MF < Ital. *carnaggio* < LL *carnaticum* flesh, meat < L *caro, carnis*]

car·nal (kär′nəl) *adj.* **1.** Relating to bodily appetites; sensual: the *carnal* sin of gluttony. **2.** Sexual: to have *carnal* knowledge of a woman. **3.** Not spiritual; worldly. [< LL *carnalis* fleshly < L *caro, carnis* flesh] — **car′nal·ist** *n.* — **car·nal·i·ty** (kär·nal′ə·tē) *n.* — **car′nal·ly** *adv.*

car·nal·lite (kär′nəl·īt) *n.* A milk-white, hydrous chloride of magnesium and potassium, an important source of potassium. [after R. von *Carnall,* 1804–74, German mineralogist]

Car·nar·von·shire (kär·när′vən·shir) See CAERNARVON-SHIRE.

car·nas·si·al (kär·nas′ē·əl) *Zool. adj.* Adapted for tearing flesh; sectorial: said of the last upper premolar and first lower molar in carnivores. — *n.* A carnassial tooth. [< F *carnassier* carnivorous < Provençal *carnacier,* ult. < L *caro, carnis* flesh]

Car·nat·ic (kär·nat′ik) A region of SE Madras State, India.

car·na·tion (kär·nā′shən) *n.* **1.** The perennial, herbaceous,

fragrant flower of any of the many cultivated varieties of the pink family (genus *Dianthus*): the State flower of Ohio. **2.** A light pink, bright rose, or scarlet color. **3.** *Obs.* In painting, the flesh tints of human skin. [< F, flesh color < L *carnatio, -onis* fleshiness < *caro, carnis* flesh]

car·nau·ba (kär·nou′bə) *n.* **1.** The wax palm (def. 2). **2.** The greenish or yellow wax from its leaves, used as a polish, insulating material, etc. [< Pg. < Tupi]

Car·ne·gie (kär·nā′gē, -neg′ē, kär′nə·gē), **Andrew,** 1835–1919, U.S. industrialist and philanthropist born in Scotland.

car·nel·ian (kär·nēl′yən) *n.* A clear red chalcedony, often cut as a gem: also *cornelian.* [Earlier *cornelian* < MF *corneline* < Med.L *corneolus, cornelius* chalcedony; infl. in form by L *caro, carnis* flesh]

car·ni·fy (kär′nə·fī) *v.t. & v.i.* **·fied, ·fy·ing** To form into flesh or a fleshlike consistency. [< L *carnificare* < *caro, carnis* flesh + *facere* to make] — **car′ni·fi·ca′tion** *n.*

Car·ni·o·la (kär·nē·ō′lə) A former duchy of Austria; 3,845 sq. mi.; since 1947 included in Yugoslavia: German *Krain.* Slovenian *Kranj.*

car·ni·val (kär′nə·vəl) *n.* **1.** An amusement show, usually one that travels, with merry-go-round, Ferris wheel, side shows, etc. **2.** Any gay festival, wild revel, or merrymaking. **3.** A period of festivity immediately preceding Lent. Compare MARDI GRAS. [< Ital. *carnevale* < Med.L *carnelevarium* < L *caro, carnis* flesh + *levare* to remove]

car·ni·vore (kär′nə·vôr, -vōr) *n.* **1.** Any of an order (*Carnivora*) of flesh-eating mammals, including cats, dogs, bears, seals, etc. **2.** An insectivorous plant.

car·niv·o·rous (kär·niv′ə·rəs) *adj.* **1.** Eating or living on flesh. **2.** Of or pertaining to the *Carnivora.* [< L *carnivorus* < *caro, carnis* flesh + *vorare* to eat, devour] — **car·niv′o·rous·ly** *adv.* — **car·niv′o·rous·ness** *n.*

car·nos·i·ty (kär·nos′ə·tē) *n. pl.* **·ties** *Pathol.* An abnormal fleshy growth or excrescence upon any bodily organ. [< MF *carnosité* < Med.L *carnositas, -tatis* < L *carnosus* fleshy]

Car·not cycle (kär·nō′) *Physics* A thermodynamic cycle consisting of four reversible changes in the operation of an ideal heat engine working at maximum efficiency. [after N. L. S. *Carnot,* 1796–1832, French physicist]

car·no·tite (kär′nə·tīt) *n.* A yellow, earthy vanadate containing potassium, uranium, and slight traces of radium, found in western Colorado, a source of uranium. [after M. A. *Carnot,* 1839–1920, an inspector general of mines in France]

car·ob (kar′əb) *n.* **1.** A caesalpinaceous evergreen tree (*Ceratonia siliqua*) of the Mediterranean region: also called *locust.* **2.** Its long, sickle-shaped, fleshy pods, used for fodder: sometimes called *algarroba, St. John's bread:* also **carob bean.** [< F *carobe, caroube* < Arabic *kharrūbah* bean pods]

ca·roche (kə·rōch′, -rōsh′) *n.* A stately carriage of the 16th and 17th centuries: also spelled *carroch.* Also **ca·roach′, ca·roch′.** [< MF *carroche* < Ital. *carroccio,* aug. of *carro* chariot < L *carrus* wagon]

car·ol (kar′əl) *n.* **1.** A song of joy or praise; especially, a Christmas song. **2.** *Obs.* A dance performed in a circle, or the song accompanying it. — *v.* **car·oled** or **·olled, car·ol·ing** or **·ol·ling** *v.i.* **1.** To sing, especially in a joyous strain; warble. — *v.t.* **2.** To utter in song; sing. **3.** To celebrate or praise in song. [< OF *carole,* prob. ult. < L *choraules* flutist < Gk. *choraulēs* < *choros* a dance + *auleein* to play the flute < *aulos* a flute] — **car′ol·er** or **car′ol·ler** *n.*

Car·ol II (kar′əl), 1893–1953, king of Rumania 1930–40; abdicated.

Car·o·li·na (kar′ə·lī′nə) An English colonial settlement, divided in 1729 into what is now North and South Carolina. — **the Carolinas** North and South Carolina.

Carolina parakeet An extinct parakeet (*Conuropsis carolinensis*) of the SE United States.

Carolina pinkroot See under PINKROOT.

Carolina potato The common sweet potato (which see).

Car·o·line (kar′ə·lin, -lin) *adj.* **1.** Pertaining to Charles I and II of England and their times. Also **Car·o·le·an** (kar′ə·lē′ən). **2.** Carolingian. [< Med.L *Carolinus* < *Carolus* Charles]

Caroline Islands A group of over 500 islands and islets in the Pacific east of the Philippines; 550 sq. mi.; part of the UN Trust Territory of the Pacific Islands: formerly *New Philippines.*

Car·o·lin·gi·an (kar′ə·lin′jē·ən) *adj.* Of or pertaining to the dynasty of Charlemagne. — *n.* A member of the house of Charlemagne, or a sovereign in that line. Also *Carlovingian.*

Car·o·lin·i·an (kar′ə·lin′ē·ən) *adj.* **1.** Of or pertaining to North or South Carolina. **2.** Carolingian. **3.** Caroline. — *n.* A native or inhabitant of North or South Carolina.

car·o·lus (kar′ə·ləs) *n. pl.* **·lus·es** or **·li** (-lī) An old English gold coin worth about twenty shillings. [< Med.L *Carolus* Charles; because first issued under Charles I]

car·om (kar′əm) *n.* **1.** In billiards, a shot in which the cue ball strikes against two other balls in succession: in England called a *cannon;* also, a similar shot in pool, curling, etc.: also called *billiard.* **2.** Any impact followed by a rebound. — *v.i.* **1.** To hit and rebound: The car *caromed* off the wall. — *v.t.* **2.** To cause to make a carom. Also spelled *carrom.* [Earlier *carambole* < F]

car·o·tene (kar′ə·tēn) *n. Biochem.* A deep yellow or red crystalline hydrocarbon, $C_{40}H_{56}$, that acts as a plant pigment, especially in carrots, and occurs also in various animal tissues, where it is changed to vitamin A: also spelled *carotin.* Also **car′o·tin** (-tin). [< L *carota* carrot + -ENE]

ca·rot·e·noid (kə·rot′ə·noid) *n. Biochem.* One of a large variety of nitrogen-free, light yellow to deep red lipochrome pigments found in plant and animal tissues. — *adj.* Of or pertaining to carotene or carotenoids. Also **ca·rot′i·noid.** [< CAROTENE + -OID]

ca·rot·id (kə·rot′id) *adj. Anat.* Of, pertaining to, or near one of the two major arteries on each side of the neck. Also **ca·rot′i·dal.** [< Gk. *karōtides,* pl. < *karoein* to stupefy < *karos* stupor; so called from the belief that pressure on them would cause unconsciousness]

ca·rou·sal (kə·rou′zəl) *n.* A riotous or boisterous drinking party; a jovial feast or banquet.

ca·rouse (kə·rouz′) *v.i.* **·roused, ·rous·ing** To drink freely and boisterously; engage in a carousal. — *n.* **1.** A carousal. **2.** *Obs.* The draining of a full bumper of liquor. [< G *gar aus* (*trinken*) (to drink) all out] — **ca·rous′er** *n.*

car·ou·sel (kar′ə·sel′, -zel′) *n.* **1.** A merry-go-round (def. 1). **2.** A tournament in which horsemen perform elaborate exercises. Also spelled *carrousel.* [< F *carrousel* < Ital. *carosello* tournament]

carp¹ (kärp) *v.i.* To find fault unreasonably; complain; cavil. [< ON *karpa* to boast] — **carp′er** *n.*

carp² (kärp) *n. pl.* **carp** or **carps 1.** A fresh-water food fish (*Cyprinus carpio*), originally of China but now widely distributed in Europe and America. **2.** Any of various other cyprinoid fishes, as dace, minnows, and goldfish. [< OF *carpe* < LL *carpa*]

carp. Carpentry.

-carp *combining form* Fruit; fruit (or seed) vessel: *pericarp.* [< Gk. *karpos* fruit]

car·pal (kär′pəl) *Anat. adj.* Of, pertaining to, or near the wrist. — *n.* A carpale. [< NL *carpalis* < L *carpus* wrist < Gk. *karpos*]

car·pa·le (kär·pā′lē) *n. pl.* **·li·a** (-lē-ə) *Anat.* A bone of the carpus or wrist; especially, one articulating with the metacarpal bones: also *carpal.* [< NL, neut. of *carpalis.* See CARPAL.]

Car·pa·thi·an Mountains (kär·pā′thē·ən) A range of central and eastern Europe, enclosing the Great Hungarian Plain; highest peak, Gerlachovka, 8,737 ft. Also **the Car·pa′thi·ans.**

Car·pa·tho-U·kraine (kär·pā′thō·yōō·krān′) See TRANS-CARPATHIAN OBLAST.

car·pe di·em (kär′pē dī′em) *Latin* Enjoy the present; seize today's opportunities; literally, seize the day.

car·pel (kär′pəl) *n. Bot.* A simple pistil or seed vessel. Also **car·pel·lum** (kär·pel′əm). For illustration see FRUIT. [< NL *carpellum* < Gk. *karpos* fruit] — **car·pel·lar·y** (kär′pə·ler′ē) *adj.*

car·pel·late (kär′pə·lāt) *adj. Bot.* Possessing carpels.

Car·pen·tar·i·a (kär′pən·târ′ē·ə), **Gulf of** A large inlet of the Arafura Sea in NE Australia.

car·pen·ter (kär′pən·tər) *n.* A workman who builds and repairs wooden structures, as houses, ships, etc. — *v.i.* **1.** To work as a carpenter. — *v.t.* **2.** To make or build as a carpenter. [< AF *carpentier* < LL *carpentarius* carpenter, wagonmaker < L *carpentum* two-wheeled carriage] — **car′·pen·ter·ing** *n.* — **car′pen·try** *n.*

Car·pen·ter (kär′pən·tər), **John Alden,** 1876–1951, U.S. composer.

carpenter bee A large, hairy, solitary bee (genus *Xylocopa*) that bores tunnels in wood for its nest, as the **great carpenter bee** (*X. virginica*) of the United States.

carpenter moth A large, light brown moth (*Prionoxystus robiniae*) whose larvae (**carpenter worms**) bore beneath the bark of certain trees.

car·pet (kär′pit) *n.* **1.** A heavy covering for floors, made of woven or felted fabric; also, the fabric used for it. **2.** A surface or covering suggesting this: *a carpet* of leaves. — **on the carpet 1.** Subjected to reproof or reprimand from one in authority. **2.** Under consideration or discussion. — *v.t.* To cover with or as with a carpet. [< OF *carpite* < LL *carpita* thick woolen covering < L *carpere* to pluck, card wool]

car·pet·bag (kär′pit·bag′) *n.* An old type of traveling bag, made of carpeting.

car·pet·bag·ger (kär′pit·bag′ər) *n. U.S.* **1.** One of the Northern adventurers who sought to gain advantages in the South from the unsettled conditions that prevailed there after the Civil War. Compare SCALAWAG (def. 2). **2.** Originally, an unscrupulous itinerant banker of the West. — **car′·pet·bag′ger·y, car′pet·bag′gism** *n.*

carpet beetle A beetle (*Anthrenus scrophulariae*) whose reddish brown larvae are destructive of carpets, woolen fabrics, and animal products: also called *buffalo bug.* Also **carpet bug.** For illustration see INSECTS (injurious).

car·pet·ing (kär′pit·ing) *n.* Material or fabric used for carpets; also, carpets collectively.

carpet knight A knight or soldier who lives in comfort away from battle: a contemptuous term.

carpet sweeper A hand-operated apparatus for sweeping carpets, combining a revolving brush and closed dustpan.

car·pet·weed (kär′pit·wēd′) *n.* A North American annual plant (*Mollugo verticillata*), the leaves of which, clustered in whorls, form mats on the ground.

carp·ing (kär′ping) *adj. & n.* Faultfinding. — **carp′ing·ly** *adv.*

carpo- *combining form* Fruit: *carpology.* [< Gk. *karpos* fruit]

car·pog·e·nous (kär·poj′ə·nəs) *adj. Bot.* Fruit-producing: said of the cell or groups of cells from which the spores are formed in certain algae. [< CARPO- + -GENOUS]

car·po·go·ni·um (kär′pə·gō′nē·əm) *n. pl.* **·ni·a** (-nē-ə) *Bot.* The female organ of certain algae; especially, in the red algae, the carpogenous cell or cells of the procarp that develop a sporocarp after fertilization. [< CARPO- + -GONIUM] — **car′po·go′ni·al** *adj.*

car·pol·o·gy (kär·pol′ə·jē) *n.* The department of botany that treats of fruits in general. [< CARPO- + -LOGY] — **car·po·log·i·cal** (kär′pə·loj′i·kəl) *adj.* — **car·pol′o·gist** *n.*

car·poph·a·gous (kär·pof′ə·gəs) *adj.* Fruit-eating. [< CARPO- + -PHAGOUS]

car·po·phore (kär′pə·fôr, -fōr) *n. Bot.* **1.** A portion of the receptacle prolonged between the carpels, as in geraniums and many umbelliferous plants. **2.** In fungi, any fruit-bearing structure or organ. [< CARPO- + -PHORE]

car·port (kär′pôrt, -pōrt) *n. U.S.* A shelter for an automobile, usually a roof projecting from the side of a building.

-carpous *combining form* Having a certain kind or number of fruits: *acrocarpous.* Also *-carpic.* [< Gk. *karpos* fruit]

car·pus (kär′pəs) *n. pl.* **·pi** (-pī) **1.** *Anat.* The wrist, or the carpal bones collectively. **2.** *Zool.* A part analogous to or like a wrist. [< NL < Gk. *karpos* wrist]

car·rack (kar′ək) *n.* A merchant vessel of the 14th to 16th centuries: also spelled *carack.* [< OF *carraque* < Med.L *carraca,* ? < Arabic *qaraqīr,* pl. of *qorqūr* merchant ship]

car·ra·geen (kar′ə·gēn) *n.* A stubby, purplish, edible seaweed (*Chondrus crispus*), known commercially as Irish moss and used in medicine: also spelled *carageen, caragheen, carrigeen.* Also **car′ra·gheen.** [from *Carragheen,* near Waterford, Ireland, where it grows]

Car·ran·za (kär·rän′sä), **Venustiano** 1859–1920, Mexican revolutionist; president 1915–20; assassinated.

Car·ra·ra (kə·rä′rə, *Ital.* kär·rä′rä) A city in central Italy; famous for white marble quarries; pop. about 63,300.

car·rel (kar′əl) *n.* A small space, as among the stacks in a library, for solitary study. Also **car′rell.** [Var. of CAROL.]

Car·rel (kə·rel′, kar′əl), **Alexis,** 1873–1944, French surgeon and physiologist active in the United States.

Car·rère (kə·râr′), **John Merven,** 1858–1911, U.S. architect.

car·riage (kar′ij; *for def. 7, also* kar′ē·ij) *n.* **1.** A wheeled, usually horse-drawn vehicle for carrying persons. **2.** *Brit.* A railroad passenger car. **3.** Manner of carrying the head and limbs; bearing. **4.** A moving portion of a machine carrying another part: the *carriage* of a lathe. **5.** A wheeled frame for carrying something heavy: a gun *carriage.* **6.** The act of carrying; transportation. **7.** The cost of transportation. **8.** Manner of execution; management. **9.** A baby carriage (which see). [< AF *cariage* < *carier.* See CARRY.]

carriage dog A Dalmatian.

carriage trade The wealthy patrons of a restaurant, theater, etc., so called because they came in private carriages.

car·rick bend (kar′ik) *Naut.* A knot used for joining two hawsers, etc.

carrick bitt *Naut.* One of the two posts on a ship's deck that support the ends of a windlass.

car·ried (kar′ēd) Past tense and past participle of CARRY.

Carrie Nation See NATION.

car·ri·er (kar′ē·ər) *n.* **1.** One who or that which carries. **2.** A person or company that carries persons or goods for hire. **3.** A mechanism, container, or support for carrying something. **4.** *Naval* An aircraft carrier (which see). **5.** *Med.* A person who is immune to a disease but transmits it to others by carrying the pathogens in his body. **6.** *Chem.* A material used as a catalytic agent acting to transfer an element between compounds. **7.** *Telecom.* A carrier wave. **8.** *Genetics* An individual capable of transmitting a specified gene while manifesting none of its effects.

carrier pigeon A homing pigeon (which see).

carrier wave *Telecom.* The radio-frequency wave that is varied in some respect in order to transmit intelligence.

car·ri·geen (kar′ə·gēn) See CARRAGEEN.

car·ri·ole (kar′ē·ōl) See CARIOLE.

car·ri·on (kar′ē·ən) *n.* Dead and putrefying flesh. — *adj.* **1.** Feeding on carrion. **2.** Like or pertaining to carrion; putrefying. [< AF *caroigne,* ult. < L *caro, carnis* flesh]

carrion crow The common crow (*Corvus corone*) of Europe.

car·ritch (kar′ich) *n. Scot.* A catechism.

car·roch (kə·roch′, -rōsh′) See CAROCHE.

Car·roll (kar′əl), **Charles,** 1737–1832, American patriot;

signer of the Declaration of Independence. — **Lewis** Pseudonym of *Charles Lutwidge Dodgson*, 1832–98, English mathematician and author of *Alice in Wonderland*. — **Paul Vincent**, 1900–1968, Irish playwright.

car·rom (karˈəm) See CAROM.

car·ro·ma·ta (käˈrō·mäˈtä) *n.* In the Philippines, a two-wheeled, horse-drawn vehicle. [< Sp. *carromato* < *carro* cart]

car·ro·nade (karˈə·nādˈ) *n.* Formerly, a short iron cannon of large caliber, used for close-range firing. [after the *Carron* ironworks, Scotland]

car·ron oil (karˈən) A mixture of limewater and linseed oil, used for burns. [after the *Carron* ironworks, Scotland]

car·rot (karˈət) *n.* **1.** The long, reddish yellow, edible root of an umbelliferous plant (*Daucus carota*). **2.** The plant itself. [< F *carotte* < L *carota* < Gk. *karōton*]

car·ro·tin (karˈə·tin) See CAROTENE.

car·rot·y (karˈət·ē) *adj.* **1.** Like a carrot, especially in color. **2.** Having red hair.

car·rou·sel (karˈə·selˈ, -zelˈ) See CAROUSEL.

car·ry (karˈē) *v.* **·ried**, **·ry·ing** *v.t.* **1.** To bear from one place to another; transport; convey. **2.** To serve as a medium of conveyance for; transmit: The wind *carries* sounds. **3.** To have or bear upon or about one's person: to *carry* a watch. **4.** To bear the weight, burden, or responsibility of. **5.** To give support to; corroborate; confirm. **6.** To bear as a mark or attribute; imply; involve: Her words *carried* conviction. **7.** To be pregnant with. **8.** To bear (the body, or a part of it) in a specified manner: *Carry* your head high! **9.** To conduct or comport (oneself). **10.** To take by force or effort; capture; win: to *carry* a fortress. **11.** To win the support or interest of: His bold words *carried* the crowd. **12.** To gain victory or acceptance for: to *carry* a point; also, to achieve success in: to *carry* an election. **13.** To cause to go or come; urge; move: Love of art *carried* him abroad. **14.** To extend; continue: to *carry* a viaduct to a city. **15.** To have or keep for sale: This store *carries* magazines. **16.** To transfer, as a number or figure, to another column. **17.** To bear as crops; yield; also, to sustain (cattle). **18.** To maintain on one's account books for a future settlement. **19.** *U.S.* To sing or play (a part or melody). **20.** *Southern U.S.* To lead or escort; accompany. **21.** In golf, to cover or pass, as a distance or object, in one stroke. **22.** In hunting, to keep to and follow (a scent). —*v.i.* **23.** To act as bearer or carrier: to fetch and *carry*. **24.** To have or exert propelling or projecting power: The rifle *carries* more than half a mile. **25.** To hold the neck and head habitually in a particular manner: This horse *carries* well. **26.** To gain victory or acceptance: The motion *carried*. — **to carry all before one** To meet with uniform success. — **to carry arms 1.** To belong to the army. **2.** To bear weapons. **3.** To hold a weapon in a prescribed position against the shoulder. — **to carry away** To move the feelings greatly; enchant, as with passion or rapture. — **to carry forward 1.** To progress or proceed with. **2.** In bookkeeping, to transfer (an item, etc.) to the next column or page. — **to carry off 1.** To cause to die: Pneumonia *carried* him *off*. **2.** To win, as a prize or honor. **3.** To face consequences boldly; brazen out. **4.** To abduct. — **to carry on 1.** To keep up; keep going; continue. **2.** To behave in a wild, excited, or foolish manner. **3.** To engage in; manage; conduct. — **to carry out** To accomplish; bring to completion. — **to carry over 1.** In bookkeeping, to repeat (an item, etc.) on another page or in another column. **2.** To postpone; put off. — **to carry through 1.** To carry to completion or success. **2.** To sustain or support to the end. — *n. pl.* **·ries 1.** Range, as of a gun: also, the distance covered by a projectile, golf ball, etc. **2.** *U.S.* A portage, as between navigable streams. **3.** The act of carrying. [< AF *carier* < LL *carricare* < L *carrus* cart. Doublet of CHARGE.] — **Syn.** (verb) **1.** See CONVEY. **3.** *Carry* and *bear* both mean to sustain in the hands or on the person. We *carry* a load only when moving, but we may *bear* a load while standing still: Father Time *carries* a scythe, Atlas *bears* the world on his shoulders.

car·ry·all¹ (karˈē·ôlˈ) *n.* **1.** A one-horse, four-wheeled covered vehicle. **2.** A closed automobile having two facing passenger seats arranged lengthwise. [Alter. of CARIOLE]

car·ry·all² (karˈē·ôlˈ) *n.* A large basket or bag.

carrying charge In installment buying, the interest charged on the unpaid balance.

carrying place *Canadian* A portage (def. 2).

car·ry·o·ver (karˈē·ōˈvər) *n.* **1.** Something left over or kept until later. **2.** In bookkeeping, a sum carried forward.

carse (kärs) *n. Scot.* Alluvial land along a river.

car·sick (kärˈsik) *adj.* Nauseated from riding in a car.

Car·son (kärˈsən) An unincorporated place in SW California; pop. 71,150.

Car·son (kärˈsən), **Christopher**, 1809–68, U.S. frontiersman: called **Kit Carson**. — **Edward Henry**, 1854–1935, Baron Carson of Duncairn, Irish politician: opposed Home Rule.

Carson City The capital of Nevada, in the western part; pop. 15,468.

Car·stensz (kärˈstənz), **Mount** A peak in west central New Guinea; about 16,400 feet.

cart (kärt) *n.* **1.** A heavy two-wheeled vehicle, for carrying loads. **2.** A light, two-wheeled vehicle with springs, used for business or pleasure. **3.** Loosely, any two- or four-wheeled vehicle. — *v.t.* **1.** To convey or carry in or as in a cart. — *v.i.* **2.** To drive or use a cart. [ON *kartr*] — **cartˈer** *n.*

cart·age (kärˈtij) *n.* The act of or charge for carting.

Car·ta·ge·na (kärˈtə·jēˈnə, *Sp.* kärˈtä·hāˈnä) **1.** A port city in SE Spain; pop. 123,301 (est. 1959). **2.** A port city in northern Colombia, on the **Bay of Cartagena**, an inlet of the Caribbean; pop. 179,250 (est. 1961).

carte¹ (kärt) *n.* **1.** A menu. **2.** *Scot.* A playing card. [< F, card]

carte² (kärt) See QUARTE.

Carte (kärt), **Richard D'Oy·ly** See D'OYLY CARTE.

carte blanche (kärtˈ blänshˈ, *Fr.* kȧrt blänshˈ) *pl.* **cartes blanches** (kärtsˈ blänshˈ, *Fr.* kȧrt blänshˈ) **1.** A signed paper granting its possessor the freedom to write his own conditions. **2.** Unrestricted authority. [< F, white card]

carte de vi·site (kärtˈ də vē·zētˈ) *pl.* **cartes de visite** (kärt) A visiting card. [< F]

car·tel (kär·telˈ, kärˈtəl) *n.* **1.** An international syndicate or trust that aims at monopolistic control of a particular market. Compare MONOPOLY, SYNDICATE, TRUST. **2.** An official agreement between governments, especially for the exchange of prisoners. **3.** In some European countries, a political bloc. **4.** A challenge to single combat. — **Syn.** See CONTRACT. [< F < Ital. *cartello*, dim. of *carta* paper]

Car·ter (kärˈtər), **Howard**, 1873–1939, English archeologist. — **Jimmy (James Earl, Jr.)**, born 1924, governor of Georgia 1971–74, 39th president of the United States, 1977–.

Car·ter·et (kärˈtər·it), **John**, 1690–1763, first Earl Granville, British statesman.

Car·te·sian (kär·tēˈzhən) *adj.* Of or pertaining to René Descartes, French philosopher and mathematician, or to his doctrines and methods. — *n.* A follower of Descartes or his doctrines. [< NL *Cartesianus* < *Cartesius*, Latinized form of *Descartes*]

Cartesian coordinate system *Geom.* A system for indicating the curve of an equation graphically by means of two axes, graduated in both directions from the origin, or for indicating the shape of a solid by means of three planes intersecting at right angles to one another at the origin: also called *rectangular coordinate system*.

Car·te·sian·ism (kär·tēˈzhən·izˈəm) *n.* The philosophy of Descartes, who maintained that genuine knowledge must be based on infallible intuitions of clear and distinct ideas, and who defended a thoroughgoing dualism between thought (or mind) and extension (the subject matter of physical science).

Car·thage (kärˈthij) An ancient city-state in North Africa near modern Tunis; destroyed by the Romans in 146 B.C. Ancient **Car·tha·go** (kär·thäˈgō, -täˈ/-). — **Car·tha·gin·i·an** (kärˈthə·jinˈē·ən) *adj. & n.*

Carthaginian peace A peace on drastically severe terms, in allusion to the Roman destruction of Carthage (146 B.C.).

Carthaginian Wars The Punic Wars. See table for WAR.

Car·thu·sian (kär·thōōˈzhən) *n.* A monk or nun of a contemplative order founded at Chartreuse in the French Alps by St. Bruno in 1084. — *adj.* Of or pertaining to the Carthusians. [< Med.L *Cartusianus* < *Carturissium* Chartreuse]

Car·tier (kȧr·tyāˈ), **Sir George Étienne**, 1814–73, Canadian statesman. — **Jacques**, 1491–1557, French seafarer and explorer; discovered the St. Lawrence River 1535.

car·ti·lage (kärˈtə·lij) *n. Zool.* **1.** A tough, elastic form of connective tissue in man and animals, composed of cells embedded in a translucent matrix, either homogeneous or fibrous; gristle. **2.** A structure or part consisting of cartilage. [< MF < L *cartilago* gristle]

cartilage bone *Anat.* A bone originating in the connective tissue of which cartilage is formed: distinguished from *membrane bone*.

car·ti·lag·i·nous (kärˈtə·lajˈə·nəs) *adj.* **1.** Of or like cartilage; gristly. **2.** Having a gristly skeleton, as sharks.

Car·tist (kärˈtist) *n.* A supporter of the constitution in Spain or Portugal. [< Sp. *carta* charter]

cart·load (kärtˈlōd) *n.* As much as a cart can hold.

car·to·gram (kärˈtə·gram) *n.* A map giving statistical information by means of shading, dots, etc. [< F *cartogramme*]

car·tog·ra·phy (kär·togˈrə·fē) *n.* The science or art of drawing or compiling maps or charts: also spelled *chartography*. [< *carto-* map (< L *charta*) + -GRAPHY] — **car·togˈra·pher** *n.* — **car·to·graphˈic** (kärˈtə·grafˈik) or **·i·cal** *adj.*

car·ton (kärˈtən) *n.* **1.** A cardboard box; also, the amount it holds. **2.** A paper or plastic container for liquids. Abbr. *c.*, *C.* **3.** A white disk within the bull's-eye of a target, or a shot striking it. [< F, pasteboard. See CARTOON.]

car·toon (kär·tōōnˈ) *n.* **1.** A drawing or caricature, as in a newspaper or periodical, depicting a humorous situation, or commenting satirically, on some topic of public interest. **2.** A comic strip. **3.** A motion-picture film (**animated cartoon**) produced by photographing a series of drawings, each of which represents a minute advancement in the action of the film. **4.** A full-size sketch for a fresco, mosaic, etc. — *v.t.* **1.** To make a caricature or cartoon of. — *v.i.* **2.** To make cartoons. [< F *carton* < Ital. *cartone* pasteboard, aug. of *carta* card < L *charta* paper] — **car·toon'ist** *n.*

car·touche (kär·tōōsh') *n.* **1.** An oblong or oval figure containing a royal or divine name, as on ancient Egyptian monuments. **2.** *Archit.* An ornamental tablet or panel with a space in the center for an inscription or emblem; a scroll-like design. **3.** A cartridge (def. 1), or a cartridge box. **4.** The case containing the flammable materials in some fireworks. Also **car·touch'.** [< F < Ital. *cartoccio*, aug. of *carta* card < L *charta* paper]

car·tridge (kär'trij) *n.* **1.** A casing of metal, pasteboard, or the like, containing a charge of powder for a firearm and, usually, the projectile or shot and the primer. **2.** Any small similar container, as the removable case in a tone arm containing the pickup and stylus of a record player. **3.** *Photog.* A roll of protected sensitized film. [Alter. of CARTOUCHE]

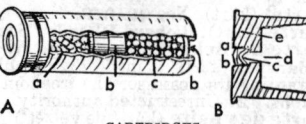

CARTRIDGES
A Shotgun shell: *a* Powder, *b* Wad, *c* Shot.
B Section of rifle or pistol cartridge case: *a* Primer cup, *b* Percussion composition, *c* Anvil, *d* Vent, *e* Base.

cartridge belt A belt having loops or pockets for cartridges or cartridge clips.

cartridge clip A metal container holding cartridges for a rapid-fire gun, as an automatic rifle.

car·tu·lar·y (kär'chŏō·ler'ē) *n. pl.* **·lar·ies** A record or register of deeds, etc.; also, a place for such records, or an officer in charge of them: also spelled *chartulary.* [< LL *cartularium* < L *cartula,* dim. of *carta, charta* paper]

cart·wheel (kärt'hwēl') *n.* **1.** A sideways handspring. **2.** *U.S. Informal* A large coin, especially a silver dollar.

Cart·wright (kärt'rīt), **Edmund,** 1743–1823, English clergyman; inventor of the power loom.

car·un·cle (kar'ung·kəl, kə·rung'kəl) *n.* **1.** *Zool.* A fleshy excrescence, as a cock's comb. **2.** *Bot.* A protuberant growth on the coat of a seed at or near the hilum. Also **ca·run·cu·la** (kə·rung'kyə·lə). [< MF < L *caruncula,* dim. of *caro, carnis* flesh] — **ca·run·cu·lar** (kə·rung'kyə·lər), **ca·run·cu·lous** *adj.*

ca·run·cu·late (kə·rung'kyə·lit, -lāt) *adj.* Having a caruncle or caruncles. Also **ca·run·cu·lat·ed.**

Ca·ru·so (kə·rōō'sō, *Ital.* kä·rōō'zō), **Enrico,** 1873–1921, Italian operatic tenor.

carve (kärv) *v.* **carved, carv·ing** *v.t.* **1.** To make by cutting, or as if by cutting. **2.** To create, design, or fashion by cutting. **3.** To cut up, as cooked meat; divide. — *v.i.* **4.** To make carved work. **5.** To cut up meat. — *n.* A cut or stroke in carving. [OE *ceorfan*] — **carv'er** *n.*

car·vel (kär'vəl) *n.* A caravel.

car·vel-built (kär'vəl·bilt') *adj. Naut.* Built with the hull planks laid flush. For illustration see CLINKER–BUILT.

carv·en (kär'vən) *adj. Poetic* or *Archaic* Carved.

Car·ver (kär'vər), **George Washington,** 1864?–1943, U.S. botanist and chemist. — **John,** 1575–1621, Pilgrim settler; first governor of Plymouth Colony.

carv·ing (kär'ving) *n.* **1.** The act of one who carves. **2.** Carved work; a carved figure or design.

Car·y (kâr'ē), **Alice,** 1820–71, U.S. poet and novelist. — **Henry Francis,** 1772–1844, English clergyman and translator. — **Joyce,** 1888–1957, English novelist: full name **Arthur Joyce Lunel Cary.** — **Phoebe,** 1824–71, U.S. poet; sister of Alice.

car·y·at·id (kar'ē·at'id) *n. pl.* **·at·ids** or **·at·i·des** (-at'ə·dēz) *Archit.* A supporting column in the form of a sculptured female figure. [< L *Caryatis, -ides* < Gk. *Karyatis* a priestess of Artemis at Karyai in Laconia, Greece] — **car'y·at'i·dal** (-ə·dəl), **car'y·at'i·de·an** (-ə·dē'ən), **car'y·a·tid'ic** (-ə·tid'ik) *adj.*

caryo- See KARYO-.

car·y·o·phyl·la·ceous (kar'ē·ō·fi·lā'shəs) *adj. Bot.* **1.** Pertaining or belonging to a family (*Caryophyllaceae*) of herbs, the pink family, characterized by opposite entire leaves, and perfect or dioecious flowers: also *silenaceous.* **2.** Having a tubular calyx with five long-clawed petals. [< NL < Gk. *karyophyllon* clove tree < *karyon* nut + *phyllon* leaf]

car·y·op·sis (kar'ē·op'sis) *n. pl.* **·op·ses** (-op'sēz) or **·op·si·des** (-op'sə·dēz) *Bot.* A seedlike, one-celled, dry fruit, as the grains of wheat and rye: also spelled *cariopsis.* [< NL < Gk. *karyon* nut + -OPSIS]

car·y·o·tin (kar'ē·ō'tin) See KARYOTIN.

ca·sa·ba (kə·sä'bə) *n.* A winter variety of muskmelon with sweet white flesh and yellow rind: also spelled *cassaba.* Also **casaba melon.** [from *Kasaba,* a town in western Turkey]

Cas·a·blan·ca (kas'ə·blang'kə, kä'sə·bläng'kə) The largest city in Morocco, a port on the NW coast; pop. 1,320,000 (est. 1969). Arabic *Dar-el-Beida.*

Cas·a Gran·de National Monument (kas'ə gran'dē) An area in southern Arizona that includes prehistoric ruins; 473 acres; established 1918.

Ca·sals (kä·säls'), **Pablo,** born 1876, Spanish violoncellist, conductor, and composer.

Cas·a·no·va (kas'ə·nō'və, kaz'-; *Ital.* kä'sä·nô'vä), **Giovanni Giacomo,** 1725–98, Italian adventurer; known for his *Memoirs:* full surname **Casanova de Sein·galt** (dä sin'gält).

Ca·sau·bon (kə·sô'bən, *Fr.* kä·zō·bôn'), **Isaac,** 1559–1614, French Protestant theologian and scholar.

ca·sa·va (kə·sä'və) See CASSAVA.

Cas·bah (käz'bä) The native quarter of Algiers or of other cities with a large Arab population: also *Kasbah.*

cas·ca·bel (kas'kə·bel) *n.* **1.** A knob at the rear of a muzzle-loading cannon; also, the entire rear part. **2.** A rattlesnake. Also **cas'ca·ble** (-bəl). [< Sp., little bell]

cas·cade (kas·kād') *n.* **1.** A fall of water over steep rocks, or one of a series of such falls. **2.** Anything resembling a waterfall, as the zigzag fall of lace trimming on a dress. **3.** *Chem.* A connection in series of two or more electrolytic cells or tanks so arranged as to produce a flow of the electrolyte from higher to lower levels. **4.** *Physics* A successive operation, as cooling a gas by utilizing the effect of a previously expanded gas. **5.** *Electronics* An arrangement of simple and similar subordinate sections or stages within a complex circuit such that the output of one circuit becomes the input of the next. — *v.i.* **cad·ed, cad·ing 1.** To fall in the form of a waterfall; form cascades. **2.** *Electronics* To arrange in cascade. [< F < Ital. *cascata* < *cascare* to fall < L *cadere*]

Cascade Range A range of mountains in Oregon, Washington, and British Columbia; highest peak, Mount Rainier, 14,408 ft.

cas·car·a (kas·kâr'ə) *n.* **1.** A buckthorn (*Rhamnus purshiana*) of the NW United States, yielding cascara sagrada: also called *bearwood.* Also **cascara buckthorn. 2.** Cascara sagrada. [< Sp. *cáscara* bark]

cascara sa·gra·da (sə·grä'də) A laxative obtained from the bark of the cascara: also called *cascara.*

cas·ca·ril·la (kas'kə·ril'ə) *n.* **1.** The aromatic bark of a West Indian shrub (*Croton eluteria*) of the spurge family, sometimes used as a tonic. Also **cascarilla bark. 2.** The shrub. [< Sp., dim. of *cáscara* bark]

Cas·co Bay (kas'kō) An inlet of the Atlantic in SW Maine, including Portland harbor.

case¹ (kās) *n.* **1.** A particular instance or occurrence: a *case* of mistaken identity. **2.** The actual circumstance or state of affairs; the fact or facts: Such is not the *case.* **3.** An instance of disease or injury; also, a patient. **4.** A set of arguments, reasons, etc.: the *case* for capital punishment. **5.** A question or problem: a *case* of conscience. **6.** *Law* a An action or suit at law. **b** The set of facts offered in support of a claim. **7.** Condition or situation; plight. **8.** *Informal* A peculiar or exceptional person. **9.** *Gram.* a The syntactical relationship of a noun, pronoun, or adjective to other words in a sentence, generally indicated by declensional endings in inflected languages or by prepositions and word order in non-inflected languages. **b** The form of a word indicating this relationship. **c** These relationships or forms collectively. — **in any case** No matter what; regardless. — **in case** In the event that; if. — **in case of** In the event of: *in case* of fire. — *v.t.* **cased, cas·ing** *U.S. Slang* To look over carefully, especially with intent to rob: to *case* a bank. [< OF *cas* < L *casus* event < *cadere* to fall; the grammatical cases (def. 9) were thought of as "falling" from the nominative]

case² (kās) *n.* **1.** A box, sheath, bag, etc., for containing something. **2.** A box and its contents. **3.** A set or pair: a *case* of pistols. **4.** *Printing* A tray with compartments for holding type, commonly made in pairs and called *upper case* or *cap case* for capital letters, and *lower case* for small letters. **5.** The covers and spine in which a book, when sewed, is bound. **6.** An outer or protective part, as of a watch. **7.** A frame or casing, as for a door. **8.** The head cavity of a sperm whale, containing the spermaceti. Abbr. *c., C., cs., C/S.* — *v.t.* **cased, cas·ing** To put into or cover with a case; incase. [< AF *casse* < L *capsa* box < *capere* to take, hold]

ca·se·ase (kā'sē·ās) *n. Biochem.* An enzyme of bacterial origin that dissolves casein and hastens ripening in cheese. [< CASE(IN) + -ASE]

ca·se·ate (kā'sē·āt) *v.i.* **·at·ed, ·at·ing** To become cheesy; undergo caseation. [< L *caseatus* mixed with cheese < *caseus* cheese]

ca·se·a·tion (kā'sē·ā'shən) *n.* **1.** Conversion into cheese or curd; coagulation. **2.** *Pathol.* Degeneration into a granular, cheeselike substance, as of the tissues.

ca·se·fy (kā'sə·fī) *v.t. & v.i.* **·fied, ·fy·ing** To make or become like cheese. [< L *caseus* cheese + -FY]

case·hard·en (kās'här'dən) *v.t.* **1.** *Metall.* To harden by carburizing the surface of (low-carbon steel), followed by quenching. **2.** To make callous, especially in feelings.

case history A record of an individual or a family unit, in which salient facts on health, ancestry, economic status, and the like, are collected for use in medical, psychiatric, sociological, or similar studies. Also **case study.**

ca·se·in (kā′sē·in, -sēn) *n. Biochem.* A phosphoprotein found especially in milk and constituting the principal ingredient in cheese, used in the manufacture of plastics and synthetic resins. [< L *caseus* cheese + -IN] — **ca·se·ic** (kā′sē·ik) *adj.*

ca·se·in·o·gen (kā′sē·in′ə·jən, kā·sē′nə-) *n. Biochem.* The casein-bearing protein of milk. [< CASEIN + -GEN]

case knife **1.** A knife kept in a sheath. **2.** A table knife.

case law The body of law based on judicial decisions, as distinguished from that based on statute or other sources of law.

case·mate (kās′māt) *n.* A bombproof shelter in a fortification, or an armored compartment on a warship, for a gun and its crew. [< MF < Ital. *casamatta,* ? < Gk. *chasmata,* pl. of *chasma* opening] — **case′mat′ed** *adj.*

case·ment (kās′mənt) *n.* **1.** The sash of a window that opens on hinges at the side, or a window having such sashes. **2.** A case; covering. [? < CASE² + -MENT. Cf. also OF *encassement,* Med.L *casamentum* frame of a house] — **case′ment·ed** *adj.*

Case·ment (kās′mənt), **Sir Roger David,** 1864–1916, Irish patriot; hanged by the British for treason.

ca·se·ose (kā′sē·ōs) *n. Biochem.* An intermediary product in the hydration of caseins, either artificial or in the digestive process; a proteose. [< L *caseus* cheese + -OSE²]

ca·se·ous (kā′sē·əs) *adj.* Of or like cheese; cheesy.

ca·sern (kə·zûrn′) *n.* A barrack for soldiers in a garrison town. Also **ca·serne′.** [< F *caserne* < Sp. *caserna* small hut < L *quaterna* four each]

case shot An assortment of small shot, as shrapnel or canister, enclosed in a metal case.

case system A system of teaching law in which selected cases form the basis for study, supplemented by textbooks.

case·work (kās′wûrk′) *n.* The investigation and guidance by a social worker of maladjusted individuals and families. — **case′work′er** *n.*

case·worm (kās′wûrm′) *n.* The larva of a caddis fly.

Ca·sey Jones (kā′sē jōnz′) Nickname of **John Luther Jones,** 1864–1900, U.S. railroad hero who died in a train wreck.

cash¹ (kash) *n.* **1.** Current money in hand or readily available. **2.** Money paid down; immediate payment. — **Syn.** See MONEY. — *v.t.* To convert into ready money, as a check; give or receive money for. — **to cash in** **1.** In gambling, to turn in one's chips and receive cash. **2.** *U.S. Slang* To die. — **to cash in on** *U.S. Informal* **1.** To make a profit from. **2.** To turn to advantage. [< F *caisse* cash box, cash < Ital. *cassa* < L *capsa* box] — **cash′a·ble** *adj.*

cash² (kash) *n., pl.* **cash** Any of various coins of low value of the East Indies and China; especially, a Chinese coin of copper and lead, with a square hole in the middle. [< Pg. *caixa* < Tamil *kāsu* small coin]

cash-and-car·ry (kash′ən·kar′ē) *adj.* Operated on a system of cash purchase and no delivery.

ca·shaw (kə·shô′) See CUSHAW.

cash basis A system of bookkeeping that includes only cash receipts as income and only cash payments as expense; opposed to *accrual basis.*

cash·book (kash′book′) *n.* A book in which a record is kept of money taken in and paid out.

cash crop A crop grown for sale, often the chief product of a country or region.

cash discount A discount from the purchase price allowed the buyer if he pays within a stipulated period. *Abbr. c.d.*

cash·ew (kash′oo, kə·shoo′) *n.* **1.** A tropical American tree (genus *Anacardium*) of the sumac family, now naturalized in Africa and Asia, that yields a gum. **2.** Its small, kidney-shaped, edible fruit: also **cashew nut.** [< F *acajou* < Pg. *acajú* < Tupi *acajoba*]

cash·ier¹ (ka·shir′) *n.* **1.** One employed to collect cash payments, as in a restaurant. **2.** In a bank, an executive officer responsible for the bank's assets. [< F *caissier* < *caisse.* See CASH¹.]

cash·ier² (ka·shir′) *v.t.* **1.** To dismiss in disgrace, as a military officer. **2.** To discard. [< Du. *casseren* < F *casser* < LL *cassare* to annul and L *quassare* to destroy]

cashier's check A check drawn by a bank's cashier upon its own funds. *Abbr. c.c., C.C.*

cash·mere (kash′mir, kazh′-) *n.* **1.** A fine wool obtained from Cashmere goats. **2.** A soft fabric made from this or similar wool. **3.** A dress, shawl, etc., made of cashmere. Also spelled *kashmir.* [after *Kashmir,* India]

Cash·mere (kash·mir′, kash′mir) See KASHMIR.

Cashmere goat A variety of goat originally native in Kashmir.

cash on delivery Immediate payment to the bearer on delivery of goods. *Abbr. c.o.d., C.O.D.*

ca·shoo (kə·shoo′) *n.* Catechu.

cash register A device usually with a money drawer attached, that records, adds, and displays the amount of cash received.

cas·i·mere, cas·i·mire (kas′ə·mir) See CASSIMERE.

cas·ing (kā′sing) *n.* **1.** A protective case or covering. **2.** A framework, as about a door or window. **3.** The intestines of cattle, hogs, etc., cleaned and used as sausage containers. **4.** *U.S.* The shoe of a pneumatic tire. [< CASE²]

ca·si·no (kə·sē′nō) *n., pl.* **·nos** **1.** A room or building for public amusement, dancing, gambling, etc. **2.** In Italy, a summerhouse; also, a country house. **3.** Cassino. [< Ital., dim. of *casa* house]

cask (kask, käsk) *n.* **1.** A barrel-shaped wooden vessel, made of staves, hoops, and flat heads. **2.** The quantity a cask will hold. **3.** *Obs.* A casket. *Abbr.* (def. 1, 2) *ck.,* (pl. *cks.*), *csk.* [< Sp. *casco* skull, potsherd, cask, ? ult. < L *quassare* to break. Related to CASQUE.]

cas·ket (kas′kit, käs′-) *n.* **1.** *U.S.* A coffin. **2.** A small box or chest, as for jewels. — *v.t.* To enclose in a casket. [Orig. uncertain]

Cas·lon (kaz′lən) *n.* A style of type created by the English type founder **William Caslon,** 1692–1766.

Cas·par (kas′pər) Traditionally, one of the three Magi: also called *Gaspar.*

Cas·per (kas′pər) A city in central Wyoming; pop. 39,361.

Cas·pi·an Sea (kas′pē·ən) The largest salt-water lake and inland sea in the world, between SE Europe and SW Asia in the Soviet Union and Iran; 163,800 sq. mi.: *ancient* **Cas′pi·um Ma′re.**

casque (kask) *n.* A helmet; heaume. [< F, ult. < L *quassare.* Related to CASK.] — **casqued** (kaskt) *adj.*

Cass (kas), **Lewis,** 1782–1866, U.S. statesman.

cas·sa·ba (kə·sä′bə) See CASABA.

Cas·san·dra (kə·san′drə) In Greek mythology, a daughter of Priam whose prophecies were fated by Apollo to be true but never believed. — *n.* Anyone who utters unheeded prophecies of disaster.

CASQUE (Surmounted by crest)

cas·sa·reep (kas′ə·rēp) *n.* A condiment made from the juice of the cassava. [< F *cachiri* < Tupi]

cas·sa·tion (ka·sā′shən) *n.* The act of making null; abrogation; cancellation, as of a decree. [< F < LL *cassatio, -onis* < *cassare* to annul < L *cassus* empty]

Cas·satt (kə·sat′), **Mary,** 1845–1926, U.S. painter

cas·sa·va (kə·sä′və) *n.* **1.** One of several tropical American shrubs or herbs (genus *Manihot*), cultivated for their edible roots; especially, the **sweet cassava** (*M. dulcis*) and the **bitter cassava** (*M. esculenta*): also called *manioc.* **2.** A starch made from the roots of these plants, the source of tapioca. Also spelled *casava.* [< F *cassave* < Taino *casavi*]

Cas·se·grai·ni·an telescope (kas′ə·grā′nē·ən) *Astron.* A reflecting telescope having a hyperbolic mirror within the prime focus to reflect an image through an aperture in the primary mirror at the base of the focus tube. [after N. *Cassegrain,* 17th c. French physician, who invented it in 1672]

Cas·sel (kas′əl, *Ger.* käs′əl) See KASSEL.

cas·se·role (kas′ə·rōl) *n.* **1.** An earthenware or glass dish in which food is baked and served. **2.** Any food so prepared and served. **3.** A small dish with a handle, used by chemists. **4.** *Brit.* A saucepan. — **en casserole** Designating food cooked and served in an earthenware or glass dish. [< F, ult. < *casse* pan, bowl]

cas·sette (kə·set′, ka-) *n.* **1.** *Photog.* A lightproof magazine for holding a sensitized plate or film in a camera or X-ray device. **2.** *Electronics* A small cartridge containing magnetic tape for use in a tape recorder. [< F, lit., small box]

cas·sia (kash′ə, kas′ē·ə) *n.* **1.** A coarse variety of cinnamon obtained from the bark (**cassia bark**) of a tree (*Cinnamomum cassia*) native in China. **2.** The tree itself. **3.** Any of a large genus (*Cassia*) of leguminous shrubs, herbs, and trees of tropical regions, especially one (*C. fistula*), whose dried pods (**cassia pods**) yield a mild laxative. [< L < Gk. *kasia* < Hebrew *qetsi'* < *qātsa'* to strip off bark]

cas·si·mere (kas′ə·mir) *n.* A woolen cloth for men's wear: also called *kerseymere*: also spelled *casimere, casimire.* [< F *casimir* cashmere]

cas·si·no (kə·sē′nō) *n.* A game of cards for from two to four players: also spelled *casino.* [Var. of CASINO]

Cas·si·no (kə·sē′nō, *Ital.* käs·sē′nō) A town in central Italy; site of a Benedictine abbey (**Monte Cassino**): formerly *San Germano.*

Cas·si·o·do·rus (kas′ē·ō·dō′rəs), **Flavius Magnus Aurelius,** died A.D. 575?, Roman statesman and historian.

Cas·si·o·pe·ia (kas′ē·ə·pē′ə) In Greek mythology, the wife of Cepheus and mother of Andromeda. — *n.* A constellation: also **Cassiopeia's Chair.** See CONSTELLATION.

cas·sis (kä·sēs′) *n.* **1.** The European black currant (*Ribes nigrum*). **2.** A cordial made from black currants. [< F]

cas·sit·e·rite (kə·sit′ə·rīt) *n.* A tetragonal, brown to black tin dioxide, SnO₂, the most important ore of tin: also called *tinstone.* [< Gk. *kassiteros* tin]

Cas·sius Lon·gi·nus (kash′əs lon·jī′nəs), **Gaius,** died 42 B.C., Roman general; conspirator against Caesar.

cas·sock (kas'ək) *n.* **1.** *Eccl.* A close-fitting vestment, usually black, reaching to the feet, and worn by clergymen, acolytes, choir singers, etc. **2.** A short garment or loose jacket worn under a Geneva gown. **3.** A clergyman. [< MF *casaque* < Ital. *casacca* greatcoat] — **cas·socked** (kas'əkt) *adj.*

cas·so·war·y (kas'ə-wer'ē) *n. pl.* **·war·ies** A large, three-toed, flightless bird (genus *Casuarius*) of Australia and New Guinea, related to the emu. [< Malay *kasuārī*]

cast (kast, käst) *v.* **cast, cast·ing** *v.t.* **1.** To throw or hurl with force; fling. **2.** To put with violence or force: They *cast* him into jail. **3.** To throw down; throw to the ground; defeat, as in wrestling. **4.** To cause to fall upon or over something or in a particular direction; project: to *cast* a shadow. **5.** To direct, as a glance of the eyes. **6.** To let down; drop: to *cast* anchor. **7.** To throw forth or out: to *cast* a net. **8.** To throw off; lose; also, to shed; molt. **9.** To throw aside; reject or dismiss. **10.** To give birth to, especially prematurely; drop. **11.** To deposit; give: He *cast* his vote. **12.** To draw by chance; throw, as dice. **13.** In the theater, movies, etc., to assign the parts of (a play) or a part in a play to (an actor). **14.** To throw up, as with a shovel: to *cast* a mound of earth. **15.** To calculate mathematically; add. **16.** To compute astrologically: to *cast* a horoscope. **17.** To arrange by some system or into divisions. **18.** To contrive; devise. **19.** *Metall.* To shape in a mold; make a cast of; found. **20.** *Printing* To stereotype or electroplate. **21.** To twist; warp. **22.** *Naut.* To turn (a ship); tack. — *v.i.* **23.** To make a throw, as with dice, a fishing line, etc. **24.** To revolve something in the mind; deliberate; also, to scheme. **25.** To conjecture; forecast. **26.** To make arithmetical calculations; compute; add. **27.** *Metall.* To take shape in a mold. **28.** To warp, as timber. **29.** *Naut.* To veer; fall off; also, to tack; put about. — **to cast about** To consider ways and means; scheme. — **to cast away 1.** To discard. **2.** To shipwreck or maroon. — **to cast down 1.** To overthrow; destroy. **2.** To cause to feel dejection; discourage; depress. — **to cast off 1.** To reject or discard. **2.** To let go, as a ship from a dock. **3.** *Printing* To estimate the number of pages, columns, etc., a manuscript will yield. — **to cast up 1.** To eject; vomit. **2.** To compute; add. **3.** To drive ashore. **4.** To direct upward. — *n.* **1.** The act of casting or throwing. **2.** The distance to which a thing may be thrown: a stone's *cast*. **3.** The throwing of a line or fishing net into the water. **4.** A throw of dice; also, the number thrown. **5.** Anything thrown out, off, or away, as an insect's skin, the earth excreted by an earthworm, etc. **6.** The actors who portray the characters in a play, movie, etc. **7.** *Surg.* A rigid dressing or bandage, usually made of plaster of Paris, for preventing movement of fractured bones. **8.** In angling, a leader, sometimes including the flies. **9.** In hunting, a scattering of the dogs in search of the scent. **10.** A pair of hawks or other birds. **11.** The act of casting or founding. **12.** An impression made of anything; a mold. **13.** Something shaped or formed in a mold, as of bronze, plaster, etc.; a casting. **14.** The material poured into molds at one operation. **15.** The form in which a thing is made or fashioned; arrangement. **16.** Kind; sort; type: He is of the *cast* of your father. **17.** The appearance or form of something, as of facial features. **18.** A tinge; shade. **19.** A fixed turn or twist to one side; squint: a *cast* in one's eye. **20.** A glance; look. **21.** A warp: a *cast* in a plank. **22.** A calculation or computation; also, a forecast or conjecture. **23.** A stroke of fortune; lot. **24.** *Pathol.* A plastic substance formed in and often taking the shape of hollow, diseased cavities and organs: a renal *cast.* [< ON *kasta* to throw] — **Syn.** (verb) **1.** throw, toss. **8.** slough. **9.** discard.

Cas·ta·li·a (kas-tā'lē-ə) A fountain on Mount Parnassus, near Delphi, sacred to Apollo and the Muses, and supposed to give inspiration to those who drank of it. Also **Cas·ta·ly** (kas'tə-lē). — **Cas·ta'li·an** *adj.*

cas·ta·net (kas'tə-net') *n.* One of a pair of small concave disks of wood or ivory, clapped together with the fingers, as a rhythmical accompaniment to song or dance. [< Sp. *castañeta,* dim. of *castaña* < L *castanea* chestnut]

cast·a·way (kast'ə-wā', käst'-) *adj.* **1.** Adrift; shipwrecked. **2.** Thrown away; discarded. — *n.* **1.** One who is shipwrecked. **2.** An outcast.

caste (kast, käst) *n.* **1.** In India, one of the hereditary social classes into which Hindus are divided. **2.** Any social class in which membership is based on heredity, wealth, religion, etc. **3.** The system or principles of such class divisions. **4.** The position conferred by such a system: to lose *caste.* [< Pg. *casta* unmixed breed < L *castus* pure]

cas·tel·lan (kas'tə-lan) *n.* A chatelain. [< AF *castelain* < L *castellanus* < *castellum* castle]

cas·tel·la·ny (kas'tə-lā'nē) *n. pl.* **·nies 1.** The office or jurisdiction of a castellan. **2.** The lands belonging to a castle.

cas·tel·lat·ed (kas'tə-lā'tid) *adj.* **1.** Having battlements and turrets; built like a castle. **2.** Having many castles. [< Med.L *castellatus,* pp. of *castellare* to build a castle < L *castellum* castle] — **cas'tel·la'tion** *n.*

Cas·tel·ros·so (käs-tel'rōs'sō) See KASTELLORIZO.

cast·er (kas'tər, käs'-) *n.* **1.** One who or that which casts. **2.** One of a set of small, swiveling wheels or rollers, fastened under articles of furniture, or the like, to allow them to be moved about. **3.** A cruet for condiments; also, a stand for such cruets. Also (for defs. 2 and 3) *castor.*

cas·ti·gate (kas'tə-gāt) *v.t.* **·gat·ed, ·gat·ing** To rebuke or chastise severely; criticize. — **Syn.** See CHASTEN. [< L *castigatus,* pp. of *castigare* to chasten, ult. < *castus* pure] — **cas'ti·ga'tion** *n.* — **cas'ti·ga'tor** *n.*

Cas·ti·glio·ne (käs'te-lyô'nā), **Conte Baldassare,** 1478–1529, Italian diplomat and writer.

Cas·tile (kas-tēl') A region and former kingdom in northern and central Spain. *Spanish* **Cas·til·la** (käs-tē'lyä).

Castile soap (kas'tēl, kas-tēl') A hard, white, odorless soap made with olive oil and soda. Also **cas'tile soap.** [after *Castile,* where first made]

Cas·til·ian (kas-til'yən) *n.* **1.** A native or citizen of Castile. **2.** The standard form of Spanish as spoken in Spain, originally the dialect of Castile. — *adj.* Of or pertaining to Castile, its people, language, or culture.

cast·ing (kas'ting, käs'-) *n.* **1.** The act of one who or that which casts. **2.** That which is cast, as an article formed in a mold.

casting vote A deciding vote, given by the chairman of an assembly in cases where the votes of the members tie.

cast-i·ron (kast'ī'ərn, käst'-) *adj.* **1.** Made of cast iron. **2.** Like cast iron; rigid or strong; unyielding.

cast iron Iron having a high carbon content, and usually hard, brittle, and not malleable.

cas·tle (kas'əl, käs'-) *n.* **1.** In feudal times, the fortified dwelling of a prince or noble. **2.** Any large, imposing house. **3.** A place of refuge; stronghold. **4.** A small defensive tower, as on the back of an elephant. **5.** In chess, a rook. — **Syn.** See FORT. — *v.* **·tled, ·tling** *v.t.* **1.** To place in a castle; fortify. **2.** In chess, to move (the king) two squares to the right or left and place the rook from that side on the square over which the king has passed. — *v.i.* **3.** In chess, to move the rook and king in this manner. [Fusion of OE *castel* village and AF *castel* castle, both < L *castellum,* dim. of *castrum* camp, fort]

cas·tled (kas'əld, käs'-) *adj.* **1.** Having or furnished with a castle or castles. **2.** Castellated; fortified.

castle in the air A fanciful, impractical scheme; daydream. Also **castle in Spain.**

Cas·tle·reagh (kas'əl-rā, käs'-), **Viscount,** 1769–1822, Robert Stewart, second Marquis of Londonderry, British statesman.

cast-off (kast'ôf', -of', käst'-) *adj.* Thrown or laid aside; discarded: *castoff* garments. — *n.* **1.** One who or that which is no longer wanted or used. **2.** *Printing* A calculation of the amount of printed matter a manuscript will yield.

cas·tor¹ (kas'tər, käs'-) *n.* **1.** An oily, odorous secretion of beavers, used in medicine and perfumery: also **cas·to·re·um** (kas-tôr'ē-əm, -tō'rē-əm). **2.** A hat of beaver or other fur. **3.** A heavy, all-wool fabric used for coats. **4.** *Rare* A beaver. [< L < Gk. *kastōr* beaver]

cas·tor² (kas'tər, käs'-) See CASTER (defs. 2 and 3).

Cas·tor and Pol·lux (kas'tər, käs'-; pol'əks) **1.** In Greek mythology, the Dioscuri, twin sons of Leda and brothers of Helen and Clytemnestra, set by Zeus among the stars. **2.** *Astron.* The two brightest stars in the constellation Gemini.

castor bean 1. The seed of the castor-oil plant. **2.** The castor-oil plant.

castor oil A viscid oil extracted from castor beans and used as a cathartic and lubricant.

cas·tor-oil plant (kas'tər-oil', käs'-) A herbaceous plant (*Ricinus communis*) of the spurge family, native in India but widely naturalized, yielding the castor bean.

cas·trate (kas'trāt) *v.t.* **·trat·ed, ·trat·ing 1.** To remove the testicles from; emasculate; geld. **2.** To remove the ovaries from; spay. **3.** *Rare* To expurgate, as a book; mutilate. [< L *castratus,* pp. of *castrare* to castrate] — **cas·tra'tion** *n.*

Cas·tri·o·ta (kas'trē-ō'tə), **George** See SCANDERBEG.

Cas·tro (käs'trō, kas'-), **Fidel,** born 1926, Cuban revolutionary leader; premier 1959–: full name **Fidel Castro Ruz** (rōōth).

Cas·tro Valley (käs'trō) An unincorporated place in western California; pop. 44,760.

cast steel *Metall.* Steel cast in molds to form machine parts or other articles that are not rolled or forged.

cas·u·al (kazh'ōō-əl) *adj.* **1.** Occurring by chance; accidental: a *casual* meeting. **2.** Irregular; occasional: *casual* visits. **3.** Without intention or plan; haphazard; offhand: a *casual* question. **4.** Negligent or unconcerned; nonchalant: a *casual* manner. **5.** Designed for informal wear: *casual* clothes. **6.** *Med.* Pertaining to accidents or accidental injuries. **7.** *Brit.* Of or pertaining to persons who receive temporary charity. **8.** *Obs.* Precarious. — **Syn.** See ACCIDENTAL. — *n.* **1.** One who is employed at irregular intervals. **2.** An occasional visitor. **3.** *Brit.* One who receives occasional, temporary charity. **4.** *Mil.* A soldier temporarily attached to a unit or duty while awaiting permanent assignment. [< MF *casuel* < L *casualis* < *casus* accident < *cadere* to fall] — **cas'u·al·ly** *adv.* — **cas'u·al·ness** *n.*

CASTANETS
a Outer and inner sides.
b Position in use.

cas·u·al·ism (kazh′ŏŏ-əl-iz′əm) n. The doctrine that chance prevails in all things. **— cas′u·al·ist** n.

cas·u·al·ty (kazh′ŏŏ-əl-tē) n. pl. **·ties 1.** One who or that which is destroyed, injured, or otherwise made ineffective by an accident. **2.** Mil. A soldier who is killed, wounded, captured, or otherwise lost to his command through combat action. **3.** An accident, especially a fatal or serious one.

casualty insurance Insurance of property against accidental loss, damage, or injury.

cas·u·ist (kazh′ŏŏ-ist) n. One who studies or resolves ethical problems or cases of conscience: often used for one who rationalizes about such matters. [< F casuiste < L casus event, case]

cas·u·is·tic (kazh′ŏŏ-is′tik) adj. **1.** Pertaining to casuists or casuistry. **2.** Sophistical; equivocal; specious. Also **cas′·u·is′ti·cal. — cas′u·is′ti·cal·ly** adv.

cas·u·ist·ry (kazh′ŏŏ-is·trē) n. pl. **·ries 1.** The science or doctrine of ambiguous cases of conscience or questions of right and wrong. **2.** Sophistical or equivocal reasoning, especially in cases of conscience. **— Syn.** See FALLACY.

ca·sus (kā′səs) n. Law An occurrence or event; case. [< L]

ca·sus bel·li (kā′səs bel′ī) Latin A cause justifying war.

cat (kat) n. **1.** A domesticated carnivorous mammal (Felis domestica) of wide distribution in various breeds and colors, having retractile claws, and valued because it kills mice and rats. **2.** Any other animal of the cat family (Felidae), as a lion, tiger, lynx, ocelot, etc. **3.** A gossiping or backbiting woman. **4.** A piece of wood used in the game of tipcat; also, the game. **5.** A game of ball, called from the number of batters **one old** (or **o′**) **cat, two old cat,** etc. **6.** Naut. **a** A tackle for hoisting an anchor to the cathead. **b** A catboat. **7.** A cat-o′-nine-tails. **8.** A catfish. **9.** U.S. Slang A man; guy; especially, a jazz musician or fan. **10.** U.S. & Canadian A caterpillar tractor. **— to let the cat out of the bag** To divulge a secret. **—** v.t. **cat·ted, cat·ting 1.** To hoist and fasten at the cathead. **2.** To flog with a cat-o′-nine-tails. **—** v.i. **3.** Brit. to vomit. [OE cat, catte]

cat. 1. Catalogue. **2.** Catechism.

cata- prefix **1.** Down; against; upon: cataclysm. **2.** Back; over: cataphonic. Also, before vowels, **cat-:** also cath-. Also spelled kata-. [< Gk. kata- < kata down, against, back]

cat·ab·a·sis (kə-tab′ə-sis) n. pl. **·ses** (-sēz) **1.** A going downward; descent: opposed to anabasis. **2.** Pathol. The decreasing of a disease. [< Gk. katabasis < kata- down + bainein to go] **— cat·a·bat·ic** (kat′ə-bat′ik) adj.

ca·tab·o·lism (kə-tab′ə-liz′əm) n. Biol. The process by which tissue material breaks down into simpler and more stable substances; destructive metabolism: opposed to anabolism. Also spelled katabolism. [< Gk. katabolē destruction < kata- down + ballein to throw] **— cat·a·bol·ic** (kat′ə-bol′ik) adj. **— cat·a·bol′i·cal·ly** adv.

ca·tab·o·lite (kə-tab′ə-līt) n. Any product of catabolism.

cat·a·caus·tic (kat′ə-kôs′tik) Optics adj. Denoting a caustic curve formed by reflected light rays: opposed to diacaustic. **—** n. Such a curve. [< CATA- + CAUSTIC (def. 3)]

cat·a·chre·sis (kat′ə-krē′sis) n. **1.** Misuse of words, or the use of a mixed metaphor. **2.** The use of a wrong form of a word, as sparrow grass for asparagus: see FOLK ETYMOLOGY. [< L < Gk. katachrēsis < kata- against + chraesthai to use] **— cat·a·chres·tic** (kat′ə-kres′tik) or **·ti·cal** adj. **— cat·a·chres′ti·cal·ly** adv.

cat·a·cli·nal (kat′ə-klī′nəl) adj. Geol. Running in the direction of the dip: said of a valley: distinguished from anaclinal. [< Gk. kataklinēs sloping < kata- down + klinein to bend]

cat·a·clysm (kat′ə-kliz′əm) n. **1.** Any violent upheaval or change, as a war, revolution, etc. **2.** Any violent disturbance of the earth's surface, as an earthquake. **3.** An overwhelming flood; deluge. **— Syn.** See DISASTER. [< MF cataclysme < Gk. kataklysmos flood < kata- down + klyzein to wash] **— cat·a·clys′mic, cat′a·clys′mal** (-məl) adj.

cat·a·comb (kat′ə-kōm) n. Usually pl. An underground place of burial, consisting of passages and small rooms with excavations in their sides for tombs. [< F catacombe < LL catacumbas, ult. origin uncertain]

ca·tad·ro·mous (kə-tad′rə-məs) adj. Zool. Pertaining to fishes that go down rivers to the sea to spawn: opposed to anadromous. [< CATA- + -DROMOUS]

cat·a·falque (kat′ə-falk) n. A structure supporting the coffin of a deceased person during a funeral. Also **cat′a·fal′co.** [< F catafalco < Ital. catafalco; ult. origin unknown]

Cat·a·lan (kat′ə-lan, -lən) adj. Of or pertaining to Catalonia, its people, or their language. **—** n. **1.** A native or inhabitant of Catalonia. **2.** The Romance language of Catalonia and Valencia, closely related to Provençal.

cat·a·lase (kat′ə-lās) n. Biochem. An enzyme that decomposes hydrogen peroxide into water and oxygen. [< CATAL(YSIS) + -ASE]

cat·a·lec·tic (kat′ə-lek′tik) adj. In prosody, designating a line of verse ending in an incomplete foot. [< LL catalectic-us < Gk. katalēktikos < kata- wholly + lēgein to stop]

cat·a·lep·sy (kat′ə-lep′sē) n. Psychiatry An abnormal maintenance of physical postures, accompanied by extreme muscular rigidity and irresponsiveness to stimuli, common in hysteria and schizophrenia. [< Med.L catalepsia < Gk. katalēpsis < kata- upon + lēpsis seizure < lambanein to grasp] **— cat′a·lep′tic** (-lep′tik) adj. & n.

Cat·a·li·na Island (kat′ə-lē′nə) See SANTA CATALINA.

cat·a·lo (kat′ə-lō) n. pl. **·loes** or **·los** A fertile hybrid between the bison and the domestic cow: also spelled cattalo. [< CAT(TLE) + (BUFF)ALO]

cat·a·log (kat′ə-lôg, -log) n., v.t., & v.i. **·loged, ·log·ing** Catalogue: the standard spelling in library work. **— cat′a·log′·er, cat′a·log′ist** n.

cat·a·logue (kat′ə-lôg, -log) n. **1.** A list or enumeration of names, objects, etc., usually in alphabetical order and often with accompanying description. **2.** A publication containing such a list, as of articles for sale. **3.** A card catalogue (which see). Abbr. cat. **—** v.t. & v.i. **·logued, ·logu·ing** To make a catalogue (of); enter (items) in a catalogue. [< F < LL catalogus < Gk. katalogos list < kata- down + legein to select, choose] **— cat′a·logu′er, cat′a·logu′ist** n.

Cat·a·lo·nia (kat′ə-lō′nē-ə) A region of NE Spain; 12,332 sq. mi. Spanish **Ca·ta·lu·ña** (kä′tä-lōō′nyä). Catalan **Ca′ta·lu′nya.**

ca·tal·pa (kə-tal′pə) n. A tree (genus Catalpa) of China, Japan, and North America, having large, ovate leaves, fragrant flowers, and long, slender pods. [< N. Am. Ind.]

ca·tal·y·sis (kə-tal′ə-sis) n. pl. **·ses** (-sēz) Chem. An increase in the rate of a chemical reaction, caused by the presence of a substance that is not permanently altered by the reaction: also spelled katalysis. [< Gk. katalysis dissolution < kata- wholly, completely + lyein to loosen]

cat·a·lyst (kat′ə-list) n. **1.** Chem. Any substance that causes catalysis. Also **cat′a·lyz′er.** Compare ACCELERATOR, INHIBITOR, RETARDER. **2.** Any person or thing that has a social or other effect analogous with catalysis.

cat·a·lyt·ic (kat′ə-lit′ik) Chem. adj. Pertaining to or effecting catalysis. **—** n. A catalyst.

cat·a·lyze (kat′ə-līz) v.t. **·lyzed, ·lyz·ing** To submit to or decompose by catalysis.

cat·a·ma·ran (kat′ə-mə-ran′) n. Naut. **1.** A long, narrow raft of logs, often with an outrigger. **2.** A boat having twin hulls. **3.** Canadian In Newfoundland, a heavy-duty wooden sled. [< Tamil katta-maram tied wood]

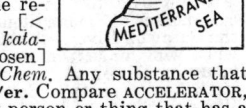
CATAMARAN (def. 2) (Tahitian war canoe)

cat·a·me·ni·a (kat′ə-mē′nē-ə) n.pl. Physiol. Menstruation. [< Gk. katamēnia, neut. pl. of katamēnios monthly < kata- by + mēn month] **— cat′a·me′ni·al** adj.

cat·a·mite (kat′ə-mīt) n. A boy used in sodomy. [< L Catamitus, alter. of Gk. Ganymēdēs Ganymede]

cat·am·ne·sis (kat′əm-nē′sis) n. Med. The history of a patient after his recovery: distinguished from anamnesis. [< NL < Gk. kata- down + -mnēsis recollection < mimnēskein to remember] **— cat′am·nes′tic** (-nes′tik) adj.

cat·a·mount (kat′ə-mount) n. **1.** U.S. The puma; also, the lynx. **2.** A catamountain. [Short form of CATAMOUNTAIN]

cat·a·moun·tain (kat′ə-moun′tən) n. One of various wild felines, as the leopard or wildcat: also cat-o′-mountain.

Ca·ta·nia (kä-tä′nyä) A Province of eastern Sicily; 1,377 sq. mi.; pop. 889,125 (1961); capital, Catania, on the Gulf of Catania, an inlet of the Ionian Sea; pop. 361,466.

cat·a·pho·re·sis (kat′ə-fə-rē′sis) n. **1.** The movement of medicinal substances in or through living tissue under the influence of an electric field. **2.** Electrophoresis (which see). [< NL < Gk. kata- down + phorēsis carrying < pherein to bear, carry] **— cat′a·pho·ret′ic** (-ret′ik) adj.

cat·a·phyll (kat′ə-fil) n. Bot. A rudimentary or scalelike leaf, as of a bud. [< CATA- + Gk. phyllon leaf]

cat·a·plasm (kat′ə-plaz′əm) n. A soothing poultice, often medicated. [< MF cataplasme, ult. < Gk. kataplasma]

cat·a·pult (kat′ə-pult) n. **1.** An ancient military engine for throwing stones, arrows, etc. **2.** Aeron. A device for launching an airplane at flight speed, as from the deck of a ship. **3.** A slingshot. **—** v.t. **1.** To hurl from or as from a catapult. **—** v.i. **2.** To hurtle through the air. [< L catapulta < Gk. katapeltēs < kata- down + pallein to brandish, hurl]

cat·a·ract (kat′ə-rakt) n. **1.** A waterfall of great size. **2.** A heavy downpour or flood of water; deluge. **3.** Pathol. **a** Opacity of the lens of the eye, causing partial or total blindness. **b** The opaque area. [< MF cataracte < L cataracta < Gk. kataraktēs < kata- down + arassein to fall headlong]

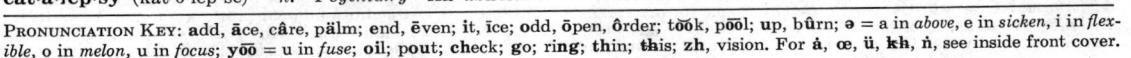

ca·tarrh (kə·tär′) n. Pathol. Inflammation of the mucous membrane, especially of the air passages in the throat and head, characterized by excessive secretion of mucus. [< MF catarrhe < L catarrhus < Gk. katarrhoos < kata- down + rheein to flow] — **ca·tarrh′al, ca·tarrh′ous** adj.

cat·ar·rhine (kat′ə·rīn, -rin) adj. **1.** Having a narrow or slender nose: also leptorrhine. **2.** Zool. Designating or belonging to a former group (Catarrhini) of primates, the cercopithecoid monkeys, characterized by a relatively narrow septum between the nostrils: distinguished from platyrrhine. [< NL < Gk. kata- down + rhis, rhinos the nose]

ca·tas·ta·sis (kə·tas′tə·sis) n. pl. ·ses (-sēz) In ancient drama, the heightened part of the action preceding the catastrophe. [< Gk. katastasis settled condition < kata- down + stasis a settling < histanai to stand]

ca·tas·tro·phe (kə·tas′trə·fē) n. **1.** A great and sudden disaster; calamity. **2.** A sudden, violent change or upheaval, as in the surface of the earth; cataclysm. **3.** In a drama, the conclusion or revelation of the plot; dénouement. — **Syn.** See DISASTER. [< Gk. katastrophē < kata- over, down + strephein to turn]

cat·a·stroph·ic (kat′ə·strof′ik) adj. Resulting from or like a catastrophe; disastrous. — **cat′a·stroph′i·cal·ly** adv.

ca·tas·tro·phism (kə·tas′trə·fiz′əm) n. Geol. A former theory attributing the principal geological changes of the earth to sudden and violent physical upheavals, as distinct from gradual changes. — **ca·tas′tro·phist** n.

cat·a·to·ni·a (kat′ə·tō′nē·ə) n. Psychiatry A complex of symptoms in a type of schizophrenia, characterized by stupor, muscular rigidity, and occasional mental agitation. [< NL < Gk. kata- down + tonos tension, tone < teinein to stretch] — **cat′a·ton′ic** (-ton′ik) adj. & n.

Ca·taw·ba (kə·tô′bə) n. **1.** One of a tribe of North American Indians of Siouan linguistic stock, formerly living along the Catawba River. **2.** An American red grape; also, a dry white wine made from it.

Catawba River A river rising in North Carolina and flowing 295 miles south to South Carolina, where it is called the Wateree.

cat·bird (kat′bûrd′) n. A small, slate-colored North American songbird (Dumetella carolinensis), related to the mockingbird, and having a catlike cry. **2.** Either of two Australian birds (genus Ailuroedus) having a similar cry.

cat·boat (kat′bōt′) n. Naut. A small sailboat, having its mast stepped well forward and carrying a single fore-and-aft sail with boom and gaff.

cat·brier (kat′brī′ər) n. The green briar (which see).

cat·call (kat′kôl′) n. A shrill, discordant call or whistle expressing impatience or derision. — v.t. **1.** To deride or show contempt for with catcalls. — v.i. **2.** To utter catcalls.

catch (kach) v. caught, catch·ing v.t. **1.** To take, seize, or come upon, as something departing or fleeing; take captive. **2.** To take by trapping; ensnare: to catch fish. **3.** To surprise in the act; detect unexpectedly: We caught him lying. **4.** To take hold of suddenly so as to detain: He caught my arm as I passed. **5.** To grip; entangle: The nail caught her dress. **6.** To arrest the motion of; grasp and retain: to catch a ball; to catch rain water in a barrel. **7.** To overtake: We were caught by the storm. **8.** To reach in time to board: to catch a train. **9.** To reach with a blow; strike: She caught him a box on the ear. **10.** To check (oneself) in speaking: He caught himself before revealing his plans. **11.** To become affected with, as by contagion: to catch cold; to catch the spirit of an occasion. **12.** To take; get (something fleeting or sudden): to catch a nap; to catch fire. **13.** To apprehend or perceive: I don't catch the meaning; also, to apprehend so as to reproduce accurately: The artist has not caught her expression. **14.** To captivate, as an audience. **15.** To seize (the senses, etc.) suddenly or momentarily: The sound of music caught my ear; also, to perceive fleetingly: to catch a glimpse. **16.** U.S. Informal To see (a motion picture, television program, etc.). — v.i. **17.** To make a movement of grasping or seizing. **18.** In baseball, to act as catcher. **19.** To become entangled or fastened. **20.** To be communicated or communicable, as a disease or enthusiasm. **21.** To take fire; kindle; ignite. **22.** Naut. To catch the wind: The sails began to catch. — **to catch it** Informal To receive a reprimand, scolding, thrashing, or the like. — **to catch on** Informal **1.** To understand. **2.** To become popular or fashionable. **3.** To start suddenly, as a fire. — **to catch one's breath 1.** To check the breath suddenly, as in fear. **2.** To draw a breath; to rest. — **to catch one's eye** To meet one's glance, intentionally or otherwise. — **to catch up 1.** To snatch or pick up suddenly. **2.** To raise by attaching something; loop up: a dress caught up with ribbons. **3.** To come from behind; regain lost ground. **4.** To discover (someone) in error. **5.** To take up completely; absorb: caught up in one's work. — **to catch up with (or up to)** To overtake. — n. **1.** The act of catching; a grasping and holding. **2.** That which catches; a fastening. **3.** That which is caught; a quantity taken, as of fish. **4.** Informal One who is worth catching, as in marriage. **5.** Informal An artful or hidden condition; trick: What's the catch? **6.** In sports, the catching of a thrown or batted

ball before it touches the ground. **7.** A scrap or fragment: catches of song. **8.** A stoppage; break, as in the voice. **9.** Music A round, especially one designed for humorous effect. — adj. **1.** Attracting or meant to attract attention: a catch phrase. **2.** Tricky. [< AF cachier < LL captiare, freq. of L capere to take, hold. Doublet of CHASE.]
— **Syn.** (verb) **1.** Catch, capture, nab, apprehend, bag, and seize mean to lay hold of someone or something in flight, motion, or active resistance. Catch suggests dexterity or ingenuity: to catch a flying ball. Capture implies the overcoming of resistance: to capture an enemy fort. Nab and apprehend both suggest physical seizure, but apprehend is often used figuratively: to nab or apprehend a fugitive, to apprehend an idea. Bag refers to the catching of game, which is then put into a bag; in its extended sense, the word suggests a triumphant feeling: She bagged a minor poet for her salon. One seizes a thing by taking hold of it strongly, by physical force or force of authority. Compare GRASP. — **Ant.** lose, miss, release.

catch·all (kach′ôl′) n. **1.** A bag or the like to hold odds and ends. **2.** Anything that covers a wide range of situations, etc., as a phrase or doctrine.

catch basin A filter at the entrance to a drain or sewer to stop matter that might clog the pipes.

catch crop Agric. A quick-growing crop raised between two main crops, when the ground would otherwise be idle.

catch·er (kach′ər) n. **1.** One who or that which catches. **2.** In baseball, the player stationed behind home plate to catch balls that pass the batter. Abbr. (def. 2) c., C.

catcher's mitt See under MITT.

catch·fly (kach′flī′) n. Any of various plants (genus Silene) of the pink family, having a sticky stem and calyx.

catch·ing (kach′ing) adj. **1.** Infectious. **2.** Attractive.

catch·ment (kach′mənt) n. **1.** The catching and collecting of water, etc. **2.** A structure or drainage system that catches and collects water. **3.** The water so collected.

catchment basin Geog. The area drained by a river or river system. Also **catchment area.**

catch·pen·ny (kach′pen′ē) adj. Designed merely to sell; cheap and showy. — n. pl. ·nies A catchpenny article.

catch·pole (kach′pōl) n. One who arrests for debt; a bailiff. Also **catch·poll.** [< Med.L cacepollus chaser of fowl]

catch·up (kach′əp, kech′-) See KETCHUP.

catch·weight (kach′wāt′) n. In certain sports, the weight of a contestant as determined by chance or by his own discretion, rather than by rule or agreement.

catch·word (kach′wûrd′) n. **1.** A word or phrase taken up and often repeated, especially as a political slogan. Also **catch phrase.** **2.** Printing A word at the head of a page or column, as in a dictionary or encyclopedia, identifying the first or last article on the page. **3.** In old books, the first word of a page printed at the bottom of the preceding page. **4.** An actor's cue.

catch·y (kach′ē) adj. catch·i·er, catch·i·est **1.** Attractive; catching the fancy; also, easily remembered: catchy tunes. **2.** Deceptive; tricky. **3.** Fitful: catchy winds.

cate (kāt) n. Usually pl. Archaic Choice food; a delicacy. [Earlier acate < AF acat provision, purchase < acater to buy]

cat·e·che·sis (kat′ə·kē′sis) n. pl. ·ses (-sēz) Oral instruction, as of a catechumen. [< L < Gk. katēchēsis instruction < kata- thoroughly + ēcheein to sound, resound, talk]

cat·e·chet·ic (kat′ə·ket′ik) adj. Pertaining to oral instruction, especially by question and answer. Also **cat′e·chet′i·cal.**

cat·e·chin (kat′ə·chin, -kin) n. Chem. An amorphous yellow powder, $C_{15}H_{14}O_6$, contained in catechu, and used in dyeing. [< CATECH(U) + -IN]

cat·e·chism (kat′ə·kiz′əm) n. **1.** A short manual giving, in the form of questions and answers, an outline of the principles of a religious creed. Abbr. cat. **2.** Any similar manual giving instruction in other subjects. **3.** Examination by questions and answers, as of a political candidate. **4.** Obs. Catechetic instruction. [< Med.L catechismus < Gk. katēchizein to instruct]

cat·e·chist (kat′ə·kist) n. One who catechizes; especially, an instructor of catechumens. Also **cat′e·chiz′er, cat′e·chis′er.** — **cat′e·chis′tic** or **·ti·cal** adj.

cat·e·chize (kat′ə·kīz) v.t. ·chized, ·chiz·ing **1.** To instruct, especially in the principles of Christianity, by asking a series of set questions and discussing the answers. **2.** To question searchingly and at length. Also **cat′e·chise.** — **Syn.** See ASK. [< L catechizare to instruct < Gk. katēchizein] — **cat′e·chi·za′tion** n.

cat·e·chol (kat′ə·chōl, -kōl) n. Chem. Pyrocatechol (which see). [< CATECH(U) + -OL¹]

cat·e·chu (kat′ə·chōō, -kyōō) n. A resinous astringent and tanning extract prepared from the wood of various Asian and East Indian plants, especially Acacia catechu. Also called cachou, cashoo, cutch. [< NL < Malay kachu]

cat·e·chu·men (kat′ə·kyōō′mən) n. **1.** One who is under instruction in the elements of Christianity; a neophyte or convert. **2.** One undergoing elementary instruction in any subject, set of opinions, etc. [< L catechumenus < Gk. katēchoumenos, ppr. passive of katēcheein to instruct] — **cat′e·chu′me·nal, cat·e·chu·men·i·cal** (kat′ə·kyōō·men′i·kəl) adj.

cat·e·gor·i·cal (kat′ə·gôr′i·kəl, -gor′-) adj. **1.** Without qualification; absolute; unequivocal. **2.** Of, pertaining to, or included in a category. — **cat·e·gor/i·cal·ly** adv. — **cat/. e·gor·i·cal·ness** n.

categorical imperative *Philos.* The principle established by Immanuel Kant, stating, "Act in such a way that the maxim of your will can simultaneously apply as the basis for a universal law."

cat·e·go·rize (kat/ə·gə·rīz/) v.t. **·rized, ·riz·ing** To put into a category; classify.

cat·e·go·ry (kat/ə·gôr/ē, -gō/rē) n. pl. **·ries 1.** A division in any system of classification; a class: Drama is a *category* of literature. **2.** *Logic* Any of the fundamental concepts or classifications into which all forms of knowledge can be placed: also called *predicament*. [< L *categoria* < Gk. *katēgoria* < *katēgoreein* to allege, predicate < *kata-* against + *agora* public assembly]

ca·te·na (kə·tē/nə) n. pl. **·nae** (-nē) A chain or closely connected series; especially, a series of excerpts from the works of the Fathers of the Church. [< L, chain]

cat·e·nar·y (kat/ə·ner/ē, kə·tē/nər·ē) n. pl. **·nar·ies** *Math.* The curve formed by a flexible, inextensible cord suspended from two points not in the same vertical line. — adj. Relating to or like a catenary or a chain: also **cat·e·nar·i·an** (kat/ə·nâr/ē·ən). [< L *catenarius* < *catena* chain]

cat·e·nate (kat/ə·nāt) v.t. **·nat·ed, ·nat·ing** To connect like the links of a chain; form into a chain. — **cat/e·na/tion** n.

cat·e·noid (kat/ə·noid) n. *Math.* The surface formed by the rotation of a catenary about its axis of symmetry.

ca·ten·u·late (kə·ten/yə·lāt, -lit) adj. Chainlike in form or arrangement. [< L *catenula*, dim. of *catena* chain]

ca·ter (kā/tər) v.i. **1.** To furnish food or entertainment. **2.** To provide for the gratification of any need or taste. — v.t. **3.** To furnish food for: to *cater* a party. [< AF *acater* to buy < LL *accaptare* < L *ad-* toward + *captare* to grasp, seize]

cat·er·an (kat/ər·ən) n. A marauder or brigand of the Scottish Highlands. [< dial. E (Scottish) *catherein* < Scottish Gaelic *ceathairne* peasantry]

cat·er-cor·nered (kat/ər·kôr/nərd) adj. Diagonal. — adv. Diagonally. Also *catty-cornered, kitty-cornered.* Also **cat/er·cor/ner.** [< dial. E *cater* diagonally < F *quatre* four < L *quattuor* + CORNERED]

ca·ter·cous·in (kā/tər·kuz/ən) n. *Archaic* **1.** A cousin or relative. **2.** An intimate friend. [Origin uncertain]

ca·ter·er (kā/tər·ər) n. One who caters; especially, one whose occupation is the providing of food and services for social functions. — **ca/ter·ess** n.fem.

cat·er·pil·lar (kat/ər·pil/ər) n. The larva of a butterfly or moth, or of certain other insects, as the sawfly. — adj. Moving or fitted with treads mounted on endless belts: a *caterpillar* tractor. [ME *catepel* < AF *catepelose* < L *catta* cat + *pilosus* < *pilum* hair; infl. in form by obs. *piller* plunderer]

CATERPILLARS

a Swallowtail butterfly. *b* Mourning cloak. *c* Emperor moth. *d* Eyed hawk moth. *e* Great peacock moth. *f* Pale tussock moth. *g* Puss moth.

Cat·er·pil·lar (kat/- ər·pil/ər) n. A tractor that moves by means of two endless metal tracks running along each side, enabling it to be used on soft or rough terrain: a trade name. Also **cat/er·pil/lar, caterpillar tractor.**

caterpillar hunter Any of a genus (*Calosoma*) of carabid beetles that prey on caterpillars. For illustration see INSECTS (beneficial).

cat·er·waul (kat/ər·wôl) v.i. **1.** To utter the discordant cry of cats at rutting time. **2.** To make any discordant screeching. **3.** To argue or dispute noisily. — n. The cry of cats at rutting time; also, any similar cry. [ME *caterwawen* < *cater* cat (cf. G *kater* tomcat) + *wawen* to wail, howl]

cat·face (kat/fās/) n. A lesion on the surface of a tree caused by an injury or wound that has not completely healed.

cat·fall (kat/fôl/) n. *Naut.* The tackle for raising an anchor to the cathead.

cat·fish (kat/fish/) n. pl. **·fish** or **·fish·es** Any of numerous silurid fishes having sensitive barbels around the mouth.

cat·gut (kat/gut/) n. A very tough cord made from the intestines of certain animals, as sheep, and used for stringing musical instruments, making surgical ligatures, etc.

cath. Var. of CATA-.
cath. Cathedral.
Cath. Catholic.

ca·thar·sis (kə·thär/sis) n. **1.** *Med.* Purgation, especially of the alimentary canal. **2.** A purifying or purging of the emotions through the effect of art, as through the arousal of pity and terror on witnessing tragic drama. **3.** *Psychoanal.* A method of psychotherapy that induces the discharge of re-

pressed or painful emotions: compare ABREACTION. Also spelled *katharsis.* [< Gk. *katharsis* a cleansing < *katharos* pure]

ca·thar·tic (kə·thär/tik) adj. Purgative; purifying. Also **ca·thar/ti·cal.** — n. A medicine emptying the bowels; a laxative. [< Gk. *kathartikos* < *katharos* pure]

Ca·thay (ka·thā/) *Poetic* or *Archaic* China.

cat·head (kat/hed/) n. *Naut.* A beam projecting over the bow, by which the anchor is supported clear of the ship.

ca·the·dra (kə·thē/drə, kath/ə-) n. **1.** A bishop's seat or throne in the cathedral or chief church of his diocese. **2.** The see or office of a bishop. **3.** The chair of one in authority, as of a professor. [< L < Gk. *kathedra* < *kata-* down + *hedra* seat. Doublet of CHAIR.]

ca·the·dral (kə·thē/drəl) n. **1.** The church containing the cathedra or official chair of a bishop. **2.** Loosely, any large or important church. — adj. **1.** Pertaining to or containing a bishop's chair or see. **2.** Authoritative; dogmatic. **3.** Of, pertaining to, or resembling a cathedral.

ca·thep·sin (kə·thep/sin) n. *Biochem.* Any of a class of intracellular proteolytic enzymes found in animal tissues, and catalyzing the hydrolysis of peptides into amino acids.

Cath·er (kath/ər), **Willa Sibert,** 1876–1947, U.S. author.

Cath·e·rine (kath/rin, -ər·in), **Saint** Fourth-century Christian martyr of Alexandria.

Catherine I, 1684?–1727, empress of Russia; wife of Peter the Great.

Catherine II, 1729–96, empress of Russia: called **Catherine the Great.**

Catherine de'Medici See (Catherine de') MEDICI.

Catherine of Aragon, 1485–1536, first wife of Henry VIII of England.

Catherine of Braganza, 1638–1705, queen of Charles II of England.

catherine wheel A firework similar to a pinwheel.

cath·e·ter (kath/ə·tar) n. *Med.* A slender, flexible tubular instrument for introduction into body cavities or passages, for purposes of examination or drainage, especially one passed through the urethra to draw urine from the bladder. [< L < Gk. *kathetēr* < *kata-* down + *hienai* to send, let go]

cath·e·ter·ize (kath/ə·tə·rīz/) v.t. **·ized, ·iz·ing** To introduce a catheter into.

ca·thex·is (kə·thek/sis) n. *Psychoanal.* **1.** Concentration of psychic energy upon a person, fantasy, idea, or object. **2.** The investment or charging of an idea or emotion with significance. [< Gk. *kathexis* a holding < *kata-* thoroughly + *echein* to hold, have; trans. of G *besetzung*]

cath·ode (kath/ōd) n. *Electr.* **1.** The negatively charged electrode that receives electrons from an outside source of current during electrolysis, and toward which cations migrate. **2.** The element of an electron tube from which electrons escape. Also spelled *kathode.* Abbr. *C., ca., ka.* [< Gk. *kathodos* a way down < *kata-* down + *hodos* road, way] — **ca·thod·ic** (kə·thod/ik) or **·i·cal** adj.

cathode rays *Physics* A stream of electrons that pass from a cathode to the opposite wall of an evacuated electron tube when it is excited by a current of electricity, or by a series of spark discharges.

cathode-ray tube *Electronics* A special type of electron tube in which a beam of electrons is focused by an electric or magnetic field and deflected so as to impinge upon a sensitized screen, forming an image, as on a television receiver.

cath·o·lic (kath/ə·lik, kath/lik) adj. **1.** Broad-minded, as in belief or tastes; liberal; comprehensive; large. **2.** Universal in reach; general. [< L *catholicus* < Gk. *katholikos* universal < *kata-* thoroughly + *holos* whole] — **ca·thol·i·cal·ly** (kə·thol/ik·lē) adv.

— **Syn. 2.** universal, cosmic, cosmopolitan. — **Ant. 1.** narrow, intolerant. **2.** limited.

Cath·o·lic (kath/ə·lik, kath/lik) adj. **1.** Since the Reformation: **a** Of or pertaining to the Roman Catholic Church. **b** Designating those churches that claim to have the apostolic doctrine, discipline, orders, and sacraments of the ancient, undivided church, and including the Anglican, Old Catholic, Orthodox, and Roman Catholic churches. **2.** Of the ancient, undivided Christian church; being in accordance with the decrees of the seven ecumenical councils: the *Catholic* fathers; a *Catholic* creed. **3.** Designating the western or Latin Church as opposed to the eastern or Greek Church after their final separation in 1472; not Orthodox. **4.** Of, pertaining to, belonging or addressed to all Christians: a *Catholic* epistle. — n. A member of any Catholic church; especially, a Roman Catholic. Abbr. *C., Cath.*

Catholic Church The Roman Catholic Church (which see).

Ca·thol·i·cism (kə·thol/ə·siz/əm) n. The doctrine, system, and practice of a Catholic church, especially of the Roman Catholic Church. Also **Cath·o·lic·i·ty** (kath/ə·lis/ə·tē).

cath·o·lic·i·ty (kath/ə·lis/ə·tē) n. **1.** The state or quality of being catholic; freedom from narrowness; liberality. **2.** Universal prevalence or acceptance; universality.

ca·thol·i·cize (kə·thol/ə·sīz) *v.t.* & *v.i.* ·cized, ·ciz·ing To make or become catholic or Catholic.

ca·thol·i·con (kə·thol/ə·kən) *n.* A supposed universal remedy; a panacea. [< LL < Gk. *katholikos* universal]

cath·o·lyte (kath/ə·līt) *n. Chem.* The liquid formed near the cathode during electrolysis. [< CATHO(DE) + (ELEC-TRO)LYTE]

cat·house (kat/hous/) *n. U.S. Slang.* A bordello; brothel.

Cat·i·line (kat/ə·lin) Anglicized name of **Lucius Sergius Catilina**, 108?–62 B.C., Roman conspirator.

cat·i·on (kat/ī·ən) *n. Chem.* The electropositive ion of an electrolyte, that moves toward the cathode in electrolysis: opposed to *anion:* also spelled *kation.* [< Gk. *kation*, ppr. neut. of *katienai* < *kata-* down + *ienai* to go] **— cat/i·on·ic** (-ī·on/ik) *adj.*

cat·kin (kat/kin) *n. Bot.* A deciduous, scaly spike of flowers, as in the willow: also called *ament.* For illustration see INFLORESCENCE, WEEPING WILLOW. [MDu. *katteken*, dim. of *katte* cat]

cat·like (kat/līk/) *adj.* Like a cat; noiseless; stealthy.

cat·ling (kat/ling) *n.* 1. Catgut. 2. *Surg.* A long, double-edged knife used in amputation: also *cat/lin.* 3. A kitten.

cat nap A short, light nap; doze.

cat·nip (kat/nip/) *n.* An aromatic herb (*Nepeta cataria*) of the mint family, of which cats are fond. Also *Brit.* **cat/mint/.** [< CAT + dial. E *nep* catnip]

Ca·to (kā/tō), **Marcus Porcius**, 234–149 B.C., Roman statesman: called **the Elder** or **the Censor**. **— Marcus Porcius**, 95–46 B.C., Roman patriot and Stoic philosopher; greatgrandson of the preceding: called **U·ti·cen·sis** (yōō/ti·ken/səs) or **the Younger**.

cat-o'-moun·tain (kat/ə·moun/tən) See CATAMOUNTAIN.

cat-o'-nine-tails (kat/ə·nīn/tālz/) *n.* A whip with nine knotted lines fastened to a handle.

Cat·ons·ville (kat/nz·vil) An unincorporated place in central Maryland; pop. 54,812.

ca·top·trics (kə·top/triks) *n.pl.* (*construed as sing.*) The branch of optics that treats of the reflection of light and the formation of images by mirrors. [< Gk. *katoptrikos* of a mirror < *katoptron* mirror] **— ca·top/tric** or **·tri·cal** *adj.*

cat owl The great horned owl (which see).

cat rig The rig of a catboat, consisting of one mast far forward and one sail with a long boom and a gaff. **— cat·rigged** (kat/rigd/) *adj.*

cat's cradle A game played with a loop of string stretched in an intricate arrangement over the fingers and then transferred to another player's hands in a changed form.

cat's-eye (kats/ī/) *n.* 1. A gemstone, usually chrysoberyl or quartz, that shows a line of light across the dome when cut en cabochon. 2. A small metal or glass reflector.

Cats·kill Mountains (kats/kil) A range of the Appalachians in SE New York; highest peak, Slide Mountain, 4,204 feet. Also **the Catskills**.

cat·skin·ner (kat/skin/ər) *n. U.S. & Canadian* One who operates a caterpillar tractor.

cat's-paw (kats/pô/) *n.* 1. A person used as a tool or dupe. 2. A light wind that barely ruffles the water. 3. *Naut.* A twisting hitch in the bight of a rope. Also **cats/paw/.**

cat·sup (kat/səp, kech/əp) See KETCHUP.

Catt (kat), **Carrie Chapman**, 1859–1947, U.S. suffragist.

cat·tail (kat/tāl/) *n.* A marsh plant (genus *Typha*), having flowers in cylindrical terminal spikes and long leaves used for making mats, chair seats, etc.: also called *reed-mace.*

cat·ta·lo (kat/ə·lō) See CATALO.

Cat·te·gat (kat/ə·gat) See KATTEGAT.

Cat·tell (kə·tel/), **James McKeen**, 1860–1944, U.S. psychologist and editor.

cat·tle (kat/l) *n.* 1. Domesticated bovine animals, as cows, bulls, and steers. 2. Formerly, all livestock, as horses, sheep, etc. 3. Human beings: a contemptuous term. 4. *Obs.* Vermin, birds, etc. [< AF *catel* < LL *captale* < L *capitale* capital, wealth. Doublet of CHATTEL.]

cat·tle·man (kat/l·mən) *n. pl.* **·men** (-mən) One who raises or tends cattle.

cat·tle·ya (kat/lē·ə) *n.* Any of a genus (*Cattleya*) of tropical American orchids, widely cultivated for their showy flowers. [< NL, after William *Cattley*, English botanist]

cat·ty¹ (kat/ē) *n. pl.* **·ties** An Asian weight equivalent to about 1½ pounds avoirdupois: also called *chang.* Also **cat/tie.** [< Malay *kātī*]

cat·ty² (kat/ē) *adj.* **·ti·er, ·ti·est** 1. Like or pertaining to cats. 2. Slyly malicious; spiteful. **— cat/ti·ly** *adv.* **— cat/ti·ness** *n.*

cat·ty-cor·nered (kat/ē-kôr/nərd) *adj.* Cater-cornered.

Ca·tul·lus (kə·tul/əs), **Gaius Valerius**, 84?–54? B.C., Roman lyric poet.

cat·walk (kat/wôk/) *n.* Any narrow walking space, as at the side of a bridge.

cat whisker *Electronics* A fine wire used to make contact on the surface of a crystal detector. Also **cat's whisker.**

Cau·ca (kou/kä) A river in western Colombia, flowing about 600 miles north to the Magdalena.

Cau·ca·sian (kô·kā/zhən, -shən, -kash/ən) *n.* 1. A member of the Caucasoid division of the human species, so called from a skull found in the Caucasus, which was taken as es-

tablishing the type. 2. A member of the native peoples of the Caucasus region. 3. A family of languages spoken in the Caucasus region, including Georgian and Circassian. **—** *adj.* 1. Of or pertaining to the region of the Caucasus, its inhabitants, or their languages. 2. Caucasoid. Also **Cau·cas·ic** (kô·kas/ik) *adj.*

Cau·ca·soid (kô/kə·soid, -zoid) *Anthropol. adj.* 1. Of, pertaining to, or belonging to a major ethnic division of the human species, characterized by skin color ranging from very light to brown, hair varying from straight to curly, etc. 2. Resembling, related to, or characteristic of Caucasoids. **—** *n.* A Caucasoid person.

Cau·ca·sus (kô/kə·səs) 1. A mountain range between the Black and Caspian seas; highest peak, Mount Elbrus, 18,481 feet: also *Greater Caucasus.* 2. A physiographic region of the SW Soviet Union between the Black and Caspian seas; divided by the Caucasus mountains into Northern Caucasus and Transcaucasia: also **Cau·ca·sia** (kô·kā/zhə, -shə, -kash/ə).

Caucasus In·di·cus (in/di·kəs) The ancient name for the HINDU KUSH.

cau·cus (kô/kəs) *n.* 1. A meeting of members of a political party to select candidates, plan a campaign, etc. 2. *Brit.* A political committee in charge of shaping policy, etc. **—** *v.i.* **cau·cused** or **·cussed, cau·cus·ing** or **·cus·sing** To meet in or hold a caucus. [after the *Caucus* Club, Boston, Mass., prob. < Algonquian *caucawasu* adviser]

cau·dad (kô/dad) *adv. Zool.* Toward the tail: opposed to *cephalad.* [< L *cauda* tail + *ad* toward]

cau·dal (kôd/l) *adj. Zool.* 1. Of, pertaining to, or near the tail or posterior part of the body. 2. Taillike. [< NL *caudalis* < L *cauda* tail] **— cau/dal·ly** *adv.*

cau·date (kô/dāt) *adj. Zool.* Having a tail or taillike appendage. Also **cau/dat·ed.** [< L *caudatus* < *cauda* tail]

cau·dex (kô/deks) *n. pl.* **·di·ces** (-də·sēz) or **·dex·es** *Bot.* 1. The woody axis or trunk of a tree. 2. The woody base of a perennial plant. [< L, var. of *codex* trunk of a tree]

cau·dil·lo (kou·thē/lyō, -thē/yō) *n. Spanish* A leader. **— el Caudillo** Title of Francisco Franco.

Cau·dine Forks (kô/dīn) Two narrow passes in the Apennines, southern Italy; site of a defeat of the Romans by the Samnites, 321 B.C.

cau·dle (kôd/l) *n.* A warm drink of gruel with wine, eggs, sugar, spices, etc., for invalids. [< AF *caudel* < Med.L *caldellum*, dim. of L *caldum, calidum* warm, hot]

caught (kôt, kot) Past tense and past participle of CATCH.

caul (kôl) *n.* The part of the amniotic sac that sometimes envelops the head of a child at birth, formerly thought to be a good omen: also called *veil.* [< OF *cale* cap]

Cau·lain·court (kō·laṅ·kōōr/), **Marquis Armand Augustine Louis de**, 1772–1827, French general and diplomat.

cauld (kôld, käld, kôd) *adj.* & *n. Scot.* Cold.

caul·dron (kôl/drən) *n.* A large kettle or boiler: also spelled *caldron.* [< AF *caudron* < L *caldria* kettle < *calidus* hot]

cau·les·cent (kô·les/ənt) *adj. Bot.* Having a clearly defined stem. [< L *caulis* stem + -ESCENT]

cau·li·cle (kô/li·kəl) *n. Bot.* A little stem; especially, the rudimentary stem in the embryo of a seed. [< L *cauliculus*, dim. of *caulis.* See CAULIS.]

cau·li·flow·er (kô/lə·flou/ər, kol/i-) *n.* 1. The fleshy, edible head formed by the young flowers of a variety of cabbage (*Brassica oleracea botrytis*). 2. The plant bearing this. [Earlier *colieflorie*, alter. of NL *cauliflora* flowering cabbage; infl. in form by *flower*]

cauliflower ear An ear that has been deformed by blows, usually in boxing.

cau·li·form (kô/lə·fôrm) *adj. Bot.* Shaped like a stem.

cau·line (kô/lin, -līn) *adj. Bot.* Of, pertaining to, or growing on a stem. [< NL *caulinus* < L *caulis.* See CAULIS.]

cau·lis (kô/lis) *n. pl.* **·les** (-lēz) *Bot.* The stem of a plant. [< L < Gk. *kaulos* stem of a plant]

caulk (kôk) *v.t.* 1. *Naut.* To make tight, as a boat's seams, by plugging with soft material, such as oakum or hemp fiber. 2. To hammer or fasten together, as the edges of a boiler's plates. 3. To plug the crevices of, as a window frame. Also spelled *calk.* [< OF *cauquer* < L *calcare* to tread] **— caulk/ing** *n.*

caulk·er (kô/kər) *n.* 1. One who caulks. 2. A tool used for caulking. Also spelled *calker.*

caus·al (kô/zəl) *adj.* Pertaining to, constituting, involving, or expressing a cause. **—** *n. Gram.* A form expressing cause or reason, as the conjunction *therefore.* [< L *causalis* of a cause < *causa* cause] **— caus/al·ly** *adv.*

cau·sal·gi·a (kô·zal/jē·ə) *n. Pathol.* A burning pain, such as often follows injuries of the nerves; neuralgia with severe local pain. [< NL < Gk. *kausos* heat < *kaiein* to burn + *-algia* pain < *algeein* to hurt]

cau·sal·i·ty (kô·zal/ə·tē) *n. pl.* **·ties** 1. The relation of cause and effect. 2. Causal character or agency.

cau·sa si·ne quan·on (kô/zə si/nē kwä non/) *Latin* An indispensable condition; literally, cause without which not.

cau·sa·tion (kô·zā/shən) *n.* 1. The act of causing. 2. That which produces an effect; cause. 3. The relation of cause and effect. [< Med.L *causatio, -onis* < L, an excuse, pretext < *causari* to bring about < *causa* cause]

caus·a·tive (kô′zə·tiv) *adj.* **1.** Effective as a cause. **2.** *Gram.* Expressing cause or agency; indicating that the subject causes the action: *en-* in *enfeeble* is a *causative* prefix; *to lay* (to cause to lie) is a *causative* verb. — *n. Gram.* A form that expresses or suggests causation. [< MF *causatif* < L *causativus* < *causa* cause] — **caus′a·tive·ly** *adv.* — **caus′a·tive·ness** *n.*

cause (kôz) *n.* **1.** The agent or force producing an effect; a person, occasion, condition, etc., giving rise to a result or action. **2.** A ground for choice or action; reason; motive: *cause* for complaint. **3.** Sufficient ground; good reason: no *cause* to strike. **4.** An aim, object, or principle advocated and supported by an individual or group, especially one inspired by moral motives: the *cause* of liberty. **5.** *Law* **a** A ground of action; the matter to be decided in court. **b** An action or suit; case. **6.** A matter under discussion or in dispute. — *v.t.* **caused, caus·ing** To be the cause of; produce; effect; induce; compel. [< MF < L *causa* cause, legal case] — **caus′a·ble** *adj.* — **cause′less** *adj.* — **caus′er** *n.*
— **Syn.** (noun) **1, 2.** *Cause, determinant, antecedent, motive,* and *reason* refer to events or circumstances prior to others. A *cause,* in strict usage, produces a necessary and invariable effect; more loosely, it may be used in the sense of *determinant* to mean one of the prior factors that influence the form, details, or character of an effect without being its sole *cause*: Friction is the *cause* of wear in machine parts; soil sterility is a *cause* of poor harvests, and a *determinant* of the size of a particular crop. An *antecedent* refers merely to that which goes before in time, and does not necessarily imply any causal relationship: the medieval *antecedents* of the violin. A *motive* is the inner impulse that guides intelligent action; a *reason,* the explanation given for a fact, an action, or a state of affairs. *Reason* and *motive* are often used interchangeably: to give one's *reasons* (or *motives*) for coming; and *reason* is also used for *cause* in its strict sense, when the latter is known: Laziness was the *reason* for (or *cause* of) his failure. Compare REASON.

cause cé·lè·bre (kôz sā·leb′r′) *French* **1.** A famous legal case. **2.** Any well-known controversial issue.

cau·se·rie (kō′zə·rē′, *Fr.* kōz·rē′) *n.* **1.** An informal conversation; a chat. **2.** A short, chatty piece of writing. [< F]

cause·way (kôz′wā′) *n.* **1.** A raised road or way, as over marshy ground. **2.** A paved way; a highway. — *v.t.* **1.** To make a causeway for or through, as a marshy tract. **2.** To pave, as a road. [Earlier *causeyway* < AF *caucie* < LL *calciata,* fem. pp. of *calciare* to tread, stamp down < L *calx, calcis* heel + WAY]

cau·sey (kô′zē) *n. pl.* **·seys** *Scot. & Brit. Dial.* A paved way, street, or highway.

caus·tic (kôs′tik) *adj.* **1.** Capable of corroding or eating away tissues; burning; corrosive. **2.** Sarcastic; biting: *caustic* wit. **3.** *Optics* **a** Designating a surface to which all rays emitted from one point and reflected or refracted from a curved surface are tangents. **b** Designating a curve formed by such a surface. — *n.* **1.** A caustic substance. **2.** *Optics* A caustic curve or surface. [< L *causticus* < Gk. *kaustikos* < *kaustos* burning < *kaiein* to burn] — **caus′ti·cal·ly** *adv.* — **caus·tic·i·ty** (kôs·tis′ə·tē) *n.*

caustic potash Potassium hydroxide.

caustic soda Sodium hydroxide.

cau·ter·ant (kô′tər·ənt) *adj.* Of or pertaining to cautery or a caustic. — *n.* A cauterizing substance.

cau·ter·ize (kô′tə·rīz) *v.t.* **·ized, ·iz·ing** To sear with a caustic agent or heated iron. Also *Brit.* **cau′ter·ise.** [< LL *cauterizare* < L *cauterium.* See CAUTERY.] — **cau′ter·i·za′tion** *n.*

cau·ter·y (kô′tər·ē) *n. pl.* **·ter·ies** *Med.* **1.** The destruction of tissue by the application of a caustic substance or a searing iron. **2.** A cauterizing agent. [< L *cauterium* branding iron < Gk. *kauterion* < *kaiein* to burn]

cau·tion (kô′shən) *n.* **1.** Care to avoid injury or misfortune; prudence; wariness; discretion. **2.** An admonition or warning. **3.** *Archaic Informal* One who or that which alarms, astonishes, etc. — *v.t.* To advise to be prudent; warn. [< OF < L *cautio, -onis* < *cavere* to beware, take heed]

cau·tion·ar·y (kô′shən·er′ē) *adj.* Constituting or conveying a warning; admonitory; cautionary signals.

cau·tious (kô′shəs) *adj.* Exercising or manifesting extreme care or prudence; reluctant to incur danger; wary. — **cau′tious·ly** *adv.* — **cau′tious·ness** *n.*

Cau·ve·ry (kä′vûr·ē) A river in southern India flowing 475 miles, generally SE, to the Bay of Bengal; regarded as sacred by Hindus: also *Kaveri.*

cav. **1.** Cavalier. **2.** Cavalry.

cav·al·cade (kav′əl·kād′, kav′əl·kād) *n.* **1.** A company of horsemen on the march or in procession. **2.** A procession; parade. [< MF < Ital. *cavalcata* < *cavalcare* to ride on horseback < LL *caballicare* < L *caballus* horse]

cav·a·lier (kav′ə·lir′) *n.* **1.** A horseman; knight. **2.** A courtly or dashing gentleman; a gallant; also, a lady's escort. Also *Obs.* **cav·a·le·ro** (kav′ə·lā′rō), **cav′a·lie′ro** (-lyā′rō). *Abbr. cav.* — *adj.* **1.** Haughty; supercilious. **2.** Free and easy; offhand. — *v.i.* To behave in a cavalier fashion; show arrogance. [< MF < Ital. *cavaliere* < LL *caballarius* < L *caballus* horse, nag. Doublet of CHEVALIER.]

Cav·a·lier (kav′ə·lir′) *n.* A supporter of Charles I of England; a Royalist. Compare ROUNDHEAD. — *adj.* Pertaining to the Cavaliers. — **Cav′a·lier′ism** *n.*

cav·a·lier·ly (kav′ə·lir′lē) *adv.* In a cavalier manner; disdainfully; arrogantly. — *adj.* Characteristic of a cavalier; haughty.

Cavalier poets A group of English lyric poets, mainly at the court of Charles I, including Herrick, Carew, Lovelace, and Suckling.

ca·val·la (kə·val′ə) *n. pl.* **·las** or **·la** The king mackerel. Also **ca·val′ly.** [< Sp. *cavalla* horse mackerel < L *caballus* horse]

cav·al·ry (kav′əl·rē) *n. pl.* **·ries** **1.** Troops trained primarily to maneuver and fight on horseback or, more recently, in armored motor vehicles. *Abbr. cav.* **2.** Riders or horses, collectively. [< MF *cavallerie* < Ital. *cavalleria* < LL *caballarius* horseman < L *caballus* horse. Doublet of CHIVALRY.] — **cav′al·ry·man** (-mən) *n.*

cav·a·ti·na (kav′ə·tē′nə, *Ital.* kä′vä·tē′nä) *n. Music* **1.** A short song, usually without a second part or repeat. **2.** Loosely, a lyric composition for instruments. [< Ital.]

cave (kāv) *n.* **1.** A chamber beneath the earth, in a mountain or mountainside, etc. ◆ Collateral adjective: *spelean.* **2.** *Brit.* Secession from a political party, or the faction that secedes. — **Syn.** See HOLE. — *v.* **caved, cav·ing** *v.t.* **1.** To hollow out. — *v.i.* **2.** *Informal* To fall in or down; give way. — **to cave in 1.** To fall in or down, as when undermined; cause to fall in. **2.** *Informal* To yield utterly; give in, as to argument, hardship, or strain. [< OF < L *cava* < *cavus* hollow]

ca·ve·at (kā′vē·at) *n. Law* A formal notification given by an interested party to a court or officer, either judicial or ministerial, not to do a certain act. **2.** A caution or warning. [< L, let him beware]

ca·ve·at emp·tor (kā′vē·at emp′tôr) *Latin* Let the buyer beware, implying that the purchase is made at his own risk.

ca·ve·a·tor (kā′vē·ā′tər) *n.* One who enters a caveat.

ca·ve ca·nem (kā′vē kā′nəm) *Latin* Beware of the dog.

cave·fish (kāv′fish′) *n. pl.* **·fish** or **·fish·es** A blindfish (which see).

cave-in (kāv′in′) *n.* A collapse or falling in, as of a mine or tunnel; also, the site of such a collapse.

Cav·ell (kav′əl), **Edith Louisa,** 1865–1915, English nurse; executed by the German army in World War I.

cave man 1. A Paleolithic man; prehistoric cave dweller; troglodyte (def. 1). **2.** *Informal* A man who is rough and brutal, especially in his approach to women.

cav·en·dish (kav′ən·dish) *n.* Tobacco that has been softened, sweetened with molasses, and pressed into plugs. [after *Cavendish,* proper name]

Cav·en·dish (kav′ən·dish), **Henry,** 1731?–1810, English chemist; discovered chemical composition of water. — **Willi·m,** 1640–1707, first Duke of Devonshire, English statesman.

cav·ern (kav′ərn) *n.* A cave, especially one that is large or extensive. — *v.t.* **1.** To shut in or as in a cavern. **2.** To hollow out. [< MF *caverne* < L *caverna* < *cavus* hollow]

cav·ern·ous (kav′ər·nəs) *adj.* **1.** Full of caverns. **2.** Characteristic of a cavern. **3.** Hollow. **4.** Full of cavities; of a porous texture. — **cav′ern·ous·ly** *adv.*

ca·vet·to (kə·vet′ō, *Ital.* kä·vet′tō) *n. pl.* **·ti** (-tē) or **·tos** *Archit.* A concave molding of not more than 90° curvature, with a projection usually about equal to its height. For illustration see MOLDING. [< Ital., dim. of *cavo* hollow < L *cavus*]

cav·i·ar (kav′ē·är, kä′vē-) *n.* The roe of sturgeon or other fish, salted and sometimes pressed. Also **cav′i·are.** — **caviar to the general** Something too refined or exquisite to appeal to popular taste. [< F < Turkish *khāvyār*]

cav·i·corn (kav′ə·kôrn) *Zool. adj.* Having hollow horns. [< L *cavus* hollow + *cornu* horn]

ca·vie (kā′vē) *n. Scot.* A hencoop. [? < MDu. *kevie*]

cav·il (kav′əl) *v.* **cav·iled** or **·illed, cav·il·ing** or **·il·ling** *v.i.* **1.** To raise trivial objections; argue captiously; carp: with *at* or *about.* — *v.t.* **2.** To find fault with. — *n.* A captious objection. [< MF *caviller* < L *cavillari* < *cavilla* a jeering, a scoffing] — **cav′il·er** or **cav′il·ler** *n.* — **cav′il·ing·ness** or **cav′il·ling·ness** *n.* — **cav′il·ing·ly** or **cav′il·ling·ly** *adv.*

cav·i·ta·tion (kav′ə·tā′shən) *n. Physics* The formation and collapse of low-pressure vapor cavities in a flowing liquid, often resulting in serious damage to pumps, ship propellers, etc. [< CAVITY]

Ca·vi·te (kä·vē′tä) A Province of the Philippines, on southern Luzon; 498 sq. mi.; pop. 315,620 (est. 1958); capital, Cavite, pop. 43,759 (est. 1960).

cav·i·ty (kav′ə·tē) *n. pl.* **·ties 1.** A hollow or sunken space; hole. **2.** A natural hollow in the body. **3.** A hollow place in a tooth; especially, one caused by decay. — **Syn.** See HOLE. [< MF *cavité* < LL *cavitas, -tatis* a hollow < L *cavus* hollow]

ca·vort (kə·vôrt′) *v.i. U.S.* To prance about; caper; frisk. [Origin unknown]

Ca·vour (kä·vōōr′) **Count Camillo Benso di,** 1810–61, Italian statesman.

CAVU *Aeron.* Ceiling and visibility unlimited.

ca·vy (kā′vē) *n. pl.* **·vies** A small South American rodent with the tail absent or rudimentary, as the guinea pig (*Cavia cobaya*), the **restless cavy** (*C. porcellus*), the **southern cavy** (*C. australis*), common on the Patagonian coast, and the harelike **Patagonian cavy** (*Dolichotis patagonica*). — **giant cavy** The capybara. [< NL *Cavia* < Carib]

caw (kô) *v.i.* To make the high harsh sound of a crow, rook, etc. — *n.* The cry of a crow, raven, etc. [Imit.]

Cax·ton (kak′stən) *n.* **1.** Any book printed by **William Caxton,** 1422?–91, English printer, who introduced printing into England. **2.** *Printing* A style of type imitating the black letter of Caxton.

cay (kā, kē) *n.* A coastal reef or sandy islet, as in the Gulf of Mexico. See KEY². [< Sp. *cayo* shoal]

Cay·enne (kī·en′, kā-) The capital of French Guiana, a port city in the northern part; pop. 19,668 (1967).

cayenne pepper A hot, biting red powder made from the fruit of various capsicums: also called *Guinea pepper*, *red pepper*. Also **cay·enne′.**

Cayes (kā) See LES CAYES.

cay·man (kā′mən) *n. pl.* **·mans** A tropical American crocodilian (genus *Caiman*) closely related to the alligator, as the **spectacled cayman** (*C. sclerops*), having prominent ridges above the upper eyelid: also spelled *caiman*. [< Sp. *caiman* < Carib]

Cay·mans (kā′mənz, kī·mänz′) A British Colony comprising a West Indies island group; 93 sq. mi.; pop. 12,000 (est. 1969). Also **Cayman Islands.**

Ca·yu·ga (kā·yōō′gə, kī-) *n. pl.* **·ga** or **·gas** One of a tribe of North American Indians of Iroquoian stock formerly dwelling around Cayuga Lake, N.Y.

Ca·yu·ga Lake (kā·yōō′gə, kī-) One of the Finger Lakes in west central New York.

cay·use (kī·yōōs′) *n. U.S.* An Indian pony.

Cay·use (kī·yōōs′) *n.* A member of a tribe of North American Indians formerly inhabiting Oregon.

ca·zique (kə·zēk′) See CACIQUE.

c.b. **1.** Center of buoyancy. **2.** Confined to barracks.

Cb **1.** *Chem.* Columbium. **2.** *Meteorol.* Cumulonimbus.

CB **1.** Citizens band. **2.** *Mil.* Construction Battalion.

C.B. **1.** Bachelor of Surgery (L *Chirurgiae Baccalaureus*). **2.** *Brit.* Companion of the Bath. **3.** *Brit.* County borough.

CBC Canadian Broadcasting Corporation.

C.B.D. or **c.b.d.** Cash before delivery.

CBI China, Burma, India.

CBS Columbia Broadcasting System.

cc. **1.** Chapters. **2.** Cubic centimeter(s): also **c.c., cc**

Cc *Meteorol.* Cirrocumulus.

CC Cyanogen chloride.

C.C. Cape Colony.

C.C. or **c.c.** **1.** Carbon copy. **2.** Cashier's check. **3.** Chief clerk. **4.** Circuit court. **5.** City council; city councilor. **6.** Common councilman. **7.** Consular clerk. **8.** Contra credit. **9.** County clerk. **10.** County commissioner. **11.** County council. **12.** County court. **13.** Current account (F *compte courant*).

CCA Commission for Conventional Armaments.

C.C.A. **1.** Chief Clerk of the Admiralty. **2.** Circuit Court of Appeals.

CCC **1.** Civilian Conservation Corps. **2.** Commodity Credit Corporation.

C clef See under CLEF.

cd. Cord.

c.d. Cash discount.

Cd *Chem.* Cadmium.

C.D. Civilian Defense.

cd. ft. Cord foot (feet).

CDR or **Cdr.** *Mil.* Commander.

Ce *Chem.* Cerium.

CE **1.** Corps of Engineers. **2.** Council of Europe.

C.E. **1.** Chemical Engineer. **2.** Chief Engineer. **3.** Christian Endeavor. **4.** Church of England. **5.** Civil Engineer.

CEA Council of Economic Advisers.

Ce·a·rá (sā′ä·rä′) **1.** A State in NE Brazil; 57,102 sq. mi.; pop. 3,314,000 (est. 1958); capital, Fortaleza. **2.** See FORTALEZA.

Ceará rubber The coagulated latex of a manihot tree.

cease (sēs) *v.* **ceased, ceas·ing** *v.t.* **1.** To leave off or discontinue, as one's own actions. — *v.i.* **2.** To come to an end; stop; desist. — *n.* End; stopping: now only in the phrase **without cease.** [< MF *cesser* < L *cessare* to stop < *cedere* to withdraw, yield] — **cease′·less** *adj.* — **cease′less·ly** *adv.*

— **Syn.** (verb) *Cease, stop, discontinue,* and *desist* refer to the suspension of motion or activity, or to the ending of a thing's existence. *Cease* is applied chiefly to conditions or states of being: My joy shall never *cease.* That which advances or is in progress *stops*; sustained activity and operations are *discontinued*: Our train *stops* here; work on the new bridge *stopped*; we have *discontinued* publication of the paper. *Desist* is applied to an active agency and implies forbearance: to *desist* from false advertising. Compare ABANDON, DIE, END, REST.

cease-fire (sēs′fīr′) *n.* An armistice; truce.

ceb·a·dil·la (seb′ə·dil′ə) *n.* Sabadilla (which see).

ce·boid (sē′boid) *Zool. adj.* Pertaining to or describing any member of a superfamily (*Ceboidea*) of monkeys, including the marmosets, capuchins, tamarins, sapajous, and spider monkeys. — *n.* A member of the *Ceboidea*: also **cebid** (sē′bid, seb′id). [< NL < Gk. *kēbos*, a longtailed monkey]

Ce·bu (sā·bōō′) **1.** One of the Visayan Islands in the central Philippines; 1,702 sq. mi.; pop. 1,402,090; chief city, **Cebu,** pop. 209,111 (est. 1960).

Ce·cil (ses′əl, sis′-), **(Edgar Algernon) Robert,** 1864–1958, Viscount Cecil of Chelwood, British statesman; active in formation of League of Nations. — **Lord David,** born 1902, English biographer and critic. — **Robert,** 1563?–1612, first Earl of Salisbury, English statesman; son of William. — **Robert Arthur Gascoyne** See (Marquis of) SALISBURY — **William,** 1520–98, first Lord Burghley, English statesman.

Ce·cil·ia (si·sēl′yə), **Saint,** died 230?, Roman woman who suffered martyrdom; patroness of music.

ce·cro·pi·a moth (si·krō′pē·ə) A large, strikingly marked moth (*Samia cecropia*) common in the eastern United States. [< NL *Cecropia,* genus of mulberry, named after *Cecrops*]

Ce·crops (sē′krops) In Greek legend, the first king of Attica and founder of Athens, represented as half man, half dragon.

ce·cum (sē′kəm) *n. pl.* **ce·ca** (sē′kə) *Anat.* A pouch, or cavity, open at one end, especially that situated between the large and small intestines: also called *blind gut*: also spelled *caecum.* For illustration see INTESTINE. [< L < *caecus* blind] — **ce′cal** *adj.*

ce·dar (sē′dər) *n.* **1.** A large tree (genus *Cedrus*) of the pine family, having evergreen leaves and fragrant wood. There are several species, as the **cedar of Lebanon** (*C. libani*), **deodar cedar** (*C. deodara*), etc. **2.** The red cedar (def. 1). **3.** Spanish cedar (which see). **4.** The wood of these and related trees. — *adj.* Pertaining to or made of cedar: also *Poetic* **ce′darn** (-dərn). [< OF *cedre* < L *cedrus* < Gk. *kedros*]

ce·dar·bird (sē′dər·bûrd) *n.* The cedar waxwing. See under WAXWING.

cedar chest A storage chest for woolens, made of cedarwood for protection from moths.

Cedar Rapids A city in eastern Iowa; pop. 110,642.

ce·dar·wood (sē′dər·wood′) *n.* The wood from any cedar.

cedarwood oil A colorless to pale yellow essential oil distilled from cedarwood and used in perfumes and insecticides.

cede (sēd) *v.t.* **ced·ed, ced·ing 1.** To yield or give up. **2.** To surrender title to; transfer: to *cede* land. — **Syn.** See RELINQUISH. [< MF *céder* < L *cedere* to withdraw, yield]

ce·di (sē′dē) *n.* The monetary unit of Ghana, equivalent to 100 pesewas.

ce·dil·la (si·dil′ə) *n.* A mark put under the letter *c* (ç) before *a, o,* or *u* in some French words, as in *français,* to indicate that it is to be sounded as (s), and used also in the Turkish version of the Latin alphabet. [< Sp. dim. of *zeda,* the letter *z* < Gk. *zēta*; orig. a small *z* placed next to a *c* to indicate its sound]

ced·u·la (sej′oo·lə, *Sp.* thā′thoo·lä) *n.* **1.** Any of various permits, certificates, etc., issued by the government in certain Spanish-American countries. **2.** In the Philippines, a personal registration tax certificate; also, the tax itself. [< Sp. *cédula* note, bill]

cee (sē) *n.* The letter C.

CEGEP (sē′zhep, -jep) *n. Canadian* A provincial junior college in Quebec offering general and vocational courses. [< F (C)ollège d' (E)nseignement (G)énéral (e)t (P)rofessionel]

ce·i·ba (sā′i·bä, sē′bä) *n.* A West Indian and Mexican tree (*Ceiba pentandra*) yielding kapok. [< Sp. < Arawakan]

ceil (sēl) *v.t.* To furnish with a ceiling. [< F *ciel* roof, canopy < L *caelum* heaven, sky]

ceil·ing (sē′ling) *n.* **1.** The overhead covering or lining of a room. **2.** An upper limit; maximum, as one set on prices or wages. **3.** *Naut.* The inside planking of a vessel. **4.** *Aeron.* **a** The maximum height to which a given aircraft can be flown. **b** The greatest altitude from which the earth is visible at a given time, usually measured in hundreds of feet between the ground and the base of an overcast.

ceil·om·e·ter (sē·lom′ə·tər) *n. Meteorol.* A photoelectric device used to determine the ceiling height of clouds under all weather conditions. [< CEIL(ING) + -METER]

Cel. Celsius.

Ce·lae·no (se·lē′nō) In Greek mythology, one of the Pleiades. — *n. Astron.* A visible star in the Pleiades.

cel·an·dine (sel′ən·dīn) *n.* **1.** A plant (*Chelidonium majus*) of the poppy family, with yellow flowers: also called *swallowwort.* **2.** A crowfoot (*Ranunculus ficaria*) having tuberous roots and yellow flowers: also called *pilewort.* [< OF *celidoine* < L *chelidonia* < Gk. *chelidonion* < *chelidōn* a swallow]

-cele¹ *combining form* Tumor or hernia: *gastrocele.* [< Gk. *kēlē* tumor]

-cele² *combining form* Cavity; hollow space: *blastocele*: also spelled *-coele.* [< Gk. *koilos* hollow]

Cel·e·bes (sel′ə·bēz, sə·lē′bēz) An island of Indonesia, east of Borneo; 69,277 sq. mi.; pop. 7,665,000 (est. 1970): Indonesian *Sulawesi.* See map of INDONESIA.

Celebes Sea The part of the Pacific between Celebes and the Philippines.

cel·e·brant (sel′ə·brənt) *n.* **1.** One who participates in a celebration. **2.** The officiating priest at the Eucharist. [< L *celebrans, -antis,* ppr. of *celebrare.* See CELEBRATE.]

cel·e·brate (sel′ə·brāt) *v.* **·brat·ed, ·brat·ing** *v.t.* **1.** To observe, as a festival or occasion, with demonstrations of respect or rejoicing. **2.** To make known or famous; extol. **3.** To perform (a ceremony) publicly and as ordained. — *v.i.* **4.** To observe or commemorate a day or event. **5.** To perform a religious ceremony. [< L *celebratus,* pp. of *celebrare* to celebrate, honor < *celeber* famous] — **cel′e·bra′tor** *n.*
— **Syn. 1.** *Celebrate, commemorate, solemnize, observe,* and *keep* refer to the festivities or ceremonies of special or appointed days, especially public holidays. *Celebrate* is used for joyous occasions: to *celebrate* a religious holiday or the birthday of a respected person. *Commemorate* refers to the solemnity of an event, as does *solemnize,* but *commemorate* looks to the past, often with sorrow, while *solemnize* refers to the seriousness of a present occasion: to *commemorate* a great man's death, a monument to *commemorate* a national disaster, to *solemnize* a marriage. A regular holiday or season is *observed* or *kept; observe* is more general, and suggests merely the performance of any actions appropriate to the day, while *keep* emphasizes the careful performance of prescribed or conventional acts: to *observe* a holiday by not working, to *keep* Lent with fasting and prayer. **2.** See PRAISE.

cel·e·brat·ed (sel′ə·brā′tid) *adj.* Well-known; much publicized: a *celebrated* murder trial.
— **Syn.** famous, renowned, noted. Compare ILLUSTRIOUS.

cel·e·bra·tion (sel′ə·brā′shən) *n.* **1.** The act of celebrating. **2.** That which is done in commemoration of any event.

ce·leb·ri·ty (sə·leb′rə·tē) *n. pl.* **·ties 1.** A famous or celebrated person. **2.** Fame or notoriety; renown. — **Syn.** See FAME. [< L *celebritas, -tatis* fame < *celeber* famous]

ce·ler·i·ty (sə·ler′ə·tē) *n.* Quickness of motion; speed; rapidity. [< F *célérité* < L *celeritas, -tatis* < *celer* swift]

cel·er·y (sel′ər·ē, sel′rē) *n.* A biennial herb (*Apium graveolens*), whose blanched stems are used as a vegetable or salad. [< F *céleri* < dial. Ital. *sellari,* pl. of *sellaro* < L *selinon* parsley < Gk.]

ce·les·ta (sə·les′tə) *n.* A musical instrument having a keyboard and steel plates struck by hammers. [< F *célesta*]

ce·les·tial (sə·les′chəl) *adj.* **1.** Of or pertaining to the sky or heavens. **2.** Of heaven; divine. **3.** *Often cap.* Of or pertaining to the former Chinese Empire or the Chinese people. — *n.* **1.** A heavenly being. **2.** *Often cap.* A Chinese: a humorous term. [< OF < L *caelestis* heavenly < *caelum* sky, heaven] — **ce·les′tial·ly** *adv.*

celestial body A star, planet, comet, etc.

Celestial Empire The former Chinese Empire: translation of *Tien Chao,* Heavenly Dynasty.

celestial equator *Astron.* The great circle in which the plane of the earth's equator cuts the celestial sphere: also called *equinoctial line.*

celestial globe A globe whose surface depicts the geography of the heavens, fixed stars, constellations, etc.

celestial latitude See under LATITUDE.

celestial longitude See under LONGITUDE.

celestial navigation Navigation in which position is determined by observation of celestial bodies: also called *astronavigation, celonavigation.*

celestial pole Either of the two points where the earth's axis of rotation pierces the celestial sphere.

celestial sphere *Astron.* The imaginary spherical surface on which the heavenly bodies seem to lie, commonly conceived as of infinite diameter and enclosing the universe.

Cel·es·tine V (sel′is·tēn, sə·les′tīn), **Saint,** 1215–96, pope 1294–46: original name **Pietro di Mur·ro·ne** (dē mŏŏr·rō′ne).

cel·es·tite (sel′is·tīt) *n.* A vitreous, white, often bluish orthorhombic strontium sulfate, SrSO₄. Also **cel′es·tine** (-tin, -tīn). [< L *caelestis* heavenly; from its blue color]

ce·li·ac (sē′lē·ak) *adj.* Of or pertaining to the abdomen. Also spelled *coeliac.* [< L *coeliacus* < Gk. *koiliakos* < *koilia* belly, abdomen < *koilos* hollow]

celiac disease *Pathol.* A chronic intestinal disorder of young children, characterized by abdominal distention, diarrhea, emaciation of the groin, and nutritional disturbances.

cel·i·ba·cy (sel′ə·bə·sē) *n.* The state of being unmarried; especially, abstinence from marriage in accordance with religious vows. [< L *caelibatus* < *caelebs* unmarried]

cel·i·bate (sel′ə·bit, -bāt) *n.* One who remains unmarried, especially by vow. — *adj.* Unmarried, especially by vow.

cell (sel) *n.* **1.** A small room, as for a prisoner or monk; cubicle. **2.** A small compartment, receptacle, or cavity. **3.** A body of persons forming a single unit in an organization of similar groups. **4.** *Biol.* **a** The fundamental structural unit of plant and animal life, consisting of a small, usually microscopic mass of cytoplasm, variously differentiated in com-

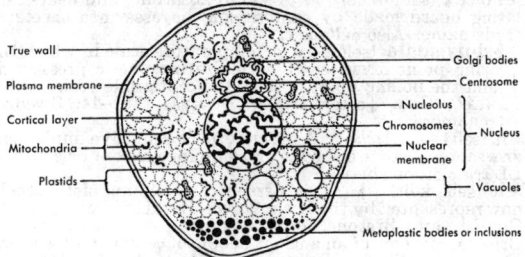

GENERALIZED CELL

position, structure, and function, usually enclosing a central nucleus and surrounded by a cell membrane (animal) or a cell wall (plant). **b** One of the cases or cuplike cavities containing an individual zoospore. **5.** *Entomol.* **a** A small space or cavity bounded by the veins or nerves on the surface of an insect's wing. **b** A single compartment of a honeycomb. **6.** *Bot.* **a** The cavity of an anther, containing pollen. **b** The seed-bearing cavity of an ovary or pericarp. **7.** *Electr.* The unit composing all or part of a battery, consisting of electrodes in contact with an electrolyte and in which a current is generated by means of chemical action. **8.** A small monastery or nunnery dependent on a larger one. — **daughter cell** *Biol.* One of two or more complete units into which a cell divides. — **dry cell** *Electr.* A primary cell with its electrolyte distributed in plaster or other porous substance. [< OF *celle* < L *cella* cell, small room]

cel·la (sel′ə) *n. pl.* **cel·lae** (sel′ē) *Archit.* The enclosed interior of an ancient Greek or Roman temple, containing a statue of the deity: also called *naos.* [< L, small room]

cel·lar (sel′ər) *n.* **1.** A room or enclosed space wholly or partly underground and usually beneath a building, used for storage, etc. **2.** A wine cellar; also, a stock of wines. — *v.t.* To put or keep in a cellar. [< AF *celer,* OF *celier* < L *cellarium* pantry < *cella* cell, small room]

cel·lar·age (sel′ər·ij) *n.* **1.** Space in or for a cellar. **2.** The charge for storing goods in a cellar.

cel·lar·er (sel′ər·ər) *n.* The keeper of a cellar, as the steward in a monastery.

cel·lar·et (sel′ə·ret′) *n.* A case or small cabinet for wine and liquor bottles, decanters, glasses, etc. Also **cel′lar·ette′.**

cell-block (sel′blok′) *n.* In prisons, a unit comprising a number or cells.

Cel·li·ni (chə·lē′nē, *Ital.* chel·lē′nē), **Benvenuto,** 1500–71, Italian sculptor and goldsmith; known for his autobiography.

cel·list (chel′ist) *n.* One who plays the cello. Also **'cel′list.**

cell membrane *Biol.* The delicate, semipermeable layer of protoplasmic material enclosing a living plant or animal cell.

cel·lo (chel′ō) *n. pl.* **·los** A bass instrument of the violin family, having four strings tuned an octave lower than the viola, and held between the performer's knees when played: also called *violoncello.* Also **'cel′lo.** [Short for VIOLONCELLO]

cel·loi·din (sə·loi′din) *n.* A substance composed of pyroxylin, used for embedding microscopic specimens so that they may be cut in thin sections. [< CELL(ULOSE) + -OID + -IN]

cel·lo·phane (sel′ə·fān) *n.* A specially treated regenerated cellulose that has been processed in thin, transparent, and impermeable strips or sheets. [< CELL(ULOSE) + -PHANE]

cel·lu·lar (sel′yə·lər) *adj.* **1.** Of, pertaining to, or like a cell or cells. **2.** Consisting of or characterized by cells: *cellular* tissue. [< NL *cellularis* < L *cellula.* See CELLULE.]

cel·lule (sel′yool) *n.* A small cell. [< L *cellula,* dim. of *cella* cell, small room]

cel·lu·li·tis (sel′yə·lī′tis) *n. Pathol.* A diffuse, often rapidly spreading inflammation of the tissues, especially of the skin and of the subcutaneous structures. [< NL]

Cel·lu·loid (sel′yə·loid) *n.* A hard, elastic, flammable plastic, made by subjecting guncotton mixed with camphor and other substances to hydraulic pressure: a trade name. Also **cel′lu·loid.**

cel·lu·lose (sel′yə·lōs) *n. Biochem.* An amorphous white carbohydrate, isomeric with starch, insoluble in all ordinary solvents, and forming the fundamental material of the structure of plants. [< L *cellula.* See CELLULE.]

cellulose acetate *Chem.* **1.** An acetic acid ester of cellulose, used in making artificial leather and synthetic textile yarns and fabrics. **2.** Acetate rayon.

cellulose nitrate *Chem.* A nitric acid ester of cellulose, used in the manufacture of explosives and lacquers: also called *nitrocellulose.*

cel·lu·lous (sel′yə·ləs) *adj.* Consisting or full of cells.

cell wall *Bot.* The relatively thick layer of cellulose surrounding the cell membrane of plant cells, of which it serves as a support during plant growth.

CELESTIAL EQUATOR
e Equator. *n* North Pole. *s* South Pole.

ce·lom (sē′ləm) See COELOM.
cel·o·nav·i·ga·tion (sel′ō-nav′ə-gā′shən) *n.* Celestial navigation (which see). [< L *caelum* sky + NAVIGATION]
Cel·o·tex (sel′ə-teks) *n.* A sound-absorbing and heat-insulating board made by compressing bagasse into sheets: a trade name. Also **cel′o·tex.**
Cel·si·us scale (sel′sē-əs) A temperature scale in which the freezing point of water at normal atmospheric pressure is 0° and the boiling point is 100°; the centigrade scale. Abbr. *C., Cel., Cels.* [after Anders *Celsius,* 1701–44, Swedish astronomer]
celt (selt) *n. Archeol.* A prehistoric or primitive implement or weapon made of stone or bronze, resembling an ax or chisel. [< LL *celtis* stone chisel]
Celt (selt, kelt) *n.* **1.** A person of Celtic linguistic stock, now represented by the Irish, Welsh, Highland Scots, Manx, Cornish, and Bretons, formerly by the ancient Gauls and Britons. **2.** One of an ancient people of central and western Europe, described as being fair and tall. Also spelled **Kelt. Celt.** Celtic.
Celt·ic (sel′tik, kel′-) *n.* A subfamily of the Indo-European family of languages, including ancient Gaulish, the Brythonic or Cymric branch (Cornish, Welsh, Breton), and the Goidelic or Gaelic branch (Irish, Scottish Gaelic, Manx). — *adj.* Of or pertaining to the Celtic peoples, their languages, or culture. Also spelled *Keltic.* Abbr. *C., Celt.*
Celtic cross An upright cross having a circle behind the crossbeam. For illustration see CROSS.
ce·ment (si-ment′) *n.* **1.** A substance, usually made from burned limestone and clay, that is applied as a mortar and by hardening will bind stones or bricks together, provide a smooth, waterproof surface, etc. When it will harden under water, it is called **hydraulic cement. Portland cement** is a hydraulic cement made by calcining limestone with chalk, mud, etc. **2.** Any soft material, as a preparation of glue, that, when hardened, will bind objects together. **3.** Something that unites. **4.** *Metall.* The finely divided metal or other substance used in cementation. **5.** The groundmass of igneous rock. **6.** *Dent.* An adhesive material used in filling teeth and in other dental work. **7.** *Anat.* Cementum. — *v.t.* **1.** To unite or join with or as with cement; bind firmly: to *cement* two pieces of wood; to *cement* a friendship. **2.** To cover or coat with cement, as a cistern. — *v.i.* **3.** To become united by means of cement; cohere. [< OF *ciment* < L *caementum* rough stone, stone chip < *caedere* to cut] — **ce·men′ter** *n.*
ce·men·ta·tion (sē′mən·tā′shən, sem′ən-) *n.* **1.** The act or result of cementing. **2.** *Metall.* The process of heating a solid with a finely powdered substance until they are closely combined into a desired material, as iron into steel.
ce·ment·ite (si-men′tīt) *n. Metall.* Iron carbide, Fe₃C, as used to harden steel.
cement mixer A concrete mixer (which see).
ce·ment·um (si-men′təm) *n. Anat.* The layer of bony tissue developed over the roots of the teeth about the fifth month after birth: also called *cement.* For illustration see TOOTH. [< L]
cem·e·ter·y (sem′ə-ter′ē) *n. pl.* **·ter·ies** A place for burying the dead; graveyard. [< L *coemeterium* < Gk. *koimētērion* < *koimaein* to put to sleep]
cen. **1.** Central. **2.** Century.
cen·a·cle (sen′ə-kəl) *n.* A small supper room, usually on an upper story. — **the Cenacle** The upper chamber in which Christ ate the Last Supper with his disciples. [< F *cénacle* < L *cenaculum* < *cena* dinner]
-cene *combining form Geol.* Recent; new: used in the names of geological periods: *Pliocene.* [< Gk. *kainos* new]
ce·nes·the·sia (sē′nis·thē′zhə, -zhē-ə, sen′is-) *n. Psychol.* The diffuse internal awareness of bodily existence, caused by the interaction of numerous unlocalized sensations whose aggregate expression may be of any degree of pain or pleasure: also spelled *coenesthesia.* Also **ce′nes·the′sis.** [< CEN(O)- + Gk. *aisthēsis* feeling] — **ce′nes·thet′ic** (-thet′ik) *adj.*
Ce·nis (sə·nē′), **Mont** (môn) See MONT CENIS.
ceno- *combining form* Common: *cenesthesia.* Also spelled *coeno-:* also, before vowels, **cen-.** [< Gk. *koinos* common]
cen·o·bite (sen′ə·bīt, sē′nə-) *n.* A member of a religious community: distinguished from *anchorite:* also spelled *coenobite.* [< LL *coenobita* < *coenobium* < Gk. *koinobion* convent < *koinos* common + *bios* life] — **cen′o·bit′ic** (-bit′ik) or **·i·cal** *adj.* — **cen·o·bit·ism** (sen′ə·bīt·iz′əm, sē′nə-) *n.*
ce·no·gen·e·sis (sē′nə·jen′ə·sis, sen′ə-) *n. Biol.* A form of development in which an individual organism is not typical of the group to which it belongs: opposed to *palingenesis.* Also spelled *coenogenesis, kenogenesis.* [< Gk. *kainos* new + *genesis* origin] — **ce·no·ge·net·ic** (sē′nə·jə·net′ik, sen′ə-) *adj.*
cen·o·taph (sen′ə·taf, -täf) *n.* An empty tomb; a monument erected to the dead but not containing the remains. [< MF *cenotaphe* < L *cenotaphium* < Gk. *kenotaphion* < *kenos* empty + *taphos* tomb] — **cen′o·taph′ic** *adj.*
Ce·no·zo·ic (sē′nə·zō′ik, sen′ə-) *Geol. adj.* Of or pertaining to the fourth and latest of the eras of geologic time, following the Mesozoic, and extending to and including the present.

See chart for GEOLOGY. — *n.* The Cenozoic period. Also *Caenozoic, Cainozoic.* [< Gk. *kainos* new + *zōē* life]
cense (sens) *v.t.* **censed, cens·ing** **1.** To perfume with incense. **2.** To offer burning incense to. [< INCENSE²]
cen·ser (sen′sər) *n.* A vessel for burning incense, especially in religious ceremonies: also called *thurible.* [< OF *censier,* short for *encensier* < Med.L *incensarium* < *incensum* incense]
cen·sor (sen′sər) *n.* **1.** An official examiner of manuscripts, plays, etc., empowered to suppress them, wholly or in part, if politically or morally objectionable. **2.** An official who examines dispatches, letters, etc., and may prohibit forwarding or publication, especially in time of war. **3.** Anyone who censures or arraigns. **4.** In ancient Rome, one of two magistrates who drew up the census and supervised public manners and morals. **5.** *Psychoanal.* Censorship. — *v.t.* To act as censor of; delete; suppress. [< L *censere* to judge]
cen·so·ri·al (sen·sôr′ē·əl, -sō′rē-) *adj.* Of or pertaining to a censor.
cen·so·ri·ous (sen·sôr′ē·əs, -sō′rē-) *adj.* **1.** Given to censure; judging severely; faultfinding. **2.** Containing or involving censure, as remarks. — **cen·so′ri·ous·ly** *adv.* — **cen·so′ri·ous·ness** *n.*
cen·sor·ship (sen′sər·ship) *n.* **1.** The action of censoring. **2.** The office or power of a censor. **3.** A system of censoring. **4.** *Psychoanal.* The aggregate of selective agencies that suppress unpleasant memories and thoughts and inhibit impulses and behavior deemed improper: also called *censor.*
cen·sur·a·ble (sen′shər·ə·bəl) *adj.* Deserving censure. — **cen′sur·a·ble·ness** *n.* — **cen′sur·a·bly** *adv.*
cen·sure (sen′shər) *n.* The expression of disapproval or blame; adverse or hostile criticism; reprimand. — **Syn.** See REPROOF. — *v.* **sured, ·sur·ing** *v.t.* **1.** To express disapproval of; condemn; blame. **2.** *Obs.* To pass judgment on. — *v.i.* **3.** To express disapproval or condemnation. [< F < L *censura* < *censere* to judge] — **cen′sur·er** *n.* — **Syn.** (noun) **1.** See REPROOF. — (verb) **1.** reprove, reprimand; blame; denounce. — **Ant.** (verb) praise, commend, approve.
cen·sus (sen′səs) *n. pl.* **·sus·es** **1.** An official count of the people of a country or district, with statistics as to age, sex, employment, etc. **2.** In ancient Rome, a similar enumeration, with special reference to property, in order to determine taxation. [< L < *censere* to assess] — **cen·su·al** (sen′shŏŏ·əl) *adj.*
cent (sent) *n.* **1.** The hundredth part of a dollar; also, a coin of this value: symbol *¢.* **2.** The hundredth part of a standard unit in other monetary systems, as of a guilder in the Netherlands. **3.** A hundred: used only in *percent, per cent.* Abbr. *c., C., ct.* (pl. *cts.*). [< F < L *centum* hundred]
cent. **1.** Centered. **2.** Centigrade. **3.** Centimeter(s).
cen·tal (sen′təl) *n. Rare* A hundredweight. [< L *centum* hundred]
cen·tare (sen′târ, *Fr.* sän·târ′) *n.* A measure of land area, equal to one square meter: also *centiare.* Abbr. *ca.* See table inside back cover. [< F *centi-* hundredth (< L *centum* hundred) + *are.* See ARE².]
cen·taur (sen′tôr) *n.* In Greek mythology, one of a race of monsters, having the head, arms, and torso of a man united to the body and legs of a horse. [< L *Centaurus* < Gk. *Kentauros*]

Cen·tau·rus (sen·tôr′əs) *n.* A constellation, the Centaur, containing the bright star Rigil Centaurus. Also **Cen′taur.** See CONSTELLATION.
cen·tau·ry (sen′tô·rē) *n. pl.* **·ries** One of certain small herbs (genera *Centaurium* and *Sabatia*) with opposite leaves and clusters of rose, purple, or pink flowers, especially *C. umbellatum,* reputed to have medicinal properties. [< Med.L *centauria,* ult. < Gk. *kentaureion* < *kentauros* centaur; because the centaur Chiron reputedly discovered its medicinal properties]

CENTAUR

cen·ta·vo (sen·tä′vō) *n. pl.* **·vos** (-vōz, *Sp.* -vōs) **1.** A small coin of the Philippines and various Spanish-American countries, equal to one hundredth of the monetary unit, usually of the peso. **2.** A similar coin of Portugal, the hundredth part of an escudo, and of Brazil, the hundredth part of a cruzeiro. [< Sp.]
cen·te·nar·i·an (sen′tə·nâr′ē·ən) *n.* One who is 100 years old. — *adj.* **1.** Of the age of 100 years. **2.** Pertaining to a period of 100 years.
cen·te·nar·y (sen′tə·ner′ē, sen·ten′ə·rē) *adj.* **1.** Of or pertaining to 100 or 100 years. **2.** Occurring every 100 years. — *n. pl.* **·nar·ies** **1.** A period of 100 years. **2.** A centennial. [< L *centenarius* a hundredfold < *centum* hundred]
cen·ten·ni·al (sen·ten′ē·əl) *adj.* **1.** Of an age or duration of 100 years. **2.** Of or marking a period of 100 years or its completion. **3.** Occurring every 100 years. — *n.* A 100th anniversary or its celebration. [< L *centum* hundred + *annus* year, on analogy with *biennial*] — **cen·ten′ni·al·ly** *adv.*
Centennial State Nickname of COLORADO.
cen·ten·ni·um (sen·ten′ē·əm) *n.* A century.
cen·ter (sen′tər) *n.* **1.** The point or place equally distant from the extremities or sides of anything; the middle part or

point: the *center* of a lake. **2.** *Geom.* **a** The point within a circle or sphere equidistant from every point on the circumference or surface. **b** The point within a regular polygon equidistant from the vertices. **3.** A point, axis, line, etc., about which a thing revolves. **4.** A place or point at which activity is concentrated or toward which people seem to converge: a *center* of interest. **5.** A point from which effects, influences, etc., proceed; source: the *center* of infection. **6.** *Mil.* The part of an army occupying the front between the wings. **7.** *Often cap.* A group, party, etc., having moderate views or tendencies; especially, in Europe, the moderate parties whose members are seated in front of the presiding officer in a deliberative assembly. **8.** In football, basketball, etc., a player who occupies a middle position, as in the forward line. **9.** *Physiol.* Any group of nerve cells controlling a specific bodily function: the respiratory *center*. **10.** The part of a target next to the bull's-eye, or a shot striking it. **11.** *Mech.* **a** One of two points, as in a lathe, between which an object is held and rotated. Compare DEAD CENTER, LIVE CENTER. **b** The depression in a piece of work into which such a center is inserted. — *v.t.* **1.** To place in or at the center; fix at the center. **2.** To direct toward one place; concentrate. **3.** To determine or mark the center of. **4.** To shape (a lens) so as to have it thickest in the center. **5.** In football, to pass (the ball) from the line to a backfield player. — *v.i.* **6.** To be centered or concentrated. — *adj.* Central; middle. Also, *Brit.*, *centre.* Abbr. (n., adj.) *c.*, *C.*, *ctr.* [< L *centrum* < Gk. *kentron* point (i.e., around which a circle is described)] — **Syn.** (noun) **1.** *Center*, *middle*, and *midst* all refer to an inner position away from the boundaries of a thing. Strictly, the *center* is a point, while the *middle* is an area that may be only approximately central: at the *center*, in the *middle*. *Midst* commonly im plies a group or multitude of surrounding objects: in the *midst* of the battle. — **Ant.** boundary, perimeter, rim.

center bit A carpenter's bit having a sharp point to guide the cutting edge.

cen·ter·board (sen′tər-bôrd′, -bōrd′) *n.* *Naut.* In flat-bottomed sailboats, a board or plate so hung that it can be lowered below the bottom through a watertight slot to prevent leeway. Also *Brit.* **cen′tre·board′.**

cen·ter·ing (sen′tər-ing) *n.* **1.** The act of placing in or converging toward a center; focusing. **2.** A temporary framework for an arch, dome, or vault while under construction. Also *Brit.* **cen′tring.**

center of buoyancy *Physics* In a freely-floating body, a point that is identical with the center of gravity of the displaced liquid.

center of gravity *Physics* The point about which a body freely acted upon by the earth's gravity, is in equilibrium in all positions. Abbr. *c.g.*, *C.G.*

center of mass *Physics* That point in a body at which all its mass could be concentrated without altering the effect upon it of a uniform gravitational field.

cen·ter·piece (sen′tər-pēs′) *n.* A piece at the center of anything; especially, an ornament in the center of a table, ceiling, etc. Also *Brit.* **cen′tre·piece′.**

cen·tes·i·mal (sen·tes′ə-məl) *adj.* **1.** Hundredth. **2.** Pertaining to or divided into hundredths. [< L *centesimus* hundredth] — **cen·tes′i·mal·ly** *adv.*

cen·tes·i·mo (sen·tes′ə-mō; *Ital.* chän·tā′sē·mō, *Sp.* sen·tes′ē-mō) *n.* *pl.* **·mi** (-mē) for def. 1, **·mos** (-mōz, *Sp.* -mōs) for defs. 2 & 3 **1.** An Italian coin, the hundredth part of a lira. **2.** A small Uruguayan coin, the hundredth part of a peso. **3.** A small Panamanian coin, the hundredth part of a balboa.

centi- *combining form* **1.** Hundred: *centipede*. **2.** In the metric system and in technical usage, one hundredth of (a specified unit): *centiliter*. [< L *centum* hundred]

cen·ti·are (sen′tē-âr) See CENTARE.

cen·ti·grade (sen′tə-grād) *adj.* Graduated to a scale of a hundred. [< F < L *centum* hundred + *gradus* step, degree]

centigrade scale A temperature scale in which the freezing point of water at normal atmospheric pressure is 0° and the boiling point is 100°: also called *Celsius scale*. Abbr. *c.*, *C.*, *cent.* See TEMPERATURE. For illustration see THERMOMETER.

cen·ti·gram (sen′tə-gram) *n.* In the metric system, the hundredth part of a gram. Also **cen′ti·gramme.** Abbr. *cg*, *cg.*, *cgm.* See table inside back cover.

cen·tile (sen′til, -tīl) *n.* Percentile (which see).

cen·ti·li·ter (sen′tə-lē′tər) *n.* In the metric system, the hundredth part of a liter. Also *esp. Brit.* **cen′ti·li′tre.** Abbr. *cl*, *cl.* See table inside back cover.

cen·time (sän′tēm, *Fr.* sän·tēm′) *n.* A small coin, the hundredth part of a franc. Abbr. *c.*, *C.* (pl. *cts.*). [< F < OF *centisme* < L *centesimus* hundredth]

cen·ti·me·ter (sen′tə-mē′tər) *n.* In the metric system, the hundredth part of a meter. Also *esp. Brit.* **cen′ti·me′tre.** Abbr. *c.*, *C.*, *cent.*, *cm*, *cm.* See table inside back cover.

cen·ti·me·ter-gram-sec·ond (sen′tə-mē′tər-gram′sek′ənd) *adj.* See CGS.

cen·ti·mo (sen′tə-mō) *n.* *pl.* **·mos** Any of various small coins, the hundredth part of a peseta, guarani, bolivar, or colon.

cen·ti·pede (sen′tə-pēd) *n.* An elongate, chiefly nocturnal myriapod (class *Chilopoda*) having a pair of legs to each segment, the front pair being modified into poison fangs. [< F, < L *centipeda* < *centum* hundred + *pes*, *pedis* foot.]

cen·ti·stere (sen′tə-stir) *n.* A hundredth of a stere. See table inside back cover. [< F *centistère*]

cent·ner (sent′nər) *n.* **1.** The hundredweight of various European countries, or 110.23 pounds, equal to 50 kilograms. **2.** *Metall.* A hundred pounds. **3.** In assaying, one dram. [< G *centner* hundred-weight < L *centenarius* of a hundred]

cen·to (sen′tō) *n.* *pl.* **·tos** **1.** A literary work, as a poem, patched together from the work of several authors. **2.** Any medley. **3.** *Obs.* Patchwork. [< L, patchwork cloak]

cen·tral (sen′trəl) *adj.* **1.** At, in, or near the center. **2.** Of or constituting the center. **3.** That exercises a controlling influence; dominant. **4.** Most important; principal; chief: a *central* event. **5.** *Anat.* **a** Designating a major division of the nervous system. **b** Of or pertaining to a centrum. **6.** *Phonet.* Formed with the tongue in a position intermediate between front and back: said of vowels. Abbr. *cen.* — *n.* A telephone exchange; also, an operator in such an exchange. [< L *centralis* < *centrum* center] — **cen′tral·ly** *adv.*

Central African Republic An independent Republic in central Africa; 238,224 sq. mi.; pop. 1,518,000 (1969); capital, Bangui: formerly *Ubangi-Shari.* French *République Centrafricaine.*

Central America The southernmost part of North America, bounded by Mexico and Colombia on the north and south, respectively. — **Central American** *adj.*

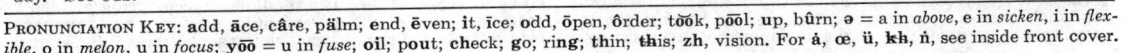

central angle *Geom.* An angle whose vertex is the center of a circle and whose sides are radii.

Central Asia See SOVIET CENTRAL ASIA.

central heating A system of heating a building by piping hot steam, water, or air from a central source to heat distributors located in separate rooms, etc.

Central India A former group of Indian states under British supervision; 51,946 sq. mi. Also **Central India Agency.**

cen·tral·ism (sen′trəl·iz′əm) *n.* A centralizing tendency or system; concentration of control in a central authority. — **cen′tral·ist** *n.* & *adj.* — **cen′tral·is′tic** *adj.*

cen·tral·i·ty (sen·tral′ə-tē) *n.* **1.** The state of being central. **2.** Tendency toward or situation at a center.

cen·tral·ize (sen′trəl·īz) *v.* **·ized, ·iz·ing** *v.t.* **1.** To bring to a center; make central; especially, to bring under a central authority. — *v.i.* **2.** To come to a center; concentrate. — **cen′tral·i·za′tion** *n.* — **cen′tral·iz′er** *n.*

Central Kar·roo (kə·rōō′) See GREAT KARROO.

central nervous system *Anat.* That part of the nervous system consisting of the brain and spinal cord. Abbr. *CNS, C.N.S.*

Central Powers The countries opposed to the Allies in World War I, consisting of Germany and Austria-Hungary, with their allies, Bulgaria and Turkey.

Central Provinces and Be·rar (bā-rär′) The former name for MADHYA PRADESH.

central spindle *Biol.* The fibrous portions of protoplasm lying between the asters in the mitotic division of a cell, and about which the chromosomes are grouped.

Central Standard Time See STANDARD TIME. Abbr. *c.s.t., CST, C.S.T.*

Central Valley The great trough in California between the Coast Ranges and the Sierra Nevada: also *Great Valley.*

cen·tre (sen′tər) *n.*, *adj.*, *v.t.* & *v.i.* **·tred, ·tring** *Brit.* Center.

centri- *combining form* Center: used in words of Latin origin, as in *centriole.* Compare CENTRO-. [< L *centrum* center]

cen·tric (sen′trik) *adj.* **1.** At, relating to, or having a center. **2.** *Physiol.* Related to or connected with a nerve center. Also **cen′tri·cal.** [< Gk. *kentrikos* < *kentron* center] — **cen′tri·cal·ly** *adv.* — **cen·tric·i·ty** (sen·tris′ə-tē) *n.*

cen·trif·u·gal (sen·trif′yə-gəl, -trif′ə-gəl) *adj.* **1.** Directed or tending away from a center; radiating: opposed to *centripetal.* **2.** Employing centrifugal force: a *centrifugal* pump. **3.** *Bot.* Developing from the center or apex outward. **4.** *Physiol.* Leading away from the central nervous system: efferent. — *n.* A machine employing centrifugal force; also, a rotary part in such a machine. [< NL *centrifugus* < L *centrum* center + *fugere* to flee] — **cen·trif'u·gal·ly** *adv.*

cen·trif·u·gal force *Physics* The inertial reaction by which a body tends to move away from a center about which it revolves.

cen·tri·fuge (sen'trə·fyōoj) *n.* A rotary machine with accessory containers, etc., for the separation by centrifugal force of substances having different densities. — *v.t.* **·fuged, ·fug·ing** To subject to the action of a centrifuge. [< F] — **cen·trif·u·ga·tion** (sen·trif'yə·gā'shən, -ə·gā'-) *n.*

cen·tri·ole (sen'trē·ōl) *n. Biol.* A minute structure, enclosed within the centrosome of the cell aster in cell division, and with which it makes up the central spindle. [< CENTRI- + -OLE²]

cen·trip·e·tal (sen·trip'ə·təl) *adj.* 1. Directed, tending, or drawing toward a center: opposed to *centrifugal.* 2. Acting by drawing toward a center: a *centripetal* pump. 3. *Bot.* Developing from without toward the center or in the direction of the apex. 4. *Physiol.* Conducting toward the central nervous system; afferent. [< NL *centripetus* < L *centrum* center + *petere* to seek] — **cen·trip'e·tal·ly** *adv.*

cen·trip·e·tal force *Physics* A force attracting a body toward a center around which it revolves.

cen·trist (sen'trist) *n.* One who takes a moderate position in politics, especially in France.

centro- *combining form* Center: used in words of Greek origin, as in *centrosphere.* Also, before vowels, **centr-.** Compare CENTRI-. [< Gk. *kentron* center]

cen·troid (sen'troid) *n.* 1. *Physics* Center of mass. 2. *Mech.* The point at which the area of a body may be concentrated without altering the moment of any line in its plane, as the center of a square or the intersections of the median lines of a triangle. [< CENTR(O)- + -OID]

cen·tro·some (sen'trə·sōm) *n. Biol.* The small area of protoplasm external to the nucleus of the cell containing the centrioles, at the center of each aster in mitosis. For illustration see CELL. [< CENTRO- + -SOME²] — **cen'tro·som'ic** (-som'ik) *adj.*

cen·tro·sphere (sen'trə·sfir') *n.* 1. *Geol.* The central portion of the earth. 2. *Biol.* In living cells, the sphere from which the astral rays diverge, and which surrounds the centrosome, if any. [< CENTRO- + -SPHERE]

cen·trum (sen'trəm) *n. pl.* **·trums** or **·tra** (-trə) 1. A center or central mass. 2. *Anat.* The body of a vertebra. [< L]

cen·tum languages (ken'təm) The Indo-European languages, including the Hellenic, Italic, Celtic, and Germanic subfamilies, Cuneiform Hittite, and Tocharian, in which the velar stop (k) of primitive Indo-European (or Indo-Hittite) is retained as a velar, as in Latin *centum* "hundred." Compare SATEM LANGUAGES.

cen·tu·ple (sen'tə·pəl, sen·tōo'pəl, -tyōo'-) *v.t.* **·pled, ·pling** To increase a hundredfold. — *adj.* Increased a hundredfold. [< F < LL *centuplus* hundredfold]

cen·tu·pli·cate (*v.* sen·tōo'plə·kāt, -tyōo'-; *adj. & n.* sen·tōo'plə·kit, -tyōo'-) *v.t.* **·cat·ed, ·cat·ing** To multiply by a hundred; centuple. — *adj. & n.* Hundredfold. [< LL *centuplicatus,* pp. of *centuplicare* to increase a hundredfold < L *centuplex* hundredfold] — **cen·tu·pli·ca'tion** *n.*

cen·tu·ri·al (sen·tōor'ē·əl, -tyōor'-) *adj.* Of or pertaining to a century in the Roman army, or to a period of 100 years.

cen·tu·ried (sen'chə·rēd) *adj.* Centuries old.

cen·tu·ri·on (sen·tōor'ē·ən, -tyōor'-) *n.* In the ancient Roman army, a captain of a century. [< L *centurio, -onis*]

cen·tu·ry (sen'chə·rē) *n. pl.* **·ries** 1. One hundred consecutive years. 2. A period of 100 years in any system of chronology, especially in reckoning from the first year of the Christian era. 3. In ancient Rome: a **a** A body of foot soldiers, originally of 100 men. **b** One of 193 electoral divisions. 4. A group or series of a hundred. *Abbr.* (defs. 1, 2) *c., C., cen.* [< L *centuria* < *centum* hundred]

century plant A succulent plant (*Agave americana*) of the amaryllis family, flowering in twenty to thirty years and then dying, popularly supposed to bloom once in a century: also called *American aloe.*

ceorl (cheôrl, kyûrl) *n.* In ancient England, a freeman of the lowest rank; a churl. [OE] — **ceorl'ish** *adj.*

Ce·os (sē'os) The ancient name for KEOS.

ce·pha·e·line (si·fā'ə·lēn, -lin) *n. Chem.* A white, crystalline alkaloid, $C_{28}H_{38}O_4N_2$, from ipecac, regarded as more powerful than emetine. [< NL *Cephaelis,* genus name of ipecac + -INE²]

ceph·a·lad (sef'ə·lad) *adv. Zool.* Toward the head: opposed to *caudad.* [< Gk. *kephalē* head + L *ad* toward]

ce·phal·ic (sə·fal'ik) *adj.* 1. Of or pertaining to the head. 2. At, on, in, or near the head. 3. Performing the functions of a head. [< F *céphalique,* ult. < Gk. *kephalikos* < *kephalē* head]

-cephalic *combining form* Head; skull: *brachycephalic.* [See CEPHALIC.]

cephalic index *Anat.* The ratio of the greatest breadth of the human head from side to side, multiplied by 100, to the greatest length from the glabella to the occiput. On the living, such indices are usually designated as *brachycephalic, mesocephalic,* and *dolichocephalic.* Compare CRANIAL INDEX.

ceph·a·li·za·tion (sef'ə·lə·zā'shən, -lī·zā'-) *n. Zool.* Concentration or localization of functions, powers, or parts in or toward the head: the *cephalization* of the vertebrate nervous system.

cephalo- *combining form* Head: *cephalometer.* Also, before vowels, **cephal-.** [< Gk. *kephalē* head]

ceph·a·lo·chor·date (sef'ə·lō·kôr'dāt) *Zool. adj.* Denoting any of a subphylum (*Cephalochordata*) of chordates having the notochord continued into the head, as the lancelets. Also **ceph·a·lo·chor'dal.** — *n.* A member of this group. [< NL *Cephalochordata* < CEPHALO- + CHORDATA]

ceph·a·lom·e·ter (sef'ə·lom'ə·tər) *n.* An instrument for measuring the head or skull; craniometer. [< CEPHALO- + -METER] — **ceph'a·lom·e·try** *n.*

Ceph·a·lo·ni·a (sef'ə·lō'nē·ə, -lōn'yə) The largest of the Ionian Islands, western Greece; 289 sq. mi.: Greek *Kephallenia.*

ceph·a·lo·pod (sef'ə·lə·pod') *Zool. n.* Any one of a class of highly developed marine mollusks (*Cephalopoda*), such as squids, cuttlefishes, octopuses, etc., having a clearly defined head and eyes, beaked mouth, ink sac, and tentacles or arms in the place of feet. — *adj.* Of or pertaining to the *Cephalopoda:* also **ceph'a·lo·pod'ic, ceph·a·lop·o·dous** (sef'ə·lop'ə·dəs). — **ceph·a·lop·o·dan** (sef'ə·lop'ə·dən) *n. & adj.* [< NL *Cephalopoda* < CEPHALO- + -PODA]

ceph·a·lo·tho·rax (sef'ə·lō·thôr'aks, -thō'raks) *n. Zool.* The anterior portion of certain arthropods, as crustaceans and arachnids, consisting of the united head and thorax. For illustration see SHRIMP. [< CEPHALO- + THORAX] — **ceph'a·lo·tho·rac'ic** (-thə·ras'ik) *adj.*

ceph·a·lous (sef'ə·ləs) *adj.* Having a head.

-cephalous *combining form* Headed: *hydrocephalous.* [< Gk. *kephalē* head]

Ceph·e·id variable (sef'ē·id) *Astron.* Any of a class of variable stars characterized by cycles of brightness associated with corresponding internal changes.

Ce·pheus (sē'fyōos, -fē·əs) In Greek legend, a king of Ethiopia, husband of Cassiopeia and father of Andromeda. — *n.* A constellation near Draco and Cassiopeia. See CONSTELLATION.

cer- *Var.* of CERO-.

ce·ra·ceous (si·rā'shəs) *adj.* Waxy. [< L *cera* wax]

Ce·ram (si·ram', *Du.* sā'räm) An island of Indonesia, in the Banda Sea west of New Guinea; 6,622 sq. mi.: also *Serang.* See map of INDONESIA.

ce·ram·al (sə·ram'əl) *n. Metall.* A combination of metals with ceramic materials, developed to provide resistance to very high temperatures: also called *cermet.* [< CERAM(IC) AL(LOY)]

ce·ram·ic (sə·ram'ik) *adj.* Pertaining to pottery and to articles made of fired and baked clay: also *keramic.* [< Gk. *keramikos* < *keramos* potter's clay]

ce·ram·ics (sə·ram'iks) *n.pl.* (*construed as sing. in def. 1.*) 1. The art of molding, modeling, and baking in clay. 2. Objects made of fired and baked clay. — **cer·a·mist** (ser'ə·mist) *n.*

ce·rar·gy·rite (sə·rär'jə·rīt) *n.* An isometric, easily sectile mineral, silver chloride, AgCl: also called *horn silver.* [< Gk. *keras* horn + *argyros* silver]

ce·ras·tes (sə·ras'tēz) *n.* A horned viper (*Cerastes cornutus*) of the Near East. [< L < Gk. *kerastēs* < *keras* horn]

ce·rate (sir'āt) *n.* A medicated ointment of oil or lard mixed with resin, wax, etc., and intermediate in consistency between ointments and plasters. [< L *ceratus,* pp. of *cerare* to smear with wax < *cera* wax]

ce·rat·ed (sir'ā·tid) *adj.* Covered with wax.

cerato- *combining form* Horn; of or like horn: *ceratodus.* Also, before vowels, **cerat-.** [< Gk. *keras, -atos* horn]

ce·rat·o·dus (sə·rat'ə·dəs, ser'ə·tō'dəs) *n.* The barramunda, a fish. [< NL < CERATO- + Gk. *odous* tooth]

cer·a·toid (ser'ə·toid) *adj.* Horny; horn-shaped.

Cer·ber·us (sûr'bər·əs) In classical mythology, the three-headed dog guarding the portals of Hades. — **Cer·be·re·an** (sər·bir'ē·ən) *adj.*

cer·car·i·a (sər·kâr'ē·ə) *n. pl.* **·car·i·ae** (-kâr'i·ē) *Zool.* A larval, parasitic form of a trematode worm, originating as a bud from a birth stage and having a tail that is lost in the adult. [< NL < Gk. *kerkos* tail] — **cer·car'i·al** *adj.*

cer·co·pi·the·coid (sûr'kō·pith'ə·koid, -pi·thē'koid) *Zool. adj.* Relating to or describing any of a superfamily or group (*Cercopithecoidea,* formerly *Catarrhini*) of Old World monkeys, including macaques, mandrills, baboons, langurs, and Barbary apes. — *n.* A member of this group. [< NL < L *cercopithecus* < Gk. *kerkopithēkos* < *kerkos* tail + *pithēkos* ape]

cere¹ (sir) *v.t.* **cered, cer·ing** 1. To wrap in cerecloth. 2. *Obs.* To coat with wax. [< MF *cirer* < L *cerare* to smear with wax < *cera* wax]

cere² (sir) *n. Ornithol.* In parrots and birds of prey, a waxlike, fleshy area about the bill, containing the nostrils. [< F *cire* < L *cera* wax]

ce·re·al (sir'ē·əl) *n.* 1. An edible, starchy grain yielded by certain plants of the grass family, as rice, wheat, rye, oats, etc. 2. Any of the plants yielding such grains. 3. A breakfast food made from a cereal grain. — *adj.* Of or pertaining to edible grains, or to the grasses that produce them. [< L *cerealis* of grain < *Ceres*, goddess of grain]

cer·e·bel·lum (ser′ə·bel′əm) *n. pl.* **·bel·lums** or **·bel·la** (-bel′ə) *Anat.* The massive, dorsally located part of the brain below and behind the cerebrum. It consists of a central lobe and two lateral lobes and acts as the coordination center of voluntary movements, posture, and equilibrium. Also called *epencephalon*. [< L, dim. of *cerebrum* brain] — **cer′·e·bel′lar** *adj.*

cer·e·bral (ser′ə·brəl, sə·rē′-) *adj.* **1.** Of or pertaining to the cerebrum or the brain. **2.** Appealing to or involving the intellect; intellectual. **3.** *Phonet.* Cacuminal. — *n. Phonet.* A cacuminal consonant. [< F *cérébral* < L *cerebrum* brain]

cerebral hemisphere *Anat.* One of the two halves into which the brain is divided.

cerebral palsy *Pathol.* Any paralysis affecting the ability to control movement and caused by brain lesions resulting from prenatal defect or birth injury.

cer·e·brate (ser′ə·brāt) *v.i.* **·brat·ed, ·brat·ing 1.** To have or manifest brain action. **2.** To think. [Back formation < *cerebration* < L *cerebrum* brain]

cer·e·bra·tion (ser′ə·brā′shən) *n.* **1.** The functional activity of the cerebrum. **2.** The act of thinking; thought.

cerebro- *combining form* Brain: *cerebrospinal.* Also, before vowels, **cerebr-.** [< L *cerebrum* brain]

cer·e·bro·side (ser′ə·brō·sīd) *n. Biochem.* A nitrogenous fatty substance containing a carbohydrate group and found in brain and nerve tissue. [< CEREBR(O)- + -OSE² + -IDE]

cer·e·bro·spi·nal (ser′ə·brō·spī′nəl) *adj. Anat.* Of or pertaining to the brain and the spinal cord, with their associated nerve structures. [< CEREBRO- + SPINAL]

cerebrospinal meningitis *Pathol.* An acute inflammation of the enveloping membranes of the brain and spinal cord, caused by various microorganisms and accompanied by fever, severe headaches, often red blotches on the skin, etc. Also **cerebrospinal fever.**

cer·e·brum (ser′ə·brəm, sə·rē′brəm) *n. pl.* **·bra** (-brə) *Anat.* The upper anterior part of the brain above the pons and the cerebellum, consisting of two hemispherical masses enclosed within the cortex and connected at the base by the corpus callosum. It constitutes the chief bulk of the brain in man and is assumed to be the seat of conscious processes. [< L] — **cer·e·bric** (ser′ə·brik, sə·rē′-) *adj.*

cere·cloth (sir′klôth′, -kloth′) *n.* Cloth treated with wax or the like, used especially to wrap the dead; a winding sheet. [Orig. *cered cloth* < CERE¹]

cer·e·ment (ser′ə·mənt) *n. Usually pl.* **1.** A cerecloth. **2.** A shroud. [< F *cirement* a waxing < MF *cirer.* See CERE¹.]

cer·e·mo·ni·al (ser′ə·mō′nē·əl) *adj.* Of, pertaining to, or characterized by ceremony; ritual; formal. — *n.* **1.** A prescribed set of ceremonies for some particular occasion; ritual. **2.** A rite; ceremony. — **cer′e·mo′ni·al·ism** *n.* — **cer′e·mo′ni·al·ist** *n.* — **cer′e·mo′ni·al·ly** *adv.*

cer·e·mo·ni·ous (ser′ə·mō′nē·əs) *adj.* **1.** Given to ceremony; studiously or overly polite. **2.** Characterized by or conducted with ceremony; formal: a *ceremonious* occasion. — **cer′e·mo′ni·ous·ly** *adv.* — **cer′e·mo′ni·ous·ness** *n.* — **Syn. 1.** punctilious, proper, decorous; conventional. Compare CEREMONIAL. — **Ant.** informal; unconventional.

cer·e·mo·ny (ser′ə·mō′nē) *n. pl.* **·nies 1.** A formal act or ritual, or a series of them, performed in a prescribed manner. **2.** Formal observances collectively; ritual. **3.** A rite that has lost all meaning; empty ritual. **4.** Adherence to forms; formality: with much *ceremony.* **5.** An act of formal courtesy. — **to stand on** (or **upon**) **ceremony** To insist upon formalities. [< OF *cerymonie* < L *caerimonia* awe, veneration]

Ce·ren·kov effect (se·ren′kôf) *Physics* Radiation from a charged particle passing through a medium at a velocity greater than that of light in the medium, detected by a **Cerenkov counter.** Also **Cerenkov radiation.** [after P. A. *Cerenkov,* Soviet physicist]

Ce·res (sir′ēz) In Roman mythology, the goddess of grain and harvests: identified with the Greek Demeter. — *n.* The first of the asteroids to be discovered, 1801.

ce·re·us (sir′ē·əs) *n.* Any of a genus (*Cereus*) of very tall, often nocturnal cactuses having large lateral tubular flowers, as the **night-blooming cereus** (*Selenicereus grandiflorus*). [< L *cereus* waxy < *cera* wax]

ce·ri·a (sir′ē·ə) *n. Chem.* An infusible compound, CeO_2, used in the manufacture of gas mantles. [< CERIUM]

ce·ric (sir′ik) *adj. Chem.* Containing cerium in its higher valence.

ce·rif·er·ous (sə·rif′ər·əs) *adj.* Yielding or producing wax. [< L *cera* wax + *ferre* to bear]

Ce·ri·go (chā′rē·gō) The Italian name for KYTHERA.

cer·iph (ser′if) See SERIF.

ce·rise (sə·rēz′, -rēs′) *n. & adj.* Vivid red; cherry. [< F, *cherry*]

ce·rite (sir′īt) *n.* A hydrous cerium silicate. [< CERIUM]

ce·ri·um (sir′ē·əm) *n.* A silver-white, ductile, highly reactive and electropositive element (symbol Ce) of the lanthanide series. See ELEMENT. [after the asteroid *Ceres*]

cerium metals A subgroup of the lanthanide series of elements, generally considered as extending from cerium to samarium.

cer·met (sûr′met) *n.* Ceramal. [< CER(AMIC) + MET(AL)]

CERN European Council for Nuclear Research (F *Centre Européen des Recherches Nucléaires*).

Cer·nă·uți (cher′nə·ōōts′) The Rumanian name for CHERNOVTSY.

cer·nu·ous (sûr′nyōō·əs) *adj. Bot.* Drooping or nodding, as a flower. [< L *cernuus* stooping]

ce·ro (sir′ō) *n. pl.* **·ros 1.** The king mackerel. **2.** A food fish (*Scomberomorus regalis*) of the Atlantic: also called *kingfish, pintado.* [< Sp. *sierra* < L *serra* saw]

cero- *combining form* Wax: *cerotype.* Also, before vowels, **cer-.** [< L *cera* or Gk. *kēros* wax]

ce·rog·ra·phy (si·rog′rə·fē) *n.* **1.** The art of engraving or writing on wax. **2.** Encaustic painting. [< Gk. *kērographia* < *kēros* wax + *graphein* to write] — **ce·ro·graph** (sir′ə·graf, -gräf) *n.* — **ce′ro·graph′ic** or **·i·cal** *adj.* — **ce·rog′·ra·phist** *n.*

ce·ro·plas·tic (sir′ə·plas′tik) *adj.* **1.** Pertaining to wax modeling. **2.** Modeled in wax. [< Gk. *kēroplastikos* < *kēros* wax + *plassein* to mold]

ce·rot·ic (si·rot′ik) *adj.* Of, pertaining to, or derived from beeswax, as **cerotic acid,** $C_{26}H_{53}COOH$. [< Gk. *kērotos* waxed < *kēros* wax]

ce·ro·type (sir′ə·tīp′, ser′-) *n.* **1.** A process of engraving in which a metal plate is coated with wax, the wax cut away according to some design, and the plate then used as a mold for electrotyping. **2.** A printing plate so produced. [< CERO- + TYPE]

ce·rous (sir′əs) *adj. Chem.* Of, pertaining to, or containing cerium in its lower valence.

Cer·ro de Pas·co (ser′rō thä päs′kō) A city in central Peru; a mining center; pop. about 28,000.

cert. or **certif.** Certificate; certificated.

cer·tain (sûr′tən) *adj.* **1.** Absolutely confident; convinced: He is *certain* of success. **2.** Sure; destined: He is *certain* to succeed. **3.** Beyond doubt or question; indisputable. **4.** Sure in its workings or results; dependable; also, unerring. **5.** Fixed; determined. **6.** Not explicitly stated or identified, but assumed to be determinable: on *certain* occasions. **7.** Some, or some at least: a *certain* improvement. — *n.* An indefinite number or quantity: *Certain* of the students were absent. — **for certain** Without doubt; surely. [< OF, ult. < L *certus*, orig. pp. of *cernere* to determine] — **Syn.** (adj.) **1.** confident, positive. **2.** inevitable; predestined. — **Ant.** uncertain, doubtful, dubious.

cer·tain·ly (sûr′tən·lē) *adv.* Without doubt; surely.

cer·tain·ty (sûr′tən·tē) *n. pl.* **·ties 1.** The state, quality, or fact of being certain. **2.** Something beyond doubt; a known fact.

— **Syn. 1.** *Certainty, certitude, assurance,* and *conviction* mean freedom from doubt. *Certainty* arises from examination of evidence and rigorous reasoning: a scientific *certainty. Certitude* is sometimes interchangeable with *certainty,* but more often is in use of unreasoning but profound faith and approaches more closely to *assurance.* Both *certitude* and *assurance* refer to a high degree of confidence and stress subjective experience rather than objective reality: the *certitude* of faith, *assurance* of victory. *Conviction* often implies the overcoming of previous doubt or skepticism: a deep *conviction* of a man's honesty. — **Ant.** conjecture, doubt.

cer·tes (sûr′tēz) *adv. Archaic* Truly; certainly; verily. [< OF < *a certes* < L *certus.* See CERTAIN.]

cer·tif·i·cate (*n.* sər·tif′ə·kit; *v.* sər·tif′ə·kāt) *n.* An official or sworn document stating fact; as: **a** *Law* A writing made in court and legally authenticated. **b** A bank's statement that a person has a specified sum on deposit: also **certificate of deposit. c** A statement that a ship has been legally registered: also **certificate of registry. d** A document showing completion of a course of study not leading to a diploma. **e** A document authorizing some professional pursuit: teaching *certificate.* **f** A document (**stock certificate**) showing an investment in a corporation: also **certificate of stock.** — *v.t.* **·cat·ed, ·cat·ing** To furnish with or attest by a certificate. Abbr. *cert., certif.* (pl. *certifs., cts.*). [< Med.L *certificatus,* pp. of *certificare.* See CERTIFY.] — **cer·tif′i·ca′tor** (-kā′tər) *n.* — **cer·tif′i·ca·to·ry** (-tôr′ē, -tō′rē) *adj.*

cer·ti·fi·ca·tion (sûr′tə·fi·kā′shən) *n.* **1.** The act of certifying or guaranteeing. **2.** The state of being certified. **3.** That which guarantees or vouches for. **4.** A certificate.

cer·ti·fied (sûr′tə·fīd) *adj.* **1.** Vouched for in writing; endorsed. **2.** Affirmed or guaranteed by a certificate. **3.** Legally committed to a mental institution.

certified check A check issued by a bank that guarantees that it is drawn on an account having sufficient funds.

certified public accountant See under ACCOUNTANT.

cer·ti·fy (sûr′tə·fī) *v.* **·fied, ·fy·ing** *v.t.* **1.** To give certain information of; attest. **2.** To testify to in writing; vouch for. **3.** To endorse as meeting set standards or requirements. **4.** To guarantee in writing on the face of (a check) that the account drawn on has sufficient funds for payment: said of banks. **5.** To make certain; assure. **6.** To declare insane; commit to a mental institution. — *v.i.* **7.** To make attestation; vouch (*for*) or testify (*to*). [< OF *certefier* < Med.L *certificare* to attest < L *certus* certain + *facere* to make] — **cer'ti·fi'a·ble** *adj.* — **cer'ti·fi'er** *n.*

cer·ti·o·ra·ri (sûr'shē·ə·râr'ē, -râr'ī) *n.* *Law* A writ from a superior to an inferior court, directing that a certified record of its proceedings in a designated case be sent up for review. [< LL, to be certified]

cer·ti·tude (sûr'tə·tood, -tyood) *n.* Complete confidence; certainty. — **Syn.** See CERTAINTY. [< MF < LL *certitudo* < L *certus*. See CERTAIN.]

ce·ru·le·an (sə·roo'lē·ən, -lyən) *adj. & n.* Sky blue; vivid blue. [< L *caeruleus* dark blue]

ce·ru·men (sə·roo'mən) *n.* Earwax. [< NL < L *cera* wax] — **ce·ru'mi·nous** *adj.*

ce·ruse (sir'oos, sə·roos') *n.* White lead used as a pigment. [< F *céruse* < L *cerussa*]

ce·rus·site (sir'ə·sīt) *n.* An orthorhombic, white to grayish-black lead carbonate, PbCO₃: also called *white lead.* Also **ce'-ru·site.** [< L *cerussa* white lead + -ITE¹]

Cer·van·tes (sər·van'tēz, *Sp.* ther·vän'tās), **Miguel de,** 1547–1616, Spanish novelist and dramatist; author of *Don Quixote*: full surname **Cervantes Sa·a·ve·dra** (sä'ä·vä'thrä).

cer·vi·cal (sûr'vi·kəl) *adj. Anat.* Of, pertaining to, in, or near the neck or the cervix uteri. [< L *cervix, -icis* neck]

cervico- *combining form* Neck: *cervicofacial.* Also, before vowels, **cervic-**. [< L *cervix, -icis* neck]

cer·vi·co·fa·cial (sûr'vi·kō·fā'shəl) *adj. Anat.* Pertaining to the neck and the face.

cer·vine (sûr'vīn, -vin) *adj.* **1.** Deerlike. **2.** Of or pertaining to deer or to the subfamily (*Cervinae*) of deer representing the typical deer. [< L *cervinus* < *cervus* deer]

cer·vix (sûr'viks) *n. pl.* **cer·vix·es** or **cer·vi·ces** (sər·vī'sēz, sûr'və·sēz) *Anat.* **1.** The neck. **2.** The cervix uteri. **3.** A necklike part. [< L]

cervix u·ter·i (yoo'tə·rī) *Anat.* The constricted neck of the uterus that distends during parturition. [< L]

ce·sar·e·an (si·zâr'ē·ən) *Surg.* *n.* A cesarean section. — *adj.* Of or pertaining to a cesarean section. Also spelled *caesarean, caesarian*: also **ce·sar'i·an.**

Ce·sar·e·an (si·zâr'ē·ən), **Ce·sar·i·an** See CAESAREAN.

cesarean section *Surg.* The birth of a child by section of the abdominal walls and the uterus: reputed to have been performed at the birth of Julius Caesar. Also **cesarean operation.** [< L *sectio caesarea* < *caesus,* pp. of *caedere* to cut]

ce·sar·e·vitch (si·zär'ə·vich) See CZAREVITCH.

ce·si·um (sē'zē·əm) *n.* A steel gray, ductile metallic element (symbol Cs) of the alkali group that includes potassium and rubidium: also spelled *caesium.* See ELEMENT. [< NL < L *caesius* bluish gray]

Čes·ké Bu·dě·jo·vi·ce (ches'ke boo'dye·yô'vi·tse) A city in western Czechoslovakia, on the Vltava; pop. 64,104 (est. 1957): German *Budweis.*

Čes·ko·slo·ven·sko (ches'kô·slō·ven'skô) The Czech name for CZECHOSLOVAKIA.

ces·pi·tose (ses'pə·tōs) *adj. Bot.* Growing in tufts or clumps, as a plant; matted; turfy: also spelled *caespitose.* [< L *caespes, caespitis* turf] — **ces'pi·tose·ly** *adv.*

cess (ses) *n. Irish* Luck; success: usually in the phrase **bad cess** to Bad luck to. [? Short for SUCCESS]

ces·sa·tion (se·sā'shən) *n.* A ceasing; stop; pause. [< L *cessatio, -onis* < *cessare* to stop]

ces·sion (sesh'ən) *n.* **1.** The act of ceding; a giving up, as of territory or rights, to another. **2.** A ceded territory. [< L *cessio, -onis* surrender < *cessus,* pp. of *cedere* to yield]

ces·sion·ar·y (sesh'ən·er'ē) *n. pl.* **·ar·ies** One to whom something is transferred or assigned; assignee or grantee.

cess·pool (ses'pool') *n.* **1.** A covered well or pit for the drainage from sinks, toilets, etc. **2.** Any repository of filth. Also spelled *sesspool*: also **cess/pit'.** [Origin uncertain]

c'est·à·dire (se·tà·dēr') *French* That is to say; namely.

c'est la guerre (se là gâr') *French* That's war.

c'est la vie (se là vē') *French* That's life.

ces·tode (ses'tōd) *n.* A tapeworm. — *adj.* Of or pertaining to the tapeworm. [< NL *Cestoda,* the tapeworms < Gk. *kestos* girdle]

ces·toid (ses'toid) *adj.* Ribbonlike, as the tapeworm.

ces·tus¹ (ses'təs) *n. pl.* **·tus** A wrapping of thongs, often weighted, worn about the hands by boxers in ancient Rome: also spelled *caestus.* [< L *caedere* < *caedere* to kill]

ces·tus² (ses'təs) *n. pl.* **·ti** (-tī) **1.** A belt or girdle. **2.** In classical mythology, the girdle of Aphrodite, which could awaken love in whoever beheld it. [< L < Gk. *kestos*]

CESTUS¹

ce·su·ra (si·zhoor'ə, -zyoor'ə) See CAESURA.

ce·ta·cean (si·tā'shən) *adj.* Of or belonging to an order

(*Cetacea*) of aquatic mammals, especially those of a fishlike form with teeth conic or absent, including the whales, dolphins, and porpoises. Also **ce·ta'ceous.** — *n.* A cetacean animal. [< NL *cetacea* < L *cetus* < Gk. *kētos* whale]

ce·tane (sē'tān) *n. Chem.* A saturated hydrocarbon of the methane series, C₁₆H₃₄, used as fuel for diesel engines. [< L *cetus* whale + -ANE²]

cetane number *Chem.* A measure of the performance characteristics of diesel engine fuels. It is the percentage of cetane (value = 100) in a mixture of cetane and *alpha*-methylnaphthalene (value = 0) that gives the same ignition performance as the fuel being tested. Compare OCTANE NUMBER.

Ce·ta·tea Al·bă (che·tä'tyä äl'bə) The Rumanian name for BYELGOROD–DNIESTROVSKI.

ce·te·ris pa·ri·bus (set'ər·is par'i·bəs) *Latin* Other things being equal. Abbr. *cet. par.*

Ce·tin·je (tse'tēn·ye) A town in Southern Yugoslavia; formerly the capital of Montenegro; pop. about 10,000: also *Tsetinye.*

ce·tol·o·gy (si·tol'ə·jē) *n.* The branch of zoology dealing with whales. [< Gk. *kētos* whale + -LOGY] — **ce·to·log·i·cal** (sē'tə·loj'i·kəl) *adj.* — **ce·tol'o·gist** *n.*

Ce·tus (sē'təs) *n.* A constellation, the Sea Monster. See CONSTELLATION. [< L]

Ceu·ta (syoo'tə, soo'-; *Sp.* thä'oo·tä) A Spanish enclave in Morocco, a fortified port city on the Strait of Gibraltar; pop. 88,000 (est. 1970).

cev·a·dil·la (sev'ə·dil'ə) *n.* Sabadilla (which see).

Cé·vennes (sā·ven') A mountain range in Southern France; highest peak, Mt. Mézenc, 5,755 feet.

Cey. Ceylon.

Cey·lon (si·lon') An island south of India, an independent member of the British Commonwealth; officially, *Sri Lanka*; 25,332 sq. mi.; pop. 13,341,000 (est. 1973); capital, Colombo. — **Cey·lon·ese** (sēl'ən·ēz, -ēs) *adj. & n.*

Ceylon moss A red seaweed (*Gracilaria lichenoides*) of the East Indies, a principal source of agar-agar.

Ce·yx (sē'iks) In Greek mythology, the husband of Alcyone.

Cé·zanne (sā·zàn'), **Paul,** 1839–1906, French painter.

Cf *Chem.* Californium.

cf. **1.** Calif. **2.** Compare (L *confer*).

c/f Carried forward (bookkeeping).

c.f. or **cf** Center field; center fielder (baseball).

C.F. or **c.f.** Cost and freight.

C.F.I. or **c.f.i.** Cost, freight, and insurance.

c.f.m. or **cfm** Cubic feet per minute.

c.f.s. or **cfs** Cubic feet per second.

cg or **cg.** or **cgm.** Centigram(s).

CG **1.** Commanding general. **2.** Coast Guard: also **C.G.**

C.G. or **c.g.** **1.** Center of gravity. **2.** Consul general.

C.G.H. Cape of Good Hope.

cgs The centimeter-gram-second system of measurement in which the unit of length is the centimeter, the unit of mass is the gram, and the unit of time is one second. Also **c.g.s.,** **CGS, C.G.S.**

C.G.T. (French) General Federation of Labor (F *Confédération Générale du Travail*).

ch. or **Ch.** **1.** Chain. **2.** Champion. **3.** Chancery. **4.** Chaplain. **5.** (*pl.* **chs.**) Chapter. **6.** Check (in chess). **7.** Chestnut. **8.** Chief. **9.** Child; children. **10.** Chirurgeon. **11.** Church. **12.** Of surgery (L *chirurgiae*).

Ch. **1.** Chaldean; Chaldee. **2.** China; Chinese.

C.H. *Brit.* Companion of Honor.

C.H. or **c.h.** **1.** Clearing-house. **2.** Courthouse. **3.** Customhouse.

chab·a·zite (kab'ə·zīt) *n.* A rhombohedral, white or flesh-colored hydrous silicate of calcium and aluminum. Also **chab'a·site** (-sīt). [< F *chabazie,* alter. of Gk. *chalazios,* a precious stone < *chalaza* hail + -ITE¹]

Cha·blis (shà·blē') *n.* A dry, white, Burgundy wine made in the region of Chablis, a town in north central France.

cha·bouk (chà'book) *n.* A horsewhip; especially, a long whip used in the Orient for corporal punishment. Also **cha'-buk.** [< Persian *chābuk* horsewhip]

chac·ma (chak'mə) *n.* A large, black-and-gray South African baboon (*Papio porcarius*). [< Hottentot]

Cha·co (chä'kō), **El** See GRAN CHACO.

cha·conne (shà·kôn') *n.* A musical form, important in the Baroque period, consisting of variations over a ground bass or a reiterated harmonic scheme, usually in slow triple meter, probably derived from a 16th century Spanish colonial dance: often called *passacaglia.* [< F < Sp. *chacona*]

cha·cun à son goût (shà·kœn nà sôn goo') *French* Each to his own taste.

Chad (chad) An independent Republic in north-central Africa; formerly an autonomous member of the French Community; 495,752 sq. mi.; pop. 3,977,000 (est. 1973); capital, Fort Lamy: French *Tchad.*

Chad (chad), **Lake** A lake in NW central Africa; 4,000–8,000 sq. mi., varying with rainfall.

Chad·wick (chad'wik), **Sir James,** 1891–1974, English physicist.

Chaer·o·ne·a (ker'ə·nē'ə) A town of ancient Boeotia, central Greece; scene of victories of Philip II of Macedon over

Athens and Thebes, 338 B.C., and of Sulla over Mithridates, 86 B.C.

chae·ta (kē′tə) *n. pl.* **·tae** (-tē) *Zool.* A bristle or seta. [< NL < Gk. *chaitē* hair]

chaeto- *combining form* Hair: *chaetopod.* Also, before vowels, **chaet-**. [< Gk. *chaitē* hair, bristle]

chae·tog·nath (kē′tog-nath) *n. Zool.* Any of a phylum (*Chaetognatha*) of small, active, widely distributed marine animals having characteristic bristles around the mouth and elongate, arrow-shaped, almost transparent bodies. [< NL < CHAETO- + Gk. *gnathos* jaw]

chae·to·pod (kē′tə-pod) *n. Zool.* Any of a class (*Chaetopoda*) of annelid worms having conspicuous segments provided with locomotor organs and setae, including clamworms and earthworms. [< NL < CHAETO- + -POD]

chafe (chāf) *v.* **chafed, chaf·ing** *v.t.* **1.** To abrade or make sore by rubbing. **2.** To make warm by rubbing. **3.** To irritate; annoy. — *v.i.* **4.** To rub. **5.** To be irritated; fret; fume: *to chafe* under the abuse. **— to chafe at the bit** To be impatient and irritable because of delay. — *n.* **1.** Soreness or wear from rubbing; friction. **2.** Irritation or vexation. [< OF *chaufer* to warm < L *calefacere* < *calere* to be warm + *facere* to make]

chaf·er (chā′fər) *n.* The cockchafer or other scarabaeid beetle. Also **chaf·fer** (chaf′ər). [OE *ceafor*]

chaff[1] (chaf, chäf) *n.* **1.** The external envelopes or husks of grain. **2.** Straw or hay cut fine. **3.** Any light refuse or rubbish. **4.** Any trivial or worthless matter. [OE *ceaf*] — **chaff′y** *adj.*

chaff[2] (chaf, chäf) *v.t. & v.i.* To poke fun (at). — *n.* Good-natured raillery. [Origin uncertain] — **chaff′er** *n.*

Chaf·fee (chaf′ē), **Adna Romanza,** 1884–1941, U.S. major general; organized the first mechanized brigade.

chaf·fer (chaf′ər) *v.i.* **1.** To haggle about price; bargain. **2.** To talk idly; chatter. — *v.t.* **3.** To say idly; bandy. **4.** *Obs.* To deal in; barter. — *n.* **1.** A haggling about terms; bargaining. **2.** *Obs.* Trade; traffic. [ME *chapfare* trade < OE *cēap* bargain + *faru* going] — **chaf′fer·er** *n.*

chaf·finch (chaf′finch) *n.* A song finch (*Fringilla caelebs*) of Europe, popular as a cage bird. [< CHAFF[1] + FINCH]

chafing dish A vessel with a heating apparatus beneath it, to cook or keep food warm at the table.

Cha·gall (shə-gäl′), **Marc,** born 1887, Russian painter active in France and the United States.

Cha·gas disease (chä′gäs) *Pathol.* A form of trypanosomiasis prevalent in South and Central America, communicated by the bite of the assassin bug. [after C. *Chagas,* 1879–1934, Brazilian physician]

Cha·gres (chä′gres) A river in central Panama flowing SW, through Gatun Lake in the Canal Zone, and NW to the Caribbean.

Chagres fever *Pathol.* A malignant malaria endemic along the Chagres.

cha·grin (shə-grin′) *n.* Distress or vexation caused by disappointment, failure, etc.; mortification. — *v.t.* To humiliate; mortify: used in the passive. [< F. See SHAGREEN.]
— **Syn.** (noun) *Chagrin, disappointment, humiliation, mortification,* and *vexation* are sorrowful states of mind. We feel *chagrin* if we have contributed to our own *disappointment* or *humiliation. Disappointment* suggests that one's expectations have not been fulfilled, but does not necessarily imply grief or self-reproach. *Humiliation* refers to a loss of esteem in the opinion of others, whatever the cause, while *mortification* is a severe or keenly distressing *humiliation. Vexation* is mild resentment or irritation, and may be directed at things entirely beyond one's control.

chain (chān) *n.* **1.** A series of connected rings or links, usually of metal, serving to bind, drag, hold, or ornament. **2.** *pl.* Anything that confines or restrains; shackles; bonds. **3.** *pl.* Bondage. **4.** Any connected series; a succession: *a chain* of events. **5.** A range of mountains. **6.** A series of stores, banks, etc., under a common management or ownership. **7.** *Chem.* A series of atoms or radicals of the same or different kinds, linked together and acting as a unit. **8.** A measuring line or tape of 100 links: the **engineer's** (or **Ramden's**) **chain** is 100 feet long; the **surveyor's** (or **Gunter's**) **chain** is 66 feet long. Abbr. (def. 8) *ch.,* Ch. — *v.t.* **1.** To fasten or connect with a chain. **2.** To fetter; bind. [< OF *chaeine* < L *catena*] — **chain′less** *adj.*

Chain (chān), **Ernst Boris,** born 1906, German pathologist active in England.

chain gang A gang of convicts chained together while doing hard labor.

chain letter A letter intended to be sent on from one to another in a series of recipients.

chain lightning Forked or jagged lightning.

chain mail Flexible armor consisting of interlinked metal chains, rings, or scales.

CHAIN
a Chain shot.
b Chain stitch.

chain·man (chān′mən) *n. pl.* **·men** (-mən) In surveying, a man who carries one end of the measuring chain. Also **chain′bear′er.**

chain pump A pump that raises water by means of buckets or disks on an endless chain passing under water and up over a wheel.

chain reaction **1.** *Physics* The self-sustaining fission of atomic nuclei, in which neutrons released by one fission induce fission in neighboring nuclei, as in a nuclear bomb or reactor. **2.** Any series of reactions or events, each of which develops from the preceding one.

chain shot Shot formed of two cannon balls or half balls linked by a short chain.

chain smoker One who smokes cigarettes or cigars in rapid succession.

chain stitch An ornamental stitch resembling a chain, used in sewing, crocheting, etc.

chain store *U.S.* One of a number of retail stores under the same ownership and selling similar merchandise.

chair (châr) *n.* **1.** A seat, usually having four legs and a back, for one person. **2.** A seat of office, authority, etc., as that of a professor or bishop. **3.** The office or dignity of one who presides or is in authority. **4.** A presiding officer; chairman. **5.** The electric chair (which see). **6.** A sedan chair (which see). **7.** An iron block for holding railroad track in place. **8.** A position in an orchestra. **— to take the chair** To assume the duties of a presiding officer; to preside at or open a meeting. — *v.t.* **1.** To seat in a chair. **2.** To install in office. **3.** To preside over (a meeting). **4.** *Brit.* To carry aloft in triumph, usually in a chair. [< AF *chaere,* OF *chaiere* < L *cathedra.* Doublet of CATHEDRA.]

chair car A parlor car (which see).

chair·man (châr′mən) *n. pl.* **·men** (-mən) **1.** One who presides over an assembly, committee, etc. Abbr. *chm., chmn.* **2.** One employed to wheel or carry others in a chair.

chair·wom·an (châr′wŏŏm′ən) *n. pl.* **·wom·en** (-wim′ən) A woman who presides over an assembly, committee, etc.

chaise (shāz) *n.* **1.** A two-wheeled, one-horse vehicle for two persons, having a calash top. **2.** A similar carriage with four wheels. **3.** A post chaise (which see). Also, *Dial., shay.* [< F, var. of *chaire* chair]

chaise longue (shāz′ lông′, *Fr.* shez lôṅg′) A couchlike chair having the seat prolonged to support the sitter's outstretched legs. [< F, lit., long chair]

Chal. Chaldaic; Chaldean; Chaldee.

cha·la·za (kə-lā′zə) *n. pl.* **·zas** or **·zae** (-zē) **1.** *Biol.* One of the two spirally twisted albuminous threads attached to each end of the lining membrane of an egg. For illustration see EGG. **2.** *Bot.* The part of an ovule where the coats are united to each other and to the nucellus. [< NL < Gk., hailstone, small lump]

Chal·ce·don (kal′sə-don, kal-sē′dən) An ancient Greek port in Asia Minor, on the Bosporus; site of modern *Kadiköy.*

chal·ced·o·ny (kal-sed′ə-nē, kal′sə-dō′nē) *n. pl.* **·nies** A waxy, translucent variety of quartz, often of a pale blue or grayish color: also spelled *calcedony.* [after *Chalcedon*]

chal·ced·o·nyx (kal-sed′ə-niks, kal′sə-don′iks) *n.* A variety of agate in which white and gray layers alternate. [< CHALCED(ONY) + ONYX]

chal·cid (kal′sid) *n.* A tiny hymenopterous fly (family *Chalcididae*) whose larvae are parasitic on the larvae of other insects. Also **chalcid fly.** [< NL < Gk. *chalkos* copper; with ref. to its color]

Chal·cid·i·ce (kal-sid′ə-sē) A peninsula of NE Greece extending into the Aegean. *Greek* **Chal·ki·di·ki** (khäl′kē-the̅-kē′), *Khalkídiki.*

chalco- *combining form* Copper; brass: *chalcography.* [< Gk. *chalkos* copper]

chal·co·cite (kal′kə-sīt) *n.* A metallic, blackish gray copper sulfide, Cu₂S: also called *copper glance.* [< Gk. *chalkos* copper + -ITE[2]]

chal·cog·ra·phy (kal-kog′rə-fē) *n.* The art of engraving on copper or brass. [< CHALCO- + -GRAPHY] — **chal·cog′ra·pher, chal·cog′ra·phist** *n.* — **chal′co·graph′ic** *adj.*

chal·co·py·rite (kal′kə-pī′rīt, -pir′īt) *n.* A tetragonal, metallic, yellow sulfide of copper and iron, CuFeS₂: also called *copper pyrites.* [< CHALCO- + PYRITE]

Chald. Chaldaic; Chaldean; Chaldee.

Chal·de·a (kal-dē′ə) In Biblical times, the southernmost Tigris and Euphrates valley, sometimes including Babylonia. Also **Chal·dae′a.**

Chal·de·an (kal-dē′ən) *n.* **1.** One of an ancient people of Chaldea, who conquered and ruled Babylon. **2.** One versed in the occult learning of the Chaldeans; an astrologer; sorcerer; soothsayer. **3.** The Semitic language of the Chaldeans. — *adj.* Of or pertaining to Chaldea, the Chaldeans, or their language or culture: also **Chal·da·ic** (kal-dā′ik). Also **Chal·dae′an.** Abbr. *Ch., Chal., Chald.*

Chal·dee (kal-dē′, kal′dē) *n.* **1.** A Chaldean. **2.** Biblical Aramaic: an erroneous use. — *adj.* Chaldean. Abbr. *Ch., Chal., Chald.*

chal·dron (chôl′drən) *n.* An old English weight or measure for coal and coke, equaling 32 to 36 bushels. [Var. of CAL-DRON]

cha·let (sha·lā′, shal′ā) *n.* **1.** A Swiss cottage with a gently sloping, projecting roof; also, any cottage built in this style. **2.** A herdsman's hut of the Alpine regions of Europe, especially in Switzerland. [< F; ult. origin uncertain]

Cha·lia·pin (shä·lyä′pin), Feodor Ivanovich, 1873–1938, Russian operatic bass.

chal·ice (chal′is) *n.* **1.** A drinking cup or goblet. **2.** *Eccl.* In the Eucharist: **a** A cup or vessel in which the wine is consecrated. **b** The consecrated wine. **3.** A cup-shaped flower. [< OF < L *calix, calicis* a cup]

chal·iced (chal′ist) *adj.* Having a cup-shaped flower.

chal·i·co·there (kal′i·kō·thir′) *n. Paleontol.* One of a family (*Chalicotheriidae*) of extinct ungulates related to both the horse and rhinoceros and having three-clawed hoofs. [< NL < Gk. *chalix* gravel + *thēr* wild beast]

chalk (chôk) *n.* **1.** A soft, grayish white or yellowish compact limestone, largely composed of the shells of foraminifers. **2.** A piece of soft limestone or similar material, frequently colored, used for marking or drawing. **3.** A score, tally, or notation of credit given. — *v.t.* **1.** To write or draw with chalk. **2.** To mark with chalk; record. **3.** To treat or dress with chalk. **4.** To make pale; blanch. — **to chalk up** To score; credit. — *adj.* Made with chalk. [OE *cealc* < L *calx* limestone] — **chalk′i·ness** *n.* — **chalk′y** *adj.*

chalk·stone (chôk′stōn′) *n. Pathol.* Tophus.

chalk talk A lecture during which the speaker makes diagrams or illustrations on a blackboard.

chal·lah (khä′lə, hä′-) See HALLAH. Also **cha′leh.**

chal·lenge (chal′ənj) *v.* **·lenged, ·leng·ing** *v.t.* **1.** To demand a contest with; summon to personal combat. **2.** To demand defiantly. **3.** To call in question; dispute. **4.** *Law* To object to; demand the rejection of, as a juror. **5.** To claim as due; demand: Such actions *challenge* respect. **6.** *Mil.* To stop and demand the countersign from. **7.** *U.S.* To claim that (a person) is not qualified to vote, or that (a vote) is invalid. — *v.i.* **8.** To make a challenge. **9.** To cry on picking up the scent: said of hunting dogs. — *n.* **1.** An invitation or dare to participate in a contest; a summons to personal combat. **2.** *Mil.* A sentry's call, requiring one to halt and give the countersign. **3.** A calling in question; dispute. **4.** *U.S.* A claim that a voter is not qualified, or that a vote is not valid. **5.** *Law* A formal objection, as to a juror. **6.** *Telecom.* An electromagnetic signal requesting identification, as in radar communication. [< OF *chalenger* < L *calumniari* to accuse falsely < *calumnia* slander. Doublet of CALUMNY.] — **chal′lenge·a·ble** *adj.* — **chal′leng·er** *n.*

chal·lis (shal′ē) *n.* A light fabric, usually of printed wool, rayon, etc. Also **chal′lie.** [Origin uncertain]

Chal·mers (chä′mərz), Alexander, 1759–1834, Scottish biographer and editor.

chal·one (kal′ōn) *n. Physiol.* An endocrine secretion that inhibits physiological activity. [< Gk. *chalōn*, ppr. of *chalein* to slacken]

Châ·lons-sur-Marne (shä·lôṅ′sür·märn′) A city in northern France; scene of the defeat of Attila, A.D. 451; pop. 48,558 (1968).

Cha·lon-sur-Saône (shä·lôṅ′sür·sōn′) A city in eastern France; pop. 47,004 (1968).

chal·u·meau (shal′yə·mō′, Fr. shà·lü·mō′) *n.* **1.** The lowest register of the clarinet. **2.** An old, single-reed wind instrument from which the clarinet developed. [< F < OF *chalemel* < L *calamellus*, dim. of *calamus* reed]

cha·lutz (khä·lōots′) See HALUTZ.

Chal·y·be·an (kal′ə·bē′ən, kə·lib′ē·ən) *adj.* Of or pertaining to the ancient **Chal·y·bes** (kal′ə·bēz), a people of Asia Minor, famous for their work in iron and steel. [< L *chalybeius*, ult. < Gk. *chalyps, chalybos* steel]

cha·lyb·e·ate (kə·lib′ē·āt, -it) *adj.* **1.** Impregnated with compounds of iron, as mineral waters. **2.** Tasting of iron. — *n.* A medicine or water containing iron in solution. [< NL *chalybeatus* < L *chalybeius.* See CHALYBEAN.]

chal·y·bite (kal′ə·bīt) *n.* Siderite (def. 1).

cham (kam) *n. Archaic* A Tatar or Mogul ruler; a khan. [< F < Turkic *khān* lord]

cha·made (shə·mäd′) *n. Mil.* A signal, made with drum or trumpet, for a parley. [< F < Pg. *chamada* < *chamar* < L *clamare* to cry out, shout]

cham·ber (chām′bər) *n.* **1.** A room in a house; especially, a bedroom. **2.** *pl.* An office or suite of rooms, as: **a** The office of a judge. **b** *Brit.* A set of rooms for one living alone. **3.** A room where a great personage holds audiences. **4.** A hall where an assembly, especially a legislative assembly, meets; also, the assembly itself: the lower *chamber.* **5.** A council; board: *chamber* of commerce. **6.** An enclosed space or cavity; compartment. **7.** An enclosed space at the breech of a gun for the explosive charge, or in the cylinder of a revolver for a cartridge. **8.** A chamber pot. — *v.t.* **1.** To provide with a chamber. **2.** To fit into or as into a chamber. [< F *chambre* < L *camera* vaulted room < Gk. *kamara.* Doublet of CAMERA.]

chamber concert A concert of chamber music.

cham·bered nautilus (chām′bərd) See under NAUTILUS.

cham·ber·lain (chām′bər·lin) *n.* **1.** An official charged with the domestic affairs of a monarch or lord; a chief steward. **2.** A high officer of a royal court. **3.** An official who receives the rents and fees of a municipality; a treasurer. **4.** *Archaic* The chamber attendant of a monarch or lord. [< OF *chamberlenc* < OHG *chamarlinc* < *chamara* room < *camera.* See CHAMBER.] — **cham′ber·lain·ship′** *n.*

Cham·ber·lain (chām′bər·lin) A prominent English family, including **Joseph,** 1836–1914, British statesman, and his sons, **Sir (Joseph) Austen,** 1863–1937, British statesman, and **(Arthur) Neville,** 1869–1940, British statesman; prime minister 1937–40.

Cham·ber·lin (chām′bər·lin), **Thomas Chrowder,** 1843–1928, U.S. geologist.

cham·ber·maid (chām′bər·mād′) *n.* A female servant who cleans and tends bedrooms in a house, hotel, etc.

chamber music Music composed for a small group of instruments, originally for performance in a private home or small concert hall.

chamber of commerce An association of merchants and businessmen for the regulation and promotion of business in a city or locality. Abbr. *C. of C.*

chamber pot A portable vessel used in a bedroom as a receptacle for urine, etc.

Cham·bers (chām′bərz), **Robert,** 1802–71, Scottish publisher and editor.

Cham·bord (shän·bôr′) A village in north central France; site of a celebrated chateau built by Francis I.

cham·bray (sham′brā) *n.* A strong, lightweight cotton fabric woven with colored warp and white filling. [after *Cambrai,* France]

cha·me·le·on (kə·mē′lē·ən, -mēl′yən) *n.* **1.** Any of various lizards (genus *Chamaeleon*), having the ability to change color. **2.** A person of changeable disposition or habits. [< L *chamaeleon* < Gk. *chamaileōn* < *chamai* on the ground + *leōn* lion] — **cha·me·le·on·ic** (kə·mē′lē·on′ik) *adj.*

Cha·me·le·on (kə·mē′lē·ən, -mēl′yən) *n.* A constellation. Also **Cha·mae′le·on.** See CONSTELLATION.

cham·fer (cham′fər) *v.t.* **1.** To cut away the corner of (a timber, etc.); bevel. **2.** To cut a furrow in; flute. — *n.* A surface produced by chamfering; a bevel. [< F *chanfrein* < OF *chanfraindre* to cut off an edge]

cham·fron (cham′frən) *n.* Armor for the front of a horse's head. Also **cham·frain** (cham′frin). [< OF *chanfrain*]

Cha·mi·nade (shà·mē·nàd′), **Cécile Louise Stéphanie,** 1861–1944, French composer.

cham·ois (sham′ē, Fr. shà·mwä′) *n. pl.* **·ois 1.** A mountain antelope (*Rupicapra rupicapra*) of Europe, the Caucasus, and western Asia. **2.** A soft leather originally prepared from the skin of the chamois, now from sheep, goats, deer, etc.: also spelled *shammy, shamois*: also **cham′my. 3.** The color of this leather, a yellowish beige. — *v.t.* To dress (leather or skin) like chamois. [< MF]

cham·o·mile (kam′ə·mīl) See CAMO-MILE.

Cha·mo·nix (sham′ə·nē, Fr. shà·mô·nē′) The valley of the Arve north of Mont Blanc, eastern France; site of **Chamonix-Mont-Blanc,** a resort town; pop. about 3,000. Also **Cha·mou·ni** (sham′ōō·nē, Fr. shà·mōō·nē′).

CHAMOIS
(2 feet high at shoulder; 45 inches long)

Cha·mor·ro Var·gas (chä·môr′rō vär′gäs) **Emiliano,** 1871–1966, Nicaraguan general; president 1917–20, 1926.

champ¹ (champ) *v.t.* **1.** To crush and chew noisily; munch. **2.** To bite upon restlessly. **3.** *Scot.* To mash; trample. — *v.i.* **4.** To make a biting or chewing movement with the jaws. — *n.* The action of chewing or biting. [Prob. imit.]

champ² (champ) *n. Slang* Champion.

cham·pagne (sham·pān′) *n.* **1.** A sparkling white wine made in the area of Champagne; also, any wine made in imitation of this. **2.** A still white wine from this region. **3.** The color of champagne, a pale or greenish yellow. — *adj.* Pertaining to this wine or to its color.

Cham·pagne (sham·pān′, Fr. shäṅ·pàn′y′) A region and former province of NE France.

cham·paign (sham·pān′) *n.* Flat and open country; a plain. — *adj.* Flat and open. [< OF *champaigne* < LL *campania.* See CAMPAIGN.]

Cham·paign (sham·pān′) A city in east central Illinois; pop. 56,532.

cham·pak (cham′pak, chum′puk) *n.* An Indian tree (*Michelia champaca*) of the magnolia family, having yellow, fragrant flowers and wood that yields a camphorlike substance. Also **cham′pac.** [< Hind. *campak* < Skt. *campaka*]

cham·per·ty (cham′pər·tē) *n. pl.* **·ties** *Law* An illegal bargain made by an outsider with one of the parties to a suit whereby the former undertakes to bear the expense or render services in consideration of receiving a share of the matter sued for. [< F *champart* < OF < L *campi pars* share of the field] — **cham′per·tous** (-təs) *adj.*

cham·pi·gnon (sham-pin′yən, *Fr.* shän-pē-nyôṅ′) *n.* An edible mushroom, especially the field mushroom (*Agaricus campestris*). [< MF, ult. < LL *campania* a field < L *campus*]

cham·pi·on (cham′pē-ən) *n.* **1.** One who has defeated all opponents and is ranked first, especially in a sport. **2.** Anything awarded first place. **3.** One who fights for another or defends a principle or cause. **4.** A fighter; warrior. *Abbr. ch., Ch.* — *adj.* Having won first prize or rank; superior to all others. — *v.t.* **1.** To fight in behalf of; defend; support. **2.** *Obs.* To challenge; defy. [< OF < LL *campio, -onis* fighter < L *campus* field] — **cham′pi·on·ess** *n. fem.*

cham·pi·on·ship (cham′pē-ən-ship′) *n.* **1.** The state of being a champion; supremacy. **2.** The position or honor of a champion. **3.** The act of championing; advocacy; defense.

Cham·plain (sham-plān′), **Lake** A lake between New York and Vermont, extending into Canada ; 600 sq. mi.; 125 mi. long.

Cham·plain (sham-plān′, *Fr.* shän-plaṅ′), **Samuel de,** 1567–1635, French explorer; founder of Quebec.

Cham·pol·lion (shäṅ-pô-lyôṅ′), **Jean François,** 1790–1832, French Egyptologist; deciphered the Rosetta stone.

— **Champollion-Fi·geac** (-fē-zhàk′), **Jean Jacques,** 1778–1867, French archeologist; brother of the preceding.

Champs É·ly·sées (shän zā-lē-zā′) A fashionable avenue in Paris. [< F, lit., Elysian fields]

chance (chans, chäns) *n.* **1.** The unknown or undefined cause of events; fortune; luck. **2.** An unusual and unexplained event; a happening: We saw him *by chance*. **3.** The probability of anything happening; possibility: There is a *chance* he will come. **4.** An opportunity: Now is your *chance* to see him. **5.** A risk or gamble; hazard. ʲ **6.** A ticket in a lottery. **7.** In baseball, an opportunity to make a play, counted as an error if not successful. **8.** *Archaic* An unfortunate event; a mischance. — *v.* **chanced, chanc·ing** *v.i.* **1.** To occur accidentally; happen. — *v.t.* **2.** To take the chance of; risk: I'll *chance* it. — **to chance upon** (or **on**) To find or meet unexpectedly or undesignedly. — *adj.* Occurring by chance: a *chance* acquaintance. [< OF *cheance* < LL *cadentia* a falling. Doublet of CADENCE, CADENZA.]

— **Syn.** (noun) **1.** *Chance, accident,* and *hazard* are compared as they denote the unknown or undetermined cause of an event. We ascribe to *chance* those events whose causes we cannot trace. *Accident* may be a close equivalent of *chance*: to meet a friend by *chance* (or by *accident*); more often, *accident* emphasizes lack of planning or purpose: to disclose a secret by *accident*. *Hazard* is applied to partially known or predictable causes: fearful of the *hazards* of old age. **4.** See OPPORTUNITY. — (verb) **1.** See HAPPEN.

chance·ful (chans′fəl, chäns′-) *adj.* **1.** Full of chance or chances; eventful. **2.** *Obs.* Dependent on chance.

chan·cel (chan′səl, chän′-) *n.* The space near the altar of a church reserved for the officiating clergy and the choir, often set apart by a screen or railing. [< OF < LL *cancellus* < L *cancelli,* pl., lattice, railing; because it is so enclosed]

chan·cel·ler·y (chan′sə-lər-ē, -slər-ē, chän′-) *n. pl.* **·ler·ies 1.** The office or dignity of a chancellor. **2.** The building or room in which a chancellor has his office. **3.** The office of an embassy or legation. Also **chan·cel·ry** (chan′səl-rē, chän′-).

chan·cel·lor (chan′sə-lər, -slər, chän′-) *n.* **1.** In some European countries, a chief minister of state. **2.** The chief secretary of an embassy. **3.** A secretary, as of a nobleman or ruler. **4.** The head of some universities. **5.** *U.S.* A judge of a court of chancery or equity. Also **chan′cel·or.** *Abbr. C.* — **Lord High Chancellor** *Brit.* The highest judicial officer of the crown: also **Lord Chancellor.** [< OF *chancelier* < LL *cancellarius* one who stands at the bar in a court < L *cancelli.* See CHANCEL.] — **chan′cel·lor·ship′** *n.*

Chan·cel·lor (chan′sə-lər, -slər, chän′-) A village in NE Virginia; scene of a Confederate victory in the Civil War (1863); pop. 3,175: formerly **Chan′cel·lors·ville′** (-lərz-vil′)

Chancellor of the Exchequer The minister of finance in the British cabinet.

chance-med·ley (chans′med′lē, chäns′-) *n.* **1.** *Law* A sudden affray, especially one resulting in unpremeditated homicide in self-defense. **2.** Inadvertent or random action. [< OF *chance medlee* mixed case or event < *chance* chance + *medlee,* pp. of *medler* to mix]

chan·cer·y (chan′sər-ē, chän′-) *n. pl.* **·cer·ies 1.** In the United States: **a** A court of equity, as distinguished from a court of common law. Also **court of chancery. b** Equity, or proceedings in equity. **2.** *Brit.* Before 1873, the highest court next to the House of Lords, presided over by the Lord High Chancellor, and since 1873, one of the five divisions of the High Court of Justice. **3.** A chancellery. **4.** A court of records; archives. *Abbr. c., C., ch., Ch.* — **in chancery 1.** *Law* Pending in a court of chancery; in litigation. **2.** In wrestling, with the head caught and held under an opponent's arm. **3.** In a hopeless predicament. [< OF *chancelerie* < *chancelier.* See CHANCELLOR.]

chan·cre (shang′kər) *n. Pathol.* A primary syphilitic lesion resembling a sore with a hard base. [< F < L *cancer* crab, ulcer. Doublet of CANKER.] — **chan·crous** (shang′krəs) *adj.*

chan·croid (shang′kroid) *n. Pathol.* A nonsyphilitic, localized venereal lesion of the genitals, caused by infection with a bacterium (*Hemophilus ducreyi*): also called *soft chancre*.

chanc·y (chan′sē, chän′-) *adj.* **chanc·i·er, chanc·i·est 1.** *Informal* Subject to chance; risky. **2.** *Scot.* Favored by chance; auspicious. — **chan′ci·ly** *adv.*

chan·de·lier (shan′də-lir′) *n.* A branched support for a number of lights, suspended from a ceiling. [< F < Med.L *candelarius* < L *candela* candle]

chan·delle (shan-del′) *n. Aeron.* An abrupt climbing turn of an airplane, utilizing momentum to gain altitude while the direction of flight is reversed or changed. [< F]

Chan·der·na·gore (chun′dər-nə-gôr′) A city in south central West Bengal, India; formerly a French settlement; pop. about 50,000.

Chan·di·garh (chun′dē-gär′) The new capital (1953) of Punjab, India, a newly constructed city in the eastern part of the State; pop. about 80,000.

chan·dler (chan′dlər, chän′-) *n.* **1.** A trader; dealer: ship *chandler.* **2.** One who makes or sells candles. **3.** *Brit.* A retailer of groceries, etc.; shopkeeper. [< OF *chandelier* chandler, candlestick. See CHANDELIER.]

chan·dler·y (chan′dlər-ē, chän′-) *n. pl.* **·dler·ies 1.** The goods, shop, or business of a chandler. **2.** A place for storing candles.

Chan·dra·gup·ta I (chun′drə-gŏŏp′tə) Fourth-century B.C. Indian ruler of the Maurya kingdom: also *Sandrocottus.*

chang (chang) *n.* A catty, an Asian weight.

Ch'ang-chou (chäng′jō′) A port city in southern Kiangsu Province, China; pop. 300,000 (est. 1958): also *Changchow, Wutsin.*

Chang·chow (chäng′jō′) **1.** A former name for LUNGKI. **2.** Ch'ang-chou.

Chang·chun (chäng′chŏŏn′) The capital of Kirin Province, China, in the western part; pop. 975,000 (est. 1957) formerly *Hsinking.* Also **Ch'ang/ch'un′.** See MANCHUKUO.

change (chānj) *v.* **changed, chang·ing** *v.t.* **1.** To make different; alter; transmute. **2.** To exchange; interchange: to *change* places. **3.** To give or obtain the equivalent of, as money in smaller units or foreign currency. **4.** To put other garments, coverings, etc., on: to *change* the bed. — *v.i.* **5.** To become different; vary. **6.** To enter upon a new phase: The moon has *changed.* **7.** To make a change or exchange. **8.** To transfer from one train, etc., to another. **9.** To put on other garments. — **to change color 1.** To blush. **2.** To turn pale. — **to change front 1.** *Mil.* To alter the direction of a line of attack. **2.** To alter one's attitude or principles. — **to change hands** To pass from one possessor to another. — *n.* **1.** The act of fact of changing; alteration; transformation. **2.** A substitution of one thing for another. **3.** Something new or different; variety; diversity. **4.** A passing from one phase, form, place, etc., to another: the *change* of the moon. **5.** A clean or different set of clothes. **6.** The amount returned when a coin or bill of greater value than the sum due has been tendered. **7.** Money of lower denomination given in exchange for higher. **8.** Small coins. **9.** *Music Usually pl.* Any order in which a peal of bells may be struck. **10.** A place for transacting business; an exchange: also **'change. 11.** *Obs.* Fickleness; caprice. — **to ring the changes 1.** To operate a chime of bells in every possible order. **2.** To repeat something with every possible variation. [< OF *changer* < LL *cambiare* to exchange] — **chang′er** *n.*

— **Syn.** (verb) **1.** *Change, modify, alter, vary, convert, transform,* and *transmute* mean to make different. *Change* means to make radically different, or to replace with something else: to *change* a pumpkin into a coach, to *change* horses. *Modify,* in a strict sense, means to limit: An adjective *modifies* a noun; but it is loosely used in the sense of *alter* or to make only slightly different. Weather *varies,* because it is different from one day to another in different ways. *Convert* implies the equivalence of the objects involved: to *convert* paper money into gold. We *transform* a thing by changing its appearance while leaving its substance the same; we *transmute* by changing its qualities: a face *transformed* by a disguise; lead *transmuted* into gold. Compare ADAPT.

change·a·ble (chān′jə-bəl) *adj.* **1.** Likely to change or vary; inconstant; fickle. **2.** Capable of being changed; alterable. **3.** Reflecting light so as to appear of different color from different points of view. — **change·a·bil·i·ty** (chān′jə-bil′ə-tē), **change′a·ble·ness** *n.* — **change′a·bly** *adv.*

change·ful (chānj′fəl) *adj.* Full of or given to change; variable. — **change′ful·ly** *adv.* — **change′ful·ness** *n.*

change·less (chānj′lis) *adj.* Free from change; enduring; unchanging. — **change′less·ly** *adv.* — **change′less·ness** *n.*

change·ling (chānj′ling) *n.* **1.** A child secretly left in place of another. **2.** *Archaic* One apt to change; a waverer. **3.** *Archaic* An idiot; simpleton.

change of life The menopause.

change·o·ver (chānj′ō′vər) *n.* A shift, transition, or alteration, as of methods, activities, etc.

change ringing The production of every possible variation in the ringing of a set of bells.

Chang·jin (chăng·jin) A river in North Korea, flowing about 160 miles, generally NE to the Yalu; **Changjin reservoir**, in its upper course, was the scene of fierce fighting in the Korean War (1950): Japanese *Chosin*.

Chang·sha (chăng/shä′) The capital of Hunan Province, eastern China, a port city on the Siang; pop. 703,000 (est. 1957). Also **Ch'ang/sha′**.

Chang·teh (chäng/du′) A city in NW Hunan province, central China; pop. about 94,800.

Chang Tso·lin (jäng′ tsō/lin′), 1873–1928, Chinese general.

chan·nel[1] (chan/əl) *n.* **1.** The bed of a stream. **2.** A wide strait: the English *Channel*. **3.** *Naut.* The deep part of a river, harbor, etc.; also, a navigable passage between the shallow parts. **4.** A tubular passage, as for liquids. **5.** The course through which anything moves or passes: to turn one's thoughts into other *channels*. **6.** *pl.* The official or proper routes of communication: to put a request through *channels*. **7.** *Telecom.* **a** A path for the transmission of telegraph, telephone, or radio communications. **b** A range of frequencies assigned for television transmission. **8.** A groove or furrow. **9.** A metal beam or bar having a bracket-shaped section: also **channel bar, channel iron.** — *v.t.* **chan·neled** or **·nelled, chan·nel·ing** or **·nel·ling 1.** To cut or wear channels in. **2.** To direct or convey through or as through a channel: to *channel* one's emotions. [< OF *chanel* < L *canalis* groove. Doublet of CANAL.]

chan·nel[2] (chan/əl) *n. Naut.* A thick plank or ledge attached to the outside of a vessel, to spread the shrouds and keep them clear of the bulwarks. [Alter. of *chainwale* < CHAIN + WALE[1] (def. 2)]

Channel Islands A group of British islands in the English Channel off the coast of Normandy, including Jersey, Guernsey, Alderney, and Sark; 75 sq. mi.; pop. 104,398 (1961).

Chan·ning (chan/ing), **William Ellery**, 1780–1842, U.S. Unitarian minister and writer.

chan·son (shan/sən, *Fr.* shän·sôn′) *n.* A song. [< F < L *cantio, -onis* song < *canere* to sing]

chan·son de geste (shän·sôn′ də zhest′) An Old French epic tale in verse, dealing with history and legend. [< F, song of noble deeds]

chant (chant, chänt) *n.* **1.** A simple melody in which a varying number of syllables are sung or intoned on each note. **2.** A psalm or canticle so sung or intoned. **3.** A song; melody. **4.** Any measured monotonous singing or shouting of words, as from a mob or spectators at a sports event. **5.** A singing intonation in speech. — *v.t.* **1.** To sing to a chant; intone, as in public worship. **2.** To celebrate in song. **3.** To recite or say in the manner of a chant. — *v.i.* **4.** To sing chants. **5.** To make melody; sing. **6.** To talk monotonously and continuously. Also, *Archaic*, **chaunt.** [< OF *chanter* < L *cantare*, freq. of *canere* to sing]

chant·age (chan/tij, chän/-; *Fr.* shän·täzh′) *n.* Blackmail. [< F. Cf. slang *faire chanter* to make (someone) sing, to make pay]

chant·er (chan/tər, chän/-) *n.* **1.** One who chants or sings; especially, a chorister or precentor. **2.** A priest or singer in a chantry. **3.** The pipe of a bagpipe on which the melody is played. For illustration see BAGPIPE. Also **chan/tor.**

chan·te·relle (shan/tə·rel′, chan′-) *n.* An edible yellow mushroom (*Cantharellus cibarius*). [< F < NL *cantharellus*, dim. of *cantharus* drinking cup < Gk. *kantharos*]

chan·teuse (shän·tœz′) *n. French* A woman singer.

chant·ey (shan/tē, chan/-) *n. pl.* **·eys** A rhythmical working song of sailors: also spelled *shantey, shanty.* Also **chant/y.** [Alter. of F *chantez*, imperative of *chanter* to sing]

chan·ti·cleer (chan/tə·klir) *n.* A cock: used as a proper name. [< OF *Chantecler* (name of the cock in the medieval epic *Reynard the Fox*) < *chanter* to sing, crow + *cler* aloud]

Chan·til·ly (shan·til/ē, *Fr.* shän·tē·yē′) A town in northern France; famous for its fine lace; pop. about 7,000.

chan·try (chan/trē, chän/-) *n. pl.* **·tries 1.** An endowment for the singing of daily masses for someone's soul; also, a chapel or altar so endowed. **2.** A chapel for subsidiary services. [< OF *chanterie* < *chanter*. See CHANT.]

Cha·nu·kah (khä/noo·kə) See HANUKKAH.

Chao·an (chou/än′) A city in SE China, on the Han; pop. about 300,000. Formerly **Chao·chow** (chou/jō′).

cha·os (kā/os) *n.* **1.** Utter disorder and confusion; also, anything so characterized. **2.** The supposed unformed original state of the universe. **3.** *Obs.* A vast chasm; abyss. [< L < Gk., abyss < *chainein* to gape, yawn]

cha·ot·ic (kā·ot/ik) *adj.* Utterly disordered and confused. Also **cha·ot/i·cal.** — **cha·ot/i·cal·ly** *adv.*

chap[1] (chap) *n.* **1.** *Informal* A fellow; lad. **2.** *Dial.* A buyer; purchaser. **3.** *Southern U.S.* A child. [Short for CHAPMAN]

chap[2] (chap) *v.* **chapped** or **chapt, chap·ping** *v.t.* **1.** To cause to split, crack, or become rough: The cold has *chapped* my hands. — *v.i.* **2.** To split, crack, or redden. — *n.* **1.** A crack or roughened place in the skin. **2.** *Scot.* A blow; rap. [ME *chappen.* Akin to CHIP[1], CHOP[1].]

chap[3] (chap, chop) *n.* **1.** A jaw. **2.** *pl.* The mouth and cheeks. Also spelled **chop.** [Cf. ME *chaft* jaw]

cha·pa·re·jos (chä/pä·rā/hōs) *n.pl. SW U.S.* Chaps. Also **cha·pa·ra·jos** (chä/pä·rä/hōs). [< Sp.]

chap·ar·ral (chap/ə·ral′) *n.* A thicket of dwarf oak, low thorny shrubs, etc. [< Sp. < *chaparra* evergreen oak]

chaparral cock The roadrunner. Also **chaparral hen.**

chaparral pea A thorny shrub (*Pickeringia montana*) of the pea family, growing densely over chaparrals.

chap·book (chap/book′) *n.* A small book containing tales, ballads, etc., formerly peddled by chapmen.

chape (chāp) *n.* **1.** A metal tip or trimming, as at the point of a scabbard. **2.** The piece by which a buckle is fastened to a strap. [< MF < LL *capa, cappa* cap]

cha·peau (sha·pō′, *Fr.* shä·pō′) *n. pl.* **·peaux** (-pōz′, *Fr.* -pō′) or **·peaus** (-pōz′) A hat. [< F]

chap·el (chap/əl) *n.* **1.** A place of worship subordinate to, and usually smaller than, a church. **2.** A recess or enclosed part of a church, for small or special services. **3.** *Brit.* A place of worship not connected with the established church. **4.** A building or room in a college, school, etc., for religious services; also, the services. **5.** A choir or orchestra attached to a chapel, court, etc. **6.** *Archaic* A printing house. **7.** A workers' association of printers. [< OF *chapele* < Med.L *cappella*, dim. of *cappa* cloak; orig., a sanctuary where the cloak of St. Martin was kept as a relic]

chap·el·mas·ter (chap/əl·mas/tər, -mäs/-) *n.* A Kapellmeister.

chap·er·on (shap/ə·rōn) *n.* **1.** An older woman who, for propriety, accompanies a young unmarried woman in public. **2.** An older person who accompanies and supervises a group of young people. — *v.t.* To act as chaperon to. Also **chap/er·one.** [< F, hood < *chape* cape; because she acts as a protector] — **chap·er·on·age** (shap/ə·rōn/nij) *n.*

chap·fall·en (chap/fô/lən, chop/-) *adj.* Dejected; crestfallen. Also *chopfallen.*

chap·i·ter (chap/i·tər) *n. Archit.* A capital. [< F *chapitre.* See CHAPTER.]

chap·lain (chap/lin) *n.* **1.** A clergyman who conducts religious services in a legislative assembly, for a military unit, etc. **2.** A clergyman attached to a chapel. Abbr. *ch., Ch.* [< OF *chapelain* < Med.L *cappellanus* < *cappella.* See CHAPEL.] — **chap·lain·cy, chap/lain·ship** *n.*

chap·let (chap/lit) *n.* **1.** A wreath or garland for the head. **2.** A rosary, or, more strictly, one third of a rosary. **3.** A string of beads, or anything resembling it, as an astragal molding, or a rope of frog or toad spawn. **4.** A device to hold a foundry mold in place. [< OF *chapelet*, double dim. of *chape* hood < LL *cappa* hooded cape]

Chap·lin (chap/lən), **Charles Spencer**, born 1889, English motion-picture actor and producer formerly active in the United States: called **Charlie Chaplin.**

chap·man (chap/mən) *n. pl.* **·men** (-mən) **1.** *Brit.* A peddler; hawker. **2.** *Archaic* A merchant; trader. [OE *cēapman* < *cēap* business + *man* man]

Chap·man (chap/mən), **Frank Michler**, 1864–1945, U.S. ornithologist. — **George**, 1559?–1634, English dramatic poet; translator of Homer. — **John**, 1775–1847, American pioneer: called *Johnny Appleseed.* — **John Jay**, 1862–1933, U.S. writer.

chaps (chaps, shaps) *n.pl. U.S.* Leather overalls without a seat, worn over trousers by cowboys to protect the legs: also called *chaparejos.* [Short for CHAPAREJOS]

chap·ter (chap/tər) *n.* **1.** A main division of a book or treatise, usually numbered. Abbr. *cap.* (L *caput*). **2.** A branch of a society or fraternity. **3.** *Eccl.* **a** A meeting of the canons of a cathedral or collegiate church; also, the canons collectively. **b** A meeting of the monks of a monastery or of an entire religious order. **4.** In certain church services, a short Scriptural passage read immediately after the psalms. **5.** Any period or portion of time, experience, development, etc.: an important *chapter* in history; a *chapter* of one's life. Abbr. *c., C., cc., ch., Ch.* (pl. *chs.*). — *v.t.* To divide into chapters, as a book. [< F *chapitre* < OF *chapitle* < L *capitulum*, dim. of *caput* head, capital, chapter]

chapter house 1. A place of assembly for a cathedral or monastery chapter. **2.** The house of a fraternity or sorority.

Cha·pul·te·pec (chə·pul/tə·pek, *Sp.* chä·pōōl/tā·pek′) A fortified hill SW of Mexico City; captured (1847) by U.S. forces in the Mexican War.

cha·que·ta (chä·kā/tä) *n. SW U.S.* A jacket, usually of leather, worn by cowboys. [< Sp.]

char[1] (chär) *v.* **charred, char·ring** *v.t.* **1.** To burn or scorch the surface of, as timber. **2.** To convert into charcoal by incomplete combustion. — *v.i.* **3.** To become charred. — **Syn.** See BURN[1]. — *n.* Charcoal. [? < CHARCOAL]

char[2] (chär) *n. pl.* **chars** or **char** Any of various salmonoid fishes (genus *Salvelinus*), allied to the lake trout; especially, the **Arctic char** (*S. alpinus*) of Canada and Europe: also spelled *charr.* [< Scottish Gaelic *ceara* blood red]

char[3] (chär) *Brit. n.* **1.** A chore; especially, a household task: also called *chare.* **2.** A charwoman. — *v.i.* **charred, char·ring** To do chores; work by the day; work as a charwoman. Also *chare.* [OE *cerr* turn of work]

char·a·banc (shar/ə·bangk, -bang) *n. pl.* **·bancs** *Brit.* A long, open vehicle with rows of seats facing forward. Also **char′-a-banc.** [< F *char à bancs* car with benches]

char·a·cin (kar′ə·sin) *n. Zool.* Any of a large and diversified family of fishes (*Characinidae*) native to South America and Africa, including the voracious piranha and many popular aquarium species. [< NL *Characinidae* < Gk. *charax*, a sea fish < *charassein* to sharpen, whet]

char·ac·ter (kar′ik·tər) *n.* **1.** The combination of qualities or traits that distinguishes an individual or group; personality. **2.** Any distinguishing attribute; characteristic; property. **3.** Moral force; integrity: He has no *character*. **4.** Reputation; also, good reputation. **5.** Status; capacity: in his *character* as president. **6.** A personage. **7.** A person in a play, novel, etc. **8.** *Informal* An eccentric or humorous person. **9.** A detailed description of a person's qualities or abilities. **10.** A written recommendation given by an employer to a former employee. **11.** A figure engraved, written, or printed; mark; sign; letter. **12.** Style of handwriting or printing. **13.** A form of secret writing; a cipher. **14.** *Genetics* Any structural or functional trait in a plant or animal resulting from the interaction of genes and regarded as hereditary in origin. **— in** (or **out of**) **character** In keeping (or not in keeping) with the general character or role. — *v.t.* **1.** To write, print, or engrave. **2.** *Archaic* To represent; portray. [< MF *caractere* < L *character* < Gk. *charaktēr* stamp, mark < *charassein* to sharpen, engrave, carve] — **char′ac·ter·less** *adj.*

character actor An actor who portrays characters markedly different from himself in age, temperament, etc.

char·ac·ter·is·tic (kar′ik·tə·ris′tik) *adj.* Indicating or constituting the distinctive quality, character, or disposition; typical: a *characteristic* gesture. — *n.* **1.** A distinctive feature or trait. **2.** *Math.* The integral part of a logarithm; index. — **char′ac·ter·is′ti·cal·ly** *adv.*
— **Syn.** (noun) *Characteristic, peculiarity, trait,* and *property* refer to qualities we discern in persons or things. A *characteristic* is that by which we recognize something for what it is; a hump is one of a camel's *characteristics*. A *peculiarity* is a *characteristic* that distinguishes one individual or kind from another. We speak of the qualities of persons as *traits*, and of the qualities of objects or substances as *properties*. Compare ATTRIBUTE, MARK[1].

char·ac·ter·i·za·tion (kar′ik·tər·ə·zā′shən) *n.* **1.** The act or result of describing qualities or peculiarities; representation; description. **2.** The creation of characters in writing or by acting.

char·ac·ter·ize (kar′ik·tə·rīz′) *v.t.* **·ized, ·iz·ing** **1.** To describe by qualities or peculiarities; designate. **2.** To be a mark or peculiarity of; distinguish. **3.** To give character to, as in writing or acting. — **char′ac·ter·iz′er** *n.*

character sketch **1.** A literary profile of a person or a type of personality. **2.** In the theater, a short impersonation.

char·ac·ter·y (kar′ik·tər·ē, -trē) *n. pl.* **·ter·ies** *Archaic* The expression of thought by characters or symbols; also, the characters collectively.

cha·rades (shə·rādz′, *Brit.* shə·rädz′) *n.pl.* (construed as *sing.*) A game in which words and phrases are to be guessed, sometimes syllable by syllable, from their representation in pantomime. [< F < Provençal *charrado* chatter < *charra* to chatter, prattle]

char·coal (chär′kōl′) *n.* **1.** A black, porous substance obtained by the imperfect combustion of organic matter, as wood, used as a fuel, adsorbent, filter, etc. **2.** A drawing pencil or crayon made of charcoal dust. **3.** A drawing made with such a pencil or crayon. — *v.t.* To write, draw, mark, or blacken with charcoal. [ME *charcole*; origin unknown]

Char·cot (shàr·kō′), **Jean Martin,** 1825–93, French physician and neurologist.

chard (chärd) *n.* A variety of white beet (*Beta vulgaris cicla*) cultivated for its large leaves and leafstalks, used for salad and as a vegetable: also called *Swiss chard, leaf beet.* [Var. of obs. *card* < F *carde* < L *carduus* thistle]

Char·din (shàr·daň′), **Jean Baptiste Siméon,** 1699–1779, French painter.

chare (châr) *n.* Char[3] (def. 1.) — *v.i.* **chared, char·ing** Char[3].

charge (chärj) *v.* **charged, charg·ing** *v.t.* **1.** To place a load upon. **2.** To place in or on (a thing) what it is intended or able to receive: to *charge* a furnace with ore. **3.** To load (a firearm). **4.** To diffuse something throughout; saturate, as water with carbon dioxide or air with electricity. **5.** To fill as if with electricity; make vibrant: to *charge* the air with tension. **6.** To supply (a storage battery) with a quantity of electricity. **7.** To accuse; impute something to: They *charged* him with murder. **8.** To command; enjoin. **9.** To instruct, exhort, or warn solemnly or authoritatively: to *charge* a jury. **10.** To entrust with a duty, responsibility, etc.; burden, as with care. **11.** To set or state as a price: to *charge* a dollar. **12.** To require payment from; make financially liable. **13.** To set down or record as a debt to be paid: to *charge* a purchase. **14.** To attack forcefully; rush violently upon or toward: to *charge* a fort. **15.** To place (a weapon) in position for use. **16.** *Heraldry* To place a bearing on. — *v.i.* **17.** To make an onset; rush violently. **18.**

To demand or fix a price. **19.** To make a charge or entry to one's debit. **20.** To crouch or lie down at command: said of dogs. **— Syn.** See ACCUSE. **— to charge off** To regard as a loss. — *n.* **1.** A load or burden. **2.** The quantity of anything that an apparatus or receptacle can hold at one time. **3.** The amount of explosive to be detonated at one time. **4.** The quantity of static electricity present in or on an apparatus, as a saturated storage battery. **5.** Care and custody; superintendence: to have *charge* of supplies. **6.** A person or thing entrusted to one's care. **7.** A responsibility or duty. **8.** An accusation; allegation. **9.** An address of instruction or admonition given by a judge to a jury at the close of a trial. **10.** An order or injunction; command. **11.** The expense or cost of something; price. **12.** Any pecuniary burden; tax; lien; expense. **13.** A debt or charged purchase, or an entry recording it. **14.** An onslaught or attack; also, the signal for this. **15.** *Heraldry* A figure or device; bearing. **16.** *Physics* The energy, measured in electrostatic units, present in an atomic particle, as the proton, electron, meson, etc. Abbr. (n. 11, 12, 13) *chg.* (pl. *chgs.*). **— Syn.** See PRICE. **— in charge of 1.** Having responsibility for or control of. **2.** Under the supervision or control of. ◆ The ambiguity of this phrase can be resolved by the use of *in the charge of*: The prisoner was *in the charge of* the detective. [< OF *chargier* < LL *carricare* to carry < L *carrus* cart. Doublet of CARRY.]

charge·a·ble (chär′jə·bəl) *adj.* **1.** That may be or is liable to be charged, as with a crime. **2.** Properly to be charged: This fee is not *chargeable* to my account. **3.** Liable to become a public charge, duty, or responsibility.

charge account A retail credit account to which purchases or services may be charged for future payment.

char·gé d'af·faires (shär·zhā′ də·fâr′, *Fr.* shär·zhā′ dà·fâr′) *pl.* **char·gés d'af·faires** (shär·zhāz′ də·fâr′, *Fr.* shär·zhā′ dà·fâr′) **1.** One who temporarily heads a diplomatic mission in the absence of the ambassador or minister: in full **chargé d'affaires ad interim. 2.** A diplomatic representative of the lowest rank, accredited to the foreign minister of a country to which his government does not accredit an ambassador or minister. Also **char·gé′.**

charg·er[1] (chär′jər) *n.* **1.** One who or that which charges. **2.** A horse trained for use in battle; a war horse. **3.** An apparatus for charging storage batteries.

charg·er[2] (chär′jər) *n. Archaic* A large shallow dish for meat. [ME *chargeour*]

Cha·ri (shä′rē) See SHARI.

char·i·ly (châr′ə·lē) *adv.* In a chary manner; carefully; sparingly; stingily.

char·i·ness (châr′ē·nis) *n.* **1.** The quality of being chary; carefulness; frugality; stinginess. **2.** *Obs.* Integrity.

Char·ing Cross (châr′ing) A district of Westminster metropolitan borough, central London, England.

char·i·ot (char′ē·ət) *n.* **1.** An ancient two-wheeled vehicle used in war, racing, processions, etc. **2.** A four-wheeled carriage. — *v.t. & v.i.* To convey, ride, or drive in a chariot. [< OF, aug. of *char* car < L *carrus* cart, wagon]

char·i·o·teer (char′ē·ə·tir′) *n.* One who drives a chariot.

Char·i·o·teer (char′ē·ə·tir′) *n.* The constellation Auriga. See CONSTELLATION.

cha·ris·ma (kə·riz′mə) *n.* **1.** *Theol.* An extraordinary spiritual gift or grace granted to individuals for the benefit of others, as the power to heal, etc.; loosely, any spiritual grace. **2.** A unique personal power conceived of as belonging to those exceptional individuals capable of securing the allegiance of large numbers of people. Also **char·ism** (kar′iz·əm). [< Gk., grace, favor]

char·is·mat·ic (kar′iz·mat′ik) *adj.* **1.** Spiritually endowed; divinely inspired. **2.** Having the power to command.

char·i·ta·ble (char′ə·tə·bəl) *adj.* **1.** Generous in giving gifts to the poor; beneficent. **2.** Inclined to judge others leniently; kindly; tolerant. **3.** Of or concerned with charity: a *charitable* enterprise. [< OF < *charité.* See CHARITY.] — **char′i·ta·ble·ness** *n.* — **char′i·ta·bly** *adv.*
— **Syn. 1.** benevolent. **2.** indulgent, kind, lenient, merciful. **3.** philanthropic.

char·i·ty (char′ə·tē) *n. pl.* **·ties 1.** The providing of help to the poor; almsgiving; also, public provision for the poor. **2.** That which is given to help the needy; alms. **3.** An institution, organization, or fund to aid those in need. **4.** Inclination to think well of others; tolerance; leniency. **5.** An act or feeling of benevolence or good will. **6.** Spiritual benevolence; brotherly love. **— Syn.** See BENEVOLENCE. [< OF *charite* < L *caritas, -tatis* love < *carus* dear]

cha·ri·va·ri (shə·riv′ə·rē′, shiv′ə·rē′, shä′rē·vä′rē) *n. pl.* **·ris** A mock serenade, as to a newly married couple, performed with tin pans, horns, kettles, etc.: also *chivaree, shivaree.* [< MF; ult. origin unknown]

chark (chärk) *Dial. v.t.* To char; turn into charcoal. — *n.* Charcoal. [Back formation < CHARCOAL]

char·kha (chûr′kə, chär′-) *n.* In India, a spinning wheel. Also **char′ka.** [< Hind. *carkhā*]

char·la·tan (shär′lə·tən) *n.* One who makes claim to skill and knowledge he does not possess; an impostor; quack. [< F < Ital. *ciarlatano* babbler < *ciarlare* to babble < *ciarla* chat, idle talk] — **char′la·tan′ic** (-tan′ik) *adj.* — **char′la·tan·ism, char′la·tan·ry** *n.*

Char·le·magne (shär′lə·mān), 742?–814, king of the Franks 768–814; emperor of the West as **Charles I,** 800–814: called **Charles the Great.**

Char·le·roi (shär′l-rwä′) A commune in SW Belgium; site of the first battle of World War I (1914); pop. 25,491 (est. 1959). Also **Char·le·roy′.**

Charles (chärlz), **Cape** The northern point at the entrance of Chesapeake Bay, Virginia.

Charles I (chärlz), 823–877, king of France; emperor as Charles II, 875–877: called **the Bald.**

Charles I, 1600–49, Charles Stuart, king of England 1625–1649; beheaded.

Charles II, 1630–85, king of England 1660–85.

Charles V, 1337–80, king of France 1364–80: called **the Wise.**

Charles V, 1500–58, emperor of Germany 1519–56, and king of Spain (as **Charles I**) 1516–56.

Charles VI, 1368–1422, king of France 1380–1422: called **the Mad,** the **Well-Beloved.**

Charles VII, 1403–61, king of France 1422–61: called **the Victorious.**

Charles IX, 1550–74, king of France 1560–74.

Charles X, 1757–1836, king of France 1824–30.

Charles XII, 1682–1718, king of Sweden 1697–1718.

Charles XIV John See under BERNADOTTE.

Charles Edward Stuart See (Charles Edward) STUART.

Charles Francis Joseph, 1887–1922, emperor of Austria (as **Charles I**), king of Hungary (as **Charles IV**) 1916–18.

Charles Mar·tel (mär·tel′), 688?–741, king of the Franks; grandfather of Charlemagne: called **the Hammer.**

Charles River (chärlz) A river in eastern Massachusetts, flowing about 60 miles to Boston Harbor.

Charles's law (chärl′ziz) *Physics* The statement that the volume of a gas kept at constant pressure varies directly with the absolute temperature: also called *Gay-Lussac's law.* [after J. A. C. *Charles,* 1746–1823, French physicist]

Charles's Wain (chärlz) The constellation Ursa Major.

Charles·ton (chärl′stən) *n.* A fast dance in ¼ time, popular in the 1920's. [after *Charleston,* S.C.]

Charles·ton (chärl′stən) **1.** The capital of West Virginia, in the central part; pop. 71,505. **2.** A port city in SE South Carolina; pop. 66,945.

Charles·town (chärlz′toun) Formerly a city, now part of Boston, Massachusetts; site of Bunker Hill.

char·ley horse (chär′lē) *U.S. Informal* A severe muscular stiffness or cramp in the arm or leg. [Origin unknown]

char·lock (chär′lək) *n.* Any of several herbs (genus *Brassica*) of the mustard family; especially, *B. kaber,* often a troublesome weed: also called *wild mustard.* [OE *cerlic*]

char·lotte (shär′lət) *n.* A dish made of fruits, whipped cream, custard, or the like, enclosed in a mold of cake, bread, or crumbs. [< F, from a feminine personal name]

Char·lotte (shär′lət) A city in south central North Carolina; pop. 241,178.

Char·lot·te A·ma·li·e (shär·lot′ə ə·mä′lē·ə) The capital of the Virgin Islands of the United States, a port city on southern St. Thomas; pop. 12,372 (est. 1970): formerly *St. Thomas.*

Char·lot·ten·burg (shär·lot′n·bûrg, *Ger.* shär·lôt′n·bŏŏrkh) The chief residential district of Berlin, a western suburb.

charlotte russe (rōōs) A dessert consisting of a mold of sponge cake with a filling of whipped cream or custard. [< F, *Russian charlotte*]

Char·lottes·ville (shär′ləts·vil) A city in central Virginia; pop. 38,880.

Char·lotte·town (shär′lət·toun) The capital of Prince Edward Island, Canada, a port city on the southern coast of the island; pop. 18,631.

charm¹ (chärm) *n.* **1.** The power to allure or delight; pleasing quality; fascination: the *charm* of poetry. **2.** Any fascinating or alluring quality or feature. **3.** A small ornament worn on a necklace, bracelet, etc. **4.** Something worn to ward off evil or ensure good luck; an amulet. **5.** Any formula or action supposed to have magic power; a spell. **6.** Originally, the chanting of a magic verse; incantation. **7.** *Physics* A property of a fundamental particle, such as its electric charge, that survives a reaction intact. — *v.t.* **1.** To attract irresistibly; delight; fascinate. **2.** To cast a spell upon

or influence as if by a spell; bewitch. **3.** To protect by or as by magic power: a *charmed* life. — *v.i.* **4.** To be pleasing or fascinating. **5.** To act as a charm. **6.** To use spells or incantations. [< F *charme* < L *carmen* song, incantation] — **charm′er** *n.*
— **Syn.** (noun) See TALISMAN. — (verb) **1.** captivate, enrapture. — **Ant.** disgust, repel.

charm² (chärm) *n. Archaic* Singing, especially of birds; also, song or melody. [ME *cherme,* var. of *chirm.* See CHIRM.]

char·meuse (shär·mœz′) *n.* A soft, light fabric with a satin finish. [< F, fem., *charmer*]

charm·ing (chär′ming) *adj.* **1.** Delightful; very attractive. **2.** Magically powerful. — **charm′ing·ly** *adv.*

char·nel (chär′nəl) *n.* A charnel house (which see). — *adj.* Suggesting or fit for receiving the dead; sepulchral; ghastly. [< OF < LL *carnalis* fleshy < L *caro, carnis* flesh]

charnel house A room or vault where bones or bodies of the dead are placed.

Charn·wood (chärn′wŏŏd), **Baron,** 1864–1945, Godfrey Rathbone Benson, English biographer.

Char·on (kâr′ən, kar′-) In Greek mythology, the ferryman who carried the dead over the river Styx to Hades. — *n.* A ferryman: a humorous use.

Char·pen·tier (shär·pän·tyā′), **Gustave,** 1860–1956, French composer. — **Marc-Antoine,** 1634–1704, French composer.

char·poy (chär′poi′) *n.* The typical bedstead or cot of India, usually having a wooden frame. Also **char·pai** (chär′pī′). [< Hind. *charpāī* < *chār* four + *pāī* foot]

char·qui (chär′kē) *n.* Jerky, a kind of meat. [< Sp. *charqui* < Quechua *echarqui* dried beef]

charr (chär) See CHAR².

char·ry (chär′ē) *adj.* **·ri·er, ·ri·est** Like charcoal.

chart (chärt) *n.* **1.** A map, especially one for the use of mariners. **2.** An outline map on which other than strictly geographical information can be shown, as climatic data, military operations, etc. **3.** A sheet showing facts graphically or in tabular form. **4.** A graph showing changes and variation of temperature, population, prices, wages, etc. — *v.t.* To lay out on a chart; map out. [< OF *charte* < L *charta* < Gk. *chartēs* leaf of paper. Doublet of CARD¹.]

char·ter (chär′tər) *n.* **1.** A document of incorporation of a municipality, institution, or the like, specifying its privileges and purposes. **2.** A formal document by which a sovereign or government grants special rights or privileges to a person, company, or the people. **3.** An authorization to establish a branch or chapter of some larger organization. **4.** A contract for the lease of the whole or part of a vessel for the conveyance of goods: also **charter party. 5.** Any hiring or leasing of transportation, as of an airplane. **6.** A written evidence of agreement or contract; a deed. **7.** A special privilege; immunity. — *v.t.* **1.** To hire or lease by charter. **2.** To hire (an airplane, train, etc.). **3.** To establish by charter; give a charter to. [< OF *chartre* < L *chartula,* dim. of *charta* paper] — **char′ter·er** *n.*

char·ter·age (chär′tər·ij) *n.* The act or business of chartering, especially vessels; also, a shipbroker's fee.

charter colony In American history, a colony established under a royal charter freeing it from direct parliamentary control, as Massachusetts.

char·tered accountant (chär′tərd) *Brit.* A member of an institute of accountants with royal charter. Abbr. *c.a., C.A.*

char·ter·house (chär′tər·hous′) *n.* A Carthusian monastery. [< MF *chartrouse*]

Charterhouse A school and asylum established in London in 1611 on the site of a Carthusian monastery.

charter member An original member of a corporation, order, or society.

Charter of the United Nations The charter adopted at San Francisco, April–June, 1945, making the United Nations a permanent organization.

Chart·ism (chär′tiz·əm) *n.* A movement in England (1838–1848) advocating social and political reform, based on principles embodied in the **People's Charter** of 1838; also, the principles of this movement. — **Chart′ist** *n. & adj.*

chart·less (chärt′lis) *adj.* Not mapped: a *chartless* ocean.

char·tog·ra·phy (kär·tog′rə·fē) See CARTOGRAPHY.

Chartres (shär′tr′) A city in north central France; famous for its Gothic cathedral; pop. about 29,000.

char·treuse (shär·trœz′; *for def. 2,* also shär·trooz′) *n.* **1.** A yellow, pale green, or white liqueur made by the Carthusian monks. **2.** A pale, yellowish green color. — *adj.* Of the color chartreuse. [< F < *La Grande Chartreuse,* chief Carthusian monastery in France]

char·tu·lar·y (kär′chŏŏ·ler′ē) See CARTULARY.

char·wom·an (chär′wŏŏm′ən) *n. pl.* **·wom·en** (-wim′ən) *Brit.* A woman employed to do housework, or cleaning and scrubbing, as in office buildings. [< CHAR³ + WOMAN]

char·y (châr′ē) *adj.* **char·i·er, char·i·est 1.** Cautious; careful; wary: *chary* of strangers. **2.** Fastidious; particular: *chary* of one's food. **3.** Sparing; frugal; stingy: *chary* of praise. [OE *cearig* sorrowful, sad < *cearu* care]

Cha·ryb·dis (kə·rib′dis) In Greek mythology, a monster dwelling in a whirlpool on the Sicilian coast opposite the cave of Scylla; also, the whirlpool. See SCYLLA.

chase[1] (chās) *v.* **chased, chas·ing** *v.t.* **1.** To pursue with intent to catch, capture, overtake, or harm. **2.** To follow regularly or persistently; run after. **3.** To put to flight; drive; dispel: often with *away, out,* or *off.* — *v.i.* **4.** To follow in pursuit. **5.** *Informal* To rush; go hurriedly. — *n.* **1.** The act of chasing or pursuing. **2.** The sport of hunting: preceded by *the.* **3.** That which is pursued; prey; quarry. **4.** In Great Britain: **a** An unenclosed private game preserve. **b** The right to hunt or keep game on a certain tract. — **to give chase** To pursue. [< OF *chacier* < LL *captiare,* freq. of L *capere* to take, hold. Doublet of CATCH.]

chase[2] (chās) *n.* **1.** *Printing* A rectangular metal frame into which pages of type are fastened for printing or plate-making. **2.** The part of a cannon between the trunnions and the swell of the muzzle. **3.** A groove or slot; hollow; trench. **4.** A longitudinal groove for a tenon or tongue. — *v.t.* **chased, chas·ing 1.** To indent or groove. **2.** To ornament by embossing; engrave. [Fusion of F *chasse* and *chas,* both ult. < L *capsa* box; *v.* def. 2 < ENCHASE] — **chas′er** *n.*

Chase (chās), **Mary Ellen,** 1887–1973, U.S. educator and author. — **Salmon Portland,** 1808–73, U.S. jurist; chief justice of the Supreme Court 1864–73. — **Samuel,** 1741–1811, American patriot; signer of the Declaration of Independence; associate justice of the Supreme Court 1796–1811.

chas·er (chā′sər) *n.* **1.** One who chases or pursues; a hunter. **2.** A pursuing vessel. **3.** A cannon at the bow (*bow chaser*) or stern (*stern chaser*) of a ship, for use during pursuit of or by another vessel: also **chase gun. 4.** *U.S. Informal* A drink of water or the like taken after strong liquor.

chasm (kaz′əm) *n.* **1.** A yawning crack in the earth's surface; a deep gorge. **2.** An abrupt interruption of continuity; a gap or void. **3.** Any great difference of opinion, sentiment, loyalty, etc. [< Gk. *chasma* < *chainein* to gape, open wide] — **chas·mal** (kaz′məl) *adj.*

chas·sé (sha·sā′) *n.* A sideward movement in dancing consisting of a series of quick, gliding steps in which the same foot always leads. — *v.i.* **chas·séd, chas·sé·ing** To perform a chassé. [< F, pp. of *chasser* to chase]

chasse·pot (shȧs·pō′) *n.* A French type of needle gun. [after A. A. *Chassepot,* 1833–1905, French inventor]

chas·seur (sha·sûr′) *n.* **1.** One of a body of light cavalry or infantry trained for rapid maneuvers, as in the French army. **2.** A liveried servant or attendant. **3.** A huntsman. [< F, hunter < *chasser* to chase < OF *chacier.* See CHASE[1].]

Chas·si·dim (khä·sē′dim) *n.* *pl.* of **Chas·sid** (khä′sid) A sect of Jewish mystics: also spelled *Hasidim.* [< Hebrew, pious] — **Chas·si·dic** (khä·sē′dik) *adj.*

chas·sis (shas′ē, chas′ē) *n.* *pl.* **chas·sis** (shas′ēz, chas′ēz) **1.** The flat, rectangular frame that supports the body of a motor vehicle and includes the wheels, springs, motor, etc. **2.** *Aeron.* The landing gear of an aircraft as the wheels, floats, or other structures that support the main weight. **3.** *Telecom.* **a** The metal framework to which the tubes and other components of a radio receiver, amplifier, etc., are attached. **b** The assembled framework and components. **4.** A movable frame on which the top carriage of a gun moves backward and forward. [< F *chassis* < *chas.* See CHASE[2].]

chaste (chāst) *adj.* **1.** Not guilty of unlawful sexual intercourse; virtuous. **2.** Pure in character or conduct; not indecent. **3.** Pure in artistic or literary style; simple. [< OF < L *castus* pure] — **chaste′ly** *adv.* — **chaste′ness** *n.*

chas·ten (chā′sən) *v.t.* **1.** To discipline by punishment or affliction; chastise. **2.** To moderate; soften; temper. **3.** To refine; purify. [Earlier *chaste* < OF *chastier* < L *castigare* to correct. See CASTIGATE.] — **chast′en·er** *n.*

— **Syn. 1.** *Chasten, correct, discipline, chastise,* and *castigate* suggest various degrees of punishment inflicted to cause a person to change his conduct. *Chasten, correct,* and *discipline* imply success in this effort, with *chasten* serving as a general term to cover mild or severe punishment, whether physical or moral. *Correct* suggests mild punishment or sometimes mere verbal reproof. *Discipline,* like *correct,* looks to future conduct, and stresses training rather than punishment: to *correct* an unruly child, to *discipline* soldiers. *Chastise* and *castigate* refer to corporal punishment as retribution for past misconduct rather than as a corrective measure; of the two, *castigate* is harsher and more severe. Compare REPROVE, SCOLD.

chas·tise (chas·tīz′) *v.t.* **·tised, ·tis·ing 1.** To punish, especially by beating. **2.** *Archaic* To refine; chasten. — **Syn.** See CHASTEN. [ME *chastisen*] — **chas·tis′a·ble** *adj.* — **chas·tise·ment** (chas′tiz·mənt, chas·tīz′-) *n.* — **chas·tis′er** *n.*

chas·ti·ty (chas′tə·tē) *n.* **1.** The state or quality of being chaste; purity. **2.** Virginity or celibacy: a vow of *chastity.* [< OF *chastete* < L *castitas, -tatis* purity < *castus* pure]

chastity belt In the Middle Ages, a girdlelike device locked on a woman to prevent sexual intercourse during her husband's absence.

chas·u·ble (chaz′yə·bəl, chas′-) *n.* A long, sleeveless vestment worn over the alb by a priest when celebrating the Eucharist. [< F < Med.L *casubula,* var. of *casula* cloak < L, dim. of *casa* house]

chat[1] (chat) *v.i.* **chat·ted, chat·ting** To converse in an easy or gossipy manner; talk familiarly. — **Syn.** See TALK. — *n.* **1.** Easy, informal conversation. **2.** Any of several singing birds: so called from their notes. — **Syn.** See CONVERSATION. [Short for CHATTER]

chat[2] (chat) *n.* *Bot.* The inflorescence, catkin, or seed of various plants, as the ament of the pine, the samara of the maple, etc. [< F, cat; so called from its appearance]

cha·teau (sha·tō′, *Fr.* shä·tō′) *n.* *pl.* **·teaux** (-tōz′, *Fr.* -tō′) **1.** A French castle or manor house. **2.** A house on a country estate, particularly one resembling a French castle. Also *French* **châ·teau′.** [< F < OF *chastel* < L *castellum.* See CASTLE.]

Cha·teau·bri·and (shä·tō·brē·än′), **François René,** 1768–1848, Vicomte de Chateaubriand, French writer.

Châ·teau-Thier·ry (shä·tō′tye·rē′) A commune in northern France; scene of heavy fighting (1918) in World War I; pop. about 10,858 (1968).

château wine A wine made from the grapes of a specified French chateau, especially one in the Bordeaux region, and usually bottled on the estate.

chat·e·lain (shat′ə·lān) *n.* The keeper of a castle: also called *castellan.* [< F *châtelain*]

chat·e·laine (shat′ə·lān) *n.* **1.** A chain hanging from a woman's belt to hold small articles, as keys; also, a clasp to hold a watch or purse. **2.** The mistress of a chateau, castle, or any fashionable household. [< F *châtelaine,* fem. of *châtelain* < OF *chastelain,* AF *castelain.* See CASTELLAN.]

Cha·tel·per·ro·ni·an (sha·tel′pə·rō′nē·ən) *adj.* *Anthropol.* Designating a culture stage developing at the beginning of the Upper Paleolithic. [after *Chatelperron,* town in southern France where artifacts were found]

Chat·ham (chat′əm) A municipal borough in northern Kent, England, a port on the Medway river estuary; pop. 55,460 (est. 1969).

Chat·ham (chat′əm), **Earl of** See PITT.

Chatham Islands Two islands of New Zealand, **Chatham** and **Pitt,** east of South Island; 372 sq. mi.

cha·toy·ant (shə·toi′ənt, *Fr.* shȧ·twȧ·yän′) *adj.* Possessing a changeable luster, like that of a cat's eye in the dark. — *n.* A stone having such a luster; cat's-eye. [< F, ppr. of *chatoyer* to change, as a cat's eye < *chat* cat] — **cha·toy′an·cy** *n.*

Cha·tri·an (shȧ·trē·än′), **Alexandre** See ERCKMANN-CHATRIAN.

Chat·ta·hoo·chee River (chat′ə·hōō′chē) A river, 436 miles long, forming the southern part of the boundary between Alabama and Georgia, and flowing south to the Apalachicola River.

Chat·ta·noo·ga (chat′ə·nōō′gə) A city in SE Tennessee, scene of Union victories (1863) in the Civil War; pop. 119,082.

chat·tel (chat′l) *n.* **1.** *Law* **a** An article of personal property; a movable: called a **chattel personal. b** Any interest or right in land less than a freehold: called a **chattel real. 2.** *Archaic* A slave; serf. [< OF *chatel* < L *capitale* property < *caput* head. Doublet of CATTLE.]

chattel mortgage A mortgage on movable property as security for a debt or obligation.

chat·ter (chat′ər) *v.i.* **1.** To click together rapidly, as the teeth in shivering. **2.** To talk rapidly and trivially. **3.** To utter a rapid series of short, inarticulate sounds, as a squirrel. **4.** To clatter or vibrate while operating, as a power tool. — *v.t.* **5.** To utter in a trivial or chattering manner. — *n.* **1.** Idle or foolish talk; prattle. **2.** Jabbering, as of a monkey. **3.** A rattling of the teeth. **4.** The jar or vibration of a chattering tool. [Imit.]

— **Syn.** (verb) **2.** prate, jabber. **3.** gibber.

chat·ter·box (chat′ər·boks′) *n.* An incessant talker.

chat·ter·er (chat′ər·ər) *n.* **1.** One who or that which chatters. **2.** Any of a large number of tropical, chiefly fruit-eating American birds (family *Cotingidae*), varying in size and coloration.

chatter marks 1. *Mech.* Irregular markings caused by vibration of a tool. **2.** *Geol.* Transverse crescent-shaped marks in a continuous series, sometimes occurring in deeply gouged glacial striae as the result of vibration.

Chat·ter·ton (chat′ər·tən), **Thomas,** 1752–70, English poet.

chat·ty (chat′ē) *adj.* **·ti·er, ·ti·est 1.** Given to chat; loquacious. **2.** Easy and familiar; informal: a *chatty* style of writing. — **chat′ti·ly** *adv.* — **chat′ti·ness** *n.*

Chau·cer (chô′sər), **Geoffrey,** 1340?–1400, English poet.

Chau·ce·ri·an (chô·sir′ē·ən) *adj.* Of, related to, or characteristic of the writings of Chaucer. — *n.* **1.** A specialist in Chaucer's works. **2.** Any of a group of 15th-century Scottish poets imitating Chaucer.

chauf·fer (chô′fər, shô′-) *n.* A small, portable furnace. Also **chau′fer.** [Var. of obs. *chafer* saucepan]

chauf·feur (shō′fər, shō·fûr′) *n.* One who is employed as the driver of an automobile. — *v.t.* To serve as driver for. [< F, stoker < *chauffer* to warm]

chaul·moo·gra (chôl·mōō′grə) *n.* An East Indian and Malayan tree (*Taraktogenos kurzii*) whose seeds yield the yellowish **chaulmoogra oil**, formerly used in treating leprosy and other skin diseases. Also **chaul·mu′gra.** [< Bengali *cāulmugrā*]

chaunt (chônt, chänt) See CHANT.

chausses (shōs) *n.pl.* A medieval garment for the legs and feet, especially one made of mail. [< OF *chauces* < L *calceus* boot < *calx*, *calcis* heel]

Chaus·son (shō·sôn′), **Ernest**, 1855–99, French composer.

chaus·sure (shō·sür′) *n. French* Foot covering.

chau·tau·qua (shə·tô′kwə) *n. Often cap. U.S.* An educational assembly resembling those held at Chautauqua, New York.

Chau·tau·qua (shə·tô′kwə) A summer resort town in western New York on **Lake Chautauqua** (18 miles long); seat of a summer educational association offering lectures, home study, concerts, etc.; pop. 4,376.

chau·vin·ism (shō′vən·iz′əm) *n.* 1. Militant glorification of one's country; vainglorious patriotism. 2. Unreasoning attachment to one's race, group, etc. [after Nicholas *Chauvin*, a devoted soldier and overzealous supporter of Napoleon Bonaparte] — **chau′vin·ist** *n.* — **chau·vin·is′tic** *adj.* — **chau·vin·is·ti·cal·ly** *adv.*

Cha·vannes (shà·vàn′) See PUVIS DE CHAVANNES.

chaw (chô) *n., v.t. & v.i. Dial.* Chew.

cha·zan (khä′zən) See HAZZAN.

Ch.B. Bachelor of Surgery (L *Chirurgiae Baccalaureus*).

Ch.E. Chemical Engineer.

cheap (chēp) *adj.* 1. Bearing or bringing a low price; inexpensive. 2. Charging low prices, as a store. 3. Obtainable at a low price in proportion to its value. 4. Easily obtained; costing little trouble. 5. Of money: *a* Obtainable at a low rate of interest. *b* Depreciated in exchange value or purchasing power. 6. Being of little value; poor; inferior. 7. Not esteemed. 8. Vulgar; mean: a *cheap* thing to do. 9. *Informal* Stingy: a *cheap* person. 10. Embarrassed; sheepish: to feel *cheap.* — *n. Obs.* A market. — *adv.* At a low price; cheaply. [Earlier *good cheap* a bargain < OE *cēap* business, trade] — **cheap′ly** *adv.* — **cheap′ness** *n.*
— **Syn.** (adj.) 4. easy. 8. low, petty, base, ignoble. — **Ant.** expensive, valuable.

cheap·en (chē′pən) *v.t.* 1. To make cheap or cheaper; bring into contempt; belittle; disparage. — *v.i.* 2. To become cheap. — **cheap′en·er** *n.*

Cheap·side (chēp′sīd) A street and district of London, formerly a market; site of the Mermaid Tavern.

cheap·skate (chēp′skāt) *n. U.S. Slang* A miserly person.

cheat (chēt) *v.t.* 1. To swindle or defraud. 2. To mislead or delude; trick. 3. To elude or escape; foil. — *v.i.* 4. To practice fraud or act dishonestly. 5. *U.S. Slang* To be sexually unfaithful. — *n.* 1. A fraud; swindle. 2. One who cheats or defrauds. 3. An article of fictitious value; a sham. 4. *Law* The obtaining of property by imposture. 5. *Chess*[2] (def. 1). [ME *chete*, short for *achete* to confiscate, deprive] — **cheat′er** *n.* — **cheat′ing·ly** *adv.*

che·bec (chi·bek′) *n.* The least flycatcher. See under FLYCATCHER.

che·cha·ko (chē·chä′kō) See CHEECHAKO.

Che·chiang (chē′kyang′, *Chinese* ju′jyäng′) See CHEKIANG.

check (chek) *n.* 1. A break in progress or advance; a stopping; rebuff; delay. 2. One who or that which stops or controls. 3. Control maintained to secure accuracy, honesty, etc.; supervision. 4. A test, examination, or comparison. 5. A mark to show that something has been verified or investigated. 6. An order, in writing, upon a bank or banker to pay a designated sum: also, *Brit.*, *cheque.* Abbr. *ck.,* (pl. *cks.*). 7. *U.S.* A tag, slip, or the like, issued for identification: a baggage *check.* 8. *U.S.* A slip listing the amount one owes, as in a restaurant. 9. A counter used in various games; a chip. 10. A square in a checkered surface; also, a checkered pattern, as on a chessboard. 11. A fabric having a checkered pattern. 12. In hockey, a defensive impeding or harrying of the puck-carrier by use of the body or stick. 13. In chess, the condition of a king that is subject to capture on the next opposing move. 14. A crack, as in timber or steel. 15. A notch or rabbet into which a piece fits. 16. *Mining* A slight fault. 17. A check-rein. 18. *Obs.* Rebuke; reproof. — **in check** Under control or restraint. — *v.t.* 1. To bring to a stop suddenly or sharply; halt. 2. To hold back; curb; restrain. 3. To test or verify as to accuracy, completeness, etc.; also, to investigate. 4. To mark with a check, as to indicate correctness. 5. To mark with squares or crossed lines; checker. 6. To deposit or accept for temporary safe-keeping: to *check* luggage. 7. In hockey, to impede (the puck-carrier) by use of the body or stick. 8. In chess, to put (an opponent's king) in check. 9. To cause to crack. 10. *Agric.* To plant so as to form checkrows. — *v.i.* 11. To come to a stop; pause. 12. *U.S.* To agree item for item; correspond accurately. 13. In hockey, to impede the puck-carrier by use of the body or stick. 14. In chess, to put an opponent's king in check. 15. *U.S.* To draw on a checking account. 16. To crack, as paint. 17. In hunting, to pause to locate a lost scent: said of dogs. 18. In falconry, to for-

sake proper quarry for a baser game: with *at.* — **to check in** *U.S.* To register as a guest at a hotel, etc. — **to check on** (or **up on**) *U.S.* To inquire into; investigate. — **to check out** *U.S. Informal* 1. To pay one's bill and leave, as from a hotel; also, to depart; die. 2. To investigate or confirm. 3. To be true or as expected, upon investigation. 4. To count and charge for (merchandise). 5. To test the performance of. — *interj.* In chess, an exclamation proclaiming that an opponent's king is in check. — *adj.* 1. *Chiefly Brit.* Formed or marked in a pattern of checks. 2. Serving to verify or check. Abbr. (n. 12, v. 7, 12) *ch., Ch.* [< OF *eschec* defeat, check < Arabic *shāh* king < Persian; orig. from chess, indicating the king was in danger] — **check′a·ble** *adj.*

check·book (chek′bŏŏk′) *n.* A book of blank bank checks.

checked (chekt) *adj.* 1. Marked with squares: *checked* gingham. 2. Kept in check; restrained. 3. Stopped.

check·er (chek′ər) *n.* 1. A piece used in the game of checkers, usually a small disk. 2. One of the squares in a checkered surface; also, a pattern of such squares. 3. One who checks; especially, one who inspects, counts, or supervises the disposal of merchandise in a commercial establishment. 4. The checker tree. 5. The fruit of the checker tree. — *v.t.* 1. To mark with squares or crossed lines. 2. To fill with variations or vicissitudes. Also, *Brit., chequer.* [< ME *escheker* < OF *eschaquier* chessboard < OF *eschec.* See CHECK.]

check·er·ber·ry (chek′ər·ber′ē) *n. pl.* **·ries** 1. The wintergreen (def. 1). 2. The spiceberry. 3. Loosely, the partridgeberry.

check·er·board (chek′ər·bôrd′, -bōrd′) *n.* A board divided into 64 squares, used in playing checkers or chess.

check·ered (chek′ərd) *adj.* 1. Divided into squares. 2. Marked by light and dark patches. 3. Marked by alternations; eventful: a *checkered* career.

check·ers (chek′ərz) *n.pl.* (*construed as sing.*) A game played by two persons on a checkerboard, each player starting with twelve pieces: in England usually called *draughts.*

checker tree The service tree (def. 1).

check·ing account (chek′ing) A bank account against which a depositor may draw checks.

check list A list by which something may be confirmed, identified, or verified.

check·mate (chek′māt′) *v.t.* **·mat·ed, ·mat·ing** 1. In chess, to put (an opponent's king) in check from which no escape is possible, thus winning the game. 2. To defeat by a skillful maneuver. — *n.* 1. In chess: *a* The move that checkmates a king. *b* The condition of a king when checkmated. 2. Utter defeat. — *interj.* In chess, an exclamation announcing that an opponent's king is checkmated. Also *mate.* Abbr. (v. 1, n. 1) *chm.* [< OF *eschec mat* < Arabic *shāh māt* the king is dead < Persian]

check·off (chek′ôf′, -of′) *n.* The collection of trade-union dues by deduction from the pay of each employee, the employer then transmitting them to the union.

check·out (chek′out′) *n.* 1. The series of actions by which the parts of a machine, apparatus, etc., are tested for adequate performance. 2. The operation of examining and charging for a customer's purchases, as in a supermarket.

check·rein (chek′rān′) *n.* 1. A rein from the bit to the saddle of a harness to keep a horse's head up: also called *bearing rein.* For illustration see HARNESS. 2. A rein connecting the driving rein of one horse to the bit of his mate in a double team. Also **check′line′.**

check·room (chek′rōōm′, -rŏŏm′) *n.* A room in which packages, coats, etc., may be left temporarily.

check·row (chek′rō′) *n.* In agriculture, one of a series of rows, especially of corn, dividing the land into squares to permit easier cultivation between adjacent plants and adjacent rows. — *v.t.* To plant in checkrows.

checks and balances Complementary or balanced powers among the branches of a government, as among the legislative, executive, and judiciary branches.

check·up (chek′up′) *n.* A thorough examination or testing: a medical *checkup.*

check valve *Mech.* A one-way valve, as in a boiler, that closes automatically to prevent return of fluid passing through it.

Ched·dar (ched′ər) *n.* Any of several types of white to yellow, hard, smooth cheese. Also **ched′dar, Cheddar cheese.** [after *Cheddar,* Somerset, England, where originally made]

ched·ite (ched′īt, shed′-) *n.* An explosive used in blasting. [after *Chedde,* a town in eastern France + -ITE[1]]

chee·cha·ko (chē·chä′kō) *n.* In Alaska and the Yukon, a newcomer; tenderfoot: also spelled *chechako.* [< Chinook *t'shi* new + *chakho* to come]

cheek (chēk) *n.* 1. Either side of the face below the eye and above the mouth. ♦ Collateral adjectives: *buccal, jugal.* 2. A side or part analogous to the side of the face: the *cheek* of a vise. 3. *Naut.* One of two projections on a mast, supporting the trestletrees. 4. *pl.* The buttocks. 5. *Informal* Impudent self-assurance. — *v.t. Informal* To confront or address impudently. [OE *cēce, cēace*]

cheek·bone (chēk′bōn′) *n.* Either of two bony prominences of the cheek below the eye socket: also called *malar*, *zygomatic bone*. For illustration see SKULL.

cheek by jowl Side by side; in close intimacy.

cheek pouch A distensible bag in the cheeks of certain rodents and other animals, adapted for holding food.

Cheek·to·wa·ga (chēk′tə-wä′gə) An unincorporated place in western New York, adjoining Buffalo on the east; formerly Cheektowaga-Northwest; pop. 113,844.

cheek·y (chē′kē) *adj.* **cheek·i·er, cheek·i·est** *Informal* Impudent; brazen. **— cheek′i·ly** *adv.* **— cheek′i·ness** *n.*

cheep (chēp) *v.t.* & *v.i.* To make, or utter with, a faint, shrill sound, as a young bird. *— n.* A weak chirp or squeak. [Imit.] **— cheep′er** *n.*

cheer (chir) *n.* **1.** A shout of acclamation or encouragement; also, a set of words or sounds used at athletic events to give encouragement or acclamation. **2.** Gladness or gaiety; joy; mirth. **3.** State of mind; mood: Be of good *cheer*. **4.** That which promotes happiness or joy; encouragement. **5.** Provisions for a feast; fare. **6.** Warm hospitality. **7.** *Obs.* Expression of the face. *— v.t.* **1.** To make cheerful, hopeful, or glad: often with *up*. **2.** To acclaim with cheers. **3.** To urge; incite: often with *on*. *— v.i.* **4.** To become cheerful, hopeful, or glad: often with *up*. **5.** To utter cries of encouragement, approval, etc. **6.** *Obs.* To fare or feel. [< OF *chiere*, *chere* face, countenance < LL *cara*] **— cheer′er** *n.* **— cheer′ing·ly** *adv.*

— Syn. (noun) **1.** applause, roar. — (verb) **1.** See CONSOLE[1]. **2.** applaud, acclaim. **5.** root, shout.

cheer·ful (chir′fəl) *adj.* **1.** In good spirits; joyous; lively. **2.** Pleasant; cheering: a *cheerful* color. **3.** Willing; ungrudging: a *cheerful* giver. **— cheer′ful·ly** *adv.* **— cheer′ful·ness** *n.*

— Syn. blithe, cheery, happy, jocund, joyous, sprightly.

cheer·i·o (chir′ē-ō′) *interj.* & *n. pl.* **cheer·i·os** *Brit. Informal* **1.** Hello. **2.** Good-by. Also **cheer′o.**

cheer·lead·er (chir′lē′dər) *n.* A person who leads organized cheering at an athletic event. Also **cheer leader.**

cheer·less (chir′lis) *adj.* Destitute of cheer; gloomy. **— cheer′less·ly** *adv.* **— cheer′less·ness** *n.*

cheer·y (chir′ē) *adj.* **cheer·i·er, cheer·i·est** Abounding in or promoting cheerfulness; bright; gay. **—cheer′i·ly** *adv.* **— cheer′i·ness** *n.*

cheese[1] (chēz) *n.* **1.** The pressed curd of milk, variously prepared and flavored; also, a cake or mass of this substance. **2.** Any of various substances like cheese in consistency or shape, as headcheese. [OE *cēse* < L *caseus* cheese]

cheese[2] (chēz) *v.t.* **cheesed, chees·ing** *Slang* To stop: especially in the phrase **cheese it!** Look out! Run! [< CEASE]

cheese[3] (chēz) *n. Slang* Personage: a big *cheese*. [? < Urdu *chīz* thing]

cheese·burg·er (chēz′bûr′gər) *n.* A hamburger with melted cheese on top of the meat.

cheese·cake (chēz′kāk′) *n.* **1.** A cake containing sweetened curds, eggs, milk, etc.: also **cheese cake.** **2.** *Slang* A photograph featuring a pretty girl's legs and figure; also, such photographs collectively.

cheese·cloth (chēz′klôth′, -kloth′) *n.* A thin, loosely woven cotton fabric, originally used for wrapping cheese.

cheese·par·ing (chēz′pâr′ing) *adj.* Miserly; parsimonious. *— n.* **1.** A paring of cheese. **2.** Something of no value. **3.** A mean or stingy practice.

chees·y (chē′zē) *adj.* **chees·i·er, chees·i·est** **1.** Of or like cheese. **2.** *U.S. Slang* Inferior. **— chees′i·ness** *n.*

chee·tah (chē′tä) *n.* An animal (*Acinonyx jubatus*) of the cat family, resembling the leopard, native to SW Asia and northern Africa, often trained to hunt antelope: also called *hunting leopard*: also spelled *chetah*. [< Hind. *chītā* leopard < Skt. *chitraka* speckled]

chef (shef) *n.* A head cook; also, any cook. [< F *chef* (*de cuisine*) head (of the kitchen) < OF. See CHIEF.]

chef de cui·sine (də kwē-zēn′) *French* Chief cook.

chef-d'oeu·vre (she-dœ′vr′) *n. pl.* **chefs-d'oeu·vre** (she-) *French* A masterpiece, especially of an artist, writer, etc.

Che·foo (chē′fōō′) See YENTAI. Also *Chihfu*.

cheg·oe (cheg′ō) *n.* The chigoe (def. 1).

cheilo- See CHILO-.

cheiro- See CHIRO-.

Chei·ron (kī′ron) See CHIRON.

Che·ju (chä-jōō) An island of South Korea, in the East China Sea; 710 sq. mi.; pop. 336,694 (1966): formerly *Quelpart*.

Che·ka (che′kä) *n.* A Soviet commission working as secret police against counterrevolution, superseded by the OGPU in 1922. [< Russian *Che* C + *Ka* K, initials of *Chrezvychainaya Komissya* extraordinary commission]

Che·khov (chek′ôf), **Anton Pavlovich**, 1860–1904, Russian dramatist and story writer: also *Tchekhov*. Also *Che′kov*.

Che·kiang (che′kyang′, *Chinese* ju′jyäng′) A province of eastern China; 40,000 sq. mi.; pop. 25,280,000 (est. 1957); capital Hangchow: also *Chechiang*.

che·la[1] (chā′lä) *n. Anglo-Indian* A disciple of a holy man. [< Hind. *chelā* disciple < Skt. *chetaka* servant, slave]

che·la[2] (kē′lä) *n. pl.* **·lae** (-lē) *Zool.* A pincerlike claw in crustaceans and arachnids. [< NL < Gk. *chēlē* claw]

che·late (kē′lāt) *adj. Zool.* Having a chela. *— n. Chem.* A compound that has been subjected to chelation. *— v.t.* **·la·ted, ·la·ting** *Chem.* To subject a compound to chelation.

che·la·tion (kē-lā′shən) *n. Chem.* The inactivation of metallic ions in a solution by an organic reagent with whose molecules the metallic ions are strongly bound in a relatively inactive ring structure. [< Gk. *chēlē* claw]

che·li·form (kē′lə-fôrm, kel′ə-) *adj. Zool.* Having the form of a chela; pincerlike.

Chel·le·an (shel′ē-ən) *adj. Anthropol.* Denoting a culture stage of the Lower Paleolithic period, now more frequently assigned to the Abbevillian. [after *Chelles*, France, where artifacts were first found]

Chelm (khelm) A city in eastern Poland: Russian *Kholm*.

che·loid (kē′loid) See KELOID.

che·lo·ni·an (ki-lō′nē-ən) *adj.* Of or belonging to an order of reptiles (*Chelonia*) having external skeletons and toothless jaws, including tortoises and turtles. *— n.* A member of this order. [< NL < Gk. *chelōnē* tortoise]

Chel·sea (chel′sē) **1.** A metropolitan borough of SW London, England; pop. 47,085 (1961). **2.** A city in eastern Massachusetts; pop. 30,625.

Chel·ten·ham (chelt′nəm for def. 1, chel′tən·ham′ for def. 2.) **1.** A municipal borough in north central Gloucester, England; pop. 76,000 (1969). **2.** An urban township in SE Pennsylvania, a suburb of Philadelphia; pop. 40,238.

Che·lya·binsk (chi-lyä′binsk) A city in the west central Russian S.F.S.R.; pop. 874,000 (1970). Also **Che·lia·binsk.**

Che·lyus·kin (chi-lyōōs′kin), **Cape** The northernmost point of Asia, on the Taimur Peninsula in the Soviet Union.

chem- Var. of CHEMO-.

chem. Chemical; chemist; chemistry.

chemi- See CHEMO-.

chem·ic (kem′ik) *adj. Archaic* **1.** Chemical. **2.** Alchemic. *— n. Obs.* A chemist.

chem·i·cal (kem′i-kəl) *adj.* Of or pertaining to chemistry or its phenomena, laws, operations, or results: *chemical* analysis. *— n.* A substance obtained by or used in a chemical process. Abbr. *chem.* [< F *chimique* < Med.L *alchimicus* of alchemy] **— chem′i·cal·ly** *adv.*

chemical bond The force, usually exerted by shared electrons, that holds atoms together in a molecule.

chemical engineer A professional engineer who studies, develops, and supervises the applications of chemistry to industrial processes. Abbr. *C.E.*, *Ch.E.*

chemical warfare The technique of using poisonous and irritant substances, as smoke screens, gases, incendiary materials, etc., in warfare.

chem·i·lu·mi·nes·cence (kem′i·lōō′mə·nes′əns) *n.* The emission of light from a substance undergoing a chemical reaction. **— chem′i·lu′mi·nes′cent** *adj.*

che·min de fer (shə·man′ də fâr′) *French* **1.** A railroad; literally, road of iron. **2.** A form of baccarat.

che·mise (shə·mēz′) *n.* **1.** A woman's loose undergarment resembling a short slip. **2.** A dress hanging straight from the shoulders. [< OF < LL *camisia* shirt]

chem·i·sette (shem′i·zet′) *n.* An ornamental dickey formerly worn by women. [< F, dim. of *chemise*. See CHEMISE.]

chem·ism (kem′iz·əm) *n. Rare* **1.** Chemical affinity or attraction. **2.** Chemical properties or activities collectively.

chem·ist (kem′ist) *n.* **1.** One versed in chemistry. Abbr. *chem.* **2.** *Brit.* A druggist. **3.** *Obs.* An alchemist. [< ALCHEMIST]

chem·is·try (kem′is·trē) *n. pl.* **·tries** **1.** The science that treats of the structure, composition, and properties of substances and of their transformations. Abbr. *chem.* **2.** Chemical composition or processes. For symbols used in chemistry see Special Signs and Symbols section.

Chem·nitz (kem′nits) The former name for KARL-MARX-STADT.

chemo- *combining form* Chemical; of or with chemicals or chemical reactions: *chemotherapy*. Also spelled *chemi-*. Also, before vowels, *chem-*. [< CHEMICAL]

chem·o·sphere (kem′ə·sfir, kē′mō-) *n. Meteorol.* A region of the atmosphere from 26 to 70 miles above the earth, marked by predominant photochemical activity. [< CHEMO- + -SPHERE] **— chem′o·spher′ic** (-sfir′ik, -sfer′-) *adj.*

chem·o·stat (kem′ō·stat, kē′mō-) *n.* An apparatus for growing a very homogeneous bacterial culture at a constant rate by automatic control of one growth nutrient.

chem·o·syn·the·sis (kem′ō·sin′thə·sis, kē′mō-) *n.* The formation of organic compounds from inorganic constituents by the energy derived from chemical changes. [< CHEMO- + SYNTHESIS] **— chem′o·syn·thet′ic** (kem′ō·sin·thet′ik) *adj.* **— chem′o·syn·thet′i·cal·ly** *adv.*

chem·o·tax·is (kem′ō·tak′sis, kē′mō-) *n. Biol.* The property that certain motile living cells possess of approaching (**positive chemotaxis**) or moving away from (**negative chemotaxis**) chemical substances: also called *chemotropism*. [<

CHEMO- + Gk. *taxis* order < *tattein* to arrange] — **chem'o·tac'tic** (-tak'tik) *adj.* — **chem'o·tac'ti·cal·ly** *adv.*

chem·o·ther·a·py (kem'ō·ther'a·pē, kē'mō-) *n. Med.* The treatment of diseases by the disinfection of affected tissues through the use of chemically synthesized drugs having a specific action against certain pathogenic microorganisms. Also **chem'o·ther'a·peu'tics.** [< CHEMO- + THERAPY] — **chem'o·ther'a·peu'tic** *adj.* — **chem'o·ther'a·pist** *n.*

che·mot·ro·pism (ki·mot'rə·piz'əm) *n. Biol.* 1. The response of a plant or animal organism to a chemical reaction, as by unequal growth or directed movements. 2. Chemotaxis. [< CHEMO- + TROPISM] — **chem·o·trop·ic** (kem'ō·trop'ik) *adj.*

Che·mul·po (che·mŏŏl'pō) See INCHON. Also **Che·mul·pho.**

chem·ur·gy (kem'ər·jē) *n.* The chemical exploitation of organic raw materials, especially agricultural products, in the industrial development of new products. [< CHEM(O)- + -URGY] — **chem·ur·gic** (kem·ûr'jik) or **·gi·cal** *adj.*

Che·nab (chi·näb') A river of NW India, flowing generally west about 675 miles to the Sutlej.

Chen-chiang (jun'jyäng') See CHINKIANG. Also **Chen'-kiang'.**

Cheng·teh (chung'du') A city in the Inner Mongolian Autonomous Region, NE China; pop. about 93,000: also *Jehol.* Also **Ch'eng'-te'.**

Cheng·tu (chung'dōō') The capital of Szechwan province, south central China, in the central part of the province; pop. 1,107,000 (est. 1957). Also **Ch'eng'-tu'.**

Ché·nier (shā·nyā'), **André Marie de,** 1762–94, French poet; guillotined.

che·nille (shə·nēl') *n.* 1. A soft, fuzzy cord of silk, rayon, cotton, or worsted, used for embroidery, fringes, etc. 2. A fabric made with filling of this cord, used for rugs, bedspreads, or the like. [< F, caterpillar < L *canicula,* dim. of *canis* dog; from its fuzzy appearance]

Chen·nault (shə·nôlt'), **Claire Lee,** 1891–1958, U.S. aviator; major general in World War II.

che·no·pod (kē'nə·pod, ken'ə-) *n.* Any plant of the goosefoot family (*Chenopodiaceae*), including spinach, beets, orach, and wormseed. [< NL *chenopodium* < Gk. *chēn, chēnos* goose + *pous, podos* foot] — **che·no·po·di·a·ceous** (kē'nə·pō'dē·ā'shəs, ken'ə-) *adj.*

Che·ops (kē'ops) Egyptian king of the fourth dynasty (about 2900 B.C.); builder of the Great Pyramid at Giza: also *Khufu.*

cheque (chek) *n. Brit.* A check (def. 6).

chequ·er (chek'ər) *n. Brit.* A checker.

Cher (shâr) A river in central France, flowing 200 miles NW to the Loire.

Cher·bourg (sher'bŏŏrg, *Fr.* sher·bōōr') A port city in northern France, on the English Channel; pop. 37,933 (1968).

Cherbourg Peninsula See COTENTIN PENINSULA.

cher·chez la femme (sher·shā' là fàm') *French* Seek the woman: used to imply that a woman is the motive for a specified action.

cher·ish (cher'ish) *v.t.* 1. To hold dear; treat with tenderness; foster. 2. To entertain fondly, as a hope or an idea. [< OF *cheriss-,* stem of *cherir* to hold dear < *cher* dear < L *carus*] — **cher'ish·er** *n.* — **cher'ish·ing·ly** *adv.*
— **Syn.** 1. harbor, nourish, nurture, shelter. 2. prize, treasure, value. — **Ant.** neglect, forsake, abandon.

Cher·nov·tsy (cher·nôf'tsē) A city in the western Ukrainian S.S.R., on the Prut; pop. 145,000 (1959): Rumanian *Cernăuţi.* German *Czernowitz.*

cher·no·zem (cher'nə·zem) *n.* A soil typical of temperate subhumid grasslands, consisting of a rich, black surface layer overlying a layer of accumulated lime. [< Russian *chernozem* black soil]

Cher·o·kee (cher'ə·kē, cher'ə·kē') *n. pl.* **·kee** or **·kees** 1. One of a great tribe of Iroquoian Indians formerly occupying northern Georgia and North Carolina, now dwelling in Oklahoma. 2. The Iroquoian language of this tribe.

Cherokee rose A trailing rose (*Rosa laevigata*) of China having large, solitary white flowers, naturalized in the United States and the West Indies: the State flower of Georgia.

che·root (shə·rōōt') *n.* A cigar cut square at both ends: also spelled *sheroot.* [< F *cheroute* < Tamil *shuruṭṭu* roll, cigar]

cher·ry (cher'ē) *n. pl.* **·ries** 1. Any of various trees (genus *Prunus*) of the rose family, related to the plum and the peach and bearing small, round or heart-shaped drupes enclosing a smooth pit; especially, the **sweet** or **mazzard cherry** (*P. avium*), the **sour cherry** (*P. cerasus*), and the **wild black cherry** (*P. serotina*). 2. The wood or fruit of a cherry tree. 3. A bright red color resembling that of certain cherries: also **cherry red.** — *adj.* 1. Bright red. 2. Made of or with cherries: *cherry brandy.* 3. Made of cherry wood. [ME *chery,* back formation from AF *cherise* (mistaken for a plural) < L *cerasus* cherry tree < Gk. *kerasos*]

cher·ry·stone (cher'ē·stōn') *n. U.S.* A small quahog. Also **cherrystone clam.**

cher·so·nese (kûr'sə·nēz, -nēs) *n.* A peninsula. — **the Chersonese** Gallipoli Peninsula. [< L *chersonesus* < Gk. *chersonēsos* < *chersos* dry + *nēsos* island]

chert (chûrt) *n.* A dull-colored cryptocrystalline quartz or chalcedony: also called *hornstone.* [Origin uncertain]

cher·ub (cher'əb) *n. pl.* **cher·ubs** or **cher·u·bim** (cher'ə·bim, -yə·bim) *for def. 1,* **cherubs** *for def. 2,* **cherubim** *for defs. 3 & 4* 1. A representation of a beautiful winged child, the accepted type of the angelic cherub. 2. A beautiful child; also, a chubby, innocent-looking adult. 3. *pl. Theol.* The second of the nine orders of angels. See ANGEL. 4. In Scripture, a celestial being. *Ps.* xviii 10; *Ezek.* x; *Heb.* ix 5. [< LL < Hebrew *kerūb,* an angelic being] — **che·ru·bic** (chə·rōō'bik) or **·bi·cal** *adj.*

Che·ru·bi·ni (kā'rōō·bē'nē), **Maria Luigi,** 1760–1842, Italian composer.

cher·vil (chûr'vəl) *n.* 1. Either of two European garden herbs (*Anthriscus cerefolium* or *Chaerophyllum bulbosum*) of the parsley family, the young leaves of which are used for soups, salads, etc. 2. Any of several other plants of the same family, as the **great** or **sweet chervil** (*Myrrhis odorata*). [OE *caerfille* < L *chaerephyllum* < Gk. *chairephyllon*]

cher·vo·nets (cher·vō'nets) *n. pl.* **·vont·si** (-vŏnt'sē) A former gold monetary unit of the U.S.S.R., equivalent to ten rubles. [< Russian]

Ches. or **Chesh.** Cheshire.

Ches·a·peake Bay (ches'ə·pēk) An inlet of the Atlantic, about 195 miles long, located in Virginia and Maryland.

Chesh·ire (chesh'ər, -ir) *n.* A crumbly type of Cheddar cheese: also **Cheshire cheese.** [after *Cheshire,* England]

Chesh·ire (chesh'ər, -ir) A county in western England: 1,015 sq. mi.; pop. 904,600 (1976); county seat, Chester: also *Chester.*

Cheshire cat In Lewis Carroll's *Alice's Adventures in Wonderland,* a grinning cat that gradually faded away until only its grin remained.

chess¹ (ches) *n.* A game of skill played on a chessboard by two persons, with 16 pieces on each side. The aim of each player, proceeding by alternate moves, is to checkmate his opponent's king. [< OF *esches,* pl. of *eschec.* See CHECK.]

chess² (ches) *n.* 1. Any of several kinds of bromegrass, especially *Bromus secalinus,* a weed found in grain fields: also called *cheat.* 2. The darnel. [Origin uncertain]

chess³ (ches) *n.* One of the planks in the floor of a pontoon bridge. [Origin uncertain]

chess·board (ches'-bôrd', -bōrd') *n.* A board divided into 64 alternately colored squares, used in playing chess.

chess·man (ches'-man', -mən) *n. pl.* **·men** (-men', -mən) One of the pieces used in playing chess.

CHESSBOARD

B—Bishop. Kt (or N)—Knight. Q—Queen. K—King. P—Pawn. R—Rook.
In chess notation the ranks (horizontal rows of squares) are numbered 1–8 reading away from each player, and each file (vertical row) is named for the piece standing at its head. The symbol for each piece is opposite the square it occupies at the beginning of the game, excepting the pawns, which are indicated at each end of the pawn rows. Bishops, knights, and rooks are named for the king or queen, according to their positions at the start. Pawns are named for the pieces they stand in front of.

chest (chest) *n.* 1. The part of the body enclosed by the ribs; thorax. ◆ Collateral adjective: *pectoral.* 2. A box, usually with a hinged lid, for storing or protecting articles, as tools, jewelry, etc. 3. The treasury or coffers of a public institution; also, the funds contained there. 4. A case in which to transport certain commodities, as tea; also, the quantity contained in such a chest. 5. A receptacle for gas, liquid, etc.: a steam *chest.* 6. A chest of drawers (which see). [OE *cest* < L *cista* < Gk. *kistē* basket, box]

Ches·ter (ches'tər) 1. The county seat of Cheshire, England, a county borough in the western part of the county; pop. 117,000 (1976): ancient *Deva, Devana Castra.* 2. A city on the Delaware River in SE Pennsylvania; pop. 56,331. 3. See CHESHIRE.

ches·ter·bed (ches'tər·bed') *n. Canadian* A sofa bed.

ches·ter·field (ches'tər·fēld') *n.* 1. A single-breasted topcoat, generally with concealed buttons. 2. *Chiefly Canadian* A sofa. [after a 19th c. Earl of *Chesterfield*]

Ches·ter·field (ches'tər·fēld), **Lord,** 1694–1773, Philip Dormer Stanhope, fourth Earl of Chesterfield, English statesman and author.

Ches·ter·field·i·an (ches'tər·fēl'dē·ən) *adj.* 1. Of or pertaining to Lord Chesterfield. 2. Suave; polished; elegant.

Ches·ter·ton (ches'tər·tən), **Gilbert Keith,** 1874–1936, English author.

Chester white One of a breed of white pigs first developed in Chester County, Pa.

chest·nut (ches'nut', -nət) *n.* **1.** The edible nut of various trees (genus *Castanea*) of the beech family, growing in a prickly bur; also, a tree that bears this nut. **2.** One of certain similar trees, or their fruit, as the horse chestnut. **3.** A reddish brown color: also **chestnut brown**. **4.** A horse of this color. **5.** *Informal* **a** A stale joke. **b** Anything trite, as a story, song, etc. **6.** A small, horny callosity on the inner surface of the leg of a horse. — *adj.* Reddish brown. Abbr. *ch., Ch.* [ME *chesten*, var. of *chesteine* chestnut < OF *chastaine* < L *castanea* < Gk. *kastanea* + NUT]

chest of drawers A piece of furniture consisting of a frame containing a set of drawers for storing linens, clothing, etc.

chest-on-chest (chest'on-chest') *n.* A chest of drawers placed upon another that is wider and has feet.

chest register The lower tones of the human voice. Also **chest voice.**

chest·y (ches'tē) *adj.* **chest·i·er, chest·i·est** *Informal* **1.** Self-assertive; proud. **2.** Large in the chest.

che·tah (chē'tə) See CHEETAH.

cheth (kheth) See HETH.

Chet·nik (chet'nik) *n. pl.* **Chet·ni·ci** (chet·nē'tsē) or **Chet·niks** In World War II, any of a group of Serbian guerrillas in Yugoslavia. [< Serbo-Croatian]

che·val-de-frise (shə·val'də·frēz') *n. pl.* **che·vaux-de-frise** (shə·vō'-) **1.** A portable obstacle of barbed wire supported on a sawhorse construction. **2.** Formerly, an obstacle of projecting spikes used against cavalry. **3.** A protecting line, as of broken glass or spikes, on top of a wall. [< F, lit., horse of Friesland; because first used by the Frisians]

che·val glass (shə·val') A long mirror mounted on horizontal pivots in a frame.

chev·a·lier (shev'ə·lir') *n.* **1.** A member of certain orders of knighthood or honor, as of the French Legion of Honor. **2.** A knight or cavalier. **3.** A chivalrous man; a gallant. **4.** In France, formerly, a noble of the lowest rank, or a cadet who entered the army. [< AF *chevaler*, OF *chevalier* < LL *caballarius*. Doublet of CAVALIER.]

che·ve·lure (shəv·lür') *n. French* A head of hair.

chev·i·ot (shev'ē·ət) *n.* A rough cloth of twill weave, used for suits, overcoats, etc., originally made from Cheviot wool.

Chev·i·ot (chev'ē·ət, chē'vē-) *n.* One of a breed of large sheep, originating in the Cheviot Hills, esteemed for their wool (**Cheviot wool**).

Chev·i·ot Hills (chev'ē·ət, chē'vē-) A range, 35 miles long, on the boundary between Scotland and England; highest peak, **The Cheviot**, 2,676 ft.

chev·ron (shev'rən) *n.* **1.** An emblem or insignia usually consisting of stripes meeting at an angle, worn on a uniform sleeve to indicate rank, length of service, etc., used by military, naval, and police forces. **2.** Any V-shaped mark or zigzag pattern, especially as used in architecture. For illustration see MOLDING. **3.** *Heraldry* A charge shaped like an inverted V. [< OF, chevron, rafter, ult. < L *caper* goat]

CHEVRONS (def. 1)

Sergeant—Army *a* United States. *b* Great Britain. *c* France (gold, regular army).

chev·ro·tain (shev'rə·tān, -tin) *n.* A small, deerlike, hornless ruminant (family *Tragulidae*) of Africa and Asia: also called *mouse deer*. [< F < OF *chevrot*, dim. of *chèvre* she goat < L *capra*, fem. of *caper* goat]

chev·y (chev'ē) *n. pl.* **chev·ies** *Brit.* **1.** A hunt, or a shout in hunting. **2.** *Prisoner's base*, a game. — *v.* **chev·ied, chev·y·ing** *v.t.* **1.** To chase about; hunt. **2.** To harass; worry. — *v.i.* **3.** To race; scamper. Also *chivy, chivvy*. [Prob. < *Chevy Chase*]

Chev·y Chase (chev'ē) An old English ballad dealing with the battle of Otterburn.

chew (chōō) *v.t.* **1.** To crush or grind with the teeth; masticate. **2.** To meditate upon; consider carefully. — *v.i.* **3.** To work the jaws and teeth; champ. **4.** To meditate. **5.** *Informal* To use chewing tobacco. — **to chew out** *U.S. Slang* To reprimand severely; berate. — *n.* **1.** The act of chewing. **2.** That which is chewed; a quid; cud: a *chew* of tobacco. [OE *cēowan*] — **chew'er** *n.*

chew·ing gum (chōō'ing) A preparation of some natural gum, usually chicle, flavored and sweetened for chewing.

che·wink (chi·wingk') *n.* The towhee, a bird. [Imit.]

chew·y (chōō'ē) *adj.* **chew·i·er, chew·i·est** Relatively soft and requiring chewing: Caramels are *chewy*.

Chey·enne (shī·en') *n. pl.* **·enne** or **·ennes** One of a tribe of North American Indians of Algonquian stock, formerly inhabiting Wyoming, Nebraska, and the western Dakotas, now in Montana and Oklahoma.

Chey·enne (shī·an', -en') The capital of Wyoming, in the SE part; pop. 40,914.

Cheyenne River A river in Wyoming and South Dakota, flowing 290 miles NE to the Missouri.

Chey·ne (chā'nē), **Thomas Kelly**, 1841–1915, English Biblical scholar and editor.

chez (shā) *prep. French* At; at the home of; by.

chg. (*pl.* **chgs.**) Charge.

chgd. Charged.

chi (kī) *n.* The twenty-second letter in the Greek alphabet (X, χ), transliterated as *ch*. See ALPHABET. [< Gk.]

chi·a (chē'ə) *n. SW U.S.* A Californian and Mexican herb (*Salvia columbariae*) of the mint family, whose seeds yield a beverage and an oil (**chia oil**). [< Sp. < Nahuatl]

Chi·an (kī'ən) *adj.* Of, pertaining to, or produced in Chios: *Chian* wine. — *n.* A native of Chios.

Chiang Kai-shek (chyäng' kī'shek', chang'; *Chinese* jyäng'), 1886 –1975, Chinese generalissimo and statesman; head of the Nationalist government of the Republic of China: original name **Chiang Chung-cheng**. — **Madame Chiang Kai-shek** See under SOONG.

Chi·an·ti (kē·an'tē, *Ital.* kyän'tē) *n.* A dry, red, Italian wine from the Monti Chianti region; also, any similar wine.

Chian·ti (kyän'tē), **Mon·ti** (môn'tē) A small range of the Apennines in central Italy; highest peak, Monte San Michele, 2,930 ft.

Chi·a·pas (chē·ä'päs) A State in SE Mexico; 28,732 sq. mi.; pop. 1,578,180 (1970); capital, Tuxtla Gutiérrez.

chi·a·ro·scu·ro (kē·är'ə·skyŏŏr'ō) *n. pl.* **·ros** **1.** The distribution and treatment of light and shade in a picture. **2.** A kind of painting or drawing using only light and shade. **3.** An artist's treatment of light and shade. Also called *clair-obscure*: also **chi·a·ro·o·scu·ro** (kē·är'ə·ō·skyŏŏr'ō). [< Ital. < *chiaro* clear (< L *clarus*) + *oscuro* dim, obscure < L *obscurus*] — **chi·a'ro·scu'rist** *n.*

chi·asm (kī'az·əm) *n.* **1.** *Anat.* An intersecting or X-like commissure that unites the optic nerves at the base of the brain. **2.** *Genetics* The point of intersection of two chromosomes. Also **chi·as·ma** (kī·az'mə). [< NL *chiasma* < Gk. crossing < *chiazein* to mark crosswise] — **chi·as'mal, chi·as'mic** *adj.*

chi·as·ma·ty·py (kī·az'mə·tī'pē) *n. Genetics* The intertwining of two homologous chromosomes during meiosis, which may result in a crossing over. [< Gk. *chiasma* crossing + *typos* impression] — **chi·as'ma·type'** *adj. & n.*

chi·as·mus (kī·az'məs) *n.* In rhetoric, a contrast by reverse parallelism, as in "They fall successive, and successive rise." [< Gk. *chiasmos* < *chiazein* to mark crosswise]

chi·as·to·lite (kī·as'tə·līt) *n. Mineral.* An andalusite in which the crystals in transverse section show a checkered pattern because of the arrangement of its impurities. [< Gk. *chiastos* crossed]

chiaus (chous, choush) *n.* A Turkish official messenger or sergeant at arms: also *choush*. [< Turkish *chāush*]

Chi·ba (chē·bä) A city on central Honshu island, Japan, on Tokyo Bay; pop. 407,000 (est. 1968).

Chib·cha (chib'chə) *n. pl.* **·cha** A member of an extinct, culturally advanced tribe of Colombian Indians.

Chib·chan (chib'chən) *n.* **1.** A stock of South and Central American Indians, including the Chibcha. **2.** The family of languages spoken by these people. — *adj.* Of or pertaining to this ethnic stock or linguistic family.

chi·bouk (chi·bŏŏk', -bŏŏk') *n.* A Turkish tobacco pipe having a long straight stem, and a bowl of red clay. Also **chi·bouque'**. [< Turkish *chibūk*]

chic (shēk, shik) *adj.* Smart; stylish; elegant. — *n.* Originality, elegance, and taste, especially in dress. [< F]

Chi·ca·go (shə·kä'gō, -kô'-) A city in NE Illinois on Lake Michigan; second largest city in the United States; pop. 3,366,957.

Chicago Heights A city in NE Illinois; pop. 40,900.

chi·ca·lo·te (chē'kä·lō'tä) *n.* A prickly poppy (*Argemone platyceras*) of the SW United States and Mexico. [< Sp. < Nahuatl *chicalotl* thorny]

chi·cane (shi·kān') *v.* **·caned, ·can·ing** *v.t.* **1.** To deceive by chicanery; trick. **2.** To quibble about. — *v.i.* **3.** To resort to chicanery; use tricks. — *n.* **1.** Chicanery. **2.** A bridge or whist hand containing no trumps. [< F *chicaner*]

chi·can·er·y (shi·kā'nər·ē) *n. pl.* **·er·ies** **1.** Trickery and subterfuge; sophistry; quibbling. **2.** A trick; quibble. — **Syn. 1.** deceit, deception, underhandedness, cunning.

Chi·ca·no (chē·kä'nō) *n. pl.* **·nos** or **·noes** A Mexican-American. [< (*Me*)*xicano*]

chic·co·ry (chik'ər·ē) See CHICORY.

Chich·a·gof Island (chich'ə·gôf) An island in the Alexander Archipelago, SE Alaska; 2,104 sq. mi.

Chi·chén-It·zá (chē·chen'ēt·sä') A ruined Mayan city in Yucatán, Mexico.

Chich·es·ter (chich'is·tər) The county seat of West Sussex, England, a municipal borough in the SW part of the county; pop. 93,610 (1976).

chi·chi (shē'shē) *adj. Informal* Ostentatiously stylish or elegant. [< F, frill]

chick (chik) *n.* **1.** A young chicken. **2.** Any young bird. **3.** A child. **4.** *U.S. Slang* A young woman; girl.

---

chick·a·dee (chik′ə-dē) *n.* An American titmouse (genus *Parus*) without a crest and with the top of the head and the throat black or dark colored; especially, the **black-capped chickadee** (*P. atricapillus*) of eastern North America. [Imit. of its cry]

CHICKADEE
(5¾ inches long; tail 2⅝ inches; wing-spread 8½ inches)

Chick·a·mau·ga (chik′ə-mô′gə) A city in NW Georgia, on **Chickamauga Creek**; scene of a Confederate victory in the Civil War, 1863; pop. 1,842.

chick·a·ree (chik′ə-rē) *n.* The red squirrel. See under SQUIRREL. [Imit. of its cry]

Chick·a·saw (chik′ə-sô) *n. pl.* **·saw** or **·saws** One of a tribe of Muskhogean North American Indians formerly occupying the country along the Mississippi River and eastward but now living in Oklahoma.

chick·en (chik′ən) *n.* **1.** The young of the common domestic fowl. **2.** A cock or hen of any age, or its flesh. **3.** *Informal* A child; a young, inexperienced person: now chiefly in the phrase **no chicken**, one no longer young. **4.** *U.S. Slang* A young woman. — *adj. U.S. Slang* **1.** Afraid; cowardly. **2.** Adhering narrowly and nastily to the rules. — *v.i. U.S. Slang* To lose one's nerve: often with *out.* [OE *cicen*]

chicken colonel *U.S. Slang* A colonel as distinguished from a lieutenant colonel. [after his eagle insignia]

chicken breast *Pathol.* Pigeon breast (which see). — **chick·en-breast·ed** (chik′ən-bres′tid) *adj.*

chicken feed *Slang* **1.** Small change, as pennies, nickels, dimes, etc. **2.** Low wages or other remuneration.

chicken hawk Any of various hawks that prey on poultry, especially Cooper's hawk.

chick·en-heart·ed (chik′ən-här′tid) *adj.* Timid or cowardly.

chick·en-liv·ered (chik′ən-liv′ərd) *adj.* Cowardly.

chicken louse One of a species of wingless insects (order *Mallophaga*) parasitic on chickens. For illustration see INSECTS (injurious).

chicken pox *Pathol.* A contagious disease, principally of children, characterized by skin eruptions, a slight fever, and a typically brief course: also called *varicella, water pox.*

chick·pea (chik′pē′) *n.* **1.** A plant (*Cicer arietinum*) of Mediterranean regions and central Asia. **2.** Its seed, widely used as a food in Asia, Latin America, and southern Europe. Also called *garbanzo.* [Alter. of ME *chichpease* < F *pois chiche* < *pois* base + *chiche* < L *cicer,* a small pea]

chick·weed (chik′wēd′) *n.* A spreading, Old World stitchwort (*Stellaria media*), having white flowers and used for feeding caged birds.

chic·le (chik′əl) *n.* The milky juice or latex of the sapodilla, used as the basic principle of chewing gum. Also **chicle gum**. [< Sp. < Nahuatl *chictli*]

chi·co (chē′kō) *n. pl.* **·cos** The greasewood. [< Sp. *chicalote*. See CHICALOTE.]

Chic·o·pee (chik′ə-pē) A city in SW Massachusetts; pop. 66,676.

chic·o·ry (chik′ər-ē) *n. pl.* **·ries 1.** A perennial herb (*Cichorium intybus*) of the composite family, having usually blue flowers, naturalized in the United States and used as a salad plant. **2.** Its dried, roasted, and ground roots, used for mixing with coffee or as a coffee substitute. Also called *succory*: also spelled *chiccory.* [< MF *cichorée* < L *cichorium* < Gk. *kichora*]

chide (chīd) *v.t. & v.i.* **chid·ed** or **chid** (chid), **chid·ed** or **chid** or **chid·den** (chid′n), **chid·ing** To speak reprovingly (to); scold. [OE *cīdan*] — **chid′er** *n.* — **chid′ing·ly** *adv.*
— **Syn.** rebuke, reprimand, criticize, censure, upbraid. — **Ant.** commend, compliment, praise.

chief (chēf) *n.* **1.** *Often cap.* The person highest in rank or authority, as the leader or head of a tribe, band, police force, government bureau, etc. Abbr. *c., C., ch., Ch.* **2.** *Usually cap.* A ship's chief engineer; also, a chief petty officer. **3.** *Slang* A boss. **4.** *Heraldry* The upper part of a shield. **5.** *Archaic* The main or most valuable part. **6.** *Obs.* A head; upper part. — **in chief 1.** Having the highest authority: commander *in chief.* **2.** Chiefly. — *adj.* **1.** Highest in rank or authority. **2.** Most important or eminent; leading. — *adv. Archaic* Chiefly. [< OF *chef, chief* < L *caput* head]
— **Syn.** (noun) *Chief, head, chieftain, leader, master,* and *commander* mean a person in authority over others. *Chief* is a general term for one who occupies an office of authority over a group, large or small: the *chief* of state, the *chief* of police. *Head,* like *chief,* is also a general term, but is often used of those who hold subordinate offices: the *head* of the accounting department. *Chieftain,* originally the *head* of a Scottish clan, now refers to the *head* of a more or less primitive tribe. A *leader* is one who is followed because of his ability to control, or because he has been chosen by a group or party to be its *head.* A *master* or a *commander* has authority to enforce obedience; *commander,* however, is generally restricted to military and naval usage: the *master* of a ship, or of a slave, the *commander* of a regiment. — **Ant.** follower, retainer, subordinate.

chief commissioner's state Any of the constituent states of the Republic of India administered by the central government through chief commissioners.

chief justice The presiding judge of a court composed of several justices. Abbr. *Ch.J., C.J.*

Chief Justice of the United States The official head of the U.S. Supreme Court.

chief·ly (chēf′lē) *adv.* **1.** Most of all; above all; especially. **2.** Principally; mainly.

chief of staff *U.S.* The principal staff officer who assists the commanding officer of a major military or naval organization, as a division or its equivalent, or higher levels.

Chief of Staff *U.S.* The ranking officer in the Army or Air Force, responsible to the Secretary of his department. Abbr. *C of S*

chief·tain (chēf′tən) *n.* **1.** The head of a clan or tribe. **2.** Any chief; leader. — **Syn.** See CHIEF. [< OF *chevetaine* < LL *capitaneus* < L *caput* head. Doublet of CAPTAIN.] — **chief′tain·cy, chief′tain·ship** *n.*

chiel (chēl) *n. Scot.* A young man; lad. Also **chield** (chēld).

chiff·chaff (chif′chaf′, -chäf′) *n.* A small, brownish white, Old World warbler (*Phylloscopus collybita*). [Imit. of its cry]

chif·fon (shi-fon′, shif′on) *n.* **1.** A sheer silk or rayon fabric. **2.** *pl.* Ornamental adjuncts of feminine attire, as ribbons or lace. — *adj.* **1.** Of or pertaining to chiffon. **2.** In cooking, having a light, fluffy texture like a soufflé. [< F, dim. of *chiffe* rag]

chif·fo·nier (shif′ə-nir′) *n.* A high chest of drawers, often with a mirror at the top. Also **chif′fon·nier′.** [< F < *chiffon.* See CHIFFON.]

chif·fo·robe (shif′ə-rōb) *n. U.S.* A wardrobe with drawers at one side. [< CHIFFO(NIER) + (WARD)ROBE]

chig·e·tai (chig′ə-tī) *n.* The dziggetai, a wild ass.

chig·ger (chig′ər) *n.* **1.** The larva of various mites (family *Trombidiidae*) of the southern United States, that attaches itself to the skin, causing intense itching: also called *chigoe, jigger, redbug.* **2.** The chigoe (def. 1). [Alter. of CHIGOE]

chi·gnon (shēn′yon, *Fr.* shē-nyôn′) *n.* A knot or roll of hair worn at the back of the head by women. [< F]

chig·oe (chig′ō) *n.* **1.** A flea (*Tunga penetrans*) of the West Indies and South America, of which the female burrows under the skin, especially of the feet, causing sores: also called *chegoe, chigger, jigger.* **2.** A chigger (def. 1) [< Carib]

Chih·fu (chē′foo′) See CHEFOO.

Chih·li (chē′lē′, Chinese ju′lē′), **Gulf of** See PO HAI.

Chi·hua·hua (chi-wä′wä) *n.* One of an ancient breed of very small, smooth-coated dogs with large, pointed ears, originally native to Mexico. [from *Chihuahua,* Mexico]

Chi·hua·hua (chi-wä′wä) **1.** A State in northern Mexico, on the Rio Grande; 94,830 sq. mi.; pop. 730,012 (1970); capital, **Chihuahua**, pop. 144,653 (1970).

chil- Var. of CHILO-.

chil·blain (chil′blān) *n. Pathol.* An inflammation of the hands or feet caused by exposure to cold. [< CHILL + BLAIN]

child (chīld) *n. pl.* **chil·dren 1.** An offspring of human parents; a son or daughter. **2.** A boy or girl, most commonly one between infancy and youth. **3.** A descendant: the *Children* of Israel. **4.** A childish person. **5.** A person or thing considered as a result or product of a specified condition, quality, etc.: a *child* of sorrow. **6.** *Brit. Dial.* A female infant. **7.** *Law* A legitimate son or daughter. **8.** *Archaic* A childe. Abbr. (def. 1, 2, 3) *c., C., ch., Ch.* — **with child** Pregnant. [OE *cild*] — **child′less** *adj.*

child-bear·ing (chīld′bâr′ing) *n.* The bringing forth of children.

child·bed (chīld′bed′) *n.* The state of a woman giving birth to a child.

child·birth (chīld′bûrth′) *n.* Parturition.

childe (chīld) *n. Archaic* A youth of noble birth. [Var. of CHILD]

Chil·der·mas (chil′dər·məs) *n.* Holy Innocents' Day. Also **Childermas Day**. [OE *cildra,* genitive pl. of *cild* child + *mæsse* Mass]

child·hood (chīld′hŏŏd) *n.* The state or time of being a child. [OE *cildhād*]

child·ing (chīl′ding) *adj.* **1.** *Archaic* Pregnant. **2.** *Bot.* Having young blossoms clustered around an older blossom.

child·ish (chīl′dish) *adj.* **1.** Of, like, or proper to a child. **2.** Unduly like a child; immature; puerile; weak. [OE *cildisc*] — **child′ish·ly** *adv.* — **child′ish·ness** *n.*
— **Syn. 1.** *Childish, childlike,* and *infantile* refer to the qualities of very young children, *childish* to the undesirable, *childlike* to the lovable ones: a *childish* fit of temper, a *childlike* candor. *Infantile* is often used in the sense of *childish* to express even greater disapproval or scorn. — **Ant.** manly, mature.

child labor The full-time employment of minors under a legally defined age. Standards concerning child labor differ in various States, but Federal law (1938) sets the minimum legal age at 16.

child·like (chīld′līk′) *adj.* Like, characteristic of, or appropriate to a child; artless, docile, etc. Also *Rare* **child′ly**. — **Syn.** See CHILDISH. — **child′like′ness** *n.*

chil·dren (chil′drən) Plural of CHILD.

Children of Israel The descendants of Jacob; the Jews.

child's play Something easy to do.

Chil·e (chil′ē, *Sp.* chē′lä) A Republic on the western coast of South America south of Peru; 286,397 sq. mi.; pop. 9,556,000 (1969); capital, Santiago: officially **Republic of Chile.** — **Chil′e·an** *adj. & n.*

Chile saltpeter   Caliche (def. 1).

chil·i (chil′ē) *n. pl.* **chil·ies 1.** The acrid red pod or fruit of certain peppers, especially *Capsicum frutescens*, used as a seasoning. **2.** Chili con carne. Also **chil′e, chil′li.** [< Sp. < Nahuatl *chilli*]

chil·i·ad (kil′ē·ad) *n.* **1.** A thousand. **2.** A period of a thousand years. [< L *chilias* < Gk. *chilias, -ados* < *chilioi* thousand]

chil·i·arch (kil′ē·ärk) *n.* In Greek antiquity, a commander of a thousand men. [< Gk. *chiliarchos* < *chilioi* thousand + *archos* leader]

chil·i·asm (kil′ē·az′əm) *n. Theol.* The doctrine that Christ will reign upon earth a thousand years. [< Gk. *chiliasmos* < *chilias*. See CHILIAD.] — **chil′i·ast** *n.* — **chil′i·as′tic** *adj.*

chili con car·ne (kon kär′nē) A highly seasoned dish made with meat, chili, and often beans. [< Sp., chili with meat]

chili sauce A spiced condiment sauce made with tomatoes and chili.

Chil·koot Pass (chil′kōot) A mountain pass from SE Alaska to the Yukon valley; elevation, 3,502 ft.

chill (chil) *n.* **1.** A sensation of cold, as that which precedes fever, often with shivering. **2.** A moderate degree of coldness. **3.** A check to enthusiasm, joy, etc. **4.** A numbing sensation of dread or anxiety. **5.** *Metall.* A metal mold in which to chill castings: also called *coquille*. — *v.t.* **1.** To reduce to a low temperature. **2.** To affect with cold; seize with a chill. **3.** To check, as ardor; dispirit. **4.** To harden the surface of (metal) by sudden cooling. — *v.i.* **5.** To become cold. **6.** To be stricken with a chill. **7.** To become hard by sudden cooling, as metal. — *adj.* **1.** Moderately or unpleasantly cold. **2.** Affected by or shivering with cold. **3.** Cold in manner; distant. **4.** Dispiriting; discouraging. [OE *ciele, cele*] — **chill′ing·ly** *adv.* — **chill′ness** *n.*

chill·er (chil′ər) *n.* **1.** That which chills. **2.** A horror story or movie.

Chil·lon (shi·lon′, *Fr.* shē·yôṅ′) A castle on the eastern shore of the Lake of Geneva, once used as a prison.

chill·y (chil′ē) *adj.* **chill·i·er, chill·i·est 1.** Causing chill; cold or chilling. **2.** Feeling cold; affected by chill. **3.** Lacking warmth; disheartening; unfriendly. — **chill′i·ly** *adv.* — **chill′i·ness** *n.*
— **Syn.** (adj.) cool, cold, chill, gelid, icy, frigid.

chilo- *combining form* Lip: *chilopod*. Also spelled *cheilo-*: also, before vowels, *chil-*. [< Gk. *cheilos* lip]

chi·lo·pod (kī′lə·pod) *n. Zool.* One of a class (*Chilopoda*) of arthropods with numerous legs; a centipede. [< NL CHILO- + -POD] — **chi·lop·o·dan** (kī·lop′ə·dən) *adj. & n.*

Chil·tern Hundreds (chil′tern) *Brit.* An ancient, now purely nominal office under the crown for which members of Parliament apply when they wish to resign.

Chi·lung (jē′lŏŏng′) See KEELUNG.

chi·mae·ra (kə·mir′ə, kī-) *n.* **1.** Any of a genus (*Chimaera*) of fishes related to the sharks and rays, having smooth skin, and a short anterior dorsal fin with a spine in front. **2.** See CHIMERA. [Var. of CHIMERA]

Chim·bo·ra·zo (chim′bō·rä′zō, *Sp.* chēm′bō·rä′sō) An inactive volcano in central Ecuador; 20,577 ft.

chime[1] (chīm) *n.* **1.** *Often pl.* A set of bells, as in a bell tower, tuned to a scale **2.** A single bell: the *chime* of a clock. **3.** A metal tube or set of tubes producing bell-like sounds when struck. **4.** *Often pl.* The sounds or music produced by a chime. **5.** A mechanism for playing a chime or chimes. **6.** Harmonious sound. **7.** Agreement; accord. — *v.* **chimed, chim·ing** *v.t.* **1.** To cause to sound musically by striking; ring. **2.** To announce (the hour) by the sound of bells. **3.** To summon, welcome, or send by chimes. **4.** To say rhythmically; prate. — *v.i.* **5.** To sound musically. **6.** To ring chimes. **7.** To harmonize; agree: with *with*. — **to chime in 1.** To join in harmoniously. **2.** To join, and so interrupt, a conversation. [ME *chimbe*, chime, alter. of OE *cimbal* < L *cymbalum* cymbal] — **chim′er** *n.*

chime[2] (chīm) *n.* The rim of a cask, barrel, etc., formed by the projecting ends of the staves: also called *chine*. Also **chimb** (chīm). [OE *cimb-* edge, as in *cimbing* joint]

chi·me·ra (kə·mir′ə, kī-) *n.* **1.** An absurd creation of the imagination; a foolish or horrible fancy. **2.** In painting, sculpture, etc., an imaginary, grotesque monster. **3.** An incongruous medley. **4.** *Biol.* A novel or unusual organism having tissue characteristic of two or more types; especially, a hybrid of mixed characteristics produced by grafting. Also spelled *chimaera*. [See CHIMERA]

Chi·me·ra (kə·mir′ə, kī-) In Greek mythology, a fire-breathing monster, part lion, part goat, and part serpent, killed by Bellerophon. Also **Chi·mae′ra** (-mir′-). [< L *chimaera* < Gk. *chimaira* she-goat]

chi·mere (chi·mir′, shi-) *n.* A loose, sleeveless outer vestment worn by Anglican bishops. Also **chim·ar** (chim′ər, shim′-), **chim′er.** [< OF *chamarre*]

chi·mer·i·cal (kə·mer′i·kəl, kī-) *adj.* **1.** Of the nature of a chimera; fantastic; imaginary. **2.** Given to fanciful dreams; visionary. Also **chi·mer′ic.** — **chi·mer′i·cal·ly** *adv.*

chim·ley (chim′lē) *n. Dial.* A chimney.

chim·ney (chim′nē) *n.* **1.** A flue to conduct gases and smoke from a fire to the outer air. **2.** A structure containing such a flue, usually vertical and rising above the roof of a building. **3.** A smokestack; funnel. **4.** A tube, usually of glass, for enclosing the flame of a lamp. **5.** A slender tube in an organ pipe, serving to sharpen the sound. **6.** *Geol.* **a** A formation of rock suggesting a chimney. **b** A long spur or pipe of ore. **7.** A vent of a volcano. **8.** *Dial.* A fireplace; hearth. [< OF *cheminee* < LL *caminata* < L *caminus* furnace, oven < Gk. *kaminos*]

chimney piece 1. A mantel. **2.** *Obs.* An ornament placed over a fireplace.

chimney pot A pipe placed on the top of a chimney to improve the draft and prevent smoking.

chimney swallow 1. The chimney swift. See under SWIFT. **2.** The European swallow (*Hirundo rustica*).

chimney sweep One whose occupation is the cleaning of soot from inside chimneys. Also **chimney sweeper.**

chimney swift See under SWIFT.

chi·mo (chē′mō) *interj. Canadian* A greeting, originally associated with the Eskimos, now sometimes used as a toast. [< Eskimo]

chim·pan·zee (chim′pan·zē′, chim·pan′zē) *n.* An arboreal anthropoid ape (*Pan troglodytes*) of equatorial Africa, having large ears and dark brown hair, and characteristically smaller, less erect, and more intelligent than the gorilla. [< native West African name]

chin (chin) *n.* **1.** The lower part of the face, between the mouth and the neck. **2.** *Anat.* The central and anterior part of the lower jaw. — *v.* **chinned, chin·ning** *v.t.* **1.** To lift (oneself) while grasping an overhead bar until the chin is level with the hands. — *v.i.* **2.** *U.S. Informal* To talk idly. **3.** To chin oneself. [OE *cin*]

CHIMPANZEE
(About 5 feet
high; weight,
170 pounds)

Chin. China; Chinese.

chi·na (chī′nə) *n.* **1.** Fine porcelain or ceramic ware, originally made in China. **2.** Any crockery. Also **chi′na·ware′.**

Chi·na (chī′nə) A country of eastern Asia, the most populous and third largest in the world; divided (1949) into the **People's Republic of China** on the mainland; 3,760,000 sq. mi. (est.); pop. 760 million (est. 1970); capital, Peking, and the **Republic of China** on Taiwan and several smaller islands; 13,890 sq. mi.; pop. 14 million (est. 1970); temporary capital, Taipei.

China aster An erect, hairy plant (*Callistephus chinensis*) of the composite family, with terminal heads and rayed flowers, cultivated in many varieties.

china bark Cinchona (def. 2).

chi·na·ber·ry (chī′nə·ber′ē) *n. pl.* **·ries 1.** Either of two trees (*Sapindus saponaria* and *S. marginatus*) of the soapberry family, found in Mexico and the SW United States. Also **China tree. 2.** Its berrylike fruit. **3.** The azedarach.

Chi·na·man (chī′nə·mən) *n. pl.* **·men** (-mən) A Chinese: an offensive term.

Chi·nan (jē′nän′) See TSINAN.

China Sea The part of the Pacific bordering on China. See EAST CHINA SEA, SOUTH CHINA SEA.

China squash The cushaw.

Chi·na·town (chī′nə·toun′) The Chinese quarter of any

city outside China, especially of San Francisco and New York City.

chin·ca·pin (ching′kə·pin)   See CHINQUAPIN.

chinch (chinch)   *n.* **1.** A small, typically brown and black hemipterous insect (*Blissus leucopterus*), destructive to grain. Also **chinch bug.** **2.** The bedbug.   [< Sp. *chinche* < L *cimex* bug]

chin·chil·la (chin·chil′ə)   *n.* **1.** A small rodent (*Chinchilla laniger*) native in the Andes, about the size of a squirrel. **2.** The soft, valuable, pearl gray fur of the chinchilla. **3.** A closely woven, twilled fabric having a tufted surface.   [< Sp., ? alter. of Quechua *sinchi* strong]

chin·cough (chin′kôf′, -kof′)   *n.* Whooping cough (which see).

Chin·dwin (chin′dwin′)   A river in Upper Burma, flowing over 500 miles, generally south, to the Irrawaddy.

chine[1] (chīn)   *n.* **1.** *Naut.* The line of intersection between the sides and bottom of a boat. **2.** The spine, backbone, or back. **3.** A piece of meat including all or part of the backbone. **4.** *Rare* A ridge. — *v.t.* **chined, chin·ing** *Archaic* To cut through the backbone of; cut into chines.   [< OF *eschine* backbone < Gmc.]

chine[2] (chīn)   *n.* Chime[2].

chine[3] (chīn)   *n.* *Brit. Dial.* A ravine formed by running water.   [OE *cinu*]

Chi·nese (chī·nēz′, -nēs′)   *adj.* Of or pertaining to China, its people, or their languages. — *n. pl.* **·nese** **1.** A native of China, or a person of Chinese ancestry. **2.** The standard language of China, based on the language spoken in Peking; Mandarin. **3.** A subfamily of the Sino-Tibetan family of languages, including the many languages and dialects spoken in China, as those of Peking, Canton, Amoy, Foochow, etc. **4.** Any of these languages or dialects, some of which are mutually unintelligible. Abbr. *Ch., Chin.*

Chinese blue   Prussian blue (which see).

Chinese Chippendale   See under CHIPPENDALE.

Chinese Empire   China as ruled by various imperial dynasties until the founding of the Republic of China, 1912.

Chinese ink   India ink (which see).

Chinese lantern   A collapsible lantern made of thin paper.

Chinese puzzle   **1.** An intricate puzzle originally made by the Chinese. **2.** Any problem difficult to solve.

Chinese red   **1.** Chrome red (which see).   **2.** Vermilion. Also **Chinese vermilion.**

Chinese Republic   See CHINA.

Chinese Revolution   See REVOLUTION

Chinese Turkestan   See under TURKESTAN.

Chinese Wall   See GREAT WALL OF CHINA.

Chinese wax   The yellowish white, waxy secretion of a scale insect (*Ceroplastes ceriferus*), deposited on the branches and twigs of a certain Chinese ash tree.

Chinese white   **1.** A pigment composed of barium sulfate. **2.** Very thick zinc oxide used as a pigment.

Chinese windlass   A differential windlass (which see).

Chinese wood oil   Oil from the tung tree.

Chinese yellow   One of various bright ocher pigments.

Ching·hai (ching′hī′)   See TSINGHAI.

Chin Hills (chin)   A mountainous region of Upper Burma; highest point, Mt. Victoria, 10,018 ft.

chink[1] (chingk)   *n.* A small, narrow cleft; crevice. — *v.t.* **1.** To make cracks or fissures in. **2.** To fill the cracks of, as a wall; plug up.   [ME *chynke*] — **chink′y** *adj.*

chink[2] (chingk)   *n.* **1.** A short, sharp, metallic sound. **2.** *Slang* Coin; cash. — *v.t. & v.i.* To make or cause to make a sharp, clinking sound.   [Imit.]

Chink (chingk)   *n.* *Slang* A Chinese: an offensive term.

Chin·kiang (chin′kyang′)   A port city in eastern China, on the Yangtze; pop. 250,000 (1970): also *Chen-chiang, Chen-kiang.*

Chin·ne·reth (kin′ə·reth), **Sea of**   The Old Testament name for the (Sea of) GALILEE.

chi·no (chē′nō)   *n.* **1.** A strong cotton fabric with a twilled weave. **2.** *pl.* Boys′ or mens′ trousers of this material.   [< Sp., toasted; with ref. to the original tan color]

Chino-   *combining form* Belonging to or connected with China: *Chino-Japanese.* Compare SINO-.

chi·noi·se·rie (shē·nwàz·rē′)   *n. French* **1.** An example of Chinese art, etc. **2.** Intricate complexity; red tape.

chi·nook (chi·nŏŏk′, -nŏŏk′)   *n.* *U.S. & Canadian* **1.** A warm wind of the Oregon and Washington coasts. **2.** A warm, dry wind that blows off the eastern slopes of the Rocky Mountains in the NW United States and western Canada: also called *snow-eater.* [after *Chinook*]

Chi·nook (chi·nŏŏk′, -nŏŏk′)   *n. pl.* **·nook** or **·nooks** **1.** One of a tribe of North American Indians speaking Chinookan languages, formerly occupying the region of the Columbia River, Oregon. **2.** The language of this tribe.

Chi·nook·an (chi·nŏŏ′kən, -nŏŏk′ən)   *n.* A North American Indian linguistic family of the Penutian phylum. — *adj.* Of or pertaining to the Chinook, their culture, or their language.

Chinook jargon   A lingua franca comprising words from Chinook and other Indian languages, mixed with English and French, once used by traders and Indians from Oregon to Alaska.

Chinook salmon   A salmon (*Oncorhyncus tschawy′tscha*) of North Pacific coastal waters: also called *king salmon, quinnat, tyee.*

chin·qua·pin (ching′kə·pin)   *n.* **1.** Any of several trees (genus *Castanea*) of North America; especially, *C. pumila*: also called *dwarf chestnut.* **2.** A related tree, the **giant chinquapin** (*Castanopsis chrysophylla*) of the Pacific coast. **3.** The edible nut of these trees. Also spelled *chincapin*: also **chin′ka·pin.**   [< N. Am. Ind.]

chintz (chints)   *n.* A cotton fabric usually glazed and printed in bright colors. Also **chints.**   [Orig. *chints*, pl. of Hind. *chīnt* < Skt. *chitra* variegated]

chintz·y[1] (chints′ē)   *adj.* **chintz·i·er, chintz·i·est** Of, relating to, or displaying chintz.

chintz·y[2] (chints′ē)   *adj.* **chintz·i·er, chintz·i·est** *U.S. Informal* Cheap; trashy; measly.   [? < CHINTZ + -Y[2]]

Chi·os (kī′os, *Greek* khē′ôs)   An island of Greece, in the Aegean off the west coast of Asia Minor; 321 sq. mi.: also *Khios.*

chip[1] (chip)   *n.* **1.** A small piece cut or broken off. **2.** A small disk or counter used in certain games, as in poker. **3.** A crack or imperfection caused by chipping. **4.** A thinly sliced morsel: potato *chips.* **5.** *pl. Brit.* French fried potatoes. **6.** *Usually pl.* Dried animal droppings used as fuel. **7.** Anything of little or no value; also, anything dried up or tasteless. **8.** Wood, palm leaves, etc., cut into strips for weaving. **9.** In golf, a chip shot (which see). — **a chip off** (or **of**) **the old block** One who resembles either of his parents in behavior, appearance, etc. — **a chip on one′s shoulder** A willingness to take offense; belligerent manner. — **in the chips** *Slang* Possessing money; affluent. — *v.* **chipped, chip·ping** *v.t.* **1.** To break off small pieces of, as china. **2.** To chop or cut, as with an ax. **3.** To shape by cutting off pieces. — *v.i.* **4.** To become chipped. **5.** In golf, to make a chip shot. — **to chip in** **1.** *Informal* To contribute, as to a fund. **2.** In poker, to put up one′s ante or bet. **3.** *Informal* To interpose (a remark); interrupt.   [ME *chippe.* Related to CHAP[2], CHOP[1].] — **chip′per** *n.*

chip[2] (chip)   *v.t. & v.i.* **chipped, chip·ping** To cheep. — *n.* A squeak or weak chirp, as of a bird.   [Imit.]

chip[3] (chip)   *n.* In wrestling, a trick to throw one′s opponent.   [Cf. ON *kippa* a pull, sudden motion]

Chip·e·wy·an (chip·ə·wī′ən)   *n.* **1.** One of a tribe of North American Indians living in NW Canada. **2.** The Athapascan language of this tribe.

chip·munk (chip′mungk)   *n.* Any of various striped North American rodents of the squirrel family; especially *Tamias striatus* of the eastern United States and Canada, and the genus *Eutamias* of the West, having many subspecies: also called *ground squirrel, hackee, striped squirrel.* Also **chip·muck** (chip′-muk), **chipping squirrel.**   [< N. Am. Ind.]

chipped beef (chipt)   Beef smoked and sliced thin.

Chip·pen·dale (chip′ən·dāl)   *adj.* Designating a graceful, rococo style of furniture made by, or in the manner of, Thomas Chippendale, 1718–79, English cabinetmaker. — **Chinese Chippendale** Denoting Chippendale furniture characterized by adaptations of Chinese forms and motifs.

chip·per (chip′ər)   *adj.* *U.S. Informal* **1.** Brisk; cheerful. **2.** Smartly dressed; spruce. — *v.i.* **1.** To chirp, as a bird; twitter. **2.** To chatter; babble.   [? < CHIP[2]]

Chip·pe·wa (chip′ə·wä, -wä, -wə)   *n. pl.* **·wa** or **·was** Ojibwa. Also **Chip·pe·way** (chip′ə·wā).

chipping sparrow   A small sparrow (*Spizella passerina*) of eastern North America, with a reddish brown cap.

chip·py (chip′ē)   *n. pl.* **·pies** **1.** The chipping sparrow (which see).   **2.** A chipmunk.   **3.** *Slang* A young woman of easy morals; also, a prostitute. — *adj. Canadian Slang* Quarrelsome; truculent: also **chip′pie.**

chips (chips)   *n. Often cap. Informal* A ship′s carpenter.

chip shot   In golf, a short, lofted shot made in approaching the green.

Chi·ri·co (kē′rē·kō), **Giorgio di,** born 1888, Italian painter.

chirk (chûrk)   *v.i. Scot.* To make a screeching or gritting noise; creak; shriek. — **to chirk up** *Informal* To cheer up.   [OE *cearcian* to creak]

chirm (chûrm)   *n.* Twittering or din, as of many birds. — *v.i.* To make a chirm.   [OE *cirm < cirman* to cry out]

chiro-   *combining form* Hand; of or with the hand: *chirography.* Also spelled *cheiro-.* Also, before vowels, **chir-.**   [< Gk *cheir, cheiros* hand]

chi·rog·ra·phy (kī·rog′rə·fē)   *n.* The art, style, or character of handwriting.   [< CHIRO- + -GRAPHY] — **chi·rog′ra·pher** *n.* — **chi·ro·graph·ic** (kī′rə·graf′ik) or **·i·cal** *adj.*

chi·ro·man·cy (kī′rə·man′sē)   *n.* Palmistry.   [< F *chiromancie,* ult. < Gk. *cheiromanteia < cheir* hand + *manteia* divination] — **chi′ro·man′cer** *n.*

Chi·ron (kī′ron)   In Greek mythology, a wise centaur, tutor of Achilles and other heroes: also *Cheiron.*

chi·ro·plas·ty (kī′rə·plas′tē)   *n.* Plastic surgery of the hand.   [< CHIRO- + -PLASTY]

CHIPMUNK

(About 6½ inches long; tail 4½ inches)

chi·rop·o·dy (kə·rop/ə·dē, kī-)   n. The branch of medicine that deals with ailments of the foot, as bunions, corns, etc.: also called *pedicure, podiatry*. [< CHIRO- + Gk. *pous, podos* foot] — **chi·rop/o·dist** *n*.

chi·ro·prac·tic (kī/rə·prak/tik)   n. A method of therapy based on the theory that disease is mainly due to a malfunction of the nerves that may be corrected by manipulation of bodily structures, especially the spinal column. [< CHIRO- + Gk. *praktikos* effective < *prattein* to do, act] — **chi·ro·prac·tor** (kī/rə·prak/tər) *n*.

chi·rop·ter (kī·rop/tər)   n. *Zool.* Any of an order (*Chiroptera*) of flying mammals; a bat. [< NL < CHIRO- + Gk. *pteron* wing] — **chi·rop/ter·an** *adj. & n*.

chirp (chûrp)   v.i. 1. To give a short, acute cry, as a sparrow or locust; cheep, as a young bird. 2. To make a similar sound. 3. To talk in a quick and shrill manner. — *v.t.* 4. To utter with a quick, sharp sound. — *n.* The sound of chirping. [Var. of CHIRK] — **chirp/er** *n*.

chirr (chûr)   v.i. To make a sharp trilling sound, as that of the grasshopper, cicada, and some birds. — *n.* The trilling sound of crickets, locusts, etc. Also **chirre**. [Imit.]

chir·rup (chir/əp)   v.i. 1. To chirp continuously or repeatedly, as a bird. 2. To chirp with the lips, as in urging a horse. — *v.t.* 3. To utter with chirps. — *n.* A sound of chirruping. [< CHIRP] — **chir/rup·y** *adj*.

chi·rur·geon (kī·rûr/jən)   n. *Archaic* A surgeon. Abbr. *ch., Ch.* [< OF *cirurgien*, ult. < L *chirurgia* surgery < Gk. *cheirourgia* < *cheir* hand + *ergon* work] — **chi·rur/ger·y** *n.* — **chi·rur/gic** or **·gi·cal** *adj*.

chis·el (chiz/əl)   n. A cutting tool with a beveled edge, used for cutting, engraving, or mortising metal, stone, or wood. — *v.* **chis·eled** or **·elled, chis·el·ing** or **el·ling** *v.t.* 1. To cut, engrave, or carve with or as with a chisel. 2. *Slang* To cheat; swindle; also, to obtain by dishonest or unfair methods. — *v.i.* 3. To use a chisel. 4. *Slang* To use dishonest or unfair methods. [< AF, ult. < L *caedere* to cut] — **chis/el·er** or **chis/el·ler** *n*.

chis·eled (chiz/əld)   adj. 1. Cut or shaped with or as with a chisel. 2. Finely formed; distinctly outlined. Also *Brit.* **chis/elled**.

Chi·shi·ma Ret·to (chē·shē·mä ret·tō) The Japanese name for the KURILE ISLANDS.

Chis·holm Trail (chiz/əm) An old cattle trail from San Antonio, Texas, to Abilene, Kansas.

Chi·si·nău (kē/shē·nä/) Rumanian name for KISHINEV.

Chis·leu (kis/lef) See KISLEW.

chi-square test (kī/skwâr/) *Stat.* A test of the reliability of using a particular frequency distribution to fit the data.

chit¹ (chit)   n. 1. A voucher of a sum owed, as for food. 2. *Brit.* A short letter; note; memorandum: also **chit/ty**. [< Hind. *chiṭṭhī* note]

chit² (chit)   n. A pert child, girl, or young woman. [ME *chitt.* ? Related to CAT.]

Chi·ta (chē·tä/) A city in the southern Russian S.F.S.R., on the Trans-Siberian Railway; pop. 171,000 (1959).

chit-chat (chit/chat/)   n. 1. Informal or familiar talk. 2. Gossip. [Reduplication of CHAT¹]

chi·tin (kī/tin)   n. *Biochem.* A colorless, horny, amorphous substance, the principal constituent of the hard covering of insects and crustaceans. [< F *chitine* < Gk. *chitōn* tunic]. — **chi/tin·ous** *adj*.

chi·ton (kī/tən)   n. 1. A gown or tunic worn by men and women in ancient Greece. 2. Any of a genus (*Chiton*) of marine mollusks found mostly on rocks. [< Gk. *chitōn*]

Chit·ta·gong (chit/ə·gong) The main port city of Bangladesh, in the SE part on the Karnaphuli river; pop. 363,000 (1961).

chit·ter (chit/ər)   v.i. 1. To twitter. 2. *Dial.* To shiver, as with cold. [Var. of CHATTER]

chit·ter·ling (chit/ər·ling)   n. 1. *pl.* The small intestines of pigs, especially as used for food; also **chit/lin** (chit/lin), **chit/ling**. 2. *Obs.* A short frill; ruff. [Cf. G *kutteln* entrails]

chiv·al·ric (shiv/əl·rik, shi·val/rik)   adj. 1. Of or pertaining to chivalry. 2. Chivalrous.

chiv·al·rous (shiv/əl·rəs)   adj. 1. Having the qualities of the ideal knight; gallant, courteous, generous, etc. 2. Pertaining to chivalry. [< OF *chevalereus* < *chevalier* knight] — **chiv/al·rous·ly** *adv.* — **chiv/al·rous·ness** *n*.

chiv·al·ry (shiv/əl·rē)   n. 1. The feudal system of knighthood. 2. The spirit or principles of this system; knight-errantry. 3. The ideal qualities of knighthood, as courtesy, valor, charity, skill in arms, etc. 4. A body of knights, warriors, gallant gentlemen, etc. 5. *Obs.* The rank of a knight; knighthood. [< OF *chevalerie*, ult. < LL *caballarius* cavalier. Doublet of CAVALRY.]

chiv·a·ree (shiv/ə·rē/) See CHARIVARI.

chive (chīv)   n. A perennial herb (*Allium schoenoprasum*) allied to the leek and onion, used as a flavoring in cooking. Also **chive garlic**. [< AF < L *cepa* onion]

chiv·y (chiv/ē), **chiv·vy** See CHEVY (def. 1).

Ch. J. Chief Justice.

Chka·lov (chkä/ləf) A former name for ORENBURG.

chlam·y·date (klam/ə·dāt)   adj. *Zool.* Having a mantle, as certain mollusks. [< L *chlamydatus* cloaked < Gk. *chlamys, -ydos* cloak]

chla·myd·e·ous (klə·mid/ē·əs)   adj. *Bot.* Pertaining to the floral envelope of a plant. [< Gk. *chlamys, -ydos* cloak]

chla·mys (klā/mis, klam/is)   n. pl. **chla·mys·es** or **ch'am·y·des** (klam/ə·dēz) A short cloak caught up on the shoulder, worn by men in ancient Greece. [< Gk.]

Chlod·wig (klōt/vik) See CLOVIS.

Chlo·e (klō/ē) See DAPHNIS AND CHLOE.

chlor- Var. of CHLORO-.

chlor·a·cet·o·phe·none (klôr/ə·set/ə·fi·nōn/, klōr/-)   n. *Chem.* A colorless, crystalline compound, C_8H_7ClO, with an odor of apple blossoms, used as a tear gas. Symbol, CN.

chlo·ral (klôr/əl, klō/rəl)   n. *Chem.* 1. A colorless, oily, liquid compound, $CCl_3·CHO$, with a penetrating odor, obtained variously, as by the action of chlorine on alcohol. 2. A white, crystalline, pungent compound, $CCl_3CHO·H_2O$, used medicinally as a hypnotic: also **chloral hydrate**. [< CHLOR(INE) + AL(COHOL)]

chlo·ra·mine (klôr/ə·mēn, klō/rə-)   n. *Chem.* A colorless, volatile liquid compound, NH_2Cl, derived from ammonia. [< CHLOR- + -AMINE]

chlo·ram·phen·i·col (klôr/am·fen/i·kōl, -kol, klō/ram-)   n. *Chem.* A crystalline nitrogenous compound, $C_{11}H_{12}Cl_2O_5N_2$, obtained from a soil bacillus (*Streptomyces venezuelae*) and also made synthetically, used as an antibiotic against certain viral, bacterial, and rickettsial diseases. [< CHLOR- + AM(IDE) + PHE(NOL) + NI(TROGEN) + (GLY)COL]

chlo·rate (klôr/āt, klō/rāt)   n. *Chem.* A salt of chloric acid.

chlor·dane (klôr/dān, klōr/-)   n. *Chem.* A viscous, odorless, toxic compound of chlorine, $C_{10}H_6Cl_8$, used in various concentrations as a fumigant and insecticide, especially against cockroaches. Also **chlor/dan** (-dan).

chlo·rel·la (klə·rel/ə)   n. *Bot.* Any of a genus (*Chlorella*) of unicellular green algae, some species of which yield large amounts of proteins, carbohydrates, and fats suitable for use as human food. [< NL, dim. of Gk. *chlóros* green]

chlo·ren·chy·ma (klə·reng/kə·mə)   n. *Bot.* Stem tissue of a plant containing chlorophyll. [< CHLOR(OPHYLL) + (PAR)-ENCHYMA]

chlo·ric (klôr/ik, klō/rik)   adj. *Chem.* Of, pertaining to, or combined with chlorine in its higher valence.

chloric acid *Chem.* A monobasic, pungent acid, $HClO_3$, existing only in solution.

chlo·ride (klôr/īd, -id, klō/rīd, -rid)   n. *Chem.* A compound of chlorine with a more positive element or radical. Also **chlo·rid** (klôr/id, klō/rid). — **chlo·rid·ic** (klə·rid/ik) *adj*.

chloride of lime *Chem.* A disinfecting and bleaching agent made by the action of chlorine on slaked lime; bleaching powder.

chlo·rin·ate (klôr/ə·nāt, klō/rə-)   v.t. **·at·ed, ·at·ing** *Chem.* To treat, impregnate, or cause to combine with chlorine, as in purifying water, whitening fabrics, or separating gold from ore. — **chlo/rin·a/tion** *n.* — **chlo/rin·a/tor** *n*.

chlo·rine (klôr/ēn, -in, klō/rēn, -rin)   n. A greenish yellow, poisonous, readily liquefiable gaseous element (symbol Cl) of the halogen group, with a suffocating odor, obtained principally from common salt, and widely used in industry, medicine, etc. Also **chlo·rin** (klôr/in, klō/rin). See ELEMENT. [< Gk. *chlóros* green]

chlo·rin·i·ty (klô·rin/ə·tē)   n. A measure of the total amount of chlorine per kilogram of sea water. Compare SALINITY.

chlo·rite¹ (klôr/īt, klō/rīt)   n. Any of several green hydrous silicates, closely related to the micas. [< Gk. *chlóritis* greenstone < *chlóros* green]

chlo·rite² (klôr/īt, klō/rīt)   n. *Chem.* A salt of chlorous acid. [< CHLOR- + -ITE]

chloro- combining form 1. Light green: *chlorophyll*. 2. Chlorine: *chlorohydrin*. Also, before vowels, *chlor-*. [< Gk. *chlóros* green]

chlo·ro·a·ce·tic acid (klôr/ō·ə·sē/tik, -ə·set/ik, klō/rō-) *Chem.* A colorless, corrosive compound, $CH_2ClCOOH$, derived from acetic acid, used in synthesizing dyestuffs and in medicine as a caustic.

chlo·ro·form (klôr/ə·fôrm, klō/rə-)   n. *Chem.* A colorless, volatile, sweetish liquid compound, $CHCl_3$, used as an anesthetic and solvent. — *v.t.* 1. To administer chloroform to. 2. To anesthetize or kill with chloroform. [< CHLORO- + FORM(YL)]

chlo·ro·hy·drin (klôr/ə·hī/drin, klō/rə-)   n. *Chem.* Any of a group of organic compounds containing the hydroxyl radical and chlorine. [< CHLORO- + HYDR- + -IN]

Chlo·ro·my·ce·tin (klôr/ə·mī·sē/tən, klō/rə-)   n. Proprietary name for a brand of chloramphenicol, used as an antibiotic: also **chlo/ro·my·ce/tin**.

chlo·ro·phane (klôr/ə·fān, klō/rə-)   n. A variety of fluorite

CHLAMYS

emitting a green phosphorescence when heated. [< CHLORO- + Gk. *phainein* to appear]

chlo·ro·phyll (klôr′ə·fil, klō′rə-) *n. Biochem.* The green nitrogenous coloring matter contained in the chloroplasts of plants, essential to the production of carbohydrates by photosynthesis. It occurs in two forms, the bluish green **chlorophyll-A**, $C_{55}H_{72}O_5N_4Mg$, the most abundant form, and the yellowish green **chlorophyll-B**, $C_{55}H_{70}O_6N_4Mg$. Some derivatives are used as dyes, in cosmetics, and in medicine for healing wounds. Also **chlo′ro·phyl.** [< CHLORO- + Gk. *phyllon* leaf] — **chlo·ro·phyl·la·ceous** (klôr′ə·fi·lā′shəs, klō′rə-), **chlo′ro·phyl′lose** (-fil′ōs), **chlo·ro·phyl′lous** (-fil′əs) *adj.*

chlo·ro·plast (klôr′ə·plast, klō′rə-) *n. Bot.* One of the flattened bodies or plastids containing chlorophyll. Also **chlo′ro·plas′tid.** [< CHLORO- + PLAST(ID)]

chlo·ro·prene (klôr′ə·prēn, klō′rə-) *n. Chem.* A colorless liquid, C_4H_5Cl, synthesized from acetylene and chlorine, that, in its polymerized forms, yields neoprene. [< CHLORO- + (ISO)PRENE]

chlo·ro·sis (klə·rō′sis) *n.* **1.** *Pathol.* An anemic disease affecting young women, characterized by a greenish pallor, hysteria, etc.; greensickness. **2.** *Bot.* The blanching or etiolation of plants, usually resulting from a lack of iron and other mineral salts. [< NL < Gk. *chlōros* green] — **chlo·rot·ic** (klə·rot′ik) *adj.*

chlo·rous (klôr′əs, klō′rəs) *adj. Chem.* Of, pertaining to, or combined with chlorine in its lower valence.

chlor·pic·rin (klôr·pik′rin, klōr-) *n. Chem.* A colorless, oily liquid, CCl_3NO_2, having a nauseous vapor and used as an insecticide and chemical warfare agent. Also **chlo′ro·pic′rin.** [< CHLOR- + PICR(IC ACID) + -IN]

chlor·pro·ma·zine (klôr·prō′mə·zēn, -zin, klōr-) *n.* A synthetic tranquilizing drug used to control severe excitement in certain mental disorders. [A composite word from dimethyl amino*propyl chlor*ophenothi*azine* hydrochloride]

chlor·tet·ra·cy·cline (klôr′tet·rə·sī′klin, klōr′-) *n. Chem.* An organic compound chemically related to tetracycline, obtained from a soil bacillus (*Streptomyces aureofaciens*), and used as an antibiotic. [< CHLOR- + TETRACYCLINE]

chm. **1.** Checkmate. **2.** Chairman: also **chmn.**

Ch.M. Master of Surgery (L *Chirurgiae Magister*).

cho·an·o·cyte (kō·an′ə·sīt) *n.* Collar cell. [< Gk. *choanē* funnel + -CYTE]

Choate (chōt), **Joseph Hodges,** 1832–1917, U.S. lawyer and ambassador. — **Rufus,** 1799–1859, U.S. lawyer and orator.

chock (chok) *n.* **1.** A block or wedge, so placed as to prevent or limit motion. **2.** *Naut.* **a** A heavy piece of metal or wood fastened to a deck, etc., and having jaws through which a rope or cable may pass. **b** A block or support on which to rest a boat, etc. — *v.t.* **1.** To make fast or fit with a chock or chocks. **2.** To place on chocks, as a boat. — *adv.* As far or as close as possible. [< AF *choque* log]

CHOCK (def. 2)

chock-a-block (chok′ə·blok′) *adj.* **1.** Drawn to the limit, with blocks touching: said of a tackle. **2.** Close together; jammed. — *adv.* Close; very near.

chock-full (chok′fŏŏl′) *adj.* Completely full; stuffed: also **choke-full, chuck-full.** [ME *chokke-fulle*; ult. origin uncertain]

choc·o·late (chôk′lit, chôk′ə·lit, chok′-) *n.* **1.** A preparation of cacao nuts roasted and ground without removing the fat, and usually sweetened and flavored. **2.** A beverage or confection made from this. **3.** A dark brown color. — *adj.* Flavored with, made with, or colored like chocolate. [< Sp. < Nahuatl *chocolatl*] — **choc·o·lat·y** *adj.*

Choc·taw (chôk′tô) *n. pl.* **·taw** or **·taws 1.** A member of a tribe of North American Indians of Muskhogean stock, now living in Oklahoma. **2.** The language of this tribe. **3.** *U.S. Informal* Unintelligible language; jargon.

choice (chois) *n.* **1.** The act of choosing; selection. **2.** The right or privilege of choosing; option. **3.** The person or thing chosen. **4.** A number or variety from which to choose: a great *choice* of dishes. **5.** A well-selected supply. **6.** An alternative: He had no *choice*. **7.** The best or preferred part of anything. **8.** Excellence: wine of *choice*. — *adj.* **choic·er, choic·est 1.** Meriting preference; select; excellent. **2.** Chosen with care. [< OF *chois* < *choisir* to choose] — **choice′ly** *adv.* — **choice′ness** *n.*
— **Syn.** (adj.) See EXCELLENT. — **Ant.** inferior, ordinary, poor.

choir (kwīr) *n.* **1.** An organized body of singers, especially in a church. **2.** The part of a church occupied by such singers; chancel. **3.** Any company, especially of dancers or musicians. **4.** *Theol.* Any of the nine angelic orders. — *v.i.* **1.** To sing, as in a choir. — *v.t.* **2.** To sing or utter in chorus. [< OF *cuer* < L *chorus*; infl. in form by F *choeur* choir. Doublet of CHORUS.]

choir·boy (kwīr′boi′) *n.* A boy who sings in a choir.

choir loft A gallery in a church set aside for the choir.

choir·mas·ter (kwīr′mas′tər, -mäs′-) *n.* One who directs or trains a choir.

Choi·seul (shwä·zœl′) One of the British Solomon Islands; about 1,500 sq. mi.

Choi·seul (shwä·zœl′), **Duc Étienne de,** 1719–85, French statesman.

choke (chōk) *v.* **choked, chok·ing** *v.t.* **1.** To stop the breathing of by obstructing or constricting the windpipe; strangle. **2.** To keep back; suppress. **3.** To fill completely. **4.** To obstruct or close up by filling; clog. **5.** To retard the progress, growth, or action of. **6.** To lessen the air intake of the carburetor in order to enrich the fuel mixture of (a gasoline engine). — *v.i.* **7.** To become suffocated or stifled. **8.** To become clogged, fouled, or obstructed. **9.** In sports, to assume a shortened or raised grip, as on a bat. — **to choke up 1.** To be overcome by emotion, tears, etc. **2.** To perform poorly because of tension, agitation, etc. — *n.* **1.** The act or sound of choking. **2.** A narrow, constrictive part, as in a chokebore. **3.** *Mech.* A device to control the flow of air, as to a gasoline engine. **4.** *Electr.* A choke coil. [Appar. var. of obs. *achoke* to strangle < OE *acēocian*]

choke·ber·ry (chōk′ber′ē, -bər·ē) *n. pl.* **·ries 1.** A North American shrub (genus *Aronia*) of the rose family. **2.** The small, red or purple astringent fruit of this shrub.

choke·bore (chōk′bôr′, -bōr′) *n.* In shotguns, a bore narrowed at the muzzle to concentrate the shot; also, a shotgun with such a bore.

choke·cher·ry (chōk′cher′ē) *n. pl.* **·ries** A wild cherry (*Prunus virginiana*) of North America, or its sour fruit.

choke coil *Electr.* A low-resistance coil of sufficient inductance to limit or suppress any fluctuating current without impeding the flow of a steady current.

choke·damp (chōk′damp′) *n.* **1.** Any condition of the atmosphere resulting in choking or suffocation. **2.** *Mining* Blackdamp (which see).

choke-full (chōk′fŏŏl′) See CHOCK-FULL.

chok·er (chō′kər) *n.* **1.** One who or that which chokes. **2.** *Informal* A neckcloth or necklace worn high around the throat; also, a high, tight collar. **3.** A small fur neckpiece.

choking (chō′king) *adj.* **1.** Stifling; smothering. **2.** Strained with emotion, as the voice. — **chok′ing·ly** *adv.*

chok·y (chō′kē) *adj.* **chok·i·er, chok·i·est 1.** Causing one to choke. **2.** Somewhat choked. Also **chok′ey.**

chole- *combining form* Bile; gall: *cholesterol*. Also **cholo-:** also, before vowels, **chol-.** [< Gk. *cholē* bile]

chol·e·cyst (kol′ə·sist) *n. Anat.* The gall bladder. [< NL *cholecystis* < Gk. *cholē* gall + *kystis* bladder]

chol·er (kol′ər) *n.* **1.** Anger; hastiness of temper, formerly thought to be caused by an excess of bile. **2.** Formerly: **a** Bile. Compare HUMOR (def. 7). **b** Biliousness. [< OF *colere* < L *cholera*. See CHOLERA.]

chol·er·a (kol′ər·ə) *n. Pathol.* An acute, infectious, epidemic disease characterized principally by serious intestinal disorders, caused by a bacterium (*Vibrio comma*). In its more malignant forms, as **Asiatic cholera,** it is usually fatal. [< L < Gk., cholera morbus]

cholera in·fan·tum (in·fan′təm) *Pathol.* A noncontagious, often fatal diarrhea of children, occurring in summer. [< L, cholera of infants]

cholera mor·bus (môr′bəs) *Pathol.* Acute gastroenteritis, a summer complaint. Also **cholera nos·tras** (nos′tras). [< L, cholera disease]

chol·er·ic (kol′ər·ik) *adj.* **1.** Easily provoked to anger; irascible. **2.** Of the nature of, or caused by, anger. **3.** *Obs.* Bilious or causing biliousness.

cho·les·ter·ol (kə·les′tə·rōl, -rol) *n. Biochem.* A fatty, monatomic crystalline alcohol, $C_{27}H_{45}OH$, derived principally from bile, present in most gallstones, and very widely distributed in animal fats and tissues. Also **cho·les′ter·in** (-in). [< CHOLE- + Gk. *stereos* solid + -OL²]

cho·line (kō′lēn, kol′ēn, -in) *n. Biochem.* A colorless, viscous, strongly alkaline compound, $C_5H_{15}NO_2$, found in many animal and vegetable tissues.

chol·la (chōl′yä) *n.* Any of several treelike, very spiny cacti (genus *Opuntia*) of SW United States and Mexico. [< Sp., head]

Cho·lu·la (chə·lōō′lä) A city in central Mexico; site of a pre-Columbian pyramid to Quetzalcoatl; about 8,500.

chon·dri·fy (kon′drə·fī) *v.t. & v.i.* **·fied, ·fy·ing** *Physiol.* To convert into or become cartilage. — **chon′dri·fi·ca′tion** *n.*

chon·dri·o·somes (kon′drē·ə·sōmz′) *n.pl. Biol.* Mitochondria. [< Gk. *chondrion*, dim. of *chondros* cartilage + -SOME²]

chondro- *combining form* Cartilage. Also, before vowels, **chondr-.** [< Gk. *chondros* cartilage]

chon·droid (kon′droid) *adj. Anat.* Resembling cartilage.

chon·dro·ma (kon·drō′mə) *n. pl.* **·mas** or **·ma·ta** (-mə·tə) *Pathol.* A cartilaginous tumor. [< NL]

Cho·ne·an (chō′nē·ən) *n.* Tsonecan (def. 2).

choose (chōōz) *v.* **chose, cho·sen, choos·ing** *v.t.* **1.** To select as most desirable; take by preference. **2.** To desire or have a preference for. **3.** To prefer (to do something): He has *chosen* to remain. — *v.i.* **4.** To make a choice. — **cannot choose but** Must. [OE *cēosan*] — **choos′er** *n.*
— **Syn.** *Choose, select, pick, cull,* and *prefer* mean to take one or a few things from a larger group. *Choose* implies an act of will: to *choose* sides. *Select* emphasizes careful consideration and comparison: to *select* the best apples in a basket. To *pick* is to *select* because especially well fitted or appropriate: to *pick* men for an honor guard. *Cull* means to *select* and collect at the same time: to *cull*

striking passages from a book. To *prefer* is to favor mentally, often without any overt act: to *prefer* sunshine to rain.

choos·y (chōō′zē) *adj.* **choos·i·er, choos·i·est** *Informal* Disposed to be particular or fussy in one's choices. Also **choos′ey.**

chop[1] (chop) *v.* **chopped, chop·ping** *v.t.* **1.** To cut or make by strokes of a sharp tool: to *chop* a hole in the ice. **2.** To cut up in small pieces; mince. **3.** To utter jerkily; cut short. **4.** To make a cutting, downward stroke at (the ball), as in tennis. — *v.i.* **5.** To make cutting strokes, as with an ax. **6.** To go, come, or move with sudden or violent motion. — *n.* **1.** The act of chopping. **2.** A piece chopped off; especially, a cut of meat, usually lamb, pork, or veal. **3.** A sharp, downward, cutting blow or stroke, as in boxing, tennis, cricket, etc. **4.** A quick, broken motion of waves; also, choppy water. **5.** A cleft or fissure; a crack, especially in the skin. [ME *choppen.* Akin to CHAP[2], CHIP.]
— **Syn.** (verb) **1.** hew, hack, cleave, slash. — (noun) See WAVE.

chop[2] (chop) *v.* **chopped, chop·ping** *v.i.* **1.** To veer suddenly; shift, as the wind; vacillate. **2.** *Obs.* To bargain; barter. — *v.t.* **3.** *Obs.* To barter. [ME *choppen.* Akin to CHEAP.]

chop[3] (chop) *n.* **1.** *Usually pl.* A jaw; also the part of the face about the mouth or jaws. **2.** A sudden bite or snap. — *v.t.* **chopped, chop·ping 1.** To utter in a quick, abrupt manner. **2.** To seize with the jaws; snap. [Var. of CHAP[3]]

chop[4] (chop) *n.* **1.** In India, China, etc., an official stamp or seal; also, a clearance, passport, or permit. **2.** *Anglo-Indian* Quality: first *chop,* superior quality. [< Hind. *chhāp* stamp]

chop chop (chop′chop′) In Pidgin English, quickly!

chop·fal·len (chop′fô′lən) See CHAPFALLEN.

chop·house[1] (chop′hous′) *n.* An eating house specializing in chops and steaks. [< CHOP[1] + HOUSE]

chop·house[2] (chop′hous′) *n.* A Chinese custom house. [< CHOP[4] + HOUSE]

Cho·pin (shō′pan, *Fr.* shō·paṅ′), **Frédéric François,** 1810–1849, Polish composer and pianist active in France.

cho·pine (chō·pēn′, chop′in) *n.* A type of high, woman's clog worn in Europe in the 16th and 17th centuries. Also **chop·in** (chop′in). [< Sp. *chapin* < *chapa* metal plate]

chop·per (chop′ər) *n.* **1.** One who or that which chops. **2.** *Telecom.* A device that interrupts regularly a beam of light or a radio signal. **3.** *Slang* A helicopter. **4.** *U.S. Slang* A submachine gun. [< CHOP[1]]

chop·ping[1] (chop′ing) *adj.* Choppy[2].

chop·ping[2] (chop′ing) *adj. Scot.* Stout; strapping; bouncing: said especially of a child.

chop·py[1] (chop′ē) *adj.* **·pi·er, ·pi·est 1.** Full of short, rough waves. **2.** Full of cracks or fissures. [< CHOP[1], n.]

chop·py[2] (chop′ē) *adj.* **·pi·er, ·pi·est** Variable, shifting, as wind. [< CHOP[2]]

chop·sticks (chop′stiks′) *n.pl.* Slender rods of ivory or wood, used in pairs by the Chinese, Japanese, etc., to convey food to the mouth. [< Pidgin English *chop* quick + STICK; trans. of Chinese name]

chop su·ey (sōō′ē) A Chinese-American dish consisting of bits of meat or chicken, bean sprouts, onions, mushrooms, etc., cooked in their own juices and served with rice. [< Chinese *tsa-sui,* lit., mixed pieces]

cho·ra·gus (kō·rā′gəs) *n. pl.* **·gi** (-jī) **1.** In ancient Greece, the leader of a chorus, as in a play. **2.** A leader of any chorus or band. Also **cho·re·gus** (kō·rē′gəs). [< L < Gk. *chorēgos* < *choros* chorus + *agein* to lead] — **cho·rag·ic** (kō·raj′ik, -räj′ik) *adj.*

cho·ral (kôr′əl, kō′rəl) *adj.* **1.** Pertaining to a chorus (defs. 1 and 2) or choir. **2.** Written for or sung by a chorus. [< Med.L *choralis* < L *chorus.* See CHORUS.] — **cho′ral·ly** *adv.*

cho·rale (kō·ral′, kə-) *n.* A hymn characterized by a simple melody and firm rhythm, often sung in unison. Also **cho·ral′.** [< G *choral*]

chord[1] (kôrd) *n. Music* A combination of three or more tones sounded together. [Earlier *cord,* short for ACCORD; form infl. by *chord* string]

chord[2] (kôrd) *n.* **1.** A string of a musical instrument. **2.** An emotional response or reaction. **3.** *Geom.* A straight line connecting the extremities of an arc. **b** The portion of a straight line contained by its intersections with a curve. **4.** *Engin.* One of the principal members of a bridge truss. **5.** *Anat. Rare* A cord. **6.** *Aeron.* The length from the leading edge to the trailing edge of an airfoil. [< L *chorda* < Gk. *chordē* string of a musical instrument. Doublet of CORD.] — **chord′al** *adj.*

CHORD (def. 3)
Lines *cb* and *ab* are chords respectively of arcs *cab* and *ab.*

chor·date (kôr′dāt) *Zool. n.* Any of a large phylum (*Chordata*) of the animal kingdom that includes the vertebrates and whose members are characterized by an internal skeleton (in primitive forms a notochord) and a dorsally located central nervous system. — *adj.* Of, pertaining to, or belonging to this phylum or its characteristics. [< NL *Chordata* < L *chorda.* See CHORD[2].]

chore (chôr, chōr) *n. U.S.* **1.** A small or minor job; incidental piece of work. **2.** *pl.* The routine duties of a household or farm. **3.** An unpleasant or hard task. Also, *Brit., char, chare.* [Var. of CHAR[3]]

-chore *combining form Bot.* A plant distributed in a specified manner: *anemochore.* [< Gk. *chōreein* to spread]

cho·re·a (kō·rē′ə, kō-) *n. Pathol.* An acute nervous disease of children characterized by involuntary and uncontrollable muscular twitching of the face and limbs: also called *St. Vitus' dance.* [< NL < Gk. *choreia* dance] — **cho·re′al, cho·re′ic** *adj.*

choreo- *combining form* Dance: *choreography.* Also **choro-.** [< Gk. *choreia* dance]

cho·re·og·ra·pher (kôr′ē·og′rə·fər, kō′rē-) *n.* One who devises ballet and other dance compositions.

cho·re·og·ra·phy (kôr′ē·og′rə·fē, kō′rē-) *n.* **1.** The devising of ballets and incidental dances, especially for the stage. **2.** The written representation of figures and steps of dancing. **3.** The art of dancing; ballet. Also **cho·reg·ra·phy** (kə·reg′rə·fē). [< CHOREO- + -GRAPHY] — **cho·re·o·graph·ic** (kôr′ē·ə·graf′ik, kō′rē-) *adj.*

cho·ri·am·bus (kôr′ē·am′bəs, kō′rē-) *n. pl.* **·bus·es** or **·bi** (-bī) In prosody, a metrical foot of four syllables, the second and third short and the others long (-∪∪-). Also **cho·ri·amb** (kôr′ē·amb, kō′rē-). [< L *choriambus* < Gk. *choriambos* < *choreios* trochee + *iambos* iambus] — **cho′ri·am′bic** *adj.*

cho·ric (kôr′ik, kō′rik) *adj.* Of or like a chorus (defs. 7–10).

cho·ri·on (kôr′ē·on, kō′rē-) *n. Anat.* The membrane that invests the fertilized ovum and the embryo in higher vertebrates, attaches to the uterus, and contributes to the formation of the placenta. [< Gk.]

chor·is·ter (kôr′is·tər, kor′-) *n.* **1.** A member of a choir; especially, a choirboy. **2.** A leader of a choir. **3.** Any singer, as a bird. [< AF *cueristre* < *cuer.* See CHOIR.]

cho·ri·zo (chô·rē′zō, -sō) *n.* A highly seasoned Spanish and Mexican pork sausage. [< Sp.]

cho·rog·ra·phy (kō·rog′rə·fē, kō-) *n. pl.* **·phies 1.** The delineation or mapping of regions or districts. **2.** A map or chart of a region. [< Gk. *chōros* region + -GRAPHY] — **cho·rog′ra·pher** *n.* — **cho·ro·graph·ic** (kôr′ə·graf′ik, kō′rə-) or **·i·cal** *adj.* — **cho′ro·graph′i·cal·ly** *adv.*

cho·roid (kôr′oid, kō′roid) *Anat. adj.* Resembling the chorion: said of highly vascular membranes. — *n.* The vascular tunic of the eyeball, between the sclera and the retina. For illustration see EYE. Also **cho·ri·oid** (kôr′ē·oid, kō′rē-).

chor·tle (chôr′təl) *v.t. & v.i.* **·tled, ·tling** To utter or utter with chuckles of glee. — *n.* A chuckle; joyful vocal sound. [Blend of CHUCKLE and SNORT; coined by Lewis Carroll in *Through the Looking-Glass*]

cho·rus (kôr′əs, kō′rəs) *n.* **1.** A musical composition, usually in parts, to be sung by a large group. **2.** A group of singers who perform such works. **3.** A body of singers, or singers and dancers, who perform together in opera, musical comedy, etc. **4.** A group of persons singing or speaking something simultaneously. **5.** A simultaneous utterance of words, cries, etc., by many individuals: a *chorus* of giggles. **6.** A refrain, as of a song. **7.** In ancient Greece, a ceremonial dance, usually religious, accompanied by the singing of odes. **8.** In Greek drama, a body of actors who comment upon and sometimes take part in the main action of a play. **9.** In later drama, an actor who recites the prologue and epilogue and comments on the plot. **10.** The part of a drama performed by a chorus. — *v.t. & v.i.* **cho·rused** or **·russed, cho·rus·ing** or **·rus·sing** To sing or speak in concert. [< L < Gk. *choros* dance. Doublet of CHOIR.]

chorus girl A woman in the chorus of a musical comedy, cabaret, etc. Also *U.S. Informal* **cho·rine** (kôr′ēn, kō′rēn).

Cho·rzów (khô′zhōōf) A city in southern Poland; pop. 145,400 (est. 1959): formerly *Królewska Huta.*

chose[1] (chōz) Past tense of CHOOSE.

chose[2] (shōz) *n. Law* Anything that is personal property. [< F, thing < L *causa* matter, cause]

chose ju·gée (shōz zhü·zhā′) *French* Any matter that has been decided; literally, an adjudicated case.

cho·sen (chō′zən) Past participle of CHOOSE. — *adj.* **1.** Made an object of choice; selected. **2.** *Theol.* Elect.

Cho·sen (chō′sen) The Japanese name for KOREA.

chosen people The Israelites. *Deut.* xiv 2.

Cho·sin (chō′shin) The Japanese name for CHANGJIN.

Chou (jō) A Chinese imperial dynasty (1122?–249 B.C.).

Chou En-lai (jō′ en′lī′), 1898–1976, Chinese statesman; foreign minister 1949–58, and premier of the People's Republic of China 1949–76.

chough (chuf) *n.* A European bird of the crow family, especially the **red-legged** or **Cornish chough** (*Pyrrhocorax pyrrhocorax*) with black plumage and red beak and feet. [OE *cēo*]

chouse (chous) *Archaic & Dial. v.t.* **choused, chous·ing** To cheat; swindle. — *n.* **1.** A swindle. **2.** A swindler. **3.** A dupe. Also **chowse.** [< Turkish *chaush* messenger; ? with ref. to a dishonest 17th c. Turkish agent in London]

choush (choush) See CHIAUS.

chow[1] (chou) *n.* **1.** A medium-sized dog native to China, having a thick, brown or black coat and a blue-black tongue: also **chow-chow.** **2.** *Slang* Food. [Short for CHOW-CHOW.]

chow[2] (chou) *n.* A Chinese subordinate district or its chief city: used frequently in combination in place names: *Foochow.*

chow[3] (chou) *n. Scot.* The jowl.

chow-chow (chou′chou′) *n.* **1.** A relish of chopped mixed vegetables pickled in mustard. **2.** Chow[1] (def. 1). [< Pidgin English]

CHOW (def. 1) (20 inches high at shoulder)

chow·der (chou′dər) *n.* A dish usually made of clams or fish stewed with vegetables, often in milk. [< F *chaudière* kettle < L *caldaria.* See CAULDRON.]

chow mein (chou′ mān′) A Chinese-American dish made of shredded meat, onions, celery, bean sprouts, etc., stewed and served with fried noodles. [< Chinese *ch'ao* to fry + *mein* flour]

Chr. **1.** Christ. **2.** Christian.

chres·ard (kres′ərd) *n. Ecol.* The available water of the soil: opposed to *echard.* [< Gk. *chrēsthai* to use + *ardeia* irrigation]

Chres·tien de Troyes (krā-tyaṅ′ də trwä′) Twelfth-century French poet. Also **Chré·tien′ de Troyes′.**

chres·tom·a·thy (kres-tom′ə-thē) *n. pl.* **·thies** A collection of choice extracts, especially for instruction in a language. [< Gk. *chrēstomatheia* < *chrēstos* useful + *manthanein* to learn]

chrism (kriz′əm) *n. Eccl.* **1.** Consecrated oil used in certain churches for anointing at baptism, confirmation, unction, etc. **2.** Any sacramental anointing; especially, in the Eastern Orthodox Church, the rite of confirmation. Also spelled **chrisom.** [OE *crisma* < LL *chrisma* < Gk. < *chriein* to anoint. Doublet of CREAM.] — **chris·mal** (kriz′məl) *adj.*

chris·ma·to·ry (kriz′mə-tôr′ē, -tō′rē) *n. pl.* **·ries** A vessel or container for chrism. [< Med.L *chrismatorium* < LL *chrisma* chrism]

chris·om (kriz′əm) *n.* **1.** A baptismal or christening robe. **2.** *Archaic* A child in its baptismal robe; a baby. Also **chris·om child.** **3.** Chrism. [Var. of CHRISM]

Christ (krīst) *n.* **1.** The Anointed; the Messiah: the deliverer of Israel foretold by the Hebrew prophets. **2.** Jesus of Nazareth, regarded as fulfilling this prophecy: at first a title (*Jesus the Christ*), later a proper name (*Jesus Christ*). **3.** In Christian Science, the divine manifestation of God. Abbr. *Chr.* [OE *Crist* < L *Christus* < Gk. *Christos* (< *chriein* to anoint); trans. of Hebrew *māshīaḥ* anointed] — **Christ′li·ness** *n.* — **Christ′ly** *adv.*

Christ·church (krīst′chûrch′) A city on the eastern coast of South Island, New Zealand; pop. 151,500 (est. 1960).

christ·cross (kris′krôs′, -kros′) *n.* **1.** *Archaic* The mark of the cross (✠), formerly placed before the alphabet in hornbooks, etc. **2.** *Brit. Dial.* A mark (✕) made by one who cannot sign his name. **3.** *Obs.* The alphabet. [< *Christ's cross*]

christ-cross-row (kris′krôs-rō′, -kros′-) *n. Obs.* The alphabet. Also spelled **crisscross-row.**

chris·ten (kris′ən) *v.t.* **1.** To name in baptism. **2.** To administer Christian baptism to. **3.** To give a name to; name in a ceremony analogous to baptism. **4.** *Informal* To use for the first time. [OE *cristnen* < *cristen.* See CHRISTIAN.]

Chris·ten·dom (kris′ən-dəm) *n.* **1.** Christian lands. **2.** Christians collectively. **3.** *Obs.* Christianity.

chris·ten·ing (kris′ən-ing) *n.* A Christian baptismal ceremony, especially the baptizing of an infant.

Christ·hood (krīst′hŏŏd) *n.* The condition of being the Christ.

Chris·tian (kris′chən) *adj.* **1.** Professing or following the religion of Christ; especially, affirming the divinity of Christ. **2.** Relating to or derived from Christ or his doctrine. **3.** Manifesting the spirit of Christ or of his teachings. **4.** Characteristic of Christianity or Christendom. **5.** *Informal* Human; civilized; decent. — *n.* **1.** One who believes in or professes belief in Jesus as the Christ; a member of any of the Christian churches. **2.** One who lives according to the example and teaching of Jesus. **3.** *Informal* A human being as distinguished from a brute. **4.** *Informal* A civilized, decent, or respectable person. Abbr. *Chr.* [OE *cristen* < LL *christianus* < L *Christus.* See CHRIST.] — **Chris′tian·ly** *adv.*

Christian The hero in Bunyan's *Pilgrim's Progress.*

Christian X, 1870–1947, king of Denmark 1912–47.

Christian Brothers A Roman Catholic lay order founded in 1684, devoted to education: full name **Brothers of the Christian Schools.**

Christian era The era beginning at the approximate date of Christ's birth, but now considered four to six years too late. Dates in this era are denoted *A.D.*, those before it, *B.C.*

Chris·ti·a·ni·a (kris′tē-ä′nē-ə, kris′chē-an′ē-ə) *n.* In skiing, any of several turns, especially one in which the parallel skis are swung around as the weight is removed from them by a downward crouch: also called *Christy.* Also **Christiania turn.**

Chris·tia·ni·a (kris-tyä′nē-ä) A former name for OSLO.

Chris·ti·an·i·ty (kris′chē-an′ə-tē) *n.* **1.** The Christian religion. **2.** Christians collectively. **3.** The state of being a Christian.

Chris·tian·ize (kris′chən-īz) *v.* **·ized,** **·iz·ing** *v.t.* **1.** To convert to Christianity. **2.** To imbue with Christian ideas, principles, and faith. — *v.i.* **3.** *Rare* To adopt Christianity. — **Chris′tian·i·za′tion** *n.* — **Chris′tian·iz′er** *n.*

Christian Mission See under SALVATION ARMY.

Christian name A baptismal name (which see).

Christian Science A religion and system of healing, founded in 1866 by Mary Baker Eddy and based on her exposition of the Scriptures: officially called the **Church of Christ, Scientist.** Abbr. *C.S.* — **Christian Scientist**

Chris·ti·na (kris-tē′nə), 1626–89, queen of Sweden 1632–54.

Christ·less (krīst′lis) *adj.* **1.** Without Christ or his spirit. **2.** Unchristian. — **Christ′less·ness** *n.*

Christ·like (krīst′līk′) *adj.* Resembling Christ; having the spirit of Christ. — **Christ′like′ness** *n.*

Christ·mas (kris′məs) *n.* **1.** December 25, held as the anniversary of the birth of Jesus Christ and widely observed as a holy day or a holiday. In Great Britain, it is the winter quarter day. Also **Christmas Day.** **2.** A church festival observed annually at this date in memory of the birth of Jesus Christ. The season of Christmas extends from Christmas Eve (Dec. 24) to Epiphany (Jan. 6): also **Christ′mas·tide′.** (-tīd′). [< CHRIST + MASS]

Christmas Eve The evening before Christmas; also, loosely, the day before Christmas.

Christmas Island **1.** An island SW of Java, administered by Australia; 64 sq. mi.; pop. 2,626 (est. 1958). **2.** The largest atoll in the Line Islands district of the Gilbert and Ellice Islands Colony; atomic testing center 1962; 222 sq. mi.

Christmas rose The white-flowering black hellebore: so called because it blooms from December to February.

Christmas tree An evergreen tree decorated with ornaments and lights at Christmas.

Chris·tol·o·gy (kris-tol′ə-jē) *n. pl.* **·gies** *Theol.* **1.** The study of the person and attributes of Christ. **2.** Any theory or doctrine concerning Christ. [< CHRIST + -LOGY] — **Chris·to·log·i·cal** (kris′tə-loj′i-kəl) *adj.*

Chris·tophe (krēs-tôf′), **Henri,** 1767–1820, king of Haiti 1811–20.

Chris·to·pher (kris′tə-fər), **Saint** Third-century Christian martyr.

Christ's-thorn (krīsts′thôrn′) *n.* **1.** A Palestinian shrub (*Paliurus spina-christi*) of the buckthorn family, with long sharp thorns, so called from a belief that Christ's crown of thorns was made of it. **2.** The jujube (def. 2).

Chris·ty (kris′tē) *n.* A Christiania.

Chris·ty (kris′tē), **Howard Chandler,** 1873–1952, U.S. illustrator and painter.

chrom- Var. of CHROMO-.

chro·ma (krō′mə) *n.* The purity of a color determined by the degree of absence of white or gray; color intensity. See COLOR (def. 1). [< Gk. *chrōma* color]

chro·mate (krō′māt) *n. Chem.* A salt of chromic acid.

chro·mat·ic (krō-mat′ik) *adj.* **1.** Pertaining to color or colors. **2.** *Music* **a** Pertaining to or designating a tone, often modified by an accidental, that is not a normal part of a scale or mode. **b** Designating chords or harmony using tones foreign to the given scale or mode. **c** Denoting a progression in half-steps, as F to F#. **d** Of or pertaining to a chromatic scale, or to an instrument that can play such a scale. Compare DIATONIC. — **chro·mat′i·cal·ly** *adv.*

chromatic aberration See under ABERRATION.

chromatic color See under COLOR.

chro·mat·i·cism (krō-mat′ə-siz′əm) *n.* **1.** The state or quality of being chromatic. **2.** *Music* **a** The extensive use of chromatic harmony. **b** Chromatic progression.

chro·mat·ics (krō-mat′iks) *n.pl.* (construed as *sing.*) The science of colors.

chromatic scale *Music* A scale proceeding by semitones.

chro·ma·tid (krō′mə-tid) *n. Biol.* One of the members of a tetrad formed by the longitudinal splitting of a chromosome during meiosis. [< CHROMAT(O)- + -ID[1]]

chro·ma·tin (krō′mə-tin) *n. Biol.* The readily stainable substance in the protoplasm of the cell nucleus, developing into chromosomes during mitosis. For illustration see CELL. [< CHROMAT(O)- + -IN]

chromato- *combining form* Color; coloring or pigmentation: *chromatophore.* Also, before vowels, **chromat-.** [< Gk. *chrōma, -atos* color]

chro·mat·o·gram (krō-mat′ə-gram) *n. Chem.* The complete array of distinctively colored bands produced by chromatography.

chro·ma·tog·ra·phy (krō′mə-tog′rə-fē) *n. Chem.* A method for the analysis of mixtures, in which a solution is passed through a column of finely divided powder that selectively adsorbs the constituents in one or more sharply defined, often colored bands. [< CHROMATO- + -GRAPHY] — **chro·mat·o·graph·ic** (krō-mat′ə-graf′ik) *adj.*

chro·ma·tol·o·gy (krō′mə-tol′ə-jē) *n. pl.* **·gies** The science of colors; chromatics. [< CHROMATO- + -LOGY]

chro·ma·tol·y·sis (krō′mə-tol′ə-sis) *n. Biol.* The solution and disappearance of chromatin from the nucleus of a cell. [< CHROMATO- + -LYSIS]

chro·ma·to·phore (krō′mə·tə·fôr′, -fōr′) n. 1. Biol. One of the pigment-bearing sacs by which changes of color are effected in various animals, as in chameleons: also called pigment cell. 2. Bot. A pigment-bearing plastid found in diatoms and other plants. [< CHROMATO- + -PHORE] — **chro·ma·to·phor·ic** (krō′mə·tə·fôr′ik, -fōr′-), **chro·ma·toph·o·rous** (krō′mə·tof′ər·əs) adj.

chrome (krōm) n. 1. Chrome yellow. 2. Chromium. — v.t. **chromed, chrom·ing** 1. To plate with chromium. 2. To subject to the action of a solution of potassium dichromate, as in dyeing. [< F < Gk. chrōma color]

-chrome combining form 1. Color; colored: polychrome. 2. Chem. Chromium: ferrochrome. [< Gk. chrōma color]

chrome alum Chem. Any double sulfate of chromium with potassium, sodium, or ammonium, especially that containing ammonium, $Cr_2(SO_4)_3(NH_4)_2SO_4·24H_2O$, a dark, violet-red compound used as a mordant in dyeing.

chrome green. 1. A green pigment derived from chromic oxide. 2. The color of this, a dull, dark green.

chrome red A pigment made from basic lead chromate: also called Chinese red.

chrome steel Metall. A very hard steel alloyed with chromium. Also **chromium steel.**

chrome yellow Chem. Any of various shades of a yellow to deep orange pigment consisting of chromate of lead, barium, or zinc.

chro·mic (krō′mik) adj. Chem. 1. Of, from, or pertaining to chromium. 2. Pertaining to compounds of chromium in its higher valence.

chromic acid Chem. An acid, H_2CrO_4, existing only in solution and forming chromates.

chromic oxide Chem. A green compound, Cr_2O_3, used as a pigment.

chro·mite (krō′mīt) n. Chromic iron ore, $FeCr_2O_4$, a valuable source of chromium.

chro·mi·um (krō′mē·əm) n. A grayish white, very hard metallic element (symbol Cr), used in electroplating, making alloys and pigments, as a mordant, etc. See ELEMENT. [< NL < F chrome < Gk. chrōma color; so called from its many brightly colored, poisonous compounds]

chro·mo (krō′mō) n. pl. ·mos A chromolithograph.

chromo- combining form 1. Color; in or with color: chromophotography. 2. Chem. Chromium. Also, before vowels, chrom-. [< Gk. chrōma color]

chro·mo·gen (krō′mə·jen) n. 1. Chem. Any organic coloring matter or substance capable of yielding a dye. 2. Biol. Any substance in an animal or plant that under certain conditions becomes colored or deepens its hue. [< CHROMO- + -GEN] — **chro′mo·gen′ic** (-jen′ik) adj.

chro·mo·lith·o·graph (krō′mō·lith′ə·graf, -gräf) n. A print in colors obtained by chromolithography.

chro·mo·li·thog·ra·phy (krō′mō·li·thog′rə·fē) n. The process of reproducing a color print by lithography. — **chro′mo·li·thog′ra·pher** n. — **chro·mo·lith·o·graph·ic** (krō′mō·lith′-ə·graf′ik) adj.

chro·mo·mere (krō′mə·mir) n. Biol. One of the granules of chromatin forming the chromosome. [< CHROMO- + -MERE]

chro·mo·phore (krō′mə·fôr, -fōr) n. Chem. A group of atoms or electrons so linked within a molecule as to produce certain colors when combined under proper conditions. [< CHROMO- + -PHORE] — **chro·mo·phor·ic** (krō′mə·fôr′ik, -fō′rik), **chro·moph·o·rous** (krō·mof′ər·əs) adj.

chro·mo·pho·to·graph (krō′mō·fō′tə·graf, -gräf) n. A photograph in colors.

chro·mo·pho·tog·ra·phy (krō′mō·fə·tog′rə·fē) n. Photography in colors. — **chro·mo·pho·to·graph·ic** (krō′mō·fō′tə·graf′ik) adj.

chro·mo·plast (krō′mə·plast) n. Bot. A protoplasmic granule of a color other than green. [< CHROMO- + -PLAST]

chro·mo·some (krō′mə·sōm) n. Biol. One of the deeply staining, rod- or loop-shaped bodies into which the chromatin of the cell nucleus divides during cell division, and in which the genes are located. [< CHROMO- + -SOME²]

chromosome map Biol. A schematic representation of the linear order of genes in a specified type of chromosome: also called crossover map.

chromosome number Biol. The number of chromosomes characteristic of each biological species, every body cell having twice the number present in the reproductive cells, the full complement of chromosomes being restored in the fertilization of the egg by the sperm.

chro·mo·sphere (krō′mə·sfir′) n. Astron. 1. An incandescent, gaseous envelope, consisting mostly of hydrogen and helium, that surrounds the sun beyond the photosphere. 2. A similar envelope surrounding a star. [< CHROMO- + -SPHERE] — **chro′mo·spher′ic** (-sfir′ik, -sfer′-) adj.

chro·mous (krō′məs) adj. Chem. Of or pertaining to chromium in its lower valence.

chron. or **chronol.** Chronological; chronology.

Chron. Chronicles.

chro·nax·y (krō′nak·sē) n. pl. ·nax·ies Physiol. The minimum time required by an electric current of twice the rheobase to excite a muscle, nerve fiber, etc. Also **chro′nax·ie, chro·nax·i·a** (krō·nak′sē·ə). [< CHRON(O)- + Gk. axia value]

chron·ic (kron′ik) adj. 1. Continuing for a long period; constant: chronic unrest. 2. Prolonged; lingering; also, recurrent: said of a disease: opposed to acute. 3. Long affected by a disease, or given to a habit; confirmed: a chronic alcoholic. [< F chronique < L chronicus < Gk. chronikos of time < chronos time] — **chron′i·cal·ly** adv. — Syn. 3. habitual, inveterate. — Ant. occasional.

chron·i·cle (kron′i·kəl) n. A register of events in the order of time; a chronological historical record. — Syn. See ACCOUNT, HISTORY. — v.t. ·cled, ·cling To record in, or in the manner of, a chronicle. [< AF cronicle < L chronica, neut. pl. of chronicus. See CHRONIC.] — **chron′i·cler** n.

Chron·i·cles (kron′i·kəlz) n.pl. (construed as sing.) Either of two historical books, I and II Chronicles, of the Old Testament: also, in the Douai Bible, called I and II Paralipomenon.

chrono- combining form Time: chronograph. Also, before vowels, chron-. [< Gk. chronos time]

chron·o·gram (kron′ə·gram) n. 1. A record of a chronograph. 2. An inscription, phrase, etc., in which certain conspicuous letters, when read as Roman numerals, record a date. [< CHRONO- + -GRAM]

chron·o·graph (kron′ə·graf, -gräf) n. An instrument for recording graphically the moment or duration of an event, measuring intervals of time, etc. [< CHRONO- + -GRAPH] — **chron′o·graph′ic** adj.

chron·o·log·i·cal (kron′ə·loj′i·kəl) adj. 1. Arranged according to sequence in time, as a series of events. 2. Pertaining to or occupied with chronology. Also **chron′o·log′ic.** Abbr. chron., chronol. — **chron′o·log′i·cal·ly** adv.

chronological age See under AGE.

chro·nol·o·gy (krə·nol′ə·jē) n. pl. ·gies 1. The science of determining the proper sequence and dating of historical events. 2. Arrangement or relationship according to order of occurrence. 3. A chronological list or table. Abbr. chron., chronol. [< NL chronologia < Gk. chronos time + -logia study] — **chro·nol′o·ger, chro·nol′o·gist** n.

chro·nom·e·ter (krə·nom′ə·tər) n. A timekeeping instrument of high precision for use in navigation and scientific work. [< CHRONO- + -METER] — **chron·o·met·ric** (kron′-ə·met′rik) or **·ri·cal** adj. — **chron′o·met′ri·cal·ly** adv.

chro·nom·e·try (krə·nom′ə·trē) n. The science or method of measuring time or periods of time.

chron·o·scope (kron′ə·skōp) n. An instrument for measuring a minute interval of time. [< CHRONO- + -SCOPE] — **chron·o·scop·ic** (kron′ə·skop′ik) adj.

-chroous combining form Having (a certain) color: isochroous. [< Gk. chrōs, chroos color]

chrys·a·lid (kris′ə·lid) Entomol. n. A chrysalis. — adj. Of, pertaining to, or like a chrysalis: also **chry·sal·i·dal** (kri·sal′ə·dal).

chrys·a·lis (kris′ə·lis) n. pl. **chrys·a·lis·es** or **chry·sal·i·des** (kri·sal′ə·dēz) 1. Entomol. The capsule-enclosed pupa from which the butterfly or moth develops. 2. Anything in an undeveloped or transitory state. [< L < Gk. chrysallis golden sheath of a butterfly < chrysos gold]

chrys·an·the·mum (kri·san′thə·məm) n. 1. Any of a genus of perennials (Chrysanthemum) of the composite family, some cultivated varieties of which have large heads of showy flowers. 2. The flower. [< L < Gk. chrysanthemon marigold, lit., golden flower]

Chrys·e·is (krī·sē′is) In the Iliad, the daughter of a priest of Apollo, captured and given to Agamemnon, and returned after Apollo sent a plague upon the Greeks.

chrys·e·le·phan·tine (kris′el·ə·fan′tin, -tīn) adj. Made or covered with gold and ivory, as certain ancient Greek statues. [< Gk. chryselephantinos of gold and ivory < chrysos gold + elephas, elephantos ivory]

chryso- combining form Gold; of a golden color: chrysotile. Also, before vowels, **chrys-.** [< Gk. chrysos gold]

chrys·o·ber·yl (kris′ə·ber′əl) n. A vitreous, yellowish or greenish, transparent to translucent beryllium aluminate, $BeAl_2O_4$, used as a gem. [< L chrysoberyllus < Gk. chrysoberyllos < chrysos gold + beryllos beryl]

chrys·o·lite (kris′ə·līt) n. A variety of olivine. [< OF crisolite < Med.L crisolitus < L crysolithus < Gk. chrysolithos < chrysos gold + lithos stone] — **chrys·o·lit·ic** (kris′-ə·lit′ik) adj.

chrys·o·prase (kris′ə·prāz) n. A semiprecious, apple-green variety of chalcedony, colored by nickel oxide, used as a gem. [< OF crisopace < L chrysoprasus < Gk. chrysoprasos < chrysos gold + prason leek]

Chrys·os·tom (kris′əs·təm, kris·os′təm), **Saint John,** 345?–407, patriarch of Constantinople 398–404; a Greek church father.

chrys·o·tile (kris′ə·til) *n.* A fibrous, silky variety of serpentine. [< CHRYSO- + Gk. *tilos* hair, fiber]

chs. Chapters.

chtho·ni·an (thō′nē·ən) *adj.* In ancient mythology, pertaining to the gods and spirits of the underworld. Also **chthon·ic** (thon′ik). [< Gk. *chthōn* the earth]

chub (chub) *n. pl.* **chubs** or **chub** 1. A carplike fish (*Leuciscus cephalus*) common in European rivers. 2. One of various other fishes, as the fallfish, tautog, whitefish, etc. [ME *chubbe*; origin unknown]

chu·bas·co (choo·bäs′kō) *n. Meteorol.* A violent thunder squall along the west coast of Central America. [< Sp.]

chub·by (chub′ē) *adj.* **·bi·er, ·bi·est** Plump; rounded. —**chub′bi·ness** *n.*
—**Syn.** portly, chunky, hefty, rotund, buxom. Compare FAT.

chuck[1] (chuk) *v.t.* 1. To pat or tap affectionately or playfully, especially under the chin. 2. To throw or pitch: to *chuck* a baseball. 3. *Informal* To throw away; discard. 4. *Informal* To eject forcibly: with *out*. 5. *Slang* To quit: He *chucked* his job. —*n.* 1. A playful pat under the chin. 2. A throw; toss. [Cf. F *choquer* shake, jolt]

chuck[2] (chuk) *n.* 1. The cut of beef extending from the neck to the shoulder blade. 2. *Mech.* A clamp, chock, or wedge used to hold a tool or work in a machine, as in a lathe. [Var of CHOCK]

chuck[3] (chuk) *n.* 1. A short, clucking sound. 2. *Archaic* A term of endearment. —*v.i.* To cluck, as a chicken. [Imit.]

chuck (chuk) *n. U.S. Informal* Woodchuck.

chuck-a-luck (chuk′ə·luk′) *n.* A gambling game employing three dice. Also **chuck′-luck′**.

chuck·full (chuk′fŏŏl′) See CHOCK-FULL.

chuck·hole (chuk′hōl′) *n. U.S. Dial.* A mudhole in a road.

chuck·le[1] (chuk′əl) *v.i.* **·led, ·ling** 1. To laugh quietly and with satisfaction, especially to oneself. 2. To cluck, as a hen. —*n.* A low, mildly amused laugh. [Freq. of CHUCK[3]] —**chuck′ler** *n.*

CHUCKS (def. 2)
a Geared scroll. *b* Planer. *c* Drill. *d* Tapping. *e* Independent reversible-jaw lathe. *f* Beach drill. *g* Sectional view of drill chuck.

chuck·le[2] (chuk′əl) *adj.* Stupid or clumsy. [? < CHUCK[2], in dial. sense of "lump, chunk"]

chuck·le·head (chuk′əl·hed′) *n. Informal* A stupid fellow; blockhead. —**chuck′le·head′ed** *adj.*

chuck wagon *U.S.* A wagon fitted with cooking equipment and provisions for cowboys, harvest hands, etc.

chuck·wal·la (chuk′wol′ə) *n.* A large, herbivorous lizard (*Sauromalus ater*) of the deserts of the SW United States. Also **chuck·a·wal·la** (chuk′ə·wol′ə). [< N. Am. Ind.]

chuck·will's-wid·ow (chuk′wilz′wid′ō) *n.* A large goatsucker (*Antrostomus carolinensis*) of the southern United States. [Imit. of its cry]

chuck·y (chuk′ē) *n. pl.* **·ies** *Scot.* A little chick.

chud·dar (chud′ər) *n. Anglo-Indian* A large, square shawl made in India. Also **chud·dah** (chud′ə), **chud′der.** [< Hind. *chadar* square piece of cloth]

Chud·sko·ye O·ze·ro (choot′skə·yə ô′zyi·rə) The Russian name for (Lake) PEIPUS.

chu·fa (choo′fə) *n.* 1. A sedge (*Cyperus esculentus*) whose tuberous roots are eaten in southern Europe. 2. One of the tubers. [< Sp.]

chuff (chuf) *Brit. Dial. n.* 1. A rustic; boor. 2. A miser. —*adj.* Gruff.

chuf·fy (chuf′ē) **·fi·er, ·fi·est** *adj.* 1. *Scot. & Brit. Dial.* Chubby; plump. 2 *Brit. Dial.* Gruff.

chug (chug) *n.* A dull, explosive sound, as of the exhaust of an engine. —*v.i.* **chugged, chug·ging** To move or operate with a series of such sounds. [Imit.]

Chu-Kiang (joo′jyäng′) The Chinese name for the CANTON (river).

chuk·ker (chuk′ər) *n.* In polo, one of the periods of continuous play, lasting 7½ minutes. Also **chuk′kar.** [< Hind. *chakkar* < Skt. *chakra* wheel]

Chu·la Vis·ta (choo′lə vis′tə) A city in SW California; pop. 67,901.

Chu·lym (choo·lim′) A river in the west central R.S.F.S.R., flowing 1,177 miles, generally NE to the Ob. Also **Chu·lim′.**

chum[1] (chum) *n.* 1. An intimate companion. 2. Originally, a roommate. —**Syn.** See FRIEND. —*v.i.* **chummed, chum·ming** 1. To associate very closely with another. 2. To share the same room. [? Short for *chamber fellow*]

chum[2] (chum) *n.* Fish bait, usually pieces of oily fish, scattered around the lines. [Origin uncertain]

chum·my (chum′ē) *adj.* **·mi·er, ·mi·est** *Informal* Friendly; intimate. —**chum′mi·ly** *adv.*

chump[1] (chump) *n.* 1. *Informal* A stupid or foolish person. 2. A chunk of wood. 3. The thick end of anything, as of a loin of mutton. 4. *Slang* The head. —**off one's chump** *Brit. Slang* Out of one's senses. [? Var. of CHUNK]

chump[2] (chump) *v.t. & v.i.* To chew; munch. [< CHAMP[1]]

Chung·king (chŏŏng′king′) A port city in south central China; the capital of China during World War II; pop. 3,500,000 (est. 1970). Also **Chung-ch'ing** (jŏŏng′ching′).

chunk (chungk) *n.* 1. A thick mass or piece of anything, as of wood. 2. A considerable quantity of something. 3. *U.S. Informal* A strong, stocky person or animal. [Var. of CHUCK[2]]

chunk·y (chung′kē) *adj.* **chunk·i·er, chunk·i·est** 1. Short and thickset; stocky. 2. In chunks. —**chunk′i·ness** *n.*

Chur (kŏŏr) A town in eastern Switzerland, capital of Graubünden canton; pop. about 20,400. *French* **Coire** (kwär).

church (chûrch) *n.* 1. A building for Christian worship. 2. Regular religious services; public worship. 3. A local congregation of Christians. 4. *Usually cap.* A distinct body of Christians having a common faith and discipline; a denomination. Abbr. *c., C., ch., Ch.* 5. All Christian believers collectively. 6. Ecclesiastical organization and authority, as distinguished from secular authority: the separation of *church* and state. 7. The clerical profession; holy orders. 8. A non-Christian religious body, society, or place of worship. 9. In Christian Science, whatever rests upon and proceeds from divine Principle. —**Syn.** See RELIGION. —*v.t.* 1. To call to account before the congregation; subject to church discipline. 2. To conduct a religious service for (a person, especially a woman after childbirth). [OE *circe,* ult. < Gk. *kyriakon* (dōma) the Lord's (house) < *kyrios* Lord]

Church·ill (chûrch′il, -əl) A port village in northern Manitoba, Canada, at the mouth of the **Churchill River,** that flows 1,000 miles, generally NE, to Hudson Bay; pop. 3,039.

Church·ill (chûrch′il, -əl), **John** See MARLBOROUGH, DUKE OF. —**Lord Randolph (Henry Spencer),** 1849–95, British statesman. —**Winston,** 1871–1947, U.S. novelist. —**Sir Winston (Leonard Spencer),** 1874–1965, British statesman and author; prime minister 1940–45, 1951–55; son of Lord Randolph.

church key A leverlike contrivance with a bottle opener at one end and, at the other, a sharp, pointed device for puncturing canned beverages.

church·ly (chûrch′lē) *adj.* Of, pertaining to, or suitable to a church. —**church′li·ness** *n.*

church·man (chûrch′mən) *n. pl.* **·men** (-mən) 1. A devoted supporter or member of a church, especially of an established church. 2. A clergyman. —**church′man·ly** *adj.* —**church′man·ship** *n.* —**church′wom′an** *n.fem.*

church mouse A mouse that lives in a church: usually in the phrase **poor as a church mouse,** very poor.

Church of Christ, Scientist See CHRISTIAN SCIENCE.

Church of England The national church of England, established by law in the 16th century, claiming to be an independent branch of the ancient Catholic church, and repudiating papal authority: also called *Anglican Church.* Abbr. *C.E.*

Church of Jesus Christ of Latter-day Saints The Mormon Church: its official name.

Church of Rome The Roman Catholic Church.

Church Slavic, Church Slavonic See under SLAVIC.

church text *Brit. Printing* Black letter.

church·war·den (chûrch′wôr′dən) *n.* 1. In the Church of England, an elected lay officer who assists in the administration of a parish, and acts as its legal representative. 2. In the Protestant Episcopal Church, one of two elected lay officers of a vestry. 3. A long-stemmed clay pipe. Also **church warden.**

church·yard (chûrch′yärd′) *n.* The ground surrounding or adjoining a church, often used as a cemetery.

churl (chûrl) *n.* 1. A rude or surly person. 2. A stingy, niggardly person; miser. 3. A rustic; countryman. 4. In Anglo-Saxon England, a freeman of low birth. [OE *ceorl.* Akin to CARL.]

churl·ish (chûr′lish) *adj.* 1. Of or like a churl; rude; boorish; niggardly. 2. Hard to work or manage; intractable. —**churl′ish·ly** *adv.* —**churl′ish·ness** *n.*

churn (chûrn) *n.* 1. A vessel in which milk or cream is agitated to separate the oily globules and gather them as butter. 2. A similarly shaped vessel, pump, etc. A state of unrest or agitation. —*v.t.* 1. To stir or agitate (cream or milk), as in a churn, to make butter. 2. To make in a churn, as butter. 3. To agitate violently: The oars *churned* the water. —*v.i.* 1. To work a churn. 5. To move with violent agitation; seethe. [OE *cyrin*] —**churn′er** *n.*

churn·ing (chûr′ning) *n.* 1. The act of one who churns. 2. The butter churned at one time.

churr (chûr) *n.* A low, vibrant trill or whir made by certain birds and insects. —*v.i.* To make this sound. [Imit.]

chute (shōōt) *n.* 1. An inclined trough or vertical passage down which water, coal, etc., may pass. 2. A steep, narrow watercourse; a rapid; shoot. **3.** A narrow pen for branding or controlling cattle. **4.** A slide, as for toboggans. **5.** *Informal* A parachute. [Fusion of F *chute* a fall and SHOOT, n.]

Chu Teh (joo′ du′), 1886–1976, Chinese general; commander in chief of the army, People's Republic of China.

chut·ney (chut′nē) *n.* A piquant relish of fruit, spices, etc. Also **chut′nee.** [< Hind. *chatnī*]

chutz·pah (hoots′pə, khoots′-) *n.* *U.S. Slang* Brazen effrontery; gall: also spelled *hutzpah.* [< Yiddish < Hebrew]

Chu·vash (choo′väsh, *Russ.* choo-väsh′) *n.* *pl.* **·vash·es** or **·vash 1.** One of a Tatar people living chiefly in the Chuvash A.S.S.R. **2.** The Turkic language of these people.

Chuvash A.S.S.R. A division of the western R.S.F.S.R.; 7,066 sq. mi.; pop. 1,224,000 (1970); capital, Cheboksary. Also **Chuvash Republic, Chu·vash·i·a** (choo-väsh′i-ə). *Russian* **Chu·vash/ska/ya A.S.S.R.** (-skä-yä).

chyle (kīl) *n.* *Physiol.* The milky emulsion of lymph and fat taken up from the small intestine by the lacteals during digestion and passed from the thoracic duct into the veins. [< F < L *chylus* < Gk. *chylos* juice < *cheein* to pour] — **chy·la·ceous** (kī-lā′shəs), **chy·lous** (kī′ləs) *adj.*

chyme (kīm) *n.* *Physiol.* The partly digested food in semiliquid form as it passes from the stomach into the small intestine. [< L *chymus* < Gk. *chymos* juice < *cheein* to pour] — **chy·mous** (kī′məs) *adj.*

chym·ic (kim′ik), **chym·ist** (kim′ist), etc. Archaic spellings for CHEMIC, CHEMIST, etc.

chy·mo·sin (kī′mə·sin) *n.* *Biochem.* Rennin.

Ci. *Meteorol.* Cirrus.

C.I. Channel Islands.

Cia. or **cia.** Company (Sp. *compañia*).

CIA Central Intelligence Agency.

Cia·no (chä′rō), **Count Ga·le·az·zo** (gä′lä-ät′tsō), 1903–44, Italian di lo nat; Fascist foreign minister 1936–43; son-in-law of Mussolini.

Cib·ber (sib′ər), **Colley,** 1671–1757, English dramatist; poet laureate 1730–57.

cib·ol (sib′əl) *n.* The Welsh onion (*Allium fistulosum*), having hollow stems and a very small bulb: also called *sybo.* Also **cib′oule.** [< F *ciboule* < LL *cepula* bed of onions < L *cepa* onion]

ci·bo·ri·um (si·bôr′ē·əm, -bō′rē-) *n.* *pl.* **·bo·ri·a** (-bôr′ē-ə, -bō′rē-ə) **1.** An arched canopy over an altar, especially a permanent one. **2.** A covered receptacle for the consecrated bread of the Eucharist. [< Med.L < Gk. *kibōrion* cup]

CIC *Mil.* Counterintelligence Corps.

ci·ca·da (si·kā′də, -kä′-) *n.* *pl.* **·das** or **·dae** (-dē) A large homopterous insect (family *Cicadidae*), the male of which is equipped at the base of the abdomen with vibrating membranes that produce a loud, shrill sound: often called *locust.* [< L]

CICADA
(1 to 1½ inches long)

cicada killer A digger wasp (*Sphecius speciosus*) that preys upon the cicada. For illustration see INSECTS (beneficial).

ci·ca·la (si·kä′lə) *n.* A cicada. [< Ital.]

cic·a·tric·le (sik′ə·trik′əl) *n.* *Biol.* **1.** The germinating point in the yolk of an egg or in the embryo of a seed. **2.** A cicatrix. [< L *cicatricula*, dim. of *cicatrix* scar]

cic·a·trix (sik′ə·triks) *n.* *pl.* **cic·a·tri·ces** (sik′ə·trī′sēz) **1.** *Med.* A scar or seam consisting of new tissue formed in the healing of wounded or ulcerous parts and remaining after their cure. **2.** *Biol.* A scar or scarlike marking, as that left by the removal of an organ or by the fall of a leaf. Also **cic·a·trice** (sik′ə·tris). [< L] — **cic·a·tri·cial** (sik′ə·trish′əl), **ci·cat·ri·cose** (si·kat′ri·kōs) *adj.*

cic·a·trize (sik′ə·trīz) *v.t.* & *v.i.* **·trized, ·triz·ing** To heal or be healed by the forming of a scar. — **cic′a·tri·za/tion** *n.*

cic·e·ly (sis′ə·lē) *n.* *pl.* **·lies** A fragrant perennial herb (*Myrrhis odorata*) of the parsley family. [< L *seselis* < Gk.; infl. in form by *Cecily*, a feminine name]

cic·e·ro (sis′ə·rō) *n.* *Printing* A unit of typographical measurement in Europe, slightly larger than the pica. [after an edition of *Cicero* printed in 1458]

Cic·e·ro (sis′ə·rō) A city in NE Illinois, a suburb of Chicago; pop. 67,058.

Cic·e·ro (sis′ə·rō), **Marcus Tullius,** 106–43 B.C., Roman statesman, orator, and author: also called *Tully.*

cic·e·ro·ne (sis′ə·rō′nē, *Ital.* chē′chä·rō′nä) *n.* *pl.* **·nes,** *Ital.* **·ni** (-nē) A guide who explains to tourists the curiosities and antiquities of a place. [< Ital., Cicero; with ref. to the usual talkativeness of a guide]

Cic·e·ro·ni·an (sis′ə·rō′nē·ən) *adj.* Of or pertaining to Cicero, or to his rhetorical style; eloquent.

cich·lid (sik′lid) *n.* *pl.* **·lids** or **·li·dae** (-dē) One of a family (*Cichlidae*) of spiny-finned fresh-water fishes with a compressed body, found in tropical waters of Asia, Africa, and South America. [< NL *Cichlidae* < Gk. *kichlē*, a sea fish]

ci·cho·ri·a·ceous (si·kōr′ē·ā′shəs) *adj.* Of or pertaining to a former family (*Cichoriaceae*) of composite herbs and shrubs, especially chicory. [< NL *Cichoriaceae* < L *cichorium* chicory < Gk. *kichórion*]

ci·cis·be·o (si·sis′bē·ō, *Ital.* chē′chēz·bä′ō) *n.* *pl.* **·be·i** (-bi·ē, *Ital.* -bä′ē) The acknowledged lover or gallant of a married woman. [< Ital.]

ci·co·ree (sēk′ə·rə) *n.* *Obs.* Chickoree.

Cid (sid, *Sp.* thēth), **the,** 1044?–99, Rodrigo Díaz de Bivar, Spanish epic hero; champion in the wars against the Moors: also called **El Cid Cam·pe·a·dor** (käm′pä·ä·thôr′).

C.I.D. *Brit.* Criminal Investigation Dept.

-cidal *combining form* Killing; able to kill: *homicidal.* [< L *caedere* to kill]

-cide *combining form* **1.** Killer or destroyer of: *regicide.* **2.** Murder or killing of: *parricide.* [def. 1 < L *-cida* killer < *caedere* to kill; def. 2 < L *-cidium* slaughter < *caedere*]

ci·der (sī′dər) *n.* The expressed juice of apples used to make vinegar, and as a beverage before fermentation (**sweet cider**), or after fermentation (**hard cider**). [< OF *sidre* < LL *sicera* strong drink < Hebrew *shēkār*]

cider press A press for squeezing apples for cider.

ci·de·vant (sē·də·vän′) *adj.* *French* Former.

Cie. or **cie.** Company (F *compagnie*).

Cien·fue·gos (syen·fwä′gōs) A port city in southern Cuba, on **Cienfuegos Bay,** an inlet of the Caribbean; pop. 91,800 (1967).

C.I.F. or **c.i.f.** Cost, insurance, and freight.

ci·gar (si·gär′) *n.* A small roll of tobacco leaves prepared and shaped for smoking. [< Sp. *cigarro*]

cig·a·rette (sig′ə·ret′, sig′ə·ret) *n.* A small roll of finely cut tobacco for smoking, usually enclosed in thin paper. Also *U.S.* **cig′a·ret′.** [< F, dim. of *cigare* cigar]

cigar fish A carangoid food fish (*Decapterus punctatus*) found in the West Indies and along the Atlantic coast of the United States: also called *round scad.*

cil·i·a (sil′ē·ə) Plural of CILIUM.

cil·i·ar·y (sil′ē·er′ē) *adj.* **1.** *Biol.* Of, pertaining to, or like cilia. **2.** *Anat.* **a** Pertaining to or situated near the eyelashes. **b** Pertaining to the muscle fibers attached to ligaments supporting the lens of the eye. [< L *cilium* eyelid]

cil·i·ate (sil′ē·it, -āt) *adj.* *Biol.* Having cilia. Also **cil′i·at′ed.** — *n.* *Zool.* One of a class (*Ciliata*, formerly *Infusoria*) of protozoans possessing cilia in both young and adult stages.

cil·ice (sil′is) *n.* **1.** A very coarse cloth, originally made of goat's hair. **2.** A shirt made of this; a hair shirt. [< F < L *cilicium* < Gk. *Kilikia* Cilicia, where the cloth was originally woven] — **cil·i·cious** (si·lish′əs) *adj.*

Ci·li·cia (si·lish′ə) An ancient country in SE Asia Minor. — **Ci·li′cian** *adj.* & *n.*

Cilician Gates The ancient name for GÜLEK BOGHAZ.

cil·i·o·late (sil′ē·ə·lit, -lāt) *adj.* Fringed with minute cilia.

cil·i·um (sil′ē·əm) *n.* *pl.* **cil·i·a** (sil′ē·ə) **1.** *Biol.* A vibratile, microscopic, hairlike process on the surface of a cell, organ, plant, etc. **2.** An eyelash. [< L, eyelid]

Ci·ma·bu·e (chē′mä·boo′ā), **Giovanni,** 1240?–1302?, Florentine painter.

Cim·ar·ron River (sim′ə·rōn, -ron) A river flowing 692 miles from NE New Mexico through Colorado and Kansas to the Arkansas River in NE Oklahoma.

Cim·bri (sim′brī) *n.pl.* A Germanic people of central Europe, defeated by Marius in northern Italy in 101 B.C. [< L < Gmc.] — **Cim·bri·an** (sim′brē·ən), **Cim′bric** *adj.*

ci·mex (sī′meks) *n.* *pl.* **cim·i·ces** (sim′ə·sēz) An insect (genus *Cimex*), the bedbug. [< L, bug]

Cim·me·ri·an (si·mir′ē·ən) *adj.* **1.** Of or pertaining to the Cimmerians, a mythical people mentioned by Homer as living in perpetual darkness. **2.** Densely dark; gloomy.

Ci·mon (sī′mən), 507?–449 B.C., Athenian general and statesman.

CINC or **C in C** *Mil.* Commander in Chief.

cinch¹ (sinch) *n.* *U.S.* **1.** A girth used to fasten a saddle or pack onto an animal. For illustration see SADDLE. **2.** *Informal* A tight grip. **3.** *Slang* Something easy or sure. — *v.t.* **1.** To fasten a saddle girth around. **2.** *Slang* To get a tight hold upon. **3.** *Slang* To make sure of. — *v.i.* **4.** To tighten a saddle girth: often with *up.* [< Sp. *cincha* girth < L *cingula* girdle < *cingere* to bind]

cinch² (sinch) *n.* A game of cards in which the five of trumps is the most important card. [Prob. < Sp. *cinco* five]

cin·cho·na (sin·kō′nə) *n.* **1.** Any of various Peruvian trees and shrubs (genus *Cinchona*) of the madder family, now widely cultivated in India and Java as a source of quinine and related alkaloids. **2.** The bark of any of these trees: also called *china bark, Jesuits' bark, Peruvian bark.* [after the Countess of Chinchón, 1576–1639, wife of the viceroy of Peru] — **cin·chon·ic** (sin·kon′ik) *adj.*

cin·cho·nine (sin′kə·nēn, -nin) *n.* *Chem.* A crystalline alkaloid, $C_{19}H_{22}N_2O$, derived from cinchona. [< CINCHON(A) + -INE²]

cin·cho·nism (sin′kə·niz′əm) *n.* *Pathol.* An abnormal condition caused by overdoses of cinchona, characterized by giddiness, deafness, and temporary loss of sight.

cin·cho·nize (sin′kə·nīz) *v.t.* **·nized, ·niz·ing** To treat with cinchona or quinine. — **cin′cho·ni·za/tion** *n.*

Cin·cin·nat·i (sin′sə·nat′ē, nat′ə) A city on the Ohio River in SW Ohio; pop. 452,524.

Cin·cin·na·tus (sin′sə·nā′təs), **Lucius Quinctius**, 519?–439? B.C., Roman patrician and patriot.

cinc·ture (singk′chər) *n.* **1.** A belt, cord, etc., put around the waist; especially, a white or colored cord with tassels, used to secure an alb. **2.** Anything that encircles or encloses. **3.** The act of girding or surrounding. — *v.t.* **·tured, ·tur·ing** To surround with a cincture; gird; encompass. [< L *cinctura* < *cingere* to bind, gird]

cin·der (sin′dər) *n.* **1** Any partly burned substance, not reduced to ashes and incapable of further combustion. **2.** A thoroughly charred bit of wood, coal, etc., that can burn further but without flame. **3.** *pl.* That which is left after burning; ashes. **4.** *pl. Geol.* Scoria ejected from a volcano during an eruption. **5.** A scale of iron oxide thrown off in forging; slag. — *v.t.* To burn or reduce to a cinder. [OE *sinder*; infl. in form by L *cinis, cineris* ash] — **cin′der·y** *adj.*

cinder block A large, bricklike, partially hollow block made of cinders and cement, used to build walls, foundations for buildings, etc.

Cin·der·el·la (sin′də·rel′ə) *n.* **1.** The heroine of a popular fairy tale, who is treated as a menial drudge by her stepmother and stepsisters but eventually marries a prince. **2.** Any girl who achieves happiness after a period of neglect.

cinder track A race track covered with fine cinders.

cine- *combining form* Cinema. [< CINEMA]

cin·e·ma (sin′ə·mə) *n.* **1.** A motion picture (def. 2). **2.** A motion-picture theater. — **the cinema** Motion pictures collectively; also, the art or business of making motion pictures. [Short for CINEMATOGRAPH] — **cin·e·mat·ic** (sin′ə·mat′ik) *adj.* — **cin′e·mat′i·cal·ly** *adv.*

cin·e·mat·o·graph (sin′ə·mat′ə·graf, -gräf) *n.* A motion-picture camera or projector. — *v.t. & v.i.* To take photographs (of) with a motion-picture camera: also **cin·e·ma·tize** (sin′ə·mə·tīz′). Also **kinematograph.** [< Gk. *kinēma, -atos* movement + -GRAPH]

cin·e·ma·tog·ra·phy (sin′ə·mə·tog′rə·fē) *n.* The art and process of making motion pictures. — **cin′e·ma·tog′ra·pher** *n.* — **cin·e·mat′o·graph·ic** (sin′ə·mat′ə·graf′ik) *adj.* — **cin′·e·mat′o·graph′i·cal·ly** *adv.*

cin·e·ol (sin′ē·ōl, -ol) *n.* Eucalyptol. Also **cin′e·ole** (-ōl). [Transposition of NL *ole(um) cin(ae)* oil of wormwood]

cin·e·rar·i·a (sin′ə·râr′ē·ə) *n.* A cultivated, ornamental plant (*Senecio cruentus*) of the composite family, originally from the Canary Islands, having heart-shaped leaves and showy white, red, or purple flowers. [< NL < L, fem. of *cinerarius* ashy < *cinis, cineris* ash]

cin·e·rar·i·um (sin′ə·râr′ē·əm) *n. pl.* **·rar·i·a** (-râr′ē·ə) A place for keeping the ashes of a cremated body. [< L] — **cin·er·ar·y** (sin′ə·rer′ē) *adj.*

cin·er·a·tor (sin′ə·rā′tər) *n.* A furnace for cremating dead bodies; crematory. [Short for INCINERATOR]

ci·ne·re·ous (si·nir′ē·əs) *adj.* Of the nature or color of ashes; ashen; ash gray. [< L *cinereus* ashes]

cin·gu·lum (sing′gyə·ləm) *n. pl.* **·la** (-lə) *Zool.* A band, zone, or girdlelike part, as of color. [< L < *cingere* to gird] — **cin·gu·late** (sing′gyə·lit, -lāt) or **cin′gu·lat′ed** *adj.*

cin·na·bar (sin′ə·bär) *n.* **1.** A heavy, crystallized red mercuric sulfide, HgS, the chief ore of mercury. **2.** Vermilion. [< L *cinnabaris* < Gk. *kinnabari*, ult. < Persian *zanjifrah*]

cin·nam·ic (si·nam′ik, sin′ə·mik) *adj.* Of, pertaining to, or derived from cinnamon. Also **cin·na·mon·ic** (sin′ə·mon′ik).

cinnamic acid *Chem.* A colorless, crystalline, volatile compound, $C_9H_8O_2$, contained in cinnamon and various balsams, and also made synthetically.

cin·na·mon (sin′ə·mən) *n.* **1.** The aromatic inner bark of any of several tropical trees of the laurel family, used as a spice. **2.** Any tree that yields this bark, especially the Ceylon cinnamon (*Cinnamomum zeylanicum*). **3.** A shade of light reddish brown. [< L *cinnamomum* < Gk. *kinnamōmon* < Hebrew *quinnāmōn*]

cinnamon bear A cinnamon-colored variety of the American black bear.

cinnamon stone Essonite.

cin·na·myl (sin′ə·mil) *n. Chem.* The univalent radical C_9H_9, an important constituent of many compounds used in making soap, perfumes, drugs, etc. [< CINNAM(ON) + -YL]

cin·quain (sing·kān′) *n.* A stanza of five lines. [< F]

cinque (singk) *n.* The number five, in cards or dice. [< F *cinq* < L *quinque* five]

cin·que·cen·tist (ching′kwə·chen′tist) *n.* An Italian artist or writer of the 16th century. [< Ital. *cinquecentista* < *cinquecento* five hundred, short for *mil cinque cento* fifteen hundred, i.e., the 16th century]

cin·que·cen·to (ching′kwə·chen′tō) *n.* The 16th century, especially with reference to Italy, its arts and literature.

cinque·foil (singk′foil) *n.* **1.** *Archit.* A five-cusped ornament or window. **2.** Any of several species of a genus (*Potentilla*) of plants of the rose family, with five-lobed leaves: also called *five-fingers*. **3.** *Heraldry* A five-leaved clover. [< F < L *quinquefolium* < *quinque* five + *folium* leaf]

Cinque Ports (singk) An association of maritime towns in southern England, including Dover, Hastings, Hythe, Rom-

ney, and Sandwich, that formerly furnished men and ships for the king's service in return for special privileges. [< OF *cinq porz* five ports]

CIO or **C.I.O.** Congress of Industrial Organizations.

ci·on (sī′ən) *n.* A twig or shoot cut from a plant or tree, especially for grafting: also spelled *scion*. [Var. of SCION]

-cion Var. of -TION.

Ci·pan·go (si·pang′gō) *Poetic* Japan: the name used by Marco Polo.

CINQUE-FOIL (def. 1)

ci·pher (sī′fər) *n.* **1.** The figure 0, the symbol of the absence of quantity; zero. **2.** A person or thing of no value or importance. **3.** Any system of making a secret written message by a prearranged scheme or key. Compare CODE (def. 4). **4.** A message in cipher; also, its key. **5.** A character consisting of interlaced letters; monogram. **6.** Any Arabic numeral; a number. — *v.t.* **1.** To calculate arithmetically. **2.** To write in characters of hidden meaning; encipher. — *v.i.* **3.** To work out arithmetical examples. **4.** To sound continuously, as an organ pipe. Also spelled *cypher*. [< OF *cyfre* < Arabic *ṣifr*. Doublet of ZERO.]

cip·o·lin (sip′ə·lin) *n.* An Italian marble having layers of alternating white and green. [< F < Ital. *cipollino*, dim. of *cipolla* onion; with ref. to its layered structure]

circ. or **cir.** **1.** About (L *circa, circiter, circum*). **2.** Circular. **3.** Circulation. **4.** Circumference.

cir·ca (sûr′kə) *prep. Latin* About; around; used before approximate date or figures. Abbr. *c., C., ca., cir., circ.*

cir·ca·di·an (sər·kā′dē·ən) *n. Biol.* Pertaining to or designating those vital processes in plants and animals that tend to recur in cycles of approximately 24 hours. [< L *circa* around + *dies* day]

Cir·cas·sia (sər·kash′ə, -kash′ē·ə) A region of the NW Caucasus, R.S.F.S.R.

Cir·cas·sian (sər·kash′ən, -kash′ē·ən) *n.* **1.** A member of one of a group of tribes of the Caucasus region. **2.** The Northwest Caucasian language of these tribes. — *adj.* Of or pertaining to Circassia, its people, or their language: also **Cir·cas·sic** (sər·kas′ik).

Circassian walnut See under WALNUT.

Cir·ce (sûr′sē) In the *Odyssey*, an enchantress who changed Odysseus's companions into swine by a magic drink.

Cir·ce·an (sər·sē′ən) *adj.* **1.** Of, pertaining to, or characteristic of Circe. **2.** Bewitching and degrading.

cir·ci·nate (sûr′sə·nāt) *adj.* **1.** Ringed; ring-shaped. **2.** *Bot.* Rolled inward from the apex into a coil. [< L *circinatus*, pp. of *circinare* to make round < *circinus* circle] — **cir′ci·nate·ly** *adv.*

Cir·ci·nus (sûr′si·nəs) *n.* A constellation, the Compass. See CONSTELLATION. [< L]

cir·cle (sûr′kəl) *n.* **1.** A plane figure bounded by a curved line every point of which is equally distant from the center. **2.** The circumference of such a figure. **3.** Something having the form of a circle, as a crown, halo, or ring. **4.** A round or spherical body; an orb. **5.** A group of persons united by some common interest or pursuit; a set; coterie. **6.** The domain or scope of a special influence or action. **7.** A gallery or tier of seats in a theater: the family *circle*. **8.** A series or process that finishes at its starting point or that repeats itself without end: the *circle* of the seasons. **9.** A circular path or course; circuit. **10.** *Astron.* The orbit of a heavenly body; also, its period of revolution. **11.** An astronomical or other instrument whose important parts are graduated circles. **12.** *Logic* An invalid form of argument in which the conclusion is assumed to prove the premise, and the premise to prove the conclusion: also called *vicious circle*. **13.** *Geog.* A parallel of latitude. **14.** In some European countries, an administrative governmental district. — **Syn.** See CLIQUE. — *v.* **·cled, ·cling** *v.t.* **1.** To enclose in a circle; encompass. **2.** To move around, as in a circle. — *v.i.* **3.** To move in a circle. [< L *circulus*, dim. of *circus* ring] — **cir′cler** *n.*

cir·clet (sûr′klit) *n.* A small ring or ring-shaped object, especially one worn as an ornament. [< F *cerclet*, dim. of *cercle* ring; infl. in form by *circle*]

cir·cuit (sûr′kit) *n.* **1.** A moving or traveling round; a circular route or course: the earth's *circuit* of the sun. **2.** A periodic journey from place to place, as by a judge or minister, in the discharge of duties; also, the persons making such trips. **3.** The route traversed, or the district visited, in such a journey; especially, a division assigned to a judge for holding court at stated intervals. **4.** A group of associated theaters presenting plays, films, etc., in turn. **5.** The line or distance around an area; circumference; also, the area enclosed. **6.** *Electr.* **a** The entire course traversed by an electric current. When complete, it is a **made** or **closed circuit**, and when interrupted, it is a **broken** or **open circuit**. **b** The complete assembly of generators, conductors, electron tubes, switches, etc., by which an electric current is transmitted. **7.** *Telecom.* A transmission and reception system. — *v.t. & v.i.* To go or move (about) in a circuit. [< F < L *circuitus* < *circumire* < *circum-* around + *ire* to go]

circuit binding A style of bookbinding in which flexible projections (**circuit edges**) protect the edges of the pages.

circuit breaker *Electr.* A switch or relay for breaking a circuit under specified or abnormal conditions of current flow: also called *overload.*

circuit court A court of law that sits in various counties or districts over which its jurisdiction extends. Abbr. *c.c., C.C.*

Circuit Court of Appeals The highest U.S. court of appellate jurisdiction below the Supreme Court.

circuit judge A judge of a circuit court.

cir·cu·i·tous (sər·kyōō′ə·təs) *adj.* Roundabout; indirect. — **cir·cu′i·tous·ly** *adv.* — **cir·cu′i·tous·ness** *n.*

circuit rider A minister who preaches at churches on a circuit or district route.

cir·cuit·ry (sûr′kit·rē) *n. Electr.* The design and arrangement of circuits in any device, instrument, or system carrying a current.

cir·cu·i·ty (sər·kyōō′ə·tē) *n. pl.* **·ties** Roundabout procedure or speech; indirectness.

cir·cu·lar (sûr′kyə·lər) *adj.* **1.** Shaped like a circle; round. **2.** Moving in or describing a circle: a *circular* path. **3.** Of or referring to the mathematical circle: *circular* measure. **4.** Ending at or constantly returning to the starting point. **5.** Roundabout; indirect; devious: *circular* reasoning. **6.** Addressed to several persons, or intended for general circulation. — *n.* A statement, notice, or advertisement printed in quantity for general distribution. Abbr. *cir., circ.* [< AF *circuler* < L *circularis* < *circulus*. See CIRCLE.] — **cir·cu·lar·i·ty** (sûr′kyə·lar′ə·tē), **cir′cu·lar·ness** *n.* — **cir′cu·lar·ly** *adv.*

cir·cu·lar·ize (sûr′kyə·lə·rīz′) *v.t.* **·ized**, **·iz·ing 1.** To make circular. **2.** To make into a circular. **3.** To distribute circulars to. — **cir′cu·lar·i·za′tion** *n.* — **cir′cu·lar·iz′er** *n.*

circular measure A system of measurement for circles.

circular mil A unit of measurement for determining the area of wire in cross section, equal to the area of a circle having a diameter of 1 mil. Abbr. *c.m.*

circular sailing Great-circle sailing (which see).

circular saw A disk-shaped saw having a toothed edge, rotated at high speed by a motor.

circular triangle *Geom.* A triangle each of whose sides is an arc of a circle.

cir·cu·late (sûr′kyə·lāt) *v.* **·lat·ed**, **·lat·ing** *v.i.* **1.** To move by a circuitous course back to the starting point, as the blood through the body. **2.** To pass from place to place or person to person; spread or travel about: to *circulate* in society; Rumors *circulate* quickly. **3.** To be in free motion; become diffused, as air. — *v.t.* **4.** To hand or pass around, as money, news, etc.; disseminate. **5.** To cause (a fluid, etc.) to move through an enclosed area or system. [< L *circulatus*, pp. of *circulari* to form a circle < *circulus*. See CIRCLE.] — **cir·cu·la·tive** (sûr′kyə·lā′tiv) *adj.* — **cir′cu·la′tor** *n.*

circulating decimal A repeating decimal (which see).

circulating library A library from which books may be borrowed or rented: also called *lending library.*

circulating medium Currency used as a medium of exchange.

cir·cu·la·tion (sûr′kyə·lā′shən) *n.* **1.** A moving around or through something back to the starting point; circular or circuitous motion. **2.** The motion of the blood to and from the heart through the arteries and veins. **3.** The similar transmission of nutritive matter to the cells of plants. **4.** A transmission or spreading from one person or place to another; dissemination. **5.** The extent or amount of distribution of a periodical; the number of copies distributed, as of a magazine. Abbr. *cir., circ.* **6.** In libraries, the lending of books for use outside; also, the library department managing such loans. **7.** A current medium of exchange, as coin; currency. [< L *circulatio, -onis* < *circulari*. See CIRCULATE.]

cir·cu·la·to·ry (sûr′kyə·lə·tôr′ē, -tō′rē) *adj.* Of, pertaining to or affecting circulation: a *circulatory* disorder.

circum- *prefix* **1.** About; around; on all sides; surrounding: *circumfluent, circumnavigate.* **2.** Revolving around: *circumsolar.* [< L *circum-* around, about < *circus* circle]

cir·cum·am·bi·ent (sûr′kəm·am′bē·ənt) *adj.* Encompassing; surrounding. — **cir′cum·am′bi·ence, cir′cum·am′bi·en·cy** *n.*

cir·cum·am·bu·late (sûr′kəm·am′byə·lāt) *v.t. & v.i.* **·lat·ed**, **·lat·ing** To walk around. [< L *circumambulatus,* pp. of *circumambulare* < *circum-* around + *ambulare* to walk] — **cir′cum·am′bu·la′tion** *n.* — **cir′cum·am′bu·la′tor** *n.*

cir·cum·ben·di·bus (sûr′kəm·ben′di·bəs) *n.* A roundabout course; a circumlocution: a humorous usage. [Coined from CIRCUM- + BEND + L *-bus*]

cir·cum·cise (sûr′kəm·sīz) *v.t.* **·cised**, **·cis·ing 1.** To cut off all or part of the prepuce of, either as a religious rite or as a prophylactic operation. **2.** To excise the clitoris of. **3.** In the Bible, to purify from sin; cleanse spiritually. [< OF *circonciser* < L *circumcisus,* pp. of *circumcidere* < *circum-* around + *caedere* to cut] — **cir′cum·cis′er** *n.*

cir·cum·ci·sion (sûr′kəm·sizh′ən) *n.* **1.** The act, operation, or ritual of circumcising. **2.** Spiritual purification. — **the Circumcision** A church festival observed on January 1, commemorating the circumcision of Jesus Christ.

cir·cum·fer·ence (sər·kum′fər·əns) *n.* **1.** The boundary line of any area; especially, the boundary of a circle. **2.** The length of such a line; distance around; compass. Abbr. *cir., circ.* — **Syn.** See PERIMETER. [< L *circumferentia* < *circum-* around + *ferre* to bear; trans. of Gk. *periphereia.* See PERIPHERY.] — **cir·cum·fer·en·tial** (sər·kum′fə·ren′shəl) *adj.* — **cir·cum′fer·en′tial·ly** *adv.*

cir·cum·flex (sûr′kəm·fleks) *n.* A mark (^, ˆ, ˇ) written over a letter in ancient Greek to indicate the combination of a rising with a falling tone, and later, in other languages, to mark a long vowel, contraction, etc., or used as a diacritical mark in phonetic transcription. ◆ In the pronunciations in this dictionary, the circumflex is used over *a* to indicate the vowel sound in *care* (kâr), over *o* for the vowel in *fall* (fôl), and over *u* for the vowel in *earn* (ûrn). — *adj.* **1.** Pronounced or marked with the circumflex accent. **2.** *Physiol.* Bent or curving around, as certain vessels and nerves. — *v.t.* **1.** To pronounce or mark with a circumflex. **2.** To wind around; bend about. [< L *circumflexus,* pp. of *circumflectere* < *circum-* around + *flectere* to bend] — **cir·cum·flex·ion** (sûr′kəm·flek′shən) *n.*

cir·cum·flu·ous (sər·kum′flōō·əs) *adj.* **1.** Flowing around; surrounding. Also **cir·cum·flu·ent** (sər·kum′flōō·ənt). **2.** Surrounded by or as by water. [< L *circumfluus,* pp. of *circumfluere* < *circum-* around + *fluere* to flow]

cir·cum·fuse (sûr′kəm·fyōōz′) *v.t.* **fused**, **fus·ing 1.** To pour, scatter, or spread about. **2.** To surround, as with a liquid. [< L *circumfusus,* pp. of *circumfundere* < *circum-* around + *fundere* to pour] — **cir·cum·fu·sion** (sûr′kəm·fyōō′zhən) *n.*

cir·cum·gy·rate (sûr′kəm·jī′rāt) *v.t. & v.i.* **·rat·ed**, **·rat·ing** To circle about. [< CIRCUM- + L *gyratus,* pp. of *gyrare* to spin] — **cir′cum·gy·ra′tion** *n.*

cir·cum·ja·cent (sûr′kəm·jā′sənt) *adj.* Bordering on all sides; surrounding. [< L *circumjacens, -entis,* ppr. of *circumjacere* < *circum-* around + *jacere* to lie]

cir·cum·lo·cu·tion (sûr′kəm·lō·kyōō′shən) *n.* Indirect or roundabout expression; the use of superfluous words; also, an example of this. [< L *circumlocutio, -onis* < *circum-* around + *locutio* speaking < *loqui* to speak] — **cir·cum·loc·u·to·ry** (sûr′kəm·lok′yə·tôr′ē, -tō′rē) *adj.*

— **Syn.** *Circumlocution, periphrasis, pleonasm, tautology, prolixity, diffuseness, verbiage, verbosity,* and *wordiness* refer to an excess of words. In *circumlocution* and the less common *periphrasis* the excess is felt because the same idea could be expressed more directly. *Pleonasm* and *tautology* are repetitious. *Pleonasm* repeats what is implicit and may be acceptable for emphasis, as in "I saw with my own eyes." *Tautology* repeats what is explicit, as in "All the members agreed unanimously," and so is to be avoided as useless. *Prolixity* goes into endless petty details, without selection or perspective. *Diffuseness* tends to obscure ideas by diluting them with too many words, while *verbiage* is the use of mere words without ideas. *Verbosity* and *wordiness* denote an excess of words in proportion to the thoughts expressed. — **Ant.** brevity, conciseness, condensation, directness, succinctness, terseness.

cir·cum·nav·i·gate (sûr′kəm·nav′ə·gāt) *v.t.* **·gat·ed**, **·gat·ing** To sail around. [< L *circumnavigatus,* pp. of *circumnavigare* < *circum-* around + *navigare* to sail] — **cir′cum·nav′i·ga′tion** *n.* — **cir·cum·nav·i·ga·ble** (sûr′kəm·nav′ə·gə·bəl) *adj.* — **cir′cum·nav′i·ga′tor** *n.*

cir·cum·nu·tate (sûr′kəm·nōō′tāt, -nyōō′-) *v.t. Bot.* To turn or move with a circular, spiral, or elliptical motion, as the growing tips of tendrils, stems, roots, etc. [< CIRCUM- + L *nutare* to nod] — **cir′cum·nu·ta′tion** *n.*

cir·cum·po·lar (sûr′kəm·pō′lər) *adj.* **1.** Near or surrounding one of the terrestrial or celestial poles. **2.** Of stars, revolving about either pole without setting.

cir·cum·ro·tate (sûr′kəm·rō′tāt) *v.i.* **·tat·ed**, **·tat·ing** To revolve, as a wheel. [< L *circumrotatus,* pp. of *circumrotare* < *circum-* around + *rotare* to turn] — **cir·cum·ro·ta·to·ry** (sûr′kəm·rō′tə·tôr′ē, -tō′rē) *adj.* — **cir′cum·ro·ta′tion** *n.*

cir·cum·scis·sile (sûr′kəm·sis′il) *adj. Bot.* Opening, as a capsule, in a transverse circular line, so that the top separates like a lid. [< L *circumscissus,* pp. of *circumscindere* < *circum-* around + *scindere* to cut]

cir·cum·scribe (sûr′kəm·skrīb′, sûr′kəm·skrīb′) *v.t.* **scribed**, **·scrib·ing 1.** To mark out the limits of; define; especially, to confine within bounds. **2.** To draw a line or figure around; encompass. **3.** *Geom.* **a** To draw (a figure) about another figure so that it touches at every possible point without intersecting: to *circumscribe* a circle about a triangle. **b** To surround (another figure) in this way. [< L *circumscribere* < *circum-* around + *scribere* to write] — **cir′cum·scrib′a·ble** *adj.* — **cir′cum·scrib′er** *n.*

cir·cum·scrip·tion (sûr′kəm·skrip′shən) *n.* **1.** The act of circumscribing, or the state of being limited or bounded; limitation; restriction. **2.** Anything that limits or encloses. **3.** The line marking the bounds of an object; periphery. **4.** A space marked out or bounded. **5.** An inscription around a coin, medallion, etc. **6.** *Obs.* Definition; description. [< L *circumscriptio, -onis* < *circumscribere.* See CIRCUMSCRIBE.] — **cir′cum·scrip′tive** *adj.*

cir·cum·so·lar (sûr/kəm·sō/lər) *adj.* Revolving about or surrounding the sun.

cir·cum·spect (sûr/kəm·spekt) *adj.* Attentive to everything; watchful in all directions, as against danger or error; cautious; wary. [< L *circumspectus*, orig. pp. of *circumspicere* < *circum-* around + *specere* to look] — **cir/cum·spect/ly** *adv.* — **cir/cum·spect/ness** *n.*

cir·cum·spec·tion (sûr/kəm·spek/shən) *n.* Cautious and prudent observation or action. — **cir/cum·spec/tive** *adj.*

cir·cum·stance (sûr/kəm·stans) *n.* **1.** A factor connected with an act, event, or condition, either as an incidental accessory or as a determining or modifying element: a *circumstance* attending a crime. **2.** *Often pl.* The conditions, influences, etc., surrounding and affecting persons or actions: a victim of *circumstances.* **3.** *pl.* Condition in life; relative prosperity: in poor *circumstances.* **4.** An event or happening; occurrence: a happy *circumstance.* **5.** Detail, especially superfluous detail, as in narrative. **6.** Formal display: pomp and *circumstance.* — **under no circumstances** Never; under no conditions. — **under the circumstances** Since such is (or was) the case. — *v.t.* **·stanced**, **·stanc·ing 1.** To place in or under limiting circumstances or conditions. **2.** *Obs.* To relate with details. [< OF < L *circumstantia* < *circumstare* < *circum-* around + *stare* to stand]
— **Syn. 1.** *Circumstance, situation, accompaniment,* and *concomitant* all refer to one fact or event in its relation to another. A *circumstance* may be any event, fact, state of affairs, detail, etc., that modifies or illuminates another; it may be in part a cause or occasion, but never an effect. All the *circumstances* affecting a principal fact or event form a *situation.* An *accompaniment* is united with the principal matter, but is not necessary to it, while a *concomitant* is joined to the principal matter by natural necessity, and is often a consequence of it. Compare CAUSE. **4.** See EVENT.

cir·cum·stanced (sûr/kəm·stanst) *adj.* Being in or under certain conditions.

cir·cum·stan·tial (sûr/kəm·stan/shəl) *adj.* **1.** Pertaining to or dependent on circumstances. **2.** Incidental; not essential. **3.** Full of details; minutely particular. **4.** Relating to material welfare: *circumstantial* prosperity. **5.** Full of formal display. — **cir/cum·stan/tial·ly** *adv.*

circumstantial evidence *Law* Evidence consisting of circumstances that furnish reasonable ground for believing or deciding as to the existence of a fact, or the guilt or innocence of an accused person.

cir·cum·stan·ti·al·i·ty (sûr/kəm·stan/shē·al/ə·tē) *n. pl.* **·ties 1.** The quality of being particular, detailed, or minute. **2.** A particular matter; detail.

cir·cum·stan·ti·ate (sûr/kəm·stan/shē·āt) *v.t.* **·at·ed, ·at·ing** To set forth or establish by circumstances or in detail. — **cir/cum·stan/ti·a/tion** *n.*

cir·cum·val·late (sûr/kəm·val/āt) *v.t.* **·lat·ed, ·lat·ing** To surround with a rampart or a trench. — *adj.* Enclosed by or as by a wall: *circumvallate* papillae. [< L *circumvallatus,* pp. of *circumvallare* < *circum-* around + *vallare* to fortify < *vallum* rampart] — **cir/cum·val·la/tion** *n.*

cir·cum·vent (sûr/kəm·vent/) *v.t.* **1.** To surround or entrap, as an enemy, by craft or stratagem. **2.** To gain an advantage over, as by craft, artifice, or fraud; outwit. **3.** To go around: to *circumvent* a town. **4.** To avoid: to *circumvent* disaster. [< L *circumventus,* pp. of *circumvenire* < *circum-* around + *venire* to come] — **cir/cum·vent/er** or **cir/cum·ven/tor** *n.* — **cir/cum·ven/tive** *adj.* — **cir/cum·ven/tion** *n.*
— **Syn. 2.** outsmart. Compare BAFFLE. **4.** escape, evade.

cir·cum·vo·lu·tion (sûr/kəm·və·lōō/shən) *n.* **1.** A turning round an axis or center; also, a complete turn. **2.** A winding or folding around something; also, a single fold so made. **3.** A winding course; sinuosity. [< L *circumvolutus,* pp. of *circumvolvere* < *circum-* around + *volvere* to turn, spin]

cir·cum·volve (sûr/kəm·volv/) *v.t. & v.i.* **·volved, ·volv·ing** To revolve. [< L *circumvolvere.* See CIRCUMVOLUTION.]

cir·cus (sûr/kəs) *n.* **1.** A traveling show of acrobats, clowns, trained animals, etc.; also, a performance of such a show. **2.** A circular, usually tented area with tiers of seats around it, used for such shows. **3.** In ancient Rome, an oblong enclosure with tiers of seats around three sides, used for races, games, etc. **4.** *Brit.* An open place, usually circular, at the junction of several streets. **5.** *U.S. Informal* A noisy frolic; also, something or someone uproariously entertaining. [< L, a ring, racecourse < Gk. *kirkos.* Doublet of CIRQUE.]

Cir·cus Max·i·mus (sûr/kəs mak/si·məs) A large arena of ancient Rome, used for chariot races.

Ci·re·na·i·ca (chē/rā·nä/ē·kä) The Italian name for CYRENAICA.

Ci·re·ne (chē·rā/nā) Italian name for CYRENE.

cirque (sûrk) *n.* **1.** A circular space or enclosure; especially, a circular valley with precipitous walls. **2.** *Poetic* A circlet; ring. [< F < L *circus.* Doublet of CIRCUS.]

cir·rate (sir/āt) *adj.* Having cirri. [< L *cirratus* < *cirrus* curl]

cir·rho·sis (si·rō/sis) *n. Pathol.* A disease of the liver, characterized by an abnormal formation of connective tissue with progressive cellular alteration and breakdown. [< NL < Gk. *kirrhos* tawny; with ref. to the color of the cirrhotic liver] — **cir·rhot·ic** (si·rot/ik) *adj.*

cir·ri (sir/ī) Plural of CIRRUS.

cir·ri·ped (sir/ə·ped) *Zool. n.* One of an order (*Cirripedia*) of crustaceans that become sessile or parasitic in the adult stage, as the barnacle. — *adj.* Of or pertaining to this order. [< NL *Cirripedia* < L *cirrus* curl + *pes, pedis* foot]

cirro- *combining form* Cirrus: *cirrostratus.* Also **cirri-**. [< L *cirrus* curl]

cir·ro·cu·mu·lus (sir/ō·kyōōm/yə·ləs) *n. Meteorol.* A mass of fleecy, globular cloudlets (Symbol Cc) in contact with one another; mackerel sky. See table for CLOUD.

cir·ro·stra·tus (sir/ō·strā/təs) *n. Meteorol.* A fine, whitish veil of cloud (Symbol Cs), often giving a hazy appearance to the sky. See table for CLOUD.

cir·rous (sir/əs) *adj.* **1.** Having or like cirri. **2.** Of or pertaining to a cirrus cloud. Also **cir·rose** (sir/ōs).

cir·rus (sir/əs) *n. pl.* **cir·ri** (sir/ī) **1.** *Meteorol.* A type of white, wispy cloud (Symbol Ci), usually consisting of ice crystals and seen in tufts or feathery bands across the sky. See table for CLOUD. **2.** *Bot.* A tendril. **3.** *Zool.* A threadlike appendage serving as an organ of touch. [< L, ringlet, curl]

cir·soid (sûr/soid) *adj.* **1.** Resembling a varix. **2.** Varicose. [< Gk. *kirsos* a dilated vein]

cir·sot·o·my (sər·sot/ə·mē) *n. pl.* **·mies** *Surg.* The incision of varicose veins. [< Gk. *kirsos* dilated vein + -TOMY]

cis- *prefix* **1.** On this side of: *cisatlantic:* opposed to *trans-* or *ultra-.* **2.** Since; following: *cis-Elizabethan:* opposed to *pre-.* [< L *cis* on this side]

cis·al·pine (sis·al/pīn, -pin) *adj.* On the Roman side of the Alps. [< L *cisalpinus* < *cis* on this side + *Alpes* the Alps]

Cisalpine Gaul An ancient name for northern Italy.

cis·at·lan·tic (sis/ət·lan/tik) *adj.* On this side of the Atlantic.

Cis·cau·ca·sia (sis/kô·kā/zhə, -shə) See NORTHERN CAUCASUS.

cis·co (sis/kō) *n. pl.* **·coes** or **·cos** *U.S. & Canadian* A whitefish (genus *Coregonus* or *Leucichthys*) of North America; especially, the lake herring. [? < N. Am. Ind.]

cis·lu·nar (sis·lōō/nər) *adj.* On this side of the moon.

cis·mon·tane (sis·mon/tān) *adj.* On this side of the mountains; especially, on this side of the Alps: opposed to *ultramontane.* [< L *cismontanus* < *cis* on this side + *mons, montis* mountain]

cis·pa·dane (sis/pə·dān, sis·pā/dān) *adj.* On this (the southern) side of the river Po, as viewed from Rome. [< CIS- on this side + L *Padus* the Po]

cis·soid (sis/oid) *Math. n.* A curve having a cusp at one end of a diameter and intersecting the circumference at the same points as does the perpendicular bisector of the diameter. — *adj.* Contained within the concave sides of two intersecting curves: said of an angle: opposed to *sistroid.* [< Gk. *kissoeidēs* like ivy < *kissos* ivy + *eidos* form]

cist[1] (sist) *n.* In classical antiquity, a chest, usually for sacred utensils. [< L *cista.* See CHEST.]

cist[2] (sist, kist) *n.* A prehistoric tomb or casket, usually of rock slabs: also spelled *kist.* [< Welsh, chest < L *cista.* See CHEST.]

cis·ta·ceous (sis·tā/shəs) *adj. Bot.* Designating the rockrose family (*Cistaceae*) of shrubby or herbaceous plants. [< NL *Cistaceae* < Gk. *kistos* rockrose]

Cis·ter·cian (sis·tûr/shən) *n.* A monk of a very strict contemplative order founded in 1098 at Cistercium (modern Cîteaux), France, as an offshoot of the Benedictines. — *adj.* Of or pertaining to this order.

cis·tern (sis/tərn) *n.* **1.** An artificial reservoir, as a tank, for holding water or other liquids. **2.** *Anat.* A large lymph space; a sac. [< OF *cisterne* < L *cisterna* < *cista* chest]

cit. 1. Citation; cited. **2.** Citizen.

cit·a·del (sit/ə·del, -del) *n.* **1.** A fortress commanding a city. **2.** Any fortress or stronghold. **3.** The heavily plated casemate in a war vessel. — **Syn.** See FORT. [< MF *citadelle* < Ital. *cittadella,* dim. of *città* city]

ci·ta·tion (sī·tā/shən) *n.* **1.** A citing or quoting, as for substantiation; also, a passage or authority so cited. **2.** A public commendation for outstanding achievement. **3.** A summons, as to appear in court. **4.** *Law* A citing of former court decisions or authoritative books. **5.** A recounting; enumeration, as of facts. Abbr. *cit.* [< OF < L *citatio, -onis* < *citare.* See CITE.] — **ci·ta·to·ry** (sī/tə·tôr/ē, -tō/rē) *adj.*

cite (sīt) *v.t.* **cit·ed, cit·ing 1.** To quote as authority or illustration. **2.** To bring forward or refer to as proof or support. **3.** *Mil.* To mention in a report, especially for bravery. **4.** To mention or enumerate. **5.** To summon to appear in court. **6.** To summon to action; rouse. [< F *citer* < L *citare* < *ciere* to set in motion] — **cit/a·ble** or **cite/a·ble** *adj.*

cith·a·ra (sith/ə·rə) *n.* **1.** An ancient Greek stringed instrument resembling a lyre. **2.** Loosely, any stringed instrument of ancient Greece. **3.** A cittern. Also spelled *kithara.* [< L < Gk. *kithara.* Doublet of GUITAR and ZITHER.]

cith·er (sith/ər) *n.* **1.** A zither. **2.** A cittern. Also **cith·ern** (sith/ərn). **3.** A cithara.

cit·ied (sit/ēd) *adj.* **1.** Occupied by a city or cities. **2.** Made into or likened to a city.

cit·i·fied (sit/i·fīd) *adj.* Having the ways, habits, fashions, etc., of city life: also spelled *cityfied.*

cit·i·zen (sit'ə-zən) *n.* **1.** A native or naturalized person owing allegiance to, and entitled to protection from, a government. Compare ALIEN, SUBJECT. Abbr. *cit.* **2.** A resident of a city or town. **3.** A civilian, as distinguished from a public officer, soldier, etc. [< AF *citezein*, var. of OF *citeain* < *cité*. See CITY.] — **cit′i·zen·ess** *n.fem.* — **Syn. 1.** subject, national. — **Ant.** alien, foreigner.

cit·i·zen·ry (sit'ə-zən-rē) *n.* *pl.* **·ries** Citizens collectively.

citizens band A set of high-frequency radio channels reserved for generalized communication, usually to and from vehicles, under easy licensing rules. Abbr. *CB.*

cit·i·zen·ship (sit'ə-zən-ship') *n.* The status of a citizen.

Cit·lal·té·petl (sēt'läl-tā'pet·l) See ORIZABA.

ci·to·la (sə-tō'lə) *n.* A cittern. Also **ci·tole′** (-tōl′).

citra- *prefix* On this side; cis-. [< L]

cit·ral (sit'rəl) *n.* *Chem.* An oily liquid aldehyde, $C_{10}H_{16}O$, contained in geranium, lemon, and other oils and used as a flavoring extract and in perfumery: also called *geranial.* [< CITR(US) + AL(DEHYDE)]

cit·rate (sit'rāt, -rit, sī'trāt) *n.* *Chem.* A salt of citric acid.

cit·rat·ed (sit'rāt·id) *adj.* Containing or treated with a citrate, as potassium citrate.

cit·re·ous (sit'rē·əs) *adj.* Having the yellow color of a citron or lemon. [< L *citreus* < *citrus* citron tree]

cit·ric (sit'rik) *adj.* Of or derived from citrus fruits.

citric acid *Chem.* A white, crystalline, sharply sour compound, $C_6H_8O_7$, occurring in various fruits.

cit·ri·cul·ture (sit'ri·kul'chər) *n.* The cultivation of citrus fruits. [< CITRUS + CULTURE] — **cit'ri·cul'tur·ist** *n.*

cit·rine (sit'rin) *adj.* **1.** Lemon yellow. **2.** Pertaining to the citron, lemon, and allied trees. — *n.* **1.** Citrine color. **2.** A light yellow, vitreous variety of quartz resembling topaz. [< F *citrin*]

cit·ron (sit'rən) *n.* **1.** A fruit like a lemon, but larger and less acid. **2.** The tree (*Citrus medica*) producing this fruit. **3.** A watermelon (*Citrullus vulgaris citroides*), with a small, hard-fleshed fruit. Also **citron melon.** **4.** The rind of either of these fruits, preserved and used in confections. [< MF, lemon < Ital. *citrone* < L *citrus* citrus tree]

cit·ron·el·la (sit'rə-nel'ə) *n.* A grass (*Cymbopogon nardus*) cultivated in Ceylon, yielding **citronella oil,** used in perfumery, in cooking, and as protection against mosquitoes. Also **citronella grass.** [< NL < CITRON; so called from its odor]

cit·ron·el·lal (sit'rə-nel'əl) *n.* *Chem.* An unsaturated aldehyde, $C_9H_{17}CHO$, found in essential oils, used in making soaps and perfumes. [< CITRONELL(A) + AL(DEHYDE)]

citron wood 1. The wood of the sandarac tree, used in cabinetwork. **2.** The wood of the citron tree.

cit·rus (sit'rəs) *adj.* Of or pertaining to a genus (*Citrus*) of trees or shrubs of the rue family, cultivated for their fruits. Also **cit'rous.** [< L, citron tree]

citrus fruit A fruit of the genus *Citrus*, as the orange, lemon, lime, citron, grapefruit, etc.

Cit·tà del Va·ti·ca·no (chēt·tä' däl vä'tē·kä'nō) The Italian name for VATICAN CITY.

cit·tern (sit'ərn) *n.* Any of a group of stringed instruments resembling a lute or guitar, used in the 13th–16th centuries: also *cithara, cither, cithern, citola, citole, gittern.* [< L *cithara* < Gk. *kithara*; perhaps modeled after GITTERN]

cit·y (sit'ē) *n.* *pl.* **cit·ies 1.** A place inhabited by a large, permanent, organized community. **2.** In the United States, a municipality of the first class with definite boundaries and with various legal powers derived from a charter granted by the State. **3.** In Canada, a municipality of high rank whose legal character varies from province to province. **4.** In Great Britain, a large incorporated town, usually the seat of a bishop, on which the title *city* has been conferred by royal authority. **5.** The people of a city, collectively. **6.** A city-state. **7.** In earlier times a central, walled place used by the dwellers in a district as a market, a place of worship or festivity, and a refuge. Abbr. (defs. 2, 3, 4) *c., C.* — **the City** See under LONDON. [< OF *cité* < L *civitas* < *civis* citizen]

city block An urban plot contained within neighboring and intersecting streets, usually four; a square; also, one side or street length of such a division.

city desk A department in a newspaper office where local news is received, rewritten, and edited.

city editor On a newspaper, the editor having charge of local news and of the reportorial staff.

city father One who directs the public affairs of a city, as a mayor, councilman, etc.

cit·y·fied (sit'i·fīd) See CITIFIED.

city manager An administrator not publicly elected but appointed by a city council to manage the city.

City of God Heaven.

City of (the) Seven Hills Rome.

city planning Public control of the physical development of a city, as by regulation of the size and use of buildings and streets, location of parks, etc. — **city planner**

cit·y·scape (sit'ē-skāp') *n.* A view or depiction of a large city, especially of its skyline. [< CITY + (LAND)SCAPE]

cit·y-state (sit'ē·stāt') *n.* A state consisting of a city and its contiguous territories, as ancient Athens.

Ciu·dad Bo·lí·var (syōō·thäth' bō·lē'vär) A port city in eastern Venezuela, on the Orinoco; pop. 63,266 (est. 1969).

Ciudad Juá·rez (hwä'rās) A city in northern Mexico, on the Rio Grande; pop. 436,054 (1970): formerly *El Paso del Norte.* Also *Juárez.*

Ciudad Tru·jil·lo (trōō·hē'yō) See SANTO DOMINGO.

civ. 1. Civil. **2.** Civilian.

civ·et (siv'it) *n.* **1.** A substance of musklike odor, secreted by the genital glands of the civet cat, used in perfumery. **2.** A dark gray, feline carnivore of Africa (genus *Viverra*), that secretes this substance. Also **civet cat.** **3.** The fur of this animal. [< MF *civette,* ult. < Arabic *zabād*]

civ·ic (siv'ik) *adj.* Of or pertaining to a city, a citizen, or citizenship; civil. [< L *civicus* < *civis* citizen]

civ·ics (siv'iks) *n.pl.* (*construed as sing.*) The division of political science dealing with the privileges and obligations of citizenship; study of civic affairs.

civ·ies (siv'ēz). See CIVVIES.

civ·il (siv'əl) *adj.* **1.** Characteristic of ordinary community life as distinguished from military or ecclesiastical affairs. **2.** Of or pertaining to the relations between citizens and government: *civil* affairs. **3.** Occurring within the state or between citizens; domestic: *civil* war. **4.** Of a citizen as a private person: *civil* rights. **5.** Proper to or befitting a citizen: *civil* duties: now often *civic.* **6.** In accordance with the requirements of civilization; civilized. **7.** Observing the recognized social amenities; proper; polite. **8.** *Law* **a** In accord with Roman civil law, or its modern derivatives. **b** Related to the rights of citizens and to legal proceedings involving these rights. **9.** According to the legal reckoning of time: *civil* day. Abbr. *civ.* — **Syn.** See POLITE. [< MF < L *civilis* under law, orderly < *civis* citizen] — **civ'il·ly** *adv.*

civil code See under CODE.

civil defense An emergency system of warning devices, shelters, and planned actions by civilian volunteers in the event of military attack or natural disaster.

civil disobedience A refusal to comply with certain civil laws, usually done as a matter of moral conviction and by means of passive resistance.

civil engineer A professional engineer trained to design, build, and maintain public works, as roads, harbors, bridges, tunnels, dams, and the like. Abbr. *C.E.*

ci·vil·ian (sə-vil'yən) *n.* **1.** One who is not in active military or naval service; also, one who is not a member of a police force or similar organization. **2.** One learned in the Roman or civil law. — *adj.* Of or pertaining to a civilian or civil life. Abbr. *civ.* [< OF *civilien* < L *civilis.* See CIVIL.]

ci·vil·i·ty (sə-vil'ə-tē) *n.* *pl.* **·ties 1.** The quality of being civil; courtesy; politeness. **2.** A polite act or speech.

civ·i·li·za·tion (siv'ə-lə·zā'shən, -lī-zā'-) *n.* **1.** A state of human society characterized by a high level of intellectual, social, and cultural development. **2.** The countries and peoples considered to have reached this stage. **3.** The cultural development of a specific people, country, or region. **4.** The act of civilizing, or the process of becoming civilized.

civ·i·lize (siv'ə-līz) *v.t.* **·lized, ·liz·ing** To bring into a state of civilization; bring out of savagery; refine; enlighten. Also *Brit.* **civ'i·lise.** [< MF *civilizer* < Med.L *civilizare* < L *civilis.* See CIVIL.] — **civ'i·liz'a·ble** *adj.* — **civ'i·liz'er** *n.*

civil law 1. The body of laws constituting the officially established legal system of a nation or state, especially in regard to the rights and privileges of private citizens. **2.** Roman law (which see). Abbr. *c.l.*

civil liberty A liberty guaranteed to the individual by the laws of a government, as distinguished from one based only upon some ideal or theory of natural law.

civil list *Brit.* The amount voted by Parliament for the personal and household expenses of the sovereign.

civil marriage A marriage solemnized by a civil or government official rather than by a clergyman.

civil rights The rights, privileges, and immunities of a citizen; especially, the rights guaranteed to all citizens of the United States by the 13th and 14th amendments to the U.S. Constitution and by certain acts of Congress.

civil servant One employed in the civil service.

civil service 1. The branches of governmental service that are not military, naval, legislative, or judicial. **2.** The body of persons employed in these branches. Abbr. *c.s., C.S.*

civil time Mean time (which see).

civil war War between parties or sections of the same country.

Civil War See table for WAR.

civil year A calendar year (which see).

civ·ism (siv'iz·əm) *n.* Good citizenship.

civ·vies (siv'ēz) *n.pl.* *Informal* Civilian clothes, as distinguished from military dress; mufti: also spelled *civies.*

C.J. 1. Corpus juris (L, body of law). **2.** Chief Judge. **3.** Chief Justice.

ck. (*pl.* **cks.**) **1.** Cask. **2.** Check. **3.** Cook.

cl. 1. Claim. 2. Class. 3. Classification. 4. Clause. 5. Clearance. 6. Clergyman. 7. Clerk. 8. Cloth.

cl. or **cl** Centiliter(s).

c.l. 1. Carload; carload lots. 2. Center line. 3. Civil law. 4. Craft loss (insurance).

Cl. *Chem.* Chlorine.

Cla. Clackmannan.

clab·ber (klab'ər) *n.* Milk curdled by souring. — *v.t. & v.i.* To curdle, as milk. [Short for BONNYCLABBER]

clach·an (klakh'ən) *n. Scot.* A hamlet. Also **clach.**

clack (klak) *v.i.* 1. To make a sharp, dry sound, as two flat pieces of wood striking together. 2. To chatter heedlessly; prate. 3. To cluck or cackle, as a hen. — *v.t.* 4. To cause to clack by striking together. 5. To utter unthinkingly; babble. — *n.* 1. A short, sharp sound duller than a clap. 2. Something that makes a clack. 3. Loud, prolonged talk; chatter. [Imit.] — **clack′er** *n.*

Clack·man·nan (klak·man′ən) A county in east central Scotland; 54.6 sq. mi.; pop. 44,084 (1969); county seat, **Clackmannan**; pop. 2,476 (1961). Also **Clack′man·nan·shire** (-shir).

clack valve *Mech.* A valve hinged at one edge, permitting flow of fluid is one direction only.

Clac·to·ni·an (klak·tō′nē·ən) *adj. Anthropol.* Pertaining to a culture stage of the Lower Paleolithic period, resembling the Abbevillian but characterized by flake stone tools. [after *Clacton*, England, where artifacts were found]

clad (klad) Alternative past tense and past participle of CLOTHE.

clad·o·phyll (klad′ə·fil) *n. Bot.* A leaflike branch stemming from the axil of a leaf. Also **clad·ode** (klad′ōd). [< Gk. *klados* branch + *phyllos* leaf]

claim (klām) *v.t.* 1. To demand on the ground of right; affirm to be one's due; assert ownership or title to. 2. To hold to be true against implied denial or doubt; maintain; assert. 3. To require or deserve: The problem *claims* our attention. — **Syn.** See DEMAND. — *n.* 1. A demand for something as due; an assertion of a right. 2. An assertion of something as true or factual: a *claim* of innocence. 3. A ground for claiming something; a right or title: a *claim* to greatness. 4. That which is claimed, as a piece of land, an insurance payment, etc. Abbr. *cl.* [< OF *clamer* to call, claim < L *clamare* to declare] — **claim′a·ble** *adj.* — **claim′er** *n.*

claim·ant (klā′mənt) *n.* One who makes a claim.

claiming race A horse race in which any entry is subject to purchase at a previously set price, the right to purchase being often restricted to those entering horses in that meeting.

claim jumper *U.S.* One who seizes another's mining claim.

clair·ob·scure (klâr′ob·skyōōr′) *n.* Chiaroscuro.

clair·voy·ance (klâr·voi′əns) *n.* 1. The alleged ability to perceive objects that are distant or hidden. 2. Insight into or knowledge of things beyond the area of normal perception; second sight. [< MF]

clair·voy·ant (klâr·voi′ənt) *adj.* Having clairvoyance or second sight. — *n.* A clairvoyant person.

clam¹ (klam) *n.* 1. Any of various bivalve mollusks; especially, the quahog, the soft clam (which see), and the **giant clam** (*Tridacna gigas*) of the Indian and Pacific oceans, whose shell may exceed three feet in length. 2. *Informal* A close-mouthed person. — *v.i.* **clammed, clam·ming** To hunt for or dig clams. — **to clam up** *U.S. Slang* To become or keep silent. [< CLAM³; from the capacity of the shells to clamp together]

clam² (klam) *n.* 1. Clamminess. 2. A sticky substance. — *adj.* Sticky. [Cf. OE *clǣman* to smear, Du. *klam* sticky]

clam³ (klam) *n.* A clamp or a vise. [OE *clamm* grip, grasp]

cla·mant (klā′mənt) *adj.* 1. Clamorous; noisy. 2. *Scot.* Urgent. [< L *clamans, -antis,* ppr. of *clamare* to cry out]

clam·a·to·ri·al (klam′ə·tôr′ē·əl, -tō′rē-) *adj. Ornithol.* Relating to a suborder (*Clamatores*) of passerine birds, as the kingbirds. [< NL *Clamatores* < L *clamare* to cry out]

clam·bake (klam′bāk′) *n. U.S.* 1. A picnic where clams and other foods are baked, usually in layers on buried hot stones and covered with seaweed. 2. *Informal* An informal gathering, especially a noisy one.

clam·ber (klam′bər, klam′ər) *v.t. & v.i.* To climb by using the hands and feet; mount or descend with difficulty. — *n.* The act of clambering. [Akin to CLIMB] — **clam′·ber·er** *n.*

clam·jam·fer·y (klam·jam′fər·ē) *n. Scot.* 1. Rubbish. 2. Rabble. Also **clam·jam·fry** (klam·jam′frē), **clam·jam′ohrie.**

clam·my (klam′ē) *adj.* **·mi·er, ·mi·est** Stickily soft and damp, and usually cold. [< CLAM², adj.] — **clam′mi·ly** *adv.* — **clam′mi·ness** *n.*

clam·or (klam′ər) *n.* 1. A loud, repeated outcry. 2. A vehement protest or demand; public outcry. 3. Any loud and continuous noise; din. — *v.i.* 1. To make loud outcries, demands, or complaints. — *v.t.* 2. To utter with clamor. 3. To move or drive by clamor. 4. *Obs.* To disturb with noise. Also *Brit.* **clam′our.** [< OF < L *clamare* to cry out] — **Syn.** (noun) 3. uproar, racket, pandemonium, hubbub.

clam·or·ous (klam′ər·əs) *adj.* Making, or made with, a clamor; noisy. — **clam′or·ous·ly** *adv.* — **clam′or·ous·ness** *n.*

clamp¹ (klamp) *n.* Any of a number of devices for holding objects together, securing a piece in position, etc.; especially, an instrument having two opposite parts that can be brought together by a screw or spring action to compress or hold something. — *v.t.* To hold or bind with or as with a clamp. — **to clamp down** *U.S. Informal* To become more strict. [Cf. OE *clamm,* M.Du. *klampe*]

clamp² (klamp) *v.i.* To walk heavily; tramp. — *n.* A heavy tread; tramp. [Imit.]

clamp·er (klam′pər) *n.* An attachment having spikes, fastened to a shoe to prevent slipping on ice.

clam·shell (klam′shel′) *n.* 1. The shell of a clam. 2. A dredging bucket hinged like a clam's shell. [See CLAM¹]

clam·worm (klam′wûrm′) *n.* Nereis.

clan (klan) *n.* 1. A united group of relatives, or families, claiming a common ancestor and having one hereditary chieftain and the same surname, especially in the Scottish Highlands. 2. In certain primitive societies, a subgroup tracing descent through either the mother or the father. 3. A clique, or set of persons; a fraternity; club. 4. Loosely, a family. [< Scottish Gaelic *clann*]

clan·des·tine (klan·des′tin) *adj.* Kept secret for a purpose, usually for something evil or illicit; surreptitious; furtive; — **Syn.** See STEALTHY. [< F < L *clandestinus* < *clam* in secret] — **clan·des′tine·ly** *adv.* — **clan·des′tine·ness** *n.*

clang (klang) *v.t. & v.i.* To make or cause to make a loud, ringing, metallic sound; ring loudly. — *n.* 1. A ringing sound, as of metal struck. 2. The ringing call of cranes or geese. [Prob. imit. Cf. L *clangere.*]

clan·gor (klang′gor, klang′ər) *n.* Repeated clanging; clamor; din. — *v.i.* To ring noisily; clang. Also *Brit.* **clan′gour.** [< L < *clangere* to clang] — **clan′gor·ous** *adj.* — **clan′gor·ous·ly** *adv.*

clank (klangk) *n.* A short, harsh, metallic sound. — *v.t. & v.i.* To emit, or cause to emit, a clank. [Blend of CLANG and CLINK]

clan·nish (klan′ish) *adj.* 1. Of or characteristic of a clan. 2. Disposed to cling together, or bound by family prejudices, traditions, etc. — **clan′nish·ly** *adv.* — **clan′nish·ness** *n.*

clans·man (klanz′mən) *n. pl.* **·men** (-mən) A member of a clan. — **clans′wom·an** (-wŏŏm′ən) *n.fem.*

clap¹ (klap) *v.* **clapped, clap·ping** *v.t.* 1. To strike the hands together with a sharp, explosive sound in applauding. 2. To make such a sound, as two boards striking together. — *v.t.* 3. To bring (the hands) together sharply and with an explosive sound. 4. To strike with the open hand, as in greeting: to *clap* someone on the back. 5. To applaud (someone or something) by clapping the hands. 6. To put, place, or fling quickly or suddenly: They *clapped* him into jail. 7. To flap, as the wings. — *n.* 1. The act or sound of clapping the hands. 2. A sudden, loud, explosive sound, especially of thunder. 3. A sudden blow with the open hand. 4. *Dial.* A stroke, especially of misfortune. [OE *clæppan*]

clap² (klap) *n. Slang* Gonorrhea: usually preceded by *the.* [< OF *clapoir* a venereal sore]

clap·board (klab′ərd, klap′bôrd′, -bōrd′) *n.* 1. A narrow board having one edge thinner than the other, nailed overlapping as siding on frame buildings: sometimes called *weatherboard.* 2. *Brit.* A size of board used for wainscoting, etc. — *v.t.* To cover with clapboards. [Partial trans. of MDu. *klapholt* barrel stave]

clap·per (klap′ər) *n.* 1. The tongue of a bell. 2. Something that claps or clacks, as one of a pair of bones. 3. One who or that which claps. 4. *Slang* The tongue.

clapper boards In motion pictures, a pair of striped boards hinged at one end and struck together in front of the camera before a take to facilitate synchronization of the sound and picture prints. Also **clap·pers** (klap′ərz).

clap·per·claw (klap′ər·klô′) *v.t. & v.i. Archaic & Dial.* 1. To scratch and claw. 2. To scold or abuse.

clap·trap (klap′trap) *n.* Pretentious language; cheap, sensational artifice. [< CLAP¹, n. + TRAP¹, n.]

claque (klak) *n.* 1. A group of hired applauders in a theater. 2. Any set of persons who praise or applaud from interested motives. [< F < *claquer* to clap]

clar. *Music* Clarinet.

clar·a·bel·la (klar′ə·bel′ə) *n.* An 8-foot organ stop. Also **clar′i·bel′la.** [< L *clarus* clear + *bellus* pretty]

Clare (klâr) A county in Munster province, western Ireland; 1,231 sq. mi.; pop. 73,702 (1969); county seat, Ennis.

Clare of Assisi (klâr), Saint, 1194–1253, Italian nun; founder of the Order of Poor Clares.

clar·ence (klar′əns) *n.* A four-wheeled, four-seated, closed carriage. [after the Duke of *Clarence,* later William IV]

Clar·en·don (klar′ən·dən), Earl of See (Edward) HYDE.

clar·et (klar′ət) *n.* 1. Red Bordeaux wine; also, loosely, dry red wine. 2. Ruby to deep purplish red. [< OF (*vin*) *claret* clear (wine) < *cler* < L *clarus* bright]

claret cup An iced beverage consisting of claret, soda, lemon juice, brandy, sugar, etc.

clar·i·fy (klar′ə·fī) *v.t. & v.i.* **·fied, ·fy·ing** 1. To make or become clear and pure, or free from impurities. 2. To make or become clear and understandable; explain; elucidate. [< OF *clarifier* < LL *clarificare* < L *clarus* clear + *facere* to make] — **clar′i·fi·ca′tion** *n.* — **clar′i·fi′er** *n.*

clar·i·net (klar/ə·net/) *n.* **1.** A cylindrical woodwind instrument having a single-reed mouthpiece, finger holes, and keys. **2.** An organ stop having a

CLARINET

sound similar to that of a clarinet. Also *Rare* **clar·i·o·net** (klar/ē·ə·net/). [< F *clarinette,* prob. < It. *clarinetto,* dim. of *clarino* trumpet] — **clar/i·net/ist** or **clar/i·net/tist** *n.*

clar·i·on (klar/ē·ən) *n.* **1.** An obsolete kind of trumpet having a shrill tone. **2.** The sound of a clarion, or any sound resembling it. — *v.t. & v.i.* To proclaim as with a clarion. — *adj.* Clear and resounding. [< OF *claron, clairon* < L *clarus* clear]

clar·i·ty (klar/ə·tē) *n.* Clearness; lucidity.

Clark (klärk), **Abraham,** 1726–94, American patriot; signer of the Declaration of Independence. — **Champ,** 1850–1921, U.S. politician: full name **James Beauchamp Clark.** — **George Rogers,** 1752–1818, American Revolutionary soldier and pioneer. — **Mark Wayne,** born 1896, U.S. general. — **Thomas Campbell,** born 1899, U.S. jurist; associate justice of the Supreme Court. — **William,** 1770–1838, brother of George Rogers; with Meriwether Lewis, led expedition to Columbia River, 1804–06.

Clarks·burg (klärks/bûrg) A city in northern West Virginia; pop. 24,864.

cla·ro (klar/ō, klä/-) *adj.* Light in color and, usually, mild: said of cigars. — *n. pl.* **·os** A claro cigar. [< Sp.]

clar·y (klâr/ē) *n. pl.* **clar·ies** Any of several species of sage, especially *Salvia sclarea* of Italy, Syria, etc.: also **clary sage.** [< Med.L *sclarea*]

clash (klash) *v.t.* **1.** To strike or dash together or against with a harsh, metallic sound. — *v.i.* **2.** To collide with loud and confused noise. **3.** To conflict; be in opposition. — *n.* **1.** A resounding, metallic noise, as of violent contact. **2.** A conflict or opposition, as of temperaments or colors. [Imit. Cf. CLAP[1], DASH.]
— **Syn.** (noun) **2.** discord, quarrel, strife, incompatibility.

clasp (klasp, kläsp) *n.* **1.** A fastening, as a hook, by which things or parts are held together. **2.** A firm grasp or embrace. **3.** A small bar affixed to the ribbon of a military decoration and indicating the specific campaign or operation in which the wearer has taken part. — *v.t.* **1.** To take hold of with an encircling grasp; embrace. **2.** To fasten with or as with a clasp. **3.** To grasp firmly in or with the hand. — **Syn.** See GRASP. [ME *claspe*; origin unknown] — **clasp/er** *n.*

clasp knife A knife with a blade that folds into the handle.

class (klas, kläs) *n.* **1.** A body of persons considered to have certain social, economic, occupational, or other characteristics in common: the educated *class*; the working *class.* **2.** The division of society by relative standing; social rank; caste. **3.** A category of objects, persons, etc., based on quality or rank: of the first *class.* **4.** A number of objects, facts, or events grouped together as having common properties; a set; category; kind. **5.** A group of students under one teacher, or pursuing a study together; also, a meeting of such a group: a history *class.* **6.** *U.S.* A group of students in a school or college having the same standing and graduating together. **7.** *Biol.* A group of plants or animals standing below a phylum and above an order. **8.** *Mil.* A group of men born in the same year, who are conscripted or liable to be conscripted together: the *class* of 1934. **9.** *Slang* Superiority; elegance. Abbr. *cl.* — **the classes** The wealthier, more educated, or higher social classes. — *v.t.* **1.** To arrange or group according to characteristics or properties; assign to a class; classify. — *v.i.* **2.** *Rare* To be placed or ranked, as in a class. [< MF *classe* < L *classis* group, class]
— **Syn.** (noun) **3.** *Class, caste, estate,* and *rank* refer to groupings in a society. *Classes* are based on such things as lineage, income, and occupation, while *caste* is hereditary. A person is able to move from one *class* to another, but cannot escape from his *caste.* An *estate* was originally one of the three *classes* of feudal society, but is now chiefly applied to a *class* having special powers or limitations with respect to government. A *rank* is one of the grades in a fixed scale of authority, power, or honor: to hold the *rank* of colonel in an army. Compare CLIQUE, COMPANY.

class. **1.** Classic; classical. **2.** Classification. **3.** Classified; classify.

class consciousness Awareness of the nature, interest, and unity of one's social group. — **class/-con/scious** *adj.*

class day *U.S.* A day set apart shortly before a school or college commencement for exercises and ceremonies conducted by the graduating class.

clas·sic (klas/ik) *adj.* **1.** Belonging to the first class or highest rank, especially in art or literature; approved as a model; also, of lasting significance or value. **2.** Adhering to standard and authoritative principles and forms in art, literature, music, etc. **3.** Of or characteristic of ancient Greece and Rome, their literature or art. **4.** In the style of ancient Greek and Roman authors and artists; balanced; formal; austere. Abbr. *class.* **5.** Having literary or historical tradi-

tions: *classic* lands. — *n.* **1.** An author, artist, or work generally recognized as a standard of excellence. **2.** *Informal* Any well-known event thought of as being typical or traditional. **3.** *Rare* A classicist. — **the classics** Ancient Greek and Roman literature. [< L *classicus* of the first rank < *classis* order, class]

clas·si·cal (klas/i·kəl) *adj.* **1.** Adhering to the esthetic principles manifested in the art and literature of ancient Greece and Rome during their period of highest culture; classic. **2.** Generally accepted as being standard and authoritative; not new or experimental: *classical* economic theory. **3.** Of ancient Greece and Rome: *classical* civilization. **4.** Versed in the Greek and Roman classics: a *classical* scholar. **5.** Consisting of or pertaining to studies based on Greek and Roman language, literature, and thought: a *classical* curriculum. **6.** *Music* **a** Following strict and established form, as a fugue or sonata. **b** Loosely, of a serious or semiserious nature, as distinguished from jazz or popular music. **7.** *Physics* Describing those physical theories based upon or derived from Newtonian mechanics, especially as distinguished from relativity theory and quantum mechanics. Abbr. *class.* — **clas/si·cal·ly** *adv.*

clas·si·cal·ism (klas/i·kəl·iz/əm) *n.* Classicism (which see). — **clas/si·cal·ist** *n.*

clas·si·cal·i·ty (klas/ə·kal/ə·tē) *n. pl.* **·ties** **1.** The quality of being classical. Also **clas/si·cal·ness.** **2.** Anything with classical qualities or characteristics. **3.** Classicism.

clas·si·cism (klas/ə·siz/əm) *n.* **1.** A group of esthetic principles (simplicity, restraint, balance, dignity, etc.) as manifested in ancient Greek and Roman art and literature: distinguished from *romanticism.* **2.** Adherence to these principles. **3.** The style of ancient Greek and Roman literature, oratory, architecture, sculpture, etc. **4.** Knowledge of ancient Greek and Roman culture; classical scholarship. **5.** A Greek or Latin idiom or form.

clas·si·cist (klas/ə·sist) *n.* **1.** One versed in the classics. **2.** An adherent or imitator of classic style. **3.** One who actively supports the study of the classics.

clas·si·cize (klas/ə·sīz) *v.* **·cized, ·ciz·ing** *v.t.* **1.** To make classic. — *v.i.* **2.** To affect the classic style.

clas·si·fi·ca·tion (klas/ə·fə·kā/shən) *n.* **1.** The act, process, or result of classifying. **2.** *Biol.* Taxonomy or systematics. Abbr. *cl., class.*

clas·si·fi·ca·to·ry (klas/ə·fə·kā/tər·ē, klə·sif/ə·kə·tôr/ē, -tō/rē) *adj.* Of or pertaining to classification; taxonomic.

classified advertisement An advertisement printed in condensed form under any of various subject headings, as in a newspaper. Also **classified ad.**

clas·si·fy (klas/ə·fī) *v.t.* **·fied, ·fy·ing** **1.** To arrange or put in a class or classes on the basis of resemblances or differences. **2.** To declare or designate as of aid to an enemy and restrict as to circulation or use, as a document, weapon, or item of information. Abbr. *class.* [< L *classis* class + -FY] — **clas/si·fi/a·ble** *adj.* — **clas/si·fi/er** *n.*
— **Syn.** **1.** group, order, categorize, sort, assort.

clas·sis (klas/is) *n. pl.* **clas·ses** (klas/ēz) **1.** In some Reformed churches, a local governing body consisting of ministers and elders. **2.** The district administered by a classis. [< L]

class·mate (klas/māt, kläs/-) *n.* A member of the same class in school or college.

class·room (klas/rōōm/, -rŏŏm/, kläs/-) *n.* A room in a school or college in which classes are held.

class struggle **1.** The conflict between classes in society. **2.** In Marxist theory, the economic and political struggle for power between the dominant class and the rising class.

class·y (klas/ē) *adj.* **class·i·er, class·i·est** *Slang* Stylish; elegant.

clas·tic (klas/tik) *adj.* **1.** *Biol.* Breaking, separating, or dividing into parts: a *clastic* cell. **2.** That may be taken apart for inspection and then reassembled: a *clastic* anatomical model. **3.** *Geol.* Composed of fragments of preexisting rocks; fragmental. [< Gk. *klastos* broken]

clath·rate (klath/rāt) *adj.* **1.** *Chem.* Of or pertaining to a stable, crystalline mixture in which the molecules of one component are held within the organic crystal lattice of the other. **2.** *Biol.* Having a latticelike appearance. [< L *clathratus,* pp. of *clathrare* to furnish with a lattice]

clat·ter (klat/ər) *v.i.* **1.** To make a rattling noise; give out short, sharp noises rapidly or repeatedly. **2.** To move with a rattling noise. **3.** To talk noisily; chatter. — *v.t.* **4.** To cause to clatter. — *n.* **1.** A rattling or clattering sound. **2.** A disturbance or commotion. **3.** Noisy talk; chatter. [OE *clatrunge* a clattering noise] — **clat/ter·er** *n.*

Clau·del (klō·del/), **Paul,** 1868–1955, French diplomat, poet, and dramatist.

Clau·di·an (klô/dē·ən) *adj.* Of or pertaining to the Roman emperors of the Claudius family (Tiberius, Caligula, Claudius, and Nero, A.D. 14–68).

Clau·di·an (klô/dē·ən), died 408?, Latin epic poet. Also *Latin* **Clau·di·us, Clau·di·a·nus** (klô/dē·əs, klô/dē·ā/nəs).

clau·di·cant (klô′di·kənt) *adj. Obs.* Limping; lame. [< L *claudicans, -antis,* ppr. of *claudicare* to limp < *claudus* lame]

clau·di·ca·tion (klô′di·kā′shən) *n.* A limp.

Clau·di·us (klô′dē·əs) In Shakespeare's *Hamlet,* king of Denmark, Hamlet's stepfather and uncle.

Claudius I, 10 B.C.–A.D. 54, Tiberius Claudius Drusus, Roman emperor 41–54.

Claudius II, 214–270, Marcus Aurelius Claudius, Roman emperor 268–270: called *Gothicus.*

claught (klôkht) *v.t. & n. Scot.* Clutch; grasp.

clause (klôz) *n.* **1.** A distinct part of a composition, as an article in a statute, will, treaty, etc. **2.** *Gram.* A group of words containing a subject and a predicate: distinguished from *phrase.* Abbr. *cl.* — **dependent clause** A clause that functions as a subject or complement (noun clause) or as a modifier (adjective or adverb clause) within a sentence: also called *subordinate clause.* — **independent clause** A clause that can stand alone as a simple sentence, or combine with other clauses to form compound or complex sentences: also called *main clause, principal clause.* [< OF < Med.L *clausa* < L *clausus,* pp. of *claudere* to close] — **claus′al** *adj.*

Clau·se·witz (klou′zə·vits), **Karl von,** 1780–1831, Prussian general and military scientist.

claus·tral (klôs′trəl) *adj.* Cloistral (which see).

claus·tro·pho·bi·a (klôs′trə·fō′bē·ə) *n. Psychiatry* Morbid fear of enclosed or confined places. [< L *claustrum* a closed place + -PHOBIA] — **claus′tro·pho′bic** *adj.*

cla·vate (klā′vāt) *adj.* Club-shaped. [< L *clavatus,* pp. of *clavare* to stud with nails; infl. in meaning by L *clava* club] — **cla′vate·ly** *adv.*

clave (klāv) Archaic past tense of CLEAVE[1] and CLEAVE[2].

cla·ver (klā′vər, klav′ər) *v.i. Scot.* To gossip; chatter. — *n.* Gossip; chatter.

clav·i·chord (klav′ə·kôrd) *n.* A keyboard musical instrument whose tones are produced by the impact of brass pins on horizontal strings, a forerunner of the piano. [< Med.L *clavichordium* < L *clavis* key + *chorda* string]

clav·i·cle (klav′ə·kəl) *n. Anat.* The bone connecting the shoulder blade and breastbone and forming part of the pectoral arch: also called *collarbone.* For illustration see THORAX. [< L *clavicula,* dim of *clavis* key] — **cla·vic·u·lar** (klə·vik′yə·lər) *adj.*

clav·i·corn (klav′ə·kôrn) *adj. Entomol.* Of, pertaining to, or belonging to a superfamily of beetles (*Staphylinoidea,* formerly *Clavicornia*) having club-shaped antennae. Also **clav·i·cor·nate** (klav′ə·kôr′nāt) [< NL *Clavicornia* < L *clava* club + *cornu* horn]

clav·i·er (klə·vir′; for defs. 1 and 3, also klav′ē·ər) *n.* **1.** A keyboard. **2.** Any keyboard stringed instrument, as a harpsichord, piano, etc. **3.** A dummy keyboard for silent practicing. [< F, keyboard < L *clavis key*]

clav·i·form (klav′ə·fôrm) *adj.* Club-shaped; clavate. [< L *clava* club + -FORM]

claw (klô) *n.* **1.** A sharp, usually curved, horny nail on the toe of a bird, mammal, or reptile. **2.** A chela or pincer of certain insects and crustaceans; also, a limb terminating in a chela. **3.** Anything sharp and hooked, as the cleft part of a hammerhead. — *v.t. & v.i.* To tear, scratch, dig, pull, etc., with or as with claws. [OE *clawu*]

claw hammer **1.** A hammer with one end of its head forked and curved like a claw for drawing nails. For illustration see HAMMER. **2.** *Informal* A swallow-tailed coat.

claw hatchet A hatchet having the head forked at one end. For illustration see HATCHET.

clax·on (klak′sən) See KLAXON.

clay (klā) *n.* **1.** A fine-grained, variously colored earth, plastic when wet, consisting of hydrated aluminum silicates mixed with other minerals and widely used in the making of bricks, tiles, pottery, etc. **2.** Earth in general; mud. **3.** Earth as a symbol of the human body; also, the body itself. — *v.t.* To cover, mix, or treat with clay. [OE *clæg*]

Clay (klā), **Henry,** 1777–1852, U.S. statesman and orator. — **Lucius Du Bignon,** born 1897, U.S. general and military administrator.

clay·bank (klā′bangk′) *n.* A yellowish brown color.

clay·ey (klā′ē) *adj.* **clay·i·er, clay·i·est** Of, like, abounding in, mixed or covered with clay.

clay·ish (klā′ish) *adj.* Like or containing clay.

clay·more (klā′môr, -mōr) *n.* **1.** A double-edged broadsword formerly used by the Scottish Highlanders. **2.** Loosely, the basket-hilted broadsword of the Highlanders. [< Scottish Gaelic *claidheamh* sword + *mor* great]

clay pigeon In trapshooting, a saucer-shaped disk, as of baked clay, projected from a trap as a flying target.

clay stone **1.** A rounded mass of rock found in alluvial clay as part of a concretion. **2.** A dull-colored igneous rock containing feldspar and clay in a compact mass.

Clay·ton (klā′tən), **John Middleton,** 1796–1856, U.S. lawyer and statesman.

clay·to·ni·a (klā·tō′nē·ə) *n.* One of a genus (*Claytonia*) of perennial wild flowers of the purslane family: also called *spring beauty.* [< NL, after John *Clayton,* 1693–1773, botanist, of Virginia]

-cle *suffix of nouns* Small; minute: *particle, corpuscle.* [< F < L *-culus,* dim. suffix]

clean (klēn) *adj.* **1.** Free from dirt or stain; unsoiled. **2.** Free from foreign or undesirable matter; unadulterated. **3.** Morally pure; wholesome; unsullied: a *clean* life. **4.** Free from imperfections, as a gem; perfect. **5.** Without obstructions, encumbrances, or restrictions: a *clean* title to land. **6.** Completely without something; having none of: *clean* of guilt. **7.** Thorough; complete: a *clean* getaway. **8.** Clever; dexterous: a *clean* jump. **9.** Well-proportioned; trim; shapely. **10.** In sports, without infractions; fair. **11.** Conforming to a ceremonial or religious law; ceremonially pure. **12.** Neat in habits. **13.** Having few alterations; legible: said of copy intended for the printer. **14.** Producing an explosion relatively free of radioactive fallout: said of an atomic or thermonuclear bomb. — *v.t.* **1.** To render free of dirt or other impurities. **2.** To prepare (fowl, game, etc.) for cooking. — *v.i.* **3.** To undergo or perform the act of cleaning. — **to clean out** **1.** To clear of trash or rubbish. **2.** *Informal* To force out; drive away. **3.** To empty (a place) of contents or occupants. **4.** *Informal* To leave without money: The depression *cleaned* him *out.* — **to clean up** **1.** To clean completely and thoroughly. **2.** *Slang* To make a large profit. **3.** *Informal* To finish: to *clean up* one's work. — *adv.* **1.** In a clean manner; cleanly. **2.** Wholly; completely. [OE *clǣne* clear, pure] — **clean′a·ble** *adj.* — **clean′ness** *n.*

clean and jerk In weightlifting, the lifting of the weight to shoulder height, holding it there a moment, and then raising it straight over the head.

clean-cut (klēn′kut′) *adj.* **1.** Cut with smooth edge or surface; well-made. **2.** Sharply defined; clear. **3.** Pleasing in appearance; wholesome; neat: a *clean-cut* young man.

clean·er (klē′nər) *n.* **1.** A person whose work is cleaning, especially clothing. **2.** Any substance or mechanical device that removes dirt.

clean-hand·ed (klēn′han′did) *adj.* Innocent; guiltless.

clean-limbed (klēn′limd′) *adj.* Having well-formed limbs.

clean·li·ness (klen′lē·nis, -li-) *n.* The state of being clean.

clean·ly (*adj.* klen′lē; *adv.* klēn′lē) *adj.* **1.** Habitually and carefully clean; neat; tidy. **2.** *Obs.* Cleansing. — *adv.* In a clean manner. — **clean·li·ly** (klen′lə·lē) *adv.*

cleanse (klenz) *v.t.* **cleansed, cleans·ing** To free from dirt or defilement; clean; purge. [OE *clǣnsian* < *clǣne* clean] — **Syn.** wash, scour, scrub, sweep, dust. — **Ant.** soil, stain, besmear; sully, besmirch, pollute.

cleans·er (klenz′ər) *n.* One who or that which cleanses; especially, a soap, detergent, etc., used for cleansing.

clean-shav·en (klēn′shā′vən) *adj.* Having the beard or hair shaved off.

Cle·an·thes (klē·an′thēz) Third-century B.C. Greek Stoic philosopher.

clean·up (klēn′up′) *n.* **1.** A complete cleaning; especially, eradication of gambling, corruption, etc. **2.** *Slang* A large profit; gain.

clear (klir) *adj.* **1.** Free from anything that dims or darkens; bright; unclouded. **2.** Without impurity or blemish. **3.** Of great transparency; pellucid: a *clear* stream. **4.** Free from obstructions or hindrances; open: a *clear* road. **5.** Plain to the mind; thoroughly understandable. **6.** Plain to the eye, ear, etc.; distinct. **7.** Able to discern; quick and orderly; keen: a *clear* mind. **8.** Free from uncertainty; convinced; sure: Are you *clear* on that point? **9.** Free from guilt; not to blame. **10.** Undisturbed; serene. **11.** Without qualifications or limits; complete. **12.** Without roughness, protrusions, etc.: *clear* lumber. **13.** Not in contact: usually with *of:* to stand *clear* of a fire. **14.** Freed or emptied of contents or cargo. **15.** Without deductions; net: a *clear* $5,000. **16.** Without debt or obligation. — *adv.* In a clear manner; wholly or plainly; clearly. — *v.t.* **1.** To make clear; brighten. **2.** To free from foreign matter, impurities, blemishes, or muddiness. **3.** To rid of obstruction: to *clear* a harbor. **4.** To remove, as obstacles, in making something clear. **5.** To disentangle: to *clear* a rope. **6.** To free from imputations or accusations of guilt; acquit. **7.** To free from doubt or ambiguity; make plain. **8.** To pass or get by or over without touching: to *clear* a fence. **9.** To free from debt by payment. **10.** To settle (a debt). **11.** To obtain or give clearance for. **12.** To gain over and above expenses. **13.** To pass (a check, etc.) through a clearing-house. — *v.i.* **14.** To become free from fog, cloud, or obscurity; grow bright; become fair. **15.** To pass away, as mist or clouds. **16.** To settle accounts by exchange of bills and checks, as in a clearing-house. **17.** To obtain clearance. — **to clear away** (or **off**) **1.** To remove out of the way. **2.** To disperse; disappear. — **to clear out** **1.** *Informal* To go away. **2.** To empty of contents. — **to clear the air** To dispel emotional tensions; settle differences. — **to clear up** **1.** To make clear. **2.** To grow fair, as the weather. **3.** To free from confusion or mystery. **4.** To put in order; tidy. — *n.* **1.** An unobstructed space. **2.** Inside measurements; clearance. — **in the clear** **1.** Free from limitations or obstructions. **2.** *Informal* Free from guilt or involvement; not under suspicion. [< OF *cler* < L *clarus* clear, bright] — **clear′a·ble** *adj.* — **clear′ly** *adv.*

— **Syn.** (adj.) **1, 3.** *Clear, lucid, pellucid, transparent, translucent,* and *limpid* refer to ease of vision. A thing is *clear* when it presents no obstructions to the sight; it is *lucid* or *pellucid* when brightly illuminated: *clear* moonlight, *lucid* stars, a *pellucid* lake. We see objects clearly through something *transparent*; that which is *translucent* allows the passage of light, but may obscure form and color. *Limpid* refers to the transparency of a colorless liquid. **5, 6.** *Clear, plain, distinct,* and *intelligible* mean easy to understand. A *clear* thing or matter is open to view, while something that is *plain* is free of complexities that tend to conceal or deceive. That which is *distinct* has a well-defined outline; that which is *intelligible* can be understood by interpreting what is perceived. Compare APPARENT, VIVID. — **Ant.** cloudy, dim, indistinct, mysterious, muddled, obscure, opaque, turbid, vague.

clear·ance (klir'əns) *n.* **1.** The act or instance of clearing. **2.** A space cleared. **3.** The space by which a moving object clears something. **4.** Permission for a ship, airplane, truck, etc., to proceed, as after a check of its equipment or load. **5.** A certificate granting a ship permission to sail. Also **clearance papers.** **6.** Permission for an article to be entered into a country, region, or place. **7.** Approval of a person as trustworthy, loyal, safe, etc., usually accompanied by the granting of specified privileges: *clearance* for secret information. **8.** Disposal of merchandise, as in a sale. **9.** The passage of checks, bank drafts, etc. through a clearinghouse. Abbr. (defs. 3, 9) *cl.*

Cle·ar·chus (klē·är'kəs), died 401 B.C., Spartan general; executed by the Persians.

clear-cut (klir'kut') *adj.* **1.** Distinctly and sharply outlined. **2.** Plain; evident; obvious.

clear-eyed (klir'īd') *adj.* **1.** Having bright, clear eyes; keen-sighted. **2.** Mentally acute; perceptive.

Clear Grit *Canadian* A member of a radical reformist party originating in the 1850's.

clear-head·ed (klir'hed'id) *adj.* Not mentally confused; clear in thought; sensible. — **clear'-head'ed·ly** *adv.* — **clear'-head'ed·ness** *n.*

clear·ing (klir'ing) *n.* **1.** A making or becoming clear. **2.** That which is clear or cleared, as a tract of land. **3.** The exchange between banks of checks and drafts and the adjustment of differences arising from it. **4.** *pl.* The total of checks, drafts, etc., presented daily at a clearing-house.

clear·ing-house (klir'ing·hous') *n.* An office where bankers exchange drafts and checks and adjust balances. Abbr. *c.h., C.H.* Also **clear'ing·house'.**

clear·ness (klir'nis) *n.* The state or quality of being clear.

clear-sight·ed (klir'sī'tid) *adj.* **1.** Having accurate perception and good judgment; discerning. **2.** Having keen vision. — **clear'-sight'ed·ly** *adv.* — **clear'-sight'ed·ness** *n.*

clear·starch (klir'stärch') *v.t.* To stiffen with clear or pure starch.

clear·sto·ry (klir'stôr'ē, -stō'rē) See CLERESTORY.

Clear·wa·ter (klir'wô'tər, -wot'ər) A city in western Florida, on the Gulf of Mexico; pop. 52,074.

clear·wing (klir'wing') *n.* Any of various moths (family *Aegeriidae*) having nearly transparent wings.

cleat (klēt) *n.* **1.** A strip of wood or iron fastened across a surface to strengthen or support. **2.** A piece of metal or wood with arms on which to wind or secure a rope. **3.** *Naut.* A wedgelike piece of wood fastened to a spar to keep rigging from slipping. **4.** A piece of rubber or metal fastened to the underside of a shoe to prevent slipping or retard wear. **5.** A spurlike attachment used to grip a pole or tree in climbing. — *v.t.* **1.** To furnish or strengthen with a cleat or cleats. **2.** *Naut.* To fasten (rope, etc.) to or with a cleat. [ME *clete.* Akin to CLOT.]

CLEATS
(def. 2)
a Pole.
b Surface.
c Deck.

cleav·age (klē'vij) *n.* **1.** A cleaving or being cleft. **2.** A split or cleft. **3.** *Mineral.* A tendency in certain rocks or crystals to split in certain directions. **4.** *Biol.* The process of division of a fertilized ovum by which the original single cell becomes a mass of smaller cells. **5.** *Informal* The space between a woman's breasts, especially when visible at a low neckline.

cleave¹ (klēv) *v.* **cleft** or **cleaved** or **clove** (*Archaic* **clave**), **cleft** or **cleaved** or **clo·ven** (*Archaic* **clove**), **cleav·ing** *v.t.* **1.** To split or sunder, as with an ax or wedge. **2.** To make or achieve by cutting: to *cleave* a path. **3.** To pass through; penetrate: to *cleave* the air. — *v.i.* **4.** To part or divide along natural lines of separation. **5.** To make one's way; pass: with *through.* [OE *clēofan*] — **cleav'a·ble** *adj.*

cleave² (klēv) *v.i.* **cleaved** (*Archaic* **clave, clove**), **cleaved, cleav·ing 1.** To stick fast; adhere: with *to.* **2.** To be faithful: with *to.* [Fusion of OE *clifan* and *clīfian*]

cleav·er (klē'vər) *n.* **1.** One who or that which cleaves. **2.** A butcher's heavy, axlike knife. [< CLEAVE¹]

cleav·ers (klē'vərz) *n.pl.* (*Usually construed as sing.*) A species of bedstraw (*Galium avarine*), having hooked prickles on stem and fruit: also called *clivers.* [< CLEAVE²]

cle·don·ism (klē'də·niz'əm) *n.* Avoidance of words considered unlucky. [< Gk. *klēdōn* omen]

cleek (klēk) *v.t. & v.i. Scot.* **1.** To clutch; hook. **2.** To marry. — *n.* **1.** A hook. **2.** A golf club with a wooden head.

clef (klef) *n. Music* A symbol placed on the staff to show the pitch of the notes on the various lines and spaces. A **G clef** locates G above middle C, a **C clef** middle C, and an **F clef** F below middle C. The **treble clef** places G on the second, the **bass clef** places F on the fourth line, the **alto clef** places C on the third line, and the **tenor clef** places C on the fourth line. [< MF < L *clavis* key]

CLEFS
1. G clef. 2. F clef. 3. C clef. 4. Treble clef. 5. Bass clef. 6. Alto clef. 7. Tenor clef. (Note heads show middle C.)

cleft (kleft) Past tense and past participle of CLEAVE¹. — *adj.* **1.** Divided partially or completely. **2.** *Bot.* Having deep, narrow divisions, as leaves. — *n.* **1.** A fissure; crevice; rift. **2.** An indentation or division between two parts, as of the chin, a hoof, etc. [ME *clift.* Related to CLEAVE¹.]

cleft palate A congenital longitudinal fissure in the roof of the mouth.

Cleis·the·nes (klīs'thə·nēz) Sixth-century B.C. Athenian statesman. Also *Clisthenes.*

cleisto- *combining form* Closed: *cleistogamy.* Also, before vowels, **cleist-.** [< Gk. *kleistos* closed < *kleiein* to close]

cleis·tog·a·my (klīs·tog'ə·mē) *n. Bot.* The condition of having small, closed, self-fertilizing flowers, usually in addition to the regular flowers, as in the pansy and some violets: also spelled *clistogamy.* [< CLEISTO- + -GAMY] — **cleis·to·gam·ic** (klīs'tə·gam'ik), **cleis·tog'a·mous** *adj.*

clem·a·tis (klem'ə·tis) *n.* **1.** Any plant of a genus (*Clematis*) of perennial shrubs or vines of the crowfoot family. **2.** Any vine of a related genus (*Atragene*). [< Gk. *klēmatis*, dim. of *klēma* vine]

Cle·men·ceau (klem'ən·sō', *Fr.* kle·män·sō'), **Georges Eugène**, 1841–1929, French statesman; premier 1906–09, 1917–1920: called *the Tiger.*

clem·en·cy (klem'ən·sē) *n. pl.* **·cies 1.** Mildness of temper, especially toward offenders; leniency; mercy. **2.** An act of mercy or leniency. **3.** Mildness of weather, etc. — **Syn.** See MERCY. — **Ant.** harshness, severity. [< L *clementia* < *clemens* mild]

Clem·ens (klem'ənz), **Samuel Langhorne** See MARK TWAIN.

clem·ent (klem'ənt) *adj.* **1.** Lenient or merciful in temperament; compassionate. **2.** Mild: said of weather. [< L *clemens, -entis* mild, merciful] — **clem'ent·ly** *adv.*

Clem·ent I (klem'ənt) First-century bishop of Rome; pope 88–97: called *Clement of Rome, Saint Clement.*

Clement V, 1264–1314, pope 1305–14: original name *Bertrand de Got* (də gō') or *d'A·goust* (dá·gōost').

Clement VII, 1478–1534, pope 1523–34: original name *Giulio de' Medici.*

Clement XIV, 1705–74, pope 1769–74: original name *Giovanni Gang·a·nel·li* (gäng·gä·nel'lē).

Clement of Alexandria, died 215?, Greek Christian theologian: original name *Titus Flavius Clem·ens* (klem'ənz).

clench (klench) *v.t.* **1.** To grasp or grip firmly. **2.** To close tightly or lock, as the fist or teeth. **3.** To clinch, as a nail. **4.** *Naut.* To fasten by making a clinch. — *n.* **1.** A tight grip. **2.** Anything that clenches or grips, as a mechanical device. [OE *-clenc(e)an* in *beclencan* to hold fast]

cle·o·me (klē·ō'mē) *n.* Any of a genus (*Cleome*) of plants of the caper family, with showy, variously colored flowers: also called *spiderflower.* [< NL < LL, a plant]

Cle·om·e·nes III (klē·om'ə·nēz), died 219? B.C., Spartan king.

Cle·on (klē'on) Fifth-century B.C. Athenian demagogue.

Cle·o·pa·tra (klē'ə·pat'rə, -pā'trə, -pä'trə), 69–30 B.C., queen of Egypt 51–49 B.C., 48–30 B.C.; mistress of Julius Caesar and Mark Antony; committed suicide after Antony's defeat by Octavian at Actium.

Cleopatra's Needle Popularly, either of two Egyptian obelisks, one in New York City, the other in London.

clepe (klēp) *v.t.* **cleped** or **clept, clep·ing** *Archaic* To name; call: in the past participle also spelled *ycleped, yclept.* [OE *clipian, cleopian*]

clep·sy·dra (klep'sə·drə) *n. pl.* **·dras** or **·drae** (-drē) An ancient instrument for measuring time by the regulated flow of water: also called *water clock.* [< L < Gk. *klepsydra* < *kleptein* to steal + *hydōr* water]

clep·to·ma·ni·a (klep'tə·mā'nē·ə) See KLEPTOMANIA.

clere·sto·ry (klir'stôr'ē, -stō'rē) *n. pl.* **·ries 1.** *Archit.* The highest story of the nave and choir of a church, with windows opening above the aisle roofs, etc. **2.** A similar part in other structures, for light and ventilation. Also spelled *clearstory*: also **clere'sto'rey.** [< earlier *clere* clear + STORY]

cler·gy (klûr′jē) *n. pl.* **·gies 1.** The whole body of men set apart by ordination for the service of God: distinguished from *laity.* **2.** *Brit.* The ministers of the Church of England. [< OF *clergie* < *clerc* clerk, cleric < LL *clericus.* See CLERK.]

cler·gy·man (klûr′jē·mən) *n. pl.* **·men** (-mən) One of the clergy; an ordained minister. Abbr. *cl.*

cler·ic (kler′ik) *adj.* Clerical. — *n.* A member of the clergy. [< LL *clericus.* See CLERK.]

cler·i·cal (kler′i·kəl) *adj.* **1.** Of or related to clerks or office workers or their work: a *clerical* error. **2.** Belonging to or characteristic of the clergy. **3.** Advocating great political influence for the clergy: a derogatory term. — *n.* **1.** A clergyman. **2.** *pl.* The distinctive dress of a clergyman. **3.** A member of a clerical party. — **cler′i·cal·ly** *adv.*

clerical collar A stiff, white collar that stands up around the neck, is fastened at the back, and is worn without a tie by clergymen: also called *roman collar.*

cler·i·cal·ism (kler′i·kəl·iz′əm) *n.* **1.** Principles or policies relating to clergymen. **2.** Excessive clerical influence in politics or secular affairs; also, advocacy of such influence. — **cler′i·cal·ist** *n.*

cler·id (kler′id) *n. Entomol.* Any of a family (*Cleridae*) of small, slender, soft-bodied, variously colored coleopterous insects. [< NL *Cleridae* < Gk. *klēros,* a type of beetle]

cler·i·hew (kler′ə·hyōō) *n.* A satiric or comic poem usually in two couplets. [after Edmund *Clerihew* Bentley, 1875–1956, English writer, the originator]

cler·i·sy (kler′ə·sē) *n.* The well-educated class; the literati. [< Med.L *clericia*]

clerk (klûrk, *Brit.* klärk) *n.* **1.** A worker in an office or commercial establishment who keeps records or accounts, attends to correspondence, etc. **2.** An official or employee of a court, legislative body, or the like, charged with the care of records, etc. **3.** *U.S.* A salesperson in a store. **4.** A hotel employee who assigns guests to their rooms. **5.** In the Church of England, a lay minister who assists the parish clergyman in his duties: also called *parish clerk.* **6.** *Archaic* A clergyman. **7.** *Archaic* Any person able to read or write; also, a scholar. Abbr. *cl., clk.* — *v.i.* To work or act as clerk. [OE *clerc* < LL *clericus* < Gk. *klēros* lot, portion] — **clerk′ly** (klûrk′lē, *Brit.* klärk′-) *adj.* **clerk·li·er, clerk·li·est 1.** Of a clerk: *clerkly* duties. **2.** *Archaic* Scholarly; learned. — *adv.* In the manner of a clerk. — **clerk′li·ness** *n.*

Cler·mont-Fer·rand (kler·môn′fe·rän′) A city in central France; pop. 145,856 (1968).

cleve·ite (klev′īt) *n.* A radioactive variety of uraninite. [after Per *Cleve.* 1840–1905, Swedish chemist]

Cleve·land (klēv′lənd) **1.** A city in NE Ohio, on Lake Erie; pop. 750,903. **2.** A county in NE England; 225 sq. mi.; pop. 565,600 (1976); county seat, Middlesbrough.

Cleve·land (klēv′lənd), **(Stephen)** Grover, 1837–1908, 22nd and 24th president of the United States 1885–89, 1893–97.

Cleveland Heights A city in NE Ohio, near Cleveland; residential suburb; pop. 60,767.

clev·er (klev′ər) *adj.* **1.** Mentally keen; intelligent; quick-witted. **2.** Physically adroit, especially with the hands; dexterous. **3.** Ingeniously made, said, done, etc.: a *clever* remark. **4.** *U.S. Dial.* Good-natured; friendly. **5.** *Dial.* Handsome; well-made. **6.** *Obs.* Handy; convenient. [Cf. ME *cliver* adroit] — **clev′er·ly** *adv.* — **clev′er·ness** *n.*

clev·is (klev′is) *n.* A U-shaped metal fastening pierced for a bolt, used to attach chains, cables, etc. [Akin to CLEAVE[1]]

clew (klōō) *n.* **1.** In legends, a ball of thread that guides through a maze. **2.** Something that serves as a guide in solving a problem or mystery: in this sense now usually spelled *clue.* **3.** *Naut.* A lower corner of a square sail or the lower aft corner of a fore-and-aft sail; also, a loop at the corner. For illustration see SAIL. **4.** *pl.* The cords by which the two ends of a hammock are slung. **5.** A ball of yarn, thread, or the like. — *v.t.* **1.** To coil into a ball. **2.** To guide or track by or as by a clew. **3.** *Naut.* To raise the clews of (a square sail) for furling: with *up.* [OE *cliwen*]

clew line *Naut.* A rope by which the clew of a sail is run up to the yards.

cli·ché (klē·shā′) *n.* **1.** A trite or hackneyed expression, action, etc. **2.** Formerly, an electrotype or stereotype plate. [< F, pp. of *clicher* to stereotype] — **Syn. 1.** platitude, commonplace, bromide.

Cli·chy (klē·shē′) A city in north central France; a suburb of Paris; pop. 52,398 (1968). Also **Cli·chy′-la-Ga·renne′** (-là·gà·ren′), **Cli·chy′-sous-Bois′** (-sōō·bwä′).

click (klik) *n.* **1.** A short, sharp, nonresonant metallic sound, as that made by a latch. **2.** *Mech.* A detent or stop; pawl. **3.** *Phonet.* One of a group of speech sounds produced on the inhaled breath by closing the oral cavity at the front and back and withdrawing the tongue suddenly from some part of the mouth, characteristic of certain African languages: also called *suction stop.* — *v.t.* **1.** To cause to make a click or clicks. — *v.i.* **2.** To produce a click or succession of clicks. **3.** *Slang* To succeed: The show *clicked.* **4.** *Slang* To suit exactly: agree. [Imit.] — **click′er** *n.*

click beetle An elaterid beetle that, by a quick, snapping movement, is able to right itself when on its back: also called *snapping beetle.* For illustration see INSECTS (injurious).

cli·ent (klī′ənt) *n.* **1.** One in whose interest a lawyer acts. **2.** One who engages the services of any professional adviser. **3.** A customer. **4.** A dependent or follower, as of an ancient Roman patrician. [< L *cliens, -entis,* var. of *cluens,* ppr. of *cluere* to hear, listen] — **cli·en·tal** (klī·en′təl, klī′ən·təl) *adj.*

cli·en·tele (klī′ən·tel′) *n.* A body of clients, patients, dependents, customers, or adherents; a following. Also **cli·ent·age** (klī′ən·tij). [< F]

cliff (klif) *n.* A high steep face of rock; a precipice. Also *Obs.* **clift.** [OE *clif*]

cliff dweller 1. One of certain aboriginal North American Indian tribes of the SW United States and NW Mexico who lived in recesses in the sides of cliffs and canyons, and who were the antecedents of the Pueblo Indians. **2.** *U.S. Informal* A person who lives in a city apartment house. — **cliff dwelling**

cliff·hang·er (klif′hang′ər) *n. Informal.* **1.** A serialized motion picture in which each episode cuts off at a point of imminent peril. **2.** A tense situation of which the outcome is uncertain. — **cliff′hang·ing** *adj. & n.*

cliff swallow A North American swallow (*Petrochelidon pyrrhonota*) that builds mud nests under the eaves of buildings or against cliffs: also called *mud dauber.*

cliff·y (klif′ē) *adj.* Abounding in or resembling cliffs; craggy.

Clif·ton (klif′tən) A city in NE New Jersey; pop. 82,437.

cli·mac·ter·ic (klī·mak′tər·ik, klī′mak·ter′ik) *n.* **1.** An age or period of life characterized by marked physiological change, formerly believed to occur at ages that are multiples of seven and an odd number. **2.** The menopause. **3.** Any critical year or period. — *adj.* Pertaining to a critical year or period: also **cli·mac·ter·i·cal** (klī′mak·ter′i·kəl). [< L *climactericus* < Gk. *klimaktērikos* < *klimaktēr* rung of a ladder]

cli·mac·tic (klī·mak′tik) *adj.* Pertaining to or constituting a climax. Also **cli·mac′ti·cal.**

cli·mate (klī′mit) *n.* **1.** The combination of temperature, precipitation, winds, etc., characteristic of a locality or region over an extended period of time. **2.** A region characterized by a certain average temperature, rainfall, dryness, etc. **3.** A prevailing trend or condition in human affairs: the *climate* of opinion. [< OF *climat* < LL *clima* < Gk. *klima, -atos* region, zone < *klinein* to slope] — **cli·mat·ic** (klī·mat′ik) or **·i·cal** *adj.* — **cli·mat′i·cal·ly** *adv.*

climato- *combining form* Climate; pertaining to climate or climatic conditions: *climatology.* Also, before vowels, **climat-.** [< Gk. *klima, -atos* region]

cli·ma·tol·o·gy (klī′mə·tol′ə·jē) *n.* The branch of science dealing with the phenomena of climate. — **cli·ma·to·log·ic** (klī′mə·tə·loj′ik) or **·i·cal** *adj.* — **cli·ma·tol′o·gist** *n.*

cli·max (klī′maks) *n.* **1.** The point of greatest intensity or fullest development; culmination; acme. **2.** In drama, the scene or moment of action that determines the dénouement. **3.** In rhetoric: **a** A passage consisting of statements or parts in increasing order of force or intensity. **b** The last statement or part in such a series. **4.** *Ecol.* A relatively stable community of plants and animals dominant in a given locality. — *v.t. & v.i.* To reach or bring to a climax. [< L < Gk. *klimax* ladder]

climb (klīm) *v.* **climbed** (*Archaic* **clomb**), **climb·ing** *v.t.* **1.** To ascend or mount (something), especially by means of the hands and feet; go up by holding or by getting a foothold. — *v.i.* **2.** To rise or go up, especially by using the hands and feet. **3.** To rise or advance in status, rank, etc. **4.** To incline or slope upward. **5.** To rise during growth, as certain vines, by entwining a support or clinging by means of tendrils. — **to climb down 1.** To descend or move down, especially by using the hands and feet. **2.** *Informal* To give up or abandon a position, etc. — *n.* **1.** The act or process of climbing; ascent. **2.** A place ascended by climbing. [OE *climban*] — **climb′a·ble** *adj.*

climb·er (klī′mər) *n.* **1.** One who or that which climbs. **2.** *Bot.* A plant that supports its growth by its tendrils, rootlets, or the like. **3.** *Informal* A person who constantly strives for a higher social or professional position.

climbing fish The anabas.

climbing irons Iron bars bearing spur points, strapped to the legs to aid in climbing telegraph poles, trees, etc. Also **climb·ers** (klī′mərz).

clime (klīm) *n. Poetic* A country, region, or climate. [< LL *clima.* See CLIMATE.]

cli·nan·dri·um (kli·nan′drē·əm) *n. pl.* **·dri·a** (-drē·ə) *Bot.* A depression in the summit of the column in certain orchids, in which the anther is lodged: also called *androclinium.* [< NL < Gk. *klinē* bed + *anēr, andros* man, male (with ref. to the stamen)]

cli·nan·thi·um (kli·nan′thē·əm) *n. pl.* **·thi·a** (-thē·ə) *Bot.* The receptacle of a composite flower. [< NL < Gk. *klinē* bed + *anthos* flower]

clinch (klinch) *v.t.* **1.** To secure firmly, as a driven nail or staple, by bending down the protruding point. **2.** To fasten together by this means. **3.** To make sure; settle. **4.** *Naut.* To fasten by making a clinch. — *v.i.* **5.** To take a hold; grapple, as combatants. **6.** *Slang* To embrace, as lovers.

n. **1.** The act of clinching. **2.** That which clinches; especially, a clinched nail or bolt; a clamp. **3.** *Naut.* A knot in a rope made by a half hitch and seizings. **4.** A grip or struggle at close quarters, as in boxing. **5.** *Slang* A close embrace. [Var. of CLENCH]

clinch·er (klin′chər) *n.* **1.** One who or that which clinches. **2.** A nail made for clinching. **3.** *Informal* A deciding statement, point, etc.

cline (klīn) *n. Ecol.* A graded series of changes in a biotype, induced by corresponding gradual environmental alterations within a large area. [< Gk. *klinein* to slope, bend]

cling (kling) *v.i.* **clung, cling·ing 1.** To hold fast to something, as by grasping, sticking, embracing, or winding round; adhere closely: His wet coat *clung* to his back. **2.** To remain in contact; resist separation: with *together.* **3.** To remain attached in thought or practice; hold on: to *cling* to memories. — *n.* A clingstone peach. [OE *clingan*] — **cling′er** *n.*

cling·fish (kling′fish′) *n. pl.* **·fish** or **·fish·es** Any of a group of small marine fishes (family *Gobiesocidae*) having a large central suction disk by which they cling to rocks, shells, etc.

clinging vine *Informal* A woman who displays extreme dependence on a man.

Cling·mans Dome (kling′mənz) Highest point of the Great Smoky Mountains, on the border between Tennessee and North Carolina; 6,642 ft.

cling·stone (kling′stōn′) *n.* A variety of peach in which the pulp adheres to the stone: also called *cling.*

cling·y (kling′ē) *adj.* Tending to cling or adhere, as a fabric.

clin·ic (klin′ik) *n.* **1.** An infirmary, usually connected with a hospital or medical school, for the treatment of nonresident patients. **2.** The teaching of medicine and surgery by treating patients in the presence of a class; also, a class receiving such instruction. **3.** A place where patients are studied and treated by specialists. **4.** An organization that offers advice or treats specific problems: a marriage *clinic.* [< F *clinique* < Gk. *klinikē* (*technē*) (art) of the sickbed < *klinē* bed < *klinein* to recline]

clin·i·cal (klin′i·kəl) *adj.* **1.** Of or pertaining to a clinic. **2.** Concerned with the observation and treatment of patients in clinics, as distinguished from laboratory experimentation. **3.** Coldly scientific or detached. **4.** Administered to one on a deathbed or sickbed: *clinical* baptism. — **clin′i·cal·ly** *adv.*

clinical thermometer An accurately calibrated thermometer used for determining body temperature.

cli·ni·cian (kli·nish′ən) *n.* A physician trained in clinical methods, or one who gives instruction in clinics.

clink[1] (klingk) *v.t. & v.i.* **1.** To make or cause to make a short, slight, ringing sound. **2.** To rhyme; jingle. — *n.* **1.** A slight ringing or tinkling sound. **2.** *Scot.* Money. **3.** The shrill note of certain birds, as the whinchat. **4.** A rhyme or jingle. [Imit. Cf. MDu. *klinken.*]

clink[2] (klingk) *n. Slang* A prison. [? after *Clink* prison in London]

clink·er (kling′kər) *n.* **1.** The fused, earthy residue left by coal, etc., in burning. **2.** *Metall.* A scale of black iron oxide formed by the heating of iron in air. **3.** A very hard brick. **4.** A partially vitrified brick, or a mass of fused bricks. **5.** *U.S. Slang* A mistake or error, especially in a musical performance. — *v.i.* To form clinkers, as coal in burning. [Earlier *clinkard* < Du. *klinckaerd,* kind of brick]

clink·er-built (kling′kər·bilt′) *adj.* Built with overlapping and riveted planks or plates, as a boat. [< *clink* Scot. var. of CLINCH + BUILT]

clink·stone (kling′stōn′) *n.* A variety of phonolite that clinks like metal when struck. [Trans. of G *klingstein*]

clino- combining form Bend; slope; incline: *clinometer.* [< Gk. *klinein* to bend]

cli·nom·e·ter (klī·nom′ə·tər, kli-) *n.* An instrument for determining angular inclination, as of guns, slopes, etc.: also called *anglemeter.* [< CLINO- + -METER] **cli·no·met·ric** (klī′nə·met′rik) *adj.* Of or measured by a clinometer. Also **cli′no·met′ri·cal.**

clin·quant (kling′kənt) *adj.* Glittering as with gold or silver; tinseled. — *n.* Imitation gold leaf; tinsel. [< F, ppr. of *clinquer* to ring, glitter]

Clin·ton (klin′tən) A New York family prominent in American history, including **James,** 1733–1812, Revolutionary general: **George,** 1739–1812, brother of James, first governor of New York, and vice president of the United States 1805–1812; **De Witt,** 1769–1828, son of James, lawyer and statesman. — **Sir Henry,** 1738?–95, British general; commander in chief in the American Revolution 1778–82.

Clin·ton (klin′tən) A city in eastern Iowa on the Mississippi River; pop. 34,719.

clin·to·ni·a (klin·tō′nē·ə) *n.* A plant of a small genus (*Clintonia*) of perennial herbs of the lily family, having broadly lanceolate leaves and bearing white or yellow flowers succeeded by berries. [after De Witt *Clinton*]

CLINKER-
BUILT (A) and
CARVEL–BUILT
(B)

Cli·o (klī′ō) The Muse of history. [< Gk. *kleein* to celebrate, make famous]

clip[1] (klip) *n.* **1.** A device that clasps, grips, or holds articles together, as letters or papers. **2.** A cartridge clip (which see). **3.** A flange on a horseshoe, projecting upward above the calk. **4.** *Med.* An appliance for stopping the bleeding of arteries, etc. — *v.t.* **clipped, clip·ping 1.** To fasten with or as with a clip; hold tightly. **2.** *Archaic* To clasp; embrace. [OE *clyppan* to clasp]

clip[2] (klip) *v.* **clipped, clip·ping** *v.t.* **1.** To cut with shears or scissors, as hair or fleece; trim. **2.** To snip a part from, as a coin. **3.** To cut short; curtail: to *clip* the ends of words. **4.** *Informal* To strike with a sharp blow. **5.** In football, to block (an opponent who is not carrying the ball) from the rear. **6.** *U.S. Slang* To cheat or defraud. — *v.i.* **7.** To cut or trim. **8.** *Informal* To run or move swiftly. — **to clip the wings of** To check the aspirations or ambitions of. — *n.* **1.** The act of clipping, or that which is clipped off. **2.** The wool yielded at one shearing or during one season. **3.** A sharp blow; punch. **4.** *Informal* A quick pace: at a good *clip.* **5.** *pl.* Shears. [< ON *klippa*]

clip·board (klip′bôrd′, -bōrd′) *n.* A board that provides a solid foundation for writing and has a spring clip attached at the top for holding the paper.

clip joint *U.S. Slang* A restaurant, night club, store, etc., where prices are unconscionably high.

clipped form A shortened form of a polysyllabic word, as *bus* for *omnibus.* Also **clipped word.**

clip·per (klip′ər) *n.* **1.** *pl.* An instrument or tool for clipping or cutting. **2.** A sailing vessel of the mid-19th century, built for speed, and having tall masts and sharp, overhanging bows: also **clipper ship.** **3.** One who clips. **4.** Something that moves swiftly, as a fast horse or sled.

clip·ping (klip′ing) *n.* **1.** The act of one who or that which clips. **2.** *Chiefly U.S.* That which is cut off or out by clipping: a newspaper *clipping.* — *adj.* That cuts or clips.

clique (klēk, klik) *n.* An exclusive or clannish set; a narrow coterie. — *v.i.* **cliqued, cli·quing** To unite in a clique; act clannishly. [< MF, a claque < *cliquer* to click, clap] — **Syn.** *Clique, coterie, circle,* and *set* denote a group of persons having a common interest. *Clique* suggests that this interest is selfish or hostile to a larger group, whereas *coterie* suggests amiable congeniality. A *circle* centers upon a person or an activity, and may be small or large: a sewing *circle,* scientific *circles. Set* suggests a large and loosely bound group: the fashionable *set.*

cli·quish (klē′kish, klik′ish) *adj.* Inclined to form cliques; exclusive. Also **cli′quey, cli′quy.** — **cli′quish·ly** *adv.* — **cli′quish·ness** *n.*

Clis·the·nes (klis′thə·nēz) See CLEISTHENES.

clis·tog·a·my (klis·tog′ə·mē, klis-) See CLEISTOGAMY.

cli·to·ris (klī′tə·ris, klit′ə-) *n. Anat.* A small erectile organ at the upper part of the vulva, the homologue of the penis. [< NL < Gk. *kleitoris*] — **clit′o·ral** (-rəl) *adj.*

Clive (klīv), **Robert,** 1725–74, Baron Clive of Plassey, English general; founded British India.

clo·a·ca (klō·ā′kə) *n. pl.* **·cae** (-sē) **1.** *Zool.* The common cavity into which the various ducts of the body open in certain fishes, reptiles, birds, and some mammals. **2.** A sewer or a privy. [< L, a drain] — **clo·a′cal** *adj.*

cloak (klōk) *n.* **1.** A loose outer garment, usually without sleeves. **2.** Something that covers or hides; a pretext; disguise; mask. — *v.t.* **1.** To cover with a cloak. **2.** To conceal; disguise. [< OF *cloaque, cloke* < Med.L *cloca* bell, cape; so called from its bell-like shape. Doublet of CLOCK[1].]

cloak·room (klōk′rōōm′, -rŏŏm′) *n.* A room where hats, coats, luggage, etc., are left temporarily, as in a theater.

clob·ber (klob′ər) *v.t. U.S. Slang* **1.** To beat severely; trounce; maul. **2.** To defeat utterly. [? Freq. of CLUB[1], v.]

cloche (klōsh, *Fr.* klôsh) *n.* **1.** A woman's close-fitting, bell-shaped hat. **2.** A bell-shaped glass cover. [< F, bell]

clock[1] (klok) *n.* **1.** An instrument for measuring and indicating time; especially, a sizable mechanism having pointers that move over a dial marked off in hours: distinguished from *watch.* Abbr. *clk.* **2.** Any clocklike registering device for recording distance, output, etc. — *v.t.* To ascertain the speed or the time of with a stopwatch. [< MDu. *clocke* < OF *cloaque, cloche* bell < Med.L *cloca.* Doublet of CLOAK.]

clock[2] (klok) *n.* An embroidered or woven ornament on the side of a stocking or sock at the ankle. — *v.t.* To ornament with clocks. [Origin uncertain]

Clock (klok) *n.* The constellation Horologium.

clock·mak·er (klok′mā′kər) *n.* One who makes or repairs clocks.

clock·wise (klok′wīz′) *adj. & adv.* Going in the direction traveled by the hands of a clock.

clock·work (klok′wûrk′) *n.* The machinery of a clock, or any similar mechanism, usually driven by a spring. — **like clockwork** With regularity and precision.

clod (klod) *n.* **1.** A lump of earth, clay, etc. **2.** Anything earthy, as the body compared with the soul. **3.** A dull, stupid person; dolt. **4.** The cut of beef high on the shoulder.

[Var. of CLOT] — **clod′dish** adj. — **clod′dish·ness** n. — **clod′dy** adj.

clod·hop·per (klod′hop/ər) n. **1.** Informal A rustic; hick; lout. **2.** pl. Large, heavy shoes.

clod·pate (klod′pāt′) n. A blockhead; a stupid person. Also **clod·poll** (klod′pōl′), **clod/pole′**.

clog (klog) n. **1.** Anything that impedes motion; an obstruction; hindrance. **2.** A block or weight attached, as to a horse, to hinder movement. **3.** A wooden-soled shoe. **4.** A clog dance. — v. **clogged**, **clog·ging** v.t. **1.** To choke up or obstruct. **2.** To impede; hinder. **3.** To fasten a clog to; hobble. — v.i. **4.** To become clogged or choked. **5.** To adhere in a mass; coagulate. **6.** To perform a clog dance. [ME clogge block of wood] — **clog/gi·ness** n. — **clog′gy** adj.

clog dance A dance performed with clogs or other shoes whose clatter emphasizes the rhythm of the music.

cloi·son·né (kloi′zə·nā′) n. **1.** A method of producing designs in enamel by laying out the pattern with metal strips on edge and filling the interstices with enamel. **2.** The ware so produced. — adj. Of, pertaining to, or made by this method. [< F < cloison partition]

clois·ter (klois′tər) n. **1.** A covered walk along the inside walls of buildings in a quadrangle, as in a monastery or college. **2.** A building devoted to religious seclusion; a monastery; convent. **3.** Any place of quiet seclusion. **4.** Monastic life. — v.t. To seclude; confine, as in a cloister. [OF cloistre < L claustrum enclosed place]
— **Syn.** (noun) **2.** Cloister, convent, nunnery, monastery, friary, abbey, priory, and hermitage are places of seclusion for a religious community. Cloister is the most general term; it refers to a retreat for either sex, and stresses loneliness. Convent emphasizes the association of its inmates; it was originally a general term, but is now usually restricted to a retreat for women, replacing the former nunnery. Monasteries and friaries are cloisters for men. Abbeys and priories are cloisters governed respectively by abbots and priors. A hermitage, at first the dwelling of a single recluse, is now applied to a collection of hermits' cells.

clois·tered (klois′tərd) adj. **1.** Living in cloisters: cloistered nuns. **2.** Concealed or withdrawn from the world.

clois·tral (klois′trəl) adj. **1.** Of, pertaining to, or living in a cloister. **2.** Like a cloister; secluded; solitary. Also claustral.

clomb (klōm) Archaic past tense and past participle of CLIMB.

clone (klōn) n. **1.** A group of organisms derived from a single individual by asexual means, including, theoretically, identical human beings from body cells. **2.** One of the organisms so derived. — v.t. & v.i. **cloned**, **clon·ing** To reproduce in the form of a clone. [< Gk. klōn sprout, twig] — **clon′al** adj. — **clon′al·ly** adv.

clo·nus (klō′nəs) n. Pathol. A form of muscular spasm in which contraction and relaxation rapidly alternate. [< NL < Gk. klonos motion, turmoil] — **clon·ic** (klon′ik) adj. — **clo·nic·i·ty** (klō·nis/ə·tē) n. — **clo′nism** n.

Cloot (klōōt) Scot. The devil. Also **Cloo·tie** (klōō/tē), **Cloots**.

clop (klop) v.i. **clopped**, **clop·ping** To produce or move with a hollow percussive sound, as of a horse's hoof striking pavement. — n. The sound made by clopping.

close (adj., adv., n. defs. 4 and 5 klōs; v., n. defs. 1–3 klōz) adj. **clos·er**, **clos·est** **1.** Near or near together in space, time, etc. **2.** Having the component parts or members near to each other; dense; compact: a close weave; a close arrangement. **3.** Near to the surface; short: a close haircut. **4.** Near to the mark: a close shot. **5.** Nearly even or equal: said of contests. **6.** Fitting tightly or snugly: a close cap. **7.** Conforming to or approximating an original: a close resemblance. **8.** Logically exact; precise: close reasoning. **9.** Thorough; rigorous: close attention; a close search. **10.** Bound by strong affection, loyalty, common interests, etc.: a close friend. **11.** Enclosed or partly enclosed; shut in or about; not open. **12.** Confined in space; narrow; cramped: close quarters. **13.** Open only to a few; restricted: a close corporation: now usually closed. **14.** Strictly guarded or confined, as a prisoner. **15.** Concealing one's thoughts or feelings; reticent; secretive. **16.** Hidden from observation; secluded: close secrecy. **17.** Not liberal; close-fisted; stingy. **18.** Difficult to obtain; scarce: said of money or credit. **19.** Ill-ventilated; stifling, as a room; also, oppressive: close weather. **20.** Phonet. Of vowels, pronounced with a part of the tongue relatively close to the palate, as (ē): opposed to open. — v. **closed**, **clos·ing** v.t. **1.** To shut, as a door. **2.** To fill or obstruct, as an opening or passage. **3.** To bring the parts of together, as a knife or book. **4.** To bring into contact; join, as parts of an electric circuit. **5.** To bring to an end; terminate. **6.** To shut in; enclose. — v.i. **7.** To become shut or closed. **8.** To come to an end. **9.** To grapple; come to close quarters. **10.** To join; coalesce; unite. **11.** To come to an agreement. **12.** To be worth at the end of a business day: Stocks closed three points higher. — **to close down 1.** To suppress. **2.** To cease operations, as a factory. **3.** To come down; blanket the sight, as night. — **to close in** To advance from all sides so as to prevent escape. — **to close out** U.S. To sell all of, usually at reduced prices. — **to close up 1.** To close completely. **2.** To come nearer together, as troops. — n. **1.** The end; conclusion. **2.** A junction; meeting. **3.** A closing in battle; grapple. **4.** An enclosed place; enclosure; especial-

ly, enclosed land about a cathedral or building. **5.** Scot. & Brit. Dial. A lane or entry; also, a courtyard. — adv. In a close manner; nearly; closely. [< OF clos, pp. of clore to close < L claudere to close] — **close·ly** (klōs/lē) adv. — **close·ness** (klōs/nis) n. — **clos·er** (klō′zər) n.
— **Syn.** (adj.) **1.** near, nigh, neighboring. **15.** See TACITURN. **17.** frugal, miserly. Compare STINGY.[1] — (verb) **5.** stop, conclude. Compare END, FINISH.

close call (klōs) U.S. Informal A narrow escape.

closed chain (klōzd) Chem. An organic compound in which the carbon atoms are arranged in a cyclical form, as in benzene and aromatic compounds: distinguished from open chain.

closed circuit 1. Electr. A circuit through which current flows. **2.** Telecom. A form of television in which broadcasts are transmitted by cable to a restricted number of receivers.

closed corporation A business enterprise in which the stock is owned by a few persons. Also **close corporation**.

closed-end investment company (klōzd/end′) See under INVESTMENT COMPANY.

closed primary A direct primary election in which only those voters who qualify for party membership may vote.

closed season That part of the year during which it is unlawful to catch or kill certain varieties of fish or game.

closed shop An establishment where only union members are employed: opposed to open shop.

close-fist·ed (klōs/fis′tid) adj. Stingy; miserly. — **close′-fist′ed·ness** n.

close-fit·ting (klōs/fit′ing) adj. Fitting snugly.

close-grained (klōs/grānd′) adj. Compact in growth or structure; solid, as certain woods, crystals, etc.

close-hauled (klōs/hôld′) adj. & adv. Naut. With sails set for sailing as close to the wind as possible.

close-lipped (klōs/lipt′) adj. Taciturn; close-mouthed.

close-mouthed (klōs/mouthd′, -moutht′) adj. Not given to speaking; taciturn; uncommunicative.

close-or·der drill (klōs/ôr′dər) Mil. A systematic exercise in formation marching and in the formal handling of arms.

close quarters (klōs) **1.** In fighting, an encounter at close range or hand-to-hand. **2.** A small, confined space.

close shave (klōs) U.S. Informal A narrow escape.

close stitch (klōs) The buttonhole stitch (which see).

clos·et (kloz/it) n. **1.** Chiefly U.S. A small room or recess for storing clothes, linen, etc. **2.** A small, private room. **3.** A ruler's council chamber. **4.** A water closet; toilet. — v.t. To shut up or conceal in or as in a closet, especially for privacy: usually reflexive. — adj. **1.** Private; confidential. **2.** Based on theory rather than practice: closet strategy. [< OF, dim. of clos. See CLOSE.]

closet drama A play written solely, or chiefly, for reading rather than performance.

close-up (klōs/up′) n. **1.** A picture taken at close range, or with a telescopic lens. **2.** A close look or view.

clos·trid·i·um (klos·trid/ē·əm) n. pl. **·trid·i·a** (-trid/ē·ə) Bacteriol. Any of a genus (Clostridium) of rod-shaped, spore-bearing, anaerobic bacteria, including those causing botulism and tetanus. [< NL < Gk. klōstēr spindle]

clo·sure (klō′zhər) n. **1.** A closing or shutting up. **2.** That which closes or shuts. **3.** An end; conclusion. **4.** Cloture. — v.t. & v.i. **·sured**, **·sur·ing** To cloture. [< OF < L clausura a closing < claudere to close]

clot (klot) n. A thick, viscid, or coagulated mass, as of blood. — v.t. & v.i. **clot·ted**, **clot·ting** To form into clots; coagulate; mat, fill, or cover with clots. [OE clott lump, mass]

cloth (klôth, kloth) n. pl. **cloths** (klôthz, klothz, klôths, kloths) **1.** A woven, knitted, or felted fabric of wool, cotton, rayon, etc.; also, a piece of such fabric. Abbr. cl. **2.** A piece of cloth for a special use, as a tablecloth. **3.** Naut. **a** Sails; canvas. **b** A sail. **4.** Professional attire, especially of the clergy. **5.** Obs. Raiment; clothing. — **the cloth** The clergy collectively. [OE clâth]

clothe (klōth) v.t. **clothed** or **clad**, **cloth·ing** **1.** To cover or provide with clothes; dress. **2.** To cover as if with clothing; invest. [Fusion of OE clâthian and clǣthan]

clothes (klōz, klōthz) n.pl. **1.** The articles of dress worn by human beings; garments; clothing. **2.** Bedclothes (which see). [OE clâthas, pl. of clâth cloth]

clothes·horse (klōz/hôrs′, klōthz/-) n. **1.** A frame on which to hang or dry clothes. **2.** U.S. Slang A person regarded as excessively concerned with dress.

clothes·line (klōz/līn′, klōthz/-) n. A cord, rope, or wire on which to hang clothes to dry.

clothes moth Any of various moths, especially of the family Tineidae, whose larvae destroy wool, fur, etc. For illustration see INSECTS (injurious).

clothes·pin (klōz/pin′, klōthz/-) n. A forked peg or clamp with which to fasten clothes on a line.

clothes pole A pole for holding up a clothesline.

clothes-press (klōz/pres′, klōthz/-) n. A closet or chest for clothes; wardrobe.

clothes tree A stand having arms or hooks on which to hang hats, coats, etc.: also called hall tree.

cloth·ier (klōth/yər) n. One who makes or sells cloths or clothing.

cloth·ing (klō′thing) *n.* **1.** Dress collectively; apparel. **2.** A covering.

Clo·tho (klō′thō) One of the three Fates or Moirai. [< Gk. *klōthein* to spin]

cloth yard A unit for measuring cloth, formerly 27 inches, now equal to the standard yard of 36 inches.

clot·ty (klot′ē) *adj.* **1.** Full of clots. **2.** Tending to clot.

clo·ture (klō′chər) *n.* A parliamentary device to stop debate in a legislative body in order to secure a vote. Compare PREVIOUS QUESTION. — *v.t.* To stop (debate) by cloture. Also *closure.* [< F *clôture*]

cloud (kloud) *n.* **1.** A mass of visible vapor or an aggregation of watery or icy particles floating in the atmosphere. In the International Code, clouds have been classified into four families and ten genera, according to height and typical formation. See table below. **2.** Any visible collection of particles in the air, as steam, smoke, or dust. **3.** A cloudlike mass of things in motion, especially in flight: a *cloud* of gnats. **4.** Something that darkens, obscures, or threatens. **5.** A dark vein or thread, as in marble; a flaw or blemish. **6.** A dimness or milkiness, as in glass or liquids. — **in the clouds 1.** In the realm of the unreal or fanciful. **2.** Impractical. — **under a cloud 1.** Overshadowed by reproach or distrust. **2.** Troubled or depressed. — *v.t.* **1.** To cover with or as with clouds; dim; obscure. **2.** To render gloomy or troubled. **3.** To cover with calumny or disgrace; sully, as a reputation. **4.** To mark with different colors; variegate. — *v.i.* **5.** To become overcast, as with clouds: often with *up* or *over.* [OE *clūd* rocky mass, hill] — **cloud′less** *adj.*

CLOUD TABLE—INTERNATIONAL CODE
Families: A: high clouds, from 20,000 feet up; B: middle clouds, 6,500–20,000 feet; C: low clouds, near surface to 6,500 feet; D: vertical displacement clouds, 1,600–20,000 feet.

Type	Symbol	Family	Av. ht. miles
Altocumulus	Ac	B	2½
Altostratus	As	B	3½
Cirrocumulus	Cc	A	5
Cirrostratus	Cs	A	6
Cirrus	Ci	A	7
Cumulonimbus	Cb	D	4
Cumulus	Cu	D	2
Nimbostratus	Ns	C	¼
Stratocumulus	Sc	C	1
Stratus	St	C	¼

The following variations of the International Code are also accepted in the U.S. Weather Bureau procedure: *altocumulus castellatus* (Acc), *cumulonimbus mammatus* (Cm), *fractocumulus* (Fc), and *fractostratus* (Fs).

cloud·ber·ry (kloud′ber′ē) *n. pl.* **·ries** A raspberry (*Rubus chamaemorus*) producing an amber-colored fruit: also called *bakeapple, bake apple, baked-apple berry, salmonberry.*

cloud·burst (kloud′bûrst′) *n.* A sudden, heavy downpour.

cloud-capped (kloud′kapt′) *adj.* Having clouds encircling the top.

cloud chamber *Physics* An enclosed receptacle containing air or gas saturated with water vapor whose sudden cooling indicates the presence of ions by the tracks of water droplets they produce: also called *fog chamber, Wilson Cloud Chamber.*

cloud·land (kloud′land′) *n.* The realm of fancy and dreams or of theory and speculation.

cloud·let (kloud′lit) *n.* A little cloud.

cloud rack A mass of clouds driven by the wind.

cloud·y (kloud′ē) *adj.* **cloud·i·er, cloud·i·est 1.** Overspread with clouds. Abbr. *c., C.* **2.** Of or like a cloud or clouds. **3.** Marked with cloudlike spots. **4.** Not limpid or clear. **5.** Obscure; vague; confused: *cloudy* thinking. **6.** Full of foreboding; gloomy; sullen: *cloudy* looks. [OE *clūdig*] — **cloud′i·ly** *adv.* — **cloud′i·ness** *n.*
— **Syn. 1.** murky, hazy, overcast.

Clou·et (klōō·e′), **François,** 1516?–72?, son of Jean; court painter to King Francis I. — **Jean,** 1485?–1541?, French painter.

clough (kluf, klou) *n.* A gorge or ravine. [ME *clough, cloghe,* < OE (assumed) *clōh*]

Clough (kluf), **Arthur Hugh,** 1819–61, English poet.

clour (klōōr) *n. & v.t. Scot.* Knock; bump.

clout (klout) *n.* **1.** *Informal* A heavy blow or cuff with the hand. **2.** In baseball slang, a long hit. **3.** In archery, the center of a target, or a shot that strikes it. **4.** *Archaic & Dial.* A piece of cloth or leather; patch; rag. **5.** A type of flat-headed nail: also **clout nail.** **6.** *U.S. Informal* Influence. — *v.t.* **1.** *Informal* To hit or strike, as with the hand. **2.** *Archaic & Dial.* To patch or bandage crudely. [OE *clūt*]

clout·ed (klou′tid) *adj. Brit. Dial.* Clotted: said of cream.

clove¹ (klōv) *n.* A dried flower bud of a tropical evergreen tree (*Syzygium aromaticum* or *Eugenia aromatica*) of the myrtle family, used as a spice. [< OF *clou* (de *girofle*) nail (of clove) < L *clavus* nail; so called from its shape]

clove² (klōv) *n. Bot.* One of the small bulbs formed in the axis of the scale of a mother bulb, as in garlic. [OE *clufu*]

clove³ (klōv) **1.** Alternative past tense and archaic past participle of CLEAVE¹. **2.** Archaic past tense of CLEAVE².

clove hitch *Naut.* A knot consisting of two half hitches, with the ends of the rope going in opposite directions, used for fastening a rope around a spar. For illustration see HITCH.

clo·ven (klō′vən) Alternative past participle of CLEAVE¹. — *adj.* Parted; split.

cloven hoof 1. A hoof divided or cleft, as in cattle. **2.** The sign of Satan, depicted with cloven hoofs. Also **cloven foot.**

cloven-hoofed (klō′vən-hōoft′, -hōoft′) *adj.* **1.** Having the foot cleft or divided, as cattle. **2.** Satanic; devilish. Also **clo′ven-foot′ed.**

clove pink Any of several varieties of pink (*Dianthus caryophyllus*) having a sweet, clovelike odor.

clo·ver (klō′vər) *n.* **1.** Any of several species of leguminous plants (genus *Trifolium*) having dense flower heads and trifoliolate leaves; especially, the **red clover** (*T. pratense*) used for forage and adopted as the State flower of Vermont. **2.** Any of certain other plants of the legume family, as meliot. — **in clover 1.** Originally, in good pasture. **2.** In a prosperous or luxurious condition. [OE *clǣfre* trefoil]

clo·ver·leaf (klō′vər-lēf′) *n. pl.* **·leafs** A type of intersection resembling a four-leaf clover, in which two highways crossing at different levels are connected by a system of curving ramps, enabling a vehicle to change roads without interference.

Clo·vis (klō′vis), 466?–511, king of the Franks 481–511; traditional founder of the French kingdom: also *Chlodwig.*

CLOVERLEAF

clown (kloun) *n.* **1.** A professional buffoon in a play or circus, who entertains by jokes, tricks, etc.; a zany; jester. **2.** A coarse or vulgar person; boor. **3.** A countryman. — *v.i.* To behave like a clown. [Earlier *cloune* < MLG. Cf. Du. *kloen,* dial. Frisian *klönne* lout, boor.] — **clown′er·y** *n.*
— **Syn.** (noun) **1.** fool, antic, comic, merry-andrew. **2.** lout, churl, clodhopper.

clown·ish (klou′nish) *adj.* **1.** Of or like a clown. **2.** Foolish or rude. — **clown′ish·ly** *adv.* — **clown′ish·ness** *n.*

cloy (kloi) *v.t.* **1.** To gratify beyond desire, especially with richness or sweetness; surfeit. — *v.i.* **2.** To cause a feeling of surfeit. [Var. of earlier *accloy* < OF *encloyer* to nail up, block, overload < LL *inclavare* to nail < L *clavus* a nail] — **cloy′ing·ly** *adv.* — **cloy′ing·ness** *n.*

C.L.U. Chartered Life Underwriter.

club¹ (klub) *n.* **1.** A stout stick or staff; a cudgel; truncheon. **2.** A stick or bat used in games to strike a ball; especially, a stick with a curved head used in golf. **3.** In card games: **a** A black marking on a playing card, shaped like a three-leaf clover. **b** A card so marked. **c** *pl.* The suit so marked. **4.** *Biol.* A clavate organ or part. — *v.* **clubbed, club·bing** *v.t.* **1.** To beat, as with a club. **2.** To use (a rifle, musket, etc.) as a club by grasping the barrel. **3.** *Archaic* To gather into a clublike mass, as hair. — *v.i.* **4.** *Archaic* To form into a mass. [< ON *klubba*]

club² (klub) *n.* **1.** A group of persons organized for some mutual aim or pursuit, especially a group that meets regularly. **2.** A house or room reserved for the meetings of such an organization. — *v.* **clubbed, club·bing** *v.t.* **1.** To contribute for a common purpose: to *club* resources. — *v.i.* **2.** To combine or unite, as for a common purpose; form a club: often with *together.* [Special use of CLUB¹]
— **Syn.** (noun) **1.** society, association, circle.

club·ba·ble (klub′ə·bəl) *adj. Informal* Having tastes or qualities suited to club life; sociable. Also **club′a·ble.**

club car A railroad passenger car furnished with easy chairs, tables, a buffet or bar, etc.

club·foot (klub′fōot′) *n. pl.* **·feet** *Pathol.* **1.** Congenital distortion of the foot: also called *talipes.* **2.** A foot so affected. — **club′foot′ed** *adj.*

club·hand (klub′hand′) *n.* **1.** A deformity of the hand, analogous to clubfoot: also called *talipomanus.* **2.** A hand so deformed.

club·haul (klub′hôl′) *v.t. Naut.* To put (a vessel) about when in danger of drifting on a lee shore by dropping the lee anchor, hauling to windward by the cable, and cutting the cable when the sails are filled on the new tack.

club·house (klub′hous′) *n.* The building occupied by a club.

club·man (klub′mən, -man′) *n. pl.* **·men** (-mən, -men′) A man who is a member or frequenter of fashionable clubs.

club moss Any of a widely distributed genus (*Lycopodium*) of perennial evergreen herbs allied to the ferns.

club sandwich A sandwich consisting of three slices of toast and layers of various meats, lettuce, tomatoes, etc.

club steak A small beefsteak cut from the loin.

club topsail *Naut.* A gaff topsail, extended at its foot by a small spar. For illustration see SCHOONER.

club·wom·an (klub′woŏm′ən) *n. pl.* **·wom·en** (-wim′ən) A woman who is a member of a club or clubs, especially one who devotes much time to club activities.

cluck (kluk) *v.i.* **1.** To give the low, guttural cry of a brooding hen, or of one calling her chicks. **2.** To utter any similar sound, as in urging a horse. — *v.t.* **3.** To call by clucking. **4.** To express with a like sound: to *cluck* disapproval. — *n.* **1.** The low, guttural sound made by a brooding hen; also, any sound similar to this. **2.** *U.S. Slang* A stupid or inept person. [OE *cloccian;* imit.]

clue (kloō) *n.* Something that leads to the solution of a problem or mystery. — *v.t.* **clued, clu·ing 1.** To clew. **2.** *U.S. Informal* To give (someone) information. [Var. of CLEW.]

Cluj (kloozh) A city in west central Rumania; former capital of Transylvania; pop. 162,419 (est. 1959): German *Klausenburg,* Hungarian *Kolozsvár.*

Clum·ber spaniel (klum′bər) A spaniel having a long, low body, silky white coat, and orange or lemon markings. Also **clum′ber.** [after *Clumber,* estate of the second Duke of Newcastle, where originally bred]

clump (klump) *n.* **1.** A thick cluster: a *clump* of bushes. **2.** A heavy, dull sound, as of tramping. **3.** An irregular mass; a lump. **4.** *Bacteriol.* A mass of bacteria in a state of rest, as by the agency of agglutinins. — *v.i.* **1.** To walk clumsily and noisily. **2.** *Bacteriol.* To form clumps. — *v.t.* **3.** To place or plant in a clump. **4.** *Bacteriol.* To cause to form clumps. [Var. of CLUB¹] — **clump′y, clump′ish** *adj.*

clum·sy (klum′zē) *adj.* **·si·er, ·si·est 1.** Lacking dexterity, ease, or grace; awkward. **2.** Rudely constructed; ungainly or unwieldy. **3.** Ineptly said or done; ill-contrived: a *clumsy* excuse. — **Syn.** See AWKWARD. [< obs. *clumse* to be numb with cold (< Scand. Cf. dial Sw. *klumsen* benumbed.) + -Y¹] — **clum′si·ly** *adv.* — **clum′si·ness** *n.*

clung (klung) Past tense and past participle of CLING.

Clu·ny (klü′nē′) A town in east central France; site of remains of a medieval Benedictine abbey; pop. 4,000.

Clu·ny lace (kloō′nē) A bobbin lace made of heavy linen thread, usually in a large, open design. [after *Cluny,* France]

Clu·pe·id (kloō′pē·id) *n.* Any of a family of teleost fishes (*Clupeidae*) having compressed bodies, including the herrings, shads, etc. — *adj.* Pertaining to the *Clupeidae.* [< NL *Clupeidae* < L *clupea,* a kind of small fish]

clu·pe·oid (kloō′pē·oid) *adj.* Herringlike. — *n.* A fish of the herring family.

clus·ter (klus′tər) *n.* **1.** A collection of objects of the same kind growing or fastened together. **2.** A number of persons or things close together; group. — *v.t. & v.i.* To grow or form into a cluster or clusters: animals that *clustered* together for warmth. [OE *cluster*] — **clus′tered** *adj.* — **clus′ter·y** *adj.*

— **Syn.** (noun) **1.** bunch. **2.** gathering, assemblage, congeries, aggregation, association, company, gang, party, troop.

clutch¹ (kluch) *v.t.* **1.** To seize eagerly; snatch, as with hands or talons. **2.** To grasp and hold firmly. — *v.i.* **3.** To attempt to seize, snatch, or reach: with *at.* — Syn. See GRASP. — *n.* **1.** A tight grip; grasp. **2.** *pl.* Power or control: in the *clutches* of the police. **3.** A talon, claw, or paw that clutches. **4.** *Mech.* **a** Any of a number of variously constructed devices for coupling two working parts, as the engine and driveshaft of an automobile. **b** A lever or pedal for operating such a device. **5.** A contrivance for gripping. **6.** *Slang* Emergency; pinch. [ME *clucchen,* var. of *clicche* < OE *clyccan* to grasp]

CLUTCH
(*n. def.* 4)
a Fixed member.
b Movable and splined member.
c Collar. *d* Fork. *e* Lever.

clutch² (kluch) *n.* **1.** The number of eggs laid at one time. **2.** A brood of chickens. — *v.t.* To hatch. [Var. of dial. *cletch* < *cleck* to hatch < ON *klekja* hatch]

clut·ter (klut′ər) *n.* **1.** A disordered state or collection; litter. **2.** A clattering, confused noise; chattering. **3.** *Telecom.* Interference resulting from fixed objects within range of a radar set. — *v.t.* **1.** To litter, heap, or pile in a confused manner. — *v.i.* **2.** To run or move with bustle or confusion. **3.** To make a clatter. **4.** To speak hurriedly and inexactly. [Var. of earlier *clotter,* orig. freq. of CLOT.]

— **Syn.** (noun) **1.** jumble. muddle. mess. chaos, snarl.

Clwyd (kloō′id) A county in northern Wales; 936 sq. mi.; pop. 373,300 (1976); county seat, Mold.

Clyde (klīd) A river in SW Scotland, flowing 106 miles generally NW, to the **Firth of Clyde,** its delta.

Clyde (klīd), **Baron** See (Sir Colin) CAMPBELL.

Clyde·bank (klīd′bangk) A burgh in western Scotland, on the Clyde; pop. 49,654 (1961).

Clydes·dale (klīdz′dāl) *n.* A breed of draft horses originating in the valley of the Clyde, Scotland.

Clydesdale terrier A small terrier having a long, silky coat and related to the Skye terrier.

Cly·mer (klī′mər), **George,** 1739–1813, American patriot; signer of the Declaration of Independence.

clyp·e·ate (klip′ē·āt) *adj.* **1.** Shield-shaped. Also **clyp·e·i-**

form (klip′ē·ə·fôrm′). **2.** Having a clypeus. Also **clyp′e·at′ed.**

clyp·e·us (klip′ē·əs) *n. pl.* **clyp·e·i** (klip′ē·ī) **1.** *Entomol.* A shieldlike plate on the front part of the head of an insect. **2.** *Bot.* A band encircling the perithecium of certain fungi. [< L, shield] — **clyp′e·al** *adj.*

clys·ter (klis′tər) *n. Med.* An enema. [< OF *clystere* < Gk. *klyster* < *klyzein* to wash out, rinse]

Cly·tem·nes·tra (klī′təm·nes′trə) The wife of Agamemnon, daughter of Leda and Tyndareus. See ORESTES. Also **Cly′·taem·nes′tra.**

Cm 1. *Chem.* Curium. **2.** *Meteorol.* Cumulonimbus mammatus.

cm. or **cm** Centimeter(s).

c.m. 1. Church missionary. **2.** Circular mil. **3.** Common meter. **4.** Corresponding member. **5.** *Physics* Center of mass.

CM *Mil.* Court martial.

C.M. Master of Surgery (L *Chirurgiae Magister*).

Cmdr. Commander.

C.M.G. Companion (of the Order) of St. Michael and St. George.

cml. Commercial.

CmlC *Mil.* Chemical Corps.

Cn *Meteorol.* Cumulonimbus.

C/N or **c.n. 1.** Circular note. **2.** Credit note.

Cni·dus (nī′dəs) An ancient Greek city in SW Asia Minor.

CNO *Mil.* Chief of Naval Operations.

Cnos·sus (nos′əs) See KNOSSOS.

CNS or **C.N.S.** *Med.* Central nervous system.

Cnut (knoōt) See CANUTE.

Co *Chem.* Cobalt.

co-¹ *prefix* With; together; joint or jointly: used with verbs, nouns, adjectives, and adverbs. [< L *co-* var. of *com-* before *gn, h,* and vowels < *cum* with]

Following is a list of self-explanatory words containing the prefix *co-*:

coadequate	cocreate	coinheritor
coadminister	cocreator	coinmate
coadministration	cocreditor	coinspire
coadministrator	cocurator	cointer
coadmiration	codebtor	cointerest
coadmire	codefendant	cointersect
coadmit	codelinquent	coinventor
coadventure	coderive	coinvolve
coagency	codescendant	colaborer
coagent	codiscoverer	colegatee
coagitate	codominion	colegislator
coagitation	coeditor	colessee
coagitator	coeffect	colessor
coagriculturist	coembody	comortgagee
coambassador	coembrace	comourner
coanimate	coeminency	co-oblige
coannex	coemperor	co-occupy
coannihilate	coemploy	co-organize
coappear	coenact	co-original
coappearance	coenactor	co-owner
coappriser	coenamor	co-ownership
coapprove	coendure	coparent
coarbiter	coepiscopacy	copartner
coarrange	coequate	copassionate
coarrangement	coequation	copastor
coassessor	coerect	copatentee
coassignee	coestablish	copatron
coassist	coestablishment	copetitioner
coassistance	coexchange	coplaintiff
coassistant	coexchangeable	coplot
coassume	coexecutant	coproject
coattend	coexecutor	copromote
coattest	coexert	coproprietor
coattestation	coexertion	coredeem
coattribute	coheir	coregency
coattribution	coheritage	coregnant
coauditor	coincline	coreign
coauthor	coinclude	corejoice
coauthority	coincorporate	corenounce
coauthorship	coindemnify	coresidence
cobeliever	coindicate	corevolve
cocapital	coinfer	cosovereign
coconnection	coinhabit	cospecies
coconspirator	coinhabitant	cotenant
coconstituent	coinhere	cotrustee
cocontractor	coinheritance	

co-² *prefix* **1.** *Math.* Of the complement: *cosine.* **2.** *Astron.* Complement of: *codeclination.* [< L *co mplementum* complement]

c.o. or **c/o 1.** Care of. **2.** Carried over.

Co. or **co.** (*pl.* **cos.**) **1.** Company. **2.** County.

CO or **C.O. 1.** *Mil.* Commanding Officer. **2.** Conscientious objector.

C/O Cash order.

co·ac·er·vate (kō·as′ər·vāt′) *n. Chem.* The colloid phase in the process of coacervation: also **coazerate.**

co·ac·er·va·tion (kō·as′ər·vā′shən) *n. Chem.* The separation of certain colloids into two liquid phases by the addition of a third component that precipitates an aqueous solution: also *coazervation.*

coach (kōch) *n.* **1.** A large, four-wheeled closed carriage. **2.** A passenger bus. **3.** Air coach (which see). **4.** A railroad passenger car; especially, one having only seats and offering the cheapest travel. **5.** An enclosed, two-door automobile. **6.** A private tutor. **7.** A trainer or director in athletics, dramatics, etc. **8.** In baseball, a person standing near first or third base to advise his team's base runners. — *v.t.* **1.** To tutor or train; act as coach to. — *v.i.* **2.** To study with or be trained by a coach. **3.** To act as coach. **4.** To ride or drive in a coach. [< MF *coche* < Hung. *kocsi* (*szeker*) (*wagon*) of Kocs, the village where first used]

coach-and-four (kōch′ən-fôr′, -fōr′) *n.* A coach drawn by four horses.

coach dog A Dalmatian.

coach·man (kōch′mən) *n. pl.* **·men** (-mən) **1.** One who drives a coach. **2.** In angling, a variety of artificial fly.

coach screw A lag screw (which see).

co·act (kō·akt′) *v.t. Obs.* To compel. [< L *cogere*] — **co·ac′tion** *n.* — **co·ac′tive** *adj.* — **co·ac′tive·ly** *adv.*

coad. Coadjutor.

co·ad·ju·tant (kō·aj′ŏō-tənt) *adj.* Cooperating. — *n.* An assistant or co-worker. [< CO-[1] + L *adjutans, -antis,* ppr. of *adjutare* to help]

co·ad·ju·tor (kō·aj′ŏō-tər, kō′ə·jŏō′tər) *n.* **1.** An assistant or co-worker. **2.** In the Anglican and Roman Catholic churches, a bishop who assists a diocesan bishop and has the right to succeed him. — **co·ad′ju·tress, co·ad′ju trix** *n.fem.*

co·ad·u·nate (kō·aj′ŏō-nit, -nāt) *adj. Biol.* Closely joined, as organs or parts, especially during growth. [< LL *coadunatus,* pp. of *coadunare* to unite < L *co-* together + *ad* to + *unus* one] — **co·ad′u·na′tion** *n.* — **co·ad′u·na′tive** *adj.*

co·ae·val (kō·ē′vəl) See COEVAL.

co·ag·u·la·ble (kō·ag′yə·lə·bəl) *adj.* Capable of being coagulated. — **co·ag′u·la·bil′i·ty** *n.*

co·ag·u·lant (kō·ag′yə·lənt) *n.* A coagulating agent, as rennet. [< L *coagulans, -antis,* ppr. of *coagulare* to curdle]

co·ag·u·late (kō·ag′yə·lāt) *v.t. & v.i.* **·lat·ed, ·lat·ing** To change from a liquid into a clot or jelly, as blood. [< L *coagulatus,* pp. of *coagulare* to curdle] — **co·ag′u·la′tion** *n.* — **co·ag′u·la′tive** *adj.* — **co·ag′u·la′tor** *n.*

co·ag·u·lum (kō·ag′yə·ləm) *n. pl.* **·la** (-lə) Any coagulated mass, as a gel, curd, or clot. [< L, that which binds together]

Co·a·hui·la (kō′ä·wē′lä) A State in northern Mexico; 58,067 sq. mi.; pop. 1,140,989 (1970); capital, Saltillo.

coal (kōl) *n.* **1.** A dark brown to black, combustible mineral of variable physical and chemical composition, produced by the carbonization of prehistoric vegetation, found in beds or veins in the earth and used as fuel and a source of hydrocarbons. Its principal varieties are *bituminous coal* (soft coal), *anthracite* (hard coal), and *lignite* (brown coal). **2.** This material crushed or broken for use. Also *Brit.* **coals.** **3.** A piece of coal. **4.** A glowing or charred fragment of wood or other fuel; an ember. — **to haul** (**rake,** etc.) **over the coals** To criticize severely; reprimand. — *v.t.* **1.** To supply with coal. **2.** To reduce to charcoal; char. — *v.i.* **3.** To take on coal. [OE *col*]

Coal may appear as a combining form or as the first element in two-word phrases; as in:

coal ashes	coal-dark	coal heaver
coal barge	coal dealer	coal-laden
coalbin	coal deposit	coal mine
coal-black	coal digger	coal miner
coal-blue	coal district	coal mining
coalbox	coal dust	coalmonger
coal bunker	coalfield	coal-producing
coal-burning	coal-fired	coal-rich
coal chute	coal furnace	coalshed
coal-consuming	coal grinder	coalyard

coal·er (kō′lər) *n.* **1.** A railroad, ship, etc., that carries or supplies coal. **2.** One who supplies coal.

co·a·lesce (kō′ə·les′) *v.i.* **·lesced, ·lesc·ing** To grow or come together into one; fuse; blend. [< L *coalescere* to unite < *co-* together + *alescere,* inceptive of *alere* to grow up] — **co′a·les′cence** *n.* — **co′a·les′cent** *adj.*

coal gas **1.** The poisonous gas produced by the combustion of coal. **2.** A gas used for illuminating and heating, produced by the distillation of bituminous coal and consisting chiefly of methane, carbon monoxide, and hydrogen.

coaling station A place where ships or trains take on coal.

co·a·li·tion (kō′ə·lish′ən) *n.* **1.** An alliance of persons, parties, or states. **2.** A fusion into one mass. — **Syn.** See ALLIANCE. [< L *coalitio, -onis* < *coalescere.* See COALESCE.] — **co′a·li′tion·ist** *n.*

Coal Measures A division of the Carboniferous series containing beds of coal.

coal oil Kerosene.

coal·pit (kōl′pit′) *n.* **1.** A pit from which mineral coal is obtained. **2.** A pit for making charcoal.

coal·sack (kōl′sak′) *n. Astron.* One of several dark regions in the Milky Way composed of great masses of nonluminous

dust, especially **the Coalsack,** near the Magellanic clouds in the Southern Cross.

coal scut·tle (skut′l) *n.* A bucketlike container in which coal may be kept or carried. Also **coal hod.**

coal tar A black, viscid liquid produced in the distillation of bituminous coal, yielding a large variety of organic compounds used in making dyestuffs, explosives, flavoring extracts, drugs, plastics, etc. — **coal′-tar′** *adj.*

coam·ing (kō′ming) *n.* A curb about a hatchway or skylight, to keep water from entering. [Origin unknown]

co·arc·tate (kō·ärk′tāt) *adj.* **1.** *Bot.* Crowded together, as a panicle of flowers; compressed. **2.** *Entomol.* Constricted within the hardened larval skin. [< L *coarctatus,* pp. of *coarctare,* var. of *coartare* to confine, constrain < *co-* together + *artus* crowded] — **co·arc·ta′tion** *n.*

coarse (kôrs, kōrs) *adj.* **1.** Lacking refinement or delicacy; vulgar; low. **2.** Inferior; base; common. **3.** Composed of large parts or particles; not fine in texture. [Adjectival use of COURSE in sense "customary sequence" (as in *of course*); hence, usual, ordinary] — **coarse′ly** *adv.* — **coarse′ness** *n.* — **Syn. 1.** gross, unrefined, earthy, crude. Compare VULGAR.

coarse-grained (kôrs′grānd′, kōrs′-) *adj.* **1.** Having a coarse grain or texture. **2.** Not delicate or refined; crude.

coars·en (kôr′sən, kōr′-) *v.t. & v.i.* To make or become coarse.

coast (kōst) *n.* **1.** The land next to the sea; the seashore. **2.** *Obs.* A frontier; boundary. **3.** A slope suitable for sliding, as on a sled; also, a slide down it. — **Syn.** See SHORE[1]. — **the Coast** *U.S.* That part of the United States bordering on the Pacific Ocean. — **the coast is clear** There is no danger or difficulty now. — *v.i.* **1.** To slide down a slope by force of gravity alone, as on a sled. **2.** To continue moving on acquired momentum alone. **3.** To sail along a coast. **4.** To move or behave aimlessly. — *v.t.* **5.** To sail along, as a coast; skirt. [< OF *coste* < L *costa* rib, flank]

coast·al (kōs′təl) *adj.* Of, at, or bordering a coast.

coast artillery Artillery, fixed or movable, for defense of coasts against ships, aircraft, etc.

coast·er (kōs′tər) *n.* **1.** One who or that which coasts, as a person or vessel engaged in the coasting trade. **2.** A sled or toboggan. **3.** A roller coaster (which see). **4.** A small disk of glass, metal, etc., set under a drinking glass to protect the surface beneath. **5.** Formerly, a tray used in passing a decanter around a table.

coaster brake A clutchlike brake on a bicycle, operated by reversing the pressure on the pedals.

coast guard **1.** Naval or military coastal patrol and police. **2.** A member of this police. Abbr. *CG, C.G.* — **United States Coast Guard** A force set up to protect life and property at sea and to enforce customs, immigration, and navigation laws. It operates in wartime within the U.S. Navy and at other times under the Department of the Treasury. Abbr. *USCG, U.S.C.G.*

coast·guards·man (kōst′gärdz-mən) *n. pl.* **·men** (-mən) A member of a coast guard.

coasting trade Trade carried on by sailing from port to port along a coast. Also **coast·ing** (kōs′ting).

coast·line (kōst′līn′) *n.* The contour or boundary of a coast.

Coast Mountains A range in western British Columbia and southern Alaska; highest point, Mt. Waddington, 13,260 ft.

Coast Ranges A mountain belt of western North America, extending along the Pacific coast from Alaska to Lower California; highest peak, Mt. Logan, 19,850 ft., the second highest peak on the continent.

coast·ward (kōst′wərd) *adj.* Directed or facing toward the coast. — *adv.* Toward the coast: also **coast′wards.**

coast·wise (kōst′wīz′) *adj.* Following, along, or sailing along the coast. — *adv.* By way of or along the coast: also **coast′ways′** (-wāz′).

coat (kōt) *n.* **1.** A sleeved outer garment for the upper part of the body, as the jacket of a suit, or an overcoat or topcoat. **2.** A natural covering or integument, as the fur of an animal, the rind of a melon, etc. **3.** Any layer covering a surface, as paint, ice, etc. **4.** *Dial.* A skirt; petticoat. **5.** *Obs.* The distinctive garb of an order, profession, etc.; cloth. — *v.t.* **1.** To cover with a surface layer, as of paint. **2.** To provide with a coat. [< OF *cote*; ult. origin uncertain] — **coat′less** *adj.*

coat·ed (kō′tid) *adj.* **1.** Having a covering, outer layer, or coat. **2.** In papermaking, having a smooth calendered surface of additional matter, as sizing or china clay.

coat·ee (kō·tē′) *n. Archaic* A short, tight-fitting coat.

Coates (kōts), **Albert,** 1882–1954, English conductor born in Russia. — **Eric,** 1886–1957, English composer. — **Joseph Gordon,** 1878–1943, New Zealand statesman; premier 1925–1928.

co·a·ti (kō·ä′tē) *n. pl.* **·tis** (-tēz) Any of various carnivorous, raccoonlike mammals (genus *Nasua*) of tropical America, with mobile snout, plantigrade feet, and a long, ringed tail. Also **co·a′ti·mon′di** (-mun′dē), **co·a′ti·mun′di** (-mun′·dē). [< Tupi]

coat·ing (kō′ting) *n.* **1.** A covering layer; coat. **2.** Cloth for coats.

coat of arms 1. A tabard or other coat blazoned with the armorial bearings of a person or family. **2.** A representation of armorial bearings; a blazon.

coat of mail *pl.* **coats of mail** A defensive garment made of chain mail; a hauberk.

coat·tail (kōt′tāl′) *n.* The loose, back part of a coat below the waist; also, either half of this in a coat split at the back.

coax (kōks) *v.t.* **1.** To persuade or seek to persuade by gentleness, tact, flattery, etc.; wheedle. **2.** To obtain by coaxing: to *coax* a promise from someone. — *v.i.* **3.** To use persuasion or cajolery. — *n.* One who coaxes. [< earlier *cokes* a fool, dupe; ult. origin unknown] — **coax′er** *n.* — **coax′ing·ly** *adv.*
— **Syn.** (*verb*) **1.** cajole, blandish.

co·ax·i·al (kō-ak′sē-əl) *adj.* **1.** Having a common axis or coincident axes. Also **co·ax·al** (kō-ak′səl). **2.** Describing a cable consisting of two or more insulated conductors enclosed within a protective sheath and capable of operating singly or in combination to transmit radio or television signals or of multiple telegraph or telephone messages. [< CO-¹ + AXIAL]

co·az·er·vate (kō-az′ər·vāt′) See COACERVATE.

co·az·er·va·tion (kō-az′ər·vā′shən) See COACERVATION.

cob¹ (kob) *n.* **1.** A corncob. **2.** A male swan. **3.** A thickset horse with short legs. **4.** A roundish mass or lump, as of coal. **5.** *Brit. Dial.* A great man; a leader. [ME *cobbe*; origin uncertain]

cob² (kob) *n.* A gull, especially the great black-backed gull (*Larus marinus*). Also **cobb.** [Cf. Du. *kobbe* gull]

co·bal·a·min (kō·bôl′ə·min) *n. Biochem.* Vitamin B₁₂. [< COBAL(T) + (VIT)AMIN]

co·balt (kō′bôlt) *n.* A tough, lustrous, pinkish gray, metallic element (symbol Co) related to iron and nickel, and seldom found in the free state. It is used as an alloy and in pigments. See ELEMENT. [< G *kobalt,* var. of *kobold* goblin; so called by early miners who thought it a worthless, injurious ore]

cobalt bloom Erythrite (def. 1).

cobalt blue 1. A permanent, deep blue pigment, made from oxides of cobalt and aluminum. **2.** An intense blue.

co·bal·tic (kō·bôl′tik) *adj. Chem.* Designating a compound containing cobalt in its higher valence.

co·bal·tite (kō·bôl′tīt, kō′bôl·tīt) *n.* A metallic, silver-white, brittle cobalt sulfide of arsenic, CoAsS. Also **co·balt·ine** (kō′bôl·tēn, -tin).

co·bal·tous (kō·bôl′təs) *adj. Chem.* Designating a compound containing cobalt in its lower valence.

Cobb (kob), **Irvin S**(hrewsbury), 1876–1944, U.S. humorist. — **Ty,** 1886–1961, U.S. baseball player: full name **Tyrus Raymond Cobb.**

Cob·bett (kob′it), **William,** 1762–1835, English pamphleteer and politician: pseudonym **Peter Porcupine.**

cob·ble¹ (kob′əl) *n.* **1.** A cobblestone. **2.** *pl.* Cob coal (which see). — *v.t.* **·bled, ·bling** To pave with cobblestones. [Akin to COB¹]

cob·ble² (kob′əl) *v.t.* **·bled, ·bling 1.** To make or repair, as boots or shoes. **2.** To put together roughly. [Origin uncertain]

cob·bler¹ (kob′lər) *n.* **1.** One who patches boots and shoes; a shoemaker. **2.** *Archaic* A clumsy workman. [< COBBLE²]

cob·bler² (kob′lər) *n.* **1.** An iced drink made of wine, sugar, fruit juices, etc. **2.** *U.S.* A deep-dish fruit pie with no bottom crust. [Origin unknown]

cob·ble·stone (kob′əl·stōn′) *n.* A naturally rounded stone, formerly used for paving. [< COBBLE¹ + STONE]

cob coal A large, round piece of coal; also, coal in such pieces.

Cob·den (kob′dən), **Richard,** 1804–65, English statesman and political economist.

co·bel·lig·er·ent (kō′bə·lij′ər·ənt) *n.* A country waging war in cooperation with another or others, but not bound by an alliance. [< CO-¹ + BELLIGERENT]

Côbh (kōv) An urban district and port in SW Ireland; pop. about 6,000: formerly *Queenstown.*

Cob·ham (kob′əm), **Lord,** died 1417, Sir John Oldcastle, English Lollard leader.

co·bi·a (kō′bē·ə) *n.* The sergeant fish (def. 1).

co·ble (kō′bəl, kob′əl) *n.* **1.** *Brit.* A flat-bottomed fishing boat having a lugsail. **2.** *Scot.* A flat-bottomed rowboat. [OE (Northumbrian) *cuopl,* < L *caupulus,* ? < Celtic]

Co·blenz (kō′blents) See KOBLENZ.

cob·nut (kob′nut′) *n.* **1.** A large nut from a cultivated variety of hazel tree (*Corylus avellana grandis*). **2.** The tree producing such nuts. [< COB¹ (def. 4) + NUT]

co·bra (kō′brə) *n.* Any of a genus (*Naja*) of very venomous snakes of Asia and Africa that when excited can dilate their necks into a broad hood; especially, the **spectacled cobra** (*N. naja*) of India, and the **king cobra** (*Ophiophagus hannah*). [< Pg. < L *colubra* snake]

co·bra-de-ca·pel·lo (kō′brə·dē·kə·pel′ō) *n. pl.* **co·bras-de-ca·pel·lo** The spectacled cobra. See under COBRA. [< Pg., snake with a hood]

cob·web (kob′web′) *n.* **1.** The network of fine thread spun by a spider; also, a single thread of this. **2.** Something like a cobweb in flimsiness, or in its ability to ensnare. — *v.t.* **·webbed, ·web·bing** To cover with or as with cobwebs. [ME *coppeweb* < *coppe* spider + WEB] — **cob′web′by** *adj.*

co·ca (kō′kə) *n.* **1.** The dried leaves of a South American shrub (genus *Erythroxylon*), yielding cocaine and other alkaloids and sometimes chewed for their stimulant properties. **2.** Either of the two species of this shrub (*E. coca* or *E. truxillense*). [< Sp. < Quechua]

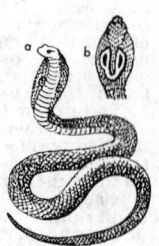
COBRA
a Indian or spectacled cobra. *b* Markings or "spectacles" on back of head. (To 6 feet long)

co·caine (kō·kān′, kō′kān; *in technical usage* kō′kə·ēn) *n.* A white, bitter, crystalline alkaloid, C₁₇H₂₁NO₄, contained in coca leaves, used in medicine as a local anesthetic and as a narcotic. Also **co·cain′** (kō·kān′, kō′kān, kō′kə·ēn). [< COCA + -INE²]

co·cain·ism (kō·kā′niz·əm, kō′kə·niz′əm) *n. Pathol.* An abnormal condition caused by the excessive use of cocaine.

co·cain·ize (kō·kā′nīz, kō′kə·nīz) *v.t.* **·ized, ·iz·ing** To bring under the specific effect of cocaine. — **co·cain′i·za′tion** *n.*

coc·cal (kok′əl) *adj.* Of, having to do with, or like a coccus.

cocci- *combining form* Berry; berry-shaped. [< Gk. *kokkos* berry, seed]

coc·cid (kok′sid) *n. Entomol.* Any member of a superfamily (*Coccoidea*) of hemipterous insects, including mealybugs and scale insects. [< NL *Coccidae,* former insect family name < Gk. *kokkos* berry]

coc·cid·i·oi·dal granuloma (kok-sid′ē·oid′l) A disease caused by a fungus (genus *Coccidioides*) and superficially resembling tuberculosis, affecting the lymph nodes of some animals including man. [< NL *Coccidioides* < Gk. *kokkos* berry + *eidos* form]

coc·cid·i·o·sis (kok-sid′ē·ō′sis) *n.* One of a group of specific infectious diseases caused by protozoan parasites (order *Coccidiomorpha*) that attack the epithelial tissue of animals, birds, and, rarely, man. [< NL *Coccidia,* a protozoan order (< Gk. *kokkos* a berry) + -OSIS]

coc·cif·er·ous (kok-sif′ər·əs) *adj. Bot.* Bearing or producing berries. [< COCCI- + -FEROUS]

coc·coid (kok′oid) *adj. Bacteriol.* Like a coccus, as certain forms of bacteria.

coc·co·lith (kok′ə·lith) *n. Geol.* A minute oval or rounded calcareous body often found in deep-sea mud. [< Gk. *kokkos* berry + -LITH]

coc·cus (kok′əs) *n. pl.* **coc·ci** (kok′sī) **1.** *Bot.* **a** One of the dry, one-seeded portions into which a schizocarp splits. **b** A spore mother cell in which the spores are contained for a time after maturity. **2.** *Bacteriol.* One of the principal forms of bacteria, characterized by an ovoid or spherical shape: often used in combination, as *streptococcus.* For illustration see BACTERIUM. **3.** *Entomol.* One of a genus (*Coccus*) of scale insects. [< NL < Gk. *kokkos* berry]

-coccus *combining form* Berry-shaped. [< Gk. *kokkos* berry, seed]

coc·cyx (kok′siks) *n. pl.* **coc·cy·ges** (kok-sī′jēz) *Anat.* The small triangular bone consisting of four or five rudimentary vertebrae at the caudal end of the spine. For illustration see PELVIS. [< L < Gk. *kokkyx* cuckoo; from a fancied resemblance to a cuckoo's bill] — **coc·cyg·e·al** (kok-sij′ē·əl) *adj.*

Co·cha·bam·ba (kō′chä·bäm′bä) A department of central Bolivia; 21,479 sq. mi.; pop. 741,100 (1969); capital, **Cochabamba,** pop. 157,000 (1962).

Co·chin (kō′chin, koch′in) *n.* A variety of large domestic fowl, of Asian origin, having heavily feathered legs. Also **Cochin china.** [after *Cochin China*]

Co·chin China (kō′chin) A former French colony on the southern Indochina peninsula; 24,750 sq. mi.; since 1949 part of South Vietnam: *French* **Co·chin·chine** (kô′shän·shēn′).

coch·i·neal (koch′ə·nēl′, koch′ə·nēl) *n.* A brilliant scarlet dye prepared from the dried bodies of the female *Dactylopius coccus,* a scale insect of tropical America and Java. [< F *cochenille* < Sp. *cochinilla* < L *coccineus* scarlet < *coccus* a berry, grain of kermes < Gk. *kokkos*]

coch·le·a (kok′lē·ə) *n. pl.* **·le·ae** (-lī·ē) *Anat.* A spirally wound tube in the internal ear, forming an essential part of the mechanism of hearing. For illustration see EAR. [< L, snail] — **coch′le·ar** *adj.*

coch·le·ate (kok′lē·āt) *adj.* Spirally twisted like a snail shell. Also **coch′le·at·ed.**

co·ci·ne·ra (kō′sē·nā′rä) *n. SW U.S.* A cook. [< Sp.]

cock¹ (kok) *n.* **1.** A full-grown male of the domestic fowl; a rooster. **2.** Any male bird. **3.** A leader; champion. **4.** A weathercock (which see). **5.** A faucet, often with the nozzle bent downward. **6.** In a firearm, the hammer; also, the condition of readiness for firing. **7.** A significant jaunty tip or upward turn, as of a hat brim. — *v.t.* **1.** To set the mechanism of (a firearm) so as to be ready for firing. **2.** To turn up or to one side alertly, jauntily, or inquiringly, as the head, eye, ears, etc. **3.** To bring to a position of readiness: He *cocked* his fist. — *v.i.* **4.** To cock a firearm. **5.** To stick up prominently. — *adj.* Male: a *cock* lobster. [OE *cocc*]

cock² (kok) *n.* A conical pile of straw or hay. — *v.t.* To arrange in piles or cocks, as hay. [< ON *kökkr* lump, heap]

cock·ade (kok-ād′) *n.* A rosette, knot of ribbon, or the like, worn on the hat, lapel, etc., as a badge or ornament. [< MF *coquarde* saucy, pert < *coq* cock] — **cock·ad′ed** *adj.*

Cockade State Nickname of MARYLAND.

cock-a-doo·dle-doo (kok′ə-dōōd′l-dōō′) *n.* The characteristic crow of a rooster. [Imit.]

cock-a-hoop (kok′ə-hōōp′, -hōōp′) *adj.* **1.** Elated; exultant. **2.** Boastful. [Origin uncertain]

cock-a-leek·ie (kok′ə-lē′kē) *n. Scot.* Soup made from chicken boiled with leeks. Also **cock′a·leek′ie, cock′ie·leek′ie.**

cock-a-lo·rum (kok′ə-lôr′əm, -lō′rəm) *n. Informal* A self-important little fellow. [Cf. Du. *kockeloeren* to crow]

cock·a·ma·mie (kok′ə-mā′mē) *adj. U.S. Slang* **1.** Ludicrous or wildly improbable; harebrained. **2.** Inferior or trifling. Also **cock′a·ma′my.** [Alter. of DECALCOMANIA]

cock-and-bull story (kok′ən-bōōl′) A highly improbable, absurd tale or account.

cock·a·tiel (kok′ə-tēl′) *n.* A crested parrot (*Leptolophus hollandicus*) of Australia. Also **cock′a·teel′.** [< Du. *kaketielje*]

cock·a·too (kok′ə-tōō′, kok′ə-tōō) *n. pl.* **-toos** Any of various brightly colored, crested parrots of the East Indies or Australia, especially one of the genus *Kakatoë.* [< Du. *kaketoe* < Malay *kakatūa*; infl. in form by COCK¹]

CRESTED COCKATOO (About 12 inches high)

cock·a·trice (kok′ə-tris) *n.* **1.** A fabulous serpent, said to be hatched from a cock's egg, deadly to those who felt its breath or met its glance. Compare BASILISK. **2.** In the Bible an unidentified species of deadly serpent. [< OF *cocatris* (infl. by *coq* cock) < Med.L *calcatrix,* lit. hunter, tracer, trans. of Gk. *ichneumōn.* See ICHNEUMON.]

cock·boat (kok′bōt) *n.* A ship's small rowboat: also called **cockle boat.** [< obs. *cock* (< MF *coque* small boat) + BOAT]

cock·chaf·er (kok′chā′fər) *n.* Any of a widely distributed group of scarabaeid beetles, especially a large European variety (*Melolontha melolontha*) destructive to vegetation. [< COCK¹ (def. 3) because of its size + CHAFER]

cock·crow (kok′krō′) *n.* Early morning.

cocked hat (kokt) A hat with the brim turned up, especially in three places; a tricorn. — **to knock into a cocked hat** To demolish or make impossible, as a theory or plan; ruin.

cock·er¹ (kok′ər) *n.* **1.** A cocker spaniel. **2.** One who keeps or matches gamecocks or attends cockfights.

cock·er² (kok′ər) *v.t.* To spoil by indulgence; coddle. [Appar. related to obs. *cockle* to cherish < Scand. or LG. Cf. Norw. *kokla* to fuss over, Du. *kokelen* to pamper.]

cock·er·el (kok′ər-əl) *n.* A cock less than a year old. [Dim. of COCK¹]

cocker spaniel A small, sturdy spaniel of solid or variegated coloring, used for hunting and as a house pet. [? Because used in hunting woodcock]

cock·eye (kok′ī) *n.* A squinting eye. [< COCK¹, v. + EYE]

cockeye bob *Austral. Slang* A willy-nilly² (def. 1).

cock·eyed (kok′īd′) *adj.* **1.** Cross-eyed. **2.** *Slang* Off center; askew. **3.** *Slang* Absurd; ridiculous. **4.** *Slang* Drunk.

cock·fight (kok′fīt′) *n.* A fight between gamecocks that are usually fitted with steel spurs. — **cock′fight′ing** *adj. & n.*

cock·horse (kok′hôrs′) *n.* A rocking horse or hobbyhorse.

cock·i·ness (kok′ē-nis) *n. Informal* Pert or swaggering self-assurance.

cock·ish (kok′ish) *adj.* Cocklike; cocky. — **cock′ish·ly** *adv.* — **cock′ish·ness** *n.*

cock·le¹ (kok′əl) *n.* **1.** A European bivalve mollusk (genus *Cardium*), especially the edible *C. edule,* with ridged, somewhat heart-shaped shells. **2.** Any of various similar mollusks. **3.** A cockleshell. **4.** A wrinkle; pucker. — **the cockles of one's heart** The depths of one's heart or feelings. — *v.t. & v.i.* **-led, ·ling** To wrinkle; pucker. [< F *coquille,* ult. < L *conchylium* shell < Gk. *konchylion,* dim. of *konchē* a shell, mussel]

cock·le² (kok′əl) *n.* A weed that grows among grain, as the darnel. [OE *coccel*]

cock·le·boat (kok′əl-bōt′) *n.* A cockboat (which see).

cock·le·bur (kok′əl-bûr′) *n.* **1.** A coarse, branching weed (genus *Xanthium*) of the composite family, having burs about an inch long. **2.** The burdock. [< COCKLE² + BUR]

cock·le·shell (kok′əl-shel′) *n.* **1.** The shell of a cockle. **2.** A scallop shell; especially, one valve of a scallop shell worn in a pilgrim's hat. **3.** A frail, light boat. [< COCKLE¹ + SHELL]

cock·loft (kok′lôft′, -loft′) *n.* A loft or attic under a roof. [Origin uncertain]

cock·ney (kok′nē) *n.* **1.** *Often cap.* A resident of the East End of London; traditionally, one born within the sound of the bells of St. Mary-le-Bow Church. **2.** The dialect or accent of East End Londoners: also **cock′ney·ese′** (-ēz′, -ēs′). — *adj.* Of or like cockneys or their speech. [ME *cokeney,* lit., cock's egg < *coken* cock's + OE *æg* egg; later, a pampered child, a soft person, a city man] — **cock′ney·ish** *adj.*

cock·ney·fy (kok′ni-fī) *v.t.* **·fied, ·fy·ing** To cause to resemble a cockney in speech or manners.

cock·ney·ism (kok′nē-iz′əm) *n.* **1.** A mannerism, idiom, or way of speaking peculiar to cockneys. **2.** The writings or literary characteristics of John Keats, Leigh Hunt, etc.: so called by their contemporary detractors.

cock of the walk **1.** The leader or chief. **2.** One who is inordinately proud and self-assured.

cock-of-the-rock (kok′əv-thə-rok′) *n.* A bird (*Rupicola rupicola*) of tropical South America, having brilliant orange plumage and a rounded crest. Also **cock of the rock.**

cock·pit (kok′pit′) *n.* **1.** An open or covered compartment in the fuselage of some airplanes, where the pilot and copilot sit. **2.** A pit or ring for cockfighting. **3.** A scene of many battles or contests. **4.** *Naut.* **a** In small vessels, a space toward the stern lower than the rest of the deck. **b** In old warships, an apartment below the water line for junior officers or, during an action, for care of the wounded. **5.** *Obs.* The pit of a theater.

cock·roach (kok′rōch′) *n.* Any of a large group of swift-running, chiefly nocturnal insects (families *Blattidae* and *Phyllodromidae*) of world-wide distribution, many of which are household pests, having flat, oval bodies, biting mouth parts, and a typically offensive odor; especially, the Croton bug, the dark brown **Oriental cockroach** (*Blatta orientalis*) and the large, winged **American cockroach** (*Periplaneta americana*). For illustration see INSECTS (injurious). [< Sp. *cucaracha*]

cocks·comb (koks′kōm′) *n.* **1.** The comb of a cock. **2.** A plant (genus *Celosia*) with showy red or yellowish flowers. **3.** A jester's cap, surmounted with a scalloped scarlet ridge. **4.** A coxcomb (def. 1). Also spelled *coxcomb.*

cock·shut (kok′shut′) *n. Obs.* or *Brit. Dial.* Nightfall; twilight.

cock·shy (kok′shī′) *n. pl.* **·shies** *Brit.* **1.** A mark to be shied or thrown at, as at fairs. **2.** A throw, as at a mark. [< COCK¹, n. + SHY², v.]

cock·spur (kok′spûr′) *n.* **1.** A spur on the leg of a cock. **2.** A kind of hawthorn (*Crataegus crusgalli*) with long thorns.

cock·sure (kok′shoor′) *adj.* **1.** Absolutely sure. **2.** Overly self-confident; presumptuously sure. — **cock′sure′ness** *n.*

cock·swain (kok′sən, -swān′) See COXSWAIN.

cock·tail¹ (kok′tāl′) *n.* **1.** Any of various chilled alcoholic drinks, consisting usually of brandy, whisky, gin, etc., mixed with other liquors, fruit juice, etc. **2.** An appetizer, as chilled, diced fruits, fruit juices, or seafood seasoned with sauce. [? Alter. of F *coquetel,* a mixed drink popular in the 18th c.]

cock·tail² (kok′tāl′) *n.* **1.** A horse with a docked tail. **2.** An underbred horse. **3.** A person of low breeding who pretends to be a gentleman. [< COCK¹ to stick up prominently + TAIL; with ref. to the appearance of a horse's docked tail]

cock·up (kok′up′) *n.* **1.** An upturned or cocked part or point of anything. **2.** A hat or cap turned up in front.

cock·y (kok′ē) *adj.* **cock·i·er, cock·i·est** *Informal* Pertly or swaggeringly self-confident; conceited. — **cock′i·ly** *adv.* — **Syn.** jaunty, chipper, perky, arrogant, vain, swaggering.

co·co (kō′kō) *n. pl.* **·cos** **1.** The coconut palm. **2.** The fruit of the coconut palm. — *adj.* Made of the fiber of the coconut. [< Pg., grinning face; with ref. to the appearance of the eyes of a coconut]

co·coa (kō′kō) *n.* **1.** A powder made from the roasted, husked seed kernels of the cacao; chocolate. **2.** A beverage made from this. **3.** The light, reddish brown color of cocoa powder. [Alter. of CACAO]

cocoa butter A hard, yellowish, fatty substance obtained from cacao seeds, used for making soap, cosmetics, etc.: also called *cacao butter.*

coco grass Nut grass (which see).

co·con·scious (kō-kon′shəs) *n. Psychol.* The aggregate of mental processes dissociated from those of the dominant personality. Also **co·con′scious·ness.** — *adj.* Of or pertaining to the coconscious. — **co·con′scious·ly** *adv.*

co·co·nut (kō′kə-nut′, -nət) *n.* The fruit of the coconut palm, a large seed having white meat enclosed in a hard shell, and containing a milky liquid. Also **co′coa·nut′.**

coconut milk The milky fluid contained within the fresh coconut.

coconut oil The oil derived from the dried meat of the coconut, used in soaps, foodstuffs, etc.

coconut palm A tropical palm tree (*Cocos nucifera*) of wide distribution, bearing coconuts: also called *coco.* Also **coco palm, coconut tree.**

co·coon (kə·kōōn′) *n.* **1.** The envelope spun by the larvae of certain insects, as silkworms, in which they are enclosed in the pupal or chrysalis state. **2.** Any of various analogous structures, as the egg case of spiders, earthworms, etc. **3.** *Mil.* A weatherproof covering of cellophane or quick drying synthetic resin in which equipment may be sealed during transport or when not in use. [< F *cocon* < *coque* shell]

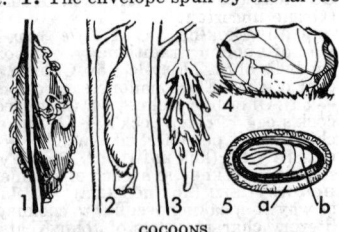

COCOONS
1. Cecropia moth. 2. Promethea moth. 3. Bagworm. 4. Polyphemus moth. 5. Bollworm (cross section): *a* Cocoon, *b* Pupa.

Co·cos Islands (kō′kōs) An island group SW of Java, a dependency of Australia; 5 sq. mi.; pop. 650 (est. 1959): also *Keeling Islands.* Also **Co′cos-Kee′ling** (-kē′ling).

co·cotte (kō·kot′, kə-) *n.* A loose woman; prostitute. [< F]

Coc·teau (kok·tō′), **Jean,** 1889–1963, French dramatist, novelist, critic, and poet.

Co·cy·tus (kō·sī′təs) In Greek mythology one of the rivers of Hades, a tributary of the Acheron.

cod[1] (kod) *n. pl.* **cod** or **cods** **1.** An important food fish (*Gadus callarias*) of the North Atlantic: also called *codfish.* **2.** Any gadoid fish. [Origin unknown]

cod[2] (kod) *n.* **1.** *Dial.* A pod or husk. **2.** *Obs.* A bag or envelope. **3.** *Scot.* A pillow or cushion. [OE *codd* bag]

Cod (kod), **Cape** A peninsula of SE Massachusetts projecting 65 miles into the Atlantic and enclosing Cape Cod Bay.

Cod. or **cod.** (*pl.* **Codd.** or **codd.**) Codex.

C.O.D. or **c.o.d.** **1.** Cash on delivery. **2.** Collect on delivery.

co·da (kō′də) *n. Music* A passage at the end of a composition or movement that brings it to a formal, complete close. [< Ital. < L *cauda* tail]

cod·der (kod′ər) *n. Canadian* A cod fisherman or his boat.

cod·dle (kod′l) *v.t.* **·dled, ·dling** **1.** To boil gently; simmer in water. **2.** To treat as a baby or an invalid; pamper. [? Akin to CAUDLE] —**cod′dler** *n.*

code (kōd) *n.* **1.** A systematized body of law. **2.** Any system of principles or regulations. **3.** A set of signals, characters, or symbols used in communication, as the Morse code. **4.** A set of symbols with arbitrary, prearranged meaning, as words, letters, or numerals, used for secrecy or brevity in transmitting messages. Compare CIPHER (*n.* def. 3). **5.** A message in code. —**civil code** A code regulating the civil relations of citizens. —**criminal** (or **penal**) **code** A code defining crimes and prescribing the method and degree of punishment. —*v.t.* **cod·ed, cod·ing** **1.** To systematize, as laws; make a digest of. **2.** To put into the symbols of a code. [< F < L *codex* writing tablet]

co·dec·li·na·tion (kō′dek·lə·nā′shən) *n. Astron.* The complement of the angle of declination: also called *polar distance.*

co·deine (kō′dēn, kō′di·ēn) *n. Chem.* A white crystalline alkaloid, $C_{18}H_{21}NO_3$, derived from morphine and used in medicine as a mild narcotic. Also **co·de·in** (kō′dē·in, kō′dēn), **co·de·ia** (kō·dē′ə). [< Gk. *kōdeia* head of a poppy + -INE[2]]

Code Na·po·lé·on (kōd nà·pō·lā·ôn′) The body of French civil law, put in force by Napoleon Bonaparte between 1804 and 1807.

co·dex (kō′deks) *n. pl.* **co·di·ces** (kō′də·sēz, kod′ə-) **1.** An ancient manuscript volume, as of Scripture. **2.** *Obs.* A code of laws. [< L, writing tablet]

Co·dex Ju·ris Ca·non·i·ci (kō′deks jŏŏr′is kə·non′ə·sī) A compilation of legislation of the Roman Catholic Church, in effect since 1918.

cod·fish (kod′fish′) *n.* The cod or its edible flesh.

codg·er (koj′ər) *n. Informal* An eccentric or testy man, especially an old one. [Prob. var. of *cadger.* See CADGE.]

cod hauler *Canadian Slang* A Newfoundlander.

co·di·ces (kō′də·sēz, kod′ə-) Plural of CODEX.

cod·i·cil (kod′ə·səl) *n.* **1.** *Law* A supplement to a will, changing or explaining something in it. **2.** An appendix; addition. [< L *codicillus,* dim. of *codex* writing tablet] —**cod·i·cil·la·ry** (kod′ə·sil′ər·ē) *adj.*

cod·i·fy (kod′ə·fī, kō′də-) *v.t.* **·fied, ·fy·ing** To systematize, as laws. [< F *codifier* < *code* system, code] —**cod′i·fi·ca′tion** *n.* —**cod′i·fi′er** *n.*

cod·ling[1] (kod′ling) *n. pl.* **·lings** (*Rare* **·ling**) **1.** A young cod. **2.** A gadoid fish (genus *Phycis*) with filamentous ventral fins of two or three rays; a hake. [Dim. of COD[1]]

cod·ling[2] (kod′ling) *n.* **1.** One of a variety of elongated, tapering cooking apples. **2.** Any hard, unripe apple for stewing. Also **cod·lin** (kod′lin). [ME *querdling;* origin uncertain]

codling moth A moth (*Carpocapsa pomonella*) whose larvae feed on the interior of apples, pears, quinces, etc. Also **codlin moth.** For illustration see INSECTS (injurious).

cod-liver oil (kod′liv′ər, kod′liv′ər) Oil from the livers of cod, used in medicine as a source of vitamins A and D.

cod·piece (kod′pēs′) *n.* A bag or flap covering an opening in the front of the tight breeches worn by men in the 15th and 16th centuries. [ME *cod* scrotum + PIECE]

Co·dy (kō′dē), **William Frederick,** 1846–1917, U.S. plainsman, army scout, and showman: called *Buffalo Bill.*

co·ed (kō′ed′) *Informal n.* A woman student at a coeducational institution. —*adj.* Coeducational. Also **co-ed′.**

co·ed·u·ca·tion (kō′ej·oō·kā′shən) *n.* The education of both sexes in the same classes or institution. [< CO-[1] + EDUCATION] —**co′ed·u·ca′tion·al** *adj.*

coef. or **coeff.** Coefficient.

co·ef·fi·cient (kō′ə·fish′ənt) *n.* **1.** *Math.* A number or letter put before an algebraic expression and multiplying it. **2.** *Physics* A number indicating the kind and amount of change in a substance, body, or process under given conditions. —*adj.* Acting together. [< CO-[1] + EFFICIENT]

coe·la·canth (sē′lə·kanth) *n. Zool.* A large-bodied, hollow-spined crossopterygian fish, extinct except for one species, *Latimeria chalumnae.* [< COEL(O)- + Gk. *akantha* spine]

-coele Var. of -CELE[2].

coe·len·ter·ate (si·len′tə·rāt) *Zool. n.* Any of a phylum (*Coelenterata*) of invertebrate animals having a cavity occupying the entire interior of the body and functioning as a vascular as well as a digestive system, including sea anemones, corals, jellyfish, and hydras. —*adj.* Belonging or pertaining to the *Coelenterata.* [< COEL(O)- + Gk. *enteron* intestine] —**coe·len·ter·ic** (sē′len·ter′ik) *adj.*

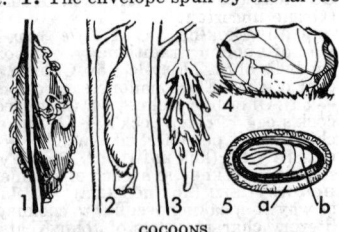

COELACANTH (4 to 5½ feet long)

coe·len·ter·on (si·len′tə·ron) *n. pl.* **·ter·a** (-tər·ə) *Zool.* The primitive intestinal cavity of coelenterates. [< NL]

coe·li·ac (sē′lē·ak) See CELIAC.

coelo- *combining form* Cavity; cavity of the body, or of an organ. Also, before vowels, **coel-.** [< Gk. *koilos* hollow]

coe·lom (sē′ləm) *n. Zool.* The body cavity of a metazoan, between the viscera and the body wall: also spelled *celom.* Also **coe·lome** (sē′lōm). [< Gk. *koilōma* cavity < *koilos* hollow]

coe·lo·stat (sē′lə·stat) *n. Astron.* A mirror so mounted and driven as to reflect the same celestial image continuously to the eyepiece of a fixed telescope. [< L *caelum, coelum* heaven + *status* a standing < *stare* to stand]

co·empt (kō·empt′) *v.t.* To obtain control of (a market, prices, etc.) by coemption.

co·emp·tion (kō·emp′shən) *n.* The buying up of the entire available supply of a commodity. [< L *coemptio, -onis* < *coemere* to buy up < *co-* completely + *emere* to buy]

coe·nes·the·sia (sē′nis·thē′zhə, -zhē·ə, sen′is-) See CENESTHESIA.

coeno- See CENO-.

coe·no·bite (sen′ə·bīt, sē′nə-) See CENOBITE.

coe·no·cyte (sē′nə·sit, sen′ə-) *n. Bot.* An aggregation of protoplasmic units enclosed within a common wall, exemplified in the lower algae and fungi. [< COENO- + -CYTE]

coe·no·gen·e·sis (sē′nə·jen′ə·sis, sen′ə-) See CENOGENESIS.

coe·nu·rus (si·nyŏŏr′əs) *n.* The larval state of various tapeworms (genus *Multiceps*), especially of one that causes the gid in sheep. Also **coe·nure** (sē′nyŏŏr). [< COEN(O)- + Gk. *oura* tail]

co·en·zyme (kō·en′zīm, -zim) *n. Biochem.* Any substance required to promote the effective functioning of certain enzymes. [< CO-[1] + ENZYME]

co·e·qual (kō·ē′kwəl) *adj.* Of the same value, age, size, etc. —*n.* The equal of another or others. [< CO-[1] + EQUAL] —**co·e·qual·i·ty** (kō′i·kwol′ə·tē) *n.* —**co·e′qual·ly** *adv.*

co·erce (kō·ûrs′) *v.t.* **·erced, ·erc·ing** **1.** To compel by force, law, authority, or fear. **2.** To restrain or repress by superior force. **3.** To bring about by forcible measures: to *coerce* compliance. [< L *coercere* < *co-* together + *arcere* to shut up, restrain] —**co·er′cer** *n.* —**co·er′ci·ble** *adj.*

co·er·cion (kō·ûr′shən) *n.* **1.** Forcible constraint or restraint, moral or physical. **2.** Government by force. —**co·er·cion·ar·y** (kō·ûr′shən·er′ē) *adj.* —**co·er′cion·ist** *n.*

co·er·cive (kō·ûr′siv) *adj.* Serving or tending to coerce. —**co·er′cive·ly** *adv.* —**co·er′cive·ness** *n.*

coercive force See under FORCE.

co·es·sen·tial (kō′i·sen′shəl) *adj.* Having the same essence; united in being. [< CO-[1] + ESSENTIAL]

co·e·ta·ne·ous (kō′i·tā′nē·əs) *adj.* Originating at the same time; of equal age; contemporary. [< LL *coaetaneus* < L *co-* together + *aetas* age] —**co′e·ta′ne·ous·ly** *adv.* —**co′e·ta′ne·ous·ness** *n.*

co·e·ter·nal (kō′i·tûr′nəl) *adj.* Equally eternal; eternally existing together. [< CO-[1] + ETERNAL] —**co′e·ter′nal·ly** *adv.*

co·e·ter·ni·ty (kō′i·tûr′nə·tē) *n.* Existence with another or others for eternity.

Coeur de Li·on (kûr′də lē′ən) See RICHARD I.

co·e·val (kō·ē′vəl) *adj.* **1.** Of or belonging to the same age, time, or duration. **2.** Contemporary. —**Syn.** See CONTEMPORANEOUS. —*n.* **1.** One of the same age. **2.** A contemporary. Also spelled *coaeval.* [< LL *coaevus* < L *co-* together + *aevum* age] —**co·e′val·ly** *adv.*

co·ex·ist (kō'ig·zist') *v.i.* To exist together, in or at the same place or time. [< co-¹ + EXIST] **— co'ex·ist'ent** *adj.*
co·ex·ist·ence (kō'ig·zis'təns) *n.* **1.** The state of existing together. **2.** The simultaneous existence, through a policy of mutual noninterference, of two or more nations or societies differing widely in ideology.
co·ex·tend (kō'ik·stend') *v.t. & v.i.* To extend through the same space or time. [< CO-¹ + EXTEND] **— co'ex·ten'sion** *n.*
co·ex·ten·sive (kō'ik·sten'siv) *adj.* Having the same limits or extent; having equal extension. **— co'ex·ten'sive·ly** *adv.*
C. of C. Chamber of Commerce.
coff (kof) *v.t.* **coft, coff·ing** *Scot.* To buy.
cof·fee (kôf'ē, kof'ē) *n.* **1.** A beverage made from the roasted and ground seeds or beans found in the dark, berrylike fruit (**coffee berries**) of a tropical evergreen shrub (genus *Coffea*). **2.** The seeds or beans of this shrub: also **coffee beans. 3.** The shrub itself, native to Asia and Africa and widely grown in Brazil. **4.** The brown color of coffee with cream. [< Ital. *caffe* < Turkish *qahveh* < Arabic *qahwah*]
coffee break *U.S.* A short recess from work during which coffee or other refreshments are taken.
coffee cake A kind of cake to be eaten with coffee, often containing raisins or nuts and topped with sugar or icing.
coffee house A public room where coffee is the main beverage, often used as a social club. Also **cof·fee·house** (kôf'ē·hous', kof'ē-).
coffee klatch (kloch, kläch), **coffee klatsch** See KAFFEEKLATSCH.
coffee maker Any of various devices for brewing coffee.
coffee mill A mill for grinding roasted coffee beans.
coffee nut Kentucky coffee.
cof·fee·pot (kôf'ē·pot', kof'ē-) *n.* A covered pot or container for preparing or serving coffee.
coffee shop A restaurant or public room where coffee and food are served. Also **coffee room.**
coffee table A low table, generally placed in front of a sofa, for serving refreshments. etc.
cof·fee-ta·ble book (kôf'ē·tā'bal, kof'ē-) A book designed primarily for display, as on a coffee table.
coffee tree 1. Any tree yielding coffee beans. **2.** The Kentucky coffee (def. 1).
cof·fer (kôf'ər, kof'-) *n.* **1.** A chest or box, especially one for valuables; a strongbox; safe. **2.** *pl.* Financial resources; a treasury. **3.** A decorative, sunken panel in a ceiling, dome, etc. **4.** A lock in a canal. **5.** A cofferdam (which see). — *v.t.* **1.** To place in a coffer. **2.** To adorn with coffers, as a ceiling. [< F *coffre* < L *cophinus*. See COFFIN.]
cof·fer·dam (kôf'ər·dam, kof'-) *n.* **1.** A temporary enclosure built in the water and pumped dry to permit work on bridge piers and the like. **2.** A watertight structure attached to a ship's side for repairs made below the water line.
cof·fin (kôf'in, kof'-) *n.* **1.** A box or case in which a corpse is buried. **2.** The part of a horse's hoof below the coronet. — *v.t.* To put into or as into a coffin. [< OF *cofin* < L *cophinus* < Gk. *kophinos* basket]
Cof·fin (kôf'in, kof'-), **Robert P(eter) Tristram,** 1892–1955, U.S. poet and writer.
coffin bone The bone of the foot of a horse or related animal, enclosed within the hoof.
cof·fle (kof'əl) *n.* A train of persons or animals fastened together, as for marching. — *v.t.* **·fled, ·fling** To form into a coffle. [< Arabic *gāfilah* caravan]
C of S Chief of Staff.
cog¹ (kog) *n.* **1.** *Mech.* A tooth or one of a series of teeth projecting from the surface of a wheel or gear to impart or receive motion. **2.** A cogwheel (which see). **3.** One who plays a minor but necessary part in a large or complex process. **4.** A projecting part on the end of a timber, used for forming a joint; tenon. [ME *cogge* < Scand. Cf. Sw. *kugge* cog.]
cog² (kog) *v.* **cogged, cog·ging** *v.t.* **1.** To load or mishandle (dice). — *v.i.* **2.** To cheat, as with loaded dice. — *n.* A trick or deception; a lie. [Origin unknown]
cog³ (kog. kôg) *n.* **1.** A small rowboat. **2.** A broad-beamed ship used before the 16th century. [< OF *cogue*]
cog. Cognate.
co·gent (kō'jənt) *adj.* Compelling belief, assent, or action; forcible: convincing. [< L *cogens, -entis,* ppr. of *cogere* to compel.] **— co'gen·cy** (kō'jən·sē) *n.*
cog·i·tate (koj'ə·tāt) *v.t. & v.i.* **·tat·ed, ·tat·ing** To give careful thought (to); ponder; meditate. [< L *cogitatus,* pp. of *cogitare* to think < *co*- together + *agitare* to consider] — **cog·i·ta·ble** (koj'ə·tə·bəl) *adj.* **— cog'i·ta'tor** *n.*
— Syn. think, deliberate, reflect, reason, cerebrate.
cog·i·ta·tion (koj'ə·tā'shən) *n.* Careful consideration; reflection; thought. [< OF *cogitaciun* < L *cogitatio, -onis* < *cogitare.* See COGITATE.]
cog·i·ta·tive (koj'ə·tā'tiv) *adj.* Capable of or given to cogitation. **— cog'i·ta'tive·ly** *adv.* **— cog'i·ta'tive·ness** *n.*
co·gi·to er·go sum (koj'i·tō ûr'gō sum') *Latin* I think, therefore I exist: the basic idea of Descartes' philosophy.

co·gnac (kōn'yak, kon'-) *n.* **1.** Brandy produced in the Cognac region of western France. **2.** Any brandy. [< F]
cog·nate (kog'nāt) *adj.* **1.** Allied by blood; kindred. Compare AGNATE, ENATE. **2.** Allied by derivation from the same source; belonging to the same stock or root: English "cold" and Latin "gelidus" are *cognate* words. **3.** Allied in characteristics; having the same nature or quality; similar; related. — *n.* A cognate person or thing. [< L *cognatus* < co- together + (*g*)*natus,* pp. of (*g*)*nasci* to be born] **— Syn.** (adj.) **3.** related, akin, affiliated, similar.
cog·na·tion (kog·nā'shən) *n.* Relationship by blood or derivation.
cog·ni·tion (kog·nish'ən) *n.* **1.** The act or faculty of knowing or perceiving. **2.** A thing known; a conception or perception. **3.** *Obs.* Knowledge. **— Syn.** See KNOWLEDGE. [< L *cognitio, -onis* knowledge < *cognoscere* to know < co- together + (*g*)*noscere* to know] **— cog·ni'tion·al** *adj.*
cog·ni·tive (kog'nə·tiv) *adj.* Pertaining to or having the power of cognition; knowing.
cog·ni·za·ble (kog'nə·zə·bəl, kon'ə-, kog·nī'zə·bəl) *adj.* **1.** Capable of being known. **2.** Capable of being tried or examined by a court. **— cog'ni·za·bly** *adv.*
cog·ni·zance (kog'nə·zəns, kon'ə-) *n.* **1.** Apprehension or perception of fact; knowledge; notice. **2.** *Law* **a** The hearing of a case by a court. **b** The right of a court to hear a case. **c** Acknowledgment of a fact or deed; confession. **3.** Range or sphere of what can be known. **4.** A distinctive badge or device, as in heraldry. **— to take cognizance of** To acknowledge; recognize; notice. [< OF *conisance, conoisance* < *conoistre* to know < L *cognoscere.* See COGNITION.]
cog·ni·zant (kog'nə·zənt, kon'ə-) *adj.* Having knowledge; aware: with *of.*
cog·nize (kog'nīz) *v.t.* **·nized, ·niz·ing** To know, perceive, or recognize. Also *Brit.* **cog'nise.** [Back formation < COGNIZANCE]
cog·no·men (kog·nō'mən) *n. pl.* **·no·mens** or **·nom·i·na** (-nom'ə·nə) **1.** A surname. **2.** In ancient Rome, the last of a citizen's three names; a family name, as *Naso* in Publius Ovidius Naso. **3.** Loosely, any name, nickname, or appellation. **— Syn.** See NAME. [< L < co- together + (*g*)*nomen* name] **— cog·nom·i·nal** (kog·nom'ə·nəl) *adj.*
cog·no·scen·te (kō'nyō·shen'tā) *n. pl.* **·ti** (-tē) A person with knowledge, especially with knowledge not widely available; insider; initiate: also *conoscente.* [< Ital.]
cog·nos·ci·ble (kog·nos'ə·bəl) *adj.* Capable of being known. [< LL *cognoscibilis* < L *cognoscere.* See COGNITION.] **— cog·nos'ci·bil'i·ty** *n.*
cog·no·vit (kog·nō'vit) *n. Law* A written acknowledgment by a defendant that the plaintiff's demand is just, made so as to avoid the expense of contending. [< L *cognovit* (*actionem*) he has acknowledged (the action)]
co·gon (kə·gōn') *n.* A tall, rank grass (*Imperata cylindrica*) of the Philippines, used for fodder and in thatching. [< Sp. *cogón* < Tagalog]
cog railway A railway operating on very steep grades, having a center rail with cogs (**cog rail**) and locomotives with matching cogwheels with which to maintain traction: also called *rack railway.* Also **cog·way** (kog'wā').
cog·wheel (kog'hwēl') *n.* A wheel with cogs, used to transmit or receive motion; a gearwheel.
co·hab·it (kō·hab'it) *v.i.* **1.** To live together as husband and wife, especially illegally. **2.** *Obs.* To inhabit together the same place or country. [< LL *cohabitare* < L co- together + *habitare* to live] **— co·hab'i·tant, co·hab'it·er** *n.* **— co·hab'i·ta'tion** *n.*
Co·han (kō·han'), **George M(ichael),** 1878–1942, U.S. playwright and entertainer.
Co·hen (kō'ən), **Morris Raphael,** 1880–1947, U.S. philosopher and logician born in Russia.
co·here (kō·hir') *v.i.* **·hered, ·her·ing 1.** To stick or hold firmly together. **2.** To be logically connected; be consistent, as the parts of a speech or story. **3.** *Obs.* To agree. [< L *cohaerere* < co- together + *haerere* to stick]
co·her·ence (kō·hir'əns) *n.* **1.** A sticking together; conjunction; cohesion. **2.** Logical connection or consistency; congruity: the *coherence* of his thoughts. **3.** *Physics* The continuity of the relationship between the phases of two or more waves or wavelike quantities, resulting in the possibility of interference phenomena. Also **co·her'en·cy.** [< MF *cohérence* < L *cohaerentia* < *cohaerere.* See COHERE.]
co·her·ent (kō·hir'ənt) *adj.* **1.** Sticking together, as particles of the same substance. **2.** Observing logical order and connection; consistent. **3.** Intelligible or articulate, as speech. **4.** *Physics* Pertaining to or characterized by coherence. [< MF *cohérent* < L *cohaerens, -entis,* ppr. of *cohaerere.* See COHERE.] **— co·her'ent·ly** *adv.*
co·her·er (kō·hir'ər) *n.* A device formerly used for detecting radio waves, in which the waves cause loosely touching metallic particles in a glass tube to cohere more closely, thus momentarily producing a local electric signaling circuit.
co·he·sion (kō·hē'zhən) *n.* **1.** The act or state of cohering.

2. *Physics* That force by which molecules of the same kind or the same body are held together: distinguished from *adhesion*. **3.** *Bot.* The joining of one part with another. [< F *cohésion* < L *cohaerere*. See COHERE.]

co·he·sive (kō·hē′siv) *adj.* Having or exhibiting cohesion. **— co·he′sive·ly** *adv.* **— co·he′sive·ness** *n.*

co·ho·bate (kō′hō·bāt) *v.t.* ·bat·ed, ·bat·ing To redistill by restoring the distillate to the retort so as to mingle again with the matter there. [< Med.L *cohobatus*, pp. of *cohobare*, ? < Arabic *ka'aba* to repeat]

co·hog (kō′hôg, -hog) See QUAHOG.

co·hort (kō′hôrt) *n.* **1.** The tenth of an ancient Roman legion, 300 to 600 men. **2.** A band or group, especially of warriors. **3.** A companion or follower. [< L *cohors, cohortis.* Doublet of COURT.]

co·hosh (kō′hosh, kō·hosh′) *n.* Either of two North American herbs, the **blue cohosh** (*Caulophyllum thalictroides*), often called *beechdrops* or *squawroot*, and the **black cohosh** (*Cimicifuga racemosa*). [< N. Am. Ind.]

co·hune (kō·hōōn′) *n.* A feather-leaved palm (*Orbignya cohune*) of Central and South America, yielding a fatty oil. Also **cohune palm.** [< native Honduran name]

coif (koif for *n. defs. 1, 2,* and *3, v. def. 1;* kwäf for *n. def. 4, v. def. 2*) *n.* **1.** A close-fitting cap or hood, as that worn by nuns under the veil. **2.** In England: **a** A skullcap of white lawn, formerly worn by barristers, and especially by sergeants at law. **b** The rank or office of a sergeant at law. **3.** Formerly, a thick skullcap of steel or leather worn under a helmet. **4.** Coiffure. *— v.t.* **1.** To cover with or as with a coif. **2.** To dress or arrange (the hair). [< OF *coife* < LL *cofea* < Gmc.]

coif·feur (kwȧ·fœr′) *n. French* A male hairdresser. **— coif·feuse** (kwȧ·fœz′) *n.fem.*

coif·fure (kwä·fyŏŏr′, *Fr.* kwȧ·für′) *n.* **1.** A style of arranging or dressing the hair. **2.** A headdress. *— v.t.* To dress (the hair). Also called *coif.* [< F. See COIF.]

coign (koin) *n.* **1.** A projecting angle or stone; a corner. **2.** A wedge. Also **coigne.** [Var. of QUOIN]

coign of vantage An advantageous position for observation or action.

coil[1] (koil) *n.* **1.** A series of concentric rings or spirals, as that formed by winding a rope. **2.** A single ring or spiral of such a series. **3.** A spiral pipe, or series of pipes, forming a continuous conduit, as in a radiator. **4.** *Electr.* **a** A conductor consisting of a number of turns of wire wound on an insulating coil. **b** An induction coil (which see). **5.** *Canadian* A small stack of hay. *— v.t.* **1.** To wind spirally or in rings; wind round and round. *— v.i.* **2.** To form rings or coils. **3.** To move in spirals, as a hawk. [< OF *ceuillir* < L *colligere.* See COLLECT.] **— coil′er** *n.*

coil[2] (koil) *n. Archaic* Confusion; tumult. [Origin unknown]

coil stamps Stamps issued in rolls and perforated either horizontally or vertically.

Coim·ba·tore (koim′bə·tōr′) A city in Tamil Nadu, India; pop. 393,145 (1971).

Co·im·bra (kō·im′brə) A city in north central Portugal, the capital of medieval Portugal; pop. 46,313 (1960).

coin (koin) *n.* **1.** A piece of metal stamped by government authority for use as money. **2.** Metal currency collectively. **3.** *Archit.* A corner or angle of a building; cornerstone: see QUOIN. **— Syn.** See MONEY. *— v.t.* **1.** To stamp (coins) from metal. **2.** To make into coins. **3.** To originate or invent, as a word or phrase. *— v.i.* **4.** *Brit. Informal* To counterfeit money. **— to coin money** *Informal* To make money rapidly or easily; be successful. [< F, wedge, die < L *cuneus* wedge] **— coin′a·ble** *adj.* **— coin′er** *n.*

coin·age (koi′nij) *n.* **1.** The act or right of making coins. **2.** The coins made; metal money. **3.** The system of coins of a country; currency. **4.** The act of fabricating or inventing anything, especially a word or phrase. **5.** Something fabricated, as an artificially created word. **— Syn.** See MONEY.

co·in·cide (kō·in·sīd′) *v.i.* ·cid·ed, ·cid·ing **1.** To have the same dimensions and position in space; be in the same place. **2.** To occur at the same time or for the same span of time. **3.** To agree exactly; accord. [< MF *coincider* < Med.L *coincidere* < L *co-* together + *incidere* to happen < *in-* upon + *cadere* to fall]

co·in·ci·dence (kō·in′sə·dəns) *n.* **1.** The fact or condition of coinciding; correspondence. **2.** A remarkable concurrence of events, ideas, etc., apparently by mere chance.

co·in·ci·dent (kō·in′sə·dənt) *adj.* **1.** Having the same position and extent. **2.** Occurring at the same time. **3.** In exact agreement; consonant: with *with.* **— co·in′ci·dent·ly** *adv.*

co·in·ci·den·tal (kō·in′sə·den′təl) *adj.* Characterized by or involving coincidence. **— co·in′ci·den′tal·ly** *adv.*

co·in·sur·ance (kō′in·shōōr′əns) *n.* **1.** Joint insurance with another or others. **2.** A form of insurance in which a person insures his property for some percentage of its full value and is understood to be his own insurer for the difference. Compensation for a partial loss is proportionate to the amount of insurance carried. [< CO-[1] + INSURANCE]

co·in·sure (kō′in·shōōr′) *v.t. & v.i.* ·sured, ·sur·ing **1.** To insure with another or others. **2.** To insure according to the specific terms of coinsurance. **— co′in·sur′er** *n.*

Coin·treau (kwän′trō, *Fr.* kwäṅ·trō′) *n.* An orange-flavored liqueur with a curaçao base: a trade name.

coir (koir) *n.* Coconut-husk fiber, used in making ropes, matting, etc.: also called *kyar.* [< Malay *kāyar* rope]

coi·stril (koi′strəl) *n. Archaic* **1.** A knight's groom. **2.** A knave; varlet. Also **coi′strel.** [? < OF *coustillier* soldier]

co·i·tion (kō·ish′ən) *n.* Sexual intercourse. Also **co·i·tus** (kō′i·təs). [< L *coitio, -onis* < *co-* together + *ire* to go]

coke[1] (kōk) *n.* A solid, carbonaceous fuel obtained by heating coal in ovens or retorts to remove its volatile constituents. *— v.t. & v.i.* coked, cok·ing To change into coke. [? ME *colke;* origin uncertain]

coke[2] (kōk) *n. Slang* Cocaine.

Coke (kōōk, kōk), **Sir Edward,** 1552–1634, Lord Coke, English jurist; lord chief justice.

col (kol) *n.* **1.** *Geog.* A depression between two mountains; a gap in a ridge, serving as a pass from one valley to another. **2.** *Meteorol.* A necklike area of low pressure between two anticyclones. Also called *saddle.* [< F < L *collum* neck]

col-[1] Var. of COM-.

col-[2] Var. of COLO-.

col. 1. Collected; collector. **2.** College. **3.** Colonial; colony. **4.** Color; colored. **5.** Column.

Col. 1. Colombia. **2.** Colonel. **3.** Colorado (unofficial). **4.** Colossians. **5.** Columbia.

co·la[1] (kō′lə) Plural of COLON[1] (def. 2).

co·la[2] (kō′lə) A small tropical tree (*Cola acuminata*) bearing cola nuts: also spelled *kola:* also called *kola nut tree.* Also **cola nut tree.** [< *kola* native African name]

cola nut The seed of the cola, yielding an extract containing caffeine and theobromine used in the manufacture of soft drinks: also spelled *kola nut.*

col·an·der (kul′ən·dər, kol′-) *n.* A perforated vessel for draining off liquids: also spelled *cullender.* [Cf. Sp. *colador* < L *colare* to strain]

co·lat·i·tude (kō·lat′ə·tōōd, -tyōōd) *n.* In astronomy and navigation, the complement of the latitude, or the difference between the latitude and 90°. [< CO-[2] + LATITUDE]

Col·bert (kôl·bâr′), **Jean Baptiste,** 1619–83, French statesman and financier.

col·can·non (kəl·kan′ən, kôl′kan·ən) *n.* An Irish dish of potatoes and cabbage or greens cooked and mashed together. [< Irish *cāl ceannain* white-headed cabbage]

Col·ches·ter (kōl′ches′tər, -chis·tər) A municipal borough of NE Essex, England; pop. 65,072 (1961).

col·chi·cine (kol′chə·sēn, kol′kə-) *n. Biochem.* A pale yellow, poisonous alkaloid, $C_{22}H_{25}O_6N$, obtained from colchicum and also made synthetically, used in medicine and to accelerate plant growth. [< COLCHIC(UM) + -INE[2]]

col·chi·cum (kol′chə·kəm, kol′kə-) *n.* **1.** A plant of a genus (*Colchicum*) of Old World bulbous plants of the lily family. **2.** The dried corms or seeds of *C. autumnale,* yielding colchicine. **3.** A medical preparation made from this. [< L < Gk. *kolchikon* < *Kolchis* Colchis, home of Medea]

Col·chis (kol′kis) A region of the western Georgian S.S.R.: identified with the legendary land of the Golden Fleece: Russian *Kolkhida.*

col·co·thar (kol′kə·thər) *n.* A dark red ferric oxide formed by heating ferrous sulfate, used as a polish and as the pigment Indian red. [< Med.L < Arabic *qolqotār*]

cold (kōld) *adj.* **1.** Having a relatively low temperature; having little or no perceptible heat: a *cold* night. **2.** Having a relatively low temperature as compared with a normal body temperature: *cold* hands. **3.** Feeling no or insufficient warmth; chilled; chilly: I'm *cold*! **4.** Without vital heat; dead. **5.** Not influenced by emotion; objective: *cold* reason. **6.** Lacking in affection; displaying no feeling. **7.** Lacking in sexual desire; frigid. **8.** Not enthusiastic or cordial; unfriendly. **9.** Chilling to the spirit; depressing. **10.** *U.S. Informal* Unconscious, as from a blow. **11.** Lacking freshness; stale; old: *cold* news; a *cold* trail. **12.** *Informal* Distant from the object sought: said of a seeker in a game, etc. **13.** In art, bluish in tone; not suggestive of warmth. **— cold feet** *Informal* Loss of courage; timidity. **— to throw cold water on** To discourage by being unenthusiastic or indifferent (about something). *— adv. U.S. Slang* **1.** Thoroughly; with certainty: to know it *cold.* **2.** Without preparation, rehearsal, etc.: He played the concerto *cold.* *— n.* **1.** The comparative lack of heat. **2.** The sensation caused by loss or lack of heat. **3.** An acute infection of the mucous membranes of the upper respiratory tract, caused by a virus, and characterized by sneezing, coughing, etc. **4.** Temperature below the freezing point. **5.** Any relatively low temperature. **— out in the cold 1.** Not provided for. **2.** Intentionally ignored. **— to catch (or take) cold** To become affected with a cold. [OE *cald*] **— cold′ly** *adv.* **— cold′ness** *n.*

cold-blood·ed (kōld′blud′id) *adj.* **1.** Unsympathetic; heartless; deliberately cruel. **2.** Sensitive to cold. **3.** *Zool.* Poikilothermal. **— cold′-blood′ed·ly** *adv.* **— cold′-blood′ed·ness** *n.*

cold chisel A chisel of tempered steel for cutting cold metal.

cold cream A cleansing and soothing ointment for the skin.

cold cuts Cooked or prepared meat or fowl, as ham, beef, bologna, salami, etc., sliced and served cold.

cold-deck (kōld′dek′) *v.t. U.S. Slang* To cheat (someone) at cards by stacking the deck. — **cold′-deck′er** *n.*

cold deck *U.S. Slang* A deck of cards prearranged to the advantage of the dealer.

cold-drawn (kōld′drôn′) *adj.* Stretched or drawn while cold, as wire.

cold frame A wooden frame with a glass top, set into the ground to protect plants and seedlings against cold.

cold front *Meteorol.* The irregular, forward edge of a cold air mass advancing beneath and against a warmer mass.

Cold Harbor A village in eastern Virginia; site of Civil War battles, 1862 and 1864.

cold-heart·ed (kōld′här′tid) *adj.* Without sympathy; unkind. — **cold′heart′ed·ly** *adv.* — **cold′heart′ed·ness** *n.*

cold light Light that is not produced by incandescence or combustion, as phosphorescent light.

cold pack **1.** *Med.* Cold, wet wrappings around the body as a means of therapy. **2.** A canning process in which raw food is packed in cans or jars and then subjected to heat.

cold rubber A synthetic rubber that has been polymerized at low temperatures to impart greater resistance to abrasion.

cold shoulder *Informal* A deliberate slight or show of indifference.

cold snap A sudden spell of very cold weather.

cold sore An eruption about the mouth or nostrils, often accompanying a cold or fever: also called *herpes labialis*.

cold storage **1.** The storage of perishable food, furs, etc., in a refrigerated chamber. **2.** *Informal* A state of temporary retirement or disuse: to put an idea in *cold storage*.

cold sweat Sweating accompanied by chill, usually a sign of fear or shock.

cold turkey *U.S. Slang* **1.** The abrupt and total deprivation of a substance, as a narcotic drug or cigarettes, from one addicted to its use. **2.** Blunt, candid talk, often unwelcome to the listener.

cold war An intense rivalry between nations, as in diplomatic strategy, falling just short of armed conflict.

cold wave *Meteorol.* An unusual drop in temperature; a spell of cold weather, usually moving along a specified course.

cole (kōl) *n.* A plant of the same genus (*Brassica*) as the cabbage, especially rape: also called *colewort*. [OE *cāl, cāwl* < L *caulis* cabbage]

co·lec·to·my (kə-lek′tə-mē) *n. pl.* **·mies** *Surg.* The excision of all or part of the colon. [< COL-² + -ECTOMY]

cole·man·ite (kōl′mən·īt) *n.* A colorless hydrous calcium borate, $Ca_2B_6O_{11}·5H_2O$, occurring massive or in monoclinic crystals, and used in manufacturing borax. [after W. T. *Coleman*, 1824–93, U.S. manufacturer of borax]

co·le·op·ter (kō′lē·op′tər, kol′ē-) *n. Entomol.* A coleopterous insect. Also **co·le·op·ter·on** (kō′lē·op′tə·ron, kol′ē-), **co·le·op·ter·an** (-tər·ən).

co·le·op·ter·ous (kō′lē·op′tər·əs, kol′ē-) *adj.* Belonging or referring to a large, cosmopolitan order of insects (*Coleoptera*), including the beetles and weevils, having horny front wings that fit as cases over the hind wings. [< NL *Coleoptera* < Gk. *koleos* sheath + *pteron* wing]

co·le·op·tile (kō′lē·op′til, kol′ē-) *n. Bot.* The first leaf appearing above the ground in grass seedlings. [< NL < Gk. *koleos* sheath + *ptilon* feather]

co·le·o·rhi·za (kō′lē·ə·rī′zə, kol′ē-) *n. pl.* **·zae** (-zē) *Bot.* The root sheath in certain plants, through which the radicle bursts in germination. [< NL < Gk. *koleos* sheath + *rhiza* root]

Cole·pep·er (kul′pep′ər), **Lord Thomas.** See CULPEPER.

Cole·ridge (kōl′rij), **Samuel Taylor,** 1772–1834, English poet and critic.

cole·seed (kōl′sēd′) *n.* Colza.

cole·slaw (kōl′slô′) *n.* A salad made of finely shredded raw cabbage: also called *slaw*. Also **cole slaw.** [< Du *kool sla* cabbage salad]

Col·et (kol′it), **John,** 1467?–1519, English humanist.

Co·lette (kō·let′) Pseudonym of **Sidonie Gabrielle Claudine Colette.** 1873–1954, French novelist.

co·le·us (kō′lē·əs) *n.* A plant of a large genus (*Coleus*) of tropical African and East Indian herbs or shrubs of the mint family. [< NL < Gk. *koleos* sheath]

cole·wort (kōl′wûrt′) *n.* Cole (which see).

col·ic (kol′ik) *n.* Acute abdominal pain resulting from muscular spasms. — *adj.* Pertaining to, near or affecting the colon. [< F *colique* < L *colicus* sick with colic < Gk. *kōlikos* < *kolon* colon]

col·ick·y (kol′ik·ē) *adj.* **1.** Subject to or suffering from colic. **2.** Resembling or productive of colic.

col·ic·root (kol′ik·rōot′, -rŏŏt′) *n.* **1.** A North American herb (*Aletris farinosa*) of the lily family, having a bitter root. **2.** Any of various other plants believed to soothe colic.

col·ic·weed (kol′ik·wēd′) *n.* One of several plants, as dutchman's-breeches or the pale corydalis.

Co·li·gny (kō·lē·nyē′), **Gaspard de,** 1519–72, French admiral and Huguenot leader. Also **Co·li·gni′.**

Co·li·ma (kō·lē′mä) **1.** A State in western Mexico; 2,010 sq. mi.; pop. 240,245 (1970); capital, **Colima. 2.** See NEVADO DE COLIMA, VOLCÁN DE COLIMA.

col·in (kol′in) *n.* **1.** The bobwhite. **2.** Any bird of a related species. [< Am. Sp. *colin* < Nahuatl]

-coline Var. of -COLOUS.

col·i·se·um (kol′ə·sē′əm) *n.* A large building, as a stadium or hall, for exhibitions, entertainments, sports events, etc.: also spelled *colosseum*.

Col·i·se·um (kol′ə·sē′əm) See COLOSSEUM.

co·li·tis (kə·lī′tis) *n. Pathol.* Inflammation of the colon: also called *colonitis*. [< COL(O)- + -ITIS]

coll. 1. Colleague. **2.** Collect; collection; collector. **3.** College; collegiate. **4.** Colloquial.

col·lab·o·rate (kə·lab′ə·rāt) *v.i.* **·rat·ed, ·rat·ing 1.** To work or cooperate with another, especially in literary or scientific pursuits. **2.** To cooperate traitorously; be a collaborationist. [< LL *collaboratus*, pp. of *collaborare* < L *com*- with + *laborare* to work] — **col·lab′o·ra′tion** *n.* — **col·lab′o·ra′tive** *adj.* — **col·lab′o·ra′tor** *n.*

col·lab·o·ra·tion·ist (kə·lab′ə·rā′shən·ist) *n.* A citizen of a country invaded or occupied by foreign troops who cooperates with the enemy.

col·lage (kə·läzh′) *n.* An artistic composition consisting of or including flat materials, as newspaper, photographs, cloth, etc., pasted on a picture surface; also, the technique of making such compositions. Compare ASSEMBLAGE. [< F, pasting < *colle* glue < L *colla* < Gk. *kolla*]

col·la·gen (kol′ə·jen) *n. Biochem.* A protein forming the chief constituent of the connective tissues and the bones. [< Gk. *kolla* glue + -GEN]

col·lapse (kə·laps′) *v.* **·lapsed, ·laps·ing** *v.i.* **1.** To give way; cave in. **2.** To fail utterly; come to naught. **3.** To assume a more compact form by being folded. **4.** To lose health or strength completely, as from exhaustion or disease. **5.** To lose all or part of its air content, as a lung. — *v.t.* **6.** To cause to collapse. — *n.* **1.** The act or process of collapsing. **2.** Extreme prostration. **3.** Utter failure; ruin. [< L *collapsus*, pp. of *collabi* < *com*- together + *labi* to fall] — **col·laps′i·ble** or **col·laps′a·ble** *adj.* — **col·laps′i·bil′i·ty** *n.*

col·lar (kol′ər) *n.* **1.** The part of a garment at the neck, often folded over. **2.** A necklace or chain worn as an ornament, badge of office, insigne, etc. **3.** An identifying or restraining band of leather or metal for the neck of an animal. **4.** A ring or band suggesting a collar, as a growth of fur about an animal's neck. **5.** A cushion placed around the neck of a draft animal to bear most of the strain of the pull. For illustration see HARNESS. **6.** *Mech.* Any of various devices encircling a rod or shaft, to limit motion, form a connection, etc. — *v.t.* **1.** To provide with a collar. **2.** To grasp by the collar. **3.** *Informal* To take or lay hold of; capture. [< OF *colier*, AF *coler* < L *collare* < *collum* neck]

col·lar·bone (kol′ər·bōn′) *n.* The clavicle.

collar cell *Zool.* A flagellate cell having the base of the flagellum surrounded by a collarlike expansion: also called *choanocyte*.

col·lard (kol′ərd) *n. Usually pl.* A variety of cabbage that does not form a head. [Alter. of *colewort*. See COLE.]

col·lar·et (kol′ə·ret′) *n.* A small collar of fur, linen, lace, etc. Also **col′lar·ette′.** [< F *collerette*, dim. of *collier* collar]

collat. Collateral.

col·late (kə·lāt′, kol′āt) *v.t.* **·lat·ed, ·lat·ing 1.** To compare critically, as writings or facts. **2.** In bookbinding, to examine (the gathered sheets to be bound) in order to verify and correct their arrangement. **3.** In library work, to examine (the pages of a book) to see that none is missing or out of order. **4.** To put together (pages of a manuscript, etc.) in proper order; also, to combine (data, etc.) into a unified whole. **5.** *Eccl.* To appoint or admit (a cleric) to a benefice. [< L *collatus*, pp. of *conferre* < *com*- together + *ferre* to bear, carry] — **col·la·tor** (kə·lā′tər, kol′ā·tər) *n.*

col·lat·er·al (kə·lat′ər·əl) *adj.* **1.** Lying or running side by side; parallel; bordering. **2.** Uniting in tendency, direction, or effect; concomitant. **3.** Tending to the same conclusion; corroborative. **4.** Lying aside from the main subject, issue, or purpose; subordinate; secondary. **5.** Additional; supporting: *collateral* security. **6.** Guaranteed by collateral security: a *collateral* loan. Abbr. *collat.* **7.** Descended from a common ancestor, but in a different line. — *n.* **1.** *U.S.* Security pledge for a loan or obligation. **2.** A collateral kinsman. **3.** An accompanying or subordinate fact, condition, or part. [< Med.L *collateralis* < L *com*- together + *lateralis* lateral < *latus, -eris* a side] — **col·lat′er·al·ly** *adv.*

collateral adjective An adjective closely related to a given noun in meaning, but not in immediate origin, as *brachial* is to *arm*.

collateral security Property, stocks, etc., deposited as security additional to one's personal or contractual obligation, and subject to forfeiture in case of default.

col·la·tion (kə·lā′shən) *n.* **1.** The act or process of collating; comparison. **2.** A description of the size, contents, pages, and other technical features of a book. **3.** *Eccl.* The presentation of a clergyman to a benefice, as in the Church of England. **4.** *Eccl.* **a** The reading or discussing of a religious book before compline. **b** A light meal permitted in place of supper on fast days, originally eaten after collation. **5.** Any light, informal meal or repast; refreshments. [< OF < L *collatio, -onis* < *conferre.* See COLLATE.]

col·league (kol′ēg) *n.* A fellow member of a profession, official body, etc.; an associate. Abbr. *coll.* — **Syn.** See ASSOCIATE. [< F *collègue* < L *collega* < *com-* together + *legere* to choose] — **col′league·ship** *n.*

col·lect[1] (kə·lekt′) *v.t.* **1.** To gather together; assemble. **2.** To bring together as a hobby or for study: to *collect* stamps. **3.** To request and obtain (payments of money): to *collect* taxes. **4.** To regain control of; bring or call back: to *collect* one's wits. — *v.i.* **5.** To assemble or congregate, as people. **6.** To accumulate, as sand or dust. **7.** To gather payments or donations. — **Syn.** See AMASS, CONVOKE. — *adj. & adv.* To be paid for by the receiver: Send it *collect*; a *collect* call. Abbr. (adj. & adv.) *coll.* [Fusion of obs. *collect* gathered, and OF *collecter* to gather taxes, both ult. < L *collectus,* pp. of *colligere* < *com-* together + *legere* to choose] — **col·lect′a·ble** or **col·lect′i·ble** *adj.*

col·lect[2] (kol′ekt) *n. Eccl.* A short, formal prayer used in several Western liturgies, usually containing a single petition and varying with the season or occasion. [< F *collecte* < L *collecta* a gathering together < *colligere.* See COLLECT[1].]

col·lec·ta·ne·a (kol′ek·tā′nē·ə) *n.pl.* Passages selected from different authors; a miscellany. [< L, (things) gathered together] — **col′lec·ta′ne·ous** *adj.*

col·lect·ed (kə·lek′tid) *adj* Composed; self-possessed. — **col·lect′ed·ly** *adv.* — **col·lect′ed·ness** *n.*

col·lec·tion (kə·lek′shən) *n.* **1.** The act or process of collecting. **2.** That which is collected; an assemblage of objects, writings, etc.: a *collection* of modern verse. **3.** That which has accumulated: a *collection* of dirt. **4.** A soliciting and collecting of money, as for church expenses or charity; also, the money. (def. 4) *coll.* [< OF < L *collectio, -onis* < *colligere.* See COLLECT[1].]

col·lec·tive (kə·lek′tiv) *adj.* **1.** Formed or gathered together by collecting. **2.** Of, relating to, or proceeding from a number of persons or things together; common: a *collective* effort. **3.** *Gram.* Denoting in the singular number a collection or aggregate of individuals: a *collective* noun. — *n.* **1.** A collective enterprise or body; especially, a collective farm. **2.** The individuals comprising such a body or enterprise. **3.** *Gram.* A collective noun (which see). [< L *collectivus* < *collectus.* See COLLECT[1].] — **col·lec′tive·ly** *adv.* — **col·lec′tive·ness** *n.*

collective bargaining Negotiation between organized workers and employers on wages, hours, etc.

collective farm A farm worked and managed by cooperative labor, and in which the machinery and buildings are owned by the state or communally. See KOLKHOZ.

collective fruit *Bot.* A fruit that is the product of a number of distinct flowers growing in a compact mass, as a mulberry or a pineapple: also called *multiple fruit.*

collective noun *Gram.* A singular noun naming a collection or group. It takes either a singular or a plural verb, depending upon whether it refers to the objects composing it as one aggregate or as separate individuals: The audience *was* large; The audience *were* divided in opinion.

collective security A system for the maintenance of world peace through the concerted action of participating countries against an aggressor.

col·lec·tiv·ism (kə·lek′tiv·iz′əm) *n.* A system in which the people as a whole, or the state, own and control the material and means of production and distribution. — **col·lec′tiv·ist** *adj. & n.* — **col·lec′tiv·is′tic** *adj.* — **Syn.** socialism, communism.

col·lec·tiv·i·ty (kol′ek·tiv′ə·tē) *n.* **1.** Collective quality or state. **2.** The whole taken together; especially, the people as a body. **3.** Collectivism.

col·lec·tiv·ize (kə·lek′tiv·īz) *v.t.* **·ized, ·iz·ing** To organize (an agricultural settlement, industry, economy, etc.) on a collectivist basis. — **col·lec′tiv·i·za′tion** *n.*

col·lec·tor (kə·lek′tər) *n.* **1.** One who or that which collects. **2.** One who collects taxes, duties, debts, etc. Abbr. *col., coll.* **3.** One who collects coins, stamps, etc., as a hobby. — **col·lec′tor·ship** *n.*

col·leen (kol′ēn, kə·lēn′) *n. Irish* A girl. [< Irish *cailín*]

col·lege (kol′ij) *n.* **1.** A school of higher learning that grants a bachelor's degree at the completion of a course of study. **2.** Any of the undergraduate divisions or schools of a university. **3.** A school for instruction in a special field or a profession, often affiliated with a university: a *college* of pharmacy. **4.** A building or buildings used by a college or university. **5.** A body of associates or colleagues engaged in a common task and having certain rights and privileges: the electoral *college.* **6.** A company or assemblage. **7.** In France, a secondary school not supported by the state. Compare LYCÉE. **8.** A clerical community living on a foundation. **9.** *Brit. Slang* A prison. Abbr. *col., coll.* [< OF *college* < L *collegium* body of associates < *collega.* See COLLEAGUE.]

College of Cardinals In the Roman Catholic Church, the body of cardinals who elect and advise the Pope, and, in his absence, administer the Holy See: also called *Sacred College.*

col·le·gian (kə·lē′jən, -jē·ən) *n.* **1.** A college student; undergraduate. **2.** A member of a college.

col·le·giate (kə·lē′jit, -jē·it) *adj.* **1.** Of or pertaining to a college. **2.** Of, characteristic of, or intended for college students: *collegiate* fashions. **3.** Like or resembling a college or colleges. Also **col·le·gi·al** (kə·lē′jē·əl). Abbr. *coll.* — *n. Canadian* **a** A collegiate institute. **b** *Informal* Any secondary school.

collegiate church **1.** A Roman Catholic or an Anglican church, not a cathedral, having a body of clergy or canons living together under a common rule. **2.** *U.S.* An association of churches having pastors in common. **3.** A member church in such an association. **4.** *Scot.* A church served jointly by two or more ministers.

collegiate institute *Canadian* A type of high school.

col·len·chy·ma (kə·leng′kə·mə) *n. Bot.* A form of thick-walled, elastic plant tissue composed of elongated cells strongly thickened at the angles. [< NL < Gk. *kolla* glue + *enchyma* infusion] — **col·len·chy·ma′tous** (-mat′əs) *adj.*

col·let (kol′it) *n.* **1.** *Mech.* A collar or clamp with jaws, used to hold a rod. **2.** The ring or rim in which a gem is set. **3.** In watchmaking, a small collar to which the inside end of a balance spring is fastened. — *v.t.* To place in or furnish with a collet. [< MF, dim. of *col* neck < L *collum*]

col·lide (kə·līd′) *v.i.* **·lid·ed, ·lid·ing** **1.** To come together with violent impact; crash. **2.** To come into conflict; clash. [< L *collidere* < *com-* together + *laedere* to strike]

col·lie (kol′ē) *n.* A large sheep dog of Scottish breed, characterized by a long, narrow head and full, long-haired coat. [Prob. < Scottish Gaelic *cuilean* puppy]

col·lier (kol′yər) *n.* **1.** *Chiefly Brit.* A coal miner. **2.** A vessel employed in carrying coal; also, one of the crew. **3.** *Obs.* A dealer in coal. [ME *colier* < OE *col* coal + *-IER*]

Col·lier (kol′yər), **Jeremy,** 1650–1726, English clergyman. — **Peter Fenelon,** 1849–1909, U.S. publisher.

col·lier·y (kol′yər·ē) *n. pl.* **·lier·ies** A coal mine.

col·lie·shang·ie (kol′ē·shang′ē) *n. Scot.* A quarrel; brawl.

col·li·gate (kol′ə·gāt) *v.t.* **·gat·ed, ·gat·ing** **1.** To tie or fasten together. **2.** *Logic* To bind together (facts) by means of some suitable conception or explanation. [< L *colligatus,* pp. of *colligare* < *com-* together + *ligare* to bind] — **col′li·ga′tion** *n.* — **col′li·ga′tive** *adj.*

col·li·mate (kol′ə·māt) *v.t.* **·mat·ed, ·mat·ing** **1.** To bring into line or make parallel, as refracted rays of light. **2.** To adjust the line of sight of (a telescope, etc.). [< L *collimatus,* pp. of *collineare* < *com-* together + *lineare* to align] — **col′li·ma′tion** *n.*

col·li·ma·tor (kol′ə·mā′tər) *n. Optics* A device used to obtain parallel rays of light, as a fixed telescope or the convex lens in a spectroscope. For illustration see SPECTROSCOPE.

col·lin·e·ar (kə·lin′ē·ər) *adj.* Lying in the same straight line. — **col·lin′e·ar·ly** *adv.*

Col·lins (kol′inz), **Michael,** 1890–1922, Irish patriot. — **William,** 1721–59, English poet. — **(William) Wilkie,** 1824–89, English novelist.

col·lin·si·a (kə·lin′sē·ə, -zē·ə) *n.* **1.** An annual or biennial plant (genus *Collinsia*) of the figwort family with whorled leaves. **2.** Any of the variously colored flowers of this plant. [after Z. *Collins,* 1764–1831, U.S. botanist]

col·li·sion (kə·lizh′ən) *n.* **1.** The act of colliding; a violent striking together. **2.** A clash of views or interests; conflict. [< LL *collisio, -onis* < L *collidere.* See COLLIDE.]

col·lo·cate (kol′ō·kāt) *v.t.* **·cat·ed, ·cat·ing** To place together or in relation; arrange. [< L *collocatus,* pp. of *collocare* < *com-* together + *locare* to place]

col·lo·ca·tion (kol′ō·kā′shən) *n.* **1.** A placing or being placed together or in relation; juxtaposition. **2.** Arrangement, as of words in a sentence; syntax.

col·lo·di·on (kə·lō′dē·ən) *n.* A solution of guncotton or pyroxylin in ether and alcohol, used as a coating for wounds and formerly for photographic plates. Also **col·lo·di·um** (kə·lō′dē·əm). [< Gk. *kollōdēs* gluelike < *kolla* glue]

col·logue (kə·lōg′) *Brit. Dial. v.i.* **·logued, ·lo·guing** To confer secretly; connive. — *n.* A private conversation. [Prob. < F *colloque* conference < L *colloquium*]

col·loid (kol′oid) *n.* **1.** Any gluelike or jellylike substance, as gelatin, starch, raw egg white, etc., that diffuses not at all or very slowly through vegetable and animal membranes: distinguished from *crystalloid.* **2.** *Chem.* A state of matter in which finely divided particles of one substance (the disperse phase) are suspended in another (the dispersion medium) in such manner that the electrical and surface properties acquire special importance. **3.** *Med.* A translucent, gelatinous substance resulting from certain forms of tissue degeneration. — *adj.* Of or pertaining to a colloid or the colloid state: also **col·loi·dal** (kə·loid′l). [< Gk. *kolla* glue + -OID] — **col·loi·dal·i·ty** (kol′oi·dal′ə·tē) *n.*

colloid system *Chem.* Any aggregate of substances exhibiting the properties of a colloid, as sols, gels, emulsions, etc.

col·lop (kol′əp) *n.* A small portion or piece, as of meat. [Cf. Sw. *kalops* slices of stewed beef]

colloq. Colloquial; colloquialism; colloquially.

col·lo·qui·al (kə-lō′kwē-əl) *adj.* **1.** Denoting a manner of speaking or writing that is characteristic of familiar conversation; informal. **2.** Conversational. Abbr. *coll., colloq.* — **col·lo′qui·al·ly** *adv.* — **col·lo′qui·al·ness** *n.*

col·lo·qui·al·ism (kə-lō′kwē-əl-iz′əm) *n.* **1.** An expression or form of speech of the type used in informal conversation. Abbr. *colloq.* **2.** Informal, conversational style.

col·lo·quy (kŏl′ə-kwē) *n., pl.* **·quies** **1.** A conversation or conference, especially one that is formally arranged. **2.** A literary work written in conversational or dialogue form. — **Syn.** See CONVERSATION. [< L *colloquium* conversation < *com-* together + *loqui* to speak] — **col′lo·quist** *n.*

col·lo·type (kŏl′ə-tīp) *n. Printing* **1.** A photomechanical process that prints from a hardened gelatin image on a glass plate: also called *photogelatin process.* **2.** A print or plate made for this process. [< Gk. *kolla* glue + -TYPE] — **col·lo·typ·ic** (kŏl′ə-tĭp′ĭk) *adj.*

col·lude (kə-lōōd′) *v.i.* **·lud·ed, ·lud·ing** To cooperate secretly; conspire; connive. [< L *colludere* < *com-* together + *ludere* to play, trick] — **col·lud′er** *n.*

col·lu·sion (kə-lōō′zhən) *n.* Secret agreement for a wrongful purpose, especially between persons wishing to defraud another or between persons who wish to appear as adversaries. [< L *collusio, -onis* < *colludere.* See COLLUDE.] — **Syn.** conspiracy, connivance, plot.

col·lu·sive (kə-lōō′sĭv) *adj.* Secretly arranged to defraud another or to circumvent the law. — **col·lu′sive·ly** *adv.* — **col·lu′sive ness** *n.*

col·ly (kŏl′ē) *Dial. n.* Coal dust; soot. — *v.t.* **·lied, ·ly·ing** To blacken; begrime. [ME *colie* < OE *col* coal]

col·lyr·i·um (kə-lĭr′ē-əm) *n. pl.* **·ri·ums** or **·ri·a** (-rē-ə) An eyewash or eye salve. [< L < Gk. *kollyrion* poultice, dim. of *kollyra* bread]

Col·mar (kŏl′mär, *Fr.* kôl·màr′) A commune in eastern France; pop. about 58,623 (1968): German *Kolmar.*

colo- *combining form* Colon: *colotomy.* Also, before vowels, **col-.** [< Gk. *kolon* colon]

Colo. Colorado.

Co·lô·a·ne (kŏō·lō′ə·nə) See MACAO.

col·o·cynth (kŏl′ə-sĭnth) *n.* **1.** A Mediterranean vine (*Citrullus colocynthis*) of the gourd family. **2.** Its small fruit, yielding a cathartic drug. Also called *bitter apple, coloquintida.* [< L *colocynthis* < Gk. *kolokynthē* gourd]

co·logne (kə-lōn′) *n.* A toilet water consisting of alcohol scented with aromatic oils: also called *eau de Cologne.* Also **Cologne water.** [after *Cologne*]

Co·logne (kə-lōn′) A city in western West Germany, on the Rhine; pop. 780,124 (est. 1959): German *Köln.*

Co·lombes (kŏ-lônb′) A commune in northern France, a suburb of Paris; pop. 80,224 (1968).

Co·lom·bi·a (kə-lŭm′bē-ə, Sp. kō-lōm′byä) A Republic in NW South America; 439,519 sq. mi.; pop. 21,117,000 (est. 1970); capital, Bogotá: officially **Republic of Colombia.** — **Co·lom′bi·an** *adj. & n.*

Co·lom·bo (kə-lŭm′bō) The capital of Ceylon; a port city on the west coast; pop. 551,200 (est. 1969).

co·lon[1] (kō′lən) *n. pl.* **co·lons** for def. **1,** **co·la** (kō′lə) for def. **2** **1.** A punctuation mark (:) indicating a pause greater than a semicolon, but less than a period, used as a sign of apposition or equality to connect one clause with another that explains it, after a word introducing a quotation, citation, etc., after the salutation in a formal letter, in expressing clock time, and in mathematical proportions. **2.** In ancient prosody, a member or section of a rhythmical period, containing from two to six feet and one principal accent. [< L < Gk. *kōlon* member, limb, clause]

co·lon[2] (kō′lən) *n. pl.* **co·lons** or **co·la** (kō′lə) *Anat.* The portion of the large intestine between the cecum and the rectum. For illustration see INTESTINE. [< L < Gk. *kolon*] — **co·lon·ic** (kə-lŏn′ĭk) *adj.*

co·lon[3] (kō-lōn′) *n. pl.* **co·lons** (kō-lōnz′), *Sp.* **co·lo·nes** (kō-lō′nās) The monetary unit of Costa Rica, equivalent to 100 centimos, and of El Salvador, equivalent to 100 centavos.

Co·lôn (kō-lōn′) A port city of Panama, an enclave at the Caribbean end of the Canal Zone; pop. 67,641 (1970).

Co·lôn Archipelago (kō-lōn′) The official name for the GALÁPAGOS ISLANDS.

colo·nel (kûr′nəl) *n. Mil.* A commissioned officer ranking next above a lieutenant colonel and next below a brigadier or brigadier general; also, the term of address for this officer and for a lieutenant colonel. See tables at GRADE. Abbr. *Col.* [Earlier *coronel* < MF < Ital. *colonnello* < *colonna* column of soldiers] — **colo′nel·cy, colo′nel·ship** *n.*

co·lo·ni·al (kə-lō′nē-əl) *adj.* **1.** Of, pertaining to, or living in a colony or colonies. **2.** Of or referring to the thirteen British colonies that became the United States. Abbr. *col.* **3.** Characteristic of colonial times. **4.** Describing a style of architecture, influenced by English Renaissance or Georgian style, that originated in the American colonies. — *n.* A citizen or inhabitant of a colony. — **co·lo′ni·al·ly** *adv.*

co·lo·ni·al·ism (kə-lō′nē-əl-iz′əm) *n.* The policy of a nation seeking to acquire, extend, or retain overseas dependencies.

col·o·nist (kŏl′ə-nĭst) *n.* **1.** A member or inhabitant of a colony. **2.** A settler or founder of a colony.

col·o·ni·tis (kŏl′ə-nī′tĭs) *n.* Colitis (which see.)

col·o·nize (kŏl′ə-nīz) *v.* **·nized, ·niz·ing** *v.t.* **1.** To set up a colony in; settle. **2.** To establish as colonists. — *v.i.* **3.** To establish or unite in a colony or colonies. **4.** To settle in colonies. Also *Brit.* **col′o·nise.** — **col′o·ni·za′tion** *n.* — **col′o·niz′er** *n.*

col·on·nade (kŏl′ə-nād′) *n. Archit.* A series of regularly spaced columns, usually supporting an entablature. [< F < *colonne* column] — **col′on·nad′ed** *adj.*

col·o·ny (kŏl′ə-nē) *n. pl.* **·nies** **1.** A body of emigrants or their descendants living in a land apart from, but under the control of, the parent country. **2.** The region thus settled. **3.** Any territory politically controlled by a distant state. Abbr. *col.* **4.** A group of individuals from the same country, of the same occupation, etc., living in a particular part of a city, state, or country: a Chinese *colony.* **5.** The region or quarter occupied by such a group. **6.** *Biol.* A group of organisms of the same species, usually from the same parent cell, functioning in close association and with varying degrees of independence, as certain bacteria, coelenterates, and algae. **7.** *Ecol.* A group of plants or animals of the same kind living in a particular locality. — **the Colonies** The British colonies that became the original thirteen States of the United States: New Hampshire, Massachusetts, Rhode Island, Connecticut, New York, New Jersey, Pennsylvania, Delaware, Maryland, Virginia, North Carolina, South Carolina, and Georgia. [< L *colonia* < *colonus* farmer] — **Syn.** **3.** possession, dominion, territory, protectorate.

col·o·phon (kŏl′ə-fon, -fən) *n.* **1.** An inscription formerly placed at the end of a book, showing the title, printer's name, date, etc. **2.** An emblematic device adopted by a publisher, usually printed on the title page of his books. [< LL < Gk. *kolophōn* summit, finishing touch]

Col·o·phon (kŏl′ə-fon) An ancient city of Asia Minor, near Ephesus.

col·o·pho·ny (kŏl′ə-fō′nē, kə-lof′ə-nē) *n.* Rosin. [< L *colophonia* (*resina*) (rosin) from Colophon]

col·o·quin·ti·da (kŏl′ə-kwĭn′ti-də) *n.* Colocynth. [< Med.L, ult. < Gk. *kolokynthē* gourd]

col·or (kŭl′ər) *n.* **1.** A visual attribute of bodies or substances distinct from their spatial characteristics and depending upon the spectral composition of the wavelengths of radiant energy capable of stimulating the retina and its associated neural structures. Colors are classified in two major categories: achromatic colors, that include black and white and the entire series of intermediate grays, varying only in *brilliance*; and chromatic colors, as green, blue, red, etc., that may vary also in *hue* and *saturation.* **2.** A paint, dyestuff, or pigment. **3.** Complexion; hue of the skin. **4.** Ruddy complexion; also, a blush. **5.** The complexion of those peoples not classed as Caucasians, especially of Negroes. **6.** *pl.* The ensign or flag of a nation, military or naval unit, etc. **7.** A color, ribbon, badge, etc., used for identification: college *colors.* **8.** *pl.* The side, or the opinions, arguments, etc., one upholds: Stick to your *colors.* **9.** Outward appearance; semblance; aspect: a *color* of reason. **10.** A false appearance; pretext; disguise: under *color* of religion. **11.** General character; sort; kind. **12.** Liveliness or vividness, especially in literary work. **13.** In art and literature, the use of characteristic details of customs, speech, dress, etc., to produce a realistic effect: local *color.* **14.** In art, the total effect of the colors in a painting. **15.** *Music* **a** The effect of music with respect to its sound quality as distinguished from its melodic, harmonic, and rhythmic content. **b** Timbre. **16.** *pl.* In the U.S. Navy, the salute made when the national flag is hoisted in the morning or lowered in the evening. **17.** *Law* An apparent or prima-facie right, authority, etc. **18.** A small particle or trace of gold, etc., found in auriferous sand or gravel. Abbr. *col.* — **to change color 1.** To turn pale. **2.** To blush. — **to lose color** To turn pale. — **to show one's (true) colors** To show one's real nature, beliefs, etc. — *v.t.* **1.** To apply or give color to, as by painting, staining, or dyeing. **2.** To misrepresent by distortion or exaggeration. **3.** To modify, influence, or change in nature or character. — *v.i.* **4.** To take on or change color, as ripening fruit. **5.** To blush. Also, *Brit., colour.* [< OF *colour* < L *color*] — **col′or·er** *n.* — **Syn.** (noun) **1.** tint, tinge, shade. **6.** banner, standard, pennant. **13.** flavor, savor, atmosphere. — (verb) **5.** flush, redden.

col·or·a·ble (kŭl′ər-ə-bəl) *adj.* **1.** That may be colored. **2.** Capable of appearing true or right. **3.** Specious or plausible; deceptive. Also *Brit.* **col′our·a·ble.** — **col′or·a·bil′i·ty, col′or·a·ble·ness** *n.* — **col′or·a·bly** *adv.*

col·o·ra·do (kŏl′ə-rä′dō) *adj.* **1.** Having medium strength and color: said of cigars. **2.** *SW U.S.* Red; reddish, used in geographic names. [< Sp., colored, red]

Col·o·ra·do (kŏl′ə-rä′dō, -rad′ō) A western State of the

United States; 104,247 sq. mi.; pop. 2,207,259. Capital, Denver; entered the Union Aug. 1, 1876: nickname *Centennial State*. Abbr. *Colo*. — **Col′o·ra′dan** *adj. & n.*

Colorado beetle The potato beetle (which see).

Colorado Desert An arid region in SE California and northern Lower California.

Colorado River 1. A river flowing about 1,400 miles from northern Colorado through Utah and Arizona to the northern tip of the Gulf of California. 2. A river in Texas, flowing 900 miles SE to the Gulf of Mexico: also *Eastern Colorado River*.

Colorado Springs A city in east central Colorado, at the base of Pikes Peak, seat of the United States Air Force Academy; pop. 135,060.

col·or·a·tion (kul′ə·rā′shən) *n.* Arrangement of colors, as in an animal or plant; coloring.

col·or·a·tu·ra (kul′ər·ə·toŏr′ə, -tyoŏr′ə) *n.* 1. In vocal music, runs, trills, or other florid decoration. 2. Music characterized by this. 3. A coloratura soprano (which see). — *adj.* Characterized by or suitable for coloratura. Also **col·or·a·ture** (kul′ər·ə·choŏr). [< Ital., coloration]

coloratura soprano 1. A soprano voice of unusually high pitch, having a wide range and great flexibility. 2. A singer with such a voice.

col·or·blind (kul′ər·blīnd′) *adj.* Affected with color blindness.

color blindness The inability to perceive chromatic color, achromatopsia, or more commonly, to distinguish one of the three primary colors, dichromatism.

col·or·cast (kul′ər·kast′, -käst′) *n.* A television broadcast in color. — *v.t. & v.i.* In television, to broadcast in color.

col·ored (kul′ərd) *adj.* 1. Having color. 2. Of a race other than the Caucasoid; especially, wholly or partially Negro. 3. Of or relating to Negroes or to the Negroid ethnic division. 4. Influenced or distorted; biased; tainted: The report was *colored* by envy. 5. False or misleading; specious.

Col·ored (kul′ərd) *n. pl.* **Col·ored** In South Africa, a person of mixed African and European or Asian parentage: also spelled *Coloured*.

col·or·fast (kul′ər·fast′, -fäst′) *adj.* Resistant to fading or running: *colorfast* fabrics.

color filter *Photog.* A layer of substance in solid, liquid, or gaseous form that absorbs a certain wavelength of light, used to change the relative intensities of impinging light waves. Also called **color screen**.

col·or·ful (kul′ər·fəl) *adj.* 1. Full of colors, especially contrasting colors. 2. Full of variety; vivid; picturesque: a *colorful* story. — **col′or·ful·ly** *adv.* — **col′or·ful·ness** *n.*

color guard The flagbearers and guards who conduct the colors in a ceremony.

col·or·if·ic (kul′ə·rif′ik) *adj.* 1. Producing or imparting color. 2. Of or pertaining to color. [< F *colorifique*]

col·or·im·e·ter (kul′ə·rim′ə·tər) *n.* An apparatus for determining the hue, purity, and brightness of a color, especially as compared with a specified standard. [< COLOR + -(I)METER] — **col·or·i·met·ric** (kul′ər·ə·met′rik) or **·ri·cal** *adj.* — **col′or·i·met′ri·cal·ly** *adv.*

col·or·im·e·try (kul′ə·rim′ə·trē) *n.* The measurement and analysis of color by comparison with a standard or in terms of physical and spectral characteristics.

col·or·ing (kul′ər·ing) *n.* 1. The act or manner of applying colors. 2. A substance used to impart color. 3. Appearance of anything as to color. 4. Characteristic tone or style. 5. False appearance.

col·or·ist (kul′ər·ist) *n.* 1. One who uses color. 2. An artist who uses colors skillfully. — **col′or·is′tic** *adj.*

col·or·less (kul′ər·lis) *adj.* 1. Without color. 2. Weak in color; pallid. 3. Lacking vividness or variety; dull; uninteresting. 4. Without bias; neutral.

color line A social, political, and economic distinction drawn between the white and other races.

color sergeant A sergeant who carries the regimental or national colors or standard.

Coloss. Colossians.

Co·los·sae (kə·los′ē) An ancient city of SW Phrygia, Asia Minor.

co·los·sal (kə·los′əl) *adj.* 1. Of immense size or extent; enormous; huge. 2. *Informal* Beyond belief or understanding: *colossal* pride. [< COLOSSUS] — **co·los′sal·ly** *adv.* — **Syn.** 1. gigantic, mammoth, titanic, vast. — **Ant.** tiny, minuscule, infinitesimal.

col·os·se·um (kol′ə·sē′əm) See COLISEUM.

Col·os·se·um (kol′ə·sē′əm) An amphitheater in Rome, built by Vespasian and Titus in A.D. 75–80: also *Coliseum*.

Co·los·sian (kə·losh′ən) *adj.* Pertaining to Colossae. — *n.* 1. A native or inhabitant of Colossae. 2. *pl.* (construed as *sing.*) A book of the New Testament, consisting of Saint Paul's epistle to the Colossians. Abbr. (n., 2) *Col.*

co·los·sus (kə·los′əs) *n. pl.* **co·los·si** (kə·los′ī) or **co·los·sus·es** 1. A gigantic statue. 2. Something of great size or stature. [< L < Gk. *kolossos* gigantic statue]

Colossus of Rhodes A gigantic bronze statue of Apollo set at the entrance to the harbor of ancient Rhodes about 285 B.C. See SEVEN WONDERS OF THE WORLD.

co·los·to·my (kə·los′tə·mē) *n. pl.* **·mies** *Surg.* The cutting of an artificial opening in the colon. [< COLO- + -STOMY]

co·los·trum (kə·los′trəm) *n.* The first milk of a mammal after parturition; beestings. [< L]

co·lot·o·my (kə·lot′ə·mē) *n. pl.* **·mies** *Surg.* Incision of the colon. [< COLO- + -TOMY]

col·our (kul′ər) British spelling of COLOR.

Col·oured (kul′ərd) See COLORED.

-colous *combining form* Dwelling in or inhabiting: *arenicolous*. Also *-coline*. [< L *colere* to dwell, inhabit]

col·pi·tis (kol·pī′tis) *n. Pathol.* Vaginitis. [< Gk. *kolpos* womb + -ITIS]

col·por·tage (kol′pôr·tij) *n.* A colporteur's work. [< F]

col·por·teur (kol′pôr·tər) *n.* A peddler of books. 2. A traveling agent who sells or gives away Bibles, etc. [< F < *colporter* to peddle < *col* neck + *porter* to carry]

colt (kōlt) *n.* 1. A young horse, donkey, etc.; especially, a young male horse. 2. A young or inexperienced person. 3. *Naut.* A piece of rope formerly used as a lash. [OE] — **colt′ish** *adj.*

Colt (kōlt) *n.* A kind of pistol: a trade name. Also **colt.** [after Samuel *Colt*, 1814–62, U.S. inventor]

col·ter (kōl′tər) *n.* A blade or disk on a plow that cuts the sod: also spelled *coulter*. [OE *culter* < L *culter* knife]

colts·foot (kōlts′foŏt′) *n. pl.* **·foots** A low, perennial, Old World herb (*Tussilago farfara*) of the composite family, bearing yellow flowers, formerly used in medicine.

col·u·brine (kol′yə·brīn, -brin) *adj.* 1. Of or like a snake. 2. Of or pertaining to a widely distributed family of snakes (*Colubridae*), especially to the subfamily *Colubrinae*, that includes the nonvenomous snakes, as the garter snake, blacksnake, etc. [< L *colubrinus* < *coluber* snake]

co·lu·go (kə·loŏ′gō) *n. pl.* **·gos** The flying lemur.

Col·um (kol′əm), **Padraic**, born 1881, Irish poet and playwright.

Co·lum·ba (kə·lum′bə) *n.* A constellation, the Dove. See CONSTELLATION. [< L]

Co·lum·ba (kə·lum′bə), **Saint**, 521–597, Irish monk; missionary to the Scots.

Co·lum·ban (kə·lum′bən), **Saint**, 545?–615, Irish monk and scholar; missionary in France, Switzerland, and Italy.

col·um·bar·i·um (kol′əm·bâr′ē·əm) *n. pl.* **·bar·i·a** (-bâr′ē·ə) 1. A dovecote; also, a pigeonhole in a dovecote. Also **col·um·bar·y** (kol′əm·ber′ē). 2. A vault for the dead with niches for cinerary urns; also, the niches. [< L < *columba* dove]

Co·lum·bi·a (kə·lum′bē·ə) *n. Poetic* The personification of the United States of America. [after Christopher *Columbus*]

Co·lum·bi·a (kə·lum′bē·ə) 1. The capital of South Carolina, in the central part; pop. 113,542. 2. A city in central Missouri; pop. 58,804.

Columbia, District of See DISTRICT OF COLUMBIA.

Co·lum·bi·an (kə·lum′bē·ən) *adj.* 1. Of or pertaining to Columbia (the United States). 2. Pertaining to Columbus.

Co·lum·bi·an (kə·lum′bē·ən) *n. Printing* Formerly, a size of type, 16-point.

Columbia River A river in SW Canada and NW United States, flowing about 1,200 miles to the Pacific Ocean.

THE COLUMBIA and Its Tributaries

col·um·bine (kol′əm·bīn) *n.* A herbaceous plant (genus *Aquilegia*) of the crowfoot family with variously colored flowers of five petals; especially, the **Colorado columbine** (*A. coerulea*), State flower of Colorado. — *adj.* Dovelike. [< F < L *columbinus* dovelike < *columba* dove; from the resemblance of its flowers to a flock of doves]

Col·um·bine (kol′əm·bīn) A stock character in pantomimes, the daughter of Pantaloon and sweetheart of Harlequin.

co·lum·bite (kə·lum′bīt) *n.* A black, brittle mineral, containing variable proportions of niobium and tantalum, associated with iron and manganese. [< COLUMB(IUM) + -ITE¹]

co·lum·bi·um (kə·lum′bē·əm) *n.* Former name for the element niobium. Abbr. *Cb* [< NL < *Columbia*, the United States]

Co·lum·bus (kə·lum′bəs) 1. The capital of Ohio, in the central part; pop. 539,677. 2. A city in western Georgia; pop. 154,168.

Co·lum·bus (kə·lum′bəs), **Christopher**, 1446?–1506, Genoese seafarer and explorer; discovered America for Spain, Oct. 12, 1492. Spanish **Cristóbal Co·lón** (kō·lōn′), Italian **Cris·to·fo·ro Co·lom·bo** (kō·lōm′bō).

Columbus Day October 12, a holiday in most of the United States commemorating the discovery of America by Christopher Columbus: also called *Discovery Day*.

col·u·mel·la (kol′yə·mel′ə) *n. pl.* **·mel·lae** (-mel′ē) *Biol.* A little rod, pillar, or central axis. Also **col·u·mel** (kol′yə·mel). [< L, dim. of *columna* column] — **col′u·mel′lar** *adj.* — **col·u·mel·li·form** (kol′yə·mel′ə·fôrm) *adj.*

col·umn (kol′əm) *n.* **1.** *Archit.* A post or pillar; especially, such a member consisting of base, shaft, and capital, serving as support or ornament. **2.** Something suggesting a column: the spinal *column*; a *column* of figures. **3.** *Printing* A section of printed matter on a page, usually narrow and enclosed by a rule or blank space. **4.** An entertaining or instructive feature article that appears regularly in a newspaper or periodical, often the work of a single writer or editor and presented under a fixed title. **5.** *Mil. & Naval* A formation in which elements of troops, vehicles ships, or aircraft are placed one behind another. *Abbr.* **col.** [< L *columna*] **—col·umned** (kol′əmd) *adj.*

co·lum·nar (kə·lum′nər) *adj.* **1.** Of, pertaining to, or resembling a column. **2.** *Geol.* Describing the hexagonal structure of basaltic rock.

col·um·ni·a·tion (kə·lum′nē·ā′shən) *n.* The use or grouping of columns in a building; also, columns collectively.

col·um·nist (kol′əm·nist, -əm·ist) *n.* One who writes or conducts a special column in a newspaper or periodical.

co·lure (kə·lyŏŏr′, kō′lyŏŏr) *n. Astron.* One of the two great circles of the celestial sphere at right angles to each other, intersecting at the poles and passing through the equinoctial and solstitial points respectively [< L *colurus* < Gk. *kolouros* < *kolos* docked + *oura* tail; because their lower parts are cut off by the horizon]

Col·ville River (kōl′vil) A river of northern Alaska, flowing about 375 miles NE to the Beaufort Sea.

co·ly (kō′lē) *n. pl.* **·lies** The mousebird (def. 1). [< NL *colius* < Gk. *kolios*, a green woodpecker]

col·za (kol′zə) *n.* The summer rape whose seeds produce rape oil: also called *coleseed*. [< F < Du. *koolzaad* < *kool* cabbage + *zaad* seed]

colza oil Rape oil (which see).

COM (kom) Computer output microfilm; a system for printing data from a computer directly onto microfilm, usually by means of a cathode ray tube.

com– *prefix* With; together: *combine, compare.* Also: *co–* before *gn, h,* and vowels; *col–* before *l,* as in *collide*; *con–* before *c, d, f, g, j, n, q, s, t, v,* as in *concur, confluence, connect, conspire*; *cor–* before *r,* as in *correspond.* [< L *com–* < *cum* with]

com. **1.** Comedy; comic. **2.** Comma. **3.** Commentary. **4.** Commerce; commercial. **5.** Common; commonly. **6.** Commune. **7.** Communication(s).

Com. **1.** Commission. **2.** Commissioner. **3.** Committee. **4.** Communist.

co·ma¹ (kō′mə) *n. pl.* **·mas** **1.** *Pathol.* A condition of profound unconsciousness caused by disease, poison, or severe physical or nervous injury. **2.** Stupor; lethargy. —**Syn.** See STUPOR. [< NL < Gk. *kōma* deep sleep]

co·ma² (kō′mə) *n. pl.* **·mae** (-mē) **1.** *Astron.* A luminous, gaseous envelope around the nucleus of a comet. **2.** *Bot.* A tuft of silky hairs. **3.** *Optics* An effect produced by the spherical aberration of a lens, resulting in a hazy, usually oval or pear-shaped border surrounding the image of the object viewed. [< L, hair < Gk. *komē*] —**co′mal** *adj.*

Co·ma Ber·e·ni·ces (kō′mə ber′ə·nī′sēz) A constellation, Berenice's Locks. See CONSTELLATION.

Co·man·che (kō·man′chē, kə–) *n. pl.* **·ches** **1.** A North American Plains Indian of Shoshonean stock, ranging between Kansas and northern Mexico, now in Oklahoma. **2.** The Uto-Aztecan language of this tribe.

Co·man·che·an (kō·man′chē·ən) *Geol. adj.* Of or pertaining to the Comanche series of rocks and to the epoch during which it was deposited. —*n.* **1.** An epoch of the Mesozoic following the Jurassic and including the Lower Cretaceous. **2.** The Comanche series.

Comanche series *Geol.* The Lower Cretaceous series of rocks in the region of the Gulf of Mexico. [after *Comanche,* a town and county of central Texas]

co·mate¹ (kō′māt) *adj. Bot.* Having a coma; hairy; fuzzy. [< L *comatus* < *coma* hair]

co·mate² (kō·māt′, kō′māt) *n.* A mate; companion. [< CO–¹ + MATE¹]

co·mat·ik (kō·mad′ik) See KOMATIK.

co·ma·tose (kō′mə·tōs, kom′ə–) *adj.* **1.** Relating to or affected with coma or unconsciousness. **2.** Lethargic; torpid. [< COMA¹] —**co′ma·tose′ly** *adv.*

co·mat·u·la (kō·mat′yə·lə) *n. Zool.* One of a genus (*Comatula*) of free-swimming crinoids, with plumelike arms: also called *feather star.* Also **co·mat′u·lid.** [< NL < *comatulus,* dim. of *comatus* having hair < *coma* hair]

comb¹ (kōm) *n.* **1.** A toothed strip of hard, often flexible material, used for smoothing, dressing, or fastening the hair. **2.** A thing resembling this in appearance or use, as a card for dressing wool or flax. **3.** The fleshy crest on the head of a fowl. **4.** Something resembling a fowl's comb in shape or position, as the crest of a wave. **5.** Honeycomb. —*v.t.* **1.** To dress or smooth with or as with a comb. **2.** To card, as wool or flax. **3.** To search carefully and exhaustively. —*v.i.* **4.** To crest and break: said of waves. [OE *camb*]

comb² (kōōm, kōm) See COOMB.

comb. Combination; combining.

com·bat (*n.* kom′bat, kum′–; *v.* kəm·bat′) *n.* A battle or fight; struggle; contest; duel. —**close combat** Hand-to-hand fighting. —**single combat** A fight between two persons; a duel. —*v.* **·bat·ed** or **·bat·ted, ·bat·ing** or **·bat·ting** *v.t.* **1.** To fight or contend with; oppose in battle. **2.** To resist. —*v.i.* **3.** To do battle; struggle: with *with* or *against.* —**Syn.** See OPPOSE. [< F < *combattre* < L *com–* with + *batuere* to fight, beat] —**com·bat·a·ble** (kəm·bat′ə·bəl, kom′bat·ə·bəl, kum′–) *adj.* —**com·bat·er** (kom′bat·ər, kum′–, kəm·bat′ər) *n.*

com·bat·ant (kəm·bat′nt, kom′bə·tənt, kum′–) *n.* One engaged in or prepared for combat or hostilities. —*adj.* **1.** Fighting; battling. **2.** Ready or disposed to fight. [< OF *combatant,* ppr. of *combattre.* See COMBAT.]

combat fatigue *Psychiatry* A psychoneurotic disorder characterized by anxiety, depression, loss of control, etc., associated with the stresses of modern warfare: formerly called *shell shock*: also called *battle fatigue.*

combat infantryman's badge *U.S.* A badge awarded in World War II and the Korean War to any infantryman who performed satisfactorily in active ground combat.

com·bat·ive (kəm·bat′iv, kom′bə·tiv, kum′–) *adj.* Inclined or eager to fight; pugnacious. —**com·bat′ive·ly** *adv.* —**com·bat′ive·ness** *n.*

combe (kōōm, kōm) See COOMB.

comb·er (kō′mər) *n.* **1.** One who or that which combs wool, flax, etc. **2.** A long, crested wave. —**Syn.** See WAVE.

com·bi·na·tion (kom′bə·nā′shən) *n.* **1.** The act of joining together or the state of being joined; union; conjunction. **2.** That which is formed by combining; compound; aggregate. **3.** An alliance, as of persons or parties, to further a common interest, activity, etc. **4.** The series of numbers or letters forming the key symbol to a combination lock; also, the mechanism of such a lock. **5.** Underwear consisting of an undershirt and underpants made in one piece. **6.** *Math.* Any selection of a group of units such that the order of selection is immaterial, as 123, 321, and 213. **7.** *Chem.* The union of elements in certain fixed proportions, or the compound resulting from this. *Abbr.* **comb.** [< MF < LL *combinatio, -onis* a joining by twos < *combinare.* See COMBINE.] —**com′bi·na′tion·al** *adj.*

combination lock A lock that can be opened only by moving a dial in a set sequence of turns, thus releasing the tumblers that secure it.

com·bi·na·tive (kom′bə·nā′tiv, kəm·bī′nə–) *adj.* Tending to combine. Also **com·bi·na·to·ri·al** (kom′bə·nə·tôr′ē·əl).

com·bine (*v.* kəm·bīn′; *n.* kom′bīn) *v.* **·bined, ·bin·ing** *v.t.* **1.** To bring together into close union; blend; merge; unite. **2.** To possess in union: a style *combining* clarity and elegance. —*v.i.* **3.** To become one, or parts of a whole; coalesce. **4.** To associate for a purpose; form an alliance. **5.** *Chem.* To enter into combination. —*n.* **1.** A combination. **2.** *U.S. Informal* A group of persons united in pursuit of selfish commercial or political ends; a trust; ring. **3.** *Agric.* A machine that reaps, threshes, and cleans grain while harvesting it. [< LL *combinare* < L *com–* together + *bini* two by two] —**com·bin′a·ble** *adj.* —**com·bin′er** *n.*

comb·ings (kō′mingz) *n.pl.* Hairs, wool, etc., removed by or from a comb.

combining form The stem of a word, usually of Greek or Latin origin, as *tele–* and *–phone* in *telephone,* or an English word unchanged, as *over* in *overeat,* used in combination with other forms to create compounds.

comb jelly A ctenophore.

com·bo (kom′bō) *n. Informal* **1.** Combination. **2.** A small jazz or dance band, usually only three or four musicians. [< COMB(INATION) + -o]

com·bust (kəm·bust′) *adj.* In astrology, obscured by proximity to the sun, as a planet or star. —*v.t. & v.i. Rare* To burn, as fuel. [< OF < L *comburere* to burn up]

com·bus·ti·ble (kəm·bus′tə·bəl) *adj.* **1.** Capable of burning; easily ignited; flammable. **2.** Easily excited; fiery. —*n.* Any substance that will readily burn, as paper or wood. —**com·bus′ti·ble·ness, com·bus′ti·bil′i·ty** *n.* —**com·bus′ti·bly** *adv.*

com·bus·tion (kəm·bus′chən) *n.* **1.** The action or operation of burning; the state of being on fire. **2.** *Chem.* **a** Oxidation of a substance, accompanied by the generation of heat and sometimes light. **b** Any chemical combination attended by the release of energy in the form of heat and light. **c** Slow oxidation, as of food in the body. **3.** Violent disturbance; tumult. — **Syn.** See FIRE. [< LL *combustio*, *-onis* < L *comburere* to burn up] — **com·bus′tive** *adj.*

combustion furnace *Chem.* A heating apparatus for determining the amounts of carbon, sulfur, and other components in a substance or material.

combustion tube *Chem.* A wide tube of heat-resistant glass, silica, or porcelain that contains the substance being analyzed in a combustion furnace.

com·bus·tor (kəm-bus′tər) *n.* The chamber of a jet-propulsion engine in which combustion occurs.

comdg. *Mil.* Commanding.

Comdr. *Mil.* Commander.

Comdt. *Mil.* Commandant.

come (kum) *v.i.* **came, come, com·ing** 1. To move to or toward the speaker; move hither; draw near; approach. 2. To arrive as the result of motion or progress: They *came* to a river. 3. To advance or move into view; become perceptible. 4. To arrive in due course or in orderly progression: when your turn *comes.* 5. To occur in time: Labor Day *came* late that year. 6. To reach or extend. 7. To arrive at some state or condition: to *come* to harm. 8. To happen; occur: *come* what may. 9. To exist as an effect or result: This *comes* of trifling. 10. To emanate or proceed; be derived. 11. To become: The wheel *came* loose. 12. To turn out or prove to be: His prediction *came* true. 13. To be offered, obtainable, or produced: The car *comes* in many colors. 14. To act as the speaker wishes: used in the imperative and expressing impatience, anger, protest, etc. — **to come about** 1. To take place; happen. 2. *Naut.* To turn to the opposite tack. — **to come across** 1. To meet with or find by chance. 2. *Slang* To give or do what is requested. — **to come again** 1. To return. 2. To repeat oneself. — **come around** (or **round**) 1. To recover or revive. 2. To change or turn, as in direction or opinion. 3. *Informal* To pay a visit. — **to come at** 1. To reach. 2. To attain. 3. To attack. — **to come back** 1. To return. 2. *Informal* To regain former status; make a comeback. 3. *Slang* To reply sharply. — **to come by** 1. To pass near. 2. To acquire; get. — **to come down** 1. To lose status, wealth, etc. 2. To descend as by inheritance. — **to come forward** 1. To offer one's services. 2. To present oneself. — **to come in** 1. To enter. 2. To arrive. 3. To be brought into use. — **to come in for** *Informal* 1. To be eligible to receive. 2. To acquire; get. — **to come into** 1. To inherit. 2. To enter into; join. — **to come of** 1. To be descended from. 2. To result from. — **to come off** 1. To become detached. 2. To happen; occur. 3. To emerge from action or trial; acquit oneself. — **to come on** 1. To meet by chance. 2. To make progress; develop. 3. To enter, as on stage. — **to come out** 1. To be made public; be published. 2. To make one's debut. 3. To speak frankly; declare oneself. 4. To result; end. — **to come out with** 1. To declare openly. 2. To offer; publish. — **to come over** 1. To take possession of; seize; happen to. 2. To change sides. — **to come through** 1. To be successful (in). 2. To survive. 3. To wear through. 4. *Informal* To give or do what is required. — **to come to** 1. To recover; revive. 2. To amount to. 3. To result in. 4. *Naut.* **a** To turn close to the wind. **b** To anchor. — **to come up** 1. To arise; appear. 2. *Naut.* **a** To come closer to the wind. **b** To slacken. — **to come upon** 1. To chance upon. 2. To attack. — **to come up to** 1. To equal; rival. 2. To reach. — **to come up with** *U.S. Informal* 1. To propose or produce: to *come up with* an idea. 2. To find or cause to emerge: to *come up with* the answer. [OE *cuman*] **come-at-a·ble** (kum-at′ə-bəl) *adj. Informal* Accessible.

come·back (kum′bak′) *n.* 1. *Informal* A return, as to health or lost position. 2. *Slang* A smart retort. 3. *U.S. Slang* Ground for complaint; recourse.

co·me·di·an (kə-mē′dē-ən) *n.* 1. An actor in comedies. 2. An entertainer specializing in jokes, comic skits, and the like. 3. One who continually tries to be funny. 4. A person who writes comedy. [< F *comédien*]

co·me·di·enne (kə-mē′dē-en′) *n.* A female comedian. [< F]

com·e·do (kom′ə-dō) *n. pl.* **com·e·dos** or **com·e·do·nes** (kom′ə-dō′nēz) A blackhead (def. 3). [< L, glutton < *comedere* to eat up < *com-* thoroughly + *edere* to eat]

come·down (kum′doun′) *n.* A descent to a lower condition or position; a humiliating or disappointing setback.

com·e·dy (kom′ə-dē) *n. pl.* **·dies** 1. A play, motion picture, etc., dealing with human folly in a light and humorous manner, and having a happy ending: opposed to *tragedy*; also, any literary composition of similar theme or treatment. 2. The branch of drama treating of such themes. 3. The art or theory of composing comedy. 4. An incident, situation, etc., resembling comedy. Abbr. *com.* [< MF *comédie* < L *comoedia* < Gk. *kōmōidia* < *kōmos* revel + *aeidein* to sing] — **co·me·dic** (kə-mē′dik, -med′ik), **co·me′di·cal** *adj.* — **co·me′·di·cal·ly** *adv.*

comedy of manners A satiric comedy portraying the manners, customs, and foibles of the fashionable world.

come-hith·er (kum′hith′ər) *adj. U.S. Slang* Alluring: a *come-hither* look.

come·ly (kum′lē) *adj.* **·li·er, ·li·est** 1. Pleasing in person; handsome; graceful. 2. Suitable; becoming. — **Syn.** See

BEAUTIFUL. [OE *cȳmlic* < *cȳme* fine] — **come′li·ly** *adv.* — **come′li·ness** *n.*

Co·me·ni·us (kō-mē′nē-əs), **John Amos,** 1592–1670, Moravian theologian; pioneer of modern pedagogy. Also **Jan Amos Ko·men·sky** (kô′men·skē).

come-on (kum′on′, -ôn′) *n. U.S. Slang* 1. Someone or something that lures or inveigles. 2. A beckoning look or gesture.

com·er (kum′ər) *n.* 1. One who comes or arrives. 2. *Informal* One who or that which shows great promise. — **all comers** All applicants, contestants, etc.

co·mes·ti·ble (kə-mes′tə-bəl) *Rare adj.* Edible. — *n.* *Usually pl.* Food. [< MF < LL *comestibilis* < L *comedere.* See COMEDO.]

com·et (kom′it) *n. Astron.* A celestial body moving in an orbit having the sun as a focus, and occasionally bright enough to be observed by the naked eye, consisting of a nucleus of more or less condensed material, accompanied by a tenuous coma pointing in a direction away from the sun. Among the better known periodic comets are **Biela's comet,** with a period of 7 years, **Encke's comet,** with a period of 3 years, and **Halley's comet,** with a period of 76 years. [OE *cometa* < L < Gk. *komētēs* long-haired < *komē* hair] — **com·et·ar·y** (kom′ə·ter′ē), **co·met·ic** (kə-met′ik) *adj.*

co·meth·er (kə-meth′ər) *n. Irish* 1. An affair; matter. 2. Friendship. — **to put the** (or **one's**) **comether on** To persuade, as by flattery; beguile. [Alter. of *come hither*]

comet seeker *Astron.* A small telescope having a wide-angle lens and mounted to search for comets. Also **comet finder.**

come·up·pance (kum′up′əns) *n. U.S. Informal* The punishment one deserves; just deserts. Also **come′up′ance.**

com·fit (kum′fit, kom′-) *n.* A sweetmeat; confection. Also **com·fi·ture** (kum′fi·chŏŏr, kom′-). [< OF *confit* < L *confectus.* Related to CONFECT.]

com·fort (kum′fərt) *n.* 1. A state of mental or physical ease, especially one free from pain, want, or other afflictions. 2. Relief from sorrow, distress, etc.; solace; consolation. 3. One who or that which gives or brings ease or consolation. 4. Help or support: aid and *comfort.* 5. *pl.* Things or conveniences bringing satisfaction or cheer: the *comforts* of home. 6. *U.S.* A bed comforter. — *v.t.* 1. To cheer in time of grief or trouble; solace; console. 2. To relieve of physical pain. 3. *Law* To aid; help. [< OF *confort* < *conforter* < LL *confortare* to strengthen < L *com-* with + *fortis* strong] — **com′fort·ing** *adj.* — **com′fort·ing·ly** *adv.* — **com′fort·less** *adj.*

— **Syn.** (noun) 1. ease, repose, relaxation. Compare HAPPINESS, SATISFACTION. — (verb) 1. See CONSOLE[1].

com·fort·a·ble (kum′fər·tə·bəl, kumf′tə·bəl, -tər-) *adj.* 1. Imparting comfort and satisfaction. 2. Free from physical or mental distress; content; at ease. 3. *Informal* Moderate; adequate: a *comfortable* income. — *n. U.S.* A comforter for a bed. [< AF *confortable* < OF *conforter.* See COMFORT.] — **com′fort·a·ble·ness** *n.* — **com′fort·a·bly** *adv.*

— **Syn.** (adj.) 1. satisfactory, agreeable. 2. contented, satisfied, cheerful. — **Ant.** uncomfortable, disagreeable, dissatisfied, cheerless, dreary.

com·fort·er (kum′fər·tər) *n.* 1. One who comforts; a consoler. 2. *U.S.* A thick, quilted bedcover: also called *comfort, comfortable.* 3. A long woolen scarf.

Com·fort·er (kum′fər·tər) The Holy Spirit.

comfort station A public toilet or rest room.

com·frey (kum′frē) *n. pl.* **·freys** 1. A rough, hairy herb (genus *Symphytum*) of the borage family. 2. Its root, containing tannin. [< OF *confirie,* appar. ult. < L *conferra*]

com·ic (kom′ik) *adj.* 1. Pertaining to, like, or connected with comedy. 2. Provoking mirth; funny; ludicrous. — *n.* 1. A comical person; especially, a comic actor or entertainer. 2. The element in art, life, etc., that excites humor or merriment. 3. *pl. Informal* Comic strips. 4. *Informal* A book of comic strips. Abbr. *com.* [< L *comicus* < Gk. *kōmikos* < *kōmos* revelry]

com·i·cal (kom′i·kəl) *adj.* 1. Causing merriment; funny; ludicrous. 2. *Obs.* Of or adapted to comedy. — **Syn.** See HUMOROUS. — **com·i·cal·i·ty** (kom′ə·kal′ə·tē), **com′i·cal·ness** *n.* — **com′i·cal·ly** *adv.*

comic book A booklet of comic strips.

comic opera An opera or operetta having a humorous plot and spoken dialogue.

comic strip A strip of cartoons printed in a newspaper, etc., relating adventurous or comic stories or incidents.

Co·mines (kô·mēn′), **Philippe de,** 1447?–1511?, French courtier and historian. Also **Commines.**

Com·in·form (kom′in·fôrm) *n.* The Communist Information Bureau, established in 1947 to coordinate the policies and activities of nine European Communist parties, and dissolved in 1956. [< COM(MUNIST) INFORM(ATION)]

com·ing (kum′ing) *adj.* 1. Approaching, especially in time: the *coming* year. 2. On the way to fame or distinction. — *n.* The act of approaching; arrival; advent.

com·ing-out (kum′ing·out′) *n. Informal* Debut into society.

Com·in·tern (kom′in·tûrn) *n.* An international organization formed at Moscow in 1919 for extending the scope of Marxist socialism, and dissolved in 1943: also called *Third International*: also spelled *Komintern*. [< COM(MUNIST) INTERN(ATIONAL)]

com·i·ta·tus (kom′ə-tā′təs) *n.* **1.** In late Roman and medieval times: **a** The armed retainers of a prince or chieftain. **b** The allegiance between such a group and their chief, for mutual security. **2.** In old English law, a county. [< L, a company < *comes, comitis* companion]

co·mi·ti·a (kə-mish′ē-ə) *n.* In ancient Rome, an assembly of the people. [< L, pl. of *comitium* a place of assembly < *com-* together + *ire* to go] — **co·mi·tial** (kə-mish′əl) *adj.*

com·i·ty (kom′ə-tē) *n.* *pl.* **·ties** Courtesy; civility. [< L *comitas, -tatis* courtesy < *comis* kind]

comity of nations **1.** The courteous recognition that one nation accords to the laws and usages of another. **2.** Loosely, the nations extending such recognition.

coml. Commercial.

comm. **1.** Commerce. **2.** Commissary. **3.** Commission. **4.** Committee. **5.** Commonwealth.

com·ma (kom′ə) *n.* **1.** A punctuation mark (,) indicating a slight separation in ideas or in grammatical construction within a sentence. Abbr. *com.* **2.** In ancient prosody: **a** A phrase or group of feet less than a colon. **b** A section of a hexameter, indicated by a cesura at beginning or end. **3.** Any pause or separation. [< L < Gk. *komma* short phrase < *koptein* to cut]

comma bacillus *Bacteriol.* A bacillus (*Vibrio comma* or *cholerae*), shaped like a comma and causing Asiatic cholera.

com·mand (kə-mand′, -mänd′) *v.t.* **1.** To order, require, or enjoin with authority. **2.** To control or direct authoritatively; rule; have at one's disposal or use. **3.** To overlook, as from a height; guard: These hills *command* the town. **4.** To exact as being due or proper: His knowledge *commands* respect. — *v.i.* **5.** To be in authority; rule. **6.** To overlook something from a superior position. — *n.* **1.** The act of commanding; bidding: We await your *command*. **2.** The power or the authority to command. **3.** That which is enjoined or commanded; an order. **4.** Dominating power as achieved through superior position; also, degree or range of one's view. **5.** Ability to control; mastery: *command* of one's emotions. **6.** *Mil. & Naval* The unit, units, or area under the command of one person. **7.** In the U.S. Air Force, a unit, usually a wing or more, directed by an officer; also, its base of operations. **8.** *Brit.* An invitation by the reigning sovereign. [< OF *comander* < LL *commandare* < L *com-* thoroughly + *mandare* to order. Related to COMMEND.] — **Syn.** (verb) **1.** bid, instruct, charge. **5.** reign, govern. — (noun) **2.** sway, dominion, sovereignty. **3.** injunction, behest.

com·man·dant (kom′ən-dant′, -dänt′) *n.* A commanding officer, as of a service school, military district, etc. Abbr. *Comdt.* [< F, orig. ppr. of *commander* to order]

com·man·deer (kom′ən-dir′) *v.t.* **1.** To force into military service. **2.** To seize for public use, especially under military necessity; sequester; confiscate. Compare ANGARY. **3.** *Informal* To take by force or constraint. [< Afrikaans *kommandeeren* to command < F *commander*]

com·mand·er (kə-man′dər, -män′-) *n.* **1.** One who commands or is in command; a leader; chief. **2.** *Mil.* The commissioned officer in command of a force or post. **3.** *Naval* A commissioned officer ranking next above a lieutenant commander and next below a captain. See table at GRADE. Abbr. *CDR., Cdr., Cmdr., Comdr.* **4.** The chief officer of various medieval orders. **5.** A high-ranking member of certain modern fraternal orders. — **Syn.** See CHIEF. [< OF *comandere* < LL *commandator* < *commandare*. See COMMAND.] — **com·mand′er·ship** *n.*

commander in chief *pl.* **commanders in chief** **1.** Often *cap.* One holding supreme command of the armed forces of a nation: in the United States, the President. Abbr. *CINC, C in C.* **2.** The officer commanding a fleet, major force, etc. **Commander Islands** See KOMANDORSKI ISLANDS.

com·mand·er·y (kə-man′dər-ē, -män′-) *n.* *pl.* **·er·ies** **1.** The district or rank of a commander, especially of an order of knights. **2.** The house or priory of an order of knights. **3.** *U.S.* A chapter or lodge of certain secret orders. Also **com·mand·ry** (kə-man′drē, -män′-). [< MF *commanderie* < Med.L *commendaria* benefice held in commendam]

com·mand·ing (kə-man′ding, -män′-) *adj.* **1.** Exercising command. Abbr. *comdg.* **2.** Impressive; imperious. **3.** Dominating, as from a height. — **com·mand′ing·ly** *adv.*

commanding officer In the Royal, Royal Canadian, and other Commonwealth navies, a commissioned officer ranking above a sub-lieutenant and below a lieutenant. See table at GRADE.

com·mand·ment (kə-mand′mənt, -mänd′-) *n.* **1.** An authoritative mandate; edict; order; law. **2.** *Sometimes cap.* One of the Ten Commandments.

command module *Aerospace* In a spacecraft, the module that serves as a home base for the astronauts.

com·man·do (kə-man′dō, -män′-) *n.* *pl.* **·dos** or **·does** **1.** A special fighting force trained for quick, destructive raids into enemy territory; especially, such a unit in the British Army in World War II. **2.** A member of such a unit. **3.** In South Africa, especially in the Boer War, a force of militia; also, a raid. [< Afrikaans < Pg., a group commanded < *commandar* to command < LL *commandare*. See COMMAND.]

command performance A theatrical or musical performance presented at the request of a ruler, etc.

command post The field headquarters of a military unit.

com·meas·ure (kə-mezh′ər) *v.t.* ·ured, ·ur·ing To be coextensive with or equal to. — **com·meas′ur·a·ble** *adj.*

com·me·dia dell' ar·te (kōm-me′dyä del är′tā) *Italian* A type of drama originating in 16th-century Italy, characterized by improvisation from a written plot, and standard characters such as Pantaloon, Harlequin, and Columbine.

comme il faut (kô mēl fō′) *French* As it should be; correct.

com·mem·o·rate (kə-mem′ə-rāt) *v.t.* **·rat·ed, ·rat·ing** To celebrate or signalize the memory of; keep in remembrance. Also **com·mem′o·rize** (-ə-rīz). — **Syn.** See CELEBRATE. [< L *commemoratus*, pp. of *commemorare* to recall < *com-* together + *memorare* to remember] — **com·mem′o·ra′tor** *n.*

com·mem·o·ra·tion (kə-mem′ə-rā′shən) *n.* **1.** The act of commemorating, or that which commemorates. **2.** A commemorative observance. — **com·mem′o·ra′tion·al** *adj.*

com·mem·o·ra·tive (kə-mem′ə-rā′tiv, -rə-tiv) *adj.* Serving to commemorate. Also **com·mem·o·ra·to·ry** (kə-mem′ər-ə-tôr′ē, -tō′rē). — *n.* Anything that commemorates.

com·mence (kə-mens′) *v.t. & v.i.* **·menced, ·menc·ing** To start; begin; originate. [< OF *comencer* < L *com-*thoroughly + *initiare* to begin] — **com·menc′er** *n.*

com·mence·ment (kə-mens′mənt) *n.* **1.** A beginning; origin. **2.** The ceremony at a college or school during which degrees are conferred; also, the day such a ceremony is held. — **Syn.** See BEGINNING.

com·mend (kə-mend′) *v.t.* **1.** To express a favorable opinion of; praise. **2.** To recommend; accredit. **3.** To present the regards of: *Commend* me to your mother. **4.** To commit with confidence; entrust. **5.** *Eccl.* To bestow in commendam; charge. Related to COMMAND.] — **com·mend′a·ble** *adj.* — **com·mend′a·ble·ness** *n.* — **com·mend′a·bly** *adv.* — **Syn.** **1.** applaud, laud, approve, compliment.

com·men·dam (kə-men′dam) *n.* *Eccl.* **1.** The right to hold a benefice. The benefice was said to be held in commendam, until a regular incumbent could be appointed. **2.** The benefice so held. [< Med.L (*dare in*) *commendam* (to give in) trust < L *commendare*. See COMMEND.]

com·men·da·tion (kom′ən-dā′shən) *n.* **1.** The act of commending; approbation. **2.** Something that commends. **3.** *Archaic* A message of good will; a greeting. [< OF < L *commendatio, -onis* < *commendare*. See COMMEND.]

Commendation Ribbon A U.S. military decoration consisting of a ribbon and medallion, awarded for meritorious achievements or service. See DECORATION.

com·mend·a·to·ry (kə-men′də-tôr′ē, -tō′rē) *adj.* **1.** Serving to commend; expressing commendation. **2.** *Eccl.* Holding a benefice in commendam.

com·men·sal (kə-men′səl) *adj.* **1.** Eating at the same table. **2.** *Zool.* Associated or living with another in close but nonparasitic relationship. — *n.* **1.** A table companion. **2.** *Zool.* A commensal organism. [< OF < Med.L *commensalis* < L *com-* together + *mensa* table] — **com·men′sal·ism, com·men·sal·i·ty** (kom′en-sal′ə-tē) *n.* — **com·men′sal·ly** *adv.*

com·men·su·ra·ble (kə-men′shər-ə-bəl, -sər-ə-) *adj.* **1.** Capable of being measured by a common standard or unit. **2.** Fitting as to proportion; proportionate. [< LL *commensurabilis* < L *com-* together + *mensurabilis* measurable] — **com·men′su·ra·bil′i·ty** *n.* — **com·men′su·ra·bly** *adv.*

com·men·su·rate (kə-men′shə-rit, -sə-rit) *adj.* **1.** Having the same measure or extent; coextensive. **2.** In proper proportion; adequate. **3.** Measurable by a common standard; commensurable. [< LL *commensuratus*, pp. of *commensurare* < L *com-* together + *mensurare* to measure] — **com·men′su·rate·ly** *adv.* — **com·men′su·rate·ness** *n.* — **com·men′su·ra′tion** *n.*

com·ment (kom′ent) *n.* **1.** A written note of explanation, illustration, or criticism, as of a literary passage. **2.** A remark made in observation or criticism. **3.** Talk; conversation; gossip. — **Syn.** See REMARK. — *v.i.* **1.** To make a comment or comments. **2.** To make comments on; annotate. [< OF < L *commentum* invention < *comminisci* to contrive] — **com′ment·er** *n.*

com·men·tar·y (kom′ən-ter′ē) *n.* *pl.* **·ries** **1.** A series or body of illustrative or explanatory notes, as on the Scriptures; an exposition. **2.** Anything serving to explain or illustrate; a comment. **3.** A series of remarks. **4.** *Usually pl.* A historical narrative or memoir; a journal of official acts: the Royal *Commentaries* of Peru. Abbr. *com.* [< L *commentarius* notebook < *commentari*, freq. of *comminisci* to contrive, devise] — **com·men·tar·i·al** (kom′ən-târ′ē-əl) *adj.* — **Syn.** **1.** annotation, exegesis, scholia, gloss.

com·men·ta·tor (kom'ən·tā'tər) *n.* **1.** One who writes commentaries. **2.** One who discusses or analyzes news events, etc. on radio or television. [< L, author, contriver < *commentari.* See COMMENTARY.]

com·merce (*n.* kom'ərs; *v.* kə·mûrs') *n.* **1.** The exchange of materials, products, etc., especially on a large scale between states or nations; extended trade. *Abbr. com., comm.* **2.** Social or intellectual intercourse. **3.** Sexual intercourse. — **Syn.** See TRAFFIC. — **Department of Commerce** An executive department of the U.S. Government (established 1913), headed by the Secretary of Commerce, that supervises transportation and shipping, the census, and food and drug laws. — *v.i.* **·merced, ·merc·ing** To have dealings; associate; commune. [< F < L *commercium* < *com-* together + *merx, mercis* wares] — **com·merc'er** *n.*

com·mer·cial (kə·mûr'shəl) *adj.* **1.** Of, relating to, or engaged in commerce; mercantile. **2.** Produced in large quantities for industry: *commercial* sulfur. **3.** Having financial gain as an object: a *commercial* novel. *Abbr. cml., com., coml.* — *n.* In radio and television, an advertisement. — **com·mer·ci·al·i·ty** (kə·mûr'shē·al'ə·tē) *n.* — **com·mer'cial·ly** *adv.*

commercial bank A bank whose chief functions are the acceptance of demand deposits and the making of short-term loans.

commercial college A business college (which see).

com·mer·cial·ism (kə·mûr'shəl·iz'əm) *n.* **1.** The spirit or methods of commerce. **2.** Commercial practices having profit as their chief aim. — **com·mer'cial·ist** *n.* — **com·mer'cial·is'tic** *adj.*

com·mer·cial·ize (kə·mûr'shəl·īz) *v.t.* **·ized, ·iz·ing** To put on a commercial basis; make a matter of business. — **com·mer'cial·i·za'tion** *n.*

commercial paper Any of various short-term negotiable papers originating in business transactions, as drafts, bills of exchange, promissory notes, etc.

commercial traveler A traveling salesman.

com·mie (kom'ē) *n. Often cap. Informal* A Communist.

com·mi·na·tion (kom'ə·nā'shən) *n.* A denunciation or threatening, especially from a divine source. [< MF < L *comminatio, -onis* < *comminari* < *com-* thoroughly + *minari* to threaten] — **com·min·a·to·ry** (kə·min'ə·tôr'ē, -tō'rē, kom'in·ə-) *adj.*

Com·mines (kô·mēn'), **Philippe de** See COMINES.

com·min·gle (kə·ming'gəl) *v.t. & v.i.* **·gled, ·gling** To mix together; mingle. [< COM- + MINGLE]

com·mi·nute (kom'ə·nōōt, -nyōōt) *v.t.* **·nut·ed, ·nut·ing** To reduce to minute particles; pulverize; triturate. [< L *comminutus,* pp. of *comminuere* < *com-* thoroughly + *minuere* to lessen] — **com'mi·nu'tion** *n.*

com·mis·er·a·ble (kə·miz'ər·ə·bəl) *adj.* Worthy of commiseration; pitiable.

com·mis·er·ate (kə·miz'ə·rāt) *v.* **·at·ed, ·at·ing** *v.t.* **1.** To feel or express sympathy for; pity. — *v.i.* **2.** To express sympathy; condole: used with *with.* [< L *commiseratus,* pp. of *commiserari* < *com-* with + *miserari* to feel pity] — **com·mis'er·a'tive** *adj.* — **com·mis'er·a'tive·ly** *adv.* — **com·mis'er·a'tor** *n.*

com·mis·er·a·tion (kə·miz'ə·rā'shən) *n.* A feeling or expression of sympathy; compassion. — **Syn.** See PITY.

com·mis·sar (kom'ə·sär, kom'ə·sär') *n.* Formerly, an official in charge of a commissariat of the Soviet government. [< Russ. *komissar* < F *commissaire* < Med.L *commissarius* < L *committere.* See COMMIT.]

com·mis·sar·i·at (kom'ə·sâr'ē·ət) *n.* **1.** The department of an army charged with providing food and daily necessities; also, the officers of such a department. **2.** The supplies provided. **3.** Any similar source of supply. **4.** Formerly, any major department of the Soviet government; a ministry. [< F < Med.L *commissarius.* See COMMISSAR.]

com·mis·sar·y (kom'ə·ser'ē) *n. pl.* **·sar·ies 1.** A store selling food, equipment, etc., as at a camp or military post. **2.** A representative of higher authority delegated for a special duty. **3.** *Eccl.* A church officer authorized to represent a bishop. **4.** In France, a police official directly under the prefect of police. **5.** In the Soviet Union, a commissar. *Abbr. comm.* [< Med.L *commissarius.* See COMMISSAR.] — **com·mis·sar·i·al** (kom'ə·sâr'ē·əl) *adj.* — **com'mis·sar'y·ship** *n.*

com·mis·sion (kə·mish'ən) *n.* **1.** The act of committing to the charge of another; an entrusting. **2.** The matter or trust so committed; a charge. **3.** Authorization or command to act as specified. **4.** A written warrant conferring a particular authority or power. **5.** *Mil.* **a** An official document conferring rank and authority on an officer in an army, navy, etc., issued in the United States by the President. **b** The rank or authority conferred. **6.** A body of persons acting under lawful authority to perform certain duties. **7.** The authority given an agent or agency to act for another or others. **8.** The fee or percentage given an agent or salesman for his services. **9.** The condition of being authorized or delegated. **10.** The act of committing, doing, or perpetrating; a positive doing: opposed to *omission.* **11.** The act committed, as a crime or error. *Abbr. Com., comm.* — **in commission** In active service or use, as a ship or an aircraft; ready for service; usable. — **out of commission** Not in active service or use; laid up for repairs, etc.; not in usable condition. — *v.t.* **1.** To give rank or authority to, as an officer. **2.** *Naval* To put into active service under a designated commander, as a ship. **3.** To appoint; empower; delegate. [< OF < L *commissio, -onis* < *committere.* See COMMIT.] — **com·mis'sion·al, com·mis·sion·ar·y** (kə·mish'-ən·er'ē) *adj.*

com·mis·sion·aire (kə·mish'ən·âr') *n. Brit. & Canadian* **1.** One who carries messages, performs minor errands, etc.; a porter or messenger. **2.** One of a body of pensioned soldiers employed as doorkeepers, etc. [< F *commissionnaire*]

commissioned officer An officer who holds a commission, ranking in the U.S. Army, Marine Corps, and Air Force from second lieutenant to general, and in the U.S. Navy and Coast Guard from ensign to admiral.

com·mis·sion·er (kə·mish'ən·ər) *n.* **1.** One who holds a commission to perform certain duties. **2.** A member of a commission. **3.** A public official in charge of a department: fire *commissioner.* **4.** In baseball, etc., an official selected by the several leagues as supreme arbiter and authority. *Abbr. Com., Comr.* — **com·mis'sion·er·ship** *n.*

commission house A business house that buys and sells goods and stocks for others on a commission basis.

commission merchant One who buys and sells goods, either as an agent for a commission or as a trader or merchant for his own account.

commission plan A form of municipal government in which the legislative and administrative powers are vested in an elected commission: also called *Galveston plan.*

com·mis·sure (kom'ə·shŏŏr) *n.* **1.** A line or place of junction; juncture; seam. **2.** *Anat.* **a** The point of union of two bodies, parts, or organs, as at the angle of the lips. **b** A connecting tract or band of nerve fibers. **3.** *Bot.* The face or edge by which two carpels adhere. [< L *commissura* a joining < *committere.* See COMMIT.] — **com·mis·su·ral** (kə·mish'ə·rəl, kom'ə·sŏŏr'əl) *adj.*

com·mit (kə·mit') *v.t.* **·mit·ted, ·mit·ting 1.** To do; perpetrate: to *commit* a crime. **2.** To place in trust or charge; entrust; consign. **3.** To consign for custody, as to a prison or mental institution. **4.** To give over, as for disposal or keeping. **5.** To consign for future reference or for preservation: to *commit* a speech to memory. **6.** To devote (oneself) unreservedly; pledge; bind. **7.** To refer, as to a committee for consideration. [< L *committere* to join, entrust < *com-* together + *mittere* to send] — **com·mit'ta·ble** *adj.*

— **Syn.** *Commit, confide, entrust,* and *consign* mean to hand over to another, usually for safekeeping. *Commit* is the most general of these words; we *commit* a person or thing to another's care, or *commit* a paper to the flames. *Confide* and *entrust* stress our confidence in the receiver. *Confide* is used chiefly of mental or spiritual things; *entrust* may also refer to material ones: to *confide* a secret to a friend; to *entrust* one's goods to someone. *Consign* occurs in commerical use: to *consign* goods to an agent. Compare TRUST.

com·mit·ment (kə·mit'mənt) *n.* **1.** The act or process of entrusting or consigning. **2.** The state of being committed, as to a hospital. **3.** An engagement or pledge to do something. **4.** The act of doing; perpetration. **5.** *Law* A warrant for imprisonment; a mittimus. **6.** The act of referring a bill or proposal to a legislative committee. **7.** Liability incurred through buying or selling stocks, bonds, etc., or by agreeing to buy or sell.

com·mit·tal (kə·mit'l) *n.* Commitment (defs. 1, 3, 4, 6).

com·mit·tee (kə·mit'ē) *n.* **1.** A group of people chosen to investigate, report, or act on a matter; also, one person so designated. **2.** *Law* One appointed by a court to care for the person or property of another. *Abbr. Com., comm.* — **in committee** Under consideration by a committee, as a proposal or bill. [< AF *commissioner,* orig. var. of *commis,* pp. of *commettre* to entrust]

com·mit·tee·man (kə·mit'ē·mən) *n. pl.* **·men** (-mən) A member of a committee. — **com·mit'tee·wom'an** *n.fem.*

committee of the whole A committee consisting of all the members present, as of a legislative body, meeting under the chairmanship of some member other than the regular presiding officer for the purpose of deliberating on some special business rather than for enacting legislation. Also **committee of the whole house.**

com·mix (kə·miks') *v.t. & v.i.* **·mixed** or **·mixt, ·mix·ing** To mix; blend. [Back formation < obs. *commixt* < L *commixtus,* pp. of *commiscere* < *com-* together + *miscere* to mix]

com·mix·ture (kə·miks'chər) *n.* A mixture; compound.

com·mode (kə·mōd') *n.* **1.** A low chest of drawers; a cabinet. **2.** A covered washstand. **3.** A low chair or cabinet enclosing a chamber pot. **4.** A woman's high headdress, worn about 1700. **5.** A toilet. [< MF < L *commodus* convenient]

com·mo·di·ous (kə·mō'dē·əs) *adj.* **1.** Containing ample room; spacious. **2.** *Archaic* Well adapted to satisfying needs. [< Med.L *commodiosus* < L *commodus* convenient] — **com·mo'di·ous·ly** *adv.* — **com·mo'di·ous·ness** *n.*

— **Syn.** ample, capacious, comfortable, roomy.

COMMODE
(*def.* 4)

com·mod·i·ty (kə-mod′ə-tē) *n. pl.* **·ties** **1.** A movable article of trade or convenience: something bought and sold. **2.** Anything of use or profit. **3.** An element of economic wealth. **4.** *Obs.* Convenience; profit. [< MF *commodité* < L *commoditas, -tatis* convenience]

commodity money The currency of a suggested financial system, the unit of which, the **commodity dollar**, has a gold value to be determined at regular intervals by an index number based on the market prices of certain commodities.

com·mo·dore (kom′ə-dôr, -dōr) *n.* **1.** In the U.S. Navy, an officer next above a captain and next below a rear admiral: a rank last used during World War II. **2.** In the Royal, Royal Canadian, and other Commonwealth navies, an officer ranking next below a rear-admiral. See table at GRADE. **3.** A title given to the senior captain of a naval squadron or of a fleet of merchantmen, or to the presiding officer of a yacht club. **COMO, Como.** [Earlier *commandore,* ? < Du. *kommandeur*]

Com·mo·dus (kom′ə-dəs), **Lucius Aelius Aurelius,** 161–192, Roman emperor 180–192.

com·mon (kom′ən) *adj.* **1.** Frequent or usual; unexceptional: a *common* occurrence. **2.** Widespread; general: *common* knowledge. **3.** Shared equally by two or more, or by all; joint; universal: our *common* heritage. **4.** Pertaining to the entire community; public. **5.** Habitual; inveterate; notorious: a *common* thief. **6.** Of low rank; ordinary: a *common* soldier. **7.** Not excellent or distinguished; commonplace; also, vulgar; low; coarse. **8.** *Gram.* **a** Of gender, applied to either sex; either masculine or feminine, as *parent, spouse, cat.* **b** Of a noun, applicable to any individual of a class of similar objects; not proper or personal, as *dog.* **9.** In prosody, either long or short; doubtful in quantity. **10.** *Math.* Referring to a number or quantity belonging equally to two or more quantities: a *common* denominator. Abbr. *com.* **11.** *Anat.* Formed by or having similar relations to two or more organs: the *common* carotid artery. — *n.* **1.** A tract of land considered as the property of the community, open to the use of all. **2.** *Law* The right of one man to take something from the lands or water of another. **3.** *Sometimes cap. Eccl.* An office or service used for any of certain classes of feast: the *common* of virgins. — **in common** Equally with another or others; jointly. [< OF *comun* < L *communis* common] — **com′mon·ness** *n.*
— **Syn.** See GENERAL, MUTUAL, TRITE. — **Ant.** unusual, rare, exceptional, infrequent.

com·mon·a·ble (kom′ən-ə-bəl) *adj.* **1.** Entitled to pasture on a common. **2.** Held in common: said of land.

com·mon·age (kom′ən-ij) *n.* **1.** A right held in common; especially, the right to pasture on a common. **2.** The state of being held in common. **3.** Land so held. **4.** The common people; commonalty.

com·mon·al·ty (kom′ən-əl-tē) *n. pl.* **·ties** **1.** The common people, as opposed to the nobility. **2.** A body corporate, or its members. **3.** The entire mass; whole: the *commonalty* of mankind. [< OF *comunalte* < *comunal.* See COMMUNAL.]

common carrier An individual or company that, for a fee, provides public transportation for goods or persons.

common council A municipal legislative body; also, a co-ordinate branch of such a body.

common denominator A number that may be divided by each of the denominators of a given group of fractions, leaving no remainder.

common divisor A number or quantity that is contained in another number or quantity without leaving a remainder.

com·mon·er (kom′ən-ər) *n.* **1.** One of the common people; a person who is not a noble. **2.** At Oxford University, a student not dependent on the university foundation for his food, tuition, etc. Compare PENSIONER (def. 2). **3.** One who has a joint right in common ground. **4.** *Rare* A member of the House of Commons.

common fraction *Math.* A fraction expressed by two numbers, a denominator, indicating the number of equal parts into which the unit is to be divided, and a numerator, indicating the number of those parts to be taken: also called *vulgar fraction.*

common gender See under GENDER.

common law **1.** A system of jurisprudence based on custom, traditional usage, and precedent, rather than codified written laws, as that of England. **2.** The system of laws generally in force in a nation, state, etc., as distinguished from regulations of local or specific application.

com·mon-law marriage (kom′ən-lô′) A marriage in which both members consent to live as man and wife without undergoing a religious or civil ceremony.

common logarithm *Math.* A logarithm having 10 as a base.

com·mon·ly (kom′ən-lē) *adv.* **1.** Ordinarily; usually. **2.** In a common manner.

common man A man of the common people; average citizen.

common market A customs union.

Common Market Any of several customs unions, especially the European Economic Community.

common measure Common time (which see).

common multiple Any number that is exactly divisible by two or more numbers, not including itself.

common noun *Gram.* A noun that names any member of a class of things, as *man, boat:* distinguished from *proper noun.*

com·mon·place (kom′ən-plās′) *adj.* Not remarkable or interesting; ordinary. — **Syn.** See TRITE. — *n.* **1.** A trite or obvious remark; platitude. **2.** Something common or ordinary. **3.** A memorable passage or fact noted for reference. [Trans. of L *locus communis* < Gk. *koinos topos* general theme or argument] — **com′mon·place′ness** *n.*

commonplace book A notebook or journal for noteworthy literary excerpts, personal memoranda, etc.

common pleas See COURT OF COMMON PLEAS.

Common Prayer The prescribed form of public worship of the Anglican Church, as contained in the Book of Common Prayer. Abbr. *C.P.*

com·mons (kom′ənz) *n.pl. Chiefly Brit.* **1.** The commonalty (def. 1). **2.** (*often construed as sing.*) Food provided for a common table, as in a college. **3.** Rations; fare. **4.** (*construed as sing.*) The dining hall of a college.

Com·mons (kom′ənz) *n.pl.* The House of Commons.

common school One of the free public elementary schools in the United States.

common sense **1.** Practical understanding; sound judgment. **2.** Ordinary mental capacity. — **com′mon-sense′** *adj.*

common stock Corporation stock the ownership of which entitles the holder to dividends or a share in the profits only after other obligations have been met and dividends rendered to holders of preferred stock.

common time *Music* Meter in which there are four quarter notes to a measure: a¹so called *common measure.*

com·mon·weal (kom′ən-wēl′) *n.* **1.** The general welfare; common good. **2.** *Obs.* A commonwealth. Also **common weal.** [< COMMON + WEAL]

com·mon·wealth (kom′ən-welth′) *n.* **1.** The whole people of a state or nation; the body politic. **2.** A state in which the sovereignty is vested in the people; a republic. Abbr. *comm.* **3.** The official title of Kentucky, Massachusetts, Pennsylvania, and Virginia; loosely, any of the United States. **4.** The official title of Puerto Rico, denoting its special status as an autonomous republic under the U.S. Government. **5.** A body of persons united by some common interest. **6.** *Obs.* The general welfare; commonweal. —

The Commonwealth The official name of the British Commonwealth of Nations. [< COMMON + WEALTH]

Commonwealth Day May 24th, the anniversary of Queen Victoria's birthday: formerly called *Empire Day.*

Commonwealth of Australia See AUSTRALIA.

Commonwealth of England The English government established after the execution of Charles I in 1649 and lasting until the beginning of Cromwell's Protectorate in 1653: also used for the whole English interregnum from 1649 until the restoration of Charles II in 1660.

Commonwealth of Nations See BRITISH COMMONWEALTH OF NATIONS.

com·mo·tion (kə-mō′shən) *n.* **1.** A violent agitation; excitement. **2.** Popular tumult; social disorder; insurrection. [< L *commotio. -onis* < *commovere* < *com-* thoroughly + *movere* to move]
— **Syn. 1.** turmoil, turbulence, fuss, disturbance. **2.** riot, uprising. Compare MUTINY. — **Ant.** calm, order.

com·move (kə-mōōv′) *v.t.* **·moved, ·mov·ing** To put in motion or commotion; disturb; unsettle. [< OF *commouvoir* < L *commovere.* See COMMOTION.]

com·mu·nal (kom′yə-nəl, kə-myōō′nəl) *adj.* **1.** Of or pertaining to a commune. **2.** Of or belonging to a community; common; public. **3.** Involving religious or ethnic groups within a country: *communal* riots. — **com′mu·nal·ly** *adv.*

com·mu·nal·ism (kom′yə-nəl-iz′əm, kə-myōō′nəl-) *n.* **1.** A theory or system of government in which the state exists merely as a federation of virtually self-governing communes. **2.** Communal ownership of goods and property. — **com′·mu·nal·ist** *n.* — **com′mu·nal·is′tic** *adj.*

com·mu·nal·ize (kom′yə-nəl-īz′, kə-myōō′nəl-īz) *v.t.* **·ized, ·iz·ing** To render communal; make municipal property of. — **com′mu·nal·i·za′tion** *n.* — **com′mu·nal·iz′er** *n.*

Com·mu·nard (kom′yə-närd) *n.* A member or adherent of the Paris Commune of 1871. [< F]

com·mune¹ (*v.* kə-myōōn′; *n.* kom′yōōn) *v.i.* **·muned, ·mun·ing** **1.** To converse or confer intimately. **2.** To partake of the Eucharist. — *n.* **1.** Intimate conversation; communion. [< OF *comuner* to share < *comun.* See COMMON.]

com·mune² (kom′yōōn) *n.* **1.** The smallest political division of France, Belgium, Italy, etc., governed by a mayor and his council. Abbr. *com.* **2.** The people or the government of such a district. **3.** Any community organized for local interests and self-government; also, its people. **4.** The common people. — **the Commune** or **the Commune of Paris** **1.** The revolutionary committee that took over the government of Paris between 1789 and 1794. **2.** The body of Communards who controlled Paris from March 18 to May 28, 1871. [< L *communa* community < *communis* common]

com·mu·ni·ca·ble (kə-myōō'ni-kə-bəl) *adj.* **1.** Capable of being communicated, as a disease. **2.** *Obs.* Communicative. — **com·mun/i·ca·bil/i·ty, com·mu/ni·ca·ble·ness** *n.* — **com·mu/ni·ca·bly** *adv.*

com·mu·ni·cant (kə-myōō'nə-kənt) *n.* **1.** One who communicates. **2.** One who partakes or has a right to partake of the Eucharist. — *adj.* Communicating. [< L *communicans, -antis,* ppr. of *communicare.* See COMMUNICATE.]

com·mu·ni·cate (kə-myōō'nə-kāt) *v.* **·cat·ed, ·cat·ing** *v.t.* **1.** To cause another or others to partake of or share in; impart. **2.** To transmit, as a disease. **3.** To convey knowledge of; tell, as one's thoughts. **4.** To administer the Eucharist to. — *v.i.* **5.** To transmit or exchange thought or knowledge: to *communicate* by gestures. **6.** To be connected: The kitchen *communicates* with the dining room. **7.** To partake of the Eucharist. [< L *communicatus,* pp. of *communicare* to share < *communis* common] — **com·mu/ni·ca·tor** *n.*

com·mu·ni·ca·tion (kə-myōō'nə-kā'shən) *n.* **1.** The act of imparting or transmitting. **2.** The transmission or exchange of ideas, information, etc., as by speech or writing. **3.** That which is communicated; a message. **4.** A means of passage or of transmitting messages between places or persons; as: **a** A line of connection; a channel. **b** *pl.* A telegraph or telephone system. **c** *pl. Mil.* The routes or methods for transporting troops and supplies. **5.** *pl.* The science or study of communicating. Abbr. *com.*

communications satellite An artificial earth satellite that is used to relay radio or television signals between distant ground points, as between continents.

com·mu·ni·ca·tive (kə-myōō'nə-kā'tiv, -kə·tiv) *adj.* **1.** Inclined to communicate freely; talkative. **2.** Of or pertaining to communication. — **com·mu/ni·ca·tive·ly** *adv.* — **com·mu/ni·ca·tive·ness** *n.*

com·mu·ni·ca·to·ry (kə-myōō'nə-kə-tôr/ē, -tō/rē) *adj.* Tending to communicate.

com·mu·ni con·sen·su (kə-myōō'nī kon·sen/sōō) *Latin* By common consent.

com·mun·ion (kə-myōōn'yən) *n.* **1.** A having or sharing in common; mutual participation. **2.** A mutual sharing of thoughts, feelings, etc.; sympathetic intercourse. **3.** Religious fellowship, as between members of a church or between autonomous churches. **4.** A body of Christians having a common faith and discipline; denomination. **5.** *Usually cap.* The Eucharist. **6.** An antiphon said or chanted after the distribution of the Eucharistic elements. [< OF < L *communio, -onis* fellowship < *communis* common]

com·mun·ion·ist (kə-myōōn'yən·ist) *n.* **1.** One holding a specified view as to who may receive Holy Communion. **2.** A communicant (def. 2).

com·mu·ni·qué (kə-myōō'nə-kā', kə-myōō'nə-kā) *n.* An official announcement or bulletin. [< F]

com·mu·nism (kom'yə-niz/əm) *n.* **1.** A social system characterized by the communal sharing of goods and services. **2.** A theory of social change conceived by Marx, directed to the ideal of a classless society. As developed by Lenin and others, it advocates seizure of power by a conspiratorial political party, maintenance of power during an interim period by stern suppression of internal opposition, centralized public ownership of almost all productive property, and the sharing of the products of labor, and commitment to the ultimate goal of a world-wide communist state. **3.** *Often cap.* The system in force in any state based on this theory, as that of the Soviet Union, the People's Republic of China, etc. [< F *commun* common, shared equally + -ISM]

com·mu·nist (kom'yə-nist) *n.* **1.** *Often cap.* A member of a Communist party. **2.** One who supports or advocates communism. **3.** *Usually cap.* A Communard. — *adj.* Pertaining to communism and communists. Abbr. *Com.* — **com·mu·nis·tic** (kom'yə-nis/tik) *adj.* — **com/mu·nis/ti·cal·ly** *adv.* — **Syn.** (noun) **1.** red, commie, Bolshevik, Bolshevist. **2.** collectivist. Compare SOCIALIST, RADICAL.

Communist Manifesto A pamphlet written in 1848 by Karl Marx and Friedrich Engels, regarded as the first statement of the principles of modern communism.

Communist Party 1. The dominant party in Russia since 1917, previously called the Bolshevik Party. **2.** Any political party advocating communism. Abbr. *C.P.*

com·mu·ni·tar·i·an (kə-myōō'nə-târ/ē-ən) *n.* A member of or a believer in a communistic community.

com·mu·ni·ty (kə-myōō'nə-tē) *n. pl.* **·ties 1.** A group of people living together or in one locality and subject to the same laws, having common interests, characteristics, etc.: a rural *community;* religious *community.* **2.** The district or area in which they live. **3.** The public; society in general. **4.** Common ownership or participation. **5.** Identity or likeness: *community* of interests. **6.** *Ecol.* **a** A group of plants or animals living under relatively similar conditions in a definite area. **b** The area in which they live. [< L *communitas, -tatis* fellowship < *communis* common] — **Syn. 1.** citizenry, constituency, denizens, inhabitants. **3.** commonalty, population. **5.** sameness.

community center A building or grounds used by a community for social and recreational activities.

community chest A welfare fund formed by individual contributions, and drawn upon by various charitable groups.

com·mu·nize (kom'yə-nīz) *v.t.* **·nized, ·niz·ing 1.** To make common; make public property. **2.** To make or cause to become communistic. — **com/mu·ni·za/tion** *n.*

com·mu·tate (kom'yə-tāt) *v.t.* **·tat·ed, ·tat·ing** *Electr.* To alter or reverse the direction of (a current).

com·mu·ta·tion (kom'yə-tā/shən) *n.* **1.** A substitution or interchange, as of one kind of payment for another. **2.** A payment or service substituted. **3.** *U.S.* Regular travel to and from work, especially over a distance by commutation ticket. **4.** *Electr.* The reversing of the direction of current. **5.** *Law* A reduction or change of the penalty imposed by a judicial sentence. [< L *commutatio, -onis* < *commutare* to change, alter < *com-* thoroughly + *mutare* change]

commutation ticket *U.S.* A railroad or other ticket issued at a reduced rate and good for a specified number of trips, or for a specified period, over a given route.

com·mu·ta·tive (kə-myōō/tə-tiv, kom'yə-tā/tiv) *adj.* **1.** Pertaining to or characterized by substitution or interchange. **2.** *Math.* Designating an operation for which the order of the quantities is irrelevant, as addition, $a + b = b + a$, or multiplication, $ab = ba$.

commutative law or **principle** *Math.* The fact that the order in which certain operations are performed will not alter the result, as 5 plus 2 is the same as 2 plus 5.

com·mu·ta·tor (kom'yə-tā/tər) *n. Electr.* **1.** Any contrivance for reversing the direction of current. **2.** An assembly of individually insulated segments connected with the armature of a dynamo or generator and serving to collect and transmit the induced current.

com·mute (kə-myōōt/) *v.* **·mut·ed, ·mut·ing** *v.t.* **1.** To exchange reciprocally for something else; interchange. **2.** To exchange for something less severe: to *commute* a sentence, debt, or payment. **3.** To pay in gross at a reduced rate, as an annuity or railroad fare, instead of in successive payments. — *v.i.* **4.** To serve as or be a substitute. **5.** To pay a railroad fare, etc., in gross at a reduced rate. **6.** To make regular trips of some distance to and from work. [< L *commutare.* See COMMUTATION.] — **com·mut/a·ble** *adj.* — **com·mut/a·ble·ness, com·mut/a·bil/i·ty** *n.*

com·mu·ter (kə-myōōt/ər) *n.* One who travels regularly some distance between home and place of work, as a suburbanite who works in the city.

com·mu·tu·al (kə-myōō/chōō-əl) *adj.* Reciprocal; mutual. [< COM- + MUTUAL]

Com·ne·nus (kom-nē/nəs) *pl.* **·ni** (-nī) A family of Byzantine sovereigns of Constantinople (1057–1185) and Trebizond (1204–1461), which included **Alexius I,** 1048–1118, emperor 1081–1118, and his daughter, Princess **Anna Comnena,** 1083–1150?.

Co·mo (kō/mō) A commune in northern Italy; pop. 82,070 (1961), on **Lake Como,** Italian *Lago di Como,* about 30 mi. long.

COMO or **Como.** *Mil.* Commodore.

Com·o·rin (kom/ə-rin), **Cape** The southernmost point of India.

Com·o·ro Islands (kom/ə-rō) A volcanic archipelago in the Indian Ocean near Madagascar, a French Overseas Territory; 863 sq. mi.; pop. 270,000 (est. 1969); capital, Moroni: French *Îles Comores, Territoire des Comores.*

co·mose (kō/mōs) *adj. Bot.* Having hairs; tufted; comate. Also **co·mous** (kō/məs). [< L *comosus* < *coma* hair]

comp. 1. Companion. **2.** Comparative. **3.** Compare. **4.** Comparison. **5.** Compilation; compiled; compiler. **6.** Complete. **7.** Composition. **8.** Compositor. **9.** Compound; compounded. **10.** Comprising.

com·pact¹ (*adj.* kəm-pakt/, kom/pakt; *v.* kəm-pakt/; *n.* kom/-pakt) *adj.* **1.** Closely and firmly united; pressed together; solid; dense; also, fine-grained. **2.** Brief and to the point; pithy; terse. **3.** Packed into a small space. **4.** Composed; made up: with *of.* — *v.t.* To pack or press closely; compress; condense. — *n.* **1.** A small, hinged box with a mirror, in which a woman carries face powder. **2.** A small automobile. [< L *compactus,* pp. of *compangere* < *com-* together + *pangere* to fasten] — **com·pact/ly** *adv.* — **com·pact/ness** *n.*

com·pact² (kom/pakt) *n.* A covenant, agreement, or contract. — **Syn.** See CONTRACT. [< L *compactum* < *compacisci* < *com-* together + *pacisci* to agree]

com·pa·dre (kom-pä/drā) *n. SW U.S.* A close male companion. [< Sp., lit., godfather]

com·pan·ion¹ (kəm-pan/yən) *n.* **1.** One who accompanies another or others; a comrade; associate. **2.** A person employed to live with, accompany, or assist another. Abbr. *comp.* **3.** One of a pair; a mate. **4.** A member of the lowest grade of an order of knighthood. Abbr. *C.* **5.** *Obs.* A worthless fellow. — **Syn.** See ASSOCIATE. — *v.t.* To be companion to; accompany; associate with. [< OF *compagnon* < LL *companio, -onis* < L *com-* together + *panis* bread]

com·pan·ion² (kəm-pan/yən) *n. Naut.* A companionway; also, the hood or covering over a companionway. [< Du. *kampanje* buarter-deck, storeroom < Med.L *campania* provisions < L *com-* with + *panis* bread; infl. by *companion¹*]

com·pan·ion·a·ble (kəm·pan′yən·ə·bəl) *adj.* Fitted for companionship; friendly; sociable. **— com·pan′ion·a·bil′i·ty** *n.* **— com·pan′ion·a·bly** *adv.*

com·pan·ion·ate (kəm·pan′yən·it) *adj.* **1.** Of or characteristic of companions. **2.** Agreed upon; shared.

companionate marriage A proposed form of marriage in which a couple agree to remain childless until marital compatibility has been assured, a simple divorce being obtainable by mutual consent before children are born.

com·pan·ion·ship (kəm·pan′yən·ship) *n.* Fellowship; association.

com·pan·ion·way (kəm·pan′yən·wā′) *n. Naut.* A staircase leading below from a ship's deck; also, the space it occupies.

com·pa·ny (kum′pə·nē) *n. pl.* **·nies** **1.** A group of people; an assemblage. **2.** A gathering of persons for social purposes; society. **3.** A guest or guests; visitors. **4.** Companionship; association; society: She kept in her mother's *company.* **5.** A number of persons associated for some common purpose, as in business: an insurance *company.* **6.** A partner or partners not named in the title of a firm. Abbr. *co., Co.,* (pl. *cos.*). **7.** A body of actors and actresses; troupe; cast. **8.** *Mil.* A body of men commanded by a captain, larger than a platoon and smaller than a battalion: the basic military unit, equivalent to a battery or troop. **9.** *Naut.* The entire crew of a ship, including the officers. **— to keep company** (**with**) **1.** To associate (with). **2.** To court, as lovers; go together. **— to part company** (**with**) To end friendship or association (with). **— v.t. & v.i. ·nied, ·ny·ing** *Archaic* To keep or go in company (with); associate (with). [< OF *compagnie* < *compagnon.* See COMPANION[1].]
— Syn. (noun) **1.** *Company, assemblage, assembly, gathering, congregation, crowd, multitude, group,* and *body* refer to a number of persons or, sometimes, things taken as a whole. *Company* implies an association, temporary or permanent, for a common purpose, as business, pleasure, travel, etc. An *assemblage* may be of persons or objects; an *assembly* is usually of persons. Both words stress the act of coming together, but *assembly* implies organization, unity of purpose, or integration of parts, while *assemblage* may be haphazard or miscellaneous. *Gathering* suggests the coming together of many persons from far and wide: the *gathering* of the clans. *Congregation* is now applied almost exclusively to a religious community. *Crowd, multitude,* and *group* designate a collection of individuals with no necessary implication of common purpose or interest: a *crowd* of bystanders, *multitudes* of insects, a *group* of pictures. *Body* is used of a number of persons so unified and organized as to be thought of as one whole. Compare ASSOCIATION, FLOCK[1]. **— Ant.** dispersion, solitude, privacy, seclusion, loneliness.

company officer *Mil.* An officer ranking below a major and serving in a company; a captain, first lieutenant, or second lieutenant.

company union A union composed of workers within one company and having no outside affiliation, usually considered to be dominated by the employer.

compar. Comparative.

com·pa·ra·ble (kom′pər·ə·bəl) *adj.* **1.** Capable of comparison. **2.** Worthy of comparison. **— com′pa·ra·ble·ness, com′pa·ra·bil′i·ty** *n.* **— com′pa·ra·bly** *adv.*

com·par·a·tive (kəm·par′ə·tiv) *adj.* **1.** Pertaining to, resulting from, or making use of comparison: *comparative* anatomy. **2.** Estimated by comparison; not positive or absolute; relative. **3.** *Gram.* Expressing a degree of an adjective or adverb higher than the positive and lower than the superlative. **— n.** *Gram.* The comparative degree, or a word or form by which it is expressed: "Better" is the *comparative of* "good." Abbr. *comp., compar.* [< L *comparativus* < *comparare.* See COMPARE.] **— com·par′a·tive·ly** *adv.*

comparative linguistics The study of the relationships among languages and dialects with emphasis upon related families, branches, etc.

com·pa·ra·tor (kom′pə·rā′tər) *n.* An instrument for automatically comparing data of length, distance, colors, etc.

com·pare (kəm·pâr′) *v.* **·pared, ·par·ing** *v.t.* **1.** To represent or speak of as similar, analogous, or equal; liken: with *to:* to *compare* a laugh to music **2.** To examine so as to perceive similarity or dissimilarity; state the resemblance or difference of: with *with.* Abbr. *cf.* or *conf.* (L *confer*), *comp., cp.* **— Syn.** See CONTRAST. **3.** *Gram.* To form or state the degrees of comparison of (an adjective or adverb). **— v.i.** **4.** To be worthy of comparison: with *with.* **5.** To vie or compete. **— n.** Comparison: usually in the phrase **beyond compare.** [< MF *comparer* < L *comparare* < *com-* together + *par* equal]

com·par·i·son (kəm·par′ə·sən) *n.* **1.** A comparing or being compared; an estimate or statement of relative likeness or unlikeness. **2.** Comparable quality or character; similarity: There is no *comparison* between them. **3.** *Gram.* That inflection of adjectives or adverbs that indicates differences of degree. There are three **degrees of comparison,** the positive, comparative, and superlative, the latter two usually expressed in words of one or two syllables by adding *-er* or *-est* to the positive, or by using *more* or *most, less* or *least,* before the positive, or by certain irregular forms. **4.** Any rhetorical

figure that compares one thing to another, as a simile or metaphor. Abbr. *comp.* **— Syn.** See SIMILE. [< OF *comparaison* < L *comparatio, -onis* < *comparare.* See COMPARE.]

com·part (kəm·pärt′) *v.t.* To divide into compartments; partition. [< OF *compartir* to divide equally < L *compartiri* < *com-* together + *partiri* to share < *pars, partis* part]

com·part·ment (kəm·pärt′mənt) *n.* **1.** One of the parts into which an enclosed space is subdivided. **2.** Any separate section or chamber: a watertight *compartment;* a passenger *compartment.* Abbr. *compt.* [< F *compartiment* < Ital. *compartimento* < L *compartiri.* See COMPART.]

com·part·men·tal·ize (kom′pärt·men′təl·īz) *v.t.* **·ized, ·iz·ing** To divide into compartments: a recent coinage.

com·pass (kum′pəs, kom′-) *n.* **1.** An instrument for determining direction, consisting essentially of a freely suspended magnetic needle that points toward the magnetic north. **2.** The reach or extent of something; area or range; scope: the *compass* of a lifetime. **3.** An enclosing line or boundary; circumference; girth. **4.** Moderate bounds; due limits. **5.** The range of tones of a voice or instrument. **6.** *Sometimes pl.* An instrument having two usually pointed legs hinged at one end, used for taking measurements, describing circles, etc.: also **pair of compasses.** **7.** *Archaic* A circular course or circuit. **— v.t.** **1.** To go round; make a circuit of. **2.** To surround; encompass. **3.** To grasp mentally; comprehend. **4.** To attain or accomplish; achieve. **5.** To plot; devise. [< OF *compas* measure, circle, compasses, appar. ult. < L *com-* together + *passus* step] **— com′pass·a·ble** *adj.*
— Syn. (noun) **2.** radius, sweep, reach, purview. **3.** periphery, perimeter. **4.** gamut. **— (verb) 1.** circumambulate. **2.** gird, ensphere. **3.** seize, apprehend. **4.** gain, reach. **5.** scheme.

Com·pass (kum′pəs, kom′-) *n.* The constellation Circinus.

compass card The circular card or dial resting on the pivot of a mariner's compass, on which the 32 points and 360 degrees of the circle are marked.

compass heading *Aeron.* A specified flight course that the pilot follows by compass indications.

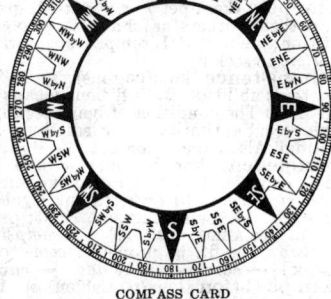

COMPASS CARD

com·pas·sion (kəm·pash′ən) *n.* Pity for the suffering or distress of another, with the desire to help or spare. **— Syn.** See PITY. [< MF < LL *compassio, -onis* < L *com-* together + *pati* to feel, suffer]

com·pas·sion·ate (*adj.* kəm·pash′ən·it; *v.* kəm·pash′ən·āt) *adj.* **1.** Feeling compassion or pity; merciful; sympathetic; charitable. **2.** *Obs.* Piteous. **— v.t.** **·at·ed, ·at·ing** To have compassion for; pity; sympathize. **— com·pas′sion·ate·ly** *adv.* **— com·pas′sion·ate·ness** *n.*

compass plant **1.** A tall, rough, bristly herb (*Silphium laciniatum*) of North American prairies, having large leaves lying in a vertical position with their edges turned north and south: also called *rosinweed.* **2.** The prickly lettuce.

com·pat·i·ble (kəm·pat′ə·bəl) *adj.* **1.** Capable of existing together; congruous; congenial: usually with *with.* **2.** In television, capable of being received in black and white on sets not adapted for color reception. [< MF < Med.L *compatibilis* < L *com-* together + *pati* to feel, suffer] **— com·pat′i·bil′i·ty, com·pat′i·ble·ness** *n.* **— com·pat′i·bly** *adv.*

com·pa·tri·ot (kəm·pā′trē·ət, -pat′rē·ət) *n.* A fellow countryman. **— adj.** Of the same country. [< F *compatriote* < LL *compatriota* < L *com-* together + *patriota* countryman < *patria* native land] **— com·pa′tri·ot′ic** (-ot′ik) *adj.* **— com·pa′tri·ot·ism** *n.*

com·peer (kəm·pir′, kom′pir) *n.* **1.** One of equal rank; a peer. **2.** A comrade; associate. **— v.t.** *Obs.* To equal; match. [< OF *comper* < L *compar* equal < *com-* with + *par* equal]

com·pel (kəm·pel′) *v.t.* **·pelled, ·pel·ling** **1.** To urge irresistibly; constrain. **2.** To obtain by force; exact. **3.** To force to yield; overpower. **4.** To drive together; herd. [OF *compeller* < L *compellere* < *com-* together + *pellere* to drive] **— com·pel′la·ble** *adj.* **— com·pel′la·bly** *adv.* **— com·pel′ler** *n.*
— Syn. 1. force, coerce, drive, oblige, necessitate. Compare ACTUATE, BIND, INFLUENCE. **— Ant.** prevent, restrain, hinder.

com·pel·la·tion (kom′pə·lā′shən) *n.* **1.** The act of addressing or greeting by name or title. **2.** The name or form used; appellation. [< L *compellatio, -onis* < *compellare* to accost]

com·pend (kom′pend) *n.* A compendium. [See COMPENDIUM.]

com·pen·di·ous (kəm·pen′dē·əs) *adj.* Stating briefly and succinctly the substance of something; concise. — **Syn.** See TERSE. [< OF *compendieux* brief < L *compendiosus* < *compendium*. See COMPENDIUM.] — **com·pen′di·ous·ly** *adv.* — **com·pen′di·ous·ness** *n.*

com·pen·di·um (kəm·pen′dē·əm) *n. pl.* **·di·ums** or **·di·a** (-dē·ə) A brief, comprehensive summary; an abridgment. — **Syn.** See ABRIDGMENT. [< L < *compendere* < *com-* together + *pendere* to weigh]

com·pen·sa·ble (kəm·pen′sə·bəl) *adj.* That may be compensated.

com·pen·sate (kom′pən·sāt) *v.* **·sat·ed, ·sat·ing** *v.t.* **1.** To make suitable amends to or for; requite; remunerate; pay; reimburse. **2.** To counterbalance or make up for; offset. **3.** To stabilize the purchasing power of (a monetary unit) by varying gold content to counteract price fluctuations. **4.** *Mech.* To provide with a device that will counteract variations, as of temperature, neutralize opposing forces, as of magnetic attraction, or maintain equilibrium. — *v.i.* **5.** To make returns or amends; serve as an equivalent or substitute. [< L *compensatus*, pp. of *compensare* < *com-* together + *pensare*, freq. of *pendere* to weigh]

com·pen·sa·tion (kom′pən·sā′shən) *n.* **1.** The act of compensating, or that which compensates; payment; amends. **2.** *Psychol.* A form of behavior whereby an individual attempts to make up for some personal lack or defect, as by the development of substitute goals or abilities. **3.** *Biol.* The offsetting of defects in the structure and functions of an organ or part by the supplementary development and action of another organ or of undamaged parts of the same organ. — **Syn.** See SALARY. — **com′pen·sa′tion·al** *adj.*

com·pen·sa·tor (kom′pən·sā′tər) *n.* **1.** One who or that which compensates. **2.** Any device or arrangement for neutralizing or offsetting something, as pressure in a gas main or the influence of local attraction on a compass needle.

com·pen·sa·to·ry (kəm·pen′sə·tôr′ē, -tō′rē) *adj.* Serving to compensate. Also **com·pen·sa·tive** (kom′pən·sā′tiv, kəm·pen′sə·tiv).

com·pete (kəm·pēt′) *v.i.* **·pet·ed, ·pet·ing** To contend with another or others, as for a prize; engage in a contest or competition; vie. [< L *competere* to strive < *com-* together + *petere* to seek]

com·pe·tence (kom′pə·təns) *n.* **1.** The state of being competent; ability. **2.** Sufficient means for comfortable living. **3.** *Law* The condition of being legally qualified or admissible; legal authority or jurisdiction: the *competence* of a tribunal. Also **com′pe·ten·cy.** — **Syn.** See ABILITY.

com·pe·tent (kom′pə·tənt) *adj.* **1.** Having sufficient ability; capable. **2.** Sufficient for the purpose; adequate: a *competent* reason. **3.** *Law* Having legal qualification; admissible; fit. **4.** Belonging as a right; permissible: with *to*. — **Syn.** See ABLE. [< MF < L *competens, -entis*, ppr. of *competere* to be fit, be proper < *com-* together + *petere* to go, seek] — **com′pe·tent·ly** *adv.* — **com′pe·tent·ness** *n.*

com·pe·ti·tion (kom′pə·tish′ən) *n.* **1.** A striving against another or others for some object, as a prize, or for superiority. **2.** A trial of skill or ability; a contest. **3.** Business rivalry between persons or firms striving for the same market. **4.** *Ecol.* The struggle for existence among living organisms. [< L *competitio, -onis* < *competere.* See COMPETE.]

com·pet·i·tive (kəm·pet′ə·tiv) *adj.* Of, pertaining to, or characterized by competition. Also **com·pet·i·to·ry** (kəm·pet′ə·tôr′ē, -tō′rē). — **com·pet′i·tive·ly** *adv.* — **com·pet′i·tive·ness** *n.*

com·pet·i·tor (kəm·pet′ə·tər) *n.* One who competes, as in games or in business. — **Syn.** See ENEMY.

Com·piègne (kôṅ·pyen′y′) A town in northern France, near the Forest of Compiègne, site of the signing of armistices between the Allies and Germany, 1918, and Germany and France, 1940; pop. about 22,000.

com·pi·la·tion (kom′pə·lā′shən) *n.* **1.** The action of compiling. **2.** Something compiled, as an anthology. Abbr. *comp.* [< MF < L *compilatio, -onis* < *compilare.* See COMPILE.]

com·pile (kəm·pīl′) *v.t.* **·piled, ·pil·ing 1.** To put together from materials collected from other sources. **2.** To gather (various materials) into a volume. **3.** To amass; collect. [< L *compilare* < *com-* thoroughly + *pilare* to strip, plunder; prob. infl. in meaning by PILE¹] — **com·pil′er** *n.*

com·pla·cen·cy (kəm·plā′sən·sē) *n. pl.* **·cies 1.** A feeling of content: satisfaction; especially, self-satisfaction; smugness. **2.** *Rare* Complaisance. Also **com·pla′cence.**

com·pla·cent (kəm·plā′sənt) *adj.* **1.** Feeling or showing satisfaction, especially self-satisfaction. **2.** Complaisant. [< L *complacens, -entis*, ppr. of *complacere* to be very pleasing < *com-* thoroughly + *placere* to please. Doublet of COMPLAISANT.] — **com·pla′cent·ly** *adv.*

com·plain (kəm·plān′) *v.i.* **1.** To express feelings of dissatisfaction, resentment. pain. etc.; grumble. **2.** To describe one's pains or ills. **3.** To make a formal accusation; present a complaint. [< OF *complaign-*, stem of *complaindre* < LL *complangere* < L *com-* thoroughly + *plangere* to beat (the breast in grief)] — **com·plain′er** *n.*

com·plain·ant (kəm·plā′nənt) *n.* One who enters a complaint, as before a magistrate. [< F *complaignant* a plaintiff, orig. ppr. of *complaindre.* See COMPLAIN.]

com·plaint (kəm·plānt′) *n.* **1.** An expression of pain, grief, grievance, or dissatisfaction. **2.** A cause for complaining; grievance. **3.** An ailment; disorder. **4.** *Law* A formal presentation charging another with the commission of an offense, as before a magistrate. — **Syn.** See DISEASE. [< F *complainte* < *complaindre.* See COMPLAIN.]

com·plai·sance (kəm·plā′zəns, kom′plə·zans) *n.* **1.** The disposition to defer to the wishes, views, or convenience of others; desire to please; obligingness. **2.** An obliging act.

com·plai·sant (kəm·plā′zənt, kom′plə·zant) *adj.* Showing a desire to please; yielding; compliant. [< MF, ppr. of *complaire* to please < L *complacere.* Doublet of COMPLACENT.] — **com·plai′sant·ly** *adv.*

com·plect (kəm·plekt′) *v.t.* To join by weaving. [< L *complecti* < *com-* together + *plecti* to twine, weave]

com·plect·ed (kəm·plek′tid) *adj. U.S. Dial.* Complexioned: used only in compounds: light-*complected*. [< earlier *complection*, var. of *complexion*]

com·ple·ment (*n.* kom′plə·mənt; *v.* kom′plə·ment) *n.* **1.** That which fills up or completes a thing; that which must be added to make up a whole. **2.** Full or complete number, allowance, or amount: The vessel has her *complement* of men. **3.** One of two parts that mutually complete each other. **4.** *Geom.* An angle that when added to another angle produces a sum of 90°. **5.** *Gram.* A word or phrase used after a verb of incomplete predication to complete the construction. A **subjective complement** describes or identifies the subject, as *president* in *He was elected president*, or *happy* in *She is happy.* An **objective complement** describes or identifies the direct object, as *president* in *They elected him president*, or *happy* in *It made her happy.* **6.** *Music* A musical interval that, with the interval already given, will complete an octave. **7.** *Bacteriol.* An unstable, heat-sensitive substance in the blood that aids in the destruction of pathogenic bacteria and materials: also called *alexin.* — *v.t.* To add or form a complement to; make complete; supply a lack in. [< L *complementum* < *complere.* See COMPLETE.]

com·ple·men·tal (kom′plə·men′təl) *adj.* Complementary.

com·ple·men·tar·i·ty (kom′plə·men·tar′ə·tē) *n. pl.* **·ties** The quality or condition of being complementary.

com·ple·men·ta·ry (kom′plə·men′tər·ē, -trē) *adj.* **1.** Serving as a complement; completing. **2.** Mutually providing each other's needs. **3.** Being a complementary color.

complementary angle *Geom.* Either of two angles whose sum is a right angle.

complementary cell *Bot.* One of the cellular components of the lenticel.

complementary color 1. Either of a pair of spectrum colors that when combined give a white or nearly white light. **2.** One of two colors or pigments whose mixture produces a third color, as blue and yellow mixed to produce green.

com·plete (kəm·plēt′) *adj.* **1.** Having all needed or normal parts; lacking nothing; entire; full. **2.** Wholly finished; ended; concluded. **3.** Perfect in quality or nature. **4.** *Archaic* Accomplished; expert. Abbr. *comp.* — *v.t.* **·plet·ed, ·plet·ing 1.** To make complete or perfect. **2.** To finish; end. [< L *completus*, pp. of *complere* < *com-* thoroughly + *plere* to fill] — **com·plete′ly** *adv.* — **com·plete′ness** *n.*

com·ple·tion (kəm·plē′shən) *n.* **1.** The act of completing, or the state of being completed. **2.** Accomplishment; fulfillment.

com·ple·tive (kəm·plē′tiv) *adj.* Serving to complete.

com·plex (*adj.* kəm·pleks′, kom′pleks; *n.* kom′pleks) *adj.* **1.** Consisting of various connected or interwoven parts; composite. **2.** Complicated, as in structure; involved; intricate. **3.** *Gram.* Designating a word containing one or more bound forms, as *quick-ly, re-ceive.* **4.** *Math.* Of, pertaining to, or involving complex numbers. — *n.* **1.** A whole made up of interwoven or connected parts. **2.** *Psychoanal.* A group of emotionally interrelated feelings, desires, memories, and ideas, that function as a unit to dominate the personality, and which, when repressed, often lead to abnormal patterns of behavior. **3.** Loosely, an excessive concern or fear; an obsession. [< L *complecti* < *com-* together + *plectere* to twist] — **com·plex′ly** *adv.* — **com·plex′ness** *n.*
— **Syn.** (adj.) **1.** *Complex, compound, composite,* and *manifold* characterize a whole by describing its parts. A thing is *complex* if its parts are numerous or diverse, and *compound* if they are chiefly alike or coordinate. Parts that display independence or striking diversity make a thing *composite*; *manifold* describes a thing composed of many like parts. **2.** *Complex, complicated, involved, tangled,* and *intricate* mean so elaborate as not to be easily understood. A matter is *complex* when it has many diverse aspects, and *complicated* when the relationships between its parts are elaborate. *Involved* suggests something rolled together and difficult to separate in thought or fact. Threads that are twisted in a confusing way are said to be *tangled*; *intricate* describes something, as a knot, which is perplexing or whose parts are difficult to follow.

complex fraction *Math.* A fraction in which either the numerator or the denominator is a fraction; also called *compound fraction.*

com·plex·ion (kəm·plek′shən) *n.* **1.** The color and appearance of the skin, especially of the face. **2.** General aspect or appearance; quality; character. **3.** *Obs.* The cast of one's mind or thought; temperament. **4.** In medieval physiology, the combination of certain qualities (cold, heat, moistness, and dryness) supposed to control the nature of plants, bodies, etc. [< F < L *complexio, -onis* the constitution of the body < *complecti* to put together. See COMPLEX.] — **com·plex′·ion·al** *adj.*

com·plex·ioned (kəm·plek′shənd) *adj.* Of a certain complexion: used in compounds: light-*complexioned*.

com·plex·i·ty (kəm·plek′sə·tē) *n. pl.* **ties. 1.** The state of being complex. **2.** Something complex.

complex number *Math.* Any number in the form $a + bi$, in which both a and b are real numbers and i is equal to $\sqrt{-1}$. Compare IMAGINARY NUMBER.

complex sentence See under SENTENCE.

com·plex·us (kəm·plek′səs) *n. Anat.* A large muscle extending from the upper thoracic vertebrae of the spine to the back of the head. [< L < *complecti*. See COMPLEX.]

com·pli·a·ble (kəm·plī′ə·bəl) *adj.* Compliant. — **com·pli′a·ble·ness** *n.* — **com·pli′a·bly** *adv.*

com·pli·ance (kəm·plī′əns) *n.* **1.** The act of complying or yielding. **2.** A disposition to comply; complaisance. Also **com·pli′an·cy.** — **in compliance with** In agreement or accordance with.
— **Syn. 1.** obedience, acquiescence, resignation, consent. **2.** easiness, pliancy, docility.

com·pli·ant (kəm·plī′ənt) *adj.* Complying; yielding. — **Syn.** See DOCILE. [< COMPLY + -ANT] — **com·pli′ant·ly** *adv.*

com·pli·ca·cy (kom′plə·kə·sē) *n. pl.* **cies 1.** The state of being complicated. **2.** A complication.

com·pli·cate (*v.* kom′plə·kāt; *adj.* kom′plə·kit) *v.* **·cat·ed, ·cat·ing** *v.t.* **1.** To make complex, difficult, or perplexing. **2.** To twist or wind around; intertwine. — *v.i.* **3.** To become complex or difficult. — *adj.* **1.** Complicated; complex. **2.** *Bot.* Folded lengthwise upon itself; conduplicate. **3.** *Zool* Folded longitudinally, as the wings of certain insects. [< L *complicatus*, pp. of *complicare* < *com-* together + *plicare* to fold]

com·pli·cat·ed (kom′plə·kā′tid) *adj.* Containing or consisting of parts or elements difficult to separate, analyze, or understand; intricate; involved. — **Syn.** See COMPLEX. — **com′pli·cat′ed·ly** *adv.* — **com′pli·cat′ed·ness** *n.*

com·pli·ca·tion (kom′plə·kā′shən) *n.* **1.** The act of complicating. **2.** An intricate or perplexing structure, condition, or relationship. **3.** Anything that complicates, as an element or condition. **4.** *Med.* A disease or condition that coexists with and aggravates the primary disease.

com·plice (kom′plis) *n. Obs.* An accomplice or close associate. [< MF < LL *complex, -icis* closely connected < stem of *complicare* to connect]

com·plic·i·ty (kəm·plis′ə·tē) *n. pl.* **·ties 1.** The state of being an accomplice, as in a wrong act. **2.** Complexity.

com·pli·er (kəm·plī′ər) *n.* One who complies.

com·pli·ment (*n.* kom′plə·mənt; *v.* kom′plə·ment) *n.* **1.** An expression of admiration, praise, or congratulation. **2.** Usually *pl.* A formal greeting or remembrance. **3.** *Archaic* A gift or gratuity. — *v.t.* **1.** To pay a compliment to. **2.** To show regard for, as by a gift. [< MF < Ital. *complimento* < Sp. *cumplimiento*, lit., completion of courtesy < L *complementum*. See COMPLEMENT.]
— **Syn.** (noun) **1.** flattery, adulation, felicitation, eulogy, panegyric. — (verb) **1.** praise, flatter, applaud. **2.** admire, commend.

com·pli·men·ta·ry (kom′plə·men′tər·ē, -trē) *adj.* **1.** Conveying, using, or like a compliment. **2.** Given free: a *complimentary* copy of a book. — **com′pli·men′ta·ri·ly** *adv.*

com·plin (kom′plin) *n. Often cap. Eccl.* Prescribed prayers constituting the last of the seven canonical hours. Also **compline** (kom′plin, -plīn), **com/plines, com/plins.** [< OF *com-plie* < L *completa (hora)* finished, last (hour) < *complere*. See COMPLETE.]

com·plot (*v.* kəm·plot′; *n.* kom′plot′) *Archaic v.t. & v.i.* **·plot·ted, ·plot·ting** To plot together. — *n.* A concerted plot; conspiracy. [< F *comploter*; ult. origin uncertain] — **com·plot′ter** *n.*

com·ply (kəm·plī′) *v.i.* **·plied, ·ply·ing 1.** To act in conformity; consent; obey: with *with.* **2.** *Obs.* To be complaisant or courteous. [< Ital. *complire* < Sp. *cumplir* complete an act of courtesy < L *complere*. See COMPLETE.]

com·po (kom′pō) *n. pl.* **·pos** A compound or mixed substance, as mortar or plaster. [Short for COMPOSITION]

com·po·nent (kəm·pō′nənt) *n.* **1.** A constituent element or part. **2.** *Chem.* In a mixture, one of the ingredients that may be present in varying proportions and without loss of its own chemical properties, as salt in water. **3.** *Physics* **a** One of the independently variable factors needed to establish equilibrium in a given material system. Compare PHASE RULE. **b** One of two or more forces, or parts of a single force, acting to produce a given resultant. — *adj.* Forming a part or ingredient; constituent. [< L *componens, -entis,* ppr. of *componere.* See COMPOSE.]

com·po·ny (kəm·pō′nē) *adj. Heraldry* Composed of two tinctures in alternate squares in one row: said of an or-

dinary. Also **com·po·né** (kəm·pō′nā, *Fr.* kôṅ·pô·nā′). [< OF *componné,* prob. < L *componere.* See COMPOSE.]

com·port (kəm·pôrt′, -pōrt′) *v.t.* **1.** To conduct or behave (oneself). — *v.i.* **2.** To be compatible; agree: with *with.* [< F *comporter* bear, behave < L *comportare* < *com-* together + *portare* to carry]

com·port·ment (kəm·pôrt′mənt, -pōrt′-) *n.* Behavior or bearing; deportment.

com·pose (kəm·pōz′) *v.* **·posed, ·pos·ing** *v.t.* **1.** To be the constituent elements of; constitute; form: usually used in the passive: Water is *composed* of hydrogen and oxygen. **2.** To make of elements or parts; fashion. **3.** To create (a literary or musical work). **4.** To make calm or tranquil; quiet: *Compose* yourself. **5.** To reconcile or settle, as differences. **6.** To arrange artistically, as elements in a painting. **7.** *Printing* To arrange (type) in lines; set. — *v.i.* **8.** To engage in composition, as of musical works. **9.** *Printing* To set type. [< MF *composer* < *com-* together + *poser.* See POSE[1].]
— **Syn. 2.** fabricate. **4.** collect. **5.** adjust, arbitrate.

com·posed (kəm·pōzd′) *adj.* Free from agitation; calm. — **com·pos·ed·ly** (kəm·pō′zid·lē) *adv.* — **com·pos′ed·ness** *n.*
— **Syn.** cool, unruffled, nonchalant, tranquil, collected.

com·pos·er (kəm·pō′zər) *n.* One who composes; especially, one who writes music.

composing room *Printing* A room where type is set.

composing stick *Printing* A tray, usually of metal and adjustable in width, in which type is set and spaced by hand.

com·pos·ite (kəm·poz′it) *adj.* **1.** Made up of separate parts or elements; combined or compounded. **2.** *Bot.* Characteristic of or pertaining to the largest, most highly developed and widely distributed family (*Compositae,* formerly *Asteraceae*) in the vegetable kingdom, consisting mostly of herbaceous plants, as the dandelion, chrysanthemum, dahlia, aster, etc., the flowers usually occurring in dense clusters opening from a central cup-shaped envelope. — *n.* **1.** That which is composed or made up of parts; a compound. **2.** *Bot.* A composite plant. [< L *compositus,* pp. of *componere* < *com-* together + *ponere* to put. Doublet of COMPOST.] — **com·pos′ite·ly** *adv.* — **com·pos′ite·ness** *n.*
— **Syn.** See COMPLEX. — (noun) **1.** synthesis, mixture, combination, blend, fusion, amalgam. — **Ant.** pure.

composite number *Math.* Any number exactly divisible by one or more numbers other than itself and 1: opposed to *prime number.*

Composite order *Archit.* A variant of the Corinthian order, having four scroll-like ornaments, like those of the Ionic order, above the acanthus leaves.

composite photograph A photograph formed by combining several photographs.

composite school *Canadian* A high school with academic, commercial, and industrial curricula: also *comprehensive school.*

com·po·si·tion (kom′pə·zish′ən) *n.* **1.** A putting together of parts, ingredients, etc., to form a whole. **2.** That which is so formed, or the condition or state resulting from such formation; compound; mixture. **3.** The manner of being put together; constitution; make-up. **4.** The arranging of words into sentences, notes into music, etc.; especially, the act or art of creating a literary, musical, or artistic work. **5.** The work so created, or its general structural arrangement or organization. **6.** A short essay, especially one written as an exercise for school. **7.** *Gram.* The formation of compounds. **8.** An agreement or settlement, especially by compromise. **9.** *Law* An agreement whereby the creditors of an insolvent debtor accept partial payment as full satisfaction for the debt; also, the sum agreed upon. **10.** *Printing* The setting of type. Abbr. *comp.* [< MF < L *compositio, -onis* < *compo-nere.* See COMPOSITE.]
— **Syn. 1.** combination, amalgamation, assembly, compounding. **2.** amalgam, blend, admixture. **8.** adjustment, bargain.

composition face *Crystall.* The face or plane by which the parts of a twin crystal are united. Also **composition plane.**

composition of forces *Physics* The joining of two or more forces, exerted in the same or different directions, into one equivalent force, the resultant.

com·pos·i·tive (kəm·poz′ə·tiv) *adj.* Having the power of compounding; synthetic.

com·pos·i·tor (kəm·poz′ə·tər) *n. Printing* A typesetter (def. 1). Abbr. *comp.*

com·pos men·tis (kom′pəs men′tis) *Latin* Of sound mind.

com·post (kom′pōst) *n.* **1.** A fertilizing mixture of decomposed vegetable matter. **2.** A mixture; compound. [< OF, mixture < L *compostum,* var. of *compositum,* pp. of *com-ponere.* Doublet of COMPOSITE.]

Com·po·ste·la (kōm′pō·stā′lä) See SANTIAGO DE COMPOSTELA.

com·po·sure (kəm·pō′zhər) *n.* **1.** Tranquillity, as of mind; calmness; serenity. **2.** *Obs.* Composition. [< COMPOSE]

com·po·ta·tion (kom′pō·tā′shən) *n.* A drinking in company; carouse. [< L *compotatio, -onis* < *com-* together + *potare* to drink]

com·pote (kom'pōt, Fr. kôṅ·pôt') n. 1. Fruit stewed or preserved in syrup. 2. A dish for holding fruits, etc. [< F < OF composte. Related to COMPOST.]

com·pound¹ (n. kom'pound; v. kom·pound', kəm-; adj. kom'pound, kom·pound') n. 1. A combination of two or more elements, ingredients, or parts. 2. Gram. a In writing, a word composed of two or more words joined with a hyphen or written in solid form, as fly-by-night, shoestring. b In speaking. two or more words connected by a reduction of stress on one and a shortening of the pause between the words, as blue'ber'ry distinguished from blue' ber'ry. Many spoken compounds are written as separate words, as air mail, life raft, street corner. 3. Chem. A definite substance resulting from the combination of specific elements or radicals in fixed proportions: distinguished from mixture. —v.t. 1. To make by combining various elements or ingredients. 2. To mix (elements or parts) to form a compound substance; combine: to compound drugs. 3. To compute (interest) on both the principal and whatever interest has accrued. 4. To complicate or intensify, as by the introduction of a new element: to compound an insult. 5. To settle for less than the sum due, as a debt; compromise. 6. Law To aid in concealing (a crime) or to agree not to prosecute, in return for a consideration: to compound a felony. 7. Electr. To place duplex windings on the field magnets of (a dynamo), one serving as a shunt and the other being in series with the main circuit, making the machine self-regulating. —v.i. 8. To agree or come to terms, especially by way of a compromise. —adj. 1. Composed of or produced by the union of two or more elements, ingredients, or parts; composite. 2. Zool. Made up of many distinct individuals functioning as a whole, as a colony of hydrozoans. Abbr. comp., cpd. [Orig. pp. of ME compounen to combine < OF compondre < L componere. See COMPOSITE.] —com·pound'a·ble adj. —com·pound'er n.
—Syn. (noun) 1. mixture, admixture, blend, composite, amalgam, fusion. —(verb) 1. compose, constitute, synthesize. 2. blend, amalgamate. 5. adjust. —(adj.). See COMPLEX.

com·pound² (kom'pound) n. 1. In the Orient, an enclosure containing a residence, factory, etc., especially one occupied by Europeans. 2. Any similar enclosed place. [< Malay kampong]

compound engine A steam or compressed-air engine in which the working fluid expands in two stages from a small, high-pressure cylinder to a larger, low-pressure cylinder.

compound eye Biol. The organ of vision in many insects and certain other arthropods. consisting of numerous photosensitive facets, each contributing to a mosaiclike image upon the retina.

compound flower Bot. The anthodium or head of the flower of a composite plant.

compound fraction Math. A complex fraction (which see).

compound fracture See under FRACTURE.

compound interest Interest computed on the original principal together with its accrued interest.

compound leaf Bot. A leaf having several distinct blades on a common leafstalk. For illustration see LEAF.

compound meter Music See under METER².

compound number Math. A quantity containing more than one unit or denomination, as 6 feet 3 inches.

compound sentence See under SENTENCE.

com·pra·dor (kom'prə·dôr') n. In China. etc., a native agent, as in a foreign business house, consulate, etc. Also **com'pra·dore'**. [< Pg. buvor, ult. < L comparare to buy]

com·pre·hend (kom'pri·hend') v.t. 1. To grasp mentally; understand fully. 2. To take in or embrace; include. —v.i. 3. To understand. —Syn. See APPREHEND. [< L comprehendere < com- together + prehendere to grasp, seize]

com·pre·hen·si·ble (kom'pri·hen'sə·bəl) adj. Capable of being comprehended; understandable: intelligible. Also **com'·pre·hend'i·ble.** —com'pre·hen·si·bil'i·ty, com·pre·hen'si·ble·ness n. —com'pre·hen'si·bly adv.

com·pre·hen·sion (kom'pri·hen'shən) n. 1. The mental grasping of ideas, facts, etc., or the power of so doing; understanding. 2. An including or taking in; comprehensiveness. 3. Logic The complete conception of a term or idea, involving all the elements of its meaning and its correlations. —Syn. See KNOWLEDGE. [< L comprehensio, -onis < comprehendere. See COMPREHEND.]

com·pre·hen·sive (kom'pri·hen'siv) adj. 1. Large in scope or content: including much; broad. 2. Having the power of fully understanding or comprehending. —com'pre·hen'·sive·ly adv. —com'pre·hen'sive·ness n.

comprehensive school Canadian A composite school (which see).

com·press (v. kəm·pres'; n. kom'pres) v.t. To press together or into smaller space; condense; compact. —n. 1. Med. A cloth or pad, sometimes medicated, for applying moisture, cold, heat, or pressure to a part of the body. 2. An apparatus for compressing bales of cotton, etc. [< OF compresser < LL compressare, freq. of L comprimere < com- together + premere to press] —com·press'i·bil'i·ty, com·press'i·ble·ness n. —com·press'i·ble adj.

com·pressed (kəm·prest') adj. 1. Pressed together or into

smaller compass; made compact. 2. Flattened laterally. 3. Biol. Reduced in breadth, as the bodies of certain fishes.
—Syn. 1. concentrated, condensed, contracted. 2. squashed.

compressed air Air reduced in volume by pressure, so that its expansive force can be utilized in various mechanisms.

com·pres·sion (kəm·presh'ən) n. 1. The act of compressing or the state of being compressed. Also **com·pres·sure** (kəm·presh'ər). 2. The process by which a confined gas is reduced in volume through the application of pressure, as in the cylinder of an internal-combustion engine. [< MF < L compressio, -onis < comprimere. See COMPRESS.]

com·pres·sive (kəm·pres'iv) adj. Tending to or having the power to compress. —com·press'ive·ly adv.

com·pres·sor (kəm·pres'ər) n. 1. One who or that which compresses. 2. Anat. A muscle that compresses a part of the body. 3. Surg. An instrument for compressing a part of the body. 4. Mech. A power-driven machine for compressing a gas in order to utilize its expansion, as for refrigeration.

com·prise (kəm·prīz') v.t. ·prised, ·pris·ing To consist of or take in; contain; include; embrace. [< MF compris, pp. of comprendre < L comprehendere. See COMPREHEND.] —com·pris'a·ble adj. —com·pri'sal n.

com·pro·mise (kom'prə·mīz) n. 1. An adjustment or settlement by mutual concession, usually involving a partial surrender of claims, purposes, or principles. 2. The result of such concessions. 3. Something lying midway between, or combining the qualities of, two different things. 4. An imperiling, as of character or reputation. —v. ·mised, ·mis·ing v.t. 1. To adjust by concessions. 2. To expose to risk, suspicion, or disrepute; imperil: to compromise one's reputation. 3. Obs. To bind or pledge mutually. —v.i. 4. To make a compromise. [< MF compromis < L compromissum a mutual agreement to accept arbitration < com- together + promittere to promise] —com'pro·mis'er n.

compt. 1. Compartment. 2. Comptometer.

compte ren·du (kôṅt rän·dü') French An official report; literally, account rendered.

Comp·tom·e·ter (komp·tom'ə·tər) n. A high-speed calculating machine: a trade name. Also **comp·tom'e·ter.**

Comp·ton (komp'tən) A city in SW California, near Los Angeles; pop. 78,611.

Comp·ton (komp'tən), **Arthur Holly**, 1892–1962, and his brother, **Karl Taylor**, 1887–1954, U.S. physicists.

comp·trol·ler (kən·trō'lər) See CONTROLLER (def. 2).

com·pul·sion (kəm·pul'shən) n. 1. The act of compelling; coercion. 2. The state of being compelled. 3. Psychol. a An irresistible impulse or tendency to perform an act. b An act or series of acts so performed. [< MF < L compulsio, -onis < compellere. See COMPEL.]
—Syn 1. constraint, force, duress. 2. necessity, obligation.

com·pul·sive (kəm·pul'siv) adj. 1. Compelling; compulsory. 2. Psychol. Of, pertaining to, or involving compulsion. —com·pul'sive·ly adv. —com·pul'sive·ness n.

com·pul·so·ry (kəm·pul'sər·ē) adj. 1. Employing compulsion; coercive. 2. Required; obligatory: compulsory education. —com·pul'so·ri·ly adv. —com·pul'so·ri·ness n.

com·punc·tion (kəm·pungk'shən) n. 1. An uneasiness of mind arising from wrongdoing; a sense of guilt or remorse. 2. A feeling of slight regret or pity. —Syn. See REPENTANCE. [< OF < LL compunctio, -onis < L com- greatly + pungere to prick, sting] —com·punc'tious adj. —com·punc'tious·ly adv.

com·pur·ga·tion (kom'pər·gā'shən) n. Formerly, the practice of clearing a person of a charge if a sufficient number of people swore to his innocence. [< LL compurgatio, -onis < L com- thoroughly + purgare to cleanse]

com·pur·ga·tor (kom'pər·gā'tər) n. One who testifies in favor of another.

com·pu·ta·tion (kom'pyə·tā'shən) n. 1. The act or method of computing. 2. A computed amount or number.

com·pute (kəm·pyōōt') v.t. & v.i. ·put·ed, ·put·ing To ascertain (an amount or number) by calculation; reckon. —Syn. See CALCULATE. —n. Computation. [< MF computer < L computare < com- together + putare to reckon. Doublet of COUNT¹.] —com·put'a·bil'i·ty n. —com·put'a·ble adj. —com·put'ist n.

com·put·er (kəm·pyōō'tər) n. 1. One who or that which computes. 2. Any of various machines equipped with keyboards, electronic and electrical circuits, storage units, and recording devices for the high-speed performance of mathematical and logical operations, or for the processing of large masses of coded information.

Comr. Commissioner.

com·rade (kom'rad, -rid, kum'-) n. 1. An intimate companion or friend. 2. A person who shares one's own occupation, interests, etc. 3. Often cap. A fellow member, as of a political party, especially of the Communist Party. —Syn. See ASSOCIATE. [Earlier camerade < MF camarade < Sp. camarada roommate < L camera room] —com'rade·ship n.

Com·stock (kum'stok, kom'-), **Anthony**, 1844–1915, U.S. crusader against immorality.

Com·stock·er·y (kum'stok/ər·ē, kom'-) n. Exaggerated censorship of literature, pictures, etc., because of alleged immorality. [after Anthony Comstock]

Com·stock Lode (kum′stok, kom′-)   A rich vein of silver and gold discovered in 1859 at Virginia City, Nevada. [after Henry *Comstock*, 1820–70, U.S. prospector]

comte (kôṅt)   *n. French* A count[2].

Comte (kôṅt, *Fr.* kôṅt), **Auguste**, 1798–1857, French philosopher; founder of positivism. **— Com·ti·an** (kom′tē-ən, kôṅ′-) *adj.*

Com·tism (kom′tiz-əm, kôṅ′-)   *n.* The philosophy of Comte; positivism. **— Com′tist** *adj. & n.*

Co·mus (kō′məs)   1. In classical mythology, the young god of revelry   2. A masque (1634) by John Milton.

Com. Ver.   Common Version (of the Bible).

con[1] (kon)   *v.t.* **conned, con·ning** To study; peruse carefully; commit to memory. [Var. of CAN[1]] **— con′ner** *n.*

con[2] (kon)   *Naut. v.t.* **conned, con·ning** To direct the steering of (a vessel). **—** *n.* The act or post of one who cons. Also spelled **conn.** [Earlier *cond* < F *conduire* to guide < L *conducere.* See CONDUCT.]

con[3] (kon)   *U.S. Slang adj.* Confidence: used in phrases: *con* man; *con* game. **—** *v.t.* **conned, con·ning** To defraud; dupe; swindle. [Short for CONFIDENCE.]

con[4] (kon)   *n.* A person, vote, proposal, etc., that is in opposition. **—** *adv.* Against. See PRO[1]. [< L *contra* against]

con[5] (kon)   *n. Slang* A convict.

con- Var. of COM-.

con.   1. Against (L *contra*).   2. *Music* Concerto.   3. Conclusion.   4. Condense.   5. Connection.   6. Consolidate.   7. Consols.   8. Continued.   9. Wife (L *conjunx*).

Con.   1. Conformist.   2. Consul.

Co·na·kry (kô-nà-krē′)   The capital of Guinea, a port city in the western part on Tombo Island; pop. 197,267 (est. 1967): also *Konakri*.

con a·mo·re (kōn ä-mō′rä)   *Music* Lovingly; with tenderness: a direction to the performer. [< Ital., with love]

Co·nant (kō′nənt), **James Bryant**, born 1893, U.S. chemist and educator; president of Harvard University 1933–53.

co·na·tion (kō-nā′shən)   *n. Psychol.* The element of volition and of conscious striving. **— Syn.** See WILL[1]. [< L *conatio, -onis* an attempt < *conari* to try]

con·a·tive (kon′ə-tiv, kō′nə-)   *adj.* 1. *Psychol.* Of, pertaining to, or having the nature of conation.   2. *Ling.* Expressing endeavor: said of a form of certain Semitic verbs.

co·nat·u·ral (kə-nach′ər-əl)   See CONNATURAL.

co·na·tus (kō-nā′təs)   *n. pl.* **·tus** 1. An attempt or endeavor; effort.   2. *Biol.* A tendency in plants and animals analogous to effort in human beings. [< L < *conari* to try]

con bri·o (kōn brē′ō)   *Music* With spirit. [< Ital.]

conc.   1. Concentrate; concentrated; concentration.   2. Concerning.

con·cat·e·nate (kon-kat′ə-nāt)   *v.t.* **·nat·ed, ·nat·ing** To join or link together; connect in a series. **—** *adj.* Joined together; connected in a series. [< L *concatenatus*, pp. of *concatenare* < *com-* together + *catena* chain]

con·cat·e·na·tion (kon-kat′ə-nā′shən)   *n.* 1. The act of linking together.   2. Union in a chainlike series.   3. A succession of things united and mutually dependent or related, as associated nerve cells, events, etc.

con·cave (*adj.* kon-kāv′, kon′kāv, kong′-; *n.* kon′kāv, kong′-; *v.* kon-kāv′)   *adj.* 1. Hollow and curving inward, as the interior of a sphere or bowl: opposed to *convex.*   2. *Obs.* Hollow. **—** *n.* A concave surface; vault. **—** *v.t.* **·caved. ·cav·ing** To make concave. [< MF < L *concavus* < *com-* thoroughly + *cavus* hollow] **— con·cave′ly** *adv.* **— con·cave′ness** *n.*

con·cav·i·ty (kon-kav′ə-tē)   *n. pl.* **·ties** 1. The state of being concave.   2. A concave surface; a hollow.

con·ca·vo-con·cave (kon-kā′vō-kon-kāv′)   *adj.* Biconcave (which see).

con·ca·vo-con·vex (kon-kā′vō-kon-veks′)   *adj.* 1. Concave on one side and convex on the other.   2. *Optics* Describing a lens in which the curvature of the concave side is greater than that of the convex: distinguished from *convexo-concave.* See illustration of LENS.

con·ceal (kən-sēl′)   *v.t.* To keep from sight, discovery, or knowledge; hide; secrete. **— Syn.** See HIDE[1]. [< OF *conceler* < L *concelare* < *com-* thoroughly + *celare* to hide] **— con·ceal′a·ble** *adj.* **— con·ceal′er** *n.*

con·ceal·ment (kən-sēl′mənt)   *n.* 1. The act of concealing, or the state of being concealed.   2. A place or means of hiding.

con·cede (kən-sēd′)   *v.* **·ced·ed, ·ced·ing** *v.t.* 1. To acknowledge as true, correct, or proper; admit.   2. To grant; yield, as a right or privilege. **—** *v.i.* 3. To make a concession; yield. **— Syn.** See CONFESS, GRANT. [< L *concedere* < *com-* thoroughly + *cedere* to yield, go away] **— con·ced′er** *n.*

con·ceit (kən-sēt′)   *n.* 1. A high opinion of one's own person or accomplishments; overweening self-esteem.   2. An ingenious, fanciful thought or expression.   3. In poetry, an elaborate, extended metaphor; also, the use of such metaphors.   4. Imagination; fancy.   5. *Archaic* A thought; conception.   6. *Obs.* The power of conceiving; understanding.

7. *Obs.* A fancy article. **— Syn.** See EGOTISM, PRIDE. **—** *v.t.* 1. *Obs.* To imagine.   2. *Dial.* To take a fancy to; regard favorably. [< CONCEIVE, on analogy with *deceit, receipt*, etc.]

con·ceit·ed (kən-sē′tid)   *adj.* 1. Having an excessively high opinion of oneself; vain.   2. *Dial.* Fanciful; whimsical. **— con·ceit′ed·ly** *adv.* **— con·ceit′ed·ness** *n.*

con·ceive (kən-sēv′)   *v.* **·ceived, ·ceiv·ing** *v.t.* 1. To become pregnant with.   2. To form in the mind; develop mentally.   3. To form a concept or notion of; imagine: to *conceive* the perfect man.   4. To understand; grasp.   5. To express in a particular way.   6. To believe or suppose; think. **—** *v.i.* 7. To form a mental image; think: with *of.*   8. To become pregnant. [< OF *conceveir* < L *concipere* < *com-* thoroughly + *capere* to grasp, take] **— con·ceiv′a·ble** *adj.* **— con·ceiv′a·bil/i·ty, con·ceiv′a·ble·ness** *n.* **— con·ceiv′a·bly** *adv.* **— con·ceiv′er** *n.*

— Syn. 3. visualize, envision, fancy. 4. apprehend, comprehend.

con·cent (kən-sent′)   *n. Archaic* 1. Concord of sounds or voices; harmony.   2. Agreement. [< L *concentus* < *con-cinere* to harmonize < *com-* together + *canere* to sing]

con·cen·ter (kon-sen′tər)   *v.t. & v.i.* To direct or come to a common point or center; focus. Also *Brit.* **con·cen′tre.** [< F *concentrer* < L *com-* together + *centrum* center]

con·cen·trate (kon′sən-trāt)   *v.* **·trat·ed, ·trat·ing** *v.t.* 1. To draw or direct to a common point; focus: to *concentrate* troops; to *concentrate* one's attention.   2. To intensify or purify by removing certain constituents; condense. **—** *v.i.* 3. To converge toward a center.   4. To become compacted, intensified, or more pure.   5. To direct one's entire attention: often with *on* or *upon.* **—** *n.* A product of concentration, as in chemistry or metallurgy. **—** *adj.* Concentrated. Abbr. **conc.** [< CONCENTER + -ATE[1]] **— con′cen·tra′tor** *n.*

— Syn. 1. gather, consolidate, unify, assemble. 2. distill, refine, rectify. 5. fasten, fix. **— Ant.** dissipate, disperse.

con·cen·tra·tion (kon′sən-trā′shən)   *n.* 1. The act of concentrating, or the state of being concentrated.   2. That which is concentrated.   3. Complete attention to some single problem, task, etc.   4. *Chem.* The amount of a substance per unit volume, as of a solute in a solution. Abbr. **conc.**

concentration camp An enclosed camp for the confinement of prisoners of war, political prisoners, aliens, etc.

con·cen·tra·tive (kon′sən-trā′tiv, kən-sen′trə-tiv)   *adj.* Tending to concentrate, or characterized by concentration. **— con′cen·tra′tive·ly** *adv.* **— con′cen·tra′tive·ness** *n.*

con·cen·tric (kən-sen′trik)   *adj.* Having a common center, as circles: opposed to *eccentric.* Also **con·cen′tri·cal.** **— con·cen′tri·cal·ly** *adv.* **— con·cen·tric·i·ty** (kon′sen-tris′ə-tē) *n.*

Con·cep·ción (kôn′sep-syōn′)   A Province of south central Chile; 2,201 sq. mi.; pop. 638,118 (est. 1970); capital, **Concepción,** pop. 189,929.

con·cept (kon′sept)   *n.* A mental image; especially, a generalized idea formed by combining the elements of a class into the notion of one object; also, a thought or opinion. **— Syn.** See IDEA. [< L *conceptus* a conceiving < *concipere.* See CONCEIVE.]

con·cep·ta·cle (kən-sep′tə-kəl)   *n. Bot.* A cavity on the surface of many algae and fungi, enclosing reproductive bodies. [< L *conceptaculum* a receptacle < *concipere.* See CONCEIVE.]

con·cep·tion (kən-sep′shən)   *n.* 1. A conceiving, or a being conceived, in the womb.   2. That which is so conceived; an embryo or fetus.   3. A beginning; commencement.   4. The act or faculty of forming concepts or contriving designs and plans; apprehension; invention.   5. That which is conceived or devised mentally; a concept, idea, plan, or design. **— con·cep′tion·al** *adj.*

con·cep·tive (kən-sep′tiv)   *adj.* Capable of conceiving mentally.

con·cep·tu·al (kən-sep′chōō-əl)   *adj.* Of or pertaining to conception or concepts. **— con·cep′tu·al·ly** *adv.*

con·cep·tu·al·ism (kən-sep′chōō-əl-iz′əm)   *n. Philos.* The doctrine, intermediate between the extremes of nominalism and realism, that universals, or abstract characteristics, have no independent reality, and exist only as ideas in the mind or as traits embodied in particular things. **— con·cep′tu·al·ist** *n.* **— con·cep′tu·al·is′tic** *adj.*

con·cern (kən-sûrn′)   *v.t.* 1. To relate or pertain to; be of interest or importance to.   2. To occupy the attention or mind of; engage; involve: used as a reflexive or in the passive, often with *in* or *with*: He *concerns* himself with petty details.   3. To affect with anxiety; trouble: often in the passive. **—** *v.i.* 4. *Obs.* To be of importance. **—** *n.* 1. That which concerns or affects one; affair; business.   2. Anxiety or interest; solicitous regard; care.   3. Relation or bearing.   4. A business enterprise; a firm.   5. *Informal* Any object, contrivance, or article: usually derogatory. **— Syn.** See CARE. [< MF *concerner* < Med.L *concernere* to regard < L *com-* thoroughly + *cernere* to see, discern]

con·cerned (kən-sûrnd′)   *adj.* 1. Interested or involved.   2. Uneasy; troubled.

---

con·cern·ing (kən·sûr'ning) *prep.* In relation to; regarding; about. *Abbr. conc.*

con·cern·ment (kən·sûrn'mənt) *n.* 1. Relation, bearing, or importance. 2. Participation; involvement. 3. A feeling of concern; anxiety. 4. Anything that relates to one; affair.

con·cert (*n.* kon'sûrt; *v.* kən·sûrt') *n.* 1. A musical performance by a number of singers or musicians appearing singly or in various combinations. 2. Agreement in effort, purpose, or feeling; accord; harmony. **— in concert** In unison; all together. **—** *adj.* Of or for concerts. **—** *v.t.* 1. To arrange or contrive by mutual agreement. 2. To plan; contrive. **—** *v.i.* 3. To act or plan together. [< MF < Ital. *concerto* harmony < *concertare* to agree, be in accord] **— Syn.** (noun) 2. cooperation, concurrence.

con·cert·ed (kən·sûr'tid) *adj.* 1. Arranged, agreed upon, or done together; combined. 2. *Music* Arranged in parts for voices or instruments. **— con·cert'ed·ly** *adv.*

con·cer·ti·na (kon'sər·tē'nə) *n.* A small bellowslike musical instrument with buttons for keys and handles on each of the two hexagonal ends. [< Ital. < *concerto.* See CONCERT.]

con·cer·ti·no (kon'cher·tē'nō) *n. pl.* ·nos or ·ni (-nē) *Music* 1. A short concerto. 2. The group of solo instruments in a concerto grosso. [< Ital., dim. of *concerto.* See CONCERT.]

con·cer·tize (kon'sər·tīz) *v.i.* ·tized, ·tiz·ing To perform music publicly, especially as a soloist.

con·cert·mas·ter (kon'sərt·mas'tər, -mäs'-) *n.* The leader of the first violin section of an orchestra, who acts as assistant to the conductor. Also con·cert·meis·ter (kon'sərt·mīs'tər, *Ger.* kôn·tsert'mīs'tər).

CONCERTINA

con·cer·to (kən·cher'tō) *n. pl.* ·tos, *Ital.* ·ti (-tē) *Music* A composition, usually of three movements, for performance by a solo instrument or instruments accompanied by an orchestra. *Abbr. con.* [< Ital. See CONCERT.]

concerto gros·so (grō'sō) *pl.* concerti gros·si (grō'sē) A concerto for a group of solo instruments and an orchestra. [< Ital., lit., big concerto]

concert pitch See under PITCH².

con·ces·sion (kən·sesh'ən) *n.* 1. The act of conceding or yielding, as to a demand, point of argument, etc. 2. Anything so yielded. 3. A right, privilege, or property granted by a government or other authority for a specific purpose. 4. *U.S.* The right to operate a subsidiary business on certain premises; also, the business so operated: a coatroom *concession.* 5. *Canadian* In Ontario and Quebec, a subdivision of land in township surveys. 6. A strip of land conceded to an alien government for its economic use, usually with the privileges of self-government and extraterritoriality. [< MF < L *concessio, -onis* < *concedere.* See CONCEDE.]

con·ces·sion·aire (kən·sesh'ən·âr') *n.* One who holds or operates a concession. Also con·ces'sion·er [< F]

con·ces·sion·ar·y (kən·sesh'ən·er'ē) *adj.* Pertaining to, or obtained by a concession. **—** *n. pl.* ·ar·ies A concession-aire.

concession road *Canadian* In Ontario and Quebec, a road following a survey line.

con·ces·sive (kən·ses'iv) *adj.* 1. Involving or implying concession. 2. *Gram.* Expressing concession, as the conjunction *though.*

conch (kongk, konch) *n. pl.* conchs (kongks) or conch·es (kon'chiz) 1. Any of various marine mollusks (order *Gastropoda*) having large, spiral, univalve shells; especially, the **giant** or **queen conch** (*Strombus gigas*), and the **fighting conch** (*S. pugilis*) of southern waters. 2. The shell of such a mollusk. 3. Such a shell blown as a horn by the Tritons. 4. *Archit.* A semidome or the plain concave surface of a dome or vault. [< L *concha* < Gk. *konchē* shell]

CONCH SHELL

conch. Conchology.

con·cha (kong'kə) *n. pl.* ·chae (-kē) 1. *Anat.* A structure of shell-like appearance, as the external ear. 2. *Archit.* A conch. [< L. See CONCH.]

con·chif·er·ous (kong·kif'ər·əs) *adj.* Bearing or producing a shell. [< L *concha* shell + -FEROUS]

Con·cho·bar (kong'kō·wər, kon'ōr) In Irish legend, a king of Ulster. See DEIRDRE.

con·choi·dal (kong·koid'l) *adj. Mineral.* Having shell-like elevations and depressions.

con·chol·o·gy (kong·kol'ə·jē) *n.* The study of shells and mollusks. [< L *concha* shell + -LOGY] **— con·cho·log·i·cal** (kong'kə·loj'i·kəl) *adj.* **— con·chol'o·gist** *n.*

con·chy (kon'chē) *n. pl.* ·chies *Slang* A conscientious objector.

con·ci·erge (kon'sē·ûrzh', *Fr.* kôn·syârzh') *n.* 1. The doorkeeper of a building; a janitor. 2. *Obs.* A custodian or warden. [< F; ult. origin unknown]

con·cil·i·ate (kən·sil'ē·āt) *v.t.* ·at·ed, ·at·ing 1. To over-

come the hostility or suspicion of; secure the friendship of; win over; placate; appease; propitiate. 2. To secure or attract by favorable measures; win. 3. To make compatible or consistent. [< L *conciliatus,* pp. of *conciliare* to unite, reconcile < *concilium* council] **— con·cil·i·a·ble** (kən·sil'ē·ə·bəl) *adj.* **— con·cil·i·a'tion** *n.* **— con·cil·i·a'tor** *n.*

con·cil·i·a·to·ry (kən·sil'ē·ə·tôr'ē, -tō'rē) *adj.* Tending to reconcile or conciliate. Also con·cil'i·a·tive. **— con·cil'i·a·to'ri·ly** *adv.* **— con·cil'i·a·to'ri·ness** *n.*

con·cin·ni·ty (kən·sin'ə·tē) *n. pl.* ·ties 1. A harmonious arrangement of parts. 2. Elegance and harmony. [< L *concinnitas, -tatis* < *concinnus* well-adjusted]

con·cise (kən·sīs') *adj.* Expressing much in brief form; compact; terse. **— Syn.** See TERSE. [< L *concisus,* pp. of *concidere* < *com-* thoroughly + *caedere* to cut] **— con·cise'ly** *adv.* **— con·cise'ness** *n.*

con·ci·sion (kən·sizh'ən) *n.* 1. Conciseness, as of style; brevity. 2. A cutting off or apart; division.

con·clave (kon'klāv, kong'-) *n.* 1. A private or secret meeting. 2. The private chambers in which the College of Cardinals meets to elect a pope; also, the meeting. 3. The cardinals assembled to elect a pope. 4. The College of Cardinals. [< F < L, a place that can be locked up < *com-* together + *clavis* key]

con·clav·ist (kon'klā·vist, kong'-) *n.* A cardinal's ecclesiastic attendant at an electoral conclave.

con·clude (kən·klood') *v.* ·clud·ed, ·clud·ing *v.t.* 1. To bring to an end; terminate; finish. 2. To arrange or settle finally; effect. 3. To form an opinion or judgment about; decide. 4. To resolve (to do); determine. 5. *Obs.* To shut in; enclose; also, to restrain. **—** *v.i.* 6. To come to an end. 7. To come to a decision or agreement. [< L *concludere* < *com-* thoroughly + *claudere* to close, shut off] **— con·clud'er** *n.*

con·clu·sion (kən·kloo'zhən) *n.* 1. The end or termination of something; close; finish. 2. A closing part, as the summing up of a speech. 3. The result of an act or process; outcome; issue. 4. A judgment or opinion obtained by reasoning; inference; deduction. 5. A final decision; resolve. 6. A final arranging; settlement, as of a treaty. 7. *Logic* **a** In a syllogism, the proposition that necessarily follows from the major and minor premises. **b** A proposition deduced from one or more premises. 8. *Law* **a** The ending of a pleading or deed. **b** An estoppel. *Abbr. con.* **— in conclusion** As a final statement or summing up. **— to try conclusions with** To engage (someone) in a contest to determine superiority. [< MF < L *conclusio, -onis* < *concludere.* See CONCLUDE.]

con·clu·sive (kən·kloo'siv) *adj.* Ending doubt or question; decisive. **—** con·clu'sive·ly *adv.* **— con·clu'sive·ness** *n.*

con·coct (kon·kokt', kən-) *v.t.* 1. To make by mixing ingredients, as food, a drink, etc. 2. To make up; devise: to *concoct* a plan. [< L *concoctus,* pp. of *concoquere* < *com-* together + *coquere* to cook, boil] **— con·coct'er** or con·coc'tor *n.* **— con·coc'tive** *adj.*

con·coc·tion (kon·kok'shən, kən-) *n.* 1. The act of concocting. 2. Something concocted, as a mixture.

con·com·i·tance (kon·kom'ə·təns, kən-) *n.* Existence or occurrence together; accompaniment: a *concomitance* of faith and doubt. Also con·com'i·tan·cy.

con·com·i·tant (kon·kom'ə·tənt, kən-) *adj.* Existing or occurring together; attendant. **—** *n.* An attendant circumstance, state, or thing. **— Syn.** See CIRCUMSTANCE. [< L *concomitans, -antis,* ppr. of *concomitari* < *com-* with + *comitari* to accompany] **— con·com'i·tant·ly** *adv.*

con·cord (kon'kôrd, kong'-) *n.* 1. Unity of feeling or interest; agreement; accord. 2. Peace; friendly relations. 3. A treaty establishing this. 4. *Music* Consonance. 5. *Gram.* Agreement of words, as in gender, number, case, or person. **— Syn.** See HARMONY. [< MF *concorde* < L *concordia* < *concors* agreeing < *com-* together + *cor, cordis* heart]

Con·cord (kong'kərd) 1. The capital of New Hampshire, in the south central part; pop. 85,164. 2. A city in western California; pop. 30,022. 3. A town in NE Massachusetts; scene of a Revolutionary War battle, April 19, 1775; pop. 16,148.

con·cor·dance (kon·kôr'dəns, kən-) *n.* 1. Agreement; concord. 2. An alphabetical index of the important words in a book as they occur in context: a *concordance* of the Bible.

con·cor·dant (kon·kôr'dənt, kən-) *adj.* Existing in concord; agreeing; harmonious. [< L *concordans, -antis,* ppr. of *concordare* to agree < *concors.* See CONCORD.] **— con·cor'dant·ly** *adv.*

con·cor·dat (kon·kôr'dat) *n.* 1. An agreement between the papacy and a national government for the regulation of ecclesiastical affairs. 2. Any official agreement or pact. [< MF < Med.L *concordatum* thing agreed upon < L *concordare* to agree < *concors.* See CONCORD.]

Concord coach A type of stagecoach first made in Concord, New Hampshire. Also **Concord wagon.**

Con·corde (kon·kôrd') A supersonic transport airplane produced jointly by British and French manufacturers.

Con·cord grape (kong'kərd, kon'kôrd) A dark blue or blackish, round, cultivated grape of eastern North America. [after *Concord,* Mass.]

con·cor·po·rate (kon·kôr'pə·rāt) *v.t. & v.i.* ·rat·ed, ·rat·ing

Archaic To unite in one body or substance. — *adj.* United in a single body. [< L *concorporatus,* pp. of *concorporare* < *com-* together + *corpus, corporis* body]

con·course (kon′kôrs, -kōrs, kong′-) *n.* **1.** A coming together; confluence. **2.** A crowd; throng. **3.** A large place, usually open, for the assembling or passage of crowds, as in a railroad station or a park. [< MF *concours* < L *concursus* < *concurrere.* See CONCUR.]

con·cres·cence (kon·kres′əns) *n. Biol.* A growing together of separate parts, as of the cells of an embryo during gastrulation. [< L *concrescentia* < *concrescere.* See CONCRETE.]

con·crete (kon′krēt; *for adj., n., & v. def. 3,* also kon·krēt′) *adj.* **1.** Relating to a specific case or object; particular or individual, as opposed to general: a *concrete* example. **2.** Belonging to or embodied in actual existence or experience; physically perceptible; objectively real. **3.** *Gram.* Naming a specific thing or class of things, rather than an abstract quality or state. *Nobility* is an abstract noun in *nobility of character,* but concrete in *the nobility of England.* **4.** Formed by the growth or coalescence of parts or particles; constituting a composite mass or substance; solid. **5.** Made of concrete. — *n.* **1.** A building material of sand and gravel or broken rock united by cement, used for roadways, bridges, walls, etc. **2.** That which is concrete: often preceded by *the:* to deal in the *concrete.* **3.** Any mass of particles united and solidified. — *v.* **·cret·ed, ·cret·ing** *v.t.* **1.** To bring together in one mass or body; cause to coalesce. **2.** To bring into concrete or specific form; concretize. **3.** To treat or cover with concrete. — *v.i.* **4.** To coalesce; solidify. [< L *concretus,* pp. of *concrescere* < *com-* together + *crescere* to grow] — **con·crete′ly** *adv.* — **con·crete′ness** *n.*

concrete mixer A machine for mixing together sand, gravel, cement, etc., to make concrete: also called *cement mixer.*

concrete noun *Gram.* A noun that names anything having actual physical existence, as *table, street:* distinguished from *abstract noun.*

concrete number *Math.* A number applied to particular objects, as *four men, ten* dollars.

con·cre·tion (kon·krē′shən) *n.* **1.** The act or process of growing or coming together; a solidifying. **2.** A concrete mass. **3.** *Geol.* A rounded body of inorganic matter found in sedimentary rock and usually formed concentrically about a nucleus, which may be a fossil. **4.** *Med.* **a** A calculus. **b** An abnormal joining of adjacent parts, as of fingers.

con·cre·tion·ar·y (kon·krē′shən·er′ē) *adj.* **1.** Pertaining to or resulting from concretion. **2.** Containing concretions.

con·cre·tive (kon·krē′tiv) *adj.* Tending to coalesce or solidify.

con·cre·tize (kon′kri·tīz) *v.t.* **·tized, ·tiz·ing** To render concrete; make specific.

con·cu·bi·nage (kon·kyōō′bə·nij) *n.* **1.** The state of being a concubine. **2.** Cohabitation without marriage.

con·cu·bi·nar·y (kon·kyōō′bə·ner′ē) *adj.* Pertaining to or living in concubinage.

con·cu·bine (kong′kyə·bīn, kon′-) *n.* **1.** A woman who cohabits with a man without being married to him. **2.** In certain polygamous societies, a secondary wife. [< F < L *concubina,* fem. of *concubinus* bedfellow < *concumbere* < *com-* with + *cumbere* to lie]

con·cu·pis·cence (kon·kyōō′pə·səns) *n.* **1.** Sexual desire; lust. **2.** Any immoderate desire. — **Syn.** See DESIRE.

con·cu·pis·cent (kon·kyōō′pə·sənt) *adj.* **1.** Overly desirous or eager. **2.** Lustful; carnal; sensual. [< L *concupiscens, -entis,* ppr. of *concupiscere,* inceptive of *concupere* < *com-* thoroughly + *cupere* to desire]

con·cur (kən·kûr′) *v.i.* **·curred, ·cur·ring** **1.** To agree or approve, as in opinion or action. **2.** To cooperate or combine. **3.** To happen at the same time; coincide. **4.** To converge to a point, as lines. — **Syn.** See ASSENT. [< L *concurrere* to meet < *com-* together + *currere* to run]

con·cur·rence (kən·kûr′əns) *n.* **1.** The act of concurring. **2.** Cooperation or combination to effect some purpose or end. **3.** Agreement in mind or opinion; assent; consent. **4.** Simultaneous occurrence; coincidence. **5.** *Rare* Competition; rivalry. **6.** *Geom.* The point where three or more lines meet. **7.** *Law* A joint power or claim. Also **con·cur′ren·cy.**

con·cur·rent (kən·kûr′ənt) *adj.* **1.** Occurring together at the same time or place; existing in close association. **2.** United in action or application; cooperating; coordinate. **3.** Having the same authority or jurisdiction. **4.** Meeting at or going toward the same point. **5.** In agreement or accordance; harmonious. — *n.* **1.** A person or thing that concurs. **2.** *Rare* A rival; competitor. [< L *concurrens, -entis,* pp. of *concurrere.* See CONCUR.] — **con·cur′rent·ly** *adv.*

concurrent resolution *U.S.* A resolution adopted by both houses of Congress, that does not have the force of law and does not require the signature of the President.

con·cuss (kən·kus′) *v.t.* **1.** To affect or injure (the brain) by concussion. **2.** To agitate; shake. [< L *concussus,* pp. of *concutere* < *com-* together + *quatere* to strike, beat]

con·cus·sion (kən·kush′ən) *n.* **1.** A violent shaking; shock; jar. **2.** *Pathol.* A violent shock to some organ, especially to the brain, by a fall, sudden blow, or blast; also, the condition resulting from this. [< L *concussio, -onis* < *concutere.* See CONCUSS.] — **con·cus·sive** (kən·kus′iv) *adj.*

cond. **1.** Condition. **2.** *Music* Conducted. **3.** Conductivity. **4.** Conductor.

Con·dé (kôn·dā′), **Prince de,** 1621–86, Louis II de Bourbon, Duc d'Enghien, French general: called **the Great Condé.**

con·demn (kən·dem′) *v.t.* **1.** To express opinion against; hold to be wrong; censure. **2.** To pronounce judicial sentence against; doom. **3.** To show the guilt of; convict: His writings *condemn* him. **4.** To pronounce or declare to be unfit for use, usually by official order. **5.** *U.S.* To appropriate for public use by judicial decree; declare forfeited. **6.** To pronounce incurable. [< L *condemnare* < *com-* thoroughly + *damnare* to condemn] — **con·dem·na·ble** (kən·dem′nə·bəl) *adj.* — **con·demn·er** (kən·dem′ər) *n.*

con·dem·na·tion (kon′dem·nā′shən) *n.* **1.** The act of condemning, or the state of being condemned. **2.** Severe censure; reproof. **3.** A cause or occasion for condemning. [< L *condemnatio, -onis* < *condemnare.* See CONDEMN.]

con·dem·na·to·ry (kən·dem′nə·tôr′ē, -tō′rē) *adj.* Expressing condemnation.

con·den·sate (kən·den′sāt) *adj. Archaic* Condensed. — *n.* A product of condensation. [< L *condensatus,* pp. of *condensare.* See CONDENSE.]

con·den·sa·tion (kon′den·sā′shən) *n.* **1.** The act of condensing, or the state of being condensed. **2.** Any product of condensing. **3.** *Physics* The reduction of a vapor or gas to a liquid or a solid, or of a liquid to a solid or semisolid. **4.** *Chem.* The rearrangement of atoms to form a molecule of greater weight, density, or complexity. **5.** *Psychoanal.* A fusion of events, thoughts, words, etc., as in dreams.

condensation trail *Aeron.* A vapor trail (which see).

con·dense (kən·dens′) *v.* **·densed, ·dens·ing** *v.t.* **1.** To compress or make dense; consolidate. **2.** To abridge or make concise, as an essay. **3.** To change from the gaseous to the liquid state, or from the liquid to the solid state, as by cooling or compression. — *v.i.* **4.** To become condensed. *Abbr.* **con.** [< L *condensare* < *condensus* thick < *com-* together + *densus* crowded, close] — **con·den′sa·bil·i·ty** or **con·den′si·bil′i·ty** *n.* — **con·den′sa·ble** or **con·den′si·ble** *adj.* — **Syn.** **1.** contract, shrink, concentrate, compact. **2.** digest, summarize, shorten. — **Ant.** disperse, attenuate, expand, dilate.

condensed milk Cow's milk, sweetened with sugar, and thickened by evaporation of its water content.

con·dens·er (kən·den′sər) *n.* **1.** One who or that which condenses. **2.** Any device for reducing a vapor to liquid or solid form. **3.** *Electr.* A capacitor. **4.** *Optics* A combination of lenses for effectively focusing light rays.

con·de·scend (kon′di·send′) *v.i.* **1.** To come down voluntarily to equal terms with inferiors; be affable. **2.** To lower oneself (to do something); deign. **3.** To behave in a superior or patronizing manner. **4.** *Obs.* To give way; yield or consent. [< MF *condescendre* < LL *condescendere* < L *com-* together + *descendere* to stoop. See DESCEND.]

con·de·scen·dence (kon′di·sen′dəns) *n.* **1.** In Scottish law, a plaintiff's statement of facts. **2.** Condescension.

con·de·scend·ing (kon′di·sen′ding) *adj.* Showing conscious courtesy toward inferiors; especially, making a display of such courtesy; patronizing. — **con′de·scend′ing·ly** *adv.*

con·de·scen·sion (kon′di·sen′shən) *n.* **1.** The act of condescending; also, a particular instance of this. **2.** Patronizing behavior. [< LL *condescensio, -onis* < *condescendere.* See CONDESCEND.]

con·dign (kən·dīn′) *adj.* **1.** Deserved; merited: said of punishment. **2.** *Obs.* Worthy. [< MF *condigne* < L *condignus* < *com-* thoroughly + *dignus* worthy] — **con·dign′ly** *adv.*

con·di·ment (kon′də·mənt) *n.* A sauce, relish, spice, etc., used to season food. [< L *condimentum* < *condire* to pickle]

con·di·tion (kən·dish′ən) *n.* **1.** The state or mode of existence of a person or thing. **2.** State of health; especially, a sound or healthful state. **3.** *Informal* An ailment: a heart *condition.* **4.** An event, fact, or circumstance necessary to the occurrence or existence of some other, though not its cause; a prerequisite: Hard work is the *condition* of success. **5.** Something stipulated or required as the prerequisite to something else; a provision. **6.** *Usually pl.* The circumstances affecting an activity or a mode of existence: poor living *conditions.* **7.** Social status. **8.** *Gram.* A dependent clause expressing a conditional or contingent circumstance, idea, etc. **9.** *Logic* A proposition upon which another proposition depends for its validity; antecedent. **10.** In a will, contract, etc., a provision allowing for modification upon the occurrence of some uncertain future event; also, the event. **11.** *Obs.* Disposition; temper. — **in** (or **out of**) **condition** Fit (or unfit) for proper performance, especially of some physical activity. — **on condition that** Provided that; if. — *v.t.* **1.** To restrict or determine by a condition or conditions: He *conditions* his going on the weather. **2.** To be a condition or prerequisite of. **3.** To specify as a condition; stipulate. **4.** To render fit or in good condition. **5.** *Psychol.* To train to a behavior pattern or conditioned response. **6.** To accustom (someone) to: Poverty *conditioned* him to hunger. — *v.i.* **8.** To bargain; stipulate. Abbr. *cond.* [< OF *condicion* < L *condicio, -onis* agreement < *condicere* to agree < *com-* together + *dicere* to say] — **con·di'tion·er** *n.*

con·di·tion·al (kən-dish'ən-əl) *adj.* **1.** Containing, imposing, or dependent upon conditions; not absolute; tentative. **2.** *Gram.* Expressing or implying a condition. — *n. Gram.* A conditional word, tense, clause, or mood. — **con·di·tion·al·i·ty** (kən-dish'ən-al'ə-tē) *n.* — **con·di'tion·al·ly** *adv.*
— **Syn.** (adj.) **1.** contingent, provisional, relative, temporary.

con·di·tioned (kən-dish'ənd) *adj.* **1.** Subject to conditions or stipulations. **2.** Placed in or existing under given conditions or circumstances; situated; environed. **3.** In good condition; fit. **4.** *Psychol.* Trained to a conditioned response. **5.** Accustomed: with *to*.

conditioned response *Psychol.* A learned response to a previously neutral stimulus that has been made directly effective through close repeated juxtaposition with the stimulus normally evoking this response. Also **conditioned reflex.**

con·di·ti·o si·ne qua non (kən-dish'ē·ō sī'nē kwä non') *Latin* An indispensable condition.

con·dole (kən-dōl') *v.* **·doled, ·dol·ing** *v.i.* **1.** To grieve or express sympathy with one in affliction: with *with*. — *v.t.* **2.** *Rare* To express sympathetic grief for. — **Syn.** See CONSOLE¹. [< LL *condolere* < L *com-* together + *dolere* to grieve] — **con·do·la·to·ry** (kən·dō'lə·tôr'ē, ·tō'rē) *adj.* — **con·dol'er** *n.* — **con·dol'ing·ly** *adv.*

con·do·lence (kən·dō'ləns, *occasionally* kon'də·ləns) *n.* **1.** Expression of sympathy with a person in pain or sorrow. Also **con·dole·ment** (kən·dōl'mənt). **2.** *pl.* A declaration of sympathy. — **Syn.** See PITY.

con do·lo·re (kōn dō·lō'rā) *Music* With sorrow; sadly. [< Ital.]

con·dom (kon'dəm, kun'-) *n.* A sheath for the penis, usually made of rubber and having an antivenereal or contraceptive function: also spelled *cundum*. [? Alter. of *Conton*, 18th c. English physician said to have invented it]

con·do·min·i·um (kon'də·min'ē·əm) *n.* **1.** Joint sovereignty or ownership. **2.** A territory jointly governed by several states under international law. **3.** *U.S.* An apartment house in which the units are owned separately by individuals and not by a corporation or cooperative; also, an apartment in such a building. [< NL < L *com-* together + *dominium* rule]

Con·don (kon'dən), **Edward Uhler,** born 1902, U.S. physicist.

con·do·na·tion (kon'dō·nā'shən) *n.* The implied forgiving or overlooking of a wrong or offense.

con·done (kən·dōn') *v.t.* **·doned, ·don·ing** To treat (an offense) as overlooked or as if it had not been committed. [< L *condonare* < *com-* thoroughly + *donare* to give] — **con·don'er** *n.*

con·dor (kon'dôr, -dər) *n.* **1.** A vulture (*Vultur gryphus*) of the high Andes, one of the largest flying birds, characterized by a fleshy comb and a white, downy neck. **2.** The California condor (which see). **3.** A former gold coin of Chile, bearing the image of a condor. [< Sp. < Quechua *cuntur*]

Con·dor·cet (kôn·dôr·se'), **Marquis de,** 1743–1794, Marie Jean de Caritat, French social philosopher and revolutionist.

con·dot·tie·re (kon'dot·tyâ'rā) *n. pl.* **·ri** (-rē) In the 14th to 16th centuries, a leader of mercenary soldiers. [< Ital. < *condotto* a mercenary < L *conductus* hired. See CONDUCT.]

CONDOR
(About 3 feet long; wingspread to 10 feet)

con·duce (kən·dōōs', -dyōōs') *v.i.* **·duced, ·duc·ing** To help or tend toward a result; contribute: with *to*. [< L *conducere* to bring together. See CONDUCT.]

con·du·cive (kən·dōō'siv, -dyōō'-) *adj.* Contributive or promotive; leading; helping: with *to*. Also **con·du·cent** (kən·dōō'sənt, -dyōō'-). — **con·du'cive·ness** *n.*

con·duct (*v.* kən·dukt'; *n.* kon'dukt) *v.t.* **1.** To accompany and show the way; guide; escort. **2.** To manage or control. **3.** To direct and lead the performance of, as an orchestra, opera, etc. **4.** To serve as a medium of transmission for; convey; transmit. **5.** To act or behave: used reflexively. — *v.i.* **6.** To serve as a conductor. **7.** To direct or lead. — *n.* **1.** The way a person acts or lives; behavior; deportment. **2.** Management, as of a business; direction; control. **3.** The act of guiding or leading. **4.** *Obs.* An escort or guide. [< L *conductus*, pp. of *conducere* < *com-* together + *ducere* to lead] — **con·duct'i·bil'i·ty** *n.* — **con·duct'i·ble** *adj.*
— **Syn.** (verb) **1.** See ACCOMPANY. **3.** administer, operate, direct. **5.** comport.

con·duc·tance (kən·duk'təns) *n. Electr.* The ability of a body to allow the passage of a current without radiating energy as heat, light, etc.: the reciprocal of *resistance*, expressed in mhos. Abbr. *g., G.*

con·duc·tion (kən·duk'shən) *n.* **1.** *Physics* The transmission of heat, sound, or electricity through matter without

motion of the conducting body as a whole. Compare CONVECTION. **2.** *Physiol.* The transference of a stimulus along nerve fibers. **3.** Transmission or conveyance in general.

con·duc·tive (kən·duk'tiv) *adj.* **1.** Having the power of conducting. **2.** Proceeding by or resulting from conduction.

con·duc·tiv·i·ty (kon'duk·tiv'ə·tē) *n.* **1.** *Physics* The capacity to transmit sound, heat, or electricity. **2.** *Electr.* The conductance between opposite parallel faces of a cubic centimeter of a given material: the reciprocal of *resistivity.* Abbr. *cond.*

con·duc·tor (kən·duk'tər) *n.* **1.** One who conducts or leads; a guide or director. **2.** *Chiefly U.S.* One who has charge of a railroad train, streetcar, bus, etc. **3.** The director of an orchestra or chorus. **4.** Any substance, material, or medium that conducts electricity, heat, etc. **5.** A lightning rod. Abbr. *cond.* — **con·duc'tor·ship** *n.* — **con·duc'tress** *n.fem.*

con·duit (kon'dit, -dōō·it) *n.* **1.** A channel or pipe for conveying water or other liquid; a canal; aqueduct. **2.** A covered passage or tube for electric wires. **3.** *Rare* A fountain. [< MF < *conduire* to lead < L *conducere*. See CONDUCT.]

con·du·pli·cate (kon·dōō'plə·kit, -dyōō'-) *adj. Bot.* Folded along the midrib with the upper face in: said of leaves in bud. [< L *conduplicatus*, pp. of *conduplicare* to double]

con·dyle (kon'dil) *n. Anat.* An enlarged, rounded prominence on the end of a bone, by which it articulates with a depression or cavity of another bone. [< MF < L *condylus* knuckle < Gk. *kondylos*] — **con·dy·lar** (kon'də·lər) *adj.*

con·dy·loid (kon'də·loid) *adj.* Of or like a condyle.

con·dy·lo·ma (kon'də·lō'mə) *n. pl.* **·ma·ta** (-mə·tə) *Pathol.* A wartlike growth, usually near the anus and external genitals. [< NL < Gk. *kondylōma* lump] — **con·dy·lom·a·tous** (kon'də·lom'ə·təs, -lō'mə·təs) *adj.*

cone (kōn) *n.* **1.** *Geom.* **a** A surface generated by a straight line passing through all the points of a nonintersecting plane curve and a fixed point (the vertex) outside the plane. **b** A solid bounded by such a surface, called a **right circular cone** if the plane curve is a circle whose plane is perpendicular to the axis from the vertex through its center, or an **oblique circular cone** if the axis is not perpendicular to the base. **2.** A thing that tapers uniformly from a circular base to a point, as any of several conical instruments or machine parts, or the brittle papery shell used to hold ice cream. **3.** *Bot.* A dry multiple fruit, as of the pine, composed of scales arranged symmetrically around an axis and enclosing seeds: also called *strobile.* **4.** *Physiol.* One of the specialized, photosensitive cells in the retina concerned with the perception of color and with daylight vision. — *v.t.* **coned, con·ing** To shape conically. [< L *conus* < Gk. *kōnos*]

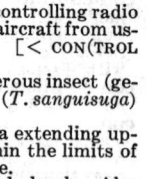

CONES
a Stone pine.
b Sequoia.
c Eastern hemlock. *d* Red spruce.

cone·flow·er (kōn'flou'ər) *n.* **1.** The rudbeckia. **2.** Any of various related plants, as the **prairie coneflower** (*Ratibida columnaris*) of western North America.

con·el·rad (kon'əl·rad) *n.* A technique for controlling radio signals from stations so as to prevent enemy aircraft from using the signals for navigation or information. [< CON(TROL OF) EL(ECTROMAGNETIC) RAD(IATION)]

cone·nose (kōn'nōz') *n.* **1.** A large hemipterous insect (genus *Triatoma*), as the **bloodsucking conenose** (*T. sanguisuga*) of the United States. **2.** An assassin bug.

cone of silence *Aeron.* A cone-shaped area extending upward from a radio transmitting station, within the limits of which signals from that station are inaudible.

co·ne·pa·te (kō'nā·pä'tē) *n.* The hognosed skunk. Also **co·ne·pa·tl** (kō'nā·pät'l). [< Nahuatl *conepatl* < *conetl* small + *epatl* fox]

Con·es·to·ga wagon (kon'is·tō'gə) *U.S.* A type of covered wagon with broad wheels, used by American pioneers for freight conveyance and for westward travel over the prairies. [after *Conestoga*, Pa., where first made]

CONESTOGA WAGON

co·ney (kō'nē, kun'ē) See CONY.

Co·ney Island (kō'nē) A seaside resort and amusement center in Brooklyn, New York City.

conf. **1.** Compare (L *confer*). **2.** *Med.* Confection. **3.** Conference. **4.** Confessor.

con·fab (kon'fab) *Informal v.i.* **·fabbed, ·fab·bing** To converse. — *n.* A conversation. [Short for CONFABULATION]

con·fab·u·late (kən·fab'yə·lāt) *v.i.* **·lat·ed, ·lat·ing** **1.** To chat; gossip; converse. **2.** *Psychol.* To compensate for loss or impairment of memory by fabrication or invention of details. [< L *confabulatus*, pp. of *confabulari* < *com-* together + *fabulari* to chat < *fabula* story] — **con·fab'u·la'tion** *n.* — **con·fab·u·la·to·ry** (kən·fab'yə·lə·tôr'ē, -tō'rē) *adj.*

con·far·re·a·tion (kon·far'ē·ā'shən) *n.* In ancient Rome, the patrician religious form of marriage, in which a cake of spelt was offered as a sacrifice. [< L *confarreatio, -onis* < *confarreare* to marry solemnly < *com-* together + *farreum* cake of spelt < *far* grain, wheat]

con·fect (*v.* kən·fekt′; *n.* kon′fekt) *v.t.* **1.** To make into a confection; preserve; prepare. **2.** To construct or put together. — *n. Obs.* A confection. [< L *confectus*, pp. of *conficere* < *com–* together + *facere* to make. Akin to COMFIT.]

con·fec·tion (kən·fek′shən) *n.* **1.** The act or process of mixing or compounding. **2.** Any of various sweet preparations, as candy or preserves. **3.** A medicinal compound, usually a drug mixed with honey or syrup; electuary. Abbr. *conf.* **4.** A frilly, stylish article of dress for women, usually ready-made. — *v.t.* To make up into a confection. [< MF *confeccion* < L *confectio, -onis* < *conficere*. See CONFECT.]

con·fec·tion·ar·y (kən·fek′shən·er′ē) *adj.* Pertaining to or like confections or their manufacture. — *n. pl.* **·ar·ies 1.** A place where confections are prepared. **2.** A confection; sweetmeat. **3.** *Rare* A confectioner.

con·fec·tion·er (kən·fek′shən·ər) *n.* One who makes or deals in confectionery.

confectioner's sugar A finely ground powdered sugar, used in icings, confections, etc.

con·fec·tion·er·y (kən·fek′shən·er′ē) *n. pl.* **·er·ies 1.** Sweetmeats collectively. **2.** A confectioner's shop, or the business of a confectioner.

Confed. 1. Confederate. **2.** Confederation.

con·fed·er·a·cy (kən·fed′ər·ə·sē) *n. pl.* **·cies 1.** A union of states or persons for mutual support or action; a league; alliance. **2.** An unlawful combination; conspiracy. — **Syn.** See ALLIANCE. — **the Confederacy** The Confederate States of America: also **Southern Confederacy.** [< AF *confederacie* < LL *confœderatio* < *confœderare*. See CONFEDERATE.]

con·fed·er·ate (*n., adj.* kən·fed′ər·it; *v.* kən·fed′ə·rāt) *n.* One who takes part in a league or plot; an associate; accomplice. — **Syn.** See ACCESSORY. — *adj.* Associated in a confederacy; confederated. — *v.t. & v.i.* **·at·ed, ·at·ing** To form or join in a confederacy. [< LL *confœderatus,* pp. of *confœderare* to join in a league < L *com–* together + *fœdus* league] — **con·fed′er·a′tive** *adj.*

Con·fed·er·ate (kən·fed′ər·it) *adj.* Pertaining to the Confederate States of America. — *n.* An adherent of the Confederate States of America. Abbr. *Confed.*

Confederate States of America A league of eleven southern States that seceded from the United States during the period from December, 1860 to May, 1861, including South Carolina, Mississippi, Florida, Alabama, Georgia, Louisiana, Texas, Virginia, Tennessee, Arkansas, and North Carolina, in the order of secession. Abbr. *C.S.A.*

con·fed·er·a·tion (kən·fed′ə·rā′shən) *n.* **1.** The act of confederating, or the state of being confederated. **2.** An association of states usually less permanent than a federation. Abbr. *Confed.* — **Syn.** See ALLIANCE.

Con·fed·er·a·tion (kən·fed′ə·rā′shən) *n.* **1.** The federation formed by Ontario, Quebec, Nova Scotia, and New Brunswick in 1867, now including ten provinces. **2.** The union of the American colonies, 1781–89, under the Articles of Confederation.

con·fer (kən·fûr′) *v.* **·ferred, ·fer·ring** *v.t.* **1.** To grant as a gift or benefit; bestow. **2.** *Obs.* To compare; collate. Abbr. *cf.* — *v.i.* **3.** To hold a conference; consult together; take counsel. — **Syn.** See CONSULT, GIVE. [< L *conferre* < *com–* together + *ferre* to bring, carry] — **con·fer′ment** *n.* — **con·fer′ra·ble** *adj.* — **con·fer′rer** *n.*

con·fer·ee (kon′fə·rē′) *n.* **1.** One who takes part in conference or a conference. **2.** One upon whom some honor, degree, etc., is conferred. Also **con·fer′ree′.**

con·fer·ence (kon′fər·əns, -frəns) *n.* A discussion or consultation on some important matter; also, a formal meeting for this. **2.** *Govt.* A meeting of committees of two branches of a legislature to settle differences. **3.** In the Methodist, Congregational, and other churches: **a** Any of several clerical, or clerical and lay, assemblies in a local area, district, etc. **b** The churches collectively represented in any of these assemblies. **4.** The act of bestowing; conferment. **5.** A league or association, as of athletic teams. Abbr. *conf.* [< MF *conférence* < Med.L *conferentia* < L *conferre*. See CONFER.] — **con·fer·en·tial** (kon′fə·ren′shəl) *adj.*

con·fer·va (kən·fûr′və) *n. pl.* **·vae** (-vē) or **·vas** *Bot.* Any of a genus (*Tribonema*) of greenish, threadlike, fresh-water algae. [< L] — **con·fer′val, con·fer′void** (-void) *adj.*

con·fess (kən·fes′) *v.t.* **1.** To acknowledge or admit, as a fault, guilt, or sin. **2.** To concede or admit to be true. **3.** To acknowledge belief or faith in. **4.** *Eccl.* **a** To admit or make known (one's sins), especially to a priest, in order to obtain absolution. **b** To hear the confession of: said of a priest. **5.** *Poetic* To make manifest. — *v.i.* **6.** To make acknowledgment, as of fault or crime: with *to.* **7.** To make confession to a priest. [< MF *confesser* < L *confessus,* pp. of *confiteri* < *com–* thoroughly + *fateri* to own, declare]

— **Syn. 1.** *Confess, acknowledge, own, admit,* and *concede* agree in meaning to say something reluctantly. *Confess* is now generally restricted to the sense of making known to others one's own error or wrongdoing: to *confess* a robbery. We *acknowledge* that for which we are responsible, often with no bad implication: to *acknowledge* a debt or one's signature. *Own* implies more reluctance than *acknowledge:* to *own* the authorship of a book. *Admit* and *concede* indicate a yielding to the assertion or wish of another; we *admit* the truth of an allegation; we *concede* a demand, claim, opposing view, etc. Compare AVOW. — **Ant.** deny, disavow, repudiate.

con·fess·ed·ly (kən·fes′id·lē) *adv.* By admission; avowedly.

con·fes·sion (kən·fesh′ən) *n.* **1.** The act of confessing; acknowledgment; admission, especially of guilt. **2.** That which is confessed. **3.** A statement, especially a formal document, in which something is confessed. **4.** *Eccl.* The contrite acknowledgment of one's sins to a priest in order to obtain absolution: in full **sacramental** or **auricular confession. 5.** A general admission of sinfulness, embodied in a set form and used in the Roman Catholic, Anglican, and other liturgies. **6.** A body of doctrine put forth as the belief of a church: also **confession of faith. 7.** A church holding a particular confession of faith. **8.** The tomb of a martyr; also, an altar erected above it, or the building enclosing them. — **Syn.** See APOLOGY. [< OF < L *confessio, -onis* < *confiteri*. See CONFESS.]

con·fes·sion·al (kən·fesh′ən·əl) *adj.* Of, pertaining to, or like confession. — *n.* A small enclosure or stall where a priest hears confessions. Also *Rare* **con·fes′sion·ar′y** (-er′ē).

con·fes·sor (kən·fes′ər) *n.* **1.** A priest who hears confessions. **2.** One who confesses. **3.** One who confesses his faith in Christianity, especially in the face of persecution. Also **con·fess′er.** Abbr. *conf.* [< L < *confiteri*. See CONFESS.]

con·fet·ti (kən·fet′ē) *n.pl.* **1.** (*construed as sing.*) Small pieces of colored paper thrown at carnivals, weddings, etc. **2.** Bonbons. [< Ital., pl. of *confetto* confection]

con·fi·dant (kon′fə·dant′, -dänt′, kon′fə·dant, -dänt) *n.* A person to whom secrets are confided. [< F *confident* < Ital. *confidente* < L *confidens,* ppr. of *confidere.* See CONFIDE.] — **con′fi·dante′** *n.fem.*

con·fide (kən·fīd′) *v.* **·fid·ed, ·fid·ing** *v.t.* **1.** To reveal in trust or confidence. **2.** To put into another's trust or keeping. — *v.i.* **3.** To have trust; impart secrets trustingly: with *in.* — **Syn.** See COMMIT. [< L *confidere* < *com–* thoroughly + *fidere* to trust] — **con·fid′er** *n.*

con·fi·dence (kon′fə·dəns) *n.* **1.** A feeling of trust in a person or thing; reliance; faith. **2.** A relationship of trustful intimacy: He spoke in *confidence.* **3.** Self-assurance; also, fearlessness. **4.** Excessive self-assurance; presumption. **5.** A feeling of certainty; expectation. **6.** Something told in trust; a secret. — *adj.* Of or pertaining to a confidence game or confidence man. — **Syn.** See TRUST. — **to take into one's confidence** To trust with one's secrets.

confidence game A swindle in which the victim is defrauded after his confidence has been won: also, *U.S. Slang,* **con game.** Also **confidence trick.**

confidence man A swindler in a confidence game.

con·fi·dent (kon′fə·dənt) *adj.* **1.** Having confidence; assured: *confident* of success. **2.** Self-assured; also, bold; presumptuous. **3.** *Obs.* Trustful. — *n.* A confidant. [< L *confidens, -entis,* ppr. of *confidere.* See CONFIDE.] — **con′fi·dent·ly** *adv.*

con·fi·den·tial (kon′fə·den′shəl) *adj.* **1.** Given or imparted in confidence; secret: *confidential* information. **2.** Enjoying another's confidence; trusted; intimate: a *confidential* clerk. **3.** Denoting intimacy or the confiding of secrets: a *confidential* manner. **4.** *U.S. Mil.* Denoting the lowest category of security classification: compare SECRET, TOP-SECRET. — **con·fi·den·ti·al·i·ty** (kon′fə·den′shē·al′ə·tē), **con·fi·den′tial·ness** *n.* — **con′fi·den′tial·ly** *adv.*

con·fid·ing (kən·fī′ding) *adj.* That trusts or confides; unsuspicious. — **con·fid′ing·ly** *adv.* — **con·fid′ing·ness** *n.*

con·fig·u·ra·tion (kən·fig′yə·rā′shən) *n.* **1.** The arrangement of the parts of a thing, or the form resulting therefrom; conformation; contour. **2.** *Psychol.* A gestalt. **3.** *Physics* The spatial arrangement of atoms in a molecule, or of nucleons and electrons in an atom. **4.** *Astron.* The relative positions of stars or planets; also, a group of stars. [< LL *configuratio, -onis* < *configurare* < L *com–* together + *figurare* to shape, fashion] — **con·fig′u·ra′tion·al, con·fig′u·ra′tive** (kən·fig′yər·ə·tiv, -yə·rā′tiv) *adj.*

— **Syn. 1.** shape, figure, disposition, placement, structure.

con·fig·u·ra·tion·ism (kən·fig′yə·rā′shən·iz′əm) *n.* Gestalt psychology.

con·fine (*v., n. defs. 2 and 3* kən·fīn′; *n. def. 1* kon′fīn) *v.* **·fined, ·fin·ing** *v.t.* **1.** To shut within an enclosure; imprison. **2.** To restrain or oblige to stay within doors. **3.** To hold within limits; restrict: to *confine* remarks. — *v.i.* **4.** *Obs.* To border; abut. — *n.* **1.** *Usually pl.* A boundary or border; frontier; limit. **2.** *Poetic* Confinement. **3.** *Obs.* Prison. [< MF *confiner* < Ital. *confinare* to limit, border < L *confinis* bordering < *com-* together + *finis* border] — **con·fin′a·ble** or **con·fine′a·ble** *adj.* — **con·fin′er** *n.*

con·fined (kən·fīnd′) *adj.* **1.** Limited; restricted. **2.** In childbed.

con·fine·ment (kən·fīn′mənt) *n.* **1.** The act of confining, or the state of being confined. **2.** A woman's lying-in; childbirth.

con·firm (kən·fûrm′) *v.t.* **1.** To assure the validity of; verify. **2.** To add firmness to; strengthen. **3.** To render valid and binding by formal approval or acceptance; ratify; sanction. **4.** To receive into the church by confirmation. [< OF *confermer* < L *confirmare* to strengthen < *com-* thoroughly + *firmus* strong] — **con·firm′a·ble** *adj.* — **con·firm′er**, *Law* **con·firm′or** (kon′fər·môr′, kən·fûr′mər) *n.*
— **Syn. 1.** *Confirm, corroborate, prove, verify, establish,* and *substantiate* mean to show or discover a thing to be true, valid, or genuine. We *confirm* that which is uncertain by removing all elements of doubt and making it firm or stable; usually the word suggests that the truth of a statement has been settled beyond a doubt. *Corroborate* is to support by additional testimony or evidence: to *corroborate* another's story. Correct reasoning from premises to conclusions *proves* a proposition or theory; examination of data or evidence *verifies* a statement by showing it to be true. To *establish* is to *prove* or *verify* beyond doubt or question, while to *substantiate* is to show to be real or valid: to *establish* one's innocence, to *substantiate* a claim for damages. **3.** See RATIFY. — **Ant.** disprove, refute, contradict, contravene.

con·fir·ma·tion (kon′fər·mā′shən) *n.* **1.** The act of confirming. **2.** That which confirms; proof. **3.** A religious rite in which a person is strengthened in his baptismal faith and admitted to all the privileges of a church.

con·firm·a·to·ry (kən·fûr′mə·tôr′ē, -tō′rē) *adj.* Serving to confirm. Also **con·firm′a·tive.**

con·firmed (kən·fûrmd′) *adj.* **1.** Firmly established; ratified. **2.** Inveterate; chronic; habitual: a *confirmed* skeptic. **3.** Having received the rites of religious confirmation.

con·fis·ca·ble (kən·fis′kə·bəl) *adj.* Liable to confiscation.

con·fis·cate (kon′fis·kāt) *v.t.* **·cat·ed, ·cat·ing 1.** To seize or appropriate for the public use or treasury, usually as a penalty. **2.** To appropriate by or as by authority. — *adj.* **1.** Appropriated or forfeited. **2.** Deprived of property through confiscation. [< L *confiscatus,* pp. of *confiscare* < *com-* together + *fiscus* chest, treasury] — **con′fis·ca′tion** *n.* — **con′fis·ca′tor** *n.*

con·fis·ca·to·ry (kən·fis′kə·tôr′ē, -tō′rē) *adj.* Of the nature of or resulting in confiscation.

Con·fit·e·or (kən·fit′ē·ôr) *n.* In the Roman Catholic Church, a prayer in which confession of sins is made, as at the beginning of the Mass. [< L, I confess: the first word]

con·fi·ture (kon′fi·choŏr) *n.* A confection; a sweetmeat or preserve. [< F]

con·fla·grant (kən·flā′grənt) *adj.* Burning fiercely. [< L *conflagrans, -antis,* ppr. of *conflagrare* < *com-* thoroughly + *flagrare* to burn]

con·fla·gra·tion (kon′flə·grā′shən) *n.* A great and disastrous fire. [< L *conflagratio, -onis* < *conflagrare.* See CONFLAGRANT.]

con·fla·tion (kən·flā′shən) *n.* A blending together, as of variant readings of a text; also, the result of this. [< LL *conflatio, -onis* < L *conflare* < *com-* together + *flare* to blow]

con·flict (*n.* kon′flikt; *v.* kən·flikt′) *n.* **1.** A struggle between opposing forces; a battle; also, a war. **2.** A condition of opposing forces and discord; mutual antagonism, as of ideas, interests, etc. **3.** A clash between contradictory impulses within an individual. **4.** A dashing together; collision. — *v.i.* **1.** To come into collision; be in mutual opposition; clash. **2.** To engage in battle; struggle. [< L *conflictus* < *confligere* < *com-* together + *fligere* to strike] — **con·flic′tive** *adj.*
— **Syn.** (noun) **1.** combat, fight, fray. **2.** disagreement, strife, disharmony, dissension. — **Ant.** harmony.

con·flu·ence (kon′floŏ·əns) *n.* **1.** A flowing together of streams; also, the place where they meet. **2.** The body or stream of water so formed. **3.** A flocking together; crowd; concourse. Also **con·flux** (kon′fluks).

con·flu·ent (kon′floŏ·ənt) *adj.* **1.** Flowing together; blended into one. **2.** *Pathol.* Merging or running together; not discrete: a *confluent* rash. **3.** *Anat.* Blended or coalesced, as two bones originally separate. — *n. Geog.* A stream that unites with another; loosely, a tributary. [< L *confluens, -entis,* ppr. of *confluere* < *com-* together + *fluere* to flow]

con·fo·cal (kon·fō′kəl) *adj.* Having the same focus or foci. [< CON- + -FOCAL]

con·form (kən·fôrm′) *v.i.* **1.** To be or act in accordance; show identity or resemblance; correspond: with *to:* to *conform* to specification. **2.** To adhere to conventional behavior. **3.** In English history, to adhere to the usages of the Church of England. — *v.t.* **4.** To make the same or similar: with *to.* **5.** To bring (oneself) into harmony or agreement: with *to.* — **Syn.** See ADAPT. [< F *conformer* < L *conformare* < *com-* together + *formare* to shape] — **con·form′er** *n.*

con·form·a·ble (kən·fôr′mə·bəl) *adj.* **1.** In agreement; har-

monious; consistent: a plan *conformable* to our interests. **2.** Corresponding in form, character, or use; similar: *conformable* to a model. **3.** Compliant or obedient; submissive. **4.** *Geol.* Parallel to one another without break, as contiguous rock strata. — **con·form′a·bil′i·ty, con·form′a·ble·ness** *n.* — **con·form′a·bly** *adv.*

con·form·ance (kən·fôr′məns) *n.* Conformity.

con·for·ma·tion (kon′fôr·mā′shən) *n.* **1.** The manner in which a thing is formed; structure or outline. **2.** The symmetrical arrangement and shaping of parts. **3.** The act of conforming, or the state of being conformed.

con·form·ist (kən·fôr′mist) *n.* **1.** One who conforms or complies. **2.** An adherent of the Church of England: opposed to *dissenter. nonconformist.* Abbr. (def. 2) *Con.*

con·form·i·ty (kən·fôr′mə·tē) *n. pl.* **·ties 1.** Correspondence in form, manner, or use; agreement; harmony; congruity. **2.** The act or habit of conforming; acquiescence. **3.** Adherence to the Church of England.

con·found (kon·found′, kən-; *for def. 4* kon′found′) *v.t.* **1.** To confuse, amaze, or bewilder. **2.** To confuse with something else; fail to distinguish. **3.** To confuse or mingle (elements, things, or ideas) indistinguishably. **4.** To damn: used as a mild oath. **5.** *Archaic* To put to shame; abash. **6.** *Archaic* To overthrow or defeat; ruin. **7.** *Obs.* To waste. [< AF *confoundre,* OF *confondre* < L *confundere.* See CONFUSE.] — **con·found′er** *n.*
— **Syn. 1.** puzzle, perplex, dumfound, mystify.

con·found·ed (kon·foun′did, kən-) *adj.* **1.** Confused or abashed. **2.** *Informal* Damned; detestable: a *confounded* cheat. — **con·found′ed·ly** *adv.*

con·fra·ter·ni·ty (kon′frə·tûr′nə·tē) *n. pl.* **·ties 1.** A body of men united for a common purpose or in some profession; especially, an organization of laymen for certain devotional, charitable, or educational purposes. **2.** Brotherly unity; brotherhood. [< Med.L *confraternitas, -tatis* < L *com-* with + *fraternitas* brotherhood < *frater* brother]

con·frere (kon′frâr) *n.* A fellow member of an association or profession; a colleague. [< MF < L *com-* with + *frater* brother]

con·front (kən·frunt′) *v.t.* **1.** To stand face to face with; face defiantly. **2.** To put face to face: to *confront* a liar with the truth. **3.** To bring together for comparison. [< F *confronter* < L *com-* together + *frons, frontis* face, forehead] — **con·front′ment** *n.* — **con·fron′ter** *n.*

con·fron·ta·tion (kon′frən·tā′shən) *n.* **1.** The act of confronting, or the state of being confronted. **2.** A direct challenge to the power of an opposing group or state, as by affirmation of policy, acts of protest, or acts or threats of violence; the provocation of conflict as a means of bringing about political change. **3.** A crisis or conflict between two opposing political groups or states: events leading toward a *confrontation* with China.

Con·fu·cian (kən·fyoō′shən) *adj.* Of or pertaining to Confucius, his teachings, or his followers. — *n.* An adherent of Confucius or his teachings.

Con·fu·cian·ism (kən·fyoō′shən·iz′əm) *n.* The ethical system taught by Confucius, emphasizing ancestor worship, devotion to family and friends, and the maintenance of justice and peace. — **Con·fu′cian·ist** *n.*

Con·fu·cius (kən·fyoō′shəs), 551?–478? B.C., Chinese philosopher and teacher. Chinese *K'ung Fu-tse.*

con·fuse (kən·fyoōz′) *v.t.* **·fused, ·fus·ing 1.** To perplex or perturb; confound; bewilder. **2.** To mix indiscriminately; jumble. **3.** To mix up mentally; mistake one for the other: He *confused* the dates of the events. **4.** *Obs.* To undo; ruin. [< L *confusus,* pp. of *confundere* < *com-* together + *fundere* to pour. Akin to CONFOUND.] — **con·fus·ed·ly** (kən·fyoō′zid·lē) *adv.* — **con·fus′ed·ness** *n.* — **con·fus′ing·ly** *adv.*

con·fu·sion (kən·fyoō′zhən) *n.* **1.** The act of confusing, or the state of being confused. **2.** Disarray; disorder. **3.** Perplexity of mind; distraction. **4.** Embarrassment; shame. **5.** *Archaic* Overthrow; ruin. — **con·fu′sion·al** *adj.*

con·fu·ta·tion (kon′fyoō·tā′shən) *n.* **1.** The act of confuting; disproof. **2.** That which confutes. [< L *confutatio, -onis* < *confutare.* See CONFUTE.]

con·fute (kən·fyoōt′) *v.t.* **·fut·ed, ·fut·ing 1.** To prove to be wrong, false, or invalid; refute successfully. **2.** To overwhelm with proofs or disproofs; prove (a person) to be in the wrong. **3.** To bring to naught; confound. — **Syn.** See REFUTE. [< L *confutare* to check, restrain] — **con·fut′er** *n.*

cong. Gallon (L *congius*).

Cong. 1. Congregational. **2.** Congress; Congressional.

con·ga (kong′gə) *n.* **1.** A dance of Latin American origin in which the dancers form a winding line. **2.** The music for this dance, in fast 4/4 time. [< Am. Sp.]

con game *U.S. Slang* A confidence game (which see).

Con·ga·ree River (kong′gə·rē′) A river in central South Carolina, flowing SE about 50 miles to the Santee River.

con·gé (kon′zhā, Fr. kôn·zhā′) *n.* **1.** Leave-taking, especially, formal leave-taking; also, permission to depart. **2.** Dismissal. **3.** *Obs.* A polite or formal bow, as at leave-taking. **4.** *Archit.* A concave molding. [< F < OF *congée* < L *commeatus* leave of absence < *commeare* to come and go < *com-* thoroughly + *ire* to go]

con·geal (kən·jēl′) *v.t. & v.i.* **1.** To change from a fluid to a solid condition, as by freezing or curdling. **2.** To clot or coagulate, as blood. [< MF *congeler* < L *congelare* < *com-* together + *gelare* to freeze < *gelum* frost] — **con·geal′a·ble** *adj.* — **con·geal′er** *n.* — **con·geal′ment** *n.*

con·ge·la·tion (kon′jə·lā′shən) *n.* **1.** A congealing. **2.** A congealed state, or something congealed. [< L *congelatio, -onis* < *congelare.* See CONGEAL.]

con·ge·ner (kon′jə·nər) *n.* A fellow member of the same genus, class, family, or kind. [< MF *congenere* < L *congener* of the same race < *com-* together + *genus, generis* race, kind]

con·ge·ner·ic (kon′jə·ner′ik) *adj.* Of the same kind, class, or genus. Also **con·gen·er·ous** (kən·jen′ər·əs).

con·gen·ial (kən·jēn′yəl) *adj* **1.** Having similar character or tastes; sympathetic. **2.** Suited to one's disposition; agreeable: a *congenial* job. [< CON- + GENIAL] — **con·ge·ni·al·i·ty** (kən·jē′nē·al′ə·tē) *n.* — **con·gen′ial·ly** *adv.*

con·gen·i·tal (kən·jen′ə·təl) *adj.* **1.** Existing prior to or at birth, but not inherited: distinguished from *hereditary*: a *congenital* defect. **2.** Loosely, disposed as if by birth: a *congenital* liar. — **Syn.** See INNATE. [< L *congenitus* < *com-* together + *genitus,* pp. of *gignere* to bear] — **con·gen′i·tal·ly** *adv.*

con·ger (kong′gər) *n.* A marine eel (*Conger conger*) from 4 to 10 feet long, used as a food fish. Also **conger eel.** [< OF *congre* < L *conger* < Gk. *gongros*]

con·ge·ries (kon′jə·rēz, kən·jir′ēz) *n.pl.* (*usually construed as sing.*) A collection of things; a mass; heap. [< L < *congerere.* See CONGEST.]

con·gest (kən·jest′) *v.t.* **1.** To collect or crowd together; overcrowd. **2.** *Pathol.* To surcharge (an organ or part) with an excess of blood. **3.** *Obs.* To accumulate. — *v.i.* **4.** To become congested. [< L *congestus,* pp. of *congerere* < *com-* together + *gerere* to bear, carry] — **con·ges′tive** *adj.*

con·ges·tion (kən·jes′chən) *n.* **1.** *Pathol.* An excessive accumulation, as of blood in an organ. **2.** An overcrowded condition.

con·glo·bate (kon·glō′bāt, kong′glō·bāt) *v.t. & v.i.* ·**bat·ed**, ·**bat·ing** To gather or form into a globe or ball-like mass. Also **con·globe** (kon·glōb′). — *adj.* Globular. [< L *conglobatus,* pp. of *conglobare* < *com-* together + *globare* to make a ball < *globus* ball] — **con′glo·ba′tion** *n.*

con·glom·er·ate (*adj., n.* kən·glom′ər·it; *v.* kən·glom′ə·rāt) *adj.* **1.** Massed or clustered. **2.** *Geol.* Consisting of loosely cemented heterogeneous material: *conglomerate* clay: also **con·glom·er·at·ic** (kən·glom′ə·rat′ik), **con·glom′er·it′ic** (-ə·rit′ik). — **Syn.** See AGGREGATE. — *n.* **1.** A heterogeneous collection; cluster. **2.** *Geol.* A rock composed of pebbles, etc., loosely cemented together. — *v.t. & v.i.* ·**at·ed,** ·**at·ing** To gather into a cohering mass. [< L *conglomeratus,* pp. of *conglomerare* < *com-* together + *glomus, glomeris* ball]

con·glom·er·a·tion (kən·glom′ə·rā′shən) *n.* **1.** A conglomerated mass. **2.** A heterogeneous collection. **3.** The act of conglomerating.

con·glu·ti·nant (kən·glōō′tə·nənt) *adj.* *Med.* Promoting healing by adhesion, as of the edges of a wound. [< L *conglutinans, -antis,* ppr. of *conglutinare.* See CONGLUTINATE.]

con·glu·ti·nate (kən·glōō′tə·nāt) *v.t. & v.i.* ·**nat·ed,** ·**nat·ing** **1.** To glue or stick together; adhere. **2.** *Med.* To reunite by adhesion, as wounds or fractures. — *adj.* Glued together; united by adhesion. [< L *conglutinatus,* pp. of *conglutinare* < *com-* together + *glutinare* to stick < *gluten, -inis* glue] — **con·glu′ti·na′tion** *n.* — **con·glu′ti·na′tive** *adj.*

con·go¹ (kong′gō) *n.* The congo snake (which see).

con·go² (kong′gō) *n.* Congou.

Con·go (kong′gō) A river rising in the SE Republic of the Congo (now Zaire) and flowing about 2,900 miles to the South Atlantic; one of the world's longest rivers.

Congo (Brazza·ville), Republic of the An independent member of the French community in central Africa; 132,000 sq. mi.; pop. 864,684 (1962); capital, Brazzaville; formerly *Middle Congo.* French *République du Congo.* — **Con·go·lese** (kong·gə·lēz′, -lēs′) *n. & adj.*

Congo Free State A former name for BELGIAN CONGO.

Congo group *Chem.* A class of direct dyes from benzidine or tolidine, mostly azo derivatives. Also **Congo dyes.**

Congo, Democratic Republic of the Before January, 1972, the name for an independent Republic in west central Africa; formerly *Congo Free State, Belgian Congo* (1908–60). See ZAIRE, REPUBLIC OF. — **Con·go·lese** ((kong·gə·lēz′, -lēs′) *n. & adj.*

Congo paper A paper dyed with Congo red, used to indicate the presence of acids.

Congo red *Chem.* A dye of the Congo group, used in dyeing cotton and wool, and as a chemical indicator showing red in neutral or alkaline solutions and blue in acid.

congo snake A tailed aquatic salamander (*Amphiuma means*) of the SE United States, of elongate eellike form with rudimentary limbs. Also **congo eel.**

con·gou (kong′gōō) *n.* A grade of black tea from China: also called *congo.* [< Chinese *kung-fu*(*ch'a*) labor (tea); tea on which labor has been spent]

con·grat·u·lant (kən·grach′ōō·lənt) *adj.* Expressing congratulations. — *n.* A congratulator. [< L *congratulans, -antis,* ppr. of *congratulari.* See CONGRATULATE.]

con·grat·u·late (kən·grach′ōō·lāt) *v.t.* ·**lat·ed,** ·**lat·ing** **1.** To express pleasure in or otherwise acknowledge the achievement or good fortune of (another); felicitate. **2.** *Obs.* To welcome; hail. [< L *congratulatus* pp. of *congratulari* < *com-* together + *gratulari* to rejoice] — **con·grat′u·la′tor** *n.*

con·grat·u·la·tion (kən·grach′ōō·lā′shən) *n.* **1.** The act of congratulating. **2.** *pl.* Expressions of pleasure and good wishes on another's fortune or success.

con·grat·u·la·to·ry (kən·grach′ōō·lə·tôr′ē, -tō′rē) *adj.* Expressing congratulations.

con·gre·gate (*v.* kong′grə·gāt; *adj.* kong′grə·git) *v.t. & v.i.* ·**gat·ed,** ·**gat·ing** To bring or come together into a crowd; assemble. — *adj.* **1.** Relating to a congregation. **2.** Gathered together; collected. [< L *congregatus,* pp. of *congregare* < *com-* together + *gregare* to crowd, collect < *grex, gregis* flock] — **con′gre·ga′tor** *n.*

con·gre·ga·tion (kong′grə·gā′shən) *n.* **1.** The act of congregating; a collecting into one mass, body, or assembly. **2.** An assemblage of people or things. **3.** A group of people met together for worship; also, the body of persons who worship in a local church; a parish. **4.** In the Old Testament, the whole body of Israel. **5.** In the Roman Catholic Church: **a** A religious community or order bound by a common rule. **b** Any of several committees of cardinals who administer departments of the papal government. **6.** In colonial New England, a town or settlement, considered as a religious community. — **Syn.** See COMPANY. — **con′gre·ga′tion·al** *adj.*

con·gre·ga·tion·al·ism (kong′grə·gā′shən·əl·iz′əm) *n.* A form of church government in which each local congregation is autonomous in all church matters.

Con·gre·ga·tion·al·ism (kong′grə·gā′shən·əl·iz′əm) *n.* The type of organization and system of beliefs of an evangelical Protestant denomination (**Congregational Christian Churches**) practicing congregationalism and forming, since 1957, part of the United Church of Christ. Abbr. *Cong.* — **Con′gre·ga′tion·al** *adj.* — **Con′gre·ga′tion·al·ist** *n.*

Congregation of the Holy Office See under HOLY OFFICE.

con·gre·ga·tive (kong′grə·gā′tiv) *adj.* Tending to congregate — **con′gre·ga′tive·ness** *n.*

con·gress (kong′gris) *n.* **1.** An assembly or conference; especially, a formal meeting of representatives, as of sovereign nations, for the settlement of certain questions. **2.** A coming together; meeting. **3.** Social intercourse. **4.** Sexual intercourse. **5.** The legislature of various nations, especially of a republic. — *v.i.* To meet at a congress. [< L *congressus* a coming together < *congredi* < *com-* together + *gradi* to walk]

Con·gress (kong′gris) *n.* The legislative body of the United States, consisting of the Senate and the House of Representatives; also, this body during one of the two-year periods between regular elections to the House of Representatives. Abbr. *C., Cong.*

congress boot *U.S.* A high shoe with elastic material in the sides. Also **congress gaiter.**

con·gres·sion·al (kən·gresh′ən·əl) *adj.* Often *cap.* *U.S.* Pertaining to a congress, especially to the United States Congress. Abbr. *Cong.*

Congressional district *U.S.* A division of a State, entitled to one representative in Congress.

con·gres·sion·al·ist (kən·gresh′ən·əl·ist) *n.* A supporter or adherent of a congress.

Congressional Medal of Honor See MEDAL OF HONOR.

Congressional Record *U.S.* An official publication containing the debates and proceedings of Congress.

con·gress·man (kong′gris·mən) *n. pl.* ·**men** (-mən) Often *cap.* A member of the U.S. Congress, especially of the House of Representatives. — **con′gress·wom′an** *n.fem.*

Congress of Industrial Organizations A former affiliation of trade unions originally organized within the American Federation of Labor in 1935, independent of it from 1938–1955, and merged with it in 1955. See AFL–CIO. Abbr. *CIO, C.I.O.*

Congress of the Confederation See under CONTINENTAL CONGRESS.

Congress of Vienna A conference of European powers, 1814–15, held after the first exile of Napoleon, and aiming, under Metternich's leadership, at territorial readjustment and restoration of monarchical governments.

Con·greve (kon'grĕv, kong'-) *n.* **1.** A variety of friction match. Also **Congreve match. 2.** A military rocket invented in 1808: also **Congreve rocket.** [after Sir William *Congreve*, 1772–1828, English engineer who invented both]

Con·greve (kon'grĕv, kong'-) **William,** 1670–1729, English dramatist.

con·gru·ence (kong'grōō·əns) *n.* Conformity; agreement. Also **con'gru·en·cy.**

con·gru·ent (kong'grōō·ənt) *adj.* **1.** Agreeing or conforming; congruous. **2.** *Geom.* Exactly coinciding when superimposed. **3.** *Math.* Of numbers, leaving the same remainders when divided by a given quantity. [< L *congruens, -entis*, ppr. of *congruere* to agree] — **con'gru·ent·ly** *adv.*

con·gru·i·ty (kən·grōō'ə·tē) *n.* *pl.* **·ties 1.** The state or quality of being congruous; agreement or fitness. **2.** An example or point of agreement. **3.** *Geom.* Exact correspondence when superimposed. — **Syn.** See HARMONY. [< L *congruitas, -tatis* < *congruus.* See CONGRUOUS.]

con·gru·ous (kong'grōō·əs) *adj.* **1.** Agreeing in nature or qualities; harmonious; concordant. **2.** Appropriate; fit. **3.** *Geom.* Congruent. [< L *congruus* < *congruere* to agree] — **con'gru·ous·ly** *adv.* — **con'gru·ous·ness** *n.*

con·ic (kon'ik) *adj.* **1.** Cone-shaped. **2.** Relating to or formed by or upon a cone. Also **con'i·cal.** — *n.* *Math.* A conic section. [< Gk. *kōnikos* < *kōnos* cone] — **con'i·cal·ly** *adv.*

conic projection A type of map in which the terrain is plotted on a conical surface, the projection then being flattened out to a plane surface.

conic section *Math.* A curve formed by the intersection of a plane with a right circular cone, being an ellipse, parabola, or hyperbola, according to the inclination of the cutting plane to the axis.

CONIC SECTIONS

conic sections The branch of mathematics that treats of the ellipse, parabola, and hyperbola. Also **con'ics.**

a Circle. *b* Parabola. *c* Hyperbola. *d* Ellipse. *e* Right-line.

co·nid·i·o·phore (kō·nid'ē·ə·fôr', -fōr') *n.* *Bot.* A branch of the hypha in the mycelium of fungi that bears the conidia. [< CONIDIUM + -PHORE]

co·nid·i·um (kō·nid'ē·əm) *n.* *pl.* **·nid·i·a** (-nid'ē·ə) *Bot.* A nonsexually produced propagative cell or spore borne upon special branches of the hypha in many species of fungi. Also **co·nid·i·o·spore** (kō·nid'ē·ə·spôr', -spōr'). [< NL < Gk. *konis* dust] — **co·nid'i·al** *adj.*

con·i·fer (kon'ə·fər, kō'nə-) *n.* Any of a large and widely distributed family of evergreen shrubs and trees (*Coniferae*), characterized by needle-shaped leaves, cones, and a resinous wood, as the pines, spruces, firs, and junipers. [< L < *conus* cone + *ferre* to bear]

co·nif·er·ous (kō·nif'ər·əs) *adj.* **1.** Cone-bearing. **2.** Of or composed of conifers: *coniferous* forests.

co·ni·ine (kō'ni·ēn, -nē·in) *n.* *Chem.* A very poisonous alkaloid, $C_8H_{17}N$, contained in poison hemlock, sometimes used locally as a narcotic to relieve pain. Also **co·nin** (kō'nin), **co·nine** (kō'nēn). [< CONI(UM) + -INE²]

conio- *combining form* Dust: *coniology.* [< Gk. *konis* dust]

co·ni·ol·o·gy (kō'nē·ol'ə·jē) *n.* The scientific study of dust, especially with reference to its effects upon plant and animal life: also spelled *koniology.* [< CONIO- + -LOGY]

co·ni·um (kō'nē·əm) *n.* Any of a genus (*Conium*) of tall, highly poisonous, biennial herbs of the parsley family; especially, the poison hemlock. [< L < Gk. *kōneion* hemlock]

conj. **1.** Conjugation. **2.** Conjunction. **3.** Conjunctive.

con·jec·tur·al (kən·jek'chər·əl) *adj.* **1.** Involving or dependent upon conjecture. **2.** Given to conjecture. — **con·jec'tur·al·ly** *adv.*

con·jec·ture (kən·jek'chər) *v.* **·tured, ·tur·ing** *v.t.* **1.** To conclude or suppose from incomplete evidence; guess; infer. — *v.i.* **2.** To make a conjecture. — **Syn.** See SUPPOSE. — *n.* **1.** Inference from incomplete or merely probable evidence. **2.** A conclusion based on this; a tentative judgment; guess; surmise. **3.** *Obs.* Divination; prediction. — **Syn.** See HYPOTHESIS. [< L *conjectura* < *conjicere* < *com-* together +*jacere* to throw] — **con·jec'tur·a·ble** *adj.* — **con·jec'tur·a·bly** *adv.* — **con·jec'tur·er** *n.*

con·join (kən·join') *v.t.* & *v.i.* To join together; associate; connect; unite. [< MF *conjoindre* < L *conjungere* < *com-* together + *jungere* to join] — **con·join'er** *n.*

con·joint (kən·joint') *adj.* **1.** Associated; conjoined. **2.** Joint. [< MF, pp. of *conjoindre.* See CONJOIN.] — **con·joint'ly** *adv.*

con·ju·gal (kon'jōō·gəl, -jə-) *adj.* Pertaining to marriage or to the relation of husband and wife; connubial. [< F < L *conjugalis* < *conjunx, conjux* spouse < *conjungere* to join in marriage] — **con·ju·gal·i·ty** (kon'jōō·gal'ə·tē) *n.* — **con'ju·gal·ly** *adv.*

con·ju·gate (kon'jōō·gāt, -jə-; *for adj., n., also* kon'jōō·git, -jə-) *v.* **·gat·ed, ·gat·ing** *v.t.* **1.** *Gram.* To give the inflections of (a verb) for person, number, tense, mood, and voice. **2.** *Rare* To join together; couple in marriage. — *v.i.* **3.**

Biol. To unite in conjugation. **4.** *Rare* To unite in sexual intercourse. — *adj.* **1.** Joined in pairs; coupled. **2.** *Math.* Reciprocally related or interchangeable with respect to certain properties. **3.** *Chem.* Containing two or more radicals acting as one. **4.** *Bot.* Composed of two leaflets: said of a pinnate leaf. **5.** Kindred in origin and, usually, meaning: said of words. — *n.* **1.** One of two or more conjugate words. **2.** A member of any conjugate pair. [< L *conjugatus*, pp. of *conjugare* < *com-* together + *jugare* to join < *jugum* yoke] — **con'ju·ga'tor** *n.*

con·ju·ga·tion (kon'jōō·gā'shən, -jə-) *n.* **1.** A joining or being joined together; conjunction; union. **2.** *Gram.* **a** The inflection of verbs. **b** A schematic presentation of the entire inflection of a verb. **c** A class of verbs that are inflected in the same manner. **3.** *Biol.* **a** The temporary fusion of two similar protozoans during which exchange of nuclear material takes place. **b** A similar fusion of gametes in certain algae and fungi. Abbr. (def. 2, 3) *conj.* — **con'ju·ga'tion·al** *adj.* — **con'ju·ga'tion·al·ly** *adv.*

con·ju·ga·tive (kon'jōō·gā'tiv, -jə-) *adj.* Of, tending to, or characterized by conjugation.

con·junct (kən·jungkt', kon'jungkt) *adj.* Joined together; conjoined. [< L *conjunctus*, pp. of *conjungere.* See CONJOIN.] — **con·junct'ly** *adv.*

con·junc·tion (kən·jungk'shən) *n.* **1.** The act of joining together, or the state of being so joined; combination; union. **2.** A simultaneous occurrence of events; concurrence; coincidence. **3.** *Astron.* **a** The position of two celestial bodies when they are in the same longitude or right ascension. **b** The position of a planet when it is on a direct line with the earth and the sun. **4.** *Gram.* A word used to connect words, phrases, clauses, or sentences; one of the eight traditional parts of speech. — **coordinate conjunction** A conjunction, as *and, but,* or, that joins words or groups of words of equal rank. — **subordinate conjunction** A conjunction, as *as, because, if, that, though,* that joins clauses of minor rank to principal clauses. Abbr. (def. 3, 4) *conj.* — **con·junc'tion·al** *adj.* — **con·junc'tion·al·ly** *adv.*

con·junc·ti·va (kon'jungk·tī'və, kən·jungk'tə·və) *n.* *pl.* **·vas** or **·vae** (-vē) *Anat.* The mucous membrane lining the eyelids and covering the front part of the eyeball. For illustration see EYE. [< NL (*membrana*) *conjunctiva* connective (membrane)] — **con'junc·ti'val** *adj.*

con·junc·tive (kən·jungk'tiv) *adj.* **1.** Joining; connective. **2.** Joined together. **3.** *Gram.* **a** Serving to unite both meaning and construction, as the conjunction *and.* **b** Of an adverb, serving to unite sentences in larger units, as *furthermore, nevertheless,* etc. — *n.* *Gram.* A conjunctive word, especially a conjunction. Abbr. *conj.* [< L *conjunctivus* < *conjungere.* See CONJOIN.] — **con·junc'tive·ly** *adv.*

con·junc·ti·vi·tis (kən·jungk'tə·vī'tis) *n.* *Pathol.* Inflammation of the conjunctiva. [< CONJUNCTIV(A) + -ITIS]

con·junc·ture (kən·jungk'chər) *n.* **1.** A combination of circumstances or events; juncture. **2.** A critical situation; crisis. **3.** *Obs.* The act of joining; union.

con·ju·ra·tion (kon'jōō·rā'shən) *n.* **1.** The doing of something by magic; originally, the conjuring of a demon to one's will. **2.** A magic spell or expression. **3.** The performing of magic. **4.** *Obs.* A solemn invocation; entreaty. [< OF < L *conjuratio, -onis* conspiracy < *conjurare.* See CONJURE.]

con·jure (*v. defs. 1 and 6* kən·jŏŏr'; *v. defs. 2–5, adj.* kon'jər, kun'-) *v.* **·jured, ·jur·ing** *v.t.* **1.** To call on or appeal to solemnly; adjure. **2.** To summon by incantation or spell, as a devil. **3.** To accomplish or effect by or as by magic. — *v.i.* **4.** To practice magic, especially legerdemain. **5.** To summon a devil or spirit by incantation. **6.** *Obs.* To conspire. — *adj.* *U.S. Dial.* Practicing or curing by magic: a *conjure* man. [< OF *conjurer* < L *conjurare* < *com-* together + *jurare* to swear]

con·jur·er (kon'jər·ər, kun'-*for def.1*; kən·jŏŏr'ər *for def. 2*) *n.* **1.** One who practices magic or legerdemain; a sorcerer, magician, or juggler. **2.** One who appeals or invokes solemnly. Also **con'jur·or.**

conk (kongk) *n.* *Slang* **1.** *U.S.* The head. **2.** The nose. — *v.t.* *U.S. Slang* To hit on the head. — **to conk out 1.** *Informal* To stall or fail: said of engines. **2.** *U.S. Slang* To become suddenly weak and tired; collapse, especially after effort or indulgence. [? < CONCH]

con man (kon) *U.S. Slang* A confidence man.

con mo·to (kōn mō'tō) *Music* With action; vivaciously. [< Ital.]

conn (kon) See CON².

Conn. Connecticut.

Con·nacht (kon'əkht, kon'ət) A Province of western Ireland; 6,611 sq. mi.; pop. 446,221 (1956). Also **Con·naught** (kon'ôt).

con·nate (kon'āt) *adj.* **1.** Born in one; innate; congenital. **2.** Born or existing together or with another; cognate. **3.** *Biol.* Congenitally or firmly united, as the parts of an organism. [< L *connatus*, pp. of *connasci,* var. of *cognasci* to be related. See COGNATE.] — **con'nate·ly** *adv.* — **con'nate·ness** *n.* — **con·na·tion** (kə·nā'shən) *n.*

con·nat·u·ral (kə·nach'ər·əl) *adj.* **1.** Innate; congenital;

inborn. **2.** Allied; cognate. Also spelled *conatural*. [< Med.L *connaturalis* < L *com-* together + *naturalis* natural] — **con·nat′u·ral·ly** *adv.*

con·nect (kə·nekt′) *v.t.* **1.** To join or fasten together; link. **2.** To associate by some relation, as in thought or action. **3.** To place in an electric circuit. **4.** To put in telephonic communication: with *with*. — *v.i.* **5.** To come into union or close relation; join or fit. **6.** To meet so that passengers can transfer from one route to another: said of trains, buses, etc. **7.** *U.S. Informal* To hit the ball, as in baseball. **8.** *U.S. Informal* To be successful; make out well. [< L *connectere*, var. of *conectere* < *com-* together + *nectere* to bind] — **con·nec′tor** or **con·nect′er** *n.*

Con·nec·ti·cut (kə·net′ə·kət) A State of the NE United States; 5,009 sq. mi.; pop. 3,032,217; capital, Hartford; entered the Union Jan. 9, 1788, one of the original thirteen States: nicknames *Constitution State, Nutmeg State.*

Connecticut River The longest river of New England, flowing 345 miles between Vermont and New Hampshire, and through Massachusetts and Connecticut to Long Island Sound.

connecting rod *Mech.* A rod joining a piston with the crankshaft in an engine, pump, etc.: also called *piston rod.*

con·nec·tion (kə·nek′shən) *n.* **1.** The act of connecting, or the state of being connected; union; combination. **2.** That which joins or relates; a bond; link. **3.** Logical sequence of words or ideas; coherence. **4.** Context: In what *connection* did he speak of them? **5.** Family relationship, especially by marriage; also, a distant relative. **6.** A group of persons united by religious affiliation; a sect. **7.** *Usually pl.* A group of persons with whom one is associated, by interests, dealings, beliefs, etc.; especially, such a group considered as influential in some way. **8.** Sexual intercourse. **9.** *Often pl.* A transfer or continuation in transit from one route or vehicle to another. **10.** *Mech.* A device or apparatus that joins separate parts, as a connecting rod. **11.** A means of communication between two stations: a telephone *connection.* Also *Brit.* **con·nex′ion.** Abbr. *con.* — **con·nec′tion·al** *adj.*

con·nec·tive (kə·nek′tiv) *adj.* Capable of connecting, or serving to connect. — *n.* **1.** That which connects. **2.** *Gram.* A connecting word or particle, as a conjunction. **3.** *Bot.* The tissue of a stamen that units the lobes of an anther. — **con·nec′tive·ly** *adv.* — **con·nec·tiv·i·ty** (kon′ek·tiv′ə·tē) *n.*

connective tissue *Anat.* The fibrous tissue that serves to unite and support the various parts of the body, as cartilage, bone, or tendon.

Con·nel·ly (kon′əl·ē), **Marc,** born in 1890, U.S. playwright: full name **Marcus Cook Connelly.**

conning tower **1.** The armored pilothouse of a warship. **2.** In submarines, an observation tower serving also as an entrance.

con·nip·tion (kə·nip′shən) *n.* *U.S. Informal* A fit of hysteria, rage, etc. Also **conniption fit.** [Cf. dial. E (Northern) *canapshus* ill-tempered]

con·niv·ance (kə·nī′vəns) *n.* **1.** The act or fact of conniving; silent or indirect assent, especially to wrongdoing. **2.** *Law* A guilty assent to or knowledge of a wrongful or criminal act. Also **con·niv′ence.**

con·nive (kə·nīv′) *v.i.* **·nived, ·niv·ing 1.** To encourage or assent to a wrong by silence or feigned ignorance: with *at*. **2.** To be in collusion: with *with*. [< L *connivere*, var. of *conivere* to wink, shut the eyes] — **con·niv′er** *n.*

con·niv·ent (kə·nī′vənt) *adj.* *Biol.* Converging, as stamens or wings. [< L *connivens, -entis,* pp. of *conivere.* See CONNIVE.]

con·nois·seur (kon′ə·sûr′) *n.* One competent to judge critically because of thorough knowledge, especially in matters of art and taste. — **Syn.** See AMATEUR. [< F, ult. < L *cognoscere* to know, understand] — **con′nois·seur′ship** *n.*

con·no·ta·tion (kon′ə·tā′shən) *n.* **1.** The suggestive or associative significance of an expression, additional to the explicit literal meaning; implication. Compare DENOTATION. **2.** *Logic* The total of the qualities constituting the signification of a term; intension. **3.** The act of connoting. [< Med.L *connotatio, -onis* < *connotare.* See CONNOTE.]

con·no·ta·tive (kon′ə·tā′tiv, kə·nō′tə·tiv) *adj.* Having or of the nature of connotation; connoting. — **con′no·ta′tive·ly** *adv.*

con·note (kə·nōt′) *v.t.* **·not·ed, ·not·ing 1.** To suggest or imply along with the literal meaning. **2.** To involve as a condition, consequence, etc. Also *Rare* **con·no·tate** (kon′ə·tāt). [< Med.L *connotare* < L *com-* together + *notare* to mark]

con·nu·bi·al (kə·nōō′bē·əl, -nyōō′-) *adj.* Pertaining to marriage or to the married state; conjugal; matrimonial. [< L *connubialis* < *connubium* marriage < *com-* together + *nubere* to marry] — **con·nu′bi·al′i·ty** *n.* — **con·nu′bi·al·ly** *adv.*

co·no·dont (kō′nə·dont, kon′ə-) *n.* *Paleontol.* A small toothlike fossil, found in Paleozoic rocks. [< Gk. *kōnos* cone + *odous, odontos* tooth]

co·noid (kō′noid) *adj.* Cone-shaped; conical. Also **co·noi′**-

dal. — *n.* **1.** Something shaped like a cone. **2.** *Geom.* A surface or solid formed by the revolution about its axis of a parabola, hyperbola, or ellipse. [< Gk. *kōnoeidēs* conical]

co·no·scen·te (kō′nō·shen′tā) See COGNOSCENTE.

con·quer (kong′kər) *v.t.* **1.** To overcome or subdue by force, as in war; vanquish. **2.** To acquire or gain control of by or as by force of arms. **3.** To overcome by mental or moral force; surmount. — *v.i.* **4.** To be victorious. [< OF *conquerre* < L *conquirere* < *com-* thoroughly + *quaerere* to search for, procure] — **con′quer·a·ble** *adj.*

con·quer·or (kong′kər·ər) *n.* One who conquers; a victor. — **the Conqueror** William I of England.

con·quest (kon′kwest, kong′-) *n.* **1.** The act of conquering. **2.** The thing conquered, as territory. **3.** A winning of another's favor or love. **4.** One whose favor or love has been won. — **the Conquest** The Norman Conquest (which see). [< OF, pp. of *conquerre.* See CONQUER.]

con·qui·an (kong′kē·ən) *n.* A two-handed card game resembling rummy, requiring 40 cards: also called *cooncan.* [< Sp. *con quién* with whom]

con·quis·ta·dor (kon·kwis′tə·dôr, -kis′-; *Sp.* kōng·kēs′tä·thōr′) *n.* *pl.* **·dors,** *Sp.* **·do·res** (-thō′rās) A conqueror; especially, any of the Spanish conquerors of Mexico and Peru in the 16th century. [< Sp. < *conquistar* to conquer]

Con·rad (kon′rad), **Joseph,** 1857–1924, English author born in Poland: original name **Teodor Józef Konrad Kor·ze·niow·ski** (kôr′ze·nyôf′skē).

cons. 1. Consecrated. **2.** Conserve. **3.** Consigned; consignment. **4.** Consolidated. **5.** Consonant. **6.** Construction. **7.** Consulting.

cons. or **Cons. 1.** Constable. **2.** Constitution; constitutional. **3.** Consul.

con·san·guin·e·ous (kon′sang·gwin′ē·əs) *adj.* Of the same blood or ancestry; akin. Also **con·san·guine** (kon·sang′gwin). [< L *consanguineus* < *com-* together + *sanguis* blood] — **con′san·guin′e·ous·ly** *adv.*

con·san·guin·i·ty (kon′sang·gwin′ə·tē) *n.* **1.** Relationship resulting from common ancestry; blood relationship. **2.** Any close affinity or connection. — **Syn.** See RELATIONSHIP.

con·science (kon′shəns) *n.* **1.** The faculty by which distinctions are made between moral right and wrong, especially in regard to one's own conduct; moral discrimination. **2.** Conformity in conduct to the prescribed moral standard: a man of *conscience.* **3.** *Obs.* Inner thoughts. **4.** *Obs.* Consciousness. — **in (all) conscience 1.** In truth; in reason and honesty. **2.** Certainly; assuredly. [< OF < L *conscientia* < *conscire* to know inwardly < *com-* together + *scire* to know] — **con′science·less** *adj.*

conscience clause A clause in a law releasing persons who have conscientious or religious scruples from performing acts required thereunder.

conscience money Money secretly paid to atone for some concealed act of dishonesty.

con·sci·en·tious (kon′shē·en′shəs, kon′sē-) *adj.* **1.** Governed by or done in accordance with conscience; scrupulous. **2.** Careful and thorough; painstaking. — **con′sci·en′tious·ly** *adv.* — **con′sci·en′tious·ness** *n.*

conscientious objector One who, on grounds of religious or moral convictions, objects to warfare and refuses to bear arms or perform military service. Abbr. *CO, C.O.*

con·scion·a·ble (kon′shən·ə·bəl) *adj.* *Obs.* Conformable to conscience or right; just. — **con′scion·a·bly** *adv.*

con·scious (kon′shəs) *adj.* **1.** Aware of one's own existence, feelings, and thoughts, or of external objects and conditions; mentally awake. **2.** Aware of some object or fact; cognizant: *conscious* of one's shortcomings. **3.** Felt by oneself; internally known: *conscious* superiority. **4.** Overly aware of oneself; self-conscious. **5.** Deliberate; intentional. **6.** *Archaic* Aware of guilt or fault. — *n. Psychoanal.* That part of mental life of which an individual is aware: also called *consciousness.* [< L *conscius* knowing inwardly < *com-* together + *scire* to know] — **con′scious·ly** *adv.*

con·scious·ness (kon′shəs·nis) *n.* **1.** The state of being conscious; awareness of oneself and one's surroundings. **2.** Awareness of some object, influence, etc.; a feeling or conviction: *consciousness* of danger. **3.** The mental and emotional experience and awareness of an individual, or of a group of persons: mob *consciousness.* **4.** *Psychoanal.* The conscio-

con·script (*n., adj.* kon′skript; *v.* kən·skript′) *n.* One ...o is compulsorily enrolled for some service or job, especi·.·y in the armed forces. — *adj.* Enlisted by compulsion; conscripted. — *v.t.* To force into military, naval, or other service. [< L *conscriptus,* pp. of *conscribere* to enroll < *com-* together + *scribere* to write]

conscript fathers (kon′skript) **1.** The senators of ancient Rome. **2.** The members of any legislative body.

con·scrip·tion (kən·skrip′shən) *n.* **1.** A compulsory enrollment of men for military or naval service; a draft. **2.** A payment of money exacted by a government in wartime.

con·se·crate (kon′sə·krāt) *v.t.* **·crat·ed, ·crat·ing 1.** To set apart as sacred; dedicate to sacred uses with appointed ceremonies. **2.** To dedicate; devote: He *consecrated* his life to the cause. **3.** To apotheosize; canonize. **4.** To make reverend or venerable; hallow: *consecrated* by time. — *adj. Archaic* Hallowed; consecrated. [< L *consecratus*, pp. of *consecrare* < *com-* thoroughly + *sacer* holy] — **con'se·cra'tor** *n.* — **con·se·cra·to·ry** (kon/sə·krə·tôr/ē, -tō/rē) *adj.*

con·se·cra·tion (kon/sə·krā/shən) *n.* The act or ceremony of consecrating, or the state of being consecrated.

con·se·cu·tion (kon/sə·kyōō/shən) *n.* **1.** Logical or grammatical sequence. **2.** A succession or series. [< L *consecutio, -onis* < *consequi*. See CONSEQUENT.]

con·sec·u·tive (kən·sek/yə·tiv) *adj.* **1.** Following in uninterrupted succession; successive. **2.** Characterized by logical sequence. **3.** *Gram.* Denoting result or consequence: a *consecutive* clause. [< L *consecutus*, pp. of *consequi*. See CONSEQUENT.] — **con·sec'u·tive·ly** *adv.* — **con·sec'u·tive·ness** *n.*

con·sen·su·al (kən·sen/shōō·əl) *adj.* **1.** *Law* Existing merely by virtue of consent. **2.** *Physiol.* Denoting instinctive and reflex actions that are stimulated by conscious actions. [< L *consensus*. See CONSENSUS.] — **con·sen'su·al·ly** *adv.*

con·sen·sus (kən·sen/səs) *n.* A collective opinion; general agreement. ◆ The phrase *consensus of opinion*, although redundant, is now widely used. [< L < *consentire* < *com-* together + *sentire* to feel, think]

con·sent (kən·sent/) *v.i.* **1.** To give assent; agree or acquiesce. **2.** *Obs.* To agree together; accord. — **Syn.** See ASSENT. — *n.* **1.** A voluntary yielding to what is proposed or desired by another; acquiescence; compliance. **2.** Agreement in opinion or sentiment; harmony; concord. [< OF *consentir* < L *consentire*. See CONSENSUS.] — **con·sent'er** *n.*

con·sen·ta·ne·ous (kon/sen·tā/nē·əs) *adj.* **1.** Unanimous. **2.** Agreeing or agreeable; suited. [< L *consentaneus* agreeing] — **con·sen·ta·ne·i·ty** (kən·sen/tə·nē/ə·tē), **con/sen·ta'·ne·ous·ness** *n.* — **con/sen·ta'ne·ous·ly** *adv.*

con·sen·tience (kən·sen/shəns) *n.* The state or quality of being in agreement or accord. — **con·sen'tient** *adj.*

con·se·quence (kon/sə·kwens, -kwəns) *n.* **1.** That which naturally follows from a preceding action or condition; result. **2.** The relation of an effect to its cause; causal sequence. **3.** A logical conclusion or inference. **4.** Distinction; note: a man of *consequence*. **5.** Importance; significance: an event of no *consequence*.

— **Syn.** See EFFECT (noun). Compare CAUSE.

con·se·quent (kon/sə·kwent, -kwənt) *adj.* **1.** Following as a natural result, or as a logical conclusion; logical. **2.** Characterized by correctness of reasoning; logical. **3.** *Geol.* Having a course or direction depending on or resulting from the original slope of the earth's surface: contrasted with *antecedent*. — *n.* **1.** That which follows something else, as in time or order, without causal relation. **2.** An outcome; result. **3.** *Logic* The conclusion of an argument, as of a syllogism; deduction; inference. **4.** *Math.* The second term of a ratio. [< L *consequens, -entis*, ppr. of *consequi* < *com-* together + *sequi* to follow]

con·se·quen·tial (kon/sə·kwen/shəl) *adj.* **1.** Following as an effect or conclusion; consequent. **2.** Of consequence; important. **3.** Having or showing self-importance. — **con·se·quen·ti·al·i·ty** (kon/sə·kwen/shē·al/ə·tē), **con/se·quen'tial·ness** *n.* — **con/se·quen'tial·ly** *adv.*

con·se·quent·ly (kon/sə·kwent/lē, -kwənt·lē) *adv.* As a result; therefore. — **Syn.** See THEREFORE.

con·ser·van·cy (kən·sûr/vən·sē) *n. pl.* **·cies** **1.** Conservation. **2.** *Brit.* A board or commission to conserve fisheries, waterways, etc. [Earlier *conservacy* < AF *conservacie*. Akin to CONSERVATION.]

con·ser·va·tion (kon/sər·vā/shən) *n.* **1.** The act of keeping or protecting from loss or injury. **2.** The preservation of natural resources, as forests, fisheries, etc., for economic or recreational use; also, an area so preserved. [< L *conservatio, -onis* < *conservare*. See CONSERVE.] — **con/ser·va'tion·al** *adj.*

con·ser·va·tion·ist (kon/sər·vā/shən·ist) *n.* One who advocates conservation of natural resources.

conservation of energy *Physics* The principle that in any closed material system the total amount of energy remains constant, though it may assume different forms successively.

con·ser·va·tism (kən·sûr/və·tiz/əm) *n.* **1.** Devotion to the existing order of things; opposition to change. **2.** The principles of people or groups so devoted.

Con·ser·va·tism (kən·sûr/və·tiz/əm) *n.* The doctrines and policies of the Conservative Party.

con·ser·va·tive (kən·sûr/və·tiv) *adj.* **1.** Inclined to preserve the existing order of things; opposed to change. **2.** Moderate; cautious: a *conservative* estimate. **3.** Conserving; preservative. — *n.* **1.** A conservative person. **2.** A preservative. — **con·ser'va·tive·ly** *adv.* — **con·ser'va·tive·ness** *n.*

Con·ser·va·tive (kən·sûr/və·tiv) *adj.* Of or pertaining to the Conservative Party. — *n.* **1.** A member of this party. **2.** A member of the Progressive-Conservative Party in Canada. Abbr. *C.*

Conservative Judaism That branch of Judaism that accepts as binding the Mosaic Laws and their rabbinical interpretations, but allows some adjustments to the changed conditions of today.

Conservative Party **1.** In Great Britain, the principal right-wing party. See TORY. **2.** In many nations of the British Commonwealth, the political party of the right wing.

con·ser·va·tor (kon/sər·vā/tər, kən·sûr/və·tər) *n.* A protector; guardian; keeper.

con·ser·va·to·ry (kən·sûr/və·tôr/ē, -tō/rē) *n. pl.* **·ries** **1.** A small greenhouse or glass-enclosed room in which plants are grown and displayed. **2.** A school of music. Also **con·ser·va·toire** (kən·sûr/və·twär/). **3.** *Obs.* A place for the preservation or protection of anything. — *adj.* Adapted to preserve.

con·serve (kən·sûrv/; *for n.*, also kon/sûrv) *v.t.* **·served**, **·serv·ing** **1.** To keep from loss, decay, or depletion; maintain; protect. **2.** To preserve with sugar. — *n. Often pl.* A kind of jam made of several fruits stewed together in sugar, often with nuts, raisins, etc. Abbr. *cons.* [< MF *conserver* < L *conservare* < *com-* thoroughly + *servare* to keep, save] — **con·serv'a·ble** *adj.* — **con·serv'er** *n.*

con·sid·er (kən·sid/ər) *v.t.* **1.** To think about or deliberate upon; examine mentally; weigh. **2.** To look upon or regard (as): think (to be): to *consider* her a genius. **3.** To hold as an opinion; believe. **4.** To make allowance for; keep in mind: *Consider* his poverty. **5.** To take into account; have regard for: to *consider* the feelings of others. **6.** To think well of; regard highly. **7.** *Archaic* To observe closely. — *v.i.* **8.** To think carefully; deliberate. [< MF *considerer* < L *considerare, ?* < *com-* thoroughly + *sidus, sideris* star; with ref. to astrology]

— **Syn.** **1.** examine, study, ponder, reflect, meditate. Compare DELIBERATE. **2.** *Consider, regard, reckon, count,* and *account* refer to one's opinion or judgment on some matter or person. *Consider* suggests a more objective judgment that has been reached after careful thought, while *regard* stresses the subjective nature of an opinion: to *consider* Milton a great poet, to *regard* someone as a fool. *Reckon, count,* and, more formally, *account* contain the idea of calculating or numbering, and indicate an evaluation or summation: to *count* a day well spent, to be *reckoned* (or *accounted*) an honest man. — **Ant.** ignore, disregard, neglect, overlook, forget.

con·sid·er·a·ble (kən·sid/ər·ə·bəl) *adj.* **1.** Somewhat large in amount, extent, etc.; much: *considerable* trouble. **2.** Worthy of consideration; important. — *n. U.S. Informal* A good deal; much. — **con·sid/er·a·bly** *adv.*

con·sid·er·ate (kən·sid/ər·it) *adj.* **1.** Thoughtful of others; kind. **2.** Deliberate; considered. **3.** *Archaic* Prudent; cautious. — **con·sid/er·ate·ly** *adv.* — **con·sid/er·ate·ness** *n.*

con·sid·er·a·tion (kən·sid/ə·rā/shən) *n.* **1.** The act of considering; careful thought; deliberation. **2.** A circumstance to be taken into account, as in forming an opinion. **3.** Thoughtful or kindly feeling or treatment; solicitude. **4.** A thought or reflection; opinion. **5.** Something given for a service; fee; recompense. **6.** *Law* That which is given, done, or promised as compensation, as in a contract. **7.** Claim to be considered; importance. **8.** High regard; esteem. — **in consideration of** In view of, or in return for. — **under consideration** Being thought about or discussed. [< OF < L *consideratio, -onis* < *considerare*. See CONSIDER.]

con·sid·ered (kən·sid/ərd) *adj.* **1.** Carefully thought about: a *considered* opinion. **2.** Highly regarded; esteemed.

con·sid·er·ing (kən·sid/ər·ing) *prep.* In view of; taking into account. — *adv. Informal* Taking all the facts into account: He came out quite well, *considering.*

con·sign (kən·sīn/) *v.t.* **1.** To entrust or commit to the care of another. **2.** To give up or turn over; transfer; relegate. **3.** To forward or deliver, as merchandise, for sale or disposal. **4.** To set apart or devote, as for a specific use. **5.** *Obs.* To impress, as with a seal; sign. — *v.i.* **6.** *Obs.* To yield oneself; consent. — **Syn.** See COMMIT. [< MF *consigner* < L *consignare* to seal < *com-* with + *signum* a seal] — **con·sign'a·ble** *adj.* — **con·sig·na·tion** (kon/sig·nā/shən) *n.*

con·sign·ee (kon/sī·nē/) *n.* One to whom goods are consigned.

con·sign·ment (kən·sīn/mənt) *n.* **1.** A consigning of something, especially of goods, for sale or disposal. **2.** That which is consigned. Abbr. *cons.* — **on consignment** Of goods, paid for by the retailer only after they have been sold.

con·sign·or (kən·sī/nər, kon/sī·nôr/) *n.* One who consigns, especially goods for sale. Also **con·sign'er.**

con·sist (kən·sist/) *v.i.* **1.** To be made up or constituted: with *of.* **2.** To have as source or basis; exist; inhere: with *in.* **3.** To be compatible; harmonize: with *with.* **4.** *Rare* To stand together; subsist. [< L *consistere* to stand still, be, exist < *com-* together + *sistere* to stand]

con·sis·ten·cy (kən·sis/tən·sē) *n. pl.* **·cies** **1.** Agreement between things, acts, or statements; logical connection. **2.** Agreement with previous acts, statements, or decisions. **3.** The condition of holding together; firmness, nearness, or density. **4.** Degree of firmness, thickness, or density. Also **con·sis'tence.**

con·sis·tent (kən·sis/tənt) *adj.* **1.** Not contradictory or self-contradictory; compatible; harmonious. **2.** Conforming to a single set of principles, or to previous action or belief. **3.** *Rare* Not loose or fluid; solid. [< L *consistens, -entis* < *consistere*. See CONSIST.] — **con·sis'tent·ly** *adv.*

con·sis·to·ry (kən·sis/tər·ē) *n. pl.* **·ries** **1.** *Eccl.* **a** The highest council of the Roman Catholic Church, composed of all the cardinals, and usually presided over by the Pope. **b** In many reformed churches, a local governing body consisting of the ministers and elders of a congregation. **c** A court of the Lutheran state churches, appointed to oversee ecclesiastical affairs. **d** A diocesan court of the Church of England, presided over by the chancellor or commissary of the diocese. **2.** The place where any such body meets, or the meeting itself. **3.** A council; assembly. [< AF *consistorie* < Med.L *consistorium* council chamber, waiting room < *consistere* to stand still, wait. See CONSIST.] **— con·sis·to·ri·al** (kon′sis-tôr′ē-əl, -tō′rē-), **con·sis·to′ri·an** *adj.*

con·so·ci·ate (kən-sō′shē-āt; *for adj., n., also* kən-sō′shē-it) *v.t. & v.i.* **·at·ed, ·at·ing** To bring or come into association; unite. **—** *adj.* Associated; united. **—** *n.* An associate; partner. [< L *consociatus*, pp. of *consociare* < *com-* together + *socius* ally, friend] **— con·so·ci·a·tion** (-sō′shē-ā′shən, -shē-) *n.*

con·so·cies (kən-sō′shēz) *n. Ecol.* A plant or animal community marked by the dominance of one species characteristic of the given environment. [< NL < L < *com-* together + *socius* ally]

consol. Consolidated.

con·so·la·tion (kon′sə-lā′shən) *n.* **1.** The act of consoling, or the state of being consoled; solace. **2.** One who or that which consoles. [< OF < L *consolatio, -onis* < *consolari.* See CONSOLE.]

con·so·la·to·ry (kən-sol′ə-tôr′ē, -tō′rē) *adj.* Providing solace; consoling.

con·sole¹ (kən-sōl′) *v.t.* **·soled, ·sol·ing** To comfort (a person) in grief or sorrow; cheer. [< MF *consoler* < L *consolari* < *com-* together + *solari* to solace] **— con·sol′a·ble** *adj.*
— Syn. *Console, comfort, solace, condole, cheer,* and *sympathize* embrace kindly words or acts by which we try to alleviate another's sorrow or suffering. We *console* a person by soothing or sustaining his fallen spirits, or *comfort* him by any act that brings relief to his mind or body. *Solace* stresses the feeling of relief that results from our actions; we may *solace* the weary as well as the grief-stricken. To *condole* is to express sympathy for another, indicating that we share his sorrow. We *cheer* another by thoughts or things that give positive pleasure, and *sympathize* with him not only in sorrow but also in joy by indicating that we share his feelings. Compare ALLEVIATE. **—Ant.** distress, grieve, sadden.

con·sole² (kon′sōl) *n.* **1.** A bracket, especially one used to support a cornice or ornamental fixture; a corbel. **2.** A console table (which see). **3.** The portion of an organ containing the manuals and stops. **4.** A cabinet for a radio, phonograph, or television set, designed to rest on the floor. [< MF, a bracket; ult. origin uncertain]

console table A table supported wholly or in part by consoles, or whose legs have the appearance of consoles.

CONSOLE²
(def. 1)

con·sol·i·date (kən-sol′ə-dāt) *v.* **·dat·ed, ·dat·ing** *v.t.* **1.** To make solid, firm, or coherent; strengthen. **2.** *Mil.* To organize and strengthen, as a newly captured position. **3.** To combine in one body or system; form a union of. Abbr. *con.* **—** *v.i.* **4.** To become united, solid, or firm. **—** *adj.* Consolidated. [< L *consolidatus,* pp. of *consolidare* < *com-* together + *solidus* solid] **— con·sol′i·da·tor** *n.*
— Syn. (verb) **1.** solidify. **3.** merge, unite. **4.** unify, concentrate. **—Ant.** disintegrate, dissipate.

Consolidated Fund *Brit.* A public fund into which the main part of the revenue is paid, and out of which is paid interest on the national debt and other charges.

Consolidated Revenue Fund *Canadian* The revenues of the federal government.

consolidated school *U.S. & Canadian* A school, usually rural, for pupils from more than one district.

con·sol·i·da·tion (kən-sol′ə-dā′shən) *n.* The act of consolidating, or the state of being consolidated.

con·sols (kon′solz, kən-solz′) *n.pl. Brit.* British governmental securities: also called *bank annuities.* Abbr. *con.* [Short for *consolidated annuities*]

con·so·lute (kon′sə-lōōt) *adj. Chem.* Completely miscible or soluble under given conditions: said of liquids. [< LL *consolutus* completely dissolved < L *com-* thoroughly + *solutus,* pp. of *solvere* to dissolve]

con·som·mé (kon′sə-mā′, *Fr.* kôṅ-sô-mā′) *n.* A clear soup made of meat and sometimes vegetables boiled in water. [< F, pp. of *consommer* to complete, finish < L *consummare.* See CONSUMMATE.]

consommé madrilène A consommé flavored with tomato and served hot or cold.

con·so·nance (kon′sə-nəns) *n.* **1.** Agreement; accord. **2.** Correspondence of sounds; especially, in prosody, resemblance of consonants but not of vowels in a stressed syllable. **3.** *Music* A simultaneous combination of tones regarded as stable and not requiring resolution; also, such combinations collectively: also called *concord.* Also **con′so·nan·cy. — Syn.** See HARMONY.

con·so·nant (kon′sə-nənt) *adj.* **1.** Being in agreement; consistent. **2.** Corresponding in sound; having consonance. **3.** Consonantal. **4.** *Music* Having the quality of consonance. **—** *n.* **1.** *Phonet.* A sound produced by contact or constriction of the speech organs resulting in deflection or complete or partial blockage of the breath stream. Distinguished from *vowels,* which are characterized primarily by the shape of the resonance cavity, consonants are described by their place of articulation (bilabial, alveolar, etc.), vibration or nonvibration of the vocal cords (voiced or voiceless), presence or absence of nasality, and manner of formation (stop, fricative, etc.). **2.** A letter or written symbol representing such a sound, as *b, f, k, s.* Abbr. *cons.* [< MF < L *consonans, -antis,* ppr. of *consonare* < *com-* together + *sonare* to sound] **— con′so·nant·ly** *adv.*

con·so·nan·tal (kon′sə-nan′təl) *adj.* **1.** Of the nature of a consonant. **2.** Having a consonant or consonants.

con·sort¹ (*n.* kon′sôrt; *v.* kən-sôrt′) *n.* **1.** A husband or wife; spouse. **2.** A companion or partner; mate; also, companionship; company. **3.** *Naut.* A vessel sailing with another. **—** *v.i.* **1.** To keep company; associate. **2.** To be in agreement; harmonize. **—** *v.t.* **3.** To join; associate. **4.** *Obs.* To accompany; escort. [< MF < L *consors, consortis* < *com-* together + *sors* share, lot]

con·sort² (kon′sôrt) *n. Archaic* **1.** A harmonious set of voices or instruments. **2.** Accord; harmony. [< F *concert*]

con·sor·ti·um (kən-sôr′shē-əm) *n. pl.* **·ti·a** (-shē-ə) **1.** A coalition, as of banks or corporations for a venture requiring vast resources. **2.** Any association or fellowship. **3.** *Law* The right of a husband to the society, assistance, and affection of his wife; also, in recent times, recognized as a right of the wife. [< L, fellowship < *consors.* See CONSORT¹.]

con·spec·tus (kən-spek′təs) *n. pl.* **·tus·es** **1.** A general view of a subject. **2.** A digest or summary. [< L < *con-spicere.* See CONSPICUOUS.]

con·spic·u·ous (kən-spik′yōō-əs) *adj.* **1.** Clearly visible; easy to be seen. **2.** Readily attracting attention; striking: a *conspicuous* fault. [< L *conspicuus* < *conspicere* < *com-* together + *specere* to look at] **— con·spic′u·ous·ly** *adv.* **— con·spic′u·ous·ness** *n.*
— Syn. 1. obvious, apparent, patent, salient, prominent.

con·spir·a·cy (kən-spir′ə-sē) *n. pl.* **·cies** **1.** An agreeing or planning of two or more persons to do an evil act in concert; also, the plan so made. **2.** *Law* A combination between two or more persons to commit any unlawful act, or to effect a legal purpose by unlawful means. **3.** An acting together: a *conspiracy* of the elements. [< CONSPIR(E) + -ACY]
— Syn. 1. *Conspiracy, plot,* and *intrigue* refer to a secret or underhand agreement. *Conspiracy* is a legal term denoting an intention to violate the law; in general use, it is applied chiefly to major crimes: a *conspiracy* to betray one's country. *Plot* emphasizes careful planning and a sinister purpose, though it may be petty in scope, while *intrigue* suggests complicated scheming and clandestine methods, and often implies a selfish rather than a criminal purpose: a political *plot,* a lovers' *intrigue.* Compare CABAL, FACTION.

con·spir·a·tor (kən-spir′ə-tər) *n.* One who is involved in a conspiracy. [< AF *conspiratour* < L *conspirator* < *conspirare* to plot. See CONSPIRE.] **— con·spir′a·tress** *n.fem.*

con·spir·a·to·ri·al (kən-spir′ə-tôr′ē-əl, -tō′rē-) *adj.* Of, pertaining to, or like conspiracy or conspirators.

con·spire (kən-spīr′) *v.* **·spired, ·spir·ing** *v.i.* **1.** To combine secretly in an evil or unlawful enterprise. **2.** To act together: The winds *conspire* against us. **—** *v.t.* **3.** To plan secretly; plot. [< MF *conspirer* < L *conspirare* < *com-* together + *spirare* to breathe] **— con·spir′er** *n.*

con spi·ri·to (kôn spē′rē-tō) *Music* With spirit and vigor. [< Ital.]

Const. or **const.** **1.** Constable. **2.** Constant. **3.** Constitution.

con·sta·ble (kon′stə-bəl, kun′-) *n.* **1.** A peace officer who arrests offenders, serves writs, executes warrants, etc. **2.** The chief officer, usually military, in medieval monarchies. **3.** The keeper or governor of a royal castle. Abbr. *cons., Cons., const., Const.* **— Lord High Constable of England** A former military and judicial officer of high rank. [< OF *conestable* < LL *comes stabuli* count of the stable, chief groom] **— con′sta·ble·ship′** *n.*

Con·sta·ble (kun′stə-bəl), **John,** 1776–1837, English landscape painter.

con·stab·u·lar·y (kən-stab′yə-ler′ē) *n. pl.* **·lar·ies** **1.** The body of constables of a city, etc. **2.** The district of a constable. **3.** A police force organized in a military fashion. **—** *adj.* Pertaining to constables or their functions. [< Med.L *constabularia* < *constabulus* chief officer, constable]

Con·stance (kon′stəns) A city in southern West Germany, on the Lake of Constance; pop. about 49,800: German *Konstanz.*

Constance, Lake of A lake in NE Switzerland, NW Austria, and southern Germany; 208 sq. mi.: German *Bodensee.*

con·stan·cy (kon′stən-sē) *n.* **1.** Steadiness or faithfulness

in purpose, action, affections, etc. **2.** Unchanging quality; stability; uniformity; consistency.
con·stant (kon′stənt) *adj.* **1.** Long-continuing, or continually recurring; persistent. **2.** Unchanging; invariable. **3.** Steady in purpose, action, affection, etc.; persevering; faithful. **4.** *Obs.* Confident; sure. — **Syn.** See CONTINUAL. — *n.* **1.** That which is permanent or invariable. **2.** *Math.* A quantity that retains a fixed value throughout a given discussion. Abbr. *k.* **3.** In the sciences, any characteristic of a substance, event, etc., numerically determined, that remains the same under specified conditions. Abbr. *C., const., Const.* [< MF < L *constans, -antis*, ppr. of *constare* < *com*- thoroughly + *stare* to stand] — **con′stant·ly** *adv.*
Con·stant (kôṅ·stäṅ′), **Jean Joseph Benjamin**, 1845–1902, French portrait painter.
Con·stan·ṭa (kôṅ·stäṅ′tsä) A city in SE Rumania, on the Black Sea; pop. 110,485 (est. 1959). Also **Con·stan′tsa.**
con·stant·an (kon′stən·tan) *n.* An alloy of nickel and copper with high thermal and electrical resistance, used in rheostats and thermocouples. [Arbitrary coinage < CONSTANT]
Con·stant (de Re·becque) (kôṅ·stäṅ′ də rə·bek′), **Benjamin**, 1767–1830, French writer and statesman.
Con·stan·tine (kon′stən·tēn, *Fr.* kôṅ·stäṅ·tēn′) A city in NE Algeria; pop. 221,000 (est. 1960).
Con·stan·tine I (kon′stən·tēn, -tīn), 288?–337, first Christian emperor of Rome; founder of the Byzantine Empire: called **the Great.**
Constantine I, 1868–1923, king of Greece 1913–17, 1920–1922.
Constantine V, 718–775, Byzantine emperor 740–775; opposed the Pope; lost Rome.
Constantine VII, 905–959, Byzantine emperor: called **Por·phy·ro·gen·i·tus** (pôr′fə·rō·jen′i·təs) ("born to the purple").
Constantine XI, 1394–1453, last Byzantine emperor: surnamed **Pa·lae·ol·o·gus** (pā′lē·ol′ə·gəs).
Con·stan·ti·no·ple (kon′stan·tə·nō′pəl) A city on the Bosporus, founded by the Roman emperor Constantine I, capital of the Byzantine Empire, and of the Ottoman Empire after 1453. See ISTANBUL.
Con·stan·ti·no·pol·i·tan Creed (kon·stan′tə·nō·pol′ə·tən) Nicene Creed (which see).
con·stel·late (kon′stə·lāt) *v.t. & v.i.* **·lat·ed, ·lat·ing** To group in constellations.

natus, pp. of *consternare*, var. of *consternere* < *com*- thoroughly + *sternere* to cast down, prostrate]
con·ster·na·tion (kon′stər·nā′shən) *n.* Sudden, paralyzing fear or amazement; panic. — **Syn.** See ALARM.
con·sti·pate (kon′stə·pāt) *v.t.* **·pat·ed, ·pat·ing** **1.** To cause constipation in. **2.** *Obs.* To crowd together. [< L *constipatus*, pp. of *constipare* < *com*- together + *stipare* to press, crowd] — **con′sti·pat′ed** *adj.*
con·sti·pa·tion (kon′stə·pā′shən) *n.* A condition of the bowels characterized by suppressed or difficult evacuation.
con·stit·u·en·cy (kən·stich′ōō·ən·sē) *n. pl.* **·cies 1.** A body of voters who elect a representative to a legislative body; also, the district represented. **2.** Any body of supporters.
con·stit·u·ent (kən·stich′ōō·ənt) *adj.* **1.** Serving to form or compose; constituting. **2.** Entitled to elect a representative. **3.** Having the power to frame or modify a constitution. — *n.* **1.** One represented politically or in business; a voter or client. **2.** A necessary part or element. **3.** *Gram.* One of the component forms of a construction. In *The boy's horse runs swiftly*, the **immediate constituents** are *the boy's horse* and *runs swiftly*; the **ultimate constituents** are *the, boy, -s, horse, run, -s, swift, -ly.* [< L *constituens, -entis*, ppr. of *constituere*. See CONSTITUTE.]
con·sti·tute (kon′stə·tōōt, -tyōōt) *v.t.* **·tut·ed, ·tut·ing 1.** To be the substance or elements of; make up; compose: Twenty cigarettes *constitute* a pack. **2.** To enact (a law, etc.). **3.** To found, as a school; establish, as an assembly, in legal form. **4.** To empower; appoint: I *constitute* you my spokesman. **5.** To make by combining elements or parts; frame. **6.** *Obs.* To place; set. [< L *constitutus*, pp. of *constituere* to set up < *com*- together + *statuere* to place, station] — **con′sti·tut′er** or **con′sti·tu′tor** *n.*
con·sti·tu·tion (kon′stə·tōō′shən, -tyōō′-) *n.* **1.** The act of constituting; a setting up or appointing. **2.** The composition or make-up of a thing; especially, physical make-up: a weak *constitution.* **3.** Mental disposition; temperament. **4.** The fundamental laws and principles that normally govern the operation of a state or association; also, a document recording such laws and principles. — **the Constitution** The Constitution of the United States, framed and adopted in 1787, subsequently ratified by each State, and put into effect March 4, 1789. Abbr. *cons., Cons., const., Const.*
Con·sti·tu·tion (kon′stə·tōō′shən, -tyōō′-) A U.S. frigate active in the War of 1812: popularly called *Old Ironsides.*

TABLE OF CONSTELLATIONS

Explanation: GROUP N includes constellations within 45 degrees of the North Pole. GROUP E includes constellations within 45 degrees of each side of the equator. GROUP S includes constellations within 45 degrees of the South Pole.

NAME	Group	On the Meridian at 9 P.M.	NAME	Group	On the Meridian at 9 P.M.	NAME	Group	On the Meridian at 9 P.M.	NAME	Group	On the Meridian at 9 P.M.
Andromeda	E	Nov.	Columba	E	Feb.	Lacerta	N	Oct.	Piscis		
Antlia	E	April	Coma			Leo	E	April	Austrinus	E	Oct.
Apus	S	July	Berenices	E	May	Leo Minor	E	April	Puppis	E	Feb.
Aquarius	E	Oct.	Corona			Lepus	E	Jan.	Pyxis	E	March
Aquila	E	Aug.	Australis	E	Aug.	Libra	E	June	Reticulum	S	Jan.
Ara	S	July	Corona			Lupus	E	June	Sagitta	E	Aug.
Aries	E	Dec.	Borealis	E	July	Lynx	N	Feb.	Sagittarius	E	Aug.
Auriga	E	Feb.	Corvus	E	May	Lyra	E	Aug.	Scorpio	E	July
Boötes	E	June	Crater	E	April	Mensa	S	Jan.	Sculptor	E	Nov.
Caelum	E	Jan.	Crux	S	May	Microsco-			Scutum	E	Aug.
Camelopar-			Cygnus	E	Sept.	pium	E	Sept.	Serpens	E	July
dalis	N	March	Delphinus	E	Sept.	Monoceros	E	March	Sextans	E	April
Cancer	E	March	Dorado	S	Jan.	Musca	S	May	Taurus	E	Jan.
Canes Venatici	E	May	Draco	N	June	Norma	S	July	Telescopium	S	Aug.
Canis Major	E	Feb.	Equuleus	E	Sept.	Octans	S	......	Triangulum	E	Dec.
Canis Minor	E	March	Eridanus	E	Dec.	Ophiuchus	E	July	Triangulum		
Capricorn	E	Sept.	Fornax	E	Dec.	Orion	E	Jan.	Australe	S	July
Carina	S	March	Gemini	E	Feb.	Pavo	S	Aug.	Tucana	S	Oct.
Cassiopeia	N	Nov.	Grus	S	Oct.	Pegasus	E	Oct.	Ursa Major	N	April
Centaurus	E	May	Hercules	E	July	Perseus	E	Dec.	Ursa Minor	N	......
Cepheus	N	Nov.	Horologium	S	Dec.	Phoenix	S	Nov.	Vela	E	March
Cetus	E	Dec.	Hydra	E	April	Pictor	S	Jan.	Virgo	E	June
Chameleon	S	April	Hydrus	S	Dec.	Pisces	E	Nov.	Volans	S	March
Circinus	S	June	Indus	S	Oct.				Vulpecula	E	Sept.

The four constellations Carina, Puppis, Pyxis, and Vela were formerly considered together as Argo Navis.

con·stel·la·tion (kon′stə·lā′shən) *n.* **1.** *Astron.* Any of various groups of stars imagined to represent the outline of a being or thing, usually mythological, and named accordingly; also, the portion of the heavens occupied by such a group. See table above. **2.** Any brilliant group of persons or things. **3.** In astrology, the aspect of the planets at the time of one's birth; also, disposition or character as influenced by one's horoscope. **4.** *Psychol.* A group of associated emotions, ideas, tendencies, etc., centering upon a dominant element. [< LL *constellatio, -onis* < *constellatus* studded with stars < L *com*- together + *stella* star] — **con·stel·la·to·ry** (kən·stel′ə·tôr′ē, -tō′rē) *adj.*
con·ster·nate (kon′stər·nāt) *v.t.* **·nat·ed, ·nat·ing** To overwhelm with terror and confusion; dismay. [< L *conster-*

con·sti·tu·tion·al (kon′stə·tōō′shən·əl, -tyōō′-) *adj.* **1.** Of or inherent in the constitution of a person or thing; essential: a *constitutional* weakness. **2.** Consistent with, protected by, or pertaining to the constitution of a state; lawful. **3.** Acting under and controlled by a constitution: a *constitutional* monarchy. **4.** Loyal to the constitution. **5.** Affecting or benefiting one's health. — *n.* A walk or exercise taken for one's health. Abbr. *const., Cons.* — **con′sti·tu′tion·al·ly** *adv.*
Constitutional amendment A legal alteration of or addition to the Constitution of the United States, ratified by three fourths of the States.
con·sti·tu·tion·al·ism (kon′stə·tōō′shən·əl·iz′əm, -tyōō′-) *n.* **1.** The principles of constitutional government. **2.** Adherence to these principles. **3.** Constitutional government.

con·sti·tu·tion·al·i·ty (kon′stə·tōō′shən·al′ə·tē, -tyōō′-) *n.* The state or quality of being in agreement with a constitution, especially that of a country, state, etc.
constitutional monarchy See under MONARCHY.
Constitution State Nickname of CONNECTICUT.
con·sti·tu·tive (kon′stə·tōō′tiv, -tyōō′-) *adj.* **1.** Forming an essential element of something; basic. **2.** Having power to enact, institute, or establish. **— con′sti·tu′tive·ly** *adv.*
constr. Construction.
con·strain (kən·strān′) *v.t.* **1.** To compel by physical or moral means; coerce. **2.** To confine, as by bonds. **3.** To restrain; compel to inaction. [< OF *constreindre* < L *constringere* < *com-* together + *stringere* to bind. Doublet of CONSTRINGE.] **— con·strain′a·ble** *adj.* **— con·strain′er** *n.*
— Syn. 1. oblige, force. **2.** bind, constrict, hold. **3.** check.
con·strained (kən·strānd′) *adj.* **1.** Subjected to or resulting from constraint; compelled. **2.** Forced; unnatural: a *constrained* smile. **— con·strain·ed·ly** (kən·strā′nid·lē) *adv.*
con·straint (kən·strānt′) *n.* **1.** The use of force; coercion; compulsion. **2.** Confinement; restriction. **3.** Repression of feelings, or the unnaturalness of manner resulting from this; awkwardness; embarrassment. **4.** The act of constraining, or the state of being constrained. **5.** Anything that constrains. [< OF *constreinte* < *constreindre*. See CONSTRAIN.]
con·strict (kən·strikt′) *v.t.* To draw together by force; cause to shrink or contract; bind; cramp. [< L *constrictus,* pp. of *constringere.* See CONSTRAIN.]
con·stric·tion (kən·strik′shən) *n.* **1.** The act of constricting, or the state of being constricted. **2.** A feeling of tightness. **3.** That which constricts or is constricted.
con·stric·tive (kən·strik′tiv) *adj.* **1.** Tending to constrict. **2.** *Phonet.* Fricative. **—** *n. Phonet.* A fricative.
con·stric·tor (kən·strik′tər) *n.* **1.** That which constricts. **2.** *Anat.* A muscle that contracts an organ of the body; especially, any of the three muscles of the pharynx. **3.** A serpent that coils about and crushes its prey.
con·stringe (kən·strinj′) *v.t.* **·stringed, ·string·ing** *Rare* To cause contraction in; shrink; compress. [< L *constringere* to bind tight. Doublet of CONSTRAIN.] **— con·strin′gen·cy** (-strin′jən·sē) *n.* **— con·strin′gent** *adj.*
con·struct (*v.* kən·strukt′; *n.* kon′strukt) *v.t.* **1.** To form by combining materials or parts; build; erect. **2.** To form mentally; devise. **3.** To form (anything) systematically. **—** *n.* **1.** Something constructed or formulated. **2.** *Psychol.* A synthesized complex of mental images and impressions. [< L *constructus,* pp. of *construere.* See CONSTRUE.] **— con·struct′er** or **con·struc′tor** *n.*
con·struc·tion (kən·struk′shən) *n.* **1.** The act of constructing; also, the business of building. **2.** Something constructed; a structure or building. **3.** The way in which a thing is formed or constructed. **4.** Interpretation given a statement, law, etc.; explanation. **5.** *Gram.* **a** The arrangement of forms syntactically, as in sentences, or morphologically, as in words. **b** Any meaningful grouping of words or morphemes. Abbr. *cons., constr.* **— con·struc′tion·al** *adj.*
con·struc·tion·ist (kən·struk′shən·ist) *n.* One who construes or interprets laws, documents, etc.
con·struc·tive (kən·struk′tiv) *adj.* **1.** Tending to build, improve, or advance; resulting in positive conclusions. **2.** Pertaining to construction; structural. **3.** Assumed by interpretation; inferred though not expressly stated. **— con·struc′tive·ly** *adv.* **— con·struc′tive·ness** *n.*
con·strue (*v.* kən·strōō′; *n.* kon′strōō) *v.* **·strued, ·stru·ing** *v.t.* **1.** To analyze the grammatical structure of (a clause or sentence); parse. **2.** To interpret; explain; also, to deduce by inference. **3.** To translate orally. **4.** *Gram.* To use syntactically: The noun "aerodynamics" is *construed* as a singular. **—** *v.i.* **5.** To determine grammatical structure. **6.** To infer; deduce. **7.** To admit of grammatical analysis. **—** *n.* An act of construing. [< L *construere* to construct < *com-* together + *struere* to build up] **— con·stru′a·ble** *adj.* **— con·stru′er** *n.*
con·sub·stan·tial (kon′səb·stan′shəl) *adj.* Having the same substance. See TRINITY. [< LL *consubstantialis* < *con-* together + *substantia* substance] **— con′sub·stan′ti·al′i·ty** *n.* **— con′sub·stan′tial·ly** *adv.*
con·sub·stan·ti·ate (kon′səb·stan′shē·āt) *v.* **·at·ed, ·at·ing** *v.t.* **1.** To unite in one common substance. **2.** To regard as being so united. **—** *v.i.* **3.** To become one in substance. **4.** To believe in the doctrine of consubstantiation. [< Med.L *consubstantiatus,* pp. of *consubstantiare* < L *com-* together + *substantia* substance]
con·sub·stan·ti·a·tion (kon′səb·stan·shē·ā′shən) *n. Theol.* The doctrine that Christ is substantially present in the consecrated Eucharistic elements, together with the unchanged substance of bread and wine: distinguished from *impanation, transubstantiation.*
con·sue·tude (kon′swi·tōōd, -tyōōd) *n.* Custom; usage. [< OF < L *consuetudo.* See CUSTOM.]
con·sue·tu·di·nar·y (kon′swi·tōō′də·ner′ē, -tyōō′-) *adj.* Customary.

con·sul (kon′səl) *n.* **1.** An officer residing in a foreign city to protect his country's commercial interests, ensure the welfare of its citizens, and perform certain administrative duties, as the issuance of passports. **2.** Either of the two chief magistrates ruling conjointly in the Roman republic. **3.** Any of the three chief magistrates of the French republic, 1799–1804. Abbr. *c., C., Con., cons., Cons.* [< L] **— con′su·lar** (-sə·lər, -syə·lər) *adj.*
consular agent A consul of the lowest rank, stationed in a foreign city of relatively little importance. Abbr. *c.a., C.A.*
con·su·late (kon′sə·lit, -syə-) *n.* **1.** The office or term of office of a consul. Also **con′sul·ship. 2.** The official place of business of a consul. **3.** Government by consuls. **— the Consulate** The government of France under the consuls, following the Directory. [< L *consulatus* < *consul* consul]
consul general A consular officer of the highest rank stationed in an important foreign commercial city, who supervises the other consuls in his district. Abbr. *c.g., C.G.*
con·sult (kən·sult′) *v.t.* **1.** To ask the advice of; go to for counsel; refer to. **2.** To have regard to in deciding or acting; consider: to *consult* one's best interests. **3.** *Obs.* To contrive or devise. **—** *v.i.* **4.** To ask advice. **5.** To compare views; take counsel: with *with.* **6.** To give professional advice, usually for a fee. [< L *consultare,* freq. of *consulere* to seek advice] **— con·sult′er** or **con·sul′tor** *n.*
— Syn. 5. *Consult* and *confer* refer to a talk between two or more persons. *Consult* indicates almost exclusively the receiving of information or opinion, whereas *confer* indicates an interchange of views. Compare DELIBERATE.
con·sult·ant (kən·sul′tənt) *n.* **1.** A person referred to for expert or professional advice. **2.** One who consults.
con·sul·ta·tion (kon′səl·tā′shən) *n.* **1.** The act or practice of consulting. **2.** A meeting of consultants.
con·sult·a·tive (kən·sul′tə·tiv) *adj.* Involving consultation; advisory. Also **con·sult′a·to′ry** (-tôr′ē, -tō′rē).
con·sult·ing (kən·sul′ting) *adj.* Giving professional advice when consulted. **—** *n.* Consultation. Abbr. *cons.*
con·sume (kən·sōōm′) *v.* **·sumed, ·sum·ing** *v.t.* **1.** To destroy, as by burning. **2.** To eat, drink, or use up. **3.** To squander, as money or time. **4.** To engross or absorb. **—** *v.i.* **5.** To be wasted or destroyed. [< L *consumere* < *com-* thoroughly + *sumere* to take up, use] **— con·sum′a·ble** *adj.*
con·sum·ed·ly (kən·sōō′mid·lē) *adv.* Excessively; unrestrainedly.
con·sum·er (kən·sōō′mər) *n.* **1.** One who or that which consumes. **2.** One who uses an article or service, as distinguished from a producer; one of the buying public.
consumer goods *Econ.* Products for satisfying people's needs rather than for producing other goods or services, as food, automobiles, etc. Also **consumers′ goods.**
con·sum·mate (*v.* kon′sə·māt; *adj.* kən·sum′it) *v.t.* **·mat·ed, ·mat·ing 1.** To bring to completion or perfection; achieve. **2.** To fulfill (a marriage) by sexual intercourse. **—** *adj.* Of the highest degree; perfect; complete. [< L *consummatus,* pp. of *consummare* to complete < *com-* together + *summa* sum, total] **— con·sum′mate·ly** *adv.* **— con′sum·ma′tive** *adj.* **— con′sum·ma′tor** *n.*
con·sum·ma·tion (kon′sə·mā′shən) *n.* The act of consummating, or the state of being consummated; fulfillment.
con·sump·tion (kən·sump′shən) *n.* **1.** The act or process of consuming; destruction, as by burning, use, etc. **2.** The amount consumed. **3.** *Econ.* The using up of consumer goods. **4.** *Pathol.* A wasting disease; especially, pulmonary tuberculosis. [< L *consumptio, -onis* < *consumere.* See CONSUME.]
con·sump·tive (kən·sump′tiv) *adj.* **1.** Tending to, causing, or designed for consumption. **2.** *Pathol.* Pertaining to, affected with, or disposed to pulmonary tuberculosis. **—** *n.* A person affected with pulmonary tuberculosis. **— con·sump′tive·ly** *adv.* **— con·sump′tive·ness** *n.*
cont. 1. Containing. **2.** Contents. **3.** Continent. **4.** Continue; continued. **5.** Contract; contraction. **6.** Contrary.
Cont. Continental.
con·tact (kon′takt) *n.* **1.** The coming together or touching of bodies; also, the relation of touching or being in touch, actually or figuratively. **2.** A potentially helpful acquaintance: He has many *contacts.* **3.** *Electr.* The touching or joining of conductors, permitting the flow of a current; also, a conducting part for completing or breaking a circuit. **4.** *Med.* One who has been exposed to a contagious disease. **—** *v.t.* **1.** To bring or place in contact; touch. **2.** *Informal* To get in touch with (someone). ◆ This informal usage, regarded with disfavor by some, is widely used. **—** *v.i.* **3.** To be or come in contact; touch: with *with.* [< L *contactus,* pp. of *contingere* < *com-* together + *tangere* to touch] **— con·tac·tu·al** (kən·tak′chōō·əl) *adj.* **— con·tac′tu·al·ly** *adv.*
contact flight *Aeron.* Flight in which a pilot can see the land or water over which he passes.
contact lens *Optics* A thin, concave disk of glass or plastic having a central lens ground to optical prescription and worn directly on the eyeball.

con·tac·tor (kon′tak·tər) *n. Electr.* A device for repeatedly opening and closing an electric circuit other than by hand.

contact print *Photog.* A positive print made by exposing a photosensitive surface in contact with the negative.

con·ta·gion (kən·tā′jən) *n.* **1.** The communication of disease by contact, direct or indirect. **2.** A disease that is or may be communicated. **3.** The medium of transmission of disease; contagium; also, a poison. **4.** Impure or corrupting influence; harmful contact: the *contagion* of graft. **5.** The communication of mental states, of ideas, etc., as by association: the *contagion* of sorrow. [< MF < L *contagio, -onis* < *contingere*. See CONTACT.]
— **Syn. 1.** *Contagion* and *infection* refer to epidemic diseases and the ways in which they spread. Originally, the two words were interchangeable. Now, in careful usage, *contagion* denotes transmission of disease from person to person by direct contact or by use of the same articles; *infection* denotes transmission through environmental factors, as air, water, food, etc.

con·ta·gious (kən·tā′jəs) *adj.* **1.** Transmissible by contact, as a disease. **2.** Spreading contagion; pestilential; harmful: *contagious* exhalations. **3.** Exciting or tending to excite similar feelings, etc., in others; spreading; catching: Laughter is *contagious.* — **con·ta′gious·ly** *adv.* — **con·ta′gious·ness** *n.*

con·ta·gi·um (kən·tā′jē·əm) *n. pl.* **·gi·a** (-jē·ə) *Med.* The specific substance, matter, or organism by which disease is communicated. [< L, var. of *contagio*. See CONTAGION.]

con·tain (kən·tān′) *v.t.* **1.** To hold or enclose. **2.** To include or comprise. **3.** To be capable of containing; be able to hold. **4.** To keep within bounds; restrain, as oneself or one's feelings. **5.** *Math.* To be exactly divisible by. **6.** To be equivalent to: A pound *contains* sixteen ounces. **7.** *Mil.* To hold or surround (enemy forces), or prevent their withdrawal. [< OF *contenir* < L *continere* to hold, hang together < *com-* together + *tenere* to hold] — **con·tain′a·ble** *adj.*

con·tain·er (kən·tā′nər) *n.* Something that contains, as a box or carton.

container ship A ship used to transport cargo that is already packaged in uniform, sealed, reusable containers.

con·tain·ment (kən·tān′mənt) *n.* The act or fact of containing; especially, the prevention of territorial or ideological expansion on the part of another power.

con·tam·i·nate (kən·tam′ə·nāt) *v.t.* **·nat·ed, ·nat·ing** To make impure by contact or admixture; taint; defile; pollute. — *adj. Archaic* Contaminated. [< L *contaminatus,* pp. of *contaminare* < *contamen, contagmen* pollution < *com-* together + *tag-,* root of *tangere* to touch] — **con·tam′i·na·tive** *adj.* — **con·tam′i·na·tor** *n.*

con·tam·i·na·tion (kən·tam′ə·nā′shən) *n.* **1.** The act of contaminating, or the state of being contaminated; pollution. **2.** Something that contaminates. **3.** *Ling.* A combination of two or more forms, producing one, as *Perish (the thought)* + *(God) forbid.*

contd. Continued.

conte (kôṅt) *n.* A short story. [< F]

con·temn (kən·tem′) *v.t.* To despise; scorn. [< OF *contemner* < L *contemnere* < *com-* thoroughly + *temnere* to slight, scorn] — **con·temn·er** (kən·tem′ər, -tem′nər) or **con·tem·nor** (kən·tem′nər) *n.*

contemp. Contemporary.

con·tem·plate (kon′təm·plāt) *v.* **·plat·ed, ·plat·ing** *v.t.* **1.** To look at attentively; gaze at. **2.** To consider thoughtfully; meditate upon. **3.** To intend or plan: to *contemplate* marriage. **4.** To consider possible: Failure is not *contemplated.* — *v.i.* **5.** To meditate; muse. — **Syn.** See SEE[1]. [< L *contemplatus,* pp. of *contemplari* < *com-* together + *templum* temple; with ref. to divination] — **con′tem·pla′·tor** *n.*

con·tem·pla·tion (kon′təm·plā′shən) *n.* **1.** The act of contemplating, meditating, or musing; meditation; consideration. **2.** Expectation or intention: in *contemplation* of war. **3.** Religious or spiritual reflection or meditation.

con·tem·pla·tive (kən·tem′plə·tiv, kon′təm·plā′tiv) *adj.* Of or given to contemplation; meditative. — *n.* **1.** One who contemplates. **2.** A member of a religious order devoted to prayer and penance rather than to teaching, caring for the sick, etc. — **con·tem′pla·tive·ly** *adv.* — **con·tem′·pla·tive·ness** *n.*

con·tem·po·ra·ne·ous (kən·tem′pə·rā′nē·əs) *adj.* Living or occurring within the same period of time: also *cotemporaneous.* [< L *contemporaneous* < *com-* together + *tempus, -oris* time] — **con·tem·po·ra·ne·i·ty** (kən·tem′pə·rə·nē′ə·tē), **con·tem′po·ra′ne·ous·ness** *n.* — **con·tem′po·ra′ne·ous·ly** *adv.*
— **Syn.** *Contemporaneous, contemporary,* and *coeval* indicate coincidence in historical time. *Contemporaneous* is used chiefly of events and facts, and *contemporary* of persons. *Coeval* refers to a broad period of time, an era or age, so that two men may have been *coeval* though not alive at the same time.

con·tem·po·rar·y (kən·tem′pə·rer′ē) *adj.* **1.** Belonging to the same age; living or occurring at the same time. **2.** Of the same age. **3.** Current; modern. — **Syn.** See CONTEMPORANEOUS. — *n. pl.* **·rar·ies** A contemporary person or thing. Also *cotemporary.* Abbr. *contemp.* [< L *com-* together + *tempus, -oris* time]

con·tem·po·rize (kən·tem′pə·rīz) *v.t. & v.i.* **·rized, ·riz·ing** To make or be equal in respect of time; synchronize.

con·tempt (kən·tempt′) *n.* **1.** The act or feeling of one who views something as mean, vile, and worthless; disdain; scorn. **2.** The state of being despised; disgrace: to be held in *contempt.* **3.** *Law* Willful disregard or disrespect of authority, as of a court. — **Syn.** See SCORN. [< L *contemptus* < *contemnere* to despise, disdain. See CONTEMN.]

con·tempt·i·ble (kən·temp′tə·bəl) *adj.* **1.** Deserving of contempt; despicable. **2.** *Obs.* Contemptuous. — **con·tempt′·i·bil′i·ty, con·tempt′i·ble·ness** *n.* — **con·tempt′i·bly** *adv.*

con·temp·tu·ous (kən·temp′chŏō·əs) *adj.* Showing or feeling contempt; disdainful; scornful. — **con·temp′tu·ous·ly** *adv.* — **con·temp′tu·ous·ness** *n.*

con·tend (kən·tend′) *v.i.* **1.** To strive in competition or rivalry; vie: to *contend* for a prize. **2.** To argue earnestly; dispute; debate. **3.** To struggle; fight. — *v.t.* **4.** To maintain in argument; assert: with a clause as object. [< L *contendere* < *com-* together + *tendere* to strive, strain] — **con·tend′er** *n.*
— **Syn. 1.** compete, contest, strive. **2.** See ARGUE. **3.** fight, battle, combat. Compare OPPOSE.

con·tent[1] (kon′tent) *n.* **1.** *Usually pl.* That which a thing contains: the *contents* of a box or book. **2.** Subject matter; substance, as of a document. **3.** The sum of elements constituting a conception, or the meaning and relations involved; loosely, basic meaning: the *content* of Donne's sonnets. **4.** Ability to contain; capacity. **5.** Extent or size; area. **6.** The quantity of a specified part: the silver *content* of a ton of ore. [< L *contentum,* pp. neut. of *continere.* See CONTAIN.]

con·tent[2] (kən·tent′) *adj.* **1.** Not inclined to complain or to desire something else; satisfied. **2.** Submissive to circumstances; resigned; accepting. — *n.* **1.** Freedom from worry or unsatisfied desires; ease of mind; satisfaction. **2.** *Brit.* An affirmative vote in the House of Lords. — *v.t.* To fulfill the hopes or expectations of; satisfy. [< L *contentus,* pp. of *continere.* See CONTAIN.]

con·tent·ed (kən·ten′tid) *adj.* Satisfied with things as they are; content. — **con·tent′ed·ly** *adv.* — **con·tent′ed·ness** *n.*

con·ten·tion (kən·ten′shən) *n.* **1.** A striving against one another, especially in controversy; strife or argument. **2.** Competition; rivalry. **3.** A point asserted in argument. — **in contention** Being contended over. [< MF < L *contentio, -onis* < *contendere.* See CONTEND.]

con·ten·tious (kən·ten′shəs) *adj.* **1.** Given to contention; quarrelsome. **2.** Involving or characterized by contention. [< MF *contentieux* < L *contentiosus*] — **con·ten′tious·ly** *adv.* — **con·ten′tious·ness** *n.*
— **Syn. 1.** warlike, pugnacious, aggressive, litigious, bellicose.

con·tent·ment (kən·tent′mənt) *n.* The state or quality of being contented; satisfaction.

con·ter·mi·nous (kən·tûr′mə·nəs) *adj.* **1.** Having a common boundary line. **2.** Contained within the same limits; coextensive. Also *coterminous:* also **con·ter′mi·nal.** — **Syn.** See ADJACENT. [< L *conterminus* < *com-* together + *terminus* limit] — **con·ter′mi·nous·ly** *adv.*

Conterminous United States See under UNITED STATES.

con·test (*n.* kon′test; *v.* kən·test′) *n.* **1.** A struggling against one another; conflict; strife. **2.** Verbal controversy; dispute. **3.** A competition, game, match, etc. — *v.t.* **1.** To fight for; strive to keep or win. **2.** To call in question; challenge: to *contest* a decision. — *v.i.* **3.** To struggle or dispute; contend: with *with* or *against.* [< F *contester* < L *contestari* to bring legal action against < *com-* together + *testari* to bear witness < *testis* witness] — **con·test′a·ble** *adj.* — **con·tes·ta·tion** (kon′tes·tā′shən) *n.* — **con·test′er** *n.*

con·test·ant (kən·tes′tənt) *n.* **1.** One who enters a contest; a competitor. **2.** One who contests or disputes (an election, will, etc.); a litigant. [< F, ppr. of *contester.* See CONTEST.]

con·text (kon′tekst) *n.* **1.** Any phrase, sentence, or passage so closely connected to a word or words as to affect their meaning. **2.** Something that surrounds and influences, as environment or circumstances. **3.** *Obs.* The whole text of a discourse or writing. [< L *contextus* connection < *contexere* < *com-* together + *texere* to weave]

con·tex·tu·al (kən·teks′chŏō·əl) *adj.* Of, belonging to, or depending on the context. — **con·tex′tu·al·ly** *adv.*

con·tex·ture (kən·teks′chər, kon-) *n.* **1.** A weaving together; also, the manner of weaving together. **2.** The structure or texture of a thing. **3.** Something made of interwoven parts: a fabric. — **con·tex′tur·al** *adj.*

Con·ti (kon′tē), **Niccolò de'** Fifteenth-century Venetian traveler and writer.

con·ti·gu·i·ty (kon′tə·gyŏō′ə·tē) *n. pl.* **·ties 1.** The state of being contiguous or in actual contact; nearness. **2.** A continuous series or mass.

con·tig·u·ous (kən·tig′yŏō·əs) *adj.* **1.** Touching at the edge or boundary. **2.** Close, but not touching; adjacent. — **Syn.** See ADJACENT. [< L *contiguus* < *contingere* to touch. See CONTACT.] — **con·tig′u·ous·ly** *adv.* — **con·tig′u·ous·ness** *n.*

contin. 1. Continued. **2.** Let it be continued. (L *continuetur.*)

con·ti·nence (kon′tə·nəns) *n.* Self-restraint, especially moderation in or abstinence from sexual intercourse. Also **con′ti·nen·cy.**

con·ti·nent (kon′tə·nənt) *n.* **1.** One of the large land masses of the earth: Africa, Australia, Europe and Asia (the conventional divisions of the Eurasian land mass), North America, South America, and, usually, Antarctica. Abbr. *cont.* **2.** *Rare* That which contains or holds. **— the Continent** Europe, as distinct from the British Isles. *— adj.* **1.** Self-restrained; moderate. **2.** Abstinent, especially sexually; chaste. **3.** *Rare* Containing; capacious. **4.** *Obs.* Restrictive. [< L *continens, -entis,* ppr. of *continere* to hang together. See CONTAIN.] **— con′ti·nent·ly** *adv.*
con·ti·nen·tal (kon′tə·nen′təl) *adj.* **1.** Of, or of the proportions of, a continent. **2.** *Often cap.* Pertaining to the European continent; European. *— n.* **1.** *Usually cap.* An inhabitant of the European continent; a European. **2.** A note of the money issued by the Continental Congress. Abbr. *cont.* **— not worth a continental** Practically valueless.
Con·ti·nen·tal (kon′tə·nen′təl) *adj.* Pertaining to the thirteen American colonies during and just after the Revolution. *— n.* A regular soldier in the Continental army.
Continental Congress The legislative and governing body of the Revolutionary American colonies, that convened in 1774, 1775–76, and 1776–81. It was de facto until 1781 when it became de jure the **Congress of the Confederation.**
Continental Divide The great ridge of the Rocky Mountain summits separating west-flowing streams from east-flowing streams in North America: also *Great Divide.*
continental drift *Geol.* The slow movement to which, according to a certain theory, the continental land masses are subject through the action of underlying molten material.
continental Morse code International Morse code (which see).
continental shelf *Geog.* The submerged border of a continent, of varying width and degree of slope, and separating the land mass from the ocean depths. The sharp declivity leading to the ocean depths is called the **continental slope.**
continental United States See under UNITED STATES.
con·tin·gence (kən·tin′jəns) *n.* **1.** Contact; a touching. **2.** Contingency.
con·tin·gen·cy (kən·tin′jən·sē) *n. pl.* **·cies 1.** Uncertainty of occurrence; the condition of being subject to chance or accident. **2.** An unforeseen but possible occurrence or condition; accident. **3.** Something incidental; an adjunct.
con·tin·gent (kən·tin′jənt) *adj.* **1.** Liable, but not certain, to happen; possible. **2.** Occurring by chance; accidental; fortuitous. **3.** Dependent upon an uncertain event or condition: with *on* or *upon.* **4.** *Logic* Not necessarily, but possibly or probably consequent. *— n.* **1.** An accidental or possible occurrence: contingency. **2.** A proportionate share or quota of something to be furnished, as of troops. **3.** A representative group in an assemblage. [< L *contingens, -entis* touching, happening, ppr. of *contingere.* See CONTACT.] **— con·tin′gent·ly** *adv.*
con·tin·u·al (kən·tin′yōō·əl) *adj.* **1.** Renewed frequently and regularly; often repeated. **2.** Continuous (in time); uninterrupted. [< OF *continuel* < L *continuus* hanging together] **— con·tin′u·al·ly** *adv.*
— Syn. *Continual, continuous, ceaseless, incessant, constant,* and *perpetual* refer to unlimited duration or extent. *Continual* is used of events in time that intermit but recur regularly or that continue unceasingly; *continuous* is used of time or space and implies complete absence of interruption: the *continual* dripping of a faucet, a *continuous* flow of water. A similar distinction is made between *ceaseless* and *incessant,* but *ceaseless* may have the further meaning of unending. *Constant* is sometimes used in the sense of *continual,* but more often it indicates unvarying value, purpose, sentiment, etc.: a *constant* advance, *constant* devotion. *Perpetual* means continuing throughout all time: a region of *perpetual* snows; informally, *perpetual* is pejorative and suggests unpleasant recurrence: a *perpetual* cough.
con·tin·u·ance (kən·tin′yōō·əns) *n.* **1.** A continuing of something, as an action or condition, or a remaining in something, as in a place or state. **2.** Continuation, as of a novel. **3.** Duration: a disease of long *continuance.* **4.** *Law* Adjournment to a future time.
con·tin·u·ant (kən·tin′yōō·ənt) *n. Phonet.* A consonant whose sound may be prolonged without a change in quality, as the fricatives (f) and (s): opposed to *stop.* [< L *continuans, -antis,* ppr. of *continuare.* See CONTINUE.]
con·tin·u·ate (kən·tin′yōō·āt) *adj. Obs.* Unbroken; uninterrupted. [< L *continuatus,* pp. of *continuare* to continue]
con·tin·u·a·tion (kən·tin′yōō·ā′shən) *n.* **1.** The act of continuing, as after an interruption; also, the state of being continued. **2.** The extension or a carrying further in time, space, or development: the *continuation* of a history. **3.** That which so extends or carries further; addition; sequel.
continuation school A school for the further education of persons already employed.
con·tin·u·a·tive (kən·tin′yōō·ā′tiv) *adj.* Denoting, causing, or expressing continuation. *— n.* That which causes or expresses continuation. **— con·tin′u·a′tive·ly** *adv.*
con·tin·u·a·tor (kən·tin′yōō·ā′tər) *n.* One who continues the work of another.

con·tin·ue (kən·tin′yōō) *v.* **·tin·ued, ·tin·u·ing** *v.i.* **1.** To go on in some action or condition; persist. **2.** To resume after an interruption. **3.** To remain in the same place, condition, or capacity. **4.** To last; endure. *— v.t.* **5.** To persevere or persist in; carry forward. **6.** To take up again after interruption. **7.** To extend or prolong in space, time, or development. **8.** To cause to last or endure; also, to keep on; retain, as in office. **9.** *Law* To postpone; grant a continuance of. Abbr. *cont.* [< OF *continuer* < L *continuare* < *continuus* continuous < *continere* to hang together. See CONTAIN.] **— con·tin′u·a·ble** *adj.* **— con·tin′u·er** *n.*
continued fraction *Math.* A number plus a fraction whose denominator is another number plus another fraction, and so on.
continued proportion *Math.* A series of three or more quantities in which the ratio is the same between each two adjacent terms, as in 2, 4, 8, where 2 is to 4 as 4 is to 8.
con·ti·nu·i·ty (kon′tə·nōō′ə·tē, -nyōō′-) *n. pl.* **·ties 1.** The state or quality of being continuous. **2.** An uninterrupted and usually changeless continuance or connection in space, time, or development. **3.** In motion pictures, television, etc., a scenario outlining the events and the sequence of scenes. **4.** The spoken parts of a radio script.
con·tin·u·ous (kən·tin′yōō·əs) *adj.* Connected, extended, or prolonged without break; uninterrupted. **— Syn.** See CONTINUAL. [< L *continuus* < *continere* to hang together. See CONTAIN.] **— con·tin′u·ous·ly** *adv.* **— con·tin′u·ous·ness** *n.*
con·tin·u·um (kən·tin′yōō·əm) *n. pl.* **·tin·u·a** (-tin′yōō·ə) **1.** Something that is continuous, of which no separate parts are discernible. **2.** *Math.* A set of numbers or points such that between any two of them a third may be interpolated. [< L, neut. of *continuus* continuous]
con·to (kon′tō) *n. pl.* **·tos** A Portuguese money of account, equal to 1,000 escudos in Portugal or 1,000 cruzeiros in Brazil.
con·tort (kən·tôrt′) *v.t. & v.i.* To twist violently; wrench out of shape or place. [< L *contortus,* pp. of *contorquere* < *com-* together + *torquere* to twist] **— con·tor′tive** *adj.*
con·tor·tion (kən·tôr′shən) *n.* **1.** The act of contorting, or the state of being contorted. **2.** A twisted position or shape.
con·tor·tion·ist (kən·tôr′shən·ist) *n.* A performer trained to twist his limbs and body into unnatural positions.
con·tour (kon′tŏŏr) *n.* **1.** The outline of a figure or body, or a line representing it. *— v.t.* **1.** To shape the contour of. **2.** To draw in outline or contour; determine the contour lines of. **3.** To construct, as a road, around the contour of a hill. *— adj.* **1.** *Agric.* Following the contours of uneven or hilly land in such a way as to minimize erosion: *contour* plowing. **2.** Shaped to fit the outline or contour of something: *contour* sheets. [< F *contourner* < LL *com-* together + *tornare* to round off, make round]
contour feathers The outer feathers that determine the outline of a bird; pennae.
contour line A line connecting points that are at the same elevation, used especially on maps.
contour map A map showing topographic configuration by contour lines, each of which is separated from the next by a definite difference in height (**contour interval**).
contr. 1. Contract; contraction. **2.** *Music* Contralto. **3.** Control.
contra- *prefix* Against; opposite; contrary: *contradict.* [< L < *contra* against]
con·tra·band (kon′trə·band) *n.* **1.** Goods that, by law or treaty, may not be imported or exported. **2.** Illegal commerce in such goods; smuggling. **3.** Goods that, by international law, a neutral may not furnish to a belligerent, and which are subject to seizure and confiscation: in full **contraband of war. 4.** During the U.S. Civil War, a fugitive slave who took refuge within Union lines. *— adj.* Prohibited by law from being imported or exported. [< Sp. *contrabanda* a smuggling < Ital. *contrabando* < *contra* against + *bando* < LL *bannum* law, proclamation]
con·tra·band·ist (kon′trə·ban′dist) *n.* A smuggler.
con·tra·bass (kon′trə·bās) *Music n.* The member of a family of instruments whose range is below the bass; especially, the double bass. *— adj.* Pitched lower than the normal bass: the *contrabass* clarinet. [< Ital. *contrabasso*] **— con·tra·bass·ist** (kon′trə·bā′sist) *n.*
con·tra·bas·so (kon′trə·bä′sō) *n.* A contrabass.
con·tra·bas·soon (kon′trə·bə·sōōn′) *n.* The double bassoon (which see).
con·tra·cep·tion (kon′trə·sep′shən) *n.* The deliberate prevention of conception. [< CONTRA- + (CON)CEPTION]
con·tra·cep·tive (kon′trə·sep′tiv) *adj.* **1.** Tending or used to prevent impregnation. **2.** Pertaining to contraception. *— n.* A contraceptive device or agent.
con·tra·clock·wise (kon′trə·klok′wīz′) *adj. & adv.* Counterclockwise (which see).
con·tract (*v.* kən·trakt′; *for v. def. 3,* also kon′trakt; *n.* kon′trakt) *v.t.* **1.** To cause to draw together; reduce in size or

duration. **2.** To wrinkle, as the brow. **3.** To arrange or settle by agreement; enter upon with reciprocal obligations. **4.** To acquire or become affected with, as a disease or habit. **5.** *Gram.* To shorten, as a word, by omitting or combining medial letters or sounds. **6.** To engage to marry; betroth. —*v.i.* **7.** To draw together or within narrower compass; become smaller. **8.** To make a contract. —*n.* **1.** A formal agreement between two or more parties, especially one that is legally binding. **2.** The paper or writing containing such an agreement. **3.** The department of law dealing with contracts. **4.** A betrothal or marriage. **5.** In bridge: **a** The highest and final bid of a hand, stating a denomination and the number of tricks to be made. **b** Contract bridge. *Abbr. cont., contr.* [< L *contractus,* pp. of *contrahere* < *com-* together + *trahere* to pull, draw] — **con·tract/i·bil/i·ty, con·tract/i·ble·ness** *n.* — **con·tract/i·ble** *adj.*
— **Syn.** (verb) **1.** condense, compact, compress, constrict. — (noun) **1.** *Contract, covenant, compact, pact, treaty,* and *cartel* are solemn agreements between persons or nations, usually written, and with some binding legal or moral force. *Contract* is the general term for such an agreement enforceable by law; it must usually be written, signed in the presence of witnesses, sealed, and accompanied by payment of money, or some other consideration: a *contract* to deliver supplies, a marriage *contract.* A *covenant* is a sworn agreement invested with religious solemnity; the idea of solemn promise is also uppermost in *compact,* an agreement resting upon the honor of the persons involved. *Pact* may be used like *compact,* but more often it is substituted for *treaty,* the general term for a signed agreement between nations; we speak of a *treaty* of alliance, or a trade *pact.* A *cartel* may be an agreement between governments, especially when they are at war: a *cartel* on the exchange of prisoners; more often it is applied to an international agreement between business firms to fix prices, divide markets, etc.
contract bridge A variety of the game of bridge in which tricks made by the declarer in excess of the contract do not count toward game. Compare AUCTION BRIDGE.
con·tract·ed (kən·trak/tid) *adj.* **1.** Having undergone contraction; shrunken. **2.** Shortened; abridged. **3.** Narrow; restricted. — **con·tract/ed·ly** *adv.* — **con·tract/ed·ness** *n.*
con·trac·tile (kən·trak/təl) *adj.* Having the power to contract or to induce contraction. — **con·trac·til·i·ty** (kon/trak·til/ə·tē) *n.*
contractile tissue *Anat.* Body tissue composed of smooth or striated muscle cells whose contraction aids in the production of movement.
con·trac·tion (kən·trak/shən) *n.* **1.** The act of contracting, or the state of being contracted. **2.** *Gram.* The shortening of a word or phrase by the omission of medial letters or sounds, as in *don't* for *do not*; also, the new word formed. **3.** *Physiol.* The drawing together and thickening of contractile tissue. *Abbr. cont., contr.* — **Syn.** See ABBREVIATION.
con·trac·tive (kən·trak/tiv) *adj.* Tending or pertaining to contraction. — **con·trac/tive·ness** *n.*
con·trac·tor (kən·trak/tər; *for def. 1, also* kon/trak·tər) *n.* **1.** One who agrees to supply materials or perform services for a sum, especially for the construction of buildings. **2.** That which contracts, as a muscle.
con·trac·tu·al (kən·trak/chōō·əl) *adj.* Connected with or implying a contract.
con·trac·ture (kən·trak/chər) *n. Med.* A permanent contraction and rigidity of muscles.
con·tra·dance (kon/trə·dans/, -däns/), **con·tra·danse** See CONTREDANSE.
con·tra·dict (kon/trə·dikt/) *v.t.* **1.** To maintain or assert the opposite of (a statement); declare to be false or incorrect. **2.** To deny a statement of (a person). **3.** To be contrary to or inconsistent with. —*v.i.* **4.** To utter a contradiction. — **Syn.** See OPPOSE. [< L *contradictus,* pp. of *contradicere* < *contra* against + *dicere* to say, speak] — **con/tra·dict/a·ble** *adj.* — **con/tra·dict/er** *or* **con/tra·dic/tor** *n.*
con·tra·dic·tion (kon/trə·dik/shən) *n.* **1.** Assertion of the opposite of a statement; denial. **2.** A statement that denies the validity of another. **3.** Obvious inconsistency, as between two statements; discrepancy. **4.** Something that contradicts itself; inconsistency; paradox.
con·tra·dic·tive (kon/trə·dik/tiv) *adj.* That contradicts or implies contradiction. — **con/tra·dic/tive·ly** *adv.*
con·tra·dic·to·ry (kon/trə·dik/tər·ē) *adj.* **1.** Involving or of the nature of a contradiction; inconsistent; contrary. **2.** Given to contradiction. —*n. pl.* **·ries** *Logic* Either of two statements so related that if one is true the other must be false. — **con/tra·dic/to·ri·ly** *adv.* — **con/tra·dic/to·ri·ness** *n.*
◆ **contradictory, contrary** In logic, two statements are *contradictory* if they cannot both be true and cannot both be false, as *I am an American* and *I am not an American. Contrary* statements cannot both be true, but they can both be false, as *I am an American* and *I am a Frenchman.* The falsity of either contrary proves nothing about the other, but the truth of one establishes the falsity of the other.
con·tra·dis·tinc·tion (kon/trə·dis·tingk/shən) *n.* Distinction by contrast or by contrasting qualities: an emperor, in *contradistinction* to a prince. — **con/tra·dis·tinct/, con/tra·dis·tinc/tive** *adj.* — **con/tra·dis·tinc/tive·ly** *adv.*
con·tra·dis·tin·guish (kon/trə·dis·ting/gwish) *v.t.* To discriminate by contrasting opposite qualities.

con·trail (kon/trāl) *n. Aeron.* A vapor trail (which see). [< *con(densation) trail*]
con·tra·in·di·cate (kon/trə·in/də·kāt) *v.t. Med.* To indicate the danger or undesirability of (a given drug or treatment). — **con/tra·in/di·cant** *n.* — **con/tra·in/di·ca/tion** *n.*
con·tral·to (kən·tral/tō) *n. pl.* **·tos** *or* **·ti** (-tē) **1.** The lowest female voice, intermediate between soprano and tenor. **2.** One having such a voice. **3.** Formerly, the highest male voice, the countertenor. — *adj.* Of or pertaining to the contralto or its range. *Abbr. contr.* [< Ital.]
con·tra·po·si·tion (kon/trə·pə·zish/ən) *n.* A placing opposite.
con·trap·tion (kən·trap/shən) *n. Informal* A contrivance or gadget. [? < CONTRIVE]
con·tra·pun·tal (kon/trə·pun/təl) *adj. Music* **1.** Of or pertaining to counterpoint. **2.** Characterized by, or constructed according to the principles of, counterpoint. [< Ital. *contrapunto* counterpoint] — **con/tra·pun/tal·ly** *adv.*
con·tra·pun·tist (kon/trə·pun/tist) *n. Music* One skilled in counterpoint. Also **con/tra·pun/tal·ist.**
con·tra·ri·e·ty (kon/trə·rī/ə·tē) *n. pl.* **·ties** **1.** The quality or state of being contrary. **2.** A quality or a proposition contrary to another; an inconsistency. [< OF *contrarieté* < LL *contrarietas, -tatis* < L *contrarius* opposite]
con·trar·i·ous (kən·trâr/ē·əs) *adj. Rare* Perverse or adverse; contrary. — **con·trar/i·ous·ly** *adv.*
con·trar·i·wise (kon/trer·ē·wīz/; *for def. 3, also* kən·trâr/ē·wīz/) *adv.* **1.** On the contrary; on the other hand. **2.** In the reverse order; conversely. **3.** Contrarily; perversely.
con·trar·y (kon/trer·ē; *for adj. def. 4, also* kən·trâr/ē) *adj.* **1.** Opposed in essence, purpose, aim, etc. **2.** Opposite as to position or direction. **3.** Adverse; unfavorable: *contrary winds.* **4.** Inclined to oppose and contradict; perverse. —*n. pl.* **·trar·ies** **1.** One of two contrary things. **2.** The opposite: The *contrary* is true. **3.** *Logic* A statement the truth of which is undetermined by the falsity of another, but which cannot be true if the latter is true. *Abbr. cont.* — **by contraries** By way of opposition; contrary to anticipated procedure. — **on the contrary** On the other hand; conversely. — **to the contrary** To the opposite effect. — *adv.* In a contrary manner; contrariwise. ◆ See note under CONTRADICTORY. [< AF *contrarie* < L *contrarius* < *contra* against] — **con/trar·i·ly** *adv.* — **con/trar·i·ness** *n.*
— **Syn.** (adj.) **1.** contradictory, opposed, opposite, antithetical, inconsistent, conflicting. **4.** balky, stubborn. Compare ALIEN (adj.), INCONGRUOUS, INIMICAL, PERVERSE. — **Ant.** complaisant.
con·trast (*v.* kən·trast/; *n.* kon/trast) *v.t.* **1.** To place in opposition so as to set off differences or discrepancies. **2.** To set (one another) off by opposition, difference, etc. —*v.i.* **3.** To reveal differences when set in opposition. —*n.* **1.** The act of contrasting, or the state of being contrasted. **2.** A dissimilarity revealed by contrasting. **3.** One who or that which shows unlikeness to another. **4.** In painting, music, poetry, etc., the use of opposite effects in close proximity. **5.** *Photog.* The difference between light and dark. [< OF *contraster* to oppose < LL *contrastare* < L *contra-* against + *stare* to stand] — **con·trast/able** *adj.*
— **Syn.** (verb) **1.** *Contrast, differentiate, discriminate,* and *compare* mean to discern or show the differences between objects. We *contrast* them by pointing out the qualities in which they are strikingly dissimilar or opposite, and *differentiate* them by enumerating the differences, point by point. To *discriminate* is to judge which differences are real and important, and which are not. In *comparing* things, we note the points of likeness as well as of difference. Compare DIFFERENCE.
con·trast·ive (kən·tras/tiv) *adj.* Yielding contrast; distinctive. — **con·trast/ive·ly** *adv.*
con·tra·val·la·tion (kon/trə·və·lā/shən) *n.* A chain of fortifications raised by besiegers around the object of their attack. [< F *contrevallation* < LL *contra-* against + *vallatio, -onis* rampart < L *vallum* wall]
con·tra·vene (kon/trə·vēn/) *v.t.* **·vened, ·ven·ing** **1.** To come into conflict with; run counter to; infringe; transgress: to *contravene* a law. **2.** To oppose or contradict. — **Syn.** See OPPOSE. [< F *contrevenir* < LL *contravenire* < L *contra-* against + *venire* to come] — **con/tra·ven/er** *n.* — **con·tra·ven·tion** (kon/trə·ven/shən) *n.*
con·tra·yer·va (kon/trə·yûr/və) *n.* **1.** The stimulant and tonic root of a tropical American plant (*Dorstenia contrajerva*) of the mulberry family. **2.** The plant. [< Sp. *contrayerba* antidote < *contra-* against + *yerba* herb < L *herba*]
contre- *prefix* Counter; against; in opposition to. [< L *contra.* See CONTRA-.]
con·tre·danse (kôn/trə·däns/) *n.* A country-dance: also *contradance, contredanse.* Also **con·tre·dance** (kôn/trə·dans/, -däns/). [< F, alter. of COUNTRY–DANCE]
con·tre·temps (kôn/trə·tän/) *n. pl.* **·temps** (-tänz/, *Fr.* -tän/) An embarrassing or awkward occurrence; a mischance. [< F]
contrib. Contribution; contributor.
con·trib·ute (kən·trib/yōōt) *v.* **·ut·ed, ·ut·ing** *v.t.* **1.** To give or furnish in common with others; give for a common purpose. **2.** To furnish (an article, story, etc.) to a publication. —*v.i.* **3.** To share in effecting a result: These causes

contributed to the king's downfall. **4.** To make a contribution. [< L *contributus*, pp. of *contribuere* < *com-* together + *tribuere* to grant, allot] **—con·trib′ut·a·ble** *adj.* **—con·trib′u·tive** *adj.* **—con·trib′u·tive·ly** *adv.* **—con·trib′u·tive·ness** *n.* **—con·trib′u·tor** *n.*

con·tri·bu·tion (kon′trə·byōō′shən) *n.* **1.** The act of contributing. **2.** Something contributed. **3.** An article, story, etc., furnished to a periodical. **4.** An impost or levy.

con·trib·u·to·ry (kən·trib′yə·tôr′ē, -tō′rē) *adj.* **1.** Contributing, as money or aid. **2.** Helping toward a result; that forms a contribution. **3.** Liable to an impost. **— Syn.** See AUXILIARY. **—** *n. pl.* **·ries** One who or that which contributes.

con·trite (kən·trīt′, kon′trīt) *adj.* **1.** Deeply and humbly sorry for one's sins; penitent. **2.** Resulting from remorse: *contrite* tears. [< OF *contrit* < L *contritus*, pp. of *conterere* to grind, crush < *com-* together + *terere* to rub] **—con·trite′ly** *adv.* **—con·trite′ness** *n.*

con·tri·tion (kən·trish′ən) *n.* **1.** Sincere sorrow for wrongdoing. **2.** *Theol.* **a** A feeling of repentance for sin, with an intention to amend, arising from love of God and consideration of his goodness (**perfect contrition**). **b** A similar feeling resulting from inferior motives, as fear of punishment (**imperfect contrition**). **— Syn.** See REPENTANCE.

con·triv·ance (kən·trī′vəns) *n.* **1.** A contriving, devising, or adapting, especially to a particular purpose; also, the ability to do this. **2.** That which is contrived, as a device or mechanical apparatus; a contraption; invention. **3.** An ingenious plan; stratagem; trick; plot.

con·trive (kən·trīv′) *v.* **·trived, ·triv·ing** *v.t.* **1.** To plan ingeniously; devise. **2.** To plot; scheme: to *contrive* treachery. **3.** To improvise; invent: He *contrived* an extra sail. **4.** To manage, as by some device or scheme: We *contrived* to leave early. **—** *v.i.* **5.** To plan, scheme, or plot. [< OF *controver* to find, invent, ? < L *com-* together + *turbare* to stir up, disclose, find] **—con·triv′a·ble** *adj.* **—con·triv′er** *n.*

con·trol (kən·trōl′) *v.t.* **·trolled, ·trol·ling** **1.** To exercise a directing, regulatory, or governing influence over. **2.** To restrain; curb. **3.** To regulate or verify, as an experiment, by comparison with a parallel experiment or other standard. **4.** To check, as an account, by means of a duplicate register; verify or rectify. **—** *n.* **1.** Power to regulate and direct; command; sway. **2.** A restraining influence; check. **3.** A standard of comparison against which to check the results of a scientific experiment. **4.** *Often pl. Mech.* A device or set of devices used for operating or guiding a machine, airplane, etc. **5.** In spiritualism, a spirit presumed to act through a medium. *Abbr. cont., contr.* [< MF *contrôler* < OF *controeller* to keep a check list < Med.L *contrarotulus* a check list < L *contra-* against + *rotulus* list] **—con·trol′·la·bil′i·ty, con·trol′la·ble·ness** *n.* **—con·trol′la·ble** *adj.*

control chart *Stat.* A chart on which the numerical values of a series of observations are plotted in the order of their occurrence and checked to determine the extent of variation from given standards of quality, quantity, performance, etc.

control experiment An experiment in which the significance of variable factors is determined by altering them one at a time under closely controlled conditions.

con·trol·ler (kən·trō′lər) *n.* **1.** One who controls, regulates, or directs. **2.** An officer responsible for fiscal planning and control, including accounting, budgeting, and tax procedures: also spelled *comptroller*. **3.** A mechanism that regulates the strength of an electric current, the speed of a machine, etc. **—con·trol′ler·ship** *n.*

control stick *Aeron.* The lever that operates the longitudinal and lateral control surfaces of an airplane.

control surface *Aeron.* Any movable airfoil, such as the aileron, rudder, flaps, etc., operated to guide or control an aircraft, rocket, guided missile, etc.

control tower A specially equipped structure at an airfield, from which aircraft traffic is directed.

con·tro·ver·sial (kon′trə·vûr′shəl) *adj.* **1.** Subject to or characterized by controversy; debatable. **2.** Given to controversy; disputatious. **—con′tro·ver′sial·ist** *n.* **—con′tro·ver′sial·ly** *adv.*

con·tro·ver·sy (kon′trə·vûr′sē) *n. pl.* **·sies** **1.** Dispute or debate regarding a matter on which opinions differ. **2.** A dispute. [< L *controversia* < *controversus* turned against, disputed < *contra-* against + *versus*, pp. of *vertere* to turn]

con·tro·vert (kon′trə·vûrt, kon′trə·vûrt′) *v.t.* **1.** To argue against; contradict; deny; oppose. **2.** To argue about: a much *controverted* problem. [< L *controversus*, on analogy with *convert, revert*, etc. See CONTROVERSY.] **—con′tro·vert′er** *n.* **—con′tro·vert′i·ble** *adj.* **—con′tro·vert′i·bly** *adv.*

con·tu·ma·cious (kon′tŏo·mā′shəs, -tyōō-) *adj.* Stubbornly and incorrigibly disobedient; insubordinate; rebellious. **—con′tu·ma′cious·ly** *adv.* **—con′tu·ma′cious·ness** *n.*

con·tu·ma·cy (kon′tŏo·mə·sē, -tyōō-) *n. pl.* **·cies** Contemptuous disobedience of authority; insolent defiance; insubordination. [< L *contumacia* < *contumax, -acis* stubborn] **—con·tu·me·ly** (kon′tŏo·mə·lē, -tyōō-, -mē′lē; kən·tŏo′mə·lē,

-tyōō′-) *n. pl.* **·lies** **1.** Insulting rudeness in speech or manner; scornful insolence. **2.** An insult, or an insulting act. [< OF *contumelie* < L *contumelia* reproach] **—con·tu·me·li·ous** (kon′tŏo·mē′lē·əs, -tyōō-) *adj.* **—con′tu·me′li·ous·ly** *adv.* **—con′tu·me′li·ous·ness** *n.*

con·tuse (kən·tŏoz′, -tyōōz′) *v.t.* **·tused, ·tus·ing** To bruise by a blow or impact. [< L *contusus*, pp. of *contundere* < *com-* together + *tundere* to beat]

con·tu·sion (kən·tŏo′zhən, -tyōō′-) *n.* **1.** An injury in which the skin remains unbroken; a bruise. **2.** The act of bruising.

co·nun·drum (kə·nun′drəm) *n.* **1.** A riddle of which the answer depends on a pun. **2.** Any problem or puzzle. **— Syn.** See PUZZLE. [Origin unknown]

con·ur·ba·tion (kon′ər·bā′shən) *n.* A large metropolitan area consisting of a cluster of suburbs and small towns that have merged together around a central city. [< CON- + L *urb(s), urb(is)* city + -ATION]

CONUS *Mil.* Continental United States.

con·va·lesce (kon′və·les′) *v.i.* **·lesced, ·lesc·ing** To recover after illness; regain good health. [< L *convalescere* < *com-* thoroughly + *valescere*, inceptive of *valere* to be strong]

con·va·les·cence (kon′və·les′əns) *n.* **1.** Gradual recovery from illness. **2.** The period of such recovery.

con·va·les·cent (kon′və·les′ənt) *adj.* **1.** Recovering from sickness. **2.** Of or pertaining to convalescence. **—** *n.* A convalescent person. [< L *convalescens, -entis*, ppr. of *convalescere*. See CONVALESCE.]

con·vec·tion (kən·vek′shən) *n.* **1.** *Physics* The transference of heat in a gas or liquid by currents resulting from unequal temperature and the consequent unequal densities. Compare CONDUCTION. **2.** *Meteorol.* A thermal process whereby atmospheric circulation is maintained through the upward or downward transfer of air masses of different temperature. **3.** The act of conveying. [< L *convectio, -onis* < *convehere* < *com-* together + *vehere* to carry] **—con·vec′·tion·al** *adj.* **—con·vec′tive·ly** *adv.*

con·ve·nance (kon′və·näns, *Fr.* kôn′və·näns′) *n.* **1.** Conventional usage; propriety. **2.** *pl.* The conventionalities. [< F < *convenir* to be proper < L *convenire* to meet, agree]

con·vene (kən·vēn′) *v.* **·vened, ·ven·ing** *v.t.* **1.** To cause to assemble; convoke. **2.** To summon to appear, as by judicial authority. **—** *v.i.* **3.** To come together; assemble. **— Syn.** See CONVOKE. [< MF *convenir* < L *convenire* < *com-* together + *venire* to come] **—con·ven′a·ble** *adj.* **—con·ven′er** *n.*

con·ven·ience (kən·vēn′yəns) *n.* **1.** The quality of being convenient; suitability. **2.** Personal comfort; ease; ready accommodation: a swimming pool for the *convenience* of guests. **3.** Anything that increases comfort or saves work. Also *Rare* **con·ven′ien·cy.** **— at one's convenience** At a time or occasion suiting one's needs or preference.

con·ven·ient (kən·vēn′yənt) *adj.* **1.** Well suited to one's purpose or needs; conducive to ease or comfort. **2.** Within easy reach; handy. [< L *conveniens, -entis*, ppr. of *convenire* to be proper. See CONVENE.] **—con·ven′ient·ly** *adv.*

con·vent (kon′vent, -vənt) *n.* **1.** A religious community, especially of nuns, living according to an established rule. **2.** The building or buildings of such a community. **— Syn.** See CLOISTER. [< AF *covent*, OF *convent* < L *conventus* meeting, assembly < *convenire*. See CONVENE.]

con·ven·ti·cle (kən·ven′ti·kəl) *n.* **1.** A meeting or assembly for religious worship; especially, a secret or illicit one, as of English dissenters in the 16th and 17th centuries. **2.** The meeting place of such an assembly. **3.** *Obs.* An assembly. [< L *conventiculum*, dim. of *conventus* assembly < *convenire*. See CONVENE.] **—con·ven′ti·cler** *n.*

con·ven·tion (kən·ven′shən) *n.* **1.** A formal meeting of delegates or members, as for political or professional purposes. **2.** The persons attending such a meeting. **3.** General consent or approval; accepted custom, rule, opinion, etc. **4.** A rule or approved technique in conduct or art; a custom or usage. **5.** Conventionality. **6.** An agreement or contract. **7.** A compact between nations, usually relating to a specific subject, as international copyright. [< L *conventio, -onis* < *convenire*. See CONVENE.]

con·ven·tion·al (kən·ven′shən·əl) *adj.* **1.** Growing out of or established by convention or custom. **2.** Following or conforming to approved or established practice. **3.** Lacking spontaneity or originality; formal; stylized. **4.** In art, simplified or abstracted for purposes of design or decoration; conventionalized. **5.** Established by general agreement or acceptance: a *conventional* symbol. **6.** *Law* Based upon agreement or contract. **7.** Of or pertaining to a convention. **—con·ven′tion·al·ist** *n.* **—con·ven′tion·al·ly** *adv.*

con·ven·tion·al·ism (kən·ven′shən·əl·iz′əm) *n.* **1.** Regard for or adherence to custom. **2.** Anything conventional.

con·ven·tion·al·i·ty (kən·ven′shən·al′ə·tē) *n. pl.* **·ties** **1.** The state or quality of being in accord with convention; adherence to established forms, customs, or usages. **2.** A conventional act, principle, custom, etc. **3.** *pl.* The accepted rules and customs of social behavior: preceded by *the*.

con·ven·tion·al·ize (kən·ven'shən·əl·īz') *v.t.* **·ized**, **·iz·ing** **1.** To make conventional. **2.** To represent in a conventional manner. **— con·ven'tion·al·i·za'tion** *n.*

con·ven·tu·al (kən·ven'chōō·əl) *adj.* Belonging or pertaining to a convent. **—** *n.* One who belongs to a convent. [< Med.L *conventualis* < *conventus* convent < L. See CONVENT.]

Con·ven·tu·al (kən·ven'chōō·əl) *n.* A member of a branch of the Franciscan order that follows a modified rule.

con·verge (kən·vûrj') *v.* **·verged**, **·verg·ing** *v.i.* **1.** To move toward one point; come together by gradual approach. **2.** To tend toward the same conclusion or result. **—** *v.t.* **3.** To cause to tend toward one point. [< LL *convergere* < L *com*-together + *vergere* to bend]

con·ver·gence (kən·vûr'jəns) *n.* **1.** The act, fact, or state of converging. **2.** The degree or point of converging. Also **con·ver'gen·cy**. **3.** *Meteorol.* The net horizontal inflow of air into a given layer of atmosphere. **4.** *Math.* The gradual approach of a series of values to a fixed limit as new values are added. **5.** *Biol.* The tendency of different organisms to develop along similar lines in response to the same environment. **— con·ver'gent** *adj.*

convergent strabismus See under STRABISMUS.

con·vers·a·ble (kən·vûr'sə·bəl) *adj.* **1.** Approachable in conversation; affable. **2.** Fond of talking. **3.** Of or adapted to conversation. [< MF < Med.L *conversabilis* < L *conversari*. See CONVERSE[1].] **— con·vers'a·ble·ness** *n.* **— con·vers'a·bly** *adv.*

con·ver·sant (kon'vər·sənt, kən·vûr'sənt) *adj.* Well acquainted or familiar, as by study: *conversant with American history.* [< OF, ppr. of *converser* < L *conversari*. See CONVERSE[1].] **— con·ver·sance** (kon'vər·səns, kən·vûr'səns), **con'ver·san·cy** *n.* **— con'ver·sant·ly** *adv.*

con·ver·sa·tion (kon'vər·sā'shən) *n.* **1.** An informal talk with another or others; colloquy. **2.** Intimate association or social intercourse. **3.** Sexual intercourse. See CRIMINAL CONVERSATION. **4.** *Rare* Acquaintance with something through study or use. **5.** *Obs.* Mode of life; conduct. [< OF < L *conversatio*, -*onis* intercourse < *conversari*. See CONVERSE[1].]

— Syn. 1. *Conversation, talk, discourse, parley, colloquy, chat,* and *dialogue* refer to communication by talking. A *conversation* is any interchange of ideas in which two or more persons participate. *Talk* may be wholly one-sided; hence, a public address is often called a *talk*, or, more formally, a *discourse*. A *parley* is a *conversation* to negotiate terms or settle differences: a *parley* between warring factions. *Colloquy* and *chat* are informal *conversations*, and a *dialogue*, strictly, a *conversation* between two persons. *Dialogue* is also used of all lines written for dramatic characters.

con·ver·sa·tion·al (kon'vər·sā'shən·əl) *adj.* **1.** Of or characteristic of conversation. **2.** Disposed to or adept at conversation. **— con'ver·sa'tion·al·ly** *adv.*

con·ver·sa·tion·al·ist (kon'vər·sā'shən·əl·ist) *n.* One who enjoys or excels in conversation. Also **con'ver·sa'tion·ist.**

conversation piece **1.** A type of painting, especially of the 18th century, depicting a group of fashionable people. **2.** Something, as a piece of furniture, that arouses comment.

con·ver·sa·zi·o·ne (kon'vär·sät'sē·ō'nē, *Ital.* kōn'vär·sä·tsyō'nä) *n. pl.* **·nes** (-nēz), *Ital.* **·ni** (-nē) *Italian* A meeting for conversation, particularly on some special topic, as art.

con·verse[1] (*v.* kən·vûrs'; *n.* kon'vûrs) *v.i.* **·versed**, **·vers·ing** **1.** To speak together informally; engage in conversation. **2.** *Obs.* To associate; commune. **— Syn.** See TALK. **—** *n.* **1.** Social interchange of thoughts; conversation. **2.** Familiar social intercourse; fellowship. [< OF *converser* to live with < L *conversari*, freq. of *convertere* < *com*- together + *vertere* to turn] **— con·vers'er** *n.*

con·verse[2] (kon'vûrs; *for adj., also* kən·vûrs') *adj.* Turned about so that two parts are interchanged; reversed; contrary. **—** *n.* **1.** That which exists in a converse relation; opposite. **2.** *Logic* A proposition that is the result of conversion. [< L *conversus*, pp. of *convertere* < *com*- thoroughly + *vertere* to turn] **— con·verse·ly** (kən·vûrs'lē, kon'vûrs·lē) *adv.*

con·ver·sion (kən·vûr'zhən, -shən) *n.* **1.** The act of converting, or a being converted in substance, condition, form, function, etc. **2.** A change in which one comes to adopt and uphold new opinions and beliefs; especially, in matters of religion, a spiritual turning to righteousness and faith. **3.** *Law* **a** Wrongful appropriation to one's own use of the goods of another. **b** The exchange of real to personal property or the reverse. **4.** *Logic* The interchange of the subject and predicate terms of a proposition so as to form another proposition. **5.** *Math.* The formation of a new proportion from four proportional terms by substituting for the second the difference between the first and second and for the fourth the difference between the third and fourth. **6.** *Psychiatry* The process by which a psychic conflict manifests itself in motor or sensory disturbances associated with and partially satisfying the repressed emotion or desire. Also **conversion hysteria.** **7.** In football, one or two extra points scored after a touchdown: see CONVERT (def. 11). [< MF < L *conversio*, -*onis* < *convertere*. See CONVERSE[2].] **— con·ver'sion·al**, **con·ver'sion·ar·y** (kən·vûr'zhən·er'ē, -shən-) *adj.*

— Syn. 1. change, transformation, metamorphosis, transmutation.

con·vert (*v.* kən·vûrt'; *n.* kon'vûrt) *v.t.* **1.** To change into another state, form, or substance; transform. **2.** To apply or adapt to a new or different purpose or use. **3.** To change from one belief, doctrine, or course of action to another. **4.** To cause to change in character; to turn from a sinful to a righteous life. **5.** To exchange for an equivalent value, as goods for money. **6.** To exchange for value of another form, as preferred for common stock. **7.** To change chemically. **8.** *Logic* To transpose the subject and predicate of (a proposition) by conversion. **9.** *Law* **a** To assume possession of illegally. **b** To change (property) from real to personal, or the reverse. **—** *v.i.* **10.** To become changed in character. **11.** In professional football, to score an extra point after the touchdown by a place kick; in college football, to score either one extra point in this manner or two extra points by rushing or passing. **—** *n.* A person who has been converted, as from one religion or set of beliefs to another. [< OF *convertir*, ult. < L *convertere*. See CONVERSE[2].]

— Syn. (verb) See CHANGE. **—** (noun) *Convert, proselyte*, and *neophyte* characterize a person who has recently adopted a religion, doctrine, or way of life. A *convert* or *proselyte* has changed his allegiance or opinion; a *convert* is a sincere believer in his new faith; *proselyte* is often used disparagingly for one who changes for expediency or mere fickleness. *Neophyte* is chiefly applied to a newcomer not yet fully indoctrinated.

con·vert·er (kən·vûr'tər) *n.* **1.** One who or that which converts. **2.** A vessel in which materials are converted; especially, a Bessemer converter (which see). **3.** *Electr.* An apparatus for converting direct into alternating current, or vice versa; inverter. **4.** One who converts raw textiles into finished products. Also **con·ver'tor.**

con·vert·i·ble (kən·vûr'tə·bəl) *adj.* Capable of being converted. **—** *n.* **1.** A convertible thing. **2.** An automobile with a folding top. **— con·vert'i·bil'i·ty, con·vert'i·ble·ness** *n.* **— con·vert'i·bly** *adv.*

con·vert·i·plane (kən·vûr'tə·plān') *n.* An aircraft built so as to perform both as a fixed-wing airplane and as a helicopter. [< *converti(ble)* (*air*)*plane*]

con·vert·ite (kon'vər·tīt) *n.* *Archaic* A convert.

con·vex (kon'veks; *for adj., also* kon·veks') *adj.* Curving outward, as the exterior of a globe: opposed to *concave*. **—** *n.* A convex surface or body; convexity. [< L *convexus* vaulted, curved < *convehere* < *com*- together + *vehere* to bring, carry] **— con·vex'ly** *adv.*

con·vex·i·ty (kon·vek'sə·tē) *n. pl.* **·ties** **1.** The state of being convex. **2.** A convex surface or thing.

con·vex·o-con·cave (kon·vek'sō·kon·kāv') *adj.* **1.** Convex on one side and concave on the other. **2.** *Optics* Describing a lens of which the convex surface has a greater curvature than the opposite concave surface: distinguished from *concavo-convex*. See illustration of LENS.

con·vex·o-con·vex (kon·vek'sō·kon·veks') *adj.* Biconvex (which see).

con·vex·o-plane (kon·vek'sō·plān') *adj.* Plano-convex.

con·vey (kən·vā') *v.t.* **1.** To carry from one place to another; transport. **2.** To serve as a medium or path for; transmit. **3.** To make known; impart; communicate. **4.** To transfer ownership of, as real estate. **5.** *Obs.* To remove or steal. [< AF *conveier* to travel with < L *com*- together + *via* road, way. Doublet of CONVOY, *v.*] **— con·vey'a·ble** *adj.*

— Syn. *Convey, transport, transmit, transfer,* and *carry* concern the moving of something from one place to another. *Convey* stresses a regular or continuous flow; a pipe *conveys* water, trucks *convey* supplies to a city; the word is also commonly used in a figurative sense: to *convey* ideas. *Transport* refers to material objects, especially those of great weight or bulk; coal and lumber are *transported* by railroad. *Transmit* emphasizes the sending out or away of something, and is chiefly used of communication; we *transmit* news, letters, or telegrams. *Transfer* is chiefly applied to the immaterial; the title to property is *transferred*. *Carry* differs from the other synonyms in that it does not necessarily imply delivery to a destination, though it may be so used; generally it means merely to bear as a burden; a train *carries* passengers, a man *carries* a cane or an air of distinction. **— Ant.** keep, retain, hold.

con·vey·ance (kən·vā'əns) *n.* **1.** The act of conveying; communication; transportation. **2.** Something used for conveying, as a truck or bus. **3.** *Law* The transfer of title to property; also, the document whereby title is transferred.

con·vey·anc·ing (kən·vā'ən·sing) *n.* *Law* The business of preparing conveyances of property, including the investigation of titles. **— con·vey'anc·er** *n.*

con·vey·er (kən·vā'ər) *n.* **1.** One who or that which conveys, transports, or transfers. **2.** Any mechanical contrivance for conveying articles or materials, as an endless belt, a series of rollers, etc. Also (*especially for def. 2*) **con·vey'or.**

conveyor belt A conveyor consisting of an endless belt.

con·vict (*v., adj.* kən·vikt'; *n.* kon'vikt) *v.t.* **1.** To prove guilty; find guilty after a judicial trial. **2.** To awaken to a sense of guilt or sin. **—** *n.* **1.** One serving a sentence in prison. **2.** One found guilty of a crime. **—** *adj.* *Archaic* Convicted. [< L *convictus*, pp. of *convincere*. See CONVINCE.]

con·vic·tion (kən·vik'shən) *n.* **1.** The state of being convinced; firm belief. **2.** A firm belief. **3.** A convincing, as of a truth. **4.** A convicting; a pronouncing or being guilty. **— Syn.** See BELIEF, CERTAINTY. **— con·vic'tion·al** *adj.*

con·vic·tive (kən·vik′tiv) *adj.* Serving to convince or convict. **— con·vic′tive·ly** *adv.*

con·vince (kən·vins′) *v.t.* **·vinced, ·vinc·ing** **1.** To cause to believe something, as by proof; bring to belief: often with *of.* **2.** *Obs.* To convict. **3.** *Obs.* To overcome. [< L *convincere* to overcome < *com-* thoroughly + *vincere* to conquer] **— con·vince′ment** *n.* **— con·vinc′er** *n.* **— con·vin′ci·ble** *adj.*

— Syn. 1. *Convince* and *persuade* agree in the sense of making one's view or will prevail over another's. A man is *convinced* by argument or evidence addressed to his intellect; he is *persuaded* by appeals to his affections or will. In strict usage, we *convince* a man of a truth, but *persuade* him to act.

con·vinc·ing (kən·vin′sing) *adj.* **1.** Satisfying by evidence: *convincing* testimony. **2.** Credible or believable: a *convincing* act. **— con·vinc′ing·ly** *adv.* **— con·vinc′ing·ness** *n.*

con·viv·i·al (kən·viv′ē·əl) *adj.* **1.** Fond of feasting and good fellowship; jovial; sociable. **2.** Of or befitting a feast; festive. [< L *convivialis* < *convivium* a feast, banquet < *convivere* < *com-* together + *vivere* to live] **— con·viv′i·al·ist** *n.* **— con·viv·i·al·i·ty** (kən·viv′ē·al′ə·tē) *n.* **— con·viv′i·al·ly** *adv.*

con·vo·ca·tion (kon′vō·kā′shən) *n.* **1.** A calling together; a summoning to assemble. **2.** A group of persons summoned to meet; an assembly; meeting. **3.** In the Anglican Church, a body similar to a synod, but meeting only when called. **4.** In the Protestant Episcopal Church, a meeting of clergy and laity of part of a diocese; also, the district represented. [< L *convocatio, -onis* < *convocare.* See CONVOKE.] **— con′vo·ca′tion·al** *adj.* **— con′vo·ca′tor** *n.*

con·voke (kən·vōk′) *v.t.* **·voked, ·vok·ing** To call together; summon to meet. [< F *convoquer* < L *convocare* < *com-* together + *vocare* to call, summon] **— con·vok′er** *n.*

— Syn. *Convoke, convene, summon, muster, assemble, call, gather,* and *collect* refer to an order or request to others to meet. *Convoke,* and the slightly less formal *convene,* suggest the serious nature of the meeting, or the authority of the person issuing the order; *summon* is a close synonym of *convoke,* but implies greater authority: to *convoke* a general church council, to *convene* the student body, to *summon* jurymen to serve. *Muster* almost always refers to a military force: to *muster* troops for war. *Assemble* stresses the unity or definite purpose of the meeting, and *call* emphasizes the order itself: to *assemble* the cast for a play, to *call* workers together. *Gather,* and less frequently *collect,* when used in the sense here compared, suggest some degree of necessity or compulsion: to *gather* (or *collect*) the people together in one place. **— Ant.** disband, disperse, dissolve, separate, dismiss, discharge.

con·vo·lute (kon′və·lōōt) *adj.* **1.** Rolled one part over another or inward from one side. **2.** *Bot.* Coiled longitudinally, as the petals of the wallflower. **— *v.t. & v.i* ·lut·ed, ·lut·ing** To coil up intricately. [< L *convolutus,* pp. of *convolvere.* See CONVOLVE.] **— con′vo·lute′ly** *adv.*

con·vo·lu·tion (kon′və·lōō′shən) *n.* **1.** A coiled or convoluted state. **2.** A fold or twist in something convoluted. **3.** *Anat.* One of the folds of the surface of the brain; a gyrus.

con·volve (kən·volv′) *v.t. & v.i.* **·volved, ·volv·ing** To roll together; coil up, wind, or twist. [< L *convolvere* < *com-* together + *volvere* to spin, twist]

con·vol·vu·la·ceous (kən·vol′vyə·lā′shəs) *adj. Bot.* Designating the morning-glory family (*Convolvulaceae*) of gamopetalous, chiefly climbing plants with alternate leaves and showy flowers. [< NL *Convolvulaceae*]

con·vol·vu·lus (kən·vol′vyə·ləs) *n.* Any of a genus (*Convolvulus*) of twining herbs with large, showy, trumpet-shaped flowers: also called *bindweed, corn lily.* [< L, bindweed]

con·voy (kon′voi; *for v.,* also kən·voi′) *n.* **1.** A protecting escort, as for ships at sea. **2.** A formation of ships, baggage train, etc., traveling under escort. **3.** A group of military vehicles organized for control. **4.** The act of convoying, or the state of being convoyed. **— *v.t.*** To act as convoy to; escort. **— Syn.** See ACCOMPANY. [< MF *convoyer* < L *com-* together + *via* road. Doublet of CONVEY.]

con·vulse (kən·vuls′) *v.t.* **·vulsed, ·vuls·ing 1.** To affect with violent movements; agitate or shake. **2.** To throw into convulsions. **3.** To cause to laugh violently. [< L *convulsus,* pp. of *convellere* < *com-* together + *vellere* to pull]

con·vul·sion (kən·vul′shən) *n.* **1.** Often *pl. Pathol.* A violent and involuntary contraction or series of contractions of the voluntary muscles. **2.** Any violent commotion or disturbance, as an earthquake. **3.** A violent fit of laughter.

con·vul·sion·ar·y (kən·vul′shən·er′ē) *adj.* Affected with, attended by, or of the nature of convulsions. **— *n. pl.* ·ar·ies** One subject to or affected with convulsions.

con·vul·sive (kən·vul′siv) *adj.* Producing, characterized by, or of the nature of convulsions: *convulsive* anger. **— con·vul′sive·ly** *adv.* **— con·vul′sive·ness** *n.*

co·ny (kō′nē, kun′ē) *n. pl.* **·nies 1.** A rabbit, especially the European rabbit. **2.** Rabbit fur. **3.** In the Bible, the hyrax or daman. **4.** The little chief hare. **5.** *Archaic* A dupe; ninny. Also spelled *coney.* [< OF *conil* < L *cuniculus* rabbit]

coo (kōō) *v.* **cooed, coo·ing** *v.i.* **1.** To utter the murmuring note of a dove. **2.** To talk amorously in murmurs: to bill and coo. **— *v.t.* 3.** To utter with a coo. **— *n.*** A murmuring sound, as of a dove. [Imit.] **— coo′er** *n.* **— coo′ing·ly** *adv.*

Co·o (kō′ō) The Italian name for Kos.

Cooch Be·har (kōōch′ bi·här′) A former state of NE India, since 1950 a district of West Bengal; 1,318 sq. mi.; pop. about 641,000; capital, **Cooch Behar:** formerly *Kooch Behar.*

coo·ee (kōō′ē) *n.* A long, shrill cry of the Australian aborigines, also used by the Australian settlers. Also **coo′ey.** **— *v.i.* within cooee** Within calling distance; close at hand. **— *v.i.* cooeed, coo·ee·ing** To make this cry. [Imit.]

cooee bird The koel.

coof (kōōf) *n. Scot.* A lout; blockhead: also *cuif.*

cook¹ (kook) *v.t.* **1.** To prepare (food) for eating by the action of heat, as by boiling, frying, or roasting. **2.** To subject to the action of heat, as tobacco in curing. **3.** *Informal* To tamper with; doctor: to *cook* a report. **4.** *Slang* To ruin; undo. **— *v.i.* 5.** To act as a cook. **6.** To undergo cooking. **— to cook up** *Informal* To invent; concoct: to *cook up* a scandal. **— *n.*** One who prepares food for eating. Abbr. *ck.* [OE *cōc* < LL *cocus* < L *coquus*] **— cook′er** *n.*

cook² (kook) *v.i. Scot.* To crouch or stoop.

Cook (kook), **Captain James,** 1728–79, English seafarer.

Cook, Mount The highest mountain in New Zealand, on South Island; 12,349 ft.: also *Aorangi.*

cook·book (kook′book′) *n.* A book containing recipes and other information about cooking.

Cooke (kook), **Jay,** 1821–1905, U.S. financier and railroad magnate.

cook·er·y (kook′ər·ē) *n. pl.* **·er·ies 1.** The art or practice of cooking. **2.** A place for cooking.

Cook Inlet An inlet of the Gulf of Alaska in southern Alaska.

Cook Islands An archipelago SW of Samoa, a dependency of New Zealand; about 89 sq. mi.; pop. 18,041 (1959); capital, Raratonga.

cook·out (kook′out′) *n. U.S. Informal* A meal cooked outdoors.

Cook Strait The passage between North Island and South Island, New Zealand; narrowest point, 16 miles.

cook·y (kook′ē) *n. pl.* **cook·ies** *U.S.* A small, thin, dry cake, usually sweetened. Also **cook′ey, cook′ie.** [< Du. *koekje,* dim. of *koek* cake]

cool (kōōl) *adj.* **1.** Moderately cold; lacking warmth. **2.** Producing a feeling of coolness: a *cool* suit. **3.** Calm in action or thought; deliberate; composed. **4.** Lacking enthusiasm or passion; not cordial; chilling: a *cool* reception. **5.** Calmly audacious; bold. **6.** Suggesting coolness: said especially of the colors blue, green, and violet. **7.** *U.S. Informal* Not exaggerated; actual: a *cool* million. **8.** *U.S. Slang* Excellent; great. **9.** *U.S. Slang* Of modern jazz, restrained and relaxed. **— *adv. U.S. Informal* Coolly. **— *v.t. & v.i.* 1.** To make or become less warm. **2.** To make or become less angry, ardent, or zealous; calm. **— *n.* 1.** A cool time, thing, place, etc.: the *cool* of dawn. **2.** Coolness. [OE *cōl*] **— cool′ly** *adv.* **— cool′ness** *n.*

cool·ant (kōō′lənt) *n.* Any substance, usually a liquid, used as a cooling medium, as for an internal-combustion engine or for high-speed cutting tools.

cool·er (kōō′lər) *n.* **1.** A vessel or apparatus that serves to cool something or to keep it cool. **2.** Anything that makes cool, as a cold drink. **3.** *Slang* A jail.

cool-head·ed (kōōl′hed′id) *adj.* Not readily excited; calm.

Coo·lidge (kōō′lij), **(John) Calvin,** 1872–1933, 30th president of the United States 1923–29. **— Julian Lowell,** 1873–1954, U.S. mathematician.

Coolidge tube An X-ray tube having a cathode whose temperature can be closely controlled. [after William David Coolidge, 1873–1975, U.S. physicist]

coo·lie (kōō′lē) *n.* An unskilled Oriental laborer working for very low wages. Also **coo′ly.** [Prob. < *Kuli,* an aboriginal Gujarat tribe; infl. by Tamil *kūli* hire, wages]

cool·ish (kōō′lish) *adj.* Somewhat cool.

Coo·mas·sie (kōō·mas′ē) A former spelling of KUMASI.

coomb (kōōm) *n. Brit.* A narrow valley: also spelled *comb, combe.* Also **coombe.** [OE *cumb,* ? < Celtic]

coon (kōōn) *n.* **1.** A raccoon. **2.** *Slang* A Negro: an offensive term. [Short for RACCOON]

coon·can (kōōn′kan′) *n.* Conquian, a card game.

coon's age *U.S. Informal* A very long time.

coon·tie (kōōn′tē) *n.* A tropical American plant (genus *Zamia*) of the cycad family, whose stems and roots yield a starch. [< Muskhogean (Seminole) *kunti* flour]

coop (kōōp, koop) *n.* **1.** An enclosure or box, as for fowls. **2.** *Slang* A jail. **— to fly the coop** *Slang* To escape from prison, etc. **— *v.t.*** To put into a coop: confine: usually with *in* or *up.* [ME *cupe* < MLG. Cf. MDu. *kupe* cask.]

co·op (kō′op, kō·op′) *n. Informal* A cooperative.

co-op. or **coop.** Cooperative.

coop·er (kōō′pər, koop′ər) *n.* One whose business it is to make and repair casks, barrels, etc. **— *v.t. & v.i.*** To make or mend (casks, barrels, etc.). [ME *couper* < LG. Cf. MDu. *kuper* < *kupe* a cask.]

PRONUNCIATION KEY: add, āce, câre, pälm; end, ēven; it, īce; odd, ōpen, ôrder; took, pool; up, bûrn; ə = a in *above,* e in *sicken,* i in *flexible,* o in *melon,* u in *focus;* yōō = u in *fuse;* oil; pout; check; go; ring; thin; this; zh, vision. For ȧ, œ, ü, kh, ṅ, see inside front cover.

Coop·er (kōō′pər, kŏŏp′ər), **Hugh Lincoln**, 1865–1937, U.S. engineer. **— James Fenimore**, 1789–1851, U.S. novelist. **— Peter**, 1791–1883, U.S. industrialist and philanthropist.

coop·er·age (kōō′pər·ij, kŏŏp′ər-) *n.* The work or workshop of a cooper; also, the charge for his services.

co·op·er·ate (kō·ŏp′ə·rāt) *v.i.* **·at·ed, ·at·ing** **1.** To work together for a common objective; act in combination. **2.** To practice economic cooperation. Also **co·op′er·ate, co·öp′er·ate**. [< L *cooperatus*, pp. of *cooperari* < *co-* together + *operari* to work < *opus* work, labor] **— co·op′er·a′tor** *n.*

co·op·er·a·tion (kō·ŏp′ə·rā′shən) *n.* **1.** A working together toward a common end; joint action. **2.** The association of laborers, farmers, small capitalists, etc., in a common endeavor for mutual economic benefit. Also **co·op′er·a′tion**. — **co·op′er·a′tion·ist** *n.*

co·op·er·a·tive (kō·ŏp′ər·ə·tiv, -ə·rā′tiv) *adj.* **1.** Acting or willing to act with others; cooperating. **2.** Pertaining to or organized for economic cooperation. — *n.* A store, apartment house, etc., organized on a basis of economic cooperation. Also **co·op′er·a·tive.** — **co·op′er·a·tive·ly** *adv.* — **co·op′er·a·tive·ness** *n.*

Cooperative Commonwealth Federation *Canadian* Former name of the NEW DEMOCRATIC PARTY.

Coop·er's hawk (kōō′pərz) A hawk (*Accipiter cooperii*) common in North America. [after William *Cooper*, 19th c. U.S. naturalist]

coop·er·y (kōō′pər·ē, kŏŏp′ər·ē) *n. pl.* **·er·ies** The trade or workshop of a cooper; also, a cooper's wares, collectively.

co·opt (kō·ŏpt′) *v.t.* **1.** To elect as a fellow member of a committee, etc. **2.** To appoint; also, to preempt. **3.** To make ineffectual as an instrument for radical change by incorporating within the established order: radicals *co-opted* into running for elective office. [< L *cooptare* < *co-* together + *optare* to choose] **— co′·op·ta′tion** or **co·op′tion** *n.* **— co·op·ta·tive** (kō·ŏp′tə·tiv) *adj.*

co·or·di·nal (kō·ôr′də·nəl) *adj.* **1.** Belonging to the same order, as in botany or zoology. **2.** *Math.* Having or defined by (a certain number of) coordinates. Also **co·or′di·nal.**

co·or·di·nate (kō·ôr′də·nāt; *for adj., n., also* kō·ôr′də·nit) *adj.* **1.** Of equal importance or rank; not subordinate. **2.** Of or pertaining to coordinates or coordination. **3.** Having separate colleges for men and women, as a university. — *n.* **1.** One who or that which is of the same order, rank, power, etc. **2.** *Math.* Any of a set of magnitudes by means of which the position of a point, line, or angle is determined with reference to fixed elements. — *v.* **·nat·ed, ·nat·ing** *v.t.* **1.** To put in the same rank, class, or order. **2.** To bring into harmonious relation or action; adjust. — *v.i.* **3.** To become coordinate. **4.** To act in harmonious or reciprocal relation. Also **co·or′di·nate.** [< Med.L *coordinatus*, pp. of *coordinare* to arrange < L *co-* together + *ordinare* to set in order < *ordo, -inis* rank] **— co·or′di·nate·ly** *adv.* **— co·or′di·nate·ness** *n.* **— co·or′di·na′tive** *adj.* **— co·or′di·na′tor** *n.*

coordinate conjunction See under CONJUNCTION.

co·or·di·na·tion (kō·ôr′də·nā′shən) *n.* **1.** The act of coordinating, or the state of being coordinated. **2.** Harmonious, integrated action or interaction. Also **co·or′di·na′tion.**

Coorg (kŏŏrg) A former chief commissioner's state in SW India, since 1956 part of Mysore; 1,593 sq. mi.: also *Kurg.*

coot (kōōt) *n.* **1.** Any of various short-winged aquatic birds (genus *Fulica*) resembling the rails; especially, the **American coot** (*F. americana*), or water hen, ranging from Canada to Hawaii. **2.** Loosely, a scoter. **3.** *Informal* A simpleton; dolt. [ME *cote* < LG. Cf. Du. *koet*.]

coot·ie (kōō′tē) *n. Slang* A louse. [? < Indonesian *kutu*, a parasitic insect; orig. nautical slang]

cop¹ (kop) *n. Informal* A policeman. **— v.t. copped, cop·ping** *Slang* **1.** To steal. **2.** To catch. **— to cop out** *U.S. Slang* To back down or turn away, as from one's responsibilities or ideals; renege. [? Var. of *cap* to catch, take < OF *caper* < L *capere*]

cop² (kop) *n.* **1.** A conical roll of thread formed on a spindle. **2.** *Obs.* A top; crest, as of a hill. [OE *copp* summit]

cop. **1.** Copper. **2.** Copyright; copyrighted.

co·pai·ba (kō·pā′bə, -pī′-) *n.* A viscous, aromatic South American balsam from some species of *Copaifera* used in varnishes and formerly in medicine. [< Sp. < Tupi *cupauba*]

co·pa·cet·ic (kō′pə·set′ik) See COPESETIC.

co·pal (kō′pəl) *n.* A hard, transparent resin exuded by various tropical trees, used in varnishes. [< Sp. < Nahuatl *copalli* incense]

co·palm (kō′päm) *n.* **1.** The sweet gum, a tree. **2.** The resin obtained from it. [Origin uncertain]

co·par·ce·nar·y (kō·pär′sə·ner′ē) *n. pl.* **·nar·ies** **1.** *Law* An estate in lands inherited by coparceners: also called *parcenary.* **2.** Partnership. Also **co·par′ce·ny** (-sə·nē).

co·par·ce·ner (kō·pär′sə·nər) *n. Law* One of two or more heirs inheriting an undivided interest in an estate: also called *parcener.* [< CO-¹ + PARCENER]

co·part·ner (kō·pärt′nər) *n.* A partner, especially an equal partner, in a business, etc. **— co·part′ner·ship** *n.*

cope¹ (kōp) *v.* **coped, cop·ing** *v.i.* **1.** To contend or strive, especially successfully: often with *with.* **2.** *Archaic* To meet or encounter: with *with.* **— v.t. 3.** *Brit. Informal* To con-

tend with. **4.** *Obs.* To meet in combat. **5.** *Obs.* To requite. [< OF *couper* to strike < *coup, colp* a blow < L *colaphus*]

cope² (kōp) *n.* **1.** A semicircular mantle worn by priests or bishops on solemn or ceremonial occasions. **2.** Something that arches overhead; a vault: the *cope* of heaven. **3.** A coping, as of a wall. **4.** *Obs.* A cloak. **— v.t. coped, cop·ing 1.** To dress in a cope or cloak. **2.** To furnish with a coping, as a wall. [< Med.L *capa* cape, cope, var. of LL *cappa*. See CAP¹.]

co·peck (kō′pek) See KOPECK.

Co·pen·ha·gen (kō′pən·hā′gən, -hä′-) The capital and largest city of Denmark, a port on the east coast of Zealand; pop. 643,242 (1969): Danish *København.*

copenhagen blue A dusty, light blue.

co·pe·pod (kō′pə·pod) *n.* One of an order (*Copepoda*) of small, free-swimming, fresh-water and marine crustaceans. — *adj.* Of or belonging to the *Copepoda.* Also **co·pep·o·dan** (kō·pep′ə·dən). [< NL < Gk. *kōpē* oar + *pous, podos* foot]

Copernican system *Astron.* The theory of the solar system of Copernicus that the earth and other planets revolve about the sun, displacing the earth from the central position given to it in the Ptolemaic system.

Co·per·ni·cus (kō·pûr′nə·kəs), **Nicholas**, Latinized name of **Mikołaj Ko·per·nik** (kô·pûr′něk), 1473–1543, Polish astronomer. **— Co·per′ni·can** *adj.*

cope·set·ic (kō′pə·set′ik) *adj. U.S. Slang* Fine; excellent: also spelled *copacetic.* Also **co′pa·set′ic, co′pe·set′tic.** [< Creole *coupesētique* capable of being coped with]

cope·stone (kōp′stōn′) *n.* **1.** The top stone of a wall or building. **2.** One of the stones of a coping. **3.** The final or crowning stroke; culmination. Also called *capstone, topstone.* [< COPE² + STONE]

cop·i·er (kop′ē·ər) *n.* **1.** An imitator. **2.** A copyist.

co·pi·lot (kō′pī′lət) *n.* The assistant or relief pilot of an aircraft.

cop·ing (kō′ping) *n.* The top course of a wall, roof, etc., usually sloping to shed water. [< COPE², v.]

coping saw A narrow-bladed saw set in a recessed frame and used for cutting curved pieces from wood.

co·pi·ous (kō′pē·əs) *adj.* **1.** Large in quantity; ample. **2.** Abundant; plentiful. **3.** Diffuse; wordy. **4.** *Obs.* Affording an abundance. **— Syn.** See PLENTIFUL. [< L *copiosus* < *copia* abundance] **— co′pi·ous·ly** *adv.* **— co′pi·ous·ness** *n.*

co·pla·nar (kō·plā′nər) *adj. Math.* Being in the same plane: said of figures.

Cop·land (kōp′lənd), **Aaron**, born 1900, U.S. composer.

Cop·ley (kop′lē), **John Singleton**, 1738–1815, American protrait painter.

co·pol·y·mer (kō·pol′ə·mər) *n. Chem.* A compound formed by the polymerization of two or more unlike substances and having properties different from those of the components taken singly.

co·pol·y·mer·ize (kō·pol′ə·mə·rīz′) *v.t. & v.i.* **·ized, ·iz·ing** To make or become a copolymer. **— co·pol·y·mer·i·za′tion** *n.*

cop-out (kop′out′) *n. U.S. Slang* **1.** A way of avoiding responsibility; especially, an easy or cowardly resolution of a problem; evasion. **2.** One who cops out. [< criminal slang *cop out, cop a plea* to plead guilty]

cop·per¹ (kop′ər) *n.* **1.** A reddish, ductile, metallic element (symbol Cu) occurring native and in combination. It is one of the best conductors of heat and electricity and is extensively used in the arts, both in the pure state and in alloys, as bronze, brass, etc.: also called *cuprum.* See ELEMENT. Abbr. *c., C., cop.* **2.** A large pot, now usually of iron, for cooking or for boiling clothes. **3.** A coin of copper, or of bronze. **4.** A lustrous, reddish brown, the color of polished copper. — *v.t.* **1.** To cover or coat with copper. **2.** *U.S. Slang* To bet against (another bet). **— adj.** Of, or of the color of, copper. [OE *coper* < LL *cuprum* < L (*aes*) *cyprium* Cyprian (metal) < Gk. *kyprios* < *Kypros* Cyprus] **— cop′per·y** *adj.*

cop·per² (kop′ər) *n. Slang* A policeman. [< COP¹]

cop·per·as (kop′ər·əs) *n.* A green, crystalline, astringent ferrous sulfate, $FeSO_4 \cdot 7H_2O$, used in dyeing, inkmaking, photography, etc.: also called *green vitriol.* [< MF *coperose* < Med.L *cuperosa, cuprosa* < (*aqua*) *cuprosa* copper (water) < LL *cuprum.* See COPPER.]

copper barilla A native copper mixed with sandstone.

copper glance Chalcocite.

cop·per·head (kop′ər·hed′) *n.* A venomous North American crotaline snake (*Agkistrodon contortrix*) having reddish brown markings on a buff-colored body.

Cop·per·head (kop′ər·hed′) *n. U.S.* During the Civil War, a Northerner who sympathized with the Confederate States.

Cop·per·mine River (kop′ər·mīn′) A river in Northwest Territories, Canada, flowing 525 miles, generally NW, to the Beaufort Sea.

COPPERHEAD
(To 40 inches long)

copper nickel Niccolite.

cop·per·plate (kop′ər·plāt′) *n.* **1.** An engraved or etched plate of copper. **2.** A print or engraving from such a plate. **3.** A fine, sharp style of handwriting.

copper pyrites Chalcopyrite.

cop·per·smith (kop′ər·smith′) *n.* One who works in copper.

copper sulfate Blue vitriol.

cop·pice (kop′is) *n.* A copse. [Alter. of COPSE]

cop·ra (kop′rə, kō′prə) *n.* The dried and broken kernel of the coconut, yielding coconut oil. Also **cop·per·ah** (kop′-ər-ə), **cop′rah, cop′pra.** [< Pg. < Malayalam *koppara*]

cop·re·mi·a (kop·rē′mē-ə) *n. Pathol.* A poisoning of the blood from retained fecal matter. Also **cop·rae′mi·a.** [< COPR(O)- + Gk. *haima* blood] — **cop·re′mic** *adj.*

copro- *combining form* Dung; feces; filth: *coprolite.* Also, before vowels, **copr-.** [< Gk. *kopros* dung]

cop·ro·lite (kop′rə-līt) *n.* The petrified dung of extinct vertebrates. [< COPRO- + -LITE]

cop·rol·o·gy (kop-rol′ə-jē) *n.* Indecency or filth in art or literature; also, the study of this. [< COPRO- + -LOGY]

cop·roph·a·gous (kop-rof′ə-gəs) *adj.* Feeding upon dung, as scarabaeid beetles. [<NL < Gk. *koprophagos* < *kopros* dung + *phagein* to eat]

cop·roph·i·lous (kop-rof′ə-ləs) *adj.* Growing readily on dung, as certain fungi. [< COPRO- + -PHILOUS]

copse (kops) *n.* A thicket of bushes or small trees: also called *coppice.* [Earlier *coppice* < OF *copeiz* < *coper* to cut]

Copt (kopt) *n.* **1.** A native Egyptian of ancient Egyptian stock. **2.** A member of the Coptic Church. [< Med.L *Coptus, Cophtus* < Arabic *quft* < Coptic *gyptios, kyptaios* < Gk. *Aigyptios* Egyptian]

Cop·tic (kop′tik) *adj.* Of or pertaining to the Copts, or to their language. — *n.* The Hamitic language of the Copts, the latest form of the ancient Egyptian, a dead language except as the liturgical language of the Coptic Church.

Coptic Church The principal Christian sect of Egypt, becoming a separate body in 451, and adhering to the Monophysitic doctrine after this was rejected by the Council of Chalcedon. See MONOPHYSITE.

cop·u·la (kop′yə-lə) *n. pl.* **·las** or **·lae** (-lē) **1.** *Gram.* A linking verb. **2.** *Logic* The link between the subject and predicate of a proposition. [< L, a link, band] — **cop′u·lar** *adj.*

cop·u·late (kop′yə-lāt) *v.i.* **·lat·ed, ·lat·ing** To unite in sexual intercourse. [< L *copulatus,* pp. of *copulare* to fasten < *copula* a link]

cop·u·la·tion (kop′yə-lā′shən) *n.* **1.** Sexual intercourse; coition. **2.** A coupling or being coupled; union.

cop·u·la·tive (kop′yə-lā′tiv, -lə-tiv) *adj.* **1.** Serving to join or unite. **2.** *Gram.* **a** Serving as a copula: a *copulative* verb. **b** Connecting words or clauses in a coordinate relationship: "And" is a *copulative* conjunction. **3.** Copulatory. — *n. Gram.* A copulative word. — **cop′u·la·tive·ly** *adv.*

cop·u·la·to·ry (kop′yə-lə-tôr′ē, -tō′rē) *adj.* Pertaining to or used in copulation: *copulatory* organs.

cop·y (kop′ē) *n. pl.* **cop·ies 1.** A reproduction or imitation of an original; duplicate; transcript. **2.** A single specimen of a book, print, etc. **3.** Written matter as distinct from graphic matter, as in advertising, newspapers, preparation of books and pamphlets, etc. **4.** Something to be reproduced or imitated; especially, an example of penmanship for a student. **5.** *Printing* Manuscript or other matter to be reproduced in type. **6.** In journalism, subject matter for an article, etc.: The president is good *copy.* **7.** *Brit. Informal* A school composition. Abbr. *c., C.* — *v.* **cop·ied, cop·y·ing** *v.t.* **1.** To make a copy of; reproduce or transcribe. **2.** To follow as a model; imitate, as in actions or opinions. — *v.i.* **3.** To make a copy or reproduction; follow an example. [< MF *copie* < Med.L *copia* transcript < L, supply, abundance] — **Syn.** (noun) **1.** See DUPLICATE. — (verb) **2.** mimic, ape.

cop·y·book (kop′ē-bŏŏk′) *n.* **1.** A book containing copies to be imitated in penmanship. **2.** A book for copies.

copy boy An errand boy in a newspaper office who delivers copy to the editor, composing room, etc.

cop·y·cat (kop′ē-kat′) *n.* An imitator: a child's term of derision.

copy desk A desk in a newspaper office where copy is edited and prepared for the typesetters.

cop·y·ed·it (kop′ē-ed′it) *v.t.* To edit (a text, page, etc.) for typesetting. — **copy editor** *n.*

cop·y·graph (kop′ē-graf, -gräf) *n.* A hectograph (which see).

cop·y·hold (kop′ē-hōld′) *n.* In English law, a tenure of lands confirmed and made authentic by being recorded in the manorial court roll.

cop·y·hold·er[1] (kop′ē-hōl′dər) *n.* **1.** One who reads copy aloud for a proofreader. **2.** A device that holds copy, as for a typesetter.

cop·y·hold·er[2] (kop′ē-hōl′dər) *n.* In English law, one who holds land by copyhold.

cop·y·ist (kop′ē-ist) *n.* **1.** One who makes copies, especially of documents. **2.** One who imitates or copies.

cop·y·read·er (kop′ē-rē′dər) *n.* A person who edits work intended for publication.

cop·y·right (kop′ē-rīt) *n.* The exclusive statutory right of authors, composers, playwrights, artists, publishers, and distributors to publish and dispose of their works for a specified period of time. In the United States this period is 28

years, with the privilege of one renewal for an additional 28 years. Abbr. *c., C., cop.* — *v.t.* To secure copyright for. — *adj.* Of or protected by copyright. — **cop′y·right′a·ble** *adj.* — **cop′y·right′er** *n.*

cop·y·writ·er (kop′ē-rī′tər) *n.* One who writes copy for advertisements.

coque·li·cot (kōk′li-kō) *n.* **1.** The corn poppy. **2.** The reddish orange color of this flower. [< F]

Coque·lin (kôk-laN′), **Benoît Constant,** 1841–1909, French actor.

co·quet (kō-ket′) *v.* **·quet·ted, ·quet·ting** *v.i.* **1.** To treat a person with pretended affection; flirt. **2.** To act in a trifling manner; dally. — *v.t.* **3.** *Obs.* To flirt with. Also spelled **coquette.** [< F *coqueter* < *coquet,* dim. of *coq* a cock; with ref. to its strutting]

co·quet·ry (kō′kə-trē, kō·ket′rē) *n. pl.* **·ries** The behavior or practices of a flirtatious woman.

co·quette (kō-ket′) *n.* A woman who tries to attract the affections of men merely to gratify her vanity; a flirt. — *v.t. & v.i.* **·quet·ted, quet·ting** To coquet. [< F, fem. dim. of *coq* a cock. See COQUET.] — **co·quet′tish** *adj.* — **co·quet′tish·ly** *adv.* — **co·quet′tish·ness** *n.*

co·quil·la nut (kō-kēl′yə, -kē′yə) The hard-shelled, oval nut of a Brazilian palm (*Attalea funifera*). [< Sp. *coquillo,* dim. of *coco* coconut]

co·quille (kō-kēl′) *n.* **1.** Any of various dishes, usually of sea food, baked in a shell. **2.** *Metall.* A chill. [< F, shell]

co·qui·na (kō-kē′nə) *n.* A soft, highly porous limestone composed of fragments of marine shells, used as building material. [< Sp., shell, ult. < L *concha*]

co·qui·to (kō-kē′tō) *n. pl.* **·tos 1.** A feather palm (*Jubaea spectabilis*) of Chile, bearing a dense crown of foliage. **2.** Its small, edible nut. [< Sp., dim. of *coco* coconut]

cor- Var. of COM-.

cor. **1.** Corner. **2.** Coroner. **3.** Corpus. **4.** Correct; corrected. **5.** Correlative. **6.** Correspondence; correspondent; corresponding. **7.** Corrupt.

Cor. Corinthians.

cor·a·ci·i·form (kôr′ə-sī′ə-fôrm) *adj.* Of or belonging to an order (*Coraciiformes*) of birds including the rollers and kingfishers. [<NL < Gk. *korax, korakis* raven + -FORM]

cor·a·cle (kôr′ə-kəl, kor′-) *n.* A small, rounded boat of hide on a wicker frame. [< Welsh *corwgl* < *corwg* boat]

cor·a·coid (kôr′ə-koid, kor′-) *Anat. adj.* Designating a bony process of the shoulder girdle in many vertebrates, uniting with the scapula to form the glenoid cavity. — *n.* **1.** The coracoid process. **2.** The chief bone of the shoulder girdle of a teleost fish. [< L *coracoides* < Gk. *korakoeidēs* < *korax, korakis* raven + *eidos* form; so called from its shape]

cor·al (kôr′əl, kor′-) *n.* **1.** The calcareous skeleton secreted in or by the tissues of various, usually compound, marine coelenterates, deposited in various forms and colors. **2.** A mass of these skeletons forming an island, reef, etc. **3.** An animal of this type. **4.** A pinkish or yellowish red. **5.** An object, as a toy or jewel, made of coral. **6.** Lobster or crab roe, so called from its appearance when cooked. — *adj.* Of, relating to, or of the color of coral. [< OF < L *coralium* < Gk. *korallion* red coral]

CORAL
a Reef. *b* Mushroom. *c* Bud. *d* Red. *e* Brain.

cor·al·ber·ry (kôr′əl-ber′ē, kor′-) *n. pl.* **·ries** A bushy American shrub (*Symphoricarpos orbiculatus*) with dark berries somewhat resembling currants.

Cor·al Ga·bles (kôr′əl gā′bəlz) A city in SE Florida, on Biscayne Bay, near Miami; pop. 42,069.

coralli- *combining form* Coral; coralliferous. Also (before vowels) **corall-.** [< Gk. *korallion* red coral]

cor·al·lif·er·ous (kôr′ə-lif′ər-əs, kor′-) *adj.* Producing or containing coral. [< CORALLI- + -FEROUS]

cor·al·line (kôr′ə-lin, -līn, kor′-) *adj.* **1.** Of, producing, or like coral. **2.** Yellowish or pinkish red. — *n.* **1.** A calcareous, corallike seaweed. **2.** A coral or corallike animal. [< L *corallinus*]

cor·al·loid (kôr′ə-loid, kor′-) *adj.* Coral-shaped; especially, branching like coral. Also **cor′al·loi′dal.**

coral reef A reef, often of great extent, formed by the gradual deposit of coral skeletons.

cor·al·root (kôr′əl-rōōt′, -rŏŏt′, kor′-) *n.* Any of a genus (*Corallorhiza*) of leafless orchids with corallike roots.

Coral Sea A SW area of the Pacific Ocean east of Australia and New Guinea; scene of U.S. naval victory over Japan in World War II, 1942.

PRONUNCIATION KEY: add, āce, câre, pälm; end, ēven; it, īce; odd, ōpen, ôrder; tŏŏk, pōōl; up, bûrn; ə = a in *above,* e in *sicken,* i in *flexible,* o in *melon,* u in *focus;* yōō = u in *fuse;* oil; pout; check; go; ring; thin; this; zh, vision. For a, œ, ü, kh, ṅ, see inside front cover.

coral snake Any of a genus (*Micrurus*) of venomous snakes of tropical America and the southern United States, noted for their brilliant red, black, and yellow rings; especially, the **South American coral snake** (*M. lemniscatus*) and the **Eastern coral snake** (*M. fulvius*) of Mexico and the southern United States: also called *harlequin snake*.

co·ram pop·u·lo (kō'ram pop'yə·lō) *Latin* In public.

cor an·glais (kôr än·gle') *French* The English horn.

co·ran·to (kə·ran'tō, -rän'-) *n. Music* A courante.

Cor·an·tyn (kôr'ən·tīn, kor'-) See COURANTYNE.

cor·ban (kôr'bən, kôr·bän') *n.* In ancient Judaism, an offering to God, as in fulfillment of a vow. [< Hebrew *qorbān*]

cor·beil (kôr'bəl) *n. Archit.* A sculptured basket of fruit or flowers. [< F *corbeille* < L *corbicula*, dim. of *corbis* basket]

cor·bel (kôr'bəl, -bel) *n. Archit.* 1. A projection from the face of a wall to support an overhanging weight. 2. A short timber placed under a girder to increase its bearing. —*v.t.* **cor·beled** or **·belled, cor·bel·ing** or **·bel·ling** To support by or furnish with corbels. [< OF < LL *corvellum*, dim. of L *corvus* crow; so called from its shape]

cor·bel·ing (kôr'bəl·ing) *n. Archit.* An arrangement of stones or bricks in which each successive course projects beyond the one below it. Also **cor'bel·ling.**

cor·bie (kôr'bē) *n. Scot.* A crow or raven. Also **cor'by.**

cor·bie-step (kôr'bē·step') *n.* One of a series of steps in the top of a gable wall, from the eaves to the apex of the roof: often called *crowstep.*

Cor·co·va·do (*Pg.* kôr'kə·vä'thōō, *Sp.* kôr'kō·vä'thō) 1. A peak near Rio de Janiero, Brazil; 2,310 ft.; topped by a large statue of Christ. 2. A volcano in southern Chile; 7,550 ft.; near the **Gulf of Corcovado,** an inlet of the Pacific: also **Corcovado Volcano.**

Cor·cy·ra (kôr·sī'rə) The ancient name for CORFU.

cord (kôrd) *n.* 1. A string or small rope of several strands twisted together; twine. 2. A flexible, insulated electric wire, usually with a plug at one end. 3. A measure for wood, usually for firewood, equaling a pile 4 × 4 × 8 feet, or 128 cubic feet. *Abbr. cd.* See table inside back cover. 4. The hangman's rope. 5. An influence that draws or restrains. 6. A raised rib in fabric; also, fabric with such ribs. 7. *pl.* Corduroy trousers. 8. *Anat.* A cordlike structure: spinal *cord:* sometimes spelled *chord.* —*v.t.* 1. To bind with cord. 2. To furnish or ornament with cords. 3. To pile (firewood) by the cord. [< MF *corde* < L *chorda* < Gk. *chordē* string of a musical instrument. Doublet of CHORD.] —**cord'er** *n.*

cord·age (kôr'dij) *n.* 1. Ropes and cords collectively, especially in a ship's rigging. 2. The amount of wood, in cords, on a given area of land. [< MF < *corde.* See CORD.]

cor·date (kôr'dāt) *adj. Bot.* Heart-shaped, as a leaf. See illustration of LEAF. [< L *cordatus* < *cor, cordis* heart] —**cor'date·ly** *adv.*

Cor·day (kôr·dā'), **Charlotte,** 1768–93, French patriot; assassinated Marat: full name **Marie Anne Charlotte Corday d'Ar·mont** (dàr·môn').

cord·ed (kôr'did) *adj.* 1. Bound or fastened with cord. 2. Striped or ribbed with cords: a *corded* fabric. 3. Piled in cords: *corded* firewood. 4. *Obs.* Made of cord or rope.

Cor·del·ia (kôr·dēl'yə, -dē'lē·ə) In Shakespeare's *King Lear,* the youngest of Lear's three daughters, the only one to remain faithful to him.

Cor·de·lier (kôr'də·lir') *n.* 1. In France, a Franciscan friar of the Observantine branch. 2. *pl.* A political club of the time of the French Revolution, whose meetings were held in an old Cordelier convent. [< F *cordelle,* dim. of *corde* a cord; with ref. to the knotted cord worn by these friars]

cor·dial (kôr'jəl, *esp. Brit.* -dyəl) *adj.* 1. Warm and hearty; sincere. 2. Giving heart; invigorating. 3. *Obs.* Of the heart. —*n.* 1. A liqueur. 2. Something that invigorates, as a medical stimulant. [< Med.L *cordialis* < L *cor, cordis* heart] —**cor'dial·ly** *adv.* —**cor'dial·ness** *n.*

cor·dial·i·ty (kôr·jal'ə·tē,-jē·al'-, *esp. Brit.* -dē·al'-) *n. pl.* **·ties** Cordial quality; sincerity of feeling; warmth.

cor·di·er·ite (kôr'dē·ə·rīt') *n. Mineral.* A bluish silicate of magnesium, aluminum, and iron, crystallizing in the orthorhombic system, used as a gemstone: also called *dichroite, iolite.* [after P. *Cordier,* 1777–1861, French geologist]

cor·di·form (kôr'də·fôrm) *adj.* Heart-shaped; cordate. [< L *cor, cordis* heart + -FORM]

cor·dil·le·ra (kôr'dil·yâr'ə, kôr·dil'ər·ə) *n. Geog.* An entire system of mountain ranges continuous within a great land mass. [< Sp. < OSp. *cordilla,* dim. of *cuerda* rope < L *chorda.* See CORD.] —**cor·dil·ler·an** (kôr'dil·yâr'ən, kôr·dil'ər·ən) *adj.*

Cor·dil·le·ras (kôr'dil·yâr'əz, kôr·dil'ər·əz; *Sp.* kôr'thē·yā'rräs) The Andes range in South America and its continuation in the Rocky Mountain system of North America.

cord·ite (kôr'dīt) *n.* A variety of smokeless powder consisting of cellulose nitrate or guncotton, nitroglycerin, and a mineral jelly. [< CORD; with ref. to its appearance]

cor·do·ba (kôr'də·bə, *Sp.* kôr'thō·vä) *n.* The monetary unit of Nicaragua, equivalent to 100 centavos. [after Francisco de *Córdoba,* 16th c. Spanish explorer]

Cór·do·ba (kôr'thō·vä) 1. A city in north central Argentina; pop. 467,419 (est. 1958). 2. A city in southern Spain, on the Guadalquivir; pop. 198,148 (1960): also **Cor·do·va** (kôr'də·və).

cor·don (kôr'dən) *n.* 1. A line, as of men or ships, stationed so as to guard or enclose an area. 2. A ribbon worn as an insignia of honor or rank, usually across the breast. 3. A cord worn as a fastening or adornment. 4. *Archit.* A stringcourse. —*v.t.* To form a cordon around: often with *off.* [< F < *corde.* See CORD.]

cor·don bleu (kôr·dôn' blœ') *French* 1. The blue ribbon formerly worn by members of the order of the Holy Ghost, the highest order of the Bourbon monarchy. 2. Any high distinction. 3. One who is highly distinguished in his field. 4. An exceptionally able cook.

cor·don sa·ni·taire (kôr·dôn' sá·nē·târ') *French* 1. A guarded barricade or line quarantining an infected district. 2. A series of buffer states serving as a barrier or deterrent against a nation considered potentially dangerous. Also called *sanitary cordon.*

cor·do·van (kôr'də·vən) *n.* A fine leather first made at Córdoba, Spain, originally of goatskin, but now usually of split horsehide. Also **cordovan leather.** —*adj.* Made of cordovan. [< OSp. *cordovan* of Córdoba]

Cor·do·van (kôr'də·vən) *adj.* Of or pertaining to Córdoba. —*n.* A native or resident of Córdoba.

cor·du·roy (kôr'də·roi, kôr'də·roi') *n.* 1. A durable fabric, usually of cotton, having a ribbed pile. 2. *pl.* Trousers made of corduroy. —*adj.* Made of corduroy. —*v.t.* To make into a corduroy road. [? < *cord* (ribbed fabric) + obs. *duroy* coarse woolen cloth; later taken as < F *corde du roi* king's cord]

corduroy road A road formed from logs laid transversely, as over miry ground.

cord·wain (kôrd'wān) *n. Archaic* Cordovan leather. [< OF *cordewan, cordoan* < OSp. *cordovan* of Córdoba]

cord·wain·er (kôrd'wā·nər) *n. Archaic* A worker in cordwain; especially, a shoemaker.

cord·wood (kôrd'wŏŏd') *n.* Firewood or pulpwood cut for stacking in a cord or sold by the cord.

core (kōr, kôr) *n.* 1. The central or innermost part of a thing; the heart or essence. 2. The fibrous or membranous central part of a fruit, containing the seeds. 3. A cylindrical mass of rock or other material. 4. *Electr.* The central iron mass of an induction coil, armature, or electromagnet. 5. The base wood to which veneers are glued. 6. A form, usually of sand, placed in a mold so as to obtain a hollow casting. —*v.t.* **cored, cor·ing** To remove the core of. [ME; origin uncertain] —**core'less** *adj.*

co·re·la·tion (kō/ri·lā'shən) See CORRELATION.

co·re·lig·ion·ist (kō'ri·lij'ən·ist) *n.* An adherent of the same religion, church, or sect as another.

Co·rel·li (kō·rel'lē), **Arcangelo,** 1653–1713, Italian composer.

Cor·en·tyn, Cor·en·tyne (kôr'ən·tīn, kor') See COURANTYNE.

co·re·op·sis (kôr'ē·op'sis, kō/rē-) *n.* A plant (genus *Coreopsis*) of the composite family, with showy yellow or reddish flowers: also called *calliopsis, tickseed.* [< NL < Gk. *koris* bug + -OPSIS; with ref. to the shape of the seed]

cor·er (kōr'ər, kô'rər) *n.* A knifelike utensil for coring apples and other fruit.

co·re·spon·dent (kō'ri·spon'dənt) *n. Law* A joint defendant; especially, in a suit for divorce, one charged with having committed adultery with the husband or wife. —**co're·spon'den·cy** *n.*

corf (kôrf) *n. pl.* **corves** (kôrvz) *Brit.* A small wagon or, formerly, a wicker basket, in which coal or ore is carried from a mine. [ME < LG. Cf. MDu. *korf* basket.]

Cor·fu (kôr·fōō', kôr'fyōō) An island of Greece in the Ionian group; 229 sq. mi.: ancient *Corcyra.* Greek *Kerkyra.*

cor·gi (kôr'gē) *n.* The Welsh corgi (which see).

Co·ri (kô'rē), **Carl Ferdinand,** born 1896, and his wife **Gerty Theresa,** 1896–1957, *née* Radnitz, U.S. biochemists born in Prague.

co·ri·a·ceous (kôr'ē·ā'shəs, kō/rē-) *adj.* Of or resembling leather. [< L *coriaceus* < *corium* leather]

co·ri·an·der (kôr'ē·an'dər, kō/rē-) *n.* 1. A plant (*Coriandrum sativum*) of the parsley family, bearing aromatic seeds used for seasoning and in medicine. 2. The seeds of this plant. [< MF *coriandre* < L *coriandrum* < Gk. *koriannon*]

Co·rin·na (kə·rin'ə) Greek lyric poetess of the early fifth century B.C.

Cor·inth (kôr'inth, kor'-) 1. An ancient city in Argolis, Greece. 2. A modern city near the site of ancient Corinth; pop. about 17,700.

Corinth, Gulf of An inlet of the Ionian Sea between the Peloponnesus and northern Greece: also *Gulf of Lepanto.*

Corinth, Isthmus of An isthmus connecting the Peloponnesus with northern Greece; traversed by a canal.

Co·rin·thi·an (kə·rin'thē·ən) *adj.* 1. Of or pertaining to ancient Corinth, noted for its luxury, licentiousness, and ornate art. 2. Given to luxury and dissipation. 3. *Archit.* Of or pertaining to an order of Greek architecture characterized by ornate, bell-shaped capitals decorated with simulated acanthus leaves. For illustration see CAPITAL. **4.** Elegantly ornate. **— n. 1.** A native or inhabitant of Corinth. **2.** A man about town. **3.** A gentleman sportsman. **4.** *Obs.* A dissolute man. **— Epistle to the Corinthians** Either of two letters addressed by Saint Paul to the Christians at Corinth, each forming a book of the New Testament. Also **Corinthians.** *Abbr. Cor.*

Cor·i·o·la·nus (kôr′ē·ə·lā′nəs, kor′-), **Gaius** (or **Gnaeus**) **Marcius** Fifth-century B.C. Roman general; champion of the patricians; hero of Shakespeare's tragedy *Coriolanus.*

Cor·i·o·lis force (kôr′ē·ō′lis) *Physics* The deflecting effect of the earth's rotation whereby freely moving air masses, aircraft, projectiles, etc., are deflected to the right in the northern hemisphere and to the left in the southern hemisphere. [after Gaspard Gustave de *Coriolis,* 1792–1843, French mathematician]

co·ri·um (kôr′ē·əm, kō′rē-) *n. pl.* **·ri·a** (-ə) **1.** *Anat.* The sensitive vascular portion of the skin beneath the epidermis: also called *cutis, cutis vera, derma, dermis.* **2.** *Entomol.* In certain insects (order *Heteroptera*), the elongated middle section or harder portion of the forewing. [< L, skin, hide]

cork (kôrk) *n.* **1.** The light, porous, elastic outer bark of the cork oak, widely used in industry and the arts. **2.** Something made of cork, especially a piece of this bark used as a bottle stopper; also, a stopper made of other material, as rubber, glass, etc. **3.** A small float used on a fishing net or line. **4.** *Bot.* A protective tissue that forms beneath and replaces the epidermis in the stems of dicotyledons. **— v.t. 1.** To stop with a cork, as a bottle. **2.** To restrain; check; repress. **3.** *U.S.* To blacken with burnt cork. [Appar. < OSp. *alcorque* cork slipper < Arabic ? < L *quercus* oak]

Cork (kôrk) The largest county in Ireland, in southern Munster province; 2,880 sq. mi.; pop. 330,443 (1966); county seat, **Cork,** a county borough and port in the SE central part, on the Lee river; pop. 77,980.

cork cambium *Bot.* Phellogen.

corked (kôrkt) *adj.* **1.** Stopped with a cork. **2.** Spoiled by tasting of cork, as wine. **3.** *U.S.* Blackened with burnt cork.

cork·er (kôr′kər) *n.* **1.** One who or that which corks. **2.** *Slang* Something outstanding or astonishing. **3.** An argument, remark, etc., that puts an end to discussion.

cork·ing (kôr′king) *Slang adj.* Excellent; splendid.

cork oak An evergreen oak (*Quercus suber*) of southern Europe and North Africa, from whose bark cork is produced.

cork·screw (kôrk′skrōo′) *n.* An instrument for drawing corks from bottles, consisting of a sharply pointed metal spiral attached to a handle. **— v.t. & v.i.** To move or cause to move like a corkscrew; twist spirally. **— adj.** Shaped like a corkscrew; twisted; spiral.

cork·wood (kôrk′wŏŏd′) *n.* **1.** Any of various trees, as the balsa, having light, porous wood; also, the wood itself. **2.** A small tree (*Leitneria floridiana*) of the SE United States, having glossy, deciduous leaves and very light wood.

cork·y (kôr′kē) *adj.* **cork·i·er, cork·i·est 1.** Of or resembling cork. **2.** *Informal* Lively; skittish. **3.** Tasting of cork; corked. **4.** *Obs.* Withered; dry. **— cork′i·ness** *n.*

corm (kôrm) *n. Bot.* A bulblike enlargement of the underground stem in certain plants, as the gladiolus. [< NL *cormus* < Gk. *kormos* tree trunk]

cor·mo·phyte (kôr′mə·fīt) *n.* Any of a former division (*Cormophyta*) of plants having stems, leaves, and roots. [< *cormo-* (< CORM) + -PHYTE] **— cor′mo·phyt′ic** (-fit′ik) *adj.*

cor·mo·rant (kôr′mər·ənt) *n.* **1.** Any of various large, web-footed aquatic birds (genus *Phalacrocorax*) of wide distribution, having a hooked bill and a pouch under the beak in which it holds fish: also called *shag.* **2.** A greedy or voracious person. **— adj.** Greedy; rapacious. [< MF *cormoran,* prob. < L *corvus marinus* sea crow]

corn¹ (kôrn) *n.* **1.** *U.S.* Any of many varieties of a tall, extensively cultivated cereal plant (*Zea mays*), bearing seeds on a large ear or cob; also, the seeds of this plant, used as food or fodder: also called *Indian corn, maize.* **2.** *Brit.* The edible seeds of various cereal plants, usually the chief cereal plant of a region, in England being chiefly wheat, and in Scotland and Ireland, oats. **3.** *Brit.* Any cereal plant. **4.** A single seed of a cereal plant; kernel; grain. **5.** *U.S. Informal* Corn whisky. **6.** *U.S. Slang* Anything regarded as trite or overly sentimental. **— v.t. 1.** To preserve in coarse salt or in brine. **2.** To feed corn to. **3.** To granulate. [OE]

corn² (kôrn) *n.* A horny thickening of the skin in a small area, commonly on a toe, caused by pressure or friction. [< OF < L *cornu.* Akin to HORN.]

Corn. Cornish; Cornwall.

cor·na·ceous (kôr·nā′shəs) *adj.* Of or belonging to a family (*Cornaceae*) of shrubs or trees including the dogwood. [< NL < L *cornus* dogwood]

Corn Belt *U.S.* The region including the chief corn-growing States, Illinois, Indiana, Iowa, Kansas, Missouri, Nebraska, and Ohio.

corn borer The larva of a moth (*Pyrausta nubilalis*) that feeds on the ears and stalks of corn.

corn bread *n.* Bread made from cornmeal. Also **corn·bread** (kôrn′bred′).

corn·cake (kôrn′kāk′) *n. U.S.* Johnnycake (which see). Also **corn cake.**

corn·cob (kôrn′kob′) *n. U.S.* The woody spike of corn around which the kernels grow. Also **corn cob.**

corncob pipe A pipe whose bowl is cut from a corncob.

corn·cock·le (kôrn′kok′əl) *n.* A tall weed (*Agrostemma githago*) of the pink family, with purple flowers: also called *corn rose, rose campion.*

corn crake A European rail (*Crex crex*), having a short bill and frequenting grainfields: also called *dakerhen.*

corn·crib (kôrn′krib′) *n.* A small building in which to store ears of corn, having slatted walls for ventilation.

corn·dodg·er (kôrn′doj′ər) *n. U.S.* A cake of cornmeal baked or fried hard.

cor·ne·a (kôr′nē·ə) *n. Anat.* The transparent anterior part of the outer coat of the eyeball, continuous with the sclera. Also **cornea lens.** For illustration see EYE. [< Med.L *cornea* horny < L *cornu* horn] **— cor′ne·al** *adj.*

corn earworm The larva of a noctuid moth (*Heliothis armigera*), very destructive of corn, cotton, tomatoes, and other plants: also called *bollworm.*

corned (kôrnd) *adj.* Preserved in salt or brine, as beef.

Cor·neille (kôr·nā′, *Fr.* kôr·nā′y′), **Pierre,** 1606–84, French dramatist.

cor·nel (kôr′nəl) *n.* Any of a genus (*Cornus*) of shrubs and small trees with hard wood, as the dogwood: also called *cornus.* [Appar. trans. of G *cornel(baum),* ? < Med.L *cornolium* < MF *cornoille* cornelberry, ult. < L *cornus* cornel]

Cor·nel·ia (kôr·nēl′yə) Second-century B.C. Roman matron; mother of the Gracchi.

cor·nel·ian (kôr·nēl′yən) *n.* Carnelian.

Cor·ne·li·us (kôr·nā′lē·ŏŏs), **Peter von,** 1783–1867, German painter.

Cor·nell (kôr·nel′), **Ezra,** 1807–74, U.S. philanthropist; founded Cornell University. **— Katharine,** born 1898, U.S. actress.

cor·ne·ous (kôr′nē·əs) *adj.* Consisting of horn; of a hornlike texture; horny. [< L *corneus* horny < *cornu* horn]

cor·ner (kôr′nər) *n.* **1.** The point or place formed by the meeting of two lines or surfaces; also, the angle so formed. **2.** The place where two streets meet. **3.** A threatening or embarrassing position. **4.** A part, region, or place, especially a remote or retired place: in every *corner* of the land. **5.** A piece for forming, ornamenting, or guarding a corner, as of a book. **6.** *Econ.* An operation in which a commodity or security is bought up by an individual or group of individuals with a view to forcing higher prices. *Abbr. cor.* **— to cut corners** To economize; reduce expenditures. **— v.t. 1.** To force into a corner; place in a dangerous or embarrassing position. **2.** To form a corner in (a stock or commodity). **3.** To furnish with corners. **4.** To place in a corner. **— v.i. 5.** To form a corner in a stock or commodity. **6.** *U.S.* To come together or be located on or at a corner. **7.** To turn, as at a corner: said of automobiles. **— adj. 1.** Located on a corner. **2.** Designed for a corner. [< AF, var. of OF *cornier,* ult. < L *cornu* horn, point]

cor·nered (kôr′nərd) *adj.* **1.** Having (a specified kind or number of) corners: used in combination: *tri-cornered.* **2.** Forced into a difficult or embarrassing position.

cor·ner·stone (kôr′nər·stōn′) *n.* **1.** A stone uniting two walls at the corner of a building. **2.** Such a stone, often inscribed and made into a repository for historical documents, etc., laid into the foundation of an edifice. **3.** Something of primary importance.

cor·ner·wise (kôr′nər·wīz′) *adv.* **1.** With the corner in front. **2.** From corner to corner, diagonally. Also **cor′ner·ways′.**

cor·net¹ (kôr·net′ *for def. 1;* kôr′nit *for defs. 2–4*) *n.* **1.** A small wind instrument of the trumpet class, with a somewhat wider bore. *Abbr. cor.* **2.** A cone-shaped paper wrapper, as for candy, nuts, etc. **3.** A woman's headdress, often cone-shaped, of the 12th to 18th centuries. **4.** A distinctive type of headdress worn by some orders of nuns. [< OF, dim. of *corn* < L *cornu* horn]

cor·net² (kôr′nit) *n.* Formerly, the lowest commissioned cavalry officer in the British army; also, a pennant carried by him. [< MF, dim. of *corne* < L *cornu* horn]

cor·net-à-pis·tons (kôr·net′ə·pis′tənz, *Fr.* kôr·ne′å·pē·stôn′) *n. pl.* **cor·nets-à-pis·tons** (kôr·nets′-, *Fr.* kôr·ne′zå·pē·stôn′) A cornet, the musical instrument.

cor·net·cy (kôr′nit·sē) *n. pl.* **·cies** The rank or commission of a cornet.

cor·net·tist (kôr·net′ist) *n.* One who plays a cornet. Also **cor·net′ist.**

corn-fed (kôrn′fed′) *adj.* **1.** Nourished on corn. **2.** *U.S. Slang* Strong and healthy, but rustic and unsophisticated.

corn·field (kôrn′fēld′) *n.* A field in which corn is grown.

corn·flow·er (kôrn′flou′ər) *n.* **1.** A hardy annual plant (*Centaurea cyanus*) of the composite family, with heads of blue, purple, pink, or white flowers: also called *bachelor's-button, bluebonnet, bluebottle*. **2.** Any of various other plants growing in grain fields.

corn·husk (kôrn′husk′) *n. U.S.* The leaves or husk enclosing an ear of corn: also called *corn shuck*.

Cornhusker State Nickname of Nebraska.

corn·husk·ing (kôrn′hus′king) *n. U.S.* **1.** The husking of corn. **2.** A social gathering for husking corn, usually followed by refreshments, dancing, etc.: also called *husking bee*. — **corn′husk′er** *n.*

cor·nice (kôr′nis) *n.* **1.** *Archit.* **a** The horizontal molded projection at the top of a building or of a component part of a building, usually under the eaves. **b** The uppermost member of an entablature. For illustration see ENTABLATURE. **2.** A molding around the walls of a room, close to the ceiling. **3.** A frame fastened to a wall or window so as to cover the rods and hooks used for hanging curtains, etc. **4.** A mass of snow projecting from a mountain ridge. — *v.t.* ·niced, ·nic·ing To provide or adorn with a cornice. [< Ital., ? < L *coronis* < Gk. *korōnis* curved line, flourish, finishing touch]

cor·nic·u·late (kôr·nik′yə·lāt, -lit) *adj.* Having horns or hornlike processes. [< L *corniculatus* < *corniculum*, dim. of *cornu* horn]

Cor·nish (kôr′nish) *adj.* Pertaining to Cornwall, England, or its people. — *n.* The former language of Cornwall, belonging to the Brythonic branch of the Celtic languages but extinct since the early 19th century and replaced by a dialect of English. — **Cor′nish·man** (-mən) *n.*

Corn Laws In English history, certain laws placing restrictions on the grain trade and especially the importation of grain, repealed in 1846.

corn lily **1.** A convulvulus. **2.** Ixia.

corn·meal (kôrn′mēl′) *n.* **1.** Meal made from corn: also called *Indian meal*. **2.** *Scot.* Oatmeal. Also **corn meal**.

Cor·no Gran·de (kôr′nō grän′dā) See MONTE CORNO.

corn picker A machine for removing and husking ears of standing corn.

corn pit An exchange devoted to business in corn.

corn pone *Southern U.S.* Bread made of cornmeal, water, and salt, usually without milk or eggs.

corn popper A utensil used for popping corn.

corn poppy The common Old World poppy (*Papaver rhoeas*) bearing bright red flowers, a symbol of the dead of World War I: also called *coquelicot, corn rose*.

corn rose **1.** The corncockle. **2.** The corn poppy.

corn salad Any of various plants (genus *Valerianella*), having leaves used for salad: also called *lamb's lettuce*.

corn shock An upright bundle of stalks of corn, often tied together at the top.

corn shuck *U.S.* A cornhusk.

corn silk The soft, silky styles on an ear of corn.

corn smut A widespread disease of corn, caused by the infection of a smut fungus (*Ustilago zeae*) and characterized by growths attached to the ears and other parts of the plant.

corn snow In skiing, snow that has melted slightly and refrozen, forming a coarse, granular surface.

corn·stalk (kôrn′stôk′) *n.* A stalk of corn. Also **corn stalk**.

corn·starch (kôrn′stärch′) *n.* **1.** Starch made from corn. **2.** A purified starchy cornmeal used in making puddings.

corn sugar Glucose obtained from corn.

corn syrup Syrup extracted from corn grains, containing glucose mixed with dextrine and maltose.

corn't (kôrnt) *adj. Scot.* Fed on oats.

cor·nu (kôr′nyōō) *n. pl.* ·nu·a (-nyōō·ə) A horn, or anything shaped like a horn: applied to various anatomical structures. [< L, horn]

cor·nu·co·pi·a (kôr′nə·kō′pē·ə) *n.* **1.** In Greek mythology, the horn of Amalthea. **2.** A symbol of prosperity, represented as a curved horn overflowing with fruit, vegetables, grains, etc. **3.** A great abundance. **4.** Any horn-shaped container. Also called *horn of plenty*. [< LL *cornucopia* < L *cornu copiae* horn of plenty] — **cor′nu·co′pi·an** *adj.*

cor·nus (kôr′nəs) *n.* A cornel.

cor·nute (kôr·nōōt′, -nyōōt′) *adj.* Having horns or hornlike processes. Also **cor·nut′ed**. [< L *cornutus* < *cornu* horn]

cor·nu·to (kôr·nōō′tō, -nyōō′-) *n. pl.* ·tos *Obs.* A cuckold. [< Ital.]

Corn·wall (kôrn′wôl, *Brit.* -wəl) A county in SW England; 1,357 sq. mi.; pop. 396,600 (1976); county seat. Truro.

Corn·wal·lis (kôrn·wôl′is, -wol′-), **Charles**, 1738–1805, first Marquis Cornwallis, English general and statesman.

corn whisky Whisky distilled from corn.

corn·y (kôr′nē) *adj.* ·corn·i·er, corn·i·est **1.** *Slang* Trite, banal, sentimental, or unsophisticated. **2.** Of, abounding in, or producing corn.

cor·o·dy (kôr′ə·dē, kor′-) *n. pl.* ·dies **1.** In English history, an allowance, as of food or clothes, provided for sustenance. **2.** A lord's right to lodging by a vassal. Also spelled *corrody*. [< Med.L *corrodium*, var. of *corredium* provision]

corol. or **coroll.** Corollary.

co·rol·la (kə·rol′ə) *n. Bot.* The second series or inner circle of flower leaves, usually colored, forming the inner floral envelope; the petals of a flower collectively. [< L, dim. of *corona* crown]

co·rol·la·ceous (kôr′ə·lā′shəs, kor′-) *adj. Bot.* Pertaining to or like a corolla.

co·rol·lar·y (kôr′ə·ler′ē, kor′-; *Brit.* kə·rol′ər·ē) *n. pl.* ·lar·ies **1.** A proposition following so obviously from another that it requires little or no proof. **2.** An inference or deduction. **3.** A natural consequence; result. — *adj.* Like a corollary; consequent. [< L *corollarium* gift, orig., money paid for a garland < *corolla* garland]

cor·ol·late (kôr′ə·lāt, kor′-) *adj. Bot.* Having a corolla.

Cor·o·man·del (kôr′ə·man′dəl, kor′-) The coast of SE India from the Kistna river to Point Calimere. Also **Coromandel Coast**.

co·ro·na (kə·rō′nə) *n. pl.* ·nas or ·nae (-nē) **1.** A crownlike structure or part, as the top of the head, the upper part of a tooth, etc. **2.** In Greek and Roman antiquity, a wreath awarded for distinguished achievement. **3.** *Astron.* **a** A luminous circle around one of the heavenly bodies, as when seen through cloud or mist. **b** The luminous envelope of ionized gases surrounding the chromosphere of the sun and visible during a total eclipse. **4.** Anything resembling a corona or halo. **5.** *Archit.* The projecting brow of a cornice. **6.** A chandelier suspended from the ceiling of a church. **7.** *Bot.* A crownlike process at the top of the tube of a corolla, as in jonquils. **8.** *Electr.* The luminous discharge appearing at the surface or between the terminals of an electrical conductor under very high voltage, caused by ionization of the air. Compare BRUSH DISCHARGE. **9.** A long cigar with blunt ends. [< L, crown]

Co·ro·na Aus·tra·lis (kə·rō′nə ôs·trā′lis) A constellation, the Southern Crown: also called the *Wreath*. See CONSTELLATION. [< L]

Corona Bo·re·a·lis (bôr′ē·al′is, -ā′lis, bō′rē-) A constellation, the Northern Crown. See CONSTELLATION. [< L]

cor·o·nach (kôr′ə·nəkh, kor′-) *n. Scot. & Irish* A dirge or lament for the dead. [< Irish *coranach*]

Co·ro·na·do (kôr′ə·nä′dō, *Sp.* kō′rō·nä′thō), **Francisco Vásquez de**, 1510–54, Spanish explorer.

co·ro·nal (kôr′ə·nəl, kə·rō′nəl, kor′-) *adj.* **1.** Of or pertaining to a corona or halo, or to a crown. **2.** *Anat.* Having the direction of the coronal suture; as a *coronal* plane. — *n.* A crown or garland. [< F < L *coronalis* < *corona* crown]

coronal suture *Anat.* The suture between the frontal and parietal bones of the skull. For illustration see SKULL.

cor·o·nar·y (kôr′ə·ner′ē, kor′-) *adj.* **1.** Pertaining to or like a crown. **2.** *Anat.* Encircling; especially, designating either of two arteries rising from the aorta and supplying blood to the heart muscle. For illustration see HEART. — *n.* Coronary thrombosis. [< L *coronarius* < *corona* crown]

coronary thrombosis *Pathol.* The formation of a thrombus, or blood clot, in one of the coronary arteries, resulting in interruption of blood supply to the heart muscle.

cor·o·na·tion (kôr′ə·nā′shən, kor′-) *n.* The act or ceremony of crowning a monarch. [< MF, ult. < L *coronare* to crown < *corona* crown]

cor·o·ner (kôr′ə·nər, kor′-) *n.* A public officer whose principal duty is the investigation, with the aid of a jury (coroner's jury), of the cause of deaths not clearly due to natural causes. Abbr. *cor.* [< AF *coruner* officer of the crown < *corune* crown < L *corona*] — **cor′o·ner·ship′** *n.*

cor·o·net (kôr′ə·net, -nit, kor′-) *n.* **1.** A small crown, denoting noble rank less than sovereign. **2.** Any chaplet or wreath for the head; especially, a headband ornamented with jewels, etc. **3.** *Vet.* The upper margin of a horse's hoof. [< OF *coronete*, dim. of *corone* crown < L *corona*]

BRITISH CORONETS

a Heir apparent. *b* Younger sons and brothers of the sovereign. *c* Nephews, etc., of the sovereign. *d* Duke. *e* Marquis. *f* Earl. *g* Viscount. *h* Baron.

cor·o·net·ed (kôr′ə·net′id, -nit·id, kor′-) *adj.* Wearing or entitled to wear a coronet. Also **cor′o·net′·ted**.

Co·rot (kô·rō′), **Jean Baptiste Camille**, 1796–1875, French painter.

corp. or **corpn.** Corporation.

cor·po·ra (kôr′pər·ə) Plural of CORPUS.

cor·po·ral¹ (kôr′pər·əl) *adj.* **1.** Belonging or related to the body: *corporal* punishment. **2.** Personal: *corporal* possession. **3.** *Obs.* Corporeal. — **Syn.** See PHYSICAL. — *n.* The linen cloth on which the elements are placed during the celebration of the Eucharist. Also **corporal cloth**, **cor·po·ra·le** (kôr′pə·rā′lē). [< L *corporalis* < *corpus, -oris* body] — **cor·po·ral·i·ty** (kôr′pə·ral′ə·tē) *n.* — **cor′po·ral·ly** *adv.*

cor·po·ral² (kôr′pər·əl, -prəl) *n.* **1.** *Mil.* A noncommissioned officer of the lowest rank, next below a sergeant. See tables at GRADE. Abbr. *cpl.* **2.** In the Royal Navy, a petty officer assisting the master-at-arms. [< MF, var. of *caporal* < Ital. *caporale* < *capo* head < L *caput*]

corporal punishment *Law* Physical punishment given a convicted offender, as death, imprisonment, or flogging.

corporal's guard 1. The squad commanded by a corporal. 2. Any small or inadequate number of persons.

cor·po·rate (kôr′pər·it) *adj.* 1. Formed by law for the transaction of business; incorporated. 2. Of or related to a corporation. 3. Combined as a whole; considered as one; collective: *corporate* responsibility. 4. Corporative (def. 2). [< L *corporatus*, pp. of *corporare* to form into a body < *corpus, -oris* body] — **cor′po·rate·ly** *adv.*

cor·po·ra·tion (kôr′pə·rā′shən) *n.* 1. A body of persons recognized by law as an individual person or entity having its own name and identity, and with rights, privileges, and liabilities distinct from those of its members. 2. Any group of persons acting as one body. 3. *Informal* A bulging abdomen; paunch.

cor·po·ra·tive (kôr′pə·rā′tiv, -pər·ə·tiv) *adj.* 1. Of or pertaining to a corporation. 2. In political systems, regimenting the major economic functions, as banking, industry, and labor, through corporate bodies of employers and employees selected from principal corporations and controlled by the government: also *corporate.* — **cor′po·ra′tive·ly** *adv.*

cor·po·ra·tor (kôr′pə·rā′tər) *n.* A member, especially an original member, of a corporation.

cor·po·re·al (kôr·pôr′ē·əl, -pō′rē·əl) *adj.* 1. Of, or of the nature of, the body; bodily; mortal. 2. Of a material nature; physical. 3. *Law* Tangible: *corporeal* hereditaments. — **Syn.** See PHYSICAL. [< L *corporeus* < *corpus, -oris* body] — **cor·po·re·al·i·ty** (kôr·pôr′ē·al′ə·tē, -pō′rē-) *n.* — **cor·po′·re·al·ly** *adv.* — **cor·po′re·al·ness** *n.*
— **Syn.** 2. tangible, actual, palpable.

cor·po·re·i·ty (kôr′pə·rē′ə·tē) *n.* Bodily or material existence. [< Med.L *corporeitas, -tatis* < L *corpus, -oris* body]

cor·po·sant (kôr′pə·zant) *n.* St. Elmo's fire. [< Pg. *corpo santo* < L *corpus sanctus* holy body]

corps (kôr, kōr) *n. pl.* **corps** (kôrz, kōrz) 1. *Mil.* a A tactical unit, intermediate between a division and an army, consisting of two or more divisions and auxiliary arms and services. b A special department or subdivision: the Transportation *Corps.* Abbr. *c., C.* 2. A number of persons acting together. [< MF, var. of OF *cors.* See CORPSE.]

corps de bal·let (kôr′ də ba·lā′, *Fr.* bȧ·le′) The ballet dancers who perform as a group and have no solo parts. [< F]

corpse (kôrps) *n.* 1. A dead body, usually of a human being. 2. *Obs.* A living body. [ME *corps,* var. of *cors* < OF < L *corpus* body]

corpse fat *Physiol.* Adipocere.

corps·man (kôr′mən, kōr′-) *n. pl.* **·men** (-mən) 1. In the U.S. Navy, an enlisted man trained as a pharmacist or hospital assistant. 2. In the U.S. Army, an enlisted man in the Medical Corps in a combat area: also called *aidman.*

cor·pu·lence (kôr′pyə·ləns) *n.* An excess accumulation of fat in the body; obesity. Also **cor′pu·len·cy.**

cor·pu·lent (kôr′pyə·lənt) *adj.* Having a great excess of fat; very fleshy. [< F < L *corpulentus* fleshy < *corpus, -oris* body] — **cor′pu·lent·ly** *adv.*
— **Syn.** stout, obese, adipose, portly, pursy. See FAT. — **Ant.** lean, skinny, thin, gaunt, slight, spare.

cor·pus (kôr′pəs) *n. pl.* **·po·ra** (-pər·ə) 1. A human or animal body. 2. A collection of writings, generally on one subject or by one author. 3. *Anat.* The main part or mass of an organ, as of the brain. 4. The principal or capital of a trust fund, estate, etc., as distinguished from the income derived from it. 5. *Ling.* A sample of recorded utterances from which a description or analysis of a language or dialect may be made or by which it may be tested. Abbr. *cor.* [< L]

corpus cal·lo·sum (kə·lō′səm) *pl.* **corpora cal·lo·sa** (kə·lō′sə) *Anat.* A large band of commissural fibers connecting the two halves of the cerebral hemispheres. [< NL, hard body]

Cor·pus Chris·ti (kôr′pəs kris′tē, -tī) In the Roman Catholic Church, a festival honoring the Eucharist on the first Thursday after Trinity Sunday. [< L, body of Christ]

Cor·pus Chris·ti (kôr′pəs kris′tē) A port city in Texas on **Corpus Christi Bay,** an inlet of the Gulf of Mexico in southern Texas; pop. 284,832.

cor·pus·cle (kôr′pəs·əl, -pus·əl) *n.* 1. *Biol.* a Any protoplasmic granule of distinct shape or characteristic function. b One of the particles forming part of the blood of vertebrates, either a **red corpuscle** or erythrocyte, or a **white corpuscle** or leucocyte. 2. A minute particle of matter. Also **cor·pus·cule** (kôr·pus′kyōōl). [< L *corpusculum,* dim. of *corpus, -oris* body] — **cor·pus·cu·lar** (kôr·pus′kyə·lər) *adj.*

cor·pus de·lic·ti (kôr′pəs di·lik′tī) 1. *Law* The essential fact of the commission of a crime, as, in a case of murder, the finding of the body of the victim. 2. Loosely, the victim's body in a murder case. [< L, the body of the offense]

corpus ju·ris (joor′is) *Latin* The body of law. Abbr. *C.J.*

Corpus Juris Ca·non·i·ci (kə·non′ə·sī) *Latin* The collective decrees and canons of the Roman Catholic Church, constituting the standard of canon law prior to 1918, when it was replaced by Codex Juris Canonici.

Corpus Juris Ci·vil·is (si·vil′is) *Latin* The collective body of Roman law, comprising the Institutes, the Pandects or Digest, the Code, and the Novels or new laws, of Justinian, promulgated 528–534.

corpus lu·te·um (loo′tē·əm) *pl.* **corpora lu·te·a** (loo′tē·ə) *Anat.* The hormone-secreting body into which a Graafian follicle is converted immediately after ovulation. [< NL < L, yellow body]

corpus stri·a·tum (strī·ā′təm) *pl.* **corpora stri·a·ta** (strī-ā′tə) *Anat.* One of two masses of ganglionic cells situated in front of the thalamus and at the base of either hemisphere of the cerebrum. [< NL < L, striped body]

corr. 1. Correct; corrected. 2. Correspondence; correspondent; corresponding. 3. Corrupt; corrupted; corruption.

cor·rade (kə·rād′) *v.t. & v.i.* **·rad·ed, ·rad·ing** *Geol.* To erode, as rocks, by the mechanical wear and abrasion of running water. [< L *corradere* < *com-* together + *radere* to scrape, rub] — **cor·ra·sion** (kə·rā′zhən) *n.*

cor·ra·di·ate (kə·rā′dē·āt) *v.i.* **·at·ed, ·at·ing** To converge to a focus, as rays of light. [< COR- + RADIATE]

cor·ral (kə·ral′) *n.* 1. An enclosed space or pen for livestock. 2. Formerly, an enclosure made of wagons for protection against attack. — *v.t.* **·ralled, ·ral·ling** 1. To drive into and enclose in a corral. 2. To arrange in the form of a corral: to *corral* wagons. 3. *U.S. Informal* To seize or capture; secure. [< Sp., a yard, an enclosed space]

cor·rect (kə·rekt′) *v.t.* 1. To make free from error or mistake; set right: to *correct* false notions. 2. To remedy or counteract (an error, malfunction, etc.); rectify. 3. To indicate the error of; mark for amendment: to *correct* proofs. 4. To punish or rebuke so as to improve: to *correct* him for his bad manners. 5. To adjust, as to a standard: to *correct* a lens. — *adj.* 1. Free from fault or mistake; true or exact; accurate. 2. Conforming to custom or other standard; proper: *correct* behavior. Abbr. *cor., corr.* [< L *correctus,* pp. of *corrigere* < *com-* together + *regere* to make straight] — **cor·rect′a·ble** or **cor·rect′i·ble** *adj.* — **cor·rect′ly** *adv.* — **cor·rect′ness** *n.* — **cor·rec′tor** *n.*
— **Syn.** (verb) See AMEND, CHASTEN. — (adj.) *Correct, right, accurate, exact,* and *precise* mean conforming to the truth or some other standard. *Correct* suggests that there are only two possible cases (*correct* and incorrect) and that discrimination between them is easy; it is applied to standards of taste and fashion as well as fact. *Right* is largely interchangeable with *correct,* but often adds a suggestion of moral approval: a *correct* (or right) answer, *correct* dress for a formal dinner, the *right* course of action. *Accurate* suggests that there are degrees of conformity to a standard, and stresses the painstaking care necessary for close conformity: an *accurate* report, an *accurate* measurement. *Exact* emphasizes rigorous agreement with the standard: to give the *exact* figures, to repeat another's *exact* words. *Precise* applies to sharpness of definition: a *precise* statement of principles. — **Ant.** incorrect, wrong, inaccurate, inexact, imprecise, erroneous, faulty.

cor·rec·tion (kə·rek′shən) *n.* 1. The act of correcting. 2. That which is offered or used as an improvement; an emendation. 3. The act or process of disciplining or chastening; punishment. 4. A quantity added or subtracted for correcting: chronometer *corrections.* — **cor·rec′tion·al** *adj.*
— **Syn.** 1. rectification, revision. 3. chastisement, castigation.

cor·rec·ti·tude (kə·rek′tə·tōōd, -tyōōd) *n.* Correctness.

cor·rec·tive (kə·rek′tiv) *adj.* Tending or intended to set right. — *n.* That which corrects. — **cor·rec′tive·ly** *adv.*

Cor·reg·gio (kōr·red′jō), **Antonio Allegri da,** 1494–1534, Italian painter.

Cor·reg·i·dor (kə·reg′ə·dôr) An island in Manila Bay; 2 sq. mi.; site of the surrender of the Philippines by U.S. forces to Japan, May, 1942, in World War II.

correl. Correlative.

cor·re·late (kôr′ə·lāt, kor′-) *v.* **·lat·ed, ·lat·ing** *v.t.* 1. To place or put in reciprocal relation: to *correlate* literature and philosophy. — *v.i.* 2. To be mutually or reciprocally related. — *adj.* Having a mutual or reciprocal relation. — *n.* Either of two things mutually related, especially when one implies the other. [< COR- + RELATE]

cor·re·la·tion (kôr′ə·lā′shən, kor′-) *n.* 1. Mutual or reciprocal relation. 2. The act of correlating. 3. *Biol.* The interplay among parts of an organism. 4. *Physiol.* The combination of nerve impulses in sensory centers resulting in adaptive reactions. 5. *Stat.* A statement of the kind and degree of relationship between two or more variables. Sometimes *corelation.* — **cor′re·la′tion·al** *adj.*

correlation coefficient *Stat.* A numerical measure of the degree of correlation between two variables.

cor·rel·a·tive (kə·rel′ə·tiv) *adj.* 1. Having correlation; especially, mutually involving or implying one another: *correlative* structures. 2. Mutually related in grammatical or logical significance: *Either . . . or* are *correlative* conjunctions. — *n.* 1. One of two correlative things; a correlate. 2. A correlative term. Abbr. *cor., correl.* — **cor·rel′a·tive·ly** *adv.* — **cor·rel′a·tive·ness, cor·rel′a·tiv′i·ty** *n.*
— **Syn.** 1. corresponding, reciprocal, complementary.

corresp. Correspondence.

cor·re·spond (kôr′ə·spond′, kor′-) *v.i.* **1.** To conform in fitness or appropriateness; be in agreement; suit: often with *with* or *to*. **2.** To be similar in character or function: with *to*: The claws of a bird *correspond* to the nails of a man. **3.** To hold communication by means of letters. [< Med.L *correspondere* < L *com-* together + *respondere* to answer]

cor·re·spon·dence (kôr′ə·spon′dəns, kor′-) *n.* **1.** The act or state of corresponding; agreement; congruity; also, analogy; similarity. Also **cor·re·spon′den·cy**. **2.** Communication by letters; also, the letters written. *Abbr. cor., corr., corresp.*

correspondence school A school that offers courses of study by mail.

cor·re·spon·dent (kôr′ə·spon′dənt, kor′-) *n.* **1.** One who communicates by means of letters. **2.** A person employed to report news, etc., from a distant place. **3.** A person or firm that carries on business with another, especially at a distance. **4.** A thing that corresponds; a correlative. — *adj.* Corresponding or suitable; conformable. *Abbr. cor., corr.*

cor·re·spond·ing (kôr′ə·spon′ding, kor′-) *adj.* **1.** That corresponds in character or place; similar or equivalent. **2.** Carrying on or handling correspondence. [< Med.L *corresponsus*, pp. of *correspondere.* See CORRESPOND.] — **cor′re·spond′ing·ly** *adv.*

cor·re·spon·sive (kôr′ə·spon′siv, kor′-) *adj. Rare* Corresponding; conformable. *Abbr. cor., corr.*

cor·ri·dor (kôr′ə·dər, -dôr, kor′-) *n.* **1.** A gallery or passageway, usually having rooms opening upon it. **2.** A strip of land across a foreign country, as one affording a landlocked nation access to the sea. **3.** A long compartment of terrain formed by features such as mountain ranges or ridges. [< MF < Ital. *corridore* < *correre* to run < L *currere*]

cor·rie (kôr′ē, kor′ē) *n. Scot.* A cirque. [< *coire* kettle]

Cor·rien·tes (kôr·ryän′tās) A Province of NE Argentina; 34,492 sq. mi.; pop. 543,226 (1960); capital, **Corrientes.**

cor·ri·gen·dum (kôr′ə·jen′dəm, kor′-) *n. pl.* **·da** (-də) **1.** Something to be corrected, as a printer's error. **2.** *pl.* A list of corrected errors, as in a printed book. [< L, gerundive of *corrigere.* See CORRECT.]

cor·ri·gi·ble (kôr′ə·jə·bəl, kor′-) *adj.* **1.** Capable of being corrected or reformed. **2.** Submissive to correction. [< MF, ult. < L *corrigere.* See CORRECT.] — **cor′ri·gi·bil′i·ty** *n.* — **cor′ri·gi·bly** *adv.*

cor·ri·val (kə·rī′vəl) *adj.* Rival. — *n. Rare* A rival. [< MF < L *corrivalis* < *com-* thoroughly + *rivalis* rival]

cor·rob·o·rant (kə·rob′ər·ənt) *adj.* Corroborating; also, strengthening, as a medicine. — *n.* Something that strengthens or corroborates. [< L *corroborans, -antis*, ppr. of *corroborare.* See CORROBORATE.]

cor·rob·o·rate (kə·rob′ə·rāt) *v.t.* **·rat·ed, ·rat·ing** To strengthen or support, as conviction; confirm. — **Syn.** See CONFIRM. [< L *corroboratus*, pp. of *corroborare* < *com-* together + *robur, -oris* strength] — **cor·rob′o·ra′tor** *n.*

cor·rob·o·ra·tion (kə·rob′ə·rā′shən) *n.* **1.** The act of corroborating or confirming. **2.** That which corroborates.

cor·rob·o·ra·tive (kə·rob′ə·rā′tiv, -ər·ə·tiv) *adj.* Tending to strengthen or confirm. Also **cor·rob·o·ra·to·ry** (kə·rob′ər·ə·tôr′ē, -tō′rē). — **cor·rob′o·ra′tive·ly** *adv.*

— **Syn.** confirming, substantiating, verifying, supporting.

cor·rob·o·ree (kə·rob′ə·rē) *n. Austral.* **1.** A tribal dance of Australian aborigines. **2.** A noisy celebration. [< native Australian name]

cor·rode (kə·rōd′) *v.* **·rod·ed, ·rod·ing** *v.t.* **1.** To eat away or destroy gradually, as by chemical action. **2.** To destroy, consume, or impair (character, strength, etc.). — *v.i.* **3.** To be eaten away. [< L *corrodere* < *com-* thoroughly + *rodere* to gnaw] — **cor·rod′i·ble** or **cor·ro·si·ble** (kə·rō′sə·bəl) *adj.*

cor·ro·dy (kôr′ə·dē, kor′-) See CORODY.

cor·ro·sion (kə·rō′zhən) *n.* **1.** An eating or wearing away. **2.** *Metall.* The gradual breakdown of metals by surface disintegration, chiefly through chemical action. **3.** A product of corrosive action, as rust. [< OF < LL *corrosio, -onis* < L *corrodere.* See CORRODE.]

cor·ro·sive (kə·rō′siv) *adj.* **1.** Having the power of corroding or eating away. **2.** Tending to impair or weaken: a *corrosive* influence. **3.** Having the power to hurt one's feelings, etc.; biting; cutting: *corrosive* wit. — *n.* A corroding substance. — **cor·ro′sive·ly** *adv.* — **cor·ro′sive·ness** *n.*

corrosive sublimate *Chem.* Mercuric chloride.

cor·ru·gate (kôr′ə·gāt, -yə-, kor′-) *v.t. & v.i.* **·gat·ed, ·gat·ing** To contract into alternate ridges and furrows; wrinkle. — *adj.* Contracted into ridges or folds; wrinkled, furrowed: also **cor′ru·gat′ed.** [< L *corrugatus*, pp. of *corrugare* < *com-* thoroughly + *rugare* to wrinkle] — **cor′ru·ga′tion** *n.*

corrugated iron Sheets of iron or steel, usually galvanized, shaped into parallel curved ridges and hollows.

corrugated paper A cardboard with parallel ridges and furrows, used for packing, etc.

cor·rupt (kə·rupt′) *adj.* **1.** Open to bribery; dishonest; venal. **2.** Immoral or perverted; depraved; wicked. **3.** Rotting; putrid. **4.** Tainted; unclean. **5.** Debased by changes or errors; altered, as a text. — *v.t.* **1.** To pervert the fidelity or integrity of, as by bribing. **2.** To destroy morally; pervert; ruin. **3.** To change from the original; debase: to *cor-*

rupt a text. **4.** To contaminate; taint. **5.** To make putrid; spoil. — *v.i.* **6.** To become corrupt; degenerate. *Abbr. cor., corr.* [< OF < L *corruptus*, pp. of *corrumpere* < *com-* thoroughly + *rumpere* to break] — **cor·rupt′er** or **cor·rup′tor** *n.* — **cor·rupt′ly** *adv.* — **cor·rupt′ness** *n.*

— **Syn.** (*adj.*) **1.** crooked. **3.** decayed, decomposed. **4.** defiled, impure. **5.** vitiated. — (*verb*) **2.** deprave. **4.** pollute, defile. **6.** decay, deteriorate, putrefy. — **Ant.** pure, clean.

cor·rupt·i·ble (kə·rup′tə·bəl) *adj.* Capable of being corrupted. — **cor·rupt′i·bil′i·ty, cor·rupt′i·ble·ness** *n.* — **cor·rupt′i·bly** *adv.*

cor·rup·tion (kə·rup′shən) *n.* **1.** The act of corrupting, or the state of being corrupt. **2.** Dishonesty and lack of integrity; also, bribery. **3.** Moral deterioration; depravity; vice. **4.** Physical decay; rot. **5.** Any corrupting influence. **6.** The changing of a text, word, etc., from the original; debasement; also, an instance of this. *Abbr. corr.*

— **Syn. 1.** defilement, perversion. **2.** cheating. **3.** vileness, debauchery. **4.** putrescence.

cor·rup·tion·ist (kə·rup′shən·ist) *n.* One who defends or is guilty of corrupt practices.

cor·rup·tive (kə·rup′tiv) *adj.* Of a corrupting character.

cor·sac (kôr′sak) *n.* A small, yellowish Asian fox (*Vulpes corsac*). also called *dog fox.* [< Turkic]

cor·sage (kôr·sazh′) *n.* **1.** A small bouquet of flowers for a woman to wear, as at the waist or shoulder. **2.** The bodice or waist of a woman's dress. [< OF < *cors* body < L *corpus*]

cor·sair (kôr′sâr) *n.* **1.** A privateer; especially, a privateer of the Barbary States. **2.** Loosely, a pirate. **3.** A corsair's vessel. [< MF *corsaire* < Med.L *cursarius* < *cursus* inroad, raid < L, a running < *currere* to run. Doublet of HUSSAR.]

corse (kôrs) *n. Poetic* A corpse. [< OF *cors.* See CORPSE.]

corse·let (kôrs′lit *for defs.1, 2*; kôr′sə·let′ *for def.3*) **1.** Body armor; also, a breastplate. Also **cors′let. 2.** *Zool.* The thorax of an arthropod. **3.** A light corset, usually without stays. [< MF, double dim. of OF *cors* body. See CORPSE.]

cor·set (kôr′sit) *n.* **1.** A close-fitting undergarment, usually tightened with laces and reinforced by stays, worn chiefly by women to give support or desired shape to the body. **2.** A close-fitting medieval garment. — *v.t.* To enclose or dress in a corset. [< OF, dim. of *cors* body. See CORPSE.]

cor·se·tier (kôr·sə·tyā′) *n. French* A maker or fitter of corsets. — **cor·se·tière** (kôr·sə·tyâr′) *n.fem.*

Cor·si·ca (kôr′si·kə) An island in the Mediterranean, a Department of France; 3,368 sq. mi.; pop. 269,831 (1968); capital, Ajaccio. *French* **Corse** (kôrs) — **Cor′si·can** *adj. & n.*

cor·tege (kôr·tezh′, -tāzh′) *n.* **1.** A train of attendants. **2.** A ceremonial procession. Also *Chiefly Brit.* **cor·tège** (-tezh′). [< F < Ital. *corteggio* < *corte* court]

Cor·tes (kôr′tiz, *Sp.* kôr·tās′) *n.* The national legislature of Spain. [< Sp. < *corte* court]

Cor·tés (kôr·tez′, *Sp.* kôr·tās′), **Hernando,** 1485–1547, Spanish conquistador; conqueror of Mexico. Also **Cor·tez′.**

cor·tex (kôr′teks) *n. pl.* **·ti·ces** (-tə·sēz) **1.** *Bot.* The outer portion of the stem, thalli, or root in plants; especially, the bark of trees or the rind of fruits. **2.** *Zool.* In animals, the outer layer of various organs. **3.** *Anat.* **a** The external layer of gray matter of the cerebrum and cerebellum. **b** The external portion of the adrenal glands, enclosing the medullae and indispensable to proper functioning. [< L, bark]

cor·ti·cal (kôr′ti·kəl) *adj.* **1.** Of, pertaining to, or consisting of a cortex, bark, or rind. **2.** *Physiol.* Designating a process, function, or condition caused by or associated with the cerebral cortex: *cortical* sensibility. [< NL *corticalis* < L *cortex, icis* bark] — **cor′ti·cal·ly** *adv.*

cor·ti·cate (kôr′ti·kit, -kāt) *adj.* Sheathed in bark or in a cortex. Also **cor′ti·cat′ed.** [< L *corticatus* < *cortex* bark]

cor·ti·cose (kôr′ti·kōs) *adj.* Having or like bark. Also **cor′ti·cous** (-kəs). [< L *corticosus* with a thick bark]

cor·ti·cos·ter·one (kôr′ti·kos′tə·rōn) *n. Biochem.* A steroid, $C_{21}H_{30}O_4$, occurring in the adrenal cortex and closely associated with its proper functioning. [< *cortico-* (< L *cortex, -icis*) + STER(OID) + (HORM)ONE]

cor·tin (kôr′tin) *n. Biochem.* A substance containing various hormones of the adrenal cortex. [< CORT(EX) + -IN]

cor·ti·sone (kôr′tə·sōn, -zōn) *n.* A powerful hormone extracted from the cortex of the adrenal gland and also made synthetically. It has a palliative effect upon some forms of rheumatoid arthritis, rheumatic fever, and certain other diseases. [Short for CORTICOSTERONE]

Co·run·na (kō·run′ə) See LA CORUÑA.

co·run·dum (kə·run′dəm) *n.* An aluminum oxide, Al_2O_3, used as an abrasive, second only to the diamond in hardness. Translucent varieties include the ruby and sapphire. [< Tamil *kurundam.* Related to Skt. *kuruvinda* ruby.]

cor·us·cate (kôr′ə·skāt, kor′-) *v.i.* **·cat·ed, ·cat·ing** To give out sparkles of light. — **Syn.** See SHINE. [< L *coruscatus*, pp. of *coruscare* to glitter] — **cor′us·ca′tion** *n.*

cor·vée (kôr·vā′) *n.* **1.** Formerly, an obligation to render feudal service. **2.** Forced labor, particularly for repairing roads. [< F < OF *corovee* < L *corrogata* (*opera*) required (work), pp. of *corrogare* < *com-* together + *rogare* to ask]

cor·vette (kôr·vet′) *n.* **1.** A small, swift warship armed with

depth charges and guns, used chiefly as an antisubmarine escort vessel. 2. Formerly, a warship equipped with sails and a single tier of guns, smaller than a frigate. Also **cor·vet** (kôr·vet′, kôr′vet). [< F < Pg. *corveta,* prob. < L *corbita* (*navis*) cargo (ship) < *corbis* basket]

cor·vi·na (kôr·vī′nə) *n.* **1.** A sciaenoid food fish (*Micropogon undulatus*) found in Atlantic waters from Cape Cod to Texas. **2.** A croaker (*Cynoscion parvipinnis*) of southern California, highly esteemed as a food fish. [< Sp.]

cor·vine (kôr′vīn, -vin) *adj.* Of or pertaining to a crow; crowlike. [< L *corvinus* < *corvus* crow]

Cor·vus (kôr′vəs) *n.* A constellation, the Crow or Raven. See CONSTELLATION.

co·ryd·a·lis (kə·rid′ə·lis) *n.* Any of a large genus (*Corydalis*) of herbs of the fumitory family, with racemes of rose, white, or yellow flowers; especially, the **pale corydalis** (*C. sempervirens*). [< NL < Gk. *korydallis, korydalos* crested lark]

cor·y·don (kôr′ə·dən, -don, kor′-) In pastoral poetry, a name for a shepherd or a rustic.

cor·ymb (kôr′imb, -im, kor′-) *n. Bot.* A flat-topped or convex open flower cluster. For illustration see INFLORESCENCE. [< F *corymbe* < L *corymbus* < Gk. *korymbos* flower cluster] — **co·rym·bose** (kə·rim′bōs) *adj.* — **co·rym′bose·ly** *adv.* — **co·rym·bous** (kə·rim′bəs) *adj.*

cor·y·phae·us (kôr′ə·fē′əs, kor′-) *n. pl.* **·phae·i** (-fē′ī) **1.** In ancient Greek drama, the leader of the chorus. **2.** The chief or leader, as of a chorus, sect, or party. [< L < Gk. *koryphaios* leader of the chorus < *koryphē* head, top]

cor·y·phée (kôr′ə·fā′, kor′-) *n.* A ballet dancer who ranks between the soloists and the corps de ballet. [< F < L *coryphaeus.* See CORYPHAEUS.]

co·ry·za (kə·rī′zə) *n.* **1.** *Pathol.* Inflammation of the mucous membrane of the nose and connecting sinuses; cold in the head. **2.** *Vet.* A contagious bacterial disease of the upper air passages of poultry, characterized by mucus secretions. [< L < Gk. *koryza* catarrh]

cos¹ (kôs, kos) *n.* A kind of lettuce with a cylindrical head of erect, oblong leaves. [after *Kos,* where first grown]

cos² (kôs) See COSS.

cos *Trig.* Cosine.

cos **1.** Companies. **2.** Counties.

Cos (kôs) See KOS.

C.O.S. or **c.o.s.** Cash on shipment.

cosec *Trig.* Cosecant.

co·se·cant (kō·sē′kant) *n. Trig.* The secant of the complement of an acute angle; also, a function of any angle, equal to the distance of a point from the origin divided by the ordinate of the point when the angle is plotted on Cartesian coordinates and the point is on the line forming the angle with the *x* axis. Abbr. *cosec, csc.* For illustration see TRIGONOMETRIC FUNCTIONS. [< CO-² + SECANT]

co·seis·mal (kō·sīz′məl, -sīs′-) *adj.* Pertaining to or designating a line on a map connecting all points at which an earthquake shock is felt at the same time.

co·sey (kō′zē) See COZY. Also **co·sie.**

Cos·grave (koz′grāv), **William Thomas,** born 1880, Irish patriot and statesman.

cosh (kosh) *Chiefly Brit. Slang n.* A blackjack. — *v.t.* To strike with a cosh; bludgeon.

cosh·er¹ (kosh′ər) *v.t.* To pamper; coddle. [? < dial. E (Northern) *cosh* snug, comfortable]

cosh·er² (kosh′ər) *v.i. Irish* To live or be entertained at another's expense. [< Irish *coisir* feast]

co·sig·na·to·ry (kō·sig′nə·tôr′ē, -tō′rē) *adj.* Signing together or jointly. — *n. pl.* **·ries** One of the joint signers of a document: also called *cosigner.* [< CO-¹ + SIGNATORY]

co·sign·er (kō′sī′nər) *n.* **1.** One who endorses the signature of another, as for a loan. **2.** A cosignatory.

co·sine (kō′sīn) *n. Trig.* The sine of the complement of an acute angle; also, a function of any angle, equal to the abscissa of a point divided by its distance from the origin when the angle is plotted on Cartesian coordinates and the point is on the line forming the angle with the *x* axis. Abbr. *cos* For illustration see TRIGONOMETRIC FUNCTIONS. [< CO-² + SINE]

cos·met·ic (koz·met′ik) *adj.* **1.** Used to beautify, especially the complexion. **2.** Tending to improve or restore facial or physical attractiveness: said of certain dental or surgical procedures. Also **cos·met′i·cal.** — *n.* A cosmetic preparation. [< Gk. *kosmētikos* skilled in decorating < *kosmos* order, ornament] — **cos·met′i·cal·ly** *adv.*

cos·me·ti·cian (koz′mə·tish′ən) *n.* One whose business is manufacturing, selling, or applying cosmetics.

cos·me·tol·o·gy (koz′mə·tol′ə·jē) *n.* The study or art of cosmetics and their application. [COSMET(IC) + -(O)LOGY] — **cos′me·tol′o·gist** *n.*

cos·mic (koz′mik) *adj.* **1.** Of or relating to the universe or cosmos. **2.** Relating to the material universe, especially that portion beyond earth or the solar system. **3.** Limitless; vast. **4.** Harmonious; orderly. Also **cos′mi·cal.** [< Gk. *kosmikos* < *kosmos* order, the universe] — **cos′mi·cal·ly** *adv.*

cosmic dust Fine particles of matter collected by the earth from outer space.

cosmic rays *Physics* Radiation of intense penetrating power and high frequency, emanating from outer space and consisting principally of high-energy rays of positively charged particles, and of rays formed from many types of atomic particles, positive and negative in charge.

cos·mism (koz′miz·əm) *n. Philos.* The doctrine that the universe is a self-existent, self-acting system whose characteristics and evolution can be explained in terms of physical science. Compare POSITIVISM (def. 2). — **cos′mist** *n.*

cosmo- *combining form* The universe: *cosmorama.* Also, before vowels, **cosm-.** [< Gk. *kosmos* the universe]

cos·mog·o·ny (koz·mog′ə·nē) *n. pl.* **·nies 1.** A theory concerning the origin, structure, and development of the material universe. **2.** The creation of the universe. [< Gk. *kosmogonia < kosmos* the universe + *-gonia < -gon,* stem of *gignesthai* to be born] — **cos·mo·gon·ic** (koz′mə·gon′ik) or **·i·cal, cos·mog′o·nal** *adj.* — **cos·mog′o·nist** *n.*

cos·mog·ra·phy (koz·mog′rə·fē) *n. pl.* **·phies 1.** The science that describes the universe, including astronomy, geology, and geography. **2.** A general description of the universe or the earth. [< Gk. *kosmographia < kosmos* the universe + *graphein* to write] — **cos·mog′ra·pher, cos·mog′ra·phist** *n.* — **cos·mo·graph·ic** (koz′mə·graf′ik) or **·i·cal** *adj.*

Cos·mo·line (koz′mə·lēn) *n.* A heavy petrolatum, used as a rust preventive: a trade name. Also **cos′mo·line.**

cos·mol·o·gy (koz·mol′ə·jē) *n. pl.* **·gies** The general philosophy of the universe considered as a totality of parts and phenomena subject to laws. [< NL *cosmologia* < Gk. *kosmos* the universe + *-logia* study] — **cos·mo·log·i·cal** (koz′mə·loj′i·kəl) or **cos′mo·log′ic** *adj.* — **cos·mol′o·gist** *n.*

cos·mo·naut (koz′mə·nôt) *n.* An astronaut (which see).

cos·mop·o·lis (koz·mop′ə·lis) *n.* A city composed of people from all parts of the world. [< COSMO- + Gk. *polis* city]

cos·mo·pol·i·tan (koz′mə·pol′ə·tən) *adj.* **1.** Common to all the world; not local or limited. **2.** At home in all parts of the world; free from local attachments or prejudices. **3.** *Biol.* Distributed widely over the world. — *n.* A cosmopolitan person. — **cos′mo·pol′i·tan·ism, cos·mop·o·lit·ism** (koz·mop′ə·līt·iz′əm) *n.*

cos·mop·o·lite (koz·mop′ə·līt) *n.* **1.** One at home everywhere; a cosmopolitan person. **2.** A plant or animal widely distributed over the world. [< Gk. *kosmopolitēs < kosmos* world + *polites* citizen < *polis* city]

cos·mo·ra·ma (koz′mə·rä′mə, -ram′ə) *n.* An exhibition of scenes from different parts of the world. [< COSMO- + Gk. *horama* sight] — **cos′mo·ram′ic** *adj.*

cos·mos (koz′məs, -mos) *n.* **1.** The world or universe considered as an orderly system. **2.** Any harmonious and complete system. **3.** Order; harmony. **4.** *Bot.* Any member of a small genus (*Cosmos*) of the composite family of plants, related to the dahlia. [< Gk. *kosmos* order, the universe]

cos·mo·scope (koz′mə·skōp) *n.* An orrery.

cos·mo·tron (koz′mə·tron) *n. Physics* An accelerator resembling the bevatron. [< *cosmo-* (< COSMIC RAYS) + (ELEC)TRON]

coss (kôs) *n.* In India, a unit of distance varying from one to three miles: also spelled *cos.* [< Hind. *kos* < Skt. *kroça*]

Cos·sack (kos′ak, -ək) *n.* One of a people of the southern U.S.S.R. in Europe and nearby Asia, famous as cavalrymen. [< Russ. *kazak* < Turkic *quzzāq* guerrilla, freebooter]

cos·set (kos′it) *v.t.* To pamper; pet. — *n.* **1.** A pet lamb. **2.** Any pet. [? OE *cot-sǣta* dweller in a cottage]

Cos·sy·ra (kə·sī′rə) The ancient name for PANTELLERIA.

cost (kôst) *v.* cost (*for def. 3, also* cost·ed), cost·ing *v.i.* **1.** To be acquirable for or have the value of a price, sum, consideration, etc. **2.** To be gained by the expenditure or sacrifice of a specified thing, as health, pain, effort, etc. — *v.t.* **3.** To estimate the amount spent for the production of. — *n.* **1.** The price paid for anything; outlay; expense; charge. **2.** Loss; suffering; detriment. **3.** *pl. Law* The charges fixed by law or allowed by the court in a lawsuit; especially, the charges payable by an unsuccessful litigant. Abbr. (n. def. 1, 3) *c., C.* — **Syn.** See PRICE. — **at all costs** (**or at any cost**) Regardless of cost; by all means. [< OF *coster* to be fixed, stand firm < *com-* together + *stare* to stand]

cos·ta (kos′tə) *n. pl.* **·tae** (-tē) **1.** A rib or a riblike structure, part, or marking. **2.** *Entomol.* A longitudinal vein along the anterior part of an insect's wing. [< L, rib]

cost accountant An accountant who keeps track of the costs incurred in production and distribution. — **cost accounting**

cos·tal (kos′təl) *adj.* Of, on, or near a rib or the ribs.

Cos·ta Me·sa (kos′tə mā′sə) A city in SW California; pop. 37,550.

co·star (*n.* kō′stär′; *v.* kō′stär′) *n.* An actor or actress given equal prominence with another or others playing the leading roles in a motion picture, play, etc. — *v.t. & v.i.* **starred, star·ring** To be or cause to be a costar. [< CO-¹ + STAR]

cos·tard (kos′tərd, kôs′-) *n.* **1.** A variety of English apple. **2.** *Archaic* The head: a humorous usage. [? < F *coste* rib; because of its riblike markings]

Cos·ta Ri·ca (kos′tə rē′kə, kôs′tə; *Sp.* kôs′tä rē′kä) A Republic of Central America; about 19,690 sq. mi.; pop. 1,800,-000 (1970); capital, San José. — **Cos′ta Ri′can** *n. & adj.*

cos·tate (kos′tāt) *adj.* Ribbed. [< L *costatus* < *costa* rib]

Cos·tel·lo (kos′tə·lō), **John Aloysius,** 1891–1975, Irish statesman; prime minister 1948–51, 1954–57.

cos·ter·mon·ger (kos′tər·mung′gər, -mong′-, kôs′-) *n. Brit.* A street hawker of vegetables, fruits, etc. Also **cos′ter.** [Earlier *costardmonger* < COSTARD + MONGER]

cos·tive (kos′tiv, kôs′-) *adj.* **1.** Constipated, or producing constipation. **2.** *Obs.* Slow. [< OF *costive* < L *constipatus.* See CONSTIPATE.] — **cos′tive·ly** *adv.* — **cos′tive·ness** *n.*

cost·ly (kôst′lē, kost′-) *adj.* **·li·er, ·li·est 1.** Costing very much; expensive. **2.** Splendid; gorgeous. **3.** *Obs.* Freehanded; lavish. — **cost′li·ness** *n.*
— **Syn. 1.** valuable, precious, dear. Compare SUMPTUOUS.

cost·mar·y (kost′mâr′ē, kôst′-) *n.* A fragrant southern European herb (*Chrysanthemum majus*), used in salads. [< L *costum,* an Eastern plant + *Maria* (the Virgin) Mary]

costo- *combining form* Rib: used in anatomical, surgical, and zoological terms: *costotomy.* Also, before vowels, **cost-.** [< L *costa* rib]

cost of living The average cost, as to an individual or family, of food, clothing, shelter, etc.

cos·tot·o·my (kos·tot′ə·mē, kôs-) *n. pl.* **·mies** *Surg.* The operation of cutting or dividing a rib. [< COSTO- + -TOMY]

cost-plus (kôst′plus′, kost′-) *n.* The cost of production plus a percentage of that cost for profit.

cos·trel (kos′trəl) *n. Archaic & Dial.* A flask or bottle with ears to hang it by, as about the person. [< OF *costerel,* ? dim. of *coster* something at the side, ult. < L *costa* rib]

cos·tume (*n.* kos′tōōm, -tyōōm; *v.* kos·tōōm′, -tyōōm′) *n.* **1.** The mode of dress, including ornaments and hair style, of a given region, time, or class, especially as imitated on the stage and at fancy balls. **2.** The dress of an actor in playing a part. **3.** A set of garments for some occasion or activity: *summer costume.* **4.** Garb; apparel, especially that of a woman. — *v.t.* **·tumed, ·tum·ing** To furnish with costumes. [< F < Ital. *costuma* fashion, guise < L *consuetudo* custom. Doublet of CUSTOM.]

cos·tum·er (kos·tōō′mər, -tyōō′-) *n.* One who makes or furnishes costumes. Also **cos·tum·ier** (kos·tōōm′yər, -tyōōm′-; *Fr.* kôs·tü·myā′).

co·sy (kō′zē) See COZY.

cot[1] (kot) *n.* A light, narrow bed, commonly of canvas stretched on a folding frame. [< Hind. *khāt* < Skt. *khatvā*]

cot[2] (kot) *n.* **1.** A small house; cottage. **2.** A cote. **3.** A protective covering, as a fingerstall. [OE]

cot *Trig.* Cotangent.

co·tan·gent (kō·tan′jənt) *n. Trig.* The tangent of the complement of an acute angle; also, a function of any angle, equal to the abscissa of a point divided by the ordinate of the point when the angle is plotted on Cartesian coordinates and the point is on the line forming the angle with the *x* axis. *Abbr. cot, ctn.* For illustration see TRIGONOMETRIC FUNCTIONS. [< CO-[2] + TANGENT] — **co·tan·gen·tial** (kō′tan·jen′shəl) *adj.*

cote[1] (kōt) *n.* **1.** A small shelter for sheep or birds: used chiefly in compounds, as *dovecote.* **2.** *Dial.* A little house; hut. [OE. Akin to COT[2].]

cote[2] (kōt) *v.t.* **cot·ed, cot·ing** *Archaic* To go around by the side of; pass. [? < F *côtoyer* < L *costa* rib, side]

co·teau (kō·tō′) *n. Canadian* Uplands. [< dial. F. *ana* (*C'dian*)]

Côte d'A·zur (kōt dä·zür′) The eastern Mediterranean coast of France. See RIVIERA.

co·tem·po·ra·ne·ous (kō·tem′pə·rā′nē·əs), **co·tem·po·rar·y** (kō·tem′pə·rer′ē), *etc.* See CONTEMPORANEOUS, etc.

co·ten·ant (kō·ten′ənt) *n. Law* One of several tenants holding the same property under the same title. [< CO-[1] + TENANT] — **co·ten′an·cy** *n.*

Co·ten·tin Peninsula (kō·tän·tan′) A peninsula of lower Normandy, extending into the English Channel; scene of landing (June 6, 1944) of Allied invasion troops in World War II: also *Cherbourg Peninsula.*

co·te·rie (kō′tə·rē) *n.* A small, exclusive group of persons who share certain interests or pursuits: a literary *coterie.* — **Syn.** See CLIQUE. [< F, earlier, an organization of tenants holding land from the same lord < *cotier* cotter < *cote* hut]

co·ter·mi·nous (kō·tûr′mə·nəs) See CONTERMINOUS.

co·thur·nus (kō·thûr′nəs) *n. pl.* **·ni** (-nī) A buskin. Also **co·thurn** (kō′thûrn, kō·thûrn′). [< L < Gk. *kothornos*]

co·ti·dal (kō·tīd′l) *adj.* **1.** Indicating simultaneity in tides. **2.** Designating lines on a chart, atlas, etc., that indicate places where high tide occurs simultaneously. [< CO-[1] + TIDAL]

co·til·lion (kō·til′yən, kə-) *n.* **1.** *U.S.* An elaborate dance marked by frequent change of partners, the execution of complex figures, and the exchange of small favors: also called *german.* **2.** *U.S.* In some cities, a formal ball at which young ladies are presented to society. **3.** A lively, quick dance similar to the quadrille. Also **co·til·lon** (kō·til′yən, kə-; *Fr.* kô·tē·yôn′). [< F *cotillon* petticoat, dim. of *cotte* coat]

Co·to·pax·i (kō′tə·pak′sē, *Sp.* kō′tō·pä′hē) A volcano in north central Ecuador; 19,344 ft.

cot·quean (kot′kwēn) *n. Archaic* **1.** A low, vulgar woman. **2.** A man who meddles with affairs regarded as belonging to women. [< COT[2] + QUEAN]

Cots·wold (kots′wōld, -wəld) *n.* A breed of sheep with long wool, originally bred in the Cotswold Hills.

Cotswold Hills A range of low hills in SW central England; highest point, Cleeve Cloud, 1,031 ft. Also **Cots′wolds.**

cot·ta (kot′ə) *n. pl.* **cot·tas** or **cot·tae** (-tē) A short surplice, with short sleeves or none. [< Med.L *cota* coat]

cot·tage (kot′ij) *n.* **1.** A small house in the suburbs or the country. **2.** *U.S.* A temporary home at a resort. **3.** A small, humble dwelling. [< COT[2]]

cottage cheese A soft, white cheese made of strained milk curds: also called *Dutch cheese, pot cheese.*

cottage pudding Plain cake covered with a sweet sauce.

cot·tag·er (kot′ij·ər) *n.* **1.** One who lives in a cottage. **2.** *Brit.* A rural laborer. **3.** *Canadian* A summer resident.

cot·ter[1] (kot′ər) *n.* **1.** *Scot.* A tenant farmer. **2.** *Irish* A cottier. **3.** A cottager. Also **cot′tar.** [< Med.L *cotarius* < *cota* cottage]

cot·ter[2] (kot′ər) *n.* A key, wedge, pin, etc., inserted to hold parts of machinery together. [Origin uncertain]

cotter pin A cotter in the form of a pin that is split lengthwise so that the ends may be spread apart to hold it in place.

Cot·ti·an Alps (kot′ē·ən) A range of the Alps on the French-Italian border; highest peak, Monte Viso, 12,602 ft.

cot·ti·er (kot′ē·ər) *n.* **1.** Formerly, in Ireland, a tenant of a house and a plot of land at a rental fixed by public competition. **2.** In Great Britain and Ireland, a peasant with a small farm. [< OF *cotier* < Med.L *cotarius.* See COTTER[1].]

cot·ton (kot′n) *n.* **1.** The soft, fibrous, white or yellowish material, of high cellulose content, attached to the seeds of the cotton plant. It is graded chiefly in accordance with the length of the fibers, long-staple and short-staple, and is widely used as a textile. **2.** The cotton plant itself (genus *Gossypium*); especially, in the United States, **upland cotton** (*G. hirsutum*) and **Sea Island cotton** (*G. barbadense*). **3.** Cotton plants collectively. **4.** Cotton cloth or thread. **5.** Any plant substance like cotton. — *adj.* Woven or composed of cotton cloth or thread. — *v.t. Obs.* **1.** To wrap in cotton. **2.** To coddle or pet. — **to cotton to** *Informal* **1.** To become friendly with. **2.** To take a liking to. — **to cotton up to** *Informal* To attempt to please by friendly overtures or flattery. [< F *coton* < OSp. < Arabic *qutun*]

COTTON
a Boll ready for picking.

Cot·ton (kot′n), **Charles,** 1630–87, English author and translator. — **John,** 1585–1652, English Puritan clergyman in America; grandfather of Cotton Mather.

cotton belt *U.S.* The region of the southern United States in which cotton is the chief crop.

cotton boll The seed capsule of the cotton plant.

cotton cake *U.S.* Cottonseed meal pressed into a cake for use as animal feed.

cotton flannel A soft, warm cotton fabric, napped on one or both sides.

cotton gin A machine used to separate the seeds from the fiber of cotton.

cotton grass One of various rushlike plants (genus *Eriophorum*) of the sedge family, bearing cottony spikes.

cot·ton-leaf worm (kot′n·lēf′) The larva of a lepidopterous insect (*Alabama argillacea*), injurious to the cotton plant. Also **cotton worm.**

cot·ton·mouth (kot′n·mouth′) *n.* The water moccasin, a snake.

cotton picker A machine designed to remove the ripe cotton from standing cotton plants.

cot·ton-pick·ing (kot′n·pik′ən) *adj. U.S. Slang* or *Dial.* Blamed; darn: Keep your *cotton-picking* hands to yourself.

cot·ton·seed (kot′n·sēd′) *n.* The seed of the cotton plant.

cottonseed meal Cottonseed ground after the oil has been expressed, used in feeding cattle and as a fertilizer.

cottonseed oil A pale yellow, viscid oil pressed from cottonseeds, used in cooking, paints, and as a lubricant.

cotton stainer Any of a genus (*Dysdercus*) of insects that puncture the developing seeds of the cotton boll and stain them with indelible yellow or red juices.

Cotton State Nickname of ALABAMA.

cot·ton·tail (kot′n·tāl′) *n.* The common American gray rabbit (genus *Sylvilagus*).

cotton tree 1. The cottonwood. **2.** An East Indian tree (*Gossypium arboreum*) that produces a silky cotton.

cot·ton·weed (kot′n·wēd′) *n.* **1.** A perennial herb (*Diotis candidissima*) of the composite family, grown in rock gardens. **2.** The cudweed (which see). Also **cot′ton·rose′.**

cot·ton·wood (kot′n·wōōd′) *n.* Any of several American

species of poplar trees whose seeds discharge a cottony substance, especially *Populus deltoides*: also called *alamo*.

cotton wool   **1.** Raw cotton.   **2.** *Brit.* Absorbent cotton.

cot·ton·y (kot′n-ē)   *adj.*   **1.** Resembling cotton; soft; fluffy.   **2.** Covered with cottonlike fibers.

cot·y·le·don (kot′ə-lēd′n)   *n.*   **1.** *Bot.* One of a pair of the first leaves from a sprouting seed: also called *seed leaf.*   **2.** One of a genus (*Cotyledon*) of ornamental herbs of the Old World.   [< L, navelwort < Gk. *kotylēdōn* socket < *kotylē* a cavity]   — **cot′y·le′do·nous, cot′y·le′do·nal** *adj.*

cot·y·loid (kot′ə-loid)   *adj.* Cup-shaped. Also **cot′y·loi′dal.**   [< Gk. *kotyloeidēs* cup-shaped, hollow]

couch (kouch)   *n.*   **1.** A piece of furniture, usually upholstered and having a back, on which several may sit or one may recline; also, a bed, or any place of repose.   **2.** The floor or frame on which barley is spread in malting.   **3.** A coat of varnish, paint, etc.   — *v.t.*   **1.** To phrase; put into words.   **2.** To imply; suggest.   **3.** To cause to recline, as on a bed.   **4.** To bend or bring down; lower.   **5.** To lower (a spear, etc.) for attack.   **6.** To embroider by laying thread flat along the surface and stitching it down at intervals.   **7.** *Surg.* To remove (a cataract) by pushing down the opaque lens of the eye with a needle until it lies below the line of vision.   **8.** In brewing, to spread out, as steeped barley, to germinate.   **9.** *Obs.* To hide.   — *v.i.*   **10.** To lie down; recline.   **11.** To lie in ambush; hide.   **12.** To lie in a heap or pile, as leaves.   [< OF < *coucher*, earlier *culcher* to put to bed < L *collocare* to set, place. See COLLOCATE.]   — **couch′er** *n.*

couch·ant (kou′chənt)   *adj.*   **1.** Lying down.   **2.** *Heraldry* Reclining with head uplifted, as a lion.   [< MF, ppr. of *coucher.* See COUCH.]

couch grass   A perennial grass (*Agropyron repens*), multiplying injuriously in cultivated grounds by its long rootstocks: also called *cutch, quack grass, quatch grass, quick grass, quitch grass, twitch grass.*   [Var. of QUITCH (GRASS)]

couch·ing (kou′ching)   *n.*   **1.** *Surg.* The operation of removing a cataract.   **2.** Embroidery done by laying heavy threads on a material and securing them with minute stitches.

Cou·é (koo·ā′), **Émile**, 1857–1926, French psychologist.

Cou·é·ism (koo·ā′iz·əm)   *n.* The principle of self-mastery by autosuggestion, advocated by Émile Coué.

cou·gar (koo′gər)   *n.* The puma.   [< F < Tupi]

cough (kôf, kof)   *v.i.*   **1.** To expel air from the lungs in a noisy or spasmodic manner.   — *v.t.*   **2.** To expel by a cough.   **3.** To express by coughing.   — **to cough up 1.** To expel by coughing.   **2.** *Slang* To surrender; hand over, as money.   — *n.* **1.** A sudden, harsh expulsion of breath.   **2.** An illness in which there is frequent coughing.   [ME *cozen, couzen.* Akin to OE *cohhetan* to cough.]   — **cough′er** *n.*

cough drop   A small, medicated lozenge to ease a sore throat or relieve coughing.

could (kood)   Past tense of CAN[1].   [ME *coude,* OE *cuthe* knew how; *l* inserted on analogy with *should* and *would*]

could·na (kood′na)   *Scot.* Could not.

could·n't (kood′nt)   Could not.

couldst (koodst)   Archaic or poetic second personal singular of COULD.

cou·lee (koo′lē)   *n.*   **1.** *U.S.* A deep gulch cut by rainstorms or melting snow.   **2.** *Geol.* A sheet of solidified lava. Also *French* **cou·lée** (koo·lā′).   [< F *coulée* < *couler* to flow]

cou·lisse (koo·lēs′)   *n.*   **1.** A grooved timber, as one in which the wings of a stage setting slide.   **2.** A flat piece of scenery at the side of a stage; also, the space between two such pieces of scenery; wing.   [< F, groove < *couler* to flow, slide]

cou·loir (koo·lwär′)   *n.* A deep gorge or gully on a mountainside.   [< F < *couler* to flow]

cou·lomb (koo′lŏm, -lom)   *n.* The practical unit of quantity in measuring electricity; the amount conveyed by one ampere in one second, equal to 6.3 × 10[18] electrons.   — **international coulomb** The quantity of electricity passing a circuit in one second when the current is one international ampere.   [after C. A. de *Coulomb,* 1736–1806, French physicist]

cou·lom·e·ter (koo·lom′ə·tər)   *n.* An electrolytic cell for measuring the quantity of electricity by the chemical action produced: also called *voltameter.* Also **coulomb meter.**   [< COULO(MB) + -METER]

coul·ter (kōl′tər)   See COLTER.

Coul·ter (kōl′tər), **John Merle**, 1851–1928, U.S. botanist.

cou·ma·rin (koo′mə·rin)   *n.* *Chem.* A fragrant crystalline compound, C₉H₆O₂, contained in Tonka beans, sweet clover, and other plants, and also made synthetically, used as a flavor extract and in perfumery: also spelled *cumarin.*   [< F *coumarine* < *coumarou* Tonka bean, ult. < Tupi]

cou·ma·rou (koo′mə·rōo)   *n.* The Tonka bean.   [< F, ult. < Tupi]

coun·cil (koun′səl)   *n.*   **1.** An assembly of persons convened for consultation or deliberation: a *council* of physicians.   **2.** A body of men elected or appointed to act in an administrative, legislative, or advisory capacity in the government of a city, colony, territory, etc.   **3.** The deliberation or consultation that takes place in a council chamber.   **4.** A gathering of ecclesiastical dignitaries and scholars for the purpose of discussing and regulating matters of church doctrine and discipline.   **5.** The Sanhedrin.   [< AF *concilie* < OF *cuncile* < L *concilium* < *com-* together + *calare* to call; infl. by AF *counseil* < L *consilium* advisory or deliberative body]

Council Bluffs   A city in SW Iowa; pop. 60,348.

coun·cil·man (koun′səl·mən)   *n. pl.* **·men** (-mən)   A member of a council, especially the governing council of a city.

coun·cil·man·ag·er plan (koun′səl·man′ij·ər)   A type of municipal government whose head is a manager chosen by the city council.

Council of Trent   A general council of the Roman Catholic Church, held at intervals in Trent, Italy, from 1545 to 1563. It defined doctrine, reformed many abuses within the church, and condemned the teachings of the Reformation.

council of war   **1.** A conference of military and naval officers to plan strategy, discuss operations, etc.   **2.** Any meeting in which plans of action are formulated.

coun·cil·or (koun′səl·ər, -slər)   *n.* A member of a council. Also *Brit.* **coun′cil·lor.**   — **coun′cil·or·ship′** *n.*

coun·sel (koun′səl)   *n.*   **1.** Mutual exchange of advice, opinions, etc.; consultation.   **2.** Advice given as the result of consultation; opinion on what to do; guidance: to give *counsel.*   **3.** A deliberate purpose; plan.   **4.** A secret intent or opinion: obsolete except in **to keep one's own counsel.**   **5.** A lawyer or lawyers engaged to give advice in a legal matter or to conduct a cause in court.   **6.** A counsel of perfection (which see).   **7.** *Archaic* Good judgment; prudence.   — *v.* **coun·seled** or **·selled, coun·sel·ing** or **·sel·ling** *v.t.*   **1.** To give advice to; advise.   **2.** To advise in favor of; recommend.   — *v.i.* **3.** To give or take counsel.   [< AF *counseil,* OF *conseil* < L *consilium* < *consulere* to deliberate]

counsel of perfection   An advisory declaration made by Christ or one of the Apostles as a guide to the highest morality: also called *evangelical counsel.*

coun·sel·or (koun′səl·ər, -slər)   *n.*   **1.** One who gives counsel; an adviser.   **2.** An attorney at law; advocate.   **3.** A member of the supervisory staff at a children's camp. Also **coun′sel·lor.**   — **Syn.** See LAWYER.

count[1] (kount)   *v.t.*   **1.** To list or call off the units of (a group or collection) one by one to ascertain the total; number; enumerate.   **2.** To list numerals in a progressive sequence up to: to *count* ten.   **3.** To consider to be; judge.   **4.** To take note of; include in a reckoning.   **5.** *Obs.* To ascribe; impute.   — *v.i.* **6.** To list numbers in sequence.   **7.** To have worth; be of importance: Every vote *counts.*   **8.** To have a specified importance: His words *count* for little.   **9.** To be accounted or included.   **10.** *Music* To keep time by counting or beating.   — **Syn.** See CONSIDER.   — **to count in** To include.   — **to count on** (or **upon**) To rely on.   — **to count out 1.** In boxing, to reach a count of ten over (a downed boxer), thus declaring him defeated.   **2.** To omit or exclude; disregard.   — *n.* **1.** The act of counting or reckoning.   **2.** The number arrived at by counting; total.   **3.** An accounting or reckoning.   **4.** *Law* A separate and distinct charge, as in an indictment.   **5.** In boxing, the counting from one to ten seconds, during which time the contestant who is down must get up or lose the fight.   **6.** *Archaic* Attention; heed.   [< OF *conter* < L *computare.* Doublet of COMPUTE.]   — **count′a·ble** *adj.*

count[2] (kount)   *n.* In some European countries, a nobleman having a rank corresponding to that of an earl in England. Abbr. *Ct.*   [< AF *counte,* OF *conte* < L *comes* an associate]

count·down (kount′doun′)   *n.* A reverse counting of time units, reaching zero at the instant when an operation, as a rocket launching, etc., is to be executed; also, the process of preparing a rocket for launching.

coun·te·nance (koun′tə·nəns)   *n.*   **1.** The face or features.   **2.** Facial expression; appearance.   **3.** An encouraging look or expression; also, approval; support.   **4.** Self-control; composure.   — **out of countenance** Disconcerted; embarrassed; abashed.   — *v.t.* **·nanced, ·nanc·ing** To approve; encourage; abet.   [< OF *contenance* < L *continentia* behavior < *continere.* See CONTAIN.]   — **coun′te·nanc·er** *n.*

coun·ter[1] (koun′tər)   *n.*   **1.** An opposite or contrary.   **2.** In boxing, a blow given while receiving or parrying another.   **3.** In fencing, a parry in which one foil follows another in a small circle.   **4.** A piece encircling the heel of a shoe to stiffen and support the outer leather. For illustration see SHOE.   **5.** *Naut.* The curved part of a vessel's stern extending from the water line to the point of fullest outward swell.   **6.** The breast of a horse.   **7.** In type-founding, the depressed part of a type between the raised lines of the character.   — *v.t.* **1.** To return, as a blow, by another blow.   **2.** To oppose; contradict; controvert.   **3.** To put a new counter on (a shoe, etc.).   — *v.i.* **4.** To give a blow while receiving or parrying one.   **5.** To make a countermove.   — *adj.* Opposing; opposite; contrary.   — *adv.* Contrary; in an opposite manner or direction.   [< F *contre* against < L *contra*]

coun·ter[2] (koun′tər)   *n.*   **1.** A board, table, or the like, on which to expose goods for sale, transact business, or serve refreshments or meals.   **2.** A piece of wood, ivory, etc., used in counting, as in billiards. **3.** A piece in chess, checkers, etc. **4.** An imitation coin; token; also, any coin. [< AF *counteour*, OF *conteoir* < Med.L *computatorium* < L *computare* to compute]

count·er³ (koun′tər)   *n.* One who or that which counts; especially, a device or machine for computing.

coun·ter⁴ (koun′tər)   *n. & v.t. Obs.* Encounter. [Aphetic var. of ENCOUNTER]

counter- *combining form* **1.** Opposing; contrary; acting in opposition or response to the action of the main element (sometimes with the idea of outdoing, checking, or reversing that action); as in:

counteraccusation	countermeasure
counteragent	counterorder
counteralliance	counterplan
counterappeal	counterpoison
counterargument	counterproject
counterattraction	counterpropaganda
counterbarrage	counterproposal
counterbid	counterreform
counterblow	counterreligion
counterdeclaration	counterresolution
counterdemand	countersiege
counterdemonstration	counterstatement
countereffort	countersuggestion
counterforce	countertendency
counterhypothesis	countertheory
counterideal	counterthreat
counterinfluence	counterthrust
counterlegislation	countervote

2. Done or acting in reciprocation or exchange; as in:

counterassurance	counterquestion
counterobligation	countersignal
counteroffer	countertoken

3. Complementing or corresponding; denoting the duplicate or parallel (often with the idea of balancing or sustaining); as in:

countercopy	countersecurity
counterfugue	counterstain
counterseal	countertally

4. Opposite in direction or position; as in:

counterapse	counterposition
counterarch	counterpressure
countercurrent	counterpull
counterflight	counterradiation
counterflow	counterstep
countermigration	counterturn

[< F *contre-* < L *contra-* against]

coun·ter·act (koun′tər·akt′)   *v.t.* To act in opposition to; check. **— coun′ter·ac′tion** *n.* **— coun′ter·ac′tive** *adj.*

coun·ter·at·tack (*n.* koun′tər·ə·tak′; *v.* koun′tər·ə·tak′)   *n.* An attack designed to counter another attack. **—** *v.t. & v.i.* To make a counterattack (against).

coun·ter·bal·ance (*v.* koun′tər·bal′əns; *n.* koun′tər·bal′əns)   *v.t.* **·anced, ·anc·ing** To oppose with an equal weight or force; offset. **—** *n.* **1.** Any power equally opposing another. **2.** A weight that balances another; counterpoise.

coun·ter·blast (koun′tər·blast′, -bläst′)   *n.* **1.** An opposing blast. **2.** An answering argument; a denunciation.

coun·ter·change (koun′tər·chānj′)   *v.t.* **·changed, ·chang·ing** **1.** To exchange; interchange. **2.** To diversify; checker. [< MF *contrechanger*]

coun·ter·charge (*n.* koun′tər·chärj′; *v.* koun′tər·chärj′)   *n.* An opposing charge or accusation. **—** *v.t. & v.i.* **·charged, ·charg·ing** To charge in return.

coun·ter·check (*n.* koun′tər·chek′; *v.* koun′tər·chek′)   *n.* **1.** Something that opposes or thwarts a course of action or another check. **2.** That which confirms a previous check, as to accuracy, etc. **—** *v.t.* **1.** To oppose or thwart by counteraction. **2.** To check again; recheck.

coun·ter·claim (*n.* koun′tər·klām′; *v.* koun′tər·klām′)   *n.* A claim that opposes another claim. **—** *v.t. & v.i.* To make or plead (as) a counterclaim. **— coun′ter·claim′ant** *n.*

coun·ter·clock·wise (koun′tər·klok′wīz′)   *adj. & adv.* Opposite in the direction taken by the hands of a clock around the dial; from right to left.

coun·ter·es·pi·o·nage (koun′tər·es′pē·ə·näzh′, -nij)   *n.* Operations and measures intended to detect and counteract enemy spying.

coun·ter·feit (koun′tər·fit)   *v.t.* **1.** To make an imitation of, as money or stamps, with the intent to defraud. **2.** To copy; imitate; also, to feign; dissemble: to *counterfeit* sorrow. **—** *v.i.* **3.** To practice deception; feign. **4.** To make counterfeits. **—** *adj.* **1.** Made to resemble some genuine thing with the intent to deceive or defraud: *counterfeit* money. **2.** Pretended; feigned; deceitful: *counterfeit* sympathy. **—** *n.* **1.** Something, as a coin, made fraudulently to resemble the genuine. **2.** Any imitation or copy. **3.** *Obs.* An imposter. [< OF *contrefet*, pp. of *contrefaire* < L *contra-* against + *facere* to make] **— coun′ter·feit′er** *n.*
— Syn. (adj.) spurious, forged, bogus, false, falsified, sham, mock. **—** (noun) See FORGERY. **— Ant.** genuine, authentic.

coun·ter·foil (koun′tər·foil′)   *n.* The part of a check, money order, etc., kept by the issuer as a record; a stub.

coun·ter·glow (koun′tər·glō′)   *n. Meteorol.* The gegenschein.

coun·ter·in·sur·gen·cy (koun′tər·in·sûr′jən·sē)   *n.* Measures, usually of a military nature, designed to combat guerrilla warfare or to suppress revolutionary activities.

coun·ter·in·tel·li·gence (koun′tər·in·tel′ə·jəns)   *n.* Activities to counter espionage, subversion, and sabotage.

coun·ter·ir·ri·tant (koun′tər·ir′ə·tənt)   *n. Med.* An agent employed to excite irritation in one place so as to counteract irritation or inflammation existing elsewhere.

coun·ter·mand (*v.* koun′tər·mand′, -mänd′; *n.* koun′tər·mand, -mänd)   *v.t.* **1.** To revoke or reverse (a command, order, etc.). **2.** To recall or order back by a contrary command. **—** *n.* An order contrary to or revoking one previously issued. [< OF *contremander* < L *contra-* against + *mandare* to order]

coun·ter·march (*n.* koun′tər·märch′; *v.* koun′tər·märch′)   *n.* **1.** A return march. **2.** *Mil.* A reversal of direction while marching. **3.** Any reversal of conduct or method. **—** *v.t. & v.i.* To execute or cause to execute a countermarch.

coun·ter·mine (*v.* koun′tər·mīn′; *n.* koun′tər·mīn′)   *v.t. & v.i.* **·mined, ·min·ing** **1.** To mine counter to (an enemy); to obstruct secretly. **2.** To destroy mines in (an area) by exploding charges nearby. **—** *n.* **1.** A mine placed so as to destroy an enemy's mines. **2.** A plot to foil another.

coun·ter·move (*n.* koun′tər·mōōv′; *v.* koun′tər·mōōv′)   *n.* A move designed to counter another move. **—** *v.t. & v.i.* **·moved, ·mov·ing** To move in opposition (to).

coun·ter·of·fen·sive (koun′tər·ə·fen′siv, koun′tər·ə·fen′siv)   *n.* A large-scale attack designed to stop the offensive of an enemy and to seize the initiative along an extended front.

coun·ter·pane (koun′tər·pān′)   *n.* A coverlet or quilt for a bed. [Alter. of COUNTERPOINT², after F *pan* quilt]

coun·ter·part (koun′tər·pärt′)   *n.* **1.** Someone or something precisely or closely resembling another. **2.** One who or that which supplements or completes another; a complement; something corresponding but in reverse, as one of a pair of gloves to its mate. **3.** *Obs.* A copy.

coun·ter·plot (*n.* koun′tər·plot′; *v.* koun′tər·plot′)   *n.* A plot designed to foil another plot. **—** *v.t. & v.i.* **·plot·ted, ·plot·ting** To oppose (a plot) by another plot.

coun·ter·point (koun′tər·point′)   *n. Music* **1.** The technique or practice of composing two or more melodic parts to be heard simultaneously; also, the arrangement of parts so composed. **2.** Any of such parts in relation to the principal or predominating part: the theme has several *counterpoints.* **3.** The condition of the melodic parts in such an arrangement: sounding together in *counterpoint.* **4.** The use of complementary or contrasting elements in any form of discourse or art; also, the items so used. [< MF *contrepoint* < Med.L (*cantus*) *contrapunctus* (melody) with contrasting notes < L *contra-* against + *punctus* point, note]

coun·ter·poise (*v.* koun′tər·poiz′; *n.* koun′tər·poiz′)   *v.t.* **·poised, ·pois·ing** **1.** To bring to a balance by opposing with an equal weight or force; counterbalance. **2.** To offset or counteract by equal effort or power. **—** *n.* **1.** A counterbalancing weight. **2.** A counterbalancing force, power, or influence. **3.** A state of equilibrium; balance. [< OF *contrepeser* < L *contra-* against + *pensare* to weigh]

coun·ter·punch (koun′tər·punch′)   *n.* In boxing, a blow or punch that counters another blow or punch. **—** *v.t. & v.i.* To make or give such a blow.

coun·ter·re·con·nais·sance (koun′tər·ri·kon′ə·səns, -säns)   *n. Mil.* Measures to prevent enemy observation.

coun·ter·ref·or·ma·tion (koun′tər·ref′ər·mā′shən)   *n.* A reformation aimed at counteracting a previous one.

Counter Reformation   The reform movement within the Roman Catholic Church in the 16th century in reaction to the Protestant Reformation.

coun·ter·rev·o·lu·tion (koun′tər·rev′ə·lōō′shən)   *n.* A revolution designed to counteract a previous revolution and to reverse its effects. **— coun′ter·rev′o·lu′tion·ar′y** *adj. & n.*

coun·ter·scarp (koun′tər·skärp′)   *n.* The outer slope of a ditch or trench in a fortification: distinguished from *escarp.* [< MF *contrescarpe*, ult. < Ital. *contra-* opposite + *scarpa* slope]

coun·ter·shaft (koun′tər·shaft′, -shäft′)   *n. Mech.* An intermediate shaft driven by a main shaft.

coun·ter·sign (*v.* koun′tər·sīn′, koun′tər·sīn′; *n.* koun′tər·sīn′)   *v.t.* To sign (a document already signed by another), as in authenticating. **—** *n.* **1.** *Mil.* A secret word or phrase to be given a sentry in order to pass; password. **2.** A secret word given in response to another. **3.** A countersignature. [< OF *contresigner*]

coun·ter·sig·na·ture (koun′tər·sig′nə·chər)   *n.* An additional, authenticating signature.

coun·ter·sink (*v.* koun′tər·singk′, koun′tər·singk′; *n.* koun′tər·singk′)   *v.t.* **·sank** or **·sunk, ·sunk** (*Obs.* **·sunk·en**), **·sink·ing** **1.** To cut the edges of (a hole) so that a screw, bolthead, etc., will lie flush with or below the surface. **2.** To sink, as a bolt or screw, into such a depression. **—** *n.* **1.** A tool for countersinking. **2.** A countersunk hole. Abbr. *csk.*

coun·ter·spy (koun′tər·spī′)   *n.* A counterintelligence agent.

coun·ter·stroke (koun′tər·strōk′)   *n.* **1.** A return stroke. **2.** Shock or injury transmitted to a part of the body removed from that which receives the blow.

coun·ter·ten·or (koun′tər-ten′ər) *n.* **1.** An adult male voice higher than the tenor. **2.** A singer with such a voice. [< MF *contreteneur*]

coun·ter·type (koun′tər-tīp′) *n.* **1.** A corresponding or analogous type. **2.** An opposite type.

coun·ter·vail (koun′tər-vāl′, koun′tər-vāl) *v.t.* **1.** To oppose with equal force or effect; avail against; counteract. **2.** To compensate or make up for; offset. **3.** *Archaic* To equal — *v.i.* **4.** To be of avail: with *against*. [< AF *countrevaloir* < L *contra valere* to avail against]

coun·ter·weigh (koun′tər-wā′) *v.t. & v.i.* To counterbalance.

coun·ter·weight (koun′tər-wāt′) *n.* Any counterbalancing weight, force, or influence; a counterpoise. — **coun′ter·weight′ed** *adj.*

counter word A word widely used without regard to its exact meaning, as *nice, awful, fix*.

coun·ter·work (*v.* koun′tər-wûrk′; *n.* koun′tər-wûrk′). *v.t. & v.i.* To work or act in opposition (to). — *n.* Any work or activity in opposition to another, as a fortification.

count·ess (koun′tis) *n.* **1.** The wife or widow of a count, or, in Great Britain, of an earl. **2.** A woman equal in rank to a count or earl. [< OF *contesse*, fem. of *conte*. See COUNT².]

count·ing house (koun′ting) A building or office in which a mercantile or other firm carries on bookkeeping, correspondence, etc. Also **count′ing-house′**.

counting room A room used as a counting house.

count·less (kount′lis) *adj.* That cannot be counted; innumerable. **Syn.** See INFINITE.

count palatine **1.** Originally, a count of the palace of the Holy Roman Empire, with wide judicial powers, and later a nobleman with certain imperial powers in his own province: also called *palsgrave*. **2.** Formerly, in England, an earl or lord who exercised royal prerogatives in his own domain.

coun·tri·fied (kun′tri-fīd) *adj.* Having the appearance, manner, etc., associated with the country or with country people; rural; rustic. Also **coun′try-fied.**

coun·try (kun′trē) *n. pl.* **·tries 1.** A land under a particular government, inhabited by a certain people, or within definite geographical limits. **2.** The land of one's birth or allegiance; fatherland. **3.** The district outside cities and towns; rural areas. **4.** A region of a specified character: mountain *country*; sheep *country*. **5.** The people of a region; the nation. **6.** *Law* A jury. Originally, a jury was summoned from the region in which the facts at issue were supposed to have occurred, the question being submitted to **trial by the country.** A litigant put himself **upon the country.** — **to go to the country** *Brit.* To dissolve Parliament and hold an election, especially after Parliament has failed to give the cabinet a vote of confidence. — **Syn.** See NATION. — *adj.* **1.** Of or pertaining to rural regions; rustic. **2.** Wanting in refinement or polish. **3.** *Dial.* Pertaining to one's country; native. [< OF *contree* < LL *contrata* the region before one, landscape < L *contra* on the opposite side]

country club A club in the outskirts of a town or city, with a clubhouse, grounds, and facilities for outdoor sports.

country cousin A relative from the country, to whom city life is new or confusing.

coun·try-dance (kun′trē-dans′, -däns′) *n.* A folk dance of English origin, in which the partners are in opposite lines.

coun·try·folk (kun′trē-fōk′) *n.pl.* **1.** People who live in the country. **2.** Compatriots; fellow countrymen.

country gentleman A landed proprietor who lives on his country estate.

coun·try·man (kun′trē-mən) *n. pl.* **·men** (-mən) **1.** A man of the same country as another; compatriot. **2.** A native of a particular country. **3.** A man living in the country; a rustic. — **coun′try·wom′an** *n.fem.*

coun·try·seat (kun′trē-sēt′) *n.* A mansion or estate in the country.

coun·try·side (kun′trē-sīd′) *n.* A rural district, or its inhabitants.

coun·ty (koun′tē) *n. pl.* **·ties 1.** A civil division of a state or kingdom, created for political, judicial, and administrative purposes. In the United States, it is the division next below a State except in Louisiana, where it is called a *parish*. In England a county is sometimes called a *shire*. Abbr. *co., Co., ct.* **2.** The people of a county. **3.** *Obs.* The domain of an earl or count. **4.** *Obs.* An earl or count. [< AF *counté*, OF *conte* < L *comitatus* < *comes* count, companion]

county palatine The province of a count palatine.

county seat The seat of government of a county.

county town *Brit.* A county seat: also called *shire town*.

coup (kōō) *n. pl.* **coups** (kōōz, *Fr.* kōō) A sudden, telling blow; a masterstroke; brilliant stratagem. [< F, ult. < L *colaphus* a blow with the fist < Gk. *kolaphos*]

coup de grâce (kōō′ də gräs′) *French* **1.** The mortal stroke, as delivered to a wounded enemy, etc.; death blow; literally, stroke of mercy. **2.** Any finishing stroke.

coup de main (kōō′ də maṅ′) *French* A sudden, vigorous stroke; a surprise; literally, stroke of hand.

coup de maî·tre (kōō′ də me′tr′) *French* A masterstroke.

coup de so·leil (kōō′ də sô-lā′y′) *French* Sunstroke.

coup d'es·sai (kōō′ des-se′) *French* A first attempt; a trial.

coup d'é·tat (kōō′dā-tá′) *French* An unexpected stroke of policy; especially, a sudden seizure of government, often accompanied by violence; literally, stroke of state.

coup de thé·â·tre (kōō′ də tā-ä′tr′) *French* **1.** A theatrical hit. **2.** A theatrical or sensational trick.

coup d'oeil (kōō′ dœ′y′) *French* A quick, comprehensive glance; literally, stroke of eye.

coupe (kōōp, *occasionally still* kōō-pā′) *n.* A closed automobile with two doors, seating two to six persons: also *coupé*. [< COUPÉ]

cou·pé (kōō-pā′) *n.* **1.** A low, four-wheeled, closed carriage with a seat for two and an outside seat for the driver. **2.** A half compartment at the end of a European railway carriage. **3.** A coupe. [< F, pp. of *couper* to cut]

Cou·pe·rin (kōō-praṅ′), **François**, 1668–1733, French composer; called **le Grand.**

Cou·pe·rus (kōō-pā′rəs), **Louis**, 1863–1923, Dutch novelist.

cou·ple (kup′əl) *n.* **1.** Two of a kind; a pair. **2.** Two persons of opposite sex, wedded or otherwise paired, as in dances, games, etc. **3.** *Informal* A few: a *couple* of hours. **4.** Something joining two things together, as a leash for two dogs; coupler; link. **5.** *Mech.* A pair of equal forces acting in opposite and parallel lines, tending to turn a body around without moving it from its place. **6.** A voltaic couple (which see). — *v.* **·led, ·ling** *v.t.* **1.** To join, as one thing to another; link; unite in pairs. **2.** To join in wedlock; marry. **3.** *Electr.* To connect (two currents or circuits) magnetically or directly. — *v.i.* **4.** To copulate. **5.** To form a pair or pairs; pair. [< OF *cople* < L *copula* band, bond]

coup·ler (kup′lər) *n.* **1.** One who or that which couples. **2.** A device that connects objects; especially: **a** A contrivance for linking railroad cars by means of interlocking jaws. **b** A device enabling two or more organ keys or keyboards to play together. **3.** *Electronics* A device for transferring energy from one circuit to another.

coup·let (kup′lit) *n.* **1.** Two successive lines of verse, usually rhymed and in the same meter, forming a single unit. **2.** A pair of similar things. [< MF, dim. of *couple* pair]

coup·ling (kup′ling) *n.* **1.** The act of one who or that which couples. **2.** A linking device; especially, a device for joining railroad cars. **3.** The part of the body of a quadruped joining the hindquarters to the forequarters. **4.** *Electr.* A connection between two circuits, permitting transfer of power from one to the other.

cou·pon (kōō′pon, kyōō′-) *n.* **1.** One of a number of dated certificates attached to a bond, representing interest accrued and payable at stated periods. **2.** A section or detachable portion of a ticket, advertisement, etc., or a certificate given with merchandise, entitling the holder to something in exchange. Abbr. *cps.* [< F < *couper* to cut]

cour·age (kûr′ij) *n.* **1.** That quality of mind or spirit enabling one to meet danger or opposition with fearlessness, calmness, and firmness; bravery. **2.** *Obs.* Heart; spirit; disposition. — **the courage of one's convictions** The courage to act in accordance with what one feels to be right. [< OF *corage*, ult. < L *cor* heart]
— **Syn. 1.** boldness, intrepidity, gallantry, valor, fearlessness, pluck, resolution. — **Ant.** cowardice, timidity, timorousness, fear, fright.

cou·ra·geous (kə-rā′jəs) *adj.* Possessing or characterized by courage; brave; daring: *courageous* words. — **Syn.** See BRAVE. — **cou·ra′geous·ly** *adv.* — **cou·ra′geous·ness** *n.*

cou·rante (kōō-ränt′) *n. Music* **1.** An old, lively dance in triple measure. **2.** The music for such a dance. Also *coranto*: also **cou·rant, cou·ran·to** (kōō-rän′tō). [< F, lit., running (dance) < *courir* to run]

Cour·an·tyne (kûr′ən-tīn) A river on the border of British Guiana and Surinam, flowing about 450 miles north to the Atlantic. Also *Corantyn, Corentyn, Corentyne*.

Cour·bet (kōōr-be′), **Gustave**, 1819–77, French painter.

Cour·be·voie (kōōr′bə-vwä′) A commune in northern France, a suburb of Paris; pop. 57,998 (1968).

cou·reur de bois (kōō-rœr′ də bwä′) *pl.* **cou·reurs de bois** (kōō-rœr′) *French* Formerly, a French or half-breed trapper of Canada and contiguous United States.

cou·ri·er (kŏŏr′ē-ər, kûr′-) *n.* **1.** A messenger; especially: **a** One traveling in haste on an urgent errand. **b** One dispatched on official diplomatic business. **2.** An attendant who arranges the details of a journey for travelers. [Fusion of OF *coreor* runner (< LL *curritor*) and MF *courier* messenger < Ital. *corriere*, both ult. < L *currere* to run]

cour·lan (kŏŏr′lən) *n.* The limpkin, a bird. [< F < S. Am. Ind.]

Cour·land (kŏŏr′land) A region of western and southern Latvia, on the **Courland Lagoon**, a Baltic coastal lagoon: also *Kurland*.

course (kôrs, kōrs) *n.* **1.** Onward movement in a certain direction; advance; progress: to continue our *course*. **2.** The

path or ground passed over: the *course* of a river; a golf *course*. **3.** Line of motion; direction: to take an eastward *course*. **4.** Passage or duration in time: in the *course* of a week. **5.** Advance from one condition or stage to another; progression: the *course* of evolution. **6.** Natural or customary way of proceeding; usual development: The disease must run its *course*. **7.** A series of actions, events, etc., constituting a unit: a *course* of lectures; a *course* of treatment. **8.** Line of conduct: a wise *course*. **9.** A prescribed curriculum of studies leading to a degree: a liberal arts *course*; also, any unit of study in a school curriculum: a history *course*. **10.** A portion of a meal served at one time. **11.** A horizontal row or layer, as of stones in a wall. **12.** *Naut.* **a** A sail bent to the lower yard of a square-rigged mast. **b** A point of the compass. **13.** The pursuit of game with hounds. **14.** A charge or onset of two knights in a tournament. **15.** *pl.* Menstruation. — **in due course** In the proper sequence; at the right time. — **of course** As might be expected; naturally. **2.** Certainly. — *v.* **coursed, cours·ing** *v.t.* **1.** To run through or over. **2.** To run after; pursue. **3.** To hunt (hares, etc.) with hounds. **4.** To cause (hounds) to chase game. — *v.i.* **5.** To move swiftly; race. **6.** To take a direction; follow a course. **7.** To hunt game with hounds. **8.** *Obs.* To engage in a hunt or joust. [Fusion of OF *cours* running (< L *cursus*) and MF *course*, both ult. < L *currere* to run]
cours·er¹ (kôr′sər, kōr′-) *n.* **1.** One who courses dogs. **2.** A dog used in coursing. [< COURSE, *v.* + -ER¹]
cours·er² (kôr′sər, kōr′-) *n. Poetic* A fleet, spirited horse. [< F *coursier* < OF *corsier*, ult. < L *currere* to run]
cours·er³ (kôr′sər, kōr′-) *n.* Any of various ploverlike birds (genus *Cursorius*) of arid regions of the Old World, capable of running rapidly. [< L *cursorius* able to run]
cours·ing (kôr′sing, kōr′-) *n.* The sport of chasing game with hounds that follow by sight instead of scent.
court (kôrt, kōrt) *n.* **1.** An open space surrounded by buildings or walls; a courtyard. **2.** A short street or alley enclosed by buildings on three sides. **3.** An open area or section in a museum or exhibition hall, often roofed with glass. **4.** Formerly, a large building or group of buildings set in a courtyard: now only in proper names. **5.** The residence of a sovereign; palace. **6.** A sovereign together with his council and retinue. **7.** A formal assembly held by a sovereign. **8.** A place where justice is judicially administered. **9.** A tribunal possessing civil, military, or ecclesiastical jurisdiction, and duly constituted to hear cases and render judgments based on law. **10.** The regular session of a judicial tribunal. **11.** A level space laid out for tennis, basketball, squash, or similar games; also, a subdivision of such a space. **12.** Flattering attention paid another to win favor; homage. **13.** Wooing; courtship. **14.** A group of officials or directors of a corporation, company, etc. **15.** A local branch of certain fraternal orders. Abbr. *C., ct.* — **out of court 1.** Without a trial. **2.** Without claim to a hearing. — *v.t.* **1.** To try to gain the favor of. **2.** To seek the love of; woo. **3.** To attempt to gain: to *court* applause. **4.** To invite or tempt: to *court* disaster. — *v.i.* **5.** To engage in courtship. — *adj.* Of or pertaining to a court. [< OF *cort* < L *cohors, cohortis* yard, troop of soldiers. Doublet of COHORT.]
court-bar·on (kôrt′bar′ən, kōrt′-) *n. pl.* **courts-baron** Formerly, a local court held by the steward or lord of a manor. Also **court baron.**
court card *Brit.* A face card (which see). [Alter. of *coat card*]
cour·te·ous (kûr′tē·əs) *adj.* Showing courtesy; polite. — **Syn.** See POLITE. [< OF *corteis* befitting a court < *cort.* See COURT.] — **cour′te·ous·ly** *adv.* — **cour′te·ous·ness** *n.*
cour·te·san (kôr′tə·zən, kōr′-, kûr′-) *n.* **1.** A woman who prostitutes herself to men of wealth and high rank. **2.** Any prostitute. Also **cour′te·zan.** [< MF *courtisane* < Ital. *cortigiana*, fem. of *cortigiano* courtier]
cour·te·sy (kûr′tə·sē) *n. pl.* **·sies 1.** Habitual politeness; good manners. **2.** A courteous favor or act. **3.** Common consent or allowance, as opposed to right: an aunt by *courtesy.* **4.** A curtsy. [< OF *corteisie* < *corteis* courteous]
courtesy title A title of address of no legal validity, given by social custom to the children of peers.
court hand The Gothic or Saxon handwriting formerly used in English public records.
court·house (kôrt′hous′, kōrt′-) *n.* **1.** A public building occupied by judicial courts and public administrative offices. **2.** *U.S. Dial.* A county seat. Abbr. *c.h., C.H.*
court·i·er (kôr′tē·ər, -tyər, kōrt′-) *n.* **1.** A member of a sovereign's court. **2.** One who seeks favor by flattery and complaisance. [< AF *corteour*, OF *cortoyeur* (assumed forms) < OF *cortoyer* to be at court]
court-leet (kôrt·lēt′, kōrt′-) *n. pl.* **courts-leet.** Leet (which see). Also **court leet.**
court·ly (kôrt′lē, kōrt′-) *adj.* **·li·er, ·li·est 1.** Pertaining to or befitting a court. **2.** Elegant in manners; stately; refined. **3.** *Rare* Fawning; servile. — **Syn.** See POLITE. — *adv.* In a courtly manner. — **court′li·ness** *n.*
court-mar·tial (kôrt′mär′shəl, kōrt′-) *n. pl.* **courts-mar·tial 1.** A military court convened to try persons subject to military law. **2.** A trial by such a court. Abbr. *CM.* — *v.t.*

-mar·tialed or **·tialled, -mar·tial·ing** or **·tial·ling** To try by court-martial.
— **general court-martial** The highest military court, consisting of a law officer and five or more members, convened to try the gravest offenses and empowered to deliver a death sentence, a dishonorable discharge, or any other punishment not barred by law.
— **special court-martial** A court-martial, consisting of three or more members, that tries offenses not warranting a general court-martial and delivers sentences of limited imprisonment, forfeiture of pay, or a bad conduct discharge.
— **summary court-martial** The least formal court-martial, presided over by one officer, that tries enlisted men for minor offenses and imposes limited penalties.
Court of Appeals A high court of justice to which cases from lower courts are taken for rehearing. Abbr. *C.A.*
Court of Claims A court at Washington, D.C., having jurisdiction over claims against the government.
Court of Common Pleas 1. A common-law court of record, having original jurisdiction over civil and criminal matters. **2.** Formerly, an English court with exclusive jurisdiction in various classes of civil cases.
Court of Exchequer Formerly, in England, a common-law court dealing with matters concerning the public revenue, and now merged in the Court of King's Bench.
Court of King's Bench In England, a division of the high court of justice, formerly the supreme court of common-law jurisdiction consisting of a chief justice and four puisne or associate justices: when a queen is the reigning sovereign, called **Court of Queen's Bench.** Abbr. *K.B.* (or *Q.B.*)
Court of St. James's See (Court of) ST. JAMES'S.
court plaster Adhesive tape.
Cour·trai (kōōr·trā′) A commune in western Belgium; pop. 42,542 (est. 1959): Flemish *Kortrijk.*
court·room (kôrt′rōōm′, -rŏŏm′, kōrt′-) *n.* A room in which judicial proceedings are held.
court·ship (kôrt′ship, kōrt′-) *n.* **1.** The act or period of courting or wooing. **2.** *Obs.* Courtly behavior.
court tennis See under TENNIS.
court·yard (kôrt′yärd′, kōrt′-) *n.* An enclosed yard adjoining a building or surrounded by buildings or walls; a court.
cous·in (kuz′ən) *n.* **1.** One collaterally related by descent from a common ancestor, but not a brother or sister. Children of brothers and sisters are **first** or **full cousins** to each other; children of first cousins are **second cousins** to each other. A **first cousin once removed** is the child of one's first cousin; a **first cousin twice removed** is the grandchild of one's first cousin, etc. A **second cousin once removed** is the child of one's second cousin, etc. A first cousin once removed is sometimes called a second cousin, a second cousin once removed called a third cousin, and so on. **2.** One of a kindred group or nation: our English *cousins.* **3.** A title of address used by a sovereign to a noble or a fellow sovereign. [< OF *cosin* < L *consobrinus* child of a maternal aunt] — **cous′in·hood, cous′in·ship** *n.* — **cous′in·ly** *adj. & adv.*
cous·in-ger·man (kuz′ən-jûr′mən) *n. pl.* **cous·ins-ger·man** A first or full cousin. [< F *cousin germain*]
cous·in·ry (kuz′ən·rē) *n. pl.* **·ries** Cousins or kindred.
cou·teau (kōō·tō′) *n. pl.* **·teaux** (-tōz′, *Fr.* -tō′) A knife; especially, a long, double-edged knife of the Middle Ages. [< F < OF *coutel, coltel* < L *culter* knife]
couth (kōōth) *adj. Obs.* Known; familiar. Compare UN-COUTH. [OE *cūth*, pp. of *cunnan* to know, be able]
cou·tu·ri·er (kōō·tü·ryā′) *n.* A male dressmaker. [< F] — **cou·tu·riè·re** (kōō·tü·ryâr′) *n.fem.*
cou·vade (kōō·väd′) *n.* A custom among some primitive peoples in which the father of a newly born child observes certain taboos, typically going to bed as though he had borne the child. [< F *couver* to brood < L *cubare* to lie down]
co·va·lence (kō′vā′ləns) *n. Chem.* **1.** A bond formed by the sharing of electrons between the atoms of a compound. **2.** The number of pairs of electrons that can be shared between the atoms of different elements. Distinguished from *electrovalence.* [< CO-¹ + VALENCE] — **co′va′lent** *adj.*
Co·var·ru·bias (kō′vär·rōō′byäs), **Miguel,** 1902–57, Mexican artist and illustrator.
cove¹ (kōv) *n.* **1.** A small bay or baylike recess in a shoreline. **2.** A recess among hills, in a wood, etc.; also, a gap; pass, as through mountains. **3.** A cave in a mountain; cavern. **4.** *Archit.* **a** A concave vault. For illustration see VAULT. **b** A concave molding. **c** A concave curved portion where a ceiling meets a wall. — *v.t.* **coved, cov·ing** To curve over or inward. [OE *cofa* chamber, cave]
cove² (kōv) *n. Brit. Slang* A boy or man; fellow. [< Romany *covo* that man]
cov·en (kuv′ən, kōv′-) *n.* A group of witches; especially, a congregation of thirteen. [< OF *covent* < L *conventus* assembly]
cov·e·nant (kuv′ə·nənt) *n.* **1.** An agreement entered into by two or more persons or parties; a compact. **2.** A solemn pledge made by members of a church to maintain its faith, ordinances, etc. **3.** *Theol.* The promise of God to bless those who obey him or fulfill some other condition. **4.** *Law* **a** A written agreement, as a contract, under seal. **b** A modifying

clause within a contract or deed. **c** An action to recover damages for breach of contract. **— Syn.** See CONTRACT. **— Covenant of the League of Nations** The first twenty-six articles of the Treaty of Versailles. **— National Covenant** An agreement extensively signed by Presbyterians in Scotland, in 1638, to resist by force the introduction of episcopacy by Charles I. **— Solemn League and Covenant** An agreement (1643) between the English and Scottish Parliaments to support Protestantism. *— v.t. & v.i.* To promise by or in a covenant. [< OF, orig. ppr. of *covenir* to agree < L *convenire* to meet together, agree]

cov·e·nant·al (kuv′ə-nan′təl) *adj.* Of or pertaining to a covenant. **— cov·e·nant′al·ly** *adv.*

cov·e·nant·ee (kuv′ə-nan-tē′) *n.* The party to a covenant to whom the promise is made.

cov·e·nant·er (kuv′ə-nən-tər) *n.* One who makes a covenant.

Cov·e·nant·er (kuv′ə-nən-tər, kuv′ə-nan′tər) *n.* A Scottish Presbyterian who adhered to the National Covenant.

cov·e·nan·tor (kuv′ə-nən-tər) *n.* The party to a covenant who assumes its obligations.

Cov·ent Garden (kuv′ənt) A district in central London; site of the Royal Opera House, a theater, and important markets.

Cov·en·try (kuv′ən-trē) A city and county borough in West Midlands, England; pop. 335,000 (1976). **— to send to Coventry** To banish from society; ostracize.

cov·er (kuv′ər) *v.t.* **1.** To place something over or upon, as to protect or conceal. **2.** To provide with a cover or covering; clothe; enwrap. **3.** To invest as if with a covering: *covered* with confusion. **4.** To hide or keep from view; conceal, as actions, facts, or crimes: often with *up*. **5.** To provide shelter or protection for, as from evil or danger. **6.** To occupy the surface of; serve as a cover or covering for; overlay: Snow *covered* the house. **7.** To allow for or have provision for; treat of; include: His speech *covered* the tax problem. **8.** To be sufficient to pay, defray, or offset, as a debt, expense, or loss. **9.** To protect or guarantee against the risk or loss of (life, property, etc.) with insurance. **10.** To incubate or sit on, as eggs. **11.** To copulate with (a female): said of animals. **12.** To travel over; traverse: to *cover* 200 miles in a day. **13.** To aim directly at, as with a firearm. **14.** *Mil.* **a** To provide protective fire for (another person, unit, etc.). **b** To march or stand directly behind (another man). **15.** In journalism, to report the details of, as an event or meeting. **16.** In sports, to guard the activity of (an opponent); also, to protect (an area or position), as one temporarily vacated by another player: The pitcher *covered* first base. **17.** To provide the equivalent of; equal, as the wager of an opponent. **18.** In card games, to play a higher card than (the one previously played). **19.** To place a hat, cap, or the like, on (one's head). **20.** *Archaic* To pardon (an injury, etc.), as by putting out of one's memory. *— v.i.* **21.** To spread over so as to overlay or conceal something. **22.** To put on a hat, cap, or the like. **23.** In card games, to play a higher card than the one led. *— n.* **1.** That which covers or is laid over something else. **2.** Shelter; protection; concealment, as from enemy fire. **3.** Shrubbery, underbrush, etc., that shelters game and wild animals; covert. **4.** Something that veils or disguises; a pretext. **5.** In stamp collecting, an envelope or wrapper that bears a postmark. **6.** The table articles, as plate, silverware, napkin, etc., for one person. **7.** *U.S.* A cover charge (which see). **— to break cover** To come from hiding. **— under cover 1.** Protected. **2.** Secret or secretly. **3.** Within an envelope. [< OF *covrir* < L *cooperire* < *co-* thoroughly + *operire* to hide] **— cov′er·er** *n.*

cov·er·age (kuv′ər-ij) *n.* **1.** The extent to which anything is covered, included, or reported. **2.** The protection afforded by an insurance policy. **3.** The amount, especially in gold, held in reserve to meet liabilities.

cov·er·alls (kuv′ər-ôlz) *n.pl.* A one-piece work garment with sleeves, worn to protect the clothes. Also **cov′er·all.**

cover charge A fixed charge added to the bill at cabarets, hotels, etc., for entertainment or service.

cover crop *Agric.* A crop sown to protect the ground through winter and to enrich it when plowed under in the spring.

Cov·er·dale (kuv′ər-dāl), **Miles,** 1488–1569, English theologian; translated the Bible into English.

covered wagon *U.S.* A large wagon covered with canvas stretched over hoops, used especially by American pioneers for prairie travel; prairie schooner; Conestoga wagon.

cover girl A female model who poses for magazine cover illustrations.

cov·er·ing (kuv′ər-ing) *n.* That which covers, protects, etc.

cov·er·let (kuv′ər-lit) *n.* The outer covering of a bed; a bedspread. Also **cov′er·lid.**

Cov·er·ley (kuv′ər-lē), **Sir Roger de 1.** The principal character in a series of sketches in *The Spectator* by Addison and Steele, an idealized country gentleman of the early 18th century. **2.** An old English country-dance.

covers. *Trig.* Coversed sine.

co·versed sine (kō′vûrst) *Trig.* The versed sine of the complement of an angle or arc equal to one minus the sine: also *versed cosine.* Also **co·ver·sine** (kō′vər-sīn).

cov·ert (kuv′ərt, kō′vərt) *adj.* **1.** Concealed; secret. **2.** Covered over; sheltered. **3.** *Law* Under protection of a husband. *— n.* **1.** A covering. **2.** A shelter or hiding place. **3.** A thicket where game is likely to hide. **4.** Covert cloth. **5.** *pl. Ornithol.* Small feathers overlying the bases of tail and wing quills. For illustration see BIRD. [< OF, pp. of *covrir*. See COVER.] **— cov′ert·ly** *adv.* **— Syn.** (adj.) **1.** clandestine, hidden, stealthy, surreptitious. **— Ant.** overt, open.

covert cloth (kō′vərt, kuv′ərt) A twilled, chiefly woolen cloth of speckled appearance, used for suits, overcoats, etc.

covert coat A short overcoat made of covert cloth.

cov·er·ture (kuv′ər-chər) *n.* **1.** *Law* The legal status of a married woman. **2.** A covering; especially, a shelter or disguise; concealment. [< OF]

cov·et (kuv′it) *v.t.* **1.** To desire eagerly; long for; especially, to desire something belonging to another. *— v.i.* **2.** To feel desire; long or lust. **— Syn.** See DESIRE. [< OF *cuveiter, coveiter,* ult. < L *cupiditas* eager desire < *cupere* to desire] **— cov′et·a·ble** *adj.* **— cov′et·er** *n.*

cov·et·ous (kuv′ə-təs) *adj.* Excessively desirous (of something); avaricious; greedy. **— Syn.** See ENVIOUS. [< OF *coveitus*] **— cov′et·ous·ly** *adv.* **— cov′et·ous·ness** *n.*

cov·ey (kuv′ē) *n., pl. ·eys* **1.** A flock of quails or partridges. **2.** A company; set; bevy. **— Syn.** See FLOCK[1]. [< OF *covee,* pp. of *cover* to brood, ult. < L *cubare* to lie down]

Cov·ing·ton (kuv′ing-tən) A city in northern Kentucky, on the Ohio River; pop. 52,535.

cow[1] (kou) *n., pl.* **cows** (*Archaic* **kine**) **1.** The mature female of a bovine animal (genus *Bos*), especially of the domesticated species. **2.** The mature female of some other animals, as of the whale, elephant, moose, etc. [OE *cū*]

cow[2] (kou) *v.t.* To overawe; intimidate; daunt. **— Syn.** See INTIMIDATE. [< ON *kūga* to tyrannize over]

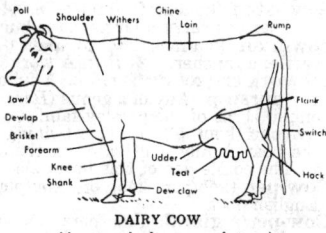

DAIRY COW
(Anatomical nomenclature)

cow[3] (kou, kō) *v.t. Scot.* To cut short; lop off. [Appar. alter. of obs. *coll* to shear]

cow·age (kou′ij) See COWHAGE.

cow·ard (kou′ərd) *n.* One who yields unworthily to fear of pain or harm; a craven. *— adj.* Cowardly. [< OF *couard* < *coue* tail < L *cauda;* with ref. to a dog with its tail between its legs]

Cow·ard (kou′ərd), **Noël,** 1899–1973, English playwright, actor, and composer.

cow·ard·ice (kou′ər-dis) *n.* Lack of courage in the face of danger, pain, opposition, etc.; unworthy timidity. [< OF *couardise* < *couard* coward]

cow·ard·ly (kou′ərd-lē) *adj.* **1.** Lacking courage; ignobly fearful. **2.** Befitting a coward: a *cowardly* lie. *— adv.* Like a coward; meanly. **— cow′ard·li·ness** *n.* **— Syn.** (adj.) **1.** craven, pusillanimous, spineless, yellow. Compare TIMID, FEARFUL. **— Ant.** See BRAVE.

cow·bane (kou′bān′) *n.* **1.** The water hemlock. **2.** A similar plant (*Oxypolis rigidior*) of the eastern United States.

cow·bell (kou′bel′) *n.* **1.** A bell hung around a cow's neck to indicate her whereabouts. **2.** The bladder campion.

cow·ber·ry (kou′ber′ē, -bər-ē) *n., pl.* **·ries** Any of a species (*Vaccinium vitis-idaea*) of trailing evergreen shrubs of the heath family, bearing acid red berries.

cow·bind (kou′bīnd′) *n.* Any of various species of bryony.

cow·bird (kou′bûrd′) *n.* An American blackbird (*Molothrus ater*), often found with cattle. Also **cow blackbird.**

cow·boy (kou′boi′) *n. U.S.* A man, usually working on horseback, who herds and tends cattle on a ranch.

cow camp *U.S.* The camp of a working group of cowboys.

cow·catch·er (kou′kach′ər) *n.* An iron frame on the front of a locomotive or streetcar for clearing the track: also called *pilot.*

cow·er (kou′ər) *v.i.* To crouch, as in fear; tremble; quail. [ME *couren,* prob. < Scand.]

Cowes (kouz) An urban district on the northern coast of the Isle of Wight; a port and resort center; pop. 16,974 (1961).

cow·fish (kou′fish′) *n., pl.* **·fish** or **·fish·es 1.** Any of various small cetaceans, as the grampus, dolphin, etc. **2.** A sirenian. **3.** Any of various trunkfishes with horny projections over the eyes.

cow·girl (kou′gûrl′) *n.* A girl who helps to herd and tend cattle or who dresses like a cowboy.

cow·hage (kou′ij) *n.* **1.** The stinging hairs on the pods of a tropical climbing plant (genus *Stizolobium* or *Mucuna*) of the bean family. **2.** The pods themselves. **3.** The plant. Also spelled *cowage*. [Alter. of Hind. *kawāch*, short for *kawānch*]

cow·hand (kou′hand′) *n.* A cowboy.

cow·herb (kou′ûrb′, -hûrb′) *n.* A smooth-leaved Old World annual (*Saponaria vaccaria*).

cow·herd (kou′hûrd′) *n.* One who herds cattle: also, *Archaic*, *neatherd*.

cow·hide (kou′hīd′) *n.* **1.** The skin of a cow, either before or after tanning. **2.** A heavy, flexible whip, usually of braided leather. — *v.t.* **·hid·ed**, **·hid·ing** To whip as with a cowhide.

cow killer A large, antlike wasp (*Dasymutilla occidentalis*) found in the SW United States.

cowl[1] (koul) *n.* **1.** A monk's hood; also, a hooded garment. **2.** A hood-shaped top for a chimney, to increase the draft. **3.** *Aeron.* A cowling. **4.** The part of an automobile body to which the windshield, instrument board, and the rear end of the hood are attached. — *v.t.* **1.** To cloak with a cowl. **2.** To make a monk of. **3.** To cover with or as with a cowl. [OE *cugele* < LL *cuculla* < L *cucullus* hood]

cowl[2] (koul) *n. Archaic* A large vessel for carrying water. [< OF *cuvele* < L *cupella*, dim. of *cupa* cask, vat]

cowled (kould) *adj.* **1.** Wearing a cowl; hooded. **2.** Shaped like a cowl.

Cow·le·ian ode (kou′lē-ən, -kōō′-) A pseudo-Pindaric ode (which see). [after Abraham *Cowley*]

Cow·ley (kou′lē, kōō′-), **Abraham**, 1618–67, English poet.

cow·lick (kou′lik′) *n.* A tuft of hair turned up as if licked by a cow.

cowl·ing (kou′ling) *n. Aeron.* The covering over or around any section or component of an aircraft. [< COWL[1]]

cowl·staff (koul′staf′, -stäf′) *n. Archaic* A pole by which two persons carry a large water bucket or cowl.

cow·man (kou′mən) *n. pl.* **·men** (-mən) **1.** One who owns cattle; a rancher. **2.** *Brit.* A worker who tends cows.

co-work·er (kō′wûr′kər) *n.* A fellow worker.

cow parsnip Any of a genus (*Heracleum*) of tall, stout, perennial herbs of the parsley family.

cow·pea (kou′pē′) *n.* **1.** A twining herb (*Vigna sinensis*) of the bean family, cultivated in the southern United States. **2.** The edible pea of this herb: also called *black-eyed pea.*

Cow·per (kōō′pər, kŏŏp′ər, kou′pər), **William**, 1731–1800, English poet.

Cow·per's glands (kou′pərz, kōō′-) *Anat.* In males, two small glands near the base of the prostate, that discharge a mucous secretion into the urethra. [after William *Cowper*, 1666–1709, English anatomist]

cow pilot *n.* The pintano, a fish.

cow pony *U.S.* A small horse used in herding cattle.

cow·pox (kou′poks′) *n. Vet.* An acute contagious disease of cows, forming pustules containing a virus that is used in making smallpox vaccine: also called *vaccinia.*

cow·punch·er (kou′pun′chər) *n. U.S. Informal* A cowboy. Also **cow′poke′**.

cow·ry (kou′rē) *n. pl.* **·ries** **1.** A glossy seashell formed by a mollusk (genus *Cypraea*) of warm seas; especially, the **money cowry** (*C. moneta*), used as money in Africa and southern Asia. **2.** The mollusk itself. Also **cow′rie**. [< Hind. *kaurī*]

cow shark A large shark (*Hexanchus griseus*) of European and West Indian waters.

cow·shed (kou′shed′) *n.* A shelter for cows.

cow·skin (kou′skin′) *n.* **1.** The hide of a cow. **2.** Leather made from it.

cow·slip (kou′slip′) *n.* **1.** An English wildflower (*Primula veris*) of the primrose family. **2.** The marsh marigold of the United States. [OE *cūslyppe* < *cū* cow + *slyppe* dung; because it commonly grows in pastures]

cox (koks) *n. Informal* Coxswain. — *v.t. & v.i.* To act as coxswain to (a boat).

cox·a (kok′sə) *n. pl.* **cox·ae** (kok′sē) **1.** *Entomol.* The first joint or body joint of the leg in arthropods. **2.** *Anat.* The hip or hip joint. [< L, hip] — **cox′al** *adj.*

cox·al·gi·a (kok·sal′jē-ə) *n. Pathol.* Pain in the hip. Also **cox′al·gy** (-jē). [< NL < L *coxa* hip + Gk. *algos* pain] — **cox·al′gic** *adj.*

cox·comb (koks′kōm′) *n.* **1.** A pretentious and conceited fop. **2.** A cockscomb. [Var. of *cockscomb*] — **cox·comb′i·cal** (koks·kom′i·kəl, -kō′mi-) *adj.* — **cox·comb′i·cal·ly** *adv.*

cox·comb·ry (koks′kōm′rē) *n. pl.* **·ries** Vain, foppish behavior; silly conceit; also, an instance of this.

cox·swain (kok′sən, kok′swān′) *n.* One who steers or has charge of a small boat or a racing shell: also spelled *cockswain*. [< *cock* (see COCKBOAT) + SWAIN]

coy (koi) *adj.* **1.** Shy and retiring; shrinking from notice: said chiefly of women. **2.** Feigning shyness to attract attention; coquettishly shy. **3.** *Obs.* Disdainful. **4.** *Obs.* Quiet. — *v.i.* **1.** *Archaic* To act coyly. — *v.t.* **2.** *Obs.* To smoke. **3.** To caress. [< MF *coi* < OF *quei* < L *quietus*. Doublet of QUIET.] — **coy′ish** *adj.* — **coy′ly** *adv.* — **coy′ness** *n.*

coy·o·te (kī-ō′tē, kī′ōt) *n.* A small wolf (*Canis latrans*) of western North America: also called *prairie wolf*. [< Am. Sp. < Nahuatl]

Coyote State Nickname of SOUTH DAKOTA.

co·yo·til·lo (kō′yō-tēl′yō, kī′ō-) *n. pl.* **·los** A small shrub (*Karwinskia humboldtiana*) of the buckthorn family, producing poisonous fruit, native in northern Mexico and the SW United States. [< Am. Sp., dim of *coyote*. See COYOTE.]

coy·pu (koi′pōō) *n. pl.* **·pus** or **·pu** A South American aquatic, beaverlike rodent (*Myocastor coypus*), that yields the fur known as nutria: sometimes called *nutria*. Also **coy′pou** (-poo). [< Am. Sp. < native name]

coz (kuz) *n. Informal* A cousin.

coz·en (kuz′ən) *v.t. & v.i.* To cheat, especially in a petty way; deceive. [< F *cousiner* to deceive by claiming kinship < *cousin*. See COUSIN.] — **coz′en·er** *n.*

coz·en·age (kuz′ən·ij) *n.* **1.** The practice of cheating; deception. **2.** A deception; fraud.

co·zy (kō′zē) *adj.* **·zi·er**, **·zi·est** Snugly comfortable. — *n.* A padded cap or cover for a teapot to keep it hot: also called *tea cozy*. Also spelled *cosey, cosie, cosy*: also **co′zey**, **co′zie**. [< dial. E (Scottish) *cosie*, prob. < Scand. Cf. Norw. *kose* comfortable.] — **co′zi·ly** *adv.* — **co′zi·ness** *n.*

cp or **c.p.** Candlepower.

cp. Compare.

CP *Mil.* Command Post.

C.P. **1.** Cape Province. **2.** Chief Patriarch. **3.** Common Prayer. **4.** Communist Party.

C.P. or **c.p.** **1.** Chemically pure. **2.** Court of probate.

CPA or **C.P.A.** Certified Public Accountant.

cpd. Compound.

C.P.H. Certificate in Public Health.

Cpl. *Mil.* Corporal.

cpm or **c.p.m.** Cycles per minute.

CPO or **C.P.O.** Chief Petty Officer.

cps or **c.p.s.** Cycles per second.

cps. Coupons.

CQ *Mil.* Charge of Quarters.

cr. **1.** Created. **2.** Credit; creditor. **3.** Creek. **4.** Crown(s).

Cr *Chem.* Chromium.

C.R. Costa Rica.

craal (kräl) See KRAAL.

crab[1] (krab) *n.* **1.** Any of various species of ten-footed crustaceans (suborder *Brachyura* in the order *Decapoda*), characterized by a small abdomen folded under the body, a flattened carapace, and the ability to walk in any direction without turning, but usually moving sideways. **2.** The hermit crab (which see). **3.** The horseshoe crab (which see). **4.** A crab louse. See under LOUSE. **5.** *Aeron.* The lateral slant of an aircraft needed to maintain a flight line in a crosswind. **6.** Any of various mechanisms for lifting or pulling heavy loads. **7.** *pl.* The lowest throw of a pair of dice. — **to catch a crab** In rowing, to become unbalanced because one's oar has missed the water in making a stroke or has not cleared the water in recovering. — *v.* **crabbed**, **crab·bing** *v.i.* **1.** To take or hunt crabs. **2.** *U.S. Informal* To back out. **3.** *Naut.* To drift sideways. — *v.t.* **4.** *Aeron.* To head (an aircraft) across a contrary wind to compensate for drift. [OE *crabba*. Akin to CRAB[3].]

crab[2] (krab) *n.* **1.** The crab apple or crab tree. **2.** An ill-tempered or querulous person. — *v.* **crabbed**, **crab·bing** *v.i.* **1.** *Informal* To find fault; complain. — *v.t.* **2.** *Informal* To spoil or ruin: he *crabbed* my act. **3.** *Informal* To criticize; disparage. **4.** *Obs.* To anger; irk. [? < Scand. Cf. dial Sw. *scrabba* wild apple.]

crab[3] (krab) *v.i.* **crabbed**, **crab·bing** To claw each other: said of hawks. [< MDu. *crabben* to scratch]

Crab (krab) *n.* The constellation and sign of the zodiac Cancer.

crab apple **1.** A kind of small, sour apple, some varieties of which are used for jellies and preserves: also called *crab*. **2.** A tree (genus *Malus*) bearing crab apples: also called *crab*, *crab tree*.

Crabb (krab), **George**, 1778–1851, English philologist.

Crabbe (krab), **George**, 1754–1832, English poet.

crab·bed (krab′id) *adj.* **1.** Sour-tempered; surly; perverse. **2.** Hard to understand; abstruse. **3.** Irregular in form; cramped: *crabbed* handwriting. [< CRAB[1], n. (def. 1); infl. in meaning by *crab*[2]] — **crab′bed·ly** *adv.* — **crab′bed·ness** *n.*

crab·ber (krab′ər) *n.* **1.** One who fishes for crabs. **2.** A boat used for crab fishing.

crab·by (krab′ē) *adj.* **·bi·er**, **·bi·est** Ill-tempered; peevish. [See CRABBED]

crab grass A low-growing grass (genus *Digitaria*) with freely rooting stems, especially *D. sanguinalis*, a lawn pest.

crab·stick (krab′stik′) *n.* **1.** A cudgel made of crab-tree wood; also, any cudgel. **2.** An ill-tempered person.

crab tree **1.** A tree, as the dogbane, having a bitter bark that is used medicinally. **2.** The crab apple.

crack (krak) *v.i.* **1.** To break without separation of parts; form fissures; also, to break apart or to pieces. **2.** To make a sharp snapping sound, as in breaking. **3.** To change tone abruptly to a higher register; also, to become hoarse: said of the voice. **4.** *Informal* To break down; fail. **5.** *Slang* To speak flippantly; make remarks. **6.** *Dial. & Scot.* To gossip; chat. **7.** *Archaic* To boast. — *v.t.* **8.** To produce fissures in; break partially or completely. **9.** To cause to give forth a short, sharp sound, as in breaking or snapping: to *crack* a whip. **10.** *Informal* To break into; open: to *crack* a safe; to *crack* a bottle. **11.** *Informal* To find the solution of: to *crack* a code. **12.** To cause (the voice) to crack. **13.** *Informal* To strike sharply or with a sharp sound. **14.** *Slang* To tell (a joke). **15.** To break mentally; derange. **16.** To impair or injure, as a reputation. **17.** To reduce by distillation, as petroleum. **— to crack a book** *U.S. Slang* To open, as a textbook, and read or study. **— to crack a smile** *Slang* To smile. **— to crack down** *U.S. Informal* To take severe repressive measures: with *on*. **— to crack up** *Informal* **1.** To smash or destroy, as an airplane or automobile; also,to be in an automobile or airplane accident. **2.** To have a breakdown, nervous or physical. **3.** To praise highly; extol. **4.** *U.S. Slang* To become convulsed with laughter; also, to cause (someone) to laugh uproariously: They *crack* him up. **— to crack wise** *U.S. Slang* To wisecrack. **— n. 1.** A partial break, in which parts are not completely separated; a fissure. **2.** A narrow space: Open the door a *crack*. **3.** A sudden sharp sound, as of a rifle discharging. **4.** *Informal* A resounding blow. **5.** A mental or physical defect; flaw. **6.** A cracked tone of the voice, as when changing at puberty. **7.** *Informal* An attempt; try: He took a *crack* at lifting the weight. **8.** *Informal* A witty or sarcastic remark. **9.** *Informal* A moment; instant: I'll come in a *crack*. **10.** *Informal* One of high skill or excellence. **11.** *Slang* A burglar; also, a burglary. **12.** *Scot.* A chat. **13.** *Archaic* A boast; boasting. **— adj.** *Informal* Of superior excellence; first-class: a *crack* shot. [OE *cracian*]

crack·brain (krak′brān′) *n.* A weak-minded person.

crack·brained (krak′brānd′) *adj.* Foolish; crazy.

crack·down (krak′doun′) *n. U.S. Informal* Swift disciplinary or corrective action.

cracked (krakt) *adj.* **1.** Having a crack or cracks. **2.** Broken to pieces: *cracked* ice. **3.** Damaged or blemished. **4.** *Informal* Mentally deranged. **5.** Uneven in tone: said of the voice.

crack·er (krak′ər) *n.* **1.** *U.S.* A thin, crisp biscuit, usually unsweetened. **2.** *U.S.* A firecracker. **3.** *U.S.* A cylindrical paper roll containing candy, etc., and a weak explosive set off by pulling strips of paper at either end: also **cracker bonbon**. **4.** A person or thing that cracks. **5.** An impoverished white person of parts of the SE United States: a contemptuous term. **6.** *Obs.* A noisy boaster.

crack·er-bar·rel (krak′ər-bar′əl) *adj.* Characteristic of the informal, rambling discussions of those habitually gathered in a country store: *cracker-barrel* philosophy.

crack·er·jack (krak′ər-jak′) *Slang adj.* Of exceptional quality; excellent. **— n.** A person or thing of exceptional merit or skill. Also **crack′a·jack′**.

crack·ers (krak′ərz) *adj. Brit. Slang* Crazy.

Cracker State Nickname of GEORGIA.

crack·hemp (krak′hemp′) *n. Obs.* A gallows bird.

crack·ing (krak′ing) *n. Chem.* A process by which the molecular structure of petroleum or other complex hydrocarbons is changed under pressure by heat, distillation, or catalytic action, so that fractions of high boiling point are broken down to those of low boiling point, important in the production of high-octane gasoline.

crack·le (krak′əl) *v.* **·led, ·ling** *v.i.* **1.** To make a succession of light, sharp sounds. **— v.t.** **2.** To crush or crumple, as paper, with such sounds. **3.** To cover, as china, with a delicate network of cracks. **— n.** **1.** A sound of crackling. **2.** A network of fine cracks produced in the glaze of china, porcelain, etc. **3.** Ware having such an appearance: also **crack′le·ware′** (-wâr′). [Freq. of CRACK, v.]

crack·ling (krak′ling) *n.* **1.** The giving forth of small sharp sounds in rapid succession. **2.** The crisp browned skin of roasted pork. **3.** *pl.* The crisp remains of fat after rendering.

crack·ly (krak′lē) *adj.* Likely to crackle; brittle.

crack·nel (krak′nəl) *n.* **1.** A hard, brittle biscuit. **2.** *pl.* Bits of crisply fried fat pork. [Alter. of F *craquelin*]

crack of doom **1.** The signal announcing the dawn of Judgment Day. **2.** Doomsday; the end of the world.

crack·pot (krak′pot′) *Slang n.* A weak-minded or eccentric person; a crank. **— adj.** Eccentric; foolish; insane.

crack shot *Informal* An excellent marksman.

cracks·man (kraks′mən) *n. pl.* **·men** (-mən) *Slang* A burglar; especially, a safecracker.

crack·up (krak′up′) *n.* **1.** A crash, as of an airplane or automobile. **2.** *Informal* A physical or mental breakdown.

crack·y (krak′ē) *interj.* An exclamation of surprise or delight: usually in the phrase **by cracky**.

Crac·ow (krak′ou, krä′kō) A city in southern Poland, on the Vistula; capital of Poland 1320–1609; pop. 540,200 (est. 1968): Polish *Kraków*.

-cracy *combining form* Government or authority: *democracy.* [< Gk. *-krateia* power < *krateein* to rule]

cra·dle (krād′l) *n.* **1.** A small bed for an infant, usually on rockers. **2.** A place of birth or origin: the *cradle* of liberty. **3.** A framework for supporting something, as a ship while under construction or repair, or a dirigible while being inflated. **4.** A frame to protect an injured limb. **5.** The electrically connected holder for the handset of a telephone. **6.** A scaffolding suspended by ropes. **7.** A frame attached to a scythe to catch the cut grain so it can be laid evenly; also, a scythe with such a frame attached. **8.** *Mining* A box on rockers for washing metal-bearing dirt; a rocker. **9.** A low frame on casters for a mechanic to lie on while working under an automobile. **10.** *Mil.* The part of a gun carriage upon which the gun slides in recoil. **11.** A serrated tool for making mezzotint grounds on a metal plate. **— to rob the cradle** *Informal* To marry or take as a sweetheart one much younger than oneself. **— v. ·dled, ·dling** *v.t.* **1.** To put into or rock in or as in a cradle; soothe. **2.** To nurse in infancy; nurture. **3.** To cut or reap (grain) with a cradle. **4.** To place or support in a cradle, as a ship. **5.** *Mining* To wash, as goldbearing gravel, in a cradle. **— v.i. 6.** To lie in or as in a cradle. **7.** To cut or reap. [OE *cradol*]

cra·dle·song (krād′l·sông′, -song′) *n.* A lullaby (def. 1).

craft (kraft, kräft) *n.* **1.** Skill or proficiency, especially in hand work; loosely, art. **2.** Skill in deception; guile; cunning. **3.** An occupation or trade, usually one calling for manual skill. **4.** The membership of a particular trade or society; a guild. **5.** A vessel or an aircraft: also used collectively. **— Syn.** See OCCUPATION. [OE *cræft* skill, art, strength, courage]

-craft *combining form* Skill; trade; art of: *woodcraft.* [< CRAFT]

crafts·man (krafts′mən, kräfts′-) *n. pl.* **·men** (-mən) One engaged in a craft; a skilled artisan; also, one skilled in the techniques of an art, as in writing. **— crafts′man·ship** *n.*

craft union A labor union limited to workers who perform the same type of work: also called *horizontal union*. Compare INDUSTRIAL UNION.

craft·y (kraf′tē, kräf′-) *adj.* **craft·i·er, craft·i·est** **1.** Skillful in deceiving; cunning; artful. **2.** *Archaic* Skillful; dexterous. **— craft′i·ly** *adv.* **— craft′i·ness** *n.* **— Syn. 1.** shrewd, sly, tricky, wily, foxy.

crag (krag) *n.* A rough, steep, or prominently projecting rock. [ME *cragg* < Celtic. Cf. Irish *creag,* Welsh *craig.*]

crag·gy (krag′ē) *adj.* **·gi·er, ·gi·est** Having numerous crags. Also **crag·ged** (krag′id). **— crag′gi·ness** *n.*

crags·man (kragz′mən) *n. pl.* **·men** (-mən) One who is skilled in climbing crags or cliffs.

Craig·av·on (krāg·av′ən), Viscount, 1871–1940, James Craig, first Viscount Craigavon, Irish statesman; first prime minister of Northern Ireland 1921–40.

Crai·gie (krā′gē), **Sir William Alexander,** 1867–1957, British lexicographer.

Craik (krāk), **Dinah Maria,** 1826–87, English novelist. Also *Miss Mulock.*

Cra·io·va (krä·yō′vä) A city in southern Rumania; pop. 106,276 (est. 1959).

crake (krāk) *n.* Any of various small, harsh-voiced birds of the rail family, as the corn crake. [< ON *kraka* crow]

cram (kram) *v.* **crammed, cram·ming** *v.t.* **1.** To force into an inadequate space; stuff. **2.** To fill or pack tightly. **3.** To feed to excess. **4.** To force (information) into the mind, or to fill (a person or his mind) with information, as in intensive study for an examination. **— v.i. 5.** To eat greedily; stuff oneself with food. **6.** To engage in intensive, hurried study. **— n. 1.** The act or process of cramming. **2.** A crowded condition; a crush. **3.** Knowledge gained by cramming. [OE *crammian* to stuff] **— cram′mer** *n.*

Cram (kram), **Ralph Adams,** 1863–1942, U.S. architect.

cram·bo (kram′bō) *n.* **1.** A word game in which a rhyme must be found to a word or line given by another. **2.** Rhyme: a contemptuous use. [Alter. of L *crambe* cabbage (< Gk. *krambē*) in phrase *crambe repetita* an unpleasant repetition, lit., cabbage served over]

cram·oi·sy (kram′oi·zē, kram′ə·zē) *Archaic adj.* Crimson. **— n.** Crimson cloth. Also **cram/oi·sie.** [< OF *crameisi, cramoisi,* ult. < Arabic *qirmazī.* See CRIMSON.]

cramp¹ (kramp) *n.* **1.** An involuntary, sudden, painful muscular contraction, as in a leg, often caused by strain or sudden chill. **2.** A paralysis of local muscles caused by continued overexertion: writer's *cramp.* **3.** *pl.* Acute abdominal pains. **— v.t.** To affect with a cramp. [< OF *crampe* < LG. Related to CRAMP².]

cramp² (kramp) *n.* **1.** An iron bar bent at both ends, used to bind two stones, timbers, etc., together: also **cramp iron. 2.** An adjustable frame in which pieces may be held or forced together, as in making a joint; a clamp. **3.** Anything that presses or confines; also, a confined position or state. **— v.t. 1.** To fasten with a cramp. **2.** To restrain or confine; hamper. **3.** To deflect (the wheel of a vehicle) in making a turn; also, to jam (a wheel) by turning too short. **— to cramp one's style** *Slang* To hamper one's customary skill or self-confidence. — *adj.* **1.** Narrowed; contracted. **2.** Difficult to make out; crabbed, as handwriting. [ME, appar. < LG. Cf. MDu. *krampe* hook.]

cramp·fish (kramp′fish′) *n. pl.* **·fish** or **·fish·es** The electric ray.

cram·pon (kram′pən) *n.* **1.** A pair of hooked pieces of iron for raising heavy stones, etc. **2.** *Usually pl.* An iron attachment for the shoe to aid in walking on ice or in climbing. Also **cram·poon** (kram-pōōn′). [< MF *crampe* hook < LG. Related to CRAMP².]

CRAMPON (def. 2)

Cra·nach (krä′näkh), **Lucas,** 1472–1553, German painter and engraver. Also *Kranach.*

cran·ber·ry (kran′ber′ē, -bər-ē) *n. pl.* **·ries 1.** The edible, scarlet, acid berry of a plant (*Vaccinium macrocarpum*) growing in marshy land. **2.** The plant itself. — **small cranberry** The common Old World cranberry (*V. oxycoccus*). [Prob. < LG. Cf. *kranebere.*]

cranberry tree The guelder-rose. Also **cranberry bush.**

crane (krān) *n.* **1.** One of a family (*Gruidae*) of large, long-necked, long-legged birds, as the **sandhill crane** (*Grus canadensis*), and the rare **whooping crane** (*G. americana*) of North America. **2.** Loosely, any of various herons or cormorants, as the great blue heron. **3.** A hoisting machine, usually having a projecting movable arm, by which a heavy object can be raised and moved. **4.** Any arm swinging horizontally, by which something is suspended, as a pot over a fire. — *v.* **craned, cran·ing** *v.t.* **1.** To stretch out (one's neck) as a crane does. **2.** To lift or move by or as if by a crane. — *v.i.* **3.** To stretch out one's neck. **4.** To halt and lean forward, as a horse at a jump; also, to hesitate. [OE *cran*]

Crane (krān) *n.* The constellation Grus.

Crane (krān), **(Harold) Hart,** 1899–1932, U.S. poet. — **(Robert) Bruce,** 1857–1937, U.S. painter. — **Stephen,** 1871–1900, U.S. novelist and short-story writer. — **Walter,** 1845–1915, English painter and illustrator.

crane·bill (krān′bil′) *n.* Any species of geranium; especially, the **spotted cranebill** (*Geranium maculatum*), the root of which is used in medicine: also called *alumroot.* Also **cranes·bill′** (krānz′bil′), **crane's′-bill′.** [< CRANE + BILL², so called from the appearance of its fruit]

crane fly A fly (family *Tipulidae*) with very long, slender legs, resembling a large mosquito: in England often called *daddy-longlegs.*

Cran·ford (kran′fərd) An urban township in eastern New Jersey; pop. 27,391.

cra·ni·al (krā′nē·əl) *adj.* Of or pertaining to the skull.

cranial index A measure analogous to the cephalic index, but taken against the skull instead of the head.

cra·ni·ate (krā′nē·it, -āt) *adj.* Having a cranium. — *n.* Any of a primary division (*Craniata*) of the phylum *Chordata*, that includes all vertebrates having a skull, as fishes, reptiles, birds, and mammals. [< NL *craniata* < Med.L *cranium.* See CRANIUM.]

cranio- *combining form* Cranium; cranial: *craniometer.* Also, before vowels, **crani-.** [< Med.L *cranium* skull < Gk. *kranion*]

craniol. Craniological; craniology.

cra·ni·ol·o·gy (krā′nē·ol′ə·jē) *n.* The branch of anatomy and medicine that treats of the structure and characteristics of skulls. [< CRANIO- + -LOGY] — **cra·ni·o·log·i·cal** (krā′nē·ə·loj′i·kəl) *adj.* — **cra·ni·ol′o·gist** *n.*

craniom. Craniometry.

cra·ni·om·e·ter (krā′nē·om′ə·tər) *n.* An instrument for measuring skulls. [< CRANIO- + -METER] — **cra·ni·o·met·ric** (krā′nē·ə·met′rik) or **·ri·cal** *adj.* — **cra·ni·o·met′ri·cal·ly** *adv.* — **cra·ni·om′e·try** *n.*

cra·ni·o·sa·cral (krā′nē·ō·sā′krəl) *adj.* Parasympathetic.

cra·ni·ot·o·my (krā′nē·ot′ə·mē) *n. pl.* **·mies** *Surg.* An operation on the cranium, as for brain surgery. [< CRANIO- + -TOMY]

cra·ni·um (krā′nē·əm) *n. pl.* **·ni·ums** or **·ni·a** (-nē-ə) **1.** The skull of an animal. **2.** The part of the skull enclosing the brain; the brainpan. [< Med.L < Gk. *kranion* skull]

crank¹ (krangk) *n.* **1.** A device for transmitting motion, usually a handle attached at right angles to a shaft. **2.** *Informal* One given to eccentric or hostile behavior. **3.** *Informal* A grouchy, ill-tempered person. **4.** A fantastic turn of speech; conceit. **5.** A perverse notion or action; whim. **6.** *Obs.* A bend. — *v.t.* **1.** To bend into the shape of a crank. **2.** To furnish with a crank. **3.** To start or operate by a crank. — *v.i.* **4.** To turn a crank. **5.** *Obs.* To bend; twist. [OE *cranc*, as in *crancstæf* a weaving comb]

crank² (krangk) *adj. Naut.* Liable to heel or capsize: also **cranky.** [Earlier *crank-sided* < Du. *krengd* heeled over < *krengan* to push]

crank³ (krangk) *adj. Dial.* Spirited; lively. [Origin uncertain]

crank-case (krangk′kās′) *n. Mech.* The case enclosing an engine crankshaft, as of an automobile.

cran·kle (krang′kəl) *n.* A bend; crinkle. — *v.t. & v.i.* **·kled, ·kling** To bend; crinkle. [Dim. of CRANK¹]

crank·ous (krang′kəs) *adj. Scot.* Irritable; cranky.

crank·pin (krangk′pin′) *n. Mech.* The round pin that joins a connecting rod to the crankshaft.

crank·shaft (krangk′shaft′, -shäft′) *n. Mech.* A shaft driven by or driving a crank.

crank·y (krang′kē) *adj.* **crank·i·er, crank·i·est 1.** Irritable; peevish. **2.** Eccentric; queer. **3.** Loose and rickety; shaky. **4.** Full of turns; crooked. **5.** *Naut.* Liable to heel; top-heavy: also *crank.* [< CRANK¹] — **crank′i·ly** *adv.* — **crank′i·ness** *n.*
— **Syn. 1.** cross, irascible, testy.

Cran·mer (kran′mər), **Thomas,** 1489–1556, English church reformer; Anglican archbishop of Canterbury; executed.

cran·nog (kran′əg) *n.* In Scotland and Ireland, an ancient lake dwelling built on pilings or on an island. [< Irish < *crann* tree, timber]

cran·ny (kran′ē) *n. pl.* **·nies** A narrow opening; a crevice, or chink. [? < OF *cran, cren* notch] — **cran′nied** *adj.*

Cran·ston (kran′stən) A city in eastern Rhode Island; pop. 66,766.

crap (krap) *U.S. n.* **1.** The game of craps. **2.** A losing throw in craps, as a two, three, or twelve. **3.** *Slang* Statements that lie, mislead, or exaggerate; bull. **4.** *Slang* Anything worthless or inferior; junk. **5.** *Slang* Excrement. — **to crap out 1.** In craps, to throw a seven before making one's point, thereby losing the throw and the dice. **2.** *Slang* To fail in any way. [See CRAPS]

crape (krāp) See CREPE.

crape·hang·er (krāp′hang′ər) See CREPEHANGER.

crap·pie (krap′ē) *n. pl.* **·pies** or **·pie** An edible fresh-water fish (*Pomoxis annularis*) of the central United States: also called *bachelor.* [Origin unknown]

craps (kraps) *n.pl.* (construed as sing.) *U.S.* A game of chance, played with two dice. [< F *crabs, craps* < E *crabs,* the lowest throw (two aces) in hazard]

crap·shoot·er (krap′shoo′tər) *n. U.S.* One who plays the game of craps.

crap·u·lence (krap′yoo·ləns) *n.* **1.** Sickness caused by eating or drinking too much. **2.** Gross intemperance, especially in drinking.

crap·u·lent (krap′yoo·lənt) *adj.* **1.** Grossly intemperate in eating or drinking; drunken; gluttonous. **2.** Sick from eating or drinking too much. Also **crap′u·lous.** [< LL *crapulentus* very drunk < L *crapula* drunkenness < Gk. *kraipalē* drunken headache]

crash¹ (krash) *v.i.* **1.** To break to pieces with a loud noise. **2.** To suffer damage or destruction, as by falling to earth or by striking an obstacle: said of an airplane, automobile, etc. **3.** To make a loud, sharp noise of clattering or breaking. **4.** To move with such a noise: to *crash* through the sound barrier. **5.** To fail or come to ruin; collapse. — *v.t.* **6.** To dash violently to pieces; smash. **7.** To force or drive with a sound of crashing. **8.** To cause (an airplane, automobile, etc.) to crash. **9.** *Informal* To enter without invitation or without paying admission: to *crash* a party. — *n.* **1.** A loud noise, as of things being violently broken. **2.** A sudden crashing or breaking. **3.** A sudden collapse, as of a business enterprise. **4.** The act of crashing, as of an airplane, automobile, etc. — *adj. U.S. Informal* Of, pertaining to, or resembling a crash program. [Imit.]

crash² (krash) *n.* A coarse fabric woven of thick, uneven yarns, used for towels, etc. [? < Russian *krashenina*]

Crash·aw (krash′ô), **Richard,** 1613?–49, English poet.

crash dive *Naval* The quick submergence of a submarine, usually to escape detection or attack.

crash helmet A heavy, padded helmet worn to prevent injury from impact.

crash landing A landing of an airplane, especially in an emergency, in which the airplane suffers damage.

crash pad A room or apartment maintained by one or more tenants as an emergency stopping place for friends and acquaintances.

crash program *U.S. Informal* An intensive emergency undertaking in government, science, etc., having priority over all others. Also **crash project.**

cra·sis (krā′sis) *n.* Syneresis (def. 1). [< Gk. *krasis* mixture]

crass (kras) *adj.* **1.** Grossly vulgar or stupid. **2.** Coarse or thick. [< L *crassus* thick] — **crass′ly** *adv.* — **crass′ness** *n.*

cras·si·tude (kras′ə·tood, -tyood) *n.* **1.** Gross ignorance; extreme stupidity. **2.** Grossness; coarseness.

cras·su·la·ceous (kras′yoo·lā′shəs) *adj. Bot.* Of or pertaining to the orpine family (*Crassulaceae*) of usually succulent herbs, including the sedums and houseleeks. [< NL *Crassulaceae* < L *crassus* thick]

Cras·sus (kras′əs), **Marcus Licinius,** 115?–53 B.C., Roman financier and triumvir with Julius Caesar and Pompey.

-crat *combining form* A supporter or member of a social class or of a type of government: *democrat, aristocrat.* See -CRACY. [< F *-crate* < Gk. *-kratēs* < *krateein* to rule, govern]

cratch (krach) *n. Dial.* A crib or rack for fodder; a manger. [< OF *creche.* Akin to CRIB.]

crate (krāt) *n.* **1.** A protective case or framework of slats in which to pack something for shipment. **2.** A packing box.

3. A large wickerwork hamper. **4.** *Slang* A decrepit vehicle. — *v.t.* **crat·ed, crat·ing** To pack in a crate. [Prob. < L *cratis* wickerwork. Doublet of GRATE².] — **crat'er** *n.*

cra·ter (krā'tər) *n.* **1.** A bowl-shaped depression at the outlet of a volcano or hot spring. **2.** Any similar cavity, as one resulting from the explosion of a mine, bomb, or shell. **3.** In antiquity, a large bowl in which wine was mixed with water before serving. [< L < Gk. *kratēr* bowl < *kra-*, stem of *kerannynai* to mix]

Cra·ter (krā'tər) *n.* A constellation, the Cup. See CONSTELLATION. [< Gk. *kratēr* bowl]

Crater Lake National Park An area in SW Oregon; 251 sq. mi.; established 1902; contains **Crater Lake**, a lake (20 sq. mi., about 2,000 ft. deep) on the site of an extinct volcano.

craunch (krônch, kränch) *n. & v. Rare* Crunch.

cra·vat (krə·vat') *n.* **1.** A necktie. **2.** A scarf. [< F *cravate* < *Cravate* a Croatian < G *Krabate* < Croatian *Hrvat*; with ref. to the neckcloths worn by the 17th c. Croatian soldiers]

crave (krāv) *v.* **craved, crav·ing** *v.t.* **1.** To long for; desire greatly. **2.** To be in need of; require. **3.** To ask for earnestly; beg. — *v.i.* **4.** To desire or long: with *for* or *after*. — **Syn.** See DESIRE. [OE *crafian*] — **crav'er** *n.*

cra·ven (krā'vən) *adj.* Conspicuously lacking in courage; cowardly. — *n.* A base coward. — *v.t.* To make cowardly. [? < OF *cravant*, ppr. of *craver, crever* to burst < L *crepare* to creak, break] — **cra'ven·ly** *adv.* — **cra'ven·ness** *n.*

Crav·en·ette (krav'ə·net', krā'və-) *n.* **1.** A chemical process for waterproofing garments: a trade name. **2.** A fabric treated by this process. — *v.t.* **·et·ted, ·et·ting** To make (fabric) waterproof by this process. Also **crav'en·ette'**.

crav·ing (krā'ving) *n.* A yearning or desire; intense longing. — **crav'ing·ly** *adv.* — **crav'ing·ness** *n.*

craw¹ (krô) *n.* **1.** The crop of a bird. **2.** The stomach of any animal. — **to stick in one's craw** To be displeasing or unacceptable. [ME *crawe.* Akin to Du. *kraag* neck.]

craw² (krô) *n. Scot.* A rook or crow. [See CROW¹]

craw·dad (krô'dad') *n. U.S. Dial.* A crayfish.

craw·fish (krô'fish') *n. pl.* **·fish** or **·fish·es** A crayfish (which see). — *v.i. U.S. Informal* To back out or retreat, as from a position or a promise. [Var. of CRAYFISH]

Craw·ford (krô'fərd), **Francis Marion**, 1854–1909, U.S. novelist.

crawl¹ (krôl) *v.i.* **1.** To move along slowly with the body on or close to the ground, as a snake or an infant. **2.** To move slowly, feebly, or cautiously. **3.** To be covered with things that crawl. **4.** To feel as if covered with crawling things: His skin *crawled.* **5.** To behave with servility; fawn or cringe. **6.** *Informal* To back down from a declared position. **7.** To grow by extending branches, etc., as a vine. — *n.* **1.** The act of crawling; a creeping motion. **2.** A swimming stroke performed face down, combining an overarm stroke with a flutter kick, the face being turned to one side for brief intakes of breath. Variants are the **American crawl**, combining a six-beat flutter kick with each stroke, and the **Australian crawl**, combining an eight-beat flutter kick with each stroke. [Prob. < ON *krafla* to paw] — **crawl'ing·ly** *adv.*

crawl² (krôl) *n.* A pen in shallow water for confining fish, turtles, etc. [Alter. of Du. *kraal.* See KRAAL.]

crawl·er (krô'lər) *n.* **1.** One who or that which crawls. **2.** *U.S.* A hellgrammite: a term used by fishermen.

crawl·y (krô'lē) *adj.* **crawl·i·er, crawl·i·est** *Informal* Creepy.

cray·fish (krā'fish') *n. pl.* **·fish** or **·fish·es** **1.** Any of a family (*Astacidae*) of fresh-water decapod crustaceans resembling the lobster; especially, one of a genus (*Cambarus*) common in eastern North America. **2.** Loosely, the spiny lobster. Also called *crawfish.* [Earlier *crevice* < OF < OHG *krebiz*; infl. in form by *fish*]

cray·on (krā'ən, -on) *n.* **1.** A stick of colored wax, chalk, etc., for use in drawing. **2.** A drawing made with crayons. — *v.t. & v.i.* To sketch or draw with crayons. [< F, pencil < *craie* chalk < L *creta*] — **cray'on·ist** *n.*

craze (krāz) *v.* **crazed, craz·ing** *v.t.* **1.** To render insane or demented. **2.** To make full of minute intersecting cracks, as the glaze of pottery. **3.** *Obs.* To impair or weaken; also, to break. — *v.i.* **4.** To become insane. **5.** To become full of minute cracks. — *n.* **1.** A brief fashion or fad; rage. **2.** An extravagant liking or enthusiasm. **3.** Mental disorder; insanity. **4.** A minute flaw in the glaze of pottery, etc. [ME *crasen*, prob. < Scand. Cf. Sw. *krasa* to break.]

crazed (krāzd) *adj.* **1.** Insane; maddened. **2.** Having minute cracks in the glaze, as some pottery.

cra·zy (krā'zē) *adj.* **·zi·er, ·zi·est 1.** Disordered in mind; insane; demented; mad; maniacal. **2.** *Informal* Very enthusiastic or excited. **3.** *Informal* Unpredictable or inexplicable; odd or unconventional: a *crazy* driver; a *crazy* way to talk. **4.** Dilapidated; rickety; unsound. — **cra'zi·ly** *adv.* — **cra'zi·ness** *n.*

crazy bone The funny bone (which see).

crazy quilt A patchwork quilt made of pieces of various sizes, shapes, and colors.

cra·zy·weed (krā'zē·wēd') *n.* Locoweed (which see).

creak (krēk) *n.* A sharp, squeaking sound, as from friction. — *v.t. & v.i.* To produce or cause to produce a creak. [Imit.]

creak·y (krē'kē) *adj.* **·i·er, ·i·est 1.** Creaking. **2.** Likely to creak: a *creaky* step. — **creak'i·ly** *adv.* — **creak'i·ness** *n.*

cream (krēm) *n.* **1.** An oily, yellowish substance contained in milk, composed chiefly of fatty globules that rise and gather on the surface, and combine into butter when churned. **2.** The best or most significant part. **3.** The yellowish white color of cream. **4.** A delicacy made with or resembling cream; also, a candy with a creamlike filling. **5.** A creamed purée: *cream* of mushroom soup. **6.** Something resembling cream. **7.** A soft, oily cosmetic for cleansing or protecting the skin. — *v.t.* **1.** To skim cream from. **2.** To take the best part from. **3.** To add cream to, as coffee. **4.** To permit (milk) to form cream. **5.** To beat, as butter and sugar, to a creamy consistency. **6.** To cook or prepare (food) with cream or cream sauce. **7.** *U.S. Slang* To defeat decisively. — *v.i.* **8.** To froth or foam. **9.** To form cream. [< OF *cresme* < LL *chrisma.* Doublet of CHRISM.]

cream cheese Soft, white cheese made of cream or a mixture of cream and milk.

cream-col·ored (krēm'kul'ərd) *adj.* Having the characteristic yellowish white color of cream.

cream·cups (krēm'kups') *n.* An ornamental annual (*Platystemon californicus*) of the poppy family, with cream-colored flowers: sometimes called *California poppy.*

cream·er (krē'mər) *n.* **1.** A small pitcher used for serving cream. **2.** A refrigerator in which milk is placed to accelerate the rising of cream. **3.** Any device in which cream is separated.

cream·er·y (krē'mər·ē) *n. pl.* **·er·ies 1.** A place where milk and cream are prepared for market. **2.** An establishment at which butter and cheese are made or where milk and milk products are sold.

cream of tartar Potassium bitartrate.

cream puff 1. A shell of pastry filled with whipped cream or custard. **2.** *Slang* A sissy; weakling.

cream·y (krē'mē) *adj.* **cream·i·er, cream·i·est 1.** Containing cream. **2.** Resembling cream in consistency, color, or richness. — **cream'i·ness** *n.*

crease¹ (krēs) *n.* **1.** A mark or line made by folding or wrinkling. **2.** In cricket, any of the lines limiting the position of the bowler or the batsman, or the space so limited. For illustration see CRICKET². **3.** In hockey, a clearly marked rectangle in front of the goal, that opposing players may enter only under special conditions. — *v.* **creased, creas·ing** *v.t.* **1.** To make a crease, line, or fold in; wrinkle. **2.** To graze with a bullet. — *v.i.* **3.** To become wrinkled. [ME *creaste,* ? var. of *creste* crest, ridge] — **creas'er** *n.*

crease² (krēs) See KRIS.

creas·y (krē'sē) *adj.* **creas·i·er, creas·i·est** Creased; wrinkled.

cre·ate (krē·āt') *v.t.* **·at·ed, ·at·ing 1.** To cause to come into existence; originate. **2.** To be the cause of; occasion: The speech *created* much interest. **3.** To produce (a work of art, etc.) by one's own thought and imagination. **4.** To be the first to portray, as a character or part. **5.** To invest with new office, rank, etc.; appoint. — *adj. Poetic* Created. [< L *creatus*, pp. of *creare* to produce, create]

cre·a·tine (krē'ə·tēn, -tin) *n. Biochem.* A nitrogenous compound, $C_4H_9N_3O_2$, found in the muscle tissue, brain, and blood of all vertebrate animals, and also made synthetically. Also **cre'a·tin** (-tin). [< Gk. *kreas, -atos* flesh + -INE²]

cre·a·tion (krē·ā'shən) *n.* **1.** The act of creating, or the fact of being created. **2.** Anything created; especially, an original product of human intelligence or imagination. **3.** *Usually cap.* The act of God in bringing the universe into existence. **4.** The world or the universe; also, all living creatures. — **cre·a'tion·al** *adj.*

cre·a·tion·ism (krē·ā'shən·iz'əm) *n. Theol.* **1.** The doctrine that the universe and all matter and forms of being within it are the result not of evolution but of God's direct and instantaneous creation. **2.** The doctrine that God creates an entirely new soul for each human being: distinguished from *infusionism* and *traducianism.* — **cre·a'tion·ist** *n.*

cre·a·tive (krē·ā'tiv) *adj.* **1.** Having the power or ability to create. **2.** Characterized by originality of thought and execution. **3.** Productive: with *of.* — **cre·a'tive·ly** *adv.* — **cre·a'tive·ness, cre·a·tiv·i·ty** (krē'ā·tiv'ə·tē, krē·ā·tiv'-) *n.*

cre·a·tor (krē·ā'tər) *n.* One who or that which creates. — **the Creator** God. — **cre·a'tor·ship** *n.*

crea·tur·al (krē'chər·əl) *adj.* Relating to or of the nature of a creature or creatures. Also **crea'ture·ly.**

crea·ture (krē'chər) *n.* **1.** A living being; especially, an animal. **2.** A person, especially when regarded with scorn, pity, etc. **3.** That which has been created. **4.** One who is dependent upon, influenced by, or subordinate to something or someone; puppet; tool. **5.** *U.S.* A domestic animal; critter. — **the creature** Strong drink; whisky; a humorous term. [< OF < LL *creatura* < L *creare* to produce]

creature comforts Things or conveniences that comfort or refresh the body.

Cré·bil·lon (krä·bē·yôn′), **Prosper Jolyot de,** 1674–1762, French dramatist. — **Claude Prosper Jolyot de,** 1707–77, French novelist; son of the preceding: called **Crébillon fils.**

crèche (kresh, krāsh) n. 1. A group of figures representing the scene in the stable at the Nativity. 2. A foundling asylum. 3. Brit. A public day nursery. [< F, crib, cradle]

Cré·cy (krā·sē′) A village in northern France; scene of an English victory over French forces, August, 1346: also Cressy. Also **Cré·cy-en-Pon·thieu** (krä·sē′än·pôn·tyœ′).

cre·dence (krēd′ns) n. 1. Belief, especially as based upon the evidence or reports of others. 2. Recommendation or accreditation: letters of credence. 3. Eccl. A small table or shelf near the altar to hold the cruets and other articles used in the celebration of the Mass. [< MF crédence < Med.L credentia < L credere to believe]

cre·den·da (kri·den′də) n. pl. of **cre·den·dum** (kri·den′dəm) Eccl. Articles of faith or belief: distinguished from agenda. [< L, neut. pl. gerundive of credere to believe]

cre·dent (krēd′nt) adj. Archaic 1. Believing. 2. Believable. [< L credens, -entis, ppr. of credere to believe]

cre·den·tial (kri·den′shəl) n. 1. That which entitles one to authority or confidence. 2. Usually pl. A certificate or letter giving evidence of one's authority, identity, or claim to confidence. — adj. Giving title to credit and confidence. [< Med.L credentia belief + -AL¹]

cre·den·za (kri·den′zə) n. A sideboard or buffet, often without legs. [< Ital. < Med.L credentia < L credere to believe; orig., in the Renaissance, a table where food was tested for poison before serving]

credibility gap The difference between that which is presented as truth, such as a governmental statement, and the amount of it believed to be true by the public.

cred·i·ble (kred′ə·bəl) adj. 1. Capable of being believed. 2. Worthy of confidence; reliable: a credible witness. [< L credibilis < credere to believe] — **cred′i·bil′i·ty, cred′i·ble·ness** n. — **cred′i·bly** adv.

cred·it (kred′it) n. 1. Belief in the genuineness or truth of something; trust; faith. 2. The quality or condition of being credible or trustworthy. 3. A reputation for trustworthiness; credibility; good name; formerly, reputation; repute. 4. A source of honor or good repute: a credit to one's family. 5. Approval or commendation for some action or quality. 6. Influence derived from the good opinion of others. 7. Usually pl. Acknowledgment of those who have assisted in the preparation or production of a book, motion picture, play, etc. 8. Confidence in the ability and disposition of an individual, firm, etc., to fulfill financial obligations: to buy on credit. 9. Reputation for solvency and commercial integrity. 10. The time extended for payment of a liability. 11. In bookkeeping: a The entry of any amount paid by a debtor, or the amount entered. b The right-hand side of an account, where values received are entered; also, an entry on this side, or the total of such entries. Compare DEBIT. 12. In an account, the balance in one's favor. 13. An amount placed by a bank at a customer's disposal, against which he may draw. 14. U.S. Official certification that a student has passed a course of study; also, a unit of academic study. Abbr. cr. — v.t. 1. To give credit for; accept as true. 2. To ascribe, as intelligence or honor, to: with with. 3. Archaic To reflect credit upon. 4. In bookkeeping, to give credit for or enter as credit to. 5. U.S. To give educational credits to (a student). — Syn. See ATTRIBUTE. [< MF crédit, ult. < L creditum a loan < credere to believe, trust]

cred·it·a·ble (kred′it·ə·bəl) adj. 1. Deserving credit or esteem; praiseworthy. 2. Obs. Credible. — **cred′it·a·bil′i·ty, cred′it·a·ble·ness** n. — **cred′it·a·bly** adv.

credit card A card entitling its holder to credit, as by virtue of membership in an organization having such an arrangement with certain hotels, restaurants, etc.

credit line A listing of those to whom credit is due for work done, as in a news report, motion picture, etc.

cred·i·tor (kred′i·tər) n. 1. One to whom money is owed. 2. In bookkeeping, the credit side of an account. Abbr. (def. 2) cr. [< AF creditour < L creditor < credere to believe, trust]

credit rating An estimate or rating of the solvency or commercial integrity of a person or company.

credit standing Reputation for paying debts.

credit union A cooperative group for making loans to its members at low rates of interest.

cre·do (krē′dō, krā′-) n. pl. **·dos** 1. A set of beliefs; a creed. 2. Often cap. The Apostles' Creed or the Nicene Creed; also, a musical setting for this. [< L, I believe; the opening word of the Creed]

cre·du·li·ty (krə·dōō′lə·tē, -dyōō′-) n. Readiness to believe on slight evidence; gullibility. [< L credulitas, -tatis < credulus. See CREDULOUS.]

cred·u·lous (krej′ōō·ləs) adj. 1. Disposed to believe on slight evidence. 2. Arising from credulity: credulous superstitions. [< L credulus < credere to believe] — **cred′u·lous·ly** adv. — **cred′u·lous·ness** n.

Cree (krē) n. pl. Cree or Crees 1. One of an Algonquian tribe of North American Indians formerly dwelling in Manitoba and Saskatchewan. 2. The language of this tribe.

creed (krēd) n. 1. A formal and authoritative statement of religious belief or doctrine; a confession of faith. 2. Any organized system or statement of beliefs, principles, etc. — Syn. See DOCTRINE. — **the Creed** The Apostles' Creed. [OE crēda < L credo I believe. See CREDO.]

creek (krēk, krik) n. 1. U.S. A stream intermediate in size between a brook and a river. 2. Chiefly Brit. A narrow inlet or cove in a shoreline. 3. Obs. A winding or narrow passage. Abbr. cr. — **up the creek** U.S. Informal 1. In a state of uncertainty or bewilderment. 2. Out of luck. [ME creke, crike < Scand. Cf. Sw. krik cove, inlet.]

Creek (krēk) n. 1. A confederacy of chiefly Muskhogean tribes of North American Indians, once occupying parts of Georgia, Alabama, and northern Florida. 2. An Indian of any of these tribes. 3. Their Muskhogean language.

creel (krēl) n. 1. An angler's wicker basket for carrying fish. 2. A cage of wickerwork for catching lobsters. 3. A frame in a spinning machine that holds the bobbins. [Appar. related to OF greille grating. See GRILLE.]

creep (krēp) v.i. **crept, creep·ing** 1. To move with the body close to or touching the ground; crawl. 2. To move imperceptibly, stealthily, or timidly. 3. To act servilely; cringe. 4. To grow along a surface or support, as a vine. 5. To have a sensation of being covered with creeping things. 6. To slip out of place; be displaced. 7. To slip or move slightly lengthwise, as railroad tracks under pressure of traffic. — n. 1. The act of creeping; a slow movement. 2. pl. Informal A sensation as of insects creeping on the flesh; also, uneasy apprehension. 3. Metall. A slow slipping or flow of metal when subjected to critical temperature or stresses. 4. Geol. The gradual movement of rock waste and soil down a weathered slope. 5. Slang A repugnant person. [OE crēopan]

creep·er (krē′pər) n. 1. One who or that which creeps. 2. Bot. A plant growing along or across a surface by sending out short, flowering stems, as ivy and the Virginia creeper. 3. Any of various small birds adapted for creeping about trees. 4. pl. A baby's garment resembling overalls. 5. A type of grapnel. 6. A device with sharp points attached to a shoe or boot to prevent slipping. 7. Mech. An apparatus for conveying material in, to, or from a machine. 8. One of a breed of domestic fowl having very short legs. 9. The lowest gear, as in a truck: also **creeper gear.**

creep·ie (krē′pē, krip′ē) n. Scot. A low stool.

creep·y (krē′pē) adj. **creep·i·er, creep·i·est** 1. Having or producing a feeling of fear or repugnance, as of things crawling on the skin. 2. Characterized by a creeping motion. — **creep′i·ly** adv. — **creep′i·ness** n.

creese (krēs) See KRIS.

creesh (krēsh) Scot. n. Grease. — v.t. To grease. [< OF craisse, var. of graisse grease]

cre·mate (krē′māt, kri·māt′) v.t. **·mat·ed, ·mat·ing** To burn up; reduce to ashes: to cremate a dead body. [< L crematus, pp. of cremare to burn to ashes] — **cre·ma·tion** (kri·mā′shən) n.

cre·ma·tor (krē′mā·tər, kri·mā′tər) n. 1. One who cremates bodies. 2. A furnace where bodies are cremated. 3. An incinerator for rubbish.

cre·ma·to·ry (krē′mə·tôr′ē, -tō′rē, krem′ə-) adj. Related to or connected with cremation. — n. pl. **·ries** A furnace for cremating dead bodies; also, the building containing such a furnace: also **cre·ma·to·ri·um** (-tôr′ē·əm, -tō′rē-).

crème (krem) n. French Cream: used in names of sauces and liqueurs.

crème de ca·ca·o (də kə·kā′ō, -kä′ō) French A sweet, chocolate-flavored liqueur.

crème de la crème (də là krem′) French The very best; most choice; literally, cream of the cream.

crème de menthe (də mänt) French A sweet, green or white cordial with a strong flavor of mint.

Cre·mo·na (kri·mō′nə, Ital. krä·mō′nä) n. Any violin made at Cremona, Italy, from the 16th to the 18th century, by the Amati family, Antonio Stradivari, or Giuseppe Guarneri.

Cre·mo·na (kri·mō′nə, Ital. krä·mō′nä) A province in Lombardy, northern Italy; 678 sq. mi.; pop. 350,818 (1961); capital, **Cremona;** pop. 74,242.

cre·nate (krē′nāt) adj. Bot. Scalloped or toothed with even, rounded notches, as a leaf or margin. Also **cre′nat·ed.** [< NL crenatus < crena notch]

cre·na·tion (kri·nā′shən) n. 1. A rounded projection, as on a leaf: crenature. 2. The state of being crenate.

cren·a·ture (kren′ə·chŏŏr, krē′nə-) n. A rounded projection, as on the edge of a leaf; also, the notches between.

cren·el (kren′əl) n. 1. One of the embrasures, or indentations, of a battlement. 2. A crenature. — v.t. **cren·eled** or **·elled, cren·el·ing** or **·el·ling** To crenelate. Also **cre·nelle** (kri·nel′). [< OF, dim. of cren notch]

cren·el·ate (kren′ə·lāt) v.t. **·lat·ed, ·lat·ing** To provide with battlements or crenels. — adj. Crenulate. Also Brit. **cren′el·late.**

cren·el·a·tion (kren′ə·lā′shən) n. 1. The act of crenelating, or the state of being crenelated. 2. Crenelated work, as on a battlement. 3. A notch; indentation. Also **cren′el·la′tion.**

cren·u·late (kren′yə·lit, -lāt) *adj.* Finely notched or scalloped, as some leaves. Also **cren′u·lat′ed.** [< NL *crenulatus* < *crenula*, dim. of *crena* notch]

cren·u·la·tion (kren′yə·lā′shən) *n.* **1.** The state of being crenulate. **2.** A small crenature.

cre·o·dont (krē′ə·dont) *n. Paleontol.* One of a suborder (*Creodonta*) of primitive Tertiary carnivora, having incisors with closed roots, and very small brains. [< NL *Creodonta* < Gk. *kreas* flesh + *odous, odontos* tooth]

cre·ole (krē′ōl) *adj.* **1.** Cooked with a savory sauce containing peppers, tomatoes, onions, etc. **2.** Of, pertaining to, or characteristic of the Creoles or their patois. — *n.* **1.** A Creole (defs. 5 and 6). **2.** A creolized language.

Cre·ole (krē′ōl) *n.* **1.** A native of Spanish America or the West Indies but of European descent. **2.** A descendant of the original French settlers of the southern United States, especially of Louisiana, who retains his characteristic speech or cultural pattern: distinguished from *Cajun.* **3.** The French patois spoken by the Louisiana Creoles. **4.** A descendant of Spanish or Portuguese settlers in the Gulf States. **5.** A Negro born in the Americas, as distinguished from one brought from Africa: also **Creole Negro.** **6.** Loosely, any person having both Creole and Negro ancestors, and speaking the Creole patois. [< F *créole* < Sp. *criollo* a native < *criar* to produce, bring forth < L *creare* to create]

Creole State Nickname of LOUISIANA.

cre·o·lized language (krē′ə·līzd) A mixed language, as Gullah, resulting from close and prolonged contact between a dominant and a subject group speaking dissimilar languages, usually incorporating a simplified vocabulary from the dominant language with the grammatical system of the subject language, and becoming the only language of the subject group. Compare PIDGIN.

Cre·on (krē′on) In Greek legend, the brother of Jocasta and successor to Oedipus. See ANTIGONE.

cre·o·sol (krē′ə·sōl, -sol) *n. Chem.* A colorless, aromatic, oily liquid compound, $C_8H_{10}O_2$, derived from beech tar or guaiacum by distillation. [< CREOS(OTE) + -OL²]

cre·o·sote (krē′ə·sōt) *n. Chem.* **1.** An oily liquid consisting principally of cresol and other phenols, obtained by the destructive distillation of wood, used as an antiseptic and preservative. **2.** A similar liquid distilled from coal tar: also **coal-tar creosote.** — *v.t.* **·sot·ed, ·sot·ing** To treat or impregnate with creosote, as shingles, etc. [< Gk. *kreas* flesh + *sōtēr* preserver < *sōzein* to save]

creosote bush A shrub (*Larrea tridentata*) of the caltrop family of Mexico and the Colorado desert, having a resinous foliage that smells like creosote.

crepe (krāp) *n.* **1.** A thin fabric of silk, cotton, wool, or synthetic fiber, having a crinkled surface. **2.** Black crepe used as a sign of mourning, as in an armband: in this sense usually *crape.* **3.** Crepe paper. **4.** Crepe rubber. — *v.t.* **creped, crep·ing** To frizz (the hair). Also spelled *crape:* also **crepe.** [< F (*tissu*) *crêpe* crinkled (cloth) < L *crispus* curled]

crepe de Chine (də shēn′) A soft, thin, silk dress fabric, with a pebbly surface.

crepe hair Artificial hair, used in theatrical make-up.

crepe·hang·er (krāp′hang′ər) *n. Slang* A gloomy or pessimistic person: also spelled *crapehanger.*

crepe paper A tissue paper resembling crepe, used for decorations.

crepe rubber Rubber prepared in crinkled texture for the soles of shoes.

crêpes su·zette (krep′ soo·zet′) Thin egg pancakes rolled in a hot, orange-flavored sauce, and usually served aflame in cognac or curaçao.

crep·i·tate (krep′ə·tāt) *v.i.* **·tat·ed, ·tat·ing** To make a succession of quick snapping sounds; crackle; rattle. [< L *crepitatus*, pp. of *crepitare*, freq. of *crepare* to creak] — **crep′i·tant** *adj.* — **crep′i·ta′tion** *n.*

crept (krept) Past tense of CREEP.

cre·pus·cu·lar (kri·pus′kyə·lər) *adj.* **1.** Pertaining to or like twilight; dim; obscure. **2.** Appearing or flying in the twilight, as certain birds and insects.

cre·pus·cule (kri·pus′kyool) *n.* Twilight. Also **cre·pus·cle** (kri·pus′əl). [< MF *crépuscule* < L *crepusculum* < *creper* dark, dusky]

cres. or **cresc.** *Music* Crescendo.

cres·cen·do (krə·shen′dō, -sen′-) *Music n. pl.* **·dos** A gradual increase in volume of sound: expressed by the sign ⟨⟩: opposed to *diminuendo.* — *v.i.* **·doed, ·do·ing** To produce a crescendo. [< Ital., ppr. of *crescere* to increase < L]

cres·cent (kres′ənt) *n.* **1.** The visible part of the moon in its first or last quarter, having one concave edge and one convex edge. **2.** Something crescent-shaped. **3.** The device on the Turkish standard. **4.** A crescent-shaped roll made of yeast dough; croissant. — **the Crescent** Turkish or Moslem power. — *adj.* **1.** Increasing: said of the moon

in its first quarter. **2.** Shaped like the moon in its first quarter. [< L *crescens, -entis,* ppr. of *crescere* to increase]

cres·cive (kres′iv) *adj. Obs.* Growing; increasing. [< L *crescere* to increase + -IVE]

cre·sol (krē′sōl, -sol) *n. Chem.* Any one of three isomeric liquid or crystalline compounds, C_7H_8O, obtained by the destructive distillation of coal tar or wood tar, used as an antiseptic. [Var. of CREOSOL]

cress (kres) *n.* One of various plants of the mustard family, as watercress, pungent to taste, used in salads. [OE *cresse*]

cres·set (kres′it) *n.* A metal holder for burning oil, wood, etc., for illumination. [< OF *craicet, craisset*]

Cres·si·da (kres′i·də) In medieval legend, in Chaucer's *Troilus and Criseyde,* and in Shakespeare's *Troilus and Cressida,* a Trojan girl unfaithful to her lover Troilus: also spelled *Criseyde.* Also **Cres′sid.** See PANDARUS.

Cres·sy (kres′ē) See CRÉCY.

crest (krest) *n.* **1.** A comb, tuft, or projection on the head of an animal, especially of birds. **2.** Something resembling this in shape or position, as the top of a wave. **3.** The highest point or stage; pinnacle: the *crest* of a flood. **4.** The ridge on the neck of a horse, dog, etc.; also, the mane growing from this. **5.** The projection on the top of a helmet; a plume; also, a helmet. **6.** *Heraldry* A device placed above the shield in a coat of arms. **7.** *Archit.* **a** The ridge of a roof. **b** A cresting. **8.** *Archaic* Pride; courage. — *v.t.* **1.** To serve as a crest for; cap. **2.** To furnish with a crest. **3.** To reach the crest of: to *crest* a wave. — *v.i.* **4.** To come to a crest, as a wave prior to breaking. [< OF *creste* < L *crista* tuft] — **crest′ed** *adj.* — **crest′less** *adj.*

crested auklet A small, brownish black diving bird (*Aethia cristatella*), abundant in Alaska and the North Pacific.

crested flycatcher Any flycatcher having a conspicuous crest, especially the **great crested flycatcher** (*Myiarchus crinitus*) of eastern North America.

crest·fall·en (krest′fô′lən) *adj.* **1.** Depressed; dispirited; dejected. **2.** Having a fallen or drooping crest.

crest·ing (kres′ting) *n. Archit.* An ornamental ridge surmounting a roof, wall, etc.

cre·ta·ceous (kri·tā′shəs) *adj.* Consisting of, containing, or resembling chalk. [< L *cretaceus* < *creta* chalk < *Creta* Cretan, of Crete (where large deposits of chalk occurred)]

Cre·ta·ceous (kri·tā′shəs) *Geol. adj.* Of or pertaining to the third and last of the geologic periods of the Mesozoic era, preceded by the Jurassic and followed by the Tertiary period of the Cenozoic era. — *n.* The system of rocks deposited during this period. See chart under GEOLOGY.

Crete (krēt) An island in the eastern Mediterranean, comprising with several smaller islands an administrative division of Greece; 3,207 sq. mi.; pop. 483,075 (1961); capital, Canea: also *Candia.* Greek *Krete, Kriti.* See map of AEGEAN SEA. — **Cre′tan** *adj. & n.*

cre·tic (krē′tik) *n.* In prosody, an amphimacer. [< L (*pes*) *Creticus* Cretan (foot) < *Creta* Crete]

cre·tin (krē′tin, krēt′n) *n.* A person afflicted with cretinism. [< F *crétin,* var. of *chrétien* Christian, human being, i.e., not an animal] — **cre′tin·ous** *adj.*

cre·tin·ism (krē′tən·iz′əm) *n. Pathol.* A disease associated with thyroid deficiency and inactivity, marked by physical deformities, arrested development, goiter, and various forms of mental retardation.

cre·tonne (kri·ton′, krē′ton) *n.* A heavy, unglazed cotton, linen, or rayon fabric printed in colored patterns, used especially for draperies, chair coverings, etc. [after *Creton,* a village in Normandy]

Cre·u·sa (krē·ōō′sə) **1.** In Greek legend, the bride of Jason, killed by the jealous Medea. **2.** In the *Aeneid,* wife of Aeneas.

Creu·sot (krœ·zō′). Le See LE CREUSOT.

cre·vasse (krə·vas′) *n.* **1.** A deep fissure or chasm, as in a glacier. **2.** *U.S.* A breach in a levee. — *v.t.* **·vassed, ·vass·ing** To split with crevasses. [< F < OF *crevace.* See CREVICE]

Crève·coeur (krev·kœr′). Michel-Guillaume Jean de, 1735-1813, French author in America: pseudonym **J. Hector St. John Crèvecoeur.**

crev·ice (krev′is) *n.* A fissure or crack on or through the surface of something; cleft; chink. [< OF *crevace* < LL *crepatia* < L *crepare* to crack, creak] — **crev′iced** *adj.*

crew¹ (krōō) *n.* **1.** *Naut.* **a** The company of seamen belonging to one ship or boat, sometimes including officers, and legally including both master and officers unless specifically excepted. **b** The gang of a boatswain, gunner, or other petty officer. **2.** A body of men organized or detailed for a particular job: a repair *crew.* **3.** A group trained to handle a racing shell, consisting of oarsmen and coxswain. **4.** A company of people; crowd; gang: usually a derogatory term. **5.** A band of armed men. — **Syn.** See CABAL. [< OF *creue* an increase < *croistre* to grow < L *crescere* to increase]

crew² (krōō) Past tense of CROW.

crew cut *U.S.* A closely cropped haircut.

Crewe (krōō) A municipal borough in south central Cheshire, England; pop. 53,394 (1961)

crew·el (krōō′əl) *n.* A slackly twisted worsted yarn, used in fancywork. [Origin uncertain] — **crew′el·work′** *n.*

crib (krib) *n.* **1.** A child's bed, with side railings. **2.** A box, bin, or small building for grain, having slat or openwork sides. **3.** A rack or manger for fodder. **4.** A stall for cattle. **5.** A small house, cottage, or room. **6.** A wicker basket. **7.** A framework of wood or metal, used to retain or support something, as in mines. **8.** *Informal* A petty theft, especially of another's ideas or writings; a plagiarism. **9.** *Chiefly Brit. Informal* A translation or other unauthorized aid employed by students. **10.** In cribbage, the cards initially discarded, two from each player, that later are scored for the dealer. — *v.* **cribbed, crib·bing** *v.t.* **1.** To enclose in or as in a crib; confine closely. **2.** To line or bolster, as the walls of a pit, with timbers or planking. **3.** *Informal* To steal; also, to plagiarize. — *v.i.* **4.** *Informal* To use a crib in translating. **5.** To crib-bite. [OE *cribb*] — **crib′ber** *n.*

crib·bage (krib′ij) *n.* A game of cards for two, three, or four players, the score being kept on a small board with rows of holes into which pegs are inserted. [< CRIB, n. (def. 10)]

crib-bite (krib′bīt′) *v.i.* **-bit, -bit·ten** or **-bit, -bit·ing** To engage in crib-biting.

crib-bit·ing (krib′bī′ting) *n. Vet.* A harmful habit in which a horse bites his manger, at the same time sucking in air. Also **crib′bing.**

crib·bled (krib′əld) *adj.* Covered with small punctures or dots, as in engraving. [< F *criblé* < *crible* sieve]

crib death *Med.* The sudden death, usually during sleep, of a healthy baby for unknown reasons. Also **sudden infant death syndrome.**

crib·ri·form (krib′rə-form) *adj.* Having the form of a sieve; sievelike. [< L *cribrum* sieve + -(I)FORM]

crib·work (krib′wûrk′) *n.* A frame of logs piled one upon another, with each layer at right angles to the next.

Crich·ton (krī′tən) **James,** 1560–82?, Scottish scholar and soldier: called the Admirable Crichton.

crick[1] (krik) *n.* A painful spasm of the muscles, as of the neck; a cramp. — *v.t.* To turn or twist so as to produce a crick. [Origin uncertain]

crick[2] (krik) *n. U.S. Dial.* A creek (def. 1).

crick·et[1] (krik′it) *n.* A leaping orthopterous insect (family *Gryllidae*), having long antennae, the male of which makes a chirping sound by friction of the forewings. For illustration see INSECTS (injurious). [< OF *criquet* < LG; orig. imit.]

crick·et[2] (krik′it) *n.* **1.** An outdoor game played with bats, a ball, and wickets, between two sides of eleven each, popular in England. **2.** *Informal* Fair, gentlemanly behavior; sportsmanship. — *v.i.* To play cricket. [< F *criquet* bat, stick, ? < MDu. *cricke*] — **crick′et·er** *n.*

CRICKET FIELD

A Bowling crease. *B* Popping crease. *C* Wicket (3 stumps 8 inches apart). Field is usually 150 x 100 yards.

crick·et[3] (krik′it) *n.* A footstool. [Origin unknown]

cri·coid (krī′koid) *Anat. adj.* Designating a ringlike cartilage at the lowest part of the larynx. — *n.* The cricoid cartilage. [< NL *cricoides* < Gk. *krikoeidēs* < *krikos* ring + *eidos* shape, form]

cri·co·thy·roid (krī′kō·thī′roid) *adj. Anat.* Of or pertaining to the cricoid and thyroid cartilages. For illustration see LARYNX. [< CRICO(ID) + THYROID]

cried (krīd) Past tense and past participle of CRY.

cri·er (krī′ər) *n.* **1.** One who cries. **2.** One who makes public announcements, as of sales, news, etc. **3.** A hawker.

crime (krīm) *n.* **1.** *Law* An act or omission in violation of public law either forbidding or commanding it, for which a punishment is prescribed and which is prosecuted by the state in its own name or in the name of the people or the sovereign. **2.** Any grave offense against morality or social order; wickedness; iniquity. **3.** Unlawful activity: a wave of *crime.* **4.** *Informal* Any apparent injustice; a shame: It's a *crime* to charge such high prices. — **Syn.** See OFFENSE. [< MF < OF *crimne* < L *crimen* accusation, charge]

Cri·me·a (krī-mē′ə, kri-) A peninsula in the SE Ukrainian S.S.R., on the northern coast of the Black Sea, comprising the **Crimean Oblast;** 9,900 sq. mi.; pop. 1,814,000 (1970); center, Simferopol: ancient *Tauric Chersonese.* Russian *Krym, Krymskaya Oblast.* See map of DNEIPER. — **Cri·me′an** *adj. & n.*

Crimean War See table for WAR.

crim·i·nal (krim′ə-nəl) *adj.* **1.** Implying or involving crime or great wickedness. **2.** *Law* Pertaining to the administration of penal as opposed to civil law: a *criminal* court. **3.** Guilty of crime. — *n.* One who has committed a crime. [< OF *criminel* < L *criminalis* < *crimen* charge] — **crim′i·nal·ly** *adv.*

— **Syn.** (adj.) **2.** *Criminal, felonious, illegal,* and *unlawful* refer to actions that are contrary to law. Any offense against public law is *criminal;* it becomes *felonious* if it is one of the more serious offenses, as arson, robbery, homicide, etc., that are punishable by imprisonment or death. All *criminal* acts are *illegal* and *unlawful,*

but the latter words may also refer to offenses against private rights, as trespassing on another's land, or invading his privacy. Such actions may bring a civil suit for damages, but they are not *criminal* nor punishable by fine or imprisonment.

criminal code See under CODE.

criminal conversation *Law* Adultery.

crim·i·nal·i·ty (krim′ə-nal′ə-tē) *n., pl.* **-ties** **1.** The state or quality of being criminal. **2.** A criminal act or practice.

crim·i·nate (krim′ə-nāt) *v.t.* **·nat·ed, ·nat·ing** To accuse of or implicate in crime; incriminate. [< L *criminatus,* pp. of *criminare* to accuse of crime < *crimen* charge] — **crim′i·na′-tion** *n.* — **crim′i·na·tive, crim·i·na·to·ry** (krim′ə-nə-tôr′ē, -tō′rē) *adj.* — **crim′i·na′tor** *n.*

crim·i·nol·o·gy (krim′ə-nol′ə-jē) *n.* The scientific study and investigation of crime and the behavior of criminals. [< L *crimen, criminis* crime + -LOGY] — **crim·i·no·log·i·cal** (krim′ə-nə-loj′i-kəl) *adj.* — **crim′i·nol′o·gist** *n.*

crim·mer (krim′ər) See KRIMMER.

crimp[1] (krimp) *v.t.* **1.** To bend or press into ridges or folds; corrugate; flute. **2.** To indent and close, as a cartridge case; crease. **3.** To bend into shape, as the uppers of boots. **4.** To gash the flesh of before cooking, as fish, to make firmer and crisper. **5.** To curl or wave: to *crimp* the hair. — *n.* **1.** Something that has been crimped. **2.** *pl.* Waved or curled hair. **3.** A crimping machine. **4.** An offset in a piece of structural steel, used to fit one piece over another. **5.** A breakdown of wood fibers caused by weakness or too rapid drying. **6.** The waviness or curl in natural wool fibers. — **to put a crimp in** *Informal* To hinder or obstruct. [< MDu. *crimpen* to wrinkle, draw together] — **crimp′er** *n.*

crimp[2] (krimp) *n.* One who procures the impressment of sailors, soldiers, etc., by decoying or entrapping them. — *v.t.* To decoy or entrap into forced military or naval service. [Origin uncertain]

crim·ple (krim′pəl) *v.t. & v.i.* **·pled, ·pling** To wrinkle or crumple. [Freq. of CRIMP[1]]

crimp·y (krim′pē) *adj.* **crimp·i·er, crimp·i·est** Having a crimped appearance; wavy; curly.

crim·son (krim′zən) *n.* A deep red color having a tinge of blue, but lighter than purple. — *adj.* **1.** Of a deep red color. **2.** Bloody. — *v.t. & v.i.* To make or become crimson; redden; blush. [ME *cremesin* < Sp., var. of *carmesin, carmesi* < Arabic *qirmazī* < *qirmiz* kermes. Doublet of CARMINE.]

cringe (krinj) *v.i.* **cringed, cring·ing** **1.** To shrink or crouch in servility or cowardice. **2.** To wince as with pain or fear. **3.** To fawn. — *n.* A servile crouching. [ME *cringen, crengen.* Related to OE *cringan* to curl up, yield, fall.] — **cring′er** *n.* — **Syn.** **1.** cower. **2.** flinch. **3.** truckle, toady.

crin·gle (kring′gəl) *n. Naut.* A small loop or grommet of rope or metal, attached to the edge of a sail. [Appar. < LG. Cf. < Du. *kringel* little ring.]

cri·nite[1] (krī′nīt) *adj.* **1.** *Bot.* Having hair or bearded with long weak hairs. **2.** Resembling a tuft of hair. [< L *crinitus,* pp. of *crinire* to cover with hair < *crinis* hair]

cri·nite[2] (krī′nīt, krin′īt) *n. Paleontol.* An encrinite (which see). [< Gk. *krinon* lily + -ITE[1]]

crin·kle (kring′kəl) *v.t. & v.i.* **·kled, ·kling** **1.** To form or cause to form wrinkles, turns, etc. **2.** To rustle or crackle. — *n.* A wrinkle or fold; turn; twist. [ME *crenklen,* freq. of OE *crincan,* var. of *cringan* to curl up] — **crin′kly** *adj.*

crin·kle·root (kring′kəl-rōōt′, -rōot′) *n.* A toothwort (genus *Dentaria*) of the mustard family, especially *D. diphylla* with small white or lilac flowers and a rootstock with a pungent, aromatic taste: also called *pepperroot.*

cri·noid (krī′noid, krin′oid) *adj.* **1.** *Zool.* Of or pertaining to a class of echinoderms (*Crinoidea*) having jointed stems attached by stalks to the sea bottom, and radial arms: also called *sea lily.* **2.** Lilylike. — *n.* A crinoid echinoderm. [< NL < Gk. *krinoeidēs* lilylike < *krinon* lily + *eidos* form]

crin·o·line (krin′ə-lin, -lēn) *n.* **1.** A highly sized, stiff fabric, used in puffed sleeves, hems, interlinings, etc., originally made of horsehair and linen. **2.** A petticoat of this fabric, worn under a full skirt to make it flare. **3.** A hoop skirt. — *adj.* Resembling, or serving as, a crinoline. [< F < Ital. *crinolino* < *crino* hair (< L *crinis*) + *lino* linen (< L *linum*)]

cri·num (krī′nəm) *n.* Any of a genus (*Crinum*) of frequently cultivated tropical herbs of the amaryllis family, with tunicate bulbs, numerous long, narrow leaves, and showy, fragrant flowers. [< NL < Gk. *krinon* lily]

cri·o·sphinx (krī′ə-sfingks′) *n.* A sphinx with a ram's head. [< Gk. *krios* ram + SPHINX]

crip·ple (krip′əl) *n.* **1.** A lame or disabled person or animal; one lacking the natural use of a limb or the body. **2.** *U.S. Dial.* A thicket in low, marshy land. — *v.t.* **·pled, ·pling** **1.** To make lame. **2.** To impair or disable. [OE *crypel.* Akin to CREEP.] — **crip′pler** *n.*

Cripple Creek A city in central Colorado; former center of one of the world's richest gold-producing areas; pop. 614.

Cripps (krips), **Sir (Richard) Stafford,** 1889–1952, English statesman.

Cri·sey·de (kri-sā′də) See CRESSIDA.

cri·sis (krī′sis) *n., pl.* **·ses** (-sēz) **1.** A crucial turning point in the progress of an affair or of a series of events, as in politics, business, a story or play, etc.; a critical moment. **2.**

Pathol. Any sudden or decisive change in the course of a disease, favorable or unfavorable. [< L < Gk. *krisis* point of decision < *krinein* to decide]

crisp (krisp) *adj.* **1.** Firm and brittle; easily crumbled. **2.** Fresh and firm: *crisp* vegetables. **3.** Brisk; invigorating: a *crisp* breeze. **4.** Stimulating; lively: a *crisp* conversation. **5.** Terse or pithy; curt: a *crisp* retort. **6.** Having tight curls or waves, as hair. **7.** Rippled with minute waves or folds, as water. — *v.t. & v.i.* To make or become crisp. [OE < L *crispus* curled] — **crisp′ly** *adv.* — **crisp′ness** *n.*

cris·pate (kris′pāt) *adj.* Having a crisped or curled appearance. Also **cris′pat·ed.** [< L *crispatus,* pp. of *crispare* to curl < *crispus* curled]

cris·pa·tion (kris·pā′shən) *n.* **1.** A curling or crisping. **2.** A slight contraction or spasmodic constriction. **3.** A minute ripple of a liquid's surface, caused by vibration. Also **crisp·a·ture** (kris′pə·chŏŏr).

crisp·er (kris′pər) *n.* One who or that which makes crisp or curly.

Cris·pi (krēs′pē), **Francesco,** 1819–1901, Italian statesman; premier 1887–91, 1893–96.

Cris·pin (kris′pin), **Saint** Third-century Roman Christian martyr; patron saint of shoemakers.

crisp·y (kris′pē) *adj.* **crisp·i·er, crisp·i·est** Crisp.

cris·sal (kris′al) *adj.* **1.** Of or pertaining to the crissum. **2.** Having a bright-colored crissum.

criss·cross (kris′krôs′, -kros′) *v.t.* **1.** To cross with interlacing lines. — *v.i.* **2.** To move in crisscrosses. — *adj.* Crossing one another in different directions: said of lines or the like; also, marked by crossings. — *n.* **1.** The cross of one who cannot write. **2.** A group of intersecting lines. **3.** Ticktacktoe, a game. **4.** *Obs.* The alphabet. — *adv.* In different crossing directions; crosswise. [Alter. of CHRISTCROSS]

criss·cross-row (kris′krôs′rō′, -kros′-) See CHRISTCROSS-ROW.

cris·sum (kris′əm) *n. Ornithol.* The region or feathers about the anus of a bird. [< NL < L *crissare* to rotate the hips]

cris·tate (kris′tāt) *adj.* **1.** Crested. **2.** Forming a crest. Also **cris′tat·ed.** [< L *cristatus* < *crista* crest]

Cris·tó·bal (kris·tō′bəl, *Sp.* krēs·tō′väl) A port town in Panama at the Atlantic end of the Panama Canal; pop. 817.

crit. **1.** Critic; criticism; criticize. **2.** Critical.

cri·te·ri·on (krī·tir′ē·ən) *n. pl.* **·te·ri·a** (-tir′ē-ə) or **·te·ri·ons** A standard or rule by which a judgment can be made; a model, test, or measure. [< Gk. *kritērion* < *kritēs* judge < *krinein* to decide]

crit·ic (krit′ik) *n.* **1.** One who judges the merits of anything by some standard or criterion. **2.** A skilled judge of literary, theatrical, or other artistic creations. **3.** One who judges severely. **4.** *Obs.* A critique or review. Abbr. *crit.* [< L *criticus* < Gk. *kritikos* < *kritēs* judge. See CRITERION.]

crit·i·cal (krit′i·kəl) *adj.* **1.** Given to faultfinding or severe judgments; carping. **2.** Exhibiting careful, precise judgments and evaluations; analytical: a *critical* report. **3.** Of or characteristic of a critic or criticism. **4.** Of the nature of a crisis or turning point; crucial; decisive: a *critical* week in history. **5.** Attended with danger; risky; perilous: a *critical* lack of foresight. **6.** *Pathol.* Pertaining to or characterized by a stage of a serious illness or injury in which the patient is momentarily expected to change markedly for better or worse. **7.** Necessary for the prosecution of a war: *critical* materiel. **8.** *Physics* Designating a constant value or point indicating a decisive change in a specified condition, as temperature, pressure, speed, etc. Abbr. *crit.* — **Syn.** See ACUTE. — **crit′i·cal·ly** *adv.* — **crit′i·cal·ness** *n.*

critical angle See under ANGLE².

critical mass *Physics* The mass of nuclear fuel in a reactor just sufficient to maintain a chain reaction.

critical pressure *Physics* The pressure of a vapor at the critical temperature.

critical speed *Physics* The speed at which a rotating shaft becomes dynamically unstable, and that if maintained will result in serious vibration and resonance effects.

critical temperature *Physics* The temperature above which a substance can exist only in the gaseous state, no matter what pressure may be applied.

crit·i·cas·ter (krit′ik·as′tər) *n.* A petty, incompetent critic. [< CRITIC + -ASTER] — **crit′ic·as′try** *n.*

crit·i·cism (krit′ə·siz′əm) *n.* **1.** The act of criticizing, especially disapprovingly. **2.** A severe or unfavorable judgment. **3.** The art of making informed and discriminating judgments. **4.** The occupation or profession of a critic. **5.** A review, article, or commentary expressing a critical judgment. **6.** A detailed, scientific inquiry into the origin, history, authority, etc., of literary or historical texts. Abbr. *crit.*

crit·i·cize (krit′ə·sīz) *v.t. & v.i.* **1.** To judge severely; censure: *criticized* for wasting public funds. **2.** To pass judgment on the merits or faults of; examine critically: to *criticize* foreign policy constructively; to *criticize* a new

book. Also *Brit.* **crit/i·cise.** Abbr. *crit.* — **Syn.** See BLAME. — **crit/i·ciz/a·ble** *adj.* — **crit/i·ciz/er** *n.*

cri·tique (kri·tēk′) *n.* **1.** A critical review, especially of a work of art or literature. **2.** The art of criticism. [< F]

crit·ter (krit′ər) *n. U.S. Dial.* **1.** A domestic animal. **2.** Any living creature. [Var. of CREATURE]

croak (krōk) *v.i.* **1.** To utter a hoarse, low-pitched cry, as a frog or crow. **2.** To speak in a low, hoarse voice. **3.** To talk in a doleful tone; forbode evil; grumble. **4.** *Slang* To die. — *v.t.* **5.** To utter with a croak. **6.** *Slang* To kill. — *n.* A hoarse vocal sound, as of a frog. [Imit. Cf. OE *cræcetian* to croak.] — **croak/y** *adj.*

croak·er (krō′kər) *n.* **1.** Any of various animals that croak; especially, one of a class of marine fishes, the grunts. **2.** One who speaks dolefully or forebodes evil.

Cro·at (krō′at, -ət) *n.* **1.** A Slavic native of Croatia. **2.** The Croatian language.

Cro·a·tia (krō·ā′shə) A constituent Republic of NW Yugoslavia; 21,719 sq. mi.; pop. 4,281,000 (est. 1965); capital, Zagreb; formerly an independent kingdom. Serbo-Croatian *Hrvatska.*

Cro·a·tian (krō·ā′shən) *adj.* Pertaining to Croatia or the Croats. — *n.* **1.** A Croat. **2.** The South Slavic language of the Croats; Serbo-Croatian.

Cro·ce (krō′chā), **Benedetto,** 1866–1952, Italian philosopher, critic, and historian.

cro·ce·in (krō′sē·in) *n. Chem.* One of many artificially produced yellow and bright red dyes, generally formed of diazo and sulfonic-acid derivatives of benzene and naphthol. [< L *croceus* yellow + -IN]

cro·chet (krō·shā′) *v.t. & v.i.* **·cheted** (-shād′), **·chet·ing** (-shā′ing) To form or ornament (a fabric) by interlacing thread with a hooked needle. — *n.* A kind of fancywork produced by crocheting: now chiefly attributive, as in *crochet hook.* [< F, dim. of *croche* hook]

cro·cid·o·lite (krə·sid′ə·līt) *n.* **1.** A fibrous, silky, blue or green hydrous sodium iron silicate. **2.** A yellow alteration product of this silicate used as a gemstone; tigereye. [< Gk. *krokis, -idos* nap of cloth + -LITE]

cro·cine (krō′sin, -sēn) *adj.* Of or pertaining to the crocus. [< L *crocinos* < *crocus* crocus]

crock¹ (krok) *n.* **1.** An earthenware pot or jar. **2.** A fragment of earthenware. [OE *croc*]

crock² (krok) *n. Dial.* **1.** *Chiefly Brit.* The black product of combustion; soot. **2.** The coloring matter that rubs off from cloth. — *v.t.* To stain; soil. [Origin uncertain]

crock³ (krok) *Brit. n.* **1.** *Dial.* An old ewe. **2.** A broken-down horse. **3.** *Slang* A worthless, decrepit, or disabled person. — *v.i.* To become weak or sick. [ME *crocke* < Scand. Cf. Norw., Sw. *krake* a decrepit horse.]

crocked (krokt) *adj. U.S. Slang* Drunk.

Crock·er (krok′ər), **Charles,** 1822–88, U.S. financier.

crock·er·y (krok′ər·ē) *n.* Earthen vessels collectively.

crock·et (krok′it) *n. Archit.* A Gothic ornament usually terminating in a curve or roll of foliage, used on angles of pinnacles, spires, gables, and cornices. [< AF *croquet,* OF *crochet,* dim. of *croche* hook]

Crock·ett (krok′it), **David,** 1786–1836, American frontiersman and politician; killed defending the Alamo: called **Davy Crockett.**

croc·o·dile (krok′ə·dīl) *n.* **1.** A large, lizardlike, amphibious reptile (order *Crocodilia*) of tropical regions, with long jaws, armored skin, and webbed feet; especially, the Nile crocodile (*Crocodylus niloticus*), up to 18 feet long, and the American crocodile (*C. americanus*), up to 14 feet long. **2.** A gavial. [Earlier *cocodrille* < OF < Med.L *cocodrillus,* alter. of L *crocodilus* < Gk. *krokodilos* lizard, crocodile]

CROCODILE
(To 18 feet long)

Croc·o·dile (krok′ə·dīl) See LIMPOPO.

crocodile bird A small, black-headed plover (*Pluvianus aegyptius*) of northern Africa, that often perches on crocodiles and devours their insect parasites: also called *trochilus.*

crocodile tears False weeping; hypocritical grief: from the ancient tale that the crocodile weeps over those he devours.

croc·o·dil·i·an (krok′ə·dil′ē·ən) *adj.* **1.** Of or like a crocodile. **2.** Belonging to an order (*Crocodilia*) of reptiles that includes crocodiles, alligators, and caymans. — *n.* A crocodilian reptile. — **croc′o·dil′e·an.**

cro·co·ite (krō′kō·īt) *n.* A brilliant orange lead chromate, PbCrO₄: also called *red lead ore.* Also **cro·co·i·site** (krō·kō′ə·sīt). [< Gk. *krokoeis* saffron-colored + -ITE¹]

cro·cus (krō′kəs) *n. pl.* **cro·cus·es** or **cro·ci** (krō′sī) **1.** Any of a genus (*Crocus*) of plants of the iris family, with long grasslike leaves and large flowers. **2.** The flower of this plant. **3.** A deep orange yellow; saffron. **4.** A red or yellow polishing powder of iron oxide. [< L < Gk. *krokos*]

Croe·sus (krē′səs) Sixth-century B.C. Lydian king, noted for his wealth. — *n.* Any very wealthy man.

croft (krôft, kroft) *n. Brit.* **1.** A small field near a house. **2.** A small tenant farm. [OE, field]

croft·er (krôf′tər, krof′-) *n. Brit.* A tenant cultivating a croft.

crois·sant (krwä-sän′) *n.* A small, crescent-shaped roll made of dough and yeast. [< F, crescent]

Croix de Guerre (krwä də gâr′) A French military decoration for bravery; literally, cross of war.

cro·jik (krō′jik) *n.* A crossjack.

Cro·ker (krō′kər), **John Wilson**, 1780–1857, English essayist and politician. — **Richard**, 1841–1922, U.S. politician: called **Boss Croker**.

Cro-Mag·non (krō-mag′non, *Fr.* krō-mȧ-nyôṅ′) *Anthropol.* *n.* A member of a prehistoric race associated with the Aurignacian culture of Europe and considered to be of the same species as modern man. — *adj.* Pertaining or belonging to the Cro-Magnon race. [after the cave in the Dordogne department, France, where their remains have been found]

Cro·mer (krō′mər), **Earl of** See (Evelyn) BARING.

crom·lech (krom′lek) *n.* **1.** An ancient monument of large standing stones arranged roughly in a circle. **2.** A dolmen. [< Welsh < *crom* bent + *llech* flat stone]

Cromp·ton (kromp′tən), **Samuel**, 1753–1827, English inventor of the spinning mule.

Crom·well (krom′wel, -wəl, krum′-), **Oliver**, 1599–1658, English general and statesman; lord protector of England 1653–58. — **Richard**, 1626–1712, English statesman; lord protector of England 1658–59; son of the preceding. — **Thomas**, 1485?–1540, English statesman.

Cromwell current A long Pacific equatorial current running eastward and terminating at the Galapagos Islands. [after T. *Cromwell*, 1922–58, U.S. oceanographer]

crone (krōn) *n.* **1.** A withered old woman. **2.** *Rare* A senile man. [Prob. < OF *carogne* carcass. Akin to CARRION.]

Cron·je (krōn′yə), **Piet Arnoldus**, 1835–1911, Boer general.

Cro·nus (krō′nəs) In Greek mythology, the youngest of the Titans, son of Uranus and Gaea, who deposed his father, married his sister, Rhea, and was himself thrown by his son Zeus into Tartarus with the other Titans: identified with the Roman *Saturn*: also spelled *Kronos*.

cro·ny (krō′nē) *n. pl.* ·**nies** A friend. — **Syn.** See FRIEND. [Orig. university slang < Gk. *chronios* contemporary]

crook (krŏŏk) *n.* **1.** A bend or curve; also, something bent or crooked. **2.** The curved or bent part of a thing: the *crook* of a branch. **3.** A bending or curving. **4.** Something with a crook in it, as a shepherd's staff or a bishop's crosier. **5.** *Informal* A thief or swindler. **6.** *Scot.* A pothook. — *v.t.* **1.** To bend; make crooked. — *v.i.* **2.** To grow crooked. — **Syn.** See BEND[1]. [< ON *krókr*]

crook·back (krŏŏk′bak′) *n.* A hunchback. — **crook′·backed′** *adj.*

crook·ed (krŏŏk′id) *adj.* **1.** Having angles or crooks; not straight. **2.** Not straightforward in conduct; tricky; dishonest. — **crook′ed·ly** *adv.* — **crook′ed·ness** *n.*

Crookes (krŏŏks), **Sir William**, 1832–1919, English physicist and chemist.

Crookes space *Physics* A dark region between the glow at the cathode and the anode in an electron tube containing a gas at low pressure. [after Sir William *Crookes*]

Crookes tube *Physics* An electron tube in which the gases are exhausted to a high degree, permitting the free movement of cathode rays.

crook·neck (krŏŏk′nek′) *n.* Any of several varieties of squash with a long, curved neck.

croon (krōōn) *v.t. & v.i.* **1.** To sing or hum in a low tone. **2.** To sing (popular songs) in a soft and sentimental manner. **3.** *Scot. & Brit. Dial.* To bellow. — *n.* A low, mournful humming or singing. [< MDu. *kronen* to sing softly, lament] — **croon′er** *n.*

crop (krop) *n.* **1.** The cultivated produce of the land, as grain or vegetables. **2.** The soil product of a particular kind, place, or season: the wheat *crop*. **3.** The seasonal yield of things other than plants: the honey *crop*. **4.** A collection or quantity of anything produced: a *crop* of graduates. **5.** A cropping, especially of the hair: a close *crop*. **6.** The result of cropping, as: **a** A style of short haircut, or a head of hair cropped short. **b** An earmark, as on cattle. **7.** An enlargement of the gullet or esophagus in front of the true stomach, as in birds; the craw. **8.** The handle of a whip. **9.** A whip having a leather loop for a lash. **10.** The entire tanned hide of an animal. — *v.* **cropped, crop·ping** *v.t.* **1.** To cut or eat off the stems or ends of, as grass. **2.** To pluck or reap. **3.** To cut off closely, as hair. **4.** To trim or clip; cut short. **5.** To raise a crop or crops on; cause to bear crops. — *v.i.* **6.** To appear above the surface; sprout: with *up* or *out*. **7.** To develop or come up unexpectedly: with *up* or *out*. **8.** To bear or yield a crop or crops. [OE]

crop-eared (krop′ird′) *adj.* **1.** Having the ears cropped. **2.** With the hair cut short above the ears.

crop·per[1] (krop′ər) *n.* **1.** One who or that which crops. **2.** *U.S.* One who cultivates another's land in return for part of the crop. **3.** A machine for shearing the nap of cloth. **4.** A plant that produces a crop: Corn is a heavy *cropper* in Iowa.

crop·per[2] (krop′ər) *n.* A bad fall, as when one is thrown over a horse's head. — **to come a cropper 1.** To fall headlong, as from a horse. **2.** To fail disastrously in an undertaking. [? < dial. *neck and crop* completely, bodily]

crop rotation *Agric.* A method of conserving soil fertility by planting dissimilar crops in alternate seasons.

cro·quet (krō-kā′) *n.* **1.** An outdoor game played by driving wooden balls through a series of wire arches by means of long-handled mallets. **2.** The act of croqueting. — *v.i.* ·**queted** (-kād′), ·**quet·ing** (-kā′ing) In croquet, to drive away the opponent's ball, after having hit it with one's own, by placing the two balls in contact and hitting one's own while keeping it in position with the foot. [< AF *croquet*, var. of *crochet*. See CROCHET.]

cro·quette (krō-ket′) *n.* A ball or cake of minced food, as meat, fowl, or vegetables, fried brown in deep fat. [< F < *croquer* to crunch]

cro·qui·gnole (krō′kə-nōl, -kin-yōl) *n.* A kind of permanent wave in which the hair is wound from the ends toward the scalp. Also **croquignole wave**. [< F, a fillip < dial. F *croquer*, var. of *crocher* to hook < *croc* a hook]

cro·quis (krō-kē′) *n. French* A rough likeness or quick sketch, especially of a fashion design.

crore (krôr, krōr) *n.* In India, ten millions (of rupees); one hundred lakhs. [< Hind. *karōr*]

cro·sier (krō′zhər) *n.* **1.** A staff surmounted by a crook or cross, borne by or before a bishop or archbishop on occasions of ceremony. **2.** *Bot.* A circinate or coiled young fern frond. Also spelled *crozier*. [< OF *crocier* staff bearer < Med.L *crociarius* < *crocia* bishop's crook]

cross (krôs, kros) *n.* **1.** An ancient instrument of execution, an upright with a horizontal piece near the top, upon which condemned persons were fastened until they died. **2.** A sacred symbol in many ancient religions, consisting basically of two intersecting lines. **3.** The emblem of Christianity, a representation of the cross upon which Christ died; also, a cross with the figure of Christ affixed to it; a crucifix. **4.** Suffering endured for Christ's sake. **5.** Any severe trial, affliction, or suffering: to bear one's *cross*. **6.** The sign of the cross, made with the right hand as a devotional act. **7.** A monument, staff, or other structure in the form of or surmounted by a cross. **8.** An ornament or medal shaped like or holding a cross, worn as a distinction. **9.** Any object or pattern formed by the intersection of two straight lines and resembling a cross, as the mark of one who cannot write, etc. **10.** Anything that resembles or is intermediate between two other things: a *cross* between poetry and prose. **11.** A mixing of varieties or breeds of plants or animals; also, the product of this mixing; a hybrid. **12.** *Slang* A game or match in which the outcome is prearranged. **13.** *Electr.* The accidental contact of two wires so that a portion of the current from one flows to the other. **14.** *Stat.* The geometric mean of two formulas: used in index numbers. **15.** *Heraldry* A figure used as a bearing. **16.** A pipe fitting with four openings, resembling a cross. **17.** An old English coin stamped with a cross. — **the Cross 1.** The cross on which Christ was crucified. **2.** The Christian religion and its adherents; Christianity. — **to take the cross** To turn crusader. — *v.t.* **1.** To move or pass from one side to the other side of; go across; traverse. **2.** To extend from side to side of; span: An overpass *crosses* a highway. **3.** To pass across or intersect, as streets or lines. **4.** To transport or convey across: The convoy *crossed* supplies. **5.** To make the sign of the cross upon or over. **6.** To draw or put a line across: to *cross* a *t*. **7.** To lay or place across or over: to *cross* the legs, fingers, etc. **8.** To meet and pass: Your *crossed* mine. **9.** To obstruct or hinder; thwart. **10.** *Biol.* To crossbreed (plants or animals). **11.** *Naut.* To put (a yard) in place across a mast. — *v.i.* **12.** To pass, move, or extend from side to side. **13.** To intersect; lie athwart. **14.** To meet and pass: Our paths *crossed*. **15.** *Biol.* To crossbreed. — **to cross one's fingers** To hope for luck or success by crossing the middle finger over the index finger. — **to cross one's heart** To promise to tell the truth by making the sign of the cross over one's heart. — **to cross one's mind** To occur to one. — **to cross someone's palm. 1.** To mark a cross on the palm with a coin, especially before paying a fortuneteller. **2.** To pay someone money

CROSSES

a Latin cross. *b* Cross of Lorraine. *c* Tau cross. *d* Ansate cross. *e* Celtic cross. *f* Papal cross. *g* Maltese cross. *h* St. Andrew's cross. *i* Greek cross; cross of St. George. *j* Cross fourchée. *k* Jerusalem cross. *l* Cross fleury. *m* Cross crosslet.

as a bribe. **— to cross swords** To oppose with swords; also, to compete with. **— to cross up** *Informal* To deceive or mislead; betray. **—** *adj.* **1.** Peevish; ill-humored; disagreeable. **2.** Lying across each other; transverse; intersecting: *cross* streets. **3.** Embodying interchange; reciprocal. **4.** Contrary; adverse: at *cross* purposes. **5.** Hybrid. **—** *adv.* **1.** Across; crosswise; transversely. **2.** Adversely; contrarily; counter. [< OE *cros* < ON *kross* < L *crux*] **— cross'ly** *adv.* **— cross'ness** *n.*

Cross (krôs, kros), **Wilbur Lucius,** 1862–1948, U.S. educator and politician.

cross·band (krôs'band', kros'-) *v.t.* To arrange (plywood) so that the grain in each layer is at right angles to the grain of the adjoining layers.

cross·bar (krôs'bär', kros'-) *n.* A transverse bar or line. **—** *v.t.* **·barred, ·bar·ring** To secure or mark with crossbars.

cross·beam (krôs'bēm', kros'-) *n.* **1.** A large beam or girder going from wall to wall. **2.** Any beam that crosses another.

cross·bed·ded (krôs'bed'id, kros'-) *adj. Geol.* Characterized by subsidiary beds or layers of rock cutting across the main stratification.

cross·bill (krôs'bil', kros'-) *n.* A finchlike bird (genus *Loxia*), having points on its mandibles that cross each other when the beak is closed.

cross·birth (krôs'bûrth', kros'-) *n. Med.* Any abnormal presentation of a fetus before delivery.

cross·bones (krôs'bōnz', kros'-) *n.* A representation of two bones crossing each other, usually surmounted by a skull, used as a symbol of death, a pirate's emblem, etc.

cross·bow (krôs'bō', kros'-) *n.* A medieval weapon consisting of a bow fixed transversely on a grooved stock along which arrows or stones are released. **— cross'bow'man** *n.*

cross bracing *Engin.* A type of bracing in which two braces cross or intersect each other at an oblique angle.

cross·breed (krôs'brēd', kros'-) *v.t. & v.i.* **·bred, ·breed·ing** *Biol.* To produce (a strain or animal) by interbreeding or blending two varieties; hybridize. **—** *n.* A strain or animal produced by crossbreeding; a hybrid; mongrel.

cross·check (krôs'chek') *v.t. & v.i.* **1.** To confirm or make certain by using parallel or additional data. **2.** In hockey, to check illegally with the stick by chopping at the puck-carrier's arms or stick. **—** *n.* The act of one who crosschecks.

cross-coun·try (krôs'kun'trē, kros'-) *adj. & adv.* **1.** Across open country and disregarding roads, lanes, etc. **2.** From one part of a country to the opposite part.

cross crosslet A cross having a small cross near the end of each arm. For illustration see CROSS.

cross-cur·rent (krôs'kûr'ənt, kros'-) *n.* **1.** A current flowing across another. **2.** A contradictory tendency or movement: *crosscurrents* of opinion.

cross-cut (krôs'kut', kros'-) *v.t. & v.i.* **·cut, ·cut·ting** To cut crosswise or through; run across; intersect. **—** *adj.* **1.** Used or made for the purpose of cutting something across: a *crosscut* saw. **2.** Cut across or on the bias: *crosscut* silk. **—** *n.* **1.** A cut across or a shortcut. **2.** *Mining* A cutting that intersects the lode or the main workings.

crosse (krôs, kros) *n.* A lacrosse stick. [< F]

cross-ex·am·ine (krôs'ig·zam'in, kros'-) *v.t. & v.i.* **·ined, ·in·ing 1.** To question anew (a witness called by the opposing party) for the purpose of testing the reliability of his previous testimony. **2.** To question again in order to test the validity of previous answers. **— cross'-ex·am'i·na'tion** *n.* **— cross'-ex·am'in·er** *n.*

cross-eye (krôs'ī', kros'-) *n.* Strabismus in which one or both eyes are turned inward.

cross-eyed (krôs'īd', kros'-) *adj.* Affected with convergent strabismus.

cross-fer·ti·li·za·tion (krôs'fûr'tə·lə·zā'shən, kros'-) *n.* **1.** *Biol.* The fertilization of an organism by the union of sexually differentiated reproductive cells or gametes, one from the ovum and one from the sperm. **2.** *Bot.* The fertilization of one plant or flower by the pollen from another.

cross-fer·ti·lize (krôs'fûr'tə·līz, kros'-) *v.t.* **·lized, ·liz·ing** To fertilize (a plant or animal) by cross-fertilization.

cross·fire (krôs'fīr', kros'-) *n.* **1.** *Mil.* Intersecting lines of fire from two or more different positions. **2.** Any similar situation in which several things or forces meet or cross: a *crossfire* of congratulations. **—** *v.i.* **·fired, ·fir·ing** To shoot from different points so that the lines of fire intersect.

cross fleu·ry (flōō'rē) A cross whose arms end in fleurs-de-lis. For illustration see CROSS.

Cross-Flor·i·da Waterway (krôs'flôr'ə·də, kros'-, -flor'-) A system of canals, rivers, etc., extending 155 miles across the Florida peninsula: also *Okeechobee Waterway.*

cross four·chée (fŏŏr·shā') A cross proportioned like the Greek cross but having each extremity forked. For illustration see CROSS.

cross-grained (krôs'grānd', kros'-) *adj.* **1.** Having the grain gnarled, or running transversely: a *cross-grained* board. **2.** Stubborn; perverse: a *cross-grained* man.

cross hair One of two fine threads or strands, as of a spider's web, crossed in the center of the focal plane of an optical instrument to define the exact point to which the readings of the circle or micrometer refer: also called *cross wire.*

cross·hatch (krôs'hach', kros'-) *v.t.* To shade, as a picture, by crossed lines. **— cross'hatch'ing** *n.*

cross·head (krôs'hed', kros'-) *n.* **1.** *Mech.* A beam across the top of something; especially, the sliding element between the connecting rod and piston of an engine. **2.** A descriptive heading placed across a column, as in a newspaper.

cross-in·dex (krôs'in'deks, kros'-) *v.t. & v.i.* To insert cross-references in (an index, etc.).

cross·ing (krôs'ing, kros'-) *n.* **1.** The act of going across or traversing. **2.** The place where something, as a road, may be crossed. **3.** Intersection, as of roads. **4.** In a cruciform church, the intersection of the transept and the nave. **5.** The act of obstructing or contradicting. **6.** Crossbreeding.

crossing over *Genetics* An interchange of parts between two homologous chromosomes in meiosis: also called *crossover.*

cross·jack (krôs'jak', kros'-) *n. Naut.* The mizzen sail: also called *crojik.*

cross-leg·ged (krôs'leg'id, -legd', kros'-) *adj.* Having one leg crossed over the other.

cross·let (krôs'lit, kros'-) *n. Heraldry* A small cross. [< AF *croiselette,* dim. of OF *crois* cross]

cros·sop·te·ryg·i·an (kro·sop'tə·rij'ē·ən) *n. Zool.* Any of a superorder (*Crossopterygii*) of bony fishes abundant in the Devonian period, having paddle-shaped, lobate fins, as the coelacanth, regarded as the direct ancestors of amphibians. [< NL *Crossopterygii* < Gk. *krossoi* fringe + *pterygia* fins, pl. dim. of *pteryx* wing]

cross-o·ver (krôs'ō'vər, kros'-) *n.* **1.** A place at which a crossing is made; also, the means of crossing; passageway; connection. **2.** *Genetics* **a** A crossing over (which see). **b** A character resulting from this. **3.** A short railroad track for switching trains from one track to another.

crossover map *Genetics* A chromosome map (which see).

cross·patch (krôs'pach', kros'-) *n. Informal* A cranky, ill-tempered person.

cross peen A chisellike peen on a hammerhead, the peen running parallel to the handle.

cross·piece (krôs'pēs', kros'-) *n.* Any piece of material that crosses another.

cross-pol·li·nate (krôs'pol'ə·nāt, kros'-) *v.t.* **·nat·ed, ·nat·ing** To cross-fertilize (a plant). **— cross'-pol'li·na'tion** *n.*

cross-pur·pose (krôs'pûr'pəs, kros'-) *n.* **1.** A purpose or aim in conflict with another. **2.** *pl.* A conversational game of questions and answers. **— to be at cross-purposes** To misunderstand or act counter to each other's purposes.

cross-ques·tion (krôs'kwes'chən, kros'-) *v.t.* To question minutely; also, to cross-examine. **—** *n.* A question asked in a cross-examination. **— cross'-ques'tion·ing** *n.*

cross-re·fer (krôs'ri·fûr', kros'-) *v.* **·ferred, ·fer·ring** *v.t.* **1.** To refer to another passage or part. **—** *v.i.* **2.** To make a cross-reference.

cross-ref·er·ence (krôs'ref'rəns, -ref'ər·əns, kros'-) *n.* A note or statement directing a reader from one part of a book, index, etc., to another part. Abbr. *x-ref.*

cross relation *Music* **1.** A chromatic progression divided between two different voices. **2.** The simultaneous occurrence of two tones with the same letter name, one of which is modified by an accidental. Also called *false relation.*

cross·road (krôs'rōd', kros'-) *n.* **1.** A road that intersects another road. **2.** A road crossing from one main road to another. Also called *crossway.*

cross·roads (krôs'rōdz', kros'-) *n.pl.* (construed as sing.) **1.** The place where roads meet: in rural areas, often a settlement. **2.** The meeting place of different cultures: Paris is one of the *crossroads* of the world. **— at the crossroads** At any critical point or moment.

cross·ruff (krôs'ruf', kros'-) *n.* In cards, a play in which each of two partners alternately trumps the other's lead.

cross section 1. A plane section of any object cut at right angles to its length; also, a piece so cut or a diagram or representation of this cutting. **2.** A sampling meant to be characteristic or typical of the whole: a *cross section* of opinion. **3.** A cutting through anything at right angles. **4.** In surveying, a vertical section of ground taken along a survey line for purposes of computing excavation and earthwork quantities.

cross-stitch (krôs'stich', kros'-) *n.* **1.** A double stitch in the form of an *x.* **2.** Needlework made with this stitch. **—** *v.t.* To make or mark with a cross-stitch.

cross·talk (krôs'tôk', kros'-) *n. Telecom.* The garbled sounds heard in a telephone receiver or on the radio as a result of interfering currents from another channel.

cross thread In hemstitching, one of the threads remaining in a fabric across the space from which a number of parallel threads have been drawn, and which are divided and fastened into clusters. For illustration see HEMSTITCH.

cross·tie (krôs'tī', kros'-) *n. Chiefly U.S.* A beam or tie laid crosswise under railroad tracks to support them; also, any similar support.

cross-town (krôs′toun′, kros′-) *adj.* Going across a town or city: a *cross-town* bus. — *adv.* Across a town or city: They headed *cross-town*.

cross-tree (krôs′trē′, kros′-) *n. Usually pl. Naut.* Pieces of wood or metal set crosswise at the head of a mast to sustain the top or to extend the topgallant shrouds.

cross-walk (krôs′wôk′, kros′-) *n.* A lane marked off for use by pedestrians in crossing a street.

cross-way (krôs′wā′, kros′-) *n.* A crossroad.

cross-wind (krôs′wind′, kros′-) *n.* 1. A wind blowing across the flight path of an aircraft or the course of a ship. 2. Any wind at an angle to a given course or direction.

cross wire 1. One wire crossing another. 2. A cross hair (which see).

cross-wise (krôs′wīz′, kros′-) *adv.* 1. Across. 2. In the form of a cross. 3. Contrarily. Also **cross′ways′** (-wāz′).

cross-word puzzle (krôs′wûrd′, kros′-) A puzzle worked on a pattern of white and black spaces, of which the white spaces are to be filled with letters that form words to agree with numbered definitions or similar clues, the words often crossing each other horizontally or vertically.

crot-a-line (krot′ə-lin, -līn, krō′tə-) *adj.* Of or pertaining to a subfamily (*Crotalinae*) of venomous snakes, including the copperhead and rattlesnake. [< NL < Gk. *krotalon* rattle]

crotch (kroch) *n.* 1. The fork or angle formed by two diverging parts, as by the branches of a tree. 2. The region of the human body where the legs separate from the pelvis. 3. A forked pole, support, etc. [? < OF *croche* crook]

crotched (krocht) *adj.* Having a crotch; forked.

crotch-et (kroch′it) *n.* 1. A whimsical or perverse notion or whim; an eccentricity. 2. A small hook or hooklike instrument, as used in surgery, etc. 3. *Entomol.* A hooklike process. 4. *Music Chiefly Brit.* A quarter note. [< MF *crochet.* See CROCHET.]

crotch-et-y (kroch′ə-tē) *adj.* 1. Full of eccentric or stubborn notions; perverse; contrary. 2. Like a crotchet. — **crotch′et-i-ness** *n.*

cro-ton (krōt′n) *n.* 1. Any member of a genus (*Croton*) of trees and shrubs of the spurge family, some species of which are used medicinally. 2. An ornamental tropical shrub (*Codiaeum variegatum*) grown for its foliage. [< NL < Gk. *krotōn* a tick; so called from the appearance of the seeds]

Cro-ton bug (krōt′n) A small, light-colored cockroach (*Blatella germanica*): also called *German cockroach, water bug.* For illustration see INSECTS (injurious). [after *Croton* Aqueduct; because the first serious infestation in New York City occurred shortly after this aqueduct was opened in 1842]

cro-ton-ic acid (krō-ton′ik, -tō′nik) *Chem.* A compound, $C_4H_6O_2$, obtained from croton oil, used in organic synthesis.

Cro-ton Lake (krōt′n) An artificial lake formed by damming the **Croton River,** a river flowing through SE New York, a source of water supply for New York City.

croton oil A yellowish viscid oil obtained from the seeds of a small East Indian tree (*Croton tiglium*), used as a purgative.

crouch (krouch) *v.i.* 1. To stoop or bend low, as an animal ready to spring. 2. To cringe; abase oneself; cower. — *v.t.* 3. To bend low. — *n.* A crouching or crouching position. [? < OF *crochir* to be bent < *croc* a hook]

croup¹ (kroop) *n. Pathol.* 1. A disease of the throat characterized by hoarse coughing, laryngeal spasm, and difficult breathing. 2. Loosely, inflammation of the larynx. [Imit.]

croup² (kroop) *n.* The rump of certain animals, especially the portion of a horse's back behind the saddle. Also **croupe.** For illustration see HORSE. [< OF *crope*]

crou-pi-er (kroo′pē-ər, *Fr.* kroo-pyā′) *n.* 1. One who collects the stakes lost and pays out those won at a gaming table. 2. The assistant chairman at a public dinner. [< F, lit., one who rides on the croup, an assistant]

croup-ous (kroo′pəs) *adj. Pathol.* Relating to or similar to croup.

croup-y (kroo′pē) *adj.* 1. Of, pertaining to, or indicating croup. 2. Having croup. — **croup′i-ness** *n.*

crouse (kroos) *adj. Scot.* Contented and jolly; frisky; saucy. [ME (northern) *crous* < Gmc.]

crou-ton (kroo′ton, kroo-ton′; *Fr.* kroo-tôn′) *n.* A small piece of toasted or fried bread used as a garnish, as in soups. [< F *croûton* < *croûte* crust]

crow¹ (krō) *n.* 1. Any of various omnivorous, raucous, oscine birds (genus *Corvus*) having glossy black plumage; especially *C. brachyrhynchos* of North America, and the carrion crow of Europe. 2. Loosely, the rook or raven. ◆ Collateral adjective: *corvine.* 3. A crowbar. — **as the crow flies** In a straight line. — **to eat crow** *Informal* To recant a statement; back down; humiliate oneself. [OE *crāwe*]

crow² (krō) *v.i.* **crowed** or (*for def. 1*) **crew, crowed, crow-ing** 1. To utter the shrill cry of a cock. 2. To exult; boast. 3. To utter sounds expressive of delight, as an infant. — *n.* 1. The cry of a cock. 2. Any shrill, inarticulate sound resembling this, as an infant's cry of pleasure. [OE *crāwan*]

Crow (krō) *n.* 1. A North American Indian of a Siouan tribe formerly inhabiting the region between the Platte and Yellowstone rivers. 2. The language of this tribe.

Crow (krō) *n.* The constellation Corvus.

crow-bar (krō′bär′) *n.* A straight iron or steel bar with a flattened point often set at an angle, used as a lever.

crow-ber-ry (krō′ber′ē, -bər′ē) *n. pl.* **-ries** 1. Any of several shrubby, evergreen plants (genus *Empetrum*) having berrylike fruit; especially, the **black crowberry** (*E. nigrum*) of alpine and arctic regions of North America. 2. The bearberry (def. 1). 3. The fruit of either of these plants. [Prob. trans. of G *krähenbeere*]

crow blackbird The grackle (def. 1).

crowd¹ (kroud) *n.* 1. A large number of persons gathered closely together; a throng. 2. The populace in general; mob. 3. *Informal* A particular set of people; a clique. 4. A collection of things gathered together: a *crowd* of paintings. — **Syn.** See COMPANY. — *v.t.* 1. To shove or push. 2. To fill to overflowing, as with a crowd; fill to excess. 3. To cram together; force into a confined space. 4. *Informal* To put pressure on, especially for payment; press annoyingly. — *v.i.* 5. To gather in large numbers; throng together. 6. To push forward; force one's way. 7. To shove or push. — **to crowd (on) sail** *Naut.* To spread a great amount of sail in order to gain speed. [OE *crūdan*] — **crowd′er** *n.*

crowd² (kroud) *n.* An ancient instrument resembling a violin, used in Ireland and Wales. [< Welsh *crwth* violin]

crowd-ed (krou′did) *adj.* 1. Filled or closely packed, as with people or things. 2. Too closely gathered together.

crow-die (krou′dē, krood′ē) *n. Scot.* Porridge. Also **crow′dy.**

crow-foot (krō′foot′) *n. pl.* **-foots** for *defs. 1 & 2,* **-feet** for *defs. 3, 4, & 5* 1. Any plant of a genus (*Ranunculus*) typical of a large family (*Ranunculaceae*) including the buttercup, columbine, delphinium, etc. 2. Any of various plants having leaves, etc., suggestive of a bird's foot. 3. *Mil.* A caltrop. 4. *Naut.* A number of divergent lines passed through the apertures of a perforated wooden block and supporting an awning. 5. *Aeron.* A crow's-foot.

crown (kroun) *n.* 1. A circlet, often of precious metal set with jewels, worn on the head as a mark of sovereign power. 2. A decorative covering for the head; garland; wreath. 3. Anything shaped like a crown, as a badge, hallmark, etc. 4. *Heraldry* A bearing representing a crown. 5. A coin stamped with a crown or a crowned head, as: **a** The English crown, worth five shillings. **b** A koruna. **c** A krona. **d** A krone. 6. The top part of the head: a bald *crown.* 7. The head itself: He cracked his *crown.* 8. The upper part of a hat. 9. The top or summit of something: The *crown* of a hill. 10. The most perfect or complete state or type: the *crown* of womanhood. 11. A reward or prize for achievement. 12. *Dent.* **a** The part of a tooth that is covered with enamel. **b** An artificial substitute for the crown of a tooth, made of gold, porcelain, or certain plastics. 13. *Naut.* The lowest or outer point of junction of the two arms of an anchor. 14. *Bot.* **a** The upper part of a tree, including the living branches and their foliage. **b** The point where stem and root unite in a seed plant. 15. The crest of an animal, especially of a bird. 16. The part of a cut gem stone above the girdle. *Abbr.* cr. — **the Crown** 1. The sovereign ruler; monarch. 2. The power or the empire of a monarch; sovereignty. — *v.t.* 1. To place a crown or garland on the head of. 2. To enthrone; make a monarch of. 3. To endow with honor or dignity. 4. To surmount; be the topmost part of. 5. To form the crown, ornament, or top to. 6. To finish or make complete; consummate. 7. *Dent.* To place a crown on (a tooth). 8. *Informal* To strike on the head. 9. In checkers, to make (a piece) into a king by placing another piece upon it. [< AF *coroune,* OF *corone* < L *corona*] — **crown′er** *n.* — **crown′less** *adj.*

HISTORIC CROWNS

a Imperial Russian crown. *b* Crown of the German Empire. *c* Iron crown of Lombardy. *d* Imperial crown of Charlemagne.

crown colony A colony of Great Britain in which the Crown retains control of legislation, usually administered by a governor with executive and legislative councils.

crown-er (krou′nər) *n. Brit. Dial.* A coroner.

crown-et (krou′nit) *n. Obs.* A coronet.

crown glass 1. Hard optical glass of low refraction. 2. Window glass blown into a bubble, then whirled flat.

crown graft In horticulture, a form of graft in which a split cion is inserted at the crown of the stock.

crown-land (kroun′land′) *n.* Formerly, one of the major administrative divisions of Austria-Hungary.

crown land 1. Land belonging by hereditary right to a reigning sovereign. 2. In certain countries of The Commonwealth, nonurban public land.

crown lens *Optics* The convex portion in an achromatic lens, made of crown glass.

crown-piece (kroun′pēs′) *n.* 1. A piece forming the top or crown of anything. 2. The strap in a bridle that goes over the horse's head and is buckled with the cheek straps. For illustration see HARNESS.

Crown Point A village in NE New York; site of two colonial forts, strategic in the French and Indian War and captured from the British in the Revolutionary War.

crown prince The male heir apparent to a throne.

crown princess 1. The wife of a crown prince. **2.** The female heir apparent to a throne.

crown saw A cylindrical saw with teeth at right angles to its plane, operated with a rotary motion.

crown vetch The axseed, a plant.

crown wheel *Mech.* A wheel with cogs at right angles to its plane, as the wheel that drives the balance in a watch.

crown·work (kroun′wûrk′) *n.* **1.** A fortification running into the field, designed to cover some advantageous position and to protect other works. **2.** *Dent.* **a** The placing of artificial crowns upon teeth. **b** An artificial crown or crowns.

crow's-foot (krōz′fŏŏt′) *n. pl.* **-feet 1.** One of the wrinkles diverging from the outer corner of the eye. **2.** An embroidery stitch forming a three-pointed design. **3.** *Aeron.* An arrangement of short ropes diverging from a main rope, used in the handling of lighter-than-air craft: also *crowfoot.*

crow's-nest (krōz′nest′) *n.* **1.** *Naut.* A small observation platform near the top of a ship's mast. **2.** Any similar look-out station, as one ashore.

crow·step (krō′step′) A corbie-step (which see).

Croy·don (kroid′n) A county borough in NE Surrey, a suburb of London; pop. 252,387 (1961).

croze (krōz) *n.* **1.** The groove in the staves of a cask in which the edge of the head is set. **2.** A cooper's tool for making a croze: also *croz′er.* [? < F *creux* < OF *croz* groove]

cro·zier (krō′zhər) See CROSIER.

crs. Credits; creditors.

cru·ces (krōō′sēz) Alternative plural of CRUX.

cruci- *combining form* Cross: *cruciform.* [< L *crux, crucis* cross]

cru·cial (krōō′shəl) *adj.* **1.** Of a critical or decisive nature: a *crucial* battle. **2.** Involving trials and difficulties; severe. **3.** Having the form of a cross. — **Syn.** See ACUTE. [< MF < L *crux, crucis* cross, torture] — **cru′cial·ly** *adv.*

cru·ci·ate (krōō′shē·it, -āt) *adj.* **1.** Cross-shaped. **2.** *Entomol.* Having the wings crossing obliquely when at rest, as certain insects. **3.** *Bot.* Having the parts arranged in the form of a cross with equal arms. [< L *cruciatus,* pp. of *cruciare* to crucify < *crux* cross]

cru·ci·ble (krōō′sə·bəl) *n.* **1.** A heat-resistant vessel for melting metals or minerals: also called *fire pot.* **2.** The hollow place in the bottom of a metallurgical furnace, in which the molten metal is received. **3.** A severely trying test or experience. [< Med.L *crucibulum* earthen pot, lamp, ? ult. < L *crux* cross. Cf. also MHG *kruse* pot.]

crucible steel *Metall.* A high-grade steel made by melting wrought iron with ferromanganese or other special steels in crucibles placed in specially designed furnaces.

cru·ci·fer (krōō′sə·fər) *n.* **1.** One who bears a cross. **2.** *Bot.* A cruciferous plant. [< LL < L *crux* cross + *ferre* to bear]

cru·cif·er·ous (krōō·sif′ər·əs) *adj.* **1.** Bearing a cross. **2.** *Bot.* Of or pertaining to a large family (*Cruciferae*) of herbaceous plants having cruciate flowers, including the mustards.

cru·ci·fix (krōō′sə·fiks) *n.* **1.** A cross bearing an effigy of Christ crucified. **2.** The cross as a Christian emblem. [< OF *crucefix* < L *cruci fixus* one hanged on a cross < *crux* cross + *figere* to fasten]

cru·ci·fix·ion (krōō′sə·fik′shən) *n.* **1.** The act of crucifying, or the state of being crucified. **2.** Extreme persecution or suffering. **3.** A painting, piece of sculpture, etc., that represents Christ's death on the cross. — **the Crucifixion** The execution of Jesus Christ on the cross.

cru·ci·form (krōō′sə·fôrm) *adj.* Cross-shaped; cruciate. [< CRUCI- + -FORM]

cru·ci·fy (krōō′sə·fī) *v.t.* **·fied, ·fy·ing 1.** To put to death by nailing or fastening the hands and feet to a cross. **2.** To mortify; subdue: to *crucify* the lusts of the flesh. **3.** To torture; torment. [< OF *crucifier,* ult. < L *cruci figere* to fasten to a cross] — **cru′ci·fi′er** *n.*

crud (krud) *n.* **1.** *Brit. Dial.* Curd. **2.** *Slang* Worthless rubbish. [ME *crud* curd; origin uncertain]

crude (krōōd) *adj.* **crud·er, crud·est 1.** In an unrefined or unprepared state: raw: *crude* oil. **2.** Immature; unripe. **3.** Showing a lack of skill or knowledge: a *crude* effort. **4.** Roughly made; unfinished. **5.** Lacking tact, refinement, or taste; uncultured; rude. **6.** Undisguised; bare: the *crude* truth. — *n.* Petroleum as it comes from the well; unrefined petroleum and hydrocarbons. [< L *crudus* rough, immature. Akin to CRUEL.] — **crude′ly** *adv.* — **crude′ness** *n.* — **Syn. 4.** unpolished, simple, rude. **5.** vulgar, uncouth, gross.

Cru·den (krōō′dən), **Alexander,** 1701–70, Scottish compiler of a Biblical concordance.

cru·di·ty (krōō′də·tē) *n. pl.* **·ties 1.** The state or quality of being crude. **2.** A crude act, remark, etc.

cru·el (krōō′əl) *adj.* **cru·el·er** or **·el·ler, cru·el·est** or **·el·lest 1.** Disposed to inflict pain or hardship; indifferent to or enjoying the suffering of others; pitiless: a *cruel* master. **2.** Inflicting mental or physical suffering; painfully harsh. [< OF < L *crudelis* severe. Akin to CRUDE.] — **cru′el·ly** *adv.* — **cru′el·ness** *n.*

cru·el·ty (krōō′əl·tē) *n. pl.* **·ties 1.** The quality or condition of being cruel; mercilessness; inhumanity. **2.** That which causes suffering; an inhuman act; brutal treatment.

cru·et (krōō′it) *n.* A small glass bottle for vinegar, oil, etc. [< AF, dim. of OF *crue* pot]

Cruik·shank (krŏŏk′shangk), **George,** 1792–1878, English caricaturist.

cruise (krōōz) *v.* **cruised, cruis·ing** *v.i.* **1.** To sail about with no fixed destination, as for pleasure or for reconnaissance purposes. **2.** To travel about at a moderate speed, as a police squad car. **3.** To move at the optimum speed for sustained travel: said of aircraft, ships, etc. — *v.t.* **4.** To cruise over. — *n.* A cruising trip, especially a voyage at sea. [< Du. *kruisen* to cross, traverse < *kruis* a cross < L *crux*]

cruis·er (krōō′zər) *n.* **1.** One who or that which cruises. **2.** A fast, maneuverable warship, having long cruising radius, with medium tonnage and armament. **3.** A small power vessel equipped with living facilities: also called *cabin cruiser.*

cruising radius The maximum distance from base that a ship or aircraft can go and return without refueling.

cruising speed The optimum speed for sustained travel of a ship, aircraft, etc.

crul·ler (krul′ər) *n.* A small cake of sweetened dough, fried in deep fat: also spelled *kruller.* [< Du. < *krullen* to curl]

crumb (krum) *n.* **1.** A tiny fragment of bread, cake, or the like. **2.** A bit or scrap of anything: *crumbs* of information. **3.** The soft inner part of bread, as distinguished from the crust. **4.** *U.S. Slang* A contemptible person. — *v.t.* **1.** To break into small pieces; crumble. **2.** In cooking, to dress or cover with bread crumbs. [OE *cruma; b* added on analogy with *dumb, lamb,* etc.]

crum·ble (krum′bəl) *v.* **·bled, ·bling** *v.t.* **1.** To cause to break into tiny parts, as by crushing. — *v.i.* **2.** To fall to small pieces; fall into decay; disintegrate. — **Syn.** See DECAY. — *n. Archaic* Any crumbly substance. [ME *crimble,* ult. < OE *cruma* crumb; infl. in form by *crumb*]

crum·bly (krum′blē) *adj.* **·bli·er, ·bli·est** Apt to crumble; friable. — **crum′bli·ness** *n.*

crumb·y (krum′ē) *adj.* **crumb·i·er, crumb·i·est 1.** Full of crumbs. **2.** Soft, like the inner part of bread. **3.** *U.S. Slang* Crummy.

crum·mie (krum′ē, krōōm′ē) *n. Scot.* A cow with crooked horns. [< obs. *crum* crooked < OE *crumb*]

crum·my (krum′ē) *adj.* **crum·mi·er, crum·mi·est** *U.S. Slang* Inferior; cheap; shabby.

crump (krump) *v.i.* To make a crunching sound. — *adj. Scot & Brit. Dial.* Crisp; crusty; brittle. [Imit.]

crum·pet (krum′pit) *n.* A thin, leavened batter cake baked on a gridiron and usually toasted and buttered. [Short for *crumpet cake* < ME *crompid,* pp. of *crompen* to curl up]

crum·ple (krum′pəl) *v.* **·pled, ·pling** *v.t.* **1.** To press into wrinkles; rumple. — *v.i.* **2.** To become wrinkled; shrivel. **3.** *Informal* To collapse. — *n.* Anything crumpled; a wrinkle. [Freq. of obs. *crump,* var. of CRIMP]

crunch (krunch) *v.t.* **1.** To chew with a crushing or crackling sound. **2.** To crush or grind noisily. — *v.i.* **3.** To chew noisily. **4.** To move or advance with a crushing sound. **5.** To emit a crushing sound. — *n.* A crunching, or the sound of crunching. Also, *Rare, craunch.* [Imit.]

cru·node (krōō′nōd) *n. Math.* A point at which a curve crosses itself and therefore has two tangents. [< L *crux* cross + NODE] — **cru·no′dal** *adj.*

cru·or (krōō′ôr) *n.* Clotted blood; gore. [< L]

crup·per (krup′ər) *n.* **1.** The looped strap that goes under a horse's tail. For illustration see HARNESS. **2.** The rump of a horse; croup. [< AF *cropere,* OF *cropiere* < *crope* croup²]

cru·ra (krŏŏr′ə) Plural of CRUS.

cru·ral (krŏŏr′əl) *adj.* Of or pertaining to the leg or the thigh. [< L *cruralis* < *crus* leg]

crus (krus) *n. pl.* **cru·ra** (krŏŏr′ə) *Anat.* **1.** The part of the leg between the knee and ankle; shank. **2.** *Usually pl.* Stalks or peduncles, as the compact masses of fibers that connect different parts of the brain. **3.** Any part resembling or likened to a leg. [< L, leg]

cru·sade (krōō·sād′) *n.* **1.** *Usually cap.* Any of the military expeditions undertaken by European Christians from the 11th through the 13th century to recover the Holy Land from the Moslems. See table for WAR. **2.** Any expedition under papal sanction against heathens or heretics. **3.** Any vigorous concerted movement or cause, especially a reform movement. — *v.i.* **·sad·ed, ·sad·ing** To engage in a crusade. [< Sp. *cruzada* < Med.L *cruciata* a crossing < *cruciare* to mark with a cross < L *crux* a cross; infl. in form by related F *croisade*] — **cru·sad′er** *n.*

cru·sa·do (krōō·sā′dō) *n. pl.* **·does** or **·dos** A former Portuguese gold or silver coin: also spelled *cruzado.* [< Pg., lit., marked with a cross]

cruse (krōōz, krōōs) *n.* A small bottle, flask, or jug; cruet. [? < MDu. *cruyse* jar, pot]

cru·set (krōō′sit) *n.* A goldsmith's melting pot. [< MF *creuset*; ult. origin uncertain]

crush (krush) *v.t.* 1. To press or squeeze out of shape; mash. 2. To smash or grind into fine particles. 3. To obtain or extract by pressure. 4. To press upon; crowd. 5. To rumple or press out of shape. 6. To put down; subdue; conquer. 7. *Archaic* To burden or oppress. 8. *Rare* To drink. —*v.i.* 9. To become broken or misshapen by pressure. 10. To move ahead by crushing or pressing. — *Syn.* See BREAK. —*n.* 1. The act of crushing; extreme compression. 2. The state of being crushed, as in a crowd. 3. A crowd or throng; jam. 4. A substance obtained by or as if by crushing: orange *crush*. 5. *Informal* An infatuation, or the object of it. [< OF *croissir* to break < Gmc. Cf. MHG *krosen* to crush, crack.] — **crush′a·ble** *adj.* — **crush′er** *n.*

Cru·soe (krōō′sō), **Robinson** See ROBINSON CRUSOE.

crust (krust) *n.* 1. The hard outer part of bread, as distinguished from the crumb. 2. A piece of bread consisting mostly of crust (def. 1); also, any dry, hard piece of bread. 3. The pastry shell of a pie, tart, etc. 4. Any hard, crisp surface, as of snow. 5. A hard coating deposited by wine on the interior of bottles. 6. *Slang* Insolence; impertinence. 7. *Geol.* The solid, cool exterior shell or zone of the earth. 8. *Biol.* The hard integument of certain organisms, as lichens, crustaceans, etc. 9. A coating of dry, hard blood, pus, etc.; a scab. —*v.t. & v.i.* 1. To cover with or acquire a crust. 2. To form into a crust. [< OF *crouste* < L *crusta*]

crus·ta·cean (krus·tā′shən) *n.* One of a class of arthropods (*Crustacea*) having crustlike shells, and generally aquatic, including lobsters, crabs, barnacles, sow bugs, etc. —*adj.* Of or pertaining to the *Crustacea*. [< NL *Crustacea* < L *crusta* crust; with ref. to the shell]

crus·ta·ceous (krus·tā′shəs) *adj.* 1. Petaining to, of the nature of, or having a crustlike shell. 2. Crustacean.

crus·tal (krus′təl) *adj.* Of or pertaining to a crust, especially the earth's crust.

crust·y (krus′tē) *adj.* **crust·i·er, crust·i·est** 1. Like or having a crust. 2. Harshly curt in manner or speech; surly. — **crust′i·ly** *adv.* — **crust′i·ness** *n.*

crutch (kruch) *n.* 1. A staff used by the lame as a support in walking, especially one having a crosspiece to fit under the armpit and a grip for the hand. 2. Anything that gives support: *Liquor was his crutch.* 3. Any of various devices resembling a crutch in shape or function, as a forked leg rest on a sidesaddle. 4. The crotch of the human body. 5. *Naut.* A forked support for a swinging boom when not in use. —*v.t.* To prop up or support, as on crutches. [OE *crycc*]

crutched (krucht) *adj.* Bearing the sign of the cross: the *Crutched* Friars. [Earlier *crouched*, pp. of obs. *crouch* to mark with a cross]

crux (kruks) *n. pl.* **crux·es** or **cru·ces** (krōō′sēz) 1. A pivotal, fundamental, or vital point. 2. A cross. 3. A tormenting or baffling problem. [< L. *crux*]

Crux (kruks) *n.* A constellation, the Southern Cross, containing the bright star Acrux. See CONSTELLATION.

crux an·sa·ta (an·sā′tə) An ansate cross (which see).

cru·za·do (krōō·sā′dō) See CRUSADO.

cru·zei·ro (krōō·zā′rō, *Pg.* -rōō) *n.* The monetary unit of Brazil, equivalent to 100 centavos. [< Pg < *cruz* cross < L *crux*]

cry (krī) *v.* **cried, cry·ing** *v.i.* 1. To utter sobbing sounds of grief, pain, fear, etc., usually accompanied by tears; weep; also, to shed tears inaudibly. 2. To call out or appeal loudly; shout: often with *out.* 3. To make characteristic calls: said of animals. —*v.t.* 4. To utter loudly or shout out; exclaim. 5. To advertise loudly and publicly: to *cry* one's wares. 6. To affect (oneself) in some specified way by weeping: to *cry* oneself to sleep. 7. To beg for; implore: to *cry* mercy. — **to cry down** 1. To belittle; disparage. 2. To silence or put down by cries. — **to cry off** To back out of a promise or undertaking. — **to cry up** To praise highly. — *n. pl.* **cries** 1. A loud or emotional utterance; shout; call. 2. A fit of weeping: *She had a long cry.* 3. An appeal; entreaty. 4. Advertisement by outcry: a vender's *cry.* 5. General report or rumor; public opinion. 6. A rallying call; battle cry. 7. A political slogan; catchword. 8. A demand; clamor: a *cry* for better housing. 9. The characteristic call of a bird or animal. 10. A pack of hounds. — **a far cry** 1. A long distance away. 2. Something very unlike: *a far cry* from the original. — **in full cry** In full pursuit, as a pack of hounds. [< OF *crier* < L *quiritare* to call out]

cry·ba·by (krī′bā′bē) *n. pl.* **·bies** A person, especially a child, given to crying or complaining.

cry·ing (krī′ing) *adj.* 1. That cries: a *crying* child. 2. Calling for immediate action or remedy: a *crying* shame.

cryo- *combining form* Cold; frost: *cryogen.* [< Gk. *kryos* frost]

cry·o·chore (krī′ə·kôr, -kōr) *n. Ecol.* The region of perpetual ice and snow. [< CRYO- + Gk. *chōrē* region] — **cry′o·chor′ic** *adj.*

cry·o·gen (krī′ə·jən) *n.* A mixture that induces freezing. [< CRYO- + -GEN]

cry·o·gen·ics (krī′ə·jen′iks) *n.pl.* (*construed as sing.*) The branch of physics dealing with very low temperatures. — **cry′o·gen′ic** *adj.*

cry·o·hy·drate (krī′ə·hī′drāt) *n.* A eutectic mixture of a salt and water in such proportions that the melting and freezing points are at a minimum.

cry·o·lite (krī′ə·līt) *n.* A vitreous, snow-white, translucent fluoride of sodium and aluminum, used in the production of aluminum, soda, and glass, to which it gives a milky hue: also spelled *kryolite, kryolith.* [< CRYO- + -LITE]

cry·om·e·ter (krī·om′ə·tər) *n.* An instrument for measuring a lower temperature than the ordinary mercury thermometer will indicate, as an alcohol thermometer.

cry·o·scope (krī′ə·skōp) *n.* An instrument used for determining the freezing point of liquids and other substances. [< CRYO- + -SCOPE]

cry·os·co·py (krī·os′kə·pē) *n.* The study of the freezing points of solutions, especially in relation to the lowered freezing point of the solute.

cry·o·stat (krī′ə·stat) *n.* An apparatus for automatically maintaining very low temperatures. [< CRYO- + -STAT]

cry·o·ther·a·py (krī′ə·ther′ə·pē) *n. Med.* The use of low or freezing temperatures as a therapeutic measure: also called *frozen sleep, psychrotherapy.* Also **cry′mo·ther′a·py** (krī′mə-).

cry·o·tron (krī′ə·tron) *n. Electronics* A device for utilizing the superconductivity of certain metals at temperatures approaching that of liquid helium. [< CRYO- + (ELEC)TRON]

crypt (kript) *n.* 1. A chamber or vault, especially one beneath a church, used as a place of burial. 2. *Physiol.* A small pit or cavity opening on the skin, a membrane, etc. [< L *crypta* < Gk. *kryptē* < *kryptos* hidden. Doublet of GROTTO.]

cryp·tan·al·y·sis (krip′tə·nal′ə·sis) *n. pl.* **-ses** (-sēz) The scientific study and conversion into plain text of cryptograms, ciphers, codes, etc., to which the key is not known. [< CRYPT(O)- + ANALYSIS] — **cryp·tan·a·lyst** (krip·tan′ə-list) *n.* **cryp′tan·a·lyt′ic** *adj.*

cryp·tes·the·sia (krip′təs·thē′zhə, -zhē·ə) *n.* Any of various modes of supernormal sensibility, as clairvoyance, telepathy, etc. [< CRYPT(O)- + ESTHESIA]

cryp·tic (krip′tik) *adj.* 1. Secret or hidden; occult. 2. Puzzling; mystifying: a *cryptic* remark. 3. *Zool.* Protective; concealing: *cryptic* coloration. Also **cryp′ti·cal.** [< LL *crypticus* < Gk. *kryptikos* < *kryptos* hidden]

crypto- *combining form* Hidden; secret: *cryptogram.* Also, before vowels, **crypt-.** [< Gk. *kryptos* hidden]

cryp·to·clas·tic (krip′tō·klas′tik) *adj. Geol.* Composed of microscopic fragmental grains. [< CRYPTO- + CLASTIC]

cryp·to·crys·tal·line (krip′tō·kris′tə·lin, -lēn) *adj. Mineral.* Possessing a crystalline structure that cannot be resolved into distinct individuals even under the microscope: opposed to *phanerocrystalline.* [< CRYPTO- + CRYSTALLINE]

cryp·to·gam (krip′tə·gam) *n. Bot.* 1. Any of a former division (*Cryptogamia*) of plants that have no pistils or stamens, but propagate by spores, as algae, fungi, ferns, and mosses. 2. A plant lacking true seeds and flowers: distinguished from *phanerogam.* Also called *cryptophyte.* [< F *cryptogame*, ult. < Gk. *kryptos* hidden + *gamos* marriage] — **cryp′to·gam′ic, cryp·tog·a·mous** (krip·tog′ə·məs) *adj.*

cryp·tog·a·my (krip·tog′ə·mē) *n. Bot.* The state or condition of being cryptogamic or having concealed fructification.

cryp·to·gen·ic (krip′tə·jen′ik) *adj.* Of obscure origin: used mainly of diseases. [< CRYPTO- + Gk. *genos* race, origin]

cryp·to·gram (krip′tə·gram) *n.* A message written in code or cipher, or in some combination of the two. [< CRYPTO- + GRAM] — **cryp′to·gram′mic** *adj.*

cryp·to·graph (krip′tə·graf, -gräf) *n.* 1. A cryptogram. 2. A system of cipher writing; a cipher. [< CRYPTO- + -GRAPH]

cryp·tog·ra·phy (krip·tog′rə·fē) *n.* 1. The art or process of writing in or reconverting cipher. 2. Any system of writing in secret characters. — **cryp·tog′ra·pher, cryp·tog′ra·phist** *n.* — **cryp·to·graph·ic** (krip′tə·graf′ik) *adj.*

cryp·tol·o·gy (krip·tol′ə·jē) *n.* 1. Cryptography and cryptanalysis. 2. Enigmatic language [< NL *cryptologia* < Gk. *kryptos* hidden + -*log*, stem of *legein* to speak]

cryp·tom·ne·sia (krip′təm·nē′zhə, -zhē·ə) *n.* A mental condition in which ideas based on past experiences appear as completely new. [< CRYPTO- + Gk. *mnasthai* to remember]

cryp·to·nym (krip′tə·nim) *n.* A secret name. [< CRYPTO- + Gk. *onoma, onyma* name]

cryp·ton·y·mous (krip·ton′ə·məs) *adj.* Anonymous.

cryp·to·phyte (krip′tə·fīt) *n. Bot.* A cryptogam. [< CRYPTO- + -PHYTE]

cryp·to·zo·ic (krip′tə·zō′ik) *adj. Geol.* Of or pertaining to those eras of the earth's history now generally included in the pre-Cambrian period. [< CRYPTO- + Gk. *zōē* life]

crys·tal (kris′tal) *n.* 1. The solid form assumed by many minerals. 2. Colorless transparent quartz, or rock crystal. 3. *Physics* A homogeneous solid body, exhibiting a definite and symmetrical internal structure, with geometrically arranged cleavage planes and external faces that assume any of a group of patterns associated with peculiarities of atomic structure. 4. Flint glass, or any fine clear glass, especially as made into tableware, etc. 5. Anything transparent and colorless. 6. A glass or plastic covering over the face of a watch. **7.** A specially shaped and ground piece of quartz or similar material, used to improve radio reception. — *adj.* **1.** Composed of crystal. **2.** Like crystal; extremely clear; limpid: *crystal waters.* [< OF *cristal* < L *crystallum* < Gk. *krystallos* ice, crystal < *krystainein* to freeze < *kryos* frost] — **crys'tal·like'** *adj.*

crystal ball A ball of crystal or glass used in crystal gazing.

crystal detector *Telecom.* A device consisting of metal electrodes in contact with suitable crystal materials, used to rectify incoming radio signals in a crystal set.

CRYSTALS
a Tetragonal pyramid.
b Tetragonal prism.
c Dodecahedron.
d Deltahedron.

crystal gazing The act of looking intently into a crystal ball in order to induce a vision of distant objects or future events; also, the ability to do this. — **crys·tal-gaz·er** (kris'təl·gā'zər) *n.*

crystall. or **cryst.** Crystallography.

crys·tal·lif·er·ous (kris'tə·lif'ər·əs) *adj.* Producing or containing crystals. Also **crys·tal·lig·er·ous** (kris'tə·lij'ər·əs). [< L *crystallum* clear ice, crystal + -FEROUS]

crys·tal·line (kris'tə·lin, -lēn) *adj.* **1.** Of, pertaining to, or like crystal or crystals. **2.** Transparent; clear; pure. **3.** Composed of crystal or crystals. [< F *cristallin* < L *crystallinus* < Gk. *krystallinos* < *krystallos*. See CRYSTAL.]

crystalline lens *Anat.* Lens.

crys·tal·lite (kris'tə·līt) *n. Mineral.* One of certain minute bodies not truly crystalline but resulting from a crystallizing process, found in igneous rock. [< Gk. *krystallos* crystal + -ITE[1]]

crys·tal·lize (kris'tə·līz) *v.* **·lized**, **·liz·ing** *v.t.* **1.** To cause to form crystals or become crystalline. **2.** To bring to definite and permanent form: to *crystallize* one's plans. **3.** To coat with sugar. — *v.i.* **4.** To assume the form of crystals. **5.** To assume definite and permanent form. Also **crys'ta·lize.** — **crys'tal·liz'a·ble** *adj.* — **crys'tal·li·za'tion** *n.*

crystallo- *combining form* Crystal: *crystallography.* Also, before vowels, **crystall-.** [< Gk. *krystallos* crystal]

crys·tal·lo·graph·ic (kris'tə·lə·graf'ik) *adj.* Of or pertaining to crystallography. Also **crys'tal·lo·graph'i·cal.** — **crys'·tal·lo·graph'i·cal·ly** *adv.*

crys·tal·log·ra·phy (kris'tə·log'rə·fē) *n.* The science of crystals, including the study of their geometrical, physical, and chemical structure. [< NL *crystallographia* < Gk. *krystallos* crystal + *graphein* to write]

crys·tal·loid (kris'tə·loid) *adj.* Like or having the nature of a crystal or a crystalloid. Also **crys'tal·loi'dal.** — *n.* **1.** *Chem.* One of a class of substances, usually crystallizable, whose solutions pass easily through membranes: distinguished from *colloid.* **2.** *Bot.* A crystallike protein body found in plant cells. [< Gk. *krystalloeidēs* like crystal]

crystal pickup A pickup that utilizes a piezoelectric crystal to transform mechanical motion into sound, etc., often used in electric record players. Compare MAGNETIC PICKUP.

crystal set A radio receiving set operating with a crystal detector but without electron tubes.

crystal system Any of the fundamental patterns by which crystals are identified on the basis of imaginary axes drawn from each face or edge though the center of the crystal. The six major systems are the isometric or cubic, tetragonal, hexagonal, orthorhombic, monoclinic, and triclinic, to which some authorities add a seventh, the trigonal.

crystal violet A derivative of rosaniline, used as an indicator in medicine and bacteriology.

crystal vision The ability to see or predict events by looking into a crystal ball; also, that which is alleged to be seen.

Cs 1. *Chem.* Cesium. **2.** *Meteorol.* Cirrostratus.

C/S or **cs.** Case(s).

C.S. Christian Science; Christian Scientist.

C.S. or **c.s. 1.** Capital stock. **2.** Civil service.

C.S.A. Confederate States of America.

csc *Trig.* Cosecant.

CSC Civil Service Commission.

csk. 1. Cask. **2.** Countersink.

CSS Commodity Stabilization Service.

CST or **C.S.T.** or **c.s.t.** Central Standard Time.

ct. 1. Cent(s). **2.** County. **3.** Court. **4.** One hundred (L *centum*).

Ct. 1. Connecticut. **2.** Count.

CT or **C.T.** or **c.t.** Central Time.

cte·nid·i·um (tə·nid'ē·əm) *n. pl.* **·nid·i·a** (-nid'ē·ə) *Zool.* **1.** One of the comblike respiratory organs of mollusks. **2.** One of the comblike structures situated on the toes of some birds. [< NL < Gk. *ktenidion*, dim. of *kteis, ktenos* comb]

cteno- *combining form Zool.* A comblike structure. Also, before vowels, **cten-.** [< Gk. *kteis, ktenos* comb]

cten·oid (ten'oid, tē'noid) *adj. Biol.* Having a comblike

margin, as certain plants, or having comblike plates, as in ctenophores. [< Gk. *ktenoeidēs* like a comb]

cten·o·phore (ten'ə·fôr, -fōr, tē'nə-) *n.* One of a phylum (*Ctenophora*) of free-swimming marine coelenterates having transparent gelatinous bodies on which are eight longitudinal rows of comblike plates: also called *comb jelly.* [< NL *Ctenophora* < Gk. *kteis, ktenos* comb + *pherein* to bear]

Ctes·i·phon (tes'ə·fon) A ruined city in Iraq, on the Tigris; capital of ancient Parthia.

ctn *Trig.* Cotangent.

ctr. Center.

cts. 1. Centimes. **2.** Cents. **3.** Certificates.

cu. or **cu** Cubic.

Cu 1. *Chem.* Copper (L *cuprum*). **2.** *Meteorol.* Cumulus.

cub (kub) *n.* **1.** The young of the bear, fox, wolf, and certain other carnivores; a whelp. **2.** A rough, awkward, or ill-mannered youth. **3.** A beginner or learner; an apprentice. **4.** A cub scout (which see). [Origin uncertain] — **cub'bish** *adj.* — **cub'bish·ly** *adv.*

Cu·ba (kyōō'bə, *Sp.* kōō'bä) The largest of the Caribbean islands, comprising (with the Isle of Pines) a Republic; 44,217 sq. mi.; pop. 8,553,395 (est. 1970); capital, Havana. — **Cu'ban** *adj. & n.*

Cuba li·bre (lē'brə) A drink made of rum, lemon juice, and a cola beverage. Also **cu'ba li'bre.** [< Sp., free Cuba]

cu·ba·ture (kyōō'bə·chŏŏr) *n.* **1.** The process of determining the cubic contents of a solid. **2.** Cubic contents. Also **cu·bage** (kyōō'bij). [< L *cubus* cube, on analogy with QUADRATURE]

cub·by·hole (kub'ē·hōl') *n.* A small, enclosed space. Also **cub'by.** [< *cubby*, dim. of dial. E *cub* shed + HOLE]

cube[1] (kyōōb) *n.* **1.** *Geom.* A solid bounded by six equal squares and having all its angles right angles. **2.** *Math.* The third power of a quantity: the *cube* of 3 is 27, or $3^3 = 3 \times 3 \times 3 = 27$. — *v.t.* **cubed, cub·ing 1.** To raise (a number or quantity) to the third power. **2.** To find the cubic capacity of. **3.** To form or cut into cubes or cubelike shapes; dice: to *cube potatoes.* [< OF < L *cubus* < Gk. *kybos* cube, die[2]]

cu·be[2] (kōō'bā) *n.* A substance extracted from the roots of a leguminous plant (*Lonchocarpus nicou*), used as a fish poison. Also **cu'bé.** [< Sp. *quibey* < native name]

cu·beb (kyōō'beb) *n.* A berry of an East Indian shrub (*Piper cubeba*) of the pepper family, used in treating urinary and bronchial diseases and often smoked in the form of cigarettes. [< OF *cubèbe*, ult. < Arabic *kabābah*]

cube root The number that, taken three times as a factor, produces a number called its cube: 4 is the *cube root* of 64.

cu·bic (kyōō'bik) *adj.* **1.** Shaped like a cube. **2.** Having three dimensions, or pertaining to three-dimensional content: said especially of a given linear unit to denote a volume equal to a cube with the given unit as its edge: a *cubic* foot (a volume equal to a cube with edges of one foot). Abbr. *c., C., cu., cu.* **3.** *Math.* Of the third power or degree: a *cubic* equation. **4.** *Crystall.* Isometric. [< OF *cubique* < L *cubicus* < Gk. *kybikos* < *kybos* cube]

cu·bi·cal (kyōō'bi·kəl) *adj.* Shaped like a cube. — **cu'bi·cal·ly** *adv.* — **cu'bi·cal·ness** *n.*

cu·bi·cle (kyōō'bi·kəl) *n.* **1.** A bedroom, especially a partially enclosed section in a dormitory. **2.** Any small room or partitioned area, as a carrell. [< L *cubiculum* bedroom < *cubare* to lie down]

cubic measure A unit or system of units for measuring volume, or the amount of space occupied in three dimensions. See table inside back cover.

cu·bic·u·lum (kyōō·bik'yə·ləm) *n. pl.* **·la** (-lə) A burial chamber, as in the Roman catacombs. [< L. See CUBICLE.]

cu·bi·form (kyōō'bə·fôrm) *adj.* Shaped like a cube.

cu·bism (kyōō'biz·əm) *n.* A movement in modern art, about 1907–25, concerned with the abstract and geometric interpretation of form, rather than with a realistic representation of nature. — **cu'bist** *adj. & n.* — **cu·bis'tic** *adj.*

cu·bit (kyōō'bit) *n.* An ancient measure of length, originally represented by the length of the forearm, but usually about 18 to 20 inches. [< L *cubitum* elbow]

cu·bi·tal (kyōō'bə·təl) *adj.* **1.** Of or pertaining to the ulna or to the forearm. **2.** Of the measure of a cubit.

cu·boid (kyōō'boid) *adj.* **1.** Shaped like a cube. **2.** *Anat.* Of or pertaining to the outer distal bone of the tarsus. Also **cu·boi'dal.** — *n.* **1.** *Anat.* The cuboid bone. **2.** *Geom.* A rectangular parallelepiped. [< Gk. *kyboeidēs* cubelike]

cub reporter A young, inexperienced newspaper reporter.

cub scout A member of a subdivision of the Boy Scouts, comprising boys eight to ten years of age.

Cu·chu·lain (kōō·khōō'lən) A legendary Irish hero.

cuck·ing stool (kuk'ing) A chair in which disorderly women, scolds, and dishonest tradesmen were tied, left to public derision, and sometimes ducked. [< obs. *cuck* to defecate]

cuck·old (kuk'əld) *n.* The husband of an unfaithful wife. — *v.t.* To make a cuckold of. [< OF *cucuault* < *cucu* cuckoo; with ref. to the cuckoo's habit of laying its eggs in another bird's nest]

cuck·old·ry (kuk'əl·drē) *n.* The cuckolding of a husband.
cuck·oo (kŏŏk'ōō; *for adj., also* kŏŏ·kōō') *n.* **1.** A bird belonging to a large family (*Cuculidae*), many species of which, as the common European cuckoo (*Cuculus canorus*), deposit their eggs in the nests of other birds. **2.** Any of various similar or related birds, as the **yellow-billed cuckoo** (*Cocyzus americanus*), and the **black-billed cuckoo** (*C. erythrophthalmus*) of America. **3.** A simpleton; fool. **4.** A cuckoo's cry. — *v.* ·**ooed**, ·**oo·ing** *v.t.* **1.** To repeat without cessation. — *r.i.* **2.** To utter or imitate the cry of the cuckoo. — *adj. Slang* Crazy; silly. [< OF *cucu, coucou*; imit.]
cuckoo clock A clock in which a mechanical cuckoo announces the hours.
cuck·oo-flow·er (kŏŏk'ōō·flou'ər) *n.* **1.** A species of cress (*Cardamine pratensis*) with showy flowers: also called *lady's smock.* **2.** The ragged robin.
cuck·oo-pint (kŏŏk'ōō·pīnt') *n.* A European herb (*Arum maculatum*) resembling the jack-in-the-pulpit: also called *wake-robin.*
cuckoo spit 1. A frothy secretion exuded upon plants by the larvae of certain insects, as froghoppers: also called *frog spit, toad spit.* **2.** An insect that secretes such froth; a froghopper.
cu. cm. Cubic centimeter(s).
cu·cu·li·form (kyŏŏ·kyŏŏ'lə·fôrm) *adj. Ornithol.* Of or pertaining to an order of birds (*Cuculiformes*), including the cuckoos and roadrunners. [< NL *Cuculiformes* < L *cuculus* cuckoo + *forma* shape]
cu·cul·late (kyŏŏ·kə·lāt, kyŏŏ·kul'āt) *adj.* **1.** Shaped like a hood or cowl. **2.** *Bot.* Having a hoodlike part, as certain leaves; cowled. Also **cu·cul·lat·ed** (kyŏŏ'kə·lā'tid, kyŏŏ·kul'·ā·tid). [< LL *cucullatus* < L *cucullus* hood]
cu·cum·ber (kyŏŏ'kum·bər) *n.* **1.** The cylindrical, hard-rinded fruit of a creeping plant (*Cucumis sativus*) of the gourd family, cultivated as a vegetable. **2.** The plant. [< OF *cocombre* < L *cucumis, -eris*]
cucumber tree 1. A straight, tall tree (*Magnolia acuminata*) of the eastern United States, bearing a fruit resembling a small cucumber. **2.** A tree (*Averrhoa bilimbi*) of the East Indies cultivated for its edible acid berries and its flowers.
cu·cu·mi·form (kyŏŏ·kyŏŏ'mə·fôrm) *adj.* Having the form of a cucumber. [< L *cucumis* cucumber + -FORM]
cu·cur·bit (kyŏŏ·kûr'bit) *n.* **1.** The body of an alembic, originally gourd-shaped. For illustration see STILL². **2.** Any cucurbitaceous plant. [< F *cucurbite* < L *cucurbita* gourd]
cu·cur·bi·ta·ceous (kyŏŏ·kûr'bə·tā'shəs) *adj.* Denoting any of a family (*Cucurbitaceae*) of plants, the gourd family, many of which have edible fruit, as the pumpkin, squash, etc. [< NL *Cucurbitaceae* < L *cucurbita* gourd]
cud (kud) *n.* Food forced up into the mouth from the first stomach of a ruminant and chewed over again. [OE *cwidu*]
cud-bear (kud'bâr) *n.* A purplish red dyestuff made from certain lichens (genus *Lecanora*), and used as a coloring for foods and drugs. [Coined from his first name by Dr. *Cuthbert* Gordon, who first made it]
cud·dle (kud'l) *v.* ·**dled**, ·**dling** *v.t.* **1.** To caress fondly within a close embrace; fondle. — *v.i.* **2.** To lie close; hug one another; nestle together. — *n.* An embrace or caress; a hug. [? < dial. E (Northern) *couth* snug, cozy] — **cud'dle·some** (-səm) *adj.* — **cud'dly** *adj.*
cud·dy¹ (kud'ē) *n. pl.* ·**dies 1.** *Naut.* A small cabin or a cook's galley. **2.** Any small room, cupboard, or pantry. [Origin unknown]
cud·dy² (kud'ē, kŏŏd'ē) *n. Scot.* A donkey. Also **cud'die.** [Origin uncertain]
cudg·el (kuj'əl) *n.* A short, thick club. — **to take up the cudgels** To enter into a contest or controversy. — *v.t.* **cudg·eled** or ·**elled, cudg·el·ing** or ·**el·ling** To beat with a cudgel. — **to cudgel one's brains** To think hard; puzzle. [OE *cycgel*] — **cudg'el·er** or **cudg'el·ler** *n.*
cud·weed (kud'wēd) *n.* Any one of various woolly-leaved plants (genus *Gnaphalium* or *Helichrysum*) of the composite family: also called *cottonweed.* [< CUD + WEED]
cue¹ (kyōō) *n.* **1.** A long, tapering rod, used in billiards, pool, etc., to strike the cue ball. **2.** A queue of hair. **3.** A queue, as of persons, awaiting their turn. — *v.t.* **cued, cu·ing 1.** To twist, braid, or tie into a cue: to *cue* the hair. **2.** In billiards, etc., to hit with a cue. [< F *queue* tail]
cue² (kyōō) *n.* **1.** In plays, movies, and the like, any action, word, or sound that signals the commencement of another action, speech, etc. **2.** Anything that serves as a signal to begin: a musical *cue.* **3.** A hint or suggestion; reminder. **4.** An action made necessary by or thought proper to the circumstances: His *cue* is to deny it. **5.** State of mind; mood; disposition. **6.** *Psychol.* A secondary, often obscure, stimulus that elicits responses, influences behavior, etc. — *v.t.* **cued, cu·ing** To call a cue to (an actor); prompt. [Earlier *Q, qu,* said to have been an abbreviation of L *quando* when, written in actors' copies of plays to mark their entrances]
cue³ (kyōō) *n.* The letter Q.
cue ball The ball struck by the cue in billiards or pool.
Cuen·ca (kweng'kä) A city in south central Ecuador; pop. 66,800 (est. 1960).

cues·ta (kwes'tə) *n. SW U.S.* A ridge or hill that has a steep descent on one side and a gentle slope on the other. [< Sp.]
cuff¹ (kuf) *n.* **1.** A band or fold at the lower end of a sleeve. **2.** *U.S.* The turned-up fold on the bottom of a trouser leg. **3.** A detachable band of fabric worn about the wrist, either under or over the sleeve. **4.** The portion of a long glove or gauntlet covering the wrist. **5.** A handcuff (which see). — **off the cuff** *U.S. Slang* Without preparation; spontaneously. — **on the cuff** *U.S. Slang* On credit; with payment postponed. [ME *cuffe, coffe*; origin unknown]
cuff² (kuf) *v.t.* **1.** To strike, as with the open hand; buffet. — *v.i.* **2.** To scuffle or fight; box. — *n.* A blow, especially with the open hand. — **Syn.** See BLOW², STRIKE. [? < Scand. Cf. Sw. *kuffa* to push.]
cuff links A pair of linked buttons or the like, used to fasten shirt cuffs.
Cu·fic (kyōō'fik) See KUFIC.
Cu·fra (kōō'frä) The Italian name for KUFRA.
cu. ft. Cubic foot or feet.
Cu·i (kü·ē'), **César Antonovich,** 1835–1918, Russian composer.
Cu·ia·bá (kōō'yä·bä') The capital of Mato Grosso, Brazil, in the central part of the State, a port on the **Cuiabá river,** that flows about 300 miles SW to the São Lourenço; pop. about 24,000: formerly *Cuyaba.*
cui bo·no (kwē' bō'nō, kī') *Latin* For whose benefit? Also, inaccurately, for what purpose?
cuif (kōōf, kuf) See COOF.
cu. in. Cubic inch(es).
cui·rass (kwi·ras') *n.* **1.** A piece of defensive armor consisting of a breastplate and backplate; also, the breastplate alone. **2.** *Zool.* A cuirasslike covering, as the bony plates of a mailed fish. — *v.t.* To equip with a cuirass. [< MF, ult. < L *coriacea* leathern < *corium* leather]
cui·ras·sier (kwi'rə·sir') *n.* A mounted soldier wearing a cuirass.
cui·sine (kwi·zēn') *n.* **1.** The style or quality of cooking. **2.** The food prepared. **3.** The cooking department and its staff, as at a restaurant; the kitchen. [< F < L *coquina* kitchen < *coquere* to cook]
cuisse (kwis) *n.* A piece of plate armor for the thigh. Also **cuish** (kwish). [< OF *cuissel* < *cuisse* thigh < L *coxa* hip]
culch (kulch) *n.* **1.** Gravel, empty shells, etc., used to form a bed to which the spawn of oysters may adhere. **2.** Oyster spawn. **3.** Refuse; rubbish. Also spelled *cultch.* [? < OF *culche* bed, layer]
cul-de-sac (kul'də·sak', kŏŏl'-; *Fr.* kü'də·sàk') *n. pl.* **cul-de-sacs,** *Fr.* **culs-de-sac** (kü'-) **1.** A passage open only at one end; blind alley; trap. **2.** *Anat.* A saclike cavity or part open only at one end. **3.** *Mil.* The position of a force surrounded by hostile lines. [< F, bottom of the bag]
-cule *suffix of nouns* Small; little: *animalcule.* [< F < L *-culus,* dim. suffix]
Cu·le·bra Cut (kōō·lā'brə, -lē'-) A former name for the GAILLARD CUT.
cu·let (kyōō'lit) *n.* **1.** The small, flat bottom of a gem when cut as a brilliant. **2.** *Often pl.* One of the plates of armor for the lower part of the back. [< OF, dim. of *cul* bottom < L *culus* buttock]
cu·li·cine (kyōō'lə·sin, -sīn) *adj.* Pertaining or belonging to a widely distributed family (*Culicidae*) of dipterous insects, the mosquitoes. — *n.* A mosquito. Also **cu·lic·id** (kyōō'lis·id).
cu·li·nar·y (kyōō'lə·ner'ē, kul'-) *adj.* Of or pertaining to cookery or the kitchen. [< L *culinarius* < *culina* kitchen]
Cu·lion Island (kōō'lyōn') An island in the western Philippines; 153 sq. mi.; site of **Culion Reservation,** a leper colony.
cull (kul) *v.t.* **1.** To pick or sort out; select. **2.** To gather: to *cull* flowers. **3.** To pick over and divide as to quality. — **Syn.** See CHOOSE. — *n.* Something picked or sorted out, especially something rejected as inferior. [< OF *cuillir* < L *colligere* to collect] — **cull'er** *n.*
cul·lay (kə·lā') See QUILLAI.
Cul·len (kul'ən), **Coun·tee** (koun'tē), 1903–46, U.S. poet.
cul·len·der (kul'ən·dər) See COLANDER.
cul·let (kul'it) *n.* Broken or refuse glass, gathered for remelting. [< F *collet,* dim. of *col* neck < L *collum*; with ref. to the neck of glass left on the pipe after blowing]
Cul·li·nan diamond (kul'ə·nən) One of the world's largest diamonds, originally 3,106 metric carats, discovered in South Africa in 1905. [after Sir T. M. *Cullinan,* owner of the diamond mine where found]
cul·lion (kul'yən) *n. Archaic* A base, despicable fellow. [< F *couillon* base fellow, testicle < L *coleus* testicle]
cul·lis (kul'is) *n. Archit.* A gutter in a roof. [< F *coulisse*]
cul·ly (kul'ē) *n. pl.* ·**lies** *Brit.* **1.** Archaic One who is tricked; a dupe. **2.** *Slang* Fellow; pal. — *v.t.* ·**lied,** ·**ly·ing** *Obs.* To trick; dupe. [? < CULLION]
culm¹ (kulm) *n. Bot.* The jointed, usually hollow, stem or straw of grasses. — *v.i.* To form a culm. [< L *culmus* stalk] — **cul·mif·er·ous** (kul·mif'ər·əs) *adj.*
culm² (kulm) *n.* **1.** Coal refuse or dust. **2.** An inferior anthracite coal. [Var. of dial. *coom* soot]

cul·mi·nant (kul′min·ənt) *adj.* Culminating; highest.

cul·mi·nate (kul′min·āt) *v.i.* **·nat·ed, ·nat·ing** **1.** To reach the highest point or degree; come to a final result or effect: with *in.* **2.** *Astron.* To reach the meridian, or the point of greatest or least altitude. [< LL *culminatus,* pp. of *culminare* to mature < L *culmen* top, highest point]

cul·mi·na·tion (kul′mə·nā′shən) *n.* **1.** The act of culminating. **2.** That in which something culminates; the highest point, condition, or degree. **3.** *Astron.* The passage of a heavenly body over the meridian.

culm measures . *Geol.* A rock formation belonging to the Lower Carboniferous era, alternating marine fossil beds with plant fossil beds.

cu·lottes (kyŏŏ·lots′, kŏŏ-; *Fr.* kü·lôt′) *n.pl.* A woman's trouserlike garment cut to resemble a skirt. [< F]

cul·pa (kul′pə) *n. Law* A fault, especially of negligence. [< L]

cul·pa·ble (kul′pə·bəl) *adj.* Deserving of blame or censure. [< OF < L *culpabilis* < *culpa* fault] — **cul′pa·bil′i·ty, cul′-pa·ble·ness** *n.* — **cul′pa·bly** *adv.*

Cul·pep·er (kul′pep′ər), **Lord Thomas**, 1635–89, English colonial governor of Virginia 1680–83. Also *Colepeper.*

cul·prit (kul′prit) *n.* **1.** One guilty of some offense or crime; offender. **2.** One charged with or arraigned for a crime. [< AF *cul prit,* short for *culpable* guilty (< L *culpabilis*) + *prit* ready for trial < OF *prist, prest* < L *praesto* at hand, orig., prosecutor's reply to plea of "not guilty"]

cult (kult) *n.* **1.** A system of religious rites and observances: the *cult* of Aphrodite. **2.** Zealous devotion to a person, ideal, or thing. **3.** The object of this devotion. **4.** The followers of a cult; a sect. — **Syn.** See RELIGION. [< F *culte* < L *cultus* < *colere* to cultivate, cherish, worship]

cultch (kulch) See CULCH.

cul·ti·va·ble (kul′tə·və·bəl) *adj.* Capable of cultivation. Also **cul′ti·vat′a·ble** (-vā′tə·bəl). [< F < *cultiver* to cultivate] — **cul′ti·va·bil′i·ty** *n.*

cul·ti·var (kul′tə·vär) *n. Bot.* A horticultural variety of plant or flower. [< CULTI(VATED) + VAR(IETY)]

cul·ti·vate (kul′tə·vāt) *v.t.* **·vat·ed, ·vat·ing** **1.** To make fit for raising crops, as by plowing, fertilizing, etc.; till. **2.** To care for (plants, etc.) so as to promote growth and abundance. **3.** To raise from seeds, bulbs, etc., for later planting. **4.** To produce or improve (plants, etc.) by selective breeding or other techniques. **5.** To improve or develop by study, exercise, or training; refine: to *cultivate* one's mind. **6.** To give one's attention to in order to acquire: to *cultivate* a friendship, a habit, good manners, etc. **7.** To promote the development or advancement of: to *cultivate* the sciences. **8.** To seek intimacy or acquaintance with; court the friendship of. [< Med.L *cultivatus,* pp. of *cultivare* < *cultivus* tilled < L *cultus,* pp. of *colere* to care for, cherish]

cul·ti·vat·ed (kul′tə·vā′tid) *adj.* **1.** Prepared for seed; tilled. **2.** Developed or grown by cultivation: a *cultivated* rose. **3.** Cultured; refined: a *cultivated* person.

cul·ti·va·tion (kul′tə·vā′shən) *n.* **1.** The act of cultivating the ground, plants, etc. **2.** The improvement or development of anything through study and effort. **3.** Culture; refinement. — **Syn.** See REFINEMENT.

cul·ti·va·tor (kul′tə·vā′tər) *n.* **1.** One who cultivates. **2.** *Agric.* A machine for cultivating, commonly having several blades that loosen the ground and destroy weeds.

cul·trate (kul′trāt) *adj.* Sharp-edged and pointed. Also **cul′trat·ed.** [< L *cultratus* < *culter* knife]

cul·tur·al (kul′chər·əl) *adj.* **1.** Of, pertaining to, or developing culture: *cultural* studies. **2.** Produced by breeding, as certain varieties of fruits or plants. — **cul′tur·al·ly** *adv.*

cultural lag *Sociol.* A marked retardation in the rate of development of certain features of a culture as compared with others. Also **culture lag.**

cul·ture (kul′chər) *n.* **1.** The cultivation of plants or animals, especially with a view to improvement of the breed or stock. **2.** The training, development, and refinement of mind, morals, or taste. **3.** The condition thus produced; refinement; enlightenment. **4.** A specific stage or period in the development of a civilization. **5.** Cultivation of the soil. **6.** *Anthropol.* The sum total of the attainments and learned behavior patterns of any specific period, race, or people, regarded as expressing a traditional way of life subject to gradual but continuous modification by succeeding generations. **7.** *Biol.* **a** The development of microorganisms in artificial media. **b** The organisms so developed. — **Syn.** See REFINEMENT. — *v.t.* **·tured, ·tur·ing** **1.** To cultivate (plants or animals). **2.** *Biol.* **a** To develop or grow (microorganisms) in an artificial medium. **b** To inoculate with a prepared culture. **3.** *Obs.* To educate or refine. [< F < L *cultura* < *colere* to care for]

culture area *Sociol.* A region characterized by similar cultural patterns among the groups inhabiting it.

culture complex *Sociol.* A collection of cultural traits clustered about a central, dominant trait, thereby forming an interrelated whole.

cul·tured (kul′chərd) *adj.* **1.** Possessing or manifesting culture. **2.** Created or grown by cultivation.

cultured pearl A pearl artificially cultivated by inserting a suitable core within the shell or mantle of a mollusk.

culture medium *Biol.* Any substance or material suitable for the growth of microorganisms.

culture pattern *Sociol.* A complex of culture traits within a particular culture.

culture trait *Sociol.* Any socially transmitted element or feature within a culture.

cul·tur·ist (kul′chər·ist) *n.* **1.** One who cultivates. **2.** An advocate of cultural development.

cul·tus (kul′təs) *n. pl.* **·tus·es** or **·ti** (-tī) A cult (defs. 1 & 2). [< L. See CULT.]

cul·ver (kul′vər) *n.* A pigeon or dove. [OE *culfer*]

Cul·ver City (kul′vər) A city in SW California, near Los Angeles; pop. 31,035.

cul·ver·in (kul′vər·in) *n.* **1.** A long cannon used in the 16th and 17th centuries. **2.** An early form of musket. [< F *coulevrin* < *couleuvre* serpent]

Cul·ver's root (kul′vərz) A tall plant (*Veronicastrum virginicum*) having roots used as an aperient and tonic.

cul·vert (kul′vərt) *n.* An artificial, covered channel for water, as under a road. [Origin uncertain]

Cu·mae (kyŏŏ′mē) An ancient city on the coast of Campania, Italy; the earliest Greek colony in Italy.

Cu·mae·an (kyŏŏ·mē′an) *adj.* Of or pertaining to Cumae.

Cumaean sibyl In Roman legend, a sibyl who prophesied to Aeneas and brought the Sibylline books to Rome.

cu·ma·rin (kŏŏ′mə·rin) See COUMARIN.

Cumb. or **Cumb** Cumberland.

cum·ber (kum′bər) *v.t.* **1.** To hinder; obstruct; hamper. **2.** To weigh down; burden. **3.** *Obs.* To harass; trouble. — *n.* **1.** A hindrance or encumbrance. **2.** *Obs.* Distress; perplexity. [Cf. OF *encombrer* to hinder]

Cum·ber·land (kum′bər·lənd) **1.** A former county in NW England on the Scottish border; 1,521 sq. mi.; pop. 292,009 (1971); county seat, Carlisle. **2.** A city in NW Maryland, on the Potomac; pop. 29,724.

Cumberland Gap A natural passage through the Cumberland Mountains between Virginia and Tennessee.

Cumberland Mountains The SW division of the Appalachian Mountains, extending from SW West Virginia to NW Alabama. Also **Cumberland Plateau.**

Cumberland River A river in Kentucky and Tennessee, flowing 693 miles west to the Ohio River.

Cumberland Road A national highway, first constructed in the early 19th century from Cumberland, Maryland, westward to the Ohio River: also *National Road.*

cum·ber·some (kum′bər·səm) *adj.* **1.** Unwieldy; clumsy. **2.** Vexatious; burdensome. — **cum′ber·some·ly** *adv.* — **cum′ber·some·ness** *n.*

cum·brance (kum′brəns) *n.* **1.** An encumbrance. **2.** Trouble.

Cum·bri·a (kum′brē·ə) A county in NW England; 2,658 sq. mi.; pop. 475,700 (1976); county seat, Carlisle.

cum·brous (kum′brəs) *adj.* Cumbersome. — **cum′brous·ly** *adv.* — **cum′brous·ness** *n.*

cum gra·no sa·lis (kum grā′nō sā′lis) *Latin* With a grain of salt; with some reservation; not literally.

cum·in (kum′in) *n.* **1.** An annual (*Cuminum cyminum*) of the parsley family, with fennellike leaves. **2.** Its seeds, used as a condiment. Also **cum′min.** [OE *cymen* < L *cuminum* < Gk. *kyminon* < Semitic]

cum lau·de (kum lô′dĕ, kŏŏm lou′de) *Latin* With praise: used on diplomas to denote the special merit of the recipient's work. — **magna cum laude** With ;h praise. — **summa cum laude** With highest praise.

cum·mer (kum′ər) *n. Scot.* **1.** A godmother. **2.** A female friend. **3.** A woman or girl.

cum·mer·bund (kum′ər·bund) *n.* A broad sash worn as a waistband; also, a girdle; belt: sometimes spelled *kummerbund.* [< Persian *kamar-band* < *kamar* loin + *band* band]

Cum·mings (kum′ingz), **E(dward) E(stlin)**, 1894–1962, U.S. poet, author, and artist: name usually written by him as **e. e. cummings.**

cum·quat (kum′kwot) See KUMQUAT.

cum·shaw (kum′shô) *n.* Something given as a present; a tip; baksheesh. [< Chinese *ka ṇ hsieh* grateful thanks]

cu·mu·late (kyŏŏm′yə·lāt; *for adj.* also kyŏŏm′yə·lit) *v.t. & v.i.* **·lat·ed, ·lat·ing** To collect into a heap; accumulate. — *adj.* Massed; heaped; accumulated. [< L *cumulatus,* pp. of *cumulare* to heap up < *cumulus* a heap]

cu·mu·la·tion (kyŏŏm′yə·lā′shən) *n.* **1.** An accumulating. **2.** A heap or mass.

cu·mu·la·tive (kyŏŏm′yə·lā′tiv, -lə·tiv) *adj.* **1.** Gathering volume, strength, or value; steadily increasing. **2.** Gained or acquired by accumulation: *cumulative* knowledge. **3.** Increasing or accruing, as unpaid interest or dividends, to be paid in the future. **4.** *Law* Reinforcing or proving previous evidence. — **cu′mu·la′tive·ly** *adv.*

cumulative voting A system of voting in which each elector may vote as many times as there are candidates to vote for, giving his votes to one, several, or all of the candidates.

cu·mu·li·form (kyōōm′yə·lə·fôrm′) *adj. Meteorol.* Having the characteristic form of cumulus clouds. [< L *cumulus* heap + -FORM]

cu·mu·lo·cir·rus (kyōōm′yə·lō·sir′əs) *n. Meteorol.* Alto-cumulus.

cu·mu·lo·nim·bus (kyōōm′yə·lō·nim′bəs) *n. Meteorol.* A heavy, massive cloud formation (Symbol Cb) rising vertically in the shape of mountains or turrets, and producing thunder and showers. Abbr. *Cn* See table for CLOUD.

cumulonimbus mammatus *Meteorol.* A cumulonimbus cloud formation (Symbol Cm), having pouchlike protuberances beneath. Also called *mammato-cumulus.*

cu·mu·lo·stra·tus (kyōōm′yə·lō·strā′təs) *n. Meteorol.* Stratocumulus.

cu·mu·lous (kyōōm′yə·ləs) *adj.* Like cumulus; heaped; piled: said of clouds.

cu·mu·lus (kyōōm′yə·ləs) *n. pl.* **·li** (-lī) **1.** A mass; pile. **2.** *Meteorol.* A dense, usually white cloud formation (Symbol Cu) with dome-shaped upper surfaces and horizontal bases, seen in fair weather. See table under CLOUD. [< L]

Cu·nax·a (kyōō·nak′sə) A town in Babylonia, near the Euphrates; scene of a battle between Cyrus the Younger and Artaxerxes II, 401 B.C.

cunc·ta·tion (kungk·tā′shən) *n.* Delay. [< L *cunctatio, -onis* < *cunctari* to delay] — **cunc·ta·tive** (kungk′tə·tiv) *adj.*

cunc·ta·tor (kungk·tā′tər) *n.* One who delays.

cun·dum (kun′dəm) See CONDOM.

cu·ne·al (kyōō′nē·əl) *adj.* Wedge-shaped. [< Med.L *cunealis* < L *cuneus* wedge]

cu·ne·ate (kyōō′nē·it, -āt) *adj.* Wedge-shaped: said especially of leaves. Also **cu′ne·at′ed, cu·ne·at·ic** (kyōō′nē·at′ik). [< L *cuneatus,* pp. of *cuneare* to make wedge-shaped < *cuneus* wedge] — **cu′ne·ate·ly** *adv.*

cu·ne·i·form (kyōō·nē′ə·fôrm, kyōō′nē·ə·fôrm′) *adj.* **1.** Wedge-shaped, as the characters in some ancient Sumerian, Assyrian, Babylonian, and Persian inscriptions. **2.** *Anat.* Designating a wedge-shaped bone in the wrist, or one of three in the human foot. For illustration see FOOT. — *n.* Cuneiform writing. Also **cu·ni·form** (kyōō′nə·fôrm). [< L *cuneus* wedge + -FORM]

CUNEIFORM
a Earth. *b* Woman. *c* Man. *d* Food.

Cuneiform Hittite See under HITTITE.

Cun·ha (kōō′nyə), **Tristão da,** 1460?–1540?, Portuguese seafarer and explorer.

cun·ner (kun′ər) *n.* A small, edible fish (*Tautogolabrus adspersus*), abundant along the North Atlantic shores of America: also called *bluefish.* [Origin uncertain]

cun·ning (kun′ing) *n.* **1.** Skill in deception: craftiness; guile. **2.** Knowledge combined with manual skill; dexterity. — *adj.* **1.** Crafty or shrewd; artful; guileful. **2.** Executed with skill; ingenious. **3.** *U.S.* Innocently amusing; cute. **4.** *Obs.* Knowing; adept. — **Syn.** See ASTUTE. [OE *cun* *nung* knowledge < *cunnan* to know, be able. Akin to CAN¹.] — **cun′ning·ly** *adv.* — **cun′ning·ness** *n.*

cup (kup) *n.* **1.** A small, open vessel, often with a handle, used chiefly for drinking from. **2.** The contents of a cup; a cupful: as a measure of capacity, equal to 8 ounces or 16 tablespoonfuls. **3.** The bowl of a drinking vessel that has a stem and base. **4.** In the Eucharist, the chalice, or its contents. **5.** One's lot in life; portion: the bitter *cup* of exile. **6.** Intoxicating drink, or the habit of drinking: the pleasures of the *cup.* **7.** An alcoholic beverage, usually chilled and served with herbs, fruits, etc.: a claret *cup.* **8.** A cup-shaped object or part, as of a flower. **9.** *Med.* A glass used in cupping. **10.** An ornamental cup-shaped vessel given as a prize, especially in sports: the Davis *Cup.* **11.** In golf, a hole, or the metal receptacle within it. — **in one's cups** Drunk. — *v.t.* **cupped, cup·ping 1.** To shape like a cup: to *cup* one's hands. **2.** To place in or as in a cup. **3.** *Med.* To perform cupping on. [OE *cuppe* < LL *cuppa* cup, var. of L *cupa* tub, cask]

Cup (kup) The constellation Crater.

cup·bear·er (kup′bâr′ər) *n.* One who serves drinks.

cup·board (kub′ərd) *n.* **1.** A closet or cabinet with shelves, as for dishes. **2.** Any small cabinet or closet.

cupboard love Love professed for selfish reasons.

cup·cake (kup′kāk′) *n.* A small individual cake baked in a cup-shaped receptacle.

cu·pel (kyōō′pəl, kyōō·pel′) *v.t.* **cu·peled** or **·pelled, cu·pel·ing** or **·pel·ling** To separate from base metals by cupellation. — *n.* **1.** A shallow, absorbent vessel used in assaying gold and silver ores. **2.** The movable bottom in a silver-refining furnace. [< MF *coupelle* < Med.L *cupella,* dim. of LL *cuppa* cup]

cu·pel·la·tion (kyōō′pə·lā′shən) *n.* The process of refining gold or silver by subjecting an alloy to a high heat in a cupel. [< F]

cup·ful (kup′fŏŏl′) *n. pl.* **·fuls** The quantity held by a cup; in measuring, half a pint.

Cu·pid (kyōō′pid) In Roman mythology, the god of love:

identified with the Greek *Eros.* — *n.* **1.** A representation of the god of love as a naked, winged boy with a bow and arrow. **2.** One who arranges or who helps to arrange meetings between lovers: chiefly in the phrase **to play Cupid.** [< L *Cupido* < *cupido* passion, desire]

cu·pid·i·ty (kyōō·pid′ə·tē) *n.* Eager desire for possession, especially of wealth; avarice; greed. [< L *cupiditas, -tatis*]

cup of tea *Informal* That which suits one; a favorite or preferred object, activity, etc.

cu·po·la (kyōō′pə·lə) *n.* **1.** *Archit.* A rounded roof; dome. **b** A small, vaulted structure, usually hemispherical, rising above the roof of a building. **2.** A revolving gun turret on a battleship. **3.** *Metall.* An upright cylindrical furnace used for melting cast iron. **4.** Any of various structures, organs, etc., shaped like a dome. — *v.t.* **-laed, ·la·ing** To provide with or shape like a cupola. [< Ital. < LL *cupula,* dim. of L *cupa* tub, cask]

cupped (kupt) *adj.* Cup-shaped; concave.

cup·per (kup′ər) *n. Med.* One who performs cupping.

cup·ping (kup′ing) *n. Med.* The process of drawing blood to the surface of the skin by creating a vacuum at that point, with or without scarification or heat.

cupping glass *Med.* A cup, generally of glass, applied to the skin in the operation of cupping.

cup plant Rosinweed (def. 1).

cu·pre·ous (kyōō′prē·əs) *adj.* Of, pertaining to, containing, or resembling copper. [< LL *cupreus* < L *cuprum* copper]

cu·pric (kyōō′prik) *adj. Chem.* Of or pertaining to copper, especially in its highest valence: *cupric* oxide, CuO.

cu·prif·er·ous (kyōō·prif′ər·əs) *adj.* Containing copper.

cu·prite (kyōō′prīt) *n.* A red, translucent cuprous oxide, Cu_2O, constituting an important ore of copper.

cupro- *combining form* Copper: *cupronickel.* Also, before vowels, **cupr-.** [< L *cuprum* copper]

cu·pro·nick·el (kyōō′prō·nik′əl) *n.* Any of several alloys of copper and nickel.

cu·prous (kyōō′prəs) *adj. Chem.* Of or pertaining to copper, especially in its lowest valence: *cuprous* oxide, Cu_2O.

cu·prum (kyōō′prəm) *n.* Copper. [< L]

cu·pu·late (kyōō′pym̄·lāt) *adj.* **1.** Cup-shaped. **2.** Having a cupule. Also **cu′pu·lar.**

cu·pule (kyōō′pyōōl) *n.* **1.** A concave or cup-shaped depression. **2.** *Bot.* A cup-shaped part, as the receptacle that holds an acorn. [< LL *cupula.* See CUPOLA.]

cur (kûr) *n.* **1.** A mongrel dog. **2.** A mean or despicable person. [Short for earlier *kur-dogge.* Cf. dial. Sw. *kurre* dog.]

cur. 1. Currency. **2.** Current.

cur·a·ble (kyōōr′ə·bəl) *adj.* Capable of being cured. — **cur′a·bil′i·ty, cur′a·ble·ness** *n.* — **cur′a·bly** *adv.*

cu·ra·çao (kyōōr′ə·sō′, kōō′rä·sou′) *n.* A liqueur made by distilling spirits with the peel of the sour orange. Also **cu′ra·çoa′** (-sō′). [after *Curaçao*]

Cu·ra·çao (kyōōr′ə·sō′, kōō′rä·sou′) The largest island in the western group of the Netherlands Antilles; 171 sq. mi.; pop. 196,170 (est. 1970); capital, Willemstad.

cu·ra·cy (kyōōr′ə·sē) *n. pl.* **·cies** The position, duties, or term of office of a curate.

cur·agh See CURRACH.

cu·ra·re (kyōō·rä′rē) *n.* **1.** A blackish, resinous extract of certain South American trees, especially *Strychnos toxifera* and *Chondrodendron tomentosum,* that, when introduced into the blood stream, paralyzes the motor nerves. It is used as an arrow poison, to reduce muscular spasms, and in general anesthesia. **2.** A plant from which this is extracted. Also called *oorali, ourari, urare, urari, woorali, woorari:* also **cu·ra·ra** (kyōō·rä′rə), **cu·ra′ri.** [< Sp. *curaré* < Tupi]

cu·ra·rine (kyōō·rä′rēn, -rin) *n. Chem.* A poisonous alkaloid, $C_{19}H_{26}N_2O$, obtained from curare. [< CURARE + -INE²]

cu·ra·rize (kyōōr′ə·rīz, kyōō·rä′rīz) *v.t.* **·rized, ·riz·ing 1.** To poison by the use of curare. **2.** To administer curare to, as for paralyzing the motor nerves. — **cu′ra·ri·za′tion** *n.*

cu·ras·sow (kyōōr′ə·sō, kyōō·ras′ō) *n.* A large, turkeylike bird (family *Cracidae*) of South and Central America: also *carassow.* [after *Curaçao*]

cu·rate (kyōōr′it) *n.* A clergyman assisting a parish priest, rector, or vicar. [< Med.L *curatus* < L *cura* care, cure]

cur·a·tive (kyōōr′ə·tiv) *adj.* **1.** Having the power or tendency to cure. **2.** Relating to the cure of diseases. — *n.* A remedy. — **cur′a·tive·ly** *adv.* — **cur′a·tive·ness** *n.*

cu·ra·tor (kyōō·rā′tər) *n.* **1.** A person in charge of a museum or similar institution. **2.** A custodian; superintendent. **3.** *Law* A guardian appointed to take charge of the property of a person not legally qualified to act for himself. [< L *curare* to care for < *cura* care] — **cu·ra·to·ri·al** (kyōōr′ə·tôr′ē·əl, -tō′rē-) *adj.* — **cu·ra′tor·ship** *n.*

curb (kûrb) *n.* **1.** Anything that restrains or controls: a *curb* on inflation. **2.** A border of concrete or stone along the edge of a street: also, *Brit., kerb.* **3.** A chain or strap bracing a bit against the lower jaw of a horse, used to check the horse when the reins are pulled. For illustration see HARNESS. **4.** An enclosing or confining framework, margin, etc., as at the top of a well. **5.** *U.S.* The curb exchange (which see). **6.** A hard swelling on the hind leg of a horse. — *v.t.* **1.** To control, as with reins and curb; restrain. **2.** To protect by or provide with a curb. [< F *courbe*, orig. adj., curved < L *curvus*]

curb bit A horse's bit with a curb chain or strap attached.

curb exchange 1. An organization for the sale of securities not listed on the regular stock exchange. **2.** The building in which this market operates. [< CURB, orig. the street as a market for selling securities out of hours + EXCHANGE n. def. 5]

curb·ing (kûr′bing) *n.* Material constituting or used for making a curb.

curb roof *Archit.* A roof consisting of two slopes of varying pitch; a mansard or gambrel roof.

curb·stone (kûrb′stōn′) *n.* A stone, row of stones, etc., on the outer edge of a sidewalk. Also, *Brit.*, **kerbstone.**

curch (kûrch) *n. Scot.* A kerchief worn on the head.

cur·cu·li·o (kûr·kyōō′lē·ō) *n. pl.* **·os** Any of various weevils (family *Curculionidae*) having the head prolonged into a beak, many species of which are injurious to fruits and nuts: also called *snout beetle*. [< L, weevil]

cur·cu·ma (kûr′kyōō·mə) *n.* Any of several plants (genus *Curcuma*) of the ginger family, especially those of which the rootstocks yield turmeric and a variety of arrowroot. [< NL < Arabic *kurkum* saffron]

curcuma paper Turmeric paper (which see).

curd (kûrd) *n.* **1.** *Often pl.* The coagulated portion of milk, of which cheese is made, as distinct from the watery whey. **2.** Any similar coagulation. — *v.t. & v.i.* To form into or become curd. [Metathetic var. of CRUD] — **curd′y** *adj.*

cur·dle (kûr′dəl) *v.t. & v.i.* **·dled, ·dling** To change or turn to curd; coagulate; congeal; thicken. [Freq. of CURD]

cure (kyōōr) *n.* **1.** A restoration to a sound or healthy condition. **2.** That which restores health or removes an evil. **3.** A special method or course of remedial or medicinal treatment. **4.** Spiritual care, especially of a clergyman for the members of his congregation: also **cure of souls. 5.** A manner or process of preserving food or other products. — *v.* **cured, cur·ing** *v.t.* **1.** To restore to a healthy or sound condition. **2.** To remedy or eradicate: to *cure* a bad habit. **3.** To preserve, as by salting, smoking, or aging. **4.** To vulcanize (rubber). **5.** To subject (synthetic plastics) to chemical action or heat in order to render infusible or chemically inert. — *v.i.* **6.** To bring about recovery. **7.** To be or become cured by a preserving process. [< OF < L *cura* care] — **cure′less** *adj.* — **cur′er** *n.*

cu·ré (kyōō·rā′) *n.* A parish priest, especially in France. [< F, curate]

cure-all (kyōōr′ôl′) *n.* Something supposedly curing all diseases or evils; a panacea.

cu·ret·tage (kyōō·ret′ij, kyōōr′ə·täzh′) *n. Med.* A scraping of a body cavity, as the uterus, by a curette.

cu·rette (kyōō·ret′) *Med. n.* A small instrument resembling a spoon or scoop, used for scraping growths, tissue, etc., from a body cavity. — *v.t.* **·ret·ted, ·ret·ting** To scrape or treat with a curette. [< F < *curer* to cure, restore]

cur·few (kûr′fyōō) *n.* **1.** A police or military regulation requiring persons to keep off the streets after a designated hour; also, a similar order applying to children. **2.** A medieval regulation requiring fires to be put out at the tolling of a bell. **3.** The bell itself. **4.** The hour of ringing such a bell. **5.** The ringing of a bell at a certain hour in the evening. [< AF *coeverfu*, OF *cuevrefu* < *couvrir* to cover + *feu* fire]

cu·ri·a (kyōōr′ē·ə) *n. pl.* **cu·ri·ae** (kyōōr′ē·ē) **1.** A court of justice. **2.** *Often cap.* The governing body of officials of the papal government: also **Cu′ri·a Ro·ma·na** (rō·mā′nə). **3.** Among the ancient Romans, a tribal division; also, its meeting place. **4.** The Roman senate house, or the senate of any Italian city. [< L] — **cu′ri·al** *adj.*

Cu·ri·a·ti·i (kyōōr′ē·ā′shē·ī) In Roman legend, three brothers killed by the Horatii.

cu·rie (kyōōr′ē, kyōō·rē′) *n. Physics* **1.** The unit of radioactivity, equal to 3.70×10^{10} disintegrations per second, of any radioactive nuclide. **2.** The quantity of radon emanation in equilibrium with one gram of radium: also called **cu′·rie·gram** (-gram). [after Marie *Curie*]

Cu·rie (kyōōr′ē, kyōō·rē′; *Fr.* kü·rē′), **Marie,** 1867–1934, *née* Sklodowska, born in Poland, and her husband **Pierre,** 1859–1906, French physicists, discoverers of radium.

Curie point *Physics* The temperature at which the transformation of ferromagnetism into paramagnetism takes place.

Curie-Weiss law (kyōōr′ē·wīs′, kyōō·rē′–; kü·rē′·vīs′) *Physics* The statement that paramagnetic substances are magnetically susceptible in inverse proportion to the absolute temperature. [after Pierre *Curie* and Pierre *Weiss*, 1865–1940, French physicist]

cu·ri·o (kyōōr′ē·ō) *n. pl.* **·os** A rare or curious art object, piece of bric-a-brac, etc. [Short for CURIOSITY]

cu·ri·o·sa (kyōōr′ē·ō′sə) *n.pl.* Books or other writings on unusual, especially pornographic, subjects. [< L, neut. pl. of *curiosus* curious, prying]

cu·ri·os·i·ty (kyōōr′ē·os′ə·tē) *n. pl.* **·ties 1.** Eager desire

for knowledge of something, especially of something novel or unusual. **2.** Interest in the private affairs of others. **3.** That which excites interest by its strangeness or rarity. **4.** *Obs.* Overcarefulness; fastidiousness.

cu·ri·ous (kyōōr′ē·əs) *adj.* **1.** Eager for information or knowledge. **2.** Given to prying or meddling. **3.** Attracting interest because of novelty or unusualness; odd; strange. **4.** Obscene; pornographic: said of books. **5.** Executed with ingenuity or skill; elaborate. **6.** *Rare* Involving special care or pains. **7.** *Obs.* Hard to please; fastidious. — **Syn.** See INQUISITIVE. [< OF *curios, curius* < L *curiosus* < *cura* care] — **cu′ri·ous·ly** *adv.* — **cu′ri·ous·ness** *n.*

Cu·ri·ti·ba (kōō′rē·tē′və) The capital of Paraná, Brazil, in the SE part of the State; pop. 616,500 (est. 1968).

cu·ri·um (kyōōr′ē·əm) *n.* An unstable radioactive element (symbol Cm), produced originally, with americium, by the bombardment of uranium and plutonium with alpha particles. See ELEMENT. [after Marie and Pierre *Curie*]

curl (kûrl) *v.t.* **1.** To twist into ringlets or curves, as the hair. **2.** To form into a curved or spiral shape. **3.** *Obs.* To adorn with curls. — *v.i.* **4.** To form ringlets, as the hair. **5.** To become curved; take a spiral shape. **6.** To play at the game of curling. — **to curl up 1.** To assume a position with the back curved and the legs drawn close to the body. **2.** *Informal* To break down completely; give up. — *n.* **1.** Something coiled or spiral, as a ringlet of hair. **2.** A curled or circular shape or mark: a *curl* in wood. **3.** The act of curling, or the state of being curled. **4.** A disease that attacks the leaves of plants, causing them to curl. [Metathetic var. of ME *crollid, crulled* curled < *crull* curly < MLG]

curl·er (kûr′lər) *n.* **1.** One who or that which curls. **2.** One who plays the game of curling.

cur·lew (kûr′lōō) *n.* **1.** A shore bird (family *Scolopacidae*), with a long bill and long legs, as *Numenius arquatus* of Europe and the **Hudsonian curlew** (*Phaeopus hudsonicus*). **2.** Any bird resembling the curlew. [< OF *corlieu, courlieus*; orig. imit., infl. in form by OF *courlieu* messenger]

curl·i·cue (kûr′li·kyōō) *n.* Any fancy curl or twist, as a flourish with a pen. Also **curl′y·cue.** [< CURLY + CUE¹]

curl·ing (kûr′ling) *n.* A game played on ice in which the opposing players slide heavy, smooth, circular stones (**curling stones**) toward a goal or tee at either end.

curling iron An implement of metal, used when heated for curling or waving the hair. Also **curling irons.**

curl paper A small strip of paper on which a lock of hair is rolled up to make it curl.

CURLING STONE

curl·y (kûr′lē) *adj.* **curl·i·er, curl·i·est 1.** Having curls. **2.** Tending to curl. **3.** Containing curllike marks: *curly* maple. — **curl′i·ness** *n.*

cur·mudg·eon (kər·muj′ən) *n.* **1.** A gruff or irritable person, especially an elderly man. **2.** *Archaic* A miserly, grasping person. [Origin unknown] — **cur·mudg′eon·ly** *adj.*

curn (kûrn) *n. Scot.* **1.** A grain. **2.** A small quantity.

curr (kûr) *v.i. Scot. & Brit. Dial.* To coo or purr, as a dove, cat, etc. [< ON *kurra* murmur]

cur·rach (kûr′əkh, kûr′ə) *n. Scot. & Irish* A coracle. Also spelled *curagh*: also **cur′ragh.**

cur·ra·jong (kûr′ə·jong) See KURRAJONG.

cur·rant (kûr′ənt) *n.* **1.** A round, acid berry, used for making jelly. **2.** The bush (genus *Ribes*) producing this berry; especially, the **red** or **white currant** (*R. sativum*) and the **black currant** (*R. nigrum*). **3.** A small seedless raisin of the Levant. [Back formation < *Corauntz*, taken as pl. in AF (*raisins de*) *Corauntz* (raisins from) Corinth]

cur·ren·cy (kûr′ən·sē) *n. pl.* **·cies 1.** The current medium of exchange; money, both metal and paper. Abbr. *cur.* **2.** General acceptance or circulation; prevalence; vogue: The story gained wide *currency*. **3.** The time during which something is current: the *currency* of a law. — **Syn.** See MONEY.

cur·rent (kûr′ənt) *adj.* **1.** Belonging to the immediate present; in progress: the *current* year. Abbr. *cur.* **2.** Passing from person to person; circulating, as money or news. **3.** Generally accepted; prevalent. **4.** *Rare* Moving; running; flowing. — *n.* **1.** A continuous onward movement, as of water; a flowing. **2.** The part of any body of water or air that has a more or less steady flow in a definite direction: an ocean *current*. **3.** Any perceptible course, movement, or trend; tendency: main *currents* in American thought. **4.** *Electr.* **a** A movement or flow of electricity passing through a conductor. **b** The rate at which it flows. Abbr. (n. def. 4) *c., C.* — **alternating current** *Electr.* A current that periodically reverses its direction of flow, each complete cycle having the same value. Abbr. *AC, a.c., A.C.* — **direct current** *Electr.* A current flowing in one direction. Abbr. *DC, d.c., D.C.* [< OF *curant*, ppr. of *corre* < L *currere* to run; infl. in form by L *currens, -entis*, ppr. of *currere*] — **cur′rent·ly** *adv.* — **cur′rent·ness** *n.*

current density *Electr.* Density (def. 5b).

current expenses Any expenses necessary for the regular, daily maintenance of a business.

cur·ri·cle (kûr′i·kəl) n. An open, two-wheeled carriage drawn by two horses abreast. [< L *curriculum* race < *currere* to run]

cur·ric·u·lum (kə·rik′yə·ləm) n. pl. ·lums or ·la (-lə) 1. All the courses of study offered at a university or school. 2. A regular or particular course of study. [< L, a race < *currere* to run] — **cur·ric′u·lar** adj.

cur·ric·u·lum vi·tae (kə·rik′yə·ləm vī′tē) Latin 1. Course of life; career. 2. A short biographical statement giving one's date of birth, schooling, etc.: also called *vita*.

cur·ri·er (kûr′ē·ər) n. 1. One who curries leather. 2. One who curries horses, etc.

Cur·ri·er and Ives (kûr′ē·ər; īvz) 1. A U.S. firm of lithographers, founded in 1835 by **Nathaniel Currier**, 1813–88, later joined by **James Merritt Ives**, 1824–95. 2. Any print issued by this firm, the subjects of which were scenes of American life, manners, and history.

cur·ri·er·y (kûr′ē·ər·ē) n. pl. ·er·ies The trade or occupation of a currier, or a currier's shop.

cur·rish (kûr′ish) adj. Of or like a cur; snarling; mean.

cur·ry[1] (kûr′ē) v.t. ·ried, ·ry·ing 1. To rub down and clean with a currycomb; groom (a horse, etc.). 2. To dress (tanned hides) by soaking, scouring, smoothing, etc. 3. To beat or pummel. — **to curry favor** To seek favor by flattery, etc. [< OF *correier, conreder* to make ready, prepare]

cur·ry[2] (kûr′ē) n. pl. ·ries 1. A pungent sauce of East Indian origin, used as a relish for meats, rice, etc. Also **curry sauce.** 2. A dish of meat, fish, etc., cooked with this sauce. 3. Curry powder. — v.t. ·ried, ·ry·ing To flavor with curry. [< Tamil *kari* sauce]

cur·ry·comb (kûr′ē·kōm′) n. A comb consisting of a series of teeth or upright serrated ridges, for grooming horses, etc. — v.t. To comb with a currycomb.

curry powder A condiment prepared from pungent spices, turmeric, etc., used in making curry and curried dishes.

curse (kûrs) n. 1. An appeal for evil or injury to befall another, as through the intercession of God or gods. 2. The evil or injury so invoked. 3. Any profane oath; imprecation. 4. A source of calamity or evil. 5. Something cursed. 6. Eccl. An excommunication or severe censure; anathema. — **the curse** Informal Menstruation. — v. **cursed** (kûrst) or **curst, curs·ing** v.t. 1. To invoke evil or injury upon; damn. 2. To swear at; execrate. 3. To cause evil or injury to; afflict. — v.i. 4. To utter curses; swear; blaspheme. [OE *cursian* < OIrish *cursagim* to blame]

— **Syn.** (noun) *Curse, imprecation, malediction,* and *anathema* mean the calling down of evil upon a person. A *curse* is an appeal to a supernatural power to punish a wrongdoer or an enemy; it may also be applied to any affliction that is regarded as sent by a deity or by fate. *Imprecation* suggests anger or strong hatred rather than moral indignation. A *malediction* is usually public, and is intended to arouse general abhorrence of the person against whom it is pronounced. An *anathema* is an ecclesiastical *curse,* usually pronounced against heretics.

curs·ed (kûrst; for adj., also kûr′sid) A past tense and past participle of CURSE. — adj. 1. Under a curse. 2. Deserving a curse; wicked; detestable. 3. Dial. Ill-tempered; vicious: in this sense usually *curst.* Also **curst.** — **curs·ed·ly** (kûr′sid·lē) adv. — **curs′ed·ness** n.

cur·sive (kûr′siv) adj. Running; flowing: said of writing or printing in which the letters are joined. — n. 1. A letter or character used in cursive writing. 2. Printing A kind of type in which the letters are shaped as in handwriting. [< Med.L *cursivus* < L *cursus* < *currere* to run] — **cur′sive·ly** adv.

cur·so·ri·al (kûr·sôr′ē·əl, -sō′rē-) adj. 1. Adapted for running or walking: said of the limbs of certain animals. 2. Having, or performed by, such limbs.

cur·so·ry (kûr′sər·ē) adj. Rapid and superficial; not thorough; hasty. [< LL *cursorius* pertaining to running < *cursor* a runner < L *currere* to run] — **cur′so·ri·ly** adv. — **cur′so·ri·ness** n.

curt (kûrt) adj. 1. Brief and abrupt; especially, rudely brief: *a curt* nod. 2. Short or shortened. — **Syn.** See BLUNT. [< L *curtus* shortened] — **curt′ly** adv. — **curt′ness** n.

cur·tail (kər·tāl′) v.t. To cut off or cut short; abbreviate; lessen; reduce. [< CURTAL; infl. in form by *tail*] — **cur·tail′er** n. — **cur·tail′ment** n.

curtail step The bottom step or steps of a flight of stairs when extended and rounded at the outer ends.

cur·tain (kûr′tən) n. 1. A piece or pieces of cloth, etc. hanging in a window or opening as a decoration or screen, usually capable of being drawn to the sides or raised. 2. Something that conceals or separates like a curtain: the *curtain* of darkness. 3. In theaters, the hanging drapery that conceals the stage. 4. The raising of the curtain at the opening of an act or scene, or the lowering of the curtain at the close. 5. The speech or situation in a play occurring immediately before the curtain falls. 6. The part of a rampart or wall connecting two bastions or towers. 7. Archit. A portion of a wall between two towers, piers, etc. 8. pl. Slang Ruin; death. — v.t. To provide, shut off, or conceal with or as with a curtain. [< OF *curtine* < LL *cortina*]

curtain call Prolonged applause of an audience at the end of a play, scene, etc., as a call for the performers to reappear and acknowledge it; also, their reappearance.

curtain lecture A private scolding given by a wife to her husband, with reference to the old-fashioned curtained bed.

curtain raiser 1. A short play or sketch presented before a longer or more important play. 2. Any introductory event.

curtain wall Archit. An outside wall providing enclosure but giving no structural support.

cur·tal (kûr′təl) Obs. adj. 1. Cut short, as an animal's tail. 2. Wearing a short frock, as a friar. — n. 1. An animal with a docked tail. 2. Anything cut short. [< OF *curtald*]

curtal ax Obs. A cutlass. [Alter. of CUTLASS]

cur·tate (kûr′tāt) adj. Shortened. [< L *curtatus,* pp. of *curtare* to shorten < *curtus* shortened]

cur·te·sy (kûr′tə·sē) n. Law The life tenure in which a man holds his dead wife's estates when issue capable of inheriting them was born during the marriage. [Var. of COURTESY]

cur·ti·lage (kûr′tə·lij) n. Law The enclosed ground adjacent to a dwelling house. [< AF, var. of OF *cortillage* < *cortil,* dim. of *cortis, cort.* See COURT.]

Cur·tis (kûr′tis), **Charles,** 1860–1936, U.S. statesman; vice president 1929–33. — **Cyrus Hermann,** 1850–1933, U.S. publisher.

Cur·tiss (kûr′tis), **Glenn Hammond,** 1878–1930, U.S. pioneer aviator and inventor.

Cur·ti·us (kûr′tsē-ŏŏs), **Ernst,** 1814–96, German archeologist and educator.

curt·sy (kûrt′sē) n. pl. ·sies A bending of the knees and lowering of the body as a gesture of civility or respect, performed by women: sometimes spelled *courtesy.* — v.i. ·sied, ·sy·ing To make a curtsy. Also **curt′sey.** [Var. of COURTESY]

cu·rule (kyŏŏr′ōōl) adj. Privileged to sit in a curule chair; of the highest rank. [< L *curulis* < *currus* chariot]

curule chair The official seat of an ancient Roman magistrate of the highest rank, originally like a campstool with curved legs, later highly ornamented. Also **curule seat.**

cur·va·ceous (kûr·vā′shəs) adj. U.S. Informal Having voluptuous curves; shapely: said of a woman.

cur·va·ture (kûr′və·chər) n. 1. The act of curving or bending, or the state of being curved. 2. Math. The rate of change in the deviation of a given arc from any tangent to it. 3. Something curved or bent. 4. Physiol. A curving, especially when abnormal: *curvature* of the spine. [< L *curvatura* < *curvare* to bend]

curve (kûrv) n. 1. A line continuously bent, as the arc of a circle. 2. A curving, or something curved. 3. An instrument for drawing curves, used by draftsmen. 4. Math. The locus of a point moving in such a way that its course can be defined by an equation. 5. Stat. Any line that, plotted against coordinates, represents variations in the values of a given quantity, force, characteristic, etc.: The population *curve* is rising. 6. A grading system in which students are ranked according to their standing in the tested group, with high, average, and low marks being assigned on the basis of a theoretical frequency distribution. 7. In baseball, a ball pitched with a spin that causes it to veer to one side; also, the course of such a ball. — v. **curved, curv·ing** v.t. 1. To cause to assume the form of or move in the path of a curve. — v.i. 2. To assume the form of a curve. 3. To move in a curve. — adj. Curved. [< L *curvum* < *curvus* bent] — **curv·ed·ly** (kûr′vid·lē) adv. — **curv′ed·ness** n.

cur·vet (n. kûr′vit; v. kər·vet′, kûr′vit) n. A light, low leap of a horse, made so that all four legs are off the ground at one time. — v. **cur·vet·ted** or **·vet·ed, cur·vet·ting** or **·vet·ing** v.i. 1. To make a curvet. 2. To prance; frisk. — v.t. 3. To cause to curvet. [< Ital. *corvettare* < *corvetta,* dim. of *corva* bent < L *curvus*]

curvi- combining form Curved. [< L *curvus* curved]

cur·vi·fo·li·ate (kûr′və·fō′lē·it, -āt) adj. Bot. Having curved leaves.

cur·vi·lin·e·ar (kûr′və·lin′ē·ər) adj. Formed or enclosed by curved lines. Also **cur′vi·lin′e·al.**

Cur·zon (kûr′zən), **George Nathaniel,** 1859–1925, first Marquess Curzon of Kedleston, English statesman.

Cus·co (kōōs′kō) See CUZCO.

cu·sec (kyōō′sek) n. A cubic foot per second, a unit for measuring the rate of flow of a liquid. [< CU(BIC) + SEC(OND)]

Cush (kush) In the Old Testament, a son of Ham. Gen. x 6.

Cush (kush) A region referred to in the Bible as settled by the descendants of Cush, identified as Ethiopia: also *Kush.*

cush·at (kush′ət, kŏŏsh′-) n. The European ringdove (*Columba palumbus*), having a cream-colored mark around the neck: also called *wood pigeon.* [OE *cûscote*]

cu·shaw (kə·shô′) n. A variety of crookneck squash: also spelled *cashaw:* also called *China squash.* [< N. Am. Ind.]

Cush·ing (kŏŏsh′ing), **Caleb,** 1800–79, U.S. jurist and diplomat. — **Harvey Williams,** 1869–1939, U.S. surgeon.

cush·ion (kŏŏsh′ən) n. 1. A flexible bag or casing filled with some soft or elastic material, as feathers, air, etc., used for lying or resting on. 2. Anything resembling a cushion in appearance or use; especially, any device to deaden the jar or impact of parts, as padding, inserted rubber, or a column of air or steam. **3.** The elastic rim of a billiard table. **4.** A pillow used in making lace. **5.** *Canadian* The ice of a hockey rink. — *v.t.* **1.** To seat or arrange on or as on a cushion; prop up. **2.** To provide with a cushion. **3.** To cover or conceal, as with a cushion. **4.** To pad, as with a cushion; absorb the shock or effect of. **5.** *Mech.* To compress, as exhaust steam or other motive fluid, by closing the exhaust outlet of a cylinder. [< L *coxa* hip, thigh] — **cush/ion·y** *adj.*

Cush·it·ic (kŏŏsh·it/ik) *n.* A group of Hamitic languages spoken in Ethiopia and Somaliland. — *adj.* Pertaining to this group of languages. Also spelled *Kushitic.*

Cush·man (kŏŏsh/mən), **Charlotte Saunders,** 1816–76, U.S. actress.

cush·y (kŏŏsh/ē) *adj.* *Slang* **cush·i·er, cush·i·est** Comfortable; agreeable; easy. [< CUSHION; orig. Brit. slang]

cusk (kusk) *n.* *pl.* **cusks** or **cusk 1.** An edible, codlike fish (*Brosmius brosme*) of northern seas. **2.** The burbot. [Origin unknown]

cusp (kusp) *n.* **1.** A point or pointed end. **2.** *Astron.* Either point of a crescent moon. **3.** *Geom.* A point at which two branches of a curve meet and end, with a common tangent. **4.** *Archit.* The figure formed at the point where two arcs intersect, as in medieval tracery. **5.** *Anat.* **a** A prominence or point, as on the crown of a tooth. **b** The pointed fold forming a segment of the cardiac valves. **6.** *Bot.* A sharp, stiff point, as of a leaf. [< L *cuspis, -idis* a point]

cus·pate (kus/pāt) *adj.* **1.** Having a cusp or cusps. **2.** Cusp-shaped. Also **cus/pat·ed, cusped** (kuspt).

cus·pid (kus/pid) *n.* A canine tooth.

cus·pi·date (kus/pə·dāt) *adj.* **1.** Having a cusp or cusps. **2.** *Bot.* Ending in a cusp, as a leaf. Also **cus·pi·dal** (kus/pə·dəl), **cus/pi·dat/ed.**

cus·pi·da·tion (kus/pə·dā/shən) *n.* *Archit.* Decoration with cusps.

cus·pi·dor (kus/pə·dôr) *n.* A spittoon. [< Pg., spitter < *cuspir* to spit < L *conspuere* < *com-* thoroughly + *spuere* to spit]

cus·pis (kus/pis) *n.* *pl.* **·pi·des** (-pə·dēz) *Latin* A cusp.

cuss (kus) *U.S. Informal v.t. & v.i.* To curse. — *n.* **1.** A curse. **2.** A queer or perverse person or animal: a humorous or contemptuous term. [Var. of CURSE]

cuss·ed (kus/id) *adj.* *U.S. Informal* **1.** Cursed. **2.** Mean; perverse. — **cuss/ed·ly** *adv.* — **cuss/ed·ness** *n.*

cus·so (kus/ō) *n.* **1.** An Abyssinian tree (*Hagenia abyssinica*) of the rose family. **2.** The flowers of this tree, used as a vermifuge. Also spelled *kousso, kusso.* [< native name]

cus·tard (kus/tərd) *n.* A mixture of milk, eggs, sugar, and flavoring, either boiled or baked. [Alter. of earlier *crustarde, crustade* < F *croustade,* a type of pie < L *crusta* crust]

custard apple 1. The soft, edible, pulpy fruit of a tropical American tree (*Annona reticulata*). **2.** The tree bearing this fruit. **3.** The papaw.

Cus·ter (kus/tər), **George Armstrong,** 1839–76, Union general in the Civil War and Indian fighter; killed by the Sioux at the Little Bighorn River.

cus·to·di·al (kus·tō/dē·əl) *adj.* Pertaining to custody.

cus·to·di·an (kus·tō/dē·ən) *n.* A guardian; caretaker. — **cus·to/di·an·ship/** *n.*

cus·to·dy (kus/tə·dē) *n.* *pl.* **·dies 1.** A keeping; guardianship. **2.** The state of being held in keeping or under guard. — **to take into custody** To arrest. [< L *custodia* < *custos* guardian]

cus·tom (kus/təm) *n.* **1.** The habitual practice of a community or a people; established usage; convention: the *custom* of shaking hands. **2.** An ordinary or usual manner of doing or acting; habit. **3.** *Law* An old and general usage that has obtained the force of law. **4.** Habitual patronage, as of a hotel, store, etc. **5.** *pl.* A tariff or duty upon imported or, rarely, exported goods; also, the agency of the government that collects such duties. **6.** Rent, service, or tribute given to a feudal lord by his tenant. — **Syn.** See HABIT. — *adj.* **1.** Made to order. **2.** Specializing in made-to-order goods. [< OF *custume, costume* < L *consuetudo* < *com-* thoroughly + *suescere* to become used to. Doublet of COSTUME.]

cus·tom·a·ble (kus/təm·ə·bəl) *adj.* Subject to customs or tariffs; dutiable.

cus·tom·ar·y (kus/tə·mer/ē) *adj.* **1.** Conforming to or established by custom; usual; habitual. **2.** *Law* Holding or held by custom, as a feudal estate. — *n. pl.* **·ar·ies** A written statement of laws and customs. [< Med.L *customarius* < OF *custume.* See CUSTOM.] — **cus·tom·ar·i·ly** (kus/tə·mer/ə·lē, kus/tə·mer/ə·lē) *adv.* — **cus/tom·ar/i·ness** *n.*

cus·tom-built (kus/təm-bilt/) *adj.* Built to order or to individual specifications: a *custom-built* boat.

cus·tom·er (kus/təm·ər) *n.* **1.** One who buys something; especially, one who deals regularly at a given establishment. **2.** *Informal* One to be dealt with: a queer *customer.*

cus·tom·house (kus/təm·hous/) *n.* The government office where duties are collected and vessels cleared for entering or leaving. Also **custom house.** *Abbr.* **c.h., C.H.**

cus·tom-made (kus/təm·mād/) *adj.* Made to order.

cus·toms union (kus/təmz) An association of nations that remove tariff restrictions among themselves and have a common tariff policy toward other nations: also *common market.*

cus·tos (kus/tos) *n.* *pl.* **cus·to·des** (kus·tō/dēz) **1.** A custodian; keeper. **2.** The superior in certain religious houses. [< L, guardian]

custos mo·rum (môr/əm, mō/rəm) *Latin* Guardian of morals.

cus·tu·mal (kus/chŏŏ·məl, -tyŏŏ-) *adj.* Belonging to the customs of a city, manor, etc. — *n.* A written collection of the customs of a city, manor, etc.; a customary.

cut (kut) *v.* **cut, cut·ting** *v.t.* **1.** To open or penetrate with a sharp edge; make an incision in; gash; pierce. **2.** To divide with a sharp edge into parts or segments; sever, carve, or slice. **3.** To remove or sever from the main part: usually with *off.* **4.** To make or shape by cutting: to *cut* gems. **5.** To hollow out; excavate. **6.** To fell or hew: often with *down.* **7.** To strike sharply, as with a whip; lash. **8.** To cause mental pain to; hurt the feelings of. **9.** *Informal* To pretend not to know; snub. **10.** *Informal* To absent oneself from: to *cut* a class. **11.** To cross or intersect: One line may *cut* another. **12.** To shorten and trim, as hair, or prune, as a hedge; clip; pare. **13.** To shorten or edit by removing parts. **14.** To prepare for sound reproduction: to *cut* a record. **15.** To mow or reap (wheat, rye, etc.). **16.** To reduce or lessen; curtail: to *cut* prices, noise, etc. **17.** To dilute or weaken: to *cut* whisky. **18.** To dissolve or break down: to *cut* grease. **19.** To have (a new tooth) grow through the gum. **20.** In certain sports and games, to strike (the ball) so that it will spin and bound irregularly, or be deflected to one side. **21.** To divide (a pack of cards), as before dealing. **22.** To perform; present: to *cut* a caper or a figure. **23.** To castrate; geld. — *v.i.* **24.** To make an incision; act as a sharp edge. **25.** To admit to being severed or cut. **26.** To use a sharp edge. **27.** To penetrate like a knife: The wind *cut* through his sweater. **28.** To veer sharply in one's course: He *cut* to the right. **29.** To go by the shortest or most direct route: with *across, through,* etc. **30.** In certain sports and games, to deflect the ball. **31.** To grow through the gum: said of teeth. **32.** To divide a pack of cards, as before dealing. — **cut and run** To cut the moorings of a vessel and sail hastily. **2.** To dash off suddenly; flee. — **to cut back 1.** To shorten by removing the end. **2.** To reduce or curtail. **3.** To reverse one's direction. **4.** To flash back (which see). — **to cut down 1.** To reduce; curtail. **2.** To kill, as with a sword. — **to cut in 1.** To move into a line or queue abruptly or out of turn. **2.** To interrupt a dancing couple so as to take the place of one partner. **3.** To break in, as on a conversation; interrupt. — **to cut off 1.** To remove or detach by cutting. **2.** To put an end to; stop. **3.** To interrupt. **4.** To intercept. **5.** To disinherit. — **to cut out 1.** To remove by cutting; excise. **2.** To shape by cutting. **3.** To be suited for: He's not *cut out* for the work. **4.** To move sharply from one's course, as in traffic. **5.** To oust and supplant, as a rival. **6.** *Slang* To stop doing; cease. — **to cut up 1.** To cut in pieces. **2.** To affect deeply; distress. **3.** *Informal* To behave in an unruly manner. — *n.* **1.** A severing, slashing, or piercing stroke: a clean *cut.* **2.** The opening or wound made by such a stroke; gash; cleft. **3.** A part cut off; especially, the part of a meat animal: the shoulder *cut.* **4.** A deletion or excision of a part: to make *cuts* in a manuscript. **5.** A passage or channel that has been cut or dug out. **6.** A direct route: a short *cut.* **7.** Something that hurts the feelings, as an insult. **8.** *Informal* A refusal to recognize an acquaintance. **9.** The manner in which a thing is cut; fashion; style: the *cut* of a suit. **10.** A reduction in prices, wages, etc.; also, the amount reduced. **11.** *U.S. Slang* A share or commission. **12.** *Informal* An absence from a class at school. **13.** *Printing* An engraved block or plate; also, an impression made from this. **14.** *U.S.* The season's output, especially of lumber. **15.** A stroke imparting spin to a ball, as in tennis, billiards, etc. **16.** A cutting of a deck of cards. **17.** One of the pieces used in drawing lots. **18.** *Chem.* A fraction, as of petroleum, obtained in distillation. — **a cut above** A degree better than. — *adj.* **1.** That has been cut off, into, or through: *cut* flowers; a *cut* finger. **2.** Dressed or finished by a tool, as stone or glass. **3.** Reduced, as rates or prices. **4.** Diluted, as whisky. **5.** Castrated. **6.** *Bot.* Incised or cleft. — **cut and dried 1.** Prepared or arranged beforehand. **2.** Lacking interest or suspense; routine; dull. [ME *cutten, kytten* < Scand. Cf. dial. Sw. *kuta,* Norw. *kutte.*]

cu·ta·ne·ous (kyŏŏ·tā/nē·əs) *adj.* Of, pertaining to, affecting, or like skin. [< Med.L *cutaneus* < L *cutis* skin]

cut·a·way (kut/ə·wā/) *n.* A man's formal daytime coat, having the front corners cut slopingly away from the waist down to the tails at the back: also **cutaway coat.**

cut·back (kut/bak/) *n.* **1.** A sharp reduction, as in personnel or scheduled production. **2.** In movies, novels, etc., a flashback. **3.** In football, a sudden change in a player's running direction.

cutch[1] (kuch) *n.* Couch grass. [Var. of COUCH(GRASS)]

cutch[2] (kuch) *n. Anglo-Indian* Catechu.

cut·cher·ry (kə-cher′ē) *n. pl.* **·ries** *Anglo-Indian* A hall of justice; also, any public administrative office. Also **cutch·er·y** (kuch′ər·ē).

cute (kyōōt) *adj.* **cut·er, cut·est** **1.** *U.S. Informal* Pretty, dainty, or attractive. **2.** *Dial.* Clever or shrewd. [Var. of ACUTE] — **cute′ly** *adv.* — **cute′ness** *n.*

cut glass Glass that has been shaped or ornamented by cutting on a wheel of stone, iron, copper, etc.

cut·grass (kut′gras′, -gräs′) *n.* A swamp grass (*Leersia oryzoides*) with flat leaves edged with tiny hooks that cut the flesh when drawn against it.

Cuth·bert (kuth′bərt), **Saint,** died 687, English monk.

cu·ti·cle (kyōō′ti·kəl) *n.* **1.** *Anat.* The epidermis. **2.** Any superficial covering. **3.** The crescent of toughened skin around the base of a fingernail or toenail. **4.** *Bot.* A transparent film covering the surface of a plant, derived from the layers of epidermal cells. **5.** *Zool.* A thick lining membrane, as the integument of arthropods: also **cu·tic·u·la** (kyōō·tik′yə·lə). [< L *cuticula,* dim. of *cutis* skin] — **cu·tic′u·lar** *adj.*

cu·tie (kyōō′tē) *n. U.S. Informal* Someone cute. Also **cu′tey.**

cu·tin (kyōō′tin) *n.* **1.** *Bot.* A variety of fatty or waxy protective cuticle of leaves, stems, etc., of plants. **2.** *Med.* A material prepared from animal membrane, used for dressing and protecting wounds. [< L *cutis* skin + -IN]

cut-in (kut′in′) *n.* In motion pictures and television, a scene inserted in order to break the action or show in close-up some significant object: also called *insert.*

cu·tin·i·za·tion (kyōō′tən-ə-zā′shən, -ī-zā′-) *n. Bot.* The modification of cell walls by the presence of cutin, making them waterproof.

cu·tin·ize (kyōō′tən-īz) *v.t. & v.i.* **·ized, ·iz·ing** To undergo or cause to undergo cutinization.

cu·tis (kyōō′tis) *n. Anat.* The corium. Also **cutis vera.** [< L]

cut·lass (kut′ləs) *n.* A short, swordlike weapon, often curved, formerly used chiefly by sailors. Also **cut′las.** [< F *coutelas,* aug. of *couteau* knife < L *culter*]

CUTLASSES

a British, 10th century. *b* German, 15th century. *c* Mariner's, 17th century.

cutlass fish Any of various long, eel-like fish (genus *Trichiurus*) of North American waters, especially the **Atlantic cutlass fish** (*T. lepturus*), and the **Pacific cutlass fish** (*T. nitens*): also called *scabbard fish.*

cut·ler (kut′lər) *n.* One who makes repairs, or deals in cutlery. [< OF *coutelier* < Med.L *cultellarius* maker of knives < L *cultellus,* dim. of *culter* knife]

cut·ler·y (kut′lər·ē) *n.* **1.** Cutting instruments collectively, especially those for use at the dinner table. **2.** The occupation of a cutler. [< OF *coutelerie* < *coutelier.* See CUTLER.]

cut·let (kut′lit) *n.* **1.** A thin piece of meat for frying or broiling, usually veal or mutton cut from the leg or sometimes from the ribs. **2.** A flat croquette of chopped meat, fish, etc. [< F *côtelette,* double dim. of *côte* rib, side < L *costa* rib; infl. in form by CUT]

cut-off (kut′ôf′, -of′) *n.* **1.** The prescribed termination or limit of a process or series. **2.** *U.S.* A shorter road or route that cuts across something. **3.** *U.S.* A new channel cut by a river across a bend: also, the part thus cut off. **4.** *Mech.* **a** A stopping or cutting off of the flow of something, as fluid or steam. **b** The mechanism that does this. **c** The point at which it is done. **5.** *Music* A cessation of sound; also, a conductor's gesture indicating this.

cut·out (kut′out′) *n.* **1.** Something cut out or intended to be cut out. **2.** *Electr.* A device that cuts off the current when the flow reaches an unsafe level. **3.** A device to let the exhaust gases from an internal-combustion engine pass directly to the air without going through the muffler.

cut·o·ver (kut′ō′vər) *adj.* Cleared of timber, as land.

cut-price (kut′prīs′) *adj.* Sharply reduced in price.

cut·purse (kut′pûrs′) *n.* A pickpocket; formerly, one who cut away purses that were attached to a girdle or belt.

cut-rate (kut′rāt′) *adj.* Sold or selling at reduced prices.

cut·tage (kut′ij) *n.* The propagation of plants by means of slips or cuttings.

cut·ter (kut′ər) *n.* **1.** One who cuts, especially one who shapes, fits, decorates, or edits by cutting. **2.** A device that cuts. **3.** *Naut.* **a** A single-masted, fast-sailing vessel of narrow beam and deep draft, and normally spreading no more than four sails. **b** A small, swift, armed, and engined vessel, as used by the Coast Guard for coastal patrol, etc. **c** A small to medium-sized boat either employed by or carried on a larger vessel (such as a warship) and used to discharge passengers, transport stores, etc. **4.** A small sleigh.

CUTTER (def. 4)

cut·throat (kut′thrōt′) *n.* **1.** Bloodthirsty; murderous. **2.** Ruinous; merciless: *cutthroat competition.* **3.** Played by three players: said of poker and other card games. — *n.* One who cuts throats; a murderer.

cut·ting (kut′ing) *adj.* **1.** Adapted to cut; edged. **2.** Disagreeably penetrating; sharp; chilling. **3.** Tending to wound the feelings; sarcastic. — *n.* **1.** The act of one who or that which cuts. **2.** Something obtained or made by cutting. **3.** In motion pictures, the putting together of film in its proper or most effective sequence. **4.** An excavation made through a hill or high piece of ground for the construction of a railroad, canal, etc. **5.** *Bot.* A young plant shoot cut off for rooting or for propagation. **6.** *Brit.* A newspaper clipping.

cut·tle (kut′l) *n.* **1.** A cuttlefish. **2.** Cuttlebone. [OE *cudele*]

cut·tle·bone (kut′l·bōn′) *n.* The internal calcareous plate of a cuttlefish, used as a dietary supplement for birds and, when powdered, as a polishing agent.

cut·tle·fish (kut′l·fish′) *n. pl.* **·fish** or **·fish·es** A carnivorous marine cephalopod (genus *Sepia*), having lateral fins, ten sucker-bearing arms, an internal calcareous skeleton, and concealing itself by ejecting an inky fluid.

cut·ty (kut′ē, kŏŏt′ē) *Scot. adj.* Short; hasty; quick. — *n. pl.* **·ties** **1.** Anything cut short, as a spoon or tobacco pipe. **2.** A thickset girl. **3.** A slattern. [< CUT]

cutty sark (särk) *Scot.* A short chemise.

cutty stool *Scot.* **1.** A little stool. **2.** A seat in church where offenders, especially against chastity, used to sit and be publicly rebuked.

cut-up (kut′up′) *n. Informal* A person who tries to seem funny, as a practical joker.

cut·wa·ter (kut′wô′tər, -wot′ər) *n.* **1.** The forward part of the prow of a vessel. **2.** The sharp edge of a bridge pier, designed to resist the current, break up ice, etc.

cut·work (kut′wûrk′) *n.* Openwork embroidery with cut-out edges.

cut·worm (kut′wûrm′) *n.* Any of several nocturnal caterpillars (family *Noctuidae*) that cut off plants at the surface of the ground. For illustration see INSECTS (injurious).

Cu·vier (kōō′vē·ā, kyōō′-; *Fr.* kü·vyā′), **Baron Georges,** 1769–1832, French naturalist.

Cux·ha·ven (kŏŏks′hä·fən) A port city in West Germany, at the mouth of the Elbe; pop. 45,218 (est. 1970).

Cu·ya·bá (kōō′yä·bä′) See CUIABÁ.

Cuy·a·hog·a Falls (kə·hog′ə, kī′ə·hog′ə, -hô′gə, -hō′gə) A city in NE Ohio; pop. 49,678.

cu. yd. Cubic yard(s).

Cuyp (koip), **Albert,** 1620–91, Dutch painter. Also *Kuyp.*

Cuz·co (kōōs′kō) A city in southern Peru; formerly capital of the Inca Empire; pop. 108,900 (est. 1970): also *Cusco.*

c/v Catalogue value.

C.V. Common Version (of the Bible).

Cwm·ry (kŏŏm′rē) See CYMRY.

CWO *Mil.* **1.** Chief Warrant Officer. **2.** Commissioned Warrant Officer.

C.W.O. or **c.w.o.** Cash with order.

cwt. Hundredweight.

-cy *suffix* Forming nouns: **1.** (*from adjectives*) Quality, state, or condition of: *secrecy, bankruptcy.* **2.** (*from nouns*) Rank, order, or condition of: *chaplaincy.* [< F *-cie, -tie* < L *-cia, -tia* < Gk. *-kia, -keia, -tia, -teia;* or directly < L or < Gk.]

cyan- Var. of CYANO-.

cy·an·a·mide (sī·an′ə·mīd, -mid, sī′ə·nam′īd, -id) *n. Chem.* A white crystalline compound, CH_2N_2, formed from calcium cyanamide or by the action of cyanogen chloride on ammonia. Also **cy·an·a·mid** (sī·an′ə·mid, sī′ə·nam′id). [< CYAN- + AMIDE]

cy·a·nate (sī′ə·nāt) *n. Chem.* A salt or ester of cyanic acid. [< CYAN- + -ATE³]

cy·an·ic (sī·an′ik) *adj.* **1.** Of, pertaining to, or containing cyanogen. **2.** Blue.

cyanic acid *Chem.* A volatile, poisonous liquid compound, HCNO, with a penetrating pungent odor and caustic properties, stable only at low temperatures.

cy·a·nide (sī′ə·nīd) *n. Chem.* A compound of cyanogen with a metallic element or radical, especially potassium cyanide, KCN. Also **cy′a·nid** (-nid). — *v.t.* **·nid·ed, ·nid·ing** *Metall.* To subject to the action of cyanide: to extract gold by *cyaniding* the ore. [< CYAN- + -IDE] — **cy′a·ni·da′tion** *n.*

cy·a·nin (sī′ə·nin) *n.* Anthocyanin (which see). [< CYAN- + -IN]

cy·a·nine (sī′ə·nēn, -nin) *n. Chem.* Any of a group of bluish green, crystalline dyes related to quinoline, used in photography as a sensitizer and indicator. [< CYAN- + -INE¹]

cy·a·nite (sī′ə·nīt) *n.* A blue, gray, or black aluminum silicate, occurring in long, bladelike, triclinic crystals or fibrous columnar masses, used as a refractory: also *kyanite.* [< CYAN- + -ITE¹]

cyano- *combining form* **1.** Characterized by bluish coloring: *cyanosis.* **2.** *Chem.* Cyanide: *cyanotype.* Also, before vowels, *cyan-.* [< Gk. *kyanos* dark blue]

cy·an·o·gen (sī·an′ə·jən) *n. Chem.* **1.** A colorless, intensely poisonous, liquefiable gas, C_2N_2, having an almondlike odor and burning with a purple flame. **2.** The univalent radical CN. [< F *cyanogène*]

cy·a·no·hy·drin (sī′ə·nō·hī′drin) *n. Chem.* Any of a class of organic compounds in which an aldehyde is combined with both the cyanogen and hydroxyl radicals.

cy·a·no·sis (sī'ə-nō'sis) *n. Pathol.* A disordered condition of the circulation due to inadequate oxygenation of the blood, causing the skin to look blue. Also **cy·a·no·chroi·a** (sī'ə-nō-kroi'ə), **cy·a·no·der·ma** (-dûr'mə), **cy·a·nop·a·thy** (-nop'ə-thē). [< CYAN- + -OSIS] — **cy·a·not·ic** (sī'ə-not'ik) *adj.*

cy·an·o·type (sī·an'ə-tīp') *n.* A photographic picture, as a blueprint, made with a cyanide. [< CYANO- + -TYPE]

cy·a·nu·ric acid (sī'ə-nŏŏr'ik, -nyŏŏr'-) *Chem.* An acid, $C_3H_3O_3N_3\cdot2H_2O$, obtained variously, as by the dry distillation of uric acid. [< CYAN- + URIC]

Cyb·e·le (sib'ə-lē) In Phrygian mythology, the goddess of nature: identified with the Greek *Rhea*: also *Great Mother.*

cy·ber·net·ics (sī'bər-net'iks) *n. pl. (construed as sing.)* The science that treats of the principles of control and communication as they apply both to the operation of complex machines and the functions of organisms. [< Gk. *kybernētēs* steersman + -ICS] — **cy·ber·net·ic** *adj.*

cyc. Cyclopedia; cyclopedic.

cy·cad (sī'kad) *n.* Any of a small family (*Cycadaceae*) of primitive, seed-bearing, mostly tropical plants of fernlike or palmlike appearance. [< NL *Cycas, -adis* < Gk. *kykas*, a copyist's error for *koïkas*, accusative pl. of *koïx* a palm tree] — **cyc·a·da·ceous** (sik'ə-dā'shəs) *adj.*

Cyc·la·des (sik'lə-dēz) An island group in the southern Aegean, a Department of Greece; 1,023 sq. mi.; pop. 99,959 (1961); capital, Hermoupolis: Greek *Kikladhes, Kyklades.*

cyc·la·men (sik'lə-mən, -men) *n.* An Old World bulbous flowering herb (genus *Cyclamen*) of the primrose family, with white, pink, or crimson flowers: also called *sowbread.* [< NL < *L cyclaminos* < Gk. *kyklaminos, kyklamis*, ? < *kyklos* a circle; with ref. to the shape of the root]

cy·cle (sī'kəl) *n.* **1.** A recurring period within which certain events or phenomena occur and complete themselves in a definite sequence; a round of years or ages. **2.** A completed round of events or phenomena in which there is a final return to the original state. **3.** A pattern of regularly recurring events; a series that repeats itself: the business *cycle.* **4.** A vast period of time; an eon. **5.** A body of traditional poems or stories relating to a real or legendary person, or to a particular period: the Arthurian *cycle.* **6.** A sequence of miracle plays: the Chester *cycle.* **7.** A bicycle, tricycle, etc. **8.** *Astron.* The orbit of a celestial body: the lunar *cycle.* **9.** *Biol.* Any recurrent sequence of phenomena in plants or animals: the growth *cycle.* **10.** *Physics* A recurring series of changes in a material system leading to a restoration of the initial condition, as in an internal-combustion engine. **11.** *Electr.* A full period of an alternating current. **12.** *Telecom.* A completed series of variations in electromagnetic waves of a given frequency, as in radio transmission. — *v.i.* **·cled, ·cling 1.** To pass through cycles. **2.** To ride a bicycle, tricycle, etc. [< OF < LL *cyclus* < Gk. *kyklos* circle]

cycle car A light, open vehicle with three or four wheels, resembling a motorcycle.

cy·clic (sī'klik, sik'lik) *adj.* **1.** Pertaining to or characterized by cycles; recurring in cycles. **2.** *Chem.* Of, pertaining to, or characterized by a closed chain or ring formation, as benzene, naphthalene, anthracene, etc. **3.** *Bot.* Having parts arranged in whorls, as a flower. Also **cy·cli·cal.**

cyclic rate The rate at which a weapon fires automatically.

cy·clist (sī'klist) *n.* One who rides a bicycle, tricycle, etc. Also **cy'cler.**

cyclo- *combining form* **1.** Circular: *cyclograph.* **2.** *Chem.* A saturated cyclic hydrocarbon compound: *cyclopropane.* Also, before vowels, **cycl-.** [< Gk. *kyklos* circle]

cy·clo·graph (sī'klə-graf, -gräf) *n.* **1.** An arcograph (which see). **2.** A camera capable of taking a panoramic view of an object. [< CYCLO- + -GRAPH]

cy·clo·hex·ane (sī'klō-hek'sān) *n. Chem.* A saturated hydrocarbon, C_6H_{12}, made by the hydrogenation of benzene and occurring in petroleum, composed of six methylene radicals arranged in cyclic form. [< CYCLO- + HEXANE]

cy·cloid (sī'kloid) *adj.* **1.** Resembling a circle or somewhat circular. **2.** Of fish scales, having concentric rings and smooth edges. **3.** *Psychiatry* Exhibiting cyclothymia. — *n. Geom.* The curve described by a point on the circumference of a circle rolling along a straight line in a single plane. [< Gk. *kykloeidēs* circular] — **cy·cloi'dal** *adj.*

CYCLOID
As the circle *c* rolls along the line *bd*, point *a* traces the cycloid *bad.*

cy·clom·e·ter (sī-klom'ə-tər) *n.* **1.** An instrument for recording the rotations of a wheel to show speed and distance traveled; a speedometer. **2.** A device for measuring circular arcs. [< CYCLO- + -METER]

cy·clom·e·try (sī-klom'ə-trē) *n.* The measuring of circles.

cy·clone (sī'klōn) *n.* **1.** *Meteorol.* A system of winds circulating about a center of relatively low barometric pressure, and advancing at the earth's surface with clockwise rotation in the Southern Hemisphere, counterclockwise in the Northern. **2.** Loosely, any violent and destructive whirling wind-

storm. — **Syn.** See WHIRLWIND. [< Gk. *kykloōn*, ppr. of *kykloein* to whirl, move in a circle < *kyklos* circle] — **cy·clon·ic** (sī-klon'ik) or **·i·cal** *adj* — **cy·clon'i·cal·ly** *adv.*

cyclone cellar An underground shelter adapted for use during cyclones and tornadoes: also called *storm cellar.*

cy·clo·pe·an (sī'klə-pē'ən) *adj.* **1.** *Usually cap.* Of or pertaining to the Cyclopes. **2.** Gigantic: a *cyclopean* task. **3.** Designating an ancient style of architecture characterized by the use of massive blocks of stone.

cy·clo·pe·di·a (sī'klə-pē'dē-ə) *n.* An encyclopedia (which see). Also **cy'clo·pae'di·a.** Abbr. *cyc.* [Short for ENCYCLOPEDIA]

cy·clo·pe·dic (sī'klə-pē'dik) *adj.* Embracing a wide range of knowledge; encyclopedic. Also **cy'clo·pae'dic.** Abbr. *cyc.* — **cy'clo·pe'di·cal·ly** *adv.*

cy·clo·pe·dist (sī'klə-pē'dist) *n.* One who makes or contributes to a cyclopedia. Also **cy'clo·pae'dist.**

cy·clo·pen·tane (sī'klə-pen'tān) *n. Chem.* A relatively inert liquid compound, C_5H_{10}, obtained from some mineral oils. [< CYCLO- + PENTANE]

cy·clo·ple·gi·a (sī'klə-plē'jē-ə) *n. Pathol.* Paralysis of the ciliary muscle of the eye. [< *cyclo-* (< Gk. *kyklos* circle, eyeball) + -PLEGIA] — **cy·clo·ple'gic** *adj.*

cy·clo·pro·pane (sī'klə-prō'pān) *n. Chem.* A colorless, pungent, inflammable gas, C_3H_6, used as an anesthetic. [< CYCLO- + PROPANE]

Cy·clops (sī'klops) *n. pl.* **Cy·clo·pes** (sī-klō'pēz) **1.** In Homeric legend, any of a race of one-eyed giants inhabiting Sicily. **2.** In Hesiodic legend, any of the three Titans who forged Zeus's thunderbolts.

cy·clo·ram·a (sī'klə-ram'ə, -rä'mə) *n.* **1.** A series of pictures on the interior of a cylindrical surface, appearing in natural perspective to a spectator standing in the center. **2.** A backdrop curtain, often concave, used on theater stages. [< CYCLO- + Gk. *horama* a view] — **cy·clo·ram·ic** (sī'klə-ram'ik) *adj.*

cy·clo·stome (sī'klə-stōm) *Zool. n.* Any of a class (*Cyclostomata*) of primitive, carnivorous, aquatic vertebrates, the lampreys and hagfishes, having round, suctorial mouths devoid of jaws, and a single nostril. — *adj.* **1.** Pertaining to the cyclostomes. **2.** Having a round mouth. Also **cy·clos·to·mate** (sī-klos'tə-māt), **cy·clo·stom·a·tous** (sī'klə-stom'ə-təs, -stō'mə-) *adj.* [< NL *Cyclostomata* < CYCLO- + -STOME]

cy·clo·style (sī'klə-stīl) *n.* An apparatus for duplicating writing, etc., by means of a rough-edged wheel that punctures holes in specially prepared paper, producing a kind of stencil. [< Gk. *kyklos* circle, wheel + STYLE (n. def. 13)]

cy·clo·thy·mi·a (sī'klə-thī'mē-ə) *n. Psychiatry* A mild form of manic-depressive psychosis characterized by frequent fluctuations of mood from gaiety to depression. [< CYCLO- + -THYMIA] — **cy'clo·thy'mic** *adj.*

cy·clo·tron (sī'klə-tron) *n. Physics* An apparatus in which atomic nuclei are accelerated to high energies by a voltage that alternates in synchronism with their motion on a spiral path to which they are constrained by a magnetic field. [< CYCLO- + -TRON]

Cyd·nus (sid'nəs) The ancient name for the TARSUS.

Cy·do·ni·a (sī-dō'nē-ə) The ancient name for CANEA.

cyg·net (sig'nit) *n.* A young swan. [< MF *cygne* a swan < L *cycnus* < Gk. *kyknos* + -ET]

Cyg·nus (sig'nəs) *n.* A constellation, the Swan, containing the bright star Deneb: also called *Northern Cross.* See CONSTELLATION. [< L]

cyl. Cylinder; cylindrical.

cyl·in·der (sil'in-dər) *n.* **1.** *Geom.* **a** A solid figure described by the circumference of a circle whose center moves along a straight line, the ends of the figure being equal, parallel circles. It is called a **right cylinder** if the center moves along a line perpendicular to the plane of the circle, and otherwise an **oblique cylinder.** **b** Any curved surface generated by a straight line that remains parallel to a fixed straight line while constantly intersecting a given curve. **2.** Any object or container resembling a cylinder in form. **3.** *Mech.* In a reciprocating engine, the chamber in which the pistons move. **4.** In a revolver, the rotating part that holds the cartridges. For illustration see REVOLVER. **5.** In a printing press, a rotating cylindrical part that carries the plates, or receives the impression or ink. **6.** The barrel of a pump. **7.** *Archeol.* A cylindrical stone or clay tablet with an incised design or a cuneiform inscription, used as a seal, amulet, etc. — *v.t.* To press or fit with a cylinder. Abbr. *cul.* [< L *cylindrus* < Gk. *kylindros* roller < *kylindein* to roll]

cylinder head In an internal-combustion engine, a detachable cover forming the ends of the cylinders.

cylinder stop The mechanism that locks each chamber in the cylinder of a revolver in alignment with the barrel. For illustration see REVOLVER.

cy·lin·dri·cal (si-lin'dri-kəl) *adj.* **1.** Of or pertaining to a cylinder. **2.** Shaped like a cylinder. Also **cy·lin'dric.** Abbr. *cul.* — **cy·lin·dri·cal·i·ty** (si-lin'dri-kal'ə-tē) *n.* — **cy·lin'dri·cal·ly** *adv.*

cyl·in·droid (sil′in·droid) *n.* A solid body resembling a cylinder but having equal and parallel elliptical bases. — *adj.* Like a cylinder. [< Gk. *kylindroeidēs*]

cy·lix (sī′liks, sil′iks) See KYLIX.

Cyl·le·ni·an (si·lē′nē·ən) *adj.* Relating to Hermes. [after Mount *Cyllene*, Greece, his supposed birthplace]

cy·ma (sī′mə) *n. pl.* **·mae** (-mē) **1.** *Archit.* A curved molding with a partly concave and partly convex profile. The **cyma rec·ta** (rek′tə) has the convex part nearest the wall; the **cyma re·ver·sa** (ri·vûr′sə) has the concave part nearest the wall. For illustration see MOLDING. **2.** *Bot.* A cyme. [< NL < Gk. *kyma* a wave]

cy·mar (si·mär′) See SIMAR.

cy·ma·ti·um (si·mā′shē·əm) *n. pl.* **·ti·a** (-shē·ə) *Archit.* **1.** A cyma. **2.** A molding that caps a division of an entablature. [< L < Gk. *kymation,* dim. of *kyma* a wave]

cym·bal (sim′bəl) *n.* One of a pair of concave metal plates clashed or beaten to produce a musical ringing sound. [OE *cymbal* and OF *cymble,* both < L *cymbalum* < Gk. *kymbalon* < *kymbē* cup, hollow of a vessel] — **cym′bal·ist** *n.*

Cym·be·line (sim′bə·lēn) In Shakespeare's drama of the same name, a king of Britain.

cyme (sīm) *n. Bot.* A flat-topped flower cluster in which the central flowers bloom first: also called *cyma.* For illustration see INFLORESCENCE. [< F < L *cyma* a wave, a sprout < Gk. *kyma*]

cy·mene (sī′mēn) *n. Chem.* One of three isomeric liquid compounds, $C_{10}H_{14}$, with lemonlike odor, contained in several volatile oils, as cumin, wild thyme, etc. Also **cy·mol** (sī′mōl, -mol). [< Gk. *kyminon* cumin + -ENE]

cym·lin (sim′lin) *n.* A kind of round, flat squash with a scalloped edge: also called *pattypan squash:* also spelled *simlin.* Also **cym′bling, cym′ling.** [Var. of *simlin,* an alter. of SIMNEL]

cymo- *combining form* Wave. [< Gk. *kymo-* < *kyma* wave]

cy·mo·gene (sī′mə·jēn) *n. Chem.* A volatile, flammable distillate of petroleum, consisting of hydrocarbons with a high butane content. [< Gk. *kyminon* cumin + -GENE]

cy·mo·graph (sī′mə·graf, -gräf) *n.* **1.** An instrument for tracing outlines of architectural moldings. **2.** A kymograph (which see). [< CYMO- + -GRAPH] — **cy′mo·graph′ic** *adj.*

cy·moid (sī′moid) *adj.* Resembling a cyma or a cyme.

cy·mo·phane (sī′mə·fān) *n.* A variety of chrysoberyl having a changeable luster. [< CYMO- + -PHANE]

cy·mose (sī′mōs, sī·mōs′) *adj. Bot.* Pertaining to, bearing, or like a cyme. Also **cy·mous** (sī′məs). — **cy′mose·ly** *adv.*

Cym·ric (kim′rik, sim′-) *adj.* Of or pertaining to the Cymry; Brythonic. — *n.* **1.** The Welsh language. **2.** The Brythonic branch of the Celtic languages. Also spelled *Kymric.*

Cym·ry (kim′rē, sim′-) *n.* A collective name for the Welsh and their Cornish and Breton kin: also *Cwmry, Kymry.* Also **Cym′ri.** [< Welsh *Cymry* the Welsh, pl. of *Cymro* a Welshman]

Cyn·e·wulf (kin′ə·wŏolf) Eighth-century Anglo-Saxon poet: also *Kynewulf.* Also **Cyn′wulf.**

cyn·ic (sin′ik) *n.* A sneering, faultfinding person; especially, one who believes that all men are motivated by selfishness. — *adj.* **1.** Cynical. **2.** Pertaining to Sirius, the Dog Star. [< L *cynicus* < Gk. *kynikos,* lit., doglike < *kyōn, kynos* dog]

Cyn·ic (sin′ik) *n.* One of a sect of Greek philosophers of the fifth and fourth centuries B.C., who held that virtue was the goal of life. Their doctrine eventually came to represent insolent self-righteousness. — *adj.* Pertaining to or characteristic of the Cynics: also **Cyn′i·cal.**

cyn·i·cal (sin′i·kəl, -ə-) *adj.* Distrusting or contemptuous of virtue in others; sneering; sarcastic. — **cyn′i·cal·ly** *adv.*

cyn·i·cism (sin′ə·siz′əm, -i-) *n.* **1.** Cynical character or attitude; contempt for or disbelief in the virtues of others. **2.** A cynical remark, action, etc. Also **cyn′i·cal·ness.**

cy·no·sure (sī′nə·shŏŏr, sin′ə-) *n.* **1.** An object that attracts notice and admiration; a center of attraction. **2.** Something that serves as a guide. [< MF < L *cynosura* < Gk. *kynosoura* the constellation Ursa Minor, lit., dog's tail < *kyōn, kynos* dog + *oura* tail]

Cy·no·sure (sī′nə·shŏŏr, sin′ə-) *n.* **1.** The constellation Ursa Minor, containing the polestar. **2.** Polaris (def. 1).

Cyn·thi·a (sin′thē·ə) Artemis. — *n. Poetic* The moon.

Cyn·thus (sin′thəs), **Mount** A mountain in Delos, Greece, anciently regarded as sacred to Artemis and Apollo.

C.Y.O. Catholic Youth Organization.

cy·per·a·ceous (sī′pə·rā′shəs, sip′ə-) *adj. Bot.* Pertaining or belonging to the sedge family (*Cyperaceae*) of grasslike or rushlike herbs. [< NL *Cyperaceae* < Gk. *kypeiros* sedge]

cy·pher (sī′fər) See CIPHER.

cy pres (sē′ prā′) *Law* As nearly as possible: designating the doctrine whereby a gift or trust impossible to administer as the testator directed may be used as nearly as possible in accordance with his intentions. [< OF *si pres* as near as]

cy·press¹ (sī′prəs) *n.* **1.** Any of various evergreen trees (genus *Cupressus*) of the pine family, having flat, scalelike foliage and durable wood. **2.** Any of various related trees, as the white cedar or bald cypress. **3.** The wood of these trees. **4.** Branches of cypress used to symbolize mourning. [< OF *cypres* < LL *cypressus* < Gk. *kyparissos*]

cy·press² (sī′prəs) *n. Obs.* A transparent, black lawn fabric formerly worn as mourning. Also **cy′prus.** [< OF *Cipre, Cypres* Cyprus]

cypress vine An annual, twining plant (*Quamoclit pennata*) with leaves parted into linear, parallel lobes, and narrow, funnel-shaped, scarlet or white flowers.

Cyp·ri·an (sip′rē·ən) *adj.* **1.** Of or pertaining to Cyprus. **2.** Pertaining to or characteristic of the worship of Aphrodite on ancient Cyprus; lewd; wanton. — *n.* **1.** A Cypriote. **2.** *Rare* A lewd person; especially, a prostitute. [< L *Cyprius* < Gk. *Kyprios* < *Kypros* Cyprus]

Cyp·ri·an (sip′rē·ən), **Saint,** 200?–258, Christian theologian; bishop of Carthage.

cyprino- *combining form* Carp: *cyprinodont.* Also, before vowels, **cyprin-.** [< Gk. *kyprinos* carp]

cy·prin·o·dont (si·prin′ə·dont, si·prī′nə-) *n.* Any of a family (*Cyprinodontidae*) of fishes with flattish heads, including the killifishes, guppies, and minnows. [< NL *Cyprinodon,* generic name < Gk. *kyprinos* carp + Gk. *odous, odontos* tooth]

cyp·ri·noid (sip′rə·noid, si·prī′-) *adj.* Of or pertaining to the *Cyprinidae;* carplike. — *n.* Any fish of the carp family (*Cyprinidae*), including barbels, breams, goldfishes, and many of the fresh-water minnows. Also **cy·pri·nid** (si·prī′nid, sip′rə·nid). [< Gk. *kyprinos* carp + -OID]

Cyp·ri·ote (sip′rē·ōt) *n.* **1.** A native or inhabitant of Cyprus. **2.** The ancient or modern Greek dialect of Cyprus. — *adj.* Of or pertaining to Cyprus. Also **Cyp·ri·ot** (sip′rē·ət). [< F *cypriote*]

cyp·ri·pe·di·um (sip′rə·pē′dē·əm) *n.* Any of a genus (*Cypripedium*) of orchids having fibrous roots, and large flowers with a pouchlike lip: also called *lady's-slipper.* [< NL < Gk. *Kypris* Aphrodite + *podion* slipper, dim. of *pous, podos* foot]

Cy·prus (sī′prəs) An island in the Mediterranean, south of Turkey, comprising an independent Republic; 3,572 sq. mi.; pop. 649,000 (est. 1970); capital, Nicosia.

cyp·se·la (sip′sə·lə) *n. pl.* **·lae** (-lē) *Bot.* An achene in plants of the composite family, as the sunflower. [< NL < Gk. *kypselē* hollow vessel]

Cyr·a·no de Ber·ge·rac (sir′ə·nō də bûr′zhə·rak, Fr. sē·rà·nō′ də ber·zhə·ràk′), **Savinien de,** 1620?–55, French writer and swordsman famous for his large nose; hero of a drama by Edmond Rostand.

Cyr·e·na·ic (sir′ə·nā′ik, sī′rə-) *adj.* **1.** Of or pertaining to the hedonistic school of philosophy founded by Aristippus of Cyrene. **2.** Of or pertaining to Cyrene or to Cyrenaica. — *n.* **1.** A disciple of Cyrenaic philosophy. **2.** A native or inhabitant of Cyrenaica.

Cyr·e·na·i·ca (sir′ə·nā′i·kə, sī′rə-) The eastern division of Libya on the Mediterranean; 330,258 sq. mi.; pop. 450,954 (est. 1964); capital, Benghazi: Italian *Cirenaica.*

Cy·re·ne (sī·rē′nē) A town in western Cyrenaica, an ancient Greek colony; pop. about 500: Italian *Cirene.*

Cyr·il (sir′əl), **Saint,** 315?–386?, Christian theologian; bishop of Jerusalem.

Cyril, Saint, 376–444, Christian theologian; archbishop of Alexandria.

Cyril, Saint, 827–869, Christian scholar and missionary: called **Apostle of the Slavs.**

Cy·ril·lic (si·ril′ik) *adj.* Of or pertaining to Saint Cyril.

Cyrillic alphabet An old Slavic alphabet based mainly on that of the Greeks, ascribed traditionally to Saint Cyril, but most likely devised in the tenth century by Bulgarian scholars. In its modern forms it is used for Russian, Bulgarian, Serbo-Croatian, Ukrainian, Byelorussian, Mongolian, and Macedonian. See ALPHABET.

Cy·rus (sī′rəs), died 529 B.C., king of Elam; founder of the Persian Empire: called **the Great.**

Cy·rus (sī′rəs) The ancient name for the KURA.

Cyrus the Younger, died 401 B.C., Persian satrap. See ANABASIS.

cyst (sist) *n.* **1.** *Pathol.* Any abnormal sac or vesicle in which matter may collect and be retained. **2.** *Biol.* **a** Any membranous sac or vesicle containing liquid or semi-solid material. **b** A resistant surrounding capsule formed by certain micro-organisms as they enter an inactive or resting stage, often in response to unfavorable environmental conditions; also, the capsule and its contents; spore (def. 2). **c** A capsule surrounding an inactive parasite, as a trichina. **3.** *Zool.* **a** A bladderlike sac, as that with which an embryonic tapeworm surrounds itself. **b** An organism forming such a sac, as a bladderworm. **4.** *Bot.* **a** A receptacle for oil in the rind of the orange and like fruits. **b** A cell or cavity containing reproductive bodies in certain cryptogams. **c** The spore case of a seaweed. [< Med.L *cystis* < Gk. *kystis* bladder < *kyein* to contain]

cys·tec·to·my (sis·tek′tə·mē) *n. pl.* **·mies** *Surg.* **1.** An operation to remove a cyst. **2.** Removal of the gall bladder or part of the urinary bladder. [< CYST(O) + -ECTOMY]

cys·te·ine (sis′ti·ēn, -in) *n.* An amino acid, $C_3H_7NO_2S$, derived from cystine. Also **cys·te·in** (sis′tē·in). [< CYSTEINE]

cys·tic (sis′tik) *adj.* **1.** Of, like, or containing a cyst or cysts. **2.** *Anat.* Pertaining to the gall bladder or to the urinary bladder. **3.** *Zool.* Encysted.

cys·ti·cer·cus (sis/tə·sûr/kəs) *n. pl.* **·ci** (-sī) *Zool.* A cyst that develops from the larva of a tapeworm and gives rise to its scolex. It was formerly regarded as a distinct genus. [< CYSTI- + Gk. *kerkos* tail] **— cys/ti·cer/coid** *adj.*

cys·tine (sis/tēn, -tin) *n. Biochem.* An amino acid, C_6H_{12}-$N_2O_4S_2$, produced by the digestion of proteins in the body, and isolated in the form of white hexagonal crystals. [< CYST(O)- + -INE¹]

cys·ti·tis (sis·tī/tis) *n. Pathol.* Inflammation of the bladder. [< CYST(O)- + -ITIS]

cysto- *combining form* Bladder; cyst: *cystoscope.* Also, before vowels, **cyst-:** also **cysti-.** [< Gk. *kystis* bladder]

cys·to·carp (sis/tə·kärp) *n. Bot.* The sporocarp in certain red algae. [< CYSTO- + -CARP] **— cys/to·car/pic** *adj.*

cys·to·cele (sis/tə·sēl) *n. Pathol.* A hernia or rupture of the urinary bladder. [< CYSTO- + -CELE¹]

cys·toid (sis/toid) *adj.* Shaped like a cyst. **—** *n.* A cystoid growth.

cys·to·lith (sis/tə·lith) *n. Bot.* A mineral concretion in the epidermal cells of some leaves. [< CYSTO- + -LITH]

cys·to·scope (sis/tə·skōp) *n. Med.* A catheter with a device for introducing light into the bladder to permit visual examination and treatment. [< CYSTO- + -SCOPE] **— cys·to·scop·ic** (sis/tə·skop/ik) *adj.*

cys·tos·to·my (sis·tos/tə·mē) *n. pl.* **·mies** *Surg.* The making of an artificial outlet from the bladder. [< CYSTO- + -STOMY]

cys·tot·o·my (sis·tot/ə·mē) *n. pl.* **·mies** *Surg.* 1. A cutting into the bladder. 2. The operation of puncturing an encysted tumor. [< CYSTO- + -TOMY]

-cyte *combining form* Cell: *phagocyte.* [< Gk. *kytos* hollow vessel]

Cy·the·ra (si·thir/ə) The Latin name for KYTHERA.

Cyth·e·re·a (sith/ə·rē/ə) Aphrodite. [after the island of *Kythera,* near which she is fabled to have risen from the sea] **— Cyth/e·re/an** *adj.*

cyto- *combining form* Cell: *cytogenesis.* Also, before vowels, **cyt-.** [< Gk. *kytos* hollow vessel < *kyein* to contain, be pregnant with]

cy·to·gen·e·sis (sī/tō·jen/ə·sis) *n. Biol.* The formation of cells. Also **cy·tog·e·ny** (sī·toj/ə·nē). **— cy/to·ge·net/ic** *adj.*

cy·to·ge·net·ics (sī/tō·jə·net/iks) *n.pl.* (*construed as sing.*) The scientific investigation of the role of cells in the phenomena of heredity and evolution.

cy·to·ki·ne·sis (sī/tō·ki·nē/sis, -kī-) *n. Biol.* The changes that take place in the cytoplasm of the cell during mitosis, meiosis, and fertilization. [< CYTO- + Gk. *kinēsis* motion]

cy·tol·o·gy (sī·tol/ə·jē) *n.* The scientific study of the structure, organization, and function of cells. [< CYTO- + -LOGY] **— cy·to·log·ic** (sī/tə·loj/ik) or **·i·cal** *adj.* **— cy/to·log/i·cal·ly** *adv.* **— cy·tol/o·gist** *n.*

cy·tol·y·sin (sī·tol/ə·sin) *n. Biochem.* An antibody serving to dissolve bacteria or red blood cells in the presence of the complement: also called *amboceptor.*

cy·tol·y·sis (sī·tol/ə·sis) *n. Biol.* The dissolution of cells. [< CYTO- + Gk. *lysis* a loosing] **— cy/to·lyt/ic** (-lit/ik) *adj.*

cy·to·plasm (sī/tə·plaz/əm) *n. Biol.* All the protoplasm of a cell except that in the nucleus. **— cy/to·plas/mic** *adj.*

cy·to·plast (sī/tə·plast) *n. Biol.* Cytoplasm. **— cy/to·plas/tic** *adj.*

Cyz·i·cus (siz/i·kəs) 1. An ancient city at the southern end of Kapıdağı Peninsula, Turkey. 2. The ancient name for the Kapıdağı Peninsula.

C.Z. Canal Zone, Panama.

czar (zär) *n.* 1. An emperor or king; especially, one of the former emperors of Russia. 2. An absolute ruler; despot. 3. *Informal* One in authority; chief: a *czar* of industry. Also *tsar, tzar.* [< Russ. *tsar',* ult. < L *Caesar* Caesar]

czar·das (chär/däsh) *n.* A Hungarian dance consisting of a slow, melancholy section followed by a quick, fiery one. [< Hung. *csárdás*]

czar·dom (zär/dəm) *n.* 1. The territory ruled by a czar. 2. The position or power of a czar. Also *tsardom, tzardom.*

czar·e·vitch (zär/ə·vich) *n.* The eldest son of a czar: also *cesarevitch, tsarevitch, tzarevitch.* [< Russ. *tsarevich*]

cza·rev·na (zä·rev/nə) *n.* 1. The wife of the czarevitch. 2. Formerly, the title of any daughter of the czar. Also *tsarevna, tzarevna.* [< Russ. *tsarevna*]

cza·ri·na (zä·rē/nə) *n.* The wife of a czar; an empress of Russia: also *tsarina, tzarina.* Also **cza·rit·za** (zä·rit/sə). [< G *czarin,* for Russ. *tzaritsa*]

czar·ism (zär/iz·əm) *n.* Absolutism in government; despotism; autocracy; especially, the government of Russia under the czars: also *tsarism, tzarism.* **— czar/ist** *adj. & n.*

Czech (chek) *n.* 1. A member of the western branch of Slavs, including the peoples of Bohemia and Moravia. 2. The West Slavic language of the Czechs, formerly called Bohemian. **—** *adj.* Relating to Czechoslovakia, the Czechs, or their language: also **Czech/ic, Czech/ish.**

Czech. Czechoslovakia (n).

Czech·o·slo·vak (chek/ə·slō/vak, -väk) *n.* A Czech or Slovak inhabiting Czechoslovakia. **—** *adj.* Of or pertaining to the Czechoslovaks.

Czech·o·slo·va·ki·a (chek/ə·slō·vä/kē·ə, -vak/ē·ə) A Republic of east central Europe; 49,368 sq. mi.; pop. 14,497,000 (est. 1970); capital, Prague: Czech *Československo.* Officially **Czechoslovak Socialist Republic.**

Czech·o·slo·va·ki·an (chek/ə·slō·väk/ē·ən, -vak/ē·ən) *n.* A Czechoslovak. **—** *adj.* Of or pertaining to Czechoslovakia or its inhabitants, or to the Czech or Slovak languages.

Czer·no·witz (chûr/nə·vits) The German name for CHERNOVTSY.

Czę·sto·cho·wa (cheń/stô·khô/vä) A city in south central Poland; pop. 179,400 (est. 1968).

D

d, D (dē) *n. pl.* **d's** or **ds, D's** or **Ds, dees** (dēz) 1. The fourth letter of the English alphabet. The shape of the Phoenician *daleth* was adopted by the Greeks as *delta* and became Roman *D.* Also *dee.* 2. The sound represented by the letter *d,* usually a voiced alveolar stop. 3. Anything shaped like the letter D or a half circle. **— symbol** 1. The Roman numeral for 500. 2. *Music* **a** The second tone in the natural scale of C; re. **b** The pitch of this tone, 293.7 cycles per second or this value multiplied by any power of 2, in standard pitch. **c** A written note representing it. **d** The scale built upon D. 3. *Math.* Differential. 4. The fourth in a series or group: vitamin D. 5. Pence (*d.,* from Latin *denarii*). 6. *Chem.* Deuterium (symbol D). 7. *Physics* Density. 8. *U.S.* The lowest passing grade for school work.

d. or **D.** 1. Dam (in animal pedigrees). 2. Date. 3. Daughter. 4. Day(s). 5. Dead. 6. Decree. 7. Degree. 8. Democrat(ic). 9. Deputy. 10. Diameter. 11. Died. 12. Dinar. 13. Director. 14. Dollar. 15. Door (stage). 16. Dose. 17. Dowager. 18. Drachma. 19. Dyne. 20. *Med.* Give (L *da*).

D. 1. December. 2. Department. 3. Deus. 4. Doctor. 5. Dominus. 6. Don (Sp.). 7. Duchess. 8. Duke. 9. Dutch.

da 1. Daughter. 2. Day(s). 3. Deciare.

D.A. District Attorney.

dab¹ (dab) *n.* 1. Any of various flounders; especially, the American **sand dab** (*Limanda ferruginea*) of the Atlantic and Pacific coasts. 2. Any flatfish. [Origin uncertain]

dab² (dab) *n. Informal* An expert. [Origin uncertain]

dab³ (dab) *n.* 1. A gentle blow; pat. 2. A quick stroke; a peck. 3. A soft, moist lump or patch: a *dab* of paint. 4. A little bit. **—** *v.t. & v.i.* **dabbed, dab·bing** 1. To strike softly; tap. 2. To peck. 3. To pat with something soft and damp. 4. To apply (paint. etc.) with light strokes. [ME *dabben.* Cf. G *tappe* footprint, MDu. *dabben* to fumble, dabble.]

dab·chick (dab/chik) *n.* A small grebe (*Podiceps ruficollis*) of Europe, or the pied-billed grebe of North America: also called *didapper, helldiver.* [? < DAB³ + CHICK]

dab·ber (dab/ər) *n.* 1. One who or that which dabs. 2. A printer's or engraver's pad for applying ink, color, etc.

dab·ble (dab/əl) *v.* **·bled, ·bling** *v.i.* 1. To play in a liquid, as with the hands; splash gently. 2. To engage oneself slightly or superficially: to *dabble* in art. **—** *v.t.* 3. To wet slightly; bespatter. [Freq. of DAB³, v.] **— dab/bler** *n.*

dab·ster (dab/stər) *n.* 1. *Brit. Dial.* A handy person; adept. 2. *Informal* A dabbler or bungler. [< DAB³]

da ca·po (dä kä/pō) *Music* From the beginning: a direction to repeat the opening section of a piece. Abbr. *D.C.*

Dac·ca (dak/ə) The capital of Bangladesh, in the central part; pop. 556,712 (est. 1966).

d'ac·cord (dà·kôr/) *French* In accord; agreed.

dace (dās) *n. pl.* **dac·es** or **dace** 1. A small cyprinoid fresh-water fish (*Leuciscus leuciscus*) of Europe. **2.** A fresh-water fish (genus *Rhinichthys*) of North America. [< OF *dars*, a small fish, lit., dart; from its movements]

da·cha (dä′chə) *n.* A Russian cottage or villa. [< Russ., a giving, gift]

Da·chau (dä′khou) A town in central Upper Bavaria, West Germany; site of a Nazi concentration camp; pop. 25,000.

dachs·hund (däks′hŏŏnt′, daks′hŏŏnd′, dash′-) *n.* A breed of dog native to Germany, having a long, compact body, short legs, and a short coat, usually of red, tan, or black and tan. [< G < *dachs* badger + *hund* dog]

Da·cia (dā′shə) An ancient kingdom and province of the Roman Empire corresponding roughly to modern Rumania. — **Da′cian** *adj. & n.*

DACHSHUND
(7 to 9 inches high at shoulder)

dack·er (dak′ər) *Scot. & Brit. Dial. v.i.* **1.** To waver. **2.** To saunter; stroll. — *n.* **1.** A sauntering walk. **2.** A contest. Also *daiker*. [Appar. < M Flemish *daeckeren*]

da·coit (də·koit′) *n.* A member of a robber band in India or Burma: also spelled *dakoit*. [< Hind. *dakait* < *dākā* robbery by a gang]

da·coit·y (də·koi′tē) *n.* Robbery by a band of dacoits.

Da·cron (dā′kron, dak′ron) *n.* A synthetic polyester textile fiber of high tensile strength, having great resistance to stretching and wrinkling: a trade name. Also **da′cron.**

dac·tyl (dak′təl) *n.* **1.** In prosody, a metrical foot consisting of one long or accented syllable followed by two short or unaccented ones (— ⌣⌣). **2.** A line of verse made up of or characterized by such feet: Nŏw in thĕ | ĕarth ăll thĕ | sĕeds ăre ăt | rĕst. **3.** *Zool.* A finger or toe; digit. [< L *dactylus* < Gk. *daktylos* finger, dactyl]

dac·ty·late (dak′tə·lāt) *adj.* Having fingerlike processes.

dac·tyl′ic (dak·til′ik) *adj.* Of, pertaining to, or characterized by dactyls. — *n.* A dactylic verse.

dactylo- *combining form* Finger; toe: *dactylology.* Also, before vowels, **dactyl-.** [< L *dactylus* < Gk. *daktylos* finger]

dac·tyl·o·gram (dak·til′ə·gram) *n.* A fingerprint. [< DACTYLO- + -GRAM]

dac·ty·log·ra·phy (dak′tə·log′rə·fē) *n.* The scientific study of fingerprints. [< DACTYLO- + -GRAPHY] — **dac·ty·lo·graph·ic** (dak′tə·lə·graf′ik) *adj.*

dac·ty·lol·o·gy (dak′tə·lol′ə·jē) *n.* The use of the fingers in communicating ideas, as in the deaf-and-dumb alphabet. [< DACTYLO- + -LOGY]

dad (dad) *n. Informal* Father. Also **dad·dy** (dad′ē). [Origin unknown]

da·da (dä′dä, -də) *n. Often cap.* A movement in art and literature, occurring especially in France, Germany, and Switzerland about 1916–20, that violently satirized all previous art. Also **da′da·ism.** [< F *dada*, a nonsense word] — **da′da·ist** *n.* — **da·da·ist′ic** *adj.*

dad·dle (dad′l) *v.t. & v.i.* **·dled, ·dling** Diddle[1].

dad·dy-long·legs (dad′ē·lông′legz′, -long′-) *n. pl.* **·legs** **1.** A longlegged arachnid of the order *Phalangida*, resembling a spider: also called *harvestman*. **2.** *Brit.* The crane fly.

da·do (dā′dō) *n. pl.* **·does** **1.** *Archit.* The part of a pedestal between the base and the cornice; the die. **2.** The lower part of an interior wall, often ornamented. [< Ital., a die, a cube < L *datum*. See DIE[2].]

dae·dal (dē′dəl) *adj.* **1.** Cunning; ingenious: a *daedal* mind. **2.** Skillfully contrived; intricate. Also spelled *dedal.* [< L *daedalus* < Gk. *daidalos* skillful, cunning]

Daed·a·lus (ded′ə·ləs, *Brit.* dē′də-) In Greek mythology, an Athenian architect and inventor who devised the Cretan Labyrinth in which he was later imprisoned with his son Icarus, and from which they escaped by artificial wings. — **Dae·da·li·an, Dae·da·le·an** (di·dā′lē·ən, -dāl′yən) *adj.*

dae·mon (dē′mən) *n.* A demon (def. 4).

daff[1] (daf, däf) *v.t.* **1.** *Archaic* To thrust aside; discard. **2.** *Obs.* To doff; take off. [Var. of DOFF]

daff[2] (daf, däf) *v.i. Scot.* To play the fool; talk foolishly. [< dial. E (Northern) *daff* fool, simpleton]

daf·fo·dil (daf′ə·dil) *n.* A plant (*Narcissus pseudo-narcissus*) of the amaryllis family, with solitary yellow flowers. Also *Dial.* or *Poetic* **daf·fa·dil·ly** (daf′ə·dil′ē), **daf·fa·down·dil·ly** (daf′ə·doun·dil′ē), **daf·fy·down·dil·ly** (daf′ē-). [Var. of ME *affodille* < Med.L *affodillus* < L *asphodelus.* Doublet of ASPHODEL.]

daf·fy (daf′ē) *adj.* **daf·fi·er, daf·fi·est** *Informal* Crazy; silly; zany. [< DAFF[2]]

daft (daft, däft) *adj.* **1.** *Chiefly Brit.* Insane. **2.** *Chiefly Brit.* Foolish; silly. **3.** *Scot.* Frolicsome. [OE *gedæfte* mild, meek. Akin to DEFT.] — **daft′ly** *adv.* — **daft′ness** *n.*

dag (dag) *n.* A loose-hanging point, lock, or shred. [ME *dagge*; origin uncertain]

Da·gan (dä′gän) The Babylonian god of the earth.

Dag·en·ham (dag′nəm) A municipal borough in SW Essex, England, near London: pop. 108,363 (1961).

Da·ges·tan (da′gəs·tan′, *Russ.* də·gyis·tän′) A division of the SE R.S.F.S.R.; 19,400 sq. mi.; pop. 1,429,000 (1970); capital, Makhachkala. Also **Da·ghes·tan′, Dagestan A.S.S.R.** *Russian* **Da·ges·tan′ska·ya A.S.S.R.** (-ska-yə).

dag·ger (dag′ər) *n.* **1.** A short, pointed and edged weapon for stabbing. **2.** *Printing* A reference mark (†): the second in a series. — **double dagger** *Printing* A reference mark (‡); a diesis: the third in a series. — **to look daggers (at)** To glare or scowl (at). — *v.t.* **1.** To pierce with a dagger; stab. **2.** *Printing* To mark with a dagger. [? ME *dag* to pierce; stab. Cf. F *dague* dagger.]

dag·gle (dag′əl) *v.t. & v.i.* **·gled, ·gling** *Archaic* To trail or draggle in mud or water. [Freq. of dial. *dag* to bemire]

dag·lock (dag′lok′) *n.* A dirty or tangled lock, as of wool on a sheep. [< dial. *dag* to bemire + LOCK[2]]

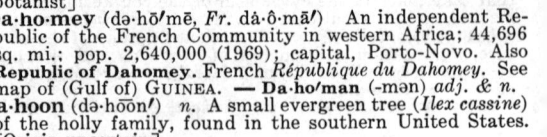

DAGGERS

da·go (dā′gō) *n. pl.* **·gos** or **·goes** *U.S. Slang* An Italian, or less commonly, a Spaniard or Portuguese: an offensive term. [Alter. of Sp. *Diego*, a personal name]

Dago (dä′gə) The Russian name for HIIUMA.

da·go·ba (dä′gə·bə) *n.* A dome-shaped Buddhist shrine containing sacred relics. [< Singhalese *dāgaba*]

Da·gon (dā′gon) A national god of the Philistines and later of the Phoenicians, represented as half man and half fish. [< Hebrew *dāg* fish]

da·guerre·o·type (də·ger′ə·tīp′, -ē·ə·tīp′) *n.* **1.** An early photographic process using silver-coated metallic plates that were sensitive to light and then were developed by mercury vapor. **2.** A picture made by this process. [after Louis Jacques Mandé *Daguerre*, 1789–1851, French inventor, + TYPE] — **da·guerre′o·typ′er, da·guerre′o·typ′ist** *n.* — **da·guerre′o·typ·y** *n.*

da·ha·be·ah (dä′hə·bē′ə) *n.* A passenger boat of the Nile, originally equipped with lateen sails, and now generally propelled by engines. Also **da′ha·bee′yah, da′ha·bi′ah, da·ha·bi′eh, da/ha·bi′yeh.** [< Arabic *dhahabīyah* golden < *dhahab* gold; with ref. to a gilded royal Egyptian barge]

Dahl·gren (dal′grən), **John Adolphus Bernard**, 1809–70, U.S. admiral; designer of a smoothbored naval cannon.

dahl·ia (dal′yə, däl′-, dāl′-) *n.* **1.** A tender perennial plant (genus *Dahlia*) of the composite family, having tuberous roots and showy red, purple, yellow, or white flowers. **2.** The flower or root of this plant. [after Anders *Dahl*, 18th c. Swedish botanist]

DAHABEAH

Da·ho·mey (də·hō′mē, *Fr.* då·ô·mā′) An independent Republic of the French Community in western Africa; 44,696 sq. mi.; pop. 2,640,000 (1969); capital, Porto-Novo. Also **Republic of Dahomey.** French *République du Dahomey.* See map of (Gulf of) GUINEA. — **Da·ho′man** (-mən) *adj. & n.*

da·hoon (də·hōōn′) *n.* A small evergreen tree (*Ilex cassine*) of the holly family, found in the southern United States. [Origin uncertain]

dai·ker (dā′kər) *v. & n.* Dacker.

Dail Ei·reann (dô·əl âr′ən) The lower house of the legislature of Ireland.

dai·ly (dā′lē) *adj.* Of, occurring, or appearing every day or every weekday. — *n. pl.* **·lies** A daily publication. — *adv.* Day after day; on every day. [OE *dæglic* < *dæg* day]

— **Syn.** *Daily* and *diurnal* refer to the period of the day, *daily* being the popular term and *diurnal* the scientific. *Diurnal* refers to the hours of daylight; a *diurnal* flower is one that opens or blooms only in daylight. *Daily* means occurring once every twenty-four hours; a *daily* broadcast may take place in the evening, and *daily* rest refers to the hours of sleep.

daily double In horse racing, a single bet won only by choosing the winners of two specified races in one day.

dai·men (dā′min) *adj. Scot.* Occasional; scattered. [Origin unknown]

dai·mio (dī′myō) *n. pl.* **·mio** or **·mios** Formerly, a hereditary feudal baron of Japan. Also **dai′myo.** [< Japanese < Chinese *dai* great + *mio, myo* name]

dai·mon (dī′mōn) *n.* A demon (def. 4). [< Gk.]

Dai Nip·pon (dī nēp·pōn′) A Japanese name for JAPAN.

dain·ty (dān′tē) *adj.* **·ti·er, ·ti·est** **1.** Delicately pretty or graceful. **2.** Of pleasing taste; delicious. **3.** Of fine sensibilities; fastidious; also, too fastidious; overnice. — **Syn.** See ELEGANT. — *n. pl.* **·ties** Something tasty or delicious; a delicacy. [< OF *daintie* < L *dignitas.* Doublet of DIGNITY.] — **dain′ti·ly** *adv.* — **dain′ti·ness** *n.*

dai·qui·ri (dī′kər·ē, dak′ər·ē) *n.* A cocktail made of rum, lime or lemon juice, and sugar. [after *Daiquiri*, Cuba, where a type of rum was made]

Dai·ren (dī′ren′) See LÜ-TA.

dair·y (dâr′ē) *n. pl.* **·ies** **1.** A commercial establishment that processes or manufactures milk products, and sells them. **2.** A room or building on a farm where milk and cream are kept and processed. **3.** A dairy farm. **4.** A herd of dairy cattle. **5.** Dairying. [ME *deierie* < *deie* dairymaid < OE *dæge*]

dairy cattle Cows of a breed specially adapted for milk production. Also **dairy cows.**

dairy farm A farm for producing dairy products.

dair·y·ing (dâr′ē·ing) *n.* The business of a dairy.

dair·y·maid (dâr′ē·mād′) *n.* A female worker in a dairy.

dair·y·man (dâr′ē·mən) *n. pl.* **·men** (-mən) A man who works in or owns a dairy.

da·is (dā′is, dās) *n.* A raised platform in a room or hall on which a speaker, eminent guests, etc., may sit or stand. [< OF *deis* < LL *discus* table. Doublet of DESK, DISH, DISK.]

dai·sy (dā′zē) *n. pl.* **·sies** 1. Any of various plants of the composite family; especially, the **oxeye daisy** (*Chrysanthemum leucanthemum*), common in the United States and having a yellow disk and white rays, and the **English daisy** (*Bellis perennis*), having a small yellow disk and numerous white or rose rays. 2. *Slang* Something excellent or exceptional. [OE *dæges ēage* day's eye] **— dai′sied** *adj.*

dak (dôk, däk) *n. Anglo-Indian* 1. Transport for passengers and mail by relays of men and horses. 2. The mail. Also spelled *dawk*. [< Hind. *ḍāk*]

Dak. Dakota.

Da·kar (dä·kär′, də-) The capital of Senegal, a port on the Cape Verde Peninsula; pop. 550,000 (est. 1969).

da·ker·hen (dā′kər·hen′) *n.* The corn crake. [Origin unknown]

Da·kin's solution (dā′kinz) A dilute, mildly basic solution of sodium hypochlorite, used as an antiseptic. [after Henry Drysdale *Dakin*, 1880–1952, English chemist]

da·koit (də·koit′) See DACOIT.

Da·ko·ta (də·kō′tə) *n.* 1. A member of the largest division of the Siouan stock of North American Plains Indians, now on reservations in North and South Dakota, Minnesota, and Montana. 2. The Siouan language of the Dakotas. 3. A Sioux Indian. **— Da·ko′tan** *adj. & n.*

Da·ko·ta (də·kō′tə) A former territory of the United States, comprising what is now North and South Dakota.

Dakota River See JAMES RIVER.

dal. or **dal** Decaliter.

Da·la·dier (dà·là·dyā′) **Édouard**, 1884–1970, French political leader; premier 1933, 1934, 1938–40.

Da·lai La·ma (dä·lī′ lä′mə) The pontiff of the principal Buddhist faith in Tibet, and traditional chief of state: also called *Grand Lama*. The 14th Dalai Lama, born 1934, was installed in 1940 and has been in exile since 1959. See LAMAISM.

da·la·si (dä·lä′sē) *n.* The monetary unit of Gambia, equivalent to 100 bututs.

dale (dāl) *n.* A small valley. [OE *dæl*. Akin to DELL.]

Dale (dāl), **Sir Henry** (**Hallett**), 1875–1968, English physiologist. **— Sir Thomas**, died 1619, English colonial governor of Virginia.

dales·man (dālz′mən) *n. pl.* **·men** (-mən) One living in a dale, especially in the north of England.

da·leth (dä′leth) *n.* The fourth letter in the Hebrew alphabet. See ALPHABET.

Dal·hou·sie (dal·hōō′zē) **Earl of**, 1770–1838, George Ramsay, British general and colonial administrator. **— Marquis of**, 1812–60, James Andrew Ramsay, British governor general of India 1848–56.

Da·li (dä′lē) **Salvador**, born 1904, Spanish surrealist painter.

Dal·las (dal′əs) A city in northern Texas; pop. 844,401.

Dal·las (dal′əs) **George Mifflin**, 1792–1864, U.S. statesman; vice president 1845–49.

dalles (dalz) *n.pl.* In the western United States, rapids running between steep rock walls; also, steep rock walls on either side of a ravine: also *dells*. [< F *dalle* trough, gutter]

dal·li·ance (dal′ē·əns) *n.* 1. Amorous play, flirting, or fondling. 2. Idle wasting of time; trifling.

dal·ly (dal′ē) *v.* **·lied**, **·ly·ing** *v.i.* 1. To make love sportively; frolic. 2. To play; trifle: to *dally* with death. 3. To waste time. **— *v.t.*** 4. To waste (time): with *away*. [< OF *dalier* to converse, chat] **— dal′li·er** *n.*

Dal·ma·tia (dal·mā′shə) A region of Croatia, western Yugoslavia; 4,954 sq. mi.; pop. 750,000 (est. 1959); capital, Split. *Serbo-Croatian* **Dal·ma·ci·ja** (däl·mä′tsē·yä).

Dal·ma·tian (dal·mā′shən) *n.* 1. A large, short-haired dog, white with black spots: also called *carriage dog, coach dog*. 2. One of the Slavic people of Dalmatia. **—** *adj.* Of or pertaining to Dalmatia or its people.

dal·mat·ic (dal·mat′ik) *n.* 1. *Eccl.* A wide-sleeved vestment worn by a deacon over the alb, as at High Mass. 2. A similar robe worn by English kings at their coronation. [< OF *dalmatique* < L *dalmatica* (*vestis*) Dalmatian (robe)]

Dal·rym·ple (dal·rim′pəl, dal′rim′pəl) **James**, 1619–95, first Viscount Stair, Scottish jurist. **— Sir David**, Lord Hailes, 1726–92, Scottish jurist and historian; great-grandson of the preceding.

dal se·gno (däl sā′nyō) *Music* From the sign: a direction to repeat from the sign :S: to a point designated as the end. Abbr. *d.s.*, *D.S.* [< Ital.]

Dal·ton (dôl′tən) **John**, 1766–1844, English chemist and physicist. **— Dal·to·ni·an** (dôl·tō′nē·ən) *adj.*

dal·ton·ism (dôl′tən·iz′əm) *n.* Color blindness, especially to the colors red and green. [after John *Dalton*, who was color blind]

Dal·ton plan (dôl′tən) In education, a system in which a student organizes his own assignments and advances as fast as his ability allows. [after *Dalton*, Mass., where first used]

Dal·ton's law (dôl′tənz) *Physics* The statement that the total pressure of a mixture of gases equals the sum of the separate pressures exerted by each gas if it occupied the same volume as the mixture at the same temperature.

Da·ly (dā′lē), **John Augustin**, 1838–99, U.S. playwright and producer.

Da·ly City (dā′lē) A city in western California, south of San Francisco; pop. 66,922.

dam¹ (dam) *n.* 1. A barrier to obstruct or control the flow of water. 2. The water held back by such a barrier. 3. Any obstruction. **—** *v.t.* **dammed**, **dam·ming** 1. To erect a dam in; obstruct or confine by a dam. 2. To keep back; restrain: with *up* or *in*. [ME. Akin to OE *demman* to block.]

dam² (dam) *n.* A female parent: said of animals. Abbr. *d.*, *D.* [Var. of DAME]

Dam (däm), (**Carl Peter**) **Henrik**, born 1895, Danish biochemist.

dam·age (dam′ij) *n.* 1. Injury to person or property; harm; loss. 2. *pl. Law* Money to compensate for an injury or wrong. 3. *Sometimes pl. Informal* Price or expense. **—** *v.* **·aged**, **·ag·ing** *v.t.* 1. To cause damage to. **—** *v.i.* 2. To be susceptible to damage. **— Syn.** See INJURE. [< OF < *dam* loss < L *damnum*] **— dam′age·a·ble** *adj.*

dam·an (dam′ən) *n.* A small, hyracoid, hoofed mammal (genus *Procavia*) with rhinoceroslike molar teeth; especially, *P. syriaca* of Asia Minor: in the Bible called *cony*. [< Arabic *damān* (*isrāīl*) sheep (of Israel)]

Da·man·hur (dä′män·hoor′) A city in northern Lower Egypt; pop. 126,100 (est. 1959).

Da·mão (də·mou′) A former Portuguese territory comprising three small enclaves in western India; annexed by India in 1961; 211 sq. mi.; pop. 72,040 (est. 1956); capital, Damão. Also **Da·man** (də·män′).

Da·ma·ra·land (dä·mä′rə·land′, də-) A region in central South-West Africa.

dam·as·cene (dam′ə·sēn, dam′ə·sēn′) *v.t.* **·cened**, **·cen·ing** To ornament (iron, steel, etc.) with wavy patterns or by inlaying or etching. Also **dam·as·keen** (dam′ə·skēn, dam′ə·skēn′). **—** *adj.* Relating to damascening or to damask. **—** *n.* Work ornamented by damascening.

Da·mas·cus (də·mas′kəs) The capital of Syria, an ancient city in the SW part; pop. 836,179 (est. 1970): Arabic *Dimashq*, *Es Sham*. *French* **Da·mas** (dà·mäs′). **— Dam·a·scene** (dam′ə·sēn, dam′ə·sēn′) *adj. & n.*

Damascus steel A steel with wavy markings formerly used in swords made at Damascus. Also **damask steel.**

dam·ask (dam′əsk) *n.* 1. A rich, reversible, elaborately patterned fabric, originally made of silk. 2. A fine, twilled table linen. 3. Damascus steel, or the wavy pattern on such steel. 4. A deep pink or rose color. **—** *adj.* 1. Of or from Damascus. 2. Made of Damascus steel or of damask. 3. Deep pink or rose-colored. **—** *v.t.* 1. To damascene. 2. To weave or ornament with rich patterns. 3. To make deep pink or rose. [after *Damascus*]

damask rose A large pink rose (*Rosa damascena*) of the Near East, noted for its fragrance.

dame (dām) *n.* 1. A mature woman; matron. 2. A woman of high social rank; a lady. 3. *U.S. Slang* A woman. 4. In Great Britain: **a** A title of the Order of the British Empire conferred on women, equivalent to that of knight. Abbr. *D.B.E.* **b** The legal title of the wife of a knight or baronet. 5. *Archaic* A schoolmistress. [< OF < L *domina* lady, fem. of *dominus* master. Doublet of DUENNA.]

dame·wort (dām′wûrt′) *n.* A plant (*Hesperis matronalis*) of the mustard family, having fragrant purplish flowers. Also **dame's rocket** (dāmz), **dame's violet.**

Da·mien de Veus·ter (dà·myan′ də vœs·târ′), **Joseph**, 1840–1888, Belgian Roman Catholic missionary to the lepers in Molokai: called **Father Da·mi·en** (dā′mē·ən).

Dam·i·et·ta (dam′ē·et′ə) A city in NE Egypt, in the Nile delta; pop. 77,200 (est. 1959). Arabic *Dumyat*.

dam·mar (dam′ər) *n.* 1. An oleoresinous gum yielded by various evergreen trees (genus *Agathis*) of Australia, India, and Asia, used as a varnish. 2. A similar resin from other plant sources. Also **dam′ar**, **dam′mer**. [< Malay *damar*]

damn (dam) *v.t.* 1. To pronounce worthless, bad, a failure, etc.: to *damn* a play. 2. To curse or swear at. 3. *Theol.* To condemn to eternal punishment. 4. To pronounce guilty; bring ruin upon: His words *damned* him. 5. *Obs.* To adjudge guilty; doom. **—** *v.i.* 6. To swear; curse. **— to damn with faint praise** To praise so reluctantly as to imply adverse criticism. **—** *n.* 1. The saying of "damn" as an oath. 2. The smallest, most contemptible bit: not worth a *damn*. **—** *interj.* An oath expressive of irritation, disappointment, etc. **—** *adj. & adv. Informal* Damned. [< OF *damner* < L *damnare* to condemn to punishment]

dam·na·ble (dam′nə·bəl) *adj.* Meriting damnation; detestable; outrageous. [< OF < L *damnabilis* < *damnare* to condemn] **—dam′na·ble·ness** *n.* **—dam′na·bly** *adv.*

dam·na·tion (dam-nā′shən) *n.* **1.** The act of damning, or the state of being damned. **2.** *Theol.* **a** Condemnation to eternal punishment; also, eternal punishment. **b** A cause for this; a mortal sin. **3.** Ruin by adverse criticism. **—** *interj.* Damn. [< F < L *damnatio, -onis* < *damnare*. See DAMN.]

dam·na·to·ry (dam′nə-tôr′ē, -tō′rē) *adj.* Tending to convict or condemn; damning: *damnatory* actions.

damn·dest (dam′dist) *Informal adj.* **1.** Most detestable or outrageous: the *damndest* lie. **2.** Most extraordinary. **—** *n.* The utmost: Do your *damndest*. Also **damned′est.**

damned (damd, *poetic or rhetorical* dam′nid) *adj.* **1.** Doomed; condemned, especially to eternal punishment. **2.** Deserving damnation or condemnation; detestable; outrageous: a *damned* fool. **—** *adv. Informal* Very: *damned* funny.

dam·ni·fy (dam′nə-fī) *v.t. Law* To cause injury, hurt, or damage to. [< OF *damnifier* < L *damnificare* to injure]

damn·ing (dam′ing, dam′ning) *adj.* That damns or condemns; inculpating: *damning* evidence. **—damn′ing·ly** *adv.*

Dam·o·cles (dam′ə-klēz) In Greek legend, a courtier who overpraised the happiness of the tyrant Dionysius the Elder, and was forced to sit at a banquet under a sword suspended by a single hair that he might learn the perilous nature of that happiness. **—sword of Damocles** Any impending calamity. **—Dam·o·cle·an** (dam′ə-klē′ən) *adj.*

Da·mon and Pyth·i·as (dā′mən; pith′ē-əs) In Roman legend, two devoted friends. Damon served as hostage for the condemned Pythias (Phintias) who wished to visit his home before dying.

dam·o·sel (dam′ə-zel) *n. Archaic* A damsel. Also **dam·oi·selle** (dam′ə-zel′), **dam·o·zel.** [Var. of DAMSEL]

damp (damp) *adj.* **1.** Somewhat wet; moist. **2.** *Archaic* Dejected. **—** *n.* **1.** Moisture or moistness; vapor; mist. **2.** Foul air or poisonous gas, especially in a mine. **3.** Depression of spirits. **4.** A discouragement; check. **—** *v.t.* **1.** To make damp; moisten. **2.** To discourage or dull (energy, ardor, etc.). **3.** To stifle, as with poisonous gas; choke. **4.** To bank, as a fire. **5.** *Music* To check the vibrations of (a string, etc.); deaden. **6.** *Physics* To reduce the amplitude of (a series of waves). [< MDu., vapor, steam] **—damp′ly** *adv.* **—damp′ness** *n.*

damp·en (dam′pən) *v.t.* **1.** To make damp; moisten. **2.** To check; depress, as ardor or spirits. **—** *v.i.* **3.** To become damp. **—damp′en·er** *n.*

damp·er (dam′pər) *n.* **1.** One who or that which damps, depresses, or checks. **2.** A flat plate in the flue of a stove, furnace, etc., for controlling the draft. **3.** *Music* **a** A mechanism for stopping the vibrations of the strings in a piano. **b** In brass instruments, a mute. **4.** *Electr.* A device for reducing or checking oscillations, as of a pendulum, electric current, or magnetic needle.

Damp·ier (dam′pyər, dam′pē-ər, -pir), **William,** 1652–1715, English adventurer and seafarer.

damp·ish (dam′pish) *adj.* Slightly damp.

Dam·rosch (dam′rosh), **Walter (Johannes),** 1862–1950, U.S. musician and conductor born in Germany.

dam·sel (dam′zəl) *n.* A young unmarried woman; maiden. Also, *Archaic,* **damosel.** [< OF *dameisele* gentlewoman, ult. < L *domina.* See DAME.]

damsel fly A slender-bodied dragonfly (order *Odonata*) with four similar elongate wings that are folded together over the back when at rest. For illustration see INSECTS (beneficial).

dam·son (dam′zən, -sən) *n.* **1.** An oval purple plum of Syrian origin. **2.** The tree (*Prunus institia*) producing it. Also **damson plum.** [ME *damascene* < L (*prunum*) *Damascenum* (plum) from Damascus]

dam·yan·kee (dam′yang′kē, dam′-) *n. U.S. Informal* A Northerner: a contemptuous term used by Southerners since the Civil War. Also **damned Yankee, damn Yankee.**

Dan (dan) *n. Obs.* Sir; mister: a title of honor: *Dan* Cupid. [< OF < L *dominus* master]

Dan (dan) In the Old Testament, a son of Jacob and Bilhah. *Gen.* xxx 6. **—** *n.* The tribe of Israel descended from him.

Dan (dan) **1.** In Biblical times, a city at the northern extremity of Palestine. **2.** A settlement in NE Israel, near the reputed site of the Biblical city. **—from Dan to Beersheba** From end to end, Dan and Beersheba being respectively the extreme northern and southern cities of Palestine.

Dan. 1. Daniel. **2.** Danish. **3.** Danzig.

Da·na (dā′nə), **Charles Anderson,** 1819–97, U.S. editor. **— Edward Salisbury,** 1849–1935, U.S. mineralogist. **— James Dwight,** 1813–95, U.S. geologist. **—Richard Henry,** 1815–82, U.S. lawyer and writer.

Dan·a·ë (dan′ī-ē) In Greek mythology, the mother of Perseus by Zeus, who loved her in the form of a shower of gold.

Dan·a·id (dan′ē-id) *n.* One of the Danaides.

Da·na·i·des (də-nā′ə-dēz) *n.pl.* In Greek mythology, the fifty daughters of Danaus who, except for Hypermnestra, murdered their husbands on their bridal night at their father's command, and who were punished in Hades by having to draw water in a sieve forever. **—Dan·a·id·e·an** (dan′ē-id′ē-ən, dan′ē-ə-dē′ən) *adj.*

Dan·a·us (dan′ī-əs) In Greek mythology, a king of Argos.

dance (dans, däns) *v.* **danced, danc·ing** *v.i.* **1.** To move the body and feet rhythmically, especially to music. **2.** To move about lightly or excitedly; leap about. **3.** To move up and down jerkily; bob. **—** *v.t.* **4.** To perform the steps of (a waltz, tango, etc.). **5.** To cause to be as specified by dancing: to *dance* one's cares away. **6.** To cause to dance. **—to dance attendance** To wait upon another constantly and tediously. **—** *n.* **1.** A series of regular rhythmic steps or movements, usually performed to music. **2.** An act or instance of dancing. **3.** A musical composition for dancing, as a waltz. **4.** A gathering of people for dancing; a ball. **—the dance** Dancing as an art. [< OF *danser*] **—danc′er** *n.*

dance fly A small or medium-sized, slender, predatory fly (genus *Empis,* family *Empididae*) that mates in dancing swarms. For illustration see INSECTS (beneficial).

dance of death An allegory, common in medieval art, representing Death as a skeleton leading people to the grave: also, *French, danse macabre.*

dan·de·li·on (dan′də-lī′ən, -dē-) *n.* A widespread plant (*Taraxacum officinale*) of the composite family, having yellow flower heads and deeply toothed, edible leaves. [< F *dent de lion* lion's tooth; with ref. to the shape of the leaves]

dan·der¹ (dan′dər) *n. U.S. Informal* Ruffled temper; anger. **—to get one's dander up** To make one angry. [? Var. of Scottish *dunder* to ferment]

dan·der² (dan′dər) *v.i. Scot.* To saunter: also *daunder.*

dan·der³ (dan′dər) *n.* Small, loose particles of hair or fur. [? Akin to DANDRUFF]

Dan·die Din·mont terrier (dan′dē din′mont) A shortlegged, long-bodied terrier with drooping ears. Also **Dandie Dinmont.** [after a Scottish farmer, portrayed in Scott's *Guy Mannering,* who claimed to have started the breed]

dan·di·fy (dan′də-fī) *v.t.* **·fied, ·fy·ing** To cause to resemble a dandy or fop. **—dan′di·fi·ca′tion** *n.*

dan·di·prat (dan′dē-prat) *n. Obs.* **1.** A little boy; urchin. **2.** A small English coin of the 16th century. Also **dan′dy·prat.** [Origin unknown]

dan·dle (dan′dəl) *v.t.* **·dled, ·dling 1.** To move up and down lightly on the knees or in the arms, as an infant or child. **2.** To fondle; caress. [Cf. Ital. *dandolare*] **—dan′dler** *n.*

dan·druff (dan′drəf) *n.* A fine scurf that forms on the scalp and comes off in small scales. [Origin unknown]

dan·dy¹ (dan′dē) *n. pl.* **·dies 1.** A man who is excessively interested in fine clothes and elegant appearance; a fop. **2.** *Informal* A particularly fine specimen of its kind. **3.** A dandy roll (which see). **4.** A yawl (def. 1). **—** *adj.* **1.** Like a dandy; foppish. **2.** *U.S. Informal* Excellent; very fine. [Alter. of *Andy* < *Andrew,* a personal name. Cf. MERRY-ANDREW.] **—dan′dy·ish** *adj.* **—dan′dy·ism** *n.*

dan·dy² (dan′dē) *n.* Dengue. Also **dandy fever.**

dandy roll A cylinder of wire gauze by which a web of paper pulp is given a watermark. Also **dandy roller.**

Dane (dān) *n.* A native or inhabitant of Denmark, or a person of Danish descent. [< ON *Danir* the Danes]

Dane·geld (dān′geld′) *n.* An annual tax levied in Britain from the 10th to 12th centuries to pay for protection against the Danes, later continued as a land tax. Also **Dane′gelt′** (-gelt′). [< Scand. Cf. ODan. *Danegjeld.*]

Dane·law (dān′lô′) *n.* A ninth-century code of laws established by Danish settlers in NE England; also, the region of England under these laws. Also **Dane′lagh′** (-lô′). [OE *Denalagu* Danes' law]

dane·wort (dān′wûrt′) *n.* The dwarf elder, a plant. Also **Dane's′-blood′, dane′weed′.**

dang (dang) *adj., adv., & v.t. Informal* Damn: a euphemism.

dan·ger (dān′jər) *n.* **1.** Exposure to evil, injury, or loss; peril; risk. **2.** A cause or instance of peril or risk. **3.** *Obs.* Power; control; ability to injure. [< OF, power of a lord, power to harm < L *dominium* lordship < *dominus* lord]

— Syn. *Danger, peril, risk, jeopardy,* and *hazard* denote liability to misfortune. *Danger* is the widest term; we speak of the *danger* of skidding on an icy road, or the *danger* of buying unlisted stocks. *Peril* suggests a more imminent or concrete threat: the *perils* of polar exploration. *Risk* often refers to the uncertainties of business: the *risk* of an investment. *Jeopardy* is chiefly legal, while *hazard* emphasizes the element of chance; a man being tried for murder is in *jeopardy* of his life; a soldier in battle is exposed to the *hazards* of warfare. **— Ant.** safety, security.

dan·ger·ous (dān′jər-əs) *adj.* Attended with danger; perilous; unsafe. **—dan′ger·ous·ly** *adv.* **—dan′ger·ous·ness** *n.*

dan·gle (dang′gəl) *v.* **·gled, ·gling** *v.i.* **1.** To hang loosely; swing to and fro. **2.** To follow or hover near someone as a suitor or hanger-on. **—** *v.t.* **3.** To hold so as to swing loosely. **—** *n.* **1.** Manner or act of dangling. **2.** Something that dangles. [< Scand. Cf. Dan. *dangle.*] **—dan′gler** *n.*

dan·gle·ber·ry (dang′gəl·ber′ē) *n.* The tangleberry (which see).

dangling participle See under PARTICIPLE.

Dan·iel (dan′yəl) In the Bible, a young Hebrew prophet, captive in Babylon. *Dan.* i 3–6. **—** *n.* A book of the Old Testament, containing the story of Daniel and the prophecies attributed to him. Abbr. *Dan., Danl.*

Dan·iel (dan′yəl), **Samuel,** 1562–1619, English poet.

Dan·iels (dan′yəlz), **Josephus**, 1862–1948, U.S. journalist and statesman.
Dan·ish (dā′nish) *adj.* Of or pertaining to Denmark, the Danes, or their language. — *n.* The North Germanic language of the Danes. Abbr. *Dan.* [OE *Denisc*]
Danish pastry A rich, flaky pastry made with raised dough, often filled with fruit, cheese, etc.
Danish West Indies A former name for the VIRGIN ISLANDS OF THE UNITED STATES.
Dan·ite (dan′īt) *n.* **1.** A descendant of Dan. **2.** One of a reputed secret brotherhood of Mormons.
dank (dangk) *adj.* Unpleasantly damp; cold and wet. [ME *danke* < Scand. Cf. Sw. *dank* marshy ground.] — **dank′ly** *adv.* — **dank′ness** *n.*
Danl. Daniel.
Dan·mark (dan′märk) The Danish name for DENMARK.
D'An·nun·zio (dän·nōon′tsyō), **Gabriele**, 1863–1938, Italian poet and patriot.
Da·no-Nor·we·gian (dā′nō-nôr·wē′jən) *n.* Riksmål.
danse ma·ca·bre (däns mà·kä′br′) *French* Dance of death.
dan·seuse (dän·sœz′) *n. pl.* **·seus·es** (-sœ′ziz, *Fr.* -sœz′) A female ballet dancer. [< F, fem. of *danseur*]
Dan·te A·li·ghie·ri (dän′tä ä′lē·gyä′rē, dan′tē) 1265–1321, Italian poet; author of the *Divine Comedy*: original name **Durante Alighieri.**
Dan·tesque (dan·tesk′) *adj.* Pertaining to or in the style of Dante Alighieri; especially, characterized by solemn purpose and fervent expression. Also **Dan·te·an** (dan′tē·ən, dan·tē′ən). [< Ital. *dantesco* < *Dante*]
Dan·ton (dän·tôn′), **Georges Jacques**, 1759–94, French Revolutionary leader; guillotined.
Dan·u (thän′ōō) In ancient Irish mythology, the goddess of death and mother of the gods.
Dan·ube (dan′yōōb) A river in central and SE Europe, flowing about 1,750 miles eastward from Baden, Germany, to the Black Sea: German *Donau*, Hungarian *Duna*, Rumanian *Dunărea*, Serbo-Croatian, Bulgarian *Dunav*. — **Dan·u·bi·an** (dan·yōō′bē·ən, də·nōō′-) *adj.*

THE DANUBE and Its Tributaries

GERMANY, POLAND, CZECHOSLOVAKIA, U.S.S.R., SWITZERLAND, AUSTRIA, HUNGARY, ITALY, RUMANIA, YUGOSLAVIA, BULGARIA

Dan·ville (dan′vil) **1.** A city in eastern Illinois; pop. 42,570. **2.** A city in southern Virginia; pop. 46,391.
Dan·zig (dan′sig, *Ger.* dän′tsikh) The German name for GDAŃSK.
dap (dap) *v.i.* **dapped, dap·ping 1.** To dip lightly or suddenly into water, as a bird. **2.** To fish by dropping a baited hook gently on the water. **3.** To bounce or skip, as over the surface of water. [Prob. var. of DAP³]
daph·ne (daf′nē) *n.* Any of a genus (*Daphne*) of shrubs having fragrant flowers. [< NL < Gk. *daphnē*]
Daph·ne (daf′nē) In Greek mythology, a nymph changed into a laurel tree to escape the pursuit of Apollo.
Daph·nis (daf′nis) In Greek mythology, a Sicilian shepherd, son of Hermes and inventor of bucolic poetry.
Daphnis and Chloe A pair of lovers in a Greek pastoral romance attributed to Longus.
Da Pon·te (dä pōn′tä), **Lorenzo**, 1749–1838, Italian poet and librettist; born *Emanuele Coneigliano*.
dap·per (dap′ər) *adj.* **1.** Smartly dressed; trim; natty. **2.** Small and active. — **Syn.** See NEAT¹. [< MDu., strong, energetic]
dap·ple (dap′əl) *v.t.* **·pled, ·pling** To make spotted or variegated in color. — *adj.* Spotted; variegated: also **dap′pled.** — *n.* **1.** A spot or dot, as on the skin of a horse. **2.** An animal marked with spots. [Origin uncertain]
dap·ple-gray (dap′əl·grā′) *adj.* Gray with a pattern of variegated rounded markings: usually said of horses.
Dap·sang (dup′sung) See K2.
DAR or **D.A.R.** Daughters of the American Revolution.
darb (darb) *n. Canadian Slang* Something considered extraordinary, excellent, etc.
dar·bies (där′bēz) *n.pl. Brit. Slang* Handcuffs. [? < *Darby*, a surname]
d'Ar·blay (där′blā) See BURNEY.
Dar·by and Joan (där′bē; jōn) A happily married, elderly couple. [from an 18th-century English ballad]
d'Arc, Jeanne (zhän därk) French name of Joan of Arc.
Dar·dan (där′dən) *adj. & n.* Trojan. Also **Dar·da·ni·an** (där·dā′nē·ən).
Dar·da·nelles (där′də·nelz′) A narrow strait in NW Turkey connecting the Sea of Marmara with the Aegean; length, 37 mi.: ancient *Hellespont.* Turkish *Çanakkale Boğazı.* See maps of AEGEAN SEA, BOSPORUS.
Dar·da·nus (där′də·nəs) In Greek mythology, a son of Zeus and ancestor of the Trojans.

dare¹ (dâr) *v.* **dared** (*Archaic* **durst**), **dar·ing** *v.t.* **1.** To have the courage or boldness to undertake; venture on. **2.** To challenge (someone) to attempt something as proof of courage, etc. **3.** To oppose and challenge; defy. — *v.i.* **4.** To have the courage or boldness to do or attempt something; venture. — **I dare say** I have no reason to doubt (it); I believe (it): also **I dare·say** (dâr′sā). — *n.* A challenge; taunt: to do something on a *dare.* [OE *durran*] — **dar′er** *n.*
◆ The third person singular present indicative appears in two forms: *dare*, with the infinitive without *to*, or the infinitive understood, as in *He dare not return*, and *dares*, a later development, as in *He dares to defy them.*
dare² (dâr) *v.* **dared**, **dar·ing** *Obs. v.t.* **1.** To daunt; scare. **2.** To bedazzle. — *v.i.* **3.** To be in fear. [OE *darian* to lurk]
Dare (dâr) **Virginia**, born 1587, first child born of English parents in America.
dare·dev·il (dâr′dev′əl) *n.* One who is recklessly bold. — *adj.* Rash; reckless. — **dare′dev′il·ry, dare′dev′il·try** *n.*
Dar-el-Bei·da (där′el-bī-dä′, -bā-dä′) The Arabic name for CASABLANCA.
Dar es Sa·laam (där′ es sə·läm′) The capital of Tanzania, a port on the Indian Ocean; pop. 272,821 (1967).
Dar·fur (där·fōor′) A Province of the western Sudan; 191,-650 sq. mi.; pop. 1,328,765 (1956); capital, El Fasher.
dar·ic (dar′ik) *n.* An ancient Persian gold coin. [< Gk. *Dareîkos* coin of Darius]
Dar·i·en (dâr′ē·en′, där′ē·en; *Sp.* dä·ryän′) The eastern part of Panama between the Gulf of San Miguel and the **Gulf of Darien**, a bight of the Caribbean Sea in the east coast of Panama.
Darien, Isthmus of See (Isthmus of) PANAMA.
da Ri·mi·ni (dä rē′mē·nē), **Francesca** See FRANCESCA DA RIMINI.
dar·ing (dâr′ing) *adj.* **1.** Brave and adventurous; bold; fearless. **2.** Audacious; presuming. — *n.* Adventurous courage; bravery. — **dar′ing·ly** *adv.* — **dar′ing·ness** *n.*
Da·ri·us I (də·rī′əs), 558?–486? B.C., king of Persia 521–486? B.C.; defeated at Marathon: called **Darius the Great.** Also **Darius Hys·tas·pes** (his·tas′pēz).
Darius III 380?–330 B.C., king of Persia 336–330 B.C.; defeated by Alexander the Great.
Dar·jee·ling (där·jē′ling) A resort town in northern West Bengal State, India; pop. 40,651 (1961).
dark (därk) *adj.* **1.** Having little or no light; dim: a *dark* cave. **2.** Giving off or reflecting little light; gloomy: a *dark* day. **3.** Of a deep shade; black, or almost black: a *dark* color. **4.** Brunet in complexion; not light or fair. **5.** Cheerless or disheartening; dismal; threatening. **6.** Sullen in disposition or appearance; frowning; dour. **7.** Unenlightened in mind or spirit; ignorant. **8.** Evil or sinister; wicked; atrocious: a *dark* deed. **9.** Not understandable; mysterious; obscure: a *dark* saying. **10.** Not known; concealed; secret. — *n.* **1.** Lack of light. **2.** A place or condition of little or no light. **3.** Night; nightfall. **4.** Obscurity; secrecy. **5.** Ignorance; lack of culture. **6.** A dark shadow or color, as in a painting. — **in the dark 1.** In secret. **2.** Ignorant; uninformed. — *v.t. & v.i. Obs.* To darken. [OE *deorc*]
— **Syn.** (adj.) **1.** *Dark, black, obscure, shadowy, shady, dim,* and *murky* refer to the absence of light. Strictly, *dark* means destitute of light, while *black* means destitute of color, but this distinction is often ignored, as when we speak of a *black* night. *Obscure, shadowy,* and *shady* describe something from which light is more or less cut off. *Obscure* stresses the inadequacy of the available light: an *obscure* corner; the other two words suggest some obstruction to light, with *shadowy* often bearing a sinister connotation and *shady* a pleasant one: a *shadowy* doorway, a *shady* garden. Something *dim* is not clear in outline, because of distance, poor light, mist, etc., while *murky* means both *obscure* and gloomy. — **Ant.** light, bright, shining, luminous. Compare LIGHT.
Dark Ages The period in European history between the fall of the Western Roman Empire (A.D. 476) and the Italian Renaissance; the Middle Ages, especially the early part: so called because the period was considered to be characterized by ignorance and reaction.
Dark Continent Africa: so called because little was known about it until the 19th century.
dark·en (där′kən) *v.t.* **1.** To make dark or darker; deprive of light. **2.** To make dark in color; make black. **3.** To fill with gloom; sadden. **4.** To obscure; confuse. **5.** To blind. — *v.i.* **6.** To grow dark or darker; become obscure. **7.** To grow clouded or flushed: His face *darkened* with anger. **8.** To become blind. — **dark′en·er** *n.*
dark-field illumination (därk′fēld′) *Optics* The lighting of the field of a microscope from the side instead of from below, so as to reveal the specimen against a dark background.
dark horse 1. A little-known horse, runner, etc., unexpectedly winning a race. **2.** A political candidate unexpectedly nominated.
dark·ish (där′kish) *adj.* Somewhat dark.
dark lantern A lantern having a case with one transparent side that can be covered by a shield to hide the light.
dar·kle (där′kəl) *v.i.* **·kled, ·kling 1.** To appear indistinctly;

be in darkness. **2.** To grow gloomy or dark. [Back formation < DARKLING, adv.]

dark·ling (därk′ling) *Poetic adj.* Occurring or being in the dark; dim. — *adv.* In the dark. [< DARK + -LING²]

dark·ly (därk′lē) *adv.* **1.** In a dark manner. **2.** Obscurely; mysteriously.

dark·ness (därk′nis) *n.* **1.** Total or partial absence of light; gloom. **2.** Blindness. **3.** Ignorance. **4.** Wickedness; evil. **5.** Lack of clarity; obscurity; secrecy. **6.** The quality of being dark in color.

dark·room (därk′room′, -room′) *n. Photog.* A room equipped to exclude actinic rays, for treating plates, films, etc.

dark·some (därk′səm) *adj. Poetic* Dark; darkish.

dark star *Astron.* An invisible, nonshining or dimly shining star, known only through spectrum analysis, gravitational effect, or during eclipsing action.

dark·y (därk′kē) *n. pl.* **dark·ies** *Informal* A Negro: an offensive term. Also **dark′ey, dark′ie.**

Dar·lan (där-län′), **Jean François,** 1881–1942, French admiral and politician; assassinated.

dar·ling (där′ling) *n.* **1.** A person tenderly loved: often a term of address. **2.** A person in great favor. — *adj.* Beloved; very dear. [OE *dēorling,* dim. of *dēor* dear]

Dar·ling River (där′ling) A river in SE Australia, flowing 1,910 miles, generally SW, to the Murray River.

Dar·ling·ton (där′ling-tən) A county borough in south Durham, England; pop. 84,162 (1961).

Dar·ling·ton (där′ling-tən), **Cyril Dean,** born 1903, English geneticist.

Darm·stadt (därm′shtät) A city in southern Hesse, West Germany; pop. 141,075 (est. 1970).

darn¹ (därn) *v.t. & v.i.* To repair (a garment or a hole) by filling the gap with interlacing stitches. — *n.* **1.** A place mended by darning. **2.** The act of darning. [? OE *dernan* to conceal < *derne* hidden] — **darn′er** *n.*

darn² (därn) *v.t., adj., n., & interj. U.S. Informal* Damn: a euphemism. [Alter. of DAMN]

darn·dest (därn′dist) *n. & adj. U.S. Informal* Damndest: a euphemism. Also **darned′est.**

dar·nel (där′nəl) *n.* An annual grass (*Lolium temulentum*), often found in grain fields: also called *chess, cockle, ryegrass.* [< dial. F *darnelle*]

darning needle 1. A large-eyed needle used in darning. **2.** A dragonfly. **3.** A related but slightly larger insect. For illustration see INSECTS (beneficial).

Darn·ley (därn′lē), **Lord,** 1546–67, Henry Stuart (or Stewart), second husband of Mary Queen of Scots; murdered.

Dar·row (dar′ō), **Clarence Seward,** 1857–1938, U.S. lawyer.

dart (därt) *n.* **1.** A thin, pointed weapon, as a javelin or arrow, to be thrown or shot. **2.** Anything like a dart in appearance or effect, as the small, pointed missile thrown in darts. **3.** A sudden, rapid motion. **4.** The stinger of an insect. **5.** A tapering tuck made in a garment to fit it to the figure. — *v.i.* **1.** To move suddenly like a dart; rush. — *v.t.* **2.** To throw or emit suddenly or swiftly. [< OF < Gmc. Cf. OHG *tart* javelin.]

dart·er (där′tər) *n.* **1.** One who or that which moves with swift, sudden movements. **2.** A small American percoid fish (genus *Estheostoma*). **3.** The snakebird.

dar·tle (där′təl) *v.t. & v.i.* **·tled, ·tling** To dart repeatedly.

Dart·moor (därt′moor) A wild upland in south Devonshire, England; 350 sq. mi.; includes Dartmoor Prison.

darts (därts) *n.pl.* (*construed as sing.*) A game of skill in which small darts are thrown at a bull's-eye target.

Dar·win (där′win) The capital of the Northern Territory, Australia, a port on the northern coast; pop. 18,042 (1966): formerly *Palmerston.*

Dar·win (där′win), **Charles Robert,** 1809–82, English naturalist. — **Erasmus,** 1731–1802, English physician and writer; grandfather of the preceding.

Dar·win·i·an (där-win′ē-ən) *adj.* Pertaining to Charles Darwin, or to Darwinism. — *n.* An advocate of Darwinism: also **Dar′win·ite** (-īt).

Dar·win·ism (där′win-iz′əm) *n.* The biological doctrine of the origin of species through descent by natural selection with variation, advocated by Charles Darwin. See NATURAL SELECTION. — **Dar′win·ist** *n. & adj.* — **Dar′win·is′tic** *adj.*

dash (dash) *v.t.* **1.** To strike with violence, especially so as to break or shatter. **2.** To throw, thrust, or knock suddenly and violently: usually with *away, out, down,* etc. **3.** To splash; bespatter. **4.** To do, write, etc., hastily: with *off* or *down.* **5.** To frustrate; confound: to *dash* hopes. **6.** To daunt or discourage. **7.** To put to shame; abash. **8.** To adulterate; mix: with *with:* to *dash* with salt. **9.** *Brit.* To damn: a euphemism: often used in the imperative: *Dash* it all! — *v.i.* **10.** To strike; hit: The waves *dashed* against the shore. **11.** To rush or move impetuously. — *n.* **1.** A sharp blow or stroke; a collision; impact. **2.** The splashing of water or other liquid against an object; also, the sound of this. **3.** A small addition of some other ingredient: a *dash* of bitters. **4.** A hasty stroke, as with a pen or brush. **5.** A check or hindrance. **6.** A sudden advance or onset; a short rush. **7.** A short race run at full speed: the 100-yard *dash.* **8.** Spirited action; impetuosity. **9.** Vigor of style; verve. **10.** A

horizontal line (—) used as a mark of punctuation to set off words or phrases in a sentence, to indicate an abrupt breaking off, to mark omissions of words or letters, etc. **11.** *Telecom.* The long sound in the Morse or similar code, used in combination with the dot to represent letters or numbers. **12.** A dashboard. — **to cut a dash** To make a showy appearance. [ME *daschen* < Scand. Cf. Dan. *daske* a slap.]

dash·board (dash′bôrd′, -bōrd′) *n.* **1.** The instrument panel of an automobile. **2.** An upright screen on the front of a vehicle to intercept mud, spray, etc.

da·sheen (da-shēn′) *n.* A tropical plant (*Colocasia esculenta*) related to the taro, the root of which is a staple food of the tropics. [? < F *de Chine* of China]

dash·er (dash′ər) *n.* **1.** One who or which dashes. **2.** A lively or showy person. **3.** The plunger of a churn. **4.** A dashboard.

dash·ing (dash′ing) *adj.* **1.** Spirited; bold; impetuous. **2.** Ostentatiously showy or gay. — **dash′ing·ly** *adv.*

Dasht-i-Ka·vir (dasht′ē-kä-vēr′) A salt desert of the central Iranian plateau; 200 mi. wide. Also **Dasht′-e-Ka-vir′.**

Dasht-i-Lut (dasht′ē-loot′) A desert of eastern Iran; 200 mi. long, 100 mi. wide. Also **Dasht′-e-Lut′.**

dash·y (dash′ē) *adj.* **dash·i·er, dash·i·est** Stylish; showy; dashing.

das·tard (das′tərd) *n.* A base coward; a sneak. — *adj.* Dastardly. [? ME *dased, dast,* pp. of *dasen* to daze, stupefy + -ARD]

das·tard·ly (das′tərd-lē) *adj.* Base; cowardly. — **das′-tard·li·ness** *n.*

das·y·ure (das′ē-oor) *n.* **1.** An arboreal marsupial (genus *Dasyurus*); especially, the **spotted dasyure** (*D. maculatus*) of Tasmania and southern Australia. **2.** The Tasmanian devil. [< NL *dasyrus* < Gk. *dasys* hairy + *oura* tail]

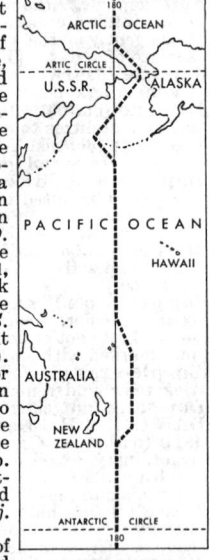

DASYURE
(Body 1 to 1½ feet long)

dat. *Gram.* Dative.

da·ta (dā′tə, dat′ə, dä′tə) *n. orig. pl. of* **datum** Facts or figures from which conclusions may be drawn. ◆ Those who continue to regard *data* as a Latin plural use it with a plural verb (These data *are* new), but its use with a singular verb (This data *is* new) is widespread. [< L, neut. pl. of *datus,* pp. of *dare* to give]

DATA Defense Air Transportation Administration.

data processing The operations involved in handling and storing information, using computers and other machines.

da·ta·ry (dā′tə-rē) *n. pl.* **·ries** **1.** In the Roman Catholic Church, a cardinal in charge of a department of the Curia that examines the fitness of candidates for papal benefices. **2.** The office or work of this cardinal. [< Med. L. *datarius,* ult. < L *dare* to give, grant]

date¹ (dāt) *n.* **1.** A particular point of time; especially, the time of the occurrence of an event. **2.** The part of a writing, inscription, coin, statue, etc., that tells when, or where and when, it was written or made. **3.** The age or period to which a thing belongs: a town of ancient *date.* **4.** The term or duration of a thing. **5.** The day of the month. **6.** *Informal* A social appointment or engagement for a specified time. **7.** *Informal* A person of the opposite sex with whom such an appointment is made. Abbr. *d., D.* — **to date** Up to and including the present day; till now. — *v.* **dat·ed, dat·ing** *v.t.* **1.** To furnish or mark with a date. **2.** To ascertain the time or era of; assign a date to. **3.** *U.S. Informal* To make an appointment with (a member of the opposite sex). — *v.i.* **4.** To have origin in an era or time: usually with *from:* This coin *dates* from the Renaissance. **5.** To reckon time. **6.** *Informal* To have appointments with members of the opposite sex. [< F < L *data,* fem. pp. of *dare* to give; from first word of Latin formula giving a letter's date and place of writing] — **dat′a·ble** *adj.* — **dat′er** *n.*

date² (dāt) *n.* **1.** The sweet fruit of the date palm, enclosing a single hard seed. **2.** A palm (*Phoenix dactylifera*) bearing this fruit: also **date palm.** [< OF < L *dactylus* < Gk. *daktylos* finger; with ref. to its shape]

dat·ed (dā′tid) *adj.* **1.** Marked with a date. **2.** Antiquated; old-fashioned.

date·less (dāt′lis) *adj.* **1.** Bearing no date. **2.** Without end or limit. **3.** Immemorial. **4.** Of permanent interest.

date line 1. The line containing the date of publication of a periodical or of any contribution printed in it. **2.** An imaginary line roughly corresponding to 180° longitude from Greenwich, internationally agreed upon as determining

DATE LINE

those points on the earth's surface where a day is dropped on crossing it from west to east and added on crossing from east to west: also called *International Date Line*.

da·tive (dā′tiv) *n. Gram.* **1.** In inflected Indo-European languages, the case of a noun, pronoun, or adjective denoting the indirect object. It is expressed in English by *to* or *for* with the objective or by word order, as in *I told the story to him, I told him the story.* **2.** A word in this case. — *adj.* **1.** *Gram.* Pertaining to or designating the dative case or a word in this case: also **da·ti·val** (dā·tī′val). **2.** *Law* **a** That may be disposed of at will. **b** Removable, as distinguished from perpetual. [< L *dativus*, trans. of Gk. (*ptōsis*) *dotikē* (the case of) giving < *didonai* to give] — **da′tive·ly** *adv.*

dat·to (dä′tō) *n. pl.* ·**tos** **1.** In the Philippines, a chief of a Moslem Moro tribe. **2.** The headman of a barrio or Malay tribe. Also **da′to.** [< Malay *dātoa* grandfather]

da·tum (dā′təm, dat′əm, dä′təm) *n. pl.* ·**ta** (-tə) **1.** A known, assumed, or conceded fact from which an inference is made. **2.** The point from which any reckoning or scale starts. [< L, neut. sing. of *datus*. See DATA.]

datum plane The horizontal plane from which heights and depths are measured. Also **datum level.**

da·tu·ra (də·tŏŏr′ə, -tyŏŏr′ə) *n.* One of a genus (*Datura*) of plants of the nightshade family, having large funnel-shaped flowers. [< NL < Hind. *dhātūrā* a plant]

dau. Daughter.

daub (dôb) *v.t. & v.i.* **1.** To smear or coat (something), as with plaster, grease, etc. **2.** To paint without skill. — *n.* **1.** Any sticky application, as of mud, plaster, clay, etc. **2.** A smear or spot. **3.** A poor painting. **4.** An instance or act of daubing. [< OF *dauber* < L *dealbare* to whitewash] — **daub′er** *n.* — **daub′y** *adj.*

daub·er·y (dô′bər·ē) *n.* Bad or inexpert painting. Also **daub·ry** (dô′brē).

Dau·bi·gny (dō·bē·nyē′), **Charles François,** 1817–78, French landscape painter.

Dau·det (dō·de′), **Alphonse,** 1840–97, French novelist. — **Léon,** 1867–1942, French journalist and novelist; son of the preceding.

Dau·ga·va (dou′gä·vä) The Latvian name for the DVINA (def. 2).

Dau·gav·pils (dou′gäf·pils) A port city in SE Latvia, on the Western Dvina; pop. 65,000 (1959): German *Dünaburg,* Russian *Dvinsk.*

daugh·ter (dô′tər) *n.* **1.** A female child, considered in relationship to either or both of her parents. *Abbr. d., D., da., dau.* **2.** A female descendant. **3.** A woman or girl considered to be in a relationship like that of a daughter: a *daughter* of nobility. **4.** Anything regarded as a female descendant: French is a *daughter* of Latin. [OE *dohtor*]

daugh·ter-in-law (dô′tər·in·lô′) *n. pl.* **daugh·ters-in-law** The wife of one's son.

daugh·ter·ly (dô′tər·lē) *adj.* Of, like, or befitting a daughter. — **daugh′ter·li·ness** *n.*

Daughters of the American Revolution A society of women descended from patriots in the American Revolution. *Abbr. DAR, D.A.R.*

Dau·mier (dō·myā′), **Honoré,** 1808–79, French painter and caricaturist.

daun·der (dôn′dər, dän′-) See DANDER[2].

daunt (dônt, dänt) *v.t.* To dishearten or intimidate; cow. — **Syn.** See INTIMIDATE. [< OF *danter, donter* < L *domitare, freq. of *domare* to tame]

daunt·less (dônt′lis, dänt′-) *adj.* Fearless; intrepid. — **daunt′less·ly** *adv.* — **daunt′less·ness** *n.*

dau·phin (dô′fin, *Fr.* dō·faň′) *n.* The eldest son of a king of France, a title used from 1349 to 1830. [< F, a dolphin; used as a personal name and title]

Dau·phi·né (dō·fē·nā′) A region and former province of SE France. Also **Dau′phi·ny′.**

dau·phin·ess (dô′fin·is) *n.* The wife of a dauphin. Also **dau′phine** (-fēn)

daut (dôt, dät) *v.t. Scot.* To fondle: also spelled *dawt.*

daut·ie (dô′tē) *n. Scot.* A little pet: also spelled *dawtie.*

DAV or **D.A.V.** Disabled American Veterans.

Da·vao (dä·vou′) A port city on Davao Gulf, a large inlet on the SE coast of Mindanao, Philippines; pop. 138,899 (est. 1960).

Dav·e·nant (dav′ə·nənt), **Sir William,** 1606–68, English poet and dramatist; poet laureate 1638–68. Also **D'Av′e·nant.**

dav·en·port (dav′ən·pôrt, -pōrt) *n.* **1.** *U.S.* A large, upholstered sofa, often usable as a bed. **2.** *Brit.* A small writing desk. [Prob. from the name of the first manufacturer]

Dav·en·port (dav′ən·pôrt, -pōrt) A city in eastern Iowa on the Mississippi River; pop. 98,469.

Dav·en·port (dav′ən·pôrt, -pōrt), **John,** 1597–1670, English Puritan clergyman.

Da·vid (dā′vid), 1040?–970? B.C., second king of Judah and Israel 1010?–970? B.C., succeeded Saul: son of Jesse and father of Solomon. — **Da·vid·ic** (də·vid′ik) *adj.*

Da·vid (dà·vēd′), **Gerard,** 1460?–1523, Flemish painter. — **Jacques Louis,** 1748–1825, French painter. — **Pierre Jean,** 1789–1856, French sculptor: called **David d'An·gers** (däň· zhā′).

David, Saint Sixth-century bishop; patron of Wales.

David, star of Mogen David (which see).

David I, 1084–1153, king of Scotland 1124–53.

Da·vid·son (dā′vid·sən), **Jo,** 1883–1952, U.S. sculptor.

da Vin·ci (də vin′chē, *Ital.* dä vēn′chē), **Leonardo,** 1452–1519, Florentine painter, sculptor, and architect; pioneer in biology, geology, engineering, and military science.

Da·vis (dā′vis), **Jefferson,** 1808–89, U.S. statesman; president of the Confederacy 1862–65. — **Norman Hezekiah,** 1878–1944, U.S. financier and diplomat. — **Owen,** 1874–1956, U.S. dramatist. — **Richard Harding,** 1864–1916, U.S. journalist and novelist. — **William Stearns,** 1877–1930, U.S. educator and historian.

Davis Cup A trophy cup presented to the nation whose team wins the International Lawn Tennis Championship. [after Dwight F. *Davis,* 1879–1945, who instituted the tournament in 1900]

Da·vis·son (dā′vis·ən), **Clinton Joseph,** 1881–1958, U.S. physicist.

Davis Strait The strait connecting Baffin Bay with the Atlantic.

dav·it (dav′it, dā′vit) *n. Naut.* One of a pair of small cranes on a ship's side for hoisting its boats, stores, etc. [Appar. from *David,* proper name]

DAVIT

a Position on deck. *b* Position when lowering lifeboat.

Da·vout (dà·vōō′), **Louis Nicolas,** 1770–1823, Duc d'Auerstädt, Prince d'Eckmühl, French marshal.

da·vy (dā′vē) *n. pl.* ·**vies** A safety lamp (def. 1). [after Sir Humphry *Davy,* who invented it] Also **Davy lamp.**

Da·vy (dā′vē), **Sir Humphry,** 1778–1829, English scientist.

Da·vy Jones (dā′vē jōnz′) The spirit of the sea.

Davy Jones's locker The bottom of the ocean, especially as the grave of the drowned.

daw (dô) *n.* **1.** A jackdaw (which see). **2.** *Obs.* A simpleton. [ME *dawe*]

daw·dle (dôd′l) *v.t. & v.i.* ·**dled,** ·**dling** To waste (time) in slow trifling; loiter: often with *away.* [? Var. of DADDLE] — **daw′dler** *n.*

Dawes (dôz), **Charles Gates,** 1865–1951, U.S. financier and statesman; vice president 1925–29.

dawk (dôk, däk) See DAK.

dawn (dôn) *n.* **1.** The first appearance of light in the morning; daybreak. ◆ Collateral adjective: *auroral.* **2.** An awakening, as of a new era; a beginning or unfolding. — *v.i.* **1.** To begin to grow light in the morning. **2.** To begin to be understood: with *on* or *upon:* The truth has just *dawned* on me. **3.** To begin to expand or develop. [Back formation < *dawning,* ME *dawenyng* daybreak < Scand. Cf. Sw. *dagning.*]

Daw·son (dô′sən) A city in western Yukon, Canada; formerly the capital of the territory; pop. 745.

Daw·son (dô′sən), **Sir John (William),** 1820–99, Canadian geologist and naturalist.

Dawson Creek A city in eastern British Columbia; the southern terminal of the Alaska Highway; pop. 11,488.

dawt (dôt, dät) See DAUT.

daw·tie (dô′tē) See DAUTIE.

Dax (däks) A resort town in SW France; pop. about 15,000.

day (dā) *n.* **1.** The period of light from dawn to dark; daylight. **2.** The interval represented by one rotation of the earth upon its axis; twenty-four hours; also, this period as a unit in computing time. ◆ Collateral adjective: *diurnal.* **3.** A portion of a day spent in a particular way or place: a shopping *day*; a *day* outdoors. **4.** The hours of a day devoted to work: a seven-hour *day.* **5.** A time or period; age; epoch: in Caesar's *day.* **6.** *Usually cap.* A particular day: Labor *Day.* **7.** A day as a point of time: the third *day.* **8.** *Often pl.* A lifetime, or a prominent part of it, as one's youth: the rest of his *days*; in my *day.* **9.** A period of success, influence, accomplishment, etc.: Your *day* will come. **10.** The contest or battle of the day: to win the *day.* **11.** Loosely, the period during which a heavenly body rotates once about its axis. *Abbr. d., D., da.* — **day after day** Every day. — **day by day** Each day. — **day in, day out** Every day. — **(from) day to day** From one day to the next: not long-range. — **to have seen better days** To be past one's prime: look or be worn out: Those shoes *have seen better days.* [OE *dæg*]

Day·ak (dī′ak) See DYAK.

day bed A lounge or couch that can be converted into a bed.

day blindness *Pathol.* Hemeralopia.

day·book (dā′bŏŏk′) *n.* **1.** In bookkeeping, the book in which transactions are recorded in the order of their occurrence. **2.** A diary or journal.

day·break (dā′brāk′) *n.* The time each morning when daylight replaces darkness.

day coach A railroad car without special accommodations, as distinguished from a sleeping car, dining car, etc.

day·dream (dā'drēm') n. A dreamlike thought, as of a future or desired event, situation, etc.; reverie. — v.i. To have daydreams. **— day'dream'er** n.

day·flow·er (dā'flou'ər) n. Any of various plants (genus *Commelina*), having typically blue, short-lived flowers.

day·fly (dā'flī') n. A May fly (which see).

day labor Labor hired and paid for by the day. **— day laborer**

day letter A telegram sent during the day, slower and cheaper than a regular telegram.

Day-Lew·is (dā'lōō'is), **Cecil,** 1904–72, British poet and critic; poet laureate 1968–72. Also **Day Lewis.**

day·light (dā'līt') n. **1.** The light received from the sun; the light of day. **2.** Insight into or understanding of something formerly puzzling. **3.** Exposure to view; publicity. **4.** The period of light during the day. **— to see daylight** To near the end of a difficult situation or undertaking.

day·lights (dā'līts') n.pl. *Slang* Consciousness; wits: to shake the *daylights* out of someone.

day·light-sav·ing time (dā'līt'sā'ving) Time in which more daylight is obtained at the end of each working day by setting clocks one or more hours ahead of standard time, especially during the summer months. Abbr. *DST, D.S.T*

day·lil·y (dā'lil'ē) n. pl. **·lil·ies 1.** Any of several plants (genus *Hemerocallis*) of the lily family, with lanceolate leaves, and large, showy flowers that usually last only one day. **2.** The plantain lily (which see).

day·long (dā'lông', -long') adj. Lasting all day. — adv. Through the entire day.

day nursery A place for the care of small children, especially those of working mothers, during the day.

Day of Atonement Yom Kippur

Day of Judgment *Theol.* Judgment Day.

day school 1. A school that holds classes during the daytime, as distinguished from night school. **2.** A school attended by pupils who live at home: distinguished from *boarding school.*

days·man (dāz'mən) n. pl. **·men** (-mən) *Archaic* An umpire; arbiter. [ME *dayes*, genitive of *day*, time set for judgment + MAN]

days of grace Days (usually three) allowed for the payment of a note or bill of exchange after it falls due.

day·spring (dā'spring') n. *Poetic* The early dawn.

day·star (dā'stär') n. **1.** The morning star. **2.** *Poetic* The sun.

day·time (dā'tīm') n. The time of daylight; the time between sunrise and sunset.

Day·ton (dā'tən) A city in SW Ohio, on the Miami River; pop. 243,601.

Day·to·na Beach (dā·tō'nə) A resort city on the eastern coast of Florida; pop. 45,327.

daze (dāz) v.t. **dazed, daz·ing** To stupefy or bewilder; stun. — n. The state of being dazed. [ME *dasen.* Akin to ON *dasask* to become weary.] **— daz·ed·ly** (dā'zid·lē) adv.

daz·zle (daz'əl) v. **·zled, ·zling** v.t. **1.** To blind or dim the vision of by excess of light. **2.** To bewilder or charm, as with brilliant display. — v.i. **3.** To be blinded by lights or glare. **4.** To excite admiration. — n. **1.** The act of dazzling; dazzled condition. **2.** Something that dazzles; brightness. [Freq. of DAZE] **— daz'zling·ly** adv.

db or **db.** or **dB** Decibel(s).

d.b.a. Doing business as.

D.B.E. Dame (Commander, Order) of the British Empire.

d.b.h. In forestry, diameter at breast height.

D.Bib. Douai Bible.

dbl. Double.

DC *Mil.* Dental Corps.

DC or **D.C.** or **d.c.** *Electr.* Direct current.

D.C. 1. District of Columbia. **2.** Doctor of Chiropractic. **3.** Da capo.

D.C.L. 1. Doctor of Canon Law. **2.** Doctor of Civil Law.

D.C.M. *Brit.* Distinguished Conduct Medal.

D.C.S. 1. Deputy Clerk of Sessions. **2.** Doctor of Christian Science. **3.** Doctor of Commercial Science.

dd. or **d/d** Delivered.

D/D or **D/d** or **d.d. 1.** Days after date. **2.** Day's (or days') date.

D.D. Doctor of Divinity (L *Divinitatis Doctor*).

D.D. or **D/D** Demand draft.

D-day (dē'dā') n. In military operations, the unspecified date of the launching of an attack; especially, June 6, 1944, the day on which the Allies invaded France in World War II.

D.D.S. Doctor of Dental Surgery.

D.D.Sc. Doctor of Dental Science.

DDT A powerful insecticide effective on contact. [< D(I-CHLORO)D(IPHENYL)T(RICHLOROETHANE)]

de (də) *prep. French* Of; from: used in names and phrases, as in Cyrano de Bergerac; coup de grace.

de- *prefix* **1.** Away; off: *deflect, decavitate.* **2.** Down: *decline, descend.* **3.** Completely: utterly: *derelict, denude.* **4.** The undoing, reversing, or ridding of (the action, condition or substance expressed by the main element: *decode, decen-*

tralization, decarbonization. [< L *de* from, away, down; also < F *dé-* < L *de-,* or < OF *des-* < L *dis-* (see DIS-¹)]

Following is a list of self-explanatory words containing the prefix *de-* (def. 4):

deacetylate	deflea	depolish
deacidification	defluorinate	depopularize
deacidify	deforest	deproteinization
deaerate	degerm	deproteinize
deair	deglaze	derat
dealkalization	deglamorization	derestrict
dealkalize	deglamorize	desand
deash	deglorification	desaturate
debug	deglorify	desex
dechlorinate	dehypnotize	desilver
dechristianize	delead	despecialization
declassify	delime	despecialize
decolor	demast	despiritualize
decondition	demesmerize	destigmatize
decongest	demineralize	desugar
decrown	denasalization	desuperheat
dedifferentiate	denasalize	detribalize
dedifferentiation	deozonize	dewater
defeminization	depalatalization	dewax
defeminize	depalatalize	dewool

DE *Mil.* Destroyer Escort.

D.E. 1. Doctor of Engineering. **2.** Doctor of Entomology.

dea·con (dē'kən) n. **1.** A lay church officer or subordinate minister. **2.** In the Anglican, Eastern Orthodox, and Roman Catholic churches, a clergyman ranking next below a priest. **3.** Any cleric who acts as chief assistant at a High Mass; a gospeler. — v.t. *U.S. Informal* **1.** To read aloud a line or two of (a hymn) at a time, as an aid to congregational singing. **2.** To arrange (produce) for sale with only the best showing. **3.** To adulterate. [OE < L *diaconus* < Gk. *diakonos* servant, minister] **— dea'con·ship** n.

dea·con·ess (dē'kən·is) n. A woman appointed or chosen as a lay church worker or officer.

dea·con·ry (dē'kən·rē) n. pl. **·ries 1.** The position of a deacon. **2.** Deacons collectively.

de·ac·ti·vate (dē·ak'tə·vāt) v.t. **·vat·ed, ·vat·ing 1.** To render inactive or ineffective, as an explosive, chemical, etc. **2.** *Mil.* To release (a military unit, ship, etc.) from active duty; demobilize. **— de·ac·ti·va'tion** n.

dead (ded) adj. **1.** Having ceased to live; lifeless. Abbr. *d., D.* **2.** Resembling death; deathlike: a *dead* faint. **3.** Not alive; inanimate; inorganic. **4.** Not responsive; insensible: with to: *dead* to pity. **5.** Lacking sensation; numb. **6.** No longer in existence or use; extinct: a *dead* language. **7.** No longer in force; ineffective: a *dead* law. **8.** Not productively employed: *dead* capital. **9.** Without spiritual life or vitality: a *dead* conscience. **10.** *Informal* Exhausted; worn out. **11.** Barren; sterile: *dead* fields. **12.** Lacking activity, excitement, or interest: a *dead* town. **13.** Giving no light or heat; extinguished: a *dead* fire. **14.** Without luster; not bright: said of colors. **15.** Without resonance; muffled: said of sounds. **16.** Without resilience or elasticity. **17.** Tasteless; flat: *dead* beer. **18.** Complete; absolute: utter: *dead* silence. **19.** Having full or unrelieved force: a *dead* weight. **20.** Having no outlet or opening: a *dead* end. **21.** Perfect; exact: *dead* center. **22.** Unerring; sure; certain: a *dead* shot. **23.** In certain games, out of play: said of the ball. **24.** Deprived of civil life, as a prisoner for life. **25.** *Electr.* Not carrying a charge or current; unconnected. **26.** *Printing* Not required for further use, as composed type. **— Syn.** See LIFELESS. — n. **1.** A dead person, or dead persons collectively: preceded by *the*: the quick and the *dead.* **2.** The coldest, darkest, or most intense part: the *dead* of winter. — adv. **1.** Completely; absolutely. **2.** Directly: *dead* ahead. [OE *dēad*] **— dead'ness** n.

— Syn. (adj.) See LIFELESS. **— Ant.** alive, living, animate.

dead-beat (ded'bēt') n. *U.S. Slang* **1.** One who avoids paying his bills. **2.** A sponger. — adj. Beating without recoil, as a watch movement; also, stopping without oscillation.

dead center *Mech.* **1.** One of two points in the motion of a crank, at which the crank and connecting rod are in alignment and the connecting rod has no power to turn the crank: also called *dead point.* **2.** A center that does not rotate, as in a lathe.

dead·en (ded'n) v.t. **1.** To diminish the sensitivity, force, or intensity of. **2.** To impede the velocity of; retard. **3.** To render soundproof. **4.** To make dull or less brilliant in color. — v.i. **5.** To become dead. **— dead'en·er** n.

dead end 1. An end of a passage, street, etc., having no outlet. **2.** A point or condition from which no progress can be made.

dead·en·ing (ded'n·ing) n. **1.** The act of making less sensitive or intense. **2.** A material used in soundproofing. **3.** A material or process for lessening gloss or luster.

dead·eye (ded'ī') n. *Naut.* A wooden disk pierced by holes through which lanyards are passed, and having a grooved circumference, used to set up shrouds, stays, etc. For illustration see SHROUD².

dead·fall (ded'fôl') n. **1.** A trap operated by a weight that falls upon and kills or holds an animal: also called *downfall.* **2.** *U.S.* Fallen trees, etc.

dead hand *Law* Mortmain.

dead-head (ded′hed′) *Informal* *n.* **1.** One who is admitted, entertained, or accommodated free of charge; especially, a passenger who rides without paying fare. **2.** A railroad car, bus, etc., carrying no passengers or freight. **3.** A dull, stupid person. — *v.t. & v.i.* To treat or act as a deadhead. — *adj.* Traveling without passengers or freight. Abbr. *d.h.*

dead heat A race in which two or more competitors finish together; a tie.

dead letter **1.** A letter that, after lying unclaimed or undelivered for a certain length of time, has been sent to the **dead-letter office**, a department of the general post office where such letters are examined and returned to their senders or destroyed. **2.** A law, issue, etc., no longer valid or enforced, though still formally in effect.

dead-light (ded′līt′) *n.* **1.** *Naut.* **a** A strong shutter, usually of iron, protecting a cabin window or porthole in stormy weather. **b** A round, thick glass window in the side or deck of a ship. **2.** A skylight that does not open.

dead-line (ded′līn′) *n.* **1.** A time limit, as for the completion of newspaper copy or other work, payment of debts, etc. **2.** Originally, within the limits of a prison, a boundary line that prisoners might not cross under penalty of being shot.

dead load *Engin.* The fixed and permanent load of a structure, as the weight of a building or bridge.

dead-lock (ded′lok′) *n.* A standstill or stoppage of activity resulting from the unrelenting opposition of equally powerful forces. — *v.t. & v.i.* To cause or come to a deadlock.

dead-ly (ded′lē) *adj.* **·li·er**, **·li·est** **1.** Likely or certain to cause death; fatal: a *deadly* wound. **2.** Seeking to kill; implacable; mortal: a *deadly* enemy. **3.** Resembling death; deathly: *deadly* pallor. **4.** *Theol.* Causing or involving spiritual death: a *deadly* sin. **5.** Excessive: *deadly* deliberation. — *adv.* **1.** As in death; deathly: *deadly* cold. **2.** *Informal* Very. — **dead′li·ness** *n.*

deadly nightshade Belladonna.

deadly sins The seven deadly sins (which see).

dead man's float In swimming, the act of floating in a prone position with the arms and legs extended.

dead march A piece of solemn funeral music, especially one played for a military funeral.

dead-pan (ded′pan′) *U.S. Slang* *adj.* Having a blank or unrevealing facial expression. — *adv.* Without betraying emotion; expressionlessly. — *v.i.* **·panned**, **·pan·ning** To act, speak, etc., without showing or expressing emotion.

dead pan *U.S. Slang* A completely expressionless face.

dead point *Mech.* Dead center (def. 1).

dead reckoning *Naut.* The computation of a vessel's position at sea by log and compass without astronomical observations. Abbr. *d.r.*, *D/R* *D.R.*

Dead Sea A salt lake on the Israel-Jordan border; 49 mi. long; 405 sq. mi.; 1,292 ft. below sea level. See map of ISRAEL.

Dead Sea Scrolls A number of scrolls of parchment, leather, or copper, dating from about 100 B.C. to A.D 100, containing Hebrew and Aramaic texts of Biblical works and liturgical and communal writings, found in 1947 and after in clay jars in caves at various sites near the Dead Sea.

dead set *Informal* **1** Firmly determined: with *on* or *against*. **2.** A resolute attempt or attack: with *at*.

dead storage Storage of vehicles, equipment, etc., for an indefinite period.

dead weight **1.** A heavy weight or load, as of something inert. **2.** An oppressive burden: the *dead weight* of ignorance. **3.** In shipping, freight charged for by weight instead of by bulk. **4.** In railway transportation, the weight of rolling stock as distinguished from its load.

dead-wood (ded′wŏŏd′) *n.* **1.** Wood dead on the tree. **2.** *U.S.* Worthless material; a useless person or thing. **3.** *Naut.* A mass of timber built up above the keel of a vessel at each end to support the cant timbers.

deaf (def) *adj.* **1.** Partly or completely lacking the power to hear. **2.** Determined not to hear; unwilling to listen. [OE *dēaf*] — **deaf′ly** *adv.* — **deaf′ness** *n.*

deaf-and-dumb alphabet (def′ən-dum′) Manual alphabet (which see).

deaf-en (def′ən) *v.t.* **1.** To make deaf. **2.** To confuse, stupefy, or overwhelm, as with noise. **3.** To drown (a sound) by a louder sound. **4.** To make soundproof.

deaf-mute (def′myŏŏt′) *n.* A deaf person who cannot speak, usually because of deafness from early life. Also **deaf mute.**

deal¹ (dēl) *v.* **dealt** (delt), **deal·ing** *v.t.* **1.** To distribute among a number of persons; mete out, as playing cards. **2.** To apportion to (one person) as his or her share. **3.** To deliver or inflict, as a blow. — *v.i.* **4.** To conduct oneself; behave toward: with *with*. **5.** To be concerned or occupied: with *in* or *with*: to deal in facts. **6.** To consider, discuss, or take action with *with*: The court will *deal* with him. **7.** To trade; do business with *in*, *with*, or *at*. **8.** In card games, to act as dealer. — **Syn.** See DISTRIBUTE. — *n.* **1.** The act of distributing; sharing; apportionment. **2.** In card games: **a**

The distribution of the cards to the players. **b** The right or turn to distribute the cards. **c** The cards distributed to a player; a hand. **d** A single round of play. **3.** An indefinite amount, degree, extent, etc.: a great *deal* of time. **4.** *Informal* A business transaction; sale; also, a favorable transaction; bargain: to close a *deal*; the best *deal* in town. **5.** *Informal* A secret arrangement, as in politics, between apparently hostile parties. **6.** *Informal* A plan, agreement, or treatment: a rough *deal.* [OE *dǣlan.* Akin to DOLE¹.]

deal² (dēl) *n.* **1.** A fir or pine plank of varying dimensions. A plank three inches thick, nine inches wide, and twelve feet long is called **standard deal. 2.** Such planks collectively. **3.** Wood, as fir, for deals. [< MDu. *dele* board, plank]

deal·er (dē′lər) *n.* **1.** A trader engaged in a specified business. **2.** In card games, the player who deals. Abbr. *dlr.*

deal·fish (dēl′fish′) *n.* *pl.* **·fish** or **·fish·es** A ribbonfish (*Trachipterus arcticus*) of northern seas.

deal·ing (dē′ling) *n.* **1.** The act of distributing. **2.** *Usually pl.* Transactions or relations with others. **3.** Method or manner of treatment: honest *dealing.*

dealt (delt) Past tense and past participle of DEAL.

de·am·i·na·tion (dē-am′ə-nā′shən) *n.* *Chem.* The elimination of the amino group, NH_2, from an organic compound. Also **de·am′i·ni·za′tion.**

dean (dēn) *n.* **1.** An officer of a college or university, having jurisdiction over a particular class, group of students, area of study, or acting as head of a faculty: *dean* of men; *dean* of the law school. **2.** The senior member, in length of service, of an association or class of men: the *dean* of American composers. **3.** The chief ecclesiastical officer of a cathedral or of a collegiate church. **4.** *Chiefly Brit.* An ecclesiastical officer acting as a deputy of a bishop or archdeacon in the administration of part of a diocese: also called *rural dean.* [< OF *deien* < LL *decanus* head of ten men < L *decem* ten] — **dean′ship** *n.*

Deane (dēn), **Silas,** 1737–89. American Revolutionary patriot and diplomat.

dean·er·y (dē′nər·ē) *n.* *pl.* **·er·ies** The office, revenue, jurisdiction, or place of residence of a dean.

dean's list A list of students of high academic standing published by a college or university usually at the end of a semester.

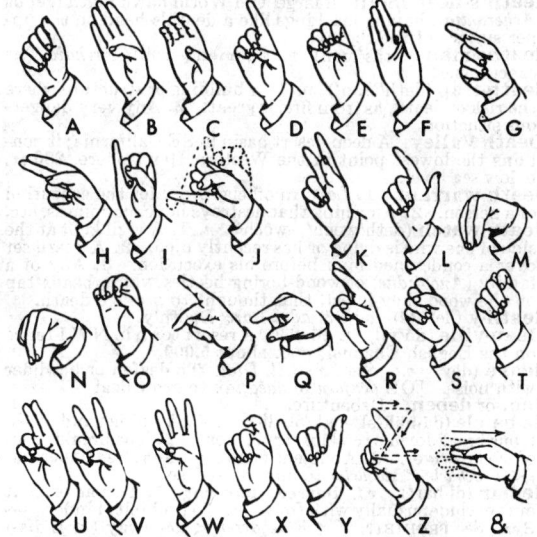

ONE-HANDED MANUAL ALPHABET OF THE DEAF

dear¹ (dir) *adj.* **1.** Beloved; precious. **2.** Highly esteemed: used in letter salutations. **3.** Expensive; costly. **4.** Characterized by high prices. **5.** Intense; earnest: our *dearest* wish. **6.** *Obs.* Noble; glorious. — *n.* One who is much beloved; a darling. — *adv.* Dearly. — *interj.* An exclamation of regret, surprise, etc. [OE *dēore*] — **dear′ness** *n.*

dear² (dir) *adj.* *Obs.* Severe; dire; difficult: also spelled *dere.* [OE *dēor* wild]

Dear·born (dir′bôrn′, -bərn) A city in SE Michigan, near Detroit; pop. 104,199.

dear·ly (dir′lē) *adv.* **1.** With much affection; fondly. **2.** At great cost. **3.** Earnestly; deeply.

dearth (dûrth) *n.* Scarcity; lack; famine. [ME *derthe*]

dear·y (dir′ē) *n.* *pl.* **dear·ies** *Informal* Darling; dear. Also **dear′ie.**

death (deth) *n.* **1.** The permanent cessation of all vital

functions in an animal or plant. **2.** The condition of being dead. **3.** *Usually cap.* A personification or symbolic representation of death, usually a skeleton holding a scythe. **4.** The extinction of anything; destruction. **5.** The cause or occasion of dying. **6.** The time or manner of dying: to meet a tyrant's *death*. **7.** Absence of spiritual life; eternal ruin. **8.** Civil death (which see). **9.** Great carnage or bloodshed; murder; slaughter. **10.** Something considered as terrible as death. **11.** *Obs.* A fatal plague; pestilence. **12.** In Christian Science, the unreal and untrue. ◆ Collateral adjectives: *lethal, mortal.* **— at death's door** Almost dead. **— to death** Very much: He frightened me *to death*. **— to put to death** To kill; execute. [OE *dēath*]
death·bed (deth′bed′) *n.* **1.** The bed on which a person dies or died. **2.** The last hours of life.
death bell A bell rung to announce a death: also called *passing bell.*
death·blow (deth′blō′) *n.* That which causes the death or the end of a person or thing.
death camass **1.** Any of several herbaceous plants (genus *Zigadenus*) of the lily family, common in the western United States. **2.** The poisonous root of these plants
death·cup (deth′kup′) *n.* A common, extremely poisonous mushroom (*Amanita phalloides*) having a usually white, olive, or umber cap.
death duties *Brit.* Inheritance tax.
death·ful (deth′fəl) *adj.* **1.** Fatal. **2.** Like death.
death house That part of a prison, as a block of cells, in which prisoners condemned to death are confined.
death·less (deth′lis) *adj.* Not liable to die; perpetual; immortal. **— death′less·ly** *adv.* **— death′less·ness** *n.*
death·ly (deth′lē) *adj.* **1.** Resembling or suggesting death. Also **death′like′.** **2.** Causing death; fatal. **3.** *Poetic* Pertaining to death. **— adv. 1.** In a deathlike manner. **2.** Extremely; very: *deathly* ill.
death mask A cast of the face taken just after death.
death rate The number of persons per thousand of population who die within a given time.
death rattle The rattling sound caused by the breath passing through mucus in the throat of one dying.
death's-head (deths′hed′) *n.* A human skull, or a representation of it, as a symbol of death.
death's-head moth A large, Old World hawk moth (genus *Acherontia*), having markings like a death's-head on the upper surface of the thorax.
deaths·man (deths′mən) *n.* *pl.* **·men** (-mən) *Archaic* The executioner.
death·trap (deth′trap′) *n.* **1.** A building or structure where the risk of death, as from fire, is great. **2.** Any very dangerous situation.
Death Valley A deep desert basin in SE California; it contains the lowest point in the Western Hemisphere, 280 ft. below sea level.
death warrant **1.** *Law* An official order for the execution of a person. **2.** Anything that destroys hope, happiness, etc.
death·watch (deth′woch′, -wôch′) *n.* **1.** A vigil kept at the side of one who is dying or has recently died. **2.** A guard set over a condemned man before his execution. **3.** Any of a family (*Anobiidae*) of wood-boring beetles whose heads tap on the wood they infest, thus thought to presage death.
death·y (deth′ē) *adj. & adv.* *Rare* Deathly.
Deau·ville (dō′vil, *Fr.* dō-vēl′) A resort town in NW France on the English Channel; pop. about 5,000.
deave (dēv) *v.t.* *Scot. & Brit. Dial.* To deafen or bewilder with noise. [OE *dēafian* in *adēafian* to grow deaf]
deb. or **deben.** Debenture.
de·ba·cle (dā-bäk′əl, -bak′əl, di-) *n.* **1.** A sudden and disastrous breakdown or collapse; ruin; rout. **2.** The breaking up of ice in a river. **3.** A violent flood. **— Syn.** See DISASTER. [< F *débâcle* < *débâcler* to unbar, set free]
de·bar (di-bär′) *v.t.* **·barred,** **·bar·ring** **1.** To bar or shut out; exclude: usually with *from.* **2.** To prohibit; hinder. **— Syn.** See PROHIBIT. [< F *débarrer* < *dé-* away (< L *dis-*) + *barrer* to bar] **— de·bar′ment** *n.*
de·bark (di-bärk′) *v.t.* **1.** To put ashore or unload from a ship or aircraft. **— v.i. 2.** To go ashore; disembark. [< F *débarquer* < *dé-* away, from + *barque* ship] **— de·bar·ka·tion** (dē′bär·kā′shən) *n.*
de·base (di-bās′) *v.t.* **·based,** **·bas·ing** **1.** To lower in character, quality, or worth; degrade. **2.** *Obs.* To lower in rank or esteem. **— Syn.** See ABASE, POLLUTE. [< DE- + obs. *base,* var. of ABASE] **— de·base′ment** *n.* **— de·bas′er** *n.*
de·bat·a·ble (di-bā′tə·bəl) *adj.* **1.** Capable of being discussed. **2.** Open to dispute; questionable.
de·bate (di-bāt′) *n.* **1.** A discussion of any question; argument; dispute. **2.** Deliberation. **3.** A formal contest in argumentation conducted between persons taking opposite sides of a question. **4.** *Obs.* Combat; strife. **— v.** **·bat·ed,** **·bat·ing** *v.t.* **1.** To argue about; discuss or dispute, as in a public meeting. **2.** To deliberate upon; consider, as alternatives. **3.** To discuss in formal debate. **4.** *Obs.* To fight or contend for. **— v.i. 5.** To engage in argument; discuss a question. **6.** To take part in a formal debate. **7.** To deliberate; ponder. **8.** *Obs.* To fight; contend. **— Syn.** See AR-

GUE. [< OF *debatre* < *de-* down (< L *de-*) + *batre* < L *battuere* to strike] **— de·bat′er** *n.*
de·bauch (di-bôch′) *v.t.* **1.** To corrupt in morals; seduce; deprave. **2.** *Obs.* To cause to forsake allegiance. **— v.i. 3.** To indulge in debauchery; dissipate. **— n. 1.** An act or period of debauchery. **2.** Debauchery. [< F *débaucher* to lure from work < OF *desbaucher*] **— de·bauch·ed·ly** (di·bô′chid·lē) *adv.* **— de·bauch′er** *n.* **— de·bauch′ment** *n.*
deb·au·chee (deb′ô·chē′, -shē′) *n.* One habitually profligate, drunken, or lewd; a libertine.
de·bauch·er·y (di·bô′chər·ē) *n. pl.* **·er·ies 1.** Gross sensual indulgence. **2.** Seduction from virtue, duty, or fidelity.
de Beau·voir (də bō·vwär′), **Simone** See BEAUVOIR.
de·ben·ture (di·ben′chər) *n.* **1.** A certificate given as acknowledgment of debt. **2.** A bond, usually without security, issued by a corporation and often convertible into common stock. Also **debenture bond.** **3.** A customhouse certificate providing for a drawback. Abbr. *deb., deben.* [< L *debentur* there are owing < *debere* to owe]
debenture stock *Brit.* A debenture of a corporation or public body issued in the form of stock, the certificates of which are usually transferable but not redeemable and entitle the holder to a perpetual annuity.
de·bil·i·tate (di·bil′ə·tāt) *v.t.* **·tat·ed,** **·tat·ing** To make feeble or languid; weaken. [< L *debilitatus,* pp. of *debilitare* < *debilis* weak] **— de·bil′i·ta′tion** *n.* **— de·bil′i·ta′tive** *adj.*
de·bil·i·ty (di·bil′ə·tē) *n. pl.* **·ties** Abnormal weakness; languor; feebleness. [< F *débilité* < L *debilitas* < *debilis* weak]
deb·it (deb′it) *n.* **1.** An item of debt recorded in an account. **2.** An entry of debt in an account, or the sum of such entries. **3.** The left-hand side of an account, where debts are recorded. Abbr. *dr.* **— v.t. 1.** To enter (a debt) in an account. **2.** To charge with a debt. Compare CREDIT. [< L *debitum,* pp. of *debere* to owe. Doublet of DEBT.]
deb·o·nair (deb′ə·nâr′) *adj.* **1.** Urbane; nonchalant. **2.** Pleasantly gracious. **3.** Cheerful; lively; gay. Also **deb′o·naire′,** **deb′on·naire′.** [< OF *de bon aire* of good mien] **— deb′o·nair′ly** *adv.* **— deb′o·nair′ness** *n.*
de bonne grâce (də bun gräs′) *French* With good grace.
Deb·o·rah (deb′ər·ə, deb′rə) A prophetess of Mount Ephraim, who judged Israel. *Judg.* iv 4.
de·bouch (di·boosh′) *v.i.* **1.** *Mil.* To march from a narrow passage, wood, etc., into the open. **2.** To come forth; emerge; issue. **— v.t. 3.** To cause to emerge. **— n. 1.** An opening, especially in military works, for the passage of troops. **2.** An outlet, as for commerce. Also *French* **dé·bou·ché** (dā·boo·shā′) *n.* [< F *déboucher* < *dé-* from (< L *dis-*) + *bouche* a mouth < L *bucca* cheek]
de·bouch·ment (di·boosh′mənt) *n.* **1.** *Geog.* The opening out of a valley, stream, etc. **2.** The act of debouching. Also *French* **dé·bou·chure** (dā·boo·shür′).
De·bre·cen (de′bre·tsen) A city in eastern Hungary; pop. 129,671 (1960). Formerly **De′bre·czen.**
dé·bride·ment (dā·brēd·män′, di·brēd′mənt) *n.* *Surg.* The removal of foreign matter and diseased or dead tissue from a wound to prevent infection. [< F *débrider* to unbridle]
de·brief (dē′brēf′) *v.t.* *Mil.* To question or instruct (a pilot, agent, etc.) at the end of a mission or period of service.
de·brief·ing (dē′brēf′ing) *n.* *Mil.* The process of being debriefed; also, the meeting or interview involved.
de·bris (də·brē′, dā′brē; *Brit.* deb′rē) *n.* **1.** Fragments, or scattered remains, as of something destroyed; ruins; rubble. **2.** *Geol.* An accumulation of detached fragments of rocks. Also **dé·bris′.** [< F *débris* < OF *debrisier* to break away]
de Bro·glie (də brô·glē′, *Fr.* də brô′y′) See (de) BROGLIE.
Debs (debz), **Eugene Victor,** 1855–1926, U.S. labor leader; Socialist presidential candidate 1900, 1904, 1908, 1912, 1920.
debt (det) *n.* **1.** That which one owes, as money, goods, or services. **2.** The obligation to pay or render something to another. **3.** The condition of owing something. **4.** *Theol.* A sin; trespass. [< OF *dette* < L *debitum.* Doublet of DEBT.]
debt of honor A debt that depends for its payment solely on the honor of the debtor, as a gambling debt.
debt·or (det′ər) *n.* One under obligation to another, as for money or services. Abbr. *dr.* [< OF *dettor* < L *debitor* < *debere* to owe]
de·bug (dē·bug′) *v.* **·bugged,** **bug·ging** *v.t.* *Informal* **1.** To find and correct faults in (computer programs, electronic equipment, etc.). **2.** To find and remove hidden electronic listening devices from (a room).
de·bunk (di·bungk′) *v.t.* *Informal* To expose or deride the sham, false pretensions, etc., of. [< BUNK²]
De·bus·sy (də·byoo′sē, *Fr.* də·bü·sē′), **Claude (Achille),** 1862–1918, French composer.
de·but (di·byoo′, dā-, dā′byoo) *n.* **1.** A first public appearance, as on the stage. **2.** A formal introduction to society, as of a debutante. **3.** The beginning, as of a career. Also **dé·but′.** [< F *début* < *débuter* to begin, lead off]
deb·u·tante (deb′yoo·tänt′, deb′yoo·tänt) *n.* A young woman making a debut in society. Also **dé′bu·tante′.** [< F *débutante,* fem. ppr. of *débuter* to begin] **— deb′u·tant′** *n.masc.*
dec. 1. Deceased. **2.** Declaration. **3.** Declension. **4.** Declination. **5.** Decrease. **6.** Decrescendo.

dec. Decimeter.
Dec. or **Dec** December.
deca- *combining form* **1.** Ten: *decapod.* **2.** In the metric system, deka-. Also, before vowels, **dec-.**
dec·ade (dĕk′ād, de·kād′) *n.* **1.** A period of ten years. **2.** A group or set of ten. [< MF < L *decas, decadis* a group of ten < Gk. *dekas < deka* ten]
de·ca·dence (di·kād′ns, dĕk′ə·dəns) *n.* **1.** A process of deterioration; decay. **2.** A condition or period of decline, as in art or morals. [< F *décadence* < Med.L *decadentia* < L *decadere < de-* down + *cadere* to fall]
dec·a·dent (di·kād′nt, dĕk′ə·dənt) *adj.* **1.** Falling into, or characteristic of, decay and decline. **2.** Of or pertaining to the decadents. **—** *n.* **1.** One in a state or process of mental or moral decay. **2.** One of a group of French or English writers and artists of the late 19th century whose work was overrefined in style and preoccupied with the morbid, neurotic, or abnormal. **— de·ca′dent·ly** *adv.*
dec·a·gon (dĕk′ə·gon) *n. Geom.* A polygon with ten sides and ten angles. [< Gk. *dekagōnon < deka* ten + *gōnia* angle] **— de·cag′o·nal** (di·kag′ə·nəl) *adj.* **— de·cag′o·nal·ly** *adv.*
dec·a·gram (dĕk′ə·gram) See DEKAGRAM.
dec·a·he·dron (dĕk′ə·hē′drən) *n. pl.* **·drons** or **·dra** (-drə) *Geom.* A polyhedron bounded by ten plane faces. [< DECA- + Gk. *hedra* seat] **— dec′a·he′·dral** *adj.*
de·cal (dē′kal, di·kal′) *n.* A decalcomania.
de·cal·ci·fy (dē·kal′sə·fī) *v.t.* **·fied, ·fy·ing** To remove lime or calcareous matter from (bones, teeth, etc.). **— de·cal′ci·fi·ca′tion** *n.*
de·cal·co·ma·ni·a (di·kal′kə·mā′nē·ə, -mān′yə) *n.* **1.** A process of transferring prints, designs, etc., from specially prepared paper to glass, porcelain, or other material. **2.** The design or print to be transferred. [< F *décalcomanie < décalquer* to transfer a tracing + *-manie* -mania]
de·ca·les·cence (dē′kə·les′əns) *n. Physics* The sudden absorption of heat by a metal or alloy when the rising temperature reaches a certain critical point: opposed to *recalescence.* [< L *decalescens, -entis,* ppr. of *decalescere < de-* intens. + *calescere* to grow hot] **— de′ca·les′cent** *adj.*
dec·a·li·ter (dĕk′ə·lē′tər) See DEKALITER.
Dec·a·logue (dĕk′ə·lôg, -log) *n.* The Ten Commandments. *Ex.* xx 2–17. Also **Dec′a·log.** [< Gk. *dekalogos < deka* ten + *logos* word]
De·cam·er·on (di·kam′ər·ən) A collection of 100 stories by Boccaccio (published 1353). [< Ital. *decamerone* < Gk. *deka* ten + *hēmera* day]
dec·a·me·ter (dĕk′ə·mē′tər) See DEKAMETER.
de·camp (di·kamp′) *v.i.* **1.** To leave a camping ground; break camp. **2.** To leave suddenly or secretly; run away. **Syn.** See ESCAPE. **— de·camp′ment** *n.*
dec·a·nal (dē·kā′nəl, di·kā′nəl) *adj.* Pertaining to a dean or deanery. [< LL *decanus.* See DEAN.] **— dec′a·nal·ly** *adv.*
de·can·drous (di·kan′drəs) *adj. Bot.* Having ten stamens. [< DEC(A)- + Gk. *anēr, andros* man]
dec·ane (dĕk′ān) *n. Chem.* Any of several isomeric hydrocarbons, C₁₀H₂₂, of the methane series, variously derived from coal tar, etc. [< DEC(A)- + -ANE²]
de·cant (di·kant′) *v.t.* **1.** To pour off (a liquid) without disturbing its sediment. **2.** To pour from one container into another. [< F *décanter* < Med.L *decanthare < de-* from + *canthus* lip of a jug < Gk. *kanthos*] **— de·can·ta·tion** (dē′kan·tā′shən) *n.*
de·cant·er (di·kan′tər) *n.* A vessel for decanting; especially, a decorative, stoppered bottle for serving wine, etc.
de·cap·i·tate (di·kap′ə·tāt) *v.t.* **·tat·ed, ·tat·ing** To cut off the head of; behead. [< Med.L *decapitare < de-* off + *caput* head] **— de·cap′i·ta′tion** *n.* **— de·cap′i·ta′tor** *n.*
dec·a·pod (dĕk′ə·pod) *adj.* **1.** Ten-footed or ten-armed. **2.** *Zool.* Of or pertaining to an order of crustaceans (*Decapoda*) having five pairs of legs, including the crabs, lobsters, shrimps, etc. **—** *n.* **1.** Any ten-legged crustacean. **2.** Any ten-armed cephalopod, as a cuttlefish or squid. [< Gk. *dekapous, -podos < deka* ten + *pous* foot] **— de·cap′o·dal** (di·kap′ə·dəl), **de·cap′o·dous** *adj.*
De·cap·o·lis (di·kap′ə·lis) A region in the north of ancient Palestine containing a confederacy of ten cities. *Matt.* iv 25.
de·car·bon·ate (dē·kär′bən·āt) *v.t.* **·at·ed, ·at·ing** To free from carbon dioxide. **— de·car′bon·a′tor** *n.*
de·car·bon·ize (dē·kär′bən·īz) *v.t.* **·ized, ·iz·ing** To decarburize. **— de·car·bon·i·za′tion** *n.* **— de·car′bon·iz′er** *n.*
de·car·box·y·la·tion (dē′kär·bok′sə·lā′shən) *n. Chem.* The elimination of one or more carboxyl radicals from an organic acid, with the release of carbon dioxide, as in certain amino acids. [< DE- + CARBOXYL]
de·car·bu·rize (dē·kär′byə·rīz) *v.t.* **·rized, ·riz·ing** To remove carbon from (molten steel or the cylinders of an internal-combustion engine). **— de·car′bu·ri·za′tion** *n.*

dec·are (dĕk′âr, dek·âr′) See DEKARE.
dec·a·stere (dĕk′ə·stir) See DEKASTERE.
dec·a·syl·la·ble (dĕk′ə·sil′ə·bəl) *n.* A line of verse having ten syllables. **— dec·a·syl·lab·ic** (dĕk′ə·si·lab′ik) *adj.*
de·cath·lon (di·kath′lon) *n.* An athletic contest consisting of ten different track and field events in all of which each contestant participates. [< DEC(A)- + Gk. *athlon* a contest]
De·ca·tur (di·kā′tər) **1.** A city in central Illinois; pop. 90,397. **2.** A city in northern Alabama, on the Tennessee River; pop. 38,044.
De·ca·tur (di·kā′tər), **Stephen,** 1779–1820, U.S. naval officer.
de·cay (di·kā′) *v.i.* **1.** To fail slowly in health, beauty, quality, or any form of excellence. **2.** To decompose; rot. **—** *v.t.* **3.** To cause to decay. **—** *n.* **1.** A falling into a ruined or reduced condition; gradual decline, as in health or mental power. **2.** Decomposition, as of a dead organism. **3.** Rottenness; corruption. **4.** *Physics* The disintegration of a radioactive element or isotope. [< OF *decair,* var. of *decaoir* < L *decidere < de-* -down + *cadere* to fall]
— Syn. (verb) **2.** *Decay, putrefy, rot, spoil, disintegrate, molder,* and *crumble* refer to a destructive change in substance. Dead organic matter *decays* by the action of bacteria. The word is also used figuratively; a great mind may *decay* with age. *Putrefy* is used only of animal matter, and stresses the foul aspects of decay, as does the strong, direct *rot. Spoil* is a less forceful word, and suggests mild decay or taint; food *spoils* if not refrigerated. A thing *decomposes* when its chemical constituents separate; it *disintegrates* when its physical parts separate. *Molder* and *crumble* mean to break down into small fragments, and refer to the visible signs of decomposition or disintegration.
Dec·can Plateau (dĕk′ən) A triangular tableland covering most of peninsular India; average height about 2,000 ft.
Deccan States A group of former princely states within Maharashtra State, India.
decd. Deceased.
de·cease (di·sēs′) *v.i.* **·ceased, ·ceas·ing** To die. **—** *n.* Death. [< OF *deces* < L *decessus < decedere < de-* away + *cedere* to go]
de·ceased (di·sēst′) *adj.* Dead. Abbr. *dec., decd.* **— Syn.** See LIFELESS. **— the deceased** The dead person or persons.
de·ce·dent (di·sēd′nt) *n. Law* A person deceased. [< L *decedens, -entis,* ppr. of *decedere.* See DECEASE.]
de·ceit (di·sēt′) *n.* **1.** The act of deceiving; concealment or misrepresentation of the truth. **2.** An instance of deception or a device that deceives; a trick; artifice. **3.** The quality of being deceptive; falseness; full of *deceit.* [< OF *deceite* < *deceveir.* See DECEIVE.]
de·ceit·ful (di·sēt′fəl) *adj.* **1.** Given to deceiving; lying or treacherous. **2.** Tending to deceive; false. **— Syn.** See DECEPTIVE. **— de·ceit′ful·ly** *adv.* **— de·ceit′ful·ness** *n.*
de·ceive (di·sēv′) *v.* **·ceived, ·ceiv·ing** *v.t.* **1.** To mislead by falsehood; lead into error; delude. **2.** *Obs.* To while away (time). **—** *v.i.* **3.** To practice deceit. [< OF *deceveir* < L *decipere < de-* away, down + *capere* to take] **— de·ceiv′er** *n.* **— de·ceiv′ing·ly** *adv.*
— Syn. 1. mislead, delude, dupe, trick, beguile, betray.
de·cel·er·ate (dē·sel′ə·rāt) *v.t. & v.i.* **·at·ed, ·at·ing** To diminish in speed. [< DE- + L *celeratus,* pp. of *celerare* to hasten < *celer* quick] **— de·cel′er·a′tor** *n.*
de·cel·er·a·tion (dē·sel′ə·rā′shən) *n.* A decrease in speed.
De·cem·ber (di·sem′bər) *n.* The twelfth month of the year, having 31 days. Abbr. *D., Dec, Dec.* [< L < *decem* ten; December was the tenth month in the old Roman calendar]
De·cem·brist (di·sem′brist) *n.* One who conspired against Czar Nicholas I of Russia on his accession, Dec., 1825.
de·cem·vir (di·sem′vər) *n. pl.* **·virs** or **·vi·ri** (-və·rī) A member of any body of ten magistrates; especially one commissioned to codify the laws of Rome in 451 B.C. [< L < *decem* ten + *vir* man] **— de·cem′vi·ral** *adj.*
de·cem·vi·rate (di·sem′və·rit, -rāt) *n.* **1.** A body of ten men in authority. **2.** The government of such a body.
de·cen·a·ry (di·sen′ər·ē) *adj.* Of or pertaining to a tithing. **—** *n.* A tithing. Also spelled *decennary.* [< Med.L *decenarius < decena* a tithing < L *decem* ten]
de·cen·cy (dē′sən·sē) *n. pl.* **·cies 1.** The quality or state of being decent; propriety in conduct, speech, or dress; regard for decorum. **2.** *Usually pl.* Those things that are proper or decent. **3.** *pl.* The requirements for a proper or comfortable manner of life. [< *decens < decens.* See DECENT.]
de·cen·na·ry¹ (di·sen′ər·ē) *adj.* Of or pertaining to a period of ten years. **—** *n. pl.* **·ries** A decennium. [< L *decennis* < *decem* ten + *annus* year]
de·cen·na·ry² (di·sen′ər·ē) See DECENARY.
de·cen·ni·al (di·sen′ē·əl) *adj.* **1.** Of or continuing for ten years. **2.** Occurring every ten years. **—** *n.* An anniversary observed every ten years. **— de·cen′ni·al·ly** *adv.*
de·cen·ni·um (di·sen′ē·əm) *n. pl.* **·cen·ni·ums** or **·cen·ni·a** (-sen′ē·ə) A period of ten years; decade. [< L < *decem* ten + *annus* year]
de·cent (dē′sənt) *adj.* **1.** Characterized by propriety of conduct, speech, or dress; proper; respectable. **2.** Free of coarse-

ness or indelicacy; modest; chaste. **3.** Adequate; passable; satisfactory: a *decent* meal. **4.** Generous; kind. **5.** *Informal* Adequately or properly clothed. **6.** *Archaic* Appropriate; also, comely. [< L *decens, -entis*, ppr. of *decere* to be fitting, proper] — **de·cent·ly** *adv.* — **de·cent·ness** *n.*

de·cen·ter (dē-sen′tər) *v.t.* To put out of center; make eccentric. Also *Brit.* **de·cen′tre.**

de·cen·tral·ize (dē-sen′trəl-īz) *v.t.* **·ized, ·iz·ing** To undo the centralization of; reorganize into smaller and more dispersed parts. — **de·cen′tral·i·za′tion** *n.*

de·cep·tion (di-sep′shən) *n.* **1.** The act of deceiving; deceit. **2.** The state of being deceived. **3.** Anything that deceives or is meant to deceive; a delusion. [< L *deceptio, -onis* < *decipere.* See DECEIVE.]
— **Syn. 1.** *Deception, trickery, deceit,* and *fraud* denote misrepresentations or falsehoods that are intended to mislead. *Deception* and *trickery* are not always bad; a magician uses them both to entertain. *Deception* usually refers to the fact of misleading, and *trickery,* to the means: to profit from *deception,* to gain gold by *trickery. Deceit* is always bad, and suggests a trait or quality: a transaction marked by *deceit. Fraud* is the misleading of another for one's own gain, and is usually criminal; the sale of property which one does not own is *fraud.* Compare LIE.

de·cep·tive (di-sep′tiv) *adj.* Having power or tendency to deceive. — **de·cep′tive·ly** *adv.* — **de·cep′tive·ness** *n.*

de·cer·e·brate (*v.* dē-ser′ə-brāt; *adj.* dē-ser′ə-brit) *v.t.* **·brat·ed, ·brat·ing** To remove the brain from. — *adj.* Having had the brain removed. [< DE- + L *cerebrum* brain] — **de·cer′e·bra′tion** *n.*

de·cern (di-sûrn′) *v.t.* **1.** In Scottish law, to decree; adjudge. **2.** To discern. [< F *décerner* < L *decernere* to decide < *de-* down + *cernere* to decide]

deci- *combining form* In the metric system, one tenth of (a specified unit): *decimeter.* [< L *decimus* tenth < *decem* ten]

dec·i·are (des′ē-âr) *n.* In the metric system, one tenth of an are. Abbr. *da.* [< F *déciare*]

dec·i·bel (des′ə-bel) *n. Physics* One tenth of a bel, the common unit of power ratio: a measure of sound intensity. Abbr. *db, db.*

de·cide (di-sīd′) *v.* **·cid·ed, ·cid·ing** *v.t.* **1.** To determine; settle, as a controversy, contest, etc.; arbitrate. **2.** To determine the issue or conclusion of: The charge *decided* the battle. **3.** To bring (someone) to a decision. — *v.i.* **4.** To give a decision or verdict; pronounce a judgment. **5.** To make a decision. [< MF *décider* < L *decidere* < *de-* down, away + *caedere* to cut] — **de·cid′a·ble** *adj.*

de·cid·ed (di-sī′did) *adj.* **1.** Free from uncertainty; definite; unquestionable: a *decided* improvement. **2.** Exhibiting determination; resolute; emphatic: a *decided* manner. — **de·cid′ed·ly** *adv.* — **de·cid′ed·ness** *n.*

de·cid·u·a (di-sij′ŏŏ-ə) *n. Physiol.* The mucous membrane lining the uterus that is modified for pregnancy and in some mammals is cast off during menstruation or at parturition. [< NL (*membrana*) *decidua* (membrane) that falls off < L *deciduus.* See DECIDUOUS.] — **de·cid′u·al** *adj.*

de·cid·u·ous (di-sij′ŏŏ-əs) *adj.* **1.** *Bot.* **a** Falling off or shed at maturity or at specific seasons, as petals, fruit, or leaves. **b** Characterized by such a falling off: distinguished from *evergreen.* **2.** *Zool.* Liable to be shed at periodical times, as antlers, hair, teeth, wings of insects, etc. **3.** Not enduring; short-lived. Compare PERSISTENT. [< L *deciduus* < *decidere* < *de-* down, away + *cadere* to fall] — **de·cid′u·ous·ly** *adv.* — **de·cid′u·ous·ness** *n.*

dec·i·gram (des′ə-gram) *n.* In the metric system, the tenth part of a gram. Also **dec′i·gramme.** Abbr. *dg, dg.* See table inside back cover.

dec·ile (des′il) *n. Stat.* One of the parts or intervals of a frequency distribution, each of which contains one tenth of the cases in the complete series. [< F *décile* < L *decem* ten]

dec·i·li·ter (des′ə-lē′tər) *n.* In the metric system, the tenth part of a liter. Also *esp. Brit.* **dec′i·li·tre.** Abbr. *dl, dl.* See table inside back cover.

de·cil·lion (di-sil′yən) *n.* **1.** *U.S.* A thousand nonillions, written as 1 followed by thirty-three zeros: a cardinal number. **2.** *Brit.* A million nonillions (def. 2), written as 1 followed by sixty zeros: a cardinal number. — *adj.* Being a decillion in number. [< DEC(A)- + (M)ILLION]

de·cil·lionth (di-sil′yənth) *adj.* **1.** Having the number one decillion: the ordinal of *decillion.* **2.** Being one of a decillion equal parts. — *n.* **1.** One of a decillion equal parts. **2.** That which is numbered one decillion.

decim. Decimeter.

dec·i·mal (des′ə-məl) *adj.* **1.** Pertaining to or founded on the number 10. **2.** Proceeding by tens. — *n.* A decimal fraction or one of its digits. [< Med.L *decimalis* of tenths < L *decimus* tenth < *decem* ten]

decimal fraction *Math.* A fraction whose denominator is any power of 10 and which may be expressed in decimal form, as 7/10 (0.7), 3/100 (0.03), etc.

dec·i·mal·ize (des′ə-məl-īz′) *v.t.* **·ized, ·iz·ing** To reduce to a decimal system. — **dec′i·mal·i·za′tion** *n.*

decimal point A dot used before a decimal fraction.

decimal system A system of reckoning by tens or tenths.

dec·i·mate (des′ə-māt) *v.t.* **·mat·ed, ·mat·ing 1.** To destroy or kill a large proportion of. **2.** To select by lot and kill one out of every ten of. **3.** *Obs.* To take a tenth part of. [< L *decimatus,* pp. of *decimare* to take a tenth part from < *decem* ten] — **dec′i·ma′tion** *n.* — **dec′i·mat′or** *n.*

dec·i·me·ter (des′ə-mē′tər) *n.* In the metric system, the tenth part of a meter. Also *esp. Brit.* **dec′i·me′tre.** Abbr. *dec., decim., dm, dm.* See table inside back cover.

de·ci·pher (di-sī′fər) *v.t.* **1.** To determine the meaning of (something obscure, illegible, etc.); make out; interpret: to *decipher* an inscription. **2.** To translate from cipher or code into plain text; decode. **3.** *Obs.* To portray; depict. — **de·ci′pher·a·ble** *adj.* — **de·ci′pher·er** *n.* — **de·ci′pher·ment** *n.*

de·ci·sion (di-sizh′ən) *n.* **1.** The act of deciding (an issue, question, etc.). **2.** A conclusion or judgment reached by deciding; a verdict. **3.** The making up of one's mind. **4.** Firmness in judgment, action, or character; determination. **5.** In boxing, a victory decided on points when there has not been a knockout. — **Syn.** See DETERMINATION. [< F *décision* < L *decisio, -onis* < *decidere.* See DECIDE.]

de·ci·sive (di-sī′siv) *adj.* **1.** Ending uncertainty or dispute; conclusive: a *decisive* blow. **2.** Characterized by decision and firmness; prompt; determined. **3.** Unquestionable; unmistakable. — **de·ci′sive·ly** *adv.* — **de·ci′sive·ness** *n.*

dec·i·stere (des′ə-stir) *n.* In the metric system, a cubic decimeter, or the tenth part of a stere. Abbr. *ds.*

De·cius (dē′shəs, desh′əs,) Gaius Messius Quintus Trajanus, 201–251, Roman emperor 249–251.

deck (dek) *n.* **1.** *Naut.* **a** A platform covering or extending horizontally across a vessel, and serving as both floor and roof. **b** The space between two such platforms. **2.** Any similar flat surface. **3.** *U.S.* A pack of playing cards. — **to clear the deck** To clear away that which impedes free action; to prepare for action. — **to hit the deck** *Slang* **1.** To rise from bed; get up. **2.** To prepare for action. **3.** To drop to a prone position. — **on deck** *Slang* **1.** Present and ready for action. **2.** Waiting one's turn, as to bat in a baseball game. — *v.t.* **1.** To dress or decorate elegantly; adorn: to *deck* the halls. **2.** *Naut.* To furnish with a deck. **3.** *Obs.* To cover; clothe. — **Syn.** See ADORN. [< MDu. *dek* roof, covering]

deck·er (dek′ər) *n.* Something with one or more decks, layers, levels, etc.: usually in combination: a *double-decker.*

Deck·er (dek′ər), **Thomas** See DEKKER.

deck hand A common sailor employed on deck.

deck·house (dek′hous′) *n.* A compartment or cabin built on an upper deck of a ship.

deck·le (dek′əl) *n.* **1.** In making paper by hand, a frame that limits the size of the sheet by confining the paper pulp to a definite area on the mold. **2.** The ragged edge of handmade paper: also **deckle edge.** Also **deck′el.** [< G *deckel,* dim. of *decke* cover]

deck·le-edged (dek′əl-ejd′) *adj.* Having a deckle edge.

decl. Declension.

de·claim (di-klām′) *v.i.* **1.** To speak loudly and rhetorically. **2.** To give a formal, set speech or recitation. **3.** To condemn or attack verbally and vehemently: with *against.* — *v.t.* **4.** To utter rhetorically. [< L *declamare* < *de-* completely + *clamare* to shout] — **de·claim′er** *n.*

dec·la·ma·tion (dek′lə-mā′shən) *n.* **1.** The act or art of declaiming. **2.** A prepared speech or recitation to be performed publicly. **3.** Bombastic or empty oratory. **4.** *Music* The technique of performing vocal passages that are half sung and half spoken, as recitatives.

de·clam·a·to·ry (di-klam′ə-tôr′ē, -tō′rē) *adj.* **1.** Characterized by or pertaining to declamation. **2.** Emptily rhetorical; bombastic. — **de·clam′a·to′ri·ly** *adv.*

dec·la·ra·tion (dek′lə-rā′shən) *n.* **1.** A formal, explicit, or emphatic statement; also, a document containing such a statement. **2.** The act of declaring or proclaiming. **3.** That which is declared; a proclamation. **4.** A statement of goods liable to taxation. **5.** *Law* **a** The written statement of a plaintiff's causes and claims. **b** A solemn statement made in place of an oath, under the same penalties of perjury if violated. **6.** In some card games, an announcement of points made; in bridge, a contract. Abbr. *dec.*

Declaration of Independence The manifesto of the Second Continental Congress that formally declared the political independence of the American colonies from Great Britain. It was written by Thomas Jefferson and adopted July 4, 1776.

de·clar·a·tive (di-klar′ə-tiv) *adj.* Making a declaration or statement; affirmative: a *declarative* sentence. Also **de·clar·a·to·ry** (di-klar′ə-tôr′ē, -tō′rē).

de·clare (di-klâr′) *v.* **·clared, ·clar·ing** *v.t.* **1.** To make known or clear; especially, to announce formally; proclaim. **2.** To say emphatically; assert; avow. **3.** To reveal; prove: His actions *declare* him a saint. **4.** To make full statement of, as goods liable to duty. **5.** In some card games, to show (points made); in bridge, to make a bid designating (a trump suit or no-trump). — *v.i.* **6.** To make a declaration. **7.** To proclaim a choice or opinion: with *for* or *against.* — **Syn.** See ASSERT. [< L *declarare* < *de-* completely + *clarare* to make clear < *clarus* clear] — **de·clar′er** *n.*

de·clared (di-klârd′) *adj.* Openly avowed; proclaimed: a *declared* enemy. — **de·clar·ed·ly** (di-klâr′id-lē) *adv.*

de·class (dē-klas′, -kläs′) *v.t.* To lower in status; degrade.
dé·clas·sé (dā-klȧ-sā′) *adj. French* Fallen or lowered in social status, class, rank, etc. Also **de·classed** (dē-klast′, -kläst′). — **dé·clas·sée′** *adj. fem.*
de·clen·sion (di-klen′shən) *n.* 1. *Gram.* **a** The inflection of nouns, pronouns, and adjectives according to case, number, and gender. **b** A class of words similarly inflected: *Stella* and *nauta* are Latin nouns of the first *declension.* Abbr. *dec., decl.* 2. A sloping downward; descent. 3. A falling off; decline. 4. Deviation, as from a belief. [< L *declinatio, -onis* < *declinare.* See DECLINE.] — **de·clen′sion·al** *adj.*
dec·li·na·tion (dek′lə-nā′shən) *n.* 1. The act of inclining or bending downward. 2. Deviation, as in direction or conduct. 3. The angular difference in direction between true north and either magnetic north (**magnetic declination**) or grid north (**grid declination**). 4. *Astron.* The angular distance of a heavenly body north or south from the celestial equator; celestial latitude. 5. Decline in quality; deterioration. 6. A polite refusal. Abbr. *dec.*
de·cli·na·to·ry (di-klī′nə-tôr′ē, -tō′rē) *adj.* Of or involving declination; especially, conveying a refusal.
de·cli·na·ture (di-klī′nə-chər) *n.* The act of declining an offer or request; refusal.
de·cline (di-klīn′) *v.* **·clined, ·clin·ing** *v.i.* 1. To refuse politely to accept, comply with, or do something. 2. To lessen or fail gradually, as in health. 3. To draw to an end, as the day; wane. 4. To lower oneself; stoop, as to a mean action. 5. To bend or incline downward or aside. — *v.t.* 6. To refuse politely to accept, comply with, or do. 7. To cause to bend or incline downward or aside. 8. *Gram.* To give the inflected forms of (a noun, pronoun, or adjective). — *n.* 1. The act or result of declining; deterioration; decay. 2. A period of declining and approaching a close. 3. A condition in which one's mental or physical faculties weaken or deteriorate. 4. Any disease that weakens one gradually. 5. A downward slope. [< OF *decliner* < L *declinare* to lean down] — **de·clin′a·ble** *adj.* — **de·clin′er** *n.*
dec·li·nom·e·ter (dek′lə-nom′ə-tər) *n.* An instrument for measuring declination. [< DECLINE + -(O)METER]
de·cliv·i·tous (di-kliv′ə-təs) *adj.* Somewhat steep.
de·cliv·i·ty (di-kliv′ə-tē) *n. pl.* **·ties** A downward slope or descending surface; opposed to *acclivity.* [< L *declivitas, -tatis* < *declivis* < *de-* down + *clivus* hill, slope]
de·cli·vous (di-klī′vəs) *adj.* Sloping downward.
de·coct (di-kokt′) *v.t.* To extract by boiling; boil down; condense. [< L *decoctus,* pp. of *decoquere* < *de-* down + *coquere* to cook]
de·coc·tion (di-kok′shən) *n.* 1. The act of boiling anything, especially in water, to extract its soluble properties; distinguished from *infusion.* 2. A solution prepared by boiling an animal or vegetable substance; an essence.
de·code (dē-kōd′) *v.t.* **·cod·ed, ·cod·ing** To convert from code into plain language. — **de·cod′er** *n.*
de·col·late (di-kol′āt) *v.t.* **·lat·ed, ·lat·ing** To behead. [< L *decollatus,* pp. of *decollare* < *de-* down, from + *collum* neck] — **de·col·la·tion** (dē′kə-lā′shən) *n.* — **de·col′la·tor** *n.*
dé·colle·tage (dā-kôl′täzh′) *n. French* 1. Lowness of neckline in a garment. 2. A décolleté costume.
dé·colle·té (dā′kol-tā′, *Fr.* dā-kôl-tā′) *adj.* 1. Cut low in the neck, as a gown. 2. Having the neck and shoulders bare; wearing a low-necked garment. [< F, pp. of *décolleter* to bare the neck < *dé-* from (< L *de-*) + *collet,* dim. of *col* neck, shoulder < L *collum*]
de·col·or (dē-kul′ər) *v.t.* To deprive of color; bleach. Also *Brit.* **de·col′our.** — **de·col·o·ra′tion** *n.*
de·col·or·ant (dē-kul′ər-ənt) *adj.* Bleaching. — *n.* A bleaching substance.
de·col·or·ize (dē-kul′ə-rīz) *v.t.* **·ized, ·iz·ing** To decolor. Also *Brit.* **de·col′our·ise.** — **de·col·or·i·za′tion** *n.* — **de·col′or·iz′er** *n.*
de·com·mis·sion (dē′kə-mish′ən) *v.t.* To take out of active service, as a ship; retire from use.
de·com·pose (dē′kəm-pōz′) *v.t. & v.i.* **·posed, ·pos·ing** 1. To separate into constituent parts or elements. 2. To decay; putrefy. — **Syn.** See DECAY. — **de′com·pos′a·ble** *adj.* — **de·com·pos′er** *n.*
de·com·pos·ite (dē′kəm-poz′it) *adj.* 1. Formed of compounds, as a word. 2. *Bot.* Decompound.
de·com·po·si·tion (dē′kom-pə-zish′ən) *n.* The act, process, or result of decomposing.
de·com·pound (dē′kəm-pound′) *v.t.* 1. To compound with (things already compound). 2. To decompose. — *adj.* 1. Formed by compounding things already compound. 2. *Bot.* Having or designating parts that are themselves already compounded, as some leaves.
de·com·press (dē′kəm-pres′) *v.t.* 1. To free of pressure. 2. To remove the pressure on (divers, caisson workers, etc.), as in an air lock or decompression chamber.
de·com·pres·sion (dē′kəm-presh′ən) *n.* The reduction or removal of pressure, especially in connection with work under high atmospheric pressure.

decompression chamber An enclosed chamber for decompression, or for reducing normal pressure.
decompression sickness Caisson disease.
de·con·tam·i·nate (dē′kən-tam′ə-nāt) *v.t.* **·nat·ed, ·nat·ing** 1. To rid of contamination. 2. To make (a contaminated object or area) safe by destroying or neutralizing poisonous chemicals, radioactivity, etc.
de·con·trol (dē′kən-trōl′) *v.t.* **·trolled, ·trol·ling** To remove from control. — *n.* The removal of controls.
dé·cor (dā′kôr, dā-kôr′) *n.* 1. The scheme or style of decoration in a room, home, club, etc. 2. In the theater, scenic decoration. Also **de′cor.** [< F *décorer* to decorate]
dec·o·rate (dek′ə-rāt) *v.t.* **·rat·ed, ·rat·ing** 1. To embellish or furnish with things beautiful; adorn. 2. To confer a decoration or medal upon. — **Syn.** See ADORN. [< L *decoratus,* pp. of *decorare* < *decus, decoris* grace, embellishment]
Decorated style A style of English Gothic architecture prevailing from the end of the 13th to the last part of the 14th century. Also **Decorated architecture.**
dec·o·ra·tion (dek′ə-rā′shən) *n.* 1. The act, process, or art of decorating. 2. A thing or group of things that decorate or embellish; ornamentation. 3. A badge or emblem conferred as a mark of honor; a medal. ◆ The U.S. military decorations in order of precedence are: Medal of Honor, Distinguished Service Cross or Navy Cross (Navy and Marine Corps), Distinguished Service Medal, Silver Star, Legion of Merit, Distinguished Flying Cross, Soldier's Medal, Bronze Star, Air Medal, Commendation Ribbon, and Purple Heart.
Decoration Day Memorial Day (which see).
dec·o·ra·tive (dek′ər-ə-tiv, dek′rə-tiv, dek′ə-rā′tiv) *adj.* Of, pertaining to, or suitable for decoration; ornamental. — **dec′o·ra·tive·ly** *adv.* — **dec′o·ra·tive·ness** *n.*
dec·o·ra·tor (dek′ə-rā′tər) *n.* One who decorates; especially, an interior decorator.
dec·o·rous (dek′ər-əs, di-kôr′əs, -kō′rəs) *adj.* Marked by decorum; seemly; proper. [< L *decorus* < *decus, decoris* grace] — **dec′o·rous·ly** *adv.* — **dec′o·rous·ness** *n.*
de·cor·ti·cate (di-kôr′tə-kāt) *v.t.* **·cat·ed, ·cat·ing** 1. To strip off the bark or outer coat of; peel. 2. *Surg.* To strip off a portion of the cortical substance of (the brain, etc.). [< L *decorticatus,* pp. of *decorticare* < *de-* down + *cortex, corticis* bark] — **de·cor′ti·ca′tion** *n.* — **de·cor′ti·ca′tor** *n.*
de·co·rum (di-kôr′əm, -kō′rəm) *n.* 1. Conformity to the requirements of good taste or social convention; propriety in behavior, dress, etc.; seemliness. 2. *Usually pl.* The proprieties. [< L, neut. of *decorus.* See DECOROUS.]
de·cou·page (dā-kōō-päzh′) *n.* 1. The art of decorating a surface with cutouts of foil, paper, etc. 2. Something done in decoupage. [< F < OF *decouper* to cut out]
de·coy (*n.* di-koi′, dē′koi; *v.* di-koi′) *n.* 1. A person or thing that lures into danger, deception, or similar trap. 2. A bird or animal, or the likeness of one, used to lure game into a snare or net or within gunshot. 3. An enclosed place into which game may be lured for capture. — *v.t. & v.i.* To lure or be lured into danger or a trap. [Earlier *coy* < Du. *kooi* a cage < L *cavea* < *cavus* hollow] — **de·coy′er** *n.*

DECOY (def. 2)

de·crease (*v.* di-krēs′; *n.* dē′krēs, di-krēs′) *v.t. & v.i.* **·creased, ·creas·ing** To grow, or cause to grow, less or smaller; diminish, especially by a gradual process; abate; reduce. — *n.* 1. The act, process, or state of decreasing. 2. The amount or degree of decreasing. Abbr. *dec.* [< OF *decreiss-,* stem of *decreistre* < L *decrescere* < *de-* down + *crescere* to grow] — **de·creas′ing·ly** *adv.*
— **Syn.** *Decrease, lessen, dwindle, abate, subside, diminish,* and *reduce* mean to make or become smaller or less. In the main, *decrease* is applied to amount, *lessen* to number, *dwindle* to size, *abate* to force, and *subside* to position. To *diminish* is to grow smaller by the removal of a part. *Reduce* is used in all the foregoing senses, but is usually transitive: to *reduce* a load or the temperature of a room.
de·cree (di-krē′) *n.* 1. A formal and authoritative order or decision; a law or ordinance. 2. *Theol.* A foreordained and eternal purpose of God. Abbr. *d., D.* — *v.* **·creed, ·cree·ing** *v.t.* 1. To order, adjudge, ordain, or appoint by law or edict. — *v.i.* 2. To issue an edict or decree. [< OF *decre, decret* < L *decretum,* neut. pp. of *decernere.* See DECERN.]
dec·re·ment (dek′rə-mənt) *n.* 1. The act or process of decreasing or waning. 2. The amount lost by decrease or waste. 3. *Math.* A decrease in value of a variable quantity. [< L *decrementum* < *decrescere.* See DECREASE.]
de·crep·it (di-krep′it) *adj.* Enfeebled or worn out by old age or excessive use. [< L *decrepitus* < *de-* completely + *crepare* to creak] — **de·crep′it·ly** *adv.*
de·crep·i·tate (di-krep′ə-tāt) *v.* **·tat·ed, ·tat·ing** *v.t.* 1. To heat (salt, minerals, etc.) so as to cause a crackling sound or until this sound ceases. — *v.i.* 2. To crackle when heated, as salt. [< NL *decrepitatus,* pp of *decrepitare* < L *de-* completely + *crepitare,* freq. of *crepare* to creak] — **de·crep′i·ta′tion** *n.*

de·crep·i·tude (di-krep′ə-tōōd, -tyōōd) n. A decrepit or enfeebled condition, as from infirmity or old age.
decresc. Decrescendo.
de·cre·scen·do (dē′krə-shen′dō) n. & v.i. Music Diminuendo. Abbr. dec., decresc.
de·cres·cent (di-kres′ənt) adj. Decreasing; waning. [< L decrescens, -entis, ppr. of decrescere. See DECREASE.] **— de·cres′cence** n.
de·cre·tal (di-krēt′l) n. A decree; especially, a papal decree or letter determining some point in ecclesiastical law. **Decretals** The collection of papal laws and decisions forming part of the canonical laws of the Church, especially the collection authorized by Gregory IX in 1234. **—** adj. Of or pertaining to a decree. [< F décrétale < Med.L decretale < L decretum. See DECREE.]
de·cre·tist (di-krē′tist) n. One versed in canon law.
de·cre·tive (di-krē′tiv) adj. Pertaining to or having the force or nature of a decree. **— de·cre′tive·ly** adv.
dec·re·to·ry (dek′rə-tôr′ē, -tō′rē) adj. Pertaining to, resulting from, or established by a decree; judicial; definitive.
de·cri·al (di-krī′əl) n. The act of decrying; condemnation.
de·cry (di-krī′) v.t. ·cried, ·cry·ing 1. To condemn or disparage openly; denounce. 2. To depreciate or condemn officially, as foreign coins. **— Syn.** See DISPARAGE. [< F décrier < dé- down (< L de-) + crier to cry] **— de·cri′er** n.
de·crypt (dē-kript′) v.t. To convert (a cryptogram) into plain text by decoding or deciphering.
dec·u·man (dek′yōō-mən) adj. Very large; principal: said especially of waves, from the theory that the tenth wave in a series is the largest. [< L decumanus, var. of decimanus of the tenth part, large < decimus tenth]
de·cum·bence (di-kum′bəns) n. A decumbent or prostrate state or position. Also **de·cum′ben·cy.**
de·cum·bent (di-kum′bənt) adj. 1. Lying down; recumbent. 2. Bot. Prostrate: said of stems, shoots, etc., growing along the ground. [< L decumbens, -entis, ppr. of decumbere < de- down + cumbere to lie, recline]
dec·u·ple (dek′yōō-pəl) adj. Tenfold. **—** n. A number or quantity ten times as large as another, or ten times repeated. **—** v.t. ·pled, ·pling To increase tenfold. [< F décuple < L decuplus < decem ten]
de·cu·ri·on (di-kyōōr′ē-ən) n. 1. In ancient Rome, an officer who commanded ten soldiers or a decury. 2. A member of the senate in an ancient Roman colony or municipal town. [< L decurio, -onis < decem ten]
de·cur·rent (di-kûr′ənt) adj. Bot. Extending or running downward into another structure, as the base of a leaf along a plant stem. [< L decurrens, -entis, ppr. of decurrere < de- down + currere to run] **— de·cur′rent·ly** adv.
de·curve (di-kûrv′) v.t. & v.i. ·curved, ·curv·ing To curve downward.
dec·u·ry (dek′yōō-rē) n. pl. ·ries 1. In ancient Rome, a company of soldiers, originally ten. 2. A division or class, as of ancient Roman senators. [< L decuria < decem ten]
de·cus·sate (v. di·kus′āt, dek′ə-sāt; adj. di·kus′āt, -it) v.t. & v.i. ·sat·ed, ·sat·ing To cross in the form of an X; intersect. **—** adj. 1. Crossed; intersected. 2. Bot. Having each pair of leaves at right angles with the pair below or above. See illustration of LEAF. [< L decussatus, pp. of decussare to mark with an X < decussis the number ten, X] **— de·cus′sate·ly** adv. **— de·cus·sa·tion** (dē′kə-sā′shən, dek′ə-) n.
de·dal (dēd′l) See DAEDAL.
de·dans (də′dəns, Fr. də-dän′) n. 1. In tennis, a screened gallery for spectators. 2. The spectators. [< F, inside]
De·de·a·gach (de-de′ä-gäch′) A former name for ALEXANDROUPOLIS.
ded·i·cate (ded′ə-kāt, -i-) v.t. ·cat·ed, ·cat·ing 1. To set apart for sacred uses; consecrate. 2. To set apart for or devote to any special use, duty, or purpose. 3. To inscribe (a work of literature, etc.) to someone as a mark of affection or esteem. 4. To commit (oneself) to a certain course of action or thought. 5. To open or unveil (a bridge, statue, etc.) to the public, especially with a formal ceremony. **—** adj. Archaic Dedicated; devoted. [< L dedicatus, pp. of dedicare < de- down + dicare to proclaim]
ded·i·ca·tion (ded′ə-kā′shən, -i-) n. 1. The act of dedicating or the state of being dedicated. 2. An inscription dedicating a literary work, etc., to someone or something.
ded·i·ca·tive (ded′ə-kā′tiv, -i-) adj. That dedicates.
ded·i·ca·to·ry (ded′ə-kə-tôr′ē, -tō′rē, -i-) adj. Constituting, containing, or serving as a dedication: a dedicatory preface.
de·duce (di-dōōs′, -dyōōs′) v.t. ·duced, ·duc·ing 1. To derive as a conclusion by reasoning; infer; conclude. 2. To trace, as derivation or origin. [< L deducere < de- down + ducere to lead] **— de·duc′i·ble** adj.
de·duct (di-dukt′) v.t. To take away or subtract. [< L deductus, pp. of deducere. See DEDUCE.] **— de·duct′i·ble** adj.
de·duc·tion (di-duk′shən) n. 1. The act of deducing. 2. Logic Reasoning from the general to the particular; also, reasoning from stated premises to conclusions formally or necessarily implied by such premises. Compare INDUCTION. 3. An inference; conclusion. 4. The act of deducting. 5. A subtraction; abatement. **— Syn.** See INFERENCE.
de·duc·tive (di-duk′tiv) adj. 1. Of or reached by deduction.

2. Based on or involving deduction. **— de·duc′tive·ly** adv.
dee (dē) n. The letter D.
Dee (dē) 1. A river in NE Scotland, flowing 87 miles east to the North Sea at Aberdeen. 2. A river in northern Wales and England, flowing 70 miles NE to the Irish Sea.
deed (dēd) n. 1. Anything done; an act. 2. A notable achievement; feat; exploit. 3. Action in general, as opposed to words. 4. Law Any written, sealed instrument of bond, contract, transfer, etc., especially of real estate conveyance. **— Syn.** See ACT. **— in deed** In fact; in truth; actually. **—** v.t. To transfer by deed. [OE dǣd] **— deed′less** adj.
deed·ed (dē′did) adj. Law Conveyed by a deed.
deem (dēm) v.t. & v.i. To judge; think; believe. [OE dēman to judge]
de·em·pha·size (dē-em′fə-sīz) v.t. ·sized, ·siz·ing To treat with less importance; minimize. **— de·em′pha·sis** n.
deem·ster (dēm′stər) n. Either of the two highest judicial officers in the Isle of Man: also called dempster. [ME demestre] **— deem′ster·ship** n.
deep (dēp) adj. 1. Extending or situated far from a surface. 2. Extending far inward or backward, or to either side. 3. Having a (specified) depth or dimension below a surface, or inward or backward: six feet deep. 4. Rising to the level of; also, sunk or immersed to the level of: used in combination: knee-deep. 5. Coming from or penetrating to a depth: a deep sigh. 6. Difficult to understand; obscure. 7. Learned and penetrating; wise. 8. Of great intensity: extreme: deep sorrow. 9. Of intense or dark hue. 10. Of low, sonorous tone; full-toned. 11. Much involved; absorbed: deep in thought. 12. Artful; cunning. **— to go off the deep end** Informal 1. To act rashly. 2. To become excited or hysterical. **—** n. 1. A place or thing of great depth; an abyss, as of the sea. 2. The most intense or profound part: the deep of night. 3. Naut. The interval between two successive marked fathoms on a sounding line. **— the deep** Poetic The sea or ocean. **—** adv. 1. Deeply. 2. Far along in time. [OE dēop. Akin to DIP.] **— deep′ly** adv. **— deep′ness** n.
deep-dish pie (dēp′dish′) A pie baked in a deep dish and having only a top crust.
deep-dyed (dēp′dīd′) adj. Thoroughgoing; absolute: a deep-dyed villain.
deep·en (dē′pən) v.t. & v.i. To make or become deep or deeper.
deep·freeze (dēp′frēz′) n. 1. A refrigerator for freezing and storing foods for long periods of time at temperatures approximating 0° F. 2. Storage, especially of long duration. **—** v.t. ·froze or ·freezed, ·fro·zen or ·freezed, ·freez·ing To place or store in or as in a deepfreeze.
deep-fry (dēp′frī′) v.t. -fried, -fry·ing To fry in deep fat or oil.
deep-laid (dēp′lād′) adj. Made with extreme care and cleverness, usually in secret: deep-laid plans.
deep-root·ed (dēp′rōō′tid, -rŏŏt′id) adj. 1. Having roots that reach far below the surface. 2. Firmly held: said of beliefs, prejudices, etc.
deep-sea (dēp′sē′) adj. Of, in, or pertaining to the deeper parts of the sea.
deep-seat·ed (dēp′sē′tid) adj. Established far within; difficult to remove, as a fear or disease.
deep-set (dēp′set′) adj. 1. Deeply placed, as eyes.
Deep South The old cotton belt, including parts of South Carolina, Georgia, Alabama, Louisiana, and Mississippi.
deer (dir) n. pl. deer 1. Any of a family (Cervidae) of ruminant animals that typically have deciduous antlers, usually in the male only, as the moose, elk, and reindeer. ◆ Collateral adjective: cervine. 2. Any of the smaller species of similar animals. [OE dēor beast]
deer fly A bloodsucking fly (genus Chrysops), similar to a horsefly but smaller. For illustration see INSECTS (injurious).
deer·grass (dir′gras′, -gräs′) n. A forage grass (Muhlenbergia rigens) of Mexico and the SW United States.
deer·hound (dir′hound′) n. A breed of sporting dog, having a long, flat head and a shaggy, dark gray or brindle coat: also called staghound. Also **Scottish deerhound.**
deer lick U.S. A place where deer come to lick naturally or artificially salted earth.
deer mouse A species (Peromyscus maniculatus) of white-footed mice of North America.
deer·skin (dir′skin′) n. A deer's hide, or leather made from it.
deer·stalk·er (dir′stô′kər) n. 1. One who hunts deer by stalking. 2. A double-visored cloth cap with earflaps.
deer·weed (dir′wēd′) n. A branching, leguminous herb (Lotus scoparius) found in Arizona and southern California, sometimes used for cattle food. Also **deer′vetch′** (-vech′).
de·es·ca·late (dē-es′kə-lāt) v.t. & v.i. ·lat·ed, ·lat·ing To decrease or be decreased gradually, as in scope, effect, or intensity: to de-escalate a war. **— de·es′ca·la′tion** n.
dee·wan (di-wän′) See DEWAN.
def. 1. Defective. 2. Defendant. 3. Defense. 4. Deferred. 5. Defined. 6. Definite. 7. Definition.

DEERHOUND
(28 to 32 inches high at shoulder)

de·face (di-fās′) *v.t.* ·faced, ·fac·ing 1. To mar the surface or appearance of; disfigure. 2. To obliterate wholly or partially, as an inscription; efface. [< obs. F *defacer* < OF *desfacier* < des- down, away + *face* face < L *facies*] — de·face′a·ble *adj.* — de·face′ment *n.* — de·fac′er *n.*

de fac·to (dē fak′tō) *Latin* Actually or really existing, with or without legal sanction, as a government: distinguished from *de jure.*

de·fal·cate (di-fal′kāt) *v.i.* ·cat·ed, ·cat·ing To misappropriate; embezzle. [< Med.L *defalcatus*, pp. of *defalcare* to lop off < L *de-* down, away + *falx, falcis* scythe] — de·fal′ca·tor *n.*

de·fal·ca·tion (dē′fal-kā′shən) *n.* 1. A fraudulent appropriation of money held in trust; embezzlement; also, the amount. 2. *Obs.* A deducting or the amount deducted.

def·a·ma·tion (def′ə-mā′shən) *n.* The act of defaming; slander; aspersion; calumny. [< L *diffamatio, -onis* a speaking against < *diffamare*. See DEFAME.]

de·fam·a·to·ry (di-fam′ə-tôr′ē, -tō′rē) *adj.* Slanderous.

de·fame (di-fām′) *v.t.* ·famed, ·fam·ing 1. To attack the good name or reputation of; slander; libel. 2. *Obs.* To indict; accuse. — Syn. See ASPERSE. [< L *diffamare* < *dis-* away, from + *fama* a report, reputation] — de·fam′er *n.*

de·fault (di-fôlt′) *n.* 1. A failure or neglect to fulfill an obligation or requirement, as to pay money due, to appear in court, or to appear for or finish a contest. 2. *Obs.* A fault; transgression. — in default of Owing to lack or failure of. — *v.i.* 1. To fail to do or fulfill something required. 2. To fail to meet financial obligations. 3. *Law* To fail to appear in court; also, to lose a case by default. 4. In sports, to fail to compete or to complete a game, etc.; also, to lose or forfeit a game, etc., by default. — *v.t.* 5. To fail to perform or pay. 6. To declare in default, especially legally. 7. In sports, to fail to compete in, as a game; also, to forfeit by default. [< OF *defaut* < *defaillir* < L *de-* down + *fallere* to deceive] — de·fault′er (di-fôl′tər) *n.* 1. One who defaults; as: **a** One who fails to appear in court. **b** One who fails to account for trust money. **c** One who fails to pay debts. 2. *Brit.* A soldier who has committed an offense against military law.

de·fea·sance (di-fē′zəns) *n.* 1. A making null or void; an annulment. 2. *Law* A condition in a deed or collateral instrument by the performance of which the deed is rendered void. [< OF *defesance* an undoing < *desfaire*. See DEFEAT.]

de·fea·si·ble (di-fē′zə-bəl) *adj.* Capable of being rendered void. — de·fea′si·ble·ness, de·fea′si·bil′i·ty *n.*

de·feat (di-fēt′) *v.t.* 1. To overcome in any conflict or competition; vanquish. 2. To prevent the successful outcome of; baffle; thwart; frustrate: to *defeat* someone's purpose. 3. *Law* To make void; annul. 4. *Obs.* To destroy; ruin. — *n.* 1. The act or result of defeating; an overthrow; failure to win or succeed. 2. Frustration; bafflement. 3. *Law* An annulment. 4. *Obs.* Destruction. [< OF *defeit*, pp. of *desfaire* < *des-* not (< L *dis-*) + *faire* to do < L *facere*]

de·feat·ism (di-fē′tiz-əm) *n.* The policy, practice, or state of mind of those who are prone to accept defeat as inevitable. — de·feat′ist *n. & adj.*

def·e·cate (def′ə-kāt) *v.* ·cat·ed, ·cat·ing *v.i.* 1. To discharge excrement. 2. To become free of dregs. — *v.t.* 3. To clear of dregs or impurities; refine; purify. [< L *defaecatus*, pp. of *defaecare* < *de-* down, away + *faex* dregs] — def′e·ca′tion *n.* — def′e·ca′tor *n.*

de·fect (*n.* di-fekt′, dē′fekt; *v.* di-fekt′) *n.* 1. Lack of something necessary for perfection or completeness. 2. A blemish; failing; fault. — Syn. See BLEMISH. — *v.i.* To desert. [< L *defectus*, pp. of *deficere* to fail < *de-* not + *facere* to do]

de·fec·tion (di-fek′shən) *n.* 1. Abandonment of allegiance, duty, principles, etc.; apostasy; desertion. 2. Failure.

de·fec·tive (di-fek′tiv) *adj.* 1. Having a defect; imperfect; faulty. 2. *Gram.* Lacking one or more of the inflected forms normal for its class: *Can* is a *defective* verb. 3. *Psychol.* Having less than normal intelligence. — *n.* One who or that which is imperfect; especially, a mentally defective person. Abbr. *def.* — de·fec′tive·ly *adv.* — de·fec′tive·ness *n.*

de·fec·tor (di-fek′tər) *n.* One who deserts an allegiance, army, political party, etc.

de·fend (di-fend′) *v.t.* 1. To shield from danger, attack, or injury; protect. 2. To justify or vindicate; support. 3. *Law* **a** To act in behalf of (an accused). **b** To contest (a claim, charge, or suit). 4. *Obs.* To forbid. — *v.i.* 5. To make a defense. [< L *defendere* < *de-* down, away + *fendere* to strike] — de·fend′a·ble *adj.* — de·fend′er *n.*

de·fend·ant (di-fen′dənt) *n. Law* A person against whom an action is brought: opposed to *plaintiff.* Abbr. *def.* — *adj.* 1. Making a defense. 2. *Obs.* Defensive. [< F *défendant*, ppr. of *défendre* to defend]

Defender of the Faith The English form of the title *Fidei Defensor* given in 1521 by Pope Leo X to Henry VIII of England for writing against Luther, and still used by English sovereigns. Abbr. *D. F*

de·fen·es·tra·tion (dē-fen′ə-strā′shən) *n.* The act of throwing out of a window. [< L *de-* out of + *fenestra* window]

de·fense (di-fens′) *n.* 1. The act of defending against danger or attack; protection. 2. Anything that defends or serves to defend. 3. A plea or argument in justification or support of something. 4. *Law* **a** The defendant's denial of the validity or truth of a complaint; also, whatever is alleged or pleaded in such denial. **b** A defendant and his legal counsel, collectively. 5. The act or science of protecting oneself, one's side, or a goal, as in sports. Also *Brit.* de·fence′. Abbr. *def.* — Department of Defense An executive department of the U.S. government (established 1949), headed by the Secretary of Defense, that supervises military and civil defense operations. [< OF < L *defensus* pp. of *defendere*. See DEFEND.] — de·fense′less *adj.* — de·fense′less·ly *adv.* — de·fense′less·ness *n.*

defense mechanism 1. *Psychoanal.* An unconscious adjustment of behavior or mental attitude directed toward shutting out painful emotions and unacceptable impulses: also *escape mechanism.* 2. *Physiol.* Any self-protective reaction of an organism, as in resistance to bacteria.

de·fen·si·ble (di-fen′sə-bəl) *adj.* Capable of being defended, maintained, or justified. — de·fen′si·bil′i·ty, de·fen′si·ble·ness *n.* — de·fen′si·bly *adv.*

de·fen·sive (di-fen′siv) *adj.* 1. Intended or suitable for defense. 2. Carried on for the purpose of defense: distinguished from *offensive.* 3. Of or for defense: a *defensive* statement. 4. Having an attitude of defense. — *n.* 1. An attitude or position of defense. 2. A means of defense; safeguard. — de·fen′sive·ly *adv.* — de·fen′sive·ness *n.*

de·fer¹ (di-fûr′) *v.t. & v.i.* ·ferred, ·fer·ring To delay or put off to some other time; postpone. — Syn. See POSTPONE. [< OF *differer* < L *differre.* Doublet of DIFFER.] — de·fer′ra·ble *adj.*

de·fer² (di-fûr′) *v.i.* ·ferred, ·fer·ring To yield to the opinions or decisions of another: with *to.* [< MF *déférer* < L *deferre* < *de-* down + *ferre* to bear, carry] — de·fer′rer *n.* — Syn. *Defer, submit,* and *yield* agree in referring to the setting aside of our own views or wishes in favor of those of another. We *defer* to those whom we respect, and *submit* to those who have superior power or authority. We may *yield* for any reason, as from affection, persuasion, or compulsion. Compare OBEY, VENERATE.

def·er·ence (def′ər-əns) *n.* 1. Submission or yielding to the will, opinions, etc., of another. 2. Respectful regard. — Syn. *Deference, respect,* and *regard* characterize our attitude toward a person whom we honor. We give *deference* to one we consider superior in position, ability, or attainment. *Respect* is shown to those who are felt worthy, and *regard* for those who are admirable.

def·er·ent¹ (def′ər-ənt) *adj.* Deferential; respectful.

def·er·ent² (def′ər-ənt) *adj.* 1. Carrying off or away; also, adapted to carry or convey. 2. *Anat* Pertaining to certain ducts, as the vas deferens. — *n.* In the Ptolemaic system, the circle on the circumference of which the center of the epicycle was supposed to move. For illustration see EPICYCLE. [< L *deferens, -entis*, ppr. of *deferre.* See DEFER².]

def·er·en·tial (def′ə-ren′shəl) *adj.* Marked by deference; respectful; courteous. — def′er·en′tial·ly *adv.*

de·fer·ment (di-fûr′mənt) *n.* Act of deferring or delaying; postponement. Also de·fer′ral.

de·ferred (di-fûrd′) *adj.* 1. Postponed. 2. With benefits or payments held back for a specific time: *deferred* stock. 3. Temporarily exempted from military draft. Abbr. *def.*

de·fi (dā′fē) *n.* A defy.

de·fi·ance (di-fī′əns) *n.* 1. Bold opposition; disposition to oppose or resist; contemptuous disregard of authority or opposition. 2. A challenge to meet in combat.

de·fi·ant (di-fī′ənt) *adj.* Showing or characterized by defiance. [< OF, ppr. of *defier.* See DEFY.] — de·fi′ant·ly *adv.*

de·fi·cien·cy (di-fish′ən-sē) *n. pl.* ·cies 1. The state of being deficient. 2. A lack. Also *Rare* de·fi′cience.

deficiency disease *Pathol.* A disease, such as pellagra, rickets, scurvy, etc., caused by insufficiency or lack of some necessary dietary element in the body.

deficiency judgment *Law* A judgment in favor of a creditor for that amount of a debt, secured by a mortgage, not satisfied by foreclosure and sale.

de·fi·cient (di-fish′ənt) *adj.* 1. Lacking an adequate or proper supply; insufficient. 2. Lacking some essential; incomplete; imperfect; defective. [< L *deficiens, -entis*, ppr. of *deficere.* See DEFECT.] — de·fi′cient·ly *adv.*

def·i·cit (def′ə-sit) *n.* The amount by which an expected or required sum of money falls short. [< L, it is lacking]

deficit financing *Econ.* The practice of financing a national deficit by borrowing against the issue of government securities.

deficit spending *Econ.* The practice of spending in excess of income, especially by a government seeking to stimulate the economy.

de fi·de (dē fī′dē) *Latin* Of the faith: said of a teaching of the Roman Catholic Church.

de·fi·er (di-fī′ər) *n.* One who defies.

def·i·lade (def′ə-lād′) *v.t.* ·lad·ed, ·lad·ing *Mil.* To construct fortifications and arrange troops so as to give protection from enfilading fire or fire from nearby elevations. — *n.* 1. The act of defilading. 2. The protection offered by defilading. [< F *défilade* < *défiler* to unthread < *dé-* away (< L *dis-*) + *fil* thread < L *filum*]

de·file¹ (di-fīl′) *v.t.* ·**filed**, ·**fil·ing** 1. To make foul or dirty; pollute. 2. To tarnish or sully the brightness of; corrupt the purity of. 3. To sully or profane (a name, reputation, etc.). 4. To render ceremonially unclean. 5. To violate the chastity of. — **Syn.** See POLLUTE. [< OF *defouler* < *de-* down < L *de-*) + *fouler* to trample; infl. in form by ME *filen* to soil, OE *fȳlan* < *fūl* foul] — **de·file′ment** *n.* — **de·fil′er** *n.*

de·file² (di-fīl′, dē′fīl) *v.i.* ·**filed**, ·**fil·ing** To march in a line or by files. — *n.* 1. A long, narrow pass, as between mountains. 2. A marching in file. [< MF *défiler* < *dé-* down (< L *de-*) + *file* row]

de·fine (di-fīn′) *v.t.* ·**fined**, ·**fin·ing** 1. To state precisely the meaning of (a word, etc.). 2. To describe the nature or properties of; explain; interpret. 3. To determine the boundary or extent of. 4. To bring out the outline of; show clearly. 5. To fix with precision; specify, as the limits of power. — *v.i.* 6. To make definitions. [< OF *definer* < L *definire* < *de-* down + *finire* to finish < *finis* end] — **de·fin′a·ble** *adj.* — **de·fin′er** *n.*

def·i·nite (def′ə-nit) *adj.* 1. Having precise limits, quantity, etc.: a *definite* sum. 2. Known for certain; positive: It is *definite* that he won. 3. Clearly defined; explicit; precise. 4. *Gram.* Limiting; particularizing: the *definite* article. Abbr. *def.* 5. *Bot.* Determinate. [< L *definitus*, pp. of *definire*. See DEFINE.] — **def′i·nite·ly** *adv.* — **def′i·nite·ness** *n.* — **Syn.** 1. specific, particular. 2. clear, plain.

definite article *Gram.* In English, the article *the*, which limits or particularizes the noun before which it stands.

def·i·ni·tion (def′ə-nish′ən) *n.* 1. The act of stating what a word, phrase, set of terms, etc., means or signifies. 2. A statement of the meaning of a word, phrase, etc. 3. The determining of the outline or limits of anything. 4. The state of being clearly outlined or determined. 5. *Optics* The power of a lens to give a distinct image at whatever magnification. 6. *Telecom.* The clarity of detail in a televised image, or of sounds received in a radio set. Abbr. *def.* — Syn. See EXPLANATION.

de·fin·i·tive (di-fin′ə-tiv) *adj.* 1. Sharply defining or limiting; precise; explicit. 2. Bringing to an end; conclusive and unalterable; final. 3. Most nearly accurate and complete: a *definitive* edition of Chaucer. — *n. Gram.* A word that defines or limits, as the definite article. — **de·fin′i·tive·ly** *adv.* — **de·fin′i·tive·ness** *n.*

de·fin·i·tude (di-fin′ə-tōōd, -tyōōd) *n.* The quality of being definite; precision. [< L *definitus* definite + -TUDE]

def·la·grate (def′lə-grāt) *v.t. & v.i.* ·**grat·ed**, ·**grat·ing** To burn quickly with great heat and light. [< L *deflagratus*, pp. of *deflagrare* < *de-* completely + *flagrare* to burn] — **def·la·gra·ble** (def′lə-grə-bəl) *adj.* — **def′la·gra′tion** *n.*

de·flate (di-flāt′) *v.* ·**flat·ed**, ·**flat·ing** *v.t.* 1. To cause to collapse by removing contained air or gas. 2. To take the conceit, confidence, or self-esteem out of. 3. *Econ.* To reduce or restrict (money supply or spending) so that prices decline. — *v.i.* 4. To become deflated. [< L *deflatus*, pp. of *deflare* < *de-* down + *flare* to blow] — **de·fla′tor** *n.*

de·fla·tion (di-flā′shən) *n.* 1. The act of deflating, or the state of being deflated. 2. *Econ.* A decline in prices caused by a decrease in money supply or spending. Compare IN-FLATION. — **de·fla′tion·ar·y** (-er′ē) *adj.* — **de·fla′tion·ist** *n. & adj.*

de·flect (di-flekt′) *v.t. & v.i.* To turn aside; swerve or cause to swerve from a course. [< L *deflectere* < *de-* down + *flectere* to bend] — **de·flec′tive** *adj.* — **de·flec′tor** *n.*

de·flec·tion (di-flek′shən) *n.* 1. The act of deflecting, or the state of being deflected; deviation. 2. The amount of deviation. 3. *Physics* The deviation from zero of the indicator of an instrument, as of a galvanometer needle. Also *Brit.* **de·flex′ion.** — Syn. See DEVIATION.

def·lo·ra·tion (def′lə-rā′shən) *n.* 1. The act of deflowering. 2. A culling of the choicest part.

de·flow·er (di-flou′ər) *v.t.* 1. To despoil of flowers. 2. To deprive (a woman) of virginity. 3. To violate; rob of beauty, charm, etc. Also **de·flo·rate** (di-flôr′āte, -flō′rāte). [< OF *desflorer, desflouer* < LL *deflorare* < L *de-* down, away + *flos, floris* flower; infl. in form by *flower*]

de·flux·ion (di-fluk′shən) *n. Pathol.* The discharge of fluids, as in catarrh. [< LL *defluxio, -onis* < L *defluere* < *de-* down + *fluere* to flow]

De·foe (di-fō′), **Daniel,** 1660?–1731, English novelist and political journalist. Also **De Foe.**

de·fo·li·ate (dē-fō′lē-āt) *v.* ·**at·ed**, ·**at·ing** *v.t.* 1. To deprive or strip of leaves. 2. To lose leaves. [< Med.L *de-foliatus*, pp. of *defoliare* < L *de-* down + *folium* leaf] — **de·fo′li·a′tion** *n.* — **de·fo′li·a′tor** *n.*

de·force (di-fôrs′, -fōrs′) *v.t.* ·**forced**, ·**forc·ing** *Law* 1. To withhold (something) by force from lawful possession. 2. To prevent (someone) by force from obtaining lawful possession. [< AF *deforcer*, var. of OF *deforcier* < *de-* down, away (< L *de-*) + *forcier* to force] — **de·force′ment** *n.*

de·for·ciant (di-fôr′shənt, -fōr′-) *n. Law* A person chargeable with deforcement.

de·for·est (dē-fôr′ist, -for′-) *v.t.* To clear of forests or trees. — **de·for′es·ta′tion** *n.* — **de·for′est·er** *n.*

De For·est (di fôr′ist, for′-), **Lee,** 1873–1961, U.S. inventor; pioneer in radio transmission.

de·form (di-fôrm′) *v.t.* 1. To distort the form of; render misshapen. 2. To mar the beauty or excellence of; disfigure; spoil. 3. *Mech.* To cause to undergo deformation. — *v.i.* 4. To become deformed or disfigured. [< L *deformare* < *de-* away, down + *forma* figure, form] — **de·form′a·bil′i·ty** *n.* — **de·form′a·ble** *adj.* — **de·form′er** *n.*

de·for·ma·tion (dē′fôr·mā′shən, def′ər-) *n.* 1. The act of deforming, or the state of being deformed; distortion; disfigurement. 2. A change in form or condition for the worse. 3. An altered form or shape. 4. *Mech.* An alteration in the form of a body subjected to stress or pressure.

de·formed (di-fôrmd′) *adj.* 1. Marred in form; misshapen. 2. Morally distorted; perverted; warped. — **de·form·ed·ly** (di-fôr′mid-lē) *adv.* — **de·form′ed·ness** *n.*

de·form·i·ty (di-fôr′mə-tē) *n. pl.* ·**ties** 1. A deformed condition; disfigurement; unsightliness. 2. An abnormally shaped part, as of the body. 3. A deformed person or thing. 4. Moral defect; also, depravity. [< OF *deformite* < L *deformitas* < *deformis* < *de-* away, down + *forma* figure, form]

de·fraud (di-frôd′) *v.t.* To take or withhold from by fraud; cheat; swindle. [< OF *defrauder* < L *defraudare* < *de-* completely + *fraus, fraudis* a cheat] — **de·fraud·a·tion** (dē′frô-dā′shən), **de·fraud′ment** *n.* — **de·fraud′er** *n.*

de·fray (di-frā′) *v.t.* To pay (the costs, expenses, etc.). [< F *défrayer* < OF *defraier* < *de-* away (< L *de-*) + *fraier* to spend < *frai* cost, charge] — **de·fray′a·ble** *adj.* — **de·fray′al, de·fray′ment** *n.* — **de·fray′er** *n.*

de·frock (dē-frok′) *v.t.* To unfrock (which see).

de·frost (dē-frôst′, -frost′) *v.t.* To remove ice or frost from.

de·frost·er (dē-frôs′tər, -fros′-) *n.* A device for removing ice or frost, or for preventing their formation.

deft (deft) *adj.* Neat and skillful in action; dexterous; adroit. [OE *gedæfte* meek, gentle. Akin to DAFT.] — **deft′ly** *adv.* — **deft′ness** *n.*

de·funct (di-fungkt′) *adj.* Dead; deceased; extinct. — **Syn.** See LIFELESS. — **the defunct** The dead person. [< L *defunctus*, pp. of *defungi* < *de-* not + *fungi* to perform]

de·fy (*v.* di-fī′; *n.* dē′fī) *v.t.* ·**fied**, ·**fy·ing** 1. To resist or confront openly and boldly. 2. To resist or withstand successfully. 3. To challenge (someone) to do something; dare. 4. *Archaic* To invite to combat. — *n. pl.* ·**fies** *U.S.* A challenge; defiance: also *defi.* [< OF *defier* < M d.L *diffidare* < L *dis-* not + *fidare* to be faithful < *fidus* loyal]

deg. Degree(s).

dé·ga·gé (dā·gá·zhā′) *adj. French* Free or easy in manner.

de·ga·me (də·gä′mə) *n.* Lemonwood. [< Sp. *dagame* < native name]

de·gas (dē·gas′) *v.t.* ·**gassed**, ·**gas·sing**; he, she, or it **de·gas·ses** or **de·gas·es** 1. To remove noxious gas from (areas or persons). 2. To exhaust the gas from (electron tubes).

De·gas (də·gä′), **(Hilaire Germain) Edgar,** 1834–1917, French impressionist painter.

De Gas·pe·ri (dā gäs′pā·rē), **Alcide,** 1881–1954, Italian statesman; premier 1945.

de Gaulle (də·gôl′, *Fr.* də·gōl′), **Charles André Joseph Marie,** 1890–1970, French general and statesman; president 1944–45, 1959–1969.

de·gauss (dē·gous′) *v.t.* To make (a ship) safe against the action of magnetic mines, especially by the use of a **degaussing cable** fitted around the hull to neutralize the magnetic field set up by the ship. [< DE- + GAUSS]

de·gen·er·a·cy (di·jen′ər·ə·sē) *n.* 1. The process of degenerating; deterioration. 2. The state of being degenerate.

de·gen·er·ate (*v.* di·jen′ə·rāt; *adj., n.* di·jen′ər·it) *v.i.* ·**at·ed**, ·**at·ing** 1. To become worse, inferior, or more debased. 2. *Biol.* To revert to a lower type; decline; deteriorate. — **Syn.** See RETROGRESS. — *adj.* Having become worse, inferior, or debased; degraded. — *n.* 1. A deteriorated or degraded individual, animal or human. 2. A morally degraded person. [< L *degeneratus*, pp. of *degenerare* < *de-* down, away + *generare* to create] — **de·gen′er·ate·ly** *adv.* — **de·gen′er·ate·ness** *n.*

de·gen·er·a·tion (di·jen′ə·rā′shən) *n.* 1. The process of degenerating. 2. A degenerate condition. 3. *Biol.* The gradual reversion of a group of organisms into a less complex type. 4. *Pathol.* Progressive deterioration of an organ, tissue, or part. 5. *Telecom.* A reduction of signal strength by feedback: compare REGENERATION.

de·gen·er·a·tive (di·jen′ə·rā′tiv, -ər·ə·tiv) *adj.* Causing, exhibiting, or tending to degeneration.

de·glu·ti·nate (dē·glōō′tə·nāt) *v.t.* ·**nat·ed**, ·**nat·ing** To remove the gluten from (wheat, etc.). — **de·glu′ti·na′tion** *n.*

de·glu·ti·tion (dē′glōō·tish′ən) *n. Physiol.* 1. The act of swallowing. 2. The ability to swallow. [< F *déglutition* < L *deglutitio, -onis* < *de-* down + *glutire* to swallow]

deg·ra·da·tion (deg′rə·dā′shən) *n.* 1. The act of degrading. 2. The state of being reduced in rank, honor, quality etc. 3. *Geol.* Disintegration of the earth's surfaces by erosion.

de·grade (di·grād′) *v.t.* **·grad·ed**, **·grad·ing 1.** To debase or lower in character, morals, etc. **2.** To bring into contempt; dishonor. **3.** To reduce in rank; remove from office, dignity, etc. **4.** To reduce in quality, intensity, etc. **5.** *Biol.* To reduce from a higher to a lower type. **6.** *Geol.* To reduce the height of by erosion. — **Syn.** See ABASE. [< OF *degrader* < LL *degradi* < L *de-* down + *gradi* to step]

de·grad·ed (di·grā′did) *adj.* Deteriorated; debased. — **de·grad′ed·ly** *adv.* — **de·grad′ed·ness** *n.*

de·grad·ing (di·grā′ding) *adj.* Debasing; humiliating. — **de·grad′ing·ly** *adv.* — **de·grad′ing·ness** *n.*

de·gree (di·grē′) *n.* **1.** One of a succession of steps or stages. **2.** Relative extent, amount, or intensity. **3.** Relative dignity or rank; social or official position. **4.** Relative condition, manner, or respect. **5.** An academic title conferred by an institution of learning upon the completion of a course of study, or as an honorary distinction. **6.** A division or unit of a scale for measurement, as of a thermometer. **7.** A step in a line of genealogical descent or consanguinity. **8.** *Law* Measure of culpability, in U.S. law fixed by statute with specific maximum punishments: murder in the first *degree*. **9.** *Geom.* One 360th of the circumference of a circle; one 90th of a right angle. **10.** *Math.* **a** The sum of the exponents of the unknowns (or variables) of an algebraic term: x^3 and xy^2 are both of the third *degree*. **b** The exponent of the highest degree term in a polynomial or equation: $x^4 + 2x^3$ is of the fourth *degree*. **11.** *Geog.* A line or point of the earth's surface defined by its angular distance from 0° to 180° east or west of a standard meridian, or from 0° to 90° north or south of the equator. **12.** *Astron.* Any of two similar sets of lines or points on the celestial sphere. **13.** *Gram.* One of the forms of comparison (positive, comparative, or superlative) of an adjective or adverb. **14.** *Music* **a** A single note of a scale. **b** The interval between consecutive tones of a scale, especially the diatonic. **c** A line or space in a staff. Abbr. *d.*, *D.*, *deg.* — **by degrees** Little by little; gradually. — **to a degree 1.** Somewhat. **2.** Greatly. [< OF *degre* < *de-* down (< L *de-*) + *gre* < L *gradus* a step]

de·gree-day (di·grē′dā′) *n.* A unit representing a declination in the mean outside temperature for one day of one degree from a standard temperature of (about) 65° F., used to estimate fuel requirements in the heating of buildings.

degree mill *U.S.* A quasi-educational organization that confers degrees without the usual requirements.

degree of freedom 1. *Stat.* One of the free (randomly sampled) variables entering into a statistic. **2.** Variance (def. 5).

de·gres·sion (di·gresh′ən) *n.* **1.** Decrease by steps; descent. **2.** The decreasing of the tax rate in degressive taxation. [< LL *degressio*, *-onis* < *degradi.* See DEGRADE.]

de·gres·sive taxation (di·gres′iv) Taxation in which the tax rate is constant on sums over a certain amount but decreases as sums decrease below this amount.

de·gum (dē·gum′) *v.t.* **·gummed**, **·gum·ming** To free from gum.

de·gust (di·gust′) *v.t. & v.i. Rare* To taste, especially with care. Also **de·gus′tate.** [< L *degustare* < *de-* completely + *gustare* to taste] — **de′gus·ta′tion** *n.*

de gus·ti·bus non est dis·pu·tan·dum (dē gus′ti·bəs non est dis′pyōō·tan′dəm) *Latin* There is no disputing about tastes.

de·hisce (di·his′) *v.i.* **·hisced**, **·hisc·ing** To split open, as the capsule of a plant. [< L *dehiscere* < *de-* down + *hiscere*, inceptive of *hiare* to gape, yawn]

de·his·cence (di·his′əns) *n. Biol.* A splitting open, as of a capsule when discharging seeds.

de·his·cent (di·his′ənt) *adj.* Bursting open; gaping.

de·horn (dē·hôrn′) *v.t.* To remove the horns of (cattle).

de·hort (di·hôrt′) *v.t. Obs.* To try to divert by persuasion; deter. [< L *dehortari* < *de-* away + *hortari* to entreat, urge] — **de·hor·ta·tion** (dē′hôr·tā′shən) *n.* — **de·hor·ta·to·ry** (di·hôr′tə·tôr′ē, -tō′rē), **de·hor′ta·tive** *adj.*

de·hu·man·ize (dē·hyōō′mən·īz) *v.t.* **·ized**, **·iz·ing 1.** To divest or deprive of human qualities or attributes; make brutelike. **2.** To make mechanical, abstract, or artificial. — **de·hu′man·i·za′tion** *n.*

de·hu·mid·i·fi·er (dē′hyōō·mid′ə·fī′ər) *n.* An apparatus by which moisture is removed from the air.

de·hu·mid·i·fy (dē′hyōō·mid′ə·fī) *v.t.* **·fied**, **·fy·ing** To render less humid; remove moisture from. — **de·hu·mid′i·fi·ca′tion** *n.*

de·hy·drate (dē·hī′drāt) *v.* **·drat·ed**, **·drat·ing** *v.t.* **1.** To deprive of water, as a chemical compound. **2.** To remove water from, as vegetables, so as to preserve. — *v.i.* **3.** To suffer loss of water; dry up. — **de′hy·dra′tion** *n.*

de·hy·dro·gen·ize (dē·hī′drə·jən·īz′) *v.t.* **·ized**, **·iz·ing** *Chem.* To remove hydrogen from (a compound).

de·hyp·no·tize (dē·hip′nə·tīz) *v.t.* **·tized**, **·tiz·ing** To awaken (a person) from the hypnotic state.

De·ia·ni·ra (dē′yə·nī′rə) In Greek mythology, the wife of Hercules. See NESSUS.

de·ice (dē·īs′) *v.t.* **·iced**, **·ic·ing** To free from ice.

de·ic·er (dē·ī′sər) *n.* A mechanical or thermal device which breaks up formations of ice, as on an airplane wing.

de·i·cide (dē′ə·sīd) *n.* **1.** The killing of a god. **2.** The slayer of a god. [< L *deus* god + -CIDE]

deic·tic (dīk′tik) *adj.* **1.** *Logic* Proving by direct argument: distinguished from *elenctic.* **2.** *Gram.* Demonstrative: a *deictic* pronoun. [< Gk. *deiktikos* able to show < *deiknynai* to show, prove] — **deic′ti·cal·ly** *adv.*

de·if·ic (dē·if′ik) *adj.* **1.** Making, or tending to make, divine. **2.** Divine. Also **de·if′i·cal.**

de·i·fi·ca·tion (dē′ə·fə·kā′shən) *n.* **1.** The act of deifying, or the state of being deified. **2.** One who or that which is or has been deified.

de·i·form (dē′ə·fôrm) *adj.* In the form of a god; like a god. [< Med.L *deiformis* < L *deus* god + *forma* form]

de·i·fy (dē′ə·fī) *v.t.* **·fied**, **·fy·ing 1.** To make a god of; rank as a deity. **2.** To regard or worship as a god. **3.** To glorify, exalt, or idealize: to *deify* the masses. [< F *déifier* < LL *deificare* < L *deus* god + *facere* to make] — **de′i·fi′er** *n.*

deign (dān) *v.i.* **1.** To think it befitting oneself (to do something); condescend. — *v.t.* **2.** To condescend to grant or allow: He *deigned* no reply. **3.** *Obs.* To condescend to accept. [< OF *deignier* < L *dignari* < *dignus* worthy]

De·i gra·ti·a (dē′ī grā′shē·ə, dā′ē grā′tē·ä) *Latin* By the grace of God. Abbr. *D.G.*

deil (dēl) *n. Scot.* **1.** The devil. **2.** A mischievous fellow.

De·iph·o·bus (dē·if′ə·bəs) In Greek legend, a son of Priam who married Helen after Paris was killed; slain by Menelaus.

deip·nos·o·phist (dīp·nos′ə·fist) *n.* One who talks learnedly at the table: from the *Deipnosophistae* by the third-century Greek author Athenaeus. [< Gk. *deipnosophistēs* < *deipnon* dinner + *sophistēs* a wise man < *sophia* wisdom]

de·ip·o·tent (dē·ip′ə·tənt) *adj.* Having divine power.

Deir·dre (dir′drə) In Irish legend, the heroine who killed herself after her lover, Naoise, had been murdered by King Conchobar.

de·ism (dē′iz·əm) *n.* **1.** Belief in the existence of a personal God, based solely on the testimony of reason and rejecting supernatural revelation; natural religion. **2.** Belief that God created the world and set it in motion, subject to natural laws, but takes no interest in it. Compare PANTHEISM, THEISM. [< L *deus* a god + -ISM] — **de·is′tic** or **·ti·cal** *adj.* — **de·is′ti·cal·ly** *adv.*

de·ist (dē′ist) *n.* One who subscribes to or professes deism.

de·i·ty (dē′ə·tē) *n. pl.* **·ties 1.** A god, goddess, or divine person. **2.** Divine nature or status; godhead; divinity. — **the Deity** God. [< F *déité* < LL *deitas* < L *deus* a god]

dé·jà vu (dā·zhà vü′) *Psychol.* A distortion of memory in which a new situation or experience is regarded as having happened before. [< F, lit., already seen]

de·ject (di·jekt′) *v.t.* **1.** To depress in spirit; dishearten. **2.** *Archaic* To throw down. — *adj. Archaic* Dejected. [< L *dejectus*, pp. of *dejicere* < *de-* down + *jacere* to throw]

de·jec·ta (di·jek′tə) *n.pl. Med.* Excrements.

de·ject·ed (di·jek′tid) *adj.* Depressed in spirits; disheartened. — **de·ject′ed·ly** *adv.* — **de·ject′ed·ness** *n.*

de·jec·tion (di·jek′shən) *n.* **1.** A state or condition of being dejected; lowness of spirits; depression; melancholy. **2.** *Med.* **a** Evacuation of the bowels. **b** Excrement.

dé·jeu·ner (dā·zhœ·nā′) *n.* **1.** A late breakfast. **2.** Luncheon. [< F, breakfast < *dé-* away (< L *de-*) + *jeun* fasting < L *jejunus* empty, barren]

de ju·re (dē jōōr′ē) *Latin* By right; rightfully or legally: distinguished from *de facto.*

deka- *combining form* In the metric system, ten times (a specified unit): *dekagram.* Also, before vowels, **dek-.** [< Gk. *deka* ten]

dek·a·gram (dek′ə·gram) *n.* In the metric system, a measure of weight equal to 10 grams: also spelled *decagram.* Also **dek′a·gramme.** Abbr. *dkg*, *dkg.* See table inside back cover.

De Kalb (di kalb′), **Baron Johann**, 1721–80, French general born in Germany; served in the American Revolution.

dek·a·li·ter (dek′ə·lē′tər) *n.* In the metric system, a measure of capacity equal to 10 liters: also spelled *decaliter.* Also *esp. Brit.* **dek′a·li′tre.** Abbr. *dal*, *dal.*, *dkl*, *dkl.* See table inside back cover.

dek·a·me·ter (dek′ə·mē′tər) *n.* In the metric system, a measure of length equal to 10 meters: also spelled *decameter.* Also *esp. Brit.* **dek′a·me′tre.** Abbr. *dkm*, *dkm.*, *dm*, *dm.* See table inside back cover.

dek·are (dek′âr) *n.* In the metric system, a thousand square meters or 10 ares: also spelled *decare.*

dek·a·stere (dek′ə·stir) *n.* In the metric system, a measure of volume equal to 10 steres: also spelled *decastere.* Abbr. *dks*, *dks.*

deke (dēk) *v.t.* **deked**, **dek·ing** *Canadian Slang* In hockey, to draw (a defensive player) out of position by a feint. [< DECOY]

Dek·ker (dek′ər), **Thomas**, 1572?–1632?, English dramatist. Also *Decker.*

De Ko·ven (di kō′vən), **(Henry Louis) Reginald**, 1859–1920, U.S. composer, critic, and conductor.

de Kruif (də krīf′), **Paul**, 1890–1971, U.S. bacteriologist and writer.

del. 1. Delegate. 2. Delete. 3. Delineavit. 4. Deliver.

Del. Delaware.

De·la·croix (də·là·krwä′), **(Ferdinand Victor) Eugène**, 1799–1863, French painter.

Del·a·go·a Bay (del′ə·gō′ə) An inlet of the Indian Ocean in the south coast of Mozambique; length, 55 mi.

de·laine (də·lān′) n. A light wool, or cotton and wool, dress fabric. [< F (mousseline) de laine (muslin) of wool]

De la Mare (də lə mâr′, del′ə·mâr), **Walter (John)**, 1873–1956, English poet and novelist.

de·lam·i·nate (dē·lam′i·nāt) v.t. & v.i. ·nat·ed, ·nat·ing To split into thin layers.

de·lam·i·na·tion (dē·lam′i·nā′shən) n. Biol. A splitting into layers: said especially of the separation of the blastoderm into two layers of cells.

De·la·roche (də·là·rôsh′), **Hippolyte Paul**, 1797–1856, French painter.

de·late (di·lāt′) v.t. ·lat·ed, ·lat·ing 1. Scot. To bring a charge against; accuse. 2. To publish or spread abroad. [< L delatus, pp. of deferre to bring down, denounce. See DEFER[2].] **— de·la′tion** n. **— de·la′tor** n.

De·la·vigne (də·là·vēn′y′), **(Jean François) Casimir**, 1793–1843, French poet and dramatist.

Del·a·ware (del′ə·wâr) n. 1. A confederacy of Algonquian tribes of North American Indians, formerly occupying the whole Delaware River valley. 2. The language of these people. Also called Lenape, Leni-Lenape, Lenni-Lenape. **— Del′a·war′e·an** adj.

Del·a·ware (del′ə·wâr) n. A small, sweet, reddish, hybrid grape. ⌈after Delaware⌉

Del·a·ware (del′ə·wâr) n. 1. A State of the United States; 1,978 sq. mi.; pop. 548,104; capital, Dover; entered the Union Dec. 7, 1787, one of the original thirteen States: nickname Diamond State. Abbr. Del. 2. An urban township in NW New Jersey; pop. 31,522.

Delaware Bay An inlet of the Atlantic Ocean between Delaware and New Jersey.

Delaware River A river separating Pennsylvania and Delaware from New York and New Jersey, flowing SE 315 miles to Delaware Bay.

Delaware Water Gap A resort borough in eastern Pennsylvania, located at the scenic gorge of the same name where the Delaware River cuts through the Kittatinny Mountains.

De La Warr (del′ə·wâr, Brit. -wər), **Baron**, 1577–1618, Thomas West, English administrator; first colonial governor of Virginia: called **Lord Delaware**. Also **Del′a·ware**.

de·lay (di·lā′) v.t. 1. To put off to a future time; postpone; defer. 2. To cause to be late; detain. **— v.i.** 3. To linger; procrastinate. **— n.** 1. The act of delaying. 2. The fact or condition of being delayed. [< OF delaier] **— de·lay′er** n.

de·layed-ac·tion (di·lād′ak′shən) adj. Designating a kind of bomb, fuse, or mine designed to explode at a set time after it has been armed or put into action.

Del·cas·sé (del·kà·sā′), **Théophile**, 1852–1923, French statesman.

de·le (dē′lē) v.t. ·led, ·le·ing Printing To take out; delete: usually an imperative represented by a sign (ϑ). Compare STET. [< L, imperative of delere to erase]

de·lec·ta·ble (di·lek′tə·bəl) adj. Giving great pleasure; delightful. [< OF < L delectabilis < delectare. See DELIGHT.] **— de·lec′ta·ble·ness, de·lec′ta·bil′i·ty** n. **— de·lec′ta·bly** adv.

de·lec·tate (di·lek′tāt) v.t. ·tat·ed, ·tat·ing To charm; delight. [< L delectatus, pp. of delectare. See DELIGHT.]

de·lec·ta·tion (dē′lek·tā′shən) n. Delight; enjoyment; amusement. **— Syn.** See PLEASURE.

De·led·da (dā·led′dä), **Grazia**, 1875–1936, Italian novelist.

del·e·ga·cy (del′ə·gə·sē) n. pl. ·cies 1. The act of delegating, or the state of being delegated. 2. The office or authority given a delegate. 3. A body of delegates.

del·e·gate (n. del′ə·gāt, -git; v. del′ə·gāt) n. 1. A person sent with authority to represent or act for another or others; a deputy; representative. 2. U.S. a A person elected or appointed to represent a Territory in the House of Representatives, where he has the right to speak but not to vote. b A member of the lower house (House of Delegates) of the legislature in Maryland, Virginia, and West Virginia. Compare BURGESS. Abbr. del. **— v.t.** ·gat·ed, ·gat·ing 1. To send as a representative, with authority to act; depute. 2. To commit or entrust (powers, authority, etc.) to another as an agent or representative. 3. To assign (a debtor of one's own) to one's creditor to satisfy a claim. [< L delegatus, pp. of delegare < de- down + legare to send] **— Syn.** (noun) 1. Delegate, deputy, representative, proxy, and substitute denote a person who takes the place of another. A delegate usually transmits the views or decisions of his principal, with little voice in them: a delegate to the United Nations; a deputy usually acts for another in the latter's absence. Both delegate and deputy are also used in the sense of representative, the general term for an elected legislator. We speak of representatives in Congress, deputies in the French national assembly, and delegates to a national convention. Proxy is chiefly applied to one who is empowered to cast another's vote, as in a legislature or a stockholders' meeting. A substitute, in most contexts, replaces another and acquires all his rights and responsibilities: a substitute in a ball game.

del·e·ga·tion (del′ə·gā′shən) n. 1. The act of delegating, or the state of being delegated; deputation. 2. A person or persons appointed to represent others; delegates collectively.

de·len·da est Car·tha·go (di·len′də est kär·thä′gō) Latin Carthage must be destroyed: ascribed to Cato the Elder.

de·lete (di·lēt′) v.t. ·let·ed, ·let·ing To take out (written or printed matter); cancel. Abbr. del. **— Syn.** See CANCEL. [< L deletus, pp. of delere to erase, destroy]

del·e·te·ri·ous (del′ə·tir′ē·əs) adj. Causing moral or physical injury; hurtful. **— Syn.** See PERNICIOUS. [< NL deleterius < Gk. dēlētērios < dēleesthai to hurt] **— del′e·te′ri·ous·ly** adv. **— del′e·te′ri·ous·ness** n.

de·le·tion (di·lē′shən) n. 1. The act of deleting, or the fact of being deleted. 2. Erased or canceled matter.

Del·fi (del′fī) See DELPHI.

delft (delft) n. 1. A glazed earthenware, usually white or blue, first made at Delft, Holland, about 1310. 2. Any tableware resembling this. Also **delf** (delf), **delft′ware′**.

Delft (delft) A commune in the western Netherlands; pop. 83,700 (est. 1970).

Del·ga·do (del·gä′dō), **Cape** A headland of northernmost Mozambique.

Del·hi (del′ē) 1. A territory of NE central India containing New Delhi; 573 sq. mi. 2. Its capital, the capital of India from 1912–1931; pop. (including New Delhi) 3,469,698 (1968). Also Old Delhi.

De·li·an (dē′lē·ən) adj. Of or pertaining to Delos. **— n.** A native or inhabitant of Delos.

de·lib·er·ate (v. di·lib′ə·rāt; adj. di·lib′ər·it) v. ·at·ed, ·at·ing v.i. 1. To consider carefully and at length. 2. To take counsel together so as to reach a decision. **— v.t.** 3. To think about or consider carefully; weigh. **— adj.** 1. Carefully thought out; intentional. 2. Slow and cautious in determining or deciding. 3. Leisurely in movement or manner; unhurried; slow. [< L deliberatus, pp. of deliberare < de- completely + librare to weigh < libra a scale] **— de·lib′er·ate·ly** adv. **— de·lib′er·ate·ness** n. **— Syn.** (verb) 1. Deliberate, ponder, reflect, meditate, and muse mean to think deeply, usually in silence. Deliberate emphasizes slowness; ponder is literally to weigh or judge, and suggests the careful consideration of all possibilities, and comparison of their individual merits. To reflect is to turn the mind back to past events. We ponder a course of action, but reflect over the meaning of a statement. Meditate implies clearness of purpose or organization of thought about some central idea, while muse suggests absence of a fixed aim and freely wandering thoughts: to meditate on virtue, to muse on love. 2. consult, confer, argue, debate.

de·lib·er·a·tion (di·lib′ə·rā′shən) n. 1. Careful and prolonged consideration. 2. Often pl. Examination and discussion of the arguments for and against a measure. 3. Slowness and care in decision or action.

de·lib·er·a·tive (di·lib′ə·rā′tiv, -rə·tiv) adj. 1. Involved in deliberation: a deliberative body. 2. Characterized by deliberation; having the form of, or a place in, argument or debate: a deliberative speech.

De·libes (də·lēb′), **(Clément Philibert) Léo**, 1836–91, French composer.

del·i·ca·cy (del′ə·kə·sē) n. pl. ·cies 1. The quality of being delicate; fineness of texture, construction, finish, etc. 2. Frailty or weakness of body or health. 3. Refinement of feeling, manner, appreciation, etc.; sensitivity. 4. Consideration for the feelings of others. 5. Nicety of touch or execution. 6. Sensitivity in reaction, as of instruments. 7. Need of cautious, tactful treatment: a subject of great delicacy. 8. Something choice and dainty, as an item of food. 9. Obs. Voluptuousness; luxuriousness.

del·i·cate (del′ə·kit) adj. 1. Exquisite and fine in workmanship, texture, shape, etc. 2. Daintily pleasing, as in taste, aroma, or color; soft; light. 3. Easily injured or destroyed; fragile; frail. 4. Requiring tactful treatment: a delicate topic. 5. Gentle and skilled: a delicate touch. 6. Sensitive and subtle in feeling, perception, or expression: a delicate eye for color. 7. Showing a fine appreciation for what is proper and becoming; modest; seemly: delicate manners. 8. Considerate of the feelings of others. 9. Sensitively accurate: a delicate thermometer. 10. Barely perceptible; subtle: a delicate distinction. 11. Obs. Voluptuous; luxurious. **— n.** Obs. A delight; a luxury. [< L delicatus pleasing] **— del′i·cate·ly** adv. **— del′i·cate·ness** n.

del·i·ca·tes·sen (del′ə·kə·tes′ən) n.pl. 1. (often construed as sing.) Cooked or preserved foods, as cooked meats, canned goods, salads, cheeses, pickles, etc. 2. (construed as sing.) A store that sells such foods. [< G, pl. of delicatesse delicacy]

de·li·cious (di·lish′əs) adj. Extremely pleasant or enjoyable; affording great pleasure, especially to the taste. [< OF < LL deliciosus < L delicia delight] **— de·li′cious·ly** adv. **— de·li′cious·ness** n. **— Syn.** Both delicious and luscious refer primarily to something pleasant to the taste, but are extended to the other senses as well. We speak of a delicious meal or a delicious piece of music of a luscious dessert or a person's *luscious* appearance. *Delicious* suggests a refined taste; *luscious*, something that is excessively sweet. Compare PLEASANT, SAVORY. — **Ant.** unsavory, unpalatable.

De·li·cious (di-lish'əs) *n.* A cultivated North American variety of sweet, red apple.

de·lict (di-likt') *n.* In civil law, a crime; misdemeanor; tort. [< L *delictum* < *delinquere*. See DELINQUENT.]

de·light (di-līt') *n.* 1. Great pleasure; gratification; joy. 2. That which gives extreme pleasure. 3. *Poetic* The quality of delighting; charm. — *v.i.* 1. To take great pleasure; rejoice: with *in* or the infinitive. 2. To give great enjoyment. — *v.t.* 3. To please or gratify highly. [< OF *delit* < *deliter* < L *delectare*, freq. of *delicere* < *de-* away + *lacere* to entice] — **Syn.** (noun) See PLEASURE. — (verb) please, charm, entertain. — **Ant.** (noun) disappointment, distress. — (verb) displease.

de·light·ed (di-lī'tid) *adj.* 1. Highly pleased; joyfully gratified. 2. *Obs.* Delightful. — **de·light'ed·ly** *adv.*

de·light·ful (di-līt'fəl) *adj.* Affording delight; extremely pleasing. — **de·light'ful·ly** *adv.* — **de·light'ful·ness** *n.* — **Syn.** pleasant, pleasing, pleasurable, agreeable, charming.

de·light·some (di-līt'səm) *adj.* *Archaic* Delightful. — **de·light'some·ly** *adv.* — **de·light'some·ness** *n.*

De·li·lah (di-lī'lə) A Philistine woman, the mistress of Samson, who betrayed him to the Philistines by cutting off his hair, thus depriving him of his strength. *Judg.* xvi 4–20. — *n.* A voluptuous but treacherous woman.

de·lim·it (di-lim'it) *v.t.* To prescribe the limits of; bound. Also **de·lim'i·tate**. [< F *délimiter* < L *delimitare* < *de-* completely + *limitare* to bound < *limes* boundary] — **de·lim'i·ta'tion** *n.* — **de·lim'i·ta·tive** *adj.*

de·lin·e·ate (di-lin'ē-āt) *v.t.* **·at·ed**, **·at·ing** 1. To draw in outline; trace out. 2. To represent by a drawing; depict. 3. To portray verbally; describe. [< L *delineatus*, pp. of *delineare* < *de-* completely + *lineare* to draw a line < *linea* a line] — **de·lin'e·a·tive** *adj.*

de·lin·e·a·tion (di-lin'ē-ā'shən) *n.* 1. The act or art of delineating. 2. A representation either by word or pictorial image.

de·lin·e·a·tor (di-lin'ē-ā'tər) *n.* 1. One who sketches or delineates. 2. A tailor's adjustable pattern for cutting garments of various sizes.

de·lin·e·a·vit (di-lin'ē-ā·vit) *Latin* He (or she) drew it.

de·lin·quen·cy (di-ling'kwən-sē) *n.* *pl.* **·cies** 1. Neglect of duty; failure to do what is required. 2. A fault; offense; misdemeanor. 3. Juvenile delinquency (which see).

de·lin·quent (di-ling'kwənt) *adj.* 1. Neglectful of or failing in duty or obligation; guilty of an offense. 2. Due and unpaid, as taxes. — *n.* 1. One who fails to perform a duty or who commits a fault. 2. A juvenile delinquent (which see). [< L *delinquens*, *-entis*, pp. of *delinquere* < *de-* down, away + *linquere* to leave] — **de·lin'quent·ly** *adv.*

del·i·quesce (del'ə·kwes') *v.i.* **·quesced**, **·quesc·ing** 1. To melt or pass away gradually. 2. To become liquid by absorption of moisture from the air, as certain salts. 3. *Bot.* **a** To become lost by repeated branching, as stems. **b** To become fluid at maturity, as certain fungi. [< L *deliquescere* < *de-* completely + *liquescere* to melt]

del·i·ques·cence (del'ə·kwes'əns) *n.* 1. The act or process of deliquescing. 2. The liquid that results from deliquescing. — **del'i·ques'cent** *adj.*

del·i·ra·tion (del'ə·rā'shən) *n.* Mental derangement; delirium. [< L *deliratio*, *-onis* < *delirare*. See DELIRIUM.]

de·lir·i·ous (di-lir'ē-əs) *adj.* 1. Suffering from delirium; raving. 2. Characteristic of delirium: *delirious* dreams. 3. Wildly excited: *delirious* with joy. — **de·lir'i·ous·ly** *adv.* — **de·lir'i·ous·ness** *n.*

de·lir·i·um (di-lir'ē-əm) *n.* 1. A sporadic or temporary mental disturbance associated with fever, intoxication, shock, or injury and marked by restlessness, excitement, hallucinations, and general incoherence. 2. Wild emotion or excitement. — **Syn.** See FRENZY. [< L *delirare* to be deranged < *de-* down, away + *lira* furrow, track]

delirium tre·mens (trē'mənz) A violent form of delirium caused especially by excessive use of alcoholic liquors and narcotic drugs, and characterized by tremblings, acute mental distress, and hallucinations. Abbr. *d.t.* [< NL, trembling delirium]

del·i·tes·cent (del'ə·tes'ənt) *adj.* Concealed; latent. [< L *delitescens*, *-entis*, ppr. of *delitescere* < *de-* away + *litescere*, inceptive of *latere* to lie hidden] — **del'i·tes'cence** *n.*

De·li·us (dē'lē-əs, dēl'yəs) Frederick, 1862–1934, English composer.

de·liv·er (di-liv'ər) *v.t.* 1. To hand over; give up; transfer; surrender. 2. To carry and distribute: to *deliver* newspapers. 3. To give forth; send forth; emit; discharge: to *deliver* a blow. 4. To give forth in words; utter. 5. To throw or pitch: to *deliver* a ball. 6. To free from restraint, evil, danger, etc.; set free; rescue. 7. To relieve of offspring in childbirth; also, to assist in the birth of (offspring). — **to be delivered of** To give birth. — **to deliver oneself of** To put into words; express. — *adj.* *Archaic* Nimble; active. [< OF

délivrer < LL *deliberare* < L *de-* down, away + *liberare* to set free < *liber* free] — **de·liv'er·a·ble** *adj.* — **de·liv'er·er** *n.* — **Syn.** (verb) 1. give, cede. 3. fire, emit. 6. release, liberate.

de·liv·er·ance (di-liv'ər-əns) *n.* 1. The act of delivering, or the state of being delivered. 2. An expression of opinion.

de·liv·er·y (di-liv'ər-ē) *n.* *pl.* **·er·ies** 1. The act of delivering or distributing something. 2. That which is distributed, as mail. 3. The act of setting free or liberating; release; rescue. 4. A transferring or handing over. 5. The bringing forth of offspring; parturition. 6. Manner of utterance, as in public speaking. 7. The act or manner of giving forth or discharging a ball, a blow, etc. 8. *Law* The transfer of a deed, etc. Abbr. *dlvy.*

de·liv·er·y·man (di-liv'ər-ē-man') *n.* *pl.* **·men** (-men') A man who delivers merchandise to stores or consumers, especially according to a regular schedule.

dell (del) *n.* A small, secluded, usually wooded valley; glen; dale. [ME. Akin to DALE.]

del·la Rob·bia (del'lä rôb'byä) See ROBBIA.

dells (delz) *n.pl.* Dalles.

Del·mar·va Peninsula (del·mär'və) A peninsula between Chesapeake and Delaware bays, including Delaware and parts of Maryland and Virginia.

de·lo·cal·ize (dē-lō'kəl-īz) *v.t.* **·ized**, **·iz·ing** 1. To remove from a locality. 2. To free from local and limiting influences; enlarge the scope of. — **de·lo'cal·i·za'tion** *n.*

De Long (də lông'), **George Washington**, 1844–81, U.S. Arctic explorer.

De·lorme (də-lôrm'), **Marion**, 1612?–50, French courtesan. Also **de Lorme**. — Philibert, 1510–70, French court architect. Also **de l'Orme**.

De·los (dē'los) The smallest island of the Cyclades, Greece; 1.2 sq. mi.; regarded as the birthplace of Apollo and Artemis. Greek *Dhilos*.

de·louse (dē-lous') *v.t.* **·loused**, **·lous·ing** To remove lice or other insect vermin from.

Del·phi (del'fī) An ancient city in Phocis, Greece; famous for its oracle: also *Delfi.* — **Del·phi·an** (del'fē-ən) *adj. & n.* — **Del·phic** (del'fik) *adj.* 1. Relating to Delphi or to Apollo's oracle there. 2. Oracular; ambiguous. Also **Del·fi·an** (del'fē-ən).

Delphic oracle The oracle of Apollo at Delphi, priestess of which, the Pythia, uttered ambiguous statements.

del·phi·nine (del'fə-nēn, -nin) *n.* A poisonous crystalline alkaloid, $C_{33}H_{45}NO_9$, found in the seeds of various larkspurs. Also **del'phi·nin** (-nin). [< DELPHIN(IUM) + -INE[2]]

del·phin·i·um (del-fin'ē-əm) *n.* Any of a genus (*Delphinium*) of perennial plants of the crowfoot family, having large, spurred flowers, usually blue; the larkspur. [< NL < Gk. *delphinion* larkspur, dim. of *delphis* dolphin; so called from the shape of the nectary]

Del·phi·nus (del-fī'nəs) *n.* A constellation, the Dolphin. See CONSTELLATION. [< L < Gk.]

Del·sarte system (del-särt') A system of exercises for the development of bodily grace, voice, and dramatic expression. [after François Alexandre *Delsarte*, 1811–71, French singer and elocutionist] — **Del·sar'tian** (-shən) *adj.*

del Sar·to (dāl sär'tō), **Andrea** See SARTO.

del·ta (del'tə) *n.* 1. The fourth letter in the Greek alphabet (Δ, δ), corresponding to English *d*. See ALPHABET. 2. *Geog.* An alluvial, typically triangular-shaped, silt deposit at or in the mouth of a river. 3. Anything triangular. [< Gk.]

del·ta·he·dron (del'tə-hē'drən) *n.* *pl.* **·dra** (-drə) *Crystall.* A crystal form having twelve equal, trapezoidal faces. Also **del'to·he'dron**. For illustration see CRYSTAL.

del·ta·ic (del-tā'ik) *adj.* Of, resembling, or forming a delta.

del·toid (del'toid) *n.* *Anat.* A triangular muscle covering the shoulder joint and serving to extend the arm out from the side. — *adj.* Shaped like a delta; triangular. [< Gk. *deltoeidēs* triangular < *delta* the letter Δ + *eidos* form]

de·lude (di-lōōd') *v.t.* **·lud·ed**, **·lud·ing** 1. To mislead the mind or judgment of; deceive. 2. *Obs.* To evade; elude. 3. *Obs.* To frustrate. [< L *deludere* < *de-* from, away + *ludere* to play] — **de·lud'er** *n.* — **de·lud'ing·ly** *adv.*

del·uge (del'yōōj) *v.t.* **·uged**, **·ug·ing** 1. To flood with water; inundate; submerge. 2. To overwhelm; besiege; swamp: *deluged* with telegrams. — *n.* 1. A great flood or inundation; downpour. 2. Something that overwhelms or engulfs: a *deluge* of tears. — **the Deluge** The flood in the time of Noah. *Gen.* vii. [< OF < L *diluvium* < *diluere* < *dis-* away + *luere* to wash]

de·lu·sion (di-lōō'zhən) *n.* 1. The act of deluding. 2. The state of being deluded or led astray. 3. A false belief, especially when persistent. 4. *Psychiatry* A false, fixed belief, held in spite of evidence to the contrary. [< L *delusio*, *-onis* < *deludere*. See DELUDE.] — **de·lu'sion·al** *adj.* — **Syn.** 3. *Delusion*, *illusion*, *hallucination*, and *mirage* denote something that is false but is taken to be true. A *delusion* is a mistaken conviction; an *illusion* is a mistaken perception. A *hallucination* is a false image or belief, completely subjective and usually suggesting a mental disorder or aberration. A *mirage* is an optical *illusion* in which a distant object is seen apparently displaced as a result of the reflection of light rays by an air layer.

de·lu·sive (di-lōō′siv) *adj.* **1.** Tending to delude; misleading; deceptive. **2.** Like a delusion; unreal. Also **de·lu·so·ry** (di-lōō′sər-ē). **— de·lu′sive·ly** *adv.* **— de·lu′sive·ness** *n.*

de·luxe (di-lōōks′, di·luks′; *Fr.* də-lüks′) *adj.* Of superfine quality; elegant. Also **de luxe.** [< F, lit., of luxury]

delve (delv) *v.* **delved, delv·ing** *v.i.* **1.** To make careful investigation; search for information: to *delve* into a crime. **2.** *Archaic & Dial.* To engage in digging, as with a spade. **— v.t.** **3.** *Archaic & Dial.* To turn over or dig (ground). [OE *delfan*] **— delv′er** *n.*

Dem. Democrat; Democratic.

de·mag·net·ize (dē-mag′nə-tīz) *v.t.* **·ized, ·iz·ing** To deprive (a substance) of magnetism. **— de·mag′net·i·za′tion** *n.* **— de·mag′net·iz′er** *n.*

dem·a·gog·ic (dem′ə-goj′ik, -gog′ik) *adj.* Pertaining to or like a demagogue; given to unprincipled political agitation. Also **dem′a·gog′i·cal. — dem′a·gog′i·cal·ly** *adv.*

dem·a·gogue (dem′ə-gôg, -gog) *n.* **1.** One who leads the populace by appealing to prejudices and passions; an unprincipled politician. **2.** Formerly, any popular leader or orator. Also **dem′a·gog.** [< Gk. *dēmagogos* < *dēmos* people + *agein* to lead]

dem·a·gogu·er·y (dem′ə-gôg′ər-ē, -gog′ər-ē) *n.* The spirit, method, or conduct of a demagogue. Also **dem′a·gog′ism, dem′a·gogu′ism.**

dem·a·go·gy (dem′ə-gō′jē, -gôg′ē, -gog′ē) *n.* **1.** Demagoguery. **2.** The rule of a demagogue. **3.** Demagogues collectively.

de·mand (di-mand′, -mänd′) *v.t.* **1.** To ask for boldly or peremptorily. **2.** To claim as due; ask for authoritatively. **3.** To ask to know; inquire formally. **4.** To have need for; require. **5.** *Law* **a** To summon to court. **b** To make formal claim to (property). **— v.i. 6.** To make a demand. **— n. 1.** The act of demanding. **2.** That which is demanded, especially with authority or firmness. **3.** A claim or requirement: the *demands* on one's time. **4.** A desire to obtain; call: a *demand* for fiction. **5.** An inquiry. **6.** *Law* A request or claim. **7.** *Econ.* **a** The desire to possess combined with the ability to purchase. **b** The potential amount of certain goods that will be purchased at a given time for a given price. **— in demand** Desired; sought after. **— on demand** On presentation: a note payable *on demand.* [< F *demander* < L *demandare* < *de-* down, away + *mandare* to command, order] **— de·mand′a·ble** *adj.* **— de·mand′er** *n.*

— Syn. (verb) **1, 2.** *Demand, require, claim,* and *exact* mean to ask or request with some insistence or authority. Insistence is uppermost in *demand; require* indicates either the authority to ask peremptorily, or the need for the thing requested: to *demand* payment of a bill, to *require* a witness to appear in court. One *claims* what is due, and *exacts* from another by compulsion that which he lacks power to withhold: to *claim* an inheritance, to *exact* tribute.

de·man·dant (di-man′dənt, -män′-) *n. Law* The plaintiff in a real action; also, any plaintiff.

demand bill A bill or draft payable on demand.

demand deposit A bank deposit available to the depositor without advance notice.

demand loan A call loan (which see). *Abbr. D/L*

demand note A note payable on demand.

de·man·toid (di-man′toid) *n.* A bright green variety of andradite, sometimes used as a gemstone. [< G *demant* diamond + -OID]

de·mar·cate (di-mär′kāt, dē′mär-kāt) *v.t.* **·cat·ed, ·cat·ing** **1.** To mark the bounds or limits of; delimit. **2.** To differentiate; separate. [Back formation < DEMARCATION]

de·mar·ca·tion (dē′mär-kā′shən) *n.* **1.** The fixing or marking of boundaries or limits. **2.** The limits or boundaries fixed. **3.** A limiting or separating. [< Sp. *demarcación* < *demarcar* < *de-* down (< L *de-*) + *marcar* to mark a boundary < Gmc.]

dé·marche (dā-märsh′) *n. French* **1.** A manner of approach or mode of procedure. **2.** In diplomacy, a change in plan of action.

de·ma·te·ri·al·ize (dē′mə-tir′ē-əl-īz) *v.t. & v.i.* **·ized, ·iz·ing** To lose or cause to lose material qualities or form. **— de′ma·te′ri·al·i·za′tion** *n.*

Dem·a·vend (dem′ə-vend′) The highest peak of the Elburz Mountains, northern Iran; 18,603 ft. Also **Mount Demavend, Dem·a·vand** (dä′mä-vänd′).

deme (dēm) *n.* One of the districts into which Attica was divided by Cleisthenes. [< Gk. *dēmos* people]

de·mean[1] (di-mēn′) *v.t.* To behave or conduct (oneself) in a particular way. [< OF *demener* < *de-* down (< L *de-*) + *mener* to lead < LL *minare* to threaten, drive]

de·mean[2] (di-mēn′) *v.t.* To lower in dignity or reputation; debase; degrade. **— Syn.** See ABASE. [< DE- + MEAN[2]]

de·mean·or (di-mē′nər) *n.* The manner in which one behaves or bears oneself; deportment; mien. Also *Brit.* **de·mean′our.** **— Syn.** See AIR, BEHAVIOR. [See DEMEAN[1]]

de·ment (di-ment′) *v.t.* To deprive of mental powers; make insane. [< L *dementare* < *de-* away + *mens, mentis* mind]

de·ment·ed (di-men′tid) *adj.* Deprived of reason; insane. **— de·ment′ed·ly** *adv.* **— de·ment′ed·ness** *n.*

de·men·tia (di-men′shə, -shē-ə) *n. Psychiatry* Unsoundness of mind resulting from organic or functional disorders, and leading to loss or serious impairment of the faculty of coherent thought. **— Syn.** See INSANITY. [< L, madness]

dementia pre·cox (prē′koks) *Psychiatry* Schizophrenia: a former name. Also **de·men′tia prae′cox.**

dementia se·ni·lis (si-nī′lis) *Psychiatry* Senile dementia (which see).

Dem·e·rar·a (dem′ə-râr′ə, -rä′rə) A river in British Guiana, flowing north about 200 miles to the Atlantic Ocean.

de·mer·it (di-mer′it) *n.* **1.** That which deserves blame or moral condemnation; a fault. **2.** In schools, etc., a mark for failure or misconduct. [< Med.L *demeritum* fault < L, pp. of *demerere < de-* down, away + *merere* to deserve]

Dem·e·rol (dem′ə-rōl, -rôl) *n.* Proprietary name for a brand of meperidine hydrochloride. Also **dem′e·rol.**

de·mesne (di-mān′, -mēn′) *n.* **1.** In feudal law, lands held in one's own power. **2.** A manor house and the adjoining lands in the immediate use and occupation of the owner of the estate. **3.** The grounds belonging to any residence, or any landed estate. **4.** Any region over which sovereignty is exercised; domain. [< AF *demeyne*, OF *demeine, demaine.* Doublet of DOMAIN.]

De·me·ter (di-mē′tər) The Greek goddess of agriculture, marriage, and fertility: identified with *Ceres.*

demi- *prefix* **1.** Half; intermediate: *demilune.* **2.** Inferior or less in size, quality, etc.; partial: *demigod.* [< F *demi* < L *dimidius* half < *dis-* from, apart + *medius* middle]

dem·i·bas·tion (dem′ē-bas′chən, -tē-ən) *n.* A fortification consisting of half a bastion, having a single flank and face.

dem·i·god (dem′ē-god′) *n.* **1.** An inferior or lesser deity. **2.** In classical mythology, a hero, supposed to be the offspring of a god and a mortal. **3.** A man with the attributes of a god. **— dem′i·god′dess** *n.fem.*

dem·i·john (dem′ē-jon′) *n.* A narrow-necked jug, often enclosed in wickerwork. [< F *dame-jeanne,* lit., Lady Jane; a folk etymology]

de·mil·i·ta·rize (dē-mil′ə-tə-rīz′) *v.t.* **·rized, ·riz·ing** **1.** To remove military characteristics from; free from militarism. **2.** To transfer from military to civilian control. **3.** To move military equipment and troops from and declare neutral, as an area or zone. **4.** To render (equipment) ineffectual for military use. **— de·mil′i·ta·ri·za′tion** *n.*

De Mille (də mil′), **Cecil B**(lount), 1881–1959, U.S. motion-picture producer and director.

dem·i·lune (dem′ē-lōōn′) *n.* **1.** A crescent or crescent-shaped object, formation, etc. **2.** *Mil.* A crescent-shaped outwork in front of a fort. [< F *demi-* half + *lune* moon]

dem·i·mon·daine (dem′ē-mon-dān′) *n.* A woman of the demimonde. Also **dem·i·rep** (dem′ē-rep′). [< F]

dem·i·monde (dem′ē-mond, dem′ē-mond′) *n.* The class of women who have lost social position and repute as a result of equivocal or scandalous behavior. [< F *demi-* half, partial + *monde* world; coined by A. Dumas *fils*]

dem·i·pique (dem′ē-pēk) *n.* Formerly, a military saddle with a pommel half the height of earlier ones. [< DEMI- + PEAK; infl. in form by F *pique* pike]

dem·i·re·lief (dem′ē-ri-lēf′) *n.* Mezzo-relievo (which see). Italian **de·mi·ril·ie·vo** (dā′mē-rē-lyä′vō).

de·mise (di-mīz′) *n.* **1.** Death; decease. **2.** *Law* **a** Decease involving as a result the transfer of an estate. **b** A transfer or conveyance of rights or an estate. **3.** The immediate transfer of a sovereign's rights at his death or abdication to his successor. **— v.** **·mised, ·mis·ing** *v.t.* **1.** To bestow by will; bequeath: said especially of sovereignty on the death or abdication of a ruler. **2.** *Law* To lease or transfer (an estate) for a term of years. **— v.i. 3.** To pass by will or inheritance. [< OF, fem of *demis,* pp. of *demettre* to send away < L *demittere.* See DEMIT.] **— de·mis′a·ble** *adj.*

dem·i·sem·i·qua·ver (dem′ē-sem′ē-kwā′vər) *n. Music Chiefly Brit.* A thirty-second note.

de·mis·sion (di-mish′ən) *n.* A giving up or relinquishment, as of an office; resignation. [< L *demissio, -onis* < *demittere.* See DEMIT.]

de·mit (di-mit′) *v.* **·mit·ted, ·mit·ting** *v.t.* **1.** To resign (an office or dignity). **2.** *Obs.* To dismiss. **— v.i. 3.** To resign. [< L *demittere < de-* down, away + *mittere* to send]

dem·i·tasse (dem′ē-tas′, -täs′) *n.* **1.** A small cup in which after-dinner coffee is served. **2.** Coffee served in such a cup. [< F, a half cup]

dem·i·urge (dem′ē-ûrj) *n.* **1.** In Plato's philosophy, the creator of the material universe. **2.** In the Gnostic systems, a deity regarded as an emanation of the Supreme Being, considered to be the creator of the material world and sometimes the creator of evil. **3.** In certain ancient Greek states, one of a class of public officers or magistrates. Also **dem′i·ur′gus** (-ûr′gəs), **dem′i·ur′gos.** [< Gk. *dēmiourgos* skilled or public worker < *dēmos* people + *ergein* to work] **— dem′i·ur′geous** (-jəs), **dem′i·ur′gic, dem′i·ur′gi·cal** *adj.*

dem·i·vierge (dem′ē·vyerzh′) *n.* A woman who behaves suggestively but retains her virginity. [< F, half-virgin]

dem·i·volt (dem′ē-vōlt′) *n.* In horseback riding, a half turn made by a horse on its hind legs. Also **dem′i·volte′.** [< F *demi-volte < demi-* half + *volte* a leap]

demo- *combining form* People: *demography.* [< Gk. *dēmos* people]

de·mob (dē-mob′) *v.t.* **·mobbed, ·mob·bing** *Brit. Informal* To demobilize. — *n.* **1.** Demobilization. **2.** One who has been demobilized.

de·mo·bi·lize (dē-mō′bə-līz) *v.t.* **·lized, ·liz·ing** To disband (an army or troops). — **de·mo′bi·li·za′tion** *n.*

de·moc·ra·cy (di·mok′rə-sē) *n. ·pl. ·cies* **1.** A form of government in which political power resides in all the people and is exercised by them directly (**pure democracy**), or is given to elected representatives (**representative democracy**), with each citizen sharing equally in political privilege and duty, and with his right to do so protected by free elections and other guarantees. **2.** A state so governed. **3.** The spirit or practice of political, legal, or social equality. **4.** The common people. [< F *démocratie* < Med.L *democratia* < Gk. *dēmokratia* < *dēmos* people + *krateein* to rule]

De·moc·ra·cy (di·mok′rə-sē) *n.* The principles of the Democratic Party; also, the party, or its members collectively.

dem·o·crat (dem′ə-krat) *n.* **1.** One who favors a democracy. **2.** One who believes in political and social equality. *Abbr. d.*

Dem·o·crat (dem′ə-krat) *n.* A member of the Democratic Party in the United States. *Abbr. D., Dem.*

dem·o·crat·ic (dem′ə-krat′ik) *adj.* **1.** Of, pertaining to, or characterized by the principles of democracy. **2.** Existing or provided for the benefit or enjoyment of all. **3.** Practicing social equality. *Abbr. d.* — **dem′o·crat′i·cal·ly** *adv.*

Dem·o·crat·ic (dem′ə-krat′ik) *adj.* Of, pertaining to, or characteristic of the Democratic Party. *Abbr. D., Dem.*

Democratic Party One of the two major political parties in the United States, dating from 1828.

Dem·o·crat·ic-Re·pub·li·can Party (dem′ə-krat′ik-ri·pub′li·kən) See under REPUBLICAN PARTY.

de·moc·ra·tize (di·mok′rə-tīz) *v.t. & v.i.* **·tized, ·tiz·ing** To make or become democratic. — **de·moc′ra·ti·za′tion** *n.*

De·moc·ri·tus (di·mok′rə-təs), 460?–352? B.C., Greek philosopher; propounded the theory of atomism. — **De·moc·ri·te·an** (di·mok′rə-tē′ən), **Dem·o·crit·i·cal** (dem′ə-krit′i·kəl) *adj.*

dé·mo·dé (dā·mō·dā′) *adj. French* Outmoded; out-of-date.

de·mod·ed (dē·mō′did) *adj.* Out of fashion.

de·mod·u·late (dē·moj′ōō-lāt) *v.t.* **·lat·ed, ·lat·ing** *Telecom.* To detect. — **de·mod′u·la′tion** *n.*

de·mog·ra·phy (di·mog′rə-fē) *n.* The study of vital and social statistics, as of births, deaths, disease, etc. [< DEMO- + -GRAPHY] — **de·mog′ra·pher, de·mog′ra·phist** *n.* — **dem·o·graph·ic** (dem′ə-graf′ik) or **·i·cal** *adj.* — **dem′o·graph′i·cal·ly** *adv.*

dem·oi·selle (dem′wä-zel′) *n.* **1.** A damsel. **2.** A crested crane (*Anthropoides virgo*) of Europe, Asia, and Africa, named from its graceful form and carriage: also called *Numidian crane.* **3.** A dragonfly (family *Agridae*). [< F, var. of *damoiselle* < OF *dameisele*. See DAMSEL.]

de·mol·ish (di·mol′ish) *v.t.* **1.** To tear down; raze, as a building. **2.** To destroy utterly; ruin. [< F *démoliss-*, stem of *démolir* < L *demoliri* < *de-* down + *moliri* to build < *moles* heap, mass] — **de·mol′ish·er** *n.* — **de·mol′ish·ment** *n.*

DEMOISELLE
(def. 2)
(About 4 feet high)

— **Syn.** *Demolish, raze, ruin,* and *destroy* agree in the sense of pulling down or tearing to pieces more or less completely. A building is *demolished* if smashed to fragments, and *razed* if leveled to the ground. It is *ruined* if made unfit for habitation or use, though much of its structure may remain. *Destroy* is a very general term, covering all these senses; it may also mean to dissolve so completely that nothing remains. Compare ABOLISH, BREAK. — **Ant.** construct, build, make, restore.

dem·o·li·tion (dem′ə-lish′ən) *n.* The act or result of demolishing; destruction. — **dem·o·li′tion·ist** *n.*

demolition bomb A high-explosive bomb used to destroy buildings and installations.

de·mon (dē′mən) *n.* **1.** An evil spirit; devil. **2.** A very wicked or cruel person. **3.** *Informal* A person of great skill or zeal: *a demon with a gun.* **4.** In ancient Greek religion, a supernatural being of secondary rank; also, a guardian spirit; genius: also called *daimon, daemon.* [< L *daemon* evil spirit (orig., spirit, god) < Gk. *daimōn*]

demon. Demonstrative.

de·mon·e·tize (dē·mon′ə·tīz) *v.t.* **·tized, ·tiz·ing** **1.** To deprive (currency) of standard value. **2.** To withdraw from use, as currency. — **de·mon′e·ti·za′tion** *n.*

de·mo·ni·ac (di·mō′nē·ak) *adj.* **1.** Of, like, or befitting a demon or evil spirit; devilish. **2.** Influenced or produced by or as by demons; mad; violent; frenzied. Also **de·mo·ni·a·cal** (dē′mə·nī′ə·kəl). — *n.* **1.** One possessed of a demon or evil spirit. **2.** A maniac; lunatic. — **de′mo·ni′a·cal·ly** *adv.*

de·mon·ic (di·mon′ik) *adj.* **1.** Of or like a demon. Also **de·mo·ni·an** (di·mō′nē·ən). **2.** Inspired, as by a demon.

de·mon·ism (dē′mən·iz′əm) *n.* **1.** Belief in demons. **2.** Demonolatry. **3.** Demonology. — **de′mon·ist** *n.*

de·mon·ize (dē′mən·īz) *v.t.* **·ized, ·iz·ing** **1.** To make a demon of. **2.** To bring under demonic influence.

demono- *combining form* Demon: *demonology.* Also, before vowels, **demon-.** [< Gk. *daimōn* spirit, god]

de·mon·ol·a·ter (dē′mən·ol′ə·tər) *n.* One who worships demons.

de·mon·ol·a·try (dē′mən·ol′ə·trē) *n.* The worship of demons. [< DEMONO- + Gk. *latreia* worship]

de·mon·ol·o·gy (dē′mən·ol′ə·jē) *n.* The study of demons or of belief in demons; also, a treatise embodying such a study. [< DEMONO- + -LOGY] — **de′mon·ol′o·gist** *n.*

Demon Star Algol.

de·mon·stra·ble (di·mon′strə-bəl, dem′ən-) *adj.* Capable of being demonstrated or proved. — **de·mon′stra·bil′i·ty, de·mon′stra·ble·ness** *n.* — **de·mon′stra·bly** *adv.*

de·mon·strance (di·mon′strəns) *n. Obs.* Demonstration.

de·mon·strant (di·mon′strənt) *n.* One who makes, furthers, or takes part in a public demonstration.

dem·on·strate (dem′ən-strāt) *v.* **·strat·ed, ·strat·ing** *v.t.* **1.** To explain or describe by use of experiments, examples, etc. **2.** To prove or show by reasoning; make evident. **3.** To exhibit or show clearly; manifest: to *demonstrate* one's love. — *v.i.* **4.** To take part in a public demonstration. **5.** To make a show of military force. **6.** To teach by using examples, etc. — **Syn.** See EXPLAIN. [< L *demonstratus,* pp. of *demonstrare* < *de-* completely + *monstrare* to show, point out]

dem·on·stra·tion (dem′ən-strā′shən) *n.* **1.** The act of making known or evident; a pointing out or proving. **2.** Undeniable proof or evidence. **3.** An exhibition and explanation of a subject, theory, commercial product, etc., by means of examples, experiments, displays, or the like **4.** A show or expression: a *demonstration* of love. **5.** A display of public feeling, as a mass meeting or parade. **6.** A show of military force or readiness. **7.** *Logic* A system of reasoning showing how, from given premises, a certain conclusion must follow. — **Syn. 1.** proof, substantiation, verification. **4.** display.

de·mon·stra·tive (di·mon′strə-tiv) *adj.* **1.** Serving to demonstrate or point out **2.** Able to prove beyond doubt; convincing and conclusive. **3.** Inclined to strong expression. **4.** *Gram.* Indicating the person or object referred to. — *n. Gram.* A demonstrative pronoun. *Abbr. demon.* — **de·mon′stra·tive·ly** *adv.* — **de·mon′stra·tive·ness** *n.*

demonstrative pronoun *Gram.* A pronoun that directly points out its antecedents, as *this, those.*

dem·on·stra·tor (dem′ən-strā′tər) *n.* **1.** One who or that which demonstrates. **2.** Something used as a model or sample for demonstration.

de·mor·al·ize (di·môr′əl·īz, -mor′-) *v.t.* **·ized, ·iz·ing** **1.** To corrupt or deprave. **2.** To undermine or destroy the courage, confidence, etc., of; dishearten. **3.** To throw into disorder. — **de·mor′al·i·za′tion** *n.* — **de·mor′al·iz′er** *n.*

De Mor·gan (di môr′gən), **William Frend,** 1839–1917, English potter and novelist.

de mor·tu·is nil ni·si bo·num (dē môr′chōō·is nil nī′sī bō′nəm) *Latin* Of the dead (say) nothing but good.

de·mos (dē′mos) *n.* **1.** The people of an ancient Greek state. **2.** *Rare* The common people. [< Gk. *dēmos*]

De·mos·the·nes (di·mos′thə·nēz), 384?–322 B.C., Athenian orator and patriot.

de·mote (di·mōt′) *v.t.* **·mot·ed, ·mot·ing** To reduce to a lower grade or rank: opposed to *promote.* [< DE- + (PRO)-MOTE] — **de·mo′tion** *n.*

de·mot·ic (di·mot′ik) *adj.* **1.** Of or pertaining to the common people of a region; popular. **2.** Designating the simplified form of the hieratic alphabet of ancient Egypt. **3.** Designating the spoken standard of Modern Greek based on popular usage. [< Gk. *dēmotikos* < *dēmos* people]

de·mot·ics (di·mot′iks) *n.pl.* (*construed as sing.*) Sociology in its most inclusive sense.

de·mount (dē·mount′) *v.t.* To remove, as a motor, from its mounting, setting, etc. — **de·mount′a·ble** *adj.*

demp·ster (demp′stər) *n.* A deemster (which see).

de·mul·cent (di·mul′sənt) *adj.* Soothing. — *n. Med.* A soothing substance, especially one to relieve irritated mucous membranes. [< L *demulcens, -entis,* ppr. of *demulcere* < *de-* down + *mulcere* to soothe]

de·mur (di·mûr′) *v.i.* **·murred, ·mur·ring** **1.** To offer objections; take exception. **2.** To delay; hesitate. **3.** *Law* To interpose a demurrer. — *n.* **1.** The act of demurring. **2.** An objection, as to proposed action; an exception taken. **3.** A delay. **4.** *Obs.* A demurrer. [< OF *demourer* < L *demorari* < *de-* completely + *morari* to delay < *mora* a delay] — **de·mur′ra·ble** *adj.*

de·mure (di·myŏŏr′) *adj.* **·mur·er, ·mur·est** **1.** Having a sedate or sober demeanor; grave; reserved. **2.** Affecting modesty; prim; coy. [ME *mure* < OF *meur* < L *maturus* mature, discreet] — **de·mure′ly** *adv.* — **de·mure′ness** *n.*

de·mur·rage (di·mûr′ij) *n.* **1.** The detention of a vessel, railway freight car, or other commercial conveyance, beyond the specified time for departure, as a result of loading, unloading, etc. **2.** Compensation for such delay. [< OF *demourage* < *demourer* < L *demorari* to delay. See DEMUR.]

de·mur·ral (di·mûr′əl) *n.* Demur.

de·mur·rer (di·mûr′ər) *n.* **1.** *Law* A pleading that allows the truth of the facts stated by the opposite party, but denies that they are sufficient to constitute a good cause of action or defense in law. **2.** Any objection or exception taken. **3.** One who demurs. [< AF]

de·my (di·mī′) *n. pl.* **·mies** **1.** Any of several sizes of paper, in the United States about 16 x 21 inches. **2.** A foundation scholar of Magdalen College, Oxford. [< DEMI-]

den (den) *n.* **1.** The cave or retreat of a wild animal; a lair. **2.** A site or dwelling: used pejoratively: a *den* of thieves. **3.** A small, private room for relaxation or study. — *v.i.* **denned, den·ning** To dwell in or as in a den. [OE *denn*]

Den. Denmark.

de·nar·i·us (di·nâr′ē·əs) *n. pl.* **·nar·i·i** (-nâr′ē·ī) **1.** The most important coin of ancient Rome, made of silver; the penny of the New Testament. **2.** A gold coin, the **denarius aureus,** worth 25 silver denarii. **3.** The Latin name of the English penny, the initial of which (*d.*) is preserved in monetary notation. [< L *denarius* (*nummus*) denary (coin); because it was worth ten asses]

den·a·ry (den′ər·ē, dē′nər·ē) *adj.* **1.** Containing ten. **2.** Proceeding by ten; decimal. [< L *denarius* < *deni* by tens < *decem* ten]

de·na·tion·al·ize (dē·nash′ən·əl·īz′) *v.t.* **·ized, ·iz·ing** **1.** To deprive of national character, status, or rights. **2.** To change the nationality of. Also *Brit.* **de·na′tion·al·ise′.** — **de·na′tion·al·i·za′tion** *n.*

de·nat·u·ral·ize (dē·nach′ər·əl·īz′) *v.t.* **·ized, ·iz·ing** **1.** To take away the nature of; render unnatural. **2.** To deprive of naturalization or citizenship. Also *Brit.* **de·nat′u·ral·ise′.** — **de·nat′u·ral·i·za′tion** *n.*

de·na·ture (dē·nā′chər) *v.t.* **·tured, ·tur·ing** **1.** To change the nature of. **2.** To adulterate (alcohol, fat, etc.) so as to make unfit for drinking or eating without destroying other useful properties. **3.** *Biochem.* To alter the original state of (a protein) by physical or chemical means. Also **de·na′tur·ize.** — **de·na′tur·ant** *n.* — **de·na′tur·a′tion** *n.*

denatured alcohol Alcohol made unfit for drinking by the addition of certain poisonous substances, as methanol.

de·na·zi·fy (dē·nät′sə·fī, -nat′-) *v.t.* **·fied, ·fy·ing** To rid of Nazi influences or of Nazism. — **de·na′zi·fi·ca′tion** *n.*

Denb. or **Denbh.** Denbighshire.

Denbighshire (den′bē·shir) A former county in NE Wales; 669 sq. mi.; pop. 184,824 (1971); county seat, Denbigh. Also **Den′bigh.**

den·dri·form (den′drə·fôrm) *adj.* Like a tree in form. [< DENDRI- + -FORM]

den·drite (den′drīt) *n.* **1.** *Mineral.* Any mineral crystallizing in a branching, treelike form; a rock or mineral with treelike markings. **2.** *Physiol.* A threadlike, branching process of a nerve cell that conducts impulses toward the cell body. See AXON, NEURON. [< Gk. *dendritēs* of a tree < *dendron* tree]

den·drit·ic (den·drit′ik) *adj.* **1.** Resembling a tree; dendriform. **2.** Of or pertaining to a dendrite. Also **den·drit′i·cal.** — **den·drit′i·cal·ly** *adv.* [< DENDRIT(E) + -IC]

dendro- *combining form* Tree: *dendrology.* Also **dendr-** (before vowels), **dendri-.** [< Gk. *dendron* tree]

den·dro·chro·nol·o·gy (den′drō·krə·nol′ə·jē) *n.* The determination of the approximate dates of past events and of periods of time by a study of the growth rings on trees.

den·droid (den′droid) *adj.* Like a tree; dendritic. Also **den·droi′dal.** [< Gk. *dendroeidēs* < *dendron* tree + *eidos* shape]

den·dro·lite (den′drə·līt) *n.* *Bot.* A petrified or fossil plant, or part of a plant. [< DENDRO- + -LITE]

den·drol·o·gy (den·drol′ə·jē) *n.* The branch of botany and forestry that deals with trees. [< DENDRO- + -LOGY] — **den·dro·log·ic** (den′drō·loj′ik) or **·i·cal, den·drol·o·gous** (den·drol′ə·gəs) *adj.* — **den·drol′o·gist** *n.*

den·dron (den′dron) *n.* *Physiol.* A dendrite. [< Gk., tree]

-dendron *combining form* Tree: *philodendron.* [< Gk. *dendron* tree]

dene (dēn) *n.* *Brit.* A sandy stretch of land or a low, sandy hill near the sea. [ME; origin uncertain]

Den·eb (den′eb) *n.* One of the 20 brightest stars, 1.26 magnitude; Alpha in the constellation Cygnus. See STAR.

De·neb·o·la (di·neb′ə·lə) *n.* A star, Beta in the constellation Leo; 2.2 magnitude.

den·e·ga·tion (den′ə·gā′shən) *n.* A denial or refusal. [< MF *dénégation* < L *denegare* to deny]

den·gue (deng′gē, -gā) *n.* *Pathol.* An acute, tropical, frequently epidemic virus disease transmitted by the bite of a mosquito (genus *Aëdes*) and characterized by fever, eruptions, and severe pains in the joints: also called *breakbone, dandy.* [< Sp., ult. < Swahili]

Den Haag (dən häкн) A Dutch name for (The) HAGUE.

Den·ham (den′əm), **Sir John,** 1615–68?, English poet.

de·ni·a·ble (di·nī′ə·bəl) *adj.* That can be denied. — **de·ni′a·bly** *adv.*

de·ni·al (di·nī′əl) *n.* **1.** Declaration that a statement is untrue; contradiction. **2.** Refusal to believe a doctrine, etc. **3.** Refusal to acknowledge; a disowning or disavowal. **4.** Refusal to grant, give, or allow. **5.** Self-denial (which see).

de·nic·o·tin·ize (dē·nik′ə·tin·īz′) *v.t.* **·ized, ·iz·ing** To remove nicotine from. Also **de·nic′o·tine.**

de·ni·er[1] (di·nī′ər) *n.* One who makes denial.

de·ni·er[2] (den′yər, də·nir′ *for def. 1,* də·nir′ *for def. 2;* *Fr.* də·nyā′) *n.* **1.** A unit of weight for denoting the coarseness or fineness of rayon, nylon, or silk yarns, based on a standard weight of five centigrams per 450 meters of silk. **2.** A former French silver coin. [< F < L *denarius.* See DENARIUS.]

den·i·grate (den′ə·grāt) *v.t.* **·grat·ed, ·grat·ing** **1.** To slander or defame. **2.** To make black; blacken. [< L *denigratus,* pp. of *denigrare* < *de-* completely + *nigrare* to blacken < *niger* black] — **den′i·gra′tion** *n.* — **den′i·gra′tor** *n.*

De·ni·ker (də·nē·kâr′), **Joseph,** 1852–1918, French anthropologist.

den·im (den′əm) *n.* **1.** A strong, twilled cotton used for overalls, uniforms, etc.; also, a finer grade of this fabric used for hangings, upholstery, etc. **2.** *pl.* Garments made of this material. [< F (*serge*) *de Nîmes* (serge) of Nîmes]

Den·is (den′is, *Fr.* də·nē′) Third-century Christian martyr; patron of France. Also **Den′ys.**

de·ni·trate (dē·nī′trāt) *v.t.* **·trat·ed, ·trat·ing** *Chem.* To remove nitrogen, nitric or nitrous acid, nitrates, or nitrogen oxide from. — **de/ni·tra′tion** *n.*

de·ni·tri·fy (dē·nī′trə·fī) *v.t.* **·fied, ·fy·ing** *Chem.* **1.** To remove nitrogen or its compounds from. **2.** To reduce (nitrates) to nitrites, nitrogen, or ammonia, as by certain bacteria. — **de/ni′tri·fi·ca′tion** *n.*

den·i·zen (den′ə·zən) *n.* **1.** One who lives in a place; a citizen; inhabitant. **2.** One who frequents a place; an habitué. **3.** *Brit.* An alien permitted to enjoy certain privileges of citizenship. **4.** A person, animal, or thing at home or naturalized in a region or condition not native to it. — *v.t.* *Brit.* **1.** To admit to the rights of citizenship. **2.** To make (someone or something) a denizen. [< AF *deinzein* < *deinz* inside < *de intus* from within] — **den′i·zen·a′tion** *n.*

Den·mark (den′märk) A Kingdom of NW Europe; 16,619 sq. mi.; pop. 5,035,800 (est. 1973); capital, Copenhagen. Danish *Danmark.* See map of BALTIC SEA.

Denmark Strait A channel between Greenland and Iceland, connecting the Atlantic with the Greenland Sea; length about 300 mi.

denom. Denomination.

de·nom·i·nate (*v.* di·nom′ə·nāt; *adj.* di·nom′ə·nit) *v.t.* **·nated, ·nat·ing** To give a name to; call. — *adj.* Made up of units of a designated kind: Three pounds is a *denominate* number. [< L *denominatus,* pp. of *denominare* < *de-* down + *nomen* name] — **de·nom′i·na·ble** (-nə·bəl) *adj.*

de·nom·i·na·tion (di·nom′ə·nā′shən) *n.* **1.** The act of naming or calling by name. **2.** The name by which a thing or a class of things is known; appellation or category. **3.** Any specifically named class or group of things or people: There were many *denominations* of criminals. **4.** A religious group; a sect. **5.** A specific class of units in a system of measures, weights, money, etc. — **Syn.** See RELIGION.

de·nom·i·na·tion·al (di·nom′ə·nā′shən·əl) *adj.* **1.** Of or pertaining to a name. **2.** Of, pertaining to, or supported by a religious denomination or sect; sectarian: a *denominational* college. — **de·nom′i·na′tion·al·ly** *adv.*

de·nom·i·na·tion·al·ism (di·nom′ə·nā′shən·əl·iz′əm) *n.* **1.** A disposition to divide into or form denominations. **2.** Rigid adherence or devotion to a denomination or sect; sectarianism. — **de·nom′i·na′tion·al·ist** *n. & adj.*

de·nom·i·na·tive (di·nom′ə·nā′tiv, -nə·tiv) *adj.* **1.** That gives or constitutes a name; appellative. **2.** *Gram.* Derived from a noun or adjective. — *n.* *Gram.* A word, especially a verb, derived from a noun or adjective, as the verb *to garden.* — **de·nom′i·na′tive·ly** *adv.*

de·nom·i·na·tor (di·nom′ə·nā′tər) *n.* *Math.* The term of a fraction indicating the number of equal parts into which the unit is divided; divisor. In a common fraction it appears below or to the right of the line. Compare NUMERATOR.

de·no·ta·tion (dē′nō·tā′shən) *n.* **1.** The specific meaning of, or the object or objects designated by, a word as distinct from that which it suggests: distinguished from *connotation.* **2.** The act of denoting. **3.** That which indicates, as a sign. **4.** That which is signified; meaning.

de·no·ta·tive (di·nō′tə·tiv, dē′nō·tā′tiv) *adj.* Having power to denote; significant. — **de·no′ta·tive·ly** *adv.*

de·note (di·nōt′) *v.t.* **·not·ed, ·not·ing** **1.** To point out or make known; mark. **2.** To serve as a symbol for; signify; indicate. **3.** To designate: mean: said of words, symbols, etc. [< L *denotare* < *de-* down + *notare* to mark] — **de·not′a·ble** *adj.*

dé·noue·ment (dā·noo′·män′) *n.* **1.** The final unraveling or solution of the plot of a play, novel, etc. **2.** The point in the plot where this occurs. **3.** Any final solution; outcome. [< OF < *desnouer* < *des-* away (< L *dis-*) + *nouer* to knot < L *nodare* < *nodus* a knot]

de·nounce (di·nouns′) *v.t.* **·nounced, ·nounc·ing** **1.** To attack or condemn openly and vehemently; inveigh against.

2. To inform against; accuse. **3.** To announce as a threat; proclaim menacingly. **4.** To give formal notice of the termination of (a treaty, etc.). **5.** *Obs.* To announce; foretell. [< OF *denoncer* < L *denuntiare* < *de-* down + *nuntiare* to announce] **— de·nounce'ment** *n.* **— de·nounc'er** *n.*

de no·vo (dē nō'vō) *Latin* From the beginning; anew.

dense (dens) *adj.* **dens·er, dens·est** **1.** Having its parts crowded together; compact; thick; close. **2.** Hard to penetrate; profound; intense: *dense* ignorance. **3.** Stupid; dull: a *dense* person. **4.** *Photog.* Opaque when developed; strongly contrasted in lights and shades: said of a negative. [< L *densus*] **— dense'ly** *adv.* **— dense'ness** *n.*

den·si·tom·e·ter (den'sə·tom'ə·tər) *n. Photog.* An apparatus for determining density. [< DENSITY + -METER]

den·si·ty (den'sə·tē) *n. pl.* **·ties** **1.** The state or quality of being dense; closeness of parts; compactness. **2.** Stupidity. **3.** *Physics* The mass of a substance per unit of its volume. *Abbr. d, D* **4.** *Sociol.* The number of specified units, as persons, families, or dwellings, per acre or square mile. **5.** *Electr.* **a** The quantity of current flowing through a given cross section of a conductor. **b** The rate of flow of a current, expressed in terms of amperes per square centimeter or square inch: also called *current density.* [< MF *densité* < L *densitas, -tatis* < *densus* thick]

dent¹ (dent) *n.* A small depression made by striking or pressing; indentation. **— v.t. 1.** To make a dent in. **— v.i. 2.** To become dented. [Var. of DINT]

dent² (dent) *n.* A toothlike part, as of a comb, gearwheel, etc. [< F < L *dens, dentis* tooth]

dent. Dental; dentist; dentistry.

den·tal (den'təl) *adj.* **1.** Of or pertaining to the teeth. **2.** Of or pertaining to dentistry. *Abbr. dent.* **3.** *Phonet.* Produced with the tip of the tongue against or near the upper front teeth, as French *t* and *d*. The English alveolars (t) and (d) are sometimes classed as dentals. **— n.** *Phonet.* A dental consonant. [< NL *dentalis* < L *dens, dentis* tooth]

dental floss A strong thread for cleaning between the teeth.

dental plate A denture.

den·tate (den'tāt) *adj.* **1.** Having teeth or toothlike processes; toothed; notched. **2.** *Bot.* Having a notched edge resembling teeth, as certain leaves. [< L *dentatus* having teeth] **— den'tate·ly** *adv.*

dent·a·tion (den·tā'shən) *n.* **1.** A toothlike formation. **2.** The state or quality of being dentate.

denti- *combining form* Tooth: *dentiform.* Also, before vowels, **dent-.** [< L *dens, dentis* tooth]

den·ti·cle (den'ti·kəl) *n.* **1.** A small tooth or toothlike projection. **2.** *Dent.* A small, calcified mass in the pulp cavity of a tooth. [< L *denticulus,* dim. of *dens, dentis* tooth]

den·tic·u·late (den·tik'yə·lit, -lāt) *adj.* **1.** Finely dentate or toothed. **2.** *Archit.* Formed into or having dentils. Also **den·tic'u·lat'ed.** **— den·tic'u·late·ly** *adv.*

den·tic·u·la·tion (den·tik'yə·lā'shən) *n.* **1.** The condition of being denticulate. **2.** A denticle or set of denticles.

den·ti·form (den'tə·fôrm) *adj.* Tooth-shaped.

den·ti·frice (den'tə·fris) *n.* A preparation, as a powder or paste, for cleaning the teeth. [< MF < L *dentifricium* < *dens, dentis* tooth + *fricare* to rub]

den·til (den'til) *n.* **1.** *Archit.* One of a series of small blocks that project like a row of teeth, as beneath some cornices. **2.** *Heraldry* A notch or indentation. [< MF *dentille,* dim. of *dent* tooth]

DENTILS (def. 1)

den·ti·la·bi·al (den'ti·lā'bē·əl) *adj. & n. Phonet.* Labiodental.

den·ti·lin·gual (den'ti·ling'gwəl) *adj. & n. Phonet.* Interdental.

den·tine (den'tēn, -tin) *n. Anat.* The hard, calcified substance forming the body of a tooth, situated just beneath the enamel and cementum. Also **den'tin** (-tin). For illustration see TOOTH. **— den'tin·al** *adj.*

den·ti·phone (den'tə·fōn) *n.* An instrument for hearing sounds by means of vibrations transmitted through the teeth to the auditory nerve. Also **den'ta·phone.**

den·tist (den'tist) *n.* One who practices dentistry. *Abbr. dent* [< F *dentiste* < *dent* a tooth]

den·tist·ry (den'tis·trē) *n.* **1** The branch of medicine concerned with the diagnosis, prevention, and treatment of diseases affecting the teeth and their associated structures. **2.** The work of a dentist. *Abbr. dent.*

den·ti·tion (den·tish'ən) *n.* **1.** The process or period of cutting teeth; teething. **2.** *Biol.* The kind and number of teeth characteristic of man and other animals, and the manner in which they are arranged in the jaws. [< L *dentitio, -onis* teething < *dentire* to cut teeth < *dens, dentis* tooth]

dento- *combining form* Dental. [< L *dens, dentis* tooth]

den·toid (den'toid) *adj.* Like a tooth.

Den·ton (den'tən) A city in northern Texas; pop. 26,844.

D'En·tre·cas·teaux Islands (dän'trə·kàs·tō') An island group SE of New Guinea; part of Papua New Guinea; 1,200 sq. mi.; pop. 32,000 (1966).

den·ture (den'chər) *n.* A set of teeth; especially, a set of artificial teeth, either partial or full: also called *dental plate.* [< F < *dent* tooth] **— den'tur·al** *adj.*

de·nu·date (di·nōō'dāt, -nyōō'-, den'yōō·dāt) *adj.* Stripped of foliage or other covering; naked. **— v.t.** **·dat·ed, ·dat·ing** To lay bare; denude. [< L *denudatus,* pp. of *denudare.* See DENUDE.]

den·u·da·tion (den'yōō·dā'shən, dē'nōō-, -nyōō-) *n.* **1.** The act of denuding, or the state of being denuded. **2.** *Geol.* **a** The laying bare of land, especially by erosion. **b** The slow disintegration of rock surfaces by weathering.

de·nude (di·nōōd', -nyōōd') *v.t.* **·nud·ed, ·nud·ing** **1.** To strip the covering from; make naked. **2.** *Geol.* To wear away or remove overlying matter from, and so expose to view. [< L *denudare* < *de-* down, completely + *nudare* to strip < *nudus* bare, naked]

de·nu·mer·a·ble (di·nōō'mər·ə·bəl, -nyōō'-) *adj. Math.* Capable of being put in a one-to-one correspondence with positive integers. **— de·nu'mer·a·bly** *adv.*

de·nun·ci·ate (di·nun'sē·āt, -shē-) *v.t. & v.i.* **·at·ed, ·at·ing** To denounce. [< L *denuntiatus,* pp. of *denuntiare.* See DE-NOUNCE.] **— de·nu'nci·a'tor** *n.*

de·nun·ci·a·tion (di·nun'sē·ā'shən, -shē-) *n.* **1.** Open disapproval or condemnation of a person or action. **2.** Accusation before public authorities; arraignment. **3.** A declaration in the form of a threat or warning. **4.** Formal notice that a treaty is to be terminated.

de·nun·ci·a·to·ry (di·nun'sē·ə·tôr'ē, -tō'rē, -shē-) *adj.* Of the nature of or containing denunciation; accusing or threatening.

Den·ver (den'vər) The capital of Colorado, in the central part; pop. 514,678.

de·ny (di·nī') *v.t.* **·nied, ·ny·ing** **1.** To declare to be untrue; contradict. **2.** To refuse to believe; declare to be false or invalid, as a doctrine. **3.** To refuse to give; withhold. **4.** To refuse (someone) a request. **5.** To refuse to acknowledge; disown; repudiate. **6.** To refuse access to. **7.** *Obs.* To refuse to accept; decline. **— to deny oneself** To refuse oneself something desired; practice self-denial. [< OF *denier* < L *denegare* < *de-* completely + *negare* to say no, refuse] **— Syn. 1.** gainsay. **2.** reject, discredit.

de·o·dand (dē'ə·dand) *n.* In early English law, any personal property instrumental in causing the death of a person, and therefore forfeited to the crown for pious uses. [< LL *deodandum* < L *deus* god + *dandum,* gerundive of *dare* to give]

de·o·dar (dē'ə·där) *n.* The East Indian cedar (*Cedrus deodara*), prized for its durable, light red wood. [< Hind. < Skt. *devadāru* divine tree < *deva* god + *dāru* wood]

de·o·dor·ant (dē·ō'dər·ənt) *adj.* Destroying, absorbing, or disguising bad odors. **— n.** A deodorant substance; especially, a cosmetic used to absorb or counteract body odors. [< DE- + L *odorans, -antis,* ppr. of *odorare* to have an odor]

de·o·dor·ize (dē·ō'dər·īz) *v.t.* **·ized, ·iz·ing** To modify, destroy, or disguise the odor of. **— de·o'dor·i·za'tion** *n.* **— de·o'dor·iz'er** *n.*

De·o fa·ven·te (dē'ō fə·ven'tē) *Latin* With God's favor.

De·o gra·ti·as (dē'ō grā'shē·əs) *Latin* Thanks to God.

De·o ju·van·te (dē'ō jōō·van'tē) *Latin* With God's help.

de·on·tol·o·gy (dē'on·tol'ə·jē) *n.* The science of moral obligation or duty; ethics. [< Gk. *deon, deontos* necessary, orig. ppr. neut. of *deein* to lack, need + -LOGY] **— de·on·to·log·i·cal** (dē·on'tə·loj'i·kəl) *adj.* **— de'on·tol'o·gist** *n.*

De·o vo·len·te (dē'ō vō·len'tē) *Latin* God willing. *Abbr. D.V.*

de·ox·i·dize (dē·ok'sə·dīz) *v.t.* **·dized, ·diz·ing** **1.** To remove oxygen from. **2.** To reduce from the state of an oxide. **— de·ox'i·di·za'tion** *n.* **— de·ox'i·diz'er** *n.*

de·ox·y- *combining form* Containing less oxygen than: *deoxyribonucleic acid.* Also **desoxy-.**

de·ox·y·gen·ate (dē·ok'sə·jə·nāt') *v.t.* **·at·ed, ·at·ing** To remove oxygen from. Also **de·ox'y·gen·ize'.** **— de·ox'y·gen·a'tion** *n.*

de·ox·y·ri·bo·nu·cle·ic acid (dē·ok'sē·rī'bō·nōō·klē'ik, -nyōō-) *Biochem.* A nucleic acid of complex molecular structure forming a principal constituent of the genes and known to play an important role in the genetic action of the chromosomes. *Abbr. DNA.*

dep. **1.** Department. **2.** Departs; departure. **3.** Deponent. **4.** Depot. **5.** Deputy.

Dep. **1.** Dependency. **2.** Deposit (banking): also **dep.**

de·paint (di·pānt') *v.t. Obs.* To depict; portray.

de·part (di·pärt') *v.i.* **1.** To go away; leave. **2.** To deviate; differ; vary: with *from:* to *depart* from tradition. **3.** To die. **— v.t. 4.** To leave: now archaic except in the phrase **to depart this life. — n.** *Obs.* Departure; death. [< OF *departir* < *de-* away < L *dis-*) + *partir* to divide < L *partire* < *pars, partis* a part]

de·part·ed (di·pär'tid) *adj.* **1.** Gone; past. **2.** Dead. **— Syn.** See LIFELESS. **— the departed** The dead person, or the dead collectively.

de·part·ment (di·pärt'mənt) *n.* **1.** A distinct part or division of something extensive and organized, as of a large business: the public relations *department*. **2.** *Usually cap. U.S.* An executive division of the federal government, headed by a cabinet officer: the State *Department*. **3.** In schools and colleges, a division devoted to a certain area of knowledge. **4.** In France, an administrative district. **5.** *Informal* An area of interest, knowledge, or responsibility. Abbr. *D.*, *dep.*, *dept.*, *dpt.* [< OF *departir*. See DEPART.]

de·part·men·tal (dē′pärt·men′təl) *adj.* **1.** Of or pertaining to a department or departments. **2.** Organized into departments. **— de′part·men′tal·ly** *adv.*

de·part·men·tal·ism (dē′pärt·men′təl·iz′əm) *n.* The tendency or practice of dividing an organization so extensively that its efficiency is impaired.

de·part·men·tal·ize (dē′pärt·men′təl·īz) *v.t. & v.i.* **·ized,** **·iz·ing** To divide into departments. **— de′part·men·tal·i·za′tion** *n.*

department store A large retail establishment selling various types of merchandise and service, and organized by departments.

de·par·ture (di·pär′chər) *n.* **1.** The act of going away or taking leave. **2.** Deviation from an accepted or ordinary method, belief, or course of action; divergence. **3.** *Naut.* **a** Distance east or west of a given meridian. **b** The position of a ship taken at the start of a voyage as a basis for calculations by dead reckoning. **4.** *Archaic* Death. Abbr. *dep.*

de·pas·ture (dē·pas′chər, -päs′-) *v.* **·tured,** **·tur·ing** *v.t.* **1.** To denude (land) of herbage by grazing. **2.** To pasture (cattle). **— v.i. 3.** To graze.

de·pend (di·pend′) *v.i.* **1.** To have full reliance; trust: with *on* or *upon.* **2.** To be conditioned or determined; be contingent: with *on* or *upon.* **3.** To rely for maintenance, support, etc.: with *on* or *upon.* **4.** To hang down: with *from.* **5.** To be pending, undecided, or in suspension. [< OF *dependre* < L *dependere* < *de-* down + *pendere* to hang]

de·pend·a·ble (di·pen′də·bəl) *adj.* That can be depended upon; trustworthy. **— Syn.** See RELIABLE. **— de·pend′·a·bil′i·ty,** **de·pend′a·ble·ness** *n.* **— de·pend′a·bly** *adv.*

de·pen·dence (di·pen′dəns) *n.* **1.** The state of relying on something or someone, as for support. **2.** Reliance or trust. **3.** The state of being contingent on or determined by something else. **4.** Subjection to the control or guidance of another. **5.** The object of one's reliance. Also **de·pen′dance.**

de·pen·den·cy (di·pen′dən·sē) *n.* *pl.* **·cies 1.** The state of being dependent; dependence. **2.** That which is dependent or subordinate. **3.** A territory or state subject to the dominion of another state or country from which it is geographically separated. Also **de·pen′dan·cy.** Abbr. (def. 3) *Dep.*

de·pen·dent (di·pen′dənt) *adj.* **1.** Conditioned by or contingent upon something else: The reward is *dependent* on your success. **2.** Subject to outside control; subordinate. **3.** Relying on someone or something for support or aid. **4.** Hanging down; pendent: often with *from.* **— n.** One who depends on another for support or favor. Also **de·pen′dant.**

dependent clause *Gram.* See under CLAUSE.

De·pew (də·pyōō′), **Chauncey Mitchell,** 1834–1928, U.S. lawyer, orator, and politician.

de·pict (di·pikt′) *v.t.* **1.** To portray or represent by or as by drawing, sculpturing, painting, etc. **2.** To portray in words; describe. [< L *depictus,* pp. of *depingere* < *de-* down + *pingere* to paint] **— de·pic′tion** *n.*

de·pic·ture (di·pik′chər) *v.t.* **·tured,** **·tur·ing** To represent in words or pictures.

dep·i·late (dep′ə·lāt) *v.t.* **·lat·ed,** **·lat·ing** To remove hair from. [< L *depilatus,* pp. of *depilare* < *de-* away + *pilus* hair] **— dep′i·la′tion** *n.* **— dep′i·la′tor** *n.*

de·pil·a·to·ry (di·pil′ə·tôr′ē, -tō′rē) *adj.* Having the power to remove hair. **— n.** *pl.* **·ries** A depilatory agent.

de·plane (dē·plān′) *v.i.* **·planed,** **·plan·ing** To alight from an airplane: to *deplane* in Boston.

de·plete (di·plēt′) *v.t.* **·plet·ed,** **·plet·ing 1.** To reduce or lessen, as by use, exhaustion, or waste. **2.** To empty completely or partially: to *deplete* the treasury. **3.** *Med.* To lessen or withdraw the fluid contents of (an organ or vessel). [< L *depletus,* pp. of *deplere* < *de-* not + *plere* to fill]

de·ple·tion (di·plē′shən) *n.* **1.** The act of depleting, or the state of being depleted. **2.** Reduction in value, as of a partially consumed asset.

de·ple·tive (di·plē′tiv) *adj.* Inducing or causing depletion. Also **de·ple·to·ry** (di·plē′tər·ē). **— n.** That which depletes.

de·plor·a·ble (di·plôr′ə·bəl, -plō′rə-) *adj.* **1.** To be deplored; lamentable. **2.** Wretched; sad. **— de·plor′a·ble·ness,** **de·plor′a·bil′i·ty** *n.* **— de·plor′a·bly** *adv.*

de·plore (di·plôr′, -plōr′) *v.t.* **·plored,** **·plor·ing** To have or show regret or sadness over; lament. **— Syn.** See MOURN. [< L *deplorare* < *de-* completely + *plorare* to bewail]

de·ploy (di·ploi′) *v.t. & v.i.* **1.** To place or position (forces, people, etc.) according to a plan. **2.** *Mil.* To spread out (troops, etc.), in battle formation. [< F *déployer* < OF *desployer, despleier* < LL *displicare* < L *dis-* from + *plicare* to fold. Doublet of DISPLAY.] **— de·ploy′ment** *n.*

de·plu·mate (dē·plōō′mit) *adj.* *Ornithol.* Bare of feathers.

de·plume (dē·plōōm′) *v.t.* **·plumed,** **·plum·ing 1.** To strip the plumage or feathers from. **2.** To strip; despoil, as of

honors or wealth. [< F *déplumer* < *dé-* away (< L *dis-*) + *plume* feather < L *pluma*] **— de′plu·ma′tion** *n.*

de·po·lar·ize (dē·pō′lə·rīz) *v.t.* **·ized,** **·iz·ing** To deprive of polarity or of polarization. **— de·po·lar·i·za′tion** *n.* **— de·po′lar·iz′er** *n.*

de·pone (di·pōn′) *v.t. & v.i.* **·poned,** **·pon·ing** *Archaic* To testify, especially under oath; depose. [< L *deponere* < *de-* down + *ponere* to place, put]

de·po·nent (di·pō′nənt) *adj.* In Latin and Greek grammar, denoting a verb that has the form of the passive or middle voice but is active in meaning. **— n. 1.** A deponent verb. **2.** *Law* One who gives sworn testimony, especially in writing. Abbr. *dep., dpt.*

de·po·u·late (dē·pop′yə·lāt; *for adj., also* dē·pop′yə·lit, -lāt) *v.t.* **·lat·ed,** **·lat·ing** To remove the inhabitants from, as by massacre, famine, eviction, etc. **— adj.** *Obs.* Depopulated. [< L *depopulatus,* pp. of *depopulari* < *de-* down + *populari* to lay waste < *populus* people] **— de·pop′u·la′tion** *n.* **— de·pop′u·la′tor** *n.*

de·port (di·pôrt′, -pōrt′) *v.t.* **1.** To expel from a country; banish. **2.** To behave or conduct (oneself). **— Syn.** See BANISH. **— n.** *Obs.* Deportment. [< OF *deporter* < L *deportare* < *de-* away + *portare* to carry]

de·por·ta·tion (dē′pôr·tā′shən, -pōr-) *n.* The act of deporting; especially, the banishment of an undesirable alien to his native country.

de·por·tee (dē′pôr·tē′, -pōr-) *n.* One who is sentenced to deportation. [< F *déporté* a banished person]

de·port·ment (di·pôrt′mənt, -pōrt′-) *n.* Conduct or behavior; demeanor; bearing. **— Syn.** See BEHAVIOR.

de·pos·al (di·pō′zəl) *n.* The act of deposing from office.

de·pose (di·pōz′) *v.* **·posed,** **·pos·ing** *v.t.* **1.** To deprive of rank or office; oust, as a king. **2.** *Law* To declare under oath, especially in an affidavit. **— v.i. 3.** *Law* To give testimony under oath, especially in writing. [< OF *deposer* < *de-* down (< L *de-*) + *poser.* See POSE[1].] **— de·pos′a·ble** *adj.*

de·pos·it (di·poz′it) *v.t.* **1.** To set down; place; put. **2.** To put down in the form of a layer, as silt; precipitate. **3.** To entrust (money, valuables, etc.) for safekeeping, as in a bank. **4.** To give as partial payment or security. **— v.i. 5.** To be collected or precipitated: Sediments *deposit* in layers. **— n. 1.** Something entrusted for safekeeping, especially money placed in a bank. Abbr. *dep., Dep.* **2.** The state of being placed for safekeeping: chiefly in the phrase **on deposit. 3.** A depository. **4.** Anything given as partial payment or security. **5.** That which is or has been deposited or cast down, as sediment. **6.** A layer of metal formed by electrolytic action. **7.** *Geol.* An accumulated mass of iron, coal, oil, etc. [< L *depositus,* pp. of *deponere.* See DEPONE.]

de·pos·i·tar·y (di·poz′ə·ter′ē) *n.* *pl.* **·tar·ies 1.** One entrusted with anything for safekeeping. **2.** A depository.

dep·o·si·tion (dep′ə·zish′ən, dē′pə-) *n.* **1.** The act of deposing, as from an office. **2.** The act of depositing; also, that which is deposited. **3.** *Law* The written testimony of a witness who is under oath, often used in court when oral testimony cannot be obtained. **— Syn.** See TESTIMONY.

de·pos·i·tor (di·poz′ə·tər) *n.* One who makes a deposit.

de·pos·i·to·ry (di·poz′ə·tôr′ē, -tō′rē) *n.* *pl.* **·ries** **1.** A place where anything is deposited. **2.** A depositary.

de·pot (dē′pō, *Mil. & Brit.* dep′ō) *n.* **1.** A warehouse or storehouse. **2.** *U.S.* A railroad station. **3.** *Mil.* **a** An installation that manufactures, procures, stores, or repairs military materiel. **b** An installation for the reception, classification, and processing of personnel. Abbr. *dep.* **— Syn.** See STATION. [< F *dépôt* < OF *depost* < L *depositum* a pledge < *deponere.* See DEPONE.]

dep·ra·va·tion (dep′rə·vā′shən) *n.* The act of depraving, or the state of being depraved; corruption.

de·prave (di·prāv′) *v.t.* **·praved,** **·prav·ing 1.** To render bad or worse, especially in morals; corrupt; pervert. **2.** *Obs.* To vilify; slander. [< L *depravare* < *de-* completely + *pravus* corrupt, wicked] **— de·prav′er** *n.*

de·praved (di·prāvd′) *adj.* Morally debased; corrupt.

de·prav·i·ty (di·prav′ə·tē) *n.* *pl.* **·ties 1.** The state of being depraved; wickedness. **2.** A depraved act or habit. **— Syn. 1.** corruption, badness, degeneracy. **2.** perversion, vice.

dep·re·cate (dep′rə·kāt) *v.t.* **·cat·ed,** **·cat·ing 1.** To express disapproval of or regret for; plead earnestly against. **2.** To disparage or belittle; depreciate. **3.** *Archaic* To desire or pray for deliverance from. [< L *deprecatus,* pp. of *deprecari* < *de-* away + *precari* to pray] **— dep′re·cat′ing·ly** *adv.* **— dep′re·ca′tion** *n.* **— dep′re·ca′tor** *n.* **— Syn. 1.** remonstrate, protest, expostulate.

dep·re·ca·tive (dep′rə·kā′tiv) *adj.* Deprecatory. **— dep′·re·ca′tive·ly** *adv.*

dep·re·ca·to·ry (dep′rə·kə·tôr′ē, -tō′rē) *adj.* Tending to deprecate; apologetic.

de·pre·ci·ate (di·prē′shē·āt) *v.* **·at·ed,** **·at·ing** *v.t.* **1.** To lessen the value of; lower the price or rate of. **2.** To disparage; belittle. **— v.i. 3.** To become less in value, etc. **— Syn.** See DISPARAGE. [< L *depretiatus,* pp. of *depretiare* < *de-* down + *pretium* price] **— de·pre′ci·a′tor** *n.*

de·pre·ci·a·tion (di·prē′shē·ā′shən) *n.* **1.** A loss in value or efficiency resulting from deterioration, usage, age, etc. **2.**

In accounting, the estimation of, and the allowance made for, such loss. **3.** A decline in the purchasing value of money. **4.** A disparagement or belittling.

de·pre·ci·a·to·ry (di-prē'shē-ə-tôr'ē, -tō'rē) *adj.* Tending to depreciate. Also **de·pre'ci·a'tive.**

dep·re·date (dep'rə-dāt) *v.t. & v.i.* **·dat·ed, ·dat·ing** To prey upon; pillage; plunder. [< LL *depraedatus*, pp. of *depraedari* < L *de-* completely + *praeda* booty, prey] — **dep're·da'tor** *n.* — **dep·re·da·to·ry** (dep'rə-dā'tər-ē, di·pred'ə-tôr'ē, -tō'rē) *adj.*

dep·re·da·tion (dep'rə-dā'shən) *n.* A plundering or despoiling; robbery.

de·press (di-pres') *v.t.* **1.** To lower the spirits of; make gloomy; sadden. **2.** To lessen in vigor, force, or energy; weaken; make dull. **3.** To lower in price or value. **4.** To press or push down; lower. **5.** *Music* To lower the pitch of. **6.** *Obs.* To subjugate; suppress. [< OF *depresser* < L *depressus*, pp. of *deprimere* < *de-* down + *primere* to press] — **Syn. 1.** deject, dispirit, discourage. **2.** diminish. **3.** reduce.

de·pres·sant (di-pres'ənt) *Med. adj.* Tending to lessen nervous or functional activity. — *n.* A drug or other substance which calms or soothes; a sedative.

de·pressed (di-prest') *adj.* **1.** Sad; dejected. **2.** Pressed down, as from above; flattened. **3.** Lowered in position; sunk even with or below the general surface: a *depressed* roadway. **4.** Reduced in power, amount, value, etc. **5.** *Zool.* Broader than high, as the bill of a flycatcher. **6.** *Bot.* Flattened from above.

depressed area A region characterized by unemployment and a low standard of living: also called *distressed area.*

de·press·ing (di-pres'ing) *adj.* Disheartening; sad. — **de·press'ing·ly** *adv.*

de·pres·sion (di-presh'ən) *n.* **1.** The act of depressing, or the state of being depressed. **2.** Low spirits or vitality; dejection; melancholy. **3.** A low or depressed place or surface; a hollow. **4.** A severe decline in business, accompanied by increasing unemployment, falling prices, etc.; also, the period during which such a decline lasts. **5.** A decrease or reduction in power, activity, amount, etc. **6.** *Med.* A decrease in functional activity. **7.** *Psychiatry* A deep dejection of spirit characterized by withdrawal, lack of response to stimulation, etc. **8.** *Meteorol.* **a** A region of low atmospheric pressure. **b** The indication of this by the fall of mercury in a barometer. **9.** *Astron.* The angular distance of a heavenly body below the horizon. **10.** In surveying, the angular distance of an object below the horizontal plane through the point of observation. **11.** *Music* The flatting of a note. — **the Depression** The economic crisis and decline of the 1930's. — **Syn. 2.** despondency, sadness, gloom. **3.** cavity, dip.

de·pres·sive (di-pres'iv) *adj.* **1.** Causing or tending to depression. **2.** Characterized by depression, especially mental depression. — **de·pres'sive·ly** *adv.* — **de·pres'sive·ness** *n.*

de·pres·so·mo·tor (di-pres'ō-mō'tər) *adj. Physiol.* Diminishing the capacity for movement; retarding motor activity. — *n. Med.* An agent that lowers the activity of the motor centers, as a bromide.

de·pres·sor (di-pres'ər) *n.* **1.** One who or that which depresses. **2.** *Physiol.* A depressor nerve. **3.** *Anat.* One of several muscles that depress or contract a part. **4.** *Med.* An instrument for pressing down a part, as the tongue.

depressor nerve *Physiol.* An afferent nerve connected with the heart, controlling heart rate and blood pressure.

dep·ri·va·tion (dep'rə-vā'shən) *n.* **1.** The act of depriving, or the state of being deprived. **2.** A taking away of rank, office, etc. **3.** Privation; loss. Also **de·priv·al** (di-prī'vəl).

de·prive (di-prīv') *v.t.* **·prived, ·priv·ing 1.** To take something away from; dispossess; divest. **2.** To keep from acquiring, using, or enjoying something. **3.** *Obs.* To put an end to. [< OF *depriver* < L *de-* completely + *privare* to strip, remove] — **de·priv'a·ble** *adj.*

De Pro·fun·dis (dē prō-fun'dis) The 130th psalm (in the Vulgate and Douai versions, the 129th): from the first words of the Latin version. [< L, out of the depths]

de pro·pri·o mo·tu (dē prō'prē-ō mō'tōō) *Latin* Of its own accord.

dep·side (dep'sīd, -sid) *n. Chem.* One of a group of aromatic compounds formed from phenol carboxylic acids, found chiefly in lichens or made synthetically. [< Gk. *depsein* to soften, tan + -IDE]

dept. 1. Department. **2.** Deputy.

Dept·ford (det'fərd) A metropolitan borough of SE London; pop. 68,267 (1961).

depth (depth) *n.* **1.** The state or degree of being deep; deepness. **2.** Extent or distance downward, inward, or backward. **3.** Profundity of thought or feeling. **4.** *Usually pl.* An extremely remote, deep, or distant part: the *depths* of the sea. **5.** *Usually pl.* An intense state of being or feeling: the *depths* of sorrow. **6.** The most intense part or stage: the *depth* of night. **7.** Richness or intensity of color, sound, etc. **8.** Lowness of pitch. [ME *depthe*]

depth charge A drum-shaped bomb that explodes under water at a desired depth, used against underwater mines and submarines. Also **depth bomb.**

dep·u·rate (dep'yə-rāt) *v.t. & v.i.* **·rat·ed, ·rat·ing** To free or become free from morbid matter or impurities. [< Med.L *depuratus*, pp. of *depurare* < L *de-* completely + *purus* pure] — **dep'u·ra'tion** *n.* — **dep·u·ra·tor** *n.*

dep·u·ra·tive (dep'yə-rā'tiv) *adj.* Purifying; purgative. — *n.* A purifying agent.

dep·u·ta·tion (dep'yə-tā'shən) *n.* **1.** A person or persons acting for another or others; a delegation. **2.** The act of deputing, or the state of being deputed.

de·pute (di-pyōot') *v.t.* **·put·ed, ·put·ing 1.** To appoint as an agent, deputy, or delegation; send with authority. **2.** To transfer (authority, etc.) to another. [< OF *deputer* < LL *deputare* < L *de-* away + *putare* to think]

dep·u·tize (dep'yə-tīz) *v.* **·tized, ·tiz·ing** *v.t.* **1.** To appoint as a deputy. — *v.i.* **2.** To act as a deputy.

dep·u·ty (dep'yə-tē) *n. pl.* **·ties 1.** One appointed to act for another: a sheriff's *deputy.* **2.** A member of a legislative assembly in certain countries. Abbr. *d., D., dep., dept.* — **Syn.** See DELEGATE. — *adj.* Acting as deputy. [< F *député*, pp. of *députer* < OF *deputer.* See DEPUTE.]

De Quin·cey (di kwin'sē), **Thomas,** 1785–1859, English essayist.

der. Derivation; derivative; derived.

de·rac·i·nate (di-ras'ə-nāt) *v.t.* **·nat·ed, ·nat·ing 1.** To pull up by the roots; uproot. **2.** To separate; dislocate; extirpate. [< F *déraciner* < *dé-* away (< L *dis-*) + *racine* a root < L *radix*] — **de·rac·i·na'tion** *n.*

de·raign (di-rān') *v.t. Obs.* To determine or maintain (a claim, right, etc.) by judicial argument or wager of battle. [< OF *deraisnier* < *de-* down (< L *de-*) + *raisnier* to reason < L *ratio, -onis* reason] — **de·raign'ment** *n.*

de·rail (dē-rāl') *v.t.* **1.** To cause (a train, etc.) to run off the rails. — *v.i.* **2.** To run off the rails. [< F *dérailler* < *dé-* from (< L *de-*) + *rail* rail] — **de·rail'ment** *n.*

De·rain (də-raṅ'), **André,** 1880–1954, French painter.

de·range (di-rānj') *v.t.* **·ranged, ·rang·ing 1.** To disturb the arrangement or order of. **2.** To disturb the functions of, as an organism, or put into a disordered condition, as a machine. **3.** To unbalance the reason of; render insane. [< F *déranger* < *dé-* away (< L *dis-*) + *ranger.* See RANGE.]

de·ranged (di-rānjd') *adj.* **1.** Insane. **2.** Disordered.

de·range·ment (di-rānj'mənt) *n.* **1.** Disorder; confusion. **2.** Severe mental disorder; insanity.

de·ray (di-rā') *n. Obs.* Disorderly revelry. [< OF *desrei* < *desreer* to disorder < *des-* away (< L *dis-*) + *rei* order]

der·by (dûr'bē) *n. pl.* **·bies** A stiff felt hat with a curved, narrow brim and round crown: also, *Brit.,* bowler. [< DERBY]

Der·by (dûr'bē, *Brit.* där'bē) *n.* **1.** An annual horse race for three-year-olds run at Epsom Downs in Surrey, England, since 1780. **2.** Any similar horse race, as the Kentucky Derby. [after the 12th Earl of *Derby,* the founder]

Derby. Derbyshire.

Der·by·shire (dûr'bē-shir, *Brit.* där'bē-) A county in central England; 1,006 sq. mi.; pop. 902,820 (1976); chief city, Derby; pop. 217,800 (1976). Also **Der'by.**

dere (dir) See DEAR[2].

de rè·gle (də re'gl') *French* According to rule; in proper form.

der·e·lict (der'ə-likt) *adj.* **1.** Neglectful of obligation; remiss. **2.** Deserted or abandoned. — *n.* **1.** That which is deserted or abandoned, as a ship at sea. **2.** A social outcast, vagrant, etc. **3.** One who neglects a duty. **4.** Land exposed by the permanent receding of the sea. [< L *derelictus*, pp. of *derelinquere* < *de-* completely + *relinquere* to abandon]

der·e·lic·tion (der'ə-lik'shən) *n.* **1.** Neglect or willful omission; failure in duty. **2.** Voluntary abandonment of a charge or property. **3.** The state or fact of being abandoned. **4.** *Law* **a** A gain of land by a permanent receding of water. **b** The land thus gained. — **Syn.** See NEGLECT.

de·ride (di-rīd') *v.t.* **·rid·ed, ·rid·ing** To treat with scornful mirth; ridicule. [< L *deridere* < *de-* completely + *ridere* to laugh, mock] — **de·rid'er** *n.* — **de·rid'ing·ly** *adv.*

de ri·gueur (də rē·gœr') *French* Necessary according to etiquette; required by good form.

der·in·ger (der'in·jer) See DERRINGER.

de·ris·i·ble (di-riz'ə-bəl) *adj.* Provoking or deserving derision.

de·ri·sion (di-rizh'ən) *n.* **1.** The act of deriding; ridicule; mockery. **2.** An object of ridicule or scorn. [< L *derisio, -onis* < *deridere.* See DERIDE.]

de·ri·sive (di-rī'siv) *adj.* Expressive of or characterized by derision; mocking. Also **de·ri·so·ry** (di-rī'sər·ē). — **de·ri'sive·ly** *adv.* — **de·ri'sive·ness** *n.*

deriv. Derivation; derivative; derived.

der·i·va·tion (der'ə-vā'shən) *n.* **1.** The act of deriving, or the condition of being derived. **2.** That which is derived; a derivative. **3.** Origin or descent. **4.** The tracing of a word from its original form and meaning; also, a statement of this; an etymology. **5.** *Gram.* The formation of new words by the addition of affixes to existing words or roots. **6.** *Math.* The process of obtaining a differential. Abbr. *der., deriv.* — **der'-i·va'tion·al** *adj.*

de·riv·a·tive (di-riv'ə-tiv) *adj.* **1.** Resulting from or characterized by derivation. **2.** Not original or primary; based on or originating in other sources. — *n.* **1.** That which is derived. **2.** *Gram.* A word developed from another, as by the addition of a prefix or suffix or by phonetic change: "Functional" is a *derivative* of "function." **3.** *Chem.* A compound formed or regarded as being formed from a specified substance or another compound, usually by partial substitution: a benzene *derivative.* **4.** *Math.* The instantaneous rate of change of a function with reference to a variable: also called *differential coefficient.* Abbr. *der., deriv.* — **de·riv'a·tive·ly** *adv.*

de·rive (di-rīv') *v.* **·rived, ·riv·ing** *v.t.* **1.** To draw or receive, as from a source or principle. **2.** To deduce, as from a premise; draw, as a conclusion. **3.** To trace the source or derivation of (a word, etc.). **4.** *Chem.* To obtain (a compound) from another, as by partial substitution. **5.** *Obs.* To cause to come; bring: with *on, to,* or *upon.* — *v.i.* **6.** To have derivation; originate; proceed. [< L *derivare* < *de-* from + *rivus* stream] — **de·riv'a·ble** *adj.* — **de·riv'er** *n.*

derm- Var. of DERMO-.

-derm *suffix* Skin: endoderm. Also **der·mis** (dûr'mis). [< Gk. *derma* skin]

der·ma (dûr'mə) *n. Anat.* The corium. [< Gk., skin]

der·mal (dûr'məl) *adj.* Of or pertaining to the skin; cutaneous. Also **der'mic.**

der·map·ter·ous (dər-map'tər-əs) *adj. Entomol.* Of or pertaining to an order (*Dermaptera*) of small, elongate, terrestrial insects, including the earwigs. Also **der·map'ter·an.** [< DERM(O)- + Gk. *a-* without + *pteron* wing]

der·ma·ti·tis (dûr'mə-tī'tis) *n. Pathol.* Inflammation of the skin. [< DERMAT(O)- + -ITIS]

dermato- *combining form* Skin: dermatology. Also, before vowels, **dermat-.** [< Gk. *derma, dermatos* skin]

der·mat·o·gen (dər-mat'ə-jən, dûr'mə-tō'jən) *n. Bot.* The outermost layer of cells in plants, forming the permanent epidermal tissue: also called *protoderm.*

der·ma·toid (dûr'mə-toid) *adj.* Resembling skin; skinlike. Also **der'moid.**

der·ma·tol·o·gy (dûr'mə-tol'ə-jē) *n.* The branch of medical science that relates to the skin and its diseases. — **der·ma·to·log·i·cal** (dûr'mə-tə-loj'i-kəl) *adj.* — **der'ma·tol'o·gist** *n.*

der·ma·to·phyte (dûr'mə-tō-fīt') *n. Bot.* A plant living parasitically upon the skin, as certain fungi which produce ringworm, favus, etc. — **der·ma·to·phyt'ic** (-fit'ik) *adj.*

der·ma·to·phy·to·sis (dûr'mə-tō-fī-tō'sis) *n. Pathol.* Athlete's foot.

der·ma·to·plas·ty (dûr'mə-tō-plas'tē) *n. Surg.* The replacement of destroyed skin by skin grafts.

dermo- *combining form* Skin. Also, before vowels, **derm-.** [< Gk. *derma* skin]

dermoid cyst *Pathol.* A cyst or tumor lined with skin tissue and sometimes containing hair follicles, sweat glands, etc.

der·ni·er (dûr'nē-ər, *Fr.* der-nyā') *adj.* Last; final. [< F]

der·nier cri (der-nyā'krē') *French* The newest thing; the latest fashion; literally, the last cry.

der·o·gate (*v.* der'ə-gāt; *adj.* der'ə-git, -gāt) *v.* **·gat·ed, ·gat·ing** *v.i.* **1.** To take away; detract: with *from.* **2.** To become inferior in character or status: with *from.* — *v.t.* **3.** *Archaic* To take away (something) so as to cause loss or impairment: with *from.* **4.** *Rare* To disparage. — *adj. Rare* Lessened in value; degraded. [< L *derogatus,* pp. of *derogare* < *de-* away + *rogare* to ask, propose a law] — **der'o·ga'tion** *n.*

de·rog·a·tive (di-rog'ə-tiv) *adj.* Tending to derogate or detract; derogatory. — **de·rog'a·tive·ly** *adv.*

de·rog·a·to·ry (di-rog'ə-tôr'ē, -tō'rē) *adj.* Having the effect of lessening or detracting; belittling; disparaging. — **de·rog'a·to'ri·ly** *adv.* — **de·rog'a·to'ri·ness** *n.*

der·rick (der'ik) *n.* **1.** An apparatus for hoisting and swinging heavy weights into place, usually consisting of a tackle at the end of a boom or mast. **2.** The framework over the mouth of an oil well or similar drill hole. [after *Derrick,* 17th c. London hangman]

der·ri·ère (der'ē-er', *Fr.* de-ryâr') *n. French* The rear; hind parts; buttocks.

der·ring-do (der'ing-dōō') *n.* Courageous or daring action. [ME *dorryng don* daring to do; mistaken for a noun phrase by Spenser]

der·rin·ger (der'in-jər) *n.* A pistol having a short barrel and a large bore: also spelled *deringer.* [after Henry *Deringer,* 19th c. U.S. gunsmith, who invented it]

der·ris (der'is) *n.* Any of a genus (*Derris*) of woody, climbing plants of the East Indies; especially, *D. triplica* and *D. elliptica,* that yield rotenone. [< NL < Gk., a covering]

der·ry (der'ē) *n. pl.* **·ries** A meaningless word used as a refrain in old songs. Also **der'ry-down'.**

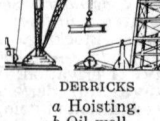

DERRICKS
a Hoisting.
b Oil-well.

Der·ry (der'ē) See LONDONDERRY.

der·vish (dûr'vish) *n.* A member of any of various Moslem orders vowed to poverty and chastity, some of whom express their devotion in whirling, howling, etc. [< Turkish < Persian *darvēsh*]

Der·went (dûr'wənt) **1.** Any of four small rivers in England. **2.** A river in southern Tasmania flowing 120 miles SE to the Tasman Sea.

de·sal·in·i·za·tion (dē-sal'in-ə-zā'shən, -ī-zā', -sā'lin-) *n.* The process of removing salt from water; desalting.

de·salt (dē-sôlt') *v.t.* To remove the salt from, as sea water, to make potable. — **de·salt'er** *n.* — **de·salt'ing** *n.*

desc. Descendant.

des·cant (*n.* des'kant; *v.* des-kant', dis-) *n.* **1.** A discussion or a series of remarks. **2.** *Music* **a** A varied melody or song. **b** Formerly, an ornamental variation of the main subject. **c** A counterpoint above the cantus firmus. **d** The composition or singing of such counterpoint. **e** The upper part in part music. — *v.i.* **1.** To discourse at length; hold forth: with *on* or *upon.* **2.** *Music* **a** To make or perform a descant. **b** To sing. Also *discant.* [< AF < Med.L *discantus* < L *dis-* away + *cantus* a song < *canere* to sing]

Des·cartes (dā-kärt'), **René,** 1596–1650, French mathematician and philosopher.

de·scend (di-send') *v.i.* **1.** To move from a higher to a lower point; go or come down; sink. **2.** To slope or incline downward, as a path. **3.** To lower oneself; stoop: to *descend* to begging. **4.** To come by inheritance; be inherited. **5.** *Biol.* To be derived by heredity. **6.** To pass from the general to the specific. **7.** To arrive or come in great numbers or force, so as to overwhelm. **8.** *Astron.* To move southward or toward the horizon, as a star. — *v.t.* **9.** To move from an upper to a lower part of; go down, as stairs. [< OF *descendre* < L *descendere* < *de-* down + *scandere* to climb]

de·scen·dant (di-sen'dənt) *n.* One who is descended lineally from another; offspring. — *adj.* See DESCENDENT. [< F, ppr. of *descendre.* See DESCEND.]

de·scen·dent (di-sen'dənt) *adj.* **1.** Proceeding downward; descending. **2.** Issuing by descent, as from an ancestor. Also spelled *descendant.* [< L *descendens, -entis,* ppr. of *descendere.* See DESCEND.]

de·scend·er (di-sen'dər) *n.* **1.** One who or that which descends. **2.** *Printing* The part of certain letters that extends below the bottom of most letters, as in *g, j, p,* etc.; also, any of the letters themselves.

de·scend·i·ble (di-sen'də-bəl) *adj.* **1.** That can be descended. **2.** That can be inherited. Also **de·scend'a·ble.**

de·scent (di-sent') *n.* **1.** The act of descending; any downward motion. **2.** A decline or deterioration: the *descent* of courtesy. **3.** The way leading down; declivity; slope. **4.** Ancestral derivation; lineage. **5.** In genealogy, a generation. **6.** *Law* The succession of property or title by inheritance. **7.** A sudden onslaught or attack. [< OF *descente* < *descendre.* See DESCEND.]

Des·chutes River (dā-shōōt') A river in central Oregon, flowing 240 miles NE to the Columbia River.

de·scribe (di-skrīb') *v.t.* **·scribed, ·scrib·ing** **1.** To present in spoken or written words; give a verbal account of. **2.** To give a mental picture or idea of by means of words; depict. **3.** To draw the figure of; trace; outline. **4.** Erroneously, to descry. [< L *describere* < *de-* down + *scribere* to write] — **de·scrib'a·ble** *adj.* — **de·scrib'er** *n.*

de·scrip·tion (di-skrip'shən) *n.* **1.** The act or technique of describing; verbal depiction or presentation. **2.** An account that describes; a portrayal in words. **3.** A drawing or tracing, as of an arc. **4.** Sort, kind, or variety: birds of every *description.* — **Syn.** See EXPLANATION. [< OF < L *descriptio, -onis* < *describere.* See DESCRIBE.]

de·scrip·tive (di-skrip'tiv) *adj.* **1.** Characterized by or containing description; serving to describe. **2.** *Gram.* **a** Of an adjective, expressing the nature or quality of something, as *beautiful* and *gray* in *a beautiful view, a gray car.* **b** Nonrestrictive. — **de·scrip'tive·ly** *adv.* — **de·scrip'tive·ness** *n.*

descriptive geometry Any of several geometric systems by which the representations of solids are projected so that their spatial properties can be accurately deduced.

descriptive linguistics The study of the structure of a language or languages at a specific stage of development: also called *synchronic linguistics.*

descriptive science Any science that emphasizes the classification and description of the material it deals with.

de·scry (di-skrī') *v.t.* **·scried, ·scry·ing** **1.** To discover with the eye, as something distant or obscure; discern; detect. **2.** To discover by observation or investigation. [< OF *descrier* < *des-* away (< L *dis-*) + *crier* to cry] — **de·scri'er** *n.*

Des·de·mo·na (dez'də-mō'nə) The heroine of Shakespeare's *Othello.*

des·e·crate (des'ə-krāt) *v.t.* **·crat·ed, ·crat·ing** To divert from a sacred to a common use; treat sacrilegiously; profane. [< DE- (def. 4) + L *sacratus,* pp. of *sacrare* to make holy < *sacer* holy] — **des'e·crat'er** or **des'e·cra'tor** *n.*

des·e·cra·tion (des'ə-krā'shən) *n.* The act of desecrating or the condition of being desecrated; profanation. — **Syn.** See PROFANATION.

de·seg·re·gate (dē-seg'rə-gāt) *v.t.* ·gat·ed, ·gat·ing To eliminate racial segregation in.

de·seg·re·ga·tion (dē'seg-rə-gā'shən) *n.* The process of
ending the separation or segregation of races, as of Negroes
and whites, in schools, public facilities, etc.

de·sen·si·tize (dē-sen'sə-tīz) *v.t.* ·tized, ·tiz·ing 1. To make
less sensitive. 2. *Photog.* To make (a film) less sensitive to
light. 3. *Med.* To lessen or eliminate the sensitiveness of
(an individual, organ, tissue, etc.), as to an allergen or other
substance. — **de·sen'si·ti·za'tion** *n.* — **de·sen'si·tiz'er** *n.*

des·ert[1] (*n., adj. def. 1* dez'ərt; *adj. def. 2* di·zûrt') *n.* 1. A
region so lacking in rainfall, moisture, and vegetation as to
be almost uninhabitable by any plant or animal population.
2. Any region that is uncultivated and desolate because of
deficient moisture, barren soil, or permanent frost. — *adj.*
1. Of or like a desert; uninhabited; barren. 2. *Archaic* Deserted; forsaken. [< OF < LL *desertum* < L, pp. neut. of
deserere < *de-* away + *serere* to join]

de·sert[2] (di·zûrt') *v.t.* 1. To forsake or abandon. 2. To forsake in violation of one's oath or orders, as a service, post,
etc. — *v.i.* 3. To abandon one's post, duty, etc. 4. *Mil.* To
be absent without leave with the intention of not returning.
— **Syn.** See ABANDON. [< F *déserter* < LL *desertare*, freq.
of L *deserere.* See DESERT[1].]

de·sert[3] (di·zûrt') *n.* 1. *Often pl.* That which is deserved or
merited: to get one's just *deserts.* 2. The state of deserving
reward or punishment. 3. Deserving of reward; also, a
worthy act. [< OF *deserte* < *deservir.* See DESERVE.]

de·sert·er (di·zûr'tər) *n.* One who forsakes a duty friends,
etc.; especially, one who deserts from a military service.

de·ser·tion (di·zûr'shən) *n.* 1. The act of deserting. 2.
The state of being deserted; desolation. 3. *Law* The willful
abandonment, without legal justification, of one's spouse or
children, or both.

de·serve (di·zûrv') *v.* ·served, ·serv·ing *v.t.* 1. To be entitled to or worthy of; merit; earn. — *v.i.* 2. To be worthy.
[< OF *deservir* < L *deservire* < *de-* completely + *servire* to
serve] — **de·serv'er** *n.*

de·served (di·zûrvd') *adj.* Earned or merited. — **de·serv·
ed·ness** (di·zûr'vid·nis) *n.*

de·serv·ed·ly (di·zûr'vid·lē) *adv.* According to merit; justly.

de·serv·ing (di·zûr'ving) *adj.* Worthy; meritorious: *deserving* of praise. — *n.* Merit or demerit; desert. — **de·serv'·
ing·ly** *adv.* — **de·serv'ing·ness** *n.*

de·sex (dē·seks') *v.t.* To remove or cut out the reproductive
organs; castrate or spay.

des·ha·bille (dez'ə·bēl') *n.* Dishabille (which see).

des·ic·cant (des'ə·kənt) *adj.* Producing dryness; desiccat-
ing, as a medicine. — *n.* A drying agent or substance.

des·ic·cate (des'ə·kāt) *v.* ·cat·ed, ·cat·ing *v.t.* 1. To dry
thoroughly. 2. To remove the moisture from (foods) in
order to preserve. — *v.i.* 3. To become dry. [< L *desicca-
tus,* pp. of *desiccare* < *de-* completely + *siccare* to dry out <
siccus dry] — **des'ic·ca'tion** *n.* — **des'ic·ca'tive** *adj. & n.*

des·ic·ca·tor (des'ə·kā'tər) *n.* 1. One who or that which
desiccates. 2. An apparatus for drying meat, vegetables,
etc. 3. A device for absorbing moisture in chemicals, etc.

de·sid·er·ate (di·sid'ə·rāt) *v.t.* ·at·ed, ·at·ing To feel desire
or need for; feel the lack of. [< L *desideratus,* pp. of *desiderare.* See DESIRE.] — **de·sid'er·a'tion** *n.*

de·sid·er·a·tive (di·sid'ə·rā'tiv) *adj.* Having, implying, or
expressing desire. — *n.* 1. Something desired; desideratum.
2. *Gram.* A verb derived from another verb and indicating
desire to perform the action expressed in the original verb,
as Latin *esurio* I wish to eat, I am hungry, from *edo* I eat.

de·sid·er·a·tum (di·sid'ə·rā'təm) *n.* *pl.* ·ta (-tə) Something needed or regarded as desirable. [< L]

de·sign (di·zīn') *v.t.* 1. To draw or prepare preliminary
plans or sketches of. 2. To plan and make with skill, as a
work of art. 3. To form or make (plans, schemes, etc.) in
the mind; conceive; invent. 4. To intend; purpose. 5. *Archaic* To mark out; designate. — *v.i.* 6. To make original
drawings or plans; be a designer. 7. To plan; conceive. —
n. 1. A preliminary sketch or outline; pattern. 2. The arrangement and coordination of the parts or details of any
object, by means of which the whole achieves a certain effect
or impression, or produces a certain result: the *design* of a
postage stamp; the *design* of a jet airplane. 3. A piece of
artistic or decorative work. 4. The art of making designs.
5. A visual pattern or composition. 6. A plan or project; an
undertaking. 7. An object or reason; purpose: the *design* of
a course of study. 8. *Often pl.* A sinister scheme or plot, as
to gain possession of something: with *on* or *against*: He had
designs on my job. 9. Intelligent, purposeful, or discoverable pattern, as opposed to chaos. [< MF *désigner* to designate < L *designare.* See DESIGNATE.] — **Syn.** See PUR-
POSE. — **de·sign'a·ble** *adj.*

des·ig·nate (*v.* dez'ig·nāt; *for adj., also* dez'ig·nit) *v.t.* ·nat·
ed, ·nat·ing 1. To indicate or make recognizable by some
mark, sign, or name; specify. 2. To name or entitle; characterize. 3. To select or appoint for a specific purpose, duty,

etc. — *adj.* Designated; selected. [< L *designatus,* pp. o
designare < *de-* completely + *signare* to mark < *signum* a
sign] — **des'ig·na'tive** (-nā'tiv) *adj.* — **des'ig·na'tor** *n.*

des·ig·na·tion (dez'ig·nā'shən) *n.* 1. A distinctive mark,
name, or title. 2. The act of indicating something. 3. Appointment or nomination. — **Syn.** See NAME.

de·sign·ed·ly (di·zī'nid·lē) *adv.* By design; intentionally.

des·ig·nee (dez'ig·nē') *n.* A person designated.

de·sign·er (di·zī'nər) *n.* 1. One who creates designs, as for
dresses, machinery, etc. 2. A schemer; contriver.

de·sign·ing (di·zī'ning) *n.* 1. The act or art of making designs. 2. The act of plotting or scheming. — *adj.* 1. Artful; scheming. 2. Exercising foresight; heedful. — **de·sign'·
ing·ly** *adv.*

des·i·nence (des'ə·nəns) *n.* 1. Termination; ending. 2.
Gram. An inflectional ending. [< MF *désinence* < Med.L
desinentia < L *desinere* to leave off < *de-* away + *sinere* to
leave]

de·sir·a·ble (di·zīr'ə·bəl) *adj.* Worthy of or exciting desire.
— **de·sir'a·bil'i·ty, de·sir'a·ble·ness** *n.* — **de·sir'a·bly** *adv*

de·sire (di·zīr') *v.t.* ·sired, ·sir·ing 1. To wish or long for;
covet; crave. 2. To express a wish for; ask for; request. —
n. 1. A longing or craving. 2. A request or wish. 3. An
object desired. 4. Sexual appetite; passion; lust. [< OF
desirer < L *desiderare,* ? < *de-* from + *sidus, sideris* star;
with ref. to astrology] — **de·sir'er** *n.*
— **Syn.** (verb) 1. *Desire, wish, want, crave,* and *covet* indicate
longing to possess something. *Desire* expresses ardent feeling, and
is so often applied to sexual longing that *wish* is commonly substituted for it to avoid that implication. *Wish* is also used of things
remote or unattainable: to *wish* to be king. *Want* originally indicated urgent need, but is now used to express less intense feeling
than *wish,* or simply preference. *Crave* is stronger than *wish* or
desire, and suggests a compulsive appetite: to *crave* liquor. We
covet that which belongs to another, with inordinate and often
reprehensible longing. — (noun) 4. *Desire, passion, lust, concu-
piscence, appetite, appetence, hankering,* and *yen* are here compared
as they apply to sexual longing. *Desire* embraces all aspects, and
includes the longing for companionship and affection as well as for
sexual satisfaction. It is usually not pejorative, nor is *passion,* the
greater ardor that distinguishes lovers from friends. *Lust* and *con-
cupiscence,* however, refer to undue carnal desire, and are always
used in a bad sense. *Appetite* suggests a great capacity as well as
desire for animal pleasure; *appetence* describes an *appetite* that is
natural. *Hankering* and the informal *yen* suggest the gnawing pangs
of unsatisfied *desire.* — **Ant.** antipathy, distaste, indifference.

de·sir·ous (di·zīr'əs) *adj.* 1. Having desire; experiencing a
wish or craving; eager. 2. *Obs.* Exciting desire; desirable.

de·sist (di·zist') *v.i.* To cease, as from an action or proceeding; forbear; stop: often with *from.* — **Syn.** See CEASE. [<
L *desistere* < *de-* from + *sistere* to stop, cease] — **de·sis'-
tance** or **de·sis'tence** *n.*

desk (desk) *n.* 1. A table or case adapted for writing or
studying, usually having compartments or drawers and a
flat or sloping surface. 2. A table or stand to hold that from
which one reads or preaches in a church; also, a pulpit. 3.
A division or post in an organization: the service *desk.* 4.
U.S. A department in a newspaper office: the copy *desk.* 5.
Music An orchestral music stand; also, two orchestral string
players reading from the same music stand. [< Med.L
desca < LL *discus.* Doublet of DAIS, DISH, DISK.]

D. ès L. Doctor of Letters (F *Docteur ès Lettres*).

des·man (des'mən) *n.* *pl.* ·mans (-mənz) An aquatic, shrew-
like, insectivorous mammal (family *Talpi-
dae*), valued for its fur; especially, *Des-
mana moschata* of SE Russia and *Galemys
pyrenaicus* of the Pyrenees. [< Sw.
desman musk]

des·mid (des'mid) *n.* *Bot.* Any of a
family (*Desmidiaceae*) of bright green,
unicellular, fresh-water algae. [< NL
Desmidium, the typical genus < Gk. *desmos* a band, chain] — **des·mid'i·an** *adj.*

DESMAN
(Body to 10
inches long;
tail about
6 inches)

des·moid (des'moid) *adj. Anat.* 1. Re-
sembling a ligament; ligamentous. 2.
Fibrous. — *n. Pathol.* A tough, very hard fibrous tumor.
[< Gk. *desmos* band + -OID]

Des Moines (də moin') The capital of Iowa, in the south
central part on the Des Moines River; pop. 201,404.

Des Moines River A river in Minnesota and Iowa, flowing
535 miles SE to the Mississippi.

Des·mou·lins (dā·mōō·lan'), (Lucie Simplice) **Camille** Benoît, 1760–94, French Revolutionary journalist.

des·o·late (*adj.* des'ə·lit; *v.* des'ə·lāt) *adj.* 1. Destitute of
inhabitants or dwellings; deserted; abandoned 2. Made
unfit for habitation; laid waste. 3. Gloomy; dreary. 4.
Without friends; forlorn; lonely. — *v.t.* ·lat·ed, ·lat·ing 1.
To deprive of inhabitants. 2. To lay waste; devastate. 3.
To make sorrowful, wretched, or forlorn. 4. To forsake;
abandon. [< L *desolatus,* pp. of *desolare* < *de-* completely
+ *solus* alone] — **des'o·late·ly** *adv.* — **des'o·late·ness** *n.*
— **des'o·lat'er** or **des'o·la'tor** *n.*

des·o·la·tion (des/ə·lā/shən) *n.* **1.** The act of making desolate; a laying waste; devastation. **2.** The condition of being ruined or deserted. **3.** Loneliness; dreariness; sadness.

de·sorp·tion (dē·sôrp/shən) *n. Chem.* The liberation or removal of a substance, usually gaseous, from the surface of adsorbing material.

De So·to (də sō/tō), **Hernando,** 1500?–42, Spanish explorer; discovered the Mississippi River, 1541.

des·ox·y- Var. of DEOXY-.

de·spair (di·spâr/) *v.i.* **1.** To lose or abandon hope; be or become hopeless: with *of.* —*v.t.* **2.** *Obs.* To lose hope in. —*n.* **1.** Utter hopelessness and discouragement. **2.** That which causes despair or which is despaired of. [< OF *desperer* < L *desperare* < *de-* away + *sperare* to hope < *spes* hope]
—**Syn.** (noun) **1.** *Despair, desperation, despondency,* and *hopelessness* signify the loss of hope. *Despair* is the utter abandonment of hope that leaves the mind apathetic or numb. *Desperation* is energized *despair,* vigorous in action and reckless of consequences. *Despondency* is paralyzing *despair* coupled with deep sorrow or chagrin. The mere absence of hope is *hopelessness;* this word is more often used to characterize circumstances than a state of mind. —**Ant.** hope, expectation, confidence.

de·spair·ing (di·spâr/ing) *adj.* Given up to or showing despair. —**de·spair/ing·ly** *adv.* —**de·spair/ing·ness** *n.*

des·patch (di·spach/) See DISPATCH.

des·patch·er (di·spach/ər) See DISPATCHER.

des·per·a·do (des/pə·rä/dō, -rä/dō) *n. pl.* **·does** or **·dos** A desperate or violent criminal; ruffian. [< OSp., pp. of *desperar* < L *desperare.* See DESPAIR.]

des·per·ate (des/pər·it) *adj.* **1.** Without care for danger; reckless, as from despair. **2.** Resorted to in desperation; frantic; violent: *desperate* measures. **3.** Regarded as almost hopeless; very bad; critical: a *desperate* sickness. **4.** Extreme; very great: in *desperate* need of food. **5.** *Obs.* Despairing. [< L *desperatus,* pp. of *desperare.* See DESPAIR.] —**des/per·ate·ly** *adv.* —**des/per·ate·ness** *n.*

des·per·a·tion (des/pə·rā/shən) *n.* **1.** The state of being desperate; also, the recklessness growing out of despair. **2.** *Obs.* The act of despairing. —**Syn.** See DESPAIR.

des·pi·ca·ble (des/pi·kə·bəl, di·spik/ə·bəl) *adj.* That is to be despised; contemptible; mean; vile. [< L *despicabilis* < L *despicere.* See DESPISE.] —**des/pi·ca·bil/i·ty, des/pi·ca·ble·ness** *n.* —**des/pi·ca·bly** *adv.*

de·spise (di·spīz/) *v.t.* **·spised, ·spis·ing** To regard as contemptible or worthless; disdain; scorn. [< OF *despis-,* stem of *despire* < L *despicere* < *de-* down + *specere* to look at]

de·spite (di·spīt/) *prep.* In spite of; notwithstanding: Persevere *despite* opposition. —**Syn.** See NOTWITHSTANDING. —*n.* **1.** Contemptuous defiance. **2.** An act of defiance, malice, or injury. **3.** *Archaic* Contempt; scorn; hatred. —**in despite of** In defiance of; in spite of; notwithstanding. —*v.t.* **·spit·ed, ·spit·ing 1.** *Archaic* To show contempt for. **2.** *Obs.* To vex; offend. [< OF *despit* < L *despectus* a looking down, contempt < *despicere.* See DESPISE.]

de·spite·ful (di·spīt/fəl) *adj. Archaic* Full of spite; malicious. —**de·spite/ful·ly** *adv.* —**de·spite/ful·ness** *n.*

des·pit·e·ous (des·pit/ē·əs) *adj. Archaic* Stirred with malicious scorn or hate; despiteful. —**des·pit/e·ous·ly** *adv.*

Des Plaines (des plānz/) A city in NE Illinois; pop. 57,259.

Des Plaines River A river in Wisconsin and Illinois, flowing about 110 miles SW to the Illinois River.

de·spoil (di·spoil/) *v.t.* To strip or deprive of possessions; plunder; rob. [< OF *despoillier* < L *despoliare* < *de-* completely + *spoliare* to rob < *spolium* plunder] —**de·spoil/er** *n.* —**de·spoil/ment** *n.*

de·spo·li·a·tion (di·spō/lē·ā/shən) *n.* The act of despoiling, or the state of being despoiled; plunder; robbery. [< LL *despoliatio, -onis* < L *despoliare.* See DESPOIL.]

de·spond (di·spond/) *v.i.* To lose spirit, courage, or hope. —*n. Archaic* Despondency. [< L *despondere* < *de-* away + *spondere* to promise] —**de·spond/ing·ly** *adv.*

de·spon·den·cy (di·spon/dən·sē) *n.* Dejection of spirits from loss of hope or courage. Also **de·spon/dence.**

de·spon·dent (di·spon/dənt) *adj.* Dejected in spirit; disheartened. —**de·spon/dent·ly** *adv.*

des·pot (des/pət, -pot) *n.* **1.** An absolute monarch; autocrat. **2.** A tyrant. **3.** Originally, master or lord, a title given to Byzantine emperors, to bishops and patriarchs of the Orthodox Church, etc. [< OF < Gk. *despotēs* master]

des·pot·ic (di·spot/ik) *adj.* Of or like a despot or despotism; tyrannical; autocratic. —**Syn.** See ABSOLUTE. —**des·pot/i·cal·ly** *adv.*

des·pot·ism (des/pə·tiz/əm) *n.* **1.** Unlimited authority; absolute power. **2.** Any tyrannical control.

des·pu·mate (des/pyōō·māt, di·spyōō/māt) *v.* **·mat·ed, ·mat·ing** *v.t.* **1.** To remove scum or impurities from; skim. —*v.i.* **2.** To throw off impurities. [< L *despumatus,* pp. of *despumare* < *de-* away + *spumare* to skim < *spuma* scum] —**des/pu·ma/tion** *n.*

des·qua·mate (des/kwə·māt) *v.i.* **·mat·ed, ·mat·ing** *Pathol.* To peel or scale off. [< L *desquamatus,* pp. of *desquamare* < *de-* away + *squama* a scale] —**des/qua·ma/tion** *n.*

D. ès S. Doctor of Sciences (F *Docteur ès Sciences*).

Des·saix (des·sā/), **Comte Joseph Marie,** 1764–1834, French general under Napoleon.

Des·sa·lines (des·sȧ·lēn/), **Jean Jacques,** 1758–1806, emperor of Haiti 1805–06: called **Jean Jacques I.**

Des·sau (des/ou) A city in East Germany, former capital of Saxony-Anhalt; pop. 95,682 (est. 1966).

des·sert (di·zûrt/) *n.* **1.** *U.S.* A serving of pastry, ice cream, etc., as the last course of lunch or dinner. **2.** *Brit.* Fruits, nuts, sweetmeats, etc., served after a dinner. [< F < *desservir* to clear a table < *des-* away + *servir* to serve]

des·sert·spoon (di·zûrt/spōōn) *n.* A spoon intermediate in size between a teaspoon and a tablespoon. —**des·sert/spoon/ful** *n.*

des·si·a·tine (des/yə·tēn) *n.* A Russian unit of area, equal to 2.698 acres. [< Russ. *desyatina*]

de-Sta·lin·i·za·tion (dē/stä/lin·ə·zā/shən) *n.* The act or process of eliminating or counteracting Stalinism.

de·ster·i·lize (dē·ster/ə·līz) *v.t.* **·lized, ·liz·ing 1.** To bring back from a sterilized or inactive condition. **2.** *Econ.* To put (sterile gold) into activity as a basis for credit and additional issues of currency. —**de·ster/i·li·za/tion** *n.*

Des·têr·ro (dish·tä/rōō) The former name for FLORIANÓPOLIS.

de Stijl (də stēl/, -stīl/) A transitional school of art, founded in 1917 in the Netherlands, that influenced Bauhaus and was marked by the use of rectangular forms and primary colors. [< Du., the style, the name of a journal published by these artists]

des·ti·na·tion (des/tə·nā/shən) *n.* **1.** The point or place set for a journey's end, or to which something is directed. **2.** The purpose or end for which anything is created or intended. **3.** The act of designating or appointing.

des·tine (des/tin) *v.t.* **·tined, ·tin·ing 1.** To design for or appoint to a distinct purpose or end. **2.** To determine the future of, as by destiny or fate. [< OF *destiner* < L *destinare* to make fast, ult. < *de-* completely + *stare* to stand]

des·tined (des/tind) *adj.* **1.** Bound for or assigned to a designated place. **2.** Intended for a particular purpose or use. **3.** Fated; ordained.

Des·ti·nies (des/tə·nēz) In classical mythology, the Fates.

des·ti·ny (des/tə·nē) *n. pl.* **·nies 1.** The fate or fortune to which a person or thing is destined; lot. **2.** The preordained or predetermined ordering of events. **3.** Fate. [< OF *destinee* < *destiner.* See DESTINE.]
—**Syn. 1.** *Destiny, fate, lot, portion,* and *fortune* refer to the future course of things. *Destiny* and *fate* preserve the implication of a guiding external force that has largely faded from the other terms. *Destiny* embraces the whole of the foreordained future; *fate* tends to be limited to the final condition or present inescapable circumstances. *Lot* and *portion* refer to one's share in the distribution of favors, whether by some higher power, or by blind chance. *Fortune* may mean the same as *destiny:* to read someone's *fortune* from his palm; or it may refer to what a person can achieve by his own efforts: to seek one's *fortune* abroad.

des·ti·tute (des/tə·tōōt, -tyōōt) *adj.* **1.** Not having or possessing; entirely lacking: with *of.* **2.** Being in want; extremely poor. **3.** *Obs.* Abandoned; forsaken. [< L *destitutus,* pp. of *destituere* to abandon < *de-* down + *statuere* to set, place]

des·ti·tu·tion (des/tə·tōō/shən, -tyōō/-) *n.* **1.** Extreme poverty. **2.** Deficiency; lack. —**Syn.** See POVERTY.

des·tri·er (des/trē·ər, des·trir/) *n. Archaic* A war horse. [< AF *destrer,* OF *destrier* < LL *(equus) dextrarius* (horse) led by the right hand < L *dexter* right]

de·stroy (di·stroi/) *v.t.* **1.** To ruin utterly; consume; dissolve. **2.** To tear down; demolish; raze. **3.** To put an end to; do away with. **4.** To kill. **5.** To make ineffective or useless. —**Syn.** See DEMOLISH. [< OF *destruire,* ult. < L *destruere* < *de-* down + *struere* to arrange, construct]

de·stroy·er (di·stroi/ər) *n.* **1.** One who or that which destroys. **2.** A speedy war vessel, smaller than a cruiser, equipped with guns, torpedo tubes, depth charges, and antiaircraft batteries, widely used as an escort vessel.

DESTROYER (U.S. Navy, World War II)

destroyer escort A U.S. Navy vessel smaller and slower than a destroyer, used against submarines. *Abbr. DE*

de·struct (di·strukt/) *n. Aerospace* The act of destroying a defective or dangerous missile or rocket after launch.

de·struc·ti·ble (di·struk/tə·bəl) *adj.* Liable to destruction; capable of being destroyed. —**de·struc/ti·bil/i·ty, de·struc/ti·ble·ness** *n.*

de·struc·tion (di·struk/shən) *n.* **1.** The act of destroying, or the state of being destroyed; demolition; ruin. **2.** That which destroys, or is a means of destroying. [< OF < L *destructio, -onis* < L *destruere.* See DESTROY.]

de·struc·tion·ist (di·struk/shən·ist) *n.* One who favors destruction, especially of existing institutions; a nihilist.

de·struc·tive (di·struk/tiv) *adj.* **1.** Causing destruction; tending to destroy; ruinous: with *of* or *to: destructive* of health;

destructive to property. **2.** Tending to tear down or discredit: *destructive* criticism. **— de·struc′tive·ly** *adv.* **— de·struc′tive·ness, de·struc·tiv′i·ty** (dē′struk·tiv′ə·tē) *n.*

destructive distillation *Chem.* The distillation of organic substances, as wood and coal, in such a way as to decompose them chemically: also called *dry distillation.*

de·struc·tor (di·struk′tər) *n.* **1.** *Brit.* An incinerator. **2.** *Aerospace* The explosive used in destruct procedure.

des·ue·tude (des′wə·tōōd, -tyōōd) *n.* A condition of disuse. [< MF *désuétude* < L *desuetudo* < *desuescere* < *de-* away + *suescere* to be used to]

de·sul·fur·ize (dē·sul′fə·rīz) *v.t.* **·ized, ·iz·ing** To remove sulfur from. Also **de·sul′fur, de·sul′fur·ate, de·sul′phur·ize.** **— de·sul′fur·i·za′tion** *n.* **— de·sul′fur·iz′er** *n.*

des·ul·to·ry (des′əl·tôr′ē, -tō′rē) *adj.* **1.** Passing abruptly from one thing to another; disconnected; unmethodical. **2.** Occurring by chance; random: a *desultory* idea. [< L *desultorius* < *desultor* leaper < *de-* down + *sultus,* pp. of *salire* to leap, jump] **— des′ul·to′ri·ly** *adv.* **— des′ul·to′ri·ness** *n.*

det. **1.** Detach; detachment. **2.** Detail.

de·tach (di·tach′) *v.t.* **1.** To unfasten and separate; disconnect; disunite. **2.** To send off for special duty, as a regiment or a ship. Abbr. (def. 2) *det.* [< F *détacher* < *de-* away (< L *dis-*) + OF *tache* nail] **— de·tach′a·bil′i·ty** *n.* **— de·tach′a·ble** *adj.* **— de·tach′er** *n.*

de·tached (di·tacht′) *adj.* **1.** Separated from others; disconnected: a *detached* house. **2.** Free from emotional or intellectual involvement; unconcerned; impartial.

detached retina *Pathol.* A disconnection of the inner layers of the retina from the pigment layer.

de·tach·ment (di·tach′mənt) *n.* **1.** The act of detaching or separating. **2.** The state of being detached. **3.** Dissociation from surroundings or worldly affairs; indifference; aloofness. **4.** Absence of prejudice or partiality. **5.** *Mil.* **a** A part of a unit separated from its parent organization for duty. **b** A special permanent unit. Abbr. (def. 5) *det.*

de·tail (*n.* di·tāl′, dē′tāl; *v.* di·tāl′; *Mil.* dē′tāl) *n.* **1.** A separately considered part or item; particular. **2.** A dealing with particulars: to go into *detail.* **3.** A narrative account giving particulars. **4.** In art, architecture, etc., a minor or secondary part, yet essential to the completeness and finish of a work. **5.** *Mil.* A small detachment designated to perform a particular task. **— in detail** Item by item; with particulars. **—** *v.t.* **1.** To report or narrate minutely; enter into or give the particulars of. **2.** *Mil.* To select and send off for a special service, duty, etc. Abbr. *det.* [< F *détailler* to cut into pieces < *dé-* completely + *tailler* to cut up]

detail drawing A drawing of parts or features of a structure, machine, or design, made to a large scale or full size.

de·tain (di·tān′) *v.t.* **1.** To keep from going on; stop; delay. **2.** To withhold (what belongs to another). **3.** To hold in custody. **— Syn.** See RETAIN. [< OF *detenir* < L *detinere* < *de-* away + *tenere* to hold] **— de·tain′ment** *n.*

de·tain·er (di·tā′nər) *n. Law* **1.** The wrongful holding of the property or person of another. **2.** A writ directing the continued holding of a prisoner in custody pending action.

de·tect (di·tekt′) *v.t.* **1.** To discover, perceive, or find, as something obscure: to *detect* an error in spelling. **2.** To expose or uncover, as a crime or a criminal. **3.** *Telecom.* To recover (the signal, audio component, etc.) from a modulated carrier wave; demodulate. **— Syn.** See DISCOVER. [< L *detectus,* pp. of *detegere* < *de-* away, off + *tegere* to cover] **— de·tect′a·ble** or **de·tect′i·ble** *adj.* **— de·tect′er** *n.*

de·tec·tion (di·tek′shən) *n.* **1.** The act of detecting, or the fact of being detected; discovery, as of things hidden or obscure. **2.** *Telecom.* Any method of operating on a modulated signal wave so as to obtain the signal imparted to it; a process of demodulation of incoming electrical signals.

de·tec·tive (di·tek′tiv) *n.* A person, often a policeman, whose work is to investigate crimes, discover evidence, capture criminals, etc. **—** *adj.* **1.** Belonging or pertaining to detectives or their work. **2.** Fitted for or used in detection.

de·tec·tor (di·tek′tər) *n.* **1.** One who or that which detects. **2.** A device for detecting, as for showing low water in a boiler, etc. **3.** *Electr.* **a** A device for discovering the presence of electric waves. **b** A portable galvanometer. **4.** *Telecom.* A device for obtaining the signal from a modulated carrier.

de·tent (di·tent′) *n. Mech.* A device that either stops or releases a movement, as a catch or pin on a ratchet wheel. [< F *détente* < *détendre* to slacken < *dé-* away (< L *dis-*) + *tendre* to stretch < L *tendere*]

dé·tente (dā·tänt′) *n.* An easing, as of discord between nations. [< F]

de·ten·tion (di·ten′shən) *n.* **1.** The act of detaining; a restraining or confining. **2.** The state of being detained; delay. [< L *detentio, -onis* < *detinere.* See DETAIN.]

de·ter (di·tûr′) *v.t.* **·terred, ·ter·ring** To prevent or discourage (someone) from acting or proceeding by arousing fear, uncertainty, etc. [< L *deterrere* < *de-* away + *terrere* to frighten] **— de·ter′ment** *n.*

de·terge (di·tûrj′) *v.t.* **terged, ·terg·ing** To cleanse or

wipe off. [< L *detergere* < *de-* away + *tergere* to wipe]

de·ter·gen·cy (di·tûr′jən·sē) *n.* Cleansing power. Also **de·ter′gence.**

de·ter·gent (di·tûr′jənt) *adj.* Having cleansing or purging qualities. **—** *n.* A cleansing agent; especially, any of a class of surface-active chemical compounds having strong cleansing effects. **— Syn.** See SOAP.

de·te·ri·o·rate (di·tir′ē·ə·rāt′) *v.t. & v.i.* **·rat·ed, ·rat·ing** To make or become worse in quality, character, etc.; depreciate. [< L *deterioratus,* pp. of *deteriorare* < *deterior* worse]

de·te·ri·o·ra·tion (di·tir′ē·ə·rā′shən) *n.* The process of gradual worsening; depreciation. **— de·te′ri·o·ra′tive** *adj.*

de·ter·mi·na·ble (di·tûr′mi·nə·bəl) *adj.* **1.** That may be found out, settled, or decided. **2.** *Law* Liable to be ended.

de·ter·mi·nant (di·tûr′mə·nənt) *adj.* Determinative. **—** *n.* **1.** That which influences or determines. **2.** *Math.* A numerical value assigned to a square matrix. **— Syn.** See CAUSE.

de·ter·mi·nate (di·tûr′mə·nit) *adj.* **1.** Definitely limited or fixed; specific; distinct. **2.** Settled and conclusive; decided; final. **3.** Fixed in purpose; resolute. **4.** Known or fixed, as a mathematical quantity. **5.** *Bot.* Terminating in a flower or bud, as each axis of an inflorescence: also *definite.* **— de·ter′mi·nate·ly** *adv.* **— de·ter′mi·nate·ness** *n.*

de·ter·mi·na·tion (di·tûr′mə·nā′shən) *n.* **1.** The act of reaching a decision; formation of a fixed purpose; also, the decision reached; a firm resolve. **2.** The quality of being firm in purpose or action; resoluteness. **3.** The act of concluding a dispute, suit, etc., by an authoritative opinion or decision; also, the opinion or decision arrived at. **4.** The determining or fixing of the quality, extent, position, degree, etc., of anything; also, the result of this; a conclusion or solution. **5.** A decisive tendency or movement toward some object or end. **6.** *Logic* The limiting or qualifying of a concept or proposition; also, that which limits or qualifies. **7.** *Biol.* **a** The classification of plants and animals. **b** The process whereby the cells of a developing organism become differentiated in structure and function.

— Syn. 2. *Determination, decision,* and *resolution* are here compared as they relate to firmness of mind. *Determination* suggests vigorous action to achieve a purpose; *decision* emphasizes promptness in making up one's mind, and subsequent freedom from doubt or wavering. *Resolution* includes both *determination* and *decision,* and refers to an unswerving adherence to a chosen course.

de·ter·mi·na·tive (di·tûr′mə·nā′tiv, -mə·nə·tiv) *adj.* Tending or having power to determine or fix; deciding; shaping. **—** *n.* **1.** That which determines. **2.** *Ling.* In certain languages, an interpolated element between the base and inflectional ending of a verb that modifies its aspect, as *-sc-* in Latin *calesco* I grow warm, from *caleo* I am warm. **— de·ter′mi·na·tive·ly** *adv.* **— de·ter′mi·na′tive·ness** *n.*

de·ter·mine (di·tûr′min) *v.* **·mined, ·min·ing** *v.t.* **1.** To settle or decide, as an argument, question, or debate. **2.** To ascertain or fix, as after thought or observation. **3.** To cause to reach a decision. **4.** To fix or give definite form to; influence; direct; shape. **5.** To give aim, purpose, or direction to. **6.** To set bounds to; limit in extent, variety, etc. **7.** *Logic* To limit or define by adding differences. **8.** *Law* To limit; terminate: to *determine* a contract. **—** *v.i.* **9.** To come to a decision; resolve. **10.** *Law* To come to an end. [< OF *determiner* < L *determinare* < *de-* completely + *terminare* to end < *terminus* limit]

de·ter·mined (di·tûr′mind) *adj.* Having or showing fixed purpose; resolute; firm. **— de·ter·mined·ly** (di·tûr′mind·lē, -min·id·lē) *adv.* **— de·ter′mined·ness** *n.*

de·ter·min·er (di·tûr′mə·nər) *n.* **1.** One who or that which determines. **2.** *Gram.* Any of a class of words, including articles and possessive adjectives, whose presence in a phrase, often before a descriptive adjective, indicates that the head word is a noun or substantive. In *his old coat,* "his" is a determiner.

de·ter·min·ism (di·tûr′mə·niz′əm) *n. Philos.* The doctrine that every event is the inevitable result of antecedent conditions, and, in particular, that every human choice and act is the result of inherited or environmental factors. Compare FREE WILL.

de·ter·rent (di·tûr′ənt) *adj.* Tending or serving to deter. **—** *n.* Something that deters. **— de·ter′rence** *n.*

de·ter·sion (di·tûr′zhən) *n.* A cleansing, as of a wound. [< LL *detersio, -onis* < L *detergere.* See DETERGE.]

de·ter·sive (di·tûr′siv) *adj. & n.* Detergent.

de·test (di·test′) *v.t.* To dislike with intensity; hate; abhor. **— Syn.** See HATE. [< MF *détester* < L *detestari* to denounce < *de-* away + *testis* a witness] **— de·test′er** *n.*

de·test·a·ble (di·tes′tə·bəl) *adj.* Deserving to be detested; extremely hateful; abominable. **— de·test·a·bil′i·ty, de·test′a·ble·ness** *n.* **— de·test′a·bly** *adv.*

de·tes·ta·tion (dē′tes·tā′shən) *n.* **1.** Extreme dislike; hatred; abhorrence. **2.** One who or that which is detested.

de·throne (dē·thrōn′) *v.t.* **·throned, ·thron·ing** To remove from the throne; depose. **— de·throne′ment** *n.* **— de·thron′er** *n.*

det·i·nue (det'i·nyōō) *n. Law* 1. An action to recover personal property wrongfully detained; also, the writ used in such action. 2. *Obs.* The act of detaining wrongfully. [< OF *detenue*, pp. of *detenir*. See DETAIN.]

det·o·nate (det'ə·nāt) *v.* ·nat·ed, ·nat·ing *v.t.* 1. To cause to explode suddenly and with violence. — *v.i.* 2. To explode suddenly with a loud report. [< L *detonatus*, pp. of *detonare* < *de-* down + *tonare* to thunder]

det·o·na·tion (det'ə·nā'shən, dē'tə-) *n.* 1. The act of detonating. 2. A violent and sudden explosion.

det·o·na·tor (det'ə·nā'tər, dē'tə-) *n.* 1. Any contrivance, as a primer or fuse, for detonating the main charge of a projectile, bomb, etc. 2. An explosive.

de·tour (dē'tŏŏr, di·tŏŏr') *n.* A roundabout way; a deviation from a direct route or course of action; especially, a byroad used when a main road is temporarily impassable. — *v.t. & v.i.* To go or cause to go by a roundabout way. [< F *détour* < *détourner* < *dé-* away + *tourner* to turn]

de·tox·i·cate (dē·tok'sə·kāt) *v.t.* ·cat·ed, ·cat·ing To destroy the toxic properties of. [< DE- + (IN)TOXICATE]

de·tract (di·trakt') *v.i.* 1. To take away a part; diminish; lessen: with *from*: Poor health *detracts* from appearance. — *v.t.* 2. To take away (a part); diminish. 3. To distract; divert. 4. *Obs.* To disparage. [< L *detractus*, pp. of *detrahere* < *de-* away + *trahere* to draw, pull]

de·trac·tion (di·trak'shən) *n.* The act of detracting from a person's reputation; slander; defamation.

de·trac·tive (di·trak'tiv) *adj.* Given to detraction; tending to detract; disparaging. — **de·trac'tive·ly** *adv.*

de·trac·tor (di·trak'tər) *n.* One who detracts or disparages.

de·train (dē·trān') *v.t. & v.i. Chiefly Brit.* To leave or cause to leave a railroad train. — **de·train'ment** *n.*

det·ri·ment (det'rə·mənt) *n.* 1. Damage or loss. 2. Something that impairs, injures, or causes loss. [< L *detrimentum* < *deterere* < *de-* away + *terere* to rub]

det·ri·men·tal (det'rə·men'təl) *adj.* Causing damage or loss; injurious; harmful. — **Syn.** See PERNICIOUS. — **det'ri·men'tal·ly** *adv.*

de·tri·tal (di·trīt'l) *adj.* Of or pertaining to detritus.

de·tri·tion (di·trish'ən) *n.* The act of rubbing or wearing off particles.

de·tri·tus (di·trī'təs) *n.* 1. *Geol.* Loose fragments or particles separated from masses of rock by erosion, glacial action, or other forces. 2. Any mass of disintegrated material; debris. [< L < *deterere*. See DETRIMENT.]

De·troit (di·troit') A city in SE Michigan, a port on the Detroit River; pop. 1,512,893.

Detroit River A river about 31 miles long, connecting Lake St. Clair with Lake Erie and forming part of the boundary between the United States and Canada.

de trop (də trō') *French* Too much or too many; superfluous; not wanted.

de·trude (di·trōōd') *v.t.* ·trud·ed, ·trud·ing 1. To thrust away or out. 2. To push down forcibly. [< L *detrudere* < *de-* away + *trudere* to thrust] — **de·tru'sion** *n.*

de·trun·cate (di·trung'kāt) *v.t.* ·cat·ed, ·cat·ing To shorten by cutting off a part. [< L *detruncatus*, pp. of *detruncare* < *de-* from + *truncare* to cut off] — **de'trun·ca'tion** *n.*

de·tu·mes·cence (dē'tŏō·mes'əns, -tyŏō-) *n.* The act or process of becoming less tumid or swollen, as an organ.

Deu·ca·li·on (dōō·kā'lē·ən, dyōō-) In Greek mythology, a son of Prometheus who, with his wife Pyrrha, was the only survivor of a deluge sent to punish the world's wickedness.

deuce¹ (dōōs, dyōōs) *n.* 1. Two; especially, a card or side of a die having two spots. 2. In tennis, a condition of the score when it is tied at 40 or at five or more games each and either side must win two successive points for the game or two successive games for the set. [< F *deux* < OF *deus* < L *duos*, accusative of *duo* two]

deuce² (dōōs, dyōōs) *n. Informal* The devil; bad luck: a mild oath used with or without the article. [Prob. < LG *de duus* the deuce (lowest throw at dice); but cf. DEUCE¹]

deu·ced (dōō'sid, dyōō'-, dōōst, dyōōst) *Informal adj.* Devilish; confounded; excessive. — *adv.* Deucedly.

deu·ced·ly (dōō'sid·lē, dyōō'-) *Archaic adv.* Extremely; devilishly; confoundedly.

De·us (dē'əs, dā'ŏōs) *n. Latin* God. Abbr. *D.*

de·us ex ma·chi·na (dē'əs eks mak'ə·nə) 1. In classical drama, a god brought to the stage in a mechanical contrivance to intervene in a difficult situation. 2. Any unexpected or improbable person or event introduced in a play, story, etc., to untangle the plot. [< L, a god from a machine]

Deus vo·bis·cum (vō·bis'kəm) *Latin* God be with you.

Deus vult (vult') *Latin* God wills it: the battle cry of the First Crusade.

Deut. Deuteronomy.

deu·ter·ag·o·nist (dōō'tər·ag'ə·nist, dyōō'-) *n.* In ancient Greek drama, the actor next in importance to the protagonist. [< Gk. *deuteragōnistēs* < *deuteros* second + *agōnistēs* actor]

deu·te·ric (dōō·tir'ik, dyōō-) *adj. Chem.* Pertaining to an acid containing deuterium.

deu·ter·ide (dōō'tə·rīd, dyōō'-) *n. Chem.* A compound of deuterium analogous to a hydride.

deu·te·ri·um (dōō·tir'ē·əm, dyōō-) *n.* The isotope of hydrogen having the atomic weight 2.01 (symbol, D or H²): also called *heavy hydrogen.* [< NL < Gk. *deuteros* second]

deuterium oxide Heavy water.

deutero- *combining form* Second; secondary: *deuterogamy.* Also, **deuter-** (before vowels), **deuto-**. [< Gk. *deuteros* second]

deu·ter·o·ca·non·i·cal (dōō'tər·ō·kə·non'i·kəl, dyōō'-) *adj.* Belonging to a second canon: applied to books of the Bible whose authenticity and inspiration were contested and later approved by the Roman Catholic Church, but that in Protestant churches are considered apocryphal. See APOCRYPHA.

deu·ter·og·a·my (dōō'tə·rog'ə·mē, dyōō'-) *n.* A second legal marriage; also, the practice of contracting such marriages. [< DEUTERO- + Gk. *gamos* marriage] — **deu'ter·og'a·mist** *n.*

Deu·ter·o-I·sa·iah (dōō'tər·ō·ī·zā'ə, dyōō'-) The presumed author of *Isaiah* xl–lxvi, a postexilian Hebrew writer.

deu·ter·on (dōō'tə·ron, dyōō'-) *n. Physics* The nucleus of a deuterium atom. [< NL < Gk., neut. sing. of *deuteros* second]

Deu·ter·on·o·my (dōō'tə·ron'ə·mē, dyōō'-) The fifth book of the Old Testament, containing a second statement of the Mosaic law. [< Gk. *deuteronomion* < *deuteros* second + *nomos* law]

deu·to·plasm (dōō'tə·plaz'əm, dyōō'-) *n. Biol.* The nutritive material formed within the cytoplasm of a cell; the food yolk of an ovum or egg cell. Also **deu·ter·o·plasm** (dōō'tər·ō·plaz'əm, dyōō'-). — **deu'to·plas'mic** or **deu'to·plas'tic** *adj.*

deut·sche·mark (doi'chə·märk') *n.* 1. The standard monetary unit of West Germany, equivalent to 100 pfennigs; also, a coin of this value. 2. The standard monetary unit of East Germany. See MARK² (def. 1). Also **deutsche mark.** Abbr. *Dm., DM.*

Deutsch·land (doich'länt) The German name for GERMANY.

Deutsch·land ü·ber al·les (doich'länt ü'bər ä'les) *German* Germany above all: a nationalist song and slogan.

de·va (dā'və) *n.* In Hindu mythology, a god or good spirit. Also **dev** (dāv). [< Skt., lit., bright or shining one]

De·va (dē'və) An ancient name for CHESTER.

De Va·le·ra (de'və·lâr'ə, dā'və·lir'ə), **Eamon,** 1882–1975, Irish statesman born in the United States; prime minister 1937–48, 1951–54, 1957–59; president 1959–73.

de·val·u·ate (dē·val'yōō·āt) *v.t.* ·at·ed, ·at·ing 1. To reduce or annul the value or worth of. 2. To establish the value of (a currency) at some point below par. Also **de·val'ue.** — **de·val'u·a'tion** *n.*

De·va·na Cas·tra (di·vā'nə kas'trə) An ancient name for CHESTER.

De·va·na·ga·ri (dā'və·nä'gə·rē) *n.* The script in which Sanskrit and much of the literature of the modern Indic languages are written: also called *Nagari.*

dev·as·tate (dev'ə·stāt) *v.t.* ·tat·ed, ·tat·ing 1. To lay waste, as by war, fire, flood, etc.; make desolate; ravage. 2. *Informal* To confound; crush. [< L *devastatus*, pp. of *devastare* < *de-* completely + *vastare* to lay waste < *vastus* waste] — **dev'as·tat'ing·ly** *adv.* — **dev'as·ta'tor** *n.*

dev·as·ta·tion (dev'ə·stā'shən) *n.* The act of devastating, or the condition of having been devastated; destruction.

de·vein (dē·vān') *v.t.* To remove the dorsal vein from, as from a shrimp.

dev·el (dev'əl) *Scot. v.t.* To strike with a heavy blow. — *n.* A stunning blow. [Origin unknown]

devel. Development.

de·vel·op (di·vel'əp) *v.t.* 1. To expand or bring out the potentialities, capabilities, etc., of. 2. To work out in detail; enlarge upon: to *develop* an idea. 3. To reveal or unfold gradually: to *develop* a plot. 4. To bring into active existence: to *develop* patience. 5. *Photog.* a To make visible (the hidden image) upon a sensitized plate that has been exposed to the action of light. b To subject (a plate or film) to a developer. 6. *Biol.* To cause to evolve to a higher stage, as in function or structure. 7. *Music* To elaborate on (a theme). 8. *Math.* To expand (an expression) in the form of a series. 9. *Geom.* To change the form of (a surface) as if by bending or unbending. 10. *Obs.* To disclose; reveal. — *v.i.* 11. To increase in capabilities, maturity, etc. 12. To advance from a lower to a higher stage; grow; evolve. 13. To be disclosed; become apparent, as events, a plot, etc. 14. To come into existence: Some tastes *develop* slowly. [< F *développer* < *dé-* away (< L *dis-*) + OF *voluper* to fold, wrap up] — **de·vel'op·a·ble** *adj.*

de·vel·op·er (di·vel'əp·ər) *n.* 1. One who or that which develops. 2. *Photog.* A chemical bath or reagent used to develop photographs.

de·vel·op·ment (di·vel'əp·mənt) *n.* 1. The act of developing. 2. The state or condition of that which has been developed. 3. A result or product of developing. 4. An event or occurrence: a political *development.* 5. *U.S.* A group of generally similar dwellings, usually constructed by the same builder: also called *tract.* 6. *Music* Melodic, harmonic, or rhythmic variation of a theme, as in a fugue or sonata form. — **Syn.** See PROGRESS.

de·vel·op·men·tal (di·vel′əp·men′təl) *adj.* Of or pertaining to development; evolutionary. **— de·vel′op·men′tal·ly** *adv.*
Dev·e·reux (dev′ə·rōō), **Robert** See (Earl of) ESSEX.
de·vest (di·vest′) *v.t.* **1.** *Law* To take away, as a title or estate. **2.** *Obs.* To undress; strip. [< OF *devester, desvestir* < *de-* from (< L *dis-*) + *vestir* to clothe < L *vestire* < *vestis* garment.]
De·vi (dā′vē) In Hinduism, the great mother goddess and consort of Siva, worshiped also as Kali, Maya, and Shakti. [< Skt., goddess, lit., bright or shining one]
de·vi·ate (*n.* dē′vē·it; *v.* dē′vē·āt) **—** *n.* **1.** One whose actions and beliefs differ considerably from the standards of his society. **2.** A sexual pervert. Also **de·vi·ant** (dē′vē·ənt). **—** *v.* **·at·ed, ·at·ing** *v.i.* **1.** To turn aside from a straight or appointed way or course; diverge. **2.** To differ, as in thought or belief. **—** *v.t.* **3.** To cause to turn aside. [< LL *deviatus,* pp. of *deviare* < L *de-* from + *via* road] **— de′vi·a′tor** *n.*
de·vi·a·tion (dē′vē·ā′shən) *n.* **1.** The act of deviating, or its result. **2.** *Stat.* The difference between one value in a series of observations and the arithmetic mean of the series.
— Syn. 2. *Deviation, deflection, aberration,* and *divergence* denote a turning aside from a course. *Deviation,* the widest term, implies some standard of reference that is usually specified: the *deviation* of a compass needle from the magnetic meridian. *Deflection* is a bending aside, especially from a straight line: the *deflection* of a beam under stress. *Aberration* in general implies mental or moral instability; in scientific usage it is applied to constant or inherent *deviations*: the spherical *aberration* of a lens. *Divergence* usually refers to no fixed standard, but to the moving apart of two or more things: the *divergence* of two lines, a *divergence* of opinion.
de·vi·a·tion·ism (dē′vē·ā′shən·iz′əm) *n.* In Communist ideology, departure from official party doctrine or policy. **— de′vi·a′tion·ist** *n. & adj*
de·vice (di·vīs′) *n.* **1.** Something devised or constructed for a specific purpose; an invention; contrivance. **2.** A scheme or plan, especially a crafty or evil one; plot; stratagem; trick. **3.** An ornamental design or pattern, as in embroidery. **4.** An emblem, often with a motto, in a coat of arms; also, any emblem or motto. **5.** *Archaic* The act, state, or power of devising; inventive skill. **— to leave (someone) to his own devices** To allow (someone) to do as he wishes. [< OF *devis* division, desire, will < *deviser*; infl. by OF *devise* emblem, design. See DEVISE.]
dev·il (dev′əl) *n.* **1.** *Sometimes cap.* In Jewish and Christian theology, the prince and ruler of the kingdom of evil; Satan. **2.** Any subordinate evil spirit; a demon. **3.** In Christian Science usage, evil; a lie; error; neither corporeality nor mind; opposite of Truth; a belief in sin, sickness, and death; animal magnetism or hypnotism. **4.** A wicked, malicious, or ill-natured person. **5.** A wretched fellow: poor *devil.* **6.** A person of great energy, daring or effrontery. **7.** A machine for any of various purposes, as for cutting or tearing up rags. **8.** A printer's apprentice or errand boy: also called *printer's devil.* **— between the devil and the deep blue sea** Between equally bad alternatives; in a dilemma. **— the devil** An exclamation of anger, disgust, surprise, etc. **— the devil to pay** Trouble to be expected as a consequence. **— to give the devil his due** To acknowledge the ability or success of even a bad or disliked person, antagonist, etc. **—** *v.t.* **dev·iled** or **·illed, dev·il·ing** or **·il·ling 1.** To prepare for eating by seasoning highly and sometimes broiling or frying. **2.** To cut up (cloth, etc.) in a devil. **3.** To annoy or harass. [OE *dēofol* < LL *diabolus* < Gk. *diabolos* slanderer; later, the devil < *diaballein* to slander < *dia-* across + *ballein* to throw]
dev·il·fish (dev′əl·fish′) *n. pl.* **·fish** or **·fish·es 1.** The manta. **2.** Any of various large cephalopods, as the octopus.
dev·il·ish (dev′əl·ish, dev′lish) *adj.* **1.** Having the qualities of the devil; diabolical; malicious. **2.** *Informal* Excessive; extreme. **—** *adv. Informal* Excessively; very. **— dev′il·ish·ly** *adv.* **— dev′il·ish·ness** *n.*
dev·il·kin (dev′əl·kin) *n.* An imp; little devil.
dev·il·may·care (dev′əl·mā·kâr′) *adj.* Careless; reckless.
dev·il·ment (dev′əl·mənt) *n.* Impish conduct; mischief.
devil's advocate (dev′əlz) **1.** In the Roman Catholic Church, an official appointed to argue against a candidate for beatification or canonization. **2.** One who argues perversely or for a bad cause.
dev·il's-darn·ing-nee·dle (dev′əlz·där′ning·nēd′l) *n.* **1.** A dragonfly. **2.** The Venus's-comb. Also **dev′il's-darn′ing-nee′dle.**
dev·il's-food cake (dev′əlz·fōōd′) A chocolate cake.
Devil's Island A rocky island off the coast of French Guiana; formerly a penal colony: French *Île du Diable.*
devil's tattoo A drumming or pounding with the feet or hands.
dev·il·try (dev′əl·trē) *n. pl.* **·tries 1.** Wanton or malicious mischief. **2.** Wickedness or cruelty. **3.** Evil magic. Also *Brit.* **dev′il·ry** (-rē).
dev·il·wood (dev′əl·wōōd′) *n.* A small tree (*Osmanthus americanus*) of the southern Atlantic States, having a fine-grained, hard wood: also called *wild olive.*

de·vi·ous (dē′vē·əs) *adj.* **1.** Winding or leading away from the regular, straight, or direct course; rambling; swerving. **2.** Straying from the proper way; erring. [< L *devius* < *de-* from + *via* way] **— de′vi·ous·ly** *adv.* **— de′vi·ous·ness** *n.*
de·vis·a·ble (di·vī′zə·bəl) *adj.* **1.** *Law* That can be devised, or given by will. **2.** That can be contrived or invented.
de·vi·sal (di·vī′zəl) *n.* A contriving or bequeathing.
de·vise (di·vīz′) *v.* **·vised, ·vis·ing** *v.t.* **1.** To form in the mind; invent; contrive; plan. **2.** *Law* To transmit (real estate) by will. Compare BEQUEATH. **3.** *Obs.* To distribute. **4.** *Obs.* To guess. **—** *v.i.* **5.** To form a plan. **—** *n. Law* **1.** The act of bequeathing lands. **2.** A gift of lands by will. **3.** A will, or a clause in a will, conveying real estate. [< OF *deviser* to divide, distinguish, contrive < L *dividere* to separate, part < *dis-* apart + *videre* to see] **— de·vis′er** *n.*
de·vi·see (di·vī′zē′, dev′ə·zē′) *n. Law* The person to whom a devise is made.
de·vi·sor (di·vī′zər, -zôr) *n. Law* One who devises property.
de·vi·tal·ize (dē·vīt′l·īz) *v.t.* **·ized, ·iz·ing** To destroy the vitality of; make weak. **— de·vi′tal·i·za′tion** *n.*
de·vi·ta·min·ize (dē′vī′tə·min·īz′) *v.t.* **·ized, ·iz·ing** To deprive (food) of vitamins, as by cooking.
de·vit·ri·fy (dē·vit′rə·fī) *v.t.* **·fied, ·fy·ing 1.** To remove the glassy quality of. **2.** To render (glass, etc.) opaque and hard by long-continued heat. **— de·vit′ri·fi·ca′tion** *n.*
de·vo·cal·ize (dē·vō′kəl·īz) *v.t.* **·ized, ·iz·ing** *Phonet.* To deprive of voice or of vocal quality. **— de·vo′cal·i·za′tion** *n.*
de·voiced (dē·voist′) *adj. Phonet.* Unvoiced; voiceless.
de·void (di·void′) *adj.* Not possessing; destitute; empty: with *of.* [ME *devoided,* pp. of obs. *devoid* to empty out < OF *desvoidier* < *des-* down (< L *de-*) + *voidier* to void]
de·voir (də·vwär′, dev′wär) *n.* **1.** *Usually pl.* Courteous attentions; respects: to pay one's *devoirs* to the king. **2.** *Archaic* Duty. [< OF *deveir* < L *debere* to owe]
dev·o·lu·tion (dev′ə·lōō′shən) *n.* **1.** A passing down from one stage to another. **2.** The passing of authority, property, etc., to a successor. **3.** *Biol.* Degeneration: opposed to *evolution.* [< Med.L *devolutio, -onis* < L *devolvere.* See DE-VOLVE.]
de·volve (di·volv′) *v.* **·volved, ·volv·ing** *v.t.* **1.** To cause (authority, duty, etc.) to pass to a successor or substitute. **2.** *Archaic* To roll down. **—** *v.i.* **3.** To pass to a successor or substitute: with *on, upon,* or *to.* [< L *devolvere* < *de-* down + *volvere* to roll] **— de·volve′ment** *n.*
Dev·on (dev′ən) *n.* A valuable breed of small, hardy cattle originating in Devonshire, England.
Dev·on·shire (dev′ən·shir) A county in SW England; 2,611 sq. mi.; pop. 928,800 (1976); county seat, Exeter. Also **Dev·on.**
De·vo·ni·an (di·vō′nē·ən) *adj.* **1.** Of or pertaining to Devon in England. **2.** *Geol.* Of or pertaining to the fourth of the periods in the Paleozoic era, following the Silurian, and succeeded by the Mississippian, or Lower Carboniferous, period. See chart for GEOLOGY. **—** *n. Geol.* The Devonian period or its characteristic rock system. [after *Devon,* England; with ref. to rocks and fossils first found there]
de·vote (di·vōt′) *v.t.* **·vot·ed, ·vot·ing 1.** To give or apply (attention, time, or oneself) completely to some activity, purpose, etc. **2.** To set apart; dedicate; consecrate. **3.** *Obs.* To curse or doom. [< OF *devot* < L *devotus,* pp. of *devovere* < *de-* completely + *vovere* to vow] **— de·vote′ment** *n.*
de·vot·ed (di·vō′tid) *adj.* **1.** Feeling or showing devotion; ardent; zealous; devout. **2.** Set apart, as by a vow; consecrated. **3.** *Obs.* Doomed. **— Syn.** See ADDICTED, FAITHFUL. **— de·vot′ed·ly** *adv.* **— de·vot′ed·ness** *n.*
dev·o·tee (dev′ə·tē′) *n.* **1.** One who is deeply devoted to anything. **2.** One who is marked by religious ardor; a votary. **— Syn.** See ENTHUSIAST. **— dev′o·tee′ism** *n.*
de·vo·tion (di·vō′shən) *n.* **1.** Strong attachment or affection, as to a person or cause. **2.** Ardor or zeal in the performance of religious acts or duties. **3.** *Usually pl.* An act of worship or prayer, especially when private. **4.** The act of devoting, or the state of being devoted. **— Syn.** See LOVE.
de·vo·tion·al (di·vō′shən·əl) *adj.* **1.** Of or pertaining to devotion. **2.** Used in worship. **— de·vo′tion·al·ly** *adv.*
De Vo·to (də vō′tō), **Bernard Augustine,** 1897–1956, U.S. author and critic.
de·vour (di·vour′) *v.t.* **1.** To eat up greedily. **2.** To destroy; waste: The disease *devoured* him. **3.** To take in greedily with the senses or the intellect: He *devoured* the book. **4.** To engross the attention of. **5.** To engulf; absorb. [< OF *devorer* < L *devorare* < *de-* down + *vorare* to gulp, swallow] **— de·vour′er** *n.* **— de·vour′ing·ly** *adv.*
de·vout (di·vout′) *adj.* **1.** Earnestly religious; pious; reverent. **2.** Warmly devoted; heartfelt; sincere. **3.** Containing or expressing devotion. [< OF *devot* < L *devotus.* See DEVOTE.] **— de·vout′ly** *adv.* **— de·vout′ness** *n.*
De Vries (də vrēs′), **Hugo,** 1848–1935, Dutch botanist.
dew (dōō, dyōō) *n.* **1.** Moisture condensed from the atmosphere in small drops upon cool surfaces **2.** Anything moist, gentle, pure, or refreshing as dew: the *dew* of youth. **3.**

Moisture generally, especially that which appears in minute drops, as perspiration, tears, etc. — *v.t.* To wet with or as with dew; bedew. [OE *dēaw*]

de·wan (di·wän′, -wŏn′) *n.* In India and Moslem countries, any of various government officials: also spelled *deewan, diwan*. [< Hind. < Persian *diwān* register. See DIVAN.]

Dew·ar (dyōō′ər), **Sir James**, 1842–1923, Scottish scientist: invented the **Dewar vessel** or **flask**, prototype of the thermos bottle.

dew·ber·ry (dōō′ber′ē, -bər·ē, dyōō′-) *n. pl.* **·ries 1.** The fruit of several species of trailing blackberry (genus *Rubus*). **2.** A plant bearing this fruit; especially *R. flagellaris*, of North America, and *R. caesius*, of Europe.

dew·claw (dōō′klô′, dyōō′-) *n.* **1.** A rudimentary toe in some dogs and other mammals. **2.** The false hoof above the true hoof of hogs, deer, etc. — **dew′clawed′** *adj.*

dew·drop (dōō′drop′, dyōō′-) *n.* A drop of dew.

De Wet (də vet′), **Christiaan Rudolph**, 1854–1922, Boer general.

Dew·ey (dōō′ē, dyōō′ē), **George**, 1837–1917, U.S. admiral in the Spanish-American War. — **John**, 1859–1952, U.S. philosopher, psychologist, and educator. — **Melvil**, 1851–1931, U.S. librarian. — **Thomas E**(dmund), 1902–71, U.S. politician and lawyer.

Dewey decimal system A number code devised by Melvil Dewey for classifying books, etc., according to subject.

dew·fall (dōō′fôl′, dyōō′-) *n.* **1.** The formation of dew. **2.** The time of evening when dew appears.

De Witt (di wit′), **Jan**, 1625–72, Dutch statesman.

dew·lap (dōō′lap′, dyōō′-) *n.* **1.** The pendulous skin under the throat of cattle, certain dogs, etc. **2.** Any similar pendulous part, as the wattles of a turkey, or the flaccid skin under the chin of an aged person. [ME *dewlappe* < *dew*, origin uncertain + *lappe*, OE *læppe* pendulous piece, lobe, fold] — **dew′lapped′** *adj.*

DEW line A chain of radar stations in North America at about the 70th parallel, maintained by the United States in cooperation with Canada. [< *D*(*istant*) *E*(*arly*) *W*(*arning*)]

dew point The temperature at which dew forms or condensation of vapor occurs.

Dews·bur·y (dōōz′ber·ē) A county borough in southern Yorkshire, England; pop. 52,942 (1961).

dew-worm (dōō′wûrm′, dyōō-) *n. Canadian* A night crawler.

dew·y (dōō′ē, dyōō′ē) *adj.* **dew·i·er, dew·i·est 1.** Moist, as with dew. **2.** Of, resembling, or forming dew. **3.** Fresh; unblemished. **4.** *Poetic* Refreshing and gentle as dew: *dewy slumber*. — **dew′i·ness** *n.*

dex·ter (dek′stər) *adj.* **1.** Of or situated on the right side. **2.** *Heraldry* Being on the wearer's right, and thus on the observer's left: opposed to *sinister*. See illustration of ESCUTCHEON. **3.** *Obs.* Favorable; propitious. [< L, right]

dex·ter·i·ty (dek·ster′ə·tē) *n.* **1.** Skill and ease in using the hands or body. **2.** Mental adroitness. **3.** *Rare* Right-handedness. [< L *dexteritas, -tatis* skill < *dexter* on the right] — **Syn.** *Dexterity, adroitness, handiness,* and *skill* refer to ease and expertness in doing. Both *dexterity* and *adroitness* are, literally, "right-handedness," or proficiency in manual tasks. In extended use, *dexterity* has remained close to this base, being applied to technical proficiency in the use of tools, methods, etc.: the *dexterity* of a magician. *Adroitness* has become cleverness in dealing with people or in handling situations: the *adroitness* of a debater. *Handiness* applies chiefly to manual work; *skill* is acquired, at least in part and sometimes wholly, by mental training: the *skill* of the sculptor, the *skill* of the lexicographer. See EASE.

dex·ter·ous (dek′stras, -stər·əs) *adj.* **1.** Possessing dexterity; skillful or adroit; artful. **2.** Done with dexterity. Also **dex·trous** (dek′stras). — **dex′ter·ous·ly** *adv.* — **dex′ter·ous·ness** *n.*

dex·tral (dek′stral) *adj.* **1.** Of or pertaining to, or turned toward the right side; right-hand. **2.** Right-handed. — **dex·tral·i·ty** (dek·stral′ə·tē) *n.* — **dex′tral·ly** *adv.*

dex·tran (dek′stran) *n. Biochem.* A white, gumlike substance produced by bacterial action in milk, molasses, beet juice, etc. [< DEXTR(O)- + -AN(E)]

dex·trin (dek′strin) *n. Biochem.* A gummy, water-soluble substance formed by the action of acids, heat, or diastase on starch, and used as a substitute for gum arabic. Also **dex·trine** (dek′strin, -strēn). [< DEXTR(O)- + -IN]

dextro- *combining form* Turned or turning to the right, or clockwise; used especially in chemistry and physics: *dextrorotatory*. Also, before vowels, **dextr-**. [< L *dexter* right]

dex·tro·gy·rate (dek′strō·jī′rāt) *adj.* Dextrorotatory.

dex·tro·ro·ta·tion (dek′strō·rō·tā′shən) *n. Optics* Clockwise rotation of the plane of polarization of light.

dex·tro·ro·ta·to·ry (dek′strō·rō′tə·tôr′ē, -tō′rē) *adj. Optics* Causing the plane of polarization of light to rotate to the right or clockwise: said of certain crystals and compounds: opposed to *levorotatory*: also **dextrogyrate**. Also **dex·tro·ro·ta·ry** (dek′strō·rō′tər·ē).

dex·trorse (dek′strôrs, dek·strôrs′) *adj. Bot.* Twining spirally toward the right, as certain climbing plants: opposed to *sinistrorse*. Also **dex·tror′sal**. [< L *dextrorsum, dextrovorsum* < *dexter* right + *vertere* to turn] — **dex′trorse·ly** *adv.*

dex·trose (dek′strōs) *n. Biochem.* The dextrorotatory form of glucose: also called *grape sugar*. Also **dex·tro·glu·cose** (dek′strō·glōō′kōs). [< DEXTR(O)- + (GLUC)OSE]

dey (dā) *n.* **1.** The title of a governor of Algiers before the French conquest of 1830. **2.** Formerly, the title of a ruler of Tunis or Tripoli. [< F < Turkish *dāi* maternal uncle]

Dezh·nev (dyezh′nyef), **Cape** The northeasternmost point of Asia, projecting into the Bering Strait: also *East Cape*.

de·zinc·i·fy (dē·zingk′ə·fī) *v.t.* **·fied, ·fy·ing** To remove zinc from. Also **de·zinc′, de·zink′i·fy**. — **de·zinc′i·fi·ca′tion** *n.*

DF or **D/F** or **D.F.** *Telecom.* Direction finding; direction finder.

D.F. 1. Dean of the Faculty. **2.** Defender of the Faith. **3.** Federal District (Pg. *Districto Federal*; Sp. *Distrito Federal*).

DFC *Mil.* Distinguished Flying Cross.

dg or **dg.** Decigram(s).

D.G. Dei gratia.

d.h. 1. Deadhead. **2.** That is to say; i.e. (G *das heisst*).

Dhah·ran (dä·rän′) A town in eastern Saudi Arabia; an oil center; pop. about 75,000: also *Zahran*.

dhak (däk, dôk) *n.* A tree (*Butea frondosa*) of India and Burma, having trifoliate leaves and bright orange-red flowers. [< Hind.]

dhar·ma (där′mə, dûr′-) *n.* In Hinduism and Buddhism, right behavior; conformity to law; virtue, truth, and righteousness. [< Skt., law, custom]

dhar·na (där′nə, dûr′-) *n.* In India, a method of claiming justice by sitting before the door of the oppressor and fasting until death or until satisfaction is received. Also **dhur′na**. [< Hind. *dharnā*, placing, act of sitting in restraint]

Dhau·la·gi·ri (dou′lə·gir′ē) A peak of the Himalayas in central Nepal; 26,810 ft.

Dhi·los (thē′lôs) The Greek name for DELOS.

dhole (dōl) *n.* A wild dog (genus *Cuon*) of SE Asia that hunts in packs, attacking large game. [Origin uncertain]

dho·ti (dō′tē) *n. pl.* **·tis** A loincloth worn by Hindu men. Also **dhoo·ti** (dōō′tē). [< Hind. *dhotī*]

dhour·ra (dōōr′ə) See DURRA.

dhow (dou) *n.* An Arabian coasting vessel usually having one mast and lateen rigging. [< Arabic *dāw*]

di-[1] Var. of DIS-[1].

di-[2] *prefix* **1.** Twice; double: *digraph*. **2.** *Chem.* Containing two atoms, molecules, radicals, etc.: *dichloride*. Also, before *s, dis-*, as in *dissyllable*. [< Gk. *di-* < *dis* twice]

di-[3] Var. of DIA-.

di. or **dia.** Diameter.

Di *Chem.* Didymium.

dia- *prefix* **1.** Through; across; between; apart: *diagonal, diastole*. **2.** Thoroughly; completely: *dialysis*. Also, before vowels, **di-**. [< Gk. *dia-* through]

di·a·base (dī′ə·bās) *n. Geol.* A granular igneous rock, composed essentially of plagioclase, feldspar, and augite: sometimes called *dolerite*. [< Gk. *diabasis* a crossing over < *dia-* across + *bainein* to go] — **di·a·ba′sic** *adj.*

di·a·be·tes (dī′ə·bē′tis, -tēz) *n. Pathol.* **1.** A disease, **diabetes mel·li·tus** (mə·lī′təs), associated with deficient insulin secretion, leading to excess sugar in the blood and urine, accompanied by progressive emaciation, extreme hunger and thirst, and metabolic failure. **2.** A metabolic disorder, **diabetes in·sip·i·dus** (in·sip′ə·dəs), characterized by great thirst and copious urine, without excess sugar. [< NL < Gk. *diabētēs* a passer through < *dia-* through + *bainein* to go]

di·a·bet·ic (dī′ə·bet′ik, -bē′tik) *Med. adj.* Of, pertaining to, or affected with diabetes. Also **di·a·bet′i·cal**. — *n.* One who has diabetes.

di·a·ble·rie (dē·ä′blə·rē, *Fr.* dyȧ·blə·rē′) *n.* **1.** Dealings with the devil; sorcery. **2.** Folklore regarding devils. **3.** Diabolical conduct; deviltry. Also **di·a·ble·ry**. [< F < *diable* devil]

di·a·bol·ic (dī′ə·bol′ik) *adj.* **1.** Of, belonging to, or proceeding from the devil; satanic; infernal. **2.** Befitting the devil; atrociously wicked or inhuman; fiendish: a *diabolic* crime. Also **di·a·bol′i·cal**. [< OF *diabolique* < LL *diabolicus* < Gk. *diabolikos* < *diabolos*. See DEVIL.] — **di·a·bol′i·cal·ly** *adv.* — **di·a·bol′i·cal·ness** *n.*

di·a·bo·lism (dī·ab′ə·liz′əm) *n.* **1.** The raising of evil spirits; sorcery; witchcraft. **2.** Worship of or possession by the devil or devils. **3.** Conduct befitting or inspired by the devil; devilishness. **4.** Devilish character. — **di·ab′o·list** *n.*

di·a·bo·lize (dī·ab′ə·līz) *v.t.* **·lized, ·liz·ing 1.** To render devilish or diabolical. **2.** To bring under diabolical influence. **3.** To represent as devilish.

di·a·bo·lo (dē·ab′ə·lō) *n.* A game played with a spool or top that is spun on a cord tied to two sticks, thrown into the air, and caught again on the cord. [< Ital.]

di·a·caus·tic (dī′ə·kôs′tik) *Optics adj.* Denoting a caustic curve formed by refracted rays: opposed to *catacaustic*. — *n.* A diacaustic surface or curve. [< DIA- + CAUSTIC (def. 3)]

DHOW

DIABOLO

di·ac·e·tyl·mor·phine (dī·as/ə·təl·môr/fēn) *n.* Heroin.
di·a·chron·ic (dī/ə·kron/ik) *adj.* **1.** Existing through time. **2.** *Ling.* Pertaining to the study of language or a linguistic feature in a chronological or developmental scale; historical: distinguished from *synchronic.* [< DIA- + Gk. *chronos* time]
diachronic linguistics Historical linguistics (which see).
di·ach·y·lon (dī·ak/ə·lon) *n.* An adhesive plaster formed by combining lead oxide, olive oil, and water. Also **di·ach/y·lum** (-ləm). [< Med.L *diachylum* < L *diachylon* < Gk. *dia chylōn* made of juices; orig. an ointment so made]
di·ac·id (dī·as/id) *adj. Chem.* Capable of combining with two molecules of a monoacid: said of bases and alcohols.
di·ac·o·nal (dī·ak/ə·nəl) *adj.* Of, pertaining to, or befitting a deacon or the diaconate. [< LL *diaconus* deacon]
di·ac·o·nate (dī·ak/ə·nit, -nāt) *n.* **1.** The office or rank of a deacon. **2.** Deacons collectively. [< LL *diaconatus*]
di·a·crit·ic (dī/ə·krit/ik) *n.* A diacritical mark. — *adj.* **1.** Diacritical. **2.** *Med.* Diagnostic. [< Gk. *diakritikos* distinguishing < *diakrinein* < *dia-* between + *krinein* to distinguish]
di·a·crit·i·cal (dī/ə·krit/i·kəl) *adj.* Serving to mark a distinction, as between phonetic values assigned to a letter; distinguishing. — **di/a·crit/i·cal·ly** *adv.*
diacritical mark A mark, point, or sign attached to a letter to indicate its phonetic value, or to distinguish it from another letter: also called *diacritic.* Also **diacritical sign.**
di·ac·tin·ic (dī/ak·tin/ik) *adj.* Capable of transmitting actinic or chemical rays. — **di·ac/tin·ism** *n.*
di·a·del·phous (dī·ə·del/fəs) *adj. Bot.* Having stamens united by their filaments so as to form two sets. Also **di/a·del/phi·an** (-fē·ən). [< Gk. *di-* two + *adelphos* brother]
di·a·dem (dī/ə·dem) *n.* **1.** A crown or headband worn as a symbol of royalty or honor. **2.** Regal power; sovereignty. — *v.t.* To adorn with or as with a diadem. [< OF *diademe* < L *diadema* < Gk. *diadēma* < *dia-* across + *deein* to bind]
di·aer·e·sis (dī·er/ə·sis) See DIERESIS.
diag. Diagram.
Dia·ghi·lev (dyä/gi·lef), **Sergei Pavlovich,** 1872–1929, Russian ballet producer.
di·ag·nose (dī/əg·nōs, -nōz, dī/əg·nōs/, -nōz/) *v.* **·nosed, ·nos·ing** *v.t.* **1.** To examine or distinguish by diagnosis. — *v.i.* **2.** To make a diagnosis of a person, disease, etc. [Back formation < DIAGNOSIS]
di·ag·no·sis (dī/əg·nō/sis) *n. pl.* **·ses** (-sēz) **1.** *Med.* **a** The act or process of recognizing diseases by their characteristic symptoms. **b** A summary of symptoms and the conclusion arrived at. **2.** Any similar examination, summary, and conclusion: a *diagnosis* of an election. **3.** *Biol.* Scientific discrimination between similar or related things or conditions for the purpose of classification. [< NL < Gk. *diagnōsis* < *diagignōskein* < *dia-* between + *gignōskein* to know]
di·ag·nos·tic (dī/əg·nos/tik) *adj.* **1.** Of or pertaining to a diagnosis. **2.** Aiding in diagnosis. — *n. Med.* **1.** A diagnosis. **2.** A symptom by which a particular disease or class of diseases is diagnosed. — **di·ag·nos/ti·cal·ly** *adv.*
di·ag·nos·ti·cian (dī/əg·nos·tish/ən) *n.* One who makes a diagnosis, especially a medical diagnosis.
di·ag·nos·tics (dī/əg·nos/tiks) *n.pl. (construed as sing.)* The science or principles of diagnosis.
di·ag·o·nal (dī·ag/ə·nəl) *adj.* **1.** Having an oblique direction; crossing obliquely from corner to corner or from side to side. **2.** Marked by oblique lines, ridges, etc. **3.** *Geom.* **a** Joining two nonadjacent angles of a figure: a *diagonal* line. **b** Joining, as a plane, two nonadjacent edges of a solid. — *n.* **1.** *Geom.* A diagonal straight line or plane. **2.** A fabric with diagonal ridges or lines. Also **diagonal cloth. 3.** Anything running diagonally. [< L *diagonalis* < Gk. *diagōnios* < *dia-* across + *gōnia* angle] — **di·ag/o·nal·ly** *adv.*
Di·ag·o·ras (dī·ag/ə·rəs) Fifth-century B.C. Greek poet and philosopher: called **the Atheist.**
di·a·gram (dī/ə·gram) *n.* **1.** An outline figure or scheme of lines, spaces, points, etc., intended to demonstrate a geometrical proposition, represent an object or area, show the relation between parts or places, etc. **2.** A graph or chart. — *v.t.* **di·a·gramed** or **·grammed, di·a·gram·ing** or **·gram·ming** To represent or illustrate by a diagram. [< Gk. *diagramma* < *dia-* across + *graphein* to write]
di·a·gram·mat·ic (dī/ə·grə·mat/ik) *adj.* **1.** Having the form of a diagram; schematic. **2.** Lacking detail; sketchy. Also **di/a·gram·mat/i·cal.** — **di/a·gram·mat/i·cal·ly** *adv.*
di·a·graph (dī/ə·graf, -gräf) *n.* A protractor and scale combined for drawing diagrams. [< DIA- + -GRAPH]
di·al (dī/əl, dīl) *n.* **1.** Any graduated circular plate or face upon which pressure, temperature. etc., is indicated by means of a pointer or needle. **2.** The face of a watch or clock; also, a sundial. **3.** A numbered disk or movable indicator on a radio or television set, used to tune in stations. **4.** A rotating disk on a plate bearing letters and numbers, used to make connections in an automatic telephone system. **5.** A miner's compass for underground surveying. — *v.* **di·aled** or **·alled, di·al·ing** or **·al·ling** — *v.t.* **1.** To measure

or survey with a dial. **2.** To turn to or indicate by means of a dial. **3.** To call by means of a dial telephone. **4.** To adjust a radio or television set to (a station, program, etc.). — *v.i.* **5.** To use a dial, as in telephoning. [< Med.L *dialis* daily < L *dies* day] — **di/al·er** or **di/al·ler, di/al·ist** or **di/al·list** *n.*
dial. Dialect; dialectal.
di·a·lect (dī/ə·lekt) *n.* **1.** A variety of speech distinguished from the standard or literary language by variations of idiom, vocabulary, phonology, and morphology peculiar to a particular region: the Yorkshire *dialect* of England. **2.** Any of the regional forms of the standard language: the Southern *dialect* of American English. **3.** A manner of speech characteristic of the members of a particular class, trade, or profession: the *dialect* of the cultured. **4.** An imperfect use of the standard language by those to whom another language is native. **5.** A language developed from an earlier language; a linguistic branch: the Romance languages are *dialects* of Latin. Abbr. *dial.* [< MF *dialecte* < L *dialectus* < Gk. *dialektos* conversation, way of speaking < *dialegesthai* < *dia-* across + *legein* to speak]
— **Syn. 1, 2.** *Dialect, patois, vernacular, argot, jargon, cant,* and *slang* denote variations from the accepted standard of a language. A *dialect* is peculiar to a region or a class; it is often older than the standard language, having developed from the same source. *Patois* is applied to the hybrid language spoken by the minority group in a bilingual country, as by the French-Canadians. *Vernacular* was originally the native language of a people as distinguished from Latin, the then universal language of scholars; it is now the common speech of the people as distinguished from the standard literary language. *Argot* is the vocabulary of the underworld; *jargon,* the vocabulary of technical words peculiar to a science, profession, etc., much of which is unintelligible to the layman. The patter of the beggar was called *cant;* hence, the word came to denote any hypocritical speech. In extended use it now refers to a professional vocabulary consisting largely of stereotypes: the *cant* of the headline writer. *Slang* consists of newly coined words that have gained currency in common speech but not in serious writing; some slang words pass into the standard language, but most of them die out or are supplanted by new slang words.
di·a·lec·tal (dī/ə·lek/təl) *adj.* Of or characteristic of a dialect. Abbr. *dial.* — **di·a·lec/tal·ly** *adv.*
dialect atlas A collection of linguistic maps showing the areas within which are found various distributions of particular features of pronunciation, vocabulary, syntax, etc.: also called *linguistic atlas.*
dialect geography Linguistic geography (which see).
di·a·lec·tic (dī/ə·lek/tik) *n.* **1.** *Often pl.* The art or practice of examining statements logically, as by question and answer, to establish validity. **2.** A specific logical mode of argument: Hegel's *dialectic.* **3.** Formerly, logic. — *adj.* **1.** Pertaining to or using dialectic. **2.** Dialectal. [< OF *dialectique* < L *dialectica* < Gk. *dialektikē* (*technē*) (art) of dialectic, discussion by question and answer < *dialektos.* See DIALECT.]
di·a·lec·ti·cal (dī/ə·lek/ti·kəl) *adj.* Dialectic. — **di/a·lec/ti·cal·ly** *adv.*
dialectical materialism *Philos.* The doctrine of Karl Marx and Friedrich Engels, combining materialism with Hegel's logical dialectic in which the conflict between two entities or forces, thesis and antithesis, is resolved by the formation of a new entity or force, the synthesis. See MARXISM.
di·a·lec·ti·cian (dī/ə·lek·tish/ən) *n.* **1.** A logician. **2.** One who specializes in the study of dialects.
di·a·lec·ti·cism (dī/ə·lek/tə·siz/əm) *n.* **1.** The character or nature of a dialect. **2.** A dialectal word or peculiarity.
di·a·lec·tics (dī/ə·lek/tiks) *n.pl. (construed as sing.)* Dialectic (def. 1).
di·a·lec·tol·o·gy (dī/ə·lek·tol/ə·jē) *n.* The study of dialects.
di·al·ing (dī/əl·ing) *n.* **1.** The act of one who dials. **2.** The measurement of time by sundials. **3.** Underground surveying with a dial, especially in mines. Also **di/al·ling.**
di·al·lage (dī/ə·lij) *n. Mineral.* A brown, gray, or green, foliated variety of pyroxene, crystallizing in the monoclinic system. [< F < Gk. *diallagē* an interchange < *dia-* across + *allassein* to change. exchange]
di·a·lo·gism (dī·al/ə·jiz/əm) *n.* **1.** A dialogue or discussion; especially, a discourse with oneself: a soliloquy. **2.** *Logic* An inference with a single premise and disjunctive conclusion.
di·a·lo·gist (dī·al/ə·jist) *n.* One who writes or takes part in a dialogue. — **di·a·lo·gis·tic** (dī/ə·lō·jis/tik) or **·ti·cal** *adj.*
di·a·lo·gize (dī·al/ə·jīz) *v.i.* **·gized, ·giz·ing** To carry on a dialogue.
di·a·logue (dī/ə·lôg, -log) *n.* **1.** A conversation in which two or more take part. **2.** The conversation in a play, novel, etc. **3.** A literary work in which two or more characters are represented as conversing: a Platonic *dialogue.* **4.** An exchange of opinions or ideas; free interchange of different points of view; discussion. — **Syn.** See CONVERSATION. — *v.* **·logued, ·logu·ing** *v.t.* **1.** To express in dialogue form. — *v.i.* **2.** To carry on a dialogue. [< F < L *dialogus* < Gk. *dialogos* < *dialegesthai* to converse. Akin to DIALECT.]
— **di/a·log/uer** or **di/a·log/er** *n.*

dial tone A low, steady, humming sound indicating to the user of a dial telephone that a call may be made.

di·al·y·sis (dī-alʹə-sis) *n. pl.* **·ses** (-sēz) **1.** Separation of parts previously or normally joined together. **2.** *Chem.* The separating of solutions of mixed substances of unequal diffusibility by means of moist membranes or septa; especially, the separation of a colloid from a crystalloid. [< Gk. *dialysis* < *dialyein* < *dia-* completely + *lyein* to loosen]

di·a·lyt·ic (dī-ə-litʹik) *adj.* **1.** Pertaining to or characterized by dialysis. **2.** Having the power or property of separating. — **di·a·lytʹi·cal·ly** *adv.*

di·a·lyze (dīʹə-līz) *v.t.* **·lyzed, ·lyz·ing** *Chem.* To subject to or prepare by dialysis; separate by dialysis.

di·a·lyz·er (dīʹə-lī/zər) *n. Chem.* An apparatus used for dialysis, especially a membranous septum stretched over a gutta-percha ring.

diam. Diameter.

di·a·mag·net·ic (dī/ə-mag·netʹik) *Physics adj.* **1.** Pertaining to or designating the property of substances that tend to lie at right angles to the poles of a magnet. **2.** Having a negative magnetic susceptibility, or a permeability less than that of a vacuum, as bismuth or copper. — *n.* A substance that possesses such properties. — **di/a·mag·netʹi·cal·ly** *adv.* — **di/a·magʹnet·ism** *n.*

di·am·e·ter (dī-amʹə-tər) *n. Math.* **1.** A straight line passing through the center of a circle or sphere and terminating at the circumference or surface. **2.** The length of such a line. **3.** The straight line connecting the two most separated points on the boundary of a figure. **4.** *Optics* A unit used to measure the magnifying power of binoculars, microscopes, etc. Abbr. *d., D., di., dia., diam.* [< OF *diametre* < L *diametrus* < Gk. *diametros* < *dia-* through + *metron* measure]

di·a·met·ri·cal (dī/ə-metʹri-kəl) *adj.* **1.** Of, pertaining to, or coinciding with a diameter. Also **di·am·e·tral** (dī-amʹə-trəl). **2.** Directly opposite; as far removed as possible: *diametrical* motives. Also **di·a·metʹric.**

di·a·met·ri·cal·ly (dī/ə-metʹrik·lē) *adv.* **1.** In the direction of or along a diameter. **2.** Irreconcilably; completely: *diametrically* opposed.

di·am·ine (dī-amʹēn, -in, dī/ə-mēn, -min) *n. Chem.* Any of a group of compounds containing two amino (NH₂) radicals; a double amine. Also **di·am·in** (dī-amʹin, dī/ə-min).

di·a·mond (dīʹmənd, dī/ə-) *n.* **1.** A mineral of great hardness and refractive power, consisting of carbon crystallized in the isometric system under great pressure and temperature; also, this mineral when used as a valuable gem. **2.** The uncut face of this stone, used in cutting glass, etc.; also, the tool in which such a diamond is used. **3.** *Geom.* A figure bounded by four equal straight lines, having two of the angles acute and two obtuse; a rhomb or lozenge. **4.** In card games: **a** A red, lozenge-shaped spot on a playing card. **b** A card with such a mark. **c** *pl.* A suit of cards so marked. **5.** In baseball, the infield or a baseball field; also, the entire field. **6.** *Printing* A size of type next above brilliant, 4- or 4½-point. — *adj.* Made of or like diamonds. — *v.t.* To adorn with or as with diamonds. [< OF *diamant* < LL *diamas, -antis,* ? alter. of L *adamas.* Doublet of ADAMANT.] — **diaʹmond·ed** *adj.*

DIAMOND CUTS
a,b,c American brilliant (top, bottom, and side views). *d* Marquise. *e* Regent or Pitt. *f* Kohinoor. *g* Double rose (side view). *h* Rose. *i* Briolette.

diamond anniversary A 60th or 75th anniversary.

di·a·mond·back (dīʹmənd·bak/, dī/ə-) *n.* **1.** An edible turtle (*Malaclemys centrata*) inhabiting salt marshes of the southern United States, having diamond-shaped markings on the shell. Also **diamond-back terrapin. 2.** A large rattlesnake (*Crotalus adamanteus*) of the SE United States, having diamond-shaped markings on the back: also **dia/mond-rat/tler** (-rat/lər).

DIAMONDBACK TERRAPIN
(Upper shell 5 to 7½ inches long)

Diamond Head A promontory on the SE shore of Oahu, Hawaii.

Diamond State Nickname of DELAWARE.

Di·an·a (dī-anʹə) In Roman mythology, goddess of the hunt, virginity, and the moon: identified with the Greek *Artemis.* — *n.* The moon.

Diana of the Ephesians An Asian goddess of fertility, confused with the Roman Diana. *Acts* xix 21.

di·an·drous (dī-anʹdrəs) *adj. Bot.* Having two stamens. [< NL *diandrus* < Gk. *di-* two + *anēr, andros* man, male]

di·a·no·et·ic (dī/ə-nō-etʹik) *adj. Logic* Of or pertaining to a rational or discursive faculty. [< Gk. *dianoētikos* of thinking < *dia-* through + *noein* to think < *nous* mind]

di·an·thus (dī-anʹthəs) *n.* Any plant of an extensive genus (*Dianthus*) of ornamental herbs of the pink family, as the carnation and the sweet william. [< NL < Gk. *Dios* of Zeus + *anthos* flower]

di·a·pa·son (dī/ə-pāʹsən, -zən) *n.* **1.** In a pipe organ, either of two principal stops (the **open diapason** and the **stopped diapason**) that extend throughout the entire compass of the instrument and produce its fundamental tone. **2.** A tuning fork; also, the standard pitch given by a tuning fork. **3.** In old Greek music, an octave. **4.** The entire compass of an instrument or voice. **5.** A vast and majestic outpouring of sound or harmony. [< L < Gk. *dia pasōn (chordōn)* through all (the notes)]

di·a·per (dīʹə-pər; *for n. defs. 1 and 2, v. def. 1, also* dī/pər) *n.* **1.** A folded piece of soft fabric used as a baby's breechcloth. **2.** A decorative pattern consisting of a system of repeated figures or designs. **3.** In the Middle Ages, a fine figured silk or linen cloth. — *v.t.* **1.** To put a diaper on (a baby). **2.** To decorate with a repeated figure or similar figures. [< OF *diapre,* earlier *diaspre* < Med.Gk. *diaspros* < *dia-* completely + *aspros* white]

DIAPER (def. 2)

di·a·pha·ne·i·ty (dī/ə-fə-nēʹə-tē) *n.* Transparency.

di·aph·a·nous (dī-afʹə-nəs) *adj.* Showing light through its substance; transparent; translucent. [< Med.L *diaphanus* < Gk. *diaphanēs* < *dia-* through + *phainein* to show] — **di·aphʹa·nous·ly** *adv.* — **di·aphʹa·nous·ness** *n.*

di·aph·o·ny (dī-afʹə-nē) *n. pl.* **·nies 1.** *Music* Organum; also, a looser form of organum in which intervals other than fourths and fifths were permitted. **2.** Anciently, dissonance: opposed to *symphony.* [< LL *diaphonia* dissonance < Gk. *diaphōnia* < *dia-* across + *phōneein* to sound < *phōnē* a sound] — **di·a·phon·ic** (dī/ə-fonʹik) *adj.*

di·a·pho·re·sis (dī/ə-fə-rēʹsis) *n. Med.* Copious perspiration, especially when produced artificially. [< LL < Gk. *diaphorēsis* < *diaphoreein* to perspire < *dia-* across, through + *phoreein* to carry]

di·a·pho·ret·ic (dī/ə-fə-retʹik) *Med. adj.* Producing perspiration. — *n.* A diaphoretic drug or agent.

di·a·phragm (dīʹə-fram) *n.* **1.** *Anat.* A muscular wall separating the thoracic and abdominal cavities in mammals. **2.** Any membrane or partition that separates or divides. **3.** Any device resembling a diaphragm in appearance or elasticity, as the thin vibrating disk of a telephone. **4.** A contraceptive device of soft rubber placed over the cervix uteri. **5.** *Chem.* The porous cup of a voltaic cell. **6.** *Optics* A disk with an adjustable aperture that can control the amount of light passing through the lens of a camera, telescope, etc. — *v.t.* To act upon or furnish with a diaphragm. [< LL *diaphragma* < Gk. *dia-* across + *phragma* fence]

di·a·phrag·mat·ic (dī/ə-frag-matʹik) *adj.* Of, pertaining to, or like a diaphragm. — **di/a·phrag·matʹi·cal·ly** *adv.*

di·aph·y·sis (dī-afʹə-sis) *n. pl.* **·ses** (-sēz) *Anat.* The shaft of a long bone. [< NL < Gk., a growing through < *dia-* through + *phyein* to grow, produce] — **di·a·phys·i·al** (dī/ə-fiz/ē-əl) *adj.*

di·a·poph·y·sis (dī/ə-pofʹə-sis) *n. pl.* **·ses** (-sēz) *Anat.* The transverse process of a vertebra. [< DI-³ + APOPHYSIS] — **di·ap·o·phys·i·al** (dī/ap-ə-fiz/ē-əl) *adj.*

Di·ar·bekr (dē-är/bek/ər) See DIYARBEKIR.

di·ar·chy (dīʹär-kē) *n. pl.* **·chies** A government in which two persons have joint power to rule, as that of William and Mary in England: also spelled *dyarchy.* [< DI-² + -ARCHY]

di·a·rist (dīʹə-rist) *n.* One who keeps a diary.

di·ar·rhe·a (dī/ə-rēʹə) *n. Pathol.* A disorder of the intestine marked by abnormally frequent and fluid evacuation of feces. Also **di·ar·rhoeʹa.** [< L *diarrhoea* < Gk. *diarrhoia* < *dia-* through + *rheein* to flow] — **di·ar·rheʹal** or **rhoeʹal, di/ar·rhe/ic** or **·rhoe/ic, di/ar·rhet/ic** or **·rhoet/ic** (-ret/ik) *adj.*

di·ar·thro·sis (dī/är-thrōʹsis) *n. pl.* **·ses** (-sēz) *Anat.* A type of articulation in which the ends of the bones are surrounded by a capsule and covered by cartilage, permitting maximum free movement of a joint. [< NL < Gk. *diarthrōsis* < *dia-* completely + *arthrōsis* an articulation < *arthron* joint] — **di/ar·thro/di·al** (-dē-əl) *adj.*

di·a·ry (dīʹə-rē, dī/rē) *n. pl.* **·ries 1.** A record of daily events; especially, a personal record of one's activities, experiences, or observations; journal. **2.** A book for keeping such a record. [< L *diarium* < *dies* day]

Di·as (dēʹəs), **Bartholomeu**, 1450?–1500, Portuguese seafarer and explorer; discovered Cape of Good Hope. Also *Diaz.*

Di·as·po·ra (dī-as/pər-ə) *n.* **1.** The dispersion of the Jews among the Gentiles after the Exile. **2.** The Jews so dispersed. **3.** In the New Testament, the Jewish Christians living outside Palestine. I *Pet.* i 1. [< Gk., dispersion < *dia-* completely + *speirein* to sow, scatter]

di·a·spore (dīʹə-spôr, -spōr) *n.* A variously colored, translucent to subtranslucent aluminum hydroxide, AlO·OH. [< Gk. *diaspora* dispersion (see DIASPORA); so called from its rapid crackling and dispersion when heated]

di·a·stal·sis (dī/ə-stôlʹsis, -stal/-) *n. pl.* **·ses** (-sēz) *Physiol.* A downward contraction forming part of the peristaltic action of the digestive tract. [< NL < Gk. *dia-* through + *stellein* to place, send] — **di/a·stal/tic** *adj.*

di·a·stase (dīʹə-stās) *n. Biochem.* An enzyme that converts starch and glycogen into dextrin and sugar (chiefly maltose), found in germinating grain and in various animal fluids. [<

F < Gk. *diastasis* separation < *dia-* apart + *histanai* to set, cause to stand] — **di·a·sta·sic, di·a·stat·ic** (-stat′ik) *adj.*

di·as·ter (dī-as′tər) *n. Biol.* **1.** That stage of cell division in which the chromosomes have separated to form two groups of starlike radiations at the poles. **2.** One of the groups of radiations so formed. [< DI-² + Gk. *astēr* star]

di·as·to·le (dī-as′tə-lē) *n.* **1.** *Physiol.* The usual rhythmic dilatation and relaxation of the heart, especially of the ventricles, after each contraction. Compare SYSTOLE. **2.** In Greek and Latin prosody, the lengthening of a syllable that is naturally short. [< LL < Gk. *diastolē* a separation, lengthening < *dia-* apart + *stellein* to send, put] — **di·as·tol·ic** (dī′ə-stol′ik) *adj.*

di·as·tro·phism (dī-as′trə-fiz′əm) *n. Geol.* **1.** Any of the processes through which the earth's crust is deformed, producing continents, mountains, etc. **2.** Any deformation resulting from this. [< Gk. *diastrophē* < *dia-* apart + *strephein* to turn] — **di·a·stroph·ic** (dī′ə-strof′ik) *adj.*

di·a·tes·sa·ron (dī′ə-tes′ə-ron) *n.* **1.** In ancient music, a perfect fourth. **2.** A harmony of the four Gospels arranged to make one continuous narrative. [< OF < L < Gk. *dia tessarōn* made of four]

di·a·ther·man·cy (dī′ə-thûr′mən-sē) *n. Physics* The property of transmitting infrared rays. [< F *diathermansie* < Gk. *dia-* through + *thermansis* a heating] — **di·a·ther·ma·nous** (dī′ə-thûr′mə-nəs) *adj.*

di·a·ther·my (dī′ə-thûr′mē) *n. pl.* **·mies** *Med.* **1.** The generation of heat in the body tissues through their resistance to the passage of high-frequency electric currents. **2.** The apparatus used. Also **di·a·ther·mi·a** (dī′ə-thûr′mē-ə). [< NL *diathermia* < Gk. *dia-* through + *thermē* heat]

di·ath·e·sis (dī-ath′ə-sis) *n. pl.* **·ses** (-sēz) *Med.* A predisposition to certain forms of disease. [< NL < Gk. *diathēsis* arrangement, disposition < *dia-* in order + *tithenai* to place] — **di·a·thet·ic** (dī′ə-thet′ik) *adj.*

di·a·tom (dī′ə-tom, -təm) *n.* A marine and fresh-water plankton, unicellular or colonial, belonging to the family *Chlorophyceae* of microscopic green algae, characterized by bivalve walls containing silica. [< NL *diatoma* < Gk. *dia-* through + *temnein* to cut]

di·a·to·ma·ceous earth (dī′ə-tə-mā′shəs) A fine, variously colored earth, derived from deposits of the cell walls of diatoms, used as an absorbent, a polishing powder, etc.: also called *kieselguhr.* Also **di·at·o·mite** (dī-at′ə-mīt).

di·a·tom·ic (dī′ə-tom′ik) *adj. Chem.* **1.** Containing only two atoms. **2.** Containing two replaceable univalent atoms; bivalent. [< DI-² + ATOMIC]

di·a·ton·ic (dī′ə-ton′ik) *adj. Music* **1.** Pertaining to the order of intervals in a major scale or a minor scale in which no accidentals are used. **2.** Designating chords or harmony using few accidentals or none at all. **3.** Designating a half-step, as F ♯ to G. Compare CHROMATIC. [< MF *diatonique* < LL *diatonicus* < Gk. *diatonikos* < *dia-* through, at the interval of + *tenein* to stretch] — **di′a·ton′i·cal·ly** *adv.* — **di·a·ton·i·cism** (dī′ə-ton′i·siz′əm) *n.*

di·a·tribe (dī′ə-trīb) *n.* A bitter or malicious harangue; an abusive discourse. [< MF < L *diatriba* < Gk. *diatribē* a spending of time < *dia-* thoroughly + *tribein* to rub]

di·at·ro·pism (dī-at′rə-piz′əm) *n. Bot.* The propensity of some plant organs to arrange themselves transversely to the line of action of an external stimulus. [< DIA- + TROPISM] — **di·a·trop·ic** (dī′ə-trop′ik) *adj.*

Di·az (dē′äs), **Bartholomeu** See DIAS.

Di·az (dē′äs), **Porfirio**, 1830–1915, Mexican general and statesman; president 1877–80, 1884–1911.

Di·az de Bi·var (dē′äth thä bē-vär′) See CID.

di·a·zine (dī′ə-zēn, -zin, dī-az′in) *n. Chem.* One of three isomeric cyclic hydrocarbon compounds, $C_4H_4N_2$, the ring of which contains two nitrogen and four carbon atoms. Also **di·a·zin** (dī′ə-zin, dī-az′in). [< DIAZ(O)- + -IN]

diazo- *combining form* Of or denoting a diazo compound: *diazomethane.* Also, before vowels, **diaz-**. [< DI-² + AZO(TE)]

di·az·o compound (dī-az′ō, dī-ā′zō) *Chem.* Any of a group of compounds in which two nitrogen atoms are united to a hydrocarbon radical.

di·a·zole (dī′ə-zōl, dī-az′ōl) *n. Chem.* Any member of a class of heterocyclic hydrocarbon compounds, the ring of which contains two nitrogen and three carbon atoms. [< DIAZ(O)- + -OLE¹]

di·az·o·meth·ane (dī-az′ō-meth′ān, dī-ā′zō-) *n. Chem.* An odorless, poisonous gas, CH_2N_2, used in organic syntheses.

di·a·zo·ni·um (dī′ə-zō′nē-əm) *n. Chem.* A basic organic radical that forms aromatic nitrogen compounds. [< DI-AZ(O)- + (AMM)ONIUM]

diazonium salt *Chem.* Any of a group of salts formed by the action of nitrous acid at low temperature upon a salt of a primary aromatic amine.

di·az·o·tize (dī-az′ə-tīz) *v.t.* **·tized, ·tiz·ing** *Chem.* To bring about chemical reactions or changes that form a diazo compound or derivative. — **di·az′o·ti·za′tion** *n.*

di·ba·sic (dī-bā′sik) *adj. Chem.* **1.** Of an acid, containing two atoms of hydrogen replaceable by a base or basic radical, as sulfuric acid. **2.** Of or derived from such an acid: said of salts. Also *bibasic.* — **di·ba·sic·i·ty** (dī′bā-sis′ə-tē) *n.*

dib·ble¹ (dib′əl) *n.* A gardener's pointed tool for planting seeds, setting slips, etc. Also **dib·ber** (dib′ər). — *v.t.* **bled, ·bling** To make holes for seeds or plants in (soil) with a dibble. [ME, ? < *dib,* var. of DAB³] — **dib′bler** *n.*

dib·ble² (dib′əl) *v.i.* **·bled, ·bling** *Brit. Dial.* **1.** In angling, to let the bait bob gently in the water. **2.** To dabble; dibber. Also **dib.** [Freq. of *dib,* var. of DAB³]

di·bran·chi·ate (dī-brang′kē-it, -āt) *n.* Any of an order (*Dibranchiata*) of cephalopods including the squids and octopuses. — *adj.* Of or pertaining to the *Dibranchiata.* [< NL *Dibranchiata* < Gk. *di-* two + *branchia* gills]

di·bro·mide (dī-brō′mīd, -mid) *n. Chem.* A compound containing two atoms of bromine.

di·car·box·yl·ic acid (dī-kär′bok-sil′ik) *Chem.* Any of a group of dibasic organic acids having two carboxyl radicals.

di·cast (dī′kast, dik′ast) *n.* In ancient Athens, one of the citizens selected annually to serve as a judge of the high court: also called *heliast.* [< Gk. *dikastēs* < *dikē* justice] — **di·cas′tic** *adj.*

dice (dīs) *n. pl. of* **die** **1.** Small cubes of bone, ivory, etc., having the sides marked with spots from one to six. **2.** A game of chance played with such cubes. — *v.* **diced, dic·ing** *v.t.* **1.** To cut into small cubes. **2.** To decorate with a dicelike pattern. **3.** To gamble away or win with dice. — *v.i.* **4.** To play at dice. [See DIE²] — **dic′er** *n.*

di·cen·tra (dī-sen′trə) *n.* Any of a genus (*Dicentra*) of perennial herbs with a raceme of nodding flowers, as the bleeding heart and dutchman's-breeches. [< NL < Gk. *dikentros* < *di-* two + *kentron* sharp point, spur]

di·ceph·a·lous (dī-sef′ə-ləs) *adj.* Having two heads.

di·cha·si·um (dī-kā′zhē-əm, -zē-əm) *n. pl.* **·si·a** (-zhē-ə, -zē-ə) *Bot.* A cymose inflorescence in which two lateral branches grow from the primary axis, each branch then repeating the division. [< NL < Gk. *dichasis* division < *dicha* in two] — **di·cha′si·al** *adj.*

di·chlor·eth·yl sulfide (dī′klôr·eth′əl, -klō·reth′-) *Chem.* Mustard gas.

di·chlo·ride (dī-klôr′īd, -id, -klō′rīd, -rid) *n. Chem.* A compound having two atoms of chlorine; a bichloride. Also **di·chlo·rid** (dī-klôr′id, -klō′rid).

di·chlo·ro·di·phen·yl·tri·chlor·o·eth·ane (dī-klôr′ō-dī-fen′əl·trī·klôr′ō·eth′ān, -klō′rō-) *n.* DDT.

dicho- *combining form* In two; in pairs: *dichotomy.* Also, before vowels, **dich-**. [< Gk. *dicha* in two < *dis* twice]

di·chog·a·mous (dī-kog′ə-məs) *adj. Bot.* Having pistils and stamens that mature at different times, thus making possible cross-fertilization between hermaphrodite flowers: opposed to *homogamous* (def. 2). [< DICHO- + -GAMOUS]

di·chog·a·my (dī-kog′ə-mē) *n. Bot.* The state of being dichogamous. [< DICHO- + -GAMY]

di·chot·o·mize (dī-kot′ə-mīz) *v.* **·mized, ·miz·ing** *v.t.* **1.** To cut or part into two sections; subdivide or separate and classify into pairs. — *v.i.* **2.** To be or become separated into two parts. — **di·chot′o·mist** *n.* — **di·chot′o·mi·za′tion** *n.*

di·chot·o·mous (dī-kot′ə-məs) *adj.* **1.** Pertaining to or involving dichotomy. **2.** Dividing into two parts or branches. Also **di·cho·tom·ic** (dī′kə-tom′ik). — **di·chot′o·mous·ly** *adv.*

di·chot·o·my (dī-kot′ə-mē) *n. pl.* **·mies** **1.** Division into two parts or by pairs; a cutting in two. **2.** *Logic* The division of a class into two mutually exclusive subclasses, as minerals into gold and not-gold. **3.** *Astron.* The aspect of the moon, Mercury, or Venus, when half the disk is visible. **4.** *Bot.* A system of branching in which each successive axis forks into two equally developed branches. [< Gk. *dichotomia* < *dicho-* in two + *temnein* to cut]

di·chro·ic (dī-krō′ik) *adj.* **1.** Exhibiting dichroism. **2.** Dichromatic. Also **di·chro·it·ic** (dī′krō-it′ik).

di·chro·ism (dī′krō-iz′əm) *n.* **1.** *Crystall.* The property of showing different colors when viewed in different directions, exhibited by doubly refracting crystals. **2.** *Chem.* The property of being differently colored in different degrees of concentration, as a solution. [< Gk. *dichroos* two-colored < *di-* two + *chrōs* color + -ISM]

di·chro·ite (dī′krō-īt) *n. Mineral.* Cordierite. [< Gk. *di-chroos* two-colored + -ITE¹]

di·chro·mate (dī-krō′māt) *n. Chem.* A salt of dichromic acid: also called *bichromate.*

di·chro·mat·ic (dī′krō-mat′ik) *adj.* **1.** Having two colors. **2.** *Zool.* Having two color phases within the species apart from changes due to age or sex. **3.** *Pathol.* Able to see only two of the three primary colors. Also *dichroic, dichromic.*

di·chro·ma·tism (dī-krō′mə-tiz′əm) *n.* The state of being dichromatic, especially with reference to color blindness. Also **di·chro′mism.**

di·chro·mic (dī-krō′mik) *adj.* **1.** Containing two atoms of chromium or their equivalents. **2.** Dichromatic.

dichromic acid *Chem.* A dibasic acid, $H_2Cr_2O_7$, known only through its salts, the dichromates.

di·chro·scope (dī′krə·skōp) *n.* An instrument for examining dichroism, as of crystals. Also **di·chro·o·scope** (dī·krō′ə·skōp). [< Gk. *dichroos* two-colored + -SCOPE] — **di·chro·scop·ic** (dī′krə·skop′ik) *adj.*

dick (dik) *n. U.S. Slang* A detective. [? < Am. slang *dick* to look about sharply; infl. by *d(et)ec(tive)*]

Dick (dik), **George Frederick**, 1881–1967, and his wife, **Gladys**, 1881–1963 *née* Henry, U.S. physicians.

dick·cis·sel (dik·sis′əl) *n.* A bird, the bunting (*Spiza americana*), of the Mississippi region, distinguished by its black throat and lively call. Also **dick·sis′sel**. [Imit.]

dick·ens (dik′ənz) *n. Informal* Devil: a euphemism: What the *dickens* is wrong?

Dick·ens (dik′ənz), **Charles (John Huffam)**, 1812–70, English novelist: pseudonym *Boz.*

Dick·en·si·an (di·ken′zē·ən) *adj.* Of or characteristic of Charles Dickens, his writing, or his style.

dick·er (dik′ər) *U.S. v.i.* **1.** To make a petty trade; haggle. **2.** In politics, to work toward a deal; bargain. — *v.t.* **3.** To barter; exchange. — *n.* The act of dickering; also, a petty trade; a bargain. [ME *dyker* lot of ten, esp. skins or hides, ult. < L *decuria* a group of ten]

dick·ey (dik′ē) *n. pl.* **·eys** **1.** A blouse front worn by women under a jacket or low-necked sweater or dress. **2.** A detachable shirt front for a man. **3.** A shirt collar. **4.** A child's bib or pinafore. **5.** A donkey. **6.** Any small bird. Also **dick′ey·bird′, dick′y·bird′** (-bûrd′). **7.** A driver's outside seat on a carriage; also, a seat for servants in the rear. Also **dick′y.** [< *Dicky*, double dim. of *Richard*, a personal name]

Dick·in·son (dik′ən·sən) **Emily (Elizabeth)**, 1830–86, U.S. poet. — **John**, 1732–1808, American statesman.

Dick test *Med.* A test of susceptibility to scarlet fever, consisting of subcutaneous injections of streptococcus toxins of the disease. [after George and Gladys *Dick*]

di·cli·nous (dī′kli·nəs, dī·klī′-) *adj. Bot.* Having stamens in one flower and pistils in another; unisexual. [< DI-² + Gk. *klinē* bed]

di·cli·ny (dī′kli·nē, dī·klī′nē) *n. Bot.* The condition of being diclinous. Also **di·cli·nism** (dī′kli·niz′əm).

di·cot·y·le·don (dī′kot·ə·lēd′n, dī·kot′-) *n. Bot.* **1.** A plant having two cotyledons or seed leaves. **2.** A member of the subclass *Dicotyledones.*

di·cot·y·le·do·nous (dī′kot·ə·lēd′n·əs, dī·kot′-) *adj. Bot.* Belonging or pertaining to the largest, most important subclass (*Dicotyledones*) of flowering plants, characterized by having seeds with two cotyledons.

di·crot·ic (dī·krot′ik) *adj. Physiol.* Having an abnormal heartbeat, with a double pulse beat to each systole of the heart. Also **di·cro·tal** (dī·krō′təl), **di·cro·tous** (dī′krə·təs). [< Gk. *dikrotos* < *di-* two + *krotos* noise sound] — **di·cro·tism** (dī′krə·tiz′əm) *n.*

dict. **1.** Dictation. **2.** Dictator. **3.** Dictionary.

dic·ta (dik′tə) Plural of DICTUM.

Dic·ta·phone (dik′tə·fōn) *n.* A type of phonographic instrument that records and reproduces speech, as for dictation to a stenographer: a trade name. Also **dic′ta·phone.**

dic·tate (dik′tāt; *for v., also* dik·tāt′) *v.* **·tat·ed, ·tat·ing** *v.t.* **1.** To utter or read aloud (something) to be recorded by another. **2.** To prescribe authoritatively, as commands, terms, rules, etc. — *v.i.* **3.** To utter aloud something to be recorded by another. **4.** To give orders. — *n.* An authoritative suggestion, rule, or command: the *dictates* of reason. [< L *dictatus*, pp. of *dictare*, freq. of *dicere* to say, speak] — **Syn.** (verb) **2.** command, decree, direct, order, require.

dic·ta·tion (dik·tā′shən) *n.* **1.** The act of dictating material to a copyist. **2.** That which is dictated. **3.** Authoritative direction. Abbr. *dict.* — **dic·ta′tion·al** *adj.*

dic·ta·tor (dik′tā·tər, dik·tā′tər) *n.* **1.** A person having absolute powers of government in a state; especially, such a person considered as a tyrant or oppressor. **2.** A person who rules, prescribes, or suggests authoritatively: a *dictator* of fashion. **3.** One who dictates. **4.** In ancient Rome, a chief magistrate with supreme authority, appointed in cases of emergency. Abbr. *dict.* — **dic·ta·tress** (dik·tā′tris) *n.fem.*

dic·ta·to·ri·al (dik′tə·tôr′ē·əl, -tō′rē-) *adj.* **1.** Given to dictating; overbearing. **2.** Of or pertaining to a dictator; autocratic. — **dic′ta·to′ri·al·ly** *adv.* — **dic′ta·to′ri·al·ness** *n.*

dic·ta·tor·ship (dik′tā·tər·ship′, dik·tā′tər·ship′) *n.* **1.** The office or term of office of a dictator. **2.** A state under the rule of a dictator. **3.** Supreme or despotic control.

dic·tion (dik′shən) *n.* **1.** The use, choice, and arrangement of words in writing and speaking. **2.** The manner of uttering speech sounds; enunciation. [< L *dictio, -onis* speech < *dicere* to say, speak]
— **Syn.** **1.** *Diction, wording, phraseology, vocabulary,* and *parlance* are here compared as they refer to choice of words. *Diction* is applied to the broad aspects of such choice: His *diction* is lofty and sententious. *Wording* and *phraseology* are used of limited passages, and often emphasize the preference shown for a particular word or turn of phrase: the *wording* of a letter, the *phraseology* of a contract. A person's *vocabulary* is the total number of words he knows or commonly uses; by extension, it refers to his broad preferences: Hardy's *vocabulary* was largely Anglo-Saxon. *Parlance* is often

used in the sense of jargon: In military *parlance*, this device was called a petard.

dic·tion·ar·y (dik′shən·er′ē) *n. pl.* **·ar·ies** **1.** A reference work containing selected and alphabetically arranged words of a language, together with statements of their meanings, and often syllabications, pronunciations, etymologies, and other pertinent information; a lexicon. **2.** A lexicon whose words and their definitions are given in one language together with their equivalents in another language: a French-English *dictionary*. **3.** A reference work containing information relating to a special branch of knowledge and arranged alphabetically under various headings or key words: a chemical *dictionary*. Abbr. *dict.* [< Med.L *dictionarium* a collection of words and phrases < L *dictio.* See DICTION.]

Dic·to·graph (dik′tə·graf, -gräf) *n.* A telephonic device capable of reproducing or recording sounds made at a considerable distance from the transmitter, used to transmit or overhear conversations: a trade name. Also **dic′to·graph.**

dic·tum (dik′təm) *n. pl.* **·ta** (-tə) **1.** An authoritative, dogmatic, or positive utterance; pronouncement. **2.** *Law* An obiter dictum (which see). **3.** A popular saying; maxim. [< L < *dicere* to say]

Di·cu·ma·rol (dī·kōō′mə·rôl, -rol, -kyōō′-) *n.* Proprietary name for a derivative of coumarin found in spoiled sweet clover and prepared synthetically, used in medicine as an anticoagulant.

did (did) Past tense of DO¹.

Did·a·che (did′ə·kē) *n.* The teaching of the Twelve Apostles, the title of a church manual of the second century. [< Gk., a teaching]

di·dac·tic (dī·dak′tik, di-) *adj.* **1.** Intended to instruct; expository. **2.** Morally instructive; preceptive. **3.** Overly inclined to teach or moralize; pedantic. Also **di·dac′ti·cal.** [< Gk. *didaktikos* apt to teach < *didaskein* to teach] — **di·dac′ti·cal·ly** *adv.* — **di·dac′ti·cism** (-siz-əm) *n.*

di·dac·tics (dī·dak′tiks, di-) *n.pl.* (*construed as sing.*) The science or art of instruction or education.

di·dac·tyl (dī·dak′təl) *adj. Zool.* Having only two digits at the end of each limb. [< DI- + DACTYL]

di·dap·per (dī′dap′ər) *n.* The dabchick, a bird. [Short for *divedapper*]

did·dle¹ (did′l) *v.* **·dled, ·dling** *Informal v.t.* **1.** To cheat. — *v.i.* **2.** To dawdle; pass time idly. Also *daddle.* [? < DIDDLE²] — **did′dler** *n.*

did·dle² (did′l) *v.t. & v.i.* **·dled, ·dling** To jerk up and down or back and forth; jiggle. [? Var. of dial. *didder*, ME *diddiren* to quiver, shake, tremble]

Di·de·rot (dē·drō′), **Denis**, 1713–84, French philosopher and encyclopedist.

did·n't (did′nt) Did not.

di·do (dī′dō) *n. pl.* **·dos** or **·does** *Informal* A caper; antic. [Origin unknown]

Di·do (dī′dō) In Roman legend, a Tyrian princess, founder and queen of Carthage. In the *Aeneid*, she falls in love with Aeneas and kills herself when he leaves her.

didst (didst) *Archaic* second person singular past tense of DO¹: used with *thou.*

di·dy (dī′dē) *n. pl.* **·dies** *Informal* A baby's diaper. [< DIAPER]

di·dym·i·um (dī·dim′ē·əm, di-) *n.* A mixture of the elements neodymium and praseodymium of the lanthanide series, found in cerite and formerly regarded as one of the elements. Abbr. *Di* [< NL < Gk. *didymos* double]

did·y·mous (did′ə·məs) *adj. Biol.* Formed in pairs; twin. [< Gk. *didymos* double]

Did·y·mus (did′ə·məs) A name of the apostle Thomas. *John* xi 16. Also *Greek* **Did′y·mos.** [< Gk. *didymos* twin]

die¹ (dī) *v.i.* **died, dy·ing** **1.** To suffer death; expire. **2.** To suffer the pains of death: The coward *dies* many times. **3.** To lose energy or power; pass gradually: with *away, down,* or *out.* **4.** To cease to exist; fade away: The smile *died* on his lips. **5.** To become extinct: often with *out* or *off.* **6.** To become indifferent or insensible: with *to:* to *die* to the world. **7.** *Informal* To desire exceedingly: He's *dying* to meet her. **8.** To stop functioning, as an engine. **9.** To faint. **10.** *Theol.* To suffer spiritual death. — **to die hard** To resist death or defeat to the end. — **to die off** To be removed one after another by death. [< ON *deyja*]
— **Syn.** **1.** decease, depart. **3.** **4.** decline, wane, wither.

die² (dī) *n. pl.* **dies** for *defs. 1 and 5;* **dice** for *defs. 2, 3, and 4* **1.** *Mech.* Any of various hard metal devices for stamping, shaping, or cutting out some object; as: **a** Any one of several parts that, when fitted together in a diestock, are used for cutting threads on a nut, bolt, etc. **b** An engraved stamp for pressing a design into metal, as in coining money. **c** A block or counter having a hole through which a punch passes, as in cutting out sheet metal. **d** A metal block containing one or more holes through which wire, etc., is drawn or extruded. **2.** A small marked cube. See DICE. **3.** A cast, as in playing dice; stake; hazard. **4.** Any small cube or block. **5.** *Archit.* The cubical dado of a pedestal. — **the die is cast** The choice is made that commits one to an irrevocable course of action. — *v.t.* **died, die·ing** To cut, stamp, or shape with or as with a die. [< OF *de* < L *datum* something given]

die·back (dī′bak′) *n.* Arrested growth in the twigs of certain woody plants, sometimes a normal stage in development but also caused by parasites, fire, frost, etc.: also called *twig blight.*

die casting *Metall.* **1.** The process of giving a metal or alloy a desired shape by forcing the molten material into a mold under pressure. **2.** A metal object so made.

di·e·cious (dī-ē′shəs), etc. See DIOECIOUS, etc.

die-hard (dī′härd′) *n.* One who obstinately refuses to abandon or modify his views; especially, a political conservative. — *adj.* Characterized by obstinate resistance. Also **die′hard′**.

di·e·lec·tric (dī′ə·lek′trik) *Electr. adj.* **1.** Nonconducting. **2.** Capable of sustaining an electric field, as by induction. Also **di′e·lec′tri·cal.** — *n.* A dielectric substance, medium, or material. — **di′e·lec′tri·cal·ly** *adv.*

Dien Bien Phu (dyen byen foo) A town in North Vietnam; besieged and captured from the French by North Vietnamese forces in 1954. Also **Dien·bien·phu.**

di·en·ceph·a·lon (dī′en·sef′ə·lon) *n. Anat.* That part of the brain forming the posterior part of the prosencephalon; the interbrain: also called *thalamencephalon.* [< NL < Gk. *di(a)-* between + *enkephalos* brain]

-diene *suffix Chem.* Denoting an open-chain unsaturated hydrocarbon compound having two double bonds: *butadiene.* [< DI-² + -ENE]

Di·eppe (dē·ep′, *Fr.* dyep) A port city in northern France, on the English Channel; pop. 29,829 (1968).

di·er·e·sis (dī·er′ə·sis) *n. pl.* **-ses** (-sēz) **1.** Two dots (¨) placed over the second of two adjacent letters to indicate that two separate vowel sounds are to be pronounced, as in *coöperate.* **2.** The separation of two adjacent vowels into two syllables. **3.** In the pronunciations in this book, a diacritic used over *a* to indicate the vowel sound in *palm* (päm). See also Pronunciation Key in front matter. **4.** A slight pause occurring in a line of verse when the end of a metrical foot coincides with the end of a word. Also spelled *diaeresis.* Compare SYNERESIS. [< LL *diaeresis* < Gk. *diairesis* a division < *diairein* < *dia-* apart + *hairein* to take, seize] — **di·e·ret·ic** (dī′ə·ret′ik) *adj.*

di·es (dī′ēz, dē′ās) *n. pl.* **di·es** (dī′ēz, dē′ās) *Latin* Day.

die·sel engine (dē′zəl) An internal-combustion engine in which fuel oil is sprayed directly into the cylinder, where it is ignited by the high temperature of the air held within the cylinder at a constant pressure. Also **Die·sel engine.** [after Rudolf *Diesel,* 1858–1913, German inventor]

die·sink·er (dī′singk′ər) *n.* One who engraves metal dies, as for coining.

Di·es I·rae (dī′ēz ī′rē) The name of a medieval Latin hymn on the Day of Judgment, used in masses for the dead: so called from its opening words. [< L, day of wrath]

di·e·sis (dī′ə·sis) *n. pl.* **-ses** (-sēz) *Printing* The double dagger (‡). [< L < Gk. *diesis,* quarter tone, formerly so marked < *diïenai* < *dia-* through + *hienai* to send, release] *adj.*

di·es non ju·ri·di·cus (dī′ēz non′ joo-rid′ə-kəs) *Law* A day on which courts are not in session. Also **di′es non′.** [< L, a day not juridical]

die·stock (dī′stok′) *n. Mech.* A device for holding dies that are used to cut threads on screws, bolts, etc.

di·es·trus (dī-es′trəs, -ēs′-) *n. Zool.* The quiescent interval between the rutting periods of female mammals: also spelled *dioestrus, dioestrum.* Also **di·es′trum.** [< NL < Gk. *dia-* between + *oistros* gadfly, passion, frenzy]

DIESTOCK

di·et¹ (dī′ət) *n.* **1.** A regulated course of eating and drinking, especially one followed for medical or hygienic reasons. **2.** The daily fare. **3.** Food, as regards its nutritive value or its effects on the body. — *Syn.* See FOOD. — *v.t.* **1.** To regulate or restrict the food and drink of. — *v.i.* **2.** To take food and drink according to a regimen. **3.** To eat. [< OF *diete* < L *diaeta* < Gk. *diaita* a way of living] — **di′et·er** *n.*

di·et² (dī′ət) *n.* **1.** A legislative assembly. **2.** *Scot.* A single session, as of a court; a day appointed for a session. [< Med.L *dieta* < L *dies* a day]

Di·et (dī′ət) *n.* **1.** The legislature of certain countries, as Japan. **2.** The semiannual meeting of the estates of the Holy Roman Empire. See (Diet of) SPIRES, (Diet of) WORMS.

di·e·tar·y (dī′ə·ter′ē) *adj.* Pertaining to diet. — *n. pl.* **·tar·ies 1.** A system or regimen of dieting. **2.** A standard or regulated allowance of food.

di·e·tet·ic (dī′ə·tet′ik) *adj.* Relating to diet or the regulation of diet. Also **di′e·tet′i·cal.** — **di′e·tet′i·cal·ly** *adv.*

di·e·tet·ics (dī′ə·tet′iks) *n.pl.* (construed as *sing.*) The branch of hygiene that treats of diet and dieting and the feeding of individuals or of great numbers.

di·eth·yl·stil·bes·trol (dī-eth′əl·stil·bes′trōl) *n. Biochem.* A synthetic sex hormone, $C_{18}H_{22}O_2$, similar in action to but more potent than the naturally occurring estrogens: also called *stilbestrol.* [< DI- + ETHYL + STILBESTROL]

di·e·ti·tian (dī′ə·tish′ən) *n.* One skilled in the principles of dietetics. Also **di·e·tet·ist** (dī′ə·tet′ist), **di′e·ti′cian.**

diet kitchen A kitchen, as in a hospital, where special diets are prepared.

Dieu a·vec nous (dyœ′ à·vek′ noo′) *French* God with us.

Dieu et mon droit (dyœ′ ā môn′ drwà′) *French* God and my right: motto of the royal arms of Great Britain.

dif- Assimilated var. of DIS-.

diff. Difference; different.

dif·fer (dif′ər) *v.i.* **1.** To be unlike in quality, degree, form, etc.: often with *from.* **2.** To disagree; dissent: often with *with.* **3.** To quarrel. [< OF *differer* < L *differre* < *dis-* apart + *ferre* to carry. Doublet of DEFER¹.]

dif·fer·ence (dif′ər·əns, dif′rəns) *n.* **1.** The state, quality, or degree of being unlike or different; dissimilarity; variation. **2.** A specific instance of such unlikeness. **3.** A distinguishing characteristic or peculiarity. **4.** A disagreement or controversy; quarrel; dispute. **5.** A discrimination: She makes no *difference* between truth and falsehood. **6.** *Math.* **a** The amount by which one quantity differs from another. **b** The amount remaining after subtracting one number from another. **7.** *Logic* The specific difference; differentia. **8.** *Heraldry* An addition to or change in a coat of arms to distinguish between two or more branches of the same family. *Abbr. diff.* — **to make a difference 1.** To affect or change the case or situation; matter. **2.** To distinguish between. — **to split the difference 1.** To divide equally what remains. **2.** To compromise. — *v.t.* **·enced, ·enc·ing 1.** To make or mark as different; distinguish. **2.** *Heraldry* To add a mark of difference to.

— *Syn.* (noun) **1.** *Difference, dissimilarity, unlikeness, divergence, diversity, variation,* and *distinction* denote lack of complete equality or correspondence between things. *Difference* is the widest term; it may be used whatever the basis of comparison. *Dissimilarity* and *unlikeness* point to *difference* in some aspect between things that are alike in other aspects. *Divergence,* too, implies initial similarity that grows into *dissimilarity* by progressive change. *Diversity* is *difference* among more than two objects. *Variation* is *difference* between specimens of the same class, or between the states of the same object at different times. Whereas *differences* lie in the objects, *distinctions* are made in the mind, and therefore are often details perceived only by careful comparison. — *Ant.* similarity, likeness, resemblance, identity.

dif·fer·ent (dif′ər·ənt, dif′rənt) *adj.* **1.** Marked by a difference; unlike; dissimilar: Their dispositions are *different.* **2.** Not the same; separate; distinct; other: There is a *different* clerk there now. **3.** Differing from the ordinary; unusual. *Abbr. diff.* [< OF *different* < L *differens, -entis,* ppr. of *differre.* See DIFFER.] — **dif′fer·ent·ly** *adv.* — **dif′fer·ent·ness** *n.*

◆ **different from, than, to** In American usage, *from* is established as the idiomatic preposition to follow *different;* when, however, a clause follows the connective, *than* is gaining increasing acceptance: a result *different than* (= *from that which* or *from what*) had been expected. This last is established British usage, which also sometimes accepts *to* on a par with *from:* She is *different to* her sister.

dif·fer·en·ti·a (dif′ə·ren′shē·ə) *n. pl.* **·ti·ae** (-shi-ē) *Logic* A specific difference; a characteristic attribute distinguishing a species from others of the same genus. [< L, neut. pl. of *differens.* See DIFFERENT.]

dif·fer·en·ti·a·ble (dif′ə·ren′shē·ə·bəl) *adj.* **1.** That can be differentiated. **2.** *Math.* Belonging to or having a differential coefficient. — **dif′fer·en′ti·a·bil′i·ty** *n.*

dif·fer·en·tial (dif′ə·ren′shəl) *adj.* **1.** Relating to, indicating, or exhibiting a difference or differences: a *differential* diagnosis. **2.** Constituting or creating a difference; distinctive. **3.** Based on a difference or distinction: *differential* import duties. **4.** *Math.* Pertaining to or involving differentials or differentiation. **5.** *Mech.* Of or having a construction in which a movement is obtained by the difference in two motions in the same direction. — *n.* **1.** *Math.* **a** An infinitesimal increment of a quantity: indicated by the symbol *d.* **b** The derivative of a function multiplied by the increment of the independent variable. **2.** *Mech.* A differential gear. **3.** *Electr.* One of two resistance coils, the current of which flows in a direction opposite to that of the other. **4.** In commerce, a difference in rates charged. — **dif′fer·en′tial·ly** *adv.*

differential calculus See under CALCULUS.

differential coefficient *Math.* A derivative.

differential equation *Math* An equation in which derivatives or differentials of an unknown function appear.

differential gear or **gearing** *Mech.* A coupling consisting of an epicyclic train of gears used to connect two or more shafts, as in the driving axle of an automobile, so that the wheels can move at different speeds on curves.

DIFFERENTIAL GEAR
a Drive shaft. *b* Drive-shaft gear. *c* Axles. *d* Ring gear. *e* Epicyclic train of gears.

differential windlass *Mech.* A windlass having two drums of different diameters on the same axis: also called *Chinese windlass.* For illustration see WINDLASS.

dif·fer·en·ti·ate (dif′ə·ren′shē·āt) *v.* **·at·ed, ·at·ing** *v.t.* **1.** To constitute the difference between; serve to distinguish between. **2.** To perceive and indicate the differences in or between. **3.** *Biol.* To cause to become unlike; develop differences in, as a species. **4.** *Math.* To find the derivative of (a function). — *v.i.* **5.** To acquire a distinct character; become specialized. **6.** To perceive a difference; discriminate. **7.** *Biol.* Of cells during embryological growth, to diversify and develop into organs and tissues with specialized functions. — **Syn.** See CONTRAST, DISCRIMINATE. — **dif′fer·en′ti·a′tion** *n.*

dif·fi·cile (dif′ə·sēl′, *Fr.* dē·fē·sēl′) *adj. French* Difficult.

dif·fi·cult (dif′ə·kult, -kəlt) *adj.* **1.** Hard to do, accomplish, or deal with; demanding effort or great care; arduous. **2.** Not easy to understand; perplexing; obscure. **3.** Hard to please: a *difficult* customer. **4.** Hard to persuade; stubborn. [Back formation < DIFFICULTY] — **dif′fi·cult·ly** *adv.* — **Syn.** 1, 2. *Difficult, hard, arduous, laborious,* and *perplexing* mean not easy to do. A *difficult* task may tax the mental or physical powers, or both, but it always requires skill and perseverance. *Hard* is closely synonymous with *difficult* in this sense, but stresses more directly the contrast with easy. The *arduous* or *laborious* task requires great exertion; a *perplexing* problem confuses the mind, and puzzles the judgment, thus hindering purposeful activity. — **Ant.** easy, facile.

dif·fi·cul·ty (dif′ə·kul′tē, -kəl-) *n. pl.* **·ties 1.** The state, fact, or quality of being difficult. **2.** That which is difficult to do, overcome, or understand. **3.** *Usually pl.* A troublesome state of affairs, especially financial embarrassment. **4.** A dispute. **5.** Reluctance or objection. **6.** A trouble; worry. [< L *difficultas, -tatis* < *difficilis* < *dis-* away, not + *facilis* easy < *facere* to do, make]

dif·fi·dence (dif′ə·dəns) *n.* Want of confidence in oneself; self-distrust; timidity; shyness.

dif·fi·dent (dif′ə·dənt) *adj.* **1.** Lacking confidence in oneself; timid; shy. **2.** *Obs.* Distrustful of others. [< L *diffidens, -entis,* ppr. of *diffidere* < *dis-* away + *fidere* to trust < *fides* faith] — **dif′fi·dent·ly** *adv.*

dif·fract (di·frakt′) *v.t.* **1.** To separate into parts. **2.** To subject to diffraction. [< L *diffractus,* pp. of *diffringere* < *dis-* away + *frangere* to break] — **dif·frac′tive** *adj.* — **dif·frac′tive·ly** *adv.* — **dif·frac′tive·ness** *n.*

dif·frac·tion (di·frak′shən) *n. Physics* **1.** A modification of light rays when partially cut off by any obstacle or passing near the edges of an opening, or through a minute hole, generally accompanied by light and dark, or colored, bands due to interference. **2.** An analogous modification of other kinds of wave motion, as of sound, electricity, X-rays, etc.

diffraction grating *Physics* A device consisting of a series of very fine parallel grooves cut in the surface of polished glass or metal, and used in spectrum analysis.

dif·fuse (*v.* di·fyōōz′; *adj.* di·fyōōs′) *v.t.* & *v.i.* **·fused, ·fus·ing 1.** To pour or send out so as to spread in all directions; spread abroad; circulate; permeate. **2.** To subject to or spread by diffusion. — *adj.* **1.** Characterized by the excessive use of words; verbose; wordy. **2.** Widely spread out; dispersed. [< L *diffusus,* pp. of *diffundere* < *dis-* away, from + *fundere* to pour] — **dif·fuse′ly** (di·fyōōs′lē) *adv.* — **dif·fuse·ness** (di·fyōōs′nis) *n.*

dif·fus·er (di·fyōō′zər) *n.* One who or that which diffuses. Also **dif·fu′sor.**

dif·fus·i·ble (di·fyōō′zə·bəl) *adj.* Capable of being diffused. — **dif·fus′i·bil′i·ty, dif·fus′i·ble·ness** *n.*

dif·fu·sion (di·fyōō′zhən) *n.* **1.** The act or process of diffusing, or the state of being diffused; dissemination; dispersion. **2.** Imprecision of verbal expression; wordiness; verbosity. **3.** *Physics* **a** The intermingling by thermal agitation of the molecules of two fluids, as of gases. **b** The scattering and crisscrossing of light rays, producing general illumination rather than direct radiation. **4.** *Anthropol.* The transmission of culture traits from one area or group to another.

dif·fu·sive (di·fyōō′siv) *adj.* Having the property of diffusing; tending to diffuse; marked by diffusion. — **dif·fu′sive·ly** *adv.* — **dif·fu′sive·ness** *n.*

dig (dig) *v.* **dug** (*Archaic* **digged**), **dig·ging** *v.t.* **1.** To break up, turn up, or remove (earth, etc.), as with a spade, claws, or the hands. **2.** To make or form by or as by digging: to *dig* a well. **3.** To take out or obtain by digging: to *dig* clams. **4.** To thrust or force, as a tool, heel, or elbow. **5.** To discover or bring out by careful effort or study: often with *up* or *out.* **6.** *U.S. Slang* To understand or like. — *v.i.* **7.** To break or turn up earth, etc. **8.** To force or make a way by or as by digging. **9.** *U.S. Informal* To study hard and steadily; plod. — **to dig in 1.** To dig trenches. **2.** *U.S. Informal* To entrench (oneself). **3.** *U.S. Informal* To begin to work intensively. — *n. Informal* **1.** A thrust; poke. **2.** A sarcastic remark; gibe; slur. **3.** An archeological excavation. **4.** *U.S.* A hard-working student. **5.** *pl. Brit. Informal* Lodgings: also *diggings.* [< MF *diguer* < Gmc. Akin to DIKE.]

dig. Digest.

di·gam·ma (dī·gam′ə) *n.* The sixth letter in the early

Greek alphabet (ϝ), equivalent in sound to *W,* but in form to *F.* [< Gk. < *di-* two + *gamma,* the letter G]

dig·a·my (dig′ə·mē) *n.* Remarriage after the death or divorce of the first spouse; a second legal marriage. [< LL *digamia* < Gk. < *di-* two + *gamos* a marriage] — **dig′a·mist** *n.* — **dig′a·mous** *adj.*

di·gas·tric (dī·gas′trik) *adj. Anat.* Having two bellies or parts joined by a tendon: said of a muscle. — *n.* A digastric muscle of the lower jaw. [< DI-² + Gk. *gastēr* belly]

Dig·by (dig′bē), **Sir Kenelm,** 1603–65, English naval commander, diplomat, and philosopher.

di·gen·e·sis (dī·jen′ə·sis) *n. Biol.* Metagenesis (which see). [< DI-² + GENESIS] — **di·ge·net·ic** (dī′jə·net′ik) *adj.*

di·gest (*v.* di·jest′, dī-; *n.* dī′jest) *v.t.* **1.** *Physiol.* To change (food) chemically in the alimentary canal into material suitable for assimilation by the body. **2.** To take in or assimilate mentally. **3.** To arrange in systematic form, usually by condensing; summarize and classify. **4.** To tolerate patiently; endure. **5.** *Chem.* **a** To soften or decompose with heat or moisture. **b** To treat, as wood, with chemical agents under pressure so as to obtain a desired result. — *v.i.* **6.** To be assimilated, as food. **7.** To assimilate food. **8.** To be subjected to heat, moisture, chemical agents, or pressure. — *n.* **1.** A systematically arranged collection or summary of literary, scientific, or other material; a compilation; synopsis. **2.** *Law* A compilation of statutes systematically arranged; a brief synopsis of the adjudications of courts. — **the Digest** The Pandects. — **Syn.** See ABRIDGEMENT. [< L *digestus,* pp. of *digerere* to divide, arrange, digest < *dis-* away + *gerere* to carry, arrange]

di·gest·er (di·jes′tər, dī-) *n.* **1.** One who makes a digest, analysis, or summary. **2.** A digestant. **3.** A vessel in which substances are exposed to moisture and heat to soften or decompose them, or to extract some ingredient.

di·gest·i·ble (di·jes′tə·bəl, dī-) *adj.* Capable of being digested. — **di·gest′i·bil′i·ty, di·gest′i·ble·ness** *n.* — **di·gest′i·bly** *adv.*

di·ges·tion (di·jes′chən, dī-) *n.* **1.** *Physiol.* **a** The act, process, or function of digesting. **b** The condition resulting from this process. **c** The ability to digest. **2.** Mental reception and assimilation. **3.** Exposure of a substance to heat and moisture in a digester.

di·ges·tive (di·jes′tiv, dī-) *adj.* Pertaining to or promoting digestion: *digestive* tract. — *n.* A medicine to aid digestion. Also **di·ges·tant** (dī·jes′tənt).

digged (digd) *Archaic* past tense and past participle of DIG.

dig·ger (dig′ər) *n.* **1.** One who digs. **2.** Any implement or part of a machine for digging. **3.** *Informal* A soldier from Australia or New Zealand.

Dig·ger (dig′ər) *n.* **1.** Originally, one of a tribe of agricultural North American Indians of Utah. **2.** An Indian of any root-eating tribe of the American Northwest.

digger wasp A wasp (family *Sphecidae*) that digs a hole in the ground for its nest, especially one of the common American genera (*Sphex* or *Ammophila,* and *Bembidula*). For illustration see INSECTS (beneficial).

dig·gings (dig′ingz) *n.pl.* **1.** A place of excavation; especially, a mining region. **2.** The materials dug out of such a region. **3.** *Brit. Informal* Lodgings.

dight (dīt) *v.t.* **dight** or **dight·ed, dight·ing 1.** *Archaic* To dress; adorn; equip; prepare. **2.** *Dial.* To cleanse or dry. [OE *dihtan* to arrange, prepare < L *dictare.* See DICTATE.]

dig·it (dij′it) *n.* **1.** A finger or toe. **2.** Any one of the ten Arabic numeral symbols, 0 to 9: so named from counting upon the fingers. **3.** An old measure of length, equal to the breadth of a finger, or about three fourths of an inch. **4.** The twelfth part of the diameter of the sun or moon. **5.** *Electronics* One of a set of characters by which, singly or in combination, a digital computer processes required information. [< L *digitus* finger]

dig·i·tal (dij′ə·təl) *adj.* **1.** Of, pertaining to, or like the fingers or digits. **2.** Having digits. **3.** Digitate. — *n.* A key on a piano, organ, etc. — **dig′i·tal·ly** *adv.*

digital computer A computer that processes discrete numbers, usually in the binary system with one digit (0 or 1) represented by the "on" state of an electronic device and the other by the "off" state. Compare ANALOG COMPUTER.

dig·i·tal·in (dij′ə·tal′in, -tā′lin) *n.* **1.** A crystalline, poisonous glycoside, $C_{36}H_{56}O_{14}$, contained in the leaves of the foxglove, of which it is the active principle. **2.** Any of several different extracts of foxglove. [< DIGITAL(IS) + -IN]

dig·i·tal·is (dij′ə·tal′is, -tā′lis) *n.* **1.** Any of a genus (*Digitalis*) of tall, Old World herbs of the figwort family, including the foxglove: sometimes called *fairy gloves.* **2.** The dried leaves of foxglove, containing several glycosides, some of which are used as a heart stimulant. [< NL < L, finger-shaped < *digitus* finger]

dig·i·tal·ism (dij′ə·təl·iz′əm) *n. Pathol.* The bodily condition resulting from the excessive administration of digitalis.

dig·i·tate (dij′ə·tāt) *adj.* **1.** *Bot.* Having parts, as leaflets, arranged like the fingers of a hand. See illustration of LEAF. **2.** *Zool.* Having fingerlike processes. Also **dig′i·tat′ed.** [< L *digitatus* < *digitus* finger] — **dig′i·tate·ly** *adv.*

dig·i·ta·tion (dij/ə·tā/shən) *n.* **1.** The state of being digitate. **2.** A fingerlike process.

digiti- *combining form* Finger; toe: *digitiform.* [< L *digitus* finger, toe]

dig·i·ti·form (dij/ə·tə·fôrm/) *adj.* Having the form or arrangement of a finger or fingers.

dig·i·ti·grade (dij/ə·tə·grād/) *Zool. adj.* Walking on the toes, without resting on the whole sole of the foot, as dogs and cats. — *n.* A digitigrade animal. Distinguished from *plantigrade.* [< DIGITI- + L *gradus,* a step, going]

dig·i·tox·in (dij/ə·tok/sin) *n.* A powerful form of digitalin. [< DIGI(TALIS) + TOXIN]

di·glot (dī/glot) *adj.* Bilingual. — *n.* A bilingual version or book. [< Gk. *diglōttos* < *di-* two + *glōtta* tongue]

dig·ni·fied (dig/nə·fīd) *adj.* Characterized by or invested with dignity; stately. — **dig/ni·fied·ly** *adv.*

dig·ni·fy (dig/nə·fī) *v.t.* **·fied, ·fy·ing** **1.** To impart or add dignity to; honor; ennoble. **2.** To give a high-sounding name to: to *dignify* lust. [< OF *dignefier* < Med.L *dignificare* < L *dignus* worthy + *facere* to make]

dig·ni·tar·y (dig/nə·ter/ē) *n. pl.* **·tar·ies** One having high official position, as in the government or church.

dig·ni·ty (dig/nə·tē) *n. pl.* **·ties** **1.** Stateliness and nobility of manner; serenity of demeanor; gravity. **2.** The state or quality of being excellent, worthy, or honorable: the *dignity* of labor. **3.** Relative importance or position; rank. **4.** A high rank, title, or office, especially in the church. **5.** One who holds high rank or position; a dignitary. **6.** Persons of high rank or position collectively: preceded by *the.* [< OF *dignete* < L *dignitas* < *dignus* worthy. Doublet of DAINTY.]

di·graph (dī/graf, -gräf) *n.* A combination of two characters representing a single sound, as *oa* in *boat, sh* in *she.* Compare DIPHTHONG.

di·gress (di·gres/, dī-) *v.i.* **1.** To turn aside from the main subject. **2.** To ramble; wander. [< L *digressus,* pp. of *digredi* < *di-* away, apart + *gradi* to go, step]

di·gres·sion (di·gresh/ən, dī-) *n.* **1.** The act of digressing. **2.** That which digresses, as a part of a speech, etc. — **di·gres/sion·al** *adj.*

di·gres·sive (di·gres/iv, dī-) *adj.* Given to, of the nature of, or marked by digression. — **di·gres/sive·ly** *adv.* — **di·gres/sive·ness** *n.*

Di·gul (dē/gōōl) A river in Western New Guinea, flowing about 400 miles south and west to the Arafura Sea. Also **Di/goel.**

di·he·dral (dī·hē/drəl) *adj.* **1.** Two-sided; formed by or having two plane faces. **2.** Pertaining to or having a dihedral angle. — *n. Aeron.* The upward or downward inclination of an airplane's supporting surfaces. [< DI-² + Gk. *hedra* base, face of a regular solid]

dihedral angle *Geom.* The angle formed by two intersecting planes.

Di·jon (dē·zhôn/) A city in eastern France; pop. 143,120 (1968).

dik·dik (dik/dik/) *n.* A NE African antelope (genera *Madoqua* and *Rhynchotragus*), about a foot tall. [< native East African name]

dike (dīk) *n.* **1.** An embankment to protect low land from being flooded. **2.** A bank formed by earth thrown up during the excavation of a ditch. **3.** A ditch. **4.** A causeway. **5.** A barrier or obstruction. **6.** *Brit. Dial.* A low wall for dividing or enclosing land. **7.** *Mining* A fissure filled with solid material other than the ore through which it cuts. **8.** *Geol.* A mass of igneous rock intruded into a fissure in other rocks. **9.** *U.S. Slang* A lesbian of the masculine type. — *v.t.* **diked, dik·ing** **1.** To surround or furnish with a dike. **2.** To drain by ditching. Also, *Chiefly Brit., dyke.* [OE *dīc.* Akin to DITCH.] — **dik/er** *n.*

DIK-DIK
(12 to 14 inches high)

di·lac·er·ate (di·las/ə·rāt, dī-) *v.t.* **·at·ed, ·at·ing** To tear to pieces. [< L *dilaceratus,* pp. of *dilacerare* < *dis-* apart + *lacerare* to tear] — **di·lac/er·a/tion** *n.* — **di·lac/er·a·tive** *adj.*

Di·lan·tin (di·lan/tin) *n.* Proprietary name for a brand of diphenylhydantoin sodium. Also **di·lan/tin.**

di·lap·i·date (di·lap/ə·dāt) *v.t. & v.i.* **·dat·ed, ·dat·ing** To fall or cause to fall into partial ruin or decay. [< L *dilapidatus,* pp. of *dilapidare* < *dis-* away, apart + *lapidare* to throw stones < *lapis* a stone]

di·lap·i·dat·ed (di·lap/ə·dā/tid) *adj.* Fallen into decay or partial ruin; neglected.

di·lap·i·da·tion (di·lap/ə·dā/shən) *n.* **1.** The process of falling into decay. **2.** A ruined or decayed condition.

di·la·tant (di·lā/tənt, di-) *adj.* Dilating. — *n.* A dilating substance or instrument. — **di·la/tan·cy** *n.*

di·la·tate (di·lā/tāt, dī/lə·tāt) *adj.* Dilated.

dil·a·ta·tion (dil/ə·tā/shən, dī/lə-) *n.* **1.** The act or process of dilating. **2.** The state or being dilated. **3.** That which is dilated. **4.** *Pathol.* An excessive enlargement of an organ, orifice, or part.

di·late (dī·lāt/, di-) *v.* **·lat·ed, ·lat·ing** *v.t.* **1.** To make wider or larger; cause to swell or expand. — *v.i.* **2.** To become

larger or wider; expand. **3.** To speak or write diffusely; enlarge; expatiate: with *on* or *upon.* [< F *dilater* < L *dilatare* to spread out < *dis-* apart + *latus* wide] — **di·lat/a·ble** *adj.* — **di·lat/a·bil/i·ty, di·lat/a·ble·ness** *n.* — **di·lat/a·bly** *adv.*

di·la·tion (dī·lā/shən, di-) *n.* **1.** Dilatation. **2.** *Med.* The expanding of an abnormally small canal or orifice.

di·la·tive (dī·lā/tiv, di-) *adj.* Tending to dilate; causing expansion or distention.

dil·a·tom·e·ter (dil/ə·tom/ə·tər) *n.* An apparatus for measuring the mechanical or chemical expansion of substances. [< DILATE + -(O)METER]

di·la·tor (dī·lā/tər, di-) *n.* **1.** One who or that which dilates. **2.** *Med.* An instrument for expanding a wound, aperture, or cavity. Also **di·la·ta·tor** (dī/lə·tā/tər, dil/ə-), **di·lat/er.**

dil·a·to·ry (dil/ə·tôr/ē, -tō/rē) *adj.* **1.** Given to or characterized by delay; tardy; slow. **2.** Tending to cause delay. [< LL *dilatorius* < L *dilator* < *dilatus,* pp. of *differe* to delay, defer] — **dil/a·to/ri·ly** *adv.* — **dil/a·to/ri·ness** *n.*
— **Syn. 1.** *Dilatory, laggard, tardy,* and *slow* are here compared as applied to persons who do not accomplish things quickly. The *dilatory* person wastes time by delaying what he could or should do promptly. The *laggard* person falls behind others in progress, generally through laziness. The *tardy* person is late in completing a task or arriving at a destination, but not necessarily through his own fault. A person may be *slow* for any of several different reasons, some blameworthy and some excusable; the term usually indicates no more than not fast in progress or not prompt in action.
— **Ant.** prompt, diligent.

di·lem·ma (di·lem/ə) *n.* **1.** A situation requiring a choice between equally undesirable alternatives; a perplexing predicament. **2.** *Logic* An argument that presents an antagonist with two (or more) alternatives, but is equally conclusive against him, whichever alternative he chooses. — **Syn.** See PREDICAMENT. — **the horns of a dilemma** The equal and usually undesirable alternatives between which a choice must be made. [< LL < Gk. *dilēmma* < *di-* two + *lēmma* a premise] — **di·lem·mat·ic** (dil/ə·mat/ik) *adj.*

dil·et·tan·te (dil/ə·tan/tē, dil/ə·tänt/) *n. pl.* **·ti** (-tē) or **·tes** **1.** One who interests himself in a subject superficially or merely for amusement; a dabbler. **2.** One who loves the fine arts. — **Syn.** See AMATEUR. — *adj.* Pertaining to or like a dilettante. [< Ital., ppr. of *dilettare* to delight < L *delectare* < *de-* away + *lacio* to allure] — **dil/et·tan/tish** or **dil/et·tan/te·ish** *adj.* — **dil/et·tan/tism** or **dil/et·tan/te·ism** *n.*

Di·li (dil/ē) The capital of Portuguese Timor, in the northern part; pop. about 7,000. Also **Dil/li, Dil/ly.**

dil·i·gence[1] (dil/ə·jəns) *n.* **1.** Persistent application to one's work or duty; persevering effort. **2.** Proper heed; care.

dil·i·gence[2] (dil/ə·jəns, *Fr.* dē·lē·zhäns/) *n.* A public stagecoach used in the 18th century in Europe, especially France. Also **dil·ly** (dil/ē). [< F *(carrosse de) diligence* fast coach]

dil·i·gent (dil/ə·jənt) *adj.* **1.** Showing perseverance and application in whatever is undertaken; industrious. **2.** Pursued with painstaking effort: a *diligent* search. — **Syn.** See BUSY. [< OF < L *diligens, -entis* attentive; orig. ppr. of *diligere* to choose, care for] — **dil/i·gent·ly** *adv.*

DILIGENCE²

dill (dil) *n.* **1.** An Old World annual (genus *Anethum*) of the parsley family, with yellow flowers and aromatic seeds, used medicinally and for flavoring. **2.** The seeds or leaves of this plant. [OE *dile*]

dill pickle A cucumber pickled in vinegar and flavored with dill.

dil·ly-dal·ly (dil/ē·dal/ē) *v.i.* **·dal·lied, ·dal·ly·ing** To waste time, especially in indecision; loiter or trifle. [Varied reduplication of DALLY]

dil·u·ent (dil/yoo·ənt) *adj.* Serving to dilute. — *n.* A diluent agent. [< L *diluens, -entis,* ppr. of *diluere.* See DILUTE.]

di·lute (di·lōōt/, dī-; *for adj., also* dī/lōōt) *v.t.* **·lut·ed, ·lut·ing** **1.** To make weaker or more fluid by adding a liquid, as water. **2.** To weaken or reduce the intensity, strength, or purity of, as by introducing another element: to *dilute* courage with cowardice. — *adj.* Weak; diluted. [< L *dilutus,* pp. of *diluere* < *dis-* away + *luere* to wash]

di·lu·tion (di·lōō/shən, dī-) *n.* **1.** The act of diluting, or the state of being diluted. **2.** Something diluted.

di·lu·vi·al (di·lōō/vē·əl) *adj.* **1.** Of or pertaining to a flood, especially the Noachian deluge (*Gen.* vii). **2.** *Geol.* a Produced by a deluge or by floods. b Consisting of or related to diluvium. Also **di·lu/vi·an.**

di·lu·vi·um (di·lōō/vē·əm) *n. Geol.* Coarse rock material transported and deposited by glaciers; glacial drift. [< NL < L, a flood < *diluere* to wash away. See DILUTE.]

dim (dim) *adj.* **dim·mer, dim·mest** **1.** Obscured or darkened from faintness of light: a *dim* street. **2.** Not clearly seen or recognized; indistinct; shadowy: a *dim* figure. **3.** Not clear to the understanding or memory; vague; indefinite: a *dim* recollection. **4.** Not perceiving clearly; obtuse. **5.** Not seeing clearly; purblind: said of the eye. **6.** Lacking luster or brilliance: a *dim* yellow. **7.** Faint: a *dim* sound. **8.** Discouraging; pessimistic: to take a *dim* view. **— Syn.** See DARK. **—** *v.t. & v.i.* **dimmed, dim·ming** To render or grow dim. [OE *dimm, dim*] **— dim′ly** *adv.* **— dim′ness** *n.*

dim. Dimension(s).

dim. or **dimin.** **1.** *Music* Diminuendo. **2.** Diminutive.

Di·mashq (dē-mäshk′) An Arabic name for DAMASCUS.

dime (dīm) *n.* A silver coin of the United States and Canada, equal to ten cents or one tenth of a dollar. [< OF *disme* < L *decima*, fem. of *decimus* a tenth part < *decem* ten]

di·men·hy·drin·ate (dī′mən-hī′drə-nāt) *n. Chem.* A white, crystalline compound, $C_{24}H_{27}ClN_5O_3$, resembling the antihistamines in action, used for motion sickness. [< DIME-(THYL-) + (AMI)N(E) + (DIPHEN)HYDR(AM)IN(E) + -ATE[3]]

dime novel *Chiefly U.S.* **1.** A cheap, sensational novel, originally costing a dime. **2.** Any trashy novel.

di·men·sion (di-men′shən) *n.* **1.** Any measurable extent, as length, breadth, or thickness. **2.** *Usually pl.* Extent or magnitude: the *dimensions* of the case. **3.** *Math.* A factor used to characterize a term: $a^2b^3c^4$ is a term of nine *dimensions*, counting all the exponents. [< MF < L *dimensio, -onis* < *dis-* apart + *metiri* to measure] **— di·men′sion·al** *adj.*

di·mer (dī′mər) *n. Chem.* A compound formed by the polymerization of two molecules of the same substance. [< DI-[2] + Gk. *meros* a part]

di·mer·cap·rol (dī′mər·kap′rol) *n. Chem.* A colorless liquid, $C_3H_8OS_2$, containing two sulfhydryl radicals, used in medicine. [< DI-[2] + MERCA(PTAN) + PR(OPANE) + -OL[1]]

dim·er·ous (dim′ər-əs) *adj.* **1.** Composed of two members or parts. **2.** *Bot.* Composed of two members in each circle or whorl: often written **2-merous**. **3.** *Entomol.* Having two-jointed tarsi. [< DI-[2] + Gk. *meros* part] **— dim′er·ism** *n.*

dime store A five-and-ten-cent store (which see).

dim·e·ter (dim′ə-tər) *n.* In prosody, a line of verse consisting of two metrical feet: Thĕ stărs │ ăre cōld. [< LL < Gk. *dimetros* of two measures < *di-* two + *metron* a measure]

di·meth·yl (dī-meth′əl) *n. Chem.* An alkyl radical, $(CH_3)_2$, generally occurring in combination with other compounds, used in the making of drugs, dyestuffs, solvents, etc.

di·met·ric (dī-met′rik) *adj. Crystall.* Tetragonal.

di·mid·i·ate (di-mid′ē-āt, di-) *adj.* Divided in half. **—** *v.t.* **·at·ed, ·at·ing** To cut in half. [< L *dimidiatus*, pp. of *dimidiare* to halve < *dimidium* half < *dis-* apart + *medius* middle] **— di·mid′i·a′tion** *n.*

di·min·ish (di-min′ish) *v.t.* **1.** To make smaller or less; decrease, as in size, amount, or degree. **2.** To reduce in rank, power, or authority; degrade; belittle. **3.** *Archit.* To cause to taper. **—** *v.i.* **4.** To grow smaller or less; dwindle; decrease. **— Syn.** See DECREASE. [Fusion of ME *diminuen* to lessen (< OF *diminuer* < L *diminuere* < *de-* down + *minuere* to lessen < *minus* less) and ME *menusen* < OF *menusier*. See MINISH.] **— di·min′ish·a·ble** *adj.*

di·min·ished (di-min′isht) *adj. Music* **1.** One semitone smaller than the corresponding minor or perfect interval. **2.** Designating a theme or motif that has been subjected to diminution.

dim·in·ish·ing return (dim-in′ish-ing) *Econ.* The theory that beyond a certain point added production factors, as capital and labor, will yield a lower increase in production.

di·min·u·en·do (di-min′yŏŏ-en′dō) *Music n. pl.* **·dos** A gradual lessening in volume: expressed by the sign ——: opposed to *crescendo*. Abbr. *dim., dimin.* **—** *v.i.* **·doed, ·do·ing** To produce a diminuendo. Also *decrescendo*. [< Ital., ppr. of *diminuire* to lessen < L *diminuere*. See DIMINISH.]

dim·i·nu·tion (dim′ə-nŏŏ′shən, -nyŏŏ′-) *n.* **1.** The act of diminishing or the condition of being diminished; decrease; reduction. **2.** *Music* The repetition of a theme in notes of smaller time value than those first used: opposed to *augmentation*. [< AF *diminuciun* < L *diminutio, deminutio, -onis* < *diminuere*. See DIMINISH.]

di·min·u·tive (di-min′yə-tiv) *adj.* **1.** Of relatively small size; small; little. **2.** Diminishing or tending to diminish. **3.** *Gram.* Expressing diminished size: said of certain suffixes. **— Syn.** See SMALL. **—** *n.* **1.** *Gram.* A word formed from another to express diminished size, familiarity, affection, etc.: *Johnny* is a *diminutive* of *John*. **2.** Anything very small. Abbr. *dim., dimin.* **— dim·in′u·tive·ly** *adv.*

dim·is·so·ry (dim′ə-sôr′ē, -sō′rē, də-mis′ər-ē) *adj.* Granting leave to go away, as to another diocese: a *dimissory* letter. [< LL *dimissorius* < L *dimittere*. See DISMISS.]

Di·mi·trov (dē-mē′trôf), **Georgi Mihailov**, 1882–1949, Bulgarian Communist leader; first premier of Bulgarian People's Republic 1946–49.

dim·i·ty (dim′ə-tē) *n. pl.* **·ties** A sheer cotton fabric woven with stripes, cords, or checks, used to make dresses, curtains, etc. [< Ital. *dimito* < ML *dimitum* < Gk. *dimitos* having a double thread < *di-* two + *mitos* thread]

dim·mer (dim′ər) *n.* A rheostat used for varying the intensity of illumination, as in a theater lighting system.

di·morph (dī′môrf) *n.* A form exhibiting dimorphism.

di·mor·phic (dī-môr′fik) *adj.* Existing or occurring in two forms; characterized by dimorphism. Also **di·mor′phous**.

di·mor·phism (dī-môr′fiz-əm) *n.* **1.** *Bot.* The existence of

two distinct forms of the same organ on the same plant or the same species of plant. **2.** *Zool.* A difference in form, color, etc., between individuals of the same species, characterizing two distinct types. **3.** *Crystall.* Crystallization of the same substance in two forms. [< Gk. *dimorphos* < *di-* two + *morphē* form]

dim-out (dim′out′) *n.* A form of modified lighting in a city, etc., to make it less visible from the air, used as a precautionary measure against aerial attack. Compare BLACKOUT.

dim·ple (dim′pəl) *n.* **1.** A slight depression in the surface of the human body, especially one made visible in the cheek by smiling. **2.** A similar depression in any smooth surface. **—** *v.t. & v.i.* **·pled, ·pling** To mark with or form dimples. [ME *dympull*; cf. OHG *tumphilo* pool] **— dim′ply** *adj.*

dim·wit (dim′wit′) *n. Slang* A stupid or simple-minded person. **— dim′wit′ted** *adj.* **— dim′wit′ted·ly** *adv.*

din (din) *n.* A loud, continuous noise or clamor; a rattling or clattering sound. **—** *v.* **dinned, din·ning** *v.t.* **1.** To assail with confusing noise. **2.** To urge or press with repetition or insistence. **—** *v.i.* **3.** To make a din. [OE *dyne*]

din. Dinar.

di·nar (di-när′) *n.* **1.** An ancient gold coin of Moslem areas. **2.** An Iranian monetary unit, the hundredth part of a rial. **3.** The monetary unit of Algeria, equivalent to 100 centimes. **4.** The monetary unit of Bahrein, Iraq, Jordan, Kuwait, and Yemen, equivalent to 1000 fils. **5.** The monetary unit of Libya, equivalent to 1000 dirhams. **6.** The monetary unit of Tunisia, equivlaent to 1000 millimes. **7.** The monetary unit of Yugoslavia, equivalent to 100 para. Abbr. *d., D., din.* [< Arabic *dīnār* < LGk. *dēnarion* < L *denarius*. See DENARIUS.]

Di·nar·ic Alps (di-nar′ik) The SE division of the eastern Alps, mostly in Yugoslavia along the eastern coast of the Adriatic; highest point, Djeravica Peak, 8,714 ft.

din·dle (din′dəl, din′əl) *Scot. & Brit. Dial. v.t. & v.i.* **·dled, ·dling** To tingle as with pain or cold; vibrate. **—** *n.* A tingling; thrill. [ME; prob. imit.]

d'In·dy (daṅ-dē′), **(Paul Marie Théodore) Vincent**, 1851–1931, French composer.

dine (dīn) *v.* **dined, din·ing** *v.i.* **1.** To eat dinner. **2.** To eat any meal. **3.** To eat; feed: with *on* or *upon*. **—** *v.t.* **4.** To entertain at dinner. **—** *n. Obs.* Dinner. [< F *dîner* < OF *disner*, prob. < L *dis-* away + *jejunus* fast]

din·er (dī′nər) *n.* **1.** One who dines. **2.** A dining car (which see). **3.** A restaurant resembling a railroad car.

di·ner·ic (dī-ner′ik) *adj. Chem.* Of or relating to the interface separating two contiguous liquids, as oil and water, in the same container. [< DI-[2] + Gk. *nēros* water + -IC[1]]

di·ne·ro (dē-nä′rō) *n. pl.* **·ros** **1.** A former Peruvian silver coin, one tenth of a sol. **2.** *U.S. Slang* Money. [< Sp. money, coin < L *denarius*. See DENARIUS.]

Din·e·sen (dē′nə-sən), **Isak** Pseudonym of *Baroness Karen Blixen*, 1885–1962, Danish author.

di·nette (dī-net′) *n.* An alcove or small room used as a dining room. [< DINE + -ETTE]

di·neu·tron (dī-nōō′tron, -nyōō′-) *n. Physics* A short-lived atomic particle consisting of two neutrons produced by tritons in a nuclear reaction.

ding (ding) *v.t.* **1.** To sound, as a bell; ring. **2.** *Informal* To instill by constant repetition; din. **—** *v.i.* **3.** To ring or sound. **4.** *Informal* To speak with constant repetition. **—** *n.* The sound of a bell, or a sound resembling this. [Imit.]

ding·bat (ding′bat′) *n. Informal* **1.** Any small object, especially one hurled at another object. **2.** A dingus. **3.** *Printing* A typographical ornament or symbol. [Origin uncertain]

ding-dong (ding′dông′, -dong′) *n.* **1.** The peal of a bell. **2.** Any monotonous repetition. [Imit.]

din·ghy (ding′gē, ding′ē) *n. pl.* **·ghies** Any of various kinds of small rowing boats, as a clinker-built skiff, a ship's boat, etc. Also **din′gey, din′gy**. [< Hind. *dīngī* boat]

din·gle (ding′gəl) *n.* A narrow, wooded valley; dell. [ME]

din·go (ding′gō) *n. pl.* **·goes** The native wild dog (*Canis dingo*) of Australia, having a foxlike face, bushy tail, and reddish brown color. [< native name]

din·gus (ding′əs) *n. Informal* A thing or device of which the name is unknown or forgotten; a gadget or thingamabob. [< Afrikaans < Du. *ding* thing]

din·gy (din′jē) *adj.* **·gi·er, ·gi·est** Darkened or discolored, as if soiled; dull; grimy; shabby. [Origin unknown] **— din′gi·ly** *adv.* **— din′gi·ness** *n.*

dining car A railway car in which meals are served en route.

dining room A room, as in a house, apartment, hotel, dormitory, etc., where meals are served.

dinitro- *combining form Chem.* Having two nitro groups, as certain isomeric compounds.

di·ni·tro·ben·zene (dī-nī′trō-ben′zēn) *n. Chem.* One of three isomeric compounds, $C_6H_4(NO_2)_2$, formed by heating benzene with a mixture of nitric and sulfuric acids.

dink (dingk) *Scot. v.t.* To array. **—** *adj.* Neat; trim; tidy.

Din·ka (ding′kä) *n.* **1.** A member of a Negroid tribe of the southern Sudan. **2.** The Sudanic language of this tribe.

dink·ey (ding′kē) *n. pl.* **dink·eys** *U.S.* A small locomotive used for shunting freight, etc.: also spelled *dinky*. [< DINKY]

dink·y (ding′kē) *adj.* **dink·i·er, dink·i·est** *Informal* **1.** *U.S.*

Small; insignificant. **2.** *Brit.* Little; cute; neat. — *n. pl.*
din·kies A dinkey. [< DINK + -Y]
Din·mont (din′mont) See DANDIE DINMONT TERRIER.
din·na (din′nə) *Scot.* Do not.
din·ner (din′ər) *n.* **1.** The principal meal of the day, taken usually at some hour between noon and nine P.M. **2.** A banquet in honor of a person or event. [< F *dîner.* See DINE.]
dinner coat or **jacket** A tuxedo jacket.
din·ner·ware (din′ər·wâr′) *n.* Dishes, etc., used in serving meals.
dino- *combining form* Terrible; huge: *dinosaur.* [< Gk. *deinos* terrible]
di·noc·er·as (dī·nos′ər·əs) *n. Paleontol.* The uintathere.
[< DINO- + Gk. *keras* horn]
di·no·saur (dī′nə·sôr) *n. Paleontol.* One of a group of extinct reptiles (orders *Saurischia* and *Ornithischia*) widely distributed during the Mesozoic period, and including the largest known land animals. [< DINO- + Gk. *sauros* lizard]
di·no·sau·ri·an (dī′nə·sôr′ē·ən) *adj.* Of, pertaining to, or characteristic of a dinosaur. — *n.* A dinosaur.
di·no·there (dī′nə·thir) *n. Paleontol.* One of a genus (*Dinotherium*) of elephantlike mammals of the Miocene and Pleistocene epochs, having huge tusks extending downward from the lower jaw. [< DINO- + Gk. *thēr* wild beast]
dint (dint) *n.* **1.** Active agency; means; force: to win by *dint* of effort. **2.** A dent. — *v.t.* **1.** To make a dent in. **2.** To drive in forcibly. [OE *dynt* a blow]
Din·wid·die (din′wid·ē), **Robert,** 1693–1770, British administrator; colonial governor of Virginia.
di·o·bol (dī·ō′bəl) *n.* A silver coin of ancient Greece equal to two oboli. Also **di·ob·o·lon** (dī·ob′ə·lon). [< Gk. *diōbolon* < *di-* two + *obolos* obol]
dioc. Diocesan; diocese.
di·oc·e·san (dī·os′ə·sən, dī′ə·sē′sən) *adj.* Of or pertaining to a diocese. — *n.* A bishop in charge of a diocese. Abbr. *dioc.*
di·o·cese (dī′ə·sēs, -sis) *n.* The territory or the churches under a bishop's jurisdiction. Abbr. *dioc.* [< OF *diocise* < Med.L *diocesis* < L *dioecesis* district < Gk. *dioikēsis,* orig., management of a house < *dia-* completely + *oikeein* to dwell, manage]
Di·o·cle·tian (dī′ə·klē′shən), **Gaius Aurelius Valerius,** 245–313, Roman emperor 284–305.
di·ode (dī′ōd) *n.* An electron tube or semiconductor device that has two terminals, and, in addition to its other properties, acts as a rectifier. [< DI(A)- + -ODE¹]
di·oe·cious (dī·ē′shəs) *adj. Bot.* Having the male and female organs borne by different plants; unisexual: also spelled *diecious.* Also **di·oi·cous** (dī·oi′kəs). [< DI-² + Gk. *oikia* house, dwelling] — **di·oe′cious·ly** *adv.* — **di·oe′cious·ness** *n.*
di·oes·trus (dī·es′trəs, -ēs′-), **di·oes·trum** (-trəm) See DI-ESTRUS.
Di·og·e·nes (dī·oj′ə·nēz), 412?–323 B.C., Greek Cynic philosopher, reputed to have lived in a tub and to have sought for an honest man at midday with a lantern.
Di·o·mede Islands (dī′ə·mēd) Two small islands in Bering Strait, one part of Alaska, the other part of the R.S.F.S.R.
Di·o·me·des (dī′ə·mē′dēz) In Greek legend, a king of Argos at the siege of Troy who helped Odysseus steal the Palladium. Also **Di·o·med** (dī′ə·med), **Di·o·mede** (dī′ə·mēd).
Di·o·ne (dī·ō′nē) In Greek mythology, the mother of Aphrodite by Zeus.
Di·o·nys·i·a (dī′ə·nish′ē·ə, -nis′ē·ə) *n.pl.* The Greek festivals in honor of Dionysus, especially those at Athens, in which the Greek drama had its origins.
Di·o·nys·i·ac (dī′ə·nis′ē·ak) *adj.* Pertaining to Dionysus or the Dionysia. Also **Di·o·ny·si·a·cal** (dī′ə·nə·sī′ə·kəl). — **Di′·o·ny·si·a·cal·ly** *adv.*
Di·o·nys·ian (dī′ə·nish′ən, -nis′ē·ən) *adj.* **1.** Dionysiac. **2.** Relating to or characteristic of Dionysius or Dionysus.
Di·o·nys·i·us Ex·ig·u·us (dī′ə·nish′ē·əs, -nis′ē·əs; eg·zig′-yōō·əs, ek·sig′-) Sixth-century Christian scholar; calculated traditional date of Christ's birth.
Dionysius of Alexandria, Saint Third-century Christian theologian.
Dionysius of Halicarnassus, died 7? B.C., Greek historian and rhetorician.
Dionysius the Elder, 430?–367 B.C., and his son **Dionysius the Younger,** 395?–343? B.C., tyrants of Syracuse.
Di·o·ny·sus (dī′ə·nī′səs) In Greek mythology, the god of wine, fertility, etc., worshiped with orgiastic rites: identified with the Roman *Bacchus.* Also **Di′o·ny′sos.**
di·op·side (dī·op′sīd, -sid) *n.* A grayish white or green variety of pyroxene. [< F < Gk. *di-* two + *opsis* view]
di·op·tase (dī·op′tās) *n.* A vitreous, emerald-green copper silicate, crystallizing in the hexagonal system. [< F < Gk. *dia-* through + *optos* visible]
di·op·ter (dī·op′tər) *n. Optics* The unit for measuring the refractive power of a lens, expressed as the reciprocal of its focal length in meters. Also **di·op′tre.** [< MF *dioptre* < L *dioptra* < Gk., optical instrument]
di·op·tom·e·ter (dī′op·tom′ə·tər) *n.* An optical instrumen

for measuring refraction and accommodation of the eye. [< DI(A)- + OPTOMETER] — **di′op·tom′e·try** *n.*
di·op·tric (dī·op′trik) *adj. Optics* **1.** Aiding the vision by refraction, as a lens. **2.** Of or pertaining to dioptrics. **3.** Of or pertaining to a diopter, or to the system of numbering optical glasses metrically. Also **di·op′tri·cal.** [< Gk. *dioptrikos* pertaining to the use of the dioptra. See DIOPTER.]
di·op·trics (dī·op′triks) *n.pl. (construed as sing.)* The branch of optics treating of light refraction by transparent media.
di·o·ra·ma (dī′ə·rä′mə, -ram′ə) *n.* **1.** An exhibit consisting of modeled figures, etc., set in a naturalistic foreground blended into a painted background. **2.** A picture in which changes are produced by means of cloth transparencies, arrangements of lights, etc. **3.** A building in which such a picture or group is exhibited. [< Gk. *dia-* through + *horama* a sight] — **di·o·ram·ic** (dī′ə·ram′ik) *adj.*
di·o·rite (dī′ə·rīt) *n.* A granular, crystallized, igneous rock composed of feldspar and hornblende. [< F < Gk. *diorizein* to divide < *dia-* through + *horos* a limit] — **di·o·rit·ic** (dī′ə·rit′ik) *adj.*
Di·os·cu·ri (dī′ə·skyoŏr′ī) *n.pl.* Castor and Pollux. [< Gk. *Dioskouroi* < *Dios* of Zeus + *kouros* boy, son]
di·ox·ane (dī·ok′sān) *n. Chem.* A colorless, liquid derivative, $C_4H_8O_2$, of glycol, having a faint, pleasant odor and used as a solvent for resins, oils, waxes, and organic compounds. [< DI-² + OX(A)- +- ANE²]
di·ox·ide (dī·ok′sīd, -sid) *n. Chem.* An oxide containing two atoms of oxygen to the molecule. Also **di·ox·id** (dī-ok′sid).
dip (dip) *v.* **dipped, dip·ping** *v.t.* **1.** To put or let down into a liquid momentarily. **2.** To obtain or lift up and out by scooping, bailing, etc. **3.** To lower and then raise, as a flag in salute. **4.** To baptize by immersion. **5.** To plunge (animals) into a disinfectant. **6.** To dye by immersion. **7.** *Chem.* To coat (a metallic surface) by immersion in a solution of readily decomposed salt. **8.** To make (candles) by repeatedly immersing wicks in wax or tallow. — *v.i.* **9.** To plunge into and come out of water or other liquid, especially briefly and quickly. **10.** To plunge one's hand or a receptacle into water, etc., or into a container, especially so as to take something out. **11.** To sink or go down suddenly. **12.** To incline downward; go down; decline. **13.** *Geol.* To lie at an angle to the horizon, as rock strata. **14.** *Aeron.* To drop rapidly and then climb. **15.** To engage in or inquire into something slightly or superficially; dabble. **16.** To read here and there, as in a book or magazine; browse: with *into.* — *n.* **1.** An act of dipping; a brief immersion or plunge: a *dip* in the sea. **2.** A liquid, sauce, etc., into which something is to be dipped. **3.** The quantity of something taken up at a dipping; also, the object used for dipping. **4.** A candle made by repeated immersion of a wick in melted tallow. **5.** A sloping downward; also, the degree of such a sloping. **6.** A hollow or depression. **7.** The angle that a magnetic needle makes with the horizon: also called *magnetic dip.* **8.** In surveying, the degree in which the horizon is below eye level. **9.** *Geol.* The position, other than horizontal, of rock strata, etc.; also, the angle between such strata and the horizontal plane. **10.** *Aeron.* A rapid drop of an airplane followed by a climb. **11.** In gymnastics, an exercise on parallel bars in which the gymnast, resting on his hands, lets his body down until his chin is even with the bars and then raises himself by straightening his arms. **12.** *Slang* A pickpocket. [OE *dyppan.* Akin to DEEP.]
di·pet·al·ous (dī·pet′l·əs) *adj. Bot.* Having two petals: also *bipetalous.*
di·phase (dī′fāz′) *adj. Electr.* Having two phases, as two alternating currents, the maxima and minima of which differ from one another by 90 degrees: also *quarter-phase, two-phase.* Also **di·phas·ic** (dī·fā′zik).
di·phen·yl (dī·fen′əl, dī·fē′nəl) *n.* Biphenyl (which see).
di·phen·yl·a·mine (dī·fen′əl·ə·mēn′, -am′in, -fē′nəl-) *n. Chem.* A crystalline aromatic amine, $(C_6H_5)_2NH$, obtained by heating aniline hydrochloride with aniline, used as a stabilizer in explosives, in the manufacture of dyestuffs, etc. Also **di·phen′yl·am′in** (-am′in).
di·phen·yl·am·ine·chlor·ar·sine (dī·fen′əl·am′in·klôr′-är′sēn, -sin, -fē′nəl-) *n.* Adamsite.
di·phen·yl·hy·dan·to·in sodium (dī·fen′əl·hī·dan′tō·in, -fē′nəl-) *Chem.* A white, odorless compound, $C_{15}H_{11}N_2O_2\cdot Na$, used in the treatment of epileptic convulsions.
di·phos·gene (dī·fos′jēn) *n. Chem.* A poison gas, $C_2O_2Cl_4$, related to phosgene and designed for use in chemical warfare.
diph·the·ri·a (dif·thir′ē·ə, dip-) *n. Pathol.* An acute contagious disease, caused by a bacillus (*Corynebacterium diphtheriae*) and characterized by the formation of a false membrane in the air passages, and by fever and great weakness. [< F *diphthérie* < Gk. *diphthera* leather, membrane]
diph·the·ri·al (dif·thir′ē·əl, dip-) *adj.* **1.** Of, pertaining to, or resembling diphtheria or the symptoms of diphtheria. **2.** Having diphtheria. Also **diph·the′ri·an, diph·the·ric** (dif-thir′ik, dip-), **diph·the·rit·ic** (dif′thə·rit′ik, dip′-).

diph·thong (dif′thông, -thong, dip′-) *n.* **1.** *Phonet.* A blend of two vowel sounds in one syllable, whether written with two letters, as *oi* in *coil*, or with a single letter, as *i* in *fine*. Compare DIGRAPH. **2.** Loosely, either of the ligatures æ or œ, now pronounced as a single sound, but originally pronounced as true diphthongs in classical Latin. [< F *diphthongue* < LL *diphthongus* < Gk. *diphthongos* < *di-* two- + *phthongos* sound] —**diph·thon′gal** *adj.*

diph·thong·ize (dif′thông-īz, -thong-, dip′-) *v.* **·ized, ·iz·ing** *v.t.* **1.** To make a diphthong of; pronounce as a diphthong. — *v.i.* **2.** To become a diphthong. —**diph′thong·i·za′tion** *n.*

di·phyl·lous (dī-fil′əs) *adj. Bot.* Having two leaves. [< DI- + Gk. *phyllon* leaf]

diph·y·o·dont (dif′ē-ə-dont′) *adj.* Developing a first set of teeth subsequently replaced by a permanent set, as most mammals. [< Gk. *diphyēs* double + *odous, odontos* tooth]

dipl. Diplomat; diplomatic.

di·plex (dī′pleks) *adj. Telecom.* Pertaining to or allowing the transmission or reception of two simultaneous communications over a single wire in the same direction: distinguished from *duplex*. [< DI-[2] + (DU)PLEX]

diplo- *combining form* Double: *diplococcus*. Also, before vowels, **dipl-**. [< Gk. *diploos* double]

dip·lo·car·di·a (dip′lə-kär′dē-ə) *n. Anat.* A condition in which the right and left sides of the heart are more or less separated as by a fissure. [< DIPLO- + Gk. *kardia* heart] —**dip′lo·car′di·ac** (-ak) *adj.*

dip·lo·coc·cus (dip′lə-kok′əs) *n. pl.* **·coc·ci** (-kok′sī) **1.** A microorganism consisting of two cells united. **2.** *Bacteriol.* Any of a genus (*Diplococcus*) of bacteria occurring in pairs or chains, including *D. pneumoniae*, the infective agent of lobar pneumonia. For illustration see BACTERIA.

di·plod·o·cus (di·plod′ə-kəs) *n. Paleontol.* Any of a genus (*Diplodocus*) of gigantic, herbivorous dinosaurs, fossil in the Upper Jurassic rocks of Wyoming and Colorado. [< NL < Gk. *diploos* double + *dokos* a beam]

dip·lo·e (dip′lō-ē) *n. Anat.* The spongy bony tissue between the two walls of the cranial bones. [< NL < Gk. *diploē* a double fold]

dip·loid (dip′loid) *adj.* **1.** Twofold or doubled. **2.** *Biol.* Having two sets of chromosomes, as in the nucleus of the somatic cells of all higher organisms. — *n.* **1.** A cell having double the haploid number of chromosomes. **2.** *Crystall.* An isometric crystal with 24 trapezoidal planes. [< DIPLO- + -OID]

di·plo·ma (di·plō′mə) *n.* **1.** A certificate given by a school, college, or university testifying that a student has earned a degree or completed a course of study. **2.** A certificate conferring some honor or privilege. **3.** An official document; a charter. [< L < Gk. *diplōma* paper folded double, a letter < *diploos* double]

di·plo·ma·cy (di·plō′mə·sē) *n. pl.* **·cies** **1.** The art, science, or practice of conducting negotiations between nations. **2.** Skill or tact in dealing with others or in managing some affair. [< F *diplomatie* < *diplomate*. See DIPLOMAT.]

dip·lo·mat (dip′lə-mat) *n.* **1.** One engaged in diplomacy. **2.** Any individual possessing skill or tact in dealing with others. Abbr. *dipl.* [< F *diplomate* < *diplomatique* < NL *diplomaticus* < L *diploma*. See DIPLOMA.]

dip·lo·mate (dip′lə-māt) *n.* The holder of a diploma: especially, a physician certified as a specialist.

dip·lo·mat·ic (dip′lə-mat′ik) *adj.* **1.** Of, pertaining to, or connected with diplomacy. **2.** Possessing skill or tact in dealing with people. Also **dip′lo·mat′i·cal.** Abbr. *dipl.* —**dip′lo·mat′i·cal·ly** *adv.*

diplomatic corps The corps of officials, as ambassadors and envoys, who are assigned to represent their country and promote its interests in the central governmental seat of another country. Also **diplomatic body.**

diplomatic immunity Exemption of the members of a diplomatic corps and of their staffs and premises from the ordinary processes of local law.

dip·lo·mat·ics (dip′lə-mat′iks) *n. pl.* (*construed as sing.*) **1.** Diplomacy. **2.** The science of deciphering ancient writings and of determining their authenticity, age, etc.

di·plo·ma·tist (di·plō′mə·tist) *n. Brit.* A diplomat.

di·plo·pia (di·plō′pē-ə) *n. Pathol.* A defect of vision in which objects appear to be double. [< NL < Gk. *diploos* double + *ōps* eye] —**di·plop·ic** (-plop′ik) *adj.*

dip·lo·pod (dip′lə-pod) *n. Zool.* Any of a class (*Diplopoda*) of segmented terrestrial arthropods; a millipede. [< NL *Diplopoda* < Gk. *diploos* double + *pous, podos* foot]

di·plo·sis (di·plō′sis) *n. Genetics* The doubling of two haploid sets of chromosomes by the union of the male and female gametes. [< DIPL(O)- + -OSIS]

dip·lo·ste·mo·nous (dip′lə-stē′mə-nəs) *adj. Bot.* Having twice as many stamens as petals. [< DIPLO- + Gk. *stēmōn* thread (taken as *stēma* stamen)]

dip needle A magnetic needle pivoted to swing vertically to indicate the inclination of the earth's magnetic field: also called *inclinometer.*

dip·no·an (dip′nō-ən) *Zool. adj.* Of or belonging to a group (*Dipnoi*) of fishes with regular gills, a single or double lung, and internal nostrils connecting with the mouth.

— *n.* A dipnoan fish: also called *lungfish.* [< NL *Dipnoi* < Gk. *dipnoos* < *di-* two + *pnoē* breath]

dip·o·dy (dip′ə-dē) *n. pl.* **·dies** In prosody, a dimeter. [< L *dipodia* < Gk. < *di-* two + *pous, podos* foot]

di·pole (dī′pōl) *n.* **1.** *Physics* Any material system having two electric charges, equal in magnitude but of unlike sign, or having two equal but opposite magnetic poles. **2.** *Chem.* A molecule exhibiting separation of positive and negative charges. —**di·po′lar** *adj.*

dip·per (dip′ər) *n.* **1.** One who dips. **2.** A long-handled cup used to dip liquids. **3.** Any of several American birds that are quick divers; especially, the pied-billed grebe and the small bufflehead duck. **3.** The water ouzel.

Dip·per (dip′ər) *n.* **1.** *U.S.* Either of two northern constellations, the Big Dipper (Ursa Major) or the Little Dipper (Ursa Minor). **2.** A Dunker or member of any other immersionist religious sect: a contemptuous term.

dip·py (dip′ē) *adj.* **·pi·er, ·pi·est** *Slang* Crazy; eccentric.

dip·sas (dip′səs) *n. pl.* **·sa·des** (-sə-dēz) **1.** A serpent whose bite was fabled to produce extreme thirst. **2.** Any of several tropical colubrine snakes (subfamily *Dipsadomorphinae*). [< L < Gk. < *dipsa* thirst]

dip·so·ma·ni·a (dip′sə-mā′nē-ə) *n.* A recurrent, uncontrollable craving for alcoholic drink. [< Gk. *dipsa* thirst + -MANIA]

dip·so·ma·ni·ac (dip′sə-mā′nē-ak) *n.* A person affected with dipsomania. — *adj.* Pertaining to or affected with dipsomania: also **dip·so·ma·ni·a·cal** (dip′sə-mə-nī′ə-kəl).

dip·ter·al (dip′tər-əl) *adj.* **1.** *Archit.* Having or resembling two rows of columns. **2.** Dipterous. [< L < Gk. *dipteros.* See DIPTEROUS.]

dip·ter·an (dip′tər-ən) *n.* A dipterous insect. Also **dip′ter·on** (-on).

dip·ter·ous (dip′tər-əs) *adj.* **1.** *Entomol.* Of or pertaining to an order (*Diptera*) of insects having a single pair of membranous wings with a posterior pair of balancers, and a sucking proboscis, including the flies, gnats, mosquitoes, etc. **2.** *Bot.* Two-winged, as a seed or fruit. [< Gk. *dipteros* two-winged < *di-* twice + *pteron* wing]

dip·tych (dip′tik) *n.* **1.** A double tablet; especially, an ancient Greek or Roman hinged double writing tablet. **2.** A double picture or carving, often depicting a religious subject. Also **dip′ty·ca** (-ti-kə), **dip′ty·chon** (-ti-kon). [< LL *diptycha* < Gk., pair of tablets; orig. neut. pl. of *diptychos* folded < *di-* twice + *ptyssein* to fold]

dir. Director.

Di·rac (di-rak′), **Paul Adrien Maurice,** born 1902, English physicist and mathematician.

DIPTYCH (*def.* 2)

dire (dīr) *adj.* **dir·er, dir·est** Calamitous; dreadful; terrible. [< L *dirus* awful] —**dire′ly** *adv.* —**dire′ness** *n.*

di·rect (di·rekt′, dī-) *v.t.* **1.** To control or conduct the affairs of; manage; govern. **2.** To order or instruct with authority; command: often with a clause as object: to *direct* him to go there. **3.** *Music* To lead as a conductor. **4.** To tell (someone) the way. **5.** To cause to move or face in a desired direction; aim: to *direct* one's gaze. **6.** To indicate the destination of, as a letter. **7.** To intend, as remarks or insults, to be heard by a person; address. **8.** To guide or supervise (the performance of a play, film, etc.). — *v.i.* **9.** To give commands or guidance. **10.** To guide the production or interpretation of a play, film, etc. — *adj.* **1.** Having or being the straightest course; straight; shortest; nearest. **2.** Free from intervening agencies or conditions; immediate. **3.** Straightforward, as in meaning, statement, or intention; clear; candid; plain. **4.** Complete; absolute: the *direct* antithesis. **5.** In a continuous line of descent; lineal. **6.** In the exact words of the speaker or writer: a *direct* quote. **7.** *Govt.* By the efforts of the people through referendum, etc., without the intervention of delegates or representatives. **8.** *Electr.* **a** Continuous as opposed to alternating, as a current. **b** Having the same direction as the primary: said of an induced current. **9.** *Astron.* Designating motion on the celestial sphere from west toward east, in the direction of the sun's movement among the stars: opposed to *retrograde.* **10.** *Chem.* Of or pertaining to direct dyes. **11.** *Stat.* Positive. — *adv.* In a direct line or manner; directly. [< L *directus,* pp. of *dirigere* to arrange, direct < *dis-* apart + *regere* to guide, conduct] —**di·rect′ness** *n.*

di·rect-ac·tion (di-rekt′ak′shən, dī-) *adj. Mech.* Having no transmitting mechanism, such as gearwheels, between the part driven and the power that drives it.

direct action An attempt, as by labor, to achieve demands by means of demonstrations, strikes, sabotage, or the like.

direct current See under CURRENT.

direct discourse See under DISCOURSE.

direct dye A dye that colors by simple immersion and does not require a mordant: also called *substantive dye.*

di·rec·ted number (di-rekt′id, dī-) *Math.* A number preceded by a plus (+) or minus (−) sign: also called *signed number.*

di·rec·tion (di-rek′shən, dī-)   *n.*   **1.** The act of directing. **2.** The course or position of an object or point as it moves, turns, faces, etc., in relation to another object or point: in the *direction* of Chicago. **3.** *Usually pl.* Instructions about how to do or use something, reach a destination, etc. **4.** An order, command, or regulation. **5.** Management, control, or administration: to be under the *direction* of a new official. **6.** Supervision and organization of the elements of a play, film, or similar production into an integrated whole. **7.** Tendency or movement toward a particular end or stage of development: the *direction* of his writings toward realism. **8.** The address on a letter, parcel, etc., that indicates the intended recipient. **9.** *Music* A word, phrase, or sign that indicates how a particular note or passage is to be played. **10.** *Naut.* The angle between true north and a given line or course, measured in degrees from the north point clockwise to the given line or course.

di·rec·tion·al (di-rek′shən-əl, dī-)   *adj.*   **1.** Pertaining to direction in space. **2.** *Telecom.* **a** Adapted for indicating from which of several directions signals are received. **b** Describing an antenna that radiates or receives radio waves more effectively in or from some directions than from others.

directional signal   A pair of flashing lights or metal arrows on a motor vehicle, used to indicate turns.

direction finder   *Telecom.*   A receiving device with which, by the use of a loop antenna, the direction of incoming radio signals may be determined. Abbr. *DF, D/F, D.F.*

di·rec·tive (di-rek′tiv, dī-)   *n.*   An order or regulation; especially, a governmental or military pronouncement. — *adj.* That directs or points out, rules, or governs.

di·rect·ly (di-rekt′lē, dī-)   *adv.*   **1.** In a direct line or manner. **2.** Without medium, agent, or go-between: taken *directly* from nature. **3.** As soon as possible; immediately. **4.** Exactly; precisely. — **Syn.** See IMMEDIATELY. — *conj. Brit.* As soon as: She saw him *directly* she entered the room.

direct object   See under OBJECT.

di·rec·tor (di-rek′tər, dī-)   *n.*   **1.** One who directs, as the head member of a corporation, the conductor of an orchestra, the chief supervisor of a play, film, or similar production, or one who acts as a spiritual guide. **2.** *Mil.* An apparatus that systematically computes firing data for use against moving targets. Abbr. *d., D., dir.* — **di·rec′tress** *n.fem.*

di·rec·tor·ate (di-rek′tər-it, dī-)   *n.*   **1.** A body of directors. **2.** The office or power of a director: also **di·rec′tor·ship.**

di·rec·to·ri·al (di-rek′tôr′ē-əl, -tō′rē-, dī-)   *adj.*   **1.** That directs; directive. **2.** Pertaining to a director or directorate.

di·rec·to·ry (di-rek′tər-ē, dī-)   *n.*   *pl.* **·ries**   **1.** An alphabetical or classified list, as of the names and addresses of the inhabitants or businesses of a city. **2.** A collection of rules; especially, a book of directions for church worship. **3.** A body of directors; directorate. — *adj.* Serving to direct.

Di·rec·to·ry (di-rek′tər-ē, dī-)   *n.*   The five executives of the French government from October 26, 1795 to November 9, 1799. Also **Di·rec·toire** (dē-rek-twär′).

direct primary   *Govt.*   A preliminary election in which a party chooses its candidates for public office by direct vote.

direct proportion   *Math.*   The relationship of two variables when one equals the other multiplied by a constant.

di·rec·trix (di-rek′triks, dī-)   *n.*   *pl.* **·trix·es** or **·tri·ces** (dī′rek-trī′sēz)   **1.** *Geom.* A line that so determines the motion of another line that the latter describes some surface or curve. **2.** *Mil.* In gunnery, the median line in the plane of fire. **3.** *Rare* A directress. [< NL]

direct tax   A tax, as on income, property, etc., that is charged directly to the taxpayer and cannot be passed on to another: distinguished from *indirect tax.*

dire·ful (dīr′fŏŏl, -fəl)   *adj.*   Dreadful; terrible; dire. — **dire′ful·ly** *adv.* — **dire′ful·ness** *n.*

dirge (dûrj)   *n.*   **1.** A song or melody expressing mourning; a lament. **2.** A hymn or choral service at a funeral. [< L *dirige* (imperative of *dirigere* to direct), the first word of the antiphon (*Ps.* v 8) of matins in the Latin burial office] — **dirge′ful** *adj.*

dir·ham (dir-ham′)   *n.*   A monetary unit of Morocco, equivalent to 100 centimes.

dir·i·gi·ble (dir′ə-jə-bəl)   *n.*   A lighter-than-air aircraft that may be steered in any direction by means of its own motive power; an airship. — *adj.* That can be directed toward a particular point. [< L *dirigere* to direct + -IBLE]

DIRIGIBLE

di·ri·go (dir′i-gō)   *Latin* I direct: motto of Maine.

dir·i·ment (dir′ə-ment)   *adj.*   Rendering absolutely void; nullifying. [< L *dirimens, -entis,* ppr. of *dirimere* to part, divide < *dis-* apart + *emere* to take]

diriment impediment of marriage   In the Roman Catholic Church, a sufficient cause for rendering a marriage null and void from the start.

dirk (dûrk)   *n.*   A dagger. — *v.t.* To stab with a dirk. [Origin uncertain]

dirl (dirl, dûrl)   *v.t. & v.i. Scot.*   To tingle; vibrate.

dirn·dl (dûrn′dəl)   *n.*   **1.** A woman's dress with a full skirt gathered to a tight bodice. **2.** The skirt of such a dress: also **dirndl skirt.** [< G *dirndl,* dim. of *dirne* girl]

dirt (dûrt)   *n.*   **1.** Any foul or filthy substance, as mud, dust, excrement, etc. **2.** Loose earth or soil; loam. **3.** Something contemptible, mean, or of small worth. **4.** Obscene speech, pictures, or writing; pornography. **5.** Rude or vilifying language. **6.** Gossip. **7.** *Mining* Washed-down earth, broken ore or rock, etc., containing precious metal. — *adj.* Made of earth: a *dirt* road. [Metathetical var. of ME *drit* < ON, dirt, bird droppings]

dirt-cheap (dûrt′chēp′)   *adj.*   Very inexpensive. — *adv.* At a very low price.

dirt farmer   *U.S. Informal*   A farmer who does his own work.

dirt·y (dûr′tē)   *adj.* **dirt·i·er, dirt·i·est**   **1.** Soiled with or as with dirt; unclean; filthy. **2.** Imparting dirt; making filthy. **3.** Indecent; obscene: *dirty* jokes. **4.** Despicable; mean: a *dirty* trick. **5.** Lacking brightness or clarity; muddy: said of colors. **6.** Unsettled or stormy: *dirty* weather. **7.** Producing or marked by excessive radioactive fallout: a *dirty* atomic bomb. — *v.t. & v.i.* **dirt·ied, dirt·y·ing** To make or become dirty. — **dirt′i·ly** *adv.* — **dirt′i·ness** *n.*

dirty work   **1.** *Informal* Trickery; deceit; foul play. **2.** A difficult job or the most difficult part of a job.

dis-[1]   *prefix*   **1.** Away from; apart: *disembody, dislodge, dismiss.* **2.** The reverse of or the undoing of (what is expressed in the rest of the word): *disband, disconnect, disrobe, disown.* **3.** Deprivation of some quality, power, rank, etc.: *disable, disbar, disenfranchise.* **4.** Not: *disadvantageous, disloyal, distasteful.* **5.** Completely; thoroughly (simple intensive with an already negative word): *disannul.* Also: *di-* before *b, d, l, m, n, r, s, v,* and usually before *g,* as in *digress, direct, diverge* (in Late Latin this was often changed back to the full form, as in *dismiss, disrupt*); *dif-* before *f,* as in *differ.* The living English prefix is always in the form *dis-.* [< L *dis-,* sometimes replacing OF *des-* (see DE-), ult. < *duo* two]

dis-[2]   *prefix*   Var. of DI-[2]. [< MF, ult. < Gk. *dis* twice]

Dis (dis)   In Roman mythology: **a** God of the lower world: identified with *Pluto.* **b** The kingdom of the dead: identified with the Greek *Hades.*

dis·a·bil·i·ty (dis′ə-bil′ə-tē)   *n.*   *pl.* **·ties**   **1.** That which disables. **2.** Lack of ability; inability. **3.** Legal incapacity or inability to act.

disability clause   In insurance policies, a clause providing benefits, such as suspended premiums with continued insurance, for a policyholder who becomes disabled.

dis·a·ble (dis-ā′bəl)   *v.t.* **·bled, ·bling**   **1.** To render incapable or unable; cripple; impair. **2.** To render legally incapable, as of inheriting property, etc. — **dis·a′ble·ment** *n.*

dis·a·buse (dis′ə-byōōz′)   *v.t.* **·bused, ·bus·ing**   To free from false or mistaken ideas; undeceive.

di·sac·cha·ride (dī-sak′ə-rīd, -rid)   *n.*   *Biochem.* One of a series of carbohydrates, as lactose and maltose, yielding two monosaccharides on hydrolysis. Also **di·sac′cha·rid** (-rid). [< DI-[2] + SACCHARIDE]

dis·ac·cord (dis′ə-kôrd′)   *n.*   Lack of accord; disharmony. — *v.i.* To lack accord or agreement; clash. [< OF *desacorder < des-* away (< L *dis-*) + *acorder.* See ACCORD.]

dis·ac·cus·tom (dis′ə-kus′təm)   *v.t.*   To free of a habit or of anything to which one has become accustomed.

dis·ad·van·tage (dis′əd-van′tij, -vän′-)   *n.*   **1.** An unfavorable condition or situation. **2.** That which interferes with success or produces an unfavorable condition or situation; drawback; handicap. **3.** Loss, injury, or detriment: This will be to your *disadvantage.* — **at a disadvantage** In an unfavorable condition or situation. — *v.t.* **·taged, ·tag·ing** To subject to a disadvantage. [< OF *desavantage < des-* away (< L *dis-*) + *avantage.* See ADVANTAGE.]

dis·ad·van·taged (dis′əd-van′təjd)   *adj.*   Having less than what is regarded as basic or minimal for decent living, as money, social position, etc.; underprivileged.

dis·ad·van·ta·geous (dis·ad′van-tā′jəs)   *adj.*   Attended with disadvantage; detrimental; inconvenient. — **dis·ad′van·ta′geous·ly** *adv.* — **dis·ad′van·ta′geous·ness** *n.*

dis·af·fect (dis′ə-fekt′)   *v.t.*   To destroy or weaken the affection or loyalty of; alienate; estrange. — **dis·af·fec′tion** *n.*

dis·af·fect·ed (dis′ə-fek′tid)   *adj.*   Alienated in feeling or loyalty; estranged; unfriendly. — **dis·af·fect′ed·ly** *adv.*

dis·af·fil·i·ate (dis′ə-fil′ē-āt)   *v.t. & v.i.* **·at·ed, ·at·ing** To sever affiliation (with).

dis·af·firm (dis′ə-fûrm′)   *v.t.*   **1.** To deny; contradict. **2.** *Law* **a** To set aside, as a decision; reverse. **b** To disclaim, as a contract; repudiate.

dis·af·fir·ma·tion (dis′af-ər-mā′shən)   *n.*   The act of disaffirming; denial. Also **dis·af·firm·ance** (dis′ə-fûr′məns).

dis·af·for·est (dis′ə-fôr′ist, -for′-)   *v.t. Brit. Law* To reduce from the privileges of a forest to common ground; disallow as a forest: also *disforest.* [< Med.L *disafforestare < dis-* away + *afforestare.* See AFFOREST.] **—dis'af·for'es·ta'·tion, dis'af·for'est·ment** *n.*

dis·a·gree (dis'ə·grē') *v.i.* **·greed, ·gree·ing** **1.** To vary in opinion; differ; dissent. **2.** To quarrel; argue. **3.** To fail to agree or harmonize, as facts. **4.** To be unacceptable or unfavorable: with *with:* Heat *disagreed* with him. [< OF *desagreer < des-* away (< L *dis-*) + *agreer.* See AGREE.]

dis·a·gree·a·ble (dis'ə·grē'ə·bəl) *adj.* **1.** Repugnant or offensive; not agreeable; unpleasant. **2.** Of unpleasant disposition; quarrelsome; bad-tempered. **—dis'a·gree'a·bil'·i·ty, dis'a·gree'a·ble·ness** *n.* **—dis'a·gree'a·bly** *adv.*

dis·a·gree·ment (dis'ə·grē'mənt) *n.* **1.** Failure to agree. **2.** Dissimilarity; inconsistency; discrepancy. **3.** Difference in views; dissent. **4.** A quarrel; dispute.

dis·al·low (dis'ə·lou') *v.t.* **1.** To refuse to allow. **2.** To reject as untrue or invalid. [< OF *desalouer* to blame < *des-* away (< L *dis-*) + *alouer.* See ALLOW.] **—dis'al·low'ance** *n.*

dis·an·nul (dis'ə·nul') *v.t.* To annul completely. **—dis'·an·nul'ment** *n.*

dis·a·noint (dis'ə·noint') *v.t.* To invalidate the consecration of.

dis·ap·pear (dis'ə·pir') *v.i.* **1.** To pass from sight; fade away; vanish. **2.** To cease to exist.

dis·ap·pear·ance (dis'ə·pir'əns) *n.* The act of disappearing; a vanishing or ceasing to exist.

dis·ap·point (dis'ə·point') *v.t.* **1.** To fail to fulfill the expectation, hope, or desire of (a person). **2.** To prevent the fulfillment of (a hope or plan); frustrate. [< OF *desappointer < des-* away (< L *dis-*) + *appointer.* See APPOINT.] **—dis'ap·point'ing·ly** *adv.*

dis·ap·point·ed (dis'ə·poin'tid) *adj.* Frustrated in one's expectations or hopes.

dis·ap·point·ment (dis'ə·point'mənt) *n.* **1.** The act of disappointing. **2.** The state or feeling of being disappointed. **3.** One who or that which disappoints. **— Syn.** See CHAGRIN.

dis·ap·pro·ba·tion (dis'ap·rə·bā'shən) *n.* Disapproval; condemnation; censure.

dis·ap·prov·al (dis'ə·prōō'vəl) *n.* The act of disapproving; the withholding of approval; censure.

dis·ap·prove (dis'ə·prōōv') *v.* **·proved, ·prov·ing** *v.t.* **1.** To regard with disfavor or censure; condemn. **2.** To refuse to approve. **—** *v.i.* **3.** To have or express an unfavorable opinion: often with *of.* **—dis'ap·prov'ing·ly** *adv.*

dis·arm (dis·ärm') *v.t.* **1.** To deprive of weapons or of any means of attack or defense; make helpless or harmless. **2.** To overcome the suspicion, antagonism, etc., of; make well-disposed or friendly. **3.** To allay or reduce (suspicion, antagonism, etc.). **—** *v.i.* **4.** To lay down arms. **5.** To reduce or eliminate one's armed forces, military equipment, or weapons of war. [< OF *desarmer < des-* away (< L *dis-*) + *armer* to arm < L *armare < arma* arms]

dis·ar·ma·ment (dis·är'mə·mənt) *n.* The act of disarming; especially, the elimination, reduction, or limitation of armed forces, military equipment, or weapons of war.

dis·arm·ing (dis·är'ming) *adj.* Tending to overcome suspicion, antagonism, etc.; winning: a *disarming* smile. **— dis·arm'ing·ly** *adv.*

dis·ar·range (dis'ə·rānj') *v.t.* **·ranged, ·rang·ing** To disturb the arrangement of; disorder. **— dis'ar·range'ment** *n.*

dis·ar·ray (dis'ə·rā') *n.* **1.** Lack of orderly arrangement, as of troops; disorder; confusion. **2.** Disorder of clothing. **—** *v.t.* **1.** To throw into disarray. **2.** *Archaic* To undress.

dis·ar·tic·u·late (dis'är·tik'yə·lāt) *v.* **·lat·ed, ·lat·ing** *v.t.* **1.** To separate the joints of; disjoint. **—** *v.i.* **2.** To become disjointed. **— dis'ar·tic'u·la'tion** *n.* **— dis'ar·tic'u·la'tor** *n.*

dis·as·sem·ble (dis'ə·sem'bəl) *v.t.* **·bled, ·bling** To take apart.

dis·as·sem·bly (dis'ə·sem'blē) *n.* The act of disassembling, or the state of being disassembled.

dis·as·so·ci·ate (dis'ə·sō'shē·āt) *v.t.* **·at·ed, ·at·ing** To dissociate. **— dis·as·so'ci·a'tion** *n.*

dis·as·ter (di·zas'tər, -zäs'-) *n.* **1.** An event causing great distress or ruin; sudden and crushing misfortune. **2.** *Obs.* The unfavorable aspect of a star or planet. [< MF *desastre < des-* away + *astre* a star < L *astrum* < Gk. *astron*]

—Syn. *Disaster, calamity, debacle, catastrophe,* and *cataclysm* refer to an event regarded as a great misfortune. A *disaster* is an accident or misadventure bringing great loss of life or property, as the great fire in Chicago in 1871. A *calamity* causes widespread distress, rather than loss of life, and is often a natural event, as a drought or great flood. Any large-scale breakdown, as of an army or a government, that results from inherent weakness is called a *debacle. Catastrophe* may refer to an unfortunate outcome or result: Inflamed nationalism hastened the *catastrophe* of war; or it may be used as a close synonym of *cataclysm,* a violent upheaval that brings profound changes. A volcanic eruption may be spoken of as a *catastrophe,* to stress its unhappy results, or as a *cataclysm,* to emphasize its violence and resultant geologic changes.

dis·as·trous (di·zas'trəs, -zäs'-) *adj.* **1.** Causing or accompanied by disaster; calamitous. **2.** *Archaic* Threatening disaster. **— dis·as'trous·ly** *adv.* **— dis·as'trous·ness** *n.*

dis·a·vow (dis'ə·vou') *v.t.* To disclaim responsibility for or approval of; refuse to acknowledge; repudiate. [< OF *desavouer < des-* away (< L *dis-*) + *avouer.* See AVOW.]

dis·a·vow·al (dis'ə·vou'əl) *n.* The act of disavowing or disowning; repudiation.

dis·band (dis·band') *v.t.* **1.** To break up the organization of; dissolve; especially, to break up (an army or similar unit) by dismissing the members from service. **—** *v.i.* **2.** To become disbanded. [< MF *desbander < des-* away (< L *dis-*) + *bander* to tie < *bande* a band] **— dis·band'ment** *n.*

dis·bar (dis·bär') *v.t.* **·barred, ·bar·ring** To expel officially from the legal profession; deprive of the right to practice law. **— dis·bar'ment** *n.*

dis·be·lief (dis'bi·lēf') *n.* Lack of belief. **— Syn.** See DOUBT.

dis·be·lieve (dis'bi·lēv') *v.t. & v.i.* **·lieved, ·liev·ing** To withhold belief (from); reject. **— dis'be·liev'er** *n.*

dis·bos·om (dis·bōoz'əm) *v.t. Archaic* To make known; confess.

dis·branch (dis·branch', -bränch') *v.t.* **1.** To deprive of branches, as a tree. **2.** To cut off, as a branch.

dis·bur·den (dis·bûr'dən) *v.t.* **1.** To relieve of a burden; unburden. **2.** To unload or get rid of (a burden). **—** *v.i.* **3.** To put off a load or burden. Also *Obs.* **dis·bur'then** (-thən). **— dis·bur'den·ment** *n.*

dis·burse (dis·bûrs') *v.t.* **·bursed, ·burs·ing** To pay out; expend. [< OF *desbourser < des-* away (< L *dis-*) + *bourse* a purse] **— dis·burs'a·ble** *adj.* **— dis·burs'er** *n.*

dis·burse·ment (dis·bûrs'mənt) *n.* **1.** The act of disbursing. **2.** That which is expended; money paid out.

disc (disk) *n.* **1.** See DISK. **2.** *Anat.* Any approximately flat, circular outgrowth, organ, or structure, as of cartilage between the joints of certain bones. [Var. of DISK]

disc. **1.** Discount. **2.** Discover(ed).

dis·calced (dis·kalst') *adj.* Barefooted, as certain orders of monks. Also **dis·cal·ce·ate** (dis·kal'sē·it, -āt). [< L *discalceatus < dis-* not + *calceatus* a shoe, orig. pp. of *calceare* to shoe]

dis·cant (dis'kant, dis·kant') See DESCANT.

dis·card (*v.* dis·kärd'; *n.* dis'kärd) *v.t.* **1.** To cast aside as useless or undesirable; reject; dismiss. **2.** In card games, to throw out (a card or cards) from one's hand; also, to play (a card, other than a trump, not of the suit led). **—** *v.i.* **3.** In card games, to throw out a card or cards. **—** *n.* **1.** The act of discarding, or the state of being discarded. **2.** A card or cards discarded. **3.** One who or that which is discarded.

dis·case (dis·kās') *v.t.* **·cased, ·cas·ing** To remove the case or covering of; unsheathe.

dis·cept (di·sept') *v.i. Archaic* To dispute or debate. [< L *disceptare < dis-* apart + *captare* to lay hold of, seize]

dis·cern (di·sûrn', di·zûrn') *v.t.* **1.** To perceive, as with sight or mind; recognize; apprehend. **2.** To recognize as separate and different; discriminate mentally. **—** *v.i.* **3.** To distinguish or discriminate something. [< OF *discerner* < L *discernere < dis-* apart + *cernere* to separate] **— dis·cern'er** *n.*

dis·cern·i·ble (di·sûr'nə·bəl, -zûr'-) *adj.* Capable of being discerned; perceptible. **— dis·cern'i·ble·ness** *n.* **— dis·cern'i·bly** *adv.*

dis·cern·ing (di·sûr'ning, -zûr'-) *adj.* Quick to discern; discriminating; penetrating. **— dis·cern'ing·ly** *adv.*

dis·cern·ment (di·sûrn'mənt, -zûrn'-) *n.* **1.** The act or process of discerning. **2.** The mental power of discerning; keenness of judgment; insight. **— Syn.** See SENSE.

dis·cerp·ti·ble (di·sûrp'tə·bəl) *adj.* Capable of being torn into parts; divisible. [< L *discerpere < dis-* apart + *carpere* to pluck, snatch]

dis·charge (dis·chärj'; *n. also* dis'chärj) *v.* **·charged, ·charg·ing** *v.t.* **1.** To remove the contents of; unload: to *discharge* a ship. **2.** To remove by unloading: to *discharge* cargo. **3.** To send forth; emit (fluid). **4.** To shoot or fire, as a gun, bow, shot, or arrow. **5.** To dismiss from office or employment. **6.** To release; set at liberty, as a prisoner or patient. **7.** To relieve of duty or obligation: to *discharge* a jury. **8.** To perform or fulfill the functions and duties of (a trust, office, etc.). **9.** To pay (a debt) or meet and satisfy (an obligation or duty). **10.** To set aside legally; annul. **11.** In dyeing, to remove (color) from textiles, as by chemical bleaching. **12.** *Electr.* To free of an electrical charge. **13.** *Archit.* **a** To receive and apportion, as the weight of a wall above a door. **b** To relieve (a part) from the weight of the wall above. **—** *v.i.* **14.** To get rid of a load, burden, etc. **15.** To go off, as a cannon. **16.** To give or send forth contents: The wound *discharges* constantly. **17.** To run or blur, as a dye. **18.** *Electr.* To lose a charge of electricity. **—** *n.* **1.** The act of removing a load or charge. **2.** The firing of a weapon or missile. **3.** An issuing forth; emission; ejection. **4.** The rate or amount of outflow. **5.** That which is discharged or released, as pus. **6.** A relieving or freeing from burden or obligation. **7.** The payment of a debt. **8.** Fulfillment; execution: the *discharge* of one's duty. **9.** Release or dismissal from service, employment, or custody. **10.** Something that releases or dismisses, as a certificate separating one from military service. **11.** An annulment or dismissal, as of a court order. **12.** *Electr.* **a** The equalization of difference of potential between terminals of a condenser or of a current source, when connected by a conductor, or placed in very near contact. **b** The removal of an electrostatic charge, as from a battery. [< OF *deschargier* < *des-* away (< L *dis-*) + *chargier*. See CHARGE.] **— dis·charge′a·ble** *adj.* **—dis.charg′er** *n.*

dis·ci·ple (di·sī′pəl) *n.* **1.** One who accepts and follows a teacher or a doctrine. **2.** One of the twelve chosen companions and apostles of Jesus Christ. **— Syn.** See ADHERENT. **—** *v.t.* **·pled, ·pling** *Archaic* To cause to become a disciple. [OE *discipul* < L *discipulus* < *discere* to learn; infl. in form by OF *deciple, disciple*] **— dis·ci′ple·ship** *n.*

Disciples of Christ A religious body organized in Pennsylvania in 1809 by Thomas and Alexander Campbell, seeking the unity of all Christians on the basis of the Bible alone, rejecting all creeds, and practicing baptism by immersion.

dis·ci·plin·a·ble (dis′ə·plin′ə·bəl) *adj.* **1.** Deserving or needing discipline. **2.** Capable of improvement by training.

dis·ci·pli·nal (dis′ə·plī′nəl, dis′ə·plin·əl) *adj.* Of, pertaining to, or of the nature of discipline.

dis·ci·plin·ant (dis′ə·plin·ənt) *n.* One who disciplines himself.

Dis·ci·plin·ant (dis′ə·plin·ənt) *n.* One of a former Spanish religious order whose members publicly scourged and otherwise tortured themselves.

dis·ci·pli·nar·i·an (dis′ə·plə·nâr′ē·ən) *n.* One who administers or advocates the maintenance of discipline. — *adj.* Disciplinary.

dis·ci·pli·nar·y (dis′ə·plə·ner′ē) *adj.* Of, relating to, or of the nature of discipline; used for discipline.

dis·ci·pline (dis′ə·plin) *n.* **1.** Training of the mental, moral, and physical powers by instruction, control, and exercise. **2.** The state or condition of orderly conduct, etc., resulting from such training. **3.** Systematic training in obedience to rules and authority, as in the armed forces. **4.** The state of order and control that results from subjection to rule and authority. **5.** Punishment or disciplinary action for the sake of training or correction; chastisement. **6.** Knowledge or training gained from misfortune, troubles, etc. **7.** A system of rules, or method of practice, as of a church. **8.** A branch of knowledge or instruction. **9.** A penitential instrument; a scourge. **— Syn.** See EDUCATION. **—** *v.t.* **·plined, ·plin·ing 1.** To train to obedience or subjection. **2.** To drill; educate. **3.** To punish. **— Syn.** See CHASTEN, TEACH. [< OF < L *disciplina* instruction < *discipulus*. See DISCIPLE.] **— dis′ci·plin·er** *n.*

disc jockey See DISK JOCKEY.

dis·claim (dis·klām′) *v.t.* **1.** To disavow any claim to, connection with, or responsibility for; disown. **2.** To reject or deny the claim or authority of. **3.** *Law* To renounce a right or claim to. **—** *v.i.* **4.** *Law* To renounce or repudiate a legal claim. [< AF *desclamer* < *des-* away (< L *dis-*) + *clamer* to claim < L *clamare* to declare]

dis·claim·er (dis·klā′mər) *n.* **1.** One who disclaims. **2.** A disclaiming act, notice, or instrument.

dis·cla·ma·tion (dis′klə·mā′shən) *n.* The act of disclaiming; a disavowal.

dis·close (dis·klōz′) *v.t.* **·closed, ·clos·ing 1.** To expose to view; lay bare; uncover. **2.** To make known; divulge. [< OF *desclos-,* stem of *desclore* < *des-* not (< L *dis-*) + *clore* to close < L *claudere*] **— dis·clos′er** *n.*

dis·clo·sure (dis·klō′zhər) *n.* **1.** The act or process of disclosing. **2.** That which is disclosed.

Dis·co (dis′kō) See DISKO.

dis·cob·o·lus (dis·kob′ə·ləs) *n. pl.* **·li** (-lī) A discus thrower. Also **dis·cob′o·los.** **— the Discobulus** A famous Greek statue of a discus thrower, attributed to Myron. [< L < Gk. *diskobolos* < *diskos* a discus + *ballein* to throw]

dis·cog·ra·phy (dis·kog′rə·fē) *n. pl.* **·phies** A systematic listing of phonograph records, giving titles, composers, performers, dates and places of issue, etc.

dis·coid (dis′koid) *adj.* **1.** Having the form of a disk. **2.** *Bot.* Disk-shaped; rayless, as the tubular central florets of a composite flower, such as the sunflower. Also **dis·coi′dal.** **—** *n.* A disk or disklike object. [< L *discoïdes* < Gk. *diskoeidēs* < *diskos* discus + *eidos* form]

dis·col·or (dis·kul′ər) *v.t.* **1.** To change or destroy the color of; stain. **—** *v.i.* **2.** To become discolored. Also *Brit.* **dis·col′our.** [< OF *descolorer* < *des-* away (< L *dis-*) + *colorer* to color < L *colorare* < *color* color]

dis·col·or·a·tion (dis·kul′ə·rā′shən) *n.* **1.** The act of discoloring, or the state of being discolored. **2.** A stain or discolored spot. Also **dis·col′or·ment.**

dis·com·bob·u·late (dis′kəm·bob′yə·lāt) *v.t.* **·lat·ed, ·lat·ing** *U.S. Slang* To throw into confusion; upset. Also **dis′com·bob′er·ate** (-ə·rāt). [Origin uncertain]

dis·com·fit (dis·kum′fit) *v.t.* **1.** To defeat the plans or purposes of; frustrate. **2.** To throw into confusion; disconcert. **3.** To rout in battle; vanquish. **— Syn.** See EMBARRASS. [< OF *desconfit,* pp. of *desconfire* to defeat < *des-* away (< L *dis-*) + *confire* to prepare < L *conficere.* See CONFECT.]

dis·com·fi·ture (dis·kum′fi·chər) *n.* The act of discomfiting, or the state of being discomfited; defeat; frustration.

dis·com·fort (dis·kum′fərt) *n.* **1.** Lack of ease or comfort; disquietude. **2.** That which interferes with comfort. **—** *v.t.* To make uneasy; distress. **— Syn.** See SUFFERING. [< OF *desconfort* < *desconforter* < *des-* away (< L *dis-*) + *conforter.* See COMFORT.]

dis·com·fort·a·ble (dis·kum′fər·tə·bəl) *adj.* **1.** *Rare* Uncomfortable. **2.** *Archaic* Producing discomfort.

discomfort index Temperature-humidity index (which see).

dis·com·mend (dis′kə·mend′) *v.t.* **1.** *Rare* To express disapproval of. **2.** *Obs.* To cause to be regarded unfavorably. **— dis′com·mend′a·ble** *adj.* **— dis′com·men·da′tion** *n.*

dis·com·mode (dis′kə·mōd′) *v.t.* **·mod·ed, ·mod·ing** To cause inconvenience to; trouble; disturb. [< DIS-¹ + L *commodus* fit, suitable, convenient]

dis·com·mod·i·ty (dis′kə·mod′ə·tē) *n. pl.* **·ties 1.** Inconvenience. **2.** That which causes inconvenience.

dis·com·mon (dis·kom′ən) *v.t.* **1.** *Law* To change from the condition of a common, as land; make private property of. **2.** To take away privileges from; especially, in some English universities, to deprive (a tradesman) of the privilege of dealing with students.

dis·com·pose (dis′kəm·pōz′) *v.t.* **·posed, ·pos·ing 1.** To disturb the composure of; make uneasy. **2.** To disorder or disarrange. **— dis′com·pos′ed·ly** *adv.* **— dis′com·pos′ing·ly** *adv.*

dis·com·po·sure (dis′kəm·pō′zhər) *n.* The state of being discomposed; agitation; perturbation.

dis·con·cert (dis′kən·sûrt′) *v.t.* **1.** To disturb the self-possession or composure of; confuse; upset. **2.** To throw into confusion; frustrate, as a plan. **— Syn.** See EMBARRASS. [< MF *desconcerter* < *dis-* apart + *concerter* to agree] **— dis′con·cert′ing·ly** *adv.* **— dis′con·cer′tion** *n.*

dis·con·cert·ed (dis′kən·sûr′tid) *adj.* Confused; perturbed; discomposed. **— dis′con·cert′ed·ly** *adv.* **— dis′con·cert′ed·ness** *n.*

dis·con·form·i·ty (dis′kən·fôr′mə·tē) *n. pl.* **·ties 1.** Lack of conformity; nonconformity. **2.** *Geol.* A type of unconformity in which the discontinuity is between rock strata lying parallel to each other.

dis·con·nect (dis′kə·nekt′) *v.t.* To break the connection of or between. **— dis′con·nec′tion** *n.*

dis·con·nect·ed (dis′kə·nek′tid) *adj.* **1.** Not connected; disjointed. **2.** Incoherent; rambling. **— dis′con·nect′ed·ly** *adv.* **— dis′con·nect′ed·ness** *n.*

dis·con·sid·er (dis′kən·sid′ər) *v.t. Archaic* To lower in the estimation of others.

dis·con·so·late (dis·kon′sə·lit) *adj.* **1.** Destitute of consolation; inconsolable; dejected. **2.** Producing or marked by gloominess; cheerless; saddening: *disconsolate* days. [< Med.L *disconsolatus* < L *dis-* not + *consolatus,* pp. of *consolari* to cheer, console. See CONSOLE¹.] **— dis·con′so·late·ly** *adv.* **— dis·con′so·late·ness, dis′con·so·la′tion** *n.*

dis·con·tent (dis′kən·tent′) *adj.* Discontented. **—** *n.* Lack of contentment; dissatisfaction; uneasiness: also **dis′con·tent′ment.** **—** *v.t.* To make discontent.

dis·con·tent·ed (dis′kən·ten′tid) *adj.* Restless; uneasy in mind, as through frustration; dissatisfied. **— dis′con·tent′ed·ly** *adv.* **— dis′con·tent′ed·ness** *n.*

dis·con·tin·u·ance (dis′kən·tin′yōō·əns) *n.* **1.** The act of discontinuing, or the state of being discontinued; cessation. **2.** *Law* A plaintiff's interruption or termination of a suit either by written notice or failure to follow through.

dis·con·tin·u·a·tion (dis′kən·tin′yōō·ā′shən) *n.* Discontinuance (def. 1).

dis·con·tin·ue (dis′kən·tin′yōō) *v.* **·tin·ued, ·tin·u·ing** *v.t.* **1.** To break off or cease from; stop. **2.** To cease using, receiving, etc.: to *discontinue* a subscription. **3.** *Law* To bring about discontinuance of. **—** *v.i.* **4.** To come to an end; cease. **— Syn.** See CEASE. [< OF *discontinuer* < Med.L *discontinuare* < L *dis-* not + *continuare.* See CONTINUE.] **— dis′con·tin′u·er** *n.*

dis·con·ti·nu·i·ty (dis′kon·tə·nōō′ə·tē, -nyōō′-) *n. pl.* **·ties 1.** Lack of continuity. **2.** A gap or break.

dis·con·tin·u·ous (dis′kən·tin′yōō·əs) *adj.* Not continuous; characterized by interruptions or breaks. **— dis′con·tin′u·ous·ly** *adv.* **— dis′con·tin′u·ous·ness** *n.*

disc·o·phile (dis′kə·fīl) *n.* A collector or connoisseur of phonograph recordings. [< L *discus* disk + -PHILE]

dis·cord (*n.* dis′kôrd; *v.* dis·kôrd′) *n.* **1.** Lack of agreement or concord; contention; conflict; strife. **2.** A harsh or disagreeable mingling of noises; din. **3.** *Music* Dissonance. **—** *v.i.* To be out of accord or harmony; clash. [< OF *descord* < *descorder* to disagree < L *discordare* < *discors* at variance < *dis-* apart + *cor, cordis* heart]

dis·cor·dance (dis·kôr′dəns) *n.* **1.** An inharmonious condition or quality; disagreement; incongruity. **2.** Discord of sounds. Also **dis·cor′dan·cy.**

dis·cor·dant (dis·kôr′dənt) *adj.* **1.** Characterized by lack of agreement or concord; differing; clashing. **2.** Dissonant, harsh, or disagreeable in sound. [< OF *descordant*, ppr. of *descorder*. See DISCORD.] **— dis·cor′dant·ly** *adv.*

dis·co·thèque (dis·kə·tek′) *n.* A night club offering recorded music for dancing instead of music played by a band of live musicians. [< F, lit., record library]

dis·count (*v.* dis′kount, dis·kount′; *n.* dis′kount) *v.t.* **1.** To deduct (an indicated sum or percent) from the full amount that would otherwise be charged or owed. **2.** To buy or sell (a bill, note, or other negotiable paper), less the amount of interest to be accumulated before maturity. **3.** To lend money on (negotiable notes, etc., not immediately payable), deducting the interest. **4.** To reduce the cost or value of: to *discount* merchandise. **5.** To take little or no account of; attach little importance to, or wholly disregard: *Discount* what she says. **6.** To allow for exaggeration, prejudice, etc., in; accept with reservation: to *discount* stories of great heroism. **7.** To take into account in advance and so lessen the full intensity or effect of. — *v.i.* **8.** To lend money, deducting the interest beforehand. — *n.* **1.** A deduction of a particular sum or percent, as one made for immediate cash payment. **2.** The interest deducted beforehand in buying, selling, or lending money on negotiable notes, etc. **3.** The rate of interest so deducted: also **discount rate.** **4.** The act of discounting negotiable notes, etc. *Abbr. disc.* **— at a discount** Below the amount regularly charged; at less than face value. [< MF *descompte, desconte* < OF *descompter* < Med.L *discomputare* < L *dis-* away + *computare.* See COMPUTE.] **— dis′count·a·ble** *adj.* **— dis′count·er** *n.*

dis·coun·te·nance (dis·koun′tə·nəns) *v.t.* **·nanced, ·nanc· ing** **1.** To look upon with disfavor; disapprove of. **2.** To abash; disconcert. [< MF *descontenancer* < OF *des-* not (< L *dis-*) + *contenancer* to favor. See COUNTENANCE.]

discount house An establishment where merchandise is sold at a price lower than the common retail price.

dis·cour·age (dis·kûr′ij) *v.t.* **·aged, ·ag·ing** **1.** To weaken the courage or lessen the confidence of; dishearten. **2.** To deter or dissuade: with *from.* **3.** To obstruct; hinder: Malnutrition *discourages* growth. **4.** To attempt to repress or prevent by disapproval. [< OF *descoragier* < *des-* away (< L *dis-*) + *corage* courage] **— dis·cour′ag·er** *n.* **— dis· cour′ag·ing·ly** *adv.*

dis·cour·age·ment (dis·kûr′ij·mənt) *n.* **1.** The act of discouraging, or the state of being discouraged. **2.** That which discourages.

dis·course (*n.* dis′kôrs, -kōrs, dis·kôrs′, -kōrs′; *v.* dis·kôrs′, -kōrs′) *n.* **1.** Connected communication of thought; continuous expression or exchange of ideas; conversation; talk. **Direct discourse** is spoken or written language quoted exactly, as in *I will leave*; it is contrasted with **indirect discourse,** in which speech or writing is reported with change of person and tense, as in *He said he would leave.* **2.** A formal, extensive, oral or written treatment of a subject; a dissertation, treatise, sermon, etc. **3.** *Archaic* The process of reasoning; ratiocination. **— Syn.** See CONVERSATION, SPEECH. **— *v.* ·coursed, ·cours·ing** *v.i.* **1.** To set forth one's ideas concerning a subject: with *on* or *upon.* **2.** To converse; confer. — *v.t.* **3.** *Archaic* To discuss. **4.** *Archaic* To give forth (musical sounds). **— Syn.** See TALK. [< F *discours* < L *discursus* < *dis-* apart + *cursus* a running, pp. of *currere* to run] **— dis·cours′er** *n.*

dis·cour·te·ous (dis·kûr′tē·əs) *adj.* Impolite; rude. **— dis· cour′te·ous·ly** *adv.* **— dis·cour′te·ous·ness** *n.*

dis·cour·te·sy (dis·kûr′tə·sē) *n. pl.* **·sies** **1.** Lack of courtesy; rudeness. **2.** An act of discourtesy.

dis·cov·er (dis·kuv′ər) *v.t.* **1.** To be first to find, find out, come upon, or make known: to *discover* a comet. **2.** To find, find out, come upon, or notice for the first time: to *discover* the pleasure of reading. **3.** *Archaic* To act or speak so as to expose or betray, especially unwittingly. **4.** *Archaic* To reveal; disclose. *Abbr. disc.* [< OF *descovrir* < *des-* away (< L *dis-*) + *covrir.* See COVER.] **— dis·cov′er·a·ble** *adj.* **— dis·cov′er·er** *n.*

— Syn. 1. *Discover, find, ascertain, detect,* and *unearth* mean to see or learn something not previously known. We may *discover* by accident or design, but we *find* as a result of searching. To *ascertain* is to *discover* through close examination or measurement. We *detect* that which has been hidden; to *unearth* suggests the discovery of something after digging deeply into a subject.

dis·cov·ert (dis·kuv′ərt) *adj. Law* Having no husband; not covert: said of a widow, divorcée, or spinster. [< OF *descovert,* pp. of *descovrir.* See DISCOVER.]

dis·cov·er·y (dis·kuv′ər·ē) *n. pl.* **·er·ies** **1.** The act of discovering. **2.** Something discovered.

Discovery Day Columbus Day (which see).

Discovery Inlet An inlet of the Ross Sea in Antarctica.

dis·cred·it (dis·kred′it) *v.t.* **1.** To harm the credit or reputation of; bring into disrepute. **2.** To cause to be doubted, disbelieved, or distrusted. **3.** To refuse to believe (something asserted). — *n.* **1.** Lack or loss of credit, reputation, etc. **2.** Something that discredits. **3.** Doubt; distrust.

dis·cred·it·a·ble (dis·kred′it·ə·bəl) *adj.* Resulting in or causing discredit. **— dis·cred′it·a·bly** *adv.*

dis·creet (dis·krēt′) *adj.* Tactful and judicious, especially in

dealing with others; careful not to say or do the wrong thing; prudent; circumspect. [< OF *discret* < LL *discretus* learned, orig. pp. of L *discernere* to discern] **— dis·creet′ly** *adv.* **— dis·creet′ness** *n.*

dis·crep·an·cy (dis·krep′ən·sē) *n. pl.* **·cies** **1.** Lack of agreement or consistency, as between alleged facts; conflicting variation or divergence; contradiction. **2.** An instance of this. Also **dis·crep′ance.** **— Syn.** See DISPARITY.

dis·crep·ant (dis·krep′ənt) *adj.* Lacking agreement or consistency; conflicting. [< OF < L *discrepans, -antis* < *dis-* apart + *crepare* to creak, make a noise] **— dis·crep′ant·ly** *adv.*

dis·crete (dis·krēt′) *adj.* **1.** Disconnected from others; distinct or separate. **2.** Made up of distinct parts or separate units; discontinuous. [Var. of DISCREET] **— dis·crete′ly** *adv.* **— dis·crete′ness** *n.*

dis·cre·tion (dis·kresh′ən) *n.* **1.** The quality of being discreet; tactfulness; prudence. **2.** Freedom or power to make one's own judgments and decisions and to act as one sees fit. **— Syn.** See ADDRESS, SENSE. **— at one's discretion** According to one's own judgment; at will. [< OF < L *discretio, -onis* < *discernere* to discern]

dis·cre·tion·al (dis·kresh′ən·əl) *adj.* Discretionary. **— dis·cre′tion·al·ly** *adv.*

dis·cre·tion·ar·y (dis·kresh′ən·er′ē) *adj.* Left to or determined by one's discretion: *discretionary* powers. **— dis· cre′tion·ar′i·ly** *adv.*

dis·crim·i·nate (*v.* dis·krim′ə·nāt; *adj.* dis·krim′ə·nit) *v.* **·nat·ed, ·nat·ing** *v.i.* **1.** To act toward someone or something with partiality or prejudice: to *discriminate* against a minority; to *discriminate* in favor of one's friends. **2.** To draw a clear distinction; distinguish: to *discriminate* between good and evil. — *v.t.* **3.** To draw or constitute a clear distinction between: differentiate: to *discriminate* good and evil. **4.** To recognize as being different. — *adj.* Discriminating. [< L *discriminatus,* pp. of *discriminare* < *discrimen, -inis* distinction < *dis-* apart + *crimen* judgment] **— dis·crim′i· nate·ly** *adv.* **— dis·crim′i·na′tor** *n.*

— Syn. (verb) **2.** *Discriminate, differentiate,* and *distinguish* are here compared in the sense of noting a difference between or among things. *Discriminate* means to compare in one aspect, or in fine details of difference. *Differentiate* usually implies enumeration of many differences, while *distinguish* frequently means merely to note the different identities of objects. **3.** See CONTRAST.

dis·crim·i·nat·ing (dis·krim′ə·nā′ting) *adj.* **1.** Able to draw clear distinctions; discerning: a *discriminating* intellect. **2.** Fastidious; particular: *discriminating* in one's choice of friends. **3.** Serving to distinguish; individualizing; differentiating: a *discriminating* mark. **4.** Differential, as a tariff setting special rates in favor of the exports of certain countries. **— dis·crim′i·nat′ing·ly** *adv.*

dis·crim·i·na·tion (dis·krim′ə·nā′shən) *n.* **1.** The act of discriminating. **2.** The power or ability to perceive distinctions or differences; discernment. **3.** Prejudice or partiality in attitudes, actions, etc.: *discrimination* against minorities.

dis·crim·i·na·tive (dis·krim′ə·nā′tiv) *adj.* Discriminating. **— dis·crim′i·na′tive·ly** *adv.*

dis·crim·i·na·to·ry (dis·krim′ə·nə·tôr′ē, -tō′rē) *adj.* **1.** Characterized by or showing prejudice or bias: *discriminatory* practices. **2.** Making or capable of making distinctions; discriminating. **— dis·crim′i·na·to′ri·ly** *adv.*

dis·crown (dis·kroun′) *v.t.* To deprive of a crown; depose.

dis·cur·sive (dis·kûr′siv) *adj.* **1.** Passing quickly or disjointedly from one subject to another; wandering from the main point; digressive. **2.** Reaching conclusions through reasoning, as opposed to intuition. [< L *discursus.* See DISCOURSE.] **— dis·cur′sive·ly** *adv.* **— dis·cur′sive·ness** *n.*

dis·cus (dis′kəs) *n. pl.* **dis·cus·es** or **dis·ci** (dis′ī) **1.** A flat, heavy disk, as of metal or stone, hurled for distance in athletic contests. **2.** The act or contest of hurling this disk. [< L < Gk. *diskos*]

dis·cuss (dis·kus′) *v.t.* **1.** To have as the subject of conversation or writing; treat or consider formally. **2.** In civil law, to exhaust proceedings against (a principal debtor) before proceeding against the surety or sureties. **3.** *Rare* To consume (food or drink). **4.** *Obs.* To cause to be known; reveal. **— Syn.** See ARGUE. [< L *discussus,* pp. of *discutere* to discuss < *dis-* apart + *quatere* to shake] **— dis·cuss′er** *n.* **— dis·cuss′i·ble** *adj.*

dis·cuss·ant (dis·kus′ənt) *n.* One who takes part in a discussion; a participant in a symposium.

dis·cus·sion (dis·kush′ən) *n.* The act of discussing; examination or consideration of a subject in speech or writing. [< OF < LL *discussio, -onis* < L *discutere.* See DISCUSS.]

dis·dain (dis·dān′) *v.t.* **1.** To consider unworthy of one's regard or notice; treat with contempt or scorn: to *disdain* a coward. **2.** To consider unworthy of one's position or character; refuse scornfully: to *disdain* to beg for food. — *n.* A feeling or attitude of superiority and dislike; proud contempt. **— Syn.** See SCORN. [< OF *desdeignier* < L *dedignare* < *dis-* away + *dignare* to design. See DEIGN.]

dis·dain·ful (dis·dān′fəl) *adj.* Filled with or expressing disdain; scornful. **— Syn.** See ARROGANT. **— dis·dain′ful·ly** *adv.* **— dis·dain′ful·ness** *n.*

dis·ease (di·zēz′) *n.* **1.** A condition of ill health or malfunctioning in a living organism; especially, a disordered physical condition or process having particular symptoms, and affecting the whole or a part of an animal or plant. **2.** Any disordered or unwholesome condition. **3.** In Christian Science, the effect of error made manifest on the body. — *v.t.* **·eased**, **·eas·ing** To cause disease in; derange by or as by infecting; make unhealthy; cause to malfunction. [< AF, OF *desaise* < *des-* away (< L *dis-*) + *aise*. See EASE.]
— **Syn. 1.** *Disease, malady, ailment, complaint, disorder,* and *affection* denote an abnormal, often painful or distressing, physical condition. A *disease* is any of the abnormal conditions that may afflict humans, animals, or plants. *Malady* is chiefly applied to chronic or deep-seated human *diseases.* An *ailment* or *complaint* causes distress, but may not be serious. *Disorder* and *affection* are applied to mildly abnormal conditions. Compare SICK.

dis·eased (di·zēzd′) *adj.* **1.** Affected with an illness or disorder, especially a chronic one. **2.** Deranged; disturbed: a *diseased* mind.

dis·em·bark (dis′em·bärk′) *v.t.* & *v.i.* To put or go ashore from a ship; land; unload. [< MF *desembarquer* < *des-* away (< L *dis-*) + *embarquer*. See EMBARK.] — **dis·em′·bar·ka′tion** *n.*

dis·em·bar·rass (dis′em·bar′əs) *v.t.* To free from embarrassment, entanglement, etc. — **dis′em·bar′rass·ment** *n.*

dis·em·bod·y (dis′em·bod′ē) *v.t.* **·bod·ied**, **·bod·y·ing** To free from the body or from physical existence: a *disembodied* spirit. — **dis′em·bod′i·ment** *n.*

dis·em·bogue (dis′em·bōg′) *v.t.* & *v.i.* **·bogued**, **·bo·guing** To pour out or discharge (waters) at the mouth; empty: said of rivers, streams, etc. [< Sp. *desembocar* < *des-* not (< L *dis-*) + *embocar* to put into the mouth < L *in-* in + *bucca* cheeks, mouth] — **dis′em·bogue′ment** *n.*

dis·em·bos·om (dis′em·bo͝oz′əm) *v.t.* **1.** To reveal (a secret). **2.** To unburden (oneself) of a secret.

dis·em·bow·el (dis′em·bou′əl, -boul′) *v.t.* **·bow·eled** or **·elled**, **·bow·el·ing** or **·el·ling** To take out the bowels or entrails of; eviscerate. — **dis′em·bow′el·ment** *n.*

dis·en·a·ble (dis′en·ā′bəl) *v.t.* **·bled**, **·bling** To make unfit; disable.

dis·en·chant (dis′en·chant′, -chänt′) *v.t.* To free from enchantment; disillusion. [< OF *desenchanter* < *des-* not (< L *dis-*) + *enchanter*. See ENCHANT.] — **dis′en·chant′er** *n.* — **dis′en·chant′ment** *n.*

dis·en·cum·ber (dis′en·kum′bər) *v.t.* To free from encumbrance. [< OF *desencombre, desencombrer* < *des-* away (< L *dis-*) + *encombre*. See ENCUMBER.]

dis·en·dow (dis′en·dou′) *v.t.* To take away an endowment from. — **dis′en·dow′er** *n.* — **dis′en·dow′ment** *n.*

dis·en·fran·chise (dis′en·fran′chīz) *v.t.* **·chised**, **·chis·ing** To disfranchise (which see). — **dis′en·fran′chise·ment** (-chīz·mənt, -chīz-) *n.*

dis·en·gage (dis′en·gāj′) *v.* **·gaged**, **·gag·ing** *v.t.* **1.** To break the connection or attachment of; set free; detach. **2.** To free from entanglement, obligation, occupation, etc. — *v.i.* **3.** To free oneself; get loose.

dis·en·gage·ment (dis′en·gāj′mənt) *n.* **1.** The act of disengaging, or the state of being disengaged. **2.** Freedom from toil or care; leisure; ease.

dis·en·tail (dis′en·tāl′) *v.t. Law* To free from or break the entail of, as an estate. — **dis′en·tail′ment** *n.*

dis·en·tan·gle (dis′en·tang′gəl) *v.* **·gled**, **·gling** *v.t.* **1.** To free or relieve of entanglement, perplexity, confusion, etc.; untangle. — *v.i.* **2.** To become disentangled. — **dis′en·tan′gle·ment** *n.*

dis·en·thrall (dis′en·thrôl′) *v.t.* **·thralled**, **·thrall·ing** To release from thralldom or bondage; set free. Also **dis′en·thral′.** — **dis′en·thrall′ment** or **dis′en·thral′ment** *n.*

dis·en·throne (dis′en·thrōn′) *v.t.* **·throned**, **·thron·ing** To dethrone; depose. — **dis′en·throne′ment** *n.*

dis·en·ti·tle (dis′en·tīt′l) *v.t.* **·tled**, **·tling** To deprive of title, right, or claim.

dis·en·tomb (dis′en·to͞om′) *v.t.* To take from or as from a tomb. — **dis′en·tomb′ment** *n.*

dis·en·trance (dis′en·trans′, -träns′) *v.t.* **·tranced**, **·tranc·ing** To arouse from a trance. — **dis′en·trance′ment** *n.*

dis·en·twine (dis′en·twīn′) *v.t.* & *v.i.* **·twined**, **·twin·ing** To untwine; disentangle.

di·sep·a·lous (dī·sep′ə·ləs) *adj. Bot.* Having two sepals. [< DI-² + SEPALOUS]

dis·es·tab·lish (dis′es·tab′lish) *v.t.* **1.** To deprive of fixed or established status or character. **2.** To take away government support from (a state church). — **dis′es·tab′lish·ment** *n.*

dis·es·teem (dis′es·tēm′) *v.t.* To regard with little esteem; have a low opinion of. — *n.* Lack of esteem.

di·seuse (dē·zœz′) *n. French* A woman entertainer who performs dramatic impersonations, monologues, etc.

dis·fa·vor (dis·fā′vər) *n.* **1.** Lack of favor; disapproval; dislike. **2.** The state of being frowned upon, disliked, or opposed. **3.** *Archaic* An unkind act. — *v.t.* To treat or regard without favor; oppose. Also *Brit.* **dis·fa′vour.**

dis·fea·ture (dis·fē′chər) *v.t.* **·tured**, **·tur·ing** To mar the features of; disfigure; deface.

dis·fig·ure (dis·fig′yər) *v.t.* **·ured**, **·ur·ing** To mar or destroy the appearance or form of; make unsightly; deform. [< OF *desfigurer* < *des-* away (< L *dis-*) + *figurer* < L *figurare* to form, fashion < *figura* a shape] — **dis·fig′ur·er** *n.*

dis·fig·ure·ment (dis·fig′yər·mənt) *n.* **1.** The act of disfiguring or the state of being disfigured. **2.** That which disfigures; a deformity or blemish. Also **dis·fig′u·ra′tion.**

dis·for·est (dis·fôr′ist, -for′-) *v.t.* **1.** To clear of forest; deforest. **2.** *Brit. Law* To disafforest. — **dis·for′es·ta′tion** *n.*

dis·fran·chise (dis·fran′chīz) *v.t.* **·chised**, **·chis·ing** **1.** To deprive (a citizen) of a right or privilege, especially of the ballot. **2.** To deprive of a franchise, privilege, or right, as a corporation. Also *disenfranchise.* — **dis·fran′chise·ment** (-chīz·mənt, -chīz-) *n.* — **dis·fran′chis·er** *n.*

dis·frock (dis·frok′) *v.t.* To unfrock (which see).

dis·fur·nish (dis·fûr′nish) *v.t. Archaic* To strip of furnishings or belongings. [< OF *desfourniss-*, stem of *desfournir* < *des-* away (< L *dis-*) + *fournir*. See FURNISH.] — **dis·fur′nish·ment** *n.*

dis·gorge (dis·gôrj′) *v.t.* **·gorged**, **·gorg·ing** **1.** To throw out, as from the throat or stomach; eject; vomit. **2.** To give up unwillingly. **3.** To empty (oneself) of something. — *v.i.* **4.** To disgorge something. [< OF *desgorger* < *des-* from (< L *dis-*) + *gorge* throat]

dis·grace (dis·grās′) *n.* **1.** A condition of shame, dishonor, or infamy; ignominy. **2.** Anything that brings about dishonor or shame. **3.** A state of being out of favor: in *disgrace* at court. — *v.t.* **·graced**, **·grac·ing** **1.** To bring reproach or shame upon. **2.** To dismiss from favor; treat with dishonor. [< MF *disgracier* < Ital. *disgraziare* < *disgrazia* < *dis-* away (< L *dis-*) + *grazia* < L *gratia* favor] — **dis·grac′er** *n.*

dis·grace·ful (dis·grās′fəl) *adj.* Characterized by or causing disgrace; shameful; disreputable. — **dis·grace′ful·ly** *adv.* — **dis·grace′ful·ness** *n.*

dis·grun·tle (dis·grun′təl) *v.t.* **·tled**, **·tling** To make dissatisfied or sulky; put out of humor.

dis·guise (dis·gīz′) *v.t.* **·guised**, **·guis·ing** **1.** To alter the appearance of so as to make recognition difficult or impossible; conceal the identity of: to *disguise* one's voice. **2.** To conceal or obscure the actual nature of by false representation: to *disguise* the facts. — *n.* **1.** The act of disguising or the state of being disguised. **2.** Something that disguises, as a mask or costume. [< OF *desguisier* < *des-* down (< L *de-*) + *guise*. See GUISE.] — **dis·guis′er** *n.*

dis·gust (dis·gust′) *v.t.* **1.** To affect with nausea or loathing. **2.** To offend the sensibilities, moral values, or good taste of; sicken. — *n.* Strong aversion aroused by something offensive. — **Syn.** See ABHORRENCE. [< MF *desgouster* < *des-* not (< L *dis-*) + *gouster* to taste < L *gustare*]

dis·gust·ed (dis·gus′tid) *adj.* Affected with disgust. — **dis·gust′ed·ly** *adv.* — **dis·gust′ed·ness** *n.*

dis·gust·ful (dis·gust′fəl) *adj.* Disgusting. — **dis·gust′ful·ly** *adv.* — **dis·gust′ful·ness** *n.*

dis·gust·ing (dis·gus′ting) *adj.* Provoking disgust; repugnant; revolting; offensive. — **dis·gust′ing·ly** *adv.*

dish (dish) *n.* **1.** An open, concave, usually shallow container, as of earthenware or glass, typically used for holding or serving food. **2.** Something contained or served in a dish. **3.** A particular kind or preparation of food: a delicious *dish.* **4.** The amount contained or served in a dish; dishful. **5.** Anything resembling a dish in shape or function. **6.** A hollow or depression like that in a dish. **7.** *Informal* Anything one particularly enjoys or does with ease. **8.** *Slang* An attractive woman or girl. — *v.t.* **1.** To put (food, etc.) into a dish; serve: usually with *up* or *out.* **2.** To hollow out (a surface). **3.** *Brit. Slang* To cheat or ruin. — **to dish it out** *Slang* **1.** To administer severe punishment or reproof. **2.** To talk glibly. [OE *disc* < L *discus.* Doublet of DAIS, DESK, DISK.] — **dish′like′** *adj.*

dis·ha·bille (dis′ə·bēl′) *n.* **1.** A state of being partially or negligently dressed. **2.** The garments worn in this state. Also *deshabille.* [< F *déshabillé*, pp. of *deshabiller* to undress < *des-* away (< L *dis-*) + *habiller* to dress]

dis·ha·bit·u·ate (dis′hə·bich′o͞o·āt) *v.t.* **·at·ed**, **·at·ing** *Rare* To make unaccustomed.

dis·hal·low (dis·hal′ō) *v.t.* To profane; desecrate.

dis·har·mo·ni·ous (dis′här·mō′nē·əs) *adj.* Not harmonious; discordant. — **dis·har·mo′ni·ous·ly** *adv.*

dis·har·mo·nize (dis·här′mə·nīz) *v.t.* & *v.i.* **·nized**, **·niz·ing** To make or be inharmonious.

dis·har·mo·ny (dis·här′mə·nē) *n. pl.* **·nies** Lack of harmony or agreement; discord.

dish·cloth (dish′klôth′, -kloth′) *n.* A cloth used in washing dishes: also called *dishrag.*

dishcloth gourd A loofah.

dish·clout (dish′klout′) *n. Archaic* A dishcloth.

dis·heart·en (dis·här′tən) *v.t.* To weaken the spirit or courage of; discourage. — **dis·heart′en·ing·ly** *adv.* — **dis·heart′en·ment** *n.*

dished (disht) *adj.* **1.** Of wheels, having the rim slanted inward or outward with reference to the hub. **2.** *Slang* Worn out; exhausted.

dis·helm (dis·helm′) *v.t. Poetic* **1.** To deprive of the helm, as of a ship. **2.** To remove the helmet from.

dis·her·it (dis·her′it) *v.t. Archaic* To disinherit. [< OF *desheriter* < LL *dis-* away + *heriditare* to inherit < L *heres, heredis* heir]

di·shev·el (di·shev′əl) *v.t.* **di·shev·eled** or **·elled**, **di·shev·el·ing** or **·el·ling 1.** To muss up, disarrange, or rumple (the hair or clothing). **2.** To disorder the hair or clothing of. [< MF *descheveler* < *des-* away (< L *dis-*) + *chevel* hair < L *capillus*] — **di·shev′el·ment** *n.*

di·shev·eled (di·shev′əld) *adj.* **1.** Tousled or rumpled. **2.** Untidy; unkempt. Also **di·shev′elled.**

dish·ful (dish′fŏŏl′) *n.* As much as a dish holds.

dis·hon·est (dis·on′ist) *adj.* **1.** Not honest; given to lying, cheating, or stealing. **2.** Showing or marked by a lack of honesty: a *dishonest* act. [< OF *deshoneste* < LL *dis-* away + *honestus* honest] — **dis·hon′est·ly** *adv.*

dis·hon·es·ty (dis·on′is·tē) *n. pl.* **·ties 1.** Lack of honesty or integrity. **2.** A dishonest act or statement.

dis·hon·or (dis·on′ər) *v.t.* **1.** To deprive of honor; disgrace; insult. **2.** To decline or fail to pay, as a note. — *n.* **1.** Lack or loss of honor or of honorable character. **2.** That which causes a loss of honor; an insult, indignity, taint, etc. **3.** Refusal or failure to pay a note, etc., when due. Also *Brit.* **dis·hon′our.** [< OF *deshonnorer* < L *dis-* away + *honor*. See HONOR.] — **dis·hon′or·er** *n.*

dis·hon·or·a·ble (dis·on′ər·ə·bəl) *adj.* **1.** Characterized by or bringing dishonor or reproach; discreditable: a *dishonorable* act. **2.** Lacking honor or honorableness: a *dishonorable* lawyer. — **dis·hon′or·a·ble·ness** *n.* — **dis·hon′or·a·bly** *adv.*

dish·pan (dish′pan′) *n.* A pan for washing dishes.

dish·rag (dish′rag′) *n.* A dishcloth.

dish·tow·el (dish′tou′əl) *n. U.S.* A towel for drying dishes.

dish·wash·er (dish′wôsh′ər, -wosh′-) *n.* **1.** A machine that washes dishes. **2.** A person who washes dishes.

dish·wa·ter (dish′wô′tər, -wot′-) *n.* Water in which dishes and kitchen utensils have been washed.

dis·il·lu·sion (dis′i·lōō′zhən) *v.t.* To free from illusion; disenchant. Also **dis′il·lu′sion·ize.** — *n.* The state or process of being disillusioned.

dis·il·lu·sion·ment (dis′i·lōō′zhən·mənt) *n.* The act of disillusioning, or the state of being disillusioned.

dis·il·lu·sive (dis′i·lōō′siv) *adj.* Tending to dispel illusion.

dis·im·pas·sioned (dis′im·pash′ənd) *adj.* Free from the influence of passion; dispassionate; tranquil.

dis·im·pris·on (dis′im·priz′ən) *v.t.* To free from imprisonment. — **dis·im·pris′on·ment** *n.*

dis·in·cli·na·tion (dis·in′klə·nā′shən) *n.* Distaste; aversion; unwillingness.

dis·in·cline (dis′in·klīn′) *v.t. & v.i.* **·clined, ·clin·ing** To make or be unwilling or averse.

dis·in·fect (dis′in·fekt′) *v.t.* To cleanse (a room, clothing, etc.) of disease germs; sterilize. — **dis·in·fec′tor** *n.*

dis·in·fec·tant (dis′in·fek′tənt) *n.* A substance or agent used to disinfect. — *adj.* Capable of disinfecting.

dis·in·fec·tion (dis′in·fek′shən) *n.* The act of disinfecting.

dis·in·fla·tion (dis′in·flā′shən) *n. Econ.* The planned reduction or leveling off of prices in an economy in order to maintain purchasing power and avoid deflation. Compare DEFLATION.

dis·in·gen·u·ous (dis′in·jen′yōō·əs) *adj.* Lacking simplicity, frankness, or sincerity; not straightforward; crafty. — **dis′in·gen′u·ous·ly** *adv.* — **dis′in·gen′u·ous·ness** *n.*

dis·in·her·it (dis′in·her′it) *v.t.* To deprive of an inheritance or of a hereditary right, as by disowning.

dis·in·her·i·tance (dis′in·her′ə·təns) *n.* The act of disinheriting, or the state of being disinherited.

dis·in·te·grate (dis·in′tə·grāt′) *v.* **·grat·ed, ·grat·ing** *v.t.* **1.** To break or reduce into component parts or particles; destroy the wholeness of. — *v.i.* **2.** To become reduced to fragments or particles; crumble. — **Syn.** See DECAY. — **dis·in′te·gra·ble** (-grə·bəl) *adj.* — **dis·in′te·gra′tor** *n.*

dis·in·te·gra·tion (dis·in′tə·grā′shən) *n.* **1.** The act of disintegrating, or the state of being disintegrated; a breaking up into fragments or particles, as of rocks under the action of rain or frost. **2.** *Physics* The breakdown of the atoms of a radioactive element or isotope through the emission of nucleons, with corresponding changes in atomic structure.

dis·in·ter (dis′in·tûr′) *v.t.* **·terred, ·ter·ring 1.** To dig up, as from a grave; exhume. **2.** To bring to light or life as if from a grave. [< MF *désenterrer* < *des-* away + *enterrer*. See INTER.] — **dis′in·ter′ment** *n.*

dis·in·ter·est (dis·in′tər·ist, -trist) *n.* **1.** Freedom from self-seeking and personal bias; impartiality. **2.** Lack of interest; indifference. — *v.t.* To rid of private interest.

dis·in·ter·est·ed (dis·in′tər·is·tid, -tris·tid, -tə·res′tid) *adj.* **1.** Free from self-seeking and personal bias; impartial and objective. **2.** Loosely, not interested; uninterested. — **dis·in′ter·est·ed·ly** *adv.* — **dis·in′ter·est·ed·ness** *n.*

◆ A person is *disinterested* if he does not stand to profit by the way he acts in a particular instance: *disinterested* advice; a *disinterested* bystander. A person is *uninterested* if he is simply without interest, as from boredom or indifference. Both words may in some contexts suggest aloofness or detachment, but the aloofness of a *disinterested* person does not stem from lack of interest but from the desire to be impartial or objective.

dis·ject (dis·jekt′) *v.t.* To split apart forcibly; break asunder; scatter about. [< L *disjectus*, pp. of *disjicere* < *dis-* apart + *jacere* to throw]

dis·jec·ta mem·bra (dis·jek′tə mem′brə) *Latin* Scattered fragments or parts, especially of literary quotations.

dis·join (dis·join′) *v.t.* **1.** To undo or prevent the joining of; separate. — *v.i.* **2.** To become divided or separated. [< OF *desjoindre* < *des-* not (< L *dis-*) + *joindre*. See JOIN.]

dis·joint (dis·joint′) *v.t.* **1.** To take apart at the joints; dismember. **2.** To put out of joint; dislocate. **3.** To separate forcibly; disunite. **4.** To upset or destroy the coherence, connection, or sequence of. — *v.i.* **5.** To come apart at the joints; fall apart. **6.** To get out of joint. — *adj. Obs.* Disjointed. [< OF *desjoint*, pp. of *desjoindre*. See DISJOIN.]

dis·joint·ed (dis·join′tid) *adj.* **1.** Taken apart at the joints: a *disjointed* fowl. **2.** Dislocated: a *disjointed* knee. **3.** Lacking coherence or orderliness; rambling and incoherent: a *disjointed* lecture. — **dis·joint′ed·ly** *adv.* — **dis·joint′ed·ness** *n.*

dis·junct (dis·jungkt′) *adj.* **1.** Not connected; detached. **2.** *Entomol.* Having the head, thorax, and abdomen separated by constrictions. [< L *disjunctus*, pp. of *disjungere* < *dis-* not + *jungere* to join]

dis·junc·tion (dis·jungk′shən) *n.* **1.** The act of disjoining, or the state of being disjointed; separation. Also **dis·junc′ture** (-chər). **2.** *Biol.* The moving apart of each pair of homologous chromosomes during the anaphase of cell mitosis. **3.** *Logic* A disjunctive proposition, or the relation of its terms to each other.

dis·junc·tive (dis·jungk′tiv) *adj.* **1.** Serving to disconnect or separate; dividing. **2.** *Gram.* Indicating alternation or opposition, as *either* or *in* either *you* or I. **3.** *Logic* Involving choice between two or more predicates in a proposition. — *n.* **1.** That which disjoins. **2.** *Gram.* A disjunctive conjunction. **3.** *Logic* A disjunctive proposition. — **dis·junc′tive·ly** *adv.*

disk (disk) *n.* **1.** A fairly flat, circular plate. **2.** *Biol.* A disc. **3.** *Bot.* The center of a flower head in certain composite plants, as in the daisy or sunflower. **4.** A phonograph record. **5.** A discus. **6.** *Astron.* The figure of a heavenly body as it appears to the naked eye. — *v.t. & v.i.* To break up or plow (land) with a disk harrow. Also, *esp. Brit., disc.* [< L *discus* < Gk. *diskos* disk, platter. Doublet of DAIS, DESK, DISH.]

disk harrow A harrow consisting of a series of rolling, saucer-shaped disks set on edge and at an angle along one or more axles, used for pulverizing the soil, covering seeds, etc.

DISK HARROW

disk jockey *U.S. Informal* An announcer and commentator on a radio program presenting recorded music.

Dis·ko (dis′kō) An island of Denmark in Davis Strait near Greenland; 3,312 sq. mi.: also *Disco.*

disk wheel A wheel having a solid outer surface from hub to rim, used on many automobiles.

dis·like (dis·līk′) *v.t.* **·liked, ·lik·ing** To regard with aversion; feel repugnance for; consider disagreeable. — *n.* A feeling of repugnance or distaste. — **dis·lik′a·ble** *adj.*

dis·limn (dis·lim′) *v.t. Poetic* To obliterate the outlines of; efface (a picture, etc.).

dis·lo·cate (dis′lō·kāt, dis·lō′kāt) *v.t.* **·cat·ed, ·cat·ing 1.** To put out of proper place or order; displace; disarrange. **2.** *Med.* To displace an organ or part, especially a bone from a joint. [< Med.L *dislocatus*, pp. of *dislocare* < *dis-* away + *locare* to set, place < *locus* a place] — **dis·lo·ca′tion** *n.*

dis·lodge (dis·loj′) *v.* **lodged, lodg·ing** *v.t.* **1.** To remove or drive out, as from an abode, hiding place, or firm position. — *v.i.* **2.** To leave a place of abode; move. — **Syn.** See EXPEL. [< OF *desloger, deslogier* < *dis-* away + *loger*. See LODGE.] — **dis·lodg′ment** or **dis·lodge′ment** *n.*

dis·loy·al (dis·loi′əl) *adj.* Not loyal; false to one's allegiance or obligations; faithless. — **Syn.** See PERFIDIOUS. [< OF *desloial* < *des-* not (< L *dis-*) + *loial.* See LOYAL.] — **dis·loy′al·ly** *adv.*

dis·loy·al·ty (dis·loi′əl·tē) *n. pl.* **·ties 1.** The quality of being disloyal; unfaithfulness. **2.** A disloyal action.

dis·mal (diz′məl) *adj.* **1.** Cheerless and depressing; dark and gloomy: a *dismal* day. **2.** Devoid of joy; bleak: to feel *dismal.* **3.** Disastrously bad; calamitous: a *dismal* failure. **4.** *Obs.* Ill-fated; unlucky. — *n.* **1.** *pl. Rare* Low spirits; the blues. **2.** *Southern U.S.* A tract of swampy land. [ult. < L *dies mali* evil or unpropitious days] — **dis′mal·ly** *adv.* — **dis′mal·ness** *n.*

— **Syn. 1.** somber. **2.** mournful, depressed. **3.** catastrophic.

Dismal Swamp A coastal swamp in SE Virginia and NE North Carolina; about 20 miles long.

dis·man·tle (dis·man′təl) *v.t.* ·tled, ·tling 1. To strip of furniture or equipment. 2. To raze. 3. To disassemble. [< MF *desmanteller* < *des*- away + *manteller* to cover with a cloak < *mantel* a cloak] — **dis·man′tle·ment** *n.*

dis·mast (dis·mast′, -mäst′) *v.t. Naut.* To deprive of masts; break off the masts of.

dis·may (dis·mā′) *v.t.* 1. To fill with consternation or apprehension; petrify with uneasiness; appall. 2. To make downhearted or greatly troubled; dishearten and depress. — **Syn.** See INTIMIDATE. — *n.* An onrush of consternation or downheartedness. — **Syn.** See ALARM. [ME *dismayen*, prob. < OF < Gmc.]

dis·mem·ber (dis·mem′bər) *v.t.* 1. To cut off or pull off the limbs or members of. 2. To divide forcibly into pieces. 3. To partition, as an empire. [< OF *desmembrer* < L *dis*- apart + *membrum* limb, member] — **dis·mem′ber·ment** *n.*

dis·miss (dis·mis′) *v.t.* 1. To discharge, as from a job. 2. To tell or allow to go or disperse. 3. To get rid of: to *dismiss* all fear. 4. To reject; repudiate: to *dismiss* the whole idea. 5. To cease consideration or treatment of; drop. 6. To have done with quickly: He *dismissed* the matter in a few words. 7. *Law* To put out of court without further hearing: The case was *dismissed*. — **Syn.** See EXPEL. [< LL *dismissus* < L *dimissus*, pp. of *dimittere* to send away]

dis·miss·al (dis·mis′əl) *n.* 1. The act of dismissing, or the state of being dismissed. 2. A notice of discharge.

dis·miss·i·ble (dis·mis′ə·bəl) *adj.* Subject to discharge.

dis·mount (dis·mount′) *v.i.* 1. To get off, as from a horse; alight. — *v.t.* 2. To remove from a setting, support, etc. 3. To disassemble. 4. To knock off or throw down, as from a horse; unseat. — **dis·mount′a·ble** *adj.*

dis·na·ture (dis·nā′chər) *v.t.* ·tured, ·tur·ing To deprive of natural character or quality. [< OF *desnaturer* < L *dis*- away + *natura* nature]

Dis·ney (diz′nē), **Walt(er Elias)**, 1901–1966, U.S. motion-picture producer; famous for animated cartoons.

Dis·ney·land (diz′nē·land′) 1. A large amusement center created by Walt Disney at Anaheim, Calif. 2. Any place or situation that is characterized by fantasy.

dis·o·be·di·ence (dis′ə·bē′dē·əns) *n.* Refusal or failure to obey; lack of obedience; insubordination.

dis·o·be·di·ent (dis′ə·bē′dē·ənt) *adj.* Not obedient; refusing or failing to obey; refractory; insubordinate. [< OF *desobedient* < L *dis*- not + *obediens*, *-entis*. See OBEDIENT.] — **dis′o·be′di·ent·ly** *adv.*

dis·o·bey (dis′ə·bā′) *v.t. & v.i.* To refuse or fail to obey. [< OF *desobeir* < L *dis*- not + L *obedire*. See OBEY.] — **dis′o·bey′er** *n.*

dis·o·blige (dis′ə·blīj′) *v.t.* ·bliged, ·blig·ing 1. To act contrary to the wishes of. 2. To slight. 3. *Dial.* To inconvenience. [< OF *desobliger* < L *dis*- not + *obligare*. See OBLIGE.]

dis·o·blig·ing (dis′ə·blī′jing) *adj.* Not disposed to oblige; unaccommodating. — **dis′o·blig′ing·ly** *adv.*

dis·or·der (dis·ôr′dər) *n.* 1. Lack of good order; disarrangement or confusion. 2. Disturbance of proper civic order; tumult; riot. 3. Derangement of physical or mental health or functions; sickness; ailment. 4. An act, occurrence, or condition marked by disorder; an instance of disorder. — *v.t.* 1. To put out of order; throw into disorder; disarrange. 2. To disturb or upset the normal health or functions of. [< MF *desordre* < L *dis*- away from, out of + *ordo* order] — **Syn.** (noun) 1. confusion, clutter, irregularity, derangement, disturbance. 2. riot, insurrection, rebellion, anarchy. 4. See DISEASE. — **Ant.** order, regularity.

dis·or·dered (dis·ôr′dərd) *adj.* 1. Put out of order; disarranged. 2. Disturbed in normal health or functions.

dis·or·der·ly (dis·ôr′dər·lē) *adj.* 1. Devoid of good order or arrangement; full of disorder. 2. Devoid of method; unsystematic. 3. Undisciplined and unruly; tumultuous: a *disorderly* mob. 4. Violating public order or decency. — *adv.* In a disorderly manner. — **dis·or′der·li·ness** *n.*

disorderly conduct *Law* A petty violation of public order or decency.

disorderly house An establishment that violates public order or decency; especially, a house of prostitution.

dis·or·gan·i·za·tion (dis·ôr′gən·ə·zā′shən, -ī·zā′-) *n.* 1. The act of disorganizing; destruction of organization. 2. The condition of being disorganized; loss or lack of organization. — **Syn.** 1, 2. confusion, derangement, disarrangement.

dis·or·gan·ize (dis·ôr′gən·īz) *v.t.* ·ized, ·iz·ing 1. To destroy the organization of; break up the systematic arrangement or unity of. 2. To throw into confusion; disorder.

dis·or·gan·ized (dis·ôr′gən·īzd) *adj.* Devoid of organization or order; confused; jumbled; muddled; disordered.

dis·o·ri·ent (dis·ôr′ē·ent′, -ō′rē-) *v.t.* To mix up; confuse; especially, to cause to lose one's sense of direction, perspective, or time; throw out of adjustment to one's environment. [< F *désorienter* < *des*- away (< L *dis*-) + *orienter*. See ORIENT.] — **dis·o′ri·en·ta′tion** *n.*

dis·own (dis·ōn′) *v.t.* To refuse to acknowledge or to admit responsibility for or connection with; deny; repudiate.

dis·par·age (dis·par′ij) *v.t.* ·aged, ·ag·ing 1. To treat or speak of with disrespect or contempt; belittle. 2. To bring discredit upon; cause to have less esteem. [< OF *desparagier* to match unequally < *des*- down, away (< L *dis*-) + *parage* equality of rank] — **dis·par′ag·er** *n.* — **Syn.** 1. *Disparage, decry, belittle,* and *depreciate* mean to express a low opinion of a person or thing. To *disparage* is to slight indirectly rather than to condemn openly. We *disparage* a person by conceding his claimed merits but regarding them as trivial. Actions, persons, or things are *decried* by open condemnation and censure. *Belittle* and *depreciate* both mean to represent as small in importance or worth; *belittle* suggests direct assertion, and *depreciate* some more indirect means. Compare ASPERSE. — **Ant.** praise, extol, laud.

dis·par·age·ment (dis·par′ij·mənt) *n.* 1. The act of disparaging; detraction. 2. Lowering or loss of esteem; discredit. 3. Something that belittles or discredits.

dis·par·ag·ing (dis·par′ij·ing) *adj.* Belittling; slighting. — **dis·par′ag·ing·ly** *adv.*

dis·pa·rate (dis·par′ət, dis′pər·it) *adj.* Essentially different; altogether dissimilar; totally distinct in kind. [< L *disparatus*, pp. of *disparare* < *dis*- apart + *parare* to make ready; infl. in meaning by L *dispars*, *-partis* unequal] — **dis′pa·rate·ly** *adv.* — **dis′pa·rate·ness** *n.*

dis·par·i·ty (dis·par′ə·tē) *n. pl.* ·ties 1. Lack of equality, as in age or rank. 2. Unlikeness; dissimilarity. 3. An instance of inequality or unlikeness. [< MF *disparité* < L *dis*- apart + *paritas* equality] . — **Syn.** *Disparity, discrepancy,* and *inequality* are applied to difference where we would expect to find likeness or equality. *Disparity* is a difference in some measurable quantity, as weight, strength, power, or importance: the *disparity* between the armed forces of two nations. A *discrepancy* is a difference due to a lack or shortage: a *discrepancy* between sales slips and cash on hand. *Inequality* is a general term and stresses that equality is the normal or expected condition. Compare DIFFERENCE.

dis·part (dis·pärt′) *v.t. & v.i. Archaic* To divide into distinct parts; separate. [Prob. < Ital. *dispartire* < L *dis*- away + *partire* to divide < *pars, partis* a part, share]

dis·pas·sion (dis·pash′ən) *n.* Freedom from passion or bias; objectivity; impartiality.

dis·pas·sion·ate (dis·pash′ən·it) *adj.* Free from passion or bias; calmly objective; impartial; unbiased. — **dis·pas′sion·ate·ly** *adv.* — **dis·pas′sion·ate·ness** *n.*

dis·patch (dis·pach′) *v.t.* 1. To send off, as a messenger, telegram, or vehicle, to a particular destination. 2. To dispose of quickly, as a business matter. 3. To kill summarily. — *v.i.* 4. *Obs.* To hurry. — *n.* 1. The act of dispatching. 2. Efficient quickness; promptness; speed: to finish a job with *dispatch*. 3. A message, usually in writing, sent with speed; especially, an official communication, as a military report. 4. A news story sent to a newspaper. 5. A service, as an agency, or a means, as telegraphy, for the speedy transmission of messages or delivery of goods: to send by special *dispatch*. Also spelled *despatch*. [< Ital. *dispacciare* or Sp. *despachar*; ult. origin uncertain]

dis·patch·er (dis·pach′ər) *n.* 1. One who dispatches. 2. One who sends out trains, buses, etc., at the time fixed by schedule. Also spelled *despatcher*.

dis·pel (dis·pel′) *v.t.* ·pelled, ·pel·ling To drive away by or as by scattering; disperse: to *dispel* darkness, fear, rumors, etc. [< L *dispellere* < *dis*- away, apart + *pellere* to drive]

dis·pend (dis·pend′) *v.t. Obs.* To spend; especially, to squander. [< OF *despendre* < L *dispendere*. See DISPENSE.]

dis·pen·sa·ble (dis·pen′sə·bəl) *adj.* 1. That can be relinquished or dispensed with; not essential; unimportant. 2. That can be distributed or administered to others. 3. That can be removed by dispensation; pardonable, as a sin. — **dis·pen′sa·bil′i·ty, dis·pen′sa·ble·ness** *n.*

dis·pen·sa·ry (dis·pen′sər·ē) *n. pl.* ·ries A place where medicines and medical advice are given out without charge or at a nominal fee.

dis·pen·sa·tion (dis′pən·sā′shən) *n.* 1. The act of dispensing; a dealing out; distribution. 2. That which is dispensed or distributed. 3. A specific plan, order, or system of dispensing or administering. 4. A special exemption from something, as from a law, rule, or obligation; especially, an exemption by ecclesiastical authority from a vow or similar obligation or from church law; also, the document containing such an exemption. 5. *Theol.* a The arrangement or ordering of events, as by a divine Providence. b A religious or moral system viewed as divinely established: the Mosaic *dispensation*. c The period during which such a system is operative: during the Christian *dispensation*. [< OF < L *dispensatio, -onis* < *dispensare*. See DISPENSE.] — **dis′pen·sa′tion·al** *adj.*

dis·pen·sa·tor (dis′pen·sā′tər) *n. Obs.* A dispenser.

dis·pen·sa·to·ry (dis·pen′sə·tôr′ē, -tō′rē) *adj.* Of or pertaining to dispensing or dispensation. — *n. pl.* ·ries 1. A book in which medicinal substances are described; a pharmacopoeia. 2. *Archaic* A dispensary.

---

dis·pense (dis·pens′) *v.* **·pensed**, **·pens·ing** *v.t.* **1.** To give or deal out in portions; distribute: to *dispense* patronage. **2.** To compound and give out (medicines). **3.** To administer, as laws. **4.** To excuse or exempt, as from an obligation, especially a religious obligation. — *v.i.* **5.** To grant exemption or dispensation. — **Syn.** See DISTRIBUTE. — **to dispense with 1.** To get along without; forgo. **2.** To dispose of; get rid of; do away with. [< OF *despenser* < L *dispensare*, freq. of *dispendere* < *dis-* away + *pendere* to weigh]

dis·pens·er (dis·pen′sər) *n.* One who or that which dispenses, manages, or administers: a soap *dispenser*.

dis·peo·ple (dis·pē′pəl) *v.t.* **·pled**, **·pling** *Rare* To depopulate.

di·sper·mous (dī·spûr′məs) *adj. Bot.* Two-seeded. [< DI-² + Gk. *sperma* a seed]

dis·per·sal (dis·pûr′səl) *n.* The act or result of dispersing; dispersion.

dis·perse (dis·pûrs′) *v.* **·persed**, **·pers·ing** *v.t.* **1.** To cause to scatter in various directions. **2.** To drive away; dispel: The sun *dispersed* the mists. **3.** To spread abroad; diffuse. **4.** To separate (light) into a spectrum. — *v.i.* **5.** To scatter in various directions; dissipate. [< MF *disperser* < L *dispersus*, pp. of *dispergere* < *dis-* away + *spargere* to scatter] — **dis·pers′er** *n.* — **dis·pers′i·ble** *adj.*

dis·pers·ed·ly (dis·pûr′sid·lē) *adv.* In a scattered way; here and there.

dis·per·sion (dis·pûr′zhən, -shən) *n.* **1.** The act of dispersing, or the state of being dispersed. **2.** *Mil.* The pattern of hits made, as by bombs, under the same conditions and from a single source. **3.** *Physics* The separation of white or complex light into different colors by passing it through a prism that refracts the component wavelengths of the light at different angles. **b** A process of sorting out emissions, as of electrons in a magnetic field, in accordance with some characteristic property, as frequency, wavelength, etc. **4.** *Chem.* The condition of the components making up a colloid system. **5.** *Stat.* The arrangement of a series of values around the median or mean of a distribution. — **the Dispersion** The Diaspora.

dis·per·sive (dis·pûr′siv) *adj.* Tending to disperse.

dis·pir·it (dis·pir′it) *v.t.* To make downhearted or depressed; dishearten. — **dis·pir′it·ing·ly** *adv.*

dis·pir·it·ed (dis·pir′it·id) *adj.* Cast down in spirit; dejected. — **dis·pir′it·ed·ly** *adv.* — **dis·pir′it·ed·ness** *n.*

dis·pit·e·ous (dis·pit′ē·əs) *adj. Archaic* Without pity or mercy.

dis·place (dis·plās′) *v.t.* **·placed**, **·plac·ing 1.** To remove or shift from the usual or proper place. **2.** To take the place of; supplant. **3.** To remove from a position or office; discharge. **4.** *Chem.* To release from combination by taking the place of: Zinc *displaces* the hydrogen of an acid. **5.** *Physics* To have a displacement of. [< OF *desplacer* < *des-* away (< L *dis-*) + *placer* to place]
— **Syn. 1.** move, transfer, derange, disarrange. **2.** replace, supersede. **3.** dismiss, oust. Compare EXPEL.

displaced person A person made homeless by war and forced to live in a foreign country. *Abbr. DP, D.P.*

dis·place·ment (dis·plās′mənt) *n.* **1.** The act of displacing, or the state of being displaced. **2.** *Astron.* An apparent change of position, as of a star. **3.** *Physics* The weight of a fluid displaced by a floating body, this weight being equal to the weight of the body; also, the total weight of a ship and its contents expressed in displacement tons. **4.** The relation between the position of a moving object at any time and its original position. **5.** *Geol.* A fault. **6.** *Psychoanal.* Transference of an emotion or attitude to something other than the object originally arousing it, in an unrecognized effort to escape social or moral censure.

displacement ton See TON¹ (def. 2).

dis·plant (dis·plant′, -plänt′) *v.t. Obs.* **1.** To take (a plant) from the ground; uproot. **2.** To dislodge; displace. [< OF *desplanter* < L *dis-* away + *plantare* to plant]

dis·play (dis·plā′) *v.t.* **1.** To make evident or obvious; make noticeable; reveal: to *display* ignorance. **2.** To expose to the sight; cause to be seen; exhibit: The flag *displays* the national colors. **3.** To make a prominent or ostentatious show of: She *displayed* her jewels. **4.** To unfurl so as to be seen: to *display* a flag. **5.** *Printing* To make (printed matter) stand out prominently, as by the use of large type or wide spacing. — *n.* **1.** The act of displaying; exhibition; manifestation. **2.** That which is exhibited or displayed. **3.** Ostentatious show: a vulgar *display* of jewels. **4.** *Printing* **a** A style or arrangement of type designed to make printed matter stand out prominently. **b** Printed matter that stands out prominently. [< OF *despleier* < LL *displicare* to scatter < *dis-* apart + *plicare* to fold, add. Doublet of DEPLOY.]
— **Syn.** (verb) **1.** exhibit, demonstrate, manifest, evince. **3.** parade, flaunt.

dis·please (dis·plēz′) *v.* **·pleased**, **·pleas·ing** *v.t.* **1.** To cause displeasure in or annoyance to; vex; offend. — *v.i.* **2.** To cause displeasure or annoyance. [< OF *desplaisir*, *desplaire*, ult. < L *displicere* < *dis-* not + *placere* to please] — **dis·pleas′ing·ly** *adv.*

dis·pleas·ure (dis·plezh′ər) *n.* **1.** The state of being dis-

pleased; annoyance. **2.** *Archaic* Discomfort. **3.** *Archaic* An offensive action. — *v.t. Archaic* To displease.

dis·plode (dis·plōd′) *v.t. & v.i.* **·plod·ed**, **·plod·ing** *Obs.* To explode. [< L *displodere* < *dis-* apart + *plaudere* to clap, burst]

dis·plume (dis·plōōm′) *v.t.* **·plumed**, **·plum·ing** *Rare* To deplume.

dis·port (dis·pôrt′, -pōrt′) *v.t.* **1.** To divert or amuse (oneself); occupy (oneself) pleasurably. — *v.i.* **2.** To frisk about playfully; frolic. — *n.* Diversion; pastime; sport. [< OF *desporter* < L *dis-* away + *portare* to carry]

dis·pos·a·ble (dis·pō′zə·bəl) *adj.* **1.** Capable of being disposed of; especially, designed to be discarded after use. **2.** Free to be used as occasion may require: *disposable* funds.

dis·po·sal (dis·pō′zəl) *n.* **1.** A particular ordering or arrangement; distribution; disposition. **2.** A particular way of attending to or settling something, as business affairs. **3.** Transfer of something to another, as by gift or sale. **4.** A getting rid of something, as by throwing away; also, the means for doing this. **5.** Liberty to deal with or dispose of in any way: The money is at your *disposal*.

dis·pose (dis·pōz′) *v.* **·posed**, **·pos·ing** *v.t.* **1.** To give a tendency or inclination to; put into a receptive frame of mind for: The news *disposed* them to accept the offer. **2.** To condition toward something; especially, to make susceptible: Fatigue *disposes* a person to colds. **3.** To put or set in a particular arrangement or position: to *dispose* books about a room. **4.** To put into proper, definitive, or final shape; settle: to *dispose* business affairs. — *v.i.* **5.** To control the course of events: Man proposes, God *disposes*. — **to dispose of 1.** To attend to; deal with. **2.** To finish up with; settle. **3.** To transfer to another, as by gift or sale. **4.** To get rid of; throw away. **5.** To consume (food or drink). — *n. Obs.* Disposal; disposition. [< OF *disposer* < *dis-* apart (< L *dis-*) + *poser*. See POSE.] — **dis·pos′er** *n.*

dis·posed (dis·pōzd′) *adj.* Having a particular inclination, frame of mind, or mood: *disposed* to take offense.

dis·po·si·tion (dis′pə·zish′ən) *n.* **1.** One's usual frame of mind, or one's usual way of reacting, as to persons or situations: a kindly *disposition*. **2.** Acquired tendency or inclination, especially when habitual: a *disposition* to drink. **3.** Natural organic tendency or inclination: the *disposition* of flowers to turn toward the sun. **4.** A particular ordering, arrangement, or distribution, as of troops. **5.** Management, adjustment, or settlement, as of business affairs. **6.** Transfer of something to another, as by gift or sale. **7.** A getting rid of something, as by throwing away. **8.** Liberty to deal with or dispose of in any way. **9.** A particular way of dealing with or disposing of something; dispensation. [< F < L *dispositio, -onis* < *dis-* away + *ponere* to place]

dis·pos·sess (dis′pə·zes′) *v.t.* To deprive of possession of something, as a house or land; oust. [< OF *despossesser* < *des-* away (< L *dis-*) + *possesser*. See POSSESS.] — **dis·pos·ses′sion** (-zesh′ən) *n.* — **dis·pos·ses′sor** *n.*

dis·po·sure (dis·pō′zhər) *n. Rare* Disposal.

dis·praise (dis·prāz′) *v.t.* **·praised**, **·prais·ing** To express disapproval or censure of; disparage. — *n.* The expression of unfavorable opinion; disparagement; censure. [< OF *despreisier* < *des-* not (< L *dis-*) + *preisier*. See PRAISE.] — **dis·prais′er** *n.* — **dis·prais′ing·ly** *adv.*

dis·pread (dis·pred′) *v.t. & v.i.* **·pread**, **·pread·ing** *Rare* To spread out; extend: also spelled *disspread*.

dis·prize (dis·prīz′) *v.t.* **·prized**, **·priz·ing** *Archaic* To hold in low esteem. [< OF *despriser*, var. of *despreisier*. See DISPRAISE.]

dis·proof (dis·prōōf′) *n.* **1.** The act of disproving. **2.** Something that disproves, as evidence.

dis·pro·por·tion (dis′prə·pôr′shən, -pōr′-) *n.* **1.** Lack of proportion or symmetry; disparity. **2.** An instance of this. — *v.t.* To make disproportionate.

dis·pro·por·tion·al (dis′prə·pôr′shən·əl, -pōr′-) *adj.* Disproportionate. — **dis′pro·por′tion·al·ly** *adv.*

dis·pro·por·tion·ate (dis′prə·pôr′shən·it, -pōr′-) *adj.* Out of proportion, as in size, form, or value. — **dis′pro·por′tion·ate·ly** *adv.* — **dis′pro·por′tion·ate·ness** *n.*

dis·prove (dis·prōōv′) *v.t.* **·proved**, **·proved** or **·prov·en**, **·prov·ing** To prove (a statement, claim, etc.) to be false, invalid, or erroneous. — **Syn.** See REFUTE. [< OF *desprouver* < *des-* not (< L *dis-*) + *prouver* to prove] — **dis·prov′a·ble** *adj.* — **dis·prov′al** *n.*

dis·put·a·ble (dis·pyōō′tə·bəl, dis′pyōō·tə·bəl) *adj.* Open to being disputed or called into question; arguable; debatable. — **dis·put′a·bil′i·ty** *n.* — **dis·put′a·bly** *adv.*

dis·pu·tant (dis′pyōō·tənt, dis·pyōō′tənt) *adj.* Engaged in controversy; disputing. — *n.* One who disputes; a debater. [< L *disputans, -antis*, ppr. of *disputare*. See DISPUTE.]

dis·pu·ta·tion (dis′pyōō·tā′shən) *n.* **1.** The act of disputing; argumentation; controversy. **2.** A formal debate; especially, formal argumentation of some point in philosophy or theology. **3.** *Obs.* A discussion or conversation. [< L *disputatio, -onis* < *disputare*. See DISPUTE.]

dis·pu·ta·tious (dis′pyōō·tā′shəs) *adj.* Given to disputing; argumentative; contentious. — **dis′pu·ta′tious·ly** *adv.* — **dis′pu·ta′tious·ness** *n.*

dis·pu·ta·tive (dis·pyōō′tə·tiv) *adj.* Disputatious.

dis·pute (dis-pyo͞ot′) v. ·put·ed, ·put·ing v.t. **1.** To argue about; debate. **2.** To question the validity, genuineness, etc., of. **3.** To strive or contest for, as a prize. **4.** To resist; oppose. — v.i. **5.** To argue. **6.** To quarrel; wrangle. — n. **1.** A controversial discussion; debate. **2.** An altercation; quarrel. [< OF desputer < L disputare < dis- away + putare to think] — **dis·put′er** n. — **Syn.** (verb) **2.** See OPPOSE. **5.** See ARGUE.

dis·qual·i·fi·ca·tion (dis-kwol′ə-fə-kā′shən) n. **1.** The act of disqualifying, or the state of being disqualified. **2.** Something that disqualifies.

dis·qual·i·fy (dis-kwol′ə-fī) v.t. ·fied, ·fy·ing **1.** To make unqualified or unfit; incapacitate. **2.** To pronounce unqualified or ineligible. **3.** In sports, to deprive of a prize or bar from competition because of rule infractions, etc.

dis·qui·et (dis-kwī′ət) n. An unsettled or disturbed condition; lack of tranquillity; uneasiness. — **Syn.** See ALARM. — v.t. To make anxious or uneasy; disturb; alarm. — adj. Rare Restless; uneasy; impatient. — **dis·qui′et·ly** adv.

dis·qui·et·ing (dis-kwī′ət·ing) adj. Causing disquiet; making uneasy. — **dis·qui′et·ing·ly** adv.

dis·qui·e·tude (dis-kwī′ə-to͞od, -tyo͞od) n. A state of unrest; uneasiness.

dis·qui·si·tion (dis′kwi-zish′ən) n. A formal treatise or discourse; dissertation. [< L disquisitio, -onis investigation < dis- thoroughly + quaerere to seek, ask]

Dis·rae·li (diz-rā′lē), Benjamin, 1804–81, first Earl of Beaconsfield, English statesman and novelist; prime minister 1868, 1874–80.

dis·rate (dis-rāt′) v.t. ·rat·ed, ·rat·ing To lower in rating or rank, as a petty officer.

dis·re·gard (dis′ri-gärd′) v.t. **1.** To pay no attention to; ignore. **2.** To treat as undeserving of consideration, respect, or attention; slight. — **Syn.** See NEGLECT. — n. Lack of notice or due regard, especially when deliberate; neglect, as of something not deserving notice. — **dis′re·gard′er** n.

dis·re·gard·ful (dis′ri-gärd′fəl) adj. Showing disregard.

dis·rel·ish (dis-rel′ish) v.t. To have some distaste for. — n. Distaste; dislike.

dis·re·mem·ber (dis′ri-mem′bər) v.t. & v.i. U.S. Informal To be unable to recall; forget.

dis·re·pair (dis′ri-pâr′) n. The state of being out of repair.

dis·rep·u·ta·ble (dis-rep′yə-tə-bəl) adj. **1.** Not in good repute; not esteemed: a disreputable author. **2.** Not respectable: a disreputable tavern. **3.** Causing ill repute; discreditable. — **dis·rep′u·ta·ble·ness** n. — **dis·rep′u·ta·bly** adv.

dis·re·pute (dis′ri-pyo͞ot′) n. **1.** Lack or loss of good repute; discredit: to fall into disrepute. **2.** Unfavorable regard; disfavor. Also Archaic **dis·rep′u·ta′tion.**

dis·re·spect (dis′ri-spekt′) n. Lack of courtesy or respect. — v.t. To treat or regard with lack of respect.

dis·re·spect·a·ble (dis′ri-spek′tə-bəl) adj. Lacking respectability. — **dis·re·spect′a·bil′i·ty** n.

dis·re·spect·ful (dis′ri-spekt′fəl) adj. Having or showing a lack of proper respect; impolite; rude. — **dis′re·spect′ful·ly** adv. — **dis′re·spect′ful·ness** n.

dis·robe (dis-rōb′) v.t. & v.i. ·robed, ·rob·ing To undress. — **dis·robe′ment** n.

dis·root (dis-ro͞ot′, -ro͝ot′) v.t. To uproot or dislodge.

dis·rupt (dis-rupt′) v.t. **1.** To throw into disorder; upset. **2.** To halt or impede the movement of, procedure of, etc. **3.** To break or burst apart. — v.i. **4.** To break; burst. [< L disruptus, pp. of disrumpere < dis- apart + rumpere to burst] — **dis·rupt′er** or **dis·rup′tor** n.

dis·rup·tion (dis-rup′shən) n. **1.** The act or process of disrupting. **2.** The state of being disrupted. **3.** A rupture; break.

dis·rup·tive (dis-rup′tiv) adj. Producing, tending to, or pertaining to disruption. — **dis·rup′tive·ly** adv.

disruptive discharge Electr. A strong discharge of electrical current in or through an insulating medium, caused by a breakdown of the medium under electrostatic stress.

dis·sat·is·fac·tion (dis′sat·is-fak′shən) n. **1.** A dissatisfied state or feeling; discontent. **2.** That which dissatisfies.

dis·sat·is·fac·to·ry (dis′sat·is-fak′tər-ē) adj. Causing dissatisfaction; unsatisfactory.

dis·sat·is·fied (dis-sat′is-fīd) adj. **1.** Not satisfied; displeased; discontented. **2.** Showing dissatisfaction.

dis·sat·is·fy (dis-sat′is-fī) v.t. ·fied, ·fy·ing To fail to satisfy; disappoint; displease.

dis·seat (dis-sēt′) v.t. To unseat.

dis·sect (di-sekt′, dī-) v.t. **1.** To cut apart or divide, as an animal body or a plant, in order to examine the structure; anatomize. **2.** To analyze critically; examine in detail. [< L dissectus, pp. of dissecare < dis- apart + secare to cut]

dis·sect·ed (di-sek′tid, dī-) adj. **1.** Cut in pieces; separated at the joints. **2.** Geol. Cut into ridges, as a plateau. **3.** Bot. Deeply cut into lobes or segments, as a leaf.

dis·sec·tion (di-sek′shən, dī-) n. **1.** The act of dissecting. **2.** A dissected object, as an animal or plant being studied. **3.** A detailed critical analysis.

dis·sec·tor (di-sek′tər, dī-) n. **1.** One who dissects. **2.** An instrument used in dissecting.

dis·seize (dis-sēz′) v.t. ·seized, ·seiz·ing Law To oust unlawfully from the possession of an estate. Also **dis·seise′**. [< AF disseisir, OF dessaisir < des- away (< L dis-) + saisir to seize. See SEIZE.] — **dis·sei′zor** (-zər, -zôr) n.

dis·sei·zee (dis′sē·zē′, dis·sē′zē′) n. One who is disseized. Also **dis′seis·ee′.**

dis·sei·zin (dis-sē′zin) n. Law Unlawful dispossession. Also **dis·sei′sin, dis·seiz·ure** (dis·sē′zhər). [< AF disseisine < disseisir. See DISSEIZE.]

dis·sem·blance (di-sem′bləns) n. **1.** The act of dissembling; dissimulation. **2.** Lack of resemblance; dissimilarity.

dis·sem·ble (di-sem′bəl) v. ·bled, ·bling v.t. **1.** To conceal or disguise the actual nature of (intentions, feelings, etc.); cover up; dissimulate. **2.** To make a false show of; feign: to dissemble madness. **3.** Obs. To ignore. — v.i. **4.** To conceal one's true nature, intentions, etc.; act hypocritically. [Var. of earlier dissimule < OF dissimuler < L dissimulare < dis- not, away + similis alike; infl. in form by resemble] — **dis·sem′bler** n. — **dis·sem′bling·ly** adv.

dis·sem·i·nate (di-sem′ə-nāt) v.t. ·nat·ed, ·nat·ing To scatter, as if sowing; diffuse far and wide: to disseminate knowledge. [< L disseminatus, pp. of disseminare < dis- away + seminare to sow < semen, seminis seed] — **dis·sem′i·na′tion** n. — **dis·sem′i·na′tive** adj. — **dis·sem′i·na′tor** n.

dis·sen·sion (di-sen′shən) n. **1.** Difference of opinion, especially arising from dissatisfaction or anger; discord; strife. **2.** A heated quarrel or disagreement.

dis·sent (di-sent′) v.i. **1.** To differ in thought or opinion: with from. **2.** To withhold approval or consent. **3.** To refuse adherence to an established church. — n. **1.** Difference of opinion; disagreement. **2.** Refusal to conform to an established church; nonconformity. [< L dissentire < dis- apart + sentire to think, feel]

dis·sent·er (di-sen′tər) n. **1.** One who dissents or disagrees. **2.** Often cap. One who refuses assent to the doctrines or usages of an established or state church, especially the Church of England: opposed to conformist. — **Syn.** See HERETIC.

dis·sen·tient (di-sen′shənt) adj. Dissenting. — n. A dissenter. [< L dissentiens, -entis, ppr. of dissentire. See DISSENT.] — **dis·sen′tience** n.

dis·sent·ing (di-sen′ting) adj. Expressing disagreement: a dissenting opinion. — **dis·sent′ing·ly** adv.

dis·sen·tious (di-sen′shəs) adj. Quarrelsome; disputatious.

dis·sep·i·ment (di·sep′ə-mənt) n. Biol. A septum or partition, as one dividing a compound ovary into two or more cells. [< L dissaepimentum < dis- apart + saepire to fence in < saepes fence, hedge]

dis·ser·tate (dis′ər-tāt) v.i. ·tat·ed, ·tat·ing Rare To discourse or write in a learned or formal manner. Also **dis·sert′.** [< L dissertatus, pp. of dissertare, freq. of dissere < dis- apart + serere to join, connect] — **dis′ser·ta′tor** n.

dis·ser·ta·tion (dis′ər·tā′shən) n. An extended formal treatise or discourse; especially, a written treatise required of a candidate for the doctorate; thesis.

dis·serve (dis-sûrv′) v.t. ·served, ·serv·ing To serve poorly or treat badly; do an ill turn to.

dis·ser·vice (dis-sûr′vis) n. Ill service; an ill turn; injury.

dis·sev·er (dis-sev′ər) v.t. **1.** To divide; separate. **2.** To separate into parts. — v.i. **3.** To become separated. [< AF deseverer, OF dessevrer < LL disseparare < L dis- apart + separare. See SEPARATE.] — **dis·sev′er·ance, dis·sev′er·ment** n.

dis·si·dence (dis′ə-dəns) n. Disagreement; dissent.

dis·si·dent (dis′ə-dənt) adj. Dissenting; differing. — n. A dissenter. [< L dissidens, -entis, ppr. of dissidere < dis- apart + sedere to sit]

dis·sil·i·ent (di-sil′ē-ənt) adj. Springing or bursting apart, as some pods. [< L dissiliens, -entis, ppr. of dissilire < dis- apart + salire to leap] — **dis·sil′i·en·cy** n.

dis·sim·i·lar (di-sim′ə-lər) adj. Not similar; unlike; different: sometimes with to. — **dis·sim′i·lar·ly** adv.

dis·sim·i·lar·i·ty (di-sim′ə-lar′ə-tē) n. pl. ·ties **1.** Lack of similarity; unlikeness; difference. **2.** An instance or example of this. — **Syn.** See DIFFERENCE.

dis·sim·i·late (di-sim′ə-lāt) v.t. & v.i. ·lat·ed, ·lat·ing **1.** To make or become unlike. **2.** Phonet. To undergo or cause to undergo dissimilation. [< DIS-¹ + L similis alike]

dis·sim·i·la·tion (di-sim′ə·lā′shən) n. **1.** The act or process of making or becoming dissimilar. **2.** Phonet. The process whereby one of two or more similar sounds in a word is omitted, as in the pronunciation (lī′bər/ē) for library, or replaced by another sound, as in the English form turtle from Latin turtur.

dis·si·mil·i·tude (dis′si·mil′ə-to͞od, -tyo͞od) n. **1.** Lack of resemblance; unlikeness. **2.** An instance of this. [< L dissimilitudo < dissimilis < dis- not + similis alike]

dis·sim·u·late (di-sim′yə-lāt) v.t. & v.i. ·lat·ed, ·lat·ing To conceal (intentions, feelings, etc.) by pretense; dissemble. [< L *dissimulatus*, pp. of *dissimulare*. See DISSEMBLE.] — **dis·sim′u·la′tive** *adj.* — **dis·sim′u·la′tor** *n.*

dis·sim·u·la·tion (di-sim′yə-lā′shən) *n.* False pretense; hypocrisy. — **Syn.** See HYPOCRISY.

dis·si·pate (dis′ə-pāt) *v.* **·pat·ed, ·pat·ing** *v.t.* **1.** To disperse or drive away; dispel. **2.** To spend wastefully; squander. — *v.i.* **3.** To become dispersed; scatter. **4.** To engage in excessive or dissolute pleasures. [< L *dissipatus*, pp. of *dissipare* < *dis-* away + *supare* to throw about, scatter] — **dis′si·pat′er** or **dis′si·pa′tor** *n.* — **dis′si·pa′tive** *adj.*

dis·si·pat·ed (dis′ə-pā′tid) *adj.* **1.** Wasted; scattered. **2.** Pursuing pleasure to excess; dissolute. — **dis′si·pat′ed·ly** *adv.* — **dis′si·pat′ed·ness** *n.*

dis·si·pa·tion (dis′ə-pā′shən) *n.* **1.** The act of dissipating, or the state of being dissipated; dispersion; scattering. **2.** Excessive indulgence, especially in dissolute pleasures. **3.** Distraction or diversion, as of the mind.

dis·so·cia·ble (di-sō′shə-bəl, -shē-ə- *for defs. 1 and 3*; di-sō′-shə-bəl *for def. 2*) *adj.* **1.** Capable of being separated or dissociated. **2.** Unsociable. **3.** Incongruous; ill-assorted. — **dis·so′cia·bil′i·ty, dis·so′cia·ble·ness** *n.* — **dis·so′cia·bly** *adv.*

dis·so·cial (di-sō′shəl) *adj.* Unsocial; unfriendly.

dis·so·ci·ate (di-sō′shē-āt, -sē-) *v.* **·at·ed, ·at·ing** *v.t.* **1.** To break the association of; disconnect; separate. **2.** To regard as separate in concept or nature. **3.** To subject to dissociation. — *v.i.* **4.** To break an association. **5.** To undergo dissociation. Also *disassociate.* [< L *dissociatus*, pp. of *dissociare* < *dis-* apart + *sociare* to join together < *socius* companion] — **dis·so′ci·a′tive** *adj.*

dis·so·ci·a·tion (di-sō′sē-ā′shən, -shē-ā′-) *n.* **1.** The act of dissociating, or the state of being dissociated. **2.** *Chem.* **a** The resolution of a compound into simpler constituents by a change in physical state, as by heat or pressure, with recombination when the original conditions are restored. **b** Dissolution of an electrolyte into ions. **3.** *Psychol.* **a** The process whereby a set of ideas, feelings, etc., loses most of its relationships with the rest of the personality, functioning somewhat independently. **b** An example or result of this.

dis·sol·u·ble (di-sol′yə-bəl) *adj.* Capable of being dissolved or decomposed. [< L *dissolubilis* < *dissolvere*. See DISSOLVE.] — **dis·sol′u·bil′i·ty, dis·sol′u·ble·ness** *n.*

dis·so·lute (dis′ə-lōōt) *adj.* Not governed by moral restraints; abandoned; debauched. [< L *dissolutus*, pp. of *dissolvere*. See DISSOLVE.] — **dis′so·lute′ly** *adv.* — **dis′so·lute·ness** *n.*

dis·so·lu·tion (dis′ə-lōō′shən) *n.* **1.** Separation into parts; disintegration. **2.** Change from a solid to a fluid form; liquefaction. **3.** The breaking up or liquidation of a formal or legal union, bond, or tie, as of a marriage or a business enterprise. **4.** Dismissal of a meeting or assembly. **5.** Termination or destruction: the *dissolution* of the king's power. **6.** Separation of soul and body; death. — **dis′so·lu′tive** *adj.*

dis·solve (di-zolv′) *v.* **·solved, ·solv·ing** *v.t.* **1.** To cause to pass into solution. **2.** To overcome or melt, as by emotion. **3.** To break up into parts; disintegrate. **4.** To put an end to; destroy: to *dissolve* a partnership. **5.** To dismiss (a meeting or assembly). **6.** To destroy the power or control of: to *dissolve* a spell. **7.** *Law* To set aside; annul, as an injunction. — *v.i.* **8.** To pass into solution. **9.** To be overcome; melt: to *dissolve* in tears. **10.** To come to an end; break up; disperse. **11.** To dwindle away; be dissipated. **12.** To fade away or vanish, as an image. **13.** In motion pictures and television, to change gradually from one picture or scene to another by overlapping two shots. — *n.* A lap dissolve (which see). [< L *dissolvere* < *dis-* apart + *solvere* to loosen] — **dis·solv′a·ble** *adj.* — **dis·solv′er** *n.*

dis·sol·vent (di-zol′vənt) *adj.* Having the power to dissolve. — *n.* A solvent.

dissolving view The continuous image thrown on a screen by a slide projector that fades one picture into the next.

dis·so·nance (dis′ə-nəns) *n.* **1.** A discordant mingling of sounds; discord. **2.** Harsh disagreement; incongruity. **3.** *Music* A simultaneous combination of tones that seem to clash and require resolution; also, such combinations collectively. Also **dis′so·nan·cy.**

dis·so·nant (dis′ə-nənt) *adj.* **1.** Harsh in sound; inharmonious. **2.** Naturally hostile; incongruous. **3.** *Music* Consisting of or containing a dissonance. [< L *dissonans*, -*antis*, ppr. of *dissonare* < *dis-* away + *sonare* to sound] — **dis′so·nant·ly** *adv.*

dis·spread (dis-pred′) See DISPREAD.

dis·suade (di-swād′) *v.t.* **·suad·ed, ·suad·ing 1.** To change or alter the plans or intentions of (someone) by persuasion or advice: with *from.* **2.** *Rare* To advise against (a course of action). [< L *dissuadere* < *dis-* away + *suadere* to persuade] — **dis·suad′er** *n.*

dis·sua·sion (di-swā′zhən) *n.* The act of dissuading. [< L *dissuasio*, -*onis* < *dissuadere*. See DISSUADE.]

dis·sua·sive (di-swā′siv) *adj.* Tending or intended to dissuade. — *n.* A dissuading argument, fact, or consideration. — **dis·sua′sive·ly** *adv.* — **dis·sua′sive·ness** *n.*

dis·syl·la·ble (di-sil′ə-bəl, dis′sil′ə-bəl) *n.* A word of two

syllables: also spelled *disyllable*. [< F < L *disyllabus* < Gk. *disyllabos* < *di-* two + *syllabē* syllable. See SYLLABLE.] — **dis′syl·lab′ic** *adj.*

dis·sym·me·try (dis-sim′ə-trē) *n.* *pl.* **·tries** Lack of symmetry. — **dis·sym·met′ric** or **·ri·cal** *adj.* — **dis′sym·met′ri·cal·ly** *adv.*

dist. 1. Distance; distant. **2.** Distinguish(ed). **3.** District.

dis·taff (dis′taf, -täf) *n.* *pl.* **·taffs** or *Rare* **·taves** (-tāvz) **1.** A rotating vertical staff that holds a bunch of flax or wool for use in spinning by hand. **2.** Women in general; woman. **3.** Woman's work or domain. [OE *distæf* < *dis* bundle of flax + *stæf* staff]

distaff side The maternal branch or female line of a family: opposed to *spear side.*

dis·tain (dis-tān′) *v.t. Archaic* **1.** To stain; dye. **2.** To sully; disgrace. [< OF *desteindre* < *des-* completely (< L *dis-*) + *teindre* < L *tingere* to stain, dye]

dis·tal (dis′təl) *adj.* *Anat.* Relatively remote from the center of the body or point of attachment; peripheral: opposed to *proximal.* [< DIST(ANT) + -AL¹] — **dis′tal·ly** *adv.*

dis·tance (dis′təns) *n.* **1.** The extent of spatial separation between things, places, or locations. **2.** The extent of separation between points of time; interval. **3.** The state or fact of being separated from something else, especially to a notable extent, in space, time, or condition. **4.** A gap, as in relationship or rank, between persons or things. **5.** Remoteness; especially, reserve or aloofness of manner: to keep one's *distance.* **6.** A point or location removed from another, especially to a notable extent. **7.** In art, the part of a painting that represents things as distant. **8.** *Music* The interval between two tones. **9.** In horse racing, a marked place set back from the finish line that must be reached before the winner reaches the finish line in order to qualify for later heats. Abbr. *dist.* — *v.t.* **·tanced, ·tanc·ing 1.** To leave behind, as in a race; outstrip; outdo; excel. **2.** To cause to appear distant. **3.** To hold off or place at some distance.

dis·tant (dis′tənt) *adj.* **1.** Separated or apart by a specified amount of space or time; away: often with *from*: They are 90 miles *distant* from here. **2.** Remote in time or space: a *distant* star; a *distant* event. **3.** At, from, or to a distance: a *distant* journey. **4.** Not closely related; far apart; remote, as to similarity, kinship, etc. **5.** Reserved or unapproachable; cold; aloof. Abbr. *dist.* [< F < L *distans*, -*antis*, ppr. of *distare* < *dis-* apart + *stare* to stand] — **dis′tant·ly** *adv.*

dis·taste (dis-tāst′) *n.* Dislike; aversion: a *distaste* for work. — *v.t.* **·tast·ed, ·tast·ing** *Rare* **1.** To dislike. **2.** To displease; offend.

dis·taste·ful (dis-tāst′fəl) *adj.* Causing dislike; offensive; disagreeable. — **dis·taste′ful·ly** *adv.* — **dis·taste′ful·ness** *n.*

dist. atty. or **Dist. Atty.** District attorney.

dis·tem·per¹ (dis-tem′pər) *n.* **1.** *Vet.* Any of several infectious diseases of animals; especially, a catarrhal disease of puppies associated with a filterable virus. **2.** A disorder of the mind or body; illness. **3.** Political or civil disturbance; riot; disorder. — *v.t.* **1.** To derange the faculties or functions of; disorder. **2.** To ruffle; disturb. [< Med.L *distemperare* < L *dis-* away + *temperare* to regulate, mix]

dis·tem·per² (dis-tem′pər) *n.* **1.** Tempera. **2.** A painting medium in which size is the only agent used to bind the pigments. **3.** The art or method of using this medium. **4.** A painting done in distemper. **5.** *Brit.* Calcimine. — *v.t.* **1.** To mix (colors or pigments) with a binding medium, such as casein. **2.** To paint in distemper. [< OF *destemprer* < Med.L *distemperare* < L *dis-* apart + *temperare* to mix, mingle, soak]

dis·tem·per·a·ture (dis-tem′pər-ə-chər, -prə-chər) *n.* *Archaic* A disordered state of mind or body.

dis·tend (dis-tend′) *v.t. & v.i.* **1.** To expand by or as by pressure from within. **2.** To stretch out; swell. [< L *distendere* < *dis-* apart + *tendere* to stretch]

dis·ten·si·ble (dis-ten′sə-bəl) *adj.* Capable of being distended. — **dis·ten′si·bil′i·ty** *n.*

dis·tent (dis-tent′) *adj. Poetic* Distended.

dis·ten·tion (dis-ten′shən) *n.* The act of distending or the state of being distended; dilation; expansion. Also **dis·ten′sion.** [< L *distentio*, -*onis* < *distendere*. See DISTEND.]

dis·tich (dis′tik) *n.* In prosody, a couplet; especially, a couplet used in a classical elegiac. [< L *distichon* < Gk., neut. sing. of *distichos* < *di-* two + *stichos* a row, line]

dis·ti·chous (dis′ti·kəs) *adj. Bot.* Arranged in two longitudinal rows on opposite sides of a common axis, as leaves. [< L *distichus* < Gk. *distichos*. See DISTICH.] — **dis′ti·chous·ly** *adv.*

dis·till (dis-til′) *v.* **·tilled, ·till·ing** *v.t.* **1.** To subject to or as to distillation so as to purify, concentrate, or refine. **2.** To extract volatile substances from by distillation: to *distill* corn. **3.** To extract or produce by distillation: to *distill* whisky. **4.** To give forth or send down in drops: The clouds *distill* rain. — *v.i.* **5.** To undergo distillation. **6.** To exude in drops. Also *Brit.* **dis·til′.** [< L *distillare*, var. of *destillare* < *de-* down + *stillare* to drop, trickle] — **dis·till′a·ble** *adj.*

dis·til·late (dis′tə-lit, -lāt) *n.* The condensed product separated by distillation: also called *distillation.* [< L *distillatus*, pp. of *distillare*. See DISTILL.]

dis·til·la·tion (dis/tə·lā/shən) *n.* **1.** The act or process of separating the more volatile parts of a substance from those less volatile by heating in a retort or still and then condensing the vapor thus produced by cooling it in a retort or worm. **2.** The purification or rectification of a substance by this process. **3.** A distillate. **4.** The essential or abstract quality of anything. Also *distillment.*

dis·tilled (dis·tild/) *adj.* Made or obtained by distillation.

dis·til·ler (dis·til/ər) *n.* **1.** One who distills; especially, a maker of distilled liquors. **2.** A condenser for distilling.

dis·til·ler·y (dis·til/ər·ē) *n. pl.* **·ler·ies** An establishment for distilling, especially alcoholic liquors.

dis·till·ment (dis·til/mənt) *n.* **1.** Distillation. **2.** A product of distillation. Also *Brit.* **dis·til/ment.**

dis·tinct (dis·tingkt/) *adj.* **1.** Recognizably not the same; clearly different. **2.** Differentiated by individualizing features; different in nature or qualities. **3.** Sharp and clear to the senses or mind; unmistakable; definite. **4.** Undeniably such; unquestionable: a *distinct* step forward. **5.** *Poetic* Distinctively decorated. — **Syn.** See CLEAR. [< L *distinctus,* pp. of *distinguere.* See DISTINGUISH.] — **dis·tinct/ness** *n.*

dis·tinc·tion (dis·tingk/shən) *n.* **1.** The act of distinguishing; discrimination. **2.** A difference that may be distinguished: the *distinction* between thrift and avarice. **3.** The state of being different or distinguishable. **4.** A characteristic difference or distinctive quality: The *distinction* of the tunnel is its length. **5.** A mark of honor; a symbol of recognition. **6.** A distinguishing superiority or preeminence: to serve with *distinction.* — **Syn.** See DIFFERENCE.

dis·tinc·tive (dis·tingk/tiv) *adj.* **1.** Serving to distinguish; individualizing; characteristic. **2.** *Ling.* Relevant. — **dis·tinc/tive·ly** *adv.* — **dis·tinc/tive·ness** *n.*

dis·tinct·ly (dis·tingkt/lē) *adv.* **1.** In a clear, precise manner: Speak *distinctly.* **2.** Unmistakably; undoubtedly.

dis·tin·gué (dis/tang·gā/, *Fr.* dēs·tan·gā/) *adj.* Eminently well-bred and dignified; having an air of distinction. [< F, pp. of *distinguer.* See DISTINGUISH.] — **dis/tin·guée/** *adj.fem.*

dis·tin·guish (dis·ting/gwish) *v.t.* **1.** To indicate the differences of or between; mark as different. **2.** To be an outstanding or individualizing characteristic of: Honesty *distinguished* his career. **3.** To recognize as separate or distinct; discriminate. **4.** To divide into classes or categories; classify. **5.** To bring fame, celebrity, or credit upon. **6.** To perceive with the senses. — *v.i.* **7.** To make or discern differences; discriminate: often with *among* or *between.* Abbr. *dist.* — **Syn.** See DISCRIMINATE. [< MF *distinguiss-,* stem of *distinguer* < L *distinguere* to separate] — **dis·tin/guish·a·ble** *adj.* — **dis·tin/guish·a·bly** *adv.* — **dis·tin/guish·er** *n.*

dis·tin·guished (dis·ting/gwisht) *adj.* **1.** Conspicuous for qualities of excellence; celebrated; eminent; famous. **2.** Having an air of distinction; distingué.

Distinguished Conduct Medal A British military decoration awarded for gallantry under battle conditions. Abbr. *D.C.M.*

Distinguished Flying Cross **1.** A U.S. military decoration awarded for heroism or exceptional achievement in aerial flight. See DECORATION. **2.** A British military decoration awarded to R.A.F. officers for gallantry while flying in combat. Abbr. *DFC, D.F.C.*

Distinguished Service Cross **1.** A U.S. military decoration awarded for extraordinary heroism in combat. See DECORATION. **2.** A British military decoration awarded to members of the Royal Navy for gallantry under battle conditions. Abbr. *DSC, D.S.C.*

Distinguished Service Medal **1.** A U.S. military decoration awarded for meritorious service in a duty of great responsibility. See DECORATION. **2.** A British military decoration awarded to members of the Royal Navy for distinguished service in war. Abbr. *DSM, D.S.M.*

Distinguished Service Order A British military decoration awarded to members of all three branches for distinguished service in the field. Abbr. *D.S.O.*

dis·tort (dis·tôrt/) *v.t.* **1.** To twist or bend out of shape; make crooked or misshapen. **2.** To twist the meaning of; misrepresent; pervert. [< L *distortus,* pp. of *distorquere* < *dis-* apart + *torquere* to twist] — **dis·tort/er** *n.*

dis·tort·ed (dis·tor/tid) *adj.* Twisted. — **dis·tort/ed·ly** *adv.* — **dis·tort/ed·ness** *n.*

dis·tor·tion (dis·tôr/shən) *n.* **1.** The act of distorting. **2.** The condition of being distorted; deformity. **3.** That which is distorted, as a misleading statement. **4.** *Telecom.* A

change in the wave form of a signal caused by nonuniform transmission at different frequencies. — **dis·tor/tion·al** *adj.*

distr. Distribute; distribution; distributor.

dis·tract (dis·trakt/) *v.t.* **1.** To draw or divert (the mind, etc.) from something claiming attention. **2.** To turn or draw (the mind or attention) in conflicting directions; bewilder; confuse. **3.** To make frantic; craze. [< L *distractus,* pp. of *distrahere* < *dis-* away + *trahere* to draw] — **dis·tract/er** *n.* — **dis·tract/i·ble** *adj.*

dis·tract·ed (dis·trak/tid) *adj.* **1.** Bewildered or harassed. **2.** Mentally deranged; mad. — **dis·tract/ed·ly** *adv.*

dis·tract·ing (dis·trak/ting) *adj.* Serving or tending to distract. Also **dis·trac/tive.** — **dis·tract/ing·ly** *adv.*

dis·trac·tion (dis·trak/shən) *n.* **1.** The act of distracting or the state of being distracted. **2.** Something that distracts. **3.** Strong emotional conflict or mental distress, as caused by severe grief or pain. **4.** *Rare* Madness; frenzy.

dis·train (dis·trān/) *Law v.t.* **1.** To seize and detain (personal property) as security for a debt, claim, etc. **2.** To subject (a person) to the seizure of personal property so as to compel payment of debts, etc. — *v.i.* **3.** To distrain something or someone. [< OF *destreindre* to distress < L *distringere* to detain, hinder < *di-* apart + *stringere* to draw together] — **dis·train/a·ble** *adj.* — **dis·train/ment** *n.* — **dis·train/or** or **dis·train/er** *n.*

dis·train·ee (dis/trā·nē/) *n. Law* One whose property has been distrained.

dis·traint (dis·trānt/) *n. Law* The act of distraining; distress.

dis·trait (dis·trā/, *Fr.* dēs·tre/) *adj.* Absent-minded. [< F, pp. of *distraire* to distract < L *distrahere.* See DISTRACT.] — **dis·traite** (dis·trāt/, *Fr.* dēs·tret/) *adj.fem.*

dis·traught (dis·trôt/) *adj.* **1.** Deeply agitated in mind; worried, tense, and bewildered. **2.** Driven insane; crazed. [Var. of earlier *distract,* pp. of DISTRACT]

dis·tress (dis·tres/) *v.t.* **1.** To inflict suffering upon; cause agony or worry to; afflict; harass. **2.** To constrain by suffering or pain. **3.** *Law* To distrain. — *n.* **1.** Acute or extreme suffering or its cause; pain; trouble. **2.** An afflicted, wretched, or exhausted condition; a state of extreme need: a ship in *distress.* **3.** *Law* **a** The act of distraining. **b** The goods distrained. — **Syn.** See SUFFERING. [< AF *destresser,* OF *destrecier* < LL *districtiare* < L *districtus.* See DISTRAIN.]

dis·tressed area (dis·trest/) A depressed area (which see).

dis·tress·ful (dis·tres/fəl) *adj.* **1.** Full of or causing distress. **2.** Denoting distress: *distressful* groans. — **dis·tress/ful·ly** *adv.* — **dis·tress/ful·ness** *n.*

dis·tress·ing (dis·tres/ing) *adj.* Causing distress. — **dis·tress/ing·ly** *adv.*

dis·trib·u·tar·y (dis·trib/yōō·ter/ē) *n. pl.* **·tar·ies** A river branch flowing away from the main branch and not returning to it: opposed to *tributary.*

dis·trib·ute (dis·trib/yōōt) *v.t.* **·ut·ed, ·ut·ing** **1.** To divide and deal out in shares; apportion; allot. **2.** To divide and classify; categorize: to *distribute* plants into orders. **3.** To scatter or spread out, as in an area or over a surface; diffuse. **4.** To divide and arrange into distinctive parts or functions. **5.** *Logic* To use (a term) in its full extension, so as to include all members of the class denoted. **6.** *Printing* To separate and return (type) to the proper boxes. Abbr. *distr.* [< L *distributus,* pp. of *distribuere* < *dis-* away, apart + *tribuere* to give, allot] — **dis·trib/ut·a·ble** *adj.*
— **Syn.** **1.** *Distribute, divide, deal,* and *dispense* agree in meaning to give out portions of a whole. *Distribute,* the most general term, includes the senses of *dividing* the whole into parts and of *dealing* these parts to recipients. When we *distribute* or *deal,* we give to others; when we *divide,* we may take a share for ourselves. To *dispense* is to give out in carefully measured quantity or degree; a taproom *dispenses* liquor, a court *dispenses* justice.

dis·trib·u·tee (dis·trib/yə·tē/) *n. Law* An individual entitled to share in the estate of one who died intestate.

dis·tri·bu·tion (dis/trə·byōō/shən) *n.* **1.** The act of distributing or the state of being distributed. **2.** The manner in which something is distributed: random *distribution.* **3.** That which is distributed. **4.** *Econ.* The division of the aggregate income and goods of a society among the members of the society. **5.** In commerce, the system of distributing goods among consumers. **6.** *Stat.* Frequency: symbolized by *t.* Abbr. *distr.* — **dis/tri·bu/tion·al** *adj.*

distribution curve *Stat.* A frequency curve (which see).

dis·trib·u·tive (dis·trib/yə·tiv) *adj.* **1.** Pertaining to or caused by distribution. **2.** Serving or tending to distribute. **3.** *Gram.* Singling out the separate individuals of a group: *Each* and *every* are *distributive* adjectives. **4.** *Math.* Designating an operation that when performed on a set of quantities is equivalent to performing the operation on the individual members of the set and combining the results, as multiplication, $a(b + c) = ab + ac$. **5.** *Logic* Distributed throughout a particular proposition: said of a term. — *n. Gram. & Logic* A distributive word or expression. — **dis·trib/u·tive·ly** *adv.* — **dis·trib/u·tive·ness** *n.*

dis·trib·u·tor (dis-trib′yə-tər, -tôr) *n.* **1.** One who or that which distributes, or sells merchandise, usually of a specific type or category. **2.** In a gasoline engine, a device that directs, in an orderly sequence, the electrical current to the spark plugs. Also **dis·trib′ut·er** (-yə-tər). *Abbr. distr.*

dis·trict (dis′trikt) *n.* A particular region or locality; especially, an area, as within a city or state, set off from the surrounding territory for special reasons, as for administrative or judicial purposes: an electoral *district*; a residential *district. Abbr. dist.* — *v.t.* To divide into districts. [< MF < Med.L *districtus* jurisdiction < L *distringere.* See DISTRAIN.]

district attorney The prosecuting officer of a Federal or State judicial district. See PROSECUTING ATTORNEY. *Abbr. D.A., Dist. Atty.*

district court 1. A U.S. court serving a Federal judicial district. **2.** A State court serving a State judicial district.

district judge A judge who presides over a Federal or State district court.

District of Columbia A Federal district in the eastern part of the United States, coextensive with the capital city of Washington on the Potomac River; 69 sq. mi.; pop. 756,510. *Abbr. D.C.*

Dis·tri·to Fe·de·ral (dēs-trē′tō fā′thā-räl′) *Spanish* Federal District. *Abbr. D.F.*

dis·trust (dis-trust′) *v.t.* To feel no trust for or confidence in; doubt; suspect. — *n.* Lack of confidence or trust; doubt; suspicion. — **Syn.** See DOUBT.

dis·trust·ful (dis-trust′fəl) *adj.* Full of distrust or suspicion; doubtful; suspicious: *distrustful* of promises. — **dis·trust′ful·ly** *adv.* — **dis·trust′ful·ness** *n.*

dis·turb (dis-tûrb′) *v.t.* **1.** To destroy or interfere with the repose, tranquillity, or peace of. **2.** To agitate the mind of; disquiet; trouble. **3.** To upset the order, system, or progression of. **4.** To interrupt; break in on. **5.** To inconvenience. [< OF *destorber* < L *disturbare* < *dis-* completely + *turbare* to disorder < *turba* tumult, crowd] — **dis·turb′er** *n.*

dis·tur·bance (dis-tûr′bəns) *n.* **1.** The act of disturbing, or the state of being disturbed. **2.** Something that disturbs. **3.** A tumult or commotion; especially, a public disorder. **4.** A disordered condition of the mind; mental agitation or distraction. [< OF *destorbance* < *destorber.* See DISTURB.]

dis·turbed (dis-tûrbd′) *adj.* **1.** Characterized by disturbance. **2.** Troubled emotionally or mentally; neurotic.

di·sul·fate (dī-sul′fāt) *n. Chem.* **1.** A pyrosulfate (which see). **2.** A bisulfate (which see). Also **di·sul′phate.**

di·sul·fide (dī-sul′fīd) *n. Chem.* A sulfide containing two atoms of sulfur to the molecule: also called *bisulfide.* Also **di·sul′fid** (-fid), **di·sul′phide.**

di·sul·fur·ic acid (dī-sul-fyŏŏr′ik) *Chem.* Pyrosulfuric acid (which see).

dis·un·ion (dis-yōōn′yən) *n.* **1.** The state of being disunited; severance; rupture. **2.** A condition of disagreement.

dis·un·ion·ist (dis-yōōn′yən-ist) *n.* **1.** An advocate of disunion. **2.** In U.S. history, one who favored the dissolution of the Union before or during the Civil War period; a Secessionist. — **dis·un′ion·ism** *n.*

dis·u·nite (dis′yōō-nīt′) *v.* **·nit·ed, ·nit·ing** *v.t.* **1.** To break the union of; separate; part. **2.** To alienate; estrange. — *v.i.* **3.** To come apart. [< DIS-¹ + UNITE]

dis·u·ni·ty (dis-yōō′nə-tē) *n. pl.* **·ties** Lack of unity.

dis·use (*n.* dis-yōōs′; *v.* dis-yōōz′) *n.* The state of not being used; out of use. — *v.t.* **·used, ·us·ing** To stop using.

dis·u·til·i·ty (dis′yōō-til′ə-tē) *n.* **1.** Lack of usefulness. **2.** Harmfulness.

dis·val·ue (dis-val′yōō) *v.t.* **·val·ued, ·val·u·ing** *Rare* To treat as of little value; disparage.

di·syl·la·ble (dī-sil′ə-bəl) See DISSYLLABLE.

di·ta (dē′tə) *n.* A Philippine forest tree (*Alstonia scholaris*) of the dogbane family, the bark of which yields a poisonous alkaloid similar to curare. [< Tagalog]

di·tat De·us (dī′tat dē′əs) *Latin* God enriches: motto of Arizona.

ditch (dich) *n.* A long, narrow trench or channel dug in the ground, typically used for irrigation or drainage. — *v.t.* **1.** To make a ditch in. **2.** To surround with a ditch. **3.** To throw into or as into a ditch. **4.** *U.S.* To derail (a train). **5.** *U.S. Slang* To get rid of; also, to get away from. — *v.i.* **6.** To make a ditch. **7.** *Slang* To bring down a disabled airplane into water. [OE *dīc.* Related to DIKE.] — **ditch′er** *n.*

di·the·ism (dī′thē-iz′əm) *n. Theol.* Belief in two coequal gods; dualism. **2.** Belief in two antagonistic principles of good and evil, as in Zoroastrianism. [< DI-² + Gk. *theos* God] — **di′the·ist** *n.* — **di′the·is′tic** *adj.*

dith·er (dith′ər) *n.* A state of nervous excitement or anxiety, or of trembling agitation. — *v.i.* To be in a dither. [Var. of earlier *didder* to tremble, shake; origin uncertain]

dith·y·ramb (dith′ə-ram, -ramb) *n.* **1.** In ancient Greece, a wild, passionate choric hymn or chant sung in honor of Dionysus and constituting the direct forerunner of Greek drama. **2.** A highly emotional or rhapsodic speech or piece of writing. [< L *dithyrambus* < Gk. *dithyrambos*]

dith·y·ram·bic (dith′ə-ram′bik) *adj.* **1.** Pertaining to or resembling a dithyramb. **2.** Passionately or wildly lyrical; rhapsodic. — *n.* A dithyramb.

Dit·mars (dit′märz), **Raymond Lee,** 1876–1942, U.S. zoologist.

dit·ta·ny (dit′ə-nē) *n. pl.* **·nies 1.** A perennial American herb (*Cunila origanoides*) of the mint family, with small, purplish or lilac blossoms: also called *stonemint.* **2.** Any of various plants of the mint family, as the **Cretan dittany** (*Origanum dictamnus*). **3.** Fraxinella. [< OF *ditan, dictamne* < L *dictamnus* < Gk. *diktamnon,* ? < *Dikté,* a mountain in Crete where it grew]

dit·to (dit′ō) *n. pl.* **·tos 1.** The same thing (as something written above or mentioned or done before), usually symbolized, as in a list, by ditto marks. *Abbr. do.* **2.** A duplicate or copy of something. **3.** Ditto marks. — *adv.* As written above or as mentioned before. — *interj. Informal* I agree. — *v.t.* **·toed, ·to·ing 1.** To repeat. **2.** To duplicate. [< Ital. *detto, ditto* said, aforesaid < L *dictum.* See DICTUM.]

dit·tog·ra·phy (di-tog′rə-fē) *n. pl.* **·phies 1.** Unintentional repetition of written letters or words. **2.** A passage showing this. [< Gk. *dittos* double + -GRAPHY] — **dit′to·graph′ic** *adj.*

ditto marks Two small marks (″) placed beneath something previously written to indicate that it is to be repeated. Also **ditto mark.**

dit·ty (dit′ē) *n. pl.* **·ties** A short, simple song. [< OF *dittie, ditie* < L *dictatum* a thing said < *dictare.* See DICTATE.]

ditty bag A sailor's bag for needles, thread, personal belongings, etc. [Origin uncertain]

ditty box A small box used like a ditty bag.

Di·u (dē′ōō) A district of former Portuguese India comprising an island off the coast of NW India and two small areas on the mainland; 14 sq. mi.; pop. 14,280 (1961); capital, Diu; annexed by India in 1961.

di·u·re·sis (dī′yŏŏ-rē′sis) *n. Pathol.* Excessive secretion of urine. [< NL < Gk. *dia-* thoroughly + *ourēsis* urination]

di·u·ret·ic (dī′yŏŏ-ret′ik) *adj.* Increasing the secretion and flow of urine. — *n.* A diuretic medicine.

di·ur·nal (dī-ûr′nəl) *adj.* **1.** Of, belonging to, or occurring each day; daily. **2.** Of, belonging to, or occurring during the daytime; not nocturnal. **3.** More active during the day than at night: *diurnal* animals. **4.** *Bot.* Opening during the day and closing at night: *diurnal* flowers. — **Syn.** See DAILY. — *n.* **1.** *Eccl.* A breviary containing all or most of the canonical hours except matins. **2.** *Archaic* A diary. **3.** *Archaic* A daily newspaper. [< L *diurnalis* < *diurnus* daily < *dies* day. Doublet of JOURNAL.] — **di·ur′nal·ly** *adv.*

diurnal parallax See under PARALLAX.

div. 1. Divided. **2.** Dividend. **3.** Division; divisor. **4.** Divorce(d).

di·va (dē′və) *n. pl.* **·vas** or **·ve** (-vā) A celebrated female operatic singer; a prima donna. [< Ital., fem. of *divo* divine < L *divus*]

di·va·gate (dī′və-gāt) *v.i.* **·gat·ed, ·gat·ing 1.** To wander or stray aimlessly. **2.** To digress. [< L *divagatus,* pp. of *divagari* < *dis-* about, in different directions + *vagari* to wander] — **di′va·ga′tion** *n.*

di·va·lent (dī-vā′lənt, div′ə-) *adj. Chem.* Bivalent (which see).

di·van (di-van′, dī′van) *n.* **1.** A sofa or couch; especially, a long, low, cushioned seat without arm rests or back. **2.** A room set aside for smoking or drinking. **3.** In the Near East, a room used for councils of state or similar formal functions; also, a council of state. **4.** In Persia, a collection of poems by one writer: also spelled *diwan.* [< Turkish *divan* < Persian *dēvān,* orig. a collection of poems, a register; later, a council, chamber, bench]

di·var·i·cate (*v.* di-var′ə-kāt, dī-; *adj.* di-var′ə-kit, -kāt, dī-) *v.* **·cat·ed, ·cat·ing** *v.i.* **1.** To spread apart or branch out at a wide angle from a common point; diverge. — *v.t.* **2.** To cause to diverge widely. — *adj.* Widely divergent. [< L *divaricatus,* pp. of *divaricare* < *dis-* apart + *varicare* to straddle < *varicus* straddling] — **di·var′i·cate·ly** *adv.*

di·var·i·ca·tion (di-var′ə-kā′shən, dī-) *n.* **1.** The act of spreading apart or branching out. **2.** A divergence of opinion. **3.** *Biol.* A crossing of fibers at different angles.

di·var·i·ca·tor (di-var′ə-kā′tər, dī-) *n.* **1.** One who or that which diverges or causes to diverge. **2.** *Zool.* A muscle that causes the shells of a bivalve to open wide.

dive (dīv) *v.* **dived** or **dove, dived, div·ing** *v.i.* **1.** To plunge, especially, headfirst, as into water. **2.** To go under water or to the bottom, as in a diving suit; submerge, as a submarine. **3.** To plunge downward at a sharp angle. **4.** To dart away into something: to *dive* into a forest. **5.** To leap into something: to *dive* into bed. **6.** To rush into and become deeply involved or engrossed in something. **7.** To reach into something with abrupt eagerness: to *dive* into a box of candy. — *v.t.* **8.** To cause to plunge; especially, to cause (an airplane) to move swiftly downward at a sharp angle. — *n.* **1.** A plunge, as into water. **2.** A sharp, swift descent, as of an airplane. **3.** *Informal* A cheap, disreputable place, as a squalid drinking establishment. — **to take a dive** *U.S. Slang* In boxing, to allow an opponent to win by prearrangement. [Blend of OE *dūfan* to dive and *dȳfan* to immerse]

dive bomber An airplane designed to bomb a target while in a steep dive.

div·er (dī'vər) *n.* **1.** One who dives from a diving board or platform, often in competition. **2.** One who dives to salvage sunken cargo, etc. **3.** A bird that dives, as a loon or grebe.

di·verge (di·vûrj', dī-) *v.* **·verged, ·verg·ing** *v.i.* **1.** To move or extend outward in different directions from a common point or from each other, as rays of light: opposed to *converge*. **2.** To deviate, as from a norm. **3.** To differ, as in opinion. — *v.t.* **4.** To cause to diverge. [< NL *divergere* < L *dis-* apart + *vergere* to incline]

di·ver·gence (di·vûr'jəns, dī-) *n.* **1.** The act of diverging, or the state of being divergent. **2.** Deviation, as from a norm. **3.** Difference, as of opinion. **4.** *Meteorol.* An atmospheric condition marked by a net outflow of air from a given region. Also **di·ver'gen·cy.** — **Syn.** See DEVIATION, DIFFERENCE.

di·ver·gent (di·vûr'jənt, dī-) *adj.* **1.** Moving or extending outward in different directions: opposed to *convergent*. **2.** Deviating, as from a norm. **3.** Differing, as in opinion. Also **di·verg'ing.** [< NL *divergens, -entis,* ppr. of *divergere.* See DIVERGE.] — **di·ver'gent·ly** *adv.*

divergent strabismus See under STRABISMUS.

di·vers (dī'vərz) *adj.* **1.** Several. **2.** Various. **3.** *Archaic* Diverse. — **Syn.** See SEVERAL. [< OF < L *diversus* different, orig. pp. of *divertere.* See DIVERT.]

di·verse (di·vûrs', dī-, dī'vûrs) *adj.* **1.** Marked by distinct differences; not alike. **2.** Varied in kind or form; diversified. [< OF < L *diversus.* See DIVERS.] — **di·verse'ly** *adv.* — **di·verse'ness** *n.*

di·ver·si·fied (di·vûr'sə·fīd, dī-) *adj.* Varied; variegated.

di·ver·si·form (di·vûr'sə·fôrm, dī-) *adj.* Varying in form.

di·ver·si·fy (di·vûr'sə·fī, dī-) *v.t.* **·fied, ·fy·ing** **1.** To make diverse; give variety to; vary. **2.** To make or distribute (investments) among different types of securities so as to minimize risk. — **di·ver·si·fi·ca·tion** (di·vûr'sə·fə·kā'shən, dī-) *n.*

di·ver·sion (di·vûr'zhən, -shən, dī-) *n.* **1.** The act of diverting or turning aside, as from a course. **2.** *Mil.* An attack or feint intended to draw the attention and force of the enemy from the principal point of operation. **3.** Something that diverts or distracts, as from worry or labor; amusement.

di·ver·sion·ar·y (di·vûr'zhən·er'ē, -shən-, dī-) *adj.* Pertaining to a diversion; especially, designed to distract the enemy from the principal point of operation: *diversionary* tactics.

di·ver·si·ty (di·vûr'sə·tē, dī-) *n. pl.* **·ties** **1.** The state or quality of being diverse; unlikeness; difference; also, an instance of this. **2.** Variety; multiplicity: a *diversity* of interests. — **Syn.** See DIFFERENCE.

di·vert (di·vûrt', dī-) *v.t.* **1.** To turn aside, as from a set course; deflect. **2.** To distract the attention of. **3.** To amuse; entertain. — **Syn.** See ENTERTAIN. [< L *divertere* < *dis-* apart + *vertere* to turn]

di·vert·ing (di·vûr'ting, dī-) *adj.* Amusing; entertaining. — **di·vert'ing·ly** *adv.*

di·ver·tic·u·lum (dī'vər·tik'yə·ləm) *n. pl.* **·la** (-lə) *Anat.* A blind pouch or structure, as the cecum, leading off from a larger canal or cavity. [< L *diverticulum, deverticulum* by-path < *divertere.* See DIVERT.] — **di'ver·tic'u·lar** *adj.*

di·ver·ti·men·to (di·ver'ti·men'tō) *n. pl.* **·ti** (-tē) *Music* A light and graceful instrumental composition in several movements. [< Ital., diversion]

di·ver·tisse·ment (dē·ver·tēs·män') *n.* **1.** A diversion; amusement. **2.** *Music* A divertimento. **3.** A short ballet or similar presentation performed during or between the parts of a longer work, as in an opera or play. [< MF]

Di·ves (dī'vēz) The rich man of the parable in *Luke* xvi 19–31. — *n.* Any rich, worldly man. [< L, rich]

di·vest (di·vest', dī-) *v.t.* **1.** To strip, as of clothes. **2.** To deprive, as of rights or possessions. **3.** *Law* To devest. [< Med.L *divestire, disvestire* < OF *desvestir.* See DEVEST.]

di·vest·i·ture (di·ves'tə·chər, dī-) *n.* The act of divesting, or the state of being divested. Also **di·vest'ment, di·ves'ture.**

di·vide (di·vīd') *v.* **·vid·ed, ·vid·ing** *v.t.* **1.** To separate into pieces or portions, as by cutting. **2.** To distribute the pieces or portions of: to *divide* candy among children. **3.** To separate into sections: to *divide* a room with a partition. **4.** To separate into groups; classify. **5.** To split up into opposed sides; cause dissent in; disunite. **6.** To cause to be apart; cut off: The sea *divided* them from civilization. **7.** *Math.* a To subject to the process of division. **b** To be an exact divisor of. **8.** *Mech.* To mark dividing lines on (a sextant, etc.); graduate; calibrate. — *v.i.* **9.** To become separated into parts; branch; diverge. **10.** To split up through disagreement; be at variance. **11.** *Brit.* In Parliament and other legislative bodies, to separate into two groups in order to vote, one group being for and one against a measure. **12.** To share. **13.** To perform mathematical division. — **Syn.** See DISTRIBUTE. — *n.* A mountain range or area of high land separating one drainage system from another; watershed. [< L *dividere* to separate, divide] — **di·vid'a·ble** *adj.*

di·vid·ed (di·vī'did) *adj.* **1.** Separated into parts; parted. **2.** Shared; distributed. **3.** Split up, as by conflicting opinions; disunited. **4.** *Bot.* Having incisions or indentations extending to the base or the midrib, as in certain leaves.

di·vi·de et im·pe·ra (div'ə·dē et im'pər·ə) *Latin* Divide and rule.

div·i·dend (div'ə·dend) *n.* **1.** *Math.* A quantity divided, or to be divided, into equal parts. **2.** A sum of money, as that accruing from profits or sales, that is to be distributed according to some fixed proportion, as to stockholders or creditors. **3.** The portion of such a sum given to each individual. **4.** In insurance, a refund in money or a reduction in premium payments given to the insured as a form of profit sharing. Abbr. *div.* [< L *dividendum* thing to be divided < *dividere* to separate, divide]

di·vid·er (di·vī'dər) *n.* **1.** One who or that which divides, separates, or apportions. **2.** *pl.* A pair of compasses typically used for measuring or marking off short intervals.

div·i·di·vi (div'ē·div'ē) *n.* **1.** A small tree or shrub (*Caesalpinia coriaria*) of tropical America. **2.** Its brown pods, used for dyeing and tanning. **3.** A related species (*C. tinctoria*) whose pods are similarly used. [< Sp. < Carib]

di·vid·u·al (di·vij'ōō·əl) *adj.* **1.** Divided or divisible into parts. **2.** Separate or separable. **3.** Distributed. [< L *dividuus* divisible < *dividere* to divide] — **di·vid'u·al·ly** *adv.*

div·i·na·tion (div'ə·nā'shən) *n.* **1.** The act or art of foretelling the future or of discovering by supernatural or intuitive means that which is hidden or unknown. **2.** That which is foretold; a prophecy. **3.** A successful or clever guess. — **Syn.** See MAGIC. — **di·vin·a·to·ry** (div·in'ə·tôr'ē, -tō'rē) *adj.*

di·vine (di·vīn') *adj.* **1.** Of or pertaining to God or a god; also, of or pertaining to theology: *divine* studies. **2.** Given by or derived from God or a god: a *divine* vision. **3.** Directed or devoted to God or a god; sacred; religious: *divine* worship. **4.** Reflecting the attributes or suggestive of God or a god; godlike: *divine* beauty. **5.** Extraordinarily perfect; excellent to the highest degree: the *divine* poets of antiquity. **6.** *Informal* Altogether delightful: She said it was a *divine* party. — *n.* **1.** A clergyman. **2.** A theologian. — *v.* **·vined, ·vin·ing** *v.t.* **1.** To foretell (the future) or find out (what is obscure) by occult means. **2.** To locate (water, etc.) by means of a divining rod. **3.** To conjecture or surmise by insight or instinct. **4.** *Archaic* To make known; disclose. **5.** *Archaic* To indicate in advance; foreshow; portend; presage. — *v.i.* **6.** To practice divination. **7.** To conjecture something; guess. — **Syn.** See AUGUR. [< OF *devin, divin* < L *divinus* < *divus* < *deus* god] — **di·vine'ly** *adv.* — **di·vine'ness** *n.*

Divine Comedy A narrative poem in 100 cantos, written (1307–21) in Italian by Dante Alighieri, dealing with the poet's imaginary journey through hell, purgatory, and paradise.

Divine Office The canonical hours.

di·vin·er (di·vī'nər) *n.* One who divines.

divine right of kings Royal authority considered as God-given.

diving beetle Any aquatic, predacious beetle (family *Dytiscidae*), the larva of which is called a *water tiger*.

diving bell A large, hollow, inverted vessel supplied with air under pressure, in which men may work under water.

diving board A flexible board upon which divers jump in order to gain height or impetus for the dive: also called *springboard*.

diving duck Any of various ducks (subfamily *Aythyinae*) that dive under water to feed, as the eider, scaup, scoter, and canvasback.

diving suit A waterproof garment with detachable helmet worn by divers doing underwater work, supplied with air through a hose from the surface or from portable tanks.

divining rod A forked twig or branch, usually of hazel or willow, popularly asserted to indicate underground water or metal resources by bending downward when held by the tips and carried about an area: also called *dowsing rod*.

di·vin·i·ty (di·vin'ə·tē) *n. pl.* **·ties** **1.** The state or quality of being divine; especially, the state or quality of being God or a god; godhead. **2.** A godlike character or attribute; especially, supreme excellence. **3.** A god or goddess; deity. **4.** Theology. **5.** A soft, creamy candy usually made of sugar, egg whites, corn syrup or honey, flavoring, and nut meats. — **the Divinity** God. [< OF *devinite* theology < L *divinitas* godhead, deity < *divinus.* See DIVINE.]

div·i·nize (div'ə·nīz) *v.t.* **·nized, ·niz·ing** To make or treat as divine; deify. — **div'i·ni·za'tion** *n.*

di·vis·i·ble (di·viz'ə·bəl) *adj.* **1.** Capable of being divided. **2.** *Math.* That can be divided and leave no remainder. — **di·vis'i·bil'i·ty, di·vis'i·ble·ness** *n.* — **di·vis'i·bly** *adv.*

di·vi·sion (di·vizh'ən) *n.* **1.** The act of dividing; separation. **2.** The state of being divided. **3.** One of the parts into which a thing is divided; section. **4.** A part or section of a country, government, business organization, etc., that has been divided for administrative, political, or other reasons. **5.** Something that divides or separates, as a partition or boundary line. **6.** The state of being at variance, as in opinion; disagreement; discord. **7.** The act of distributing or sharing; distribution: a *division* of labor. **8.** *Math.* The operation of finding how many times a number or quantity (the *divisor*) is contained in another number or quantity (the *dividend*), the number or quantity found being called the *quotient*. **9.** A voting of a legislative body, especially when the members rise and go into affirmative and negative lobbies, as in the British Parliament. **10.** *Mil.* A major administrative and tactical unit that combines in itself the necessary arms and services for sustained combat, is larger than a regiment and smaller than a corps, and is normally commanded by a major general. **11.** In the U.S. Navy, a number of ships of similar type grouped for operational and administrative command. **12.** In the U.S. Air Force, an air combat organization normally consisting of two or more combat wings with appropriate service units. **13.** *Zool.* A category of animals having common characters but no established rank in taxonomy. Abbr. *div.* — **Syn.** See PORTION. [< OF < L *divisio, -onis* < *dividere* to divide] — **di·vi′sion·al** *adj.*

division sign *Math.* The symbol (÷) placed between two numbers or quantities to denote a division of the first by the second, as 6 ÷ 2 = 3.

di·vi·sive (di·vī′siv) *adj.* **1.** Causing or expressing division or distribution. **2.** Creating division, dissension, or strife.

di·vi·sor (di·vī′zər) *n. Math.* **1.** A number or quantity by which another number or quantity is divided. **2.** A common divisor (which see). Abbr. *div.*

di·vorce (di·vôrs′, -vōrs′) *n.* **1.** Dissolution of a marriage bond by legal process or by accepted custom. **2.** Legal separation of a husband and wife without dissolution of the marriage. **3.** A judicial declaration dissolving a marriage. **4.** Any radical or complete separation. Also **di·vorce′ment.** — *v.* **·vorced, ·vorc·ing** *v.t.* **1.** To dissolve the marriage of. **2.** To free oneself from (one's husband or wife) by divorce. **3.** To separate; cut off; disunite. — *v.i.* **4.** To get a divorce. [< MF < L *divortium* < *divertere* to divert]

di·vor·cé (di·vôr′sā′, -vōr′-, di·vôr′sā, -vōr′-) *n.* A divorced man. [< F, pp. of *divorcer* to divorce] — **di·vor′cée′** *n.fem.*

di·vor·cee (di·vôr′sē′, -vōr′-) *n.* A divorced person.

div·ot (div′ət) *n.* **1.** A piece of turf torn from the sod by the stroke of a golf club. **2.** *Scot.* An oblong piece of turf or sod.

di·vul·gate (di·vul′gāt) *v.t.* **·gat·ed, ·gat·ing** To make known. [< L *divulgatus*, pp. of *divulgare*. See DIVULGE.] — **di·vul′gat·er** *n.* — **di·vul·ga·tion** (div′əl·gā′shən) *n.*

di·vulge (di·vulj′) *v.t.* **·vulged, ·vulg·ing** To tell, as a secret; disclose; reveal. [< L *divulgare* < *dis-* away + *vulgare* to make public] — **di·vulge′ment** *n.* — **di·vulg′er** *n.*

di·vul·gence (di·vul′jəns) *n.* Disclosure.

div·vy (div′ē) *Slang n. pl.* **·vies** A share; portion. — *v.t.* **·vied, ·vy·ing** To divide: often with *up.* [Short for DIVIDE]

di·wan¹ (di·wän′, -wön′) See DEWAN.

di·wan² (di·wän′, -wön′) *n.* Divan (def. 4).

Dix·ie (dik′sē) **1.** Traditionally, those States that comprised the Confederacy during the Civil War; the Southern United States. Also **Dixie Land.** **2.** A song composed by D. D. Emmett in 1859, adopted by the Confederate army as a marching song.

Dix·ie·crat (dik′sē·krat) *n.* Formerly, a member of the States' Rights Party. [< DIXIE + (DEMO)CRAT]

Dix·ie·land (dik′sē·land′) *n.* A style of jazz in two-beat or four-beat rhythm, originally played in New Orleans.

dix·it (dik′sit) *n.* A statement or a declaration made upon personal authority. [< L, he has spoken]

Di·yar·be·kir (dē·yär′be·kir′) A city in SE Turkey, on the Tigris; pop. 80,645 (1960): also *Diarbekr*. Also **Di·yar′ba·kir′.**

diz·en (diz′ən, dī′zən) *v.t.* To dress in finery; deck out; bedizen. [< M.Du. *disen* to put flax on a distaff] — **diz′en·ment** *n.*

diz·zy (diz′ē) *adj.* **·zi·er, ·zi·est** **1.** Having a feeling of whirling or confusion, with a tendency to fall; giddy. **2.** Causing or inclined to cause giddiness: a *dizzy* height. **3.** *Informal* Silly; stupid. — *v.t.* **·zied, ·zying** To make giddy; confuse. [OE *dysig* foolish, stupid] — **diz′zi·ly** *adv.* — **diz′zi·ness** *n.*

Djai·lo·lo (ji·lō′lō) See HALMAHERA.

Dja·kar·ta (jä·kär′tä) See JAKARTA.

djeb·el (jeb′əl) See JEBEL.

Dji·bou·ti (ji·bōō′tē) The capital of the French Territory of the Afars and Issas; pop. 41,200 (est. 1969): also *Jibuti*.

djin·ni (ji·nē′) See JINNI, etc.

Djok·ja·kar·ta (jōk′yə·kär′tə) See JOGJAKARTA.

dkg or dkg. Dekagram(s).

dkl or dkl. Dekaliter(s).

dkm or dkm. Dekameter(s).

dks or dks. Dekastere(s).

dl or dl. Deciliter(s).

D/L Demand loan.

D layer A region of the atmosphere, lying just below the Heaviside layer, that reflects very long radio waves.

D.Lit. or D.Litt. Doctor of Letters (or Literature) (L *Doctor Lit(t)erarum*).

dlr. Dealer.

D.L.S. Doctor of Library Science.

dlvy Delivery.

dm or dm. **1.** Decameter(s). **2.** Decimeter(s).

DM. or Dm. Deutschemark.

D.M. Deputy Master.

D.M.D. Doctor of Dental Medicine (L *Dentariae Medicinae Doctor*).

DME Distance Measuring Equipment.

D.Mus. Doctor of Music.

DMZ Demilitarized zone.

D.N. Our Lord (L *Dominus Noster*).

DNA *Biochem.* Deoxyribonucleic acid.

DNB or D.N.B. *Brit.* Dictionary of National Biography.

Dnie·per (dnye′pər, nē′pər) A river in the SW Soviet Union, flowing 1,420 miles, generally SE, to the Black Sea. *Russian* **Dnie·pr** (dnye′pr). Also **Dne′per.**

Dnie·pro·dzer·zhinsk (dnye′prə·dzer·zhinsk′, *Russ.* dnye′pro·dzir·zhēnsk′) A city in the Ukrainian S.S.R., on the Dnieper; pop. 227,000 (1970): formerly *Kamienskoye*. Also **Dne′pro·dzer·zhinsk′.**

Dnie·pro·ges (dnye′pro·ges′) A dam in the Ukrainian S.S.R., on the Dnieper; 200 ft. high, 5 mi. long; site of a hydroelectric power station. Also **Dne′pro·ges′.** Formerly **Dnie′pro·stroi′, Dne′pro·stroi′** (-stroi′). [< Russian *Dnie·pro(vskaya)g(idro)e(lektricheskaya)s(tantsiya)*]

Dnie·pro·pye·trovsk (dnye′prə·pə·trofsk, *Russ.* dnye′pro·pye·trovsk′) A city in the SW Ukrainian S.S.R., on the Dnieper; pop. 863,000 (1970): formerly *Yekaterinoslav, Ekaterinoslav*. Also **Dne′pro·pe·trovsk′.**

Dnies·ter (dnyes′tər, nēs′tər) A river in the SW Soviet Union, flowing 876 miles, generally SE to the Black Sea. *Russian* **Dnies·tr** (dnyes′tr). Also **Dnes′ter.**

do¹ (dōō) *v.* **did, done, do·ing** Present: *sing.* do, do (*Archaic* thou do·est or dost), does (*Archaic* do·eth or doth), *pl.* do; past: **did** (*Archaic* thou didst); pp. **done**; ppr. **do·ing** *v.t.* **1.** To perform, as an action; fabricate or compose, as a piece of work. **2.** To fulfill; complete; accomplish. **3.** To deal with or take care of: to *do* chores. **4.** To cause or produce; bring about: to *do* no wrong. **5.** To exert; put forth: He *did* his best. **6.** To give; render: to *do* homage. **7.** To work at: She *does* sewing for a living. **8.** To work out, as a problem; solve. **9.** To translate: to *do* Dante into English. **10.** To present (a play, reading, etc.): They are *doing* Ibsen. **11.** To enact the part of: to *do* Ophelia. **12.** To cover (a distance); travel. **13.** *Informal* To make a tour of; visit: to *do* the Louvre. **14.** To serve the needs of; be sufficient for: Five dollars will *do* me. **15.** *Informal* To serve, as a term in prison. **16.** *Informal* To cheat; swindle. — *v.i.* **17.** To exert oneself; be active; strive: to *do* or die. **18.** To conduct or behave oneself. **19.** To fare; get along: I *did* badly in the race. **20.** To serve the purpose; suffice. — **to do away with** **1.** To throw away; discard; abolish. **2.** To kill; destroy. — **to do by** To act toward. — **to do for** **1.** To provide for; care for. **2.** *Informal* To ruin; kill. — **to do in** *Slang* To kill. — **to do over** *Informal* To redecorate. — **to do up** **1.** To wrap or tie up, as a parcel. **2.** To roll up or arrange, as the hair. **3.** To clean; repair. **4.** To tire out. — **to do without** To exist without or get along without. — **to have to do with** To be involved with or have a relation with. — **to make do** To get along with (whatever is available). — *auxiliary* As an auxiliary, *do* is used: **1.** Without specific meaning in negative, interrogative, and inverted constructions: I *do* not want it; *Do* you want to leave?; Little *did* he know. **2.** To add force to imperatives: *Do* hurry. **3.** To express emphasis: I *do* believe you. **4.** As a substitute for another verb to avoid repetition: I will not affirm, as some *do*; Did he come? Yes, he *did*. — *n. pl.* **do's** or **dos** **1.** *Informal* A trick; cheat. **2.** Deed; duty: chiefly in the phrase **to do one's do.** **3.** *Informal* Festivity; celebration. **4.** *Dial.* Bustle; stir. **5.** *pl.* That which ought to be done: used chiefly in the expression **do's and don'ts.** [OE *dōn*] — **Syn.** **1.** perform, execute, accomplish, achieve, effect.

do² (dō) *n. Music* The first of the syllables used in solmization; the keynote of a major scale; also, the tone C. [< Ital.]

do. Ditto.

D.O. Doctor of Osteopathy.

do·a·ble (dōō′ə·bəl) *adj.* Capable of being done.

do-all (dōō′ôl′) *n.* A general helper; factotum.

dob·ber (dob′ər) *n. U.S. Dial* A float on a fishing line. [< Du., float, cork]

dob·bin (dob′in) *n.* A horse, especially a plodding or patient one; a workhorse. [after *Dobbin*, var. of *Robin* < *Robert*, a personal name]

dob·by¹ (dob′ē) *n. pl.* **·bies** A mechanical attachment on a loom for weaving small designs known as **dobby weave.** [Dim. of *Dobbin.* See DOBBIN.]

dob·by² (dob'ē) *n. pl.* **·bies** *Brit. Dial.* A sprite; brownie. [? < DOBBIN]

Do·ber·man pinscher (dō'bər-mən) A breed of large, short-haired dogs originally developed in Germany, usually black, brown, or gray-blue, with rust markings. [after Ludwig *Dobermann,* its first breeder]

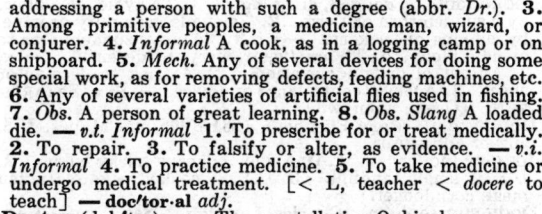

DOBERMAN PINSCHER
(26 to 28 inches high at shoulder)

do·bie (dō'bē) *n. pl.* **·bies** *SW U.S.* Adobe. Also **do'by.** [See ADOBE.]

Do·bie (dō'bē), **J**(ames) **Frank,** 1888–1964, U.S. writer and folklorist.

do·bla (dō'blä) *n.* An ancient Spanish gold coin. [< Sp. < *doble* double < L *duplus*]

do·blon (də-blōn') *n. pl.* **·blo·nes** (-blō'-nas) A former Spanish and Spanish-American gold coin. [< Sp. *doblon.* See DOUBLOON.]

do·bra (dō'brə) *n.* Any of several former Portuguese gold coins. [< Pg. < *dobre* double < L *duplus*]

Do·bro guitar (dō'brō) A type of Hawaiian guitar much used by hillbilly musicians: a trade name. Also **do'bro guitar.**

Do·bru·ja (dō'brōō-jä) A region of SE Rumania and NE Bulgaria along the Black Sea; about 9,000 sq. mi. Also **Do'·bru·dja,** *Rumanian* **Do·bro·gea** (dō'brō-jä), *Bulgarian* **Do·bru·dzha** (dō'brōō-jä).

dob·son (dob'sən) *n.* The hellgrammite. [? from *Dobson,* a surname]

Dob·son (dob'sən), **(Henry) Austin,** 1840–1921, English poet, essayist, and biographer.

dobson fly A large, North American megalopterous insect (*Corydalis cornutus*), the adult of the dobson.

Dob·zhan·sky (dōb·zhän'skē), **Theodosius,** 1900–75, U.S. geneticist born in Russia.

doc. document.

do·cent (dō'sənt) *n.* A teacher, lecturer, or tutor without regular faculty rank, as in some U.S. universities. [< G (*Privat*)*dozent* < L *docens, -entis,* ppr. of *docere* to teach]

doc·ile (dos'əl, *Brit.* dō'sīl) *adj.* **1.** Amenable to training; easy to manage; tractable. **2.** Easily worked or handled. [< MF < L *docilis* able to be taught < *docere* to teach] — **doc'ile·ly** *adv.* — **do·cil·i·ty** (do·sil'ə·tē, dō-) *n.*
— **Syn. 1.** *Docile, tractable, pliant, compliant,* and *amenable* mean submissive to the will of another. The *docile* person is easy to teach; the *tractable* person easy to lead. A *pliant* man can easily be bent in any direction; *compliant* stresses ease of persuasion, and *amenable* describes the person who is disposed to be obedient. — **Ant.** intractable, obstinate, willful, fractious, inflexible.

dock¹ (dok) *n.* **1.** The water space between two adjoining piers or wharves where ships can remain for loading, unloading, or repair. **2.** A wharf or pier. **3.** *Often pl.* A group of wharves or piers together with their adjoining waterways, sometimes roofed over. **4.** A shipping or loading platform, as for trucks, trains, etc. — **Syn.** See WHARF. — *v.t.* To bring (a vessel, truck, etc.) into or next to a dock. — *v.i.* To come into a dock. [< MDu. *docke*]

dock² (dok) *n.* **1.** The fleshy part of an animal's tail. **2.** The stump of a tail that remains after clipping. — *v.t.* **1.** To cut off the end of (a tail, etc.), or clip short the tail of. **2.** To take a part from (wages, etc.). **3.** To take from the wages, etc. of. [Cf. ME *docken* to cut short; OE *-docca,* as in *fingir-docca* finger muscle; ON *dockr* tail]

dock³ (dok) *n.* An enclosed space for the defendant in a criminal court. [< Flemish *dok* cage]

dock⁴ (dok) *n.* **1.** Any of various plants (genus *Rumex*) of the sorrel or buckwheat family, as the **sour dock** (*R. acetosa*). **2.** Any plant resembling these. [OE *docce*]

dock·age¹ (dok'ij) *n.* **1.** A charge for docking (a ship, etc.). **2.** Facilities for docking a vessel. **3.** The act of docking.

dock·age² (dok'ij) *n.* **1.** Curtailment, as of wages; deduction. **2.** Waste matter in grain, easily separated by cleaning.

dock·er¹ (dok'ər) *n.* One who or that which docks.

dock·er² (dok'ər) *n.* A dock laborer; longshoreman.

dock·et (dok'it) *n.* **1.** A summary, usually written on the back of a document; an abstract. **2.** *Law* A formal record of court judgments. **b** The book in which such a record is kept. **c** A court calendar of the cases still pending. **3.** Any calendar of things to be done. **4.** A tag or label attached to a parcel, listing contents, directions, etc. — *v.t.* **1.** To enter in a docket. **2.** To put a tag or label on (a parcel, etc.). [ME; origin uncertain]

dock·yard (dok'yärd') *n.* **1.** An area of docks, warehouses, etc., where ships are built, repaired, or fitted out. **2.** *Brit.* A navy yard (which see).

doc·tor (dok'tər) *n.* **1.** One who is trained in and licensed to practice medicine or one of its branches; a physician, surgeon, psychiatrist, dentist, veterinarian, etc. **2.** A person who has received a diploma of the highest degree, as in law, literature, divinity, etc. (abbr. *D.*); also, the title used in

addressing a person with such a degree (abbr. *Dr.*). **3.** Among primitive peoples, a medicine man, wizard, or conjurer. **4.** *Informal* A cook, as in a logging camp or on shipboard. **5.** *Mech.* Any of several devices for doing some special work, as for removing defects, feeding machines, etc. **6.** Any of several varieties of artificial flies used in fishing. **7.** *Obs.* A person of great learning. **8.** *Obs. Slang* A loaded die. — *v.t. Informal* **1.** To prescribe for or treat medically. **2.** To repair. **3.** To falsify or alter, as evidence. — *v.i. Informal* **4.** To practice medicine. **5.** To take medicine or undergo medical treatment. [< L, teacher < *docere* to teach] — **doc'tor·al** *adj.*

Doctor (dok'tər) *n.* The constellation Ophiuchus.

doc·tor·ate (dok'tər·it) *n.* The degree, status, or title of a doctor. •

doc·tri·naire (dok'trə·nâr') *adj.* Theoretical; visionary. — *n.* One whose views are derived from theories rather than from facts; an impractical theorist. — **doc'tri·nair'ism** *n.*

doc·tri·nal (dok'trə·nəl, *Brit. also* dok·trī'nəl) *adj.* Pertaining to or characterized by doctrine. — **doc'tri·nal·ly** *adv.*

doc·tri·nar·i·an (dok'trə·nâr'ē·ən) *n.* A doctrinaire. — **doc'tri·nar'i·an·ism** *n.*

doc·trine (dok'trin) *n.* **1.** That which is presented for acceptance or belief; teachings, as of a religious or political group. **2.** A particular principle or tenet that is taught, or a body of such principles or tenets. [< OF < L *doctrina* teaching < *docere* to teach]
— **Syn.** *Doctrine, theory, dogma, belief, creed,* and *tenet* refer to religious, philosophical, or scientific principles accepted by some body of persons. *Doctrine* primarily signifies that which is taught. A *theory* is a proposition regarded as susceptible of verification, and thus is usually scientific. Both a *doctrine* and a *theory* may be defended by reasoning, but a *dogma* rests as well on authority, such as the decision of a church council. Any *doctrine* is a *belief* on the part of those who accept it, but *belief* more often suggests matters of faith rather than of reason. A *creed* is the list of *doctrines* or *dogmas* of a religion or church; any single item of such a list is a *tenet.*

doc·u·ment (*n.* dok'yə·mənt; *v.* dok'yə·ment') *n.* **1.** Something written or printed that furnishes conclusive information or evidence, as an original, legal, or official paper or record. Abbr. **doc. 2.** *Obs.* Evidence or proof. **3.** *Obs.* An admonition or warning. — *v.t.* **1.** To furnish with documents. **2.** To support by conclusive information or evidence. **3.** To supply (a book, etc.) with citations or examples that prove or support what is stated. [< OF < L *documentum* lesson < *docere* to teach]

doc·u·men·ta·ry (dok'yə·men'tər·ē) *adj.* **1.** Pertaining to, consisting of, or based upon documents. **2.** That presents factual material objectively without fictionalizing: a *documentary* book. Also **doc'u·men'tal.** — *n. pl.* **·ries** A motion picture dealing with events, circumstances, etc., in a factual way, typically filmed apart from a studio and without the use of professional actors.

doc·u·men·ta·tion (dok'yə·men·tā'shən) *n.* **1.** The preparation, citation, or supplying of documents, references, records, etc. **2.** Documentary evidence. **3.** The collection, storage, and dissemination of recorded information in an integrated system for efficient use and easy accessibility.

DOD or **DoD** Department of Defense.

dod·der¹ (dod'ər) *v.i.* **1.** To tremble or totter, as from age. **2.** To move or progress with shaky or feeble steps. [Cf. ME *didder* to tremble]

dod·der² (dod'ər) *n.* Any of several leafless, twining herbs (genus *Cuscuta*), parasitic on various plants to which they adhere by suckers: also called *lovevine.* [ME *doder*]

dod·dered (dod'ərd) *adj.* **1.** Having lost the top or branches through age or decay: said of trees. **2.** Feeble; infirm. [ME *dodden* to poll, take the top off a tree]

dod·der·ing (dod'ər·ing) *adj.* Shaky; infirm, especially from age; senile.

dodeca- *combining form* Twelve; of or having twelve: *dodecagon.* Also, before vowels, **dodec-.** [< Gk. *dōdeka* twelve]

do·dec·a·gon (dō-dek'ə·gon) *n. Geom.* A polygon having twelve sides and twelve angles. [< Gk. *dōdekagōnon*] — **do·de·cag·o·nal** (dō'de·kag'ə·nəl) *adj.*

do·dec·a·he·dron (dō'dek·ə·hē'drən) *n. pl.* **·drons** or **·dra** (-drə) *Geom.* A polyhedron bounded by twelve plane faces. For illustration see CRYSTAL. [< Gk. *dōdekahedron,* neut. sing. of *dōdekahedros* < *dōdeka* twelve + *hedra* face of a solid] — **do·dec·a·he'dral** *adj.*

DODECAHEDRA
a Rhombic.
b Pentagonal.

Do·dec·a·nese (dō·dek'ə·nēs', -nēz', dō'dek·ə-) A group of islands in the Aegean comprising a Department of Greece; 1,036 sq. mi.; pop. 121,480 (1951); capital, Rhodes. *Greek* **Do·de·ka·ne·sos,** **Do·de·ka·ni·sos** (dō'de·ka·nē'sōs).

do·dec·a·phon·ic (dō'dek·ə·fon'ik) *adj. Music* Twelve-tone (def. 1). — **do·dec'a·phon'ism'** *n.* — **do·dec'a·phon'·ist** *n.* — **do·dec'a·phon'y** *n.*

dodge (doj) *v.* **dodged, dodg·ing** *v.t.* **1.** To avoid, as a blow, by a sudden turn or twist. **2.** To evade, as a duty or issue, by cunning or trickery. — *v.i.* **3.** To move suddenly, as to avoid a blow. **4.** To practice trickery; be deceitful. — *n.* **1.** An act of dodging; evasion. **2.** A trick to deceive or cheat. **3.** A clever contrivance or device. — **Syn.** See ARTIFICE. [Origin unknown]

Dodge (doj), **Mary Elizabeth,** 1831–1905, *née* Mapes, U.S. author and editor.

dodg·er (doj'ər) *n.* **1.** One who dodges; a tricky fellow. **2.** *U.S.* A small handbill. **3.** *U.S.* A cooked cake of Indian meal; corndodger.

Dodg·son (doj'sən), **Charles Lutwidg**: See (Lewis) CARROLL.

do·do (dō'dō) *n.* *pl.* **·does** or **·dos** **1.** A large, extinct bird (genus *Raphecus*) of Mauritius and Réunion, about the size of a turkey, with rudimentary, functionless wings. **2.** *Informal* One who is slow to respond to new developments, as from dullness or senility. [< Pg. *doudo*]

Do·do·na (dō-dō'nə) An ancient town in Epirus, Greece; site of a temple and oracle of Zeus. — **Do·do·nae·an** or **Do·do·ne·an** (dō'də-nē'ən), **Do·do'ni·an** *adj.*

doe (dō) *n.* **1.** The female of the deer, antelope, rabbit, kangaroo, and certain other animals. **2.** Loosely, the female of the moose or elk (properly called *cow*) or of the red deer (properly called *hind*). [OE *dā*]

Doe·nitz (dœ'nits), **Karl,** born 1891, German admiral; successor to Hitler at the fall of the Third Reich in 1945.

do·er (dōo'ər) *n.* One who acts, does, or performs; an agent.
— **Syn.** *Doer, actor, performer, executive, agent, factor,* and *operator* are compared as they denote one who is the principal in some action. The *doer* of a deed is solely responsible. *Actor* and *performer* are sometimes used in the same sense, but more often denote one of several participants in an activity. In government and business, one who puts laws, plans, etc., into effect is an *executive.* Strictly speaking, an *agent* is the prime mover of an action, but more often the word means one who carries out the orders of another, and is a close synonym of *factor.* An *operator* may be the independent head of a commercial enterprise; the word is also used to denote a skilled worker of a machine.

does (duz) Present tense, third person singular, of DO[1].

doe·skin (dō'skin') *n.* **1.** The skin of the female deer. **2.** Leather made from this, used especially for gloves. **3.** A heavy, short-napped, woolen fabric; also, a heavy, twilled, cotton fabric napped on one side.

does·n't (duz'ənt) Does not. ◆ See note under DON'T.

doff (dof, dôf) *v.t.* **1.** To take off or remove, as clothing. **2.** To take off (the hat) in salutation. **3.** To throw away; discard. [Contraction of *do off*; cf. DON] — **doff'er** *n.*

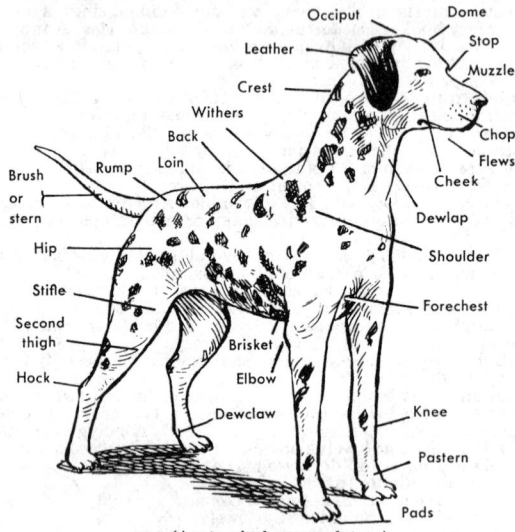

DOG (Anatomical nomenclature)

Labels: Occiput, Dome, Stop, Leather, Muzzle, Crest, Chop, Withers, Flews, Back, Cheek, Brush or stern, Rump, Loin, Dewlap, Hip, Shoulder, Stifle, Forechest, Second thigh, Brisket, Hock, Elbow, Dewclaw, Knee, Pastern, Pads

dog (dôg, dog) *n.* **1.** A domesticated, carnivorous mammal (*Canis familiaris*) of many varieties. ◆ Collateral adjective: *canine.* **2.** Any of various other species of this family (*Canidae*), as wolves, foxes, etc. **3.** The male of any of these species: opposed to *bitch.* **4.** One of various animals, as the prairie dog or the dogfish, having an appearance suggestive of a dog. **5.** A despicable person; wretch. **6.** *Informal* A man or boy; fellow: a lucky *dog.* **7.** An andiron. **8.** *Mech.* One of several devices for gripping or holding logs, etc. **9.** *Meteorol.* A sundog or fogdog. **10.** *Informal* A hot dog. **11.** *pl. U.S. Slang* The feet. — **to go to the dogs** *Informal* To go to ruin; deteriorate. — **to put on the dog** *U.S. Informal* To make a pretentious display. — *adv.* Very; utterly: used in combination: *dog-tired.* — *v.t.* **dogged, dog·ging** **1.** To

follow after or pursue persistently; hound. **2.** *Mech.* To grip or fasten (a log, etc.) with a dog. [OE *docga*]

Dog (dôg, dog) *n.* **1.** Either of two constellations, Canis Major (the Greater Dog) or Canis Minor (the Little Dog), located near Orion. **2.** The star Sirius.

dog-ape (dôg'āp', dog'-) *n.* A baboon or similar ape.

dog·bane (dôg'bān', dog'-) *n.* Any of a genus (*Apocynum*) of smooth, reddish-stemmed herbs having an acrid, milky juice; especially, the **spreading dogbane** (*A. androsaemifolium*) of North America, used in medicine. The dogbane typifies a family (*Apocynaceae*), including the oleanders and periwinkles. [DOG + BANE]

dog·ber·ry (dôg'ber'ē, dog'-) *n.* *pl.* **·ries** **1.** The red dogwood of Europe; also, its fruit. See under DOGWOOD. **2.** The bearberry (def. 1). **3.** The dog rose.

dog biscuit A hard biscuit made with meat scraps, ground bones, etc., for feeding dogs.

dog·cart (dôg'kärt', dog'-) *n.* **1.** A one-horse vehicle, usually two-wheeled, with two seats set back to back and, originally, an enclosed space for dogs beneath the rear seat. **2.** A cart hauled by one or more dogs.

DOGCART

dog·catch·er (dôg'kach'ər, dog'-) *n.* *U.S.* A person employed or elected to pick up and impound stray dogs.

dog days The hot, sultry days of July and early August, so called because during this period Sirius, the Dog Star, rises and sets with the sun.

doge (dōj) *n.* The elective chief magistrate in the former republics of Venice and Genoa. [< Ital. < L *dux, ducis* chief. Doublet of DUKE.] — **doge'dom, doge'ship** *n.*

dog-ear (dôg'ir', dog'-) *n.* A turned-down corner of a book page. — *v.t.* To turn down the corner of (a page). Also *dog's-ear.* — **dog'-eared** *adj.*

dog-eat-dog (dôg'ēt·dôg', dog'ēt·dog') *adj.* Intensely or viciously competitive.

dog·face (dôg'fās', dog'-) *n.* *U.S. Slang* A soldier in the U.S. Army; especially, an infantryman.

dog·fen·nel (dôg'fen'əl, dog'-) *n.* **1.** Mayweed. **2.** The heath aster.

dog·fight (dôg'fīt', dog'-) *n.* **1.** A fight between or as between dogs. **2.** *Mil.* A battle between fighter planes.

dog·fish (dôg'fish', dog'-) *n.* *pl.* **·fish** or **·fish·es** One of various small, littoral sharks, as the common **spiny dogfish** (*Squalus acanthias*) of North American waters, and the **smooth dogfish** (*Mustelus canis*): also called *grayfish.*

dog fox **1.** A male fox. **2.** The corsac.

dog·ged (dôg'id, dog'-) *adj.* Stubborn; obdurate. — **Syn.** See OBSTINATE. — **dog'ged·ly** *adv.* — **dog'ged·ness** *n.*

dog·ger (dôg'ər, dog'-) *n.* A two-masted fishing vessel with a broad beam and a fish well in the center, used in the North Sea. [ME *doggere*: origin uncertain]

Dogger Bank A submerged sand shoal in the North Sea between Denmark and England; scene of a German naval defeat in World War I (1915).

dog·ger·el (dôg'ər·əl, dog'-) *n.* Trivial, awkwardly written verse, usually comic or burlesque. — *adj.* Of or composed of such verse. Also **dog'grel.** [ME; origin unknown]

dog·ger·y (dôg'ər·ē, dog'-) *n.* *pl.* **·ies** **1.** Mean or malicious behavior. **2.** Dogs collectively. **3.** The rabble.

dog·gish (dôg'ish, dog'-) *adj.* **1.** Relating to or suggestive of a dog. **2.** Bad-tempered; snappish. **3.** *U.S. Informal* Pretentiously stylish. — **dog'gish·ly** *adv.* — **dog'gish·ness** *n.*

dog·gone (dôg'gôn', dog'gon') *U.S. Informal interj.* Damn!; darn!: a mild oath. — *v.t.* **·goned, ·gon·ing** To damn: a euphemism. [? Alter. of *God damn,* or perh. *dog on it*]

dog·gy (dôg'ē, dog'ē) *n.* *pl.* **·gies** A dog; especially, a small dog or a pet dog. Also **dog'gie.** — *adj.* **dog·gi·er, dog·gi·est** **1.** Of or like a dog. **2.** *U.S. Informal* Showily fashionable.

dog·house (dôg'hous', dog'-) *n.* A small house for a dog. — **in the doghouse** *U.S. Informal* In disfavor with someone.

do·gie (dō'gē) *n.* In the western United States, a stray or motherless calf: also spelled *dogy.* [Origin unknown]

dog in the manger One who keeps others from using or enjoying something he cannot use or enjoy.

dog Latin **1.** Barbarous or incorrect Latin. **2.** A jargon imitating Latin.

dog·ma (dôg'mə, dog'-) *n.* *pl.* **·mas** or **·ma·ta** (-mə·tə) **1.** *Theol.* A doctrine or system of doctrine maintained by a religious body as true and necessary of belief. **2.** A belief, principle, tenet, etc., more or less formally stated and held to be authoritative. **3.** A system of such beliefs or principles: the *dogmas* of art. — **Syn.** See DOCTRINE. [< L < Gk. *dogma, -atos* opinion, tenet < *dokeein* to think, deem right]

dog·mat·ic (dôg·mat'ik, dog-) *adj.* **1.** Of the nature of or pertaining to dogma. **2.** Marked by authoritative, often arrogant, assertion of opinions or beliefs; positive; overbearing. Also **dog·mat'i·cal.** — **dog·mat'i·cal·ly** *adv.* — **Syn.** **1.** authoritarian. **2.** opinionated, dictatorial, domineering, imperious.

dog·mat·ics (dôg·mat'iks, dog-) *n.pl.* (*construed as sing.*) The systematic study of religious dogmas, especially in the Christian church. Also **dogmatic theology.**

dog·ma·tism (dôg′mə·tiz′əm, dog′-) *n.* **1.** Positive or arrogant assertion, as of opinions or beliefs. **2.** *Philos.* Uncritical reliance on principles arrived at by reason alone and not sufficiently tested by evidence: opposed to *skepticism.*

dog·ma·tist (dôg′mə·tist, dog′-) *n.* **1.** One given to dogmatic assertions. **2.** One who sets forth dogma.

dog·ma·tize (dôg′mə·tīz, dog′-) *v.* **·tized, ·tiz·ing** *v.i.* **1.** To express oneself dogmatically. — *v.t.* **2.** To declare or assert as a dogma. — **dog′ma·ti·za′tion** *n.* — **dog′ma·tiz′er** *n.*

do-good·er (dōō′gŏŏd′ər) *n. Informal* An idealistic philanthropist or reformer: a derisive term.

dog rose The wild brier (*Rosa canina*) of European hedges and thickets, bearing single pink flowers: also *dogberry.*

dog's age (dôgz) *U.S. Informal* A long time.

dog's-ear (dôgz′ir′, dogz′-) *n.* Dog-ear (which see).

dog sled A sled drawn by one or more dogs. Also **dog sledge.**

dog's letter A name for the letter *r*, especially when representing a trill. [Trans. of L *litera canina*; so called because its sound resembles a dog's growl]

dog's life *Informal* A wretched existence.

dog's-tail (dôgz′tāl′, dogz′-) *n.* An Old World perennial grass (genus *Cynosurus*) with flat leaves and spikelets in dense clusters; especially the **crested dog's-tail** (*C. cristatus*), naturalized in eastern North America. Also **dog′tail′.**

Dog Star The star Sirius.

dog's-tongue (dôgz′tung′, dogz′-) *n.* Hound's-tongue (def. 1).

dog tag 1. A pendant or small metal plate on the collar of a dog, usually indicating ownership. **2.** *U.S. Informal* A soldier's identification tag, worn on a chain around the neck.

dog·tooth (dôg′tōōth′, dog′-) *n.* **1.** A canine tooth. **2.** *Archit.* An ornament, popular in the 13th century, generally composed of four radiating leaves, suggesting a dog's tooth.

dogtooth violet 1. A European herb (*Erythronium dens-canis*) of the lily family, bearing yellow, purple, or white flowers: also called *adder's tongue.* **2.** One of various American plants, as *E. albidum*, bearing pinkish flowers, or the yellow-flowered *E. americanum.* Also **dog's-tooth violet.**

dog·trot (dôg′trot′, dog′-) *n.* A regular and easy trot.

dog·vane (dôg′vān′, dog′-) *n. Naut.* A small vane, as of bunting, placed on the weather gunwale of a vessel to indicate the direction of the wind.

dog·watch (dôg′woch′, dog′-) *n. Naut.* Either of two short watches aboard ship, from 4 to 6 or 6 to 8 P.M.

dog·wood (dôg′wŏŏd′, dog′-) *n.* Any of certain trees or shrubs (family *Cornaceae*); especially, the **red dogwood** (*Cornus sanguinea*) of Europe, the **flowering dogwood** and **Virginia dogwood** (*C. florida*) of the United States, the state flower of Virginia, with large, decorative, white or pink flowers, and the **red-osier dogwood** (*C. stolonifera*) with dark reddish branches and bluish or white fruit: also called *cornel.*

do·gy (dō′gē) See DOGIE.

doiled (doild) *adj. Scot. & Brit. Dial.* Stunned; dazed.

doi·ly (doi′lē) *n.* *pl.* **·lies 1.** A small, ornamental piece of lace, etc., used to protect surfaces on which dishes or other objects are placed. **2.** A small dessert napkin. Also spelled *doyley, doyly.* [after *Doily* or *Doyley*, 17th c. English draper]

do·ings (dōō′ingz) *n.pl.* **1.** Activities or proceedings. **2.** Behavior; conduct.

doit (doit) *n.* **1.** A former small copper coin of the Netherlands. **2.** A tiny sum or quantity. [< Du. *duit* coin]

doit·ed (doi′tid, -tit) *adj. Scot.* Old and feeble.

do-it-your·self (dōō′it-yŏŏr·self′) *adj. U.S. Informal* Designed to be used or done without special or hired help, as in constructing, decorating, repairing, etc.

dol (dol) *n. Psychol.* A unit of pain intensity based on the sensation of heat rays on the skin. [< L *dolor* pain]

dol. 1. *Music* Dolce. **2.** Dollar(s).

do·lab·ri·form (dō-lab′rə-fôrm) *adj.* Having a shape suggestive of an ax or hatchet. [< L *dolabra* ax + -FORM]

dol·ce (dōl′chä) *Music adj.* Smooth and sweet in performance. Abbr. *dol.* — *adv.* Sweetly; softly. — *n.* A soft-toned organ stop. [< Ital. < L *dulcis* sweet]

dol·ce far nien·te (dōl′chä fär nyen′te) *Italian* Pleasant idleness; literally, (it is) sweet to do nothing.

dol·drums (dol′drəmz, dōl′-) *n.pl.* **1.** Those parts of the ocean near the equator where calms or baffling winds prevail. **2.** A becalmed state. **3.** A dull, depressed, or bored condition of mind; the dumps. [Cf. OE *dol* dull, stupid]

dole¹ (dōl) *n.* **1.** That which is distributed, especially in charity; a small gift of food or money for the poor. **2.** A giving out of something, especially of charitable gifts. **3.** A sum of money officially paid to an unemployed person for sustenance; in Great Britain, government relief for the unemployed. **4.** *Archaic* One's lot in life; fate. — **on the dole** Receiving relief payments from the government. — *v.t.* **doled, dol·ing** To dispense in small quantities; distribute: usually with *out.* [OE *dāl.* Akin to DEAL¹.]

dole² (dōl) *n. Archaic* Grief; mourning. [< OF *dol* < LL *dolium* grief < L *dolere* to feel pain]

dole·ful (dōl′fəl) *adj.* Melancholy; mournful. [< DOLE²] — **dole′ful·ly** *adv.* — **dole′ful·ness** *n.*

dol·er·ite (dol′ə·rīt) *n.* **1.** A coarse basalt or other igneous rock, as diabase. **2.** *U.S.* Any similar igneous rock not readily identified except by microscopic examination. [< Gk. *doleros* deceptive < *dolos* deceit + -ITE¹; so called because not easily identified] — **dol′er·it′ic** (-rit′ik) *adj.*

dole·some (dōl′səm) *adj. Archaic* Doleful.

dol·i·cho·ce·phal·ic (dol′i·kō·sə·fal′ik) *adj.* Having a long skull, the breadth less than one third of the length, the cephalic index being 76 or less; longheaded. Also **dol′i·cho·ceph′a·lous** (-sef′ə·ləs). [< Gk. *dolichos* long + *kephalē* head] — **dol′i·cho·ceph′a·lism, dol′i·cho·ceph′a·ly** *n.*

doll (dol) *n.* **1.** A child's toy made to resemble the human figure. **2.** A pretty but superficial woman. **3.** A pretty or lovable child. **4.** *Slang* An attractive or charming person of either sex. — *v.t. & v.i. Informal* To adorn or dress smartly: with *up.* [from *Doll*, nickname for *Dorothy*, a proper name] — **doll′ish** *adj.* — **doll′ish·ly** *adv.* — **doll′ish·ness** *n.*

dol·lar (dol′ər) *n.* **1.** The standard monetary unit of the United States, equivalent to 100 cents. **2.** The monetary unit of Australia, Bahamas, Barbados, Belize, Bermuda, Brunei, Canada, Cayman, Ethiopia, Fiji, Grenada, Guyana, Hong Kong, Jamaica, Liberia, New Zealand, Rhodesia, Singapore, Taiwan, and Trinidad and Tobago, equivalent to 100 cents. **3.** A gold or silver coin or a piece of paper currency equivalent to any of these. **4.** Loosely, any piece of currency of similar value, as the Mexican peso. **5.** A taler. Symbol $ or $. Abbr. *d., D., dol.* [< earlier *daler* < LG < G *taler, thaler*, short for *Joachimstaler*, a coin of *Joachimstal*, a village in Bohemia where first minted, 1519]

dol·lar-a-year (dol′ər·ə·yir′) *adj. U.S.* Designating a government employee, job, etc., having only token pay.

dollar diplomacy A practice or policy whereby a government protects or encourages investments by its private citizens in foreign countries or uses public or private funds to advance its own interests abroad.

dol·lar·fish (dol′ər·fish′) *n. pl.* **·fish** or **·fish·es** The butterfish (which see).

dollar sign The symbol $ or $, meaning dollar or dollars when placed before a number. Also **dollar mark.**

Doll·fus (dōl′fōōs), **Engelbert**, 1892–1934, Austrian statesman; premier 1932–34; assassinated.

dol·lop (dol′əp) *n. Informal* A portion, serving, etc., of indefinite form or amount, as of a soft substance or liquid.

dol·ly (dol′ē) *n. pl.* **·lies 1.** A doll: a child's term. **2.** A low, flat frame set on small wheels or rollers, propelled by hand and used for moving heavy loads. **3.** A similar device for moving a motion-picture or television camera about a set. **4.** A small locomotive running on narrow-gauge tracks, used in railroad yards, etc. **5.** A tool used to hold one end of a rivet while a head is being formed at the other. **6.** A short length of wood or metal that is set on the head of a pile while the pile is being driven. **7.** *Brit. Dial.* A wooden instrument for beating or stirring clothes that are being washed. — *v.i.* **·lied, ·ly·ing** To move a motion-picture or television camera mounted on a dolly toward or away from the action being photographed or televised. [< DOLL + -Y³]

Dolly Var·den (vär′dən) **1.** A flowered dress having a skirt gathered up in loops over a brightly colored petticoat. **2.** A woman's flower-trimmed hat having a wide brim turned down at one side. **3.** A fish (*Salvelinus malma*) of Pacific Coast streams, having red spots on its back and sides: also **Dolly Varden trout.** [after *Dolly Varden*, a character in Dickens's *Barnaby Rudge*]

dol·man (dol′mən) *n.* **1.** A long Turkish outer garment. **2.** A woman's coat with dolman sleeves or capelike arm pieces. **3.** The capelike uniform jacket of a hussar. [< F *doliman* < Turkish *dōlāmān* long robe]

dolman sleeve A sleeve tapering from a wide opening at the armhole to a narrow one at the wrist.

dol·men (dol′mən) *n.* A prehistoric monument made of two or more large, rough stones set on end and capped with a single huge stone or several stones: sometimes called *cromlech.* [< F, < Breton *tol* table + *men* stone]

dol·o·mite (dol′ə·mīt) *n.* **1.** A brittle calcium magnesium carbonate, occurring abundantly in white to pale pink rhombohedral crystals. **2.** A rock consisting principally of this and resembling marble. [after D. de *Dolomieu*, 1750–1801, French geologist] — **dol′o·mit′ic** (-mit′ik) *adj.*

Dol·o·mites (dol′ə·mīts) An eastern division of the Alps in northern Italy; highest peak, Marmolada, 10,964 ft. Also **Dolomite Alps.**

do·lor (dō′lər) *n. Poetic* Sorrow; anguish. Also *Brit.* **do′lour.** [< OF < L, pain]

dol·or·im·e·try (dol′ə·rim′ə·trē) *n. Psychol.* The measurement of the intensity of pain in terms of dols. [< L *dolor, -oris* pain + -METRY]

do·lo·ro·so (dō′lə·rō′sō) *Music adj.* Having a sorrowful or plaintive quality. — *adv.* With sorrow or a plaintive quality. [< Ital., sorrowful]

do·lor·ous (dō′lər·əs, dol′ər-) *adj.* **1.** Sad; mournful. **2.** Painful. **— do′lor·ous·ly** *adv.* **— do′lor·ous·ness** *n.*

dol·phin (dol′fin) *n.* **1.** Any of various cetaceans (family *Delphinidae*) with beaklike snouts; especially, the **common dolphin** (*Delphinus delphis*), of the Mediterranean and temperate Atlantic, and the bottlenose: loosely called *porpoise.*

DOLPHIN (*def.* 1)
(To 8 feet long)

2. A fish (genus *Coryphaena*) of southern waters, noted for colors that become brighter and vary when the fish is taken out of water: also called *dorado.* **3.** *Naut.* Any of several devices to which a boat can be moored, as a buoy or post. [< OF *daulphin* < L *delphinus* < Gk. *delphis, -inos*]

Dol·phin (dol′fin) *n.* The constellation Delphinus.

dolphin striker *Naut.* **1.** A vertical spar under a bowsprit, used in guying stays: also called *martingale.* **2.** The spearlike point of this spar.

dolt (dōlt) *n.* A stupid person; blockhead; dunce. [ME *dold* dulled, stupid. Cf. OE *dol.*] **— dolt′ish** *adj.* **— dolt′ish·ly** *adv.* **— dolt′ish·ness** *n.*

Dom (dom) *n.* **1.** In Portugal and Brazil, a title of respect: used with the given name. **2.** A title given to certain Roman Catholic monks and church dignitaries. [< L *dominus* master]

dom. **1.** Domain. **2.** Domestic. **3.** Dominion.

-dom *suffix of nouns* **1.** State or condition of being: *freedom.* **2.** Domain of: *kingdom.* **3.** Rank of: *earldom.* **4.** The totality of those having a certain rank, state, or condition: *Christendom.* [OE *-dōm* state, condition]

Dom. Dominican.

Do·magk (dō′mäk), **Gerhard,** 1895–1964, German chemist.

do·main (dō·mān′) *n.* **1.** A territory over which dominion is exercised, as by a sovereign; realm. **2.** A sphere or field of action, interest, knowledge, etc.: the *domain* of science. **3.** A landed estate. **4.** *Law* **a** Eminent domain (which see). **b** Absolute ownership and control of land. **5.** *Math.* A set of numbers that includes the sum, difference, product, and quotient (except division by zero) in the set, as all rational numbers, all real numbers, etc. *Abbr.* dom. [< MF *domaine* < OF *demeine, demaine* < L *dominicum,* neut. sing. of *dominicus* of a lord < *dominus* lord. Doublet of DEMESNE.]

dome (dōm) *n.* **1.** A roof resembling an inverted cup or hemisphere, formed by grouped, rounded arches or vaults rising from a round or many-sided base. **2.** Something shaped like this: the *dome* of a mountain. **3.** *Poetic* A large, majestic building. **4.** *Slang* The head. **5.** *Crystall.* In the orthorhombic, monoclinic, and triclinic crystal systems, a form whose faces intersect the vertical axis and one lateral axis. **— *v.* domed, dom·ing** *v.t.* **1.** To furnish or cover with a dome. **2.** To shape like a dome. **— *v.i.* 3.** To rise or swell upward like a dome. [< MF *dome* < Ital. *duomo* < L *domus* house]

dome fastener *Canadian* A snap fastener.

domes·day (dōōmz′dā′) *n.* See DOOMSDAY.

Domes·day Book (dōōmz′dā′) A book containing a record of the English landowners, the extent and value of their estates, livestock, etc., made in 1085–86 by order of William the Conqueror: also *Doomsday Book.*

do·mes·tic (də·mes′tik) *adj.* **1.** Of or pertaining to the home or family. **2.** Given to or fond of things concerning the home or family. **3.** Adapted to living with or near man; tame; domesticated: *domestic* animals. **4.** Of or pertaining to a particular country, especially one's own country: *domestic* and foreign issues. **5.** Produced or existing within a particular country, especially one's own country: *domestic* goods. **— *n.* 1.** A household servant. **2.** *pl.* Native products. *Abbr.* (adj. def. 4, 5) dom. [< MF < L *domesticus* < *domus* house] **— do·mes′ti·cal·ly** *adv.*

do·mes·ti·cate (də·mes′tə·kāt) *v.* **·cat·ed, ·cat·ing** *v.t.* **1.** To train for domestic use; tame. **2.** To civilize. **3.** To cause to feel at ease or at home; make domestic. **— *v.i.* 4.** To become domestic. Also **do·mes′ti·cize.** [< Med.L *domesticatus,* pp. of *domesticare* to live in a house < L *domus* house] **— do·mes′ti·ca′tion** *n.*

do·mes·tic·i·ty (dō′mes·tis′ə·tē) *n. pl.* **·ties** **1.** Life at home with one's family. **2.** Devotion to home and family. **3.** *pl.* Domestic matters.

do·mi·cal (dō′mi·kəl, dom′i-) *adj.* Pertaining to, resembling, or having a dome. Also **do′mic.** **— do′mi·cal·ly** *adv.*

dom·i·cile (dom′ə·səl, -sīl) *n.* **1.** A settled place of abode; a home, house, or dwelling. **2.** The place where one has one's legal abode. **— Syn.** See HOME. **— *v.* ·ciled, ·cil·ing** *v.t.* **1.** To establish in a place of abode. **— *v.i.* 2.** To have one's abode; dwell: also **dom·i·cil·i·ate** (-sil′ē·āt). Also **dom′i·cil** (-səl). [< MF < L *domicilium* < *domus* house]

dom·i·cil·i·ar·y (dom′ə·sil′ē·er′ē) *adj.* Pertaining to a fixed or a private residence.

dom·i·nance (dom′ə·nəns) *n.* The state or fact of being dominant; control; ascendancy. Also **dom′i·nan·cy.**

dom·i·nant (dom′ə·nənt) *adj.* **1.** Exercising the chief control or authority; ruling; governing. **2.** Conspicuously prominent or commanding, as in position. **3.** *Genetics* Designating one of a pair of hereditary characters that, appearing in hybrid offspring, masks a contrasting character: opposed to *recessive.* See MENDEL'S LAWS. **4.** *Music* Of or based upon the dominant. **— *n.* 1.** *Genetics* A dominant character. **2.** *Music* The fifth tone of a diatonic scale, a perfect fifth above the tonic. [< MF < L *dominans, -antis,* ppr. of *dominari.* See DOMINATE.] **— dom′i·nant·ly** *adv.*

— Syn. (adj.) *Dominant, predominant, paramount,* and *preponderant* mean superior to others in power, position, influence, etc. We speak of the *dominant* member of a group, or the *dominant* feature of a picture. *Predominant* differs from *dominant* only in that it sometimes implies a temporary ascendancy: escape was the *predominant* thought in his mind. Something *paramount* is first in importance or regard, while *preponderant* refers to that which has greater weight, force, quantity, etc.

dom·i·nate (dom′ə·nāt) *v.* **·nat·ed, ·nat·ing** *v.t.* **1.** To exercise control over; govern. **2.** To tower above; loom over: The city *dominates* the plain. **— *v.i.* 3.** To be dominant, as in power or position. [< L *dominatus,* pp. of *dominari* to rule, dominate < *dominus* lord] **— dom′i·na′tor** *n.*

dom·i·na·tion (dom′ə·nā′shən) *n.* **1.** The act of dominating, or the state of being dominated. **2.** Control; authority; dominion. **3.** *pl. Theol.* The fourth of the nine orders of angels: also called *dominions:* see ANGEL.

dom·i·na·tive (dom′ə·nā′tiv) *adj.* Dominating; controlling.

dom·i·ne (dom′ə·nē, dō′mə-) *n. Obs.* Lord or master: a title of address. [< L, vocative of *dominus* lord]

Do·mi·ne, di·ri·ge nos (dom′i·nē dir′i·jē nōs) *Latin* Lord, direct us: motto of the City of London.

dom·i·neer (dom′ə·nir′) *v.t. & v.i.* **1.** To rule arrogantly or insolently; tyrannize; bully. [< Du. *domineren* < F *dominer* < L *dominus* lord]

dom·i·neer·ing (dom′ə·nir′ing) *adj.* Overbearing; tyrannical. **— dom′i·neer′ing·ly** *adv.*

Dom·i·nic (dom′ə·nik), **Saint,** 1170–1221, Spanish friar; founded the Dominican Order: original name **Domingo de Guz·mán** (gōōth·män′).

Dom·i·ni·ca (dom′ə·nē′kə, də·min′i·kə) An island and former British colony; member of the West Indies Associated States; 305 sq. mi.; pop. 70,300 (est. 1970); capital, Roseau.

do·min·i·cal (də·min′i·kəl) *adj.* **1.** Relating to Christ as the Lord. **2.** Relating to Sunday as the Lord's day. [< LL *dominicalis* of the Lord < L *dominicus* < *dominus* lord]

dominical letter A letter chosen from the first seven letters of the alphabet to designate the Sundays of a given year in ecclesiastical calendars.

Do·min·i·can (də·min′i·kən) *adj.* **1.** Of or pertaining to St. Dominic. **2.** Belonging to a monastic order or institution founded by St. Dominic. **3.** Of the Dominican Republic. **— *n.* 1.** In the Roman Catholic Church, a member of the mendicant monastic order founded in 1216 by St. Dominic. **2.** A native of the Dominican Republic. *Abbr.* Dom.

Dominican Republic A Republic on the eastern part of Hispaniola; 18,700 sq. mi.; pop. 4,011,589 (1970); capital, Santo Domingo: Spanish *República Dominicana.*

dom·i·nie (dom′ə·nē) *n.* **1.** *Scot.* A schoolmaster. **2.** *U.S.* A minister of the Dutch Reformed Church. **3.** *U.S. Informal* Any minister. [Var. of DOMINE]

do·min·ion (də·min′yən) *n.* **1.** Sovereign or supreme authority; the power of ruling or governing; domination. **2.** *Law* Dominium. **3.** A country under a particular government. **4.** A self-governing member of the British Commonwealth of Nations. **5.** *pl. Theol.* Dominations. *Abbr.* dom. **— the Dominion** Canada. [< F < L *dominium* property, right of ownership < *dominus* lord]

Dominion Day In Canada, July 1, the anniversary of Canada's federation into a dominion, 1867: a legal holiday.

dominion government The federal government of Canada.

Dom·i·nique (dom′ə·nēk′) *n.* An American breed of domestic fowl, with gray-barred plumage, yellow legs, and rose comb. Also **Dom·i·nick** (dom′ə·nik). [< F, Dominica]

do·min·i·um (də·min′ē·əm) *n. Law* The absolute right of ownership and control of property, especially of land. [< L < *dominus* lord]

dom·i·no[1] (dom′ə·nō) *n. pl.* **·noes** or **·nos** **1.** A small mask for the eyes. For illustration see MASK[1]. **2.** A loose robe, hood, and mask worn at masquerades. **3.** A person wearing this. **4.** A hooded garment forming an outer ecclesiastical vestment. [< MF, hood worn by clerics < L *dominus* lord]

dom·i·no[2] (dom′ə·nō) *n. pl.* **·noes** or **·nos** **1.** A small, oblong piece of wood, plastic, etc., with the upper side marked into halves, each half being either blank or marked with one to six dots. **2.** *pl.* (*construed as sing.*) A game usually played with a set of 28 of these pieces. [? < DOMINO[1]]

Dom·i·nus (dom′ə·nəs) *n. Latin* The Lord. *Abbr.* D.

Dom·i·nus vo·bis·cum (dom′ə·nəs vō·bis′kəm) *Latin* The Lord be with you.

Do·mi·tian (də·mish′ən) A.D. 51–96, Roman emperor 81–96: full name **Titus Flavius Do·mi·ti·a·nus Augustus** (dō·mish′ē·ā′nəs).

Dom·re·my (dôṅ·rə·mē′) A village in NE France; birthplace of Joan of Arc. Also **Dom·re·my′·la·Pu·celle′** (-là-pü·sel′).

don[1] (don) *n.* **1.** A Spanish gentleman or nobleman. **2.** *Archaic* An important personage. **3.** *Brit. Informal* A head, fellow, or tutor of a college. [< Sp. < L *dominus* lord]

don[2] (don) *v.t.* **donned, don·ning** To put on, as a garment. [Contraction of *do on*; cf. DOFF]

Don (don) *n.* Sir: a title of respect or address, used with the given name in Spanish-speaking countries. Abbr. *D.*

Don (don, *Russ.* dôn) **1.** A river in the SW R.S.F.S.R. flowing 1,222 miles, generally south to the Sea of Azov: ancient *Tanais.* See maps of DNIEPER, VOLGA. **2.** A river in NE Scotland flowing 82 miles east to the North Sea. **3.** A river in NE England flowing 70 miles NE to the Ouse.

do·na (dô′nə) *n.* A Portuguese lady or noblewoman. [< Pg. < L *domina* mistress]

Do·na (dô′nə) *n.* Lady; Madam: a title of respect or address used with the given name in Portuguese-speaking countries.

do·ña (dô′nyä) *n.* A Spanish lady or noblewoman. [< Sp. < L *domina* mistress]

Do·ña (dô′nyä) *n.* Lady; Madam: a title of respect or address used with the given name in Spanish-speaking countries.

Do·nar (dô′när) In Germanic mythology, the god of thunder: identified with the Norse *Thor.*

do·nate (dô′nāt, dō·nāt′) *v.t.* **·nat·ed, ·nat·ing** *Chiefly U.S.* To give, as to a charitable organization; contribute. — **Syn.** See GIVE. [Back formation < DONATION] — **do′na·tor** *n.*

Don·a·tel·lo (don′ə·tel′ō; *Ital.* dô′nä·tel′lō), 1386?-1466, Florentine sculptor: original name **Donato di Niccolò di Bet·to Bar·di** (dē bät′tō bär′dē).

do·na·tion (dō·nā′shən) *n.* **1.** The act of giving, as charity. **2.** A gift; grant; offering. [< F *donatio, -onis* < *donare* to give]

Don·a·tist (don′ə·tist) *n.* One of a fourth-century Christian schismatic sect of North Africa. [< Med.L *Donatista* after *Donatus,* 4th c. North African bishop, founder of the sect] — **Don′a·tism** *n.*

Do·nau (dô′nou) The German name for the DANUBE.

Don·cas·ter (dong′kas·tər, *Brit.* -kəs-) A county borough in South Yorkshire, England; pop. 280,830 (1976).

done (dun) Past participle of DO[1]. — *adj.* **1.** Completed; finished; ended; agreed. **2.** Cooked sufficiently.

do·nee (dō·nē′) *n.* One who receives a gift. [< DON(OR) + -EE]

done for *U.S. Informal* **1.** Ruined; finished; exhausted. **2.** Dead or about to die.

Don·e·gal (don′i·gôl, don′i·gôl′) A county in Ulster province, Ireland; 1,865 sq. mi.; pop. 113,842 (1969); county seat, Lifford.

done in *U.S. Informal* **1.** Utterly exhausted; worn out with fatigue. Also **done up. 2.** Killed; destroyed.

Do·nets (do·nets′, *Russian* do·nyets′) A river in the SW Soviet Union, flowing 631 miles SE to the Don. Also **Do·niets** (do·nyets′).

Donets Basin A principal industrial region of the Soviet Union SW of the lower Donets; 10,000 sq. mi. *Russian* **Do·niet·skiy Bas·syein** (do·nyet′skē bəs·sän′). Also **Don·bas, Don·bass** (don·bäs′).

Do·netsk (do·nyetsk′) A city in the SE Ukrainian S.S.R., in the Donbas; pop. 879,000 (1970): formerly *Stalino, Yuzovka.* Also **Do·nietsk′.**

dong (dong) *n.* **1.** Formerly, the monetary unit of South Vietnam, equivalent to 100 centimes. **2.** The monetary unit of the Socialist Republic of Vietnam, equivalent to 10 chao and 100 sau.

Don·go·la (dong′gə·lə) A town in Northern Province, Sudan, on the Nile; former capital of the **Christian Kingdom of Dongola** (6th to 14th centuries); pop. about 3,400.

Don·i·zet·ti (don′ə·zet′ē, *Ital.* dô′nē·dzet′tē), **Gaetano,** 1797-1848, Italian operatic composer.

don·jon (dun′jən, don′-) *n.* The main tower or keep of a castle. [< OF, the lord's tower, ult. < L *dominus* lord]

Don Juan (don wän′; *for def. 3,* don jōō′ən) **1.** A legendary Spanish nobleman and seducer of women, the hero of many poems, operas, plays, etc. **2.** Any rake or seducer. **3.** An unfinished epic satire by Lord Bryon, published 1819-24.

don·key (dong′kē, dung′-) *n.* **1.** The ass. **2.** A stupid or stubborn person. [? after *Duncan,* a personal name]

donkey engine A small subsidiary engine for pumping, hoisting, etc.

don·na (don′ə, *Ital.* dôn′nä) *n.* An Italian lady or noblewoman. [< Ital. < L *domina* mistress, lady]

DONJON
(Chateau de Vi-viennes, France)

Don·na (don′ə, *Ital.* dôn′nä) *n.* Lady; Madam, a title of respect or address used with the given name in Italian-speaking countries.

Donne (dun), **John,** 1573-1631, English poet and clergyman.

don·nered (don′ərd) *adj. Scot.* Dazed; stunned; stupefied. Also **don′nerd, don′nert** (-ərt).

don·nish (don′ish) *adj.* **1.** Of or suggestive of a university don. **2.** Formal; pedantic. — **don′nish·ness** *n.*

don·ny·brook (don′ē·brŏŏk′) *n.* A brawl marked by roughness and abusive language; free-for-all. [after *Donnybrook Fair,* an annual event known for its brawls, held in Donnybrook, Ireland]

do·nor (dō′nər) *n.* **1.** One who gives, contributes, or bestows. **2.** *Med.* One who furnishes blood, skin tissue, etc., for another's use. [< AF *donour,* OF *doneur* < L *donator* a giver < *donare* to give]

do·noth·ing (dōō′nuth′ing) *n.* An idler; procrastinator. — *adj.* Idle; procrastinating.

Don·o·van (don′ə·vən), **William Joseph,** 1883-1959, U.S. general and lawyer: called **Wild Bill Donovan.**

Don Quix·ote (don kwik′sət, kē·hō′tē; *Sp.* dôn kē·hō′tä) **1.** A novel by Cervantes that satirizes chivalric romances. **2.** The hero of this novel, a naive, dreamy, befuddled idealist who dons the attire of a knight and attempts to combat evil and oppression. Also **Don Qui·jo·te** (kē·hō′tē, *Sp.* kē·hō′tä). See QUIXOTIC.

don·sie (don′sē) *adj. Scot.* **1.** Neat. **2.** Restive. **3.** Unlucky. Also **don′sy.** [Origin unknown]

don′t (dōnt) Do not. ◆ *Don't* in place of *doesn't* as in *He don't want any,* is now nonstandard in general American speech. However, it is still heard in educated informal speech in the eastern United States. The locution is nonstandard in formal contexts and writing.

don·zel (don′zəl) *n. Archaic* A young squire or page. [< Ital. *donzello* < LL *domnicellus,* dim. of L *dominus* lord]

doo·dad (dōō′dad) *n. Informal* **1.** A small ornament; bauble. **2.** A doohickey. [Humorous coinage; extension of DO]

doo·dle (dōōd′l) *Informal v.t. & v.i.* **·dled, ·dling** To draw or scribble in an aimless, preoccupied way. — *n.* A design, figure, picture, etc., made in an aimless, preoccupied way. [Cf. dial. E *doodle* to be idle, trifle, perh. < LG *dudeltopf* simpleton]

doo·dle·bug (dōōd′l·bug′) *n.* **1.** *U.S. Informal* A divining rod or similar device. **2.** *U.S. Dial.* The larva of several insects, especially the ant lion. **3.** Any droning insect, as the tumblebug. **4.** *Brit.* A robot bomb, especially a V-1. [? < dial. E *doodle* idler, fool + BUG]

doo·hick·ey (dōō′hik′ē) *n. pl.* **·eys** *U.S. Informal* A gadget or small object whose exact name is not known or cannot be recalled. [Humorous coinage; extension of DO]

doo·lee (dōō′lē) *n. Anglo-Indian* A light litter. Also **doo′·lie, doo′ly.** [< Hind. *dōlī,* dim. of *dōlā* litter < Skt.]

Doo·lit·tle (dōō′lit′l), **Hilda,** 1886-1961, U.S. poet: pseudonym *H. D.* — **James Harold,** born 1896, U.S. general.

doom (dōōm) *v.t.* **1.** To pronounce judgment or sentence upon; condemn. **2.** To destine to an unhappy fate. *Archaic* To decree (a judicial sentence, etc.). — *n.* **1.** An unhappy fate or destiny. **2.** An adverse judicial sentence. **3.** Death or ruin. **4.** The Last Judgment. [OE *dōm*]

doom palm A palm (*Hyphaene thebaica*) of northern Africa, the fruit of which has the flavor of gingerbread: also called *gingerbread tree*: also spelled *doum palm.* [< F *doum* < Arabic *dawm*]

dooms·day (dōōmz′dā′) *n.* **1.** The day of the Last Judgment, supposedly the end of the world. **2.** Any day of final judgment. Also spelled *domesday.* [OE *dōmes dæg* judgment day < *dōm* doom + *dæg* day]

Doomsday Book See DOMESDAY BOOK.

Doon (dōōn) A river in southern Scotland, flowing 27 miles NW to the Firth of Clyde.

door (dôr, dōr) *n.* **1.** A hinged, sliding, folding, or rotating structure, as of wood, used for closing or opening an entrance to a house, building, vehicle, room, etc. **2.** A doorway, often representing an entire building or room: to live six *doors* away. **3.** Any means of entrance, exit, or approach: access. — **Syn.** See ENTRANCE[1]. [Fusion of OE *duru* pair of doors and *dor* gate]

door·bell (dôr′bel′, dōr′-) *n.* An electric bell or chime actuated by a button at a doorway; also, a manually operated bell or chime at a doorway.

door·jamb (dôr′jam′, dōr′-) *n.* A vertical piece at the side of a doorway supporting the lintel.

door·keep·er (dôr′kē′pər, dōr′-) *n.* A guardian or keeper of a doorway.

door·knob (dôr′nob′, dōr′-) *n.* A handle used in opening a door.

door·man (dôr′man′, -mən, dōr′-) *n. pl.* **·men** (-men′, -mən) An attendant at the door of a hotel, apartment house, etc., who assists persons entering and leaving the building.

door mat A mat placed at an entrance for wiping the shoes.

Doorn (dōrn) A village in central Netherlands; residence of William II of Germany, 1919–41.

door·nail (dôr′nāl′, dōr′-) *n.* A large-headed nail, formerly used in the construction and ornamentation of doors. — **dead as a doornail** Unquestionably dead.

door·plate (dôr′plāt′, dōr′-) *n.* A metal plate on a door, with the occupant's name, street number, etc.

door·post (dôr′pōst′, dōr′-) *n.* A doorjamb.

door·sill (dôr′sil′, dōr′-) *n.* The sill or threshold of a door.

door·step (dôr′step′, dōr′-) *n.* A step or one of a series of steps leading to a door.

door·stop (dôr′stop′, dōr′-) *n.* A device to keep a door open or to keep it from slamming.

door·way (dôr′wā′, dōr′-) *n.* The passage for entrance and exit into and out of a building, room, etc. — **Syn.** See EN-TRANCE[1].

door·yard (dôr′yärd′, dōr′-) *n.* A yard around, or especially in front of, a house.

dope (dōp) *n.* 1. A viscid substance or unusually thick liquid; as: **a** Axle grease or some other lubricant. **b** A filler, varnish, or similar preparation used for protecting and making taut the fabric of airplane wings, etc. 2. A material used for absorbing and retaining a liquid, as the sawdust impregnated with nitroglycerin in dynamite. 3. *Photog.* A developer. 4. *Slang* A drug or narcotic. 5. *Slang* A dull-witted or incapable individual. 6. *Slang* Inside information. — *v.t.* **doped, dop·ing** 1. To apply dope to. 2. To adulterate or treat (a substance) with another. 3. *Slang* To give drugs to; drug: often with *up*. 4. *Slang* To plan or solve; work out; figure out: usually with *out*. 2. Stupid. Also **do′py**. [Orig. U.S., prob. < Du. *doop* a dipping, sauce < *doopen* to dip]

dope addict *Slang* A habitual user of a narcotic drug. Also **dope fiend.**

dope ring *Slang* A combination of persons trafficking illegally in narcotics.

dope sheet *Slang* An information sheet on horses in the day's races, giving their pedigree, past performance, etc.: also called *scratch sheet*.

do·pey (dō′pē) *adj.* **·pi·er, ·pi·est** *Slang* 1. Lethargic from or as from narcotics. 2. Stupid. Also **do′py**.

Dop·pel·gäng·er (dôp′əl·geng′ər) *n.* *German* A ghostly apparition or double, especially of someone not yet dead: also called *doubleganger*.

Dop·pler (dop′lər), **Christian Johann**, 1803–53, German physicist and mathematician active in Austria.

Doppler effect *Physics* The change in the frequency of a sound, light, or other wave caused by movement of its source relative to the observer. Also **Doppler shift.** [after C. J. *Doppler*]

Doppler navigation A method of determining the velocity, position, and course of an aircraft by beaming directional radar signals on a given frequency and interpreting the returning frequencies on the principle of the Doppler effect: sometimes called *DOVAP.*

dor[1] (dôr) *n.* A black European dung beetle (genus *Geotrupes*) known by its droning flight. Also **dor′bee·tle** (-bēt′l), **dor′bug′** (-bug′), **dorr, dorr′bee′tle**. [OE *dora* bumblebee]

dor[2] (dôr) *n.* *Obs.* Ridicule; mockery. [? < ON *dār* a scoff]

Dor. 1. Dorian. 2. Doric.

do·ra·do (də·rä′dō) *n.* A dolphin (def. 2). [< Sp., gilded < LL *deauratus*, pp. of *deaurare* to gild < L *de-* completely + *aurum* gold]

Do·ra·do (də·rä′dō) *n.* A constellation, the Swordfish. See CONSTELLATION.

Dor·cas society (dôr′kəs) A woman's society, usually connected with a church, for supplying garments to the poor. [after *Dorcas*, a female disciple. See *Acts* ix 36.]

Dor·ches·ter (dôr′ches·tər, -chis-) The county seat of Dorsetshire, England, a municipal borough in the southern part of the county; pop. 12,266.

Dor·dogne (dôr·dôn′y′) A river in central and SW France flowing about 300 miles, generally SW, to the Garonne.

Dor·drecht (dôr′drekht) A commune in the SW Netherlands, on the Meuse; pop. 81,909 (est. 1960): also *Dort.*

Do·ré (dô·rā′), **Paul Gustave**, 1833–83, French painter, illustrator, and engraver.

Do·ri·an (dôr′ē·ən, dō′rē-) *adj.* Pertaining to Doris, its inhabitants, or their culture. — *n.* 1. A member of one of the major tribes of ancient Greece. 2. A resident or native of Doris. Abbr. *Dor.*

Dor·ic (dôr′ik, dor′-) *adj.* 1. Dorian. 2. *Archit.* Of or pertaining to the simplest of the three orders of Greek architecture. For illustration see CAPITAL. — *n.* A dialect of ancient Greek, spoken by the Dorians in northern Greece, the Peloponnesus, Crete, Sicily, etc., used by Pindar and other lyric poets. Abbr. *Dor.*

Dor·is (dôr′is, dōr′-) In Greek mythology, wife of Nereus and mother of the Nereids.

Dor·is (dôr′is, dor′-) A small, mountainous district of west central Greece, traditionally the home of the Dorians.

Dor·king (dôr′king) *n.* One of a breed of domestic fowls characterized by five toes on each foot and a large, heavy body. [from *Dorking*, a town in Surrey, England]

dorm (dôrm) *n.* *Informal* A dormitory.

dor·man·cy (dôr′mən·sē) *n.* The state of being dormant.

dor·mant (dôr′mənt) *adj.* 1. Asleep or as if asleep; motionless through sleep or torpidity. 2. Not active; inoperative: *dormant* energies. 3. Not erupting: a *dormant* volcano. 4. *Biol.* Marked by partial suspension of vital processes, as many animals and plants in winter. 5. Not asserted or enforced, as claims. 6. *Heraldry* Lying down in a sleeping position: compare COUCHANT, RAMPANT. [< OF, ppr. of *dormir* < L *dormire* to sleep]

dor·mer (dôr′mər) *n.* 1. A vertical window set in a small gable that projects from a sloping roof. Also **dormer window.** 2. The roofed projection or gable itself. [< OF *dormeor* < L *dormitorium.* See DORMITORY.]

DORMER WINDOW

dor·mi·to·ry (dôr′mə·tôr′ē, -tō′rē) *n.* *pl.* **·ries** 1. A large room with sleeping accommodations for many persons. 2. A building providing sleeping and living accommodations, especially at a school, college, or resort. [< L *dormitorium* < *dormire* to sleep]

dor·mouse (dôr′mous′) *n.* *pl.* **·mice** One of various small, arboreal European rodents (family *Gliridae*), resembling squirrels in aspect and habits. [ME ? dial. E *dorm* to doze + MOUSE]

dor·my (dôr′mē) *adj.* In golf, being as many holes ahead of an opponent as there are holes still to play. Also **dor′mie.** [< dial. E *dorm* to doze, ult. < L *dormire* to sleep; so called because no further holes need be won]

dor·nick[1] (dôr′nik) *n.* A heavy damask cloth, used for hangings, carpets, etc. Also **dor′nock** (-nok). [< Flemish *Doornik* Tournai, where originally made]

dor·nick[2] (dôr′nik) *n.* *U.S.* A small cobblestone or pebble. [Prob. < Irish *dornóg* a small, round stone]

DORMOUSE
(6 inches long)

dorp (dôrp) *n.* *Obs.* A village. [< Du. Akin to THORP.]

Dor·pat (dôr′pät) The German name for TARTU.

Dorr (dôr), **Thomas Wilson,** 1805–54, U.S. political reformer; instigated **Dorr's Rebellion** in Rhode Island, 1842.

Dors. or **Dorset.** Dorsetshire.

dor·sad (dôr′sad) *adv.* *Anat.* Toward the back. [< L *dorsum* back + *ad* toward]

dor·sal (dôr′səl) *adj.* 1. *Anat.* **a** Of, pertaining to, situated on or near the back. **b** On or toward the posterior part of the body. 2. *Bot.* Designating the under surface, as of a leaf. 3. *Phonet.* Articulated with the back of the tongue, as (k) in *cool.* — *n.* A dosser (def. 1). [< Med.L *dorsalis* < L *dorsum* back] — **dor′sal·ly** *adv.*

dorsal fin The long, unpaired fin along the backbone of fish and other aquatic vertebrates. For illustration see FISH.

Dor·set (dôr′sit), **Earl of** See SACKVILLE.

Dorset Horn A large-horned breed of English sheep, having a tightly textured fleece of medium length.

Dor·set·shire (dôr′sit·shir) A county in SW England; 973 sq. mi.; pop. 570,500; county seat, Dorchester. Also **Dor′set.**

dorsi- *combining form* 1. On, to, or of the back: *dorsiferous.* 2. Dorso-. [< L *dorsum* back]

dor·sif·er·ous (dôr·sif′ər·əs) *adj.* *Bot.* Borne on the back, as the sori of ferns. [< DORSI- + -FEROUS]

dor·si·ven·tral (dôr′si·ven′trəl) *adj.* 1. *Bot.* Having distinct surfaces on both sides, as most leaves. 2. *Zool.* Dorsoventral. [DORSI- + VENTRAL]

dorso- *combining form* Dorsal; dorsal and: *dorsoventral.* [< L *dorsum* back]

dor·so·ven·tral (dôr′sō·ven′trəl) *adj.* 1. *Bot.* Dorsiventral. 2. *Zool.* Extending from the back to the ventral side. [DORSO- + VENTRAL] — **dor′so·ven′tral·ly** *adv.*

dor·sum (dôr′səm) *n.* *pl.* **·sa** (-sə) 1. *Anat.* **a** The back. **b** Any part of an organ corresponding to or resembling the back. 2. *Phonet.* The back of the tongue. [< L]

Dort (dôrt) See DORDRECHT.

Dort·mund (dôrt′mənd, *Ger.* dôrt′mŏont) A city in North Rhine–Westphalia, West Germany; pop. 648,880 (est. 1970).

dort·y (dôr′tē) *adj.* *Scot.* Sulky; haughty. [? < Scottish Gaelic *dort* to sulk]

Do·rus (dō′rus) In Greek legend, son of Hellen and ancestor of the Dorians.

do·ry[1] (dôr′ē, dō′rē) *n.* *pl.* **·ries** A deep, flat-bottomed rowboat with a sharp prow, used especially by North Atlantic fishermen. [< native Honduran name]

do·ry[2] (dôr′e, dō′rē) *n.* *pl.* **·ries** 1. The wall-eyed pike. 2. The John Dory (which see). [< F *dorée*, pp. fem. of *dorer* to gild < LL *deaurare.* See DORADO.]

dor·y·line ant (dôr′ē·līn′, dō′rē-) The driver ant (which see).

dos-à-dos (dō·zà·dō′; *for def. 2, usually* dō′sē·dō′) *adv. French* Back to back. — *n. pl.* **dos-à-dos** (-dōz′, *Fr.* -dō′) 1. An open vehicle, sofa, etc., made so the occupants sit back to back. 2. In square dances, a movement in which the dancers pass each other, back to back; also, a call directing the dancers to make such a movement.

dos·age (dŏ′sij) *n.* **1.** The administering of medicine in prescribed quantity. **2.** The total amount of medicine to be given. **3.** The process of adding sugar, liqueur, etc., to wines to improve quality and flavor or to increase strength.

dose (dōs) *n.* **1.** A particular quantity of medicine or of other remedial treatment, given or prescribed to be given at one time. Abbr. *d.*, *D.* **2.** *Informal* A particular amount of something usually disagreeable or painful. **3.** A particular quantity of sugar, liqueur, etc., added to wine to improve it. **4.** *Slang* Infection with a venereal disease, especially gonorrhea. — *v.* **dosed**, **dos·ing** *v.t.* **1.** To give medicine, etc., to in doses. **2.** To give, as medicine or drugs, in doses. **3.** To add sugar, etc., to (wine). — *v.i.* **4.** To take medicines. [< MF < Med.L *dosis* < Gk., orig., a giving] — **dos′er** *n.*

do·sim·e·ter (dō-sim′ə-tər) *n. Med.* An instrument for measuring the total amount of radiation absorbed in a given time: also called *quantimeter.* [< Gk. *dosis* dose + -METER]

do·sim·e·try (dō-sim′ə-trē) *n. Med.* **1.** The accurate measurement of doses. **2.** A method for the regular administration of alkaloids of definite strength, usually in granular form. — **do·si·met·ric** (dō′si-met′rik) *adj.*

Dos Pas·sos (dōs pas′ōs), **John Roderigo**, 1896–1970, U.S. novelist.

doss (dos) *n. Brit. Slang* **1.** A bed, especially in a cheap lodging house. Also **doss house.** **2.** Sleep. [< F *dos* back < L *dorsum*]

dos·sal (dos′əl) *n.* A dosser (def. 1). Also **dos′sel.** [< Med.L *dossalis*, var. of *dorsalis* of the back < L *dorsum*]

dos·ser (dos′ər) *n.* **1.** A rich hanging, as of silk, for the back of an altar, throne, etc., or for walls, as of a hall or chancel: also called *dorsal.* **2.** A basket to be carried on the back; pannier. [< F *dossier* < *dos* back < L *dorsum*]

dos·si·er (dos′ē-ā, dos′ē-ər; *Fr.* dô-syā′) *n.* A collection of papers, documents, etc., relating to a particular matter or person. [< F, bundle of papers]

dos·sil (dos′əl) *n.* **1.** *Printing* A cloth roll for wiping ink from an engraved plate. **2.** A small wad, as of cotton, used for cleaning a wound or as a compress. [< OF *dosil* spigot, plug < LL *duciculus*, ult. < L *ducere* to conduct]

Dos·so Dos·si (dôs′sō dôs′sē), 1479?–1542, Italian painter: original name **Giovanni de Lu·te·ri** (lōō-târ′ē).

dost (dust) *Do:* archaic or poetic second person singular, present tense of DO[1]: used with *thou.*

Dos·to·ev·ski (dŏs′tô-yef′skē), **Feodor Mikhailovich**, 1821–81, Russian novelist. Also **Dos′to·yev′sky.**

dot[1] (dot) *n.* **1.** A tiny, usually round, mark; a speck, spot, or point. **2.** Anything resembling a small spot or mark, as a small amount. **3.** In writing and printing, a point used as a part of a letter, in punctuation, etc. **4.** *Music* **a** A point written after a note or rest that increases its time value by half. **b** A point placed over a note to indicate staccato treatment. **5.** *Telecom.* A signal in Morse code that is of shorter duration than the dash. **6.** *Math.* **a** A multiplication symbol. **b** A decimal point. — **on the dot** At exactly the specified time. — *v.* **dot·ted**, **dot·ting** *v.t.* **1.** To mark with a dot or dots. **2.** To make by means of dots; stud. **3.** To be scattered thickly over or about: Trees *dot* the plains. — *v.i.* **4.** To make a dot or dots. — **to dot one's i's and cross one's t's** To be exact or correct. [OE *dott* head of a boil] — **dot′ter** *n.*

dot[2] (dot, *Fr.* dô) *n.* A woman's marriage portion; dowry. [< F < L *dos, dotis*] — **do·tal** (dōt′l) *adj.*

do·tage (dō′tij) *n.* **1.** Feebleness of mind as a result of old age; senility. **2.** Foolish and excessive affection. [< DOTE + -AGE]

do·tard (dō′tard) *n.* An old person whose mind is impaired by age. [< DOTE + -ARD]

do·ta·tion (dō-tā′shən) *n.* Endowment. [< OF < L *dotatio, -onis* < *dotare* to endow]

dote (dōt) *v.i.* **dot·ed**, **dot·ing** **1.** To lavish extreme fondness: with *on* or *upon.* **2.** To be feeble-minded as a result of old age. **3.** To decay, as trees, from age, etc. [ME *doten.* Cf. MDu. *doten* to be silly.] — **dot′er** *n.*

doth (duth) *Does:* archaic or poetic third person singular, present tense of DO[1].

Do·than (dō′thən) A city in SE Alabama; pop. 36,733.

dot·ing (dō′ting) *adj.* **1.** Extravagantly or foolishly fond. **2.** Feeble-minded; senile. **3.** Decaying from age: said of plants. — **dot′ing·ly** *adv.*

dot·se·quen·tial (dot′si-kwen′shəl) *adj.* Pertaining to a system of color television in which the three primary colors are dissected, projected, transmitted, and received in sequence as a series of dots interwoven to produce the original image.

dot·ted (dot′id) *adj.* **1.** Marked with dots; spotted. **2.** Distinguished by a dot or dots.

dotted swiss A sheer, crisp, cotton fabric, having embroidered, woven, or applied dots.

dot·ter·el (dot′ər-əl) *n.* **1.** A migratory plover (genus *Eudromias*) of northern Europe and Asia. **2.** *Dial.* A dupe. Also **dot′trel** (-rəl). [ME *dotrelle.* Akin to DOTE.]

dot·tle (dot′l) *n.* The plug of tobacco ash left in a pipe after smoking. Also **dot′tel.** [? Dim. of DOT[1]]

dot·ty (dot′ē) *adj.* ·ti·er, ·ti·est **1.** Consisting of or marked with dots. **2.** *Informal* Of unsteady or feeble gait. **3.** *Informal* Slightly demented; mentally weak.

do·ty (dō′tē) *adj.* ·ti·er, ·ti·est Stained by decay, as trees. [< DOTE, def. 3]

Dou (dou), **Gerard**, 1613–75, Dutch painter. Also *Dow.*

Dou·ai (dōō-ā′, *Fr.* dwä) A town in northern France; pop. about 47,347 (1968). Formerly **Dou·ay′.**

Douai Bible An English translation of the Vulgate Bible made by Roman Catholic scholars at Reims and Douai and completed in 1610. A revision of the New Testament was published in 1941. Also **Douay Bible.** Abbr. *D.Bib., D.V.*

Dou·a·la (dōō-ä′lə) A port city in SW Cameroon; pop. 230,000 (est. 1969). Also **Du·a′la.**

dou·ble (dub′əl) *adj.* **1.** Combined with another usually identical one; repeated: a *double* consonant. **2.** Two together; two combined: *double* lines. **3.** Having two parts, applications, functions, etc.; twofold; duple. **4.** More than one; not single; dual: a *double* role. **5.** Consisting of two layers. **6.** Made for two: a *double* bed. **7.** Twice as great, as large, as many, etc.: *double* fare. **8.** Extra heavy, large, wide, etc.: a *double* blanket. **9.** Marked by duplicity; twofaced: a *double* life. **10.** *Music* Producing tones one octave lower than the notes indicated on a score: said of an instrument. **11.** *Bot.* Having the petals increased in number. — *n.* **1.** Something that is twice as much. **2.** One who or that which closely resembles another; duplicate. **3.** A player or singer who can substitute for another; understudy. **4.** In motion pictures, one who substitutes for a star in performing dangerous feats. **5.** A sharp or backward turn, as of a hunted fox. **6.** A trick or stratagem. **7.** A fold or pleat. **8.** *Eccl.* A feast at which the antiphon is said both before and after the psalms. **9.** *pl.* In tennis, etc., a game having two players on each side. **10.** In baseball, a fair hit that enables the batter to reach second base without benefit of an error. **11.** In bridge, the act of challenging an opponent's bid by increasing its value and thus the penalty if the contract is not fulfilled; also, a hand warranting such an act. — **on** (or **at**) **the double 1.** In double time. **2.** *Informal* Quickly. — *v.* **·led**, **·ling** *v.t.* **1.** To make twice as great in number, size, value, force, etc. **2.** To be twice the quantity or number of. **3.** To fold or bend one part of upon another; make of two thicknesses: usually with *over, up, back.* **4.** To clench (the fist): often with *up.* **5.** *Naut.* To sail around: to *double* a cape. **6.** *Music* To duplicate a voice or part in unison or in another octave. **7.** In baseball, to advance (a base runner) by making a two-base hit: He *doubled* him home. **8.** In bridge, to challenge (an opponent) by announcing a double. — *v.i.* **9.** To become double; increase by an equal amount. **10.** To turn and go back on a course: often with *back.* **11.** To act or perform in two capacities. **12.** To serve as a double: to *double* for an actress. **13.** In baseball, to make a two-base hit. **14.** In bridge, to announce a double. — **to double in brass** *U.S. Slang* **1.** To be useful or adept in another capacity apart from one's (or its) specialty. **2.** Originally, of musicians, to play a second instrument in addition to the regular one. — **to double back 1.** To fold back. **2.** To turn and go back on the same or a parallel course. — **to double up 1.** To bend over or cause to bend over, as from pain or laughter. **2.** *U.S. Informal* To share one's quarters, bed, etc., with another. **3.** In baseball, to complete a double play upon. — *adv.* In pairs; twofold; doubly. Abbr. (adj. & n.) *dbl.* [< OF < L *duplus* double]

double bar *Music* A double vertical line on a staff, indicating the end of a piece of music or of a section of it.

doub·le-bar·reled (dub′əl-bar′əld) *adj.* **1.** Having two barrels, as a shotgun. **2.** Having two purposes. **3.** Ambiguous, as a remark. Also, *Brit.,* **doub′le-bar′relled.**

double bass 1. The largest and deepest-toned of the stringed instruments played with a bow: also called *bass viol, string bass.* **2.** The contrabass (which see).

double bassoon A double-reed instrument pitched an octave below the ordinary bassoon: also called *contrabassoon.*

double bed A bed wide enough for two people.

double boiler A cooking utensil consisting of two pots, one fitting into the other. Food in the upper pot is cooked by the heat from water boiling in the lower pot.

doub·le-breast·ed (dub′əl-bres′tid) *adj.* Having two rows of buttons and fastening so as to provide a double thickness of cloth across the breast: said of a coat or vest.

double chin A fat, fleshy fold under the chin.

double concave Biconcave (which see).

double convex Biconvex (which see).

doub·le-cross (*v.* dub′əl-krôs′, -kros′; *n.* dub′əl-krôs′, -kros′) *Slang v.t.* To betray by failing to act as promised. — *n.* A betrayal; a treacherous act. — **doub′le-cross′er** *n.*

double dagger See under DAGGER.

doub·le-date (dub′əl-dāt′) *v.i.* -dat·ed, -dat·ing *U.S. Informal* To make or go out on a double date.

double date *U.S. Informal* A social engagement of two couples.

doub·le-deal·er (dub′əl-dē′lər) *n.* One who acts with duplicity.

doub·le-deal·ing (dub′əl-dē′ling) *adj.* Treacherous; deceitful. — *n.* Treachery; duplicity.

doub·le-deck·er (dub′əl-dek′ər) *n.* **1.** *Naut.* A ship with two decks above the water line. **2.** *U.S.* A bus or streetcar with an upper floor. **3.** *U.S.* Two beds or bunks built one above the other in a unit. **4.** *U.S. Informal* A sandwich made with three slices of bread and two layers of filling.

double decomposition *Chem.* A form of decomposition in which each of two compounds exchanges an element or radical with the other: also called *metathesis.*

double drum A bass drum (which see).

double Dutch Unintelligible language; gibberish.

double eagle A gold coin of the United States with a face value of $20, withdrawn from circulation in 1934.

doub·le-edged (dub′əl-ejd′) *adj.* **1.** Having two cutting edges. **2.** Applicable both for and against: a *double-edged* argument.

dou·ble-en·ten·dre (dōō-blän-tän′dr′) *n.* A word or phrase of double meaning, the less obvious one often of doubtful propriety. [Alter. of F *double entente*]

dou·ble en·tente (dōō-blän-tänt′) *French* A double meaning.

double entry A method of bookkeeping in which every transaction is made to appear as both a debit and a credit.

double exposure *Photog.* The act of exposing the same film or plate twice, as in making a composite photograph; also, a print developed from a film or plate so exposed.

doub·le-faced (dub′əl-fāst′) *adj.* **1.** Having two faces. **2.** Having a pattern or finished nap on each side: said of a fabric. **3.** Deceitful; hypocritical; two-faced.

double feature A program of two full-length motion pictures.

double first *Brit.* A university degree with the highest honors in two subjects; also, a student who obtains it.

double flat A character (♭♭) that, placed before a note, lowers the pitch one whole tone; also, a note so lowered.

doub·le-gang·er (dub′əl-gang′ər) *n.* A Doppelgänger.

doub·le-head·er (dub′əl-hed′ər) *n.* **1.** In baseball, two games played in succession on the same day by the same two teams. **2.** A train pulled by two locomotives.

double indemnity A clause in a life insurance policy by which a payment of double the face value of the policy is made in the event of accidental death.

double jeopardy The peril under which a defendant is placed when he is tried more than once for the same offense.

doub·le-joint·ed (dub′əl-join′tid) *adj.* Having very flexible joints that permit the bones to move freely backward and forward so that limbs, fingers, etc., can be bent at unusual angles.

doub·le-mind·ed (dub′əl-mīn′did) *adj.* **1.** Undecided; wavering. **2.** Deceitful.

double negative See under NEGATIVE.

doub·le-ness (dub′əl-nis) *n.* **1.** The state or quality of being double. **2.** Duplicity; deceitfulness.

doub·le-park (dub′əl-pärk′) *v.t. & v.i.* To park (a motor vehicle) alongside another already parked at the curb.

double play In baseball, a play in which two base runners are put out during one continuous play of the ball.

double pneumonia Pneumonia affecting both lungs.

doub·le-quick (dub′əl-kwik′) *adj.* Very quick. — *n.* Double time (def. 1). — *v.t. & v.i.* To march or cause to march in double time.

doub·le-reed (dub′əl-rēd′) *adj. Music* Designating a group of wind instruments having a reed consisting of two segments united at the lower end and separated at the upper, as the oboe and bassoon.

double refraction See under REFRACTION.

doub·le-rip·per (dub′əl-rip′ər) *n.* A coasting sled composed of two small sleds fastened together, one behind the other, by a long board. Also **doub′le-run′ner** (-run′ər).

double salt *Chem.* A salt formed by crystallization from a solution containing two salts.

double sharp A character (×, ⚹) that, placed before a note, raises the pitch one whole tone; also, a note so raised.

double standard A moral standard that permits men greater freedom than women, especially in sexual behavior.

double star *Astron.* Two stars so near one another as to be almost indistinguishable except when viewed through a telescope.

doub·le-stop (dub′əl-stop′) *v.i.* -stopped, -stop·ping **1.** *Music* To produce two tones simultaneously on a stringed instrument, as a violin, by drawing the bow over two strings, one or both of which are stopped by the fingers or left open. **2.** Loosely, to produce chords on a violin, viola, etc. — *n.* **1.** The tones produced by double-stopping. **2.** Written or printed notes indicating double-stopping.

doub·let (dub′lit) *n.* **1.** A short, close-fitting outer garment, with or without sleeves, worn by men during the Renaissance. **2.** A pair of like things; a couple. **3.** An imitation gem consisting of a real stone cemented to a piece of colored glass; also, a paste jewel mounted with a thin face of a genuine jewel. **4.** *Ling.* One of a pair of words derived from the same original but entering a language through different routes, as *regal* and *royal*. **5.** *Usually pl.* A pair of dice that, when thrown, show on the upper surface the same number of spots. **6.** *Optics* A pair of lenses joined so as to eliminate the distortion caused by either lens used alone. [< OF, something folded, orig. dim. of *double*. See DOUBLE.]

DOUBLET
(def. 1)

double take Delayed reaction to a joke or unusual situation, characterized by blank acceptance initially and then sudden, startled realization of the actual significance.

double talk **1.** Apparently intelligible but actually nonsensical speech made up of a rapid flow of actual words mixed with meaningless syllables. **2.** Ambiguous talk meant to deceive.

dou·ble·think (dub′əl·thingk′) *n.* A way of rationalizing conflicting facts so that two opposing viewpoints can be held at the same time.

dou·ble-time (dub′əl·tīm′) *v.t. & v.i.* -timed, -tim·ing **1.** To march or cause to march in double time. **2.** To run or jog.

double time **1.** In the U.S. Army, a fast marching step at the rate of 180 three-foot steps per minute: also called *double-quick*. **2.** A doubled wage rate, as for overtime. Abbr. *d.t.*

doub·le-tongue (dub′əl·tung′) *v.i.* -tongued, -tongu·ing *Music* To apply the tongue rapidly to the teeth and hard palate alternately, as in playing a rapid series of repeated notes on the flute, cornet, etc.

doub·le-tongued (dub′əl·tungd′) *adj.* Characterized by duplicity of speech.

doub·le·tree (dub′əl·trē′) *n. U.S.* In a wagon, carriage, etc., the bar or crosspiece to the ends of which two swingletrees are fastened. For illustration see WHIFFLETREE.

double window *Canadian* Storm window (which see).

doub·le-you (dub′əl·yōō) *n.* The letter W.

doub·loon (du·blōōn′) *n.* A former Spanish gold coin, originally worth about 16 dollars. [< Sp. *doblón*, aug. of *doble* double; orig. worth two pistoles]

dou·blure (dōō-blür′) *n.* The lining of a book cover, especially when ornamental. [< F < *doubler* to line]

doub·ly (dub′lē) *adv.* **1.** In twofold degree; twice. **2.** In pairs. **3.** In twice the quantity.

Doubs (dōō) A river in eastern France, flowing 270 miles to the Saône.

doubt (dout) *v.t.* **1.** To hold the truth, validity, or reliability of as uncertain; hesitate to believe or accept. **2.** *Archaic* To be apprehensive or suspicious of. — *v.i.* **3.** To be unconvinced or mistrustful. — *n.* **1.** Lack of certainty about the truth or fact of something. **2.** A condition or state of affairs giving rise to uncertainty: Their fate was in *doubt*. **3.** An unresolved point or matter; difficulty: to clear up *doubts*. **4.** *Obs.* Fear; dread. — **beyond doubt** Unquestionably; certainly. — **no doubt 1.** Certainly. **2.** Most likely; probably. — **without doubt** Certainly. [< OF *duter, douter* < L *dubitare*; spelling refashioned after L] — **doubt′er** *n.*

— Syn. (verb) **1.** question, distrust, mistrust. — (noun) **1.** *Doubt, uncertainty, indecision, skepticism, incredulity, disbelief, suspicion, distrust,* and *misgiving* refer to a state of mind that causes suspension of judgment or action. *Doubt* may be simple *uncertainty* about facts or truth, but usually combines also *indecision* about what action to take. *Skepticism* is a disposition to question, to demand evidence or proof before rendering judgment; it falls short of *incredulity,* which is unwillingness to believe what seems unlikely, and *disbelief,* which is the positive rejection of something alleged to be true or valid. We direct *suspicion* toward that which may be evil or wrong; *distrust* toward that which may be treacherous or deceitful. *Misgiving* is *doubt* about the outcome of an action. — **Ant.** certainty, assurance, confidence, trust, belief, conviction.

doubt·ful (dout′fəl) *adj.* **1.** Subject to or causing doubt; uncertain; unsettled. **2.** Having or experiencing doubt; undecided. **3.** Indistinct or obscure in appearance, meaning, etc.; vague; ambiguous. **4.** Of questionable character: a *doubtful* reputation. — **doubt′ful·ly** *adv.* — **doubt′ful·ness** *n.*

Doubting Thomas A confirmed skeptic. *John* xx 25.

doubt·less (dout′lis) *adv.* **1.** Unquestionably. **2.** Probably. Also **doubt′less·ly.** — *adj.* Free from uncertainty.

douce (dōōs) *adj. Scot.* Sedate. [< F, sweet < L *dulcis*]

dou·ceur (dōō-sœr′) *n.* **1.** *Archaic* Money given as a tip or bribe. **2.** *Obs.* Amiability. [< F < LL *dulcor, -oris* sweetness < *dulcis* sweet]

douche (dōōsh) *n.* **1.** A jet of water or other fluid directed into or onto some part of the body for cleansing or medicinal purposes. **2.** A cleansing or medicinal treatment of this kind. **3.** A syringe or other device for administering a douche. — *v.* douched, douch·ing *v.t.* **1.** To cleanse or treat medicinally with a douche. — *v.i.* **2.** To administer a douche. [< F < Ital. *doccia* water pipe, ult. < L *ducere* to lead]

dough (dō) *n.* **1.** A soft mass of moistened flour or meal and other ingredients, mixed for making bread, pastry, etc. **2.** Any soft, pasty mass. **3.** *Slang* Money. [OE *dāh*]

dough·boy (dō′boi′) *n.* **1.** A dumpling of raised dough. **2.** *U.S. Informal* An infantryman of World War I.

dough·nut (dō'nut') *n.* A small cake of usually leavened and sweetened dough, cooked by frying in deep fat, and typically shaped with a hole through the center.

dough·ty (dou'tē) *adj.* **·ti·er, ·ti·est** Valiant; brave: chiefly humorous. [OE *dyhtig, dohtig*] —**dough'ti·ly** *adv.* — **dough'ti·ness** *n.*

Dough·ty (dou'tē), **Charles Montagu**, 1843–1926, English traveler and author.

dough·y (dō'ē) *adj.* **dough·i·er, dough·i·est** Resembling dough in consistency or appearance; soft, pasty, pale, etc.

Doug·las (dug'ləs) The capital of the Isle of Man, a port town in the SE part; pop. 19,517 (est. 1969).

Doug·las (dug'ləs) A family prominent in Scottish history, especially **Sir William**, died 1298, first Lord of Douglas: called **the Hardy**; **Sir James**, 1286–1330, his son: called **James the Good** and **the Black Douglas**; **William**, 1327?–84, first Earl of Douglas and Mar; **Archibald**, 1449?–1514, fifth Earl of Angus: called **the Great Earl**; **Gawin**, 1474?–1522, his son, bishop and poet.
— **Stephen Arnold**, 1813–61, U.S. senator; opposed Lincoln in a series of debates, 1858.
— **William Orville**, born 1898, U.S. jurist; associate justice of the Supreme Court 1939–.

Douglas fir A large timber tree (*Pseudotsuga taxifolia*) of the pine family, growing on the Pacific coast of the United States: often called **red fir, Oregon fir, Nootka fir.** Also **Douglas hemlock, Douglas pine, Douglas spruce.** [after David *Douglas*, 1798–1834, Scottish botanist]

Doug·las-Home (dug'ləs-hyōōm'), **Sir Alec (Frederick)**, former Earl of Home, born 1903, British statesman; prime minister, 1963–1964.

Doug·lass (dug'ləs), **Frederick**, 1817?–95, U.S. Negro abolitionist and statesman: original name **Frederick Augustus Washington Bai·ley** (bā'lē).

Douk (dōōk) *n. Canadian Slang* A Dukhobor.

Dou·kho·bors (dōō'kə-bôrz) See DUKHOBORS.

Dou·ma (dōō'mä) See DUMA.

Dou·mergue (dōō-merg'), **Gaston**, 1863–1937, French statesman; president 1924–31.

doum palm (dōōm) See DOOM PALM.

dour (dōōr, dour) *adj.* **1.** Forbidding and surly; morosely stern; ill-tempered. **2.** *Scot.* Unyielding; obstinate; stubborn. [< L *dur* hard < L *durus*] —**dour'ly** *adv.* —**dour'ness** *n.*

dou·ra (dōōr'ə) See DURRA.

dou·ri·cou·li (dōō'ri·kōō'lē) *n. pl.* **·lis** A nocturnal monkey (genus *Aotes*) of South America. [< S.Am.Ind.]

dou·rine (dōō·rēn') *n. Vet.* An infectious disease of horses: also called *equine syphilis.* [< F < Arabic *darin* unclean]

Dou·ro (dō'rōō) A river in Spain and Portugal, flowing about 475 miles, generally west, to the Atlantic: Spanish *Duero.*

douse¹ (dous) *v.* **doused, dous·ing** *v.t.* **1.** To plunge into water or other liquid; dip suddenly; duck. **2.** To drench with water or other liquid. —*v.i.* **3.** To become drenched or immersed. —*n.* A ducking or drenching. Also spelled *dowse.* [Origin unknown]

douse² (dous) *v.t.* **doused, dous·ing 1.** *Informal* To put out; extinguish. **2.** *Informal* To take off, as clothes. **3.** *Naut.* To take in or haul down quickly, especially a sail. **4.** *Obs.* To strike; give a blow to. [Cf. MDu. *dossen* to beat, strike]

douse³ (dous) See DOWSE².

douze·pers (dōōz'pârz') *n.pl.* of **douze·per** (-pâr') **1.** In medieval legend, twelve knights chosen to attend Charlemagne. **2.** In French history, the twelve chief spiritual and temporal peers. [< OF *douze pers* twelve peers]

DO·VAP (dō'vap) *n.* Doppler navigation. [< Do(ppler) v(elocity) a(nd) p(osition)]

dove¹ (duv) *n.* **1.** Any bird of the pigeon family (*Columbidae*), especially the mourning dove, turtle dove, etc. **2.** *Usually cap.* A symbol of the Holy Ghost. **3.** A symbol of peace. **4.** One who seeks to resolve a war primarily by means of limited military action, negotiation, or unilateral withdrawal: opposed to *hawk¹* (def. 3). **5.** A gentle, innocent, tender person. [ME *duve.* Cf. ON *dufā.*]

dove² (dōv) *Informal* Alternative past tense of DIVE.

Dove (duv) *n.* The constellation Columba.

dove·cote (duv'kōt', -kot') *n.* A house or houselike box set on a pole or high on a building, used for breeding and taming pigeons. Also **dove'cot'** (-kot').

dove hawk The goshawk (which see).

dove·kie (duv'kē) *n.* **1.** The little auk (*Plautus alle*), an arctic bird about 7½ inches long, black above, white below: also called *rotche.* **2.** A European name for the black guillemot. Also **dove'key.**

Do·ver (dō'vər) **1.** A municipal borough and port in eastern Kent, England, on the **Strait of Dover** (French *Pas de Calais*), a strait 21 miles wide at the eastern end of the English Channel; pop 35,217 (1961). **2.** The capital of Delaware, in the central part; pop. 17,488.

Dover's powder A preparation of ipecac, opium, and sugar of milk, formerly used to ease pain and induce sweating. [after Thomas *Dover*, 1660–1742, English physician]

dove·tail (duv'tāl') *n.* **1.** A tenon shaped like a wedge and designed to interlock with a mortise of similar shape. **2.** A joint formed by interlocked tenons and mortises of this kind. —*v.t. & v.i.* **1.** To interlock or join by dovetails. **2.** To fit together closely or harmoniously.

dov·ish (duv'ish) *adj.* Being or characteristic of a dove¹ (def. 4); disposed to rely on conciliation to resolve a war: opposed to *hawkish.*

Dow (dou), **Gerard** See DOU.

Dow. or **dow.** Dowager.

dow·a·ble (dou'ə-bəl) *adj.* Entitled to dower.

dow·a·ger (dou'ə·jər) *n.* **1.** In English law, a widow holding property or title derived from her deceased husband. Abbr. *d., D., dow., Dow.* **2.** *Informal* An elderly woman of dignified bearing. [< OF *douagiere*, ult. < L *dotare* to give]

Dow·den (dou'dən), **Edward**, 1843–1913, Irish scholar and critic.

dow·dy (dou'dē) *adj.* **·di·er, ·di·est** Notably devoid of trimness and smartness in dress; frumpish. —*n. pl.* **·dies 1.** A dowdy woman. **2.** A deep-dish fruit pie; pandowdy. [ME *doude* slut] —**dow'di·ly** *adv.* —**dow'di·ness** *n.*

dow·el (dou'əl) *n.* A pin or peg fitted tightly into adjacent holes of two pieces so as to hold them together. Also **dowel pin.** —*v.t.* **dow·eled** or **·elled, dow·el·ing** or **·el·ling** To furnish or fasten with dowels. [ME, ? < MLG *dovel* plug]

dow·er (dou'ər) *n.* **1.** The part of a deceased man's estate that is assigned by law to his widow for life. **2.** A natural talent or endowment. **3.** A dowry. —*v.t.* **1.** To provide with a dower. **2.** To endow, as with a talent or quality. [< OF *douaire* < LL *dotarium* < L *dos, dotis* dowry]

dow·er·y (dou'ər·ē) See DOWRY.

dow·ie (dou'ē, dō'ē) *adj. Scot.* Dreary. [? OE *dol*]

dow·itch·er (dou'ich·ər) *n.* **1.** A long-billed shore bird (*Limnodromus griseus*) of eastern North America resembling the snipe. **2.** A related bird, the **long-billed dowitcher** (*L. griseus scolopaceus*). [< N.Am.Ind.]

down¹ (doun) *adv.* **1.** From a higher to a lower place, level, position, etc.: to come *down* from a ladder. **2.** In or on a lower place, level, etc.: The flag is *down.* **3.** On or to the ground: The house burned *down.* **4.** To or toward the south. **5.** To or in a place regarded as distant or outlying: *down* on the farm. **6.** Below the surface or horizon. **7.** From an upright to a prone or prostrate position: to knock a man *down.* **8.** To lesser bulk, heavier consistency, etc.: The mixture boiled *down.* **9.** To less activity, intensity, etc.: Things quieted *down.* **10.** To a lower amount, rate, etc.: Prices have gone *down.* **11.** In or into subjection or control: to put the rebels *down.* **12.** In or into a depressed or prostrate physical or mental state. **13.** With earnestness: to get *down* to work. **14.** Completely; fully: loaded *down* with honors. **15.** From an earlier time or individual: This heirloom came *down* from my grandmother. **16.** In cash as partial payment: five dollars *down.* **17.** In writing: Take *down* his name. — **down with** (Let us) do away with or overthrow: *Down with* tyranny. —*adj.* **1.** Directed downward: a *down* curve. **2.** *Informal* Downcast; depressed. **3.** Given in cash as a partial amount: a *down* payment. **4.** In games, behind an opponent by a specified number of points, strokes, etc. **5.** In football, not in play: said of the ball. **6.** In baseball, put out. —**down and out 1.** In a completely miserable state, as of poverty or desolation. **2.** In boxing, knocked to the floor. —**down on** *Informal* Annoyed with or hostile to: He's *down on* me for refusing to lend him some money. —*prep.* **1.** In a descending direction along, upon, or in. **2.** During the course of: *down* the years. —*v.t.* **1.** To knock, throw, or put down. **2.** *Informal* To swallow quickly; gulp. —*v.i.* **3.** *Rare* To go, fall, or sink down. —*n.* **1.** A downward movement; descent. **2.** A reverse of fortune: chiefly in the phrase **ups and downs. 3.** In football, any of the four consecutive plays during which a team must advance the ball at least ten yards to keep possession of it; also, the declaring of the ball as out of play, or the play immediately preceding this declaration. [OE *dūne*, aphetic var. of *adūne* < *of dūne* from the hill]

down² (doun) *n.* **1.** The fine, soft plumage of birds under the feathers, especially that on the breast of water birds. **2.** The first feathering of a bird. **3.** The soft hairs that first appear on the human face. **4.** *Bot.* **a** Soft, short hairs; pubescence, as on plants or fruits. **b** The pappus of some seeds. **5.** Any feathery, fluffy substance. [< ON *dūnn*]

down³ (doun) *n.* **1.** *pl.* Turf-covered, undulating tracts of upland, especially in southern and SE England. **2.** A hill, especially of sand; dune. [OE *dūn.* Akin to DUNE.]

Down (doun) A county in SE Northern Ireland; 952 sq. mi.; pop. 300,800 (est. 1969); county seat, Downpatrick.

down·beat (doun'bēt') *n. Music* **1.** The first accent of each measure. **2.** The downward gesture made by the conductor to indicate this accent.

down-bow (doun′bō′) *n. Music* On the violin, etc., a stroke of the bow across the strings, going from the nut toward the tip: expressed by the sign ⌐: opposed to *up-bow*.

down·cast (doun′kast′, -käst′) *adj.* **1.** Directed downward: *downcast eyes.* **2.** Low in spirits; dejected; depressed. — *n.* **1.** The act of casting down; ruin. **2.** A shaft, as in a mine, down which fresh air passes.

down·com·er (doun′kum′ər) *n.* A pipe or other conduit for conveying liquids, gases, etc., downward.

Down East *Informal* New England, especially Maine. Also **down East.** — **down-east** (doun′ēst′) *adj.* — **down′-east′er** *n.*

Downes (dounz), (**Edwin**) **Olin**, 1886–1955, U.S. music critic.

Dow·ney (dou′nē) A city in SW California, a suburb of Los Angeles; pop. 88,445.

down·fall (doun′fôl′) *n.* **1.** A sudden descent, as in reputation or fortune; collapse; ruin. **2.** A sudden, heavy fall of rain, snow, etc. **3.** A deadfall (def. 1).

down·fall·en (doun′fô′lən) *adj.* Fallen; ruined.

down·grade (doun′grād′) *n.* A descending slope, as of a hill or road. — **on the downgrade** Declining in health, reputation, status, etc. — *adj.* Downhill. — *v.t.* **·grad·ed, ·grad·ing** To reduce in status, salary, etc.

down·haul (doun′hôl′) *n. Naut.* A rope for hauling down sails.

down·heart·ed (doun′här′tid) *adj.* Dejected; discouraged. — **down′heart′ed·ly** *adv.* — **down′heart′ed·ness** *n.*

down·hill (*adv.* doun′hil′; *adj.* doun′hil′) *adv.* In a downward direction; toward the bottom of a hill. — **to go downhill** To decline, as in success or health. — *adj.* Descending.

Down·ing Street (dou′ning) **1.** A street in Westminster, London; site of the official residences of the Prime Minister (No. 10), the Chancellor of the Exchequer, and the Foreign and Colonial Offices. **2.** *Informal* The British government or cabinet.

down·lead (doun′lēd′) *n. Brit.* A lead-in.

down payment In installment buying, the initial payment on a purchase.

down·pour (doun′pôr′, -pōr′) *n.* A heavy fall of rain.

down·right (doun′rīt′) *adj.* **1.** Thorough; absolute; utter: *downright* nonsense. **2.** Straightforward. **3.** *Archaic* Going straight down. — *adv.* **1.** Thoroughly; utterly: *downright* terrified. **2.** *Obs.* Frankly; plainly. **3.** *Obs.* Straight down.

Downs (dounz), **The 1.** A sheltered roadstead in the English Channel off the SE coast of Kent. **2.** Two parallel ranges of low chalk hills in southern England.

down·spout (doun′spout′) *n.* A pipe for draining rain water from a roof or from a gutter along a roof.

Down's syndrome (dounz) Mongolism. [after John Langdon-*Down*, 19th c. English physician]

down·stage (*adv.* doun′stāj′; *adj.* doun′stāj′) *adv.* Toward, near, or on the front half of a stage. — *adj.* Pertaining to the front half of a stage.

down·stairs (*adv.* doun′stârz′; *adj. & n.* doun′stârz′) *adv.* **1.** Down the stairs. **2.** On or to a lower floor. — *adj.* Situated on a lower floor: also **downstair′.** — *n.* The downstairs part of a house or other building.

down·stream (*adv.* doun′strēm′; *adj.* doun′strēm′) *adv.* Down the stream. — *adj.* In the direction of the current.

down·throw (doun′thrō′) *n.* **1.** Overthrow. **2.** *Geol.* A downward displacement of rock on one side of a fault.

down·town (*adv.* doun′toun′; *adj.* doun′toun′) *adv.* To, toward, or in the geographically lower section of a town or city. — *adj.* Located in the geographically lower section of a town or city, usually the chief business section.

down·trod·den (doun′trod′n) *adj.* **1.** Trampled under foot. **2.** Subjugated; oppressed. Also **down′trod′.**

down under *Informal* Australia or New Zealand.

down·ward (doun′wərd) *adv.* **1.** From a higher to a lower level, position, etc. **2.** From an earlier or more remote time, place, etc. Also **down′wards,** occasionally **down′ward·ly.** — *adj.* **1.** Descending from a higher to a lower level. **2.** Descending in course from that which is more remote.

down·y (dou′nē) *adj.* **down·i·er, down·i·est 1.** Of, like, or covered with down. **2.** Soft; quiet. — **down′i·ness** *n.*

downy mildew Grape rot.

dow·ry (dou′rē) *n. pl.* **·ries 1.** The money or property a wife brings to her husband at marriage: also called *portion.* **2.** A natural talent or endowment. **3.** *Archaic* The dower of a widow. **4.** *Archaic* A marriage gift from a man to his bride or her family. Also spelled *dowery.* [< AF *dowarie,* var. of OF *douaire.* See DOWER.]

dowse¹ (dous) See DOUSE¹.

dowse² (douz) *v.i.* **dowsed, dows·ing** To search for underground water, etc., with a divining rod: also spelled *douse.* [? < DOUSE² (def. 4)] — **dows′er** *n.*

dowsing rod A divining rod (which see).

Dow·son (dou′sən), **Ernest Christopher,** 1867–1900, English poet.

dox·ol·o·gy (dok·sol′ə·jē) *n. pl.* **·gies 1.** A hymn or verse of praise to God, specifically applied to a stanza beginning "Praise God, from whom all blessings flow." **2.** A formula

of praise, used as the closing words of a sermon. — **greater doxology** The Gloria in excelsis Deo. — **lesser doxology** The Gloria Patri. [< Med.L *doxologia* < Gk. < *doxa* praise + *legein* to speak] — **dox·o·log·i·cal** (dok′sə·loj′i·kəl) *adj.* — **dox′o·log′i·cal·ly** *adv.*

dox·y¹ (dok′sē) *n. pl.* **dox·ies** *Archaic Slang* A loose wench; prostitute. [? < obs. E *docke* rump, tail. See DOCK².]

dox·y² (dok′sē) *n. pl.* **dox·ies** A doctrine; belief, especially a religious one. [< *-doxy,* as in *orthodoxy, heterodoxy*]

doy·en (doi′ən, *Fr.* dwä·yaǹ′) *n.* The eldest or senior member of a group. [< F < LL *decanus.* See DEAN.] — **doy·enne** (doi′en, *Fr.* dwä·yen′) *n.fem.*

Doyle (doil), **Sir Arthur Conan,** 1859–1930, English physician and novelist; creator of *Sherlock Holmes.*

doy·ley, doy·ly (doi′lē) See DOILY.

D'Oy·ly Carte (doi′lē kärt′), **Richard,** 1844–1901, English theatrical impresario.

doz or **doz.** Dozen(s).

doze (dōz) *v.* **dozed, doz·ing** *v.i.* **1.** To sleep lightly or be drowsy for brief periods of time; nap. — *v.t.* **2.** To spend (time) in napping or in being half asleep. — **to doze off** To fall into a light, brief sleep. — *n.* A light, brief sleep; nap. [< Scand., ? ult. < ON *dūsa* to doze]

doz·en¹ (duz′ən) *n. pl.* **doz·ens**; *when preceded by a number,* **doz·en** A group or set of twelve things. Abbr. *doz, doz., dz.* [< OF *dozeine* < *douze* twelve < L *duodecim* < *duo* two + *decem* ten]

doz·en² (dō′zən) *v.t. Scot.* To stun; stupefy. [See DOZE]

doz·enth (duz′ənth) *adj. & n.* Twelfth.

do·zy (dō′zē) *adj.* **·zi·er, ·zi·est** Drowsy. — **do′zi·ly** *adv.* — **do′zi·ness** *n.*

DP or **D.P. 1.** *Chem.* Degree of polymerization. **2.** Diametrical pitch. **3.** Displaced person.

D.Ph. or **D.Phil.** Doctor of Philosophy.

D.P.H. Doctor of Public Health.

D.P.Hy. Doctor of Public Hygiene.

dpt. 1. Department. **2.** Deponent.

D.P.W. Department of Public Works.

dr Dram(s).

dr. 1. Debit. **2.** Debtor. **3.** Drachma. **4.** Dram(s). **5.** Drawer.

Dr. 1. Doctor. **2.** Drive.

D.R. or **d.r.** or **D/R 1.** Dead reckoning. **2.** Deposit receipt.

drab¹ (drab) *adj.* **drab·ber, drab·best 1.** Lacking brightness or sparkle; dull and monotonous. **2.** Having a dull, yellowish brown color. **3.** Made of a thick, woolen, yellowish brown cloth. — *n.* **1.** A dull, yellowish brown color. **2.** A thick, woolen, yellowish brown cloth. [< F *drap* cloth < LL *drappus,* ? < Celtic] — **drab′ly** *adv.* — **drab′ness** *n.*

drab² (drab) *n.* **1.** A slipshod, untidy woman. **2.** A prostitute; slut. — *v.i.* **drabbed, drab·bing 1.** To associate with prostitutes. **2.** To be a prostitute. [? < Celtic. Cf. Irish *drabog.*]

drab·bet (drab′it) *n. Brit.* A coarse linen fabric of drab color. [< DRAB¹ + -ET]

drab·ble (drab′əl) *v.t. & v.i.* **·bled, ·bling** To draggle. [< LG *drabbeln* to walk in water or mud, splash]

dra·cae·na (drə·sē′nə) *n.* One of various tropical shrubs and small trees (genera *Dracaena* and *Cordyline*) of the lily family, grown as ornamental plants. [< NL < Gk. *drakaina,* fem. of *drakōn* dragon]

drachm (dram) *n.* **1.** A dram. **2.** A drachma. [< F *drachme* < L DRACHMA.]

drach·ma (drak′mə) *n. pl.* **·mas** or **·mae** (-mē) **1.** An ancient Greek silver coin. **2.** The standard monetary unit of Greece, equivalent to 100 lepta; also, a coin of this value. **3.** An ancient Greek unit of weight. **4.** Any of several modern weights, as the dram. Abbr. *d., D., dr.* [< L *drachma* < Gk. *drachmē* a handful. Doublet of DRAM.]

Dra·co (drā′kō) *n.* A constellation, the Dragon. See CONSTELLATION. [< L *draco* < Gk. *drakōn*]

Dra·co (drā′kō) Seventh-century B.C. Athenian legislator; reputed author of the first Athenian written code of laws.

Dra·co·ni·an (drā·kō′nē·ən) *adj.* **1.** Pertaining to Draco or his laws. **2.** Harsh; inflexible; severe.

dra·con·ic (drā·kon′ik) *adj.* **1.** Of or resembling a dragon. [< L *draco, -onis* < Gk. *drakōn* + -IC]

Dra·con·ic (drā·kon′ik) *adj.* Draconian. — **Dra·con′i·cal·ly** *adv.*

draff (draf) *n.* Refuse grain from breweries and distilleries; also, lees or dregs. [ME *draf.* Akin to ON and MDu. *draf.*]

draff·ish (draf′ish) *adj.* Worthless. Also **draff′y.**

draft (draft, dräft) *n.* **1.** The act or process of selecting an individual or individuals for some special duty or purpose; especially, the selection of men for compulsory military service; conscription; levy. **2.** The condition of being selected for some special duty or purpose; also, those selected. **3.** A current of air. **4.** A device for controlling the airflow, as in a furnace. **5.** A written order, as of an individual, bank, or company, directing the payment of money; a check. **6.** A sketch, plan, or design of something to be made. **7.** A preliminary or rough version of a writing. **8.** A quantity of liquid for drinking; a drink: a *draft* of ale. **9.** The act of drinking; also, the amount of liquid taken at one drink. **10.** The drawing of liquid from its container, as beer from a cask. **11.** The act of drawing in a fishnet; also, the amount of fish taken with one drawing of a net. **12.** The act of drawing air, smoke, etc., into the lungs; also, the quantity of air, etc., taken in. **13.** The pulling or drawing of something, as a loaded wagon; also, the load pulled or drawn. **14.** A heavy demand or drain on something. **15.** *pl.* Draughts. **16.** *Naut.* The depth of water required for a ship to float, especially when loaded. **17.** An allowance made for waste or loss of weight. **18.** The total sectional area of the openings of a turbine wheel or sluice gate. **19.** A line or border chiseled on a stone to guide in its dressing. **20.** *Metall.* The taper given to the pattern for a casting so that it may more easily be drawn from the mold. **— on draft** Ready to be drawn, as beer, from a cask, etc. **—** *v.t.* **1.** To draw up in preliminary form, especially in writing. **2.** To select and draw off, as for military service; conscript. **3.** To draw off or away. **4.** To cut a draft on (a stone). **—** *adj.* **1.** Suitable to be used for pulling heavy loads: a *draft* animal. **2.** Not bottled, as beer; drawn from a cask. Also *(usually only for n. defs. 3, 4, 8–12, 16, and adj. def. 2)* **draught.** Also *Brit.* **draught.** [ME *draht* < OE *dragan* to draw]

draft board An official board of civilians that selects men for compulsory service in the U.S. armed forces.

draft dodger One who avoids or attempts to avoid conscription into military service.

draft·ee (draf·tē′, dräf-) *n.* A person drafted for service in the armed forces.

drafts·man (drafts′mən, dräfts′-) *n. pl.* **·men** (-mən) **1.** One who draws or prepares designs or plans of buildings, machinery, etc. **2.** One who draws up documents, as deeds. **3.** An artist especially skilled in drawing. Also spelled *draughtsman.* **— drafts′man·ship** *n.*

draft·y (draf′tē, dräf′-) *adj.* **draft·i·er, draft·i·est** Having or exposed to drafts of air: a *drafty* room. Also spelled *draughty.* **— draft′i·ly** *adv.* **— draft′i·ness** *n.*

drag (drag) *v.* **dragged, drag·ging** *v.t.* **1.** To pull along by main force; haul. **2.** To sweep or search the bottom of, as with a net or grapnel; dredge. **3.** To catch or recover, as with a grapnel or net. **4.** To draw along heavily and wearily. **5.** To harrow (land). **6.** To continue tediously; protract: often with *on* or *out.* **7.** To introduce (an irrelevant subject or matter) into a discussion, argument, etc.: usually with *in.* **—** *v.i.* **8.** To be pulled or hauled along; trail to or as to the ground. **9.** To move heavily or slowly. **10.** To lag behind. **11.** To pass slowly. **12.** To use a grapnel, drag, or dredge. **13.** To cause a feeling of clutching or tugging: *Worry dragged* at him. **— to drag one's feet** *U.S. Informal* To act or work with deliberate slowness. **—** *n.* **1.** The act of dragging. **2.** The amount of resistance encountered in dragging: a heavy *drag* on the left wheel. **3.** A slow, heavy, usually impeded motion or movement **4.** Something that slows down movement, as a clog on a wheel. **5.** Something heavy that is dragged. **6.** A contrivance, as a dragnet, for dragging through water to find or bring up something. **7.** Anything that hinders; an impediment. **8.** A stagecoach, usually drawn by four horses, with seats inside and on the top. **9.** The scent or trail left by a fox. **10.** An artificial scent used in hunting. **11.** A drag hunt (which see). **12.** *Aeron.* That component of the total forces exerted upon an aircraft in flight that is opposite to the direction of motion and parallel to the relative wind. **13.** *U.S. Slang* Influence that brings special favors; pull. **14.** *Slang* A puff on a cigarette, cigar, or pipe. **15.** *U.S. Slang* One who or that which is tedious, boring, or colorless. **16.** *U.S. Slang* A drag race (which see). [ME *draggen,* prob. < OE *dragan;* infl. in form by ON *draga.* Akin to DRAW.]

dra·gée (drȧ·zhā′) *n. French* A piece of candy, or a pill, coated with sugar.

drag·gle (drag′əl) *v.* **·gled, ·gling** *v.t.* **1.** To make soiled or wet by dragging in mud or over damp ground; muddy. **—** *v.i.* **2.** To become wet or soiled; drag in the mud. **3.** To follow slowly; lag. [Freq. of DRAG]

drag·gle·tail (drag′əl·tāl) *n.* An untidy person.

drag·gle·tailed (drag′əl·tāld′) *adj.* Bedraggled from or as if from having the garments trailing in the wet or mud.

drag·hound (drag′hound′) *n.* A hound trained to follow an artificial scent.

drag hunt A hunt in which an artificial scent is used.

drag·line (drag′līn′) *n.* **1.** A line used for dragging. **2.** A dredge that uses a dragline. **3.** A dragrope or guiderope.

drag link *Mech.* A link for connecting the cranks of two shafts.

drag·net (drag′net′) *n.* **1.** A net to be drawn along the bottom of the water or along the ground, to find or capture something. **2.** Any device or plan for catching a criminal.

DRAG (*n.,* def. 8)

drag·o·man (drag′ə·mən) *n. pl.* **·mans** (-mənz) or **·men** (-mən) An interpreter or guide for travelers in the Near East. [< F < LGk. *dragoumanos* < Arabic *tarjumān* translator]

drag·on (drag′ən) *n.* **1.** A mythical, serpentlike, winged monster. **2.** In the Bible, a word variously understood as a large reptile, a marine monster, a jackal, etc. **3.** A fierce, violent person. **4.** An overbearing, watchful woman. **5.** A short, large-bored firearm of the 17th century, as carried by a dragoon. **6.** *Bot.* Any of various plants of the arum family, as the jack-in-the-pulpit. **7.** *Zool.* Any of several small, arboreal, Asian lizards (genus *Draco*), capable of gliding by means of winglike expansions of the skin: also called *flying lizard.* [< OF < L *draco, -onis* < Gk. *drakōn* serpent]

Drag·on (drag′ən) *n.* The constellation Draco.

drag·on·et (drag′ən·it) *n.* **1.** Any of a family (*Callionymidae*) of small, often brightly colored marine fishes of tropical and temperate waters, as *Callionymus calliuris* of the Florida coast. **2.** A small dragon. [< OF, dim. of *dragon* dragon]

drag·on·fly (drag′ən·flī′) *n. pl.* **·flies** A predatory insect (order *Odonata*), having a slender body, four finely veined wings, and strong jaws: also called *darning needle, devil's-darning-needle.* For illustration see INSECTS (beneficial).

drag·on·head (drag′ən·hed′) *n.* Any of a genus (*Dracocephalum*) of hardy annual or perennial herbs of the mint family. Also **drag′on's-head′.**

drag·on·nade (drag′ə·nād′) *n.* **1.** In French history, the quartering of dragoons on Protestant families by Louis XIV as a means of persecution. **2.** Any military persecution. [< F < *dragon* dragoon]

dragon's blood One of various reddish brown resins used as a pigment, especially those obtained from the fruit of a Malayan rattan palm (*Daemonorops draco*).

dragon's head *Astron.* The point where the ecliptic is intersected by the ascending orbit of the moon or of a planet: symbol ☊.

dragon's tail *Astron.* The point where the ecliptic is intersected by the descending orbit of the moon or of a planet: symbol ☋.

dragon tree A gigantic tree (*Dracaena draco*) of the Canary Islands, yielding dragon's blood.

dragon withe A West Indian climbing plant (genus *Banisteriopsis* or *Heteropteris*), bearing winged fruit.

dra·goon (drə·gōon′) *n.* **1.** In some European armies, a cavalryman. **2.** Formerly, a soldier who served either on horseback or on foot and who carried a short musket. **—** *v.t.* **1.** To harass by dragoons. **2.** To coerce; browbeat. [< F *dragon* dragon (def. 5)]

drag race *Slang* A race between hot rods to test acceleration, usually held on a short, straight course (**drag strip**).

drag·rope (drag′rōp′) *n.* **1.** A rope used to pull something, as a gun carriage. **2.** *Aeron.* A rope dragged by a balloon over the ground, to check speed, regulate ascent, etc.

drag sail *Naut.* A sea anchor made from a sail. Also **drag sheet.**

drain (drān) *v.t.* **1.** To draw off (water, etc.) gradually. **2.** To draw water, etc., from: to *drain* a swamp. **3.** To empty (a glass, cup, etc.) by drinking. **4.** To use up gradually; exhaust: Dissipation *drained* his strength. **5.** To filter. **—** *v.i.* **6.** To flow off gradually. **7.** To become dry by the flowing off or away of liquid. **8.** To discharge waters contained: said of an area: The region *drains* into the lake. **—** *n.* **1.** A pipe, trench, or similar device for draining. **2.** *Surg.* A substance or appliance, as gauze or tubing, inserted into a wound or cavity to afford a channel for discharge. **3.** A continuous outflow, expenditure, or depletion: a *drain* on our funds. **4.** The act of draining. [OE *drēahnian*] **— drain′er** *n.*

drain·age (drā′nij) *n.* **1.** The act or method of draining. **2.** A system of drains. **3.** That which is drained off; waste water. **4.** The area drained; drainage basin. **5.** *Surg.* The gradual drawing off of fluids from wounds.

drainage basin A large surface area whose waters are drained off into a principal river system.

drain·pipe (drān′pīp′) *n.* A pipe used for draining.

drake¹ (drāk) *n.* **1.** A male duck. **2.** A flat stone used in the game of ducks and drakes. [ME. Cf. dial. G *draak.*]

drake² (drāk) *n.* **1.** A May fly, used as bait in angling. Also **drake fly.** **2.** A small, obsolete, brass cannon. **3.** *Obs.* A dragon. [OE *draca* < L *draco.* See DRAGON.]

Drake (drāk) **Sir Francis,** 1540?–96, English admiral; first Englishman to circumnavigate the globe.

Dra·kens·berg (drä′kənz·bûrg) A mountain range in eastern South Africa; highest peak, Thabantshonyana, 11,425 ft.: also *Quathlamba.*

Drake Passage A strait joining the South Pacific and the South Atlantic between Cape Horn and the South Shetland Islands; length, about 500 mi.

dram (dram) *n.* **1.** An apothecaries' weight equal to 60 grains, 3.89 grams, or one eighth of an ounce. Abbr. *dr.* **2.** An avoirdupois measure equal to 27.34 grains, 1.77 grams, or one sixteenth of an ounce. See table inside back cover.

3. A fluid dram (which see). **4.** A drink of alcoholic liquor. **5.** A drachma. **6.** A small portion; bit. Also spelled *drachm.* — *v.* **drammed, dram·ming** *v.t.* **1.** To ply with liquor. — *v.i.* **2.** To use intoxicants freely. [< OF *drame* < L *drachma* < Gk. *drachmē* a handful. Doublet of DRACHMA.]

dra·ma (drä′mə, dram′ə) *n.* **1.** A literary composition written to be performed upon a stage, telling a story, usually of human conflicts and emotions, by means of dialogue and action; a play. Compare CLOSET DRAMA. **2.** Stage plays as a specific branch of literature: the classical *drama.* **3.** The art or profession of writing, acting, or producing plays. **4.** A series of actions, events, etc., having dramatic quality. **5.** The state or quality of being dramatic. [< LL, a play < Gk., deed, action < *draein* to act, do]

Dram·a·mine (dram′ə·mēn) *n.* Proprietary name of a brand of dimenhydrinate, used especially for motion sickness. Also **dram′a·mine.**

dra·mat·ic (drə·mat′ik) *adj.* **1.** Of, connected with, or like the drama. **2.** Characterized by the action or spirit of the drama, especially when involving conflict; theatrical; vivid. **3.** *Music* Having a singing voice of heavy quality and more than average loudness: a *dramatic* tenor. Also *Rare* **dra·mat′i·cal.** — **dra·mat′i·cal·ly** *adv.*

dra·mat·ics (drə·mat′iks) *n.pl.* (*usually construed as sing. in def. 2*) **1.** Dramatic performance, especially by amateurs. **2.** The art of staging or acting plays.

dram·a·tis per·so·nae (dram′ə·tis pər·sō′nē) *Latin* The characters of a play; also, a list of these.

dram·a·tist (dram′ə·tist) *n.* One who writes plays.

dram·a·ti·za·tion (dram′ə·tə·zā′shən, -tī·zā′-) *n.* **1.** The act or process of dramatizing. **2.** A dramatized version of something, as of a novel or historical event.

dram·a·tize (dram′ə·tīz) *v.* **·tized, ·tiz·ing** *v.t.* **1.** To present in dramatic form; adapt for performance, as a play, motion picture, etc. **2.** To represent or interpret (events, oneself, etc.) in a theatrical manner. — *v.i.* **3.** To be suitable for dramatization. Also *Brit.* **dram′a·tise.**

dram·a·turge (dram′ə·tûrj) *n.* A dramatist. Also **dram·a·tur′gist.** [< F < Gk. *dramatourgos* < *drama, -atos* a play + *ergein* to work]

dram·a·tur·gy (dram′ə·tûr′jē) *n.* The art of writing or producing plays, or of acting in them; dramatics. — **dram·a·tur′gic** (dram′ə·tûr′jik) or **·gi·cal** *adj.*

dram·shop (dram′shop′) *n.* A saloon; bar.

Drang nach Ost·en (dräng näkh ôs′tən) *German* The imperialistic policy of extending German influence to the east and south; literally, drive to the east.

drank (drangk) Past tense of DRINK.

drape (drāp) *v.* **draped, drap·ing** *v.t.* **1.** To cover or adorn in a graceful fashion, as with drapery or clothing. **2.** To arrange in graceful folds. **3.** *Informal* To dispose in a leisurely or sloppy manner: He *draped* himself over the rail. — *v.i.* **4.** To hang in folds. — *n.* **1.** *U.S. & Canadian Usually pl.* Drapery; curtains. **2.** The way in which cloth hangs, as in clothing. [< F *draper* to weave < *drap* cloth]

drap·er (drā′pər) *n.* **1.** *Brit.* A dealer in cloth or dry goods. **2.** Formerly, a manufacturer of cloth.

Dra·per (drā′pər) *n.* **Henry,** 1837–82, U.S. astronomer. — **John William,** 1811–82, U.S. chemist, physiologist, and historian born in England.

drap·er·y (drā′pər·ē) *n. pl.* **·er·ies 1.** Loosely hanging attire, especially on figures in painting, sculpture, etc. **2.** *Often pl.* Hangings or curtains arranged in loose folds. **3.** Cloth in general. **4.** *Brit.* The business of a draper.

dras·tic (dras′tik) *adj.* Acting vigorously; violently effective; extreme. [< Gk. *drastikos* effective < *draein* to act, to do] — **dras′ti·cal·ly** *adv.*

drat (drat) *interj.* A mild exclamation of anger or annoyance. [Alter. of *God rot*]

drat·ted (drat′id) *adj. Informal* Darned; confounded.

draught (draft, dräft) See DRAFT.

draughts (drafts, dräfts) *n.pl.* (*construed as sing.*) *Brit.* The game of checkers: also spelled *drafts.* [ME < OE *draht,* pp. of *dragan,* to draw, pull]

draughts·man (drafts′mən, dräfts′-) *n. pl.* **·men** (-mən) **1.** *Brit.* One of the pieces used in the game of checkers; a checker. **2.** See DRAFTSMAN.

draught·y (draf′tē, dräf′-) See DRAFTY.

Dra·va (drä′vä) A river in south central Europe, flowing about 450 miles SE to the Danube: *German* **Drau** (drou). Hungarian **Dráva** (drä′vo). Also **Dra′ve** (drä′və).

drave (drāv) Archaic past tense of DRIVE.

Dra·vid·i·an (dra·vid′ē·an) *n.* **1.** A member of the oldest indigenous people of southern India. **2.** A family of languages spoken primarily in southern India and northern Ceylon, including Tamil, Malayalam, Kanarese, and Telugu. — *adj.* Of the Dravidians or their languages: also **Dra·vid′ic.**

draw (drô) *v.* **drew, drawn, draw·ing** *v.t.* **1.** To cause to move toward or to follow behind an agent exerting physical force; pull; drag. **2.** To acquire or obtain, as from a receptacle: to *draw* water. **3.** To extract or take out, as a tooth, cork, etc. **4.** To cause to flow forth: to *draw* blood. **5.** To bring forth; evoke; elicit: to *draw* praise. **6.** To take or pull off, on, or out, as a sword, gloves, etc. **7.** To portray with

lines or words; sketch; delineate: to *draw* a portrait. **8.** To deduce or extract by a mental process; formulate: to *draw* a conclusion. **9.** To attract or allure; entice: Honey *draws* flies. **10.** To pull tight, as a rope or bowstring. **11.** To make or manufacture by stretching or hammering, as wire or dies. **12.** To take in, as air or a liquid, by inhaling or sucking. **13.** To close or shut as curtains. **14.** To disembowel: to *draw* a chicken. **15.** To cause (an abscess, etc.) to soften and drain by applying a poultice. **16.** To shrink or wrinkle; contract. **17.** To extract (essence) by infusion, distillation, etc.: to *draw* tea. **18.** To select or obtain, as by chance; also, to win (a prize) in a lottery. **19.** To get or receive; earn, as a salary or interest. **20.** To take out or withdraw, as money from a bank. **21.** To write out; draft (a check). **22.** *Naut.* Of a vessel, to sink to (a specified depth) in floating. **23.** To leave undecided, as a game or contest. **24.** In card games: **a** To take or get (a card or cards). **b** To cause (a card or cards) to be played: to *draw* trumps. **25.** In billiards, to cause (the cue ball) to recoil after impact. **26.** In cricket, to deflect (the ball) by a slight turn of the bat. **27.** In curling, to play (the stone) gently. — *v.i.* **28.** To practice the art of drawing; sketch. **29.** To exert a pulling or drawing force. **30.** To approach or retreat: to *draw* near or away. **31.** To exert an attracting influence: This movie does not *draw.* **32.** To pull out or unsheathe a weapon for action: usually with *on.* **33.** To shrink or become contracted, as a wound. **34.** To cause redness or irritation of the skin, as a poultice or blister. **35.** To obtain by making an application to some source; make a draft or demand on something: with *on* or *upon:* to *draw* on one's credit; to *draw* on one's experience. **36.** To produce a current of air: This chimney *draws* well. **37.** To end a contest without a decision; tie. **38.** In hunting: **a** To track game by scent. **b** To approach game slowly after pointing: said of hounds. — **to draw a blank** To be unsuccessful. — **to draw and quarter** In medieval executions: **a** To disembowel and dismember after hanging. **b** To tie each of the victim's arms and legs to a different horse and drive the horses in different directions. — **to draw on** To approach: Evening is *drawing* on. — **to draw oneself up** To straighten up or stiffen, as in anger or indignation. — **to draw out 1.** To prolong. **2.** To cause (someone) to talk freely. — **to draw the line** To fix a limit and refuse to go further. — **to draw up 1.** To write out in proper form: to *draw up* a deed. **2.** To bring or come to a standstill, as horses. **3.** To come alongside. — *n.* **1.** The act of drawing, as by pulling or tugging. **2.** The act of drawing out a weapon for action: quick on the *draw.* **3.** Something drawn, as a ticket in a lottery. **4.** Something that attracts a large audience. **5.** A stalemate; tie. **6.** *U.S.* A gully or ravine into which water drains. [OE *dragan.* Akin to DRAG.]

draw·back (drô′bak′) *n.* **1.** Anything that hinders progress, success, etc.; a disadvantage. **2.** A refund on money paid, especially on duties for imported goods being exported again, or on excess payment for freight.

draw·bar (drô′bär′) *n.* **1.** The bar used to couple railroad cars. **2.** On a tractor, the bar to which implements are coupled.

draw·bore (drô′bôr′, -bōr′) *n.* In carpentry, a hole in a tenon and mortise for a pin (**drawbore pin**) to pass through and thus join them tightly.

draw·bridge (drô′brij′) *n.* A bridge of which the whole or a part may be raised, let down, or drawn aside.

DRAWBRIDGE

draw·ee (drô′ē′) *n.* One on whom an order for the payment of money is drawn.

draw·er (drô′ər *for def. 1;* drôr *for def. 2*) *n.* **1.** One who draws; as: **a** A draftsman. **b** One who draws a check or money order. **c** A bartender, or someone else who draws beer, etc. **2.** A sliding receptacle, as in a desk, that can be drawn out and pushed back. Abbr. *dr.*

draw·ers (drôrz) *n.pl.* An undergarment covering the lower part of the body and having separate coverings for all or part of each leg; underpants.

draw·ing (drô′ing) *n.* **1.** The act of drawing. **2.** That which is drawn. **3.** The art of representing something, usually by pen, pencil, or crayon. **4.** The picture, sketch, or design produced by this art. **5.** A lottery.

drawing account An account from which a partner, employee, or salesman may draw cash for expenses or cash advanced against his expected income, salary, or commissions.

drawing board A smooth, flat board to which paper, etc., is attached for making drawings.

drawing card Something, as a popular entertainer, that attracts a large audience.

drawing pin *Brit.* A thumbtack.

drawing room 1. A room in which visitors are received and entertained. **2.** *Chiefly Brit.* A reception in a drawing room, especially when formal; also, the company assembled at such a reception. **3.** *U.S.* A private compartment in a sleeping car on a train. [Short for WITHDRAWING ROOM]

draw·knife (drô'nīf') *n. pl.* **·knives** (-nīvz') A knife with a handle at each end, used for shaving over a surface with a drawing motion. Also **drawing knife.**

drawl (drôl) *v.t. & v.i.* To speak or pronounce slowly, especially with a drawing out of the vowels. — *n.* The act of drawling; a lengthening of sounds, giving an impression of slowness of speech. [? Freq. of DRAW] — **drawl'er** *n.* — **drawl'ing·ly** *adv.* — **drawl'y** *adj.*

drawn (drôn) Past participle of DRAW.

drawn butter *U.S.* A sauce of melted butter, often thickened with flour mixed with hot water.

drawn work Ornamental openwork made by pulling out threads of fabric and forming by needlework various patterns with the remaining threads.

draw·plate (drô'plāt') *n.* A hard plate with holes of diminishing diameters for drawing out metal rods or wire.

draw·shave (drô'shāv') *n. U.S.* A drawknife.

draw·string (drô'string') *n.* A string, ribbon, or cord run through a casing or hem, as of the mouth of a bag, and when pulled draws together and closes an opening.

draw·tube (drô'tōōb', -tyōōb') *n.* A tube that slides within another tube, as the moving eyepiece tube of a microscope.

dray (drā) *n.* A low, strong cart with removable sides, for carrying heavy articles. — *v.t.* To transport by dray. [OE *dræge* dragnet < *dragan* to draw]

dray·age (drā'ij) *n.* **1.** The act of conveying in a dray. **2.** The charge for draying.

dray·man (drā'mən) *n. pl.* **·men** (-mən) A man who drives a dray.

Dray·ton (drā'tən), **Michael**, 1563–1631, English poet.

dread (dred) *v.t.* **1.** To anticipate with great fear or anxiety. **2.** *Archaic* To hold in awe. — *adj.* **1.** Causing great fear; terrible. **2.** Exciting awe or reverential fear. — *n.* **1.** A terrifying anticipation, as of evil or danger; great fear. **2.** Fear mixed with deep respect; awe. **3.** A person or thing inspiring fear or awe. — **Syn.** See ALARM, FEAR. [ME *dreden* < OE *ondrǣdan*]

dread·ful (dred'fəl) *adj.* **1.** Inspiring dread or awe; terrible. **2.** *Informal* Disgusting; shocking; very bad; awful. — *n. Brit. Informal* A penny dreadful (which see). — **dread'·ful·ly** *adv.* — **dread'ful·ness** *n.*

dread·nought (dred'nôt') *n.* **1.** One of a class of heavily armed battleships formerly used in the Royal Navy, typified by the **Dreadnought**, built in 1906. **2.** A heavy cloth, or an outer garment made of such cloth. **3.** One who fears nothing. Also **dread'naught'.**

dream (drēm) *n.* **1.** A series of thoughts or images passing through the mind in sleep; also, the mental state in which this occurs. **2.** A fancy or vision more or less freely entertained while awake; a daydream; reverie. **3.** A cherished or vain hope or ambition. **4.** Anything of dreamlike quality, especially of unreal beauty or charm. **5.** *Informal* Something so perfect, wonderful, etc., that it can hardly be accepted as real. — *v.* **dreamed** or **dreamt** (dremt), **dream·ing** *v.t.* **1.** To see or imagine in a dream. **2.** To envision, as in a dream. **3.** To spend (time) in idle reverie: with *away*. — *v.i.* **4.** To have a dream or dreams. **5.** To indulge in fancies or daydreams. **6.** To consider something as possible; be able to imagine something: with *of*: I would not *dream* of staving. — **to dream up** *Informal* To concoct or create, as by ingenuity or cleverness. [ME *dreme* < OE *drēam* joy; infl. by ON *draumr* a dream] — **dream'ful** *adj.* — **dream'ful·ly** *adv.* — **dream'ing·ly** *adv.* — **dream'less** *adj.* — **dream'less·ly** *adv.* — **dream'like'** *adj.*

— **Syn.** (noun) *Dream, vision, hallucination,* and *trance* are here compared in their extended senses. *Dream* is applied chiefly to idle hopes, but sometimes, like *vision,* it may be used of picturization of the ideal: *dreams* of amorous conquests, a *vision* of a new social order. *Hallucination* is applied to delusion or self-deception, and *trance* to a bemused state of mind in which judgment is impaired.

dream·er (drē'mər) *n.* **1.** One who dreams. **2.** A visionary.

dream·land (drēm'land') *n.* The realm of dreams.

dream world A world of illusions.

dream·y (drē'mē) *adj.* **dream·i·er, dream·i·est** **1.** Of, pertaining to, or causing dreams. **2.** Appropriate to dreams; shadowy; vague. **3.** Given to dreams; visionary. **4.** Soothing; soft; ethereal. **5.** *Informal* Wonderful; perfect. — **dream'i·ly** *adv.* — **dream'i·ness** *n.*

drear (drir) *adj. Poetic* Dreary.

drear·y (drir'ē) *adj.* **drear·i·er, drear·i·est** **1.** Causing or manifesting sadness or gloom; dismal. **2.** Dull or monotonous; lifeless. **3.** *Archaic* Sad; melancholy. [OE *drēorig* sad, bloody < *drēor* gore] — **drear'i·ly** *adv.* — **drear'i·ness** *n.*

dredge¹ (drej) *n.* **1.** A large, powerful scoop or suction apparatus for clearing out or deepening channels, harbors, etc., by removing the mud or gravel from their bottoms. Also **dredging machine.** **2.** Any smaller device for bringing up something from under water, as a dragnet. — *v.* **dredged, dredg·ing** *v.t.* **1.** To clear or widen by means of a dredge.

2. To remove, catch, or gather with a dredge. — *v.i.* **3.** To use a dredge. [ME *dreg.* Akin to DRAW.]

dredge² (drej) *v.t.* **dredged, dredg·ing** To sprinkle or dust with a powdered substance, especially flour. — *n. Obs.* A sweetmeat. [ME *drage* sweetmeat < OF *dragie* < L *tragemata* spices < Gk.]

FLOATING DREDGE

dredg·er¹ (drej'ər) *n.* **1.** One who dredges. **2.** A dredge. **3.** A boat engaged in dredging.

dredg·er² (drej'ər) *n.* In cookery, a box with a perforated lid used for sprinkling flour, etc. Also **dredging box.**

dredg·ing (drej'ing) *n.* **1.** The act of using a dredge. **2.** That which is taken up with a dredge.

dree (drē) *Scot. v.t.* To suffer; endure. — **to dree one's weird** To endure one's fate. — *adj.* Tedious: also **dreigh** (drēkh). [OE *drēogan*]

dreg·gy (dreg'ē) *adj.* **·gi·er, ·gi·est** Containing or full of dregs; foul. — **dreg'gi·ness** *n.* — **dreg'gish** *adj.*

dregs (dregz) *n.pl.* **1.** The sediment of liquids, especially of beverages; lees. **2.** Coarse, worthless residue: the *dregs* of society. **3.** (*construed as sing.*) A small amount left over. [ME *dregges* < ON *dregg*]

Drei·bund (drī'bōont) *n.* A triple alliance, especially that of Germany, Austria-Hungary, and Italy (1882–1915). [< G *drei* three + *bund* alliance]

Drei·ser (drī'sər, -zər), **Theodore (Herman Albert)**, 1871–1945, U.S. novelist.

drench (drench) *v.t.* **1.** To wet thoroughly; soak. **2.** *Vet.* To administer a potion to; force to swallow a draft. — *n.* **1.** *Vet.* A large draft or quantity of fluid. **2.** A water solution for drenching. **3.** The act of drenching. — **drench'er** *n.* [OE *drencan* to cause to drink]

Drep·a·num (drep'ə-nəm) The ancient name for TRAPANI.

Dres·den (drez'dən) *n.* A fine china made in Dresden, Germany. Also **Dresden china.**

Dres·den (drez'dən, *Ger.* drās'dən) A city in southern East Germany, on the Elbe; pop. 499,848 (est. 1968).

dress (dres) *v.* **dressed** or **drest, dress·ing** *v.t.* **1.** To put clothes on; clothe. **2.** To supply with clothing. **3.** To trim or decorate; adorn, as a store window. **4.** To treat medicinally, as a wound or sore. **5.** To comb and arrange (hair). **6.** To curry (a horse). **7.** To prepare (stone, timber, fabrics, etc.) for use or sale. **8.** To clean (fowl, game, fish, etc.) for cooking. **9.** To till, trim, or prune. **10.** To put in proper alignment, as troops. — *v.i.* **11.** To put on or wear clothing, especially formal clothing. **12.** To come into proper alignment. — **to dress down** *Informal* To rebuke severely; scold. — **to dress ship** *Naut.* To display the national colors, all signal flags, and bunting, as in honor of an individual or event. — **to dress up** To put on or wear formal attire or clothing more elaborate than is usually worn. — *n.* **1.** An outer garment for a woman or child, consisting of a skirt and waist, usually in one piece. **2.** Covering for the body; clothing collectively. **3.** Formal or fashionable clothing. **4.** External adornment or appearance. — *adj.* **1.** Of, pertaining to, or suitable for a dress. **2.** To be worn on formal occasions: a *dress* suit. [< OF *dresser* to arrange, set up, ult. < L *directus*. See DIRECT.]

— **Syn.** (noun) *Dress, clothing, clothes, garments, raiment, vesture, array, habit, vestment, apparel, attire, garb,* and *costume* refer to coverings worn on the body. *Dress* is the outer covering, especially when suitable for some occasion: court *dress,* evening *dress. Clothing* denotes the entire covering taken as a whole; *clothes* and *garments* view it as composed of separate parts. These three terms, as well as *raiment,* include underclothes as well as outer; all others here listed are applied only to outer *clothes. Raiment, vesture,* and *array* are not in common use, and have a somewhat archaic or poetic flavor. *Habit* has a few restricted applications: a riding *habit,* a monk's *habit. Vestment* is rare except in ecclesiastical use. *Apparel* and *attire* are chiefly used of complete and elegant outer *clothing* though *dress* has largely supplanted them in this sense. *Garb* is the *clothing* characteristic of some class, profession, or the like: the *garb* of a priest. In several other senses, a characteristic *dress* is called a *costume*: the *costume* of an actor, a 16th-century *costume,* the national *costume* of Bulgaria.

dres·sage (dres'ij, *Fr.* dre-säzh') *n.* The guiding of a trained horse through a set of paces or maneuvers by the rider's imperceptible bodily signals. [< F]

dress circle A section of seats in a theater or concert hall, usually the first gallery behind and above the orchestra.

dress coat The coat of a man's dress suit.

dress·er¹ (dres'ər) *n.* **1.** One who dresses something. **2.** One who assists another in dressing. **3.** One who dresses well or in a particular way: a fancy *dresser.* **4.** A tool used in dressing stone, leather, etc. **5.** *Brit.* A surgical assistant.

dress·er² (dres'ər) *n.* **1.** A chest of drawers for articles of clothing. **2.** A piece of furniture for holding dishes, silverware, etc.; buffet. [< OF *dresseur* < *dresser* to dress]

dress goods Fabrics for dresses.

dress·ing (dres′ing) *n.* **1.** The act of one who or that which dresses. **2.** That with which something is dressed. **3.** Medicated bandages, etc., applied to a wound or sore. **4.** Manure or other material used for dressing soil. **5.** A mixture of bread, seasonings, etc., used for stuffing poultry or roasts. **6.** A sauce for salads, vegetables, and the like.
dress·ing-down (dres′ing-doun′) *n. U.S. Informal* **1.** A severe scolding. **2.** A beating.
dressing gown A loose gown worn while lounging at home or before dressing.
dressing room A room for dressing, as backstage in a theater.
dressing station *Mil.* A medical field station for giving immediate aid to the wounded: also *aid station.*
dressing table A small table or stand with a mirror, used while putting on make-up, grooming the hair, etc.
dress·mak·er (dres′mā′kər) *n.* One who makes women's dresses or other articles of clothing. — *adj.* Not severely tailored, but having soft, feminine lines: a *dressmaker* suit. — **dress′mak′ing** *n.*
dress parade A formal military parade in dress uniform.
dress rehearsal A final rehearsal of a play, done with the costumes, lighting, etc., to be used in the public performance.
dress shield A piece of fabric worn to protect clothes from underarm perspiration.
dress suit A man's suit for formal evening wear, characterized by a low-cut vest and swallow-tailed coat.
dress uniform A military uniform worn at social or ceremonial events.
dress·y (dres′ē) *adj.* **dress·i·er, dress·i·est** *Informal* **1.** Having or giving an appearance of smart elegance; stylish; chic. **2.** Fond of dressing up. — **dress′i·ness** *n.*
drew (drōō) Past tense of DRAW.
Drew (drōō), **John,** 1853–1927, U.S. actor.
Drex·el (drek′səl), **Anthony Joseph,** 1826–93, U.S. banker and philanthropist.
Drey·fus (drā′fəs, drī′-; *Fr.* dre-füs′), **Alfred,** 1859–1935, French army officer; wrongfully convicted of treason in 1894; vindicated in 1906.
drib (drib) *v.t.* **dribbed, drib·bing** *Obs.* **1.** To let fall in drops. **2.** To do or say little by little. — *n. Dial.* Driblet. — **dribs and drabs** Small quantities. [Var. of DRIP]
drib·ble (drib′əl) *v.t. & v.i.* **·bled, ·bling 1.** To fall or let fall in drops; drip. **2.** To drool; drivel. **3.** In basketball, to propel (the ball) by bouncing with the hand. **4.** In soccer, to propel (the ball) by successive kicks. — *n.* **1.** A small quantity of a liquid falling in drops or flowing in a scanty and broken stream. **2.** In soccer and basketball, the act of dribbling. **3.** *Scot.* A drizzle. [Freq. of DRIB] — **drib′bler** *n.*
drib·let (drib′lit) *n.* **1.** A small drop of water or other liquid. **2.** A tiny quantity of something; bit. Also **drib′blet.** [< DRIB + -LET]
dried (drīd) Past tense and past participle of DRY.
dri·er (drī′ər) Comparative of DRY. — *n.* **1.** One who or that which dries. **2.** A substance added to paint, etc., to make it dry more quickly. **3.** A mechanical device for drying. Also spelled *dryer.*
dri·est (drī′ist) Superlative of DRY: also spelled *dryest.*
drift (drift) *n.* **1.** The act of moving along, or the fact of being carried along, in or as in a current of water, air, etc. **2.** A force or influence that drives something along steadily in a particular direction. **3.** The course along which something is directed, or the direction in which it tends; tendency or intent: the *drift* of a conversation. **4.** A usually slow, broad current of water, as in some parts of an ocean. **5.** The rate at which a current of water moves. **6.** The direction in which a current of water moves. **7.** Something driven along or heaped up by air currents or water currents: a cloud *drift*; a snow *drift*. **8.** Material, as rock particles, etc., carried along from one place to another, as by a glacier or river. **9.** The act of driving something along. **10.** *Naut.* The distance a vessel is driven from her direct course by wind, sea, etc. **11.** The lateral divergence of an aircraft, missile, or projectile from its projected line of heading because of crosswind or, in the case of a projectile, because of rotation about its axis. **12.** *Mech.* A cylindrical tool, sometimes with cutting edges, for enlarging or smoothing the edges of a hole in metal plate. **13.** *Mining* A horizontal or nearly horizontal passage in a mine; also, the direction of a passage or gallery. — *v.i.* **1.** To move along in or as in a current. **2.** To become heaped up by air currents or water currents. **3.** To be borne along by the force of circumstances; move along aimlessly. — *v.t.* **4.** To cause to drift. [ME < OE *drīfan* to drive]
drift·age (drif′tij) *n.* **1.** The act or process of drifting. **2.** Deviation caused by drifting. **3.** Something carried along or deposited by air currents or water currents.
drift anchor A sea anchor (which see).
drift angle *Aeron.* The angular difference between an aircraft's projected line of heading and its actual flight path.
drift·er (drif′tər) *n.* **1.** One who or that which drifts; especially, one who moves aimlessly from one job or place to another. **2.** A fishing boat with nets that drift with the

current or tide; also, a similar boat used in mine sweeping.
drift tube *Electronics* An enclosure, usually cylindrical and forming part of a klystron, in which electrons are maintained at a constant potential and velocity.
drift·wood (drift′wŏŏd′) *n.* Wood floated or drifted by water; especially, wood washed up on a seashore.
drift·y (drif′tē) *adj.* **drift·i·er, drift·i·est** Forming or full of drifts.
drill[1] (dril) *n.* **1.** A tool used for boring holes in metal, stone, wood, or other hard substances, usually by a rotary cutting or abrasive action or by punching. **2.** A mollusk (*Urosalpinx cinerea*) that kills oysters by drilling holes in their shells. **3.** Disciplined training process marked by the in-

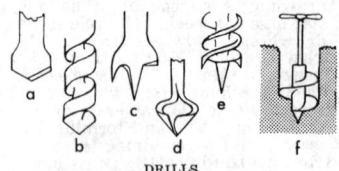

DRILLS
a Flat (metal). *b* Twist (metal). *c* Center bit (wood). *d* Countersink (wood or metal). *e* Twist bit (wood). *f* Earth borer.

culcation of fixed procedures and the use of much repetition, as in training in military or naval procedures, in gymnastics, in arithmetic, etc. **4.** The act or method of teaching through such training; also, a particular exercise forming a part of such training. — **Syn.** See PRACTICE. — *v.t.* **1.** To pierce or bore with as with a drill. **2.** To make (a hole) with a drill. **3.** To train in military procedures, etc. **4.** To teach by drill. — *v.i.* **5.** To make a hole with or as with a drill. **6.** To take part in a drill, as in military exercises. **7.** To train or teach someone by drill. — **Syn.** See TEACH. [< Du. *dril, drille* < *drillen* to bore]
drill[2] (dril) *Agric. n.* **1.** A machine for planting seeds in rows. **2.** A small furrow in which seeds are sown. **3.** A row of seeds so planted. — *v.t.* **1.** To plant in rows. — *v.i.* **2.** To sow or plant in rows. [? < DRILL[1]]
drill[3] (dril) *n.* Heavy, twilled linen or cotton cloth. Also called *drilling*. [Short for DRILLING[2] < G *drillich* cloth with three threads < L *trilix* < *tres* three + *licium* thread]
drill[4] (dril) *n.* A baboon (*Mandrillus leucophaeus*) of West Africa, similar to the mandrill. [? < native name]
drill·er (dril′ər) *n.* One who or that which drills.
drill·ing[1] (dril′ing) *n.* The act of one who or that which drills.
drill·ing[2] (dril′ing) *n.* Drill[3].
drill·mas·ter (dril′mas′tər, -mäs′-) *n.* One who teaches or trains by drilling; especially, a trainer in military exercises.
drill press A machine tool used in drilling holes.
drill·stock (dril′stok′) *n.* The part of a tool or machine that holds the shank of a drill used in boring holes.
dri·ly (drī′lē) See DRYLY.
drink (dringk) *v.* **drank** (*Archaic* **drunk**), **drunk** (*Archaic* **drunk·en** or **drank**), **drink·ing** *v.t.* **1.** To take into the mouth and swallow (a liquid). **2.** To soak up or absorb (liquid or moisture): often with *up* or *in*. **3.** To receive or absorb eagerly through the senses or the mind: often with *in*. **4.** To swallow the contents of (a glass, etc.). **5.** *Archaic* To honor with a toast. — *v.i.* **6.** To swallow a liquid. **7.** To drink alcoholic liquors, especially to excess or habitually. **8.** To drink a toast: with *to*. — **to drink the health of** To offer homage or good wishes to by a toast. — *n.* **1.** A drinkable liquid; beverage. **2.** A portion of liquid swallowed, as a glassful. **3.** Alcoholic liquor. **4.** The practice of drinking alcoholic liquor to excess. **5.** *Slang* A body of water. [OE *drincan*]
drink·a·ble (dringk′ə-bəl) *adj.* Capable of or suitable for use as a drink; potable. — *n. Usually pl.* A beverage.
drink·er (dringk′ər) *n.* **1.** One who drinks. **2.** One who drinks alcoholic liquors habitually or to excess.
Drink·wa·ter (dringk′wô′tər, -wot′ər), **John,** 1882–1937, English poet and playwright.
drip (drip) *n.* **1.** The formation and falling of drop after drop of liquid. **2.** Liquid falling in drops. **3.** The sound made by a liquid that falls in drops. **4.** Melted fat exuded from meat being roasted or fried. Also **drip′pings.** **5.** *Archit.* A projecting molding, as on a cornice, for shedding rainwater. **6.** *U.S. Slang* A disagreeable, insipid, or inept individual. — *v.t.* & *v.i.* **dripped** or **dript, drip·ping** To fall in drops or to let (liquid) fall in drops. [OE *dryppan*]
drip-dry (drip′drī′) *adj.* Designating or pertaining to a garment or fabric that is treated to dry quickly after being hung while dripping wet, to retain its shape, and to require little or no ironing. — *v.i.* **-dried, -dry·ing** To dry after being hung while dripping wet: said especially of drip-dry garments or fabrics.
drip grind A fine grind of coffee used in a dripolator.
drip·o·la·tor (drip′ə-lā′tər) *n.* A coffeepot in which boiling water seeps through the finely ground coffee. Also **drip coffee maker.** [< DRIP + (PERC)OLATOR]
dripping pan A pan for catching drippings or for holding meat being roasted.
drip·py (drip′ē) *adj.* **·pi·er, ·pi·est 1.** That drips or tends to drip: a *drippy* faucet. **2.** Very wet; rainy: a *drippy* day. **3.** *U.S. Slang* Obnoxious, stupid, or inept.

drip·stone (drip′stōn′) *n.* **1.** *Archit.* A stone projection, as on a cornice, for shedding rainwater. **2.** Calcium carbonate in the form of stalactites or stalagmites.

drive (drīv) *v.* **drove** (*Archaic* **drave**), **driv·en, driv·ing** *v.t.* **1.** To push or propel onward with force; urge or press forward; impel. **2.** To force to work or activity, especially excessively; overwork. **3.** To thrust or goad by force or compulsion: Failure *drove* him to despair. **4.** To cause to penetrate by force: to *drive* a nail into a wall. **5.** To produce or form by forcible penetration: to *drive* a well. **6.** To cause to go rapidly by striking or throwing with force: to *drive* a ball over the fence. **7.** To control the operation, movement, and direction of (a vehicle). **8.** To transport in a vehicle: to *drive* someone home. **9.** To provide the motive power for and cause to operate; make function: Steam *drives* the mechanism. **10.** To carry through without letup to a conclusion: to *drive* a hard bargain. **11.** In hunting, to chase (game) from cover or into traps, etc.; also, to search (an area) for game in this way. — *v.i.* **12.** To move along rapidly before an impelling force: The ship *drove* before the wind. **13.** To rush along; dash; speed. **14.** To strike, throw, or impel a ball, etc., with force. **15.** To drive a car or other vehicle. **16.** To be transported in a car or other vehicle. **17.** To work toward a particular objective or meaning: with *at*: What are you *driving* at? — **to drive home 1.** To force in all the way, as a nail. **2.** To make evident with force or emphasis: to *drive* home one's meaning. — **to let drive** To aim or release (a blow, shot, etc.). — *n.* **1.** The act of driving. **2.** A road for driving; also, a driveway. Abbr. *Dr.* **3.** A journey or trip in a car or other vehicle. **4.** Urgent pressure or rush, as of business. **5.** The gathering together and forcing onward of cattle, logs, etc. **6.** A herd of cattle, collection of logs, etc., being driven along. **7.** An organized campaign: a *drive* for money. **8.** *U.S. Informal* Energy; aggressiveness; also, initiative. **9.** *Psychol.* A strong, motivating power or stimulus: the sex *drive*. **10.** *Mil.* A large-scale, forceful, and sustained attack. **11.** *Mech.* A means of transmitting power, as from the motor of an automobile to the wheels. **12.** In certain games, as golf, the act of driving the ball, or the stroke by which the ball is driven. [OE *drīfan*]
— **Syn.** (verb) **1.** thrust, shove, press.

drive-in (drīv′in′) *n.* **1.** An outdoor motion-picture theater having a large screen designed for viewing from parked cars. **2.** A restaurant, shop, etc., serving patrons who remain in their cars. — *adj.* Designed for giving service to patrons in cars.

driv·el (driv′əl) *v.* **driv·eled** or **·elled, driv·el·ing** or **·el·ling** *v.i.* **1.** To let saliva flow from the mouth; slobber. **2.** To flow like saliva. **3.** To talk foolishly. — *v.t.* **4.** To let flow from the mouth. **5.** To say in a foolish manner. — *n.* **1.** A flow of saliva from the mouth. **2.** Senseless talk; twaddle. [OE *dreflian*] — **driv′el·er** or **driv′el·ler** *n.*

driv·en (driv′ən) Past participle of DRIVE.

driv·er (drī′vər) *n.* **1.** One who drives, as a vehicle, animals, logs, etc.; a chauffeur, coachman, drover, or the like. **2.** Something used for driving, as a hammer or mallet. **3.** In golf, a wooden-headed club with full-length shaft, for driving from the tee. For illustration see GOLF CLUB. **4.** *Mech.* Any of various parts that transmit motion or power.

Dri·ver (drī′vər), **Samuel Rolles**, 1846–1914, English Hebraic and Biblical scholar.

driver ant Any of a subfamily (*Dorylinae*) of carnivorous, stinging ants of tropical Africa and South America, that live in temporary nests and raid the countryside in huge armies: also called *army ant, doryline ant, legionary ant.*

drive shaft *Mech.* A shaft for transmitting power from an engine to the working parts of machinery.

drive·way (drīv′wā′) *n.* **1.** A private road providing access to a garage, house, or other building. **2.** A road for driving.

driv·ing (drī′ving) *adj.* **1.** Transmitting power or motion. **2.** Violent and intense: a *driving* rain. **3.** Active and energetic: a *driving* personality.

driving wheel A wheel used to communicate power or motion to some part of a machine, as in a locomotive. Also **drive wheel, driver wheel.**

driz·zle (driz′əl) *v.t.* & *v.i.* **·zled, ·zling** To rain steadily in fine drops. — *n.* A light rain. [? Freq. of ME *dresen*, OE *drēosan* to fall] — **drizz′ly** *adj.*

Dro·ghe·da (drô′ə-də, dro′hē-də) A municipal borough and port in NE Ireland; inhabitants massacred by Cromwell 1649; pop. about 17,000.

droit (droit, *Fr.* drwä) *n.* **1.** A legal right or claim. **2.** That to which one has a legal claim. **3.** *pl.* Customs duties. [< F, a right < LL *directum* < L *dirigere* to set straight]

droit des gens (drwä dā zhän′) *French* Law of nations; international law.

droll (drōl) *adj.* Humorously odd; charmingly amusing; comical; funny. — **Syn.** See HUMOROUS. — *n.* A prankster; clown. — *v.i.* To clown. [< MF *drolle* < MDu. *drol* a jolly little man] — **droll′ly** *adv.*

droll·er·y (drō′lər-ē) *n.* *pl.* **·er·ies 1.** The quality of being droll; humor. **2.** An amusing way of acting or talking. **3.** Something droll, as a funny remark.

-drome *combining form* Place for running; racecourse: *hippodrome.* [< Gk. *dromos* a running < *dramein* to run]

drom·e·dar·y (drom′ə-der′ē, drum′-) *n.* *pl.* **·dar·ies** The swift, one-humped Arabian camel (*Camelus dromedarius*), trained for riding. [< OF *dromedaire* < LL *dromedarius* < L *dromas* < Gk., a running]

drom·ond (drom′ənd, drum′-) *n.* A swift medieval ship propelled by oars and sails. Also **drom·on** (drom′ən, drum′-). [< AF *dromund*, OF *dromon* < LL *dromon* < L Gk. *dromōn* < Gk. *dromos* a running < *dramein* to run]

-dromous *combining form* Running: *catadromous.* [< -DROME + -OUS]

drone[1] (drōn) *v.* **droned, dron·ing** *v.i.* **1.** To make a dull, humming sound; hum. **2.** To speak monotonously. — *v.t.* **3.** To utter in a monotonous tone. — *n.* **1.** A dull humming sound, as of a bee. **2.** One of the single-note reed pipes of the bagpipe; also, a bagpipe or similar instrument. For illustration see BAGPIPE. **3.** *Music* A sustained sound or note in the bass, usually of fixed pitch. **4.** A drawling or monotonous speaker. [ME *dronen* < *drone* male bee]

drone[2] (drōn) *n.* **1.** The male of the bee, especially of the honeybee, having no sting and gathering no honey. **2.** A loafer who lives by the help or labor of others; an idler. **3.** *Aeron.* An unmanned airplane piloted by remote control. — *v.i.* **droned, dron·ing** To live in idleness. [OE *drān*]

dron·go (drong′gō) *n.* *pl.* **·gos** A crowlike, insectivorous bird (*Dicrurus forficatus*) of the East Indies and Africa, with a long, forked tail. Also **drongo shrike.** [< Malagasy]

drool (drōōl) *v.t.* & *v.i.* To drivel; slaver. — *n.* **1.** Spittle. **2.** *Informal* Foolish talk; twaddle. [Contraction of DRIVEL]

droop (drōōp) *v.i.* **1.** To sink down; hang downward. **2.** To lose vigor or vitality; languish. **3.** To become dejected; lose spirit. — *v.t.* **4.** To let hang or sink down. — *n.* A drooping. [< ON *drūpa*] — **droop′ing·ly** *adv.*

droop·y (drōō′pē) *adj.* **droop·i·er, droop·i·est 1.** That droops or tends to droop. **2.** Despondent; gloomy; forlorn. — **droop′i·ly** *adv.* — **droop′i·ness** *n.*

drop (drop) *n.* **1.** A small quantity of liquid, shaped like a tiny ball or pear; globule. **2.** A very small amount of anything, especially of a liquid. **3.** *pl.* A liquid medicine given in drops. **4.** Something resembling a drop of liquid in shape, size, etc., as a small piece of hard candy or a pendant of a chandelier. **5.** Something designed to fall, slide, or hang down from a higher point, as a trap door or drop curtain. **6.** A slot or other aperture, as in a mailbox, through which letters, etc., are pushed so as to fall into a receptacle. **7.** A sudden or quick downward movement; a rapid descent or fall. **8.** A sudden or quick decrease or slump: a *drop* in prices. **9.** The vertical distance from a higher to a lower level. **10.** A falling off or away of a supporting surface: a sheer *drop* at the edge of a cliff. **11.** An incline or slope, especially when abrupt or steep: a sudden *drop* in the road. **12.** A parachuting of men or supplies. **13.** *Naut.* The vertical length of a course on its central line. — **at the drop of a hat** With little or no hesitation or provocation; at once. — **to have** (or **get**) **the drop on** To have (or get) the advantage over; especially, to have (a person) covered with a gun before he can draw his. — *v.* **dropped** or **dropt, drop·ping** *v.i.* **1.** To fall in drops, as a liquid. **2.** To fall or descend rapidly. **3.** To fall down exhausted, injured, or dead. **4.** To decline or decrease, as in amount: Prices *dropped.* **5.** To crouch, as a hunting dog at the sight of game. **6.** To fall into some state or condition: to *drop* into a habit. **7.** To come to an end; cease; stop: to let the matter *drop.* — *v.t.* **8.** To let fall by letting go of. **9.** To let fall in drops. **10.** To sprinkle with drops; spot. **11.** To give birth to: said of animals. **12.** To utter in or as in a casual way: to *drop* a hint. **13.** To write and send (a note, etc.) in a casual way. **14.** To cause to fall, as by striking, tackling, or shooting. **15.** To have no more to do with; have done with; dismiss: to *drop* an unpleasant subject. **16.** To let out or deposit at a particular place: *Drop* your friend off at her house. **17.** To parachute (soldiers, supplies, etc.). **18.** To leave out; omit, as a word, line, or stitch. **19.** *U.S.* To discharge (an employee). **20.** To move down; lower. **21.** To poach (an egg). **22.** *Slang* To lose (money, etc.), as in gambling. **23.** *Naut.* To outdistance. **24.** In football, to drop-kick (the ball); also, to score (a goal) by drop-kicking. — **to drop behind** (or **back**) To fall behind or lag behind purposely or by necessity. — **to drop in** To make a casual or unexpected visit. — **to drop off 1.** To decline or decrease. **2.** To go to sleep. — **to drop out** To withdraw from membership or participation. [OE *dropa*]

drop curtain A stage curtain that can be raised and lowered.

drop·forge (drop′fôrj′) *v.t.* **·forged, ·forg·ing** To forge (metal) between dies by a machine employing the mechanical force of a dropped weight. — **drop′forg′ing** *n.*

drop hammer A machine for forging, stamping, etc., in which a heavy weight sliding between vertical guides hammers the metal beneath it. Also **drop press.**

drop-kick (drop′kik′) *v.t.* & *v.i.* To give a drop kick (to).

drop kick In football, a kick given the ball just as it is rebounding after being dropped by the kicker; also, the consequent flight of the ball, or the distance covered by it.

drop leaf A hinged section of a table that can be folded down when not in use.

drop-let (drop′lit) *n.* A tiny drop.

drop letter *U.S.* A letter delivered from the same post office at which it is posted.

drop-light (drop′līt′) *n.* An electric lamp, etc., that hangs suspended and can be raised or lowered.

drop-out (drop′out′) *n.* *U.S. & Canadian* A child who leaves school as soon as attendance is not compulsory.

drop-per (drop′ər) *n.* **1.** One who or that which drops. **2.** A glass tube with a suction bulb at one end and a narrow opening at the other for dispensing a liquid in drops.

drop-ping (drop′ing) *n.* **1.** The act of falling or letting fall in drops. **2.** *Usually pl.* Falling drops, or that which has fallen in drops. **3.** *pl.* The dung of animals.

drop shot 1. Shot made by dropping molten metal from a height into water. **2.** In tennis, etc., a softly stroked return that barely clears the net.

drop-sonde (drop′sond′) *n.* *Meteorol.* A radiosonde that is dropped by parachute. [< DROP + (RADIO)SONDE]

drop-sy (drop′sē) *n.* **1.** *Pathol.* An abnormal accumulation of serous fluid. **2.** A disease of certain plants resulting from an excess of water. [Short for HYDROPSY] — **drop′si-cal** (-si-kəl), **drop′sied** (-sēd) *adj.* — **drop′si-cal-ly** *adv.*

dropt (dropt) Alternative spelling of DROPPED.

drop-wort (drop′wûrt′) *n.* **1.** A perennial plant (*Filipendula hexapetala*) of the rose family, with interruptedly pinnate leaves and white or reddish, odorless flowers. **2.** A North American marsh plant (*Oxypolis rigidior*) of the parsley family.

drosh-ky (drosh′kē, drôsh′-) *n.* *pl.* **·kies**
1. A light, open, four-wheeled Russian carriage. **2.** Any of several similar carriages. Also **dros-ky** (dros′kē, drôs′-). [< Russ. *drozhki*, dim. of *drogi* wagon]

dro-soph-i-la (drō-sof′ə-la, dra-) *n.* *pl.* **·lae** (-lē) The fruit fly (def. 2). [< NL < Gk. *drosos* dew + *phileein* to love]

DROSHKY

dross (drôs, dros) *n.* **1.** *Metall.* Refuse or impurity in melted metal; slag; cinders. **2.** Waste matter; refuse. [OE *drōs*] — **dross′i-ness** *n.* — **dross′y** *adj.*

drought (drout) *n.* **1.** Long-continued dry weather; lack of rain. **2.** Scarcity; dearth. **3.** *Dial.* Thirst. Also **drouth** (drouth). [OE *drūgath.* Akin to DRY.]

drought-y (drou′tē) *adj.* **1.** Marked by or suffering from drought. **2.** *Dial.* Thirsty. Also **drouth-y** (drou′thē).

drouk (drook) *v.t.* *Scot.* To drench. [Origin uncertain. Cf. ON *drukna* to be drowned.]

drove¹ (drōv) Past tense of DRIVE.

drove² (drōv) *n.* **1.** A number of animals driven or herded for driving. **2.** A moving crowd of human beings. **3.** A stonemason's broad-edged chisel. Also **drove chisel.** **4.** The surface of stone smoothed by a drove: also **drove′work** (-wûrk′). — **Syn.** See FLOCK. — *v.t.* **droved, drov·ing 1.** To drive (cows, etc.) for some distance. **2.** To dress (stone) with a broad-edged chisel. [OE *drāf.* Akin to DRIVE.]

drov-er (drō′vər) *n.* One who drives animals in droves to market; a cattle or sheep dealer.

drown (droun) *v.i.* **1.** To die by suffocation with water or other liquid. — *v.t.* **2.** To kill by suffocation with water or other liquid. **3.** To cover with or as with a flood; inundate. **4.** To lessen or obliterate the sound of by greater volume; muffle. **5.** To submerge so as to lessen or extinguish: He *drowned* his grief in drink. ♦ The variant form *drownded* for *drowned* is not acceptable in standard English. [ME *drounen.* Cf. ON *drukna* to be drowned.]

drowse (drouz) *v.* **drowsed, drows·ing** *v.i.* **1.** To be only half awake; doze. — *v.t.* **2.** To make sleepy, dull, or lethargic. **3.** To pass (time) in drowsing. — *n.* The state of being half asleep; doze. [OE *drūsian* to become sluggish]

drow-si-head (drou′zē-hed′) *n.* *Archaic* Drowsiness. Also **drow′si-hood′** (-hood′).

drow-sy (drou′zē) *adj.* **·si-er, ·si-est 1.** Heavy with sleepiness; dull. **2.** Produced by sleepiness or lethargy. **3.** Making sleepy; soporific. — **drow′si-ly** *adv.* — **drow′si-ness** *n.*

drub (drub) *v.t.* **drubbed, drub·bing 1.** To beat, as with a stick; cudgel; thrash. **2.** To vanquish; overcome. **3.** To stamp (the feet). — *n.* A blow; thump. [? < Arabic *ḍarb* a beating < *ḍaraba* to beat] — **drub′ber** *n.*

drub-bing (drub′ing) *n.* **1.** A thrashing; a beating. **2.** Utter defeat, as in a sports contest; a rout.

drudge (druj) *v.i.* **drudged, drudg·ing** To work hard at wearisome, monotonous, or menial tasks. — *n.* One who drudges. [Prob. akin to OE *drēogan* work, labor] — **drudg′er** *n.* — **drudg′ing·ly** *adv.*

drudg-er-y (druj′ər-ē) *n.* *pl.* **·er-ies** Dull, wearisome, or menial work. — **Syn.** See TOIL¹.

drug (drug) *n.* **1.** Any chemical compound or biological substance, other than food, intended for use in the treatment, prevention, or diagnosis of disease in man or other animals. **2.** Formerly, any substance used in chemistry, dyeing, the arts, etc. **3.** A narcotic (def. 1). **4.** A commodity that is overabundant or in excess of demand: a *drug* on the market. — *v.t.* **drugged, drug·ging 1.** To mix drugs with (food, drink, etc.), especially narcotic or poisonous drugs. **2.** To administer drugs to. **3.** To stupefy or poison with or as with drugs. [ME *drogge* < MF *drogne*, ? < MLG *droge(vate)* a dry (cask). Cf. MDu. *droge* dry.]

drug addict One who uses narcotics habitually.

drug-get (drug′it) *n.* **1.** A coarse woolen or wool-and-cotton fabric for rugs, etc. **2.** A rug made of this material. **3.** Formerly, a kind of woolen or part-woolen dress fabric. [< MF *droguet* cheap cloth; dim. of *drogue*]

drug-gist (drug′ist) *n.* **1.** One who compounds prescriptions and sells drugs; a pharmacist. **2.** A dealer in drugs. [MF *droguiste* < *drogue* dry]

drug-store (drug′stôr′, -stōr′) *n.* *U.S.* A place where prescriptions are compounded, and drugs and miscellaneous merchandise are sold; pharmacy. Also **drug store.**

dru-id (drōō′id) *n.* One of an order of priests or teachers of an ancient Celtic religion. [< MF *druide* < L *druidae, druides* < Celtic, ? ult. from a root meaning "oak" or a word meaning "greatly learned"] — **dru′id·ess** *n.fem.* — **dru-id·ic** (drōō-id′ik) or **·i·cal** *adj.* — **dru′id·ism** *n.*

drum¹ (drum) *n.* **1.** A hollow percussion instrument, typically shaped like a cylinder or hemisphere, having a membrane stretched tightly over one or both ends, and played by beating the membrane with sticks, the hands, etc. **2.** A booming, thumping, or tapping sound produced by or as by a drum. **3.** Something resembling a drum in shape; as: **a** A metal cylinder around which cable, wire, etc., is wound. **b** A cylindrical metal container, as for oil. **c** A cylindrical section forming part of a pillar. **d** A circular wall or other rounded structure. **4.** The drumfish (which see). **5.** *Anat.* The middle ear, or the tympanic membrane. **6.** *Archaic* A drummer. **7.** *Obs.* A social gathering in a private home. — *v.* **drummed, drum·ming** *v.i.* **1.** To beat a drum. **2.** To tap or thump continuously or rhythmically, as with the fingers. **3.** To make a booming or thumping noise: said especially of the beating wings of partridge, etc. — *v.t.* **4.** To perform on or as on a drum. **5.** To summon by beating a drum. **6.** To force upon or into by constant repetition: to *drum* rules into a person's head. **7.** To work up (business or trade) by advertising, canvassing, etc.: usually with *up.* **8.** To expel in disgrace: usually with *out.* [Prob. < MDu. *tromme*]

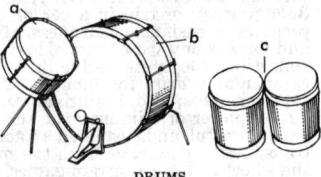

DRUMS

a Snare. *b* Bass. *c* Bongo.

drum² (drum) *n.* **1.** *Scot. & Irish* A hill or elevation. **2.** A drumlin. [< Irish or Scottish Gaelic *druim* ridge]

drum-beat (drum′bēt′) *n.* The sound of a drum.

drum-ble (drum′bəl) *v.i.* *Dial.* To move sluggishly. [< Obs. *drumble,* var. of *dummel* stupid < DUMB]

drum-fire (drum′fīr′) *n.* Gunfire so rapid and continuous as to sound like drums.

drum-fish (drum′fish′) *n.* *pl.* **·fish** or **·fish·es 1.** A sciaenoid fish (*Pogonias cromis*) of the North American Atlantic coast that makes a drumming sound, especially in the breeding season. **2.** Any of various similar fishes, as the freshwater drum (*Aplodinotus grunniens*) of the Great Lakes and the Mississippi: also called *sheepshead.*

drum-head (drum′hed′) *n.* **1.** The membrane stretched over the end of a drum. **2.** *Naut.* The circular top of a capstan. For illustration see CAPSTAN. **3.** *Anat.* The tympanic membrane.

drumhead court-martial A court-martial called for summary trial of an offense committed on the line of march or in action, formerly with a drumhead used as a table.

drum-lin (drum′lin) *n.* *Geol.* A long oval mound of unstratified glacial debris: also called *drum.* [< Irish *druim*]

drum-ly (drum′lē) *adj.* *Scot.* **1.** Turbid. **2.** Dark and gloomy. [Variation of obs. *drubly*]

drum major One who instructs or leads a band or drum corps. — **drum ma·jor·ette** (mā′jə-ret′) *fem.*

drum-mer (drum′ər) *n.* **1.** One who or that which drums. **2.** *U.S.* A traveling salesman.

Drum-mond (drum′ənd), **William,** 1585–1649, first laird of Hawthornden, Scottish poet: called **Drummond of Hawthornden.**

Drummond light The calcium light (which see). [after *T. Drummond,* 1797–1840, British engineer]

drum-stick (drum′stik′) *n.* **1.** A stick for beating a drum. **2.** The lower joint of the leg of a cooked fowl.

drunk (drungk) Past participle and archaic past tense of DRINK. — *adj.* **1.** Affected with alcoholic drink to the

extent of having lost normal control over bodily and mental faculties; intoxicated; inebriated. **2** Overwhelmed by some powerful stimulus or influence: *drunk* with joy. — *n. Informal* **1.** One who is drunk. **2.** One who habitually drinks alcoholic beverages to excess. **3.** A bout of drinking; binge.
— **Syn.** (adjective) **1.** intoxicated, inebriated, tight, potted. **2.** intoxicated. — (noun) **1.** inebriate. **2.** dipsomaniac, alcoholic, sot. **3.** bender.

drunk·ard (drungk′ərd) *n.* One who habitually drinks alcoholic beverages to excess.

drunk·en (drungk′ən) Archaic past participle of DRINK. — *adj.* **1.** Habitually drunk: a *drunken* husband. **2.** Relating to, showing the effects of, or occurring during the state of being drunk: a *drunken* stupor. — **drunk′en·ly** *adv.*

drunk·en·ness (drungk′ən·nis) *n.* The state of being drunk.

drunk·om·e·ter (drung·kom′ə·ter) *n.* A device, usually used by police, to test a sample of a driver's breath in order to measure the amount of alcohol in his blood.

dru·pa·ceous (droo·pā′shəs) *adj. Bot.* Of, like, or bearing drupes.

drupe (droop) *n. Bot.* A soft, fleshy fruit, as a peach or cherry, enclosing a hard-shelled stone or seed. [< NL *drupa* < L *drupa* (*oliva*) an overripe (olive) < Gk. *dryppa*]

drupe·let (droop′lit) *n. Bot.* A little drupe.

Dru·ry Lane (droor′ē) A street in London, known in the 17th and 18th centuries for its theaters.

druse (drooz) *n. Geol.* A crust of small crystals lining a cavity in a rock of similar composition. [< G]

Druse (drooz) *n.* One of a religious sect mostly of Syrians. [< Arabic *Durūz*, pl., after Ismail al-*Darazi*, who founded the sect] — **Dru·si·an** (droo′zē·ən) or **Dru′se·an** *adj.*

Dru·sus (droo′səs), Caesar, 13? B.C.–A.D. 23, Roman general; son of the emperor Tiberius: called **Drusus Junior.** — **Nero Claudius,** 38–9 B.C., Roman general; brother of the emperor Tiberius: called **Drusus Senior.**

dry (drī) *adj.* **dri·er** or, occasionally, **dry·er, dri·est** or, occasionally, **dry·est. 1.** Devoid of moisture; not wet or damp. **2.** Marked by little or no rainfall: a *dry* season. **3.** Marked by the absence of normal moisture: a *dry* region. **4.** Not lying under water: to step off a ship onto *dry* land. **5.** Parched or withered through absence of moisture: the *dry* desert. **6.** Having all or nearly all the water drained away or evaporated: a *dry* stream. **7.** Having all or nearly all the water exhausted: a *dry* well. **8.** No longer giving milk: *dry* breasts. **9.** Devoid of tears: *dry* eyes. **10.** Thirsty: to feel *dry*. **11.** Eaten or served without butter, jam, etc.: *dry* toast. **12.** Unaccompanied by the discharge of phlegm, etc.: a *dry* cough. **13.** Consisting of or pertaining to commodities, etc., that are not liquids: *dry* provisions. **14.** Lacking sweetness: said of wines in which the sugar has been decomposed during fermentation. **15.** Plain; unadorned; bare: the *dry* facts. **16.** Devoid of interest and life; dull; boring: a *dry* lecture. **17.** Devoid of warmth, color, or emotion; cold and stiff: a *dry* welcome. **18.** Crisp, quietly shrewd, and impersonal: *dry* humor. **19.** *U.S. Informal* Opposing or prohibiting the sale of or indulgence in alcoholic beverages: a *dry* State. — *v.* **dried, dry·ing** *v.t.* **1.** To make dry. **2.** To preserve (meat, fish, etc.) by removing moisture. — *v.i.* **3.** To become dry. — **to dry up 1.** To become thoroughly dry: also **dry out. 2.** To become unproductive: His imagination *dried up.* **3.** *Slang* To stop talking. — *n. pl.* **drys** *U.S. Informal* A prohibitionist. [OE *drȳge*]

dry·ad (drī′əd, -ad) *n.* In classical mythology, a nymph dwelling in or presiding over woods and trees. [< L *dryas*, -*adis* < Gk. < *drys, dryos* tree] — **dry·ad′ic** *adj.*

dry·as·dust (drī′əz·dust′) *n.* An uninteresting, pedantic writer or speaker; a dull pedant. — **dry′-as-dust′** *adj.*

dry battery *Electr.* A battery composed of one or more dry cells. Also **dry-cell battery** (drī′sel′).

dry-bone ore (drī′bōn′) Smithsonite (def. 1).

dry-bulb thermometer (drī′bulb′) *Meteorol.* An ordinary thermometer, especially when used in a psychrometer with a wet-bulb thermometer.

dry cell *Electr.* A primary cell containing an electrolyte of liquid and powder combined to form a paste.

dry-clean (drī′klēn′) *v.t.* To clean (clothing, etc.) with solvents other than water, such as carbon tetrachloride. Also **dry′-cleanse′.** — **dry cleaner** — **dry cleaning**

Dry·den (drīd′n), **John,** 1631–1700, English poet, critic, and dramatist; poet laureate 1670–88.

dry distillation *Chem.* Destructive distillation (which see).

dry-dock (drī′dok′) *v.t.* **1.** To put into dry dock. — *v.i.* **2.** To go into dry dock.

dry dock A floating or stationary structure from which

water can be removed, used for repairing and cleaning ships.

dry·er (drī′ər) Alternative comparative of DRY. — *n.* A drier.

dry·est (drī′ist) Alternative superlative of DRY.

dry-eyed (drī′īd′) *adj.* Not weeping; tearless.

dry farming In an arid country, the raising of crops without irrigation, mainly by saving the moisture of the soil and by raising drought-resisting crops. — **dry farmer**

dry fog *Meteorol.* Haze formed from a suspension of fine dust or smoke particles in the atmosphere.

dry goods Textile fabrics, as distinguished from groceries, hardware, etc.

Dry Ice Solid carbon dioxide, having a temperature of about −110° F., and passing directly to the gaseous state, widely used as a refrigerant: a trade name: also called *carbon dioxide snow.* Also **dry ice.**

dry·ing (drī′ing) *adj.* **1.** Able to draw out or absorb moisture; causing evaporation; absorbent. **2.** Becoming dry rapidly, as certain oils.

dry kiln A heated oven or chamber for drying and seasoning lumber.

dry law *U.S.* A law prohibiting the sale of alcoholic beverages.

dry·ly (drī′lē) *adv.* In a dry manner: also spelled *drily.*

dry measure A unit or system of units for measuring the volume of dry commodities, as fruits or grains. See table inside back cover.

dry·ness (drī′nis) *n.* The state or quality of being dry.

dry-nurse (drī′nûrs′) *v.t.* **-nursed, -nurs·ing** To be a dry nurse to.

dry nurse 1. A nurse who rears a child without suckling it. **2.** One who trains another; especially, one who instructs a new or inexperienced superior.

dry point 1. A fine, hard etching needle used to incise fine lines on copperplate without the use of acid; also, the process of using this needle. **2.** An engraving made from copperplate incised with this needle.

dry rot 1. A fungous disease of timber, causing it to crumble into powder. **2.** A disease of potato tubers and other vegetables. **3.** Inward and gradual corruption, as of morals.

dry run 1. *Mil.* A practice exercise in combat skills without using live ammunition. **2.** Any rehearsal or trial run.

dry-salt (drī′sôlt′) *v.t.* To preserve (food) by salting and removing moisture.

dry·salt·er (drī′sôl′tər) *n. Brit.* A dealer in chemical preparations, dyestuffs, etc.

dry·salt·er·y (drī′sôl′tər·ē) *n. pl.* **·er·ies** *Brit.* The business or stock of a drysalter.

dry-shod (drī′shod′) *adj. & adv.* Having the shoes or feet dry; without getting the feet wet: to cross a brook *dry-shod.*

Dry Tor·tu·gas (tôr·tōō′gəz) A group of Florida islets west of the Marquesas Keys: also *Tortugas.*

dry wash Laundry washed and dried but not ironed.

d.s. Decistere.

d.s. or **D.S.** *Music* Dal segno.

D.S. or **D.Sc.** Doctor of Science (L *Doctor Scientiae*).

DSC *Mil.* Distinguished Service Cross.

DSM *Mil.* Distinguished Service Medal.

D.S.O. *Brit.* **1.** (Companion of the) Distinguished Service Order. **2.** District Staff Officer.

d.s.p. Died without issue (L *decessit sine prole*).

DST or **D.S.T.** Daylight Saving Time.

D.S.T. Doctor of Sacred Theology.

d.t. 1. Delirium tremens. **2.** Double time.

D.Th. or **D.Theol.** Doctor of Theology.

Du. 1. Duke. **2.** Dutch.

du·ad (dōō′ad, dyōō′-) *n.* A pair of objects considered as a single unit. [< Gk. *dyas*, -*ados* the number two]

du·al (dōō′əl, dyōō′-) *adj.* **1.** Denoting or relating to two. **2.** Composed of two: twofold; double; binary. **3.** *Gram.* In some languages, as Sanskrit and Greek, of or designating a word form that denotes two: distinguished from *singular, plural.* — *n. Gram.* The dual number, or a word form having this number. [< L *dualis* < *duo* two]

Du·a·la (dōō·ä′lä) *n.* **1.** One of a Bantu people inhabiting the Cameroons, West Africa. **2.** The language of this people.

Dual Alliance An alliance (1879) between Germany and Austria-Hungary against Russia.

du·al·ism (dōō′əl·iz′əm, dyōō′-) *n.* **1.** The state of being twofold; duality. **2.** *Philos.* The theory that the universe is composed of two principles, as mind and matter. **3.** *Psychol.* The theory that man's body and mind are two different entities, but intimately correlated and interacting. **4.** *Theol.* The doctrine that there are two eternal and opposing principles or beings, one good and the other evil. — **du′al·ist** *n.*

du·al·is·tic (dōō′əl·is′tik, dyōō′-) *adj.* **1.** Of or pertaining to dualism. **2.** Dual in nature. — **du′al·is′ti·cal·ly** *adv.*

du·al·i·ty (dōō·al′ə·tē, dyōō′-) *n. pl.* **·ties** The state, character, or quality of being two or composed of two.

du·al-pur·pose (dōō′əl·pûr′pəs, dyōō′-) *adj.* Having two functions or uses.

FLOATING DRY DOCK
a Water line when ship is floated in.
b Water line after water is pumped out.
c Block supports for ship. *d* Shoring for side support. *e* Watertight compartment.

dub[1] (dub) *v.t.* **dubbed, dub·bing** **1.** To confer knighthood upon by tapping on the shoulder with a sword. **2.** To name or style; call: They *dubbed* him Speedy. **3.** To smooth or rub; dress, as timber. [OE *dubbian*]

dub[2] (dub) *v.t. & v.i.* **dubbed, dub·bing** **1.** To push or thrust. **2.** To beat (a drum). — *n.* The act of dubbing. [Prob. imit.]

dub[3] (dub) *U.S. Informal n.* A clumsy, blundering person. — *v.t.* **dubbed, dub·bing** To bungle. [? < DUB[1]]

dub[4] (dub) *v.t.* **dubbed, dub·bing** **1.** To rerecord (a record, tape, etc.) in order to edit or add portions or to change volume, frequency, or tonal quality. **2.** To insert a new sound track into a film. — **to dub in 1.** In motion pictures, to insert (a new sound track) into a film. **2.** To blend (new sounds, music, etc.) into a record, the sound track of a film, or into a radio or television broadcast. — *n.* New dialogue, music, etc., added to a sound track. [Short for DOUBLE]

dub[5] (dub) *n. Scot.* A pool or puddle. [Origin uncertain]

Du Bar·ry (dōō bar′ē, dyōō; *Fr.* dü bȧ·rē′), **Comtesse**, 1746?–1793, Marie Jeanne Bécu, mistress of Louis XV; guillotined.

dub·bing[1] (dub′ing) *n.* **1.** Material for softening leather and making it waterproof. Also **dub·bin** (dub′in). **2.** The material of the body of a fishing fly. [< DUB[1]]

dub·bing[2] (dub′ing) *n.* The rerecording of a record, tape, etc., in whole or in part; especially, the synchronized conversion of a motion-picture sound track from the language of the original into some other language. [< DUB[4]]

Dub·he (dōōb′he) *n.* A star, Alpha in the constellation Ursa Major. [< Arabic *dubb* bear]

du·bi·e·ty (dōō·bī′ə·tē, dyōō-) *n. pl.* **·ties 1.** The state of being dubious. **2.** Something doubtful. Also **du·bi·os·i·ty** (dōō′bē·os′ə·tē, dyōō′-). [< LL *dubietas, -tatis* < L *dubius* doubtful]

du·bi·ous (dōō′bē·əs, dyōō′-) *adj.* **1.** Unsettled in judgment or opinion; doubtful. **2.** Causing doubt; equivocal: a *dubious* compliment. **3.** Not predictable in outcome or result; uncertain. **4.** Open to criticism, objection, or suspicion; questionable: a *dubious* reputation. [< L *dubiosus* < *dubium* doubt] — **du′bi·ous·ly** *adv.* — **du′bi·ous·ness** *n.*

du·bi·ta·ble (dōō′bi·tə·bəl, dyōō′-) *adj.* Open to doubt or debate; questionable; uncertain. — **du′bi·ta·bly** *adv.*

du·bi·ta·tion (dōō′bə·tā′shən, dyōō′-) *n.* Doubt. [< F L *dubitatio*]

du·bi·ta·tive (dōō′bə·tā′tiv, dyōō′-) *adj.* **1.** Feeling doubt; hesitant. **2.** Expressing doubt or hesitation. — **du′bi·ta′tive·ly** *adv.*

Dub·lin (dub′lin) **1.** The capital of Ireland, in the eastern part, a port on **Dublin Bay**, an inlet of the Irish Sea; pop. 567,866 (1971). **2.** A county of Leinster Province, eastern Ireland; 356 sq. mi.; pop. 718,332 (1966); county seat, Dublin. Irish *Baile Átha Cliath*.

Du Bois (dōō bois′), **W(illiam) E(dward) B(urghardt)**, 1868–1963, U.S. educator and scholar.

Du·bon·net (dōō′bə·nā′, *Fr.* dü·bô·ne′) *n.* **1.** A fortified French wine used as an apéritif: a trade name. **2.** A reddish purple, the color of red Dubonnet. Also **du′bon·net′**.

Du·brov·nik (dōō′brôv·nik) A port city in southern Yugoslavia, on the Adriatic; pop. 19,400 (est. 1959): Italian *Ragusa*.

Du·buque (də·byōōk′) A city in eastern Iowa, on the Mississippi; pop. 56,606.

duc (dük) *n. French* Duke.

du·cal (dōō′kəl, dyōō′-) *adj.* Pertaining to a duke or a duchy. [< MF < LL *ducalis* < L *dux* leader] — **du′cal·ly** *adv.*

Du Cange (dü känzh′), **Sieur**, 1610–88, Charles du Fresne, French historian and philologist.

duc·at (duk′ət) *n.* **1.** Any of several gold or silver coins, ranging in value from about $2.34 to 83 cents, formerly current in Europe; especially, the Dutch or Venetian gold coin. **2.** *Slang* A piece of money. **3.** *Slang* A ticket, as to a show. [< MF < Ital. *ducato* a coin with a picture of a duke (doge) < LL *ducatus* < L *dux* leader]

Duc·cio (dōōt′chō), 1260?–1319?, Sienese painter; called **Duccio di Buo·nin·se·gna** (dē bwô·nēn·sā′nyä).

du·ce (dōō′chā) *n. Ital.* Leader; commander. — **il Duce** The title assumed by Benito Mussolini as leader of the Fascist Italian state.

Du Chail·lu (dü shȧ·yü′) **Paul Belloni**, 1835–1903, U.S. explorer born in France.

Du·champ (dü·shän′), **Marcel**, 1887–1968, French painter.

duch·ess (duch′is) *n.* **1.** The wife or widow of a duke. **2.** The female sovereign of a duchy. Abbr. *D.* [< OF *duchesse* < L *ducissa* < L *dux* leader]

duch·y (duch′ē) *n. pl.* **duch·ies** The territory of a duke or duchess; dukedom. [< OF *duché* < L *dux* leader]

duck[1] (duk) *n.* **1.** Any of various aquatic birds (family *Anatidae*), both wild and domesticated, with short legs, webbed feet, and broad bills. **2.** The female of this bird. The male is called a **drake. 3.** The flesh of the duck used as food. **4.** *Chiefly Brit. Informal* A dear; darling. **5.** *U.S. Slang* A person; fellow. [OE *dūce* diver]

duck[2] (duk) *v.t.* **1.** To thrust suddenly under water. **2.** To

lower quickly; bob, as the head. **3.** *Informal* To dodge; evade (a blow or punishment). **4.** To avoid (a duty, person, etc.). — *v.i.* **5.** To submerge suddenly under water. **6.** *Informal* To move quickly and abruptly, as in dodging. — *n.* The act of ducking; especially, a quick plunge under water. [ME *douken, duken* to dive, ult. < Gmc.]

duck[3] (duk) *n.* **1.** A strong, tightly woven linen or cotton fabric similar to canvas. **2.** *pl.* Trousers made of this fabric. [< Du. *doek* cloth]

duck[4] (duk) *n. Mil.* An amphibious truck of World War II, equipped with a propeller and rudder for traveling on water. [< DUKW, code word for this type of vehicle]

duck·bill (duk′bil′) *n.* A platypus. Also **duck·billed** (-bild′) platypus.

duck·board (duk′bôrd′, -bōrd′) *n.* A board or section of boarding laid on supports, as over a wet floor or muddy ground, to form a surface for walking.

duck·er[1] (duk′ər) *n.* **1.** One who or that which ducks. **2.** A grebe, loon, or other bird that dives.

duck·er[2] (duk′ər) *n.* **1.** A duck hunter. **2.** One who rears ducks.

duck·foot·ed (duk′fŏŏt′id) *adj.* Having the back toe pointing nearly forward: said of poultry.

duck hawk The peregrine falcon (def. 2).

duck·ing stool (duk′ing) A chair or stool on which a culprit was tied and plunged into water, formerly used as a punishment, especially for quarrelsome women.

duck·ling (duk′ling) *n.* A young duck.

duck·pin (duk′pin′) *n.* **1.** A pin 9 inches high and 3½ inches in diameter at the body, used in a variation of the game of tenpins. **2.** *pl.* (construed as sing.) The game played with such pins.

ducks and drakes A game in which one skims or skips flat stones, shells, etc., along the surface of water. — **to make ducks and drakes of or play (at) ducks and drakes with** To throw away or squander; also, to deal recklessly with.

duck soup *U.S. Slang* Something that is very simple to do.

duck·weed (duk′wēd′) *n.* Any of several small, stemless aquatic plants (genus *Lemna*) that float free on ponds and streams. Also **duck′s-meat** (duks′mēt′).

duck·y (duk′ē) *adj.* **duck·i·er, duck·i·est** *Slang* Delightful; excellent.

duct (dukt) *n.* **1.** Any tube, canal, or passage by which a fluid, gas, etc., is conveyed. **2.** *Anat.* A tubular passage for fluid, especially one by which a secretion is carried away from a gland: the nasal *duct.* **3.** *Electr.* A tubular channel for carrying electric power, telegraph cables, or telephone cables. [< L *ductus* a leading < *ducere* to lead]

duc·tile (duk′təl, -til) *adj.* **1.** Capable of being hammered into thin layers, drawn out into wire or otherwise subjected to stress without breaking, as certain metals. **2.** Easily molded or shaped; plastic. **3.** Ready to obey; easily led; tractable. — **Syn.** See PLASTIC. [< F < L *ductilis* < *ducere* to lead] — **duc·til·i·ty** (duk·til′ə·tē) *n.*

duct·less gland (dukt′lis) *Physiol.* A gland that has no excretory duct but releases its secretions directly into the blood or lymph, as the thyroid gland, etc. See ENDOCRINE GLAND.

dud (dud) *n.* **1.** *Mil.* A bomb or shell that fails to explode. **2.** *Informal* A failure. [< Du. *dood* dead]

dud·die (dud′ē) *adj. Scot.* Tattered. Also **dud′dy.** [ME *dudde*]

dude (dōōd, dyōōd) *n. U.S.* **1.** A man who dresses in a flashy or extremely fastidious manner; dandy; fop. **2.** *Informal* A city person, especially one who is vacationing on a ranch. [Origin unknown] — **dud′ish** *adj.*

du·deen (dōō·dēn′) *n. Irish* A short-stemmed tobacco pipe. [< Irish *dúidín*]

dude ranch *U.S.* A ranch operated as a resort for tourists.

Du·de·vant (dü·də·vän′), **Baroness** See SAND.

dudg·eon[1] (duj′ən) *n.* Sullen displeasure; resentment: to leave in high *dudgeon.* [Origin unknown]

dudg·eon[2] (duj′ən) *n.* **1.** *Obs.* A kind of wood much used for the handles of daggers, knives, etc.; also, a hilt made of this wood. **2.** *Archaic* A dagger with a hilt of this wood: also **dudgeon dagger.** [< AF *digeon*; ult. origin unknown]

Dud·ley (dud′lē) A borough in West Midlands, England; pop. 298,700 (1976).

Dud·ley (dud′lē), **Robert** See (Earl of) LEICESTER. — **Thomas**, 1576–1653, English administrator; governor of Massachusetts Bay colony.

duds (dudz) *n.pl. Informal* **1.** Clothing. **2.** Belongings in general. [ME *dudde* cloak; origin uncertain]

due (dōō, dyōō) *adj.* **1.** Subject to demand for payment; especially, payable because of the arrival of a stipulated date. **2.** That should be rendered or given; proper; appropriate: the honor *due.* **3.** Adequate; sufficient: *due* cause for alarm. **4.** Appointed or expected to arrive, be present, or be ready: The bus is *due.* **5.** That may be charged or attributed; ascribable: with *to:* The mistake was *due* to carelessness. ◆ **Due to** as a locution introducing an adverbial phrase, though widely used, is still questioned by some, who prefer *because of* or *on account of,* as We were delayed *because of* (not *due to*) flooded roads. This is to be distinguished from the accepted use of *due* as an adjective, as in The delay was *due to* rain. — *n.* **1.** That which is owed or rightfully required; a debt or obligation. **2.** *pl.* Charge or fee: club *dues.* — *adv.* **1.** Directly; exactly: *due east.* **2.** *Archaic* Duly. [< OF *deü,* pp. of *devoir* to owe < L *debere*]

due bill A mere written acknowledgment of indebtedness, not payable to the order of the person named and not transferable by endorsement.

du·el (dōō′əl, dyōō′-) *n.* **1.** A prearranged combat between two persons, usually fought with deadly weapons in the presence of witnesses or seconds. **2.** A struggle between two contending parties. — *v.t. & v.i.* **du·eled** or **·elled, du·el·ing** or **·el·ling** To fight, or fight with, in a duel. [< F < Ital. *duello* < L *duellum,* earliest form of *bellum* war; by folk etymology explained as a fight between two (L *duo*)] — **du′el·er** or **du′el·ler, du′el·ist** or **du′el·list** *n.*

du·el·lo (dōō·el′ō, dyōō-) *n.* *pl.* **·los 1.** The art, practice, or code of dueling. **2.** *Obs.* A duel. [< Ital.]

du·en·na (dōō·en′ə, dyōō-) *n.* **1.** In Spain and Portugal, an elderly woman who serves as a companion and protector to a young girl. **2.** A chaperon. [< Sp. < L *domina* lady. Doublet of DAME.]

due process of law The legally prescribed method for determining whether a person is guilty of a civil or criminal offense, incorporating rules and forms that protect his private rights. Also **due process.**

Due·ro (dwā′rō) The Spanish name for DOURO.

du·et (dōō·et′, dyōō-) *n.* A musical composition for two performers. [< Ital. *duetto,* dim. of *duo,* duet < L *duo* two]

duff[1] (duf) *n.* A thick flour pudding boiled in a cloth bag. [Var. of DOUGH]

duff[2] (duf) *n.* **1.** *Scot. & U S.* Fallen leaves, branches, etc., in a forest. **2.** Small or fine coal. [Origin uncertain]

duf·fel (duf′əl) *n.* **1.** A coarse woolen fabric napped on both sides. **2.** Equipment or supplies, especially for camping. Also **duf′fle.** [after *Duffel,* a town near Antwerp]

duffel bag A sack, usually of canvas or duck, used to carry clothing and personal possessions. Also **duffle bag.**

duf·fer (duf′ər) *n.* **1.** *Brit. Informal* A dull-witted or clumsy person. **2.** *Brit. Dial.* A peddler or hawker. **3.** *Slang* Any counterfeit or sham. [Origin uncertain]

Du·fy (dü·fē′), Raoul, 1878–1953, French painter.

dug[1] (dug) Past tense and past participle of DIG.

dug[2] (dug) *n.* A teat or udder. [Cf. Dan. *dægge* to suckle]

Du Gard (dü gàr′), Roger Martin See MARTIN DU GARD.

Dug·dale (dug′dāl), Richard Louis, 1841–83, U.S. sociologist.

du·gong (dōō′gong) *n.* A herbivorous marine mammal (genus *Dugong*) of the Indian Ocean and Western Pacific, having flippers and a paddlelike tail: also called *sea cow.* [< Malay *duyong*]

DUGONG
(To 8 feet long)

dug·out (dug′out′) *n.* **1.** A canoe made by hollowing out a log. For illustration see CANOE. **2.** An excavated shelter or dwelling for protection against storms, bombs, etc. **3.** In baseball, a low structure, usually with a floor below ground level and set back from the diamond, in which team members sit when not at bat or in the field.

Du Gues·clin (dü ge·klan′), Bertrand, 1320?–80, French military commander; constable of France.

Du·ha·mel (dü·a·mel′), Georges, 1884–1966, French poet, dramatist, and novelist.

dui·ker (dī′kər) *n.* A small antelope (genus *Cephalophus*) of southern Africa. Also **dui·ker·bok** (dī′kər·bok′). [< Du. < *duiker* ducker, diver; from its habit of plunging through thickets]

Duis·burg (düs′bŏŏrkh) A port city in North Rhine–Westphalia, West Germany, on the Rhine; pop. 457,900 (est. 1970): from 1929–35 **Duis·burg-Ham·born** (-häm′bôrn).

Du·kas (dü·kà′), Paul, 1865–1935, French composer.

duke (dōōk, dyōōk) *n.* **1.** In Great Britain and certain other European countries, a nobleman having hereditary rank immediately below that of a prince and above that of a marquis. **2.** A European prince ruling over a duchy. Abbr. *D., Du.* [< F *duc* < L *dux* leader]

Duke (dōōk, dyōōk), Benjamin Newton, 1855–1929, and his brother, James Buchanan, 1856–1925, U.S. tobacco magnates and philanthropists.

duke·dom (dōōk′dəm, dyōōk′-) *n.* **1.** A duchy. **2.** The office or title of a duke.

dukes (dōōks, dyōōks) *n.pl. Slang* The fists. [Short for *Duke of Yorks,* orig. rhyming slang for *forks;* later, fingers, hands, fists]

Du·kho·bors (dōō′kə·bôrz) *n.pl.* A religious sect of Russian peasants who emigrated in 1898 to escape persecution, and settled in Canada: also spelled *Doukhobors.* [< Russ. *dukhobortsy < dukh* spirit + *bortsy* wrestlers]

dul·cet (dul′sit) *adj.* **1.** Pleasing to the ear; melodious; also, soothing; pleasant. **2.** *Obs.* Sweet-tasting. — *n.* An organ stop resembling the dulciana, but an octave higher. [< OF dim. of *douz,* sweet, refashioned after L *dulcis* sweet]

dul·ci·an·a (dul′sē·an′ə) *n.* An organ stop of soft and delicate tone. [< Med.L *dulciana* < L *dulcis* sweet]

dul·ci·fy (dul′sə·fī) *v.t.* **·fied, ·fy·ing 1.** To please; mollify. **2.** *Obs.* To sweeten. — **dul′ci·fi·ca′tion** *n.*

dul·ci·mer (dul′sə·mər) *n.* **1.** A stringed instrument played with two padded hammers or plucked with the fingers. **2.** In Biblical times, a form of harp. *Dan.* iii 10. [< OF *doulcemer, doulce-mele,* ? < LL *dulcemelos < dulcis* sweet + *melos* a song < Gk.]

Dul·cin·e·a (dul·sin′ē·ə, dul′sə·nē′ə) A peasant girl whom Don Quixote imagines to be a beautiful noblewoman. — *n.* A sweetheart.

DULCIMER
(def. 1)

Dul·heg·gia (dul·hej′ə) *n.* The twelfth month of the Moslem year. See (Moslem) CALENDAR.

du·li·a (dōō·lī′ə, dyōō-) *n.* In the Roman Catholic Church, a secondary kind of worship, used in the sense of veneration of the saints and angels: distinguished from *latria, hyperdulia.* [< Gk. *douleia* service < *doulos* slave]

Dul·kaa·da (dul·kä′də) *n.* The eleventh month of the Moslem year. See (Moslem) CALENDAR.

dull (dul) *adj.* **1.** Lacking in intelligence or understanding; stupid. **2.** Wanting in perception, sensibility, or responsiveness: a *dull* audience. **3.** Not brisk or active: Trade is *dull.* **4.** Without spirit; listless; depressed. **5.** Having a blunt edge or point; not sharp. **6.** Exciting little or no interest; tedious: a *dull* book. **7.** Not acute or intense: a *dull* pain. **8.** Cloudy; gloomy. **9.** Not bright, clear, or vivid: a *dull* color. **10.** Unclear in sound; muffled. — *v.t. & v.i.* To make or become dull. [ME *dul.* Akin to OE *dol* foolish.] — **dull′ish** *adj.* — **dull′ness** or **dul′ness** *n.* — **dul′ly** *adv.* — **Syn. 1.** dense, doltish. **2.** apathetic. **3.** sluggish, slow **4.** lifeless. **6.** uninteresting. **8.** overcast, leaden. **10.** deadened.

dull·ard (dul′ərd) *n.* A stupid person; dolt.

Dul·les (dul′əs), John Foster, 1888–1959, U.S. lawyer and diplomat; secretary of state 1953–59.

dulse (duls) *n.* A reddish brown seaweed (*Rhodymenia palmata*) sometimes eaten as a vegetable. [< Irish *duileasg*]

Du·luth (də·lōōth′, dōō-) A port city in NE Minnesota, on Lake Superior; pop. 100,578.

du·ly (dōō′lē, dyōō′-) *adv.* **1.** In due or proper manner; fitly. **2.** At the proper time. **3.** To an adequate degree.

Du·ma (dōō′mä) *n.* The former Russian national assembly elected indirectly by the people, created by an imperial decree in 1905, and dissolved during the revolution of 1917. Also spelled *Douma.* [< Russian]

Du·mas (dōō·mä′, dōō′mä; *Fr.* dü·mà′), Alexandre, 1802–1870, **Dumas père,** and his son Alexandre, 1824–95, **Dumas fils,** French novelists and dramatists.

Du Mau·ri·er (dōō′môr′ē·ā, dyōō′-) Daphne, born 1907, English novelist. — George (Louis Palmella Busson), 1834–96, English illustrator and novelist born in France; grandfather of the preceding.

dumb (dum) *adj.* **1.** Having no power of speech; mute. **2.** Temporarily speechless: *dumb* with grief. **3.** Not inclined to speak; silent; uncommunicative. **4.** *U.S. Informal* Stupid; dull-witted. **5.** Made or done without speech, as a pantomime. **6.** Not having the usual characteristics, symptoms, properties, etc.: *dumb* piano keys. [OE; cf. G *dumm* stupid] — **dumb′ly** *adv.* — **dumb′ness** *n.*

Dumb. Dumbarton.

dumb ague *Pathol.* A form of malarial fever characterized by slight periodicity and the absence of well-marked chills.

Dum·bar·ton (dum·bär′tən) **1.** The county seat of Dunbarton, in the southern part; pop. 25,900 (est. 1956). **2.** See DUNBARTON: also **Dum·bar·ton·shire** (-shir).

Dum·bar·ton Oaks (dum′bär·tən, dum·bär′tən) An estate in Washington, D.C., at which conferences were held, August-October 1944, leading to proposals for the organization of the United Nations.

dumb·bell (dum′bel′) *n.* **1.** A gymnastic hand instrument used for exercising, consisting of a wood or metal handle with a weighted ball at each end. **2.** *U.S. Slang* A stupid person.

dumb show 1. Gestures without words; pantomime. **2.** In early English drama, part of a play acted in pantomime.

dumb·wait·er (dum′wāt′ər) *n.* **1.** *U.S.* A small elevator for conveying food, dishes, garbage, etc., from one floor to another. **2.** *Brit.* A movable serving stand, sometimes with revolving shelves, placed near a dining table.

dum·dum bullet (dum′dum′) A small-arms bullet having a soft point or a jacket cut across at the point so that it will expand on impact and tear a gaping wound. [from *Dumdum,* a town near Calcutta, India, where first made]

Dumf. Dumfries.

dum·found (dum′found′) *v.t.* To strike dumb; confuse; amaze. Also **dumb′found′.** [Blend of DUMB and CONFOUND]

Dum·fries (dum·frēs´) A county in southern Scotland; 1,072 sq. mi.; pop. 87,276 (1969); county seat, **Dumfries**; pop. 28,149 (1969). Also **Dum·fries´shire** (-shir).

dum·my (dum´ē) *n.* *pl.* **·mies** **1.** A figure representing the human form, used for displaying clothing, for tackling in football practice, etc. **2.** An imitation object made to resemble the real thing, as a false drawer. **3.** One who is dumb; a mute. **4.** *Slang* A stupid person; a dolt. **5.** One who seems to be acting for his own interests while secretly representing another. **6.** *Printing* **a** A sample book or magazine, usually blank, made up to specification as a model of the final product. **b** A model page form for the printer, made up of proofs pasted into position. **7.** In certain card games, especially bridge: **a** An exposed hand played in addition to his own by the person sitting opposite it. **b** The inactive player who has exposed such a hand. — **double dummy** Whist or bridge as played by two persons, each playing two hands, one of which is exposed. — *adj.* **1.** Sham; counterfeit; imitation: a *dummy* door. **2.** Silent; mute. **3.** Ostensibly acting for oneself, but actually acting for another. **4.** Played with a dummy, as certain card games. [< DUMB]

du·mor·ti·er·ite (dōo·môr´tē·ə·rīt´, dyōo-) *n.* An aluminum borosilicate mineral used in making refractories. [after E. *Dumortier*, French paleontologist]

dump¹ (dump) *v.t.* **1.** To drop or throw down heavily or abruptly. **2.** To empty out, as from a container. **3.** To empty (a container), as by overturning. **4.** To get rid of; throw away, as rubbish. **5.** To put up (goods) for sale cheaply and in large quantities, especially in a foreign market. — *v.i.* **6.** To fall or drop suddenly. **7.** To unload. **8.** To offer large quantities of goods for sale at low prices. — *n.* **1.** A dumping area, as for rubbish. **2.** That which is dumped. **3.** *Mil.* A temporary storage place, in or near the field, for ammunition and supplies. **4.** *U.S. Slang* A shabby, poorly kept place. [ME < Scand.; prob. imit. Cf. Norw. *dumpa* to fall suddenly and ON *dumpa* to thump]

dump² (dump) *n.* **1.** *pl.* A gloomy state of mind: now only in the phrase **in the dumps.** **2.** *Obs.* A slow, melancholy dance, or the music for it. [Cf. MDu. *domp* haze]

dump³ (dump) *n. Brit.* A shapeless leaden counter used by boys in certain games. [Origin uncertain]

dump·cart (dump´kärt) *n.* A cart so built that its body can be tilted or the bottom opened to discharge its load.

dump·ish (dump´ish) *adj.* Depressed in spirits; sad; morose. — **dump´ish·ly** *adv.* — **dump´ish·ness** *n.*

dump·ling (dump´ling) *n.* **1.** A ball of biscuit dough filled with fruit and baked or steamed. **2.** A small mass of dough dropped into boiling soup or stew. **3.** *Informal* A short, plump person or animal.

dump truck A truck for hauling gravel, coal, etc., that unloads by tilting back the cargo bin and opening the tailboard.

dump·y¹ (dump´ē) *adj.* **dump·i·er, dump·i·est** Sullen or discontented; sulky. [See DUMP².]

dump·y² (dump´ē) *adj.* **dump·i·er, dump·i·est** Short and thick; squat. — **dump´i·ly** *adv.* — **dump´i·ness** *n.* [See DUMP³.]

dumpy level A surveyor's level consisting of a short telescope rigidly attached to a horizontally rotating table.

Dum·yat (dōom·yät´) The Arabic name for DAMIETTA.

dun¹ (dun) *v.t. & v.i.* **dunned, dun·ning** To press (a debtor) for payment; importune; pester. — *n.* **1.** One who duns. **2.** A repeated demand for payment. [Prob. var. of DIN.]

dun² (dun) *adj.* Of a grayish brown or reddish brown color. — *n.* **1.** Dun color. **2.** A dun-colored horse. **3.** A dun fly (which see). — *v.t.* **dunned, dun·ning** **1.** To make duncolored. **2.** *U.S.* To cure (fish) by salting and packing in a dark place. [OE *dunn*]

Du·na (dōo´no) The Hungarian name for the DANUBE.

Dü·na (dü´nä) The German name for the DVINA (def. 2).

Dü·na·burg (dü´nä·bŏŏrkh) The German name for DAUGAVPILS.

Du·nant (dü·näṅ´), **Jean Henri,** 1828–1910, Swiss philanthropist; founded the Red Cross Society, 1864.

Du·nă·rea (dōo´no·ryä) The Rumanian name for the Danube.

Du·nav (dōo´näv) The Serbo-Croatian and Bulgarian name for the DANUBE.

Dun·bar (dun·bär´) A burgh in eastern Scotland, on the North Sea; scene of Cromwell's victory over the Scots, 1650; pop. about 4,000.

Dun·bar (dun´bar), **Paul Laurence,** 1872–1906, U.S. poet. **William,** 1460?–1525?, Scottish friar and poet.

Dun·bar·ton (dun·bär´tən) A county in west central Scotland; 246 sq. mi.; pop. 277,635 (est. 1969); county seat, Dumbarton: also *Dumbarton, Dumbartonshire.* Also **Dun·bar´ton·shire** (-shir).

Dun·can (dung´kən), **Isadora,** 1878–1927, U.S. dancer.

Dun·can I (dung´kən), died 1040?, king of Scotland 1034?–1040?; murdered by Macbeth.

Dun·can Phyfe (dung´kən fīf´) Of or like the furniture designed by Duncan Phyfe. See PHYFE.

dunce (duns) *n.* A stupid or ignorant person. [Earlier *Dunsman,* a follower of John *Duns* Scotus, a pedantic opponent of Humanism; later, any opponent of learning]

dunce cap A conical cap, formerly placed on the head of a dull student. Also **dunce's cap.**

dunch (dunsh, dōonsh) *n. Scot. & Brit. Dial.* A push or jog. [ME; origin uncertain]

Dun·ci·ad (dun´sē·ad) A satirical poem (1728–42) by Alexander Pope.

Dun·dalk (dun·dôk´, -dôlk´) An unincorporated place in central Maryland, a suburb of Baltimore; pop. 85,377.

Dun·dee (dun·dē´) A burgh in eastern Scotland, a port on the Firth of Tay; pop. 182,959 (1961).

dun·der·head (dun´dər·hed´) *n.* A blockhead; dunce. Also **dun´der·pate´** (-pāt´). [? < dial. E (Scottish) *dunder* thunder, noise + HEAD] — **dun´der·head´ed** *adj.*

dune (dōon, dyōon) *n.* A hill of loose sand heaped up by the wind. [< F < MDu. *dūne*. Akin to DOWN³.]

Dun·e·din (dun·ē´din) **1.** A port city in SE South Island, New Zealand; pop. 103,300 (est. 1960). **2.** The Scottish Gaelic name for EDINBURGH.

Dun·ferm·line (dun·fûrm´lin) A burgh in SW Fife, Scotland; pop. 47,159 (1961).

dun fly An artificial fly resembling the May fly, used in angling.

dung¹ (dung) *n.* **1.** Animal excrement; manure. **2.** Anything foul. — *v.t.* To cover or enrich with or as with dung. [OE] — **dung´y** *adj.*

dung² (dung, dōong) *adj. Scot.* Exhausted; finished. [Pp. of dial. E *ding* to bang, smash]

dun·ga·ree (dung´gə·rē´) *n.* **1.** A coarse cotton cloth, originally from the East Indies, used for work clothes, tents, sails, etc. **2.** *pl.* Trousers or overalls made of this fabric. [< Hind. *dungrī*]

dung beetle Any of various scarabaeid beetles that breed in dung, as the tumblebug and the scarab of Egypt. Also **dung chafer.**

dun·geon (dun´jən) *n.* **1.** A dark confining prison or cell, especially one underground. **2.** A donjon. For illustration see DONJON. [< DONJON]

dung·hill (dung´hil´) *n.* **1.** A heap of manure. **2.** A vile thing, abode, or condition.

dun·ie·was·sal (dōo´nē·wos´əl) *n. Scot.* **1.** A yeoman. **2.** A gentleman; especially, a younger son of a family of rank. [< Gaelic *duine uasal* gentleman < *duine* man + *uasal* noble]

dunk (dungk) *v.t. & v.i.* To dip or sop (bread, doughnuts, etc.) into tea, coffee, soup, etc. [< G *tunken* to dip. ? Akin to L *tingere* to moisten] — **dunk´er** *n.*

Dun·ker (dung´kər) *n.* One of a body of German-American Baptists opposing military service and the taking of legal oaths: officially called *German Baptist Brethren.* Also **Dun´kard.** [< G *tunker* < *tunken* to dip]

Dun·kirk (dun´kûrk) A port town in northern France, on the North Sea; scene of the evacuation of British forces in World War II, May 26–June 4, 1940; pop. 26,038 (1968). French **Dun·kerque** (dœṅ·kerk´).

Dun Laoghai·re (dun lär´ē) A city borough and port in SE County Dublin, Ireland, on the Irish Sea; pop. 47,792 (1966). Formerly **Dun·lea·ry** (dun·lir´ē).

dun·lin (dun´lin) *n.* A sandpiper (*Erolia alpina*) of wide distribution, having in summer plumage a black belly and a reddish back. [Var. of *dunling* < DUN² + -LING¹]

Dun·lop (dun´lop, dun·lop´), **John Boyd,** 1840–1921, Scottish inventor.

dun·nage (dun´ij) *n.* **1.** *Naut.* Mats and battens used to protect cargo. **2.** Baggage. [? < DUN² + -AGE]

Dunne (dun), **Finley Peter,** 1867–1936, U.S. journalist and humorist.

dun·nite (dun´īt) *n.* An explosive made of ammonium picrate. [after Major B. W. *Dunn,* 1860–1936, U.S. inventor]

Du·nois (dü·nwä´), **Jean,** 1403?–68, French commander under Joan of Arc; natural son of the Duke of Orléans: called **the Bastard of Orléans.**

Dun·sa·ny (dun·sā´nē), **Lord,** 1878–1957, Edward John Moreton Drax Plunkett, eighteenth Baron Dunsany, Irish poet and dramatist.

Dun·si·nane (dun´sə·nän´, dun´sə·nān) A hill in SE Perth, Scotland; reputed scene of Macbeth's defeat, 1054; height, 1,012 ft.

Duns Sco·tus (dunz skō´təs), **John,** 1265?–1308, Scottish scholastic theologian: called the Subtle Doctor.

Dun·stan (dun´stən), **Saint,** 910?–988, English monk and statesman; archbishop of Canterbury 961–988.

dunt (dunt, dōont) *Scot. & Dial. n.* **1.** A blow. **2.** An injury from a blow. — *v.t. & v.i.* To smite. [Var. of DINT]

du·o (dōo´ō, dyōo´ō) *n. pl.* **du·os** or **du·i** (-ē) *Music* An instrumental duet. [< Ital. < L *duo* two]

duo- *combining form* Two: *duologue.* [< L *duo* two]

du·o·dec·i·mal (dōo´ō·des´ə·məl, dyōo´-) *adj.* **1.** Pertaining to twelve or twelfths. **2.** Reckoning by twelves. — *n.* **1.** One of the numbers used in duodecimal arithmetic; a twelfth. **2.** *pl.* A method of computing by twelves instead of by tens. [< L *duodecimus* twelfth < *duodecim* twelve]

du·o·dec·i·mo (dōo´ō·des´ə·mō, dyōo´-) *adj.* **1.** Having twelve pages or leaves to one sheet of printing paper. **2.** Measuring about 5 x 7¾ inches in size: said of a page or book. — *n. pl.* **·mos** The size of a page folded twelve to a sheet;

also, a page or a book of this size. Also *twelvemo*. Also written **12 mo., 12°**. [< L (*in*) *duodecimo* (in) twelfth]

du·o·dec·u·ple (dōō′ō-dek′yŏŏ-pəl, dyōō′-) *adj.* Consisting of twelve; having twelve parts; twelvefold; also, taken by twelves. — *n.* A number or sum twelve times as great as another. [< L *duodecim* twelve; infl. in form by *decuple*]

du·o·de·cu·pli·cate (*adj., n.* dōō′ō-de-kyōō′plə-kit, dyōō′-; *v.* dōō′ō-de-kyōō′plə-kāt, dyōō′-) *adj.* **1.** Twelvefold. **2.** Raised to the twelfth power. — *v.t.* **·cat·ed, ·cat·ing** To multiply by twelve. — *n.* One of twelve like things. — **du′o·de·cu′pli·cate·ly** *adv.*

du·o·de·nal (dōō′ə-dē′nəl, dyōō′-, dōō·od′ə-nəl) *adj.* Of or pertaining to the duodenum.

du·o·den·a·ry (dōō′ō-den′ər-ē, -dē′nər-ē, dyōō′-) *adj.* Pertaining to or determined by the number twelve; duodecimal. [< L *duodenarius* containing twelve]

du·o·de·ni·tis (dōō′ə-də-nī′tis, dyōō′-) *n. Pathol.* Inflammation of the duodenum.

duodeno- *combining form* Of or pertaining to the duodenum. Also, before vowels, **duoden-**. [< DUODENUM]

du·o·de·num (dōō′ə-dē′nəm, dyōō′-; dōō·od′ə-nəm) *n. pl.* **·na** (-nə) *Anat.* The part of the small intestine extending from the stomach to the jejunum. For illustration see INTESTINE. [< Med.L *duodenum* (*digitorum*) of twelve (fingers) < *duodecim* twelve; with ref. to its length]

du·o·logue (dōō′ə-lôg, -log, dyōō′-) *n.* **1.** A dramatic piece for two performers. **2.** A conversation involving two speakers; dialogue. Also **du′o·log.** [< DUO- + (MONO)LOGUE]

duo·mo (dwō′mō) *n. pl.* **·mi** (-mē) *Italian* A cathedral.

du·o·tone (dōō′ō-tōn′, dyōō′-) *n. Printing* **1.** An illustration in two tones of the same color. **2.** The process by which such prints are made.

dup (dup) *v.t. Obs.* To open. [Contraction of *do up*]

dup. or **dupl.** Duplicate.

dupe (dōōp, dyōōp) *n.* One who is easily deceived or misled. — *v.t.* **duped, dup·ing** To make a dupe of; deceive; trick. [< OF *duppe* < *d'uppe* of a hoopoe < *huppe* hoopoe (a bird thought to be stupid) < L *upupa*] — **dup′a·bil′i·ty** *n.* — **dup′a·ble** *adj.* — **dup′er** *n.*

dup·er·y (dōō′pər-ē, dyōō′-) *n. pl.* **·er·ies** **1.** The act or practice of duping. **2.** The state of one who is duped.

du·ple (dōō′pəl, dyōō′-) *adj.* Double; twofold. [< L *duplus.* See DOUBLE.]

Du·pleix (dü·pleks′), **Joseph François,** 1697–1763, Marquis Dupleix, French general; governor in India.

duple meter *Music* See under METER².

Du·ples·sis-Mor·nay (dü·ple·sē′môr·nā′) See MORNAY.

du·plex (dōō′pleks, dyōō′-) *adj.* **1.** Having two parts; double; twofold. **2.** *Mech.* Having two similar parts placed in one framework so that each part can operate independently or in conjunction with the other. **3.** *Telecom.* Pertaining to or allowing the transmission of two messages simultaneously over a single wire and in opposite directions: distinguished from *diplex*. — *n.* A duplex apartment or house. [< L < *duo* two + stem of *plicare* to fold] — **du·plex′i·ty** *n.*

duplex apartment **1.** *U.S.* An apartment having rooms on two floors. **2.** *Canadian* A two-story building having an apartment on each floor.

duplex house *U.S. & Canadian* A house having two one-family units.

du·pli·cate (*adj., n.* dōō′plə-kit, dyōō′-; *v.* dōō′plə-kāt, dyōō′-) *adj.* **1.** Made like or corresponding exactly to an original: a *duplicate* key. **2.** Growing or existing in pairs; double; twofold. **3.** In card-playing, replayed by other players with the same hands as originally dealt: *duplicate* bridge. — *n.* **1.** An exact copy. **2.** A double or counterpart. **3.** A duplicate game of cards. — *v.t.* **·cat·ed, ·cat·ing** **1.** To copy exactly; reproduce. **2.** To double; make twofold. **3.** To do a second time; repeat. [< L *duplicatus,* pp. of *duplicare* to double < *duplex* twofold] — **du′pli·cate·ly** *adv.*

— **Syn.** (noun) *Duplicate, copy, transcript, facsimile, replica,* and *imitation* denote an object that is closely like another. A *duplicate* is exactly like the original and can be used in its place; a *copy* is as nearly like the original as the copyist can make it, but it may be somewhat inaccurate: a *duplicate* of a key, a *copy* of the Mona Lisa. In law, a *transcript* is an official *copy* of a document, attested as accurate by the seal of a court. A *facsimile* is like the original in appearance, as a printed picture of the design on a coin. A *replica* is a *copy* of a work of art by the maker of the original; an *imitation* is a *copy* of a thing by someone else, and is regarded as inferior. — **Ant.** original, prototype, archetype, pattern, model.

du·pli·ca·tion (dōō′plə-kā′shən, dyōō′-) *n.* **1.** The act or process of duplicating, or the state of being duplicated. **2.** A duplicate. — **du′pli·ca′tive** *adj.*

du·pli·ca·tor (dōō′plə-kā′tər, dyōō′-) *n.* A mechanical device for making duplicates.

du·plic·i·ty (dōō·plis′ə-tē, dyōō′-) *n. pl.* **·ties** Tricky deceitfulness; double-dealing. [< OF *duplicite* < LL *duplicitas, -tatis* doubleness < L *duplex* twofold]

du Pont (dōō pont′, dyōō′; *Fr.* dü pôn′) A family of U.S. industrialists, especially **Eleuthère Irénée,** 1771–1834, founder of E. I. du Pont de Nemours Company.

du Pont de Ne·mours (dōō pont′ də nə·mōōr′, dyōō pont′; *Fr.* dü pôn′ də nə·mōōr′), **Pierre Samuel,** 1739–1817, French politician and economist.

Dur. Durham.

du·ra (dōōr′ə) See DURRA.

du·ra·bil·i·ty (dōōr′ə·bil′ə·tē, dyōōr′-) *n. pl.* **·ties** The quality of being durable; the power of long resistance to decay or change. Also **du′ra·ble·ness.**

du·ra·ble (dōōr′ə·bəl, dyōōr′-) *adj.* **1.** Able to withstand decay or wear; lasting. **2.** Not easily changed or upset; stable. — **Syn.** See PERMANENT. [< OF < L *durabilis* < *durare* to endure < *durus* hard] — **du′ra·bly** *adv.*

du·ral (dōōr′əl, dyōōr′-) *adj.* Of, pertaining to, or derived from the dura mater.

Du·ral·u·min (dōō·ral′yə·min, dyōō-) *n.* A light, strong alloy of aluminum and copper, with addition of magnesium and manganese: a trade name. Also **du·ral′u·min.**

du·ra ma·ter (dōōr′ə mā′tər, dyōōr′ə) *Anat.* The tough fibrous membrane forming the outermost of the three coverings of the brain and spinal cord. Also **du′ra.** [< Med.L < L *dura* hard + *mater* mother, trans. of Arabic term]

du·ra·men (dōō·rā′min, dyōō-) *n. Bot.* The heartwood, or darker central portion, of an exogenous stem or tree trunk. For illustration see EXOGEN. [< L, a ligneous vine branch]

dur·ance (dōōr′əns, dyōōr′-) *n.* **1.** Forced confinement or imprisonment. **2.** *Archaic* Duration; continuance. [< OF, duration < *durer* to last < L *durare*]

Du·ran·go (dōō·räng′gō) A State in northern Mexico; 47,691 sq. mi.; pop. 919,381 (1970); capital, **Durango;** pop. 192,934 (1970).

du·ran·te vi·ta (dyōō·rän′tē vī′tə) *Latin* During life.

du·ra·tion (dōō·rā′shən, dyōō-) *n.* **1.** The period of time during which anything lasts. **2.** Continuance in time. — **for the duration** Until the end of a trying time, especially of World War II. [< LL *duratio, -onis* < L *durare* to endure, last]

dur·a·tive (dōōr′ə·tiv, dyōōr′-) *Gram. adj.* Designating an aspect of a verb that expresses action as continuous; imperfective. — *n.* The durative aspect, or a verb in this aspect. Example: Oranges *grow* in Florida.

Du·raz·zo (dōō·rät′tsō) The Italian name for DURRËS.

Dur·ban (dûr′bən) A port city in eastern Natal, Republic of South Africa; pop. 655,370 (1960).

dur·bar (dûr′bär) *n. Anglo-Indian* **1.** Formerly, a reception given by a native ruler or by a high British official in India; a state levee. **2.** The place in which such a reception was held. **3.** The court of a native Indian ruler. [< Hind. < Persian *darbār* court < *dar* door + *bār* assembly]

dure (dōōr, dyōōr) *Archaic v.t. & v.i.* To endure. — *adj.* Severe; hard; rough. [< OF *durer* < L *durare* to endure < *durus* hard]

Dü·rer (dü′rər), **Albrecht,** 1471–1528, German painter and engraver.

du·ress (dōō·res′, dyōō-, dōōr′is, dyōōr′-) *n.* **1.** Constraint by force or fear; compulsion. **2.** *Law* **a** Coercion to do or say something against one's will or judgment. **b** Imprisonment without full legal sanction. [< OF *duresse* hardness, constraint < L *duritia* < *durus* hard]

D'Ur·fey (dûr′fē), **Thomas,** 1653–1723, English dramatist and songwriter.

Dur·ham (dûr′əm) *n.* One of a breed of short-horned beef cattle. [after *Durham,* England]

Dur·ham (dûr′əm) **1.** A county of NE England; 1,015 sq. mi.: pop. 610,900 (1976); county seat, **Durham;** pop. 88,200 (1976). **2.** A city in north central North Carolina; pop. 95,438.

du·ri·an (dōōr′ē·ən) *n.* **1.** A tall forest tree (*Durio zibethinus*) cultivated throughout the Malay Peninsula. **2.** Its edible fruit. Also **du′ri·on.** [< Malay < *duri* a thorn]

dur·ing (dōōr′ing, dyōōr′-) *prep.* **1.** Throughout the time, existence, or action of: The noise continued *during* the night. **2.** In the course of; at some period in. [Orig. ppr. of DURE]

Durk·heim (dûrk′hīm, *Fr.* dür·kem′), **Émile,** 1858–1917, French sociologist and philosopher.

dur·mast (dûr′mast, -mäst) *n.* A European oak (*Quercus petraea*), valuable for its tough, elastic wood. [< *dun mast* (*oak*) < DUN² + MAST²]

du·ro (dōō′rō) *n. pl.* **·ros** The Spanish and Spanish-American silver dollar. [< Sp. (*peso*) *duro* hard (peso) < L *durus* hard]

dur·ra (dōōr′ə) *n.* A variety of sorghum of southern Asia and northern Africa: also spelled *dhoora, dhourra, doura, dura*: also called *Guinea corn.* Also **durr** (dōōr). [< Arabic *dhura*]

Dur·rës (dōōr′rəs) A port city in western Albania, on the Adriatic; pop. 32,300 (est. 1958): ancient *Dyrrachium.* Italian *Durazzo.*

durst (dûrst) *Archaic* past tense of DARE.

du·rum (dōōr′əm, dyōōr′-) *n.* A species of wheat (*Triticum durum*) widely grown for macaroni and spaghetti products. [< L, neut. sing. of *durus* hard]

Du·ru·y (dü-rü-ē′), **Victor**, 1811–94, French historian.

Du·se (dōō′zā), **Eleonora**, 1859–1924, Italian actress.

dusk (dusk) *n.* 1. The partial darkness between day and night, usually considered darker than twilight. 2. Any degree of light or dark resembling this. — *adj.* Somewhat dark or dim; shadowy. — *v.t. & v.i.* To make, grow, or appear shadowy or dim; darken. [OE *dox*] — **dusk′ish** *adj.*

dusk·y (dus′kē) *adj.* **dusk·i·er, dusk·i·est** 1. Somewhat dark; dim; obscure. 2. Rather dark in shade or coloring; swarthy. 3. Gloomy. — **dusk′i·ly** *adv.* — **dusk′i·ness** *n.*

Düs·sel·dorf (düs′əl-dôrf) A port city in North Rhine–Westphalia, West Germany, on the Rhine; pop. 680,800 (est. 1970).

dust (dust) 1. Earthy matter reduced to particles so fine as to be easily borne in the air. 2. Any substance reduced to fine powder. 3. A cloud of powdered earth or other fine particles. 4. Confusion; turmoil; stir. 5. Earth, especially as the receptacle of the dead. 6. The disintegrated remains of a human body. 7. A low or despised condition. 8. Something worthless. 9. *Brit.* Sweepings, ashes, or other refuse. 10. Pollen. 11. Gold dust (which see). 12. *Slang* Money. — **to bite the dust** To be killed or injured. — **to lick the dust** 1. To be defeated; humble oneself; grovel. 2. To be killed or wounded. — **to throw dust in someone's eyes** To deceive; mislead. — *v.t.* 1. To wipe or brush dust from: to *dust* furniture. 2. To sprinkle with powder, insecticide, etc.: to *dust* plants. 3. To sprinkle (powder, etc.) over something. 4. To soil with dust. — *v.i.* 5. To wipe or brush dust from furniture, etc. 6. To cover oneself with dust, as a bird. 7. To become dusty. [OE *dūst*] — **dust′less** *adj.*

dust·bin (dust′bin′) *n. Brit.* A container for refuse.

dust bowl An area subject to dust storms and drought. — **the Dust Bowl** A region in the south central United States where the eroded topsoil was blown away by dust storms during the droughts of 1934–37.

dust·cloth (dust′klôth′, -kloth′) *n.* A cloth or rag used for dusting furniture, etc. Also **dust′rag′** (-rag′).

dust devil A small whirlwind that lifts dust, leaves, etc., to considerable heights.

dust·er (dus′tər) *n.* 1. One who or that which dusts. 2. A cloth or brush for removing dust. 3. A device for sprinkling a powder, insecticide, condiments, etc., over something. 4. An outer garment worn to protect clothing from dust. 5. A woman's loose-fitting housecoat of the same length as a dress. 6. *U.S. Informal* In baseball, a pitch purposely thrown close to a batter.

dust jacket A removable paper cover, usually printed and ornamented, that protects the binding of a book: also called *book jacket.* Also **dust cover.**

dust·man (dust′man, -mən) *n. pl.* **·men** (mən) 1. *Brit.* One whose business is the removal of ashes and refuse. 2. The sandman (which see).

dust·pan (dust′pan′) *n.* An implement resembling a short-handled shovel into which dust from a floor is swept.

dust·proof (dust′prōōf′) *adj.* Resistant to dust.

dust storm A windstorm of arid regions that carries clouds of dust with it.

dust·y (dus′tē) *adj.* **dust·i·er, dust·i·est** 1. Covered with or full of dust. 2. Like dust; powdery. 3. Of the color of dust. 4. Having a grayish or dull cast: *dusty* pink. — **dust′i·ly** *adv.* — **dust′i·ness** *n.*

Dutch (duch) *adj.* 1. Of or relating to the Netherlands, its people, culture, or language. 2. Loosely, German. — *n.* 1. The people of the Netherlands: preceded by *the.* 2. Loosely, the German people: preceded by *the.* 3. The language of the Netherlands, belonging to the West Germanic branch, closely related to Flemish with the usual regional variations in pronunciation and vocabulary. Abbr. *D., Du.* 2. Pennsylvania Dutch (which see). — **in Dutch** *U.S. Informal* In trouble or disgrace. — **to beat the Dutch** *U.S. Informal* To be most unusual or surprising. — **to go Dutch** *U.S. Informal* To have each participant in a meal or entertainment pay his own expenses. [< MDu. *dutsch* Germanic, Dutch]

Dutch Belted A breed of dairy cattle originating in the Netherlands and characterized by a wide white band around the middle of the body.

Dutch Borneo See under BORNEO.

Dutch cheese 1. A round, cured cheese, as Edam cheese. 2. Cottage cheese (which see).

Dutch courage Courage inspired by intoxicating drink.

Dutch door A door divided horizontally in the middle, allowing either half to open individually.

Dutch East Indies See NETHERLANDS EAST INDIES.

Dutch elm disease A fungus disease of elms attacking the leaves, causing defoliation, decay, and death.

Dutch Guiana See SURINAM.

Dutch Harbor A village and U.S. naval base on a small island off Unalaska Island, Aleutian Islands.

dutch·man (duch′mən) *n. pl.* **·men** (-mən) *U.S.* A piece inserted, as in a wooden joint, to hide a bad fitting or to replace another piece that has been broken off.

DUTCH DOOR

Dutch·man (duch′mən) *n. pl.* **·men** (-mən) 1. A native of the Netherlands. 2. Loosely, a German. 3. A Dutch ship.

dutch·man's-breech·es (duch′mənz-brich′iz) *n. sing. & pl.* A low herb (*Dicentra cucullaria*) with widely spreading spurs: also called *colicweed.* Also **dutch′mans·breech′es.**

dutch·man's-pipe (duch′mənz-pīp′) *n.* A North American climbing shrub (*Aristolochia durior*) having a calyx tube shaped like the bowl of a pipe.

Dutch metal A malleable alloy of copper, tin, and zinc, used in the form of thin leaves as a substitute for gold leaf; tombac: also called **Dutch foil, Dutch gold, Dutch leaf.**

Dutch New Guinea A former name for WEST NEW GUINEA.

Dutch oven 1. A cast-iron kettle with a tight-fitting cover, used for meats, stews, etc. 2. A metal box with an open side, set before a fire for cooking by reflected heat. 3. A brick oven preheated for baking.

Dutch treat *U.S. Informal* An entertainment or meal at which each person pays his own bill.

Dutch uncle A very frank and severe critic or adviser.

Dutch West Indies A former name for the NETHERLANDS ANTILLES.

du·te·ous (dōō′tē-əs, dyōō′-) *adj.* Obedient; dutiful. — **du′te·ous·ly** *adv.* — **du′te·ous·ness** *n.*

du·ti·a·ble (dōō′tē-ə-bəl, dyōō′-) *adj.* Subject to impost duty.

du·ti·ful (dōō′ti-fəl, dyōō′-) *adj.* 1. Performing one's duties; obedient. 2. Expressive of a sense of duty; respectful: *dutiful* attentions. — **du′ti·ful·ly** *adv.* — **du′ti·ful·ness** *n.*

Du·tra (dōō′trə), **Eurico Gaspar**, born 1885, Brazilian general; president 1946–51.

du·ty (dōō′tē, dyōō′-) *n. pl.* **·ties** 1. That which one is morally or legally bound to do; obligation. 2. The impelling or controlling force of such obligations or responsibilities: *Duty* calls. 3. Action or conduct required by one's profession or position: the *duty* of a doctor. 4. Specific obligatory service or function, especially of military personnel: overseas *duty.* 5. A tax on imported or exported goods; tariff. 6. *Agric.* The quantity of water necessary to irrigate a definite area: also **duty of water.** 7. *Mech.* **a** The efficiency of an engine or motor under stated conditions. **b** The efficiency of an engine expressed in terms of its fuel consumption. — **off duty** Temporarily not at work. — **on duty** At work or at one's post. [< AF *duete* < *dû.* See DUE.]

— **Syn.** 1. *Duty, obligation,* and *responsibility* denote an action that one is bound to perform. In origin, *duty* is that which is owed or due; *obligation,* that by which one is bound; *responsibility,* that for which one must answer. *Duty* arises from external circumstances; *responsibility,* from one's own undertakings: the *duty* of a soldier to his country, the *responsibility* of a captain for his ship. *Obligation* is used in both senses: the *obligation* of a child to its parents, the *obligation* of a debtor to pay his bills.

du·ty-free (dōō′tē-frē′, dyōō′-) *adj. & adv.* Exempt from customs duties. .

du·um·vir (dōō-um′vər, dyōō-) *n. pl.* **·virs** or **·vi·ri** (-vi-rī) One of two ancient Roman magistrates holding an office jointly. [< L < *duo* two + *vir* man] — **du·um′vi·ral** *adj.*

du·um·vi·rate (dōō-um′və-rit, dyōō-) *n.* 1. The joint governmental office or authority of two men. 2. A pair of men jointly holding the same office.

Du·ve·neck (dōō′və-nek), **Frank**, 1848–1919, U.S. painter and art teacher: original name **Frank Decker.**

du·ve·tyn (dōō′və-tēn, dōō′və-tēn′) *n.* Twill-weave fabric with a napped surface, made of wool, rayon, cotton, or silk. Also **du′ve·tine, du′ve·tyne.** [< F *duvet* down]

D.V. 1. Deo volente. 2. Douai Version (of the Bible).

Dvi·na (dvē′nə) 1. A river in the NW R.S.F.S.R. flowing 455 miles NW to Dvina Bay: also *Northern Dvina.* Russian *Severnaya Dvina.* 2. A river in the western Soviet Union flowing 633 miles, generally SW to the Gulf of Riga: also *Western Dvina.* Russian *Zapadnaya Dvina.* German *Düna.* Latvian *Daugava.*

Dvina Bay An inlet of the White Sea in the NW R.S.F.S.R.: also *Archangel Bay.* Also **Dvina Gulf, Gulf of Dvinsk.** *Russian* **Dvi·na Gu·ba** (dvyē′nə gōō-bä′).

Dvinsk (dvyēnsk) The Russian name for DAUGAVPILS.

D.V.M. Doctor of Veterinary Medicine.

D.V.M.S. Doctor of Veterinary Medicine and Surgery.

Dvo·řák (dvôr′zhäk), **Anton**, 1841–1904, Czech composer.

D/W Dock warrant.

dwarf (dwôrf) *n.* A human being, animal, or plant that is stunted in its growth and often has abnormal physical proportions. Compare MIDGET, PYGMY. — *v.t.* 1. To prevent the natural development of; stunt. 2. To cause to appear small or less by comparison. — *v.i.* 3. To become stunted; grow smaller. — *adj.* Diminutive; stunted. [OE *dweorh*]

dwarf alder A species of buckthorn (*Rhamnus elnifolia*) having leaves resembling those of the alder.

dwarf chestnut The chinquapin.

dwarf cornel A woody perennial herb (genus *Cornus*) of the dogwood family, especially the bunchberry.

dwarf elder A species of Old World elder (*Sambucus ebulus*) naturalized in the United States, having fragrant white and roseate flowers and black fruit: also called *danewort.*

dwarf·ish (dwôr′fish) *adj.* Like a dwarf; diminutive; stunted. — **dwarf′ish·ly** *adv.* — **dwarf′ish·ness** *n.*

dwarf·ism (dwôr′fiz·əm) *n. Pathol.* A condition of arrested physical development, variously caused.

dwarf mallow See under MALLOW.

dwarf star *Astron.* Any of a class of stars that have reached their greatest luminosity and are in the phase of contraction, including the sun.

dwell (dwel) *v.i.* **dwelt** or **dwelled, dwell·ing** 1. To have a fixed abode; reside. 2. To linger, as on a subject: with *on* or *upon.* 3. To continue in a state or place. — **Syn.** See LIVE. [OE *dwellan* to go astray; infl. by ON *dvelja* to delay, stop] — **dwell′er** *n.*

dwell·ing (dwel′ing) *n.* A place of residence; abode; house. Also **dwelling place.** — **Syn.** See HOME. — *adj.* Having or characterized by a (specified kind of) habitat: used in combination: *tree-dwelling.*

Dwight (dwīt), Timothy, 1752–1817, American clergyman and educator; president of Yale College 1795–1817.

dwin·dle (dwin′dəl) *v.t. & v.i.* **·dled, ·dling** To diminish or become less; make or become smaller. — **Syn.** See DE-CREASE. [Freq. of DWINE]

dwine (dwīn) *v.i. Scot.* or *Obs.* To pine or waste away; languish. [OE *dwīnan* to waste away]

dwt. Pennyweight.

DX or **D.X.** Distance; distant.

Dy *Chem.* Dysprosium.

dy·ad (dī′ad) *adj.* 1. *Chem.* Having a combining power of two; bivalent. 2. Dyadic. — *n.* 1. A pair of units; duad. 2. *Chem.* An atom, radical, or element that has a combining power of two. 3. *Biol.* **a** One of a pair of chromosomes, especially in the prophases of the second division in the formation of gametes. **b** A secondary unit made up of an aggregate of monads. [< LL *dyas, dyadis* < Gk. *dyas* the number two]

dy·ad·ic (dī·ad′ik) *adj.* 1. Of or pertaining to a dyad. 2. Based on or relating to the number 2; binary.

Dy·ak (dī′ak) *n.* One of the aboriginal people of Borneo, linguistically akin to the Malays, but differing from them in stature, type, and culture: also spelled *Dayak.*

Dya·ko·vi·tsa (dyä·kō′vi·tsä) See DJAKOVICA.

dy·ar·chy (dī′är·kē) See DIARCHY.

dyb·buk (dib′ək) *n.* In medieval Jewish legend, the spirit of a dead person that enters into and acts through a human being; also, a demon that similarly takes possession of a living human being. Also **dib′buk.** [< Hebrew *dābaq* to cling]

dye (dī) *v.* **dyed, dye·ing** *v.t.* 1. To fix a color in (cloth, hair, etc.), especially by soaking in liquid coloring matter. — *v.i.* 2. To take or give color: This cloth *dyes* badly. — *n.* A coloring matter used for dyeing; also, the color so produced. [OE *dēagian* to dye < *dēag* dye] — **dyer′** *n.*

dyed-in-the-wool (dīd′in·thə·wŏŏl′) *adj.* 1. Dyed before being woven. 2. Thoroughgoing; complete: a *dyed-in-the-wool* scoundrel.

dye·ing (dī′ing) *n.* The act, process, or trade of fixing colors in cloth or the like.

dy·er's-broom (dī′ərz·brŏŏm′, ·brŏŏm′) *n.* A shrub (*Genista tinctoria*) yielding a yellow dye that with woad becomes green: also called *woadwaxen, woodwaxen.* Also **dye′weed′.**

dy·er's-weed (dī′ərz·wēd′) *n.* Any of several plants that yield dyeing matter, such as woad.

dye·stuff (dī′stuf′) *n.* Any material used for dyeing.

dye·wood (dī′wŏŏd′) *n.* A wood that yields dyestuff.

Dy·fed (duv′ed) A county in SW Wales; 2,226 sq. mi.; pop. 320,100 (1976); county seat, Carmarthen.

dy·ing (dī′ing) *adj.* 1. Near death; expiring: a *dying* man. 2. Coming to a close; destined to end: a *dying* civilization. 3. Given, uttered, or manifested just before death: a *dying* wish. — *n.* Death.

dyke (dīk) See DIKE.

dyn. or **dynam.** Dynamics.

dyna- *combining form* Power: *dynatron.* Also, before vowels, **dyn-.** [< Gk. *dynamis* power]

dy·nam·e·ter (dī·nam′ə·tər) *n. Optics* A device for measuring the magnifying power of telescopes.

dy·nam·ic (dī·nam′ik) *adj.* 1. Of or pertaining to forces not in equilibrium, or to motion as the result of force: opposed to *static.* 2. Pertaining to or characterized by mechanical force. 3. Producing or involving change or action. 4. Characterized by energy or forcefulness: a *dynamic* personality. 5. *Music* Of, pertaining to, or indicating dynamics. Also *Rare* **dy·nam′i·cal.** [< Gk. *dynamikos* powerful < *dynamis* power] — **dy·nam′i·cal·ly** *adv.*

dy·nam·ics (dī·nam′iks) *n.pl.* (*construed as sing. in defs. 1, 2, and 4*) 1. The branch of physics that treats of the motion of bodies and the effects of forces in producing motion, including kinetics. Compare STATICS. 2. The science that treats of the action of forces, whether producing equilibrium or motion: in this sense including both statics and kinetics. 3. The forces producing or governing activity or movement of any kind; also, the methods of such activity: spiritual *dynamics.* 4. *Music* **a** The aggregation of words, abbrevia-

tions, and symbols used to indicate varying degrees of loudness; also **dynamic marks. b** The technique, practice, or possibility of producing varying degrees of loudness.

dy·na·mism (dī′nə·miz′əm) *n. Philos.* Any of various doctrines that explain the phenomena of the universe in terms of force or energy. — **dy′na·mist** *n.* — **dy′na·mis′tic** *adj.*

dy·na·mite (dī′nə·mīt) *n.* An explosive composed of nitroglycerin held in some absorbent substance. — *v.t.* **·mit·ed, ·mit·ing** 1. To blow up or shatter with or as with dynamite. 2. To charge with dynamite, as a mine. [< Gk. *dynamis* power] — **dy′na·mit′er** *n.*

dy·na·mo (dī′nə·mō) *n. pl.* **·mos** A generator for converting mechanical energy into electrical energy by electromagnetic induction. [Short for *dynamoelectric machine*]

dynamo- *combining form* Force; power: *dynamometer.* [< Gk. *dynamis* power]

dy·na·mo·e·lec·tric (dī′nə·mō·i·lek′trik) *adj.* Pertaining to the conversion of mechanical energy into electrical energy, or the reverse. Also **dy′na·mo·e·lec′tri·cal.**

dy·na·mom·e·ter (dī′nə·mom′ə·tər) *n.* An instrument for measuring force or power. [< DYNAMO- + -METER] — **dy·na·mo·met·ric** (dī′nə·mō·met′rik) or **·ri·cal** *adj.*

dy·na·mom·e·try (dī′nə·mom′ə·trē) *n.* The act or art of measuring the expenditure of power.

dy·na·mo·tor (dī′nə·mō′tər) *n.* A dynamoelectric machine having one field magnet, one armature core, and two armature windings, each having a commutator and being insulated from the other. [< DYNA(MO) + MOTOR]

dy·nast (dī′nast, ·nəst; *Brit.* din′əst) *n.* A ruler, especially a hereditary one; monarch. [< L *dynastes* < Gk. *dynastēs* < *dynasthai* to be powerful]

dy·nas·ty (dī′nəs·tē, *Brit.* din′əs·tē) *n. pl.* **·ties** 1. A succession of sovereigns in one line of descent; also, the length of time during which one family is in power. 2. A group or family whose power or prominence endures over a period of time as though inherited from one generation to the next: a political *dynasty.* — **dy·nas·tic** (dī·nas′tik, di-) or **·ti·cal** *adj.* — **dy·nas′ti·cal·ly** *adv.*

dy·na·tron (dī′nə·tron) *n. Electronics* A tetrode operated in the range of plate voltages where secondary emission of electrons causes the plate current to decrease as plate voltage increases, used as an oscillator. [< DYNA- + (ELEC)TRON]

dyne (dīn) *n. Physics* The fundamental unit of force in the cgs system that, if applied to a mass of one gram, would give it an acceleration of one centimeter per second per second. Abbr. *d., D.* [< F < Gk. *dynamis* power]

Dy·nel (dī·nel′) *n.* 1. A copolymer of vinyl chloride and acrylonitrile: a trade name. 2. A fabric made of Dynel.

Dyr·ra·chi·um (di·rā′kē·əm) The ancient name for DURRËS.

dys- *combining form* Bad; defective; difficult; hard: *dysgenic.* [< Gk. *dys-* bad, difficult]

dys·en·ter·y (dis′ən·ter′ē) *n. Pathol.* A severe inflammation of the mucous membrane of the large intestine, attended with bloody evacuations, griping pains, and some fever. [< OF *dysenterie* < L *dysenteria* < Gk. < *dys-* bad + *enteron* intestine] — **dys·en·ter′ic** or **·i·cal** *adj.*

dys·func·tion (dis·fungk′shən) *n. Med.* Deterioration of the natural action of a part; malfunction, as of an organ.

dys·gen·ic (dis·jen′ik) *adj.* Relating to or causing the biological deterioration of a strain or type, especially of man.

dys·gen·ics (dis·jen′iks) *n.pl.* (*construed as sing.*) The science dealing with the factors producing biological, especially genetic, deterioration in offspring: also called *cacogenics.*

dys·lo·gis·tic (dis′lō·jis′tik) *adj.* Conveying disapproval or censure. [< DYS- + (EU) LOGISTIC] — **dys′lo·gis′ti·cal·ly** *adv.*

dys·men·or·rhe·a (dis·men′ə·rē′ə) *n. Pathol.* Difficult or painful menstruation. Also **dys·men′or·rhoe′a.** [< NL < Gk. *dys-* hard + *mēn, mēnos* month + *rheein* to flow]

dys·pep·sia (dis·pep′shə, -sē·ə) *n.* Difficult or painful digestion, usually chronic. Also *Dial.* **dys·pep·sy** (dis·pep′sē). [< L < Gk. < *dys-* hard + *peptein* to cook, digest]

dys·pep·tic (dis·pep′tik) *adj.* 1. Relating to or suffering from dyspepsia. 2. Gloomy; peevish. Also **dys·pep′ti·cal.** — *n.* A dyspeptic person. — **dys·pep′ti·cal·ly** *adv.*

dys·pha·gi·a (dis·fā′jē·ə) *n.* Difficulty in swallowing. [< NL < Gk. *dys-* hard + *phagein* to eat] — **dys·phag′ic** (-faj′ik) *adj.*

dys·pha·sia (dis·fā′zhə, -zhē·ə) *n.* Difficulty in speaking or sometimes in understanding speech, resulting from damage to the brain. [< NL < Gk. *dys-* hard + *-phasia* utterance < *phanai* to speak]

dys·pho·ni·a (dis·fō′nē·ə) *n.* Difficulty in uttering articulate sounds. [< NL < Gk. *dysphōnia* < *dys-* hard + *phōnē* sound] — **dys·phon′ic** (-fon′ik) *adj.*

dys·pho·ri·a (dis·fôr′ē·ə, -fō′rē·ə) *n. Psychol.* A chronic feeling of illness and discontent. [< NL < Gk *dysphoria* < *dys-* hard + *pherein* to bear, endure]

dysp·ne·a (disp·nē′ə) *n. Pathol.* Labored breathing. Also **dysp·noe′a.** [< NL < L *dyspnoea* < Gk. *dyspnoia* < *dys-* hard + *pneein* to breathe] — **dysp·ne′al** or **dysp·ne′ic** *adj.*

dys·pro·si·um (dis·prō′sē·əm, -shē-) *n.* A highly magnetic element (symbol Dy) of the lanthanide series. See ELEMENT. [< NL < Gk. *dysprositos* < *dys-* hard + *prosienai* to approach]

dys·tax·i·a (dis·tak′sē·ə) *n. Pathol.* Muscular tremor resulting from disorder of the spinal cord. [< NL < Gk. *dys-* hard, defective + *taxis* arrangement]

dys·tel·e·ol·o·gy (dis′tel·ē·ol′ə·jē, -tē·lē-) *n.* **1.** The doctrine of purposelessness or of absence of final cause. Compare TELEOLOGY. **2.** Purposelessness, as the presence of apparently useless organs or parts. — **dys′tel·e·o·log′i·cal** (-ē-ə·loj′i·kəl) *adj.*

dys·thy·mi·a (dis·thī′mē·ə) *n. Psychiatry* A state of anxiety and depression. [< DYS- + Gk. *thymos* the mind]

dys·to·ci·a (dis·tō′shē·ə) *n. Med.* Prolonged or difficult labor and delivery in childbirth. [< DYS- + Gk. *tokos* birth]

dys·to·ni·a (dis·tō′nē·ə) *n. Pathol.* A condition of disordered tonicity of muscle tissue. [< DYS- + Gk. *teinein* to stretch]

dys·to·pi·a (dis·tō′pē·ə) *n. Pathol.* The faulty placement of an organ or part. [< DYS- + Gk. *topos* place, position]

dys·tro·phy (dis′trə·fē) *n.* Defective or perverted nutrition. Also **dys·tro·phi·a** (dis·trō′fē·ə) [< NL *dystrophia* < Gk. *dys-* hard, defective + *trophē* nourishment]

dys·u·ri·a (dis·yŏŏr′ē·ə) *n. Pathol.* Difficult, painful, or incomplete urination. [< LL < Gk. *dysouria* < *dys-* hard + *ouron* urine] — **dys·u′ric** *adj.*

Dy·u·la (dē′ŏŏ·lə, dyŏŏ′lə) *n. pl.* **Dy·u·la** or **Dy·u·las** **1.** A scattered African tribe who live and trade among other tribes on the Ivory Coast, the Upper Volta, and other parts of West Africa. **2.** The language of these people, widely used in trading.

Dyu·sham·be (dyōō·shäm′bə) The capital of the Tadzhik S.S.R., in the eastern part; pop. 374,000 (est. 1970): from 1929–1961 *Stalinabad.*

dy·vour (dē′vər) *n. Scot.* A bankrupt person. [Origin uncertain]

dz. Dozen(s).

Dzer·zhinsk (dyir·zhinsk′) A city in the western R.S.F. S.R., on the Oka; pop. 221,000 (est. 1970).

Dzhu·ga·shvi·li (jōō′gä·shvē′lē), **Iosif Vissarionovich** See STALIN.

dzig·ge·tai (dzig′ə·tī) *n.* A species of Mongolian wild ass: also called *chigetai.* [< Mongolian *dschiggetei* long-eared < *tchikhi* ear]

Dzun·gar·i·a (zŏŏng·gâr′ē·ə) A semidesert plateau region in the northern Sinkiang-Uighur Autonomous Region, China.

E

e, E (ē) *n. pl.* **e's, E's** or **es, Es, ees** (ēz) **1.** The fifth letter of the English alphabet. The shape of the Phoenician consonant *he* was adopted by the Greeks as *epsilon* and became the Roman *E.* **2.** Any sound represented by the letter *e.* — *symbol* **1.** *Music* **a** The third tone in the natural scale of C, *mi.* **b** The pitch of this tone, 329.6 cycles per second or this value multiplied by any power of 2, in standard pitch. **c** A written note representing it. **d** The scale built upon E. **2.** *Math.* The limit of the expression $(1 + 1/n)^n$, as *n* increases without limit: 2.7182818284+: the base to which Napierian logarithms are calculated: written *e.* **3.** The medieval Roman numeral for 250. **4.** *U.S.* A grade indicating failure in school work.

e 1. *Physics* Erg. **2.** Error(s) (baseball).

e- Reduced var. of EX-.

e. 1. East; eastern. **2.** Eldest. **3.** Engineer; engineering. **4.** Entrance (theater). **5.** Error(s) (baseball).

E 1. East; eastern. **2.** *Physics* Energy. **3.** English. **4.** Excellent.

E. 1. Earl. **2.** Earth. **3.** East; eastern. **4.** Engineer; engineering. **5.** English.

ea. Each.

E·a (ā′ä) In Babylonian mythology, one of the supreme deities and god of the waters.

EA or **E.A.** *Psychol.* Emotional age.

each (ēch) *adj.* Being one of two or more individuals that together form an aggregate; every. — **Syn.** See EVERY. — *pron.* Every one of any number or group considered individually; each one. ◆ The pronoun *each* is usually treated as a singular, as *Each* did *his* own work. — *adv.* For or to each person, article, etc.; apiece: one dollar *each.* Abbr. *ea.* [OE *ǣlc* < *ā* ever + *gelic* alike]

each other A compound reciprocal pronoun used in oblique cases: They saw *each other* (that is, Each saw the other). The possessive case is *each other's.* ◆ Some grammarians restrict the use of *each other* to two and use *one another* when reference is made to more than two; however, these phrases are commonly used interchangeably.

Eads (ēdz), **James Buchanan,** 1820–87, U.S. civil engineer.

Ead·ward (ad′wərd) or **Ead·weard** (ad′werd) See EDWARD.

ea·ger (ē′gər) *adj.* **1.** Impatiently desirous of something: *eager* to work. **2.** Showing impatient or intense feeling or desire: an *eager* glance. **3.** *Obs.* Sour; tart; pungent. [< OF *aigre* < L *acer* sharp] — **ea′ger·ly** *adv.* — **ea′ger·ness** *n.*

eager beaver *U.S. Slang* A zealous or diligent person.

ea·gle (ē′gəl) *n.* **1.** A very large diurnal bird of prey (family *Accipitridae*). Typical examples are: the **golden eagle** (*Aquila chrysaëtos canadensis*), ranging throughout northern regions, dark brown with a cowl of golden feathers; the **bald** (or **American**) **eagle** (genus *Haliaeetus*), dark brown, with the head, neck, and tail white, the national emblem of the United States; and the **imperial eagle** (*Aquila heliaca*) of Europe. ◆ Collateral adjective: *aquiline.* **2.** Any national seal or standard that bears an eagle as symbol. as the seal of the United States. **3.** A former gold coin of the United States having a value of $10. **4.** In golf, a score of two under par on any hole. [< OF *egle, aigle* < L *aquila*]

Ea·gle (ē′gəl) *n.* The constellation Aquila.

ea·gle-eyed (ē′gəl-īd′) *adj.* Having keen sight.

eagle owl A large predatory European owl (*Bubo bubo*).

eagle scout A boy scout of the highest rank.

ea·gle·stone (ē′gəl·stōn′) *n.* A yellow clay ironstone occurring as hollow oval nodules.

ea·glet (ē′glit) *n.* A young eagle.

ea·gle·wood (ē′gəl·wŏŏd′) *n.* Agalloch.

ea·gre (ē′gər, ā′-) *n.* A sudden flood of the tide in an estuary: also spelled **eager.** [ME *higre* < ML *higra* flood]

Ea·ker (ā′kər), **Ira Clarence,** born 1896, U.S. aviator and general.

Ea·kins (ā′kinz), **Thomas,** 1844–1916, U.S. painter.

eal·dor·man (ôl′dər·mən) *n.* The chief officer of a shire in pre-Norman England. Also **eal′der·man.** [Var. of ALDERMAN]

Eal·ing (ē′ling) A municipal borough of Middlesex, England, near London; pop. 183,151 (1961).

EAM In World War II, a Greek leftist organization formed as an underground party to resist the Nazi occupation. [< Mod.Gk. *E(thniko) A(pelevtherotiko) M(etopo)* National Liberation Front]

E. & O.E. or **e. and o.e.** Errors and omissions excepted.

ear¹ (ir) *n.* **1.** The organ of hearing in its entirety. ◆ Collateral adjective: *aural.* **2.** The fleshy or cartilaginous external part of the organ of hearing. **3.** The sense of hearing. **4.** The ability to perceive the refinements of music, poetry, or the like. **5.** Attentive consideration; heed. **6.** Something resembling the external ear in shape or position, as a projecting piece on a vase. **7.** In newspapers, a box in either of the upper corners of the front page, containing a motto, the weather report, etc. — **to be all ears** To be eagerly attentive. — **to be up to the ears** To be submerged in work, problems, etc. — **to have an ear to the ground** To listen to or heed current public opinion. — **to lend an ear** To pay attention. — **to play by ear** To play an instrument without the aid of musical notation. [OE *ēare*] — **ear′less** *adj.*

Incus (anvil) Semicircular canals
Malleus (hammer) Groove for auditory nerves
Auditory canal to outer ear
Tympanic membrane (eardrum) Tympanic cavity Cochlea Eustachian tube
Stapes (stirrup)

HUMAN EAR, FRONTAL SECTION
(Anatomical nomenclature)

ear² (ir) *n.* The fruit-bearing part of a cereal plant; the head. — **in** (or **on**) **the ear** On the cob, as corn; unhusked, as grain. — *v.i.* To form ears, as grain. [OE *ēar*]

ear·ache (ir′āk′) *n.* Pain in the middle or internal ear.

ear·drop (ir′drop′) *n.* An earring with a pendant.

ear·drum (ir′drum′) *n.* The tympanic membrane.

eared (ird) *adj.* **1.** Having ears or earlike appendages; auriculate. **2.** Having or characterized by a (specified kind of) ear or (a specified number of) ears: *lop-eared; one-eared.*

eared seal Any of a family (*Otariidae*) of seals, including the sea lion and the fur seals, having external ears.

ear flap (ir′flap′) *n.* An earlap (def. 1).

ear·ful (ir′fŏŏl′) *n. U.S. Informal* **1.** Something heard and considered enough or too much: *Did you get an earful?* **2.** Surprising or important news or gossip. **3.** A scolding.

Ear·hart (âr′härt), **Amelia,** 1898–1937, Mrs. George Palmer Putnam, U.S. aviatrix.

ear·ing (ir′ing) *n. Naut.* A small line used to fasten the corners of a sail to a yard. [< EAR¹]

earl (ûrl) *n.* A member of the British nobility next in rank above a viscount and below a marquis. *Earl* is the equivalent of the Norman *count*, which title superseded it in England as long as Norman French was spoken, and is still retained in the feminine form *countess.* Abbr. *E.* [OE *eorl* nobleman]

ear·lap (ir′lap′) *n.* **1.** One of two flaps attached to a cap for protecting the ears from the cold. **2.** The external ear; especially, the ear lobes.

earl·dom (ûrl′dəm) *n.* The rank or territory of an earl.

earl marshal A British officer of state, head of the Heralds′ College and director of official ceremonies: hereditary office of the dukes of Norfolk.

ear lobe The soft, fleshy protuberance at the lower part of the external ear.

ear·ly (ûr′lē) *adj.* **·li·er, ·li·est** **1.** Coming near the beginning of any specified period of time or of any series of related things: *an early Shaw play.* **2.** Belonging to a distant time or stage of development. **3.** Occurring ahead of the usual or arranged time: *an early dinner.* **4.** Occurring in the near future: *An early truce is expected.* — *adv.* **1.** Near the beginning of any specified period or series of things. **2.** Far back in time. **3.** Before the usual or arranged time. [OE *līce* < *ǣr* before + *-līce* -ly] — **ear′li·ness** *n.*

Ear·ly (ûr′lē), **Jubal Anderson,** 1816–94, Confederate General in the Civil War.

early bird *Informal* One who rises or arrives early.

ear·mark (ir′märk′) *n.* **1.** A distinctive mark made on an animal′s ear to denote ownership. **2.** Any mark of identification. — *v.t.* **1.** To put an earmark on. **2.** To set aside, as money, for a particular purpose.

ear·mind·ed (ir′mīn′dĭd) *adj.* Showing a marked response to and preference for auditory stimuli.

ear·muff (ir′mŭf′) *n. U.S.* One of a pair of adjustable coverings for the ears, worn as protection against the cold.

earn¹ (ûrn) *v.t.* **1.** To receive or deserve as recompense for labor, service, or performance. **2.** To acquire as a consequence: *to earn a bad name.* **3.** To produce as profit. — **Syn.** See GET [OE *earnian*] — **earn′er** *n.*

earn² (ûrn) *v.i. Obs.* To yearn. [Var. of YEARN]

earned income See under INCOME.

ear·nest¹ (ûr′nist) *adj.* **1.** Intent and direct in purpose; zealous: *an earnest student.* **2.** Marked by deep feeling or conviction: *an earnest apology.* **3.** Of a serious or important nature. — **in earnest** With serious intent or determination. [OE *eornoste*] — **ear′nest·ly** *adv.* — **ear′nest·ness** *n.*

ear·nest² (ûr′nist) *n.* **1.** *Law* Money paid in advance to bind a contract. Also **earnest money.** **2.** An assurance or token of something to come. [Prob. < OF *erres* < L *arra, arrhabo* < Gk. *arrhabōn* < Hebrew ′*ērābōn* pledge; infl. by EARNEST¹]

earn·ings (ûr′ningz) *n. pl.* That which is earned; wages.

ear·phone (ir′fōn′) *n.* A radio or telephone listening or hearing device held at or inserted into the ear.

ear·plug (ir′plug′) *n.* A rubber or plastic mold inserted into the ear to exclude water or noise.

ear·ring (ir′ring′) *n.* A ring or ornament for the ear lobe.

ear shell An abalone.

ear·shot (ir′shŏt′) *n.* The distance at which sounds may be heard.

ear·split·ting (ir′splĭt′ing) *adj.* Painfully loud or high-pitched; deafening.

ear·stone (ir′stōn′) *n.* An otolith. Also **ear stone.**

earth (ûrth) *n.* **1.** The dry land surface of the globe, as distinguished from the oceans and sky; ground. **2.** The softer, loose part of land, as distinguished from rock; soil; dirt. **3.** The planet on which man dwells; also, the people who inhabit it: *All the earth mourned his death.* **4.** The abode of mortal man, as opposed to heaven and hell. **5.** Worldly or temporal affairs, as contrasted with spiritual ones. **6.** The mortal body. **7.** The hole or lair of a burrowing animal. **8.** *Electr.* The ground that forms part of an electric circuit. **9.** *Chem.* A rare-earth element. **10.** *Obs.* A country; land. — **down to earth** Realistic; practical; unaffected. — **to run to earth** To hunt down and find, as a fox. — *v.t.* **1.** To heap up (plants, etc.) with soil for protection. **2.** To chase (an animal) into hiding. **3.** *Electr.* To ground. **4.** To burrow or hide in the earth, as a fox. [OE *eorthe*]

Earth (ûrth) *n.* The third planet from the sun and fifth in order of size, having an area of about 196 million square miles and a mass of 6.57 sextillion tons (6.57 × 10²¹) See PLANET. Abbr. *E.*

earth-bor·er (ûrth′bôr′ər, -bō′rər) *n.* An auger for boring into the ground. For illustration see DRILL¹.

earth·born (ûrth′bôrn′) *adj.* Born out of the earth; of earthly origin; also, mortal.

earth·bound (ûrth′bound′) *adj.* **1.** Having only material interests. **2.** Fixed in or on the earth.

earth color Any of several pigments or paints prepared from naturally occurring earth materials, as umber, ocher, chalk.

earth current An electric current that circulates within the earth′s crust.

earth·en (ûr′thən) *adj.* Made of earth or baked clay.

earth·en·ware (ûr′thən-wâr′) *n.* Dishes, pots, and the like, made of a coarse grade of baked clay.

earth flax **1.** Asbestos. **2.** Amianthus.

earth inductor *Electr.* An induction coil that may be sharply rotated in the earth′s magnetic field in order to determine the intensity of the field by the strength of the induced current as read on a galvanometer.

earth inductor compass A compass equipped with an induction coil actuated by the earth′s magnetic field.

earth·i·ness (ûr′thē-nis) *n.* The quality of being earthy.

earth·light (ûrth′līt′) *n. Astron.* Earthshine.

earth·ling (ûrth′ling) *n.* **1.** A dweller on earth; mortal. **2.** One devoted to worldly things; worldling.

earth·ly (ûrth′lē) *adj.* **1.** Of or relating to the earth and its material qualities; worldly; secular. **2.** Possible; imaginable: *of no earthly use.* — **earth′li·ness** *n.*

earth·nut (ûrth′nut′) *n.* **1.** Any of various underground tubers or nutlike pods, as the peanut. **2.** Either of two European herbs (genus *Carum*) of the parsley family: also called *hognut.* **3.** A truffle.

earth·pea (ûrth′pē′) *n.* The hog peanut.

earth·quake (ûrth′kwāk′) *n.* A vibration or sudden undulation of a portion of the earth′s crust, caused by the splitting or faulting of a mass of rock or by volcanic or other disturbances. ◆ Collateral adjective: *seismic.*

earth·rise (ûrth′rīz′) *n.* **1.** As seen from the moon, the rising of the earth above the horizon. **2.** The time when this occurs.

earth science Any of a group of sciences concerned primarily with the origin, structure, composition, and other physical features of the earth, as geology, geography, etc.

earth·set (ûrth′set′) *n.* **1.** As seen from the moon, the setting of the earth below the horizon. **2.** The time when this occurs.

earth·shine (ûrth′shīn′) *n. Astron.* That portion of sunlight reflected from the earth′s surface and faintly illuminating parts of the moon not reached directly by the sun′s rays.

earth·star (ûrth′stär′) *n.* A fungus (genus *Geaster*) having the outer coat split into divisions and suggestive of a star.

earth·ward (ûrth′wərd) *adv.* Toward the earth. Also **earth′wards.** — *adj.* Moving toward the earth.

earth wax Ozocerite.

earth·work (ûrth′wûrk′) *n.* **1.** *Mil.* A fortification made largely or wholly of earth. **2.** *Engin.* The work of excavating and preparing the earth preliminary to construction.

earth·worm (ûrth′wûrm′) *n.* **1.** Any of a family (*Lumbricidae*) of burrowing annelids whose activity stirs and aerates the soil, used as fishing bait. **2.** A low, groveling person.

earth·y (ûr′thē) *adj.* **earth·i·er, earth·i·est** **1.** Composed of or resembling earth. **2.** Characteristic of earth. **3.** Unrefined; coarse. **4.** Natural; robust; lusty. **5.** Worldly.

ear trumpet A trumpet-shaped instrument that collects and concentrates sound, used as an aid in hearing.

ear·wax (ir′waks′) *n.* A substance secreted by glands lining the passages of the external ear: also called *cerumen.*

ear·wig (ir′wig′) *n.* **1.** An insect (family *Forficulidae*) with horny forewings and a caudal pair of forceps, erroneously believed to enter the human ear. For illustration see INSECTS (injurious). **2.** *U.S.* A small centipede. — *v.t.* **·wigged, ·wig·ging** To insinuate against in secret. [OE *ēarwicga*]

ease (ēz) *n.* **1.** Freedom from physical discomfort or mental agitation. **2.** Freedom from great effort or difficulty; facility: *to run with ease.* **3.** Freedom from affectation or embarrassment; naturalness; poise. — *v.* **eased, eas·ing** *v.t.* **1.** To relieve the mental or physical pain or oppression of; comfort. **2.** To make less painful or oppressive; alleviate. **3.** To lessen the pressure, weight, tension, etc., of: *to ease an axle.* **4.** To make easier; facilitate. **5.** To move, lower, or put in place slowly and carefully. — *v.i.* **6.** To lessen in severity, tension, speed, etc.: often with *up* or *off.* — **to ease the helm** *Naut.* To put the helm a trifle to midships so as to reduce the strain on the rudder. [< OF *aise* < L *adjacens, -entis* close at hand, within easy reach]

— **Syn.** (noun) *Ease, facility, dexterity,* and *readiness* refer to aptitude in doing something. *Ease* is largely negative, denoting absence of effort, strain, hesitation, uncertainty, etc. *Facility* and *dexterity* are ability to do, acquired by practice; *dexterity* implies the greater degree of skill. *Readiness* is the ability to deal with whatever comes, and so implies alertness, promptness, and quickness. Compare DEXTERITY. — **Ant.** effort, exertion.

ease·ful (ēz′fəl) *adj.* Giving ease or quiet; restful; peaceful. **— ease′ful·ly** *adv.* **— ease′ful·ness** *n.*

ea·sel (ē′zəl) *n.* A folding frame or tripod used to support an artist's canvas, a painting being displayed, etc. [< Du. *ezel* easel, orig. an ass, beast of burden]

ease·ment (ēz′mənt) *n.* **1.** Anything that gives ease or comfort. **2.** Relief. **3.** *Law* The privilege or right of making limited use of another's adjacent property.

eas·i·ly (ē′zə·lē) *adv.* **1.** In an easy manner; without difficulty, discomfort, or anxiety. **2.** Beyond question; certainly: This is *easily* his best novel. **3.** Very possibly: He may *easily* be wrong.

eas·i·ness (ē′zi·nis) *n.* The state of being at ease, or of being easy to do.

east (ēst) *n.* **1.** The direction of the sun in relation to an observer on earth at sunrise. **2.** One of the four cardinal points of the compass, directly opposite *west* and 90° clockwise from *north.* See COMPASS CARD. **3.** Any direction near this point. **4.** *Sometimes cap.* Any region east of a specified point. **— the East 1.** Asia and its adjacent islands; the Orient. **2.** In the United States: **a** The region east of the Mississippi and north of the Ohio. **b** The region east of the Allegheny Mountains and north of Maryland. **3.** The Soviet Union and its associates in world politics. *— adj.* **1.** To, toward, facing, or in the east; eastern. **2.** Coming from the east: the *east* wind. **3.** Near the altar of a church as seen from the nave. *— adv.* In or toward the east; eastward. Abbr. *E, e., E.* [OE *ēast*]

East (ēst), **Edward Murray,** 1879–1938, U.S. biologist.

East Africa Protectorate A former name for KENYA.

East An·gli·a (ang′glē·ə) An ancient Anglo-Saxon kingdom in SE England, comprising Norfolk and Suffolk counties.

East Bengal See under BENGAL.

East Berlin See under BERLIN.

east·bound (ēst′bound′) *adj.* Going eastward. Also **east′-bound′.**

East·bourne (ēst′born, -bərn) A county borough in East Sussex, England; pop. 73,300 (1976).

east by north A point on the mariner's compass, seven points or 78° 15′ clockwise from due north. See COMPASS CARD. Abbr. *EBN*

east by south A point on the mariner's compass, nine points or 101° 15′ clockwise from due north. See COMPASS CARD Abbr. *EBS*

East Cape See (Cape) DEZHNEV.

East Chicago A city in the NW corner of Indiana, on Lake Michigan near the Illinois border; pop. 46,982.

East China Sea The NE part of the China Sea, bounded by Korea, Japan, Taiwan, and China.

East Cleveland A city in NE Ohio, a suburb of Cleveland; pop. 39,600.

East Detroit A city in SE Michigan, near Detroit; pop. 45,920.

East End A heavily populated section of eastern London, comprising industrial and slum districts.

east·er (ēs′tər) *n.* A wind or storm from the east.

East·er (ēs′tər) *n.* **1.** A Christian festival commemorating the resurrection of Christ. **2.** The day on which this festival is celebrated, the Sunday immediately after the first full moon that occurs on or after March 21: also **Easter Sunday** [OE *Eastre* goddess of spring]

Easter egg A decorated egg, or imitation of an egg, given as a present at Easter.

Easter Island An island of Chile in the South Pacific; 45.5 sq. mi.; known for its numerous stone monuments: native name *Rapa Nui.* Spanish *Isla de Pascua.*

east·er·ly (ēs′tər·lē) *adj.* **1.** In, of, toward, or pertaining to the east. **2.** From the east, as a wind. *— adv.* Toward or from the east. *— n. pl.* **·lies** A wind or storm from the east.

Easter Monday The day following Easter.

east·ern (ēs′tərn) *adj.* **1.** To, toward, or in the east. **2.** Native to or inhabiting the east: an *eastern* species. **3.** *Sometimes cap.* Of, pertaining to, or characteristic of the east or the East. **4.** From the east, as a wind. Abbr. *E, e., E.*

Eastern Church 1. The church of the Byzantine Empire, including the patriarchates of Constantinople, Alexandria, Antioch, and Jerusalem, that separated from the Western Church in 1054: also called *Greek Church.* **2.** The Eastern Orthodox Church. **3.** The Uniat Church.

Eastern Colorado River See COLORADO RIVER.

Eastern Empire The Byzantine Empire (which see).

east·ern·er (ēs′tərn·ər) *n.* **1.** One who is native to or lives in the east. **2.** *Usually cap.* One who lives in or comes from eastern United States.

Eastern Hemisphere See under HEMISPHERE.

east·ern·most (ēs′tərn·mōst′) *adj.* Farthest east.

Eastern Orthodox Church The modern churches derived from the medieval Eastern Church, including various autonomous bodies, as the Greek and Russian Orthodox churches, that agree in faith and order with the patriarch of Constantinople: also called *Eastern Church, Orthodox Church,* or loosely *Greek Church.*

Eastern rite Any of the liturgical rites of the Uniat Church as distinguished from the rite of the Latin Church.

Eastern Roman Empire The Byzantine Empire (which see).

Eastern Samoa See under SAMOA.

Eastern Security Treaty A collective defense pact between Albania, Bulgaria, Czechoslovakia, East Germany, Hungary, Poland, Rumania, and the Soviet Union, signed in Warsaw May 14, 1955: also called *Warsaw Pact.*

Eastern Shore 1. The eastern coast of Chesapeake Bay; especially, the tidewater region of Maryland. **2.** Often, the Delmarva peninsula.

Eastern Standard Time See under STANDARD TIME. Abbr. *EST, E.S.T., e.s.t.*

Eastern Townships *Canadian* The part of Quebec south of the St. Lawrence River valley and west of a line between Quebec City and the U.S. border.

East·er·tide (ēs′tər·tīd′) *n.* **1.** The season of Easter, a period extending in various churches from Easter to Ascension Day, Whitsunday, or Trinity Sunday. **2.** The week beginning with and immediately following Easter. [< EASTER + TIDE¹ (def. 4)]

East Flanders A province of NW Belgium; 1,147 sq. mi.; pop. 1,310,638 (est. 1970); capital, Ghent: Flemish *Oost-Vlaanderen.* French *Flandre Orientale.*

East Germanic See under GERMANIC.

East Germany See under GERMANY.

East Ham A county borough in SW Sussex, England, on the Thames; pop. 105,359 (1961).

East Hartford A town in north central Connecticut, near Hartford; pop. 57,583.

East India Company The name of various mercantile associations organized in the 17th and 18th centuries by Europeans to carry on trade with the East Indies, notably the British, Dutch, and French companies.

East Indies 1. The Malay Archipelago; also, occasionally, the Malay Archipelago together with India and Indochina. **2.** The islands of the Republic of Indonesia (formerly Netherlands East Indies). **3.** Formerly, India. Also **East India.** **— East Indian**

east·ing (ēs′ting) *n.* **1.** *Naut.* The distance traversed by a ship running on an easterly course. **2.** The distance eastward from a given meridian. **3.** A shifting or moving east.

East Lansing A city in south central Michigan, near Lansing; pop. 47,504.

East London A port city in SE South Africa, on the Indian Ocean; pop. 134,100 (est. 1967): Afrikaans *Oos-Londen.*

East Los Angeles An unincorporated place in SW California, a suburb of Los Angeles; pop. 105,033.

East Lo·thi·an (lō′thē·ən) A county in SE Scotland; 267 sq. mi.; pop. 55,070 (est. 1969): county seat, Haddington: formerly *Haddington, Haddingtonshire.*

East·man (ēst′mən), **George,** 1854–1932, U.S. industrialist; **— Max (Forrester),** 1883–1969, U.S. editor and writer.

East Meadow An unincorporated place in SE New York on Long Island, near Hempstead; pop. 46,252.

East Midland See under MIDLAND.

east-north-east (ēst′nôrth′ēst′) *n.* **1.** The direction midway between east and northeast. **2.** A point on the mariner's compass, 6 points or 67°30′ clockwise from due north. See COMPASS CARD. Abbr. *ene, ENE, e.n.e., E.N.E.* *— adj. & adv.* In, toward, or from the east-northeast.

Eas·ton (ēs′tən) A city in eastern Pennsylvania, on the Delaware River; pop. 30,256.

East Orange A city in NE New Jersey, near Newark; pop. 75,471.

East Pakistan See BANGLADESH.

East Point A city in central Georgia, near Atlanta; pop. 39,315.

East Providence A town in eastern Rhode Island, a suburb of Providence; pop. 48,151.

East Prussia A former province of Prussia in NE Germany; capital, Königsberg: German *Ostpreussen.*

East Riding A former administrative county of SE Yorkshire, England; 1,185 sq. mi.; pop. 542,556 (1971); county seat, Beverley.

East River A navigable tidal strait connecting Long Island Sound and New York Bay; length, about 16 mi. See map of NEW YORK BAY.

East Semitic See under SEMITIC.

East Slavic See under SLAVIC.

east-south-east (ēst′south′ēst) *n.* **1.** The direction midway between east and southeast. **2.** A point on the mariner's compass, ten points or 112°30′ clockwise from due north. See COMPASS CARD. Abbr. *ese, ESE, e.s.e., E.S.E.* *— adj. & adv.* In, toward, or from the east-southeast.

East St. Louis A city in SW Illinois, on the Mississippi River opposite St. Louis, Missouri; pop. 69,996.

East Sussex A county in southern England; 693 sq. mi.; pop. 661,100 (1976); county seat, Lewes.

east·ward (ēst′wərd) *adv.* Toward the east. Also **east′-wards.** *— adj.* To, toward, facing, or in the east. *— n.* An eastward direction or point; also, an eastern part or region.

east·ward·ly (ēst′wərd·lē) *adj. & adv.* **1.** Toward the east. **2.** Coming from the east, as a wind.

eas·y (ē′zē) *adj.* **eas·i·er, eas·i·est 1.** Requiring little work or effort; offering few difficulties: an *easy* task; an *easy* language.   **2.** Free from discomfort, trouble or anxiety: an *easy* mind.   **3.** Characterized by or conducive to rest or comfort: an *easy* life.   **4.** Not stiff or formal; relaxed: an *easy* manner.   **5.** Not strict; lenient; indulgent.   **6.** Easily persuaded; yielding; credulous: an *easy* victim.   **7.** Complacent; easygoing.   **8.** Unhurried; gentle: an *easy* trot.   **9.** Not burdensome; moderate: to buy on *easy* terms.   **10.** Well-to-do; affluent: in *easy* circumstances.   **11.** *Econ.* **a** Readily available: said of a commodity. **b** Available for loan at low interest rates: said of money. **c** Characterized by relaxed demand; quiet; slow: said of a market: opposed to *tight*. **— to be on easy street** *Informal* To be well-to-do; live in comfort. **— adv.** *Informal* In an easy manner; easily. **— to go easy on** *Slang* **1.** To use with moderation, as liquor.   **2.** To be lenient with.   **3.** To be tactful about. **— to take it easy** *Informal* **1.** To avoid exertion; relax.   **2.** To remain calm. [< OF *aisie*, pp. of *aisier*, *aiser* to put at ease]

easy chair A large, comfortable, usually padded armchair.
eas·y·go·ing (ē'zē-gō'ing) *adj.* **1.** Not inclined to effort or worry.   **2.** Moving at an easy pace, as a horse.
easy mark *Informal* One easily fooled or victimized.
eat (ēt) *v.* **ate** (āt, *Brit.* et) or *Archaic* **eat** (et, ēt), **eat·en**, **eat·ing** *v.t.* **1.** To take in through the mouth as nourishment; especially, to chew and swallow.   **2.** To consume or destroy by or as by eating: usually with *away* or *up*.   **3.** To wear away; waste: His body was *eaten* by disease.   **4.** To make (a hole, etc.) by gnawing or corroding. — *v.i.* **5.** To take food; have a meal.   **6.** To wear away by or as by gnawing or corroding: with *through* or *into*. **— to eat one's words** To retract what one has said. [OE *etan*] **— eat'er** *n.*
eat·a·ble (ē'tə-bəl) *n.* *Often pl.* Something fit for food. *adj.* Fit to be eaten; edible.
eat·ing (ē'ting) *n.* **1.** The act of taking food.   **2.** Food: Brook trout are good *eating*.
Eaton (ēt'n), **Theophilus**, 1590?–1658, English administrator in America; first governor of New Haven Colony 1639–58.
eats (ēts) *n.pl.* *U.S. Slang* Food.
eau (ō) *n.pl.* **eaux** (ō) Water: a word designating various perfumes, cordials, etc. [< F < L *aqua* water]
Eau Claire (ō klâr') A city in west central Wisconsin, on the Chippewa River; pop. 44,619.
eau de Co·logne (ō' də kə·lōn') Cologne, a toilet water.
eau de vie (ō' də vē') *French* Brandy; literally, water of life.
eaves (ēvz) *n.* (*orig. sing., now construed as pl.*) The lower projecting edge of a sloping roof. [OE *efes* edge]
eaves·drop (ēvz'drop') *v.i.* **·dropped**, **·drop·ping** To listen secretly, as to a private conversation. — *n.* **1.** Water that drops from the eaves.   **2.** The ground on which the water drops from the eaves. **— eaves'drop'per** *n.*
eaves trough A gutter (def. 3): also **eave trough.**
ebb (eb) *v.i.* **1.** To recede, as the tide: opposed to *flow*.   **2.** To decline or weaken; fail. — *n.* **1.** The flowing back of tidewater to the ocean: opposed to *flood*. Also **ebb tide.**   **2.** A condition or period of decline or decay. [OE *ebbian*]
E·bert (ā'bərt), **Friedrich**, 1871–1925, German statesman; first president of the German republic 1919–25.
Eb·lis (eb'lis) In Moslem mythology, the devil: also *Iblees*. [< Arabic *Iblīs* < Gk. *Diabolos* devil]
EbN East by north.
E-boat (ē'bōt') *n.* *Brit.* A fast German torpedo boat. [< *e*(*nemy*) *boat*]
eb·on (eb'ən) *Poetic adj.* **1.** Of ebony.   **2.** Black. — *n.* Ebony.
eb·on·ite (eb'ən·īt) *n.* Vulcanite, a rubber product.
eb·on·ize (eb'ən·īz) *v.t.* **·ized**, **·iz·ing** To stain or polish in imitation of ebony.
eb·on·y (eb'ən·ē) *n.* *pl.* **·ies** **1.** A hard, heavy wood, usually black, used for cabinetwork, etc. It is furnished by various species of a tropical genus (*Diospyros*) of hardwood trees.   **2.** Any tree of this genus, especially *D. ebenum* of Ceylon and southern India. — *adj.* **1.** Made of ebony.   **2.** Like ebony, especially in color; black. [< L *hebeninus* < Gk. *ebeninos* of ebony < *ebenos* ebony < Egyptian *hehni*]
Eb·or·a·cum (eb'ə·rā'kəm) The capital of Roman Britain. See YORKSHIRE.
e·brac·te·ate (ē·brak'tē·āt) *adj.* *Bot.* Without bracts. [< NL *ebracteatus* < L *e-* without + *bractea* plate, bract]
E·bro (ē'brō, *Sp.* ā'brō) A river in NE Spain, flowing about 500 miles SE to the Mediterranean.
EbS East by south.
e·bul·lient (i·bul'vənt) *adj.* **1.** Bubbling over with enthusiasm or excitement; exuberant.   **2.** Boiling or bubbling up. [< L *ebulliens*, *-entis*, ppr. of *ebullire* < *e-* out + *bullire* to boil] **— e·bul'lient·ly** *adv.* **— e·bul'lience, e·bul'lien·cy** *n.*
eb·ul·li·tion (eb'ə·lish'ən) *n.* **1.** The bubbling of a liquid; boiling.   **2.** Any sudden or violent agitation, as of emotions. [< L *ebullitio*, *-onis* < *ebullire*. See EBULLIENT.]
eb·ur·na·tion (eb'ər·nā'shən) *n.* *Pathol.* **1.** Ossification of joint cartilage.   **2.** Condensation of a bone structure to the hardness of ivory. [< L *eburnus* ivory + *-ATION*]

ec- Var. of EX-²
ECA Economic Commission for Africa
ECAFE Economic Commission for Asia and the Far East.
é·car·té (ā'kär·tā') *n.* A game of cards for two persons. [< F, pp of *écarter* to discard]
Ec·bat·a·na (ek·bat'ə·nə) The capital of ancient Media. See HAMADAN.
ec·bol·ic (ek·bol'ik) *Med. adj.* Causing contraction of the uterus and thus inducing abortion or promoting parturition. — *n.* An ecbolic drug. [< Gk. *ekbolē* a casting out (< *ek-* out + *ballein* to throw) + *-IC*]
ec·ce ho·mo (ek'sē hō'mō, ek'ē) Behold the man: in the Vulgate, the words of Pontius Pilate when he presented Christ to his accusers. *John* xix 5. [< L]
Ecce Homo A representation of Christ crowned with thorns.
ec·cen·tric (ek·sen'trik) *adj.* **1.** Departing from conventional custom or practice; differing conspicuously in behavior, appearance, or opinions.   **2.** Not situated in the center, as an axis.   **3.** Deviating from a perfect circle: said chiefly of an elliptical orbit.   **4.** *Math.* Not having the same center: opposed to *concentric*. — *n.* **1.** One who or that which deviates markedly from the regular or expected course of behavior; an odd or erratic individual.   **2.** *Mech.* A machine element for converting rotary into reciprocating motion, consisting of a disk attached off center to a driving shaft and able to revolve freely within a fixed collar or strap connected with a rod. [< LL *eccentricus* < Gk. *ekkentros* < *ek-* out, *away* + *kentron* center] **— ec·cen·tri·cal·ly** *adv.*
ec·cen·tric·i·ty (ek'sen·tris'ə·tē) *n.* *pl.* **·ties 1.** Deviation from what is regular or expected; irregularity.   **2.** An act or characteristic marked by oddity; a peculiarity.   **3.** The quality of being eccentric: the *eccentricity* of an orbit.   **4.** The degree of being eccentric.   **5.** The distance between the centers of two eccentric circles or objects.
ec·chy·mo·sis (ek'i·mō'sis) *n.* *pl.* **·ses** (-sēz) *Med.* A discoloration, as a black-and-blue spot resulting from the rupture of small blood vessels by a blow or contusion. [< NL < Gk. *ekchymōsis* < *ek-* out + *chymos* humor (def. 7a)] **— ec'chy·mot'ic** (-mot'ik) *adj.*
eccl. or **eccles.** Ecclesiastical.
Ec·cles (ek'əlz), **Marriner Stoddard**, born 1890, U.S banker and economist.
Eccles. or **Eccl. 1.** Ecclesiastes.   **2.** Ecclesiastical.
ec·cle·si·a (i·klē'zhē·ə, -zē·ə) *n.* *pl.* **·ae** (-ē) **1.** The legislative assembly in ancient Greek states   **2.** A church; congregation. [< L < Gk. *ekklēsia* < *ekkaleein* < *ek-* out + *kaleein* to call]
ec·cle·si·arch (i·klē'zē·ärk) *n.* A church ruler, especially one in high authority. [< ECCLESIA + Gk. *archos* chief]
Ec·cle·si·as·tes (i·klē'zē·as'tēz) *n.* A book of the Old Testament, formerly attributed to King Solomon: also, *Hebrew*, *Koheleth*. [< Gk. *ekklēsiastēs*, trans. of Hebrew *qōhēleth* preacher]
ec·cle·si·as·tic (i·klē'zē·as'tik) *adj.* Ecclesiastical. — *n.* One officially in the service of the church; a cleric; churchman. [< Gk. *ekklēsiastikos* for the assembly < *ekklēsia*. See ECCLESIA.]
ec·cle·si·as·ti·cal (i·klē'zē·as'ti·kəl) *adj.* Of or pertaining to the church, especially as an organized and governing power. **— ec·cle'si·as'ti·cal·ly** *adv.*
ec·cle·si·as·ti·cism (i·klē'zē·as'tə·siz'əm) *n.* **1.** The principles, practices, and organization of the church.   **2.** Devotion to these; also, the spirit leading to such devotion.
Ec·cle·si·as·ti·cus (i·klē'zē·as'ti·kəs) *n.* One of the didactic books of the Old Testament Apocrypha, accepted as canonical by the Roman Catholic Church: also called *Wisdom of Jesus, Son of Sirach.*
ec·cle·si·ol·a·try (i·klē'zē·ol'ə·trē) *n.* Worship of the church; extreme veneration for the authority, forms, and traditions of the church. [< Gk. *ekklēsia* church + *latreia* worship] **— ec·cle'si·ol'a·ter** *n.*
ec·cle·si·ol·o·gy (i·klē'zē·ol'ə·jē) *n.* The study of church architecture and decoration. **— ec·cle·si·o·log·ic** (i·klē'zē·ə·loj'ik) or **·i·cal** *adj.*
Ecclus. Ecclesiasticus.
ec·dys·i·ast (ek·diz'ē·ast, -əst) *n.* A stripteaser. [< Gk. *ekdusis* a shedding of the skin; coined by H. L. Mencken]
ec·dy·sis (ek'də·sis) *n.* *pl.* **·ses** (-sēz) The shedding of an integument, as in snakes and insects. [< NL < Gk. *ek-* off + *dyein* to enter, dress]
e·ce·sis (i·sē'sis) *n.* *Ecol.* The adjustment of a plant to a new habitat; establishment of a migrant organism. [< NL < Gk. *oikēsis* a dwelling]
ECG *Med.* Electrocardiogram.
ec·hard (ek'härd) *n.* *Ecol.* The nonavailable water of the soil: opposed to *chresard*. [< Gk. *echthos* outside + *ardeia* irrigation]
eche (ēch) *v.t.* *Obs.* To increase or enlarge. [OE *ēcan*]
E·che·ga·ray y Ei·za·guir·re (ā'chā·gä·rī' ē ā'thä·gir'rā), **José**, 1832–1916, Spanish dramatist and mathematician.

ech·e·lon (esh'ə·lon) n. 1. A troop, fleet, or airplane formation resembling a series of steps, in which each rank, ship, or airplane extends behind and slightly to the right or left of the preceding one. 2. *Mil.* **a** One of the different fractions of a command arranged from front to rear, to which a particular combat mission is assigned: assault *echelon*; support *echelon*. **b** One of the various subdivisions from front to rear of a military headquarters: forward *echelon*; rear *echelon*. **c** Level of command: command *echelon*; subordinate *echelon*. 3. *Optics* A diffraction grating made of glass plates forming a stair-like pattern. — *v.t. & v.i.* To form in echelon. [< F *échelon* < *échelle* ladder < L *scala*]

e·chid·na (i·kid'nə) n. pl. **·nae** (-nē) An egg-laying monotreme (family *Tachyglossidae*) of Australia, Tasmania, and New Guinea, having a wormlike tongue, long snout, digging claws, and strong spines intermixed with fur: also called *porcupine anteater*, *spiny anteater*. [< NL < Gk., viper]

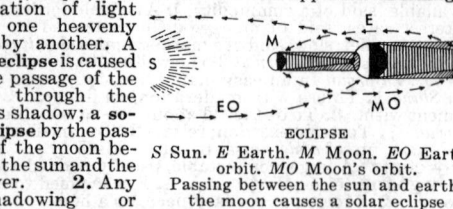

ECHIDNA
(About 15 inches long)

ech·i·na·ce·a (ek/ə·nā/shē·ə) n. Any of a genus (*Echinacea*) of hardy perennial plants of the composite family native in the United States. [< NL < Gk. *echinos* hedgehog]

ech·i·nate (ek/ə·nāt) adj. Set or armed thickly with prickles; bristly; spiny. Also **ech/i·nat/ed.**

e·chi·ni·form (i·kī/nə·fôrm) adj. Resembling a sea urchin.

echino- *combining form* Spiny; prickly: *echinoderm*. Also **echin-** (before vowels), **echini-.** [< Gk. *echinos* hedgehog]

e·chi·no·derm (i·kī/nə·dûrm) *Zool.* n. Any of a phylum (*Echinodermata*) of marine animals characterized by radial symmetry, calcareous exoskeletons, provided usually with spiny processes, body cavities, and a well-developed digestive system, including the starfishes, sea cucumbers, and sea urchins. — adj. Of or pertaining to the *Echinodermata*.

e·chi·no·der·mal (i·kī/nə·dûr/məl) adj. Having the surface of the body covered with spines.

e·chi·noid (i·kī/noid) n. A sea urchin. — adj. Echiniform.

e·chi·nus (i·kī/nəs) n. pl. **·ni** (-nī) 1. *Archit.* The cushion-like molding below the abacus in the capital of a Doric column, or the corresponding part in some other order. For illustration see CAPITAL². 2. A sea urchin. [< L < Gk. *echinos* hedgehog, sea urchin]

ech·o (ek/ō) n. pl. **ech·oes** 1. The repetition of a sound by the reflection of sound waves from an opposing surface; also, the sound so produced. 2. The repetition or reproduction of the views, style, etc., of another. 3. One who imitates another or repeats his words. 4. Prompt, sympathetic response. 5. *Telecom.* A retarded sound wave in radio reception, received in addition to or later than the expected one. 6. *Music* **a** The repetition in a softer tone of a note or phrase. **b** An echo stop. **c** An echo organ. 7. In poetry, the repetition of certain syllables or sounds; also, a refrain. 8. In whist and bridge, a signal to one's partner by the play of a high card and subsequently of a lower card of the same suit. — v.t. 1. To repeat or send back (sound) by echo: The walls *echoed* the shot. 2. To repeat the words, opinions, etc., of. 3. To repeat (words, opinions, etc.) in imitation of another. — v.i. 4. To give back sound; reverberate. 5. To be repeated or given back. [< L < Gk. *ēchō* < *ēche* sound, noise] — **ech'o·er** n.

Ech·o (ek/ō) In Greek mythology, a nymph who, because of love for Narcissus, pined away until only her voice was left.

e·cho·ic (e·kō/ik) adj. 1. Formed in imitation of natural sounds; onomatopoeic. 2. Like an echo.

ech·o·ism (ek/ō·iz/əm) n. The formation of words by the repetition or imitation of natural sounds; onomatopoeia.

ech·o·la·li·a (ek/ō·lā/lē·ə) n. *Psychiatry* The senseless repetition of words. [< NL < Gk. *echō* echo + *lalein* to babble]

ech·o·lo·ca·tion (ek/ō·lō·kā/shən) n. *Electronics* The determination of the distance and position of objects by the interpretation of sound waves transmitted to and returned from them. Also **ech·o·la·tion** (ek/ō·lā/shən).

echo organ A group of pipes or stops of a pipe organ, set apart from the main instrument and enclosed for echo effects.

echo stop On a pipe organ, a stop with pipes enclosed so as to echo the tones produced.

echo verse A poetic form wherein a line starts with the terminal syllable or syllables of the preceding line.

Eck (ek), **Johann,** 1486–1543, German Roman Catholic theologian; opponent of Luther: original name **Johann Mayer.**

Eck·hart (ek/härt), **Johannes,** 1260?–1327?, German theologian and mystic: called **Meister Eckhart.** Also **Eck/ardt.**

ECLA Economic Commission for Latin America.

é·clair (ā·klâr/, i·klâr/) n. A small oblong pastry shell filled with custard or whipped cream and usually iced with chocolate. [< F, lit., flash of lightning]

é·clair·cisse·ment (ā·klâr·sēs·män/) n. *French* A clearing up of something obscure; a full explanation.

ec·lamp·si·a (ek·lamp/sē·ə) n. *Pathol.* A sudden convulsive seizure, especially during pregnancy or childbirth. [< NL < Gk. *eklampsis* shining forth, sudden development < *ek-* forth + *lampein* to shine]

é·clat (ā·klä/, i·klä/) n. 1. Brilliance of action or effect; conspicuous success. 2. Splendor of reputation; renown; also, notoriety. 3. Acclaim. [< F < *éclater* to burst out]

ec·lec·tic (ek·lek/tik, ik-) adj. 1. Selecting what is considered best from different systems or sources. 2. Composed of elements selected from diverse sources. — n. One favoring no particular belief or practice, as in philosophy or art, but selecting from all. [< Gk. *eklektikos* < *ek-* out + *legein* to select] — **ec·lec/ti·cal·ly** adv. — **ec·lec/ti·cism** n.

e·clipse (i·klips/) n. 1. *Astron.* The apparent dimming or elimination of light from one heavenly body by another. A **lunar eclipse** is caused by the passage of the moon through the earth's shadow; a **solar eclipse** by the passage of the moon between the sun and the observer. 2. Any overshadowing or dimming, as of power or reputation. — v.t. **e·clipsed, e·clips·ing** 1. To cause an eclipse of; darken. 2. To obscure the beauty, fame, worth, etc., of; overshadow; surpass. [< OF < L *eclipsis* < Gk. *ekleipsis* < *ek-* out + *leipein* to leave]

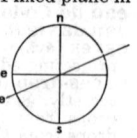

ECLIPSE

S Sun. *E* Earth. *M* Moon. *EO* Earth's orbit. *MO* Moon's orbit.
Passing between the sun and earth, the moon causes a solar eclipse total to observers within the umbra (vertically shaded portions) of the moon's shadow and partial to those within the penumbra (diagonally shaded portions). Passing into the earth's shadow, the moon undergoes partial or total eclipse.

e·clip·sis (i·klip/sis) n. pl. **·ses** (-sēz) or **·sis·es** 1. Ellipsis. 2. In the Celtic languages, a phonetic change undergone by the initial consonant of a word under the influence of a preceding word or form. [< L. See ECLIPSE.]

e·clip·tic (i·klip/tik, ē-) n. 1. *Astron.* **a** The plane, passing through the center of the sun, that contains the orbit of the earth: also called **plane of the ecliptic.** Compare illustration for TROPIC. **b** The great circle in which this plane intersects the celestial sphere; the apparent path of the sun around the celestial sphere. 2. A great circle on a terrestrial globe drawn tangent to the tropics, used when a terrestrial globe is employed for a celestial. — **fixed ecliptic** A fixed plane in the position of the ecliptic at some standard epoch. — adj. Pertaining to eclipses or to the ecliptic: also **e·clip/ti·cal.** — **e·clip/ti·cal·ly** adv.

ec·lo·gite (ek/lə·jīt) n. A rock consisting of red garnet, greenish pyroxene, and emerald-green smaragdite. [< Gk. *eklogē* selection < *ek-* out + *legein* to select]

ec·logue (ek/lôg, -log) n. A short pastoral poem; bucolic; especially, a pastoral dialogue. [< F *éclogue* < L *ecloga* < Gk. *eklogē.* See ECLOGITE.]

PLANE OF THE ECLIPTIC (pe)

n, s North, south poles.
e Equator.
ns Greenwich meridian.

ecol. Ecological; ecology.

é·cole (ā·kôl/) n. *French* School.

e·col·o·gy (i·kol/ə·jē, ē-) n. 1. The division of biology that treats of the relations between organisms and their environment: also called *bionomics*. 2. *Sociol.* The study of human populations in terms of physical environment, spatial distribution, and cultural characteristics. [< Gk. *oikos* home + -LOGY] — **ec·o·log·ic** (ek/ə·loj/ik) or **·i·cal** adj. — **ec/o·log/i·cal·ly** adv. — **e·col/o·gist** n.

econ. Economic; economics; economy.

e·con·o·met·rics (i·kon/ə·met/riks) n. pl. (construed as sing.) The use of statistical and mathematical methods for developing and testing economic theories. [< ECONO(MY) + METRICS] — **e·con·o·met·ric** or **·ri·cal** adj.

ec·o·nom·ic (ek/ə·nom/ik, ē/kə-) adj. 1. Of or pertaining to the development and management of the material wealth of a government or community: the French *economic* policy. 2. Relating to the science of economics: *economic* theory. 3. Of or pertaining to financial matters. 4. Of practical use or application; utilitarian. Abbr. *econ.* [< L *oeconomicus* < Gk. *oikonomia.* See ECONOMY.]

ec·o·nom·i·cal (ek/ə·nom/i·kəl, ē/kə-) adj. 1. Prudent in management; frugal. 2. Economic. — Syn. See FRUGAL.

ec·o·nom·i·cal·ly (ek/ə·nom/ik·lē, ē/kə-) adv. 1. In a thrifty manner. 2. From an economic standpoint.

economic determinism The theory that all human activities and institutions have economic origins.

economic geography A division of geography that deals with the relationship between natural resources and human economic activity.

ec·o·nom·ics (ek/ə·nom/iks, ē/kə-) n.pl. 1. (construed as sing.) The science that treats of the production, distribution, and consumption of wealth, and of the means of supplying the material needs of mankind. Abbr. *econ.* 2. Economic questions or matters.

e·con·o·mist (i·kon/ə·mist) n. 1. One who is proficient in economics. 2. One who is careful and thrifty.

e·con·o·mize (i·kon/ə·mīz) v. **·mized, ·miz·ing** v.i. 1. To be sparing in expenditure; manage thriftily. — v.t. 2. To use sparingly or to best advantage. Also *Brit.* **e·con'o·mise.** — e·con'o·miz'er *n.*

e·con·o·my (i·kon'ə·mē) *n. pl.* **·mies 1.** Frugal management of money, materials, resources, and the like; freedom from extravagance; thrift: *economy* of words; also, an example of this. **2.** The practical administration of the material resources of a country, community, or establishment: the national *economy*; also, a particular system for developing and managing material resources: a slave *economy.* **3.** The orderly distribution and interplay of parts in a structure or system: the *economy* of nature. **4.** *Theol.* **a** The divine plan of creation and redemption. **b** Any specific method or era of divine government. Abbr. *econ.* [< L *oeconomia* < Gk. *oikonomia* < *oikos* house + *nemein* to manage]

ECOSOC Economic and Social Council (of the UN).

e·co·spe·cies (ē'kō·spē'shēz, ek'ə-) *n. Ecol.* A species of plant, natural or cultivated, interfertile, and highly adapted to its habitat. [< Gk. *oikos* home + SPECIES]

eco·sys·tem (ek'ō·sis'təm) *n. Ecol.* The basic unit in ecology, including both the organisms and the nonliving environment. [< Gk. *oikos* home + SYSTEM]

e·co·tone (ē'kō·tōn, ek'ə-) *n. Ecol.* The zone wherein two different forms of vegetable life contend for dominance; a transition area between two communities. [< Gk. *oikos* home + *tonos* stress, tension]

e·co·type (ē'kə·tīp, ek'ə-) *n. Ecol.* A subspecies or variety adapted to specific environmental conditions. [< ECO- + TYPE] — **ec·o·typ·ic** (ek'ə·tīp'ik) *adj.* — **ec'o·tip'i·cal·ly** *adv.*

é·cra·seur (ā·krä·zœr') *n. Surg.* An instrument in the form of a fine chain, wire, or cord, for tightening around a tumor, etc., as a means of removal. [< F < *écraser* to crush]

ec·ru (ek'rōō, ā'krōō) *adj.* Of the color of unbleached linen. — *n.* **1.** The color of unbleached linen; a light, yellowish brown. **2.** Goods made of unbleached linen. Also **é'cru.** [< F *écru* < OF *escru* < L *ex-* thoroughly + *crudus* raw]

ECSC European Coal and Steel Community.

ec·sta·sy (ek'stə·sē) *n. pl.* **·sies 1.** The state of being beside oneself through some overpowering emotion: in an *ecstasy* of anticipation. **2.** Intense delight; rapture: dissolved in *ecstasy.* **3.** A trance or frenzy thought to attend prophetic, mystic, or poetic inspiration. — **Syn.** See PLEASURE. [< OF *extasie* < LL *ecstasis* < Gk. *ekstasis* displacement < *ek-* out + *histanai* to place]

ec·stat·ic (ek·stat'ik) *adj.* **1.** Pertaining to, of the nature of, or exciting to ecstasy; rapturous. **2.** In a state of ecstasy; transported; enraptured. Also **ec·stat'i·cal.** — *n.* **1.** A person subject to ecstasies or trances. **2.** *pl.* Rapturous emotions; transports. — **ec·stat'i·cal·ly** *adv.*

ec·thy·ma (ek·thī'mə) *n. pl.* **·thym·a·ta** (-thim'ə·tə) *Pathol.* A virus disease characterized by the formation on the skin of ulcerating pustules whose discharge produces vesicular lesions. [< Gk. *ekthyma* blister < *ek-* out + *thyein* to seethe]

ecto- *combining form* Without; outside; external: *ectoderm.* Also, before vowels, **ect-.** [< Gk. *ekto-* < *ektos* outside]

ec·to·blast (ek'tə·blast) *n. Biol.* The embryonic stage of the ectoderm. [< ECTO- + -BLAST] — **ec'to·blas'tic** *adj.*

ec·to·derm (ek'tə·dûrm) *n. Biol.* The outermost of the three primary germ layers in the embryo of metazoan animals, developing into the skin, sense organs, and nervous system: also *epiblast.* Compare ENDODERM, MESODERM. [< ECTO- + -DERM] — **ec'to·der'mal, ec'to·der'mic** *adj.*

ec·to·en·zyme (ek'tō·en'zīm, -zim) *n. Biochem.* An enzyme functioning outside of the cell and acting directly upon the surrounding blood or tissue: opposed to *endoenzyme.* Also called *exoenzyme.* Also **ec'to·en'zym** (-zim).

ec·tog·e·nous (ek·toj'ə·nəs) *adj. Biol.* Capable of development outside of the host, as certain bacteria. Also **ec·to·gen·ic** (ek'tə·jen'ik). [< ECTO- + -GENOUS]

ec·to·mere (ek'tə·mir) *n. Biol.* One of the blastomeres derived from the ovum during the development of the ectoderm. [< ECTO- + -MERE] — **ec'to·mer'ic** (-mer'ik) *adj.*

ec·to·morph (ek'tə·môrf) *n.* An ectomorphic person.

ec·to·mor·phic (ek'tə·môr'fik) *adj.* Characterized by a lean body structure as developed from the ectodermal layer of the embryo, associated with a predominance of the nervous system. [< ECTO- + -MORPHIC] — **ec'to·mor'phy** *n.*

-ectomy *combining form* Removal of a part by cutting out: used in surgical terms to indicate certain kinds of operations: *appendectomy.* [< Gk. *ektomē* < *ek-* out + *temnein* to cut]

ec·to·par·a·site (ek'tō·par'ə·sīt) *n. Biol.* A parasite that lives upon the exterior of its host, as a louse.

ec·to·pi·a (ek·tō'pē·ə) *n. Pathol.* Displacement of parts or organs, especially when congenital. [< NL < Gk. *ek-* out, from + *topos* place] — **ec·top·ic** (ek·top'ik) *adj.*

ectopic pregnancy *Pathol.* Development of the embryo and fetus outside of the womb, as in a Fallopian tube.

ec·to·plasm (ek'tə·plaz'əm) *n.* **1.** *Biol.* The firm outer layer of the cytoplasm of a unicellular organism or of a plant cell. **2.** The substance alleged to emanate from the body of a spiritualist medium during a trance: also called *teleplasm.* [< ECTO- + -PLASM] — **ec'to·plas'mic** *adj.*

ec·to·sarc (ek'tə·särk) *n. Biol.* The ectoplasm of protozoans. [< ECTO- + Gk. *sarx* flesh]

ec·tos·to·sis (ek'tos·tō'sis) *n. Pathol.* Ossification around the exterior of a cartilage. [< ECT(O)- + OST(EO)- + -OSIS]

ec·type (ek'tīp) *n.* An imitation or reproduction of an original: opposed to *prototype.* [< Gk. *ektypos* < *ek-* out + *typos* impression < *typtein* to strike] — **ec·ty·pal** (ek'tə·pəl) *adj.*

é·cu (ā·kü') *n. pl.* **é·cus** (ā·kü'). **1.** Any of several French gold or silver coins of varying value, especially a silver coin of the 17th and 18th centuries. **2.** A small triangular shield carried by a mounted man-at-arms in the Middle Ages. [< F, orig., shield < L *scutum*]

Ecua. Ecuador.

Ec·ua·dor (ek'wə·dôr, *Sp.* ā'kwä·thôr') A Republic in NW South America; 104,306 sq. mi.; pop. 6,144,000 (est. 1970); capital, Quito: officially **Republic of Ecuador.** See map of AMAZON. — **Ec'ua·do'ri·an** or **Ec'ua·do're·an** *adj. & n.*

ec·u·men·i·cal (ek'yōō·men'i·kəl) *adj.* **1.** World-wide in scope or application; general; universal. **2.** Belonging to, representing, or accepted by the Christian church throughout the world: an *ecumenical* council. **3.** Of, desiring, or promoting world-wide Christian unity: an *ecumenical* movement. Also spelled *oecumenical*: also **ec'u·men'ic.** [< LL *oecūmenicus* < Gk. *oikoumenikos* < *oikeein* to inhabit] — **ec'u·men'i·cal·ly** *adv.*

ec·u·men·ism (ek'yōō·men'iz·əm) *n.* The beliefs, principles, or practices of those who desire and work for world-wide unity and cooperation among all Christian churches. Also **ec'u·men'i·cal·ism** (ek'yōō·men'ə·kəl·iz·əm), **ec'u·men'i·cism** (ek'yōō·men'ə·siz'əm).

ec·ze·ma (ek'sə·mə, eg'zə·mə, eg·zē'mə) *n. Pathol.* An inflammatory disease of the skin attended by itching, watery discharge, and the appearance of lesions. [< Gk. *ekzema* < *ek-* out + *zeein* to boil] — **ec·zem·a·tous** (eg·zem'ə·təs) *adj.*

ed. (*pl.* **eds.**) **1.** Edited. **2.** Edition. **3.** Editor.

-ed[1] *suffix* Forming the past tense of regular verbs: *walked, killed, played.* [OE *-ede, -ode, -ade*]

-ed[2] *suffix* **1.** Forming the past participle of regular verbs: *clothed, washed.* **2.** Forming adjectives from adjectives in *-ate,* with the same general meaning: *bipinnated.* [OE *-ed, -ad, -od*]

-ed[3] *suffix* Forming adjectives from nouns, with the senses: **1.** Having; possessing; characterized by: *toothed, green-eyed.* **2.** Like; resembling: *bigoted.* [OE *-ede*]

e·da·cious (i·dā'shəs) *adj.* Given to eating; voracious. [< L *edax, edacis* < *edere* to eat] — **e·da'cious·ly** *adv.*

e·dac·i·ty (i·das'ə·tē) *n.* Excess in eating; gluttony.

Edam (ē'dam, ē'dam) A commune and port in the NW Netherlands, on the Ijsselmeer; pop. 13,168 (est. 1956).

Edam cheese A mild curd cheese, originally from Edam, in a round, flattened shape usually coated with red paraffin.

e·daph·ic (i·daf'ik) *adj. Ecol.* Pertaining to or affected by the soil rather than the climate. [< Gk. *edaphos* soil]

Ed.B. Bachelor of Education.

Ed.D. Doctor of Education.

Ed·da (ed'ə) *n.* Either of two collections of Old Icelandic, or Old Norse, literature: the **Elder** or **Poetic Edda,** a collection of mythological and heroic poetry of the 10th–13th centuries; and the **Younger** or **Prose Edda,** a commentary on Norse mythology and composition by Snorri Sturluson. [< ON] — **Ed·da·ic** (e·dā'ik), **Ed'dic** *adj.*

Ed·ding·ton (ed'ing·tən), **Sir Arthur Stanley,** 1882–1944, English mathematician, astronomer, and astrophysicist.

ed·dy (ed'ē) *n. pl.* **·dies 1.** A backward-circling current of water or air; whirlpool. **2.** Figuratively, a turning aside or departure from the main current of thought or life. — *v.t. & v.i.* **·died, ·dy·ing** To move, or cause to move, in or as in an eddy. [Prob. < ON *idha*]

Ed·dy (ed'ē), **Mary Baker,** 1821–1910, *née* Mary Morse Baker, U.S. religious leader; founder of Christian Science.

Ed·dy·stone Rocks (ed'i·stōn') A dangerous reef in the English Channel, 14 miles SW of Plymouth; site of **Eddystone lighthouse;** height, 133 ft.; visible for 17 mi.

e·del·weiss (ā'dəl·vīs) *n.* A small, perennial herb (*Leontopodium alpinum*) of the composite family, growing chiefly in the Alps, with white, woolly leaves suggesting a flower. [< G *edel* noble + *weiss* white]

e·de·ma (i·dē'mə) *n. pl.* **·ma·ta** (-mə·tə) *Pathol.* An abnormal accumulation of serous fluid in various organs, cavities, or tissues of the body; swelling: also spelled *oedema.* [< NL < Gk. *oidēma* a tumor < *oidein* to swell] — **e·dem·a·tous** (i·dem'ə·təs), **e·dem'a·tose** (-tōs) *adj.*

EDELWEISS
(To 4 inches high)

E·den (ēd'n) *n.* **1.** In the Bible, the garden that was the first home of Adam and Eve: often called *Paradise.* **2.** Any delightful region or abode; a paradise. **3.** A state of perfect bliss. [< Hebrew *ēden* delight]

E·den (ēd'n), **Sir (Robert) Anthony,** 1897–1977, English statesman; prime minister 1955–57.

e·den·tate (ē·den'tāt, i·den'-) *adj.* **1.** Of or pertaining to an order of placental mammals (*Edentata* or *Xenarthra*), some of which lack teeth, including sloths, anteaters, and armadillos. **2.** Toothless. — *n.* One of the *Edentata*. [< L *edentatus* < *e-* without + *dens, dentis* tooth]

e·den·tu·lous (ē-den'choo-ləs, i-den'-) *adj.* Having no teeth. Also **e·den'tu·late** (-lit, -lāt).

E·des·sa (i-des'ə) The ancient name for URFA.

Ed·fu (ed'foo) See IDFU.

Ed·gar (ed'gər) See table for ENGLAND.

edge (ej) *n.* **1.** A bounding or dividing line; also, the part along a boundary; border; margin: the *edge* of a lawn. **2.** A verge or brink; rim: the *edge* of a cliff. **3.** The line where two surfaces of a solid meet: the *edge* of a cube. **4.** The thin, sharp, cutting side of a blade. **5.** Sharpness; keenness: to give *edge* to an appetite. **6.** *U.S. Informal* Advantage; superiority: Our team has the *edge* on them. — **Syn.** See BOUNDARY. — **on edge 1.** Keenly sensitive; tense; irritable. **2.** Eager; impatient. — *v.* **edged, edg·ing** *v.t.* **1.** To sharpen. **2.** To furnish with an edge or border. **3.** To push sidewise or by degrees: to *edge* one's way — *v.i.* **4.** To move sidewise or by degrees. [OE *ecg*] — **edge'less** *adj.*

edged (ejd) *adj.* **1.** Having an edge or edges, as a cutting tool. **2.** Having or characterized by a (specified kind of) edge or (a specified number of) edges: used in combination: *keen-edged, two-edged.*

Edge·hill (ej'hil') A ridge in southern Warwickshire, England; site of a battle between Charles I and Parliamentary forces, 1642. Also **Edge Hill.**

edge tool A sharp, cutting tool, as a chisel.

edge·wise (ej'wīz') *adv.* **1.** With the edge forward. **2.** On, by, with, or toward the edge. Also **edge'ways** (-wāz').

Edge·worth (ej'wərth), **Maria,** 1767–1849, English novelist.

edg·ing (ej'ing) *n.* Something serving as or attached to an edge; trimming; border.

edg·y (ej'ē) *adj.* **edg·i·er, edg·i·est 1.** Tense, nervous, or irritable. **2.** Having a sharp edge. **3.** Having outlines that are too sharp, as a piece of sculpture. — **edg'i·ness** *n.*

edh (eth) *n.* The name of the letter ð, capital Ð, used in Old English to represent both voiceless *th*, as in *thin*, and voiced *th*, as in *then*, and in Icelandic and the International Phonetic Alphabet to represent voiced *th*: also spelled *eth.* Compare THORN (def. 5).

ed·i·ble (ed'ə-bəl) *adj.* Fit to eat. — *n.* Usually *pl.* Something suitable for food. [< LL *edibilis* < L *edere* to eat] — **ed'i·bil'i·ty, ed'i·ble·ness** *n.*

e·dict (ē'dikt) *n.* **1.** An official decree publicly proclaimed. **2.** Any formal command or prohibition. [< L *edictum*, pp. neut. of *edicere* to proclaim < *e-* out + *dicere* to say] — **e·dic·tal** (ē-dik'təl) *adj.* — **dic'tal·ly** *adv.*

ed·i·fi·ca·tion (ed'ə-fə-kā'shən) *n.* Intellectual or moral enlightenment and improvement. [< L *aedificatio, -onis* < *aedificare.* See EDIFY.]

ed·i·fice (ed'ə-fis) *n.* A building or other structure, especially one that is large and imposing. [< F *édifice* < L *aedificium* < *aedes* building + *facere* to make] — **ed·i·fi·cial** (ed'ə-fish'əl) *adj.*

ed·i·fy (ed'ə-fī) *v.t.* **·fied, ·fy·ing** To enlighten and benefit, especially morally or spiritually. [< OF *edifier* < L *aedificare* < *aedes* building + *facere* to make] — **ed'i·fi'er** *n.*

ed·i·fy·ing (ed'ə-fī'ing) *adj.* That enlightens and uplifts; instructive, as by good example. — **ed'i·fy'ing·ly** *adv.*

e·dile (ē'dīl) See AEDILE.

E·di·na (i-dī'nə) A city in SE Minnesota, near Minneapolis; pop. 44,046.

Ed·in·burgh (ed'ən-bûr'ə) The capital of Scotland, in the eastern part on the Firth of Forth; pop. 465,421 (1969): Scottish Gaelic *Dunedin.*

E·dir·ne (e-dir'ne) See ADRIANOPLE.

Ed·i·son (ed'ə-sən) An urban township in eastern New Jersey; pop. 67,120.

Ed·i·son (ed'ə-sən), **Thomas Alva,** 1847–1931, U.S. inventor.

ed·it (ed'it) *v.t.* **1.** To correct and prepare for publication: to *edit* a manuscript. **2.** To compile, arrange, and emend for publication: to *edit* a collection of poems. **3.** To direct the preparation, publication, and editorial policies of (a newspaper, magazine, etc.). [Back formation < EDITOR]

edit. **1.** Edited. **2.** Edition. **3.** Editor.

e·di·tion (i-dish'ən) *n.* **1.** The particular form in which a book, magazine, or other literary work is published: a three-volume *edition.* **2.** The total number of copies of a publication issued at any one time and printed from the same plates, etc.: a new *edition*; the morning *edition*: also, a copy belonging to this printing: a first *edition.* Abbr. **ed., edit.** [< F < L *editio, -onis* < *edere* < *e-* out + *dare* to give]

e·di·ti·o prin·ceps (i-dish'ē-ō prin'seps) *Latin* A first edition.

ed·i·tor (ed'i-tər) *n.* **1.** One who edits manuscript, copy, etc., for publication. **2.** One in charge of a publication or of one of its departments: a newspaper *editor*; the book *editor* of a magazine. **3.** A writer of editorials. Abbr. *ed., edit.* [< L]

ed·i·to·ri·al (ed'i-tôr'ē·əl, -tō'rē-) *n.* An article in a newspaper, magazine, or the like, published as the periodical's official expression of opinion on some issue. — *adj.* **1.** Of or pertaining to an editor or editing: *editorial* policy. **2.** Writ-

ten or approved by an editor: the *editorial* page of a newspaper. **3.** Used by or expressed in the manner of an editor: the *editorial* plural; *editorial* comment.

ed·i·to·ri·al·ize (ed'i·tôr'ē·əl·īz', -tō'rē-) *v.t. & v.i.* **·ized, ·iz·ing 1.** To express opinions (on a subject) editorially. **2.** To insert editorial opinions (into a news item, etc.).

ed·i·to·ri·al·ly (ed'i·tôr'ē·əl·ē, -tō'rē-) *adv.* **1.** In the capacity or manner of an editor. **2.** In an editorial.

editorial plural The editorial "we"; the first person plural substituted for the first person singular.

editor in chief *pl.* **editors in chief** The chief editor of a publication, who establishes its policy and supervises operations.

ed·i·tor·ship (ed'i-tər-ship') *n.* The position, functions, or direction of an editor.

Ed. M. Master of Education.

Ed·mon·ton (ed'mən-tən) **1.** The capital of Alberta, Canada, in the central part of the province; pop. 434,116. **2.** A municipal borough in Middlesex, England, near London; pop. 92,062 (1961).

Ed·mund I (ed'mund) See table for ENGLAND.

Edmund II, 989?–1016, king of Wessex 1016: called **Ironside.**

E·do (e-dō) A former name for TOKYO.

E·dom (ē'dəm) An ancient country SE of Palestine: also called *Idumaea, Idumea.*

E·dom (ē'dəm) In the Old Testament, Esau. *Gen.* xxv 30.

E·dom·ite (ē'dəm·īt) *n.* **1.** A descendant of Esau. **2.** An inhabitant of Edom. — **E'dom·it'ish** (-ī'tish) *adj.*

EDP Electronic data processing.

Ed·red (ed'rəd) See table for ENGLAND.

EDT or **E.D.T.** or **e.d.t.** Eastern daylight time.

educ. Education; educational.

ed·u·ca·ble (ej'oo-kə-bəl) *adj.* Capable of being educated. [< EDUC(ATE) + -ABLE]

ed·u·cate (ej'oo-kāt) *v.t.* **·cat·ed, ·cat·ing 1.** To develop or train the mind, capabilities, or character of by instruction or study; give knowledge or skill to; teach. **2.** To train for some special purpose: He was *educated* for the ministry. **3.** To develop or train (taste, special ability, etc.). **4.** To provide schooling for. [< L *educatus*, pp. of *educare* to bring up < *educere* See EDUCE.]

ed·u·cat·ed (ej'oo-kā'tid) *adj.* **1.** Developed and informed by education; instructed trained. **2.** Having a cultivated mind, speech, manner, etc.

ed·u·ca·tion (ej'oo-kā'shən) *n.* **1.** The act of educating; systematic development or training of the mind, capabilities, or character through instruction or study. **2.** Acquisition of knowledge or skills; especially, formal schooling in an institution of learning. **3.** Knowledge, skills, or cultivation acquired through instruction or study. **4.** The study of teaching methods and problems, the learning process, and other matters related to the classroom; pedagogy. Abbr. *educ.*

— **Syn.** *Education, instruction, training, discipline,* and *schooling* refer to the imparting of knowledge and skill. *Education* is the development and cultivation of the innate powers of the mind; *instruction,* the giving of information and guidance. *Education* may be gained by one's own efforts, but *instruction* is always imparted by another. *Training* is *education* aimed at producing a particular ability or character: military *training. Discipline* is rigorous and systematic *training,* with the idea of subjection to authority and perhaps of punishment. *Schooling* is formal *training,* such as that received in a school or college.

ed·u·ca·tion·al (ej'oo-kā'shən-əl) *adj.* **1.** Of or pertaining to education. **2.** Imparting education: an *educational* trip. Abbr. *educ.* — **ed'u·ca'tion·al·ly** *adv.*

ed·u·ca·tion·al·ist (ej'oo-kā'shən-əl-ist) *n.* A specialist in the field of education. Also **ed'u·ca'tion·ist.**

ed·u·ca·tive (ej'oo-kā'tiv) *adj.* **1.** That educates or tends to educate; educational. **2.** Of or relating to education.

ed·u·ca·tor (ej'oo-kā'tər) *n.* **1.** A teacher or school administrator. **2.** An educationalist.

ed·u·ca·to·ry (ej'oo-kə-tôr'ē, -tō'rē) *adj.* Educative.

e·duce (i-doos', i-dyoos') *v.t.* **e·duced, e·duc·ing 1.** To call forth; bring out; elicit. **2.** To infer or develop from data; deduce. [< L *educere* < *e-* out + *ducere* to lead] — **e·duc'i·ble** *adj.*

e·duct (ē'dukt) *n.* **1.** That which is educed. **2.** A substance derived without chemical change from another: distinguished from *product.* [< L *eductum* < *educere.* See EDUCE.]

e·duc·tion (i-duk'shən) *n.* **1.** The act or process of educing. **2.** An educt. — **e·duc'tive** *adj.*

e·dul·co·rate (i-dul'kə-rāt) *v.t.* **·rat·ed, ·rat·ing 1.** To sweeten or soften. **2.** *Chem.* To cleanse or free from soluble acids, salts, etc., by washing with water. [< LL *edulcoratus*, pp. of *edulcorare* < *e-* out + *dulcorare* to sweeten < *dulcor* sweetness < *dulcis* sweet] — **e·dul'co·ra'tion** *n.* — **e·dul'co·ra'tive** *adj.*

Ed·ward (ed'wərd), 870?–924, king of the West Saxons 901–924; son of Alfred the Great: called **the Elder.** Also *Eadward, Eadweard.*

Edward, 963–978, king of the West Saxons 975–978; murdered: called **the Martyr.** Also *Eadward.*

Edward, 1004?–66, king of England 1042–66: called the **Confessor.**

Edward, 1330–76, Prince of Wales; son of Edward III; fought at Crécy and Poitiers: called the *Black Prince.*

Edward I, 1239–1307, king of England 1272–1307: called **Edward Long·shanks** (lông′shangks′, long′-).

Edward II, 1284–1327, king of England 1307–27; defeated by Robert the Bruce at Bannockburn.

Edward III, 1312–77, king of England 1327–77; defeated the Scots and French.

Edward IV, 1442–83, king of England 1461–70, 1471–83; overthrew the Lancastrians.

Edward V, 1470–83, king of England 1483; murdered in the Tower of London.

Edward VI, 1537–53, king of England 1547–53; son of Henry VIII and Jane Seymour.

Edward VII, 1841–1910, king of England 1901–10; called **the Peacemaker.**

Edward VIII, 1894–1972, succeeded his father George V as king of England, Jan. 20, 1936; abdicated Dec. 10, 1936; became the Duke of Windsor.

Edward, Lake A lake in Africa between the Republic of Zaire and Uganda; 830 sq. mi. Also **Edward Ny·an·za** (nī·an′zə, nē-; nyän′zə).

Ed·ward·i·an (ed·wôr′dē·ən) *adj.* Of, relating to, or typical of the reigns of any of the English kings named Edward; especially, stiffly ornate, highly mannered, or overly genteel in a manner often associated with the times of Edward VII.

Ed·wards (ed′wərdz), **Jonathan,** 1703–58, American theologian and philosopher.

Ed·win (ed′win), 585?–633, king of Northumbria 617–633.

Ed·wy (ed′wē) See table for ENGLAND.

e.e. Errors excepted.

-ee *suffix of nouns* **1.** One who undergoes, or benefits from, some action: used especially in legal terms, and opposed to *-er, -or,* as in *grantor, grantee.* **2.** One who is described by the main element: *absentee.* [< AF *-é,* suffix of pp. < L *-atus*]

E.E. **1.** Early English. **2.** Electrical Engineer; electrical engineering.

E.E. & M.P. Envoy Extraordinary and Minister Plenipotentiary.

E.E.C. or **EEC** European Economic Community.

EEG *Med.* Electroencephalogram.

eel (ēl) *n. pl.* **eels** or **eel 1.** A teleost fish (order *Apodes*), having a snakelike body, usually without scales or pelvic fins, and of both marine and fresh-water habitat; especially, the **American eel** (*Anguilla rostrata*), and the **European eel** (*A. anguilla*). **2.** Any of certain other fishes, as the lamprey and the electric eel. **3.** An eelworm. [OE *æl*] —**eel′y** *adj.*

eel·grass (ēl′gras′, -gräs′) *n.* An herb (*Zostera marina*) of the pondweed family, of grasslike appearance, growing wholly under water, used as a sound insulator, for packing, etc.

eel·pout (ēl′pout′) *n. pl.* **·pouts** or **·pout** Any of various marine fishes (family *Zoarcidae*) having an eellike body tapering backward; especially, *Zoarces anguillaris* of North America. **2.** The ocean pout (which see). [OE *ælepūta*]

eel·worm (ēl′wûrm′) *n.* **1.** A threadworm or nematode, especially *Ascaris lumbricoides,* parasitic in the human digestive tract. **2.** The vinegar eel.

e'en¹ (ēn) *adv. Poetic* Even.

e'en² (ēn) *n. Poetic & Dial.* Evening.

e'er (âr) *adv. Poetic* Ever.

-eer *suffix of nouns and verbs* **1.** One who is concerned with, works with, or makes something indicated: *engineer, profiteer.* **2.** Be concerned with; work at: *electioneer.* [< F *-ier* < L *-arius*]

ee·rie (ir′ē, ē′rē) *adj.* **1.** Inspiring fear; weird; ghostly. **2.** Affected by superstitious fear. Also **ee′ry.** [ME *eri* timid, var. of *erg* < OE *earg*] —**ee′ri·ly** *adv.* —**ee′ri·ness** *n.*

ef- Assimilated var. of EX-¹.

eff (ef) *n.* The letter F.

ef·fa·ble (ef′ə·bəl) *adj. Archaic* That can be uttered or expressed. [< L *effabilis* < *ex-* out + *fari* to speak]

ef·face (i·fās′) *v.t.* **·faced, ·fac·ing 1.** To rub out, as written characters; erase; cancel. **2.** To obliterate or destroy, as a memory. **3.** To make (oneself) inconspicuous or insignificant. —**Syn.** See CANCEL. [< F *effacer* < L *ex-* out + *facies* face] —**ef·face′a·ble** *adj.* —**ef·face′ment** *n.* —**ef·fac′er** *n.*

ef·fect (i·fekt′) *n.* **1.** Something brought about by some cause or agency; result; consequence: the *effect* of an explosion. **2.** Capacity to produce some result; efficacy: a statement of little *effect.* **3.** The state of being operative; condition or fact of being in active force: to put a law into *effect.* **4.** The state of being actually accomplished or realized: to carry plans into *effect.* **5.** The particular way in which something affects or influences something else: the *effect* of morphine on the body. **6.** The overall reaction or impression produced by something seen, heard, or done: the *effect* of a work of art. **7.** A technique used in art, literature, music, etc., to achieve a certain result or produce a distinctive impression. **8.** The actual or basic meaning intended or conveyed; purport: usually with *to:* She said something to that effect. **9.** *pl.* Movable goods; belongings. —**in effect**

1. In actual fact. **2.** For all practical purposes; virtually. **3.** In active force or operation. —**to take effect** To begin to act upon something; be or become operative. —*v.t.* To bring about; produce as a result; cause; especially, to accomplish; achieve: to *effect* an escape. ◆ *Effect,* to bring about, accomplish, should be carefully distinguished from *affect,* to act upon, influence: The course of treatment *effected* an early cure; Long illness has *affected* his mind. [< L *effectus,* pp. of *efficere* to bring about < *ex-* out + *facere* to do, make] —**ef·fect′er** *n.* —**ef·fect′i·ble** *adj.*
—**Syn.** (noun) **1.** *Effect, consequence, result, outcome,* and *upshot* refer to events or circumstances produced by some agency. *Effect* stresses most strongly the presence and force of an agency, since its correlative is cause. Popular usage often substitutes *consequence* for *effect,* though strictly a *consequence* is merely that which comes afterward in time, and is not necessarily connected causally with its antecedents. *Result* suggests finality, or that *effect* with which the operation of a cause terminates. *Outcome* suggests a *result* that makes visible or evident the working of an agency, and *upshot* suggests a decisive or climactic *result.* Compare CAUSE.

ef·fec·tive (i·fek′tiv) *adj.* **1.** Producing or adapted to produce the proper result; efficient: an *effective* instrument. **2.** Being in force; operative, as a law. **3.** Producing a striking impression; impressive: an *effective* speaker. **4.** Ready for action, as an army. —**Syn.** See EFFICIENT. —*n.* **1.** One who is fit for duty. **2.** The number of men available for military service. —**ef·fec′tive·ly** *adv.* —**ef·fec′tive·ness** *n.*

ef·fec·tor (i·fek′tər) *n. Physiol.* A specialized structure at the periphery of a motor nerve, as a muscle or gland, serving to transform efferent nerve impulses into physical action.

ef·fec·tu·al (i·fek′chōō·əl) *adj.* **1.** Producing or having adequate power to produce an intended effect; efficacious: *effectual* measures. **2.** Legally valid or binding. —**Syn.** See EFFICIENT. [< OF *effectuel* < LL *effectualis* < L *effectus.* See EFFECT.] —**ef·fec′tu·al·ness, ef·fec′tu·al′i·ty** (-al′ə·tē) *n.*

ef·fec·tu·al·ly (i·fek′chōō·əl·ē) *adv.* In an effectual manner; with the intended effect; thoroughly.

ef·fec·tu·ate (i·fek′chōō·āt) *v.t.* **·at·ed, ·at·ing** To bring about; accomplish; effect. [< F *effectuer* < L *effectus.* See EFFECT.] —**ef·fec′tu·a′tion** *n.*

ef·fem·i·na·cy (i·fem′ə·nə·sē) *n.* The state or quality of being effeminate.

ef·fem·i·nate (i·fem′ə·nit) *adj.* **1.** Having womanlike traits or qualities to a degree unbefitting a man; womanish; unmanly. **2.** Characterized by weakness or self-indulgence; soft: an *effeminate* civilization. —**Syn.** See FEMININE. [< L *effeminatus,* pp. of *effeminare* < *ex-* out + *femina* a woman] —**ef·fem′i·nate·ly** *adv.* —**ef·fem′i·nate·ness** *n.*

ef·fen·di (i·fen′dē) *n.* Sir; master: a title of respect in Turkey. [< Turkish *efendi,* ult. < Gk. *authentēs* master]

ef·fer·ent (ef′ər·ənt) *adj. Physiol.* Carrying or carried outward: said especially of impulses transmitted from the central nervous system to muscles, etc.; discharging: opposed to *afferent.* —*n.* **1.** *Physiol.* An efferent duct, vessel, or nerve. **2.** A stream carrying off water, as from a pond. [< L *efferens, -entis,* ppr. of *efferre* < *ex-* out + *ferre* to carry]

ef·fer·vesce (ef′ər·ves′) *v.i.* **·vesced, ·vesc·ing 1.** To give off bubbles of gas, as water charged with carbon dioxide. **2.** To issue out in bubbles, as a gas. **3.** To show exhilaration or lively spirits. [< L *effervescere* < *ex-* out + *fervescere* to boil, inceptive of *fervere* to be hot]

ef·fer·ves·cence (ef′ər·ves′əns) *n.* **1.** The act or state of bubbling up; foaming. **2.** Sparkling vivacity; gaiety; exuberance. Also **ef′fer·ves′cen·cy.** [< L *effervescens, -entis,* ppr. of *effervescere.* See EFFERVESCE.]

ef·fer·ves·cent (ef′ər·ves′ənt) *adj.* **1.** Giving off bubbles of gas; bubbling up. **2.** Vivacious; lively.

ef·fete (i·fēt′) *adj.* **1.** Having lost strength or virility; lacking vigor. **2.** Incapable of further production; barren, as an animal, plant, or the soil. [< L *effetus* worn out < *ex-* out + *fetus* a breeding] —**ef·fete′ly** *adv.* —**ef·fete′ness** *n.*

ef·fi·ca·cious (ef′ə·kā′shəs) *adj.* Producing or capable of producing an intended effect; having efficacy. —**Syn.** See EFFICIENT. [< L *efficax, -cacis* < *efficere.* See EFFECT.] —**ef′fi·ca′cious·ly** *adv.* —**ef′fi·ca′cious·ness** *n.*

ef·fi·ca·cy (ef′ə·kə·sē) *n. pl.* **·cies** Power to produce a desired or intended result.

ef·fi·cien·cy (i·fish′ən·sē) *n. pl.* **·cies 1.** The quality of being efficient; effectiveness. **2.** The ratio of the work done or energy expended by an organism or machine to the energy supplied in the form of food or fuel.

ef·fi·cient (i·fish′ənt) *adj.* **1.** Productive of results with a minimum of wasted effort. **2.** Producing an effect; causative. [< L *efficiens, -entis,* ppr. of *efficere.* See EFFECT.] —**ef·fi′cient·ly** *adv.*
—**Syn.** *Efficient, effective, effectual,* and *efficacious* mean successful in producing an effect or result. An *efficient* machine is one which has a relatively high ratio of output in work to input in energy. Similarly, an *efficient* person is competent or productive in a high degree upon some actual or imagined scale. An *effective* person or thing succeeds more or less in producing a desired effect.

Effectual is rarely applied to persons, but rather characterizes a thing which is completely successful in achieving a purpose: an *effectual* political machine. *Efficacious* is applied only to things and characterizes that which has the qualities or power to be *effectual*.

ef·fi·gy (ef'ə-jē) *n. pl.* **·gies** **1.** A likeness or representation; especially, a sculptured portrait. **2.** A crude image of a disliked person. **— to burn** (or **hang**) **in effigy** To display and burn or hang publicly a crude image of a disliked person. [< F *effigie* < L *effigies* < *ex-* out + *fingere* to fashion]

ef·flo·resce (ef'lō-res', -lō·res') *v.i.* **·resced, ·resc·ing** **1.** To blossom, bloom, or flower. **2.** *Chem.* **a** To become powdery, wholly or in part, and lose crystalline structure through loss of water of crystallization on exposure to the air. **b** To become covered with a crust of saline particles left by evaporation or by chemical change. [< L *efflorescere* < *ex-* thoroughly + *florescere* to bloom < *flos, floris* a flower]

ef·flo·res·cence (ef'lôr·es'əns, -lō·res'-) *n.* **1.** The act or season of flowering; a blooming forth. **2.** *Chem.* The act or process of efflorescing; also, the crystalline deposit that results from this. **3.** *Pathol.* A rash on the skin.

ef·flo·res·cent (ef'lôr·es'ənt, -lō·res'-) *adj.* **1.** Blossoming out; blooming. **2.** *Chem.* **a** Forming into white threads or powder. **b** Covered with efflorescence. [< L *efflorescens, -entis*, ppr. of *efflorescere*. See EFFLORESCE.]

ef·flu·ence (ef'lōō-əns) *n.* **1.** A flowing out. **2.** Emanation.

ef·flu·ent (ef'lōō-ənt) *adj.* Flowing out. **—** *n.* An outflow, as of water from a lake, industrial sewage, etc. [< L *effluens, -entis*, ppr. of *effluere* < *ex-* out + *fluere* to flow]

ef·flu·vi·um (i-flōō'vē-əm) *n. pl.* **·vi·a** (-vē-ə) or **·vi·ums** **1.** An invisible emanation; especially, a foul-smelling exhalation, as from decaying matter. **2.** A supposed imponderable agent formerly regarded as the source of electric and magnetic forces. [< L, a flowing out] **— ef·flu'vi·al** *adj.*

ef·flux (ef'luks) *n.* **1.** A flowing out. **2.** That which flows forth; emanation. [< L *effluxus* < *ex-* out + *fluere* to flow]

ef·fort (ef'ərt) *n.* **1.** Expenditure of physical or mental energy to get something done; exertion. **2.** Something produced by exertion: a new theatrical *effort*. **3.** *Mech.* Force exerted against the inertia of a body. [< F < OF *esfort* < *esforcier* to force oneself < L *ex-* thoroughly + *fortis* strong]

ef·fort·less (ef'ərt·lis) *adj.* **1.** Requiring or displaying little or no effort; easy. **2.** Passive. **— ef'fort·less·ly** *adv.*

ef·fron·ter·y (i-frun'tər-ē) *n. pl.* **·ies** Shameless or insolent boldness; audacity; impudence. **— Syn.** See IMPUDENCE. [< F *effronterie* < L *effrons* shameless, barefaced < *ex-* out + *frons, frontis* forehead, face]

ef·fulge (i-fulj') *v.t. & v.i.* **·fulged, ·fulg·ing** To shine forth; radiate. [< L *effulgere* < *ex-* out + *fulgere* to shine]

ef·ful·gence (i-ful'jəns) *n.* Radiance; splendor.

ef·ful·gent (i-ful'jənt) *adj.* Shining brilliantly; radiant; splendid. [< L *effulgens, -entis*, ppr. of *effulgere*. See EFFULGE.] **— ef·ful'gent·ly** *adv.*

ef·fuse (*adj.* i-fyōōs'; *v.* i-fyōōz') *adj.* **1.** *Bot.* Spreading out loosely or flat. **2.** *Zool.* Having the lips separated by a groove, as certain shells. **3.** *Obs.* Poured out freely; profuse. **—** *v.* **·fused, ·fus·ing** *v.t.* **1.** To pour forth; shed. **—** *v.i.* **2.** To emanate; exude. **3.** *Physics* To flow through a porous diaphragm or aperture under pressure: said of gases. [< L *effusus*, pp. of *effundere* < *ex-* out + *fundere* to pour]

ef·fu·sion (i-fyōō'zhən) *n.* **1.** The act of pouring forth. **2.** That which is poured forth. **3.** An outpouring of fervid or unrestrained language, sentiment, etc. **4.** *Pathol.* The escape of blood, etc., from normal containment into adjacent tissues or cavities; also, the fluid that escapes. **5.** *Physics* The flow of gases under pressure through openings in a container.

ef·fu·sive (i-fyōō'siv) *adj.* **1.** Overflowing with sentiment; demonstrative; gushing. **2.** Pouring forth; overflowing. **— ef·fu'sive·ly** *adv.* **— ef·fu'sive·ness** *n.*

Ef·ik (ef'ik) *n. pl.* **·ik** **1.** One of a Negro people inhabiting SE Nigeria. **2.** The language of these people.

eft[1] (eft) *n.* **1.** A newt. **2.** Formerly, a lizard. [OE *efeta*]

eft[2] (eft) *adv. Archaic* **1.** Again. **2.** Afterward. [OE]

eft·soon (eft'sōōn') *adv. Archaic* **1.** Soon afterward. **2.** Quickly or immediately. **3.** Again. **4.** Often. Also **eft'·soons'**. [OE *eftsōna* immediately afterward]

e.g. For example. (L *exempli gratia*).

Eg. Egypt.

e·gad (i-gad', ē-gad') *interj.* By God!: a mild oath. [Prob. alter. of *ah, God!*]

e·gal·i·tar·i·an (i-gal'ə-târ'ē-ən) *adj.* Of, relating to, or believing in political and social equality. **—** *n.* One who believes in or advocates political and social equality. Also **equalitarian**. [< F *égalitaire*] **— e·gal'i·tar'i·an·ism** *n.*

é·ga·li·té (ā·gà·lē·tā') *n. French* Equality.

Eg·bert (eg'bərt), 775?–839, king of Wessex 802–839; king of England 829–839.

E·ge·an (i·jē'ən) See AEGEAN.

E·ger (ā'gər) The German name for the OHŘE.

E·ge·ri·a (i·jir'ē·ə) In Roman legend, a nymph who was the adviser of Numa Pompilius. **—** *n.* Any woman adviser.

e·gest (ē-jest') *v.t.* To eject or void, as feces or perspiration; excrete. [< L *egestus*, pp. of *egerere* < *e-* out + *gerere* to carry] **— e·ges'tion** *n.* **— e·ges'tive** *adj.*

e·ges·ta (ē-jes'tə) *n.pl.* Matter egested; excreta: opposed to *ingesta*. [< L, neut. pl. of *egestus*. See EGEST.]

egg[1] (eg) *n.* **1.** The round or oval reproductive body produced by female birds, insects, and most reptiles and fishes, consisting of the germ and a nutritive yolk, enclosed in a membranous or shell-like covering. **2.** *Biol.* The reproductive cell of female animals; ovum: also **egg cell.** **3.** The egg of the domestic hen, eaten raw or cooked. **4.** Something oval like a hen's egg. **5.** Figuratively, an early or formative stage, idea, etc. **6.** *U.S. Slang* Person; fellow: He's a good *egg.* **7.** *U.S. Slang* A bomb, grenade, or torpedo. **— to lay an egg** *U.S. Slang* To be a complete failure; fall flat. **— to put** (or **have**) **all one's eggs in one basket** To risk all in a single venture; have all one's property in one place. **—** *v.t.* **1.** To cover with beaten egg before cooking. [< ON *egg*; OE *æg*]

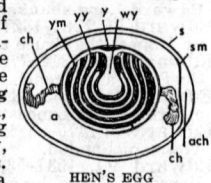

HEN'S EGG
a Albumen. *ch* Chalaza. *ym* Yolk membrane. *yy* Yellow food yolk. *y* Germinal vesicle. *wy* White yolk. *s* Shell. *sm* Amnion. *ach* Air chamber.

egg[2] (eg) *v.t.* To instigate or incite; urge: usually with *on*. [< ON *eggja*]

egg-and-dart (eg'ən-därt') *n. Archit.* An ornamental molding carved with a series of egg-shaped forms alternating with forms shaped like a dart, an anchor (**egg-and-anchor**), or a tongue (**egg-and-tongue**).

egg·beat·er (eg'bē'tər) *n.* A kitchen utensil for beating eggs, cream, etc.

EGG-AND-DART MOLDING

eg·ger (eg'ər) *n.* Any of several moths (family *Lasiocampidae*) whose larvae are known as tent caterpillars. Also **eg'gar**. [Prob. < EGG, with ref. to the shape of the cocoon]

Eg·gerts·ville (eg'ərts-vil) An unincorporated place in western New York, near Buffalo; pop. 55,000.

egg foo yong (fōō' yung') A Chinese-American dish consisting of eggs beaten and cooked with pork, seafood, minced vegetables, etc. [< Chinese *foo yong* hibiscus]

egg·head (eg'hed') *n. U.S. Slang* An intellectual; highbrow: often derisive.

Eg·gle·ston (eg'əl-stən), **Edward**, 1837–1902, U.S. clergyman and novelist.

egg·nog (eg'nog') *n.* A drink made of beaten eggs and milk with sugar and nutmeg and sometimes with brandy, rum, or other liquor. [< EGG + NOG[2]]

egg·plant (eg'plant', -plänt') *n.* **1.** A widely cultivated herb (*Solanum melongena*) of the nightshade family, with large, egg-shaped, usually purple-skinned fruit. **2.** The fruit of this plant, used as a vegetable.

egg roll A Chinese-American dish consisting of an envelope of egg dough around a combination of minced pork, seafood, vegetables, etc., and deep-fried.

egg·shell (eg'shel') *n.* The hard, brittle covering of a bird's egg. **—** *adj.* **1.** Thin and fragile. **2.** Pale yellow or ivory. **eggshell china** A very thin and delicate porcelain. Also **eggshell porcelain.**

egg white The uncooked albumen of an egg.

e·gis (ē'jis) See AEGIS.

eg·lan·tine (eg'lən-tīn, -tēn) *n.* Any of various fragrant wild roses. Also *Archaic* **eg·la·tere** (eg'lə·tir'). [< F *églantine* < OF *aiglent*, ult. < L *acus* needle]

Eg·mont (eg'mont, *Flemish* ekh'mônt), **Lamoral**, 1522–68, Count of Egmont, Flemish general and statesman.

e·go (ē'gō, eg'ō) *n. pl.* **e·gos** **1.** The thinking, feeling, and acting self that is conscious of itself and aware of its distinction from the selves of others and from the objects of its thought and other operations. **2.** *Philos.* **a** In scholastic philosophy, the entire man viewed as composed of soul, mind, and body. **b** In later philosophy, the part of the self that is the enduring, conscious subject of varying experiences. **3.** *Psychoanal.* The conscious aspect of the psyche that develops through contact with the external world and protects the organism by resolving conflicts between the id and the superego so as to conform best with reality. **4.** *Informal* Self-centeredness; conceit; egotism. [< L, I]

e·go·cen·tric (ē'gō-sen'trik, eg'ō-) *adj.* **1.** Regarding oneself as the center and object of all experience and acts; relating everything to oneself; self-centered. **2.** *Philos.* Having existence only as viewed by the individual. **—** *n.* An egocentric person. **— e'go·cen·tric'i·ty** (-sen·tris'ə·tē) *n.*

ego ideal *Psychoanal.* Traits that are regarded by an individual as ideal and that he consciously or unconsciously attempts to incorporate within his own personality.

e·go·ism (ē'gō·iz'əm, eg'ō-) *n.* **1.** Inordinate concern for one's own welfare and interests; selfishness. **2.** Self-conceit; egotism. **3.** In ethics, the doctrine that all individual conduct is rightly motivated by self-interest. **— Syn.** See EGOTISM. [< L *ego* I + -ISM]

e·go·ist (ē'gō·ist, eg'ō-) *n.* **1.** One who is completely devoted to his own interests; a selfish person. **2.** A conceited person; egotist. **3.** An adherent of the doctrine of egoism.

e·go·is·tic (ē'gō·is'tik, eg'ō-) *adj.* **1.** Concerned only with one's own interests; selfish. **2.** Conceited; egotistic. **3.** Of or pertaining to ethical egoism. Also **e′go·is′ti·cal.** — **e′go·is′ti·cal·ly** adv.

e·go·ma·ni·a (ē′gō·mā′nē·ə, -mān′yə, eg′ō-) n. Abnormal or excessive egotism. — **e′go·ma′ni·ac** (-ak) n.

e·go·tism (ē′gə·tiz′əm, eg′ə-) n. **1.** Excessive reference to oneself in speech or writing; self-conceit; boastfulness. **2.** Selfishness; egoism. [< EGO + -t- + -ISM]

— **Syn.** Egotism, egoism, selfishness, conceit, vanity, and self-esteem refer to preoccupation with oneself. Egotism and egoism are sometimes interchanged because of similarity in form and in area of meaning. Ordinarily, egotism is reserved for the braggart's inflated state of vanity and self-importance. Egoism, a less common word, insists upon self-interest as a valid motive in all personal conduct. Thus, a man sworn to egoism may not be stamped by the boastfulness that attends egotism. Selfishness is the putting of egoism into action, by showing little regard for the rights or feelings of others. Conceit is overestimation of one's abilities, qualities, or worth, while vanity is undue pride in one's possessions or attributes. Self-esteem is justifiable pride, and may suggest a reasonable concept of the self; more frequently, however, it is applied to exaggerated pride just short of conceit or vanity.

e·go·tist (ē′gə·tist, eg′ə-) n. **1.** One characterized by egotism; a conceited person. **2.** A selfish person; egoist.

e·go·tis·tic (ē′gə·tis′tik, eg′ə-) adj. **1.** Addicted to self-esteem; conceited; boastful. **2.** Selfish; egoistic. Also **e′go·tis′ti·cal.** — **e′go·tis′ti·cal·ly** adv.

e·gre·gious (i·grē′jəs, -jē·əs) adj. **1.** Conspicuously bad; glaring; flagrant. **2.** Obs. Distinguished; prominent. [< L egregius outstanding < e-out + grex, gregis herd] — **e·gre′gious·ly** adv. — **e·gre′gious·ness** n.

e·gress (ē′gres) n. **1.** A going out, as from a building; emergence; also, the right of going out. Also **e·gres′sion.** **2.** A place of exit. **3.** Astron. The emergence of a heavenly body from eclipse or occultation. [< L egressus < e- out + gradi to walk]

e·gret (ē′grit, eg′rit) n. **1.** One of various herons characterized in the breeding season by long and loose plumes drooping over the tail; especially, the **common egret** (Casmerodius albus) and the **snowy egret** (Leucophoyx thula). **2.** Aigrette (def. 1). [Var. of AIGRETTE]

E·gypt (ē′jipt) A Republic of NE Africa; 386,198 sq. mi.; pop. 33,329,000 (est. 1970); capital, Cairo; divided into **Lower Egypt,** the Nile Delta, and **Upper Egypt,** the Nile Valley between a point a few miles south of Cairo and the Sudan: officially **Arab Republic of Egypt.**

Egypt. Egyptian.

E·gyp·tian (i·jip′shən) adj. Of or pertaining to Egypt, its people, or their culture. — n. **1.** One of the people of Egypt. **2.** The ancient Hamitic language of Egypt, in its final stage called Coptic. **3.** Obs. A gypsy.

E·gyp·tol·o·gist (ē′jip·tol′ə·jist) n. A student of or authority on Egyptology.

E·gyp·tol·o·gy (ē′jip·tol′ə·jē) n. The study of the antiquities of Egypt. — **E·gyp·to·log·i·cal** (ē·jip′tə·loj′i·kəl) adj.

eh (ā, e) interj. What: used as an interrogative or to express uncertainty or surprise.

Eh·ren·burg (ā′rən·bŏŏrkh), **Ilya Grigorievich,** 1891–1967, Soviet writer.

Ehr·lich (âr′likh), **Paul,** 1854–1915, German biochemist and bacteriologist.

E.I. East India; East Indian. **2.** East Indies.

EIB or **E.I.B.** Export-Import Bank.

ei·der (ī′dər) n. A large sea duck (genus Somateria) of northern regions, having plumage mostly white above and black below. Also **eider duck.** [< ON ædhr- in ædhar-dūn eider-down; infl. in form by Sw. eider eider]

ei·der·down (ī′dər·doun′) n. **1.** The down of the eider used for stuffing pillows and quilts; also, a quilt or comforter filled with this down. **2.** A warm, lightweight cotton or woolen fabric with a woolen nap. [< ON ædhardūn]

ei·det·ic (ī·det′ik) adj. Psychol. Of or pertaining to the faculty, especially in childhood, of clearly visualizing objects previously seen. [< Gk. eidētikos < eidos form]

eidetic imagery Psychol. Clear, persistent visualization of previously seen objects.

ei·do·lon (ī·dō′lon) n. pl. **·la** (-lə) **1.** An image. **2.** A phantom. [< Gk. eidolon image]

Eif·fel (ī′fəl, Fr. ā·fel′), **Alexandre Gustave,** 1832–1923, French engineer; pioneer in aerodynamics.

Eiffel Tower An iron tower in Paris, 984.25 feet high, designed for the Exposition of 1889 by A. G. Eiffel.

eight (āt) n. **1.** The sum of seven and one: a cardinal number. **2.** Any symbol of this number, as 8, viii, VIII. **3.** Anything consisting of or representing eight units, as a team, playing card, etc. — adj. Being one more than seven. [OE eahta]

eight ball A black pool ball bearing a figure 8, and, in certain games, incurring a penalty on the player who pockets it. — **behind the eight ball** U.S. Slang In a disadvantageous or undesirable position.

eight·een (ā′tēn′) n. **1.** The sum of seventeen and one: a cardinal number. **2.** Any symbol of this number, as 18, xviii, XVIII. **3.** Anything consisting of or representing eighteen units, as an organization, game token, etc. — adj. Being one more than seventeen. [OE eahtatiene]

eight·eenth (ā′tēnth′) adj. **1.** Next after the seventeenth: the ordinal of eighteen. **2.** Being one of eighteen equal parts. — n. **1.** One of eighteen equal parts. **2.** That which follows the seventeenth.

eight·een·mo (ā′tēn′mō′) adj. & n. Octodecimo. [English reading of 18mo]

Eighteenth Amendment An amendment to the Constitution of the United States prohibiting the manufacture, sale, and transportation of intoxicating beverages: put into effect in 1920; repealed in 1933: also called Prohibition Amendment. Compare VOLSTEAD ACT.

eighth (ātth, āth) adj. **1.** Next after the seventh: the ordinal of eight. **2.** Being one of eight equal parts. — n. **1.** One of eight equal parts. **2.** That which follows the seventh.

eighth note Music A note having one eighth the time value of a whole note: also, Chiefly Brit., quaver. For illustration see NOTE.

eight·i·eth (ā′tē·ith) adj. **1.** Tenth in order after the seventieth: the ordinal of eighty. **2.** Being one of eighty equal parts. — n. **1.** One of eighty equal parts. **2.** That which is tenth in order after the seventieth.

eight·vo (āt′vō) adj. & n. Octavo.

eight·y (ā′tē) n. pl. **·ies 1.** The sum of seventy and ten: a cardinal number. **2.** Any symbol of this number, as 80, lxxx, LXXX. **3.** Anything consisting of or representing eighty units as an organization, game token, etc. — adj. Being ten more than seventy. [OE eahtatig]

Eijk·man (īk′män), **Christiaan,** 1858–1930, Dutch physician; pioneer in nutritional diseases.

ei·kon (ī′kon) See ICON.

-ein Var. of -IN.

Eind·ho·ven (īnt′hō·vən) A city in the southern Netherlands, on the Dommel; pop. 188,631 (est. 1970).

ein·korn (īn′kôrn) n. A one-grained variety of wheat (Triticum monococcum) with narrow, slender, curved spikelets. [< G ein one + korn grain]

Ein·stein (īn′stīn), **Albert,** 1879–1955, U.S. physicist born in Germany; developed the theory of relativity. — **Ein·stein·i·an** (īn·stī′nē·ən) adj.

ein·stein·i·um (īn·stī′nē·əm) n. A radioactive element (symbol Es), originally detected in the debris of a thermonuclear explosion and artificially produced by the irradiation of plutonium. See ELEMENT. [after Albert Einstein]

Eint·ho·ven (īnt′hō·vən), **Willem,** 1860–1927, Dutch physiologist.

Eir·e (âr′ə) The Irish Gaelic name for IRELAND (def. 2).

Ei·sen·ach (ī′zə·näkh) A city in SW East Germany; pop. about 50,230 (est. 1966).

Ei·sen·how·er (ī′zən·hou′ər), **Dwight David,** 1890–1969, 34th president of the United States 1953–61; Allied commander in chief in Europe in World War II, 1943–45.

Ei·ser·nes Tor (ī′zer·nəs tôr) The German name for IRON GATE.

eis·tedd·fod (ā·steth′vod, es·teth′-) n. pl. **eis·tedd·fods** or **eis·tedd·fod·au** (ā′steth·vod′ī, es′teth-) An assembly of poets and musicians, held yearly in Wales. [< Welsh, session < estedd to sit]

ei·ther (ē′thər, ī′thər) adj. **1.** One or the other of two: Use either foot. **2.** Each of two; one and the other: They sat on either side of him. — pron. One or the other: Choose either. — conj. In one of two or more cases, indeterminately or indifferently: a disjunctive correlative introducing a first alternative, the second, and any other alternatives being preceded by or: Either I shall go or he will come. — adv. Any more so: used after the denial of an alternative, or to emphasize a preceding negative: He could not speak, and I could not either; I shall leave, and you can't stop me either. [OE ǣgther]

◆ **either, neither** Either, like neither, is singular and in formal writing takes a singular verb: Either of them is suitable. In informal speech and writing, however, a plural verb is commonly used: Are either of you going to the party? When there are two subjects of differing number, the verb agrees with the nearer: Neither he nor they are ever there.

e·jac·u·late (i·jak′yə·lāt) v. **·lat·ed, ·lat·ing** v.t. **1.** To utter suddenly, as a brief exclamation; exclaim. **2.** To discharge suddenly and quickly, as seminal fluid. — v.i. **3.** To ejaculate something. — n. That which is ejaculated. — **Syn.** See EXCLAIM. [< L ejaculatus, pp. of ejaculari < e- out + jaculari to throw] — **e·jac′u·la′tive** (-lā′tiv, -lə·tiv) adj. — **e·jac′u·la·tor** n.

e·jac·u·la·tion (i·jak′yə·lā′shən) n. **1.** A brief utterance or exclamation. **2.** A short, pious utterance; a brief prayer. **3.** A sudden, quick discharge, as of seminal fluid; emission. **4.** The act of ejaculating.

e·jac·u·la·to·ry (i·jak′yə·lə·tôr′ē, -tō′rē) adj. **1.** Capable of or adapted to a sudden, quick discharge: an *ejaculatory* duct. **2.** Of the nature of a quick, brief utterance: an *ejaculatory* prayer.

e·ject (i-jekt′) *v.t.* **1.** To throw out with sudden force. **2.** To put forcibly outside; expel: to *eject* an intruder. **3.** *Law* To dispossess; evict. — **Syn.** See EXPEL. [< L *ejectus*, pp. of *ejicere* < *e-* out + *jacere* to throw]

e·jec·ta (i-jek′tə) *n.pl.* Matter or refuse cast out, as by a volcano or the body. [< L, neut. pl. of *ejectus*. See EJECT.]

e·jec·tion (i-jek′shən) *n.* **1.** The act of ejecting, or the state of being ejected. **2.** Ejected matter.

ejection seat An airplane seat, usually in a military fighter, that in an emergency ejects with its occupant clear of the aircraft and is parachuted to the ground: also **ejector seat.**

e·jec·tive (i-jek′tiv) *adj.* Relating to or causing ejection: *ejective* forces. — **e·jec′tive·ly** *adv.*

e·ject·ment (i-jekt′mənt) *n.* **1.** Dispossession; eviction. **2.** *Law* An action to recover possession of real estate, together with damages for wrongful withholding.

e·jec·tor (i-jek′tər) *n.* **1.** One who or that which ejects. **2.** *Mech.* A device that ejects used material; especially, a mechanism that ejects spent cartridges or shells from a gun.

E·ka·te·rin·burg, etc. (yi-kə·tyi·ryin-bŏŏrk′) See YEKA-TERINBURG, etc.

eke[1] (ēk) *v.t.* **eked, ek·ing 1.** To piece out; supplement: usually with *out*: to *eke* out an income. **2.** To make a (living) with difficulty: usually with *out*. **3.** *Archaic* To lengthen; increase. [Var. of ECHE]

eke[2] (ēk) *adv. & conj. Archaic* Likewise; also. [OE *ēac*]

EKG *Med.* Electrocardiogram.

e·kue·le (e·kwä′lā) *n.* The monetary unit of Equatorial Guinea, equivalent to 100 centimos.

el[1] (el) *n. U.S. Informal* An elevated railroad or train.

el[2] (el) See ELL[2] (def. 2).

el- Assimilated var. of EN-[2].

el. Elevation.

E.L. East Lothian.

e·lab·o·rate (*adj.* i-lab′ər·it; *v.* i-lab′ə-rāt) *adj.* Worked out with great thoroughness or exactness; developed in minute detail; painstaking: *elaborate* precautions; an *elaborate* carving. — *v.* **·rat·ed, ·rat·ing** *v.t.* **1.** To work out in detail; develop carefully and thoroughly. **2.** To produce by labor; fashion. — *v.i.* **3.** To add details or embellishments: with *on* or *upon*: to *elaborate* on a subject. [< L *elaboratus*, pp. of *elaborare* < *e-* out + *laborare* to work] — **e·lab′o·rate·ly** *adv.* — **e·lab′o·rate·ness** *n.* — **e·lab′o·ra′tor** *n.*

e·lab·o·ra·tion (i-lab′ə-rā′shən) *n.* **1.** The act or process of elaborating. **2.** The state or quality of being elaborate. **3.** Something elaborate, as a product or effect.

e·lab·o·ra·tive (i-lab′ə-rā′tiv, -ər·ə·tiv) *adj.* Serving or tending to elaborate.

el·ae·op·tene (el′ē·op′tēn) *n. Chem.* The liquid hydrocarbon or terpene constituent of an essential oil: distinguished from *stearoptene*. Also spelled *eleoptene*. [< Gk. *elaion* oil + *ptēnos* flying]

El·a·gab·a·lus (el′ə-gab′ə·ləs) See HELIOGABALUS.

e·la·in (i·lā′ən) *n. Chem.* Olein.

E·laine (i·lān′) In Arthurian legend, the mother of Galahad.

elaio- *combining form* Oil: *elaioplast.* Also **elaeo-, eleo-.** [< Gk. *elaion* olive oil]

el·ai·o·plast (el′ē·ə·plast′) *n. Bot.* One of the highly refractive, oil-secreting, protoplasmic granules found near the nuclei of plant cells: also spelled *eleoplast.* Also **el′ae·o·plast′.** [< ELAIO- + -PLAST]

E·lam (ē′ləm) An ancient country of SW Asia between the Persian Gulf and the Caspian Sea: also *Susiana. Gen.* xiv 1.

E·lam·ite (ē′ləm·īt) *n.* **1.** One of the inhabitants of Elam. **2.** An extinct language, or group of languages, spoken in Elam, and unrelated to any other language: also called *Susian.* — *adj.* Of or pertaining to Elam, its inhabitants, or their language: also **E′lam·it′ish** (-ī′tish).

E·lam·it·ic (ē′lə·mit′ik) *n.* The Elamite language or languages. — *adj.* Elamite.

e·lan (ā·län′) *n.* Enthusiasm; dash; vivacity. [< F < *élancer* < *é-* out + *lancer* to throw, shoot forth]

e·land (ē′lənd) *n.* A large, oxlike African antelope with twisted horns (genus *Taurotragus*): especially, *T. oryx* of SE Africa. [< Du., elk]

élan vi·tal (vē·tàl′) *French* Life force; literally, vital energy. See BERGSONISM.

el·a·phine (el′ə·fin, -fīn) *adj.* **1.** Of or pertaining to a genus (*Elaphodus*) of deer native in China. **2.** Describing the antlers characteristic of this genus: for illustration see ANTLER. [< L *elaphus* < Gk. *elaphos* stag]

el·a·pine (el′ə·pīn, -pin) *adj. Zool.* Of or pertaining to a family (*Elapidae*) of tropical snakes, including the coral snake, cobra, and harlequin snake. [< NL < Gk. *elaps,* var. of *ellops,* a kind of serpent]

e·lapse (i·laps′) *v.i.* **e·lapsed, e·laps·ing** To slip by; pass away: said of time. [< L *elapsus,* pp. of *elabi* < *e-* out, away + *labi* to glide]

ELAND
(5 to 6 feet high at shoulder)

e·las·mo·branch (i·las′mō-brangk, i·laz′-) *n. Zool.* One of a class or subclass (*Elasmobranchii*) of sharks, rays, and other aquatic vertebrates having placoid scales, cartilaginous skeletons, and brains with optic nerves forming a chiasm. [< NL < Gk. *elasmos* metal plate + *branchia* gills]

e·las·tic (i·las′tik) *adj.* **1.** Spontaneously regaining former size, shape, or bulk after compression, extension, or other distortion: said of solids; also, capable of indefinite expansion: said of gases. **2.** Adjusting readily to fit the circumstances; flexible; adaptable: an *elastic* budget. **3.** Recovering quickly, as from emotional or physical distress; resilient: an *elastic* temperament. **4.** Marked by a springy motion; bouncy: an *elastic* stride. — *n.* **1.** Fabric made stretchable by interwoven threads of rubber. **2.** An article manufactured of this fabric, as a garter or suspender. **3.** A rubber band. [< NL *elasticus* < Gk. *elastikos* driving, propulsive < *elaunein* to drive] — **e·las′ti·cal·ly** *adv.*

— **Syn.** (adj.) *Elastic, resilient, springy,* and *flexible* mean able to undergo deformation without permanent change. In scientific usage, *elastic* is applied to seemingly rigid bodies that nevertheless return to shape after slight deformation: steel is highly *elastic*. In popular usage, the word means having the power to return to shape after great deformation. *Resilient* characterizes that which returns to shape spontaneously after compression, as a rubber ball. *Springy* stresses the rapidity of *resilient* recovery. Something *flexible* can be bent or twisted without injury, but the word does not necessarily imply the power to spring back to original shape. In extension, the *elastic* person can recover from severe setbacks, the *resilient* person is undismayed by adverse fortune, and the *flexible* person accommodates easily to new circumstances. — **Ant.** rigid, stiff, inflexible.

e·las·tic·i·ty (i·las′tis′ə·tē, ē′las-) *n. pl.* **·ties 1.** The property or quality of being elastic; flexibility; buoyancy; resilience. **2.** *Physics* The tendency of a body to return to its original shape after deformation.

e·las·tin (i·las′tin) *n. Biochem.* The albuminoid substance found in tendons, cartilage, connective tissue, and bone. [< ELAST(IC) + -IN]

e·las·to·mer (i·las′tə·mər) *n. Chem.* One of a class of polymerized compounds characterized by elastic, rubberlike properties, as the synthetic rubbers and various plastics. [< ELAST(IC) + -o- + Gk. *meros* part]

e·late (i·lāt′) *v.t.* **e·lat·ed, e·lat·ing** To raise the spirits of; cause to feel joyful or triumphant; stimulate; excite. — *adj. Poetic* Elated. [< L *elatus,* pp. of *efferre* < *ex-* out + *ferre* to bear]

e·lat·ed (i·lā′tid) *adj.* Filled with joy or triumph, as over success or good fortune; exultant; jubilant. — **e·lat′ed·ly** *adv.* — **e·lat′ed·ness** *n.*

el·a·ter (el′ə·tər) *n.* **1.** *Entomol.* An elaterid. **2.** *Bot.* An elastic, twisted filament for the dispersion of spores. [< NL < Gk. *elatēr* < *elaunein* to drive]

el·a·ter·id (i·lat′ər·id) *adj.* Of or pertaining to a family (*Elateridae*) of beetles with serrate antennae, including the click beetles or snapping beetles. — *n.* An elaterid beetle. [< NL < Gk. *elatēr.* See ELATER.]

el·a·ter·in (i·lat′ər·in) *n. Chem.* A bitter, crystalline compound, $C_{20}H_{28}O_5$, contained in elaterium and having a powerful cathartic effect. [< ELATER(IUM) + -IN]

el·a·ter·ite (i·lat′ə·rīt) *n.* An elastic, resinous, dark brown natural asphalt found in soft masses. [< obs. *elater* elasticity (< Gk. < *elaunein* to drive) + -ITE[1]]

el·a·te·ri·um (el′ə·tir′ē·əm) *n.* The grayish green sediment from the juice of the squirting cucumber. [< L < Gk *elaterion* a purgative < *elaunein* to drive]

e·la·tion (i·lā′shən) *n.* Exalted feeling, as from success; triumphant joy; exultation. Also *Obs.* **e·late′ment.**

E layer The Heaviside layer (which see).

El·ba (el′bə) The largest island of the Tuscan Archipelago; 86 sq. mi.; a sovereign principality under the exiled Napoleon Bonaparte, 1814–15.

El·be (el′bə) A river of central Europe, flowing 725 miles, generally NW, to the North Sea: Czech *Labe.*

El·bert (el′bərt), **Mount** A peak in central Colorado, highest in the Rocky Mountains of the conterminous United States; 14,431 ft.

El·ber·ta (el·bûr′tə) *n.* A freestone peach of the eastern United States.

El·bing (el′bing) A port city in northern Poland, on the Vistula; pop. about 65,000. Polish **El·bląg** (el′blôngk).

el·bow (el′bō) *n.* **1.** The joint at the bend of the arm between the forearm and the upper arm; especially, the projecting outer side of this joint. **2.** The joint corresponding to an elbow in the shoulder or hock of a quadruped. **3.** Something having an angle or bend like an elbow; as: **a** A sharply turned length of pipe. **b** A projection at the side of a piece of furniture, designed to support the arm. **c** A sharp bend, as in a river. — **at one's elbow** Within easy reach. — **out at the elbows** Shabby; impoverished. — **to rub elbows with** To associate closely with (celebrities, etc.). — **up to the elbows (in)** Deeply immersed (in); much occupied (with). — *v.t.* **1.** To push or jostle with or as with the elbows. **2.** To make (one's way) by such pushing. — *v.i.* **3.** To push one's way along. [OE *elnboga*]

elbow grease *Informal* Strong physical effort.

el·bow·room (el′bō·rōōm′, -rŏŏm′) *n.* Enough room to move or work without hindrance; scope for free activity.

El·brus (el′brōōs), **Mount** A peak in the Caucasus mountains in the NW Georgian S.S.R.; the highest peak in Europe; 18,481 ft. Also **El′′brus, El′′bruz.**

El·burz (el·bŏŏrz′) A mountain range in northern Iran; highest peak Demavend, 18,603 ft: also **Alborz.**

El Ca·jon (el kä·hōn′) A city in SW California, near San Diego; pop. 52,273.

El Cap·i·tan (el kap·i·tan′) A peak in the Yosemite Valley, California; 7,564 ft.

El Cer·ri·to (el sə·rē′tō) A city in western California, on San Francisco Bay near Oakland; pop. 25,190.

El Cha·co (el chä′kō) See GRAN CHACO.

eld (eld) *n.* **1.** *Archaic* Old times; antiquity. **2.** *Dial.* Age; especially, old age. [OE *eldo* old age]

eld·er[1] (el′dər) *adj.* **1.** Of earlier birth; older; senior. **2.** Superior or prior in rank, office, etc. **3.** Pertaining to a previous time; earlier; former. — *n.* **1.** *Often pl.* An older person; one's senior; also, a forefather or predecessor. **2.** An influential senior member of a family, community, etc. **3.** *Eccl.* A governing or counseling officer in certain Christian churches. See PRESBYTER. **4.** An aged person. [OE *eldra*] — **eld′er·ship** *n.*

el·der[2] (el′dər) *n.* **1.** A shrub (genus *Sambucus*) of the honeysuckle family, with white flowers and purple-black or red berries. **2.** Any one of various trees or plants resembling this shrub, as the poison elder (*Rhus vernix*). [OE *ellærn*]

el·der·ber·ry (el′dər·ber′ē, -bər·ē) *n. pl.* **·ber·ries 1.** The berry of the elder, used to make wine. **2.** The elder.

eld·er·ly (el′dər·lē) *adj.* Rather advanced in age; approaching old age; quite old. — **Syn.** See OLD.

elder statesman 1. An elderly man, retired from public life, who acts as unofficial adviser, especially on governmental matters. **2.** A member of the Japanese genro.

eld·est (el′dist) *adj.* Alternative superlative of OLD. Abbr. *e.* [OE *eldest(a)*]

El Do·ra·do (el də·rä′dō) **1.** A legendary South American city or realm rich in gold and jewels, long sought by early explorers. **2.** Any region or opportunity rich in gold or promise: applied particularly to California during and after the gold rush of 1848–49. Also **El′do·ra′do.**

El Do·ra·do (el′ də·rä′dō) A city in southern Arkansas; pop. 25,283.

el·dritch (el′drich) *adj. Archaic & Poetic* Ghastly; weird. [< earlier E *elrish* < OE *ælf* elf]

E·le·a (ē′lē·ə) An ancient town in Lucania, Italy.

El·ea·nor of Aquitaine (el′ə·nər, -nôr), 1122?–1204, queen of France, and later of England. Also **Eleanor of Guienne.**

E·le·at·ic (el′ē·at′ik) *adj.* Pertaining or or characteristic of Elea or the school of philosophy founded there by Xenophanes and Parmenides. — *n.* **1.** A native of Elea. **2.** A disciple of the Eleatic school of philosophy, that developed the concept of the universal unity of being. [< L *Eleaticus* < *Elea* Elea] — **El′e·at′i·cism** *n.*

el·e·cam·pane (el′i·kam·pān′) *n.* **1.** A tall perennial herb of the composite family (*Inula helenium*), having large leaves, yellow flowers, and a root yielding a tonic. **2.** A coarse candy flavored with an extract from the root of this herb. [< Med.L *enula* elecampane + *campana* of the field]

e·lect (i·lekt′) *v.t.* **1.** To choose (a person or persons) for an office by vote. **2.** To pick out; select. **3.** *Theol.* To set aside by divine will for salvation: used in the passive voice. — *v.i.* **4.** To make a choice. — *adj.* **1.** Chosen; selected; picked out. **2.** Elected to office, but not yet inducted: used as the second element in compounds: president-*elect*. **3.** *Theol.* Chosen by God for salvation. — *n.* **1.** One who is favored or preferred. **2.** *Theol.* A person, or body of persons, chosen by God for salvation. [< L *electus*, pp. of *eligere* < *e*- out + *legere* to choose]

e·lec·tion (i·lek′shən) *n.* **1.** The formal choice of a person or persons for any position or dignity, usually by ballot. **2.** A popular vote upon any question officially proposed. **3.** The act of choosing. **4.** In Calvinism, the predestination of individuals to salvation. — **Syn.** See ALTERNATIVE.

e·lec·tion·eer (i·lek′shən·ir′) *v.i.* To work for votes for a particular candidate or political party.

e·lec·tive (i·lek′tiv) *adj.* **1.** Of or pertaining to a choice by vote. **2.** Obtained, bestowed, or settled by election. **3.** Having the power to elect. **4.** Subject to choice; optional. **5.** *Chem.* Having a tendency to attract and combine with some substances and not with others: *elective* absorption. — *n. U.S.* An optional subject or course of study in a school or college curriculum. — **e·lec′tive·ly** *adv.*

e·lec·tor (i·lek′tər) *n.* **1.** One who elects; a person qualified to vote. **2.** *U.S.* A member of the electoral college. **3.** *Usually cap.* One of the German princes who formerly elected the Holy Roman emperor.

e·lec·tor·al (i·lek′tər·əl) *adj.* Of, relating to, or composed of electors.

electoral college A body of electors, chosen by the voters

in the States and the District of Columbia, that formally elects the president and vice president of the United States.

e·lec·tor·ate (i·lek′tər·it) *n.* **1.** The whole body of voters. **2.** A district of voters. **3.** The rank or territory of an elector in the Holy Roman Empire.

electr. or **elec.** or **elect. 1.** Electricity. **2.** Electric; electrical. **3.** Electrician.

E·lec·tra (i·lek′trə) **1.** In Greek legend, a daughter of Agamemnon and Clytemnestra who persuaded her brother Orestes to kill their mother and their mother's lover Aegisthus to avenge their father's murder. See ORESTES. **2.** In Greek mythology, one of the Pleiades. Also *Elektra*. — *n. Astron.* One of the six visible stars in the Pleiades cluster.

Electra complex *Psychoanal.* A compulsive, strongly repressed sexual attachment of a daughter to her father. Compare OEDIPUS COMPLEX.

e·lec·tress (i·lek′tris) *n.* **1.** A woman voter. **2.** *Usually cap.* The wife or widow of an Elector (def. 3).

e·lec·tric (i·lek′trik) *adj.* **1.** Relating to, derived from, produced by, or operated by electricity: an *electric* current. **2.** Producing or carrying electricity: an *electric* cable. **3.** Thrillingly exciting or magnetic: an *electric* personality. — *n.* **1.** A streetcar, train, or automobile run by electricity. **2.** Any substance or material, as amber or resin, that can be given an electric charge by friction. Abbr. *elec., electr.* [< NL *electricus* < L *electrum* amber < Gk. *ēlektron*]

e·lec·tri·cal (i·lek′tri·kəl) *adj.* **1.** Electric (defs. 1 and 2). **2.** Concerned with the use of electricity: *electrical* engineering. Abbr. *elec., elect., electr.* — **e·lec′tri·cal·ly** *adv.*

electrical transcription *Telecom.* A transcription.

electric calamine Hemimorphite.

electric chair A chair in which a condemned prisoner is strapped to be executed by the passage of an electric current through his body; also, the electrocution itself.

electric eel A cyprinoid, eellike, fresh-water fish (*Electrophorus electricus*) of tropical America, that sometimes reaches a length of six feet, and has organs capable of delivering powerful electric shocks.

electric eye A photoelectric cell.

electric field A field of force surrounding a charged object or a moving magnet.

electric furnace 1. A furnace in which high temperatures are obtained by the use of an electric arc or by induction. **2.** A smelting furnace in which the heat is produced by an electric current.

electric guitar A guitar designed to transmit its tones to a loudspeaker through an electrical pickup on the bridge.

e·lec·tri·cian (i·lek′trish′ən, ē′lek-) *n.* A technician who designs, installs, operates, or repairs electrical apparatus. Abbr. *elec., elect., electr.*

e·lec·tric·i·ty (i·lek′tris′ə·tē, ē′lek-) *n.* **1.** A fundamental property of matter, associated with atomic particles whose movements, free or controlled, lead to the development of fields of force and the generation of kinetic or potential energy. **2.** A current or charge of energy so generated. **3.** The science that deals with the phenomena, laws, theory, and application of electric energy. **4.** The property of many substances, as amber or fur, to attract or repel each other when subjected to friction. **5.** A state of great tension or excitement. Abbr. *elec., elect., electr.*

electric motor A machine for transforming electric energy into mechanical power: distinguished from *generator*: also called *electromotor*.

electric needle A high-frequency, needle-shaped electrode used in surgery for simultaneous cutting and cautery.

electric organ An organ in which audio signals are produced electromechanically, amplified, and converted to sound.

electric ray An elasmobranch fish having muscles modified for the storage and discharge of electricity: also called *crampfish, numbfish, torpedo.*

electric shaver An electrically-powered device for shaving the beard or body hair. Also **electric razor.**

e·lec·tri·fy (i·lek′trə·fī) *v.t.* **·fied, ·fy·ing 1.** To charge with or subject to electricity. **2.** To equip, as a house, for the use of electricity. **3.** To adapt for operation by electric power, as a railroad. **4.** To arouse; startle; thrill. — **e·lec′tri·fi′·a·ble** *adj.* — **e·lec′tri·fi·ca′tion** *n.* — **e·lec′tri·fi′er** *n.*

e·lec·trize (i·lek′trīz) *v.t.* **·trized, ·triz·ing** To electrify (defs. 1, 2, and 3). — **e·lec′tri·za′tion** *n.* — **e·lec′triz′er** *n.*

e·lec·tro (i·lek′trō) *n. pl.* **·tros 1.** An electrotype. **2.** Electroplating. — *v.t.* **·troed, ·tro·ing** To electrotype or electroplate. [Short for ELECTROTYPE]

electro- *combining form* **1.** Electric; by, with, or of electricity: *electrocardiogram*. **2.** Electrolytic: *electroanalysis*. Also, before vowels, sometimes **electr-.** [< Gk. *ēlektron* amber]

e·lec·tro·a·cous·tics (i·lek′trō·ə·kōōs′tiks) *n.pl.* (*construed as sing.*) The branch of acoustics that deals with equipment used in the transmission of sound, as microphones, loudspeakers, tape recorders, etc. — **e·lec′tro·a·cous′tic** or **·ti·cal** *adj.* — **e·lec′tro·a·cous′ti·cal·ly** *adv.*

e·lec·tro·a·nal·y·sis (i·lek′trō·ə·nal′ə·sis) *n.* Chemical analysis by electrolytic methods using significant amounts of current. — **e·lec′tro·an·a·lyt′ic** or **·i·cal** *adj.*

e·lec·tro·car·di·o·gram (i·lek′trō·kär′dē·ə·gram′) *n. Med.* The record made by an electrocardiograph. Abbr. *EKG.*

e·lec·tro·car·di·o·graph (i·lek′trō·kär′dē·ə·graf′, grăf′) *n. Med.* An instrument for recording the electric current produced by the action of the heart muscle, used in the diagnosis of diseases affecting the heart. — **e·lec·tro·car·di·og·ra·phy** (i·lek′trō·kär′dē·og′rə·fē) *n.*

e·lec·tro·chem·is·try (i·lek′trō·kem′is·trē) *n.* The branch of chemistry that treats of electricity as active in effecting chemical change. — **e·lec′tro·chem′i·cal** *adj.* — **e·lec′tro·chem′i·cal·ly** *adv.* — **e·lec′tro·chem′ist** *n.*

e·lec·tro·cute (i·lek′trə·kyōōt) *v.t.* **·cut·ed, ·cut·ing** **1.** To execute in the electric chair. **2.** To kill by electricity. [< ELECTRO- + (EXE)CUTE] — **e·lec′tro·cu′tion** *n.*

e·lec·trode (i·lek′trōd) *n. Electr.* **1.** Any terminal connecting a conventional conductor, as copper wire, with a nonconventional one, as an electrolyte. **2.** Any of the elements in an electron tube, transistor, etc., that emit, collect, or control the movement of electrons. [< ELECTR(O)- + -ODE¹]

e·lec·tro·de·pos·it (i·lek′trō·di·poz′it) *v.i.* To precipitate metal from an electrolyte containing it in ionic form, causing it to deposit on the cathode by means of an electric current. — *n.* That which is precipitated by electrolysis. — **e·lec′tro·dep′o·si′tion** (-dep′ə·zish′ən, -dē′pə-) *n.*

e·lec·tro·dy·nam·ic (i·lek′trō·dī·nam′ik) *adj.* Relating to the forces of attraction and repulsion produced by electric currents. Also **e·lec′tro·dy·nam′i·cal.**

e·lec·tro·dy·nam·ics (i·lek′trō·dī·nam′iks) *n.pl.* (*construed as sing.*) The branch of physics that deals with the forces of electrical attraction and repulsion and with the energy transformations of magnetic fields and electric currents.

e·lec·tro·dy·na·mom·e·ter (i·lek′trō·dī′nə·mom′ə·tər) *n.* An instrument for measuring the strength of an electric current, as by the interaction of two wire coils.

e·lec·tro·en·ceph·a·lo·gram (i·lek′trō·en·sef′ə·lə·gram′) *n. Med.* An electroencephalographic record. Abbr. *EEG*

e·lec·tro·en·ceph·a·lo·graph (i·lek′trō·en·sef′ə·lə·graf′, -gräf′) *n. Med.* An instrument for recording electrical impulses in the brain, used in the diagnosis of epilepsy and other brain disorders. — **e·lec′tro·en·ceph′a·lo·graph′ic** *adj.* — **e·lec′tro·en·ceph′a·log′ra·phy** (-log′rə·fē) *n.*

e·lec·tro·form·ing (i·lek′trō·fôr′ming) *n.* The production of metal tubing, medals, etc., by the electrolytic deposition of metal upon a mold of the desired shape or pattern.

e·lec·tro·graph (i·lek′trō·graf, -gräf) *n.* **1.** The linear record of an electrometer. **2.** An apparatus for tracing a design on metal plates to be used in printing wallpaper, calico, etc. **3.** An X-ray photograph. **4.** A device used in phototelegraphy. — **e·lec′tro·graph′ic** *adj.* — **e·lec·trog·ra·phy** (i·lek′trog′rə·fē, ē′lek-) *n.*

e·lec·tro·ki·net·ics (i·lek′trō·ki·net′iks) *n.pl.* (*construed as sing.*) A branch of physics that deals with the motion of electrically charged particles. [< ELECTRO- + KINETIC] — **e·lec′tro·ki·net′ic** *adj.*

e·lec·tro·lu·mi·nes·cence (i·lek′trō·lōō′mə·nes′əns) *n.* The emission of light from a coated surface subjected to an alternating current. — **e·lec′tro·lu′mi·nes′cent** *adj.*

e·lec·trol·y·sis (i·lek′trol′ə·sis) *n.* **1.** The application of a direct current to an electrolyte so as to attract its positive ions to the cathode and its negative ions to the anode. **2.** The removal of hair by treating the follicle with an electrically charged needle. [< ELECTRO- + -LYSIS]

e·lec·tro·lyte (i·lek′trə·līt) *n.* **1.** *Chem.* A compound that when in solution or a fluid state conducts electricity by the dissociation of its constituents into free ions. **2.** A solution that conducts electricity; especially, the solution used in a cell or battery. [< ELECTRO- + -LYTE] — **e·lec·tro·lyt·ic** (i·lek′trə·lit′ik) or **·i·cal** *adj.* — **e·lec′tro·lyt′i·cal·ly** *adv.*

e·lec·tro·lyze (i·lek′trə·līz) *v.t.* **·lyzed, ·lyz·ing** To decompose by electric current. [< ELECTRO- + -LYZE] — **e·lec′tro·ly·za′tion** *n.* — **e·lec′tro·lyz′er** *n.*

e·lec·tro·mag·net (i·lek′trō·mag′nit) *n.* A device in which a core of soft iron or the like temporarily becomes a magnet during the passage of an electric current through a coil of wire surrounding it: distinguished from *permanent magnet.*

electromagnetic wave *Physics* Any of a class of waves propagated by a system of electric and magnetic fields and including all forms of radiant energy from radio and light waves to gamma and cosmic rays.

e·lec·tro·mag·net·ism (i·lek′trō·mag′nə·tiz′əm) *n.* **1.** Magnetism developed by electricity. **2.** The science that treats of the relations between electricity and magnetism and the resulting phenomena. — **e·lec′tro·mag·net′ic** (-mag·net′ik) *adj.* — **e·lec′tro·mag·net′i·cal·ly** *adv.*

e·lec·tro·me·chan·i·cal (i·lek′trō·mə·kan′i·kəl) *adj.* Denoting a transducer that operates with electrical and mechanical energy. — **e·lec′tro·me·chan′i·cal·ly** *adv.*

e·lec·tro·met·al·lur·gy (i·lek′trō·met′ə·lûr′jē, -mə·tal′ər·jē) *n.* The conduct of metallurgical operations by electrical means. — **e·lec′tro·met′al·lur′gi·cal** *adj.* — **e·lec′tro·met′al·lur′gist** *n.*

e·lec·trom·e·ter (i·lek′trom′ə·tər, ē′lek-) *n.* An instrument for measuring the voltage of an electric current by the electrostatic forces exerted between two charged bodies.

e·lec·trom·e·try (i·lek′trom′ə·trē, ē′lek-) *n.* The science of making electrical measurements. — **e·lec·tro·met·ric** (i·lek′trō·met′rik) or **·ri·cal** *adj.*

e·lec·tro·mo·tive (i·lek′trə·mō′tiv) *adj.* Producing, or tending to produce, a flow of electric current.

electromotive force 1. That which tends to produce a flow of electricity from one point to another. **2.** Difference of electrical potential between two points in a circuit, a battery, etc.; voltage. Abbr. *emf, e.m.f., E.M.F.*

electromotive series An arrangement of the elements in a series in such a way that each will generally, under suitable conditions, replace from its compounds any element listed after it: also called *activity series.*

e·lec·tro·mo·tor (i·lek′trə·mō′tər) *n.* **1.** An electric motor. **2.** Any electric source, as a battery.

e·lec·tron (i·lek′tron) *n.* An atomic particle carrying a unit charge of negative electricity, estimated at 4.8×10^{-10} cgs electrostatic unit, and having a mass approximately one eighteen-hundredth (more exactly 1/1837) of that of the proton. [< Gk. *ēlektron* amber]

e·lec·tro·neg·a·tive (i·lek′trō·neg′ə·tiv) *adj.* **1.** Appearing at the positive electrode in electrolysis. **2.** Having the property of becoming negatively electrified by contact or chemical action. **3.** Nonmetallic.

electron gun An apparatus, usually in the form of a slender tube with thermionic filaments, used in a cathode-ray tube for directing a steady stream of electrons in a given direction.

e·lec·tron·ic (i·lek′tron′ik, ē′lek-) *adj.* **1.** Of or pertaining to electrons. **2.** Operating or produced by the movement of free electrons, as in radio and radar. **3.** Pertaining to electronics. — **e·lec′tron′i·cal·ly** *adv.*

electronic music See under MUSIC.

electronic organ An organ in which audio signals are produced electronically, amplified, and converted to sound.

e·lec·tron·ics (i·lek′tron′iks, ē′lek-) *n.pl.* (*construed as sing.*) The branch of engineering and technology that deals with the design and manufacture of devices, as radios, television sets, computers, etc., that contain electron tubes, transistors, or related components.

electron lens A device that establishes an electric or magnetic field around the path of an electron beam such that the beam may be focused.

electron microscope A microscope that projects onto a fluorescent screen the greatly enlarged image of an object held in the path of a sharply focused electron beam, thus permitting visual examination of objects smaller than the wavelengths of visible light used by an optical microscope.

electron optics The control of electron beams by properly adjusted magnetic or electric fields so that they will simulate the effect of light rays in an optical instrument.

electron tube A device in which conduction by electrons takes place through a vacuum or a rarefied gas in a gas-tight envelope, with operation controlled by the voltage applied at the electrodes.

electron volt A unit of energy equal to that acquired by an electron that passes through a potential difference of one volt: expressed as 1.602×10^{-12} erg. Abbr. *ev, e.v.*

e·lec·trop·a·thy (i·lek′trop′ə·thē, ē′lek-) *n.* Electrotherapeutics. — **e·lec′tro·path′ic** (-trə·path′ik) *adj.*

e·lec·tro·pho·re·sis (i·lek′trō·fə·rē′sis) *n. Chem.* The slow movement of the electrically charged colloidal particles dispersed in a fluid, when under the influence of an electric field: also called *cataphoresis.*

e·lec·troph·o·rus (i·lek′trof′ər·əs, ē′lek-) *n. pl.* **·ri** (-rī) An instrument for generating static electricity by induction. Also **e·lec′tro·phore** (i·lek′trə·fôr, -fōr). [< ELECTRO- + -PHORUS. See -PHORE.]

e·lec·tro·phys·i·ol·o·gy (i·lek′trō·fiz′ē·ol′ə·jē) *n.* The branch of physiology that studies the electrical properties and phenomena of living tissue. — **e·lec′tro·phys′i·o·log′i·cal** (-ə·loj′i·kəl) *adj.* — **e·lec′tro·phys′i·ol′o·gist** *n.*

e·lec·tro·plate (i·lek′trə·plāt′) *v.t.* **·plat·ed, ·plat·ing** To coat (an object) with metal by electrodeposition. — *n.* An electroplated article. — **e·lec′tro·plat′er** *n.*

e·lec·tro·plat·ing (i·lek′trə·plā′ting) *n.* **1.** The process of coating objects with metal by electrodeposition. **2.** The metal coating so deposited.

e·lec·tro·pos·i·tive (i·lek′trō·poz′ə·tiv) *adj.* **1.** Appearing at the negative electrode in electrolysis. **2.** Having the property of becoming positively electrified by contact or chemical action. **3.** Basic; not acid.

e·lec·tro·scis·sion (i·lek′trō·sizh′ən) *n. Surg.* The cutting or division of tissues by an electric needle, etc.

e·lec·tro·scope (i·lek′trə·skōp) *n.* An instrument for detecting the presence of an electric charge upon a conductor

ELECTROSCOPE

Metal pole (*m*), charged by (*e*), conducts the charge to strips (*s*), which then undergo electrostatic repulsion.

by the attraction or repulsion of pith balls or strips of gold leaf. — **e·lec'tro·scop'ic** (-skop'ik) *adj.*

e·lec·tro·shock (i·lek'trō·shok') *n. Psychiatry* A form of shock therapy in which a carefully controlled electric current is passed through the brain of the patient.

e·lec·tro·stat·ics (i·lek'trō·stat'iks) *n.pl.* (*construed as sing.*) A branch of physics that deals primarily with electric charges, fields, induction in conductors, and polarization in dielectrics. [< ELECTRO- + STATIC] — **e·lec'tro·stat'ic** or **·i·cal** *adj.* — **e·lec'tro·stat'i·cal·ly** *adv.*

electrostatic unit An electric charge that, if concentrated at one point in a vacuum, would repel, with a force of 1 dyne, an equal and like charge 1 centimeter away. Abbr. *esu, e.s.u.*

e·lec·tro·tax·is (i·lek'trō·tak'sis) *n. Biol.* The response of an organism to an electric stimulus. Also **e·lec·trot·ro·pism** (-trot'rə·piz'əm, e'lek-). — **e·lec'tro·tac'tic** (-tak'tik) *adj.*

e·lec·tro·ther·a·peu·tics (i·lek'trō·ther'ə·pyōo'tiks) *n.pl.* (*construed as sing.*) **1.** The treatment of disease by means of electricity. **2.** The principles and procedures of such treatment. Also called *electropathy*: also **e·lec'tro·ther'a·py.** — **e·lec'tro·ther'a·peu'tic** or **·ti·cal** *adj.*

e·lec·tro·ther·a·pist (i·lek'trō·ther'ə·pist) *n.* A practitioner of electrotherapeutics. Also **e·lec'tro·ther'a·peu'tist.**

e·lec·trot·o·nus (i·lek'trot'ə·nəs, e'lek-) *n. Physiol.* The change in the activity of a nerve or muscle when an electric current passes through it. [< NL < ELECTRO- + Gk. *tonos* tension] — **e·lec·tro·ton·ic** (i·lek'trō·ton'ik) *adj.*

e·lec·tro·type (i·lek'trə·tīp') *n.* **1.** A metallic copy, made by electrodeposition, of any surface, especially of a page of type for printing. **2.** An impression from an electrotype. **3.** The process of forming electrotypes. — *v.t.* **·typed, ·typ·ing** To make an electrotype of. — **e·lec'tro·typ'er, e·lec'tro·typ'ist** *n.* — **e·lec'tro·typ'ic** *adj.*

e·lec·tro·typ·ing (i·lek'trə·ti'ping) *n.* The process of forming electrotypes. Also **e·lec'tro·typ'y** (-ti'pē).

e·lec·tro·va·lence (i·lek'trō·vā'ləns) *n. Chem.* **1.** A bond formed by the transfer of electrons from the atoms of one element to the atoms of another during the formation of a compound. **2.** The number of electrons so transferred. Distinguished from *covalence.* — **e·lec'tro·va'lent** *adj.*

e·lec·trum (i·lek'trəm) *n.* **1.** German silver or other similar alloy. **2.** Native gold containing a large percentage of silver. [< L < Gk. *ēlektron* amber]

e·lec·tu·ar·y (i·lek'chōo·er'ē) *n. pl.* **·ar·ies** A medicine mixed with honey or syrup to form a paste. [< LL *electuarium* < Gk. *ekleikton* < *ek* out + *leichein* to lick]

el·ee·mos·y·nar·y (el'ə·mos'ə·ner'ē, el'ē·ə-) *adj.* **1.** Of or pertaining to charity or alms. **2.** Aided by or dependent upon charity. **3.** Done or given as a charitable act. [< Med.L *eleemosynarius* < LL *eleemosyna.* See ALMS.]

el·e·gance (el'ə·gəns) *n.* **1.** The state or quality of being elegant or refined; tasteful opulence. **2.** Something elegant, as a fastidiously chosen word or phrase. Also **el'e·gan·cy.**

el·e·gant (el'ə·gənt) *adj.* **1.** Tastefully ornate in dress, furnishings, etc. **2.** Marked by grace and refinement, as in style, manners, or taste; refined. **3.** Marked by ingenuity and simplicity: an *elegant* solution. **4.** *Informal* Excellent; first-rate. [< F *élégant* < L *elegans, -antis* < *e-* out + *legare* to choose] — **el'e·gant·ly** *adv.*

— **Syn.** *Elegant, exquisite,* and *dainty* are applied to things regarded as satisfying a refined taste. *Elegant* originally implied lightness, delicacy, and classical simplicity, but it has now become a word of indiscriminate approval. *Exquisite* implies perfection of workmanship and refinement of detail. *Dainty* now has some of the original meaning of *elegant,* and describes that which is at once slight, delicate, and pleasing.

el·e·gi·ac (el'ə·jī'ak, i·lē'jē·ak) *adj.* **1.** Pertaining to elegies. **2.** Of the nature of an elegy; sad; plaintive; lamenting. **3.** In classical prosody, written in distichs, the first line of which is a hexameter, and the second a pentameter. — *n.* Usually *pl.* Verse composed in elegiac form.

el·e·gist (el'ə·jist) *n.* One who writes elegies.

e·le·git (i·lē'jit) *n. Law* A writ of execution issued against a debtor by which part or all of the debtor's goods are delivered to the plaintiff until the debt is settled. [< L]

el·e·gize (el'ə·jīz) *v.* **·gized, ·giz·ing** *v.i.* **1.** To write elegiac verse. — *v.t.* **2.** To lament or commemorate in elegy.

el·e·gy (el'ə·jē) *n. pl.* **·gies 1.** In classical prosody, a poem written in elegiac verse. **2.** Any meditative poem of lamentation, especially for the dead. **3.** *Music* A song or instrumental work of lamentation or mourning. [< F *élégie* < L *elegia* < Gk. *elegeia* < *elegos* a song of lament]

E·lei·a (ē·lyē'ä) The Greek name for ELIS.

E·lek·tra (i·lek'trə) See ELECTRA.

elem. 1. Element(s). **2.** Elementary.

el·e·ment (el'ə·mənt) *n.* **1.** A relatively simple constituent that is a basic part of a complex whole; a primary, integral part; essential; fundamental; rudiment: the *elements* of democracy; the *elements* of poetry. **2.** A group or class of people distinguished from a larger group to which it belongs by its own peculiar beliefs, attitudes, behavior, etc.:

the conservative *element* in the party; a rowdy *element.* **3.** One of four substances (earth, air, fire, water) anciently viewed as composing the physical universe. **4.** Earth, air, fire, or water viewed as a proper or natural environment. **5.** The surrounding conditions best suited to some person or thing: to be out of one's *element.* **6.** *pl.* Atmospheric powers or forces; weather conditions. **7.** A principle, factual item, etc., essential to the solution of some problem or to proper calculation. **8.** *Physics & Chem.* One of a limited number of substances, as gold or carbon, each of which is composed entirely of atoms having an invariant nuclear charge, and none of which may be decomposed by ordinary chemical means. **9.** *Math.* **a** An infinitely small portion of a magnitude; a generatrix. **b** One of the terms of an algebraic expression. **c** One of a class of objects in a regular or symmetrical whole. **10.** *Geom.* One of the points, lines, etc., that together form a figure. **11.** *Electr.* **a** An integral part of a device, machine, or instrument necessary to its proper functioning, as the grid of an electron tube. **b** One of the dissimilar substances in a voltaic cell or battery, etc. **12.** *Mil.* **a** A subdivision of a unit. **b** *Canadian* One of three major categories into which the Canadian Forces are divided: the land, sea, and air elements, formerly the army, navy, and air force, respectively. **13.** *Eccl.* The bread or wine of the Eucharist. Abbr. *elem.* [< L *elementum* first principle]

TABLE OF ELEMENTS
(See also PERIODIC TABLE OF ELEMENTS)

NAME	Symbol	Atomic No.	Atomic Wt.
Actinium	Ac	89	227
Aluminum	Al	13	26.9815
Americium	Am	95	243
Antimony (*stibium*)	Sb	51	121.75
Argon	Ar	18	39.948
Arsenic	As	33	74.9216
Astatine	At	85	210
Barium	Ba	56	137.34
Berkelium	Bk	97	249
Beryllium	Be	4	9.0122
Bismuth	Bi	83	208.98
Boron	B	5	10.811
Bromine	Br	35	79.909
Cadmium	Cd	48	112.40
Calcium	Ca	20	40.08
Californium	Cf	98	251
Carbon	C	6	12.01115
Cerium	Ce	58	140.12
Cesium	Cs	55	132.905
Chlorine	Cl	17	35.453
Chromium	Cr	24	51.996
Cobalt	Co	27	58.9332
Columbium	(Cb)		
See NIOBIUM			
Copper (*cuprum*)	Cu	29	63.54
Curium	Cm	96	247
Dysprosium	Dy	66	162.50
Einsteinium	Es	99	254
Erbium	Er	68	167.26
Europium	Eu	63	151.96
Fermium	Fm	100	253
Fluorine	F	9	18.9984
Francium	Fr	87	223
Gadolinium	Gd	64	157.25
Gallium	Ga	31	69.72
Germanium	Ge	32	72.59
Glucinum			
See BERYLLIUM			
Gold (*aurum*)	Au	79	196.967
Hafnium	Hf	72	178.44
Helium	He	2	4.0026
Holmium	Ho	67	164.93
Hydrogen	H	1	1.00797
Indium	In	49	114.82
Iodine	I	53	126.9044
Iridium	Ir	77	192.2
Iron (*ferrum*)	Fe	26	55.847
Krypton	Kr	36	83.80
Lanthanum	La	57	138.91
Lawrencium	Lw	103	257?
Lead (*plumbum*)	Pb	82	207.19
Lithium	Li	3	6.939
Lutetium	Lu	71	174.97
Magnesium	Mg	12	24.312
Manganese	Mn	25	54.938
Mendelevium	Md	101	256
Mercury (*hydrargyrum*)	Hg	80	200.59
Molybdenum	Mo	42	95.94
Neodymium	Nd	60	144.24
Neon	Ne	10	20.183
Neoytterbium			
See YTTERBIUM			
Neptunium	Np	93	237
Nickel	Ni	28	58.71
Niobium	Nb	41	92.906
			(*continued*)

NAME	Symbol	Atomic No.	Atomic Wt.
Niton	See RADON		
Nitrogen	N	7	14.0067
Nobelium	No	102	253
Osmium	Os	76	190.2
Oxygen	O	8	15.9994
Palladium	Pd	46	106.4
Phosphorus	P	15	30.9738
Platinum	Pt	78	195.09
Plutonium	Pu	94	242
Polonium	Po	84	210
Potassium (kalium)	K	19	39.102
Praseodymium	Pr	59	140.90
Promethium	Pm	61	147
Protactinium	Pa	91	231
Radium	Ra	88	226.05
Radon	Rn	86	222
Rhenium	Re	75	186.20
Rhodium	Rh	45	102.905
Rubidium	Rb	37	85.47
Ruthenium	Ru	44	101.07
Samarium	Sm	62	150.35
Scandium	Sc	21	44.956
Selenium	Se	34	78.96
Silicon	Si	14	28.086
Silver (argentum)	Ag	47	107.87
Sodium (natrium)	Na	11	22.9898
Strontium	Sr	38	87.62
Sulfur	S	16	32.064
Tantalum	Ta	73	180.948
Technetium	Tc	43	99
Tellurium	Te	52	127.60
Terbium	Tb	65	158.924
Thallium	Tl	81	204.37
Thorium	Th	90	232.038
Thulium	Tm	69	168.934
Tin (stannum)	Sn	50	118.69
Titanium	Ti	22	47.90
Tungsten	W	74	183.85
Uranium	U	92	238.03
Vanadium	V	23	50.942
Wolfram	See TUNGSTEN		
Xenon	Xe	54	131.30
Ytterbium	Yb	70	173.04
Yttrium	Y	39	88.90
Zinc	Zn	30	65.37
Zirconium	Zr	40	91.22

el·e·men·tal (el′ə·men′təl) *adj.* **1.** Of or relating to an element or elements. **2.** Fundamental and relatively simple; basic. **3.** Relating to or concerned with first principles; rudimentary. **4.** Of, belonging to, or suggestive of the powerful forces at work in nature or in man. **5.** Chemically uncombined; not compounded. — **el′e·men′tal·ly** *adv.*

el·e·men·ta·ry (el·ə·men′tər·ē, -men′trē) *adj.* **1.** Of or relating to an element or elements; elemental. **2.** Relating to or concerned with what is fundamental; relating to or concerned with basic or introductory material: an *elementary* course in physics. **3.** Simple and rudimentary: an *elementary* knowledge of astronomy. *Abbr. elem.* — **el′e·men′ta·ri·ly** *adv.* — **el′e·men′ta·ri·ness** *n.*

elementary education Education preceding secondary school, from about six to eight years in length and dealing with the fundamentals of knowledge.

elementary school A school giving a course of education of from six to eight years, pupils usually entering at about six years of age: also called *grade school, grammar school.*

el·e·mi (el′ə·mē) *n.* Any one of several gum resins obtained from tropical trees of various genera, used in drugs and varnishes. [< Sp. *elemi,* prob. < Arabic *al-lāmī*]

e·len·chus (i·leng′kəs) *n. pl.* **·chi** (-kī) **1.** A syllogism used to refute an argument by proving the opposite of the argument's concluding proposition. **2.** A false refutation; sophism. [< L < Gk. *elenchos* cross-examination]

e·lenc·tic (i·lengk′tik) *adj.* Logic Serving to refute by proving the opposite: distinguished from *deictic.* Also **e·len·chic** (i·leng′kik).

el·e·o·plast (el′ē·ə·plast′) See ELAIOPLAST.

el·e·op·tene (el′ē·op′tēn) See ELAEOPTENE.

el·e·phant (el′ə·fənt) *n.* **1.** A massively built, almost hairless ungulate mammal (family *Elephantidae*) of Asia and Africa, the largest of existing land animals, having a flexible proboscis or trunk, and the upper incisors developed as tusks and valued as the chief source of ivory. There are two genera, the **Asian elephant** (*Elephas maximus*) having relatively small ears, and the **African elephant** (*Loxodonta africana*) having large, flapping ears. **2.** A size of paper, 23 by 38 inches or somewhat larger. [< OF *olifant* < L *elephantus* < Gk. *elephas, -antos* ivory, elephant; ult. origin unknown]

AFRICAN ELEPHANT
(To 12 feet high)

Elephant Butte Dam The main unit of the Rio Grande reclamation project in SW New Mexico; 306 ft. high; 1,674 ft. long; impounding **Elephant Butte Reservoir.**

el·e·phan·ti·a·sis (el′ə·fən·tī′ə·sis) *n. Pathol.* A filariasis caused by a parasitic nematode worm (*Wuchereria bancrofti*), characterized by a thickening and hardening of the skin, and an enormous enlargement of the part affected, usually the lower extremities. [< L < Gk. < *elephas* elephant]

el·e·phan·tine (el′ə·fan′tin, -tēn, -tīn) *adj.* **1.** Of or pertaining to an elephant. **2.** Enormous; unwieldy; ponderous.

El·e·phan·ti·ne (el′ə·fan·tī′nē) An island in the Nile opposite Aswan; site of Egyptian and Roman ruins.

elephant's ear The taro.

el·e·phant's-foot (el′ə·fənts·fŏŏt′) *n.* A South African twining vine (*Testudinaria elephantipes*) of the yam family, having a conical, cormlike stem covered with a barky substance: also called *Hottentot bread.* Also **elephant foot.**

Eleusinian mysteries The secret religious rites originated at Eleusis and later absorbed by the Athenian state religion.

E·leu·sis (i·lōō′sis) In Greek mythology, the son of Hermes.

E·leu·sis (i·lōō′sis) A port town in east central Greece, on the **Bay of Eleusis,** an inlet of the Saronic Gulf; former site of an ancient Attic city; pop. about 11,000. *Greek* **E·lev·sis** (â′lâf·sēs′). — **El·eu·sin′i·an** (el′yŏŏ·sin′ē·ən) *n. & adj.*

El·eu·the·ri·a (el′yŏŏ·thir′ē·ə) *n.* A quadrennial festival kept by the Greeks after the battle of Plataea in honor of Zeus in his aspect of **Eleutherios** (the Deliverer).

elev. Elevation.

el·e·vate (el′ə·vāt) *v.t.* **·vat·ed, ·vat·ing 1.** To lift up; raise. **2.** To raise in rank, status, etc.; promote. **3.** To raise the spirits of; cheer; elate. **4.** To raise the pitch or loudness of (the voice). **5.** To raise the moral character or intellectual level of, as a conversation. [< L *elevatus,* pp. of *elevare* < *e-* out + *levare* to lighten, raise]

— **Syn.** *Elevate, erect, raise, rear, lift,* and *hoist* all mean to place in a higher position. *Elevate* is a somewhat formal term implying either a literal rise in position or altitude or a figurative rise in rank or distinction. *Erect* is used chiefly to indicate a structural rise or shift to a vertical position; a building or a flagpole may be *erected* on a specified site. *Raise* commonly implies a physical gesture or activity, while *rear* suggests a forceful or emphatic motion, often figuratively; a person *raises* his hand or his aim, while vice or a horse *rears* its head. *Lift* suggests the use of physical effort in moving something to a higher position, and *hoist* often signifies lifting by mechanical means.

el·e·vat·ed (el′ə·vā′tid) *adj.* **1.** Raised up; high: an *elevated* plateau. **2.** Lofty in character; sublime: *elevated* sentiments. **3.** In high spirits; elated. — **Syn.** See HIGH. — *n. U.S. Informal* An overhead railroad.

el·e·va·tion (el′ə·vā′shən) *n.* **1.** The act of elevating, or the state of being elevated. **2.** An elevated place. **3.** Height above sea level. **4.** Loftiness of thought, feeling, station, etc.; dignity; exaltation. **5.** In dancing, the ability to leap into the air in formal movements or steps. **6.** *Often cap. Eccl.* The raising of the eucharistic elements for adoration during the Mass. **7.** *Astron.* The angular distance of a celestial body above the horizon. **8.** In drafting, a side, front, or rear view of a machine or other structure. *Abbr. el., elev.*

el·e·va·tor (el′ə·vā′tər) *n.* **1.** One who or that which elevates. **2.** A mechanism for hoisting grain. **3.** *U.S.* A granary equipped with mechanisms for raising grain. **4.** *U.S.* A movable platform or car that carries passengers or freight up and down, as inside a building. **5.** *Aeron.* A control surface attached to the horizontal stabilizer of an airplane that makes the tail go up or down.

e·lev·en (i·lev′ən) *n.* **1.** The sum of ten and one: a cardinal number. **2.** Any symbol of this number, as 11, xi, XI. **3.** Anything consisting of or representing eleven units, as a team, game token, etc. — *adj.* Being one more than ten. [OE *endleofan* one left over (after ten)]

e·lev·enth (i·lev′ənth) *adj.* **1.** Next after the tenth: the ordinal of *eleven.* **2.** Being one of eleven equal parts. — *n.* **1.** One of eleven equal parts. **2.** That which follows the tenth.

eleventh hour The latest or last time possible.

el·e·von (el′ə·von) *n. Aeron.* A combined elevator and aileron. [< ELEV(ATOR) + (AIL)ERON]

elf (elf) *n. pl.* **elves** (elvz) **1.** In folklore, a dwarfish sprite with magical powers, usually intent upon playful mischief. **2.** Any mischievous creature. **3.** A tiny person. [OE *ælf*]

El Fai·yum (el·fī·yōōm′) See FAIYUM.

El Fer·rol del Cau·di·llo (el fer·rōl′ thel kou·thē′lyō) A port city in NW Spain; pop. 82,639 (est. 1959). Formerly **El Fer·rol′.**

elf·in (el′fin) *adj.* Elfish. — *n.* An elf.

elf·ish (el′fish) *adj.* **1.** Of or pertaining to elves. **2.** Suggestive of or resembling an elf; mischievous; impish. Also *elvish.* — **elf′ish·ly** *adv.* — **elf′ish·ness** *n.*

elf·lock (elf′lok′) *n.* A lock of hair tangled as if by elves.

El·gar (el′gär) **Sir Edward,** 1857–1934, English composer.

El·gin (el′gin *for defs. 1 & 2,* el′jin *for def. 3*) **1.** A burgh, county seat of Moray, Scotland in the northern part of the county; pop. 16,416 (1961). **2.** A former name for MORAY. Also **El′gin·shire** (-shir). **3.** A city in NE Illinois; pop. 55,691.

El·gin marbles (el′gin) A collection of Greek sculpture in the British Museum, London, formerly on the Acropolis at Athens. [after the Earl of *Elgin,* who had the sculptures brought to England, 1803–12]

El Gi·zeh (el gē′zə) See GIZA.

El·gon (el′gon), **Mount** An extinct volcano on the Uganda-Kenya border NE of Lake Victoria; 14,178 ft.

El Grec·o (el grek′ō, grā′kō) See GRECO.

El Ha·sa (el hä′sə) A Province and eastern dependency of Nejd, Saudi Arabia; about 22,500 sq. mi.; pop. about 2 million; capital, Hofuf: also *Al Ahsa, Hasa*. Also **El Ha·za** (hä′zä).

E·li (ē′lī) A Biblical high priest and judge. 1 *Sam.* i–iv. [< Hebrew, high]

E·li·a (ē·lyē′ä) The Greek name for ELIS.

E·li·a (ē′lē·ä) See (Charles) LAMB.

E·li·as (i·lī′əs) See ELIJAH.

e·lic·it (i·lis′it) *v.t.* **1.** To draw out or forth; evoke: to *elicit* a reply. **2.** To bring to light; educe: to *elicit* the truth. [< L *elicitus*, pp. of *elicere* < *e-* out + *lacere* to entice] — **e·lic′i·ta′tion** *n.* — **e·lic′i·tor** *n.*

e·lide (i·līd′) *v.t.* **e·lid·ed, e·lid·ing** **1.** To omit (a vowel or syllable) in pronunciation. **2.** To suppress; omit; ignore. **3.** *Law* To annul. [< L *elidere* < *e-* out + *laedere* to strike] — **e·lid′i·ble** *adj.*

el·i·gi·bil·i·ty (el′ə·jə·bil′ə·tē) *n.* *pl.* **·ties** **1.** The quality of being eligible; suitableness. **2.** *pl.* Qualities that make a person or thing eligible.

el·i·gi·ble (el′ə·jə·bəl) *adj.* **1.** Capable of and qualified for an office, position, function, etc. **2.** Fit for or worthy of choice or adoption. **3.** Agreeable to have; suitable; especially, qualified and desirable for marriage: an *eligible* young man. — *n.* An eligible person. [< F *éligible* < L *eligere*. See ELECT.] — **el′i·gi·bly** *adv.*

E·li·hu (el′ə·hyoō) A young man who visits Job. *Job* xxxii.

E·li·jah (i·lī′jə) Ninth-century B.C. Hebrew prophet: also *Elias*. [< Hebrew, Jehovah is my God]

e·lim·i·nate (i·lim′ə·nāt) *v.t.* **·nat·ed, ·nat·ing** **1.** To get rid of or do away with; strike out: to *eliminate* poverty and disease. **2.** To disregard as irrelevant; ignore. **3.** To remove (a contestant, team, etc.) from further competition by defeating. **4.** *Physiol.* To void; excrete. **5.** *Math.* To remove (a quantity) from a system of algebraic equations. — **Syn.** See CANCEL. [< L *eliminatus*, pp. of *eliminare* to expel < *e-* out + *limen* threshold] — **e·lim′i·na′tive, e·lim′i·na·to′ry** (-nə·tôr′ē, -tō′rē) *adj.*

e·lim·i·na·tion (i·lim′ə·nā′shən) *n.* The act or process of eliminating, or the state of being eliminated.

Eli·ot (el′ē·ət), **Charles William,** 1834–1926, U.S. educator; president of Harvard 1869–1909. — **George** Pseudonym of *Mary Ann Evans,* 1819–80, English novelist. — **John,** 1604–1690, English clergyman in America: called **the Apostle of the Indians.** — **Sir John,** 1592–1632, English statesman and patriot. — **T(homas) S(tearns),** 1888–1965, British poet, dramatist, and critic born in the United States.

E·lis (ē′lis) A Department of Greece in the western Peloponnesus, in part, the ancient country of Elis; 1,153 sq. mi.; pop. 188,274 (1951); capital, Pyrgos: Greek *Eleia, Elia, Ilia.*

E·lis·a·beth·ville (i·liz′ə·bəth·vil′) A former name for LUBUMBASHI.

E·li·sha (i·lī′shə) Ninth-century B.C. Hebrew prophet, successor of Elijah. [< Hebrew, God is Salvation]

e·li·sion (i·lizh′ən) *n.* Omission of a vowel or syllable, especially at the ends of words in poetry, as in "th′ imperial towers." [< L *elisio, -onis* < *elidere*. See ELIDE.]

e·lite (ā·lēt′, i·lēt′) *n.* **1.** The choicest part, as of a particular social group. **2.** A size of typewriter type, equivalent to 10-point, with 12 characters to the inch. Also **é·lite′.** [< F *élite* < *élire* < L *eligere*. See ELECT.]

e·lix·ir (i·lik′sər) *n.* **1.** A sweetened alcoholic medicinal preparation; formerly, a compound tincture. **2.** In alchemy and ancient philosophy: **a** A substance sought by alchemists for changing base metals into gold. **b** A cordial supposedly able to prolong life indefinitely: also **elixir vi·tae** (vī′tē). **3.** The essential principle of anything; quintessence. **4.** A cure-all; panacea. [< Med.L < Arabic *al-iksīr* < Gk. *xērion* medicated powder < *xēros* dry]

E·liz·a·beth (i·liz′ə·bəth) The mother of John the Baptist: called **Saint Elizabeth.** *Luke* i 5–14.

Elizabeth, born 1900, queen mother of England; wife of George VI; queen 1937–52.

Elizabeth A city in NE New Jersey; pop. 107,698.

Elizabeth I, 1533–1603, queen of England 1558–1603; daughter of Henry VIII and Anne Boleyn.

Elizabeth II, born 1926, queen of England 1952– ; daughter of George VI; married to Prince Philip.

E·liz·a·be·than (i·liz′ə·bē′thən, -beth′ən) *adj.* Of or pertaining to Elizabeth I of England, or to her era. — *n.* An Englishman living during the reign of Elizabeth I; especially, a writer or other notable person active during her reign.

Elizabethan sonnet A Shakespearean sonnet (which see).

Elizabeth of Hungary, Saint, 1207–31, Hungarian princess; queen of Thuringia 1221–27.

Elizabeth Pe·trov·na (pe·trôv′nə), 1709–62, empress of Russia 1741–62.

E·li·za·vet·pol (yi·lyi·zə·vyit·pôly′′), etc. See YELIZAVET-POL, etc.

elk (elk) *n.* *pl.* **elks** or **elk** **1.** A large deer of northern Europe and Asia (genus *Alces*), having palmated antlers and an upper lip adapted to browsing upon trees. **2.** A large North American deer; the wapiti. **3.** A pliant leather of calfskin, horsehide, etc., tanned and finished to look like elk hide. [ME *elke* < OE *elh*]

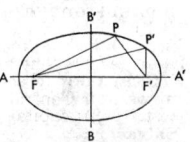

ELK (def. 2)
(About 6 feet high at shoulder)

El Kha·lil (el·kä·lēl′, khä-) The Arabic name for HEBRON.

Elk·hart (elk′härt) A city in northern Indiana; pop. 43,152.

elk·hound (elk′hound′) *n.* A medium-sized, robust dog of Norwegian origin, with a thick, gray coat and broad head.

ell[1] (el) *n.* A measure of length now rarely used: in England, 45 inches or 1.114 meters. [OE *eln* an arm's length]

ell[2] (el) *n.* **1.** The letter L. **2.** Anything shaped like the letter L: also spelled *el.* **3.** A room or extension built at right angles to the main part of a house, etc.

El·las (â·läs′) The Greek name for GREECE.

Elles·mere Island (elz′mir) An island in the northern Northwest Territories, Canada; 77,392 sq. mi.

El·lice Islands (el′is) An island group SE of the Gilbert Islands, part of the Gilbert and Ellice Islands Colony; 9.5 sq. mi.: formerly *Lagoon Islands.*

el·lipse (i·lips′) *n.* *Geom.* A plane curve such that the sum of the distances from any point of the curve to two fixed points, called *foci,* is a constant; a conic section. [< L *ellipsis.* See ELLIPSIS.]

el·lip·sis (i·lip′sis) *n.* *pl.* **·ses** (-sēz) **1.** *Gram.* The omission of a word or words necessary for the complete grammatical construction of a sentence, but not required for the understanding of it. **2.** Marks (. . . or * * *) indicating omission. Also called *eclipsis.* [< L < Gk. *elleipsis* < *en-* in + *leipsis* a leaving < *leipein* to leave]

ELLIPSE
A A′ Major axis. *BB′* Minor axis. *F, F′* Foci. *P, P′* Points on curve.
$$(FP + F'P = FP' + F'P')$$

el·lip·soid (i·lip′soid) *n.* *Math.* A solid of which every plane section is an ellipse or a circle. — *adj.* Resembling an ellipsoid: also **el·lip·soi·dal** (ē′lip·soid′l). [< ELLIPSE + -OID]

el·lip·tic (i·lip′tik) *adj.* **1.** Of, pertaining to, or shaped like an ellipse; oblong with rounded ends. **2.** *Gram.* Characterized by ellipsis; shortened. Also **el·lip′ti·cal.** — **el·lip′ti·cal·ly.** *adv.* [< Gk. *elleiptikos* < *elleipsis.* See ELLIPSIS.]

el·lip·tic·i·ty (el′lip·tis′ə·tē, i·lip′-) *n.* **1.** The state of being elliptic. **2.** The degree of deviation of an ellipse from a circle or of a spheroid from a sphere.

El·lis (el′is), **Alexander John,** 1814–90, English philologist and phonetician. — (**Henry**) **Havelock,** 1859–1939, English psychologist and author.

Ellis Island (el′is) An island in upper New York Bay; former site of the chief United States immigration station.

Ells·worth (elz′wərth) **Lincoln,** 1880–1951, U.S. polar explorer. — **Oliver,** 1745–1807, American jurist.

elm (elm) *n.* **1.** A deciduous shade tree (genus *Ulmus*) of America, Europe, and Asia, having a broad, spreading, or overarching top; especially, the **American elm** (*U. americana*) and the slippery elm (which see). **2.** The wood of this tree. [OE] — **elm′y** *adj.*

El·man (el′mən), **Mischa,** 1891–1967, U.S. violinist born in Russia.

elm-bark beetle (elm′bärk′) Any of various beetles (family *Scolytidae*) destructive to elm trees, especially a European species (*Scolytus multistratus*) introduced into America, that transmits the fungus of Dutch elm disease.

Elm·hurst (elm′hûrst) A city in NE Illinois; pop. 36,991.

El·mi·ra (el·mī′rə) A city in southern New York, near the Pennsylvania border; pop. 39,945.

El Mis·ti (el mēs′tē) A volcano in southern Peru; 19,110 ft.

elm-leaf beetle (elm′lēf′) A coleopterous insect (*Galerucella xanthomelaena* or *luteola*), yellowish green with dark lateral spots, injurious to elm trees.

El·mont (el′mont) An unincorporated place in SE New York on Long Island; pop. 29,363.

E·lo·bey (ā′lō·bā′), **Great** and **Little** Two small islands in the Bight of Biafra, part of Río Muni; 1.5 sq. mi.

el·o·cu·tion (el′ə·kyoō′shən) *n.* **1.** The art of public speaking, including vocal delivery and gesture. **2.** Manner of speaking. [< L *elocutio, -onis* < *eloqui* < *e-* out + *loqui* to speak] — **el′o·cu′tion·ar′y** *adj.* — **el′o·cu′tion·ist** *n.*

E·lo·him (e·lō·him′, -lō′him) God: Hebrew name used in the Old Testament. [< Hebrew *'Elōhīm,* pl. of *'Elōah* God]

E·lo·hist (e·lō′hist) *n.* The author of those portions of the Hexateuch that are characterized by the use of *Elohim* for God instead of *Yahweh* or *Jehovah.* Compare YAHWIST.

El·o·his·tic (el'ō·his'tik) *adj.* **1.** Of or pertaining to those portions of the Hexateuch where *Elohim* occurs in the Hebrew text and not *Yahweh* or *Jehovah.* **2.** Written by the Elohist.

e·loign (i·loin') *v.t. Law* To remove to a distance; remove beyond the jurisdiction of. Also **e·loin'.** [< OF *esloignier* to remove < LL *elongare.* See ELONGATE.]

E. long. or **e. long.** East longitude.

e·lon·gate (i·lông'gāt, i·long'-) *v.t. & v.i.* **·gat·ed, ·gat·ing** To increase in length; stretch. — *adj.* Drawn out; lengthened. [< LL *elongatus*, pp. of *elongare* < L *e-* out + *longe* far off]

e·lon·ga·tion (ē'lông·gā'shən, ē'long-, i·lông'gā'shən, i·long'-) *n.* **1.** The act of elongating, or the state of being elongated. **2.** That which adds to the length of something; an extension.

e·lope (i·lōp') *v.i.* **e·loped, e·lop·ing** **1.** To run away with a lover, usually to get married. **2.** To abscond. [< AF *aloper.* Cf. OE *ūthlēapan* to flee.] — **e·lope'ment** *n.* — **e·lop'er** *n.*

el·o·quence (el'ə·kwəns) *n.* **1.** Fluent, polished, and effective use of language, especially in public speaking. **2.** The quality of being moving, forceful, or persuasive.

el·o·quent (el'ə·kwənt) *adj.* **1.** Possessed of or manifesting eloquence; fluent and convincing in speech or writing. **2.** Visibly expressive of emotion: *eloquent* tears. [< L *eloquens, -entis,* ppr. of *eloqui.* See ELOCUTION.] — **el'o·quent·ly** *adv.*

El Pas·o (el pas'ō) A city in the western extremity of Texas, on the Rio Grande; pop. 322,261.

El Pa·so del Nor·te (el pä'sō thel nōr'tā) A former name for CIUDAD JUÁREZ.

El·phin·stone (el'fin·stōn, -stən), **Mountstuart,** 1779–1859, British historian and statesman. — **William,** 1431–1514, Scottish bishop; founded Aberdeen University.

El·sa (el'sä) The heroine of Wagner's opera *Lohengrin.*

El Sal·va·dor (el sal'və·dôr, *Sp.* el säl'vä·thōr') A Republic in western Central America; 8,260 sq. mi.; pop. 3,390,000 (est. 1969); capital, San Salvador. Officially **Republic of El Salvador.**

El·sass (el'zäs) The German name for ALSACE.

El·sass-Lo·thring·en (el'zäs·lō'tring·ən) The German name for ALSACE–LORRAINE.

else (els) *adv.* **1.** In a different place, time, or way; instead: Where *else?* How *else?* **2.** If the case or facts were different; otherwise: Hurry, or *else* you will be caught. — *adj.* Additional; different: somebody *else.* [OE *elles.* Akin to L *alius*].
◆ In modern writing, *someone else, anyone else,* etc., are treated as compound pronouns, and the possessive forms are *someone else's, anyone else's,* etc. *Whose else,* a survival of such older forms as *someone's else,* is sometimes used, but when followed by a noun, *else* takes the inflection, as *who else's* hat.

else·where (els'hwâr') *adv.* In or to another place or places; somewhere or anywhere else.

El·si·nore (el'sə·nôr, -nōr) Helsingør, Denmark: so called in Shakespeare's *Hamlet.*

e·lu·ci·date (i·lōō'sə·dāt) *v.* **·dat·ed, ·dat·ing** *v.t.* **1.** To make clear; explain. — *v.i.* **2.** To clarify something. — **Syn.** See EXPLAIN. [< LL *elucidatus,* pp. of *elucidare* < L *e-* out + *lucidus* clear] — **e·lu'ci·da'tion** *n.* — **e·lu'ci·da'tive** *adj.* — **e·lu'ci·da'tor** *n.*

e·lude (i·lōōd') *v.t.* **e·lud·ed, e·lud·ing** **1.** To avoid or escape from by dexterity or artifice; evade. **2.** To escape the notice or understanding of: The meaning *eludes* me. — **Syn.** See ESCAPE. [< L *eludere* < *e-* out + *ludere* to play]

El Uk·sor (al ōōk'sōr) The Arabic name for LUXOR.

E·lul (e·lōōl', el'ōōl) *n.* The twelfth month of the Hebrew year. See (Hebrew) CALENDAR.

e·lu·sion (i·lōō'zhən) *n.* The act of eluding; escape; evasion. [< Med.L *elusio, -onis* < L *eludere.* See ELUDE.]

e·lu·sive (i·lōō'siv) *adj.* Tending to slip away; hard to grasp or perceive: an *elusive* fragrance. Also **e·lu'so·ry** (-sər·ē). — **e·lu'sive·ly** *adv.* — **e·lu'sive·ness** *n.*

e·lu·tri·ate (i·lōō'trē·āt) *v.t.* **·at·ed, ·at·ing** To purify or separate by washing and straining or decanting. [< L *elutriatus,* pp. of *elutriare* to wash off] — **e·lu'tri·a'tion** *n.*

e·lu·vi·a·tion (i·lōō'vē·ā'shən) *n.* The process, mechanical or chemical, by which the fine particles of the topsoil are moved from one area to another: distinguished from *illuviation.* [< L *eluvies* a washing away + -ATION]

e·lu·vi·um (i·lōō'vē·əm) *n. Geol.* A deposit of soil and dust particles remaining where they were formed by the decomposition of rock masses. [< NL < L *eluvies* < *eluere* < *e-* away + *luere* to wash] — **e·lu'vi·al** *adj.*

el·ver (el'vər) *n.* A young eel. [Var. of *eelfare* the journey of young eels upstream < EEL + FARE]

elves (elvz) Plural of ELF.

elv·ish (el'vish) *adj.* Elfish. — **elv'ish·ly** *adv.*

E·ly (ē'lē) An urban district in the Isle of Ely; site of a 12th-century cathedral; pop. 9,815 (1961).

Ely, Isle of An administrative county of Cambridgeshire, England; 375 sq. mi.; county seat, March.

El·y·ot (el'ē·ət, el'yət), **Sir Thomas,** 1490?–1546, English scholar and diplomat.

E·lyr·i·a (i·lir'ē·ə) A city in northern Ohio; pop. 53,427.

E·ly·sée (ā·lē·zā') The official residence of the president of France, in Paris.

E·ly·sian (i·lizh'ən, -ē·ən) *adj.* **1.** Belonging to, or like, Elysium. **2.** Blissful; delightful.

E·ly·si·um (i·lizh'ē·əm, i·liz'-) **1.** In Greek mythology, the land of the blessed dead, represented as in Hades, or in the Islands of the Blest in the Western Ocean. Also **Elysian Fields.** **2.** A place or condition of supreme delight; paradise. [< L < Gk. *Ēlysion (pedion)* the Elysian (field)]

el·y·tra (el'ə·trə) Plural of ELYTRON.

el·y·troid (el'ə·troid) *adj.* Resembling an elytron.

el·y·tron (el'ə·tron) *n. pl.* **·tra** *Entomol.* One of the pair of thickened forewings of certain insects, as beetles, serving to cover or protect the hind wings. Also **el'y·trum** (-trəm). [< Gk. *elytron* case < *eilyein* to wrap up]

El·ze·vir (el'zə·vir) *adj.* **1.** Belonging or related to Louis Elzevir, his successors, or their firm. **2.** Denoting the type face used by the Elzevirs. — *n.* **1.** A book printed by the Elzevirs. **2.** A compact, modern printing type.

El·ze·vir (el'zə·vir), **Louis,** 1540?–1617, and his son **Bona·venture,** 1583–1652, Dutch printers; famous for fine editions of the classics. Also **El'ze·vier.**

em (em) *n.* **1.** The letter M. **2.** *Printing* The square of the body size of a type; especially, a pica em, about ⅙ of an inch, used as a standard unit of measurement: originally, the space occupied by the letter M in a font.

em-[1] Var. of EN-[1].

em-[2] Var. of EN-[2].

'em (əm, m) *pron. Informal* Them. [OE *heom,* dative pl. of *he* he]

Em. *Physics* Emanation.

EM *Mil.* Enlisted man (men).

e·ma·ci·ate (i·mā'shē·āt) *v.t.* **·at·ed, ·at·ing** To make abnormally lean; cause to lose flesh. [< L *emaciatus,* pp. of *emaciare* to waste away < *e-* away + *maciare* < *macies* leanness] — **e·ma'ci·a'tion** *n.*

e·ma·ci·at·ed (i·mā'shē·ā'tid) *adj.* Very thin; wasted away.

em·a·nate (em'ə·nāt) *v.i.* **·nat·ed, ·nat·ing** To flow forth from a source; issue. [< L *emanatus,* pp. of *emanare* < *e-* out + *manare* to flow]

em·a·na·tion (em'ə·nā'shən) *n.* **1.** The act of emanating. **2.** Something that emanates; efflux; effluence. **3.** *Physics* A gaseous product of disintegration in certain radioactive substances, as radon and thoron. — **em'a·na'tive** *adj.*

e·man·ci·pate (i·man'sə·pāt) *v.t.* **·pat·ed, ·pat·ing** **1.** To release from bondage, oppression, or authority; set free. **2.** *Law* To free (a child) from paternal control. [< L *emancipatus,* pp. of *emancipare* < *e-* out + *manus* hand + *capere* to take] — **e·man'ci·pa'tive** *adj.* — **e·man'ci·pa'tor** *n.*

e·man·ci·pa·tion (i·man'sə·pā'shən) *n.* The act of emancipating, or the state of being emancipated; liberation.

Emancipation Proclamation A proclamation issued by President Abraham Lincoln on January 1, 1863, declaring free all Negro slaves in all States and territory still in rebellion against the Union.

e·mar·gi·nate (i·mär'jə·nit, -nāt) *adj. Bot.* Having the margin or apex notched: said of leaves, petals, etc. Also **e·mar'gi·nat'ed.** [< L *emarginatus,* pp. of *emarginare* < *e-* off, away + *margo, -inis* border, edge]

e·mas·cu·late (*v.* i·mas'kyə·lāt; *adj.* i·mas'kyə·lit) *v.t.* **·lat·ed, ·lat·ing** **1.** To deprive of procreative power; castrate; geld. **2.** To deprive of masculine strength and vigor; make effeminate; weaken. **3.** To impair the vigor of (a literary work, etc.) by cutting or censoring. — *adj.* Emasculated; effeminate; weakened. [< L *emasculatus,* pp. of *emasculare* < *e-* away + *masculus* male] — **e·mas'cu·la'tion** *n.* — **e·mas'cu·la'tor** *n.* — **e·mas'cu·la·to·ry** (i·mas'kyə·lə·tôr'ē, -tō'rē), **e·mas'cu·la'tive** *adj.*

em·balm (im·bäm') *v.t.* **1.** To preserve (a dead body) from decay by treatment with balsams, chemicals, etc. **2.** To preserve or keep in memory. **3.** *Poetic* To perfume. Also spelled *imbalm.* [< F *embaumer* < *em-* in (< L *in-*) + *baume.* See BALM.] — **em·balm'er** *n.* — **em·balm'ment** *n.*

em·bank (im·bangk') *v.t.* To confine or protect with a bank, dike, or the like. [EM-[1]- + BANK]

em·bank·ment (im·bangk'mənt) *n.* **1.** A mound or bank raised to hold back water, support a roadway, etc. **2.** The act of embanking.

em·bar (im·bär') *v.t.* **·barred, ·bar·ring** **1.** To enclose within bars; fasten in; imprison. **2.** To stop; check, as by a bar. [< F *embarrer*] — **em·bar'ment** *n.*

em·bar·go (im·bär'gō) *n. pl.* **·goes** **1.** An order by a government restraining merchant vessels from leaving or entering its ports. **2.** Authoritative stoppage of foreign commerce or of any special trade. **3.** A restraint or prohibition. — *v.t.* **·goed, ·go·ing** To lay an embargo upon. [< Sp. < *embargar* ult. < LL *barra* bar]

em·bark (im·bärk') *v.t.* **1.** To put or take aboard a vessel. **2.** To invest (money) or involve (a person) in a venture. — *v.i.* **3.** To go aboard a vessel for a voyage. **4.** To engage in a venture. Also spelled *imbark.* [< F *embarquer* < LL *imbarcare* < *in-* in + *barca* boat] — **em·bark'ment** *n.*

em·bar·ka·tion (em'bär·kā'shən) *n.* The act of embarking. Also **em'bar·ca'tion.**

em·bar·rass (im·bar'əs) *v.t.* **1.** To make self-conscious and uncomfortable; abash; disconcert. **2.** To involve in finan-

cial difficulties. **3.** To hamper; impede. **4.** To render difficult; complicate. [< F *embarrasser* < *em-* in (< L *in-*) + *barre* < OF. See BAR.]
— **Syn.** Embarrass, abash, disconcert, discomfit, rattle, and *faze* mean to check by making uneasy or confused. We may be *embarrassed* in feeling or in action, as by ridicule or some material obstacle; we are *abashed* only in feeling, through the sudden loss of self-confidence. We are *disconcerted* by any unexpected hostility or rebuff, which leaves us momentarily uncertain how to proceed. To *discomfit* is to vanquish, as in a battle of wits; a defiant witness may be *discomfited* by a sharp cross-examination. *Rattle* and *faze* are both informal; *rattle* is close to *disconcert*, but with greater stress on the disorganization of the mental faculties, while *faze* (usually used negatively) includes *embarrass*, *abash*, and *disconcert*.

em·bar·rass·ing (im·bar′əs·ing) *adj.* That embarrasses. — **em·bar′rass·ing·ly** *adv.*

em·bar·rass·ment (im·bar′əs·mənt) *n.* **1.** The state of being embarrassed. **2.** That which embarrasses.

em·bas·sa·dor (im·bas′ə·dər, -dôr) *n.* *Archaic* Ambassador.

em·bas·sage (em′bə·sij) *n.* *Archaic* Embassy.

em·bas·sy (em′bə·sē) *n.* *pl.* **·sies** **1.** An ambassador together with his staff. **2.** The mission, function, or position of an ambassador. **3.** The official residence or headquarters of an ambassador. [Var. of earlier *ambassy* < OF *ambasse* < Med.L *ambactia* < L *ambactus*. See AMBASSADOR.]

em·bat·tle[1] (em·bat′l) *v.t.* **·tled**, **·tling** To form in line of battle; prepare or equip for battle. [< OF *embataillier* < *em*[1]- in (< L *in-*) + *bataille*. See BATTLE.]

em·bat·tle[2] (em·bat′l) *v.t.* **·tled**, **·tling** To furnish with battlements. [< EM-[1] + BATTLE in obs. sense of "fortify" < OF *bastillier* to build]

em·bay (em·bā′) *v.t.* **1.** To put or force (a ship, etc.) into a bay. **2.** To shut in by arms of land.

em·bay·ment (em·bā′mənt) *n.* **1.** A bay or baylike enclosure. **2.** The process of forming a bay.

em·bed (im·bed′) *v.t.* **bed·ded**, **bed·ding** **1.** To set firmly in surrounding matter. **2.** To place in or as in a bed. **3.** To fix in the memory. Also spelled *imbed*. — **em·bed′ment** *n.*

em·bel·lish (im·bel′ish) *v.t.* **1.** To beautify by adding ornamental features; decorate. **2.** To heighten the interest of (a narrative) by adding fictitious details. — **Syn.** See ADORN. [< OF *embelliss-*, stem of *embellir* to beautify < *em-* in (< L *in-*) + *bel* beautiful < L *bellus*]

em·bel·lish·ment (im·bel′ish·mənt) *n.* **1.** The act of embellishing, or the state of being embellished. **2.** Something that embellishes, as a fictitious detail added to a narrative.

em·ber (em′bər) *n.* **1.** A live coal or unextinguished brand. **2.** *pl.* A dying fire. [OE *æmerge*]

Ember days *Eccl.* Three days of fasting and prayer observed quarterly on the Wednesday, Friday, and Saturday after the first Sunday in Lent, after Whitsunday, after September 14, and after December 13 by the Roman Catholic, Anglican, and other Christian churches. [OE *ymbrene*, *ymbryne* circuit, cycle < *ymb* around + *ryne* a running]

Ember week A week including Ember days.

em·bez·zle (im·bez′əl) *v.t.* **·zled**, **·zling** To appropriate fraudulently to one's own use, as money or securities entrusted to one's care. [< AF *embesiler* < *em-* in + *besiler* to destroy] — **em·bez′zle·ment** *n.* — **em·bez′zler** *n.*

em·bit·ter (im·bit′ər) *v.t.* To make bitter, unhappy, or resentful: also spelled *imbitter*. — **em·bit′ter·ment** *n.*

em·blaze[1] (em·blāz′) *v.t.* **·blazed**, **·blaz·ing** **1.** To illuminate or make glow. **2.** To kindle or set on fire. Also spelled *imblaze*. [< EM-[1] + BLAZE[1]]

em·blaze[2] (em·blāz′) *v.t.* **·blazed**, **·blaz·ing** To emblazon: also spelled *imblaze*. [< EM-[1] + BLAZE[3]]

em·bla·zon (em·blā′zən) *v.t.* **1.** To adorn magnificently, especially with heraldic devices; set off in bright colors. **2.** To extol; celebrate. — **em·bla′zon·er** *n.*

em·bla·zon·ment (em·blā′zən·mənt) *n.* **1.** The act of emblazoning. **2.** That which is emblazoned.

em·bla·zon·ry (em·blā′zən·rē) *n.* **1.** The act or art of emblazoning. **2.** Heraldic devices collectively; also, any brilliantly colored representation or embellishment.

em·blem (em′bləm) *n.* **1.** An object or pictorial device that serves to represent something more or less abstract with which it has become connected; symbol. **2.** A distinctive badge or figured object. **3.** An allegorical picture, usually having a motto of moral nature. **4.** *Obs.* An inlaid or inserted ornament. [< L *emblema* inlaid work < Gk. *emblēma* an insertion < *em-* in + *ballein* to throw]
— **Syn. 1.** *Emblem*, *symbol*, *sign*, and *token* agree in denoting a visible representation, usually of something intangible. An *emblem* appeals most strongly to the eye. In its strict sense, it is a pictorial device, as a seal, badge, flag, etc., or, less frequently, some object which represents or suggests a religious, familial, political, or similar group, either through natural fitness or historical connection: The wild rose was the *emblem* of the house of York. In less strict use, *emblem* is sometimes interchanged with *symbol*, a word with much broader application: The Cross is the *emblem* (or *symbol*) of Christianity. A *symbol* may be pictorial or not; its connection with its original may be historical, conventional, or purely arbi-

trary: The scepter is a *symbol* of royal authority, Sb is the *symbol* for antimony. A *sign* may be an arbitrary *symbol*, or it may be the outward manifestation of inward character: Courtesy is a *sign* of good breeding. *Token* is applied chiefly to a *symbol* which represents a pledge: A kiss is a *token* of love.

em·blem·at·ic (em′blə·mat′ik) *adj.* Of, pertaining to, or serving as an emblem; symbolic. Also **em′blem·at′i·cal.** — **em′blem·at′i·cal·ly** *adv.*

em·blem·a·tize (em·blem′ə·tīz) *v.t.* **·tized**, **·tiz·ing** **1.** To serve as an emblem of. **2.** To represent by an emblem.

em·ble·ments (em′blə·mənts) *n.pl.* *Law* **1.** Growing crops. **2.** The right to such crops or to the profits from them. [< OF *emblaement* < *emblaer* to sow with grain < LL *imbladare* < L *in-* in + *bladum* grain]

em·blem·ize (em′blə·mīz) *v.t.* **·ized**, **·iz·ing** To represent by an emblem; make into an emblem.

em·bod·i·ment (im·bod′i·mənt) *n.* **1.** The act of embodying, or the state of being embodied. **2.** That which embodies, or in which something is embodied: He is the *embodiment* of patriotism.

em·bod·y (im·bod′ē) *v.t.* **bod·ied**, **bod·y·ing** **1.** To invest with or as with a body; put into visible or concrete form: to *embody* ideals in action. **2.** To collect into, or make part of, an organized whole; incorporate: to *embody* a verbal agreement in a contract. Also spelled *imbody*.

em·bold·en (im·bōl′dən) *v.t.* To make bold or bolder; give courage to; encourage: also spelled *imbolden*.

em·bo·lec·to·my (em′bə·lek′tə·mē) *n.* *pl.* **·mies** *Surg.* Removal of an embolus. [< EMBOL(US) + -ECTOMY]

em·bol·ic (em·bol′ik) *adj.* *Pathol.* Of, pertaining to, or caused by embolism or an embolus: *embolic* abscesses. **2.** *Biol.* Growing or pushing inward: *embolic* invagination.

em·bo·lism (em′bə·liz′əm) *n.* **1.** *Pathol.* The stopping up of a vein or artery by an embolus. **2.** Intercalation, as of days, for the adjustment of a calendar. [< LL *embolismus* < Gk. *embolismos* intercalary < *embolos*. See EMBOLUS.] — **em′bo·lis′mic** *adj.*

em·bo·lus (em′bə·ləs) *n.* *pl.* **·li** (-lī) *Pathol.* A foreign body that forms an obstruction in a blood vessel, as a piece of fibrin, a blood clot, or an air bubble. [< L < Gk. *embolos* peg < *en-* in + *ballein* to throw]

em·bon·point (äṅ·bôṅ·pwaṅ′) *n.* *French* Stoutness; plumpness.

em·bos·om (em·boōz′əm, -boō′zəm) *v.t.* **1.** To take to the bosom; embrace. **2.** To cherish. **3.** To enclose protectively; shelter. Also spelled *imbosom*.

em·boss[1] (im·bôs′, -bos′) *v.t.* **1.** To cover or adorn (a surface) with raised figures, designs, etc. **2.** To raise or represent (designs, figures, etc.) from or upon a surface. **3.** To decorate sumptuously. [Origin unknown] — **em·boss′er** *n.* — **em·boss′ment** *n.*

em·boss[2] (im·bôs′, -bos′) *v.t.* *Obs.* **1.** To cover with foam. **2.** To drive (a hunted animal) to exhaustion. [ME *embose*, ? < EN-[1] of *bois* woods, thicket]

em·bou·chure (äm·boō·shoōr′, *Fr.* äṅ·boō·shür′) *n.* **1.** The mouth of a river. **2.** The opening out of a river valley into flat land. **3.** *Music* **a** The mouthpiece of a wind instrument. **b** The position or application of the lips and tongue in playing a wind instrument. [< F < *emboucher* < *em-* in (< L *in-*) + *bouche* mouth < L *bucca* cheek]

em·bow (em·bō′) *v.t.* To bend or curve like a bow; arch. — **em·bow′ment** *n.*

em·bowed (em·bōd′) *adj.* Bent like a bow; curved; arched.

em·bow·el (em·bou′əl, -boul′) *v.t.* **bow·eled** or **·elled**, **bow·el·ing** or **·el·ling 1.** To disembowel. **2.** *Obs.* To embed deeply. [Def. 1 < OF *enboweler*, alter. of *esboueler* < *es-* out (< L *ex-*) + *boel* (see BOWEL); def. 2 < EN-[1] + BOWEL]

em·bow·er (em·bou′ər) *v.t. & v.i.* To cover or shelter in or as in a bower: also spelled *imbower*.

em·brace[1] (im·brās′) *v.* **·braced**, **·brac·ing** *v.t.* **1.** To clasp or infold in the arms; hug. **2.** To accept willingly; adopt, as a religion or doctrine. **3.** To avail oneself of: to *embrace* an offer. **4.** To surround; encircle. **5.** To include; contain. **6.** To take in visually or mentally. **7.** To have sexual intercourse with. — *v.i.* **8.** To hug each other. — **Syn.** See GRASP. — *n.* The act of embracing; a clasping in the arms; hug. [< OF *embracer*, ult. < L *in-* in + *bracchium* arm] — **em·brace′ment** *n.* — **em·brac′er** *n.*

em·brace[2] (em·brās′) *v.t. & v.i.* **braced**, **brac·ing** *Law* To influence, or attempt to influence, corruptly. [Back formation < EMBRACER]

em·brac·er (em·brā′sər) *n.* *Law* One guilty of embracery. Also **em·brace′or.** [< OF *embraceor* < *embraser* to kindle, incite < *em-* in + *braise* charcoal]

em·brac·er·y (em·brā′sər·ē) *n.* *Law* The act of corruptly influencing, or attempting so to influence, a jury, judge, etc.

em·branch·ment (em·branch′mənt, -bränch′-) *n.* A branching out or off, as of an arm of a river; a branch or division.

em·bran·gle (em·brang′gəl) *v.t.* **·gled**, **·gling** To entangle; complicate; confuse. [< EM-[2] + dial. *brangle* brawl] — **em·bran′gle·ment** *n.*

---

em·bra·sure (em-brā′zhər) *n.* **1.** *Archit.* An opening in a wall, as for a window or door, sloped or beveled so as to enlarge its interior outline. **2.** An opening that enlarges inwardly or outwardly in a parapet, battlement, or wall, through which a gun may be fired. For illustration see BASTION, BATTLEMENT. [< F < *embraser* (*ébraser*) to widen < *em-* in (< L *in-*) + *braser* to bevel]

em·bro·cate (em′brō·kāt) *v.t.* **·cat·ed, ·cat·ing** To moisten and rub (a part of the body) with liniment or oil. [< Med.L *embrocatus,* pp. of *embrocare* < *embrocha* ointment < Gk. *embrochē* < *en-* in + *brechein* to wet]

em·bro·ca·tion (em′brō·kā′shən) *n.* **1.** The act of embrocating. **2.** The liniment or oil used.

em·broi·der (im·broi′dər) *v.t.* **1.** To ornament (cloth) with designs in needlework. **2.** To execute (a design) in needlework. **3.** To embellish or adorn; exaggerate, as a narrative with fictitious details. — *v.i.* **4.** To make embroidery. [< EN-¹ + BROIDER] — **em·broi′der·er** *n.*

em·broi·der·y (im·broi′dər·ē) *n.* *pl.* **·der·ies 1.** Ornamental needlework, or the art of producing such work. **2.** Any elaborate ornamentation; embellishment.

em·broil (em·broil′) *v.t.* **1.** To involve in dissension or strife. **2.** To throw into uproar or tumult. **3.** To complicate or confuse. [< F *embrouiller* < *em-* in (< L *in-*) + *brouiller* to confuse] — **em·broil′ment** *n.*

em·brown (em·broun′) *v.t. & v.i.* **1.** To make or become brown or dusky. **2.** To darken. Also spelled *imbrown.*

em·brue (em·brōō′) See IMBRUE.

em·bry·ec·to·my (em′brē·ek′tə·mē) *n.* *pl.* **·mies** *Surg.* An operation for removing an embryo through an incision in the abdomen.

em·bry·o (em′brē·ō) *n.* *pl.* **·os 1.** *Biol.* **a** The earliest stages in the development of an organism, before it has assumed its distinctive form. **b** The germ of a viviparous animal in the first stages of its existence as an individual organism, that is, in the human species, the first seven weeks. **2.** *Bot.* The rudimentary plant within the seed, appearing soon after fertilization of the ovule. **3.** The rudimentary form or stage of anything. Also **em′bry·on** (-on). — **in embryo** In an undeveloped or incipient stage or state; not yet developed or advanced, as a project. — *adj.* Rudimentary; incipient. [< Gk. *embryon* < *en-* in + *bryein* to swell]

embryo- *combining form* Embryo; embryonic: *embryogeny.* Also, before vowels, **embry-.** [< Gk. *embryon* embryo]

em·bry·og·e·ny (em′brē·oj′ə·nē) *n.* The development of an organism from its embryonic stage. Also **em·bry·o·gen·e·sis** (em′brē·ō·jen′ə·sis). — **em·bry·o·gen·ic** (em′brē·ō·jen′ik) or **em·bry·o·ge·net·ic** *adj.*

em·bry·ol·o·gy (em′brē·ol′ə·jē) *n.* The science that deals with the origin, structure, and development of the embryo. — **em·bry·o·log·i·cal** (em′brē·ə·loj′i·kəl) or **em·bry·o·log′ic** *adj.* — **em·bry·o·log′i·cal·ly** *adv.* — **em·bry·ol′o·gist** *n.*

em·bry·o·nal (em′brē·ə·nəl) *adj.* Embryonic.

em·bry·on·ic (em′brē·on′ik) *adj.* Of, pertaining to, or in the state of an embryo; rudimentary; immature; undeveloped.

embryo sac *Bot.* In seed-bearing plants, the large cell in the ovule in which the embryo is developed: also called *macrospore, megaspore.*

em·cee (em′sē′) *Informal n.* Master of ceremonies. — *v.t. & v.i.* **·ceed, ·cee·ing** To act as master of ceremonies. Abbr. *mc, MC, m.c., M.C.* [< M(*aster of*) C(*eremonies*)]

em dash *Printing* A dash one em long.

Em·den (em′dən) A port city in Lower Saxony, West Germany, on the Ems; pop. 44,500 (1960).

eme (ēm) *n.* *Brit. Dial.* An uncle; also, a friend or neighbor. [OE *ēam.* Akin to G *oheim.*]

e·meer (ə·mir′) See EMIR.

e·mend (i·mend′) *v.t.* **1.** To make corrections or changes in (a literary work, etc.), especially after scholarly study. **2.** To free from faults. — **Syn.** See AMEND. [< L *emendare* < *e-* out + *menda* fault] — **e·mend′a·ble** *adj.*

e·men·date (ē′men·dāt) *v.t.* **·dat·ed, ·dat·ing** To emend (a text). [< L *emendatus,* pp. of *emendare.* See EMEND.] — **e·men·da·tor** (ē′men·dā′tər, em′en-) *n.*

e·men·da·tion (ē′men·dā′shən, em′en-) *n.* **1.** The act of emending. **2.** A correction or improvement; especially, a critical alteration made in a text. — **e·mend·a·to·ry** (i·men′də·tôr′ē, -tō′rē) *adj.*

em·er·ald (em′ər·əld, em′rəld) *n.* **1.** A bright green variety of beryl, valued as a jewel. **2.** A rich green. **3.** *Printing* A size of type intermediate between nonpareil and minion, 6½ point. — *adj.* **1.** Of, pertaining to, or like the emerald. **2.** Of a rich green color. [< OF *emeraude, esmeralde* < L *smaragdus* < Gk. *smaragdos.* Doublet of SMARAGD.]

emerald green A brilliant green, highly poisonous pigment made from copper and arsenic.

Emerald Isle Ireland: so called from its green landscape.

emerald nickel Zaratite.

e·merge (i·mûrj′) *v.i.* **e·merged, e·merg·ing 1.** To come forth from something that envelops, as from water. **2.** To come forth from concealment, obscurity, or depressed circumstances: to *emerge* from retirement, poverty, etc. **3.** To come to light; become apparent: New facts *emerged* during the trial. [< L *emergere* < *e-* out + *mergere* to dip]

e·mer·gence (i·mûr′jəns) *n.* **1.** The process or result of emerging. **2.** *Bot.* An outgrowth, as a prickle growing from the surface of a plant. **3.** The appearance of something new and unpredictable in the process of organic evolution.

e·mer·gen·cy (i·mûr′jən·sē) *n.* *pl.* **·cies** A sudden and unexpected turn of events calling for immediate action.

e·mer·gent (i·mûr′jənt) *adj.* **1.** Coming forth from or as from an enveloping fluid or covering; issuing forth; coming into view. **2.** Demanding immediate action; urgent; pressing. **3.** In the evolutionary process, new and unpredictable. [< L *emergens, -entis,* ppr. of *emergere.* See EMERGE.]

emergent evolution A philosophical theory holding that at certain critical stages in the evolutionary process new types of organisms, modes of behavior, life, and consciousness will appear that cannot be predicted.

e·mer·i·tus (i·mer′ə·təs) *adj.* Retired from active service, usually because of age, but retained in an honorary position: *professor emeritus.* — *n.* *pl.* **·ti** (-tī) One who is emeritus. [< L, pp. of *emerere* < *e-* out + *merere* to earn]

em·er·od (em′ər·od) *n.* *Obs.* **1.** A tumor; boil; hemorrhoid. **2.** In the Bible, an infectious disease, perhaps bubonic plague. 1 *Sam.* v 6. Also **em′er·oid.** [*Var.* of HEMORRHOID]

e·mersed (ē·mûrst′) *adj. Bot.* Standing above and out of water, as the stems and leaves of aquatic plants. [< L *emersus,* pp. of *emergere.* See EMERGE.]

e·mer·sion (ē·mûr′shən, -zhən) *n.* **1.** The act or process of emerging. **2.** *Astron.* The reappearance of a heavenly body after being eclipsed or occulted.

Em·er·son (em′ər·sən), **Ralph Waldo,** 1803–82, U.S. essayist, philosopher, and poet. — **Em·er·so·ni·an** (em′ər·sō′nē·ən) *adj.*

em·er·y (em′ər·ē, em′rē) *n.* A very hard, black or grayish black variety of corundum mixed with magnesite and other minerals, used as an abrasive. [< F *émeri* < OF *esmeril* < LL *smericulum* < Gk. *smēris* emery powder]

emery board A small, flat strip of wood or cardboard covered with powdered emery, used for filing the fingernails.

emery cloth Cloth coated with powdered emery, used for fine abrading and polishing.

Em·e·sa (em′ə·sə) The ancient name for HOMS.

em·e·sis (em′ə·sis) *n.* Vomiting. [< NL < Gk. < *emeein* to vomit]

e·met·ic (i·met′ik) *adj.* Tending to produce vomiting. — *n.* An emetic agent. [< Gk. *emetikos* < *emeein* to vomit]

em·e·tine (em′ə·tēn, -tin) *n.* *Chem.* A white crystalline alkaloid, $C_{29}H_{40}O_4N_2$, obtained from the ipecac root, used in certain conditions of amebic dysentery. Also **em′e·tin** (-tin). [< Gk. *emetos* vomiting + -INE²]

e·meu (ē′myōō) See EMU.

é·meute (i·myōōt′, *Fr.* ā·mœt′) *n. French* A seditious outbreak; popular uprising.

E.M.F. or **e.m.f.** or **emf** Electromotive force.

-emia *combining form Med.* Blood; condition of the blood: used in names of diseases: *leukemia.* Also spelled *-aemia, -haemia, -hemia.* [< Gk. *haima* blood]

em·i·grant (em′ə·grənt) *adj.* Moving from one place or country to settle in another. Compare IMMIGRANT. — *n.* A person who emigrates. [< L *emigrans, -antis,* ppr. of *emigrare.* See EMIGRATE.]

em·i·grate (em′ə·grāt) *v.i.* **·grat·ed, ·grat·ing** To move from one country, or section of a country, to settle in another. — **Syn.** See MIGRATE. [< L *emigratus,* pp. of *emigrare* < *e-* out + *migrare* to move]

em·i·gra·tion (em′ə·grā′shən) *n.* **1.** The act of emigrating. **2.** Emigrants collectively.

é·mi·gré (em′ə·grā, *Fr.* ā·mē·grā′) *n.* An emigrant; especially, one who fled to escape the French or Russian revolution. [< F, pp. of *émigrer* < L *emigrare.* See EMIGRATE.]

E·mi·lia-Ro·ma·gna (ā·mē′lyä·rō·mä′nyä) A Region of north central Italy; 8,543 sq. mi.; pop. 3,646,507 (1961); capital, Bologna. Formerly **E·mi′lia.**

em·i·nence (em′ə·nəns) *n.* **1.** Superiority in rank, power, achievement, etc.; elevated or exalted position. **2.** A high place or elevation, as a hill. Also **em′i·nen·cy.** [< L *eminentia* < *eminere* to stand out < *e-* out + *minere* to jut out]

Em·i·nence (em′ə·nəns) *n.* A title for cardinals of the Roman Catholic Church: often preceded by *His, Your,* etc.

em·i·nent (em′ə·nənt) *adj.* **1.** High in station, merit, or esteem; distinguished; prominent: an *eminent* scholar. **2.** Noteworthy; conspicuous: *eminent* valor. **3.** High; lofty: an *eminent* tower. [< L *eminens, -entis,* ppr. of *eminere* to stand out] — **em′i·nent·ly** *adv.*

eminent domain *Law* The right or power of the state to take private property for public use, or to control its use, usually at an adequate compensation.

e·mir (ə·mir′) *n.* **1.** An independent Moslem prince or commander, especially in Arabia. **2.** A descendant of Mohammed through his daughter Fatima. **3.** A high Turkish official. Also spelled *emeer.* [< Arabic *amīr* ruler]

e·mir·ate (ə·mir′it) *n.* The jurisdiction of an emir.

em·is·sar·y (em′ə·ser′ē) *n.* *pl.* **·sar·ies** A person sent on a mission, especially as a secret agent, to advance certain interests. — **Syn.** See SPY. — *adj.* Of, pertaining to, or serving as an emissary. [< L *emissarius* < *emittere.* See EMIT.]

e·mis·sion (i·mish′ən) *n.* **1.** The act of emitting. **2.** That which is emitted; discharge; emanation. **3.** The issuance of currency, notes, shares, etc. **4.** *Physiol.* A discharge of body fluids, especially semen. **5.** *Electronics* The ejection of electrons from the heated cathode or filament of an electron tube. [< L *emissio, -onis* < *emittere.* See EMIT.]

emission spectrum *Physics* A spectrum indicating the type of radiation emitted by a given source, often showing bright lines at wavelengths indicated by dark lines in an absorption spectrum.

e·mis·sive (i·mis′iv) *adj.* Sending or sent forth; emitting.

emissive power *Physics* The rate at which a body at a given temperature will radiate energy per unit of surface area.

em·is·siv·i·ty (em′ə·siv′ə·tē) *n. Physics* The total emissive power of a radiating surface, expressed as a ratio to that of a black body of identical area and temperature.

e·mit (i·mit′) *v.t.* **e·mit·ted, e·mit·ting 1.** To send forth or give off (light, heat, sound, etc.); discharge. **2.** To give expression to; utter, as an opinion. **3.** To issue authoritatively, as an edict. **4.** To put into circulation, as money. [< L *emittere* < *e-* out + *mittere* to send] — **e·mit′·ter** *n.*

Em·man·u·el (i·man′yōō·əl) See IMMANUEL.

em·men·a·gogue (i·men′ə·gŏg, -gog, i·mē′nə-) *n.* An agent that stimulates the menstrual flow. [< Gk. *emmēna* the menses + *agōgos* drawing forth. See -AGOGUE.]

em·mer (em′ər) *n.* Amelcorn. [< dial. G < OHG *amari*]

em·met (em′it) *n. Archaic* An ant. [OE *æmete.* Doublet of ANT.]

Em·met (em′it), **Robert,** 1778–1803, Irish patriot; executed.

em·me·tro·pi·a (em′ə·trō′pē·ə) *n.* The condition of the eye characterized by normal refraction and focusing of light rays upon the retina. [< NL < Gk. *emmetros* (< *en-* in + *metron* measure) + *ōps* eye] — **em′me·trop′ic** (-trop′ik) *adj.*

Em·my (em′ē) *n. pl.* **·mys** or **·mies** One of the gold-plated statuettes awarded annually since 1949 by the Academy of Television Arts and Sciences for exceptional performances and productions. [Alter. of *immy,* short for *image orthicon tube,* the basis of modern television. See under ORTHICON.]

e·mol·lient (i·mol′yənt, -ē·ənt) *adj.* Softening or relaxing; soothing, especially to the skin. — *n. Med.* A softening or soothing medicament. [< L *emolliens, -entis,* ppr. of *emollire* < *e-* thoroughly + *mollire* to soften < *mollis* soft]

e·mol·u·ment (i·mol′yə·mən) *n.* The salary or fee connected with any office, occupation, or service. — **Syn.** See SALARY. [< L *emolumentum, emolimentum* profit, advantage < *emolere* to grind out < *e-* out + *molere* to grind]

e·mote (i·mōt′) *v.i.* **e·mot·ed, e·mot·ing** *Informal* To exhibit an exaggerated emotion, as in acting: a humorous use. [Back formation < EMOTION]

e·mo·tion (i·mō′shən) *n.* **1.** A strong surge of feeling marked by an impulse to outward expression and often accompanied by complex bodily reactions; any strong feeling, as love, hate, or joy. **2.** The power of feeling; sensibility. [< L *emotio, -onis* < *emovere* < *e-* out + *movere* to move]

e·mo·tion·al (i·mō′shən·əl) *adj.* **1.** Of, pertaining to, or expressive of emotion. **2.** Easily or excessively affected by emotion. **3.** Arousing the emotions. — **e·mo′tion·al·ly** *adv.*

e·mo·tion·al·ism (i·mō′shən·əl·iz′əm) *n.* **1.** The tendency to overindulge the emotions or to be too much affected by them. **2.** A display of emotion. **3.** Appeal to the emotions.

e·mo·tion·al·ist (i·mō′shən·əl·ist) *n.* **1.** One whose emotions are easily aroused. **2.** One who aims to influence others through the emotions. **3.** In ethics, one who bases his theory of conduct on the emotions.

e·mo·tion·al·i·ty (i·mō′shən·al′ə·tē) *n.* Emotional nature.

e·mo·tion·al·ize (i·mō′shən·əl·īz′) *v.t.* **·ized, ·iz·ing** To make emotional; treat in an emotional manner. — **e·mo′·tion·al·i·za′tion** *n.*

e·mo·tive (i·mō′tiv) *adj.* Characterized by, expressing, or tending to excite emotion: *emotive* eloquence. — **e·mo′tive·ly** *adv.* — **e·mo′tive·ness, e·mo·tiv·i·ty** (ē′mō·tiv′ə·tē) *n.*

Emp. 1. Emperor; Empress. **2.** Empire.

em·pale (im·pāl′) See IMPALE.

em·pan·el (im·pan′əl) See IMPANEL.

em·path·ic (em·path′ik) *adj.* Characterized by or pertaining to empathy. — **em·path′i·cal·ly** *adv.*

em·pa·thize (em′pə·thīz) *v.t. & v.i.* **·thized, ·thiz·ing** To regard with or feel empathy.

em·pa·thy (em′pə·thē) *n. Psychol.* **1.** Intellectual or imaginative apprehension of another's condition or state of mind without actually experiencing the feelings of the other. **2.** Attribution of the feelings aroused by some external object, as a work of art, to the object itself. [< Gk. *empatheia* < *en-* in + *pathos* feeling; trans. of G *Einfühlung*]

Em·ped·o·cles (em·ped′ə·klēz) Fifth-century B.C. Greek poet and philosopher.

em·pen·nage (em′pi·nij, *Fr.* äṅ·pe·näzh′) *n. Aeron.* The tail assembly of an airplane, used to steer or steady it. [< F *empenner* to provide with feathers < *em-* in (< L *in-*) + *penne* < L *pinna* feather]

em·per·or (em′pər·ər) *n.* **1.** The sovereign of an empire. Abbr. *Emp.* **2.** One of various moths, as the **emperor moth** (*Samia cecropia*), or butterflies, as the **purple emperor** (*Apatura iris*) or the **tawny emperor** (*Asterocampa clyton*). [< OF *empereor* < L *imperator* commander < *imperare* to order] — **em′per·or·ship′** *n.*

em·per·y (em′pər·ē) *n. pl.* **·ies** *Poetic* **1.** Absolute dominion; sovereignty. **2.** The domain of an emperor. [< OF *emperie* < L *imperium* empire]

em·pha·sis (em′fə·sis) *n. pl.* **·ses** (-sēz) **1.** Special significance or importance assigned to something. **2.** Stress given by voice or rhetorical contrivance to a particular syllable, word, or phrase. **3.** Force or intensity of meaning, action, etc. **4.** Sharpness in outline. [< L < Gk *emphainein* to indicate < *en-* in + *phainein* to show]

em·pha·size (em′fə·sīz) *v.t.* **·sized, ·siz·ing** To give emphasis to; make specially prominent or important; stress.

em·phat·ic (em·fat′ik) *adj.* **1.** Spoken or done with emphasis; forcibly expressive. **2.** Characterized by forcefulness or intensity; positive; direct: an *emphatic* personality. **3.** Striking; decisive. [< Gk. *emphatikos,* var. of *emphantikos* < *emphainein.* See EMPHASIS.] — **em·phat′i·cal·ly** *adv.*

em·phy·se·ma (em′fə·sē′mə) *n. Pathol.* A puffed condition in the organs or tissues of the body, especially a condition of the lungs marked by difficulty in breathing because of enlargement and consequent loss of elasticity of the air sacs. [< NL < Gk. *emphysēma* inflation; *en-* in + *physaein* to blow] — **em′phy·sem′a·tous** (-sem′ə-tes) *adj.*

em·pire (em′pīr) *n.* **1.** A state, or union of states, governed by an emperor; also, the historical period of such government. **2.** A union of dispersed states and unrelated peoples under one rule. **3.** Wide and supreme dominion. Abbr. *Emp.* [< F < L *imperium* rule, authority]

Em·pire (em′pīr; *for def. 3, also* äṅ·pêr′) *adj.* **1.** Of or pertaining to the French Empire, 1804–15, under Napoleon Bonaparte. **2.** Designating a type of massive furniture of the first French Empire, having grandiose embellishments of fabrics and brass. **3.** Designating a type of woman's costume of the first French Empire, marked by a high waistline, décolleté bodice, and straight, loose skirt.

Empire Day The former name for COMMONWEALTH DAY.

Empire State Nickname of NEW YORK.

em·pir·ic (em·pir′ik) *n.* **1.** One who believes practical experience alone is the source of knowledge. **2.** A charlatan. — *adj.* Empirical. [< L *empiricus* < Gk. *empeirikos* < *empeiria* experience < *en-* in + *peira* trial]

em·pir·i·cal (em·pir′i·kəl) *adj.* **1.** Relating to or based upon direct experience or observation alone: *empirical* knowledge. **2.** Relying on practical experience without benefit of scientific knowledge or theory, especially in medicine: *empirical* treatment. — **em·pir′i·cal·ly** *adv.*

empirical formula See under FORMULA.

em·pir·i·cism (em·pir′ə·siz′əm) *n.* **1.** Empirical method or practice. **2.** *Philos.* The doctrine that all knowledge is derived from experience. **3.** Reliance on observation and experiment as the bases of knowledge. — **em·pir′i·cist** *n.*

em·place·ment (im·plās′mənt) *n.* **1.** The position assigned to guns or to a battery within a fortification; also, a gun platform, the parapet, or the like. **2.** A setting in place; location. [< F < *emplacer* to put into position]

em·ploy (im·ploi′) *v.t.* **1.** To engage the services of; hire. **2.** To provide work and livelihood for. **3.** To make use of as a means or instrument: to *employ* cunning. **4.** To devote or apply: to *employ* one's energies in research. — *n.* The state of being employed; service. [< F *employer* < L *in-* in + *plicare* to fold. Doublet of IMPLY.] — **em·ploy′a·ble** *adj.*

em·ploy·ee (im·ploi′ē, em′ploi·ē′) *n.* One who works for another in return for salary, wages, or other consideration. Also **em·ploy′e, em·ploy′é.**

em·ploy·er (im·ploi′ər) *n.* **1.** One who employs. **2.** A person or business firm that employs persons for wages or salary.

em·ploy·ment (im·ploi′mənt) *n.* **1.** The act of employing, or the state of being employed. **2.** The work upon which one is or may be engaged; occupation; trade.

em·poi·son (em·poi′zən) *v.t.* **1.** To taint or corrupt. **2.** *Obs.* To poison. — **em·poi·son·ment** *n.*

em·po·ri·um (em·pôr′ē·əm, -pō′rē-) *n. pl.* **·po·ri·ums** or **·po·ri·a** (-pôr′ē·ə, -pō′rē·ə) **1.** A store carrying general merchandise. **2.** A trading or market center. — **Syn.** See SHOP. [< L < Gk. *emporion* market < *emporos* merchant, traveler < *en-* in + *poros* way]

em·pov·er·ish (im·pov′ər·ish) See IMPOVERISH.

em·pow·er (im·pou′ər) *v.t.* **1.** To authorize; delegate authority to. **2.** To enable; permit. Also spelled *impower.* — **em·pow′er·ment** *n.*

em·press (em′pris) *n.* **1.** A woman who rules an empire. **2.** The wife or widow of an emperor. **3.** A powerful mistress. Abbr. (def. 1, 2) *Emp.* [< OF *emperesse,* fem. of *emperere,* var. of *empereor.* See EMPEROR.]

Empress Augusta Bay An inlet of the South Pacific in SW Bougainville, Solomon Islands; width, 15 mi.

---

em·presse·ment (äṅ·pres·mäṅ′) *n. French* Animated earnestness; demonstrative cordiality.

em·prise (em·prīz′) *n. Archaic* **1.** Enterprise; adventure. **2.** Chivalric prowess. Also **em·prize′.** [< OF, orig. pp. of *emprendre* to undertake < L *in-* in + *prehendere* to take]

emp·tins (emp′tinz) *n.pl. U.S.* The lees of beer, etc., used as yeast. Also **emp′tings.** [Alter. of *emptyings,* n.]

emp·ty (emp′tē) *adj.* **·ti·er, ·ti·est 1.** Containing nothing; void; vacant; especially, devoid of the usual or proper contents, as food or inhabitants: an *empty* pitcher; an *empty* room. **2.** Without value, substance, or significance; unsubstantial; hollow: *empty* promises; *empty* dreams. **3.** Carrying nothing: *empty* hands. **4.** Destitute or devoid: with *of:* *empty* of compassion. **5.** *Informal* Hungry. — *v.* **·tied, ·ty·ing** *v.t.* **1.** To make empty; remove the contents of: to *empty* a house. **2.** To transfer the contents of (a container): to *empty* a bucket onto a fire. **3.** To pour out or draw off (the contents of something): to *empty* milk into a bowl. **4.** To unburden; clear: with *of:* to *empty* oneself of despair. — *v.i.* **5.** To become empty. **6.** To discharge itself or its contents: The river *empties* into the bay. — *n. pl.* **·ties** An empty container, vehicle, etc. [OE *æmetig* < *æmetta* leisure < *æ-* not + root of *mot* a meeting] **—emp′ti·ly** *adv.* **—emp′ti·ness** *n.*

emp·ty-hand·ed (emp′tē-han′did) *adj.* Having or carrying nothing.

emp·ty-head·ed (emp′tē-hed′id) *adj.* Without sense or discretion; foolish; brainless.

Empty Quarter See RUB AL KHALL.

em·pur·ple (em·pûr′pəl) *v.t.* **·pled, ·pling** To color purple.

em·py·e·ma (em′pi·ē′mə, -pī-) *n. pl.* **·e·ma·ta** (-ē′mə·tə, -em′ə·tə) *Pathol.* A collection of pus, especially in the pleural cavity, often associated with various bacterial infections. [< NL < Gk. *empyēma* suppuration < *en-* in + *pyon* pus]

em·pyr·e·al (em·pir′ē·əl, em′pə·rē′əl, -pī-) *adj.* **1.** Of or pertaining to the highest region of heaven. **2.** Of or pertaining to the sky; celestial. **3.** Sublime; superior. **4.** Formed of pure fire; fiery. [< Med. L *empyreus* < Gk. *empyros* < *en-* in + *pyr* fire]

em·py·re·an (em′pə·rē′ən, -pī-) *n.* **1.** The highest heaven; the abode of God and the angels, anciently conceived as a region of pure fire. **2.** The firmament; also, cosmic space. — *adj.* Empyreal.

e·mu (ē′myōō) *n.* A flightless, three-toed Australian bird (genus *Dromiceius*) related to the ostrich and cassowary. Also spelled *emeu.* [Prob. < Pg. *ema* ostrich]

EMU
(About 5 feet high)

E.M.U. or **e.m.u.** or **emu** Electromagnetic unit(s).

em·u·late (em′yə·lāt) *v.t.* **·lat·ed, ·lat·ing 1.** To try to equal or surpass. **2.** To rival or vie with successfully. [< L *aemulatus,* pp. of *aemulari* to rival < *aemulus* jealous] **—em′u·la·tive** *adj.* **—em′u·la·tive·ly** *adv.* **—em′u·la·tor** *n.*

em·u·la·tion (em′yə·lā′shən) *n.* **1.** Effort or ambition to equal or excel another. **2.** *Obs.* Selfish rivalry.

em·u·lous (em′yə·ləs) *adj.* **1.** Eager to equal or excel another; competitive. **2.** Pertaining to or arising from emulation: *emulous* motives. **3.** *Obs.* Envious; jealous. — **Syn.** See AMBITIOUS. **—em′u·lous·ly** *adv.* **—em′u·lous·ness** *n.*

e·mul·si·fy (i·mul′sə·fī) *v.t.* **·fied, ·fy·ing** To make into an emulsion. **—e·mul′si·fi·ca′tion** *n.* **—e·mul′si·fi′er** *n.*

e·mul·sion (i·mul′shən) *n.* **1.** A liquid mixture in which a fatty or resinous substance is suspended in minute globules, as butter in milk. **2.** Any milky liquid. **3.** *Photog.* A light-sensitive coating for film, plates, papers, etc., usually a silver salt in gelatin. **4.** *Physics* A colloid system, consisting of the particles of one liquid finely dispersed in another. [< LL *emulsio, -onis* < L *emulgere* < *e-* out + *mulgere* to milk]

e·mul·sive (i·mul′siv) *adj.* **1.** Capable of emulsifying. **2.** Having the nature of an emulsion.

e·munc·to·ry (i·mungk′tər·ē) *adj.* Serving to remove waste matter. — *n. pl.* **·ries** An organ or part of the body that serves to remove waste matter, as the kidneys, intestines, etc. [< NL *emunctorius* < L *emunctorium* snuffer < *emungere* < *e-* out + *mungere* to blow the nose. Cf. MUCUS.]

em·yd (em′id) *n.* A fresh-water tortoise of North America (*Emys blandingii*) having a black carapace covered with pale yellow spots. Also **em·yde** (em′īd). [< Gk. *emys, emydos*]

en (en) *n.* **1.** The letter N. **2.** *Printing* A space half the width of an em.

en-¹ *prefix* Forming transitive verbs: **1.** (from nouns) To cover or surround with; place into or upon: *encircle.* **2.** (from adjectives and nouns) To make; cause to be or to resemble: *enable, enfeeble.* **3.** (from verbs) Often with simple intensive force, or used to form transitive verbs from intransitives: *enact, encompass.* Also *em-* before *b, p,* and sometimes *m,* as in *embark.* Many words in *en-* or *em-* have variant forms in *in-* or *im-* respectively, as a result of the confusion between Old French *en-,* Latin *in-,* and native English *in-.* Compare IN-². [< OF < L *in-* < *in* in, into]

en-² *prefix* In; into; on: *endemic.* Also *el-* before *l,* as in *ellipse; em-* before *b, m, p, ph,* as in *embolism, empathy; er-* before *r,* as in *errhine.* [< Gk. *en-* < *en* in, into]

-en¹ *suffix* Forming verbs: **1.** (from adjectives) Cause to be; become: *deepen, harden.* **2.** (from nouns) Cause to have; gain: *hearten, strengthen.* [OE *-nian*]

-en² *suffix of adjectives* Made of; resembling: *woolen, brazen.* [OE]

-en³ *suffix* Used in the past participles of many strong verbs: *broken, beaten.* [OE]

-en⁴ *suffix* Used in the plurals of certain nouns: *oxen, children.* [OE *-an,* plural ending of the weak declension]

-en⁵ *suffix* Small; little: *chicken, kitten.* [OE]

en·a·ble (in·ā′bəl) *v.t.* **·bled, ·bling 1.** To supply with adequate power, means, or opportunity; make able: A grant *enabled* him to continue his research. **2.** To make possible or practicable: Rockets *enable* travel in outer space.

en·act (in·akt′) *v.t.* **1.** To make into a law; decree. **2.** To carry out in action; perform. **3.** To represent in or as in a play; act the part of. **—en·act′a·ble** *adj.* **—en·ac′tor** *n.*

en·ac·tive (in·ak′tiv) *adj.* Having power to enact.

en·act·ment (in·akt′mənt) *n.* **1.** The act of enacting, or the state of being enacted. **2.** That which is enacted; a law.

en·ac·to·ry (in·ak′tər·ē) *adj.* Connected with the enactment of law.

en·am·el (in·am′əl) *n.* **1.** A vitreous, usually opaque material applied by fusion to surfaces of metal, glass, or porcelain as a decoration, a surface for encaustic painting, or a protective lining. **2.** A piece executed in enamel. **3.** A paint, varnish, or lacquer that dries to form a hard, glossy surface. **4.** Any lustrous, hard coating resembling enamel. **5.** *Anat.* The hard, glossy, calcareous outer layer of the teeth. For illustration see TOOTH. — *v.t.* **en·am·eled** or **·elled, en·am·el·ing** or **·el·ling 1.** To cover or inlay with enamel. **2.** To surface with or as with enamel. **3.** To adorn with different colors, as if with enamel. [< AF *enamayller* < *en-* on + *amayl,* OF *esmail* enamel < Gmc.] **—en·am′-el·er** or **en·am′el·ler, en·am′el·ist** or **en·am′el·list** *n.*

en·am·el·ing (in·am′əl·ing) *n.* **1.** The art or occupation of one who enamels. **2.** An ornamentation or coating of enamel. Also **en·am′el·ling.**

en·am·el·ware (in·am′əl·wâr′) *n.* Enameled kitchenware.

en·am·or (in·am′ər) *v.t.* To inflame with love; also, to charm; fascinate: chiefly in the passive, followed by *of:* He is *enamored* of his cousin. Also *Brit.* **en·am′our.** [< OF *enamourer* < *en-* in (< L *in-*) + *amour* love < L *amor*] **—en·am′ored** *adj.*

en ar·rière (äṅ nà·ryâr′) *French* **1.** In the rear; behind. **2.** In arrears.

en·ar·thro·sis (en′är·thrō′sis) *n. pl.* **·ses** *Anat.* An articulation in which the rounded head of a bone is received into a corresponding cavity; a ball-and-socket joint, as the hip joint. [< NL < Gk. *enarthrōsis* < *enarthros* jointed < *en-* in + *arthron* joint] **—en′ar·thro′di·al** (-dē·əl) *adj.*

e·nate (ē′nāt, i·nāt′) *adj.* **1.** Growing out. **2.** Related on the mother's side: compare AGNATE, COGNATE. — *n.* A relative in the female line. [< L *enatus,* pp. of *enasci* < *e-* out + *nasci* to be born] **—e·nat·ic** (i·nat′ik) *adj.*

en a·vant (äṅ nà·väṅ′) *French* Forward; onward.

en bloc (äṅ blôk′) *French* In one lump; as a whole.

en bro·chette (äṅ brō·shet′) *French* Broiled on skewers.

enc. Enclosed; enclosure(s).

en·cae·ni·a (en·sē′nē·ə, -sēn′yə) *n.pl.* (*sometimes construed as sing.*) Ceremonies commemorating the founding of a city or the consecration of a church; also, **Encaenia,** annual ceremonies held in June at Oxford University in commemoration of founders and benefactors. [< L < Gk. *enkainia* feast of dedication < *en-* in + *kainos* new]

en·cage (in·kāj′) *v.t.* **·caged, ·cag·ing** To shut up in or as in a cage: also spelled *incage.*

en·camp (in·kamp′) *v.i.* **1.** To go into camp; live in a camp. — *v.t.* **2.** To place in a camp.

en·camp·ment (in·kamp′mənt) *n.* **1.** The act of pitching a camp. **2.** A camp, or the persons occupying it.

en·car·nal·ize (in·kär′nəl·īz) *v.t.* **·ized, ·iz·ing 1.** To invest with flesh and blood; embody. **2.** To make gross or sensual.

en·case (in·kās′) See INCASE.

en cas·se·role (äṅ kàs·rôl′) *French* Prepared and served in a casserole.

en·caus·tic (en·kôs′tik) *adj.* Having the pigments burned in: *encaustic* tile. — *n.* Encaustic painting. [< L *encausticus* < Gk. *enkaustikos* < *en-* in + *kaiein* to burn]

encaustic painting A method of painting statues or architectural details with colored wax which is later fused with hot irons: also called *cerography.*

-ence *suffix of nouns* Forming nouns of action, quality, state, or condition from adjectives in *-ent,* as *diffidence, prominence.* Compare -ENCY. See note under -ANCE. [< F *-ence* < L *-entia,* suffix used to form nouns from present participles; or directly < L]

en·ceinte¹ (en·sānt′, *Fr.* äṅ·saṅt′) *adj.* With child; pregnant. [< F < L *inciens, -entis* pregnant, ? < Gk. *kyeein* to be pregnant]

en·ceinte² (en·sānt′, *Fr.* äṅ·saṅt′) *n.* **1.** A girdle of works encircling a fortified place. **2.** The place so encircled. **3.** A close or precinct, as of an abbey. [< F *enceindre* < L *cingere* < *in-* on + *cingere* to bind]

En·cel·a·dus (en·sel′ə·dəs)   In Greek mythology, a giant who, after revolting against the gods, was killed by the lightning of Zeus and buried under Mt. Etna.

en·ce·phal·ic (en′sə·fal′ik)   *adj.*   **1.** Of or pertaining to the brain. **2.** Situated within the cranial cavity.

en·ceph·a·li·tis (en′sef·ə·lī′tis, en·sef′-)   *n. Pathol.* Inflammation of the brain.   **— en·ceph·a·lit·ic** (-lit′ik) *adj.*

encephalitis le·thar·gi·ca (li·thär′ji·kə)   *Pathol.* An acute, frequently epidemic, virus form of encephalitis, deeply involving the central nervous system and accompanied by fever, lethargy, and numerous sensory disturbances: also called *epidemic encephalitis, sleeping sickness.*

en·ceph·a·li·za·tion (en·sef′ə·lə·zā′shən, -lī·zā′-)   *n. Anat.* The processes resulting in the formation of the head and the development of the cerebral cortex.

encephalo-   *combining form*   The brain: *encephalogram.* Also, before vowels, **encephal-.**   [< Gk. *enkephalos* the brain < *en-* in + *kephalē* head]

en·ceph·a·lo·gram (en·sef′ə·lə·gram′)   *n.* An X-ray photograph of the brain.   **— en·ceph′a·log′ra·phy** (-log′rə·fē) *n.*

en·ceph·a·lol·o·gy (en·sef′ə·lol′ə·jē)   *n.* The study of the anatomy, physiology, and pathology of the brain.   **— en·ceph′a·lol′o·gist** *n.*

en·ceph·a·lo·ma (en·sef′ə·lō′mə)   *n.*   *pl.* **·ma·ta** (-mə·tə) *Pathol.* A growth upon the brain; brain tumor.   [< ENCEPHALO- + -OMA]

en·ceph·a·lo·my·e·li·tis (en·sef′ə·lō·mī′ə·lī′tis)   *n. Pathol.* One of a number of inflammatory diseases affecting the brain and the spinal cord of men and certain animals, especially horses.   [< ENCEPHALO- + MYEL(O)- + -ITIS]

en·ceph·a·lon (en·sef′ə·lon)   *n.*   *pl.* **·la** (-lə) *Anat.* The brain.   [< NL < Gk. *enkephalos*]   **— en·ceph′a·lous** *adj.*

en·chain (in·chān′)   *v.t.*   **1.** To bind with or as with a chain. **2.** To hold fast or captive, as attention.   **— en·chain′ment** *n.*

en·chant (in·chant′, -chänt′)   *v.t.*   **1.** To put a spell upon; bewitch. **2.** To charm completely; delight.   [< F *enchanter* < L *incantare* < *in-* in + *cantare* to sing]

en·chant·er (in·chan′tər, -chän′-)   *n.* One who enchants, especially by magical means.

en·chant·ing (in·chan′ting, -chän′-)   *adj.* Having power to enchant; charming; fascinating.   **— en·chant′ing·ly** *adv.*

en·chant·ment (in·chant′mənt, -chänt′-)   *n.*   **1.** The act of enchanting, or the state of being enchanted. **2.** That which enchants; irresistible allure; charm.

en·chant·ress (in·chan′tris, -chän′-)   *n.*   **1** A sorceress. **2.** An attractive or fascinating woman.

en·chase (en·chās′)   *v.t.* **·chased, ·chas·ing**   **1.** To incase in a setting, as a jewel in gold. **2.** To enrich or decorate with engraved, chased, or inlaid work. **3.** To engrave or work (figures, designs, etc.) on a surface.   [< F *enchâsser* < *en-* in (< L *in-*) + *châsse* case < L *capsa*]

en·chi·la·da (en′chi·lä′də)   *n.*   *SW U.S.* A Mexican dish consisting of a rolled tortilla stuffed with meat or cheese and flavored with chili.   [< Sp.]

en·chi·rid·i·on (en′ki·rid′ē·ən, -kə-)   *n.*   *pl.* **·i·ons** or **·i·a** (-ē·ə) A handbook; manual.   [< Gk. *encheiridion* < *en-* in + *cheir* hand + *-idion*, dim. suffix]

en·chon·dro·ma (en′kon·drō′mə)   *n.*   *pl.* **·ma·ta** (-mə·tə) or **·mas** *Pathol.* A cartilaginous tumor; chondroma.   [< NL < Gk. *en-* in + CHONDR(O)- + -OMA]   **— en·chon·drom·a·tous** (en′kon·drom′ə·təs, -drō′mə-) *adj.*

en·cho·ri·al (en·kôr′ē·əl, -kō′rē-)   *adj.* Peculiar to a country; native; indigenous; especially, demotic: *enchorial* writing. Also **en·chor·ic** (en·kôr′ik, -kor′-).   [< Gk. *enchōrios* native < *en-* in + *chōra* country]

en·ci·na (en·sē′nə)   *n.* A live oak; especially, *Quercus agrifolia,* of the Pacific coast of the United States.   [< Sp. < LL *ilicina* < L *ilex, ilicis* oak]   **— en·ci′nal** *adj.*

en·ci·pher (en·sī′fər)   *v.t.* To convert (a message, report, etc.) from plain text into cipher.

en·cir·cle (en·sûr′kəl)   *v.t.* **·cled, ·cling**   **1.** To form a circle around. **2.** To go around; make a circuit of.   **— en·cir′cle·ment** *n.*

encl. Enclosed; enclosure(s).

en·clasp (en·klasp′, -kläsp′)   *v.t.* To hold in or as in a clasp; embrace: also spelled *inclasp.*

en·clave (en′klāv)   *n.*   **1.** A territory that is completely or partially enclosed by the territory of a power to which it is not politically subject, as San Marino and Vatican City in Italy. ◆ See note under EXCLAVE. **2.** A district, as in a city, inhabited by a minority group.   [< F < *enclaver* to enclose < LL *inclavare* < L *in-* in + *clavis* key]

en·clit·ic (en·klit′ik)   *adj.*   **1.** Having no independent accent, but pronounced as part of a preceding word, as English *is* in *Tom's going,* French *je* in *ai-je,* Latin *-que* in *hominesque.* **2.** *Med.* Having the planes of the fetal head inclined to those of the maternal pelvis: distinguished from *synclitic.*   *— n.*

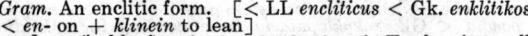

Caption of map: Florence, Arno, Rimini, SAN MARINO, ADRIATIC SEA, Tiber, Ancona, Rome, **ENCLAVE OF SAN MARINO**

Gram. An enclitic form.   [< LL *encliticus* < Gk. *enklitikos* < *en-* on + *klinein* to lean]

en·close (in·klōz′)   *v.t.* **·closed, ·clos·ing**   **1.** To close in on all sides; fence in; surround. **2.** To transmit within the cover of a letter: We have *enclosed* our price list. **3.** To contain: This letter *encloses* our check. Also spelled *inclose.*   [< EN-¹ + CLOSE, after OF *enclos,* pp. of *enclore* to shut in]

en·clo·sure (in·klō′zhər)   *n.*   **1.** The act of enclosing, or the state of being enclosed. **2.** An enclosed object or area. **3.** That which encloses, as a fence or wall. Also spelled *inclosure.* Abbr. *enc., encl., inc., incl.*

en·code (en·kōd′)   *v.t.* **·cod·ed, ·cod·ing** To convert (a message, document, etc.) from plain text into code.

en·co·mi·ast (en·kō′mē·ast)   *n.* One who speaks or writes an encomium; eulogist.

en·co·mi·as·tic (en·kō′mē·as′tik)   *adj.* Containing an encomium; eulogistic. Also **en·co′mi·as′ti·cal.**

en·co·mi·um (en·kō′mē·əm)   *n.*   *pl.* **·mi·ums** or **·mi·a** (-mē·ə) A formal expression of praise; eulogy.   — *Syn.* See EULOGY.   [< L < Gk. *enkōmion* eulogy]

en·com·pass (in·kum′pəs)   *v.t.*   **1.** To form a circle around; encircle; surround. **2.** To enclose; contain. **3.** *Obs.* To outwit.   **— en·com′pass·ment** *n.*

en·core (äng′kôr, -kōr, än′-)   *interj.* Again! once more!   *— n.* The call by an audience, as by means of prolonged applause, for repetition of some part of the program or for an additional performance; also, that which is performed in response to this call.   *— v.t.* **·cored, ·cor·ing** To call for a repetition of (a performance) or by (a performer).   [< F]

en·coun·ter (in·koun′tər)   *n.*   **1.** A meeting with a person or thing, especially when casual or unexpected. **2.** A hostile meeting; battle; contest. **3.** *Obs.* Manner of meeting; style of address.   *— v.t.*   **1.** To meet, especially casually or unexpectedly; come upon. **2.** To meet in conflict; face in battle. **3.** To be faced with or contend against (opposition, difficulties, etc.).   *— v.i.*   **4.** To meet each other casually or unexpectedly. **5.** To meet each other in conflict.   [< OF *encontrer* < LL *incontrare* < L *in-* in + *contra* against]

en·cour·age (in·kûr′ij)   *v.t.* **·aged, ·ag·ing**   **1.** To inspire with courage, hope, or resolution; hearten. **2.** To help or foster; be favorable toward.   [< OF *encoragier* < *en-* in (< L *in-*) + *corage.* See COURAGE.]   **— en·cour′ag·er** *n.*

en·cour·age·ment (in·kûr′ij·mənt)   *n.*   **1.** The act of encouraging, or the state of being encouraged. **2.** That which encourages.

en·cour·ag·ing (in·kûr′ij·ing)   *adj.* Giving, or tending to give, courage or confidence.   **— en·cour′ag·ing·ly** *adv.*

en·crim·son (en·krim′zən)   *v.t.* To make crimson; redden.

en·cri·nite (en′krə·nīt)   *n. Paleontol.* A fossil crinoid, especially one with cylindrical stem and developed arms: also called *crinite.*   [< NL *Encrinus,* name of the genus (< Gk. *en-* in + *krinon* lily) + -ITE¹]

en·croach (in·krōch′)   *v.i.*   **1.** To intrude stealthily or gradually upon the possessions or rights of another; trespass: with *on* or *upon.* **2.** To advance beyond the proper or usual limits; make inroads: The water is *encroaching* on the land.   [< OF *encrochier* < *en-* in + *croc* hook]   **— en·croach′er** *n.*

en·croach·ment (in·krōch′mənt)   *n.*   **1.** The act of encroaching. **2.** That which is gained by encroaching.

en·crust (in·krust′), etc. See INCRUST.

en·cul·tu·ra·tion (en·kul′chə·rā′shən)   *n. Sociol.* The process whereby individuals are conditioned by, adjusted to, and integrated with the cultural norms of their society.   **— en·cul′tu·ra′tive** *adj.*

en·cum·ber (in·kum′bər)   *v.t.*   **1.** To hinder in action or motion, as with a burden; impede. **2.** To block up; choke; crowd, as with obstacles or useless additions. **3.** To weigh down, as with debts. Also spelled *incumber.*   [< OF *encombrer* < LL *incombrare* < *in-* in + *combrus* obstacle]

en·cum·brance (in·kum′brəns)   *n.*   **1.** That which encumbers; something burdensome or superfluous; a hindrance; impediment. **2.** A dependent, especially a child. **3.** *Law* A lien attached to real property. Also spelled *incumbrance.*   — *Syn.* See IMPEDIMENT.   [< OF *encombrance* < *encombrer.* See ENCUMBER.]

en·cum·branc·er (in·kum′brən·sər)   *n.*   *Law* One who holds an encumbrance, as a mortgagee.

ency. or **encyc.** or **encycl.** Encyclopedia.

-ency   *suffix of nouns* A variant of -ENCE, as in *decency, urgency,* used to form words expressing quality, state, or condition, the earlier form being reserved largely for nouns of action.   [< L *-entia*]

en·cyc·li·cal (en·sik′li·kəl, -sī′kli-)   *adj.* Intended for general circulation; circular: said of letters. Also **en·cyc′lic.**   — *n.* A circular letter addressed by the Pope to the bishops of the world.   [< LL *encyclicus* < Gk. *enkyklios* circular, general < *en-* in + *kyklos* circle]

en·cy·clo·pe·di·a (en·sī′klə·pē′dē·ə)   *n.*   **1.** A comprehensive work made up of systematically arranged articles broadly covering the whole range of knowledge or treating of one particular field. Abbr. *ency., encyc., encycl.* **2.** The entire circle of knowledge. Also **en·cy'clo·pae'di·a**. [< NL *encyclopaedia* < Gk. *enkyklopaideia*, a misreading for *enkyklios paideia* a general education]

en·cy·clo·pe·dic (en·sī'klə·pē'dik) *adj*. Pertaining to, of the character of, or proper to an encyclopedia; comprehending a wide range of topics or knowledge. Also **en·cy'clo·pae'dic**, **en·cy'clo·pe'di·cal**. — **en·cy'clo·pe'di·cal·ly** *adv*.

en·cy·clo·pe·dism (en·sī'klə·pē'diz·əm) *n*. **1.** Encyclopedic learning. **2.** *Usually cap.* The advanced, enlightened doctrines of the Encyclopedists. Also **en·cy'clo·pae'dism**.

en·cy·clo·pe·dist (en·sī'klə·pē'dist) *n*. A writer for or compiler of an encyclopedia. Also **en·cy'clo·pae'dist**. — **the Encyclopedists** The writers of the French Encyclopedia (1751–72), including the two editors, Diderot and d'Alembert, and various contributors, as Voltaire and Rousseau.

en·cyst (en·sist') *v.t. & v.i. Biol.* To enclose or become enclosed in a cyst or sac. — **en·cyst'ment, en/cys·ta'tion** *n*.

end (end) *n*. **1.** The terminal point or part of anything that has length; either extremity of a line, space, or object extended longitudinally: the *end* of a log; the *end* of a street. **2.** The extreme limit of the space occupied by any extended object; boundary: the *ends* of the earth. **3.** The point in time at which something ceases; termination; conclusion: the *end* of the year. **4.** The purpose of an action; aim. **5.** An inevitable or natural consequence. **6.** Ultimate state. **7.** The termination of existence; death; destruction. **8.** Fragment; remnant: odds and *ends*. **9.** In football, either of the outermost linemen. — **to end up** To be ultimately: He *ended up* a great painter. — **to make** (both) **ends meet** To live within one's income. — **to the end that** In order that. — *v.t.* **1.** To bring to a finish or termination; conclude. **2.** To be the end of. **3.** To cause the death of; kill. — *v.i.* **4.** To come to an end. **5.** To die. [OE *ende*] — **Syn.** (noun) **4.** See PURPOSE.

end-all (end'ôl') *n*. The end of everything or that which ends everything: the be-all and *end-all*.

en·dam·age (en·dam'ij) *v.t.* **·aged, ·ag·ing** To cause damage to; injure.

en·da·me·ba (en'də·mē'bə) *n*. Any of a genus (*Endamoeba*) of endoparasitic amebas; especially, *E. histolytica*, causing dysentery and liver abscess: also called *entameba, entamoeba*. Also **en/da·moe'ba**. [< END(O) + AMEBA]

en·dan·ger (in·dān'jər) *v.t.* To expose to danger; imperil.

en dash *Printing* A dash one en long.

end·brain (end'brān') *n*. The telencephalon.

en·dear (in·dir') *v.t.* **1.** To make dear or beloved: He has *endeared* himself to us all. **2.** *Obs.* To make higher in price.

en·dear·ing (in·dir'ing) *adj*. **1.** Making dear or beloved. **2.** Manifesting affection; caressing. — **en·dear'ing·ly** *adv*.

en·dear·ment (in·dir'mənt) *n*. **1.** The act of endearing, or the state of being endeared. **2.** A loving word, act, etc.

en·deav·or (in·dev'ər) *n*. An attempt or effort to do or attain something; earnest exertion for an end. — *v.t.* **1.** To make an effort to do or effect; try: usually with an infinitive as object. — *v.i.* **2.** To make an effort; strive. Also *Brit.* **en·deav'our**. [ME *endeveren* < EN-¹ + DEVOIR]

En·de·cott (en'di·kot, -kət), **John**, 1589?–1665, English colonial administrator; first governor of Massachusetts. Also **En'di·cott**.

en·dem·ic (en·dem'ik) *adj*. **1.** Peculiar to a particular country or people. **2.** *Ecol.* Native to a restricted area: said of plants and animals. **3.** *Med.* Confined to or characteristic of a given locality: said of a disease. Also **en·de·mi·al** (en·dē'mē·əl), **en·dem/i·cal**. — **Syn.** See NATIVE. [< Gk. *endēmos* native < *en-* in + *dēmos* people]

en·de·mic·i·ty (en'də·mis'ə·tē) *n*. The quality or state of being endemic. Also **en·de·mism** (en'də·miz'əm).

En·der·by Land (en'dər·bē) A region on the coast of Antarctica south of Africa.

en·der·mic (en·dûr'mik) *adj. Med.* Acting by being absorbed in or through the skin. [< EN-² + Gk. *derma* skin]

en dés·ha·bil·lé (än dā·zà·bē·yā') *French* In dishabille.

end·ing (en'ding) *n*. **1.** The act of bringing or coming to an end. **2.** The concluding or final part; end; extremity. **3.** One or more concluding letters or syllables added to the base of a word, especially to indicate an inflection.

en·dive (en'div, än'dēv) *n*. **1.** An herb (*Cichorium endivia*) allied to chicory. There are many varieties, divided into two groups, the **curled** or **narrow-leaved endive** and the **broad-leaved** **2.** The blanched leaves of this herb, used as a salad. [< F < L *intibus* endive]

end·less (end'lis) *adj*. **1.** Enduring forever; eternal. **2.** Having no end in space; boundless; infinite. **3.** Continually recurring; incessant. **4.** Forming a closed loop or circle; continuous. — **Syn.** See EVERLASTING. — **end/less·ly** *adv*. **end/less·ness** *n*.

end line In football, the boundary line at each end of the playing field. See illustration at FOOTBALL.

end long (end'lông', -long') *adv*. **1.** Lengthwise. **2.** On end.

end man The man who sits at either end of the company in a minstrel troupe and engages in comic dialogue with the interlocutor.

end·most (end'mōst') *adj*. Placed or being at the extreme end; most remote; farthest.

endo- *combining form* Within; inside: *endocarp*. Also, before vowels, **end-**. [< Gk. < *endon* within]

en·do·blast (en'dō·blast) *n. Biol.* The endoderm. — **en/do·blas'tic** *adj*. [< ENDO- + -BLAST]

en·do·car·di·al (en'dō·kär'dē·əl) *adj. Anat.* **1.** Situated within the heart. **2.** Of or pertaining to the endocardium. Also **en/do·car/di·ac** (-ak).

en·do·car·di·tis (en'dō·kär·dī'tis) *n. Pathol.* Inflammation of the endocardium. — **en/do·car·dit/ic** (-dit/ik) *adj*.

en·do·car·di·um (en'dō·kär'dē·əm) *n. Anat.* The delicate endothelial membrane lining the chambers of the heart. [< NL < Gk. *endo-* within + *kardia* heart]

en·do·carp (en'dō·kärp) *n. Bot.* The inner layer of a pericarp, as of a cherry stone. [< ENDO- + -CARP]

en·do·cen·tric (en'dō·sen'trik) *adj. Ling.* Denoting a syntactic construction that as a unit has the same function as one or more of its immediate constituents: in the endocentric construction *the good books, books* has the same function as the entire construction: opposed to *exocentric*.

en·do·crine (en'dō·krin, -krēn, -krīn) *Physiol. n.* **1.** The internal secretion of a gland. **2.** An endocrine gland. — *adj*. **1.** Secreting internally. **2.** Of or pertaining to an endocrine gland or its secretion. Also **en/do·cri'nal** (-krī'nəl), **en/do·crin/ic** (-krin'ik), **en·doc·ri·nous** (en·dok'rə·nəs) *adj*. [< ENDO- + Gk. *krinein* to separate]

endocrine gland One of several ductless glands, as the thyroid, pituitary, and suprarenal glands, whose secretions, released directly into the blood or lymph, have a critical importance in many phases of physiological activity.

en·do·cri·nol·o·gy (en'dō·kri·nol'ə·jē, -krī-) *n*. The branch of medicine dealing with the endocrine glands and the various internal secretions. — **en/do·cri·nol/o·gist** *n*.

en·do·derm (en'dō·dûrm) *n. Biol.* The innermost of the three germ layers of the metazoan embryo, developing into the digestive and respiratory systems: also called *endoblast, entoblast, entoderm*. Compare ECTODERM, MESODERM. [< ENDO- + -DERM] — **en/do·der'mal, en/do·der'mic** *adj*.

en·do·don·tics (en'dō·don'tiks) *n. pl.* (*construed as sing.*) The branch of dentistry concerned with the prevention, diagnosis, and treatment of diseases of the tooth pulp, as root canal work. Also **en·do·don·tia** (en'dō·don'shə, -shē·ə), **en·do·don·tol·o·gy** (en'dō·don·tol'ə·jē). [< ENDO- + Gk. *odons, odontos* tooth + -ICS] — **en/do·don/tist** *n*.

en·do·en·zyme (en'dō·en'zīm, -zim) *n. Biochem.* An enzyme or ferment acting from within the cell, as zymase: opposed to *ectoenzyme*. Also **en/do·en'zym** (-zim)

en·dog·a·my (en·dog'ə·mē) *n. 1. Anthropol.* Marriage within the group, class, caste, or tribe; inbreeding: opposed to *exogamy*. **2.** *Bot.* Fertilization by pollination between two flowers on the same plant. [< ENDO- + -GAMY] — **en·dog'a·mous, en·do·gam·ic** (en'dō·gam'ik) *adj*.

en·do·gen (en'dō·jen) *n. Bot.* A monocotyledonous plant formerly supposed to grow from within by the growth of new tissue: opposed to *exogen*. [< ENDO- + -GEN]

en·dog·e·nous (en·doj'ə·nəs) *adj. 1. Bot.* Of, pertaining to, or like an endogen. **2.** *Biol.* Originating or growing from within. **3.** *Physiol.* Designating the anabolic processes within cells and tissues. — **en·dog'e·nous·ly** *adv*.

en·dog·e·ny (en·doj'ə·nē) *n*. Growth from within, as in cell formation. [< ENDO- + -GENY]

en·do·lymph (en'dō·limf) *n. Anat.* The fluid filling the membranous labyrinth of the ear. [< ENDO- + LYMPH]

en·do·morph (en'dō·môrf) *n. 1. Mineral.* A mineral enclosed within another, as a crystal of tourmaline in quartz. **2.** An endomorphic person. [< ENDO- + -MORPH]

en·do·mor·phic (en'dō·môr'fik) *adj. 1. Mineral.* **a** Of or pertaining to an endomorph. **b** Produced by endomorphism. **2.** Characterized by a heavy body structure as developed from the endodermal layer of the embryo, associated with a predominance of the visceral system. — **en/do·mor'phy** *n*.

en·do·morph·ism (en'dō·môr'fiz·əm) *n. Geol.* A change produced in igneous rock by underlying magmatic material.

en·do·par·a·site (en'dō·par'ə·sīt) *n. Biol.* A parasite that lives in the internal parts of its host, as an intestinal worm. — **en/do·par/a·sit/ic** (-sit'ik) *adj*.

en·do·path·ic (en'dō·path'ik) *adj. Pathol.* Originating from within the organism. [< ENDO- + -PATHIC]

en·do·phyte (en'dō·fīt) *n. Bot.* A plant living within another organism, usually as a parasite, as certain algae and fungi: also spelled *entophyte*. [< ENDO- + -PHYTE]

en·doph·y·tous (en·dof'ə·təs) *adj*. Living within wood.

en·do·plasm (en'dō·plaz'əm) *n. Biol.* The inner granular portion of the cytoplasm of the cell, enclosing the nucleus. Also **en/do·sarc** (en'dō·särk). — **en/do·plas/mic** *adj*.

end organ *Physiol.* Any organ adapted for the reception or delivery of nervous stimuli.

en·dorse (in·dôrs') *v.t.* **·dorsed, ·dors·ing 1.** To write on the back of (a paper); especially: **a** To transfer ownership or assign payment of (a check, draft, note, etc.) by signing on the reverse side. **b** To affirm or guarantee the payment, validity, receipt, etc., of (a check, note, etc.) by signing. **c** To write (one's signature) as an endorsement. **2.** To give sanction or support to: The public *endorsed* his views. Also spelled *indorse*. — **Syn.** See RATIFY. [< OF *endosser* < Med.L *in-*

dorsare < L *in-* on + *dorsum* back; partially refashioned after L] — **en·dors'a·ble** *adj.* — **en·dors'er** or **en·dor'sor** *n.*

en·dor·see (en'dôr·sē', in·dôr'sē) *n.* One to whom transference by endorsement is made.

en·dorse·ment (in·dôrs'mənt) *n.* **1.** The act of endorsing. **2.** That which endorses, as the signature on the back of a check. **3.** Confirmation; approval. Also *Canadian* **en'dor·sa'tion. 4.** An addition or amendment to a contract, legislative bill, document, etc.; rider. Also spelled *indorsement.*

endorsement in blank A blank endorsement (which see).

en·do·scope (en'də·skōp) *n. Med.* An instrument for inspecting an internal cavity or hollow organ, as the womb. — **en·dos·co·py** (en·dos'kə·pē) *n.* [< ENDO- + -SCOPE]

en·do·skel·e·ton (en'dō·skel'ə·tən) *n. Anat.* The internal supporting structure of an animal, as in all vertebrates: opposed to *exoskeleton.* — **en'do·skel'e·tal** *adj.*

en·dos·mo·sis (en'dos·mō'sis, -doz-) *n. Chem.* **1.** Osmosis in that direction in which the fluid traverses the septum most rapidly. **2.** Osmosis from an outer vessel to one within it: opposed to *exosmosis.* — **en'dos·mot'ic** (-mot'ik) *adj.*

en·do·sperm (en'dō·spûrm) *n. Bot.* The nutritive substance within the embryo sac of an ovule.

en·do·spore (en'dō·spôr, -spōr) *n. Bot.* **1.** An asexual spore formed within the membrane of a cell as in some bacteria. **2.** The delicate inner layer of the wall of a spore: also **en'do·spo'ri·um.** — **en·dos·po·rous** (en·dos'pər·əs) *adj.*

en·dos·te·um (en·dos'tē·əm) *n. pl.* **·te·a** (-tē·ə) *Anat.* The thin, vascular membrane lining the medullary cavity of a bone. [< NL < Gk. *endo-* within + *osteon* bone]

en·dos·to·sis (en'dos·tō'sis) *n. Biol.* Ossification that takes place between cartilage cells. [< END(O)- + OSTOSIS]

en·do·the·ci·um (en'dō·thē'sē·əm) *n. pl.* **·ci·a** (-sē·ə) *Bot.* **1.** The inner lining of the cell of an anther. **2.** The internal lining of the capsule of mosses. [< NL < Gk. *endo-* within + *thēkion* a small case]

en·do·the·li·o·ma (en'dō·thē'lē·ō'mə) *n. pl.* **·ma·ta** (-mə·tə) or **·mas** *Pathol.* A tumorous growth developed in or from the endothelium.

en·do·the·li·um (en'dō·thē'lē·əm) *n. pl.* **·li·a** (-lē·ə) *Anat.* A membrane composed of flat, thin cells, lining blood vessels, lymphatic tubes, and cavities. [< NL < Gk. *endo-* within + *thēlē* nipple] — **en·do·the'li·al** *adj.* — **en'do·the'li·oid** or **en·doth'e·loid** (en·doth'ə·loid) *adj.*

en·do·ther·mic (en'dō·thûr'mik) *adj. Chem.* Pertaining to, attended by, or produced from the absorption of heat: opposed to *exothermic.* Also **en'do·ther'mal.** [< ENDO- + Gk. *thermē* heat]

en·do·tox·in (en'dō·tok'sin) *n. Biochem.* A toxin produced within the cell wall of certain bacteria, and liberated by the disintegration of the cell. — **en'do·tox'ic** *adj.*

en·dow (in·dou') *v.t.* **1.** To bestow a permanent fund or income upon. **2.** To furnish or equip, as with talents or natural gifts: usually with *with.* **3.** *Obs.* To provide with a dower. Also spelled *indow.* [< OF *endouer* < *en-* in (< L *in-*) + *douer* < L *dotare* to give < *dos, dotis* marriage portion]

en·dow·ment (in·dou'mənt) *n.* **1.** Money or property given for the permanent use of an institution, person, etc. **2.** Any natural gift, as talent or beauty. **3.** The act of endowing. Also spelled *indowment.*

endowment insurance A form of life insurance paying the whole amount of the insurance directly to the insured if he survives beyond a specified date, or to a beneficiary if he dies before that time.

end·pa·pers (end'pā·pərz) *n. pl.* In bookbinding, the leaves of a folded sheet of paper placed at the front and back of a book, one leaf being pasted to the inside of the binding or cover, the other acting as a flyleaf. Also **end papers.**

end·plate (end'plāt') *n.* **1.** *Electronics* One of the electrodes of an electron tube, carrying a negative potential to prevent the escape of electrons at the anode. **2.** *Physiol.* The termination of a motor nerve, usually embedded in muscle fiber.

end product The final result or outcome of any process.

end table *U.S.* A small table to be placed beside a chair, at the end of a sofa, etc.

en·due (in·dōō', -dyōō') *v.t.* **·dued, ·du·ing 1.** To provide or endow with some quality, power, etc. **2.** To put on; don. **3.** To clothe; garb. Also spelled *indue.* [Fusion of OF *enduire* to introduce < L *inducere* (see INDUCE) and OF *enduire* to clothe < L *induere;* infl. in meaning by ENDOW]

en·dur·a·ble (in·dōōr'ə·bəl, -dyōōr'-) *adj.* That can be endured; bearable. — **en·dur'a·bly** *adv.*

en·dur·ance (in·dōōr'əns, -dyōōr'-) *n.* **1.** The act or capacity of bearing up, as under hardship or prolonged stress. **2.** The state or power of lasting; continued existence; duration. **3.** That which is endured. — **Syn.** See FORTITUDE.

en·dure (in·dōōr', -dyōōr') *v.* **·dured, ·dur·ing** *v.t.* **1.** To bear up under; stand firm against: to *endure* hardships. **2.** To put up with; tolerate: I cannot *endure* his insolence. — *v.i.* **3.** To continue to be; last. **4.** To suffer without yielding; hold out. [< OF *endurer* < L *indurare* < *in-* in + *durare* to harden < *durus* hard]

— **Syn. 1, 2.** *Endure, bear, tolerate,* and **brook** mean to sustain something unpleasant. We *endure* hardships, and the word here suggests lasting or repeated trials of our patience. We *bear* that which weights us down, as pain or responsibility, and here a test of physical or moral strength is suggested. We *tolerate* something or someone by overcoming our own repugnance through an act of the will. *Brook* is close in sense to *tolerate,* but is almost invariably used in the negative: he would *brook* no interference.

en·dur·ing (in·dōōr'ing, -dyōōr'-) *adj.* **1.** Lasting; permanent. **2.** Long-suffering. — **Syn.** See PERMANENT. — **en·dur'ing·ly** *adv.* — **en·dur'ing·ness** *n.*

end·wise (end'wīz') *adv.* **1.** With the end foremost or uppermost. **2.** On end. **3.** Lengthwise. **4.** End to end. Also **end'ways'** (-wāz').

En·dym·i·on (en·dim'ē·ən) In Greek mythology, a beautiful youth loved by Selene and granted eternal youth through eternal sleep.

end zone In football, the area between the goal line and the end line, in which a touchdown may be scored. See illustration at FOOTBALL.

ENE or **ene, E.N.E.** or **e.n.e.** East–Northeast.

-ene *suffix Chem.* **1.** Denoting an open-chain, unsaturated, hydrocarbon compound having one double bond: *ethylene.* **2.** Denoting an aromatic compound of the benzene series.

en·e·ma (en'ə·mə) *n. pl.* **en·e·mas** or **e·nem·a·ta** (e·nem'ə·tə) *Med.* **1.** A liquid injected into the rectum for cleansing, diagnostic, or nutritive purposes. **2.** The injection of such a liquid. [< Gk. < *enienai* < *en-* in + *hienai* to send]

en·e·my (en'ə·mē) *n. pl.* **·mies 1.** One who harbors hatred or malicious intent toward another; also, one who or that which opposes or works actively against a person, cause, etc.; adversary; foe. **2.** A hostile power or military force; also, a member of a hostile force. — *adj.* **1.** Of or pertaining to a hostile army or power. **2.** *Obs.* Unfriendly; hostile. [< OF *enemi* < L *inimicus* < *in-* not + *amicus* friend]

— **Syn.** (noun) *Enemy, foe, opponent, antagonist, adversary, rival,* and *competitor* denote one who opposes or vies with another. An *enemy* is one who manifests ill will, or broadly anyone on the opposite side in a struggle. Malice or rancor is more strongly emphasized in *foe,* a poetic word for *enemy.* An *opponent* may vie with one in a friendly contest, while an *antagonist* is always hostile and unfriendly: an *opponent* in a debate, a political *antagonist. Adversary* is a general word with a wide range of meaning, and may be applied to a friendly *opponent* or to the most implacable *enemy. Rivals* and *competitors* seek the same ends, but *rivals* often feel personal animosity while *competitors* may be more impersonal: *rivals* for the hand of a woman, *competitors* in a tennis match.

enemy alien An alien living in a country that is at war with his own country.

en·er·ge·sis (en'ər·jē'sis) *n. Bot.* The chemical processes within the plant cell by which energy is released through catabolic action. [< NL < Gk. *energeein* to be active.]

en·er·get·ic (en'ər·jet'ik) *adj.* Having or displaying energy; acting with prompt, effective force; forceful and efficient; strenuous. [< Gk. *energētikos* < *energeein* to be active] — **en'er·get'i·cal·ly** *adv.*

en·er·get·ics (en'ər·jet'iks) *n.pl.* (construed as *sing.*) The science of the laws and phenomena of energy.

en·er·gize (en'ər·jīz) *v.* **·gized, ·giz·ing** *v.t.* **1.** To give energy, force, or strength to; activate. — *v.i.* **2.** To be in operation; be active. — **en'er·giz'er** *n.*

en·er·gu·men (en'ər·gyōō'mən) *n.* **1.** One supposedly possessed by evil spirits. **2.** A fanatical enthusiast. [< LL *energumenus* < Gk. *energoumenos,* ppr. of *energeein* to be active]

en·er·gy (en'ər·jē) *n. pl.* **·gies 1.** Vigor or intensity of action, expression, or utterance. **2.** Capacity or tendency for vigorous action: Small boys are full of *energy.* **3.** Inherent power to produce an effect: the immeasurable *energy* of evil. **4.** *Often pl.* Power forcefully and effectively exercised: All their *energies* were thrown into the campaign. **5.** *Physics* The capacity for doing work and for overcoming inertia. **Potential energy** is that due to the position of one body relative to another, and **kinetic energy** is that manifested by bodies in motion. Abbr. (def. 5) *E* [< LL *energia* < Gk. *energia* < *energēs* active < *en-* in + *ergon* work]

energy level *Physics* Any of several discrete states in the energy of a physical system or any of its parts, transition between which is indicated by a gain or loss in quanta as determined by the forces acting within or upon it.

en·er·vate (*v.* en'ər·vāt; *adj.* i·nûr'vit) *v.t.* **·vat·ed, ·vat·ing** To sap the strength or vitality of; weaken in body or will. — *adj.* Weakened; devitalized. [< L *enervatus,* pp. of *enervare* to weaken < *e-* out + *nervus* sinew] — **en'er·va'tion** *n.* — **en'er·va'tor** *n.*

en·face (en·fās') *v.t.* **·faced, ·fac·ing** To write or print on the face of. — **en·face'ment** *n.*

en fa·mille (äṅ fȧ·mē'y') *French* Within the family; at home; informally.

en·fant per·du (äṅ·fäṅ' per·dü') *pl.* **en·fants per·dus** (äṅ·fäṅ' per·dü') *French* **1.** A soldier assigned to a position of extreme danger; literally, a lost child. **2.** *pl.* A forlorn hope.

en·fant ter·ri·ble (äṅ·fäṅ' te·rē'bl') *French* A child or willful adult whose remarks and conduct cause embarrassment; literally, a terrible child.

en·fee·ble (en·fē′bəl) *v.t.* **·bled, ·bling** To make feeble. — **en·fee′ble·ment** *n.* — **en·fee′bler** *n.*

en·feoff (en·fēf′ -fef′) *v.t.* **1.** *Law* To invest with a fee or fief. **2.** To surrender in vassalage. Also spelled *infeoff.* [< OF *enfeoffer* < *en*- in + *fief.* See FIEF.] — **en·feoff′ment** *n.*

en·fet·ter (en·fet′ər) *v.t.* To enchain.

En·field (en′fēld) **1.** An urban district in Middlesex, England, near London; pop. 109,524 (1961). **2.** A town in Connecticut, near the Massachusetts border; pop. 46,189.

Enfield rifle A .30-caliber, bolt-action, breechloading magazine rifle formerly used by the U.S. and British armies. [after *Enfield*, England, where it was first manufactured]

en·fi·lade (en′fə·lād′) *Mil. v.t.* **·lad·ed, ·lad·ing** To fire or be in a position to fire down the length of, as a trench or column of troops. — *n.* **1.** Gunfire that can rake lengthwise a line of troops, etc. **2.** A position exposed to a raking fire. [< F < *enfiler* to thread < *en*- in + *fil* thread]

en·fin (äṅ·faṅ′) *adv. French* In conclusion; finally.

en·fleu·rage (äṅ′flœ·räzh′) *n.* The extraction of perfumes by exposing odorless fats to the exhalations of flowers. [< F < *enfleurer* < *en*- in + *fleur* flower]

en·fold (in·fōld′) See INFOLD.

en·force (in·fôrs′ -fōrs′) *v.t.* **·forced, ·forc·ing 1.** To compel observance of (a law, etc.). **2.** To impose (obedience, performance, etc.) by physical or moral force. **3.** To lay stress upon; emphasize: The evidence *enforced* his guilt. [< OF *enforcier* < LL *infortiare* < L *in*- in + *fortis* strong] — **en·force′a·ble** *adj.* — **en·force′ment** *n.* — **en·forc′er** *n.*

en·frame (in·frām′) *v.t.* **·framed, ·fram·ing** To enclose in or as in a border or frame. — **en·frame′ment** *n.*

en·fran·chise (in·fran′chīz) *v.t* **·chised, ·chis·ing 1.** To endow with a franchise, as with the right to vote. **2.** To set free, as from bondage or legal liabilities. [< OF *enfranchiss-*, stem of *enfranchir* < *en*- in + *franc* free. See FRANK.] — **en·fran′chise·ment** (-chīz·mənt) *n.*

eng. 1. Engine; engineer; engineering. **2.** Engraved; engraver; engraving.

Eng. England; English.

En·ga·dine (eng′gə·dēn) The valley of the Inn river in eastern Switzerland; a resort center; 60 mi. long.

en·gage (in·gāj′) *v.* **·gaged, ·gag·ing** *v.t.* **1.** To hire or employ (a person); also, to secure or contract for (professional services, assistance, etc.). **2.** To reserve the use of, as lodgings. **3.** To hold the interest or attention of; engross. **4.** To occupy; keep busy: to *engage* one's time in revelry. **5.** To bind by a pledge, contract, etc. **6.** To betroth: usually in the passive. **7.** To win over; attract: to *engage* affection. **8.** To enter into conflict with; attack: to *engage* the enemy. **9.** *Mech.* To mesh or interlock with. — *v.i.* **10.** To occupy oneself in an undertaking: to *engage* in research. **11.** To pledge oneself; warrant. **12.** To enter into combat. **13.** *Mech.* To mesh. [< F *engager* < *en*- in + *gager* to pledge]

en·gaged (in·gājd′) *adj.* **1.** Occupied or busy **2.** Betrothed. **3.** Involved in conflict. **4.** *Mech.* Geared together; meshed. **5.** *Archit.* Partially sunk or built into another part of a structure, or so appearing.

en·gage·ment (in·gāj′mənt) *n.* **1.** The act of engaging, or the state of being engaged. **2.** Something that engages or binds, as an obligation. **3.** Betrothal. **4.** A business appointment. **5.** A salaried position; employment, especially for a limited period. **6.** A hostile encounter; battle; conflict. **7.** *Mech.* The state of being in gear. **8.** *pl.* Financial obligations. — **Syn.** See BATTLE.

en·gag·ing (in·gā′jing) *adj.* Attracting interest or affection; winning; pleasing. — **en·gag′ing·ly** *adv.*

en gar·çon (äṅ gȧr·sôṅ′) *French* In bachelorhood.

en garde (äṅ gȧrd′) *French* On guard: a fencing position.

en·gar·land (en·gär′lənd) *v.t.* To encircle with or as with garlands; wreathe.

Eng. D. Doctor of Engineering.

Eng·els (eng′əls), **Friedrich,** 1820–95, German socialist leader and theoretician; collaborated with Karl Marx.

en·gen·der (in·jen′dər) *v.t.* **1.** To cause to exist; give rise to; produce. **2.** *Rare* To beget. — *v.i.* **3.** To come into being. [< OF *engendrer* < L *ingenerare* to create < *in*- in + *genus, generis* race]

engin. Engineering.

en·gine (en′jən) *n.* **1.** A machine that converts heat energy into mechanical work: a steam *engine,* gas *engine,* etc. **2.** A locomotive. **3.** An apparatus or mechanical contrivance for producing some effect, especially of destruction: an *engine* of war. **4.** Any agency, means, or instrument. Abbr. *eng.* — **Syn.** See MACHINE. [< OF *engin* < L *ingenium* natural ability < *in*- in + *gen*-, root of *gignere* to beget]

engine driver *Brit.* A locomotive engineer.

en·gi·neer (en′jə·nir′) *n.* **1.** One versed in or practicing any branch of engineering. **2.** One who operates an engine. **3.** A skillful or shrewd manager. **4.** *Mil.* A member of a corps of men engaged in constructing forts and bridges, clearing and building roads, etc. Abbr. *e., E., eng., engr.* — *v.t.* **1.** To put through or manage by contrivance: to *engineer* a scheme. **2.** To plan and superintend as engineer.

en·gi·neer·ing (en′jə·nir′ing) *n.* **1.** The art and science concerned with the practical application of scientific knowledge, as in the design, construction, and operation of roads, bridges, harbors, buildings, machinery, lighting and communications systems, etc. Abbr. *e., E., eng., engin.* **2.** Painstaking management; maneuvering.

en·gine·ry (en′jən·rē) *n.* **1.** Engines collectively. **2.** Engines of war. **3.** Maneuvering; contrivance.

en·gi·nous (en′jə·nəs) *adj. Obs.* Ingenious; crafty. [< OF *enginus, enginos* < L *ingeniosus.* See INGENIOUS.]

en·gird (en·gûrd′) *v.t.* **·girt** or **·gird·ed, ·gird·ing** To gird; encompass. Also **en·gir′dle.**

en·gla·cial (en·glā′shəl) *adj.* **1.** Embedded within glacier ice. **2.** Occurring in a glacier.

Eng·land (ing′glənd) The southern part and largest political division of Great Britain, south of Scotland and east of Wales; 50,237 sq. mi.; pop. 46,102,300 (est. 1969); capital, London: Latin *Anglia.* See BRITISH COMMONWEALTH OF NATIONS, GREAT BRITAIN, UNITED KINGDOM.

Eng·land·er (ing′glən·dər) *n.* A native of England.

En·gle·wood (eng′gəl·wŏŏd) **1.** A city in central Colorado, a suburb of Denver; pop. 33,695. **2.** A city in NE New Jersey; pop. 24,985.

Eng·lish (ing′glish) *adj.* **1.** Of, pertaining to, or derived from England or its people. **2.** Expressed in or belonging to the English language — *n.* **1.** The people of England collectively: with *the.* **2.** The language, belonging to the West Germanic branch, spoken by the people of the British Isles and most of the British Commonwealth, and of the United States, its territories, and possessions. — **Old English** or **Anglo-Saxon** The English language from about A.D. 450 to 1050, having as its major dialects Kentish, West Saxon, Mercian, and Northumbrian, represented by the epic poem *Beowulf* and the writings of Alfred the Great. The language in this period is largely synthetic in form and consists of a basically Germanic vocabulary. Abbr. *OE, OE., O.E.* — **Middle English** The language of England after the Norman Conquest. from about 1050 to 1475, represented by the works of Chaucer. The characteristics of the language during this period are the gradual loss of inflections accompanied by a stabilizing of word order, extensive borrowings from Latin, French, and the Low German languages, and the rise of the East Midland dialect as the standard. Abbr. *ME, ME., M.E.* — **Modern English** The English language since 1475, often divided into **Early Modern English,** before 1700, and **Late Modern English,** after 1700. **3.** An English translation or equivalent: "John" is the *English* of the French "Jean." **4.** The English pronunciation, style, syntax, vocabulary, etc., of a particular region, time, or person: Chaucerian *English;* American *English.* **5.** *Printing* A size of type between pica and Columbian, 14-point. **6.** *U.S.* In billiards, a horizontal twist or spin given to the cue ball by striking it on one side. — *v.t.* **1.** To translate into English. **2.** To Anglicize, as a foreign word. **3.** *U.S.* In billiards, to apply English to. Abbr. (n.) *E. E., Eng.* [OE *Englisc* < *Engle* the Angles]

English bulldog A bulldog (def. 1).

English Canadian An English-speaking Canadian.

English Channel A strait between England and France, connecting the North Sea with the Atlantic Ocean; width, 20–100 mi.: French *La Manche.*

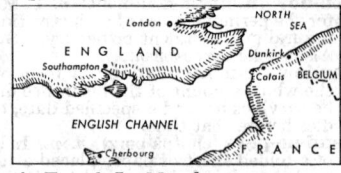

SOVEREIGNS OF ENGLAND, GREAT BRITAIN, AND THE UNITED KINGDOM

SOVEREIGNS OF ENGLAND

	Beginning of reign
ANGLO-SAXON LINE	A.D.
Egbert	829
Ethelwulf (son)	839
Ethelbald (son)[1]	858
Ethelbert (brother)	860
Ethelred I (brother)	866
Alfred *the Great* (brother)	871
Edward *the Elder* (son)	901
Athelstan (son)	924
Edmund I (brother)	940
Edred (brother)	946
Edwy (nephew)	955
Edgar (brother)	957
Edward *the Martyr* (son)	975
Ethelred II, *the Unready* (half brother)	978
Edmund II, *Ironside* (son)	1016
DANISH LINE	
Canute (son of Sweyn, a Viking)	1016
Harold I, *Harefoot* (son)	1035
Hardecanute (half brother)	1040
SAXON LINE (RESTORED)	
Edward *the Confessor* (son of Ethelred II)	1042
Harold II (son of Earl Godwin)	1066

(continued)

NORMAN LINE
William I	1066
William II (son)	1087
Henry I (brother)	1100
Stephen (nephew)	1135

PLANTAGENET LINE
Henry II (grandson of Henry I)	1154
Richard I (son)	1189
John (brother)	1199
Henry III (son)	1216
Edward I (son)	1272
Edward II (son)	1307
Edward III (son)	1327
Richard II (grandson)	1377

HOUSE OF LANCASTER
Henry IV (grandson of Edward III)	1399
Henry V (son)	1413
Henry VI (son)	1422

HOUSE OF YORK
Edward IV (great-great-grandson of Edward III)	1461
Edward V (son)	1483
Richard III (uncle)	1483

HOUSE OF TUDOR
Henry VII (great-great-great-grandson of Edward III)	1485
Henry VIII (son)	1509
Edward VI (son)	1547
Mary I (half sister)	1553
Elizabeth I (half sister)	1558

SOVEREIGNS OF GREAT BRITAIN

Beginning of reign
A.D.

STUART LINE
James I of England and VI of Scotland (son of Mary Queen of Scots, great-granddaughter of Henry VII)	1603
Charles I (son)	1625

COMMONWEALTH (the government after the execution of Charles I in 1649, directed by the House of Commons until 1653; name also applied to the period from 1649–58, including the Protectorate)

PROTECTORATE (the rule of Oliver Cromwell as Lord Protector 1653–58, succeeded by Richard Cromwell, his son, 1658–59; followed by a year of anarchy)

STUART LINE (RESTORED)
Charles II (son of Charles I)	1660
James II (brother)	1685

HOUSE OF ORANGE
William III (nephew) and Mary II (daughter of James II)	1689

STUART LINE
Anne (daughter of James II)	1702

HOUSE OF HANOVER
George I (great-grandson of James I)	1714
George II (son)	1727

SOVEREIGNS OF THE UNITED KINGDOM[2]

Beginning of reign
A.D.

George III (grandson)[3]	1760
George IV (son)	1820
William IV (brother)	1830
Victoria (niece of William IV)	1837

SAXE-COBURG LINE
Edward VII (son)	1901

HOUSE OF WINDSOR[4]
George V (son)	1910
Edward VIII (son): abdicated	1936
George VI (brother)	1936
Elizabeth II (daughter)	1952

[1]Relationship is to preceding sovereign, unless otherwise stated. [2]United in 1801. [3]Son of Frederick, Prince of Wales, who died in 1751. [4]Created by Royal Proclamation, July 17, 1917.

English daisy See under DAISY.
English horn A double-reed instrument having a pitch a fifth lower than an oboe: also called *cor anglais*.
Eng·lish·ism (ing/glish-iz/əm) *n.* 1. A Briticism. 2. Devotion to what is English in speech, manners, etc.
Eng·lish·man (ing/glish-mən) *n. pl.* **·men** (-mən) 1. A native or citizen of England. 2. An English ship.
Eng·lish·man's tie (ing/glish-mənz) *Naut.* A strong knot for heavy ropes.
English muffin A round, flat muffin made with little shortening, and usually eaten toasted.
English Revolution See under REVOLUTION.
Eng·lish·ry (ing/glish-rē) *n.* 1. People of English birth or descent collectively: applied especially to the English in Ireland. 2. The condition or fact of being an Englishman.
English setter A variety of setter, white, or white marked with black, tan, yellow, or orange, trained since the 16th century to find and point game.
English sonnet The Shakespearean sonnet (which see).
English sparrow See under SPARROW.
English springer spaniel A variously colored spaniel of medium size, used for hunting.
English walnut See under WALNUT.

Eng·lish·wom·an (ing/glish·wŏŏm/ən) *n. pl.* **·wom·en** (-wim/in) A woman who is a native or citizen of England.
en·glut (en-glut/) *v.t. Obs.* 1. To swallow greedily; gulp down. 2. To satiate; glut. [< EN-¹ + GLUT]
en·gorge (en-gôrj/) *v.t.* **·gorged**, **·gorg·ing** 1. To fill with blood, as an artery. 2. To devour or swallow greedily. 3. To satiate (oneself). [< F *engorger* < *en-* in + *gorge* throat] — **en·gorge/ment** *n.*
engr. 1. Engineer. 2. Engraved; engraver; engraving.
en·graft (en-graft/, -gräft/) *v.t.* 1. *Bot.* To graft (a cion) to another type of tree or plant for propagation. 2. To set firmly; implant. Also spelled *ingraft*. — **en·graft/ment** *n.*
en·grail (en-grāl/) *v.t.* To ornament the edge of with a series of indentations. [< OF *engresler* to indent as by hailstones < *en-* in + *gresle* hail]
en·grain (in-grān/) *v.t.* 1. To ingrain. 2. To grain in imitation of wood.
en·gram (en/gram) *n.* 1. A permanently altered state in the protoplasm of animal cells assumed to result from the temporary excitation of certain stimuli. 2. *Psychol.* A trace. [< EN-² + -GRAM]
en·grave (in-grāv/) *v.t.* **·graved**, **·grav·ing** 1. To carve or etch figures, letters, etc., into (a surface) 2. To impress deeply on the mind. 3. To cut (pictures, lettering, etc.) into metal, stone, or wood, for printing. 4. To print from plates made by such a process. [< EN-¹ + GRAVE.³ Cf. F *engraver*] — **en·grav/er** *n.*
en·grav·ing (in-grā/ving) *n.* 1. The act or art of cutting designs, etc., into a surface. 2. An engraved design; plate. 3. An impression printed from an engraved plate; print. *Abbr. eng., engr.*
en·gross (in-grōs/) *v.t.* 1. To occupy completely; absorb. 2. To copy legibly in a large hand, as a document; make a formal transcript of. 3. In business, to monopolize (goods already on the market): distinguished from *forestall*. [< AF *engrosser* < LL *ingrossare* to write large < L *in-* in + *grossus* large] — **en·gross/er** *n.*
en·gross·ing (in-grō/sing) *adj.* Holding the attention or interest completely; absorbing. — **en·gross/ing·ly** *adv.*
en·gross·ment (in-grōs/mənt) *n.* 1. The state of being completely occupied with something; absorption. 2. A document or the like that has been engrossed.
en·gulf (in-gulf/) *v.t.* To swallow up in or as in a gulf; bury or overwhelm completely: also spelled *ingulf*.
en·hance (in-hans/, -häns/) *v.t.* **·hanced**, **·hanc·ing** To heighten or increase, as in reputation, cost, beauty, quality, etc. — **Syn.** See INCREASE. [< AF *enhauncer*, prob. var. of OF *enhaucer* < *en-* in, on + *haucer* to lift, ult. < L *altus* high] — **en·hanc/er** *n.* — **en·hance/ment** *n.*
en·har·mon·ic (en/här·mon/ik) *adj. Music* 1. Having or consisting of intervals of less than a half step; especially, relating to the slight differences in pitch between tones as C♯ and D♭ when played on untempered instruments. 2. Of or relating to tones, as C♯ and D♭ having different notation but the same pitch when played on a piano or other tempered instrument. 3. Of or relating to an ancient Greek scale whose intervals were quarter tones and major thirds. [< L *enharmonicus* < Gk. *enarmonikos* < *en-* in + *harmonia*. See HARMONY.] — **en/har·mon/i·cal·ly** *adv.*
E·nid (ē/nid) A city in northern Oklahoma; pop. 44,008.
e·nig·ma (i·nig/mə) *n.* 1. An obscure or ambiguous saying; riddle. 2. Anything that puzzles or baffles. — **Syn.** See PUZZLE. [< L *aenigma* < Gk. *ainigma* < *ainissesthai* to speak in riddles < *ainos* tale]
en·ig·mat·ic (en/ig·mat/ik, ē/nig-) *adj.* Of or like an enigma; puzzling. Also **en/ig·mat/i·cal.** — **en/ig·mat/i·cal·ly** *adv.*
E·ni·sei (yen/ə·sā/) See YENISEI.
en·isle (en·īl/) *v.t.* **·isled**, **·isl·ing** *Poetic* 1. To place on an island; isolate. 2. To make an island of.
E·ni·we·tok (en/i·wē/tok, i·nē/wi·tŏk) An atoll in the Marshall Islands; U.S. proving grounds (1948) for atomic weapons; 2 sq. mi.
en·jamb·ment (en·jam/mənt, -jamb/-; *Fr.* äṅ·zhäṅb·mäṅ/) *n.* In prosody, the running over of a sentence or thought from one couplet or line to the next, without a pause at the end of the line. Also **en·jambe/ment.** [< F *enjambement* < *enjamber* to encroach < *en-* in + *jambe* leg]
en·join (in·join/) *v.t.* 1. To order authoritatively and emphatically; direct or command (a person or group) to a course of action, conduct, etc. 2. To impose (a condition, course of action, etc.) on a person or group. 3. To forbid or prohibit, especially by judicial order or injunction. ◆ In the sense of direct or command *enjoin* is followed by *to* plus an infinitive, as *I enjoined him to leave*. In the sense of forbid, it is followed by *from* plus a gerund, as *I enjoined him from leaving*. [< OF *enjoindre* < L *injungere* < *in-* on + *jungere* to join] — **en·join/er** *n.* — **en·join/ment** *n.*
en·joy (in·joi/) *v.t.* 1. To experience joy or pleasure in; receive pleasure from. 2. To have the use or benefit of. — to **enjoy oneself** To have a pleasant time. [< OF *enjoir* < *en* in (< L *in-*) + *joir* < L *gaudere* to rejoice] — **en·joy/er** *n.*

en·joy·a·ble (in-joi′ə-bəl) *adj.* Giving or capable of giving enjoyment. **— en·joy′a·ble·ness** *n.* **— en·joy′a·bly** *adv.*

en·joy·ment (in-joi′mənt) *n.* **1.** The act or state of deriving joy or pleasure from something; also, beneficial or pleasurable use or possession: the *enjoyment* of good health. **2.** Something that gives joy, pleasure, or satisfaction. **3.** Pleasure; delight; satisfaction. **— Syn.** See PLEASURE.

en·kin·dle (en-kin′dəl) *v.t.* **·dled, ·dling 1.** To set on fire; kindle. **2.** To stir to action; excite. **— en·kin′dler** *n.*

enl. 1. Enlarge(d). **2.** Enlisted.

en·lace (in-lās′) *v.t.* **·laced, ·lac·ing 1.** To bind or wrap with or as with laces. **2.** To intertwine; entangle. Also spelled *inlace.* [< OF *enlacer* < *en-* in + *lacer* < *las.* See LACE.] **— en·lace′ment** *n.*

en·large (in-lärj′) *v.* **·larged, ·larg·ing** *v.t.* **1.** To make larger; increase the amount or extent of; expand. **2.** *Photog.* To increase the size of (a photograph) by projection printing. Abbr. *enl.* **—** *v.i.* **3.** To become larger; increase; widen. **4.** To express oneself in greater detail or at greater length; expatiate: with *on* or *upon.* **— Syn.** See INCREASE. [< OF *enlarger* < *en-* in + *large* large] **— en·larg′er** *n.*

en·large·ment (in-lärj′mənt) *n.* **1.** The act of enlarging, or the state of being enlarged. **2.** An addition, expansion, increase, or extension. **3.** *Photog.* A photograph made larger than its original negative.

en·light·en (in-līt′n) *v.t.* **1.** To give revealing or broadening knowledge to; cause to know or understand; teach. **2.** *Archaic* To light up. **— en·light′en·er** *n.*

en·light·en·ment (in-līt′n-mənt) *n.* **1.** The act of enlightening, or the state of being enlightened. **— the Enlightenment** A philosophical movement of the 18th century, characterized by rationalistic methods and skepticism about established dogmas.

en·list (in-list′) *v.t.* **1.** To engage for military or naval service. **2.** To secure the active aid or participation of (a person or his services) in some cause or enterprise. **—** *v.i.* **3.** To enter military or naval service without being drafted. **4.** To join some venture, cause, etc.: with *in.*

en·list·ed man (in-lis′tid) Any male member of the armed forces who is not a commissioned officer or warrant officer; a private, seaman, noncommissioned officer, etc. Abbr. *EM*

en·list·ment (in-list′mənt) *n.* **1.** The act of enlisting, or the state of being enlisted. **2.** The term for which one enlists.

en·li·ven (in-lī′vən) *v.t.* **1.** To make lively, cheerful, or sprightly. **2.** To make active or vigorous; stimulate. **— en·li′ven·er** *n.* **— en·li′ven·ment** *n.*

en masse (en mas′, *Fr.* äṅ màs′) In a mass or body; all together. [< F]

en·mesh (en-mesh′) *v.t.* To ensnare or entangle in or as in a net: also *immesh, inmesh.*

en·mi·ty (en′mə-tē) *n. pl.* **·ties** Deep-seated unfriendliness accompanied by readiness to quarrel or fight; hostility; antagonism. [< OF *enemistie*, ult. < L *inimicus* hostile < *in-* not + *amicus* friend]
— Syn. *Enmity, hostility, antagonism, animosity,* and *rancor* denote feelings of ill will. *Enmity* is the quality or feeling that characterizes an enemy; *hostility* embraces the actions by which *enmity* is displayed. *Antagonism* suggests opposition based on temperamental differences. *Animosity* and *rancor* are stronger than *enmity,* but often less enduring; of the two, *animosity* suggests vindictive anger, and *rancor,* bitter resentment. Compare ENEMY, ANTIPATHY, HATRED. **— Ant.** amity, friendship.

en·ne·a- *combining form* Nine: *enneagon.* [< Gk. *ennea* nine]

en·ne·ad (en′ē-ad) *n.* Any system or group containing nine individuals or things. [< Gk. *enneas, enneados*]

en·ne·a·gon (en′ē-ə-gon′) *n. Geom.* A nonagon (which see). [< ENNEA- + -GON]

en·ne·a·he·dron (en′ē-ə-hē′drən) *n. pl.* **·drons** or **·dra** (-drə) *Geom.* A polyhedron bounded by nine surfaces. **— en′ne·a·he′dral** *adj.* [< ENNEA- + -HEDRON]

En·ni·us (en′ē-əs), **Quintus,** 239–169 B.C., Roman epic poet.

en·no·ble (i-nō′bəl, en-) *v.t.* **·bled, ·bling 1.** To make honorable or noble in nature, quality, etc.; dignify. **2.** To confer a title of nobility upon. [< F *ennoblir* < *en-* in (< L *in-*) + *noble.* See NOBLE.] **— en·no′ble·ment** *n.* **— en·no′bler** *n.*

en·nui (än′wē, *Fr.* äṅ-nwē′) *n.* A feeling of listless weariness and vague discontent resulting from inactivity or lack of interest; boredom. [< F< OF *ennui* < L *in odio.* See ANNOY.]

en·nuy·é (äṅ-nwē-ā′) *French adj.* Oppressed with ennui; bored. **— en·nuy·ée′** *adj.fem.*

E·noch (ē′nək) The eldest son of Cain. *Gen.* iv 17.

E·noch The father of Methuselah. *Gen.* v 21.

e·nol (ē′nol, -nōl) *n. Chem.* An organic compound in which a hydroxyl group is joined with a doubly linked carbon atom. [Prob. < Gk. *hen,* neut. of *heis* one + -OL[1]]

e·norm (i-nôrm′) *adj. Archaic* Enormous.

e·nor·mi·ty (i-nôr′mə-tē) *n. pl.* **·ties 1.** The quality of being outrageous; heinousness: the *enormity* of that crime. **2.** An outrageous offense; atrocity. [< F *énormité* < L *enormitas, -tatis* < *enormis.* See ENORMOUS.]

e·nor·mous (i-nôr′məs) *adj.* **1.** Far exceeding the usual size, amount, degree, etc.; extraordinarily large or extensive;

immense. **2.** *Archaic* Extremely wicked; atrocious; heinous. [< L *enormis* < *e-* out + *norma* rule] **— e·nor′mous·ly** *adv.* **— e·nor′mous·ness** *n.*

E·nos (ē′nəs) A son of Seth. *Gen.* iv 26. [< Hebrew *enōsh* man]

e·no·sis (e-nō′sis) *n.* Union, especially as proposed between Cyprus and Greece. [< Gk. *énōsis* union]

e·nough (i-nuf′) *adj.* Adequate for any demand or need; sufficient. **—** *n.* An ample supply; a sufficiency. **—** *adv.* **1.** So as to be sufficient; sufficiently: The house is large *enough.* **2.** Quite; very: He is glad *enough* to do it. **3.** Adequately; fairly; tolerably: I liked the play well *enough.* **—** *interj.* That's enough! [OE *genōh, genōg*]
— Syn. (*adj.*) *Enough* and *sufficient* are strictly equivalent in expressing bare adequacy. *Enough* is frequently placed after its noun, while *sufficient* comes before: to have money *enough,* to lack *sufficient* funds. *Enough* is also often used in irony or understatement to mean more than adequate, ample, or full: I've heard excuses *enough!* Compare ADEQUATE, AMPLE.

e·nounce (i-nouns′) *v.t.* **e·nounced, e·nounc·ing 1.** To make a formal statement of; announce. **2.** To give verbal expression to; utter; enunciate. [< F *énoncer* < L *enuntiare.* See ENUNCIATE.] **— e·nounce′ment** *n.*

e·now (i-nou′) *adj., n., & adv. Archaic* Enough.

en pas·sant (äṅ pà-säṅ′) *French* **1.** By the way; in passing. **2.** In chess, a capture in which a pawn that in its initial move of two squares has crossed a square that is under attack by an opposing pawn and is taken as the opposing pawn occupies the crossed square.

en·phy·tot·ic (en′fī-tot′ik) *adj. Bot.* Of regular occurrence in a locality: said of certain plant diseases. [< Gk. *en-* in + *phyton* plant]

en·plane (en-plān′) *v.i.* **·planed, ·plan·ing** To board an airplane.

en·quire (in-kwīr′), **en·quir·y** (in-kwīr′ē, in′kwər-ē) See INQUIRE, INQUIRY.

en·rage (in-rāj′) *v.t.* **·raged, ·rag·ing** To throw into a rage; infuriate. [< OF *enrager* < *en-* in + *rage.* See RAGE.]

en rap·port (äṅ rà-pôr′) *French* In sympathetic accord.

en·rapt (in-rapt′) *adj.* Rapt; enraptured.

en·rap·ture (in-rap′chər) *v.t.* **·tured, ·tur·ing** To bring into a state of rapture; delight extravagantly.

en·rav·ish (en-rav′ish) *v.t.* To enrapture.

en·reg·is·ter (en-rej′is-tər) *v.t.* To put on record; enroll; register. [< F *enregistrer*]

en re·gle (äṅ re′gl′) *French* According to rule; in due order.

en re·vanche (äṅ rə-väṅsh′) *French* In return; in revenge; by way of compensation.

en·rich (in-rich′) *v.t.* **1.** To make rich or increase the wealth of. **2.** To make more productive, as soil. **3.** To add attractive or desirable elements to; make better, more interesting, etc., by adding something. **4.** To increase the food value of, as bread. **5.** To increase the beauty of; adorn. [< OF *enrichir* < *en-* in + *riche* rich] **— en·rich′er** *n.*

en·rich·ment (in-rich′mənt) *n.* **1.** The act of enriching, or the state of being enriched. **2.** That which enriches.

en·robe (en-rōb′) *v.t.* **·robed, ·rob·ing** To dress; attire.

en·roll (in-rōl′) *v.t.* **1.** To write or record (a name) in a roll; register; list. **2.** To enlist. **3.** To place on record; record, as a document or decree. **4.** To roll up; wrap. **—** *v.i.* **5.** To place one's name on a list; register oneself. Also *Brit.* **en·rol′.** [< OF *enroller* < *en-* in + *rolle.* See ROLL.]

en·roll·ment (in-rōl′mənt) *n.* **1.** The act of enrolling, or the state of being enrolled. **2.** A record of persons or things enrolled. **3.** The number enrolled. Also **en·rol′ment.**

en·root (en-rōōt′, -rŏŏt′) *v.t.* To cause to take root; implant deeply: used chiefly in the passive.

en route (än rōōt′, *Fr.* äṅ rōōt′) On the road; on the way.

ens (enz) *n. pl.* **en·ti·a** (en′shē-ə) In scholastic philosophy, the abstract conception of being. [< LL, orig. ppr. formed from *esse* to be]

ENS or **Ens.** *Mil.* Ensign.

en·sam·ple (en-sam′pəl, -säm′-) *n. Archaic* Example.

en·san·guine (en-sang′gwin) *v.t.* **·guined, ·guin·ing** To cover or stain with or as with blood. [< EN-[1] + L *sanguis, -inis* blood]

En·sche·de (en′skhe-dā′) A commune in the eastern Netherlands; pop. 123,799 (est. 1960).

en·sconce (en-skons′) *v.t.* **·sconced, ·sconc·ing 1.** To fix securely or comfortably in some place; settle snugly. **2.** To shelter; hide. [< EN-[1] + SCONCE[1]]

en·sem·ble (än-säm′bəl, *Fr.* äṅ-säṅ′bl′) *n.* **1.** All the parts of a thing viewed together as constituting a whole. **2.** An individual's entire costume made up of two or more usually matching parts and often including accessories. **3.** The over-all effect of something, as a work of art, made up of contributing parts. **4.** The entire cast of a play, ballet, etc.; also, the appearance together of an entire cast, as during a particular scene. **5.** *Music* **a** The degree of precision, balance, and unification achieved by a group of performers. **b** A group of players or singers performing together. [< F < L *insimul* < *in-* in + *simul* at the same time]

en·sep·ul·cher (en-sep′əl-kər) *v.t.* **·chered, ·cher·ing** To put into or as into a sepulcher; entomb. Also **en·sep′ul·chre.**

en·shrine (in-shrīn′) *v.t.* **·shrined, ·shrin·ing 1.** To place in or as in a shrine. **2.** To cherish devoutly; hold sacred. Also spelled *inshrine.* **— en·shrine′ment** *n.*
en·shroud (in-shroud′) *v.t.* To shroud; conceal.
en·si·form (en′sə-fôrm) *adj.* Sword-shaped, as certain leaves; xiphoid. [< L *ensis* sword + -FORM]
en·sign (en′sīn; *also, and always for def. 2,* en′sən) *n.* **1.** A flag or banner; especially, a national standard or naval flag. **2.** In the U.S. Navy or Coast Guard, a commissioned officer of the lowest grade. See table at GRADE. Abbr. ENS, *Ens.* **3.** In the British Army, until 1871, a commissioned officer who carried the flag of a regiment or company. **4.** A badge, symbol, or distinguishing mark, as of rank, office, etc. **5.** *Obs.* A signal. [< OF *enseigne* < L *insignia* < *in-* in + *signum* mark] **— en′sign·ship, en′sign·cy** *n.*
en·si·lage (en′sə-lij) *n.* **1.** The process of preserving green fodder in closed pits or silos. **2.** Fodder preserved in silos: also called *silage.* — *v.t.* **·laged, ·lag·ing** To store in a silo for preservation: also **en·sile** (en-sīl′). [< F < *ensiler* < *en-* + *silo.* See SILO.]
en·slave (in-slāv′) *v.t.* **·slaved, ·slav·ing** To make a slave of; reduce to a condition of bondage; also, to dominate; control. **— en·slave′ment** *n.* **— en·slav′er** *n.*
en·snare (en-snâr′) *v.t.* **·snared, ·snar·ing** To catch in a snare; trick: also *insnare.* **— en·snare′ment** *n.*
en·snarl (en-snärl′) *v.t.* To tangle or involve in or as in a snarl.
en·sor·cel (en-sôr′səl) *v.t.* *Archaic* To bewitch. Also **en·sor′cell.** [< OF *ensorceler, ensorcerer.* See SORCERY]
en·soul (en-sōl′) *v.t.* **1.** To endow with a soul. **2.** To receive or put into the soul. Also *insoul.*
en·sphere (en-sfir′) *v.t.* **·sphered, ·spher·ing 1.** To enclose in a sphere. **2.** To give the form of a sphere to. Also spelled *insphere.*
en·sta·tite (en′stə-tīt) *n.* *Mineral.* A variety of orthorhombic pyroxene low in iron oxide, a constituent of many basic igneous rocks. [< Gk. *enstatēs* adversary + -ITE¹; so called from its refractory nature]
en·sue (en-sōō′) *v.* **·sued, ·su·ing** *v.i.* **1.** To follow subsequently; occur afterward. **2.** To follow as a consequence; result. — *v.t.* **3.** *Obs.* To follow after; pursue. [< OF *ensuivre* < L *insequi* < *in-* on, in + *sequi* to follow]
en suite (än swēt′) *French* In a series, set, or succession.
en·sure (en-shoor′) *v.t.* **·sured, ·sur·ing 1.** To make sure or certain: This battle *ensures* final victory. **2.** To make safe or secure: with *from* or *against*: to *ensure* liberty against tyranny. **3.** To insure (life, property, etc.). [< OF *enseurer* to make sure < *en-* in + *seur* sure]
en·swathe (en-swāth′) *v.t.* **·swathed, ·swath·ing** To wrap up, as in swaddling clothes; swathe: also spelled *inswathe.* **— en·swathe′ment** *n.*
-ent *suffix of nouns and adjectives* **1.** Having the quality, or performing the action of (the main element): *dependent.* **2.** One who or that which performs the action of (the main element): *superintendent.* Compare -ANT. [< F *-ent* < L *-ens, -entis,* suffix of present participle]
ent- See ENTO-.
en·tab·la·ture (en-tab′lə-chər) *n.* *Archit.* **1.** The uppermost member of a classical order or columnar system, consisting of the architrave, frieze, and cornice. **2.** Any projecting frieze or cornice of several members. [< MF < Ital. *intavolatura* < *in-* in + *tavola* base, table < L *tabula*]
en·ta·ble·ment (en-tā′bəl-mənt) *n.* *Archit.* **1.** An entablature. **2.** The series of platforms supporting a statue above the dado and base. [< F < *en-* in, on + *table.* See TABLE.]
en·tail (in-tāl′) *v.t.* **1.** To impose, involve, or result in by necessity: The project will *entail* much research. **2.** *Law* To restrict or leave the inheritance of (real property) to an unalterable succession of heirs. — *n.* **1.** The act of entailing, or the state of being entailed. **2.** Something entailed, as an inherited estate. **3.** A restricted line of succession or inheritance. [< OF *entaillier* < *en-* + *taillier,* to cut. See TAIL².]
en·ta·me·ba (en′tə-mē′bə) *n.* Endameba (which see). Also **en′ta·moe′ba.**
en·tan·gle (in-tang′gəl) *v.t.* **·gled, ·gling 1.** To catch in or as in a snare; hamper. **2.** To make tangled; snarl. **3.** To involve in difficulties; perplex; embarrass. **— en·tan′gler** *n.*
en·tan·gle·ment (in-tang′gəl-mənt) *n.* **1.** The act of entangling, or the state of being entangled. **2.** Something that entangles; a snare; complication.
en·ta·sis (en′tə-sis) *n.* **1.** *Archit.* A slight outward curve in

the vertical outlines of the shaft of a pilaster or of a column. **2.** *Physiol.* Spasmodic contraction of a muscle; a tonic spasm: also **en·ta·si·a** (en-tā′zhē-ə). [< NL < Gk. *entasis* stretching < *enteinein* to stretch < *en-* + *teinein*] **— en·tas·tic** (en-tas′tik) *adj.*
En·teb·be (en-teb′ē) A city in central Uganda, on Lake Victoria; pop. about 11,000.
en·tel·e·chy (en-tel′ə-kē) *n.* *pl.* **·chies** *Philos.* **1.** In Aristotle's metaphysics, completed realization, as distinguished from potentiality. **2.** In the philosophy of Bergson and other vitalists, the nonphysicochemical principle, or vital force, assumed to be responsible for life and growth. [< L *entelechia* < Gk. *entelecheia* actuality < *en telei echein* to have in (end) completion]
en·tel·lus (en-tel′əs) *n.* An East Indian monkey (genus *Presbytis*), having a short beard and a growth of hair resembling a cap: also called *hanuman.* [< NL, appar. after an athlete and boxer in the *Aeneid*]

ENTELLUS
(Body 2½ to 3 feet long; tail about 3½ feet)

en·tente (än-tänt′, *Fr.* än-tänt′) *n.* A mutual agreement; also, the parties entering into a mutual agreement. [< F]
entente cor·diale (kôr-dyàl′) Cordial understanding, as between governments; friendly agreement. [< F]
en·ter (en′tər) *v.t.* **1.** To come or go into. **2.** To make a way into; penetrate; pierce. **3.** To set in; insert: to *enter* a wedge between boards. **4.** To become a member of; join. **5.** To start out upon; embark on: to *enter* middle age. **6.** To obtain admission to (a school, etc.). **7.** To cause to be admitted to; enroll in. **8.** To write down, as in a list; record; register. **9.** To file notice of (goods, a ship, etc.) at a custom house. **10.** *Law* **a** To place (a plea, evidence, etc.) on the records of a court. **b** To go upon or into (land or other property) either by claimed right, or as a trespasser, or feloniously. **c** To file a claim to (public lands). — *v.i.* **11.** To come or go into a particular place. **12.** To come onto the stage. **13.** To begin to sing, play an instrument, etc. **— to enter into 1.** To start out on; embark on: to *enter into* a new career. **2.** To become a participant in; engage in. **3.** To take an interest in and contribute actively to: to *enter into* the plans. **4.** To form a part or constituent of: Oxygen *enters* into many compound bodies. **5.** To consider or discuss: to *enter into* particulars. **— to enter on** (or **upon**) **1.** To start out on; embark on: to *enter upon* a different sort of life. **2.** To start to have or use: to *enter upon* the privileges of an adult. [< OF *entrer* < L *intrare* < *intra* within]
en·ter·ic (en-ter′ik) *adj.* Intestinal. [< Gk. *enterikos* < *enteron* intestine < *entos* within]
enteric fever Typhoid fever (which see).
en·ter·i·tis (en′tə-rī′tis) *n.* *Pathol.* Inflammation of the intestines, chiefly the small intestine. [< ENTER(O)- + -ITIS]
entero- *combining form* Intestine. Also, before vowels, **enter-.** [< Gk. *enteron* intestine]
en·ter·o·cep·tor (en′tə-rə-sep′tər) *n.* An interoceptor (which see).
en·ter·ol·o·gy (en′tə-rol′ə-jē) *n.* The study of the intestines. [< ENTERO- + -LOGY]
en·ter·on (en′tə-ron) *n.* *pl.* **·ter·a** (-tər-ə) *Anat.* The entire intestine or alimentary canal. [< NL < Gk.]
en·ter·o·scope (en′tər-ə-skōp′) *n.* *Med.* An instrument having an electric light for examining the intestines. [< ENTERO- + -SCOPE] **— en·ter·os·co·py** (en′tə-ros′kə-pē) *n.*
en·ter·os·to·my (en′tə-ros′tə-mē) *n.* *pl.* **·mies** *Surg.* The making of an artificial passage between the intestine and the exterior of the body. [< ENTERO- + -STOMY]
en·ter·ot·o·my (en′tə-rot′ə-mē) *n.* *pl.* **·mies** *Surg.* An intestinal incision. [< ENTERO- + -TOMY]
en·ter·o·tox·e·mi·a (en′tə-rō-tok-sē′mē-ə) *n.* *Vet.* Severe intestinal poisoning of sheep caused by the toxins of certain bacteria. [< ENTERO- + TOXEMIA]
en·ter·prise (en′tər-prīz) *n.* **1.** Any project, undertaking, or task, especially when difficult, demanding, or of major importance. **2.** Boldness, energy, and venturesomeness in practical affairs. **3.** Active engagement in projects. [< OF *entreprise* < *entreprendre* < *entre-* between (< L *inter-*) + *prendre* to take < L *pre(he)ndere*]
en·ter·pris·ing (en′tər-prī′zing) *adj.* Energetic, bold, and full of initiative; venturesome. **— en′ter·pris′ing·ly** *adv.*
en·ter·tain (en′tər-tān′) *v.t.* **1.** To hold the attention of; amuse; divert. **2.** To extend hospitality to; receive as a guest. **3.** To take into consideration, as a proposal. **4.** To keep or bear in mind; maintain: to *entertain* a grudge. **5.** *Archaic* To go on with; continue. — *v.i.* **6.** To receive and care for guests. [< F *entretenir* < *entre-* between (< L *inter-*) + *tenir* to hold < L *tenere*] **— en′ter·tain′er** *n.*
— Syn. 1. *Entertain, amuse, divert, recreate,* and *beguile* refer to engagement in some pleasant occupation. That which agreeably holds one's attention *entertains;* that which brings laughter or cheer *amuses;* and that which turns one from serious thoughts or pursuits *diverts.* Anything that restores strength and energy for

serious work *recreates*. *Beguile* implies that a person has been tricked, as it were, into cheer and comfort by something that insensibly draws the thoughts away from pain or disquiet. — **Ant.** bore, tire, annoy.

en·ter·tain·ing (en′tər·tā′ning) *adj.* That entertains; amusing; diverting. — **en′ter·tain′ing·ly** *adv.* — **en′ter·tain′ing·ness** *n.*

en·ter·tain·ment (en′tər·tān′mənt) *n.* **1.** The act of entertaining. **2.** Something that entertains, as a play or concert. **3.** Diversion or amusement afforded by something entertaining. **4.** The reception and care of guests. **5.** *Obs.* Maintenance; support.

en·thal·py (en·thal′pē, en′thəl·pē) *n. Physics* The quantity of heat in a substance or physical system per unit of mass: also called *heat content*. [< Gk. *enthalpein* < *en-* in + *thalpein* to warm]

en·thet·ic (en·thet′ik) *adj. Med.* Introduced from outside: said of infectious diseases. [< Gk. *enthetikos* fit for implanting < *en-* in + *tithenai* to put]

en·thrall (in·thrôl′) *v.t.* **1.** To keep spellbound; fascinate; charm. **2.** To enslave. Also spelled *inthral.* Also **en·thral′.** — **en·thrall′ment** or **en·thral′ment** *n.*

en·throne (in·thrōn′) *v.t.* **·throned**, **·thron·ing** **1.** To put upon a throne. **2.** To invest with the authority or office of a king or bishop. **3.** To exalt; revere. Also spelled *inthrone.* — **en·throne′ment** *n.*

en·thuse (in·thōōz′) *v.* **·thused**, **·thus·ing** *U.S. Informal v.t.* **1.** To make enthusiastic. — *v.i.* **2.** To become enthusiastic; display enthusiasm. [Back formation < ENTHUSIASM]

en·thu·si·asm (in·thōō′zē·az′əm) *n.* **1.** Keen, animated interest in and preoccupation with something; eager devotion to or fondness for something; ardor; zeal. **2.** A cause or object of intense, lively interest. **3.** *Archaic* A state of exaltation viewed as supernaturally caused; also, religious fanaticism. [< LL *enthusiasmus* < Gk. *enthousiasmos*, ult. < *entheos*, *enthous* inspired, possessed < *en-* in + *theos* god] — **Syn. 1.** zeal, devotion, fanaticism. Compare ENTHUSIAST.

en·thu·si·ast (in·thōō′zē·ast, -ist) *n.* **1.** One given to or moved by enthusiasm; an ardent adherent; zealot. **2.** A religious fanatic. — **Syn.** *Enthusiast, zealot, votary, devotee, fanatic, fan,* and *bigot* denote a person who is fervently attached to a cause, occupation, or other person. Originally an *enthusiast* was one moved by frenzy or ecstasy, but now the word implies merely keen interest. *Zealot* stresses the ardor and earnestness of the attachment; in contrast, a *votary* devotes himself soberly to the service of another, especially of a deity. *Devotee* formerly also had religious associations, but is now applied to one who eagerly follows a hobby, avocation, etc. A *fanatic* is a zealot whose fervor is regarded as extravagant or irrational. *Fan* is an informal word applied especially to spectators at sports contests, and thus may imply little more than intermittent interest. A *bigot* is a zealot so devoted to his own creed, outlook, or interests as to be intolerant of all others.

en·thu·si·as·tic (in·thōō′zē·as′tik) *adj.* Full of or marked by enthusiasm; ardent. — **en·thu′si·as′ti·cal·ly** *adv.*

en·thy·meme (en′thə·mēm) *n. Logic* An argument in which the conclusion or one of the premises is not stated. [< L *enthymema* < Gk. *enthymēma* < *enthymeesthai* to think < *en-* in + *thymos* mind] — **en′thy·me·mat′ic** *adj.*

en·tice (in·tīs′) *v.t.* **·ticed**, **·tic·ing** To lead on or attract by arousing hope of pleasure, profit, etc.; allure. [< OF *enticier* to set afire < L *in-* in + *titio* firebrand] — **en·tic′er** *n.* — **en·tic′ing·ly** *adv.*

en·tice·ment (in·tīs′mənt) *n.* **1.** The act of enticing, or the state of being enticed. **2.** Something that entices.

en·tire (in·tīr′) *adj.* **1.** Having no part missing; whole; complete. **2.** Not broken; not shattered; intact. **3.** Not lessened nor impaired; full; total. **4.** Consisting wholly of one piece; not divided into sections; continuous. **5.** Not castrated. **6.** *Bot.* Having edges that are not serrated: said of leaves. **7.** *Obs.* Free from admixture; unalloyed. — *n.* **1.** The whole of something; total. **2.** An uncastrated animal. **3.** *Brit.* Porter. [< OF *entier* < L *integer* whole. Doublet of INTEGER.] — **en·tire′ness** *n.*

en·tire·ly (in·tīr′lē) *adv.* **1.** Without lessening or reservation; without diminution or exception; wholly; completely. **2.** Solely; exclusively.

en·tire·ty (in·tī′rə·tē) *n. pl.* **·ties** **1.** The state or condition of being entire; completeness. **2.** That which is entire; a whole.

en·ti·tle (in·tīt′l) *v.t.* **·tled**, **·tling** **1.** To give (a person or thing) the right to receive, demand, or do something; qualify or authorize: His rank *entitles* him to respect. **2.** To give a name or designation to. **3.** To give (a person) a title designating rank, honor, etc. Also spelled *intitle.* [< AF *entitler*, OF *entituler* < LL *intitulare* < L *in-* in + *titulus* title]

en·ti·ty (en′tə·tē) *n. pl.* **·ties** **1.** Something existing objectively or in the mind; an actual or conceivable being. **2.** Existence as opposed to nonexistence; being. **3.** Essence; substance. [< L *entitas, -tatis* < *ens*, ppr. of *esse* to be]

ento- *combining form* Within; interior: *entozoic.* Also, before vowels, *ent-*.

en·to·blast (en′tō·blast) *n. Biol.* The endoderm. — **en′to·blas′tic** *adj.*

en·to·derm (en′tō·dûrm) *n.* Endoderm (which see).

en·toil (en·toil′) *v.t. Archaic* To ensnare.

en·tomb (in·tōōm′) *v.t.* **1.** To place in or as in a tomb; bury. **2.** To serve as a tomb for. Also spelled *intomb.* [< OF *entoumber* < *en-* in + *tombe* tomb] — **en·tomb′ment** *n.*

entomo- *combining form* Insect: *entomology.* Also, before vowels, **entom-.** [< Gk. *entoma* insects, orig. neut. pl. of *entomos* cut up < *en-* in + *temnein* to cut; with ref. to their segmented body structure]

entomol. Entomological: also **entom.**

en·to·mol·o·gize (en′tə·mol′ə·jīz) *v.i.* **·gized**, **·giz·ing** **1.** To study insects. **2.** To collect insects for scientific study.

en·to·mol·o·gy (en′tə·mol′ə·jē) *n.* The branch of zoology that treats of insects. [< ENTOMO- + -LOGY] — **en·to·mo·log·i·cal** (en′tə·mə·loj′i·kəl) or **en′to·mo·log′ic** *adj.* — **en′to·mo·log′i·cal·ly** *adv.* — **en′to·mol′o·gist** *n.*

en·to·moph·a·gous (en′tə·mof′ə·gəs) *adj.* Feeding on insects. [< ENTOMO- + -PHAGOUS]

en·to·mos·tra·can (en′tə·mos′trə·kan) *Zool. adj.* Designating a subclass (*Entomostraca*) of crustaceans, including the branchiopods, copepods, etc. — *n.* A member of this subclass. [< ENTOM(O)- + Gk. *ostrakon* shell]

en·to·phyte (en′tō·fīt) *n.* Endophyte (which see).

en·top·ic (en·top′ik) *adj. Med.* Situated or occurring in its normal place. [< Gk. *entopos* in a place < *en-* in + *topos* place]

en·tou·rage (än′tōō·räzh′, *Fr.* än·tōō·räzh′) *n.* **1.** A group of followers, retainers, or attendants, especially such as surrounds an important personage; retinue. **2.** Environment. [< F < *entourer* to surround < *entour* around]

en·to·zo·an (en′tə·zō′ən) *n. Zool.* Any of a branch (*Entozoa*) of metazoans, chiefly parasitic worms, characterized by the possession of a gut cavity and a two-layered cell arrangement. — *adj.* Entozoic. [< ENTO- + Gk. *zōon* animal]

en·to·zo·ic (en′tə·zō′ik) *adj. Biol.* **1.** Living within another animal. **2.** Of, pertaining to, or caused by entozoans.

en·tr’acte (än·trakt′, *Fr.* än·träkt′) *n.* **1.** The interval between the acts of a play, opera, etc. **2.** A musical interlude, dance, or the like, performed between acts. [< F]

en·trails (en′trālz, -trəlz) *n.pl.* **1.** The internal parts of a man or animal; especially, the intestines; bowels; guts. **2.** The internal parts of anything. [< OF *entraille* < LL *intralia* intestines, ult. < L *inter* between, in the midst of]

en·train[1] (en·trān′) *v.i.* **1.** To board a train. — *v.t.* **2.** To put aboard a train. [< EN-[1] + TRAIN] — **en·train′ment** *n.*

en·train[2] (en·trān′) *v.t.* To draw along after; pull along. [< F *entraîner* < *en-* away (< L *inde*) + *traîner* to drag]

en·trance[1] (en′trəns) *n.* **1.** The act of entering. **2.** A passage, opening, or the like, affording a means of entering something: the *entrance* to a harbor. **3.** The right or power of entering; admittance. **4.** The point in a play, ballet, piece of music, etc., at which a performer is cued to enter. *Abbr. e.* [< OF < *entrer.* See ENTER.] — **Syn. 3.** *Entrance, entry, entrée, access, admittance,* and *admission* are compared as they denote the act or right of entering. *Entrance* is the widest term, indicating the passing from without to within some enclosure. Figuratively, one may make an *entrance* into a profession, career, society, etc. *Entry* is equivalent to *entrance* in these senses, but differs in some extended meanings: to make an *entry* (or *entrance*) into a building, to make an *entry* (not an *entrance*) in a ledger. *Entrée* is used chiefly of *entrance* to some exclusive place or coterie: to gain *entrée* to a palace. *Access* is approach rather than *entrance*, but is sometimes used in the latter sense: a mountain pass provided *access* to the plain. *Admittance* and *admission* refer to permission to enter; *admittance* is applied to place, *admission* to privilege, membership, position, etc.

en·trance[2] (in·trans′, -träns′) *v.t.* **·tranced**, **·tranc·ing** **1.** To fill with rapture or wonder; delight; charm. **2.** To put into a trance. [< EN-[1] + TRANCE[1]] — **en·trance′ment** *n.* — **en·tranc′ing·ly** *adv.*

en·trance·way (en′trəns·wā′) *n.* A means of entrance.

en·trant (en′trənt) *n.* **1.** One who enters; a beginner; especially, a new member of a profession, institution, etc. **2.** One who competes in a contest.

en·trap (in·trap′) *v.t.* **·trapped**, **·trap·ping** **1.** To catch in or as in a trap. **2.** To trick into danger or difficulty; deceive; ensnare. — **en·trap′ment** *n.*

en·treat (in·trēt′) *v.t.* **1.** To beseech with great intensity; implore; beg. **2.** To make an earnest request of or for; petition. **3.** *Archaic* To treat. — *v.i.* **4.** To ask earnestly. Also spelled *intreat.* [< OF *entraitier* < *en-* in + *traitier.* See TREAT.] — **en·treat′ing·ly** *adv.* — **en·treat′ment** *n.* — **Syn.** *Entreat, beseech, implore, supplicate,* and *beg* mean to ask urgently, in the face of expected refusal or reluctance. *Entreat* suggests earnest persuasiveness, and *beseech,* intense anxiety or humility. To *implore* is to ask with a show of tears; *supplicate* implies the humble demeanor of one who kneels to make a request. We *beg* for that which we cannot demand as a right, throwing ourselves upon the good will or charity of another.

en·treat·y (in·trē′tē) *n. pl.* **·ies** An earnest request; supplication.

en·tre·chat (än′trə·shä′) *n. French* In ballet, a leap upward in which the dancer repeatedly crosses his feet.

en·tre·côte (än′trə·kōt′) *n. French* Steak cut from between the ribs.

en·trée (än′trā, *Fr.* än·trā′) *n.* **1.** The act or privilege of entering; entrance; admission; also, privileged approach to some individual or place not ordinarily accessible. **2.** The principal course at a meal. **3.** In lavish or formal dinners, a dish served between the fish and meat courses or directly before the main course. Also *U.S.* **en′tree.** — **Syn.** See ENTRANCE[1]. [< F, orig. pp. of *entrer*. See ENTER.]

en·tre·mets (än′trə·mā, *Fr.* än·trə·me′) *n. pl.* **-mets** (-māz, *Fr.* -me′) **1.** A hot or cold dessert, as a custard, ice, or charlotte. **2.** Loosely, a side dish, as a vegetable. [< F]

en·trench (in·trench′) *v.t.* **1.** To fortify or protect with or as with a trench or trenches. **2.** To establish firmly: The idea was *entrenched* in his mind. — *v.i.* **3.** To encroach or trespass: with *on* or *upon*. Also spelled *intrench*.

en·trench·ment (in·trench′mənt) *n.* **1.** A defensive fortification consisting of trenches. **2.** Any fortified place or position. **3.** The act of entrenching, or the state of being entrenched. Also spelled *intrenchment*.

en·tre nous (än′tr′ nōō′) *French* Between us; in confidence.

en·tre·pôt (än′trə·pō, *Fr.* än·trə·pō′) *n.* A depot or storehouse for commercial goods. [< F < *entreposer* < *entre-* between (< L *inter-*) + *poser*. See POSE[1].]

en·tre·pre·neur (än′trə·prə·nûr′, *Fr.* än·trə·prə·nœr′) *n.* **1.** One who undertakes to start and conduct an enterprise or business, usually assuming full control and risk. **2.** An impresario. [< F < *entreprendre*. See ENTERPRISE.]

En·tre Ríos (en′trä rē′ōs) A Province of eastern Argentina; 29,427 sq. mi.; pop. 990,900 (est. 1960); capital, Paraná.

en·tre·sol (en′tər·sol, *Fr.* än·trə·sôl′) *n.* A half story or mezzanine, especially when just above the ground floor. [< F]

en·tro·py (en′trə·pē) *n.* **1.** *Physics* **a** A mathematical expression of the degree in which the energy of a thermodynamic system is so distributed as to be unavailable for conversion into work. **b** A statistical expression of the probability of a given state or arrangement of particles in a given system, as a gas. **2.** In information theory, a statistical expression of the certainty and precision of a given system, based on the frequency of use of its symbols. **3.** The irreversible tendency of a system, including the universe, toward increasing disorder and inertness; also, the final state predictable from this tendency. [< Gk. *entropia*, var. of *entropē* turning < *en-* in + *trepein* to turn]

en·trust (in·trust′) *v.t.* **1.** To give over (something) for care, safekeeping, or performance: I will *entrust* this task to you. **2.** To place something in the care or trust of; trust, as with a duty, responsibility, etc. Also spelled *intrust*. — **Syn.** See COMMIT.

en·try (en′trē) *n. pl.* **·tries 1.** The act of coming or going in; entrance. **2.** A place of entrance; a small hallway or vestibule. **3.** The act of entering anything in a register, list, etc.; also, the item entered. **4.** The act of reporting at a customhouse the arrival of a ship in port and the nature of her cargo. **5.** The act of assuming possession of lands or tenements by entering upon them. **6.** A contestant listed for a race, competition, etc. **7.** In bridge and whist, a card that will win a trick and place the lead in a specified hand: also *reentry*. — **Syn.** See ENTRANCE[1]. [< F *entrée* < *entrer*. See ENTER.]

en·try·way (en′trē·wā′) *n.* A passage, opening, or the like, giving entrance into something.

en·twine (in·twīn′) *v.t. & v.i.* **·twined, ·twin·ing** To twine around; twine or twist together: also spelled *intwine*.

en·twist (in·twist′) *v.t.* To twist together or around; entwine: also spelled *intwist*.

e·nu·cle·ate (i·nōō′klē·āt, -nyōō′-; *adj.* i·nōō′klē·it, -nyōō′-, -āt) *v.t.* **·at·ed, ·at·ing 1.** To shell, as a kernel. **2.** To explain or disclose. **3.** *Surg.* To extract from a sac without cutting, as a tumor, eyeball, etc. **4.** *Biol.* To remove the nucleus from, as a cell. — *adj.* Without a nucleus. [< L *enucleatus*, pp. of *enucleare* < *e-* out + *nucleus* kernel] — **e·nu′cle·a′tion** *n.* — **e·nu′cle·a′tor** (-ā′tər) *n.*

e·nu·mer·ate (i·nōō′mə·rāt, -nyōō′-) *v.t.* **·at·ed, ·at·ing 1.** To name one by one; list. **2.** To ascertain the number of. [< L *enumeratus*, pp. of *enumerare* < *e-* out + *numerare* to count] — **e·nu′mer·a′tive** *adj.* — **e·nu′mer·a′tor** *n.*

e·nu·mer·a·tion (i·nōō′mə·rā′shən, -nyōō′-) *n.* **1.** The act of enumerating. **2.** A list of items; catalogue.

e·nun·ci·a·ble (i·nun′sē·ə·bəl, -shē-) *adj.* That may be enunciated. — **e·nun′ci·a·bil′i·ty** *n.*

e·nun·ci·ate (i·nun′sē·āt, -shē-) *v.* **·at·ed, ·at·ing** *v.t.* **1.** To articulate (speech sounds), especially in a clear and distinct manner. **2.** To state with exactness, as a theory or dogma. **3.** To announce or proclaim. — *v.i.* **4.** To pronounce words, especially with distinct articulation. [< L *enunciatus*, pp. of *enunciare* < *e-* out + *nuntiare* to announce < *nuntius* messenger] — **e·nun′ci·a·to·ry** (-sē·ə·tôr′ē, -tō′rē) *adj.* — **e·nun′ci·a·tive·ly** *adv.* — **e·nun′ci·a′tor** *n.* — **Syn. 2.** pronounce. **3.** declare.

e·nun·ci·a·tion (i·nun′sē·ā′shən, -shē-) *n.* **1.** The utterance or mode of utterance of speech sounds. **2.** A declaration.

en·ure (in·yŏŏr′) See INURE.

en·u·re·sis (en′yə·rē′sis) *n. Pathol.* Involuntary urination, especially during sleep. [< NL < Gk. *enoureein* < *en-* in + *oureein* to urinate]

env. Envelope.

en·vel·op (in·vel′əp) *v.t.* **·oped, ·op·ing 1.** To wrap; enclose. **2.** To hide from sight or understanding; obscure. **3.** To surround. [< OF *enveloper* < *en-* in + *voluper* to wrap] — **en·vel′op·er** *n.*

en·ve·lope (en′və·lōp, än′-) *n.* **1.** A paper case or wrapper for enclosing a letter or the like, usually having a gummed flap for sealing. **2.** Any enveloping cover or wrapper. **3.** *Aeron.* **a** The outer fabric covering of a dirigible, balloon, etc. **b** The bag containing the gas, as in a free balloon. **4.** *Biol.* The enclosing membrane of an organ. **5.** *Bot.* Any covering or integument that encloses, as the calyx. **6.** *Math.* A curve or surface to which another curve or surface, varying or moving according to any law, is invariably tangent. [< F *enveloppe* < *envelopper*. See ENVELOP.]

en·vel·op·ment (in·vel′əp·mənt) *n.* **1.** The act of enveloping, or the state of being enveloped. **2.** Something that envelops; a covering. **3.** *Mil.* An attack against the flank or rear of the enemy.

en·ven·om (en·ven′əm) *v.t.* **1.** To impregnate with venom; poison. **2.** To make vindictive; embitter. [< OF *envenimer* < *en-* in + *venim* venom]

En·ver Pa·sha (en·ver′ pä·shä′), 1881?–1922, Turkish army officer, revolutionist, and political leader.

en·vi·a·ble (en′vē·ə·bəl) *adj.* So admirable or desirable as to arouse envy. — **en′vi·a·bly** *adv.*

en·vi·ous (en′vē·əs) *adj.* **1.** Full of, characterized by, or expressing envy. **2.** *Obs.* Emulous. **3.** *Obs.* Spiteful. [< OF *envieus* < L *invidiosus*. Doublet of INVIDIOUS.] — **en′vi·ous·ly** *adv.* — **en′vi·ous·ness** *n.*
— **Syn.** *Envious, covetous,* and *jealous* describe a person who begrudges the possessions of another. An *envious* man not only wishes to see the other deprived of his possession, but also wishes to obtain it for himself. A *covetous* person is greedy, but usually not malicious; he wishes only to have as much as others, without wishing to see them deprived. A *jealous* man is greatly concerned about what he himself owns or claims, and fears to see it pass from his grasp.

en·vi·ron (in·vī′rən) *v.t.* To extend around; encircle; surround. [< F *environner* < *environ* around]

en·vi·ron·ment (in·vī′rən·mənt, -vī′ərn-) *n.* **1.** The aggregate of external circumstances, conditions, and things that affect the existence and development of an individual, organism, or group. **2.** Something that environs. **3.** The act of environing, or the state of being environed. — **en·vi′ron·men′tal** *adj.*

en·vi·rons (in·vī′rənz) *n.pl.* A surrounding, outlying area, as about a city; outskirts; suburbs. [< F < *environ* around]

en·vis·age (en·viz′ij) *v.t.* **·aged, ·ag·ing 1.** To form a mental image of; visualize. **2.** To conceive of in advance; contemplate. [< EN-[1] + VISAGE] — **en·vis′age·ment** *n.*

en·vi·sion (en·vizh′ən) *v.t.* To see or foresee in the imagination: to *envision* the future. [< EN-[1] + VISION]

en·voy[1] (en′voi, än′-) *n.* **1.** A diplomatic representative of the second class ranking next below an ambassador: full title **envoy extraordinary and minister plenipotentiary.** Abbr. **E.E. & M.P. 2.** A diplomat on a special mission. **3.** Anyone entrusted with a mission. — **Syn.** See AMBASSADOR. [< F *envoyé*, pp. of *envoyer* to send < OF *envoiier* < *en voie* on the way < L *in-* + *via* way, road]

en·voy[2] (en′voi, än′-) *n.* The closing lines of a poem or prose work, often in the form of a dedication; especially, the concluding stanza of a ballade: also *l'envoie, l'envoy.* Also **envoi.** [< OF *envoye* < *envoiier*. See ENVOY[1].]

en·vy (en′vē) *n. pl.* **·vies 1.** A feeling of resentment or discontent over another's superior attainments, endowments, or possessions. **2.** A desire to possess the goods of another. **3.** Any object of envy. **4.** *Obs.* Hatred; ill will. — *v.* **·vied, ·vy·ing** *v.t.* **1.** To regard with envy; feel envy because of: I *envy* you your calm. — *v.i.* **2.** To feel or show envy. [< OF *envie* < L *invidia* < *in-* on + *videre* to see, look] — **en′vi·er** *n.* — **en′vy·ing·ly** *adv.*

en·wind (en·wīnd′) *v.t.* To wind or coil around: also spelled *inwind.*

en·womb (en·wōōm′) *v.t.* To hold in or as in the womb.

en·wrap (en·rap′) *v.t.* **·wrapped, ·wrap·ping** To wrap up; envelop: also spelled *inwrap.*

en·wreathe (en·rēth′) *v.t.* **·wreathed, ·wreath·ing** To encircle with or as with a wreath: also spelled *inwreathe.*

en·zo·ot·ic (en′zō·ot′ik) *adj.* Endemic among animals: said of a disease. — *n.* An enzootic disease. [< Gk. *en-* in + *zōion* animal + -IC]

en·zyme (en′zīm, -zim) *n. Biochem.* A protein produced by cells and having the power to initiate or accelerate specific chemical reactions in the metabolism of plants and animals; an organic catalyst; ferment. Also **en′zym** (-zim) [< L < Gk. *enzymos* leavened < *en-* in + *zymē* leaven] — **en·zy·mat·ic** (en′zī·mat′ik, -zi-) *adj.*

---

en·zy·mol·o·gy (en′zī·mol′ə·jē) *n.* The branch of biochemistry that treats of enzymes.

en·zy·mol·y·sis (en′zī·mol′ə·sis) *n.* The chemical change induced by the action of enzymes. Also **en′zy·mo′sis** (-mō′sis). [< ENZYM(E) + -LYSIS]

eo- *combining form* Earliest; early part or early representative of. [< Gk. *ēos* dawn, daybreak]

e.o. Ex officio (L).

E·o·an·thro·pus (ē′ō·an′thrə·pəs, -an·thrō′pəs) *n.* A spurious type of early man postulated from skull fragments planted by a hoaxer in Pleistocene gravel beds near Piltdown, England: also called *Piltdown man.* [< NL < Gk. *ēōs* dawn + *anthrōpos* man]

e·o·bi·ont (ē′ō·bī′ont) *n.* A type of living organism more rudimentary than the cell; especially, one produced by biopoesis. [< EO- + Gk. *biōn, biontos,* ppr. of *bioein* to live]

E·o·cene (ē′ə·sēn) *Geol. adj.* Of, pertaining to, or existing in the Early Tertiary period of the Cenozoic era, following the Paleocene and succeeded by the Oligocene. — *n.* The second epoch of the Cenozoic era, marked by a warm climate and the rise of mammals. See chart for GEOLOGY. [< EO- + Gk. *kainos* new]

E·o·gene (ē′ə·jēn) *adj. Geol.* Of or pertaining to the Paleocene, Eocene, and Oligocene epochs of the Cenozoic era: also *Paleogene.* [< EO- + -GEN(E)]

e·o·hip·pus (ē′ō·hip′əs) *n. Paleontol.* A small, primitive horse (genus *Hyracotherium,* formerly *Eohippus*), with four-toed forefeet and three-toed hindfeet, from the early Eocene of Europe and North America, ancestral to the living horse through a complete series of succeeding types. [< EO- + Gk. *hippos* horse]

e·o·li·an (ē·ō′lē·ən) See AEOLIAN.

E·o·li·an (ē·ō′lē·ən), **E·ol·ic** (ē·ol′ik) See AEO-LIAN, AEOLIC.

e·ol·i·pile (ē·ol′ə·pīl) *n.* A reaction engine consisting of a hollow sphere above a boiler with radial pipes projecting from the sphere with their openings so disposed that the forcible ejection of steam rotates the sphere in the opposite direction. Also **e·ol′o·pile.** Also spelled *aeolipile.* [< L *aeolipilae* an instrument for investigating the nature of the wind < *Aeolus* god of the winds + *pila* ball]

EOLIPILE

e·o·lith (ē′ə·lith) *n.* A stone tool of the earliest form; celt. [< EO- + Gk. *lithos* stone]

E·o·lith·ic (ē′ə·lith′ik) *adj. Anthropol.* Of or pertaining to a period of protohuman culture extending approximately from the late Pliocene to the first glacial epoch of the Pleistocene, known only by the rudest implements of bone and chipped stone.

e·o·lo·trop·ic (ē′ə·lō·trop′ik) *adj. Physics* Anisotropic; also spelled *aeolotropic.* [< Gk. *aiolos* varying + -TROPIC]

e·on (ē′on, ē′ən) *n.* **1.** An incalculable period of time; an age; eternity. **2.** *Geol.* A time interval including two or more eras. Also spelled *aeon.* [< L *aeon* < Gk. *aiōn* age]

e·o·ni·an (ē·ō′nē·ən) *adj.* Pertaining to or lasting for eons; everlasting: also spelled *aeonian.*

e·o·nism (ē′ə·niz′əm) *n.* The adoption by a male of female clothing, mannerisms, etc. Compare TRANSVESTITISM. [after Chevalier Charles *d'Eon,* 1728–1810, French diplomat]

E·os (ē′əs) In Greek mythology, the goddess of the dawn, daughter of Hyperion: identified with the Roman *Aurora.*

e·o·sin (ē′ə·sin) *n. Chem.* **1.** A reddish coloring matter, $C_{20}H_8Br_4O_5$, derived from coal tar, used for dyeing and as a stain in microscopy. **2.** Any of several analogous dyes derived from coal tar. Also **e′o·sine** (-sin, -sēn). [< Gk. *ēōs* morning red, dawn + -IN] — **e′o·sin′ic** *adj.*

e·o·sin·o·phile (ē′ə·sin′ə·fīl, -fil) *n. Biol.* A microorganism, cell, or cell substance with a special affinity for eosin stains or acid stains in general. — **e·o·si·noph·i·lous** (ē′ō·si·nof′ə·ləs), **e′o·sin′o·phil′ic** (-fil′ik) *adj.*

Eöt·vös balance (œt′vœsh) *Physics* An extremely sensitive torsion balance for detecting and measuring local irregularities in gravity. [after Roland von *Eötvös,* 1848–1919, Hungarian physicist]

-eous *suffix* Of the nature of: *vitreous.* [< L *-eus*]

E·o·zo·ic (ē′ə·zō′ik) *adj. Geol.* Of or pertaining to the later portion of the Pre-Cambrian time, immediately before the Paleozoic era, with rock formations showing the first faint signs of invertebrate life. [< EO- + Gk. *zōē* life]

ep- Var. of EPI-.

Ep. Epistle(s).

EP (ē′pē′) *adj.* Describing a phonograph record having microgrooves adjusted for a playing speed of 45 revolutions per minute and a playing time of 8 minutes. — *n.* A record so made: a trade name. [< E(*xtended*) P(*lay*).]

e·pact (ē′pakt) *n. Astron.* **1.** The excess of the solar year over 12 lunar months, generally about 11 days. **2.** The number of days in the age of the calendar moon on the first day of any particular year. [< LL *epactae* < Gk. *epaktai* (*hēmerai*) intercalary (days) fem. plur. of *epaktos* < *epi-* on + *agein* to bring]

E·pam·i·non·das (i·pam′ə·non′dəs), 418?–362 B.C., Theban general and statesman.

ep·arch (ep′ärk) *n.* **1.** The chief administrator of an eparchy. **2.** In the Greek Orthodox Church, a metropolitan or bishop. — **ep·ar′chi·al** *adj.*

ep·ar·chy (ep′är·kē) *n. pl.* **·chies 1.** In ancient Greece, a district corresponding to a Roman province. **2.** In modern Greece, a governmental subdivision of the country. **3.** In the Greek Orthodox Church, an ecclesiastical province or diocese. Also **ep′ar·chate** (-kət). [< Gk. *eparcheia* < *eparchos* < *epi-* over + *archein* to rule]

ep·au·let (ep′ə·let) *n.* **1.** *Mil.* A shoulder ornament of military and naval officers. **2.** A shoulder ornament of women's dresses. Also **ep′au·lette.** [< F *épaulette,* dim. of *épaule* shoulder < OF *espaule* < LL *spatula* shoulder, dim. of L *spatha* < Gk. *spathē* broad blade]

EPAULET

é·pée (ā·pā′) *n.* A dueling sword with a sharp point and no cutting edge. [< F < OF *espee* < L *spatha.* See EPAULET.] — **é·pée·ist** *n.*

ep·ei·rog·e·ny (ep′ī·roj′ə·nē) *n. Geol.* The process whereby great movements of uplift or subsidence in the earth's crust affect large portions of continental areas or oceanic basins: also spelled *epirogeny.* [< Gk. *ēpeiros* mainland + -GENY] — **e·pei·ric** (i·pī′rik), **e·pei·ro·gen·ic** (i·pī′rō·jen′ik), **e·pei′ro·ge·net′ic** (-jə·net′ik) *adj.*

E·pei·rus (i·pī′rəs) The Greek name for EPIRUS.

ep·en·ceph·a·lon (ep′en·sef′ə·lon) *n. pl.* **·la** (-lə) *Anat.* **1.** The embryonic rhombencephalon. **2.** The cerebellum. [< EP(I)- + ENCEPHALON] — **ep·en·ce·phal·ic** (ep′en·si·fal′ik) *adj.*

ep·en·the·sis (ep·en′thə·sis) *n. pl.* **·ses** (-sēz) *Ling.* **1.** The evolution of a new vowel, or especially of a consonant within a sound group, generally serving to facilitate the transition between sounds, as the development of the *d* in *thunder* (Old English *thunor*). **2.** The phonetic change resulting from the transference of a semivowel to the syllable preceding, as in the change of Greek *karjo* to *kairo.* [< LL < Gk. < *epi-* upon + *en-* in + *tithenai* to place] — **ep·en·thet·ic** (ep′en·thet′ik) *adj.*

e·pergne (i·pûrn′, ā·pârn′) *n.* A centerpiece for a dinner table, often consisting of several grouped dishes for fruit, flowers, etc. [? < F *épargne* economy, thrift]

ep·ex·e·ge·sis (ep·ek′sə·jē′sis) *n.* Something added by way of further elucidation; fuller statement. [< Gk. *epexēgēsis* < *epi-* upon + *exēgēsis.* See EXEGESIS.] — **ep·ex·e·get′ic** (-jet′ik) or **·i·cal** *adj.* — **ep·ex·e·get′i·cal·ly** *adv.*

eph- Var. of EPI-.

Eph. Ephesians: also **Ephes.**

e·phah (ē′fə) *n.* A Hebrew unit of dry measure equal to a little over a bushel. Also **e′pha.** [< Hebrew]

e·phe·bic (e·fē′bik) *adj.* **1.** Of or pertaining to an ephebus. **2.** Of or relating to the adult stages of an organism.

e·phe·bus (e·fē′bəs) *n. pl.* **·bi** (-bī) In ancient Greece, a youth newly entered upon manhood or newly enrolled as a citizen. Also **e·phebe** (e·fēb′, ē·fēb′), **e·phe·bos** (e·fē′bos, -bəs). [< L < Gk. *ephēbos* < *epi-* upon + *hēbē* youth]

e·phed·rine (i·fed′rin, ef′ə·drēn) *n. Chem.* An alkaloid, $C_{10}H_{15}ON$, isolated from plants of the genus *Ephedra,* and also made synthetically, used for relief of asthma, hay fever, nasal congestion of colds, and in some cases of low blood pressure. Also **e·phed·rin** (i·fed′rin, ef′ə·drin). [< NL *Ephedra,* a genus of plants + -INE²]

e·phem·er·a (i·fem′ər·ə) *n. pl.* **·er·as** or **·er·ae** (-ə·rē) **1.** An ephemerid or May fly. **2.** Anything of very short life or duration. [< Gk. *ephēmeros* for a day < *epi-* on + *hēmera* day]

e·phem·er·al (i·fem′ər·əl) *adj.* **1.** Lasting but a short time; transitory. **2.** Living one day only, as certain insects. — **Syn.** See TRANSIENT. — *n.* Anything lasting for a very short time. — **e·phem′er·al·ly** *adv.*

e·phem·er·id (i·fem′ər·id) *n.* A May fly. [< NL *Ephemerida* < Gk. *ephēmeros.* See EPHEMERA.]

e·phem·er·is (i·fem′ər·is) *n. pl.* **eph·e·mer·i·des** (ef′ə·mer′ə·dēz) **1.** A table showing the calculated positions and motions of a heavenly body from day to day or at regular intervals. **2.** A collection of such tables, or a publication giving such tables; an astronomical almanac. **3.** *Obs.* An almanac or calendar. **4.** *Obs.* A diary or journal. [< L, diary < Gk. *ephēmeris* < *ephēmeros.* See EPHEMERA.]

e·phem·er·on (i·fem′ə·ron) *n. pl.* **·er·a** (-ər·ə) **1.** An ephemerid. **2.** Anything short-lived.

E·phe·sian (i·fē′zhən) *adj.* Of or pertaining to Ephesus. — *n.* A citizen of Ephesus.

E·phe·sians (i·fē′zhəns) *n.pl.* (*construed as sing.*) A book of the New Testament, consisting of St. Paul's epistle to the church at Ephesus. Abbr. *Eph., Ephes.*

Eph·e·sus (ef′ə·səs) An ancient Greek city in western Asia Minor; site of a noted temple of Artemis.

eph·od (ef′od, ē′fod) *n.* A Jewish priestly vestment. [*Ex.* xxviii 31. < Hebrew *ēphōd* < *āphad* to gird on]

eph·or (ef′ôr, -ər) *n. pl.* **·ors** or **·o·ri** (-ə·rī) **1.** In ancient Greece, one of a body of supervising magistrates at Sparta and other Doric towns. **2.** In modern Greece, a supervisor of public works. [< L *ephorus* < Gk. *ephoros* < *ephoraein* < *epi-* over + *horaein* to see]

E·phra·im (ē′frē·əm, ē′frəm) In the Old Testament, Joseph's younger son, who obtained the birthright. *Gen.* xlvi 20. — *n.* The tribe of Israel descended from this son. *Josh.* xiv 4.

E·phra·im (ē′frē·əm, ē′frəm) 1. A hilly region of Palestine between the Mediterranean and the Plain of Jezreel, occupied by the Ephraimites: also **Mount Ephraim.** 2. The kingdom of Israel.

E·phra·im·ite (ē′frē·əm·īt) *n.* A descendant of Ephraim or a member of the tribe of Ephraim.

epi- *prefix* 1. Upon; above; among; outside: *epidermis.* 2. Besides; over; in addition to: *epilogue.* 3. Near; close to; beside: *epifocal.* Also: *ep-,* before vowels, as in *eponym; eph-,* before an aspirate, as in *ephemeral.* [< Gk. *epi-, ep-, eph-* < *epi* upon, on, besides]

ep·i·blast (ep′ə·blast) *n.* 1. *Biol.* The ectoderm. 2. *Bot.* A small, scalelike appendage in front of the embryo in the seed of certain grasses. [< EPI- + -BLAST] — **ep′i·blas′tic** *adj.*

e·pib·o·ly (e·pib′ə·lē) *n. Biol.* The inclusion of one set of cells within another through the more rapid division of the latter. Also **e·pib′o·lism.** [< Gk. *epibolē* < *epi-* upon + *ballein* to throw] — **ep·i·bol·ic** (ep′ə·bol′ik) *adj.*

ep·ic (ep′ik) *n.* 1. A long, formal, narrative poem in elevated style, typically having as its subject heroic exploits and achievements or grandiose events. 2. A novel, drama, etc., that in scale or subject resembles such a poem. — *adj.* 1. Of, pertaining to, or suitable as a theme for an epic. 2. Full of grandeur; majestically impressive; heroic; grandiose. Also **ep′i·cal** *adj.* [< L *epicus* < Gk. *epikos* < *epos* word, tale, song] — **ep′i·cal·ly** *adv.*

ep·i·ca·lyx (ep′ə·kā′liks, -kal′iks) *n. pl.* **·ca·lyx·es** or **·ca·ly·ces** (-kā′lə·sēz, -kal′ə-) *Bot.* An involucre resembling an accessory calyx and lying outside the true calyx of a flower.

ep·i·can·thus (ep′ə·kan′thəs) *n. pl.* **·thi** (-thī) A small fold of skin over the inner corner of the eye, formed by an extension of the upper lid and typical of Mongoloid peoples. Also **epicanthic fold.** [< Gk. *epi-* upon + *kanthos* corner of the eye] — **ep′i·can′thic** *adj.*

ep·i·car·di·um (ep′ə·kär′dē·əm) *n. pl.* **·di·a** (-dē·ə) *Anat.* The inner portion of the pericardium that is directly united with the substance of the heart. [< NL < Gk. *epi-* upon + *kardia* heart] — **ep′i·car′di·ac** (-ak), **ep′i·car′di·al** *adj.*

ep·i·carp (ep′ə·kärp) *n. Bot.* The outer layer of a pericarp: also called *exocarp.*

ep·i·ce·di·um (ep′ə·sē′dē·əm) *n. pl.* **·di·a** (-dē·ə) A funeral hymn; dirge. [< L < Gk. *epikēdeion,* neut. sing. of *epikēdeios* funereal < *epi-* upon + *kēdos* grief, funeral]

ep·i·cene (ep′ə·sēn) *adj.* 1. *Gram.* a Of Greek and Latin names of animals, including both sexes but having only one grammatical gender, as Latin *lepus* a male or female hare, always of masculine gender. b Of common gender, as English *bird, rat.* 2. Belonging to or partaking of the characteristics of both sexes; hermaphrodite. 3. Sexless. 4. Effeminate. — *n.* 1. *Gram.* An epicene noun. 2. An epicene person. [< L *epicoenus* < Gk. *epikoinos* < *epi-* upon + *koinos* common] — **ep′i·cen·ism** *n.*

ep·i·cen·ter (ep′ə·sen′tər) *n. Geol.* The point or area on the earth's surface directly above the focus of an earthquake. Also **ep′i·cen′tre.** [< EPI- + CENTER] — **ep′i·cen′tral** *adj.*

ep·i·cen·trum (ep′ə·sen′trəm) *n. pl.* **·tra** (-trə) *Geol.* An epicenter.

ep·i·cot·yl (ep′ə·kot′l) *n. Bot.* The part of the young stem of a plant seedling above the cotyledons. [< EPI- + COTYL-(EDON)]

e·pic·ri·sis (i·pik′rə·sis) *n. pl.* **·ses** (-sēz) 1. An elaborate or detailed literary criticism. 2. *Med.* Critical discussion and analysis of a disease subsequent to its termination. [< Gk. *epikrisis* < *epi-* upon + *krinein* to judge]

ep·i·crit·ic (ep′ə·krit′ik) *adj. Physiol.* Of or pertaining to cutaneous sensibility responsive to very delicate variations in touch and temperature stimuli: distinguished from *protopathic.* [< Gk. *epikritikos* < *epikrisis.* See EPICRISIS.]

Ep·ic·te·tus (ep′ik·tē′təs), A.D. 60?–120?, Greek Stoic philosopher.

ep·i·cure (ep′ə·kyŏŏr) *n.* One given to luxurious living and discriminating gratification of the senses; a sensualist; especially, a fastidious devotee of good food and drink; a gourmet. — **Syn.** See GOURMET. [after *Epicurus*]

ep·i·cu·re·an (ep′ə·kyŏŏ·rē′ən) *adj.* Of, relating to, or typical of an epicure. — *n.* An epicure.

Ep·i·cu·re·an (ep′ə·kyŏŏ·rē′ən) *adj.* Of, relating to, or typical of Epicurus or his teachings. — *n.* A follower of Epicurus.

ep·i·cu·re·an·ism (ep′ə·kyŏŏ·rē′ən·iz′əm) *n.* The manner of living of an epicure. Also **ep′i·cur·ism.**

Ep·i·cu·re·an·ism (ep′ə·kyŏŏ·rē′ən·iz′əm) *n.* 1. The teachings of Epicurus. 2. Adherence to these teachings. Also **Ep′i·cur·ism.**

Ep·i·cu·rus (ep′ə·kyŏŏr s), 342?–270? B.C., Greek philosopher; taught that the c ief good of life is the peace of mind and freedom from pain ttained by the pursuit of cultural in-

terests, development of inner serenity, and temperance in sensual pleasure.

ep·i·cy·cle (ep′ə·sī′kəl) *n.* 1. In the Ptolemaic system, a small circle whose center moves on the circumference of a larger circle having the earth as its center (the deferent), while its own circumference describes the orbit of a planet. 2. *Geom.* A circle that rolls upon the exterior or interior of the circumference of another circle. [< L *epicyclus* < Gk. *epikyklos* < *epi-* upon + *kyklos* circle] — **ep′i·cy′clic** (-sī′klik, -sik′lik) or **·cli·cal** *adj.*

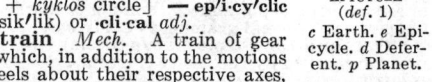

EPICYCLE
(def. 1)

c Earth. *e* Epicycle. *d* Deferent. *p* Planet.

epicyclic train *Mech.* A train of gear wheels in which, in addition to the motions of the wheels about their respective axes, one has a fixed axis about which the other axes revolve.

ep·i·cy·cloid (ep′ə·sī′kloid) *n. Math.* The curve traced by a point on the circumference of a circle that rolls on the outside of the circumference of a fixed circle. — **ep′i·cy·cloi′dal** (-sī·kloid′l) *adj.*

epicycloidal wheel *Mech.* One of the wheels in an epicyclic train.

ep·i·dem·ic (ep′ə·dem′ik) *adj.* 1. Breaking out suddenly and more or less unpredictably in a particular area in such a way as to affect many individuals at the same time: used especially of contagious diseases. Also **ep′i·dem′i·cal.** Compare ENDEMIC. — *n.* 1. An epidemic disease. 2. Anything temporarily widespread, as a fad. 3. The rapid spread of something epidemic. [< F *épidémique* < *épidémie* a plague < LL *epidemia* < Gk. *epidēmia* < *epi-* among + *dēmos* people] — **ep′i·dem′i·cal·ly** *adv.*

epidemic encephalitis *Pathol.* Encephalitis lethargica.

ep·i·de·mi·ol·o·gy (ep′ə·dē′mē·ol′ə·jē, -dem′ē-) *n.* The branch of medicine that treats of epidemic diseases. [< EPI-DEMI(C) + -LOGY] — **ep′i·de′mi·o·log′ic** (-dē′mē·ə·loj′ik) or **·i·cal** *adj.* — **ep′i·de′mi·ol′o·gist** *n.*

ep·i·der·mis (ep′ə·dûr′mis) *n.* 1. *Anat.* The outer, nonvascular covering of the skin, overlying the corium: also called *cuticle, scarfskin.* 2. Any integument or tegumentary covering; especially, the outer covering of the shell of many mollusks. 3. *Bot.* The outermost layer of cells covering the surface of a plant when there are several layers of tissue. Also **ep′i·derm.** [< NL < Gk. < *epi-* upon + *derma* skin] — **ep′i·der′mal, ep′i·der′mic** *adj.*

ep·i·der·moid (ep′ə·dûr′moid) *adj.* Of the nature of epidermis. Also **ep′i·der·moi′dal.**

ep·i·di·a·scope (ep′ə·dī′ə·skōp) *n.* A device for projecting the images of opaque or transparent objects upon a screen. [< EPI- + DIA- + -SCOPE]

ep·i·did·y·mis (ep′ə·did′ə·mis) *n. pl.* **ep·i·di·dym·i·des** (ep′-ə·di·dim′ə·dēz) *Anat.* An oblong structure attached to the back of each testicle and composed of the first, convoluted portion of the excretory ducts of the testicles. [< NL < Gk. < *epi-* upon + *didymos* testicle] — **ep′i·did′y·mal** *adj.*

ep·i·dote (ep′ə·dōt) *n.* A monoclinic, greenish to black aluminum calcium silicate. [< F *épidote* < Gk. *epididonai* to increase < *epi-* upon + *didonai* to give; from the enlarged base of its crystals] — **ep′i·dot′ic** (-dot′ik) *adj.*

ep·i·fo·cal (ep′ə·fō′kəl) *adj. Geol.* Of, pertaining to, or situated near the focus of an earthquake; epicentral.

ep·i·gas·tric (ep′ə·gas′trik) *adj. Anat.* 1. Relating to the anterior walls of the abdomen. 2. Of or pertaining to the epigastrium or the abdomen generally. Also **ep′i·gas′tri·al.**

ep·i·gas·tri·um (ep′ə·gas′trē·əm) *n. pl.* **·tri·a** (-trē·ə) *Anat.* The upper part of the abdomen; especially, the region over and in front of the stomach. For illustration see ABDOMINAL. [< NL < Gk. *epigastrion* < *epi-* upon + *gaster* stomach]

ep·i·ge·al (ep′ə·jē′əl) *adj.* 1. *Bot.* Epigeous. 2. *Zool.* Living close to the ground, as certain insects. Also **ep′i·ge′an.**

ep·i·gene (ep′ə·jēn) *adj. Geol.* Produced or occurring at or near the surface of the earth: opposed to *hypogene.* [< F *épigène* < Gk. *epigenēs* born after < *epi-* upon, after + *gen-,* root of *gignesthai* to be born]

ep·i·gen·e·sis (ep′ə·jen′ə·sis) *n.* 1. *Biol.* The theory that the structure, organization, and development of organisms, as in embryos, is the result of new formations through successive interactions between male and female cells subsequent to fertilization: opposed to *syngenesis.* 2. *Geol.* An alteration in the character of rocks due to external forces or agents. 3. *Med.* An accessory or secondary symptom of a disease. — **ep′i·ge·net′ic** (-jə·net′ik) *adj.*

e·pig·e·nous (i·pij′ə·nəs) *adj. Bot.* Growing on the surface, especially the upper surface, as fungi on leaves. [< EPIGENE + -OUS]

ep·i·ge·ous (ep′ə·jē′əs) *adj. Bot.* 1. Growing on or above the surface of the ground. 2. Rising above the ground after germination: said of cotyledons. [< Gk. *epigeios* < *epi-* upon + *gē* earth]

ep·i·glot·tis (ep′ə·glot′is) *n. Anat.* A leaf-shaped, cartilaginous lid at the base of the tongue that covers the windpipe during the act of swallowing. For illustration see LARYNX, LUNG, MOUTH, THROAT. [< NL < Gk. *epiglōttis* < *epi-* upon + *glōtta* tongue] —**ep′i·glot′tal** *adj.*

E·pig·o·ni (i·pig′ə·nī) *n.pl.* In Greek legend, the sons of the Seven against Thebes who successfully attacked Thebes.

ep·i·gram (ep′ə·gram) *n.* **1.** A brief, clever, pointed remark or observation typically marked by antithesis. **2.** A short, pithy piece of verse with a witty, often satirical point. **3.** Epigrammatic expression. [< L *epigramma* < Gk., an inscription < *epi-* upon + *graphein* to write]

ep·i·gram·mat·ic (ep′i·grə·mat′ik) *adj.* **1.** Of, relating to, or resembling an epigram. **2.** Fond of or marked by the use of epigrams. —**ep′i·gram·mat′i·cal·ly** *adv.*

ep·i·gram·ma·tism (ep′ə·gram′ə·tiz′əm) *n.* Literary expression marked by the use of epigrams.

ep·i·gram·ma·tist (ep′ə·gram′ə·tist) *n.* One who makes epigrams.

ep·i·gram·ma·tize (ep′ə·gram′ə·tīz) *v.* **·tized**, **·tiz·ing** *v.t.* **1.** To make an epigram of; express in an epigram. —*v.i.* **2.** To write or speak in epigrams; make an epigram.

ep·i·graph (ep′ə·graf, -gräf) *n.* **1.** An inscription on a monument, tomb, etc. **2.** A quotation or motto prefixed to a book, etc. [< Gk. *epigraphē* < *epi-* upon + *graphein* to write]

ep·i·graph·ic (ep′ə·graf′ik) *adj.* Of or relating to epigraphs or epigraphy. Also **ep′i·graph′i·cal.** —**ep′i·graph′i·cal·ly** *adv.*

e·pig·ra·phy (i·pig′rə·fē) *n.* **1.** The science that treats of the study, interpretation, etc., of inscriptions. **2.** Epigraphs collectively. —**e·pig′ra·pher, e·pig′ra·phist** *n.*

e·pig·y·nous (i·pij′ə·nəs) *adj. Bot.* Having floral organs adnate to and near the summit of the ovary. [< EPI- + -GY-NOUS]

e·pig·y·ny (i·pij′ə·nē) *n. Bot.* The state of being epigynous.

ep·i·lep·sy (ep′ə·lep′sē) *n. Pathol.* A disorder of cerebral function marked primarily by recurring attacks of unconsciousness with or without convulsions. See GRAND MAL, PETIT MAL. [< OF *epilepsie* < LL *epilepsia* < Gk. *epilēpsia* < *epi-* upon + *lambanein* to seize]

ep·i·lep·tic (ep′ə·lep′tik) *adj.* **1.** Of, relating to, or resembling epilepsy. **2.** Affected with epilepsy. —*n.* One affected with epilepsy. —**ep′i·lep′ti·cal·ly** *adv.*

ep·i·lep·toid (ep′ə·lep′toid) *adj.* Resembling epilepsy.

ep·i·logue (ep′ə·lôg, -log) *n.* **1.** A short section appended to a novel, poem, etc., by way of amplification or commentary. **2.** A short speech or piece of verse appended to a play and designed to be delivered by one of the performers; also, the performer. Also **ep′i·log.** [< F < L *epilogus* < Gk. *epilogos* a peroration < *epi-* in addition + *legein* to say]

Ep·i·me·the·us (ep′ə·mē′thē·əs) In Greek mythology, a Titan, the brother of Prometheus and husband of Pandora.

ep·i·mor·pha (ep′ə·môr′fə) *n.pl. Zool.* Larvae having all their segments fully formed before hatching. [< NL < Gk. *epi-* on, upon + *morphē* form]

ep·i·mor·pho·sis (ep′ə·môr·fō′sis) *n. Biol.* The rapid growth of new tissue preceding the regeneration of a part, as in many invertebrate animals. [< EPI- + MORPHOSIS]

ep·i·nas·ty (ep′ə·nas′tē) *n. Bot.* Downward curvature of a plant member, induced by a more active growth on its upper side: distinguished from *hyponasty*. [< EPI- + Gk. *nastos* compact] —**ep′i·nas′tic** *adj.*

ep·i·neph·rine (ep′ə·nef′rin, -rēn) *n. Chem.* The active principle of the medullary portion of the adrenal glands, $C_9H_{13}O_3N$, used as a heart stimulant: also called *adrenalin*. Also **ep′i·neph′rin** (-rin). [< EPI- + Gk. *nephros* kidney]

ep·i·neu·ri·um (ep′ə·nŏŏr′ē·əm, -nyŏŏr′-) *n. pl.* **·neu·ri·a** (-nŏŏr′ē·ə, -nyŏŏr′ē·ə) *Anat.* The sheath of connective tissue that surrounds a nerve trunk. [< NL < Gk. *epi-* upon + *neuron* nerve, sinew] —**ep′i·neu′ri·al** *adj.*

e·piph·a·ny (i·pif′ə·nē) *n. pl.* **·nies** An appearance or manifestation, as of a deity. [< OF *epiphanie* < Gk. *epiphainein* to manifest < *epi-* to, unto + *phainein* to show]

E·piph·a·ny (i·pif′ə·nē) *n. Eccl.* A festival, held on January 6, commemorating the manifestation of Christ to the Gentiles as represented by the Magi: also called *Twelfth day*.

ep·i·phe·nom·e·nal (ep′i·fə·nom′ə·nəl) *adj.* Of or pertaining to an epiphenomenon.

ep·i·phe·nom·e·nal·ism (ep′i·fə·nom′ə·nəl·iz′əm) *n. Philos. & Psychol.* The theory or doctrine that mental processes are merely epiphenomena caused by physical or neural processes.

ep·i·phe·nom·e·non (ep′i·fə·nom′ə·non) *n. pl.* **·na** (-ə·nə) **1.** A secondary phenomenon occurring with or accompanying another, but having no power in itself to produce effects. **2.** *Pathol.* An added condition accompanying, but not always directly related to, the initial disease.

e·piph·y·sis (i·pif′ə·sis) *n. pl.* **·ses** (-sēz) *Anat.* **1.** The extremity of a long bone that at first is separated from the bone by cartilage but later consolidated with it by ossification. **2.** The pineal body. [< NL < Gk., an outgrowth < *epi-* upon + *phyein* to grow] —**ep·i·phys·ial** (ep′ə·fiz′ē·əl) or **ep′i·phys′e·al** *adj.*

ep·i·phyte (ep′ə·fīt) *n. Bot.* A plant growing upon, but not receiving its nourishment from, another plant, as an orchid, moss, or lichen: also called *aerophyte, air plant.* —**ep′i·phyt′ic** (-fit′ik) or **·i·cal** *adj.*

ep·i·phy·tot·ic (ep′ə·fī·tot′ik) *adj. Bot.* Attacking or effecting plants within a wide area: said of plant diseases and parasites. [< EPI- + PHYTO- + -(O)TIC]

ep·i·rog·e·ny (ep′ə·roj′ə·nē) See EPEIROGENY.

E·pi·rus (i·pī′rəs) An administrative division of NW Greece, formerly an independent kingdom and republic; 3,573 sq. mi.; pop. 330,543 (1951); capital, Ioannina: Greek *Epeirus.*

Epis. **1.** Episcopal: also **Episc.** **2.** Epistle(s).

e·pis·co·pa·cy (i·pis′kə·pə·sē) *n. pl.* **·cies** **1.** Government of a church by bishops: distinguished from *presbytery.* **2.** The rank, office, or incumbency of a bishop; episcopate. **3.** Bishops collectively. [< LL *episcopatus* < *episcopus.* See BISHOP.]

e·pis·co·pal (i·pis′kə·pəl) *adj.* **1.** Of, pertaining to, or governed by bishops. **2.** Advocating episcopacy. [< LL *episcopalis* < *episcopus.* See BISHOP.] —**e·pis′co·pal·ly** *adv.*

E·pis·co·pal (i·pis′kə·pəl) *adj.* Belonging or pertaining to any Anglican Church. Abbr. *Epis., Episc.*

Episcopal Church The Protestant Episcopal Church (which see).

e·pis·co·pa·li·an (i·pis′kə·pā′lē·ən, -pāl′yən) *n.* An advocate of episcopacy. —*adj.* Pertaining to or favoring episcopal government; episcopal.

E·pis·co·pa·li·an (i·pis′kə·pā′lē·ən, -pāl′yən) *n.* A member of the Protestant Episcopal Church. —*adj.* Belonging to the Protestant Episcopal Church, etc.; Episcopal. —**E·pis′co·pa′li·an·ism** *n.*

e·pis·co·pal·ism (i·pis′kə·pəl·iz′əm) *n.* That view of the constitution of the church that gives the supreme power to a body of bishops, and recognizes no single supreme head.

e·pis·co·pate (i·pis′kə·pit, -pāt) *n.* **1.** The office, dignity, or term of office of a bishop. **2.** A bishopric. **3.** Bishops collectively.

ep·i·sode (ep′ə·sōd) *n.* **1.** A section of a novel, poem, etc., complete in itself and contributing to the main plot or theme; incident. **2.** A unified part forming a continuation of a serialized story, play, etc.; installment. **3.** An incidental, usually notable occurrence in a person's life or during a course of events. **4.** A portion of a Greek tragedy occurring between two choric songs. **5.** *Music* A passage that separates statements of a recurrent theme. —**Syn.** See EVENT. [< Gk. *epeisodion* < *epeisodios* coming in besides < *epi-* beside + *eisodos* entrance < *eis-* into + *hodos* way, road]

ep·i·sod·ic (ep′ə·sod′ik) *adj.* **1.** Of, relating to, or resembling an episode. **2.** Broken up into episodes; especially, not smoothly integrated; disjointed. Also **ep′i·sod′i·cal.** —**ep′i·sod′i·cal·ly** *adv.*

ep·i·spas·tic (ep′ə·spas′tik) *adj.* Raising blisters; vesicatory. —*n.* An agent that raises blisters; vesicatory. [< NL *epispasticus* < Gk. *epispastikos* < *epi-* on + *spaein* to draw]

Epist. Epistle(s).

e·pis·ta·sis (i·pis′tə·sis) *n. pl.* **·ses** (-sēz) **1.** *Genetics* The masking of one factor in Mendelian inheritance by another not allelomorphic to it. **2.** *Med.* Stoppage of a hemorrhage or other fluid discharge of the body. [< NL < Gk., stoppage < *epi-* upon + *histanai* to place] —**ep·i·stat·ic** (ep′ə·stat′ik) *adj.*

ep·i·stax·is (ep′ə·stak′sis) *n. Pathol.* Nosebleed. [< NL < Gk. *epistazein* to bleed from the nose < *epi-* upon + *stazein* to drop, drip]

e·pis·te·mol·o·gy (i·pis′tə·mol′ə·jē) *n. pl.* **·gies** The branch of philosophy that investigates critically the nature, grounds, limits, criteria, or validity of human knowledge; also, a particular theory of cognition. [< Gk. *epistēmē* knowledge + -LOGY] —**e·pis·te·mo·log·i·cal** (i·pis′tə·mə·loj′i·kal) *adj.* —**e·pis′te·mo·log′i·cal·ly** *adv.* **e·pis′te·mol′o·gist** *n.*

ep·i·ster·num (ep′ə·stûr′nəm) *n. pl.* **·na** (-nə) *Anat.* The manubrium (def. 1a). [< EPI- + STERNUM]

e·pis·tle (i·pis′əl) *n.* **1.** A letter, especially when long or formal. **2.** *Usually cap. Eccl.* **a** One of the letters written by an apostle. Abbr. *Ep., Epis., Epist.* **b** A selection taken from one of these letters and read as part of a service. [OE *epistol* < L *epistola* < Gk. *epistolē* < *epi-* to + *stellein* to send]

e·pis·tler (i·pis′lər) *n.* **1.** One who writes epistles. **2.** *Usually cap. Eccl.* One appointed to read the Epistle in a service. Also **e·pis·to·ler** (i·pis′tə·lər).

e·pis·to·lar·y (i·pis′tə·ler′ē) *adj.* **1.** Of or relating to a letter or an Epistle. **2.** Included in or maintained by a letter.

e·pis·tro·phe (i·pis′trə·fē) *n. Bot.* The arrangement of chlorophyll granules, as on the upper and under walls of leaf cells, when exposed to diffused light: opposed to *apostrophe.* [< EPI- + Gk. *strophē* turning about]

ep·i·style (ep′ə·stīl) *n. Archit.* An architrave (def. 1). [< L *epistylium* < Gk. *epystylion* < *epi-* upon + *stylos* pillar]

ep·i·taph (ep′ə·taf, -täf) *n.* **1.** An inscription on a tomb or monument in memory of the dead. **2.** Any short piece of prose or verse eulogizing someone deceased. [< L *epitaphium* eulogy < Gk. *epitaphios* at a tomb < *epi-* upon, at + *taphos* a tomb] —**ep′i·taph′ic** (-taf′ik) *adj.*

e·pit·a·sis (i·pit′ə·sis) *n.* The central part of classical drama in which the plot is developed, following the protasis and preceding the catastrophe. [< NL < Gk., *epileinein* to intensify < *epi-* in addition + *teinein* to stretch]

ep·i·tha·la·mi·um (ep'ə·thə·lā'mē·əm) *n.* *pl.* **·mi·ums** or **·mi·a** (-mē·ə) A nuptial poem or song in honor of the bride and bridegroom. Also **ep'i·tha·la'mi·on** (-mē·ən). [< L < Gk. *epithalamion* < *epi-* at + *thalamos* bridal chamber]

ep·i·the·li·al (ep'ə·thē'lē·əl) *adj.* Of or relating to epithelium.

ep·i·the·li·oid (ep'ə·thē'lē·oid) *adj.* *Biol.* Resembling epithelium.

ep·i·the·li·o·ma (ep'ə·thē'lē·ō'mə) *n.* *pl.* **·ma·ta** (-mə·tə) or **·mas** *Pathol.* A malignant growth originating in or affecting epithelial tissue; especially, cancer of the skin. — **ep·i·the·li·om·a·tous** (ep'ə·thē'lē·om'ə·təs) *adj.*

ep·i·the·li·um (ep'ə·thē'lē·əm) *n.* *pl.* **·li·ums** or **·li·a** (-lē·ə) *Biol.* A membranous tissue consisting of one or more layers of cells compactly joined and serving to line the canals, cavities, and ducts of the body and the free surfaces exposed to the air. [< NL < Gk. *epi-* upon + *thēlē* nipple]

ep·i·thet (ep'ə·thet) *n.* 1. An adjective or other descriptive word or phrase qualifying or used in place of the usual name of a person or thing, as *rosy-fingered* in "the rosy-fingered dawn" or *the Bold* in "Philip the Bold." 2. Loosely, any disparaging name, especially for a person. — **Syn.** See NICKNAME. [< L *epitheton* < Gk. < *epitithenai* to add < *epi-* upon + *tithenai* to place] — **ep'i·thet'ic** or **·i·cal** *adj.*

e·pit·o·me (i·pit'ə·mē) *n.* 1. A typical example or representative; embodiment: the *epitome* of arrogance. 2. An extreme example; climax or culmination: a TV commercial described as the *epitome* of gutter politics. 3. A concise summary; abridgement. — **Syn.** See ABRIDGEMENT. [< L < Gk. *epitomē* < *epi-* upon + *temnein* to cut]

e·pit·o·mize (i·pit'ə·mīz) *v.t.* **·mized, ·miz·ing** 1. To be the epitome of; represent or embody. 2. To make an epitome of; summarize concisely. Also *Brit.* **e·pit'o·mise.** — **e·pit'o·miz'er** *n.*

ep·i·zo·on (ep'ə·zō'on) *n.* *pl.* **·zo·a** (-zō'ə) An animal parasite living on the outside of the body. [< Gk. *epi-* on + *zōon* animal]

ep·i·zo·ot·ic (ep'ə·zō·ot'ik) *adj.* Affecting many animals within a wide area: said especially of diseases. — *n.* An epizootic disease: also **ep'i·zo'o·ty** (-zō'ə·tē).

e plu·ri·bus u·num (ē plŏŏr'ə·bəs yōō'nəm) *Latin* One out of many: motto of the United States.

ep·och (ep'ək, *Brit.* ē'pok) *n.* 1. A point in time marked by the beginning of a new development or state of things: the atomic *epoch* in history. 2. An interval of time memorable for extraordinary events, important influences, unusual circumstances, etc. 3. *Geol.* A minor subdivision of ti ne; a time interval less than a period: the Pleistocene *epoch.* See chart for GEOLOGY. 4. *Astron.* A moment of ti ne when a planet reaches a certain known position in relation to the sun, selected arbitrarily and thereafter used as a reference point in computing the positions of stars, etc. [< Gk. *epochē* stoppage, point of time < *epi-* upon + *echein* to hold]

ep·och·al (ep'ə·kəl) *adj.* 1. Of or pertaining to an epoch. 2. Characteristic of or marking an epoch.

ep·och-mak·ing (ep'ək·mā'king, *Brit.* ē'pok-) *adj.* Opening up a new era: an *epoch-making* event.

ep·ode (ep'ōd) *n.* 1. That part of a Pindaric ode following the strophe and antistrophe. 2. A kind of poem in which a long verse is followed by a short one. [< F *épode* < L *epodos* < Gk. *epōidos* incantation < *epi-* after + *aidein* to sing]

ep·o·nym (ep'ə·nim) *n.* A real or legendary personage from whom a nation, city, epoch, theory, etc., is reputed to derive its name. — **Syn.** See NAME. [< Gk. *epōnymos* < *epi-* upon + *onyma* name]

e·pon·y·mous (i·pon'ə·məs) *adj.* Of, relating to, or constituting an eponym. Also **e·pon·ym·ic** (ep'ə·nim'ik).

e·pon·y·my (i·pon'ə·mē) *n.* Derivation of the name of a nation, city, etc., from a real or legendary personage.

ep·o·pee (ep'ə·pē, ep'ə·pē') *n.* 1. An epic poem. 2. Epic poetry in general. Also **ep·o·poe·ia** (ep'ə·pē'ə). [< F *épopée* < Gk. *epopoiia* < *epos* word, song + *poieein* to make]

ep·os (ep'os) *n.* 1. An epic poem. 2. Epic poetry in general. 3. A sequence of epic events. [< L < Gk., word song]

e·pox·y (e·pok'sē) *n.* *Chem.* The radical -O-, especially as bonded to different atoms already joined in different ways, to form the durable, thermosetting **epoxy resins** much used for varnishes and adhesives. [< EP(I)- + OXY-²]

Ep·ping (ep'ing) An urban district of western Essex, England; on the edge of **Epping Forest,** which once included all Essex and is now a park of 5,600 acres; pop. 9,998 (1961).

ep·si·lon (ep'sə·lon) *n.* The fifth letter and second vowel in the Greek alphabet (E, ε), corresponding to English short *e.* See ALPHABET. [< Gk. *epsilon* < *e* ε + *psilon* simple]

Ep·som (ep'səm) A town in north central Surrey, England, famous for its racecourse **Epsom Downs;** pop. 71,177 (1961).

Epsom salts A hydrous magnesium sulfate, used as a purge or to reduce inflammation. Also **Epsom salt.**

Ep·stein (ep'stīn), **Sir Jacob,** 1880–1959, British sculptor born in the United States.

eq. 1. Equal. 2. Equation. 3. Equator. 4. Equivalent.

e·qua·bil·i·ty (ek'wə·bil'ə·tē, ē'kwə-) *n.* The quality of being equable; uniformity; evenness. Also **eq'ua·ble·ness.**

eq·ua·ble (ek'wə·bəl, ē'kwə-) *adj.* 1. Not changing or varying greatly; steady; even: an *equable* temperature. 2. Not easily upset; serene; tranquil: an *equable* disposition. 3. Evenly proportioned; uniform. [< L *aequabilis* < *aequare* to make equal] — **eq'ua·bly** *adv.*

e·qual (ē'kwəl) *adj.* 1. Identical in size, extent, etc.: His share is *equal* to yours. 2. Having the same rights, rank, etc.: All men are *equal* before the law. 3. Having the same abilities, degree of excellence, etc.: *equal* in talent. 4. Evenly proportioned; not disproportionate; balanced. 5. Affecting all alike; uniform in application. 6. Shared by all alike: *equal* rights. 7. Having the requisite ability, power, etc.; adequate: with *to*: *equal* to the task. 8. Sufficient in amount, extent, etc.: with *to*: wealth *equal* to the cost. 9. *Archaic* Equitable. 10. *Archaic* Tranquil; equable. 11. *Archaic* Having a flat, regular surface; level. — **Syn.** See ADEQUATE. — *v.t.* **e·qualed** or **e·qualled, e·qual·ing** or **e·qual·ling** 1. To be equal to; match. 2. To do or produce something equal to. 3. To recompense in full. 4. *Archaic* To make equal; equalize. — *n.* A person or thing equal to another. [< L *aequalis* < *aequus* even] — **e'qual·ly** *adv.*

◆ The use of *equally* in such sentences as "He is *equally* as guilty as I" is redundant and is avoided in careful writing.

e·qual-ar·e·a (ē'kwəl·âr'e·ə) *adj.* Designating a map or map projection in which the relationship between a unit area of the map and a corresponding area of the earth remains constant regardless of location.

e·qual·i·tar·i·an (i·kwol'ə·târ'ē·ən) *adj. & n.* Egalitarian. — **e·qual·i·tar'i·an·ism** *n.*

e·qual·i·ty (i·kwol'ə·tē) *n.* *pl.* **·ties** The state or quality of being equal; also, an instance of this.

Equality State Nickname of WYOMING.

e·qual·ize (ē'kwəl·īz) *v.t.* **·ized, ·iz·ing** To make equal or uniform. Also *Brit.* **e'qual·ise.** — **e'qual·i·za'tion** *n.*

e·qual·iz·er (ē'kwəl·ī'zər) *n.* 1. One who or that which equalizes. 2. *Mech.* A device for equalizing pressure or strain between parts of a structure. 3. *Electr.* **a** A conductor of low resistance used to join the currents of two generators and equalize their voltage. **b** Any contrivance for equalizing the pull of electromagnets.

equal sign A sign (=) denoting numbers, quantities, etc., equal to one another.

e·qua·nim·i·ty (ē'kwə·nim'ə·tē, ek'wə-) *n.* Evenness of mind or temper; composure; calmness. [< L *aequanimitas, -tatis* < *aequus* even + *animus* mind]

e·quan·i·mous (i·kwan'ə·məs) *adj.* Even-tempered.

e·quate (i·kwāt') *v.t.* **e·quat·ed, e·quat·ing** 1. To make equal; treat or consider as equivalent. 2. To reduce to an average; correct so as to reduce to a common standard. 3. *Math.* To indicate the equality of; express as an equation. [< L *aequatus,* pp. of *aequare* to make even < *aequus* even]

e·qua·tion (i·kwā'zhən, -shən) *n.* 1. The process or act of making equal. 2. The state of being equal; equality. 3. *Math.* A statement expressing (usually by =) the equality of two quantities. 4. *Chem.* A symbolic representation of a chemical reaction, as $Na_2CO_3 + H_2SO_4 \rightarrow Na_2SO_4 + CO_2 + H_2O$. The first member includes the substances reacting, the second, the products. 5. Personal equation (which see). Abbr. *eq.* — **e·qua'tion·al** *adj.* — **e·qua'tion·al·ly** *adv.*

e·qua·tor (i·kwā'tər) *n.* 1. The great circle of the earth, a line lying in a plane perpendicular to the earth's polar axis. 2. Any similar circle, as of the sun or a planet. 3. *Astron.* The celestial equator (which see). Abbr. *eq.* [< LL (*circulus*) *aequator* equalizer (circle); so called because day and night are equal when the sun crosses the equator]

e·qua·to·ri·al (ē'kwə·tôr'ē·əl -tō'rē-) *adj.* 1. Of, pertaining to, or like the equator. 2. Relating to conditions prevailing at the earth's equator: *equatorial* heat. — *n. Astron.* A telescope turning on two axes at right angles to each other, one being parallel to the axis of the earth.

Equatorial Current A massive surface current flowing westward in the oceans along the equator.

Equatorial Guin·ea A Republic in western Africa, comprising the provinces of Río Muni and Fernando Po; formerly *Spanish Guinea;* 10,830 sq. mi.; pop. 300,000 (est. 1970); capital, Santa Isabel.

Equatorial Islands See LINE ISLANDS.

eq·uer·ry (ek'wər·ē) *n.* *pl.* **·ries** 1. An officer in charge of the horses of a prince or nobleman. 2. A personal attendant on a member of the royal household of England. [Confusion of F *écurie* stable (< OF *escuerie,* ? ult. < Gmc.) with OF *escuier* esquire; infl. by L *equus* horse]

e·ques·tri·an (i·kwes'trē·ən) *adj.* 1. Pertaining to horses or horsemanship. 2. Mounted on horseback; also, representing someone as being on horseback: an *equestrian* portrait. 3. Composed of or pertaining to Roman *equites* or knights. — *n.* A rider on horseback, especially when skilled. [< L *equester, -tris* < *eques* horseman < *equus* horse]

e·ques·tri·an·ism (i·kwes'trē·ən·iz'əm) *n.* Horsemanship.

e·ques·tri·enne (i·kwes'trē·en') *n.* A female equestrian.
equi- *combining form* Equal; equally: *equidistant.* [< L *aequus* equal]
e·qui·an·gu·lar (ē'kwē·ang'gyə·lər) *adj.* Having equal angles.
e·qui·dis·tance (ē'kwə·dis'təns) *n.* Equal distance.
e·qui·dis·tant (ē'kwə·dis'tənt) *adj.* Equally distant. — **e'qui·dis'tant·ly** *adv.*
e·qui·lat·er·al (ē'kwə·lat'ər·əl) *n.* **1.** A side of equal length with another. **2.** A geometric figure with equal sides. — *adj.* Having all the sides equal. — **e'qui·lat'er·al·ly** *adv.*
e·quil·i·brant (i·kwil'ə·brənt) *n. Physics* A force or system of forces that counteracts another force or system and produces equilibrium. [< F *équilibrant,* ppr. of *équilibrer* to balance < *équilibre* equilibrium < L *aequilibrium*]
e·qui·li·brate (ē'kwə·lī'brāt, i·kwil'ə·brāt) *v.t. & v.i.* **·brat·ed, ·brat·ing 1.** To bring into or be in a state of equilibrium. **2.** To counterpoise. [< L *aequilibratus* level < *aequus* equal + *libratus* level < *libra* a balance] — **e'qui·li·bra'tion** *n.*
e·qui·li·bra·tor (ē'kwə·lī'brā·tər, i·kwil'ə-) *n.* A device for establishing equilibrium.
e·quil·i·brist (i·kwil'ə·brist) *n.* One skilled in balancing, as a tightrope walker. — **e·quil'i·bris'tic** *adj.*
e·qui·lib·ri·um (ē'kwə·lib'rē·əm) *n.* **1.** *Physics* **a** A state of balance between two or more forces acting within or upon a body such that there is no change in the state of rest or motion of the body. **b** Stability. **2.** *Chem.* The state in a reversible reaction when the rates of the forward and reverse reactions are equal and the concentrations of the reactants are constant. **3.** Any state of balance, compromise, or adjustment between opposites or opposing forces. **4.** A state of balance in the mind or feelings. **5.** *Biol.* Homeostasis. [< L *aequilibrium* < *aequus* equal + *libra* balance]

EQUILIBRIUM
A Stable. *B* Unstable. *C* Neutral. *g* Center of gravity.

e·quine (ē'kwīn) *adj.* Of, pertaining to, or like a horse. — *n.* A horse. [< L *equinus* < *equus* horse]
equine syphilis *Vet.* Dourine.
e·qui·noc·tial (ē'kwə·nok'shəl) *adj.* **1.** Occurring at or near the time when the sun crosses the celestial equator. **2.** Of or pertaining to the equinox, or equality of day and night. **3.** *Bot.* Opening and closing at regular hours: said of certain flowers, as the four-o'clock. **4.** Of or pertaining to the equator or equatorial regions. — *n.* **1.** *Meteorol.* A severe storm occurring usually at or near the time of the equinox. Also, *U.S. Dial., line storm.* **2.** The celestial equator. [< L *aequinoctialis* < *aequinoctium.* See EQUINOX.]
equinoctial line *Astron.* The celestial equator.
equinoctial points The points of intersection of the celestial equator and the ecliptic; the equinoxes.
equinoctial time Time reckoned from the moment at which the sun passes the vernal equinox.
equinoctial year An astronomical year (which see).
e·qui·nox (ē'kwə·noks) *n.* One of two opposite points at which the sun crosses the celestial equator, when the days and nights are equal; also, the time of this crossing (about March 21, the **vernal** or **spring equinox,** and Sept. 21, the **autumnal equinox.** [< F *équinoxe* < L *aequinoctium* < *aequus* equal + *nox* night]
e·quip (i·kwip') *v.t.* **e·quipped, e·quip·ping 1.** To furnish, endow, or fit out with whatever is needed for any purpose or undertaking. **2.** To dress or attire; array. [< F *équiper* OF *esquiper,* prob. < ON *skipa* to outfit a vessel < *skip* ship]
e·qui·page (ek'wə·pij) *n.* **1.** The equipment for a camp, army, etc. **2.** A carriage, especially when outfitted with horses, attendants, etc. **3.** *Archaic* A group of attendants; retinue. **4.** *Archaic* A set of small articles, as dishes; also, a case containing such a set. [< F *équiper.* See EQUIP.]
e·quip·ment (i·kwip'mənt) *n.* **1.** The act of equipping, or the state of being equipped. **2.** Material with which a person or organization is provided for some special purpose or service. **3.** Personal knowledge or skill, as of an instructor, diplomatist, etc. **4.** The rolling stock and apparatus for operating a railroad or other transportation system.
e·qui·poise (ē'kwə·poiz, ek'wə-) *n.* **1.** Equality of weight; equal balance. **2.** A counterpoise. [< EQUI- + POISE]
e·qui·pol·lence (ē'kwə·pol'əns) *n.* The state or quality of being equipollent. Also **e'qui·pol'len·cy.**
e·qui·pol·lent (ē'kwə·pol'ənt) *adj.* **1.** Equal in weight, power, effect, etc. **2.** Equivalent in meaning and force. — *n.* An equivalent. [< F *équipollent* < L *aequipollens, -entis* < *aequus* equal + *pollere* to be strong]
e·qui·pon·der·ance (ē'kwə·pon'dər·əns) *n.* Equality of weight; equipoise. — **e·qui·pon'der·ant** *adj.*
e·qui·pon·der·ate (ē'kwə·pon'də·rāt) *v.t.* **·at·ed, ·at·ing 1.** To counterbalance. **2.** To make balanced. [< Med. L *aequiponderatus,* pp. of *aequiponderare* < L *aequus* equal + *ponderare* to weigh]
e·qui·po·ten·tial (ē'kwə·pō·ten'shəl) *adj.* **1.** Having equal power or influence. **2.** *Electr.* Of equal potential.
e·qui·prob·a·ble (ē'kwə·prob'ə·bəl) *adj.* Having an equal chance of occurring. — **e'qui·prob'a·bil'i·ty** *n.*

eq·ui·se·tum (ek'wə·sē'təm) *n. pl.* **·tums** or **·ta** (-tə) Any of a widely distributed genus (*Equisetum*) of rushlike plants that do not bear seeds; the horsetail. [< NL < L *equus* horse + *seta* bristle]
eq·ui·ta·ble (ek'wə·tə·bəl) *adj.* **1.** Marked by equity; impartially just, fair, and reasonable. **2.** *Law* Of, relating to, or valid in equity as distinguished from statute law and common law. [< F *équitable* < *équité.* See EQUITY.] — **eq'ui·ta·ble·ness** *n.* — **eq'ui·ta·bly** *adv.*
eq·ui·tant (ek'wə·tənt) *adj. Bot.* Overlapping, as a leaf whose base embraces the leaf next within or above it. [< L *equitans, -antis,* ppr. of *equitare* to ride on horseback < *eques, -itis* horseman < *equus* horse]
eq·ui·ta·tion (ek'wə·tā'shən) *n.* Horsemanship. [< L *equitatio, -onis* < *equitare.* See EQUITANT.]
eq·ui·tes (ek'wə·tēz) *n.pl.* A privileged military class of ancient Rome, consisting originally of the cavalry. [< L, pl. of *eques* horseman < *equus* horse]
eq·ui·ty (ek'wə·tē) *n. pl.* **·ties 1.** Fairness or impartiality; justness. **2.** Something that is fair or equitable. **3.** *Law* a Justice administered between litigants that is based on the concepts of ethics and fairness. **b** A system of jurisprudence administered by courts of equity as opposed to courts of law, and designed primarily to mitigate the rigors or inadequacies of common law, from which it differs in origin, theory, and methods. **c** A right recognized or enforced by a court of equity. **4.** In business or property, the value remaining in excess of any liability or mortgage. — **Syn.** See JUSTICE. [< F *équité* < L *aequitas* < *aequus* equal]
equity of redemption The equitable right accorded to a mortgagor to redeem his mortgaged premises on payment of the sum due, even though the time appointed for payment has passed.
equiv. Equivalent.
e·quiv·a·lence (i·kwiv'ə·ləns) *n.* **1.** The state of being equivalent or of having equal values. **2.** *Chem.* The property of having equal valence. Also **e·quiv'a·len·cy.**
e·quiv·a·lent (i·kwiv'ə·lənt) *adj.* **1.** Equal in value, force, meaning, effect, etc. **2.** *Geom.* Equal in area, but not identical or congruent. **3.** *Chem.* Having the same valence or the same combining weight. — *n.* **1.** That which is equivalent. **2.** *Chem.* The weight of an element that combines with or displaces 1.008 grams of hydrogen. Abbr. *eq., equiv.* [< LL *aequivalens, -entis,* ppr. of *aequivalere* < L *aequus* equal + *valere* to be worth] — **e·quiv'a·lent·ly** *adv.*
e·quiv·o·cal (i·kwiv'ə·kəl) *adj.* **1.** Having a doubtful meaning; susceptible of varying interpretations; ambiguous. **2.** Of uncertain origin, character, value, etc.; dubious. **3.** Questionable or suspicious: *equivocal* kindness. [< LL *aequivocus* < L *aequus* equal + *vox, vocis* voice] — **e·quiv'o·cal·ly** *adv.* — **e·quiv'o·cal·ness** *n.*
e·quiv·o·cate (i·kwiv'ə·kāt) *v.i.* **·cat·ed, ·cat·ing** To use ambiguous language with intent to mislead or deceive. [< LL *aequivocatus,* pp. of *aequivocare* to call by the same name < *aequivocus.* See EQUIVOCAL.] — **e·quiv'o·ca'tor** *n.*
e·quiv·o·ca·tion (i·kwiv'ə·kā'shən) *n.* **1.** The act of equivocating. **2.** *Logic* A fallacy arising from the use of a word of double meaning. — **e·quiv'o·ca·to'ry** (-kə·tôr'ē, -tō'rē) *adj.*
eq·ui·voque (ek'wə·vōk) *n.* **1.** An ambiguous term or expression; equivocal word or phrase. **2.** A play on words; pun. **3.** A double meaning; ambiguity. Also **eq'ui·voke.** [< F *équivoque* < LL *aequivocus.* See EQUIVOCAL.]
E·quu·le·us (i·kwōō'lē·əs) *n.* A constellation, the Colt. See CONSTELLATION. [< L, dim. of *equus* horse]
er or **e.r.** Earned runs (baseball).
er- Assimilated var. of EN-².
-er¹ *suffix of nouns* **1.** A person or thing that performs the action of the root verb: *maker, reaper.* See -EE (def. 1). **2.** A person concerned with or practicing a trade or profession: *geographer, hatter.* **3.** One who lives in or comes from: *New Yorker, southerner.* **4.** A person, thing, or action related to or characterized by: *three-decker.* ◆ Nouns of agency are generally formed in English by adding *-er* to a verb, as in *leader,* but some such nouns, either borrowed from Latin or on analogy with Latin, have the suffix *-or,* as in *creditor, elevator.* [OE *-ere, -are* < L *-arius, -arium*]
-er² *suffix of nouns* A person or thing connected with: *grocer, jailer.* [< AF *-er,* OF *-ier* < L *-arius, -arium*]
-er³ *suffix* Forming the comparative degree of adjectives and adverbs: *harder, later.* [OE *-ra, -or*]
-er⁴ *suffix* Repeatedly: used in frequentative verbs: *stutter.* [OE *-rian*]
-er⁵ *suffix of nouns* Denoting the action expressed by the root word: *rejoinder, waiver.* [< F *-er,* infinitive ending]
Er *Chem.* Erbium.
E.R. 1. East Riding, Yorkshire. **2.** King Edward (L *Eduardus Rex*) or Queen Elizabeth (L *Elizabeth Regina*).
e·ra (ir'ə, ē'rə) *n.* **1.** An extended period of time reckoned from some fixed point in the past and used as the basis of a chronology: the Christian *era.* **2.** A period of time characterized by certain events, conditions, influences, etc., occurring or existing throughout it: the Elizabethan *era.* **3.** The beginning of a particular period; an epoch: Air flight marks an *era* in history. **4.** *Geol.* A division of geological history of

highest rank: the Cenozoic *era.* See chart for GEOLOGY. [< LL *aera* counters, orig. pl. of L *aes* brass, money]

e·ra·di·ate (i·rā′dē·āt) *v.t. & v.i.* ·**at·ed**, ·**at·ing** To radiate. — **e·ra′di·a′tion** *n.*

e·rad·i·cate (i·rad′ə·kāt) *v.t.* ·**cat·ed**, ·**cat·ing** **1.** To pull up by the roots; root out. **2.** To destroy utterly; extirpate; erase. — **Syn.** See ABOLISH. [< L *eradicatus,* pp. of *eradicare* < *e-* out + *radix -icis* a root] — **e·rad′i·ca·ble** (-kə·bəl) *adj.* — **e·rad′i·ca′tive** *adj.*

e·rad·i·ca·tion (i·rad′ə·kā′shən) *n.* The act of eradicating, or the state of being eradicated; extirpation; extermination.

e·rad·i·ca·tor (i·rad′ə·kā′tər) *n.* One who or that which eradicates; especially, a preparation for removing ink, etc.

e·rase (i·rās′) *v.t.* **e·rased**, **e·ras·ing** **1.** To obliterate, as by scraping or rubbing out; efface. **2.** To remove written or recorded matter from: to *erase* a tape. **3.** *U.S. Slang* To kill. — *v.i.* **4.** To permit or yield to the action of erasing. — **Syn.** See CANCEL. [< L *erasus,* pp. of *eradere* < *e-* out + *radere* to scrape] — **e·ras′a·ble** *adj.*

e·ras·er (i·rā′sər) *n.* Something used for erasing, as a piece of rubber for removing pencil or ink marks, or a piece of felt or cloth for removing chalk marks.

e·ra·sion (i·rā′zhən) *n.* **1.** The act of erasing. **2.** *Surg.* The operation of scraping away diseased material.

E·ras·mus (i·raz′məs), **Desiderius,** 1466?–1536, Dutch theologian, classical scholar and humanist: original name **Geert Geerts** (gerts) or **Gerhard Ger·hards** (ger′härts).

E·ras·tian·ism (i·ras′chən·iz′əm, -tē·ən-) *n.* The doctrine that the church is entirely subservient to the authority of the state. [after Thomas *Erastus,* to whom this doctrine is improperly attributed] — **E·ras′tian** *adj. & n.*

E·ras·tus (i·ras′təs), **Thomas,** 1524–83, German physician and Protestant theologian.

e·ra·sure (i·rā′shər, -zhər) *n.* **1.** The act of erasing, or the state of being erased. **2.** That which is erased. **3.** A mark left on a surface by erasing something.

Er·a·to (er′ə·tō) The Muse of lyric and love poetry.

Er·a·tos·the·nes (er·ə·tos′thə·nēz), 276?–195? B.C., Greek astronomer and geographer at Alexandria.

Er·bil (ir′bil) A town in northern Iraq on the site of ancient Arbela; pop. about 34,000.

er·bi·um (ûr′bē·əm) *n.* A metallic element (symbol Er) of the lanthanide series, found in gadolinite and some other minerals. See ELEMENT. [< NL < (*Ytt*)*erby,* town in Sweden where first found.]

Er·ci·yas Da·ği (er′jē·yäs′ dä·ï′) A mountain in central Turkey; 12,848 ft.: formerly *Erjias Dağı.*

Erck·mann-Cha·tri·an (erk·mǎn′shà·trē·äṅ′)· Pseudonym of **Émile Erckmann,** 1822–99, and **Alexandre Chatrian,** 1826–90, French literary collaborators.

ere (âr) *Archaic & Poetic prep.* Prior to; before in time. — *conj.* **1.** Before. **2.** Sooner than; rather than. [OE *ǣr*]

Er·e·bus (er′ə·bəs) In Greek mythology, a dark region under the earth through which the shades of the dead pass on their way to Hades.

Er·e·bus (er′ə·bəs), **Mount** A volcano on Ross Island, Antarctica; 13,200 ft.

Er·ech·the·um (er′ək·thē′əm) A temple on the Acropolis of Athens, completed about 407 B.C., famous as an example of Ionic architecture. *Greek* **Er′ech·thei′on** (-thī′on).

E·rech·theus (i·rek′thyōōs, -thē·əs) A legendary king of Athens, honored at the Erechtheum.

e·rect (i·rekt′) *v.t.* **1.** To put up (a building, etc.); construct; build. **2.** To assemble the parts of; set up. **3.** To set upright; lift up; raise. **4.** To establish or found: to *erect* an empire. **5.** To work out or formulate, as a theory or system; devise. **6.** To make into; form; constitute: with *into:* The dependency was *erected* into a sovereign state. **7.** *Physiol.* To cause (an organ of the body, etc.) to become upright, especially rigidly. **8.** *Geom.* To draw upon a given base, as a figure. **9.** *Optics* To cause (an inverted image) to become upright. **10.** *Obs.* To exalt. — *v.i.* **11.** *Physiol.* To become rigidly upright, as through an influx of blood. — **Syn.** See ELEVATE. — *adj.* **1.** Marked by a vertical position or posture; not inclined or bent; upright. **2.** Directed or pointed upward. **3.** *Archaic* Elated. **4.** *Archaic* Wideawake; alert. [< L *erectus,* pp. of *erigere* < *e-* out + *regere* to direct] — **e·rect′ly** *adv.* — **e·rect′ness** *n.*

e·rec·tile (i·rek′təl, -til) *adj.* Capable of becoming erected.

e·rec·tion (i·rek′shən) *n.* **1.** The act of erecting, or the state of being erected. **2.** Something erected, as a building. **3.** *Physiol.* **a** The raising up or stiffening of a part through the accumulation of blood in erectile tissue, especially in the penis. **b** The state of being so raised and stiffened.

e·rec·tive (i·rek′tiv) *adj.* Tending to erect.

e·rec·tor (i·rek′tər) *n.* **1.** One who or that which erects. **2.** *Anat.* Any of various muscles that stiffen or hold up a part of the body. Also **e·rect′er.**

ere·long (âr′lông′, -long′) *adv. Archaic & Poetic* Before much time has passed; soon.

er·e·mite (er′ə·mīt) *n.* A hermit or anchorite. [< LL *ere-*

mita < LGk. *eremitēs* < Gk. *erēmia* desert < *erēmos* deserted] — **er·e·mit·ic** (er′ə·mit′ik) or ·**i·cal,** **er′e·mit′ish** (-mī′tish) *adj.*

ere·now (âr′nou′) *adv. Archaic & Poetic* Before this time; heretofore.

er·e·thism (er′ə·thiz′əm) *n. Physiol.* Abnormal excitability or irritability in any part of the body. [< Gk. *erethismos* < *erethizein* to irritate] — **er′e·this′mic** *adj.*

E·re·van (yi·ryi·vän′) See YEREVAN.

ere·while (âr′whīl′) *adv. Archaic & Poetic* Some time ago; heretofore. Also **ere′whiles′.**

Er·furt (er′fŏōrt) A city in SW East Germany; pop. 186,066 (est. 1959).

erg (ûrg) *n. Physics* In the cgs system, the unit of work and of energy, being the work done in moving a body one centimeter against the force of one dyne. Abbr. *e* [< Gk. *ergon* work]

er·gas·to·plasm (er·gas′tə·plaz′əm) *n. Biol.* A netlike system of channels dispersed within the cytoplasm of a living cell, believed to transport fluids within and outside the cell. [< Gk. *ergastos* < *ergazesthai* to work + -PLASM]

er·gate (ûr′gāt) *n. Entomol.* A worker ant. [< Gk. *ergalēs* workman]

er·go (ûr′gō) *conj. & adv. Latin* Hence; therefore.

er·gos·ter·ol (ûr·gos′tə·rōl, -rol) *n. Biochem.* An inert sterol, $C_{28}H_{44}O$, obtained from ergot, yeast, etc., and converted by irradiation of ultraviolet rays into calciferol. [< ERGO(T) + STEROL]

er·got (ûr′gət) *n.* **1.** A fungus (*Claviceps purpurea*) sometimes replacing the grain in rye and other cereal grasses. **2.** The disease caused by this fungus growth. **3.** The dried sclerotia of rye ergot, used in medicine to contract involuntary muscle and to check hemorrhage. [< F < OF *argot* spur of a cock, from the shape of the fungus]

er·got·in·ine (ûr·got′ə·nēn, -nin) *n. Chem.* A crystalline mixture of alkaloids, obtained from ergot.

er·got·ism (ûr′gə·tiz′əm) *n. Pathol.* A diseased condition produced by eating grain affected with ergot or by improper use of ergot drugs.

Er·hard (er′härt), **Ludwig,** born 1897, German statesman; chancellor, 1963–, of the Federal Republic of Germany.

er·i·ca·ceous (er′ə·kā′shəs) *adj. Bot.* Of or relating to the heath family (*Ericaceae*) of plants. [< NL *Ericaceae* < *Erica,* name of a genus < L *erice* heath < Gk. *ereikē*]

Er·ic·son (er′ik·sən), **Leif** Eleventh-century Scandinavian adventurer; son of Eric the Red; probably discovered North America about 1000. Also **Er′ics·son.**

Er·ics·son (er′ik·sən), **John,** 1803–89, U.S. engineer and inventor born in Sweden.

Er·ic the Red (er′ik), born 950?, Scandinavian adventurer; colonizer of Greenland.

E·rid·a·nus (i·rid′ə·nəs) *n.* A constellation, the River, containing the bright star Achernar. See CONSTELLATION. [< L, the Po river]

E·rie (ir′ē) *n.* pl. **E·rie** or **E·ries** One of a tribe of North American Indians of Iroquoian stock, formerly inhabiting the southern shores of Lake Erie.

E·rie (ir′ē) A port city in NW Pennsylvania, on Lake Erie; pop. 129,231.

Erie, Lake The southernmost and fourth largest of the Great Lakes; 241 by 57 mi.; 9,940 sq. mi.

Erie Canal A historic waterway in New York, extending 350 miles from Buffalo to Albany; later made part of the New York State Barge Canal.

E·rig·e·na (i·rij′ə·nə), **Johannes Scotus** Ninth-century Irish philosopher active in France.

e·rig·er·on (i·rij′ə·ron) *n.* Any of a large genus (*Erigeron*) of plants of the composite family, having flowers with numerous white or purple rays. Certain species yield **oil of erigeron,** used as a hemostatic drug. [< L, groundsel < Gk. *ērigerōn* < *ēri* early + *gerōn* old (man); with ref. to the hoary growth on some species]

Er·in (âr′in, ir′in) *Chiefly Poetic* Ireland.

er·i·na·ceous (er′ə·nā′shəs) *adj.* Of or like a hedgehog. [< L *erinaceus* hedgehog]

e·rin·go (i·ring′gō) See ERYNGO.

E·rin·y·es (i·rin′i·ēz) *n.* pl. of **E·rin·ys** (i·rin′is, i·rī′nis) In Greek mythology, the Furies. [< L < Gk. *Erinys*]

E·ris (ir′is, er′is) In Greek mythology, the goddess of discord.

e·ris·tic (e·ris′tik) *adj.* **1.** Relating to controversy. **2.** Prone to dispute; argumentative. — *n.* A person given to controversy. [< Gk. *eristikos* < *eris* strife]

E·ri·tre·a (er′i·trē′ə) A province of Ethiopia; formerly an Italian colony; federated with Ethiopia in 1952; became province in 1962; 45,000 sq. mi.; pop. 1,589,400 (est. 1967); capital, Asmara. — **Er′i·tre′an** *adj. & n.*

E·ri·van (yi·ryi·vän′) See YEREVAN.

Er·ji·as Da·ği (er′jē·yäs′ dä·ï′) See ERCIYAS DAGI.

Er·lang·en (er′läng·ən) A city in north central Bavaria, West Germany; pop. 67,300 (1960).

Er·lang·er (ûr′lang·ər), **Joseph**, 1874–1965, U.S. physiologist and pathologist.

Er·len·mey·er flask (ûr′lən·mī′ər) A conical glass flask with a narrow neck and broad base, used in laboratory work. [after Emil *Erlenmeyer*, 1825–1909, German chemist]

erl·king (ûrl′king′) *n.* In Germanic folklore, an evil spirit, malicious toward children. [< G *erlkönig*, wrong translation of Dan. *ellerkonge, elverkonge* king of the elves]

er·mine (ûr′min) *n.* **1.** One of several weasels (genus *Mustela*) of the northern hemisphere, having brown fur that in winter turns white with a black tip on the tail. See STOAT. **2.** The white fur of the ermine, used in Europe for the facings of the official robes of judges, etc. **3.** The rank or functions of a judge. [< OF *(h)ermine,* ? < Gmc., or perhaps confused with L *(mus) Armenius* Armenian (mouse)]

ERMINE (def. 1)
(Body 9 to 12 inches long; tail 3 to 3½ inches)

er·mined (ûr′mind) *adj.* Wearing or decorated with ermine.

erne (ûrn) *n.* Any of various sea eagles; especially, the gray sea eagle. See under SEA EAGLE. Also **ern.** [OE *earn*]

e·rode (i·rōd′) *v.* **e·rod·ed, e·rod·ing** *v.t.* **1.** To wear away gradually by constant friction; wear down by scraping, rubbing, etc.: rocks *eroded* by the wind. **2.** To eat into; corrode: The acid *eroded* the metal. **3.** To make (a channel, gully, etc.) by wearing away or eating into. — *v.i.* **4.** To become eroded. [< L *erodere* < *e-* off + *rodere* to gnaw]

e·ro·dent (i·rōd′nt) *adj.* Erosive.

e·rog·e·nous (i·roj′ə·nəs) *adj.* Exciting or tending to excite sexual desire Also **e·ro·gen·ic** (er′ə·jen′ik) [< Gk. *erōs* love + -GENOUS]

Er·os (ir′os, er′os) In Greek mythology, the god of love, son of Aphrodite: identified with the Ro nan *Cupid*. — *n.* *Astron.* An asteroid of the sixth magnitude.

e·rose (i·rōs′) *adj.* **1.** Appearing as if gnawed. **2.** *Bot.* Having an irregularly toothed margin as some leaves. [< L *erosus*, pp. of *erodere*. See ERODE.]

e·ro·sion (i·rō′zhən) *n.* **1.** The act of eroding, or the state of being eroded. **2** *Geol* The wearing away of the earth's surface by the action of wind, water. glaciers, etc.

e·ro·sive (i·rō′siv) *adj* **1.** Eroding or tending to erode. **2.** Caustic or corrosive.

e·rot·ic (i·rot′ik) *adj.* **1.** Of, pertaining to, or concerned with sexual love; amatory: an *erotic* poem. **2.** Designed to arouse sexual desire: an *erotic* photograph. **3.** Strongly moved by sexual desire; amorous: an *erotic* individual. — *n.* **1.** An erotic person. **2.** An erotic poem. [< Gk. *erōtikos* < *erōs, -erōtos* love] — **e·rot′i·cal·ly** *adv.*

e·rot·i·ca (i·rot′i·kə) *n.pl.* Erotic pictures, books, etc. [< Gk. *erōtika* neut. pl. of *erōtikos*. See EROTIC.]

e·rot·i·cism (i·rot′ə·siz′əm) *n.* **1.** Erotic tendency or character. **2.** *Psychoanal.* Erotism.

er·o·tism (er′ə·tiz′əm) *n.* *Psychoanal.* Sexual excitement or erotic sensations; also, excessive preoccupation with sex.

e·ro·to·gen·ic (i·rō′tə·jen′ik, i·rot′ə-) *adj.* Erogenous. [< Gk. *erōs, erōt-* love + -GENIC]

e·ro·to·ma·ni·a (i·rō′tə·mā′nē·ə i·rot′ə-) *n.* *Psychiatry* Inordinate sexual desire [< EROS + -MANIA]

err (ûr, er) *v.i.* **erred, err·ing 1.** To make a mistake; be wrong. **2.** To go astray morally; sin. **3.** *Obs.* To wander; stray. [< OF *errer* < L *errare* to wander]

er·ran·cy (er′ən·sē) *n.* **1.** The condition of erring. **2.** Tendency to err.

er·rand (er′ənd) *n.* **1.** A trip made to carry a message or perform some task, usually for someone else. **2.** The business or purpose of such a trip. [OE *ærende* message, news]

er·rant (er′ənt) *adj.* **1.** Roving or wandering, especially in search of adventure; itinerant. **2.** Straying from the proper course or correct standard. **3.** *Obs.* Arrant. [< OF *errant*, ppr. of *errer* to travel < L *iter* journey; confused with OF *errant* < *errer* to wander. See ERR.] — **er′rant·ly** *adv.*

er·rant·ry (er′ənt·rē) *n* The conduct or career of a knight errant; knight-errantry.

er·ra·re hu·ma·num est (e·rä′re hyoo·mä′nəm est, e·rä′rä hyoo·mä′nəm est) *Latin* To err is human.

er·ra·ta (i·rä′tə, i·rä′tə) *n.* Plural of ERRATUM. ◆ *Errata* can be used as a singular to refer to a list of errors and, in this usage, has a regular plural, *erratas*.

er·rat·ic (i·rat′ik) *adj.* **1.** Not conforming to usual standards; irregular; eccentric. **2.** Lacking a fixed or certain course; wandering; straying. **3.** *Geol.* Transported from the original site by glaciers, currents, etc.: *erratic* rocks. — *n.* An erratic person or thing. [< L *erraticus* < *errare* to wander] — **er·rat′i·cal·ly** *adv.*

er·ra·tum (i·rä′təm, i·rā′təm) *n.* *pl.* **·ra·ta** (-rä′tə, -rā′tə) An error, as in writing or printing. [< L]

er·rhine (er′īn, -in) *Med. adj.* Promoting sneezing and nasal discharges. — *n.* An errhine substance used like snuff. [< NL *errhinum* < Gk. *errhinon* < *en-* in + *rhīs, rhīnos* nose]

err·ing (ûr′ing, er′ing) *adj.* **1.** Exhibiting error; mistaken; erroneous. **2.** Morally wrong; sinful. — **err′ing·ly** *adv.*

erron. Erroneous; erroneously.

er·ro·ne·ous (ə·rō′nē·əs e·rō′-) *adj.* Marked by error; incorrect; mistaken. — **er·ro′ne·ous·ly** *adv.* — **er·ro′ne·ous·ness** *n.*

er·ror (er′ər) *n.* **1.** Something done, said, or believed incorrectly; a mistake. **2** The condition of deviating from what is correct or true in judgment, belief, or action. **3.** An offense against morals; sin. **4.** In baseball, a misplay by a member of the team not batting, so designated by the official scorer Abbr. *e, e.* **5.** *Math.* **a** The difference between the observed value of a magnitude and the true or mean value. **b** Any deviation from the true or mean value not due to gross blunders of observation or measurement. **6.** In Christian Science, the contradiction of truth; a belief without understanding. [< OF < L *errare* to wander]
— **Syn. 1.** mistake, blunder. **2.** untruth, falsity, fallacy. **3.** See OFFENSE.

ers (ûrs) *n.* *pl.* **er·ses** (-səz) The bitter vetch. See under VETCH. [< F < L *ervum*]

er·satz (er·zäts′, er′zäts) *adj.* Substitute, and usually inferior: *ersatz* leather. — *n.* A usually inferior substitute. [< G < *ersetzen* to replace]

Erse (ûrs) *n.* **1.** Scottish Gaelic. **2.** Irish Gaelic. — *adj.* Of or pertaining to the Celts of Ireland or Scotland or their language. [Var. of IRISH]

Er·skine (ûr′skin), **John**, 1509–91 Scottish Reformation leader: called **Erskine of Dun.** — **John**, 1879–1951, U.S. educator and writer.

erst (ûrst) *Archaic adv.* **1.** Formerly; long ago. **2.** In the beginning. — *adj.* First. [OE *ærest*, superl. of *ær* before]

erst·while (ûrst′hwīl′) *adj.* Former: an *erstwhile* colleague. — *adv.* Archaic Formerly.

er·u·bes·cence (er′oo·bes′əns) *n.* The process or condition of growing red; redness; blush. [< LL *erubescentia* < L *erubescere* to blush] — **er·u·bes′cent** *adj.*

e·ruct (i·rukt′) *v.t. & v.i* To belch. Also **e·ruc′tate.** [< L *eructare* < *e-* out + *ructare* to belch]

e·ruc·ta·tion (i·ruk′tā′shən, ē′ruk-, er′ək-) *n.* **1.** The act of belching. **2.** That which is belched forth. [< L *eructatus*, pp. of *eructare*. See ERUCT.] — **e·ruc·ta·tive** (i·ruk′tə·tiv) *adj.*

e·ru·dite (er′yoo·dīt, er′oo-) *adj.* Very learned; scholarly. [< L *eruditus*, pp of *erudire* to instruct < *e-* out + *rudis* untrained] — **er′u·dite·ly** *adv.* — **er′u·dite·ness** *n.*

er·u·di·tion (er′yoo·dish′ən, er′oo-) *n* Great learning; scholarship. — **Syn.** See KNOWLEDGE.

e·rum·pent (i·rum′pənt) *adj. Bot.* Bursting forth, as the spore clusters of certain fungi. [< L *erumpens, -entis*, ppr of *erumpere*. See ERUPT.]

e·rupt (i·rupt′) *v.i.* **1.** To cast forth lava, steam, etc., as a volcano or geyser. **2.** To be cast forth from a volcano, geyser, etc., as lava or steam. **3.** To burst forth suddenly and violently: The argument *erupted* into a full-scale riot. **4.** To show a rash or become covered with pimples, etc., as the skin. **5.** Of new teeth, to break through the gums. — *v.t.* **6.** To make erupt. **7.** To cast forth (lava, etc.). [< L *eruptus*, pp. of *erumpere* < *e-* out + *rumpere* to burst]

e·rup·tion (i·rup′shən) *n* **1.** A breaking or bursting forth with violence; an outbreak, as of a disease. **2.** The violent ejection of lava, steam, or other material from a volcano, geyser, etc. **3.** A breaking out, as in a rash; also, the rash or skin affection itself.

e·rup·tive (i·rup′tiv) *adj.* **1.** Breaking out or tending to break out. **2.** Of or like an eruption. **3.** Resulting from or formed by an eruption: *eruptive* rock. **4.** *Pathol.* Pertaining to or attended by a breaking out of the skin: *eruptive* fevers. — *n.* An eruptive rock. — **e·rup′tive·ly** *adv.*

E.R.V. English Revised Version (of the Bible).

Er·vine (ûr′vin), **St. John Greer**, 1883–1971, Irish novelist and playwright.

-ery *suffix of nouns* **1.** A business, place of business, or place where something is done: *brewery*. **2.** A place or residence for: *nunnery*. **3.** A collection of things: *finery pottery*. **4.** The qualities, principles, or practices of: *snobbery* **5.** An art, trade or profession: *cookery*. **6.** A state, or condition of being: *slavery*. Also **-ry**, as in *jewelry*. [< OF *-erie* < *-ier* (< L *-arius*) + *-ie* < L *-ia*. See -ARY, -Y²]

Er·y·man·thi·an (er′ə·man′thē·ən) *adj.* Of or relating to Mount Erymanthus.

Erymanthian Boar In Greek mythology, a savage boar captured alive by Hercules.

Er·y·man·thus (er′ə·man′thəs), **Mount** A mountain between Arcadia and Achaea in Greece; 7,294 ft. *Greek* **Er·y·man·thos** (â·rē′män·thôs).

e·ryn·go (i·ring′gō) *n.* *pl.* **·goes 1.** Any of various coarse herbs (genus *Eryngium*), the roots of which are used in medicine. **2.** *Obs.* The candied root of the sea holly, once thought to be an aphrodisiac. Also spelled *eringo.* [? Alter. of Ital. *eringio* < L *eryngion* < Gk. *ēryggion*, dim. of < *ēryggos*]

er·y·sip·e·las (er′ə·sip′ə·ləs, ir′ə-) *n.* *Pathol.* An acute infectious disease of the skin, accompanied by inflammation, chills, and fever; also called *St. Anthony's fire.* [< NL < Gk. < *erythros* red + *pella* skin] — **er·y·si·pel·a·tous** (er′ə·si·pel′ə·təs, ir′ə-) *adj.*

er·y·sip·e·loid (er′ə·sip′ə·loid, ir′ə-) *n. Pathol.* A localized dermatitis caused by infection with a bacterium.

er·y·the·ma (er′ə·thē′mə) *n. Pathol.* A superficial skin disease or condition characterized by abnormal redness. [< NL < Gk. *erythēma* redness < *erythros* red] — **er′y·them′a·tous** (-them′ə·təs, -thē′mə-), **er·y·the·ma·tic** (-thi·mat′ik), **er′y·the′mic** *adj.*

e·ryth·rism (i·rith′riz·əm) *n.* Abnormal or excessive redness, especially of the plumage and hair of animals. — **er·y·thris·mal** (er′ə·thriz′məl) *adj.*

e·ryth·rite (i·rith′rīt) *n.* A red hydrous cobalt arsenate, found amorphous and also crystallized in the monoclinic system: also called *cobalt bloom.*

erythro- *combining form* Red: *erythrocyte.* Also, before vowels, **erythr-.** [< Gk. *erythros* red]

e·ryth·ro·blast (i·rith′rō·blast) *n. Anat.* One of the nucleated cells in bone marrow, from which the red corpuscles of the blood are developed. — **e·ryth′ro·blas′tic** *adj.*

e·ryth·ro·cyte (i·rith′rō·sīt) *n. Anat.* A red blood cell formed in the red bone marrow and, in all mammals, lacking a nucleus. It contains hemoglobin and transports oxygen to all tissues of the body. — **e·ryth·ro·cyt·ic** (-sit′ik) *adj.*

e·ryth·ro·cy·tom·e·ter (i·rith′rō·sī·tom′ə·tər) *n.* A device for counting the red blood cells.

e·ryth·ro·phyll (i·rith′rō·fil) *n.* Anthocyanin. [< ERYTHRO- + Gk. *phyllon* leaf]

Erz·ge·bir·ge (erts′gə·bir′gə) A mountain range on the German-Czech border; highest peak, Klinovec Mountain, 4,080 ft.

Er·zu·rum (er′zə·rōōm) A Province of NE Turkey; 9,244 sq. mi.; pop. 574,848 (est. 1960); capital, **Erzurum.** Also **Er′ze·rum.**

es- *prefix* Out: used in words borrowed from Old French: *escape, escheat.* It was often later refashioned to *ex-* after Latin, as in *exchange,* formerly *eschange.* [< OF < L *ex-.* See EX-[1].]

-es[1] An inflectional ending used to form the plural of nouns ending in a sibilant (*glasses, fuses, fishes*), an affricate (*witches, judges*), or, in some cases, a vowel. After consonants it represents a separate syllable; after vowels, as in *potatoes,* it represents a mere extension of the final syllable. Compare -S[1]. [OE *-as*]

-es[2] An inflectional ending used to form the third person singular present indicative of verbs ending in a sibilant, affricate, or vowel: *goes, kisses, poaches.* Compare -S[2]. [ME *-es*]

Es *Chem.* Einsteinium.

E·sau (ē′sô) The eldest son of Isaac, who sold his birthright to his brother Jacob. *Gen.* xxv 25. Sometimes called *Edom.* [< Hebrew '*ēsāw* hairy]

ESC Economic and Social Council.

es·ca·drille (es′kə·dril′, *Fr.* es·kà·drē′y′) *n.* **1.** In France, a unit of military airplanes. **2.** A squadron of naval vessels. [< F, dim. of *escadre* squadron; infl. by Sp. *escuadrilla,* dim. of *escuadra* squadron; both ult. < L *ex-* completely + *quadrare* to make square < *quadra* square < *quattuor* four]

es·ca·lade (es′kə·lād′) *v.t.* **·lad·ed, ·lad·ing** To attack and force a way into or over (a fort, rampart, etc.) by means of ladders. — *n.* A military attack to scale ramparts, etc. [< F < Sp. *escalada* < *escalar* to climb < L *scala* ladder]

es·ca·late (es′kə·lāt) *v.t. & v.i.* **·lat·ed, ·lat·ing 1.** To ascend or raise on an escalator. **2.** To increase or be increased gradually, as in size, scope, effort, seriousness, etc.: to *escalate* a war. **3.** To determine the upward trend of material and labor costs in adjusting (price contracts). [Back formation < ESCALATOR] — **es′ca·la′tion** *n.*

es·ca·la·tor (es′kə·lā′tər) *n.* A moving stairway built on the conveyor-belt principle, used in stores, railroad stations, etc. [< ESCALA(DE)· + -(ELEVA)TOR]

escalator clause *U.S.* A clause in a contract stipulating an increase or decrease in wages, prices, etc., under certain specified conditions.

es·cal·lop (e·skol′əp, e·skal′-) *n.* Scallop. — *v.t.* To scallop.

es·ca·pade (es′kə·pād) *n.* **1.** A brief piece of reckless behavior or prankish disregard of convention; fling; spree. **2.** An act of getting away from rigid restraint or confinement. [< F < Sp. *escapada* < *escapar* to escape]

es·cape (ə·skāp′, e·skāp′) *v.* **·caped, ·cap·ing** *v.i.* **1.** To get free from confinement, restraint, or capture; get away: to *escape* from prison; to *escape* from pursuers. **2.** To manage to avoid or remain untouched by some imminent or present evil: to *escape* from being injured. **3.** To come out gradually from a container or enclosure, as by seeping, leaking, etc.: Fumes *escaped* from the pipe. **4.** To fade away and disappear; vanish: All remembrance of him had *escaped* from her mind. **5.** *Bot.* To grow wild, as a newly introduced plant. — *v.t.* **6.** To break out of (prison, etc.) or break free from (captors, etc.); get away from. **7.** To succeed in avoiding (capture, harm, etc.); manage to miss or sidestep. **8.** To get away from the notice, observation, or recollection of; slip by: No detail *escaped* him. **9.** To slip

out from inadvertently or unintentionally: A cry *escaped* his lips. — *n.* **1.** The act of escaping, or the fact of having escaped; successful flight. **2.** A means of escaping reality, boredom, etc.: Drinking is an *escape* for him. **3.** Gradual emergence, as by leaking or seeping: an *escape* of gas. **4.** *Bot.* A plant growing wild after being cultivated. — *adj.* **1.** That provides a means of getting away from reality, etc.; escapist: *escape* literature. **2.** That provides a means of lessening or avoiding liability, etc.: an *escape* clause in a contract. [< AF *escaper* < L *ex-* out + *cappa* cloak] — **es·cap′a·ble** *adj.* — **es·cap′er** *n.*

— **Syn.** (verb) **1, 2.** *Escape, flee, fly, decamp,* and *abscond* mean to run away. To *escape* is to depart from a dangerous place or situation. *Flee* and *fly* refer to sudden and hasty departure. *Decamp* suggests a strategic withdrawal to avoid capture, arrest, embarrassment, etc., and is often applied humorously to petty intrigues. To *abscond* is to depart secretly, especially to escape the consequences of wrongdoing. **6, 7.** *Escape, elude, evade, avoid, shun,* and *eschew* agree in meaning to get away from or keep away from. We *escape* confinement or circumstances that threaten our safety. We *elude* a pursuer by cunning or wiliness; in extended uses, ideas or words may *elude* the mind. An unpleasant encounter is *evaded* by clever, adroit maneuvering. *Escape, elude,* and *evade* imply a sense of urgency in the face of present or imminent danger; this implication is lacking in *avoid, shun,* and *eschew.* To *avoid* is to stay away from, with or without awareness, and with no imputation of good or bad motives. *Shun* implies avoidance due to aversion, and *eschew* implies prudence or moral principles.

escape cock *Mech.* **1.** A cock or bearing in a watch to support the escape wheel. **2.** A cock or faucet in an engine cylinder to draw off condensed steam.

es·cap·ee (es′kā·pē′, ə·skā′pē, e·skā′pē) *n.* One who has escaped, as from prison.

escape hatch A means of emergency exit, as from an aircraft or submarine.

escape lung A flexible bag containing oxygen and an adsorbent, connected to a tightly fitting mask so as to permit underwater respiration, and used especially in escaping from submarines.

escape mechanism *Psychoanal.* A defense mechanism (which see).

es·cape·ment (ə·skāp′mənt, e·skāp′-) *n.* **1.** *Mech.* A device used in timepieces for securing a uniform movement, consisting of an escape wheel and a detent or lock, through which periodical impulses are imparted to the balance wheel. **2.** A typewriter mechanism controlling or regulating the horizontal movement of the carriage. **3.** *Rare* The act of escaping, or a means of escape.

escape velocity *Physics* The minimum velocity that allows a body to escape from a gravitational field without further propulsion, about 7 miles per second from the earth's surface. See table for PLANET.

escape wheel *Mech.* A toothed wheel in an escapement: also called *scape wheel.* For illustration see ESCAPEMENT, PENDULUM.

ESCAPEMENT OF A WATCH

a Anchor. *l* lever or fork. *ip* Impulse pallet. *r* Roller. *ew* Escape wheel. *lp* Locking pallet

es·cap·ism (ə·skā′piz·əm, e·skā′-) *n.* **1.** A desire or tendency to escape unpleasant reality by resorting to diversions, or by indulging in daydreaming. **2.** Behavior marked by or originating from this desire or tendency. — **es·cap·ist** (ə·skā′pist, e·skā′-) *adj.* Catering to or providing a means of indulging in escapism: *escapist* literature. — *n.* One given to escapism.

es·car·got (es·kàr·gō′) *n. French* An edible snail.

es·ca·role (es′kə·rōl) *n.* A variety of endive whose leaves are used for salads. [< F < ML *escariola* < *escarius* fit for eating < *esca* food < *edere* to eat]

es·carp (e·skärp′) *n.* A steep slope; an escarpment or scarp; especially, the inner wall or side of the ditch at the foot of a rampart: distinguished from *counterscarp.* — *v.t.* **1.** To cause to slope steeply. **2.** To provide with an escarp or escarpment. [< F *escarpe* < Ital. *scarpa* a scarp]

es·carp·ment (es·kärp′mənt) *n.* **1.** A precipitous artificial slope about a fortification or position. **2.** A steep slope or drop; especially, the precipitous face of a line of cliffs.

Es·caut (es·kō′) The French name for the SCHELDT.

-esce *suffix of verbs* To become or grow; begin to be or do (what is indicated by the main element): *phosphoresce.* [< L *-escere,* suffix of inceptive verbs]

-escence *suffix of nouns* Forming nouns of state or quality corresponding to adjectives in *-escent: effervescence.* [< L *-escentia*]

-escent *suffix of adjectives* Beginning to be, have, or do (what is indicated by the main element): *effervescent.* [< L *-escens, -escentis,* suffix of ppr. of inceptive verbs]

esch·a·lot (esh′ə·lot, esh′ə·lot′) *n.* A shallot. [< F *eschalotte,* dim. of *eschalogne* onion. See SCALLION.]

es·char (es′kär) *n. Med.* A hard, dry scab or slough that forms over skin tissue injured by burning or by a corrosive or caustic substance. [< L *eschara* < Gk. *eschara* hearth]

es·cha·rot·ic (es/kə·rot/ik) *Med. adj.* Able to destroy living tissue and form an eschar; corrosive or caustic. — *n.* A corrosive or caustic drug, etc.

es·cha·tol·o·gy (es/kə·tol/ə·jē) *n.* The branch of theology that treats of death, judgment, and the future state of the soul. [< Gk. *eschatos* last + -LOGY] — **es/cha·to·log/i·cal** (-tə·loj/i·kal) *adj.* — **es/cha·tol/o·gist** *n.*

es·cheat (es·chēt/) *Law n.* **1.** Reversion of property to the state or to the crown in default of legal heirs or other qualified claimants. **2.** Reversion of lands to a feudal lord in default of heirs or service. **3.** Property entering possession of the state, etc., by this process. **4.** The right of the state, etc., to take possession of property in default of legal heirs or other qualified claimants. — *v.i. & v.t.* To revert or cause to revert to the state, etc., by escheat. [< OF *eschete, escheoite* < *escheoir* < *es-* out (< L *ex-*) + *cheoir* < L *cadere* to fall] — **es·cheat/a·ble** *adj.*

es·cheat·age (es·chē/tij) *n. Law* Escheat (def. 4).

Esch·en·bach (esh/ən·bäkh), **Wolfram von** See WOLFRAM VON ESCHENBACH.

es·chew (es·chōō/) *v.t.* To shun, as something unworthy or injurious. — **Syn.** See ESCAPE. [< OF *eschiver,* ult. < Gmc. Akin to SHY[1].] — **es·chew/al** *n.*

Es·co·ri·al (es·kôr/ē·əl, -kō/rē-; *Sp.* es/kō·ryäl/) A huge structure comprising a monastery, church, and royal residence, built by Philip II in the 16th century; 27 mi. NW of Madrid. Also **Es·cu·ri·al** (es·kyŏor/ē·əl).

es·cort (*n.* es/kôrt; *v.* es·kôrt/) *n.* **1.** An individual or group of individuals accompanying another so as to give protection or guidance or out of courtesy, respect, etc.; especially, a male who takes a girl or woman to a dance, party, etc. **2.** A guard accompanying persons or property in transit. **3.** One or more planes, ships, cars, etc., moving along with another so as to give protection, guidance, or help, or as a mark of honor to some personage. **4.** Vigilant protection or safeguard: to travel under *escort.* — *v.t.* To accompany in the capacity of an escort. — **Syn.** See ACCOMPANY. [< F *escorte* < Ital. *scorta* < *scorgere* to lead < L *ex-* out + *corrigere.* See CORRECT.]

es·cri·toire (es/kri·twär/) *n.* A writing desk. [< OF < LL *scriptorium* place for writing. Doublet of SCRIPTORIUM.]

es·crow (es/krō, es·krō/) *n. Law* A written deed, contract, etc., placed in the custody of a third party and effective when delivered by the third party to the grantee upon fulfillment of a stipulated condition. **2.** The condition of being an escrow: a bond in *escrow.* [< AF *escrowe,* OF *escroe* scroll < Gmc.]

es·cu·do (es·kōō/dō; *Pg.* ish·kōō/thōō; *Sp.* es·kōō/thō) *n. pl.* **·dos** (-dōz; *Pg.* -thōōs; *Sp.* -thōs) **1.** The monetary unit of Portugal, containing 100 centavos. **2.** The monetary unit of Chile. **3.** An obsolete Spanish silver coin equal to ten reals. [< Pg. < L *scutum* shield]

Es·cu·la·pi·an (es/kyōō·lā/pē·ən) See AESCULAPIAN.

es·cu·lent (es/kyə·lənt) *adj.* Suitable for food; edible. — *n.* Anything suitable for food; especially, an edible plant; vegetable. [< L *esculentus* < *esca* food < *edere* to eat]

es·cutch·eon (i·skuch/ən) *n.* **1.** *Heraldry* A usually shield-shaped surface carrying armorial bearings; also, a shield whose surface carries armorial bearings. **2.** An ornamented plate about a keyhole, or one to which a door knocker is attached. **3.** *Naut.* The part of a ship's stern on which the name is inscribed. Also *scutcheon.* — **a blot on one's escutcheon** Something that detracts from one's honor or reputation. [< AF *escuchon* < L *scutum* shield]

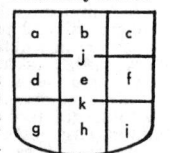

ESCUTCHEON
a Dexter chief.
b Middle chief.
c Sinister chief.
d Dexter flank.
e Fess point.
f Sinister flank.
g Dexter base.
h Middle base.
i Sinister base.
j Honor point.
k Nombril point.

Esd. Esdras.

Es·dra·e·lon (ez/drə·ē/lən) See (Plain of) JEZREEL.

Es·dras (ez/drəs) The Douai Bible name for EZRA. — *n.* In the Douai Bible, either of two books of the Old Testament. I Esdras corresponds to the book of Ezra, and II Esdras corresponds to the book of Nehemiah. [< Gk. See EZRA.]

-ese *suffix of nouns and adjectives* **1.** A native or inhabitant of: *Milanese.* **2.** The language or dialect of: *Chinese.* **3.** Originating in; denoting the inhabitants or language of: *Tirolese.* **4.** The manner or style of: *journalese.* [< OF *-eis, -ese* < L *-ensis*]

ESE or **ese, E.S.E.,** or **e.s.e.** East-southeast.

E·se·nin (yi·syä/nyin) **Sergei Aleksandrovich,** 1895-1925, Russian poet.

es·er·ine (es/ə·rēn, -rin) *n.* Physostigmine.

E·sher (ē/shər) An urban district in NE Surrey, England; pop. 60,586 (1961).

Esk. Eskimo.

es·ker (es/kər) *n. Geol.* A ridge of roughly stratified gravel and sand, probably deposited by a subglacial stream: also called *os.* Also **es·kar** (es/kär -kər). [< Irish *eiscir* ridge]

Es·ki·mo (es/kə·mō) *n. pl.* **·mos** or **·mo** **1.** One of a Mongoloid people indigenous to the Arctic coasts of North America, Greenland, and NE Siberia. **2.** The language of the Eskimos, belonging to the Eskimo-Aleut family. — *adj.* Of or relating to the Eskimos, their language, or their culture. Also spelled *Esquimau.* [< Dan. (< F *Esquimaux*) < N. Am. Ind., eaters of raw flesh]

Es·ki·mo-A·le·ut (es/kə·mō·al/ē·ōōt) *n.* A family of languages spoken along the shores of Greenland, the coasts of Labrador, in the Hudson Bay area, along the Arctic coast of North America, in western and northern Alaska the Chukchi peninsula of NE Siberia, and the Aleutian Islands.

Es·ki·mo·an (es/kə·mō/ən) *adj.* Eskimo. Also **Es/ki·mau/an.**

Eskimo dog One of a breed of large, sturdy, broad-chested dogs used by the Eskimos to draw sledges

Es·ki·şe·hir (es/kē·she·hir/) A Province of west central Turkey; 5,245 sq. mi.; pop. 389,129 (1960); capital, Eskişehir. Also **Es/ki·she·hir/.**

e·soph·a·gus (i·sof/ə·gəs) *n. pl.* **·gi** (-jī) *Anat.* The tube in animals through which food passes from the mouth to the stomach; gullet: also spelled *oesophagus.* For illustration see MOUTH, THROAT. [< NL < Gk *oisophagos* < *oisein* fut. for *pherein* to carry + *phagein* to eat] — **e·so·phag·e·al** (ē/sō·faj/ē·əl, i·sof/ə·jē/əl) or **e·soph/a·gal** (-ə·gəl) *adj.*

es·o·ter·ic (es/ə·ter/ik) *adj.* **1.** Understood by or meant for only a few specially instructed or initiated individuals: *esoteric* doctrine: opposed to *exoteric.* **2.** Lying beyond ordinary comprehension; abstruse: an *esoteric* treatise. **3.** Not openly admitted or publicized; kept secret: an *esoteric* motive. — **Syn.** See MYSTERIOUS. [< Gk. *esōterikos* inner < *esōterō,* compar. of *esō* inside] — **es/o·ter/i·cal·ly** *adv.*

es·o·ter·i·ca (es/ə·ter/ə·kə) *n. pl.* Esoteric ideas, matters, or things.

esp. or **espec.** Especially.

ESP Extrasensory perception.

es·pa·drille (es/pə·dril/) *n.* A sandal having a canvas upper part and a rubber or twisted-rope sole. [< F < Provençal *espardilho,* dim. of *espart.* See ESPARTO]

es·pal·ier (es·pal/yər) *n.* **1.** A trellis or other flat framework or surface on which small fruit trees, shrubs, etc., are trained to grow flattened out. **2.** A tree or row of plants trained to grow flat on a trellis, etc. — *v.t.* To train on or furnish with an espalier, as small trees. [< F < Ital. *spalliera* < *spalla* shoulder < L *spatula*]

Es·pa·ña (es·pä/nyä) The Spanish name for SPAIN.

Es·par·te·ro (es/pär·tā/rō) **Baldomero,** 1792-1879, Spanish statesman and general; premier 1854-56.

es·par·to (es·pär/tō) *n.* A hardy, perennial, rushlike grass (genera *Lygeum* and *Stipa*) of sandy regions in northern Africa and southern Spain, used for weaving and for making paper. Also **esparto grass** [< Sp. < L *spartum* < Gk. *sparton* fiber rope < *spartos* Spanish broom]

es·pe·cial (es·pesh/əl) *adj.* **1.** Preeminent in place or degree; very special: an *especial* friend. **2.** Belonging or relating to one particular person or thing in a very special way: in his *especial* case. ◆ *Especial* has generally the same senses as *special,* but it is sometimes preferred when emphasis is placed on the idea of preeminence or of individuality. Unlike *special,* which may be used attributively or predicatively, *especial* is now always attached to the noun it qualifies. [< OF < L *specialis* < *species* kind, type]

es·pe·cial·ly (es·pesh/əl·ē) *adv.* To a very special extent or degree; particularly; especially frequent; especially good.

Es·pe·ran·to (es/pə·rän/tō, -ran/tō) *n.* An artificial language invented in 1887 by Dr. L. Zamenhof, a Russian scholar, having a vocabulary based on words in the major European languages and a simple, regularized phonetic and inflectional system. [after Dr. *Esperanto,* pseudonym of the inventor < Sp. *esperanza* hope] — **Es/pe·ran/tist** *n.*

es·pi·al (es·pī/əl) *n.* **1.** The act of catching sight of or noticing something, or the fact of being seen or noticed. **2.** The act of spying upon; secret observation. [< OF *espiaille* < *espier.* See ESPY.]

es·piè·gle (es·pye/gl/) *adj French* Roguish; playful.

es·piè·gle·rie (es·pye·glə·rē/) *n. French* Roguishness; playfulness.

es·pi·o·nage (es/pē·ə·nij/, -näzh/; *Fr.* es·pyô·näzh/) *n.* **1.** The practice of spying. **2.** The work of spies. [< F *espionnage* < *espier* to spy]

Es·pí·ri·to San·to (is·pē/rē·tōō sun/tōō) A State in eastern Brazil; 15,281 sq. mi.; pop. 964,000 (est. 1958); capital Vitória.

Es·pí·ri·tu San·to (es·pē/rē·tōō sän/tō) The largest island of the New Hebrides group; 1,875 sq. mi.; formerly *Marina.*

es·pla·nade (es/plə·nād/, -näd/) *n.* **1.** A level, open stretch of land, as along a shore, used especially as a public walk. **2.** An open embankment or level area before a fortress, designed to expose attackers. [< F < Sp. *esplanada* < *esplanar* to level < L *explanare* < *ex-* out + *planus* level]

es·pou·sal (es·pou/zəl) *n.* **1.** Adoption or support, as of a cause. **2.** A betrothal. **3.** *Often pl.* A marriage ceremony.

es·pouse (es·pouz/) *v.t.* **·poused, ·pous·ing** **1.** To make one's own; support, as a cause or doctrine. **2.** To take as ao spouse; marry. **3.** To give in marriage. [< OF *espouser* < L *sponsare* < *sponsus*. See SPOUSE.] **—es·pous′er** *n.*

es·pres·so (es·pres′ō) *n. pl.* **·sos** Coffee brewed from darkly roasted, finely pulverized beans by steam pressure and served in a demitasse cup. [< Ital. (*caffè*) *espresso*]

es·prit (es·prē′) *n.* Spirit; wit. [< F < L *spiritus*]

esprit de corps (də kôr) *French* A spirit of enthusiastic devotedness to and support of the common goals of a group to which one belongs.

es·py (es·pī′) *v.t.* **·pied, ·py·ing** To catch sight of (something distant or hidden); see; descry. [< OF *espier* < Gmc. Cf. L *specere* to look.]

Esq. or **Esqr.** Esquire.

-esque *suffix of adjectives* Having the manner or style of; resembling; like: *picturesque, arabesque*. [< F < Ital. *-esco* < L *-iscus*, ? ult. < Gmc. Cf. E *-ish*.]

Es·qui·line (es′kwə·lïn) *n.* One of the Seven Hills of Rome.

Es·qui·mau (es′kə·mō) *n. pl.* **·maux** (-mōz) Var. of ESKIMO.

es·quire (es·kwïr′; *for n., also* es′kwïr) *n.* **1.** A title of courtesy or respect sometimes used to replace *Mr.* or *Dr.* and written abbreviated and capitalized after a man's surname: John Smith, *Esq.* **2.** In England, a man ranking just below a knight. **3.** A squire; especially: **a** A young candidate for knighthood, who served a medieval knight as his attendant. **b** *Rare* A male escort. **c** *Archaic* A country gentleman. **—** *v.t. Rare* To accompany (a girl or woman) as an escort; squire. [< OF *esquier* < LL *scutarius* shield-bearer < L *scutum* shield]

ess (es) *n.* **1.** The letter *S.* **2.** Something shaped like an *S.* [< L *es* letter *s*]

-ess *suffix* Used to form the feminine of many nouns: *goddess, lioness.* [< F *-esse* < LL *-issa* < Gk.]

Ess. Essex.

es·say (*n. def. 1* es′ā; *n. defs. 2 and 3* es′ā, e·sā′; *v.* e·sā′) *n.* **1.** A short composition dealing with a single topic and typically personal in approach. **2.** An attempt to get something done; endeavor. **3.** A tentative trying out or testing of something; trial. **—** *v.t.* **1.** To attempt to do or accomplish; try. **2.** To test the nature, quality, etc., of; try out. [< OF *essai*. Doublet of ASSAY.] **—es·say′er** *n.*

es·say·ist (es′ā·ist) *n.* **1.** A writer of essays. **2.** *Rare* One who makes an attempt.

Es·sen (es′ən) A city in North Rhine-Westphalia, West Germany; pop. 704,769 (est. 1970).

Es·sen (es′ən) **Count Hans Henrik,** 1755–1824, Swedish field marshal and statesman.

es·sence (es′əns) *n.* **1.** That which makes something what it is; that in which the real nature of a thing consists; intrinsic or fundamental nature. **2.** The distinctive quality or qualities of something. **3.** *Philos.* That in which the attributes of something inhere; substance. **4.** An existent being; especially, an immaterial being; spirit. **5.** An extract, as of a plant or food, containing the distinctive properties of the plant, etc., in concentrated form. **6.** An alcoholic solution of an extract derived from a plant, etc.; especially, an alcoholic solution of a volatile oil. **7.** A perfume. [< F < L *essentia* < *esse* to be]

Es·sene (es′ēn, e·sēn′) *n.* A member of an ancient Jewish sect that existed from about the second century B.C. to about the second century A.D. and that stressed rigorous asceticism and a distinctive kind of mysticism. [< L *Esseni* < Gk. *Essēnoi* ? < Hebrew *şenü′m* the humble, pious ones] **— Es·se·ni·an** (e·sē′nē·ən), **Es·sen·ic** (e·sen′ik) *adj.*

es·sen·tial (ə·sen′shəl) *adj.* **1.** Of, belonging to, or constituting the intrinsic nature of something; fundamental and inherent; basic: the *essential* qualities of an intelligent being. **2.** That cannot be done without or disregarded; extremely important; vital; indispensable: an *essential* need. **3.** Derived from or having the nature of the extract of a plant, etc.: an *essential* oil. **4.** Fulfilled, realized, or existent to the greatest possible extent; complete, total, or absolute: afflicted with *essential* poverty. **— Syn.** See INHERENT, NECESSARY. **—** *n.* Something fundamental, indispensable, or extremely important. [< LL *essentialis* < L *essentia*. See ESSENCE.] **—es·sen′tial·ly** *adv.*

es·sen·ti·al·i·ty (ə·sen′shē·al′ə·tē) *n. pl.* **·ties** **1.** The state or quality of being essential. **2.** Something essential.

essential oil Any of a group of volatile oils that give to plants their characteristic odors, etc., and that are used in the making of perfumes and flavors.

Es·se·qui·bo (es′ə·kwē′bō) A river in British Guiana flowing about 600 miles north to the Atlantic.

Es·sex (es′iks) **1.** A county of SE England; 1,528 sq. mi.; pop. 1,397,840 (1976); county seat, Chelmsford. **2.** An unincorporated place in northern Maryland, a suburb of Baltimore; pop. 38,193.

Es·sex (es′iks), **Earl of,** 1567?–1601, Robert Devereux, English courtier; favorite of Elizabeth I; beheaded.

Esh Sham (esh shäm) An Arabic name for DAMASCUS.

es·so·nite (es′ə·nīt) *n.* A variety of grossularite, yellow to brown in color: also called *cinnamon stone, hessonite.* [< Gk.

hēssōn lesser, inferior + -ITE[1]; because it is softer than some similar minerals]

est. **1.** Established. **2.** Estate. **3.** Estimated. **4.** Estuary.

-est[1] *suffix* Forming the superlative degree of adjectives and adverbs: *hardest, latest.* [OE *-ast, -est, -ost*]

-est[2] An archaic inflectional ending used in the second person singular present and past indicative, with *thou*: *eatest, walkest.* Also, in contracted forms, *-st,* as in *hast, didst.* [OE *-est, -ast*]

Est. Estonia.

EST or **E.S.T.** or **e.s.t.** Eastern standard time.

estab. Established.

es·tab·lish (ə·stab′lish) *v.t.* **1.** To make secure, stable, or permanent; fix firmly in a particular place or condition. **2.** To set up, found, or institute on a firm or lasting basis: to *establish* a government, colony, or business. **3.** To cause to be securely or permanently settled in a particular place, position, occupation, etc.; install: to *establish* oneself in a new home. **4.** To introduce (a law, custom, practice, etc.) and gain lasting acceptance for; initiate and cause to last: to *establish* a precedent. **5.** To cause to be widely or unquestioningly recognized and accepted: to *establish* oneself as a writer. **6.** To clear from doubt; demonstrate convincingly; prove: to *establish* one's innocence. **7.** To find out, figure out, or make clear from available evidence: They were unable to *establish* where she had been. **8.** To cause to be the official church or religion of a state or nation. **9.** In card games, to get control of (a particular suit) so that all subsequent tricks can be won. **— Syn.** See CONFIRM. [< OF *establiss-,* stem of *establir* < L *stabilire* < *stabilis*. See STABLE[1].] **—es·tab′lish·er** *n.*

established church A church, as the Church of England, recognized by a government and supported in part by public funds: also called *national church.* Abbr. *E.C.*

es·tab·lish·ment (ə·stab′lish·mənt) *n.* **1.** The act of establishing, or the state or fact of being established. **2.** Something established; as: **a** The place of business or the staff of a firm. **b** A residence, institution, etc., or the persons living or working there. **c** *Usually cap.* An established church. **d** An established government, social order, colony, etc. **e** An organized civil, military, or naval force. **3.** A secure position in life, business, marriage, etc. **4.** A regular income or allowance that assures security. **— the Establishment** Those collectively who occupy positions of influence and status in a society.

Es·taing (des·tan′), **Comte d′,** 1729–94, **Jean Baptiste Charles Hector,** French military and naval commander; active in the American Revolution.

es·ta·mi·net (es·tá·mē·nā′) *n. French* A café.

es·tan·cia (es·tän′syä) *n. SW U.S.* A large estate or cattle ranch. [< Sp.]

es·tate (ə·stāt′) *n.* **1.** A usually extensive piece of landed property or the residence built on it: a country *estate.* **2.** One's entire property and possessions; fortune: especially, the property and possessions of a deceased person or of a bankrupt. **3.** A particular condition or state, as with regard to the extent of one's wealth or to the degree of one's rank, social standing, etc.: to rise to high *estate.* **4.** A notably high degree of rank or prosperity in life; high station: a man of *estate.* **5.** A particular stage of development in life: to arrive at man's *estate.* **6.** A particular class of persons with distinct political or social status, rights, and powers in a nation; especially, one of the Estates of the Realm. **7.** *Law* The degree, nature, and extent of interest to which one is lawfully entitled with regard to the ownership or use of property; rights of ownership and disposal. **8.** *Archaic* Pomp; display. Abbr. *est.* **— Syn.** See CLASS. **—** *v.t.* **·stat·ed, ·stat·ing** *Archaic* To set up in or as in an estate. [< OF *estat* < L *status.* See STATE.]

Estates-General The States-General (def. 3).

Estates of the Realm The clergy, nobility, and common people, the three principal social and political classes in Europe, especially in medieval and early modern times.

Es·te (es′tā) An Italian noble family of Modena and Ferrara, notably Niccolò d'Este III, 1393–1441; **Lionello d'Este,** 1407–50, and his brothers, **Borso,** 1413–71, and **Ercole,** 1431–1505; **Beatrice,** 1475–97, and her sister, **Isabella,** 1474–1539, daughters of Ercole.

es·teem (ə·stēm′) *v.t.* **1.** To have a high opinion of; look upon with appreciation or respect; value greatly: to *esteem* their efforts. **2.** To think of as; regard as; rate: to *esteem* the project worthwhile. **—** *n.* **1.** High regard or respect; great appreciation: to have *esteem* for a person. **2.** Judgment; opinion: It is worth little in his *esteem.* [< F *estimer* < L *aestimare* to value]

— Syn. (verb) **1.** appreciate, prize, value. See ADMIRE. **—** (noun) **1.** admiration, favor, honor.

es·ter (es′tər) *n. Chem.* Any of a class of organic compounds formed by the reaction of an acid with an alcohol, with the elimination of water. [Coined by Leopold Gmelin, 1788–1853, German chemist]

---

es·ter·ase (es′tə·rās) *n. Biochem.* A hydrolytic enzyme that accelerates the decomposition of esters, as lipase.

Es·ter·ha·zy (es·ter·a·zē′), **Marie Charles Ferdinand Walsin**, 1847–1923, French army officer; forged evidence against Alfred Dreyfus.

es·ter·i·fy (es·ter′ə·fī) *v.t. & v.i.* **·fied, ·fy·ing** To make or change into an ester. — **es·ter′i·fi·ca′tion** *n.*

Es·tes Park (es′tēz) A resort town in northern Colorado; headquarters of Rocky Mountain National Park; pop. 1,616.

Esth. Esther.

Es·ther (es′tər) In the Old Testament, the Jewish queen, wife of King Ahasuerus (Xerxes) of Persia, who saved her people from massacre. — *n.* A book of the Old Testament containing her story. [< Hebrew *ester*, ? < Babylonian]

es·the·sia (es·thē′zhə, -zhē·ə) *n.* The ability to experience sensation; sensibility: also spelled *aesthesia.* [< NL < Gk. *aisthēsis* perception < *aisthanesthai* to perceive]

es·the·sis (es·thē′sis) *n. pl.* **·ses** (-sēz) Esthesia: also spelled *aesthesis.*

es·thete (es′thēt) *n.* **1.** One who is very responsive to and deeply appreciative of beauty in art, nature, etc **2.** One who habitually cultivates and displays an extravagant, usually artificial admiration for beauty and art. Also, *Brit.*, *aesthete.* [< Gk. *aisthētēs* one who perceives]

es·thet·ic (es·thet′ik) *adj.* **1.** Of or relating to esthetics. **2.** Of or relating to the beauty in art, nature, etc. **3.** Keenly responsive to and appreciative of beauty in art, nature, etc.; artistic. Also spelled *aesthetic:* also **es·thet′i·cal.** [< Gk. *aisthētikos* perceptive] — **es·thet′i·cal·ly** *adv.*

es·the·ti·cian (es′thə·tish′ən) *n.* A specialist in or devotee of esthetics: also spelled *aesthetician.*

es·thet·i·cism (es·thet′ə·siz′əm) *n.* **1.** A particular theory or outlook relating to the nature and forms of beauty. **2.** The assumption that esthetic values outweigh other considerations in importance. **3.** The principles or spirit of an esthete or of a group of esthetes. **4.** Keen responsiveness to and appreciation of beauty in art, etc. Also spelled *aestheticism.*

es·thet·ics (es·thet′iks) *n.pl.* (construed as *sing.*) **1.** A branch of philosophy relating to the nature and forms of beauty especially as found in the fine arts. **2.** Study of the mental and emotional responses to the beauty in art, etc. Also spelled *aesthetics.*

Es·tho·ni·a (es·tō′nē·ə, -thō′-) See ESTONIA.

Es·tienne (es·tyen′) A family prominent in the early history of French printing and publishing, especially **Henri**, 1460?–1520, and his sons, **François**, 1502–50?, **Robert**, 1503–59, and **Charles**, 1504?–64. Also *Étienne.*

es·ti·ma·ble (es′tə·mə·bəl) *adj.* **1.** Deserving to be esteemed; worthy of respect or admiration· *estimable* qualities. **2.** That may be estimated or calculated: *estimable* costs. — **es′ti·ma·ble·ness** *n.* — **es′ti·ma·bly** *adv.*

es·ti·mate (*v.* es′tə·māt; *n.* es′tə·mit) *v.* **·mat·ed, ·mat·ing** *v.t.* **1.** To form an approximate opinion of (size, amount, number, etc.). **2.** To form an opinion about; judge. — *v.i.* **3.** To make or submit an estimate. — *n.* **1.** A rough calculation based on opinion or incomplete data. **2.** A preliminary statement, as by a builder, etc., of the approximate cost for certain work. **3.** A judgment or opinion. [< L *aestimatus*, pp. of *aestimare* to value] — **es′ti·ma′tor** *n.*
— **Syn.** (verb) 1. rate, assess, assay, appraise, evaluate.

es·ti·ma·tion (es′tə·mā′shən) *n.* **1.** The act of estimating. **2.** A conclusion arrived at by estimating. **3.** Esteem; regard: I hold him in high *estimation.*

es·ti·ma·tive (es′tə·mā′tiv) *adj.* **1.** Capable of estimating. **2.** Relating to or based on an estimate.

Es·ti·mé (es·tē·mā′) **Dumarsais**, 1900–53, Haitian politician; president 1946–50.

e·stip·u·late (es·tē·mā′) *adj.* See EXSTIPULATE.

es·ti·val (es′tə·vəl, es·tī′-) *adj.* Of or pertaining to summer; appearing in summer· also spelled *aestival.* [< LL *aestivalis* < L *aestas* summer]

es·ti·vate (es′tə·vāt) *v.i.* **·vat·ed, ·vat·ing** **1.** To pass the summer. **2** To pass the summer in a dormant state: said of certain animals. Compare HIBERNATE. Also spelled *aestivate.* [< L *aestivatus*, pp. of *aestivare* to spend the summer < *aestas* summer] — **es′ti·va′tor** *n.*

es·ti·va·tion (es′tə·vā′shən) *n.* **1.** The act of estivating. **2.** *Zool.* The dormant condition of certain animals in summer. **3.** *Bot.* The arrangement of the parts of a flower in the bud. Also spelled *aestivation.*

Es·to·ni·a (es·tō′nē·ə) A constituent Republic of the western Soviet Union; 17,400 sq. mi.; pop. 1,357,000 (1970); capital, Tallinn. Officially **Estonian S.S.R.** *Russian* **Es·ton·ska·ya S.S.R.** (es·tôn′skä·yä). Also *Esthonia.* See map of BALTIC SEA.

Es·to·ni·an (es·tō′nē·ən) *adj.* Of or pertaining to Estonia. — *n.* **1.** One of a people inhabiting Estonia and part of Livonia. **2.** The Finno-Ugric language of this people.

es·top (es·top′) *v.t.* **·topped, ·top·ping** *Law* To check or bar by estoppel. **2.** *Archaic* To stop up; plug. [< OF *estoper < estoupe* tow < L *stuppa*] — **es·top′page** (-ij) *n.*

es·top·pel (es·top′əl) *n. Law* An impediment to a right of action, whereby one is forbidden to contradict or deny one's

own previous statement or act: also called *conclusion.* [< OF *estoupail* cork < *estouper*, var. of *estoper.* See ESTOP.]

es·to·vers (es·tō′vərz) *n.pl. Law* Necessaries allowed by law, as wood needed by a tenant, alimony for a wife, etc. [< OF *estover < estovoir* < L *est opus* it is necessary]

es·tra·di·ol (es′trə·dī′ōl, -ol) *n. Biochem.* An estrogenic hormone prepared from the urine of pregnant mares, the ovarian fluid of hogs, and estrone: also spelled *oestradiol.* [< ESTR(US) + DI- + -OL′]

es·trange (es·trānj′) *v.t.* **·tranged, ·trang·ing** **1.** To make (someone previously friendly or affectionate) indifferent or hostile; alienate. **2.** To remove or dissociate (oneself, etc.): to *estrange* oneself from society. [< OF *estranger* < L *extraneare < extraneus.* See STRANGE.] — **es·trange′ment** *n.*

es·tray (es·trā′) *n.* **1.** *Law* A stray or unclaimed domestic animal. **2.** Something that has strayed. — *v.i. Archaic* To stray. [< OF *estraié* pp. of *estraier.* See STRAY.]

es·treat (es·trēt′) *Brit. Law n.* An exact copy of or an extract from a court record, as of fines or other penalties. — *v.t.* **1.** To copy from the records of a court for use in prosecution. **2.** To levy or exact (a fine, etc.). [< AF *estrete*, OF *estrait*, pp. of *estraire* < L *extrahere.* See EXTRACT.]

Es·tre·ma·du·ra (es′trə·mə·dōōr′ə, *Pg.* esh′trə·mä·thōō′rə) **1.** A province of central Portugal; 2,059 sq. mi.; pop. 1,998,-600 (1968); capital, Lisbon. **2.** A historic region of western Spain bordering on Portugal, comprising Cáceres (**Upper Estremadura**) and Badajoz (**Lower Estremadura**) provinces; 16,059 sq. mi.: Spanish *Extremadura.*

es·tri·ol (es′trē·ōl, -ol) *n. Biochem.* An estrogen, $C_{18}H_{24}O_3$, found in the urine of pregnant mammals: also spelled *oestriol.* [< ESTRUS + -TRIOL]

es·tro·gen (es′trə·jən) *n. Biochem.* Any of various substances that influence estrus or produce changes in the sexual characteristics of female mammals, as estrone: also spelled *oestrogen.* [< ESTRUS + -GEN] — **es′tro·gen′ic** (-jen′ik) *adj.*

es·trone (es′trōn) *n. Biochem.* An estrogen, $C_{18}H_{22}O_2$, present in the ovaries, urine, and placental tissue; also called *oestrin, theelin:* also spelled *oestrone.* [< ESTRUS + -ONE]

es·trous (es′trəs, ēs′-) *adj.* Of, relating to, or involving estrus: also spelled *oestrous.* Also **es′tru·al** (-trōō·əl).

es·trus (es′trəs, ēs′-) *n.* **1.** *Biol.* **a** The entire cycle of physiological changes in female mammals, preparing the generative organs for their fertile period. **b** The peak of the sexual cycle, culminating in ovulation; heat. Also called *oestrum:* also spelled *oestrus.* Also **es′trum** (-trum). [< L *oestrus* frenzy, passion < Gk. *oistros* gadfly]

es·tu·a·rine (es′chōō·ə·rin, -rīn) *adj.* **1.** Of or pertaining to an estuary. **2.** Formed or deposited in an estuary

es·tu·a·ry (es′chōō·er′ē) *n. pl.* **·ar·ies** **1.** A wide mouth of a river where its current meets the sea and is influenced by the tides. **2.** An inlet or arm of the sea. Abbr. *est.* [< L *aestuarium < aestus* tide] — **es′tu·ar′i·al** (-âr′ē·əl) *adj*

e.s.u. or **esu** Electrostatic unit(s).

e·su·ri·ent (i·sŏŏr′ē·ənt) *adj.* Hungry; greedy [< L *esuriens, -entis*, ppr. of *esurire* to be hungry < *edere* to eat] — **e·su′ri·ence** or **e·su′ri·en·cy** *n.* — **e·su′ri·ent·ly** *adv.*

-et *suffix* Small; little: *islet:* often without appreciable force, as in *sonnet.* [< F]

e·ta (ā′tə, ē′-) *n.* The seventh letter and third vowel in the Greek alphabet (H, η), corresponding to English long *e.* See ALPHABET. ◆ In the etymologies in this dictionary, eta is transliterated as *ē.* [< Gk. *ēta* < Phoenician *hēth*]

ETA Estimated time of arrival.

é·ta·gère (ā·tà·zhâr′) *n.* An ornamental stand with shelves; a whatnot. [< F < *étage* shelf]

et al. **1.** And elsewhere (L *et alibi*). **2.** And others (L *et alii*).

et·a·mine (et′ə·mēn) *n.* A loosely woven fabric resembling bunting. Also **et′a·min** (-min). [< F *étamine* < L *stamen, -inis* thread]

é·tape (ā·tàp′) *n.* **1.** A public warehouse. **2.** A halting place, especially for troops on a march. **3.** Supplies allotted to troops during a march. **4.** The distance marched in one day. [< F < OF *estaple* < MDu. *stapel* warehouse]

etc. Et cetera.

et cet·er·a (et set′ər·ə, set′rə) And other things; and the rest; and so forth. Also **et caet′er·a.** Abbr. *etc., &c.* [< L]

et·cet·er·as (et·set′ər·əz, -set′rəz) *n.pl.* Miscellaneous extra things.

etch (ech) *v.t.* **1.** To engrave by means of acid or other corrosive fluid, especially in making a design on a plate for printing. **2.** To outline or sketch by scratching lines with a pointed instrument. — *v.i.* **3.** To engage in etching. [< Du. *etsen* < G *ätzen* < OHG *ezjan* to corrode, causative of *ezzen* to eat] — **etch′er** *n.*

etch·ing (ech′ing) *n.* **1.** A process of engraving in which lines are scratched with a needle on a plate covered with wax or other coating, and the parts exposed are subjected to the corrosive action of an acid. **2.** A figure or design formed by etching. **3.** An impression from an etched plate.

E·te·o·cles (i·tē′ə·klēz) In Greek legend, a son of Oedipus and Jocasta. See SEVEN AGAINST THEBES.

e·ter·nal (i·tûr′nəl) *adj.* **1.** Existing without beginning or end; having no beginning and no end; forever existent: belief in an *eternal* God. **2.** Begun at some point in time and lasting forever; unending: to hope for *eternal* happiness. **3.** Valid or true for and beyond all time; immutable and timeless: *eternal* truths. **4.** Seemingly endless: their *eternal* bickering. **5.** Tedious through constant repetition or indulgence: you and your *eternal* joking. — **Syn.** See EVERLASTING, INFINITE. — **the Eternal God.** [< OF < LL *aeternalis* < L *aeternus* < *aevum* age] — **e·ter'nal·ly** *adv.* — **e·ter'·nal·ness** *n.*

Eternal City Rome.

e·terne (i·tûrn') *adj. Archaic & Poetic* Eternal.

e·ter·ni·ty (i·tûr'nə·tē) *n. pl.* **·ties** **1.** Existence without beginning or end; endless duration. **2.** An extremely long or immeasurable extent of time. **3.** The endless extent of time following death. [< OF *eternité* < L *aeternitas*]

e·ter·nize (i·tûr'nīz) *v.t.* **·nized, ·niz·ing** **1.** To make eternal. **2.** To perpetuate the fame of; immortalize. Also **e·ter'nal·ize** (-nəl·īz). — **e·ter'ni·za'tion** *n*

e·te·sian (i·tē'zhən) *adj.* Recurring annually: said of certain northerly Mediterranean summer winds. [< L *etesius* < Gk. *etēsios* < *etos* year]

eth (eth) See EDH.

-eth[1] An archaic inflectional ending used in the third person singular present indicative of some verbs: *eateth, drinketh.* Also, in contracted forms, *-th*, as in *hath, doth.* [OE *-eth, -ath*]

-eth[2] *suffix* Var. of -TH[2].

Eth. **1.** Ethiopia. **2.** Ethiopic.

eth·ane (eth'ān) *n. Chem.* A colorless, odorless, gaseous hydrocarbon, C_2H_6, of the methane series contained in crude petroleum and in illuminating gas. [< ETHER]

eth·a·nol (eth'ə·nōl, -nol) *n. Chem.* An alcohol, C_2H_5OH, obtained by the distillation of certain fermented sugars or starches, the intoxicant in liquors, wines, and beers: also called *ethyl alcohol, grain alcohol.* [< ETHANE + -OL[1]]

Eth·el·bald (eth'əl·bôld) See table for ENGLAND.

Eth·el·bert (eth'əl·bûrt), 552?–616, king of Kent; converted by Augustine in 597. Also *Æthelbert.*

Ethelbert See table for ENGLAND.

Eth·el·red I (eth'əl·red') See table for ENGLAND.

Ethelred II 968?–1016, king of England 978–1016: called **Ethelred the Unready.** Also *Æthelred.*

Eth·el·wulf (eth'əl·wŏŏlf) See table for ENGLAND.

e·ther (ē'thər) *n.* **1.** Ethyl ether (which see). **2.** *Chem.* Any of a group of organic compounds in which an oxygen atom is joined with two organic radicals. **3.** A solid or semisolid, perfectly elastic medium formerly assumed to pervade all of space: also spelled *aether.* **4.** The clear, upper regions of the atmosphere or space: also spelled *aether.* [< L *aether* sky < Gk. *aithēr* < *aithein* to burn, shine]

e·the·re·al (i·thir'ē·əl) *adj.* **1.** Resembling ether or air, as in lightness; airy: an *ethereal* substance. **2.** Delicate or exquisite in line, feature, etc.: an *ethereal* face. **3.** Not belonging to earth; celestial; spiritual: *ethereal* spirits. **4.** Of or existing in the ether or upper regions of the atmosphere or of space: *ethereal* heights. **5.** *Chem.* Of or pertaining to ether. — **Syn.** See AIRY. — **e·the're·al·ly** *adv.*

e·the·re·al·ize (i·thir'ē·əl·īz') *v.t* **ized, ·iz·ing** To make ethereal; spiritualize. — **e·the're·al·i·za'tion** *n.*

e·the·re·al·ness (i·thir'ē·əl·nis) *n.* The state or quality of being ethereal. Also **e·the·re·al·i·ty** (i·thir'ē·al'ə·tē).

Eth·er·ege (eth'ə·rij), **Sir George,** 1635?–91, English dramatist.

e·ther·i·fy (i·ther'ə·fī) *v.t.* **·fied, ·fy·ing** *Chem.* To form ether from (an alcohol). — **e·ther'i·fi·ca'tion** *n.*

e·ther·ize (ē'thə·rīz) *v.t.* **·ized, ·iz·ing** **1.** To subject to the influence of ether; anesthetize. **2.** *Chem.* To etherify. — **e'ther·i·za'tion** *n.* — **e'ther·iz'er** *n.*

eth·ic (eth'ik) *n.* A philosophy or system of morals; ethics. — *adj.* Ethical; moral. [< L *ethicus* < Gk. *ēthikos* < *ēthos* character]

eth·i·cal (eth'i·kəl) *adj.* **1.** Pertaining to or treating of ethics and morality. **2.** Conforming to right principles of conduct as generally accepted by a specific profession, a given system of ethics, etc. — **eth'i·cal·ly** *adv.* — **eth'i·cal·ness, eth'i·cal'i·ty** (-kal'ə·tē) *n.*

eth·i·cize (eth'ə·sīz) *v.* **·cized, ·ciz·ing** *v.t.* **1.** To make ethical. **2.** To view from the standpoint of ethics.

eth·ics (eth'iks) *n.pl.* (construed as *sing.* in *defs. 1* and *3*) **1.** The study and philosophy of human conduct, with emphasis on the determination of right and wrong **2.** The principles of right conduct, especially with reference to a specific profession, mode of life, etc. **3.** A treatise on morals.

E·thi·op (ē'thē·op) *adj. & n. Archaic* Ethiopian. [< L *Aethiops* < Gk. *Aithiops*, ? < *aithein* to burn + *ops* face]

E·thi·o·pi·a (ē'thē·ō'pē·ə) **1.** An Empire in eastern Africa; 471,653 sq. mi.; pop. 24,769,000 (est. 1969); capital, Addis Ababa; annexed by Italy, 1936; recovered by British forces, 1941: also *Abyssinia.* Officially **Empire of Ethiopia. 2.** An ancient country south of Egypt.

E·thi·o·pi·an (ē'thē·ō'pē·ən) *adj.* **1.** Of or pertaining to Ethiopia, its people, or their language. **2.** *Ecol.* Designating a zoogeographic realm including Africa south of the Sahara,

southern Arabia, and Madagascar. **3.** Belonging to a former racial division (the **Ethiopian race**) of mankind, comprising Negroes and Negritoes. — *n.* **1.** A native or inhabitant of Ethiopia. **2.** Loosely, a Negro or Negrito. **3.** The Hamitic language of Ethiopia and regions to the south; Cushitic. **4.** Ethiopic. *Abbr. Eth.*

E·thi·op·ic (ē'thē·op'ik, -ō'pik) *n.* A Semitic language of ancient Ethiopia: also called *Geez. Abbr. Eth.* — *adj.* Ethiopian.

eth·moid (eth'moid) *Anat.* A bone situated at the base of the skull behind the nose, composed of thin plates having perforations through which the olfactory nerves pass. — *adj.* Of or pertaining to the ethmoid: also **eth·moi·dal** (eth·moid'l). [< Gk. *ēthmoeidēs* < *ēthmos* sieve + *eidos* form]

eth·narch (eth'närk) *n.* The ruler of a people or province. [< Gk. *ethnarchēs* < *ethnos* nation + *archein* to rule]

eth·nar·chy (eth'när·kē) *n. pl.* **·chies** The office, jurisdiction, or territory of an ethnarch.

eth·nic (eth'nik) *adj.* **1.** Of, belonging to, or distinctive of a particular racial, cultural, or language division of mankind; also, of or belonging to a population subdivision marked by common features of language, etc. **2.** Of or belonging to a people neither Jewish nor Christian; pagan. Also **eth'ni·cal.** [< Gk. *ethnikos* < *ethnos* nation] — **eth'ni·cal·ly** *adv.*

ethno- *combining form* Race; nation: peoples: *ethnogeny.* Also, before vowels, **ethn-.**

eth·no·cen·trism (eth'nō·sen'triz·əm) *n. Sociol.* The belief that one's own ethnic group is superior to and a basis for judging other ethnic groups. — **eth'no·cen'tric** *adj.*

ethnog. Ethnography

eth·nog·e·ny (eth·noj'ə·nē) *n. pl.* **·nies** The department of ethnology that deals with the origin of races and ethnic groups; also, a work or system dealing with this. — **eth·no·gen·ic** (eth'nō·jen'ik) *adj.*

eth·nog·ra·phy (eth·nog'rə·fē) *n. pl.* **·phies** **1.** The branch of anthropology concerned with the classification and description of regional, chiefly primitive human cultures; also, a work or system dealing with this. **2.** Loosely, ethnology. — **eth·nog'ra·pher** *n.* — **eth·no·graph·ic** (eth'nə·graf'ik) or **·i·cal** *adj.* — **eth'no·graph'i·cal·ly** *adv.*

ethnol. Ethnology.

eth·nol·o·gy (eth·nol'ə·jē) *n. pl.* **·gies** **1.** The branch of anthropology concerned with the study of racial and ethnic groups in their origins, characteristics, distribution, and cultures; also, a work or system dealing with this. **2.** Loosely, ethnography. — **eth·nol'o·gist** *n.* — **eth·no·log·ic** (eth'nə·loj'ik) or **·i·cal** *adj.* — **eth'no·log'i·cal·ly** *adv.*

e·thol·o·gy (ē·thol'ə·jē) *n.* The scientific study of the behavior patterns of animals. [< Gk. *ēthologia* < *ēthos* character + *-logia.* See -LOGY] — **e·thol'o·gist** *n.*

e·thos (ē'thos) *n.* **1.** The underlying and distinctive character or spirit of a people, group, culture, etc. **2.** In esthetics, the elements in a work of art that are objective and universal or ideal. Compare PATHOS. [< Gk. *ēthos* character]

eth·yl (eth'əl) *n. Chem.* **1.** A univalent hydrocarbon radical, C_2H_5, of the methane series. **2.** Any gasoline treated with tetraethyl lead to reduce knock. [< ETH(ER) + -YL] — **e·thyl·ic** (i·thil'ik) *adj.*

Eth·yl (eth'əl) *n.* An antiknock motor fuel containing tetraethyl lead and ethylene dibromide: a trade name.

ethyl alcohol Ethanol.

eth·y·late (eth'ə·lāt) *v.t* **·lat·ed, ·lat·ing** *Chem* To cause one or more ethyl groups to be introduced into (a compound). — *n.* A metallic derivative of ethanol. — **eth'y·la'tion** *n.*

eth·y·lene (eth'ə·lēn) *n. Chem.* A colorless, flammable, unsaturated gaseous hydrocarbon, C_2H_4, contained in coal gas: also called *olefiant gas.*

ethylene dibromide *Chem.* A volatile, toxic compound of ethylene and bromine, $(CH_2Br)_2$. Also **ethylene bromide.**

ethylene glycol *Chem.* A colorless, sweetish alcohol, $C_2H_4(OH)_2$, formed by decomposing certain ethylene compounds and used as an antifreeze mixture, lubricant, etc.

ethyl ether *Chem.* A colorless, volatile, flammable liquid compound, $(C_2H_5)_2O$, having a characteristic odor, used as an anesthetic and solvent: also called *ether.*

É·tienne (ā·tyen') See ESTIENNE.
e·ti·o·late (ē'tē·ə·lāt') *v.t. & v.i.* **·lat·ed, ·lat·ing** To whiten or turn yellowish, as a plant kept from sunlight. [< F *étioler* < OF *estieuler* to become slender or puny < *tieulé* tile-colored < L *tegula.* Cf. TILE.] — **e'ti·o·la'tion** *n.*
e·ti·ol·o·gy (ē'tē·ol'ə·jē) *n. pl.* **·gies** **1.** The science of causes or reasons. **2.** The branch of medicine that deals with the causes of diseases; also, a theory of the cause of a particular disease. **3.** The giving of a cause or reason for anything; also, the reason given. Also spelled *aetiology.* [< LL *aetiologia* < Gk. *aitiologia* < *aitia* cause + *logos* word, study] — **e·ti·o·log·i·cal** (ē'tē·ə·loj'i·kəl) *adj.* — **e'ti·o·log'i·cal·ly** *adv.* — **e'ti·ol'o·gist** *n.*
et·i·quette (et'ə·ket) *n.* The usages or rules conventionally established for behavior in polite society or in official or professional life. [< F < OF *estiquette*; orig., label, hence order, manners. Doublet of TICKET.]
et·na (et'nə) *n.* A vessel for heating liquids, consisting of a cup set in a saucer of alcohol. [after *Etna*]
Et·na (et'nə) A volcano in eastern Sicily; 10,868 ft.: ancient *Aetna.*
ETO European Theater of Operations.
Eton (ēt'n) An urban district in southern Buckinghamshire, England, on the Thames; pop. 3,901 (1961).
Eton College A public school for boys, in Eton, England.
E·to·ni·an (i·tō'nē·ən) *n.* One who is or has been a student at Eton College. — *adj.* Of or relating to Eton College.
Eton jacket **1.** A short jacket cut off square at the hips and generally worn with a wide, overlapping, stiff collar (the **Eton collar**), originally worn at Eton College. **2.** A similar jacket worn by women. Also **Eton coat.**
E·tru·ri·a (i·troor'ē·ə) An ancient country of west central Italy, now Tuscany and part of Umbria.
E·trus·can (i·trus'kən) *adj.* Of or relating to Etruria, its people, or language. Also **E·tru'ri·an.** — *n.* **1.** One of the people of Etruria. **2.** The extinct Etruscan language.
et se·quens (et sē'kwənz) *Latin* And the following (individual or thing). Abbr. *et seq.*
et se·quen·tes (et si·kwen'tēz) *Latin* And the following individuals. Abbr. *et seq., et seqq.*
et se·quen·ti·a (et si·kwen'shē·ə) *Latin* And the following things. Abbr. *et seq., et seqq.*
-ette *suffix of nouns* **1.** Little; small: *kitchenette.* **2.** Resembling; imitating: *leatherette.* **3.** Feminine: *farmerette.* [< F *-ette,* fem. of *-et,* dim. suffix]
et tu, Bru·te (et too broo'tā) *Latin* Thou also, Brutus!: exclamation attributed to Caesar on seeing his friend Brutus among his assassins.
é·tude (ā'tood, -tyood) *Fr.* ā·tüd') *n. Music* An exercise for solo instrument or voice, designed to perfect some phase of technique; also, any composition displaying one or more special aspects of technical virtuosity. [< F. See STUDY.]
é·tui (ā·twē') *n. pl.* **é·tuis** A case for carrying small articles. Also **e·twee** (e·twē', et'wē). [< F]
ety. or **etym.** or **etymol.** Etymological; etymology.
et·y·mol·o·gist (et'ə·mol'ə·jist) *n.* A student of or specialist in etymology.
et·y·mol·o·gize (et'ə·mol'ə·jīz) *v.* **·gized, ·giz·ing** *v.t.* **1.** To give the etymology of. — *v.i.* **2.** To give an etymology.
et·y·mol·o·gy (et'ə·mol'ə·jē) *n. pl.* **·gies** **1.** The history of a word as shown by breaking it down into basic elements or by tracing it back to the earliest known form and indicating its changes in form and meaning; also, a statement of this. **2.** The study of the derivation of words. [< F *étymologie* < L *etymologia* < Gk. < *etymon* true meaning + *logos* word, study] — **et·y·mo·log·i·cal** (et'ə·mə·loj'i·kəl) or **et'y·mo·log'ic** *adj.* — **et'y·mo·log'i·cal·ly** *adv.*
et·y·mon (et'ə·mon, -mən) *n. pl.* **·mons** or **·ma** (-mə) The earliest known form of a word. [< L < Gk., original meaning; orig. neut. sing. of *etymos* true, genuine]
Et·zel (et'səl) In the *Nibelungenlied,* the king of the Huns who married Kriemhild after Siegfried's death: identified with *Attila.*
eu- *prefix* Good; well; easy; agreeable: *euphony, eupnea.* [< Gk. *eu* well < *eus* good]
Eu *Chem.* Europium.
Eu·boe·a (yoo·bē'ə) An island separated from mainland Greece by the **Gulf of Euboea,** a part of the Aegean, and comprising with several smaller islands a Department of Greece; 1,552 sq. mi.; pop. 165,758 (1961); capital, Chalcis: Greek *Evvoia.* Italian *Negroponte.*
eu·caine (yoo·kān', -kän; *in technical usage* yoo'kə·ēn) *n. Chem.* An organic compound, $C_{15}H_{21}NO_2$, used as a local anesthetic. [< EU- + (CO)CAINE]
eu·ca·lyp·tol (yoo'kə·lip'tōl, -tol) *n.* A colorless liquid compound, $C_{10}H_{18}O$, contained in eucalyptus oil and having an odor similar to that of camphor, used as an antiseptic and expectorant: also called *cineol.* Also **eu·ca·lyp'tole** (-tōl). [< EUCALYPT(US) + -OL²]

eu·ca·lyp·tus (yoo'kə·lip'təs) *n. pl.* **·tus·es** or **·ti** (-tī) Any of a genus (*Eucalyptus*) of large, chiefly Australian evergreen trees of the myrtle family, widely used as timber and yielding a volatile, pungent oil (**oil of eucalyptus**) used in medicine as an antiseptic, stimulant, etc. Also **eu·ca·lypt** (yoo'kə·lipt). [< NL < Gk. *eu-* well + *kalyptos* covered < *kalyptein* to cover; from the covering of the buds]
eu·cha·ris (yoo'kə·ris) *n.* Any plant of a small genus (*Eucharis*) of bulbous South American plants of the amaryllis family, with white, fragrant flowers in umbels. [< NL < Gk. *eucharis* agreeable < *eu-* good + *charis* grace]
Eu·char·ist (yoo'kə·rist) *n.* **1.** A Christian sacrament in which bread and wine are consecrated, distributed, and consumed in commemoration of the passion and death of Christ: also called *Communion, Holy Communion.* **2.** The consecrated bread and wine of this sacrament. [< OF *eucariste* < LL *eucharistia* thanksgiving < Gk. < *eu-* well + *charizesthai* to show favor] — **Eu'cha·ris'tic** or **·ti·cal** *adj.*
eu·chre (yoo'kər) *n.* **1.** A card game for two to four players, played with 32 cards, one side choosing trumps and being required to take three to five tricks to win. **2.** An instance of euchring an opponent or of being euchred. — *v.t.* **·chred** (-kərd), **·chring** **1.** In the game of euchre, to defeat (the trump-making side) by taking three tricks. **2.** *Informal* To outwit or defeat. [Origin uncertain]
Eu·cken (oi'kən), **Rudolf Christoph,** 1846–1926, German philosopher.
eu·clase (yoo'klās) *n.* A brittle, usually pale green silicate of beryllium and aluminum. [< EU- + Gk. *klasis* breaking < *klaein* to break]
Eu·clid (yoo'klid) A city in NE Ohio, on Lake Erie adjacent to Cleveland; pop. 62,998.
Eu·clid (yoo'klid) A Greek mathematician of about the third century B.C., noted especially for his development of the basic principles of geometry. — *n.* **1.** One of the works of Euclid; especially, the basic treatise on geometry. **2.** The geometric principles developed by Euclid.
Eu·clid·e·an (yoo·klid'ē·ən) *adj.* Of or relating to the geometric principles of Euclid. Also **Eu·clid'i·an.**
eu·de·mon (yoo·dē'mən) *n.* A benevolent spirit. Also **eu·dae'mon.** [< Gk. *eudaimōn* fortunate < *eu-* good + *daimōn* spirit]
eu·de·mo·ni·a (yoo'di·mō'nē·ə) *n.* Happiness or well-being as found in a life of reason and moderation. Also **eu'dae·mo'ni·a.** [< Gk. *eudaimonia* < *eudaimōn.* See EUDEMON.]
eu·de·mon·ic (yoo'di·mon'ik) *adj.* **1.** Of, relating to, or tending to produce happiness. **2.** Of or relating to eudemonism. Also **eu'dae·mon'ic.**
eu·de·mon·ics (yoo'di·mon'iks) *n.pl.* (construed as sing.) Eudemonism. Also **eu'dae·mon'ics.**
eu·de·mon·ism (yoo·dē'mən·iz'əm) *n.* A system of ethics in which actions are evaluated morally according to their ability to produce happiness. Also **eu·dae'mon·ism.** — **eu·de'mon·ist** *n.* — **eu·de'mon·is'tic** or **·ti·cal** *adj.*
eu·di·om·e·ter (yoo'dē·om'ə·tər) *n. Chem.* A graduated glass tube used to determine the volume and composition of gases. [< Gk. *eudios* clear, fair + -METER] — **eu·di·o·met·ric** (yoo'dē·ə·met'rik) or **·ri·cal** *adj.* — **eu'di·o·met'ri·cal·ly** *adv.* — **eu'di·om'e·try** *n.*
Eu·gene (yoo·jēn') A city in western Oregon, on the Willamette River; pop. 50,977.
Eu·gène of Savoy (œ·zhen'), **Prince,** 1663–1736, François Eugène de Savoie-Carignan, Austrian general.
eu·gen·ic (yoo·jen'ik) *adj.* **1.** Of, relating to, or serving in the production of physically and mentally improved offspring or breeds, especially among human beings. **2.** Born with good physical and mental qualities. Also **eu·gen'i·cal.** [< Gk. *eugenēs* well-born (< *eu-* well + *genēs* born) + -IC] — **eu·gen'i·cal·ly** *adv.*
eu·gen·i·cist (yoo·jen'ə·sist) *n.* A specialist in or a student of eugenics. Also **eu·ge·nist** (yoo'jə·nist, yoo·jen'ist).
eu·gen·ics (yoo·jen'iks) *n.pl.* (construed as sing.) The science of improving the physical and mental qualities of human beings, through control of the factors influencing heredity, as by controlled selection of parents. Compare EUTHENICS. [Coined by Sir Francis Galton in 1883]
Eu·gé·nie (œ·zhā·nē'), 1826–1920, Eugénie Marie de Montijo de Guzmán, empress of France 1853–71; wife of Napoleon III.
eu·ge·nol (yoo'jə·nōl, -nol) *n. Chem.* A colorless oil, $C_{10}H_{12}O_2$, of spicy odor and burning taste, contained in oil of cloves, oil of bay, and other oils. [< EUGEN(IA) + -OL²]
Eu·gle·na (yoo·glē'nə) *n. Zool.* A genus of microscopic fresh-water protozoans having one flagellum and a red eyespot, used in biological laboratory work. [< NL < Gk. *eu-* good + *glēnē* eyeball]
eu·he·mer·ism (yoo·hē'mə·riz'əm, -hem'ə-) *n.* **1.** A theory advanced by Euhemerus, ascribing the origin of the gods of mythology to the deification of historical personages. **2.** Any theory that says all myths are based on actual events and personages. — **eu·he'mer·ist** *n.* — **eu·he'mer·is'tic** *adj.* — **eu·he'mer·is'ti·cal·ly** *adv.*
eu·he·mer·ize (yoo·hē'mə·rīz, -hem'ə-) *v.t.* **·ized, ·iz·ing** To explain (myths) by euhemerism.

ETON COLLAR
AND JACKET

Eu·he·mer·us (yōō·hē'mər·əs)   Fourth-century B.C. Sicilian philosopher.

Eu·ler (oi'lər), **Leonhard,** 1707–83, Swiss mathematician.

eu·la·chon (yōō'lə·kon)   *n. Canadian* The candlefish: also *oolachan.* Also **eu'la·chan.**

eu·lo·gi·a (yōō·lō'jē·ə)   *n.* **1.** In the Eastern Orthodox Church, unconsecrated bread blessed and distributed to noncommunicants after the Eucharist. **2.** In patristic writings, the Eucharist itself. [< Gk., blessing. See EULOGY.]

eu·lo·gist (yōō'lə·jist)   *n.* One who delivers or writes a eulogy. Also **eu'lo·giz'er.**

eu·lo·gis·tic (yōō'lə·jis'tik)   *adj.* Relating to or having the nature of eulogy; laudatory. Also **eu·lo·gis'ti·cal.** — **eu'lo·gis'ti·cal·ly** *adv.*

eu·lo·gi·um (yōō·lō'jē·əm)   *n. pl.* **·gi·ums** or **·gi·a** (-jē·ə)   Eulogy.

eu·lo·gize (yōō'lə·jīz)   *v.t.* **·gized, ·giz·ing** To speak or write a eulogy about; praise highly; extol. Also *Brit.* **eu'lo·gise.** — Syn. See PRAISE.

eu·lo·gy (yōō'lə·jē)   *n. pl.* **·gies 1.** A spoken or written piece of high praise, especially when formal and delivered publicly **2.** Great commendation: words of *eulogy.* [< Gk. *eulogia* praise < *eu-* well + *legein* to speak]
— **Syn.** *Eulogy, encomium,* and *panegyric* denote a public expression of praise. A *eulogy* is a formal and considered speech or writing, such as a funeral oration. *Encomium* implies warmer and more spontaneous praise, akin to applause, while a *panegyric* is an extravagant speech of praise, usually expressed in flowery words.

Eu·men·i·des (yōō·men'ə·dēz)   *n.pl.* The Furies. [< Gk., the kind ones; a euphemistic name]

eu·nuch (yōō'nək)   *n.* **1.** A castrated man employed as a harem attendant or as an Oriental palace official. **2.** Any castrated man or youth. [< L *eunuchus* < Gk. *eunouchos* chamber attendant < *eunē* bed + *echein* to keep, guard]

eu·on·y·mus (yōō·on'ə·məs)   *n.* Any of a genus (*Euonymus*) of shrubs and small trees of temperate regions, mostly deciduous, having small flowers and brightly colored pods: also called *evonymus.* [< L *euonymus* < Gk. *euōnymos* < *eu-* good + *onyma* name]

eu·pa·to·ri·um (yōō'pə·tôr'ē·əm, -tō'rē-)   *n.* Any of a large genus (*Eupatorium*) of chiefly American herbaceous or shrubby plants of the composite family, with clusters of purple or white flowers, as the joe-pye weed or boneset. [< NL < Gk. *eupatorion* agrimony; named after Mithridates VI, King of Pontus, called *Eupator,* he of noble fathers]

eu·pat·rid (yōō·pat'rid, yōō'pə·trid)   *n. pl.* **eu·pat·ri·dae** (yōō·pat'rə·dē) or **eu·pat·rids** *Sometimes cap.* A member of the hereditary aristocracy of ancient Athens and other Greek states, which in very early times composed the sole lawmaking and governing body of these states. [< Gk. *eupatridēs* of noble fathers < *eu-* good + *patēr* father]

eu·pep·si·a (yōō·pep'sē·ə, -shə)   *n.* Good digestion. [< NL < Gk. < *eu-* good + *pepsia* digestion < *peptein* to digest]

eu·pep·tic (yōō·pep'tik)   *adj.* Of, characteristic of, or having good digestion.

eu·phe·mism (yōō'fə·miz'əm)   *n.* **1.** Substitution of a mild or roundabout word or expression for another felt to be too blunt or otherwise distasteful or painful. **2.** A mild or roundabout word or expression substituted for another to avoid giving offense or pain: "The departed" is a *euphemism* for "the dead." [< Gk. *euphēmismos* < *euphēmizein* < *eu-* well + *phēmizein* < *phanai* to speak]

eu·phe·mist (yōō'fə·mist)   *n.* One who uses euphemisms.

eu·phe·mis·tic (yōō'fə·mis'tik)   *adj.* Relating to, constituting, or designed as a euphemism; full of euphemisms. Also **eu'phe·mis'ti·cal.** — **eu'phe·mis'ti·cal·ly** *adv.*

eu·phe·mize (yōō'fə·mīz)   *v.* **·mized, ·miz·ing** *v.t.* **1.** To speak or write of by using a euphemism. — *v.i.* **2.** To use euphemisms.

eu·phon·ic (yōō·fon'ik)   *adj.* **1.** Of or relating to euphony. **2.** Agreeable in sound; euphonious. Also **eu·phon'i·cal.** — **eu·phon'i·cal·ly** *adv.*

eu·pho·ni·ous (yōō·fō'nē·əs)   *adj.* Marked by euphony; agreeable and pleasant in sound. — **eu·pho'ni·ous·ly** *adv.*

eu·pho·ni·um (yōō·fō'nē·əm)   *n.* A brass instrument sometimes used in military bands, having a tone resembling that of a tuba but slightly higher in range and more mellow. [< NL < Gk. *euphōnos.* See EUPHONY.]

eu·pho·nize (yōō'fə·nīz)   *v.t.* **·nized, ·niz·ing** To give euphony to; make euphonious.

eu·pho·ny (yōō'fə·nē)   *n. pl.* **·nies 1.** The quality of being pleasant and agreeable in sound; smoothness and lack of harshness in sounds and sound combinations. **2.** Progressive change in speech sounds through phonetic assimilation or similar processes allowing greater ease of pronunciation. [< Gk. *euphōnia* < *euphōnos* < *eu-* good + *phōnē* sound]

eu·phor·bi·a (yōō·fôr'bē·ə)   *n.* Any plant of a large and widely distributed genus (*Euphorbia*) of herbs of the spurge family, characterized by their milky juice and various medicinal properties: also called *spurge.* [< NL < L *euphorbea* <

Gk. *euphorbion;* named after *Euphorbos,* a Greek physician]
— **eu·phor·bi·a·ceous** (yōō·fôr'bē·ā'shəs), **eu·phor'bi·al** *adj.*

eu·pho·ri·a (yōō·fôr'ē·ə, -fō'rē-)   *n.* **1** A feeling of well-being, relaxation, and happiness. **2.** *Psychiatry* An abnormally exaggerated sense of buoyancy and vigor. [< NL < Gk. *eu-* well + *pherein* to bear] — **eu·phor·ic** (yōō·fôr'ik, -fōr'-) *adj.*

eu·phra·sy (yōō'frə·sē)   *n.* Eyebright, an herb. [< Med.L *euphrasia* < Gk., delight < *eu-* good + *phrēn* mind]

Eu·phra·tes (yōō·frā'tēz)   A river of SW Asia, flowing from eastern Turkey about 1,700 miles to the Persian Gulf.

eu·phroe (yōō'frō, -vrō)   *n. Naut.* A block of wood with holes for reeving cords, used in adjusting shipboard awning: also spelled *uphroe.* [< Du. *juffrouw,* orig., maiden]

Eu·phros·y·ne (yōō·fros'ə·nē, -froz'-)   One of the Graces.

eu·phu·ism (yōō'fyōō·iz'əm)   *n.* **1.** An artificially elegant style of speech or writing; especially, a literary style cultivated by imitators of John Lyly and characterized by flowery paraphrasing, strained similes, and by similar affectations. **2.** An expression or rhetorical device typical of such a style. [after *Euphues,* character created by John Lyly < Gk. *euphyēs* graceful < *eu-* well + *phyein* to grow, form]

eu·phu·ist (yōō'fyōō·ist)   *n.* One who uses euphuisms.

eu·phu·is·tic (yōō'fyōō·is'tik)   *adj.* Of, relating to, or constituting a euphuism; full of euphuisms. Also **eu'phu·is'ti·cal.** — **Syn.** See RHETORICAL. — **eu'phu·is'ti·cal·ly** *adv.*

eu·plas·tic (yōō·plas'tik)   *Biol. adj.* Readily transformable into organic tissue. — *n.* A euplastic substance. [< Gk. *euplastos* easily molded < *eu-* well + *plassein* to form]

eup·ne·a (yōōp·nē'ə)   *n. Med.* Unlabored, normal breathing. Also **eup·noe'a.** [< Gk. *eupnoia* < *eu-* good + *pnoia* breath < *pneein* to breathe]

Eur. Europe; European.

Eur·a·sia (yōō·rā'zhə, -shə)   The large land mass that comprises Europe and Asia and is bounded by the Arctic, Atlantic, Indian, and Pacific oceans and the Red, Mediterranean, Bering, and Arafura seas, including adjacent islands. [< EUR(OPE) + ASIA]

Eur·a·sian (yōō·rā'zhən, -shən)   *adj.* **1.** Pertaining to Eurasia. **2.** Of European and Asian descent. — *n.* A person of mixed European and Asian parentage.

Eur·a·tom (yōō·rat'əm)   European Atomic Energy Commission, an agency formed in 1958 by nations of the European Economic Community to promote the development of nuclear energy for peaceful purposes. [< EUR(OPEAN) ATOM(IC ENERGY COMMISSION)]

Eu·re·ka (yōō·rē'kə)   A port city in NW California on Humboldt Bay; pop. 24,337.

eu·re·ka (yōō·rē'kə)   *interj.* I have found (it); often used as an exclamation upon discovering or figuring out something: the motto of the State of California. [< Gk. *heurēka*]

eu·rhyth·mic (yōō·rith'mik), **eu·rhyth·mics** (-miks), etc. See EURYTHMIC, etc.

Eu·rip·i·des (yōō·rip'ə·dēz), 480?–406? B.C., Greek tragic dramatist.

eu·ri·pus (yōō·rī'pəs)   *n. pl.* **·pi** (-pī) A swift sea channel. [< L < Gk. *euripos* strait < *eu-* good + *ripē* rush]

Eu·roc·ly·don (yōō·rok'lə·don)   *n.* A stormy northeast wind of the Levant. Also **Eu·raq·ui·lo** (yōō·räk'wə·lō), **Eu·ro·aq·ui·lo** (yōō'rō·äk'wə·lō). [< NL < Gk. *Euroklydōn* < *Euros* east wind + *klydōn* billow]

Eu·ro·dol·lars (yōōr'ə·dol'ərz)   *n. pl.* U.S. dollars held by European banks and used for short-term funding of international trade.

Eu·ro·pa (yōō·rō'pə)   In Greek mythology, a Phoenician princess abducted by Zeus, in the guise of a bull, to Crete, where she bore Minos, Rhadamanthus, and Sarpedon. — *n.* A female figure representing Europe.

Eu·rope (yōōr'əp)   The western part of the Eurasian land mass; excluding Turkey and the Soviet Union, about 1.9 million sq. mi.; pop. 644,574,000 (1969); one of the earth's continents.

Eu·ro·pe·an (yōōr'ə·pē'ən)   *adj.* Relating to or derived from Europe or its inhabitants. — *n.* **1.** A native or inhabitant of Europe. **2.** A person of European descent. Abbr. *Eur.*

European Economic Community A customs union of France, Italy, West Germany, and the Benelux nations, aiming toward eventual economic integration of the member nations: also called *Common Market.* Also **European Common Market.** Abbr. *E.E.C., EEC*

European Free Trade Area A customs union of Austria, Denmark, Great Britain, Norway, Portugal, Sweden, and Switzerland.

Eu·ro·pe·an·ize (yōōr'ə·pē'ən·īz)   *v.t.* **·ized, ·iz·ing** To make European, as in culture. — **Eu'ro·pe'an·i·za'tion** *n.*

European plan At a hotel, the system of paying for room and service separately from the charge for meals. Compare AMERICAN PLAN.

European Recovery Plan A post World War II recovery program of U.S. financial aid to certain European countries, initiated by George C. Marshall: also called *Marshall Plan.*

PRONUNCIATION KEY: add, āce, câre, pälm; end, ēven; it, īce; odd, ōpen, ôrder; tŏŏk, pōōl; up, bûrn; ə = a in *above,* e in *sicken,* i in *flexible,* o in *melon,* u in *focus;* yōō = u in *fuse;* oil; pout; check; go; ring; thin; this; zh, vision. For à, œ, ü, kh, ṅ, see inside front cover.

eu·ro·pi·um (yŏŏ-rō′pē-əm) *n.* A steel-gray, malleable metallic element (symbol Eu) of the lanthanide series. See ELEMENT. [< NL < L *Europa* Europe]

Eu·rus (yŏŏr′əs) In Greek mythology, the god of the east or southeast wind. [< L < Gk. *Euros* east wind]

eury- *combining form* Wide; broad: *eurypterid.* [< Gk. *eurys* wide]

Eu·ry·a·le (yŏŏ-rī′ə-lē) One of the Gorgons.

Eu·ryd·i·ce (yŏŏ-rid′ə-sē) In Greek mythology, the wife of Orpheus, who after death was permitted to follow her husband out of Hades, provided he did not look back at her. He failed in the test, and she was forced to remain in Hades.

eu·ryp·ter·id (yŏŏ-rip′tər-id) *Paleontol. n.* Any of an extinct order (*Eurypterida*) of scorpionlike aquatic arthropods related to the arachnids. — *adj.* Belonging to this order. [< NL *Eurypterida* < Gk. *eurys* broad + *pteron* wing]

Eu·rys·the·us (yŏŏ-ris′thē-əs) In Greek legend, a king of Argos who imposed the twelve labors upon Hercules.

eu·ryth·mic (yŏŏ-rith′mik) *adj.* **1.** Gracefully proportioned in structure or movement. **2.** Of or relating to eurythmics. Also spelled *eurhythmic.* Also **eu·ryth′mi·cal.**

eu·ryth·mics (yŏŏ-rith′miks) *n.pl.* (*construed as sing.*) A system devised by Émile Jaques-Dalcroze (1860–1950) for developing grace and rhythm through bodily movements made in response to music: also spelled *eurhythmics.*

eu·ryth·my (yŏŏ-rith′mē) *n.* Gracefully proportioned structure or movement: also spelled *eurhythmy.* [< L < Gk. *eurhythmia* harmony < *eu-* good + *rhythmos* symmetry]

Eu·se·bi·an (yŏŏ-sē′bē-ən) *adj.* **1.** Of or pertaining to **Eusebius Pam·phi·li** (pam′fi·lī), 260?–340?, bishop of Caesarea. **2.** Of or pertaining to **Eusebius**, died 341, bishop of Constantinople and Nicomedia, a leader of the Arians.

eu·spo·ran·gi·ate (yŏŏ-spə-ran′jē-āt) *adj. Bot.* Having sporangia developed from a group of cells, instead of from a single cell. [< EU- + SPORANGIA]

Eu·sta·chi·an tube (yŏŏ-stā′kē-ən, -shē-ən, -shən) *Anat.* A passage between the pharynx and the middle ear, serving to equalize air pressure between the tympanic cavity and the atmosphere: also called *syrinx.* For illustration see EAR. [after Bartolomeo *Eustachio*, died 1574, Italian anatomist]

eu·tec·tic (yŏŏ-tek′tik) *Chem. adj.* **1.** Denoting an alloy or solid solution that has the lowest possible melting or freezing point, usually below that of any of its components. **2.** Melting readily at a low temperature. — *n.* A eutectic substance. [< Gk. *eutēktos* < *eu-* well, easily + *tēkein* to melt]

eu·tec·toid (yŏŏ-tek′toid) *Chem. adj.* Resembling a eutectic substance. — *n.* A eutectic alloy.

eu·tel·e·gen·e·sis (yŏŏ-tel′ə-jen′ə-sis) *n.* Artificial insemination. [< EU- + TELE- + GENESIS] — **eu·tel′e·gen′ic,** **eu·tel′e·ge·net′ic** *adj.*

Eu·ter·pe (yŏŏ-tûr′pē) The Muse of lyric song and music.

eu·tha·na·si·a (yŏŏ-thə-nā′zhə, -zhē-ə) *n.* **1.** Painless, peaceful death. **2.** The deliberate putting to death, in an easy, painless way, of a person suffering from an incurable and agonizing disease: also called *mercy killing.* [< Gk. < *eu-* easy + *thanatos* death]

eu·then·ics (yŏŏ-then′iks) *n.pl.* (*construed as sing.*) The science of improving the physical and mental qualities of human beings, through control of environmental factors. Compare EUGENICS. [< Gk. *euthēnein* to thrive]

eu·tro·phi·ca·tion (yŏŏ-trō-fə-kā′shən) *n.* A decrease of dissolved oxygen in a body of water, such that plant life is favored over animal life. [< Gk. *eutrophein* to thrive]

eux·e·nite (yŏŏk′sə-nīt) *n.* A metallic, brownish black mineral valuable as a source of certain elements, as uranium, titanium, germanium, and cerium. [< Gk. *euxenos* hospitable < *eu* good + *xenos* stranger + -ITE¹]

Eux·ine Sea (yŏŏk′sin, -sīn) See BLACK SEA.

ev or **e.v.** Electron volt(s).

E.V. English Version (of the Bible).

e·vac·u·ant (i·vak′yŏŏ-ənt) *Med. adj.* Producing evacuation; cathartic, diuretic, or emetic. — *n.* An evacuant medicine, drug, etc.

e·vac·u·ate (i·vak′yŏŏ-āt) *v.* **·at·ed, ·at·ing** *v.t.* **1.** *Mil.* **a** To give up or abandon possession of, as a fortress or city. **b** To move out or withdraw (troops, inhabitants, etc.) from a threatened area or place. **2.** To depart from and leave vacant; vacate: to *evacuate* a burning building. **3.** To remove the contents of. **4.** *Physiol.* To discharge or eject, as from the bowels. **5.** *Physics* To remove the air from (a sealed chamber, receptacle, etc.); make a vacuum in. — *v.i.* **6.** To withdraw, as from a threatened area or place. **7.** *Physics* To be emptied of air, as an electric light bulb. [< L *evacuatus,* pp. of *evacuare* < *e-* out + *vacuare* to make empty < *vacuus* empty] — **e·vac′u·a′tor** *n.*

e·vac·u·a·tion (i·vak′yŏŏ-ā′shən) *n.* **1.** The act of evacuating, or the state of being evacuated. **2.** *Physiol.* The ejection of matter from the excretory passages, especially from the bowels; also, the matter ejected.

e·vac·u·ee (i·vak′yŏŏ-ē′) *n.* A person moved out or withdrawn from a destroyed or threatened area. [See EVACUATE]

e·vade (i·vād′) *v.* **e·vad·ed, e·vad·ing** *v.t.* **1.** To get away from by tricks or cleverness; save oneself from; escape: to *evade* pursuers. **2.** To get out of or avoid; get around: to *evade* a question or a duty. **3.** To baffle; elude: The facts *evade* explanation. — *v.i.* **4.** To dodge a question, responsibility, etc. — **Syn.** See ESCAPE. [< L *evadere* < *e-* out + *vadere* to go] — **e·vad′a·ble** or **e·vad′i·ble** *adj.* — **e·vad′er** *n.*

e·vag·i·nate (i·vaj′ə-nāt) *v.t.* **·nat·ed, ·nat·ing** *Biol.* To turn inside out, as a tubular organ; cause to protrude by eversion; unsheathe. [< LL *evaginatus,* pp. of *evaginare* < L *e-* out + *vagina* sheath] — **e·vag′i·na′tion** *n.*

E·vald (ĭ′väl), **Johannes** See EWALD.

e·val·u·ate (i·val′yŏŏ-āt) *v.t.* **·at·ed, ·at·ing** **1.** To find or determine the amount, worth, etc., of; appraise. **2.** *Math.* To find the numerical value of. [< F *évaluer* < *e-* out (< L *ex*) + *valuer* < OF *valoir.* See VALUE.] — **e·val′u·a′tion** *n.*

evan. or **evang.** Evangelical; evangelist.

ev·a·nesce (ev′ə·nes′) *v.i.* **·nesced, ·nesc·ing** To disappear by degrees; vanish gradually. [< L *evanescere* < *e-* out + *vanescere* to vanish < *vanus* empty] — **ev′a·nes′cence** *n.*

ev·a·nes·cent (ev′ə·nes′ənt) *adj.* Passing away, or liable to pass away, gradually or imperceptibly; fleeting. — **Syn.** See TRANSIENT. [< F *évanescent* < L *evanescens, -entis,* ppr. of *evanescere.* See EVANESCE.] — **ev′a·nes′cent·ly** *adv.*

e·van·gel¹ (i·van′jəl) *n.* **1.** The message of redemption through Jesus Christ. **2.** *Usually cap.* One of the four Gospels of the New Testament. **3.** Any good news or glad tidings. [< OF *evangile* < LL *evangelium* < Gk. *euangelion* good news < *eu-* good + *angellein* to announce. Cf. ANGEL.]

e·van·gel² (i·van′jəl) *n.* An evangelist. [< Gk. *euangelos* < *eu-* good + *angelos* messenger]

e·van·gel·i·cal (ē′van·jel′i·kəl, ev′an-) *adj.* **1.** Of, relating to, contained in, or in harmony with the New Testament, especially the Gospels. **2.** Of, relating to, or maintaining the doctrine that the Bible is the only rule of faith and that salvation is attained chiefly by faith in the redemptive work of Christ. **3.** Evangelistic. — *n.* A member of an evangelical church. Also **e·van·gel′ic.** Abbr. *evan., evang.* [< LL *evangelicus* < Gk. *euangelikos* < *euangelion.* See EVANGEL¹.] — **e·van·gel′i·cal·ly** *adv.*

Evangelical and Reformed Church A presbyterial Protestant denomination, first organized in 1934, and since 1957 a part of the *United Church of Christ.*

evangelical counsel Counsel of perfection (which see).

e·van·gel·i·cal·ism (ē′van·jel′i·kəl·iz′əm, ev′an-) *n.* Promulgation of or adherence to belief in the Bible as the supreme rule of faith and in salvation through faith.

e·van·gel·ism (i·van′jə·liz′əm) *n.* **1.** The zealous preaching or spreading of the gospel. **2.** Evangelicalism.

e·van·gel·ist (i·van′jə·list) *n.* **1.** *Usually cap.* One of the four writers of the New Testament Gospels: Matthew, Mark, Luke, or John. **2.** An itinerant or missionary preacher; revivalist. **3.** In the Mormon Church, a patriarch. Abbr. *evan., evang.*

e·van·gel·is·tic (i·van′jə·lis′tik) *adj.* **1.** Of or relating to an evangelist or the Evangelists. **2.** Engaged in or suited to evangelizing. **3.** Evangelical. — **e·van′gel·is′ti·cal·ly** *adv.*

e·van·gel·ize (i·van′jəl·īz) *v.* **·ized, ·iz·ing** *v.t.* **1.** To preach the gospel to. **2.** To convert to Christianity. — *v.i.* **3.** To preach or act as an evangelist. — **e·van′gel·i·za′tion** *n.* **e·van′gel·iz′er** *n.*

e·van·ish (i·van′ish) *v.i. Poetic* To fade out of existence or sight; vanish. [< OF *esvanir.* See EVANESCE.]

Ev·ans (ev′ənz), **Sir Arthur John,** 1851–1941, English archeologist. — **Mary Ann** See (George) ELIOT. — **Maurice,** born 1901, English actor active in the United States. — **Rudulph,** 1878–1960, U.S. sculptor.

Ev·ans·ton (ev′ən·stən, -ənz·tən) A city in NE Illinois on Lake Michigan, a suburb of Chicago; pop. 79,808.

Ev·ans·ville (ev′ənz·vil′) A city in SW Indiana, on the Ohio River; pop. 138,764.

e·vap·o·ra·ble (i·vap′ər·ə·bəl) *adj.* Capable of being converted into vapor. — **e·vap′o·ra·bil′i·ty** *n.*

e·vap·o·rate (i·vap′ə·rāt) *v.* **·rat·ed, ·rat·ing** *v.t.* **1.** To convert into vapor; vaporize. **2.** To remove moisture or liquid from (milk, fruit, etc.) so as to dry or concentrate. — *v.i.* **3.** To become vapor. **4.** To yield vapor. **5.** To vanish; disappear. [< L *evaporatus,* pp. of *evaporare* < *e-* out, away + *vapor.* See VAPOR.] — **e·vap′o·ra′tive** *adj.* — **e·vap′o·ra′tor** *n.*

evaporated milk Unsweetened canned milk slightly thickened by removal of some of the water.

e·vap·o·ra·tion (i·vap′ə·rā′shən) *n.* **1.** The act of evaporating, or the state of being evaporated. **2.** The product or result of evaporating.

e·vap·o·rim·e·ter (i·vap′ə·rim′ə·tər) *n.* An atmometer (which see).

e·va·sion (i·vā′zhən) *n.* **1.** The act of evading; especially, the act of dodging something difficult or distasteful, as a question or responsibility. **2.** A piece of trickery, deceit, or shrewdness used in dodging a question, etc. [< LL *evasio, -onis* < L *evadere.* See EVADE.]

e·va·sive (i·vā′siv) *adj.* **1.** Given to or characterized by evasion; not direct and frank: an *evasive* person; *evasive* promises. **2.** Escaping ready perception or understanding; elusive: The truth was *evasive.* — **e·va′sive·ly** *adv.* — **e·va′sive·ness** *n.*

Ev·att (ev′ət), **Herbert Vere,** 1894–1965, Australian jurist and political leader.

eve (ēv) *n.* **1.** The evening or the day before a church festival or saint's day· Christmas *Eve.* **2.** The time immediately preceding some event: on the *eve* of the election. **3.** *Poetic* Evening. [Var. of EVEN²]

Eve (ēv) The first woman; wife of Adam and mother of the human race. *Gen.* iii 20. [< Hebrew *hawwah* life]

e·vec·tion (i·vek′shən) *n. Astron.* Periodic irregularity in the movement of the moon through its orbit, caused by the gravitational pull of the sun. [< L *evectio, -onis* < *evehere* < *e-* out + *vehere* to carry] — **e·vec′tion·al** *adj.*

Eve·lyn (ēv′lin), **John**, 1620–1706, English Royalist author; known for his diary

e·ven¹ (ē′vən) *adj.* **1.** Extended without having one part higher or lower than another part; flat and smooth; level: an *even* surface. **2.** Extending to the same height or depth: a tree *even* with the housetop. **3.** Extending along a parallel line: a bookcase *even* with the wall **4** Having the same thickness or thinness throughout; equally distributed; uniform: an *even* coat of paint. **5.** Free from sudden changes; varying little; unfluctuating; steady. **6.** Calm and controlled; not easily excited; tranquil: an *even* disposition. **7.** Engaged in without notable superiority of one side over the other; equally matched: an *even* struggle. **8.** Being about the same for one of several alternatives or possibilities: The chances of success or failure are *even.* **9.** Being the same (score) for each side or competitor. **10.** Having the same score as the other side or as one's opponent: The teams are *even.* **11.** Having accomplished exact settlement of a debt. **12.** Having accomplished an exact measure of retaliation; fully revenged. **13.** Identical in quantity, number, measure, etc.: *even* portions; *even* weight. **14.** Complete and having no additional, fractional part; exact: to walk an *even* mile. **15.** Exactly divisible by 2: an *even* number: opposed to *odd.* **16.** Having numbers exactly divisible by 2: the *even* pages of a book; also, being the second, fourth, sixth, etc., of a series: to canvass the *even* houses on a street. **17.** Just and fair; equitable: an *even* bargain. — **to break even** *Informal* To end up with neither profit nor loss, as in a business deal. — **to get even** To exact one's full measure of revenge. — *adv.* **1.** To all the greater extent or degree; still: an *even* better plan. **2.** At the very same time; during the very same moment: with *as: Even* as they watched, the ship sank. **3.** In exactly the same way; precisely; just: with *as:* Do *even* as I do. **4.** As a matter of plain fact; in very fact; indeed; actually: to feel glad, *even* delighted **5.** Unlikely or inconceivable as it may seem: He was kind *even* to his enemies. **6.** All the way; as far as: faithful *even* to death. **7.** All the same; nevertheless; notwithstanding: *Even* with that handicap, he managed to win. **8.** Not otherwise than; right: It is happening *even* now. **9.** *Informal* In a smooth manner; evenly: to keep things running *even.* **10.** *Archaic* None other than: It was he, *even* his brother. — **even if** Although; notwithstanding. — *v.t.* **1.** To make even: often with *up* or *off:* to *even* up accounts. — *v.i.* **2.** To become even: often with *up* or *off:* The road *evens* off at that point. [OE *efen*] — **e′ven·ly** *adv.* — **e′ven·ness** *n.*

e·ven² (ē′vən) *n. Archaic* **1.** Evening. **2.** The eve before a church festival, an event, etc. [OE *æfen*]

e·ven·fall (ē′vən·fôl′) *n.* Early evening; twilight; dusk.

e·ven·hand·ed (ē′vən·han′did) *adj.* Treating all alike; impartial. — **e′ven·hand′ed·ly** *adv.* — **e′ven·hand′ed·ness** *n.*

eve·ning (ēv′ning) *n.* **1.** The latter part of day and the first part of night; especially: **a** The period extending from late afternoon or from sunset to about midnight or earlier. **b** *Dial.* The period extending from noon to nightfall. ◆ Collateral adjective: *vesperal.* **2.** An evening's entertainment or activity. **3.** The period during which something gradually draws to a close; especially, the declining years of life. [OE *æfnung* < *æfnian* to approach evening]

evening dress Formal evening wear. Also **evening clothes.**

evening gown A woman's formal dress for evening wear.

Evening Prayer In the Anglican Church, an order of worship for use in the evening: also called *evensong, vespers.*

evening primrose A stout, erect American biennial herb (*Oenothera biennis*) with conspicuous yellow flowers that open in the evening. It is typical of a family (*Onagraceae*) of small flowering plants, including the fuchsia.

evening star A bright planet visible in the west just after sunset, especially Venus. Also called *Hesperus, Vesper.*

e·ven·mind·ed (ē′vən·mīn′did) *adj.* Calm and controlled in disposition, temper, and judgment; equable.

e·ven·song (ē′vən·sông′, -song′) *n.* **1.** Evening Prayer. **2.** A song sung at evening. **3.** *Archaic* Evening. [OE *æfensang*]

e·vent (i·vent′) *n.* **1.** Something that takes place; a happening or an incident: the *events* of that period; especially, an occurrence of considerable importance: historical *events.* **2.** An actual or possible set of circumstances; a real or contingent situation: in the *event* of failure. **3.** Final outcome: In the *event,* she decided not to go. **4.** One of the items forming part of a variegated program of sports: the skating exhibi-

tion and other *events.* **5.** *Philos.* Something existing or oc curring at a particular portion of space time. — **in any event** or **at all events** Regardless of what happens; in any case; anyhow. [< OF < L *eventus* < *e-* out + *venire* to come]
— **Syn. 1.** *Event, incident, occurrence, episode,* and *circumstance* denote something that happens. In origin, an *event* is something that comes out or results; an *incident,* something that falls in or takes place. Major happenings are considered as *events,* and minor ones as *incidents:* an historical *event,* an *incident* of daily life. An *occurrence,* etymologically, is something that one runs against, without thought of its origin, connection, or tendency. An *episode* is one of a chain of *events,* or an *incident* of special interest or importance. *Circumstance* refers to one of the surrounding conditions from which an *event* emerges.

e·vent·ful (i·vent′fəl) *adj.* **1.** Marked by important events: an *eventful* era. **2.** Having important consequences; momentous: an *eventful* decision. — **e·vent′ful·ly** *adv.* — **e·vent′ful·ness** *n.*

e·ven·tide (ē′vən·tīd′) *n. Poetic* Evening.

e·vent·less (i·vent′lis) *adj.* Devoid of important events; not eventful. — **e·vent′less·ly** *adv.* — **e·vent′less·ness** *n.*

even-toed (ē′vən·tōd′) *adj.* Having an even number of toes.

e·ven·tu·al (i·ven′chōō·əl) *adj.* Occurring or resulting in due course of time. [< F *éventuel* < L *eventus.* See EVENT.]

e·ven·tu·al·i·ty (i·ven′chōō·al′ə·tē) *n. pl.* **·ties** Something that may or may not take place; a likely or possible occurrence; a conceivable outcome.

e·ven·tu·al·ly (i·ven′chōō·əl·ē) *adv.* In the due course of events; in the end; as a final outcome; ultimately.

e·ven·tu·ate (i·ven′chōō·āt) *v·i.* **·at·ed, ·at·ing 1.** To turn out finally in a particular way; result ultimately: His efforts *eventuated* in success. **2.** To happen or come into being as a final outcome: a fear that war might *eventuate.*

ev·er (ev′ər) *adv.* **1.** At any time; on any occasion· Did you *ever* see it? **2** By any possible chance: If the sun *ever* comes out, the fog will disappear. **3.** In any possible or conceivable way: Do it as fast as *ever* you can **4.** At all times; invariably: They remained *ever* on guard. **5.** Throughout the entire course of time; always; forever: now usually followed by *since, after,* or *afterward: Ever* since then, they have been content. **6.** *Archaic* At all; any: He was not *ever* the wiser. ◆ In informal speech, *ever* is often used merely to add force to an exclamation or a question: Was I *ever* glad!· How could you *ever* do anything like that? — **ever and again** *Archaic* Now and then; occasionally Also **ever and anon.** — **ever so** *Informal* To an extremely great extent or degree; extraordinarily; exceedingly: It was *ever so* pleasant. — **ever so often** *Informal* **1.** Extremely often; repeatedly. **2.** Now and then; every so often: not considered standard usage in this sense. — **for ever** *Brit.* Forever. — **for ever and ever** Forever: an intensive form. Also **for ever and a day.** [OE *æfre*]

Ev·er·est (ev′ər·ist, ev′rist), **Mount** A peak of the Himalayas in eastern Nepal, the highest known point of the earth's surface; 29,028 ft.

Ev·er·ett (ev′ər·it, ev′rit) **1.** A city in eastern Massachusetts, near Boston; pop. 42,485. **2.** A city in western Washington, on Puget Sound; pop. 53,622.

Ev·er·ett (ev′ər·it, ev′rit), **Edward,** 1794–1865. U.S. clergyman, scholar. statesman, and orator.

ev·er·glade (ev′ər·glād) *n.* A tract of low swampy land covered with tall grass. — **The Everglades** A swampy region of southern Florida; about 100 miles long, 50–75 miles wide; the southern part is included in **Everglades National Park;** 1,719 sq. mi.; established 1947.

Everglade State Nickname of FLORIDA.

ev·er·green (ev′ər·grēn′) *adj.* **1.** Having foliage that remains green until the formation of new foliage: distinguished from *deciduous:* an *evergreen* tree **2.** Of or belonging to an evergreen tree or plant: *evergreen* leaves. — *n.* **1.** An evergreen tree or plant. **2.** *pl.* Evergreen branches or twigs, especially as used for decorations.

Evergreen State Nickname of WASHINGTON.

ev·er·last·ing (ev′ər·las′ting, -läs′-) *adj.* **1.** Existing or lasting forever; eternal: belief in an *everlasting* God. **2.** Continuing for an indefinitely long period; perpetual: *everlasting* happiness. **3.** Apparently ceaseless; incessant· interminable: her *everlasting* chatter **4.** Tedious through constant repetition or indulgence: you and your *everlasting* jokes. — *n* **1.** Endless duration; eternity: to love for *everlasting* **2.** One of several plants, chiefly of the aster family, whose flowers keep their form and color when dried: also called *immortelle.* **3.** One of several durable fabrics. as prunella. **4.** A card game in which cards are matched until one player gets all of them. — **the Everlasting God** [ME] — **ev′er·last′ing·ly** *adv.* — **ev′er·last′ing·ness** *n.*
— **Syn. 1.** *Everlasting, eternal, endless,* and *interminable* agree in the sense of going on forever. *Everlasting* and *eternal* are used interchangeably, but strictly the *everlasting* may have had a beginning while the *eternal* has no beginning or end. *Endless* is applied to extent as well as to time: an *endless* belt in a machine.

Interminable is usually used to characterize that which is unduly prolonged or that which continues without intermission.

ev·er·more (ev′ər·môr′, -mōr′) *adv. Poetic* For and at all time to come; always. **— for evermore** Forever.

e·ver·sion (i·vûr′zhən) *n.* The act of everting, or the condition of being everted. [< OF < L *eversio, -onis* < *evertere.* See EVERT.] **— e·ver′si·ble** (-sə·bəl) *adj.*

e·vert (i·vûrt′) *v.t.* To turn outward or inside out. [< L *evertere* < *e-* out + *vertere* to turn]

e·ver·tor (i·vûr′tər) *n. Anat.* A muscle that serves to rotate an organ or a part outward.

eve·ry (ev′rē, ev′ər·ē) *adj.* **1.** Each without excepting any of all those that together form an aggregate; each of one after another without excluding any: *Every* guest is here. **2.** Each (member or unit singled out in some way) of a series: *every* tenth man; *every* four hours. **3.** Each possible or conceivable (thing specified) without exception: They gave him *every* chance to escape. **4.** The fullest or the greatest (thing specified); the utmost; all possible: Show him *every* consideration. **— every bit** *Informal* In all respects; altogether; quite: He is *every bit* as good as you. **— every now and then** From time to time; occasionally. Also **every now and again, every once in a while. — every other** Each alternate (specified thing): They won *every other* game. **— every so often** *Informal* From time to time; every now and then. **— every which way** *Informal* In every way or direction and with little or no order or logic. [ME *ever-ilk* < OE *æfre* ever + *ælc* each]

— Syn. *Every* and *each* are alike in that they both direct attention to one individual member after another of all the members of an aggregate without excluding any. But *every* stresses the idea that the member singled out is typical of the entire aggregate: *Every* man loves freedom; *each* stresses the individuality of the member: *Each* man made his own decision.

eve·ry·bod·y (ev′rē·bod′ē, -bud′ē) *pron.* Every person; everyone.

eve·ry·day (ev′rē·dā′, -dā′) *adj.* **1.** Happening every day; daily. **2.** Suitable for ordinary days: *everyday* clothes. **3.** Commonplace; ordinary: *everyday* folks.

eve·ry·one (ev′rē·wun′, -wən) *pron.* Every person; everybody.

every one Each individual person or thing out of the whole number, excepting none: *Every one* of the men is ill.

eve·ry·thing (ev′rē·thing′) *pron.* **1.** Whatever exists; all things whatsoever: *everything* in the whole world. **2.** Whatever is relevant, needed, or important: I have *everything.* **3.** The only thing that really matters; the essential thing: Happiness is *everything.*

eve·ry·where (ev′rē·hwâr′) *adv.* At, in, or to every place.

Eve's-cup (ēvz′kup′) *n.* An insectivorous American pitcher plant (*Sarracenia flava*) with trumpet leaves, crimson throat, and yellow flowers.

Eve·sham (ēv′shəm, ē′shəm, ē′səm) A municipal borough in SE Worcestershire, England; scene of Edward I's victory over Simon de Montfort, 1265; pop. 12,608 (1961).

e·vict (i·vikt′) *v.t.* **1.** To expel (a tenant) by legal process; dispossess; put out. **2.** To recover (property, etc.) by legal process or superior claim. **— Syn.** See EXPEL. [< L *evictus,* pp. of *evincere* < *e-* out + *vincere* to conquer] **— e·vic′tion** *n.* **— e·vic′tor** *n.*

ev·i·dence (ev′ə·dəns) *n.* **1.** That which serves to prove or disprove something; that which is used for demonstrating the truth or falsity of something; support; proof: *evidence* for the theory of evolution. **2.** That which serves as a ground for knowing something with certainty or for believing something with conviction; corroboration: *evidence* of the authorship of a book. **3.** An outward indication of the existence or fact of something: Her paleness was *evidence* of her distress. **4.** *Law* That which is properly presented before a court as a means of establishing or disproving something alleged or presumed and as an aid toward arriving at a final judgment or verdict, as the statements of witnesses. **— Syn.** See TESTIMONY. **— in evidence** In the condition of being readily seen or perceived; especially, conspicuously present: His friends were very much *in evidence.* **— to turn state's evidence** To testify in court against one's accomplices. *— v.t.* **·denced, ·denc·ing 1.** To give a clear indication of; show unmistakably. **2.** To support by oral testimony; attest.

ev·i·dent (ev′ə·dənt) *adj.* Easily perceived or recognized; clearly perceptible; plain. [< L *evidens, -entis,* ppr. of *evidere* < *e-* out + *videre* to see]

— Syn. *Evident, apparent, manifest, palpable, patent,* and *obvious* mean readily perceived. That which is *evident* is clearly indicated by facts and circumstances; something *apparent* is open to view without need for inference. Inward character is made *manifest* by outward signs: *manifest* disapproval of another's actions. A *palpable* thing is perceived by a sense other than sight, and so presumably is more certain than that which is merely visible. A similar deprecation of sight is suggested by a secondary sense of *apparent* when it refers to what appears to be rather than what actually is. Something *patent* is *manifest* to all, and is usually applied to what we would expect to find hidden or obscure: a *patent* flaw in reasoning. *Obvious* describes something too conspicuous to be concealed and too *apparent* to be disputed. **— Ant.** concealed, hidden, obscure, veiled.

ev·i·den·tial (ev′ə·den′shəl) *adj.* **1.** Relating to, furnishing, or having the nature of evidence. **2.** Based or relying on evidence. **— ev·i·den′tial·ly** *adv.*

ev·i·dent·ly (ev′ə·dənt·lē, -dent′-, ev′ə·dent′lē) *adv.* **1.** To all appearances; so far as can be seen; apparently: He is *evidently* her brother. **2.** Quite clearly; without much question; obviously: *Evidently* you don't approve.

e·vil (ē′vəl) *adj.* **1.** Morally bad; wicked: *evil* deeds. **2.** Causing injury, damage, or any other undesirable result; harmful or prejudicial: *evil* habits. **3.** Marked by, full of, or threatening misfortune or distress; unlucky or disastrous: *evil* times; an *evil* omen. **4.** Not high in public esteem; not well thought of: an *evil* reputation. **— the Evil One** Satan. *— n.* **1.** That which is evil; as: **a** That which is morally bad; wrongdoing; wickedness: to avoid *evil* and do good. **b** That which is injurious or otherwise undesirable: to be subject to *evil.* **c** That which causes suffering, misfortune, or disaster: to hate war and all other *evil.* **2.** Some particular thing, as an act, condition, or characteristic, that is evil: one of the *evils* of that political system. **3.** Scrofula. *— adv.* In an evil manner; badly: now chiefly in combinations: an *evil-smelling* plant. [OE *yfel*] **— e′vil·ly** *adv.* **— e′vil·ness** *n.*

— Syn. (adjective) **1.** sinful. **2.** pernicious, hurtful, destructive. — (noun) **1a.** immorality, sin. **2.** ill. — (adverb) ill.

e·vil·do·er (ē′vəl·dōō′ər) *n.* One who does evil. **— e′vil·do′ing** *n.*

evil eye A glance superstitiously supposed capable of inflicting misfortune or injury.

e·vil-mind·ed (ē′vəl·mīn′did) *adj.* Obsessed with vicious or depraved thoughts; especially, inclined to put a sexually indecent interpretation upon almost anything said or done. **— e′vil-mind′ed·ly** *adv.* **— e′vil-mind′ed·ness** *n.*

e·vince (i·vins′) *v.t.* **e·vinced, e·vinc·ing 1.** To indicate clearly; demonstrate convincingly; make evident; prove: His loyalty was *evinced* by this heroic act. **2.** To give an outward sign of having (a particular quality, feeling, etc.); exhibit; display: She *evinced* her pity by weeping. **3.** *Obs.* To overcome; also, to convince. [< L *evincere.* See EVICT.] **— e·vin′ci·ble** *adj.* **— e·vin′cive** *adj.*

e·vis·cer·ate (v. i·vis′ə·rāt; adj. i·vis′ər·it) *v.t.* **·at·ed, ·at·ing 1.** To disembowel. **2.** To remove the essential or vital part of. **3.** *Surg.* To remove the contents of (an organ): to *eviscerate* an eye. *— adj. Surg.* Disemboweled: an *eviscerate* abdomen. [< L *evisceratus,* pp. of *eviscerare* < *e-* out + *viscera* entrails] **— e·vis′cer·a′tion** *n.*

ev·i·ta·ble (ev′ə·tə·bəl) *adj.* Avoidable. [< L *evitabilis* < *evitare* to avoid < *e-* out + *vitare* to shun]

e·vite (i·vīt′) *v.t. Archaic* To avoid. [< L *evitare.* See EVITABLE.]

ev·o·ca·tion (ev′ə·kā′shən) *n.* **1.** The act of evoking or calling forth; a summoning, as of memories. **2.** In civil law, the transference of a suit from a lower to a higher court. [< L *evocatio, -onis* < *evocare.* See EVOKE.]

e·voc·a·tive (i·vok′ə·tiv, -vō′kə-) *adj.* Tending to evoke.

ev·o·ca·tor (ev′ə·kā′tər) *n.* One who evokes.

e·voke (i·vōk′) *v.t.* **e·voked, e·vok·ing 1.** To call or summon forth, as memories. **2.** To draw forth or produce (a response, reaction, etc.); elicit. **3.** To summon up (spirits) by or as by incantations. [< L *evocare* < *e-* out + *vocare* to call] **— ev·o·ca·ble** (ev′ə·kə·bəl, i·vō′kə·bəl) *adj.*

ev·o·lute (ev′ə·lōōt) *n. Math.* A curve that is the locus of the center of curvature of another curve, its *involute,* and therefore tangent to all its normals; a curve that is the envelope of all the normals of another curve. [< L *evolutus,* pp. of *evolvere.* See EVOLVE.]

ev·o·lu·tion (ev′ə·lōō′shən) *n.* **1.** The act or process of unfolding, growing, or developing, usually by slow stages. **2.** Anything developed by such an act or process. **3.** *Biol.* **a** The theory that all forms of life originated by descent, with gradual or abrupt modifications, from earlier forms, and so backward to the most rudimentary organisms. **b** The series of changes, as by natural selection, mutation, etc., through which a given type of organism has acquired the characteristics differentiating it from other types; phylogeny. **4.** One of a series of complex movements or formations. **5.** A moving or wheeling about, as in dancing, etc. **6.** A movement or maneuver of troops, ships, etc. **7.** The process of giving off gas, heat, sound, etc.; emission. **8.** *Math.* The operation of extracting a root: opposed to *involution.*

ev·o·lu·tion·al (ev′ə·lōō′shən·əl) *adj.* Evolutionary. **— ev′o·lu′tion·al·ly** *adv.*

ev·o·lu·tion·ar·y (ev′ə·lōō′shən·er′ē) *adj.* **1.** Of, relating to, or produced through evolution, especially biological evolution: *evolutionary* development. **2.** Agreeing with or proceeding according to the theory of biological evolution: *evolutionary* methods. **3.** Of, relating to, or marked by military maneuvers or other evolutions: *evolutionary* operations.

ev·o·lu·tion·ist (ev′ə·lōō′shən·ist) *n.* **1.** An adherent or proponent of the theory of biological evolution. **2.** One who believes in or advocates progress through gradual stages, as in political structure. *— adj.* **1.** Evolutionary. **2.** Of or relating to evolutionists. **— ev′o·lu′tion·ism** *n.*

ev·o·lu·tion·is·tic (ev′ə·lōō′shən·is′tik) *adj.* Serving to support or further evolution, especially biological evolution.

e·volve (i·volv′) v. **e·volved**, **e·volv·ing** v.t. **1.** To work out; develop gradually: to evolve a plan. **2.** Biol. To develop, as by a differentiation of parts or functions, to a more highly organized condition: usually in the passive. **3.** To give or throw off (vapor, heat, etc.): set free; emit. **4.** To unfold or expand. — v.i. **5.** To undergo the process of evolution. **6.** To open out; develop. [< L evolvere to unroll < e- out + volvere to roll] — **e·volv′a·ble** adj. — **e·volve′ment** n.

e·von·y·mus (i·von′ə·məs) n. Euonymus, a plant.

e·vul·sion (i·vul′shən) n. A plucking out; forcible extraction [< L evulsio -onis < e- out + vellere to pluck]

Ev·voia (ev·vyä′) The Greek name for EUBOEA.

ev·zone (ev′zōn) n. A modern Greek soldier, one of a corps picked from the mountainous regions. [< Mod. Gk. euzōno light infantry < Gk. euzōnoi pl. of euzōnos active, lit., well-girdled < eu- well + zōnē belt]

E·wald (i′väl), **Johannes**, 1743–81, Danish lyric poet: also Evald.

ewe (yōō, Dial. yō) n. A female sheep [OE eowu]

E·we (ā′wā, ā′vā) n. **1** One of a tribe of African Negroes of the Slave Coast **2.** The Sudanic language of this tribe.

ewe lamb The one highly valued possession of a person who has little else; a beloved or an only child.

Ew·ell (yōō′əl), **Richard Stoddert**, 1817–72 Confederate general in the Civil War.

ewe-neck (yōō′nek′) n. A neck, as of some horses, that is thin and bowed backward. — **ewe′-necked′** adj.

ew·er (yōō′ər) n. A large, wide-mouthed jug or pitcher. [ME < AF ewer, OF eviere < eve < L aqua water]

Ew·ing (yōō′ing) An urban township in western New Jersey, near Trenton; pop. 32,831.

ex¹ (eks) prep. **1.** In finance, without the right to have or participate in: ex bonus. **2.** In commerce, without charge to the purchaser until taken out of (a specified place or thing): ex dock. **3.** U.S. From a (class graduating in a specified year), but without graduating: ex '54. [< L ex out]

ex² (eks) n. pl. **ex·es** (ek′səz) The letter X.

ex-¹ prefix **1.** Out of: exit, exhale, exonerate. **2.** Thoroughly: exasperate, excruciate. **3.** Not having; lacking: excaudate. **4.** Being formerly; former; sometime: attached with a hyphen to the word it qualifies: ex-president, ex-wife. Also: e- before consonants except c, f, p, q, s, t, as in edentate, erode, evade; ef- before f, as in efferent. [< L ex- < ex from, out of]

ex-² prefix Out of; from; forth: exodus. Also, before consonants, ec-, as in eclipse. [< Gk. ex-, ek- < ex out]

ex-³ Var. of EXO .

ex. **1.** Examination; examined. **2.** Example. **3.** Except; excepted; exception. **4.** Exchange. **5.** Excursion. **6.** Executed. **7.** Executive.

Ex. Exodus.

ex·ac·er·bate (ig·zas′ər·bāt) v.t. **·bat·ed**, **·bat·ing** **1.** To make more sharp or severe; aggravate. **2.** To embitter or irritate (someone). [< L exacerbatus, pp. of exacerbare < ex- very + acerbus bitter, harsh] — **ex·ac′er·ba′tion** n.

ex·act (ig·zakt′) adj. **1.** Perfectly clear and complete in every detail; definite and precise: exact directions. **2.** Altogether accurate: to ask for an exact answer. **3.** Being precisely (what is specified); being neither more nor less than (what is required, proper, etc.): the exact amount necessary. **4.** Corresponding in every detail with something taken as a standard or model: an exact copy of a document. **5.** Proceeding along clearly defined lines; free from vagueness or fuzziness; sharp and clear: Exact thinking is necessary. **6.** Extremely careful about detail, accuracy, and good order; thorough and punctilious: an exact editor. **7.** Designed for use where the utmost precision and accuracy is required: an exact scientific instrument. **8.** Rigorously demanding: an exact schoolmaster. — **Syn.** See CORRECT. — v.t. **1.** To demand rigorously the full payment of; require as a matter of strict justice without making any concession whatsoever: to exact full compensation for an injury. **2.** To force unjustly the payment of; obtain by or as if by extorting: to exact a ridiculously high fee. **3.** To obtain by or as if by forcing out; wring; wrest: to exact a full reply. **4.** To insist upon the performance or yielding of as a strict right or obligation: to exact obedience. **5.** To call for; require: The situation exacted quick thinking. — **Syn.** See DEMAND. [< L exactus, pp. of exigere to determine < ex- out + agere to drive. Akin to EXAMINE.] — **ex·act′a·ble** adj. — **ex·ac′tor** or **ex·act′er** n.

ex·act·a (ig·zak′tə) n. In horse racing, a single bet won by choosing in exact order the first and second horses in a specified race.

ex·act·ing (ig·zak′ting) adj. **1.** Making rigorous demands; allowing no letup; severe: an exacting taskmaster. **2.** Involving constant hard work, effort, attention, etc.: an exacting profession — **ex·act′ing·ly** adv. — **ex·act′ing·ness** n.

ex·ac·tion (ig·zak′shən) n. **1.** The act of exacting something. **2.** The act of unjustly forcing the payment of something; extortion. **3.** Something, as a sum of money or an act of obedience, paid or yielded in compliance with an insistent demand or through extortion.

ex·act·ly (ig·zakt′lē) adv. **1.** In an exact manner; with great precision or accuracy. **2.** Precisely right; just so.

ex·act·ness (ig·zakt′nis) n. The quality of being exact; great precision or accuracy. Also **ex·act′i·tude** (-i·tōōd, -i·tyōōd).

exact science A science, as physics or astronomy, whose data are theoretically predictable on the basis of strict quantitative laws.

ex·ag·ger·ate (ig·zaj′ə·rāt) v. **·at·ed**, **·at·ing** v.t. **1.** To represent or look upon as greater than is actually the case; magnify beyond proportion: to exaggerate a difficulty; to exaggerate one's troubles. **2.** To make greater in size, intensity, etc., than what would be normal or expected: to exaggerate the natural color of the skin. — v.i. **3.** To overstate or overemphasize something. [< L exaggeratus, pp. of exaggerare < ex- out + agger heap] — **ex·ag′ger·a′tor** n.

ex·ag·ger·at·ed (ig·zaj′ə·rāt/id) adj. Going beyond actual fact, truth, or propriety. — **ex·ag′ger·a′tive**, **ex·ag′ger·a·to′ry** (-ər·ə·tôr′ē, -tō′rē) adj. — **ex·ag′ger·at·ed·ly** adv.

ex·ag·ger·a·tion (ig·zaj′ə·rā′shən) n. **1.** The act of exaggerating, or the state of being exaggerated; overstatement or overemphasis. **2.** A statement, narrative, etc., marked by exaggeration.

ex·alt (ig·zôlt′) v.t. **1.** To raise in rank, character, honor, etc.; elevate. **2.** To glorify or praise; pay honor to. **3** To fill with delight, pride, etc.; elate. **4.** To increase the intensity of, as colors; heighten. **5.** Archaic To raise up physically; lift up [< L exaltare < ex- out + altus high] — **ex·alt′er** n.

ex·al·ta·tion (eg′zôl·tā′shən) n. **1.** The act of exalting, or the state of being exalted; elevation. **2.** A state or feeling of great, often extreme, exhilaration and well-being; rapture or ecstasy. [< F < LL exaltatio, -onis < L exaltare. See EXALT.]

ex·alt·ed (ig·zôl′tid) adj. **1.** Elevated in rank, character, etc.: an exalted position in government. **2.** Lofty; sublime: an exalted ideal. — **ex·alt′ed·ly** adv. — **ex·alt′ed·ness** n.

ex·am (ig·zam′) n. Informal An examination.

exam. Examination; examined.

ex·a·men (ig·zā′men) n. Eccl. A searching examination of one's conscience. [< L. See EXAMINE.]

ex·am·i·nant (ig·zam′ə·nənt) n. An examiner.

ex·am·i·na·tion (ig·zam′ə·nā′shən) n. **1.** The act of examining, or the state of being examined; careful scrutiny or inquiry; inspection. **2.** Medical scrutiny and testing. **3.** A formal test of knowledge or skills; also, the questions or problems posed: a civil service examination. Abbr ex., exam. **4.** Law Inquiry by direct interrogation or testimony; also, the testimony made in such inquiry and reduced to writing. [< L examinatio, -onis < examinare. See EXAMINE.] — **ex·am′i·na′tion·al** adj.

ex·am·ine (ig·zam′in) v.t. **·ined**, **·in·ing** **1.** To inspect or scrutinize with care; investigate critically; inquire into. **2.** To subject (a person, organ, etc.) to medical scrutiny and testing. **3.** To test by questions or exercises as to qualifications, fitness, etc., as a pupil. **4.** To question formally in order to elicit facts, etc. [< OF examiner < L examinare < examen tongue of a balance < ex- out + ag-, root of agere to drive. Akin to EXACT.] — **ex·am′in·a·ble** adj. — **ex·am′in·er** n.

ex·am·i·nee (ig·zam′ə·nē′) n. One who is taking an examination or who is a candidate for an examination.

ex·am·ple (ig·zam′pəl, -zäm′-) n. **1.** A particular thing that belongs to and is typical of a group of things and that is singled out as having qualities identical with or similar to the qualities of any member of the group; a representative specimen; sample: an example of modern art. **2.** Something deserving to be imitated or copied; model; exemplar. **3.** An instance or object of punishment, reprimand, etc., designed to serve as a warning or deterrent to others. **4.** A previous case or instance that is identical with or similar to something under consideration; precedent: Such weather is without example. **5.** A particular problem or exercise in arithmetic, algebra, etc., worked out or designed to be worked out according to set rules. Abbr. ex. — **for example** By way of illustration; as a typical instance. — **to set an example** To act in such a way as to arouse others to imitation. — v.t. **·pled**, **·pling** To present an example of; show by example; exemplify: now only in the passive· Such courage has not recently been exampled. [< OF, earlier essample < L exemplum something taken out < eximere < ex- out + emere to buy, take. Doublet of SAMPLE.]

— **Syn. 2.** Example, exemplar, model, and pattern are compared as they signify a person or thing worthy to be imitated. Both example and exemplar denote primarily a sample, or a particular instance, but exemplar is usually limited to persons while example is extended to things and actions: Griselda was an exemplar of patience, glass is an example of an amorphous substance. Examples and exemplars may be cited as worthy or unworthy of imitation. The sense of imitation is stronger in both model and pattern. In technical usage, a model is a guide for constructing something similar, but not necessarily identical; a pattern is a guide for making an exact duplicate. In a general sense, a model approaches the ideal, while a pattern is highly typical: Penelope was a model of a faithful wife, Beau Nash was the very *pattern* of a bon vivant. Compare IDEAL.

ex·an·i·mate (ig·zan′ə·mit, -māt) *adj. Rare* **1.** Lifeless; dead. **2.** Dispirited; spiritless. [< L *exanimatus*, pp. of *ex- animare* to kill < *ex-* out + *animus* breath, life]

ex an·i·mo (eks an′i·mō) *Latin* From the heart; sincerely.

ex·an·the·ma (ek/san·thē′mə) *n. pl.* **·them·a·ta** (-them′ə· tə, -thē′mə·tə) or **·the·mas** (-thē′məz) *Pathol.* **1.** A skin rash or eruption symptomatic in scarlet fever, measles, or similar diseases. **2.** A disease marked by the appearance of skin rashes or eruptions and by fever. [< LL < Gk., eruption < *ex-* out + *anthos* blossom] **— ex·an·the·mat·ic** (ek·san′thi· mat′ik), **ex′an·them′a·tous** (-them′ə·təs) *adj.*

ex·arch (ek′särk) *n.* **1.** A provincial governor under the Byzantine Empire. **2.** In the Eastern Orthodox Church, the deputy of a patriarch. **3.** Formerly, in the Eastern Orthodox Church, a metropolitan or patriarch; later, a bish- op ranking below a patriarch. [< LL *exarchus* < Gk. *ex- archos* < *ex-* out + *archein* to rule]

ex·ar·chate (ek′sär·kāt, ik·sär′kāt) *n.* The office, province, or jurisdiction of an exarch. Also **ex′ar·chy.**

ex·as·per·ate (ig·zas′pə·rāt) *v.t.* **·at·ed, ·at·ing 1.** To make very annoyed or angry; irritate to the point of infuriation. **2.** To make (a disagreeable condition, feeling, etc.) still worse; exacerbate; aggravate. **— Syn.** See IRRITATE, OF- FEND. [< L *exasperatus*, pp. of *exasperare* < *ex-* out + *asper* rough] **— ex·as′per·at′er** *n.*

ex·as·per·at·ing (ig·zas′pə·rā′ting) *adj.* Most annoying; infuriating. **— ex·as′per·at′ing·ly** *adv.*

ex·as·per·a·tion (ig·zas′pə·rā′shən) *n.* **1.** The act of exas- perating, or the state of being exasperated; extreme annoy- ance or irritation. **2.** Something that exasperates.

exc. 1. Excellent. **2.** Except; excepted; exception. **3.** Ex- change. **4.** Excursion.

Exc. Excellency.

Ex·cal·i·bur (eks·kal′ə·bər) In Arthurian legend, the sword of King Arthur. [< OF *Escalibor* < Med.L *Caliburnus* < Celtic ? < Irish *Caladbolg* a legendary sword, lit. hard belly, voracious]

ex ca·the·dra (eks kə·thē′drə, kath′i-) *Latin* With au- thority; in one's official capacity; literally, from the chair.

ex·cau·date (eks·kô′dāt) *adj. Zool.* Having no tail. [< EX¹- + CAUDATE]

ex·ca·vate (eks′kə·vāt) *v.t.* **·vat·ed, ·vat·ing 1.** To make a hole or cavity in; hollow or dig out. **2.** To form or make (a hole, tunnel, etc.) by hollowing, digging out, or scooping. **3.** To remove by digging or scooping out, as soil. **4.** To un- cover by digging, as ruins; unearth. [< L *excavatus*, pp. of *excavare* < *ex-* out + *cavus* hollow]

ex·ca·va·tion (eks′kə·vā′shən) *n.* **1.** The act or process of excavating. **2.** A cavity or hollow formed by excavating. **3.** Something brought into view by excavating, as ruins. **— Syn.** See HOLE.

ex·ca·va·tor (eks′kə·vā′tər) *n.* One who or that which ex- cavates, as a steam shovel or dredging machine.

ex·ceed (ik·sēd′) *v.t.* **1.** To surpass, as in quantity or qual- ity. **2.** To go beyond the limit or extent of: to *exceed* one's income. **— *v.i.* 3.** To be superior; surpass others. [< F *excéder* < L *excedere* < *ex-* out, beyond + *cedere* to go] **— Syn. 1.** *Exceed, transcend, excel, surpass, outdo*, and *out- strip* mean to go beyond. *Exceed* is applied to quantity, measure, and limit, and *transcend* only to limit in a lofty sense: to *exceed* ten pounds in weight, to *exceed* one's authority, to *transcend* hu- man knowledge. To *excel* is to be superior in some good quality; to *surpass* is to go beyond the usual in either good or bad character- istics: to *excel* in bravery, to *surpass* in pride and arrogance. *Outdo* and *outstrip* refer to performance, especially in some activity re- quiring physical skill or endurance: to *outdo* all one's competitors, to *outstrip* one's pursuers.

ex·ceed·ing (ik·sē′ding) *adj.* Greater than usual; surpass- ing; extraordinary. **— *adv. Archaic* Exceedingly.

ex·ceed·ing·ly (ik·sē′ding·lē) *adv.* To a greater degree than usual; extremely.

ex·cel (ik·sel′) *v.* **·celled, ·cel·ling** *v.t.* **1.** To surpass, usually in some good quality or action; be better than; outstrip: to *excel* all rivals. **— *v.i.* 2.** To surpass others; be outstanding: to *excel* in knowledge of the law. **— Syn.** See EXCEED. [< OF *exceller* < L *excellere* to rise]

ex·cel·lence (ek′sə·ləns) *n.* **1.** The state or quality of ex- celling; superiority. **2.** That in which someone or something excels; a superior trait or quality. Also **ex′cel·len·cy.**

Ex·cel·len·cy (ek′sə·lən·sē) *n. pl.* **·cies** An honorary title or form of address for certain dignitaries, as some governors, ambassadors, and bishops: often preceded by *His, Her, Your*, etc. Abbr. *Exc.*

ex·cel·lent (ek′sə·lənt) *adj.* **1.** Being of the very best qual- ity; exceptionally good; very fine; first-rate: an *excellent* wine. Abbr. *E, exc.* **2.** *Archaic* Outstanding in some bad quality: an *excellent* hypocrite. **— ex′cel·lent·ly** *adv.* **— Syn. 1.** superior, first-rate, first-class, choice, select, prime, capital, fine, worthy, estimable. **— Ant.** inferior, poor, bad, base, good-for-nothing, worthless.

ex·cel·si·or (ik·sel′sē·ər) *n.* **1.** *U.S.* Long, fine wood shav- ings used as stuffing or as packing material. **2.** *Printing* A

size of type smaller than brilliant, about 3-point. [after a trade name]

Ex·cel·si·or (ek·sel′sē·ôr) Upward: motto of the State of New York. [Compar. of L *excelsus* high]

ex·cept (ik·sept′) *prep.* With the exclusion or omission of; aside from; barring: Everyone *except* him was willing. **— conj. 1.** Aside from the fact that; if one disregards the fact that: I could do it, *except* I don't want to. Also **except that. 2.** Otherwise than: He never referred to it *except* jokingly. ◆ In this sense, *except* may also be construed as a preposi- tion governing the following adverb, phrase, or clause. **3.** *Archaic* Unless: *Except* you try, you can't succeed. **— except for** If it were not for; but for. **— *v.t.* 1.** To exclude from consideration, enumeration, etc.; leave deliberately out of account: The book is very good, if you *except* some factual errors. **— *v.i.* 2.** To raise an objection, especially a formal objection: now usually with *to*: to *except* to an accusation. Abbr. *ex., exc.* [< F *excepter* < L *exceptare*, freq. of *excipere* < *ex-* out + *capere* to take]

ex·cept·ing (ik·sep′ting) *prep.* With the exclusion of; ex- cept. **— *conj. Archaic* Unless; except.

ex·cep·tion (ik·sep′shən) *n.* **1.** The act of excepting, or the state of being excepted; exclusion; omission. **2.** Something excluded from or not conforming to a general class, princi- ple, rule, etc. **3.** An objection or complaint; adverse criti- cism: a statement that is open to *exception*. **4.** *Law* A for- mal objection to the decision of a court during trial, implying that the objection may be used in a motion for a new trial or an appeal. Abbr. *ex., exc.* **— to take exception 1.** To ex- press disagreement with another's views; object; demur. **2.** To feel resentful over something. [< AF *excepcioun* < L *exceptio, -onis* < *excipere*. See EXCEPT.]

ex·cep·tion·a·ble (ik·sep′shən·ə·bəl) *adj.* Open to excep- tion or objection. **— ex·cep′tion·a·bly** *adv.*

ex·cep·tion·al (ik·sep′shən·əl) *adj.* Being an exception; be- ing out of the ordinary; unusual, uncommon, or extraordi- nary. **— ex·cep′tion·al·ly** *adv.*

ex·cep·tive (ik·sep′tiv) *adj.* **1.** Relating to, containing, or being an exception. **2.** Quick to object or criticize; captious. [< LL *exceptivus* < L *excipere*. See EXCEPT.]

ex·cerpt (*n.* ek′sûrpt; *v.* ik·sûrpt′) *n.* A passage picked out from a book, article, speech, etc., and cited separately; cita- tion; extract. **— *v.t.* To pick out and cite (a passage from a book, etc.); select for quotation. [< L *excerptus*, pp. of *excerpere* < *ex-* out + *carpere* to pluck, seize]

ex·cerp·tion (ik·sûrp′shən) *n. Rare* **1.** The act of excerpt- ing; extraction. **2.** An excerpt; extract.

ex·cess (*n.* ik·ses′, ek′ses; *adj.* ek′ses, ik·ses′) *n.* **1.** The condition or fact of going beyond what is usual, necessary, proper, etc.: to avoid *excess* in all things. **2.** An immoderate or inordinate quantity, extent, or degree of something; over- abundance: an *excess* of emotion. **3.** The quantity, extent, or degree by which one thing is over and above another thing; surplus: a large *excess* of profits over liabilities. **4.** An amount that is left over or that is greater than is wanted or necessary; superfluity: to produce an *excess* of farm products. **5.** Overindulgence, as in food or drink; intemperance. **— *adj.* 1.** Being over and above what is expected or usual; surplus; extra. **2.** Immoderate; excessive: *excess* grief. [< OF *exces* < L *excessus* departure < *excedere*. See EXCEED.] **— Ant.** shortage, deficiency, dearth, scantiness, meagerness.

ex·ces·sive (ik·ses′iv) *adj.* Going beyond what is usual, necessary, proper, etc.; inordinate; extreme: *excessive* laugh- ter; so to *excessive* lengths. **— ex·ces′sive·ly** *adv.*

excess profits Net profits exceeding the normal average for a specified period of years.

exch. 1. Exchange. **2.** Exchequer.

ex·change (iks·chānj′) *v.* **·changed, ·chang·ing** *v.t.* **1.** To give and receive reciprocally: to *exchange* gifts, opinions, etc. **2.** To give up for something taken as a replacement: to *ex- change* one job for another. **3.** To return as unsatisfactory and get a replacement for: to *exchange* something bought. **4.** To transfer the possession of to another and receive the equivalent of from the other: to *exchange* francs for dollars. **5.** To transfer to another in return for the equivalent in goods instead of in money; trade; swap. **— *v.i.* 6.** To ex- change something. **7.** To be exchanged: money that *ex- changes* at face value. **— *n.* 1.** The act of giving or receiving one thing as equivalent for another; trade; barter. **2.** A giv- ing and receiving in turn; interchange: an *exchange* of com- pliments. **3.** The substitution of one thing for another. **4.** That which is given or received in trade or substitution. **5.** A place where brokers, merchants, etc., meet to buy, sell, or trade commodities or securities: stock *exchange*. **6.** A cen- tral telephone system in a part of a city or in a town, con- necting one or more groups of telephones. **7.** The system of settling commercial debts between parties at a distance by using negotiable credit drafts, called *bills of exchange*, in place of money; also, a bill of exchange. **8.** The fee or percentage charged for bills of exchange, collecting drafts, etc. **9.** Rate of exchange (which see). **10.** The mutual giving and receiving of equal sums of money, as between two countries using different currencies, and allowing for differences in value. **11.** *pl.* Bills, drafts, checks, etc., presented to a clearing-house for exchange or settlement. **12.** *Physics* The mutual interaction between the electrons, protons, and other components of the same or different atoms. Abbr. (n.) *ex., exc., exch.* [< AF *eschaunge* < LL *excambium,* < *excambiare* < L *ex-* out + *cambiare* to exchange] — **ex·chang'er** *n.*

ex·change·a·ble (iks-chān'jə-bəl) *adj.* Capable of being exchanged. — **ex·change'a·bil'i·ty** *n.*

ex·cheq·uer (iks-chek'ər, eks'chek·ər) *n.* **1.** The treasury of a state, nation, organization, etc. Abbr. *exch.* **2.** *Informal* The extent of one's funds; total financial resources. [ME *escheker* < OF *eschaquier* chessboard, then table marked in squares for keeping of accounts < OF *eschac.* See CHECKER.]

Ex·cheq·uer (iks-chek'ər, eks'chek·ər) *n.* **1.** The department of the British government managing the public revenue. **2.** See COURT OF EXCHEQUER.

ex·cide (ik-sīd') *v.t.* **cid·ed, cid·ing** To remove by cutting out; excise. [< L *excidere.* See EXCISE².]

ex·cip·i·ent (ik-sip'ē·ənt) *n.* Any inert substance used to give drug preparations a suitable form or pleasant taste. [< L *excipiens, -entis,* ppr. of *excipere.* See EXCEPT.]

ex·cis·a·ble (ik-sī'zə-bəl) *adj.* Subject to an excise.

ex·cise¹ (*n.* ek'sīz, ik-sīz'; *v.* ik-sīz') *n.* **1.** An indirect tax on such commodities as liquor, tobacco, etc., produced, sold, used, or transported within a country. Also **excise tax. 2.** A license fee charged for various sports, trades, amusements, etc. **3.** *Brit.* A branch of the civil service having charge of the inland revenue taxes and duties. — *v.t.* **cised, cis·ing** To levy an excise upon. [< MDu. *excijs, accijs* < OF *acceis* < L *ad-* to + *census* tax]

ex·cise² (ik-sīz') *v.t.* **cised, cis·ing** **1.** To remove by cutting out, as a growth. **2.** To delete (a word, passage, etc.); expunge. [< L *excisus,* pp. of *excidere* < *ex-* out + *caedere* to cut] — **ex·ci·sion** (ik-sizh'ən) *n.*

ex·cise·man (ik-sīz'mən) *n. pl.* **·men** (-mən) *Brit.* An officer who collects excise duties.

ex·cit·a·bil·i·ty (ik-sī'tə-bil'ə-tē) *n.* **1.** The quality of being excitable; susceptibility to excitement. **2.** *Physiol.* Sensitivity to stimuli.

ex·cit·a·ble (ik-sī'tə-bəl) *adj.* **1.** Easily excited; highstrung. **2.** *Physiol.* Susceptible to stimuli. — **ex·cit'a·ble·ness** *n.* — **ex·cit'a·bly** *adv.*

ex·ci·tant (ik-sī'tənt, ek'sə·tənt) *n.* Something that excites or stimulates; stimulant. — *adj.* Tending to excite or stimulate; stimulating: also **ex·ci'ta·tive, ex·ci'ta·to·ry** (-tôr'ē, -tō'rē). [< L *excitans, -antis,* ppr. of *excitare.* See EXCITE.]

ex·ci·ta·tion (ek'sī·tā'shən) *n.* **1.** The act of exciting, or the state of being excited; disturbance; agitation. **2.** *Physics* **a** The raising of a system, as an atom, from one energy level to a higher level. **b** The electrification or magnetization of a substance. **3.** *Biol.* The action of a stimulus on a plant or animal organism. [< F < L *excitatio, -onis* < *excitare.* See EXCITE.]

ex·cite (ik-sīt') *v.t.* **cit·ed, cit·ing** **1.** To arouse (a feeling, reaction, etc.) into being or activity; evoke: to *excite* interest. **2.** To arouse strong feeling in; stimulate the emotions of: to *excite* someone to hatred. **3.** To provoke action in; stir to activity or motion; rouse: to *excite* someone to greater endeavor. **4.** To bring about; stir up: to *excite* a riot. **5.** *Physiol.* To cause increased activity in; stimulate (muscles or nerves). **6.** *Electr.* To initiate or develop a magnetic field in, as a dynamo. **7.** *Physics* To raise (a system, atom, etc.) to a higher energy level. [< OF *exciter* < L *excitare,* freq. of *exciere* < *ex-* out + *ciere* to move, arouse]
— **Syn. 1.** spark, awake, kindle. **2.** awaken, inflame, stir. **3.** inspire. **4.** animate.

ex·cit·ed (ik-sī'tid) *adj.* **1.** Passionately aroused. **2.** Stirred up; agitated. **3.** *Physics* Raised to a higher energy level. — **ex·cit'ed·ly** *adv.*

ex·cite·ment (ik-sīt'mənt) *n.* **1.** The state of being excited; agitation. **2.** That which excites.

ex·cit·er (ik-sī'tər) *n.* **1.** One who or that which excites. **2.** *Electr.* **a** An auxiliary generator that supplies energy for the field magnets of a dynamo. **b** A machine that generates electric waves of definite length by means of sparks.

ex·cit·ing (ik-sī'ting) *adj.* Causing excitement; stirring; rousing; thrilling. — **ex·cit'ing·ly** *adv.*

ex·ci·tor (ik-sī'tər) *n.* **1.** An exciter. **2.** *Physiol.* An afferent nerve exciting greater action in the part it supplies.

excl. 1. Exclamation: also **exclam. 2.** Exclusive.

ex·claim (iks-klām') *v.t. & v.i.* To cry out abruptly; speak vehemently, as in surprise or anger. [< F *exclamer* < L *exclamare* < *ex-* out + *clamare* to cry] — **ex·claim'er** *n.*
— **Syn.** *Exclaim* and *ejaculate* mean to say forcefully. *Exclaim* suggests merely vehement feeling; *ejaculate* adds a note of explosive utterance and incoherence.

ex·cla·ma·tion (eks'klə·mā'shən) *n.* **1.** The act of exclaiming. **2.** An abrupt or emphatic utterance, outcry, etc.; interjection. **3.** An exclamation mark. Abbr. *excl., exclam.*

exclamation mark A mark (!) used in punctuation to in-

dicate that the immediately preceding word, phrase, or sentence is an exclamation. Also **exclamation point.**

ex·clam·a·to·ry (iks-klam'ə·tôr'ē, -tō'rē) *adj.* **1.** Of, pertaining to, or expressing exclamation. **2.** Noisy; clamorous.

ex·clave (eks'klāv) *n.* A minor portion of a country separated from the main part and lying within alien territory. ◆ An *exclave* is considered with respect to the country to which it belongs, an *enclave* with respect to the surrounding territory: East Prussia was an *exclave* of Germany, but a German *enclave* in Poland. [< EX-¹ + (EN)CLAVE]

ex·clude (iks-klōōd') *v.t.* **clud·ed, clud·ing 1.** To keep from entering; shut out, as from a place or group; bar. **2.** To refuse to notice, consider, or allow for; leave out. **3.** To put out; eject. [< L *excludere* < *ex-* out + *claudere* to close] — **ex·clud'a·ble** *adj.* — **ex·clud'er** *n.*

ex·clu·sion (iks-klōō'zhən) *n.* **1.** The act of excluding, or the state of being excluded. **2.** That which is excluded. [< L *exclusio, -onis* < *excludere.* See EXCLUDE.]

ex·clu·sion·ist (iks-klōō'zhən·ist) *n.* One who favors excluding others, as from sharing in privileges. — **ex·clu'sion·ism** *n.*

ex·clu·sive (iks-klōō'siv) *adj.* **1.** Intended for or possessed by a single individual or group; not shared: *exclusive* rights. **2.** Belonging to or found in a single source, as a newspaper or magazine: an *exclusive* news story. **3.** Highly distinctive and having no duplicate; altogether original: an *exclusive* design. **4.** Admitting or catering to only a very select group: an *exclusive* club. **5.** Concentrated upon only one individual, thing, or group; complete and undivided; entire: one's *exclusive* attention. **6.** Excluding the other or others by reason of being completely opposed or unrelated; totally incompatible: mutually *exclusive* doctrines. **7.** Being the only one; sole: the *exclusive* owner of a business. **8.** Not including; not comprising: usually with *of*: the total expense *exclusive* of fees. **9.** Not including the items, dates, figures, etc., that are specified as the limits: from 1 to 10 *exclusive* (1 and 10 are not included). **10.** Indicating the exclusion of everything except what is specified: In the statement "He likes only this," *only* is an *exclusive* particle. — *n.* A choice news item, interview, etc., obtained for exclusive use. Abbr. *excl.* — **ex·clu'sive·ly** *adv.* — **ex·clu'sive·ness** *n.*

ex·cog·i·tate (iks-koj'ə·tāt) *v.t.* **tat·ed, tat·ing** To think out carefully; think up; devise. [< L *excogitatus,* pp. of *excogitare* < *ex-* out + *cogitare* to think] — **ex·cog'i·ta'tion** *n.* — **ex·cog'i·ta'tive** *adj.*

ex·com·mu·ni·ca·ble (eks'kə·myōō'ni·kə·bəl) *adj.* Punishable by or deserving excommunication.

ex·com·mu·ni·cate (*v.* eks'kə·myōō'nə·kāt; *adj. & n.* eks'kə·myōō'nə·kət) *v.t.* **cat·ed, cat·ing** *Eccl.* To cut off by ecclesiastical authority from sharing in the sacraments, worship, privileges, or fellowship of a church. — *adj.* Excommunicated. — *n.* An excommunicated person. [< LL *excommunicatus* pp. of *excommunicare* < *ex-* out + *communicare.* See COMMUNICATE.] — **ex'com·mu'ni·ca'tor** *n.*

ex·com·mu·ni·ca·tion (eks'kə·myōō'nə·kā'shən) *n.* **1.** The act of excommunicating, or the state of being excommunicated. **2.** The ecclesiastical censure by which one is excommunicated.

ex·com·mu·ni·ca·tive (eks'kə·myōō'nə·kā'tiv, -kə·tiv) *adj.* Relating to, favoring, or effecting excommunication. Also **ex·com·mu·ni·ca·to·ry** (eks'kə·myōō'nə·kə·tôr'ē, -tō'rē).

ex·co·ri·ate (ik-skôr'ē·āt, -skō'rē-) *v.t.* **at·ed, at·ing 1.** To tear, chafe, or burn away strips of (skin, bark, etc.). **2.** To upbraid or denounce scathingly. [< L *excoriatus,* pp. of *excoriare* < *ex-* out, off + *corium* skin]

ex·co·ri·a·tion (ik-skôr'ē·ā'shən, -skō'rē-) *n.* **1.** The act of excoriating, or the state of being excoriated. **2.** A raw, exposed spot or area on the surface of the body, etc.

ex·cre·ment (eks'krə·mənt) *n.* Refuse matter expelled from the body; especially, feces. [< L *excrementum* < *excernere.* See EXCRETE.]

ex·cre·men·tal (eks'krə·men'təl) *adj.* Of, relating to, or resembling excrement. Also **ex·cre·men·ti'tious** (-tish'əs).

ex·cres·cence (iks-kres'əns) *n.* **1.** An unnatural or disfiguring outgrowth, as a wart. **2.** Any unnatural addition or outgrowth. **3.** A natural outgrowth, as hair.

ex·cres·cen·cy (iks-kres'ən·sē) *n. pl.* **·cies 1.** The state of being excrescent. **2.** An excrescence.

ex·cres·cent (iks-kres'ənt) *adj.* **1.** Of, relating to, or constituting an excrescence. **2.** Added without being essential or useful; superfluous. **3.** *Phonet.* Intrusive. [< L *excrescens, -entis,* ppr. of *excrescere* < *ex-* out + *crescere* to grow]

ex·cre·ta (iks-krē'tə) *n.pl.* Excretions, as sweat, urine, etc. [Neut. pl. of *excretus.* See EXCRETE.] — **ex·cre'tal** *adj.*

ex·crete (iks-krēt') *v.t.* **cret·ed, cret·ing** To throw off or eliminate (waste matter or noxious material) by normal discharge from an organism or any of its tissues. [< L *excretus,* pp. of *excernere* < *ex-* out + *cernere* to separate]

ex·cre·tion (iks-krē'shən) *n.* **1.** The act of excreting. **2.** Matter excreted, particularly sweat, urine, and the juices exuded from certain plants.

ex·cre·to·ry (eks′krə·tôr′ē, -tō′rē, iks·krē′tər·ē) *adj.* Relating to or adapted for excretion. Also **ex·cre·tive** (iks·krē′tiv).

ex·cru·ci·ate (iks·krōō′shē·āt) *v.t.* **·at·ed, ·at·ing** To inflict extreme pain or agony upon; rack with pain. [< L *excruciatus*, pp. of *excruciare* < *ex*- completely + *cruciare* to torture < *crux, crucis* cross] — **ex·cru′ci·a′tion** *n.*

ex·cru·ci·at·ing (iks·krōō′shē·ā′ting) *adj.* Causing or inflicting intense pain; agonizing. — **ex·cru′ci·at′ing·ly** *adv.*

ex·cul·pate (eks′kul·pāt, ik·skul′-) *v.t.* **·pat·ed, ·pat·ing** To free from blame or prove innocent of guilt or fault; exonerate. [< EX-¹ + L *culpatus*, pp. of *culpare* to blame < *culpa* fault] — **ex·culp·a·ble** (ik·skul′pə·bəl) *adj.*

ex·cul·pa·tion (eks′kul·pā′shən) *n.* **1.** The act of exculpating or the state of being exculpated; exoneration. **2.** A means of establishing that one is not to be blamed; an excuse that clears from censure, criticism, suspicion, etc.

ex·cul·pa·to·ry (ik·skul′pə·tôr′ē, -tō′rē) *adj.* Serving as an exculpation; freeing or tending to free from blame.

ex·cur·rent (ik·skûr′ənt) *adj.* **1.** Moving or flowing outward. **2.** *Biol.* Continuing beyond the apex: an *excurrent* midrib of a leaf. [< L *excurrens, -entis,* ppr. of *excurrere* < *ex*- out + *currere* to run]

ex·cur·sion (ik·skûr′zhən, -shən) *n.* **1.** A short trip made with the intention of returning soon, as for relaxation, sightseeing, etc. **2.** A short trip on a boat, train, etc., that is available at reduced rates. **3.** A group of people making a short trip for relaxation, etc., especially when traveling at reduced rates. **4.** *Physics* **a** Either half of the total distance between two extreme points set by the oscillation or vibration of a body; also, the movement of the body through either half of this total distance. **b** The total distance traveled in the outward stroke or in the return stroke of a piston or similar moving part of a machine; also, the outward stroke or the return stroke of a piston, etc. **5.** *Archaic* A deviation or digression. **6.** *Obs.* A sudden military attack; raid. Abbr. *ex., exc.* — **Syn.** See JOURNEY. [< L *excursio, -onis* < *excurrere.* See EXCURRENT.]

ex·cur·sion·ist (ik·skûr′zhən·ist, -shən-) *n.* One who makes an excursion.

ex·cur·sive (ik·skûr′siv) *adj.* Going erratically in one direction and then another; rambling; discursive; digressive. — **ex·cur′sive·ly** *adv.* — **ex·cur′sive·ness** *n.*

ex·cur·sus (eks·kûr′səs) *n. pl.* **·sus·es** or **·sus 1.** A supplemental discussion added to a work. **2.** A wandering off; digression. [< L, *a going out,* pp. of *excurrere.* See EXCURRENT.]

ex·cus·a·ble (ik·skyōō′zə·bəl) *adj.* Capable of being pardoned, condoned, or justified. — **Syn.** See VENIAL. — **ex·cus′a·bly** *adv.*

ex·cus·a·to·ry (ik·skyōō′zə·tôr′ē, -tō′rē) *adj.* Excusing or tending to excuse; apologetic: *excusatory* words.

ex·cuse (*v.* ik·skyōōz′; *n.* ik·skyōōs′) *v.t.* **·cused, ·cus·ing 1.** To ask pardon or forgiveness for (oneself): He *excused* himself for being late. **2.** To grant pardon or forgiveness to: *Excuse* me for interrupting. **3.** To accept or overlook as being pardonable or justifiable; look upon indulgently: to *excuse* a child's mistakes. **4.** To free from censure or blame; extenuate or justify: Nothing can *excuse* this delay. **5.** To release or exempt, as from a duty or obligation: to *excuse* someone from further service. **6.** To allow to leave. — **to excuse oneself 1.** To ask forgiveness for oneself. **2.** To ask that one be released or exempted from some duty, etc. **3.** To ask for permission to leave. — *n.* **1.** A statement made or a reason given as a ground for being excused. **2.** A cause, factor, or circumstance that frees from blame or releases from obligation. **3.** *Archaic* Forgiveness; pardon. — **in excuse of** As an excuse for. — **Syn.** See APOLOGY, PARDON. [< OF *excuser* < L *excusare* < *ex*- out, away + *causa* charge, accusation]

exec. 1. Executive. **2.** Executor.

ex·e·cra·ble (ek′sə·krə·bəl) *adj.* **1.** Detestable and revolting; abominable: an *execrable* crime. **2.** Appallingly inferior; extremely bad: an *execrable* speller. — **ex′e·cra·bly** *adv.*

ex·e·crate (ek′sə·krāt) *v.* **·crat·ed, ·crat·ing** *v.t.* **1.** To call down evil upon; curse. **2.** To denounce violently. **3.** To detest; abhor. — *v.i.* **4.** To utter curses. [< L *execratus,* pp. of *execrari* to curse < *ex*- out + *sacrare* to devote to good or evil < *sacer* holy or accursed] — **ex′e·cra′tor** *n.*

ex·e·cra·tion (ek′sə·krā′shən) *n.* **1.** The act of cursing or denouncing something. **2.** A curse or denunciation. **3.** Extreme abhorrence; loathing. **4.** Something that is the object of cursing, denunciation, or abhorrence.

ex·e·cra·tive (ek′sə·krā′tiv) *adj.* **1.** Relating to, resembling, or containing execration. Also **ex·e·cra·to·ry** (ek′sə·krə·tôr′ē, -tō′rē). **2.** Given to execration.

ex·e·cu·tant (ig·zek′yə·tənt) *n.* One who carries into effect something to be done; also, one who gives a performance.

ex·e·cute (ek′sə·kyōot) *v.t.* **·cut·ed, ·cut·ing 1.** To follow or carry out fully: to *execute* an order. **2.** To put into force; administer, as a law. **3.** To put to death in accordance with legal sentence. **4.** To make (a will, deed, etc.) legal or valid by fulfilling all requirements of law. **5.** To perform (something demanding skill): to *execute* a maneuver. **6.** To produce or fashion, following a plan or design: to *execute* a portrait. — **Syn.** See KILL. [< L *executus,* var. of *exsecutus,* pp. of *exsequi* to follow through to the end < *ex*- throughout

+ *sequi* to follow] — **ex′e·cut′a·ble** *adj.* — **ex′e·cut′er** *n.*

ex·e·cu·tion (ek′sə·kyōo′shən) *n.* **1.** The act of executing, or the fact or condition of being executed; as: **a** Accomplishment or fulfillment: the *execution* of plans. **b** Administration or enforcement: the *execution* of a law. **c** Performance: the *execution* of a musical composition. **d** Production: the *execution* of a work of art. **e** Subjection to capital punishment: the *execution* of a criminal. **2.** The particular way in which something is done or performed; style or technique. **3.** *Law* **a** A judicial writ for carrying into effect a judgment or decree of a court. **b** Attendance to required formalities, as signature and delivery, of a deed or other legal instrument.

ex·e·cu·tion·er (ek′sə·kyōo′shən·ər) *n.* One who executes a death sentence.

ex·ec·u·tive (ig·zek′yə·tiv) *adj.* **1.** Relating or adapted to the putting into practical effect of plans, projects, business and work programs, etc.: the *executive* division of a business office. **2.** Relating or adapted to the execution of laws and the practical administration of judgments, decrees, etc.; administrative: the *executive* branch of a government: distinguished from *judicial, legislative.* — *n.* **1.** An individual, as a head of state, or a group managing the administrative affairs of a nation, state, or other political division. **2.** The executive branch of a government. **3.** An individual responsible for the direction and management of a business house, corporation, institution, etc. Abbr. *ex., exec.* — **Syn.** See DOER.

Executive Mansion *U.S.* **1.** The White House. **2.** The residence of the governor of a State.

executive officer *U.S.* The principal staff officer assisting a commanding officer in units smaller than a division. Compare CHIEF OF STAFF.

executive session A closed legislative session, as of the U.S. Senate, convoked to consider confidential business.

ex·e·cu·tor (ek′sə·kyōo′tər *for def. 1,* ig·zek′yə·tər *for def. 2*) *n.* **1.** One who carries plans, etc., into effect. **2.** *Law* One who is appointed by a testator to carry out the terms of the will after the testator's death. Abbr. *exec., exr.* — **ex·ec·u·to·ri·al** (ig·zek′yə·tôr′ē·əl, -tō′rē-) *adj.*

ex·ec·u·to·ry (ig·zek′yə·tôr′ē, -tō′rē) *adj.* **1.** Of, relating to, or entrusted with carrying out plans, etc.; administrative; executive. **2.** Being actually in effect; operative: an *executory* law. **3.** *Law* Designed to take effect at some future time: an *executory* contract.

ex·ec·u·trix (ig·zek′yə·triks) *n. pl.* **·trix·es** or **·tri·ces** (-trī′sēz) *Law* A female executor.

ex·e·dra (ek′sə·drə, ik·sē′drə) *n. pl.* **·drae** (-drē) **1.** In classical antiquity, a roofed area provided with rows of seats and serving as a meeting place. **2.** A curved, outdoor bench with a high back. [< L < Gk. < *ex*- out + *hedra* seat]

EXEDRA

ex·e·ge·sis (ek′sə·jē′sis) *n. pl.* **·ses** (-sēz) Critical explanation of the meaning of words and passages in a literary work; especially, Biblical exposition or interpretation. [< Gk. *exēgēsis* < *exēgeesthai* to explain < *ex*- out + *'egeesthai* < *agein* to lead]

ex·e·gete (ek′sə·jēt) *n.* One skilled in critical explanation, as of the Bible. Also **ex·e·ge·tist** (ek′sə·jē′tist).

ex·e·get·ic (ek′sə·jet′ik) *adj.* Pertaining to exegesis; expository; explanatory. Also **ex·e·get′i·cal.** [< Gk. *exēgētikos* < *exēgēsis.* See EXEGESIS.] — **ex′e·get′i·cal·ly** *adv.*

ex·e·get·ics (ek′sə·jet′iks) *n.pl.* (construed as sing.) The science of exegesis.

ex·em·plar (ig·zem′plər, -plär) *n.* **1.** A model, pattern, or original to be copied or imitated; archetype. **2.** A typical example, instance, or specimen. — **Syn.** See EXAMPLE. [< OF *exemplaire* < LL *exemplarium* < *exemplum* (see EXAMPLE); infl. in form by L *exemplar* typical < L *exemplum*]

ex·em·pla·ry (ig·zem′plər·ē) *adj.* **1.** Serving as a model or example worthy of imitation; commendable: *exemplary* conduct. **2.** Serving as a warning: *exemplary* punishment. **3.** Serving as an example, type, or typical instance; illustrative. — **ex·em′pla·ri·ly** *adv.* — **ex·em′pla·ri·ness** *n.*

ex·em·pli·fi·ca·tion (ig·zem′plə·fə·kā′shən) *n.* **1.** The act of exemplifying. **2.** That which exemplifies; an illustration; example. **3.** *Law* A certified copy, under seal, as of a record.

ex·em·pli·fy (ig·zem′plə·fī) *v.t.* **·fied, ·fy·ing 1.** To show by example; illustrate. **2.** *Law* **a** To prove by an attested copy. **b** To make an authenticated transcript from. [< Med.L *exemplificare* < L *exemplum* (see EXAMPLE) + *facere* to make] — **ex·em·pli·fi·ca·tive** (-fə·kā′tiv) *adj.*

ex·em·pli gra·ti·a (ig·zem′plī grā′shē·ə) *Latin* By way of example. Abbr. *e.g.*

ex·empt (ig·zempt′) *v.t.* To free or excuse from some obligation to which others are subject; grant immunity to: to *exempt* someone from military service. — *adj.* **1.** Free, clear, or excused, as from some liability, restriction, or burden. **2.** *Obs.* Remote; separated. — *n.* A person who is exempted, as from military service. [< L *exemptus,* pp. of *eximere* < *ex*- out + *emere* to buy, take] — **ex·empt′i·ble** *adj.*

ex·emp·tion (ig·zemp′shən) *n.* **1.** The act of exempting. **2.** The state of being exempt; immunity; dispensation. **3.** In the computation of income tax, an amount allowed for oneself and one's dependents as a deduction from one's gross annual income; also, one of the individuals claimed for such a deduction.

ex·en·ter·ate (eks·en'tə·rāt) *v.t.* **·at·ed, ·at·ing 1.** *Surg.* To take out (a part, organ, etc.). **2.** *Rare* To disembowel. [< L *exenteratus,* pp. of *exenterare* < *ex-* out + Gk. *enteron* intestine] **— ex·en'ter·a'tion** *n.*

ex·e·qua·tur (ek'sə·kwā'tər) *n.* In international law, the official recognition given to a consul or commercial agent by the government of the country to which he is assigned. [< L, let him perform]

ex·e·quy (ek'sə·kwē) *n. pl.* **·quies 1.** *pl.* Funeral ceremonies; obsequies. **2.** A funeral procession. [< OF *exequies* < L *exequiae* < *exequi, exsequi.* See EXECUTE.]

ex·er·cise (ek'sər·sīz) *v.* **·cised, ·cis·ing** *v.t.* **1.** To subject to drills, physical or mental routines, etc., so as to train or develop. **2.** To make use of; employ: to *exercise* a right. **3.** To perform or execute, as duties. **4.** To exert, as influence or authority; wield. **5.** To occupy the mind of; especially, to make anxious or fretful; worry. **—** *v.i.* **6.** To perform exercises. **—** *n.* **1.** A putting into use, action, or practice: an *exercise* of patience. **2.** Activity performed for training, physical conditioning, etc. **3.** A lesson, problem, etc., designed to train some particular function or skill: vocal *exercises;* mathematical *exercises.* **4.** *Usually pl.* A ceremony, program of speeches, etc., as at a graduation. **5.** An act of worship or devotion; religious service. **— Syn.** See PRACTICE. [< OF *exercice* < L *exercitium* < *exercere* to practice < *ex-* out, away + *arcere* to enclose] **— ex'er·cis'a·ble** *adj.*

ex·er·cised (ek'sər·sīzd) *adj.* Harassed; agitated; excited.

ex·er·cis·er (ek'sər·sī'zər) *n.* **1.** One who exercises. **2.** An apparatus for the exercise of the body.

ex·er·ci·ta·tion (ig·zûr'sə·tā'shən) *n.* **1.** The exercise or practice of certain skills, powers, etc. **2.** A display of skill, especially literary skill, as in an essay. [< CF < L *exercitatio, -onis* < *exercitare,* freq. of *exercere.* See EXERCISE.]

ex·ergue (ig·zûrg', ek'sûrg) *n.* The space below the principal design on the reverse of a coin or medal, with date, place of coining, etc. [< F < Gk. *ex-* out + *ergon* work]

ex·ert (ig·zûrt') *v.t.* **1.** To put forth or put into action, as strength, force, or influence; exercise vigorously. **2.** *Obs.* To push or thrust forth. **— to exert oneself** To put forth effort; strive. [< L *exertus,* var. of *exsertus,* pp. of *exserere* to thrust out < *ex-* out + *serere* to bind]

ex·er·tion (ig·zûr'shən) *n.* **1.** The act of exerting some power, faculty, influence, etc. **2.** Strong action or effort; vigorous exercise; labor: His *exertions* were successful.

ex·er·tive (ig·zûr'tiv) *adj.* Tending to exert; employing exertion.

Ex·e·ter (ek'sə·tər) The county seat of Devonshire, England, a county borough in the central part of the county; pop. 95,729 (1976).

ex·e·unt (ek'sē·ənt, -se·ŏont) They go out: a stage direction. [< L]

exeunt om·nes (om'nēz) All go out: a stage direction. [< L]

ex·fo·li·ate (eks·fō'lē·āt) *v.t.* & *v.i.* **·at·ed, ·at·ing 1.** To separate or peel off in scales, layers, flakes, etc., as skin, bark, or bone. **2.** *Geol.* To split off in scales or sheets, as a heated mineral or weathered rock. [< LL *exfoliatus,* pp. of *exfoliare* < L *ex-* off + *folium* leaf] **— ex·fo'li·a'tive** *adj.*

ex·fo·li·a·tion (eks·fō'lē·ā'shən) *n.* **1.** The act of exfoliating, or the state of being exfoliated. **2.** That which is exfoliated; matter scaled off.

ex·ha·lant (eks·hā'lənt, ig·zā'-) *adj.* Adapted to exhalation or emission: an *exhalant* duct. **—** *n.* A duct or similar vessel used in exhaling.

ex·ha·la·tion (eks'hə·lā'shən, eg'zə-) *n.* **1.** The act of exhaling. **2.** That which is exhaled, as air, a vapor, or an emanation. [< L *exhalatio, -onis* < *exhalare.* See EXHALE.]

ex·hale (eks·hāl', ig·zāl') *v.* **·haled, ·hal·ing** *v.i.* **1.** To expel air or vapor; breathe out. **2.** To pass off or rise as a vapor or emanation. **—** *v.t.* **3.** To breathe forth or give off, as air, vapor, or an aroma. **4.** To draw off; cause to evaporate: Heat *exhales* the earth's moisture. [< F *exhaler* < L *exhalare* < *ex-* out + *halare* to breathe] **— ex·hal'a·ble** *adj.*

ex·haust (ig·zôst') *v.t.* **1.** To make extremely tired; wear out completely. **2.** To drain of resources, strength, etc.; use up. **3.** To draw off, as gas, steam, etc., from or as from a container. **4.** To empty (a container) of contents; drain. **5.** To study, treat of, or develop thoroughly and completely: to *exhaust* a subject. **6.** In pharmacy, to remove the essential principles of (a drug, etc.) by means of a solvent, and leave an inert remainder. **—** *v.i.* **7.** To escape, as a waste gas, steam, etc. **—** *n.* **1.** The escape or discharge of waste gases, working fluid, etc., as from the cylinder of an engine after the piston has completed a stroke; also, the waste gases, etc., that escape or are discharged. **2.** A pipe or other engine part through which waste gases, etc., escape or are discharged. **3.** Creation of a partial vacuum to produce an outflow of air designed to suck out stale air, dust, etc., as from a

room. **4.** One of several devices designed to produce a partial vacuum to remove stale air, etc. **5.** Stale air, odors, etc., sucked out from an enclosure by creation of a partial vacuum. [< L *exhaustus,* pp. of *exhaurire* < *ex-* out + *haurire* to draw] **— ex·haust'i·ble** *adj.* **— ex·haust'i·bil'i·ty** *n.*

ex·haust·ed (ig·zôs'tid) *adj.* **1.** Entirely used up; drained; spent. **2.** Extremely tired. **— ex·haust'ed·ly** *adv.*

ex·haust·ing (ig·zôs'ting) *adj.* Extremely tiring; most fatiguing; wearying. **— ex·haust'ing·ly** *adv.*

ex·haus·tion (ig·zôs'chən) *n.* **1.** Extreme fatigue; utter weariness. **2.** The condition of being completely used up: *exhaustion* of supplies. **3.** The condition of being completely deprived of valuable or useful elements: *exhaustion* of the soil. **4.** The act of exhausting.

ex·haus·tive (ig·zôs'tiv) *adj.* **1.** That exhausts or tends to exhaust; exhausting. **2.** Thoroughly covering all points or details; comprehensive: an *exhaustive* discussion. **— ex·haus'tive·ly** *adv.* **— ex·haus'tive·ness** *n.*

ex·haust·less (ig·zôst'lis) *adj.* Incapable of being exhausted. **— ex·haust'less·ly** *adv.* **— ex·haust'less·ness** *n.*

exhaust steam Steam that has already performed work: distinguished from *live steam.*

exhaust velocity The velocity of exhaust gases at the moment of their expulsion from a reciprocating engine, jet engine, rocket motor, or the like.

ex·hib·it (ig·zib'it) *v.t.* **1.** To put on view, especially publicly; present for inspection, instruction, etc.; display: to *exhibit* an art collection. **2.** To present for entertainment; show: to *exhibit* a motion picture. **3.** To make evident, as by outward indications; reveal. **4.** *Law* To submit (evidence, etc.) formally or officially to a court or officer. **5.** *Med.* To give or apply (a drug, an anesthetic, etc.); administer. **—** *v.i.* **6.** To put something on display. **—** *n.* **1.** A putting on view; public presentation; display. **2.** An object or group of objects displayed, as at a fair. **3.** *Law* A document or other object formally submitted to a court or officer as a piece of evidence. [< L *exhibitus,* pp. of *exhibere* < *ex-* out + *habere* to hold, have]

— Syn. (verb) **1.** show, demonstrate. Compare FLAUNT. **3.** evince, manifest, disclose. **— Ant.** hide, conceal, suppress.

ex·hi·bi·tion (ek'sə·bish'ən) *n.* **1.** The act of exhibiting. **2.** That which is exhibited. **3.** A public display of art works, products, etc. **4.** *Brit.* A scholarship awarded to a student from university funds. [< OF *exhibicion* < L *exhibitio, -onis* < *exhibere.* See EXHIBIT.]

ex·hi·bi·tion·er (ek'sə·bish'ən·ər) *n. Brit.* A student who receives a university scholarship.

ex·hi·bi·tion·ism (ek'sə·bish'ən·iz'əm) *n.* **1.** A tendency to attract attention to oneself by exaggerated or inappropriate behavior. **2.** *Psychiatry* The tendency, usually compulsive, to obtain sexual gratification by public exposure of one's body or genitalia. **— ex'hi·bi'tion·ist** *n.*

ex·hib·i·tive (ig·zib'ə·tiv) *adj.* Serving or tending to exhibit or show forth: often with *of.*

ex·hib·i·tor (ig·zib'ə·tər) *n.* One who or that which exhibits something; as: **a** A person or organization displaying an exhibit at a fair, etc. **b** The owner of a theater in which motion pictures are presented. Also **ex·hib'it·er.**

ex·hib·i·to·ry (ig·zib'ə·tôr'ē, -tō'rē) *adj.* Of, pertaining to, or intended for exhibition.

ex·hil·a·rant (ig·zil'ər·ənt) *adj.* Causing exhilaration. **—** *n.* Something that exhilarates. [< F < L *exhilarans, -antis,* ppr. of *exhilarare.* See EXHILARATE.]

ex·hil·a·rate (ig·zil'ə·rāt) *v.t.* **·rat·ed, ·rat·ing 1.** To set aglow with happiness or elation; make buoyantly cheerful. **2.** To fill with vivacity; pep up; invigorate; stimulate. [< L *exhilaratus,* pp. of *exhilarare* to gladden < *ex-* completely + *hilarare* to gladden < *hilaris* glad] **— ex·hil'a·ra'tor** *n.*

ex·hil·a·rat·ing (ig·zil'ə·rā'ting) *adj.* That exhilarates or enlivens; stimulating. **— ex·hil'a·rat'ing·ly** *adv.*

ex·hil·a·ra·tion (ig·zil'ə·rā'shən) *n.* **1.** The state of being exhilarated; animation. **2.** The act of exhilarating.

ex·hil·a·ra·tive (ig·zil'ə·rā'tiv) *adj.* Exhilarating or tending to exhilarate. Also **ex·hil'a·ra·to'ry** (-ər·ə·tôr'ē, -tō'rē).

ex·hort (ig·zôrt') *v.t.* **1.** To urge by earnest appeal or argument; advise or recommend strongly. **—** *v.i.* **2.** To utter or give exhortation. [< L *exhortari* < *ex-* completely + *hortari* to urge] **— ex·hort'er** *n.*

ex·hor·ta·tion (eg'zôr·tā'shən, ek'sôr-) *n.* **1.** The act of exhorting. **2.** That which is said so as to exhort; an earnest plea. [< L *exhortatio, -onis* < *exhortari.* See EXHORT.]

ex·hor·ta·tive (ig·zôr'tə·tiv) *adj.* **1.** Pertaining to or like an exhortation. **2.** Serving to exhort. Also **ex·hor'ta·to'ry** (-tôr'ē, -tō'rē).

ex·hume (ig·zyōōm', iks·hyōōm') *v.t.* **·humed, ·hum·ing 1.** To dig up (a corpse or other buried thing); disinter. **2.** To bring (something hidden or uncertain) to light; reveal; disclose: to *exhume* the real facts. [< F *exhumer* < Med.L *exhumare* < L *ex-* out + *humus* ground] **— ex·hu·ma·tion** (eks'hyōō·mā'shən) *n.* **— ex·hum'er** *n.*

ex·i·gen·cy (ek'sə·jən·sē) *n. pl.* **·cies 1.** The state of being exigent; urgency. **2.** A situation that requires immediate attention, assistance, or remedy. **3.** *Usually pl.* A pressing need or necessity; urgent requirement. Also **ex′i·gence.** — **Syn. 2.** emergency, crisis.

ex·i·gent (ek′sə·jənt) *adj.* **1.** Demanding immediate aid or action; urgent. **2.** Requiring or exacting a great deal; unreasonably demanding. [< L *exigens, -entis,* ppr. of *exigere.* See EXACT.] — **ex′i·gent·ly** *adv.*

ex·ig·i·ble (ek′sə·jə·bəl) *adj.* That may be exacted, demanded, or required.

ex·ig·u·ous (ig·zig′yŏō·əs, ik·sig′-) *adj.* Small; scanty; diminutive. [< L *exiguus* scanty < *exigere* to weigh strictly] — **ex·i·gu·i·ty** (ek′sə·gyŏō′ə·tē), **ex·ig′u·ous·ness** *n.*

ex·ile (eg′zīl, ek′sīl) *n.* **1.** Separation by necessity or choice from one's native country, home, etc.; expatriation; especially, such separation imposed as a punishment by law or decree; banishment. **2.** One who is separated by necessity or choice from his native country, home, etc.; an expatriate; especially, one compelled to leave and stay away by a decree of banishment. — **the Exile** The Babylonian captivity of the Jews. — *v.t.* **·iled, ·il·ing** To cause (a person) to leave and stay away from (the person's) native country, home, etc.; especially, to force to leave by decree; banish. — **Syn.** See BANISH. [< OF *exil, essil* < L *exsilium*] — **ex·il·ic** (eg·zil′ik, ek·sil′ik) *adj.* Pertaining to exile, especially that of the Jews in Babylonia.

ex·im·i·ous (ig·zim′ē·əs) *adj.* *Rare* Most distinguished; excellent. [< L *eximius* < *eximere.* See EXEMPT.]

ex int. Without (L *ex*) interest.

ex·ist (ig·zist′) *v.i.* **1.** To have actual being or reality; be. **2.** To continue to live or be: Animal life cannot *exist* without oxygen. **3.** To be present; occur: This species now *exists* only in Australia. [< F *exister* < L *existere* < *ex-* out + *sistere* to be located < *stare* to stand]

ex·is·tence (ig·zis′təns) *n.* **1.** The state or fact of being or continuing to be; being: to doubt the *existence* of God. **2.** Possession or continuance of animate being; life: a fight for *existence.* **3.** Way or mode of living: a lonely *existence.* **4.** Presence; occurrence: the *existence* of life on Mars. **5.** Anything that exists; an entity; actuality. **6.** All that exists.

ex·is·tent (ig·zis′tənt) *adj.* **1.** Having being or existence. **2.** Now existing or occurring; present: *existent* conditions. — *n.* That which exists. [< L *existens, -entis,* ppr. of *existere.* See EXIST.]

ex·is·ten·tial (eg′zis·ten′shəl) *adj.* **1.** Of or pertaining to existence. **2.** Expressing or stating the fact of existence. — **ex′is·ten′tial·ly** *adv.*

ex·is·ten·tial·ism (eg′zis·ten′shəl·iz′əm) *n.* **1.** A movement in philosophy with roots in 19th-century German romanticism, especially in the thought of Kierkegaard and Nietzsche, whose chief exponents have been Heidegger and Jaspers in Germany and Sartre in France. It stresses the active role of the will rather than of reason in confronting problems posed by a hostile universe. The nature of man is regarded as consisting in decisive actions rather than in inner or latent dispositions. **2.** A cult of nihilism and pessimism popularized in France after World War II, supposedly based on the doctrines of Sartre and other existentialist writers. — **ex′is·ten′·tial·ist** *adj. & n.*

ex·it (eg′zit, ek′sit) *n.* **1.** A way or passage out; egress. **2.** The departure of an actor from the stage. **3.** Any departure. — *v.i.* **1.** To go out; depart. **2.** (He or she) goes out: a stage direction. [< L *exitus* a going out < *exire* < *ex-* out + *ire* to go]

ex li·bris (eks lī′bris, lē′-) *Latin* **1.** From the books (of): used as an inscription or label on a book, followed by the owner's name. **2.** A bookplate. *Abbr. ex lib.*

Ex·moor (eks′mŏŏr) A plateau in west Somersetshire and NE Devonshire, England; 30 sq. mi.

ex ni·hi·lo ni·hil fit (eks nī′hi·lō nī′hil fit) *Latin* Out of nothing comes nothing.

exo- *combining form* Out; outside; external: *exocarp.* Also, before vowels, *ex-*. [< Gk. *exo-, ex-* < *exō* outside]

ex·o·carp (ek′sō·kärp) *n. Bot.* The epicarp (which see). [< EXO- + -CARP]

ex·o·cen·tric (ek′sō·sen′trik) *adj. Ling.* Denoting a syntactic construction that as a unit functions differently from any of its immediate constituents, as *Jim laughed:* opposed to *endocentric.* [< EXO- + -CENTRIC]

Exod. Exodus.

ex·o·derm (ek′sō·dûrm) See ECTODERM.

ex·o·don·tia (ek′sō·don′shə, -shē·ə) *n.* The branch of dentistry concerned with the extraction of teeth. [< NL < Gk. *ex-* out + *odōn, odontos* tooth]

ex·o·dus (ek′sə·dəs) *n.* A going forth, as of a multitude, from a place or country. — **the Exodus** The departure of the Israelites from Egypt under the guidance of Moses, described in **Exodus** (abbr. *Ex., Exod.*), the second book of the Old Testament. [< L < Gk. *exodus* < *ex-* out + *hodos* way]

ex·o·en·zyme (ek′sō·en′zīm, -zim) See ECTOENZYME.

ex of·fi·ci·o (eks ə·fish′ē·ō) *Latin* By virtue of or because of office or position. *Abbr. e.o., ex off.*

ex·og·a·my (eks·og′ə·mē) *n.* **1.** The custom of marriage outside of the tribe, family, clan, etc.; outbreeding: opposed

to *endogamy.* **2.** *Biol.* The union of two protozoans of different ancestry, with fusion of nuclei, at the commencement of a new cycle of growth. [< EXO- + -GAMY] — **ex·og′a·mous, ex·o·gam·ic** (ek′sō·gam′ik) *adj.*

ex·o·gen (ek′sō·jen) *n. Bot.* A dicotyledonous plant that increases in size by successive concentric additions or rings outside the previous growth and beneath the bark: opposed to *endogen.* [< EXO- + -GEN]

EXOGEN
A Vertical section. *B* Cross-section. 1,2,3 Growth rings for successive years. *b* Bark. *c* Cambium layer. *s* Sapwood (alburnum). *h* Heartwood (duramen). *m* Medullary sheath. *p* Pith.

ex·og·e·nous (eks·oj′ə·nəs) *adj.* **1.** *Bot.* Of, pertaining to, or like an exogen. **2.** *Biol.* Originating or growing from without, or due to external causes. **3.** *Biochem.* Designating the catabolic processes within cells and tissues. — **ex·og′e·nous·ly** *adv.*

ex·on·er·ate (ig·zon′ə·rāt) *v.t.* **·at·ed, ·at·ing** **1.** To free from accusation or blame; acquit. **2.** To relieve or free from a responsibility or the like. — **Syn.** See ABSOLVE. [< L *exoneratus,* pp. of *exonerare* < *ex-* out, away + *onus, oneris* burden] — **ex·on′er·a′tion** *n.* — **ex·on′er·a′tive** *adj.*

exophthalmic goiter *Pathol.* A disease characterized by enlargement of the thyroid gland, protrusion of the eyeballs, anemia, and palpitation of the heart: also called *Basedow's disease, Graves' disease.*

ex·oph·thal·mos (ek′sof·thal′məs) *n. Pathol.* Abnormal protrusion of the eyeball. Also **ex′oph·thal′mi·a** (-mē·ə), **ex′oph·thal′mus.** [< NL < Gk. with prominent eyes < *ex-* out + *ophthalmos* eye] — **ex′oph·thal′mic** *adj.*

ex·o·ra·ble (ek′sər·ə·bəl) *adj.* Capable of being persuaded or moved by entreaty; capable of relenting. [< L *exorabilis* < *ex-* out, away + *orare* to pray] — **ex′o·ra·bil′i·ty** *n.*

ex·or·bi·tance (ig·zôr′bə·təns) *n.* **1.** Unreasonable excessiveness, as of prices or demands. **2.** *Archaic* Violation of law or morality. Also **ex·or′bi·tan·cy.**

ex·or·bi·tant (ig·zôr′bə·tənt) *adj.* **1.** Going beyond usual and proper limits, as in price or demand; excessive; extravagant. **2.** *Law* Lying beyond the scope of the law. [< LL *exorbitans, -antis,* ppr. of *exorbitare* to go astray < L *ex-* out + *orbita* track] — **ex·or′bi·tant·ly** *adv.*

ex·or·cise (ek′sôr·sīz) *v.t.* **·cised, ·cis·ing** **1.** To cast out (an evil spirit) by prayers or incantations. **2.** To free (a person, place, etc.) of an evil spirit. **3.** *Rare* To conjure up, as a demon. Also **ex′or·cize.** [< OF *exorciser* < LL *exorcizare* < Gk. *exorkizein* < *ex-* out + *horkos* oath] — **ex′or·cis′er** *n.*

ex·or·cism (ek′sôr·siz′əm) *n.* **1.** The act of exorcising evil spirits. **2.** A formula used in the rite of exorcising. — **ex′or·cise′ment** *n.* — **ex′or·cist** *n.*

ex·or·di·um (ig·zôr′dē·əm, ik·sôr′-) *n. pl.* **·di·ums** or **·di·a** (-dē·ə) The beginning or introductory part of anything, especially of a discourse, treatise, etc. [< L < *exordiri* < *ex-* out + *ordiri* to begin] — **ex·or′di·al** *adj.*

ex·o·skel·e·ton (ek′sō·skel′ə·tən) *n. Anat.* An external, protective structure or covering, as the hard shell of crustaceans: opposed to *endoskeleton.*

ex·os·mo·sis (ek′sos·mō′sis, -soz-) *n. Chem.* **1.** Osmosis in that direction in which the fluid permeates the dividing membrane most slowly. **2.** Osmosis from an inner to an outer vessel: opposed to *endosmosis.* — **ex′os·mot′ic** (-mot′ik), **ex·os·mic** (ek·sos′mik, -soz′-) *adj.*

ex·o·sphere (ek′sō·sfir) *n. Meteorol.* The region of the earth's atmosphere above the ionosphere, beginning at a height of about 400 miles. — **ex′o·spher′ic** (-sfir′ik, -sfer′-) *adj.*

ex·o·spore (ek′sō·spôr, -spōr) *n. Bot.* The outer coat or wall of a spore.

ex·os·to·sis (ek′sos·tō′sis) *n. pl.* **·ses** (-sēz) *Pathol.* An excessive bony outgrowth or tumor formed on a bone or on a cartilage. [< NL < Gk. < *ex-* out + *osteon* bone]

ex·o·ter·ic (ek′sə·ter′ik) *adj.* **1.** Adapted or intelligible, as a doctrine, theory, etc., to those outside the inner circle of disciples or to the uninitiated: opposed to *esoteric.* **2.** Suitable for popular comprehension. **3.** Commonplace; ordinary; simple. [< LL *exotericus* < Gk. *exōterikos* < *exōterō,* compar. of *exō* outside] — **ex′o·ter′i·cal·ly** *adv.*

ex·o·ther·mic (ek′sō·thûr′mik) *adj. Chem.* Pertaining to, attended by, or produced from the liberation of heat: opposed to *endothermic.* Also **ex′o·ther′mal.** [< EXO- + Gk. *thermē* heat]

ex·ot·ic (ig·zot′ik) *adj.* **1.** Belonging by nature or origin to another part of the world; not native; foreign: an *exotic* plant. **2.** Strangely different and fascinating: *exotic* customs. — *n.* Something exotic, as a flower. [< L *exoticus* < Gk. *exōtikos* foreign < *exō* outside] — **ex·ot′i·cal·ly** *adv.*

ex·ot·i·cism (ig·zot'ə·siz'əm) *n.* **1.** The quality of being exotic. **2.** Something exotic; especially, a foreign idiom.

ex·o·tox·in (ek'sō·tok'sin) *n. Biochem.* A toxin formed within and excreted by an organism that is not itself toxic: distinguished from *endotoxin.* — **ex'o·tox'ic** *adj.*

exp. 1. Expenses. **2.** Expiration; expired. **3.** Export; exported; exporter. **4.** Express.

ex·pand (ik·spand') *v.t.* **1.** To increase the range, scope, volume, size, etc., of: to *expand* a business. **2.** To spread out by unfolding or extending; open. **3.** To develop more fully the details or form of: to *expand* a speech; to *expand* an equation. — *v.i.* **4.** To grow larger, wider, etc.; become extended; increase. [< L *expandere* < *ex-* out + *pandere* to spread. Doublet of SPAWN.] — **ex·pand'er** *n.*

ex·pand·ed (ik·span'did) *adj. Printing* Extended.

ex·panse (ik·spans') *n.* **1.** That which lies spread out; a wide, continuous area or stretch: a blue *expanse* of sky. **2.** Expansion. [< L *expansum* < *expandere.* See EXPAND.]

ex·pan·si·ble (ik·span'sə·bəl) *adj.* Capable of being expanded; expansile. — **ex·pan/si·bil'i·ty** *n.*

ex·pan·sile (ik·span'səl) *adj.* **1.** Capable of expanding or of causing expansion. **2.** Relating to, adapted for, or marked by expansion.

ex·pan·sion (ik·span'shən) *n.* **1.** The act of expanding, or the state of being expanded. **2.** The amount or degree of increase in size, range, volume, etc. **3.** That which is expanded, spread out, or extended, as a surface or part. **4.** The extent or space over or through which a thing expands. **5.** *Physics* Increase of volume, as of steam in an engine cylinder when cut off from connection with the supply of pressure, or of the burning gas in an internal-combustion engine. **6.** *Math.* Development of a mathematical function into a series; also, the full expression as developed: the *expansion* of $(a + b)^3$ into $a^3 + 3a^2b + 3ab^2 + b^3$. — **Syn. 1.** dilation, enlargement, extension. **2.** expanse.

expansion bolt *Mech.* A bolt having an attached part that expands as the bolt is driven inward into a drilled hole.

ex·pan·sion·ism (ik·span'shən·iz'əm) *n.* A policy of constantly increasing the extent of territory possessed, of control over commerce, etc., typically at the expense of less powerful competitors or rivals. — **ex·pan'sion·ist** *n.*

ex·pan·sive (ik·span'siv) *adj.* **1.** Capable of expanding or tending to expand. **2.** Characterized by expansion or breadth; broad; extensive. **3.** Open and effusive; outgoing: an *expansive* personality. **4.** *Psychiatry* Characterized by a delusion of wealth, power, etc., accompanied by euphoria. — **ex·pan'sive·ly** *adv.* — **ex·pan'sive·ness** *n.*

ex par·te (eks pär'tē) *Latin* From or in the interest of one side only; one-sided.

ex·pa·ti·ate (ik·spā'shē·āt) *v.i.* **·at·ed, ·at·ing 1.** To speak, or write more fully or at considerable length; elaborate: with *on* or *upon.* **2.** *Rare* To roam about. [< L *ex(s)-patiatus,* pp. of *ex(s)patiari* < *ex-* out + *spatiari* to walk < *spatium* space] — **ex·pa'ti·a'tion** *n.* — **ex·pa'ti·a'tor** *n.*

ex·pa·tri·ate (*v.* eks·pā'trē·āt; *n. & adj.* eks·pā'trē·it, -āt) *v.t.* **·at·ed, ·at·ing 1.** To drive (a person) from his native land; exile; banish. **2.** To withdraw (oneself) from one's native land. — **Syn.** See BANISH. — *n.* An expatriated person. — *adj.* Banished; expatriated. [< Med.L *expatriatus,* pp. of *expatriare* < L *ex-* out + *patria* native land] — **ex·pa'tri·a'tion** *n.*

ex·pect (ik·spekt') *v.t.* **1.** To look forward to as certain or probable; anticipate. **2.** To look for as right, proper, or necessary; require: We *expect* the best from our students. **3.** *Informal* To presume; suppose. **4.** *Obs.* To wait for. [< L *ex(s)pectare* < *ex-* out + *spectare* to look at, freq. of *specere* to see]

ex·pec·tan·cy (ik·spek'tən·sē) *n. pl.* **·cies 1.** The action or state of expecting; anticipation; expectation. **2.** An object of expectation: life *expectancy.* **3.** *Law* The state of being expected; abeyance: an estate in *expectancy.* Also *Rare* **ex·pec'tance.**

ex·pec·tant (ik·spek'tənt) *adj.* **1.** Having expectations; expecting. **2.** Full of anticipation: an *expectant* moment. **3.** Awaiting the birth of a child: an *expectant* mother. — *n.* One who expects something. — **ex·pec'tant·ly** *adv.*

ex·pec·ta·tion (ek'spek·tā'shən) *n.* **1.** The action of expecting, or the state of mind of one who expects; anticipation: *expectation* of success; to wait in *expectation.* **2.** The state of being expected: preceded by *in:* a sum of money in *expectation.* **3.** *Often pl.* A prospect of some good to come. **4.** Something expected or looked forward to. **5.** The degree of probability that some event will occur. [< L *ex(s)pec-tatio, -onis* < *ex(s)pectare.* See EXPECT.]

expectation of life The average duration of life beyond any given age as determined by mortality statistics.

ex·pec·ta·tive (ik·spek'tə·tiv) *adj.* Of, pertaining to, or characterized by expectation.

ex·pec·to·rant (ik·spek'tər·ənt) *adj.* Relating to or promoting expectoration. — *n.* A medicine used to promote expectoration.

ex·pec·to·rate (ik·spek'tə·rāt) *v.t. & v.i.* **·rat·ed, ·rat·ing 1.** To discharge (phlegm, etc.) by hawking or coughing up and spitting. **2.** To spit. [< L *expectoratus,* pp. of *expec-torare* < *ex-* out + *pectus, -oris* breast]

ex·pec·to·ra·tion (ik·spek'tə·rā'shən) *n.* **1.** The act of expectorating. **2.** Matter expectorated.

ex·pe·di·en·cy (ik·spē'dē·ən·sē) *n. pl.* **·cies 1.** The state or quality of being expedient; fitness or appropriateness under given circumstances. **2.** That which is expedient. **3.** Adherence to or consideration of what is opportune or politic, with little or no regard for what is just or right. Also **ex·pe'di·ence.**

ex·pe·di·ent (ik·spē'dē·ənt) *adj.* **1.** Serving to promote a desired end; suitable, advisable, or proper under the circumstances. **2.** Pertaining to or prompted by utility, interest, or advantage rather than by what is right. **3.** *Obs.* Speedy; expeditious. — *n.* **1.** Something expedient; a means to an end. **2.** A means employed in an exigency; device; shift. [< OF < L *expediens, -entis,* ppr. of *expedire.* See EXPEDITE.] — **ex·pe'di·ent·ly** *adv.*

— **Syn.** (adj.) *Expedient, advisable, politic,* and *advantageous* refer to what seems the most prudent method or course of action to follow in a given situation. *Expedient* now often implies selfish motives, and a partial or complete disregard of principles: He found it *expedient* to conceal his past record. It is also used without derogatory implication, but *advisable* is more common in this sense: He thought it *advisable* (or *expedient*) to have the best legal advice. *Politic* refers to the exercise of prudence or good judgment, and may imply tact and thoughtfulness, as well as shrewdness or opportunism: By his *politic* words and actions, he kept the friendship of both disputants. As here compared, *advantageous* points to a course of action that is seen as clearly promising some personal benefit.

ex·pe·di·en·tial (ik·spē'dē·en'shəl) *adj.* Of or pertaining to expediency.

ex·pe·dite (ek'spə·dīt) *v.t.* **·dit·ed, ·dit·ing 1.** To speed up the process or progress of; facilitate. **2.** To do with quick efficiency. **3.** *Rare* To send or issue officially; dispatch. — *adj. Archaic* Unimpeded; prompt; expeditious. [< L *expeditus,* pp. of *expedire* to free the feet from fetters, hence to dispatch < *ex-* out + *pes, pedis* foot]

ex·pe·dit·er (ek'spə·dī'tər) *n.* One who or that which expedites; especially, one who facilitates the delivery of needed material. Also **ex'pe·di'tor.**

ex·pe·di·tion (ek'spə·dish'ən) *n.* **1.** A journey, march, or voyage for a definite purpose: an Arctic *expedition.* **2.** The body of persons engaged in such a journey, together with their equipment. **3.** The quality of being expeditious; speed; dispatch.

ex·pe·di·tion·ar·y (ek'spə·dish'ən·er'ē) *adj.* Relating to, designed for, or constituting an expedition.

ex·pe·di·tious (ek'spə·dish'əs) *adj.* Marked by or done with energy and dispatch; quick; speedy. — **Syn.** See SWIFT[1]. — **ex'pe·di'tious·ly** *adv.* — **ex'pe·di'tious·ness** *n.*

ex·pel (ik·spel') *v.t.* **·pelled, ·pel·ling 1.** To drive out by force; force out; eject: to *expel* something from the mouth. **2.** To force by decision of the proper authorities to end attendance at a school, etc., or to terminate membership in an organization, etc.; oust. [< L *expellere* < *ex-* out + *pellere* to drive, thrust] — **ex·pel'la·ble** *adj.*

— **Syn.** *Expel, eject, dislodge, evict, oust,* and *dismiss* mean to send away forcibly. A school *expels* an unruly pupil; water in the lungs must be promptly *expelled.* A rifle *ejects* a shell automatically; a squid *ejects* an inky fluid. To *dislodge* is to move something heavy or resisting from its place; an avalanche may *dislodge* a large boulder. A man is *evicted* from his house; an official is *ousted* from office; an employee is *dismissed* from his job.

ex·pel·lant (ik·spel'ənt) *adj.* Forcing out or tending to force out. — *n.* An expellant medicine. Also **ex·pel'lent.**

ex·pend (ik·spend') *v.t.* To pay out or spend; use up. [< L *expendere* < *ex-* out + *pendere* to weigh, pay]

ex·pend·a·ble (ik·spen'də·bəl) *adj.* **1.** Available for spending: *expendable* funds. **2.** *Mil.* Denoting supplies or equipment that can be sacrificed so as to gain some objective. — **ex·pend·a·bil'i·ty** *n.*

ex·pen·di·ture (ik·spen'də·chər) *n.* **1.** The act of expending; outlay. **2.** That which is expended; expense. [< Med.L *expenditus,* irreg. pp. of L *expendere.* See EXPEND.]

ex·pense (ik·spens') *n.* **1.** Outlay or consumption of money; expenditure. **2.** The amount of money required to buy or do something; cost; charge: an estimate of the *expense* of a new house. **3.** Something whose acquisition, maintenance, etc., requires or involves the spending of money: A car is an *expense.* **4.** *pl.* Funds allotted to cover incidental costs: salary plus traveling *expenses.* **5.** *pl.* Funds spent or charges anticipated: business *expenses.* **6.** Loss or injury necessarily involved in getting or doing something: preceded by *at:* to get the work done at the *expense* of one's health. Abbr. (for defs. 4, 5) *exp.* — **Syn.** See PRICE. [< AF < LL *expensa,* pp. of L *expendere.* See EXPEND.]

ex·pen·sive (ik·spen'siv) *adj.* Involving much expense; costly. — **ex·pen'sive·ly** *adv.* — **ex·pen'sive·ness** *n.*

ex·pe·ri·ence (ik·spir′ē·əns) *n.* **1.** Actual participation in or direct contact with something: *experience* in business. **2.** A particular activity or occurrence actually participated in: The *experience* was a pleasant one; especially, something unusual of this kind: A visit to that place is an *experience*. **3.** Knowledge or skill derived from actual participation or direct contact rather than from mere study, interest, etc.: to hire people with *experience*. **4.** The period of time during which one has been directly occupied in something: a long *experience* in teaching. **5.** The totality of one's judgments or reactions with regard to something directly met with or engaged in: The effort is worthwhile, in his *experience*. **6.** The accumulated variety of whatever has been actually met with or engaged in: the entire *experience* of mankind. — *v.t.* **·enced, ·enc·ing** To have experience of; be personally or directly aware of or moved by. [< OF < L *experientia* < *experiri* to try out]

ex·pe·ri·enced (ik·spir′ē·ənst) *adj.* **1.** Having had experience, especially to a considerable extent. **2.** Made skillful or proficient through actual practice, etc.

experience table In life insurance, a mortality table based on the records and reports of one or more companies.

ex·pe·ri·en·tial (ik·spir′ē·en′shəl) *adj.* Pertaining to or acquired by experience; empirical. — **ex·pe′ri·en′tial·ly** *adv.*

ex·per·i·ment (ik·sper′ə·mənt, -ment) *n.* **1.** An act or operation designed to discover, test, or illustrate a truth, principle, or effect. **2.** The conducting of such operations; experimentation. *Abbr. expt.* — *v.i.* To make experiments; make a test or trial. [< OF < L *experimentum* < *experiri* to try out] — **ex·per′i·ment′er** *n.*

ex·per·i·men·tal (ik·sper′ə·men′təl) *adj.* **1.** Pertaining to, resulting from, or known by experiment. **2.** Growing out of or based on experience; empirical. **3.** Having the nature of an experiment; provisional; tentative. *Abbr. exptl.* — **ex·per′i·men′tal·ly** *adv.*

ex·per·i·men·tal·ism (ik·sper′ə·men′təl·iz′əm) *n.* **1.** The use or theory of experimental procedure; empiricism. **2.** Preference for experimental procedure. — **ex·per′i·men′tal·ist** *n.*

ex·per·i·men·ta·tion (ik·sper′ə·men·tā′shən) *n.* The act or practice of experimenting.

experiment station A place where experiments are conducted with a view to improving methods and products.

ex·pert (*n.* ek′spûrt; *for adj. also* ik·spûrt′) *n.* **1.** One who has special skill or knowledge; a specialist. **2.** *Mil.* **a** In the U.S. Army, the highest of three grades for skill in the use of small arms. **b** A soldier having this grade. Compare MARKSMAN, SHARPSHOOTER. — *adj.* **1.** Skillful as the result of training or experience; practiced: an *expert* craftsman. **2.** Characteristic of or produced by an expert: *expert* cooking. [< OF < L *expertus*, pp. of *experiri* to try out] — **ex·pert′ly** *adv.* — **ex·pert′ness** *n.*
— **Syn.** (noun) **1.** adept, authority, master. — **Ant.** novice, beginner, bungler. Compare AMATEUR. — (adj.) See SKILLFUL.

ex·per·tise (ek′spər·tēz′) *n.* **1.** Evaluation or assessment by an expert. **2.** Expertness. [< F]

ex·pi·a·ble (ek′spē·ə·bəl) *adj.* That may be expiated or atoned for.

ex·pi·ate (ek′spē·āt) *v.t.* **·at·ed, ·at·ing** To atone for; make amends for. [< L *expiatus*, pp. of *expiare* < *ex-* completely + *piare* to appease < *pius* pious] — **ex′pi·a′tor** *n.*

ex·pi·a·tion (ek′spē·ā′shən) *n.* **1.** The act of expiating; atonement. ◆ Collateral adjective: *piacular.* **2.** The means by which atonement is made; something done in expiation. — **Syn.** See PROPITIATION.

ex·pi·a·to·ry (eks′pē·ə·tôr′ē, -tō′rē) *adj.* Having the power or character of an expiation; offered in atonement.

ex·pi·ra·tion (ek′spə·rā′shən) *n.* **1.** The termination of anything; close. **2.** The act of breathing out air from the lungs: opposed to *inspiration.* **3.** *Obs.* Death. *Abbr. exp.*

ex·pir·a·to·ry (ik·spīr′ə·tôr′ē, -tō′rē) *adj.* Pertaining to or used for the expiration of breath.

ex·pire (ik·spīr′) *v.* **·pired, ·pir·ing** *v.i.* **1.** To come to an end, as a contract. **2.** To breathe out air from the lungs; exhale. **3.** To breathe one's last breath; die. **4.** To die out, as embers. — *v.t.* **5.** To breathe out from the lungs. **6.** *Obs.* To emit (a vapor or odor). [< F *expirer* < L *ex(s)pirare* < *ex-* out + *spirare* to breathe] — **ex·pir′er** *n.*

ex·pir·y (ik·spīr′ē) *n.*, *pl.* **·ries** **1.** End; termination. **2.** *Archaic* Death.

ex·plain (ik·splān′) *v.t.* **1.** To make plain or understandable. **2.** To give the meaning of; interpret; expound. **3.** To give reasons for; account for. — *v.i.* **4.** To give an explanation. — **to explain away** To provide reasons in order to minimize or cancel out (one's conduct, words, etc.). [< L *explanare* < *ex-* out + *planare* to make level < *planus* flat] — **ex·plain′a·ble** *adj.*
— **Syn.** *Explain, expound, demonstrate,* and *elucidate* mean to show the meaning of something. *Explain* is the general term; we may *explain* by describing a thing's form or structure, tracing its origins and development, showing its operation or use, or citing its reasons and the relations of its parts. To *expound* is to set forth a subject at length and in detail, with such fullness as to make it clear. *Demonstrate* refers to an explanation made with

samples or models in order to show how a thing operates. To *elucidate* is to throw light on; we may *elucidate* one detail of a complex matter without *explaining* the whole.

ex·pla·na·tion (ek′splə·nā′shən) *n.* **1.** The act or process of explaining; elucidation; interpretation. **2.** That which explains; a statement that clarifies or accounts for something. **3.** The meaning assigned or adduced to explain something; sense; significance. **4.** A mutual clearing up of a misunderstanding; reconciliation. [< L *explanatio, -onis* < *explanare.* See EXPLAIN.]
— **Syn. 1, 2.** *Explanation, exposition, description, definition,* and *interpretation,* though not strictly synonymous, agree in referring to something said or written to make a subject clear. *Explanation* is a general term, including the senses of the other words. *Exposition* involves laying something open to view, and thus is applied to a statement of the content of a thing, or a detailed account of its inner structure and the relation of its parts. *Description* is pictorial, and concerns appearance and outward form. In *definition,* we show the limits of a word, category, science, etc., and how it is different from other things in its class. *Interpretation* clarifies what is not immediately apparent: an *interpretation* of the meaning of a dream.

ex·plan·a·to·ry (ek·splan′ə·tôr′ē, -tō′rē) *adj.* Serving or tending to explain. Also **ex·plan′a·tive.** — **ex·plan′a·to′ri·ly** *adv.*

ex·plant (eks·plant′, -plänt′) *v.t.* To place outside its habitat, as an organ of the body or bacteria in a medium, for purposes of observation and study.

ex·ple·tive (eks′plə·tiv) *n.* **1.** An exclamation, often profane. **2.** A word or syllable added solely for rhetorical or rhythmical effect or for the completion of a syntactic pattern. **3.** Something serving to fill out. — *adj.* Added merely to fill out a sentence, complete a rhythm, etc.: also **ex′ple·to′ry** (-tôr′ē, -tō′rē). [< LL *expletivus* < L *expletus,* pp. of *explere* < *ex-* completely + *plere* to fill]

ex·pli·ca·ble (eks′pli·kə·bəl, ik·splik′ə·bəl) *adj.* Capable of explanation.

ex·pli·cate (eks′pli·kāt) *v.t.* **·cat·ed, ·cat·ing** To clear from obscurity; explain. [< L *explicatus,* pp. of *explicare* < *ex-* out + *plicare* to fold] — **ex′pli·ca′tor** *n.*

ex·pli·ca·tion (eks′plə·kā′shən) *n.* **1.** The act or process of explicating. **2.** An explanation or interpretation, as of a complicated passage in a text. **3.** A detailed description.

ex·pli·ca·tive (eks′plə·kā′tiv, ik·splik′ə·tiv) *adj.* Serving to interpret or explain. Also **ex′pli·ca·to′ry** (-kə·tôr′ē, -tō′rē).

ex·plic·it (ik·splis′it) *adj.* **1.** Plainly expressed; clear: *explicit* instructions. **2.** Unreserved in expression; straightforward; outspoken: an *explicit* opponent. **3.** Developed in detail; not merely implied. [< L *explicitus,* var. of *explicatus.* See EXPLICATE.] — **ex·plic′it·ly** *adv.* — **ex·plic′it·ness** *n.*
— **Syn. 1.** *Explicit* and *express* mean said in plain words. What is *explicit* is unfolded, so that it is no longer obscure or doubtful; what is *express* is uttered so decidedly that it cannot be overlooked. An *explicit* statement is too clear to be misunderstood, while an *express* statement is too emphatic to be ignored. — **Ant.** implicit.

ex·plode (ik·splōd′) *v.* **·plod·ed, ·plod·ing** *v.t.* **1.** To cause to burst or blow up violently and with noise; detonate: to *explode* a bomb. **2.** To disprove utterly; refute: to *explode* a theory. **3.** To cause to expand violently or pass suddenly from a solid to a gaseous state: to *explode* gunpowder. **4.** *Phonet.* To articulate with an explosion. **5.** *Obs.* To drive from the stage, as an actor. — *v.i.* **6.** To burst into pieces or fragments; blow up. **7.** To make a noise as if bursting: to *explode* with laughter. **8.** To be exploded, as gunpowder. [< L *explodere,* orig., to drive off the stage, hiss < *ex-* out + *plaudere* to clap] — **ex·plod′er** *n.*

ex·ploit (*n.* eks′ploit, ik·sploit′; *v.* ik·sploit′) *n.* A deed or act, especially one marked by heroism or daring; feat. — **Syn.** See ACT. — *v.t.* **1.** To use meanly for one's own gain or advantage: to *exploit* workers. **2.** To put to practical use; utilize for profitable ends: to *exploit* water power. [< OF *esploit* < L *explicitum,* neut sing. of *explicitus.* See EXPLICIT.] — **ex·ploit′a·ble** *adj.*

ex·ploi·ta·tion (eks′ploi·tā′shən) *n.* The act of exploiting; especially, utilization of someone or something for purely selfish ends.

ex·ploi·ta·tive (ik·sploi′tə·tiv) *adj.* Relating to, marked by, or furthering exploitation.

ex·ploi·ter (ik·sploi′tər) *n.* One who exploits. — *v.t.* To exploit.

ex·plo·ra·tion (eks′plə·rā′shən) *n.* **1.** The act of exploring; especially, the exploring of unfamiliar or previously unknown regions. **2.** *Med.* The examination of internal organs or parts, as in diagnosis or preliminary surgery. [< L *exploratio, -onis* < *explorare.* See EXPLORE.]

ex·plor·a·to·ry (ik·splôr′ə·tôr′ē, ik·splō′rə·tō′rē) *adj.* Of, for, or relating to exploration. Also **ex·plor′a·tive.**

ex·plore (ik·splôr′, -splōr′) *v.* **·plored, ·plor·ing** *v.t.* **1.** To subject to a close search or examination; look through or scrutinize carefully: to *explore* the contents of a drawer. **2.** To travel through or go about (unfamiliar territory, etc.) so as to find out the natural features of, kind of life in, etc.

3. *Med.* To examine closely, as a wound or diseased part, especially by probing or preliminary surgery. — *v.i.* **4.** To make an exploration. [< L *explorare* to cry out, announce discovery, investigate < *ex-* out + *plorare* to cry out]

ex·plor·er (ik·splôr′ər, -splō′rər) *n.* **1.** One who explores; especially, one who travels in a new or strange region. **2.** Any device with which to explore or examine, as a probe.

Ex·plor·er (ik·splôr′ər, -splō′rər) *n.* One of a group of U.S. artificial satellites, the first of which, **Explorer I**, was launched Jan. 31, 1958.

ex·plo·sion (ik·splō′zhən) *n.* **1.** The act of exploding; a sudden blowing up or bursting. **2.** The sudden, loud noise produced by exploding. **3.** A sudden, violent outbreak of feeling; outburst: an *explosion* of laughter. **4.** A sudden and large increase or expansion: a population *explosion*. **5.** *Phonet.* Plosion. [< L *explosio, -onis* < *explodere*. See EXPLODE.]

ex·plo·sive (ik·splō′siv) *adj.* **1.** Pertaining to or marked by explosion. **2.** Liable to explode or to cause explosion. **3.** *Phonet.* Plosive. — *n.* **1.** Any substance or mixture of substances that, on impact or by ignition, reacts by a violent expansion of gases and the liberation of relatively large amounts of thermal energy. **2.** *Phonet.* A plosive consonant. — **ex·plo′sive·ly** *adv.* — **ex·plo′sive·ness** *n.*

ex·po·nent (ik·spō′nənt; *for def. 3, also* ek′spō·nənt) *n.* **1.** One who or that which explains or expounds. **2.** One who or that which represents or symbolizes something: an *exponent* of fair play. **3.** *Math.* A number or symbol placed as a superscript to the right of a quantity to indicate a power or the reciprocal or root of a power: 2 is an *exponent* in 3^2. [< L *exponens, -entis,* ppr. of *exponere* to explain]

ex·po·nen·tial (ek′spō·nen′shəl) *adj.* Of, relating to, or involving mathematical exponents, especially unknown or variable ones.

ex·po·ni·ble (ik·spō′nə·bəl) *adj.* Needing explanation, as a proposition in logic that must be restated to be intelligible.

ex·port (*v.* ik·spôrt′, -pōrt′, eks′pôrt, -pōrt; *n. & adj.* eks′-pôrt, -pōrt) *v.t.* To carry or send, as merchandise or raw materials, to other countries for sale or trade. — *n.* **1.** The act of exporting. **2.** That which is exported, as a commodity sent from one country to another. — *adj.* Of or pertaining to exports or exportation. *Abbr. exp.* [< L *exportare* < *ex-* out + *portare* to carry] — **ex·port′a·ble** *adj.* — **ex·port′a·bil′i·ty** *n.* — **ex·port′er** *n.*

ex·por·ta·tion (ek′spôr·tā′shən, -spōr-) *n.* **1.** The act or practice of exporting. **2.** That which is exported.

ex·po·sal (ik·spō′zəl) *n.* Exposure.

ex·pose (ik·spōz′) *v.t.* **·posed, ·pos·ing** **1.** To lay open to criticism, ridicule, etc.: to *expose* oneself to scorn. **2.** To lay open to some force, influence, etc.: to *expose* a mixture to heat. **3.** To present to view by baring; uncover to the sight: to *expose* one's shoulders. **4.** To make known (something kept hidden or obscure): to *expose* one's intentions; especially, to reveal (something evil, disgraceful, etc.): to *expose* a crime. **5.** To reveal the identity of (an evildoer, criminal, etc.); unmask. **6.** To leave outside in an unsheltered place so as to cause the death of by cold, starvation, etc.: to *expose* an unwanted infant. **7.** In the Roman Catholic Church, to put (the Host, relics, etc.) on view for prolonged public adoration or veneration. **8.** *Photog.* To admit light to (a sensitized film or plate). [< MF *exposer* < *ex-* out + *poser.* See POSE¹.] — **ex·pos′er** *n.*

ex·po·sé (ek′spō·zā′) *n.* **1.** A making known publicly of something hidden, especially something evil or disgraceful. **2.** A book, article, etc., making sensational disclosures. [< F, pp. of *exposer.* See EXPOSE.]

ex·posed (ik·spōzd′) *adj.* **1.** Being in plain view. **2.** Open to or unprotected from something, as the elements.

ex·po·si·tion (eks′pə·zish′ən) *n.* **1.** The act of presenting, explaining, or expounding facts or ideas. **2.** A detailed presentation of subject matter; also, a commentary or interpretation. **3.** A public display or show; especially, a large exhibition of arts, products, etc. **4.** The part of a play that gives the background of the characters and the initial dramatic situation. **5.** *Music* The initial statement of the themes of a movement; especially, in a fugue, the introduction of the several parts or voices. **6.** *Archaic* Exposure. — **Syn.** See EXPLANATION. [< OF < L *expositio, -onis* < *exponere.* See EXPONENT.]

ex·pos·i·tor (ik·spoz′ə·tər) *n.* One who expounds.

ex·pos·i·to·ry (ik·spoz′ə·tôr′ē, -tō′rē) *adj.* Of or pertaining to exposition; explanatory. Also **ex·pos′i·tive.**

ex post fac·to (eks pōst fak′tō) *Latin* Arising or enacted after some act, occurrence, etc., and having retroactive effect: said especially of a law.

ex·pos·tu·late (ik·spos′chŏŏ·lāt) *v.i.* **·lat·ed, ·lat·ing** To reason earnestly with a person concerning the impropriety or inadvisability of his actions, etc.; remonstrate: usually with *with.* [< L *expostulatus,* pp. of *expostulare* < *ex-* out + *postulare* to demand] — **ex·pos′tu·la′tor** *n.* — **ex·pos′tu·la·to·ry** (-lə·tôr′ē, -tō′rē), **ex·pos′tu·la′tive** *adj.*

ex·pos·tu·la·tion (ik·spos′chŏŏ·lā′shən) *n.* **1.** The act of expostulating; earnest argument or remonstrance. **2.** Something uttered or written in protest or dissuasion.

ex·po·sure (ik·spō′zhər) *n.* **1.** The act of exposing, or the state of being exposed. **2.** Situation or position in relation to the sun, elements, or points of the compass: a room with southern *exposure.* **3.** *Photog.* **a** The act of subjecting a sensitized plate or film to the action of actinic rays. **b** The time required for actinic rays to produce a desired effect. **c** A single film or plate acted upon by actinic rays. **4.** *Law* Offensive public display of one's body.

exposure meter *Photog.* An instrument that measures the amount of light falling on a subject and indicates the proper exposure time: also called *light meter.*

ex·pound (ik·spound′) *v.t.* **1.** To set forth in detail; state; declare: to *expound* a doctrine. **2.** To explain the meaning of; interpret. — **Syn.** See EXPLAIN. [< OF *espondre* < L *exponere.* See EXPONENT.] — **ex·pound′er** *n.*

ex·press (ik·spres′) *v.t.* **1.** To formulate in words; verbalize; state: to *express* an idea. **2.** To give an outward indication of; reveal: to *express* anger by frowning. **3.** To communicate through some medium other than words or signs: a musical theme that *expresses* melancholy. **4.** To indicate by means of a symbol, formula, etc., as in mathematics or chemistry: The sign × *expresses* multiplication. **5.** To squeeze out (a liquid, juice, etc.); press out. **6.** *U.S.* To send (goods, etc.) by special messenger or a system of rapid delivery. — **to express oneself** **1.** To communicate one's thoughts or opinions by words or gestures. **2.** To communicate or give vent to one's feelings, desires, etc., through music, painting, or other creative or free activity. — *adj.* **1.** Communicated or indicated in a clear and unmistakable way; explicit: This is her *express* wish. **2.** Made or intended for a precise (usually indicated) purpose: an *express* law to safeguard human rights. **3.** Designed for or operating at high speed: an *express* highway; an *express* train. **4.** Of or relating to a system of rapid delivery of goods, etc., as by railway: to send something by *express* delivery. **5.** Corresponding exactly; precise: She is the *express* image of her mother. — **Syn.** See EXPLICIT. — *adv.* **1.** By rapid delivery: to send something *express.* **2.** *Archaic* For a very precise purpose. — *n.* **1.** A system designed to convey goods, parcels, money, etc., rapidly from one point to another. **2.** Goods, parcels, etc., conveyed by this system. **3.** Any means of rapid conveyance. **4.** A company specializing in the rapid conveyance of goods, parcels, etc. **5.** A train or other conveyance operating at high speed and making few stops. **6.** A message sent with speed; also, a special messenger chosen to carry such messages. **7.** An express rifle. *Abbr. exp.* [< OF *expresser* < L *expressare* < *ex-* out + *pressare* freq. of *premere* to press] — **ex·press′er** *n.* — **ex·press′i·ble** *adj.*

ex·press·age (ik·spres′ij) *n.* **1.** The transportation of goods by express. **2.** The amount charged for such transportation.

ex·pres·sion (ik·spresh′ən) *n.* **1.** Communication of thought, opinion, etc.: Language is the principal means of *expression.* **2.** Outward indication or manifestation of some feeling, condition, quality, etc.: Her smile was an *expression* of gratitude. **3.** A conventional sign or set of signs used to indicate something; symbolization: The sign + is a mathematical *expression* of addition. **4.** A particular way of looking, speaking, etc., that is indicative of something; especially, a particular cast of the features: a serious *expression* on her face. **5.** The particular way in which one expresses oneself: discreet *expression* of disapproval. **6.** The quality of expressing oneself with understanding, insight, sensitivity, etc.: to read aloud with *expression.* **7.** A particular word, phrase, etc., used in communication: a slang *expression.* **8.** The kind of language used in communication; wording; diction: to have a talent for poetic *expression.* **9.** The ability to communicate thought, feeling, etc.: a concept beyond *expression.* **10.** The action of pressing or squeezing out juice, etc. [< F < L *expressio, -onis* < *exprimere* < *ex-* out + *premere* to press]

ex·pres·sion·ism (ik·spresh′ən·iz′əm) *n.* A movement in the arts, originating in Europe at about the time of World War I, that had as its object the free expression of the inner experience of the artist rather than the realistic representation of appearances. — **ex·pres′sion·ist** *n. & adj.* — **ex·pres′sion·is′tic** *adj.*

ex·pres·sion·less (ik·spresh′ən·lis) *adj.* Devoid of expression; showing little or no feeling, interest, etc.; blank: an *expressionless* face. — **ex·pres′sion·less·ly** *adv.*

ex·pres·sive (ik·spres′iv) *adj.* **1.** Of, pertaining to, or concerned with expression. **2.** Serving to express or indicate: a manner *expressive* of contempt. **3.** Full of special meaning or force; significant: an *expressive* sigh. — **ex·pres′sive·ly** *adv.* — **ex·pres′sive·ness** *n.*

express letter *Brit.* A special delivery letter.

ex·press·ly (ik·spres′lē) *adv.* **1.** With definitely stated intent or application. **2.** Exactly and unmistakably; in direct terms; plainly: *The conditions were expressly stated.*

express rifle A sporting rifle using a large charge of powder and a light bullet of large caliber, for use at close range.

ex·press·way (ik·spres′wā′) *n.* A road designed for rapid travel.

ex·pro·pri·ate (eks·prō′prē·āt) *v.t.* **·at·ed, ·at·ing 1.** To take or transfer (property) from the owner, especially for public use by right of eminent domain. **2.** To deprive (a person) of ownership or property. [< LL *expropriatus,* pp. of *expropriare* < L *ex-* out + *proprium* property < *proprius* one's own] **—ex·pro′pri·a′tion** *n.* **—ex·pro′pri·a′tor** *n.* **—ex·pro′pri·a·to′ry** (-ə·tôr′ē, -tō′rē) *adj.*

expt. Experiment.

exptl. Experimental.

ex·pul·sion (ik·spul′shən) *n.* **1.** The act of expelling; forcible ejection. **2.** The state or fact of being expelled. [< L *expulsio, -onis* < *expellere.* See EXPEL.]

ex·pul·sive (ik·spul′siv) *adj.* Tending or serving to expel.

ex·punc·tion (ik·spungk′shən) *n.* The act of expunging, or the state of being expunged; deletion or erasure. [< L *expunctio, -onis* < *expungere.* See EXPUNGE.]

ex·punge (ik·spunj′) *v.t.* **·punged, ·pung·ing 1.** To strike out (something written); delete; erase. **2.** To get rid of as if by erasing; wipe out. **— Syn.** See CANCEL. [< L *expungere* to prick out, mark (with dots) for deletion < *ex-* out + *pungere* to prick] **—ex·pung′er** *n.*

ex·pur·gate (eks′pər·gāt, eks·pûr′gāt) *v.t.* **·gat·ed, ·gat·ing 1.** To take out obscene or otherwise objectionable material from: *to expurgate a novel.* **2.** To remove or omit (objectionable words, lines, etc.): *to reprint a book after expurgating a few words.* [< L *expurgatus,* pp. of *expurgare* < *ex-* out + *purgare* to cleanse] **—ex′pur·ga′tion** *n.* **—ex′pur·ga′tor** *n.*

ex·pur·ga·to·ry (ik·spûr′gə·tôr′ē, -tō′rē) *adj.* **1.** Of or relating to expurgation or expurgators. **2.** Serving to expurgate. Also **ex·pur′ga·to′ri·al.**

ex·qui·site (eks′kwi·zit, ik·skwiz′it) *adj.* **1.** Marked by rare and delicate beauty, charm, color, craftsmanship, etc.: *an exquisite bracelet.* **2.** Being of a high degree of excellence; consummate; admirable: *an exquisite skill.* **3.** Highly sensitive to sounds, colors, forms, etc.; discriminating: *an exquisite eye for design.* **4.** Extremely refined; very fastidious: *exquisite taste.* **5.** Intensely keen or acute, as pleasure or pain. **6.** *Obs.* Very careful; curious. **— Syn.** See ELEGANT. **—** *n.* A person, usually a man, who is overelegant in dress, manners, etc.; fop; dandy. [< L *exquisitus,* pp. of *exquirere* < *ex-* out + *quaerere* to seek] **—ex′·qui·site·ly** *adv.* **—ex′qui·site·ness** *n.*

exr. Executor.

ex·san·guine (eks·sang′gwin) *adj.* Bloodless. Also **ex·san′·gui·nous, ex·san′gui·ous** (-gwē·əs).

ex·scind (ek·sind′) *v.t.* To cut out; excise. [< L *exscindere* < *ex-* out + *scindere* to cut]

ex·se·cant (eks·sē′kant, -kant) *n. Trig.* A function of an angle expressible as the secant of the angle minus one. [< EX(TERIOR) SECANT]

ex·sect (ek·sekt′) *v.t.* To cut out; excise. [< L *exsectus,* pp. of *exsecare* < *ex-* out + *secare* to cut] **—ex·sec′tion** *n.*

ex·sert (ek·sûrt′) *v.t.* To push out; make protrude. **—** *adj. Biol.* Exserted. [< L *exsertus.* See EXERT.] **—ex·ser′tion** *n.*

ex·sert·ed (ek·sûr′tid) *adj. Biol.* Protruding from surrounding parts; thrust out; unsheathed.

ex·ser·tile (ek·sûr′til) *adj.* Capable of being exserted.

ex·sic·cate (ek′sə·kāt) *v.t. & v.i.* **·cat·ed, ·cat·ing** To dry up or out. [< L *exsiccatus,* pp. of *exsiccare* < *ex-* out + *siccus* dry] **—ex′sic·ca′tion** *n.* **—ex′sic·ca′tive** *adj.* **—ex′sic·ca′tor** *n.*

ex·stip·u·late (eks·stip′yə·lit, -lāt) *adj. Bot.* Destitute of stipules: also **estipulate.**

ex·stro·phy (ek′strə·fē) *n. Pathol.* A congenital turning inside out of an organ or other part: also called *extroversion.* [< Gk. *ex-* out + *strephein* to turn]

ext. 1. Extension. **2.** External; externally. **3.** Extinct. **4.** Extra. **5.** Extract.

ex·tant (ek′stant, ik·stant′) *adj.* **1.** Still existing; not lost nor destroyed; surviving. **2.** *Archaic* Standing out; manifest; conspicuous. [< L *ex(s)tans, -antis,* ppr. of *exstare* < *ex-* out + *stare* to stand]

ex·tem·po·ra·ne·ous (ik·stem′pə·rā′nē·əs) *adj.* **1.** Uttered, performed, or composed with little or no advance preparation: *an extemporaneous talk.* **2.** Prepared with regard to content but not read or memorized word for word: *an extemporaneous political speech.* **3.** Skilled at or given to speaking or performing with little or no advance preparation. **4.** Made with anything immediately available; improvised to meet circumstances: *an extemporaneous lodging.* Also *Archaic* **ex·tem′po·ral** (-pər·əl). [< LL *extemporaneus* < L *ex-* out + *tempus, temporis* time] **—ex·tem′po·ra′ne·ous·ly** *adv.* **—ex·tem′po·ra′ne·ous·ness** *n.* **— Syn. 1, 2.** *Extemporaneous, impromptu, improvised, offhand,* and *unpremeditated* mean done without advance planning. *Extemporaneous* is applied chiefly to formal speeches and signifies merely that they are not read; their content may have been

planned but not their exact words. *Impromptu* emphasizes ready response to an unexpected demand; *improvised* points to construction without the usual materials and tools: *to compose an impromptu poem, to eat at an improvised table.* What is *offhand* is both *impromptu* and casual, but more often simply casual; it is chiefly used to mean brusque or unceremonious. *Unpremeditated* is a formal, often legal word denoting lack of preparation or previous consideration: *an unpremeditated killing.*

ex·tem·po·rar·y (ik·stem′pə·rer′ē) *adj.* **1.** Extemporaneous. **2.** *Obs.* Casual. **—ex·tem′po·rar′i·ly** *adv.* **—ex·tem′po·rar′i·ness** *n.*

ex·tem·po·re (ik·stem′pə·rē) *adj.* Extemporaneous. **—** *adv.* With little or no advance preparation; extemporaneously. [< L *ex tempore* out of the time]

ex·tem·po·rize (ik·stem′pə·rīz) *v.t. & v.i.* **·rized, ·riz·ing** To do, make, compose, or perform with little or no advance preparation; improvise: *to extemporize a speech.* **—ex·tem′po·ri·za′tion** *n.* **—ex·tem′po·riz′er** *n.*

ex·tend (ik·stend′) *v.t.* **1.** To open or stretch to full length. **2.** To cause to go or stretch to a specified point, in a given direction, or for a given distance; make longer. **3.** To cause to last until or for a specified time; prolong; continue. **4.** To widen or enlarge the area or space of; spread out; expand. **5.** To increase or broaden the range, scope, meaning, etc., of: *to extend the duties of an office.* **6.** To hold out or put forth, as the hand. **7.** To straighten or stretch out, as a leg or the body. **8.** To give or offer to give: *to extend hospitality.* **9.** In business, to put off the date of completion or payment of (a contract, debt, etc.) beyond that originally set. **10.** In bookkeeping, to calculate (totals) by multiplying unit rates or prices by the number of units. **11.** *Law* **a** *Brit.* To assess; appraise. **b** To seize (land, etc.) by legal order in settlement of a debt. **12.** *Obs.* To exaggerate. **—** *v.i.* **13.** To be extended; stretch. **14.** To reach, as in a specified direction: *This road extends west.* **— Syn.** See INCREASE. [< L *extendere* < *ex-* out + *tendere* to stretch] **—ex·tend′i·bil′i·ty** *n.* **—ex·tend′i·ble** *adj.*

ex·tend·ed (ik·sten′did) *adj.* **1.** Stretched out; pulled out. **2.** Spread over a wide range of time, a great area of space, etc. **3.** Increased in range of application, influence, etc. **4.** *Printing* Broad in proportion to height: said of type. **—ex·tend′ed·ly** *adv.*

ex·ten·si·ble (ik·sten′sə·bəl) *adj.* **1.** Capable of being extended. **2.** Extensile. **—ex·ten′si·bil′i·ty** *n.*

ex·ten·sile (ik·sten′sil) *adj.* **1.** Capable of being protruded, as the tongue. **2.** Extensible.

ex·ten·sion (ik·sten′shən) *n.* **1.** The act of extending, or the state of being extended. **2.** That which extends something; also, an extra outlet or facility, as an additional telephone that operates through the same line as the main telephone. **3.** The degree or range to or over which something is extended; extent. **4.** An agreement by which a creditor allows a debtor further time in which to pay a debt. **5.** *Physics* That property of matter by virtue of which it occupies space. **6.** *Anat.* The straightening of a limb: opposed to *flexion.* **7.** *Surg.* Traction of a fractured or dislocated limb in order to pull the bones, muscles, etc., back to their normal position. **8.** *Logic* The class of things to which a term or concept is correctly applicable: distinguished from *intension.* Abbr. *ext.* [< L *extensio, -onis* < *extendere.* See EXTEND.] **—ex·ten′sion·al** *adj.*

extension course A course of studies offered by many schools to individuals not enrolled in the regular student body, as in special evening classes.

ex·ten·si·ty (ik·sten′sə·tē) *n.* **1.** The quality of having extension; extensiveness. **2.** *Psychol.* An element of sensation enabling one to perceive spatial extension: compare PROTENSITY.

ex·ten·sive (ik·sten′siv) *adj.* **1.** Large in area: *an extensive farm.* **2.** Large in the number of things included; having a wide range; broad in scope: *extensive experience; extensive powers.* **3.** Widespread; far-reaching: *extensive damage.* **4.** *Physics & Logic* Of or relating to extension. **5.** *Agric.* Designating the cultivation of large areas of land by methods involving the smallest possible use of labor, tools, etc.: compare INTENSIVE. **—ex·ten′sive·ly** *adv.* **—ex·ten′sive·ness** *n.*

ex·ten·som·e·ter (eks′ten·som′ə·tər) *n. Mech.* A micrometer used for measuring the expansion of a body, as of a bar of metal. Also **ex′ten·sim′e·ter** (-sim′ə·tər).

ex·ten·sor (ik·sten′sər, -sôr) *n. Anat.* A muscle that straightens out a limb. Compare FLEXOR.

ex·tent (ik·stent′) *n.* **1.** The dimension, degree, or limit to which anything is extended; compass; reach; size. **2.** Size within given bounds; limits; scope: *the extent of his powers.* **3.** *Math.* Any continuous magnitude, as of a line, surface, or solid. **4.** *Law* **a** In Great Britain, a writ issued against the body, lands, and goods of a debtor; also, a seizure made in execution of such a writ. **b** In the United States, a writ assigning a creditor temporary ownership over his debtor's property. **5.** In British history, an assessment or tax valuation; also, the value assessed. **6.** *Logic* Extension. [< L *extentus,* pp. of *extendere.* See EXTEND.]

ex·ten·u·ate (ik·sten′yōō·āt) *v.t.* **·at·ed, ·at·ing 1.** To represent (a fault, crime, etc.) as less blameworthy; make excuses for. **2.** To cause to be or seem less serious or blameworthy; mitigate. **3.** To belittle the real, asserted, or apparent importance, value, size, etc., of. **4.** *Archaic* To emaciate. **5.** *Archaic* To thin out, dilute, or weaken. — **Syn.** See PALLIATE. [< L *extenuatus*, pp. of *extenuare* to weaken < *ex-* out + *tenuis* thin] — **ex·ten′u·a′tor** *n.*

ex·ten·u·at·ing (ik·sten′yōō·ā′ting) *adj.* Serving to extenuate; especially, tending to lessen guilt or the odiousness of a crime: *extenuating* circumstances.

ex·ten·u·a·tion (ik·sten′yōō·ā′shən) *n.* **1.** The act of extenuating, or the state of being extenuated. **2.** That which extenuates; excuse; palliation.

ex·ten·u·a·to·ry (ik·sten′yōō·ə·tôr′ē, -tō′rē) *adj.* Characterized by extenuation; tending to extenuate. Also **ex·ten′u·a′tive.**

ex·te·ri·or (ik·stir′ē·ər) *adj.* **1.** Of, pertaining to, or situated on the outside; external; outer. **2.** Coming or acting from without: *exterior* influences. **3.** Pertaining to foreign countries; foreign. — *n.* **1.** That which is outside, as an external surface, feature, or quality. **2.** The sum of one's observable qualities or traits, as in the physiognomy or demeanor. [< L *exterior*, compar. of *exterus* outside] — **ex·te′ri·or·ly** *adv.*

exterior angle *Geom.* **1.** Any of four angles formed on the outside of two nonintersecting straight lines cut by a third line. **2.** The angle formed between any side of a polygon and the extension of an adjacent side.

ex·ter·mi·nate (ik·stûr′mə·nāt) *v.t.* **·nat·ed, ·nat·ing** To destroy (living things) entirely; wipe out of existence; annihilate. — **Syn.** See ABOLISH. [< L *exterminatus*, pp. of *exterminare* to drive out < *ex-* out + *terminus* boundary] — **ex·ter′mi·na′tive, ex·ter′mi·na·to′ry** (-nə·tôr′ē, -tō′rē) *adj.*

ex·ter·mi·na·tion (ik·stur′mə·nā′shən) *n.* The act or process of exterminating; annihilation.

extermination camp A concentration camp for systematic mass executions.

ex·ter·mi·na·tor (ik·stûr′mə·nā′tər) *n.* One who or that which exterminates; as: **a** A person whose business is destroying rodents, insects, etc. **b** A chemical preparation used to destroy rodents, insects, etc.

ex·tern (*n.* eks′tûrn; *adj.* ik·stûrn′) *n.* A person connected with an institution but not resident, as a member of the medical staff of a hospital. Also **ex′terne.** — *adj. Obs.* External. [< F *externe* < L *externus* outer. See EXTERNAL.]

ex·ter·nal (ik·stûr′nəl) *adj.* **1.** Of, pertaining to, or situated on the outside; outer; exterior. **2.** Belonging to or derived from the outside; extrinsic: an *external* factor. **3.** Pertaining to the outer self; superficial: *external* polish. **4.** Pertaining to foreign countries: *external* affairs. **5.** Relating to, affecting, or meant for the outside of the body: *external* medication. **6.** *Philos.* Belonging to the material or phenomenal world as distinguished from the mind that perceives it; objective. — *n.* **1.** The outside; exterior. **2.** *Usually pl.* Outward or superficial aspects, circumstances, etc. Abbr. *ext.* [< L *externus* outer < *exter, exterus* on the outside < *ex* out of] — **ex·ter′nal·ly** *adv.*

ex·ter·nal-com·bus·tion (ik·stûr′nəl·kəm·bus′chən) *adj.* Designating a heat engine for which the fuel burns outside the engine itself, most often in a furnace.

ex·ter·nal·ism (ik·stûr′nəl·iz′əm) *n.* **1.** *Philos.* The doctrine that only things that are the objects of sense perception have reality or can be known to have reality; phenomenalism. **2.** Preoccupation with externals, especially in matters of religion. — **ex·ter′nal·ist** *n.*

ex·ter·nal·i·ty (ek′stər·nal′ə·tē) *n. pl.* **·ties** **1.** The quality or state of being external. **2.** An external object or characteristic. **3.** Overconcern with externals; externalism.

ex·ter·nal·ize (ik·stûr′nəl·iz) *v.t.* **·ized, ·iz·ing** **1.** To give external shape to; make external. **2.** To make outwardly real. — **ex·ter′nal·i·za′tion** *n.*

ex·ter·o·cep·tor (ek′stər·ō·sep′tər) *n. Anat.* A receptor, as those of sight, hearing, touch, etc., that responds to stimulation from external agents. Compare INTEROCEPTOR, PROPRIOCEPTOR. [< L *exterus* external + (RE)CEPTOR] — **ex′ter·o·cep′tive** *adj.*

ex·ter·ri·to·ri·al (eks′ter·ə·tôr′ē·əl, -tō′rē-) *adj.* Extraterritorial. — **ex′ter·ri·to′ri·al′i·ty** *n.* — **ex′ter·ri·to′ri·al·ly** *adv.*

ex·tinct (ik·stingkt′) *adj.* **1.** Extinguished; inactive; quenched: an *extinct* volcano. **2.** No longer existing; having no living successors: an *extinct* animal or species. **3.** Void; lapsed: an *extinct* title. Abbr. *ext.* — **Syn.** See LIFELESS. [< L *ex(s)tinctus*, pp. of *ex(s)tinguere.* See EXTINGUISH.]

ex·tinc·tion (ik·stingk′shən) *n.* **1.** The act of extinguishing, or the state of being extinguished; as: **a** A putting out or quenching: *extinction* of a flame, one's hopes, etc. **b** A wiping out; destruction; annihilation: complete *extinction* of the enemy. **2.** The process or condition of becoming extinct; a dying out: the *extinction* of a species. **3.** *Physics* A dim-

inution in the intensity of radiation due to absorption by or scattering in the medium. — **ex·tinc′tive** *adj.*

ex·tin·guish (ik·sting′gwish, -wish) *v.t.* **1.** To put out or quench, as a fire. **2.** To make extinct; wipe out. **3.** To obscure or throw into the shade; eclipse. **4.** *Law* To pay off and satisfy in full; nullify. [< L *ex(s)tinguere* < *ex-* completely + *stinguere* to quench] — **ex·tin′guish·a·ble** *adj.* — **ex·tin′guish·ment** *n.*

ex·tin·guish·er (ik·sting′gwish·ər, -wish-) *n.* **1.** One who or that which extinguishes. **2.** A fire extinguisher (which see).

ex·tir·pate (ek′stər·pāt, ik·stûr′-) *v.t.* **·pat·ed, ·pat·ing** To root out or up; destroy wholly; exterminate. — **Syn.** See ABOLISH. [< L *ex(s)tirpatus*, pp. of *ex(s)tirpare* < *ex-* out + *stirps, stirpis* stem, root] — **ex′tir·pa′tion** *n.* — **ex′tir·pa′tive** *adj.* — **ex′tir·pa′tor** *n.*

ex·tol (ik·stōl′, -stol′) *v.t.* **·tolled, ·tol·ling** To praise in the highest terms; exalt; laud. — **Syn.** See PRAISE. Also **ex·toll′.** [< L *extollere* < *ex-* out, up + *tollere* to raise] — **ex·tol′ler** *n.* — **ex·tol′ment** or **ex·toll′ment** *n.*

ex·tort (ik·stôrt′) *v.t.* To obtain (money, etc.) from a person by violence, threat, oppression, or abuse of authority; wring; wrest. [< L *extortus*, pp. of *extorquere* < *ex-* out + *torquere* to twist] — **ex·tort′er** *n.* — **ex·tor′tive** *adj.*

ex·tor·tion (ik·stôr′shən) *n.* **1.** The act or practice of extorting. **2.** The act of exacting an exorbitant price for something. **3.** That which has been extorted. **4.** *Law* The offense committed by an official who exacts money or something else of value that is not due. — **ex·tor′tion·ar·y, ex·tor′tion·ate** *adj.* — **ex·tor′tion·ate·ly** *adv.*

ex·tor·tion·ist (ik·stôr′shən·ist) *n.* One guilty of extortion. Also **ex·tor′tion·er.**

ex·tra (eks′trə) *adj.* **1.** Over and above what is normal, required, expected, etc.; additional. **2.** Larger or of better quality than usual. — *n.* **1.** Something beyond what is usual or required. **2.** A copy or an edition of a newspaper issued for some special purpose or at a time different from that of the regular edition. **3.** Something for which a special charge is made: Meals are an *extra.* **4.** Something of special quality. **5.** In motion pictures, a person hired for a small part, as in a mob scene. **6.** In cricket, any run resulting from a bye, leg bye, no-ball, or wide. — *adv.* Unusually: *extra* good. Abbr. *ext.* [< L, outside, beyond]

extra- *prefix* Beyond or outside the scope, area, or limits of: used chiefly in forming adjectives and usually written without a hyphen (*extracurricular, extragovernmental, extraterritorial*) except before words beginning with *a* (*extra-atmospheric*) or with a capital letter (*extra-Scriptural*) and except in the word *extra-condensed.* Following is a list of some self-explanatory adjectives formed with *extra-*:

extracellular	extrahistoric	extraparental
extraconscious	extrahuman	extraparietal
extraconstitutional	extraindustrial	extraparochial
extracosmic	extraintellectual	extraplanetary
extracultural	extrajural	extrapopular
extradialectal	extralegal	extrascholastic
extraessential	extramarital	extrasocial
extraformal	extranational	extratemporal
extragovernmental	extranuclear	extratorrid
extragrammatical	extraofficial	extravisceral

ex·tra-bold (eks′trə·bōld′) *n. Printing* Heavy boldface.

ex·tra·ca·non·i·cal (eks′trə·kə·non′i·kəl) *adj.* Being outside the canon; noncanonical: *extracanonical* writings.

ex·tra-con·densed (eks′trə·kən·denst′) *adj. Printing* Extremely narrow in proportion to height: said of type.

ex·tract (*v.* ik·strakt′; *n.* eks′trakt) *v.t.* **1.** To draw or pull out by force: to *extract* a tooth. **2.** To derive (happiness, instruction, etc.) from some source. **3.** To draw out or formulate (a principle, doctrine, etc.); deduce. **4.** To obtain by force or contrivance: to *extract* money. **5.** To obtain from a substance by any chemical or mechanical operation, as by pressure, distillation, etc.: to *extract* juice. **6.** To select or copy out (a passage, word, or the like), as for quotation. **7.** *Math.* To calculate (the root of a number). — *n.* **1.** Something extracted or drawn out. **2.** A passage selected from a book, etc., and used for some particular purpose; quotation; excerpt. **3.** A preparation containing the essence of a substance in concentrated form: vanilla *extract.* **4.** The portion of a plant or substance removed by solvents and used in solid, powdered, or liquid form. Abbr. *ext.* [< L *extractus*, pp. of *extrahere* < *ex-* out + *trahere* to draw, pull] — **ex·tract′a·ble** or **ex·tract′i·ble** *adj.*

ex·trac·tion (ik·strak′shən) *n.* **1.** The act of extracting, or the state of being extracted. **2.** That which is extracted. **3.** Lineage; descent: of European *extraction.*

ex·trac·tive (ik·strak′tiv) *adj.* **1.** That extracts or tends to extract. **2.** Capable of extraction. — *n.* **1.** Something capable of being extracted. **2.** The portion of an extract that becomes insoluble.

ex·trac·tor (ik·strak′tər) *n.* **1.** One who or that which extracts. **2.** The device in a firearm or cannon that withdraws a spent round of ammunition from the chamber prior to ejection. For illustration see REVOLVER.

ex·tra·cur·ric·u·lar (eks′trə-kə-rik′yə-lər) *adj.* Of or pertaining to those activities that are not a part of the curriculum but form a supplementary part of school or college life, as athletics, fraternities, publications, etc.

ex·tra·dit·a·ble (eks′trə-dī′tə-bəl) *adj.* Liable to or warranting extradition.

ex·tra·dite (eks′trə-dīt) *v.t.* **·dit·ed, ·dit·ing 1.** To deliver up (an accused individual, prisoner, or fugitive) to the jurisdiction of some other state, country, etc. **2.** To obtain the extradition of. [Back formation < EXTRADITION]

ex·tra·di·tion (eks′trə-dish′ən) *n.* The surrender of an accused individual, prisoner, or fugitive by one state, etc., to the jurisdiction of another. [< F < L *extraditio, -onis* < *ex*-out + *traditio* surrender. See TRADITION.]

ex·tra·dos (eks·trā′dos) *n. Archit.* The exterior curve of an arch. For illustration see ARCH. [< F < L *extra*- beyond + F *dos* the back < L *dorsum*]

ex·tra·ga·lac·tic (eks′trə-gə-lak′tik) *adj. Astron.* Situated beyond the Galaxy.

ex·tra·ju·di·cial (eks′trə-jōō-dish′əl) *adj.* Lying or occurring outside the jurisdiction of a court. **— ex′tra·ju·di′cial·ly** *adv.*

ex·tra·mun·dane (eks′trə-mun′dān, -mun-dān′) *adj.* Existing outside the world or universe.

ex·tra·mu·ral (eks′trə-myoor′əl) *adj.* **1.** Situated without or beyond the walls, as of a fortified city. **2.** Taking place beyond the boundaries of an educational institution: *extramural* games: opposed to *intramural.*

ex·tra·ne·ous (ik-strā′nē-əs) *adj.* **1.** Coming from without; foreign: *extraneous* rock. **2.** Unrelated to the matter at hand; not germane: an *extraneous* remark. [< L *extraneus* foreign, external < *extra.* Doublet of STRANGE.] **— ex·tra′ne·ous·ly** *adv.* **— ex·tra′ne·ous·ness** *n.*

ex·traor·di·nar·y (ik-strôr′də-ner′ē; *esp. for def. 3* eks′trə-ôr′də-ner′ē) *adj.* **1.** Being beyond or out of the common order, course, or method. **2.** Far exceeding the usual; exceptional; remarkable: an *extraordinary* accident. **3.** Employed for a special purpose or on an exceptional occasion; special: an envoy *extraordinary.* [< L *extraordinarius* < *extra* beyond + *ordo, ordinis* order] **— ex·traor′di·nar′i·ly** *adv.*
— **Syn. 2.** uncommon, phenomenal, rare, singular. — **Ant.** ordinary, common, commonplace, usual, frequent.

ex·tra·phys·i·cal (eks′trə-fiz′i-kəl) *adj.* Outside the scope of physical laws and methods. **— ex′tra·phys′i·cal·ly** *adv.*

ex·trap·o·late (eks-trap′ə-lāt) *v.t. & v.i.* **·lat·ed, ·lat·ing 1.** *Math.* To project (those values of a magnitude or function that lie beyond the range of known values) on the basis of values that have already been determined: distinguished from *interpolate.* **2.** To infer (a possibility) beyond the strict evidence of a series of facts, events, observations, etc. [< EXTRA- + (INTER)POLATE] **— ex·trap′o·la′tion** *n.* **— ex·trap′o·la′tive** *adj.*

ex·tra·pro·fes·sion·al (eks′trə-prə-fesh′ən-əl) *adj.* Outside the usual limits of professional duty or interest.

ex·tra·sen·so·ry (eks′trə-sen′sər-ē) *adj.* Beyond the range of normal sensory perception.

extrasensory perception Powers of perception of external objects or events not directly accessible to any of the sense organs. Abbr. *ESP*

ex·tra·ter·ri·to·ri·al (eks′trə-ter′ə-tôr′ē-əl, -tō′rē-) *adj.* **1.** Exempt from local territorial jurisdiction: the *extraterritorial* rights of an ambassador. **2.** Outside of the national territory: *extraterritorial* possessions. Also *exterritorial.* **— ex′tra·ter′ri·to′ri·al·ly** *adv.*

ex·tra·ter·ri·to·ri·al·i·ty (eks′trə-ter′ə-tôr′ē-al′ə-tē, -tō′rē-) *n.* **1.** In international law, exemption from local territorial jurisdiction, as accorded to foreign sovereigns, diplomatic representatives, etc. **2.** Jurisdiction of a country over its citizens in another country.

ex·tra·u·ter·ine (eks′trə-yōō′tər-in, -tə-rīn) *adj.* Situated or occurring outside of the uterus, as a pregnancy.

ex·trav·a·gance (ik-strav′ə-gəns) *n.* **1.** Wasteful expenditure of money. **2.** Extreme lack of moderation in behavior or speech; excess. **3.** An instance of wastefulness or excess in expenditure, behavior, or speech. Also **ex·trav·a·gan·cy.** [< F]

ex·trav·a·gant (ik-strav′ə-gənt) *adj.* **1.** Overly lavish in expenditure; wasteful. **2.** Exceeding reasonable limits; immoderate; unrestrained: *extravagant* praise. **3.** Flagrantly high; exorbitant: *extravagant* prices. **4.** *Obs.* Straying beyond bounds. [< MF < Med.L *extravagans, -antis,* ppr. of *extravagari* < L *extra* outside + *vagari* to wander] **— ex·trav′a·gant·ly** *adv.* **— ex·trav′a·gant·ness** *n.*

ex·trav·a·gan·za (ik-strav′ə-gan′zə) *n.* A fantastic and elaborate musical or dramatic composition; especially, a lavish, spectacular theatrical production. [< Ital. *estravaganza* extravagance, ult. < Med.L *extravagari.* See EXTRAVAGANT.]

ex·trav·a·gate (ik-strav′ə-gāt) *v.i.* **·gat·ed, ·gat·ing 1.** To roam at will. **2.** To exceed proper bounds. [< Med.L *extravagatus,* pp. of *extravagari.* See EXTRAVAGANT.]

ex·trav·a·sate (ik-strav′ə-sāt) *v.* **·sat·ed, ·sat·ing** *v.t.* **1.** *Pathol.* To cause or allow the escape of (blood, etc.) from the

proper vessels. **2.** *Geol.* To pour forth (lava, etc.) from a vent. **— v.i. 3.** *Pathol.* To filter or ooze into surrounding tissues, as blood from an artery or vein following a bruise. [< EXTRA- + L *vas* vessel + -ATE²]

ex·trav·a·sa·tion (ik-strav′ə-sā′shən) *n.* **1.** The act of extravasating, or the state of being extravasated. **2.** The matter extravasated.

ex·tra·vas·cu·lar (eks′trə-vas′kyə-lər) *adj. Anat.* **1.** Situated outside the vascular system. **2.** Having no blood vessels; nonvascular.

ex·tra·ver·sion (eks′trə-vûr′zhən, -shən), **ex·tra·vert** (eks′-trə-vûrt) See EXTROVERSION, EXTROVERT.

Ex·tre·ma·du·ra (es′trā-mä-thōō′rä) The Spanish name for ESTREMADURA.

ex·treme (ik-strēm′) *adj.* **1.** Being of the highest degree; exceedingly great or severe: *extreme* danger; *extreme* weakness. **2.** Going far beyond the bounds of moderation; exceeding what is considered reasonable; immoderate; radical: an *extreme* fashion; an *extreme* reactionary; also, very strict or drastic: *extreme* measures. **3.** Situated at the farthest limit; outermost: the *extreme* border of a country. **4.** Last; final: *extreme* unction. **— n. 1.** The highest degree; utmost point or verge: the *extreme* of cruelty; hospitable in the *extreme.* **2.** One of the two ends or farthest limits of anything: the *extremes* of joy and sorrow. **3.** An extreme condition, as one of great danger or distress: He is constantly in *extremes.* **4.** *Math.* The first or last term of a proportion or series. **5.** *Logic* **a** Either the subject or predicate of a proposition, as distinguished from the copula. **b** Either of the two terms of a syllogism that, separated in the premises, are joined in the conclusion. **— in the extreme** To the greatest or highest degree. **— to go to extremes** To use extreme measures; carry something to excess. [< OF < L *extremus,* superl. of *exterus* outside] **— ex·treme′ness** *n.*

ex·treme·ly (ik-strēm′lē) *adv.* Exceedingly; very.

extreme unction Unction (def. 2b).

ex·trem·ism (ik-strē′miz-əm) *n.* A tendency to go to extremes.

ex·trem·ist (ik-strē′mist) *n.* **1.** One who advocates extreme measures or holds extreme views. **2.** One who carries something to excess. **— adj.** Of or pertaining to extremism or extremists.

ex·trem·i·ty (ik-strem′ə-tē) *n. pl.* **·ties 1.** The utmost or farthest point; termination, end, or edge: the *extremity* of a line. **2.** The greatest degree: the *extremity* of grief. **3.** An extreme condition of distress, need, danger, etc.; especially, one's dying moments. **4.** *pl.* Extreme measures: to resort to *extremities.* **5.** A limb or appendage of the body; especially, *pl.,* the end parts of a limb or appendage; the hands or feet.

ex·tri·ca·ble (eks′tri-kə-bəl) *adj.* That can be extricated.

ex·tri·cate (eks′trə-kāt) *v.t.* **·cat·ed, ·cat·ing 1.** To free from entanglement, hindrance, or difficulties; disentangle. **2.** To cause to be given off; emit, as gas or moisture. [< L *extricatus,* pp. of *extricare* < *ex*- out + *tricae* trifles, troubles] **— ex′tri·ca′tion** *n.*

ex·trin·sic (ek-strin′sik) *adj.* **1.** Being outside the nature of something; not inherent or included in a thing; not essential: opposed to *intrinsic.* **2.** Derived or acting from without; extraneous. **3.** *Anat.* Originating beyond the limits of a body or limb: *extrinsic* muscles. Also **ex·trin′si·cal.** [< F *extrinsèque* < LL *extrinsecus* outwardly < *exter* outside + *secus* besides < *sequi* to follow] **— ex·trin′si·cal·ly** *adv.* **— ex·trin′si·cal·ness** *n.*
— **Syn. 1.** external, unessential, extraneous.

ex·trorse (eks-trôrs′) *adj. Bot.* Turned outward, as an anther from the axis of a flower: opposed to *introrse.* Also **ex·tror′sal.** [< F < LL *extrorsus* outward < *extra* outside + *versus* toward]

ex·tro·ver·sion (eks′trə-vûr′zhən, -shən) *n.* **1.** *Psychol.* The turning of one's interest toward objects and actions outside the self rather than toward one's own thoughts or feelings: opposed to *introversion:* also spelled *extraversion.* **2.** *Pathol.* Exstrophy. [< *extro*- outwards (< EXTRA-) + L *versio, -onis* a turning < *vertere* to turn]

ex·tro·vert (eks′trə-vûrt) *n. Psychol.* **1.** A person characterized by extroversion. **2.** Loosely, one who is gregarious, exuberant, etc. Opposed to *introvert.* **— adj.** Characterized by extroversion. Also spelled *extravert.*

ex·trude (ik-strōōd′) *v.* **trud·ed, trud·ing** *v.t.* **1.** To force, thrust, or push out. **2.** To shape (plastic, metal, etc.) by forcing through dies under pressure. **— v.i. 3.** To protrude. [< L *extrudere* < *ex*- out + *trudere* to thrust]

ex·tru·sion (ik-strōō′zhən) *n.* **1.** The act or process of extruding. **2.** *Geol.* An overflow of lava upon the earth's surface through conduits or fissures in the rocks.

ex·tru·sive (ik-strōō′siv) *adj.* **1.** Tending to extrude. **2.** *Geol.* Extruded, as outflows of igneous rocks.

ex·u·ber·ance (ig-zōō′bər-əns) *n.* **1.** The quality of being exuberant; abundance of high spirits, health, growth, etc. **2.** An instance of this. Also **ex·u′ber·an·cy.**

ex·u·ber·ant (ig-zōō′bər-ənt) *adj.* **1.** Abounding in high spirits and vitality; full of joy and vigor. **2.** Overflowing; lavish; effusive: *exuberant* praise. **3.** Growing luxuriantly: *exuberant* foliage. **4.** Exceedingly fertile: an *exuberant* imagination. [< L *exuberans, -antis* < *ex-* completely + *uber-are* to be fruitful < *uber* fertile] — **ex·u′ber·ant·ly** *adv.*

ex·u·ber·ate (ig·zōō′bə·rāt) *v.i.* ·**rat·ed,** ·**rat·ing** To be exuberant; overflow.

ex·u·date (eks′yōō·dāt) *n.* Exuded matter.

ex·u·da·tion (eks′yōō·dā′shən) *n.* 1. The act of exuding. 2. That which is exuded, as sweat. — **ex·u·da·tive** (eks·yōō′də·tiv) *adj.*

ex·ude (ig·zōōd′, -zyōōd′, ik·sōōd′, -syōōd′) *v.* ·**ud·ed, ·ud·ing** *v.i.* 1. To ooze or trickle forth through pores or gashes, as sweat, gum, etc. — *v.t.* 2. To discharge gradually in this manner: to *exude* moisture. 3. To give off as if through the pores: to *exude* confidence. [< L *ex*(*s*)*udare* < *ex-* out + *sudare* to sweat]

ex·ult (ig·zult′) *v.i.* 1. To rejoice greatly, as in triumph; be jubilant: to *exult* in victory. 2. *Obs.* To leap into the air, as in joy. [< F *exulter* < L *ex*(*s*)*ultare*, freq. of *exsilire* to leap up < *ex-* out + *salire* to leap] — **ex·ult′ing·ly** *adv.*

ex·ul·tant (ig·zul′tənt) *adj.* Jubilant; triumphant; elated. — **ex·ul′tant·ly** *adv.*

ex·ul·ta·tion (eg′zul·tā′shən, ek′sul-) *n.* The act or state of exulting; jubilation; triumph. Also **ex·ul′tan·cy, ex·ul′tance.**

ex·ur·ban·ite (eks·ûr′bən·īt) *n.* One living in the more fashionable region beyond the suburbs of the city in which he works. [Coined on analogy with *suburbanite*]

ex·ur·bi·a (eks·ûr′bē·ə) *n.* 1. A residential area lying beyond the suburbs of a city. Also **ex′urb.** 2. The social and cultural world of exurbanites.

ex·u·vi·ae (ig·zōō′vi·ē, ik·sōō′-) *n.pl.* Skins, shells, etc., cast off or shed by animals. [< L < *exuere* to cast off, undress] — **ex·u′vi·al** *adj.*

ex·u·vi·ate (ig·zōō′vē·āt, ik·sōō′-) *v.t.* & *v.i.* ·**at·ed, ·at·ing** To cast off or shed (a skin, shell, etc.). — **ex·u′vi·a′tion** *n.* **-ey** Var. of -Y[1].

ey·as (ī′əs) *n.* A young hawk; nestling. [ME *nyas* < F *niais* < L *nidus* nest; in ME *a nyas* was altered to *an eyas*]

Eyck (īk) See VAN EYCK.

eye[1] (ī) *n.* 1. The organ of vision in animals; in man, a nearly spherical mass set in a cavity of the skull and consisting of the cornea, iris, pupil, retina, and lens, with associated muscles and nerves, and protected by the eyelids, eyelashes, and eyebrows. 2. The area around the eye: a black *eye*. 3. The iris, in regard to its color: brown *eyes*. 4. A look; gaze: to cast an *eye* on something. 5. Attentive observation; watchful care: Keep an *eye* on him. 6. Sight; view; presence: in the public *eye*. 7. Capacity to see or discern with discrimination: an *eye* for beauty. 8. A particular expression; mien: an evil *eye*. 9. Interest; desire: an *eye* for money. 10. *Often pl.* A manner of viewing something; judgment; opinion: in the *eyes* of the church. 11. Focal point; center: The *eye* of the revolution was on the island. 12. *Meteorol.* The calm central area of a hurricane or cyclone. 13. Anything resembling the human eye in shape, function, or place: an electric *eye*; the *eye* of a needle; the *eye* of a peacock's feather. — **eye of the wind** *Naut.* The direction from which the wind blows. — **to catch one's eye** To get one's attention. — **to give (someone) the eye** *Slang* To look at (someone) admiringly or invitingly. — **to keep an eye on** (or **peeled**) To watch for something; keep alert. — **to lay** (or **set**) **eyes on** To catch sight of. — **to make eyes at** To look at amorously or covetously. — **to see eye to eye** To agree in all respects. — **with an eye to** With a view to; looking to: *with an eye to* one's own interests. — *v.* **eyed, ey·ing** or **eye·ing** *v.t.* 1. To look at carefully; scrutinize. 2. To make a hole in (a needle, etc.). — *v.i.* 3. *Obs.* To appear to the sight of the eye. [OE *ēage.* Cf. Du. *oog,* G *auge,* L *oculus.*]

eye[2] (ī) *n.* A brood of pheasants. [ME *nye* < OF *ni* < L *nidus* nest; in ME *a nye* was altered to *an eye*]

eye agate A variety of agate with concentric banding that, on cutting and polishing, resembles an eye.

eye·ball (ī′bôl′) *n.* The globe or ball of the eye.

eye·beam (ī′bēm′) *n.* A glance of the eye.

eye·bolt (ī′bōlt′) *n. Mech.* A bolt having, in place of a head, an eye or ring to receive a rope, hook, etc.

eye·bright (ī′brīt′) *n.* 1. A low annual herb (*Euphrasia officinalis*), formerly used in eye lotions: also called *euphrasy.* 2. The scarlet pimpernel: see under PIMPERNEL.

eye·brow (ī′brou′) *n.* 1. The bony ridge over the eyes. 2. The arch of small hairs growing on this ridge.

eye·cup (ī′kup′) *n.* 1. A small cup with a rim curved to fit the eye, used in applying lotions. 2. *Anat.* An embryonic structure that develops into the retina.

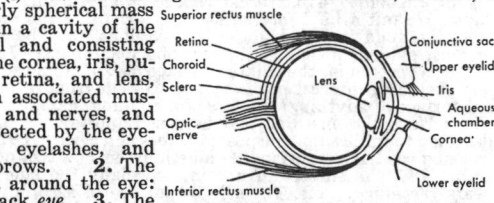

EYE (Anatomical nomenclature)

Superior rectus muscle
Retina
Choroid
Sclera
Optic nerve
Inferior rectus muscle
Conjunctiva sac
Upper eyelid
Lens
Iris
Aqueous chamber
Cornea
Lower eyelid

eyed (īd) *adj.* 1. Having an eye or eyes. 2. Having or characterized by a (specified kind of) eye or (a specified number of) eyes: used in combination: *brown-eyed; one-eyed.* 3. Having eyelike spots; ocellated.

eye·ful (ī′fŏŏl′) *n.* 1. A stare or glance involving full scrutiny of the subject. 2. An amount of something in the eye: an *eyeful* of dust. 3. *Slang* An attractive woman.

eye·glass (ī′glas′, ī′gläs′) *n.* 1. Any lens used to assist vision, as a monocle. 2. An eyepiece. 3. An eyecup.

eye·glass·es (ī′glas·iz, -gläs-) *n.pl.* A pair of corrective glass lenses mounted in a frame and held in position before the eyes by a nosepiece and two pieces that rest on the ears: also called *glasses, spectacles.*

eye·ground (ī′ground′) *n. Anat.* The fundus, or inner side of the back of the eyeball, as seen in an opththalmoscope.

eye·hole (ī′hōl′) *n.* 1. An opening through which to pass a pin, hook, rope, etc. 2. A hole through which one may look; peephole. 3. The socket containing the eye.

eye·hook (ī′hŏŏk′) *n.* A hook permanently attached to a reinforced ring at the end of a rope, chain, etc. For illustration see HOOK.

eye·lash (ī′lash′) *n.* One of the stiff, curved hairs growing from the edge of the eyelids. ◆ Collateral adjective: *ciliary.*

eye·less (ī′lis) *adj.* Lacking eyes; blind.

eye·let (ī′lit) *n.* 1. A small hole or opening, as in a wall, mask, etc. 2. A hole made in leather, canvas, etc., and lined with metal. 3. A metal ring for lining such a hole. 4. In embroidery, a small hole edged with ornamental stitches. 5. *Biol.* An ocellus. — *v.t.* ·**let·ted, ·let·ting** To make eyelets in. [< F *œillet,* dim. of *œil* eye < L *oculus*]

eye·let·eer (ī′lə·tir′) *n.* A sharp, pointed instrument for making eyelet holes; stiletto.

eye·lid (ī′lid′) *n.* Either of the movable folds of skin by which the eyes are opened or closed. ◆ Collateral adjective: *palpebral.*

eye·mind·ed (ī′mīn′did) *adj.* Showing a marked response to and preference for visual stimuli.

eye opener *U.S.* 1. That which opens the eyes or enlightens, as startling news, revelatory behavior, etc. 2. *Informal* A drink of liquor, especially one taken early in the morning.

eye·piece (ī′pēs′) *n.* The lens or combination of lenses nearest the eye in a telescope, microscope, etc.; ocular.

eye rhyme A rhyme composed of words similar in spelling but not in sound, as in *good, flood; move, love.*

eye·ser·vant (ī′sûr′vənt) *n.* One who does his duty only when watched. Also **eye′serv′er.**

eye·ser·vice (ī′sûr′vis) *n.* 1. Work performed only when the employer is watching. 2. Admiring glances.

eye shadow A cosmetic preparation, tinted blue, green, gray, etc., applied to the eyelids.

eye·shot (ī′shot′) *n.* The range or scope of one's sight.

eye·sight (ī′sīt′) *n.* 1. The power or faculty of sight. 2. Extent or range of vision; view.

eye·some (ī′səm) *adj.* Pleasant to look at.

eye·sore (ī′sôr′, ī′sōr′) *n.* Something that offends the sight.

eye splice *Naut.* A loop formed by bending back the end of a rope and splicing it into the rope. For illustration see SPLICE.

eye·spot (ī′spot′) *n.* 1. *Biol.* One of the rudimentary visual organs of many invertebrates, consisting of a few pigment cells overlying a nerve filament sensitive to light. 2. An eyelike marking.

eye·stalk (ī′stôk′) *n. Zool.* A stalk or peduncle that has an eye at its tip, as in lobsters and crabs.

eye·stone (ī′stōn′) *n.* A small, smooth, calcareous disk with one side convex, used to remove foreign matter from the eye.

eye·strain (ī′strān′) *n.* Weariness or discomfort of the eyes caused by excessive or improper use.

eye·tooth (ī′tōōth′) *n. pl.* ·**teeth** (-tēth′) One of the upper canine teeth. — **to cut one's eyeteeth** To grow old enough to gain wisdom by experience.

eye·wash (ī′wosh′, ī′wôsh′) *n.* 1. A medicinal wash for the eye. 2. *U.S. Slang* Nonsense; bunk; flattery.

eye·wa·ter (ī′wô′tər, ī′wot′ər) *n.* A wash for the eyes.

eye·wink (ī′wingk′) *n.* 1. A wink or glance. 2. An instant.

eye·wink·er (ī′wingk′ər) *n.* An eyelash.

eye·wit·ness (ī′wit′nis) *n.* One who has seen something happen and can give testimony about it. — *adj.* Of or by an eyewitness: an *eyewitness* account.

eye worm A nematode worm (*Filaria loa*), whitish in color and about half an inch long, that causes inflammation under the eyelids and is endemic in parts of Africa.

ey·ra (ī′rə) *n.* The jaguarundi. [< Tupi]

eyre (âr) *n. Obs.* 1. A circuit or journey. 2. A court of circuit judges. — **justices in eyre** Judges who prior to the time of Edward III rode a circuit periodically to hold court in the English shires. [< OF *erre* < L *iter* journey]

Eyre (âr), **Lake** A salt lake in northern South Australia, often dry; 3,430 sq. mi.

Eyre Peninsula (âr) A peninsula of South Australia, east of the Great Australian Bight. Also **Eyre's Peninsula.**

ey·rie (âr′ē, ir′ē), **ey·ry**   See AERIE.

Ez. or **Ezr.**   Ezra.

E·ze·ki·el (i·zē′kē·əl, -kyəl)   Sixth-century B.C. Hebrew prophet. — *n.* A book of the Old Testament written by him. Also, in the Douai Bible, **E·ze′chi·el.**   Abbr. **Ezek.** or **Eze.**   [< Hebrew *yeḥez-gēl* God strengthens]

E·ze·ki·el (i·zē′kē·əl, -kyəl), **Moses Jacob,** 1844–1917, U.S. sculptor and musician.

E·zo (e·zō)   See HOKKAIDO.

Ez·ra (ez′rə)   Fifth-century B.C. Hebrew high priest. — *n.* A book of the Old Testament written in part by him. Also, in the Douai Bible, *Esdras.*   [< Hebrew, help]

F

f, F (ef)   *n.*   *pl.* **f's** or **fs, F's** or **Fs, effs** (efs) **1.** The sixth letter of the English alphabet. The shape of the Phoenician *vau* (*waw*) was adopted by the Greeks as *F* (*digamma*) which, discarded from the Greek alphabet, later became the Roman *F*. Also *eff.* **2.** The sound represented by the letter *f*, usually a voiceless labiodental fricative. — *symbol* **1.** *Music* **a** The fourth tone in the musical scale of C. **b** The pitch of this tone, 349.2 cycles per second or this value multiplied by any power of 2, in standard pitch. **c** A note representing it. **d** The scale built upon F. **e** The bass clef in musical notation. **f** Forte. **2.** *Chem.* Fluorine (symbol F). **3.** *Genetics* A filial generation, usually followed by a subscript numeral, as F_1, F_2, for each successive filial generation offspring of a given mating. **4.** *U.S.* A grade indicating failure in school work.

f or **f.** **1.** Foul(s). **2.** *Math.* Function (of).

F   *Math.* Function.

F, F/, F:, f, f/, or **f:**   *Photog.* F number.

F or **F.** **1.** Fahrenheit. **2.** French.

F or **F.** or **f** **1.** *Electr.* Farad. **2.** Fathom.

F. **1.** February. **2.** Fellow. **3.** France. **4.** Friday. **5.** Son (L *filius*).

F. or **f.** **1.** Farthing. **2.** Feminine. **3.** Fine. **4.** Fluid (ounce). **5.** Folio. **6.** Following. **7.** Franc. **8.** Frequency.

fa (fä)   *n. Music* The fourth syllable used in solmization; the fourth degree of a major scale; also, the tone F.

FA   *Mil.* Field Artillery.

F.A.   Fine Arts.

F.A. or **f.a.** **1.** Free alongside. **2.** Freight agent.

FAA   Federal Aviation Agency.

F.A.A.S.   Fellow of the American Association for the Advancement of Science.

fa·ba·ceous (fə·bā′shəs)   *adj. Bot.* Of or pertaining to the bean or pea family (*Fabaceae*, or more commonly *Leguminosae*); leguminous.   [< L *fabaceus* < *faba* bean]

Fa·bi·an (fā′b·ē·ən)   *adj.* Designating, practicing, or characterized by a policy of deliberate delay. — *n.* A member of the Fabian Society. [after *Fabius* Maximus] — **Fa′bi·an·ism** *n.* — **Fa′bi·an·ist** *n. & adj.*

Fabian Society   An association formed in Great Britain in 1884, aiming at the gradual achievement of socialism.

Fa·bi·us Max·i·mus (fā′bē·əs mak′sə·məs), died 203 B.C., Roman general; foiled Hannibal in the Second Punic War by avoiding direct combat: full name **Quintus Fabius Maximus Ver·ru·co·sus** (ver′ōō·kō′səs, -yōō-): called **Cunctator.**

fa·ble (fā′bəl)   *n.* **1.** A brief tale embodying a moral and using persons, animals, or inanimate things as characters. **2.** A legend or myth. **3.** A foolish or improbable story, especially one told to deceive; a fabrication. **4.** *Archaic* The plot of an epic or dramatic poem. **5.** *Archaic* Foolish or idle talk. — **Syn.** See ALLEGORY, FICTION. — *v.t. & v.i.* **·bled, ·bling** To invent or tell (fables or stories); fabricate.   [< OF < L *fabula* < *fari* to say, speak] — **fa′bler** *n.*

fa·bled (fā′bəld)   *adj.* **1.** Recorded in or made famous by fable: a *fabled* king. **2.** Not real; invented; fictitious.

fab·li·au (fab′lē·ō, *Fr.* fȧ·blē·ō′)   *n. pl.* **·aux** (-ōz, *Fr.* -ō′) A short, comic or gay tale, usually in eight-syllable verse. The genre arose in France in the 12th and 13th centuries.   [< F, dim. of *fable*. See FABLE.]

Fa·bre (fȧ′br′), **Jean Henri,** 1823–1915, French entomologist.

fab·ric (fab′rik)   *n.* **1.** A woven, felted, or knitted material, as cloth, felt, or lace. **2.** The texture or workmanship of such material. **3.** Structure or framework: the social *fabric.* **4.** Something fabricated.   [< F *fabrique* < L *fabrica* workshop < *faber* workman. Doublet of FORGE.]

fab·ri·cant (fab′rə·kənt)   *n.* A maker or manufacturer. [< F < L *fabricans, -antis,* ppr. of *fabricare.* See FABRICATE.]

fab·ri·cate (fab′rə·kāt)   *v.t.* **·cat·ed, ·cat·ing 1.** To make or manufacture; build. **2.** To make by combining parts; assemble. **3.** To make up or invent, as a lie or story; concoct.   [< L *fabricatus,* pp. of *fabricare* to construct < *faber* workman] — **fab′ri·ca′tor** *n.*

fab·ri·ca·tion (fab′rə·kā′shən)   *n.* **1.** The art or process of fabricating. **2.** Something fabricated; especially, a falsehood, story, etc. — **Syn.** See LIE[2].

Fab·ri·koid (fab′rə·koid)   *n.* A fabric with cloth base but pyroxylin surface, impervious to water or other fluid: a trade name. Also **fab′ri·koid.**

fab·u·list (fab′yə·list)   *n.* **1.** A composer of fables. **2.** One who falsifies or fabricates.

fab·u·lous (fab′yə·ləs)   *adj.* **1.** Passing the limits of belief; incredible; astounding. **2.** Of, like, or recorded in fable; fictitious; mythical. — **fab′u·lous·ly** *adv.* — **fab′u·lous·ness** *n.*

fac. **1.** Facsimile. **2.** Factor. **3.** Factory.

fa·çade (fə·säd′)   *n.* **1.** *Archit.* The front or principal face of a building. **2.** The front or visible part of anything; especially, a false front designed to convey a favorable impression of the whole: a *façade* of respectability. Also **fa·cade′.**   [< F < Ital. *facciata* < LL *faccia* < L *facies* face]

face (fās)   *n.* **1.** The front portion of the head, comprising in man the surface between the top of the forehead and the bottom of the chin, and extending from ear to ear. **2.** The look or expression of the countenance. **3.** A grotesque or grimacing expression. **4.** External aspect or appearance; look; show: He put a bold *face* on the matter. **5.** *Informal* Effrontery; audacity: He had the *face* to tell us. **6.** The literal or most evident meaning: the *face* of a document. **7.** The value as written on the printed surface of a bond, note, etc., and excluding interest or discounts. **8.** The front or principal surface of anything: the *face* of a building, dam, etc. **9.** The surface of something that is most important or that is designed to fulfill some purpose: the *face* of a clock. **10.** The working or striking surface of something, as of a tool or golf club. **11.** The surface of a coin, especially the side that bears the effigy. **12.** The side or surface of a solid. **13.** One of the sides of any military formation, as of a square formation. **14.** The land surface or the geographical features of a region: the level *face* of the plains. **15.** *Printing* **a** The surface of a type body or printing plate that makes the impression. **b** The size or style of the letter or character on the type. **c** The letter or character itself: also *type face.* **16.** *Mining* The end of a drift or excavation where the work is either going on or has stopped. — **face to face 1.** In each other's immediate presence. **2.** In the presence of; confronting: followed by *with.* — **in the face of 1.** In the presence or sight of; confronting. **2.** In spite of; notwithstanding. — **on the face of it** Judging by all appearances; apparently. — **to fly in the face of** To act in open defiance of. — **to lose face** To lose respect, dignity, or reputation. — **to one's face** In one's presence or in plain words; openly; frankly. — **to save face** To save oneself from embarrassment or disgrace; preserve one's dignity or reputation. — **to show one's face** To put in an appearance. — *v.* **faced, fac·ing** *v.t.* **1.** To bear or turn the face toward; front upon: The house *faces* the street. **2.** To cause to turn in a given direction, as soldiers. **3.** To meet face to face; confront, as with courage or boldness. **4.** To realize or be aware of: to *face* facts. **5.** To cover with a layer or surface of another material: to *face* brick with stucco or a garment with silk. **6.** To make smooth the surface of; dress: to *face* stone. **7.** To turn face upward, as a playing card. — *v.i.* **8.** To be turned or placed with the face in a given direction: the house *faces* west. **9.** To turn in a given direction: to *face* right. — **to face down** To disconcert or prevail over by a bold, fixed gaze or an audacious denial or assertion. — **to face off** In hockey, to start play by dropping the puck between the sticks of two opposing players. — **to face out** To see to completion or endure, as by a persevering manner. — **to face the music** *U.S. Slang* To accept the consequences. — **to face up to 1.** To meet with courage; confront. **2.** To become or be made aware of; realize.   [< F, ult. < L *facies* face] — **face′a·ble** *adj.*

face card   A playing card bearing the picture of a king, queen, or jack; also, *Brit., court card.*

face-hard·en (fās′här′dən)   *v.t. Metall.* To harden the surface of (steel, iron, etc.) by the addition of carbon in conjunction with great heat.

face-height (fās′hīt′)   *n. Anat.* The distance between the gnathion and the nasion. Also **face′-length′.**

face lift·ing (lif′ting)   An operation that tightens sagging tissues or muscles in the face; plastic surgery of the face.

face-off (fās′ôf′, -of′) *n.* In hockey, the act of facing off.

face·plate (fās′plāt′) *n. Mech.* A disk that holds and rotates work, as on a lathe or boring mill.

face powder A cosmetic powder applied to the face to dull shiny skin, cover blemishes, etc.

fac·er (fā′sər) *n. Mech.* An attachment to a machine tool to hold a cutter in facing or surfacing.

face-sav·ing (fās′sā′ving) *adj.* Serving to preserve prestige.

fac·et (fas′it) *n.* **1.** One of the small plane surfaces cut upon a gem. **2.** A phase, side, or aspect of a subject or person: the many *facets* of his personality. **3.** *Archit.* A flat projection between the flutings of a column. **4.** *Zool.* A unit of a compound eye in insects and crustaceans; also, the surface or cornea of such an eye. **5.** *Anat.* A flat or abraded surface, as on a bone or tooth. — **Syn.** See PHASE. — *v.t.* **fac·et·ed** or **·et·ted, fac·et·ing** or **·et·ting** To cut or work a facet or facets upon. [< F *facette*, dim. of *face*. See FACE.]

fa·cete (fə-sēt′) *adj. Archaic* Clever; witty; humorous. [< L *facetus* elegant, facetious]

fa·ce·ti·ae (fə-sē′shi-ē) *n.pl.* **1.** Facetious sayings collectively. **2.** Coarsely witty books. [< L, pl. of *facetia* jest < *facetus* facetious]

fa·ce·tious (fə-sē′shəs) *adj.* Given to or marked by levity or flippant humor; jocular; jesting. — **Syn.** See HUMOROUS. [< F *facétieux* < *facétie* jest < L *facetiae* jests] — **fa·ce′tious·ly** *adv.* — **fa·ce′tious·ness** *n.*

face value **1.** The value stated on the face of a bond, coin, note, etc.: distinguished from *book value, market value.* **2.** Apparent value: promises taken at *face value.*

fa·cial (fā′shəl) *adj.* Of, near, or for the face. — *n. Informal* A massage or other treatment for the face. [< ML *facialis* < L *facies* face]

facial angle The angle formed between the line representing the face-height and the axis of the skull from the edge of the central incisors to the auricular point.

facial index A number expressing the ratio of the maximum breadth to the length of the face, multiplied by 100.

facial nerve *Anat.* The seventh cranial nerve, one of a pair that actuate the muscles controlling facial expression.

FACIAL ANGLE
a Glabella. *c* Edge of central incisors. *f* Auricular point. *acf* Facial angle.

fa·ci·end (fā′shē·end) *n. Math.* A multiplicand. [< L *faciendum*, neut. gerundive of *facere* to do]

-facient *suffix* Causing; making: *sorbefacient.* [< L *faciens, -entis*, ppr. of *facere* to do]

fa·ci·es (fā′shi·ēz) *n.* **1.** The general aspect or external appearance of anything. **2.** *Geol.* The aggregate of the characteristics that determine the origin, composition, and mode of formation of rock deposits. **3.** *Med.* The expression of the face in a given disease. [< L, form, face]

fac·ile (fas′əl, -il) *adj.* **1.** Requiring little effort; easily achieved or performed: a *facile* victory; *facile* work; also, showing little expenditure of effort; superficial: a *facile* prose style. **2.** Ready or quick in performance; dexterous; skillful: a *facile* tongue; also, smooth; glib: a *facile* speaker. **3.** Easily moved or persuaded; pliant; yielding. **4.** Easygoing; affable; agreeable. [< F < L *facilis* easy to do, lit., doable < *facere* to do] — **fac′ile·ly** *adv.* — **fac′ile·ness** *n.*

fa·ci·le prin·ceps (fas′ə·lē prin′seps) *Latin* Unquestionably first or foremost.

fa·ci·lis de·scen·sus A·ver·no (fas′ə·lis di·sen′səs ə·vûr′nō) or **A·ver·ni** (ə·vûr′nī) *Latin* Easy is the descent into Avernus (hell).

fa·cil·i·tate (fə·sil′ə·tāt) *v.t.* **·tat·ed, ·tat·ing** To make easier or more convenient. — **fa·cil′i·ta′tion** *n.*

fa·cil·i·ty (fə·sil′ə·tē) *n. pl.* **·ties** **1.** Ease of performance or action; freedom from impediment: *facility* of movement. **2.** Ready skill or ability; physical or mental dexterity; aptitude; talent. **3.** *Usually pl.* Something, as a building, room, area, equipment, etc., that is built or purchased to make an action or operation easier or to serve a special purpose: *facilities* for research. **4.** Readiness to comply or be persuaded; pliancy. — **Syn.** See ABILITY, EASE. [< F *facilité* < L *facilitas, -tatis* < *facilis*. See FACILE.]

fac·ing (fā′sing) *n.* **1.** A covering in front for ornament, protection against wear, etc. **2.** The lining of a garment on parts exposed by being turned back. **3.** Any heavy, durable fabric used for this. **4.** *pl.* The contrasting collars, cuffs, or trimmings on certain military uniforms.

fa·cin·o·rous (fə·sin′ər·əs) *adj. Rare* Atrocious; vile. [< L *facinorosus* criminal < *facinus* a (bad) deed]

F.A.C.P. Fellow of the American College of Physicians.

F.A.C.S. Fellow of the American College of Surgeons.

facsim. Facsimile.

fac·sim·i·le (fak·sim′ə·lē) *n.* **1.** An exact copy or reproduction. Abbr. *fac., facsim.* **2.** *Telecom.* A method of transmitting messages, drawings, or the like, by means of radio, telegraph, etc. — **Syn.** See DUPLICATE. — *adj.* **1.** Exactly copied or reproduced. **2.** Producing exact copies or facsimiles. [< L *fac simile* make like]

fact (fakt) *n.* **1.** Something that actually exists or has actually occurred; something known by observation or experience to be true or real: a scientific *fact.* **2.** Something asserted to be true or to have happened. **3.** Reality or actuality, as distinguished from conjecture or fancy: also in the phrases **as a matter of fact, in fact, in point of fact** In reality; actually. **4.** *Often pl. Law* An alleged circumstance or event presented to the jury as part of a case, considered apart from its legal interpretation by the judge. **5.** A thing done; especially, a criminal deed: now only in the legal phrases **before** (or **after**) **the fact, to deny the fact,** etc. [< L *factum* < *facere* to do. Doublet of FEAT.]

— **Syn. 1.** *Fact* and *truth* agree in denoting an assertion that corresponds to reality. A *fact* is a proposition about the material world, usually verifiable by simple perception. A *truth* requires the intervention of reasoning, either because it deals with the world beyond our senses, or because it rests upon the way we unite many *facts.* The occurrence and alternation of day and night are *facts*; that the earth revolves around its axis is a *truth.*

fact-find·ing (fakt′fīn′ding) *n.* The ascertainment of facts or conditions. — *adj.* Collecting facts and information: a *fact-finding* commission.

fac·tice (fak′tis) *n.* A fluffy, rubberlike material obtained by vulcanizing linseed oil with sulfur or sulfur chloride. [< F < L *factitius.* See FACTITIOUS.]

fac·tion (fak′shən) *n.* **1.** A group of people operating within, and often in opposition to, a larger group, to gain its own ends. **2.** Party strife; internal dissension. [< F < L *factio, -onis* < *facere* to do. Doublet of FASHION.] — **fac′tion·ist, fac′tion·ar′y** *n.* & *adj.*

— **Syn. 1.** *Faction, wing,* and *bloc* refer to subgroups, especially within political parties. *Faction* is often applied to a disruptive subgroup; *wing* refers to either of two directly opposed groups: the liberal and conservative *wings* of the Republican party. A *bloc* is a coalition that cuts across party lines: the farm *bloc.*

fac·tion·al (fak′shən·əl) *adj.* Of, pertaining to, or belonging to a faction; partisan.

fac·tion·al·ism (fak′shən·əl·iz′əm) *n.* Factional conflict or intrigue.

fac·tious (fak′shəs) *adj.* Given to or characterized by faction; promoting dissension.

fac·ti·tious (fak·tish′əs) *adj.* **1.** Not spontaneous; affected: *factitious* enthusiasm. **2.** Produced by artificial conditions or standards: a *factitious* demand for a product. [< L *factitius* artificial < *facere* to do] — **fac·ti′tious·ly** *adv.* — **fac·ti′tious·ness** *n.*

fac·ti·tive (fak′tə·tiv) *adj. Gram.* Designating a verb that takes, in addition to an object, a characterizing complement, as: They *elected* him *president*; He *called* John a *villain.* [< NL *factitivus* < L *factitare,* freq. of *facere* to do]

fac·tor (fak′tər) *n.* **1.** One of the elements or causes that contribute to produce a result. **2.** *Math.* One of two or more quantities that, when multiplied together, produce a given quantity. **3.** *Biol.* The unit of heredity; gene. **4.** *Physiol.* An element important in metabolism and nutrition, as a vitamin, enzyme, or hormone. **5.** A person or organization that undertakes to finance the operations of certain companies, as textile firms, accepting receivables as collateral. **6.** One who transacts business for another on a commission basis; a commission merchant. **7.** *Scot.* An agent who manages an estate; a bailiff or steward. **8.** *U.S.* In some States, a garnishee. — **Syn.** See DOER. — *v.t. Math.* To resolve into factors. Abbr. *fac.* [< L, maker < *facere* to make] — **fac′tor·ship** *n.*

fac·tor·age (fak′tər·ij) *n.* **1.** A factor's commission. **2.** The business of a factor.

fac·to·ri·al (fak·tôr′ē·əl, -tō′rē-) *n. Math.* The product of a series of consecutive positive integers from 1 to a given number. The *factorial* of four (written 4!) = $1 \times 2 \times 3 \times 4 = 24$. — *adj.* Pertaining to a factor or a factorial.

fac·tor·ize (fak′tə·rīz) *v.t.* **·ized, ·iz·ing** **1.** *Law* To garnishee. **2.** *Math.* To resolve into factors. — **fac′tor·i·za′tion** *n.*

fac·to·ry (fak′tər·ē) *n. pl.* **·ries** **1.** An establishment for the manufacture or assembly of goods, comprising one or more buildings and their equipment. **2.** A business establishment for factors or agents in a foreign country. Abbr. *fac.* [< Med.L *factoria* < L *factor* maker < *facere* to make]

fac·to·tum (fak·tō′təm) *n.* A man of all work. [< Med.L < L *fac,* sing. imperative of *facere* to do + *totum* everything]

fac·tu·al (fak′chōō·əl) *adj.* Pertaining to, containing, or consisting of facts; literal and exact. — **fac′tu·al·ly** *adv.*

fac·ture (fak′chər) *n. Rare* **1.** The act or manner of making something. **2.** A thing made. [< F < L *factura* a making < *facere* to make. Doublet of FEATURE.]

fac·u·la (fak′yə·lə) *n. pl.* **·lae** (-lē) *Astron.* A small spot on the sun brighter than the rest of the photosphere. [< L, dim. of *fax* torch]

fac·ul·ta·tive (fak/əl·tā/tiv) *adj.* **1.** Endowing with authority or permission; empowering but not requiring one to perform some act; permissive; optional: opposed to *obligative, obligatory.* **2.** That may or may not occur or have a specific form; contingent. **3.** *Biol.* Having the power to exist in and become adapted to changed conditions, as aerobic bacteria that can become anaerobic: opposed to *obligate.* **4.** Related or pertaining to a faculty or faculties.

fac·ul·ty (fak/əl·tē) *n. pl.* **·ties 1.** A natural or acquired power or ability; special aptitude or skill: a *faculty* for writing. **2.** One of the inherent powers or capabilities of the body or mind: the *faculty* of seeing, reasoning, speech, etc. **3.** *U.S.* The entire teaching staff at an educational institution. **4.** A department of learning or instruction at a university: the English *faculty.* **5.** The members of a learned profession collectively. **6.** Conferred power or privilege. **7.** *Eccl.* The right to perform certain ecclesiastical functions, bestowed by a prelate upon a subordinate. **8.** *Archaic* Trade; occupation. — **Syn.** See ABILITY, GENIUS. [< OF *faculté* < L *facultas* < *facilis.* See FACILE.]

fad (fad) *n.* A style, amusement, fashion, or the like, that temporarily engages the attention and interest of many people. [Origin unknown]

fad·dish (fad/ish) *adj.* **1.** Of the nature of a fad. **2.** Given to fads. Also **fad/dy.**

fad·dist (fad/ist) *n.* One interested in or given to fads.

fade (fād) *v.* **fad·ed, fad·ing** *v.i.* **1.** To lose brightness or clearness; become indistinct; dim. **2.** To vanish slowly: His smile *faded.* **3.** To lose freshness, vigor, youth, etc.; wither; wane. — *v.t.* **4.** To cause to fade. **5.** *U.S. Slang* In dice, to cover the bet of. — **to fade in** or **out** In television, motion pictures, and radio, to come into or depart from perception gradually. [< OF *fader < fade* pale, insipid, prob. < L *vapidus* stale, infl. by L *fatuus* insipid] — **Syn.** ebb, dwindle. Compare DECREASE, DIE[1].

fade-in (fād/in/) *n.* In television, motion pictures, and radio, a gradual coming into visibility or audibility.

fade·less (fād/lis) *adj.* Unfading. — **fade/less·ly** *adv.*

fade-out (fād/out/) *n.* In television, motion pictures, and radio, a gradual disappearance or fading of a sequence.

fadge (faj) *v.i.* **fadged, fadg·ing** *Brit. Dial.* **1.** To fit; suit. **2.** To succeed. [Origin unknown]

fad·ing (fā/ding) *n. Telecom.* A lessening or fluctuation in the strength of electromagnetic signals.

fae·ces (fē/sēz), **fae·cal** (fē/kəl) See FECES, FECAL.

Fa·en·za (fä·en/zə, *Ital.* fä·en/dzä) A commune in north central Italy; pop. 51,418 (est. 1960): ancient *Faventia.*

faer·ie (fâr/ē, fā/ər·ē) *Archaic n.* **1.** Fairyland. **2.** A fairy. — *adj.* Of or pertaining to fairies or fairyland. Also **faer/y.** [See FAIRY.]

Faerie Queene An allegorical, chivalric romance in verse form (1590–96) by Edmund Spenser.

Faer·oe Islands (fâr/ō) A group of 21 Danish islands in the North Atlantic; 540 sq. mi.; pop. 38,000 (est. 1969); capital, Thorshavn: also *Faroe Islands.* Also **Faer/oes.** *Danish* **Faer·ø·er·ne** (fer·œr/er·nə).

Faf·nir (fäv/nir, fäf/-) In Germanic mythology, the dragon who guards the hoard of the Nibelungs, slain by Sigurd. Also **Faf/ner.**

fag[1] (fag) *v.* **fagged, fag·ging** *v.t.* **1.** To exhaust by hard work: usually with *out*: He was *fagged out.* **2.** *Brit.* To make a fag of. — *v.i.* **3.** To weary oneself by working. **4.** *Brit.* To serve as a fag. — *n.* **1.** *Brit.* In English public schools, a boy who does menial service for another boy in a higher class. **2.** *U.S. Slang* A homosexual. Also **fag/got** (fag/ət). **3.** Drudgery. [Origin unknown]

fag[2] (fag) *n. Slang* A cigarette. [< FAG END]

fa·ga·ceous (fə·gā/shəs) *adj. Bot.* Of or pertaining to the beech family (*Fagaceæ*). [< NL *Fagaceæ* < L *fagus* beech]

fag end 1. The frayed end, as of a rope. **2.** A remnant or last part, usually of slight utility. [< FAG[1], with sense of "that which hangs down limply"]

Fa·gin (fā/gin) In Dickens's *Oliver Twist*, an old man who trained children as thieves.

F.A.G.O. Fellow of the American Guild of Organists.

fag·ot (fag/ət) *n.* **1.** A bundle of sticks, twigs, or branches, used for fuel, etc. **2.** A bundle of pieces of wrought iron or steel for working into bars, etc. — *v.t.* **1.** To make a fagot of. **2.** To ornament by fagoting. Also **fag/got.** [< OF]

fag·ot·ing (fag/ət·ing) *n.* **1.** A mode of ornamenting textile fabrics, in which a number of threads of a material are drawn out and the cross threads tied together in the middle. **2.** A kind of criss-cross hemstitch. Also **fag/got·ing.**

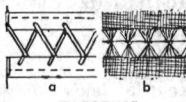

FAGOTING
a Hemstitch.
b Drawn work.

Fah. or **Fahr.** Fahrenheit.

fahl·band (fäl/band/, *Ger.* fäl/bänt/) *n. Geol.* A band or stratum of schistose rock containing finely divided sulfides, commonly intersecting metalliferous veins. [< G < *fahl* pale + *band* band]

Fahr·en·heit scale (far/ən·hīt, *Ger.* fär/ən·hīt) A temperature scale in which zero is the temperature of a mixture of equal weights of snow and common salt. On this scale, the freezing point of water is 32° and the boiling point 212°, under standard atmospheric pressure. For illustration see THERMOMETER. Abbr. *F, F., Fah., Fahr.* [after Gabriel Daniel *Fahrenheit*, 1686–1736, German physicist]

F.A.I.A. Fellow of the American Institute of Architects.

fa·ience (fī·äns/, fā-; *Fr.* fà·yäns/) *n.* **1.** A variety of glazed Italian pottery, usually highly decorated. **2.** An ancient Egyptian ceramic ware, glazed and usually greenish blue in color. [< F, pottery from Faenza]

fail (fāl) *v.i.* **1.** To turn out to be deficient or wanting, as in ability, quality, or effect; prove disappointing or unsuccessful: He *failed* in his duty. **2.** To miss doing or accomplishing something attempted, expected, requested, etc.: He *failed* to make himself clear. **3.** To prove inadequate or wholly lacking in the necessary or expected amount, supply, yield, etc.; fall short; give out: The crops *failed*; Our rations *failed.* **4.** To decline in health or strength; waste away; weaken. **5.** To fade away; die out; disappear. **6.** To become insolvent; go bankrupt. **7.** In education, to receive a grade of failure. — *v.t.* **8.** To prove of no help to; disappoint the expectations of; forsake; desert: His friends *failed* him. **9.** In education: **a** To receive a grade of failure in (a course or examination. **b** To assign a grade of failure to (a student). — *n.* Failure: in the phrase **without fail.** [< OF *faillir* < L *fallere* to deceive]

fail·ing (fā/ling) *n.* **1.** A minor fault; defect; shortcoming. **2.** The act of one who or that which fails. — *prep.* In default of; lacking: *Failing* your reply, we left. — *adj.* That fails. — **fail/ing·ly** *adv.*

faille (fāl, fil; *Fr.* fà/y) *n.* An untwilled silk dress fabric having a light grain or cord. [< F]

fail-safe (fāl/sāf/) *adj.* **1.** Utilizing a system that makes automatic adjustments in the event of operational failure to assure satisfactory performance. **2.** *Mil.* Describing a system that automatically prevents a nation's own military aircraft from carrying out planned bombing missions without specific confirming authority.

fail·ure (fāl/yər) *n.* **1.** A turning out to be unsuccessful, disappointing, or lacking: *failure* of an experiment. **2.** A falling short or giving out: *failure* of the water supply. **3.** A breaking down in health, strength, action, efficiency, etc. **4.** Nonperformance of some expected or required action; neglect: *failure* to obey the law. **5.** A becoming insolvent or bankrupt. **6.** One who or that which proves unsuccessful or disappointing: He is a *failure.* **7.** In education, a failing to pass, or the grade indicating this. [Earlier *failer* < AF, orig. var. of OF *faillir.* See FAIL.]

fain (fān) *adv. Archaic* Gladly; preferably: He would *fain* depart. — *adj.* **1.** Content to accept a substitute. **2.** Obliged or compelled. **3.** Glad; rejoiced. **4.** Eager; desirous. [OE *fægen*]

fai·naigue (fə·nāg/) *v.t. & v.i.* **·naigued, ·nai·guing** *Dial.* To finagle; cheat. [Origin unknown] — **fai·nai/guer** *n.*

fai·né·ant (fā/nē·ənt, *Fr.* fe·nā·än/) *adj.* Ineffective; lazy; useless. — *n.* An idler; do-nothing. [< F, by folk etymology < *faire* to do + *néant* nothing; actually, < F *faignant*, ppr. of *faindre* to be lazy, shirk]

faint (fānt) *v.i.* **1.** To lose consciousness; swoon: often with *away.* **2.** *Archaic* To fail in courage or hope. **3.** *Archaic* To grow weak. — *adj.* **1.** Without enthusiasm, purpose, or energy; feeble; weak: *faint* resistance. **2.** Lacking in distinctness, brightness, etc.: a *faint* sound. **3.** Ready to faint; dizzy; weak. **4.** Lacking courage; timid: *faint* heart. — *n.* A sudden, temporary loss of consciousness; swoon. [< OF, pp. of *faindre.* See FEIGN.] — **faint/er** *n.* — **faint/ish** *adj.* — **faint/ly** *adv.* — **faint/ness** *n.* — **Syn.** (adj.) **1.** irresolute, halfhearted, purposeless, faltering, fatigued, wearied, listless, languid. **2.** faded, obscure. — **Ant.** bright, strong, clear, vigorous. — (noun) See UNCONSCIOUSNESS.

faint·heart·ed (fānt/här/tid) *adj.* Cowardly; timorous; timid. — **faint/heart/ed·ly** *adv.* — **faint/heart/ed·ness** *n.*

faints (fānts) *n.pl.* The impure spirit of the first and last stages of the distillation of whisky: also spelled *feints.*

fair[1] (fâr) *adj.* **1.** Light in coloring; not dark or sallow: *fair* hair or skin. **2.** Pleasing to the eye; beautiful; comely. **3.** Free from blemish or imperfection: a *fair* name. **4.** Having no aspect of rain, snow, or hail; bright; sunny. **5.** Showing no partiality; just; upright. **6.** According to rules, principles, etc.; legitimate: a *fair* question; a *fair* win. **7.** Properly open to attack: He is *fair* game. **8.** Moderately satisfactory or acceptable; passably good or large: a *fair* crop. **9.** Likely; promising: a *fair* possibility. **10.** Apparently good and plausible, but actually false: *fair* promises. **11.** Gracious or courteous; pleasant: *fair* words. **12.** Open; unobstructed: a *fair* road. **13.** Accurately trimmed; even; regular: said of timbers, surfaces, lines, etc. **14.** Easily legible; distinct: *fair* handwriting. **15.** In baseball, situated, falling or remaining in the area bounded by the foul lines; not foul: *fair* territory. — *adv.* **1.** In a fair manner: Play *fair.* **2.** Squarely; directly: punched *fair* in the nose. — **to bid fair** To seem probable or favorable. — *v.i.* **1.** *Dial.* To become fair or clear: said of weather. **—v.t. 2.** To make smooth, as timbers. **—n.** *Archaic* **1.** A fair woman; sweetheart. **2.** Something fair. **3.** Beauty. **—for fair** For sure. [OE *fæger*] **—fair′ness** n.

fair² (fâr) n. **1.** A periodic and usually competitive exhibit of agricultural products, livestock, machinery, etc.: a county *fair*. **2.** A large exhibition or show, as of products from various countries: a world's *fair*. **3.** An exhibit and sale of fancywork, etc., for the benefit of some object or cause; a bazaar. **4.** A regularly held gathering of buyers and sellers. [< OF *feire* < L *feria* holiday]

fair and square Without deception or dishonesty.

fair ball In baseball, any batted ball that is not a foul.

Fair·banks (fâr′bangks), **Douglas**, 1883–1939, U.S. motion picture actor.

Fair·banks (fâr′bangks) A town in east central Alaska; northern terminus of the Alaska Highway; pop. 14,771.

fair catch In football, the catch of a kickoff, or of a punted ball by a defensive player who has signaled that he will not attempt a runback, and who therefore may not be tackled or interfered with without penalty.

fair copy A copy of a document after final correction.

Fair Deal *U.S.* The domestic policies of President Truman.

Fair·fax (fâr′faks), **Thomas**, 1612–71, third Baron Fairfax of Cameron, English Roundhead commander and political leader. **— Thomas**, 1692–1782, sixth Baron Fairfax of Cameron, American colonist in Virginia.

Fair·field (fâr′fēld) A town in SW Connecticut, on Long Island Sound; pop. 56,487.

fair green Fairway (def. 1).

fair·ground (fâr′ground′) n. *Often pl.* The place where a fair is held.

fair·haired (fâr′hârd′) adj. **1.** Having blond hair. **2.** Favorite: the teacher's *fair-haired* boy.

fair·ing¹ (fâr′ing) n. *Aeron.* In airplanes, an auxiliary structure or external surface designed to reduce drag or resistance: also called *fillet*. [< FAIR¹ (def. 13) + -ING¹]

fair·ing² (fâr′ing) n. *Archaic* A present bought at a fair. [< FAIR² + -ING¹]

fair·ish (fâr′ish) adj. Moderately good, well, or large.

Fair Lawn A borough in NE New Jersey, near Paterson; pop. 37,975.

fair·lead (fâr′lēd′) n. *Naut.* A ring, perforated board, or other device, through which a rope is passed to guide it or to prevent it from chafing or fouling. Also **fair′-lead·er**.

fair·ly (fâr′lē) adv. **1.** In a just manner; equitably; impartially. **2.** Moderately; somewhat: a *fairly* tall building. **3.** Positively; completely: The crowd *fairly* roared. **4.** Clearly; distinctly. **5.** *Obs.* Courteously. **6.** *Obs.* Softly. **fair·mind·ed** (fâr′mīn′did) adj. Free from bias or bigotry; open to reason; unprejudiced. **—fair′-mind′ed·ness** n.

Fair·mont (fâr′mont) A city in northern West Virginia; pop. 26,093.

Fair Oaks A locality east of Richmond, Virginia; scene of an indecisive Civil War battle, 1862: also *Seven Pines*.

fair play **1.** Fairness in playing, contending, etc. **2.** The ideal and practice of justice without prejudice or partiality.

fair sex Women.

fair·spo·ken (fâr′spō′kən) adj. Having graceful, courteous, or plausible speech.

fair to middling *U.S. Informal* Moderately good or well.

fair-trade (fâr′trād′) v.t. **-trad·ed, -trad·ing** To set a price no less than the manufacturer's minimum price on (a branded or trademarked product). **—adj.** Of or pertaining to such a price.

fair·way (fâr′wā′) n. **1.** That part of a golf course, between the tees and putting greens, where the grass is kept short: also called *fair green*. **2.** *Naut.* The navigable or usual course through a channel or harbor. [< FAIR¹ (defs. 12 and 13) + WAY]

fair-weath·er (fâr′weth′ər) adj. **1.** Suitable for or restricted to fair weather, as a racetrack. **2.** Not helpful or dependable in adversity: *fair-weather* friends.

Fair·weath·er (fâr′weth′ər), **Mount** Highest peak of the **Fairweather Range** in SE Alaska; 15,300 ft.

fair·y (fâr′ē) n. pl. **fair·ies 1.** An imaginary being, ordinarily of small and graceful human form, capable of working good or ill to mankind. Also, *Archaic*, *faerie*, *faery*. **2.** *Slang* A male homosexual. **—adj. 1.** Of or pertaining to fairies. **2.** Resembling a fairy. [< OF *faerie* fairyland < *fae*. See FAY².] **—fair′y·like′** adj.

fairy gloves Digitalis; foxglove.

fair·y·land (fâr′ē-land′) n. **1.** The fancied abode of the fairies. **2.** Any delightful, enchanting place.

fairy ring A circle in a lawn or pasture, usually caused by the spreading of the mycelia of a fungus (*Marasmius oreades*), and popularly said to be made by fairies.

fairy tale **1.** A tale about fairies. **2.** An incredible or highly imaginative story or statement.

fairy wand The blazing star (def. 1).

Fai·sal (fī′səl) See FEISAL.

---

fait ac·com·pli (fe-tȧ-kôṅ-plē′) *French* A thing done beyond recall or opposition; literally, an accomplished fact.

faith (fāth) n. **1.** Confidence in or dependence on a person, statement, or thing as trustworthy; trust. **2.** Belief without need of certain proof. **3.** Belief in God or in testimony about God as recorded in Scriptures or other religious writings. **4.** A system of religious belief: the Christian *faith*. **5.** Anything given adherence or credence: a man's political *faith*. **6.** Allegiance or fidelity. **— bad faith** Deceit; dishonesty. **— in faith** Indeed; truly. **— in good faith** With honorable intentions; honestly. **— to break faith 1.** To betray one's principles or beliefs. **2.** To fail to keep a promise. **— to keep faith 1.** To adhere to one's principles or beliefs. **2.** To keep a promise. **—interj.** In truth; indeed. [< OF *feit*, *feid* < L *fides* < *fidere* to trust] **—Syn. 1.** See TRUST. **2.** See BELIEF. **4.** See RELIGION.

faith cure **1.** The alleged cure of a disease by prayer and faith. **2.** The method used to effect such a cure.

faith·ful (fāth′fəl) adj. **1.** True or trustworthy in the performance of duty, the fulfillment of promises or obligations, etc.; constant; loyal: a *faithful* servant; *faithful* to one's agreement. **2.** Worthy of belief or confidence; truthful: a *faithful* witness; a *faithful* saying. **3.** True in detail or accurate in description: a *faithful* copy; a *faithful* account. **4.** *Obs.* Full of or firm in faith. **— the faithful 1.** The followers of a religious faith, as Christianity or Islam. **2.** The members of a church. **3.** The loyal members of any group. **—faith′ful·ly** adv. **—faith′ful·ness** n. **—Syn. 1.** *Faithful, loyal, devoted, staunch,* and *steadfast* denote constancy in attachment to a person, country, cause, etc. A person who is impelled to fulfill a pledge or obligation through strong affection or moral fervor is *faithful*: a *faithful* wife; a *loyal* person may be no less unswerving, but his allegiance is more deliberately given: a *loyal* follower of the king. *Devoted* stresses personal attachment, which may be directed toward a thing as well as toward another person: a *devoted* student of the classics, a lady's *devoted* admirer. *Staunch* and *steadfast* stress resistance to change of allegiance; *staunch* suggests firm conviction, and *steadfast*, constancy of character: a *staunch* royalist, a *steadfast* supporter of the republic. **— Ant.** unfaithful, faithless, untrustworthy, fickle.

faith healer One who seeks to heal by faith cures.

faith·less (fāth′lis) adj. **1.** Untrue to promise or obligation; unfaithful; disloyal. **2.** Not dependable or trustworthy; unreliable. **3.** Devoid of faith or trust. **4.** Lacking religious faith. **— Syn.** See PERFIDIOUS. **—faith′less·ly** adv. **—faith′less·ness** n.

fai·tour (fā′tər) n. *Obs.* A deceiver or rogue; impostor. [< AF < L *factor* a doer. See FACTOR.]

Fai·yum (fī-yōōm′) A Province of Upper Egypt; 686 sq. mi.; pop. 839,000 (1960); capital, **Faiyum**: also *Fayum*, *El Faiyum*.

fake¹ (fāk) *Informal* n. Anything or any person not genuine; a counterfeit. **— adj.** Not genuine; spurious. **— v. faked, fak·ing** v.t. **1.** To make up and attempt to pass off as genuine: to *fake* a pedigree. **2.** To simulate; feign: to *fake* gratitude. **3.** To improvise, as in music or a play. **— v.i. 4.** To practice faking. [? Var. of obs. *feague, feak* < Du. *vegen*, G *fegen* to sweep, dust off]

fake² (fāk) *Naut.* n. A single coil or turn of a rope or cable. **— v.t. faked, fak·ing** To coil, as a rope. [Origin uncertain]

fak·er (fā′kər) n. *Informal* **1.** One who fakes; a fraud. **2.** A peddler of notions or fakes. **—fak′er·y** n.

fa·kir (fə-kir′, fā′kər) n. **1.** A Moslem ascetic or religious mendicant. **2.** Loosely, any Hindu yogi or religious devotee. Also **fa·keer** (fə-kir′). [< Arabic *faqīr* poor]

fa·la (fä′lä, fä-lä′) n. **1.** A refrain in old songs. **2.** An old and simple type of part song. Also spelled *fal-la*.

Fa·lange (fā′lanj, fə-lanj′; *Sp.* fä-läng′hä) The official fascist party of the Franco regime in Spain. [< Sp., phalanx]

Fa·lan·gist (fə-lan′jist) n. A member of the Falange.

fal·ba·la (fal′bə-lə) n. *Obs.* A furbelow; flounce. [< F]

fal·cate (fal′kāt) adj. Shaped like a sickle or scythe. Also **fal′cat·ed**. [< L *falcatus* < *falx, falcis* sickle]

fal·chion (fôl′chən, -shən) n. **1.** A sword of the Middle Ages with a broad and slightly curved blade. **2.** *Poetic* Any sword. [< OF *fauchon*, ult. < L *falx, falcis* sickle]

fal·ci·form (fal′sə-fôrm) adj. Sickle-shaped; falcate.

fal·con (fal′kən, fôl′-, fô′-) n. **1.** Any of a genus (*Falco*) of diurnal birds of prey noted for their powerful wings, keen vision, and swiftness of attack upon their quarry; especially, the peregrine falcon, the male of which is called a *tercel*. **2.** Any of various other birds of the same family (*Falconidae*), having long, pointed wings, a notched bill, and strong talons, as the kestrel. **3.** A small cannon of the 15th to 17th centuries. [< OF *faucon, falcun* < LL *falco, -onis* < L *falx, falcis* sickle, because of its curved beak or wings]

FALCON
(About 15 inches long)

fal·con·er (fôl′kən·ər, fô′-, fal′-) n. One who breeds, trains, or hunts with falcons for sport.

fal·co·net¹ (fôl′kə·net, fô′-, fal′-) n. A little falcon. [< FALCON + -ET]

---

fal·co·net² (fŏl′kə·net, fô′-, fal′-) *n.* A small cannon of the 16th century. [< Ital. *falconetto*, orig., a small falcon]

fal·con·gen·tle (fŏl′kən·jen′təl, fô′, fal′-) *n.* **1.** The female of the European goshawk. **2.** Any female falcon. Also **fal′con·gen′til.** [< F *faucon gentil* lit., noble falcon]

fal·co·ni·form (fal·kŏ′nə·fôrm) *adj. Ornithol.* Belonging to the order of birds (*Falconiformes*) that includes the vultures, hawks, falcons, and eagles.

fal·co·nine (fŏl′kə·nīn, -nin) *adj.* Falconlike.

fal·con·ry (fŏl′kən·rē, fô′-, fal′-) *n.* **1.** The art of training falcons to hunt other birds and game. **2.** The sport of hunting with falcons: also called *hawking.*

fal·de·ral (fal′də·ral) *n.* **1.** Any foolish nonsense or fancy. **2.** A trifling ornament; gewgaw. **3.** A meaningless refrain used in old songs. Also spelled *folderol*: also **fal·de·rol** (fal′də·rol).

fald·stool (fôld′stool′) *n.* **1.** A portable, originally folding, seat, stool, or chair used for prayers, especially one used by a bishop when performing pontifical acts away from his own cathedral or when not seated on his throne. **2.** A folding, cushioned stool on which the sovereigns of England kneel at their coronation. **3.** A desk at which the litany is read, as in the Church of England. [< Med.L *faldistolium* < OHG *faldstuol* < *faldan* to fold + *stuol* seat]

Fa·lie·ri (fä·lyā′rē), Marino, 1278?–1355, doge of Venice 1354–55. Also **Fa·lie·ro** (fä·lyā′rō).

Fa·lis·can (fə·lis′kən) *adj.* Of or pertaining to the **Fa·lis·ci** (fə·lis′ī), an ancient people of southern Etruria. — *n.* **1.** One of the Falisci. **2.** The Italic language of the Falisci, closely related to Latin.

Fa·lis·co-La·tin·i·an (fə·lis′kō·lə·tin′ē·ən) *n.* A branch of the Italic subfamily of Indo-European languages, including Latin and its descendants and ancient Faliscan.

Fal·ken·hayn (fäl′kən·hīn), Erich von, 1861–1922, German general; chief of staff 1914–16.

Fal·kirk (fôl′kûrk, fô′-) A burgh in eastern Stirling, Scotland; scene of English defeat of Scottish forces under Wallace, 1298; pop. 38,625 (est. 1969).

Falk·land Islands (fôk′lənd) A British Crown Colony in the South Atlantic comprising **East Falkland** (2,580 sq. mi.), and **West Falkland** (2,038 sq mi.); pop. 2,000 (est. 1969); capital, Stanley. See map of (Strait of) MAGELLAN.

Falkland Islands Dependencies A former name for the BRITISH ANTARCTIC TERRITORY.

Falk·ner (fôk′nər), **William** See FAULKNER.

fall (fôl) *v.* **fell, fall·en, fall·ing** *v.i.* **1.** To drop from a higher to a lower place or position because of removal of support or loss of hold or attachment. **2.** To drop suddenly from an erect position, striking the ground with some part of the body: He *fell* to his knees; The child stumbled and *fell.* **3.** To come down in pieces; collapse: The bridge *fell.* **4.** To become less in number, intensity volume, value, etc.: The wind has *fallen*; Prices *fell.* **5.** To become less in rank, estimation, importance, etc. **6.** To drop wounded or slain, as in battle. **7.** To be overthrown; lose power, as a government. **8.** To be taken or captured: The fort *fell.* **9.** To yield to temptation; sin. **10.** To hit; land: The bombs *fell* on target. **11.** To slope downward: The road *falls* into the valley. **12.** To hang down; droop: Her veil *fell* about her shoulders. **13.** To come as though descending: Silence *fell*; Night *fell.* **14.** To pass into some specified state or condition: to *fall* asleep, sick, silent, in love, etc. **15.** To experience or show dejection: His face *fell.* **16.** To be cast down: His eyes *fell.* **17.** To come or happen by chance or lot: Suspicion *fell* on him; to *fall* among thieves. **18.** To happen; occur: Election Day *falls* on a Tuesday. **19.** To pass by right or inheritance: The estate *fell* to the oldest son. **20.** To be uttered as if accidentally: An oath *fell* from his lips. **21.** To happen or come at a specific place: The accent *falls* on the last syllable. **22.** To be classified or divided: with *into.* **23.** To be born: said of animals. — *v.t.* **24.** *U S.* To fell or cut down, as a tree. — **to fall afoul** (or **foul**) **of 1.** To come into conflict with. **2.** To collide with, as a vessel. **3.** To quarrel or argue with. — **to fall away 1.** To become lean or emaciated. **2.** To die; decline. — **to fall away from** To renounce allegiance to. — **to fall back** To recede; retreat. — **to fall back on** (or **upon**) **1.** To resort to; have recourse to. **2.** To retreat to. — **to fall behind 1.** To drop back; lose ground. **2.** To be in arrears. — **to fall down on** *U.S. Informal* To fail in. — **to fall flat** To fail to produce the intended effect or result. — **to fall for** *U.S. Informal* **1.** To be deceived by. **2.** To fall in love with. — **to fall in** *Mil.* To take proper place in a formation or group. — **to fall in with 1.** To meet and accompany. **2.** To agree with; conform to. — **to fall off 1.** To leave or withdraw. **2.** To become less: Attendance is *falling off.* **3.** *Naut.* To veer to leeward from the former course. — **to fall on** (or **upon**) **1.** To attack; assail. **2.** To find; discover. **3.** To light up: said of the eyes, the glance, etc. — **to fall out of 1.** To quarrel. **2.** To happen; result. **3.** *Mil.* To leave ranks. — **to fall short 1.** To fail to meet a standard, reach a particular place, etc.: with *of.* **2.** To be or prove deficient. — **to fall through** To come to nothing; fail. — **to fall to 1.** To set about; begin. **2.** To begin fighting. **3.** To begin

eating. **4.** To come or drop into position; shut. — **to fall under 1** To be classified as or included in. **2.** To come under (a spell, power, etc.). — *n.* **1** The act of falling; a dropping down or descending. **2.** That which falls: a *fall* of rain. **3.** The amount that falls: a *fall* of an inch an hour. **4.** The distance through which anything falls: a long *fall.* **5.** A more or less sudden descent from a vertical or erect position: the *fall* of a person, building, etc. **6.** A hanging down. **7.** A downward direction or slope: a *fall* in the ground. **8.** *Usually pl.* A waterfall; cascade. **9.** A reduction in value, price, etc. **10** A moral lapse; a yielding to temptation. **11.** A loss or diminution of esteem, reputation, worth, etc. **12.** A surrender or submission, as of a city or fort. **13.** *Often cap Chiefly U.S.* Autumn. **14.** An ornamental band or ruff for the neck. **15.** A veil hanging down over the back. **16.** In wrestling: **a** The throwing of an opponent to his back. **b** The method used. **c** A wrestling match or part thereof. **17.** A hoisting rope, or that part of it to which power is applied in hoisting. **18.** *Naut.* **a** A break in the line of a vessel between decks. **b** An apparatus for lifting or hoisting. **19.** The birth of animals. — **the fall of man** *Theol.* The disobedience of Adam and Eve that resulted in original sin. [OE *feallan*]

fal·la (fä′lä, fə·lä′) See FA-LA.

Fal·la (fä′lyä), **Manuel de,** 1876–1946, Spanish composer.

fal·la·cious (fə·lā′shəs) *adj.* **1.** Deceptive or misleading: *fallacious* documents. **2.** Containing or involving a fallacy: illogical: a *fallacious* conclusion. **3.** Delusive as a *fallacious* hope. — **fal·la′cious·ly** *adv.* — **fal·la′cious·ness** *n.*

fal·la·cy (fal′ə·sē) *n. pl.* **·cies 1.** An erroneous or misleading notion. **2.** Unsoundness or incorrectness, as of belief, judgment, etc. **3.** Deceptive quality. **4.** Any reasoning, argument, etc., contrary to the rules of logic: the *fallacy* in his argument. [< L *fallacia* < *fallax, -acis* deceptive < *fallere* to deceive]

— **Syn. 4.** *Fallacy, paralogism, sophistry,* and *casuistry* characterize errors of reasoning. *Fallacy* and *paralogism* are used chiefly in formal logic. *Sophistry* is applied to any persuasive but subtly specious reasoning. *Casuistry,* in its pejorative sense, suggests the deliberate use of false arguments.

fal·lal (fal·lal′) *n.* Any gaudy or trifling ornament or trinket. [Cf. FALBALA] — **fal·lal·er·y** (fal·lal′ər·ē) *n.*

fall dandelion An herb (*Leontodon autumnalis*) of the composite family, having yellow flowers.

fall·en (fô′lən) Past participle of FALL. — *adj.* **1.** Having come down by falling: *fallen* leaves. **2.** Brought down: *fallen* oaks. **3.** Overthrown; vanquished: a *fallen* fort **4.** Disgraced; ruined: a *fallen* woman. **5.** Slain.

fall·er (fô′lər) *n.* **1.** One who or that which falls. **2.** A machine or part that acts by falling.

fall·fish (fôl′fish′) *n. pl.* **·fish** or **·fish·es 1.** A fresh-water cyprinoid fish (genus *Semotilus*) of eastern North America. **2.** One of various other cyprinoids, as the **red fallfish** (*Notropis rubricroceus*).

fall guy *U.S. Slang* One who is left to receive the blame or penalties; a dupe; scapegoat.

fal·li·ble (fal′ə·bəl) *adj.* **1.** Liable to err. **2.** Liable to be misled or deceived. **3.** Liable to be erroneous or false [< Med.L *fallibilis* < L *fallere* to deceive] — **fal′li·bil′i·ty. fal′li·ble·ness** *n.* — **fal′li·bly** *adv.*

falling band A broad linen or lace collar worn over the shoulders in the 16th and 17th centuries.

falling leaf *Aeron.* A flight maneuver in which an airplane loses altitude by a series of lateral oscillations.

falling sickness *Rare* Epilepsy Also **falling evil.**

falling star A shooting star; meteor. Also **falling stone**

fall line *Geog.* The beginning of a plateau, as indicated by waterfalls and rapids.

Fal·lo·pi·an tube (fə·lō′pē·ən) *Anat.* One of a pair of long, slender ducts serving as a passage for the ovum from the ovary to the uterus: also called *oviduct.* [after Gabriello *Fallopio,* 1523–62, Italian anatomist]

fall·out (fôl′out′) *n. Physics* **1.** The descent of minute particles of radioactive material resulting from the explosion of an atomic or thermonuclear bomb **2.** The particles themselves. **3.** *Informal* A by-product. Also **fall′-out′.**

fal·low¹ (fal′ō) *adj.* Left unseeded after being plowed; uncultivated. — **to lie fallow** To remain unused, idle, dormant, etc. — *n.* **1.** Land left unseeded after plowing. **2.** The process of plowing or working land and leaving it unseeded for a time. — *v.t. & v.i.* To make, keep, or become fallow. [OE *fealging* fallow land] — **fal′low·ness** *n.*

fal·low² (fal′ō) *adj.* Light yellowish brown. [OE *fealu* pale. Cf. L *pallere* to be pale.]

fallow crop A crop alternated with the main crop to nourish the soil.

fallow deer A European deer (genus *Dama*), about 3 feet high at the shoulders and spotted white in the summer.

Fall River A city in SE Massachusetts, on Mt. Hope Bay; pop. 96,898.

Falls (fôlz) An urban township in NE Pennsylvania on the Susquehanna River, near Scranton; pop. 35,830.

FALLOW DEER

false (fôls) *adj.* **1.** Contrary to truth or fact; erroneous. **2.** Incorrect; irregular: *false* reasoning. **3.** Not real or genuine; artificial: *false* teeth. **4.** Deceptive or misleading: a *false* impression. **5.** Given to untruth; lying: a *false* witness. **6.** Wanting in fidelity; disloyal; faithless: a *false* husband. **7.** Supplementary; substitutive. **8.** *Music* Not correct in pitch; out of tune. **9.** *Biol.* Not properly so called, as in names of plants: *false* foxglove. — *adv.* In a false manner; falsely. [< OF *fals, faus* < L *falsus*, orig. pp. of *fallere* to deceive] — **false′ly** *adv.* — **false′ness** *n.*
— **Syn. 1.** untrue, incorrect. **6.** See PERFIDIOUS.
false bottom **1.** A partition that appears to be the bottom, as of a trunk, drawer, etc., concealing a secret compartment beneath it. **2.** The base of a container so formed as to give a deceptive notion of the capacity of the container.
false cirrus *Meteorol.* Cirrus formed from the upper frozen parts of a cumulonimbus cloud, often spreading out from the summit of a thundercloud.
false colors **1.** The flag of a country not one's own. **2.** Deceptive representation of facts or of oneself; pretense.
false face A mask.
false flax Gold-of-pleasure.
false foxglove Any of several widely distributed plants (genus *Aureolaria*) of the figwort family, with yellow flowers.
false-heart·ed (fôls′här′tid) *adj.* Treacherous; deceitful.
false hellebore **1.** Any of certain herbs (genus *Veratrum*) of the lily family; especially, the **European white false hellebore** (*V. album*), and the **American white false hellebore** (*V. viride*). **2.** The powdered roots of this herb, used as an insecticide.
false·hood (fôls′hŏŏd) *n.* **1.** Lack of accord to fact or truth; untruthfulness. **2.** An intentional untruth; lie. **3.** The act of lying; falsification. **4.** An untrue belief or idea. — **Syn.** See LIE².
false imprisonment Forcible detention of a person contrary to law.
false keel *Naut.* An extension of the true keel of a vessel for protection and greater stability.
false pretenses Willful misrepresentations made to cheat and defraud.
false relation *Music* Cross relation (which see).
false ribs *Anat.* Ribs that do not unite directly with the sternum. In man there are five on each side.
false step **1.** A stumble. **2.** An error or blunder.
fal·set·to (fôl-set′ō) *n.* *pl.* **·tos** **1.** The higher, less colorful register of a voice, especially of an adult male voice: also called *head voice.* **2.** A man who sings or speaks in this register: also **fal·set′ist.** — *adj.* Having the quality of falsetto; shrill. — *adv.* In falsetto. [< Ital., dim. of *falso* false]
false vampire Any of a group of large Old World bats (families *Nycteridae* and *Megadermidae*) wrongly supposed to suck blood.
fals·ies (fôl′sēz) *n. pl. Informal* Pads worn within a brassiere to give the breasts a fuller appearance.
fal·si·fy (fôl′sə-fī) *v.* **·fied, ·fy·ing** *v.t.* **1.** To tell lies about; misrepresent. **2.** To alter or tamper with, especially in order to deceive. **3.** To prove to be false; disprove. — *v.i.* **4.** To tell falsehoods; lie. [< F *falsifier* < LL *falsificare* < L *falsificus* making false < *falsus* false + *facere* to make] — **fal′si·fi·ca′tion** *n.* — **fal′si·fi′er** *n.*
fal·si·ty (fôl′sə-tē) *n. pl.* **·ties** **1.** The quality of being false. **2.** That which is false. — **Syn.** See ERROR.
Fal·staff (fôl′staf, -stäf), **Sir John** A fat, fun-loving old knight in Shakespeare's *Henry IV* and *The Merry Wives of Windsor*, given to ribald jest, prevarication, and drink. — **Fal·staff′i·an** *adj.*
Fal·ster (fäl′stər) An island of Denmark in the Baltic Sea; 198 sq. mi.
falt·boat (fält′bōt′) *n.* A collapsible boat resembling a kayak: also called *foldboat.* [< G *faltboot* folding boat]
fal·ter (fôl′tər) *v.i.* **1.** To be hesitant or uncertain; waver; give way. **2.** To move unsteadily; stumble. **3.** To speak haltingly; stammer. — *v.t.* **4.** To utter haltingly. — **Syn.** See VACILLATE. — *n.* **1.** An uncertainty or hesitation in voice or action. **2.** A quavering sound. [? < ON *faltrask* to be encumbered] — **fal′ter·er** *n.*
fal·ter·ing (fôl′tər·ing) *adj.* That falters. — **fal′ter·ing·ly** *adv.*
fam. 1. Familiar. **2.** Family.
F.A.M. Free and Accepted Masons.
Fa·ma·gu·sta (fä′mä-gōōs′tä) A port city in eastern Cyprus, on **Famagusta Bay,** an inlet of the Mediterranean; pop. 28,200 (est. 1959).
fame (fām) *n.* **1.** Widespread and illustrious reputation; renown. **2.** Public reputation or estimation. **3.** *Obs.* Report; rumor. — *v.t.* **famed, fam·ing** *Archaic* To speak of widely; make famous; celebrate: His deeds are *famed* in song and story. [< F < L *fama* report, reputation < *fari* to speak]
— **Syn. 1.** *Fame, renown, celebrity, reputation, repute,* and *notoriety* all refer to widespread knowledge of one's deeds, abilities,

or character. *Fame* is widest in scope, and is generally favorable; it becomes *renown* when combined with particular honor or glory: the conqueror's *fame,* the patriot's *renown. Celebrity* is more limited and local than *fame. Reputation* and *repute* denote the opinion of one's character held by other persons, and it may be good or bad. *Notoriety* is passing *fame,* acquired from some sensational or evil action.
Fa·meuse (fə-myōōz′, *Fr.* fà·mœz′) *n.* An early winter apple, having a skin striped with deep red: also called *snow apple.* [< dial. F (Canadian), fem. of *fameux* famous]
fa·mil·ial (fə-mil′yəl) *adj.* **1.** Of, pertaining to, or associated with the family. **2.** *Genetics* Transmitted within the family, as a hereditary disease. [< L *familia* family]
fa·mil·iar (fə-mil′yər) *adj.* **1.** Having thorough knowledge of something; well-acquainted: followed by *with.* **2.** Well-known; frequent; customary: Snow was a *familiar* sight there. **3.** Intimate; friendly; close. **4.** Unduly intimate; forward. **5.** Informal or unconstrained. **6.** Domesticated: said of animals. **7.** *Archaic* Familial. — *n.* **1.** A friend or close associate. **2.** A spirit supposed to attend and serve a witch, usually in animal form. **3.** In the Roman Catholic Church: **a** A domestic servant of a bishop or pope. **b** An officer of the Inquisition whose chief duty was to arrest those accused. *Abbr. fam.* [< OF *familier* < L *familiaris* of the family < *familia* family] — **fa·mil′iar·ly** *adv.*
fa·mil·i·ar·i·ty (fə-mil′ē·ar′ə·tē, -mil′yar′-) *n. pl.* **·ties** **1.** Thorough knowledge of or acquaintance with something: *familiarity* with a subject. **2.** Friendly closeness; intimacy: to be on terms of *familiarity.* **3.** Offensively familiar conduct; unwarranted intimacy. **4.** *Often pl.* An action warranted only by intimate acquaintance. [< OF *familiarite* < L *familiaritas, -tatis* < *familiaris.* See FAMILIAR.]
fa·mil·iar·ize (fə-mil′yə·rīz) *v.t.* **·ized, ·iz·ing** **1.** To make (oneself or someone) accustomed to or familiar with something. **2.** To cause (something) to be well known or familiar. — **fa·mil′iar·i·za′tion** *n.*
fam·i·ly (fam′ə·lē, fam′lē) *n. pl.* **·lies** **1.** Parents and their children. **2.** The children as distinguished from the parents. **3.** A group of persons connected by blood or marriage, including cousins, grandparents, in-laws, etc. **4.** A succession of persons connected by blood, name, etc.; a house; line; clan. **5.** Distinguished or ancient lineage or descent. **6.** A group of persons forming a household. **7.** Any class or group of like or related things. **8.** *Biol.* A taxonomic category higher than a genus: for animals, family names end in *-idae,* for plants, in *-aceae.* **9.** *Ling.* A grouping of languages assumed from certain shared characteristics to be descended from a common parent, as the Indo-European family, often subdivided into *subfamily, branch,* and *group.* — *adj.* Of, belonging to, or suitable for a family. *Abbr. fam.* [< L *familia* family < *famulus* servant]
Family Allowance *Canadian* A government money allowance for each child under sixteen: also, *Slang, baby bonus.*
family circle **1.** The members of a family. **2.** An upper balcony in a theater, containing inexpensive seats.
family name A surname.
family skeleton A hidden shame or scandal in a family.
family tree **1.** A diagram showing family descent. **2.** The ancestors and descendants of a family, collectively.
fam·ine (fam′in) *n.* **1.** A widespread scarcity of food. **2.** A great scarcity of anything; dearth: a water *famine.* **3.** Starvation. [< OF < L *fames* hunger]
fam·ish (fam′ish) *v.t. & v.i.* To suffer or die, or to cause to suffer or die, from lack of nourishment; starve. [Earlier *fame* < F *afamer* to starve; refashioned after verbs in *-ish,* as *banish, finish,* etc.] — **fam′ish·ment** *n.*
fam·ished (fam′isht) *adj.* Extremely hungry.
fa·mous (fā′məs) *adj.* **1.** Celebrated in history or public report; well-known; renowned. **2.** *Informal* Excellent; admirable: Sleep is a *famous* medicine. **3.** *Archaic* Infamous. [< OF *fameus* < L *famosus* < *fama.* See FAME.] — **fa′mous·ly** *adv.* — **fa′mous·ness** *n.*
fam·u·lus (fam′yə·ləs) *n. pl.* **·li** (-lī) An assistant or servant, as of a scholar or a magician. [< L, servant]
fan¹ (fan) *n.* **1.** A device for putting the air into motion; especially, a light, flat implement of various materials, often collapsible and opening into a wedgelike shape, a circle, etc. **2.** Anything shaped like a fan. **3.** A machine fitted with blades that revolve rapidly about a central hub, for stirring air, etc. **4.** A kind of basket formerly used for tossing grain into the air to let the chaff be blown away; also, a machine for blowing away chaff. **5.** A small sail or vane to keep the sails of a windmill at right angles to the wind. — *v.* **fanned, fan·ning** *v.t.* **1.** To move or stir (air) with or as with a fan. **2.** To direct air upon; cool or refresh with or as with a fan. **3.** To move or

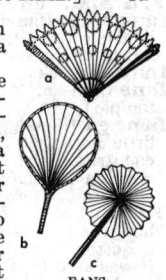

FANS
a Folding. *b* Palm leaf. *c* Collapsible.

stir to action; excite: to *fan* someone's rage. **4.** To winnow (grain or chaff). **5.** To spread like a fan. **6.** In baseball, to cause (a batter) to strike out. — *v.i.* **7.** To spread out like a fan. **8.** In baseball, to strike out. [OE *fann* < L *vannus* winnowing basket. Cf. L *ventus* wind.]

fan² (fan) *n. Informal* **1.** An enthusiastic devotee of a sport or diversion: a baseball *fan*. **2.** An ardent admirer, usually of an actor or other public figure. — **Syn.** See ENTHUSIAST. [? < FANATIC]

fa·nat·ic (fə·nat'ik) *n.* A person who is moved by a frenzy of enthusiasm or zeal; especially, a religious zealot. — **Syn.** See ENTHUSIAST. — *adj.* Fanatical. [< L *fanaticus* inspired, lit., of a temple < *fanum* temple]

fa·nat·i·cal (fə·nat'i·kəl) *adj.* **1.** Given to or actuated by extravagant or intemperate zeal; unreasonably enthusiastic. **2.** Pertaining to or characteristic of a fanatic. — **fa·nat'i·cal·ly** *adv.*

fa·nat·i·cism (fə·nat'ə·siz'əm) *n.* The spirit or conduct of a fanatic; extravagant or frenzied zeal.

fa·nat·i·cize (fə·nat'ə·sīz) *v.* **·cized, ·ciz·ing** *v.t.* **1.** To make fanatical. — *v.i.* **2.** To act like a fanatic.

fan·cied (fan'sēd) Past tense and past participle of FANCY. — *adj.* Imaginary; unreal: *fancied* insults.

fan·ci·er (fan'sē·ər) *n.* **1.** One having a special taste for or interest in something: a *fancier* of nature. **2.** A breeder of birds or animals. **3.** A dreamer; visionary.

fan·ci·ful (fan'si·fəl) *adj.* **1.** Produced by or existing only in the fancy; unreal; unsubstantial: *fanciful* schemes. **2.** Marked by fancy in design; curious in appearance: a *fanciful* costume. **3.** Indulging in fancies; whimsical: a *fanciful* mind. — **fan'ci·ful·ly** *adv.* — **fan'ci·ful·ness** *n.*
— **Syn. 1.** imaginary, chimerical. **2.** *Fanciful, fantastic,* and *grotesque* indicate some departure from the usual or normal. Anything pleasantly odd is *fanciful*: a *fanciful* Japanese flower arrangement. *Fantastic* points to something that is extravagantly different: the *fantastic* costumes of the baroque period; and *grotesque* describes anything ridiculous, as by the incongruity of its parts: the *grotesque* plumed serpent of the Incas. — **Ant.** ordinary, commonplace, prosaic, real, true.

fan·ci·less (fan'si·lis) *adj.* Lacking fancy; unimaginative.

fan·cy (fan'sē) *n. pl.* **·cies 1.** Imagination of a capricious or whimsical sort. **2.** An extravagant, odd, or whimsical invention or image. **3.** An idea or notion not based on fact or evidence; an illusion. **4.** A caprice or whim. **5.** A liking or inclination, as if resulting from caprice or whim. **6.** Taste or judgment in art, literature, style, etc. **7.** *Obs.* Love. **8.** *Obs.* A specter; phantom. — **the fancy** *Archaic* The devotees collectively of an art, sport, or amusement. — *adj.* **·ci·er, ·ci·est 1.** Adapted to please the fancy; ornamental; decorative: a *fancy* shirt. **2.** Coming from the fancy; imaginary; illusory. **3.** Capricious; whimsical; fanciful. **4.** Of higher grade than the average; choice: *fancy* fruits. **5.** Extravagant; exorbitant: *fancy* prices. **6.** Performed with exceptional grace and skill: the *fancy* bowing of a violinist. **7.** Selectively bred for certain points, as an animal: also **fan'cy·bred'.** — *v.t.* **·cied, ·cy·ing 1.** To imagine; picture: *Fancy* that! **2.** To take a fancy to; like. **3.** To believe without proof or conviction; suppose. **4.** To breed, as animals, for conventional points of symmetry or beauty. — *interj.* An exclamation of surprise. [Contraction of FANTASY]
— **Syn.** (noun) **1.** See IMAGINATION. **2.** image, idea, thought. **4, 5.** whim, mood, inclination, liking, predilection. — **Ant.** reality, actuality, fact, truth.

fancy ball A ball at which fancy dress is worn.

fancy dress Masquerade costume. — **fan'cy·dress'** *adj.*

fan·cy-free (fan'sē·frē') *adj.* **1.** Not in love. **2.** Carefree.

fancy man *Slang* A man supported by a woman, especially by a prostitute.

fancy woman *Slang* A mistress or prostitute.

fan·cy·work (fan'sē·wûrk') *n.* Ornamental needlework, as embroidery, tatting, or lacework.

F. & A.M. Free and Accepted Masons.

fan·dan·go (fan·dang'gō) *n. pl.* **·gos 1.** A Spanish dance in triple time, usually accompanied by castanets. **2.** The music for this dance. **3.** A dancing party or ball. [< Sp.]

fan delta *Geol.* An alluvial cone.

fane (fān) *n. Archaic* A sanctuary; temple. [< L *fanum* temple]

fa·ne·ga (fä·nā'gä) *n.* A Spanish dry measure equa to a little more than 1½ bushels, but variable in Latin-American countries. Also **fa·ne·ga** (fäng'gä). [< Sp.]

fa·ne·ga·da (fä·nä·gä'thä) *n.* A Spanish unit of area, equal to 6.92 ares or 7,449 square feet.

Fan·euil Hall (fan'əl, fan'yəl) A public hall and market house built in Boston, Mass., by **Peter Faneuil,** 1700–43, a Boston merchant: called the "Cradle of Liberty" because it was used by Revolutionary patriots as a meeting place.

fan·fare (fan'fâr') *n.* **1.** A short, lively call or passage, as of trumpets. **2.** A noisy or showy parade or demonstration. [< F, ? < FANFARON]

fan·fa·ron (fan'fə·ron) *n. Obs.* **1.** A braggart. **2.** A fanfare. [< F < Sp. *fanfarrón* < Arabic *farfar* talkative]

fan·fa·ron·ade (fan'fə·rə·nād') *n.* **1.** A boastful or bullying speech, style, or manner. **2.** A fanfare. — *v.i.* **·ad·ed,**
·ad·ing To swagger; bluster. [< F < Sp. *fanfarronada* < *fanfarrón*. See FANFARON.]

fang (fang) *n.* **1.** A long, pointed tooth or tusk by which an animal seizes, holds, or tears at its prey, as the canine tooth of a boar or dog. **2.** One of the long, curved, hollow or grooved, usually erectile teeth with which a venomous serpent injects its poison into its victim. **3.** One of various pointed or incurved objects, organs, or devices, especially for clutching or holding fast, as the root of a tooth or the claw or talon of a bird. [OE, a catching, seizing] — **fanged** (fangd) *adj.* — **fang'less** *adj.* **fang'like'** *adj.*

RATTLESNAKE FANG
a Anterior temporal muscles. *b* Interior pterygoid. *c* Venom gland. *d* Movable maxilla. *e* Point where venom enters channel of fang. *f* Fang.

fan·ion (fan'yən) *n.* A small flag. [< OF, var. of *fanon*. See FANON.]

fan·jet (fan'jet') *n.* A turbofan.

fan·light (fan'līt') *n. Archit.* **1.** A semicircular window containing a sash with bars radiating from the middle of its base: also called *fan window*. **2.** *Brit.* A transom.

fan mail Complimentary letters to public performers.

fan·ner (fan'ər) *n.* One who or that which fans.

fan·ny (fan'ē) *n. pl.* **·nies** *U.S. Slang* The buttocks.

fan·on (fan'ən) *n. Eccl.* **1.** A maniple worn by a celebrant at Mass. **2.** A cape worn only by the Pope, as he presides at solemn pontifical Mass. Also **fan·o** (fan'ō), **fan·um** (fan'əm). [< OF < Med.L *fano, -onis* banner, napkin < Gmc.]

fan palm Any palm with fan-shaped leaves; especially, the talipot and the palmetto.

fan·tail (fan'tāl') *n.* **1.** A variety of domestic pigeon having fanlike tail feathers. **2.** An Australian or Oriental flycatcher (genus *Rhipidura*) having fan-shaped tail feathers. **3.** Any end or tail shaped like a fan. **4.** Any of certain species of fancy-bred goldfish, having double anal and dorsal fins. **5.** *Archit.* Any fan-shaped part or member, or a combination of radiating parts. **6.** *Naut.* The overhanging stern of some ships.

FANTAIL (def. 1)

fan-tan (fan'tan') *n.* **1.** A Chinese gambling game in which the players bet on what the remainder will be after a covered pile of coins, beans, etc., has been divided by four. **2.** A game of cards played in sequence, the winner being the person who gets rid of his cards first. [< Chinese *fan t'an* repeated divisions]

fan·ta·si·a (fan·tā'zhə, -zhē·ə, fan'tə·zē'ə) *n. Music* **1.** A fanciful composition observing no strict musical form. **2.** A medley of various themes, usually with brilliant variations and embellishments. [< Ital., a fancy]

fan·ta·size (fan'tə·sīz) *v.i.* **·sized, ·siz·ing** To create mental fantasies.

fan·tasm (fan'taz·əm) See PHANTASM.

fan·tas·ma·go·ri·a (fan·taz'mə·gôr'ē·ə, -gō'rē·ə) See PHANTASMAGORIA.

fan·tas·mal (fan·taz'məl) See PHANTASMAL.

fan·tast (fan'tast) *n.* A dreamer or visionary. [< G *phantast* < Med.L *phantasta* < Gk. *phantastēs* boaster < *phantazein* to boast]

fan·tas·tic (fan·tas'tik) *adj.* **1.** Odd, grotesque, or whimsical in appearance, form, construction, etc.: a *fantastic* room. **2.** Wildly fanciful or exaggerated: *fantastic* ideas. **3.** Capricious or impulsive, as moods, actions, etc. **4.** Coming from the imagination or fancy; illusory; unreal: *fantastic* fears. — *n. Archaic* One who is fantastic in conduct or appearance. [< Med.L *fantasticus* < L *phantasticus* < Gk. *phantastikos* < *phantastēs*. See FANTAST.]
— **Syn.** queer, bizarre, extravagant. See FANCIFUL.

fan·tas·ti·cal (fan·tas'ti·kəl) *adj.* **1.** Extremely capricious, odd, or eccentric. **2.** Extravagantly fanciful, imaginative or grotesque. — **fan·tas'ti·cal·i·ty** (-kal'ə·tē), **fan·tas'ti·cal·ness** *n.* — **fan·tas'ti·cal·ly** *adv.*

fan·ta·sy (fan'tə·sē, -zē) *n. pl.* **·sies 1.** Imagination unrestrained by reality; wild fancy. **2.** An odd, unreal, or grotesque mental image; hallucination. **3.** An odd or whimsical notion. **4.** A capricious mood. **5.** An ingenious or highly imaginative creation. **6.** *Psychol.* A sequence of more or less pleasant mental images, usually serving to fulfill a need not gratified in the real world. **7.** *Music* A fantasia. — **Syn.** See IMAGINATION. — *v.t.* **·sied, ·sy·ing** To envision; imagine. Also spelled *phantasy*. [< OF *fantasie* < L *phantasia* < Gk., appearance < *phainein* to show]

Fan·tin-La·tour (fän·tan'lä·tōōr'), **Henri,** 1836–1904, French painter.

fan·toc·ci·ni (fän'tə·chē'nē) *n.pl.* **1.** Marionettes. **2.** A puppet show. [< Ital., dim. of *fantoccio* puppet < *fante* child]

fan·tom (fan'təm) See PHANTOM.

fan tracery *Archit.* Tracery diverging like a fan to form a section of fan vaulting rising from a capital or corbel, as in Henry VII's chapel, Westminster.

fan vaulting *Archit.* A system of vaulting in which the ribs spread out like a fan, used in later English Gothic.
fan window *Archit.* A fanlight.
fan·wort (fan'wûrt') *n.* An aquatic plant (*Cabomba caroliniana*) of the water-lily family, found in the southern United States: also called *fishgrass, watershield.*
FAO or **F.A.O.** Food and Agriculture Organization (of the United Nations).
F.A.P.S. Fellow of the American Physical Society.
far (fär) *adv.* **1.** At, to, or from a great distance: *far* from town; to venture *far*; to come *far*. **2.** To or at a particular distance, point, or degree: as *far* south as Naples; How *far* will he commit himself? **3.** To a great degree; very much: *far* wiser. **4.** Very remotely in time, degree, quality, etc.: *far* in the future; *far* from pleasant. **— as far as** To the distance, extent, or degree that. **— by far** In a great degree; very much. **— far and away** Very much; decidedly: He is *far and away* the best poet. **— far and wide** Distantly and extensively; everywhere. Also **far and near.** **— far be it from me** I have not the audacity or desire. **— how far** To what extent, distance, or degree. **— in so far as** To the extent that. **— so far 1.** To that extent; up to that point. **2.** Up to now. **— so far as** To the extent that. **— so far so good** Up to now everything is all right. **— to go far 1.** To accomplish much; have success. **2.** To last a long time or cover a great extent. **3.** To tend strongly. **— adj. far·ther** or **fur·ther, far·thest** or **fur·thest** (See note under FARTHER.) **1.** Very remote in space or time: a *far* country; in the *far* past. **2.** Extending widely or at length: a *far* journey. **3.** More distant: the *far* end of the garden. [OE *feor*]
far·ad (far'əd, -ad) *n.* *Electr.* The unit of capacitance; the capacitance of a condenser that retains one coulomb of charge with one volt difference of potential. Abbr. *f, F, F.* [after Michael *Faraday*]
far·a·day (far'ə-dā) *n.* *Electr.* The quantity of electricity that is required in an electrochemical reaction: usually expressed as 96,500 coulombs per gram equivalent of a metal in electrolysis. [after Michael *Faraday*]
Far·a·day (far'ə-dā), **Michael,** 1791–1867, English chemist and physicist; discovered properties of electromagnetism.
fa·rad·ic (fə·rad'ik) *adj.* Pertaining to or caused by induced electric currents. Also **far·a·da·ic** (far'ə-dā'ik).
far·a·dism (far'ə-diz'əm) *n.* **1.** The electricity of an induced current. **2.** *Med.* The treatment of a nerve or muscle with induced electric currents.
far·a·dize (far'ə-dīz) *v.t.* **·dized, ·diz·ing** To stimulate (a nerve, muscle, etc.) with induced electric currents. **— far'a·di·za'tion** *n.* **— far'a·diz'er** *n.*
far·an·dole (far'ən-dōl, *Fr.* fȧ·räṅ·dôl') *n.* **1.** A rapid dance in which the participants whirl in a circle. **2.** The music for this dance. [< F < Provençal *farandoulo*]
far·a·way (far'ə·wā') *adj.* **1.** Distant: a *faraway* town. **2.** Absent-minded; abstracted: a *faraway* look.
farce (färs) *n.* **1.** A comedy employing ludicrous or exaggerated effects or situations. **2.** A ridiculous action or situation; an absurd failure. **— v.t. farced, farc·ing 1.** To fill out with witticisms, jibes, etc., as a play. **2.** *Obs.* To stuff, as a fowl. [< F, orig., stuffing < *farcir* to stuff < L *farcire*]
far·ceur (fär·sœr') *n.* **1.** One who acts in or writes a farce. **2.** A joker; wag. Also **farc·er** (fär'sər). [< F]
far·ci·cal (fär'si·kəl) *adj.* **1.** Of or belonging to farce. **2.** Resembling farce; laughable; absurd. **— far'ci·cal·ly** *adv.* **— far'ci·cal'i·ty, far'ci·cal·ness** *n.*
far cry A long way.
far·cy (fär'sē) *n.* *Vet.* A contagious disease, primarily of the horse, affecting the lymphatic glands and characterized by abscesses, particularly on the legs: a form of glanders. [Var. of obs. *farcin* < F < L *farciminum*, a disease of horses < *farcire* to stuff]
farcy bud An abscess, as found in farcy. Also **farcy button.**
far·del (fär'dəl) *n.* *Archaic* A bundle; pack; burden. [< OF, dim. of *farde*, prob. < Arabic *fardah* bundle]
fare (fâr) *v.i.* **fared, far·ing 1.** To be in a specified state; get on: He *fares* poorly. **2.** To turn out; happen: It *fared* well with him. **3.** To be supplied with food and drink. **4.** *Archaic* To go; travel. **— n. 1.** The sum charged or paid for conveyance in a vehicle, etc. **2.** A passenger carried for hire. **3.** Food and drink; eatables; diet. **4.** *Archaic* Condition or state of things. **— Syn.** See FOOD. [OE *faran* to go, travel. Cf. G *fahren*, Du. *varen*.]
Far East The countries of eastern Asia, including China, Japan, Korea, Manchuria, and adjacent islands: sometimes extended to include all the territory east of Afghanistan.
far·er (fâr'ər) *n.* One who travels.
fare·well (n. fâr'wel'; *interj.* fâr'wel'; *adj.* fâr'wel') *n.* **1.** A parting salutation; a good-by. **2.** Leave-taking; parting. **— interj.** May you fare well; good-by. **— adj.** Parting; closing: a *farewell* speech. [Earlier *fare well.* See FARE.]
Farewell, Cape The southernmost point of Greenland.
far-fetched (fär'fecht') *adj.* Neither natural nor obvious; forced; strained: a *far-fetched* joke.

far-flung (fär'flung') *adj.* Having great range; extending over great distances.
Far·go (fär'gō) A city in SE North Dakota on the Red River; pop. 53,365.
fa·ri·na (fə·rē'nə) *n.* **1.** A meal or flour obtained chiefly from cereals, nuts, potatoes, or Indian corn, and used as a breakfast food. **2.** Starch. [< L < *far* spelt]
Fa·ri·na (fä·rē'nä), **Salvatore,** 1846–1918, Italian novelist.
far·i·na·ceous (far'ə·nā'shəs) *adj.* **1.** Consisting or made of farina. **2.** Containing or yielding starch. **3.** Mealy. [< L *farinaceus* < *farina.* See FARINA.]
far·i·nose (far'ə·nōs) *adj.* **1.** Yielding farina: *farinose* plants. **2.** *Biol.* Covered with or as if with a white meallike powder, as the under side of the leaves of certain primroses.
far·kle·ber·ry (fär'kəl·ber'ē) *n.* *pl.* **·ries** A shrub or small tree (*Vaccinium arboreum*) of the heath family, with globose black berries. [Origin unknown]
farl (färl) *n.* *Scot.* A thin oatmeal cake. Also **farle.** [Contraction for *fardel* < OE *fēortha dǣl* fourth part (of a cake)]
Far·ley (fär'lē), **James Aloysius,** 1888–1976, U.S. political leader.
farm (färm) *n.* **1.** A tract of land forming a single property and devoted to agriculture. **2.** A tract of water used for the cultivation of marine life: an oyster *farm.* **3.** In baseball, a minor-league club used by a major-league club for training its recruits. **4.** *Obs.* **a** The system of farming out revenues or taxes. **b** A fixed annual sum paid as a rent or tax. **— v.t. 1.** To cultivate (land). **2.** To take a lease of, as the use of a business or the collection of taxes, for a fixed rental, retaining the profits. **3.** To let at a fixed rental, as lands, the authority to collect taxes, etc.: usually with *out*: to *farm* out taxes. **4.** To let out the services of (a person) for hire. **5.** To agree to maintain or care for at a fixed price, as paupers. **6.** To arrange for (work) to be performed by persons or a firm not in the main organization; subcontract: with *out.* **7.** In baseball, to place (a player) with a minor-league team for training: often with *out.* **— v.i. 8.** To practice farming; be a farmer. [< F *ferme* lease < Med.L *firma* a fixed payment < L *firmare* to fix, settle < *firmus* firm]
farm·er (fär'mər) *n.* **1.** One who operates a farm. **2.** One who pays for the privilege of collecting taxes, etc. **3.** One who contracts to undertake certain duties for a sum.
farm·er·ette (fär'mə·ret') *n.* *Informal* A woman or girl who farms.
farm·er·gen·er·al (fär'mər·jen'ər·əl) *n.* *pl.* **farm·ers-gen·er·al** A member of a privileged class in France before the revolution of 1789, who farmed certain taxes. **— farm'er·gen'er·al·ship'** *n.*
Farm·er-La·bor Party (fär'mər·lā'bər) A minor U.S. political party, 1919–23, active later in Minnesota.
farm hand One who works on a farm, especially for hire.
farm·house (färm'hous') *n.* The homestead on a farm.
farm·ing (fär'ming) *n.* **1.** The business of operating a farm; agriculture. **2.** The leasing of the authority to collect taxes, etc. **— Syn.** See AGRICULTURE. **— adj.** Engaged in, suitable for, or used for agriculture: a *farming* region.
farm·stead (färm'sted) *n.* A farm and the buildings on it. Also **farm'stead·ing.**
farm·yard (färm'yärd') *n.* A space surrounded by farm buildings, and enclosed for confining stock, etc.
Far·ne·se (fär·nā'sā) An Italian noble family of Parma and Piacenza. **— Alessandro** See PAUL III. **— Alessandro,** 1545–92, military commander for Spain.
far·ne·sol (fär'nə·sōl, -sol) *n.* *Chem.* An alcohol, $C_{15}H_{26}O$, extracted from acacia, cassia oil, etc., and used in perfumery. [< NL (*Acacia*) *farnesiana*, a species of acacia + -OL[1]]
Far North *Canadian* The area north of the provincial limits.
far·o (fâr'ō) *n.* A game of cards in which the players bet against the dealer as to the order in which certain cards will appear. [Alter. of *Pharaoh*, ? from a picture originally on one of the cards]
Far·oe Islands (fâr'ō) See FAEROE ISLANDS.
Far·o·ese (fâr'ō·ēz', -ēs') *n.* **1.** *pl.* **·ese** A native or inhabitant of the Faeroe Islands. **2.** The North Germanic language spoken in these islands, closely resembling Icelandic.
far-off (fär'ôf', -of') *adj.* Distant; remote.
fa·rouche (fȧ·rōōsh') *adj.* *French* Wild; sullen; unsociable.
Fa·rouk I (fə·rōōk'), 1920–65, king of Egypt 1936–52; abdicated. Also *Faruk.*
far-out (fär'out') *adj.* *U.S. Slang* Experimental or daring, as in the arts; avant-garde: also *way-out.* Also **far out.**
Far·quhar (fär'kwər, -kər), **George,** 1678–1707, English dramatist born in Ireland.
far·rag·i·nous (fə·raj'ə·nəs) *adj.* *Rare* Formed of mixed materials or ingredients; jumbled.
far·ra·go (fə·rā'gō, -rä'-) *n.* *pl.* **·goes** A confused mixture; medley. [< L, mixed fodder < *far* spelt]
Far·ra·gut (far'ə·gət), **David Glasgow,** 1801–70, Union admiral in the Civil War.
far-reach·ing (fär'rē'ching) *adj.* Having wide influence, range, or effect.

Far·rell (far'əl), **James T**(**homas**), born 1904, U.S. novelist.
far·ri·er (far'ē-ər) *n. Brit.* **1.** One who shoes horses. **2.** A veterinarian, especially one for horses. [< OF *ferrier* < L *ferrarius* < *ferrum* iron]
far·ri·er·y (far'ē-ər-ē) *n. pl.* **·er·ies** The business or shop of a farrier.
far·row¹ (far'ō) *n.* **1.** A litter of pigs. **2.** *Obs.* A young pig. —*v.t. & v.i.* To give birth to (young): said of swine. [OE *fearh* young pig. Akin to Du. *varken* pig and L *porcus.*]
far·row² (far'ō) *adj.* Not producing young during a given year: said of cows. [Cf. Flemish *varvekoe* cow no longer fertile < Frisian *fear* barren]
Far·sa·la (fär'sä·lä) See PHARSALA.
far·see·ing (fär'sē'ing) *adj.* **1.** Having foresight; prudent; wise. **2.** Able to see distant objects clearly.
far·sight·ed (fär'sī'tid) *adj.* **1.** Able to see things at a distance more clearly than things at hand; hypermetropic. **2.** Having foresight; farseeing. —**far'sight'ed·ly** *adv.* —**far'sight'ed·ness** *n.*
fart (färt) *v.i.* To emit gas from the intestines through the anus. —*n.* An anal emission of gas. A vulgar term. [ME *farten.* Cf. OHG *ferzan.*]
far·ther (fär'thər) Comparative of FAR. —*adv.* To or at a more advanced point in space or, less often, time: I shall walk no *farther.* —*adj.* **1.** More distant or remote: the *farther* shore. **2.** Additional; more: in this sense usually *further.* [ME *ferther*; var. of FURTHER; infl. by *far*]
◆ **farther, further** When referring to literal spatial distance, *farther* and *farthest* are the preferred forms, although *further* and *furthest* are often used. The latter are always employed in figurative senses involving time, degree, or quantity: *further* in the future, *further* (= additional) damage.
Farther India See INDOCHINA.
far·ther·most (fär'thər·mōst') *adj.* Most distant; farthest.
far·thest (fär'thist) Superlative of FAR. —*adv.* To or at the greatest distance. —*adj.* **1.** Most distant or remote. **2.** Longest or most extended: the *farthest* way around. [ME *ferthest*; var. of FURTHEST; infl. by *far*]
far·thing (fär'thing) *n.* **1.** A small, bronze, English coin worth one fourth of a penny, no longer legal tender. **2.** Something of no value; a trifle. Abbr. *f., F.* [OE *fēorthung* < *fēortha* a fourth]
far·thin·gale (fär'thing·gāl) *n.* A woman's skirt of the 16th and 17th centuries, made so as to fit over a framework of hoops; also, the framework itself. [< OF *verdugale*, alter. of Sp. *verdugado* < *verdugo* rod, hoop]
Fa·ruk (fə·rook') See FAROUK I.
Fas (fäs) The Arabic name for FEZ.
FAS Foreign Agricultural Service.
F.A.S. **1.** Fellow of the Actuarial Society (Canada). **2.** *Brit.* Fellow of the Antiquarian Society. **3.** *Brit.* Fellow of the Anthropological Society.
F.A.S. or f.a.s. Free alongside ship.
F.A.S.A. Fellow of the Acoustical Society of America.
fasc. Bundle; fascicle (L *fasciculus*).
fas·ces (fas'ēz) *n.pl.* In ancient Rome, a bundle of rods enclosing an ax with the blade projecting, borne by lictors before magistrates as a symbol of power. [< L, pl. of *fascis* bundle] —**fas·ci·al** (fash'ē·əl) *adj.*
fas·ci·a (fash'ē·ə) *n. pl.* **fas·ci·ae** (fash'i·ē) **1.** *Anat.* Fibrous connective tissue forming sheets or layers beneath the skin, for enclosing or connecting muscles or internal organs. For illustration see FOOT. **2.** *Archit.* A horizontal member or band, usually in combination with other moldings, as in classical entablature. For illustration see ENTABLATURE. **3.** Something that binds together, as a fillet; a band. **4.** A bandage. **5.** *Biol.* A distinct band of color, as in certain plants and animals. [< L, band] —**fas'ci·al** *adj.*
fas·ci·ate (fash'ē·āt) *adj.* **1.** Bound with a band, fillet, or bandage. **2.** *Bot.* **a** Characterized by fasciation. **b** Formed into a cluster or bundle. **3.** *Entomol.* Marked with broad bands. **4.** Having fascicles; fasciculate. Also **fas'ci·at'ed.** [< LL *fasciatus*, pp. of *fasciare* to bind or wrap with bands < *fascia* band]
fas·ci·a·tion (fash'ē·ā'shən) *n.* **1.** The act of fastening or binding, as with bands or bandages. **2.** The state of being fasciate. **3.** *Bot.* A malformation of plants, characterized by an abnormal flattening of the stems, or by the coalescence of several stems into one.
fas·ci·cle (fas'i·kəl) *n.* **1.** A small bundle or cluster. **2.** One of the sections of a book that is published in installments. **3.** *Bot.* A cluster or bundle of leaves, flowers, or stalks. **4.** *Anat.* A fasciculus. Abbr. *fasc.* [< L *fasciculus*, dim. of *fascis* bundle] —**fas'ci·cled** (-kəld) *adj.*
fas·cic·u·lar (fə·sik'yə·lər) *adj.* **1.** Of or pertaining to a fascicle. **2.** Fasciculate.
fas·cic·u·late (fə·sik'yə·lit, -lāt) *adj.* Composed of or growing in fascicles. Also **fas·cic'u·lat'ed** (-lā'tid). —**fas·cic'u·late·ly** *adv.*
fas·cic·u·la·tion (fə·sik'yə·lā'shən) *n.* **1.** The state of being fasciculate. **2.** That which is fasciculate.

fas·cic·u·lus (fə·sik'yə·ləs) *n. pl.* **·li** (-lī) **1.** *Anat.* A bundle or cluster of fibers in the body, principally of nerve and muscle tissue. **2.** A fascicle, as of a book.
fas·ci·nate (fas'ə·nāt) *v.* **·nat·ed, ·nat·ing** *v.t.* **1.** To attract irresistibly, as by beauty or other qualities; captivate. **2.** To hold spellbound, as by terror or awe. **3.** *Obs.* To bewitch. —*v.i.* **4.** To be fascinating. [< L *fascinatus*, pp. of *fascinare* to charm < *fascinum* spell]
fas·ci·nat·ing (fas'ə·nā'ting) *adj.* Irresistibly attractive; captivating; bewitching; charming. —**fas'ci·nat'ing·ly** *adv.*
fas·ci·na·tion (fas'ə·nā'shən) *n.* **1.** The act of fascinating, or the state of being fascinated. **2.** A fascinating attraction, influence, or quality; enchantment; charm.
fas·ci·na·tor (fas'ə·nā'tər) *n.* **1.** One who or that which fascinates. **2.** A covering for the head, worn by women.
fas·cine (fa·sēn', fə·sēn') *n.* A bundle of sticks tied together and used in building earthworks and fortifications, filling ditches, etc. [< F < L *fascina* < *fascis* bundle]
fas·cism (fash'iz·əm) *n.* A one-party system of government in which each class has its distinct place, function, and representation in the government but the individual is subordinated to the state and control is maintained by military force, secret police, rigid censorship, and governmental regimentation of industry and finance. [< Ital. *fascismo* < *fascio*. See FASCISTI.]
Fas·cism (fash'iz·əm) *n.* The totalitarian system of government developed in Italy in 1919 by the Fascisti under Benito Mussolini to oppose socialism and communism: the government in Italy from 1922 to 1943, the principles of which were adapted by Adolf Hitler and the Nazi Party to include the concept of racial supremacy.
fas·cist (fash'ist) *n.* **1.** An advocate of fascism. **2.** A member of a fascist party. —*adj.* Of, advocating, or practicing fascism: a *fascist* state: also **fa·scis·tic** (fə·shis'tik).
Fas·cist (fash'ist) *n.* One of the Fascisti. —*adj.* Of or pertaining to Fascism.
Fa·scis·ti (fə·shis'tē, *Ital.* fä·shē'stē) *n. pl.* of **Fa·scis·ta** The members of the fascist party that under Benito Mussolini, took control of the government in Italy. [< Ital. < *fascio* political club < L *fascis* bundle. See FASCES.]
fash (fash) *Scot. v.t. & v.i.* To worry; fret: to *fash* one's wits. —*n.* Worry; annoyance; vexation. [< OF *fascher* to vex < LL *fastidiare* < L *fastidium* disgust]
fash·ion (fash'ən) *n.* **1.** The mode of dress, manners, living, etc., prevailing in society, especially in high society; also, compliance with the formal requirements of society; good form or style: to be in *fashion.* **2.** A current practice or usage. **3.** An object of enthusiasm among those considered, or desiring to be considered, fashionable. **4.** Fashionable people collectively; the élite. **5.** Manner; way: He walks in a peculiar *fashion.* **6.** Kind; sort: men of all *fashions.* **7.** *Archaic* Shape; form. —**Syn.** See HABIT. —**after a fashion** In some way or other; to a limited extent: He is a poet *after a fashion.* Also **in a fashion.** —*v.t.* **1.** To give shape or form to; mold; frame. **2.** To adapt, as to the occasion; accommodate. [< AF *fachon*, OF *façon* < L *factio, -onis* a (special) way of making. Doublet of FACTION.]
fash·ion·a·ble (fash'ən·ə·bəl) *adj.* **1.** Conforming to the current fashion. **2.** Associated with, characteristic of, or patronized by persons of fashion: a *fashionable* pastime, resort, etc. —*n.* A person of fashion. —**fash'ion·a·ble·ness** *n.* —**fash'ion·a·bly** *adv.*
fash·ioned (fash'ənd) *adj.* **1.** Made; shaped; formed: carefully *fashioned.* **2.** Of a certain style or fashion: usually in compounds, as *old-fashioned.*
fash·ion·er (fash'ən·ər) *n.* One who fashions, forms, or shapes anything.
fashion plate 1. One who dresses in the latest fashion. **2.** A picture representing the prevailing fashions in dress.
fash·ious (fash'əs) *adj. Scot.* Annoying; vexatious.
Fa·sho·da (fə·shō'də) A Sudanese town seized by the French (1898) causing the **Fashoda Incident,** an Anglo-French diplomatic crisis. See KODOK.
fast¹ (fast, fäst) *adj.* **1.** Firm in place; not easily moved. **2.** Firmly secured or bound. **3.** Constant; steadfast: *fast* friends. **4.** Not liable to fade: said of colors. **5.** Resistant: *acid-fast.* **6.** Sound or deep, as sleep. **7.** Acting or moving quickly; swift. **8.** Performed quickly: *fast* work. **9.** Permitting or suitable for quick movement: a *fast* track. **10.** Requiring rapidity of action or motion: a *fast* schedule. **11.** In advance of the true time: The clock is *fast.* **12.** Characterized by or given to dissipation or moral laxity: *fast* living. **13.** *Photog.* Intended for short exposure, as a high-velocity shutter or a highly sensitive film. —*adv.* **1.** Firmly; fixedly; securely. **2.** Soundly: *fast* asleep. **3.** Quickly; rapidly; swiftly. **4.** In quick succession: His thoughts came *fast.* **5.** Dissipatedly; recklessly: to live *fast.* **6.** *Archaic* Near: *fast* by. [OE *fæst.* Cf. Du. *vast*, G *fast.*]
fast² (fast, fäst) *v.i.* To abstain from food; especially, to eat sparingly or not at all or abstain from certain foods in observance of a religious duty or as a token of grief. —*n.* **1.** Abstinence from food, partial or total, or from prescribed kinds of food, particularly as a religious duty. **2.** A period prescribed for fasting. [OE *fæstan* to fasten, abstain]

fast and loose A cheating game: now chiefly in the phrase **to play fast and loose** To act in a tricky, untrustworthy, or inconstant fashion.

fast day A day set apart for fasting, as appointed by civil or ecclesiastical authority.

fas·ten (fas′ən, fäs′-) *v.t.* **1.** To attach or secure to something else; connect. **2.** To make fast; secure: to *fasten* a door. **3.** To direct (the attention, eyes, etc.) steadily. **4.** To impute or attribute. — *v.i.* **5.** To take fast hold; cling: usually with *on.* **6.** To become firm or attached. [OE *fæstnian* < *fæst* fixed] — **fas′ten·er** *n.*

fas·ten·ing (fas′ən·ing, fäs′-) *n.* **1.** The act of making fast. **2.** That which fastens, as a bolt.

fas·tid·i·ous (fas·tid′ē·əs, fəs-) *adj.* Hard to please in matters of taste; exceedingly delicate or refined; overnice; squeamish. — **Syn.** See METICULOUS. [< L *fastidiosus* < *fastidium* disgust] — **fas·tid′i·ous·ly** *adv.* — **fas·tid′i·ous·ness** *n.*

fas·ti·gi·ate (fas·tij′ē·it, -āt, fəs-) *adj.* **1.** Tapering or rising to a point. **2.** *Zool.* Forming a conical bundle. **3.** *Bot.* Nearly parallel and pointing upward, as certain branches. Also **fas·tig′i·at·ed** (-ā′tid). [< L *fastigium* top + ATE[1]]

fast·ing (fas′ting, fäs′-) *n.* Abstention from food. — **Syn.** See ABSTINENCE.

fast·ness (fast′nis, fäst′-) *n.* **1.** A fortress; stronghold. **2.** The state of being firm or fixed. **3.** Swiftness.

fat (fat) *adj.* **fat·ter, fat·test 1.** Having superfluous flesh or fat; corpulent; obese; plump. **2.** Containing much fat, oil, grease, etc. **3.** Well filled or supplied with rich or desirable elements: *fat* wood. **4.** Rich or fertile, as land. **5.** Abundant; plentiful: a *fat* profit. **6.** Yielding abundantly; profitable: a *fat* job. **7.** Thick; broad. — **a fat chance** *Slang* Very little chance; no chance at all. — **a fat lot** *Slang* Not much; nothing. — *n.* **1.** *Biochem.* Any of a large class of yellowish to white, greasy, solid or liquid substances widely distributed in plant and animal tissues. They are compounds of various fatty acids and glycerol, and are insoluble in water, but soluble in chloroform, ether, or benzene. In the pure state, fats are composed of carbon, oxygen, and hydrogen, and are generally odorless, tasteless, and colorless. **2.** Animal tissue containing large quantities of such compounds. **3.** Any vegetable or animal fat or oil used in cooking. **4.** Plumpness; obesity; corpulence. **5.** The richest or most desirable part of anything: the *fat* of the land. — **the fat is in the fire** The mischief is done. — **to chew the fat** *Slang* To talk. — *v.t. & v.i.* **fat·ted, fat·ting** To make or become fat. [OE *fæt*] — **fat′ly** *adv.* — **fat′ness** *n.*
— **Syn.** (adj.) **1.** *Fat, fleshy, stout, plump, corpulent,* and *obese* mean thick in body from abundance of flesh. *Fat* suggests overabundance or grossness, senses not always borne by *fleshy. Stout* implies bulk, whether from large bones or excess flesh, while *plump* describes a full figure with pleasant curves. *Corpulent* and *obese* refer to unsightly fatness, and often imply some glandular disorder. — **Ant.** thin, skinny, lank, lean, meager.

fa·tal (fāt′l) *adj.* **1.** Resulting in or capable of causing death; mortal; lethal. **2.** Bringing ruin or disaster; destructive. **3.** Highly significant or decisive; fateful: the *fatal* hour. **4.** Decreed or brought about by fate; destined; inevitable. **5.** Determining or controlling fate: the *fatal stars.* [< L *fatalis* < *fatum.* See FATE.]

fa·tal·ism (fāt′l·iz′əm) *n.* **1.** *Philos.* The doctrine that all things and events are predetermined and therefore unalterable. **2.** A disposition to accept every event or condition as inevitable; resignation to fate.

fa·tal·ist (fāt′l·ist) *n.* A believer in fatalism. — **fa·tal·is′tic** *adj.* — **fa·tal·is′ti·cal·ly** *adv.*

fa·tal·i·ty (fā·tal′ə·tē, fə-) *n. pl.* **·ties 1.** A death brought about through some disaster or calamity. **2.** The capability of causing death or disaster; deadliness. **3.** The state or quality of being subject to or determined by fate. **4.** A decree of fate; a destiny. **5.** A tendency to danger or disaster.

fa·tal·ly (fāt′l·ē) *adv.* **1.** So as to cause death or ruin; mortally. **2.** As decreed by fate; inevitably; unalterably.

fa·ta mor·ga·na (fä′tə môr·gä′nə) **1.** A mirage, especially as observed in the Strait of Messina. **2.** Morgan le Fay. [So called because formerly attributed to the fairy Fata Morgana (Morgan le Fay).]

fat·back (fat′bak′) *n.* **1.** The menhaden, a fish. **2.** Unsmoked salt pork.

fat·bird (fat′bûrd′) *n.* **1.** The pectoral sandpiper. **2.** The guacharo.

fat cat *U.S. Slang* A wealthy, privileged person; especially, a heavy contributor of political party funds.

fat cell *Biol.* One of a class of nucleated cells filled with fatty matter. For illustration see HAIR.

fate (fāt) *n.* **1.** A force viewed as unalterably determining in advance the way things happen; destiny. **2.** That which inevitably happens as though determined by this force; inescapable lot or outcome. **3.** Final result or outcome. **4.** An evil destiny; doom; especially, death or destruction. — **Syn.** See DESTINY. — *v.t.* **fat·ed, fat·ing** To predestine: ob-

solete except in the passive. [< L *fatum* decision, decree, orig. neut. sing. of *fatus,* pp. of *fari* to speak]

fat·ed (fā′tid) *adj.* **1.** Controlled by or subject to fate; destined. **2.** Condemned to ruin or destruction; doomed.

fate·ful (fāt′fəl) *adj.* **1.** Determining destiny; vitally affecting subsequent developments; momentous. **2.** Brought about by or as if by fate; fated. **3.** Bringing death, ruin, or disaster; fatal. **4.** Ominously prophetic; portentous. — **fate′ful·ly** *adv.* — **fate′ful·ness** *n.*

Fates (fāts) In classical mythology, the three goddesses who control human destiny: identified with the Roman *Parcae* and the Greek *Moirai* (Atropos, Clotho, and Lachesis): also called the *Destinies, Weird Sisters.*

fath. Fathom.

fat·head (fat′hed′) *n.* A dolt. — **fat′head·ed** *adj.*

fa·ther (fä′thər) *n.* **1.** A male who has begotten a child; a male parent; sire. **2.** A male who adopts a child or who otherwise holds a paternal relationship toward another. **3.** Any male ancestor; forefather. **4.** A male who originates, founds, or establishes something: the *father* of a new society. **5.** Any elderly man: used as a title of respect. **6.** One of the orthodox writers of the early Christian church. **7.** A leader or elder of a council, assembly, etc. **8.** A member of the ancient Roman senate. **9.** *Eccl.* **a** *Usually cap.* A priest or other church dignitary, as in the Roman Catholic or Anglican church: often used with or without the ecclesiastic's name as a title of respect. **b** A father confessor. Abbr. *Fr.* **10.** *Brit.* The senior member of a profession, society, etc.; doyen. **11.** In Christian Science, eternal Life; the divine Principle, commonly called God. — *v.t.* **1.** To beget. **2.** To act as a father toward. **3.** To found, create, or make. **4.** To admit oneself to be the father, author, or originator of. **5.** To fix the paternity, authorship, or origin of: with *on, upon.* **6.** To impose or attach unjustly or without basis: with *on, upon:* to *father* a false meaning on a law. [OE *fæder.* Akin to G *vater,* Du. *vader,* L *pater,* Gk. *patēr,* Skt. *pitr.*]

Fa·ther (fä′thər) *n.* **1.** God. **2.** *Theol.* The first person in the Trinity.

Father Christmas *Brit.* Santa Claus.

father confessor 1. *Eccl.* A priest who hears confessions. **2.** Anyone in whom one confides.

fa·ther·hood (fä′thər·hood) *n.* The state of being a father.

fa·ther·in·law (fä′thər·in·lô′) *n. pl.* **fa·thers·in·law 1.** The father of one's husband or wife. **2.** *Rare* A stepfather.

fa·ther·land (fä′thər·land′) *n.* **1.** The land of one's birth. **2.** The native country of one's forebears.

fa·ther·less (fä′thər·lis) *adj.* **1.** Not having a living father. **2.** Not having a known father. **3.** Deprived of a father's support, protection, or recognition.

fa·ther·ly (fä′thər·lē) *adj.* **1.** Of, pertaining to, or like a father. **2.** Showing the affection of a father; paternal. — *adv. Archaic* In a fatherly manner. — **fa′ther·li·ness** *n.*

Father's Day The third Sunday in June, a day observed in honor of fathers.

Fathers of Confederation *Canadian* Sir John Macdonald and his associates who achieved the Confederation in 1867.

Fathers of the Church The teachers and defenders of Christianity during its first seven centuries.

fath·om (fath′əm) *n. pl.* **·oms** or **·om** A measure of length, 6 feet or 1.829 meters, used principally in marine and mining measurements. See table inside back cover. Abbr. *f, F, F., fath., fm., fth., fthm.* — *v.t.* **1.** To find the depth of; sound. **2.** To understand; interpret; puzzle out. [OE *fæthm* the span of two arms outstretched] — **fath′om·a·ble** *adj.*

fath·om·less (fath′əm·lis) *adj.* **1.** Being so deep that measurement is impossible. **2.** Incapable of being understood.

fa·tid·ic (fə·tid′ik) *adj.* Relating to, marked by, or having the power of prophecy. Also **fa·tid′i·cal.** [< L *fatidicus* < *fatum* fate + *dicere* to speak]

fat·i·ga·ble (fat′ə·gə·bəl) *adj.* Subject to fatigue.

fa·tigue (fə·tēg′) *n.* **1.** The condition of being very tired as a result of physical or mental exertion; weariness; exhaustion. **2.** Something that tires or exhausts. **3.** *Physiol.* A loss of energy, lessened activity, and decreased response to stimulation, produced within an organism or any of its parts as a result of excessive exertion or stimulation. **4.** *Mech.* Structural weakness or loss of resiliency in metals or other materials, produced by excessive subjection to strain. **5.** *Mil.* **a** A special work assignment, as the digging of ditches, done by soldiers in training: also **fatigue duty. b** *pl.* Strong, durable clothes worn on fatigue duty: also **fatigue clothes.** — *v.t. & v.i.* **·tigued, ·tigu·ing 1.** To tire out; weary. **2.** To weaken, as metal. [< F < *fatiguer* to tire < L *fatigare* ? < *fatiscere* to yawn, droop and *fames* hunger.]

Fat·i·ma (fat′i·mə, fə·tē′mə), 606?–632, the daughter of Mohammed and wife of Ali.

Fat·i·ma (fat′i·mə, fə·tē′mə) The seventh and last wife of Bluebeard.

Fat·i·mid (fat′i·mid) *n.* **1.** A descendant of Fatima, daughter of Mohammed. **2.** One of a North African Arab dynasty (909–1171). — *adj.* **1.** Pertaining to or descended from

Fatima. **2.** Of or pertaining to the Fatimid dynasty. Also **Fat′i·mite** (-mīt).

fat·ling (fat′ling) *n.* A young animal fattened for slaughter.

Fat·shan (fät′shän′) A city in SE China; pop. 120,000 (est. 1970): also *Namhoi.*

fat-sol·u·ble (fat′sol′yə·bəl) *adj. Biochem.* Capable of being dissolved in fat, as certain vitamins.

fat·ten (fat′n) *v.t.* **1.** To cause to become fat; make plump or chubby; fill out. **2.** To make (land) rich or productive by fertilizing. **3.** To add to (a sum of money, etc.) so as to make larger and more attractive. — *v.i.* **4.** To grow fatter, heavier, greater, etc. — **fat′ten·er** *n.*

fat·ten·ing (fat′n·ing) *adj.* That fattens: a *fattening* food.

fat·tish (fat′ish) *adj.* Somewhat fat; plump. — **fat′tish·ness** *n.*

fat·ty (fat′ē) *adj.* **·ti·er, ·ti·est** **1.** Containing or made of fat. **2.** Having the properties of fat; greasy; oily. **3.** *Physiol.* Possessing too much fat: said of tissues, organs etc. — **fat′ti·ly** *adv.* — **fat′ti·ness** *n.*

fatty acid *Chem.* Any of a class of organic acids derived from saturated or unsaturated aliphatic hydrocarbons, and occurring as glycerides in plant and animal fats.

fatty degeneration *Pathol.* A condition in which the efficient cells in an organ are enveloped in or replaced by fat.

fatty tumor *Pathol.* A lipoma.

fa·tu·i·ty (fə·too′ə·tē, -tyoo′-) *n. pl.* **·ties** **1.** Smug stupidity; absolute foolishness; asininity. **2.** An utterly stupid action, remark, etc. **3.** *Rare* Feeble-mindedness or idiocy. [< L *fatuitē* < L *fatuitas* < *fatuus* foolish]

fat·u·ous (fach′oo·əs) *adj* **1.** Foolish and silly in a self-satisfied way; inane. **2.** Stupid; idiotic: a *fatuous* grin. **3.** *Rare* Illusory; unreal. [< L *fatuus* foolish] — **fat′u·ous·ly** *adv.* — **fat′u·ous·ness** *n.*

fat-wit·ted (fat′wit′id) *adj.* Stupid; obtuse.

fat wood Wood filled with resin.

fau·bourg (fō′boorg, *Fr.* fō·boor′) *n.* **1.** A section on the outskirts of a city; suburb. **2.** A district within a city. [< F]

fau·cal (fô′kəl) *adj.* **1.** *Anat.* Of or relating to the fauces. **2.** *Phonet.* Produced in the fauces. Also **fau·cial** (fô′shəl).

fau·ces (fô′sēz) *n.pl. Anat.* The passage from the back of the mouth to the pharynx, formed by the membranous, muscular arches extending downward from each side of the soft palate. [< L]

fau·cet (fô′sit) *n.* A fixture with an adjustable valve that controls the flow of liquids from a pipe, vat, etc.; tap; cock. [< OF *fausset*, prob. < *fausser* to break into, bore through, create a fault < L *falsare* < *falsus*. See FALSE.]

FAUCETS
a Sink. *b* Hose. *c* Mixing.

faugh (fô) *interj.* An exclamation of disgust, contempt, or rejection: also spelled *foh.*

Faulk·ner (fôk′nər), **William,** 1897–1962, U.S. novelist. Also *Falkner.*

fault (fôlt) *n.* **1.** Whatever impairs excellence; a blemish; flaw. **2.** A mistake or blunder. **3.** A slight offense; misdeed; negligence. **4.** Responsibility for some mishap, blunder, etc.; culpability; blame. **5.** *Geol.* A break in the continuity of rock strata or veins of ore, caused by movements of the earth's crust commonly associated with earthquakes. **6.** *Electr.* A deflection or leak in a current due to poor connection of circuits or defective insulation of a conductor. **7.** In tennis, squash, etc., failure to serve the ball into the prescribed area of the opponent's court; also, an improperly served ball. **8.** In hunting, loss of the trail or scent by the dogs. **9.** *Obs.* Default; lack. — **Syn.** See OFFENSE. — **at fault 1.** Open to blame; in the wrong; culpable. **2.** At a loss; perplexed; astray. **3.** Off the scent. — **in fault** Blameworthy. — **to a fault** Immoderately; excessively. — **to find fault** To seek out and complain about some imperfection, error, misdeed, etc.: often with *with.* — *v.t. Geol.* To cause a fault in. **2.** To find fault with; blame. — *v.i.* **3.** *Geol.* To crack so as to produce a fault. [< OF *faute*, ult. < L *fallere* to deceive]

FAULT (*def.* 5)

fault·find·er (fôlt′fīn′dər) *n.* A person given to complaining or finding fault; one who is excessively critical.

fault·find·ing (fôlt′fīn′ding) *n.* The act of one who finds fault. — *adj.* Inclined to find fault; critical; carping.

fault·less (fôlt′lis) *adj.* Free from faults; flawless; perfect. — **fault′less·ly** *adv.* — **fault′less·ness** *n.*

fault plane *Geol.* The fracture along which a fault occurs, commonly a curved surface.

fault·y (fôl′tē) *adj.* **fault·i·er, fault·i·est 1.** Having faults; defective; imperfect. **2.** *Obs.* Guilty of faults; blamable. — **fault′i·ly** *adv.* — **fault′i·ness** *n.*

faun (fôn) *n.* In Roman mythology, a woodland deity typically represented as a man having the ears, horns, tail, and hind legs of a goat; satyr [< L *Faunus,* a rural god < *favere* to be kindly disposed]

fau·na (fô′nə) *n. pl.* **·nas** or **·nae** (-nē) **1.** The animals living within a given area or environment or during a stated period: distinguished from *flora.* **2.** A treatise on these animals. [< NL, after L *Fauna,* a rural goddess. Introduced by Linnaeus as companion to flora.] — **fau′nal** *adj.*

Fau·nus (fô′nəs) In Roman mythology, a god of nature, patron of agriculture: identified with the Greek *Pan.*

Faure (fôr) **Élie,** 1873–1937, French art critic and historian.

Fau·ré (fō·rā′), **Gabriel Urban,** 1845–1924, French composer.

Faust (foust) **1.** In medieval legend, a philosopher who sells his soul to a devil, Mephistopheles, for wisdom and power Also **Faust·us** (fous′təs, fôs′-). **2.** The main character of Goethe's *Faust,* a two-part dramatic poem written between 1808 and 1832, of Marlowe's *Tragical History of Doctor Faustus,* 1593, and of Gounod's *Faust,* an opera first performed in 1859.

Faus·ta (fous′tə), **Flavia Maximiana,** 289?–326?, Byzantine empress; wife of Constantine the Great.

fau·teuil (fō′til, *Fr.* fô·tœ′y′) *n.* An upholstered armchair. [< F < OF *faudeteuil* < Med.L *faldistolium.* See FALDSTOOL.]

Fauves (fōv), **Les** (lā) A group of French painters, including Derain, Dufy, Matisse, and Vlaminck, who, about 1906, revolted from what they regarded as the limitations of impressionism as well as from those of academic art. [< F, wild beasts] — **Fau′vism** *n.* — **Fau′vist** *n.*

faux pas (fō pä′) *pl.* **faux pas** (fō päz′, *Fr.* fō pä′) A false step; mistake; error; especially, a breach of etiquette. [< F, lit., false step]

Fa·ven·ti·a (fə·ven′shē·ə, -shə) The ancient name for FAENZA.

fa·ve·o·late (fə·vē′ə·lāt) *adj.* Having many small pits or cavities like those of a honeycomb; alveolate. [< NL *faveolus,* dim of L *favus* honeycomb + -ATE[1]]

fa·vo·ni·an (fə·vō′nē·ən) *adj.* **1.** Of or relating to Favonius. **2.** Soft and gentle: a *favonian* breeze; also, propitious.

Fa·vo·ni·us (fə·vō′nē·əs) In Roman mythology, the west wind personified.

fa·vor (fā′vər) *n.* **1.** Something helpful, advantageous, or considerate done or granted freely as a gesture of good will, kindly interest, etc.: to do someone a *favor.* **2.** An attitude of friendliness, liking, or approbation: to look with *favor* upon a plan. **3.** The condition of being looked upon with liking or approval: to be in *favor* with the people. **4.** Special treatment prompted by friendliness, liking, or approval: to enjoy the government's *favor*; also, unfair discrimination; narrow partiality: to show *favor* in distributing benefits. **5.** Kind permission; gracious consent; leave: usually preceded by *by, with*: By your *favor,* I should like to speak. **6.** Something that helps or furthers an undertaking; aid: preceded by *by, under*: an escape made under *favor* of night. **7.** The condition of leading one's opponent in the score of a game: used with a possessive to indicate the one having the higher score: The score is 2–0, your *favor.* **8.** Some little gift or remembrance given as a token of esteem, affection, or hospitality; especially, a small gift presented to each guest on some festive occasion, as at a birthday party. **9.** *pl.* Consent to sexual intimacy. **10.** *Archaic* Attractiveness; charm. **11.** *Archaic* General appearance; look; also, the face or features. **12.** *Rare* A business letter. — **in favor** Having approval or support: a style much *in favor.* — **in favor of 1.** On the side of; giving or disposed to give approval or support to: to be *in favor of* greater liberty. **2.** To the furtherance or advantage of: The plan worked *in favor of* everyone. **3.** Made out to the benefit of: a check *in favor of* his wife. — **in one's favor** Of such a kind as to help one or promote one's interests: Everything is *in your favor.* — **out of favor** Lacking approval or support; not liked: a custom now *out of favor.* — **to find favor** To come to be looked upon with approval or liking; gain acceptance: I hope the idea will *find favor.* — *v.t.* **1.** To do a favor for; oblige. **2.** To look upon with approval or liking. **3.** To show special consideration to, often in an unfair way; show partiality to. **4.** To lean toward approving or supporting: to *favor* a plan. **5.** To increase the chances of success of; help along: Darkness would *favor* their escape. **6.** *Informal* To show a resemblance to in features; take after: The child *favors* its father. **7.** To be careful of; treat gently; spare: to *favor* an injured arm. Also *Brit.* **fa′vour.** [< OF < L *favere* < *favere* to favor] — **fa′vor·er** *n.*

fa·vor·a·ble (fā′vər·ə·bəl) *adj.* **1.** Granting something requested or hoped for: a *favorable* answer. **2.** Building up hope or confidence: a *favorable* medical diagnosis. **3.** Boding well; promising: a *favorable* indication. **4.** Expressive of approval; commendatory: a *favorable* report. **5.** Well-disposed or indulgent; friendly: to lend a *favorable* ear. **6.** Advantageous; propitious: a *favorable* wind. Also *Brit.* **fa′vour·a·ble.** — **fa′vor·a·ble·ness** *n.* — **fa′vor·a·bly** *adv.*

fa·vored (fā′vərd) *adj.* **1.** Treated with or looked upon with friendliness, liking, or approbation: a *favored* courtier. **2.** Endowed with especially good qualities; outstanding in good points or advantages: a *favored* part of the country. **3.** Having an (indicated) aspect or appearance: used in compounds: an *ill-favored* countenance. Also *Brit.* **fa′voured.**

fa·vor·ite (fā′vər·it) *adj.* Regarded with special favor; preferred. — *n.* **1.** A person or thing greatly liked or preferred. **2.** A person granted special privileges by a high official, etc.

3. In sports, the contestant considered to have the best chance of winning. Also *Brit.* **fa′vour·ite.** [< OF *favorit* < Ital. *favorito*, pp. of *favorire* to favor < L *favere*]

favorite son **1.** A man highly regarded and honored by his native city, state, etc., by reason of his accomplishments. **2.** A candidate judged by the political leaders of his native city, state, etc., to be most worthy of nomination to high office.

fa·vor·it·ism (fā′vər·ə·tiz/əm) *n.* **1.** Preferential treatment, especially when unjust or narrowly discriminating. **2.** The condition of being a favorite. Also *Brit.* **fa′vour·it·ism.**

fa·vus (fā′vəs) *n. Pathol.* A contagious disease caused by a parasitic fungus (*Achorion schönleinii*) and marked by the production of yellow, flattened scabs. [< L, honeycomb]

Fawkes (fôks), **Guy** See under GUY FAWKES DAY.

fawn¹ (fôn) *v.i.* **1.** To show cringing fondness, as a dog: often with *on* or *upon.* **2.** To show affection or seek favor by or as by cringing. [OE *fahnian,* var. of *fægnian* to rejoice] — **fawn′er** *n.* — **fawn′ing·ly** *adv.*

fawn² (fôn) *n.* **1.** A young deer; especially, a buck or doe in its first year. **2.** The light yellowish brown color of a young deer. — *adj.* Light yellowish brown. [< OF *faon,* ult. < L *fetus* offspring]

fax (faks) *v.t.* To reproduce (written, printed, or picture) material in facsimile, especially for high-speed automatic transmission to a distant point. — *n.* A facsimile reproduction. [Contraction of FACSIMILE]

fay¹ (fā) *v.t. & v.i.* To fit or join closely, as two timbers. [OE *fēgan*]

fay² (fā) *n.* A fairy. [< OF *fae* < L *fata* the Fates, pl. of *fatum* fate]

fay³ (fā) *n. Archaic* Faith: by my *fay.* [< OF *fei,* var. of *feid.* See FAITH.]

Fa·yal (fə·yäl′) An island of the central Azores; 64 sq. mi.; chief town, Horta.

fay·al·ite (fā′əl·īt, fī·äl′īt) *n.* A light green to brownish black magnetic iron silicate crystallizing in the orthorhombic system. [after *Fayal* + -ITE¹]

Fay·ette·ville (fā′it·vil) A city in south central North Carolina, on the Cape Fear River; pop. 53,510.

Fa·yum (fī·yōōm′) See FAIYUM.

faze (fāz) *v.t.* **fazed, faz·ing** *U.S. Informal* To worry; disturb; disconcert: also spelled *fease, feaze, feeze.* — **Syn.** See EMBARRASS. [Var. of dial. E *fease,* OE *fēsian* to frighten]

f.b. **1.** Freight bill. **2.** Fullback: also **fb.**

F.B.A. Fellow of the British Academy.

FBI or **F.B.I.** Federal Bureau of Investigation.

f.c. *Printing* Follow copy.

Fc *Meteorol.* Fractocumulus.

FC *Mil.* Finance Corps.

FCA Farm Credit Administration.

FCC or **F.C.C.** Federal Communications Commission.

F.C.C. **1.** Federal Council of Churches. **2.** First Class Certificate.

F clef *Music* See under CLEF.

F.D. **1.** Fidei Defensor. **2.** Fire Department.

FDA or **F.D.A.** Food and Drug Administration.

FDIC or **F.D.I.C.** Federal Deposit Insurance Corporation.

Fe *Chem.* Iron (L *ferrum*).

feal (fēl) *adj. Archaic* Faithful. [< OF, var. of *feeil* < L *fidelis* loyal]

fe·al·ty (fē′əl·tē) *n. pl.* **·ties** **1.** The obligation of fidelity owed to a feudal lord by his vassal or tenant; also, the sworn recognition of this obligation. **2.** Faithfulness; loyalty. [< OF *feaute, feaulte* < L *fidelitas.* Doublet of FIDELITY.]

fear (fir) *n.* **1.** An agitated feeling aroused by awareness of actual or threatening danger, trouble, etc.; dread; terror. **2.** An uneasy feeling that something may happen contrary to one's desires. **3.** A feeling of deep, reverential awe and dread: the *fear* of God. **4.** A continuing state or attitude of fright, dread, or alarmed concern: to live in *fear.* **5.** The possibility that something dreaded or unwanted may occur: There is no *fear* that such a thing will happen. — **for fear of** So as to avoid or keep from happening. — **for fear that** (or **lest**) So that . . . not: He held her hand *for fear that* she would fall. — *v.t.* **1.** To be in dread or terror of; be frightened of. **2.** To be uneasy or apprehensive over (an unwanted or unpleasant possibility): to *fear* death. **3.** To have a deep, reverential awe of. **4.** *Archaic* To feel fear within (oneself): I *fear* me that you don't understand. **5.** *Dial.* To frighten. — *v.i.* **6.** To feel dread or terror. **7.** To feel uneasy; have misgivings. [OE *fær* peril, sudden attack] — **fear′er** *n.*

— **Syn.** (noun) **1.** *Fear, fright, dread, terror, horror,* and *panic* are emotions aroused by imminent danger, pain, evil, violence, etc. *Fear* is the widest term. It may concern personal safety or the welfare of others and may range from mild alarm to extreme frenzy. *Fright* is a sudden onset of *fear:* to take *fright* at a loud noise. *Dread* is *fear* of future events and suggests helpless inactivity at the approach of something that cannot be avoided or changed. *Terror* is the most extreme *fear,* especially where one's own safety or well-being is concerned. Like *dread,* it may render a person unable to act or it may result in wild, frenzied activity

aimed at escaping a threatening situation. *Horror* is *fear* combined with abhorrence and frequently refers to something that is seen. *Panic* is a wave of *terror* that affects many persons; the term is also applied to individuals and, when so used, it suggests an unreasoned or senseless *fear.* Compare ALARM, ANXIETY. — **Ant.** fearlessness, courage, confidence, aplomb. Compare BRAVE.

Fear, Cape A cape at the southern end of Smith Island, off the SE coast of North Carolina at the mouth of the Cape Fear River.

fear·ful (fir′fəl) *adj.* **1.** Filled with dread or terror. **2.** Filled with uneasiness; apprehensive. **3.** Filled with deep, reverential awe. **4.** Causing dread or terror; terrifying; frightening. **5.** Showing fear; moved by fear: a *fearful* look. **6.** *Informal* Extremely bad; appalling. **7.** Going to extremes: a *fearful* drinker. — **fear′ful·ly** *adv.* — **fear′ful·ness** *n.*

fear·less (fir′lis) *adj.* Devoid of fear; not at all afraid. — **Syn.** See BRAVE. — **fear′less·ly** *adv.* — **fear′less·ness** *n.*

fear·naught (fir′nôt′) *n.* A heavy, woolen material; also, a coat made from this. Also **fear′nought′.**

fear·some (fir′səm) *adj.* **1.** Causing fear; alarming. **2.** Timid; frightened. — **fear′some·ly** *adv.* — **fear′some·ness** *n.*

fea·sance (fē′zəns) *n. Law* Performance of a duty or fulfillment of a condition, obligation, etc. [< AF *fesance* < F *faire* to do < L *facere*]

fease (fāz) See FAZE.

fea·si·ble (fē′zə·bəl) *adj.* **1.** Capable of being put into effect or accomplished; practicable: a *feasible* project. **2.** Capable of being successfully utilized; suitable: a boat *feasible* for ocean travel. **3.** Fairly probable; likely: a *feasible* explanation. [< OF *faisable* < F *faire* to do < L *facere*] — **fea′si·bil′i·ty, fea′si·ble·ness** *n.* — **fea′si·bly** *adv.*

feast (fēst) *n.* **1.** A sumptuous meal. **2.** Something affording great pleasure to the senses or intellect. **3.** An elaborate banquet for many persons. **4.** A day or days of celebration regularly set aside for a religious purpose or in honor of some person, event, or thing: also **feast day.** — *v.t.* **1.** To give a feast for; entertain lavishly. **2.** To delight; gratify. — *v.i.* **3.** To partake of a feast; eat heartily. **4.** To dwell delightedly, as on a painting. [< OF *feste* < L *festa,* neut. pl. of *festus* joyful < *feriae* holidays] — **feast′er** *n.*

feast·ful (fēst′fəl) *adj.* Festive; sumptuous.

Feast of Dedication Hanukkah

Feast of Lanterns **1.** A Chinese festival held at the first full moon of every year (January–February): so called from the use of colored lanterns. **2.** The Japanese festival, Bon.

feat¹ (fēt) *n.* **1.** A notable act or performance, as one displaying skill, or daring; an achievement. **2.** *Obs.* Any act. — **Syn.** See ACT. [< OF *fait* < L *factum.* See FACT.]

feat² (fēt) *adj. Archaic* **1.** Dexterous; neat; ingenious. **2.** Fit; befitting. [< OF *fait* shaped. fit, pp. of *faire* to make < L *facere*]

feath·er (feth′ər) *n.* **1.** One of the horny, elongated structures that form the plumage of birds, consisting essentially of a hollow tubular quill attached to the body and prolonged in a slender shaft supporting a web or vane of closely spaced barbs interlocking with barbules and barbicels. **2.** *pl.* Plumage. **3.** *pl.* Dress; attire. **4.** A lock or tuft of hair resembling a feather. **5.** The hairy fringe on the legs and tails of some dogs. **6.** A feather or feathers fastened to the shaft of an arrow to guide its flight. **7.** Something resembling a bird's feather, as a key, wedge, etc. **8.** Class or species; kind: birds of a *feather.* **9.** Condition of mind or body; mood; spirits: in fine *feather.* **10.** Anything small, of little weight, or trivial: He trembles at a *feather.* **11.** A featherlike flaw, as in a gem. **12.** The act of feathering (an oar blade or propeller). **13.** The wake of a submarine's periscope. — **a feather in one's cap** An achievement to be proud of; a thing to one's credit. — **in full feather** In full force; fully equipped. — **in high, fine,** or **good feather** In good spirits or health. — **to show the white feather** To be cowardly; back down. — *v.t.* **1.** To fit with a feather, as an arrow. **2.** To cover, adorn, line, or fringe with feathers. **3.** To join by a tongue-and-groove joint. **4.** In rowing, to turn (the oar blade) following each stroke so that the blade is more or less horizontal as it is carried back to the position for reentering the water. **5.** *Aeron.* To change the pitch of (a propeller) so that the blades are parallel with the line of flight. — *v.i.* **6.** To grow feathers or become covered with feathers. **7.** To move, spread, or expand like feathers. **8.** To feather an oar or propeller blade. — **to feather one's nest** To grow prosperous, especially by means of property entrusted to one's charge. [OE *fether*] — **feath′er·less** *adj.*

feath·er·bed (feth′ər·bed′) *adj.* Of, relating to, or promot-

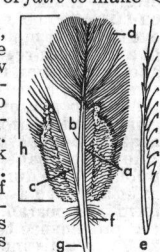

FEATHER
a Shaft.
b Shaft with barbs cut away.
c Aftershaft. *d* Barbs. *e* Barb, showing barbules. *f* Down. *g* Quill. *h* Web or vane.

ing featherbedding: *featherbed* regulations. **— v.i. ·bed·ded, ·bed·ding** To engage in or promote featherbedding.

feather bed A mattress of strong fabric stuffed with feathers or down and used on, or in place of, a bed.

feath·er·bed·ding (feth′ər·bed′ing) *n.* The practice of requiring the employment of more workers than are needed or of unnecessarily duplicating work or artificially limiting output so as to create more jobs and prevent unemployment.

feath·er·bone (feth′ər·bōn′) *n.* A substitute for whalebone, made from the quills of turkeys, geese, etc.

feath·er·brain (feth′ər·brān′) *n.* A flighty, stupid, or mentally unbalanced individual. **— feath′er·brained′** *adj.*

feath·er·cut (feth′ər·kut′) *n.* A style of cutting the hair to uneven, short lengths so that the tips curl up lightly.

feath·ered (feth′ərd) *adj.* **1.** Covered, provided, or decorated with feathers. **2.** Moving swiftly as though flying. **3.** *Aeron.* Adjusted in pitch so that the leading edge is directed in the line of flight: said of a propeller.

feath·er·edge (feth′ər·ej′) *n.* A very thin, tapering edge, as of a planed board. **— feath′er·edged′** *adj.*

feather grass **1.** An ornamental grass (*Stipa pennata*) of southern Europe with feathery awns. **2.** A related species (*S. comata*) of the United States: also called *needle grass.*

feath·er·head (feth′ər·hed′) *n.* A featherbrain. **— feath′er·head′ed** *adj.*

feath·er·ing (feth′ər·ing) *n.* **1.** Something, as plumage, made up of or resembling feathers. **2.** *Music* Light, delicate use of the bow, as of the violin, in certain passages.

feather key *Mech.* Spline.

feather palm Any of various palms with leaves that are pinnate or feathery.

feather star A comatula.

feath·er·stitch (feth′ər·stich′) *n.* An embroidery stitch resembling a feather, made by taking one or more short stitches alternately on either side of a straight line. **— v.t. & v.i.** To embroider with such a stitch.

feath·er·veined (feth′ər·vānd′) *adj. Bot.* Having the veins extending from both sides of a central midrib.

feath·er·weight (feth′ər·wāt′) *n.* **1.** A boxer or wrestler weighing more than 118 pounds and less than 127 pounds. **2.** The least weight that can be carried by a race horse in a handicap. **3.** Any person or thing relatively light in weight or size. **4.** Any person or thing of small importance. **—** *adj.* **1.** Relating to or characteristic of a featherweight. **2.** Being of small importance; insignificant; trivial.

feath·er·wood (feth′ər·wood′) *n.* A timber tree of Australia (*Polyosma cunninghami*) with a wood resembling hickory.

feath·er·y (feth′ər·ē) *adj.* **1.** Provided with or as if with feathers; feathered. **2.** Suggestive of feathers in lightness, etc. **— feath′er·i·ness** *n.*

fea·ture (fē′chər) *n.* **1.** A distinctive part of the face, as the eyes, nose, or mouth. **2.** *Usually pl.* The overall appearance of a face with regard to the natural proportions, alignment, and type of eyes, nose, etc. **3.** A prominent characteristic of something; a distinguishing mark, part, or quality. **4.** A full-length motion picture, especially when presented as a principal attraction. **5.** Anything given special prominence; as: **a** A special article, story, department, etc., as in a magazine or newspaper. **b** An item conspicuously displayed and publicized, as during a sale in a store. **c** A special attraction, as at a fair, on a variety program, etc. **6.** *Archaic* Outward form or appearance. **— v.t. ·tured, ·tur·ing 1.** To give special prominence to or present as meriting special attention. **2.** To be a distinctive characteristic of. **3.** *Informal* To resemble in facial features; take after. **4.** *Slang* To form an idea of; imagine. **5.** *Archaic* To depict; portray. [< OF *faiture* < L *factura* < *facere* to do. Doublet of FACTURE.]

fea·tured (fē′chərd) *adj.* **1.** Having (specified) facial characteristics: *hard-featured.* **2.** Presented as a special or central attraction or as meriting special attention. **3.** Given facial features or some other outward expression.

fea·ture·less (fē′chər·lis) *adj.* **1.** Lacking features. **2.** Having no prominent or distinctive characteristics; dull.

feaze¹ (fāz) See FAZE.

feaze² (fēz) *v.t. & v.i.* **feazed, feaz·ing** *Dial.* To unravel. [< LG or Du. Cf. *fæs* fringe.]

Feb. or **Feb** February.

febri- *combining form* Fever. Also, before vowels, **febr-.** [< L *febris* fever]

fe·bric·i·ty (fə·bris′ə·tē) *n.* The condition of being feverish. [< ML *febricitas*]

fe·bric·u·la (fə·brik′yə·lə) *n.* A slight, brief fever. [< L]

feb·ri·fa·cient (feb′rə·fā′shənt) *adj.* Producing fever. **—** *n.* A substance that produces fever. [< FEBRI- + L *faciens, -entis*, ppr. of *facere* to make]

fe·brif·ic (fə·brif′ik) *adj.* **1.** Causing fever. **2.** Feverish. Also **fe·brif′er·ous** (-ər·əs).

feb·ri·fuge (feb′rə·fyōōj) *n.* A medicine efficacious in reducing or removing fever. **—** *adj.* Reducing or removing fever. [< F < L *febris* + *fugare* to drive away] **— fe·brif·u·gal** (fə·brif′yə·gəl) *adj.*

fe·brile (fē′brəl, feb′rəl) *adj.* Feverish. [< F *fébrile* < L *febrilis* < *febris* fever]

Feb·ru·ar·y (feb′rōō·er′ē, feb′yōō-) *n. pl.* **·ar·ies** or **·ar·ys** The second month of the year, having twenty-eight, or, in leap years, twenty-nine days. See LEAP YEAR. *Abbr. F., Feb, Feb.* [< L *Februarius* (*mensis*) (month) of purification < *februa,* a Roman purificatory festival celebrated on Feb. 15]

fe·cal (fē′kəl) *adj.* Of, resembling, or marked by the presence of feces.

fe·ces (fē′sēz) *n.pl.* **1.** Animal excrement; ordure. **2.** Any foul refuse matter or sediment. Also spelled *faeces.* [< L< *faex, faecis* sediment]

Fech·ner (fekh′nər), **Gustav Theodor,** 1801–87, German scientist and psychophysicist.

fe·cial (fē′shəl) See FETIAL.

fe·cit (fē′sit) *Latin* He (or she) made it: formerly accompanying the artist's signature on a work. *Abbr. fec.*

feck (fek) *n. Scot.* **1.** Vigor. **2.** Value or amount.

feck·less (fek′lis) *adj.* **1.** Devoid of energy or effectiveness; feeble. **2.** Devoid of vitality; listless. **3.** Careless and irresponsible. **— feck′less·ly** *adv.* **— feck′less·ness** *n.*

feck·ly (fek′lē) *adv. Scot.* For the most part; mostly.

fec·u·la (fek′yə·lə) *n. pl.* **·lae** (-lē) **1.** Starch made by washing the ground or pulverized roots or other parts of certain plants, as potatoes, etc. **2.** The sediment yielded from a liquid in which something has been steeped. [< L *faecula* dim. of *faex* dregs]

fec·u·lence (fek′yə·ləns) *n.* **1.** The condition or quality of being feculent; muddy foulness. **2.** That which is feculent, as scummy or filthy sediment. Also **fec′u·len·cy.**

fec·u·lent (fek′yə·lənt) *adj.* Turbid or foul with impurities; filthy. [< L *faeculentus* < *faecula.* See FECULA.]

fe·cund (fē′kənd, fek′ənd) *adj.* Fruitful; fertile; prolific. [< OF *fecond* < L *fecundus* ult. < root *fe* to suckle, produce as in L *felare* to suckle. Cf. *female, fetus, filial,* etc.]

fe·cun·date (fē′kən·dāt, fek′ən-) *v.t.* **·dat·ed, ·dat·ing 1.** To make fruitful or fecund. **2.** To impregnate; fertilize. [< L *fecundatus,* pp. of *fecundare* to fertilize < *fecundus* fruitful. See FECUND.] **— fe′cun·da′tion** *n.*

fe·cun·di·ty (fi·kun′də·tē) *n.* **1.** The capacity to produce or propagate abundantly; fertility. **2.** The power to bring about fertilization. **3.** Productiveness or creativity in general.

fed (fed) Past tense and past participle of FEED. **— fed up** *Slang* Subjected to or surfeited with something to the point of being sick of it.

fed. **1.** Federal. **2.** Federated; federation.

Fe·da·yeen (fe·dä′yēn) *n.* In Arab states, a commando. [< Arabic *fidayim,* pl. of *fidayi* one who redeems his country < *fida* redemption < *faday* to redeem]

fed·er·a·cy (fed′ər·ə·sē) *n. pl.* **·cies 1.** A confederacy. **2.** *Rare* An alliance based on a treaty.

fed·er·al (fed′ər·əl) *adj.* **1.** Of, relating to, or formed by an agreement among two or more states, groups, etc., to merge into a union in which control of common affairs is granted to and maintained by a central authority established by consent of the members, with each member retaining jurisdiction over its own internal affairs; also, of, relating to, or supporting a union or central government established by such an agreement. **2.** Of or pertaining to a confederacy (def. 1). **—** *n.* An advocate or supporter of a federal union or federal government. *Abbr. fed.* [< F *fédéral* < L *foedus, -eris* compact, league < *fides* faith] **— fed′er·al·ly** *adv.*

Fed·er·al (fed′ər·əl) *adj.* **1.** Of, relating to, or supporting the central government of a specific country, as of the United States. **2.** Of, relating to, or loyal to the Union cause in the American Civil War of 1861–65. **3.** Of, relating to, or supporting the Federalist Party. **—** *n.* **1.** One who favored or fought for the Union cause in the American Civil War. **2.** A Federalist. **— Fed′er·al·ly** *adv.*

Federal Bureau of Investigation An agency of the U.S. government that investigates violations of Federal laws other than those involving counterfeiting, infringement of postal or customs regulations, or internal revenue matters specifically assigned to other agencies. *Abbr. FBI, F.B.I.*

Federal Capital Territory A former name for the AUSTRALIAN CAPITAL TERRITORY.

Federal Communications Commission An agency of the U.S. government that supervises wire, radio, and television communication. *Abbr. FCC, F.C.C.*

Federal District A district reserved by a country for the location of its national government, as the District of Columbia.

fed·er·al·ism (fed′ər·əl·iz′əm) *n.* The doctrine, system, or principle of federal union or federal government; also, advocacy or support of this doctrine, system, or principle.

Fed·er·al·ism (fed′ər·əl·iz′əm) *n.* The principles of the Federalist Party; also, advocacy or support of these principles.

fed·er·al·ist (fed′ər·əl·ist) *n.* An advocate or supporter of federalism. **—** *adj.* Of or relating to federalism or federalists: also **fed′er·al·is′tic.**

Fed·er·al·ist (fed′ər·əl·ist) *n.* **1.** One who supported the federal union of the American colonies and the adoption of the Constitution of the United States. **2.** A member of the Federalist Party. **— The Federalist** A series of 85 essays by

Alexander Hamilton, John Jay, and James Madison, explaining the Constitution of the United States and recommending its ratification. — *adj.* Of or relating to the Federalist Party or Federalists: also **Fed′er·al·is′tic.**

Federalist Party A political party (1787–1830), originally under the leadership of Alexander Hamilton, that advocated the adoption of the United States Constitution and the formation of a strong national government. Also **Federal Party.**

fed·er·al·ize (fed′ər-əl-īz′) *v.t.* ·ized, ·iz·ing To unite in a federal union; federate. — **fed′er·al·i·za′tion** *n.*

Federal Republic of Germany See under GERMANY.

Federal Reserve System A banking system created by the **Federal Reserve Act** (1913) and controlled by a **Federal Reserve Board** (abbr. *FRB*) of seven (originally eight) members, established to provide an elastic currency and to concentrate the national banking resources in a system of twelve **Federal Reserve Banks**, each designed to regulate and aid the member banks in its respective **Federal Reserve District.** Abbr. *FRS*

Federal Trade Commission An agency of the U.S. government that enforces Federal laws against unfair trade practices, such as price fixing, false advertising, etc. Abbr. *FTC, F.T.C.*

fed·er·ate (*v.* fed′ə·rāt; *adj.* fed′ə·rit) *v.t. & v.i.* ·at·ed, ·at·ing To unite in a federal union. — *adj.* Joined together in a federal union or confederacy; federal or confederate. [< L *foederatus,* pp. of *foederare* < *foedus, -eris* league]

Federated Malay States See MALAY STATES.

fed·er·a·tion (fed′ə·rā′shən) *n.* **1.** The joining together of two or more states, groups, etc., into a federal union or a confederacy. **2.** A government or political body established through federal union or as a confederacy. Abbr. *fed.* — **Syn.** See ALLIANCE.

Federation of Malaya See (Federation of) MALAYA.

Federation of Rhodesia and Nyasaland See RHODESIA.

fed·er·a·tive (fed′ə·rā′tiv, fed′ər·ə·tiv) *adj.* Belonging to, forming, or resembling a federation. — **fed′er·a′tive·ly** *adv.*

fe·do·ra (fə·dôr′ə, -dō′rə) *n.* A soft hat, usually of felt, with a curved brim and a crown creased lengthwise. [after *Fédora,* a play by V. Sardou]

fee (fē) *n.* **1.** A charge, compensation, or payment for something, especially for something not strictly computable in terms of money; as: **a** A sum charged for professional services: medical *fee.* **b** A sum charged for some privilege: membership *fee.* **c** A sum charged for admission: an entrance *fee.* **d** Money or something else given for special service, a favor, etc.; a gratuity or tip. **2.** *Law* A fee simple. **3.** In feudal law, a fief. — **Syn.** See SALARY. — **to hold in fee** To have full and absolute possession of. — *v.t.* **feed, fee·ing 1.** To pay a fee to. **2.** *Scot.* To hire for a fee. [< AF, var. of OF *fé, fief* < Med.L *feudum* fief, ult. ? < Gmc. Akin to OE *feoh,* OHG *fihu,* G *vieh,* Du. *vee,* L *pecus* all meaning cattle, hence property, money. See FEUD².]

fee·ble (fē′bəl) *adj.* ·bler, ·blest **1.** Lacking physical strength; very weak. **2.** Lacking intellectual or moral vigor: a *feeble* wit. **3.** Lacking energy, direction, or effectiveness; altogether inadequate; ineffective: *feeble* efforts; a *feeble* defense system. **4.** Lacking point or substance: a *feeble* joke. **5.** Scarcely able to be seen or heard; indistinct; faint: a *feeble* light; a *feeble* cry. [< OF *feble* < *fleible* weak < L *flebilis* lamentable < *flere* to weep. Related to FOIBLE.] — **fee′ble·ness** *n.* — **fee′bly** *adv.*

fee·ble-mind·ed (fē′bəl·mīn′did) *adj.* **1.** Lacking normal mental ability; mentally deficient. **2.** Weak-willed. — **fee′ble-mind′ed·ly** *adv.* — **fee′ble-mind′ed·ness** *n.*

feed (fēd) *v.* **fed, feed·ing** *v.t.* **1.** To give food or nourishment to; supply with food: to *feed* a hungry family. **2.** To give (something) as food or nourishment to: to *feed* carrots to rabbits. **3.** To serve as food or nourishment for: Plants *feed* many creatures; also, to produce food or nourishment for: acreage that will *feed* many. **4.** To keep supplied, as with material to be used or worked on, fuel, or some other essential or important thing: to *feed* a fire; also, to keep supplying: to *feed* data into a computing machine. **5.** To furnish with what maintains or increases: The streams are *fed* by melting snow. **6.** To keep up or make more intense or greater: to *feed* suspicions. **7.** To gratify; feast: to *feed* one's eyes on beauty. **8.** To cue (an actor, etc.) with the proper lines. **9.** In sports, to get the ball, puck, etc., to (a teammate in an advantageous position). — *v.i.* **10.** To eat: said chiefly of animals. — **to feed on** (or **upon**) **1.** To consume (something) as food; use as food: said chiefly of animals. **2.** To draw support, encouragement, etc., from: to *feed on* hope. — *n.* **1.** Food; especially, food used by animals, birds, etc.; also, the act of feeding. **2.** The amount of fodder, etc., given at one time. **3.** Material supplied, as to a machine, to be used, worked on, etc. **4.** The supplying of such material. **5.** A mechanical part, as of a sewing machine, that keeps supplying material to be worked on, etc. **6.** *Informal* A meal. — **off one's feed** *Slang* Having little appetite for food

because of some temporary ailment. [OE *fēdan* < *fōda* food]
— **Syn.** (noun) **1.** *Feed, fodder, provender,* and *forage* refer to food for lower animals. *Feed* is the general term here but is frequently restricted to grain. *Fodder* is coarse *feed,* such as cornstalks. *Provender* is dry *feed,* whether grain, hay, or straw. *Forage* is food for cattle and horses, especially when obtained by plundering or scavenging.

feed·back (fēd′bak′) *n.* The return of part of the output of a system into the input for purposes of modification and control of the output, as in electronic amplifiers, automatic machines, certain biological and psychological processes, etc.

feed·bag (fēd′bag′) *n.* A bag of canvas or similar material that holds feed for a horse or other animal and that is suspended below the animal's mouth by straps passing about the muzzle or neck: also called *nosebag.* — **to put on the feedbag** *Slang* To eat.

feed·er (fē′dər) *n.* **1.** One who or that which feeds; as: **a** A person, animal, or plant that takes in food or supplies food. **b** A worker or device that supplies material to be used, as to a machine. **c** A source of maintenance or increase. **2.** A domestic animal being fattened for slaughter. **3.** A tributary branch leading into a main line, as of a railroad. **4.** *Electr.* A conductor or group of conductors connecting different generating or distributing units of a power system.

feel (fēl) *v.* **felt, feel·ing** *v.t.* **1.** To get an impression of by touching; examine or explore with the hands, fingers, etc. **2.** To be aware of through or as if through the sense of touch: to *feel* drops of sweat on one's forehead. **3.** To experience consciously (an emotion, pain, etc.): to *feel* joy. **4.** To be emotionally affected by: to *feel* disgrace deeply; especially, to be emotionally upset or hurt by: to *feel* an insult. **5.** To perceive or be aware of through thought, bodily or emotional reactions, instinct, etc.: to *feel* the need for reform; to *feel* an atmosphere of hostility. **6.** To have as an intellectual conviction or opinion; think; suppose; judge: I *feel* that you should do this. **7.** To have one's whole being respond to through understanding, appreciation, and sensitivity: A good musician *feels* the music he plays. **8.** To be subjected to the effect of; experience the force or impact of: to *feel* the full weight of an attack. **9.** To move along (one's way) by or as if by groping: to *feel* one's way down the stairs. — *v.i.* **10.** To have or be capable of the sensation of touching or of being touched. **11.** To produce a sensory impression of being hard, soft, cold, hot, etc.: The water *feels* warm. **12.** To experience consciously the sensation or condition of being: He *feels* cold; to *feel* joyful. ◆ *He feels bad* is preferred to *He feels badly,* although the latter expression is in such common use that it can no longer be considered substandard. **13.** To produce an indicated overall condition, impression, or reaction; seem to one to be: It *feels* good to be home. **14.** To experience compassion or pity: with *for*: I *feel* for you. **15.** To have intellectual convictions or opinions: to *feel* strongly about an issue. **16.** To search for or explore something by touching; grope: to *feel* around a darkened room. — **to feel like** *Informal* To have a desire or inclination for: to *feel like* swimming. — **to feel (like) oneself** To seem to oneself to be in one's usual or normal state of health, spirits, etc. — **to feel out 1.** To try to learn indirectly and cautiously the viewpoint, opinions, etc., of (a person); sound out. **2.** To explore the nature of (a situation, etc.) in a cautious way. — **to feel up to** To seem to oneself to be capable of or ready for. — *n.* **1.** Perception by touch or contact; also, the sense of touch: Marble is cold to the *feel.* **2.** The quality of something as perceived by touch or contact: This fur has a soft *feel.* **3.** An overall sensation or impression: You get the *feel* of joy in what he writes. **4.** A deep, inward sense or appreciation of the nature, qualities, requirements, etc., of something: a *feel* for good art. [OE *fēlan.* Akin to G *fühlen,* L *palpare* to touch, and *palma* palm of the hand.]

feel·er (fē′lər) *n.* **1.** One who or that which feels. **2.** Any action, hint, proposal, etc., intended to draw out the views or intentions of another. **3.** *Zool.* An organ of touch in an animal or insect, as an antenna or tentacle.

feel·ing (fē′ling) *n.* **1.** The physical faculty or power by which one perceives sensations of pain, pressure, heat and cold, contact, etc.; the sense of touch. **2.** Any particular sensation of this sort: a *feeling* of warmth. **3.** *Psychol.* The affective aspect of mental life as distinguished from thought and from the intellectual aspects. **4.** An emotion: a *feeling* of joy, sadness, etc. **5.** A sensation or awareness of something; an impression: a *feeling* of insecurity. **6.** A capacity to feel deeply: a woman of *feeling.* **7.** *pl.* Sensibilities; sensitivities: His *feelings* are easily hurt. **8.** A generous, sympathetic attitude; compassion. **9.** An impression produced upon a person by an object, place, etc.: the peaceful *feeling* of the country. **10.** An opinion or sentiment: a *feeling* that he is wrong. **11.** A foreboding or presentiment: a *feeling* that all is not well. **12.** The depth or quality of emotion in a work of art or an artistic performance. **13.** A capacity to appreciate or understand: a *feeling* for poetry. — *adj.* **1.** Having sensation; sentient. **2.** Having warm emotions;

sympathetic: a *feeling* heart. **3.** Marked by or indicating emotion: a *feeling* reply. — **feel′ing·ly** *adv.*

fee simple *Law* **1.** An estate of land inheritable by the heirs generally of the holder of the estate without restriction to any particular class of heirs. **2.** Ownership of such an estate. Also **fee simple absolute.**

feet (fēt) Plural of FOOT. — **on one's** (or **its**) **feet 1.** In or into a condition of stability; well-established: to get a business *on its feet.* **2.** In or into a condition of restored health: to get a patient *on his feet.* **3.** Standing or walking: The work keeps him *on his feet* all day.

fee tail *Law* **1.** An estate of land restricted in inheritance to a specified individual and all direct descendants of the individual (**fee tail general**) or to a specified individual and a restricted group of direct descendants (**fee tail special**). **2.** Ownership of such an estate.

feeze¹ (fēz, fāz) See FAZE.

feeze² (fēz, fāz) *Dial. v.t.* **feezed, feez·ing** To subject to blows; chastise. — *n.* **1.** *U.S.* A state of agitation; tizzy. **2.** A heavy impact. [OE *fēsian* to drive]

feign (fān) *v.t.* **1.** To make a false show of; put on a deceptive appearance or sham: to *feign* madness. **2.** To think up (a false story, a lying excuse, etc.) and give out as true; fabricate. **3.** To imitate so as to deceive; counterfeit: to *feign* another's signature. **4.** *Rare* To portray or tell (something imagined) in story, verse, etc.; also, to conjure up in the imagination. — *v.i.* **5.** To make pretense of something. [< OF *feindre* < L *fingere* to shape] — **feign′er** *n.*

feigned (fānd) *adj.* **1.** Purely imaginary; made up; fictitious. **2.** Meant to deceive; sham; false. — **feign·ed·ly** (fā′nid·lē) *adv.*

feint (fānt) *n.* **1.** A deceptive appearance or movement; a ruse or pretense. **2.** An apparent or pretended blow or attack meant to divert attention from an attack to be made elsewhere. — *v.i.* To make a feint. — *adj. Archaic* Feigned; pretended. [< F *feinte*, pp. of *feindre.* See FEIGN.]

feints (fānts) See FAINTS.

Fei·sal I (fī′səl), 1885–1933, king of Syria 1920 and king of Iraq 1921–33: full name **Feisal** (or **Faisal**) **al-Husain.**

Feisal II, 1935–58, king of Iraq 1939–58. Also *Faisal.*

feist (fīst) See FICE.

feis·ty (fīs′tē) *adj.* **feis·ti·er, feis·ti·est** *U.S. Dial.* Frisky; spunky. [< FEIST + -Y¹]

feld·spar (feld′spär, fel′spär) *n.* Any one of a group of crystalline rock-forming materials consisting of silicates of aluminum with potassium, sodium, or calcium: sometimes spelled **felspar.** Also **feld′spath** (-spath). [Partial trans. of G *feldspat* < *feld* field + *spat* spar, by mistaken association with G *fels* rock]

feld·spath·ic (feld-spath′ik, fel-) *adj.* Of, relating to, or containing feldspar. Also **feld·spath′ose** (-ōs).

fe·li·cif·ic (fē′lə-sif′ik) *adj.* Producing happiness. [< L *felix, -icis* happy + -FIC]

fe·lic·i·tate (fə-lis′ə-tāt) *v.t.* **·tat·ed, ·tat·ing 1.** To congratulate. **2.** *Rare* To make happy. — *adj. Obs.* Made happy. [< L *felicitatus*, pp. of *felicitare* < *felix, -icis* happy]

fe·lic·i·ta·tion (fə-lis′ə-tā′shən) *n.* Congratulation.

fe·lic·i·tous (fə-lis′ə-təs) *adj.* **1.** Particularly well chosen; most appropriate; apt: a *felicitous* observation. **2.** Marked by an agreeably pertinent or effective manner or style: a *felicitous* writer. — **fe·lic′i·tous·ly** *adv.* — **fe·lic′i·tous·ness** *n.*

fe·lic·i·ty (fə-lis′ə-tē) *n. pl.* **·ties 1.** Happiness, especially when very great; bliss. **2.** An instance of happiness or bliss. **3.** A cause or source of happiness or bliss. **4.** An agreeably pertinent or effective manner or style: *felicity* of expression. **5.** An instance of this manner or style, as a pleasantly appropriate remark or observation. — **Syn.** See HAPPINESS. [< OF *felicite* < L *felicitas, -tatis* < *felix, -icis* happy]

fe·line (fē′līn) *adj.* **1.** Of or relating to an animal of the cat family (*Felidae*), that includes both the domestic cat and such wild animals as lions, tigers, and leopards. **2.** Resembling a cat, as in stealthiness. — *n.* An animal of the cat family: also **fe·lid** (fē′lid). [< L *felinus* < *felis* cat] — **fe′line·ly** *adv.* — **fe′line·ness, fe·lin·i·ty** (fə-lin′ə-tē) *n.*

fell¹ (fel) Past tense of FALL.

fell² (fel) *v.t.* **felled, fell·ing 1.** To strike and cause to fall down; knock down; prostrate: to *fell* a boxing opponent. **2.** To cut down (timber). **3.** In sewing, to finish (a seam) with a flat, smooth strip made by turning edges, folding them under, and stitching flat. — *n.* **1.** The timber cut down during one season. **2.** In sewing, a felled seam. [OE *fellan*, causative of *feallan* to fall] — **fell′a·ble** *adj.*

fell³ (fel) *adj.* **1.** Cruel; vicious; inhuman. **2.** *Archaic* Lethal; deadly: a *fell* potion. [< OF *fel* cruel, orig. nominative of *felon.* See FELON¹.] — **fell′ness** *n.*

fell⁴ (fel) *n.* **1.** The skin of an animal, especially as covered with its natural hair, wool, etc.; a hide or pelt; also, the skin of a human being. **2.** A growth of hair, especially when bushy or tangled, covering the head or body. [OE, hide]

fell⁵ (fel) *n. Brit.* **1.** A tract of wasteland; moor. **2.** A barren hill or upland level. [ME *fel* < ON *fjall*]

fel·lah (fel′ə) *n. pl.* **fel·lahs** or *Arabic* **fel·la·hin, fel·la·heen** (fel′ə-hēn′) In Arabic-speaking countries, a peasant or laborer. [< Arabic *fellāh*]

fell·er (fel′ər) *n.* **1.** One who or that which fells. **2.** A sewing-machine attachment for the felling of seams.

fell·mon·ger (fel′mung′gər, -mong′-) *n.* A dealer in the skins or furs of animals.

fel·loe (fel′ō) See FELLY¹.

fel·low (fel′ō) *n.* **1.** A man or boy: often in informal address. **2.** *U.S. Informal* The sweetheart of a woman or girl; especially, a suitor. **3.** A person in general; anybody; one: A *fellow* can only do his best. **4.** A comrade or companion. **5.** A person viewed as being of little importance or worth. **6.** A partner or accomplice: *fellows* in crime. **7.** An individual belonging to the same kind, class, or group as oneself, as one who holds the same position or dignity. **8.** Any human being: Man should treat his *fellows* with respect. **9.** Either one of a pair; counterpart; mate: to lose a shoe and its *fellow.* **10.** A member of one of several learned societies. **11.** A graduate student of a university or college who, in recognition of merit, is granted financial assistance to pursue further study **12.** *Brit.* A trustee of a university or college. Abbr. (for defs. 10, 11, 12) F. — *v.t. Rare* **1.** To put on a par with another. **2.** To produce the equal to; match. — *adj.* Being of the same kind, origin, condition, locality, organization, etc.; joined through some common occupation, interests, objectives, etc.: *fellow* citizens; *fellow* creatures. [OE *fēolaga* business partner < *fēoh* property, money + *lag-*, stem of *lecgan* to lay, orig. those who put money together]

fellow feeling A sentiment closely paralleling or harmonizing with that of another; sympathetic understanding.

fellow servant *Law* One of a group of servants hired by the same master.

fellow servant rule The common-law doctrine that an employer cannot be held responsible for any injury to an employee caused by the carelessness of another worker.

fel·low·ship (fel′ō-ship) *n.* **1.** The state of being joined to or associated with another by reason of being one of the same kind, class, or group. **2.** The condition or fact of having common interests, ideals, experiences, etc. **3.** Close association with or adoption into a body of individuals having common interests, origins, ideals, experiences, beliefs, etc.; comradeship; also, the body of individuals joined together through such interests, beliefs, etc.; brotherhood. **4.** The status of being a fellow at a university or college; also, the financial grant made to a fellow. — *v.* **·shiped** or **·shipped, ·ship·ing** or **·ship·ping** *Rare v.t.* **1.** To grant fellowship to, especially in a church group. — *v.i.* **2.** To join in fellowship with others, especially in a church group.

fellow traveler One who favors the ideology or program of a particular group without being a member; especially, a sympathizer with the ideology of the Communist Party.

fel·ly¹ (fel′ē) *n. pl.* **·lies** A segment of the rim of a wooden wheel, in which the spokes are inserted; also, the entire rim: also spelled **felloe.** [OE *felg*]

fel·ly² (fel′ē) *adv.* Harshly; fiercely. [See FELL³.]

fe·lo de se (fē′lō də sē, fel′ō) *pl.* **fe·lo·nes de se** (fel′ō-nēz) or **fe·los de se** *Law* **1.** One who commits suicide. **2.** The act of suicide. [< Med.L *felo* felon + *de* of + *se* self]

fel·on¹ (fel′ən) *n.* **1.** *Law* One who has committed a felony. **2.** *Rare* A wicked or villainous individual. — *adj. Poetic* Wicked, villainous, or cruel. [< OF *felon* base; ult. origin uncertain]

fel·on² (fel′ən) *n. Pathol.* A painful inflammation of a finger or toe occurring typically in the terminal joint or at the cuticle; whitlow. [? < FELON¹]

fe·lo·ni·ous (fə-lō′nē-əs) *adj.* **1.** *Law* **a** Of, relating to, or involving a felony: *felonious* intent. **b** Constituting, resembling, or having the nature of a felony: *felonious* assault. **2.** *Poetic* Wicked, villainous, or cruel. — **Syn.** See CRIMINAL. — **fe·lo′ni·ous·ly** *adv.* — **fe·lo′ni·ous·ness** *n.*

fel·on·ry (fel′ən·rē) *n.* Felons collectively.

fel·o·ny (fel′ə-nē) *n. pl.* **·nies** *Law* **1.** One of several grave crimes, as murder, rape, arson, or burglary, for which a punishment greater than that for a misdemeanor is provided by statute, the punishment in the United States generally ranging from a minimum of more than one year's imprisonment to a maximum of death by execution. **2.** Formerly, one of several crimes punishable by the forfeiture of lands and goods and by the infliction of some additional grave penalty, usually death; also, in early common law, any crime subject to prosecution by an appeal.

felony murder A murder committed during the perpetration of some other felony.

fel·site (fel′sīt) *n.* A finely crystalline mixture of quartz and feldspar, often containing particles of glass; a quartz porphyry. Also **fel′stone** (-stōn). [< G *fels* rock. Cf. FELDSPAR.] — **fel·sit·ic** (fel-sit′ik) *adj.*

fel·spar (fel′spär) See FELDSPAR.

felt¹ (felt) Past tense and past participle of FEEL.

felt² (felt) *n.* **1.** An unwoven fabric made by matting together fibers of wool, fur, or hair through pressure and the use of heat, chemicals, etc.; also, any fabric or material resembling this. **2.** Something made of felt, as a hat. **3.** In papermaking, a broad piece of material, usually a textile fabric, on which the freshly made sheet of paper is carried as it passes between the rollers of the machine. — *adj.* Relating to, made of, or resembling felt. **—v.t. 1.** To make into felt. **2.** To overlay with felt. **—v.i. 3.** To become matted together like felt. [OE]

felt·ing (fel′ting) *n.* **1.** The process of making felt; also, the materials used in making felt. **2.** A material made of or covered with felt.

fe·luc·ca (fə·luk′ə, fe-) *n.* A small, swift vessel propelled by lateen sails and by oars. [< Ital. < Arabic *fulk* ship]

FELUCCA

fem. Feminine; female.

fe·male (fē′māl) *adj.* **1.** Of or pertaining to the sex that brings forth young or produces ova. **2.** Typical of or suitable to this sex; feminine. **3.** Made up of women and girls: the *female* portion of the population. **4.** *Bot.* Designating a plant that has a pistil but no stamen and that is capable of being fertilized and of producing fruit; pistillate. **5.** *Mech.* Denoting or having a bore or slot designed to receive a correlated inserted part, called *male*, as some electric plugs. **6.** *Obs.* Effeminate. **— Syn.** See FEMININE. **—** *n.* **1.** A human being of the female sex; a woman or girl. **2.** A female animal or plant. Abbr. *fem.* [< OF *femelle* < L *femella*, dim. of *femina* woman. See FECUND.]

female rhyme Feminine rhyme (which see).

female suffrage Woman suffrage (which see).

feme (fem) *n.* **1.** *Law* A wife. **2.** *Obs.* A woman. [< OF]

feme cov·ert (kuv′ərt) *Law* A married woman. [< OF]

feme sole (sōl) *Law* A woman who has never married or who is widowed or divorced; a single woman. [< OF]

feme-sole trader (fem′sōl′) *Law* A married business woman independent of her husband in business and regarded at law as a single woman: sometimes called *sole trader.* Also **feme-sole merchant.**

fem·i·na·cy (fem′ə·nə·sē) *n. pl.* **·cies** *Rare* Femininity. [< L *femina* woman]

fem·i·nal·i·ty (fem′ə·nal′ə·tē) *n. pl.* **·ties** *Rare* Femininity. Also **fem′i·ne′i·ty** (-nē′ə·tē). [< OF *feminal* < L *femina* woman]

fem·i·nie (fem′ə·nē) *n. Archaic* Women collectively. [< OF]

fem·i·nine (fem′ə·nin) *adj.* **1.** Of or pertaining to the female sex; female. **2.** Of or pertaining to women and girls; typical of or appropriate to women and girls: *feminine* gentleness. **3.** Lacking manly qualities; effeminate. **4.** *Gram.* Applicable to females only or to persons or things classified, as in declension, as female. **—** *n. Gram.* **1.** The feminine gender. **2.** A word or form belonging to the feminine gender. Abbr. *f., F., fem.* [< L *femininus* < *femina* woman] **— fem′i·nine·ly** *adv.* **— fem′i·nine·ness** *n.*

— Syn. *Feminine, female, effeminate, womanly,* and *womanish* are used to describe women or their qualities. *Feminine* characterizes the qualities that are regarded as belonging particularly to women; *female* denotes sex strictly, without further implications: *feminine* modesty, a *female* voice. *Effeminate* is applied only to men, and describes attributes that are regarded as unseemly in a man, though appropriate to a woman: an *effeminate* walk. *Womanly* and *womanish* are both applied to women; *womanly* refers to things that are admirable and *womanish* to those that are not: *womanly* pity, *womanish* tears. **— Ant.** See synonyms for MASCULINE.

feminine ending 1. The termination of a line of verse with an additional and unaccented final syllable. **2.** *Gram.* A termination or final syllable indicating feminine gender.

feminine gender See under GENDER.

feminine rhyme 1. Rhyme in which the primary stress falls upon the next to the last syllable, as in *clever, never* and *concluding, protruding.* **2.** Loosely, any polysyllabic rhyme. Also called *female rhyme.*

fem·i·nin·i·ty (fem′ə·nin′ə·tē) *n. pl.* **·ties 1.** The quality or state of being feminine. **2.** A feminine trait. **3.** Women collectively; womankind.

fem·i·nism (fem′ə·niz′əm) *n.* **1.** A doctrine advocating the granting of the same social, political, and economic rights to women as the ones granted to men; also, a movement designed to support this doctrine and gain such rights. **2.** *Med.* The existence of female characteristics in the male.

fem·i·nist (fem′ə·nist) *n.* One who advocates or seeks to further feminism. **—** *adj.* Of or relating to feminism or feminists: also **fem′i·nis′tic.**

fem·i·nize (fem′ə·nīz) *v.t. & v.i.* **·nized, ·niz·ing** To make or become feminine or effeminate. **— fem′i·ni·za′tion** *n.*

femme (fàm) *n. French* Woman; wife.

femme de cham·bre (də shäṉ′br′) *French* **1.** A chambermaid. **2.** A personal maid for a woman.

femme fa·tale (fà·tàl′) *French* A dangerously seductive woman.

fem·o·ral (fem′ər·əl) *adj. Anat.* Of or pertaining to the femur or the thigh.

femto- *combining form* One quadrillionth (10⁻¹⁵) of a specified quantity or dimension: *femtovolt.*

fe·mur (fē′mər) *n. pl.* **fe·murs** or **fem·o·ra** (fem′ər·ə) *Anat.*

1. The long bone extending from the pelvis to the knee. Also called *thighbone.* For illustrations see PATELLA, PELVIS. **2.** *Entomol.* The third, strongest, and most prominent segment of an insect's leg. [< L, thigh]

fen (fen) *n.* A marsh; bog. **— the Fens** A low, flat district in Cambridgeshire, Norfolk, Huntingdonshire, and Lincolnshire, England. [OE *fenn*]

fence (fens) *n.* **1.** A structure of rails, stakes, strung wire, etc., erected as an enclosure, barrier, or boundary, as along the limits of a yard or field. **2.** Skillful use of a sword, foil, etc.; fencing. **3.** Skill at making quick, effective remarks or retorts, as in a discussion or debate. **4.** A dealer in stolen goods; also, a place where stolen goods are bought and sold. **5.** *Mech.* A guard, guide, or gauge to direct or limit the movement of a tool, machine, etc. **— on the fence** Unwilling or unable to commit oneself one way or the other. **—** *v.* **fenced, fenc·ing** *v.t.* **1.** To enclose with or as with a fence. **2.** To cause to be separated by or as by a fence. **3.** *Archaic* To ward off; keep away. **—** *v.i.* **4.** To practice the art of fencing. **5.** To avoid giving direct answers. **6.** To deal in stolen goods. [Aphetic var. of DEFENCE]

fence·less (fens′lis) *adj.* **1.** Having no fence; unenclosed. **2.** *Archaic* Having no defense. **— fence′less·ness** *n.*

fenc·er (fen′sər) *n.* **1.** One who fences, as with a foil or sword. **2.** One who builds or repairs fences.

fenc·i·ble (fen′sə·bəl) *adj. Scot.* Capable of defense. **—** *n. Archaic* A soldier enlisted for home service only.

fenc·ing (fen′sing) *n.* **1.** The art or practice of using a foil, sword, or similar weapon, in attack and defense. **2.** The art or practice of making quick, effective remarks or retorts, as in a debate, especially so as to avoid committing oneself definitely or to avoid giving direct answers. **3.** Material used in making or repairing fences; also, fences collectively.

fend (fend) *v.t.* **1.** To ward off; parry: usually with off. **2.** *Archaic* To defend. **—** *v.i.* **3.** To offer resistance; parry. **4.** *Informal* To provide; shift: with *for*: to *fend* for oneself. [Aphetic var. of DEFEND]

fend·er (fen′dər) *n.* **1.** One who or that which fends or wards off. **2.** *U.S.* A part projecting over each wheel of a car or other vehicle, as a plate of sheet metal, designed to keep water, mud, dirt, etc., from being thrown upwards: also called *mudguard.* **3.** A metal guard set before an open fire to keep the coals from slipping out and to protect from flying sparks. **4.** A part projecting from the front of a locomotive or streetcar, designed to push obstructions from the tracks. **5.** *Naut.* A padding, as of rope, used along a ship's side to cushion the impact of the ship against docks, etc.

Fé·ne·lon (fān·lôṉ′), **François de Salignac de la Mothe,** 1651–1715, French ecclesiastic and writer.

fen·es·tel·la (fen′is·tel′ə) *n. pl.* **·tel·lae** (-tel′ē) *Archit.* **1.** A small window; also, any opening suggestive of a small window. **2.** A niche in the wall of some churches, usually to the right of the altar, in which the piscina and often the credence are set. [< L, dim. of *fenestra* window]

fe·nes·tra (fə·nes′trə) *n. pl.* **·trae** (-trē) **1.** A small, natural aperture or perforation in some part of the body; especially, an oval opening leading from the tympanic cavity to the inner ear. **2.** A transparent, glassy spot, as in the wings of some insects. [< L] **— fe·nes′tral** *adj.*

fe·nes·trate (fə·nes′trit, -trāt) *adj.* **1.** *Archit.* Having windows or similar openings. **2.** Having fenestrae. Also **fe·nes′-trat·ed.** [< L *fenestratus,* pp. of *fenestrare* to furnish with windows < *fenestra* window]

fen·es·tra·tion (fen′is·trā′shən) *n.* **1.** *Archit.* The way in which the windows of a building are arranged. **2.** *Surg.* The operation of making an artificial fenestra.

Feng·tien (fung′tyen′) A former name for SHENYANG.

Fe·ni·an (fē′nē·ən, fēn′yən) *n.* **1.** A member of an organization founded in New York about 1857 to seek independence for Ireland. **2.** One sympathizing with the aims of the Fenians. **3.** One of the Fianna. **—** *adj.* Of, belonging to, or characteristic of the Fenians or the Fianna. [< OIrish *fene* Irishman, later confused with Irish *Fiann*(a) legendary band of warriors] **— Fe′ni·an·ism** *n.*

Fenian cycle A body of Old Irish tales dealing with the exploits of the Fianna.

fen·nec (fen′ek) *n.* A small, fawn-colored African fox (*Vulpes zenda*) having very large, pointed ears. [< Arabic *fanak*]

fen·nel (fen′əl) *n.* **1.** A tall, umbelliferous herb (*Foeniculum vulgare*) of the parsley family that produces aromatic seeds used in cookery and pharmacy. **2.** The seeds of this plant. **— giant fennel** An Old World herb (*Ferula communis*) of the parsley family, sometimes attaining a height of 15 feet. [OE *fenugl, fenol* < L *faeniculum* fennel, dim. of *faenum* hay, ult. < root *fe* to suckle, produce. See FECUND.]

fen·nel·flow·er (fen′əl·flou′ər) *n.* **1.** An ornamental annual herb (genus *Nigella*) of the crowfoot family, with brightly colored flowers and with seeds that are often used as a seasoning. **2.** A flower of this plant; also, its seeds.

fen·ny (fen′ē) *adj.* **1.** Relating to, typical of, or found in marshes or bogs. **2.** Having marshes or bogs: *fenny* country.

Fen·rir (fen′rir) In Norse mythology, a monstrous wolf fated to slay Odin and kept chained by the gods. Also **Fen′·ris** (-ris), **Fen′ris·wolf′** (-wŏŏlf′).

fen·u·greek (fen′yŏŏ-grēk) n. 1. An Old World herb (*Trigonella foenum-graecum*) of the pea family. 2. Its mucilaginous seeds, used in medicine and in making curry. [OE *fenograecum* < L *faenum Graecum* Greek hay]

feod (fyōōd) See FEUD².

feo·da·ry (fyōō′dər-ē) See FEUDARY.

feoff (v. fef, fēf; n. fēf) Law v.t. **feoffed, feoff·ing** To give or grant a fief to; enfeoff. — n. A fief. [< AF *feoffer*, OF *fieffer* < *fief*. See FIEF.]

feoff·ee (fef-ē′, fēf-ē′) n. Law One to whom a feoffment is made.

feof·fer (fef′ər, fēf′-) n. One who grants a feoffment. Also **feof′for.**

feoff·ment (fef′mənt, fēf′-) n. A grant of lands as a fief.

-fer combining form One who or that which bears: *conifer*. [< L < *ferre* to bear]

Fer. Fermanagh.

fe·ra·cious (fə-rā′shəs) adj. Fruitful; fertile. [< L *ferax, feracis* < *ferre* to bear] — **fe·rac·i·ty** (fə-ras′ə-tē) n.

fe·ral¹ (fir′əl) adj. 1. Not tame nor domesticated; wild; also, having become wild again after taming or domestication. 2. Of, relating to, or typical of a wild beast; savage. [< LL *feralis* < L *fera* wild beast]

fe·ral² (fir′əl) adj. Poetic 1. Of, relating to, or suggestive of the dead; sepulchral. 2. Causing death; fatal. [< L *feralis* relating to the dead or to funeral rites]

Fer·ber (fûr′bər), **Edna,** 1887–1968, U.S. writer.

fer-de-lance (fâr′də-läns′) n. A large, venomous snake (*Bothrops atrox*) of tropical South America and Martinique, related to the copperhead and rattlesnake. [< F, iron (tip) of a lance]

Fer·di·nand I (fûr′di·nand), died 1065, king of Castile and León: called **the Great.**

Ferdinand I, 1503–64, king of Bohemia and Hungary 1526–1564; emperor of the Holy Roman Empire 1558–64.

Ferdinand II, 1578–1637, king of Bohemia and Hungary; emperor of the Holy Roman Empire 1619–37; opposed Protestants in the Thirty Years' War.

Ferdinand III, 1608–57, king of Bohemia and Hungary; emperor of the Holy Roman Empire 1637–57; ended the Thirty Years' War at Westphalia in 1648; son of Ferdinand II.

Ferdinand V, 1452–1516, king of Spain; husband of Isabella I; united Aragon, Castile, Granada, and Navarre; established the Inquisition; promoted the expeditions of Columbus and Vespucci: called **the Catholic.**

fere (fir) n. Archaic 1. A companion. 2. A spouse. [OE *gefēra* < *faran* to travel. Related to FARE.]

fer·e·to·ry (fer′ə·tôr′ē, -tō′rē) n. pl. ·ries 1. A reliquary. 2. A section of a church used for keeping portable or fixed reliquaries. [Alter. of earlier *fertre* < OF *fiertre* < L *feretrum* < Gk. *pheretron* litter < *pherein* to carry]

Fer·ga·na (fer·gä′nə) See FIERGANA.

fe·ri·al (fir′ē-əl) adj. 1. Of or pertaining to a holiday. 2. Eccl. Of or pertaining to a weekday not designated as a church feast day. [< OF < LL *ferialis* < *feria* weekday, sing. of L *feriae* holidays, festivals]

fe·rine (fir′īn, -in) adj. Feral. [< L *ferinus* < *fera* wild beast]

Fe·rin·gi (fə·ring′gē) n. In India, a person of European or Eurasian descent; especially, a person of Portuguese ancestry: usually used disparagingly. Also **Fe·rin′ghee.** [< Persian *farangi* < Arabic *faranji* a Frank, European]

Fe·rish·tah (fi·rish·tä′), **Mohammed Kasim,** 1556?–1626?, Persian historian.

fer·i·ty (fer′ə-tē) n. 1. The state of being untamed or undomesticated; wildness. 2. Ferocity; also, barbarous cruelty. [< L *feritas, -tatis* < *ferus* wild, fierce]

Ferm. Fermanagh.

Fer·man·agh (fər·man′ə) A county in SW Northern Ireland; 657 sq. mi.; pop. 49,900 (est. 1969); county seat, Enniskillen.

fer·ma·ta (fer·mä′tä) n. Music A hold. [< Ital.]

Fer·ma·tian (fər·mä′shən) adj. Of or pertaining to **Pierre de Fer·mat** (fer·má′), 1601–65, French mathematician, or to the method of mathematical induction used by him.

fer·ment (n. fûr′mənt; v. fər·ment′) n. 1. Any substance or agent producing fermentation, as enzymes, yeast, certain bacteria, etc. 2. Fermentation. 3. Excitement or agitation. — v.t. 1. To produce fermentation in. 2. To excite with emotion or passion; agitate. — v.i. 3. To undergo fermentation; work. 4. To be agitated, as with emotion; seethe. [< F < L *fermentum* < *fervere* to boil] — **fer·ment′a·ble** adj. — **fer·ment′a·bil′i·ty** n.

fer·men·ta·tion (fûr′mən·tā′shən) n. 1. Chem. The gradual decomposition of organic compounds induced by the action of various ferments; specifically, the conversion of glu-

cose into ethyl alcohol through the action of zymase. 2. Commotion, agitation, or excitement.

fer·ment·a·tive (fər·men′tə·tiv) adj. Causing, capable of causing, or caused by fermentation; fermenting.

fer·mi (fer′mē, fûr′-) n. Physics A unit for the measurement of distances of the order of the radii of atomic nuclei, equal to 10⁻¹³ centimeter. [after E. *Fermi*]

Fer·mi (fer′mē), **Enrico,** 1901–54, Italian nuclear physicist active in the United States.

fer·mi·um (fer′mē-əm, fûr′-) n. A radioactive element (symbol Fm), artificially produced by the bombardment of einsteinium with alpha particles. See ELEMENT. [after E. *Fermi*]

fern (fûrn) n. Any of a widely distributed class (*Filicineae*) of plants that bear no flowers or seeds, having roots, stems, and large, feathery fronds, and reproducing by means of asexual spores growing in sacs on the underside or edges of the fronds. [OE *fearn*, ult. < root meaning feather. Cf. Gk. *pteron* feather, wing.] — **fern′y** adj.

FERNS

A *Polypodium*: rootstock and fronds. B *Asplenium tricho-manes*: fronds. C *Osmunda cinnamomea*: fertile fronds.

Fer·nán·dez (fer·nän′dāth), **Juan,** 1536?–1602?, Spanish seafarer.

Fer·nan·do de No·ro·nha (fer·nän′dŏŏ də nō·rō′nyə) An island in the South Atlantic, with adjacent islets, a Federal Territory of Brazil; 10.5 sq. mi.; a penal colony.

Fer·nan·do Po (fer·nän′dŏ pō′) An island about 20 mi. off W. Africa, in the Gulf of Guinea, forming with another island (Annóbon) a province of Equatorial Guinea; 779 sq. mi.; pop. 78,000 (est. 1970). **Fer·nan′do Po·o** (pō′ō).

Fern·dale (fûrn′dāl) A city in SE Michigan, near Detroit; pop. 30,850.

fern·er·y (fûr′nər·ē) n. pl. ·er·ies 1. A place in which ferns are grown. 2. A standing growth or bed of ferns.

fern seed Fern spores, once popularly believed capable of making invisible any person carrying them.

fe·ro·cious (fə·rō′shəs) adj. 1. Extremely savage, fierce, bloodthirsty, or cruel. 2. Informal Very intense: *ferocious heat.* [< L *ferox, ferocis* fierce + -OUS] — **fe·ro′cious·ly** adv. — **fe·ro′cious·ness** n.

fe·roc·i·ty (fə·ros′ə·tē) n. pl. ·ties The state or quality of being ferocious; fierceness or bloodthirstiness. [< F *férocité* < L *ferocitas* < *ferox* fierce]

-ferous combining form Bearing or producing: *coniferous.* [< -FER + -OUS]

Fer·ra·ra (fə·rä′rə, Ital. fer·rä′rä) A commune in north central Italy, in the Po delta; pop. 151,145 (1961).

fer·rate (fer′āt) n. Chem. A salt of ferric acid. [< L *ferrum* iron + -ATE³]

fer·rel (fer′əl) See FERRULE.

Fer·re·ro (fer·rā′rō), **Guglielmo,** 1871–1942, Italian historian.

fer·ret¹ (fer′it) n. 1. A small, red-eyed polecat of Europe (genus *Mustela*), often domesticated and used in hunting rodents and other vermin. 2. A black-footed weasel of the western United States (*M. nigripes*), that preys on prairie dogs. — v.t. 1. To search out by careful investigation: with *out*: to *ferret* out the facts. 2. To drive out of hiding or hunt with a ferret. — v.i. 3. To search. 4. To hunt by means of ferrets. [< OF *fuiret*, dim. of *fuiron* < LL *furo* robber < L *fur* thief] — **fer′ret·er** n. — **fer′ret·y** adj.

fer·ret² (fer′it) n. A narrow ribbon or tape used for binding fabrics, etc. Also **fer′ret·ing.** [< Ital. *fioretto*, dim. of *fiore* a flower < L *flos, floris*]

ferret badger A stout-bodied carnivore (genus *Helictis*) of SE Asia.

ferri- combining form Chem. Containing iron in the ferric condition: *ferricyanide.* [Var. of FERRO-]

fer·ri·age (fer′ē-ij) n. 1. The act of ferrying; conveyance by ferry. 2. The toll charged for ferrying.

fer·ric (fer′ik) adj. Chem. 1. Pertaining to iron. 2. Pertaining to or designating compounds of iron in its higher valence. [< L *ferrum* iron + -IC]

ferric acetate Chem. A reddish brown powder, FeO₅H₇C₄, used as a mordant and in certain drug preparations.

ferric acid Chem. An inorganic acid, H₂FeO₄, known only by its salts.

ferric oxide A red compound of iron and oxygen, Fe₂O₃, found naturally as hematite and also prepared chemically.

fer·ri·cy·an·ic (fer′ə-sī·an′ik) adj. Chem. Of or pertaining to a compound of iron in its higher valence and cyanogen: *ferricyanic acid,* H₃Fe(CN)₆. [< FERRI- + CYANIC]

fer·ri·cy·a·nide (fer′ə-sī′ə-nīd, -nid) n. Chem. A salt containing the trivalent negative ion radical Fe(CN)₆, as **potassium ferricyanide,** K₃Fe(CN)₆. [< FERRI- + CYANIDE]

fer·rif·er·ous (fə·rif′ər-əs) adj. Yielding iron, as rocks. [< FERRI- + -FEROUS]

FERRET
(Body about 14 inches long; tail 5 inches)

Fer·ris wheel (fer′is) *U.S.* A giant, vertical, power-driven wheel that revolves on a stationary axle and has hanging seats in which passengers ride for amusement. Also **ferris wheel.** [after G. W. G. *Ferris*, 1859–96, U.S. engineer]

fer·rite (fer′īt) *n.* **1.** *Geol.* A substance of uncertain composition that is found in igneous rocks and apparently contains iron. **2.** *Chem.* One of several compounds, often magnetic, containing ferric oxide. **3.** *Metall.* The pure metallic constituent in iron and steel. [< L *ferrum* iron + -ITE]

ferro- *combining form* **1.** Derived from, containing, or alloyed with iron: *ferroconcrete.* **2.** *Chem.* Containing iron in the ferrous condition: *ferrocyanide.* [< L *ferrum* iron]

fer·ro·al·loy (fer′ō·al′oi, -ə·loi′) *n. Metall.* An alloy of iron with certain other metals, used in the manufacture of steel.

fer·ro·chrome (fer′ō·krōm′) *n. Metall.* An alloy of iron and chromium, used in the production of especially hard steel. Also **fer′ro·chro′mi·um.**

fer·ro·con·crete (fer′ō·kon′krēt, -kon·krēt′) *n.* Reinforced concrete (which see).

fer·ro·cy·an·ic (fer′ō·sī·an′ik) *adj. Chem.* Designating a compound obtained by the treatment of ferrocyanide with acid: *ferrocyanic acid,* $H_4Fe(CN)_6$.

fer·ro·cy·a·nide (fer′ō·sī′ə·nīd, -nid) *n. Chem.* A compound containing the tetravalent radical $Fe(CN)_6$: potassium *ferrocyanide,* $K_4Fe(CN)_6$.

fer·ro·e·lec·tric (fer′ō·i·lek′trik) *adj.* Denoting a class of crystalline substances exhibiting a spontaneous electric polarization subject to reversal in an electric field. — *n.* Any member of this class.

Fer·rol (fer·rōl′), **El** See EL FERROL DEL CAUDILLO.

fer·ro·mag·ne·sian (fer′ō·mag·nē′shən) *adj. Geol.* Relating to rocks rich in iron and magnesium, as pyroxene.

fer·ro·mag·net·ic (fer′ō·mag·net′ik) *adj. Physics* Acting like iron in a magnetic field; highly magnetic. — **fer′ro·mag′ne·tism** *n.*

fer·ro·man·ga·nese (fer′ō·mang′gə·nēs, -nēz) *n.* An alloy of iron rich in manganese, used in making tough steel.

fer·ro·sil·i·con (fer′ō·sil′ə·kən, -kon) *n.* An alloy of iron and silicon added to molten iron.

fer·ro·type (fer′ō·tīp′) *n.* A tintype (which see).

fer·rous (fer′əs) *adj. Chem.* Of or pertaining to iron, especially bivalent iron, where its combining value is lowest: *ferrous* chloride, $FeCl_2$. [< L *ferrum* iron + -OUS]

fer·ru·gi·nous (fə·rōō′jə·nəs) *adj.* **1.** Of or like iron. **2.** Rust-colored. [< L *ferruginus* < *ferrugo* rust < *ferrum* iron]

fer·rule (fer′əl, -ōōl) *n.* **1.** A metal ring or cap used on or near the end of a shaft, as of a cane or a tool handle, to protect the end or reinforce the shaft. **2.** *Mech.* A bushing. — *v.t.* **·ruled, ·rul·ing** To equip with a ferrule. Also spelled *ferrel, ferule.* [< Earlier *verrel* < OF *virelle* < L *viriola*, dim. of *viriae* bracelets; infl. in form by L *ferrum* iron]

fer·rum (fer′əm) *n.* Iron [< L]

fer·ry (fer′ē) *n. pl.* **·ries 1.** A boat or other craft used in conveying people, cars, or merchandise across a river or other narrow extent of water; also, the point of embarkation on either shore. **2.** Conveyance across a narrow extent of water by or as by a boat or other craft; also, the legal right entitling an individual or group to engage in such conveyance for a fee. **3.** Delivery of a boat or other craft to a user under its own motive power. — *v.* **·ried, ·ry·ing** *v.t.* **1.** To convey across a river, etc., by a boat or other craft. **2.** To cross (a river, etc.) in a boat or other craft. **3.** To deliver by ferry (def. 3). — *v.i.* **4.** To cross a river, etc., by or as by a ferry. [OE *ferian* to carry, convey. Akin to FARE.]

fer·ry·boat (fer′ē·bōt′) *n.* A boat used as a ferry.

fer·ry·man (fer′ē·mən) *n. pl.* **·men** (-mən) One who owns or operates a ferry.

fer·tile (fûr′təl, *esp. Brit.* -tīl) *adj.* **1.** Yielding or capable of producing abundant crops or vegetation: *fertile* land. **2.** Reproducing or able to reproduce. **3.** Producing many offspring; prolific. **4.** Causing or contributing to productiveness: a *fertile* rain. **5.** Inventive or productive: a *fertile* talent. **6.** *Bot.* **a** Bearing or capable of producing fruit. **b** Capable of fertilizing or of being fertilized, as perfect anthers and pistils. **c** Productive of spore-bearing organs: said of ferns, etc. **7.** *Biol.* Capable of growth or development; productive: said of seeds or eggs. [< OF *fertil* < L *fertilis* < *ferre* to bear] — **fer′tile·ly** *adv.* — **fer′tile·ness** *n.*

Fertile Crescent 1. An arc-shaped area in the Near and Middle East in which agriculture was supposedly first practiced. **2.** An arc-shaped agricultural region extending from the Levant to modern Iraq.

fer·til·i·ty (fər·til′ə·tē) *n.* **1.** The state or quality of being fertile; productiveness. **2.** Capacity to reproduce; fruitfulness.

fer·til·i·za·tion (fûr′tə·lə·zā′shən) *n.* **1.** The act of making fertile, or the condition or fact of being made fertile. **2.** *Biol.* The fusion of a sperm cell and an egg; impregnation. **3.** *Bot.* The transfer of pollen from an anther to a stigma.

fer·til·ize (fûr′tə·līz) *v.t.* **·ized, ·iz·ing 1.** To make fertile; cause to be productive or fruitful. **2.** To cause (a female re-

productive cell or a female) to begin development of a new individual through union with or introduction of a male reproductive cell. **3.** To spread manure, nitrates, or other enriching material on (land). — **fer′til·iz′a·ble** *adj.*

fer·til·iz·er (fûr′təl·ī′zər) *n.* **1.** One who or that which fertilizes. **2.** An enriching material, as manure or nitrates, used on land to increase its productivity.

fer·u·la (fer′yōō·lə, fer′ōō-) *n. pl.* **·lae** (-lē) or **·las 1.** Any of a large genus (*Ferula*) of chiefly Mediterranean herbs of the parsley family, with dissected leaves and umbels of yellow flowers, several species of which yield medicinal products. **2.** A ferule; rod. **3.** A scepter, especially that of the Byzantine emperors. [< L, giant fennel, whip, rod]

fer·u·la·ceous (fer′yōō·lā′shəs, fer′ōō-) *adj.* Pertaining to or having a stalk like a reed or similar plant.

fer·ule[1] (fer′əl, -ōōl) *n.* **1.** A flat stick or ruler sometimes used for punishing children. **2.** Punishment; discipline. — *v.t.* **·uled, ·ul·ing** To punish with a ferule. [< L *ferula.* See FERULA.]

fer·ule[2] (fer′əl, -ōōl) *n., v.t.* **·uled, ·ul·ing** Ferrule.

fer·ven·cy (fûr′vən·sē) *n.* The state or quality of being fervent; great warmth or intensity, as of emotion.

fer·vent (fûr′vənt) *adj.* **1.** Moved by or showing great warmth or intensity, as of emotion or enthusiasm; ardent. **2.** *Poetic* Very hot; burning. [< L *fervens, -entis*, ppr. of *fervere* to boil] — **fer′vent·ly** *adv.* — **fer′vent·ness** *n.*

fer·vid (fûr′vid) *adj.* **1.** Fervent, especially to an extreme degree; most impassioned. **2.** *Poetic* Very hot; burning. [< L *fervidus* burning, violent < *fervere* to boil] — **fer′vid·ly** *adv.* — **fer′vid·ness** *n.*

Fer·vi·dor (fûr′vi·dôr, *Fr.* fer·vē·dôr′) Thermidor. See (Republican) CALENDAR.

fer·vor (fûr′vər) *n.* **1.** Great warmth or intensity, as of emotion; fervency; ardor. **2.** Heat; warmth. Also *Brit.* **fer′vour.** [< OF < L, violent heat, ardor < *fervere* to boil]

Fès (fes) See FEZ.

Fes·cen·nine (fes′ə·nīn, -nin) *adj.* **1.** Relating to the ancient festivals of **Fescennium,** a town in Etruria, and to the rude jests and licentious verses that characterized the festivals. **2.** Obscene; indelicate.

fes·cue (fes′kyōō) *n.* **1.** Any of a genus (*Festuca*) of slender, tough grasses, valuable for pasturage. **2.** *Rare* A pointer, twig, or straw, used to point out the letters to children learning to read. [< OF *festu* < L *festuca* stalk, straw]

fess (fes) *n. Heraldry* A wide horizontal band across the middle of an escutcheon. Also **fesse.** [< OF *fesse* < L *fascia* band]

Fes·sen·den (fes′ən·dən), **William Pitt,** 1806–1869, U.S. lawyer and legislator.

fess point *Heraldry* A point at the center of a fess. For illustration see ESCUTCHEON.

fess·wise (fes′wīz′) *adv. Heraldry* Horizontally. Also **fesse′wise′.**

FESS

-fest *combining form U.S. Slang* Bout; session: *gabfest.* [< G. *fest* festival]

fes·tal (fes′təl) *adj.* Pertaining to or typical of a festival, feast, or holiday. [< OF < L *festum* feast] — **fes′tal·ly** *adv.*

fes·ter (fes′tər) *v.i.* **1.** To develop pus; ulcerate. **2.** To cause infection, inflammation, and the formation of pus. **3.** To be or become rotten and foul. **4.** To be a constant source of smoldering rage, vexation, or irritation; rankle. — *v.i.* **5.** To cause to fester. — *n.* A small, ulcerous sore or wound. [< OF *festre* < L *fistula* ulcer]

fes·ti·ol·o·gy (fes′tī·ə·je) *n. pl.* **·gies** *Eccl.* A treatise on ecclesiastical festivals.

fes·ti·na len·te (fes·tī′nə len′tē) *Latin* Make haste slowly.

fes·ti·nate (fes′tə·nāt) *Obs. v.t. & v.i.* **·nat·ed, ·nat·ing** To hurry. — *adj.* Hurried. [< L *festinatus*, pp. of *festinare* to hasten]

fes·ti·na·tion (fes′tə·nā′shən) *n.* **1.** Involuntary haste in walking, as in certain nervous disorders. **2.** *Archaic* Haste.

fes·ti·val (fes′tə·vəl) *n.* **1.** A particular feast, holiday, or celebration, especially when occurring each year on a certain date: a religious *festival.* **2.** Any occasion for rejoicing or feasting, as a wedding anniversary. **3.** A period set aside for a special series of sometimes competitive performances, exhibitions, etc.: a Shakespeare *festival*; also, the series of performances, etc., held during this period. **3.** *Archaic* A time of revelry. — *adj.* Festive. [< OF < Med.L *festivalis* < L *festivus.* See FESTIVE.]

fes·tive (fes′tiv) *adj.* Of, relating to, or suitable for a feast or other celebration. [< L *festivus* < *festum* feast < *festus* joyful. Cf. FEAST.] — **fes′tive·ly** *adv.* — **fes′tive·ness** *n.*

fes·tiv·i·ty (fes·tiv′ə·tē) *n. pl.* **·ties 1.** A festival. **2.** The gladness and rejoicing typical of a feast, holiday, or other joyous occasion. **3.** *pl.* Merrymaking accompanying a festival. [< OF *festivite* < L *festivitas* < *festivus.* Cf. FESTIVE.]

fes·toon (fes·tōōn′) *n.* **1.** A decorative feature consisting of a length of flowers or leaves linked together or of a chain of colored paper, ribbon, etc., hanging in loops between two points, as from one wall to another of a room. **2.** An ornamental carving, sculpture, etc., representing this decorative feature. — *v.t.* **1.** To decorate with festoons. **2.** To fashion into festoons. **3.** To link together by festoons. [< F *feston* < Ital. *festone* < *festa* feast < L *festus*. Cf. FEAST.]

fes·toon·er·y (fes·tōō′nər·ē) *n. pl.* **·ries** **1.** A particular arrangement of festoons. **2.** Things arranged into festoons.

Fest·schrift (fest′shrift′) *n. pl.* **·schrift·en** (-shrif′ten) or **·schrifts** A volume of essays, articles, etc., written and published in honor of a noted scholar by his former students, colleagues, etc. [< G *fest* festival + *schrift* a writing]

fet (fet) *v.t.* **fet·ted, fet·ting** *Obs.* To fetch. [OE *fetian*]

fe·tal (fēt′l) *adj.* Of, pertaining to, or typical of a fetus: also spelled *foetal.*

fetal rickets Achondroplasia.

fe·ta·tion (fē·tā′shən) *n.* The development of the fetus during pregnancy: also spelled *foetation.*

fetch¹ (fech) *v.t.* **1.** To go after and bring back: to *fetch* a package for someone. **2.** To draw forth; elicit: to *fetch* a reply. **3.** To draw in (breath); also, to give forth (a sigh, groan, etc.) with or as with effort; heave. **4.** To arrive at by deducing; infer. **5.** To cost or sell for; get as a sales price: The material will *fetch* a good price. **6.** *Informal* To attract or delight. **7.** *Informal* To give or deal (a blow, slap, etc.). **8.** *Naut.* To arrive at (a port, etc.); reach. **9.** *Archaic* To execute (a leap or other movement). — *v.i.* **10.** To go after something and bring it back. **11.** To move to a particular point and stop there: usually with *up*: He *fetched* up at the door. **12.** In hunting, to retrieve game. **13.** *Naut.* To hold to a particular course; also, to swing around; veer. — **to fetch and carry** To perform menial tasks. — *n.* **1.** The act of fetching. **2.** A reaching out for something; also, the distance to which one reaches out for something, or the effort involved in so reaching. **3.** A trick; stratagem. [OE *feccan*, var. of *fetian*. Akin to FOOT.] — **fetch′er** *n.*

fetch² (fech) *n. Brit. Dial.* Wraith. [Origin uncertain]

fetch·ing (fech′ing) *adj. Informal* Very attractive or pleasing; charming. — **fetch′ing·ly** *adv.*

fete (fāt, fet) *n.* **1.** A festival. **2.** An outdoor celebration; especially, a dinner, bazaar, etc. — *v.t.* **fet·ed, fet·ing** To honor with festivities; give a feast or celebration for. Also (*Brit.* only) **fête.** [< F *fête* < OF *feste.* See FEAST.]

fête cham·pê·tre (fet shän·pe′tr′) *French* A celebration, party, dinner, etc., held out of doors.

fet·e·ri·ta (fet′ə·rē′tə) *n.* A variety of sorghum used as fodder in the United States: also called *Sudan durra.* [< native Sudanese name, prob. < Arabic *faṭīrah* unleavened bread]

fe·tial (fē′shəl) *adj.* Pertaining to the fetiales or to their office. — *n.* One of the fetiales. Also spelled *fecial.*

fe·ti·a·les (fē′shē·ā′lēz) *n. pl.* of **fe·ti·a·lis** (fē′shē·ā′lis) Twenty priests or heralds in ancient Rome who conducted the negotiations and the ceremonies attending declarations of war and peace. [? < L root *fetis* treaty]

fe·ti·cide (fē′tə·sīd) *n.* The intentional killing of a fetus; criminal abortion: also spelled *foeticide.* [< L *fetus* + -CIDE] — **fe′ti·ci′dal** *adj.*

fet·id (fet′id) *adj.* Having a foul odor as of rot or decay; stinking: also spelled *foetid.* [< L *fetidus* < *fetere* to stink] — **fet′id·ly** *adv.* — **fet′id·ness** *n.*

fe·tip·a·rous (fē·tip′ər·əs) *adj.* Designating animals, as kangaroos, giving birth to incompletely developed young: also spelled *foetiparous.* [< L *fetus* fetus + -PAROUS]

fet·ish (fet′ish, fē′tish) *n.* **1.** An object, as a stone or a tree, superstitiously regarded as being the embodiment or dwelling place of a spirit or as having magical powers that can benefit or injure human beings. **2.** Something which one cultivates or to which one is devoted excessively. **3.** *Psychiatry* Some object, as a shoe, that is not in itself erotic but that is sexually stimulating to certain individuals. Also **fetich.** — **Syn.** See TALISMAN. [< F *fétiche* < Pg. *feitiço* charm, orig. adj., artificial < L *facticius* artificial]

fet·ish·ism (fet′ish·iz′əm, fē′tish-) *n.* **1.** Superstitious belief in or worship of fetishes. **2.** Excessive or irrational cultivation of or devotion to something. **3.** *Psychiatry* Sexual stimulation produced by an object that is not in itself erotic. Also **fet′ich·ism.** — **fet′ish·ist** *n.* — **fet′ish·is′tic** *adj.*

fet·lock (fet′lok′) *n.* **1.** A tuft of hair growing at the back of the leg of a horse or similar animal just above the hoof. **2.** The part of the leg from which this tuft grows. **3.** The joint of the leg located at this projecting part: also **fetlock joint.** Also called **fetterlock.** For illustration see HORSE. [ME *fitlock, fetlak,* prob. < LG. Compound of FOOT + LOCK² (of hair). Cf. Du. *vitlok.*]

fe·tor (fē′tər, -tôr) *n.* A very bad odor; stench: also spelled *foetor.* [< L]

fet·ter (fet′ər) *n.* **1.** A chain or other bond put about the ankles to restrain movement or prevent escape; shackle. **2.** *Usually pl.* Anything checking freedom of movement or expression. — *v.t.* **1.** To put fetters upon; shackle; bind. **2.** To prevent the free movement or expression of; restrain. [OE *feter, fetor.* Cf. Du. *veter* lace. Related to FOOT.]

fetter bone The great pastern bone. See under PASTERN BONE.

fet·ter·bush (fet′ər·bŏŏsh′) *n.* **1.** An evergreen shrub (*Lyonia lucida*) of the heath family, with fragrant white

flowers, growing in the southern United States. **2.** A related shrub (*Pieris floribunda*), with white, bell-shaped flowers.

fet·ter·lock (fet′ər·lok′) *n.* A fetlock (which see).

fet·tle (fet′l) *v.t.* **·tled, ·tling** **1.** *Metall.* To line (the floor of a furnace used in making wrought iron from pig iron) with such oxidizing agents as loose ore or silica. **2.** *Brit. Dial.* **a** To put in proper order; attend to; arrange. **b** To give a good beating to; thrash. — *n.* **1.** Proper condition of health or spirits: in fine *fettle.* **2.** *Metall.* Loose material consisting of ore, silica, or other oxidizing agents used in fettling a furnace. [ME *fetlen* to prepare, lit., to gird up < OE *fetel* belt]

fet·tling (fet′ling) *n. Metall.* Fettle.

fe·tus (fē′təs) *n. pl.* **·tus·es** The individual unborn organism carried within the womb in the later stages of its development; especially, the unborn human organism from the end of the second month of pregnancy until birth. Compare EMBRYO. Also spelled *foetus.* [< L, a bringing forth, progeny]

feu (fyōō) *n.* In Scottish feudal law, the holding of land by a vassal who was required to pay rent in produce or money; also, the land so held. — *v.t.* In Scottish feudal law, to grant (land) as a feu. [< OF, var. of *fé.* See FEE.]

feu·ar (fyōō′ər) *n.* In Scottish feudal law, a vassal holding a feu.

Feucht·wang·er (foikht′väng·ər), **Lion,** 1884–1958, German novelist active in the United States.

feud¹ (fyōōd) *n.* **1.** A state of bitter hostility existing between two or more individuals, families, groups, etc., usually lasting over a long period of time and often marked by physical and verbal clashes or by bloodshed. **2.** Any venomous or revengeful quarrel or contentious outbreak resulting from or typical of such a state. — *v.i.* To take part in a feud. [ME *fede* < OF *faide, feide* < OHG *fehida* hatred, revenge]

feud² (fyōōd) *n.* In feudal law, a fief: also spelled *feod.* [< Med.L *feudum* < Gmc. See FEE.]

feu·dal (fyōōd′l) *adj.* **1.** Of, relating to, or typical of the feudal system. **2.** Of or relating to a fief or to the holding of a fief; opposed to *allodial.* — **feu′dal·ly** *adv.*

feu·dal·ism (fyōōd′l·iz′əm) *n.* The mode of life produced by the feudal system; also, the principles upon which the feudal system was based.

feu·dal·ist (fyōōd′l·ist) *n.* **1.** A supporter or promoter of the feudal system. **2.** An individual typical of those living under the feudal system. — **feu′dal·is′tic** *adj.*

feu·dal·i·ty (fyōō·dal′ə·tē) *n. pl.* **·ties** **1.** The condition or quality of being feudal. **2.** Feudalism. **3.** A fief.

feu·dal·ize (fyōōd′l·īz) *v.t.* **·ized, ·iz·ing** **1.** To subject to feudalism or the feudal system; make feudal. **2.** To make a fief of (land held). — **feu′dal·i·za′tion** *n.*

feudal system A system in medieval Europe in which vassals were granted land holdings by their lords in return for military service or the performance of other duties and in which the consequent subjection of vassals to lords profoundly affected the economic and political structure of society.

feu·da·ry (fyōō′dər·ē) *Archaic n. pl.* **·ries** **1.** A vassal holding a fief. **2.** An abject servant or subject. — *adj.* Made subject to another in or as in the feudal system. Also spelled *feodary.*

feu·da·to·ry (fyōō′də·tôr′ē, -tō′rē) *n. pl.* **·ries** **1.** A vassal holding a fief; also, the fief held. **2.** A country or state completely subject to another. — *adj.* **1.** Of, pertaining to, or typical of the relationship of a vassal to his lord. **2.** Subject to a feudal lord; also, of a country or state, subject to another.

feud·ist¹ (fyōō′dist) *n. U.S.* One who feuds with another.

feud·ist² (fyōō′dist) *n.* One who specializes in feudal law.

Feuil·lant (fœ·yän′) *n.* A member of a group of conservative French royalists who formed an association in 1791 durint the French Revolution and who were suppressed in 1792. [< F, called after the Order of the Feuillants in one of whose convents they met]

Feuil·let (fœ·ye′), **Octave,** 1821–90, French novelist and dramatist.

feuil·le·ton (fœ·yə·tôn′) *n.* **1.** The part of a page of a European newspaper, usually across the bottom, where light fiction, reviews, etc., are carried. **2.** A piece of serialized fiction printed in this part. [< F, < *feuillet,* dim. of *feuille* leaf < L *folium*]

feuil·le·ton·ist (fœ·yə·ton·ist) *n.* A writer of a feuilleton.

fe·ver (fē′vər) *n.* **1.** A disorder marked by unduly high body temperature, rapid pulse, and disturbance of body functions, often accompanied by restlessness and delirium. **2.** Any of a group of specific diseases of which high temperature is a principal symptom. **3.** Emotional excitement or restless eagerness. ◆ Collateral adjective: *febrile.* — *v.t.* To affect with fever. [OE *fēfer* < L *febris.* Akin to L *fovere* to warm.] — **fe′vered** *adj.*

fever blister A cold sore. Also **fever sore.**

fe·ver·bush (fē′vər·bŏŏsh′) *n.* The spicebush (which see).

fe·ver·few (fē′vər·fyōō′) *n.* A composite plant (*Chrysanthemum parthenium*) bearing white-rayed flowers, formerly used to make a medicinal tea. [OE

FEVERFEW
(1½ to 3 feet high)

feferfuge < LL *febrifugia* < L *febris* fever + *fugare* to drive away]

fever heat **1.** Body temperature above normal; especially, in man, body temperature above 98.6° F (37° C). **2.** Feverish excitement or eagerness.

fe·ver·ish (fē′vər·ish) *adj.* **1.** Having a fever, especially a low fever. **2.** Of or resembling a fever. **3.** Tending to produce fever or some disorder marked by fever: a *feverish* swamp. **4.** Agitated, uneasy, or restless, as if from fever. Also **fe′ver·ous.** **— fe′ver·ish·ly** *adv.* **— fe′ver·ish·ness** *n.*

fever therapy Pyretotherapy (which see).

fever tree **1.** The bluegum tree (*Eucalyptus globulus*) from which eucalyptol is obtained. **2.** An American tree (*Pinckneya pubens*) with a bark of tonic and febrifugal properties.

fe·ver·weed (fē′vər·wēd′) *n.* Any of a genus (*Eryngium*) of herbs of the parsley family having medicinal uses.

fe·ver·wort (fē′vər·wûrt′) *n.* **1.** A perennial herb (*Triosteum perfoliatum*) of the honeysuckle family, with brownish purple flowers and a root used as a purgative and emetic. Also **fe′ver·root′** (-rōōt′, -rŏŏt′). **2.** Boneset, an herb.

few (fyōō) *adj.* Small in number; not very many. ◆ **fewer,** **less** See note under LESS. **— pron. & n.** A small number; not very many. **— quite a few** A considerable number of persons or things. **— the few** The minority. [OE *fēawe*, pl. of *fea* little] **— few′ness** *n.*

fey[1] (fā) *adj.* **1.** Acting as if enchanted or under a spell. **2.** Suggestive of a sprite. [< F *fée* fairy < OF *fae.* See FAY[2].]

fey[2] (fā) *adj. Archaic & Scot.* **1.** Foredoomed to die at a certain time, especially suddenly. **2.** Being at the point of death. [OE *fǣge*]

fez (fez) *n. pl.* **fez·zes** A brimless, felt cap having the shape of an inverted cone with the tip flattened out, usually red and having a black tassel attached to the crown, often worn by Egyptian men and formerly by Turkish men. [< F < Turkish *fes*, after *Fez* in Morocco]

Fez (fez) A city in NE Morocco; pop. 280,000 (1969): also *Fès:* Arabic *Fas.*

Fez·zan (fe·zan′) A large region and former province of southwestern Libya, in the Sahara Desert; about 250,000 sq. mi.; chief town, Murzuq.

ff *Music* Fortissimo.

ff. **1.** Folios. **2.** Following.

F.F.A. Future Farmers of America.

F.F.A. or f.f.a. **1.** Free foreign agent. **2.** Free from alongside.

F.F.I. French Forces of the Interior.

F.F.V. First Families of Virginia.

F.G.S.A. Fellow of the Geological Society of America.

FHA Federal Housing Administration.

FHLBB Federal Home Loan Bank Board.

F.I. Falkland Islands.

fi·a·cre (fē·ä′kər, *Fr.* fyȧ′kr′) *n.* A small hackney coach. [after Hotel *St. Fiacre* in Paris, where they were first hired]

fi·an·cé (fē·än·sā′, fē·än′sā; *Fr.* fē·äṅ·sā′) *n.* A man to whom a woman is engaged to be married. [< F]

fi·an·cée (fē·än·sā′, fē·än′sā; *Fr.* fē·äṅ·sā′) *n.* A woman to whom a man is engaged to be married. [< F]

Fi·an·na (fē′ə·nə) *n.* **1.** The warriors of Fionn macCumhail, legendary Irish chieftain of the second and third centuries. **2.** The Fenians. Also **Fianna Eir·eann** (âr′in). [< Irish]

Fianna Fail (fôl′, foil′, fil′) An Irish political party formed in 1926 by Eamon de Valera, advocating complete political freedom from Great Britain. [< Irish *fail* company, society]

fi·ar (fē′ər) *n.* In Scottish law, the holder of a fee simple. [See FEE]

fi·as·co (fē·as′kō) *n. pl.* **·coes** or **·cos** A complete or humiliating failure. [< Ital. flask; semantic development uncertain]

fi·at (fī′at, -ət) *n.* **1.** A positive and authoritative order or decree. **2.** Authorization. [< L, let it be done]

fiat lux (fī′at luks′) *Latin* Let there be light.

fiat money Paper money made legal tender by decree, as of a government, and not based on gold or silver reserves nor necessarily convertible into coin.

fib (fib) *n.* A lie told without malice about something of little importance. **— v.i.** **fibbed,** **fib·bing** To tell a fib. [? Alter. of FABLE] **— fib′ber** *n.*

fi·ber (fī′bər) *n.* **1.** A fine, relatively long, continuous piece of something, suggestive of a thread; as: **a** One of the fine filaments combined with others to form asbestos, spun glass, etc. **b** One of the filaments of a textile or fabric. **c** *Biol.* One of the filaments of the fine, elongated bundles that together form animal or plant tissue or parts: a nerve *fiber.* **d** *Bot.* A root hair. **2.** A material made up of fine filaments; also, collectively, the filaments themselves: hemp *fiber.* **3.** The particular composition or structure of something made up of filaments: a material of coarse *fiber.* **4.** Character: to lack moral *fiber.* **5.** Vulcanized fiber (which see). Also *Brit.* **fi′bre.** [< F *fibre* < L *fibra*]

fi·ber·board (fī′bər·bôrd′, -bōrd′) *n.* **1.** A tough, pliable,

water-resistant building material made of wood fiber or other plant fiber compressed and rolled into sheets of varying thickness. **2.** A sheet of this material.

Fi·ber·glas (fī′bər·glas′, -gläs′) *n.* A flexible, nonflammable material of glass spun into filaments, used for textiles, insulation, etc.: a trade name. Also **fi′ber·glas′, fi′ber·glass′.**

fiber optics **1.** A branch of optics that investigates the structure, characteristics, and properties of optical fibers. **2.** Optical fibers.

Fi·bi·ger (fē′bē·gər), **Johannes,** 1867–1928, Danish pathologist.

fibr- See FIBRO-

fi·bri·form (fī′brə·fôrm) *adj.* Having a form or structure like that of fiber.

fi·bril (fī′brəl) *n.* **1.** A minute fiber. **2.** *Bot.* A root hair. [< NL *fibrilla*, dim. of L *fibra* fiber]

fi·bril·la (fī·bril′ə) *n. pl.* **·bril·lae** (-bril′ē) A fibril. [< NL]

fi·bril·lar (fī′brə·lər) *adj.* Of, pertaining to, resembling, or composed of fibers or fibrils. Also **fi′bril·lar·y** (-ler′ē).

fi·bril·la·tion (fī′brə·lā′shən) *n.* **1.** The formation of fibers. **2.** *Physiol.* A localized twitching of certain muscle fibers. **3.** *Pathol.* Rapid and erratic contraction of individual muscle fibers of the atrial and ventricular walls of the heart, producing weak and irregular heartbeats.

fi·bril·li·form (fī·bril′ə·fôrm) *adj* Having the form of fibrils.

fi·bril·lose (fī′brə·lōs) *adj.* Composed of, provided with, or resembling fibers or fibrils. Also **fi′bril·lous** (-ləs).

fi·brin (fī′brin) *n. Biochem.* An insoluble protein that promotes blood clotting by forming a fibrous network.

fibrino- *Combining form* Fibrin.

fi·brin·o·gen (fī·brin′ə·jən) *n. Biochem.* A complex protein of the globulin group, associated with thrombin in the formation of fibrin during coagulation.

fi·brin·o·gen·ic (fī′brə·nō·jen′ik) *adj.* Forming fibrin. Also **fi·bri·nog·e·nous** (fī′brə·noj′ə·nəs).

fi·bri·no·ly·sin (fī′brə·nō·lī′sin) *n. Biochem.* A toxic substance having the power to effect lysis in human fibrin.

fi·bri·no·sis (fī′brə·nō′sis) *n. Pathol.* A condition of excess fibrin in the blood.

fi·bri·nous (fī′brə·nəs) *adj.* Of, pertaining to, or having properties of fibrin.

fibro- *combining form* Pertaining to or composed of fibrous tissue: *fibrovascular* Also, before vowels, *fibr-.* [< L *fibra* fiber]

fi·broid (fī′broid) *adj.* Made up of or resembling fibrous tissue. **— n** *Pathol.* A fibroma.

fi·bro·in (fī′brō·in) *n. Biochem.* A white, lustrous protein forming the principal element of spider webs and raw silk.

fi·bro·ma (fī·brō′mə) *n. pl.* **·ma·ta** (-mə·tə) *Pathol.* A benign tumor made up of fibrous tissue. **— fi·brom·a·tous** (fī·brom′ə·təs, -brō′mə-) *adj.*

fi·bro·pla·sia (fī′brō·plā′zhə, -zhē·ə) *n. Med.* The development of new fibrous or connective tissue, as in the healing of wounds and in some diseased conditions.

fi·bro·sis (fī·brō′sis) *n. Pathol.* An abnormal increase of fibrous connective tissue in the body.

fi·brous (fī′brəs) *adj.* Made up of, having, or resembling fiber: *fibrous* tissue.

fi·bro·vas·cu·lar (fī′brō·vas′kyə·lər) *adj.* Made up of fibers and of vessels or ducts that convey a fluid, as sap, from one part to another: the *fibrovascular* tissue of wood.

fib·u·la (fib′yŏŏ·lə) *n. pl.* **·lae** (-lē) or **·las 1.** *Anat.* The outer and smaller of the two bones forming the lower part of the human leg from the knee to the ankle. ◆ Collateral adjective: *peroneal.* For illustration see PATELLA. **2.** *Zool.* In animals, a homologous bone of the hind leg. **3.** An ancient type of ornamental brooch, fastening like a safety pin. [< L, a clasp < *fivere*, var. of *figere* to fasten] **— fib′u·lar** *adj.*

-fic *suffix* Making, rendering, or causing: *beatific, soporific.* [< L *-ficus* < *facere* to make, render]

FICA Federal Insurance Contributions Act.

-fication *suffix* A causing to be (something indicated): *beatification, glorification.* [< L *-ficatio, -onis* < *-ficare* < *facere* to make, render]

fice (fīs) *n. U.S.* A small dog of mixed breed: also spelled *fyce:* also called *feist, fist.* [Short for *fisting dog* < obs. *fist* to break wind]

fiche (fēsh) *n.* A microfiche (which see).

Fich·te (fiḵh′tə), **Johann Gottlieb,** 1762–1814, German patriot and philosopher. **— Fich′te·an** (-tē·ən) *adj.*

Fich·te·an·ism (fiḵh′tē·ən·iz′əm) *n.* The philosophy of J. G. Fichte, according to which the ego is the only reality.

fi·chu (fish′ōō, *Fr.* fē·shü′) *n.* **1.** A triangular piece of light material worn about the neck. **2.** A three-cornered cape worn by women with the ends crossed or tied in front. [< F *ficher* to put on hastily < L *figere* to fasten]

fick·le (fik′əl) *adj.* Inconstant in feeling or purpose; changeful; capricious. [OE *ficol* crafty] **— fick′le·ness** *n.*

— Syn. changeable, shifting, wavering, vacillating. **— Ant.** constant, fixed, unchanging, steadfast.

fi·co (fē′kō) n. pl. **·coes 1.** Archaic Something of little worth; a trifle. **2.** Obs. A fig (def. 6). [< Ital. < L ficus fig]

fic·tile (fik′til) adj. **1.** Produced by being molded from earth, clay, etc. **2.** Capable of being molded into some shape; plastic. **3.** Of, relating to, or specializing in articles molded from earth, clay, etc. [< L fictilis < fingere to form]

fic·tion (fik′shən) n. **1.** A division of literature consisting of prose works in narrative form, the characters and incidents of which are wholly or partly imaginary; also, works of this category, as novels or stories. **2.** A consciously invented explanation or a deliberate falsehood. **3.** The action of arbitrarily making up an explanation, etc. **4.** Law A conventional acceptance of something as fact that in reality is not fact. [< F < L fictio a making < fingere to form]
— **Syn. 1.** Fiction, fable, legend, and myth refer to stories that depart in some sense from reality. Fiction is the general term for invented accounts or explanations that bear a semblance to the truth; fable deals with incredible events or creatures. In both senses, both words frequently refer to literary forms or productions. A legend is a story passed down (often by word of mouth) from early times and believed to have some basis in historical fact. A myth is a traditional story that has grown up among a people concerning their gods, heroes, etc. Compare LIE². **2.** fabrication, invention, falsehood. Compare LIE². — **Ant.** fact, history, reality, truth.

fic·tion·al (fik′shən·əl) adj. Belonging to or having the nature of fiction. — **fic′tion·al·ly** adv.

fic·tion·al·ize (fik′shən·əl·īz) v.t. **·ized, ·iz·ing** To make into fiction. Also **fic·tion·ize** (fik′shən·īz). — **fic′tion·al·i·za′tion** n.

fic·tion·ist (fik′shən·ist) n. One who writes fiction.

fic·ti·tious (fik·tish′əs) adj. **1.** Not corresponding to actual fact; artificially invented: to create a fictitious demand for goods; also, not genuine; not real; false: a fictitious address. **2.** Fictional. — **fic·ti′tious·ly** adv. — **fic·ti′tious·ness** n.

fic·tive (fik′tiv) adj. **1.** Fictitious. **2.** Relating to the creation of fiction: fictive ability. — **fic′tive·ly** adv. [< F fictif < L fingere to form]

fid (fid) n. Naut. **1.** A supporting bar or crosspiece to hold a topmast in place. **2.** A large, tapering wooden pin used for stretching eyes in rigging, opening ropes when splicing, etc. [Origin uncertain]

-fid combining form **1.** Divided (into an indicated number of parts): bifid. **2.** Separated into lobes (of an indicated kind): pinnatifid. [< L -fidus < findere to split]

fid·dle (fid′l) n. **1.** A violin; also, any other instrument of the violin or viol family: now chiefly in familiar or disparaging use. **2.** Naut. A frame or rack used at table during rough weather to prevent things from sliding off. — **fit as a fiddle** Enjoying perfect health. — **to play second fiddle** To have a position subordinate to that of another. — v. **·dled, ·dling** v.i. **1.** Informal To play a violin. **2.** To make nervous or restless movements, as with the hands or fingers; fidget. **3.** To talk or act carelessly, lightly, or jokingly. — v.t. **4.** Informal To play (a note or melody) on a violin. **5.** To spend (time) in a careless, light, or aimless way: usually with away: to fiddle away the hours. [OE fithele, found in fithelere fiddler < ML fidula, fidella, dim. of L fides lyre, back formation of fides string of a lyre. Akin to VIOL.]

fid·dle-de-dee (fid′l·dē·dē′) n. & interj. Nonsense.

fid·dle-fad·dle (fid′l·fad′l) n. & interj. Nonsense. — v.i. **·dled, ·dling** To occupy oneself with unimportant things; fuss. [Varied reduplication of FIDDLE]

fid·dle·head (fid′l·hed′) n. **1.** Naut. The upper part of the bow of some ships, carved decoratively like the head of a violin. **2.** U.S. & Canadian An edible fern shoot. Also **fid′dle·neck′** (-nek′).

fid·dler (fid′lər) n. **1.** One who plays a fiddle. **2.** A fiddler crab.

fiddler crab A small burrowing crab (genus Uca) found chiefly off the Atlantic coast of the United States, one of whose claws is, in the male, much larger than the other.

FIDDLER CRAB
(Carapace ½ to 1 inch wide)

fid·dle·stick (fid′l·stik′) n. **1.** A bow used on a violin, etc. **2.** Something trifling or absurd.

fid·dle·sticks (fid′l·stiks′) interj. Nonsense!

fid·dle·wood (fid′l·wŏŏd′) n. Any of several species of tropical American trees (Citharexylum and allied genera) yielding a hard, durable wood.

fi·de·i·com·mis·sar·y (fī′dē·ī·kom′ə·ser′ē) Law n. pl. **·sar·ies** A beneficiary in a fideicommissum. — adj. Relating to or having the nature of a fideicommissum.

fi·de·i·com·mis·sum (fī′dē·ī·kə·mis′əm) n. pl. **·mis·sa** (-mis′ə) Law A bequest in which the testator requests the named recipient to transfer the ownership or use of an indicated part of the inheritance to a third person. [< L < fidei, dative of fides faith + commissum, pp. neut. sing. of committere to entrust to]

Fi·de·i De·fen·sor (fī′dē·ī di·fen′sôr) Latin Defender of the Faith: a title of the British sovereign. Abbr. F.D.

fi·de·jus·sion (fī′dē·jush′ən) n. Law The condition of being bound as surety for another. [< L fidejussio, -onis < fidejubere < fide, ablative sing. of fides faith + jubere to order]

fi·del·i·ty (fī·del′ə·tē, fə-) n. pl. **·ties 1.** Faithfulness to duties, obligations, vows, etc.: marital fidelity. **2.** Undeviating loyalty. **3.** Adherence to truth or fact: to doubt the fidelity of a newspaper account. **4.** Exactness of reproductive detail: a camera ensuring complete fidelity. **5.** Electronics The extent to which a phonograph, tape recorder, etc., receives and transmits input signals without distortion. Abbr. fid. [< F fidélité < L fidelitas < fides faith]
— **Syn. 1.** honesty, integrity. **2.** loyalty, faithfulness, constancy, devotion. Compare ALLEGIANCE. — **Ant.** infidelity, disloyalty, treachery.

fidge (fij) v.i. Obs. To fidget. [ME fiken. Cf. ON fíkja to move about restlessly, fidget.]

fidg·et (fij′it) v.i. **1.** To make nervous or restless movements; stir about uneasily; also, to be nervous or restless. **2.** To toy with something nervously or restlessly. — v.t. **3.** To cause to fidget. — n. **1.** Usually pl. The condition of being restless or nervous; uneasiness. **2.** One who fidgets, especially habitually. [< FIDGE]

fidg·et·y (fij′it·ē) adj. Nervously restless; uneasy. — **fidg′et·i·ness** n.

fi·du·cial (fi·dōō′shəl, -dyōō′-) adj. **1.** Fiduciary. **2.** Prompted by or based on trust or religious faith: fiducial acceptance of a religious doctrine. **3.** Physics Fixed as a basis of measurement or reference: fiducial points of a scale. [< L fiducialis < fiducia < fidere to trust] — **fi·du′cial·ly** adv.

fi·du·ci·ar·y (fi·dōō′shē·er′ē, -shər·ē, -dyōō′-) adj. **1.** Of, pertaining to, or acting as a trustee: a fiduciary guardian; also, of, pertaining to, or having the nature of a trusteeship: fiduciary possession of property. **2.** Held in trust: a fiduciary estate. **3.** Consisting of fiat money: fiduciary currency. — n. pl. **·ar·ies** One who holds something in trust; trustee. Abbr. fid. [< L fiduciarius < fiducia < fidere to trust]

fi·dus A·cha·tes (fī′dəs ə·kā′tēz) Latin **1.** Faithful Achates. See ACHATES. **2.** Any faithful, trustworthy friend.

fie (fī) interj. An expression of impatience or disapproval. [< OF fi, fy < L fi, an expression of disgust]

fief (fēf) n. A landed estate held under feudal tenure. [< OF < Med.L feudum. See FEE.]

field¹ (fēld) n. **1.** A piece of land with few or no trees, covered with grass, weeds, or similar vegetation growing wild. ◆ Collateral adjective: campestral. **2.** A piece of cleared land covered with grass, clover, or other plants suitable for grazing animals and set aside for use as pasture land. **3.** A piece of cleared and cultivated land on which crops are grown. **4.** A large, unsettled, mostly level expanse of open country: to hunt in the field; also, any wide or open expanse: a field of snow. **5.** A particular area in which a natural resource is found: an oil field. **6.** A level, open area of land where aircraft take off and land; also, such an area with its accompanying buildings, hangars, etc.; airfield. **7.** The whole extent or a particular division of knowledge, research, study, etc.: the field of chemistry; also, a particular area of activity, experience, interest, etc.: the field of business. **8.** In sports and athletics: **a** The bounded area where a game is played or where athletic contests, exhibitions, etc., are held: a football field; also, a particular division of this area; especially, in baseball, the entire area beyond the bases (the outfield) or the left, center, or right part of this outer area. **b** The members of a football team, etc., actually engaged in active play during a game; also, as in cricket, the members of the team not at bat. **c** The competitors in a race or other contest; especially, the whole body of entrants exclusive of those favored in betting. **9.** Mil. **a** A region of active operations or maneuvers; sphere of action. **b** The area where a battle is fought; battleground; also, the battle itself. **c** Any area of operations separated from central military headquarters. **10.** In business, the area away from the home office, where company representatives contact customers. **11.** Physics An extent of space within which lines of magnetic or electric force are in operation: also called field of force. **12.** Optics The area within which objects are seen in a telescope or similar instrument. **13.** The part of a painting canvas, flag, coin, heraldic shield, etc., used for background colors, figures, etc.; also, the entire surface of a painting canvas, etc.; also, one or more of the divisions of a heraldic shield. — **to keep (or hold) the field 1.** To remain firm against opposition. **2.** To continue activity in a game, struggle, etc. — **to leave the field** U.S. Informal To back out of a contest, struggle, dispute, etc. — **to play the field** U.S. Informal To give one's energies, interest, or attention to the entire range of something. — **to take the field** To begin or take over the continuation of a game, military campaign, struggle, etc. — v.t. **1.** In baseball, cricket, etc.: **a** To catch or pick up (a ball coming to the outer field) and return to the inner field. **b** To send (a player or group of players) to a field position. — v.i. **2.** In baseball, cricket, etc.: **a** To field a ball. **b** To play in a field position. — adj. **1.** Of, pertaining to, or growing in fields: field flowers. **2.** Used or designed for use in fields: a field gun. **3.** Played or held on an open field rather than on a racetrack, etc.: field events. Abbr. fld. [OE feld. Akin to OE folde earth. Cf. PLANE.]

field² (fyeld) See FJELD.

Field (fēld), **Cyrus West,** 1819–92, U.S. merchant, promoted the first transatlantic cable, 1858. — **Eugene,** 1850–95, U.S. poet and journalist. — **Marshall,** 1834–1906, U.S. merchant and philanthropist.

field army An army (def. 3).

field artillery Artillery so mounted as to be freely movable, and suitable for use with troops in the field. — **Field Artillery** A former branch of the U.S. Army. Abbr. *FA*

field battery A battery of field artillery, containing usually four or six guns.

field cap An overseas cap (which see).

field corn Any of several kinds of corn used for feed.

field day 1. A day spent in the field, as for military maneuvers, athletic contests, or the collecting of botanical specimens. 2. A gala day full of pleasurable activity, celebration, or excitement; also, a day full of opportunity for success or satisfaction.

field·er (fēl′dər) *n.* In baseball, cricket, etc., a player in the field, especially in the outfield.

fielder's choice In baseball, the decision by a player to try to put out a man already on base rather than to try to put out the batter running to first base, in which case the batter is not credited with a hit.

field events The jumping, vaulting, and casting contests at an athletic meet: distinguished from *track events.*

field·fare (fēld′fâr′) *n.* A European thrush (*Turdus pilaris*), deep brown in color with a pearl gray head and black tail. [ME *feldefare* (< *feld* field + *faran* to go), or < *feld* field + *warian* to dwell]

field glasses A compact, portable, binocular telescope. Also **field glass.**

field goal 1. In football, a goal scored from scrimmage by a drop kick or a place kick, counting three points. 2. In basketball, a goal scored while the ball is in active play, counting two points.

field gun A field artillery cannon; a fieldpiece.

field hockey Hockey played on a field: also, *Canadian, grass hockey.*

field hospital A military hospital that may be set up near a combat zone for emergency treatment.

field ice Ice formed in fields or floes, as distinguished from icebergs.

Field·ing (fēl′ding), **Henry,** 1707–54, English novelist, dramatist, and barrister.

field jacket A lightweight, cotton, waterproof jacket of olive drab worn by soldiers in the field.

field kitchen A portable unit used to cook food for soldiers in the field.

field lark 1. The American meadowlark. 2. The English skylark. 3. Any of various larklike birds, as the pipit.

field magnet The magnet that produces the magnetic field in a generator or electric motor.

field marshal In the armies of several European nations, a general officer of high rank, usually just below the commander in chief. Abbr. *F.M.*

Field-Mar·shal (fēld′mär′shəl) *n.* In the British and Canadian armies, an officer of the highest rank. See table at GRADE.

field mouse A small rodent inhabiting fields and meadows, as the vole: also called *meadow mouse.*

field music 1. The drummers, buglers, fifers, etc., who play for military troops on the march, sound regimental calls, etc. 2. The music produced by them.

field officer *Mil.* An officer intermediate between a company officer and a general officer; a colonel, lieutenant colonel, or major.

field of force *Physics* A field in which the variable is force.

field of honor 1. The ground where a duel is fought. 2. A battlefield.

field·piece (fēld′pēs′) *n.* A cannon mounted on wheels, for use in field battles.

fields·man (fēldz′mən) *n. pl.* **·men** (-mən) In cricket, a fielder.

field spaniel A black or variegated spaniel with a long, low body, used for hunting.

field sparrow A small American sparrow (*Spizella pusilla*).

field sports 1. Outdoor sports, especially hunting, shooting, and racing. 2. Athletic events, as jumping and pole-vaulting, held on the field, as opposed to races, hurdles, and the like, held on the track.

field·stone (fēld′stōn′) *n.* Loose stone found near a construction site and used in building. — *adj.* Consisting of or having the appearance of fieldstone: a *fieldstone* house.

field trial A competitive test of hunting dogs in the field.

field trip A trip away from the classroom for direct observation and investigation.

field winding *Electr.* The winding of the field magnet coils that regulate the current of a generator or electric motor.

field·work (fēld′wûrk′) *n.* A temporary fortification thrown up in the field.

field work Observations and investigations made in the field, as by a scientist. — **field worker**

fiend (fēnd) *n.* 1. An evil spirit; devil; demon. 2. An intensely wicked or cruel person. 3. *Informal* One who is excessively engrossed or highly skilled in a certain subject, pursuit, game, etc.: a bridge *fiend.* 4. *Informal* One slavishly addicted to an injurious habit: a drug *fiend.* — **the Fiend** Satan; the devil. [OE *fēond* enemy, devil] — **fiend′like** *adj.*

fiend·ish (fēn′dish) *adj.* Exceedingly cruel or malicious; diabolical. — **fiend′ish·ly** *adv.* — **fiend′ish·ness** *n.* — **Syn.** devilish, monstrous, demoniacal.

fierce (firs) *adj.* 1. Having a violent and cruel nature or temper; savage; ferocious. 2. Violent in action or force. 3. Vehement; intense: *fierce* anger. 4. *Slang* Very disagreeable, bad, etc. [< OF *fers, fiers,* nominative sing. of *fier* proud < L *ferus* wild] — **fierce′ly** *adv.* — **fierce′ness** *n.* — **Syn.** 1. brutal, inhuman. Compare BARBAROUS. — **Ant.** docile, tame, mild.

Fier·ga·na (fyir·gä·nä′) A city in the eastern Uzbek S.S.R.; pop. 80,000 (1959): also *Fergana.*

fi·e·ri fa·ci·as (fī′ə·rī fā′shē·əs) *Law* A writ of execution commanding a sheriff to levy on the goods of a debtor to satisfy a judgment. [< L, that you cause to be made]

fier·y (fīr′ē, fī′ər·ē) *adj.* **fier·i·er, fier·i·est** 1. Containing or composed of fire. 2. Hot as fire; burning: the *fiery* sun. 3. Brightly glowing; blazing; flashing: *fiery* eyes. 4. Eager or fierce in spirit; passionate; impetuous. 5. Causing a burning sensation, as pepper. 6. Flammable. 7. Inflamed, as a boil. — **fier′i·ly** *adv.* — **fier′i·ness** *n.*

fiery cross 1. A burning cross, used by the Ku Klux Klan to inspire terror. 2. A cross with charred ends, formerly used in Scotland as a call to arms.

fiery hunter A large, black ground beetle of the United States (*Calosoma calidum*) with small coppery spots on the wing covers. For illustration see INSECTS (beneficial).

Fie·so·le (fye′zō·lā) A commune in central Italy near Florence; pop. 12,473 (est. 1960).

Fie·so·le (fye′zō·lā), **Giovanni da** See ANGELICO, FRA.

fi·es·ta (fē·es′tə, *Sp.* fyes′tä) *n.* 1. A religious festival; a saint's day. 2. Any holiday or celebration. [< Sp. < L *festa.* See FEAST.]

fife (fīf) *n.* A small, shrill-toned flute used chiefly for military music. — *v.t. & v.i.* **fifed, fif·ing** *T* play on a fife. [< G *pfeife* pipe < OHG *pfifa* < (assumed) LL *pipa* < L *pipare* to peep, chirp. Doublet of PIPE.] — **fif′er** *n.*

FIFE

Fife (fīf) A county in eastern Scotland; 504 sq. mi.; pop. 325,139 (1969); county seat, Cupar. Also **Fife′shire** (-shir, -shər).

fife rail *Naut.* A railing around a mast for holding belaying pins.

fif·teen (fif′tēn′) *n.* 1. The sum of fourteen and one: a cardinal number. 2. Any symbol of this number, as 15, xv, XV. 3. Anything consisting of or representing fifteen units, as an organization, game token, etc. — *adj.* Being one more than fourteen. [OE *fīftēne*]

fif·teenth (fif′tēnth′) *adj.* 1. Next after the fourteenth: the ordinal of fifteen. 2. Being one of fifteen equal parts. — *n.* 1. One of fifteen equal parts. 2. That which follows the fourteenth.

Fifteenth Amendment An amendment to the Constitution of the United States providing that the right of citizens to vote shall not be denied or abridged on account of "race, color, or previous condition of servitude": ratified 1870.

fifth (fifth) *adj.* 1. Next after the fourth: the ordinal of *five.* 2. Being one of five equal parts. — *n.* 1. One of five equal parts. 2. That which follows the fourth. 3. *Music* **a** The interval between a tone and another tone five steps from it in a diatonic scale or mode, counting the starting tone as one. **b** One of these tones in relation to the other, especially the one higher in pitch. **c** The fifth above the tonic; the dominant. See INTERVAL, PERFECT. 4. One fifth of a U.S. gallon, used as a measure of alcoholic liquors; also, a bottle of this size. — *adv.* In the fifth order, place, or rank: also, in formal discourse, **fifth′ly.** [OE *fīfta*]

Fifth Amendment An amendment to the Constitution of the United States guaranteeing due process of law, forbidding double jeopardy, and providing that no person "shall be compelled in any criminal case to be a witness against himself": ratified 1791.

Fifth Avenue A street in Manhattan, New York City, famous for shopping districts and wealthy residential sections.

fifth column In wartime, the civilians within defense lines who secretly assist the enemy by acting as spies, saboteurs, and propagandists: first used in the Spanish Civil War by Gen. Emilio Mola (1887–1937), who said in a radio speech that his four armed columns attacking Madrid would be helped by a *fifth column* of Franco agents and sympathizers within the city. — **fifth columnist**

Fifth Republic The republic established in France in 1958, succeeding the Fourth Republic.

fifth wheel 1. The heavy disklike device on the rear of a tractor, used as a hitch for semi-trailers. 2. A horizontal metallic circle or segment attached to the upper side of the fore axle of a carriage or wagon to give support to the body in turning. **3.** A spare wheel. **4.** A superfluous person or thing.

fif·ti·eth (fif′tē·ith) *adj.* **1.** Tenth in order after the fortieth: the ordinal of fifty. **2.** Being one of fifty equal parts. — *n.* **1.** One of fifty equal parts. **2.** That which is tenth in order after the fortieth.

fif·ty (fif′tē) *n.* *pl.* **·ties 1.** The sum of forty and ten: a cardinal number. **2.** Any symbol of this number, as 50, l, L. **3.** Anything consisting of or representing fifty units, as an organization, bill, etc. — *adj.* Being ten more than forty. [OE *fiftig*]

fifty-fifty (fif′tē·fif′tē) *Informal adj.* Sharing equally, as in benefits: *fifty-fifty* partners. — *adv.* Equally.

fig¹ (fig) *n.* **1.** The small, edible, pear-shaped fruit of a tree (genus *Ficus*), cultivated in warm climates. **2.** The tree (*F. carica*) that bears this fruit. **3.** Any tree or plant bearing a fruit somewhat like the fig; also, the fruit itself. **4.** One of several Australian trees and shrubs of the mulberry family, as *F. macrophylla*, used as fodder for cattle. **5.** A petty matter; trifle. **6.** An insulting gesture made by thrusting the thumb between two fingers or into the mouth; a fico. — *v.t.* **figged, fig·ging** *Obs.* To make a fig at; insult. [< OF *fige, figue* < L *ficus*]

fig² (fig) *v.t.* **figged, fig·ging** *Informal* To dress; deck; rig. — *n.* **1.** Dress; array: in full *fig.* **2.** Condition; form: in good *fig.* [Var. of obs. *feague* whip < G *fegen* polish]

fig. 1. Figurative(ly). **2.** Figure(s).

fig·eat·er (fig′ē′tər) *n.* **1.** A large, velvety green scarabaeid beetle (*Cotinis nitida*) common in the southern United States, injurious to ripe fruits: also called *June bug.* **2.** The beccafico.

fight (fīt) *v.* **fought, fight·ing** *v.t.* **1.** To struggle against in battle or physical combat. **2.** To struggle against in any manner. **3.** To carry on or engage in (a battle, duel, court action, etc.). **4.** To make (one's way) by struggling. **5.** To cause to fight or manage the fighting of, as boxers or game-cocks. — *v.i.* **6.** To take part in combat. **7.** To struggle in any manner. — **to fight it out** To fight until a final decision is reached. — **to fight shy of** To avoid meeting (an opponent or an issue) squarely; dodge. — *n.* **1.** Strife or struggle; battle; conflict; combat. **2.** Strife to attain an object in spite of difficulties or opposition. **3.** Power or disposition to fight; pugnacity. **4.** *Obs.* A temporary bulwark or screen on a ship when in action, to conceal the men. [OE *feohtan*] — **Syn.** (verb) See OPPOSE. — (noun) **1.** fray, affray, set-to, bout. Compare BATTLE, QUARREL, ROW³.

fight·er (fī′tər) *n.* **1.** One who fights, as a combatant or pugilist. **2.** *Mil.* A fast, highly maneuverable airplane designed to intercept and destroy enemy planes in the air: formerly called *pursuit plane*: also **fighter plane.**

fight·er-bomb·er (fī′tər·bom′ər) *n.* *Mil.* An aircraft that combines the functions of the fighter and the bomber.

fighter command In World War II, an organization of the Army Air Forces intermediate between a wing and an air force, used for interception of enemy aircraft and for support of air and ground offensive forces.

fighter strip See AIRSTRIP.

fighting chance A bare possibility of success, contingent on a hard struggle.

fighting cock 1. A gamecock. **2.** A pugnacious person.

fighting fish A brightly colored Siamese aquarium fish (*Betta splendens*), the males of which are noted for their pugnacity.

fighting top On war vessels, a platform at the lower masthead for the fire-control lookout, or for light antiaircraft guns.

fig marigold Any of several species of a South African genus of herbs (*Mesembryanthemum*) yielding a fig-shaped fruit.

fig·ment (fig′mənt) *n.* A capricious product of the mind; a fiction; fabrication. [< L *figmentum* anything made < *fingere* to form]

Fi·gue·ro·a (fē′gä·rō′ä), **Francisco de,** 1540?–1620?, Spanish poet and soldier.

fig·u·line (fig′yŏŏ·lin, -līn) *n.* **1.** A piece of pottery. **2.** Potter's clay. [< L *figulinus* < *figulus* potter < *fingere* to form]

fig·u·rant (fig′yŏŏ·rant, Fr. fē·gü·rän′) *n.* **1.** A nonfeatured ballet dancer who dances only in groups. **2.** A walk-on or supernumerary on the stage. [< F, ppr. of *figurer* to figure] — **fig·u·rante** (fig′yŏŏ·rant′, -ränt′; Fr. fē·gü·ränt′) *n.fem.*

fig·ur·ate (fig′yər·it) *adj.* **1.** Having a definite or characteristic figure or shape. **2.** *Music* Characterized by embellishments, etc.; florid; ornate. [< L *figuratus*, pp. of *figurare* to form < *figura.* See FIGURE.]

fig·u·ra·tion (fig′yə·rā′shən) *n.* **1.** The act of shaping something or of marking with a figure. **2.** Form, shape, or outline. **3.** The act of representing figuratively; also, an allegorical or figurative representation. **4.** *Music* Ornamentation, as by the addition of passing notes, etc.

fig·ur·a·tive (fig′yər·ə·tiv) *adj.* **1.** Based on, of the nature of, or involving a figure of speech: not literal; metaphorical: *figurative* language. Abbr. *fig.* **2.** Filled with or using figures of speech; flowery: a *figurative* poem. **3.** Representing by means of a form or figure; emblematic. **4.** Pertaining to

pictorial or sculptural representation. — **fig·ur·a·tive·ly** *adv.*

fig·ure (fig′yər, *Brit.* fig′ər) *n.* **1.** A character or symbol representing a number: the *figure* 5. **2.** *pl.* The use of such characters in calculating. **3.** An amount stated in numbers, as of price, population, etc. **4.** The visible form of anything; shape; outline; appearance. **5.** The human form or body. **6.** A personage or character, especially a prominent one: a well-known *figure* in the last century. **7.** The appearance or impression that a person or his conduct makes: to cut a bold *figure.* **8.** A representation or likeness, as in painting or sculpture. **9.** A pattern or design, as in a fabric. **10.** A printed illustration; a cut. Abbr. *fig.* **11.** One who or that which represents or symbolizes something: a *figure* of wisdom to the world. **12.** A figure of speech (which see). **13.** A movement or series of movements, as in a dance or in skating. **14.** *Geom.* **a** A surface enclosed by lines, as a square, triangle, etc.: called a **plane figure.** **b** A space enclosed by planes or surfaces, as a cube, sphere, etc.: called a **solid figure.** **15.** *Logic* The form of a syllogism determined by the position of the middle term. **16.** *Music* Any short succession of notes, either as melody or a group of chords, that produces a single, complete, and distinct impression. **17.** *Obs.* An imaginary form; phantasm. — *v.* **·ured, ·ur·ing** *v.t.* **1.** To compute numerically; calculate. **2.** To make an image, picture, or other representation of; depict. **3.** To ornament or mark with a design. **4.** To picture mentally; imagine. **5.** To express by a figure of speech; symbolize. **6.** *Informal* To think; believe; predict. **7.** *Music* **a** To embellish, as by adding passing notes. **b** To mark with figures above or below the bass notes, indicating accompanying chords. — *v.i.* **8.** To appear prominently; be conspicuous. **9.** To compute; reckon. — **to figure on** (or **upon**) *U.S. Informal* **1.** To count on; rely on. **2.** To plan on. — **to figure out 1.** To solve; compute. **2.** To make out; understand; ascertain. [< F < L *figura* < *fingere* to form] — **fig′ur·er** *n.*

fig·ured (fig′yərd) *adj.* **1.** Adorned or marked with figures or designs: *figured* cottons. **2.** Represented by figures; pictured. **3.** *Music* Figurate.

figured bass *Music* A bass part with numerals, etc., indicating chords: also called *basso continuo, thorough bass.*

figure eight 1. *Aeron.* A flight maneuver that consists in tracing the figure 8. **2.** A similar maneuver in ice skating. **3.** A style of knot: for illustration see KNOT.

fig·ure·head (fig′yər·hed′) *n.* **1.** A person having nominal leadership but no real power or responsibility. **2.** A carved or ornamental figure on the prow of a vessel.

figure of speech An expression that intentionally deviates from or abandons altogether the normal, literal meanings of words so as to create a more vivid or fanciful effect, as in simile, metaphor, personification, etc.

figure skating The art or sport of skating in prescribed dancelike patterns. — **figure skater.**

FIGURE-
HEAD
(*def.* 2)

fig·u·rine (fig′yə·rēn′) *n.* A small, molded or carved figure; statuette. [< F < Ital. *figurina*, dim. of *figura* < L. See FIGURE.]

fig·wort (fig′wûrt′) *n.* A plant (genus *Scrophularia*) with small, dark-colored flowers, formerly supposed to cure scrofula. It is typical of a large family (*Scrophulariaceae*) of plants including mullein eye bright, and foxglove.

Fi·ji (fē′jē) An independent member of the Commonwealth of Nations in the South Pacific comprising the **Fiji Islands** (7,039 sq. mi.) and Rotuma (18 sq. mi.); pop. 526,765 (est. 1970): capital, Suva.

Fi·ji (fē′jē) *n.* **1.** One of the native people of the Fiji Islands, mostly Melanesian with Polynesian admixture. **2.** The Melanesian language of the Fijis.

Fi·ji·an (fē′jē·ən, fi·jē′ən) *adj.* Of Fiji, its people, or their language. — *n.* A Fiji.

fil·a·gree (fil′ə·grē) See FILIGREE.

fil·a·ment (fil′ə·mənt) *n.* **1.** A fine thread, fiber, or fibril; also, any threadlike structure or appendage. **2.** *Bot.* **a** The stalk or support of an anther. For illustration see FLOWER. **b** An aggregate of cells joined in a slender thread, as in certain algae and fungi. **3.** *Electr.* The slender wire of tungsten, carbon, or other material, which, when an electric current is passed through it in a vacuum, is heated to a brilliant glow and produces light. For illustration see INCANDESCENT LAMP. **4.** *Electronics* A similar heated wire forming the cathode of an electron tube. **5.** *Ornithol.* The barb of a feather. [< F < LL *filamentum* < *filare* to spin < L *filum* thread] — **fil·a·men·ta·ry** (-men′tər·ē), **fil·a·men′tous** (-men′təs) *adj.*

fi·lar (fī′lər) *adj.* **1.** Of or pertaining to a thread or threads. **2.** *Optics* Having fine threads across the field of view, for measuring objects in the field [< L *filum* thread + -AR¹]

fi·lar·i·a (fi·lâr′ē·ə) *n.* *pl.* **·lar·i·ae** (-lâr′i·ē) A nematode (family *Filariidae*) parasitic in the blood and intestines of man and other animals. [< NL < L *filum* thread] — **fi·lar′i·al** (-əl), **fi·lar′i·an** (-ən) *adj.*

fil·a·ri·a·sis (fil′ə·rī′ə·sis) *n.* *Pathol.* **1.** Infection with nematode worms. **2.** The condition resulting from this, affecting chiefly the lymph glands and connective tissues.

fil·a·ture (fil′ə-chər) *n.* **1.** The act of forming threads or of reeling off raw silk from cocoons. **2.** An apparatus, machine, or establishment for reeling silk. [< F < LL *filare* to spin < L *filum* thread]

fil·bert (fil′bərt) *n.* **1.** The thick-shelled, edible nut of the European or the Oriental hazel (*Corylus avellana*), and also, sometimes, of the American hazel (*C. americana* and *C. cornuta*): also called *hazelnut.* **2.** The bushy shrub or small tree that bears this nut. [Earlier *filbert nut* < dial. F *noix de filbert* nut of Philibert, after St. *Philibert*, because these nuts ripen about the time of his feast day (Aug. 22)]

filch (filch) *v.t.* To steal slyly and in small amounts; pilfer. — **Syn.** See STEAL. [Origin uncertain] — **filch′er** *n.*

file¹ (fil) *n.* **1.** Any device in which papers are systematically arranged for quick reference, as a folder, drawer, or cabinet. **2.** A collection of papers or documents thus arranged. **3.** A succession or line of persons, animals, or things placed one behind another. **4.** *Mil.* **a** A formation of men arranged in a line one behind another: distinguished from *rank.* **b** A small detachment of men. **5.** A vertical row of squares running directly across a chessboard from one player to the other. **6.** *Obs.* A catalogue; roll; list. — **on file** Stored in systematic order for quick reference; in a file. — **single file** An arrangement of persons or things one behind another in a single line: also *Indian file.* — *v.* **filed, fil·ing** *v.t.* **1.** To store (papers, etc.) in systematic order. — *v.i.* **2.** To march in file, as soldiers. **3.** To make an application, as for a job. [Fusion of F *fil* thread and *file* row, both ult. < L *filum* thread] — **fil′er** *n.* — **Syn.** (verb) **1.** classify, arrange.

file² (fil) *n.* **1.** A hard steel instrument with ridged cutting surfaces, used to abrade, smooth, or polish. **2.** *Brit. Slang* A shrewd or artful person. — *v.t.* **filed, fil·ing** **1.** To cut, smooth, or sharpen with or as with a file. **2.** To remove with a file. [OE *fīl*] — **fil′er** *n.*

file³ (fil) *v.t.* *Archaic* To defile; sully. [OE *-fȳlan*, found in *befȳlan* befoul]

fi·lé (fə-lā′, fē-) *n.* Dried young sassafras leaves ground into a powder, used in Creole cooking. [< F *filer* to spin]

file clerk An employee who maintains files and records.

file·fish (fil′fish′) *n.* *pl.* ·**fish** or ·**fish·es** Any of certain fish (family *Balistidae*) with roughly granulated skin, especially the triggerfish.

file·mot (fil′ə-mot) *adj.* *Archaic* Having the color of a dead or faded leaf. [Alter. of F *feuillemorte* dead leaf]

fi·let (fi-lā′, fil′ā; *Fr.* fē-le′) *n.* **1.** Net lace having a square mesh. **2.** Fillet (def. 2). — *v.t.* **fi·leted** (fi-lād′, fil′ād), **fi·let·ing** (fi-lā′ing, fil′ā·ing) To fillet (def. 2). [< F. See FILLET.]

fi·let mi·gnon (fi-lā′ min·yon′, *Fr.* fē-le′ mē-nyôn′) A small, choice, boneless cut of beef from the inside of the loin. [< F]

fil·i·al (fil′ē-əl, fil′yəl) *adj.* **1.** Of, pertaining to, or befitting a son or daughter: *filial* devotion. **2.** *Genetics* Pertaining to a generation following the parental. The first filial generation is designated F₁, the second F₂, etc. [< LL *filialis* < L *filius* son]

fil·i·ate (fil′ē-āt) *v.t.* ·**at·ed**, ·**at·ing** **1.** To affiliate. **2.** *Law* To fix the paternity of (an illegitimate child, etc.). [< LL *filiatus*, pp. of *filiare* to have a son < L *filius* son]

fil·i·a·tion (fil′ē-ā′shən) *n.* **1.** The state or fact of being the child, especially the son, of a certain parent: correlative of *paternity.* **2.** Line of descent, as of parentage; lineage; derivation. **3.** The formation of branches, as of a language. **4.** An offshoot. **5.** *Law* Judicial assignment of paternity.

fil·i·beg (fil′ə·beg) *n.* A kilt: also spelled *philabeg, philibeg.* [< Scottish Gaelic *feileadh* kilt + *beag* little]

fil·i·bus·ter (fil′ə·bus′tər) *n.* **1.** *U.S.* **a** In a legislative body, an instance of the use of delaying tactics, especially the making of time-consuming speeches, by a member or members of the minority group in an attempt to prevent passage of a bill. **b** A legislator who obstructs the passage of a bill by dilatory tactics: also **fil′i·bus′ter·er.** **2.** A freebooter or buccaneer; pirate. **3.** An adventurer who takes part in an unlawful military expedition into a foreign country. — *v.i.* **1.** *U.S.* To obstruct legislation by long speeches and delay. **2.** To act as a freebooter or adventurer. — *v.t.* **3.** *U.S.* To block passage of (legislation) by dilatory tactics. [< Sp. *filibustero* < Du. *vrijbuiter* freebooter] — **fil′i·bus′trous** *adj.*

fil·i·cide (fil′ə·sīd) *n.* **1.** The killing of one's child. **2.** One who has killed his child. [< L *filius* son + -CIDE] — **fil′i·ci′dal** *adj.*

fil·i·cin·i·an (fil′ə·sin′ē·ən) *adj.* Of or pertaining to a large class (*Filicineae*) of pteridophyte plants; the ferns. [< NL *filicineus* < *Filicales*, an order of ferns < L *filix, filicis* fern]

fil·i·form (fil′ə·fôrm) *adj.* Threadlike.

fil·i·gree (fil′ə·grē) *n.* **1.** Delicate ornamental work formed of intertwisted gold or silver wire. **2.** Anything fanciful and delicate, but purely ornate. — *adj.* Resembling, made of, or adorned with filigree; fanciful; ornate. — *v.t.* ·**greed**, ·**gree·ing** To adorn with filigree; work in filigree. Sometimes

spelled *filagree* or *fillagree.* Also *Obs.* **fil′i·grain.** [Short for *filigreen*, var. of *filigrane* < F < Ital. *filigrana* < L *filum* thread + *granum* grain]

fil·ings (fi′lingz) *n.pl.* Particles removed by a file.

Fil·i·pine (fil′ə·pēn) See PHILIPPINE.

Fil·i·pi·no (fil′ə·pē′nō) *n.* *pl.* ·**nos** A native or inhabitant of the Philippine Islands. — *adj.* Of or pertaining to the Philippine Islands or their inhabitants.

fill (fil) *v.t.* **1.** To supply (a container, space, etc.) with as much of something as can be contained; put, pack, or pour into until no more will go in: to *fill* a glass; to *fill* a house with guests. **2.** To supply fully, as with food: to *fill* one's stomach; a head *filled* with facts. **3.** To occupy the whole of: Deer *filled* the forest; also, to be diffused throughout; pervade: Music *fills* his days. **4.** To stop up; plug: to *fill* a tooth. **5.** To put together or make up what is indicated in (an order, prescription, etc.). **6.** To satisfy or meet (a need, requirements, etc.). **7.** To occupy (an office or position). **8.** To put someone into (an office or position): to *fill* the governorship. **9.** To build up or level out (an embankment, ravine, etc.) by adding fill. **10.** *Naut.* **a** To distend (a sail): said of the wind. **b** To trim (a yard) so that the wind will distend the sail. **11.** *Obs.* To put into a receptacle so as to fill it: to *fill* wine. — *v.i.* **12.** To become full. — **to fill away** *Naut.* To turn the yards so that the sails will catch the wind. — **to fill in 1.** To fill completely, as an excavation. **2.** To insert (something omitted or for which a blank space is left): to *fill in* one's name. **3.** To complete by inserting something omitted or for which a blank space is left: to *fill in* an application. **4.** To be a substitute. — **to fill (someone) in on** *Informal* To give (someone) additional facts or details about. — **to fill out 1.** To make or become fuller or more rounded. **2.** To make complete, as an application, by inserting something. — **to fill the bill** *U.S. Informal* To do or be what is wanted or needed. — **to fill up** To make or become full. — *n.* **1.** That which fills or is sufficient to fill; a full supply: to eat one's *fill.* **2.** An embankment built up by filling in with stone, gravel, etc., over low ground. **3.** The stone, gravel, etc., used to build up low ground. [OE *fyllan* fill]

fil·la·gree (fil′ə·grē) See FILIGREE.

fille de joie (fē/y′ də zhwä′) *French* A prostitute; literally, girl of joy.

filled gold Brass, or other base metal, with a thick plate of gold welded and rolled on it.

filled milk Skim milk to which vegetable oils have been added to replace the normal cream content.

fill·er¹ (fil′ər) *n.* **1.** One who fills. **2.** That which fills; as: **a** A substance added to increase bulk, weight, etc. **b** A composition for filling pores or holes in wood before painting or varnishing. **c** Tobacco used for the inside of cigars and for plug tobacco. **d** A brief piece of writing used to fill space in a newspaper or magazine. **3.** Any device that conducts a substance into a receptacle, as a funnel. **4.** *Archit.* A plate or other piece used to fill the gap between two supporting members of a structure.

fil·lér² (fēl′lâr) *n.* *pl.* **fil·lér** A Hungarian coin, the hundredth part of a forint. [< Hungarian]

fil·let (fil′it; *for n. def. 2 and v. def. 2, also* fil′ā, fi·lā′) *n.* **1.** A narrow band or ribbon for binding the hair. **2.** A strip of boneless meat or fish; also, a strip of beef, veal, lamb, etc., rolled up and tied, as for roasts: also spelled *filet.* **3.** A narrow band of any material. **4.** *Archit.* **a** A narrow, flat molding used to separate or ornament larger moldings. For illustration see MOLDING. **b** The flat ridge or strip between the flutes of a column. **5.** *Anat.* A lemniscus extending from the medulla oblongata to the cerebrum of the brain. **6.** In bookbinding, a decorative line or band impressed upon a book cover; also, a small hand tool for making such bands. **7.** *Heraldry* A horizontal band occupying the lower fourth part of the chief. **8.** *Aeron.* Fairing¹ (def. 1). — *v.t.* **1.** To bind or adorn with a fillet or band. **2.** To slice into fillets; cook as a fillet: also spelled *filet.* [< F *filet*, dim. of *fil* thread < L *filum*]

fill-in (fil′in′) *n.* **1.** A person or thing included to fill a gap or omission. **2.** *Informal* A summary of facts given to complete one's understanding of a situation.

fill·ing (fil′ing) *n.* **1.** That which is used to fill something: a pastry *filling.* **2.** The act of making or becoming full. **3.** In weaving, the weft. **4.** *Dent.* The material put into a prepared cavity in a tooth.

filling station *U.S.* A retail station for supplying gasoline, oil, etc., to motor vehicles: also called *gas station.*

fil·lip (fil′əp) *n.* **1.** An outward snap of a finger that has been pressed down by the thumb and suddenly released; also, a smart tap with the nail of a finger so snapped. **2.** Something that serves to excite or stimulate; a stimulus; incentive. — *v.t.* **1.** To strike with a fillip; also, to rap sharply. **2.** To project by or as by a fillip. **3.** To stimulate; arouse. — *v.i.* **4.** To make a fillip. [Var. of FLIP]

fil·li·peen (fil′ə·pēn′) See PHILOPENA.

fil·lis·ter (fil/is·tər) *n. Mech.* **1.** A plane for making grooves or rabbets. **2.** A rabbet on a sash bar, for receiving the edge of the glass and the putty. **3.** A type of screw with a round head. [Origin unknown]

Fill·more (fil/môr), **Millard,** 1800–74, 13th president of the United States 1850–53.

fil·ly (fil/ē) *n. pl.* **·lies 1.** A young mare. **2.** *Informal* A spirited young girl. [< ON *fylja* < *foli* foal]

film (film) *n.* **1.** A thin covering, layer, or membrane. **2.** A thin haze or blur: a *film* of mist. **3.** *Photog.* **a** A thin coating of a light-sensitive emulsion laid on a glass plate or on a flexible base, for making photographs. **b** A sheet, roll, or strip of transparent material, usually cellulose acetate or cellulose nitrate, coated with such an emulsion. **4.** In motion pictures: **a** The film containing the pictures projected on the screen. **b** The motion picture itself. **c** *pl.* Motion pictures collectively; also, the industry engaged in making motion pictures. **5.** A delicate filament, as of a cobweb. **6.** *Pathol.* A growth on the cornea. — *v.t.* **1.** To cover or obscure by or as by a film. **2.** To photograph on a film; especially, to take motion pictures of. **3.** To make a motion picture of: to *film* a play. — *v.i.* **4.** To become covered or obscured by a film. **5.** To make a motion picture. **6.** To be adaptable for filming: His novels *film* well. [OE *filmen* membrane]

film pack *Photog.* A set of films so packaged that it may be safely handled in daylight, each individual film being exposed in turn.

film·strip (film/strip/) *n.* A length of processed film containing frames of still pictures that are projected on a screen, usually as a visual aid in lectures.

film·y (fil/mē) *adj.* **film·i·er, film·i·est 1.** Composed of or like film; gauzy. **2.** Covered with or as with a film; hazy; dim. — **film/i·ly** *adv.* — **film/i·ness** *n.*

fil·o·plume (fil/ə·plōōm/, fil/ə·) *n. Ornithol.* A feather with few or no barbs. [< L *filum* thread + *pluma* plume]

fi·lose (fi/lōs) *adj.* **1.** Threadlike. **2.** Having a threadlike appendage. [< L *filum* thread + -OSE[1]]

fils (fēs) *n. French* Son.

fil·ter (fil/tər) *n.* **1.** Any device or porous substance, as paper, cloth, or charcoal, used as a strainer for clearing or purifying liquids, air, etc. **2.** *Physics* A device that permits the passage of waves and currents of certain frequencies and limits the flow of certain others. **3.** *Photog.* A colored screen of glass, or of other translucent material, placed in front of a camera lens to control the kind and relative intensity of light waves in an exposure. — *v.t.* **1.** To pass (liquids, air, etc.) through a filter; strain. **2.** To separate or remove (impurities, etc.) by or as by a filter. **3.** To act as a filter for. — *v.i.* **4.** To pass through a filter. **5.** To leak out, as news. [< OF *filtre* < Med.L *feltrum* felt (used as a filter), ult. < Gmc. Akin to FELT[2].] — **fil/ter·er** *n.*

fil·ter·a·ble (fil/tər·ə·bəl) *adj.* **1.** Capable of being filtered. **2.** Capable of passing through a filter. Also **fil·tra·ble** (fil/trəb·əl) — **fil/ter·a·bil/i·ty** *n.*

filterable virus Virus (def. 1).

filter bed A reservoir with a sand or gravel bottom that filters and purifies large quantities of water.

filter paper A soft, porous paper suitable for filtering.

filth (filth) *n.* **1.** Anything that soils or makes foul; that which is foul or dirty. **2.** A foul condition. **3.** Moral defilement; obscenity. **4.** Obscene language. [OE *fylth*]

filth·y (fil/thē) *adj.* **filth·i·er, filth·i·est 1.** Of the nature of or containing filth; foul; dirty. **2.** Morally foul; offensive; obscene. **3.** Highly unpleasant or objectionable: *filthy* weather. — **filth/i·ly** *adv.* — **filth/i·ness** *n.*

fil·trate (fil/trāt) *v.t. & v.i.* **·trat·ed, ·trat·ing** To filter. — *n.* The liquid that has been separated by filtration. [< NL *filtratus,* pp. of *filtrare* < Med.L *filtrum* a filter]

fil·tra·tion (fil·trā/shən) *n.* **1.** The act or process of filtering. **2.** The sterilization of liquids by the mechanical removal of bacteria and other impurities.

fi·lum (fi/ləm) *n. pl.* **·la** (-lə) *Anat.* A threadlike structure. [< NL < L]

fim·ble (fim/bəl) *n.* The male hemp plant. [< Du. *femel*]

fim·bri·a (fim/brē·ə) *n. pl.* **·bri·ae** (-brī·ē) *Zool.* A fringe or fringelike structure, as around the mouth of a tube or duct in certain animals. [< NL < L, fringe] — **fim/bri·ate** (-it), **fim/bri·at·ed** (-ā/tid) *adj.* — **fim/bri·a/tion** *n.*

fim·bril·late (fim·bril/it) *adj. Biol.* Having a fine fringe or border. [< NL *fimbrilla,* dim. of L *fimbria* fringe]

fin[1] (fin) *n.* **1.** A membranous extension from the body of a fish or other aquatic animal, serving to propel, balance, or steer it in the water. For illustration see FISH. **2.** Any finlike or projecting part, appendage, or attachment. **3.** *Naut.* **a** A finlike appendage to a submarine or boat. **b** A fin keel (which see). **4.** *Aeron.* An airfoil or vane set longitudinally on an aircraft, missile, bomb, etc., for stabilization or control; especially, the vertical stabilizer of an airplane. **5.** A projecting rib or ridge, as on a radiator. **6.** *Usually pl.* A flipper (def. 2). **7.** *Slang* The hand. — *v.* **finned, fin·ning** *v.t.* **1.** To cut up or trim off the fins of (a fish). — *v.i.* **2.** To beat the water with the fins, as a whale when dying. [OE *finn*] — **fin/less** *adj.*

fin[2] (fin) *n. U.S. Slang* A five-dollar bill. [< Yiddish *finf* five]

fin. Finance; financial.

Fin. Finland; Finnish.

fin·a·ble (fi/nə·bəl) *adj.* Liable to or involving a fine: also spelled *fineable.*

fi·na·gle (fi·nā/gəl) *v.* **·gled, ·gling** *Informal v.t.* **1.** To get (something) by trickery or deceit. **2.** To cheat or trick (someone). — *v.i.* **3.** To use trickery or deceit; be sly. [Var. of FAINAIGUE] — **fi·na/gler** *n.*

fi·nal (fi/nəl) *adj.* **1.** Pertaining to, or coming at the end; ultimate; last. **2.** Precluding further action or controversy; conclusive; decisive: a *final* decree. **3.** Relating to or consisting in the end or purpose aimed at: a *final* cause. — *n.* **1.** Something that is terminal or last. **2.** *Often pl.* Something decisively final, as the last match in a tournament or the last examination of a school term. **3.** In medieval music, a tone corresponding in function to the tonic of a key: also **fi·nal·is** (fin-äl/is). [< F < L *finalis* < *finis* end]

final cause The object or end to be reached by an action or process; ultimate purpose.

fi·na·le (fi·nä/lē, -nal/ē; *Ital.* fē·nä/lā) *n.* The last part, as the final scene in a play or the concluding section of a musical composition. [< Ital., final]

fi·nal·ism (fi/nəl·iz/əm) *n. Philos.* The doctrine of final causes, stating that design or purpose actuates the universe.

fi·nal·ist (fi/nəl·ist) *n.* In games, contests, etc., a contestant who takes part in the final matches.

fi·nal·i·ty (fi·nal/ə·tē) *n. pl.* **·ties 1.** The state or quality of being final or settled; conclusiveness; decisiveness. **2.** A final or decisive act, offer, etc. **3.** *Philos.* Finalism.

fi·nal·ize (fi/nəl·īz) *v.t.* **·ized, ·iz·ing** To put into final or complete form; bring to completion. ◆ Although the use of *finalize* is frowned on by many, the word has been in established use for over twenty years.

fi·nal·ly (fi/nəl·ē) *adv.* **1.** At or in the end; in conclusion; lastly. **2.** Completely; irrecoverably; decisively.

fi·nance (fi·nans/, fi/nans) *n.* **1.** The science of monetary affairs. Abbr. **fin. 2.** *pl.* Monetary affairs; pecuniary resources; funds; revenue; income: the *finances* of a person or an empire. — *v.t.* **·nanced, ·nanc·ing 1.** To supply the money for. **2.** To manage the finances of. [< OF, payment < *finer* settle < *fin* end. See FINE[2].]

finance bill Legislation to raise revenue for the government.

fi·nan·cial (fi·nan/shəl, fi-) *adj.* **1.** Of or pertaining to finance or finances. **2.** Of or pertaining to those dealing with money and credit. Abbr. **fin.** — **fi·nan/cial·ly** *adv.*

— **Syn. 1.** *Financial, fiscal, pecuniary,* and *monetary* relate to dealings in money. *Financial* is used of large-scale dealings, whether by private individuals or by governments: *financial* backing for an expedition to Antarctica. Agencies and departments that have charge of *financial* affairs, especially in government, are described as *fiscal*; we also speak of the *fiscal* year, meaning the period for which an annual budget is prepared. Small-scale dealings are *pecuniary: pecuniary* motives, a *pecuniary* reward. We may also speak of a household's *pecuniary* problems. *Monetary* refers to the coins and bills used for money: the *monetary* value of an item, the *monetary* system of the United States.

fin·an·cier (fin/ən·sir/) *n.* **1.** One engaged in financial operations on a large scale. **2.** One skilled in financial affairs. — *v.t.* To finance.

fin·back (fin/bak/) *n.* A rorqual. Also **finback whale.**

finch (finch) *n.* A small, seed-eating bird (family *Fringillidae*), as the bunting, sparrow, grosbeak, bullfinch, goldfinch, greenfinch, canary, chaffinch, or weaverbird. ◆ Collateral adjective: *fringilline.* [OE *finc*]

find (find) *v.* **found, find·ing** *v.t.* **1.** To come upon unexpectedly; discover by chance. **2.** To discover after search or effort: to *find* a solution. **3.** To learn or become aware of by experience. **4.** To recover (something lost). **5.** To arrive at; reach; attain: The arrow *found* its target. **6.** To gain or recover the use of: He *found* his tongue. **7.** To determine by legal inquiry and declare. **8.** *Rare* To furnish or provide. — *v.i.* **9.** To express a decision after legal inquiry: to *find* for the plaintiff. — **Syn.** See DISCOVER. — **to find oneself 1.** To discover one's special abilities or one's proper vocation. **2.** To perceive oneself to be (in some specified place or condition): He *found himself* alone. — **to find out 1.** To learn; discover; ascertain. **2.** To detect the identity or true nature of. — *n.* **1.** The act of finding; discovery. **2.** Something found or discovered; especially, a valuable discovery. [OE *findan*]

find·er (fin/dər) *n.* **1.** One who or that which finds. **2.** *Astron.* A small telescope by the side of a large one, used to locate a particular object. **3.** *Photog.* A camera attachment that shows the photographer the object or scene as it appears in the field of view of the lens: also called *view finder.*

fin de siè·cle (fan də sye/kl') *French* End of the century; especially, the close of the 19th century, viewed as a period of transition in social and moral values.

fin-de-siè·cle (fan·də·sye/kl') *adj. French* Decadent.

find·ing (fin/ding) *n.* **1.** The act of one who finds; discovery. **2.** That which is found; a discovery. **3.** *Law* A conclusion arrived at before an official or a court. **4.** *pl.* The small tools and supplies of a workman.

Find·lay (fin'lē, find'-) A city in NW Ohio; pop. 35,800.

fine[1] (fīn) *adj.* **fin·er, fin·est** **1.** Superior in quality; excellent; choice. **2.** Highly satisfactory; very good: to have a *fine* time. **3.** Light or delicate in texture, workmanship, structure, etc. **4.** Composed of very small particles: *fine* powder. **5.** Very thin; slender: *fine* thread. **6.** Keen; sharp: a *fine* edge. **7.** Possessing superior ability or skill. **8.** Trained to highest efficiency: said of athletes, a horse, etc. **9.** Subtle; nice: a *fine* point in an argument. **10.** Delicate of perception; discriminating: a *fine* ear for music. **11.** Elegant; polished; fastidious: *fine* manners; also, overelegant; showy; affected. **12.** Handsome; good-looking. **13.** Cloudless; clear: *fine* weather. **14.** Free from impurities; pure: *fine* gold. **15.** Containing a given proportion of pure metal: gold 18 karats *fine*. Abbr. (for def. 15) *f.*, *F.* — *adv.* **1.** *Informal* Very well: It suits me *fine*. **2.** In billiards, in a manner so that the cue ball touches the object ball only lightly in passing. — *v.t. & v.i.* To make or become fine or finer. [< OF *fin* finished, perfected, ult. < L *finire* to complete < *finis* end]
— **Syn.** **1.** consummate, finished, perfected. **3.** dainty, exquisite. **4.** minute, comminuted. **5.** tenuous, gauzy. **12.** splendid, beautiful. **14.** clarified, clear. — **Ant.** coarse, heavy, thick, large, blunt.

fine[2] (fīn) *n.* **1.** A sum of money required as the penalty for an offense. **2.** *Law* **a** An amicable adjustment of a suit either real or fictitious, as for the final possession of lands in question. **b** A fee paid by a feudal tenant to his lord for permission to transfer the right of tenancy to another. **c** A sum of money paid by a tenant in order to keep the amount of his rent minimal. **3.** *Obs.* End; conclusion; death. — **in fine** Finally; in short. — *v.t.* **fined, fin·ing** To punish by fine; exact a fine from. [< OF *fin* settlement < L *finis* end]

fine[3] (fēn) *n.* *French* A drink of brandy.

fi·ne[4] (fē'nä) *n.* *Music* The end; finis. [< Ital.]

fine·a·ble (fī'nə-bəl) See FINABLE.

fine arts Those arts considered purely esthetic or expressive, including painting, drawing, sculpture, and architecture, and sometimes including literature, music, drama, and the dance. Abbr. *F.A.*

fine-cut (fīn'kut') *adj.* Finely shredded: said of tobacco.

fine-draw (fīn'drô') *v.t.* **-drew, -drawn, -draw·ing** **1.** To sew or close up, as a tear, so that the joining is imperceptible. **2.** To draw out to an extreme degree of fineness, tenuity, or subtlety, as a wire or an argument.

fine-drawn (fīn'drôn') *adj.* Drawn out to extreme fineness or subtlety: a *fine-drawn* distinction.

fine-grained (fīn'grānd') *adj.* Having a close, fine grain: said of some leathers and woods.

fine·ly (fīn'lē) *adv.* In a fine manner.

fine·ness (fīn'nis) *n.* **1.** The state or quality of being fine. **2.** The proportion of pure gold or silver in an alloy, expressed in number of parts per thousand or in karats.

fin·er·y[1] (fī'nər-ē) *n. pl.* **·er·ies** Elaborate adornment; showy or fine clothes or decorations.

fin·er·y[2] (fī'nər-ē) *n. pl.* **·er·ies** A hearth where cast iron is made malleable, or in which steel is made from pig iron.

fine-spun (fīn'spun') *adj.* **1.** Drawn or spun out to an extreme degree of fineness. **2.** Excessively subtle.

fi·nesse (fi-nes') *n.* **1.** Highly refined skill; subtlety of style or performance. **2.** Smoothness and tact, as in handling a delicate situation; discernment; also, artful strategy; cunning; craftiness. **3.** In bridge and other card games, an attempt on the part of a player to take a trick with a lower card when he holds a higher (as a queen when he holds the ace), in the hope that the opposing hand yet to play does not hold a taking card (as the king). — *v.* **·nessed, ·ness·ing** *v.t.* **1.** To change or bring about by finesse. **2.** In card games, to play as a finesse. — *v.i.* **3.** To use finesse. **4.** In card games, to make a finesse. [< F < *fin*. See FINE![1]]

fine-toothed comb (fīn'tōōtht') A comb with fine teeth set very close together. Also **fine'-tooth' comb.** — **to go over with a fine-toothed comb** To examine minutely.

fin·foot (fin'fōōt') *n. pl.* **·foots** Any of certain lobately web-footed aquatic birds related to the rails and coots. — **fin'-foot'ed** *adj.*

Fingal's Cave A basaltic cavern on Staffa island, Inner Hebrides, Scotland; 227 ft. long, 66 ft. high.

fin·ger (fing'gər) *n.* **1.** One of the terminating members of the hand, usually excluding the thumb. **2.** That part of a glove made to fit the finger. **3.** Anything that resembles or serves as a finger. **4.** A unit of measure based on the width of a finger (from ¾ inch to one inch); also, a measure equal to the length of (usually) the middle finger (about 4 to 4½ inches). **5.** *U.S.* A small amount of liquor filling a glass to a depth equal to the width of one finger. **6.** *Mech.* A small projecting piece of a machine. — **to burn one's fingers** To suffer the consequences of meddling or interfering. — **to have (or put) a finger in the pie** **1.** To take part in some matter. **2.** To meddle. — **to put one's finger on** To identify or indicate correctly. — **to put the finger on** *U.S.*

Slang **1.** To betray as, to the police. **2.** To point out (the victim of a planned crime). — **to twist around one's (little) finger** To influence or control with little or no effort. — *v.t.* **1.** To touch or handle with the fingers; toy with. **2.** To steal; pilfer. **3.** *Music* **a** To play (an instrument) with the fingers. **b** To mark the notes of (music) showing which fingers are to be used. **4.** *U.S. Slang* To betray, as to the police. **b** To point out (the victim of a planned crime). — *v.i.* **5.** To touch or feel anything with the fingers. **6.** *Music* **a** To use the fingers on a musical instrument in a certain manner. **b** To be arranged for playing by the fingers: said of instruments. [OE] — **fin'ger·er** *n.*

fin·ger·board (fing'gər-bôrd', -bōrd') *n.* In stringed instruments, as the violin, guitar, etc., the strip of wood upon which the strings are pressed by the fingers of the player. For illustration see VIOLIN.

finger bowl A bowl containing water for cleansing the fingers at the table after eating.

fin·ger·breadth (fing'gər-bredth', -bretth') *n.* The breadth of a finger, from ¾ inch to one inch.

fin·gered (fing'gərd) *adj.* **1.** Having fingers; digitate. **2.** Having figures to mark the fingering, as in a musical score. **3.** Marked, soiled, or touched by fingers.

fin·ger·ing (fing'gər·ing) *n.* **1.** The act of touching or feeling with the fingers. **2.** *Music* **a** The action or technique of using the fingers in playing an instrument. **b** The notation indicating what fingers are to be used.

Finger Lakes A group of long, narrow glacial lakes in west central New York.

fin·ger·ling (fing'gər·ling) *n.* **1.** A young fish, especially a salmon or trout, no bigger than a man's finger. **2.** A being of very small size: compare THUMBLING.

finger mark A mark or stain left by a finger.

fin·ger-marked (fing'gər-märkt') *adj.* Smudged with finger marks.

fin·ger·nail (fing'gər·nāl') *n.* The horny substance along the upper surface of the end of a finger.

finger painting The technique of applying paint to wet paper with the fingers and palms to form a design or picture; also, a painting made in this way.

finger post A guidepost in the shape of a hand with a pointing finger.

fin·ger·print (fing'gər·print') *n.* An impression of the skin pattern on the inner surface of a finger tip; especially, such an impression used for purposes of identification. — *v.t.* To take the fingerprints of.

fin·ger·stall (fing'gər·stôl') *n.* A protective covering for a finger.

HUMAN FINGER-NAIL
(Longitudinal section)
a Nail. *b* Matrix. *c* Nailfold. *d* Epidermis. *e* Phalange.

finger tip The extreme end of a finger. — **to have at one's finger tips** To have ready and available knowledge of or access to.

finger wave A wave shaped and set into dampened hair with the fingers, without the use of instruments or heat.

fin·i·al (fin'ē-əl) *n.* **1.** *Archit.* An ornament at the apex of a spire, pinnacle, or the like. **2.** Any terminal ornament pointing upward. [< L *finis* end + -IAL]

fin·i·cal (fin'i-kəl) *adj.* Finicky. — **fin'i·cal·ly** *adv.* — **fin'i·cal·ness, fin'i·cal·i·ty** (-kal'ə-tē) *n.*

fin·ick·ing (fin'i-king) *adj.* Finicky: also spelled *finnicking.* Also **fin·ick·in** (fin'ə-kin).

fin·ick·y (fin'i-kē) *adj.* Excessively fastidious or precise; fussy; exacting: also spelled *finnicky.* [< FINE[1] + -ICAL]

FINIAL

fin·ing (fī'ning) *n.* **1.** The removal of gas bubbles from fused glass. **2.** The purification and clarifying of wines. **3.** *pl.* Any substance used in clarifying liquids.

fin·is (fin'is, fī'nis) *n. pl.* **fin·is·es** The end; conclusion. [< L]

fin·ish (fin'ish) *v.t.* **1.** To complete or bring to an end; come to the end of: to *finish* a job; to *finish* a semester. **2.** To use up completely; consume. **3.** To perfect or complete by doing all things requisite or desirable: to *finish* a work of art. **4.** To perfect (a person) in social graces, education, etc. **5.** To give (fabric, wood, etc.) a particular surface quality or effect. **6.** *Informal* To kill, destroy, or defeat. — *v.i.* **7.** To reach or come to an end; stop. — *n.* **1.** The conclusion or last stage of anything; end. **2.** Something that completes or perfects. **3.** Completeness and perfection of detail; smoothness of execution. **4.** Perfection or polish in speech, manners, education, etc. **5.** The surface quality or appearance of textiles, paint, etc.: a rough or glossy *finish.* **6.** Woodwork, such as paneling or doors, used to complete the interior of a building. **7.** A material used in finishing: an oil *finish* on a painting. [< OF *feniss-*, stem of *fenir* to end < L *finire* < *finis* end] — **fin'ish·er** *n.*
— **Syn.** (verb) **1.** conclude, terminate, close. Compare END.

fin·ished (fin′isht) Past participle of FINISH. — *adj.* **1.** Ended; completed. **2.** Perfected to a high degree; polished. **3.** Highly accomplished or skilled: a *finished* musician.

fin·ish·ing school (fin′ish·ing) A school that prepares girls for entrance into society.

Fin·is·terre (fin′is·târ′, *Sp.* fē′nēs·ter′rä), **Cape** A headland in Galicia, the westernmost point of Spain.

fi·nite (fī′nīt) *adj.* **1.** Having bounds, ends, or limits; not infinite. **2.** That may be determined, counted, or measured. **3.** Subject to human or natural limitations: our *finite* minds. **4.** *Math.* **a** That may be equaled or completed by counting: said of numbers. **b** Limited and determinate, in theory or by observation; not infinite or infinitesimal: said of a magnitude. — *n.* Finite things collectively, or that which is finite: preceded by *the.* [< L *finitus* limited; orig. pp. of *finire* to end] — **fi′nite·ly** *adv.* — **fi′nite·ness** *n.*

finite verb *Gram.* A verb form that is limited as to person, number, tense, and mood, as distinguished from infinitives, participles, and gerunds, which have no such limitations; a verb form that can serve as a predicate.

fin·i·tude (fin′ə·tōod, -tyōod, fī′nə-) *n.* The state of being finite.

fink (fingk) *n. U.S. Slang* **1.** A strikebreaker; also, a labor spy or informer. **2.** An unsavory person; jerk. [? < FINGER, v. (def. 4)]

fin keel An extension of a yacht's keel downward, suggesting the back fin of a fish, commonly of metal and serving to ballast the yacht and to prevent lateral drifting.

Fin·land (fin′lənd) A Republic of northern Europe; 117,913 sq. mi.; pop. 4,706,000 (est. 1970); capital, Helsinki: Finnish *Suomi.* — **Fin′land·er** *n.*

Finland, Gulf of The part of the Baltic Sea between Finland and the Soviet Union.

Fin·lay (fin′lē, *Sp.* fin·lī′), **Carlos Juan,** 1833–1915, Cuban physician; discovered that yellow fever is mosquito-borne.

Finn (fin) *n.* **1.** A native or inhabitant of Finland. **2.** One whose native language is Finnish. [OE *Finnas* Finns]

Finn mac·Cool (fin′ mə·kōol′) See FIONN MACCUMHAIL.

fin·nan had·die (fin′ən had′ē) Smoked haddock. Also **fin′-nan had·dock** (had′ək). [*Findhorn* haddock, after *Findhorn,* a Scottish fishing port where originally prepared]

finned (find) *adj.* Having fins or finlike extensions.

Finn·ic (fin′ik) *n.* A branch of the Finno-Ugric subfamily of Uralic languages. — *adj.* Finnish.

fin·nick·ing (fin′ə·king), **fin·nick·y** (fin′ə·kē) See FINICKING, FINICKY.

Finn·ish (fin′ish) *adj.* Of or pertaining to Finland, the Finns, or their language. — *n.* The Uralic language of the Finns. *Abbr.* Finn.

Fin·no-U·gric (fin′ō-ōo′grik, -yōo′grik) *n.* A subfamily of the Uralic languages, embracing the Finnic (Finnish, Estonian, Lapp, etc.) and Ugric (Magyar, Ostyak, Vogul) branches. — *adj.* Pertaining to the Finns and the Ugrians, or to their languages. Also **Fin′no-U′gri·an.**

fin·ny (fin′ē) *adj.* **1.** Having fins. **2.** Resembling a fin. **3.** Of or pertaining to fish. **4.** Abounding in fish.

fi·no·chi·o (fi·nō′kē·ō) *n.* A variety of fennel (*Foeniculum vulgare dulce*) whose young sweet shoots are a food and salad. [< Ital. *finocchio* < L *faeniculum.* See FENNEL.]

fin ray One of the cartilaginous or bony rods supporting the membrane of a fish's fin: also called *ray.* For illustration see FISH.

Fin·ster·aar·horn (fin′stər·är′hôrn) The highest peak of the Bernese Alps, Switzerland; 14,032 ft.

Fi·o·na Mc·Leod (fē′nə mə·kloud′) See SHARP.

Fionn mac·Cumhail (fin′ mə·kōol′) The legendary hero of the Fenian cycle of third-century Ireland; father of the poet Ossian: also *Finn macCool.* Also **Fionn mac·Cumal.**

fiord (fyôrd, fyōrd) *n.* A long and narrow arm of the sea running between high, rocky cliffs or banks: also spelled *fjord.* [< Norw. *fjord*]

fip·pen·ny bit (fip′ə·nē, fip′nē) *U.S.* A Spanish silver coin, worth 6¼ cents, current in the United States until 1857.

fip·ple (fip′əl) *n.* A plug of wood at the mouth of certain wind instruments, as recorders. [? < ON *flipi* lip of a horse]

fipple flute A flute having a fipple.

fi·que (fē′kā) *n.* A succulent plant (*Furcraea macrophylla*) of the amaryllis family, native in tropical America, yielding a fiber similar to jute. [< Sp.]

fir (fûr) *n.* **1.** Any of several evergreen trees (genus *Abies*) of the pine family; especially, the balsam fir (which see). **2.** The wood of any of these trees. [OE *fyrh*]

Fir·dau·si (fir·dou′sē) Pseudonym of **Abul Kasim Mansur,** 941?–1020, Persian epic poet. Also **Fir·du·si** (fir·dōo′sē).

fire (fīr) *n.* **1.** The visible, active phase of combustion, manifested in light and heat. **2.** A burning mass of fuel, as in a fireplace. **3.** A destructive burning, as of a building. **4.** A substance or device that produces fire or a firelike display: Greek *fire.* **5.** A flash or spark of or as of fire: to strike *fire* from stones. **6.** A discharge of firearms: shooting: Cease *fire.* **7.** A rapid volley or series of outbursts: a *fire* of questions. **8.** Flashing brightness: brilliance: the *fire* of a diamond. **9.** *Poetic* Lightning. **10.** Intensity of spirit or feeling; ardor; passion. **11.** Vividness of thought or imagi-

nation. **12.** Warmth or heat, as of liquor. **13.** Fever or inflammation. **14.** An affliction or grievous trial: the *fires* of persecution. — **between two fires** Under attack or criticism from both sides. — **on fire 1.** Burning; ablaze. **2.** Ardent; zealous. — **to catch fire** To start to burn. — **to go through fire and water** To experience great afflictions or trials. — **to hang fire 1.** To fail to fire promptly, as a fire-arm. **2.** To be delayed, as an event. **3.** To be undecided, as a business agreement. — **to lay a fire** To arrange fuel for igniting. — **to miss fire 1.** To fail to discharge: said of fire-arms. **2.** To be unsuccessful; fail. — **to open fire 1.** To begin to shoot. **2.** To commence. — **to play with fire** To do something rash or dangerous. — **to set fire to** or **to set on fire 1.** To make burn. **2.** To inflame or excite. — **to set the world on fire** To gain great success or fame. — **to strike fire 1.** To create a fire, as with flint. **2.** To get a reaction. — **to take fire 1.** To start to burn. **2.** To become excited, angry, or enthusiastic. — **under fire 1.** Exposed to gunshot or artillery fire. **2.** Subjected to severe criticism. — *v.* **fired, fir·ing** *v.t.* **1.** To set on fire; cause to burn. **2.** To tend the fire of; put fuel in. **3.** To subject to the heat of fire. **4.** To set off, as explosives. **5.** To set off explosives within or near: to *fire* an oil well. **6.** To discharge, as a gun or bullet. **7.** *Informal* To hurl: to *fire* stones; to *fire* questions. **8.** *Informal* To dismiss from employment; discharge. **9.** To bake, as pottery, in a kiln. **10.** To cure, as tobacco, by exposure to heat. **11.** To cause to glow or shine. **12.** To inflame the emotions or passions of; inspire; excite. **13.** *Vet.* To cauterize. — *v.i.* **14.** To take fire; become ignited. **15.** To go off, as a gun. **16.** To set off firearms, a rocket, etc. **17.** *Informal* To hurl a missile. **18.** To tend a fire. **19.** To show certain effects after firing in a kiln. **20.** To become prematurely blotched or yellow, as corn or grain. — **to fire away** To start off and proceed with energy and rapidity, especially in asking questions. — **to fire up 1.** To start a fire, as in a boiler. **2.** To become excited or enraged. [OE *fŷr*] — **Syn.** (noun) **1.** *Fire, burning, combustion, flame, blaze,* and *flare* relate to the visible signs of rapid oxidation. *Fire* is a general term for the fact of burning, as well as for the light and heat evolved. *Burning* is rapid oxidation that produces marked heat, but not necessarily light. *Combustion* is the scientific term for burning. *Flame* refers to the stream of hot, and usually luminous gases given off by a *fire.* A bright *flame* is a *blaze*; a sudden outburst of *flame* or of light is a *flare.* **3.** conflagration. — (verb) **1.** ignite, light, kindle.

fire alarm 1. An alarm calling attention to a fire. **2.** An apparatus for giving an alarm of fire.

fire-and-brim·stone (fīr′ən·brim′stōn′) *adj.* Impassioned; also, threatening hell: a *fire-and-brimstone* sermon.

fire ant Any of a genus (*Solenopsis*) of destructive, mound-building red ants, especially a venomous species (*S. saevissima*) introduced into the United States from South America.

fire·arm (fīr′ärm′) *n.* Any weapon, usually small, from which a missile, as a bullet, is hurled by an explosive.

fire·ball (fīr′bôl′) *n.* **1.** A luminous meteor. **2.** Ball-shaped lightning. **3.** A hot, incandescent sphere of air and vaporized debris, formed around the center of a nuclear explosion. **4.** *U.S. Slang* A remarkably energetic person or thing. **5.** A ball or canvas sack filled with combustibles and formerly used in warfare as an explosive.

fire bed A receptacle or place for coals, as in a forge. For illustration see FORGE.

fire beetle Any of various elaterid beetles (genus *Pyrophorus*) of the West Indies.

fire·bird (fīr′bûrd′) *n.* Any of various small, brilliantly colored birds, as the Baltimore oriole, the vermilion flycatcher, and the scarlet tanager.

fire·blight (fīr′blīt′) *n.* A serious bacterial disease of various pome fruits, attacking blossoms, leaves, twigs, and fruit.

fire·board (fīr′bôrd′, -bōrd′) *n.* A board to close a fireplace not in use.

fire·boat (fīr′bōt′) *n.* A boat equipped with fire-fighting apparatus, used to protect wharves and ships.

fire·box (fīr′boks′) *n.* **1.** The chamber in which the fuel of a locomotive, furnace, etc., is burned. **2.** *Obs.* A tinderbox.

fire·brand (fīr′brand′) *n.* **1.** A piece of burning or glowing wood. **2.** One who stirs up trouble or dissension.

fire·brat (fīr′brat′) *n.* A small, wingless, scaly insect (*Thermobia domestica*), related to the silverfish, that inhabits warm houses and is destructive of wallpaper, clothing, and starchy materials. For illustration see INSECTS (injurious).

fire·break (fīr′brāk′) *n. U.S.* A strip of land that has been plowed or cleared to prevent the spread of fire.

fire·brick (fīr′brik′) *n.* A brick made of fire clay, used for lining furnaces.

fire brigade A company of firemen.

fire·bug (fīr′bug′) *n. U.S. Informal* An incendiary; pyromaniac.

fire bug The harlequin bug (which see).

fire clay A refractory material, usually a mixture of aluminum silicate, iron oxide, lime, and other constituents, used to make crucibles, furnace linings, and the like.

fire company 1. A company of men employed to extinguish fires. **2.** A company dealing in fire insurance.

fire control *Mil.* The control of the delivery of gunfire or of guided missiles by the use of special equipment.

fire·crack·er (fīr′krak′ər) *n.* A small paper cylinder charged with an explosive, used as a noisemaker.

fire-cure (fīr′kyŏŏr′) *v.t.* **-cured, -cur·ing** To cure (tobacco) with the heat and smoke of an open fire.

fire·damp (fīr′damp′) *n.* **1.** A combustible gas, chiefly methane that enters mines from coal seams. **2.** The explosive mixture formed by this gas and air.

fire department That part of the public service devoted to the prevention and extinguishing of fires. *Abbr. F.D.*

fire·dog (fīr′dôg′, -dog′) *n.* An andiron.

fire·drake (fīr′drāk′) *n.* A fire-breathing dragon of Germanic mythology. Also **fire′drag′on** (-drag′ən). [OE *fȳr-draca* < *fȳr* fire + *draca* dragon]

fire drill A practice drill or rehearsal of the prescribed procedure to be followed in case of fire.

fire-eat·er (fīr′ē′tər) *n.* **1.** A performer who pretends to eat fire. **2.** A hot-headed person eager to fight or quarrel.

fire engine A motor truck equipped with fire-fighting apparatus, especially one having power-driven pumps for throwing water and chemicals under high pressure.

fire escape A metal stairway attached to the outside of a building and furnishing a means of escape in case of fire; also, a ladder, chute, or other device similarly used.

fire extinguisher A portable apparatus containing fire-extinguishing chemicals ejected through a short hose.

fire·fang (fīr′fang′) *v.i.* To deteriorate by oxidation, as cheese, straw, or manure. [< FIRE + FANG, v.]

fire·fight·er (fīr′fī′tər) *n.* A fireman (def. 1).

fire·flaught (fīr′flôt′, -fläkht′) *n. Scot.* A flash of lightning.

fire·fly (fīr′flī′) *n. pl.* **·flies** Any of various night-flying beetles (family *Lampyridae*) emitting a phosphorescent light from an abdominal organ; especially, the North American genera *Photinus* and *Photuris*, whose females and phosphorescent larvae are called *glowworms*.

Fire-foam (fīr′fōm′) *n.* A thick, foamlike mixture of various chemicals used to smother fires: a trade name.

fire·guard (fīr′gärd′) *n.* **1.** An outdoor space cleared of all combustible matter to prevent the spread of fire. **2.** A metal screen placed before an open fire as a protection against sparks: also called *fire screen.*

fire·house (fīr′hous′) *n. U.S.* A building housing fire-fighting equipment and personnel. Also *Canadian* **fire′hall′** (-hôl′).

fire insurance Insurance covering property against loss or damage due to fire or lightning.

fire irons Poker, shovel, and tongs used in tending a fireplace.

fire·less (fīr′lis) *adj.* Having no fire.

fireless cooker A container, insulated to prevent rapid heat loss, in which hot foods may be placed to finish cooking or to be kept warm.

fire·light (fīr′līt′) *n.* The light from a fire, as from a campfire.

fire·lock (fīr′lok′) *n.* A flintlock (which see).

fire·man (fīr′mən) *n. pl.* **·men** (-mən) **1.** A member of the fire department; a man employed to prevent or extinguish fires: also called *firefighter.* **2.** One who tends fires, as on a locomotive; a stoker. **3.** In the U.S. Navy, an enlisted man of one of the three lowest grades, with a general apprenticeship in the occupational area of ship propulsion. **— visiting fireman** *U.S. Informal* An important or convivial visitor, often one of a group on a tour or convention.

fire marshal An official of the fire department who inspects fire hazards and violations and enforces their correction.

fire-new (fīr′nōō′, -nyōō′) *adj. Archaic* Fresh from the fire; brand-new.

Fi·ren·ze (fē-ren′dzā) The Italian name for FLORENCE.

fire opal A variety of opal having translucent orange-yellow to red colors suggesting streaks of flame: also called *girasol.*

fire·pan (fīr′pan′) *n.* **1.** A brazier; grate. **2.** The priming receptacle of a flintlock gun.

fire·pink (fīr′pingk′) *n.* A catchfly (*Silene virginica*) of the eastern United States, with crimson or scarlet flowers.

fire·place (fīr′plās′) *n.* A recess or structure in or on which a fire is built; especially, that part of a chimney that opens into a room.

fire·plug (fīr′plug′) *n.* A hydrant for supplying water in case of fire. *Abbr. f.p., F.P.*

fire pot **1.** That part of a stove, furnace, etc., in which the fuel is burned. **2.** A crucible.

fire·pow·er (fīr′pou′ər) *n. Mil.* **1.** Capacity for delivering fire, as from the guns of a ship, battery, etc. **2.** The amount or effectiveness of fire delivered by a given weapon or unit.

fire·proof (fīr′prōōf′) *adj.* Resistant to fire; relatively incombustible. **—** *v.t.* To make resistant to fire.

fire·proof·ing (fīr′prōō′fing) *n.* **1.** The act of making fireproof. **2.** Material used for this.

fir·er (fīr′ər) *n.* **1.** One who tends fires; a stoker. **2.** One who sets fire to something; an incendiary. **3.** One who fires

a weapon. **4.** A firearm considered with reference to its method or speed of firing: a *rapid-firer.*

fire-reels (fīr′rēlz′) *n. Canadian* A fire engine (which see). Also **fire′reel′.**

fire sale *U.S.* A bargain sale of fire-damaged goods.

fire screen A fireguard (def. 2).

fire ship A ship filled with combustibles or explosives, set afire and directed toward enemy ships, bridges, etc.

fire·side (fīr′sīd′) *n.* **1.** The hearth or space about the fireplace. **2.** Home or home life.

fire station A firehouse.

fire·stone (fīr′stōn′) *n.* **1.** Flint or pyrites formerly used for striking fire. **2.** A stone that resists fire.

fire·thorn (fīr′thôrn′) *n.* The pyracantha, a shrub.

fire tower A watchtower, usually in a wooded area, in which a lookout is posted to watch for and report fires.

fire·trap (fīr′trap′) *n.* A building notoriously flammable, or one not provided with an escape for use in case of fire.

fire wall **1.** A fireproof wall designed to block the progress of a fire. **2.** *Aeron.* A bulkhead of fire-resistant material placed between the engine of an aircraft and the rest of the structure to limit the spread of fire from the engines.

fire·war·den (fīr′wôr′dən) *n. U.S.* An officer in charge of the prevention and extinguishing of fires.

fire·wa·ter (fīr′wô′tər, -wot′ər) *n.* Whiskey: term first used by the North American Indian.

fire·weed (fīr′wēd′) *n.* The willow herb.

fire·wood[1] (fīr′wŏŏd′) *n.* Wood for fuel.

fire·wood[2] (fīr′wŏŏd′) *n.* An ironwood (*Cyrilla racemiflora*) of Central America and the SE United States.

fire·work (fīr′wûrk′) *n.* **1.** *Usually pl.* A device containing combustibles or explosives that, when ignited, produce a brilliant display of light or a loud noise. **2.** *pl.* A pyrotechnic display.

fire·worm (fīr′wûrm′) *n.* **1.** A glowworm. **2.** The larva of a tortricid moth (*Rhopobota naevana*), that devours the leaves of the cranberry, leaving the plant apparently burned.

fir·ing (fīr′ing) *n.* **1.** The act or process of applying fire or intense heat to anything, as in burning, baking, or vitrifying. **2.** The discharge of firearms. **3.** Fuel, as wood or coal.

firing line **1.** In combat, the front line from which gunfire is delivered; also, the troops stationed here. **2.** The foremost position in any activity.

firing pin The part of a firearm that strikes the primer or detonator, igniting the charge of the projectile.

firing squad **1.** A military or naval detachment assigned to execute, by shooting, a person condemned to death. **2.** A similar detachment selected to honor a deceased person by firing over his grave.

fir·kin (fûr′kən) *n.* **1.** A wooden vessel for butter, lard, etc. **2.** A measure of capacity, usually equal to one fourth of a barrel. [ME *ferdekyn* < MDu. *vierde* fourth + -KIN]

firm[1] (fûrm) *adj.* **1.** Relatively solid, compact, or unyielding to touch or pressure: *firm* snow; *firm* flesh. **2.** Difficult to move, loosen, etc.; stable: a *firm* fastening. **3.** Fixedly settled and established; immutable: a *firm* conviction. **4.** Constant and steadfast; enduring; unwavering: a *firm* friend. **5.** Full of or indicating strength or firmness; vigorous; steady: a *firm* handshake, voice, or look. **6.** Not fluctuating widely, as prices. **—** *v.t. & v.i.* To make or become firm. **—** *adv.* Solidly; resolutely; fixedly: to stand *firm* against the foe. [< L *firmus*] **— firm′ly** *adv.* **— firm′ness** *n.*

firm[2] (fûrm) *n.* **1.** A partnership of two or more persons for conducting business; business house. **2.** The name or title under which such a house carries on business. [< Ital. *firma* signature < L *firmare* to confirm < *firmus* firm]

fir·ma·ment (fûr′mə·mənt) *n.* The expanse of the heavens; sky. [< L *firmamentum* support < *firmare* to make firm] **— fir′ma·men′tal** *adj.*

fir·man (fûr′mən, fər·män′) *n. pl.* **·mans** A special decree of an Oriental sovereign. [< Persian *fermān* command]

firm·er (fûr′mər) *adj.* Designating a sturdy chisel or gouge with a thin, narrow blade, for manual use in shaping wood. **—** *n.* A firmer chisel or gouge. For illustration see GOUGE. [< F *fermoir* chisel, var. of *formoir* < *former* to shape]

firn (firn) *n. Meteorol.* Névé. [< G < *firn*, adj., of last year]

fir·ry (fûr′ē) *adj.* **1.** Of or pertaining to the fir. **2.** Made of fir. **3.** Wooded with firs.

first (fûrst) *adj.* **1.** Preceding all others in the order of numbering: the ordinal of *one.* **2.** Prior to all others in time; earliest. **3.** Nearest or foremost in place from a given point. **4.** Highest or foremost in character, rank, etc.; leading; best; chief. **5.** Denoting the forward gears with the lowest ratio in an automobile transmission. **6.** *Music* Designating one of two parts for like instruments or voices, usually the one higher in pitch or the principal one. **— in the first place** To start with. **—** *n.* **1.** One who or that which is first in time, rank, order, or position. **2.** The beginning: from *first* to last. **3.** The first day of a month; also, the first year in a period or reign. **4.** The winning position in a race or contest. **5.** The lowest forward gear of a motor vehicle; low gear. **6.** *Music* One of two parts for like instruments or voices, usually the one higher in pitch or the principal one. **7.** In English universities, the highest rank in examinations for honors; also, one winning this rank. **8.** *pl.* The best grade of certain merchandise, as of lumber, hosiery, etc. **— at first** At the beginning. **— from the first** From the beginning. **—** *adv.* **1.** Before all others in order, time, place, rank, etc.: to go *first.* **2.** In the first place: also (more formally) *firstly.* **3.** For the first time. **4.** In preference to anything else; preferably; sooner: He would die *first.* [OE *fyrst,* superl. of *fore* before]

◆ *First* usually precedes a cardinal number, as the *first ten* days. It sometimes follows the cardinal, though this order is not always considered acceptable, when it means *foremost* or *earliest,* as: They are the *two first* citizens of the state, or when the objects referred to are thought of individually, as: the *two first* books on the shelf.

— Syn. (adj.) **1.** prime, primary. **2.** original, primordial. Compare PRIMEVAL. **4.** principal, preeminent, supreme.

first aid Treatment given in an emergency before full medical care can be obtained. **— first-aid** (fûrst/ād/) *adj.*

First Amendment An amendment to the Constitution of the United States forbidding Congress to interfere with religion, free speech, a free press, the right to assemble peaceably, or the right to petition the government: ratified 1791.

first base In baseball, the base first reached by the runner, at the right-hand angle of the infield. **— to get to first base** *U.S. Slang* To succeed in the first phase of an undertaking.

first base·man (bās/mən) *n. pl.* **·men** (-mən) A baseball player stationed at or near first base.

first baseman's mitt See under MITT.

first-born (fûrst/bôrn/) *adj.* First brought forth; eldest. **—** *n.* The first-born child.

first cause 1. In Aristotelian philosophy, the prime mover. **2.** *Theol.* God as the uncaused creator of all things.

first-class (furst/klas/, -kläs/) *adj.* **1.** Of the highest rank or best quality. **2.** *U.S.* Of or pertaining to a class of sealed mail consisting wholly or partly of written matter and meeting certain governmental requirements. **3.** Of or pertaining to the most luxurious accommodations on a steamer, plane, etc. **—** *adv.* By first-class mail or conveyance.

First day Sunday: name used by the Society of Friends. **— Syn.** See SABBATH.

first estate The clergy.

first floor 1. *U.S.* The ground floor. **2.** In Britain and Europe generally, the floor just above the ground floor.

first fruit *Usually pl.* **1.** The first gatherings of a season's produce. *Ex.* xxiii 19. **2.** The first outcome, results, or rewards of anything.

first-hand (fûrst/hand/) *adj.* Direct from the original source or producer. **—** *adv.* From the original source.

first lady 1. The wife of a chief executive, especially the wife of the president of the U.S. **2.** Any outstanding or important woman in a particular profession.

first lieutenant *Mil.* A commissioned officer ranking next above a second lieutenant and next below a captain.

first light *Naut.* The beginning of morning; nautical twilight, when the sun is 12° below the horizon.

first·ling (fûrst/ling) *n.* The first or first-born.

first·ly (fûrst/lē) *adv.* In the first place: followed by *secondly, thirdly,* etc.

first mate A ship's officer ranking next below the captain.

first mortgage A mortgage having priority over all other liens.

first night The opening performance of a play, opera, etc.

first-night·er (fûrst/nī/tər) *n.* One who regularly attends opening performances at the theater.

first offender A person guilty of his first legal violation.

first officer In the merchant marine, a first mate.

first papers Documents filed by an alien, declaring intention to be naturalized as a citizen of the United States.

first person See under PERSON.

first-rate (fûrst/rāt/) *adj.* **1.** Of the finest class, quality, or character. **2.** *Informal* Excellent; very good. **—** *adv. Informal* Excellently.

First Reader In Christian Science services, a person chosen to read aloud from the works of Mary Baker Eddy.

First Republic The republic established in France in 1792 during the French Revolution, followed in 1804 by the first French Empire under Napoleon Bonaparte.

first sergeant *U.S.* The occupational title of the chief noncommissioned officer of a company, battery, troop, etc.

first water 1. The finest quality of gems, especially of diamonds and pearls. **2.** The highest grade of quality.

firth (fûrth) *n. Scot.* An arm of the sea: also spelled *frith.*

Firth of Clyde See under CLYDE.

Firth of Forth See (Firth of) FORTH.

Firth of Tay See TAY.

fisc (fisk) *n.* The treasury of a state or kingdom. [< F < L *fiscus* purse]

fis·cal (fis/kal) *adj.* **1.** Of or pertaining to the treasury or finances of a government. **2.** Financial. **—** *n.* In Spain, Portugal, and some other countries, a public prosecutor.

fiscal year A financial year at the end of which accounts are balanced; any twelve-month period used as a basis of business reckoning. *Abbr. FY*

Fisch·er (fish/ər), **Emil,** 1852–1919, German organic chemist. **— Hans,** 1881–1945, German organic chemist.

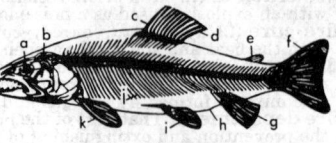

FISH
(Anatomical features of a trout)
a Eye socket. *b* Brain case. *c* Dorsal fin. *d* Fin ray. *e* Adipose fin. *f* Caudal fin. *g* Anal fin. *h* Anus. *i* Ventral fin (also called abdominal, thoracic, or jugular, according to its deviation from normal position). *j* Ribs. *k* Pectoral fin.

fish (fish) *n. pl.* **fish** or (with reference to different species) **fish·es 1.** A vertebrate, cold-blooded craniate animal with permanent gills, belonging to the superclass *Pisces* in the phylum *Chordata.* Adapted solely for aquatic life, it has a typically elongate, tapering body, usually covered with scales and provided with fins for locomotion. ◆ Collateral adjective: *piscine.* **2.** Loosely, any animal habitually living in the water. **3.** The flesh of fish used as food. **4.** *Informal* A person considered as having certain fishlike characteristics, such as lack of emotion or intelligence: a cold *fish.* **5.** A flat plate of iron, wood, etc., fastened alongside another to strengthen it, or used to join two parts. **6.** *Naut.* **a** A strip of hard wood used to strengthen a mast or yard. **b** A fish tackle. **— like a fish out of water** Out of one's proper or usual environment; not comfortable or at ease. **— neither fish, flesh, nor fowl** Neither one thing nor the other; without definite convictions, opinions, etc.; nondescript. **— to have other fish to fry** To have other and more important business to do. **—** *v.t.* **1.** To catch or try to catch fish in (a body of water). **2.** To catch or try to catch (fish, eels, etc.). **3.** To grope for and bring out: with *out* or *up:* to *fish* money out of one's pocket. **4.** *Naut.* **a** To repair or strengthen by strips fastened lengthwise: to *fish* a spar. **b** To bring the flukes of (an anchor) to the gunwale or rail. **—** *v.i.* **5.** To catch or try to catch fish. **6.** To try to get something in an artful or indirect manner: with *for:* to *fish* for compliments. **— to fish in troubled waters** To try to turn a difficult situation to one's own advantage. **— to fish out** To exhaust of fish. [OE *fisc*] **— fish/a·ble** *adj.* **— fish/like/** *adj.*

Fish (fish) *n.* The constellation and sign of the zodiac Pisces.

Fish (fish), **Hamilton,** 1808–93, U.S. statesman and lawyer.

fish and chips *Brit.* Fish fillets and potatoes sliced and French fried.

fish-ber·ry (fish/ber/ē) *n. pl.* **·ries** The berry of an East Indian vine (*Anamirta cocculus*), yielding picrotoxin.

fish-bolt (fish/bōlt/) *n.* A bolt for securing fishplates.

fish-bowl (fish/bōl/) *n.* A bowl, usually of glass, serving as a small aquarium for fish.

fish cake A fried ball or cake of chopped fish, usually salt codfish, mixed with mashed potatoes. Also **fish ball.**

fish crow A crow (*Corvus ossifragus*) of the Atlantic coast of the United States, feeding mainly on fish.

fish·er (fish/ər) *n.* **1.** One who fishes; a fisherman. **2.** A weasellike carnivore (*Martes pennanti*) of eastern North America, related to the marten: also called *pekan.* **3.** The dark brown fur of this animal.

Fish·er (fish/ər), **Dorothy Canfield,** 1879–1958, U.S. author. **— Herbert Albert Laurens,** 1865–1940, English historian. **— Irving,** 1867–1947, U.S. economist. **— John,** 1459?–1535, English bishop and scholar; executed; canonized 1935. **— Sir John Arbuthnot,** 1841–1920, Baron of Kilverstone, British admiral.

fish·er·man (fish/ər·mən) *n. pl.* **·men** (-mən) **1.** One who fishes as an occupation or for sport. **2.** A fishing boat.

fisherman's bend A knot used in bending a rope to an anchor.

fish·er·y (fish/ər·ē) *n. pl.* **·er·ies 1.** The operation or business of catching fish or other aquatic animals. **2.** The place for such an operation; a fishing ground. **3.** A fish hatchery. **4.** *Law* The right to fish in a given place at a given time.

fish flake *Canadian* A platform for drying fish.

fish-gig (fish/gig/) *n.* A staff with prongs for spearing fish: also called *fizgig.*

fish-grass (fish/gras/, -gräs/) *n.* Fanwort.

fish hatchery A place designed for the artificial propagation, hatching, and nurture of fish.

fish hawk The osprey.

fish-hook (fish/hook/) *n.* A hook, usually barbed, for catching fish.

fish·ing (fish/ing) *n.* **1.** The occupation or sport of catching fish. **2.** A place for fishing; fishery.

fishing pole A long, slender pole with a fishing line, and often a reel, attached to it.

fishing tackle Equipment for fishing, including rod, reel, leader, hooks, and harness.

fish joint A splice made by fastening two rails, beams, etc., end to end with fishplates.

fish·line (fish'līn') *n.* Line or cord used for fishing; also, a length of such line with a hook attached. Also **fishing line**.
fish·meal (fish'mēl') *n.* Ground dried fish, used as fertilizer and feed for animals.
fish·mon·ger (fish'mung'gər, -mong'-) *n.* A dealer in fish.
fish·net (fish'net') *n.* A net for catching fish.
fish·plate (fish'plāt') *n.* One of the metal plates fastened to the sides of two beams or rails, joining them end to end.
fish·pole (fish'pōl') *n.* A fishing rod.
fish·pound (fish'pound') *n. U.S.* A netlike device placed under the water to catch fish.
fish·spear (fish'spir') *n.* 1. A spear for catching or killing fish. 2. A lance for bleeding captured whales.
fish stick *U.S. & Canadian* A frozen fish filet in bar form.
fish story *Informal* An extravagant or incredible narrative.
fish tackle A tackle used to raise an anchor to the gunwale of a ship by means of an iron hook.
fish·tail (fish'tāl') *adj.* Resembling the tail of a fish in shape or action. — *v.i. Aeron.* To swing the tail of an aircraft from side to side as a retarding action; yaw.
fishtail kick In swimming, a kick in which both legs are drawn up and then thrust simultaneously backward while held together.
fish warden A local officer who enforces laws relating to the protection of fish or fisheries.
fish well A compartment, as in the hold of a fishing smack, containing water and used for storing live fish.
fish·wife (fish'wīf') *n. pl.* **·wives** (-wīvz') 1. A woman who sells fish. 2. A coarse, abusive woman.
fish·y (fish'ē) *adj.* **fish·i·er**, **fish·i·est** 1. Suggestive of, pertaining to, or like fish. 2. Abounding in fish. 3. *Informal* Improbable; unlikely: a *fishy* story. 4. *Informal* Questionable; doubtful: His accent is very *fishy*. 5. Vacant of expression; dull: *fishy* eyes. — **fish'i·ly** *adv.* — **fish'i·ness** *n.*
Fisk (fisk), **James**, 1834–72, U.S. railroad financier.
Fiske (fisk), **Bradley Allen**, 1854–1942, U.S. admiral; inventor of naval ordnance. — **John**, 1842–1901, U.S. philosopher and historian: original name **Edmund Fiske Green**. — **Minnie Maddern**, 1865–1932, *née* Davey, U.S. actress.
fis·sate (fis'āt) *adj.* Deeply cleft; fissured.
fissi- *combining form* Split; cleft: *fissirostral*. Also, before vowels, **fiss-**. [< L *fissus*, pp. of *findere* to split]
fis·sile (fis'əl) *adj.* 1. Capable of being split or separated into layers. 2. Tending to split. [< L *fissilis* < *findere* to split] — **fis·sil·i·ty** (fi·sil'ə·tē) *n.*
fis·sion (fish'ən) *n.* 1. The act of splitting or breaking apart. 2. *Biol.* Spontaneous division of a cell or organism into new cells or organisms, especially as a mode of reproduction; cell division. 3. *Physics* The disintegration of the nucleus of a heavy atom, leading to the formation of nuclei of more stable atoms and the release of energy: also called *nuclear fission*: compare FUSION. [< L *fissio*, *-onis* < *fissus*, pp. of *findere* to split]
fis·sion·a·ble (fish'ən·ə·bəl) *adj.* Capable of undergoing nuclear fission.
fis·si·pal·mate (fis'i·pal'māt) *adj.* Partially web-footed.
fis·sip·a·rous (fi·sip'ər·əs) *adj. Biol.* Reproducing or separating by fission.
fis·si·ped (fis'i·ped) *adj.* Having the toes separated: also **fis·sip·e·dal** (fi·sip'ə·dəl, fis'i·ped'l), **fis'si·pe'di·al** (-pē'dē·əl). — *n. Zool.* Any of a suborder (*Fissipedia*) of terrestrial carnivores with separate toes, as cats, bears, etc. [< LL *fissipes, -pedis*]
fis·si·ros·tral (fis'i·ros'trəl) *adj. Ornithol.* Having a wide, deeply cleft beak, as swifts, nighthawks, etc. [< FISSI- + L *rostrum* beak]
fis·sure (fish'ər) *n.* 1. A narrow opening, cleft, crevice, or furrow. 2. The act of cleaving, or the state of being cleft; cleavage. 3. *Anat.* **a** Any cleft or furrow of the body, as between the lobes of the liver. **b** One of the furrows on the surface of the brain. — *v.t. & v.i.* **·sured**, **·sur·ing** To crack; split; cleave. [< L *fissura* < *findere* to split]
fist¹ (fist) *n.* 1. The hand closed tightly, as for striking; the clenched hand; also, grip; clutch. 2. *Informal* The hand. 3. *Informal* Handwriting. 4. *Printing* The index mark ☞. — *v.t.* 1. To strike with the fist. 2. *Naut.* To grasp with the fist. [OE *fȳst*]
fist² (fist) *n.* A fice.
fist·ful (fist'fŏŏl) *n. pl.* **·fuls** *Informal* A handful.
fist·ic (fis'tik) *adj.* Of or pertaining to boxing; pugilistic.
fist·i·cuff (fis'ti·kuf') *n.* 1. *pl.* A fight with the fists. 2. *pl.* The science of boxing. 3. A blow with the fist. — *v.t. & v.i.* To beat or fight with the fists. [< FIST + CUFF²] — **fist'i·cuff'er** *n.*
fis·tu·la (fis'chŏŏ·lə) *n. pl.* **·las** or **·lae** (-lē) 1. *Pathol.* A duct or canal formed by the imperfect closing of a wound, abscess, or the like, and leading either to the body surface or from one cavity or hollow organ to another. 2. *Vet.* A deep-seated, suppurative inflammation, as in the withers of a horse. 3. *Obs.* A reed or pipe. [< L, a pipe]

fis·tu·lous (fis'chŏŏ·ləs) *adj.* 1. Of, pertaining to, or like a fistula. 2. Cylindrical and hollow like a reed. 3. Having or consisting of cylindrical or hollow parts. Also **fis'tu·lar** (-lər).
fit¹ (fit) *adj.* **fit·ter, fit·test** 1. Adapted to an end, aim, or design; suited: a machine *fit* for the job. 2. Proper or appropriate; becoming: a *fit* sentiment. 3. Possessing the proper qualifications; competent. 4. In a state of preparation; ready: ground *fit* for planting. 5. In good physical condition; healthy. 6. *Informal* Suitable: not a *fit* night for man or beast. — **Syn.** See APPROPRIATE. — *v.* **fit·ted** or **fit, fit·ting** *v.t.* 1. To be suitable or proper for: Dark days *fit* dark deeds. 2. To be of the right size and shape for. 3. To make or alter to the proper size or purpose. 4. To provide with what is suitable or necessary; equip. 5. To prepare or make ready or qualified. 6. To put in place carefully or exactly: to *fit* an arrow to a bow. — *v.i.* 7. To be suitable or proper. 8. To be of the proper size, shape, etc. — **Syn.** See ADAPT. — **to fit out** (or **up**) To supply with what is necessary; outfit. — *n.* 1. Condition or manner of fitting: a good *fit*. 2. Something that fits: This suit is a fine *fit*. 3. The act of fitting. [ME *fyt*; origin uncertain] — **fit'ness** *n.*
fit² (fit) *n.* 1. A sudden onset of an organic or functional disorder, often attended by convulsions, as in epilepsy; spasm. 2. A sudden overmastering emotion or feeling: a *fit* of rage. 3. Impulsive and irregular exertion or action: a *fit* of industry. — **by fits** or **by fits and starts** Spasmodically; irregularly. [OE *fitt* struggle]
fit³ (fit) *n. Archaic* A division of a ballad or song. [OE]
fit⁴ (fit) *n. Scot.* A foot; step.
fitch (fich) *n.* A fitchew, or its fur. [< MDu. *vitsche* polecat]
Fitch (fich), **John**, 1743–98, U.S. inventor; pioneer in steam navigation. — (**William**) **Clyde**, 1865–1909, U.S. playwright.
Fitch·burg (fich'bûrg) A city in northern Massachusetts; pop. 43,343.
fitch·ew (fich'ōō) *n.* 1. The polecat of Europe. 2. The fur of this animal. Also called *fitch*: also **fitch'et** (-it). [< OF *fissel, fissau.* Cf. MDu. *fisse, vitsche*.]
fit·ful (fit'fəl) *adj.* Characterized by irregular or spasmodic actions, moods, etc.; shifting; capricious. — **fit'ful·ly** *adv.* — **fit'ful·ness** *n.*
fit·ly (fit'lē) *adv.* In a fit manner or place, or at a fit time; properly; suitably.
fit·ter (fit'ər) *n.* 1. One who or that which fits. 2. One who adjusts pipes, as for heating. 3. One who fits and adjusts parts for a machine. 4. In dressmaking, one who fits the shape or size of the garment to the figure. 5. One who outfits or supplies things, as for an expedition.
fit·ting (fit'ing) *adj.* Fit or suitable; proper; appropriate. — **Syn.** See APPROPRIATE. — *n.* 1. The act of one who fits. 2. A piece of equipment or an appliance used in an adjustment: a gas *fitting*. 3. *pl.* Furnishings, fixtures, or decorations, as for a house. — **fit'ting·ly** *adv.* — **fit'ting·ness** *n.*
Fitz- *prefix* Son of: formerly used in forming the surnames of illegitimate children of royalty. Compare O', MAC-. [< AF, var. of OF *fiz, filz* < L *filius* son]
Fitz·Ger·ald (fits'jer'əld), **Edward**, 1809–83, English poet; translated Omar Khayyám's *Rubáiyát*.
Fitz·ger·ald (fits'jer'əld), **F**(**rancis**) **Scott** (**Key**), 1896–1940, U.S. novelist and short-story writer.
Fiu·me (fyōō'mā) The Italian name for RIJEKA.
five (fīv) *n.* 1. The sum of four and one: a cardinal number. ◆ Collateral adjective: *quinary*. 2. Any symbol of this number, as 5, v, V. 3. Anything consisting of or representing five units, as a team, playing card, etc. — *adj.* Being one more than four. [OE *fīf*]
five-and-ten-cent store (fīv'ən·ten'sent') 1. Originally, a store selling miscellaneous articles priced at five and ten cents. 2. A store selling articles priced from a few cents to one dollar or more. Also called *dime store, ten-cent store.* Also **five'-and-ten', five-and-dime** (fīv'ən·dīm').
Five Civilized Nations (or **Tribes**) The Cherokee, Chickasaw, Choctaw, Creek, and Seminole tribes of Oklahoma.
five-fin·gers (fīv'fing'gərz) *n.* 1. The cinquefoil. 2. The bird's-foot trefoil. 3. The oxlip. 4. The Virginia creeper. 5. A starfish with five arms.
Five Forks A locality in SE Virginia; scene of a Union victory in the Civil War, April 1, 1865.
five hundred A card game developed from euchre, with the joker as high card and 500 points for game.
five iron In golf, an iron with a moderately sloping face, used in lofting the ball: also called *mashie*.
Five Nations A confederacy of five tribes of Iroquois Indians, the Mohawks, Oneidas, Onondagas, Cayugas, and Senecas, within New York State. See SIX NATIONS.
five·pins (fīv'pinz') *n. Canadian* An indoor bowling game using five pins.
fiv·er (fīv'ər) *n. Informal* 1. A five-dollar bill or a five-pound note. 2. Anything counting as five.
fives (fīvz) *n.pl. Brit.* A game similar to handball.

five-spot (fīv′spot′) *n.* **1.** A small, delicate annual herb (*Nemophila maculata*) of the waterleaf family, with white, purple-spotted flowers, common in California. **2.** *Slang* A five-dollar bill.

Five-Year Plan (fīv′yir′) A plan for national economic development: a term originating with the first of such plans adopted by the Soviet Union in 1928.

fix (fiks) *v.t.* **1.** To make firm or secure; fasten so as to be immovable. **2.** To set or place permanently. **3.** To render permanent and unchangeable: to *fix* color. **4.** To place firmly in the mind. **5.** To hold or direct (the attention, gaze, etc.) steadily: He *fixed* his eyes on the door. **6.** To look at steadily or piercingly: He *fixed* her with his eyes. **7.** To settle or decide definitely: The decision *fixed* his fate. **8.** To determine or establish: The mayor *fixed* the date permanently. **9.** To place (blame or responsibility) on a person. **10.** *U.S.* To arrange or put in order; adjust, as clothing or the hair. **11.** *U.S. Informal* To repair. **12.** *U.S.* To prepare (food or a meal). **13.** *U.S. Informal* To prearrange or influence the outcome, decision, etc., of (a race, game, jury, etc.) by bribery or collusion. **14.** *U.S. Informal* To chastise or discipline: A sound thrashing will *fix* him. **15.** *U.S. Informal* To get even with: I'll *fix* him. **16.** To prepare (specimens) for microscopic study. **17.** *Chem.* To cause to form a nonvolatile or solid compound. **18.** *Photog.* To bathe (a film or plate) in chemicals that remove substances still sensitive to light, thus preventing fading. **19.** *Informal* To castrate or spay (a dog, cat, etc.). —*v.i.* **20.** To become firm or stable. **21.** *U.S. Dial.* To get ready; prepare: I'm *fixing* to go. — **to fix on** To decide upon. — **to fix up** *U.S. Informal* **1.** To repair. **2.** To arrange or put in order. **3.** To supply the needs of. —*n.* **1.** *Informal* A difficult situation; predicament. **2.** The position of a ship or aircraft as determined by reference to certain fixed points on shore, to astronomical observations, or to the point of intersection of two or more bearings. **3.** *U.S. Slang* A decision or outcome prearranged by bribery or other corrupt means. **4.** *U.S. Slang* An injection of heroin or other narcotic. — **Syn.** See PREDICAMENT. [< Med.L *fixare* to fasten < L *fixus*, pp. of *figere* to fasten] — **fix′a·ble** *adj.* — **fix′er** *n.*

fix·ate (fik′sāt) *v.t. & v.i.* **·at·ed, ·at·ing** **1.** To render or become fixed. **2.** To fix or concentrate, as the eyes or attention, upon something. **3.** *Psychoanal.* To concentrate (the libido) on a particular childhood situation or object, blocking further development or new attachment. [< Med.L *fixatus*, pp. of *fixare*. See FIX.]

fix·a·tion (fik·sā′shən) *n.* **1.** The act of fixing, or the state of being fixed. **2.** *Chem.* **a** The reduction of a volatile or fluid substance to a stable or permanent state. **b** The making permanent of a dye or color, as in a fabric or film. **c** The conversion of free nitrogen from the air into useful compounds; also, any similar process applied to an oil or a gas. **3.** *Psychoanal.* An arrested excessive attachment of the libido in a particular childhood developmental stage, hindering maturation and sometimes leading to psychoses or psychoneuroses. **4.** Loosely, a preoccupation or obsession.

fix·a·tive (fik′sə·tiv) *adj.* Serving to render permanent or fixed. —*n.* That which serves to render permanent or fixed; especially, a substance for preserving paintings or drawings.

fixed (fikst) *adj.* **1.** Placed or fastened securely; made firm in position. **2.** Steadily or intently directed; set: a *fixed* gaze. **3.** Stationary or unchanging in relative position: a *fixed* star. **4.** Definite and unalterable: a *fixed* opinion. **5.** Permanent: a *fixed* dye. **6.** *U.S. Informal* Prearranged as to outcome or decision: a *fixed* jury. **7.** *U.S. Slang* Provided with money, equipment, possessions, etc.: He's well *fixed*. **8.** *Chem.* **a** Formed into or forming part of a compound. **b** Not volatile: a *fixed* oil. **9.** *Biol.* Sessile. — **Syn.** See PERMANENT. — **fix·ed·ly** (fik′sid·lē) *adv.* — **fix′ed·ness** *n.*

fixed charge *Econ.* A charge that cannot be changed or avoided; especially, such a charge payable at fixed intervals, as rent, taxes, etc.

fixed idea *Psychiatry* An obsessional idea, often delusional, that tends to influence a person's whole attitude or mental life: also called *idée fixe.*

fixed oil *Chem.* A fatty oil that does not evaporate and leaves a stain: distinguished from *volatile oil.*

fixed star *Astron.* A star that seems to preserve the same position with respect to the stars around it.

fixed-wing (fikst′wing′) *adj. Aeron.* Designating an airplane with fixed or adjustable wings, as distinguished from a helicopter.

fix·ings (fik′singz) *n.pl. U.S. Informal* Trimmings; appurtenances.

fix·i·ty (fik′sə·tē) *n. pl.* **·ties** **1.** The state or quality of being fixed; stability; permanence. **2.** That which is fixed.

fix·ture (fiks′chər) *n.* **1.** Anything securely fixed or fastened into position; especially, a permanent part or appendage of a house: a bathroom *fixture.* **2.** A person or thing regarded as fixed in a particular place or job. **3.** *Law* **a** Any chattel or article of personal property annexed or affixed to realty with the intention that it become a part thereof and that is thereafter governed by the law of real property. **b** A chattel annexed to realty by a tenant, that can be re-

moved at any time during the tenancy without material injury to the premises. [< FIXURE; infl. in form by *mixture*]

fix·ure (fik′shər) *n. Obs.* Fixed condition; firmness. [< LL *fixura* a fastening < L *figere* to fasten]

fiz·gig[1] (fiz′gig′) *n.* **1.** A silly or flirtatious girl. **2.** A firework that makes a fizzing noise when ignited. **3.** A toplike toy that whirls rapidly; whirligig. [? < FIZZ + GIG[1]]

fiz·gig[2] (fiz′gig′) *n.* A fishgig (which see).

fizz (fiz) *v.i.* To make a hissing or sputtering noise. —*n.* **1.** A hissing or sputtering sound. **2.** An effervescent beverage. **3.** A drink made with soda water, liquor, flavoring, etc.: a gin *fizz.* **4.** *Brit.* Champagne. Also *Rare* fiz. [Imit.]

fiz·zle (fiz′əl) *v.i.* **·zled, ·zling** **1.** To make a hissing or sputtering sound. **2.** *Informal* To fail, especially after a good start: often with *out.* —*n.* **1.** A hissing or sputtering sound. **2.** *Informal* A failure; flop. [Freq. of obs. *fise* to fart]

fiz·zy (fiz′ē) *adj.* **fizz·i·er, fizz·i·est** Fizzing; effervescent.

fjeld (fyeld) *n.* In Scandinavian countries, a high, barren plateau or tableland: also spelled *field.*

fjord (fyôrd) See FIORD.

fl. **1.** Floor. **2.** Florin(s). **3.** Floruit. **4.** Flower. **5.** Fluid. **6.** *Music* Flute.

Fl *Chem.* Fluorine.

Fl. **1.** Flanders. **2.** Flemish.

Fla. Florida.

flab·ber·gast (flab′ər·gast) *v.t. Informal* To astound; confound. — **Syn.** See AMAZE. [? < FLABB(Y) + AGHAST]

flab·by (flab′ē) *adj.* **·bi·er, ·bi·est** **1.** Lacking strength or firmness; soft; flaccid: *flabby* legs or muscles. **2.** Lacking vigor or force; weak, as language, character, etc. [Var. of *flappy* < FLAP + -Y[1]] — **flab′bi·ly** *adv.* — **flab′bi·ness** *n.*

fla·bel·late (flə·bel′it, -āt) *adj. Bot. & Zool.* Fan-shaped. Also **fla·bel·li·form** (flə·bel′ə·fôrm).

flabelli- *combining form* Fan-shaped: *flabelliform.* [< L *flabellum* fan, orig. dim. of *flabrum* breeze < *flare* to blow]

fla·bel·lum (flə·bel′əm) *n. pl.* **·bel·la** (-bel′ə) **1.** A fan, especially one used ceremonially in the Greek and Roman Catholic churches. **2.** Any fan-shaped structure. [< L, fan]

flac·cid (flak′sid, flas′əd) *adj.* Lacking firmness or elasticity; limp; flabby. [< F *flaccide* < L *flaccidus* < *flaccus* limp] — **flac′cid·ly** *adv.* — **flac·cid′i·ty, flac′cid·ness** *n.*

flack (flak) *n. U.S. Slang* **1.** A press agent. **2.** Publicity from a press agent. [? < FLAK]

fla·con (flá·kôn′) *n. French* A stoppered bottle or flask.

flag[1] (flag) *n.* **1.** A piece of cloth or bunting, usually oblong and bearing various devices and colors to designate a nation, state, organization, etc., and commonly attached to a staff or halyard as a standard, symbol, or signal. **2.** The bushy part of the tail of a dog, as that of a setter. **3.** The tail of a deer. **4.** *pl. Ornithol.* The long feathers on the leg of a hawk or other bird of prey; also, those on the second joint of a bird's wing. **5.** *Music* A hook. —*v.t.* **flagged, flag·ging** **1.** To mark out or adorn with flags. **2.** To signal with or as with a flag. **3.** To send (information) by signals. **4.** To decoy (deer, etc.) by or as by waving a flag. — **to flag down** To cause to stop, as a train, by signalling with a flag or with a waving motion. [Prob. < FLAG[3]] — **flag′ger** *n.*

flag[2] (flag) *n.* **1.** Any of various irises having sword-shaped leaves and growing in moist places; especially, the **yellow flag** (*Iris pseudacorus*), and the common **blue flag** (*I. versicolor*), the State flower of Tennessee. **2.** The leaf of a flag. [Cf. Du. *vlag* iris]

flag[3] (flag) *v.i.* **flagged, flag·ging** **1.** To lose vigor; grow tired or weak: Our spirits *flagged.* **2.** To hang down; become limp. [? < obs. *flack* flutter; infl. by OF *flaquir* to droop < *flac* droopy < L *flaccus*]

flag[4] (flag) *n.* A flagstone. —*v.t.* **flagged, flag·ging** To pave with flags. [< ON *flaga* slab of stone. Akin to FLAKE.]

Flag Day June 14, the anniversary of the day in 1777 on which Congress proclaimed the Stars and Stripes the national standard of the United States.

flag·el·lant (flaj′ə·lənt, flə·jel′ənt) *n.* **1.** One who whips; especially, one who whips himself or has himself whipped from religious motives or for sexual excitement. **2.** *Often cap.* One of a medieval religious sect who practiced flagellation. Also **flag·el·la·tor** (flaj′ə·lā′tər). —*adj.* Practicing flagellation. [< L *flagellans, -antis,* ppr. of *flagellare* to scourge < *flagellum* whip]

flag·el·late (flaj′ə·lāt) *v.t.* **·lat·ed, ·lat·ing** To whip; scourge. —*adj. Biol.* **1.** Having or producing whiplike processes or branches. **2.** Shaped like a flagellum. Also **flag′el·lat′ed.** [< L *flagellatus,* pp. of *flagellare.* See FLAGELLANT.]

flag·el·la·tion (flaj′ə·lā′shən) *n.* **1.** Whipping as an abnormal incitement of sexual desire or as a means of religious discipline. **2.** *Biol.* The development of flagella.

fla·gel·li·form (flə·jel′ə·fôrm) *adj.* Long, slender, and flexible, like a whiplash. [< L *flagellum* whip + -FORM]

fla·gel·lum (flə·jel′əm) *n. pl.* **·la** (-ə) **1.** *Biol.* A lashlike appendage, as of a protozoan. **2.** A whip. [< L, whip]

flag·eo·let (flaj′ə·let′) *n.* A flutelike musical instrument blown at the end rather than at the side and having six finger holes. [< F, dim. of OF *flageol;* ult. origin uncertain]

Flagg (flag), **James Montgomery,** 1877–1960, U.S. artist.

flag·ging[1] (flag′ing) *adj.* Growing weak; failing; drooping. — **flag′ging·ly** *adv.*

flag·ging[2] (flag′ing) *n.* **1.** A pavement of flagstones; also, flagstones collectively. **2.** The act of paving with flagstones.

flag·gy[1] (flag′ē) *adj.* **·gi·er, ·gi·est** Hanging down; drooping.

flag·gy[2] (flag′ē) *adj.* **·gi·er, ·gi·est** Resembling or consisting of flagstones.

flag·gy[3] (flag′ē) *adj.* **·gi·er, ·gi·est** Covered with or made of flags (the plants).

fla·gi·tious (flə·jish′əs) *adj.* **1.** Guilty of extraordinary wickedness. **2.** Flagrantly wicked; atrocious; heinous: a *flagitious* era. [< L *flagitiosus* < *flagitium* disgraceful act] — **fla·gi′tious·ly** *adv.* — **fla·gi′tious·ness** *n.*

flag·man (flag′mən) *n. pl.* **·men** (-mən) **1.** One who carries a flag. **2.** One who signals with a flag, as on a railway.

flag officer In the U.S. Navy, an officer above the rank of captain, entitled to display a flag indicating his rank.

flag of truce A white flag displayed to the enemy to denote that a conference is desired.

flag·on (flag′ən) *n.* **1.** A vessel with a handle and a spout, and often a hinged lid, used to serve liquids. **2.** A large wine bottle. [< OF *flacon, flascon* < Med.L *flasco* < Gmc.]

flag·pole (flag′pōl′) *n.* A pole on which a flag is displayed.

fla·grant (flā′grənt) *adj.* **1.** Openly disgraceful; shockingly bad; notorious; heinous. **2.** *Obs.* Burning; blazing; also, raging. [< L *flagrans, -antis,* ppr. of *flagrare* to blaze, burn] — **fla′gran·cy, fla′grance** *n.* — **fla′grant·ly** *adv.*

— **Syn.** *Flagrant, glaring, gross,* and *rank* are intensives applied to that which is extremely offensive or evil. Anything *flagrant* draws attention to itself like the heat and light of a great fire. A *glaring* fault is one that stands in a pitiless light, as it were, and cannot be concealed, while *gross* creates a picture of something too large to be overlooked. *Rank* suggests a thing that attracts attention from its bad smell.

fla·gran·te de·lic·to (flə·gran′tē di·lik′tō) See IN FLAGRANTE DELICTO.

flag·ship (flag′ship′) *n.* The ship in a naval formation that carries a flag officer and displays his flag.

flag smut A disease of wheat caused by a smut fungus (*Urocystis tritici*), affecting the leaves and culms.

Flag·stad (flag′stad, *Norw.* fläg′stä), **Kirsten (Marie)**, 1895–1962, Norwegian operatic soprano.

flag·staff (flag′staf′, -stäf′) *n. pl.* **·staffs** or **·staves** (-stāvz′) A staff on which a flag is hung or displayed.

Flag·staff (flag′staf′, -stäf′) A city in north central Arizona; site of the Lowell Observatory; pop. 26,117.

flag station A station on a railway at which a train stops only on signal. Also **flag stop.**

flag·stone (flag′stōn′) *n.* **1.** A broad, flat stone suitable for pavements. **2.** Any fine-grained rock from which such slabs may be split. [< FLAG[4] + STONE]

flail (flāl) *n.* **1.** An implement for threshing grain by hand, consisting of a long handle to which a shorter bar (the swingle) is attached at one end so as to swing freely. **2.** A medieval weapon similar to this. — *v.t. & v.i.* To beat with or as with a flail. [OE *flygel,* prob. < L *flagellum* whip]

FLAIL (def. 2)

flair (flâr) *n.* **1.** A talent or aptitude: a *flair* for acting. **2.** Instinctive perceptiveness; discernment. **3.** *Informal* A showy or dashing style: to wear clothes with *flair.* [< OF < *flairer* to smell, scent out, ult. < L *flagrare*]

flak (flak) *n.* Antiaircraft fire. [< G *fl(ieger)* aircraft + *a(bwehr)* defense + *k(anone)* gun]

flake[1] (flāk) *n.* **1.** A small, thin piece peeled or split off from the surface of something; scale; chip. **2.** A small piece of light substance: a *flake* of snow. **3.** A stratum, layer, or lamina. — *v.t. & v.i.* **flaked, flak·ing** **1.** To peel off in flakes. **2.** To form into flakes. **3.** To spot or become spotted with flakes. — *adj. Anthropol.* Designating Paleolithic stone implements made by chipping thin flakes off the core of a large lump. [ME < Scand. Akin to FLAG[4].] — **flak′er** *n.*

flake[2] (flāk) *n.* **1.** A light rack or platform for drying fish. **2.** *Naut.* A small scaffold suspended over the side of a ship for workmen to stand on. [< ON *flaki* hurdle]

flake[3] (flāk) *n.* A flat coil of stowed cable. [Var. of FAKE[2]]

flake white Pure white lead in scales, used as a pigment.

flak·y (flā′kē) *adj.* **flak·i·er, flak·i·est 1.** Resembling or consisting of flakes. **2.** Splitting off or easily separated into flakes. — **flak′i·ly** *adv.* — **flak′i·ness** *n.*

flam[1] (flam) *Informal n.* **1.** A falsehood or deception. **2.** Humbug; sham. — *v.t. & v.i.* **flammed, flam·ming** To deceive by trick, sham, or flattery. [Short for FLIMFLAM]

flam[2] (flam) *n.* A drumbeat executed so that the two sticks strike the head almost simultaneously but are heard separately. [Prob. imit.]

flam·beau (flam′bō) *n. pl.* **·beaux** (-bōz) or **·beaus 1.** A burning torch. **2.** A large, decorated candlestick. [< F < *flambe* < OF *flamme.* See FLAME.]

flam·bée (fläṅ·bā′) *adj. French* Flaming: said of food served flaming with ignited brandy, etc. Also **flam·bé.**

flam·boy·ant (flam·boi′ənt) *adj.* **1.** Extravagantly ornate; florid; showy; bombastic: a *flamboyant* style. **2.** Brilliant in color; resplendent. **3.** *Archit.* Pertaining to a style of architecture, as French Gothic of the 15th or 16th century characterized by highly florid decoration and intricate, wavy tracery of windows and open spaces. [< F, ppr. of *flamboyer* to flame, blaze < OF *flambeiier* < *flambe.* See FLAME.] — **flam·boy′ance, flam·boy′an·cy** *n.* — **flam·boy′ant·ly** *adv.*

FLAMBOYANT ARCHITECTURE

flame (flām) *n.* **1.** A mass of burning vapor or gas rising from a fire in streams or darting tongues of light. **2.** A single tongue of flame. **3.** *Often pl.* A state of bright, intensely active combustion: The house was in *flames.* **4.** Something resembling a flame in brilliance, shape, etc. **5.** Flamelike light or coloring; brilliance. **6.** Intense passion or emotion; ardor. **7.** *Informal* A sweetheart. **8.** A bright, red-yellow color: also **flame scarlet.** — **Syn.** See FIRE. — *v.* **flamed, flam·ing** *v.i.* **1.** To give out flame; blaze; burn. **2.** To light up or burn as if on fire; flash: His face *flamed* with rage. **3.** To become enraged or excited: He *flamed* with indignation. — *v.t.* **4.** To subject to heat or flame. [< OF *flamme, flambe* < L *flamma* flame]

fla·men (flā′men) *n. pl.* **fla·mens** or **flam·i·nes** (flam′ə·nēz) In ancient Rome, a priest serving one particular deity. [< L]

fla·men·co (flə·meng′kō, -men′-, flä-) *n.* **1.** A fiery, percussive style of singing and dancing practiced particularly by the Gypsies of Andalusia. **2.** A song or dance in this style. [< Sp., Flemish, because the Gypsies were thought to be from Flanders]

flame·out (flām′out′) *n.* Cessation of burning in a jet engine, due to malfunction: also called *blowout.*

flame test *Chem.* The determination of the presence of an element or certain of its compounds by holding the substance in flame and noting the resulting color.

flame thrower *Mil.* A weapon that throws a stream of burning napalm or other gasoline mixture.

flam·ing (flā′ming) *adj.* **1.** In flames; blazing; fiery. **2.** Flamelike; brilliant. **3.** Ardent. **4.** Notorious; flagrant: a *flaming* reputation. — **flam′ing·ly** *adv.*

fla·min·go (flə·ming′gō) *n. pl.* **·gos** or **·goes** A long-necked, small-bodied wading bird (genus *Phoenicopterus*) of a pink or red color, having very long legs, webbed feet, and a bent bill. [< Pg. *flamingo* or Sp. *flamenco,* ult. < L *flamma* flame + -ING[3] (< Gmc. *-enc*)]

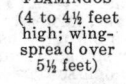

FLAMINGOS (4 to 4½ feet high; wingspread over 5½ feet)

Fla·min·i·an Way (flə·min′ē·ən) One of the chief ancient Roman roads from Rome to Cisalpine Gaul, built in 220 B.C. by Gaius Flaminius.

Flam·i·ni·nus (flam′ə·nī′nəs), **Titus Quinctius,** 230?–174? B.C., Roman general and statesman.

Fla·min·i·us (flə·min′ē·əs), **Gaius,** died 217 B.C., Roman general and politician; built the Flaminian Way.

flam·ma·ble (flam′ə·bəl) *adj.* Capable of catching fire easily; combustible; inflammable. — **flam′ma·bil′i·ty** *n.*

Flam·ma·rion (flä·má·ryôṅ′), **(Nicolas) Camile,** 1842–1925, French astronomer and writer.

flam·y (flā′mē) *adj.* **flam·i·er, flam·i·est** Pertaining to, composed of, or resembling flame; flaming; blazing.

flan (flan, *Fr.* fläṅ) *n.* **1.** A piece of metal ready to be made into a coin by receiving the stamp of the die; blank. **2.** A tart filled with cheese, cream, or fruit; also, a custard. [< F]

Flan·ders (flan′dərz) A former county in the Low Countries, divided into two Provinces of Belgium and **Flan·dre** (fläṅ′dr′), a region and former province of northern France. See EAST FLANDERS, WEST FLANDERS.

Flandre O·ri·en·tale (ô′rē·äṅ·tál′) The French name for EAST FLANDERS.

Flandre Oc·ci·den·tale (ôk′sē·däṅ·tál′) The French name for WEST FLANDERS.

flâ·ne·rie (fläṅ·rē′) *n. French* Lounging; idling; loafing.

flâ·neur (flä·nœr′) *n. French* A loafer; idler.

flange (flanj) *n.* **1.** A projecting rim or collar on a wheel, designed to keep it on a fixed track. **2.** A similar projecting part of a beam, pipe, etc., designed to aid attachment or to increase stiffness. **3.** A tool used to shape flanges. — *v.* **flanged, flang·ing** *v.t.* **1.** To provide with a flange. — *v.i.* **2.** To take the shape of a flange. [? < OF *flangir* to bend]

flank (flangk) *n.* **1.** The part between the ribs and the hip at either side of the body of an animal or human being; also, a cut of meat from this part of an animal. **2.** Loosely, the outside part of the leg between the hip and the knee; thigh. **3.** The extreme right or left part of something; side: the *flank* of a building. **4.** *Mil.* **a** The right or left section of an army, fleet, etc. **b** The right or left side of a fortification, bastion, etc. — *v.t.* **1.** To be located at the side of. **2.** *Mil.* **a** To defend or protect the flank of. **b** To launch an attack against the flank of. **c** To move around the flank of. — *v.i.* **3.** To have one side directed (toward a specified thing): with *on, upon*: The cliffs *flank* on the sea. **4.** To be located at the side of something. [< F *flanc* < Gmc.]

flank·er (flang′kər) *n.* One who or that which flanks; as: **a** A soldier in a division protecting the flank of an army. **b** A projecting extension at either side of a fortification.

flan·nel (flan′əl) *n.* **1.** A loosely woven, warm fabric made of wool or of wool and cotton to which synthetic fibers are often added. **2.** One of several very soft fabrics made chiefly of cotton, with a nap on one or both sides, and used especially for underwear, infants' garments, etc.: also **flan·nel·ette** (flan′əl·et′), **flan′nel·et′**. **3.** *pl.* A garment or garments made of flannel; especially: **a** Heavy underwear, usually of wool flannel. **b** Trousers made of light flannel. [Prob. < Welsh *gwlanen* flannel < *gwlan* wool] — **flan′nel·ly** *adj.*

flap (flap) *v.* **flapped**, **flap·ping** *v.t.* **1.** To move (wings, the arms, etc.) vigorously up and down, especially with a muffled slapping sound; beat. **2.** To cause to move with an irregular waving or rippling motion, especially with noise: The wind was *flapping* the curtains. **3.** To strike with something flat or flexible; slap. **4.** *Informal* To throw down, swing shut, or close up suddenly or noisily: to *flap* a newspaper on the floor. — *v.i.* **5.** To flap the wings, arms, etc. **6.** To have an irregular waving motion, as a flag blown by the wind. — *n.* **1.** The part of an envelope that is folded down in closing or sealing the envelope. **2.** A loosely hanging covering over the entrance to a tent, etc. **3.** A piece of material loosely covering the opening of a pocket; also, a lapel. **4.** A pendent part of a knit cap, leather helmet, etc. **5.** *Aeron.* A hinged section, as on the wings of an airplane, used to increase lift or decrease speed. **6.** *Surg.* A partially detached piece of tissue, as one to be used in grafting. **7.** The action of flapping; also, the muffled slapping sound often made by the flapping of wings, etc. **8.** A blow given with something flat or flexible; slap. **9.** *Slang* An occasion of excited activity; emergency; crisis. [Imit.]

flap·doo·dle (flap′dōōd′l) *n.* *Slang* Nonsensical talk; twaddle. [Arbitrary coinage]

flap·drag·on (flap′drag′ən) *n.* Snapdragon, a game.

flap·jack (flap′jak′) *n.* *U.S.* A griddlecake.

flap·per (flap′ər) *n.* **1.** One who or that which flaps. **2.** A broad flipper, as of a seal. **3.** A young bird not yet able to fly. **4.** *U.S. Informal* A young woman trying to appear sophisticated in dress and behavior: term current in the 1920's.

flare (flâr) *v.* **flared**, **flar·ing** *v.i.* **1.** To blaze up or burn brilliantly with a wavering light. **2.** To burst into a sudden blaze lasting a short time: often with *up*. **3.** To break out in sudden or violent emotion or action: often with *up* or *out*. **4.** To spread or gradually open outward, as the sides of a bell. — *v.t.* **5.** To cause to flare. **6.** To signal (information) with flares. — *n.* **1.** A bright, flickering light, as of a torch; brilliant, unsteady glare, usually lasting only a short time. **2.** An outburst, as of emotion: a *flare* of anger. **3.** A widening or spreading outward, as of the sides of a funnel; also, that which so flares. **4.** *Photog.* Excess light striking a film or plate, caused by internal reflection from the lens system of a camera. **5.** *Mil.* A pyrotechnic device that gives off a bright white or colored light, used for signaling or illumination. — **Syn.** See FIRE. [Origin unknown]

flare·back (flâr′bak′) *n.* **1.** Flame or gas escaping rearward from the breech of a gun through improper functioning. **2.** An outburst directed upon its source: a *flareback* of anger.

flare-up (flâr′up′) *n.* **1.** A sudden outburst of flame or light. **2.** A sudden outbreak of emotion.

flar·ing (flâr′ing) *adj.* **1.** Blazing with a bright, unsteady light. **2.** Showy; gaudy. **3.** Widening or spreading outward: *flaring* nostrils. — **flar′ing·ly** *adv.*

flash (flash) *v.i.* **1.** To burst forth suddenly or repeatedly into brilliant light or fire, as lightning. **2.** To gleam brightly; glitter: helmets *flashing* in the sunlight. **3.** To move with lightning speed: A train *flashed* by. **4.** To move suddenly into sight or perception: An idea *flashed* into his mind. — *v.t.* **5.** To cause to shine or glitter brightly: to *flash* a lantern. **6.** To emit bursts of (light, fire, etc.). **7.** To send or communicate with lightning speed: to *flash* a message by telegraph. **8.** *Informal* To show suddenly or abruptly: The policeman *flashed* his badge; also, to make an ostentatious display of: to *flash* a hundred-dollar bill. **9.** To provide (a roof, etc.) with sheet metal or other protective material; use flashing on. **10.** In glassmaking, to cover (glass) with a thin layer of differently colored glass; also, to apply (a thin layer of differently colored glass). — **Syn.** See SHINE. — **to flash back** In a novel, motion picture, etc., to break the continuity of the plot and return to an earlier episode or scene. — *n.* **1.** A sudden, quick blaze of brilliant light or fire, lasting only an instant. **2.** A sudden manifestation, as of wit, talent, or understanding. **3.** Vulgar display; ostentation. **4.** An extremely brief space of time; instant: He had the answer in a *flash*. **5.** *U.S.* A brief news dispatch sent by

radio, etc. **6.** A volatile mixture containing metal salts, used in applying a colored glaze to glass, etc.; also, a mixture made with burnt sugar, used in coloring liquors. **7.** A lock, dam, etc., used in making a greater depth of water; also, the sudden flow of water made available by such a device. **8.** *U.S. Slang* A flashlight. — **flash in the pan 1.** Explosion of the powder in the pan of a flintlock musket without ignition of the charge. **2.** A person, thing, or action that shows brilliant promise for a short time and then turns out to be a dismal failure. — *adj.* **1.** Done or occurring very quickly: *flash* flood, *flash* freezing. **2.** Vulgarly ostentatious; flashy; also, sporty. **3.** Relating to or typical of thieves, tramps, etc.: *flash* slang. [ME *flaschen*; prob. imit.] — **flash′er** *n.*

flash·back (flash′bak′) *n.* A break in the continuity of a novel, drama, motion picture, etc., to give an episode or scene occurring earlier; also, the episode or scene itself.

flash·board (flash′bôrd′, -bōrd′) *n.* A board at the top or side of a dam, used to increase the depth and pressure of the water: also called *flushboard*.

flash bulb *Photog.* Any of various electrical devices that emit an intense light of brief duration for taking photographs: also called *photoflash bulb*.

flash burn A burn caused by brief high-energy radiant heat.

flash flood A sudden, rushing flood caused by heavy rainfall.

flash gun *Photog.* A device that ignites a flash bulb.

flash·ing (flash′ing) *n.* **1.** The act of one who or that which flashes. **2.** Sheet metal or other weatherproofing or protective material used to cover joints or angles, as of a roof. **3.** The production of an artificial rush of water through a conduit, sewer, etc., so as to clean out the channel.

flash·light (flash′līt′) *n.* **1.** *U.S.* A small, portable device that emits a beam of light, consisting typically of a cylinder housing a tiny bulb powered by dry batteries. **2.** A burst of bright light artificially produced for taking photographs. **3.** A bright light flashing at intervals, as from a lighthouse.

FLASHING (def. 2)

a, b Parts of a lap joint.

flash·o·ver (flash′ō′vər) *n.* *Electr.* A disruptive leakage of current through or around an insulator.

flash point The lowest temperature at which the vapors of combustible liquids, especially lubricating oils, will ignite.

flash·y (flash′ē) *adj.* **flash·i·er**, **flash·i·est 1.** Brilliant for a moment; sparkling; flashing. **2.** Showy; cheap. — **Syn.** See GAUDY. — **flash′i·ly** *adv.* — **flash′i·ness** *n.*

flask (flask, fläsk) *n.* **1.** Any of various small containers made of glass, metal, etc., with a narrow neck; as: **a** A small, broad, flat container, especially for liquor, designed to be carried in the pocket. **b** A rounded receptacle with a long neck, used in laboratory work. **c** A powder flask (which see). **2.** A frame for holding sand molded to receive a foundry cast. [< F *flasque* < Med.L *flasca*, var. of *flasco*. See FLAGON.]

flas·ket (flas′kit, fläs′-) *n.* **1.** A very small flask. **2.** An oval, shallow basket.

flat[1] (flat) *adj.* **flat·ter**, **flat·test 1.** Extended horizontally with little or no slope. **2.** Smooth and regular with few or no hollows or projections. **3.** Stretched out level or prostrate: *flat* on one's back. **4.** Having the entire front or back surface in full contact with an even surface: *flat* against the wall. **5.** Not having high sides; shallow: a *flat* dish. **6.** Absolute and unqualified: a *flat* refusal. **7.** Lacking interest, spontaneity, or sparkle; lifeless; dull: a *flat* performance. **8.** Lacking tastiness or zestfulness: a *flat* beverage. **9.** Monotonously devoid of variety in tone: a *flat* voice. **10.** Having little or no contrast or shading: a *flat* color; also, having little or no gloss: *flat* paint. **11.** Deflated: a *flat* tire. **12.** *U.S. Informal* Having little or no money; broke. **13.** Fixed; uniform: to buy goods at a *flat* rate. **14.** Marked by little or no commercial activity: Trade was *flat*. **15.** Exact; precise: to run home in a minute *flat*. **16.** *Music* Lowered in pitch by a semitone. **b** Lower than the right, true pitch. **c** Having flats in the key signature. **17.** *Phonet.* **a** Designating the vowel sound in *man*, as opposed to the sound in *calm*. **b** Of consonants, voiced: opposed to *sharp*. **18.** *Gram.* Used as a particular part of speech without the distinguishing mark of that part of speech: The *flat* adverb *fast* lacks the adverbial ending -*ly*. **19.** *Naut.* Of a sail, etc., taut. — **Syn.** See LEVEL. — *adv.* **1.** In a flat state, position, or manner: The picture hangs *flat*. **2.** Exactly: weighing ten pounds *flat*. **3.** In finance, without interest. **4.** *Music* Below the right, true pitch: to sing *flat*. — **to fall flat** To fail to achieve a desired effect. — *n.* **1.** The flat, plane surface or part of something: the *flat* of a sword. **2.** Something that has a flat, even surface; as: **a** A piece of stage scenery, typically a length of canvas stretched on a wooden frame. **b** A railroad flatcar. **c** A flatboat. **d** A level area of land. **e** *Usually pl.* A partially submerged plain, as a marshy area near a river. **f** A shallow place in a body of water; shoal. **g** A shallow tray of earth for germinating seeds. **3.** *Informal* A tire from which most or all of the air has escaped. **4.** *pl. Informal* Women's shoes with flat heels. **5.** *Music* A sign (♭) placed before a note to indicate that the note is lowered a semitone from its normal pitch; also, the note so altered. — *v.* **flat·ted**, **flat·ting** *v.t.* **1.** To make flat. **2.** *Music* To lower (a tone), usually by a half

step. — *v.i.* **3.** To become flat. **4.** *Music* To sing or play below the right, true pitch. [< ON *flatr*] — **flat′ly** *adv.* — **flat′ness** *n.*
◆ *Flat* is the first element in many self-explaining compound adjectives: *flat-billed, flat-bottomed, flat-chested,* etc.
flat² (flat) *n.* A suite of rooms on one floor, used as a residence by an individual or family; apartment. [Var. of obs. *flet* floor, OE *flet*; infl. by *flat¹* level]
flat angle *Geom.* A straight angle (which see).
flat·boat (flat′bōt′) *n.* A large boat with a flat bottom, used on rivers. Also **flat′bot′tom** (-bot′əm).
flat·car (flat′kär′) *n. U.S.* A railroad car with no sides or roof, used for freight: also called *platform car.*
flat·fish (flat′fish′) *n. pl.* **·fish** or **·fish·es** One of several fishes, as the halibut, flounder, or sole, belonging to an order (*Heterosomata*) of fishes having a flattened body with both eyes located on the upper side in adults and swimming on one side only.
flat·foot (flat′fŏŏt′) *n.* **1.** *Pathol.* A condition in which the entire sole of the foot is in contact with the ground because of a flattened arch. **2.** *Slang* A policeman.
flat foot A foot with a completely flattened arch.
flat-foot·ed (flat′fŏŏt′id) *adj.* **1.** Having flat feet. **2.** *U.S. Informal* Direct and uncompromising; plain and resolute. — **flat′-foot′ed·ly** *adv.* — **flat′-foot′ed·ness** *n.*
Flat·head (flat′hed′) *n.* **1.** An Indian of the Salishan tribe of North America. **2.** A Chinook Indian.
flat·i·ron (flat′ī′ərn) *n.* An iron (def. 4).
flat·ling (flat′ling) *adv. Archaic & Dial.* **1.** In a prostrate position. **2.** With the flat side of a sword, etc. Also **flat′· lings.** — *adj.* Dealt with the flat side of a sword, etc.
flat out At maximum speed: to drive *flat out* on a freeway.
flat silver Flatware (def. 2).
flat spin See under SPIN.
flat·ten (flat′n) *v.t. & v.i.* **1.** To make or become flat or flatter. **2.** To make or become prostrate. — **to flatten out 1.** To flatten. **2.** *Aeron.* To resume or cause to resume a horizontal line of flight after moving at an upward or downward angle; level off. — **flat′ten·er** *n.*
flat·ter¹ (flat′ər) *v.t.* **1.** To praise excessively, especially without conviction or sincerity. **2.** To try to gain the favor of by praising in this way. **3.** To play upon the hopes or vanity of; beguile. **4.** To make pleased or gratified, as by compliments; also, to please by pampering. **5.** To show as more attractive than is actually the case: This photograph *flatters* her. — *v.i.* **6.** To flatter someone or something. — **to flatter oneself** To have the vain conviction, feeling, or notion (that): Don't *flatter yourself* (that) you will succeed. [< OF *flater* to fawn, caress. Akin to FLAT¹.] — **flat′ter·er** *n.* — **flat′ter·ing·ly** *adv.*
flat·ter² (flat′ər) *n.* One who or that which makes flat; as: **a** A worker who flattens pieces of metal, etc. **b** A die plate designed to produce flat metal strips, as for watch springs. **c** A hammer with a flat face, used by blacksmiths.
flat·ter·y (flat′ər·ē) *n. pl.* **·ter·ies 1.** The act of flattering; excessive, often insincere praise or expression of admiration. **2.** An excessively complimentary remark, speech, etc. [< OF *flaterie* < *flater* to fawn, caress]
Flat·ter·y (flat′ər·ē) **Cape** A high promontory and lighthouse at the entrance to Juan de Fuca Strait, NW Washington.
flat·ting (flat′ing) *n.* **1.** *Metall.* The process of rolling metal into flat sheets of varying size and thickness. **2.** A method of applying paint so that it dries without gloss.
flat·tish (flat′ish) *adj.* Rather flat.
flat·top (flat′top′) *n.* A U.S. naval aircraft carrier.
flat·u·lence (flach′ŏŏ·ləns, flat′yŏŏ-) *n.* **1.** An accumulation of gas in the intestinal tract. **2.** Windy pomposity or boastfulness. Also **flat′u·len·cy** [< F, ult. < L *flatus* blowing < *flare* to blow] — **flat′u·lent** *adj.* — **flat′u·lent·ly** *adv.*
fla·tus (flā′təs) *n. pl.* **·tus·es** Intestinal gas. [< L *flare* to blow]
flat·ware (flat′wâr′) *n.* **1.** Dishes that are more or less flat, as plates and saucers: distinguished from *hollowware.* **2.** Table utensils, as knives, forks, and spoons.
flat·wise (flat′wīz′) *adv.* In or into a flat position; not edgewise. Also **flat′ways′** (-wāz′).
flat·work (flat′wûrk′) *n.* Sheets, tablecloths, and similar articles that can be ironed in a mangle.
flat·worm (flat′wûrm′) *n.* A flat-bodied worm, especially a planarian.
Flau·bert (flō-bâr′), **Gustave,** 1821–80, French novelist.
flaunt (flônt) *v.i.* **1.** To make a brazen or gaudy display; parade impudently or boldly: to *flaunt* through the streets. **2.** To wave or flutter freely. — *v.t.* **3.** To show or display in an ostentatious or impudent manner. — *n.* The act of flaunting. [ME *flant* < Scand. Cf. Norw. *flanta* to gad about.] — **flaunt′er** *n.* — **flaunt′ing·ly** *adv.*
flaunt·y (flôn′tē) *adj.* **flaunt·i·er, flaunt·i·est** Marked by or given to ostentatious display; showy. — **flaunt′i·ly** *adv.* — **flaunt′i·ness** *n.*

flau·tist (flô′tist) *n.* A flutist.
fla·ves·cent (flə·ves′ənt) *adj.* Turning yellow; yellowish. [< L *flavescens, -entis,* ppr. of *flavescere* to become yellow < *flavus* yellow]
Fla·vi·an (flā′vē·ən) *adj.* Of or pertaining to the emperor Titus Flavius Vespasianus (Vespasian) or to his sons and successors Titus and Domitian.
fla·vin (flā′vən) *n. Biochem.* One of a group of yellow pigments widely distributed in plant and animal tissues and including riboflavin. [< L *flavus* yellow + -IN]
fla·vone (flā′vōn, flə·vōn′, flav′ōn) *n. Biochem.* A colorless, crystalline, vegetable pigment, C₁₅H₁₀O₂, the parent substance of certain yellow dyes, as quercetin. [< L *flavus* yellow + -ONE]
fla·vo·pro·te·in (flā′vō·prō′tē·in, -tēn) *n. Biochem.* An enzyme chemically linked with a protein and serving to oxidize nutrients in animal cells. [< FLAVIN + PROTEIN]
fla·vo·pur·pu·rin (flā′vō·pûr′pyə·rin) *n. Chem.* A crystalline coal-tar dye, C₁₄H₈O₅, isomeric with purpurin and similar to alizarin except that it produces colors with a yellowish tinge. [< L *flavus* yellow + PURPURIN]
fla·vor (flā′vər) *n.* **1.** Taste; especially, a distinctive element in the overall taste of something. **2.** Something added, as to food, to increase taste or to impart a specific taste; flavoring. **3.** A special, subtle quality pervading something: a novel that has the *flavor* of Dickens. **4.** *Archaic* Odor. — *v.t.* To give flavor to. Also *Brit.* **fla′vour.** [< OF *flaor, fleur,* prob. ult. < L *flare* to blow; *v* added on analogy with *savor*] — **fla′vor·er** *n.* — **fla′vor·less** *adj.*
fla·vor·ful (flā′vər·fəl) *adj.* Full of flavor; especially, pleasant to the taste. Also **fla′vor·ous, fla′vor·some, fla′vor·y.**
fla·vor·ing (flā′vər·ing) *n.* Something, as an essence or extract, added to heighten flavor or give a distinctive taste.
flaw¹ (flô) *n.* **1.** Something that detracts from completeness, effectiveness, or perfection; something missing or faulty; defect; also, a faulty spot as in a diamond. **2.** Something questionable or invalidating: a *flaw* in a contract. **3.** A crack or fissure; also, a torn place; rent. — *v.t.* **1.** To produce a flaw in. — *v.i.* **2.** To become cracked or torn. — **Syn.** See BLEMISH. [? < ON *flaga* slab of stone]
flaw² (flô) *n.* A sudden, brief rush of air or wind; gust; also, a brief windstorm, often accompanied by precipitation; squall. [Prob. < ON *flaga* gust]
flaw·less (flô′lis) *adj.* Devoid of flaws; absolutely perfect. — **flaw′less·ly** *adv.* — **flaw′less·ness** *n.*
flaw·y¹ (flô′ē) *adj.* Full of flaws.
flaw·y² (flô′ē) *adj.* Gusty; squally.
flax (flaks) *n.* **1.** An annual plant (genus *Linum*) with blue flowers, narrow leaves, and mucilaginous seeds, and with a slender stem that yields the fiber used in making linen. **2.** The fiber derived from the stem of this plant. **3.** One of several plants resembling flax. [OE *fleax*]
flax·en (flak′sən) **1.** Pertaining to, made of, or resembling flax. **2.** Having a light golden color like that of prepared flax fiber or straw; pale yellow; light blond. Also **flax′y.**

FLAX
(About 2
feet high)

Flax·man (flaks′mən), **John,** 1755–1826, English sculptor and draftsman.
flax·seed (flaks′sēd′, flak′sēd′) *n.* The mucilaginous seed of flax, yielding linseed oil and also used medicinally to soften and soothe irritated surfaces: also called *linseed.*
flay (flā) *v.t.* **1.** To remove all or part of the skin, hide, bark, etc., of; especially, to rip or pull off strips of skin, etc., from, as by lashing. **2.** To attack with scathing criticism. **3.** To get the money or goods of by extortion or swindling. [OE *flēan*] — **flay′er** *n.*
F layer Appleton layer (which see).
fld. Field.
fl. dr. Fluid dram(s).
flea (flē) *n.* **1.** A small, wingless, parasitic insect (order *Siphonaptera*) that sucks the blood of mammals and birds and is capable of leaping for relatively great distances. For illustration see INSECTS (injurious). ◆ Collateral adjective: *pulicene.* **2.** One of several small beetles or crustaceans that jump like fleas, as a beach flea (which see). — **a flea in one's ear 1.** A pointed hint. **2.** An upsetting or stinging rebuke, refusal, or rejection. [OE *flēa, flēah.* Akin to FLEE.]
flea·bane (flē′bān′) *n.* One of several plants of the composite family, as fleawort, popularly reputed to repel fleas.
flea·bite (flē′bīt′) *n.* **1.** The bite of a flea; also, the tiny red lesion produced by this bite. **2.** Something of tiny importance; especially, some tiny annoyance, loss, hurt, etc.
flea-bit·ten (flē′bit′n) *adj.* **1.** Bitten by fleas; also, covered with fleas. **2.** *Informal* Broken-down; decrepit. **3.** White dotted with reddish brown: said of horses.
fleam (flēm) *n. Surg.* A small, pointed instrument used especially in opening a vein. [< OF *flieme,* ult. < LL *flebotomum* < Gk. *phlebotomon.* See PHLEBOTOMY.]
flea market An outdoor market or bazaar selling secondhand or inexpensive articles.

flea·wort (flē'wûrt') *n.* **1.** A European plant (genus *Inula*) of the composite family, popularly reputed to repel fleas. **2.** A plant (*Plantago psyllium*) of the plantain family with tiny seeds used as a laxative.

flèche (flesh) *n.* **1.** *Archit.* A slender spire topping a roof, especially at a point just over the front section of the nave of a church. **2.** *Mil.* A triangular projection from the main defenses of a fortification, consisting of two walls coming to a point directed toward the assumed line of attack. [< F, arrow]

flé·chette (flā-shet') *n.* A small, pointed, steel missile to be hurled or dropped from an aircraft, used in World War I. [< F, dim. of *flèche* arrow]

fleck (flek) *n.* **1.** A tiny streak or spot. **2.** A tiny bit; speck. **3.** A minor skin blemish, as a freckle. — *v.t.* To mark with flecks. [Cf. ON *flekkr* spot]

Fleck·er (flek'ər), (**Herman**) **James Elroy**, 1884–1915, English poet.

flec·tion (flek'shən) *n.* **1.** The act of bending, or the state of being bent. **2.** A curved or bent part. **3.** *Gram.* Inflection. **4.** *Anat.* Flexion. Also (*for defs. 1 and 2*), *Brit.*, *flexion*. [< L *flexio, -onis* < *flectere* to bend] — **flec'tion·al** *adj.*

fled (fled) Past tense and past participle of FLEE.

fledge (flej) *v.* **fledged, fledg·ing** *v.t.* **1.** To furnish with feathers, as an arrow: also spelled *fletch*. **2.** To bring up (a young bird) until ready for flight. — *v.i.* **3.** To grow enough feathers for flight. [< obs. *fledge* ready to fly, ME *flegge*, OE *-flycge* in *unflycge* not ready to fly]

fledg·ling (flej'ling) *n.* **1.** A newly fledged young bird. **2.** An inexperienced person; beginner. Also **fledge'ling.**

fledg·y (flej'ē) *adj. Poetic* Having feathers; feathery.

flee (flē) *v.* **fled, flee·ing** *v.i.* **1.** To run away, as from danger or enemies. **2.** To move swiftly; leave abruptly. — *v.t.* **3.** To run away from (a person, place, etc.). — **Syn.** See ESCAPE. [OE *flēon.* Akin to FLEA.] — **fle'er** *n.*

fleece (flēs) *n.* **1.** The coat of wool covering a sheep or similar animal. **2.** The quantity of wool sheared from a sheep at one time. **3.** Anything resembling fleece in quality or appearance: a *fleece* of snow. **4.** A textile fabric with a soft, silky pile, used for linings, etc.; also, the pile. — *v.t.* **fleeced, fleec·ing 1.** To shear the fleece from. **2.** To swindle; defraud. **3.** To cover or fleck as with fleece. [OE *flēos*] — **fleec'er** *n.*

fleec·y (flē'sē) *adj.* **fleec·i·er, fleec·i·est 1.** Pertaining to, covered with, or made of fleece. **2.** Resembling fleece. — **fleec'i·ly** *adv.* — **fleec'i·ness** *n.*

fleer (flir) *v.t.* **1.** To jeer at; deride. — *v.i.* **2.** To laugh or grin coarsely or scornfully; sneer. — *n.* Derision or scorn in speech or look; sneer; jibe. [ME *flery, flerye*, prob. < Scand. Cf. Norw. *flira* to laugh, grin.] — **fleer'ing·ly** *adv.*

fleet[1] (flēt) *n.* **1.** The entire number of ships belonging to one government; navy; also, a number of ships, especially ships of war, operating together under one command in a particular area. **2.** A group of vessels, aircraft, trucks, buses, etc., organized into or viewed as a unit, or belonging to one company. [OE *flēot* ship]

fleet[2] (flēt) *adj.* **1.** Swift; quick: a *fleet* runner. **2.** *Poetic* Passing away quickly; vanishing: the *fleet* hours. **3.** *Brit. Dial.* Shallow. — **Syn.** See SWIFT. — *v.i.* **1.** To move swiftly. **2.** *Naut.* To change place; shift. **3.** *Archaic* To fade or pass away. **4.** *Obs.* To float. — *v.t.* **5.** *Rare* To while away (time). **6.** *Naut.* To change the position of. [OE *flēotan* to float] — **fleet'ly** *adv.* — **fleet'ness** *n.*

fleet[3] (flēt) *n. Dial.* An inlet or creek. [OE *flēot* estuary]

Fleet Admiral See ADMIRAL OF THE FLEET.

fleet·ing (flē'ting) *adj.* Passing quickly; transitory. — **Syn.** See TRANSIENT. — **fleet'ing·ly** *adv.* — **fleet'ing·ness** *n.*

Fleet Prison A former debtors' prison in London. Also **the Fleet.**

Fleet Street 1. An old street in London, site of many newspaper and printing firms. **2.** London journalism.

Flem. Flemish.

Flem·ing (flem'ing) *n.* **1.** A native of Flanders, especially of Belgian Flanders. **2.** A native speaker of Flemish.

Flem·ing (flem'ing), **Sir Alexander,** 1881–1955, British physician and bacteriologist; codiscoverer with Florey of penicillin. — **Sir John Ambrose,** 1849–1945, English electrical engineer and inventor.

Flem·ish (flem'ish) *adj.* Of or pertaining to Flanders, its people, or their language. — *n.* **1.** Flemings collectively: preceded by *the.* **2.** The language of the Flemings, belonging to the West Germanic branch, closely related to Dutch with the usual regional variations in pronunciation and vocabulary. Abbr. *Fl., Flem.*

flense (flens) *v.t.* **flensed, flens·ing** To strip the blubber or the skin from (a whale, seal, etc.). Also **flench** (flench). [< Dan. *flense*] — **flens'er** *n.*

flesh (flesh) *n.* **1.** The soft substance of the body of a human being or animal, especially that consisting of muscle but usually exclusive of fat. **2.** The edible substance of animals, excluding that of fish and sometimes of birds; meat. **3.** The soft, pulpy substance of fruits and vegetables, as distinguished from the core, seeds, skin, etc.; especially, this substance used as an article of food. **4.** The surface of the body of a human being or animal. **5.** The typical color of the skin of a white person, usually a moderate pink or pale orange-yellow. **6.** Plumpness; fatness; weight. **7.** The body of man as opposed to the soul or spirit; also, the physical, sensual nature of man as distinguished from or opposed to the spiritual or intellectual nature. **8.** Mankind in general; humanity; also, living creatures in general: All *flesh* must die. **9.** Kindred; kin. **10.** In Christian Science, an error of physical belief; a belief that matter has sensation. — **flesh and blood** Human nature or the human body, especially as limited by natural defects or weaknesses. — **in the flesh 1.** Physically present. **2.** Alive. — **one's (own) flesh and blood** One's blood relatives or descendants. — *v.t.* **1.** To excite the hunting instinct of (dogs, etc.) by feeding with bits of meat. **2.** To arouse or excite by giving a foretaste of something. **3.** To remove adhering flesh from (a skin or hide). — *v.i.* **4.** To become fleshy. — **flesh out** To give substance or the appearance of reality to; develop fully: to *flesh out* an idea; to *flesh out* a fictional character. [OE *flǣsc*]

flesh-col·ored (flesh'kul'ərd) *adj.* Having the typically pink or pale orange-yellow color of a white person's skin.

flesh·er (flesh'ər) *n.* One who or that which strips the flesh from hides.

flesh fly A carnivorous, dipterous insect (genus *Sarcophaga*) that deposits its eggs or larvae in living flesh.

flesh·ings (flesh'ingz) *n.pl.* **1.** Flesh-colored tights. **2.** Pieces of flesh and fat scraped from hides and used for glue.

flesh·ly (flesh'lē) *adj.* **·li·er, ·li·est 1.** Pertaining to the body; corporeal. **2.** Sensuous; carnal. **3.** Worldly. **4.** Fleshy; fat; plump. — **flesh'li·ness** *n.*

flesh·pot (flesh'pot') *n. Usually pl.* Material advantages or sensual luxuries; also, places for self-indulgence, as night clubs, brothels, etc.

flesh wound A surface wound or shallow cut.

flesh·y (flesh'ē) *adj.* **flesh·i·er, flesh·i·est 1.** Of, pertaining to, or resembling flesh. **2.** Plump; fat. **3.** Firm and pulpy: *fleshy* leaves. — **Syn.** See FAT. — **flesh'i·ness** *n.*

fletch (flech) *v.t.* To fledge (arrows). [Alter. of FLEDGE; infl. by *fletcher*]

fletch·er (flech'ər) *n. Archaic* One who makes arrows. [< OF *flechier, flecher* < *fleche* arrow]

Fletch·er (flech'ər), **John,** 1579–1625, English dramatist; collaborated with Beaumont. — **John Gould,** 1886–1950, U.S. poet and critic.

Fletch·er·ism (flech'ə·riz'əm) *n.* The practice of chewing food thoroughly as an aid to good health. [after Horace *Fletcher,* 1849–1919, U.S. dietitian]

fleur-de-lis (flœr'də-lē', -lēs', flôôr'-) *n. pl.* **fleurs-de-lis** (flœr'də-lēz', flôôr'-) **1.** *Heraldry* A device consisting of three leaves or petals resembling those of an iris or lily, bound together near the base by a bar or band. **2.** This device used as the armorial bearings of the former royal family of France. **3.** The iris flower or plant. Also called *flower-de-luce:* also **fleur'-de-lys'.** [< F, flower of lily]

fleu·ry (flôô'rē) *adj. Heraldry* Terminating in the three leaves of a fleur-de-lis: said of the arms of a cross. For illustration see CROSS.

FLEUR-DE-LIS

Fleu·ry (flœ-rē'), **André Hercule de,** 1653–1743, French cardinal and statesman; prime minister 1726–43. — **Claude,** 1640–1723, French ecclesiastical historian.

flew[1] (flōō) Past tense of FLY[1].

flew[2] (flōō) See FLUE[1].

flews (flōōz) *n.pl.* The large chops of certain dogs, especially hounds. For illustration see DOG. [Origin unknown]

flex (fleks) *v.t. & v.i.* **1.** To bend, as the arm. **2.** To contract, as a muscle. [< L *flexus,* pp. of *flectere* to bend]

flex. Flexible.

flexi- *combining form* Bent. [< L *flexus.* See FLEX.]

flex·i·ble (flek'sə·bəl) *adj.* **1.** Capable of being bent, twisted, etc., without breaking; pliant. **2.** Yielding to persuasion or influence; tractable. **3.** Able to adjust easily to change; adaptable. **4.** Capable of expressive modulations: said of the voice. Also **flex·ile** (flek'sil). — **Syn.** See ELASTIC. — **flex'i·bil'i·ty, flex'i·ble·ness** *n.* — **flex'i·bly** *adv.*

flex·ion (flek'shən) *n.* **1.** *Anat.* The bending or turning of a part, as a limb or muscle: opposed to *extension.* **2.** *Brit.* Flection (defs. 1 & 2). — **flex'ion·al** *adj.*

Flex·ner (fleks'nər), **Abraham,** 1866–1959, U.S. educator. — **Simon,** 1863–1946, U.S. pathologist and bacteriologist; brother of the preceding.

flex·or (flek'sər) *n. Anat.* A muscle that serves to bend a part of the body.

flex·u·ous (flek'shōō·əs) *adj.* **1.** Having bends or turns; winding. **2.** Unsteady; wavering. Also **flex'u·ose** (-ōs). [< L *flexuosus* < *flexus.* See FLEX.] — **flex·u·os·i·ty** (flek'shōō·os'ə·tē), **flex'u·ous·ness** *n.* — **flex'u·ous·ly** *adv.*

flex·ure (flek'shər) *n.* **1.** The act of bending, or the state of being bent. **2.** A bent part; turn; curve.

flex wing The Rogallo wing (which see).

fley (flā) *Scot. v.t.* To frighten; affright. — *n.* A fright.

flib·ber·ti·gib·bet (flib'ər·tē·jib'it) *n.* An impulsive, flighty, or gossipy person. [Imit.]

flich·ter (flikh'tər) *Scot. v.i.* To flicker. — *n.* A flicker.

flick (flik) *n.* **1.** A quick, light, snapping movement or blow. **2.** A slight, cracking sound made by such a movement or blow. **3.** A slight trace, fleck, or streak of something: a *flick* of moisture. **4.** *Usually pl. Slang* Motion pictures. — *v.t.* **1.** To strike with a quick, light stroke, as with a whip. **2.** To cause to move or snap with a quick, light movement. **3.** To strike and remove with a quick, light snap: to *flick* dust from one's cuff. — *v.i.* **4.** To move in a quick, darting manner. **5.** To flutter. [Imit.]

flick·er (flik'ər) *v.i.* **1.** To burn or shine with an unsteady or wavering light. **2.** To flash up and die away quickly, as lightning. **3.** To flutter or quiver; wave to and fro. — *v.t.* **4.** To cause to flicker. — *n.* **1.** A wavering or unsteady light. **2.** A quivering or fluttering motion. **3.** A slight stirring, as of emotion: a *flicker* of resentment. **4.** *Usually pl. Slang* Motion pictures. [OE *flicorian* to move the wings]

flick·er² (flik'ər) *n.* A woodpecker (*Colaptes auratus*) of eastern North America: also called *golden-winged woodpecker*, *high-hole*, *yellowhammer*. [Imit.]

flick·er·tail (flik'ər·tāl') *n.* A medium-sized North American ground squirrel (*Citellus richardsonii*) with a grayish coat and a short tail.

Flickertail State Nickname of NORTH DAKOTA.

flied (flīd) Past tense and past participle of FLY¹ (def. 9).

fli·er (flī'ər) *n.* **1.** One who or that which flies; as: **a** An aviator. **b** A bird. **c** A flying insect. **2.** One who or that which moves from one point to another very fast; as: **a** A fast runner. **b** An express train, bus, etc. **c** A rapidly moving part of a machine. **3.** A big leap or jump. **4.** *U.S. Informal* A risky financial investment or speculation. **5.** *U.S.* A small handbill or leaflet, as one used in advertising. **6.** One of the steps in a straight staircase. Also spelled *flyer*.

flight¹ (flīt) *n.* **1.** The act or manner of flying; also, the power of flying: a bird of swift *flight*. ◆ Collateral adjective: *volar*. **2.** Any swift movement through or as if through the air: the *flight* of a projectile. **3.** The distance traveled or the course followed by an airplane, bird, projectile, etc. **4.** A journey by airplane; also, a scheduled trip by airplane, or the airplane scheduled to make a particular trip: the noon *flight* to Paris. **5.** A group flying or projected through the air together; as: **a** A flock of birds: a *flight* of swallows. **b** A volley of missiles: a *flight* of arrows. **6.** In the U.S. Air Force, a tactical formation, usually of four or more aircraft. **7.** A soaring or an excursion above or beyond ordinary bounds: a *flight* of imagination. **8.** An ascent or continuous series of stairs or steps. **9.** A light, slender arrow for shooting at long distances: also **flight arrow**. **10.** A contest using such arrows. **11.** In angling, a device for whirling bait rapidly. — *v.i.* To migrate or move in flights, as wild fowl. [OE *flyht*. Akin to FLY.]

flight² (flīt) *n.* The act of fleeing or escaping from or as from danger. — **to put to flight** To cause to flee; rout. — **to take (to) flight** To run away; flee. [OE (assumed) *flyht*. Akin to FLEE.]

flight check *Aeron.* A test in actual flight of the proficiency of a pilot or crew member, or of the operation of a piece of aircraft equipment.

flight deck The top deck of an aircraft carrier, on which aircraft land and take off.

flight engineer *Aeron.* The crew member of an airplane in charge of mechanical performance during flight.

flight feather *Ornithol.* One of the strong, stiff feathers forming much of a bird's wing and essential to flight.

flight·less (flīt'lis) *adj.* Unable to fly, as an ostrich.

flight lieutenant (lef·ten'ənt) In the Royal, Royal Canadian, and other Commonwealth air forces, a commissioned officer ranking next below a squadron leader. See table at GRADE.

flight officer In World War II, a specially created rank in the U.S. Air Force, corresponding to a warrant officer in grade and privileges.

flight path *Aeron.* The course taken in the air by an aircraft, projectile, or guided missile.

flight pay Extra military pay received for flying duty.

flight recorder An electronic device that records automatically significant data on the performance of an airplane.

flight sergeant In the Royal, Royal Canadian, and other Commonwealth air forces, a noncommissioned officer ranking next above a sergeant. See table at GRADE.

flight strip *Aeron.* An auxiliary or emergency landing field.

flight surgeon A medical officer trained in aeromedicine.

flight·wor·thy (flīt'wûr·thē) *adj.* ·thi·er, ·thi·est Having full capability of flight within or beyond the earth's atmosphere, as an aircraft, guided missile, or spacecraft.

flight·y (flī'tē) *adj.* **flight·i·er, flight·i·est** **1.** Moving erratically from one idea or topic to another; unable to concentrate long or well; giddy. **2.** Moved by impulse or whim rather than by reason; frivolous and shallow; fickle; capricious. **3.** Not quite sane; somewhat deranged; also, not altogether clear-headed; wandering in mind: a *flighty* old lady. — **flight'i·ly** *adv.* — **flight'i·ness** *n.*

flim·flam (flim'flam') *Informal v.t.* ·flammed, flam·ming To swindle; hoax; trick. — *adj.* **1.** Frivolous; nonsensical. **2.** Deceptive. — *n.* **1.** Nonsense; silly talk. **2.** Petty trickery or deception. [Cf. Norw. *flim* lampoon, *flimta* to mock] — **flim'flam'mer** *n.*

flim·sy (flim'zē) *adj.* ·si·er, ·si·est **1.** Not strong or solid in structure; ready to fall apart or collapse. **2.** Light, thin, and delicate in texture; unsubstantial: a *flimsy* covering. **3.** Lacking real validity or effectiveness; not at all convincing or adequate; weak: a *flimsy* excuse. — *n. pl.* ·sies **1.** Thin paper used for carbon copies or transfers, as in newspaper work, telegraphy, etc. **2.** Copy written on this kind of paper. [< FILM, by metathesis; infl. in form by *clumsy*, *tipsy*, etc.] — **flim'si·ly** *adv.* — **flim'si·ness** *n.*

flinch (flinch) *v.i.* **1.** To shrink back, as from anything threatening or unpleasant; show lack of nerve; quail. **2.** To wince, as from pain. **3.** In croquet, to let the foot slip from the ball while driving away an opponent's ball. — *n.* **1.** Any act of shrinking back or wincing. **2.** A card game in which the cards are built up in certain sequences. [< OF *flenchir*, var. of *flechier* to bend; ult. origin uncertain] — **flinch'er** *n.* — **flinch'ing·ly** *adv.*

flin·der (flin'dər) *n. Usually pl.* Small fragments; splinters; shreds. [Cf. Norw. *flindra* splinter]

Flin·ders Ranges (flin'dərz) A mountain range in eastern South Australia; highest point, St. Mary's Peak, 3,900 ft.

F lines Fraunhofer lines (which see).

fling (fling) *v.* **flung, fling·ing** *v.t.* **1.** To toss or hurl, especially with violence: to *fling* a newspaper on the floor. **2.** To cast off or discard. **3.** To put abruptly or violently, as if by throwing: to *fling* someone into prison. **4.** To throw (oneself) into something completely or with energy. **5.** To throw to the ground, as in wrestling. **6.** To send forth suddenly or rapidly: to *fling* reinforcements into battle. **7.** To move (a part of the body) with sudden vigor. **8.** To give off or diffuse. — *v.i.* **9.** To move, rush, or flounce, as in anger or contempt. **10.** To make abusive remarks; speak harshly: usually with *out*. **11.** To kick and plunge: said of horses. — *n.* **1.** The act of casting out, down, or away. **2.** A sneering or contemptuous comment; taunt; gibe. **3.** A brief period of self-indulgence, unrestraint, etc. **4.** *Informal* An attempt; trial: to have a *fling* at painting. [ME *flingen* < Scand. Cf. ON *flegja* beat.] — **fling·er** (fling'ər) *n.*

flint (flint) *n.* **1.** A very hard, dull-colored variety of quartz that produces a spark when struck with steel. **2.** A piece of this stone. **3.** Anything hard, obdurate, or cruel. [OE]

Flint (flint) **1.** A city in east central Michigan; pop. 193,317. **2.** Flintshire.

flint corn A kind of Indian corn (*Zea mays indurata*) having very hard, smooth kernels that do not shrivel.

flint glass A potassium lead silicate glass of high density and good refractive power, used for lenses and in making artificial gems, cut glass, etc.: also called *lead glass*.

flint·head (flint'hed') *n.* The wood ibis, a bird.

flint·lock (flint'lok') *n.* **1.** A gunlock in which a flint is used to ignite the powder in the pan. **2.** An obsolete firearm that was equipped with such a gunlock. Also *firelock*.

Flint·shire (flint'shir, -shər) A former county in NE Wales; 256 sq. mi.; pop. 175,396 (1971); county seat, Mold: also *Flint*.

flint·y (flin'tē) *adj.* flint·i·er, flint·i·est **1.** Made of, containing, or resembling flint. **2.** Hard; cruel; obdurate. — **flint'i·ly** *adv.* — **flint'i·ness** *n.*

flip (flip) *v.* flipped, flip·ping *v.t.* **1.** To throw or move with a jerk; nick. **2.** To propel, as a coin, by an outward snap of a finger pressed down by the thumb and suddenly released. — *v.i.* **3.** To move abruptly or with a jerk. **4.** To strike lightly and quickly, with a snapping movement. **5.** *U.S. Slang* To become angry or upset; also, to become emotionally aroused. — *n.* **1.** A quick, light snapping movement, as of a lash; also, an abrupt, jerking movement. **2.** A drink made with some liquor, as sherry, mixed with egg, sugar, and spices. — *adj. Informal* Pert; saucy; impertinent. [Imit.]

flip-flop (flip'flop') *n. U.S. Informal* A somersault or hand-spring. [Varied reduplication of FLIP]

flip·pan·cy (flip'ən·sē) *n. pl.* ·cies **1.** Careless disrespect; impertinence; sauciness. **2.** An impertinent act or remark.

flip·pant (flip'ənt) *adj.* **1.** Lacking due respect or seriousness; impertinent; saucy. **2.** *Obs.* Overly talkative. [< FLIP v. + -ANT] — **flip'pant·ly** *adv.*

flip·per (flip'ər) *n.* **1.** A broad, flat limb adapted for swimming, as in seals, etc. **2.** *Usually pl.* One of a pair of rubber shoes having a long, flat, paddlelike piece projecting beyond the toes, used by skin divers and other swimmers: also called *fin*. **3.** *Slang* The hand.

flirt (flûrt) *v.i.* **1.** To act in a coquettish manner; play at love. **2.** To expose oneself to something carelessly or lightly; play; toy: to *flirt* with danger. **3.** To move about or away in a jerky or fluttering manner; dart; flit. — *v.t.* **4.** To flick suddenly or jerkily; move abruptly or briskly. **5.** To toss or snap quickly. — *n.* **1.** One who plays at love. **2.** A sudden, jerky movement; quick toss or flick. [Imit.]

flir·ta·tion (flûr·tā'shən) *n.* **1.** Coquettish behavior. **2.** A brief, casual love affair.

flir·ta·tious (flûr·tā'shəs) *adj.* **1.** Given to coquettish behavior or casual love affairs. **2.** Pertaining to or typical of flirtation. Also **flirt'y.** — **flir·ta'tious·ly** *adv.*

flit (flit) *v.* **flit·ted, flit·ting** *v.i.* **1.** To move or fly rapidly and lightly; dart; skim. **2.** To pass away quickly: Time *flits*. **3.** *Dial.* To move from one dwelling to another. — *v.t.* **4.** *Archaic* To transfer (belongings, etc.); move. — *n.* A darting, skimming, or fluttering movement. [< ON *flytja* to remove, move] — **flit'ter** *n.*

flitch (flich) *n.* **1.** A salted and smoked cut of meat from the side or back of a pig: a *flitch* of bacon; also, a strip or steak cut from the side of certain fishes, especially halibut. **2.** A piece of timber cut lengthwise from the trunk of a tree. — *v.t.* To cut into flitches. [OE *flicce*]

flite (flīt) *v.i.* **flit·ed, flit·ing** To wrangle; quarrel. — *n.* Abusive quarreling. Also spelled *flyte.*

flit·ter (flit'ər) *v.t. & v.i. Dial.* To flutter. [Freq. of FLIT]

flit·ter·mouse (flit'ər·mous') *n. pl.* **·mice** (-mīs') A bat. [Cf. G *fledermaus*]

fliv·ver (fliv'ər) *n. U.S. Slang* **1.** An old, battered car. **2.** Formerly, the Model T Ford car. [Origin unknown]

float (flōt) *v.i.* **1.** To rest on or at the surface of a liquid, supported by the upward pressure of the liquid; also, to be carried along gently on or at the surface of a liquid. **2.** To remain suspended or be carried along some distance below the surface of a liquid. **3.** To remain suspended or be carried along in the air or some other gas; also, to hover or drift as if suspended or carried along in this way. **4.** To move lightly and effortlessly, as if buoyed up: She *floated* dreamily about the dance floor. **5.** To go about from one person or thing to another in a random or unstable way: to *float* from job to job. — *v.t.* **6.** To cause to float: to *float* a ship. **7.** To put (a stock, bond, etc.) on the market. **8.** To cause (a rumor, report, etc.) to circulate. **9.** To get (a business venture, scheme, etc.) into operation; launch. **10.** To smooth the surface of (soft plaster, etc.). **11.** To irrigate by flooding. — **Syn.** See FLY¹. — *n.* **1.** An object that floats in a liquid or buoys up something in a liquid; as: **a** A buoy used to indicate the presence of submerged rocks, etc. **b** A life preserver. **c** A piece of cork or similar material attached to a fishing line to indicate by its bobbing that a fish is biting at the bait. **d** A hollow metal ball attached to a lever governing the supply of water in a tank. **e** An anchored raft. **f** *Aeron.* One of the pontoons under the wings or fuselage of an amphibious airplane. **g** *Zool.* A hollow or inflated organ that supports an animal in water. **2.** A tableau or display carried atop a wheeled platform, truck, etc., in parades or pageants. **3.** In banking, the value of checks, etc., that have not yet been presented for collection at the final bank against which they were drawn. **4.** A tool, as a plasterer's trowel, used for smoothing, leveling, or the like. **5.** *Usually pl.* In weaving, filling threads that are passed under or over several warp threads without being engaged by them. **6.** A soda or milk shake with a ball of ice cream floating in it. **7.** *Usually pl.* The footlights in a theater. **8.** *Rare* The act of floating. — **Syn.** See WHARF. [OE *flotian*] — **float'a·ble** *adj.*

float·age (flō'tij), **float·a·tion** (flō·tā'shən) See FLOTAGE, FLOTATION.

float·er (flō'tər) *n.* **1.** One who or that which floats. **2.** A person who drifts about from one job, place of residence, etc., to another. **3.** *U.S.* A nonpartisan voter; also, a voter who illegally votes in more than one district.

float-feed (flōt'fēd') *adj. Mech.* Having a floating device that automatically controls the supply of fuel, etc.

float·ing (flō'ting) *adj.* **1.** That floats or is able to float. **2.** Moving about or inclined to move about from one place, job, etc., to another. **3.** *Pathol.* Abnormally movable or detached from the usual position: a *floating* kidney. **4.** *Econ.* **a** Due at various times and in various sums; not funded: said of a debt. **b** Available for use and not assigned to any particular investment: said of capital. **5.** *Mech.* Freely suspended so as to function with little or no friction or vibration.

floating dock A type of dry dock that can be submerged to permit entry of a ship and then raised to leave the ship dry for repairs. Also **floating dry dock.**

floating heart An aquatic herb (genus *Nymphoides*) with leaves shaped like hearts.

floating island A floating mass of soil held together by vegetation and sometimes artificially anchored by poles. **2.** A dessert consisting of boiled custard with beaten egg whites or whipped cream floating on the surface.

floating rib A rib of either of the two lowest pairs of ribs in a human being, not attached to the other ribs or to the sternum but attached only to the vertebrae.

floating supply A supply of commodities, securities, etc., available on the open market.

float·y (flō'tē) *adj.* **float·i·er, float·i·est** Buoyant.

floc (flok) *n.* A floccule: also *flock.* [Short for FLOCCULE]

floc·cil·la·tion (flok'si·lā'shən) *n. Pathol.* Aimless picking at bedclothes by a delirious patient. [< NL *floccillus* (dim. of L *floccus* lock of wool) + -ATION]

floc·cose (flok'ōs, flo·kōs') *adj.* **1.** Having soft, fluffy wool or hair; flocculent. **2.** Having tiny tufts suggestive of wool. [< LL *floccosus* < L *floccus* lock of wool]

floc·cu·late (flok'yə·lāt) *v.t. & v.i.* **·lat·ed, ·lat·ing** **1.** To form into small, fluffy masses, as clouds. **2.** To form into small, soft lumps, as some soils. — **floc'cu·la'tion** *n.*

floc·cule (flok'yōōl) *n.* **1.** A tiny mass of fine particles suggestive of a tuft of wool, as in a chemical precipitate. **2.** A small tuft of wool or of woolly hair. Also **floc'cus** (flok'əs). [< NL *flocculus,* dim. of L *floccus* lock of wool]

floc·cu·lent (flok'yə·lənt) *adj.* **1.** Having soft, fluffy wool or hair; woolly or fluffy; floccose. **2.** Marked by or producing floccules. **3.** Covered with a soft, waxy secretion, as certain insects. — **floc'cu·lence** *n.* — **floc'cu·lent·ly** *adv.*

floc·cu·lus (flok'yə·ləs) *n. pl.* **·li** (-lī) **1.** A floccule. **2.** *Anat.* One of a pair of lateral lobes in the cerebellum of higher vertebrates. **3.** *Astron.* A fluffy mass of gas occurring in the atmosphere about the sun. [< NL. See FLOCCULE.]

flock¹ (flok) *n.* **1.** A group of animals of the same kind, especially sheep or goats, feeding, living, or kept together in a herd. **2.** A group of birds of the same kind, especially geese, assembled together. **3.** A group of persons who are members of the same church or congregation; also, the whole body of Christians. **4.** Any group of persons under the care or supervision of someone. **5.** A large number or assemblage of persons or things; also, a band of people traveling or otherwise grouped together. — *v.i.* To come or go in crowds: People *flocked* to the exhibition. [OE *flocc*] — **Syn.** (noun) **1, 2.** *Flock, herd, drove, bevy, covey, gaggle, gam, pack, pride, swarm, litter, hatch,* and *brood* denote an assemblage of animals. *Flock* is applied to birds and to small mammals, now usually sheep or goats. Larger animals, as cattle and elephants, form a *herd;* when gathered together to be driven, they are a *drove.* Other terms are fairly restricted in application: a *bevy* of quail, a *covey* of partridges, a *gaggle* of geese, a *gam* of whales, a *pack* of dogs or wolves, a *pride* of lions, a *swarm* of bees. All the offspring born at one time form a *litter* (of viviparous animals, as puppies) or a *hatch* or *brood* (of oviparous animals, as chicks).

flock² (flok) *n.* **1.** Finely ground wool, cloth, felt, etc., used to coat certain types of wallpaper. **2.** Refuse wool, rags, etc., cut in small pieces and used to stuff furniture. **3.** A tuft of wool, hair, etc. **4.** A floccule. — *v.t.* To cover or fill with flock. [Prob. < OF *floc* < L *floccus* lock of wool]

flock·y (flok'ē) *adj.* **flock·i·er, flock·i·est** Flocculent.

Flod·den (flod'n) A small hill in north Cumberland, England, surrounded by **Flodden Field;** scene of the defeat of James IV of Scotland by English forces, 1513.

floe (flō) *n.* A large, comparatively level field of floating ice; also, a detached section of such a field. [< ON *flō* a layer]

flog (flog, flôg) *v.t.* **flogged, flog·ging** To beat hard with a whip, rod, strap, etc. [? < L *flagellare* to whip] — **flog'ger** *n.*

flog·ging (flog'ing, flôg'-) *n.* **1.** The act of one who beats with a whip, lash, etc. **2.** An instance of such a beating.

flong (flong) *n. Printing* A sheet of specially prepared paper used for making a stereotype mold or matrix. [Var. of FLAN]

flood (flud) *n.* **1.** An unusually large flow or rise of water, especially over land not usually covered with water; inundation; deluge: high tide: opposed to *ebb:* also **flood tide.** **3.** Any copious flow or stream: a *flood* of sunshine; a *flood* of words. **4.** *Poetic* Any great body of water, as the ocean, a lake, etc. **5.** *Informal* A floodlight. — **the Flood** The deluge in the time of Noah. *Gen.* vii. — *v.t.* **1.** To cover or inundate with a flood; deluge. **2.** To fill or overwhelm with a flood: They *flooded* him with advice. **3.** To supply excessively: to *flood* an engine with gasoline. — *v.i.* **4.** To rise to a flood; overflow. **5.** To flow in a flood; gush. **6.** *Med.* **a** To bleed heavily from the uterus, especially after childbirth. **b** To suffer from excessive menstrual flow. [OE *flōd*]

flood control The use of dikes, dams, tunnels, artificial channels, and other engineering techniques as a means of regulating and controlling bodies of water that flood easily.

flood·gate (flud'gāt') *n.* **1.** A gate or valve at the head of a water channel, designed to regulate the flow or depth of the water in the channel: also called *water gate.* **2.** Something restraining or checking an outburst: to open the *floodgates* of anger.

flood·light (flud'līt') *n.* **1.** A lighting unit that throws an intensely bright, broad beam of light. **2.** The beam of light cast by this unit. — *v.t.* **·light·ed** or **·lit, ·light·ing** To illuminate with a floodlight.

flood plain A plain bordering on a river, subject to flooding by the river and often originally formed by alluvial deposits.

floor (flôr, flōr) *n.* **1.** The surface in a room or building upon which one stands or walks. **2.** The area between two adjacent levels of a building; story: the third *floor.* Abbr. **fl. 3.** The bottom surface of any cavity: the ocean *floor.* **4.** The ground surface or platform of something built, as of a bridge or pier. **5.** A level structure or platform for some special purpose: a threshing *floor.* **6.** The part of a legislative house, stock exchange, etc., where the members gather to conduct business and which is separate from the spectators' galleries. **7.** In parliamentary procedure, the right to speak to the assembly: to be given the *floor*. **8.** The lowest or minimum price paid or charged for anything. **9.** *Naut.* The more or less horizontal parts of a ship's bottom on each side of the keel. — *v.t.* **1.** To cover or provide with a floor. **2.** To knock down, as to the floor. **3.** *Informal* To puzzle completely; flabbergast; also, to reduce to stunned silence. **4.** *Informal* To vanquish; beat. [OE *flōr*] — **floor′er** *n.*

floor·age (flôr′ij) *n.* The area of a floor; floor space.

floor·board (flôr′bôrd′, flôr′bōrd′) *n.* A board in a floor.

floor·cloth (flôr′klôth′, -kloth′, flôr′-) *n.* **1.** A material used to cover floors, as linoleum. **2.** A cloth used to clean a floor.

floor·ing (flôr′ing, flō′ring) *n.* **1.** Material for the making of a floor. **2.** A floor; also, collectively, floors.

floor leader A party leader in either house of the U.S. Congress, who directs his party's business on the floor.

floor plan An architectural plan of the rooms and other spaces on one floor of a building.

floor show Entertainment consisting of dancing, singing, etc., presented on the dance floor of a night club or cabaret.

floor·walk·er (flôr′wô′kər, flōr′-) *n.* In a large store, one who supervises the sales force, helps customers, etc.: also, *Brit.*, **shopwalker**.

flooz·y (flōō′zē) *n. pl.* **flooz·ies** *U.S. Slang* A woman or girl: a contemptuous term; especially, a loose woman or a prostitute. Also **floos′y**. [Cf. FLOSSY]

flop (flop) *v.* **flopped, flop·ping** *v.i.* **1.** To move, flap, or beat about heavily or clumsily, especially with or as with dull thuds. **2.** To fall loosely and heavily; plump: to *flop* into bed. **3.** *Informal* To be completely unsuccessful. **4.** *Slang* To sleep. — *v.t.* **5.** To cause to drop or fall with or as with a dull thud. **6.** To flap in a loose, awkward, or noisy way, as wings. — *n.* **1.** The act of flopping. **2.** A dull, thudding noise. **3.** *Informal* A total failure. **4.** *Slang* A place or opportunity for sleeping. [Var. of FLAP] — **flop′per** *n.*

flop·house (flop′hous′) *n.* A cheap, shabby hotel for vagrants or derelicts.

flop·py (flop′ē) *adj.* **·pi·er, ·pi·est** *Informal* That flops or tends to flop. — **flop′pi·ly** *adv.* — **flop′pi·ness** *n.*

flor. Floruit.

Flor. Florida (unofficial).

flo·ra (flôr′ə, flō′rə) *n. pl.* **flo·ras** or **flo·rae** (flôr′ē, flō′rē) **1.** The aggregate of plants growing in and usually peculiar to a particular region or period: distinguished from *fauna*. **2.** A work systematically describing such plants. [< NL, after L *Flora*, goddess of flowers]

Flo·ra (flôr′ə, flō′rə) In Roman mythology, the goddess of flowers.

flo·ral (flôr′əl, flō′rəl) *adj.* Of, like, or pertaining to flowers. — **flo′ral·ly** *adv.*

floral envelope *Bot.* The corolla and calyx of a flower.

Flo·ré·al (flôr′ē·əl, *Fr.* flô·rā·àl′) *n.* The eighth month of the Republican calendar. See (Republican) CALENDAR. [< F < L *floreus* flowery]

Flor·ence (flôr′əns, flor′-) **1.** The capital of Tuscany, Italy, on the Arno in the central part of the Province; pop. 438,138 (1961): Italian *Firenze*. Ancient **Flo·ren·ti·a** (flō·ren′shē·ə). **2.** A city in NW Alabama, on the Tennessee River near Wilson Dam; pop. 34,031. **3.** An unincorporated place in SW California, a suburb of Los Angeles; pop. 42,895.

Flor·en·tine (flôr′ən·tēn, -tīn, flor′-) *adj.* Of or pertaining to Florence, Italy. — *n.* A native or inhabitant of Florence.

Flo·res (flō′res *for def. 1*; flō′rish *for def. 2*) **1.** An island of Nusa Tenggara, Indonesia, separated from Celebes by the **Flores Sea**, a part of the Pacific; 5,511 sq. mi. See map of INDONESIA. **2.** An island of the Azores; 55 sq. mi.

flo·res·cence (flô·res′əns, flō-) *n.* **1.** The state, period, or process of blossoming. **2.** A state or period of prosperity or success. [< NL *florescentia* < L *florescere*, inceptive of *florere* to bloom] — **flo·res′cent** *adj.*

flo·ret (flôr′it, flō′rit) *n.* **1.** A little flower. **2.** *Bot.* One of the small individual flowers that make up a cluster or head of a composite flower, as in the sunflower or dandelion. [< OF *florete*, dim. of *flor* a flower < L *flos, floris*]

Flo·rey (flôr′ē, flō′rē), **Sir Howard (Walter)**, 1898–1968, British pathologist born in Australia.

Flo·ri·an·óp·o·lis (flôr′ē·ən·op′ə·lis, flō′rē-) The capital of Santa Catarina, Brazil, a port on Santa Catarina island; pop. 98,521 (1961): formerly *Destêrro*.

flo·ri·at·ed (flôr′ē·ā′tid, flō′rē-) *adj.* Decorated with floral designs. Also **flo′re·at′ed**.

flo·ri·bun·da (flô′rə·bun′də, flôr′ə-) *n.* Any of a group of long-flowering varieties of rose with clusters of large blooms. [< NL, fem. of *floribundus* flowering freely < *flori-*.+ *-bundus* adj. suffix]

flo·ri·cul·ture (flôr′ə·kul′chər, flō′rə-) *n.* The cultivation of flowers or ornamental plants. [< L *flos, floris* flower + CULTURE] — **flo′ri·cul′tur·al** *adj.* — **flo′ri·cul′tur·ist** *n.*

flor·id (flôr′id, flor′-) *adj.* **1.** Having a ruddy color, espe-cially of the type typical of high blood pressure; flushed with redness. **2.** Ornate, especially to an excessive degree; flowery: *florid* architecture; a *florid* style. **3.** *Archaic* Vigorous. **4.** *Rare* Consisting of or covered with flowers. [< L *floridus* flowery < *flos, floris* flower] — **flor′id·ly** *adv.*

Flor·i·da (flôr′ə·də, flor′-) The southernmost Atlantic State of the United States; 58,560 sq. mi.; pop. 6,789,443; capital, Tallahassee; entered the Union March 3, 1845: nickname, *Everglade State*. Abbr. *Fla.* — **Flo·rid·i·an** (flō·rid′ē·ən, flō-, flo-), **Flor·i·dan** (flôr′ə·dən, flor′-) *adj. & n.*

Florida, Straits of A channel separating the southern tip of Florida from the Bahamas and Cuba. Also **Florida Strait**.

Florida Keys A chain of islands curving about 150 miles SW around the tip of the Florida peninsula from Virginia Key to Key West.

Florida moss Spanish moss (which see).

flo·rid·i·ty (flə·rid′ə·tē) *n. pl.* **·ties** **1.** Ruddiness. **2.** Floweriness. Also **flor′id·ness**.

flo·rif·er·ous (flô·rif′ər·əs, flō-) *adj.* Bearing flowers. [< L *florifer* bearing flowers + -OUS]

flor·in (flôr′in, flor′-) *n.* **1.** A British silver coin, equal to one tenth of a pound, or two shillings. **2.** The guilder of the Netherlands. **3.** A gold coin first issued at Florence in 1252: also **flor·ence** (flôr′əns, flor′-). **4.** A gold coin first issued in England in 1343. **5.** One of several former European coins. Abbr. *fl.* [< OF < Ital. *fiorino* < *fiore* flower < L *flos, floris* flower; so called from the figure of a lily stamped on it]

Flo·ri·o (flôr′ē·ō, flō′rē·ō), **John**, 1553?–1625, English lexicographer; translated Montaigne's *Essays*.

Flo·ris·sant (flôr′i·sənt) A city in eastern Missouri, near St. Louis; pop. 38,166.

flo·rist (flôr′ist, flō′rist, flor′ist) *n.* A grower of or dealer in flowers.

-florous *combining form Bot.* Having (a specified number, kind, etc., of) flowers: *uniflorous*. [< L *-florus* < *flos, floris* a flower]

flo·ru·it (flō′rōō·it, flôr′yōō·it) *Latin* He (or she) flourished: usually used when birth and death dates are not known. Abbr. *fl., flor.*

flos fer·ri (flos′ fer′ī) *Mineral.* A variety of aragonite resembling coral. [< L, flower of iron]

floss (flôs, flos) *n.* One of several light, silk or silklike substances or fibers; as: **a** Lustrous, untwisted thread of silk used in embroidery. **b** A similar waxed thread used in cleaning the teeth; dental floss. **c** Soft fibers produced by some plants, as tassels of corn. **d** Waste fibers of silk. **e** The outside fibers on the cocoon of a silkworm. Also **floss silk**. [< OF *flosche*]

floss·y (flôs′ē, flos′ē) *adj.* **floss·i·er, floss·i·est** **1.** Of, pertaining to, or resembling floss; silky, light, and fluffy. **2.** *U.S. Slang* Ostentatiously elegant; showy. — *n. pl.* **floss·ies** *U.S. Slang* A floozy: also **floss′ie**.

flo·tage (flō′tij) *n.* **1.** The act or state of floating; also, the ability to float; buoyancy. **2.** Floating things or material, as debris floating in water. **3.** The part of a ship's hull above the water line. Also spelled *floatage*.

flo·ta·tion (flō·tā′shən) *n.* **1.** The act or state of floating. **2.** The act of financing a business undertaking, as by an issue of stocks or bonds. **3.** *Metall.* A method of separating pulverized ores by placing them in a solution in which certain particles float and others sink. Also spelled *floatation*.

flotation gear *Aeron.* A buoyant apparatus attached to an aircraft to enable it to float.

flo·til·la (flō·til′ə) *n.* **1.** A fleet of small vessels; also, a numerically small fleet. **2.** In the U.S. Navy, an organized group of vessels of the same or related type, composed of two or more squadrons. [< Sp., dim. of *flota* fleet]

Flo·tow (flō′tō), **Friedrich von**, 1812–83, German composer.

flot·sam (flot′səm) *n.* **1.** *Law* Any goods from a wrecked or imperiled ship that are cast or swept into the sea and found floating there. Compare JETSAM, LAGAN. **2.** Any objects floating on a body of water. **3.** Vagrants or unattached persons. [< AF *floteson* < *floter* to float < OE *flotian*]

flotsam and jetsam **1.** Parts of a wrecked ship or its cargo drifting on the water or cast ashore. **2.** Worthless or trifling things; oddments. **3.** Transients; drifters.

flounce[1] (flouns) *n.* A gathered or pleated strip of material used for trimming skirts, etc., and sewn on only by its upper edge, the lower edge being left free. — *v.t.* **flounced, flounc·ing** To furnish with flounces. [Var. of FROUNCE]

flounce[2] (flouns) *v.i.* **flounced, flounc·ing** **1.** To move or go with exaggerated tosses of the body, as in anger or petulance. **2.** To plunge or flounder: said of animals. — *n.* The act of flouncing. [< Scand. Cf. dial. Sw. *flunsa* to plunge.]

flounc·ing (floun′sing) *n.* **1.** Material for flounces. **2.** A flounce; also, flounces collectively.

floun·der[1] (floun′dər) *v.i.* **1.** To struggle clumsily; move awkwardly as if mired or injured. **2.** To proceed, as in speech or action, in a stumbling, awkward, or confused manner. — *n.* A stumbling or struggling motion. [? Blend of FLOUNCE[2] and FOUNDER[2]]

---

floun·der[2] (floun′dər) *n.* **1.** Any of certain flatfish, valued as food; especially, the **winter flounder** (*Pseudopleuronectes americanus*) of the North Atlantic coast, and the **California flounder** (*Platichthys stellatus*). **2.** Any flatfish other than sole. [< AF *floundre*, prob. < Scand. Cf. Sw. *flundra*.]

flour (flour) *n.* **1.** A fine, soft, usually white powder obtained by sifting and grinding the meal of a grain, especially wheat; also, a similar substance obtained by grinding dried seeds, roots, etc. **2.** Any finely powdered substance. — *v.t.* **1.** To sprinkle or cover with flour. **2.** To make into flour by sifting and grinding. **3.** *Metall.* To break up (mercury) into tiny, noncoalescing particles. [Var. of FLOUR]

flour·ish (flûr′ish) *v.i.* **1.** To grow or fare well or prosperously; thrive. **2.** To be at the peak of success or development: Alchemy *flourished* in the Middle Ages. **3.** To move with sweeping motions; be displayed or waved about. **4.** To write with sweeping or ornamental strokes. **5.** To use elegant, flowery language. **6.** *Music* **a** To play or sing a showy passage or in a showy manner. **b** To sound a fanfare. **7.** *Obs.* To blossom. — *v.t.* **8.** To wave about or brandish, as a weapon or flag. **9.** To display ostentatiously; flaunt. **10.** To embellish, as with ornamental lines, figures, notes, etc. — *n.* **1.** A brandishing, as of a sword. **2.** A curved or decorative stroke in penmanship. **3.** Something done primarily for effect or display. **4.** Florid and ornate language. **5.** *Music* **a** A fanfare, as of trumpets. **b** A florid passage, or notes added to a passage for decorative effect. **6.** *Rare* The state of being prosperous, vigorous, or successful. **7.** *Obs.* The condition of being in flower; blooming. [< OF *floriss,-* stem of *florir* < L *florere* to bloom] — **flour′ish·er** *n.*
— **Syn.** (verb) **1, 2.** prosper, advance, increase, flower. — **Ant.** languish, decline, fail.

flour·ish·ing (flûr′ish·ing) *adj.* That flourishes; doing well; thriving. — **flour′ish·ing·ly** *adv.*

flour·y (flour′ē) *adj.* Of, pertaining to, or suggestive of flour. **2.** Sprinkled or covered with flour; white with flour.

flout (flout) *v.t.* **1.** To express scorn or contempt for; scoff at; defy with open contempt: to *flout* convention. — *v.i.* **2.** To express one's contempt; mock; jeer. — *n.* A contemptuous or mocking act or remark; gibe; scoff. [Prob. ME *flouten* to play the flute, to deride] — **flout′er** *n.* — **flout′ing·ly** *adv.*

flow (flō) *v.i.* **1.** Of water or other fluids, to move steadily and smoothly along, as through a channel or over a surface; also, of electricity or other forms of energy, to pass along or be conveyed. **2.** To move along steadily and freely as a fluid: The crowd *flowed* through the gates. **3.** To well out or pour forth: Love *flowed* from her heart. **4.** To move steadily in an agreeably effortless or rhythmic way: Conversation *flowed*. **5.** To be marked by a satisfying, harmonious continuity: The lines of the statue *flow*. **6.** To hang or ripple down in rich profusion, as hair. **7.** To be abundant in something: a heart *flowing* with joy; also, to overflow: Her eyes *flowed* with tears. **8.** Of the tide, to rise: opposed to *ebb*. — *v.t.* **9.** To cover or flood with some fluid. **10.** To cause to flow. — *n.* **1.** The act of flowing. **2.** Something that flows, as a current or stream. **3.** A continuous stream or outpouring, as of words, ideas, etc. **4.** The amount of that which flows: a daily *flow* of 500 gallons. **5.** The incoming of the tide. **6.** The manner of flowing; grace of line or movement: the *flow* of a gown. **7.** An overflowing. [OE *flōwan*]

flow·age (flō′ij) *n.* **1.** The act of flowing or overflowing, or the state of being overflowed. **2.** A liquid that flows or overflows. **3.** *Physics* Deformation of a solid body, as asphalt, by intermolecular movement or flow and without fracture.

flow chart A schematic diagram showing a sequence of operations, stages, etc., as for a computer program or industrial process: also called *flow sheet.*

flow·er (flou′ər, flour) *n.* **1.** A simple or complex cluster of petals, usually brightly colored and with an outer envelope of green leaves, at or near the tip of a seed-bearing plant or sometimes along the stem, and enclosing the reproductive parts of the plant; blossom; bloom; also, any plant that produces such a cluster. **2.** *Bot.* The reproductive structure of any plant, whether surrounded or not by such a cluster. **3.** The condition in which the reproductive parts of a plant are mature, especially when marked by brightly colored, open petals: usually preceded by *in*: a plant in *flower*. **4.** The condition of having arrived at fullest growth, development, or vigor; prime: usually preceded by *in*: to be in the *flower* of manhood. **5.** The finest or choicest part or representative of something: the *flower*

FLOWER

A Petal. *B* Pistil: *a* Stigma, *b* Style,
c Ovary. *C* Stamen: *d* Anther,
e Filament. *D* Ovule.
E Sepal. *F* Receptacle.

of youth. **6.** *Usually pl.* A decorative feature; embellishment; ornamentation: *flowers* of speech. **7.** *pl. Chem.* A powdery substance usually produced by heating a solid to a gaseous state and condensing the vapors: *flowers* of sulfur. Abbr. *fl.* — *v.i.* **1.** To produce flowers; blossom; bloom. **2.** To reach fullest growth, development, or vigor. — *v.t.* **3.** To decorate with flowers or floral designs. [< OF *flour, flor* < L *flos, floris* flower]

flow·er·age (flou′ər·ij, flou′rij) *n.* **1.** The act, process, or time of flowering. **2.** A mass of flowers or floral decorations.

flow·er-de-luce (flou′ər·də·lōōs′, flour′-) *n. pl.* **flow·ers-de-luce 1.** *Heraldry* A fleur-de-lis. **2.** The iris.

flow·ered (flou′ərd) *adj.* **1.** Dotted with flowers: a *flowered* hillside. **2.** Having a floral pattern: a *flowered* gown.

flow·er·er (flou′ər·ər) *n.* A plant that blossoms at a certain time or in a certain manner: a spring *flowerer.*

flow·er·et (flou′ər·it, flou′rit) *n.* A small flower; floret.

flow·er·fence (flou′ər·fens′, flour′-) *n.* A species of poinciana (*P. pulcherrima*) with orange-yellow flowers: also called *Barbados pride.*

flower girl 1. A girl or woman who sells flowers. **2.** A young girl who carries flowers in a procession.

flower head *Bot.* A dense cluster of tiny flowers all growing directly from the main stem of a plant.

flow·er·ing (flou′ər·ing, flour′ing) *adj.* **1.** That bears flowers. **2.** That is in flower; blooming; blossoming.

flowering ash Any of various plants (genus *Fraxinus*), especially *F. ornus* of southern Europe, having flowers with greenish petals and yielding manna: also called *manna ash.*

flowering dogwood See under DOGWOOD.

flowering maple A variety of the abutilon having maple-like leaves and orange flowers: also called *redvein maple.*

flow·er-of-an-hour (flou′ər·uv·ən·our′, flour′-) *n.* The bladder ketmia.

flow·er·pot (flou′ər·pot′) *n.* A pot for growing plants.

flowers of benzoin *Chem.* Benzoin (which see).

flow·er·y (flou′ər·ē, flour′ē) *adj.* **·er·i·er, ·er·i·est 1.** Full of or covered with flowers. **2.** Using or containing highly embellished language. **3.** Having a floral pattern. — **Syn.** See RHETORICAL. — **flow′er·i·ly** *adv.* — **flow′er·i·ness** *n.*

flow·ing (flō′ing) *adj.* **1.** Effortless and free; gracefully smooth: *flowing* movements. **2.** Harmoniously unbroken; smoothly extended: *flowing* architectural lines. **3.** Rippling down in rich profusion: *flowing* hair. — **flow′ing·ly** *adv.*

flow meter An apparatus designed to measure and record the rate of flow of a liquid or gas through pipes, etc.

flown[1] (flōn) Past participle of FLY[1].

flown[2] (flōn) *adj.* **1.** Coated with colors blended or flowing into each other: *flown* porcelain. **2.** *Naut.* Of a sail, slack. **3.** *Archaic* Elated; flushed. [< obs. pp. of FLOW]

flow sheet A flow chart (which see).

Floyd (floid), **William,** 1734–1821, American patriot; signer of the Declaration of Independence.

fl. oz. Fluid ounce(s).

flu (flōō) *n. Informal* Influenza.

flub (flub) *v.t. & v.i.* **flubbed, flub·bing** *U.S. Slang* To bungle (a job, chance, etc.). — *n.* A blunder; mistake [origin uncertain]

flub·dub (flub′dub′) *n. U.S. Informal* **1.** Pompous nonsense. **2.** Flashiness. Also **flub·dub·ber·y** [Imit.]

fluc·tu·ant (fluk′chōō·ənt) *adj.* Varying in position, condition, etc.; fluctuating; unstable.

fluc·tu·ate (fluk′chōō·āt) *v.* **·at·ed, ·at·ing** *v.i.* **1.** To change or vary often and in an irregular manner; be unsteady or unstable; waver. **2.** To move up and down; undulate. — *v.t.* **3.** To cause to fluctuate. [< L *fluctuatus,* pp. of *fluctuare* to wave < *fluctus* wave < *fluere* to flow]
— **Syn.** *Fluctuate, undulate, oscillate, vibrate,* and *vacillate* denote a wavering or varying motion. To *fluctuate* is to move up and down irregularly, like sea waves; stock prices *fluctuate.* A regular wavelike motion is indicated by *undulate;* cornstalks *undulate* in the wind. To *oscillate* is to move regularly between two positions or conditions, as the pendulum in a clock. A body *vibrates* when it quivers rapidly; the diaphragm of a telephone *oscillates* between two electrical contacts and at the same time *vibrates* to produce sound waves. To *vacillate* is to waver in mind between alternative courses of action. Compare SHAKE. — **Ant.** abide, stay, persist.

fluc·tu·a·tion (fluk′chōō·ā′shən) *n.* **1.** Frequent irregular change; vacillation. **2.** A rising and falling, as of prices. **3.** *Biol.* A variation in an organism that is not inherited.

flue[1] (flōō) *n.* **1.** A pipe or tube through which smoke, hot air, etc., is drawn off, as from a furnace or stove; also, the passage through which the smoke, etc., goes. **2.** A pipe or tube, as of a boiler, through which steam or hot air is carried so as to heat water surrounding the pipe or tube. **3.** In an organ, a flue pipe (which see); also, the passage for air in such a pipe. Also spelled *flew.* [Origin uncertain]

flue[2] (flōō) *n.* A soft, light, fluffy mass of separated fibers, as of wool. [< Flemish *vluwe* down]

flue[3] (flōō) *n.* **1.** The sharp point of a fishhook. **2.** One of the pointed tips of an anchor. **3.** One of the barbs projecting from the shaft of a feather. [Cf. Sw. *fly*]

flue[4] (flōō) *n.* One of several types of fishing net: also spelled *flew.* [ME *flew.* Cf. MDu. *vluwe* fishing net.]

flu·en·cy (floo'ən·sē) *n.* The quality of being fluent; especially, smoothness and readiness of speech.

flu·ent (floo'ənt) *adj.* **1.** Capable of speaking or writing with effortless ease. **2.** Spoken or written with effortless ease. **3.** Marked by smoothness, grace and expressiveness. **4.** Running freely, as a stream of water; also, not stable. [< L *fluens, -entis,* ppr. of *fluere* to flow] **— flu'ent·ly** *adv.*

flue pipe An organ pipe in which the tone is produced by a stream of air passing over the lips of an opening in the side of the pipe rather than by the vibration of a reed.

flue stop A stop controlling a rank of flue pipes.

fluff (fluf) *n.* **1.** A soft, light cluster, ball, or tuft of loosely gathered fibers of wool, cotton, etc., or of other fine particles; also, a number of such clusters, etc., scattered about on a surface. **2.** A mass of soft, fine feathers; down. **3.** *Informal* An error made in reading or speaking lines: said of actors, announcers, etc. **— v.t. 1.** To make (pillows, blankets, etc.) soft and light by patting or shaking. **2.** *Informal* To make an error in reading or speaking (lines). **— v.i. 3.** To become soft, light, or feathery. **4.** *Informal* To make an error in reading or speaking lines. [? Blend of FLUE² + PUFF]

fluff·y (fluf'ē) *adj.* **fluff·i·er, fluff·i·est** Of, covered with, or resembling fluff. **— fluff'i·ly** *adv.* **— fluff'i·ness** *n.*

flü·gel·horn (floo'gəl·hôrn', *Ger.* flü'gəl·hôrn') *n.* Any of a family of brass instruments similar in design to a cornet but having a wider bore and mellower tone. [< G *flügel* wing + *horn* horn; so called from its shape]

flu·id (floo'id) *adj.* **1.** Capable of flowing; not solid; liquid or gaseous. **2.** Consisting of or pertaining to liquids. *Abbr. f., F., fl.* **3.** Not firm or fixed: a *fluid* policy. **— n.** A substance capable of flowing. [< F *fluide* < L *fluidus* < *fluere* to flow] **— flu'id·i·ty** *n.* **— flu'id·ly** *adv.*

fluid dram A measure of capacity equal to one eighth of a fluid ounce, 60 minims, or 3.70 cubic centimeters. Also **fluid drachm.** *Abbr. fl. dr.* See table inside back cover.

flu·id·ex·tract (floo'id·eks'trakt) *n.* A solution in alcohol of the active principle of a vegetable drug so prepared that 1 cubic centimeter has the strength of 1 gram of the dry drug.

flu·id·ic (floo·id'ik) *adj.* Of the nature of a fluid.

flu·id·ics (floo·id'iks) *n. pl.* (*construed as sing.*) The branch of mechanical engineering and technology that deals with the principles and applications of fluids to control certain functions within a mechanical system.

fluid ounce 1. *U.S.* One sixteenth of a pint; 29.5737 cubic centimeters. **2.** *Brit.* One-twentieth of a pint; 28.413 cubic centimeters. *Abbr. fl. oz.* See table inside back cover.

fluid pressure *Physics* Pressure of a fluid, or like that of a fluid, being invariable and uniform in all directions.

flu·i·dram (floo'i·dram') *n.* A fluid dram (which see). Also **flu'i·drachm'.**

fluke¹ (flook) *n.* **1.** One of several parasitic trematode worms. **2.** A flatfish or flounder. [OE *flōc*]

fluke² (flook) *.n.* **1.** A sharp projection turned backward at an angle from the principal tip or point of an arrow, harpoon, etc.; barb; flue; also, the entire head of an arrow, harpoon, etc. **2.** The triangular head at the end of either arm of an anchor. For illustration see ANCHOR. **3.** A lobe of a whale's tail. [? < FLUKE¹; with ref. to its shape]

FLUKES²
(def. 1)

fluke³ (flook) *n.* **1.** A lucky stroke, as in the game of pool. **2.** Any piece of good luck. **3.** Anything that happens by chance, whether favorable or not. **— v. fluked, fluk·ing** *v.t.* **1.** To get, make, etc., by a fluke. **— v.i. 2.** To make or have a fluke. [Origin unknown]

fluk·y (floo'kē) *adj.* **fluk·i·er, fluk·i·est 1.** Occurring or obtained as the result of mere chance. **2.** Constantly shifting; variable: a *fluky* wind. Also **fluk'ey.**

flume (floom) *n.* **1.** *U.S.* A narrow gap in a mountain through which a torrent passes. **2.** A chute or trough for carrying water, used as a source of water power, to convey logs, etc. **— v.t. flumed, flum·ing 1.** To drain away or divert by means of a flume, as in mining. **2.** To move or transport, as logs, by means of a flume. [< OF *flum* < L *flumen* river < *fluere* to flow]

flum·mer·y (flum'ər·ē) *n. pl.* **·mer·ies 1.** One of several soft, light, easily digested foods, as a custard; originally, a dish of oatmeal. **2.** Vapid flattery; empty compliment. **3.** Utter nonsense; humbug. [< Welsh *llymru*]

flum·mox (flum'əks) *v.t. Slang* To confuse; confound; perplex. [Cf. dial. E *flummocks* to maul, mangle]

flump (flump) *Informal v.t. & v.i.* To drop heavily and clumsily; flop. **— n.** The act of flumping; also, the sound of something flopping heavily down. [Imit.]

flung (flung) Past tense and past participle of FLING.

flunk (flungk) *U.S. Informal v.t.* **1.** To fail in (an examination, course, etc.). **2.** To give a failing grade to. **— v.i. 3.** To fail, as in an examination. **4.** To back out; give up. **— to flunk out** To leave or cause to leave a class, school, or college because of failure in studies. **— n.** A failure, as in an examination. [Origin unknown]

flunk·y (flung'kē) *n. pl.* **flunk·ies 1.** An obsequious, servile fellow; toady. **2.** A manservant in livery. Also **flunk'ey.** [? Alter. of *flanker* < FLANK, *v.*] **— flunk'y·ism** *n.*

fluo- See FLUORO-.

flu·o·phos·phate (floo'ō·fos'fāt) *n. Chem.* A double salt of hydrofluoric and phosphoric acids.

flu·or (floo'ər, -ôr) *n.* Fluorite. [< NL < L, a flowing < *fluere* to flow; trans. of G *flusse*]

fluor- Var. of FLUORO-.

flu·o·resce (floo'ə·res', floor·es') *v.i.* **-resced, ·resc·ing** To become fluorescent; exhibit fluorescence. [Back formation < FLUORESCENCE]

flu·o·res·ce·in (floo'ə·res'ē·in, floor·es'-) *n. Chem.* A yellowish red crystalline compound, $C_{20}H_{12}O_5$, used in medicine and in the making of dyestuffs. Also **flu'o·res'ce·ine** (-ēn).

flu·o·res·cence (floo'ə·res'əns, floor·es'-) *n.* **1.** The property possessed by certain substances of absorbing radiation of a particular wavelength and emitting it as light while the stimulus is active: distinguished from *phosphorescence.* **2.** The light produced by substances having this property. [< FLUOR(SPAR): coined on analogy with OPALESCENCE]

flu·o·res·cent (floo'ə·res'ənt, floor·es'-) *adj.* Having or exhibiting fluorescence.

fluorescent lamp A tubular lamp in which ultraviolet light from a low-pressure mercury arc is reradiated as visible light after impact on a phosphor coating.

flu·or·ic (floo·or'ik, -or'-; floor'ik) *adj.* Pertaining to, derived from, or containing fluorine or fluorite.

fluor·i·date (floor'ə·dāt, floo'ə·ri·dāt) *v.t.* **·dat·ed, ·dat·ing** To add sodium fluoride to (drinking water), especially as a means of preventing tooth decay. **— fluor'i·da'tion** *n.*

flu·o·ride (floo'ə·rīd, -rid; floor'īd, -id) *n. Chem.* A binary compound of fluorine and another element. Also **flu'o·rid** (-rid).

flu·o·rine (floo'ə·rēn, -rin; floor'ēn, -in) *n.* A pale, greenish yellow, pungent, corrosive, and extremely reactive gaseous element (symbol F) belonging to the halogen group. See ELEMENT. Also **flu'o·rin** (-rin). *Abbr. Fl.*

flu·o·rite (floo'ə·rīt, floor'īt) *n.* A cleavable, isometric, variously colored calcium fluoride, CaF_2, used as a flux in making steel and glass: also called *fluor, fluorspar.*

fluoro- *combining form* **1.** *Chem.* Indicating the presence of fluorine in a compound. **2.** *Chem. fluoroscope.* Also, before vowels, *fluor-,* as in *fluoride:* also *fluo-,* as in *fluoborate.*

flu·o·ro·car·bon (floo'ə·rō·kär'bən, floor'ō-) *n. Chem.* Any of a group of very stable compounds of carbon and fluorine analogous in structure with hydrocarbons, and used as solvents, lubricants, insulators, and refrigerants.

flu·or·om·e·ter (floo'ə·rom'ə·tər, floor·om'-) *n. Physics* An absorbing screen used to measure the color and intensity of fluorescence, as from X-rays, radium, etc. **— flu'or·om'e·try** *n.*

fluor·o·scope (floor'ə·skōp, floo'ə·rə-) *n.* A device for observing the shadows projected upon a fluorescent screen by objects put between it and a direct beam of X-rays or other radiation. **— fluor'o·scop'ic** (-skop'ik) *adj.*

fluor·os·co·py (floor·os'kə·pē, floo'ə·ros'-) *n.* Examination conducted by means of a fluoroscope.

flu·or·o·sis (floo'ə·rō'sis, floor·ō'-) *n. Pathol.* Chronic poisoning with fluorine.

flu·or·spar (floo'ər·spär', floor·spär') *n.* Fluorite.

flu·o·sil·i·cate (floo'ō·sil'i·kit) *n. Chem.* A salt or ester of fluosilicic acid.

flu·o·sil·i·cic acid (floo'ō·si·lis'ik) *Chem.* A strong acid, H_2SiF_6, existing only in solution.

flur·ry (flûr'ē) *v.* **·ried, ·ry·ing** *v.t.* **1.** To bewilder or confuse; agitate; fluster. **— v.i. 2.** To move in a flurry. **— n. pl. ·ries 1.** A sudden commotion or excitement; nervous agitation; stir. **2.** A sudden, light gust of wind. **3.** A light, brief rain or snowfall, accompanied by small gusts. **4.** In the stock exchange, a sudden, short-lived increase in trading. [Blend of FLUTTER and HURRY]

flush¹ (flush) *v.i.* **1.** To become red in the face through a rush of blood, as from strong emotion or fever; redden; blush. **2.** To glow or shine with a reddish brightness: Dawn *flushed* in the sky. **3.** To flow or rush suddenly and copiously; flood: Blood *flushed* into his face. **4.** To become cleaned or purified through a quick, sudden flow or gush of water, etc. **— v.t. 5.** To wash out, purify, etc., as a sewer, with a quick, sudden flow or gush of water or other liquid. **6.** To cause to glow red or blush; redden. **7.** To stir up or elate with the warmth of achievement, pride, etc.: usually in the passive: to be *flushed* with success. **— n. 1.** A heightened, reddish color; warm glow; blush. **2.** A pervasive feeling of being hot; the *flush* of fever. **3.** A pervasive, warm feeling of elation, excitement, etc.: a *flush* of pride. **4.** Glowing bloom or freshness: the *flush* of youth. **5.** A sudden gush or flow of water, etc., as through a sewer. [? < FLUSH⁴; infl. in meaning by *flash, flow, blush,* etc.] **— flush'er** *n.*

flush² (flush) *adj.* **1.** Even or level with another surface:

The tiles of the floor are all *flush*. **2.** Of a line of print, even with the margin; not indented. **3.** Of the deck of a ship, extending on one plane from stem to stern. **4.** Having plenty of money on hand; also, of money, being in plentiful supply. **5.** Of a period or epoch, marked by prosperity: *flush* times. **6.** Having a heightened, reddish color: *flush* faces. **7.** Of a blow, direct; square: a *flush* hit. **8.** *Rare* Full of spirit and liveliness; also, very abundant or profuse. — *adv.* **1.** In an even position with another surface; also, in alignment with a margin. **2.** In a direct manner; squarely: to hit someone *flush* on the jaw. — *v.t.* To make even or level, as with another surface; put in alignment. [? < FLUSH¹]

flush³ (flush) *n.* In poker, etc., a hand of cards all of one suit. — **royal flush** In poker, a hand of cards made up of the ace, king, queen, jack, and ten of one suit. — **straight flush** In poker, a hand of cards made up entirely of cards of the same suit and in sequence. [Cf. F *flux* (obsolete), *flus* < L *fluxus* a flow]

flush⁴ (flush) *v.t.* **1.** To drive (an animal) from cover; especially, to startle (birds) from cover. — *v.i.* **2.** To rush out or fly from cover. [ME *flusschen*; origin uncertain]

flush-board (flush′bôrd′, -bōrd′) *n.* A flashboard.

Flush-ing (flush′ing) **1.** A port commune in the SW Netherlands, on the English Channel; pop. 40,197 (est. 1970). Dutch *Vlissingen*. **2.** A section of the Borough of Queens, New York City, including **Flushing Meadow**, site of the 1939–40 and 1964–65 World's Fair and headquarters of the United Nations, 1946–1951.

flus-ter (flus′tər) *v.t. & v.i.* To make or become confused, agitated, or befuddled. — *n.* Confusion or agitation of mind; flurry; dither. [Cf. Icel. *flaustr* to hurry]

flus-trate (flus′trāt) *v.t.* **·trat·ed, ·trat·ing** *Informal* To fluster. Also **flus′ter·ate.** [< FLUSTER + -ATE¹] — **flus.tra′tion** *n.*

flute (flōōt) *n.* **1.** A tubular, reedless, woodwind instrument of small diameter, equipped with holes and keys and with a mouthpiece located either along the side or at the end, and producing tones of a high pitch and clear, silvery quality. **2.** A flute stop in an organ. **3.** *Archit.* A groove, usually of semicircular section, as in a column. **4.** A small groove, as in pleated cloth. **5.** Anything shaped like a flute. Abbr. *ft.* — *v.* **flut·ed, flut·ing** *v.i.* **1.** To play on a flute. **2.** To produce a flutelike sound. — *v.t.* **3.** To sing, whistle, or utter with flutelike tones. **4.** To make flutes in (a column, dress, etc.). [< OF *flaüte*; ult. origin uncertain]

flut·ed (flōō′tid) *adj.* **1.** Having parallel grooves or flutes. **2.** Having the tone of a flute.

flut·er (flōō′tər) *n.* **1.** One who or that which makes fluted work. **2.** *Rare* A flutist.

flut·ing (flōō′ting) *n.* **1.** The act of making flutes in a column, ruffle, frill, etc. **2.** Flutes or grooves collectively. **3.** Fluted work; also, ornamentation with flutes. Compare REEDING. **4.** The act of playing on a flute or of singing, whistling, etc., in flutelike tones.

flut·ist (flōō′tist) *n.* A flute player: also called *flautist*.

flut·ter (flut′ər) *v.i.* **1.** To wave or flap rapidly and irregularly. **2.** To flap the wings rapidly in or as in erratic flight. **3.** To move or proceed with irregular motion: to *flutter* to the ground. **4.** To move about lightly and quickly; flit. **5.** To be excited or nervous, as with hope, fear, or expectation. **6.** To beat rapidly and sometimes unevenly, as the heart. — *v.t.* **7.** To cause to flutter; agitate. **8.** To excite or confuse; fluster. — **Syn.** See FLY. — *n.* **1.** A vibrating or quivering motion. **2.** Nervous agitation; dither. **3.** Excited interest; commotion: Her appearance caused a *flutter*. **4.** In swimming, the flutter kick. **5.** *Aeron.* A periodic oscillation set up in any part of an airplane by mechanical disturbances and maintained by inertia, structural characteristics, etc. **6.** *Telecom.* A distortion of sound caused by irregular variation in the frequency of a transmitter signal, message, or recording. **7.** *Pathol.* An abnormally rapid but rhythmical contraction of the atria of the heart. [OE *floterian*] — **flut′ter·er** *n.* — **flut′ter·y** *adj.*

flutter kick In swimming, a kick, usually performed with the crawl stroke, in which the legs are kept almost straight while being moved up and down rapidly in short strokes.

flut·y (flōō′tē) *adj.* Flutelike in tone; clear and mellow.

flu·vi·al (flōō′vē·əl) *adj.* Pertaining to, found in, or formed by a river. Also **flu·vi·a·tile** (flōō′vē·ə·til). [< L *fluvialis* < *fluvius* river]

fluvio- *combining form* River. [< L *fluvius* river]

flu·vi·o·ma·rine (flōō′vē·ō′mə·rēn′) *adj. Geol.* Formed by or pertaining to the joint action of the sea and streams.

flux (fluks) *n.* **1.** A flowing or discharge. **2.** Constant movement or change: Language is always in a state of *flux*. **3.** The flowing in of the tide. **4.** *Pathol.* An excessive and abnormal discharge of fluid matter from the body. **5.** The act or process of melting; fusion. **6.** *Metall.* **a** A substance that promotes the fusing of metals, as borax. **b** Any of various substances that by their action serve to purify metals or prevent undue oxidation of metal surfaces. **7.** *Physics* The rate of flow of fluids, heat, electricity, light, etc. — **bloody flux** Dysentery. — *v.t.* **1.** To make fluid; melt; fuse. **2.** To

treat, as metal, with a flux. **3.** *Obs.* To purge. — *v.i.* **4.** *Archaic* To flow. [< F < L *fluxus* < *fluere* to flow]

flux density *Physics* The density of electrical or magnetic lines of force as measured at a cross section of their flow.

flux·ion (fluk′shən) *n.* **1.** The act of flowing. **2.** Unceasing change. **3.** *Pathol.* Flux. **4.** *Math.* The rate of variation of a changing quantity; also, a differential. — **flux′ion·al, flux′ion·ar·y** *adj.* — **flux′ion·al·ly** *adv.*

fly¹ (flī) *v.* **flew** or (*for def.* 9) **flied, flown** or (*for def.* 9) **flied, fly·ing** *v.i.* **1.** To move through the air on wings, as a bird. **2.** To move or travel through the air by aircraft. **3.** To rush or be propelled through the air, as an arrow. **4.** To wave or flutter in the air. **5.** To move swiftly or with a rush: The door *flew* open. **6.** To pass swiftly: Time *flies*. **7.** To be used up or spent quickly, as money. **8.** To flee; escape. **9.** In baseball, to bat the ball high over the field. **10.** In falconry, to hunt with a hawk. — *v.t.* **11.** To cause to fly or float in the air. **12.** To operate (an aircraft). **13.** To transport by aircraft. **14.** To pass over in an aircraft: to *fly* the Pacific Ocean. **15.** To flee from. **16.** In falconry, to hunt with a hawk. — **to fly at** To attack suddenly or violently. — **to fly in the face of** To defy openly. — **to fly into** To enter suddenly into (an outburst of rage, etc.). — **to fly off** To leave quickly. — **to fly off the handle** To lose control of oneself through anger. — **to fly out** In baseball, to be retired by batting a ball high over the field and having it caught by an opposing player. — **to fly the coop** *U.S. Slang* To sneak off; get away; escape. — **to let fly** To utter, throw, or discharge violently: to *let fly* an oath, a stone, etc. — *n., pl.* **flies 1.** A flap of material concealing the zipper, buttons, or other fastening in a garment, especially in a pair of trousers. **2.** The flap at the entrance to a tent; also, a piece of canvas forming a second, outer roof on some tents. **3.** The flyleaf of a book. **4.** The length of a flag from the staff to its farthest edge; also, the farthest edge. **5.** In baseball, a ball batted high over the field. **6.** A device to regulate speed, consisting of vanes on a rotating shaft, used in the striking mechanism of clocks, in music boxes, etc. **7.** *Mech.* **a** A flywheel. **b** The weighted cross arm of a fly press. **c** A fly press. **8.** *Printing* A mechanism for taking single sheets from the cylinder of a press and delivering them flat on a pile. **9.** *pl.* In a theater, the space above the stage and behind the proscenium, containing drop curtains, overhead lights, etc. **10.** *Brit.* A light hackney coach. **11.** The act of flying; flight. — **on the fly 1.** While flying. **2.** *U.S. Informal* While in great haste. [OE *flēogan*]

— **Syn.** (*verb*) *Fly, flutter, soar, zoom, hover,* and *float* are here compared as they apply to the movements of birds. *Fly* is the general term for locomotion in air; birds and airplanes *fly*. A bird *flutters* by flapping its wings rapidly or irregularly; the word usually is applied to short or uncertain movements. *Soar* means to rise rapidly and refers to a long, even motion. *Zoom,* first applied to airplanes, is a close synonym of *soar,* but usually refers to a sharper and more sudden ascent. To *hover* is to stay in the air near one place, while to *float* is to be borne up by a fluid, as water or air, without any effort to progress in any direction. **3.** flit, dart, skim, scud, shoot. **8.** depart, abscond. See ESCAPE.

fly² (flī) *n., pl.* **flies 1.** Any of various small, two-winged insects (family *Muscidae*); especially, the common housefly (*Musca domestica*). For illustration see INSECTS (injurious). **2.** Any of various other flying insects not of the family *Muscidae,* as the May fly. **3.** A fishhook to which colored bits of material, feathers, etc., are attached in such a way as to resemble an insect. For illustration see LURE. — **fly in the ointment** Some small thing that detracts from the enjoyment of something. [OE *flyge*]

fly³ (flī) *adj.* **fli·er, fli·est** *Slang* Mentally sharp; quick-witted.

Fly (flī) *n.* The constellation Musca.

fly agaric A common species of poisonous mushroom (*Amanita muscaria*) with a brightly colored cap. Also **fly amanita.**

fly·a·way (flī′ə·wā′) *adj.* **1.** Disposed to flightiness; giddy. **2.** Streaming or wind-blown, as hair. — *n.* One who or that which is flighty, swift, or elusive.

fly·blow (flī′blō′) *n.* The egg or young larva of a blowfly, deposited on food, etc. — *v.t. & v.i.* **·blew, ·blown, ·blowing 1.** To taint (food) with flyblows. **2.** To spoil.

fly·blown (flī′blōn′) *adj.* **1.** Tainted with flyblows. **2.** Contaminated; corrupt.

fly·boat (flī′bōt′) *n.* **1.** A large flat-bottomed Dutch coasting boat. **2.** Any very swift vessel.

fly book A booklike case for artificial flies used in fishing.

fly-by (flī′bī′) *n., pl.* **-bys** *Aerospace* The passage of a spacecraft relatively near a heavenly body, as for obtaining photographs of its surface.

fly-by-night (flī′bī·nīt′) *adj.* Not to be trusted, especially in financial matters. — *n.* An untrustworthy person; especially, one who cheats a creditor by departing secretly.

fly·catch·er (flī′kach′ər) *n.* Any of a large order of passerine birds that typically catch insects while flying, as the **least flycatcher** (*Empidonax minimus*) or chebec.

fly·er (flī′ər) See FLIER.

fly-fish (flī′fish′) *v.i.* To fish with artificial flies as bait.

fly·ing (flī′ing) *adj.* **1.** Capable of or adapted for flight in the air. **2.** Moving or passing quickly, as if in flight: the *flying* minutes. **3.** Waving, streaming, or floating in or through the air: a *flying* banner. **4.** Hurried; hasty; rapid: a *flying* trip. **5.** Pertaining to or used in aviation: *flying* lesson. **6.** *Naut.* Pertaining to sails not secured on all sides by stays or spars. — *n.* The act of one who or that which flies.

flying boat A large seaplane having a hull for flotation.

flying buttress *Archit.* A bracing structure typically in the form of a band of stone carried by a rampant arch from a wall to an abutment. For illustration see BUTTRESS.

flying circus **1.** In World War I, a squadron of fighter planes. **2.** An exhibition of aerial acrobatics performed by several planes; also, the group giving such a performance.

flying colors **1.** Flags or banners carried aloft or waving in the air. **2.** Brilliant success: to pass with *flying colors*.

Flying Dutchman **1.** A legendary spectral Dutch ship supposed to be seen near the Cape of Good Hope in stormy weather and considered a bad omen. **2.** The captain of this ship, doomed to sail the seas until Judgment Day for his sins: the subject of an opera (1843) by Richard Wagner.

flying fatigue Aeroneurosis.

flying field A small airport.

flying fish A fish (family *Exocoetidae*) of warm and temperate seas, with large pectoral fins that enable it to glide through the air for short distances.

Flying Fish The constellation Volans.

flying fox One of several large, fruit-eating bats with snouts suggestive of foxes; especially, such a bat (genus *Pteropus*) found in the warmer parts of Europe, Asia, and Africa.

flying frog A tree frog (*Rhacophorus pardalis*) of the East Indies with greatly lengthened, webbed toes that enable it to make gliding leaps.

flying gurnard A marine fish (family *Dactylopteridae*) with very long horizontal pectoral fins that enable it to make gliding leaps out of the water.

flying jib *Naut.* A jib set out beyond the standing jib, on an extended boom called the **flying-jib boom.** For illustrations see SCHOONER, SHIP.

flying lemur An insect-eating mammal (genus *Cynocephalus*) of the East Indies, having a membrane connecting its front limbs and back limbs on each side by means of which it can make gliding leaps: also called *colugo*.

flying lizard A dragon (def. 7).

flying machine *Archaic* An airplane or similar aircraft.

flying mare A wrestling throw in which one seizes the opponent's wrist, turns around, and yanks the opponent over one's shoulder.

flying officer In the Royal, Royal Canadian, and other Commonwealth air forces, a commissioned officer ranking next below a flight lieutenant. See table at GRADE.

flying phalanger Any of several arboreal marsupials (genera *Acrobates, Petaurus, Schoinobates*) of Australia and New Guinea, having folds of skin along the sides that enable them to make long, gliding leaps from one tree to another: also called *glider, gliding possum*.

flying saucer Any of various objects of vaguely saucerlike shape, alleged to have been seen flying at high altitudes and great speeds; an unidentified flying object (UFO).

flying squirrel A squirrel (genus *Glaucomys*) having a fold of skin connecting its front limbs and back limbs on each side, enabling it to make gliding leaps.

flying start **1.** In racing, the passing of the starting post at full speed. **2.** A speedy, efficient beginning.

flying wing **1.** An airplane without a fuselage. **2.** *Canadian* In football, a player whose position varies behind the line of scrimmage.

fly·leaf (flī′lēf′) *n.* *pl.* **·leaves** (-lēvz′) A blank leaf at the beginning or end of a book, pamphlet, etc.

fly net A piece of netting designed to be hung over a window, an animal, etc., to keep insects out or off.

fly·o·ver (flī′ō′vər) *n.* **1.** A flight of planes, etc., over a given point; especially, such a flight made to demonstrate military aircraft or to display air strength. **2.** *Brit.* An overpass, as on a superhighway.

fly·pa·per (flī′pā′pər) *n.* A piece of paper coated with a sticky poisonous substance, placed so as to catch or kill flies.

Fly River The largest river in New Guinea, flowing 650 miles SE to the Gulf of Papua.

fly·speck (flī′spek′) *n.* **1.** The dot made by the excrement of a fly. **2.** Any slight speck. — *v.t.* To mark with flyspecks.

flyte (flīt) See FLITE.

fly·trap (flī′trap′) *n.* **1.** A trap for catching flies. **2.** A plant, as the Venus's-flytrap, that traps insects.

fly·weight (flī′wāt′) *n.* A boxer belonging to the lightest weight class, weighing 112 pounds or less.

fly·wheel (flī′hwēl′) *n.* A wheel heavy enough to resist sudden changes of speed, used to secure uniform motion in the working parts of a machine.

FLYING
SQUIRREL
(Body about 5
inches long;
tail 4 inches)

fm. **1.** Fathom. **2.** From.

Fm *Chem.* Fermium.

FM *Mil.* Field manual.

FM or **F.M., f-m,** or **f.m.** *Telecom.* Frequency modulation.

F.M. **1.** Field Marshal. **2.** Foreign Missions.

FMB Federal Maritime Board.

FMCS Federal Mediation and Conciliation Service.

FNMA Federal National Mortgage Association.

F number *Photog.* A number obtained by dividing the focal length of a lens by its effective diameter: the smaller the number, the wider the aperture and the shorter the exposure required: also called *F stop.* Abbr. *f, F, f:, F:, f/, F/*

Fo (fō) Buddha: the Chinese name.

F.O. Foreign Office.

foal (fōl) *n.* One of the young offspring of an animal of the horse family. — *v.t. & v.i.* To give birth to (a foal). [OE *fola*]

foam (fōm) *n.* **1.** A frothy mass of bubbles produced on the surface of a liquid by agitation, fermentation, etc. **2.** A frothy mass of saliva, sweat, etc. **3.** The frothy crest of a breaking wave. **4.** *Chem.* A colloid system of gas dispersed in a liquid. **5.** *Poetic* The sea: preceded by *the.* — *v.i.* **1.** To become foam or become covered with foam; froth. — *v.t.* **2.** To cause to foam. [OE *fām*]

foam·flow·er (fōm′flou′ər) *n.* One of a genus (*Tiarella*) of hardy perennials of the saxifrage family, with flowers that are usually white and sometimes red or purple.

foam rubber A firm, spongy rubber produced by chemical treatment of natural or synthetic rubber and used especially in mattresses, cushions, etc., and as an insulating medium.

foam·y (fō′mē) *adj.* **foam·i·er, foam·i·est** **1.** Pertaining to, consisting of, or resembling foam. **2.** Producing, covered with, or full of foam. — **foam′i·ly** *adv.* — **foam′i·ness** *n.*

fob[1] (fob) *n.* **1.** A small pocket at the front waistline of trousers or at the front of a vest, designed to hold a watch, a small amount of change, etc. **2.** *U.S.* A short chain or ribbon attached to a watch and worn dangling from such a pocket; also, a small ornament attached to the dangling end of such a chain or ribbon. [Cf. dial. G *fuppe* pocket]

fob[2] (fob) *v.t.* **fobbed, fob·bing** **1.** To dispose of by fraud or trickery: with *off*: to *fob* off worthless property on someone. **2.** To put off by lies, evasion, etc.; also, to try deceitfully to appease or satisfy: with *off*: to *fob* someone off with fair words. **3.** *Archaic* To cheat or trick. [? < FOB[1]]

F.O.B. or **f.o.b.** **1.** Free on board. **2.** Freight on board.

fo·cal (fō′kəl) *adj.* Of or pertaining to a focus. — **fo′cal·ly** *adv.*

focal distance *Optics* The distance from the center of a lens or curved mirror to the point where rays from a distant object converge. Also **focal length.**

focal infection An infection centered in a particular part of the body, as the tonsils, and often spreading from this area.

fo·cal·ize (fō′kəl·īz) *v.t. & v.i.* **·ized, ·iz·ing** **1.** To bring to a focus or become focused. **2.** *Med.* To confine or be confined to a localized area of the body. — **fo′cal·i·za′tion** *n.*

focal plane *Optics* The plane perpendicular to the principal axis of a lens or mirror and which contains the focus.

Foch (fôsh), **Ferdinand,** 1851–1929, French general; commander in chief of the Allied armies, 1918.

fo·c's'le (fōk′səl) See FORECASTLE.

fo·cus (fō′kəs) *n.* *pl.* **·cus·es** or **·ci** (-sī) **1.** *Optics* **a** The point (**real focus**) at which a system of light rays converges after passage through a lens or other optical arrangement or after reflection from a mirror. **b** The point (**virtual focus**) at which such rays appear to diverge and where they would meet if their direction were reversed. **c** The place where a visual image is clearly formed, as in the eye or a camera. **d** The adjustment of the eye, a camera lens, etc., so that a clear image is produced; also, the position of the viewed object. **e** Focal distance. **2.** Any central point, as of importance, activity, or interest. **3.** *Physics* The meeting point of any system of rays, beams, or waves. **4.** *Geom.* **a** One of two points, the sum or difference of whose distances to a conic section is a constant. **b** A point in some other curve, having similar properties. **5.** *Pathol.* A part of the body where a focal infection is originally localized before spreading to other regions. **6.** In seismology, the point where an earthquake begins. — *v.* **·cused** or **·cussed, ·cus·ing** or **·cus·sing** *v.t.* **1.** To adjust the focus of (the eye, a lens, etc.) to receive a clear image; bring into focus. **2.** To fix; concentrate: to *focus* one's mind on a problem. — *v.i.* **3.** To meet at a point of focus; become focused. [< L, hearth]

FOCUS

A Biconcave lens: light rays *a, a* refract as at *b, b* and form the virtual focus at *c.* *B* Biconvex lens: light rays *d, d* converge to the real focus at *e.*

fod·der (fod′ər) *n.* Coarse feed for horses, cattle, etc., as the stalks and leaves of field corn. — **Syn.** See FEED. — *v.t.* To feed with fodder. [OE *fōdor*]

fodg·el (foj′əl) *adj. Scot.* Plump and squat.

foe (fō) *n.* 1. One who is hostile toward another; enemy. 2. One who fights against another in war; also, a group of such individuals, as an army or a division of an army; also, a whole people or nation at war with another. 3. One who is opposed to another in viewpoint, etc., or who is opposed to a particular policy, organization, philosophy, etc. 4. One who opposes another in a game, contest, etc. 5. Something that hampers or blocks: Ignorance is a *foe* to progress. — **Syn.** See ENEMY. [Fusion of OE *fāh* hostile and *gefā* enemy]

F.O.E. Fraternal Order of Eagles.

foehn (fān, *Ger.* fœn) *n. Meteorol.* A warm, dry wind blowing down the slopes of a mountain and across the valley floor or plain: also spelled *föhn*, *fön*. [< dial. G *föhn* < L *Favonius* the west wind]

foe·man (fō′mən) *n. pl.* **·men** (-mən) One who fights against another in war; foe.

foe·tal (fēt′l), **foe·tus** (fē′təs), etc. See FETAL, FETUS, etc.

foe·tid (fē′tid, fet′id), **foe·tor** (fē′tər, -tôr) See FETID, FETOR.

fog[1] (fog, fôg) *n.* 1. Condensed watery vapor suspended in the atmosphere at or near the earth's surface. 2. *Meteorol.* A cloud of varying size formed at the surface of the earth by the condensation of atmospheric vapor and interfering to a greater or lesser extent with horizontal visibility. Compare MIST. 3. Any hazy condition of the atmosphere caused by smoke, dust particles, etc. 4. A state of mental bewilderment or blurred perception. 5. *Photog.* A dark blur clouding part or all of a developed print or plate. 6. *Chem.* A colloid system, as steam, marked by the suspension and dispersion of liquid particles in a gas. — *v.* **fogged, fog·ging** *v.t.* 1. To surround with or as with fog. 2. To confuse or bewilder. 3. *Photog.* To cloud (a print or plate) with a dark blur. — *v.i.* 4. To become enveloped by or covered with or as with fog. 5. To become confused or bewildered. 6. *Photog.* Of a print or plate, to become clouded with a dark blur. [Prob. back formation < *foggy*, in the sense "marshy" < FOG[2]; infl. in meaning by Dan. *fog* spray]

fog[2] (fog, fôg) *n.* 1. A second growth of grass after the first has been cut for hay. 2. Tall, rank grass remaining in fields after the regular season of cutting or grazing. [ME *fogge*, prob. < Scand. Cf. Norw. *fogg* long grass on wet ground.]

fog bank A mass of fog seen at a distance, especially at sea.

fog·bound (fog′bound′, fôg′-) *adj.* Prevented from traveling, sailing, flying, etc., because of fog.

fog·bow (fog′bō′, fôg′-) *n. Meteorol.* A faint, white or colored arc of light opposite the sun in fog: also called *white rainbow*.

fog chamber *Physics* A cloud chamber (which see).

fog·dog (fog′dôg′, fôg′-, -dog′) *n.* A luminous or clearing area in a fog bank: also called *seadog*.

fog·fruit (fog′froot′, fôg′-) *n.* An American creeping plant (genus *Lippia*) of the vervain family, especially *L. lanceolata*, bearing closely bracted heads of bluish white flowers.

fog·gage (fog′ij, fôg′-) *n. Scot.* 1. Fog[2]. 2. Moss.

Fog·gia (fôd′jä) A commune in southern Italy; pop. 97,504 (est. 1961).

fog·gy (fog′ē, fôg′ē) *adj.* **·gi·er, ·gi·est** 1. Full of or marked by fog. 2. Resembling fog; cloudy; murky. 3. Mentally confused; bewildered; perplexed. 4. *Photog.* Blurred; indistinct. [< FOG[1]] — **fog′gi·ly** *adv.* — **fog′gi·ness** *n.*

fog·horn (fog′hôrn′, fôg′-) *n.* 1. A horn or whistle for sounding a warning during a fog. 2. A loud, harsh voice.

fo·gy (fō′gē) *n. pl.* **·gies** A person of old-fashioned or ultra-conservative notions: usually preceded by *old.* Also **fo′gey**, **fo′gie**. [? < FOGGY] — **fo′gy·ish** *adj.* — **fo′gy·ism** *n.*

foh (fō) See FAUGH.

föhn (fān, *Ger.* fœn) See FOEHN.

foi·ble (foi′bəl) *n.* 1. A personal weakness or failing; slight fault of character. 2. The weaker portion of a sword blade, from the middle to the point: distinguished from *forte*. [< F, obs. var. of *faible*. See FEEBLE.]

foil[1] (foil) *v.t.* 1. To prevent the success of; frustrate or thwart. 2. In hunting, to cross and recross (a scent or trail) to confuse pursuers. — **Syn.** See BAFFLE. — *n.* An animal's trail. [< OF *fouler*, *fuler* to crush, trample down < LL *fullare* to full cloth < L *fullo* a fuller]

foil[2] (foil) *n.* 1. A metal, as gold or tin, hammered or rolled into very thin, pliant sheets. 2. A leaf of bright metal set beneath an artificial or inferior gem to add brilliance or color. 3. A person or thing serving by contrast to enhance or set off the qualities of another: Wit uses dullness as a *foil.* 4. The coating put on the back of a piece of glass to make a mirror. 5. *Archit.* A division, space, or piece of tracery suggestive of a leaf. — *v.t.* 1. To apply foil to; cover with foil. 2. To intensify or set off by contrast. 3. *Archit.* To adorn (windows, etc.) with foils. [< OF < L *folium* leaf]

FOILS[2] (*def.* 5)
(Foliated tracery in Gothic window)

foil[3] (foil) *n.* 1. A blunted, rapierlike implement sometimes having a button on its end, used in fencing. 2. *pl.* The art of fencing with a foil. [Origin uncertain]

foils·man (foilz′mən) *n. pl.* **·men** (-mən) One who fences with foils.

foin (foin) *Archaic v.i.* To lunge or thrust, with or as with a weapon. — *n.* A thrust or pass with a weapon. [< OF *foine* fishspear < L *fuscina*]

Fo·ism (fō′iz·əm) *n.* Chinese Buddhism. [< Fo] — **Fo′ist** *n.*

foi·son (foi′zən) *n. Archaic* 1. Power or strength. 2. *pl.* Resources. 3. Abundance; also, a bounteous harvest. [< OF, a pouring out < L *fusio* < *fundere* to pour]

foist (foist) *v.t.* 1. To impose (someone or something) slyly or wrongfully; palm off: to *foist* a candidate on a party. 2. To insert or introduce fraudulently: to *foist* a clause into a contract. [Prob. < dial. Du. *vuisten* hold in the hand, palm]

Fo·kine (fō·kēn′, *Russ.* fô′kin), **Michel**, 1880–1942, U.S. choreographer born in Russia.

Fok·ker (fok′ər), **Anthony Herman Gerard**, 1890–1939, Dutch airplane designer.

fol. 1. Folio. 2. Following.

fold[1] (fōld) *v.t.* 1. To turn back or bend over so that one part covers or lies alongside another: to *fold* a blanket. 2. To close or collapse: often with *up*: to *fold* up an umbrella. 3. To wrap up; enclose: *Fold* the picture in paper. 4. To place together and interlock: to *fold* one's hands; also, to bring (wings) close to the body. 5. To embrace; enfold: He *folded* her in his arms. 6. To wind; coil: with *about, around*, etc.: They *folded* their arms around each other. 7. In cooking, to mix (beaten egg whites, etc.) into other ingredients by gently turning one part over the other with a spoon: with *in*. 8. *Poetic* To cover completely. — *v.i.* 9. To become folded. 10. *U.S. Slang* a To fail financially; close: The show *folded*. b To collapse, as from exhaustion. — *n.* 1. One part folded over another. 2. The space between two folded parts. 3. The crease made by folding. 4. The act of folding. 5. A dip or hollow, as in hilly country. 6. A coil, as of a serpent. 7. *Anat.* A thin edge or slip of tissue folded over an organ or part; plica. 8. *Geol.* A bend in a layer of rock; anticline or syncline: for illustration see ISOCLINE. [OE *fealdan*]

fold[2] (fōld) *n.* 1. A pen, as for sheep. 2. The sheep enclosed in a pen. 3. A flock of sheep. 4. A group of people, as the congregation of a church, having a leader, a common purpose, etc. — *v.t.* To shut up in a fold, as sheep. [OE *fald*]

-fold *suffix* 1. Having (a specified number of) parts: a *three-fold* blessing. 2. (A specified number of) times as great or as much: to reward *tenfold*. 3. An amount multiplied by (a specified number): increased by a *hundredfold*. [OE *-feald* < *fealdan* to fold]

fold·boat (fōld′bōt′) *n.* A faltboat (which see).

fold·er (fōl′dər) *n.* 1. One who or that which folds. 2. A road map, timetable, or similar piece of printed material designed to be folded up into a small, compact form. 3. A large envelope or binder for loose papers.

fol·de·rol (fol′də·rol) *n.* See FALDERAL.

folding door A door made of two or more hinged panels and opened by being folded.

fold-out (fōld′out′) *n.* A gatefold.

fo·li·a (fō′lē·ə) Plural of FOLIUM.

fo·li·a·ceous (fō′lē·ā′shəs) *adj.* 1. Of, pertaining to, or resembling the leaf of a plant. 2. Having, producing, or made up of leaves or of structures resembling leaves. 3. Made up of thin, laminated sheets. [< L *foliaceus* < *folium* leaf]

fo·li·age (fō′lē·ij) *n.* 1. The growth of leaves on a tree or other plant; leafage; also, leaves collectively. 2. A representation of leaves, flowers, and branches, as in architectural ornamentation. [Earlier *foillage* < F *feuillage* < *feuille* leaf < L *folium*; refashioned after the Latin form]

fo·li·ar (fō′lē·ər) *adj.* Foliaceous (def. 1).

fo·li·ate (fō′lē·āt, *for adj., also* fō′lē·it) *adj.* 1. Having leaves; leafy. 2. Foliaceous. — *v.* **·at·ed, ·at·ing** *v.t.* 1. To roll or hammer (gold, etc.) into thin plates. 2. To divide into thin layers. 3. To coat or back (glass, etc.) with metal foil; also, to adorn with metal foil. 4. To adorn with foliage or a representation of foliage. 5. To number the leaves of (a book). — *v.i.* 6. To split into thin leaves or layers. 7. To produce leaves, as a tree. [< L *foliatus* leafy < *folium* leaf]

fo·li·a·tion (fō′lē·ā′shən) *n.* 1. *Bot.* a The act of bursting into leaf, or the state of being in leaf. b The arrangement or formation of leaves in a bud. 2. The act or process of making into foil; also, the act or process of covering or backing with foil. 3. *Archit.* a Decoration with cusps, lobes, or foliated tracery. b A cusp, lobe, etc., used in decoration. 4. *Geol.* In certain rocks, a crystalline formation into leaflike lavers; also, the layers themselves. 5. The consecutive numbering of the leaves of a book. Also **fo·li·a·ture** (fō′lē·ə·chŏŏr′).

fo·lic acid (fō′lik) *Biochem.* An orange-yellow crystalline compound, $C_{19}H_{19}N_7O_6$, having vitaminlike properties and included in the vitamin-B complex. It is found in green leaves, mushrooms, yeast, and some animal tissues and used in the treatment of anemic conditions: also *vitamin B_c*.

fo·li·o (fō′lē·ō) *n. pl.* **·li·os** 1. A sheet of paper folded once to form four pages (two leaves) of a book, the height of the pages usually ranging from 13 to 19 inches. **2.** A book, manuscript, etc., having the oversize pages made from such a sheet; also, the size of such a work. **3.** A leaf of a book, manuscript, etc., only one side of which is numbered. **4.** The page number of a book. **5.** In bookkeeping, two facing pages that are numbered alike. **6.** *Law* A set number of words (in the United States, 100; in England, 72 or 90) used as a unit in estimating the length of a document. — *v.t.* Of, pertaining to, or being of the size of a folio. — *v.t.* **li·oed**, **li·o·ing** To number in order the pages of (a book, manuscript, etc.). Abbr. (for defs. 1, 2) *F.*, (for defs. 3, 4, 5) *f.*, *fol.* [< L, ablative sing. of *folium* leaf]

fo·li·o·late (fō′lē·ə·lāt′) *adj. Bot.* Of, pertaining to, or composed of leaflets: often used in compounds: *bifoliolate.* [< L *foliolum*, dim. of *folium* leaf + -ATE¹]

fo·li·ose (fō′lē·ōs) *adj.* Bearing leaves or leaflike appendages. [< L *foliosus* < *folium* leaf]

-folious *suffix of adjectives* Leaflike or leafy. [< L *foliosus* < *folium* leaf]

fo·li·um (fō′lē·əm) *n. pl.* **·li·ums** or **·li·a** (-lē·ə) **1.** *Usually pl.* A thin layer or stratum, especially of rocks. **2.** *Geom.* A segment of a curve closed by its node; loop. [< L, leaf]

folk (fōk) *n. pl.* **folk** or **folks** **1.** A people; nation; race. **2.** *Usually pl.* People of a particular group or class: old *folks.* **3.** *pl. Informal* People in general: *Folks* disagree. **4.** *pl. Informal* One's family or relatives, especially one's parents. — **Syn.** See PEOPLE. — *adj.* Originating among or characteristic of the common people: *folk* custom; *folk* life. [OE *folc*]

folk dance **1.** A dance originating among the common people of a district or country. **2.** The music for such a dance.

Folke·stone (fōk′stən) A municipal borough, port, and resort in SE Kent, England; pop. 44,129 (1961).

Fol·ke·ting (fōl′kə·ting) *n.* The lower branch of the Danish Rigsdag or parliament. Also **Fol′ke·thing.**

folk etymology Popular modification of an unfamiliar word by catachresis resulting from an incorrect analysis of the elements and causing the word to correspond with better known forms, as *agnail* (in Middle English, a painful nail) becoming *hangnail*: also called *popular etymology.*

folk·lore (fōk′lôr′, -lōr′) *n.* **1.** The traditions, beliefs, customs, sayings, stories, etc., preserved among the common people. **2.** The study of folk cultures. — **folk′lor′ist** *n.*

folk·mote (fōk′mōt′) *n.* In early English history, a general assembly of the people of a town, county, etc. Also **folk′moot′** (-mōōt′). [OE *folcmōt* < *folc* folk + *mōt* meeting]

folk music Music created by the common people.

folk-rock (fōk′rok′) *adj.* Denoting a form of popular music derived from rock-and-roll and folk music. — *n.* Folk-rock music.

folk singer **1.** One who sings the folk songs indigenous to his region. **2.** An entertainer who sings various folk songs.

folk song **1.** A song, usually of unknown authorship, originating among the common people of a district or country and handed down orally, often in several differing versions. **2.** A song copying the style of such a song.

folk·sy (fōk′sē) *adj.* **·si·er**, **·si·est** *U.S. Informal* Friendly; sociable; unpretentious. — **folk′si·ness** *n.*

folk·ways (fōk′wāz′) *n. pl.* of **folk·way** (-wā′) *Sociol.* The traditional habits, customs, and behavior of a group, tribe, or nation.

foll. Following.

fol·li·cle (fol′i·kəl) *n.* **1.** *Anat.* A small cavity or sac in certain parts of the body, having a protective or secretory function: a hair *follicle.* For illustration see HAIR. **2.** *Bot.* **a** A dry seed vessel of one carpel. **b** A bladder on the leaves of some mosses. [< L *folliculus*, dim. of *follis* bag]

fol·lic·u·lar (fə·lik′yə·lər) *adj.* Of, having, or resembling a follicle or follicles.

fol·lic·u·lat·ed (fə·lik′yə·lā′tid) *adj.* **1.** Having a follicle. **2.** Encased in a cocoon. Also **fol·lic′u·late** (-lit).

fol·lies (fol′ēz) *n. pl.* of **fol·ly** A theatrical revue consisting of songs, dances, skits, etc., and marked typically by elaborate costumes and sets.

fol·low (fol′ō) *v.t.* **1.** To go or come after and in the same direction. **2.** To succeed in time or order. **3.** To seek to overtake or capture; pursue. **4.** To hold to the course of: to *follow* a road. **5.** To conform to; act in accordance with: to *follow* the customs of a country. **6.** To use or take as a model; imitate: to *follow* an example. **7.** To watch or observe closely: to *follow* the course of a satellite. **8.** To have an active interest in: to *follow* sports. **9.** To understand the course, sequence, or meaning of, as an explanation. **10.** To come after as a consequence or result: The effect *follows* the cause. **11.** To work at as a profession or livelihood; employ oneself in: men who *follow* the sea. **12.** To move or act in the cause of; be under the leadership or authority of: He *follows* Plato. **13.** To accompany; attend. — *v.i.* **14.** To move or come after in time. **15.** To pay attention. **16.** To understand. **17.** To come as a result or consequence. — **to follow out 1.** To follow to the end, as an argument. **2.** To comply with, as orders or instructions. — **to follow suit 1.**

In card games, to play a card of the suit led. **2.** To follow another's example. — **to follow through 1.** To swing to the full extent of the stroke after having struck the ball, as in tennis or golf. **2.** To perform fully; complete. — **to follow up 1.** To pursue closely. **2.** To bring to full completion. **3.** To increase the effectiveness of by further action. — *n.* **1.** The act of following. **2.** A stroke in billiards that causes the cue ball, after impact, to follow the object ball. [OE *folgian*]

— **Syn.** (verb) **1.** trail, shadow. **3.** chase. **5, 6.** obey, observe, imitate. **13.** See ACCOMPANY. — **Ant.** precede, lead.

fol·low·er (fol′ō·ər) *n.* **1.** One who or that which follows; as: **a** A pursuer. **b** A disciple, adherent, or supporter. **c** A subordinate or henchman. **d** A servant or attendant. **2.** *Brit. Informal* An admirer; beau. **3.** *Mech.* A part of a machine put into action by another part, as a driven pulley. — **Syn.** See ADHERENT. — **fol′low·er·ship′** *n.*

fol·low·ing (fol′ō·ing) *adj.* **1.** That comes next in time or sequence: the *following* week. Abbr. *f., F., fol., foll.* **2.** That is about to follow, be recounted, be mentioned, etc.: We need the *following* items. — *n.* A body of adherents, attendants, or disciples. — **the following** Those that are mentioned next: *The following* will attend the conference.

fol·low-through (fol′ō·throō′) *n.* **1.** In sports, the continuation and full completion of a motion; especially, in tennis and golf, the last part of the stroke after the ball has been hit. **2.** Any continuing or completion.

fol·low-up (fol′ō·up′) *n.* **1.** The act of following up. **2.** Something, as an action, procedure, letter, etc., used in following up. — *adj.* Designed to follow up: a *follow-up* visit.

fol·ly (fol′ē) *n. pl.* **·lies** **1.** The condition or state of being foolish; foolishness; senselessness. **2.** A foolish idea or action. **3.** A foolish or ruinous undertaking. **4.** *Archaic* An action viewed as immoral or criminal. **5.** *Obs.* Wickedness; especially, lewdness. [< F *folie* < *fol* fool]

Fol·som culture (fol′səm) *Anthropol.* A culture existent in North America during the Pleistocene period, attributed to **Folsom man,** and typified by the use of stone implements made of pieces chipped from rocks. [after *Folsom,* a village in NE New Mexico, near which artifacts were found]

Fo·mal·haut (fō′məl·hôt) *n.* One of the 20 brightest stars, 1.19 magnitude; Alpha in the constellation Piscis Austrinus. See STAR. [< F < Arabic *fom al-ḥūt* the whale's mouth]

fo·ment (fō·ment′) *v.t.* **1.** To stir up or instigate (rebellion, discord, etc.); incite. **2.** To treat with warm water or medicated lotions, as in applying a poultice. [< F *fomenter* < LL *fomentare* < L *fomentum* poultice < *fovere* to warm, keep warm] — **fo·ment′er** *n.*

fo·men·ta·tion (fō′men·tā′shən) *n.* **1.** Instigation or incitement, as to mutiny. **2.** Treatment with medicated lotions, poultices, etc.; also, the lotion, poultice, etc., applied.

fön (fän, *Ger.* fœn) See FOEHN.

fond¹ (fond) *adj.* **1.** Having affection (for someone or something specified): with *of*: *fond* of animals. **2.** Loving or deeply affectionate: a *fond* embrace. **3.** Unwisely or indulgently affectionate: doting: a *fond* and foolish mother. **4.** Affectionately nurtured; cherished: *fond* expectations. **5.** *Rare* Naively trusting or credulous. **6.** *Archaic* Foolish or simple; silly. [ME *fonned,* pp. of *fonnen* to be foolish] — **fond′ly** *adv.* — **fond′ness** *n.*

fond² (fond, *Fr.* fôn) *n.* A groundwork or background, especially of lace. [< F < L *fundus* bottom]

fon·dant (fon′dənt, *Fr.* fôn·dän′) *n.* A soft, creamy confection. [< F, orig. ppr. of *fondre* to melt]

Fond du Lac (fon′ də lak′, dyə lak′) A city in eastern Wisconsin, at the southern end of Lake Winnebago; pop. 35,515.

fon·dle (fon′dəl) *v.* **·dled**, **·dling** *v.t.* **1.** To handle lovingly; caress. **2.** *Obs.* To pamper; coddle. — *v.i.* **3.** To display fondness, as by caressing. [Freq. of obs. *fond* to caress] — **fon′dler** *n.*

fond·ly (fond′lē) *adv.* **1.** In a fond manner; tenderly. **2.** Dotingly. **3.** Credulously. **4.** *Archaic* Foolishly.

fond·ness (fond′nis) *n.* **1.** Tender affection; liking. **2.** Extravagant or foolish affection **3.** Strong, instinctive preference. **4.** *Archaic* Foolishness. — **Syn.** See LOVE.

fon·due (fon·doō′, *Fr.* fôn·dü′) *n.* A dish made of grated cheese, cooked with eggs, butter, etc. [< F]

Fon·se·ca (fōn·sā′kä), **Gulf of** An inlet of the Pacific in Salvador, Honduras, and Nicaragua. Also **Fonseca Bay.**

fons et o·ri·go (fonz′ et ō·rī′gō) *Latin* Source (fountain) and origin.

font¹ (font) *n.* **1.** A receptacle, often of stone, for the water used in baptism. **2.** A receptacle for holy water. **3.** The oil reservoir of a lamp. **4.** Source; origin. **5.** *Archaic* A fountain. [OE < L *fons, fontis* fountain] — **font′al** *adj.*

font² (font) *n. Printing* A full assortment of printing type of a particular face and size: also, *Brit.,* **fount.** [< F *fonte* < *fondre* to melt]

Fon·taine·bleau (fôn·ten·blō′) A town in north central France; site of the **Palace of Fontainebleau,** a former residence of French kings, now a museum; pop. 17,565 (1968).

fon·ta·nel (fon′tə·nel′) *n.* **1.** *Anat.* A soft, pulsating, unossified area in the fetal and infantile skull. **2.** *Obs.* An artificial opening for the discharge of body fluids. Also **fon'ta‧nelle'.** [< F *fontanelle*, dim. of *fontaine.* See FOUNTAIN.]

Fon‧tanne (fon‧tan'), **Lynn,** born 1887?, U.S. actress born in England; wife of Alfred Lunt.

Foo‧chow (fōō'chou', *Chinese* fōō'jō') The capital of Fukien Province, SE China, a port on the Min; pop. 900,000 (est. 1970): formerly *Minhow.* Also *Fu‧chou, Fuchow.*

food (fōōd) *n.* **1.** That which is eaten, drunk, or absorbed by an organism for the maintenance of life and the growth and repair of tissues; nourishment; nutriment. **2.** Nourishment taken in more or less solid form as opposed to liquid form: *food* and drink. **3.** A particular kind of nourishment: breakfast *food.* **4.** Anything that is used or consumed in a manner suggestive of food: intellectual *food.* [OE *fōda*]
 — **Syn.** *Food, fare, diet, victuals,* and *viands* refer to what is eaten and drunk for nourishment. *Food* is the general term; we speak of *food* for humans, fish *food,* and (figuratively) *food* for thought. *Fare* is often substituted for *food* in speaking of its nutritive value, or of the pleasures of the table: poor *fare,* sumptuous *fare. Diet* is a selection of *food* made to preserve health, and the purpose of the *diet* is usually specified in usage: a reducing *diet,* a diabetic *diet. Victuals* is a homely or dialectal word for whatever may be eaten. *Viands* is applied chiefly to meat or to choice *food* of any kind. Compare FEED.

food poi‧son‧ing (poi'zən‧ing) A gastrointestinal disorder caused by certain bacterial toxins found in rancid or decomposed food: erroneously called *ptomaine poisoning.*

food‧stuff (fōōd'stuf') *n.* **1.** Any substance suitable for food. **2.** Any substance, as fat, protein, etc., that enters into the composition of food.

foo‧fa‧raw (fōō'fə‧rô) *n.* **1.** Gaudy trimmings or ornaments. **2.** A pointless to-do. [Origin unknown]

fool[1] (fōōl) *n.* **1.** A person lacking understanding, judgment, or common sense. **2.** A clown formerly kept by noblemen for household entertainment; jester. **3.** One who has been duped or imposed upon; victim; butt. **4.** *Obs.* An imbecile; idiot. — **to be nobody's fool** *Informal* To be sharp in practical matters; shrewd. — *v.i.* **1.** To act like a fool. **2.** To act, speak, etc., in a playful or teasing manner. — *v.t.* **3.** To make a fool of; impose upon; deceive. — **to fool around** or **about** *Informal* **1.** To waste time on trifles; putter. **2.** To loiter about idly. — **to fool away** *Informal* To spend or waste foolishly; squander. — **to fool with** *Informal* **1.** To meddle with. **2.** To play or toy aimlessly with. — *adj. Informal* Stupid or silly: a *fool* idea. [< F *fou* < L *follis* a bellows; later, windbag, simpleton]
 — **Syn.** (noun) **1.** dolt, dunce, booby, boob, nincompoop, ninny, numskull, blockhead, dunderhead, saphead, sap. Compare IDIOT. **2.** clown. — (verb) **3.** delude, gull, hoodwink, hoax.

fool[2] (fōōl) *n. Brit.* Crushed stewed fruit served with whipped cream. [Prob. < FOOL[1]]

fool‧er‧y (fōō'lə‧rē) *n. pl.* **‧er‧ies** Foolish behavior, speech, etc.; also, an instance of this.

fool‧har‧di‧ness (fōōl'här'dē‧nis) *n.* The state or quality of being foolhardy. — **Syn.** See TEMERITY.

fool‧har‧dy (fōōl'här'dē) *adj.* **‧di‧er, ‧di‧est** Bold in a foolish or reckless way; rash. — **fool'har'di‧ly** *adv.*

fool hen *Canadian* The spruce grouse. See under GROUSE[1].

fool‧ish (fōō'lish) *adj.* **1.** Marked by or showing a lack of good sense; unwise; silly. **2.** Resulting from folly or stupidity: *foolish* consequences. **3.** Utterly ridiculous; absurd: a *foolish* explanation. **4.** *Archaic* Insignificant; trivial. — **fool'ish‧ly** *adv.* — **fool'ish‧ness** *n.*

foolish guillemot See under GUILLEMOT.

fool‧proof (fōōl'prōōf') *adj.* **1.** So simple and strong as to be incapable of damage or harm even through misuse. **2.** Having no weak points; infallible: a *foolproof* plan.

fools‧cap (fōōlz'kap) *n.* **1.** A writing paper measuring about 13 x 16 inches, usually folded into a page measuring about 13 x 8 inches. **2.** *Brit.* A printing paper measuring about 13½ x 17 inches, so called from the former watermark of a fool's cap and bells. **3.** A fool's cap. Abbr. (for defs. 1, 2) *fcp., fp.*

fool's cap **1.** A pointed cap, usually with bells at its tip, formerly worn by jesters. **2.** A dunce cap.

fool's errand An utterly useless or pointless undertaking.

fool's gold A metallic sulfide gold in color, as pyrite.

fool's paradise A state of deceptive happiness based on vain hopes or delusions.

fool's-parsley (fōōlz'pärs'lē) *n.* A fetid, poisonous herb (*Aethusa cynapium*) that looks like parsley.

foot (fōōt) *n. pl.* **feet** (fēt) **1.** The terminal section of the limb of a vertebrate animal, upon which it rests in standing or moving. ◆ Collateral adjective: *pedal.* **2.** Any part, as of an invertebrate animal or of a plant, piece of furniture, etc., corresponding in form, use, or position to the foot. **3.** The part of a boot or stocking that covers the wearer's foot. **4.** The lower part of anything, as contrasted with the top or head; base; bottom; especially: **a** The base of a hill or mountain. **b** The part of a bed, grave, etc., where the feet rest. **c** The bottom of a page, ladder, etc. **d** *Naut.* The lower edge of a sail. **5.** The last part of a series; final section; end. **6.** The inferior part or section: the

foot of the class. **7.** A measure of length, equivalent to 12 inches or 30.48 centimeters: symbol (*/*). Abbr. *ft.* See table inside back cover. **8.** In prosody, a group of syllables, often having a primary accent on one of the syllables and forming a major unit of poetic rhythm. **9.** Soldiers, collectively, who march or fight on foot; infantry. **10.** Step or manner of movement: a light *foot.* — **on foot** **1.** Walking or standing; not riding or sitting. **2.** In progress; proceeding; astir. — **to put one's best foot forward** **1.** To do one's best. **2.** To try to look one's best. — **to put one's foot down** To be determined; act firmly. — **to put one's foot in it** or **in one's mouth** To make an embarrassing mistake or blunder. — *v.i.* **1.** To go afoot; walk: often with indefinite *it.* **2.** To dance: often with indefinite *it.* — *v.t.* **3.** To move on or through by foot. **4.** To furnish with a foot, as a stocking. **5.** *Informal* To pay, as a bill. **6.** To add, as a column of figures, and place the sum at the bottom: often with *up.* [OE *fōt*]

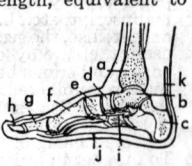

LONGITUDINAL SECTION OF HUMAN FOOT
a Tibia. *b* Astragalus. *c* Calcaneus. *d* Navicular. *e* Internal cuneiform bone. *f* First metatarsal. *g, h* Phalanges of great toe. *i* Inferior ligament. *j* Plantar fasciae, supporting the plantar arch. *k* Achilles' tendon.

foot‧age (fōōt'ij) *n.* **1.** The extent of something as measured in linear feet: the *footage* of lumber. **2.** Motion picture film exposed and, usually, processed; filmed sequences or material. **3.** *Mining* Payment by the linear foot for work done; also, the amount paid.

foot-and-mouth disease (fōōt'ən‧mouth') *Vet.* A contagious disease of cattle, swine, and some other hoofed animals, caused by a virus and marked by fever and the formation of blisters and ulcers about the mouth and hoofs.

foot‧ball (fōōt'bôl') *n.* **1.** *U.S.* A game played between two teams of eleven men on a field with goals at each end, in which points are made by carrying the ball across the opponent's goal line or by kicking the ball over the opponent's goal posts. **2.** The ball used in this game, an inflated, leather-covered ball with an ellipsoidal shape. **3.** *Canadian* A very similar game played by teams of twelve men: also called *rugby, rugby football.* **4.** *Brit.* **a** Rugby football (def. 1); also, the ball used in this game, identical with the ball used in U.S. football. **b** Soccer; also, the round, inflated ball used in this game. **5.** *Austral.* A game somewhat resembling British rugby football, played by teams of eighteen men. **6.** Something passed roughly back and forth, as an issue or problem: Each party made a political *football* of the projected tax rise.

FOOTBALL PLAYING FIELD
a Goal lines. *b* End line. *c* Goal post. *d* End zone. *e* Goal line. *f* Sideline. *g* Inbounds lines. *h* 3-yard line.
The field is marked off in lines spaced 5 yards apart.

foot‧board (fōōt'bôrd', -bōrd') *n.* **1.** A board or small platform on which to prop or rest the feet. **2.** An upright piece at the foot of a bedstead.

foot‧boy (fōōt'boi') *n.* A page; lackey.

foot brake A brake operated by pressure of the foot.

foot‧bridge (fōōt'brij') *n.* A bridge for persons on foot.

foot-can‧dle (fōōt'kan'dəl) *n.* The illumination thrown on one square foot of surface, all points of which are at a distance of one foot from one international candle: also called *candle-foot.*

foot‧cloth (fōōt'klôth', -kloth') *n.* **1.** A carpet. **2.** *Obs.* A caparison for a horse.

Foote (fōōt), **Andrew Hull,** 1806–63, Union naval officer in the Civil War.

foot‧ed (fōōt'id) *adj.* **1.** Having a foot or feet: a *footed* goblet. **2.** Having or characterized by a (specified kind of) foot or (a specified number of) feet: used in combination: *light-footed; four-footed.*

foot‧er (fōōt'ər) *n.* **1.** A person who goes on foot. **2.** A person or thing having an indicated number of linear feet in height or length: used in compounds: a *six-footer.*

foot‧fall (fōōt'fôl') *n.* The sound of a footstep.

foot‧gear (fōōt'gir') *n.* Footwear.

foot‧hill (fōōt'hil') *n.* A low hill at the base of a mountain.

foot‧hold (fōōt'hōld') *n.* **1.** A place on which the foot can rest securely, as in climbing. **2.** A good, firm position from which one can begin or carry forward some course of action.

foot‧ing (fōōt'ing) *n.* **1.** A place on which to stand, walk, or climb securely. **2.** A secure support for the foot; foothold: to lose one's *footing.* **3.** An established or secure position or foundation: Their reputation is built on a very solid *footing.* **4.** Social or professional status in relation to others; standing: to be on good *footing* with someone. **5.** The act of adding or putting a foot to something, as a shoe; also, the material used for this. **6.** The adding up of a column of figures; also, the sum obtained. **7.** *Archit.* A base or foundation wider than the structure it supports, as for a wall or pedestal.

foot·le (foot′l) *Informal v.i.* **·led, ·ling** To talk or act in a foolish or silly manner. — *adj.* Nonsensical. — *n.* Foolishness; nonsense. [Origin uncertain. Cf. FOOTY.]

foot·less (foot′lis) *adj.* **1.** Lacking feet. **2.** Having no firm support or basis. **3.** *Informal* Awkward or stupid.

foot·lights (foot′līts′) *n.pl.* **1.** Lights in a row near the front of the stage of a theater, nearly level with the performers' feet. **2.** The profession of acting on the stage.

foot·ling (foot′ling) *adj. Informal* Utterly foolish or trifling. [< FOOTLE]

foot·lock·er (foot′lok′ər) *n.* A small trunk kept at the foot of the bed and used by soldiers for personal belongings.

foot·loose (foot′loos′) *adj.* Free to travel or do as one pleases; unattached.

foot·man (foot′mən) *n. pl.* **·men** (-mən) **1.** A male servant in livery who attends a carriage, answers the door, waits at table, etc. **2.** *Rare* A pedestrian. **3.** *Archaic* A foot soldier.

foot·mark (foot′märk′) *n.* A footprint.

foot·note (foot′nōt′) *n.* An explanatory note, reference, or comment on the text, usually appearing at the bottom of a page. — *v.t.* **·not·ed, ·not·ing** To furnish with footnotes.

foot·pace (foot′pās′) *n.* **1.** A slow or walking pace. **2.** A staircase landing. **3.** A raised platform or dais.

foot·pad (foot′pad′) *n. Archaic* A highwayman on foot.

foot·path (foot′path′, -päth′) *n.* **1.** A path to be used only by persons on foot. **2.** *Brit.* A sidewalk. Also *footway.*

foot·pound (foot′pound′) *n. Mech.* A unit of measurement of energy expended, based on the amount of energy necessary to raise a one-pound mass through one linear foot. Abbr. *fp, f.p., F.P., ft-lb*

foot·pound·al (foot′poun′dəl) *n. Mech.* A unit of measurement of work done, based on the amount of work done in moving through one linear foot against a force of one poundal.

foot·print (foot′print′) *n.* The outline or impression made by a foot treading on a surface.

foot·rest (foot′rest′) *n.* Something, as a small stool or platform, on which the feet can be propped or rested.

foot·rope (foot′rōp′) *n. Naut.* **1.** A rope stretched under a yard for sailors to stand on while reefing or furling. **2.** A boltrope sewed to the lower edge of a sail.

foots (foots) *n.pl.* Sediment that settles during the refining of molasses, oil, etc.

foot soldier A soldier trained and equipped to fight on foot.

foot·sore (foot′sôr′, -sōr′) *adj.* Having sore or tired feet, as from walking.

foot·stalk (foot′stôk′) *n. Bot.* **1.** A pedicel. **2.** A peduncle.

foot·stall (foot′stôl′) *n.* **1.** The stirrup of a sidesaddle. **2.** *Archit.* The base or pedestal of a column or pillar.

foot·step (foot′step′) *n.* **1.** The action of taking a step with the foot: laborious *footsteps.* **2.** The distance covered by a foot in stepping: long *footsteps.* **3.** The sound made by a foot in stepping: loud *footsteps.* **4.** A footprint. **5.** A step of a stairway, etc. — **to follow in someone's footsteps 1.** To repeat or duplicate the work or actions of another. **2.** To succeed to another's position.

foot·stock (foot′stok′) *n. Mech.* The part of a lathe that holds the work.

foot·stone (foot′stōn′) *n.* A stone set at the foot of a grave as a marker.

foot·stool (foot′stool′) *n.* A low stool on which the feet can be rested while one is sitting.

foot·ton (foot′tun′) *n. Mech.* A unit of work equal to the energy needed to raise a long ton a distance of one foot.

foot·wall (foot′wôl′) *n.* **1.** *Mining* The layer of rock lying just beneath a vein of ore. **2.** *Geol.* That side of an inclined fault that lies below the hanging wall.

foot·way (foot′wā′) *n.* A footpath.

foot·wear (foot′wâr′) *n.* Articles worn on the feet, as shoes or slippers.

foot·work (foot′wûrk′) *n.* Use or control of the feet, as in boxing or tennis.

foot·worn (foot′wôrn′, -wōrn′) *adj.* **1.** Weary with walking. **2.** Worn down by the feet, as a path.

foot·y (foot′ē) *adj.* **foot·i·er, foot·i·est** *Informal* Foolish; insignificant; worthless. [< F *foutu,* pp. of *foutre* to damn]

foo·zle (foo′zəl) *v.t. & v.i.* **·zled, ·zling** To do awkwardly; fumble. — *n.* A misstroke or misplay, especially in golf. [Cf. dial. G *fuseln* to work badly] — **foo′zler** *n.*

fop (fop) *n.* A man overly fastidious in dress or deportment; a dandy. [Cf. Du. *foppen* to cheat]

fop·per·y (fop′ər·ē) *n. pl.* **·per·ies 1.** The conduct or ways of a fop. **2.** Something worn by or typical of a fop. Also **fop′pish·ness.**

fop·pish (fop′ish) *adj.* Characteristic of a fop; dandified. — **fop′pish·ly** *adv.*

for (fôr, *unstressed* fər) *prep.* **1.** To the extent of: The ground

is flat *for* miles. **2.** Through the duration or period of: The coupon is good *for* a week. **3.** To the number or amount of: a check *for* six dollars. **4.** At the cost or payment of: to buy a hat *for* ten dollars. **5.** On account of; as a result of: He is respected *for* his ability. **6.** In honor of: He is named *for* his grandfather. **7.** Appropriate to: a time *for* work. **8.** In place of; instead of: using a book *for* a desk. **9.** In favor, support, or approval of: a vote *for* peace. **10.** In the interest or behalf of: My lawyers will speak *for* me. **11.** Directed toward: an eye *for* bargains. **12.** As affecting (in a particular way): good *for* your health. **13.** Sent, given, or assigned to: a package *for* you. **14.** In proportion to: big *for* his age. **15.** As the equivalent to or requital of: blow *for* blow. **16.** In spite of: I believe in it *for* all your arguments. **17.** In order to reach or go toward: He left *for* his office. **18.** In order to find, keep, or obtain: looking *for* a hat. **19.** At (a particular time or occasion): to meet *for* the last time. **20.** In the character of; as being or seeming: We took him *for* an honest man. **21.** In consideration of the usual characteristics of: She is strong *for* a woman. **22.** With the purpose of: walking *for* exercise. — **O for . . . !** Would that I had!; *O for* a horse! — *conj.* Inasmuch as; because. [OE]

for-[1] *prefix* **1.** Away; off (in a privative sense): *forget, forgo.* **2.** Very; extremely: *forlorn.* [OE]

for-[2] See also words beginning FORE-.

for. 1. Foreign. **2.** Forestry.

for·age (fôr′ij, for′-) *n.* **1.** Food suitable for horses, cattle, or other domestic animals; fodder. **2.** A searching about for food or supplies; also, a raid to find or capture provisions. — **Syn.** See FEED. — *v.* **·aged, ·ag·ing** *v.i.* **1.** To search about or rummage around for something, especially for food or supplies. **2.** To make a raid so as to find or capture supplies. — *v.t.* **3.** To search through for food, supplies, etc.; also, to strip of provisions by plundering or ravaging. **4.** To obtain (food, supplies, etc.) by rummaging about. **5.** To provide with food or supplies. [< F *fourrage* < OF *feurre* fodder < Gmc.] — **for′ag·er** *n.*

forage cap *Brit.* A small, low cap worn by officers and privates when not in full dress.

foraging ant Any of various tropical ants (family *Formicidae*), as the driver ant, that leave their nests in huge hordes and ravage the countryside in search of food.

For·a·ker (fôr′ə·kər, for′-), **Mount** A mountain in the Alaska Range, south central Alaska; included in Mt. McKinley National Park; 17,280 ft.

fo·ra·men (fō·rā′mən) *n. pl.* **·ram·i·na** (-ram′ə·nə) *Biol.* A small opening or hole, usually natural, as in a bone. [< L < *forare* to bore]

foramen magnum *Anat.* The large orifice in the skull through which the spinal cord passes and becomes continuous with the medulla oblongata.

for·a·min·i·fer (fôr′ə·min′ə·fər, for′-) *n.* One of a large order (*Foraminifera*) of extremely tiny rhizopods, found chiefly in the sea, usually having bony shells perforated with many minute holes. [< L *foramen, -inis* hole + *-fer* having < *ferre* to bear] — **fo·ram·i·nif·er·al** (fə·ram′ə·nif′ər·əl), **fo·ram′i·nif′er·ous** *adj.*

for·as·much as (fôr′əz·much′) In consideration of the fact that; inasmuch as; since; because.

for·ay (fôr′ā, for′ā) *v.t. & v.i.* **1.** To plunder; pillage; raid. — *n.* An expedition or raid, as for plunder. [Prob. back formation < *forayer* raider < OF *forrier* < *forre,* var. of *feurre.* See FORAGE.] — **for′ay·er** *n.*

forb (fôrb) *n. SW U.S.* A weed or other herb that is not grass. [Appar. < Gk. *phorbē* fodder]

for·bear[1] (fôr·bâr′) *v.* **·bore, ·borne, ·bear·ing** *v.t.* **1.** To refrain or abstain from (some action): to *forbear* speaking. **2.** To cease or desist from. **3.** *Archaic* To put up with; endure. — *v.i.* **4.** To abstain or refrain. **5.** To be patient or act patiently. — **Syn.** See REFRAIN[2]. [OE] — **for·bear′er** *n.*

for·bear[2] (fôr′bâr′) See FOREBEAR.

for·bear·ance (fôr·bâr′əns) *n.* **1.** The act of forbearing; refraining or abstaining from an action. **2.** The quality of being forbearing; patience; self-control. **3.** *Law* A refraining from enforcing a right, as collection of an overdue debt.

for·bear·ing (fôr·bâr′ing) *adj.* Disposed to forbear; patient.

Forbes-Rob·ert·son (fôrbz′rob′ərt·sən), **Sir Johnston,** 1853–1937, English actor.

for·bid (fər·bid′, fôr-) *v.t.* **bade** (-bad′) or **·bad, ·bid, ·bid·den** (*Archaic* **·bid**), **·bid·ding 1.** To command (a person) not to do something, etc.; prohibit from doing, using, having, etc. **2.** To prohibit the doing, use, etc., of: to *forbid* a meeting. **3.** To have the effect of preventing; make impossible, impractical, etc.; hinder: Discretion *forbids* my saying anything. — **Syn.** See PROHIBIT. [OE *forbēodan*]

for·bid·dance (fər·bid′ns, fôr-) *n.* The act of forbidding, or the state of being forbidden. Also **for·bid′al.**

for·bid·den (fər·bid′n, fôr-) *adj.* Not allowed; prohibited.

Forbidden City 1. Lhasa, Tibet. **2.** A walled section of Peking, China, containing the royal palaces of the former Chinese Empire.

forbidden fruit 1. In the Bible, the fruit of the tree of knowledge of good and evil, forbidden to Adam and Eve. 2. Any unlawful or immoral pleasure.

for·bid·ding (fər-bid′ing, fôr-) *adj.* 1. Grim and unfriendly in appearance: a *forbidding* face. 2. Having a threatening or ominous look: a *forbidding* swamp. — **for·bid′ding·ly** *adv.*

for·bore (fôr-bôr′, -bōr′) Past tense of FORBEAR[1].

for·borne (fôr-bôrn′, -bōrn′) Past participle of FORBEAR[1].

for·by (fôr-bī′) *adv. & prep. Scot.* 1. Besides; over and above. 2. Near; hard by. 3. Past, in time. Also spelled *foreby, forebye:* also **for·bye′**.

force (fôrs, fōrs) *n.* 1. Power or energy; strength: the *force* of a gale. 2. Power exerted on any resisting person or thing; also, the use of such power; coercion. 3. The quality of anything that tends to produce an effect on the mind or will; capacity to convince or move: the *force* of his reasoning. 4. Any moral, social, or political power or influence. 5. A body of individuals belonging to or comprising one of a nation's military, naval, or air divisions: the armed *forces.* 6. Any body of individuals organized for some specific work or action: police *force.* 7. *Law* Binding effect; validity; efficacy: the *force* of a contract. 8. *Physics* Anything that changes or tends to change the state of rest or motion in a body. — **coercive force** *Physics* The power of resisting magnetization or demagnetization. — **in (full) force** 1. Still operative or enforceable, as a law; in effect. 2. With no one missing; in full number. — *v.t.* **forced, forc·ing** 1. To compel to do something; coerce. 2. To get or obtain by or as by force: to *force* an answer. 3. To bring forth or about by or as by effort: to *force* a smile. 4. To drive or move despite resistance; press: to *force* the enemy back. 5. To assault and capture, as a fortification. 6. To break open, as a door or lock. 7. To make, as a passage or way, by force. 8. To press or impose upon someone as by force: to *force* one's opinion on someone. 9. To exert to or beyond the utmost; strain, as the voice. 10. To rape. 11. To stimulate the growth of artificially, as plants in a hothouse. 12. In baseball: **a** To put out (a base runner compelled to leave one base for the next). **b** To cause (the base runner on third base) to score by walking the batter when the bases are full. **c** To allow (a run) in such a manner. 13. In card games: **a** To compel (a player) to choose between losing a trick or playing a trump from his hand. **b** To play so as to compel (a player) to reveal the strength of a hand held. **c** To compel (a player) to play (a particular card). 14. *Obs.* To put (a law, etc.) in force. [< F < L *fortis* brave, strong] — **force′a·ble** *adj.* — **forc′er** *n.*

forced (fôrst, fōrst) *adj.* 1. Done under force; compulsory: *forced* labor. 2. Strained; affected: *forced* gaiety. 3. Done in an emergency: a *forced* landing of an airplane.

forced march *Mil.* A long march at a very fast pace, with few or no pauses.

force feed A system supplying lubricating oil, under pressure, to an internal-combustion engine.

force·ful (fôrs′fəl, fōrs′-) *adj.* Full of or done with force; vigorous; strong; effective: a *forceful* blow; *forceful* speech. — **force′ful·ly** *adv.* — **force′ful·ness** *n.*

force ma·jeure (fôrs mà·zhœr′) *French* Superior and irresistible force.

force·meat (fôrs′mēt′, fōrs′-) *n.* Finely chopped, seasoned meat served separately or used as stuffing. [< *force,* alter. of FARCE, v. + MEAT]

force-out (fôrs′out′, fōrs′-) *n.* In baseball, an out made when a runner, forced from his base, fails to reach the next base before it is tagged by a fielder holding the ball.

for·ceps (fôr′səps) *n.* A pair of pincers for grasping and manipulating small or delicate objects, used by surgeons, dentists, etc. [< L < *formus* warm + *capere* to take]

force pump A pump that ejects a liquid forcibly under pressure: distinguished from *lift pump.*

for·ci·ble (fôr′sə·bəl) *adj.* 1. Accomplished or brought about by force: a *forcible* exit. 2. Characterized by or having force; vigorous; effective; cogent: a *forcible* argument; a *forcible* blow. — **for′ci·ble·ness** *n.* — **for′ci·bly** *adv.*

ford (fôrd, fōrd) *n.* A shallow place in a stream, river, etc., that can be crossed by wading. — *v.t.* To cross (a river, stream, etc.) at a shallow place. [OE] — **ford′a·ble** *adj.*

Ford (fôrd, fōrd), **Ford Madox,** 1873–1939, English novelist and critic. — **Gerald Rudolph,** born 1913, vice president of the United States 1973–74; 38th president of the United States 1974–77. — **Henry,** 1863–1947, U.S. automobile manufacturer. — **John,** 1586?–1639?, English dramatist.

for·do (fôr·dōō′) *v.t.* **·did, ·done, ·do·ing** *Archaic* 1. To kill; destroy. 2. To ruin; undo. Also spelled *foredo.* [OE *fordōn*]

for·done (fôr·dun′) *adj. Archaic* Fatigued; exhausted.

SIDE-SUCTION
FORCE PUMP

a Air chamber.
b Brake. *d, d* Discharge pipes. *p* Piston rod. *s* Stand.

fore (fôr, fōr) *adj.* Situated at or toward the front in relation to something else: the *fore* and hind legs of a horse. — *n.* 1. The front part of something. 2. That which is situated at or closest to the front. 3. *Naut.* A foremast; also, the bows of a ship. — **to the fore** 1. To or at the front part of something. 2. In or into a prominent or conspicuous position. 3. Still living or active. — *interj.* In golf, a cry made to warn anyone standing in the line of a ball about to be driven. — *adv.* 1. *Naut.* At or toward the bow of a ship. 2. *Obs.* In a former time. — *prep. & conj. Archaic* or *Dial.* Before: also **'fore.** [OE, adv. & prep.]

fore-[1] *prefix* 1. Prior in time, place, or rank; as in:

foreacquaint	foreanswer	foreconclude
foreadapt	foreassign	forenotice
fore-age	forebless	foreparent
foreannounce	forecited	foresignify

2. Situated at or near the front; as in:

forebody	forecabin	foreflank
foreboom	fore-edge	forewing

[OE *fore-, for-* before]

fore-[2] See also words beginning FOR-.

fore-and-aft (fôr′ən·aft′, fōr′-, -äft′) *adj. Naut.* Lying or going in the direction of a ship's length: a *fore-and-aft* sail.

fore and aft *Naut.* 1. In a line extending from the bow to the stern of a boat. 2. In, at, or toward both the stem and the stern of a boat.

fore-and-aft·er (fôr′ən·af′tər, fōr′-, -äf′tər) *n. Naut.* 1. A vessel having only fore-and-aft sails. 2. Anything set along the length of a ship, as a hatch beam.

fore-and-aft-rigged (fôr′ən·aft′rigd′, fōr′-, -äft′-) *adj. Naut.* Fitted with fore-and-aft sails: distinguished from *square-rigged.*

fore-and-aft sail *Naut.* A sail set in the direction of the length of the vessel and whose forward edge is set on travelers attached to the mast, with the upper edge extended on a gaff (gaff rig) or coming to a point (Marconi rig).

fore·arm[1] (fôr′ärm′, fōr′-) *n.* The part of the arm between the elbow and the wrist. ◆ Collateral adjective: *cubital.*

fore·arm[2] (fôr·ärm′, fōr′-) *v.t.* To arm beforehand.

fore·bear (fôr′bâr, fōr′-) *n.* An ancestor: also spelled *forbear.* — **Syn.** See ANCESTOR. [Earlier *for-be-er,* one who has existed previously]

fore·bode (fôr·bōd′, fōr-) *v.t. & v.i.* **·bod·ed, ·bod·ing** 1. To indicate in advance; portend. 2. To have a premonition of (something evil or harmful). — **Syn.** See AUGUR. [< FORE-[1] + BODE[2]] — **fore·bod′er** *n.*

fore·bod·ing (fôr·bō′ding, fōr-) *n.* 1. A feeling that something evil, undesirable, etc., is going to happen; presentiment. 2. An omen of misfortune, etc.; portent. — *adj.* That forebodes. — **fore·bod′ing·ly** *adv.*

fore·brain (fôr′brān′, fōr′-) *n. Anat.* The prosencephalon.

fore·by, fore·bye (fôr·bī′) See FORBY.

fore·cast (fôr′kast′, -käst′) *v.t.* **·cast** or **·cast·ed, ·cast·ing** 1. To calculate beforehand; especially, to predict (probable weather conditions) by observation and study. 2. To be an advance indication of; foreshadow. 3. To arrange or plan beforehand; also, to foresee. — **Syn.** See AUGUR. — *n.* 1. A calculated prediction of weather conditions over a given area for a specific period. 2. A prediction or prophecy. 3. *Rare* The act or power of forecasting. 4. *Obs.* A plan or preparation, as for the future.

fore·cast·er (fôr′kas′tər, -käs′-, fōr′-) *n.* One who forecasts; especially, one who forecasts the weather.

fore·cas·tle (fōk′səl) *n. Naut.* 1. That part of the upper deck of a ship located forward of the mast nearest the bow. 2. A section of a merchant ship near the bow, in which the sailors' living-quarters are located. Also spelled *fo'c's'le.*

fore·close (fôr·klōz′, fōr-) *v.* **·closed, ·clos·ing** *v.t.* 1. *Law* **a** To deprive (a mortgager in default) of the right to redeem mortgaged property. **b** To take away the power to redeem (a mortgage or pledge). 2. To shut out; exclude. 3. To hinder or preclude. 4. To settle (an objection, etc.) in advance. — *v.i.* 5. To foreclose a mortgage. [< OF *forclos,* pp. of *forclore* to exclude < *for-* outside (< L *fors*) + *clore* < L *claudere* to close] — **fore·clos′a·ble** *adj.*

fore·clo·sure (fôr·klō′zhər, fōr-) *n.* The act of foreclosing a mortgage, etc.

fore·course (fôr′kôrs′, fōr′kōrs′) *n. Naut.* The lowest sail on the mast nearest the bow of a square-rigged ship; foresail.

fore·court (fôr′kôrt′, fōr′kōrt′) *n.* 1. An enclosed area in front of a building. 2. In tennis, handball, etc., the zone nearest the net or wall.

fore·date (fôr·dāt′, fōr′-) *v.t.* **·dat·ed, ·dat·ing** To antedate.

fore·deck (fôr′dek′, fōr′-) *n. Naut.* The forward part of a deck, especially of an upper deck.

fore·do (fôr·dōō′, fōr-) See FORDO.

fore·doom (*v.* fôr·dōōm′, fōr-; *n.* fôr′dōōm′, fōr′-) *v.t.* To doom or condemn in advance. — *n.* Preordained doom or condemnation; destiny.

fore·fa·ther (fôr′fä′thər, fōr′-) *n.* An ancestor. — **Syn.** See ANCESTOR.

Forefathers' Day The anniversary of the landing of the Pilgrims at Plymouth, Mass. (Dec. 21, 1620), usually celebrated on Dec. 22.

fore·feel (fôr·fēl′, fōr-)   *v.t.* **·felt**, **·feel·ing** To have a premonition of; feel in advance.

fore·fend (fôr·fend′, fōr-)   See FORFEND.

fore·fin·ger (fôr′fing′gər, fōr′-)   *n.* The finger next to the thumb; index finger.

fore·foot (fôr′fŏŏt′, fōr′-)   *n.* *pl.* **·feet** **1.** One of the front feet of an animal, insect, etc. **2.** *Naut.* The part of a boat where the prow and keel meet.

fore·front (fôr′frunt′, fōr′-)   *n.* **1.** The very front of something. **2.** The position of most prominence, activity, etc.

fore·gath·er (fôr·gath′ər, fōr-)   See FORGATHER.

fore·glimpse (fôr′glimps′, fōr′-)   *n.* A glimpse of something before it happens.

fore·go[1] (fôr·gō′, fōr-)   *v.t.* & *v.i.* **·went**, **·gone**, **·go·ing** To go before or precede in time, place, etc. [OE *foregān*]

fore·go[2] (fôr·gō′, fōr-)   See FORGO.

fore·go·ing (fôr·gō′ing, fōr-; fôr′gō′ing, fōr′-)   *adj.* Said, written, or done previously; preceding; antecedent.

fore·gone (fôr·gôn′, fōr·gon′; fôr′gôn′, fōr′gon′)   *adj.* Already gone or finished; also, previous or past: *foregone* eras.

foregone conclusion **1.** A conclusion determined in advance of the evidence. **2.** A foreseen or inevitable result.

fore·ground (fôr′ground′, fōr′-)   *n.* **1.** The part of a landscape, picture, etc., nearest or represented as nearest to the spectator. **2.** The position of most prominence or activity.

fore·gut (fôr′gut′, fōr′-)   *n.* *Anat.* In vertebrate embryos, the front part of the alimentary canal from which develop the esophagus, pharynx, duodenum, and stomach.

fore·hand (fôr′hand′, fōr′-)   *adj.* **1.** Of or pertaining to a stroke in tennis, etc., in which the palm of the hand holding the racket faces the direction of the stroke: distinguished from *backhand.* **2.** First or foremost; leading. **3.** Done or given in advance. — *n.* **1.** A forehand stroke or the position taken for it, as in tennis. **2.** The part of a horse in front of the rider. **3.** A position of advantage or superiority.

fore·hand·ed (fôr′han′did, fōr′-)   *adj.* **1.** Forehand, as in tennis. **2.** *U.S.* Having money saved; well-to-do. **3.** *U.S.* Prudent; thrifty. **4.** Done in good time; early. — **fore′hand′ed·ness** *n.*

fore·head (fôr′id, fōr′-; *occasionally* fôr′hed′)   *n.* **1.** The part of the face from the eyebrows to the natural line of the hair. ◆ Collateral adjective: *frontal.* **2.** The front part of anything.

fore·hearth (fôr′härth′, fōr′-)   *n.* *Metall.* An independently heated reservoir in a blast furnace, designed to permit the separation of metal from slag.

for·eign (fôr′in, for′-)   *adj.* **1.** Belonging to, characteristic of, or derived from another country, region, society, etc.; not native: a *foreign* language. **2.** Located outside one's own country, state, province, etc.: a *foreign* city. **3.** Carried on or concerned with another country, state, etc.: a *foreign* correspondent; *foreign* trade. **4.** Unfamiliar; strange: Anything mechanical is *foreign* to him. **5.** Having little or no relation; not pertinent; irrelevant: Your point is *foreign* to the discussion. **6.** Belonging to, derived from, or typical of some other person or thing than the one being considered; alien: a *foreign* element in his character. **7.** Occurring in a place or body in which it is not normally found: a *foreign* body in the eye. **8.** *Law* Not subject to the laws or jurisdiction of a country or state. Abbr. (for defs. 1, 2, 3) *for.* [< F *forain,* ult. < L *foras* out of doors] — **for′eign·ness** *n.*

foreign affairs Matters of diplomacy, commerce, etc., in the dealings of one country or nation with another.

foreign bill A bill of exchange drawn in one country or state and made payable in another. Also **foreign draft.**

for·eign-born (fôr′in·bôrn′, for′-)   *adj.* Born in a foreign country or state; not native to a country or region.

for·eign·er (fôr′in·ər, for′-)   *n.* **1.** A native or citizen of a foreign country or region; alien. **2.** A ship of foreign origin; also, sometimes, a product imported from a foreign country. — Syn. See ALIEN.

foreign exchange **1.** The transaction of monetary affairs; payment of debts, etc., between citizens, companies, etc., of one country and those of another. **2.** Bills of exchange drawn in one country and made payable in another.

for·eign·ism (fôr′in·iz′əm, for′-)   *n.* **1.** A foreign peculiarity, idiom, custom, etc. **2.** Imitation or suggestion of what is foreign.

foreign legion A military unit of foreign volunteers serving in a national army.

Foreign Legion A military force in the French army composed of volunteers from many countries serving mainly in North Africa.

foreign mission **1.** A group sent to a foreign country to spread religious teaching, medical knowledge, etc. **2.** A group sent to a foreign country for diplomatic negotiations.

foreign office The department of government in charge of foreign affairs. Abbr. *F.O.*

fore·judge[1] (fôr·juj′, fōr-)   *v.t.* & *v.i.* **·judged**, **·judg·ing** To judge in advance.

fore·judge[2] (fôr·juj′, fōr-)   See FORJUDGE.

fore·know (fôr·nō′, fōr-)   *v.t.* **·knew**, **·known**, **·know·ing** To know beforehand. — **fore·know′a·ble** *adj.*

fore·knowl·edge (fôr′nol′ij, fōr′-)   *n.* Knowledge of something before it exists or takes place.

fore·la·dy (fôr′lā′dē, fōr′-)   *n.* *pl.* **·dies** A forewoman.

fore·land (fôr′land′, fōr′-)   *n.* **1.** A projecting point of land; cape. **2.** Territory situated in front: opposed to *hinterland.*

fore·leg (fôr′leg′, fōr′-)   *n.* One of the front legs of an animal, insect, etc. Also **fore/limb**[1] (-lim′).

fore·lock[1] (fôr′lok′, fōr′-)   *n.* A lock of hair growing over the forehead.

fore·lock[2] (fôr′lok′, fōr′-)   *n.* *Mech.* An iron pin or wedge passed through the end of a bolt or the like, to prevent its withdrawal.

fore·man (fôr′mən, fōr′-)   *n.* *pl.* **·men** (-mən) **1.** The overseer of a body of workmen. **2.** The chairman and spokesman of a jury. — **fore/man·ship** *n.*

fore·mast (fôr′mast′, -mäst′, -məst, fōr′-)   *n.* *Naut.* The mast that is closest to the bow of a ship.

fore·most (fôr′mōst, -məst, fōr′-)   *adj.* First in place, time, rank, or order; chief. — *adv.* In the chief or principal place, rank, etc. [OE *formest*]

fore·name (fôr′nām′, fōr′-)   *n.* One's first name or given name; the name used preceding the family name.

fore·named (fôr′nāmd′, fōr′-)   *adj.* Previously named or mentioned; aforesaid.

fore·noon (fôr′nōōn′, fōr′-; fôr·nōōn′, fōr-)   *n.* The period of daylight preceding midday, especially the later business hours; morning. — *adj.* Of or occurring in the forenoon.

fo·ren·sic (fə·ren′sik)   *adj.* **1.** Relating to, characteristic of, or used in courts of justice or public debate. **2.** Pertaining to or involving argumentation. Also **fo·ren′si·cal.** [< L *forensic* public < *forum* market place, forum] — **fo·ren′si·cal·ly** *adv.*

forensic medicine Medical jurisprudence (which see).

fore·or·dain (fôr′ôr·dān′, fōr′-)   *v.t.* **1.** To decree or appoint in advance. **2.** To fix the future or fate of in advance; predestine. — **fore/or·dain′ment, fore·or·di·na·tion** (fôr·ôr′də·nā′shən, fōr-) *n.*

fore·part (fôr′pärt′, fōr′-)   *n.* The first part in time, place, or order. Also **fore part.**

fore·past (fôr′past′, -päst′, fōr-)   *adj.* *Rare* Bygone; past. Also **fore·passed′.**

fore·peak (fôr′pēk′, fōr′-)   *n.* *Naut.* The extreme forward part of a ship's hold within the angle of the bow under the lowest deck.

fore·quar·ter (fôr′kwôr′tər, fōr′-)   *n.* **1.** The front portion of a side of beef, etc., including the leg and adjacent parts. **2.** *pl.* The forelegs and adjacent parts of an animal.

fore·rank (fôr′rangk′, fōr′-)   *n.* The front or first rank.

fore·reach (fôr·rēch′, fōr-)   *v.t.* **1.** To catch up with or get ahead of, as a ship. **2.** To win an advantage over; also, to do better than; outdo; excel; surpass. — *v.i.* **3.** To catch up with or move ahead of a ship, etc.: usually with *on, upon.*

fore·run (fôr·run′, fōr-)   *v.t.* **·ran**, **·run**, **·run·ning** **1.** To be the precursor of; foreshadow; herald. **2.** To run in advance of; precede. **3.** To forestall.

fore·run·ner (fôr·run′ər, fōr-, fôr′run′ər, fōr′-)   *n.* **1.** One who or that which precedes another, as in a particular line of research or development; predecessor; also, a forefather or ancestor. **2.** One who or that which proclaims in advance the coming of another; precursor; herald. **3.** An advance indication of something that is to take place; omen. — **the Forerunner** John the Baptist.

fore·said (fôr′sed′, fōr′-)   *adj.* Forenamed; aforesaid.

fore·sail (fôr′sāl′, -səl, fōr′-, fō′səl)   *n.* *Naut.* **1.** A square sail, bent to the foreyard, the lowest sail on the foremast of a square-rigged vessel. For illustration see SHIP. **2.** The fore-and-aft sail on a schooner's foremast, set on a boom and gaff. For illustration see SCHOONER. **3.** The forestaysail of a cutter or sloop.

fore·see (fôr·sē′, fōr-)   *v.t.* **·saw**, **·seen**, **·see·ing** To see in advance (something that is to happen, come into being, etc.); have foreknowledge of. — **fore·see′a·ble** *adj.* — **fore·se′er** (-sē′ər) *n.*

fore·shad·ow (fôr·shad′ō, fōr-)   *v.t.* To give an advance indication or suggestion of; presage. — **fore·shad′ow·er** *n.*

fore·sheet (fôr′shēt′, fōr′-)   *n.* *Naut.* **1.** A rope holding one of the clews of a foresail. **2.** *pl.* The forward space in a boat.

fore·shore (fôr′shôr′, fōr′shōr′)   *n.* That part of a shore uncovered at low tide.

fore·short·en (fôr·shôr′tən, fōr-)   *v.t.* In drawing, to shorten parts of the representation of (an object) so as to create the illusion of depth and distance while retaining the proper proportions of size and extent.

fore·show (fôr·shō′, fōr-)   *v.t.* **·showed**, **·shown**, **·show·ing** To show beforehand; reveal in advance; foreshadow.

fore·side (fôr′sīd′, fōr′-)   *n.* **1.** The front part or side of something; also, the upper part or side. **2.** *U.S.* An extent of land lying along the sea.

fore·sight (fôr′sīt′, fōr′-) *n.* **1.** The act or capacity of foreseeing; foreknowledge; also, a look directed toward something distant. **2.** Prudent anticipation of what the future may hold.

fore·sight·ed (fôr′sī′tid, fōr′-) *adj.* Marked by foresight; prudently concerned about the future. **— fore′sight′ed·ly** *adv.* **— fore′sight′ed·ness** *n.*

fore·skin (fôr′skin′, fōr′-) *n. Anat.* The prepuce.

fore·speak (fôr·spēk′, fōr-) *v.t. Rare* **1.** To speak of in advance. **2.** To foretell. **3.** To claim in advance.

fore·spent (fôr·spent′, fōr-) See FORSPENT.

for·est (fôr′ist, for′-) *n.* **1.** A large tract of land covered with a growth of trees and underbrush; also, the trees themselves. **2.** In English law, a woodland district, generally belonging to the crown, kept as a game preserve. **— *adj.*** Of, pertaining to, or inhabiting forests; sylvan. **— *v.t.*** To plant with trees; make a forest of. [< OF < Med.L (*silva*) *foresta* an unenclosed (wood) < L *foris* outside]

fore·stall (fôr·stôl′, fōr-) *v.t.* **1.** To hinder, prevent, or guard against in advance. **2.** To deal with, think of, or realize beforehand; anticipate. **3.** In business, to buy up or divert (goods not yet on the market) in order to sell at a higher price: distinguished from *engross*. **4.** Loosely, to buy up (goods) for reselling at a profit. **— Syn.** See PREVENT. [OE *foresteall* ambush] **— fore·stall′er** *n.*

for·est·a·tion (fôr′is·tā′shən, for′-) *n.* **1.** The planting of trees so as to make a forest. **2.** The science of forestry.

fore·stay (fôr′stā′, fōr′-) *n. Naut.* A wire or rope running from the head of the foremast to the stem and used primarily to support the mast.

fore·stay·sail (fôr′stā′sāl′, -səl, fōr′-) *n. Naut.* A triangular sail in front of the foremast, hoisted on the forestay: in some rigs called *foresail*.

for·est·er (fôr′is·tər, for′-) *n.* **1.** One skilled in forestry; also, one in charge of a forest. **2.** An animal dwelling in a forest. **3.** A spotted moth (family *Agaristidae*) of the United States; especially, a large black moth whose larvae feed on grapevines. **4.** A large, gray kangaroo (*Macropus giganteus*).

For·es·ter (fôr′is·tər, for′-), **C**(ecil) **S**(cott), 1899–1966, English novelist.

Forest Hills A section of Queens, New York City, site of the national lawn tennis tournaments.

for·est·ry (fôr′is·trē, for′-) *n.* **1.** The science of planting and managing forests. *Abbr.* for. **2.** Forest land.

fore·taste (*n.* fôr′tāst′, fōr′-; *v.* fôr·tāst′, fōr-) *n.* An advance experiencing or sampling of something to a limited extent, as by anticipation: a *foretaste* of happiness. **— *v.t.*** To have a foretaste of; taste in advance.

fore·tell (fôr·tel′, fōr-) *v.t. & v.i.* **·told**, **·tell·ing** **1.** To tell of or about in advance; utter a prophecy of; predict. **2.** To show or indicate in advance; be an omen of; foreshow. **— Syn.** See AUGUR, PROPHESY. **— fore·tell′er** *n.*

fore·thought (fôr′thôt′, fōr′-) *n.* **1.** Advance deliberation or consideration. **2.** Prudent anticipation of difficulties to be met, probable developments, etc.; foresight.

fore·thought·ful (fôr′thôt′fəl, fōr′-) *adj.* Marked by or given to forethought. **— fore·thought′ful·ly** *adv.*

fore·time (fôr′tīm′, fōr′-) *n.* Time gone by; the past.

fore·to·ken (*v.* fôr·tō′kən, fōr-; *n.* fôr′tō′kən, fōr′-) *v.t.* To foreshow or presage; foreshadow. **— Syn.** See AUGUR. **— *n.*** An advance indication; omen.

fore·tooth (fôr′tōōth′, fōr′-) *n. pl.* **·teeth** (-tēth′) An incisor.

fore·top (fôr′top′, fōr′-; *Naut.* fôr′təp, fōr′-) *n.* **1.** A forelock, especially of a horse. **2.** *Naut.* A platform at the top of the lower section of a foremast. **3.** *Obs.* A forelock arranged in the front part of a wig.

fore·top·gal·lant (fôr′tə·gal′ənt, fōr′-) *adj. Naut.* Of, pertaining to, or designating the mast, sail, yard, etc., immediately above the foretopmast.

fore·top·gal·lant·mast (fôr′tə·gal′ənt·mast′, -məst, fōr′-) *n. Naut.* The mast above the foretopmast.

fore·top·mast (fôr·top′məst, fōr-) *n. Naut.* The section of a mast above the foretop.

fore·top·sail (fôr·top′səl, fōr-) *n. Naut.* The sail set on the foretopmast. For illustration see SHIP.

for·ev·er (fôr·ev′ər, fər-) *adv.* **1.** Throughout eternity; to the end of time; everlastingly; always. **2.** Incessantly; constantly. Also *Brit.* **for ever.**

forever and a day Forever: an intensive form. Also **for ever and ever.**

for·ev·er·more (fôr·ev′ər·môr′, -mōr′, fər-) *adv.* Forever: an intensive form. Also **for evermore.**

fore·warn (fôr·wôrn′, fōr-) *v.t.* To warn in advance.

fore·wom·an (fôr′wŏŏm′ən, fōr′-) *n. pl.* **·wom·en** (-wim′in) **1.** A woman who supervises workers, as in a factory. **2.** The chairwoman of a jury.

fore·word (fôr′wûrd′, fōr′-, -wərd) *n.* A prefatory statement preceding the text of a book.

fore·worn (fôr·wôrn′, fōr-) See FORWORN.

fore·yard (fôr′yärd′, fōr′-) *n. Naut.* The lowest yard on the foremast of a square-rigged vessel.

For·far (fôr′fər, -fär) **1.** A former name for ANGUS. Also **For′far·shire** (-shir, -shər). **2.** The county seat of Angus, Scotland, in the central part of the county; pop. about 10,000.

for·feit (fôr′fit) *n.* **1.** Something taken away or given up as a penalty for an offense, shortcoming, error, etc.; also, the penalty fixed by law, regulation, etc. **2.** The giving up or loss of something as a penalty for an offense, etc.: the *forfeit* of their good name. **3.** *pl.* One of several games in which the players have to give up articles when they fail to do something required. **— *v.t.*** To incur the deprivation of as a penalty for an offense, mistake, etc. **— *adj.*** Taken away or liable to being taken away as a penalty for some offense, etc.: Their lives will be *forfeit*. [< OF *forfait* misdeed < Med.L *foris factum* < L *foris* outside + *factum*. See FACT.] **— for′feit·a·ble** *adj.* **— for′feit·er** *n.*

for·fei·ture (fôr′fi·chər) *n.* **1.** The giving up or loss of something by way of penalty. **2.** That which is forfeited.

for·fend (fôr·fend′) *v.t.* **1.** *U.S.* To protect; defend. **2.** *Archaic* To ward off; prevent. **3.** *Obs.* To forbid; prohibit: also spelled *forefend*.

for·fi·cate (fôr′fə·kit, -kāt) *adj.* Having a deep, V-shaped cleft in the center; deeply forked: said of the tails of certain birds. [< L *forfex*, *forficis* scissors + -ATE[1]]

for·gat (fər·gat′, fôr-) Archaic past tense of FORGET.

for·gath·er (fôr·gath′ər) *v.i.* **1.** To meet or gather together; assemble. **2.** To meet or encounter, especially by chance. **3.** To associate or converse socially. Also spelled *foregather*.

for·gave (fər·gāv′, fôr-) Past tense of FORGIVE.

forge[1] (fôrj, fōrj) *n.* **1.** An apparatus having a flat, open section in which intense heat is maintained, used for heating and softening metal to be worked into shape, as by hammering; also, a workshop in which metals are heated in such an apparatus and worked into shape; smithy. **2.** A furnace for melting or refining metals, as in the production of wrought iron from pig iron; also, an industrial plant where metals are melted and refined. **— *v.* forged, forg·ing** *v.t.* **1.** To heat (metal) in a

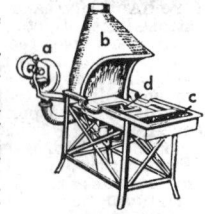

FORGE[1]
a Blower. *b* Hood.
c Water tank.
d Fire bed.

forge and work into shape; also, to produce or form as if by hammering or beating into shape. **2.** To produce, devise, change, or imitate so as to deceive; especially, to counterfeit (a signature, etc.). **— *v.i.*** **3.** To produce an imitation of or alteration in something so as to deceive; especially, to counterfeit a signature, etc. **4.** To heat metal in a forge and shape it by hammering, etc. [< OF, ult. < L *fabrica*. Doublet of FABRIC.] **— forg′er** *n.*

forge[2] (fôrj, fōrj) *v.i.* **forged, forg·ing** To move slowly but steadily forward; especially, to force one's way steadily along, in spite of difficulties, etc. [? Alter. of FORCE]

for·ger·y (fôr′jər·ē, fōr′-) *n. pl.* **·ger·ies** **1.** The act of making imitations of works of art, writings, signatures, etc., for fraudulent purposes. **2.** A fraudulent imitation. **3.** *Law* The act of falsely making or materially altering, with fraudulent intent, any writing that, if genuine, would have legal efficacy. **4.** *Obs.* Literary or fictitious invention. **— Syn. 2.** *Forgery* and *counterfeit* denote a fraudulent imitation, but differ chiefly in usage. A *forgery* is a fraudulent imitation of something written, as a document, signature, letter, etc. *Counterfeit* refers mostly to objects, as coins, bills, gems, and the like.

for·get (fər·get′, fôr-) *v.* **·got** (*Archaic* **·gat**), **·got·ten** or **·got**, **·get·ting** *v.t.* **1.** To be unable to recall (something previously known) to the mind; fail or cease to remember. **2.** To neglect (to do something) unintentionally. **3.** To fail to take through forgetfulness; leave behind accidentally. **4.** To lose interest in or regard for; overlook purposely; disregard or slight: I will never *forget* you. **5.** To leave unmentioned; fail to think of. **— *v.i.*** **6.** To lose remembrance of something. **— to forget oneself 1.** To be unselfish. **2.** To lose self-control and act in an unbecoming manner. **3.** To be lost in thought. [OE *forgietan*] **— for·get′ta·ble** *adj.* **— for·get′ter** *n.*

for·get·ful (fər·get′fəl, fôr-) *adj.* **1.** Inclined to forget; forgetting easily. **2.** Neglectful; inattentive; careless: *forgetful* of one's duty. **3.** *Poetic* Producing forgetfulness or oblivion. **— for·get′ful·ly** *adv.* **— for·get′ful·ness** *n.*

for·ge·tive (fôr′jə·tiv, fōr′-) *adj. Archaic* Creative; inventive. [? < FORGE[1], v.]

for·get-me-not (fər·get′mē·not′) *n.* Any of several small herbs (genus *Myosotis*) of the borage family that typically have blue or white flowers growing in clusters; especially, the **true forget-me-not** (*M. scorpioides*): also called *myosotis*. One species (*M. alpestris*) is the State flower of Alaska.

forg·ing (fôr′jing, fōr′-) *n.* A tool, etc., made in a forge.

for·give (fər·giv′, fôr-) *v.* **·gave, ·giv·en, ·giv·ing** *v.t.* **1.** To grant pardon for or remission of (something); cease to demand the penalty for. **2.** To grant freedom from penalty to (someone). **3.** To cease to blame or feel resentment against. **4.** To remit, as a debt. — *v.i.* **5.** To show forgiveness; grant pardon. — **Syn.** See ABSOLVE. [OE *forgiefan*] — **for·giv′a·ble** *adj.* — **for·giv′er** *n.*

for·give·ness (fər·giv′nis, fôr-) *n.* **1.** The act of forgiving, or the state of being forgiven. **2.** A disposition to forgive.

for·giv·ing (fər·giv′ing, fôr-) *adj.* Disposed to forgive; merciful. — **for·giv′ing·ly** *adv.* — **for·giv′ing·ness** *n.*

for·go (fôr·gō′) *v.t.* ·went, ·gone, ·go·ing **1.** To give up or refrain from; go without. **2.** *Archaic* To overlook or neglect; slight. **3.** *Archaic* To go from; leave. Also spelled *forego.* [OE *forgān* to pass over] — **for·go′er** *n.*

for·got (fər·got′, fôr-) Past tense and alternative past participle of FORGET.

for·got·ten (fər·got′n, fôr-) Past participle of FORGET.

fo·rint (fôr′int, *Hung.* fô·rĕnt′) *n.* The basic monetary unit of Hungary since 1946, subdivided into 100 fillér.

for·judge (fôr·juj′) *v.t.* ·judged, ·judg·ing *Law* **1.** To deprive, as of a right, by judgment of court. **2.** To expel (an attorney or officer) from court for some offense. Sometimes spelled *forejudge.* [< OF *forjugier* < *fors-* outside (< L *foris*) + *jugier* < L *judicare* to judge]

fork (fôrk) *n.* **1.** An implement consisting of a handle at the end of which are two or more prongs; as: **a** A utensil used at table to spear and convey pieces of meat, etc., to the mouth. **b** An agricultural tool used for digging, lifting, tossing, etc. **c** A tuning fork (which see). **2.** The division of something continuous, as a road or river, into two or more separately continued parts; also, the point at which this division begins, or any one of the separately continued parts. — *v.t.* **1.** To convey, lift, toss, etc., with or as with a fork: to *fork* hay into a wagon. **2.** In chess, to attack (two pieces) at the same time with one piece. **3.** To give the shape of a fork to. — *v.i.* **4.** To branch into two or more separately continued parts. — **to fork out** (or **over** or **up**) *Slang* To pay (money); also, to hand over. [OE *forca* < L *furca*]

FARM FORKS
a Spading. *b* Hay. *c* Ensilage. *d* Barley. *e* Manure.

forked (fôrkt, *Poetic* fôr′kid) *adj.* **1.** Having a fork or forking parts; also, sharply angled; zigzag. **2.** Having (a specified number of) prongs: *three-forked.*

forked tongue A lying mouth: He speaks with *forked tongue.*

fork lift A powered machine on wheels, having a two-pronged platform that can be raised and lowered for loading, unloading, and stacking heavy objects, as by stevedores on piers.

For·li (fôr·lē′) A commune in north central Italy; pop. 77,508 (1961): ancient *Forum Livii.*

for·lorn (fôr·lôrn′, fər-) *adj.* **1.** Left in distress; abandoned; deserted. **2.** Wretched; cheerless; desolate: a *forlorn* countryside. **3.** Hopeless; despairing. **4.** Bereft; deprived: with *of.* [Orig. pp. of obs. *forlese* to lose, abandon, OE *forlēosan*] — **for·lorn′ly** *adv.* — **for·lorn′ness** *n.*

forlorn hope **1.** Hope with little or no expectation of getting what is desired. **2.** An undertaking that is almost certainly doomed to failure. **3.** A small group of soldiers on some extremely risky mission. [< Du. *verloren hoop* lost troop; def. 3 orig. sense]

form (fôrm) *n.* **1.** The shape or contour of something as distinguished from its substance or color; external structure. **2.** The body of a living being with regard to its shape; figure. **3.** A mold, frame, etc., that gives shape to something. **4.** The particular state, appearance, character, etc., in which something presents itself: energy in the *form* of light. **5.** A specific type or species: Democracy is a *form* of government. **6.** The style or manner in which the parts of a poem, play, picture, etc., are expressed or organized: to use traditional *forms.* **7.** Proper arrangement or order: Your ideas are not in proper *form.* **8.** The manner in which something is done: diving *form.* **9.** Fitness of mind or body for performance: He is in good *form.* **10.** A document having spaces for the insertion of names, dates, etc.: an application *form.* **11.** An established method of doing something, usually prescribed by rule or custom. **12.** Mere outward formality; convention. **13.** A formula or draft, as of a letter, used as a model or guide. **14.** A prescribed order of words, as in legal proceedings, religious ceremonies, etc. **15.** *Philos.* The intrinsic nature of something as distinguished from the matter that embodies it; essence. **16.** *Gram.* Any of the various shapes assumed by a word in a particular context, as *talk, talks, talked, talking.* **17.** A linguistic form (which see). **18.** *Printing* The body of type and cuts secured in a chase. Also *Brit. forme.* **19.** *Brit.* A grade or class in school. **20.** *Brit.* A long bench without a back. — *v.t.* **1.** To give shape or form to; mold; fashion. **2.** To construct in the mind; devise: to *form* a plan. **3.** To combine or organize into: to *form* a club. **4.** To develop or acquire, as a habit or liking. **5.** To give a specific or exemplified shape or character to: to *form* one's ideals. **6.** To go to make up; be an element of: Guess-

work *forms* the larger part of his theory. **7.** To shape by discipline or training; mold. **8.** *Gram.* To construct (a word) by adding or combining elements: to *form* an adverb by adding *-ly* to an adjective. **9.** *Mil.* To arrange in lines or ranks. — *v.i.* **10.** To take shape; assume a specific form or arrangement. **11.** To begin to exist. [< OF *fourme* < L *forma*]

-form *combining form* Like; in the shape of: *ensiform.* [< L *-formis* -like < *forma* form]

for·mal¹ (fôr′məl) *adj.* **1.** Of, pertaining to, or based on established methods, models, or forms: *formal* procedure. **2.** Marked by and requiring more or less elaborate detail, ceremony, dress, etc.: a *formal* dinner. **3.** Appropriate for or worn at elaborate or state occasions: *formal* attire. **4.** Extremely regular and well-proportioned as to form, arrangement, design, etc.; stylized: a *formal* garden. **5.** Characterized by or given to a scrupulous adherence to rule, convention, or etiquette. **6.** Of or pertaining to external appearance, manner, or form, as distinguished from inner content or disposition: the *formal* elements of a poem. **7.** Made, done, or framed in such a way as to be binding and valid: a *formal* agreement. **8.** Pertaining to study in regular academic institutions or classes: a *formal* education. **9.** Pertaining to or characterized by language of a more complex and elaborate syntactical construction and vocabulary than that of informal speech or writing, appropriate to use on formal occasions. **10.** *Philos.* Of or pertaining to the essential nature of something rather than to its material substance. — *n.* Something formal in style or character, as an evening gown.

for·mal² (fôr·mal′) *n. Chem.* Methylal.

for·mal·de·hyde (fôr·mal′də·hīd) *n. Chem.* A colorless, pungent gas, CH_2O, used in the form of a 37% aqueous solution as an antiseptic, preservative, and disinfectant, and as the basis of various plastics. Also **for·mal′de·hyd** (-hīd). [< FORM(IC) + ALDEHYDE]

for·mal·ism (fôr′məl·iz′əm) *n.* **1.** Scrupulous observance of prescribed forms, as in religious worship, social life, art, etc. **2.** An instance of such observance. — **for′mal·ist** *n.* — **for′mal·is′tic** *adj.*

for·mal·i·ty (fôr·mal′ə·tē) *n., pl.* ·ties **1.** The state or quality of being formal, precise, stiff, or elaborately ceremonious. **2.** Adherence to rules, conventions, forms, etc. **3.** Excessive devotion to outward form. **4.** A proper or customary act, method, practice, or order of procedure. **5.** An outward observance, often devoid of real meaning.

for·mal·ize (fôr′məl·īz) *v.* ·ized, ·iz·ing *v.t.* **1.** To make formal. **2.** To give form to; reduce to form. — *v.i.* **3.** To be formal; act formally. — **for′mal·i·za′tion** *n.* — **for′mal·iz′er** *n.*

formal logic The branch of logic that deals only with the formal structure of propositions and with the operations by which conclusions are deduced from them.

for·mal·ly (fôr′məl·ē) *adv.* **1.** In a formal manner; with formality. **2.** With regard to form.

for·mant (fôr′mənt) *n.* In acoustics and phonetics, any of various frequency ranges in which the partials of a vowel sound, etc., are strongest and determine the acoustic quality or tone color of the sound.

for·mat (fôr′mat) *n.* **1.** The form, size, type face, margins, and general style of a publication, when printed and bound. **2.** The general form or arrangement of anything: the *format* of a television show. [< F < L (*liber*) *formatus* (a book) made up < *formare* to form]

for·mate (fôr′māt) *n. Chem.* A salt or ester of formic acid.

for·ma·tion (fôr·mā′shən) *n.* **1.** The act or process of forming, or the state of being formed. **2.** That which is formed. **3.** The manner in which a thing is shaped or formed; arrangement or disposition of parts. **4.** *Mil.* The disposition of troops, as in a column, line, or square. **5.** *Aeron.* A grouping or arrangement of aircraft in flight. **6.** *Geol.* Earthy or mineral deposits, or rock masses, having common physical characteristics or similar origin.

form·a·tive (fôr′mə·tiv) *adj.* **1.** Having power to shape, form, or mold: a *formative* influence. **2.** Of or pertaining to formation or development: *formative* years. **3.** *Gram.* Pertaining to a formative. — *n. Gram.* **1.** An element added to the base of a word to give it a new and special grammatical form; a derivational affix. **2.** A word formed by the addition of a new element to, or a modification of, the root.

form class *Ling.* A group of linguistic forms having certain syntactic and morphologic characteristics in common, as all words functioning as the subjects of sentences in English.

form drag *Physics* The component of fluid resistance that is due to the form of the object moving through it and that may be reduced or neutralized by streamlining.

form·er¹ (fôr′mər) *n.* One who or that which forms.

form·er² (fôr′mər) *adj.* **1.** Being the first of two persons or things referred to: often preceded by *the* and used absolutely: opposed to *latter:* I prefer the *former* version to the latter.

2. Belonging to or being of an earlier time; previous: my *former* colleague. **3.** Occurring in the past; earlier: *former* times. [ME *formere*, a back formation < *foremost*]

for·mer·ly (fôr′mər·lē) *adv.* **1.** Some time ago, or a long time ago; once. **2.** *Obs.* At a time immediately preceding the present; just now.

for·mic (fôr′mik) *adj.* **1.** Of or pertaining to ants. **2.** Designating or derived from formic acid. [< L *formica* ant]

For·mi·ca (fôr·mī′kə, fôr′mə·kə) *n.* A thermosetting phenolic resin produced in transparent or colored sheets and used as wallboard, table tops, paneling, etc.: a trade name. Also **for·mi·ca** (fôr·mī′kə, fôr′mə·kə).

formic acid *Chem.* A colorless, corrosive liquid compound, HCOOH, with a penetrating odor, occurring naturally in ants and certain other insects and in some plants, and also produced synthetically.

for·mi·car·y (fôr′mə·ker′ē) *n. pl.* **·car·ies** A nest of ants.

for·mi·cate (fôr′mə·kāt) *v.i.* **·cat·ed, ·cat·ing** **1.** To collect in swarms, as ants. **2.** To be overrun, as with ants. [< L *formicatus*, pp. of *formicare* to crawl < *formica* ant]

for·mi·ca·tion (fôr′mə·kā′shən) *n. Pathol.* A form of paresthesia producing an itching sensation like that of ants running on the skin.

for·mi·da·ble (fôr′mi·də·bəl) *adj.* **1.** Exciting fear or dread by reason of strength, size, etc.: a *formidable* adversary. **2.** Extremely difficult: a *formidable* undertaking. [< MF < L *formidabilis* < *formidare* to fear] **—for′mi·da·bil′i·ty, for′mi·da·ble·ness** *n.* **—for′mi·da·bly** *adv.*

form·less (fôrm′lis) *adj.* Lacking form or structure; shapeless. **—form′less·ly** *adv.* **—form′less·ness** *n.*

form letter One of several or many mechanically reproduced copies of a letter of information, etc., designed to be sent on one or more occasions to various groups.

For·mo·sa (fôr·mō′sə) **1.** A former name for TAIWAN. **2.** A Province of northern Argentina; 27,825 sq. mi.; pop. 178,458 (1960); capital, **Formosa.**

For·mo·san (fôr·mō′sən) *n.* **1.** A native or inhabitant of the island of Formosa (Taiwan). **2.** The Indonesian language of the Malay aborigines of Formosa. **—** *adj.* Of or pertaining to Formosa, its people, or their language.

Formosa Strait The channel between China and Taiwan.

for·mu·la (fôr′myə·lə) *n. pl.* **·las** or **·lae** (-lē) **1.** An exact or prescribed method or form for doing something; established rule. **2.** A fixed order or form of words, as used in certain religious ceremonies, legal proceedings, etc. **3.** A prescription or recipe; also, the mixture prepared by prescription or recipe. **4.** *Math.* A rule or combination expressed in algebraic or symbolic form. **5.** *Chem.* A symbolic representation of the composition and structure of a chemical compound, as an **empirical formula,** giving the quantitative values of the constituents, as H_2SO_4, or a **structural formula,** showing the linkages of each atom in the molecule, as $H-C \equiv C-H$. **6.** *Eccl.* A formal statement of doctrine or faith. [< L, dim. of *forma* form]

for·mu·lar·ize (fôr′myə·lə·rīz′) *v.t.* **·ized, ·iz·ing** To formulate. **—for′mu·lar·i·za′tion** *n.*

for·mu·lar·y (fôr′myə·ler′ē) *adj.* Pertaining to, stated in, or resembling a formula. **—** *n. pl.* **·lar·ies** **1.** A compilation or system of formulas. **2.** In pharmacy, a book listing pharmaceutical substances, their formulas, and preparation. **3.** A church ritual, or a book containing the formulas for such rituals. **4.** A prescribed form; formula.

for·mu·late (fôr′myə·lāt) *v.t.* **·lat·ed, ·lat·ing** **1.** To express in or as a formula. **2.** To put or state in exact and systematic form. **—for′mu·la′tion** *n.* **—for′mu·la′tor** *n.*

for·mu·lism (fôr′myə·liz′əm) *n.* **1.** Use of or adherence to formulas. **2.** A set of formulas. **—for′mu·lis′tic** *adj.*

for·mu·lize (fôr′myə·līz) *v.t.* **·lized, ·liz·ing** To formulate. **—for′mu·li·za′tion** *n.* **—for′mu·li′zer** *n.*

for·myl (fôr′mil) *n. Chem.* The univalent radical CHO, constituting the base of formic acid. [< FORM(IC) + -YL]

For·nax (fôr′naks) *n.* A constellation, the Oven. See CONSTELLATION. [< L]

for·ni·cate (fôr′nə·kāt) *v.i.* **·cat·ed, ·cat·ing** To commit fornication. [< L *fornicatus*, pp. of *fornicari* < *fornix, -icis* brothel, orig. vaulted chamber, vault] **—for′ni·ca′tor** *n.*

for·ni·ca·tion (fôr′nə·kā′shən) *n.* **1.** Voluntary sexual intercourse of an unmarried person with another unmarried or married person of the opposite sex. **2.** In Scriptural use: **a** Adultery, incest, or prostitution. **b** Idolatry.

for·nix (fôr′niks) *n. pl.* **for·ni·ces** (-nə·sēz) *Anat.* **1.** A vaulted or folded surface. **2.** The bands of white fibers beneath the corpus callosum of the brain, connecting the two hemispheres of the cerebellum. [< L, vault]

For·rest (fôr′ist, for′-), **Edwin,** 1806–72, U.S. actor. **— Nathan Bedford,** 1821–77, Confederate general in the Civil War.

For·res·tal (fôr′is·tôl, for′-), **James Vincent,** 1892–1949, U.S. banker; first U.S. secretary of defense 1947–49.

for·rit (fôr′it) *adv. Scot.* Forward.

for·sake (fôr·sāk′, fər-) *v.t.* **·sook** (-sŏŏk′), **·sak·en, ·sak·ing** **1.** To renounce or relinquish (an occupation, belief, etc.). **2.** To abandon; desert. **— Syn.** See ABANDON. [OE *forsacan* to repudiate, deny < *for-* away + *sacan* to renounce]

For·se·ti (fôr′se·tē) In Norse mythology, the god of justice; son of Balder. Also **For′se·te.**

for·sooth (fôr·sōōth′, fər-) *adv.* In truth; certainly: now chiefly ironical. [OE *forsōth*]

for·spent (fôr·spent′) *adj. Archaic* Tired out; exhausted: also spelled *forespent.* [Orig. pp. of *forspend* to exhaust, OE *forspendan*]

For·ster (fôr′stər), **E(dward) M(organ),** 1879–1970, English novelist.

for·swear (fôr·swâr′) *v.* **·swore, ·sworn, ·swear·ing** *v.t.* **1.** To renounce or abandon emphatically or upon oath; swear to give up completely; abjure: to *forswear* gambling. **2.** To deny absolutely or upon oath: to *forswear* a debt. **—** *v.i.* **3.** To swear falsely; commit perjury. **— to forswear oneself** To swear falsely; perjure oneself. **— Syn.** See RENOUNCE. [OE *forswerian* to swear falsely]

for·sworn (fôr·swôrn′, -swōrn′) *adj.* Perjured.

for·syth·i·a (fôr·sith′ē·ə, -sī′thē·ə, fər-) *n.* A shrub (genus *Forsythia*) of the olive family, native to China, much cultivated for its bright yellow flowers that appear early in the spring before the leaves. [after William *Forsyth*, 1737–1804, British botanist, who brought it to England]

fort (fôrt, fōrt) *n.* **1.** A fortified enclosure or structure capable of defense against an enemy; a fortification or fortress. **2.** A permanent U.S. Army post. Abbr. *ft.* [< F, orig. adj. strong < L *fortis*]
— Syn. *Fort, fortress, castle,* and *citadel* are types of military strongholds. A *fort* is a single, detached work; a *fortress* may be a *fort* or a series of *forts* and other works protecting a large area. A *castle* is a fortified residence, such as one constructed by a medieval nobleman and so serving a double purpose. *Citadel* is applied either to a *fortress* defending a town or to the most strongly fortified position in any defensive system.

fort. Fortification; fortified.

For·ta·le·za (fôr′tə·lā′zə) The capital of Ceará, NE Brazil, a port on the Atlantic; pop. 846,069 (est. 1968).

fort·a·lice (fôr′tə·lis) *n.* An outwork of a fortification; a small fort. [< Med.L *fortalitia* < L *fortis* strong]

Fort Col·lins (kol′ənz) A city in northern Colorado; pop. 43,337.

Fort Dear·born (dir′bôrn) A military post established in 1803 on the present site of Chicago, Illinois.

Fort-de-France (fôr′də·fräns′) The capital of Martinique, a port commune in the western part; pop. 100,000 (1969).

Fort Dodge (doj) A city in north central Iowa; pop. 31,263.

Fort Don·el·son National Military Park (don′əl·sən) An area in NW Tennessee; includes a Civil War fort, captured by Grant in 1862; 103 acres; established 1928.

Fort Du·quesne (dōō·kān′, dyōō-) An 18th-century French trading post on the present site of Pittsburgh, Pennsylvania. See FORT PITT.

forte[1] (fôrt, fōrt; *for def. 1, also* fôr′tā) *n.* **1.** That which one does with excellence; strong point. **2.** The strongest part of a sword blade, between the middle and the hilt: opposed to *foible.* [< F *fort.* See FORT.]

for·te (fôr′tā, -tē) *Music adj.* Loud; forceful. **—** *adv.* Loudly; forcefully. Abbr. *f, F* **—** *n.* A forte note, chord, passage, etc. [< Ital.]

forth (fôrth, fōrth) *adv.* **1.** Forward in place, time, or order. **2.** Out, as from seclusion, confinement, or inaction. **3.** Away or out, as from a place of origin; abroad. **— and so forth** And the rest; and so on. **—** *prep. Archaic* Forth from; out of. [OE]

Forth (fôrth, fōrth), **Firth of** The estuary, extending 51 miles to the North Sea, of the **Forth,** a river that flows 65 miles east in SE Scotland. The estuary is spanned by **Forth Bridge,** 3,770 ft., 8,295 ft. with approaches.

forth·com·ing (fôrth′kum′ing, fōrth′-) *adj.* **1.** Drawing near in time; approaching. **2.** Ready or about to appear, arrive, etc. **3.** Available or produced when expected or due. **—** *n.* Arrival or appearance of something due or expected.

Fort Hen·ry (hen′rē) A fort in NW Tennessee on the Tennessee River, 12 miles from Fort Donelson; captured by Union forces, 1862.

forth·right (fôrth′rīt′, fōrth′-) *adj.* **1.** Coming straight to the point; candid; frank. **2.** Going forward in a straight line; direct. **—** *adv.* **1.** In a direct course or straightforward manner. **2.** At once; straightway. **—forth′right′ness** *n.*

forth·with (fôrth′with′, -with′, fōrth′-) *adv.* Without delay; immediately. **— Syn.** See IMMEDIATELY.

for·ti·eth (fôr′tē·ith) *adj.* **1.** Tenth in order after the thirtieth: the ordinal of *forty.* **2.** Being one of forty equal parts. **—** *n.* **1.** One of forty equal parts; the quotient of a unit divided by forty. **2.** That which is tenth in order after the thirtieth.

for·ti·fi·ca·tion (fôr′tə·fə·kā′shən) *n.* **1.** The act, art, or science of fortifying. **2.** That which fortifies, as walls, ditches, etc. **3.** A military place of defense. Abbr. *fort., ft.*

fortified wine Wine having brandy added and containing 16 to 23 percent alcohol by volume, as sherry.

for·ti·fy (fôr′tə·fī) *v.* **·fied, ·fy·ing** *v.t.* **1.** To provide with defensive works; strengthen against attack. **2.** To give physical or moral strength to; invigorate or encourage. **3.** To strengthen the structure of; reinforce. **4.** To confirm;

corroborate. **5.** To strengthen, as wine, by adding alcohol. **6.** To enrich (food) by adding minerals, vitamins, etc. — *v.i.* **7.** To raise defensive works. [< F *fortifier* < L *fortificare* < *fortis* strong + *facere* to make] — **for′ti·fi′a·ble** *adj.* — **for′ti·fi′er** *n.*

for·tis (fôr′tis) *Phonet. adj.* Strongly articulated: opposed to *lenis.* — *n. pl.* **for·tes** (fôr′tēz) A consonant, usually a stop, produced with tension of the speech organs or with strong plosion. [< L, strong]

for·tis·si·mo (fôr·tis′ə·mō, *Ital.* fôr·tēs′sĕ·mō) *adj. & adv. Music* Very loud. Abbr. *ff* — *n. pl.* **-mos** A fortissimo note, chord, or passage. [< Ital., superl. of *forte* strong]

for·ti·tude (fôr′tə·tōōd, -tyōōd) *n.* **1.** Strength of mind in the face of pain, adversity, or peril; patient and constant courage. **2.** *Obs.* Physical strength or force. [< F < L *fortitudo* < *fortis* strong]
— **Syn. 1.** *Fortitude, resolution,* and *endurance* relate to firmness or strength of mind. *Fortitude* is compounded of both qualities and has no close synonym. The other words stress one aspect or the other of *fortitude. Resolution* implies a determination to be firm in conviction, faithful in allegiance, or unswerving in course, while *endurance* refers to the strength to display these qualities in the face of adversity. Compare RESOLUTION, COURAGE.

for·ti·tu·di·nous (fôr′tə·tōō′də·nəs, -tyōō′-) *adj.* Having or showing courage and endurance.

Fort Knox (noks) A military reservation in north Kentucky; site (since 1936) of Federal gold bullion depository.

Fort-La·my (fôr·lä·mē′) The capital of the Republic of Chad, in the northern part; pop. 132,500 (est. 1969).

Fort Lau·der·dale (lô′dər·dāl) A resort city in SE Florida on the Atlantic Ocean; pop. 139,590.

Fort Mc·Hen·ry National Monument (mək·hen′rē) A fort in the harbor of Baltimore, Maryland. Its bombardment by the British, Sept. 13, 1814, was the occasion of the writing of *The Star Spangled Banner* by Francis Scott Key; 48 acres.

Fort Mon·roe (mən·rō′) A military post in SE Virginia at the entrance to Hampton Roads. Also **Fortress Monroe.**

Fort Moul·trie (mōl′trē, mōōl′-, mōō′-) A fort in Charleston harbor, South Carolina; scene of battles in the Revolutionary War and the Civil War.

fort·night (fôrt′nīt′, -nit′) *n.* A period of two weeks; fourteen days. [OE *fēowertēne* fourteen + *niht* nights]

fort·night·ly (fôrt′nīt′lē) *adj.* Occurring, coming, or issued every fortnight. — *adv.* Once a fortnight. — *n. pl.* **·lies** A periodical appearing every two weeks.

Fort Peck Dam (pek) A dam in the Missouri River, NE Montana; 250 ft. high, 4 mi. long; on **Fort Peck Reservoir,** 383 sq. mi.

Fort Pierce (pirs) A city in eastern Florida, on Indian River; pop. 29,721.

Fort Pitt (pit) The British name for Fort Duquesne after they captured it from the French in 1758.

for·tress (fôr′tris) *n.* **1.** A large military stronghold; a fort, a series of forts, or a heavily fortified town. **2.** Any place of security. — **Syn.** See FORT. — *v.t.* To furnish or strengthen with a fortress; fortify. [< OF *forteresse* < L *fortis* strong]

Fort Smith (smith) A city in western Arkansas, on the Oklahoma border at the confluence of the Arkansas and Poteau rivers; pop. 62,802.

Fort Sum·ter National Monument (sum′tər) A fort in Charleston harbor, South Carolina; object of a Confederate attack, Apr. 14, 1861, that began the Civil War; 2.4 acres.

for·tu·i·tism (fôr·tōō′ə·tiz′əm, -tyōō′-) *n. Philos.* The doctrine that phenomena or events come to pass by chance rather than in accordance with intelligent design or natural law. — **for·tu′i·tist** *n. & adj.*

for·tu·i·tous (fôr·tōō′ə·təs, -tyōō′-) *adj.* Occurring by chance rather than by design; casual; accidental. — **Syn.** See ACCIDENTAL. [< L *fortuitus* < *fors* chance] — **for·tu′i·tous·ly** *adv.* — **for·tu′i·tous·ness** *n.*

for·tu·i·ty (fôr·tōō′ə·tē, -tyōō′-) *n. pl.* **·ties** Chance occurrence; also, chance.

For·tu·na (fôr·tōō′nə, -tyōō′-) In Roman mythology, the goddess of chance: identified with the Greek *Tyche.*

for·tu·nate (fôr′chə·nit) *adj.* **1.** Happening by a favorable chance; lucky. **2.** Favored with good fortune. — **for′tu·nate·ly** *adv.* — **for′tu·nate·ness** *n.*
— **Syn. 1.** *Fortunate, lucky,* and *providential* characterize a favorable event that results from factors beyond our control. *Fortunate* is the appropriate term for great matters and serves to remind us that many other persons or events may affect our destinies: a *fortunate* change in the wind prevented the spread of the fire. *Lucky* is more often used of small matters and emphasizes the element of chance: a *lucky* roll of the dice. *Providential,* strictly speaking, ascribes the favorable event to the intervention of God; more commonly it is used to mean merely very welcome or timely: a *providential* interruption of a boring conversation. **2.** happy, successful. — **Ant.** unfortunate, unlucky, unhappy, ill-starred.

for·tune (fôr′chən) *n.* **1.** That which happens or is to happen to one, whether good or bad; one's present or future lot. **2.** A power supposed to control one's future; fate; destiny; often personified. **3.** Luck or chance, especially when favor-

able. **4.** An amount of wealth or possessions: Her *fortune* was small. **5.** Great wealth or riches: to come into a *fortune.* **6.** A particular condition or state of life, usually prosperous. — **Syn.** See DESTINY. — *v.* **·tuned, ·tun·ing** *v.t.* **1.** *Rare* To bestow wealth upon. — *v.i.* **2.** *Archaic* To happen; occur by chance. [< OF < L *fortuna* < *fors* chance]

fortune hunter One who seeks to obtain wealth, especially through marriage. — **fortune hunting**

for·tune·tell·er (fôr′chən·tel′ər) *n.* One who claims to foretell events in a person's future. — **for′tune·tell′ing** *n. & adj.*

Fort Wayne (wān) A city in NE Indiana; pop. 177,671.

Fort Worth (wûrth) A city in northern Texas; pop. 393,476.

for·ty (fôr′tē) *n. pl.* **·ties 1.** The sum of thirty and ten: a cardinal number. **2.** Any symbol of this number, as 40, xl, XL. **3.** Anything consisting of or representing forty units, as an organization, game token, etc. **4.** *U.S* A tract of forty acres of land. — *adj.* Being ten more than thirty. [OE *fēowertig*]

for·ty-nin·er (fôr′tē·nī′nər) *n. U.S.* A pioneer who went to California in 1849, the year of the gold rush.

forty winks *Informal* A short nap.

fo·rum (fôr′əm, fō′rəm) *n. pl.* **fo·rums** or **fo·ra** (fôr′ə, fō′rə) **1.** The public market place of an ancient Roman city, where popular assemblies met, and most legal and political business was transacted. **2.** A tribunal; court. **3.** An assembly for discussion of public affairs. [< L]

Fo·rum Liv·i·i (fō′rəm liv′ē·ī, fō′rəm) The ancient name for FORLI.

for·ward (fôr′wərd) *adv.* **1.** Toward what is ahead or what is in front; onward. Also **for′wards. 2** At or in the front part, as of a ship. **3.** Out into a conspicuous position; to the forefront; forth: to bring *forward* an opinion. — **forward of** *U.S.* In front of. — *adj.* **1.** Being at or near the front: a *forward* position. **2.** Moving or directed toward a point lying ahead: a *forward* leap. **3.** Overstepping the usual bounds of propriety in an insolent or presumptuous way; arrogant or bold. **4.** Well-developed; not backward: a *forward* civilization. **5.** Developing or developed earlier than usual; premature; also, precocious. **6.** Extremely progressive or unconventional, as in political opinions. **7.** Ready or prompt. **8.** Made or done in advance: a *forward* contract for goods. — *n.* **1.** In football, one of the players in the front lines of attack or defense. **2.** In basketball, hockey, etc., a player who leads the offensive play. — *v.t.* **1.** To help onward or ahead; promote. **2.** To send onward or ahead; especially, to send (mail) on to a new address. **3.** In bookbinding, to supply (a book) with a cover, etc., preparatory to finishing. Abbr. (for n.) *fwd.* [OE *foreweard*]

forward delivery In commerce, delivery scheduled for a future time.

for·ward·er (fôr′wər·dər) *n.* **1.** One who or that which forwards. **2.** A person or company whose business it is to receive goods for reshipment to the proper destination.

for·ward·ly (fôr′wərd·lē) *adv.* **1.** With promptness or eagerness. **2.** Boldly or presumptuously. **3.** In a forward direction or position.

for·ward·ness (fôr′wərd·nis) *n.* **1.** Overeagerness to put oneself forward; boldness or presumptuousness. **2.** Willing readiness. **3.** The state of being well-developed, progressive, etc.; also, prematurity or precocity.

forward pass In football, the throwing or passing of the ball toward the opponent's goal. Abbr. *fp, f.p.*

forward quotation In commerce, a price set for goods to be delivered at a future time.

for·why (fôr′whī) *Archaic & Dial. adv.* Wherefore; why. — *conj.* Because.

for·worn (fôr·wôrn′, -wōrn′) *adj.* Worn out: also spelled *foreworn.* [Orig. pp. of obs. *forwear* to exhaust]

for·zan·do (fôr·tsän′dō) *adj. & adv.* Sforzando.

Fos·ca·ri (fôs·kä′rē), **Francesco,** died 1457, doge of Venice 1423–57.

Fos·dick (foz′dik), **Harry Emerson,** 1878–1969, U.S. clergyman and inspirational writer.

fos·sa (fos′ə) *n. pl.* **fos·sae** (fos′ē) *Anat.* A shallow depression or cavity in the body. [< L. See FOSSE.]

fosse (fôs, fos) *n.* An artificial ditch or moat, as in a fortification. Also **foss.** [< F < L *fossa* < *fodire* to dig]

fos·sette (fô·set′, fos-) *n. Anat.* A small depression, as a dimple. [< F, dim. of *fosse* ditch. See FOSSE.]

fos·sick (fôs′ik, fos′-) *Austral. v.i.* **1.** *Mining* To search for gold in abandoned mines, waste heaps, etc.; also, to search for surface gold. **2.** To rummage about for something: used with *about* or *around.* [Cf. dial. E *fussock* to bustle] — **fos′·sick·er** *n.*

fos·sil (fos′əl) *n.* **1.** *Paleontol.* **a** The actual remains of plants or animals, preserved in the rocks of the earth's crust. **b** Some petrified trace of the existence of an early organism, as a petrified footprint. **2.** *Geol.* One of certain inorganic objects or physical features that record natural activities or phenomena of ancient geological ages, as solidified ripple marks, etc. **3.** *Informal* One who or that which is out of date or antiquated. — *adj.* **1.** Pertaining to or of the nature of a fossil. **2.** Belonging to the past; out-of-date; antiquated. [< F *fossile* < L *fossilis* dug up < *fossa*. See FOSSE.]

fos·sil·if·er·ous (fos/əl·if/ər·əs) *adj.* Containing fossils.

fos·sil·ize (fos/əl·īz) *v.* **·ized, ·iz·ing** *v.t.* **1.** To change into a fossil; petrify. **2.** To make antiquated or out of date. — *v.i.* **3.** To become a fossil. — **fos/sil·i·za/tion** *n.*

fos·so·ri·al (fo·sôr/ē·əl, -sō/rē-) *adj.* **1.** Digging; burrowing: a *fossorial* animal. **2.** Adapted for or used in digging in the earth, as the legs and other organs of armadillos, aardvarks, etc. [< LL *fossorius* < L *fodire* to dig]

fos·ter (fôs/tər, fos/-) *v.t.* **1.** To bring up (a child); rear. **2.** To promote the growth or development of; help along: to *foster* genius. **3.** To keep alive (feelings, hopes, etc.) within oneself; cling to; cherish. **4.** *Obs.* To provide with food. — *n. Obs.* A foster parent. [OE *fōstrian* nourish]

Fos·ter (fôs/tər, fos/-), **John Watson**, 1836–1917, U.S. lawyer and diplomat. — **Stephen (Collins)**, 1826–64, U.S. song writer. — **William Z(ebulon)**, 1881–1961, U.S. Communist and labor leader.

fos·ter·age (fôs/tər·ij, fos/-) *n.* **1.** The rearing of a foster child. **2.** The condition of being reared as a foster child. **3.** Entrustment of a child to foster parents. **4.** The act of helping along the growth or development of something.

foster brother A boy in relation to the offspring of his foster parents.

foster child A child reared by a foster parent or parents.

foster daughter A girl in relation to her foster parents.

foster father A man rearing a child not his own.

foster home The home in which a foster child is reared.

foster land A country adopted as one's homeland.

fos·ter·ling (fôs/tər·ling, fos/-) *n.* A foster child.

foster mother A woman rearing a child not her own.

foster parent A man or woman rearing a child not his or her own.

foster sister A girl in relation to the offspring of her foster parents.

foster son A boy in relation to his foster parents.

Foth·er·in·ghay (foth/ər·ing·gā/) A village in NE Northamptonshire, England; site of **Fotheringhay Castle**, scene of the imprisonment and execution of Mary, Queen of Scots.

Fou·cault (fōō·kō/), **Jean Bernard Léon**, 1819–68, French physicist.

Fouc·quet (fōō·ke/) See FOUQUET.

fou·droy·ant (fōō·droi/ənt, *Fr.* fōō·drwä·yäṅ/) *adj.* Sudden and overwhelming, as lightning. [< F, ppr. of *foudroyer* to strike with lightning < *foudre* lightning]

fought (fôt) Past tense and past participle of FIGHT.

fought·en (fôt/n) *Archaic* past participle of FIGHT.

foul (foul) *adj.* **1.** Offensive or revolting to the senses; disgusting; a *foul* odor. **2.** Full of dirt or impure matter; filthy. **3.** Clogged or packed with dirt, etc.: a *foul* chimney. **4.** Spoiled or rotten, as food. **5.** Unfavorable; disagreeable; adverse: *foul* weather. **6.** Obscene, vulgar, or rude. **7.** Morally offensive; evil; wicked. **8.** Not according to rule or justice; unfair: a *foul* decision. **9.** Impeded or entangled: a *foul* anchor. **10.** In baseball, etc., of or pertaining to a foul ball or the foul lines. **11.** *Informal* Very bad; unsatisfactory. **12.** *Printing* **a** Full of errors; inaccurate. **b** Having the characters badly mixed: said of a type case. **13.** *Archaic* Ugly; homely. — *n.* **1.** An act of fouling, colliding, or becoming entangled. **2.** Something foul, as: **a** In baseball, a foul ball (which see). **b** A breach of rule in various sports and games. **c** An entanglement or collision, as of ropes, boats, etc. *Abbr.* (for def. 2) *f, f.* — *adv. Rare* In a foul manner; foully. — *v.t.* **1.** To make foul or dirty. **2.** To dishonor; disgrace. **3.** To clog or choke, as a drain. **4.** To entangle or snarl, as a rope. **5.** To cover or encumber (a ship's bottom) with barnacles, seaweed, etc. **6.** To collide with. **7.** In sports, to commit a foul against. **8.** In baseball, to bat (the ball) outside of the foul lines. — *v.i.* **9.** To become foul or dirty. **10.** To become clogged or encumbered. **11.** To become entangled. **12.** To collide. **13.** In sports, to violate a rule. **14.** In baseball, to bat a foul ball. — **to foul out** In baseball, to be retired by batting a foul ball that is caught before it strikes the ground. — **to foul up** *Slang* **1.** To throw into disorder or confusion. **2.** To blunder. [OE *fūl*] — **foul/ly** (foul/lē) *adv.*

fou·lard (fōō·lärd/) *n.* **1.** A lightweight, satiny fabric of silk, rayon, cotton, etc., usually with a printed design. **2.** A scarf, necktie, or other article made of this fabric. [< F < Swiss F *foulat* < OF *fouler*. See FOIL[1].]

foul ball In baseball: **a** A batted ball that first hits the ground outside the foul lines, even though it may later bound or roll within the lines. **b** A batted ball hitting the ground within the foul lines but passing outside the lines before reaching first or third base.

foul line **1.** In baseball, either of the two lines extending from home plate past first and third base to the limits of the field. For illustration see BASEBALL. **2.** In basketball, the free-throw line (which see). **3.** In bowling, etc., any line limiting the area of play or action.

foul·mouthed (foul/mouthd/, -moutht/) *adj.* Using abusive, profane, or obscene language.

foul·ness (foul/nis) *n.* **1.** The state or quality of being foul. **2.** Foul matter; filth. **3.** Sinfulness; evil.

foul play **1.** Unfairness; in games and sports, a violation of rule. **2.** Any unfair or treacherous action, often murder.

foul shot In basketball, a free throw.

foul tip In baseball, a pitched ball that is barely deflected by contact with the bat.

found[1] (found) *v.t.* **1.** To give origin to; set up; establish. **2.** To lay the foundation of; establish on a foundation or basis. — *v.i.* **3.** To be established or based: with *on, upon*. [< OF *fonder* < L *fundare* < *fundus* base, bottom]

found[2] (found) *v.t.* **1.** To cast, as iron, by melting and pouring into a mold. **2.** To make by casting molten metal. [< F *fondre* < L *fundere* to pour]

found[3] (found) Past tense and past participle of FIND. — *adj.* Provided with food, lodging, equipment, etc. — **and found** Plus board and lodging, as part payment.

foun·da·tion (foun·dā/shən) *n.* **1.** The act of founding or establishing. **2.** The state of being founded or established. **3.** That on which anything is founded; basis: Equality is the *foundation* of democracy. **4.** A base on which something rests: a machine's *foundation*. **5.** That part of a building or wall, wholly or partly below the surface of the ground, that constitutes a base. **6.** A fund for the maintenance of an institution; an endowment. **7.** An endowed institution, especially one that grants funds for or conducts research projects, charities, etc. **8.** A foundation garment (which see). — **foun·da/tion·al** *adj.*

foundation garment *U.S.* A girdle or corset, often combined with a brassiere.

foundation sire In horse breeding, the named stallion from which the genealogy of all horses of a given breed is traced.

found·er[1] (foun/dər) *n.* One who establishes an institution, company, society, etc.

found·er[2] (foun/dər) *n.* One who makes metal castings.

found·er[3] (foun/dər) *v.i.* **1.** To sink after filling with water, as a boat or ship. **2.** To fall or cave in, as land or buildings. **3.** To fail completely; collapse. **4.** To stumble and become lame, as a horse. **5.** *Vet.* To have founder. — *v.t.* **6.** To cause to sink. — *n.* **1.** The act of foundering. **2.** *Vet.* Inflammation of the tissue in the foot of a horse: also called *laminitis*. [< OF *fondrer* to sink < *fond* bottom < L *fundus*]

foun·der·ous (foun/dər·əs) *adj.* Causing to founder; miry.

founders' shares Shares of stock, often granting special privileges, issued to the promoters or founders of a company.

found·ling (found/ling) *n.* A deserted infant of unknown parentage. [ME *fundeling* < *funde*, pp. of *find* + -LING[1]]

foun·dry (foun/drē) *n. pl.* **·dries** **1.** An establishment in which metal, etc., is cast; also, an article made by casting. **2.** The act or operation of founding metal, etc.

foundry proof *Printing* A final proof of composed type before stereotyping or electrotyping.

fount[1] (fount) *n.* **1.** A fountain. **2.** Any source. [< F *font* < L *fons, fontis* fountain]

fount[2] (fount) British spelling of FONT[2].

foun·tain (foun/tən) *n.* **1.** A spring or jet of water issuing from the earth; especially, the source of a stream. **2.** The origin or source of anything. **3.** A jet or spray of water forced upward artificially, as to provide water for drinking. **4.** A basinlike structure designed for such a jet to rise and fall in. **5.** A reservoir or supply chamber for holding oil, ink, etc., as in a lamp, printing press, or inkstand. **6.** A soda fountain (which see). [< OF *fontaine* < LL *fontana*, orig. fem. singular of L *fontanus* of a spring < *fons, fontis* fountain]

foun·tain·head (foun/tən·hed/) *n.* **1.** A fountain or spring of water from which a stream takes its source. **2.** The source or origin of anything.

Fountain of Youth A legendary fountain said to have the power of restoring youth, sought by Ponce de León and other early explorers in Florida and the West Indies.

fountain pen A pen having a supply of ink automatically fed to the writing end from a reservoir or cartridge.

Fou·qué (fōō·kā/), **Friedrich Heinrich Karl**, 1777–1843, Baron de la Motte, German poet and dramatist: pseudonym **Pel·le·grin** (pel/ə·grin).

Fou·quet (fōō·ke/), **Jean**, 1415?–80, French painter. — **Nicolas**, 1615–80, Marquis de Belle Isle, French financier. Also *Foucquet*.

four (fôr, fōr) *n.* **1.** The sum of three and one: a cardinal number. **2.** Any symbol of this number, as 4, iv, IV. **3.** Anything consisting of or representing four units, as a team, playing card, etc. — **on all fours** **1.** On hands and knees. **2.** On all four feet. — *adj.* Being one more than three; quaternary. [OE *fēower*]

four-bag·ger (fôr/bag/ər, fōr/-) *n. Slang* In baseball, a home run.

four·chette (fōōr·shet/) *n.* **1.** A forked piece set between two adjacent fingers of a glove, uniting the front and back parts. **2.** *Ornithol.* The furculum or wishbone of a bird. **3.** *Zool.* The frog of a horse's foot. **4.** *Anat.* A fold of mucous membrane connecting the posterior section of the labia minora. [< F, dim. of *fourche* fork < L *furca*]

four-cy·cle (fôr/sī/kəl, fōr/-) *n. Mech.* A cycle of operations in an internal-combustion engine in which fuel is taken into the cylinder, compressed, burned, and exhausted in four successive strokes of the piston: also called *four-stroke cycle.* — *adj.* Having a cycle of four strokes.

four-di·men·sion·al (fôr/di·men/shən·əl, fōr/-) *adj.* **1.** Having or pertaining to four dimensions. **2.** *Math.* Relating to a system or a set of magnitudes whose elements can be completely defined only by four coordinates.

Four·drin·i·er (fŏŏr·drin/ē·ər) *adj.* Of, pertaining to, or designating a papermaking machine, the first to make a continuous web. [after Henry *Fourdrinier,* 1766–1804, British inventor] — *n.* A Fourdrinier machine.

four-eyed fish (fôr/īd/, fōr/-) The anableps.

four-flush (fôr/flush/, fōr/-) *v.i.* **1.** To bet on a poker hand containing four cards of one suit but lacking the fifth. **2.** *Slang* To bluff.

four flush A valueless poker hand containing four cards of one suit and one of another.

four-flush·er (fôr/flush/ər, fōr/-) *n. Slang.* A fake or cheat.

four-foot·ed (fôr/fŏŏt/id, fōr/-) *adj.* Having four feet.

Four Forest Cantons, Lake of the See (Lake of) LUCERNE.

Four Freedoms Freedom of speech and religion and freedom from want and fear, the world-wide goals of U.S. foreign policy stated by President Franklin D. Roosevelt in a message to Congress, January 6, 1941.

four·gon (fŏŏr·gôn/) *n. French* A covered wagon or van for carrying baggage, military supplies, etc.

four·hand·ed (fôr/han/did, fōr/-) *adj.* **1.** Designed for four players, as certain games. **2.** Designed for performance by two persons on a keyboard instrument, as a piano duet. **3.** Having four feet resembling or functioning like hands.

Four-H Club (fôr/āch/, fōr/-) A youth organization, sponsored by the Department of Agriculture, offering education in agriculture and home economics: so called because it aims at improving the head, heart, hands, and health of its members. Also **4-H Club.**

four hundred *U.S.* The most exclusive social group of a place: term originally applied to the wealthiest set in New York by Ward McAllister.

Fou·rier (fŏŏ·ryā/), **François Marie Charles,** 1772–1837, French socialist. — **Jean Baptiste Joseph,** 1768–1830, French mathematician and physicist.

Fou·ri·er·ism (fŏŏr/ē·ə·riz/əm) *n.* The social reform system advocated by F. M. C. Fourier about 1815, proposing small cooperative groups for economic production and maintenance, the achievement of social justice, and the fulfillment of individual desires. — **Fou/ri·er·ist, Fou/ri·er·ite/** *n.*

four-in-hand (fôr/in·hand/, fōr/-) *n.* **1.** A four-horse team driven by one person. **2.** A vehicle drawn by such a team. **3.** A necktie tied in a slip knot with the ends hanging vertically. — *adj.* Designating a four-in-hand.

four-leaf clover (fôr/lēf/, fōr/-) A clover plant having four leaflets, supposed to bring good luck.

four-let·ter word (fôr/let/ər, fōr/-) Any of several short English words considered obscene and unprintable.

four-mast·ed (fôr/mas/tid, -mäs/-, fōr/-) *adj. Naut.* Having four masts. — **four/-mast/er** *n.*

Four·nier d'Albe (fŏŏr/nyā dalb/), **Edmund Edward,** 1868–1933, English physicist.

four-o'clock (fôr/ə·klok/, fōr/-) *n.* **1.** An ornamental herb (*Mirabilis jalapa*) from Peru, with flowers of a great variety of colors that bloom from late afternoon till the next morning. It is typical of a family (*Nyctaginaceae*) of chiefly tropical plants that includes the bougainvillea: also called *marvel-of-Peru.* **2.** The friarbird.

four·pence (fôr/pəns, fōr/-) *n.* The sum of four English pennies; also, a silver piece worth that sum.

four-post·er (fôr/pōs/tər, fōr/-) *n.* A bedstead with four tall posts at the corners and typically with a canopy or curtains.

four·ra·gère (fŏŏ·rà·zhâr/) *n.* **1.** A metal-tipped cord of colored braid awarded to the members of a military unit for distinguished service, and worn around the left shoulder. **2.** Any similar ornament, as on a woman's dress. [< F]

four·score (fôr/skôr/, fōr/skōr/) *adj. & n.* Four times twenty; eighty.

four·some (fôr/səm, fōr/-) *n.* **1.** A game, especially of golf, in which four players take part, two on each side; also, the players in such a game. **2.** Any group of four. — *adj.* Pertaining to, consisting of, or designed for a group of four.

four·square (fôr/skwâr/, fōr/-) *adj.* **1.** Having four equal sides; square. **2.** Firm; solid. **3.** Forthright; direct. — *n.* A square. — *adv.* Squarely; bluntly.

four-stroke cycle (fôr/strōk/, fōr/-) Four-cycle (which see).

four·teen (fôr/tēn/, fōr/-) *n.* **1.** The sum of thirteen and one: a cardinal number. **2.** Any symbol of this number, as 14, xiv, XIV. **3.** Anything consisting of or representing fourteen units, as an organization, game token, etc. — *adj.* Being one more than thirteen. [OE *fēowertēne*]

Fourteen Points The peace aims set forth by President Woodrow Wilson in an address, January 8, 1918, ten months before the end of World War I. Also **Fourteen Peace Points.**

four·teenth (fôr/tēnth/, fōr/-) *adj.* **1.** Next after the thirteenth: the ordinal of *fourteen.* **2.** Being one of fourteen equal parts. — *n.* **1.** One of fourteen equal parts. **2.** That which follows the thirteenth.

Fourteenth Amendment An amendment to the Constitution of the United States (ratified 1868) giving citizenship to former slaves, and extending to state citizenship the privileges and immunities guaranteed by federal citizenship.

fourth (fôrth, fōrth) *adj.* **1.** Next after the third: the ordinal of *four.* **2.** Being one of four equal parts. — *n.* **1.** One of four equal parts. **2.** That which follows the third. **3.** *Music* **a** The interval between a tone and another tone four steps from it in a diatonic scale or mode, counting the starting tone as one. **b** One of these tones in relation to the other; especially, the fourth above the tonic; the subdominant. See INTERVAL, PERFECT. — **the Fourth** July 4th; Independence Day. — *adv.* In the fourth order, rank, or place.

fourth-class (fôrth/klas/, -kläs/, fōrth/-) *adj.* Designating mail matter consisting of merchandise, and carried at the lowest rate. — *adv.* By fourth-class mail.

fourth dimension 1. *Math.* A hypothetical, usually spatial dimension in addition to height, width, and thickness. **2.** In the theory of relativity, the temporal coordinate of space-time. — **fourth/-di·men/sion·al** *adj.*

fourth estate The public press; journalism.

fourth·ly (fôrth/lē, fōrth/-) *adv.* In the fourth place.

Fourth of July Independence Day.

Fourth Republic The republic formed in France in 1945, lasting until 1958, replaced by the Fifth Republic.

four-wheel (fôr/hwēl/, fōr/-) *adj.* **1.** Having four wheels. **2.** Affecting or controlling all four wheels: *four-wheel* drive.

fo·ve·a (fō/vē·ə) *n. pl.* **·ve·ae** (-vi·ē) *Biol.* A shallow depression in an organ or part. [< L, small pit] — **fo/ve·al** *adj.*

fovea cen·tra·lis (sen·tra/lis) *Anat.* The central pit of the retina directly in the axis of vision, the area of clearest vision.

fo·ve·ate (fō/vē·āt, -it) *adj. Biol.* Having foveae; pitted.

fo·ve·o·la (fə·vē/ə·lə) *n. pl.* **·lae** (-lē) *Biol.* A very small fovea or pit. Also **fo·ve·ole** (fō/vē·ōl), **fo/ve·o·let** (-let). [< L, dim. of *fovea* small pit]

fo·ve·o·late (fō/vē·ə·lāt) *adj. Biol.* Having foveolae or very small pits. Also **fo/ve·o·lat/ed.**

fowl (foul) *n. pl.* **fowl** or **fowls 1.** The common domestic hen or cock; a chicken. **2.** Any of various related birds, as the duck, turkey, goose, etc. **3.** The flesh of fowl, especially of the domestic hen. **4.** Birds collectively. — *v.i.* To catch or hunt wild fowl. [OE *fugol*] — **fowl/er** *n.*

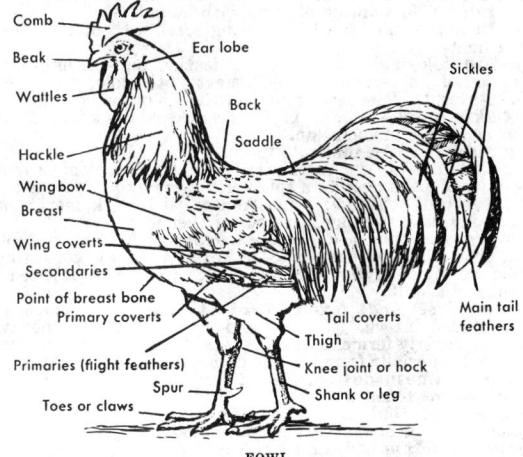

FOWL
(Anatomical nomenclature)

fowl cholera An infectious intestinal disease of domestic fowl, caused by the bacterium *Pasteurella avicida.*

Fowl·er (fou/lər), **Henry Watson,** 1858–1933, English lexicographer and authority on usage.

Fowler's solution A very poisonous, aqueous solution of potassium arsenite containing arsenious acid. [after Thomas *Fowler,* 1736–1801, English physician]

fowl·ing (fou/ling) *n.* The hunting of birds for sport.

fowling net A net for catching birds.

fowling piece A light gun used for shooting birds.

fowl pox A virus disease affecting poultry and other birds, characterized by skin lesions, tissue injuries, and sometimes diphtheria symptoms of the mucous membrane.

---

fox (foks) *n.* **1.** Any of several small, wild, canine mammals (*Vulpes* and related genera), resembling wolves though smaller in size, having long, pointed muzzles, bushy tails, and erect ears, and living typically in burrows and preying on poultry, rabbits, etc.; especially, the **red fox** (*Vulpes fulva*) of North America and a related fox (*Vulpes vulpes*) of Europe, having a reddish brown fur, and the **gray fox** (*Urocyon cinereoargenteus*) of the United States, marked by a grayish coloration and found from Pennsylvania southward. ◆ Collateral adjective: *vulpine*. **2.** The fur of the fox. **3.** A sly, crafty person. **4.** *Naut.* A small rope, made by hand, of two or more rope yarns twisted together. **5.** *Obs.* A sword. — *v.t.* **1.** To trick; outwit. **2.** To make drunk; intoxicate. **3.** To stain, as paper or timber, with a reddish color. **4.** To make sour, as beer, in fermenting. **5.** To repair or mend (shoes) with new uppers. — *v.i.* **6.** To act slyly and cunningly. **7.** To sour. **8.** To become stained with a reddish color. [OE]

NORTH AMERICAN RED FOX (Body about 2 feet long; tail 16 inches)

Fox (foks) *n.* One of an Algonquian tribe of North American Indians who formerly inhabited the neighborhood of Green Bay, Wisconsin, and who combined with the Sauks in 1760.

Fox (foks), **Charles James**, 1749–1806, English statesman and orator; opposed colonial policy of George III. — **George**, 1624–91, English preacher, founded the Society of Friends. — **Henry**, 1705–74, first Baron Holland, English politician; father of Charles James. — **John** (**William**), 1863–1919, U.S. novelist.

Foxe (foks), **John**, 1516–87, English divine and martyrologist. — **Richard**, 1448?–1528, English bishop; founded Corpus Christi College, Oxford: also **Fox**.

fox·fire (foks′fīr′) *n.* The phosphorescent light emitted by wood that has been rotted by certain fungal growths.

fox·fish (foks′fish′) *n.* The thresher (def. 2). Also **fox shark**.

fox·glove (foks′gluv′) *n.* Any plant of a genus (*Digitalis*) of the figwort family, especially the English variety (*D. purpurea*), having flowers in long one-sided racemes: the leaves are a source of digitalis. Also called *fairy gloves*.

fox grape A species of high-climbing North American grape (*Vitis labrusca*), having a purple-black fruit with a strong, sour flavor, of which the Concord grape is a cultivated variety.

fox·hole (foks′hōl′) *n.* A shallow pit dug by a combatant as cover against enemy fire.

ENGLISH FOXGLOVE

fox·hound (foks′hound′) *n.* One of a breed of large, strong, very swift dogs trained for fox hunting.

fox hunt The hunting of foxes with hounds.

fox hunting The sport of hunting foxes with hounds. — **fox hunter**

fox·ing (fok′sing) *n.* A piece of leather put on the upper leather of a shoe along the edge next to the sole.

Fox Islands The easternmost of the Aleutian Islands.

fox·skin (foks′skin′) *n.* **1.** The dressed skin of a fox. **2.** A fur cap made of such skins.

fox squirrel See under SQUIRREL.

fox·tail (foks′tāl′) *n.* **1.** The tail of a fox. **2.** Any of various species of grass bearing a spike of flowers like a fox's tail.

fox terrier A small, white terrier with dark markings, formerly used to bring foxes out of their burrows.

fox-trot (foks′trot′) *v.i.* **·trot·ted**, **·trot·ting** To do a fox trot.

fox trot **1.** A ballroom dance in 2/4 or 4/4 time, consisting of a variety of rhythmic steps. **2.** A horse's pace between a trot and a walk.

fox·y (fok′sē) *adj.* **fox·i·er**, **fox·i·est** **1.** Sly; crafty; sharp. **2.** Reddish brown. **3.** Discolored or stained, as from decay. **4.** Improperly fermented; soured: said of beer, etc. **5.** Defective, especially from age and damp. **6.** Denoting a flavor found in wine made from some American grapes. — **fox′i·ly** *adv.* — **fox′i·ness** *n.*

foy (foi) *n. Dial.* A feast or gift given before one goes on a journey, or on some other special occasion. [< MDu. *foie*, prob. < OF *voie* < L *via* road, way]

foy·er (foi′ər, foi′ā; *Fr.* fwà·yā′) *n.* **1.** A public lobby in a hotel, theater, etc. **2.** An entrance room or hall in a house or apartment. [< F < LL *focarium* hearth < L *focus*]

fp *Music* Forte piano (Ital.).

fp. Foolscap.

f.p. or **fp** Forward pass.

F.P. or **f.p.** **1.** Fireplug. **2.** Fire policy. **3.** Floating policy. **4.** Fully paid.

F.P. or **f.p.** or **fp** **1.** Foot-pound(s). **2.** Freezing point.

FPA or **F.P.A.** Foreign Press Association.

F.P.A. See (Franklin Pierce) ADAMS.

FPC or **F.P.C.** Federal Power Commission.

fpm or **f.p.m.** Feet per minute.

FPO *Mil.* Fleet post office.

fps or **f.p.s.** **1.** Feet per second. **2.** Foot-pound-second (system).

fr. **1.** Fragment. **2.** Franc. **3.** From.

Fr *Chem.* Francium.

Fr. **1.** Brother (L *Frater*). **2.** *Eccl.* Father. **3.** France. **4.** French. **5.** Friar. **6.** Friday. **7.** Wife (G *Frau*).

Fra (frä) *n.* Brother: a friar's title. [< L *frater* brother]

Fra Angelico See ANGELICO.

fra·cas (frā′kəs, *Brit.* frak′ä) *n.* A noisy disturbance, fight, or dispute; brawl; row. — **Syn.** See ROW³. [< F < Ital. *fracasso* uproar < *fracassare* to shatter]

frac·tion (frak′shən) *n.* **1.** A disconnected part of anything; small portion; fragment. **2.** *Math.* A quantity less than a unit, or one expressed as the sum of a number of aliquot parts of a unit. **3.** *Chem.* One of the components separated from a substance by fractionation. **4.** The act of breaking: said of the bread in the Eucharist. — **Syn.** See PORTION. — *v.t.* To set or separate into fractions. [< OF < L *fractio* a breaking < *fractus*, pp. of *frangere* to break]

frac·tion·al (frak′shən·əl) *adj.* **1.** Pertaining to or constituting a fraction; also, fragmentary. **2.** Small in size or importance. **3.** *Chem.* Designating a process or method of separating a complex of substances into component parts on the basis of specific properties, as solubility, boiling point, etc. **4.** In commerce, less than the unit of regular transactions. Also **frac′tion·ar′y** (-er′ē). — **frac′tion·al·ly** *adv.*

fractional currency Money or coins of any denomination less than the standard monetary unit.

frac·tion·ate (frak′shən·āt) *v.t.* **·at·ed**, **·at·ing** *Chem.* To subject (a mixture) to distillation, crystallization, etc., so as to separate into components according to boiling points, etc. — **frac′tion·a′tion** *n.*

frac·tion·ize (frak′shən·īz) *v.t. & v.i.* **·ized**, **·iz·ing** To divide into fractions. — **frac′tion·i·za′tion** *n.*

frac·tious (frak′shəs) *adj* **1.** Apt to be unruly or rebellious. **2.** Easily annoyed or angered; irritable; cranky. [< FRACTION, in obs. sense f discord, dissension] — **frac′tious·ly** *adv.* — **frac′tious·ness** *n.*

frac·to·cu·mu·lus (frak′tō·kyōō′myə·ləs) *n.* *Meteorol.* A small, low-lying, ragged variety of cumulus cloud (symbol Fc), typically associated with rain or other precipitation.

frac·to·stra·tus (frak′tō·strā′təs, -strat′əs) *n.* *Meteorol.* A wispy, shredlike variety of stratus cloud (symbol Fs), generally appearing as a darker layer below nimbostratus.

frac·tur (fräk·tŏŏr′) See FRAKTUR.

frac·ture (frak′chər) *n.* **1.** The act of breaking, or the state of being broken. **2.** A break; crack; rupture. **3.** *Med.* **a** The breaking or cracking of a bone; also, sometimes, the tearing of a cartilage. **b** Any of numerous types of bone ruptures. **4.** *Mineral.* The characteristic appearance of the freshly broken surface of a mineral. — **compound** (or **open**) **fracture** *Med.* A fracture in which the broken ends of the bone protrude through the skin. — **simple** (or **closed**) **fracture** *Med.* A bone fracture in which the skin remains unbroken. — *v.t. & v.i.* **·tured**, **·tur·ing** To break or be broken; crack. [< F < L *fractura* a breaking < *fractus*. See FRACTION.]

frae (frā) *prep. Scot.* From.

frae·num (frē′nəm) See FRENUM.

frag·ging (frag′ing) *n.* *Mil. Slang* The killing or wounding of a superior officer, as with a fragmentation grenade, by his own troops. [Alter. of FRAGMENTING]

frag·ile (fraj′əl) *adj.* Easily broken or damaged; frail; delicate. [< L *fragilis* < *frangere* to break. Doublet of FRAIL¹.] — **frag′ile·ly** *adv.* — **fra·gil·i·ty** (frə·jil′ə·tē), **frag′ile·ness** *n.* — **Syn.** *Fragile*, *frail*, *frangible*, *friable*, and *brittle* agree in meaning easily broken. That which cannot withstand even mild shocks or jars is *fragile* or, if constructed of parts poorly connected, *frail*: a *fragile* teacup, a *frail* scaffold. A *frangible* substance may be intrinsically strong but nonetheless breakable under certain conditions: *frangible* granite. *Friable* means easily pulverized, as pumice, and *brittle* is used to describe things that are hard but so rigid or inelastic that they crack under stress, as glass.

frag·ment (*n.* frag′mənt; *v.* frag·ment′) *n.* **1.** A part broken off; a small detached portion. *Abbr. fr.* **2.** A part or portion of something that has been left unfinished: a *fragment* of a novel. **3.** A separate or isolated bit; snatch: He heard *fragments* of their conversation. — *v.t. & v.i.* To break into fragments. [< F < L *fragmentum* fragment, remnant]

frag·men·tar·y (frag′mən·ter′ē) *adj.* Composed of fragments; broken; incomplete. Also **frag·men′tal**. — **frag′·men·tar′i·ly** *adv.* — **frag′men·tar′i·ness** *n.*

frag·men·ta·tion (frag′mən·tā′shən) *n.* **1.** A breaking up into fragments. **2.** *Mil.* The scattering in all directions of the fragments of an exploding grenade, shell, or bomb.

fragmentation bomb An aerial bomb that breaks into many small shrapnellike fragments upon explosion.

frag·ment·ed (frag′mən·tid) *adj.* Broken into fragments.

frag·ment·ize (frag′mən·tīz) *v.t. & v.i.* **·ized**, **·iz·ing** To fragment.

Fra·go·nard (frà·gō·nàr′), **Jean Honoré**, 1732–1806, French painter.

fra·grance (frā′grəns) *n.* **1.** The state or quality of being fragrant. **2.** A pleasant scent; sweet odor. Also *Rare* **fra′gran·cy**. — **Syn.** See SMELL.

fra·grant (frā′grənt) *adj.* Having an agreeable or sweet smell. [< L *fragrans*, *-antis*, ppr. of *fragrare* to smell sweet] — **fra′grant·ly** *adv.*

frail[1] (frāl) *adj.* **1.** Delicately constituted; lacking in strength; weak. **2.** Easily shattered or broken; fragile. **3.** Deficient in moral strength; easily tempted. — **Syn.** See FRAGILE. — *n. U.S. Slang* A girl. [< OF *fraile* < L *fragilis*. Doublet of FRAGILE.] — **frail/ly** *adv.* — **frail/ness** *n.*

frail[2] (frāl) *n.* **1.** A basket made of rushes for packing dried fruits, such as figs, raisins, etc. **2.** The weight measure, varying from 50 to 75 pounds, of dried fruits contained in such a basket. [< OF *fraiel* basket]

frail·ty (frāl/tē) *n. pl.* **·ties 1.** The state or quality of being frail; weakness. **2.** A fault or moral weakness.

fraise (frāz) *n.* **1.** A defense of pointed stakes planted in a rampart horizontally or in an inclined position. **2.** A ruff worn in Europe in the 16th century. [< F < *fraiser* to curl]

frak·tur (fräk·tŏŏr/) *n.* A form of Latin letter formerly widely used in German printing, characterized by thin shape, pointed ends, and bristling serifs: also spelled *fractur.* See ALPHABET. [< G < L *fractura* a breaking]

frame (frām) *n.* **1.** A case or border made to enclose something, as a picture. **2.** A supporting structure surrounding something, as around a window or door. **3.** A thing composed or built of parts joined and adjusted to one another; a structure serving as a support; framework; skeleton: the *frame* of a building, ship, etc. **4.** The general arrangement, structure, or constitution of a thing: the *frame* of a plan. **5.** A system or order, as of a government. **6.** Bodily structure or build, especially of the human body. **7.** A machine built in the form of or utilizing a framework: a silk *frame.* **8.** In shipbuilding, any of the girders forming the ribs of the hull and extending from the keel or bilge to the gunwale. The **square frames** are set perpendicularly to the vertical plane of the keel, and the **cant frames** at an oblique angle to it. **9.** In pool or billiards: **a** The triangular form for grouping the balls. **b** The balls placed in this form. **c** The time required to pocket all the balls. **10.** In bowling, one of the ten divisions of the game, for which the pins are set up again. **11.** *Informal* In baseball, an inning. **12.** One of the individual exposures on a roll of motion-picture film. **13.** In television, the total visual field included by one complete scanning of the electron beam. **14.** *Slang* A frame-up. — **frame of mind** Mental state; mood. — **frame of reference** The principles, circumstances, facts, values, etc., needed to inform or orient a person when thinking about, judging, or interpreting something. — **Syn.** See BODY. — *v.* **framed, fram·ing** *v.t.* **1.** To surround with or put into a frame, as a picture. **2.** To put together; construct; build: to *frame* a shelter. **3.** To put into words; utter: to *frame* a reply. **4.** To think out, conceive, or create (a theory, idea, etc.). **5.** To draw up; devise; contrive: to *frame* a law. **6.** To shape or adapt to a purpose: Traffic rules are *framed* for safety. **7.** *Slang* To incriminate falsely. **8.** *Slang* To plan or set up dishonestly in advance, as a race, contest, etc. — *v.i. Dial.* **9.** To prepare, contrive, or try to do something; also, to evidence ability to do something. **10.** To move; go; also, to progress well; flourish. [OE *framian* to be of service to, provide for] — **fram/er** *n.*

frame house A house built on a wooden framework covered on the outside by shingles, boards, stucco, etc.

frame-up (frām/up/) *n. Slang* **1.** A prearranged plan to bring about a fraudulent outcome, as in a contest. **2.** A conspiracy to convict a person on a false charge.

frame·work (frām/wûrk/) *n.* **1.** A skeleton structure for supporting or enclosing something; also, frames, collectively. **2.** The arrangement of the basic or component parts of something: the *framework* of society. **3.** Any work, such as embroidery, weaving, etc., performed by means of or on a frame.

fram·ing (frā/ming) *n.* **1.** A frame or framework. **2.** The act of erecting or fitting with frames or frameworks.

Fra·ming·ham (frā/ming·ham) A town in eastern Massachusetts; pop. 64,048.

franc (frangk) *n.* **1.** The standard monetary unit of various countries, equivalent to 100 centimes; especially: **a** The French franc: also called *new franc.* **b** The Belgian franc. **c** The Swiss franc. **d** The Luxemburgian franc. **2.** The monetary unit of Afars and Issas, Benin, Burundi, Cameroon, Central African Republic, Chad, Comoro Islands, Congo, Gabon, Ivory Coast, Madagascar, Mali, Morocco, New Caledonia, New Hebrides, Niger, Rwanda, Senegal, Togo, and Upper Volta. **3.** A French gold piece first coined in 1360; also, a silver piece first coined in 1575. *Abbr. f., Fr., fr.* [< Med.L *Franc(orum rex)* (king of the) Franks, the motto on the earliest of these coins]

France (frans, fräns) A Republic in western Europe; 212,974 sq. mi.; pop. 50,770,000 (est. 1970); capital, Paris.

France (frans, fräns), **Anatole** Pseudonym of *Jacques Anatole Thibault,* 1844–1924, French novelist and critic.

Fran·ces·ca (frän·ches/kä), **Piero della** See PIERO DELLA FRANCESCA.

Fran·ces·ca da Ri·mi·ni (frän·ches/kä dä rē/mē·nē), died 1285?, Italian lady killed for adultery, in Dante's *Inferno.*

Franche-Com·té (fränsh·kôn·tā/) A region and former province of eastern France: also *Free County of Burgundy.*

FRANCE, OLD PROVINCES

fran·chise (fran/chīz) *n.* **1.** The right to vote; suffrage. **2.** A right or privilege granted by a government or sovereign. **3.** A special privilege bestowed upon an individual or a corporate group of individuals by government grant: a *franchise* to operate a bus line. **4.** Formerly, legal exemption from certain restrictions, burdens, etc. **5.** Authorization given by a manufacturer to a distributor or retailer to sell the manufacturer's products. **6.** The territory over which any of the preceding special privileges or dispensations extend. — *v.t. Obs.* To enfranchise. [< OF < *franc, franche* free]

Fran·cis I (fran/sis, frän/-), 1494–1547, king of France 1515–1547.

Francis II, 1768–1835, last emperor of the Holy Roman Empire 1792–1806; first emperor of Austria 1804–35.

Francis Ferdinand See FRANZ FERDINAND.

Francis Joseph See FRANZ JOSEF.

Francis of Assisi, Saint, 1182?–1226, Italian friar and preacher; founded the Franciscan order: original name **Giovanni Francesco Ber·nar·do·ne** (bär/när·dō/nä).

Francis of Sales, Saint, 1567–1622, French bishop; founded the Order of the Visitation, 1610; canonized, 1665. See SALESIAN.

Francis Xavier, Saint See XAVIER.

Fran·cis·can (fran·sis/kən) *n.* A member of the mendicant order, the Gray Friars or Minorites, founded in 1209 by St. Francis of Assisi. The three branches of the order are *Capuchins, Conventuals,* and *Observantines.* See also POOR CLARE. — *adj.* **1.** Of or pertaining to St. Francis. **2.** Belonging to a religious order or institution following the rule of St. Francis.

fran·ci·um (fran/sē·əm) *n.* A radioactive element (symbol Fr), isolated from actinium, and replacing the hypothetical element formerly known as *virginium.* See ELEMENT. [after *France*]

Franck (frängk), **César Auguste,** 1822–90, French composer born in Belgium.

Fran·co (frang/kō, *Sp.* fräng/kō), **Francisco,** 1892–1975, Spanish political and military leader; chief of state 1939–75: called *el Caudillo:* full surname **Fran·co-Ba·ha·mon·de** (-bä/ä·môn/dä).

Franco- *combining form* French: *Francophile.* [< L *Francus* a Frank]

fran·co·lin (frang/kə·lin) *n.* An Old World partridge (genus *Francolinus*), having richly colored plumage and a rather long tail and bill. [< F < Ital. *francolino*]

Fran·co·ni·a (frang·kō/nē·ə) A medieval duchy in south Germany, divided into the present administrative districts of Lower, Middle, and Upper Franconia, West Germany. *German* **Fran·ken** (fräng/kən). — **Fran·co/ni·an** *adj. & n.*

Fran·co·phile (frang/kə·fil) *n.* An admirer of France or of French customs, etc. — *adj.* Kindly disposed toward France.

Fran·co·phobe (frang/kə·fōb) *n.* A person who fears or dislikes France or French things. — *adj.* Fearful of France.

Fran·co·phone (frang/kə·fōn/) *n. Often l.c. Canadian* A native speaker of French. Compare ANGLOPHONE.

Fran·co-Prus·sian War (frang/kō-prush/ən) See table for WAR.

franc·ti·reur (frän·tē·rœr′) *n.* *pl.* **francs-ti·reurs** (frän·tē·rœr′) A French soldier, one of the sharpshooters of a light infantry force. [< F < *franc* free + *tireur* shooter < *tirer* to shoot]

fran·gi·ble (fran′jə·bəl) *adj.* Easily broken; brittle; fragile. — **Syn.** See FRAGILE. [< OF < L *frangere* to break] — **fran′gi·bil′i·ty, fran′gi·ble·ness** *n.*

fran·gi·pan·i (fran′ji·pan′ē, -pä′nē) *n.* **1.** A perfume derived from or resembling that of the West Indian red jasmine (*Plumeria rubra*). **2.** The West Indian plant. **3.** A pastry made with almonds, cream, etc. Also **fran′gi·pane** (-pān). [after Marquis *Frangipani*, the inventor]

Fran·glais (frän·gle′) *n.* French that contains many loanwords from British and American English. [< F *Fr(ançais)* French + *Anglais* English]

frank[1] (frangk) *adj.* **1.** Completely honest and unreserved in speech; outspoken; candid. **2.** Marked by no effort at concealment or disguise; open: *frank* hostility. **3.** *Rare* Generous. **4.** *Obs.* Free. — **Syn.** See CANDID. — *v.t.* **1.** To mark (a letter, package, etc.), as with an official sign or signature, in indication that no charge is to be made for delivery; also, to send (a letter, etc.) without charge by marking in this way. **2.** To enable (a person) to come and go without difficulty, as by providing with some advantage, privilege, etc. **3.** To obtain immunity for; exempt. — *n.* **1.** The right to send mail, etc., without charge; also, the mark used to indicate this right. **2.** A letter, package, etc., sent without charge. [< OF *franc* frank, free]

frank[2] (frangk) *n.* *Informal* A frankfurter.

Frank (frangk) *n.* **1.** A member of one of the Germanic tribes living on the Rhine early in the Christian era. The Salian Franks conquered Gaul in the fifth century A.D. and gave their name to France. **2.** In the Near East, any European. [< L *Francus* a Frank < Gmc., a spear (cf. OE *franca* lance); named from their weapon]

Frank·en·stein (frangk′ən·stīn) The hero of Mary Wollstonecraft Shelley's *Frankenstein*, a medical student who fashions a manlike monster that slays its maker. — *n.* **1.** Any person destroyed by his own handiwork. **2.** Loosely, Frankenstein's monster. **3.** Anything that gets beyond the control of the inventor and causes its destruction.

Frank·fort (frangk′fərt) The capital of Kentucky, in the north central part on the Kentucky River; pop. 21,356.

Frankfort on the Main (mān) A city in Hesse, West Germany; pop. 660,410 (est. 1970). *German* **Frank·furt** or **Frank·furt-am-Main** (frängk′foort·äm·mīn′).

Frankfort on the O·der (ō′dər) A city in eastern East Germany; pop. 57,200 (est. 1959). *German* **Frank·furt** or **Frank·furt-an-der-O·der** (frängk′foort·än·dər·ō′dər).

frank·furt·er (frangk′fər·tər) *n.* A smoked, often highly seasoned sausage, reddish in color, made of beef or of beef and pork. Also **frank′fort·er** (-fər·tər), **frank′furt, frank′·fort** (-fərt) [after *Frankfurt*, Germany]

Frank·furt·er (frangk′fər·tər), **Felix**, 1882–1965, U.S. jurist; associate justice of the Supreme Court, 1939–62.

frank·in·cense (frangk′in·sens) *n.* An aromatic gum or resin from various trees of East Africa, especially *Boswellia carteri*, used as an incense and in medicine: also called *olibanum*. [< OF *franc* pure + *encens* incense]

Frank·ish (frang′kish) *adj.* Of or pertaining to the Franks, or, in the Near East, to Europeans in general. — *n.* The West Germanic language of the Franks.

frank·lin (frangk′lin) *n.* In late medieval England, a freeholder; a nonnoble landholder ranking below the gentry. [ME *frankeleyn* < Med.L *francus* free]

Frank·lin (frangk′lin) **1.** A temporary state, 1784–88, comprising lands of western North Carolina ceded to Congress in 1784; now part of eastern Tennessee. **2.** The northernmost district of the Northwest Territories, Canada; 549,293 sq. mi.; pop. 4,408.

Frank·lin (frangk′lin), **Benjamin**, 1706–90, American patriot, writer, scientist, and diplomat; signer of the Declaration of Independence: pseudonym **Richard Saun·ders** (sôn′dərz, sän′-). — **Sir John**, 1786–1847, English explorer.

frank·lin·ite (frangk′lin·īt) *n.* A metallic, black, slightly magnetic oxide of zinc, iron, and manganese, a valuable ore of zinc. [after *Franklin*, a town in New Jersey]

Franklin Square An unincorporated place in SE New York, on Long Island; pop. 32,156.

Franklin stove An open-faced cast-iron stove resembling a fireplace, invented by Benjamin Franklin.

frank·ly (frangk′lē) *adv.* In a frank manner; candidly; openly.

frank·ness (frangk′nis) *n.* The quality of being frank; candor; straightforwardness.

frank·pledge (frangk′plej′) *n.* **1.** In old English law, a system that required all men of a community to combine in groups of ten to stand as sureties for one another's good behavior. **2.** A member of one of the groups in this system; also, any group (*tithing*) in this system. [< AF *franc-plege*, lit., a freeman's pledge; erroneous trans. of OE *frith-borg* a pledge to keep the peace]

FRANKLIN STOVE

fran·tic (fran′tik) *adj.* **1.** Nearly driven out of one's mind, as with grief, fear, or rage. **2.** Madly excited; frenzied; wild: *frantic* gestures. **3.** *Archaic* Insane. [< OF *frenetique* < LL *phreneticus* < Gk. *phrenitikos* delirious < *phrenitis* delirium < *phrēn* mind] — **fran′ti·cal·ly, fran′tic·ly** *adv.*

Franz Fer·di·nand (fränts fûr′di·nand), 1863–1914, archduke of Austria; his assassination led to outbreak of World War I. Also *Francis Ferdinand*.

Franz Jo·sef (fränts jō′zəf, *Ger.* fränts yō′zəf), 1830–1916, emperor of Austria 1848–1916. Also *Francis Joseph*.

Franz Joseph Land An archipelago in the Arctic Ocean, the northernmost land of the Eastern Hemisphere; annexed by the Soviet Union in 1926: also *Fridtjof Nansen Land*. *Russian Zemlya Frantsa-Iosifa.*

frap (frap) *v.t.* **frapped, frap·ping** *Naut.* To draw or bind firmly. [< OF *fraper* to strike]

frap·pé (fra·pā′) *U.S. adj.* Iced; chilled. — *n.* **1.** A fruit juice or other beverage frozen to a soft, mushy consistency. **2.** A liqueur or other beverage poured over shaved ice. [< F, pp. of *frapper* to chill]

Fra·ser River (frā′zər) A river in British Columbia, flowing about 700 miles SW to the Strait of Georgia.

frat (frat) *n.* *U.S. Informal* A college fraternity.

fra·ter[1] (frā′tər) *n.* A brother; comrade. Abbr. *Fr.* [< L]

fra·ter[2] (frā′tər) *n. Obs.* A monastic dining room. [< OF *fraitur*, short for *refreitor* < Med.L *refectorium* dining hall]

fra·ter·nal (frə·tûr′nəl) *adj.* **1.** Pertaining to or befitting a brother; brotherly. **2.** Of or pertaining to a fraternal order or society. **3.** *Genetics* Designating either of a pair of human twins of the same or opposite sex that develop from separately fertilized ova and thus are distinct in hereditary characteristics: distinguished from *identical*. [< L *fraternus* < *frater* brother] — **fra·ter′nal·ly** *adv.*

fra·ter·nal·ism (frə·tûr′nəl·iz′əm) *n.* Brotherly state or feeling.

fraternal order A brotherhood of men organized to further their mutual benefit or to attain a common goal. Also **fraternal association** or **society.**

fra·ter·ni·ty (frə·tûr′nə·tē) *n.* *pl.* **·ties 1.** The state of being brothers; also, the quality or spirit of fraternal regard or affection. **2.** In U.S. schools, a society of male students, usually having a Greek letter name, and represented by chapters in many institutions. **3.** A fraternal order; especially, a group of laymen organized for charitable or pious purposes; confraternity. **4.** A body of people sharing the same interests, profession, etc.: the medical *fraternity.* [< L *fraternitas, -tatis* brotherhood < *fraternus.* See FRATERNAL.]

frat·er·nize (frat′ər·nīz) *v.* **·nized, ·niz·ing** *v.i.* **1.** To associate closely with someone in a comradely way. **2.** To mingle in a friendly or intimate way with the people of an enemy or conquered country. — *v.t.* **3.** *Rare* To bring into a brotherly or friendly relationship. — **frat′er·ni·za′tion** *n.* — **frat′er·niz′er** *n.*

frat·ri·cide (frat′rə·sīd) *n.* **1.** The killing of one's brother. **2.** One who has killed his brother. [< L *fratricida* < *frater* brother + *caedere* to kill] — **frat′ri·ci′dal** *adj.*

Frau (frou) *n.* *pl.* **Frau·en** (-ən) *German* A married woman; wife; lady: as a title, the German equivalent of *Mrs.* Abbr. *Fr.*

fraud (frôd) *n.* **1.** Willful deceit; deception; trickery. **2.** An act or instance of deception or trickery. **3.** *U.S. Informal* One who acts deceitfully; cheat; imposter. **4.** A deceptive or spurious thing. — **Syn.** See DECEPTION. [< OF *fraude* < L *fraus, fraudis* deceit]

fraud·u·lent (frô′jə·lənt) *adj.* **1.** Practicing or given to fraud; dishonest or deceitful. **2.** Proceeding from, obtained by, or characterized by fraud. [< OF < L *fraudulentus* < *fraus, fraudis* deceit] — **fraud′u·lence, fraud′u·len·cy** *n.* — **fraud′u·lent·ly** *adv.*

fraught (frôt) *adj.* Filled; laden: with *with:* a journey *fraught* with danger. — *n. Obs.* Freight or cargo; also, a load. — *v.t. Obs.* To load down with or as with freight. [Orig. pp. of ME *frahten* to freight, ult. < MDu. *vrachten*]

Fräu·lein (froi′līn) *n.* *German* An unmarried woman; a young woman: as a title, the German equivalent of *Miss.* Abbr. *Frl.*

Fraun·ho·fer (froun′hō′fər), **Joseph von**, 1787–1826, German physicist; investigated lines of the spectrum.

Fraunhofer lines A series of dark lines in a spectrum, caused by absorption or interference: also called *F lines.*

frax·i·nel·la (frak′sə·nel′ə) *n.* A Eurasian herb (*Dictamnus albus*) of the rue family, with white flowers and a powerful odor: also called *burning bush, dittany, gas plant.* [< NL, dim. of L *fraxinus* ash tree]

fray[1] (frā) *n.* **1.** Conflict; fight; melee; also a noisy, quarrelsome uproar or disturbance; brawl; row. **2.** *Obs.* A feeling of fright or alarm. — *v.i.* **1.** *Archaic* To fight; also, to disturb the peace by noisy quarreling. — *v.t.* **2.** *Obs.* To attack. **3.** *Archaic* To make frightened; scare. [Apheptic var. of AFFRAY]

fray[2] (frā) *v.t.* **1.** To cause (cloth, rope, etc.) to separate into loose threads or fibers at the edges or along the outside by friction or wear. **2.** To wear holes in (cloth, etc.) by rubbing or chafing. — *v.i.* **3.** To become frayed. —

frayed place, as of a sleeve. [< F *frayer* < L *fricare* to rub]

Fra·zer (frā′zər), **Sir James (George)**, 1854–1941, British anthropologist and author.

fraz·zle (fraz′əl) *Informal v.t. & v.i.* **·zled, ·zling 1.** To fray or become frayed; make or become tattered. **2.** To tire out; weary. **—** *n.* **1.** The state of being frazzled. **2.** A frayed end or edge; shred; remnant. **— beat to a frazzle** Overcome completely. **— worn to a frazzle 1.** Worn to shreds. **2.** Tired out; exhausted. [? Blend of FRAY[2] + obs. *fasel* to ravel]

FRB Federal Reserve Board.

F.R.C.P. Fellow of the Royal College of Physicians.

F.R.C.S. Fellow of the Royal College of Surgeons.

freak[1] (frēk) *n.* **1.** A deformed or abnormally developed human being, animal, or plant; monstrosity. **2.** Anything unusual or bizarre. **3.** A sudden whim: caprice. [Cf. OE *frician* to dance] **— to freak out 1.** To undergo intense hallucinations and other reactions after taking a psychedelic drug. **2.** To undergo experiences that resemble hallucinations, as when watching psychedelic visual effects. **3.** To become a hippie.

freak[2] (frēk) *n.* A fleck or spot of color; streak. **—** *v.t.* To mark with spots or flecks; variegate. [< FREAK[1]]

freak·ish (frēk′ish) *adj.* **1.** Pertaining to, suggestive of, or having the characteristics of a freak; odd. **2.** Marked by capriciousness; erratic and unpredictable: a *freakish* twist of fate. **— freak′ish·ly** *adv.* **— freak′ish·ness** *n.*

freak·y (frē′kē) *adj.* **freak·i·er, freak·i·est** Freakish. **— freak′i·ly** *adv.* **— freak′i·ness** *n.*

Fré·chette (frā-shet′), **Louis Honoré**, 1839–1908, Canadian poet and legislator.

freck·le (frek′əl) *n.* A small brownish or dark-colored spot on the skin. **—** *v.t. & v.i.* **·led, ·ling** To mark or become marked with freckles. [ME *fracel*, var. of *frekne* < ON *freknur* freckles] **— freck′led** (frek′əld) *adj.*

Fred·er·ick I (fred′ər·ik, fred′rik), 1123?–90, Emperor of the Holy Roman Empire 1152–90: called *Barbarossa* (Red-beard).

Frederick I, 1657–1713, elector of Brandenburg 1688–1701; first king of Prussia 1701–13.

Frederick II, 1194–1250, Emperor of the Holy Roman Empire 1215–50.

Frederick II, 1712–86, king of Prussia 1740–86: called **Frederick the Great.**

Frederick III, 1415–93, Emperor of the Holy Roman Empire 1440–93; king of Germany 1452–93.

Frederick William, 1620–88, elector of Brandenburg 1640–88: called **the Great Elector.**

Frederick William I, 1688–1740, king of Prussia 1713–40; father of Frederick the Great.

Frederick William II, 1744–97, king of Prussia 1786–97.

Frederick William III, 1770–1840, king of Prussia 1797–1840.

Frederick William IV, 1795–1861, king of Prussia 1840–61.

Fred·er·icks·burg (fred′riks·bûrg, fred′ər·iks-) A city in NE Virginia; scene of a Confederate victory in the Civil War, 1862; pop. 14,450.

Fred·er·ic·ton (fred′ər·ik·tən, fred′rik-) The capital of New Brunswick, Canada, in the central part of the Province on the St. John River; pop. 23,612.

Fre·der·iks·berg (fred′ər·iks·bûrg, fred′riks-; *Dan.* freth′·ə-rēks·berkh′) A city in Denmark, the chief suburb of Copenhagen; pop. 103,621 (1965).

free (frē) *adj.* **fre·er, fre·est 1.** Having personal liberty. **2.** Having civil, political, or religious liberty. **3.** Not controlled by a foreign power; autonomous. **4.** Not bound by restrictions or regulations: *free* trade. **5.** Released from legal charge of crime or misdeed; acquitted. **6.** Exempt from or not subject to certain regulations or impositions, as some taxes. **7.** Cleared or devoid of something: with *from, of: free* from scandal; *free* of infection. **8.** Allowed or permitted to do something: *free* to go. **9.** Not controlled, restricted, or hampered by external agents or influences: *free* will; also, altogether voluntary: *free* consent. **10.** Not given to or dominated by envy, prejudice, anger, etc.: with *from, of.* **11.** Released from or not hindered by burdens, debts, discomforts, etc.: with *from, of: free* from care. **12.** Not occupied; not busy. **13.** Available to all; open: a *free* port. **14.** Not attached, bound, fixed, or held; loose: the *free* end of a rope. **15.** Not obstructed; easy to pass through or over: The road is now *free*; also, unimpeded; profuse: a *free* flow of water. **16.** Given or provided without charge or cost: *free* seats. **17.** Easy and unconstrained: a *free* stride. **18.** Not adhering to strict form or rule: *free* verse. **19.** Not closely or literally following the original: a *free* translation. **20.** Having little regard for tradition or ceremony; informal; unconventional. **21.** Frank and honest; candid: He is very *free* in telling his faults. **22.** Unrestrained by propriety, dignity, or decency: His speech is too *free*. **23.** Generous in giving; liberal: *free* with advice.

24. *Chem.* Uncombined: *free* hydrogen. **25.** *Physics* Available for work: *free* energy. **26.** *Naut.* Favorable: applied to winds blowing from a direction more than six points away from dead ahead. **— free and clear** *Law* Pertaining to real property held without a mortgage or other encumbrance. **— to set free** To release, as from prison, slavery, or other restraint; disengage. **—** *adv.* **1.** In a free manner; easily. **2.** Without cost; gratuitously. **3.** *Naut.* With the wind more than six points away from being dead ahead. **— to make free with** To act towards (someone or something) with too much liberty or undue familiarity. **—** *v.t.* **freed, free·ing 1.** To make free; release from confinement, obligation, worry, etc. **2.** To clear or rid of obstruction or hindrance; disengage. [OE *frēo*] **— free′ness** *n.*

free alongside ship or **vessel** Delivered without charge to the pier where a ship is docked. *Abbr. f.a.s., F.A.S.*

Free and Accepted Mason A Freemason (which see).

free-and-eas·y (frē′ənd-ē′zē) *adj.* Unconventional and informal; unceremonious.

free association 1. *Psychol.* An association of ideas unrestricted by definite control or limiting factors. **2.** *Psychoanal.* A method of uncovering and resolving unconscious conflicts by encouraging spontaneous and unselective verbal association of memories, ideas, impressions, etc.

free·board (frē′bôrd′, -bōrd′) *n.* **1.** *Naut.* The side of a vessel between the water line and the main deck or gunwale. **2.** The distance between the underframe of an automobile and the ground.

free·boot (frē′boot′) *v.i.* To act as a freebooter; plunder.

free·boot·er (frē′boo′tər) *n.* One who plunders; especially, a pirate or buccaneer. [< MDu. *vrijbuiter* < *vrij* free + *buit* booty]

free·boot·y (frē′boo′tē) *n. Obs.* **1.** Loot. **2.** Pillaging.

free·born (frē′bôrn′) *adj.* **1.** Born free, not in servitude or slavery. **2.** Of or pertaining to those born free.

free city A city that has an autonomous government and is an independent state, as certain medieval cities.

free coinage The mintage of certain specified bullion brought to a mint, with or without a fixed charge.

free companion A free lance (def. 3).

free company A company of medieval mercenaries.

free diver An underwater diver not dependent, for his air, upon a connection with the surface.

freed·man (frēd′mən) *n. pl.* **·men** (-mən) An emancipated slave; especially, an emancipated American Negro after the Civil War. **— freed′wom′an** *n.fem.*

free·dom (frē′dəm) *n.* **1.** The state or condition of being free; especially, the condition of enjoying civil liberty. **2.** Political autonomy, as of a nation or people. **3.** The condition of being personally free; liberty from bondage or slavery. **4.** Liberation, as from prison or other confinement. **5.** Possession of particular privileges or immunities. **6.** Liberty to move or act without outside interference, coercion, or restriction. **7.** Liberty of personal choice, action, or thought. **8.** *Philos.* The state of the will as the first cause in human actions; self-determination. **9.** Release or immunity from any stated thing or condition: with *from: freedom* from pain. **10.** Exemption or release from obligations, ties, etc. **11.** Facility or ease, as in moving or acting. **12.** Boldness of concept or execution: the *freedom* of modern sculpture. **13.** Openness or frankness in speech and manner; informality. **14.** Excessive familiarity or candor. **15.** The right to enjoy the privileges of membership or citizenship: *freedom* of the city. **16.** The privilege of unrestricted access or use: the *freedom* of a home. [OE *frēodōm*]

— Syn. *Freedom, liberty,* and *license* refer to the right or opportunity to do as one pleases. *Freedom* is the widest term, suggesting complete absence of restraint: the *freedom* of primeval man. *Liberty* is a measure of *freedom* within restraints, granted by or as though by a sovereign power; we speak of *freedom* from arrest without warrant as a civil *liberty. License* is an exemption from restraint granted to one person but not to another; a poet exercises *license* as to the meaning of words. When the exemption is unwarranted, *license* becomes violation of law, propriety, etc.: The *license* of his speech was offensive. **— Ant.** bondage, slavery, captivity, imprisonment, servitude, constraint, restraint.

freedom of the seas The doctrine that any waters not subject to the territorial jurisdiction of any one country or nation are open to unhampered navigation by any ships or, in war, by the ships of any neutral country or nation.

free energy *Physics* The portion of the energy of a physicochemical system that is available to perform work.

free enterprise An economic system based upon private ownership and operation of business with little or no governmental control: also called *private enterprise.*

free-for-all (frē′fər-ôl′) *n.* **1.** A noisy or disorderly generalized fight. **2.** A contest, game, etc., open to anyone who wishes to participate.

free·form (frē′fôrm′) *adj.* In industrial arts, denoting a flowing design or shape not adhering to any rigid pattern.

free form *Ling.* A morpheme that can occur meaningfully in isolation, as *tree, desk:* opposed to *bound form.*

free gold   **1.** Gold held by the U.S. Treasury over and above that in the gold reserve. **2.** Pure gold found loose.

free·hand (frē′hand′) *adj.* Drawn or sketched by hand without the help of rulers, drafting instruments, etc.

free hand   Full liberty to act as one sees fit.

free·hand·ed (frē′han′did) *adj.* **1.** Having the hands free. **2.** Openhanded; generous. — **free′hand′ed·ness** *n.*

free·heart·ed (frē′här′tid) *adj.* Frank; generous; open-hearted; spontaneous.

free·hold (frē′hōld′) *n.* *Law* **1.** Tenure of an estate, or sometimes of an office or dignity, for life or as something capable of being transferred to another. **2.** The estate, office, or dignity held by such tenure. — **free′hold′er** *n.*

free-lance (frē′lans′, -läns′) *v.i.* **-lanced, -lanc·ing** To serve or work as a free lance. — *adj.* Working as a free lance.

free lance   **1.** A writer, artist, etc., whose services are not sold exclusively to any one buyer. **2.** One who supports causes without full, exclusive commitment to any one. **3.** A medieval soldier who sold his services to any state or cause; mercenary: also called *free companion.*

free list   **1.** A list of goods not subject to tariff charges. **2.** A list of persons admitted free.

free liver   One addicted to personal indulgence, as in eating and drinking.

free-living (frē′liv′ing) *adj.* **1.** Given to easygoing or self-indulgent habits of life. **2.** *Zool.* Moving freely and independently; motile; also, neither parasitic nor symbiotic.

free·load (frē′lōd′) *v.i.* *Slang* To act as a freeloader.

free·load·er (frē′lō′dər) *n.* *Slang* One who makes a practice of eating, drinking, etc., at the expense of others.

free love   The doctrine or practice of free choice in sexual relations, without legal marriage or other obligations.

free·ly (frē′lē) *adv.* In a free manner.

free·man (frē′mən) *n.* *pl.* **·men,** (-mən) **1.** A person who is free; one not in bondage of any kind. **2.** One having full political rights and privileges; citizen; also, formerly, a freeholder.

Free·man (frē′mən), **Douglas Southall,** 1886–1953, U.S. historian. — **Edward Augustus,** 1823–92, English historian. — **Mary Eleanor,** 1852–1930, U.S. writer.

free·mar·tin (frē′mär′tən) *n.* A congenitally defective, usually sterile female calf born as the twin of a male calf. [Origin uncertain]

free·ma·son (frē′mā′sən) *n.* In the Middle Ages, a stonemason belonging to a craft guild that had secret signs and passwords and that admitted honorary members who were designated *accepted masons.*

Free·ma·son (frē′mā′sən) *n.* A member of an extensive secret order or fraternity, the members denoting themselves *Free and Accepted Masons:* also called *Mason.* — **Free·ma·son·ic** (frē′mə·son′ik) *adj.*

free·ma·son·ry (frē′mā′sən·rē) *n.* Instinctive sympathy among people with a community of interests.

Free·ma·son·ry (frē′mā′sən·rē) *n.* **1.** The rites, principles, etc., of Freemasons. **2.** Freemasons collectively.

free on board   Delivered, without charge to the buyer, for shipment by a common carrier. Abbr. *f.o.b., F.O.B.*

free port   **1.** A port open to all trading vessels on equal terms. **2.** The whole or part of a port area where no customs duties are levied on foreign goods intended for transshipment rather than for import.

Free·port (frē′pôrt, -pōrt) **1.** A village in SE New York, on the southern shore of Long Island; pop. 40,374. **2.** A city in northern Illinois; pop. 27,736.

free·si·a (frē′zhē·ə, -sē·ə, -zhə) *n.* A South African plant (genus *Freesia*) of the iris family, having bell-shaped, variously colored, fragrant flowers. [< NL, after E. M. *Fries,* 1794–1878, Swedish botanist]

free silver   The free and unlimited coinage of silver, par-ticularly at a fixed ratio to gold.

free-soil (frē′soil′) *adj.* *U.S.* Pertaining to or maintaining a policy opposing the extension of slavery to the Territories during the period preceding the Civil War. — **free′-soil′er** *n.*

Free-Soil (frē′soil′) *adj.* Pertaining to the Free-Soil Party.

free soil   Territory free of slavery; especially, such territory in the United States before the Civil War.

Free-Soil·er (frē′soi′lər) *n.* A member of the Free-Soil Party.

Free-Soil Party   A U.S. political party formed in 1848 to oppose the spread of slavery to the Territories.

free-spo·ken (frē′spō′kən) *adj.* Unreserved or frank in speech. — **free-spo′ken·ness** *n.*

free·stand·ing (frē′stan′ding) *adj.* Standing apart from all other objects; independently balanced or supported: a *freestanding* sculpture.

Free State   **1.** Before the Civil War, any State where slavery was forbidden. **2.** The Irish Free State.

free·stone (frē′stōn′) *adj.* Having a pit from which the pulp easily separates, as a peach. — *n.* **1.** Any stone, as sandstone or limestone, that can be cut in any direction without breaking. **2.** A fruit easily freed from its pit.

free·style (frē′stīl′) *adj.* In swimming, employing or permitting any stroke the swimmer desires. — *n.* **1.** The use of freestyle swimming techniques. **2.** A freestyle race. **3.** A freestyle swimmer: also **free′styl·er.**

free-swim·ming (frē′swim′ing) *adj.* *Zool.* Swimming freely, as an aquatic animal: said especially of certain organisms that are attached or immovable during other stages of their development. — **free′-swim′mer** *n.*

free·think·er (frē′thing′kər) *n.* An independent thinker; especially, one who forms his own religious beliefs. — **Syn.** See SKEPTIC. — **free′think′ing** *adj.* & *n.*

free thought   Thought or belief, especially in religious matters, formed without regard for authority or convention.

free throw   In basketball, an unhindered try for a goal, given a player who has been fouled by an opposing player.

free-throw line (frē′thrō′)   The line from which a free throw is made: also called *foul line.*

Free·town (frē′toun′)   The capital of Sierra Leone, a port in the western part on the Atlantic; pop. 170,600 (est. 1969).

free trade   **1.** International commerce free from government regulations and from import and export duties. **2.** A trade system where duties are levied only for revenue and not to protect home industries. **3.** The practice, policy, or system of unrestricted trade. **4.** *Archaic* Smuggling.

free-trad·er (frē′trā′dər) *n.* **1.** One advocating or engaged in free trade. **2.** *Canadian* An independent fur trader.

free verse   Verse marked by the use of rhythmical patterns other than the conventional meters, and an absence or irregularity of rhyme: also, *French, vers libre.*

free·way (frē′wā′) *n.* A wide highway skirting populated areas and passing over or around intersections.

free wheel   *Mech.* **1.** A form of automotive transmission that allows the drive shaft to run freely when its speed exceeds that of the engine shaft. **2.** A device attached to the rear wheel of a bicycle, permitting wheel motion without pedal action, as in coasting.

free·wheel·ing (frē′hwē′ling) *n.* A free-wheel system or device. — *adj.* **1.** Pertaining to or having a free-wheel system or device. **2.** *Informal* Unhampered; unrestricted.

free·will (frē′wil′) *adj.* Made, done, or given of one's own free choice; voluntary.

free will   **1.** The power of personal self-determination. **2.** The doctrine that one's ability to choose between alternative courses of action is not completely determined by external circumstances. Compare DETERMINISM.

freeze (frēz) *v.* **froze, fro·zen, freez·ing** *v.i.* **1.** To become ice or a similar hard solid through loss of heat. **2.** To become sheeted or filled with ice, as water pipes. **3.** To become stiff or hard with cold, as wet clothes. **4.** To adhere to something by the formation of ice. **5.** To be extremely cold; especially, to be at or as if at the temperature at which water becomes ice. **6.** To be damaged or killed by great cold. **7.** To become suddenly motionless, inactive, or rigid, as through fear, shock, etc. **8.** To become icily aloof, formal, or unfriendly in manner: often with *up.* — *v.t.* **9.** To cause to become ice or a similar hard solid through loss of heat. **10.** To cause ice to form on or in. **11.** To make stiff or hard by freezing the moisture of. **12.** To make adhere by the formation of ice. **13.** To make extremely cold. **14.** To damage or kill by great cold. **15.** To make motionless or rigid, as through fear; paralyze. **16.** To make icily aloof, unfriendly, etc.; alienate. **17.** To check abruptly the ardor, enthusiasm, etc., of; discourage or squelch. **18.** To fix or stabilize (prices, wages, etc.) at a particular level. **19.** To prohibit the continued making, use, or selling of (a raw material). **20.** To make the liquidation, collection, or use of (funds or other assets) contrary to law or edict. **21.** *Med.* To anesthetize by subjecting to extreme cold: to *freeze* a tooth. — **to freeze one's blood** To fill one with terror. — **to freeze onto** (or to) To hold tightly to. — **to freeze out** *U.S. Informal* To drive away or exclude, as by unfriendliness. — *n.* **1.** The act of freezing, or the state of being frozen. **2.** A period of weather marked by freezing temperatures; frost. [OE *frēosan*]

freeze-dry (frēz′drī′) *v.t.* **-dried, -dry·ing** To dry (food, blood, etc.) under high vacuum after quick-freezing. — **freeze′-dry′ing** *n.*

freez·er (frē′zər) *n.* One who or that which freezes, as: **a** A refrigerator designed to freeze food quickly and preserve it for long periods. **b** An apparatus for freezing ice cream.

freeze-up (frēz′up′) *n.* *Canadian* The time when lakes and rivers freeze, especially in the north.

freezing point   *Physics* The temperature at which a liquid freezes under given pressure. For fresh water at sea level it is 32° F. or 0° C. Abbr. *fp, f.p., F.P.*

free zone   A section of a port or city for the receipt and storage of goods, duty free.

Frei·burg (frī′bûrg, *Ger.* frī′boorkh) **1.** A city in SW West Germany; pop. 165,960 (est. 1960); also **Freiburg-im-Breis·gau** (im brīs′gou). **2.** The German name for FRI-BOURG.

freight (frāt) *n.* **1.** In the United States and Canada: **a** The service of transporting commodities by land, air, or water; especially, ordinary transportation as opposed to express. **b** The commodities so transported. **2.** In Great Britain: **a** The service of transporting commodities by air or water. **b** The commodities so transported. Commodities transported by land are known as *goods*. **3.** The price paid for the transportation of commodities. **4.** *U.S. & Canadian* A freight train. Abbr. *frt.* — *v.t.* **1.** To load with commodities for transportation. **2.** To load; burden. **3.** To send or transport as or by freight. [< MDu. *vrecht*, var. of *vracht*. See FRAUGHT.]

freight·age (frā'tij) *n.* **1.** A cargo; freight. **2.** The price charged or paid for carrying goods. **3.** The transportation of merchandise.

freight car A railway car for carrying freight.

freight·er (frā'tər) *n.* **1.** A ship used primarily for transporting cargo. **2.** One who has freight transported. **3.** One who is engaged in receiving and transporting freight for others. **4.** One employed in loading cargo.

freight ton See under TON¹ (def. 3).

freight train *U.S.* A railroad train of freight cars.

Fre·man·tle (frē'man-təl) A port city in SW Western Australia; pop. 21,959 (1961). Nearby are its suburbs **East Fremantle** (pop. 6,520) and **North Fremantle** (pop. 2,367).

fremd (fremd) *adj. Scot.* Alien; strange.

frem·i·tus (frem'i-təs) *n. pl.* **·tus** *Pathol.* A palpable vibration, as of the wall of the chest. [< L, a roar]

Fre·mont (frē'mont) A city in western California, near Oakland; pop. 100,869.

Fré·mont (frē'mont), **John Charles**, 1813–90, U.S. army officer, explorer, and politician: called **the Pathfinder**.

French (french) *adj.* Of, pertaining to, or characteristic of France, its people, or their language; also, in Canada, pertaining to Canadian French persons, their speech, etc. — *n.* **1.** The people of France collectively: preceded by *the*; also, in Canada, the French-speaking Canadians. **2.** The Romance language of France, belonging to the Italic subfamily of Indo-European languages, also spoken extensively in Belgium, Switzerland, Canada, and Haiti. — **Old French** The French language from about 850 to 1400, descended from Vulgar Latin as it developed in Gaul. Old French had two major dialects, the *langue d'oïl*, spoken north of the Loire, and the *langue d'oc* (Provençal), spoken south of it. Modern French is derived from the former, with the central French dialect of Paris as the standard. Abbr. *OF, OF., O.F.* — **Middle French** The French language from about 1400 to 1600. Abbr. *MF, MF., M.F.* — **Modern French** The language of France after 1600. Abbr. *F, F., Fr.* [OE *Frencisc* < *Franca* a Frank]

French (french), **Daniel Chester**, 1850–1931, U.S. sculptor. — **Sir John Denton Pinkstone**, 1852–1925, first Earl of Ypres, British field marshal in World War I.

French Academy An association of forty scholars, writers, and intellectuals (the Immortals), established in 1685 by Cardinal Richelieu to exercise control over the language and literature of France. *French* **A·ca·dé·mie Fran·çaise** (à·kà·dā·mē' frän·sez').

French and Indian War The war waged in America between the English and French, 1754–63, in which the French received support from their Indian allies.

French blue Ultramarine (def. 2).

French Cameroons A former UN Trust Territory in equatorial Africa; administered by France. See CAMEROON.

French Canada **1.** The province of Quebec. **2.** French-Canadians collectively.

French-Ca·na·di·an (french'kə-nā'dē-ən) *n.* A French settler in Canada or a descendant of French settlers in Canada. Also **French Canadian.** — *adj.* Of or pertaining to the language, culture, etc., of French-speaking people in Canada.

French chalk Finely ground talc or steatite, used as a marker on fabrics or as a dry cleaner.

French chop A rib chop with the bone scraped bare.

French Community A political association formed in 1958, comprising France, its overseas territories and departments, and Central African Republic, Chad, Republic of the Congo, Gabon, Malagasy Republic, and Senegal.

French cuff A cuff of a sleeve turned back and secured with a link.

French curve A flat, often transparent device with scroll-like openings and edges, used by draftsmen, etc., as a guide in drawing curved lines.

French doors A pair of doors, usually with glass panes, attached to opposite doorjambs and opening in the middle.

French dressing A salad dressing consisting of oil, vinegar, and spices.

French Equatorial Africa A former group of French Overseas Territories in west and north central Africa. See (Republics of) CHAD, (the) CONGO, GABON, and CENTRAL AFRICAN REPUBLIC.

French fried Cooked by frying crisp in deep fat.

French Gui·an·a (gē-an'ə, -än'ə) A French Overseas Department on the NE coast of South America; about 35,000 sq. mi.; pop. 45,000 (est. 1969); capital, Cayenne.

French Guinea The former name for (the Republic of) GUINEA.

French heel A curved high heel used on women's shoes.

French horn A valved, brass instrument with a long, coiled tube, flaring widely at the end and producing a mellow tone.

FRENCH HORN

French·i·fy (fren'chə-fī) *v.t. & v.i.* **·fied, ·fy·ing** To make or become French in form or characteristics.

French India A former French Overseas Territory in India comprising Chandernagore, Karikal, Mahé, Pondicherry, and Yanam; merged with India 1949–54.

French Indochina A former name for INDOCHINA (def. 2).

French knot A decorative stitch made by twisting or winding a thread several times around a needle and then pushing the needle through the coil.

French leave An informal, secret, or hurried departure.

French·man (french'mən) *n. pl.* **·men** (-mən) **1.** A native or citizen of France. **2.** A French ship. — **French'wom'an** (-wŏŏm'ən) *n.fem.*

French Morocco A former French protectorate in NW Africa; since 1956 a part of the kingdom of Morocco.

French North Africa A former name for Algeria, French Morocco, and Tunisia.

French pastry A rich, fancy pastry often having a filling of whipped cream, custard, or preserved fruits.

French Polynesia A French Overseas Territory in the South Pacific comprising the Society, Marquesas, Gambier, Tuamotu, Austral, Leeward, and Rapa islands and Clipperton island; about 1,560 sq. mi.; pop. 109,000 (est. 1970); capital, Papeete, on Tahiti. Formerly **French Settlements in Oceania, French Oceania.**

French Republic Metropolitan France, with its overseas departments and territories. Abbr. *R.F.* (F *République française*).

French Revolution See under REVOLUTION.

French seam A seam sewed on both sides so that no raw edges are exposed.

French Shore *Canadian* The west coast and an area of the SW coast of Newfoundland.

French Somaliland The former name (1946–67) of the French Overseas Territory called French Territory of the Afars and Issas (which see.)

French Sudan A former name for the (Republic of) MALI.

French telephone A telephone with the receiver and the transmitter mounted on one handle.

French toast Bread dipped in a batter of beaten eggs and milk and fried in shallow fat.

French Togoland From 1946 to 1960, a French-administered UN Trust Territory in western Africa. See TOGOLAND, (Republic of) TOGO.

French Union A former political association (1946–58) comprising France and its overseas departments and territories: replaced by the French Community.

French West Africa A former group of French Overseas Territories in the western bulge of Africa. See (Republics of) DAHOMEY, GUINEA, IVORY COAST, MALI, NIGER, SENEGAL, UPPER VOLTA, (Islamic Republic of) MAURITANIA.

French West Indies The Caribbean islands comprising the French Overseas Departments of Guadaloupe and Martinique.

French window A casement window with adjoining sashes attached to opposite jambs and opening in the middle.

FRENCH WINDOW

French·y (fren'chē) *Informal adj.* **French·i·er, French·i·est** Having or assuming French characteristics. — *n. pl.* **French·ies** A Frenchman.

Fre·neau (fre-nō'), **Philip (Morin)**, 1752–1832, American poet: called **the Poet of the American Revolution.**

fre·net·ic (frə-net'ik) *adj.* Feverishly excited; frenzied; frantic. Also **fre·net'i·cal.** — *n.* A frenetic person. Also spelled *phrenetic.* — **fre·net'i·cal·ly** *adv.*

fre·num (frē'nəm) *n. pl.* **·nums** or **·na** (-nə) *Anat.* A restraining band or fold, as under the tongue: also spelled *fraenum.* [< L, bridle]

fren·zied (fren'zēd) *adj.* Filled with or moved by frenzy; frenetic; frantic.

fren·zy (fren'zē) *n. pl.* **·zies** **1.** A state of extreme excitement or agitation suggestive of or bordering on delirium or insanity. **2.** *Rare* Mental derangement; insanity. — *v.t.* **·zied, ·zy·ing** To throw into a frenzy; make frantic. Also, *Rare, phrensy.* — **·phren'sy.** [< OF *frenesie* < LL *phrenesis* < LGk. *phrenēsis*, var. of Gk. *phrenitis* delirium < *phrēn* mind] — **Syn.** *Frenzy, mania, delirium,* and *hysteria* agree in denoting a state of abnormal excitement. *Frenzy* denotes the state without ascribing a cause. *Mania* arises from actual insanity; *delirium,* from a temporary impairment of the brain by fever, alcohol, etc.; *hysteria,* from some functional disorder of the nerves. In extended senses, *frenzy* is often applied to any extreme, uncontrolled outburst of emotion, such as anger or terror. *Mania* refers to an obsessive idea or popular fad. *Delirium* describes foolish, nonsensical talk and *hysteria* suggests immoderate laughter or weeping.

Fre·on (frē'on) *n. Chem.* Any of a group of methane and ethane derivatives containing chlorine and fluorine, that are stable, nontoxic, and nonflammable, used as solvents, refrigerants, and aerosol propellants: a trade name.

freq. 1. Frequency. 2. Frequentative. 3. Frequent(ly).

fre·quence (frē'kwəns) *n. Rare* Frequency (defs. 1, 2, 6).

fre·quen·cy (frē'kwən·sē) *n. pl.* **·cies** 1. The state or fact of being frequent; repeated occurrence. 2. The number of times something occurs within a particular extent of time, a particular group, etc. 3. *Math.* The number of times something occurs in relation to the total number of possible occurrences. 4. *Stat.* The number of times a given case, value, or event occurs in relation to the total number of classified cases, values, or events; distribution. 5. *Physics* The number of occurrences of a periodic phenomenon, as oscillation, per unit time, usually expressed in cycles per second. 6. *Archaic* A crowd; throng. Abbr. *f., F., freq.*

frequency band *Telecom.* A channel; also, a group of channels used for the same general purpose.

frequency curve *Stat.* A graphic representation of the frequencies of the values of specified variables arranged by order of magnitude: also called *distribution curve.*

frequency distribution *Stat.* A representation, as on a graph, of the number or relative proportion of items in a specific category or range of values.

frequency modulation *Telecom.* A type of modulation in which the carrier wave of a transmitting system is varied in frequency rather than in amplitude. Abbr. *FM, f-m, f.m., F.M.*

fre·quent (*adj.* frē'kwənt; *v.* fri·kwent', frē'kwənt) *adj.* 1. Happening time after time; occurring again and again: *frequent* relapses. 2. Showing up often; appearing repeatedly: *frequent* visitors. — *v.t.* To go to repeatedly; be in or at often: to *frequent* bars. [< L *frequens, -entis* crowded] — **fre·quent'er** *n.*

fre·quen·ta·tion (frē'kwən·tā'shən) *n.* The act or practice of going or being somewhere often.

fre·quen·ta·tive (fri·kwen'tə·tiv) *Gram. adj.* Denoting repeated or habitual action. — *n.* A frequentative verb. Abbr. *freq.*

fre·quent·ly (frē'kwənt·lē) *adv.* At frequent intervals; repeatedly. Abbr. *freq.*

frère (frâr) *n. pl.* **frères** (frâr) *French* 1. Brother. 2. Friar; monk.

fres·co (fres'kō) *n. pl.* **·coes** or **·cos** 1. The art of painting on a surface of plaster, especially while the plaster is still moist. 2. A picture so painted. — *v.t.* **·coed, ·co·ing** To paint in fresco. [< Ital., fresh] — **fres'co·er, fres'co·ist** *n.*

fresh¹ (fresh) *adj.* 1. Newly made, obtained, received, etc.: *fresh* coffee; *fresh* footprints. 2. New; novel: a *fresh* approach. 3. Recent; latest: *fresh* news. 4. Additional; further: *fresh* supplies. 5. Not smoked, frozen, or otherwise preserved: *fresh* vegetables. 6. Not spoiled, stale, musty etc. 7. Retaining original vividness; not faded or worn, as colors or memories. 8. Not salt: *fresh* water. 9. Pure and clear: *fresh* air. 10. Appearing healthy or youthful. 11. Not fatigued; energetic. 12. Vivid; colorful; stimulating. 13. Inexperienced; untrained: *fresh* recruits. 14. *Meteorol.* Moderately rapid and strong: especially designating a breeze (No. 5) or a gale (No. 8) on the Beaufort scale. 15. Having a renewed supply of milk: said of a cow that has recently calved. — **fresh out of** *Slang* Having just sold out or exhausted the supply of. — *n.* 1. A freshet. 2. The early or fresh part of a day, season, etc. [OE *fersc*, infl. by OF *freis*, both ult. < Gmc.] — **fresh'ly** *adv.* — **fresh'ness** *n.* — **Syn.** 2. novel, recent. See NEW. 6. blooming, green, verdant. 7. bright, ruddy, vigorous. 13. untried, unskilled, naive. — **Ant.** decayed, dull, faded, jaded, musty, blasé.

fresh² (fresh) *adj. U.S. Informal* Saucy; impudent; disrespectful. [< G *frech* impudent]

fresh-air (fresh'âr') *adj.* Providing or organized to provide pure, invigorating air: a *fresh-air* camp.

fresh·en (fresh'ən) *v.t.* 1. To make fresh; as: **a** To pep up; invigorate. **b** To remove staleness, mustiness, etc., from. **c** To rid (fish, water, etc.) of saltiness. 2. *Naut.* To stop the chafing of (a rope, etc.) by shifting the position. — *v.i* 1. To become fresh; as: **a** To gain new pep, brightness, etc. **b** Of the wind, to become brisk. 4. To give birth to a calf. — **fresh'en·er** *n.*

fresh·et (fresh'it) *n.* 1. A sudden rise or overflow of a stream. 2. A fresh-water stream emptying into the sea.

fresh·man (fresh'mən) *n. pl.* **·men** (-mən) 1. A student during the first year of studies in a high school, college, or university. 2. A beginner; novice.

fresh-wa·ter (fresh'wô·tər, -wot'ər) *adj.* 1. Pertaining to or living in fresh water: a *fresh-water* fish. 2. Not situated on or near the seacoast; inland. 3. Lacking skill or experience. 4. *U.S.* Not well known; small: a *fresh-water* college.

Fres·nel (frā·nel'), **Augustin Jean**, 1788–1827, French physicist.

Fres·no (frez'nō) A city in central California; pop. 165,972.

fret¹ (fret) *v.* **fret·ted, fret·ting** *v.i.* 1. To be vexed, annoyed, or troubled. 2. To become worn, chafed, or corroded. 3. To bite away bit after bit of something with or as with the teeth; gnaw: with *on, upon, into.* 4. To eat through something by or as if by corrosion. 5. To rankle; fester. 6. To become rough or agitated, as water. — *v.t.* 7. To vex, annoy, or trouble. 8. To wear away or eat away by or as if by chafing, gnawing, or corrosion; also, to produce (a hole, frayed ends, etc.) in this way. 9. To roughen or agitate (the surface of water). — **Syn.** See IRRITATE. — *n.* 1. Vexation, annoyance, or uneasiness. 2. The act of chafing, gnawing, or corroding. 3. A spot worn away, chafed, etc. [OE *fretan* to devour]

fret² (fret) *n.* One of a series of ridges, as of metal, fixed across the fingerboard of a guitar, ukulele, etc., to guide the fingers in stopping the strings. — *v.t.* **fret·ted, fret·ting** To provide (a guitar, etc.) with frets. [Cf. OF *frete* ring]

FRETS³

fret³ (fret) *n.* 1. An ornamental band or border consisting of angular or sometimes curved lines symmetrically arranged. 2. Any ornamental work with a pattern like that used in such bands or borders, often done in relief or with numerous small openings. — *v.t.* **fret·ted, fret·ting** To adorn with a fret. [Prob. < OF *frette* lattice, trellis]

fret·ful (fret'fəl) *adj.* Inclined to fret; peevish or restless. — **fret'ful·ly** *adv.* — **fret'ful·ness** *n.* — **Syn.** complaining, impatient, pettish, petulant, restive.

fret saw A saw with a long, narrow blade and fine teeth, used for fretwork, scrollwork, etc.

fret·ty¹ (fret'ē) *adj.* **·ti·er, ·ti·est** Fretful; peevish.

fret·ty² (fret'ē) *adj.* Of or like fretwork.

fret·work (fret'wûrk') *n.* 1. Ornamental openwork, usually composed of frets or interlaced parts. 2. A pattern, as of light and shade, resembling such openwork.

Freud (froid), **Sigmund**, 1856–1939, Austrian neurologist; founded modern theory of psychoanalysis.

Freu·di·an (froi'dē·ən) *adj.* Of, pertaining to, or conforming to the teachings of Sigmund Freud. — *n.* An adherent of the theories of Freud. — **Freu'di·an·ism** *n.*

Frey (frā) In Norse mythology, the god of agriculture, prosperity, and peace. Also **Freyr** (frār).

Frey·a (frā'ə) In Norse mythology, the goddess of love; daughter of Njord and sister of Frey. Compare FRIGG. Also **Frey'ja.**

Frey·tag (frī'täkh), **Gustav**, 1816–95, German novelist, playwright, and historian.

F.R.G.S. Fellow of the Royal Geographical Society.

Fri. Friday.

fri·a·ble (frī'ə·bəl) *adj.* Easily crumbled or pulverized. — **Syn.** See FRAGILE. [< F < L *friabilis* < *friare* to crumble] — **fri'a·bil'i·ty, fri'a·ble·ness** *n.*

fri·ar (frī'ər) *n.* A man who is a member of one of several religious orders, especially the mendicant orders, as the Dominicans or Franciscans. Abbr. *Fr.* [< OF *frere* < L *frater* brother]

fri·ar·bird (frī'ər·bûrd') *n.* An Australian honey-eating bird (genus *Philemon*) having a bare head: also called *four-o'clock.*

friar's lantern The ignis fatuus.

Friar Tuck In medieval English legend, a jolly friar who was one of Robin Hood's associates.

fri·ar·y (frī'ər·ē) *n. pl.* **·ar·ies** 1. A monastery, especially of a mendicant order. 2. A community of friars. — **Syn.** See CLOISTER.

frib·ble (frib'əl) *v.* **·bled, ·bling** *v.t.* 1. To fritter away. — *v.i.* 2. To act in a frivolous way; trifle. — *adj.* Of little importance; frivolous. — *n.* 1. Trifling action; frivolity. 2. A trifler. [Cf. FRIVOLOUS] — **frib'bler** *n.*

Fri·bourg (frī'bûrg *Fr.* frē·bōōr') A city in west central Switzerland; pop. 32,583 (1960). German *Freiburg.*

fric·an·deau (frik'ən·dō') *n. pl.* **·deaux** (-dōz) Veal or other meat stewed and served with sauce. Also **fric'an·do'.** [< F]

fric·as·see (frik'ə·sē') *n.* A dish of meat cut small, stewed, and served with gravy. — *v.t.* **·seed, ·see·ing** To make into a fricassee. [< F *fricassée*, orig. pp. of *fricasser* to sauté]

fric·a·tive (frik'ə·tiv) *Phonet. adj.* Of consonants, produced by the passage of breath through a narrow aperture with resultant audible friction, as (f), (v), (th). — *n.* A consonant so produced. Also *spirant, constrictive.* [< NL *fricativus* < L *fricare* to rub]

Frick (frik), **Henry Clay**, 1849–1919, U.S. industrialist, art collector, and philanthropist.

fric·tion (frik'shən) *n.* 1. The rubbing of one object against another. 2. *Mech. & Physics* Resistance encountered when the surface of one body moves upon or across that of another. 3. Conflict of opinions, differences in temperament, etc.; disagreement. [< F < L *frictio, -onis* < *fricare* to rub]

fric·tion·al (frik'shən·əl) *adj.* 1. Of, pertaining to, or like friction. 2. Produced or moved by friction. — **fric'tion·al·ly** *adv.*

friction clutch *Mech.* Any of various arrangements for transferring the motion of one system of parts to another by regulating the frictional contact between designated elements. Also **friction coupling.**

friction drive *Mech.* A drive in which motion is obtained by the frictional contact of surfaces, one being connected with the power system, the other with the transmission system.

friction layer *Meteorol.* The portion of the atmosphere, from 1,500 to 3,000 feet altitude, in which air flow is strongly affected by the rotational friction of the earth.

friction match A match tipped with a chemical mixture that ignites by friction.

friction tape Cotton tape impregnated with an adhesive, moisture-resisting compound, used in electrical work.

Fri·day (frī′dē, -dā) *n.* The sixth day of the week. Abbr. *F., Fr., Fri.* [OE *Frīgedæg* Frigg's day; trans. of LL *Veneris dies* day of Venus]

Fri·day (frī′dē, -dā) In Defoe's *Robinson Crusoe*, Crusoe's native servant and companion. — *n.* Any devoted or faithful attendant or helper: man *Friday*; girl *Friday.*

fridge (frij) *n. Informal* A refrigerator.

Fridt·jof Nan·sen Land (frit′yôf nän′sən) See FRANZ JOSEF LAND.

fried (frīd) Past tense and past participle of FRY. — *adj. Slang* Intoxicated.

fried cake A small cake or doughnut fried in deep fat.

friend (frend) *n.* **1.** One who is personally well known by oneself and for whom one has warm regard or affection; intimate. **2.** One with whom one is on speaking terms; an associate or acquaintance. **3.** One who belongs to the same nation, party, etc., as oneself; also, one with whom one is united in some purpose, cause, etc. **4.** A patron or supporter: a *friend* of the arts. — **to be** (or **make**) **friends** (**with**) To be on (or enter into) friendly terms (with). — *v.t. Archaic* To befriend. [OE *frēond*]
— **Syn.** *Friend, acquaintance, intimate, chum, pal,* and *crony* denote a person, usually not a relative, with whom one is on good terms. One has regard or affection for a *friend*, and the word is frequently used of very deep or close associations. One's feelings for an *acquaintance* are less warm than for a *friend* and have more of courtesy than of affection. Both *friend* and *acquaintance* may refer to persons of the opposite sex; the other synonyms almost always refer to a person of the same sex. A *friend* whose daily life is closely associated with one's own or for whom one has a particular regard is an *intimate* or, more colloquially, a *chum* or *pal. Chum* and *pal* imply a close and continuous association, especially between young people: a school *chum*, a boyhood *pal. Crony* is closely akin to *chum* in meaning but is chiefly used of older persons or of those with whom one maintains a long-continued friendship.

Friend (frend) *n.* A member of the Society of Friends; Quaker.

friend at court An influential person well disposed toward another and able to promote the other's interests.

friend·less (frend′lis) *adj.* Having no friends. — **friend′·less·ness** *n.*

friend·ly (frend′lē) *adj.* **·li·er, ·li·est 1.** Of, pertaining to, or typical of a friend. **2.** Well-disposed; not antagonistic. **3.** Acting as a friend; showing friendship: to be *friendly* with someone. **4.** Helpful; favorable: a *friendly* wind. — *adv.* In a friendly manner: also **friend′li·ly.** — **friend′li·ness** *n.*
— **Syn. 1, 3.** neighborly, affectionate, intimate. See AMICABLE. — **Ant.** unfriendly, antagonistic, hostile, indifferent.

Friendly Islands See TONGA.

friendly society *Brit.* A benefit society (which see).

friend·ship (frend′ship) *n.* **1.** The state or fact of being friends. **2.** Mutual liking and esteem. **3.** Friendly feelings or inclinations.
— **Syn.** *Friendship, amity,* and *comity* characterize the relation between persons, nations, etc. In *friendship* there is an affectionate desire to give sympathy and aid. *Amity* refers to the absence of discord rather than to positive affection or regard. *Comity* is applied to nations or parties more often than to individuals and denotes a courteous respect for the wishes or rights of others.

fri·er (frī′ər) See FRYER.

Frie·sian (frē′zhən) See FRISIAN.

Fries·land (frēz′lənd, -land) A Province of the northern Netherlands; 1,251 sq. mi.; pop. 521,750 (est. 1970); capital, Leeuwarden.

frieze[1] (frēz) *n.* **1.** The horizontal strip running between a cornice and architrave, either plain or decorated with sculpture, scrolls, etc. For illustration see ENTABLATURE. **2.** Any decorative horizontal strip, as along the top of a wall in a room. [< MF *frise* < Med.L *frisium,* ? ult. < L *Phrygium* (*opus*) Phrygian (work, ornament)]

frieze[2] (frēz) *n.* A coarse, woolen cloth with a shaggy nap. [< MF *frise* < *friser* to curl]

frig·ate (frig′it) *n.* **1.** A sailing war vessel of medium size, in use from about the 17th to the 19th centuries. **2.** A modern ship of about 1,400 tons, used on escort and patrol missions. **3.** *Poetic* A light, fast sailboat or rowboat. [< F *frégate* < Ital. *fregata*]

frigate bird Either of two large, rapacious, web-footed marine birds (genus *Fregata*) having hooked beaks, very long wings and tail feathers, and noted for great powers of flight: also called *man-of-war bird.*

FRIGATE

Frigg (frig) In Norse mythology, the wife of Odin and the goddess of marriage: often confused with *Freya.* Also **Frig·ga** (frig′ə).

fright (frīt) *n.* **1.** Sudden, violent alarm or fear. **2.** *Informal* One who or that which is ugly, shocking, or ridiculous. — **Syn.** See FEAR. — *v.t. Poetic* To frighten. [OE *fryhto, fyrhto*]

fright·en (frīt′n) *v.t.* **1.** To make suddenly alarmed, fearful, or terrified; scare. **2.** To drive, force, etc., (away, out, into, etc.) by scaring. — *v.i.* **3.** To become afraid.
— **Syn. 1.** *Frighten, scare, startle, terrify,* and *terrorize* mean to fill with fear or apprehension. *Frighten* suggests fear that paralyzes one's thoughts, motion, etc.: The clap of thunder *frightened* her. *Scare* is more informal and suggests a milder fear such as causes one to flee: to be *scared* by the screeching of an owl. Something sudden or surprising *startles:* to be *startled* by a rabbit running across one's path. *Terrify* suggests extreme fear for one's safety; *terrorize* is used of the deliberate incitement of fear as a method of intimidation: The violence of the storm *terrified* the sailors; Rebels *terrorized* the countryside. Compare FEAR, ALARM.

fright·ened (frīt′nd) *adj.* Filled with sudden alarm or fear.

fright·en·ing (frīt′n·ing, frīt′ning) *adj.* That fills with sudden alarm or fear. — **fright′en·ing·ly** *adv.*

fright·ful (frīt′fəl) *adj.* **1.** Repulsive, shocking, or contemptible. **2.** *Informal* Most distressing; very bad: a *frightful* headache. **3.** *Informal* Excessively great: a *frightful* number of losses. **4.** Such as fills with fright; alarming or terrifying. — **fright′ful·ly** *adv.* — **fright′ful·ness** *n.*
— **Syn.** fearful, dreadful, terrible, horrible, shocking, appalling.

frig·id (frij′id) *adj.* **1.** Bitterly cold. **2.** Lacking warmth of feeling; formal. **3.** Habitually lacking sexual feeling or response: said of women. [< L *frigidus* < *frigere* to be cold] — **frig′id·ly** *adv.* — **fri·gid·i·ty** (fri·jid′ə·tē), **frig′id·ness** *n.*

Frig·id·aire (frij′i·dâr′) An electric refrigerator: a trade name.

Frigid Zone See under ZONE.

frig·o·rif·ic (frig′ə·rif′ik) *adj.* Producing cold; chilling. Also **frig′o·rif′i·cal.** [< F *frigorifique* < L *frigorificus* < *frigor* cold + *facere* to make]

fri·jol (frē′hōl) *n. pl.* **fri·joles** (frē′hōlz, *Sp.* frē·hō′lās) A bean (genus *Phaseolus*) used as food, especially by Latin-Americans. Also **fri·jole** (frē′hōl, *Sp.* frē·hō′lā). [< Sp.]

frill (fril) *n.* **1.** An ornamental strip of lace, etc., gathered together and attached along one edge and left free along the other; ruffle. **2.** *U.S. Informal* Any showy or superfluous detail of dress, manner, etc. **3.** *Zool.* A ruff of feathers about the neck of some birds or of hair about the neck of some animals. **4.** *Bot.* A thin membrane about the stem of certain fungi near the pileus or hood: also called *armilla.* **5.** *Photog.* A wrinkling along the edge of a plate or film. — *v.t.* **1.** To make into a frill. **2.** To put frills on. — *v.i.* **3.** *Photog.* To wrinkle along the edge. [Origin uncertain]

frilled lizard (frild) An arboreal lizard (*Chlamydosaurus kingii*) of Australia, about three feet long, having a broad erectile membrane on each side of the neck.

frill·ing (fril′ing) *n.* **1.** Frills collectively. **2.** A material or trimming suitable for use in a frill or frills.

frill·y (fril′ē) *adj.* **frill·i·er, frill·i·est 1.** Having a frill or frills. **2.** Suggestive of a frill or frills.

Fri·maire (frē·mâr′) *n.* The third month of the Republican calendar. See (Republican) CALENDAR. [< F *frimas* frost]

Friml (frim′əl), **Rudolf,** born 1881, U.S. composer born in Prague.

fringe (frinj) *n.* **1.** An ornamental border or trimming of hanging cords, threads, etc. **2.** Something suggestive of such a border or trimming: a *fringe* of grass along a sidewalk. **3.** The area along the edge of something; margin: the *fringes* of a city. **4.** *Optics* One of the alternate light and dark bands produced by the interference of light, as in diffraction. — *v.t.* **fringed, fring·ing 1.** To provide with or as with a fringe. **2.** To constitute a fringe on or along. — *adj.* Outer; marginal: a *fringe* area. [< OF *frenge* < *fimbria* fringe]

fringe benefit Anything of value given an employee in addition to his salary or wages, as insurance, pension, etc.

fringed orchis A hardy orchid (genus *Habenara*) with tuberous roots and flowers fringed at the lips.

fringe land   *Canadian*   Land remote from a railroad terminus.

fringe lily   A perennial herb (genus *Thysanotus*) of the lily family, having clusters of purple flowers with fringed edges, native to the western part of Australia. Also **fringed violet.**

fringe tree   A small tree (*Chionanthus virginicus*) of the olive family, producing white flowers with long, drooping petals, found chiefly in the southern United States.

frin·gil·line (frin·jil′in, -in)   *adj.* Of, pertaining to, or suggestive of a family (*Fringillidae*) of small birds of which the finches and sparrows are characteristic.   [< L *fringilla* small bird + -INE¹]

fring·y (frin′jē)   *adj.* **fring·i·er, fring·i·est** 1. Resembling a fringe. 2. Having a fringe.

frip·per·y (frip′ər·ē)   *n. pl.* **·per·ies** 1. Cheap, flashy dress or ornamentation. 2. Showiness or affectation in speech, manner, etc. 3. A collection of trivialities.   [< F *friperie* < OF *freperie* < *frepe* rag]

Fris.   Frisian.

Frisch·es Haff (frish′əs häf′)   See VISTULA.

Fris·co (fris′kō)   *Informal* San Francisco, California: not used or approved by residents.

fri·sé (fri·zā′)   *n.* An upholstery or rug fabric faced with a thick pile of uncut loops or of cut and uncut loops in design.   [< F, orig. pp. of *friser* to curl]

fri·sette (fri·zet′)   See FRIZETTE.

fri·seur (frē·zœr′)   *n. French* A hairdresser.

Fris·ian (frizh′ən, frizh′ē·ən)   *adj.* Of or pertaining to the Dutch province of Friesland, its people, or their language.   — *n.* 1. A native or inhabitant of Friesland. 2. A member of an ancient Germanic tribe of the Netherlands. 3. The Germanic language of the Frisians, closely related to English. Also spelled *Friesian*. Abbr. *Fris., Frs.*

Frisian Islands   An island chain in the North Sea, off the coasts of the Netherlands, Germany, and Denmark, divided into the **West, North,** and **East Frisian Islands.**

frisk (frisk)   *v.i.* 1. To move or leap about playfully; gambol; frolic.   — *v.t.* 2. To move with quick jerks: a lamb *frisking* its tail. 3. *U.S. Slang* To search (someone) for a concealed weapon, etc., by quickly feeling the pockets and clothing; also, sometimes, to search (premises) for narcotics, etc. 4. *Slang* To rob of valuables found through searching in this way.   — *n.* 1. A playful skipping about; frolicking movement. 2. *U.S. Slang* A search of someone for a concealed weapon, etc.   [< obs. *frisk* lively < F *frisque*; ult. origin unknown]   — **frisk′er** *n.*

fris·ket (fris′kit)   *n. Printing* A light frame to hold the printing surface between the tympan and form of a platen press.   [< F *frisquette*]

frisk·y (fris′kē)   *adj.* **frisk·i·er, frisk·i·est** Lively or playful.   — **frisk′i·ly** *adv.*   — **frisk′i·ness** *n.*

frit (frit)   *n.* 1. The material formed by the partial fusion of sand and fluxes in the process of making glass. 2. A material formed by the partial or complete fusion of alkalis, lime, etc., used as the basis for certain glazes. 3. A similar material used in making soft porcelain.   — *v.t.* To make (a mixture of sand, alkalis, etc.) into frit. Also **fritt.**   [< F *fritte* < Ital. *fritta*, pp. of *friggere* to fry]

frit fly   A small fly (*Oscinosoma frit*), destructive to cereal grains.

frith (frith)   *n. Scot.* A firth.

frit·il·lar·y (frit′ə·ler′ē)   *n. pl.* **·lar·ies** 1. One of a genus (*Fritillaria*) of arctic or north-temperate bulbous plants of the lily family with checkered pale and dark purple flowers. 2. One of various butterflies (*Argynnis, Dione,* and related genera) having wings checkered with black and light brown.   [< NL *Fritillaria* < L *fritillus* dice box; from its checkered markings]

frit·ter¹ (frit′ər)   *v.t.* 1. To waste or squander little by little, as money, time, etc.: usually with *away.* 2. *Rare* To break or tear into small pieces.   — *n. Rare* A small piece or fragment.   [Cf. OF *fraiture* < L *fractura* < *frangere* to break]

frit·ter² (frit′ər)   *n.* A small cake made of plain batter or of corn, meat, fruit, etc., covered with batter and fried in deep fat.   [< F *friture* < L *frigere* to fry]

Fri·u·li (frē·ōō′lē)   A historical region of northern Italy on the Adriatic, now partly in Yugoslavia.

Fri·u·li·an (frē·ōō′lē·ən)   *n.* 1. One of a people of Celtic origin inhabiting the region of Friuli. 2. The Rhaeto-Romanic dialect of these people.

friv·ol (friv′əl)   *v.* **friv·oled** *or* **·olled, friv·ol·ing** *or* **·ol·ling** *Informal v.i.* 1. To behave frivolously; trifle.   — *v.t.* 2. To fritter: usually with *away.*   [Back formation < FRIVOLOUS]   — **friv′ol·er** *or* **friv′ol·ler** *n.*

fri·vol·i·ty (fri·vol′ə·tē)   *n. pl.* **·ties** 1. The quality or condition of being frivolous. 2. A frivolous act or thing.

friv·o·lous (friv′ə·ləs)   *adj.* 1. Lacking importance or significance; superficial; trivial; petty. 2. Inclined to levity; not serious; silly; fickle.   [< L *frivolus* silly]   — **friv′o·lous·ly** *adv.*   — **friv′o·lous·ness** *n.*

fri·zette (fri·zet′)   *n.* A frizzed or curled fringe of hair, often artificial, worn by women as a bang: also spelled *frisette.*   [< F, little curl]

frizz¹ (friz)   *v.t. & v.i.* 1. To form into tight, crisp curls, as the hair. 2. To make or form into small, tight tufts or knots, as the nap of cloth.   — *n.* 1. That which is frizzed, as hair. 2. The condition of being frizzed. Also **friz.**   [< F *friser* to curl]   — **friz′zer** *or* **friz′er** *n.*

frizz² (friz)   *v.t. & v.i.* To fry with a sizzling noise.   [< FRY + imit. suffix]

friz·zle¹ (friz′əl)   *v.t. & v.i.* **·zled, ·zling** 1. To fry or cook with a sizzling noise. 2. To make or become curled or crisp, as by frying.   [Blend of FRY and SIZZLE; ? infl. by FRIZZLE²]

friz·zle² (friz′əl)   *v.t. & v.i.* **·zled, ·zling** To form into tight curls, as the hair; frizz.   — *n.* A crisp curl; frizz.   [? Freq. of obs. *frieze* produce a nap on < MF *frise* < *friser* to curl]

friz·zly (friz′lē)   *adj.* Having tight, crisp curls.

frizz·y (friz′ē)   *adj.* **frizz·i·er, frizz·i·est** Frizzly.   — **friz′zi·ly** *adv.*   — **friz′zi·ness** *n.*

Frl.   Fräulein.

fro (frō)   *adv.* Away from; back: used in the phrase *to* and *fro* (which see).   — *prep. Scot.* From.   [< ON *frā* from]

Fro·bish·er (frō′bish·ər), **Sir Martin,** 1535?–94, English seafarer and explorer.

Frobisher Bay   An inlet of the Atlantic in SE Baffin Island.

frock (frok)   *n.* 1. A long, loose-fitting robe with wide sleeves worn by monks; also, the clerical or priestly state. 2. Any of several types of garments; as: **a** A woman's or girl's dress. **b** A coarse, loose outer garment worn by laborers, peasants, etc.; smock. **c** A woolen jersey formerly worn by sailors. **d** Formerly, in English military service, a coat similar to a frock coat. **e** A frock coat.   — *v.t.* 1. To furnish with or clothe in a frock. 2. To invest with ecclesiastical office.   [< OF *froc*; ult. origin unknown]

frock coat   A man's dress coat, worn especially in the 19th century, having knee-length skirts and a tight-fitting, double-breasted upper part.

froe (frō)   *n.* A heavy knife with the blade at right angles to the handle, used for splitting off shingles, etc., from a block of wood: also spelled *frow.*   [Appar. < FROWARD, in sense "turned away," with ref. to the blade]

Froe·bel (frā′bəl, *Ger.* frœ′bəl), **Friedrich Wilhelm August,** 1782–1852, German educator; founded the kindergarten system.

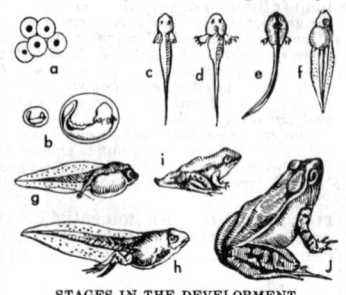

STAGES IN THE DEVELOPMENT OF THE FROG
a Eggs. *b* Embryo. *c–h* Development of the tadpole. *i* Young frog. *j* Adult frog.

frog (frog, frôg)   *n.* 1. One of a genus (*Rana*) of small, tailless, web-footed animals with short front legs and large, strong hind legs adapted to leaping. 2. One of several amphibians, as a tree frog, resembling these animals. 3. A slight irritation, accumulation of phlegm, etc., producing difficulty or hoarseness in speaking: also **frog in the** (or **one's**) **throat.** 4. A triangular prominence in the sole of a horse's foot. 5. A section of intersecting railroad tracks designed to permit wheels to pass over the junction without difficulty. 6. An ornamental piece of braid or cord, as on a jacket, often looped, so as to permit passage of a button. 7. A small holder designed to keep flowers upright, as in a bowl. 8. *Slang* A Frenchman: an offensive term.   — *v.i.* **frogged, frog·ging** To hunt frogs.   [OE *frogga*]

frog·eye (frog′ī′, frôg′ī)   *n.* A disease of tobacco leaves.

frog·fish (frog′fish′, frôg′-)   *n. pl.* **·fish, ·fish·es** The angler (def. 2).

frog·gy (frog′ē, frôg′ē)   *adj.* **·gi·er, ·gi·est** 1. Pertaining to or full of frogs. 2. Suggestive of a frog.

frog·hop·per (frog′hop′ər, frôg′-)   *n.* Any of several small, squat, leaping insects (family *Cercopidae*) that suck plant juices and whose larvae are often enclosed in a frothy mass: also called *spittle insect.*

frog kick   In swimming, a kick in which the legs are drawn up with the heels together and knees apart, extended outward, and brought together with great force.

frog lily   The yellow pond lily. See under POND LILY.

frog·man (frog′mən, -man′, frôg′-)   *n. pl.* **·men** (-mən, -men′)   An underwater reconnaissance and demolition expert, able to swim and operate under water using a scuba.

frog·mouth (frog′mouth′, frôg′-)   *n.* An East Indian nocturnal bird (genus *Podargus*) with a very broad, deeply cleft bill: found also in Australia and locally named *mopoke*: also called *goatsucker.*

frog spit   1. Cuckoo spit (which see). 2. A green freshwater alga whose filaments form foamlike floating masses.

Froh·man (frō′mən), **Charles,** 1860–1915, U.S. theatrical producer and manager.

Frois·sart (froi′särt, *Fr.* frwä·sàr′), **Jean,** 1337?–1410?, French chronicler.

frol·ic (frol'ik) n. 1. Merriness; gaiety. 2. A gay occasion or diversion. 3. A playful antic or trick. — v.i. ·icked, ·ick·ing 1. To move about or behave in a lighthearted or frisky way; cut capers. 2. To play tricks; be prankish. — adj. Archaic Merrily playful or prankish. [< Du. vrolijk merry < MDu. vro glad] — frol'ick·er n.

frol·ic·some (frol'ik·səm) adj. Gay and lighthearted. Also **frol'ick·y**. — frol'ic·some·ly adv. — frol'ic·some·ness n.

from (frum, from; unstressed frəm) prep. 1. Starting at (a particular place or time): the plane from New York; from six o'clock on. 2. With (a particular person, place or thing) as the source, origin, or instrument: a letter from your mother. 3. Out of (a holder, container, etc.): He drew a pistol from his holster. 4. Out of the control or authority of: He escaped from his captors. 5. Out of the totality of: to subtract 3 from 8. 6. At a distance in relation to: far from the city. 7. Beyond the possibility of: He kept her from falling. 8. By reason of; because of: to collapse from exhaustion. 9. As being other or another than: He couldn't tell me from my brother. Abbr. fm., fr. [OE fram, from]

fro·men·ty (frō'mən·tē) See FRUMENTY.

frond (frond) n. Bot. 1. A leaflike expansion in which the functions of stem and leaf are not fully differentiated, as the so-called leaf of ferns and seaweeds. For illustration see FERN. 2. A large leaf of tropical plants and trees, as of the palm tree. [< L frons, frondis leaf]

Fronde (frônd) n. A political party established in France during the minority of Louis XIV, opposing the court and Cardinal Mazarin, and precipitating the civil wars of 1648, 1650, and 1651. [< F, a sling]

frond·ed (fron'did) adj. Provided with fronds; leafy.

fron·des·cence (fron·des'əns) n. Bot. 1. The period or act of leafing. 2. Leaves collectively. — fron·des'cent adj.

front (frunt) n. 1. The part or side of an object or body that faces forward or is viewed as facing forward; fore part. 2. An area or position located directly ahead or before: He stood in front of her. 3. An area or position of principal or most important activity: to be at the front of scientific research. 4. Mil. a The lateral space from flank to flank occupied by a unit. b The line of contact of two opposing forces. 5. The outer side of a building, usually the side where the main entrance is. 6. An extent of land lying directly along a lake, road, etc. 7. A group or movement uniting various individuals with a common aim: the labor front. 8. One chosen to head a group, movement, etc., to give it prestige, often lacking real authority. 9. An apparently respectable person, group, business, etc., used for cloaking objectionable or illegal activities. 10. One's bearing or attitude in facing a particular situation, problem, etc.: to put on a bold front; also, sometimes, impudence. 11. Informal An outward air or pretense of wealth, social importance, etc. 12. A detachable, starched part of a man's formal dress shirt covering the chest. 13. The section of a theater in which the audience sits. 14. In hotels, the bellhop first in line. 15. Meteorol. The fore part of a mass of warm or cold air; also, the line of separation between a mass of warm air and a mass of cold air. 16. Phonet. The part of the tongue immediately behind the blade and directly below the hard palate. 17. Brit. A boardwalk along a beach. 18. Poetic The beginning of a season, month, etc. 19. Archaic The forehead; also, the face. — adj. 1. Of, pertaining to, or directed toward the front. 2. Located on, in, or at the front. 3. Phonet. Describing those vowels produced with the front of the tongue raised toward the hard palate, as (ē) in feed. — Front! In hotels, a call directing the first available bellhop to come forward and assist a guest. — v.t. 1. To face toward. 2. To meet face to face, especially with defiance. 3. To provide with a front. 4. To serve as a front for. — v.i. 5. To face toward something. [< OF < L frons, frontis forehead]

front·age (frun'tij) n. 1. The front part of a lot or building; also, the linear extent of this. 2. The direction in which something faces; exposure. 3. Land adjacent to a street, body of water, etc. 4. Land lying between the front of a building and a road, river, etc.

fron·tal[1] (frun'təl) adj. 1. Of or pertaining to the front. 2. Of or pertaining to the forehead or the frontal bone. — n. Anat. A bone of the anterior part of the skull, forming the skeleton of the forehead. For illustration see SKULL. [< NL frontalis < L frons, frontis forehead] — fron'tal·ly adv.

fron·tal[2] (frun'təl) n. 1. Eccl. A detachable hanging to cover the front of an altar. 2. Archit. A façade. 3. Obs. A band, ornament, etc., for the forehead. [< OF frontel < LL frontale < L frons, frontis forehead, front]

front bench Brit. In Parliament, the seats closest to the Speaker, reserved for the party leaders.

Fron·te·nac (fron'tə·nak, Fr. frôn·tə·nåk'), Comte Louis de Buade de, 1620–98, French governor of Canada 1672–82, 1689–98.

front foot U.S. A foot of land measured along the front of a lot.

fron·tier (frun·tir') n. 1. The part of a nation's territory lying along the border of another country. 2. The part of a settled region lying along the border of an unsettled region. 3. A new or unexplored area of thought or knowledge. — adj. Of or pertaining to a frontier. [< OF frontiere < front. See FRONT.]

fron·tiers·man (frun·tirz'mən) n. pl. ·men (-mən) One who lives on the frontier.

fron·tis·piece (frun'tis·pēs', fron'-) n. 1. A picture or drawing on the page facing the title page of a book; also, formerly, the title page itself. 2. Archit. a A façade; also, a highly decorated section of a façade. b A pediment. [Earlier frontispice < F < Med.L frontispicium face < L frons, frontis forehead + specere to look at; infl. in form by piece]

front·let (frunt'lit) n. 1. Something worn on or across the forehead; as: a A band of fabric forming part of a medieval headdress. b A phylactery. c A medieval armored plate covering the forehead and nose of a horse: also front·stall (frunt'·stôl'). 2. The forehead of an animal. 3. A bird's forehead as distinguished by coloration, etc. 4. Eccl. A decorative piece of material covering or bordering a frontal. [< OF frontelet, dim. of frontel. See FRONTAL[2].]

front line The foremost main line or space occupied by troops in war.

front matter Printing The pages preceding the actual text of a book or pamphlet, as the title page, table of contents, preface, etc., usually paginated in lower-case Roman numerals: also called preliminaries.

fronto- combining form 1. Anat. Pertaining to the frontal bone or frontal region of the skull: frontomalar. 2. Meteorol. Pertaining to a front: frontogenesis. [< L frons, frontis forehead, front]

front office The main office, or office of the highest ranking executive, in an organization.

fron·to·gen·e·sis (frun'tō·jen'ə·sis) n. Meteorol. The development of a new front between cold air and warm air masses, with corresponding changes in weather conditions.

fron·tol·y·sis (frun·tol'ə·sis) n. Meteorol. The disappearance or subsidence of a front.

fron·to·ma·lar (frun'tō·mā'lər) adj. Anat. Pertaining to the frontal and cheek bones.

front-page (frunt'pāj') adj. Appearing on or important enough to appear on the first page of a newspaper.

Front Range The easternmost range of the Rocky Mountains, in Colorado and Wyoming; highest peak, Grays Peak, 14,274 ft.

frore (frôr, frōr) adj. Archaic Frosty; frozen. [Early pp. of FREEZE]

frosh (frosh) n. pl. frosh U.S. Slang A college freshman.

frost (frôst, frost) n. 1. A feathery deposit of ice formed on the ground or on the surface of exposed objects by dew or water vapor that has frozen. 2. Rime. 3. Frozen moisture within a porous substance, as in the ground. 4. Temperature cold enough to freeze. 5. The act of freezing. 6. Coldness of manner. 7. Slang A new book, etc., given a cold reception by the public. — v.t. 1. To cover with frost. 2. To damage or kill by frost. 3. To produce a frostlike surface or effect on (glass, etc.). 4. To apply frosting to, as a cake. [OE] — frost'less adj.

Frost (frôst, frost), Robert (Lee), 1875–1963, U.S. poet.

frost·bite (frôst'bīt', frost'-) n. The condition of having some part of the body, as the ears or fingers, partially frozen, often resulting in gangrene. — v.t. ·bit, ·bit·ten, ·bit·ing To injure, as a part of the body, by partial freezing.

frost·bit·ten (frôst'bit'n, frost'-) adj. Affected by frostbite.

frost·ed (frôs'tid, fros'-) adj. 1. Covered with frost. 2. Covered with frosting, as a cake. 3. Presenting a surface resembling frost, as translucent glass. 4. Frostbitten.

frost·fish (frôst'fish', frost'-) n. pl. ·fish or ·fish·es The tomcod.

frost·flow·er (frôst'flou'ər, frost'-) n. A small bulbous plant (Milla biflora) of the lily family, bearing starlike, fragrant, white, waxy flowers, native in the SW United States; also, its flower.

frost fog Meteorol. A pogonip.

frost·ing (frôs'ting, fros'-) n. 1. A mixture of sugar, egg white, butter, etc., cooked or beaten together, and used to cover cakes. 2. The rough or lusterless surface produced on metal, glass, etc., in imitation of frost. 3. Coarsely powdered glass, etc., used for decorative work.

frost line The depth to which frost penetrates the ground.

frost·work (frôst'wûrk', frost'-) n. 1. Hoarfrost deposited in delicate tracery, as on glass or exposed objects. 2. Ornamentation, as on metal, in imitation of such an effect.

frost·y (frôs'tē, fros'-) adj. frost·i·er, frost·i·est 1. Attended with frost; freezing: frosty weather. 2. Composed of or covered with frost. 3. Lacking warmth of manner. 4. Having white hair; hoary. — frost'i·ly adv. — frost'i·ness n.

froth (frôth, froth) n. 1. A mass of bubbles resulting from fermentation or agitation; a colloid system of gas dispersed in a liquid. 2. Any foamy excretion or exudation, as of saliva. 3. Any light, unsubstantial, or trivial thing, as a foolish conversation. — *v.t.* **1.** To cause to foam. **2.** To cover with froth. **3.** To give forth in the form of foam. — *v.i.* **4.** To form or give off froth; foam. [< ON *frodha*]

froth·y (frô′thē, froth′ē) *adj.* **froth·i·er, froth·i·est 1.** Consisting of, covered with, or full of froth; foamy. **2.** Unsubstantial or trivial. — **froth′i·ly** *adv.* — **froth′i·ness** *n.*

Froude (frōod), **James Anthony,** 1818–94, English historian.

frou-frou (frōo′frōo′) *n.* **1.** A rustling, as of silk; swish. **2.** *Informal* Affected elegance; fanciness. [< F]

frounce (frouns) *Archaic v.t. & v.i.* **frounced, frounc·ing** To curl, wrinkle, or pleat. — *n.* Empty display; affectation. [< OF *froncier* < *fronce* fold, ? < Gmc.]

frow (frō) See FROE.

fro·ward (frō′ərd, -wərd) *adj.* Disobedient; intractable. [< FRO + WARD] — **fro′ward·ly** *adv.* — **fro′ward·ness** *n.*

frown (froun) *v.i.* **1.** To contract the brow, as in displeasure or concentration; scowl. **2.** To look with distaste: with *on* or *upon.* — *v.t.* **3.** To make known (one's displeasure, disgust, etc.) by contracting one's brow. **4.** To silence, rebuke, etc., by or as by a frown. — *n.* **1.** A wrinkling of the brow, as in displeasure; scowl. **2.** Any showing of displeasure. [< OF *froignier*, prob. < Gmc.] — **frown′ing·ly** *adv.*

frowst·y (frous′tē) *adj.* **frowst·i·er, frowst·i·est** *Brit. Informal* Musty; stuffy. [Cf. OF *frouste* decayed]

frow·zy (frou′zē) *adj.* **·zi·er, ·zi·est 1.** Slovenly in appearance; slatternly; unkempt. **2.** Having a disagreeable smell; musty. Also **frou′zy, frow′sy.** [? Akin to FROWSTY]

froze (frōz) Past tense of FREEZE.

fro·zen (frō′zən) Past participle of FREEZE. — *adj.* **1.** Changed into or covered with ice, as a river. **2.** Killed or damaged by cold. **3.** Extremely cold, as a climate or region. **4.** Clogged with ice, as water pipes. **5.** Preserved through quick freezing: *frozen* food. **6.** Cold and unfeeling in manner, behavior, etc. **7.** Made rigid or immobile: *frozen* with fear. **8.** *Econ.* **a** Arbitrarily maintained at a given level: said of prices, wages, etc. **b** Not readily convertible into cash: *frozen* assets. **9.** Made solid by cold: *frozen* alcohol.

frozen sleep *Med.* Cryotherapy.

FRS Federal Reserve System.

F.R.S. Fellow of the Royal Society (scientific).

F.R.S.A. Fellow of the Royal Society of Arts.

frt. Freight.

Fruc·ti·dor (fruk′ti·dôr, *Fr.* frük·tē·dôr′) *n.* The twelfth month of the French republican calendar. See (Republican) CALENDAR. [< F < L *fructus* fruit + Gk. *dōron* gift]

fruc·tif·er·ous (fruk·tif′ər·əs, frōok-) *adj.* Fruit-bearing.

fruc·ti·fy (fruk′tə·fī, frōok′-) *v.* **·fied, ·fy·ing** *v.t.* **1.** To make fruitful; fertilize. — *v.i.* **2.** To bear fruit. [< F *fructifier* < L *fructificare* < *fructus* fruit + *facere* to do, make] — **fruc′ti·fi·ca′tion** *n.*

fruc·tose (fruk′tōs, frōok′-) *n. Biochem.* A very sweet levorotatory monosaccharide, $C_6H_{12}O_6$, occurring in fruits: also called *fruit sugar, levulose.* [< L *fructus* fruit + -OSE²]

fruc·tu·ous (fruk′chōo·əs, frōok′-) *adj.* Productive; fertile; fruitful. [< OF < L *fructuosus* < *fructus* fruit]

fru·gal (frōo′gəl) *adj.* **1.** Exercising economy; avoiding waste; saving. **2.** Costing little money; meager; spare: a *frugal* meal. [< L *frugalis* < *frugi* temperate, orig. dative singular of *frux* food] — **fru′gal·ly** *adv.* — **fru′gal·ness** *n.* — **Syn. 1.** *Frugal, sparing, thrifty,* and *economical* mean careful in expenditure. The *frugal* man spends only for those things he considers necessary and regularly does without luxuries. *Sparing* describes the man who spends little, whether for necessities or luxuries. A *thrifty* person seeks both to earn and to save; *economical* refers to careful management of expenditures so as to avoid waste. — **Ant.** wasteful, prodigal.

fru·gal·i·ty (frōo·gal′ə·tē) *n. pl.* **·ties 1.** Strict economy; thrift. **2.** Wise and sparing use: *frugality* of praise.

fru·giv·o·rous (frōo·jiv′ər·əs) *adj.* Fruit-eating. [< L *frux, frugis* fruit + -VOROUS]

fruit (frōot) *n.* **1.** *Bot.* **a** The pulpy, usually edible mass covering the seeds of various plants and trees, being either *fleshy,* as in apples or oranges, *drupaceous* (having an inner stone containing the seed), as in plums or cherries, or *dry,* as in nuts or peas. **b** In flowering plants, the mature seed vessel and its contents, together with accessory parts. **c** In spore plants, the spores with their enveloping or accessory organs. ◆ In popular usage, *fruit* is usually applied only to the fleshy, juicy, and more or less sweet products of plants and trees, including many that are seedless, but not to other fleshy and juicy products, as the cucumber and tomato, which are technically fruits but are called *vegetables.* **2.** Any useful plant product, as cotton or flax. **3.** The outcome, consequence, or result of some action, effort, situation, etc.: the *fruit* of labor. **4.** *Archaic* The young borne by man or animals. **5.** *U.S.*

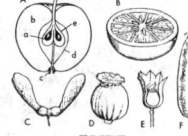

FRUIT

A Cross section of an apple: *a* Seeds, *b* Pulp, *c* Limb of calyx, *d* Core, *e* Carpels. *B* Transverse section of an orange. *C* Schizocarpous fruit of the maple. *D* Ripe poppy capsule. *E* Pyxis of henbane with outer carpel removed. *F* Legume of pea.

Slang A homosexual. — *v.i. & v.t.* To produce or cause to produce fruit. [< OF < L *fructus* < *frui* to enjoy]

fruit·age (frōo′tij) *n.* **1.** Fruit collectively. **2.** The state, process, or time of producing fruit. **3.** Any result or effect.

fruit·cake (frōot′kāk′) *n.* A rich, spiced cake containing nuts, raisins, citron, and other dried fruits.

fruit cup A mixture of cut fruits, fresh or preserved, served in a cup or glass as an appetizer or dessert.

fruit·er (frōo′tər) *n.* **1.** A ship that carries fruit; also, a fruit dealer or grower. Also *Brit.* **fruit′er·er. 2.** A fruit-bearing tree or plant.

fruit fly 1. One of various flies (family *Trypetidae*) whose larvae attack fruit; especially, a member of the tropical genera, *Ceratitis* and *Anastrepha.* **2.** A fly (genus *Drosophila*) whose larvae feed on fruit and whose species are used in research in genetics: also called *drosophila.*

fruit·ful (frōot′fəl) *adj.* **1.** Bearing fruit or offspring abundantly; prolific; productive. **2.** Favoring or causing productiveness: *fruitful* showers. **3.** Producing results: a *fruitful* discussion. — **fruit′ful·ly** *adv.* — **fruit′ful·ness** *n.*

fru·i·tion (frōo·ish′ən) *n.* **1.** The accomplishment or realization of things worked for or hoped for; fulfillment. **2.** The enjoyment of this. **3.** The bearing of fruit. [< OF < LL *fruitio, -onis* enjoyment < L *frui* to enjoy]

fruit·less (frōot′lis) *adj.* **1.** Yielding no fruit; barren. **2.** Ineffectual; useless; unproductive. — **Syn.** See FUTILE. — **fruit′less·ly** *adv.* — **fruit′less·ness** *n.*

fruit rot Leaf spot, a plant disease.

fruit sugar Fructose.

fruit tree A tree producing edible fruit.

fruit·y (frōo′tē) *adj.* **fruit·i·er, fruit·i·est 1.** Of, pertaining to, or suggestive of fruit. **2.** Having the flavor, juiciness, richness, etc., of fruit. **3.** Unctuous, ingratiating. **4.** *U.S. Slang* **a** Homosexual. **b** Crazy; wacky. — **fruit′i·ness** *n.*

fru·men·ta·ceous (frōo′mən·tā′shəs) *adj.* Of, pertaining to, or suggestive of cereal grain, as wheat. [< LL *frumentaceus* < L *frumentum* grain]

fru·men·ty (frōo′mən·tē) *n. Brit.* A dish of hulled wheat boiled in milk and sweetened with sugar, etc.: also *fromenty, furmenty, furmety.* [< OF *frumentee* < L *frumentum* grain]

frump (frump) *n.* A dowdy, sometimes ill-tempered woman. [? < MDu. *frompelen,* var. of *verrompelen* to wrinkle]

frump·ish (frum′pish) *adj.* **1.** Dowdy or old-fashioned in dress. **2.** Ill-tempered; peevish. Also **frump′y.** — **frump′ish·ly** *adv.* — **frump′ish·ness** *n.*

Frun·ze (frōon′zyə) The capital of the Kirghiz S.S.R. in the northern part; pop. 431,000 (est. 1970).

frus·trate (frus′trāt) *v.t.* **·trat·ed, ·trat·ing 1.** To keep (someone) from doing or achieving something; baffle the efforts, hopes, or desires of. **2.** To keep, as plans or schemes, from being fulfilled; bring to nothing; check. — **Syn.** See BAFFLE. — *adj. Archaic* Frustrated. [< L *frustratus,* pp. of *frustrari* to disappoint < *frustra* in vain] — **frus′trat·er** *n.*

frus·tra·tion (frus·trā′shən) *n.* **1.** The state of being frustrated or thwarted. **2.** Something that frustrates.

frus·tule (frus′chōol) *n. Bot.* The siliceous shell of a diatom. [< F < L *frustulum,* dim. of L *frustum* small piece, bit]

frus·tum (frus′təm) *n. pl.* **·tums** or **·ta** (-tə) *Geom.* **1.** That which is left of a cone or pyramid after cutting off the upper part along a plane parallel to the base. **2.** That part of a solid included between any two planes, usually parallel planes. [< L, fragment]

FRUSTUM OF A PYRAMID

fru·tes·cent (frōo·tes′ənt) *adj.* **1.** Becoming shrubby. **2.** Resembling a shrub. [< L *frutex* shrub + -ESCENT] — **fru·tes′cence** *n.*

fru·ti·cose (frōo′ti·kōs) *adj.* Having the nature or appearance of a shrub. [< L *fruticosus* < *frutex, fruticis* shrub]

fry¹ (frī) *v.t. & v.i.* **fried, fry·ing 1.** To cook in hot fat, usually over direct heat. **2.** *Archaic* To seethe or cause to seethe. — *n. pl.* **fries 1.** A dish of anything fried. **2.** A social occasion, usually a picnic, at which foods are fried and eaten: a fish *fry.* [< F *frier* < L *frigere*]

fry² (frī) *n. pl.* **fry 1.** Very young fish; also, small adult fish when together in large numbers. **2.** The young of certain animals, as of frogs, when produced in very large quantities. **3.** Young children, etc. See SMALL FRY. [< ON *frio* seed]

Fry (frī), **Christopher,** born 1907, English dramatist. — **Roger Eliot,** 1866–1934, English art critic.

fry·er (frī′ər) *n.* **1.** One who or that which fries. **2.** A young chicken suitable for frying. Also spelled *frier.*

frying pan A shallow metal pan with a long handle, for frying food.

f.s. Foot-second.

Fs *Meteorol.* Fractostratus.

F-stop (ef′stop′) *n.* F number.

ft. 1. Feet; foot. **2.** Fort. **3.** Fortification; fortified.

FTC or **F.T.C.** Federal Trade Commission.

fth. or **fthm.** Fathom.

ft-lb Foot-pound(s).

Fu·ad I (fōo·äd′), 1868–1936, sultan of Egypt 1917–22, first king of modern Egypt 1922–36: original name **Ahmed Fuad Pasha.**

fub·sy (fub′zē) *adj.* **·si·er, ·si·est** *Obs.* Plump; chubby.

Fu-chien (foo′kyen′) See FUKIEN.

Fu-chou, Fuchow (foo′chou′) See FOOCHOW.

fuch·sia (fyoo′sha, -shē·a) *n.* **1.** Any of various plants (genus *Fuchsia*) of the evening-primrose family, with red, pink, white, or purple, drooping, four-petaled flowers. **2.** The California fuchsia (which see). **3.** A bright bluish red, the typical color of the fuchsia. [after Leonhard *Fuchs*, 1501–66, German botanist]

fuch·sin (fook′sin) *n.* *Chem.* One of two deep red or violet dye compounds obtained from aniline, **fuchsin acid** or **fuchsin basic**, used as a bacterial stain, dye, etc.: also called *magenta*. Also **fuch·sine** (-sin, -sēn). [< FUCHSIA + -IN]

fu·coid (fyoo′koid) *adj.* **1.** Of, pertaining to, or resembling certain seaweeds (family *Fucaceae*), especially the rockweeds. **2.** Containing fucoids or impressions of them. Also **fu·coi′dal, fu′cous.** — *n.* **1.** A large, coarse, olive-brown seaweed. **2.** A plant that resembles a seaweed. [< FUC(US) + -OID]

fu·cus (fyoo′kas) *n.* *pl.* **·ci** (-sī) or **·cus·es 1.** Any of a genus (*Fucus*) of algae typified by certain large olive-brown seaweeds, as the rockweeds. **2.** *Obs.* A paint or dye. [< L]

fud·dle (fud′l) *v.* **·dled, ·dling** *v.t.* **1.** To confuse or make stupid with or as with liquor. — *v.i.* **2.** To tipple. [Cf. dial. G *fuddeln* to swindle]

fud·dy-dud·dy (fud′ē-dud′ē) *n.* *pl.* **-dud·dies** *Informal* **1.** An old-fashioned person. **2.** A faultfinding, fussy person. [Varied reduplication, ? < dial. E *fud* the buttocks]

fudge (fuj) *n.* **1.** A soft, cooked confection made of butter, sugar, chocolate, etc. **2.** Humbug; nonsense: commonly used as an interjection. **3.** *Printing* **a** A small section of print containing late news or other matter, that may be inserted in a newspaper without resetting the entire page. **b** An attachment used to print such sections. **c** The news printed. — *v.t.* **fudged, fudg·ing** To make, adjust, or fit together in a clumsy or dishonest manner. [Origin uncertain]

Fu·e·gi·an (fyoo·ē′jē·an, fwä′jē·an) *adj.* Of or pertaining to Tierra del Fuego or its people. — *n.* An Indian of Tierra del Fuego.

Fuehr·er (fyoor′ar, *Ger.* fü′rar) See FÜHRER.

fu·el (fyoo′al) *n.* **1.** Combustible matter used as a source of heat energy or to feed a fire. **2.** Whatever sustains or heightens emotion, etc. — *v.t.* & *v.i.* **fu·eled** or **·elled, fu·el·ing** or **·el·ling** To supply with or take in fuel. [< OF *fouaille* < LL *focalia* < L *focus* hearth] — **fu′el·er** or **fu′el·ler** *n.*

fuel cell Any of various devices for the generation of electrical energy from the chemical energy of continuously supplied fuels, chiefly hydrogen and oxygen, in contact with a suitable electrolyte.

fuel injection The providing of fuel to an engine by direct injection under pressure into the cylinders or intake passages.

fuel oil Any combustible oil used as fuel.

fu·ga·cious (fyoo-gā′shas) *adj.* **1.** Fleeting; transitory; volatile. **2.** *Bot.* Falling very early, as the petals of a poppy. [< L *fugax, fugacis* < *fugere* to flee] — **fu·ga′cious·ly** *adv.* — **fu·ga′cious·ness, fu·gac·i·ty** (fyoo-gas′a-tē) *n.*

fu·gal (fyoo′gal) *adj.* *Music* Of or pertaining to a fugue.

Fug·ger (foog′ar) A Swabian family of merchants and financiers prominent in 16th-century Europe, especially **Raymund**, 1489–1535, and his brother **Anton**, 1493–1560.

fu·gi·o (fyoo′jē·ō) *n.* A copper coin, the first U.S. coinage authorized by Congress, 1787, bearing the word *fugio* beside a meridian sun. [< L, I flee]

fu·gi·tive (fyoo′ja·tiv) *adj.* **1.** Fleeing or having fled, as from pursuit, arrest, etc. **2.** Not fixed or lasting; transient; fleeting. **3.** Treating of subjects of passing interest; occasional. **4.** Wandering about; shifting; vagabond. — *n.* **1.** One who or that which flees, as from pursuit, danger, etc.; runaway. **2.** An exile or refugee. [< F *fugitif* < L *fugitivus* < *fugere* to flee] — **fu′gi·tive·ly** *adv.* — **fu′gi·tive·ness** *n.*

FUGIO

fu·gle (fyoo′gal) *v.i.* **·gled, ·gling** *Rare* **1.** To act as fugleman. **2.** To make signals.

fu·gle·man (fyoo′gal·man) *n.* *pl.* **·men** (-man) **1.** Formerly, a soldier who stood in front of men and led them in military exercises. **2.** One who leads or sets an example in anything. [< G *flügelmann* < *flügel* wing + *mann* man]

fugue (fyoog) *n.* **1.** *Music* **a** A contrapuntal composition in which a theme is introduced by one part, repeated by other parts, and subjected to complex development. **b** The technique of fugal composition. **2.** *Psychiatry* A form of amnesia in which an individual suffers loss of memory, assumes a different identity, and performs rational actions that are forgotten upon recovery. [< F < Ital. *fuga* < L, flight]

Füh·rer (fyoor′ar, *Ger.* fü′rar) *n.* *German* Leader: a title applied to Adolf Hitler by his adherents: also spelled *Fuehrer*.

Fu·ji (foo·jē) The highest peak of Japan, an extinct volcano on Honshu island; 12,389 ft. Also **Fu·ji-no-ya·ma** (foo·jē·nō-yä′mä), **Fu·ji·san** (foo·jē·sän), **Fu·ji·ya·ma** (foo·jē-yä·mä).

Fu·kien (foo′kyen′) A Province of SE China; 45,000 sq. mi.; pop. 14,650,000 (est. 1957); capital, Foochow. Also *Fu-chien.*

Fu·ku·o·ka (foo-koo-ō·kä) A city on northern Kyushu island, Japan; pop. 812,000 (est. 1968).

-ful *suffix* **1.** Full of; characterized by: *joyful.* **2.** Able to; tending to: *helpful.* **3.** Having the character of: *manful.* **4.** The quantity or number that will fill: *cupful.* ♦ Nouns ending in *-ful* form the plural by adding *-s*, as in *cupfuls, spoonfuls.* [OE *-full, -ful* < *full* full]

Fu·la (foo′lä) *n.* **1.** One of a Moslem people of the Sudan, basically of Hamitic stock mixed with Negro. **2.** The Sudanic language of these people. Also **Fu′lah.**

Ful·bright Act (fool′brīt) A Congressional act of 1946 that provides for a large part of the proceeds from the sale of United States war surplus property in foreign countries to be used for financing the mutual exchange of students, teachers, and other cultural workers: named for **James William Fulbright**, born 1905, U.S. Senator.

ful·crum (fool′kram) *n.* *pl.* **·crums** or **·cra** (-kra) **1.** The support on which a lever rests or about which it turns when raising a weight. For illustration see LEVER. **2.** Any prop or support. **3.** *Usually pl. Zool.* In many ganoid fishes, one of the rows of spinelike scales along the forward edge of the median and paired fins. [< L, bedpost < *fulcire* to prop up]

Ful·da (fool′dä), **Ludwig**, 1862–1939, German playwright.

ful·fill (fool-fil′) *v.t.* **·filled, ·fill·ing 1.** To bring about the accomplishment of (something promised, hoped for, anticipated, etc.); make an actuality of. **2.** To execute or perform (something commanded or requested). **3.** To come up to or satisfy (something stipulated). **4.** To get through to the end of (a period of time, a task, etc.); finish up. Also *Brit.* **ful·fil′. — to fulfill oneself** To arrive at full development of one's capabilities; also, to achieve full satisfaction of one's hopes or desires. [OE *fullfyllan*] — **ful·fill′er** *n.*

ful·fill·ment (fool-fil′mant) *n.* **1.** The act of fulfilling, or the state of being fulfilled. **2.** Something that fulfills. Also **ful·fil′ment.**

ful·gent (ful′jant) *adj.* *Poetic* Shining with dazzling brightness; resplendent. Also **ful′gid** (-jid). [< L *fulgens, -entis,* ppr. of *fulgere* to gleam] — **ful′gent·ly** *adv.*

ful·gu·rant (ful′gyar·ant) *adj.* Flashing like lightning.

ful·gu·rate (ful′gya·rāt) *v.i.* **·rat·ed, ·rat·ing** To flash like lightning. [< L *fulguratus,* pp. of *fulgurare* to lighten < *fulgur* lightning]

ful·gu·rat·ing (ful′gya·rā′ting) *adj.* *Med.* Of pain sensations, sudden, sharp, and intense.

ful·gu·ra·tion (ful′gya·rā′shan) *n.* *Med.* Destruction of abnormal growths, etc., by the use of electricity.

ful·gu·rite (ful′gya·rīt) *n.* A perforation or indentation with a glassy crust, produced in sandy soil or in rock by a bolt of lightning; also, the glassy crust itself.

ful·gu·rous (ful′gyar·as) *adj.* **1.** Suggestive of lightning, as in brightness, swiftness, etc. **2.** Fulgurant.

ful·ham (fool′am) *n.* *Archaic Slang* One of a pair of dice that is loaded. Also **ful′lam.** [? after *Fulham,* a section of London once frequented by gamblers]

fu·lig·i·nous (fyoo-lij′a·nas) *adj.* **1.** Of, pertaining to, or full of smoke or soot. **2.** Dark with or as with smoke or soot. [< L *fuliginosus, -lijis* insoot] — **fu·lig′i·nous·ly** *adv.*

full¹ (fool) *adj.* **1.** Filled up with as much or as many as is possible: a *full* barrel. **2.** Containing an abundant or sufficient supply: a box *full* of money; also, containing a very large number or quantity: a garden *full* of flowers. **3.** Complete or sufficient in number, quantity, etc.; not deficient: a *full* dozen; also, whole or entire: to pay the *full* price. **4.** Maximum in size, extent, degree, etc.: a *full* load; *full* speed. **5.** Of the tide, risen to its highest level. **6.** Of the moon, having the face wholly illuminated. **7.** Having had ample food or drink. **8.** Of the face, figure, etc., not thin or scrawny; well rounded out; plump. **9.** Engrossed or pre-occupied: with *of*: *full* of plans for the future. **10.** Charged with emotion: a *full* heart. **11.** Overflowing with ideas, information, etc.: with *of*: to be *full* of one's subject. **12.** Having satisfying resonance and volume: *full* tones. **13.** Of garments, cut in ample folds; flowing: a long, *full* cape. **14.** Of an office or position, held by an incumbent. **15.** Of wines, having plenty of body. **16.** Of colors, intense or pure. **17.** Of sails, etc., distended by the wind. — **in full cry** In close pursuit: said especially of dogs. — **in full view** In a position allowing complete visibility. — *n.* The maximum size, extent, degree, etc.: now used chiefly in the phrases following. — **at (the) full 1.** At or to the maximum development, power, strength, etc. **2.** In full (def. 2). — **in full 1.** To the entire amount: paid *in full.* **2.** Without abridgment, condensation, or abbreviation: to reprint a text *in full.* — **the full of the moon** The phase of the moon when its face is wholly illuminated. — **to eat (drink, look,** etc.**) one's full** To eat (drink, look, etc.) as much as one wants. — **to the full** To the most complete extent: to enjoy something *to the full.* — *adv.* **1.** To a complete degree or extent: now chiefly in compounds: *full-fledged.*

2. Directly; straight; right: I looked him *full* in the face. **3.** Extremely; very: He knew *full* well he lied. — *v.t.* **1.** To gather, tuck, or pleat (the fabric of a garment). — *v.i.* **2.** To become full: said of the moon. [OE *ful*]

full² (fŏŏl) *v.t.* **1.** To make (cloth, yarn, etc.) thicker and more compact, as by moistening and beating or pressing. — *v.i.* **2.** Of cloth, etc., to become thicker and more compact through special treatment. [Back formation < FULLER¹.]

full and by *Naut.* Sailing with the sails full, as close to the wind as possible.

full-back (fŏŏl′bǎk′) *n.* In football, a player stationed behind the line of scrimmage, usually just behind the quarterback and the halfbacks; also, this position. Abbr. *fb*, *f.b.*

full blood 1. A person or animal of unmixed race or breed. **2.** Relationship established through descent from the same parents.

full-blood-ed (fŏŏl′blud′id) *adj.* **1.** Unmixed in race or breed; also, related to another through descent from the same parents: also **full-blood** (fŏŏl′blud′). **2.** Not anemic or effete; hearty and vigorous.

full-blown (fŏŏl′blōn′) *adj.* **1.** Blooming fully: a *full-blown* rose. **2.** Marked by the fullest or most perfect development: a *full-blown* genius.

full-bod-ied (fŏŏl′bod′ēd) *adj.* Of beverages, having a satisfying richness and strength.

full brother See under BROTHER.

full-dress (fŏŏl′dres′) *adj.* **1.** Characterized by or requiring full dress; formal: a *full-dress* dinner. **2.** Undertaken or engaged in to the fullest possible extent: a *full-dress* debate.

full dress Formal or ceremonial attire.

full-er¹ (fŏŏl′ər) *n.* One who fulls cloth, etc. [OE *fullere* < L *fullo*]

full-er² (fŏŏl′ər) *n.* **1.** A tool with a round edge, used in grooving or spreading hot iron. **2.** A groove made with this tool. — *v.t.* To groove with a fuller. [? < FULL¹, v.]

Full-er (fŏŏl′ər), **Melville Weston**, 1833–1910, U.S. jurist; chief justice of the Supreme Court 1888–1910. — **(Richard) Buckminster**, born 1895, U.S. inventor and designer. — **(Sarah) Margaret**, 1810–50, Marchioness Ossoli, U.S. writer and critic. — **Thomas**, 1608–61, English divine and historian.

Full-er-board (fŏŏl′ər-bôrd′, -bōrd′) *n.* A cardboard used as insulating material and for other protective purposes in the electrical industry: a trade name. Also **full′er-board.**

full-er's earth (fŏŏl′ərz) A soft, absorbent material resembling clay, occurring naturally as an impure hydrous aluminum silicate, used in removing grease from material to be fulled, and also as a catalyst, and in talcs, poultices, etc.

fuller's teasel A prickly herb (*Dipsacus fullonum*) with a flower head resembling that of a thistle, the dried head having been formerly used in raising a nap on cloth.

Ful-ler-ton (fŏŏl′ər-tən) A city in SW California; pop. 85,826.

full-er-y (fŏŏl′ər-ē) *n.* *pl.* **·er·ies** A place or establishment for fulling cloth, etc.

full-face (fŏŏl′fās′) *n.* *Printing* Boldface. — *adv.* With the face turned directly toward some specified point.

full-faced (fŏŏl′fāst′) *adj.* **1.** Having a plump, chubby face. **2.** Facing directly toward some specified point. **3.** *Printing* Bold-faced.

full-fash-ioned (fŏŏl′fash′ənd) *adj.* Knit to follow the contour; especially, of hosiery, knit to follow the contour of the leg and foot.

full-fledged (fŏŏl′flejd′) *adj.* **1.** Having the feathers fully grown. **2.** Completely developed or mature: a *full-fledged* adult. **3.** Completely organized and active: a *full-fledged* industry. **4.** Having full status: a *full-fledged* doctor.

full gainer A dive in which one springs forward off the board and makes a complete back somersault before plunging into the water.

full-grown (fŏŏl′grōn′) *adj.* Having reached full growth.

full house In poker, a hand made up of three cards of one kind plus two cards of another kind, as a combination of three queens and two sevens, this hand ranking below a hand in which four cards of one kind are held. Also **full hand.**

full-length (fŏŏl′lengkth′) *adj.* **1.** Showing the entire length of an object or figure: a *full-length* portrait. **2.** Being of the original or usual length; not abridged.

fulling mill A machine or mill for fulling cloth, etc.

full moon 1. The moon when the whole of its face is illuminated. **2.** The time of month when this occurs.

full-mouthed (fŏŏl′mouthd′, -moutht′) *adj.* **1.** Loud and lusty. **2.** Having all the teeth: said of cattle, etc.

full nel-son (nel′sən) A wrestling hold in which the arms are thrust under the opponent's armpits from behind and the hands are gripped at the back of the opponent's neck.

full-ness (fŏŏl′nis) *n.* The state or quality of being full: also spelled *fulness.* — **fullness of time** Completion of the time during which something has been done or accomplished.

full professor *U.S.* A college teacher of the highest rank. Compare ASSOCIATE PROFESSOR, ASSISTANT PROFESSOR.

full-rigged (fŏŏl′rigd′) *adj.* *Naut.* Completely equipped; especially, having three or more masts, each fully supplied with square sails.

full-scale (fŏŏl′skāl′) *adj.* **1.** Scaled to actual size; not reduced: a *full-scale* drawing. **2.** Engaged in or undertaken to the fullest possible extent; all-out: a *full-scale* attack.

full stop The mark used in writing to indicate the end of a sentence; period.

full swing 1. The height of activity: a party in *full swing.* **2.** Freedom of activity: to be given *full swing.*

ful·ly (fŏŏl′ē) *adv.* **1.** To the fullest extent or degree; entirely: *fully* convinced. **2.** Adequately; sufficiently: *fully* fed. **3.** At the lowest estimate: *fully* three hundred.

ful-mar (fŏŏl′mər) *n.* A large sea bird (*Fulmarus glacialis*) of the Arctic; also, the **giant fulmar** (*Macronectes giganteus*) of southern seas: also called *mallemuck.* [< ON *fūll mār* stinking mew]

ful-mi-nant (ful′mə-nənt) *adj.* **1.** Violent in denunciation. **2.** *Med.* Beginning suddenly and violently, as a fever.

ful-mi-nate (ful′mə-nāt) *v.* **·nat·ed**, **·nat·ing** *v.i.* **1.** To make loud or violent denunciations; make scathing verbal attacks; inveigh: to *fulminate* against taxes. **2.** To explode suddenly and violently, as a chemical. **3.** *Rare* To thunder and lighten. — *v.t.* **4.** To issue (decrees, censures, etc.) in scathing rebuke or condemnation; also, sometimes, to denounce scathingly **5.** To cause, as a chemical, to explode with sudden violence. — *n.* *Chem.* **1.** An explosive salt of fulminic acid. **2.** Any explosive compound: also **fulminating compound.** [< L *fulminatus*, pp. of *fulminare* to lighten < *fulmen, fulminis* lightning] — **ful′mi·na·tor** *n.*

fulminating powder *Chem.* Any explosive powder; especially, a powder made from a salt of fulminic acid.

ful-mi-na-tion (ful′mə-nā′shən) *n.* **1.** The act of fulminating. **2.** A scathing denunciation, censure, etc. **3.** A sudden, violent explosion.

ful-mi-na-to-ry (ful′mə-nə-tôr′ē, -tō′rē) *adj.* **1.** Violently denunciatory. **2.** Thundering.

ful-mine (ful′min) *v.t. & v.i.* **·mined**, **·min·ing** *Rare* To fulminate. [< F *fulminer* < L *fulminare.* See FULMINATE.]

ful-min-ic acid (ful-min′ik) *Chem.* An isomer of cyanic acid, HCNO, that unites with bases to form explosive salts.

ful-mi-nous (ful′mə-nəs) *adj.* *Rare* **1.** Of or pertaining to thunder and lightning. **2.** Violently denunciatory.

ful-ness (fŏŏl′nis) *n.* Fullness.

ful-some (fŏŏl′səm, ful′-) *adj.* **1.** Distastefully excessive in an oily or insincere way: a *fulsome* compliment. **2.** *Archaic* Gross or repulsive. [< FULL, adj. + -SOME; infl. by FOUL] — **ful′some·ly** *adv.* — **ful′some·ness** *n.*

Ful-ton (fŏŏl′tən), **Robert**, 1765–1815, U.S. engineer and inventor; developed steamboat.

ful-vous (ful′vəs) *adj.* Reddish yellow. [< L *fulvus*]

fu-mar-ic acid (fyoō-mar′ik) *Chem.* A crystalline, dibasic acid, $C_4H_4O_4$, made synthetically and occurring naturally in certain plants and fungi.

fu-ma-role (fyoō′mə-rōl) *n.* A small hole from which volcanic vapors issue. [< F *fumerolle* < LL *fumariolum*, dim. of L *fumarium* chimney < *fumus* smoke]

fu-ma-to-ri-um (fyoō′mə-tôr′ē-əm, -tō′rē-) *n.* *pl.* **·ri·ums** or **·ri·a** An airtight structure in which plants are set so as to destroy insects, etc., by chemical vapors. [< NL < L *fumare* to smoke < *fumus* smoke]

fu-ma-to-ry (fyoō′mə-tôr′ē, -tō′rē) *adj.* Of or pertaining to smoking or fumigation. — *n.* *pl.* **·ries** A fumatorium.

fum-ble (fum′bəl) *v.* **·bled**, **·bling** *v.i.* **1.** To try to locate something by groping blindly or clumsily: with *for, after.* **2.** To try awkwardly to do something: with *at.* **3.** To finger something aimlessly or abstractedly: with *with.* **4.** In football, etc., to get hold of the ball and then let it slip awkwardly from one's grasp. — *v.t.* **5.** To handle awkwardly or ineffectually; botch. **6.** To drop awkwardly (a ball in one's grasp). — *n.* The act of fumbling. [Prob. < Scand. Cf. Sw. *fumla* to grope.] — **fum′bler** *n.*

fume (fyoōm) *n.* **1.** A gaseous exhalation, especially when acrid or otherwise disagreeable. **2.** A sharply penetrating odor. **3.** Smoke having a pungent odor. **4.** Something with no more substance than smoke. **5.** A state of rage: in a *fume.* — *v.* **fumed, fum·ing** *v.i.* **1.** To give off fumes. **2.** To pass off in a mist or vapor. **3.** To be filled with or show rage, irritation, etc. — *v.t.* **4.** To subject to fumes. **5.** To give off in fumes. [< OF *fum* < L *fumus* smoke]

fumed (fyoōmd) *adj.* Treated with fumes: said especially of wood made darker by exposure to ammonia fumes.

fu-met (fyoō′met) *n.* *Obs.* **1.** The odor of long-kept game. **2.** The savory odor of meats while cooking. Also **fu-mette′.** [< F < L *fumus* smoke]

fu-mi-gant (fyoō′mə-gənt) *n.* Any substance, whose vapors are capable of destroying vermin, rats, insects, etc.

fu-mi-gate (fyoō′mə-gāt) *v.t.* **·gat·ed**, **·gat·ing 1.** To subject to smoke or fumes, as for disinfection. **2.** *Archaic* To perfume. [< L *fumigatus*, pp. of *fumigare* to smoke < *fumus* smoke + *agere* to drive] — **fu′mi·ga′tion** *n.* — **fu′mi·ga′tor** *n.*

fu-mi-to-ry (fyoō′mə-tôr′ē, -tō′rē) *n.* *pl.* **·ries** Any of a genus (*Fumaria*) typical of a family (*Fumariaceae*) of climbing herbs; especially, a low herb (*F. officinalis*), used as a source of several medicinal alkaloids. [< F *fumeterre* < Med.L *fumus terrae* smoke of the earth]

fu·mu·lus (fyōō′myə·ləs) *n. pl.* **·li** (-lī) *Meteorol.* A delicate, almost invisible veil of cloud that may form at all heights from cirrus to stratus. [< NL, dim. of L *fumus* smoke]

fum·y (fyōō′mē) *adj.* **fum·i·er, fum·i·est** Pertaining to, full of, or resembling fumes.

fun (fun) *n.* **1.** Pleasant diversion or amusement; highly enjoyable recreation; sport: Picnics are *fun.* **2.** Lighthearted playfulness; gaiety: full of *fun.* — *adj. Informal* Pleasantly diverting; full of fun: a *fun* game. — **for** (or **in**) **fun** In jest; without seriousness. — **like fun** *Informal* Absolutely not; by no means. — **to make fun of** To deride; ridicule. — *v.i.* **funned, fun·ning** *Informal* To behave or speak playfully or in jest. [< obs. *fonnen* to befool]

fu·nam·bu·list (fyōō·nam′byə·list) *n.* One skilled at walking along or doing balancing acts on a rope or cable stretched out tight or hanging slack above the ground. [< L *funambulus* < *funis* rope + *ambulare* to walk] — **fu·nam′bu·lism** *n.*

Fun·chal (fōōn·shäl′) **1.** An administrative district of Portugal comprising the Madeira Islands; 308 sq. mi. **2.** The capital of Funchal district, a port on the SE coast of Madeira; pop. 43,301 (1960).

func·tion (fungk′shən) *n.* **1.** The specific, natural, or proper action or activity of anything: the *function* of the brain. **2.** The special duties or action required of anyone in an occupation, office, or role. **3.** Any more or less formal or elaborate social gathering, entertainment, or ceremony. **4.** Any fact, quality, or thing depending upon or varying with another. **5.** *Math.* A quantity whose value is dependent on the value of some other quantity. Abbr. *f, F, f.* **6.** *Gram.* The part played by a linguistic element in a form or construction. — *v.i.* **1.** To perform as expected or required; operate properly; work. **2.** To perform the role of something else: with *as.* **3.** *Gram.* To have or perform a specific function. [< OF < L *functio, -onis* < *fungi* to perform]

func·tion·al (fungk′shən·əl) *adj.* **1.** Of or pertaining to a function or functions. **2.** Designed for or suited to a particular operation or use: *functional* architecture. **3.** Affecting the functions of an organ or part: *functional* disease: distinguished from *organic.* **4.** *Math.* Pertaining to, indicating, or depending on a function. — **func′tion·al·ly** *adv.*

functional disease *Pathol.* A disease characterized by the defective or impaired function of an organ or part, with no apparent structural change.

functional illiterate One who is unable to learn to read. — **functional illiteracy**

func·tion·al·ism (fungk′shən·əl·iz′əm) *n.* The doctrine or application of the doctrine that the function or use of an object should determine the form, structure, or material of the object. — **func′tion·al·ist** *n.*

functional shift *Ling.* The assuming of a new syntactic function by a word, without a change in form, as when an adjective serves as a noun in English. Also called **functional change.**

func·tion·ar·y (funk′shən·er′ē) *n. pl.* **·ar·ies** One who serves in a specific capacity; especially, an official.

function word *Ling.* A word that is used to indicate the function of, or the relationship between, other words in a phrase or sentence, as a preposition or conjunction.

fund (fund) *n.* **1.** A sum of money, or its equivalent, accumulated or reserved for a specific purpose. **2.** *pl.* Money readily available. **3.** A ready supply; store; stock: a *fund* of humor. **4.** *pl. Brit.* The government debt; also, government securities: with *the.* — *v.t.* **1.** In finance: **a** To convert into a long-term debt: to *fund* a debt. **b** To accumulate or furnish a fund for: to *fund* a pension plan. **c** To make into a fund, usually by investing in: to *fund* a reserve. **2.** To gather and store up a supply of. **3.** *Brit.* To invest (money) in the funds.

fun·da·ment (fun′də·mənt) *n.* **1.** The buttocks; also, the anus. **2.** *Geog.* The natural features of a region. **3.** *Obs.* A foundation, as of a building. **4.** *Obs.* An underlying principle. [< L *fundamentum* < *fundus* bottom]

fun·da·men·tal (fun′də·men′təl) *adj.* **1.** Pertaining to or constituting a foundation; basic; primary; essential. **2.** *Music* Of or pertaining to a root. **3.** *Physics* Designating the component of a wave form or other periodic oscillation on which all harmonic frequencies are based. — *n.* **1.** Anything that serves as the basis of a system, as a truth, law, principle, etc.; an essential. **2.** *Music* A root. **3.** *Physics* That frequency on which a harmonic or group of harmonics is based. — **fun′da·men′tal·ly** *adv.*
— **Syn.** (adj.) **1.** *Fundamental, basic, basal,* and *radical* refer to the foundation, basis, or lowest part of anything. *Fundamental* is used almost exclusively in the abstract: the *fundamental* principles of biology. *Basic* may be used either in the abstract or concrete and is preferred when a single element is characterized: the *basic* idea of this composition; the *basic* tier of brickwork. *Basal* is used chiefly in concrete and technical senses: the *basal* stratum of of a formation. *Radical* refers to the root; aside from technical senses, it is chiefly used in contexts referring to a change of effect brought about by modification of a cause: a *radical* measure to prevent inflation. — **Ant.** secondary, subordinate, superficial, nonessential.

fundamental bass *Music* A theoretical bass whose notes are the roots of a series of chords.

fun·da·men·tal·ism (fun′də·men′təl·iz′əm) *n.* **1.** The belief that all statements made in the Bible are to be taken literally. **2.** In the United States, a movement among Protestants holding such a belief. Compare LIBERALISM. — **fun′·da·men′tal·ist** *n. & adj.*

fund raising The activity or profession of collecting money for charitable organizations, etc. — **fund·raising** (fund′·rā′zing) *adj.*

fun·dus (fun′dəs) *n. Anat.* The inner surface constituting either the base or the internal part farthest from the opening of an organ: the *fundus* of the eye. [< L]

Fun·dy (fun′dē), **Bay of** An inlet of the Atlantic between Nova Scotia and New Brunswick and NE Maine; noted for tides rising to 70 feet.

Fü·nen (fü′nən) The German name for FYN.

fu·ner·al (fyōō′nər·əl) *n.* **1.** The burial, cremation, or other final disposal of the body of a dead person, together with accompanying services. **2.** A procession held for the final disposal of the body of a dead person. — *adj.* Of, pertaining to, or suitable for a funeral. [< OF *funeraille* < Med.L *funeralia,* neut. pl. of *funeralis* < L *funus, funeris* burial rite]

funeral director One whose profession is conducting and managing funerals.

funeral home An establishment in which the dead are prepared for burial or cremation and in which funeral services may be held. Also **funeral parlor.**

fu·ner·ar·y (fyōō′nə·rer′ē) *adj.* Of, pertaining to, or designed for a funeral: *funerary* rites.

fu·ne·re·al (fyōō·nir′ē·əl) *adj.* **1.** Depressingly sad or gloomy; melancholy; doleful: a *funereal* countenance. **2.** Pertaining to or suitable for a funeral; funerary. [< L *funereus* < *funus.* See FUNERAL.] — **fu·ne′re·al·ly** *adv.*

fu·nest (fyōō·nest′) *adj. Rare* Marked by or foreshadowing death, woe, or disaster. [< F *funeste* < L *funestus* < *funus.* See FUNERAL.]

Fünf·kir·chen (fünf′kēr′khən) The German name for PÉCS.

fun·gal (fung′gəl) *adj.* Fungous. — *n.* A fungus.

fungi- *combining form* Fungus: *fungicide.* Also, before vowels, **fung-.** [< L *fungus* mushroom]

fun·gi·ble (fun′jə·bəl) *Law adj.* Being of such a kind as to be freely exchangeable for or replaceable by another equivalent thing of the same class: Coins are *fungible.* — *n.* Something fungible. [< Med.L *fungibilis* < L *fungi* to perform] — **fun·gi·bil·i·ty** (fun′jə·bil′ə·tē) *n.*

fun·gi·cide (fun′jə·sīd, -gə-) *n.* Something, as a chemical compound, used in destroying fungi. — **fun′gi·ci′dal** *adj.*

fun·gi·form (fun′jə·fôrm, -gə-) *adj.* Having a fungoid form.

fun·gi·stat (fun′jə·stat′, -gə-) *n.* A substance that inhibits the growth of fungi without destroying them. — **fun′gi·stat′ic** *adj.*

fun·go (fung′gō) *n. pl.* **·goes** In baseball practice sessions, the hitting of a ball out to fielders by a batter who tosses the ball into the air and strikes it as it falls; also, a ball batted out to fielders by hitting it in this way. [< ?]

fun·goid (fung′goid) *adj.* Resembling or typical of fungi. — *n. Pathol.* A fungus-like growth.

fun·gous (fung′gəs) *adj.* **1.** Of, pertaining to, or having the nature of a fungus. **2.** Marked by the appearance of or caused by a fungus. **3.** Appearing or spreading rapidly and with little permanence, like mushrooms.

fun·gus (fung′gəs) *n. pl.* **fun·gus·es** or **fun·gi** (fun′jī, -gī, -gē) **1.** Any of a subdivision (*Fungi*) of thallophytes, comprising nonflowering plants that have no chlorophyll, usually reproduce asexually, and grow on dead organic matter or live parasitically, and including mushrooms, molds, and mildews. **2.** Something that appears or spreads rapidly in a manner suggestive of a mushroom, etc. **3.** *Pathol.* A soft, spongy, granular growth of morbid tissue. — *adj.* Fungous. [< L mushroom. Akin to SPONGE.]

fu·nic·u·lar (fyōō·nik′yə·lər) *adj.* **1.** Of, pertaining to, or resembling a funiculus. **2.** Moved by the pull of a cable, rope, etc., as a streetcar in a hilly section. — *n.* A railway along which cable cars are drawn: also **funicular railway.**

fu·nic·u·late (fyōō·nik′yə·lit, -lāt) *adj.* Having funiculi.

fu·nic·u·lus (fyōō·nik′yə·ləs) *n. pl.* **·li** (-lī) **1.** *Anat.* **a** A slender cord, as the umbilical cord or spermatic cord. **b** A small bundle of fibers, as of a nerve. **2.** *Bot.* A slender cord or stalk connecting an ovule or seed with the placenta of a plant. Also **fu·ni·cle** (fyōō′ni·kəl). [< L]

funk (fungk) *Chiefly Brit. Informal n.* **1.** A state of fear or panic: especially in the phrase **to be in a blue funk. 2.** One who quails with fear. — *v.t.* **1.** To shrink back from (something difficult, etc.). **2.** To cause to quail. — *v.i.* **3.** To try to evade something difficult, etc. [Cf. Flemish *fonck* fear]

Funk (fungk), **Casimir,** 1884–1967, Polish biochemist; discovered vitamins. — **Charles Earle,** 1881–1957, U.S. lexicographer. — **Isaac Kauffman,** 1839–1912; U.S. publisher and lexicographer; founded *The Literary Digest*; edited the *Standard Dictionary* and *New Standard Dictionary of the English Language*; uncle of the preceding.

funk·y[1] (fung′kē) *adj.* **funk·i·er, funk·i·est** *Informal* Frightened or terrified.

funk·y[2] (fung′kē) *adj.* **funk·i·er, funk·i·est** *Slang* Having an odor or foulness. [? < F *funkier* to smoke, stink < L *fūmigāre* to smoke < *fūmus* smoke]

fun·nel (fun′əl) *n.* **1.** A utensil, usually conical, with a wide mouth tapering to a small outlet or narrow tube, through which liquids, powders, or other free-running substances are poured into bottles, etc., having narrow necks. **2.** One of the smokestacks of a large ship or of a locomotive, etc. **3.** Any chimney, flue, or similar shaft or tube. — *v.t. & v.i.* **fun·neled** or **·nelled, fun·nel·ing** or **·nel·ling** **1.** To pass or move through or as through a funnel. **2.** To converge to or into a particular point, area, etc. [Earlier *fonel*, ult. < L *infundibulum* < *infundere* to pour < *in-* into + *fundere* to pour]

fun·nies (fun′ēz) *n.pl.* *U.S. Informal* Comic strips, or the section of a newspaper containing them.

fun·ny (fun′ē) *adj.* **·ni·er, ·ni·est** **1.** Causing one to laugh or be amused; comical. **2.** *Informal* Peculiar; strange; odd. — **fun′·ni·ly** *adv.* — **fun′ni·ness** *n.*
— **Syn. 1.** amusing, diverting, droll, risible, humorous. Compare RIDICULOUS. — **Ant.** solemn, sober, serious, sad.

funny bone The part of the elbow where the ulnar nerve joins the humerus and which, when struck, produces an unpleasant, tingling sensation: also called *crazy bone*.

funny paper *U.S. Informal* A newspaper supplement containing comic strips.

Fun·ston (fun′stən), **Frederick**, 1865–1917, U.S. army officer, botanist, and explorer.

fur (fûr) *n.* **1.** The soft, fine, hairy coat covering the skin of foxes, bears, squirrels, cats, and many other mammals; also, this coat used as a material in lining or trimming articles of apparel. **2.** An animal skin or a part of an animal skin covered with such a coat, especially when prepared for use in garments, rugs, etc.; also, such skins collectively. **3.** An article of apparel, as a cape or coat, made of such skin. **4.** A layer of foul matter, as on the tongue when the digestive tract is upset. — **to make the fur fly** *U.S. Informal* To stir up a furor, as by making accusations, revealing faults, etc. — *adj.* Made of or lined or trimmed with fur. — *v.t.* **furred, fur·ring** **1.** To cover, line or trim with fur. **3.** To clothe with fur. **3.** To cover, as the tongue, with a layer of foul matter. **4.** To put strips of wood, metal, etc., over (a wall, floor, etc.) so as to make a level surface or so as to make air spaces. [< OF *forrer* to line with fur < Gmc.]

fu·ran (fyŏŏr′an, fyŏŏ·ran′) *n. Chem.* A colorless liquid heterocyclic hydrocarbon, C_4H_4O, obtained from wood tar: also called *furfuran*. Also **fu·rane** (fyŏŏr′ān). [Short for *furfurane* < L *furfur* bran + -AN(E)[2]]

fur·be·low (fûr′bə·lō) *n.* **1.** A ruffle, frill, or similar piece of ornamentation. **2.** Any showy or pretentious bit of decoration. — *v.t.* To provide with furbelows. [Alter. of FALBALA; by popular etymology < fur below]

fur·bish (fûr′bish) *v.t.* **1.** To make bright by rubbing; burnish. **2.** To restore to brightness or beauty; renovate: often with *up.* [< OF *forbiss-*, stem of *forbir* < OHG *furban* to clean] — **fur′bish·er** *n.*

fur·cate (fûr′kāt; *for adj., also* -kit) *v.i.* **·cat·ed, ·cat·ing** To divide into branches; fork. — *adj.* Forked: also **fur′cat·ed** (-kāt·id). [< Med.L *furcatus* cloven < L *furca* fork]

fur·ca·tion (fər·kā′shən) *n.* **1.** Division into branches; forking. **2.** A forked branch or part.

fur·crae·a (fər·krē′ə) *n.* Any of a genus (*Furcraea*) of tropical American plants of the amaryllis family, one species of which (*F. macrophylla*) yields fique, a fiber resembling jute. [< NL, after A. F. *Fourcroy*, 1755–1809, French chemist]

fur·cu·la (fûr′kyə·lə) *n. pl.* **·lae** (-lē) *Anat. & Zool.* A forked bone or other part. [< L, dim. of *furca* fork]

fur·cu·lum (fûr′kyə·ləm) *n. pl.* **·la** (-lə) A furcula. [< NL, incorrectly formed as dim. of L *furca* fork]

fur·fur (fûr′fər) *n. pl.* **·fur·es** (-fə·rēz) **1.** Dandruff. **2.** *pl.* Scaly particles. [< L, bran]

fur·fur·a·ceous (fûr′fyə·rā′shəs) *adj.* **1.** Covered with dandruff; scurfy. **2.** Of or resembling bran.

fur·fur·al (fûr′fə·ral) *n. Chem.* A colorless liquid heterocyclic aldehyde, $C_5H_4O_2$, obtained by distilling the pentose sugars of corncobs, oat hulls, etc., used as a solvent and reagent, especially in the manufacture of dyes. Also **fur·fur·al·de·hyde** (fûr′fə·ral′də·hīd). [< L *furfur* bran + AL(DEHYDE)]

fur·fur·an (fûr′fə·ran) *n.* Furan. Also **fur·ane** (-rān).

Fu·ries (fyŏŏr′ēz) *n.pl.* In classical mythology, the three goddesses Alecto, Megaera, and Tisiphone, who avenge unpunished crimes: also called *Erinyes, Eumenides.*

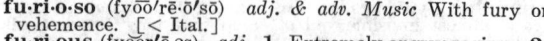

FUNNELS
a Separatory. *b* Hot-infiltration. *c* Filter. *d* Glass, with olivary tip.

fu·ri·o·so (fyŏŏ′rē·ō′sō) *adj. & adv. Music* With fury or vehemence. [< Ital.]

fu·ri·ous (fyŏŏr′ē·əs) *adj.* **1.** Extremely angry; raging. **2.** Extremely violent or intense; fierce. **3.** Pushed to the limit; extremely great: a *furious* rate of speed. [< L *furiosus* < *furere* to rage] — **fu′ri·ous·ly** *adv.* — **fu′ri·ous·ness** *n.*

furl (fûrl) *v.t.* **1.** To roll up (a sail, flag, etc.) and make secure, as to a mast or staff. — *v.i.* **2.** To become furled. — *n.* **1.** The act of furling, or the state of being furled. **2.** A rolled-up section of a sail, flag, etc. [< F *ferler* < OF *fermlier* < *ferm* close (< L *firmus*) + *lier* to bind < L *ligare*]

fur·long (fûr′lông, -long) *n.* A measure of length, equal to ⅛ mile, 220 yards, or 201.168 meters. See table inside back cover. [OE *furlang* < *furh* furrow + *lang* long]

fur·lough (fûr′lō) *n.* Official permission granted to be absent from duty, especially in the armed services; also, the period of time covered by such permission or the written form indicating such permission: the term has now been officially replaced in the U.S. services by *leave* or *leave of absence.* — *v.t.* To grant a furlough to. [< Du. *verlof*]

fur·men·ty (fûr′mən·tē), **fur·me·ty** (fûr′mə·tē) See FRUMENTY.

furn. Furnished; furniture.

fur·nace (fûr′nis) *n.* **1.** A large apparatus or structure with an enclosed chamber designed to produce intense heat for warming a building, melting metal, creating steam power, etc. **2.** Any intensely hot place. **3.** A grueling test or trial. [< OF *fornias* < L *fornax, fornacis* < *furnus* oven]

Fur·ness (fûr′nis), **Horace Howard,** 1833–1912, U.S. Shakespearean scholar.

fur·nish (fûr′nish) *v.t.* **1.** To equip, or fit out, as with fittings or furniture. **2.** To supply; provide. [< OF *furniss-*, stem of *furnir* < OHG *frumjan* to provide] — **fur′nish·er** *n.*

fur·nish·ing (fûr′nish·ing) *n.* **1.** Necessary or useful equipment. **2.** *pl.* Articles of clothing, including accessories. **3.** *pl.* Furniture, appliances, etc., for a home, office, etc.

fur·ni·ture (fûr′nə·chər) *n.* **1.** The movable articles used in a home, office, etc., as sofas, chairs, tables, or mirrors. **2.** Any necessary equipment, as for a factory or ship. **3.** *Printing* Wooden or metal strips or blocks used for holding the type in place and filling in spaces. Abbr. *furn.* [< F *fourniture* < *fournir* < OF *furnir.* See FURNISH.]

Fur·ni·vall (fûr′nə·vəl), **Frederick James,** 1825–1910, English scholar and lexicographer.

fu·ror (fyŏŏr′ôr) *n.* **1.** A great stir; commotion; rumpus. **2.** A state of intense excitement or enthusiasm. **3.** Frenzy or madness. Also **fu·rore** (fyŏŏr′ôr, fyŏŏ·rôr′ē, -rō′rē). [< L *furor* < *furere* to rage]

fu·ror lo·quen·di (fyŏŏr′ôr lō·kwen′dī) *Latin* A passion for speaking.

furor po·et·i·cus (pō·et′i·kəs) *Latin* The creative transports of a poet.

furor scri·ben·di (skri·ben′dī) *Latin* A passion for writing.

furred (fûrd) *adj.* **1.** Having or clad in fur. **2.** Made of or trimmed with fur, as garments. **3.** Coated, as the tongue.

fur·ri·er (fûr′ē·ər, -yər) *n.* **1.** One who deals in, repairs, or stores furs. **2.** One who processes furs for garments, etc.

fur·ri·er·y (fûr′ē·ər·ē) *n. pl.* **·er·ies** **1.** Furs collectively. **2.** The business of a furrier.

fur·ring (fûr′ing) *n.* **1.** A trimming or lining of fur. **2.** Furs collectively. **3.** An animal's coat of fur. **4.** A coating of foreign matter, as on the tongue. **5.** Strips of wood, metal, etc., fixed to a wall, floor, etc., so as to make a level surface or create air spaces.

fur·row (fûr′ō) *n.* **1.** A narrow channel made in the ground by or as if by a plow. **2.** Any long, narrow, deep depression, as a groove, rut, or deep wrinkle. — *v.t.* **1.** To make furrows in. **2.** To make deep wrinkles in. **3.** To plow. — *v.i.* **4.** To become furrowed or wrinkled. [OE *furh*]

fur·ry (fûr′ē) *adj.* **fur·ri·er, fur·ri·est** **1.** Of, pertaining to, or resembling fur. **2.** Covered or provided with fur. **3.** Coated, as the tongue. — **fur′ri·ness** *n.*

fur seal An eared seal that yields a fur of great commercial value; especially, a seal (*Callorhinus alascanus*) of the Pribilof Islands in the SE Bering Sea off the coast of Alaska.

Fürth (fürt) A city in central Bavaria, West Germany; pop. 98,200 (1960).

fur·ther (fûr′thər) Comparative of FAR. — *adv.* **1.** At or to a more distant or remote point in space or time. **2.** To a greater degree; more. **3.** In addition; besides; moreover. — *adj.* **1.** More distant or advanced in time or degree. **2.** More distant in space; farther. **3.** Additional. See note under FARTHER. — *v.t.* To help forward; promote. [OE *furthra*] — **fur′ther·er** *n.*

fur·ther·ance (fûr′thər·əns) *n.* **1.** The act of furthering; advancement. **2.** That which furthers.

fur·ther·more (fûr′thər·môr′, -mōr′) *adv.* In addition; moreover.

fur·ther·most (fûr′thər·mōst′) *adj.* Furthest or most remote.

fur·thest (fûr′thist) Superlative of FAR. — *adv.* **1.** At or to the most remote or distant point in space or time. **2.** To the greatest degree. — *adj.* **1.** Most distant, remote, or advanced in time or degree. **2.** Most distant in space.

fur·tive (fûr′tiv) *adj.* **1.** Done in secret; surreptitious; stealthy. **2.** Evasive; shifty; sly: a *furtive* aspect. — **Syn.** See STEALTHY. [< F *furtif* < L *furtivus* stolen < *fur* thief] — **fur′tive·ly** *adv.* — **fur′tive·ness** *n.*

fu·run·cle (fyŏŏr′ung·kəl) *n. Pathol.* A boil. [< L *furunculus*, dim. of *fur* thief] — **fu·run·cu·lar** (fyŏŏ·rung′kyə·lər), **fu·run′cu·lous** (-ləs) *adj.*

fu·ry (fyŏŏr′ē) *n., pl.* **·ries 1.** Vehement and uncontrolled anger; ungovernable rage. **2.** A fit of such anger or rage. **3.** Violent action or agitation; fierceness: the storm's *fury*. **4.** A person of violent temper, especially a woman. — **Syn.** See ANGER. — **like fury** *Informal* **1.** Violently. **2.** Rapidly. [< L *furia* < *furere* to rave]

Fu·ry (fyŏŏr′ē) *n.* One of the Furies.

furze (fûrz) *n.* A spiny evergreen shrub (*Ulex europaeus*) of the bean family, having many branches and yellow flowers: also called *gorse, whin*. [OE *fyrs*] — **furz′y** *adj.*

fu·sain (fyŏŏ·zăn′, Fr. fü·zaⁿ′) *n.* **1.** A stick of fine charcoal. **2.** A sketch or drawing made with this. [< F, spindle tree < L *fusus* spindle]

Fu·san (fōō·sän) Japanese name for PUSAN.

fus·cous (fus′kəs) *adj.* Grayish brown or tawny; dusky. [< L *fuscus* dusky]

fuse¹ (fyŏŏz) *n.* **1.** A length of combustible material passing into the charge of an explosive, designed to be lit so as to ignite the charge: also called *black match*. **2.** *Mil.* Any mechanical or electronic device designed to detonate a bomb, projectile, etc. **3.** *Electr.* A device consisting of a small strip of metal mounted in a casing and completing a circuit when put into position, the metal melting apart and so breaking the circuit if the amperage becomes excessive. — *v.t.* To attach a fuse to (a rocket, bomb, etc.). Also (especially for *n. def. 2*) spelled *fuze*. [< Ital. *fuso* < L *fusus* spindle]

FUSES
A Proximity fuse: a Radio unit, b Battery. B Aerial-bomb time fuse.

fuse² (fyŏŏz) *v.t. & v.i.* **fused, fus·ing 1.** To liquefy by heat; melt. **2.** To join by or as if by melting together. **3.** *Brit. Informal* Of an electric light or circuit, to fail or cause to fail through the melting of the metal of a fuse. — **Syn.** See MELT. [< L *fusus*, pp. of *fundere* to pour]

fu·see (fyŏŏ·zē′) *n.* **1.** A friction match with a large head capable of burning in the wind. **2.** A flare used as a railroad signal. **3.** A fuse (defs. 1 & 2). **4.** *Mech.* In old-style clocks and watches, a grooved, cone-shaped pulley that equalizes the pull of the mainspring by the differential winding and unwinding of a cord or chain connected with the cylindrical mainspring barrel. Also spelled *fuzee*. [< F *fusée* < Med.L *fusata* < L *fusus* spindle]

fu·se·lage (fyŏŏ′sə·lij, -läzh, -zə-) *n. Aeron.* The body of an airplane, containing the cockpit, cabin, etc. [< F, ult. < L *fusus* a spindle]

fu·sel oil (fyŏŏ′zəl, -səl) A volatile, poisonous, oily liquid, consisting largely of amyl alcohol, obtained from rectified corn, potato, or grape spirits and used as a solvent in various chemical processes. Also **fu′sel.** [< G *fusel* inferior spirits]

Fu·shih (fōō′shir′) A town in northern Shensi Province, China; headquarters of the Chinese Communist Party 1937–1949; pop. about 50,000: also *Yenan*.

fu·si·bil·i·ty (fyŏŏ′zə·bil′ə·tē) *n.* **1.** The quality of being fusible. **2.** The degree of this quality.

fu·si·ble (fyŏŏ′zə·bəl) *adj.* Capable of being fused or melted by heat. — **fu′si·ble·ness** *n.* — **fu′si·bly** *adv.*

fusible alloy Any alloy, as one containing bismuth, that melts at a comparatively low temperature. Also **fusible metal.**

fu·si·form (fyŏŏ′zə·fôrm) *adj.* Tapering from the middle toward each end; spindle-shaped. [< L *fusus* spindle + -FORM]

fu·sil (fyŏŏ′zəl) *n.* A flintlock musket: also spelled *fuzil*. [< F < OF *foisil* a steel for striking sparks, ult. < L *focus* hearth]

fu·sile (fyŏŏ′zəl, -səl, -sīl) *adj.* **1.** Made by melting or casting. **2.** *Obs.* Capable of being fused. [< L *fusilis* < *fundere* to pour]

fu·si·lier (fyŏŏ′zə·lir′) *n.* **1.** A soldier armed with a flintlock musket. **2.** *pl.* Soldiers of certain regiments of the British army: used in titles of the regiments. Also **fu′si·leer′.**

fu·sil·lade (fyŏŏ′sə·lād′, -läd′, -zə-, fyŏŏ′sə·lād′, -läd′, -zə-) *n.* **1.** A simultaneous or quickly repeated discharge of firearms. **2.** Anything resembling this: a *fusillade* of hail. — *v.t.* **·lad·ed, ·lad·ing** To attack or bring down with a fusillade. [< F < *fusiller* to shoot < *fusil* musket]

fu·sion (fyŏŏ′zhən) *n.* **1.** The act of fusing; a melting or blending together. **2.** The state or condition of being fused. **3.** Something formed by fusing. **4.** In politics, the union of two parties or two factions within a party; also the body of persons formed by this union. **5.** *Physics* A thermonuclear

reaction in which the nuclei of a light element undergo transformation into those of a heavier element, with the release of great energy: also called *nuclear fusion*: compare FISSION. **6.** *Ling.* A coalescing of two originally distinct words because of a similarity in form and meaning, as in the development of the verb *bid* from the Old English verbs *biddan* "to ask" and *bēodan* "to command." — **Syn.** See ALLIANCE. [< L *fusio, -onis* < *fundere* to pour]

fu·sion·ism (fyŏŏ′zhən·iz′əm) *n.* The doctrine, advocacy, or practice of fusion in politics. — **fu′sion·ist** *n.*

fuss (fus) *n.* **1.** Nervous activity; bustle; commotion. **2.** A protest or complaint. **3.** A quarrel or dispute. **4.** Excessive attention or praise. — *v.i.* **1.** To be too much concerned with trifles or small details. **2.** To criticize, scold, or argue. **3.** To worry. **4.** To flatter or watch over excessively. — *v.t.* **5.** To bother with trifles or small details. [Origin unknown] — **fuss′er** *n.*

fuss-budg·et (fus′buj′it) *n. Informal* A person who fusses.

fuss·y (fus′ē) *adj.* **fuss·i·er, fuss·i·est 1.** Too much concerned with trifles; finicky. **2.** Fidgety; fretful. **3.** Requiring meticulous attention. **4.** Having elaborate and showy trimmings, as clothing. — **fuss′i·ly** *adv.* — **fuss′i·ness** *n.*

fus·ta·nel·la (fus′tə·nel′ə) *n.* A short white skirt worn by men in modern Greece. Also **fus′ta·nelle′** (-nel′). [< Ital.]

fus·tian (fus′chən) *n.* **1.** Formerly, a kind of stout cloth made of cotton and flax; now, a coarse, twilled cotton fabric, as corduroy. **2.** Pretentious verbiage; bombast. — *adj.* **1.** Made of fustian. **2.** Pompous; bombastic. [< OF *fustaine* < Med.L (*pannus*) *fustaneus* (< L *fustis* cudgel), trans. of Gk. *xylinon* wooden < *xylon* wood]

fus·tic (fus′tik) *n.* **1.** The wood of one of several trees that yield dyes; especially, the wood of a tropical tree (*Chlorophora tinctoria*) yielding a yellow dye. **2.** The dye yielded from such wood. **3.** A tree producing such wood. [< F *fustoc* < Sp. < Arabic *fustuq*, prob. < Gk. *pistakē* pistachio]

fus·ti·gate (fus′tə·gāt) *v.t.* **·gat·ed, ·gat·ing** To beat; cudgel: now in humorous use. [< L *fustigatus*, pp. of *fustigare* < *fustis* club + *agere* to do, to drive] — **fus′ti·ga′tion** *n.*

fust·y (fus′tē) *adj.* **fust·i·er, fust·i·est 1.** Musty; moldy; rank. **2.** Old-fashioned; fogeyish. [< obs. *fust* moldy odor < OF, wine cask] — **fust′i·ly** *adv.* — **fust′i·ness** *n.*

fu·thark (fōō′thärk) *n.* The runic alphabet. Also **fu′tharc, fu′thorc** (-thôrk), **fu′thork.** [from the first six letters, *f, u, p* (*th*), *a* (or *o*), *r, c*]

fu·tile (fyŏŏ′təl, -til; *esp. Brit.* -tīl) *adj.* **1.** Being of no avail; done in vain; useless. **2.** Frivolous; trivial: *futile* chatter. [< F < L *futilis* pouring out easily, useless] — **fu′tile·ly** *adv.* — **fu′tile·ness** *n.*
— **Syn. 1.** *Futile, vain, ineffectual, bootless, fruitless,* and *abortive* mean barren of result. Misdirected effort or purposeless activity is *futile*; empty hopes or expectations are *vain*. *Ineffectual* means merely that a thing has failed to bring about a desired result but does not necessarily imply blame: an *ineffectual* medicine, an *ineffectual* plea for mercy. That which is *bootless* brings no profit or advantage. *Fruitless* suggests long and patient toil without any result except disappointment. Short-lived hopes or plans that die in the making are said to be *abortive*.

fu·til·i·tar·i·an (fyŏŏ·til′ə·târ′ē·ən) *adj.* Convinced of the futility of human enterprise. — *n.* One so convinced.

fu·til·i·ty (fyŏŏ·til′ə·tē) *n., pl.* **·ties 1.** Complete lack of effectiveness or point; uselessness. **2.** Unimportance; triviality. **3.** A futile act, event, thing, etc.

fut·tock (fut′ək) *n. Naut.* One of the curved timbers in the frame of a wooden ship. [? Alter. of FOOT HOOK]

futtock plate *Naut.* One of the iron plates attached to a mast top to hold the upper ends of the futtock shrouds.

futtock shrouds *Naut.* Short iron shrouds extending from the futtock plates to a band fitted around the lower mast.

fu·tur·al (fyŏŏ′chər·əl) *adj.* Of or pertaining to the future or futures.

fu·ture (fyŏŏ′chər) *n.* **1.** The time yet to come. **2.** What will be in time to come. **3.** A condition, usually of success or prosperity, in time to come: a man with a *future*. **4.** *Usually pl.* Any commodity or security sold or bought upon agreement of future delivery. **5.** *Gram.* **a** A verb tense denoting action that will take place at some time to come. **b** A verb in this tense. — *adj.* **1.** Such as will be in time to come. **2.** Pertaining to or expressing time to come. [< OF *futur* < L *futurus*, future participle of *esse* to be]

fu·ture·less (fyŏŏ′chər·lis) *adj.* Having no future; lacking prospects.

future life The existence of the soul after death.

future perfect *Gram.* **1.** The verb tense expressing a future action or state completed before a specified future time. Example: *He will have finished* by tomorrow. **2.** A verb in this tense.

fu·tur·ism (fyŏŏ′chə·riz′əm) *n.* A movement in art, music, and literature that originated in Italy about 1910 and rejected traditional forms in an effort to portray more vividly and directly the force, intensity, and speed of contemporary life. — **fu′tur·ist** *adj. & n.*

fu·tu·ri·ty (fyōō·tōōr'ə·tē, -tyōōr'-) *n. pl.* **·ties 1.** Time to come; the future. **2.** The state or quality of being future. **3.** A future event or possibility. **4.** A futurity race.
futurity race *U.S.* A race, as a horse race, for which entries are selected well in advance of the actual race.
futurity stakes *U.S.* Stakes in a futurity race; also, the race itself.
fuze (fyōōz) See FUSE¹.
fu·zee (fyōō·zē') See FUSEE.
fu·zil (fyōō'zəl) See FUSIL.
fuzz (fuz) *n.* **1.** Fine, loose particles, fibers, or hairs. **2.** A fluffy mass of these. — *v.i. & v.t.* To become or cause to become fuzzy. [Origin unknown]
fuzz·y (fuz'ē) *adj.* **fuzz·i·er, fuzz·i·est 1.** Having fuzz. **2.** Resembling fuzz. **3.** Lacking sharp distinctness or clarity; blurred. — **fuzz'i·ly** *adv.* — **fuzz'i·ness** *n.*

f.v. On the back of the page (L *folio verso*).
FWA, F.W.A. Federal Works Agency.
fwd. Forward.
-fy *suffix of verbs* **1.** Cause to be or become; make: *deify.* **2.** Become: *liquefy.* [< OF *-fier* < L *-ficare* < *facere* to do, to make]
FY Fiscal year.
fyce (fis) See FICE.
fyke (fik) *n.* A long, bag-shaped fish net. [< Du. *fuik* trap, snare]
fyl·fot (fil'fot) *n.* The swastika. [Appar. < FILL, v. + FOOT; so called because used to fill in the foot or base of stained glass windows]
Fyn (fün) An island of Denmark in the Baltic Sea; 1,149 sq. mi.: German *Fünen.* Also **Fyen.**
F.Z.S. Fellow of the Zoological Society.

G

g, G (jē) *n. pl.* **g's** or **gs, G's** or **Gs, gees** (jēz) **1.** The seventh letter of the English alphabet. The shape of the Phoenician *gimel* was adopted by the Greeks as *gamma* and became originally Roman *C* and then *G.* Also **gee. 2.** Any sound represented by the letter *g.* **3.** *Usually cap. U.S. Slang* One thousand dollars; a grand. — *symbol* **1.** *Music* **a** The fifth tone in the scale of C major or the seventh in the natural scale of A minor. **b** The pitch of this tone, 392.0 cycles per second or this value multiplied by any power of 2, in standard pitch. **c** A written note representing this tone. **d** A scale built upon the tone of G. **e** The treble clef. **2.** The Roman numeral for 400. **3.** *Physics* The acceleration of a body due to the earth's gravity, about 32 feet per second per second; also, a unit of acceleration equal to that due to the earth's gravity (symbol g). **4.** *Psychol.* General intelligence (symbol g). **5.** *Electr.* Conductance.
g. or **g 1.** Goalie; goalkeeper. **2.** Gram(s).
G 1. German: also **G. 2.** Gravitational force. **3.** *Mil.* Gun.
G. 1. Specific gravity. **2.** Gulf.
G. or **g. 1.** Gauge. **2.** Gourde. **3.** Grain(s). **4.** Guilder(s). **5.** Guinea(s).
G-1, G-2, G-3, G-4 See under GENERAL STAFF.
Ga *Chem.* Gallium.
Ga or **G.A. 1.** General Agent. **2.** General Assembly (of the United Nations).
Ga. 1. Gallic. **2.** Georgia.
G.A. or **G/A** or **g.a.** General average.
gab¹ (gab) *Informal v.i.* **gabbed, gab·bing** To talk, especially glibly or excessively; chatter; prate. — *n.* Glib or excessive speech. — **gift of (the) gab** An aptitude for speaking effortlessly or glibly. [Prob. < ON *gabba* to mock] — **gab'ber** *n.*
gab² (gab, gäb) *n. Scot.* The mouth.
gab·ar·dine (gab'ər·dēn, gab'ər·dēn') *n.* **1.** A firm, twilled, worsted fabric, having a diagonal raised weave, used for coats, suits, etc. **2.** A similar, softer fabric of mercerized cotton. **3.** A gaberdine. [Var. of GABERDINE]
gab·bart (gab'ərt) *n. Scot.* A sailing vessel used on inland bodies of water. Also **gab'bard** (-ərd).
gab·ble (gab'əl) *v.* **·bled, ·bling** *v.i.* **1.** To talk quickly or incoherently. **2.** To utter rapid, cackling sounds, as geese. — *v.t.* **3.** To utter rapidly or incoherently. — *n.* **1.** Glib, incoherent, or foolish talk. **2.** Cackling sounds, as of geese. — Syn. See BABBLE. [Freq. of GAB¹] — **gab'bler** *n.*
gab·bro (gab'rō) *n. pl.* **·bros** *Geol.* Any of a class of plutonic igneous rocks of granular texture, consisting essentially of monoclinic pyroxene and calcic plagioclase. [< Ital.]
gab·by (gab'ē) *adj. Informal* **·bi·er, ·bi·est** Loquacious.
ga·belle (gə·bel') *n.* In old English and French law, a tax; especially, in France, a salt tax, abolished in 1790. [< F < Med.L *gabella* < *gablum* tax < Gmc.]
gab·er·dine (gab'ər·dēn, gab'ər·dēn') *n.* **1.** A loose, coarse coat or frock. **2.** A long, loose cloak worn by Jews in medieval times. **3.** Gabardine. [< Sp. *garbardina* < MHG *wallevart* pilgrimage]
gab·er·lun·zie (gab'ər·lün'zē, -yē) *n. Scot.* A beggar who wanders about from place to place.
Ga·bès (gä'bes), **Gulf of** An inlet of the Mediterranean in eastern and SE Tunisia: ancient *Syrtis Minor.*
gab·fest (gab'fest) *n. U.S. Slang* A period or occasion of prolonged, chatty conversation. [< GAB¹ + G *fest* feast]
ga·bi·on (gā'bē·ən) *n.* **1.** *Mil.* A cylindrical wicker basket filled with earth, stones, etc., used as a defense. **2.** An open cylinder, usually of metal, filled with stones, etc., and used in the preliminary construction of dams, etc. [< F < Ital. *gabbione, aug.* of *gabbia* cage < L *cavea* cage]

ga·ble (gā'bəl) *n. Archit.* **1.** The outside, usually triangular section of a wall extending upward from the level of the eaves of an uncurved, sloped roof to the ridge pole. **2.** The wall of a building when the upper part of the wall terminates in such a section. **3.** Any architectural feature, as above a window or door, having the shape of such a section. — *v.t.* **1.** To cause to form a gable: a *gabled* roof. — *v.i.* **2.** To form a gable. [< OF, prob. < ON *gafl* gable]

GABLES

gable end One of the ends of a building when the upper section of the end terminates in a gable; also, the upper section itself.
gable roof A roof that forms a gable.
gable wall A wall that terminates in a gable.
gable window A window set in a gable wall or having a decorative gable above it.
Ga·bon (gà·bôn') An independent Republic on the west coast of central Africa; 103,346 sq. mi.; pop. 485,000 (est. 1969); capital, Libreville: formerly an Overseas Territory in French Equatorial Africa: French *République Gabonaise.* Also **Ga·boon, Ga·bun** (gə·bōōn'), **Republic of Gabon.** Officially **Gabon Republic.**
Ga·bo·riau (gà·bô·ryō'), **Emile,** 1835–73, French writer of detective stories.
Ga·bri·el (gā'brē·əl) In the Bible, one of the archangels, chosen as a special messenger of God. *Dan.* viii 16, *Luke* i 26.
gad¹ (gad) *v.i.* **gad·ded, gad·ding** To roam about restlessly or capriciously; ramble. — *n.* The act of gadding. [? Back formation < obs. *gadling* vagabond] — **gad'der** *n.*
gad² (gad) *n.* **1.** In mining, a pointed tool for breaking up ore or rock. **2.** A goad for driving cattle. — *v.t.* **gad·ded, gad·ding** To break up (ore) with a gad. [< ON *gaddr* goad, spike]
Gad (gad) *interj. & n. Archaic* God: a variant form used euphemistically in oaths.
Gad (gad) In the Old Testament, a son of Jacob and Zilpah. *Gen.* xxx 11. — *n.* The tribe descended from him, or its territory east of Jordan.
gad·a·bout (gad'ə·bout') *Informal n.* One who goes about aimlessly, frivolously, etc. — *adj.* Fond of gadding.
gad·fly (gad'flī') *n. pl.* **·flies 1.** One of various large flies (family *Tabanidae*), as a horsefly, that bite cattle, horses, etc. **2.** An irritating, bothersome individual. [< GAD² + FLY]
gadg·et (gaj'it) *n.* **1.** A device or contrivance, usually small and mechanical or electronic and often considered ingenious. **2.** Something whose name is unknown or forgotten; thingamajig. [Origin uncertain]
gadg·et·ry (gaj'it·rē) *n.* Gadgets collectively, or their use: the new electronic *gadgetry.*
Ga·dhel·ic (gə·del'ik, -dē'lik) See GOIDELIC.
ga·doid (gā'doid) *adj.* Of or belonging to a large family (*Gadidae*) of chiefly marine fishes with soft fins and wide gill openings, including the codfish, haddock, and hake. — *n.* Any gadoid fish. Also **ga'did** (-did). [< NL *gadus* codfish < Gk. *gados*, a kind of fish + -OID]
gad·o·lin·ite (gad'ə·lin·īt') *n.* A black, vitreous silicate ore that yields gadolinium and other rare-earth elements.
gad·o·lin·i·um (gad'ə·lin'ē·əm) *n.* A metallic element (symbol Gd) of the lanthanide series. See ELEMENT. [after John *Gadolin,* 1760–1852, Finnish chemist]
ga·droon (gə·drōōn') *n.* **1.** *Archit.* An ornamental molding marked by the use of notches or carved work. **2.** A decorative band used especially in silverwork and characterized by

the use of fluted work or reedings in a usually oval pattern. Also spelled *godroon*. [< F *godron* plait]

Gads·den (gadz′dən) A city in NE Alabama on the Coosa River; pop. 53,928.

Gads·den (gadz′dən), **James**, 1788–1858, U.S. politician and diplomat; secured from Mexico (1853) a tract of land (45,535 sq. mi.) known as the **Gadsden Purchase**, now part of Arizona and New Mexico.

gad·wall (gad′wôl) *n. pl.* **·walls** or **·wall** A large, wild, fresh-water duck (*Anas streptera*) found in temperate regions of the northern hemisphere. [Origin unknown]

gae¹ (gā) *v.i. Scot.* **gaed, gaen, gae·ing** To go.

gae² (gā) *Scot.* Past tense of GIVE.

Gae·a (jē′ə) In Greek mythology, the goddess of earth, mother and wife of Uranus, and mother of the Titans, etc.: identified with the Roman *Tellus*: also called *Gaia, Ge*. [< Gk. *Gaia* Earth]

Gaek·war (gīk′wär, jēk′-) *n.* Title of the native ruler of Baroda, India: also spelled *Gaikwar*. [< Marathi *Gāekvād*, a family name; lit., cowherd]

Gael (gāl) *n.* One of the Celts of Ireland or the Scottish Highlands. [< Scottish Gaelic *Gaidheal*]

Gael. Gaelic.

Gael·ic (gā′lik) *adj.* Belonging or relating to the Gaels or their languages. — *n.* **1.** The languages of the Gaels: Irish (*Irish Gaelic*), Manx, and especially, the speech of the Scottish Highlanders (*Scottish Gaelic*). **2.** The Goidelic branch of the Celtic languages.

gaff¹ (gaf) *n.* **1.** A sharp iron hook at the end of a pole, for landing a large fish; also, the pole tipped with such a hook. **2.** *Naut.* A spar for extending the upper edge of a fore-and-aft sail. **3.** A gamecock's metal spur. — *v.t.* **1.** — **to stand the gaff** *U.S. Informal* To endure hardship, ridicule, etc., patiently; be game. [< OF *gaffe*, prob. < Celtic]

gaff² (gaf) *n. Slang* Loud or annoying talk. [Cf. OE *gafsprǣc* ribald talk]

gaff³ (gaf) *n. Brit. Slang* A cheap theater or low-priced place of amusement. [Origin unknown]

gaffe (gàf) *n. French Informal* A clumsy mistake; faux pas.

gaf·fer (gaf′ər) *n.* **1.** An old man: now contemptuous or humorous. Compare GAMMER. **2.** *Brit.* A foreman. [Alter. of GODFATHER]

gaff rig *Naut.* A fore-and-aft rig having the upper edge of the sail extended on a gaff.

gaff-top·sail (gaf′top′səl, -sāl) *n. Naut.* A light sail set above a gaff, on which the sail's foot is extended.

gag (gag) *n.* **1.** Something, as a wadded cloth, forced into or bound over the mouth to prevent a person from speaking or crying out. **2.** Any restraint or suppression of free speech, as by censorship. **3.** A device to keep the jaws open, as in dentistry. **4.** *Slang* A joke or hoax. **5.** *Slang* Something interpolated by an actor or actress into a role, as a topical comment, usually made to draw laughs. — **Syn.** See JEST. — **to pull a gag** *U.S. Slang* To perform or perpetrate a practical joke, piece of deception, etc. — *v.* **gagged, gag·ging** *v.t.* **1.** To keep from speaking or crying out by means of a gag. **2.** To keep from speaking or discussing freely, as by force or authority: to *gag* the press. **3.** To cause nausea in; cause to retch. **4.** To keep (the mouth) open with a gag. **5.** *Slang* To make fun of or hoax. — *v.i.* **6.** To heave with nausea; retch; also, to choke on something. **7.** *Slang* To make jokes or speeches of an improvised nature. [ME *gaggen*; prob. imit.]

ga·ga (gä′gä′) *adj. Slang* Foolish; crazy. [< F (slang), a foolish old man]

Ga·ga·rin (gä-gä′ryin), **Yuri Alekseyevitch**, 1934–1968, Soviet air force officer; first astronaut to make a successful space flight and first man to orbit the earth, April 12, 1961.

gage¹ (gāj) See GAUGE.

gage² (gāj) *n.* **1.** Something given as security for an action to be performed; pledge. **2.** Anything, as a glove, proffered as a challenge to a duel; also. **3.** Any challenge. — *v.t.* **gaged, gag·ing** *Archaic* **1.** To bind or pledge as a guaranty or forfeit. **2.** To wager; stake. [< OF *gager* < *gage* pledge < Gmc. Doublet of WAGE.]

gage³ (gāj) *n.* One of several varieties of plum; especially, the greengage. [after Sir William *Gage*, 1777–1864, who introduced it into England]

Gage (gāj), **Thomas**, 1721–87, British general in America; commanded the British army at Bunker Hill.

gag·er (gā′jər) See GAUGER.

gag·ger (gag′ər) *n.* **1.** One who or that which gags. **2.** A piece of iron used to keep a core in its place in a mold.

gag·gle (gag′əl) *v.i.* **·gled, gling** To cackle; gabble. — *n.* **1.** A flock of geese. **2.** A chattering group of women. **3.** A cackle. — **Syn.** See FLOCK. [Imit.]

gag man A man who makes up comic routines and jokes for use by entertainers.

gag rule A rule limiting speech or discussion, as of proposed legislation. Also **gag law.**

gahn·ite (gän′īt) *n.* A green, brown, or black zinc aluminate with nearly opaque crystals. [after J. G. *Gahn*, 1745–1818, Swedish chemist]

Gai·a (gā′ə, gī′ə) See GAEA.

gai·e·ty (gā′ə·tē) *n. pl.* **·ties 1.** The state or quality of being gay; cheerfulness. **2.** Bright colorfulness or showiness, as of dress. **3.** Fun and frolic; merrymaking. Also spelled *gayety*. [< F *gaieté* < *gai.* See GAY.]

Gaik·war (gīk′wär) See GAEKWAR.

Gail·lard Cut (gā′lärd, gil·yärd′) An 8-mile section of the Panama Canal cut through a hill (Culebra Mountain) in the SE Canal Zone: formerly *Culebra Cut*. [after David Du Bose *Gaillard*, 1859–1913, American army engineer]

gail·lar·di·a (gā·lär′dē·ə) *n.* Any of a genus (*Gaillardia*) of western American herbs of the composite family with showy yellow or reddish purple flowers: also called *blanketflower*. [after *Gaillard* de Charentonneau (or Marentonneau), 18th c. French amateur botanist]

gai·ly (gā′lē) *adv.* In a gay manner: also spelled *gayly*.

gain¹ (gān) *v.t.* **1.** To come into possession of; obtain; acquire; get: to *gain* an advantage. **2.** To succeed in winning (a victory, prize, etc.). **3.** To develop an increase of; pick up: to *gain* momentum. **4.** To put on (weight). **5.** To earn (money, a living, etc.). **6.** To arrive at; get to; reach: to *gain* port. — *v.i.* **7.** To grow greater or better: to *gain* in health. **8.** To draw nearer: usually with *on* or *upon*: one runner *gaining* upon another. **9.** To increase one's lead: usually with *on, upon,* or *over*. — *n.* **1.** *Often pl.* Something obtained by way of profit, winnings, increase, etc.: small *gains*. **2.** An advantage or lead: a *gain* of one mile. **3.** An increase, as in size, amount, etc. **4.** The act of gaining. **5.** *Electronics* The ratio of output to input in a wave- or signal-transmitting circuit. [< F *gagner* < OF *gaaignier* < Gmc.] — **Syn.** (verb) **1.** See GET. **2.** attain, achieve. **7.** prosper, flourish. — (noun) See ADVANTAGE.

gain² (gān) *n.* A groove, notch, or mortise, as in a board, cut to receive a girder, joist, etc. — *v.t.* **1.** To make such a groove, etc., in. **2.** To secure with such a groove. [Origin unknown]

gain·er (gā′nər) *n.* **1.** One who or that which gains. **2.** A full gainer (which see).

Gaines·ville (gānz′vil) A city in northern Florida; pop. 64,510.

gain·ful (gān′fəl) *adj.* Yielding profit; lucrative. — **gain′-ful·ly** *adv.* — **gain′ful·ness** *n.*

gain·less (gān′lis) *adj.* Profitless. — **gain′less·ness** *n.*

gain·ly (gān′lē) *adj. Rare* Not ungainly; graceful. [< obs. *gain* fit, favorable (< ON *gegn*) + -LY] — **gain′li·ness** *n.*

gain·say (gān′sā′) *v.t.* **·said, ·say·ing 1.** To deny. **2.** To contradict; controvert. **3.** To speak or act against; oppose. — *n. Rare* A contradiction. [OE *gegn*- against + SAY²] — **gain′say′er** *n.*

Gains·bor·ough (gānz′bûr·ō, -bə·rə), **Thomas**, 1727–88, English painter.

'gainst (genst, *esp. Brit.* gānst) *prep.* Against.

Gai·se·ric (gī′zə·rik) See GENSERIC.

gait (gāt) *n.* **1.** One's particular manner of moving along on foot. **2.** One of the particular ways in which a horse steps or runs, as the pace, canter, or trot. — *v.t.* To train (a horse) to or cause to take a particular gait. [< ON *gata* way]

gait·ed (gā′tid) *adj.* Having a (specified) gait: *heavy-gaited*.

gai·ter (gā′tər) *n.* **1.** A covering of durable material, as of leather or canvas, designed to be worn over the leg from the knee to the instep, as a puttee or legging. **2.** A similar covering for the ankle and instep; a spat. **3.** One of a pair of overshoes or galoshes. **4.** An old-fashioned type of shoe with a high top. [< F *guêtre*]

Ga·ius (gā′əs, gī′-), 110?–180?, Roman jurist: also *Caius*.

gal (gal) *n. Slang* **1.** A girl. **2.** A girl friend.

gal. Gallon(s).

Gal. **1.** Galatians. **2.** Galen. **3.** Galway.

ga·la (gā′lə, gal′ə, gä′lə) *adj.* Consisting of or appropriate to a festive occasion; festive. — *n.* **1.** An occasion or celebration marked by joyous festivity and display. **2.** *Rare* Festive or ceremonial finery: used in the phrase **in gala. 3.** *Archaic* Merrymaking; frolic. [< F < Ital., holiday dress]

ga·lac·ta·gogue (gə·lak′tə·gôg, -gog) *adj.* Promoting or increasing the secretion of milk. — *n.* A galactagogue drug, etc. Also **ga·lac′ta·gog, ga·lac′to·gogue**. [< GALACT(O)- + Gk. *agogos* producing]

ga·lac·tic (gə·lak′tik) *adj. Astron.* Pertaining to galaxies or the Galaxy.

galactic circle *Astron.* The great circle passing centrally along the Milky Way.

galactic latitude *Astron.* The angular distance of a celestial body from the galactic plane.

galactic plane The plane of the galactic circle.

galactic poles The poles of the galactic circle.

galacto- *combining form* Milk; milky: *galactopoietic*. Also, before vowels, **galact-.** [< Gk. *gala, galaktos* milk]

gal·ac·tom·e·ter (gal′ək·tom′ə·tər) *n.* A lactometer.

ga·lac·to·poi·et·ic (gə-lak′tō-poi-et′ik) *adj. & n.* Galacta-gogue. [< GALACTO- + Gk. *poiētikos* capable of making]

ga·lac·tose (gə-lak′tōs) *n. Chem.* A sweet, crystalline glu-cose, $C_6H_{12}O_6$, the dextrorotatory form of which is obtained when milk sugar is treated with dilute acids.

Gal·a·had (gal′ə-had) In Arthurian legend, the noblest knight of the Round Table, son of Lancelot and Elaine, who accomplished the quest for the Holy Grail. — *n.* Any man of great purity and nobility.

ga·lan·gal (gə-lang′gəl) *n.* The aromatic rootstock of vari-ous East Indian herbs (genus *Alpinia*) of the ginger family: also spelled *galingale*. Also **gal·an·gale** (gal′ən-gāl). [< OF *galingal* < Arabic *khalanjān* < Chinese *Ko-liang-kiang* mild ginger from the province Ko]

gal·an·tine (gal′ən-tēn) *n.* A cold preparation of boned, stuffed, and seasoned chicken, veal, etc., served in its own jelly. [< F]

ga·lan·ty show (gə-lan′tē) A shadow pantomime in minia-ture, the shadows being cast by figures cut from paper. [Prob. < Ital. *galante* gallant]

Ga·lá·pa·gos Islands (gä-lä′pä-gōs) A Province of Ecuador comprising a Pacific island group 600 miles west of the main-land; 3,029 sq. mi.; pop. 1,900 (est. 1960); capital, San Cris-tóbal: officially *Colón Archipelago*.

Gal·a·ta (gä′lä-tä) A commercial part of Istanbul, Turkey.

gal·a·te·a (gal′ə-tē′ə) *n.* A strong, twilled cotton fabric, white or striped, used in making women's and children's gar-ments. [after the *Galatea*, a British warship]

Gal·a·te·a (gal′ə-tē′ə) In Greek mythology, an ivory statue of a maiden brought to life by Aphrodite after its sculptor, Pygmalion, had fallen in love with it.

Ga·la·ţi (gä-läts′, -lä′tsē) A port city in eastern Rumania on the Danube; pop. 101,878 (est. 1959). Also **Ga·latz** (gä′läts).

Ga·la·tia (gə-lā′shə, -shē-ə) An ancient country of central Asia Minor, so called from the Gauls who invaded and con-quered the region in the third century B.C. *Greek* **Ga·la·tei·a.**

Ga·la·tian (gə-lā′shən) *adj.* Belonging or relating to an-cient Galatia. — *n.* A native of ancient Galatia. — **Epistle to the Galatians** A book of the New Testament consisting of a letter written by the apostle Paul, about A.D. 56, to the Christians of Galatia. Also **Galatians.** Abbr. **Gal.**

gal·a·vant (gal′ə-vant) See GALLIVANT.

ga·lax (gā′laks) *n.* An evergreen herb (*Galax aphylla*) of the SE United States with white flowers and glistening leaves. [< NL < Gk. *gala* milk]

gal·ax·y (gal′ək-sē) *n. pl.* **·ax·ies** 1. *Astron.* Any very large system of stars, nebulae, or other celestial bodies: also called *island universe*. 2. *Usually cap.* The Milky Way. 3. Any brilliant group, as of persons. [< F *galaxie* < L *galaxias* the Milky Way < Gk. < *gala* milk]

Gal·ba (gal′bə, gôl′-), **Servius Sulpicius,** 5?B.C.–A.D. 69, Roman emperor 68–69.

gal·ba·num (gal′bə-nəm) *n.* A bitter, odorous gum resin obtained from certain herbs, especially the giant fennel, and used medicinally and in plasters. [< L *galbanum* < Gk. *chalbanē* < Hebrew *helbenah*]

gale[1] (gāl) *n.* 1. *Meteorol.* A wind stronger than a stiff breeze. See BEAUFORT SCALE. 2. *Poetic* A gentle breeze; zephyr. 3. An outburst, as of hilarity. [Origin uncertain]

gale[2] (gāl) *n.* A branching, sweet-smelling marsh shrub (*Myrica gala*) of the eastern United States. See SWEETGALE. [OE *gagel*]

Gale (gāl), **Zona,** 1874–1938, U.S. novelist and playwright.

ga·le·a (gā′lē-ə) *n. pl.* **·le·ae** (-li-ē) *Bot. & Zool.* A mem-brane or part having the shape of a helmet; especially, a part of the corolla or calyx of certain flowers. [< L, helmet]

ga·le·ate (gā′lē-āt) *adj.* 1. Resembling a helmet. 2. Hav-ing a galea. Also **ga·le·at·ed.**

ga·le·i·form (gā′lē-ə-fôrm′, gə-lē′-) *adj.* Galeate. [< L *galea* helmet + -*i*- + -FORM]

Ga·len (gā′lən), 130?–200?, Greek physician and medical writer. — **Ga·len·ic** (gə-len′ik, -lē′nik) or **·i·cal** *adj.*

ga·le·na (gə-lē′nə) *n.* A metallic, dull gray, cleavable, iso-metric lead sulfide, PbS, one of the principal ores of lead. Also **ga·le·nite** (gə-lē′nīt). [< L, lead ore]

Ga·len·ism (gā′lən-iz′əm) *n.* The theory or practice of medicine followed by Galen. — **Ga·len·ist** *n.*

Ga·ler·as Volcano (gä-ler′äs) See PASTO.

Gales·burg (gālz′bûrg) A city in western Illinois; pop. 37,243.

Ga·li·bi (gä-lē′bē) *n.* A Carib Indian, especially of the tribes in the Guianas.

Ga·li·cia (gə-lish′ə, *Polish* gä-lē′tsē-ä, *Sp.* gä-lē′thyä) 1. A region in SE Poland and the NW Ukrainian S.S.R., formerly an Austrian crownland. 2. A region and former kingdom in NW Spain.

Ga·li·cian (gə-lish′ən) *adj.* 1. Of or pertaining to Spanish Galicia, its people, or their language. 2. Of or pertaining to Polish Galicia or its native people. — *n.* 1. A native or in-habitant of Spanish Galicia. 2. The Portuguese dialect spoken in Spanish Galicia. 3. A native or inhabitant of Polish Galicia.

Gal·i·le·an (gal′ə-lē′ən) *adj.* Belonging or relating to Gali-lee. — *n.* 1. A native or inhabitant of Galilee. 2. A

Christian: so called opprobriously in ancient times by the Jews. — **the Galilean** Jesus Christ. Also **Gal′i·lae′an.**

Gal·i·le·an (gal′ə-lē′ən) *adj.* Of or pertaining to Galileo.

gal·i·lee (gal′ə-lē) *n. Chiefly Brit.* A porch or chapel at the west end of some English abbey churches.

Gal·i·lee (gal′ə-lē) A region in northern Palestine.

Galilee, Sea of A fresh-water lake in northern Palestine on the Israel-Jordan border, 64 sq. mi.: Old Testament *Sea of Chinnereth*; New Testament *Sea of Gennesaret*: also *Lake Tiberias*.

Gal·i·le·o (gal′ə-lē′ō, *Ital.* gä-lē-lā′ō), 1564–1642, Florentine astronomer and physicist, founder of the science of dy-namics; his support of Copernican ideas led to his condem-nation by the Roman Inquisition: full name **Galileo Gal·i·le·i** (gal′ə-lā′ē).

gal·i·ma·ti·as (gal′ə-mä′shē-əs, -mat′ē-əs) *n.* Confused or meaningless talk; gibberish. [< F]

gal·in·gale (gal′in-gāl) *n.* 1. A tall, perennial, rare sedge (*Cyperus longus*) of southern England, with aromatic tuber-ous roots. 2. Galangal. [See GALANGAL]

gal·i·ot (gal′ē-ət) *n.* 1. A small galley propelled by sails and oars. 2. A one- or two-masted Dutch or Flemish merchant vessel. Also spelled *galliot*. [< OF, dim. of *galie* < Med.L *galea* galley]

gal·i·pot (gal′i-pot) *n.* A white turpentine resin exuded by a pine (*Pinus pinaster*) of southern Europe: also spelled *gal-lipot*. [< F]

gal·i·vant (gal′ə-vant, gal′ə-vant′) See GALLIVANT.

gall[1] (gôl) *n.* 1. *Physiol.* The bitter fluid secreted by the liver; bile. 2. Bitter feeling; rancor. 3. Something bitter and disagreeable. 4. *Anat.* The gall bladder. 5. *U.S. Slang* Cool impudence; effrontery. [OE *gealla*]

gall[2] (gôl) *n.* 1. An abrasion or sore produced by friction. 2. Something that irritates or vexes. 3. Irritation or exas-peration. — *v.t.* 1. To make sore or injure (the skin) by friction; chafe. 2. To vex or irritate. — *v.i.* 3. To become or be chafed or irritated. [Prob. < GALL[1]]

gall[3] (gôl) *n.* An abnormal plant growth produced through localized irritation or injury, as by insects, bacteria, viruses, fungi, chemicals, etc.; especially, such a growth on certain oaks, valuable because of the tannin content. [< F *galle* < L *galla* gallnut]

gall. Gallon(s).

Gal·la (gal′ə) *n.* 1. A member of a tribe of Hamitic origin inhabiting Ethiopia. 2. The language of this tribe.

gal·lant (gal′ənt *for adj. defs.* 1, 4, 5; gə-lant′, gal′ənt *for adj. defs.* 2 & 3; *n.* gal′ənt, gə-lant′; *v.* gə-lant′) *adj.* 1. Possessing spirit and courage; intrepid; brave: *gallant* soldiers. 2. Chiv-alrously attentive to women. 3. Dashingly amorous. 4. Stately; imposing: a *gallant* fortress. 5. Gaily colorful or showy: *gallant* attire. — *n.* 1. A brave, spirited man. 2. A man chivalrously attentive to women. 3. A man who is amorous in a courtly or dashing way. 4. A suitor or para-mour. — *v.t.* 1. To be chivalrously or amorously attentive to (a woman). 2. To escort (a woman). — *v.i.* 3. To be a suitor or paramour; make love. [< OF *galant*, ppr. of *galer* to rejoice] — **gal′lant·ly** *adv.*

gal·lant·ry (gal′ən-trē) *n. pl.* **·ries** 1. Nobility and bra-very. 2. Chivalrous behavior. 3. The behavior of a dash-ingly amorous man. 4. An instance of gallant speech or be-havior. 5. *Archaic* Colorful or showy appearance or attire.

gall-apple (gôl′ap′əl) *n.* A gallnut.

Gal·la·tin (gal′ə-tin), (**Abraham Alfonse**) **Albert,** 1761–1849, U.S. statesman and financier born in Switzerland.

Gal·lau·det (gal′ə-det′), **Thomas Hopkins,** 1787–1851, U.S. educator; founded first deaf-mute institution in the United States.

gall bladder *Anat.* A small, pear-shaped muscular pouch situated beneath the liver in man and serving as a reservoir for bile conducted through the **gall duct.**

Galle (gäl) A port city in SW Ceylon; pop. 55,848 (1953): formerly *Point de Galle.*

Gal·le (gäl′ə), **Johann Gottfried,** 1812–1910, German astronomer; discoverer of Neptune, 1846.

GALLEASS

gal·le·ass (gal′ē-as, -əs) *n.* A large galley of the 15th to 17th centuries, carrying three masts, heavily armed, and used chiefly in the Mediterranean as a war vessel: also spelled *galliass*. [< F *galeace* < Ital. *galeaza*, aug. of *galea* < Med.L. See GALLEY.]

gal·le·on (gal′ē-ən) *n.* A large sailing vessel of the 15th to 17th centuries, typically with three or four decks, used in commerce and warfare. [< Sp. *galeón*, aug. of *galea* < Med.L. See GALLEY.]

gal·ler·y (gal′ər-ē) *n. pl.* **·ler·ies** 1. A roofed promenade, especially one extending along one of the inner or outer walls of a building and having an open side. 2. Any long, usu-ally narrow and enclosed area suggestive of such a passage-way, as a hall. 3. *Southern U.S.* A veranda. 4. An ele-vated floor section used as an additional seating area in a theater or other large building, projecting from the rear over the back part of the main floor; also, the area, seats, or oc-cupants of such a section. 5. A group of spectators, as of those in a grandstand. **6.** A part of the general public viewed as shallow in thought, undiscriminating, etc. **7.** A room or building in which statues, paintings, etc., are displayed. **8.** A room or building in which articles are sold to the highest bidder. **9.** A collection of art objects, photographs, etc., for exhibition. **10.** An enclosed place, as at a fair, where one shoots at targets for amusement. **11.** A tunnel

GALLEON

or other underground passage, as one connecting fortified positions or as in a mine. **12.** A balcony projecting from the stern of certain large old ships. — **to play to the gallery 1.** Of an actor, etc., to put on a performance designed to please the less discriminating part of the audience. **2.** To cater to the common crowd. — *v.t.* **·ler·ied, ·ler·y·ing** To provide with a gallery. [< F *galerie* < Med.L *galeria*, ? alter. of *galilaea* (porch)]

gal·ley (gal′ē) *n. pl.* **·leys 1.** A long, low vessel used in ancient and medieval times, propelled by oars and sails or by oars alone. **2.** A large rowboat. **3.** The kitchen of a ship. **4.** *Printing* **a** A long tray for holding composed type. **b** A galley proof. **c** An approximate unit of measurement, about 22 inches, used in composition. [< OF *galee* < Med.L *galea* < LGk. *galaia*]

galley proof *Printing* **1.** A proof taken from type composed in a galley and used for making corrections before page composition. **2.** Two or more such proofs collectively.

galley slave 1. A slave or convict condemned to row a galley. **2.** One who does monotonous work; drudge.

galley west *U.S. Informal* Completely out of shape, position, action, etc.: used chiefly in the phrase **to knock galley west.** [Cf. dial. E *collywest* contrary, crooked, askew]

gall·fly (gôl′flī′) *n. pl.* **·flies** Any of various small insects that deposit their eggs in plant tissue, with consequent production of galls.

Gal·li·a (gal′ē·ə) The Latin name for GAUL.

gal·liard (gal′yərd) *n.* **1.** A lively dance, popular in the 16th and 17th centuries. **2.** Music for or in the manner of this dance, written in triple meter. — *adj. Archaic* **1.** Full of high spirits; gay. **2.** Gallant. [< OF *gaillard*]

gal·liard·ise (gal′yər·dēz) *n. Archaic* Gaiety or revelry. [< F *gaillardise*]

gal·li·ass (gal′ē·as, -əs) See GALLEASS.

gal·lic (gal′ik) *adj. Chem.* **1.** Of, pertaining to, or derived from gallium. **2.** Relating to or derived from gallnuts.

gallic acid *Chem.* A white, odorless, crystalline organic compound, $C_7H_6O_5 \cdot H_2O$, found in many plants and used in the making of inks, dyestuffs, paper, etc. Abbr. *Ga.*

Gal·lic (gal′ik) *adj.* Of or pertaining to ancient Gaul or modern France; French. [< L *Gallicus* < *Gallus* inhabitant of Gaul]

Gal·li·can (gal′ə·kən) *adj.* **1.** Of or pertaining to Gallicanism. **2.** Gallic. — *n.* A supporter of Gallicanism.

Gal·li·can·ism (gal′ə·kən·iz′əm) *n.* A theory or movement formerly supported by large elements of the French Roman Catholic clergy and laity and formally enunciated in the **Gallican Articles** in 1682, supporting certain customs, privileges, and policies (the **Gallican Liberties**) according to which the authority of the Pope would be greatly curtailed: opposed to *Ultramontanism.*

Gal·li·cism (gal′ə·siz′əm) *n.* An idiom or turn of phrase peculiar to French.

Gal·li·cize (gal′ə·sīz) *v.t. & v.i.* **·cized, ·ciz·ing** To make or become French in character, language, etc.; Frenchify. Also *Brit.* **Gal·li·cise.**

Gal·li-Cur·ci (gäl′lē-koor′chē), **Amelita,** 1889–1963, Italian operatic soprano active in the United States.

gal·li·gas·kins (gal′i·gas′kinz) *n.pl.* **1.** Long, loose hose or breeches, worn in the 16th century; also, in humorous usage, any loose breeches. **2.** A sportsman's leather leggings. Also spelled *gallygaskins.* [Alter. of MF *garguesque,* var. of *greguesque* < Ital. *grechesca,* fem. of *grechesco* Greek]

gal·li·mau·fry (gal′i·mô′frē) *n. pl.* **·fries** A hash or hodgepodge. [< F *gallimafrée;* ult. origin unknown]

gal·li·na·cean (gal′ə·nā′shən) *n.* A gallinaceous bird. — *adj.* Gallinaceous.

gal·li·na·ceous (gal′ə·nā′shəs) *adj.* **1.** Of or pertaining to an order of birds (*Galliformes*), including the common hen, turkeys, partridges, etc. **2.** Resembling gallinaceous birds. [< L *gallinaceus* < *gallina* hen]

Gal·li·nas Point (gä·yē′näs) A cape in northern Colombia; the northernmost point of the South American continent.

gall·ing (gô′ling) *adj.* Very annoying or exasperating; most irritating. — **gall′ing·ly** *adv.*

gal·li·nip·per (gal′ə·nip′ər) *n.* A large American mosquito (*Psorophora ciliata*). [Origin uncertain]

gal·li·nule (gal′ə·nyōol, -nōol) *n.* Any of several cootlike wading birds of the rail family; especially, the **Florida gallinule** (*Gallinula chloropus cachinnans*). [< NL *gallinula,* dim. of L *gallina* hen]

gal·li·ot (gal′ē·ət) See GALIOT.

Gal·lip·o·li (gə·lip′ə·lē) A port city on the **Gallipoli Peninsula** in European Turkey, between the Gulf of Saros and the Dardanelles; pop. 36,400 (1960). Turkish *Gelibolu.*

gal·li·pot¹ (gal′i·pot) *n.* A small earthen jar, as for ointments, used especially by druggists. [? < GALLEY + POT, because orig. imported on galleys]

gal·li·pot² (gal′i·pot) See GALIPOT.

gal·li·um (gal′ē·əm) *n.* A rare, bluish white, metallic element (symbol Ga) in the aluminum group, having a low melting point (86° F.). See ELEMENT. [< NL < L *gallus* cock, trans. of *Lecoq* de Boisbaudran, 1838–1912, its discoverer]

gal·li·vant (gal′ə·vant, gal′ə·vant′) *v.i.* To roam about capriciously, as in looking for diversion: gad: also spelled *galavant, galivant.* [? Alter. of GALLANT]

gal·li·wasp (gal′i·wosp′, -wôsp′) *n.* A harmless lizard (genus *Diploglossus*) of Central America and the West Indies: also spelled *gallywasp.* [Appar. < GALLEY + WASP; orig. an insect that infested West Indian ships]

gall midge Any of various gnats (family *Cecidomyiidae*) whose larvae produce galls on plants. Also **gall gnat.** For illustration see INSECTS (injurious).

gall·nut (gôl′nut′) *n.* A gall produced on certain oaks or other plants: also called *gall-apple.*

Gallo- *combining form* Gaulish or French: *Gallo-Roman.* [< L *Gallus* Gaul]

gal·lo·glass (gal′ō·glas′, -gläs′) *n.* In ancient Ireland, an armed retainer of a chief. Also **gal′low·glass′.** [< Irish *gallóglach* < *gall* stranger + *oglach* soldier]

gal·lon (gal′ən) *n.* **1.** A liquid measure of capacity that by the United States standard (**wine gallon**) contains 231 cubic inches or 4 quarts or 3.78 liters and by the British standard (**imperial gallon**) 277.42 cubic inches or 4 imperial quarts or 5 American quarts or 4.546 liters. **2.** A dry measure that is equivalent to ⅛ bushel. **3.** A container with a capacity of 1 gallon. Abbr. *gal., gall.* See table inside back cover. [< AF *galon,* ? < Celtic]

gal·loon (gə·lōon′) *n.* A narrow braid or other trimming of worsted, silk, or rayon or sometimes of gold or silver thread. [< OF *galon* < *galonner* to adorn with ribbons]

gal·loot (gə·lōot′) See GALOOT.

gal·lop (gal′əp) *n.* **1.** The fastest gait of a horse or other quadruped, characterized by a regular succession of leaps during which all four feet are off the ground at once. **2.** A ride at a gallop. **3.** Any rapid pace. — *v.i.* **1.** To ride at a gallop. **2.** To go, run, or move very fast. — *v.t.* **3.** To cause to gallop. [< OF *galop* < *galoper* < Gmc. Doublet of WALLOP.] — **gal′lop·er** *n.*

gal·lo·pade (gal′ə·pād′) *n.* The galop, a dance.

gal·lous (gal′əs) *adj. Chem.* Designating a compound containing bivalent gallium: *gallous* bromide.

Gal·lo·way (gal′ə·wā) A district of SW Scotland comprising the counties of Wigtownshire and Kirkcudbrightshire.

Gal·lo·way (gal′ə·wā) *n.* **1.** A small horse, originally from Galloway, Scotland, now nearly or altogether extinct. **2.** A breed of dark cattle from Galloway, Scotland.

gal·low·glass (gal′ō·glas′, -gläs′) See GALLOGLASS.

gal·lows (gal′ōz) *n. pl.* **·lows·es** or **·lows 1.** A framework typically consisting of two or more upright beams supporting a crossbeam, used for executing a condemned person by hanging. Also **gallows tree. 2.** Any similar structure, as a set of crossbars. **3.** A gallows bird. [OE *galga*]

gallows bird *Informal* One who merits hanging.

gall·stone (gôl′stōn′) *n. Pathol.* A small, stony mass sometimes formed in the gall bladder or bile passages: also called *bilestone.*

Gal·lup (gal′əp), **George Horace,** born 1901, U.S. statistician and public-opinion analyst.

gal·lus (gal′əs) *pl.* **·lus·es** *Usually pl. U.S. Dial.* Suspenders for trousers. [< GALLOWS]

gall wasp A gallfly.

gal·ly·gas·kins (gal′i·gas′kinz) See GALLIGASKINS.

gal·ly·wasp (gal′i·wosp′, -wôsp′) See GALLIWASP.

ga·loot (gə·lōot′) *n. U.S. Slang* An awkward or uncouth fellow: also spelled *galloot.* [Cf. Du. *gelubt* castrated]

gal·op (gal′əp) *n.* **1.** A lively round dance, apparently of 19th century German origin. **2.** Music for or in the manner of this dance, written in duple meter. Also called *gallopade.* Also **gal·o·pade** (gal′ə·pād′). [< F, gallop]

ga·lore (gə·lôr′, -lōr′) *adv.* In great numbers or abundance: to offer bargains galore. — *n. Rare* Abundance. [< Irish *go leór,* enough]

ga·losh (gə·losh′) *n.* **1.** *Usually pl.* An overshoe reaching above the ankle and worn in snowy or wet weather. **2.** *Obs.* A heavy boot or shoe. Also spelled *golosh.* Also **ga·loshe′.** [< F *galoche,* ult. < Gk. *kalopous* wooden shoe]

gals. Gallons.

Gals·wor·thy (gôlz′wûr·the̅), **John,** 1867–1933, English novelist and playwright: pseudonym **John Sin·john** (sin′jən).

Gal·ton (gôl′tən), **Sir Francis,** 1822–1911, English scientist. — **Gal·to·ni·an** (gôl·tō′nē·ən) *adj.*

ga·lumph (gə·lumf′) *v.i.* To clump along pompously. [< GAL(LOP) + (TRI)UMPH; coined by Lewis Carroll]

galv. Galvanic; galvanism; galvanized.

Gal·va·ni (gäl·vä′nē), **Luigi,** 1737–98, Italian physiologist.

gal·van·ic (gal·van′ik) *adj.* **1.** Of, pertaining to, or caused by electricity as produced by chemical action. Abbr. *galv.* **2.** Pertaining to or resembling a reaction to an electric shock; convulsive. Also **gal·van′i·cal.** — **gal·van′i·cal·ly** *adv.*

galvanic battery *Electr.* A battery of primary cells.

galvanic cell *Electr.* A primary cell (which see).

galvanic pile *Electr.* A voltaic pile (which see).

gal·va·nism (gal′və·niz′əm) *n.* **1.** Electricity as produced by chemical action: also called *voltaism.* Abbr. *galv.* **2.** *Med.* The therapeutic application of a continuous electric current from voltaic cells. [after Luigi *Galvani* + -ISM]

gal·va·nize (gal′və·nīz) *v.t.* **·nized, ·niz·ing 1.** To stimulate to muscular action by electricity. **2.** To rouse to action; startle; excite. **3.** To provide iron, steel, etc. with a protective coating of zinc. Also *Brit.* **gal′va·nise.** — **gal′va·ni·za′tion** *n.* — **gal′va·niz′er** *n.*

galvano- *combining form* Galvanic; galvanism: *galvanometer.*

gal·va·no·cau·ter·y (gal′və·nō·kô′tər·ē) *n. pl.* **·ter·ies** *Med.* A cautery made with a wire heated by an electric current.

gal·va·nom·e·ter (gal′və·nom′ə·tər) *n. Electr.* An apparatus for indicating the presence and determining the strength and direction of an electric current. — **gal·va·no·met·ric** (gal′və·nō·met′rik, gal·van′ō-) or **·ri·cal** *adj.*

gal·va·nom·e·try (gal′və·nom′ə·trē) *n.* The science, art, or process of measuring electric currents.

gal·va·no·plas·ty (gal′və·nō·plas′tē, gal·van′ō-) *n.* The process of coating objects with metal by electrodeposition so as to reproduce their forms; electrotypy. Also **gal′va·no·plas′tics.** — **gal′va·no·plas′tic** *adj.*

gal·va·no·scope (gal′və·nō·skōp′, gal·van′ə-) *n.* An instrument for detecting an electric current and showing its direction: also called *rheoscope.* — **gal·va·no·scop·ic** (gal′və·nō·skop′ik, gal·van′ō-) *adj.*

gal·va·nos·co·py (gal′və·nos′kə·pē) *n. pl.* **·pies 1.** Use of the galvanoscope. **2.** *Med.* Diagnosis by galvanism.

gal·va·no·ther·my (gal′və·nō·thûr′mē) *n.* Production of heat by galvanism, especially as a therapeutic measure.

Gal·ves·ton (gal′vəs·tən) A port city in SE Texas, at the NE end of **Galveston Island** in **Galveston Bay,** an inlet of the Gulf of Mexico; pop. 61,809.

Galveston plan Commission plan (which see).

Gal·way (gôl′wā) A county in western Ireland; 2,293 sq. mi.; pop. 155,553 (1956); capital, **Galway,** pop. 21,219.

Galway Bay An inlet of the Atlantic in Western Ireland.

Gal·we·gian (gal·wē′jən) *adj.* Of or pertaining to Galloway, Scotland. — *n.* A native or inhabitant of Galloway.

gal·yak (gal′yak) *n.* A flat fur from the skin of a prematurely born kid or lamb. [< Russian *golyak* bare]

gam¹ (gam) *n.* **1.** A herd or school of whales. **2.** *U.S. Dial.* A social visit; especially, an exchange of visits between whaling vessels and crews. — **Syn.** See FLOCK. — *v.* **gammed, gam·ming** *v.i.* **1.** *U.S. Dial.* To visit socially; especially, to visit back and forth while at sea. — *v.t.* **2.** *U.S. Dial.* To make a visit or visits to. [? Var. of GAME¹]

gam² (gam) *n. Slang* A leg, especially of a woman. [Var. of GAMB]

Ga·ma (gam′ə, *Pg.* gä′mə), **Vasco da,** 1469?–1524, Portuguese seafarer and explorer; first European to reach India, 1498, by a sea route around Africa.

Ga·ma·li·el (gə·mā′li·əl, -māl′yəl) A Pharisee, preceptor of the apostle Paul. *Acts* v 34; xxii 3.

ga·mash·es (gə·mash′əz, -mäsh′-) *n.pl. Brit. Dial.* Leggings or high boots worn by horseback riders. [< F *gamache*]

gamb (gam) *n.* **1.** A leg; shank. **2.** *Heraldry* The entire foreleg of a beast, especially of a lion. Also **gambe.** [< OF *gambe,* var. of *jambe.* See JAMB.]

gam·ba·do¹ (gam·bā′dō) *n. pl.* **·dos** or **·does 1.** *pl.* Leather bootlike devices attached to a saddle, and serving as stirrups. **2.** A legging; gaiter. [< Ital. *gamba* leg]

gam·ba·do² (gam·bā′dō) *n. pl.* **·dos** or **·does 1.** The curvetting of a horse. **2.** Any leaping about; antic; caper. Also **gam·bade′** (-bad′). [< F *gambade*]

gam·be·son (gam′bə·sən) *n.* A medieval coat made of leather or of cloth stuffed and quilted, worn as armor. [< OF *gambison* < Gmc.]

Gam·bet·ta (gam·bet′ə, *Fr.* gäṅ·be·tá′), **Léon,** 1838–82, French statesman.

Gam·bi·a (gam′bē·ə) An independent member of the British Commonwealth in west Africa; 4,003 sq. mi.; pop. 520,000 (est. 1975); capital, Banjul. See map at GUINEA.

Gam·bier Islands (gam′bir) A part of French Polynesia at the southern end of the Tuamotu group; 12 sq. mi.; pop. about 1,600; capital, Rikitea: also *Mangareva.*

gam·bir (gam′bir) *n.* The dried extract from the leaves and twigs of an Asian woody vine (*Uncaria gambir*), used as an astringent and tonic, and in tanning, dyeing, etc. Also **gam′·bi·a** (-bē·ə), **gam′bier.** [< Malay]

gam·bit (gam′bit) *n.* **1.** In chess, an opening in which a player risks or sacrifices a piece to gain a favorable position. **2.** Any opening move, as one to promote discussion. [< F < OF *gambet,* a tripping up, ult. < LL *gamba* leg]

gam·ble (gam′bəl) *v.* **·bled, ·bling** *v.i.* **1.** To risk or bet something of value on the outcome of an event, a game of chance, etc. **2.** To take a risk to obtain a desired result. — *v.t.* **3.** To wager or bet (something of value). **4.** To lose or squander by wagering or taking risks: usually with *away.* — *n. Informal* **1.** Any risky or uncertain venture. **2.** A gambling venture or transaction. [Cf. ME *gamenen,* OE *gamenian* to sport, play] — **gam′bler** (gam′blər) *n.*

gam·boge (gam·bōj′, -boozh′) *n.* **1.** A gum resin obtained from a tropical tree (*Garcinia hanburyi*), used as a pigment and cathartic. **2.** A bright yellow or orange-yellow color. [< NL *gambogium,* after *Cambodia,* where found]

gam·bol (gam′bəl) *v.i.* **gam·boled** or **·bolled, gam·bol·ing** or **·bol·ling** To skip or leap about in play; frolic. — *n.* A skipping about in sport. [Earlier *gambald* < F *gambader* < *gambade* spring, leap < Ital. *gambata* < *gamba* leg]

gam·brel (gam′brəl) *n.* **1.** The hock of a horse or similar animal. **2.** A gambrel roof. [< OF *gamberel,* dim. of *gambe* leg < LL *gamba*]

gambrel roof *Archit.* A ridged roof with the slope broken on each side so that the lower section has the steeper pitch.

GAMBREL ROOF

game¹ (gām) *n.* **1.** A contest governed by set rules, entered into for amusement, as a test of physical or mental prowess, or for money or other stakes. **2.** *pl.* Athletic competitions: the Olympic *games.* **3.** A single contest forming an integral part of a fixed series of contests: the second *game* of a set of tennis. **4.** The number of points fixed for winning, as in tennis or cards. **5.** The score at any particular time during a contest: After ten minutes of play, the *game* was 6–6. **6.** The equipment used in playing certain games, as the board and pieces used for chess. **7.** The kind of style or degree of prowess displayed in a contest: His *game* of golf is not very good. **8.** A form of playful activity: To her, love is merely a *game.* **9.** *Informal* Any profession, business, etc.: the teaching *game.* **10.** A procedure or plan designed to attain a certain objective: to see through their *game.* **11.** Collectively, animals, birds, or fish that are hunted or taken; also, the flesh of such animals, etc., used as food. **12.** Anything hunted or pursued; quarry. **13.** A fit target for ridicule, criticism, etc.: They were fair *game* for scorn. — **to make game of** To subject to ridicule, teasing, etc. — **to play the game 1.** To act with proper honor, courtesy, consideration, etc. **2.** To act in accordance with what is expected or customary. — *v.* **gamed, gam·ing** *v.i.* **1.** To gamble at cards, dice, etc., for money or other stakes. — *v.t.* **2.** To lose or squander by gambling: with *away.* — *adj.* **1.** Of or pertaining to hunted animals, etc., or their flesh. **2.** Having a fighting spirit; plucky. **3.** *Informal* Ready; willing: to be *game* for anything. [OE *gamen*]

game² (gām) *adj. Informal* Lame: a *game* leg. [Origin uncertain]

game bird Any bird commonly hunted, as a pheasant.

game·cock (gām′kok′) *n.* A rooster bred and trained for cockfighting.

game fowl 1. One of several breeds of fowl used in cockfighting. **2.** Any bird hunted as game.

game·keep·er (gām′kē′pər) *n.* A person having the care of game, as on an estate.

game laws Laws designed to protect wild game.

game·ly (gām′lē) *adv.* In a game manner; pluckily.

game·ness (gām′nis) *n.* Pluck; bravery; endurance.

games·man·ship (gāms′mən·ship) *n.* The facetious suggestion that unethical tactics, such as distracting an opponent's attention, be used to gain an advantage or victory. Compare ONE-UPMANSHIP.

game·some (gām′səm) *adj.* Playful; sportive; gay; merry. — **game′some·ly** *adv.* — **game′some·ness** *n.*

game·ster (gām′stər) *n.* One who habitually plays cards, dice, etc., for money; gambler.

gam·e·tan·gi·um (gam′ə·tan′jē·əm) *n. pl.* **·gi·a** (jē·ə) *Bot.* The plant cell or organ in which gametes are produced. [< GAMETE + Gk. *angeion* vessel]

gam·ete (gam′ēt, gə·mēt′) *n. Biol.* Either of two mature reproductive cells, an ovum or sperm, that in uniting produce a zygote. [< NL *gameta* < Gk. *gametē* wife, or *gametēs* husband] — **ga·met·ic** (gə·met′ik) *adj.*

game theory A mathematical theory dealing with strategies in games, economics, warfare, etc., by which one tries to calculate and overcome the moves of an opponent.

gameto- *combining form* Gamete: *gametophore.* [< Gk. *gametēs* husband < *gamos* marriage]

ga·me·to·cyte (gə-mē′tə-sīt) *n. Biol.* A cell that produces gametes.

gam·e·tog·e·ny (gam′ə-toj′ə-nē) *n. Biol.* The formation of gametes. Also **gam·e·to·gen·e·sis** (gam′ə-tō-jen′ə-sis).

ga·me·to·phore (gə-mē′tə-fôr, -fōr) *n. Bot.* A modified branch or filament that bears reproductive organs or gametes, as in certain liverworts.

ga·me·to·phyte (gə-mē′tə-fīt) *n. Bot.* The phase or generation that produces the sexual organs of a plant: distinguished from *sporophyte*.

gam·ic (gam′ik) *adj. Biol.* **1.** Sexual. **2.** Capable of development only after fecundation. Opposed to *agamic*. [< Gk. *gamikos* < *gamos* marriage]

gam·i·ly (gām′ə-lē) *adv.* **1.** Gamely. **2.** In a gamy manner.

gam·in (gam′in, *Fr.* gȧ-maṅ′) *n.* A homeless youngster who wanders about the streets of a city or town. [< F]

gam·ma (gam′ə) *n.* **1.** The third letter in the Greek alphabet (Γ, γ), corresponding to *g* (as in *go*). See ALPHABET. **2.** *Physics* A unit of magnetic field intensity, equal to 10⁻⁵ gauss. **3.** A unit of weight, equal to one thousandth of a milligram. **4.** *Photog.* A number expressing the degree to which a negative has been developed as compared with the range of light values in the subject photographed.

gam·ma·di·on (gə-mā′dē-ən) *n.* **1.** A cross made of four capital gammas, especially so as to form a swastika. **2.** A Greek cross formed of four capital gammas all facing outward so that the ends of the arms of the cross are open. [< LGk. < Gk. *gamma*, the letter G]

gamma globulin *Biochem.* A globulin present in blood plasma and containing antibodies effective against certain pathogenic microorganisms.

gamma rays *Physics* A type of electromagnetic radiation of great penetrating power and having a frequency greater than that of X-rays.

gam·mer (gam′ər) *n.* An old woman: now humorous or contemptuous. Compare GAFFER. [Alter. of GODMOTHER]

gam·mon¹ (gam′ən) *n.* In backgammon, a double victory, in which one player removes all his pieces before the other player removes any. — *v.t.* To obtain a gammon over. [? ME *gamen* game]

gam·mon² (gam′ən) *Brit. Informal n.* Deceitful nonsense or trickery. — *v.t.* **1.** To hoodwink by deceitful talk. — *v.i.* **2.** To talk gammon. [Origin uncertain] — **gam′·mon·er** *n.*

gam·mon³ (gam′ən) *n.* **1.** A cured or smoked ham. **2.** The bottom part of a side of bacon. — *v.t.* To cure by salting and smoking. [< OF *gambon* < *gambe* leg < LL *gamba*]

gam·mon⁴ (gam′ən) *Naut. n.* Gammoning. — *v.t.* To make fast (the bowsprit) to the stem by means of gammoning. [Origin unknown]

gam·mon·ing (gam′ən·ing) *n. Naut.* The rope or chain that fastens the bowsprit down to the stem of a vessel.

gamo- *combining form* **1.** *Biol.* Sexually joined: *gamogenesis*. **2.** *Bot.* Fused; united: *gamophyllous*. [< Gk. *gamos* marriage]

gam·o·gen·e·sis (gam′ə-jen′ə-sis) *n. Biol.* Sexual reproduction. — **gam′o·ge·net′ic** (-jə-net′ik) *adj.* — **gam′o·ge·net′i·cal·ly** *adv.*

gam·o·pet·al·ous (gam′ə-pet′əl-əs) *adj. Bot.* Pertaining to a division of plants in which the petals are united: also *sympetalous*.

gam·o·phyl·lous (gam′ə-fil′əs) *adj. Bot.* Having leaves united along their edges. [< GAMO- + Gk. *phyllon* leaf]

gam·o·sep·al·ous (gam′ə-sep′ə-ləs) *adj. Bot.* Having the sepals more or less united; monosepalous: also *synpetalous*.

-gamous *combining form* Pertaining to marriage or union for reproduction: used in adjectives corresponding to nouns in *-gamy*: *polygamous*. [< Gk. *gamos* marriage + -OUS]

gamp (gamp) *n. Brit.* A large heavy umbrella: a humorous usage. [With ref. to one carried by Mrs. *Gamp*, a character in Dickens' *Martin Chuzzlewit*]

gam·ut (gam′ət) *n.* **1.** The whole range of anything: the *gamut* of emotions. **2.** *Music* **a** The entire range or compass of tones used in modern music. **b** The major diatonic scale. [< Med.L *gamma ut* < *gamma*, the first note of the early musical scale + *ut* (later, *do*). The names of the notes of the scale were taken from a medieval Latin hymn: *Ut queant laxis Resonare fibris, Mira gestorum Famuli tuorum, Solve polluti Labii reatum, Sancte Iohannes.*]

gam·y (gā′mē) *adj.* **gam·i·er, gam·i·est** **1.** Having the flavor or odor of game, especially game that has been kept raw until somewhat tainted. **2.** Full of pluck; disposed to fight.

-gamy *combining form* Marriage or union for reproduction: *polygamy.* [< Gk. *gamos* marriage]

gan (gan) *Archaic & Poetic* Began.

Gand (gäṅ) The French name for GHENT.

gan·der (gan′dər) *n.* **1.** A male goose. **2.** *U.S. Slang* A look or glance: to take a *gander*. [OE *gandra*]

Gan·dhi (gän′dē, gan′-), **Mohandas Karamchand,** 1869–1948, Hindu political and spiritual leader: called *Mahatma Gandhi.*

gan·dy dancer (gan′dē) *U.S. Slang* A railroad laborer.

Gan·dzha (gän′jä) A former name for KIROVABAD.

ga·nef (gä′nəf) *n. Yiddish* A thief: also spelled *ganof, gonof, gonoph.*

gang¹ (gang) *n.* **1.** A group of persons organized or associated together for disreputable or illegal purposes: a *gang* of thieves. **2.** A crew of persons who work together: a road *gang.* **3.** *Informal* A group of persons associated together for social reasons: the neighborhood *gang.* **4.** *Informal* A group of persons with similar aims, principles, ideas, etc.: a *gang* of social climbers. **5.** A set of similar tools or other devices designed or arranged to operate as a unit: a *gang* of drills. **6.** Gangue. — **Syn.** See CABAL. — *v.t.* **1.** To unite into or as into a gang. **2.** *Informal* To attack as a group. — *v.i.* **3.** To come together as a gang; form a gang. — **to gang up on** *U.S. Slang* To attack or act against together: They *ganged up on* me. [OE *gang* a going < *gangan* to go]

gang² (gang) See GANGUE.

gang³ (gang) *v.i. Scot.* To go or walk.

gang·er (gang′ər) *n. Brit.* The foreman of a gang.

Gan·ges (gan′jēz) A river in northern India and Bangladesh, flowing SE about 1,560 miles from the Himalayas to the Bay of Bengal. *Sanskrit* and *Hindi* **Gan·ga** (gung′gä).

gang hook Two or three fish hooks joined together and attached to one line.

gan·gli·at·ed (gang′glē-ā′tid) *adj.* Possessing ganglia. Also **gan′gli·ate** (-it, -āt), **gan·gli·on·at·ed** (gang′glē-ən-ā′tid).

gan·gling (gang′gling) *adj.* Awkwardly tall and lanky. Also **gan′gly.** [Cf. dial. E *gangrel* a lanky person]

ganglio- *combining form* Ganglion. Also, before vowels, **gangli-** or **ganglion-,** as in *ganglionitis.*

gan·gli·on (gang′glē-ən) *n. pl.* **·gli·ons** or **·gli·a** (glē-ə) **1.** *Physiol.* A collection of nerve cells, outside of the central nervous system. **2.** Any center of energy, activity, or strength. **3.** *Pathol.* A hard, globular tumor growing from a tendon. [< LL < Gk. *ganglion* tumor] — **gan·gli·on·ic** (gang′glē-on′ik) *adj.*

gan·gli·on·i·tis (gang′glē-ən-ī′tis) *n. Pathol.* Inflammation of a ganglion.

gang·plank (gang′plangk′) *n.* A temporary bridge for passengers between a vessel and a wharf.

gang plow A set of plowshares arranged to work simultaneously.

gan·grel (gang′grəl, -rəl) *n. Scot.* A wanderer; vagrant.

gan·grene (gang′grēn, gang·grēn′) *n. Pathol.* The death or rotting of tissue in a part of the body, caused by a failure in the circulation of the blood, as from injury, disease, infection, etc. — *v.t. & v.i.* **·grened, ·gren·ing** To cause gangrene in or become affected by gangrene. [< L *gangraena* < Gk. *gangraina*] — **gan′gre·nous** (-grə-nəs) *adj.*

gang saw An arrangement of circular saws geared to perform several cutting operations simultaneously.

gang·ster (gang′stər) *n.* A member of a criminal gang.

Gang·tok (gung′tok) The capital of Sikkim protectorate; pop. 6,848 (est. 1971).

gangue (gang) *n. Mining* The nonmetalliferous or worthless minerals found in a vein of ore: also called *veinstone*: also spelled *gang.* [< F < G *gang* vein of ore]

gang·way (*n.* gang′wā, *interj.* gang′wā′) *n.* **1.** A passageway through, into, or out of any enclosure. **2.** *Brit.* A passage between rows of seats, as in a theater. **3.** *Brit.* An aisle across the House of Commons, separating older party members from newer members. **4.** *Naut.* **a** A passage on either side of a ship's upper deck. **b** An opening in a ship's bulwarks to give entrance to passengers or freight. **c** A gangplank. **5.** *Mining* The main level in a mine. — *interj.* Get out of the way! [OE *gangweg*]

gan·is·ter (gan′is-tər) *n.* **1.** A very hard, siliceous clay stone used chiefly in lining furnaces. **2.** A furnace lining made of ground quartz and fire clay. Also **gan′nis·ter.** [< dial. G *ganster* < MHG, spark]

gan·net (gan′it) *n.* Any of several large sea birds (family *Sulidae*) related to the pelicans; especially, a white bird (*Morus bassanus*) of this group that is common along North Atlantic coasts. [OE *ganot*]

ga·nof (gä′nəf) See GANEF.

gan·oid (gan′oid) *adj.* **1.** Pertaining to the *Ganoidei*, a large division of fishes, including sturgeons, bowfins, etc. **2.** Having an enamellike appearance, as the scales of fishes of the *Ganoidei* group. — *n.* A ganoid fish. [< Gk. *ganos* brightness + -OID]

gant·let¹ (gônt′lit, gant′-) See GAUNTLET¹.

gant·let² (gônt′lit, gant′-) *n.* **1.** A former military punishment in which the offender ran between two lines of men armed with clubs, whips, etc., who struck him as he passed. **2.** An onslaught of difficulties or criticism from all sides. **3.** A section of railroad track made up of two separated lines brought close together so as to pass through a tunnel, over a bridge, etc. — **to run the gantlet 1.** To be forced to pass along between two lines of people and be beaten by clubs, whips, etc. **2.** To be subjected to a fierce onslaught, as of criticism, difficulties, etc. — *v.t.* To bring (two separate lines of railroad track) close together. Also spelled *gauntlet*. [Earlier *gantlope*, alter. of Sw. *gatlopp* a running down a lane]

gant·line (gant′līn′) *n. Naut.* A rope rove through a block at the masthead of a vessel for temporary use. [Alter. of *girtline.* See GIRT, LINE.]

gan·try (gan′trē) *n. pl.* **·tries** **1.** A bridgelike framework for holding the rails of a traveling crane or for supporting railway signals. **2.** A gantry scaffold. **3.** A frame to support a barrel or cask in a horizontal position. Also spelled *gauntry.* [Alter. of OF *gantier, chantier* < L *canterius* beast of burden, framework < Gk. *kanthēlios* pack ass]

GANTRY (def. 1)

gantry scaffold *Aerospace* A large, mobile scaffolding used to assemble and service a large rocket on its launching pad.

Gan·y·mede (gan′ə·mēd) In Greek mythology, a beautiful shepherd boy whom Zeus, in the form of an eagle, carried to Olympus to be cupbearer to the gods. — *n.* **1.** Any youth who serves drinks: a humorous use. **2.** *Astron.* The third and largest satellite of Jupiter. [< Gk. *Ganymēdēs*]

GAO General Accounting Office.

gaol (jāl) *n. Brit.* Jail. [Var. of JAIL] — **gaol′er** *n.*

gap (gap) *n.* **1.** An opening or wide crack, as in a wall; aperture. **2.** A deep notch or ravine in a mountain ridge. **3.** A break in continuity; interruption; hiatus. **4.** A difference or divergence, as in character, knowledge, opinions, etc.: a *gap* between the clergy and the layman. **5.** *Electr.* The distance between two electrodes, as in a spark plug. — *v.t.* **gapped, gap·ping** To make or adjust a breach or opening in. [< ON *gap* gap, abyss < *gapa* to gape]

gape (gāp, gap) *v.i.* **gaped, gap·ing** **1.** To stare with or as with the mouth wide open, as in awe or surprise. **2.** To open the mouth wide, as in yawning. **3.** To be or become open wide. — *n.* **1.** The act of gaping. **2.** A wide opening; gap. **3.** *Zool.* The width of the fully opened mouth or beak, as of birds, fishes, etc. — **the gapes** **1.** A fit of gaping or yawning. **2.** A disease of young fowls, caused by gapeworms that obstruct the breathing. [< ON *gapa*] — **gap′er** *n.*

gape·seed (gāp′sēd′, gap′-, gāp′-) *n. Brit.* Anything that causes wonder or astonishment.

gape·worm (gāp′wûrm′, gap′-) *n.* A nematode worm (*Syngamus trachealis*) that causes the gapes.

gap·py (gap′ē) *adj.* **·pi·er, ·pi·est** Having gaps.

gap·y (gā′pē, gap′ē) *adj.* Affected with the gapes.

gar (gär) *n.* **1.** Any of several fresh-water fishes having a spearlike snout and elongate body, as the **long-nosed gar** (*Lepisosteus osseus*) of North America. **2.** A needlefish. [Short for GARFISH]

GAR or **G.A.R.** Grand Army of the Republic.

ga·rage (gə·räzh′, -räj′; *Brit.* gar′ij) *n.* A building in which motor vehicles are stored, serviced, or repaired. — *v.t.* **·raged, ·rag·ing** To put or keep in a garage. [< F < *garer* to protect, ult. < Gmc.]

Gar·a·mond (gar′ə·mond, *Fr.* gà·rà·môn′), **Claude**, 1561, French printer; designer of the type face known by his name.

Gar·and rifle (gar′ənd, gə·rand′) *U.S. Mil.* The M-1 rifle (which see). [after J. C. *Garand*, born 1888, U.S. inventor]

garb (gärb) *n.* **1.** Clothes; especially, apparel characteristic of some office, rank, etc.: clerical *garb.* **2.** External appearance, form, or expression; dress. — **Syn.** See DRESS. — *v.t.* To clothe; dress. [< MF *garbe* gracefulness, ult. < Gmc.]

gar·bage (gär′bij) *n.* **1.** Refuse from a kitchen, etc., consisting of unwanted or unusable pieces of meat, vegetable matter, eggshells, etc. **2.** Anything worthless or offensive. [Prob. < AF. Cf. OF *garbe* sheaf of grain, animal fodder.]

gar·ban·zo (gär·bän′zō, *Sp.* gär·vän′thō, -sō) *n. pl.* **·zos** The chickpea. [< Sp.]

gar·ble (gär′bəl) *v.t.* **·bled, ·bling** **1.** To mix up or confuse (a story, facts, etc.) unintentionally. **2.** To change or distort the meaning of (facts, texts, etc.) with intent to mislead or misrepresent. **3.** *Rare* To take the best part of. **4.** *Rare* To cull or sift. — *n.* **1.** The act of garbling. **2.** That which is garbled. [< Ital. *garbellare* < Arabic *gharbala* to sift < *ghirbal* sieve, ult. < L *cribellum*, dim. of *cribrum* sieve]

gar·board (gär′bôrd′, -bōrd′) *n. Naut.* One of the planks on a ship's bottom next to the keel. Also **garboard plank, garboard strake.** [< Du. *gaarboord*]

gar·boil (gär′boil) *n. Archaic* An uproar; commotion. [< MF *garbouil* < Ital. *garbuglio*, appar. < L *bullire* to boil]

Gar·cí·a Iñí·guez (gär·thē′ä ē′nyē·gäs), **Calixto**, 1836–98, Cuban patriot and general.

Gar·cí·a Lor·ca (gär·thē′ä lôr′kä), **Federico**, 1899–1936, Spanish poet, dramatist, and essayist.

gar·çon (gàr·sôn′) *n. pl.* **·cons** (-sôn′) *French* **1.** A boy or youth. **2.** A waiter. **3.** A male servant.

Gar·da (gär′dä), **Lake** The largest lake in Italy, on the Lombardy-Veneto border; 143 sq. mi.: also *Lago di Garda, Lago di Benaco.*

gar·dant (gär′dənt) *adj. Heraldry* Turned directly toward the observer, as an animal on a shield: also spelled *guardant.* [< F, orig. ppr. of *garder* to watch]

gar·den (gär′dən) *n.* **1.** A place for the cultivation of flowers, vegetables, or small plants. **2.** Any fertile, highly cultivated territory remarkable for the beauty of its vegetation. **3.** *Often pl.* A piece of ground, commonly with ornamental plants or trees, used as a place of public resort: botanical *gardens.* — *adj.* Grown or capable of being grown in a garden. — *v.t.* **1.** To cultivate as a garden. — *v.i.* **2.** To till or work in a garden. [< AF *gardin* < Gmc.]

Gar·den (gär′dən), **Mary**, 1877–1967, U.S. operatic soprano born in Scotland.

Gar·de·na (gär·dē′nə) A city in southern California, a suburb of Los Angeles; pop. 41,021.

garden apartment An apartment unit next to or overlooking a lawn, garden, or other landscaped area.

Garden City A city in SE Michigan, near Detroit; pop. 41,864.

gar·den·er (gärd′nər, gär′dən-ər) *n.* One who tends gardens or is skilled in gardening.

gar·de·ni·a (gär·dē′nē-ə, -dēn′yə) *n.* Any of a genus (*Gardenia*) of mainly tropical shrubs or trees of the madder family, with large, fragrant, yellow or white axillary flowers. [< NL, after Alexander *Garden*, 1730–91, U.S. botanist]

gar·den·ing (gärd′ning, gär′dən-ing) *n.* Cultivation of a garden. — **Syn.** See AGRICULTURE.

Garden Grove A city in southern California; pop. 122,524.

Garden of the Gods An area of eroded sandstone formations in central Colorado.

Garden State Nickname of NEW JERSEY.

garden variety Ordinary; run-of-the-mill.

garde·robe (gärd′rōb′) *n. Archaic* **1.** A wardrobe. **2.** The articles contained in a wardrobe. **3.** A bedroom or other private chamber. [< F < *garder* to keep + *robe* robe]

Gar·di·ner (gärd′nər, gär′də-nər), **Samuel Rawson**, 1829–1902, English historian. — **Stephen**, 1483?–1555, English prelate and statesman.

Gar·eth (gar′ith) One of the knights of the Round Table.

Gar·field (gär′fēld) A city in NE New Jersey; pop. 30,722.

Gar·field (gär′fēld), **James Abram**, 1831–81, 20th president of the United States 1881; assassinated.

Garfield Heights A city in northern Ohio, a suburb of Cleveland; pop. 41,417.

gar·fish (gär′fish′) *n. pl.* **·fish** or **·fish·es** A gar. [OE *gar* spear + FISH]

gar·ga·ney (gär′gə·nē) *n.* A small duck (*Anas querquedula*) of Europe and Asia. [< Ital. *garganello*]

Gar·gan·tu·a (gär·gan′chōō-ə) The peace-loving giant prince of Rabelais' satirical romance *Gargantua* (1534), noted especially for his enormous appetite.

Gar·gan·tu·an (gär·gan′chōō-ən) *adj.* Suggestive of Gargantua; huge: a *Gargantuan* appetite.

gar·get (gär′git) *n. Vet.* An infectious inflammation of the udder in cattle, sheep, etc.; also called *mastitis.* [< OF *gargate* throat < L *gurges* whirlpool]

gar·gle (gär′gəl) *v.* **·gled, ·gling** *v.i.* **1.** To rinse the back part of the mouth and upper part of the throat with a liquid kept agitated by slowly expelling air through the liquid. **2.** To make the bubbling sound peculiar to gargling. — *v.t.* **3.** To rinse (the throat and mouth) by gargling. **4.** To utter throatily as if gargling. — *n.* A liquid used for gargling. [< OF *gargouiller* to gargle < *gargouille* throat]

gar·goyle (gär′goil) *n.* A waterspout, usually made in the form of a grotesque human or animal figure, projecting from the gutter of a building. [< OF *gargouille* throat]

gar·i·bal·di (gar′ə·bôl′dē) *n.* A loose blouse resembling those worn by the soldiers of Garibaldi.

Gar·i·bal·di (gar′ə·bôl′dē, *Ital.* gä′rē·bäl′dē), **Giuseppe**, 1807–82, Italian patriot and general; worked to unite Italy. — **Gar′i·bal′di·an** *adj. & n.*

GARGOYLES
a Cathedral of Amiens, 13th century. *b* Cathedral of St. Eustache, Paris, 16th century. *c* Church of Montmartre, Paris, 19th century. *d* Chrysler building, New York, 20th century.

gar·ish (gâr′ish) *adj.* **1.** Marked by a dazzling glare. **2.** Vulgarly showy or gaudy, as dress. **3.** Extravagantly ornate; adorned to excess. — **Syn.** See GAUDY. [Cf. obs. *gaure* to stare] — **gar′ish·ly** *adv.* — **gar′ish·ness** *n.*

gar·land (gär′lənd) *n.* **1.** A wreath or rope of flowers, leaves, vines, etc., worn or otherwise used as a token of victory, joy, or honor. **2.** Anything resembling a garland. **3.** A collection of literary pieces, especially poems, short bits of prose, etc.; anthology. **4.** *Naut.* **a** A ring of rope, wire, etc., lashed to a spar to aid in hoisting it. **b** A sailor's netted provision bag. — *v.t.* To decorate with or make into a garland. [< OF *garlande*]

Gar·land (gär′lənd) A city in northern Texas, near Dallas; pop. 81,437.

Gar·land (gär′lənd), **(Hannibal) Hamlin**, 1860–1940, U.S. writer.

gar·lic (gär′lik) *n.* **1.** A hardy bulbous perennial (*Allium sativum*) with a compound bulb made up of 10 or 12 small bulbs. **2.** The pungent bulb or one of the cloves of this perennial, used in cooking and medicine. [OE *gārlēac* < *gār* spear + *lēac* leek]

gar·lick·y (gär′lik-ē) *adj.* Containing, resembling, or having the odor or taste of garlic

gar·ment (gär′mənt) *n.* **1.** An article of clothing, especially of outer clothing. **2.** *pl.* Clothes. **3.** Outer covering. — *v.t.* To clothe: usually in the past participle. — **Syn.** See DRESS. [< OF *garnement* < *garnir* to garnish]

gar·ner (gär′nər) *v.t.* To gather or store as in a granary; accumulate. — *n.* **1.** A place for storing grain; granary. **2.** Any storage place. [< OF *gernier, grenier* < L *granarium* granary < *granum* grain]

Gar·ner (gär′nər), **John Nance**, 1869–1967, U.S. politician, vice president 1933–41.

gar·net[1] (gär′nit) *n.* **1.** Any of a group of vitreous silicate minerals containing aluminum mixed with iron, manganese, calcium, or magnesium, varying in color; especially, any of the deep red varieties, as andradite or almandite, used as gems. **2.** A deep red color. [< OF *grenat* < Med.L *granatum* < L, pomegranate; so called from its color]

gar·net[2] (gär′nit) *n. Naut.* A form of tackle for hoisting cargo, etc. [Origin uncertain]

gar·ni·er·ite (gär′nē·ə·rīt′) *n.* An amorphous, light green, hydrous silicate of nickel and magnesium, forming an important ore of nickel. [after Jules *Garnier*, French geologist]

gar·nish (gär′nish) *v.t.* **1.** To add something to by way of decoration; embellish. **2.** In cookery, to decorate (a dish) with flavorsome or colorful trimmings. **3.** *Law* To garnishee. — **Syn.** See ADORN. — *n.* **1.** Something added to served food to decorate it and enhance its flavor. **2.** An added decoration; embellishment. **3.** *Archaic* A fee or exaction. [< OF *garniss-*, stem of *garnir* to prepare. Akin to WARN.]

gar·nish·ee (gär′nish·ē′) *Law v.t.* ·nish·eed, ·nish·ee·ing **1.** To attach (any debt or property in the hands of a third person that is due or belongs to a defendant) with notice that no return or disposal is to be made until a court judgment is issued. **2.** To issue a garnishment to. — *n.* A person who has been garnisheed.

gar·nish·ment (gär′nish·mənt) *n.* **1.** The act of garnishing. **2.** That which garnishes; embellishment. **3.** *Law* A warning or summons to appear in court, issued to one who is not a litigant in the case. **b** A notice to a person holding money or effects belonging to a defendant not to return or dispose of the money or effects pending court judgment.

gar·ni·ture (gär′ni·chər) *n.* Anything used to garnish; embellishment. [< F *garnir*. See GARNISH.]

Ga·ronne (gȧ·rôn′) A river in SW France, flowing 402 miles, generally NW, to the Gironde.

gar·pike (gär′pīk′) *n.* A gar. [< GAR[1] + PIKE]

gar·ret (gar′it) *n.* A room or set of rooms in an attic. [< OF *garite* watchtower < *garir* to watch, defend < Gmc.]

gar·ret·eer (gar′ə·tir′) *n.* One who lives in a garret.

Gar·rick (gar′ik), **David**, 1717–79, English actor, manager, and author.

gar·ri·son (gar′ə·sən) *n.* **1.** The military force stationed in a fort, town, etc. **2.** The place where such a force is stationed. — *v.t.* **1.** To place troops in, as a fort or town, for defense. **2.** To station (troops) in a fort, town, etc. **3.** To occupy as a garrison. [< OF *garison* < *garir* to defend < Gmc.]

Gar·ri·son (gar′ə·sən), **William Lloyd**, 1805–79, U.S. journalist, social reformer, and abolitionist.

garrison cap *Mil.* A military cap having a round, cloth top and a stiff, shiny visor, worn with the dress uniform.

gar·rote (gə·rot′, -rōt′) *n.* **1.** A former Spanish method of execution with a cord or metal collar tightened by a screwlike device; also, the cord or collar used. **2.** Any similar method of strangulation, especially in order to rob. — *v.t.* ·rot·ed, ·rot·ing **1.** To execute with a garrote. **2.** To throttle in order to rob, silence, etc. Also **ga·rote′, ga·rotte′, gar·rotte′.** [< Sp. *garrote*, orig. a stick, cudgel < Celtic] — **gar·rot′er** *n.*

gar·ru·line (gar′ŏŏ·līn, -lin, -yŏŏ-) *adj.* Of or pertaining to a subfamily of corvine birds (*Garrulinae*) including the jays. — *n.* A garruline bird. [< NL < L *garrulus* talkative]

gar·ru·li·ty (gə·rōō′lə·tē) *n.* Glib, empty, or excessive talkativeness.

gar·ru·lous (gar′ə·ləs, -yə-) *adj.* **1.** Given to continual or glib talking; habitually loquacious. **2.** Rambling and wordy. — **Syn.** See TALKATIVE. [< L *garrulus* talkative] — **gar′ru·lous·ly** *adv.* — **gar′ru·lous·ness** *n.*

gar·ter (gär′tər) *n.* A band worn around the leg or a tab attached to an undergarment to hold a stocking in place. — *v.t.* To support or fasten with a garter. [< AF *gartier* < OF *garet* bend of the knee < Celtic]

Gar·ter (gär′tər) *n.* **1.** The distinctive badge of the **Order of the Garter**, the highest order of knighthood in Great Britain. **2.** The order itself, or membership therein.

garter snake Any of various small, harmless, viviparous, brightly striped snakes (genus *Thamnophis*).

garth (gärth) *n.* **1.** The open space or courtyard enclosed by a cloister. **2.** *Archaic* A yard. [< ON *gardhr* yard]

Gar·y (gâr′ē) A city in NW Indiana, on Lake Michigan; pop. 175,415.

Gar·y (gâr′ē), **Elbert Henry**, 1846–1927, U.S. lawyer and financier.

gas (gas) *n. pl.* **gas·es** or **gas·ses 1.** A form of matter having extreme molecular mobility and capable of diffusing and expanding rapidly in all directions. **2.** Any such form of matter other than air; as: **a** A combustible mixture used for lighting or heating: illuminating *gas.* **b** A mixture used to produce anesthesia: laughing *gas.* **c** A chemical or mixture of chemicals designed to stupefy, injure, or kill: poison *gas.* **d** An explosive mixture of air and methane, etc., sometimes accumulated in coal mines. **3.** A noxious exhalation given off by improperly digested food in the stomach or intestines; also, the accumulation of such exhalations; flatulence. **4.** *Mining* A combustible mixture of firedamp and air. **5.** *U.S. Informal* Gasoline. **6.** *Slang* Long-winded talking. **7.** *Slang* Something much out of the ordinary or very exciting, satisfying, etc.: Her parties are a real *gas* — *v.* **gassed, gas·sing**; he, she, it **gas·ses** or **gas·es** — *v.t.* **1.** To subject to or affect with gas; as: **a** To stupefy or kill with poisonous fumes. **b** To fumigate. **c** To singe (a fabric) with burning gas so as to free from loose fibers. **2.** To fill or supply with gas. **3.** *U.S. Slang* To evoke a strong reaction, as of amusement or excitement, from: His remark *gassed* them. — *v.i.* **4.** To give off gas. **5.** *Slang* To talk excessively. — **to step on** (or **give her**) **the gas 1.** To push down the accelerator of a car, truck, etc. **2.** To go faster. [Coined by J. B. van Helmont, 1577–1644, Belgian chemist, either < Du. *geest* spirit or < L < Gk. *chaos* formless mass]

gas·a·lier (gas′ə·lir′) See GASELIER.

gas attack A military attack using toxic or irritant gases as an antipersonnel weapon.

gas·bag (gas′bag′) *n.* **1.** An expansible container for holding gas. **2.** *Slang* A tiresome, talkative person.

gas black A form of soot, produced by burning natural gas.

gas bomb A bomb or shell filled with poison gas that is released when the shell explodes. Also **gas shell.**

gas burner A tube or nozzle attached to a gas fixture, for regulating the flame of the gas consumed: also called *gas jet.*

Gas·coigne (gas′koin), **George**, 1535?–77, English poet.

gas·con (gas′kən) *n.* A boaster. [< F, a native of Gascony]

Gas·con (gas′kən) *adj.* Of or pertaining to Gascony or its assertedly boastful people. — *n.* A native of Gascony.

gas·con·ade (gas′kə·nād′) *v.i.* ·ad·ed, ·ad·ing To brag; bluster. — *n.* Boastful or blustering talk. [< F *gasconnade* < *gascon*. See GASCON.] — **gas′con·ad′er** *n.*

Gas·co·ny (gas′kə·nē) A region and former province of SW France. *French* **Gas·cogne** (gȧs·kôn′y′).

gas·e·lier (gas′ə·lir′) *n.* A chandelier consisting of metal branches tipped with gas burners: also spelled *gasalier, gasolier.* [< GAS + (CHAND)ELIER]

gas engine An internal-combustion engine, especially when designed to use illuminating or natural gas.

gas·e·ous (gas′ē·əs, -yəs, gash′əs) *adj.* **1.** Of, pertaining to, or resembling gas. **2.** Light and unsubstantial.

gas fitter One who fits and puts up gas fixtures.

gas fittings The appliances designed for the use of gas in heating, etc.

gas fixture A heating or illuminating fixture, usually ornamental, designed to use gas.

gas gangrene *Pathol.* Gangrene with gas formation in the tissues of dirty wounds, caused chiefly by anaerobic bacteria.

gash (gash) *v.t.* To make a long, deep cut in. — *n.* A long, deep cut or flesh wound. [Earlier *garse* < OF *garser* to scratch]

Ga·sher·brum (gu′shər·brŏŏm) Either of two peaks in northern Kashmir, **Gasherbrum I** (also *Hidden Peak*), 26,470 ft.; or **Gasherbrum II**, 26,360 ft.

gas·house (gas′hous′) *n.* A gasworks.

gas·i·form (gas′ə·fôrm) *adj.* Having the character of a gas.

gas·i·fy (gas′ə·fī) *v.t. & v.i.* ·fied, ·fy·ing To make into or become gas. — **gas′i·fi′a·ble** *adj.* — **gas′i·fi·ca′tion** *n.* — **gas′i·fi′er** *n.*

gas jet 1. A gas burner. **2.** The jet of flame on a gas burner.

Gas·kell (gas′kəl), **Elizabeth Cleghorn**, 1810–65, *née* Stevenson, English novelist.

gas·ket (gas′kit) *n.* **1.** *Mech.* A ring, disk, or plate of packing to make a joint or closure watertight or gastight. **2.** *Naut.* A rope or cord used to confine furled sails to the yard or boom. [Cf. Ital. *gaschetta* end of rope]

gas·kin (gas′kin) *n.* **1.** The upper part of the hind leg of a horse, donkey, etc., between the stifle and the hock. For illustration see HORSE. **2.** *pl. Obs.* Galligaskins. [? < GALLIGASKINS]

gas·light (gas′līt′) *n.* **1.** Light produced by the burning of illuminating gas. Also **gas light. 2.** A gas jet or burner.

gas log An imitation log concealing a gas burner, used in a fireplace.

gas main A large gas pipe conveying gas to smaller pipes.

gas·man (gas'man') *n. pl.* **·men** (-men') **1.** A man employed to read gas meters and note the amount of gas used. **2.** A gas fitter. **3.** *Mining* One who supervises ventilation and guards against firedamp.

gas mantle A network hood composed of the salts of ceria, etc., used to give light by incandescence in burning gas, as in the Welsbach burner, gasoline camping lanterns, etc.

gas mask A protective mask with an air filter worn to prevent poisoning or irritation by noxious gases, radioactive dust, etc. Also, *Brit., respirator.*

gas meter An apparatus for measuring the quantity of gas that passes through it.

gas·o·lier (gas'ə·lir') See GASELIER.

gas·o·line (gas'ə·lēn, gas'ə·lēn') *n. U.S.* A colorless, volatile, flammable liquid hydrocarbon, made by the fractional distillation of crude petroleum and used chiefly as a fuel for internal-combustion engines and as a solvent for fats. Also **gas'o·lene.** [< GAS + -OL² + -INE²]

gas·om·e·ter (gas·om'ə·tər) *n.* An apparatus for measuring gases.

gas·om·e·try (gas·om'ə·trē) *n.* The measurement of gases. **— gas·o·met·ric** (gas'ə·met'rik) *adj.*

gasp (gasp, gäsp) *v.i.* **1.** To take in the breath suddenly and sharply, as from fear or exhaustion; breathe convulsively. **2.** To have great longing or desire: with *for* or *after*. **— v.t. 3.** To say or utter while gasping. **— n. 1.** An act of convulsive and interrupted breathing. **2.** An utterance made while gasping. [< ON *geispa* yawn]

Gas·par (gäs·pär') See CASPAR.

Gas·pé Peninsula (gäs·pā') A peninsula in eastern Quebec, Canada, in the Gulf of St. Lawrence.

gasp·er (gas'pər, gäs'-) *n. Brit. Slang* A cigarette.

gas plant The herb fraxinella.

gas·sing (gas'ing) *n.* **1.** The act of one who or that which gasses. **2.** Subjection to gas.

gas station *U.S.* A filling station (which see).

gas·sy (gas'ē) *adj.* **·si·er, ·si·est 1.** Filled with, containing, or causing the formation of gas. **2.** Resembling or suggestive of gas. **3.** *Informal* Very talkative.

gas·ter·o·pod (gas'tər·ə·pod') See GASTROPOD.

gas thermometer A thermometer that indicates temperature changes by variations in the pressure or volume of a contained gas, usually hydrogen.

gas·tight (gas'tīt') *adj.* So constructed as not to permit the entrance or escape of a gas: a *gastight* container.

Gas·to·ni·a (gas·tō'nē·ə, -tōn'yə) A city in SW North Carolina, near Charlotte; pop. 47,412.

gas·tral·gi·a (gas·tral'jē·ə) *n.* Pain in or near the stomach.

gas·trec·to·my (gas·trek'tə·mē) *n. pl.* **·mies** *Surg.* An operation to remove a portion of the stomach.

gas·tric (gas'trik) *adj.* Of or pertaining to the stomach.

gastric juice *Biochem.* A fluid secreted by stomach glands, essential to digestion and containing several enzymes.

gastric ulcer *Pathol.* An ulcer formed on the stomach lining often by excess secretion of gastric juice.

gas·trin (gas'trin) *n. Biochem.* A hormone that promotes the flow of gastric juice.

gas·tri·tis (gas·trī'tis) *n. Pathol.* Inflammation of the lining or some other part of the stomach. **— gas·trit·ic** (gas·trit'ik) *adj.*

gastro- *combining form* **1.** Stomach: *gastrolith.* **2.** Stomach and: *gastroenterology.* Also **gastero-** or, before vowels, **gastr-.** [< Gk. *gastēr* stomach]

gas·tro·en·ter·i·tis (gas'trō·en'tə·rī'tis) *n. Pathol.* Inflammation of the mucous membranes of the stomach and intestines.

gas·tro·en·ter·ol·o·gy (gas'trō·en'tə·rol'ə·jē) *n.* The study of the anatomy, physiology, and pathology of the stomach and intestines. **— gas'tro·en'ter·ol'o·gist** *n.*

gas·tro·en·ter·os·to·my (gas'trō·en'tə·ros'tə·mē) *n. pl.* **·mies** *Surg.* An operation to make a new passage between the stomach and intestine.

gas·tro·in·tes·ti·nal (gas'trō·in·tes'tə·nəl) *adj. Anat.* Of or pertaining to the stomach and intestines. Abbr. *g.i., G.I.*

gas·tro·lith (gas'trō·lith) *n. Pathol.* A small, hard, stony mass sometimes formed in the stomach.

gas·trol·o·gy (gas·trol'ə·jē) *n.* The study of the anatomy, physiology, and pathology of the stomach. **— gas·trol'o·gist** *n.*

gas·tro·nome (gas'trə·nōm) *n.* A gourmet. Also **gas·tron·o·mer** (gas·tron'ə·mər), **gas·tron'o·mist.**

gas·tro·nom·ic (gas'trə·nom'ik) *adj.* Of or pertaining to gastronomes or gastronomy. Also **gas'tro·nom'i·cal.**

gas·tron·o·my (gas·tron'ə·mē) *n.* The art of good eating; epicurism. [< F *gastronomie* < Gk. *gastronomia* < *gastēr* stomach + *nomos* law]

gas·tro·pod (gas'trə·pod) *n.* One of a large class (*Gastropoda*) of marine, fresh-water, and terrestrial mollusks, including snails, slugs, limpets, etc., usually having a univalve, spiral shell and a muscular creeping organ consisting of a ventral disk. Also spelled *gasteropod.* **— adj.** Of or pertaining to the *Gastropoda.* [< NL < Gk. *gastēr* stomach + *pous, podos* foot] **— gas·trop·o·dan** (gas·trop'ə·dən) *adj. & n.* **— gas·trop'o·dous** *adj.*

gas·tro·scope (gas'trə·skōp) *n. Med.* An apparatus for illuminating and inspecting the human stomach. **— gas'tro·scop'ic** (-skop'ik) *adj.*

gas·tros·co·py (gas·tros'kə·pē) *n. pl.* **·pies** *Med.* An examination of the stomach with a gastroscope.

gas·trot·o·my (gas·trot'ə·mē) *n. pl.* **·mies** *Surg.* An opening of or cutting into the stomach or abdomen.

gas·tro·vas·cu·lar (gas'trō·vas'kyə·lər) *adj. Physiol.* Serving both circulatory and digestive functions.

gas·tru·la (gas'trŏŏ·lə) *n. pl.* **·lae** (·lē) *Biol.* An embryonic form of metazoic animals developed from the blastula, consisting of a two-layered sac enclosing a central cavity. [< NL, dim. of Gk. *gastēr* stomach] **— gas'tru·lar** *adj.*

gas·tru·la·tion (gas'trŏŏ·lā'shən) *n.* The formation of a gastrula.

gas turbine A turbine engine in which fuel is burned under pressure and the gases sent through a rotor unit.

gas well A well from which natural gas flows.

gas·works (gas'wûrks') *n. pl.* **works** An establishment where illuminating gas or heating gas is made.

gat¹ (gat) *Archaic* Past tense of GET.

gat² (gat) *n.* A narrow channel, as between sandbars, through which a ship can pass. [< ON, opening]

gat³ (gat) *n. Slang* A pistol. [Short for GATLING GUN]

gate¹ (gāt) *n.* **1.** A movable barrier, commonly swinging on hinges, that closes or opens a passage through a wall, fence, etc. **2.** An opening for exit or entrance through a wall or fence into an enclosure **3.** The structure on either side of such an opening. **4.** Anything that gives access: the *gate* to success. **5.** A mountain gap or other natural passageway. **6.** A protective barrier capable of being raised or lowered, as at a railroad crossing. **7.** A structure or valvelike device for controlling the supply of water, oil, gas, etc., that flows through a dam, pipe, or conduit. **8.** The total paid attendance at a sports event, theatrical presentation, etc. **9.** The money collected for this attendance. **10.** A frame in which a saw (or set of saws) is set. **11.** *Electronics* A terminal through which a control signal may turn a device on or off. **— v.t. gat·ed, gat·ing** *Brit.* To keep (a college student) within school precincts as a punishment. **— to get the gate** *Slang* To be sent away or be rejected. **— to give the gate to** *Slang* To dismiss, reject, or get rid of. [OE *gatu*, pl. of *geat* opening]

gate² (gāt) *n. Metall.* **1.** A hole or channel by which molten metal enters a mold. **2.** The waste metal remaining in such a hole or channel after the casting has been made. [Cf. OE *gēotan* to pour]

gate³ (gāt) *n. Scot.* **1.** A particular way of doing something or of behaving. **2.** A course or path. [< ON *gata* way]

gate·crash·er (gāt'krash'ər) *n. Informal* One who gains admittance without paying or being invited.

gate·fold (gāt'fōld') *n.* An oversized page in a magazine or book that is folded back upon itself at the outer edge so that, when opened, it presents a larger display. Also *fold-out.*

gate hinge *Mech.* A type of hinge formed of two detachable sections, one of which pivots on a cylindrical core projecting from the other. For illustration see HINGE.

gate·house (gāt'hous') *n.* A house or other structure built at or above a gate, as a porter's lodge or a power station.

gate·keep·er (gāt'kē'pər) *n.* One in charge of a gate. Also **gate'man** (-mən).

gate-leg table (gāt'leg') A table with swinging legs that support drop leaves and fold against the frame when the leaves are let down. Also **gate-legged table** (-legd').

gate money The total amount of money received as admissions to a sports event, theatrical performance, etc.

gate·post (gāt'pōst') *n.* Either of two posts at each side of a gate, to one of which the gate is hinged.

Gates (gāts), **Horatio,** 1728–1806, American Revolutionary general. **— John Warne,** 1855–1911, U.S. stock speculator and financier: called **Bet-a-million Gates.**

Gates·head (gāts'hed) A port in Tyne and Wear, England, on the Tyne; pop. 222,300 (1976).

gate·way (gāt'wā') *n.* **1.** An entrance that is or may be closed with a gate, often with an arch or other structure built over it. **2.** That which is regarded as a means of entry or exit: the *gateway* to the Orient.

Gath (gath) In the Bible, one of the five cities of the Philistines; the home of Goliath: I *Samuel* v 17.

gath·er (gath'ər) *v.t.* **1.** To bring together into one place or group; accumulate. **2.** To bring together from various places, sources, etc. **3.** To harvest or pick, as crops, fruit, etc. **4.** To collect by picking out; cull; select. **5.** To accumulate or gain more and more of: The storm *gathered* force. **6.** To clasp or enfold: to *gather* someone into one's arms. **7.** To wrinkle (the brow). **8.** To draw into folds, as cloth on a thread; shirr. **9.** To become aware of through deduction or observation; infer. **10.** To summon up or muster, as one's energies, for an effort. **11.** In bookbinding, to arrange in consecutive order, as pages of a book. **— v.i. 12.** To come together or assemble. **13.** To increase by accumulation.   **14.** To become wrinkled or creased, as the brow. **15.** To come to a head, as a boil.   **— Syn.** See AMASS, CONVOKE.   **— to be gathered to one's fathers** To die.   **— to gather up 1.** To pick up and collect into one place.   **2.** To bring more closely together: *Gather up* all the newspapers into a bundle.   — *n. Usually pl.* A pleat or fold in cloth, held by a thread passing through the folds.   [OE *gadrian*] — **gath·er·er** *n.*

gath·er·ing (gath′ər·ing)   *n.*   **1.** The action of one who or that which gathers.   **2.** That which is gathered; accumulation; collection.   **3.** An assemblage of people; group.   **4.** A series of gathers in cloth, etc.   **5.** An abscess or boil.   **6.** In bookbinding, a collection of printed sheets in proper order.   **— Syn.** See COMPANY.

Gat·ling gun (gat′ling)   An early machine gun having barrels rotating about a central axis by the turning of a crank.   [after R. J. *Gatling*, 1818–1903, U.S. inventor]

GATT   General Agreement on Tariffs and Trade.

Gat·ti-Ca·saz·za (gät′tē·kä·zät′tsä), **Giulio**, 1869–1940, Italian operatic impresario active in the United States.

Ga·tun (gä·tōōn′)   A town in the northern Canal Zone; pop. 692. *Spanish* **Ga·tún′.**

Gatun Dam   A dam of the Panama Canal at Gatun; 7,700 ft. long, 115 ft. high; forming **Gatun Lake**, 163 sq. mi.; 85 ft. above sea level.

gauche (gōsh)   *adj.* Awkward; clumsy; boorish.   **— Syn.** See AWKWARD.   [< F, left-handed]

gauche·rie (gōsh·rē′)   *n.*   **1.** An awkward or tactless action, statement, etc.   **2.** Clumsiness; tactlessness.   [< F]

Gau·cho (gou′chō)   *n. pl.* **·chos** A cowboy of the South American pampas. Also **gau′cho.**   [< Sp.]

gaud (gôd)   *n.* An article of vulgar finery.   [< OF *gaudir* to be merry < L *gaudere* to rejoice]

gau·de·a·mus ig·i·tur (gô′dē·ä′məs ij′ə·tər, gou′dē·ä′mŏŏs ē′gi·tŏŏr)   *Latin* Therefore let us rejoice.

gaud·er·y (gô′dər·ē)   *n. pl.* **·er·ies** Showy ornamentation.

Gau·di (gou′dē), **Antonio**, 1852–1926, Spanish architect.

gaud·y¹ (gô′dē)   *adj.* **gaud·i·er, gaud·i·est** Tastelessly brilliant or showy; garish.   **— gaud′i·ly** *adv.*   **— gaud′i·ness** *n.*   **— Syn.** *Gaudy, tawdry, garish, flashy,* and *meretricious* mean showy in a vulgar way. *Gaudy* suggests poor taste; *tawdry* is similar to *gaudy* but in addition implies cheapness. Something *garish* is offensively brilliant: a *garish* electric sign. *Flashy* suggests something superficially glittering or attractive but lacking real worth. *Flashy* is often nearly equivalent to *meretricious*, which suggests something deceitfully showy and only apparently valuable or worthwhile.

gaud·y² (gô′dē)   *n. pl.* **gaud·ies** *Brit.* A feast or festival; especially, an annual dinner given by a college in an English university.   [< L *gaudium* joy]

gauf·fer (gô′fər)   See GOFFER.

gauge (gāj)   *v.t.* **gauged, gaug·ing**   **1.** To determine the dimensions, amount, force, etc., of.   **2.** To determine the contents or capacity of, as a cask.   **3.** To estimate, appraise, or judge.   **4.** To make conform to a standard measurement.   **5.** To cut or rub (stones or bricks) to uniform size.   **6.** To mix (plaster) in standard proportions.   — *n.*   **1.** A standard measurement, dimension, or quantity.   **2.** A means or standard of comparing, estimating, or judging; criterion.   **3.** Any of various instruments or devices for measuring something: a wind *gauge*; rain *gauge*; wire *gauge*.   **4.** The distance between rails in a railway.   **5.** The distance between wheel treads.   **6.** The diameter of the bore of a gun.   **7.** The length of a laid tile, slate, or shingle; also, a single row of tiles, slates, or shingles.   **8.** The amount of plaster of Paris added to common or lime plaster to speed its setting.   **9.** *Naut.* **a** The position of a vessel in relation to the wind and another vessel. **b** The draft of a vessel.   **10.** A measurement standard indicating relative fineness of hosiery, as determined by the number of needles used per inch. Also spelled *gage.* Abbr. *g., G.*   [< OF *gauger* to measure]

gaug·er (gā′jər)   *n.*   **1.** One who or that which gauges: a wind *gauger.*   **2.** An officer of the revenue service who measures the contents of casks, etc.   **3.** A tax collector.

Gau·guin (gō·gaṅ′), **Paul**, 1848–1903, French painter: full name **Eugène Henri Paul Gauguin.**

Gaul (gôl)   An ancient name for the territory south and west of the Rhine, west of the Alps, and north of the Pyrenees; roughly the area of modern France: Latin *Gallia.* See also CISALPINE GAUL, TRANSALPINE GAUL, TRANSPADANE GAUL.

Gaul (gôl)   *n.*   **1.** A native of ancient Gaul.   **2.** A Frenchman.   [< F *Gaule* < L *Gallus*]

Gau·leit·er (gou′lī·tər)   *n. German* The chief party official of a district during the Nazi regime.

Gaul·ish (gô′lish)   *adj.* Of ancient Gaul, its people, or their Celtic language.   — *n.* The extinct Celtic language of Gaul.

Gaull·ism (gô′liz·əm)   *n.* The philosophy and political policies of Charles de Gaulle, especially as applied to nationalism in France.

gaul·the·ri·a (gôl·thir′ē·ə)   *n.* Any of a large genus (*Gaultheria*) of aromatic shrubs or undershrubs, as the American

wintergreen.   [< NL, after Dr. Jean-François *Gaultier*, 1708?–56, Canadian physician and botanist]

gaunt (gônt)   *adj.*   **1.** Emaciated and hollow-eyed, as from hunger, illness, or age; haggard.   **2.** Desolate or gloomy in appearance: a *gaunt* region.   **— Syn.** See LEAN².   [? < OF *gent* elegant, infl. in meaning by ON *gand* a tall, thin person]   **— gaunt′ly** *adv.*   **— gaunt′ness** *n.*

gaunt·let¹ (gônt′lit, gänt′-)   *n.*   **1.** In medieval armor, a glove covered with metal plates to protect the hand.   **2.** Any glove with a long, often flaring extension over the wrist; also, the extension itself. Sometimes spelled *gantlet.*   **— to take up the gauntlet** To accept a challenge.   **— to throw (or fling) down the gauntlet** To challenge to combat.   [< OF *gantelet*, dim. of *gant* mitten]

GAUNTLET (def. 1)

gaunt·let² (gônt′lit, gänt′-)   See GANTLET².

gaun·try (gôn′trē)   See GANTRY.

gaur (gour)   *n.* The saladang, an ox.   [< Hind.]

gauss (gous)   *n. Physics* The electromagnetic unit of magnetic induction, equal to 1 maxwell per square centimeter.   [after K. F. *Gauss*]

Gauss (gous), **Karl Friedrich**, 1777–1855, German mathematician and astronomer.   **— Gaus·si·an** (gou′sē·ən) *adj.*

Gaussian curve   *Stat.* Normal curve (which see).

Gau·ta·ma (gô′tə·mə, gou′-)   See BUDDHA.

Gau·tier (gō·tyā′), **Théophile**, 1811–72, French poet, critic, and novelist.

gauze (gôz)   *n.*   **1.** A lightweight, transparent fabric with an open weave, made of silk, cotton, linen, etc.   **2.** Any thin, open-mesh material: wire *gauze.*   **3.** A mist or light fog.   — *adj.* Resembling or made of gauze.   [< MF *gaze*, appar. after *Gaza*, where originally made]

gauz·y (gô′zē)   *adj.* **gauz·i·er, gauz·i·est** Resembling gauze; light; transparent.   **— gauz′i·ness** *n.*

ga·vage (gə·väzh′, *Fr.* gà·väzh′)   *n.* A method of forcing nourishment on a person or animal, as through a stomach tube.   [< F < *gaver* to gorge]

gave (gāv)   Past tense of GIVE.

gav·el (gav′əl)   *n.* A mallet used by a presiding officer to call for order or attention.   [Prob. var. of KEVEL]

gav·el·kind (gav′əl·kīnd′)   *n. Brit.*   **1.** A custom formerly widespread in Great Britain of dividing an intestate's land equally among direct or collateral male heirs, the inherited land being secured by certain privileges.   **2.** Any such custom.   [OE *gafol* tribute + KIND]

ga·vi·al (gā′vē·əl)   *n.* A large crocodilian (*Gavialis gangeticus*) of India, having long, slender jaws, the upper one knobbed at the end: also, loosely, *crocodile.*   [< F < Hind. *ghariyal*]

Gav·le (yev′lə)   A port city in eastern Sweden on **Gavle Bay**, an inlet of the Gulf of Bothnia; pop. 53,916 (1960). Also *Gefle. Swedish* **Gäv′le.**

ga·votte (gə·vot′)   *n.*   **1.** A dance of French origin, popular in the 17th and 18th centuries and resembling a quick-moving minuet.   **2.** Music for or in the manner of this dance, written in duple meter. Also **ga·vot′.**   [< F < Provençal *gavoto* Alpine dance < *gavot* an inhabitant of the Alps]

Ga·wain (gä′win, gô′-)   In Arthurian legend, a knight of the Round Table, nephew of King Arthur. Also **Ga′waine.**

gawk (gôk)   *Informal v.i.*   **1.** To stare stupidly; gape.   **2.** To move about or behave awkwardly.   — *n.* An ungainly, stupid individual.   [Cf. dial. E *gawk* lefthanded]

gawk·y (gô′kē)   *adj.* **gawk·i·er, gawk·i·est** Awkward or clumsy; ungainly.   — *n. pl.* **gawk·ies** An awkward or ungainly person.   **— gawk′i·ly** *adv.*   **— gawk′i·ness** *n.*

gay (gā)   *adj.*   **1.** Happy and carefree; merry.   **2.** Brightly colorful or ornamental.   **3.** Jaunty; sporty.   **4.** Full of or given to lighthearted pleasure.   **5.** Rakish; libertine.   **6.** *Slang* Homosexual.   [< OF < Gmc.]   **— gay′ness** *n.*   **— Syn. 1.** cheerful, vivacious, merry, sprightly, lively.

Gay (gā), **John**, 1685–1732, English poet and dramatist.

Ga·ya (gī′ə)   A city in central Bihar, India; a pilgrimage center; pop. 150,884 (1961).

gay·e·ty (gā′ə·tē)   See GAIETY.

Gay Liberation   An organized movement that advocates the social acceptance of homosexuals and their activities.

Gay-Lussac (gā·lü·sàk′), **Joseph Louis**, 1778–1850, French chemist and physicist.

Gay-Lussac's law   Charles's law (which see).

gay·ly (gā′lē)   See GAILY.

Gay-Pay-Oo (gā′pä′ōō′)   *n.* The OGPU.

gay·wings (gā′wingz)   *n.* A small American herb (*Polygala paucifolia*) of eastern North America with pinkish flowers.

gaz. 1. Gazette.   **2.** Gazetteer.

Ga·za (gä′zə)   A city in SW Palestine, administered by Israel since 1967 with the **Gaza strip**, the surrounding coastal district of 100 sq. mi., pop. about 480,000.

ga·za·bo (gə·zä′bō)   *n. pl.* **·bos** or **·boes** *U.S. Slang* A man or boy; guy; fellow.   [Cf. Sp. *gazapo* a shrewd fellow]

gaze (gāz)   *v.i.* **gazed, gaz·ing** To look steadily or fixedly at something, as in wonder or admiration; stare.   — *n.* A steady or fixed look. **— Syn.** See LOOK. [ME *gasen* < Scand. Cf. dial. Sw. *gasa* stare.] **— gaz′er** *n.*

ga·ze·bo[1] (gə-zē′bō) *n. pl.* **·bos** or **·boes** A summerhouse or similar structure affording an extensive view of the surrounding landscape. [? < GAZE, imitating a Latin form]

ga·ze·bo[2] (gə-zē′bō, -zā′bō) *n. pl.* **·bos** or **·boes** *U.S. Slang* A gazabo

gaze·hound (gāz′hound′) *n.* A breed of hound that hunts its prey by means of sight and not by scent.

ga·zelle (gə-zel′) *n.* A small, delicately formed antelope of northern Africa and Arabia (genus *Gazella*), with curved horns and large eyes. [< OF < Arabic *ghazāl* gazelle]

ga·zette (gə-zet′) *n.* **1.** A newspaper or similar periodical: now used chiefly in the titles of some newspapers, etc. **2.** An official publication, as of a government or society: especially, one of several publications issued by the British government listing government appointments, public bankruptcies, etc. Abbr. *gaz.* **— v.t. ·zet·ted, ·zet·ting** To publish or announce in a gazette. [< F < Ital. *gazzetta* < dial. Ital. (Venetian) *gazeta* coin, orig. the price of the publication]

gaz·et·teer (gaz′ə-tir′) *n.* **1.** A work or section of a work listing countries, cities, rivers, etc., together with their location, size, etc. Abbr. *gaz.* **2.** A list of geographical names.

Ga·zi·an·tep (gä′zē-än-tep′) A city in southern Turkey, in Asia; pop. 160,152 (1965): formerly *Aintab.*

G.B. Great Britain.

G.B.E. (Knight or Dame) Grand (Cross or Order) of the British Empire.

GCA or **G.C.A.** Ground control approach.

G.C.B. (Knight) Grand Cross of the Bath.

G.C.D. or **g.c.d.** or **gcd** Greatest common divisor.

G.C.F. or **g.c.f.** or **gcf** Greatest common factor.

G clef *Music* See under CLEF.

G.C.L.H. Grand Cross of the Legion of Honor.

GCM *Mil.* General Court Martial.

G.C.M. or **g.c.m.** or **gcm** Greatest common measure.

GCT or **G.C.T.** Greenwich civil time.

G.C.V.O. (Knight) Grand Cross of the (Royal) Victorian Order.

Gd *Chem.* Gadolinium.

Gdańsk (gdäny′sk) A port city of northern Poland on the Gulf of Gdańsk, an inlet of the Baltic Sea between Poland and the Soviet Union; capital of the former **Free City of Danzig** (**Gdańsk**) as constituted by the Treaty of Versailles (1919); pop. 366,000 (est. 1969). German *Danzig.*

Gdańsk (gdäny′sk) The Polish name for DANZIG.

gde. Gourde.

gds. Goods.

Gdy·nia (gdē′nyä) A port city in NW Poland, on the Gulf of Danzig; pop. 143,600 (est. 1959).

Ge (jē, gē) See GAEA.

Ge (zhā) *n.* A large and important South American Indian stock of eastern and central Brazil: also called *Tapuyan.*

Ge Germanium.

ge·an·ti·cli·nal (jē-an′tə-klī′nəl) *adj.* Of or pertaining to a geanticline. **—** *n.* A geanticline.

ge·an·ti·cline (jē-an′tə-klīn) *n. Geol.* A broad, usually gently sloping anticline covering a large area. [< Gk. *gē* earth + ANTICLINE]

gear (gir) *n.* **1.** *Mech.* **a** A mechanical assembly of interacting parts that serves to transmit motion or to change the rate or direction of motion. **b** A related group of parts that work together for a special purpose: steering *gear.* **c** Loosely, a cogwheel that meshes with another toothed wheel or part. **d** The engagement and specific adjustment of toothed wheels or other parts in a mechanism: in *gear,* in high *gear.* **e** The diameter of a hypothetical wheel having a circumference equal to the distance covered by a bicycle in one complete revolution of the pedals. **2.** *Naut.* **a** The ropes, blocks, etc., used in working a spar or sail. **b** A ship's rigging or equipment. **c** The personal baggage or effects of a sailor. **3.** Any equipment, as clothing, tools, etc., used for a special purpose or task: a plumber's *gear.* **4.** *Aeron.* The landing gear of an aircraft. **5.** *Archaic* Property; possessions. **6.** *Archaic* Arms; armor. **—** *v.t.* **1.** *Mech.* **a** To put into gear. **b** To equip with gears. **c** To connect by means of gears. **2.** To regulate so as to match or suit something else: to *gear* production to demand. **3.** To put gear on; harness; dress. **— v.i. 4.** To come into or be in gear; to mesh. **— out of gear 1.** Not engaged or connected, as one gear with another. **2.** Not in working order or not in good condition. [< ON *gervi* equipment]

gear·box (gir′boks′) *n.* **1.** The gears and gearcase comprising the transmission of an automobile. **2.** A gearcase.

gear·case (gir′kās′) *n. Mech.* A metal housing for the gears of machinery.

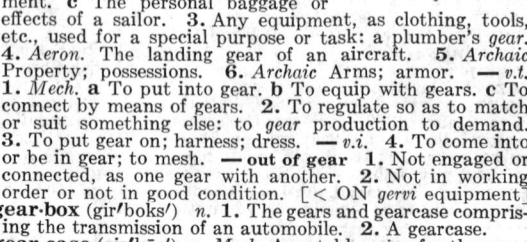

GEARS

A Spur. *B* Spur and crown. *C* Bevel. *D* Square. *E* Annular. *F* Elliptical.

gear·ing (gir′ing) *n.* **1.** *Mech.* Any system of gears or parts that transmit power or motion. **2.** *Naut.* Rope and tackle.

gear·shift (gir′shift′) *n. Mech.* A device for engaging or disengaging the gears in a power-transmission system.

gear·wheel (gir′hwēl′) *n. Mech.* A cogwheel (which see). Also **gear wheel.**

geb. Born (G *geboren*).

geck (gek) *v.t. & v.i. Scot. & Brit. Dial.* To mock derisively. **—** *n.* An object of contempt or derision; a fool; dupe.

geck·o (gek′ō) *n. pl.* **·os** or **·oes** Any of a family (*Geckonidae*) of small lizards having toes with adhesive disks: also called *wall lizard.* [< Malay *gēkoq,* imit. of its cry]

ged (ged) *n. Scot.* A pike (the fish).

Ged·des (ged′ēz), **Norman Bel,** 1893–1958, U.S. architect and designer.

gee[1] (jē) *n.* The letter G.

gee[2] (jē) *interj.* A cry used to guide horses, cattle, etc., to the right or (usually with *up*) to urge them to move forward or faster. **—** *v.t. & v.i.* **geed, gee·ing 1.** To turn to the right. **2.** To move onward or faster: usually with *up.* **3.** To evade. Opposed to *haw:* also spelled *jee.* [Origin uncertain]

gee[3] (jē) *interj.* An exclamation expressing mild surprise, sympathy, etc.: a euphemism for *Jesus.* Also **gee whiz.**

geek (gēk) *n. Slang* A carnival performer who publicly eats or swallows live animals as a sensational and horrifying spectacle. [Prob. var. of GECK]

Gee·long (jē-lông′) A port city in southern Victoria, Australia, on Corio Bay; pop. 88,160 (est. 1959).

Geel·vink Bay (khäl′vingk) A large inlet of the Pacific in NW New Guinea.

gee·pound (jē′pound′) *n. Physics* A slug, the unit of mass.

geese (gēs) Plural of GOOSE[1].

geest (gēst) *n. Geol.* Old, decayed rock material found in or near its original place of formation. [< Du., barren soil]

Ge·ez (gē·ez′, gēz) *n. Ethiopic,* an ancient Semitic language.

gee·zer (gē′zər) *n. Slang* A fellow; guy; especially, an old man. [Var. of *guiser* mummer < GUISE, v.]

ge·fül·lte fish (gə-fil′tə) A white fish, flaked and mixed with eggs, seasonings, and sometimes meal, formed into balls or oval-shaped cakes and poached in a fish stock. Also **ge·fill′te fish, ge·fil′te fish.** [< Yiddish, stuffed fish]

ge·gen·schein (gā′gən-shīn) *n. Meteorol.* A patch of faint, hazy light sometimes observable at night on the point of the ecliptic opposite the sun: also called *counterglow.* [< G]

Ge·hen·na (gi·hen′ə) *n.* **1.** In the Bible, the valley of Hinnom near Jerusalem, where refuse was thrown and fires kept burning to purify the air. **2.** A place of torment. **3.** In the New Testament, hell. [< LL < Gk. *geenna* < Hebrew *ge hinnom* valley of Hinnom]

Gei·ger (gī′gər), **Hans,** 1882–1945, German physicist.

Geiger counter *Physics* An instrument for detecting ionizing radiation by means of a sealed tube containing a gas that when struck by ionizing particles conducts an electrical impulse between two electrodes connected to a suitable counting device. Also **Geiger–Müller counter** (mü′lər), **geiger counter.** [after Hans *Geiger,* its coinventor with W. *Müller,* 20th c. German physicist]

Gei·kie (gē′kē), **Sir Archibald,** 1835–1924, Scottish geologist.

gei·sha (gā′shə, gē′-) *n. pl.* **·sha** or **·shas** A Japanese girl who has been trained to furnish entertainment by singing, dancing, conversation, etc. [< Japanese]

Geiss·ler tube (gīs′lər) *Physics* A sealed and partly evacuated glass tube containing electrodes, used for the study of electric discharges through gases. [after Heinrich *Geissler,* 1814–79, German physicist]

gel (jel) *n. Chem.* A colloidal dispersion of a solid in a liquid, typically having a jellylike consistency, as gelatin, mucilage, uncooked egg white, etc. **—** *v.t. & v.i.* **gelled, gel·ling** To change into a gel; jellify. [Short for GELATIN]

ge·län·de·sprung (gə·len′də·shprōong) *n.* In skiing, a jump made from a crouching position. [< G < *gelände* level ground + *sprung* jump]

gel·a·tin (jel′ə·tin) *n.* **1.** An almost tasteless, odorless, dried protein soluble in water and extracted by boiling the bones, tendons, skins, etc., of animals, used in food and drug preparation and in the manufacture of photographic film, plastics, etc. **2.** Any substance or product made with or resembling gelatin. Also **gel′a·tine** (-tin, -tēn). [< F *gélatine,* orig. a soup made from fish < Ital. *gelatina* < *gelata* jelly < L. See JELLY.]

ge·lat·i·nate (ji·lat′ə·nāt) *v.t. & v.i.* **·nat·ed, ·nat·ing** To change into gelatin or jelly. **— ge·lat′i·na′tion** *n.*

ge·lat·i·nize (ji·lat′ə·nīz) *v.* **·nized, ·niz·ing** *v.t.* **1.** To gelatinate. **2.** To treat or coat with gelatin. **— v.i. 3.** To be changed into gelatin or jelly. **— ge·lat′i·ni·za′tion** *n.*

ge·lat·i·nous (ji·lat′ə·nəs) *adj.* **1.** Having the nature of or resembling gelatin. **2.** Of or consisting of gelatin. Abbr. *gel.* **— ge·lat′i·nous·ly** *adv.* **— ge·lat′i·nous·ness** *n.*

ge·la·tion (ji·lā′shən) *n.* Solidification by cooling or chilling. [< L *gelatio, -onis* freezing < *gelare* to freeze]

geld[1] (geld) *n.* In early England, a tax or tribute. [OE]

geld[2] (geld) *v.t.* **geld·ed** or **gelt, geld·ing** **1.** To castrate or spay. **2.** To deprive of an essential part; weaken. [< ON *gelda* to castrate]

Gel·der·land (gel′dər·land, *Du.* khel′dər·länt) A Province of the eastern Netherlands; 1,933 sq. mi.; pop. 348,620 (est. 1970); capital, Arnhem: also *Guelderland, Guelders.*

geld·ing (gel′ding) *n.* A castrated animal; especially, a castrated horse.

Ge·lée (zhə·lā′), **Claude** See LORRAIN. Also **Gellée.**

Ge·li·bo·lu (ge′lē·bō·lōō′) The Turkish name for GALLIPOLI.

gel·id (jel′id) *adj.* Very cold; icy; frozen. [< L *gelidus*] — **ge·lid·i·ty** (ji·lid′ə·tē) *n.* — **gel′id·ly** *adv.*

gel·ig·nite (jel′ig·nīt′) *n.* An explosive composed of nitroglycerin, cellulose nitrate, ammonium nitrate, and wood pulp. [< GE(LATIN) + L *lign(um)* wood + -ITE[1]]

gel·se·mi·um (jel·sē′mē·əm) *n.* **1.** Any of a genus (*Gelsemium*) of twining plants with bright yellow flowers; especially, the yellow jasmine. **2.** The root of the yellow jasmine, used in making certain antispasmodics or sedatives. [< NL < Ital. *gelsomino* jasmine]

Gel·sen·kir·chen (gel′zən·kir′khən) A city in North Rhine-Westphalia, West Germany; 348,620 (est. 1970).

gelt (gelt) *n. U.S. Slang* Money. [< G *geld* money]

gem (jem) *n.* **1.** A cut and polished precious or semiprecious stone; jewel. **2.** One who or that which is treasured or greatly admired for perfect or nearly perfect qualities. **3.** A kind of small, light cake. **4.** *Printing Brit.* A 4-point size of type. — *v.t.* **gemmed, gem·ming** To decorate or set with or as with gems. [OE *gim* < L *gemma* jewel]

Ge·ma·ra (gə·mä′rə, -môr′ə) *n.* The second part of the Talmud, consisting of a commentary on the Mishna. [< Aramaic, completion]

gem·i·nate (jem′ə·nāt) *v.t. & v.i.* **·nat·ed, ·nat·ing** To double or become doubled; form into an identical pair. — *adj.* Formed into or appearing as a pair; doubled. [< L *geminatus,* pp. of *geminare* to double < *geminus* twin]

gem·i·na·tion (jem′ə·nā′shən) *n.* **1.** The act of geminating; doubling. **2.** The duplication of a word for rhetorical effect. **3.** *Ling.* The production of two identical sounds, especially consonants, in immediate succession.

Gem·i·ni (jem′ə·nī) *n. pl.* A constellation, the Twins; also, the third sign of the zodiac. See CONSTELLATION, ZODIAC.

gem·ma (jem′ə) *n. pl.* **gem·mae** (jem′ē) *Biol.* **1.** A bud. **2.** A part of a plant or animal that grows outward, detaches, and forms a new individual. [< L]

gem·mate (jem′āt) *adj. Biol.* Bearing or reproducing by gemmae. — *v.i.* **·mat·ed, ·mat·ing** To form or reproduce by gemmae. [< L *gemmatus,* pp. of *gemmare* to bud]

gem·ma·tion (jem·ā′shən) *n. Biol.* **1.** The process of gemmating. **2.** A particular kind or arrangement of gemmae.

gem·mip·a·rous (jem·ip′ər·əs) *adj. Biol.* Producing gemmae. [< L *gemma* bud + -PAROUS] — **gem·mip′a·rous·ly** *adv.*

gem·mu·la·tion (jem′yōō·lā′shən) *n. Biol.* Reproduction by, or formation of, gemmules.

gem·mule (jem′yōōl) *n.* **1.** *Biol.* A gemma. **2.** One of the specialized reproductive cells postulated in the theory of pangenesis. [< LL *gemmula,* dim. of L *gemma* bud]

gem·my (jem′ē) *adj.* **1.** Full of, set with, or containing gems. **2.** Suggestive of a gem, as in glittering brightness.

ge·mot (gə·mōt′) *n.* In early English history, a public meeting, assembly, or local court. Also **ge·mote′.** [OE *gemōt*]

gems·bok (gemz′bok) *n. pl.* **·bok** or **·boks** A South African antelope (*Oryx gazella*) having long, sharp horns and a tufted tail. [< Afrikaans < G *gemse* chamois + *bock* a buck]

Gem State Nickname of IDAHO.

gem·stone (jem′stōn′) *n.* A precious or semiprecious stone, especially before it is cut and polished for use as a gem.

ge·müt·lich (gə·müt′likh) *adj. German* **1.** Cozily pleasant and cheerful. **2.** Genial; cordial.

GEMSBOK
(About 3 feet high at shoulder; horns to 3 feet)

gen. **1.** Gender. **2.** Genera. **3.** General; generally. **4.** Generator. **5.** Generic. **6.** Genitive. **7.** Genus.

-gen *suffix of nouns* **1.** *Chem.* That which produces: *oxygen.* **2.** *Biol.* That which is produced: *antigen.* [< F *-gène* < Gk. *-genēs* < *gen-,* stem of *gignesthai* to be born, become]

Gen. **1.** *Mil.* General. **2.** Genesis. **3.** Geneva; Genevan.

gen·darme (zhän′därm, *Fr.* zhän·därm′) *n. pl.* **·darmes** (-därmz, *Fr.* -därm′) **1.** One of a corps of armed police, especially in France. **2.** Any policeman: a humorous use. [< F < *gens d'armes* men-at-arms]

gen·dar·me·rie (zhän′där·mə·rē, zhän·där′mə·rē; *Fr.* zhän·därm·rē′) *n.* Gendarmes collectively. Also **gen·darm′e·ry.**

gen·der (jen′dər) *n.* **1.** *Gram.* **a** One of two or more categories of words (especially nouns and pronouns) or affixes based on differences of sex or absence of sex or sometimes upon other distinctions (as of animateness or inanimateness), each category having distinctive forms for the words or affixes themselves or for the words modifying them. Thus, in English, gender is indicated by pronoun reference (*he, she,* etc.), by prefixes and suffixes (*aviator, aviatrix,* etc.), or by completely different forms (*bull, cow,* etc.). **Natural gender** is a classification based upon actual sex (**masculine gender, feminine gender**) or absence of sex (**neuter gender**). **Common gender** is a classification in which a word or affix has a form used indifferently for either masculine or feminine categories. **Grammatical gender** is a classification in which there may be partial correspondence to actual sex distinctions, but in which sexless things are arbitrarily classed as masculine, feminine or neuter. **b** Such categories collectively, or a system of such categories. **c** The distinctive form or forms used for such categories. Abbr. *gen.* **2.** *Informal* The condition or quality of being of the male or female sex; sex classification: a humorous use. **3.** *Archaic* Classification; kind; sort. — *v.t. & v.i. Archaic* To generate; beget. [< OF *gendre* < L *genus, -eris.* Doublet of GENUS, GENRE.]

gene (jēn) *n. Biol.* One of the complex protein molecules associated with the chromosomes of reproductive cells and acting, as a unit or in various biochemically determined combinations, in the transmission of specific hereditary characters from parents to offspring. [< Gk. *genea* breed, kind]

geneal. Genealogical; genealogy.

ge·ne·al·o·gist (jē′nē·al′ə·jist, jen′ē-, -nē·ol′-) *n.* One who traces genealogies or who is a student of genealogy.

ge·ne·al·o·gy (jē′nē·al′ə·jē, jen′ē-, -nē·ol′-) *n. pl.* **·gies** **1.** A record or table showing the descent of an individual or family from a certain ancestor. **2.** Descent in a direct line from a progenitor; pedigree. **3.** The study of pedigrees. [< Gk. *genea* race + -LOGY] — **ge·ne·a·log·i·cal** (jē′nē·ə·loj′i·kəl, jen′ē-) or **·log·ic** *adj.* — **ge′ne·a·log′i·cal·ly** *adv.*

gen·e·ra (jen′ər·ə) Plural of GENUS. Abbr. *gen.* [< L]

gen·er·a·ble (jen′ər·ə·bəl) *adj.* Capable of being generated. [< L *generabilis* < *generare* to generate]

gen·er·al (jen′ər·əl) *adj.* **1.** Pertaining to, including, or affecting all or the whole; not local or particular: a *general* election. **2.** Common to or current among the majority; prevalent: the *general* opinion. **3.** Extended in scope, meaning, or content; not restricted in application: a *general* principle. **4.** Not limited to a special class; miscellaneous: a *general* cargo. **5.** Not detailed or precise: a *general* idea. **6.** Usual or customary: one's *general* habit. **7.** Dealing with all branches of a business or pursuit; not specialized: a *general* practitioner. **8.** Superior in rank: a second element in some titles: attorney *general.* **9.** *Med.* Relating to or affecting the entire body. Abbr. *gen., genl.* — *n.* **1.** *Mil.* **a** In the U.S. Army, Air Force, or Marine Corps, an officer ranking next above a lieutenant general, equivalent in rank to an admiral in the Navy. **b** Any general officer, as a brigadier general, lieutenant general, etc.: a shortened form. **c** In the Canadian Army, an officer ranking next above lieutenant-general and below Field-Marshal. **d** An equivalent officer in other armies. Abbr. *Gen.* See tables at GRADE. **2.** The head of a religious order. **3.** A general statement, fact, or principle. **4.** *Archaic* The people or the public. — **in general** **1.** Without going into detail. **2.** All things considered; on the whole. **3.** Usually; commonly. [< OF < L *generalis* of a race or kind < *genus, generis* kind]

— **Syn.** (adj.) *General, universal,* and *common* come into comparison in fixing limits of inclusion or reference. *General* applies to most of the persons, things, or class named; *universal* applies to all or the whole; *common* applies to many or a large part. We may say that good health is a *general* condition, that occasional sickness is *common,* and that death is *universal.* — **Ant.** particular, individual, exceptional.

GENERAL'S INSIGNIA, U.S. ARMY
a Brigadier general. *b* Major general. *c* Lieutenant general. *d* General. *e* General of the Army.

General American American English as spoken in the United States with the exception of the South, a large part of New England, and the New York City area: a term now rejected by many linguists.

General Assembly **1.** The deliberative body of the United Nations in which every member nation is represented. Abbr. *GA, G.A.* **2.** *U.S.* The legislature in some states.

General Court **1.** During the Colonial period, a legislative body having a judicial function. **2.** The official name of the legislatures of New Hampshire and Massachusetts.

gen·er·al·cy (jen′ər·əl·sē) *n. pl.* **·cies** **1.** The rank or office of a general. **2.** Appointment to the rank of general. **3.** The time during which the rank of general is held.

general delivery *U.S.* **1.** A building or department of the post office in which an addressee's mail is kept until called for. **2.** Mail directed to this department.

general election 1. An election in which all the people vote. **2.** An election held to make a final choice for office among candidates selected in a preliminary election.

gen·er·al·is·si·mo (jen′ər·əl·is′i·mō) *n. pl.* **·mos 1.** In certain countries, one chosen as supreme commander of all the armed forces of the country. **2.** In certain countries, one chosen as supreme commander of several armies of different countries acting together in a particular campaign. [< Ital.]

gen·er·al·i·ty (jen′ə·ral′ə·tē) *n. pl.* **·ties 1.** The state or quality of being general. **2.** Something lacking detail or precision, as a statement or idea: a speech filled with *generalities*. **3.** The greater number of a group; mass.

gen·er·al·i·za·tion (jen′ər·əl·ə·zā′shən, -ī·zā′-, jen′rəl-) *n.* **1.** The act of generalizing. **2.** Something, as a broad, over-all statement or conclusion, arrived at by generalizing.

gen·er·al·ize (jen′ər·əl·īz′, jen′rəl-) *v.* **·ized, ·iz·ing** *v.t.* **1.** To make general; as: **a** To make broad in application: to *generalize* laws, principles. **b** To avoid making detailed: to *generalize* remarks. **c** To cause to be widespread. **2.** To derive a broad conclusion, principle, etc., from (particular instances, facts, etc.). — *v.i.* **3.** To write or speak without going into details or conclusions, etc.; to discuss or propose generalities. Also *Brit.* **gen′er·al·ise′.**

gen·er·al·ly (jen′ər·əl·ē, jen′rəl-) *adv.* **1.** For the most part; ordinarily: He is *generally* right. **2.** Without going into specific details or instances: *generally* speaking. **3.** Popularly; commonly: *generally* believed. Abbr. *gen.*

general officer *Mil.* Any officer ranking above a colonel, as a general, lieutenant general, major general, etc.

General of the Air Force The highest-ranking officer of the U.S. Air Force. See table at GRADE.

General of the Armies A special title and rank conferred upon John J. Pershing in 1919.

General of the Army The highest rank in the U.S. Army. See table at GRADE and see illustration under GENERAL.

general paresis *Pathol.* Chronic paralysis of syphilitic origin, characterized by degeneration of the brain tissue, physical deterioration, and progressive dementia: also called *paresis.* Also **general paralysis.** Abbr. *G.P.*

general post office A central post office having subsidiary branches within a particular city or area. Abbr. *GPO, G.P.O.*

general practitioner A physician whose practice is not limited to a medical specialty. Abbr. *G.P.*

gen·er·al-pur·pose (jen′ər·əl·pûr′pəs) *adj.* Designed for or adaptable to more than one use: a *general-purpose* flour.

general semantics A discipline for human living formulated by Alfred Korzybski and based on a critical analysis of verbal and nonverbal symbols insofar as they elicit behavioral responses.

gen·er·al·ship (jen′ər·əl·ship) *n.* **1.** A general's office or rank; generalcy. **2.** A general's military skill or management. **3.** Management or leadership of any sort.

general staff 1. A body of officers who direct the military policy and strategy of a national state. **2.** *Mil.* A group of officers who assist the commander in planning, coordination, and supervision of operations. Abbr. *GS*

general strike A strike by all or most of the workers of a particular industry or in a particular area or country.

gen·er·ate (jen′ə·rāt) *v.t.* **·at·ed, ·at·ing 1.** To produce or cause to be; bring into being. **2.** To beget; procreate. **3.** *Geom.* To trace out by motion: A moving point *generates* a line. [< L *generatus,* pp. of *generare* to generate]

gen·er·a·tion (jen′ə·rā′shən) *n.* **1.** The process of begetting offspring; reproduction. **2.** A successive step or degree in natural descent; also, the individual or individuals produced at each step: Three *generations* were present: father, son, and grandchildren. **3.** The average period between any two such successive steps, comprising about 30 years among human beings. **4.** Any group of individuals born at about the same time. **5.** Such a group regarded as having similar opinions, behavior, etc.: the Beat *Generation.* **6.** Production or origination by any process; a bringing into being: the *generation* of electricity. **7.** *Geom.* The formation of any geometrical figure by the motion of a point, line, or surface.

gen·er·a·tive (jen′ə·rā′tiv, jen′ər·ə·tiv) *adj.* **1.** Of or pertaining to generation. **2.** Having the power to produce or originate.

generative grammar *Ling.* A systematized procedure that can be used to produce every possible structural arrangement of a language and exclude structures that are not valid.

gen·er·a·tor (jen′ə·rā′tər) *n.* **1.** One who or that which generates. **2.** *Chem.* An apparatus designed to generate a gas. **3.** Any of a class of machines for the conversion of mechanical energy into electrical energy. Abbr. *gen.*

GENERATOR (*def.* 3)

gen·er·a·trix (jen′ə·rā′triks) *n. pl.* **gen·er·a·tri·ces** (jen′ər·ə·trī′sēz) **1.** *Geom.* A line, point, or figure that generates another figure by its motion. **2.** A female that generates.

ge·ner·ic (ji·ner′ik) *adj.* **1.** Pertaining to a genus or class of related things. **2.** Applicable to every member of a class or genus. **3.** Having a wide, general application; comprehensive. Also **ge·ner′i·cal.** Abbr. *gen.* [< L *genus, -eris* race, kind + -IC] — **ge·ner′i·cal·ly** *adv.*

gen·er·os·i·ty (jen′ə·ros′ə·tē) *n. pl.* **·ties 1.** The quality of being generous. **2.** Magnanimity. **3.** A generous act.

gen·er·ous (jen′ər·əs) *adj.* **1.** Marked by or showing great liberality; munificent; unselfish: a *generous* contributor. **2.** Having gracious or noble qualities; magnanimous: a *generous* nature. **3.** Abundant and overflowing; large; bountiful: a *generous* serving. **4.** Stimulating or strong, as wine. **5.** Fertile or fruitful: *generous* soil. **6.** *Archaic* Being of noble ancestry. [< F *généreux* < L *generosus* of noble birth < *genus.* See GENUS.] — **gen′er·ous·ly** *adv.* — **gen′er·ous·ness** *n.*
— **Syn. 1.** *Generous, liberal, bountiful,* and *munificent* are used to describe a person who gives freely or a gift, etc., of great worth. *Generous* emphasizes the warm feeling of sympathy, tenderness, regard, etc., that prompts the giving; *liberal* stresses the amount of the gift and points to the absence of stinginess or meanness. The *bountiful* person gives both lavishly and continuously. *Munificent* is stronger than *bountiful;* a *munificent* gift is very great in value; a *munificent* person is one who displays princely liberality. **2.** considerate, unselfish, charitable. **3.** ample, plentiful. — **Ant.** ungenerous, illiberal, close, stingy, parsimonious, meager.

Gen·e·see River (jen′ə·sē′) A river in Pennsylvania and New York that flows about 158 miles north to Lake Ontario.

gen·e·sis (jen′ə·sis) *n. pl.* **·ses** (-sēz) **1.** The act or mode of creating. **2.** Origin. [< L < Gk. *genēsis* creation, origin]

Gen·e·sis (jen′ə·sis) The first book of the Old Testament. Abbr. *Gen.*

-genesis *combining form* Development; genesis; evolution: *biogenesis.* [< Gk. *genēsis* origin]

gen·et¹ (jen′it, jə·net′) *n.* **1.** Any of certain small carnivores (genus *Genetta*) related to the civets but having only rudimentary scent glands. **2.** The fur of the genet. Also **ge·nette′.** [< F *genette* < Sp. *gineta* < Arabic *jarnait* genet]

gen·et² (jen′it) *n.* A jennet.

Ge·nêt (zhə·ne′), **Edmond Charles,** 1763–1834, French diplomat in the United States: called **Citizen Genêt.**

ge·net·ic (jə·net′ik) *adj.* **1.** Of, pertaining to, or based on genetics. **2.** Of, pertaining to, or produced by genes. **3.** Of, or pertaining to the origin, generation, or development of something. **4.** *Phonet.* Articulatory. **5.** *Ling.* Denoting those features among a group of languages that indicate descent from a common parent language. Also **ge·net′i·cal.** [< GENESIS; formed on analogy with *synthetic, antithetic,* etc.] — **ge·net′i·cal·ly** *adv.*

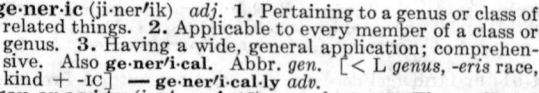

GENET¹

(About 22 inches long; tail about 18 inches)

genetic code The molecular make-up of the chromosomes of cells that determines inherited characteristics from generation to generation, with deoxyribonucleic acid being the code-bearing constituent.

ge·net·i·cist (jə·net′ə·sist) *n.* One who studies or specializes in the science of genetics.

ge·net·ics (jə·net′iks) *n.pl.* **1.** (*construed as sing.*) The science dealing with the interaction of the genes in producing similarities and differences between individuals related by descent. **2.** The inherited characteristics of an organism.

ge·ne·va (jə·nē′və) *n.* Gin, usually of Dutch manufacture. [< MDu. *genever* < OF *genevre* gin < L *juniperus* juniper]

Ge·ne·va (jə·nē′və) A city in SW Switzerland, on the Lake of Geneva; pop. 169,100 (est. 1960). *French* **Ge·nève** (zhə·nev′), *German* **Genf** (genf).

Geneva, Lake of A lake in SW Switzerland; 224 sq. mi.: also *Lake Leman.* Also **Lake Geneva.**

Geneva bands A pair of linen strips hanging from the front of the neck of some clerical or academic garments.

Geneva Convention An international agreement signed at Geneva in 1864 on the war-time treatment of prisoners and the sick and the wounded: also called *Red Cross Convention.*

Geneva cross A red St. George's or Greek cross on a white ground, worn by members of the Red Cross as a badge of neutrality. For illustration see CROSS.

Geneva gown A loose, black academic gown with large sleeves, often used as a vestment by Protestant clergy.

Ge·ne·van (jə·nē′vən) *adj.* **1.** Of or pertaining to Geneva, Switzerland. **2.** Of or pertaining to the theology taught in Geneva by Calvin; Calvinistic. — *n.* **1.** A native or inhabitant of Geneva. **2.** A Calvinist. Also **Gen·e·vese** (jen′ə·vēz′, -vēs′). Abbr. *Gen. Gen.*

Gen·e·vieve (jen′ə·vēv, jen′ə·vēv′), **Saint,** 422?–512, patron of Paris.

Gen·ghis Khan (jen′giz kän′, jeng′gis, geng′gis), 1167?–1227, Mongol conqueror; held sway from northern China to Bulgaria in 1223: original name **Te·much·in** (tə·mŏŏ′chin). Also *Jenghiz Khan.*

gen·ial¹ (jēn′yəl, jē′nē·əl) *adj.* **1.** Kindly, pleasant, or cordial in disposition or manner. **2.** Imparting warmth, comfort, or life; supporting life or growth. **3.** *Rare* Exhibiting or relating to genius. [< L *genialis* of one's tutelary deity < *genius.* See GENIUS.] — **gen′ial·ly** *adv.*

ge·ni·al[2] (jə·nī′əl) *adj. Anat.* Of, pertaining to, or near the chin. [< Gk. *geneion* chin]

ge·ni·al·i·ty (jē′nē·al′ə·tē) *n.* The quality of being genial; cheerful, kindly warmth of manner or disposition; cordiality.

gen·ic (jen′ik) *adj.* Pertaining to, characteristic of, or produced by a gene or genes.

-genic *combining form* Related to generation or production: *biogenic.* [< -GEN + -IC]

ge·nic·u·late (jə·nik′yə·lāt, -lit) *adj. Biol.* 1. Having knee-like joints or protuberances. 2. Bent abruptly, like a knee. [< L *geniculatus* < *geniculum,* dim. of *genu* knee]

ge·nic·u·la·tion (jə·nik′yə·lā′shən) *n.* 1. The state of being geniculate. 2. A knee-shaped joint or process.

ge·nie (jē′nē) See JINNI.

ge·ni·i (jē′nē·ī) Plural of GENIUS (defs. 4 and 6).

ge·ni·o·plas·ty (jə·nī′ə·plas′tē) *n.* Plastic surgery of the chin and lower cheek. [< Gk. *geneion* chin + -PLASTY]

gen·i·pap (jen′ə·pap) *n.* 1. A tropical American tree (*Genipa americana*) of the madder family. 2. Its edible fruit, about the size of an orange. [< Pg. *genipapo* < native name]

genit. Genitive.

gen·i·tal (jen′ə·təl) *adj.* Of or pertaining to the reproductive organs or the process of reproduction. [< L *genitalis* of generation < *genitus,* pp. of *gignere* to beget]

gen·i·ta·li·a (jen′ə·tā′lē·ə, -tāl′yə) *n.pl.* The genitals. [< L, neut. pl. of *genitalis.* See GENITAL.]

gen·i·tals (jen′ə·təlz) *n.pl.* The external organs of generation; sexual organs.

gen·i·ti·val (jen′ə·tī′vəl) *adj. Gram.* Pertaining to the genitive case; having a genitive form. — **gen·i·ti·val·ly** *adv.*

gen·i·tive (jen′ə·tiv) *adj.* 1. Indicating source, origin, possession, or the like. 2. *Gram.* Pertaining to a case in Latin, Greek, etc., corresponding in part to the English possessive. — *n. Gram.* 1. The genitive case. 2. A word in this case. Abbr. *gen., genit.* [< L *genitivus* < *gignere* to beget]

genito- *combining form* Genital: *genitourinary.* [< L *genitus,* pp. of *gignere* to beget]

gen·i·tor (jen′ə·tər, -tôr) *n. Rare* 1. A male parent. 2. *pl.* Parents. [< L]

gen·i·to·u·ri·nar·y (jen′ə·tō·yŏŏr′ə·ner′ē) *adj. Anat.* Of or pertaining to the genital and the urinary organs. Abbr. *g.u.*

gen·ius (jēn′yəs) *n. pl.* **gen·ius·es** for defs. 1, 2, 3, & 5; **ge·ni·i** (jē′nē·ī) for defs. 4 & 6. 1. Extraordinary intelligence surpassing that of most intellectually superior individuals; also, one who possesses such intelligence. 2. An aptitude for doing or achieving some particular thing; especially, an outstanding gift for some specialized activity: to have a *genius* for writing; also, one who possesses such an aptitude or gift. 3. The essential spirit or distinguishing characteristics of a particular individual, people, locality, era, etc. 4. In ancient mythology, a supernatural being appointed to guide a person throughout life; a guardian spirit; demon. 5. A person who exerts a strong, formative influence over another for good or evil. 6. In Moslem mythology, a jinni. [< L, tutelary spirit < *gen-,* stem of *gignere* to beget]
— **Syn.** 1, 2. *Genius, talent, gift, aptitude,* and *faculty* refer to superior mental ability. *Genius,* the strongest word, is conceived as a mental power far beyond explanation in terms of heritage or education and manifests itself by exceptional originality. *Talent* is natural readiness in learning and doing in a particular field; it is conceived of as an inborn resource that may or may not be developed. *Gift* is akin to *genius* on a lower plane; it is also an innate quality or ability that manifests itself without cultivation. *Aptitude* is special ability to learn and become proficient, while a *faculty* is a particular mental skill or knack, inborn or acquired.

ge·ni·us lo·ci (jē′nē·əs lō′sī) *Latin* 1. In ancient belief, a minor deity dwelling in or guarding a particular locality. 2. The unique quality of a place as felt by an observer.

genl. General.

Gen·nes·a·ret (jə·nes′ə·ret), **Sea of** or **Lake** The New Testament name for the Sea of GALILEE. Also **Gen·nes·a·reth.**

Gen·o·a (jen′ō·ə) A port city in NW Italy on the **Gulf of Genoa,** the NE part of the Ligurian Sea; pop. 842,764 (1968). *Italian* **Ge·no·va** (jĕ′nō·vä).

gen·o·cide (jen′ə·sīd) *n.* The systematic extermination or destruction of an entire people or national group: first used of the attempted annihilation of the Jews under the Nazi regime. [< Gk. *genos* race, tribe + -CIDE; coined by Raphael Lemkin, 1944] — **gen·o·ci′dal** *adj.*

Gen·o·ese (jen′ō·ēz′, -ēs′) *adj.* Of or pertaining to Genoa. — *n. pl.* **·ese** A native or citizen of Genoa.

gen·o·type (jen′ə·tīp) *n. Biol.* 1. The genetic constitution of an organism. 2. A group of organisms with the same genetic constitution. 3. A type species. [< Gk. *genos* race, kind + -TYPE] — **gen·o·typ·ic** (jen′ə·tip′ik) or **·i·cal** *adj.* — **gen′o·typ′i·cal·ly** *adv.*

-genous *suffix of adjectives* 1. Generating; yielding: *sporogenous.* 2. Produced or generated by: *parthogenous.* [< -GEN + -OUS]

gen·re (zhän′rə, *Fr.* zhän′r′) *n.* 1. A particular sort, kind, or category; especially, a category of art or literature charac-

terized by a certain form, style, or subject matter. 2. A class of painting or other art depicting everyday life. — *adj.* Of or pertaining to genre (def. 2). [< F < L *genus, -eris* race, kind. Doublet of GENDER, GENUS.]

gen·ro (gen′rō) *n. pl.* **·ros** 1. In Japan, a group of retired statesmen who formerly acted as informal advisers to the emperor. 2. One of these advisers: also called *elder statesman.* [< Japanese *genrō* first (of the) elders]

gens (jenz) *n. pl.* **gen·tes** (jen′tēz) 1. *Anthropol.* In primitive society, a body of blood kindred having a common descent traced through the male line. 2. In ancient Rome, a clan or house composed of several families of the same name descended through the male line. [< L]

Gen·san (gen·sän) The Japanese name for WONSAN.

Gen·ser·ic (jen′sər·ik, gen′-), died 477, king of the Vandals; conquered North Africa and Rome. Also *Gaiseric.*

gent[1] (jent) *n. Slang* A gentleman. [Short for GENTLEMAN]

gent[2] (jent) *adj. Obs.* 1. Born of good stock. 2. Pretty. [< OF < L *genitus,* orig. pp. of *gignere* to beget]

gent. Gentleman; gentlemen.

Gent (gent, кhent) The Flemish name for GHENT.

gen·teel (jen·tēl′) *adj.* 1. Well-bred or refined; elegant; polite. 2. Pertaining or appropriate to well-bred persons. 3. Stylish or fashionable. ◆ This word is now used chiefly in a derogatory or humorous sense. [< MF *gentil.* Doublet of GENTLE.] — **gen·teel′ly** *adv.* — **gen·teel′ness** *n.*

gen·tian (jen′shən) *n.* 1. Any of a large genus (*Gentiana*) of European and American flowering herbs typical of a family (*Gentianaceae*) of annual or perennial herbs with showy flowers, as the **yellow gentian** of Europe (*G. lutea*), the **fringed gentian** of America (*G. crinita*) with blue, conspicuously fringed solitary flowers, or the **closed gentian** or **bottle gentian** (*G. andrewsi*) with purple-blue flowers that do not open. 2. The root of the yellow gentian, used for making a digestant. [< L *gentiana,* appar. after *Gentius,* an Illyrian king] — **gen·tian·a·ceous** (jen′shən·ā′shəs) *adj.*

GENTIAN
a Bottle or closed.
b Fringed.

gen·tian·el·la (jen′shən·el′ə) *n.* 1. A European alpine gentian (*Gentiana acaulis*) having blue flowers. 2. A bright blue color. [< NL, dim. of L *gentiana.* See GENTIAN.]

gentian violet *Chem.* A purple dye of the rosaniline group, used as an antiseptic.

gen·tile (jen′til, -tīl; *for adj. def. 2* -til) *adj.* 1. Of or pertaining to a gens, tribe, or people. 2. Of or pertaining to Gentiles. 3. *Gram.* Of nouns and adjectives, denoting nationality or place of origin. — *n. Gram.* A gentile noun or adjective. [< F *gentil* < LL *gentilis* foreign. Doublet of GENTLE.]

Gen·tile (jen′tīl) *n.* 1. Among Jews, one not a Jew. 2. Among Christians, one not a Jew or not a Christian; a heathen or pagan; also, any Christian not of Jewish ancestry, especially when a convert from heathenism or paganism. 3. Among Mormons, one not a Mormon. — *adj.* Of, pertaining to, or being a Gentile. — **Syn.** See HEATHEN.

Gen·ti·le da Fa·bri·a·no (jän·tē′lä dä fä′brē·ä′nō), 1370?-1427?, Umbrian painter.

gen·ti·lesse (jen′tə·les) *n. Archaic* Good breeding or courtesy. [< OF < *gentil.* See GENTLE.]

gen·til·i·ty (jen·til′ə·tē) *n. pl.* **·ties** 1. The quality of being genteel or well-bred; refinement: now often used ironically. 2. Gentle birth; good extraction. 3. Well-born or well-bred persons collectively; gentry. [< OF *gentilite* < L *gentilitas, -tatis* < *gentilis.* See GENTLE.]

gen·tle (jen′təl) *adj.* **·tler** (-tlər), **·tlest** (-tlist) 1. Mild and amiable in nature or disposition; kindly; patient. 2. Not harsh, rough, or loud; soft; moderate; mild: a *gentle* voice. 3. Not steep or abrupt; gradual: a *gentle* ascent. 4. Easily managed; docile; tame. 5. Of good family and breeding; well-born. 6. Like or befitting one of good family; refined; polite. 7. *Meteorol.* Designating a moderate breeze. See BEAUFORT SCALE. 8. *Archaic* Chivalrous; noble. — *v.t.* **·tled, ·tling** 1. To make easy to control; tame. 2. *Rare* To placate. 3. *Obs.* To elevate in social rank. — *n.* 1. A bluebottle larva used as fish bait. 2. *Archaic* A person of good family or good background. [< OF *gentil* < L *gentilis* of good birth < *gens, gentis* race, clan. Doublet of GENTEEL, GENTILE.] — **gen′tly** (-tlē) *adv.* — **gen′tle·ness** *n.*

gentle craft 1. Angling. 2. *Obs.* Shoemaking.

gen·tle·folk (jen′təl·fōk′) *n.pl.* Persons of good family and good breeding. Also **gen′tle·folks′.**

gen·tle·man (jen′təl·mən) *n. pl.* **·men** (-mən) 1. A man of good birth and social position. 2. A courteous, considerate man. 3. Any man: in the plural, used as a form of address. 4. A man's personal servant; valet. 5. *Brit.* Formerly, a man above a yeoman in social rank. Abbr. *gent.*

gen·tle·man-at-arms (jen′təl·mən·ət·ärmz′) *n. pl.* **·men** (-mən) *n. Brit.* One of forty gentlemen who attend the sovereign on various state and solemn occasions.

gen·tle·man-com·mon·er (jen′təl·mən·kom′ən·ər) *n.* *pl.* **gen·tle·men-com·mon·ers** (jen′təl·mən·kom′ən·ərz) *Brit.* Formerly, a commoner at Oxford and Cambridge Universities, enjoying special privileges.

gen·tle·man-farm·er (jen′təl·mən·fär′mər) *n.* One who owns a farm but hires others to work it.

gentleman in waiting A gentleman of a royal household staff, appointed to attend the sovereign or his son.

gen·tle·man·ly (jen′təl·mən·lē) *adj.* Pertaining to or befitting a gentleman; courteous. Also **gen′tle·man·like′** (-līk′).

gentleman of fortune 1. An adventurer or gambler. 2. Formerly, a pirate.

gentleman of the road 1. A highwayman. 2. *U.S.* A hobo.

gen·tle·man's agreement (jen′təl·mənz) An understanding or arrangement about something to be done, arrived at by informal, mutual agreement and guaranteed solely by the pledged word of the parties involved. Also **gentlemen's agreement.**

gen·tle·man's gentleman (jen′təl·mənz) A personal servant for a gentleman.

gentle sex Women collectively. Also **gentler sex.**

gen·tle·wom·an (jen′təl·woom′ən) *n.* *pl.* **·wom·en** (-wim′in) 1. A woman of good family or superior social position; lady. 2. A gracious, well-mannered woman. 3. Formerly, a woman serving a lady of rank as a personal attendant.

Gen·too (jen·tōo′) *n.* *pl.* **·toos** *Archaic* A Hindu. — *adj.* Of or relating to Hindus. [< Pg. *gentio* gentile < L *gentilis*]

gen·trice (jen′tris) *n.* *Archaic* Good family or good breeding. [< OF *genterise*, var. of *gentelise* < *gentil*. See GENTLE.]

gen·try (jen′trē) *n.* 1. People of good family or superior social background; in England, the upper ranks of the middle class. 2. Individuals of a particular area, profession, etc.: the local *gentry:* now chiefly a patronizing or humorous term. 3. *Obs.* Good family or good breeding. [Appar. a back formation from GENTRICE incorrectly taken as a plural]

gen·u (jē′nōo, -nyōo) *n.* *pl.* **gen·u·a** (jē′yōo·ə) *Anat.* 1. The knee. 2. A kneelike structure or part. [< L]

gen·u·flect (jen′yə·flekt) *v.i.* To bend the knee, as in worship. [< Med.L *genuflectere* < L *genu* knee + *flectere* to bend]

gen·u·flec·tion (jen′yə·flek′shən) *n.* A bending of the knee, as in worship. Also *Brit.* **gen·u·flex′ion.**

gen·u·ine (jen′yōo·in) *adj.* 1. Being actually of the origin, authorship, or character claimed; authentic; real. 2. Not spurious, adulterated, or counterfeit; properly so named. 3. Not affected or hypocritical; frank; sincere. 4. Being of the original or true stock: a *genuine* Indian. [< L *genuinus* innate] — **gen′u·ine·ly** *adv.* — **gen′u·ine·ness** *n.*

ge·nus (jē′nəs) *n.* *pl.* **gen·e·ra** (jen′ər·ə) or, less commonly, **ge·nus·es** 1. *Biol.* A grouping or category of plants and animals ranking next above the species and next below the family or subfamily. The genus name (capitalized) immediately precedes the species name in the scientific designation of an organism or group of related organisms, as *Homo sapiens* for the human species. Abbr. *gen.* 2. *Logic* A class of things divisible into two or more subordinate classes or species. 3. A particular sort, kind, or class. [< L, race, kind]

-geny *combining form* Mode of production of; generation or development of: *anthropogeny.* [< F *-génie* < L *-genia* < Gk. *-geneia* < *gen-*, stem of *gignesthai* to become]

geo- *combining form* Earth; ground; soil: *geocentric, geology.*

ge·o·bot·a·ny (jē′ō·bot′ə·nē) *n.* Phytogeography.

ge·o·cen·tric (jē′ō·sen′trik) *adj.* 1. Calculated or viewed with relation to the earth's center: the *geocentric* latitude of a planet. 2. Formulated on the assumption that the earth is the center of the universe: ancient *geocentric* theories. Also **ge′o·cen′tri·cal** *adj.* — **ge′o·cen′tri·cal·ly** *adv.*

geocentric parallax See under PARALLAX.

ge·o·chem·is·try (jē′ō·kem′is·trē) *n.* A specialized branch of chemistry dealing with the chemical composition of the earth's crust. — **ge′o·chem′i·cal** *adj.* — **ge′o·chem′ist** *n.*

ge·o·chro·nol·o·gy (jē′ō·krə·nol′ə·jē) *n.* The science of determining the length or sequence of geological periods.

geod. Geodesy; geodetic.

ge·ode (jē′ōd) *n.* *Geol.* 1. A rock, usually globular, having a cavity lined with crystals. 2. The cavity in such a rock. [< F *géode* < L *geodes*, a precious stone < Gk. *geōdēs* earthy] — **ge·od·ic** (jē·od′ik) *adj.*

ge·o·des·ic (jē′ə·des′ik) *adj.* 1. Of or pertaining to the geometry of geodesic lines or curved surfaces. 2. Geodetic. Also **ge′o·des′i·cal.** — *n.* A geodesic line.

geodesic dome *Archit.* A light and strong hemispherical dome made of prefabricated polyhedral or triangular lattice modules and covered with a thin, strong material.

geodesic line *Math.* The shortest line connecting two points on a given, especially a curved, surface.

ge·od·e·sist (jē·od′ə·sist) *n.* One who specializes in geodesy.

ge·od·e·sy (jē·od′ə·sē) *n.* The science dealing with the determination of the shape, size, area, and curvature of the earth, with the precise mapping of continents or other large tracts, or location of specific points. Abbr. *geod.* [< F *géodésie* < NL *geodaesia* < Gk. *geodaisia* < *gē* earth + *daiein* to divide]

ge·o·det·ic (jē′ə·det′ik) *adj.* 1. Of or pertaining to geodesy. 2. Geodesic. Also **ge′o·det′i·cal.** Abbr. *geod.*

ge·o·det·ics (jē′ə·det′iks) *n.pl.* (*construed as sing.*) Geodesy.

ge·o·duck (gōo′ē·duk′) *n.* A very large, edible clam of the Pacific coast of North America: also spelled *gweduck.* [< Am. Ind.]

ge·o·dy·nam·ics (jē′ō·dī·nam′iks, -di-) *n.pl.* (*construed as sing.*) The branch of geology concerned with the forces affecting the structure of the earth.

Geof·frey IV (jef′rē), 1113–51, Count of Anjou, father of Henry II of England: called **Geoffrey of Anjou, Geoffrey Plantagenet.**

Geoffrey of Monmouth, 1100?–54?, English chronicler.

geog. Geographer; geographic(al); geography.

ge·og·no·sy (jē·og′nə·sē) *n.* The study of the materials of the earth, their structure, characteristics, and interrelationships. [< GEO- + Gk. *gnōsis* knowledge]

ge·og·ra·pher (jē·og′rə·fər) *n.* A specialist in or student of geography. Abbr. *geog.*

ge·o·graph·i·cal (jē′ə·graf′i·kəl) *adj.* 1. Of or pertaining to geography. 2. Relating to topographical facts and influences. Also **ge′o·graph′ic.** Abbr. *geog.* — **ge′o·graph′i·cal·ly** *adv.*

geographic determinism *Sociol.* The theory that attributes the forms and characteristics of a given society to geographic factors.

geographic mile See under MILE.

ge·og·ra·phy (jē·og′rə·fē) *n.* *pl.* **·phies** 1. The science that describes the surface of the earth and its associated physical, biological, economic, political, and demographic characteristics, especially in terms of large areas and the complex of interrelations obtaining among them. 2. The natural aspect, features, etc., of a place or area: the *geography* of the Arctic. 3. A particular work on or system of geography. Abbr. *geog.* [< L *geographia* < Gk. < *gē* earth + *graphein* to write, describe]

ge·oid (jē′oid) *n.* The earth considered hypothetically as an ellipsoidal solid whose surface coincides with the mean level of the ocean. [< Gk. *geoidēs* earthlike < *gē* earth + *eidos* form]

geol. Geologic(al); geologist; geology.

ge·o·log·ic (jē′ə·loj′ik) *adj.* Of or pertaining to geology. Also **ge′o·log′i·cal** *adj.* Abbr. *geol.* — **ge′o·log′i·cal·ly** *adv.*

ge·ol·o·gist (jē·ol′ə·jist) *n.* A specialist in or student of geology. Also **ge·ol′o·ger.** Abbr. *geol.*

ge·ol·o·gize (jē·ol′ə·jīz) *v.i.* **-gized, -giz·ing** 1. To study or discourse on geology. 2. To make geological investigations.

ge·ol·o·gy (jē·ol′ə·jē) *n.* *pl.* **·gies** 1. The science that treats of the origin and structure of the earth, including the physical forces which have shaped it and its physical and organic history, especially as evidenced by rocks and rock formations. 2. The structure of the earth in a given region. 3. A particular work on or system of geology. Abbr. *geol.* [< GEO- + -LOGY]

ge·o·mag·ne·tism (jē′ō·mag′nə·tiz′əm) *n.* The earth's magnetism. — **ge′o·mag·net′ic** (-mag·net′ik) *adj.*

geom. Geometrician; geometric(al); geometry.

ge·o·man·cy (jē′ō·man′sē) *n.* Divination by means of figures formed when particles of earth are thrown down at random, or by joining dots put at random on paper. [< GEO- + -MANCY] — **ge′o·man·cer** *n.* — **ge′o·man′tic** *adj.*

ge·o·med·i·cine (jē′ō·med′ə·sin) *n.* The branch of medicine that treats of the geographic factors of disease.

ge·o·met·ric (jē′ə·met′rik) *adj.* 1. Pertaining to or according to the rules and principles of geometry. 2. Forming, consisting of, or characterized by straight lines, bars, crosses, zigzags, etc., as in painting or sculpture. Also **ge′o·met′ri·cal.** Abbr. *geom.* — **ge′o·met′ri·cal·ly** *adv.*

ge·om·e·tri·cian (jē·om′ə·trish′ən, jē′ə·mə-) *n.* A specialist in geometry. Also **ge·om′e·ter** (-ə·tər). Abbr. *geom.*

geometric mean *Math.* The positive *n*th root of the product of *n* positive numbers: The *geometric mean* of 2 x 4 x 6 is the cube root of 48, or 3.6342 approximately. Compare ARITHMETIC MEAN.

geometric progression *Math.* A sequence of terms in the form $a, ar, ar^2, ar^3, \ldots ar^{n-1}$, where a is the first term, r is the ratio between any pair of adjacent terms, and n is a positive integer, as for example $2, 4, 8, 2 \times 2^{n-1}$. Compare ARITHMETIC PROGRESSION.

ge·om·e·trid (jē·om′ə·trid) *n.* Any of a family (*Geometridae*) of moths whose larvae exist as measuring worms. [< NL *Geometridae* < L *geometres* < Gk. *geōmetrēs* one who measures land]

ge·om·e·trize (jē·om′ə·trīz) *v.i.* **-trized, -triz·ing** 1. To study geometry. 2. To apply geometric methods.

ge·om·e·try (jē·om′ə·trē) *n.* *pl.* **·tries** The branch of mathematics that treats of space and its relations, especially the properties and measurement of points, lines, angles, surfaces, and solids. Abbr. *geom.* [< OF *geometrie* < L *geometria* < Gk. *geōmetria* < *gē* earth + *metreein* to measure]

ge·o·mor·phic (jē′ə·môr′fik) *adj.* Of, pertaining to, or resembling the earth's form or the configuration of its surface.

ge·o·mor·phol·o·gy (jē′ō·môr·fol′ə·jē) *n.* The study of the development, configuration, and distribution of the surface features of the earth: also called *physiography*. Also **ge′o‑mor‑phog′e‑ny** (-foj′ə‑nē). — **ge′o‑mor′pho‑log′i‑cal** (-fə‑loj′i‑kəl) *adj.*

ge‑oph‑a‑gy (jē‑of′ə‑jē) *n.* The eating of earth, clay, etc. [< GEO- + -PHAGY] — **ge‑oph‑a‑gism** (jē‑of′ə‑jiz′əm) *n.* — **ge‑oph′a‑gist** *n.*

ge‑o‑phys‑ics (jē′ō‑fiz′iks) *n.pl.* (*construed as sing.*) The study of the earth as the product of complex physico-chemical forces acting upon it internally and from outer space, es-

ge‑o‑pon‑ics (jē′ə‑pon′iks) *n.pl.* (*construed as sing.*) The art or science of agriculture.

George (jôrj) *n.* **1.** A jewelled figure of St. George slaying a dragon: an insignia of the Knights of the Garter. **2.** A former English coin with the figure of St. George on it.

George (jôrj), **David Lloyd** See LLOYD GEORGE. — **Henry,** 1839–97, U.S. economist and social reformer.

George (jôrj), **Lake** A lake in eastern New York; length about 33 mi.

GEOLOGICAL TIME SCALE

Read from bottom to top.

ERAS	TIME PERIODS ROCK SYSTEMS	TIME EPOCHS ROCK SERIES	APPROX. DURATION MILLION YEARS	APPROX. PERCENT TOTAL AGE	LIFE FORMS
CENOZOIC	QUATERNARY	RECENT PLEISTOCENE	1		Rise and dominance of Man.
CENOZOIC	UPPER TERTIARY	PLIOCENE MIOCENE	65	2	Modern animals and plants.
CENOZOIC	LOWER TERTIARY	OLIGOCENE EOCENE PALEOCENE	65		Rapid development of modern mammals, insects, and plants.
MESOZOIC	UPPER CRETACEOUS		75		Primitive mammals; last dinosaurs; last ammonites.
MESOZOIC	LOWER CRETACEOUS		75		Rise of flowering plants.
MESOZOIC	JURASSIC		45	5	First birds, first mammals. Diversification of reptiles; climax of ammonites; coniferous trees.
MESOZOIC	TRIASSIC		45		Rise of dinosaurs; cycadlike plants; bony fishes.
PALEOZOIC	PERMIAN		45		Rise of reptiles. Modern insects. Last of many plant and animal groups.
PALEOZOIC	PENNSYLVANIAN (CARBONIFEROUS)		75		First reptiles. Amphibians; primitive insects; seed ferns; primitive conifers.
PALEOZOIC	MISSISSIPPIAN (CARBONIFEROUS)		75	9	Climax of shell-crushing sharks. Primitive ammonites.
PALEOZOIC	DEVONIAN		50		First amphibians, first land snails. Primitive land plants. Climax of brachiopods.
PALEOZOIC	SILURIAN		20		First traces of land life. Scorpions. First lungfishes. Widespread coral reefs.
PALEOZOIC	ORDOVICIAN		70		First fish. Climax of trilobites. First appearance of many marine invertebrates.
PALEOZOIC	CAMBRIAN		50		First marine invertebrates, including trilobites.
PROTEROZOIC (PRE-CAMBRIAN)			About 3000	84	First signs of life. Algae.
ARCHEOZOIC (PRE-CAMBRIAN)			About 3000		

Age of oldest dated rocks: about 3,500,000,000 years.

pecially with reference to exploration of its less accessible regions. — **ge′o‑phys′i‑cal** *adj.* — **ge′o‑phys′i‑cist** *n.*

ge‑o‑phyte (jē′ə‑fīt) *n. Bot.* An earth-growing plant; especially, one whose buds, mycelia, etc., are deeply buried.

ge‑o‑po‑lit‑i‑cal (jē′ō‑pə‑lit′i‑kəl) *adj.* Of or pertaining to geopolitics. Also **ge′o‑pol′i‑tic** (-pol′ə‑tik). — **ge′o‑po‑lit′i‑cal‑ly** *adv.*

ge‑o‑pol‑i‑ti‑cian (jē′ō‑pol′ə‑tish′ən) *n.* A specialist in or student of geopolitics. Also **ge‑o‑pol′i‑tist.**

ge‑o‑pol‑i‑tics (jē′ō‑pol′ə‑tiks) *n.pl.* (*construed as sing.*) **1.** The study of political and economic geography. **2.** A doctrine, of Nazi Germany, advocating aggressive expansion: also *German* **Ge‑o‑pol‑i‑tik** (gā′ō‑pôl‑ē‑tēk′).

ge‑o‑pon‑ic (jē′ə‑pon′ik) *adj.* **1.** Pertaining to agriculture. **2.** Rustic. [< Gk. *geōponikos* < *geōponos* a farmer < *gē* earth + *ponos* labor]

George (jôrj), **Saint,** died 303?, Christian martyr; patron of England.

George (jôrj), **Stefan,** 1868–1933, German lyric poet.

George I (jôrj), 1660–1727, elector of Hanover; king of England 1714–27; founder of the Hanoverian dynasty.

George I, 1845–1913, king of Greece 1863–1913; assassinated.

George II, 1683–1760, king of England 1727–60.

George II, 1890–1947, king of Greece 1922–23, 1935–47.

George III, 1738–1820, king of England 1760–1820.

George IV, 1762–1830, king of England 1820–30.

George V, 1865–1936, king of England 1910–36.

George VI, 1895–1952, king of England 1936–52.

George V Coast A part of coastal Antarctica south of Australia.

George‑town (jôrj′toun) The capital of Guyana, a port at the mouth of the Demerara; pop. 97,190 (est. 1969).

PRONUNCIATION KEY: add, āce, câre, pälm; end, ēven; it, īce; odd, ōpen, ôrder; tŏŏk, pōōl; up, bûrn; ə = a in *above*, e in *sicken*, i in *flexible*, o in *melon*, u in *focus*; yōō = u in *fuse*; oil; pout; check; go; ring; thin; this; zh, vision. For à, œ, ü, kh, ṅ, see inside front cover.

George Town The former name of **Penang** (def. 2). Also **Georgetown.**

Geor·gette crepe (jôr·jet′) A sheer, dull fabric with a crepelike surface, originally made of silk, used for blouses, gowns, etc.: a trade name. Also **geor·gette′.** [after Mme. *Georgette* de la Plante, French modiste]

Geor·gia (jôr′jə) 1. A southern Atlantic State of the United States; 58,876 sq. mi.; pop. 4,589,575; capital, Atlanta; entered the Union Jan. 2, 1788; one of the original thirteen States: nickname, *Cracker State, Peach State:* abbr. *Ga.* 2. A constituent republic of the Soviet Union, in the southern Caucasus on the Black Sea; 26,900 sq. mi.; pop. 4,688,000 (1970); capital, Tiflis: Russian *Gruzyiya, Gruzyinskaya S.S.R.* Officially **Georgian S.S.R.**

Geor·gian (jôr′jən) adj. 1. Of or pertaining to the reigns or period of the first four Georges in England, 1714–1830, or of George V, 1910–36. 2. Of or pertaining to Georgia or Georgians. 3. Of or pertaining to the language of Georgia (def. 2.). — n. 1. A native or inhabitant of Georgia. 2. One of an ancient mountain people native to the Caucasus. 3. The Caucasian language of the Georgians of the Soviet Union. 4. A person belonging to or fond of either of the Georgian periods in England.

Georgian Bay An inlet of Lake Huron in western Ontario, Canada.

Georgia pine The longleaf pine (which see).

geor·gic (jôr′jik) adj. Pertaining to farming or rural affairs. Also **geor′gi·cal.** — n. A poem on farming. [< L *georgicus* < Gk. *geōrgikos* < *geōrgia* husbandry]

Geor·gics (jôr′jiks) A four-part poem by Vergil describing farm work and rural life.

ge·o·stat·ic (jē′ə·stat′ik) adj. Of or pertaining to the pressure of the earth.

ge·o·stat·ics (jē′ə·stat′iks) n.pl. (construed as sing.) The statics of rigid bodies in relation to balanced forces on or beneath the earth's surface.

ge·o·stroph·ic (jē′ə·strof′ik) adj. *Meteorol.* Designating a regional drift of air masses caused by the rotation of the earth. [< GEO- + Gk. *strephein* to turn]

ge·o·syn·cli·nal (jē′ō·sin·klī′nəl) adj. Of or pertaining to a geosyncline. — n. A geosyncline.

ge·o·syn·cline (jē′ə·sin′klīn) n. *Geol.* A major sinking of the earth's crust, formed during great periods of time and characterized by extensive accumulations of sedimentary and volcanic rocks.

ge·o·tax·is (jē′ə·tak′sis) n. *Biol.* The movement of an organism with respect to the force of gravitation.

ge·o·tec·ton·ic (jē′ō·tek·ton′ik) adj. *Geol.* Relating to the structure, arrangement, etc., of the rock masses of the earth's crust.

ge·o·ther·mal (jē′ə·thûr′məl) adj. Of or pertaining to the earth's internal heat. Also **ge′o·ther′mic.**

ge·ot·ro·pism (jē·ot′rə·piz′əm, jē′ō·trō′-) n. *Biol.* The growth or movement of organisms, especially plants, toward the pull of gravity (**positive geotropism**) or away from it (**negative geotropism**). — **ge·o·trop·ic** (jē′ə·trop′ik) adj. — **ge·o·trop′i·cal·ly** adv.

ger. Gerund.

Ger. German; Germany.

ge·rah (gē′rə) n. An ancient Hebrew coin and unit of weight, equal to ½₀ shekel. *Ezek.* xlv 12.

ge·ra·ni·a·ceous (ji·rā′nē·ā′shəs) adj. *Bot.* Belonging or pertaining to a widely distributed family (*Geraniaceae*) of polypetalous herbs, shrubs, and trees, the geranium family. [< NL *Geraniaceae* < L *geranium.* See GERANIUM.]

ge·ra·ni·al (ji·rā′nē·əl) n. Citral, a flavoring extract and perfume ingredient.

ge·ra·ni·ol (ji·rā′nē·ôl, -ōl) n. *Chem.* An oily colorless alcohol of the terpene group, $C_{10}H_{18}O$, found as a constituent of oil of roses, geranium, citronella, and other plants and used in the manufacture of perfumes and cosmetics.

ge·ra·ni·um (ji·rā′nē·əm) n. 1. Any plant of a large genus (*Geranium*) with showy pink or purple flowers: also called *cranebill.* 2. Any plant of a closely related genus (*Pelargonium*), originally from South Africa. 3. A very deep pink, almost red, color like that of the typical geranium. [< L < Gk. *geranion* < *geranos* crane]

ger·bil (jûr′bil) n. Any of a subfamily (*Gerbillinae*) of rodents found in Asia, Africa, and SE Europe, with long hind legs, hairy tail, and narrow incisors. Also **ger′bille.** [< F *gerbille* < NL *gerbillus,* dim. of *gerbo* jerboa]

Ger·da (gûr′dä) In Norse mythology, a giantess who was loved by Frey and became his wife.

ge·rent (jir′ənt) n. *Rare* One who governs or manages. [< L *gerens, -entis,* ppr. of *gerere* to carry on, do]

ge·re·nuk (ger′ə·nōōk) n. An East African antelope (*Lithocranius walleri*) with extremely long legs and neck and a massive head. [< native name]

ger·fal·con (jûr′fal′kən, -fôl′-, -fô′-) n. A large falcon (*Falco rusticolus*) of the arctic regions, with feathered shanks: also spelled *gyrfalcon.* [< OF *gerfaucon* < OHG *gir* vulture + OF *faucon* falcon]

ger·i·at·ric (jer′ē·at′rik) adj. Of or pertaining to geriatrics or to old people.

ger·i·a·tri·cian (jer′ē·ə·trish′ən) n. A specialist in the diseases of old age. Also **ger·i·at·rist** (jer′ē·at′rist)

ger·i·at·rics (jer′ē·at′riks) n.pl. (construed as sing.) 1. The branch of medicine that deals with the structural changes, physiology, diseases, and hygiene of old age. 2. Gerontology. [< Gk. *gēras* old age + -IATRICS]

Gé·ri·cault (zhā·rē·kō′), **Jean Louis André Théodore,** 1791–1824, French painter.

germ (jûrm) n. 1. A microorganism that causes disease; a microbe. 2. Something in its essential though rudimentary and undeveloped form: the *germ* of an idea. 3. That which gives rise to the production, growth, or development of something: to sow the *germs* of war. 4. *Biol.* a A reproductive cell; gamete. b An organism in its embryonic form. [< F *germe* < L *germen* sprig]

Germ. German; Germany.

ger·man¹ (jûr′mən) n. A cotillion (def. 1). [Short for *German cotillion*]

ger·man² (jûr′mən) adj. 1. Having the same father and mother as oneself: in the compounds *brother-german, sister-german.* 2. Related to oneself through being the child of one's uncle or aunt: in the compound *cousin-german.* 3. Germane. [< OF *germain* < L *germanus* closely related]

Ger·man (jûr′mən) adj. Of, pertaining to, or characteristic of Germany, its people, or their language. — n. 1. A native or inhabitant of Germany. 2. The language of the Germans, belonging to the West Germanic branch. Abbr. *G, G., Ger., Germ.* — **High German** The standard literary and spoken language used throughout Germany and Austria and in parts of Switzerland and Alsace: also called *New High German.* Abbr. *HG* — **Low German** 1. Collectively, the languages of the Low Countries, including Dutch, Flemish, and Frisian, and of the northern lowlands of Germany (*Plattdeutsch*). 2. The division of West Germanic that includes Dutch, Flemish, Frisian, English, etc. Abbr. *LG, LG., L.G.* — **Old High German** The language of southern Germany from about 800 to 1100. Abbr. *OHG, OHG., O.H.G.* — **Middle High German** The High German language from 1100 to 1450, as exemplified in the *Nibelungenlied.* Abbr. *MHG, MHG., M.H.G.* — **Middle Low German** The Low German language from 1100 to 1450. Abbr. *MLG, MLG., M.L.G.* [< L *Germanus,* prob. < Celtic]

German Baptist Brethren The Dunkers: official name.

German cockroach The Croton bug.

German Democratic Republic See under GERMANY.

ger·man·der (jər·man′dər) n. 1. A labiate herb (genus *Teucrium*) of the mint family, with pale purple flowers; especially, the American germander (*T. canadense*). 2. The germander speedwell: see under SPEEDWELL. [< OF *germandree* < Med.L *germandra,* alter. of LGk. *chamandrya* < Gk. *chamaidrys* < *chamai* on the ground + *drys* an oak]

ger·mane (jər·mān′) adj. Related to what is being discussed or considered; pertinent; relevant. [See GERMAN²]

German East Africa From 1885 to 1916, a German protectorate extending chiefly over Tanzania, Rwanda, and Burundi.

German Empire See under GERMANY.

ger·man·ic (jər·man′ik) adj. Containing germanium in its higher valence.

Ger·man·ic (jər·man′ik) adj. 1. Of or pertaining to a group of early Indo-European tribes living in the region between the Rhine, Danube, and Vistula rivers: later extended to include the Germans, English, Dutch, Flemings, Danes, Scandinavians, and German-Swiss. 2. Relating to the language or customs of any of these people. — n. 1. A subfamily of the Indo-European family of languages, divided into the branches **East Germanic,** including Gothic (extinct); **North Germanic** or Scandinavian, including Norwegian, Swedish, Danish, Icelandic, and Faroese; and **West Germanic,** including all the High and Low German languages and dialects, among which are German, Dutch, Flemish, Frisian, English, Yiddish, Plattdeutsch, etc. 2. The prehistoric parent of these languages: called **Primitive Germanic.** Also called *Teutonic.* Abbr. *Gmc.* [< L *Germanicus* < *Germanus.* See GERMAN.]

Ger·man·i·cus Cae·sar (jər·man′i·kəs sē′zər), 15 B.C.–A.D. 19, Roman general; son of Nero Claudius Drusus.

Ger·man·ism (jûr′mən·iz′əm) n. 1. An idiom or turn of phrase peculiar to German. 2. A custom, practice, etc., typical of Germans. 3. Admiration for or imitation of German customs, attitudes, etc.

ger·ma·ni·um (jər·mā′nē·əm) n. A grayish white, metallic element (symbol Ge) of the silicon group, used in electronics, metallurgy, and optics. See ELEMENT. [< NL < L *Germania* Germany]

Ger·man·ize (jûr′mən·īz) v. ·ized, ·iz·ing v.t. 1. To cause to conform to German speech, customs, etc. 2. To translate into German. — v.i. 3. To adopt German opinions, customs, etc. — **Ger′man·i·za′tion** n. — **Ger′man·iz′er** n.

German measles *Pathol.* A contagious virus disease accompanied by fever, sore throat, and a skin rash, and sometimes causing birth anomalies when a pregnant woman is infected: also called *rubella, rubeola.*

Germano- *combining form* German: Germanophile.

German Ocean A former name for the NORTH SEA.

Ger·man·o·phile (jər·man′ə·fīl) *n.* One who loves Germany or what is German.

Ger·man·o·phobe (jər·man′ə·fōb) *n.* One who dislikes or fears Germany or that which is German.

ger·man·ous (jûr′mən·əs) *adj.* Of or pertaining to germanium in its lower valence.

German shepherd A breed of dog with a large, strong body, thick, smooth coat, and great intelligence: also called *police dog.*

German silver A white alloy of copper, nickel, and zinc, used in the manufacture of cutlery and as a base for plated ware: also called *albata, nickel silver.* Abbr. *GS*

German Southwest Africa A former name for SOUTHWEST AFRICA.

Ger·man·town (jûr′mən·toun) A northern residential section of Philadelphia; scene of a British victory in the Revolutionary War, Oct. 4, 1777.

Ger·ma·ny (jûr′mə·nē) A country of central Europe, divided in 1949 into the **Federal Republic of Germany** (**West Germany**); 95,735 sq. mi.; pop. 61,194,-600 (est. 1970); capital, Bonn and the **German Democratic Republic** (**East Germany**); 41,479 sq. mi. (excluding East Berlin); pop. 17,177,000 (est. 1970, excluding East Berlin); capital, East Berlin. German *Deutschland.*

germ cell *Biol.* A cell specialized for reproduction: distinguished from *somatic cell.*

ger·mi·cide (jûr′mə·sīd) *n.* An agent used to destroy disease germs or other microorganisms. [< GERM + -CIDE] — **ger·mi·ci·dal** (jûr′mə·sī′dəl) *adj.*

ger·mi·nal (jûr′mə·nəl) *adj.* 1. Of, relating to, or constituting a germ or germ cell. 2. Pertaining to the earliest stage of development; embryonic. [< NL *germinalis* < L *germen, -inis* sprig]

Ger·mi·nal (jûr′mə·nəl, *Fr.* zher·mē·nàl′) *n.* The seventh month of the Republican calendar. See (Republican) CALENDAR. [< F < *germe* seed, germ]

germinal disc *Biol.* 1. A disclike area of the blastoderm of eggs of amniotic vertebrates, in which the embryo proper first appears. 2. In meroblastic eggs with much yolk, the disclike protoplasmic part that undergoes segmentation: also called *blastodisc.*

germinal vesicle 1. *Biol.* The large nucleus of the fertilized ovum before formation of the polar bodies: also called *blastocyst.*

ger·mi·nant (jûr′mə·nənt) *adj.* Germinating; sprouting.

ger·mi·nate (jûr′mə·nāt) *v.* **·nat·ed, ·nat·ing** *v.i.* 1. To begin to grow or develop; sprout. — *v.t.* 2. To cause to sprout. [< L *germinatus,* pp. of *germinare* to sprout] — **ger′mi·na·ble** (-nə·bəl) *adj.* — **ger′mi·na′tion** *n.* — **ger′mi·na′tor** *n.*

ger·mi·na·tive (jûr′mə·nā′tiv) *adj.* 1. Pertaining to or tending to produce germination; capable of germinating. 2. Capable of growing.

Ger·mis·ton (jûr′məs·tən) A city in southern Transvaal, South Africa; pop. 204,605 (1960).

germ layer *Biol.* One of the three principal layers of cells from which the embryo develops, the ectoderm, mesoderm, or endoderm.

germ plasm *Biol.* The part of the protoplasm of a germ cell that contains the chromosomes and genes.

germ theory 1. *Pathol.* The theory that infectious diseases are caused by bacteria or other microorganisms. 2. The doctrine of biogenesis.

Gé·rôme (zhā·rōm′), **Jean Léon,** 1824–1904, French painter.

Ge·ron·i·mo (jə·ron′ə·mō), 1829–1909, Apache Indian chief active in the Southwest and Mexico.

geronto- *combining form* Old age; pertaining to old people: *gerontology.* Also, before vowels, **geront-.** [< Gk. *gerōn, gerontos* old man]

ger·on·toc·ra·cy (jer′on·tok′rə·sē) *n. pl.* **·cies** 1. A government conducted by the oldest men of a people, tribe, etc. 2. A group of old men forming a governing body. — **ge·ron·to·crat·ic** (ji·ron′tō·krat′ik) *adj.*

ger·on·tol·o·gy (jer′on·tol′ə·jē) *n.* 1. The scientific study of the processes and phenomena of aging: also called *nostology.* 2. Geriatrics. — **ger′on·tol′o·gist** *n.*

-gerous *suffix* Bearing or producing: *crystalligerous.* [< L *gerere* to bear + -OUS]

Ger·ry (ger′ē), **Elbridge,** 1744–1814, American statesman; vice president of the United States 1813–1814.

ger·ry·man·der (jer′i·man′dər, ger′-) *v.t.* 1. To alter (a voting area) so as to advance unfairly the interests of a political party. 2. To adapt to one's advantage; manipulate. — *n.* The act or result of gerrymandering. [< GERRY + (SALA)MANDER; from the salamander shape of a district formed in Massachusetts while Elbridge Gerry was governor]

Gersh·win (gûrsh′win), **George,** 1898–1937, U.S. composer.

ger·und (jer′ənd) *Gram. n.* 1. In Latin, a form of a verb used like a noun in all cases of the singular except the nominative, as *canendi* in *ars canendi,* "the art of singing." 2. In English, the *-ing* form of a verb, as *doing,* or a compound tense of a verb made with the *-ing* form of an auxiliary, as *having done,* when used as the subject or object of a verb or as the object of a preposition, as *doing* in *Doing the work carefully is essential.* 3. In some other languages, a form similar to a gerund in form or function. Abbr. *ger.* [< LL *gerundium* < L *gerere* to carry on, do] — **ge·run·di·al** (jə·run′dē·əl) *adj.*

ge·run·dive (jə·run′div) *Gram. n.* 1. In Latin, a form of the verb constituting the future passive participle, having the stem of the gerund and expressing obligation, propriety, etc., as *amandus,* "to be loved," "that should be loved." 2. In some other languages, a form similar to a gerundive in form or function. — *adj.* Of, pertaining to, or resembling a gerundive, or, sometimes, a gerund. [< LL *gerundivus* < *gerundium.* See GERUND.]

Ge·ry·on (jē′rē·ən, ger′ē-) In Greek mythology, a winged monster with three bodies; killed by Hercules.

Ge·sell (gə·zel′), **Arnold Lucius,** 1880–1961, U.S. psychologist and pediatrician.

ges·so (jes′ō) *n.* 1. A mixture of plaster of Paris and glue or of some similar materials used as a ground for painting or in the making of bas-reliefs, etc. 2. A painting surface made of such a mixture. [< Ital. < L *gypsum.* See GYPSUM.]

gest[1] (jest) *n. Archaic* 1. A noteworthy deed; exploit. 2. A tale of adventure or romance; especially, a metrical romance. Also **geste.** [< OF < L *gesta* deeds, orig. neut. pl. of *gestus,* pp. of *gerere* to do]

gest[2] (jest) *n. Archaic* 1. A gesture. 2. Carriage; bearing. Also **geste.** [< OF *geste* < L *gestus* bearing < *gerere* to carry on, do]

gest. Died (G *gestorben*).

ge·stalt (gə·shtält′, -shtôlt′) *n. pl.* **·stalts** or **·stalt·en** (-shtält′ən, -shtôlt′-) A functional configuration or synthesis of separate elements of emotion, experience, etc., that constitutes more than the mechanical sum of the parts. Also **Ge·stalt′.** [< G, form]

gestalt psychology Psychology based on the theory of the gestalt.

Ge·sta·po (gə·stä′pō, *Ger.* gə·shtä′pō) *n.* The German state secret police under the Nazi regime, noted for the brutality of its methods. [< G *Ge(heime) Sta(ats) Po(lizei)* Secret State Police]

Ges·ta Ro·ma·no·rum (jes′tə rō′mə·nôr′əm, -nō′rəm) A collection of tales compiled in Latin during the 13th or 14th century, used as a source of plots by Chaucer, Shakespeare, and others. [< L, deeds of the Romans]

ges·tate (jes′tāt) *v.t.* **·tat·ed, ·tat·ing** To carry in the uterus during gestation. [< L *gestatus,* pp. of *gestare* to carry young]

ges·ta·tion (jes·tā′shən) *n.* 1. The act or period of carrying the unborn young in the uterus from conception to birth; pregnancy. 2. The development of an idea, plan, etc., in the mind. — **ges·ta·to·ry** (jes′tə·tôr′ē, -tō′rē) *adj.*

ges·tic (jes′tik) *adj.* Of or pertaining to bodily motion, especially dancing. Also **ges′ti·cal.**

ges·tic·u·late (jes·tik′yə·lāt) *v.* **·lat·ed, ·lat·ing** *v.i.* 1. To make emphatic or expressive gestures, as in speaking. — *v.t.* 2. To express by gestures. [< L *gesticulatus,* pp. of *gesticulari* < *gesticulus,* dim. of *gestus* bearing, gesture] — **ges·tic′u·la′tor** *n.* — **ges·tic′u·la′tor·y** *adj.*

ges·tic·u·la·tion (jes·tik′yə·lā′shən) *n.* 1. The act of gesticulating. 2. An energetic or expressive gesture. — **ges·tic′u·la′to·ry** *adj.*

ges·ture (jes′chər) *n.* 1. A bodily motion, as of the hands or head in speaking, used to emphasize or express some idea or emotion. 2. Such motions collectively. 3. Something said or done as a mere formality, or for effect. 4. *Obs.* Bearing; posture. — *v.* **·tured, ·tur·ing** *v.i.* 1. To make gestures; gesticulate. — *v.t.* 2. To express by gestures. [< Med.L *gestura* < L *gerere* to carry on, do] — **ges′tur·er** *n.*

Ge·sund·heit (gə·zŏŏnt′hīt) *interj. German* (Your) health: a salutation or toast, or an expression of good will to someone who has just sneezed.

---

get (get) *v.* **got** (*Archaic* **gat**), **got** or *U.S.* **got·ten, get·ting** *v.t.* **1.** To come into possession of; obtain. **2.** To go for and bring back: to *get* one's hat. **3.** To capture; seize. **4.** To cause to come, go, move, etc.: to *get* baggage through customs. **5.** To carry away; take: *Get* this out of the house. **6.** To make ready; prepare: to *get* lunch. **7.** To cause to be; bring to a state or condition: to *get* the work done. **8.** To prevail on; induce; persuade: *Get* her to sign the paper. **9.** To find out or obtain by calculation, experiment, etc.: to add the totals and *get* 100. **10.** To receive reward or punishment: to *get* a whipping. **11.** To learn or master, as by study or practice: Have you *got* your history lesson? **12.** To become sick with; contract: to *get* malaria. **13.** To establish contact or communication with: I'll *get* him on the phone. **14.** To catch, as a train; board. **15.** To beget: now said chiefly of animals. **16.** *Informal* To come to an understanding of; comprehend: I *get* the idea. **17.** *Informal* To possess: with *have* or *has*: He has *got* quite a temper. ◆ See note under GOT. **18** *Informal* To obtain the advantage over; overmaster: Drink will *get* him. **19.** *Informal* To square accounts with: I'll *get* you yet. **20.** *Informal* To be obliged or forced (to do something specified): with *have* or *has*: I have *got* to go home. See note under GOT. **21.** *Informal* To strike; hit: The shrapnel *got* him in the arm; also, to kill: That shot *got* him. **22.** *Slang* To puzzle or baffle: The remark *got* me. **23.** *Slang* To please, irritate, excite, etc.: That music *gets* me. **24.** *Slang* To take note of; observe: Did you *get* that look? **25.** To bring to or place in some specified location. — *v.i.* **26.** To arrive: When does the train *get* there? **27.** To come, go, or move: *Get* in here. **28.** To board; enter: with *on, in,* etc.: to *get* on a train. **29.** To become: to *get* drunk. **30.** To acquire profits or property: eager to *get* but not give. **— to get about 1.** To become known, as gossip or news. **2.** To move about. **3.** To be active socially. **— to get across 1.** To make or be convincing or clear, as to an audience. **2.** To be successful, as in projecting one's personality. **— to get ahead** To attain success. **— to get ahead of 1.** To move or go in front of. **2.** To be superior to; excel. **— to get along 1.** To leave; go. **2.** To manage; fare: How is he *getting along*? **3.** To be successful; succeed. **4.** To be friendly or compatible. **5.** To grow old or older. **— to get around 1.** To become known, as gossip. **2.** To move about. **3.** To attend social or public functions, etc. **4.** To flatter, cajole, etc., so as to obtain the favor of. **5.** To avoid, as by outwitting. **— to get around to** To give attention to after some delay. **— to get at 1.** To arrive at; reach: to *get at* the truth. **2.** To intend; mean: I don't see what you're *getting at*. **3.** To apply oneself to. **4.** *Informal* To influence. **— to get away 1.** To escape. **2.** To leave; go. **3.** To start, as a race horse. **— to get away with** *Slang* **1.** To do (something) without discovery, criticism, or punishment. **2.** To do something despite oneself or unintentionally: That remark *got away* with me. **— to get back** To return to a previous position. **— to get back at** *Slang* To revenge oneself on. **— to get by 1.** To pass: This *got by* the censor. **2.** *Informal* To manage to survive. **3.** *Informal* To accomplish something without discovery, blame, etc. **— to get down** To dismount or descend, as from a horse or ladder. **— to get down to** (**business, facts,** etc.) To begin to act on, investigate, or consider. **— to get in 1.** To arrive or enter. **2.** To slip in (a remark, etc.). **3.** To become involved or familiar with: He's *got in* with a fast crowd. **— to get it** *Informal* **1.** To understand. **2.** To be punished in some way. **— to get nowhere** To be unsuccessful. **— to get off 1.** To descend from; dismount. **2.** To depart. **3.** To be relieved or freed, as of a duty. **4.** To be released with a lesser penalty, etc., or none at all. **5.** To utter. **— to get (someone** or **something) off 1.** To take off: *Get* this bug *off* me. **2.** To secure the acquittal or lesser punishment of. **— to get on 1.** To mount (a horse, vehicle, etc.). **2.** To get along. **— to get out 1.** To depart or leave. **2.** To escape. **3.** To become known, as a secret. **4.** To publish. **5.** To express or utter with difficulty: He finally *got out* his thanks. **6.** To take out. **— to get out of 1.** To obtain from. **2.** To escape or help to escape. **3.** To evade or help to evade. **4.** To depart from. **— to get over 1.** To recover from (illness, surprise, anger, etc.). **2.** To get across. **— to get round** To get around (defs. 1, 2, and 5). **— to get there** *Informal* To accomplish one's purpose; succeed. **— to get through 1.** To complete. **2.** To continue to exist; survive. **— to get through (to) 1.** To establish communication (with). **2.** To make clear (to). **— to get to 1.** To begin: to *get to* telling stories. **2.** To be able to do something: I *get to* go to the theater every week now. **3.** To get through to. **— to get together 1.** To gather; assemble. **2.** To come to an agreement. **— to get up 1.** To rise, as from sleep. **2.** To mount; climb. **3.** To devise. **4.** To acquire, develop, or work up: to *get up* some enthusiasm. **5.** *Informal* To dress up; bedeck. ◆ See note under GOTTEN. **— n. 1.** The act of begetting; also, that which is begotten; breed; progeny: said of animals. **2.** In tennis, handball, etc., the retrieval of a difficult shot. [< ON *geta*]
— Syn. (verb) **1.** *Get, obtain, procure, gain, acquire,* and *earn*

mean to come into possession of some specified thing. *Get* is the widest word, ranging from seizure to simple reception of something. A man may *get* power through treachery and rebellion; he may also *get* smallpox, a ticket for speeding, or a reward for some accomplishment. We *obtain* that which we seek out: to *obtain* a loan. *Procure* implies contrivance or maneuver; *gain* suggests effort; *acquire* refers to a continuous, usually slow process: to *procure* a copy of a rare book, to *gain* a victory, to *acquire* a small fortune. *Earn* refers to that which we receive for work. See RECEIVE.

get·a·way (get′ə-wā′) *n.* **1.** An escape, as of a criminal. **2.** The start, as of an automobile, race horse, etc.

geth·sem·a·ne (geth-sem′ə-nē) *n.* A place, occasion, or period of intense suffering.

Geth·sem·a·ne (geth-sem′ə-nē) A garden outside Jerusalem at the foot of the Mount of Olives, the place where Christ began his sufferings and was arrested. *Matt.* xxvi 36. [< Gk. *Gethsēmanē* < Aramaic *gath shemānīm* oil press]

get·ter (get′ər) *n.* **1.** One who or that which gets. **2.** *Electronics* A substance, as barium, used in electron tubes, etc., to remove residual gases. **3.** *Canadian* Poisoned vermin bait.

get-to·geth·er (get′tə-geth′ər) *n. Informal* A gathering.

Get·tys·burg (get′iz-bûrg) A town in southern Pennsylvania; scene of a Union victory in the Civil War, July 1–3, 1863; site of a famous address by Abraham Lincoln, November 19, 1863, at the dedication of a national cemetery; site of **Gettysburg National Military Park**; 2,463 acres; established 1895.

get-up (get′up′) *n. Informal* **1.** Overall arrangement and appearance, especially of a book or magazine. **2.** The combination of articles of dress worn on a particular occasion; a costume; outfit. **3.** Vigorous initiative; drive: also **get′-up′-and-go′** (-ən-gō′).

gew·gaw (gyoo′gô) *n.* Some little ornamental article of small value; trinket. — *adj.* Showy; gaudy. [ME *giue-goue*; origin uncertain]

gey (gā) *Scot. adj.* Moderate; considerable. — *adv.* Very.

gey·ser (gī′zər, -sər *for def. 1*; gē′zər *for def. 2*) *n.* **1.** A natural hot spring from which intermittent jets of steam, hot water, or mud are ejected in a fountainlike column. **2.** *Brit.* A gas hot-water heater. [< Icel. *geysir* gusher, name of a hot spring < *geysan* to gush]

gey·ser·ite (gī′zər-īt) *n.* An opaline quartz deposited in various forms around geysers and other hot springs.

Ge·zi·ra (je-zē′rə) A region in east central Sudan between the Blue Nile and the White Nile.

g.gr. Great gross.

Gha·na (gä′nə) An independent Republic in the Commonwealth of Nations, comprising the former Gold Coast Colony and the protectorates of Ashanti, Northern Territories, and Togoland in western Africa; 92,100 sq. mi.; pop. 8,545,-561 (est. 1970); capital, Accra. See map of (Gulf of) GUINEA. **— Gha·na·ian** (gə-nä′ən) *adj. & n.*

ghar·ry (gar′ē) *n. pl.* **·ries** *Anglo-Indian* A cart or carriage. Also **ghar′ri.** [< Hind. *gārī* cart]

ghast·ly (gast′lē, gäst′-) *adj.* **·li·er, ·li·est 1.** Horrible; terrifying. **2.** Deathlike in appearance; pale; wan. **3.** *Informal* Very bad or unpleasant: a *ghastly* book. — *adv.* **1.** Spectral in manner or appearance. **2.** Fearfully; horribly. [ME *gastlich*, OE *gæstan* to terrify + *-lich* -LY¹] **— ghast′li·ness** *n.*
— Syn. (adj.) **1.** hideous, grisly, gruesome, grim.

ghat (gôt) *n. Anglo-Indian* **1.** A stairway or passageway leading down to the edge of a river. **2.** A mountain pass. **3.** A range or chain of mountains. Also **ghaut.** [< Hind. *ghāt*]

Ghats (gôts, gäts), **Eastern** and **Western** The two principal mountain ranges of southern India, parallel to its coasts; average height of the Western Ghats, 3,000 to 5,000 ft.; average height of the Eastern Ghats, 1,500 to 2,000 ft.

gha·zi (gä′zē) *n. pl.* **·zies** In Moslem countries, a hero; especially, one who has fought heroically against infidels. [< Arabic, orig. ppr. of *ghazā* to fight]

Ghe·ber (gā′bər, gē′-) *n.* A fire worshiper or Parsee; Zoroastrian: so called by Moslems. Also **Ghe′bre.** [< F *guèbre* < Persian *gabr.* Cf. GIAOUR.]

ghee (gē) *n. Anglo-Indian* A butterlike substance made by melting, boiling, and cooling the butterfat of buffalo milk. [< Hind. *ghi* < Skt. *ghṛta*]

Ghent (gent) A port city in NW Belgium, at the confluence of the Schelde and Lys rivers; pop. 153,301 (est. 1969). Flemish *Gent*; French *Gand*.

gher·kin (gûr′kin) *n.* **1.** A small, prickly cucumber (*Cucumis anguria*) of the southern United States, West Indies, etc., pickled and eaten as a relish. **2.** The plant producing it. **3.** Any small cucumber used for pickling. [< Du. *agurk* cucumber < G < Slavic, ult. < LGk. *angourion*]

ghet·to (get′ō) *n. pl.* **ghet·tos 1.** A section of a city, often run-down or overcrowded, inhabited chiefly by a minority group that is effectively barred from living in other communities, as because of racial prejudice or for economic or social reasons. **2.** A section of a city in certain European countries in which Jews were formerly required to live. [< Ital.]

Ghib·el·line (gib′əl-in, -ēn) *n.* In medieval Italy, a member of a political faction supporting the German emperors against the Guelphs, the papal party. — *adj.* Of or pertaining to the Ghibellines. [< Ital. *Ghibellino*, alter. of G *Waiblingen*, an imperial estate] — **Ghib'el·lin·ism** *n.*

Ghi·ber·ti (gē·ber'tē), **Lorenzo**, 1378?–1455, Florentine sculptor, painter, and goldsmith.

Ghir·lan·da·jo (gir'län·dä'yō), **Domenico**, 1449–94, Florentine painter: original name **Domenico Bi·gor·di** (bē·gôr'dē). Also **Ghir'lan·da'io.**

ghost (gōst) *n.* **1.** A disembodied spirit; a wraith, specter, or phantom. **2.** The animating spirit or soul: now only in the phrase **to give up the ghost,** to die. **3.** A haunting recollection of something: *ghosts* from the past. **4.** A mere shadow, trace, or suggestion of something: the *ghost* of a smile. **5.** *Informal* A ghostwriter (which see) **6.** *Optics* **a** A false or secondary image, as one produced by a defective lens. **b** In television, an unwanted doubling of the image on the screen. — *v.t. & v.i.* **1.** To haunt as a ghost. **2.** *Informal* To write as a ghostwriter. [OE *gāst* spirit] — **ghost'like'** *adj.*
— **Syn.** (noun) **1.** *Ghost, spirit, specter, phantom, shade, wraith, apparition, revenant,* and *spook* are alike in suggesting the visible manifestation of a person or thing in an immaterial form. *Ghost* and *spirit* are the more common terms. *Specter* emphasizes a terrifying manifestation; *phantom* stresses the possibly illusory nature of what appears to be a *ghost*. *Shade* is a rather literary word equivalent to *ghost,* while *revenant,* equally literary, avoids the often emotional associations of *ghost. Apparition* stresses the suddenness of appearance of a *spirit. Spook* is an informal term meaning a *ghost. Wraith* may indicate the manifestation of a deceased being, but it more often indicates the spectral manifestation of a person who is not actually present and who is about to die.

ghost dance A religious dance of certain North American Indian tribes to bring about communion with the dead.

ghost·ly (gōst'lē) *adj.* **·li·er, ·li·est 1.** Pertaining to apparitions; spectral. **2.** Pertaining to religion; spiritual. — **ghost'li·ness** *n.*

ghost town A deserted town, especially a former boom town.

ghost·write (gōst'rīt') *v.t. & v.i.* **·wrote, ·writ·ten, ·writ·ing** To write or act as a ghostwriter.

ghost·writ·er (gōst'rī'tər) *n.* One who writes articles, speeches, books, etc., for someone else to whom the authorship is to be attributed.

ghoul (gool) *n.* **1.** One who robs graves. **2.** One who takes pleasure in revolting things or practices. **3.** In Moslem legend, an evil spirit who preys on corpses and robs graves. [< Arabic *ghūl*] — **ghoul'ish** *adj.* — **ghoul'ish·ly** *adv.* — **ghoul'ish·ness** *n.*

GHQ, G.H.Q. *Mil.* General Headquarters.

ghyll (gil) See GILL³.

GI (jē'ī') *U.S. Informal n. pl.* **GIs** or **GI's** An enlisted man in the U.S. Army. — **the GIs** (or **GI's**) *Mil. Slang* Diarrhea. — *adj.* **1.** Of, pertaining to, or characteristic of GIs. **2.** Furnished by the government for the use of the armed forces. — *v.t.* **GIed** or **GI'ed, GIing** or **GI'ing** To clean or scrub, as for military inspection. [< *G(overnment) I(ssue)*]

GI or **G.I. 1.** General issue. **2.** Government issue.

gi. Gill(s).

G.I. or **g.i.** *Anat.* Gastrointestinal.

gi·ant (jī'ənt) *n.* **1.** In legend and folklore, a being in human form but of supernatural size and strength. **2.** In Greek mythology, one of the race of huge, manlike beings who warred against the gods of Olympus. **3.** Any person or thing of great size, strength, capability, etc.: a mental *giant.* — *adj.* **1.** Of or typical of a giant. **2.** Huge; great. [< OF *geant* < L *gigas, -antis* < Gk. *gigas, -antos*] — **gi'ant·ess** *n. fem.*

giant cactus The saguaro.

giant fennel See under FENNEL.

gi·ant·ism (jī'ənt·iz'əm) *n.* **1.** The quality or condition of being a giant. **2.** Gigantism.

giant panda The panda (def. 2).

giant powder A variety of dynamite using kieselguhr as an absorbent.

Gi·ant's Causeway (jī'ənts) A headland on the northern coast of County Antrim, Northern Ireland, consisting of thousands of small basaltic columns.

giant star *Astron.* Any of a class of stars of great mass and high luminosity that are passing through the early stages of their evolution, as Capella and Arcturus.

giaour (jour) *n.* Among Moslems, a nonbeliever; especially, a Christian. [< Turkish *giaur* < Persian *gaur,* var. of *gabr* infidel. Cf. GHEBER.]

gi·ar·di·a·sis (jē'är·dī'ə·sis) *n. Pathol.* An intestinal disorder probably caused by a parasitic protozoan (*Giardia lamblia*). [< NL *Giardia,* genus name + -IASIS]

gib¹ (gib) *Mech. n.* A piece of wood or metal, often wedge-shaped, for keeping parts of a machine tight, adjusting a bearing, etc. — *v.t.* **gibbed, gib·bing** To fasten or supply with a gib or gibs. [? < GIBBET]

gib² (gib) *n.* A cat; especially, a male cat; tomcat. [Abbr. of *Gilbert,* name for a cat.]

Gib. Gibraltar.

gib·ber (jib'ər, gib'-) *v.i. & v.t.* To talk rapidly and incoherently; jabber. — *n.* Gibberish. — **Syn.** See BABBLE. [Imit.]

gib·ber·el·lic acid (jib'ə·rel'ik) *Chem.* A derivative of gibberellin, $C_{18}H_{22}O_6$, used to promote plant growth.

gib·ber·el·lin (jib'ə·rel'in) *n. Chem.* Any of a group of closely related plant hormones that regulate certain processes in all higher plants, as flowering, germination of seeds, stem elongation, etc. [after *Gibberella fujikuroi,* a pathogenic fungus from which they were isolated]

gib·ber·ish (jib'ər·ish, gib'-) *n.* **1.** Rapid, inarticulate or unintelligible talk; gabble. **2.** Needlessly difficult, esoteric, or obscure language.

gib·bet (jib'it) *n.* An upright timber with a crosspiece projecting at right angles from its upper end, upon which criminals were formerly hanged; gallows. — *v.t.* **gib·bet·ed** or **·bet·ted, gib·bet·ing** or **·bet·ting 1.** To execute by hanging. **2.** To hang and expose on a gibbet. **3.** To hold up to public contempt. [< OF *gibet,* dim. of *gibe* staff]

gib·bon (gib'ən) *n.* A slender, long-armed arboreal anthropoid ape (genus *Hylobates*) of southern Asia and the East Indies. [< F; ult. origin uncertain]

Gib·bon (gib'ən), **Edward,** 1737–94, English historian.

Gib·bons (gib'ənz), **James,** 1834–1921, U.S. cardinal. — **Orlando,** 1583–1625, English composer and organist.

gib·bos·i·ty (gi·bos'ə·tē) *n. pl.* **·ties 1.** The state of being gibbous or convex. **2.** A rounded protuberance; hump.

gib·bous (gib'əs) *adj.* **1.** Irregularly rounded or convex, as the moon when more than half full and less than full. **2.** Hunchbacked. Also **gib·bose** (gib'ōs, gi·bōs'). [< L *gibbosus* < *gibbus* hump] — **gib'bous·ly** *adv.* — **gib'bous·ness** *n.*

BLACK-CAPPED GIBBON
(About 2½ feet tall)

Gibbs (gibz), **Josiah Willard,** 1839–1903, U.S. mathematician and physicist. — **Sir Philip,** 1877–1962, English writer.

gibe¹ (jīb) *v.* **gibed, gib·ing** *v.i.* **1.** To utter jeers or make derisive remarks. — *v.t.* **2.** To taunt; jeer at. — *n.* A derisive remark; jeer. Also spelled *jibe.* [Cf. OF *giber* to treat roughly in play] — **gib'er** *n.* — **gib'ing·ly** *adv.*

gibe² (jīb) See JIBE¹.

Gib·e·on (gib'ē·ən) A city NW of Jerusalem in ancient Palestine.

Gib·e·on·ite (gib'ē·ən·īt') *n.* One of the deceitful inhabitants of Gibeon, condemned by Joshua to do menial work for the Israelites. *Josh.* ix 27.

gib·let (jib'lit) *n. Usually pl.* Any of the parts of a fowl that are usually cooked separately; especially, the heart, liver, or gizzard. [< OF *gibelet* stew made from game]

Gi·bral·tar (ji·brôl'tər) **1.** A British crown colony, fortress, and naval base on the Rock of Gibraltar; 2.25 sq. mi.; pop. 27,000 (est. 1969), called *Key of the Mediterranean.* **2.** The Rock of Gibraltar or the Strait of Gibraltar. **3.** An impregnable fortress.

Gibraltar, Rock of A peninsula projecting from the southern part of Spain, marked by a mass of rock that rises to 1,396 feet; once called the Pillars of Hercules; strategically dominates the Strait of Gibraltar. Also **the Rock.**

Gibraltar, Strait of The passage between Spain and Africa at the western end of the Mediterranean.

Gib·ran (joob·rän'), **Kahlil,** 1883–1931, Lebanese poet active in the United States.

Gib·son (gib'sən), **Charles Dana,** 1867–1944, U.S. illustrator and painter.

Gibson Desert The central belt of the Western Australian desert, between the Great Sandy Desert and Victoria Desert.

Gibson girl An idealization of the American girl of the 1890's as portrayed by Charles Dana Gibson.

gid (gid) *n. Vet.* A disease of sheep and goats, caused by the presence in the brain or spinal cord of a bladder worm (*Coenurus cerebralis*): also called *sturdy.* [< GIDDY]

gid·dy (gid'ē) *adj.* **·di·er, ·di·est 1.** Affected by a reeling or whirling sensation; dizzy. **2.** Tending to cause such a sensation: a *giddy* precipice. **3.** Rotating rapidly; whirling. **4.** Frivolous; heedless; inconstant. — *v.t. & v.i.* **·died, ·dy·ing** To make or become dizzy or unsteady. [OE *gydig* insane] — **gid'di·ly** *adv.* — **gid'di·ness** *n.*

Gide (zhēd), **André,** 1869–1951, French writer. — **Charles,** 1847–1932, French economist; uncle of André.

Gid·e·on (gid'ē·ən) An Israelite judge. *Judg.* vi 2.

Gid·e·ons International, The (gid'ē·ənz) An association of businessmen founded in 1899 that distributes Bibles in hotels, public institutions, etc.

gie (gē) *v.t. & v.i. Scot.* To give.

gift (gift) *n.* **1.** Something that is given; present. **2.** The action of giving. **3.** A natural endowment; aptitude; talent. **4.** The right or power of giving. — *v.t.* To bestow or confer a gift or gifts upon. — **to look a gift horse in the mouth** To

find fault with a gift or favor. [OE < *gifan* to give]
— **Syn. 1.** donation, contribution, grant, boon, bounty, largess, gratuity, tip, alms, bequest, legacy. **3.** See GENIUS.

gift·ed (gif′tid) *adj.* Endowed with talent.

gift of gab See under GAB.

gift of tongues In the Bible: **a** A power given the apostles to speak to a polyglot audience so that each person understood in his own tongue. **b** An ecstatic speaking in an unintelligible tongue.

Gi·fu (gē′fōō) A city on central Honshu island, Japan; pop. 301,000 (est. 1959).

gig[1] (gig) *n.* **1.** A light, two-wheeled vehicle drawn by one horse. **2.** A machine for raising a nap on cloth. **3.** *Naut.* **a** A long ship's boat; also, a speedy, light rowboat. **b** A ship's boat reserved for the captain's use. *v.* **gigged, gig·ging** *v.i* **1.** To ride in a gig. — *v.t.* **2.** To raise the nap on (cloth). [Origin uncertain]

gig[2] (gig) *n.* An arrangement of four barbless fishhooks fastened back to back and drawn through a school of fish to catch them in the bodies. — *v.t. & v.i.* **gigged, gig·ging** To spear or catch (fish) with a gig. [< FISHGIG]

gig[3] (gig) *Slang n.* A demerit, as in the army, school, etc. — *v.t.* **gigged, gig·ging 1.** To give a demerit to. **2.** To punish with a gig. [Origin unknown]

gi·ga (jē′gä) *n.* A gigue.

giga- *combining form* A billion (10⁹) times (a specified unit): *gigacycle, gigaton.*

gi·ga·cy·cle (jig′ə·sī′kəl) A unit of frequency equal to 1 billion cycles per second.

gi·gan·tesque (jī′gən·tesk′) *adj.* Like or suited to giants. **2.** Tremendous; huge. Also **gi·gan·te·an** (jī′gan·tē′ən). [< L *gigas, -antis* giant + -IC] — **gi·gan′ti·cal·ly** *adv.*

gi·gan·tic (jī·gan′tik) *adj.* **1.** Of, like, or suited to a giant. **2.** Tremendous; huge. Also **gi·gan·te·an** (jī·gan′tē′ən). [< L *gigas, -antis* giant + -IC] — **gi·gan′ti·cal·ly** *adv.*

gi·gan·tism (jī·gan′tiz·əm) *n.* **1.** Abnormal size. **2.** *Pathol.* Excessive growth of the body due to disturbances in the pituitary gland: also called *giantism.*

giganto- *combining form* Gigantic; very large. Also, before vowels, **gigant-.** [< Gk. *gigas, -antos* giant]

gi·gan·tom·a·chy (jī′gan·tom′ə·kē) *n.* **1.** In classical mythology, the war of the giants against the gods. **2.** Any war of giants. Also **gi·gan·to·ma·chi·a** (ji·gan′tō·mā′chi·ə). [< Gk. *gigantomachia < gigas, -antos* giant + *machē* battle]

Gi·gan·to·pith·e·cus (jī·gan′tō·pith′ə·kəs) *n. Paleontol.* A giant anthropoid ape of the Middle Pleistocene, inhabiting South China. Also **Gi·gan·tan·thro·pus** (jī′gan·tan′thrə·pəs) [< NL < Gk. *gigas, -antos* giant + *pithekos* ape]

gi·ga·ton (jig′ə·tun) *n.* **1.** One billion tons. **2.** A unit equal to the explosive power of 1 billion tons of TNT.

gig·gle (gig′əl) *v.i.* **·gled, ·gling** To laugh in a high-pitched, silly, or nervous manner. — *n.* A light, convulsive laugh; titter. [Imit.] — **gig′gler** *n.*

gig·gly (gig′lē) *adj.* **·gli·er, ·gli·est** Having a tendency to giggle.

gig·let (gig′lit) *n. Brit.* A giddy girl; romp; minx. Also **gig′lot.** [Origin uncertain]

gig·o·lo (jig′ə·lō, *Fr.* zhē·gô·lō′) *n. pl.* **·los** (-lōz, *Fr.* -lō′) **1.** A professional male dancer, as in a cabaret, who dances with the women patrons. **2.** A woman's paid escort. **3.** A man who is supported by a woman to whom he is not married; a kept man. [< F, prob. < *gigolette* prostitute]

gig·ot (jig′ət) *n.* **1.** A leg-of-mutton sleeve. **2.** A cooked haunch of lamb, veal, etc. [< F]

gigue (zhēg) *n.* **1.** A jig (def. 1). **2.** *Music* A lively dance form in 6/8 or 12/8 meter, more rarely 9/8, often the final movement of a suite. Also called *giga.* [< F. See GIG.]

GI Joe *Informal* A man in the U.S. armed forces; a GI.

Gi·la monster (hē′lə) A large, venomous lizard (*Heloderma suspectum*) with a stout orange-and-black body, ranging from southern Utah and Nevada through Arizona and New Mexico into northern Mexico.

GILA MONSTER
(To 20 inches long)

Gi·la River (hē′lə) A river in New Mexico and Arizona, flowing about 650 miles SW to the Colorado River.

Gila woodpecker A woodpecker (*Centurus uropygialis*) of the SW United States, habitually nesting in the saguaro.

gil·bert (gil′bərt) *n. Electr.* The cgs unit of magnetomotive force, equal to 0.7958 ampere-turn. [after William *Gilbert*, 1540–1603, English physicist]

Gil·bert (gil′bərt), **Cass,** 1859–1934, U.S. architect. — **Sir Humphrey,** 1539?–83, English navigator. — **William,** 1540–1603, English physicist and physician. — **Sir William Schwenck,** 1836–1911, English comic poet and librettist; collaborator with Sir Arthur Sullivan.

Gilbert and Ellice Islands A British Colony in the South Pacific, comprising Ocean Island, the Gilbert Islands, the Ellice Islands, and several of the Phoenix and Line islands; about 369 sq. mi.; pop. 54,000 (est. 1969); headquarters on Tarawa.

Gil·ber·ti·an (gil·bûr′tē·ən) *adj.* Pertaining to or resembling the style or humor of Sir W. S. Gilbert.

gild[1] (gild) *v.t.* **gild·ed** or **gilt, gild·ing 1.** To coat with or as

with a thin layer of gold or gold leaf. **2.** To brighten or adorn. **3.** To give a speciously good appearance to; gloss over. **4.** *Obs.* To redden with blood. [OE *gyldan*]

gild[2] (gild) *n.* A guild.

gild·er[1] (gil′dər) *n.* One who or that which gilds.

gild·er[2] (gil′dər) *n.* A guilder.

gild·ing (gil′ding) *n.* **1.** The art or process of applying gilt. **2.** A mixture of finely divided gold, brass, or some similar substance, and a drying liquid, used as a decorative paint. **3.** A specious or superficially pleasing appearance.

Gil·e·ad (gil′ē·əd) A mountainous region of ancient Palestine east of the Jordan. *Josh.* xii 2.

Gil·e·ad·ite (gil′ē·əd·īt′) *n.* An inhabitant of Gilead. *Judg.* xii 4.

Giles (jīlz), **Saint** Seventh-century Christian hermit; patron of cripples.

Gil·ga·mesh (gil′gə·mesh) In Sumerian and Babylonian legend, a king who is the herculean hero of the **Gilgamesh epic,** an ancient Babylonian epic especially remarkable for its account of a flood suggestive of the biblical Deluge.

gill[1] (gil) *n.* **1.** *Zool.* The organ for underwater breathing of fishes, amphibians, and other aquatic vertebrates, consisting typically of leaflike or threadlike vascular processes of mucous membrane on either side of the neck. **2.** *Usually pl.* The wattles of a fowl. **3.** *pl. Informal* The area of the face and throat: usually in the phrase **green around the gills,** Sickly in appearance. **4.** *Bot.* One of the thin radial plates on the underside of the cap of a mushroom. — *v.t.* **1.** To catch by the gills, as fish in a gill net. **2.** To gut (fish). [ME *gile,* prob. < Scand. Cf. Sw. *gäl* gill.]

gill[2] (jil) *n.* A liquid measure equal to ¼ pint or 0.118 liter: also spelled *jill.* Abbr. *gi.* See table inside back cover. [< OF *gelle* measure for wine]

gill[3] (gil) *n. Brit. Dial.* **1.** A ravine or gully. **2.** A brook. Also spelled *ghyll.* [< ON *gil* gorge]

gill[4] (gil) *n.* **1.** A girl or woman: a familiar term. **2.** *Dial.* The ground ivy. [Short for *Gillian,* a personal name]

Gil·lette (ji·let′), **King Camp,** 1855–1932, U.S. industrialist; invented the safety razor. — **William Hooker,** 1855–1937, U.S. actor.

gill fungus (gil) The agaric, a mushroom.

gil·lie (gil′ē) *n. Scot.* A male servant; especially, one attending a sportsman in the field. Also **gil′ly.**

gill net (gil) A net set upright in the water, having large meshes in which fish become entangled by their gills.

gil·ly·flow·er (jil′ē·flou′ər) *n.* **1.** One of various plants of the mustard family, as the wallflower. **2.** A plant of the pink family, as the clove pink. **3.** A variety of apple. Also **gil′li·flow′er.** [Alter. of ME *gilofre* < OF, var. of *girofle* clove, ult. < Gk. *karyophyllon* clove tree]

Gil·man (gil′mən), **Daniel Coit,** 1831–1908, U.S. educator.

gil·son·ite (gil′sən·īt) *n.* Uintahite. [after S. H. *Gilson,* of Salt Lake City, Utah]

gilt[1] (gilt) Alternative past tense and past participle of GILD. — *adj.* Golden in color; gilded. — *n.* A material used in gilding. Abbr. (n.) *glt., gt.*

gilt[2] (gilt) *n.* A young sow. [< ON *gyltr*]

gilt-edged (gilt′ejd′) *adj.* **1.** Having the edges gilded, as the pages of a book. **2.** Being of the best quality or highest price: *gilt-edged* securities. Also **gilt′-edge′** (-ej′).

gim·bals (jim′bəlz, gim′-) *n.pl.* A set of three metal rings so pivoted one within the other that it maintains an object supported by it, as a ship's compass, on a horizontal plane. [Alter. of OF *gemelle* twin < L *gemellus,* dim. of *geminus* twin]

gim·crack (jim′krak) *n.* A useless, gaudy object; knick-knack. — *adj.* Cheap and showy. [Origin uncertain]

gim·crack·er·y (jim′krak·ər·ē) *n.* Worthless ornamentation or show.

GIMBALS

gim·el (gim′əl) *n.* The third letter in the Hebrew alphabet. See ALPHABET.

gim·let (gim′lit) A small, sharp tool with a cross handle and a pointed, spiral tip for boring holes. For illustration see AUGER. — *v.t.* To make a hole in with a gimlet. [< OF *guimbelet.* Akin to WIMBLE.]

gimlet eyes Eyes that probe with piercing intensity. — **gim′let-ey′ed** *adj.*

gim·mal (gim′əl) *n.* **1.** A small, circular band, as a ring for the finger, made up of two interlocked rings. **2.** A pair of connected cogs, links, etc., in a mechanism. [Cf. GIMBALS]

gim·mick (gim′ik) *n. U.S. Slang* **1.** A novel or tricky feature or detail added to or incorporated within something to increase its attractiveness or effectiveness. **2.** A hidden or deceptive device or contrivance, as one used by a magician, etc. **3.** Some little gadget the name of which is uncertain; doohickey. [Origin uncertain] — **gim′mick·ry** *n.*

gim·mick·y (gim′ik·ē) *adj. U.S. Slang* Full of gimmicks.

gimp[1] (gimp) *n.* A narrow, flat piece of fabric, often stiffened with wire, used as an ornamental trimming for clothing, curtains, etc. [Cf. OF *guimpre,* var. of *guipure,* a kind of trimming]

gimp[2] (gimp) *U.S. Slang n.* **1.** One who limps; also, a limping gait. **2.** Pep. — *v.i.* To limp. [Origin unknown]

gimp·y (gim′pē) *adj.* **gimp·i·er, gimp·i·est** *U.S. Slang*
1. Having a limp. 2. Peppy.
gin[1] (jin) *n.* An aromatic alcoholic liquor distilled from various grains, especially rye, and flavored with juniper berries or sometimes with other flavoring agents. [Short for GENEVA]
gin[2] (jin) *n.* 1. A cotton gin (which see). 2. A tripodlike machine for hoisting. 3. A type of pulley and block. For illustration see BLOCK. 4. A snare or trap. — *v.t.* **ginned, gin·ning** 1. To remove the seeds from (cotton) in a gin. 2. To trap or snare. [Aphetic var. of OF *engin* ingenuity. See ENGINE.]
gin[3] (jin) *n.* Gin rummy (which see).
gin[4] (gin) *v.t. & v.i.* **gan, gin·ning** *Archaic* To begin.
gin·gal (jing′gôl), **gin·gall** See JINGAL.
gin·ge·ley (jin′ji·lē) *n.* The sesame (def. 2) or its oil. Also **gin′ge·li, gin′gel·ly, gin′ge·ly, gin′gi·li.** [< Hind. *jingalī*]
gin·ger (jin′jər) *n.* 1. The pungent, spicy rootstock of a tropical plant (*Zingiber officinale*), used either whole or pulverized in medicine and cookery. 2. The plant itself, typical of a family (*Zingiberaceae*) of perennial tropical herbs as cardamom and curcuma. 3. A tawny, sandy, or reddish brown color. 4. *Informal* Liveliness; pep. — *v.t.* 1. To treat or spice with ginger. 2. *Informal* To make lively or piquant; enliven: often with *up.* [< OF *gingifre* < LL *gingiber* < Gk. *zingiberis*, ult. < Skt.]
ginger ale An effervescent soft drink flavored with ginger.
ginger beer An effervescent, nonalcoholic drink made with yeast and flavored with ginger, popular in England.
gin·ger·bread (jin′jər·bred′) *n.* 1. A dark, ginger-flavored cake sweetened with molasses. 2. A similarly flavored, rolled cooky cut into various shapes and usually frosted. 3. Gaudy ornamentation, as overly ornate carvings on furniture, etc. — *adj.* Cheap and tawdry; gaudy. [Alter. of OF *gingembras* preserved ginger < LL *gingiber*. See GINGER.]
gingerbread tree 1. The doom palm. 2. A tree of the rose family of West Africa (*Parinarium macrophyllum*), bearing a farinaceous fruit called the **gingerbread plum.**
gin·ger·ly (jin′jər·lē) *adv.* In a cautious, careful, or reluctant manner. — *adj.* Cautious or careful. [Cf. OF *gensor, gentchur,* compar. of *gent* delicate] — **gin′ger·li·ness** *n.*
gin·ger·snap (jin′jər·snap′) *n.* A small, flat, brittle cooky flavored with ginger and molasses.
gin·ger·y (jin′jər·ē) *adj.* 1. Having the piquantly spicy flavor of ginger. 2. Having the reddish brown color of ginger. 3. Sharply pointed or peppery, as a remark.
ging·ham (ging′əm) *n.* A firm cotton fabric, yarn-dyed, woven in solid colors, stripes, or checks. [< F *guingan,* ult. < Malay *ginggang* striped]
gin·gi·val (jin·jī′vəl, jin′jə-) *adj.* 1. Of or pertaining to the gums. 2. *Phonet.* Produced with the aid of the gums; alveolar: *gingival* sounds. [< L *gingiva* gum]
gin·gi·vi·tis (jin′jə·vī′tis) *n. Pathol.* Inflammation of the gums.
gink (gingk) *n. U.S. Slang* A man or boy; fellow; guy; especially, a peculiar man or boy. [Cf. dial. E *gink* trick]
gink·go (ging′kō, jing′kō) *n. pl.* **·goes** A large deciduous, gymnospermous tree (*Ginkgo biloba*) native to China and cultivated in the United States, with fanlike foliage and edible fruits and nuts: also called *maidenhair tree:* also spelled *jingko.* Also **ging′ko.** [< Japanese]
gin mill *Slang* A saloon.
gin·ner (jin′ər) *n.* One who operates a gin.
gin rummy A variety of rummy, in which a player may meld his hand whenever his unmatched cards are worth ten points or less.
gin·seng (jin′seng) *n.* 1. An herb (genus *Panax*) native to China and North America, having a root of aromatic and stimulant properties. 2. The root of this herb. 3. A medicinal preparation made from the root. [< Chinese *jen shen*]
Gio·con·da (jō·kôn′dä), **La** The Mona Lisa.
Gior·gio·ne (jôr·jō′nä), 1477?–1511, Venetian painter: original name **Giorgio Bar·ba·rel·li** (bär′bä·rel′lē).
Giot·to (jôt′tō), 1266?–1337, Florentine painter, architect, and sculptor: full name **Giotto di Bon·do·ne** (dē bōn·dō′nä).
gip (jip) See GYP[1].
gi·pon (ji·pon′, jip′on) See JUPON.
gip·sy (jip′sē), **Gip·sy** See GYPSY, Gypsy.
gipsy moth See GYPSY MOTH.
gi·raffe (jə·raf′, -räf′) *n. pl.* **·raffes** or **·raffe** An African ruminant (*Giraffa camelopardalis,* the tallest of all mammals, having a very long neck, long, slender limbs, and a distinctive spotted coloration. [< F, ult. < Arabic *zarāfah*]
Gi·raffe (jə·raf′, -räf′) *n.* The constellation Camelopardalis.
gir·an·dole (jir′ən·dōl) *n.* 1. A branched candlestick. 2. A rotating firework. 3. A rotating jet of water. 4. A piece of jewelry having a large stone surrounded by smaller pendent ones. 5. *Mil.* In fortifications, a con-

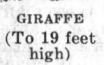

GIRAFFE
(To 19 feet high)

nection of several mines. Also **gi·ran·do·la** (ji·ran′də·lə). [< F < Ital. *girandola* < *girare* to rotate < L *gyrare.* See GYRATE.]
Gi·rard (ji·rärd′), **Stephen,** 1750–1831, U.S. banker and philanthropist born in France.
gi·ra·sol (jir′ə·sôl, -sol) *n.* 1. The fire opal. 2. Any plant of the sunflower family; especially, the Jerusalem artichoke. Also spelled *girosol:* also **gir′a·sole.** [< Ital. *girasole* sunflower < *girare* to turn + *sole* sun]
Gi·raud (zhē·rō′), **Henri Honoré,** 1879–1949, French general in World War II.
Gi·rau·doux (zhē·rō·dōō′), **Jean,** 1882–1944, French novelist and playwright.
gird[1] (gûrd) *v.t.* **gird·ed** or **girt, gird·ing** 1. To surround or make fast with a belt or girdle. 2. To encircle; surround. 3. To prepare (oneself) for action. 4. To clothe, equip, or endow, as with some quality or attribute. [OE *gyrdan*]
gird[2] (gûrd) *v.t. & v.i.* To attack with sarcasm; gibe. — *n. Archaic* A taunt; gibe. [ME *girden;* origin unknown]
gird·er (gûr′dər) *n.* A long heavy beam, as of steel or wood, that acts as a main horizontal support for the framework of a bridge or building, the joists of a floor, etc.
gir·dle[1] (gûr′dəl) *n.* 1. A belt or cord worn around the waist; sash. 2. Anything that encircles like a belt. 3. A woman's flexible undergarment worn to give support and shape to the waist and hips. 4. An encircling cut made through the bark of a tree trunk or branch. 5. The outer edge of a cut gem. 6. *Anat.* **a** The pelvic arch. **b** The pectoral arch. — *v.t.* **·dled, ·dling** 1. To fasten a girdle or belt around. 2. To encircle; encompass. 3. To make an encircling cut through the bark of (a branch or tree). [OE *gyrdle*]
gir·dler (gûrd′lər) *n.* 1. One who or that which encircles. 2. One who makes girdles. 3. *Entomol.* Any insect that bores around and into the bark of twigs and branches; especially, an American beetle (*Oncideres cingulata*) that bores into twigs to deposit its eggs: also called *twig girdler.*
girl (gûrl) *n.* 1. A female infant or child. 2. A young, unmarried woman. 3. A female servant. 4. *Informal* A sweetheart. 5. *Informal* Any woman of any age. [ME *gurle*]
girl friend 1. *Informal* A preferred female companion or intimate friend of a boy or man. 2. A female friend.
girl guide A member of a British and Canadian organization, the **Girl Guides,** resembling the Girl Scouts.
girl·hood (gûrl′hŏŏd) *n.* 1. The state or time of being a girl. 2. Girls as a group.
girl·ish (gûr′lish) *adj.* 1. Like or pertaining to a girl. 2. Suitable for a girl. — *Syn.* See YOUTHFUL. — **girl′ish·ly** *adv.* — **girl′ish·ness** *n.*
girl scout A member of an organization of girls between the ages of 7 and 17, **Girl Scouts of the U.S.A.,** founded in the United States in 1912 by Juliette Low to develop health, character, etc. Also **Girl Scout. G.S.**
girn (gûrn, girn) *Scot. v.i.* To snarl; growl. — *n.* A snarl.
gi·ro (ji′rō) *n. pl.* **·ros** An autogiro (which see).
Gi·ronde (jə·rond′, *Fr.* zhē·rônd′) An estuary in SW France formed by the Garonne and Dordogne rivers, extending about 45 miles to the Bay of Biscay.
Gi·ronde (jə·rond′, *Fr.* zhē·rônd′) A moderate republican party (1791–93) during the French Revolution, suppressed by the Jacobins. [after *Gironde,* the estuary]
Gi·ron·dist (jə·ron′dist) *n.* A member of the Gironde party. — *adj.* Of or belonging to the Gironde party.
gir·o·sol (jir′ə·sôl, -sol) See GIRASOL.
girt[1] (gûrt) Past tense and past participle of GIRD[1].
girt[2] (gûrt) *v.t. & v.i.* 1. To gird. 2. To measure in girth. — *n.* Girth. [< GIRD[1]]
girth[1] (gûrth) *n.* 1. The circumference of anything, especially the waist. 2. A band passed under the belly of a horse or other animal to make fast a saddle, harness, pack, etc. For illustration see HARNESS. 3. A girdle or band. — *v.t.* 1. To bind with a girth. 2. To encircle; girdle. — *v.i.* 3. To measure in girth. [< ON *gjordh*]
girth[2] (gûrth) *n. Chiefly Scot.* Grith.
gis·mo (giz′mō) *n. pl.* **·mos** *U.S. Slang* 1. A device or object the name or function of which is uncertain; gadget. 2. A secret procedure or formula to insure success or advantage, especially in gambling; gimmick. Also spelled *gizmo.*
Gis·sing (gis′ing), **George Robert,** 1857–1903, English novelist and critic.
gist (jist) *n.* 1. The main idea or substance, as of an argument, question, etc. 2. The ground or cause of a legal action. [< OF *giste* place of rest < *gesir* to lie < L *jacere*]
gi·ta·no (ji·tä′nō, *Sp.* hē·tä′nō) *n. pl.* **·nos** A Spanish gypsy. [< Sp.]
git·tern (git′ərn) *n.* A cittern. [< OF *guiterne* < L *cithara* < Gk. *kithara*]
Giu·lio Ro·ma·no (jōōl′yō rō·mä′nō), 1492–1546, Italian painter: original name **Guilio Pippi de' Gia·nuz·zi** (dä jä·nōōt′sē).
give (giv) *v.* **gave, giv·en, giv·ing** *v.t.* 1. To transfer freely (what is one's own) to the permanent possession of another

without asking anything in return. **2.** To transfer freely (what is one's own) to the permanent possession of another in exchange for something from the other. **3.** To transfer to the temporary possession, control, or supervision of another without change of ownership. **4.** To put into the hands of another for temporary use; hand over; let have. **5.** To put into the grasp of another: *Give* me your hand. **6.** To make available; furnish; proffer: to *give* help. **7.** To be a source of; yield as a product: Fire *gives* warmth. **8.** To grant or concede, as permission. **9.** To impart: to *give* advice. **10.** To administer (a dose of medicine, a treatment, etc.). **11.** To assign or allot: to *give* homework to a class. **12.** To deal, deliver, or inflict (a blow, beating, etc.). **13.** To transmit or communicate (a disease, etc.). **14.** To perform or do (the action indicated by the object): to *give* a frightened start. **15.** To deliver (a speech, reply, etc.). **16.** To put on, present, or execute (a play, concert, etc.). **17.** To issue (an order, etc.). **18.** To part with; relinquish or yield: He *gave* his life for his country. **19.** To devote, as oneself, to a cause, etc. — *v.i.* **20.** To make donations; make free gifts. **21.** To move down, back, etc., as under pressure; yield: The door *gave* when they pushed it. **22.** To break down, as from strain; collapse. **23.** To be springy, flexible, etc.: The bed *gives* comfortably. **24.** To furnish a view or passage; open: with *on* or *onto*. — **to give a good account of** To conduct (oneself) creditably, as in a difficult situation. — **to give and take** To exchange on equal terms. — **to give away 1.** To bestow as a gift. **2.** To hand over (the bride) to the bridegroom in the marriage ceremony. **3.** *Informal* To make known, as a secret; reveal. — **to give back** To restore or return. — **to give birth** To bear offspring. — **to give birth to 1.** To bear (offspring). **2.** To create or originate, as an idea. **3.** To result in. — **to give forth** To discharge; emit. — **to give in 1.** To yield, as to something demanded. **2.** To cease opposition; acknowledge oneself vanquished. **3.** To deliver or hand in (a report, resignation, etc.). — **to give it to** To administer a scolding, beating, etc., to. — **to give off** To send forth, as odors; emit. — **to give out 1.** To send forth; emit. **2.** To hand out or distribute. **3.** To make known; publish. **4.** To become completely used up or exhausted. — **to give over 1.** To hand over, as to another's care. **2.** To cease; desist. — **to give rise to** To cause or produce; result in. — **to give tongue** To bark or bay: said of hunting dogs in pursuit. — **to give to understand** (or **know**) To cause to understand (or know). — **to give up 1.** To surrender; cede; hand over. **2.** To stop; cease. **3.** To desist from as hopeless. **4.** To lose all hope for, as a sick person. **5.** To devote wholly: to *give* oneself *up* to art. — **to give way 1.** To collapse, bend, fail, etc., as under pressure or force. **2.** To draw back: The crowd *gave way*. **3.** To cease objecting; concede or yield. **4.** To abandon oneself, as to despair. — *n.* **1.** The quality of being resilient; elasticity. **2.** The act or process of bending or yielding, as under pressure. [Fusion of OE *giefan* and ON *gefa*] — **giv′er** *n.*

— **Syn.** (verb) **1.** *Give, present, donate, bestow,* and *confer* mean to hand over freely to another. To *give* is primarily to transfer to another's possession without compensation, but the word also has many extended senses; a boxer *gives* a blow, a clock *gives* the time, a delinquent child *gives* trouble. To *present* is to *give* formally or ceremoniously: to *present* a diploma to a graduate. We *donate* to public causes, as books to a library, or money to a health campaign. That which is greatly prized is *bestowed*: to *bestow* honors on a great poet, to *bestow* favors on a friend. To *confer* is to *give* in approval or as a reward: to *confer* knighthood, to *confer* an honorary degree. Compare GRANT. — **Ant.** withhold, receive, take.

give-and-take (giv′ən-tāk′) *n.* **1.** A system of making mutual concessions; cooperation. **2.** A smooth, unruffled interchange of ideas, repartee, etc.

give-a-way (giv′ə-wā′) *Informal n.* **1.** A disclosure or betrayal, generally unintentional; also, that which is disclosed. **2.** Something given free or at a greatly reduced price, as to promote sales, publicity, etc. — *adj.* Characterized by awards of money and prizes: said of a type of radio or television show.

giv-en (giv′ən) *adj.* **1.** Presented; bestowed. **2.** Habitually inclined; addicted: with *to*. **3.** Specified; stated: a *given* date. **4.** Issued on an indicated date: said of official documents, etc. **5.** Admitted as a fact or premise; granted. — **Syn.** See ADDICTED.

given name The name bestowed on a person at birth, or shortly thereafter, as distinguished from his surname.

Gi-za (gē′zə) A city in Upper Egypt on the Nile; site of the pyramids; pop. 177,100 (est. 1959): also *El Gizeh*. Also **Gi′-zeh.**

giz-mo (giz′mō) See GISMO.

giz-zard (giz′ərd) *n.* **1.** A second stomach in birds, in which partly digested food is finely ground. **2.** A first stomach in insects. **3.** *Informal* The human stomach: a humorous term. [< OF *gezier* < L *gigeria* cooked entrails of poultry]

Gjel-le-rup (gel′ə-rŏŏp), **Karl**, 1857–1919, Danish novelist and poet.

Gk. Greek.

Gl. *Chem.* Glucinum.

gl. 1. Glass. **2.** Gloss (sheen).

gla-bel-la (glə-bel′ə) *n.* *pl.* **-bel-lae** (-bel′ē) *Anat.* The smooth prominence on the forehead just above the nose and between the eyebrows. For illustration see FACIAL ANGLE. [< NL < L, dim. of *glaber* smooth]

gla-brate (glā′brāt) *adj.* Glabrous or becoming glabrous.

gla-brous (glā′brəs) *adj. Biol.* **1.** Devoid of hair or down. **2.** Having a smooth surface. [< L *glaber* smooth]

gla-cé (gla-sā′) *adj.* **1.** Sugared or candied, as preserved fruits. **2.** Having a glossy surface, as certain leathers. **3.** Iced; frozen. — *v.t.* **-céed, -cé-ing 1.** To cover with icing. **2.** To make smooth and glossy. [< F, pp. of *glacer* to freeze < *glace* ice]

gla-cial (glā′shəl) *adj.* **1.** Pertaining to, caused by, or marked by the presence of glaciers or similar ice masses: a *glacial* formation. **2.** Of or pertaining to a glacial epoch; especially, of or pertaining to the Pleistocene. **3.** Freezingly cold: a *glacial* wind. **4.** Chillingly indifferent, unfriendly, or antagonistic: a *glacial* stare. **5.** Marked by a rate of movement as slow as that of glaciers: a *glacial* pace. **6.** *Chem.* Having a crystalline formation suggestive of that of ice crystals: *glacial* acetic acid. [< F < L *glacialis* < *glacies* ice] — **gla′cial·ly** *adv.*

glacial deposits *Geol.* Unstratified earth materials and debris transported by glaciers and left at the place of melting.

glacial epoch *Geol.* **1.** Any portion of geological time characterized by the formation of ice sheets over large portions of the earth's surface. **2.** One of the glacial stages that succeeded one another during the Pleistocene epoch. **3.** The Pleistocene epoch.

gla-cial-ist (glā′shəl-ist) *n.* One who studies glaciers and the geological effects produced by glaciers.

glacial period 1. A glacial epoch. **2.** The portion of time comprising the four major glacial epochs.

gla-ci-ate (glā′shē-āt) *v.t.* **-at-ed, -at-ing 1.** To cover with glaciers. **2.** To subject to the action of glaciers. **3.** *Rare* To change into ice; freeze. [< L *glaciatus*, pp. of *glaciare* to freeze < *glacies* ice] — **gla′ci·a′tion** *n.*

gla-cier (glā′shər) *n.* A field of ice, formed in regions of perennial frost from compacted snow, that descends slowly through valleys (**valley glacier**) or spreads out from accumulated central masses (**continental glacier**) until it either breaks off in the sea in the form of icebergs or melts in warmer regions. [< F < L *glacies* ice]

glacier meal Rock flour (which see).

glacier milk The water of a stream issuing from a glacier, milky in appearance because of suspended silt or finely divided rock particles.

Glacier National Park A mountainous area in NW Montana containing many lakes and small glaciers; 1,560 sq. mi.; established 1910.

gla-ci-ol-o-gy (glā′sē-ol′ə-jē) *n.* The science concerned with the forms, movements, causes, and effects of glaciers. — **gla-ci-o-log-ic** (glā′sē-ə-loj′ik) or **-i-cal** *adj.* — **gla′ci-ol′o-gist** *n.*

gla-cis (glā′sis, glas′is) *n.* A slope; especially, a defensive slope in front of a fortification. For illustration see BASTION. [< F, orig., a slippery place < OF *glacier* to slip]

Glack-ens (glak′ənz), **William James**, 1870–1938, U.S. painter.

glad¹ (glad) *adj.* **glad-der, glad-dest 1.** Having a feeling of joy, pleasure, or content; gratified: often with *of* or *at*. **2.** Showing joy; brightly cheerful: a *glad* face. **3.** Giving reason to rejoice; bringing joy. — *v.t. & v.i.* **glad-ded, glad-ding** *Archaic* To gladden. [OE *glæd* shining, glad]

glad² (glad) *n. Informal* A gladiolus.

glad-den (glad′n) *v.t.* **1.** To make glad. — *v.i.* **2.** *Archaic* To be or become glad. — **glad′den-er** *n.*

glade (glād) *n.* **1.** A clearing in a wood. **2.** *U.S.* An everglade. [Prob. akin to *glad* in obs. sense of "bright, sunny"]

glad eye *Slang* A flirtatious glance: especially in the phrase *to get* (or *give*) *the glad eye.*

glad hand *Slang* A display, often insincere, of cordiality.

glad-i-ate (glad′ē-āt, -ē-ət, glā′dē-) *adj.* Sword-shaped. [< L *gladius* sword + -ATE¹]

glad-i-a-tor (glad′ē-ā′tər) *n.* **1.** In ancient Rome, a slave, captive, or paid freeman who fought other men or animals with weapons as public entertainment. **2.** One who engages in any kind of struggle. [< L < *gladius* sword]

glad-i-a-to-ri-al (glad′ē-ə-tôr′ē-əl, -tō′rē-) *adj.* Of or pertaining to gladiators or combat.

glad-i-o-la (glad′ē-ō′lə, glə-dī′ə-lə) *n.* A gladiolus (defs. 1 & 2).

glad-i-o-lus (glad′ē-ō′ləs, glə-dī′ə-ləs; *for def. 3* glə-dī′ə-ləs) *n. pl.* **-lus-es** or **-li** (-lī) **1.** Any of a large Old World genus (*Gladiolus*) of plants of the iris family with fleshy bulbs, sword-shaped leaves, and spikes of colored flowers: also called *sword grass, sword lily.* **2.** The corm or flower of one of these plants. **3.** *Anat.* The flat, narrow bone forming the lower or anterior part of the breastbone in most vertebrates: for illustration see THORAX.

glad-ly (glad′lē) *adv.* In a glad manner; with joy; willingly.

glad-ness (glad′nis) *n.* The state of being glad; joy.

glad-some (glad′səm) *adj.* Glad. — **glad′some-ly** *adv.* — **glad′some-ness** *n.*

Glad-stone (glad′stōn, -stən) *n.* **1.** A suitcase hinged to open flat and form two equal compartments. Also **Gladstone bag**. **2.** A four-wheeled pleasure carriage having two inside seats for passengers. [after W. E. *Gladstone*]

Glad·stone (glad′stōn, -stən), **William Ewart,** 1809–98, English statesman and political leader; prime minister 1868–74, 1880–85, 1886, 1892–94.

Glag·ol (glag′əl) *n.* The Glagolitic alphabet. [< Old Church Slavic *glagolŭ* word]

Glag·o·lit·ic alphabet (glag′ə·lit′ik) An ancient Slavic alphabet probably devised by Saint Cyril, still used in many Roman Catholic dioceses in Dalmatia and Croatia where Church Slavic is the liturgical language. Compare CYRILLIC ALPHABET.

glaik·it (glā′kit) *adj. Scot.* Foolish; silly. Also **glaik′et.**

glair (glâr) *n.* **1.** Raw egg white, used in making size or glaze. **2.** A glaze or size made of raw egg white. **3.** Any viscous or slimy matter. — *v.t.* To coat with glair. [< F *glaire* < L *clarus* clear]

glair·y (glâr′ē) *adj.* **glair·i·er, glair·i·est 1.** Resembling glair. **2.** Coated with glair. Also **glair·e·ous** (glâr′ē·əs). — **glair′i·ness** *n.*

glaive (glāv) *n. Archaic* A broadsword or other sword. [< OF, lance]

Glam. or **Glamorg.** Glamorganshire.

Gla·mor·gan·shire (glə·môr′gən·shir) A former county in SE Wales; 817 sq. mi.; pop. 1,255,374 (1971); county seat, Cardiff. Also **Gla·mor′gan.**

glam·or·ize (glam′ər·īz) *v.t.* **·ized, ·iz·ing** To make glamorous.

glam·or·ous (glam′ər·əs) *adj.* Full of glamour or fascination; alluring. Also **glam′our·ous.** — **glam′or·ous·ly** *adv.* — **glam′or·ous·ness** *n.*

glam·our (glam′ər) *n.* **1.** Alluring charm or fascination, often based on illusion, that transforms or glorifies a person or thing. **2.** *Archaic* A magic spell: to cast a *glamour.* Also *U.S.* **glam′or.** [< *Scot.* alter. of GRAMARYE (in sense of magic, power to bewitch). Akin to GRAMMAR.]

glance[1] (glans, gläns) *v.* **glanced, glanc·ing** *v.i.* **1.** To take a quick look. **2.** To touch briefly on some matter. **3.** To be deflected at an angle after obliquely striking or grazing a surface: The arrow *glanced* from the shield. **4.** To flash intermittently; glint. — *v.t.* **5.** To cause to strike a surface obliquely and be deflected. **6.** *Archaic* To take or get a quick look at. — *Syn.* See LOOK. — *n.* **1.** A quick look. **2.** A flash; glint. **3.** Oblique impact and deflection. **4.** In cricket, an oblique stroke to deflect the ball. [< OF *glacier* to slip, ? infl. by ME *glenten* to shine]

glance[2] (glans, gläns) *n.* A mineral, usually a sulfide, having a metallic shininess: silver *glance*. [Short for *glance ore* < Du. *glanserts* luster ore]

gland[1] (gland) *n.* **1.** *Anat.* **a** Any of various organs by means of which certain constituents are removed from the blood, either for use in the body or for elimination from it. Glands are of two types, those having ducts leading into another organ, as the pancreas, liver, etc., and those without ducts, as the adrenals, pituitary, etc., that pour their secretions directly into the bloodstream. **b** A glandlike structure: lymph *gland.* **2.** *Bot.* A special secreting organ in plants. [< F *glande* < OF *glandre* < L *glandula*, dim. of *glans, glandis* acorn]

gland[2] (gland) *n. Mech.* One of various parts of a mechanism that hold something in place; especially, a device for compressing the packing in a stuffing box to prevent leakage of a fluid under pressure. [< F < L *glans, glandis* acorn]

glan·dered (glan′dərd) *adj.* Affected with glanders.

glan·der·ous (glan′dər·əs) *adj.* **1.** Glandered. **2.** Pertaining to or suggestive of glanders.

glan·ders (glan′dərz) *n. Vet.* A contagious disease of horses and other equines, characterized by nasal discharges and ulcerative lesions of the lungs and other organs. [< OF *glandres*, pl. of *glandre* gland]

glan·dif·er·ous (glan·dif′ər·əs) *adj.* Acorn-bearing. [< L *glans, glandis* an acorn + -FEROUS]

glan·di·form (glan′də·fôrm) *adj.* Acorn-shaped.

glan·du·lar (glan′jə·lər) *adj.* **1.** Of, pertaining to, or resembling a gland. **2.** Having glands. Also **glan′du·lous.**

glandular fever Infectious mononucleosis.

glan·dule (glan′jōōl) *n.* A small gland.

glans (glanz) *n., pl.* **glan·des** (glan′dēz) *n. Anat.* The rounded head of the penis, **glans penis,** or of the clitoris, **glans cli·tor·i·dis** (kli·tôr′ə·dis, kli-). [< L, acorn]

glare[1] (glâr) *v.* **glared, glar·ing** *v.i.* **1.** To shine with a steady and dazzling intensity. **2.** To gaze or stare fiercely or in hostility. **3.** To be conspicuous or showy. — *v.t.* **4.** To express or send forth with a glare. — *Syn.* See SHINE. — *n.* **1.** A dazzling, steady light or reflection. **2.** An intense, piercing look or gaze, usually hostile. **3.** Gaudy or showy display; vulgar brilliance. [ME *glaren* < LG]

glare[2] (glâr) *U.S. n.* A glassy, smooth surface, as of ice. — *adj.* Having a glassy, smooth surface. [? < GLARE[1], n.]

glar·ing (glâr′ing) *adj.* **1.** Looking or staring fixedly or with hostility. **2.** Emitting an excessively brilliant light. **3.** Garish; gaudy. **4.** Plainly or unpleasantly conspicuous: a *glaring* mistake. — *Syn.* See FLAGRANT. — **glar′ing·ly** *adv.*

glar·y[1] (glâr′ē) *adj.* **glar·i·er, glar·i·est** Dazzling; glaring.

glar·y[2] (glâr′ē) *adj. U.S.* Slippery, as ice.

Glas·gow (glas′gō, -kō, gläs′-) A burgh and port in SW Scotland, on the Clyde; pop. 927,948 (est. 1969).

Glas·gow (glas′gō), **Ellen (Anderson Gholson),** 1874–1945, U.S. novelist.

Glas·pell (glas′pel), **Susan,** 1882–1948, U.S. novelist and dramatist.

glass (glas, gläs) *n.* **1.** A hard, amorphous, brittle, usually transparent substance made by fusing one or more of the oxides of silicon, boron, or phosphorus with certain basic oxides, followed by rapid cooling to prevent crystallization. ◆ Collateral adjective: *vitreous.* **2.** Any substance made of or resembling glass. **3.** An article made wholly or partly of glass; as: **a** A windowpane, lens, or mirror. **b** A tumbler, goblet, or other drinking vessel made of glass. **c** A bowl, jar, dish, or other container made of glass. **d** A protective covering made of glass, as for plants. **e** A tube, bulb, or other part made of glass, as in a thermometer. **f** An hourglass or other device made of glass. **g** A spyglass or telescope. **4.** Such articles collectively; glassware. **5.** The contents of a drinking glass; glassful. *Abbr.* **gl.** — *v.t.* **1.** To put in a glass container. **2.** To enclose in or cover with glass. **3.** To give a glassy surface or appearance to. **4.** *Poetic* To reflect in or as in a mirror. — *adj.* **1.** Of, pertaining to, or consisting of glass. **2.** Fitted with glass: a glass frame. [OE *glæs*]

Glass (glas, gläs), **Carter,** 1858–1946, U.S. statesman.

glass blower 1. A person engaged in glass blowing. **2.** An instrument or machine used for glass blowing.

glass blowing The art or process of directing a controlled stream of air through a tube into a mass of molten glass at the end of the tube so as to form the glass into various shapes.

glass·es (glas′iz, gläs′-) *n.pl.* Eyeglasses (which see).

glass·ful (glas′fŏŏl, gläs′-) *n. pl.* **·fuls** The amount contained in a drinking glass.

glass·house (glas′hous′, gläs′-) *n.* **1.** A factory where glass is made. **2.** *Brit.* A greenhouse (which see).

glass·ine (gla·sēn′) *n.* A tough, thin, translucent paper.

glass·mak·er (glas′mā′kər, gläs′-) *n.* One who makes glass. — **glass′mak′ing** *n.*

glass·man (glas′mən, gläs′-) *n. pl.* **·men** (-mən) **1.** One who sells glass or glassware. **2.** A glassmaker. **3.** A glazier.

glass paper Paper coated with glue and sprinkled with powdered glass, used as an abrasive.

glass snake 1. A slender, legless lizard of the southern United States (*Ophisaurus ventralis*) having a very brittle tail. **2.** A similar Old World snakelike lizard (*O. apus*).

glass·ware (glas′wâr′, gläs′-) *n.* Articles made of glass.

glass wool Fibers of spun glass of woollike appearance, used for fireproofing fabrics, and for insulation, filters, etc.

glass·work (glas′wûrk′, gläs′-) *n.* **1.** The manufacture of glass or articles made of glass. **2.** Glass as a material used in glassware, architecture, decoration, etc.; also, the particular way in which glass is used as a material. **3.** Glassware. **4.** The fitting of panes of glass; glaziery. — **glass′work′er** *n.*

GLASSWARE FOR TABLE USE

glass·works (glas′wûrks′, gläs′-) *n.pl.* (*usually construed as sing.*) A factory where glass is made.

glass·worm (glas′wûrm′, gläs′-) *n.* The arrowworm (which see).

glass·wort (glas′wûrt′, gläs′-) *n.* Any of several saline seaside herbs (genus *Salicornia*) whose ashes were formerly used in glassmaking: also called *saltwort.*

glass·y (glas′ē, gläs′ē) *adj.* **glass·i·er, glass·i·est 1.** Resembling glass in appearance or in other qualities; clear, shiny, brittle, etc., like glass. **2.** Fixed, blank, and uncomprehending: a *glassy* stare. — **glass′i·ly** *adv.* — **glass′i·ness** *n.*

Glas·ton·bur·y (glas′tən·ber′ē) A municipal borough in Somerset, England, traditionally regarded as the site of the first Christian church in England.

Glas·we·gi·an (glas·wē′jən, -jē·ən, gläs-) *adj.* Of Glasgow. — *n.* A native or inhabitant of Glasgow.

Glau·ber's salts (glou′bərz) A white crystalline sodium sulfate, used as a cathartic and diuretic. Also **Glau′ber salt.** [after Johann Rudolf *Glauber,* 1604–68, German alchemist]

glauco- *combining form* Bluish gray: *glauconite.* Also, before vowels, **glauc-.** [< Gk. *glaukos* bluish gray]

glau·co·ma (glô·kō′mə) *n. Pathol.* A disease of the eye characterized by increased pressure of fluids within the eyeball with consequent gradual loss of vision sometimes ending in total blindness. [< L < Gk. *glaukōma* < *glaukos* bluish gray] — **glau·co·ma·tous** (glô·kō′ma·təs, -kom′ə-) *adj.*

glau·co·nite (glô′kə-nīt) *n.* An amorphous, olive-green, loosely granular, massive hydrous silicate, chiefly of iron and potassium, found in greensand: also called *terre-verte.* [< Gk. *glaukon*, neut. of *glaukos* bluish gray + -ITE¹]

glau·cous (glô′kəs) *adj.* **1.** Having a yellowish green color; also, sea-green. **2.** *Bot.* Covered with a whitish bloom, as grapes. [< L *glaucus* < Gk. *glaukos* bluish gray]

glaucous gull Burgomaster (def. 2).

glaucous willow The pussy willow (which see).

glaze (glāz) *v.* **glazed, glaz·ing** *v.t.* **1.** To fit, as a window, with glass panes. **2.** To provide (a building, etc.) with windows. **3.** To coat, as pottery, with a glasslike surface applied by fusing. **4.** To cover or overspread with a thin film. **5.** To cover (foods) with a thin coating, as of syrup or egg white. **6.** To make glossy, as by polishing. **7.** In painting, to cover with a thin, transparent coating so as to modify the tone. — *v.i.* **8.** To become covered with a thin coating or film. — *n.* **1.** A thin, smooth, glossy coating; also, the substance used to make such a coating. **2.** In ceramics, the glasslike surface baked on pottery. **3.** In cooking, a substance used to coat foods, as egg white. **4.** In painting, a thin coating of a transparent substance laid on a painting to tone down the colors. **5.** A thin, filmy haze, as over the eyes. **6.** *U.S.* A thin coating of ice on trees, etc., due to freezing rain. [ME *glasen* < *glas* glass] — **glaz′er** *n.*

gla·zier (glā′zhər) *n.* **1.** One who fits windows, doors, etc., with panes of glass. **2.** One who applies glaze to pottery.

gla·zier·y (glā′zhər·ē) *n.* The work of a glazier.

glaz·ing (glā′zing) *n.* **1.** The act of setting glass, as in a window, etc. **2.** The glass used for this. **3.** A glaze. **4.** The act or art of applying a glaze.

Gla·zu·nov (glä′zŏŏ-nôf), **Alexander Konstantinovich,** 1865–1936, Russian composer.

glaz·y (glā′zē) *adj.* **glaz·i·er, glaz·i·est 1.** Covered with or as with a glaze. **2.** Resembling a glaze. — **glaz′i·ness** *n.*

gld. Guilder(s).

gleam (glēm) *n.* **1.** An intermittent or momentary ray or beam of light. **2.** A soft radiance; glow. **3.** A play of soft, reflected light over a surface: the *gleam* of polished wood. **4.** A brief or intermittent manifestation, as of humor. **5.** A faint trace or indication: a *gleam* of hope. — *v.i.* **1.** To shine with small bursts of subdued light or with a soft radiance; emit gleams. **2.** To appear briefly or intermittently in or as in a small burst of light. — *v.t.* **3.** To emit in gleams. — **Syn.** See SHINE. [OE *glǣm.* Akin to GLIM, GLIMMER.]

gleam·y (glē′mē) *adj.* **gleam·i·er, gleam·i·est 1.** Sending forth gleams. **2.** Characterized by fitful gleams of sunlight; uncertain: said of the weather.

glean (glēn) *v.t. & v.i.* **1.** To collect (facts, etc.) by patient effort. **2.** To gather (the leavings) from a field after the crop has been reaped. **3.** To gather the leavings from (a field, etc.). [< OF *glener* < LL *glenare* < Celtic] — **glean′er** *n.*

glean·ing (glē′ning) *n.* **1.** The act of a gleaner. **2.** *Usually pl.* That which is gleaned.

glebe (glēb) *n.* **1.** *Brit.* A portion of land attached to an ecclesiastical benefice as part of its endowment. **2.** *Poetic* Any field or piece of land; also, soil; earth. [< OF < L *gleba* clod]

glede (glēd) *n.* The European kite (genus *Milvus*), a bird of the hawk family. Also **gled** (gled). [OE *glida*]

glee (glē) *n.* **1.** Lively, exuberant joy or merriment. **2.** A musical composition for several male voices, without accompaniment. [OE *glēo*]

glee club A group of singers organized to sing part songs, as glees and other choral works.

gleed (glēd) *n. Obs.* A fiery coal. [OE *glēd*]

glee·ful (glē′fəl) *adj.* Feeling or exhibiting glee; mirthful. Also **glee′some** (-səm). — **glee′ful·ly** *adv.* — **glee′ful·ness** *n.*

glee·man (glē′mən) *n. pl.* **-men** (-mən) *Archaic* A wandering singer. — **Syn.** See MINSTREL.

gleet (glēt) *n. Pathol.* **1.** A mucous discharge from the urethra, resulting from infection, as in gonorrhea. **2.** Any morbid discharge. — *v.t.* To discharge gleet. [< OF *glette* mucus, pus] — **gleet′y** *adv.*

gleg (gleg) *adj. Scot.* Alert.

glen (glen) *n.* A small, secluded valley. [< Scottish Gaelic *glenn*]

Glen·coe (glen·kō′) A valley in Argyll, Scotland; scene of massacre of the MacDonalds by the Campbells and by English troops, 1692.

Glen·dale (glen′dāl) A city in SW California, near Los Angeles; pop. 132,752.

Glen·dow·er (glen′dou·ər, glen·dou′ər, glen′dŏŏr), **Owen,** 1359?–1415?, Welsh chieftain, rebelled against Henry IV.

Glen·gar·ry (glen-gar′ē) *n.* A Scottish cap having straight sides that slope backward, a crease in the crown, and often short streamers in back. Also **Glengarry bonnet.** [after *Glengarry*, a valley in Scotland]

Glen More (glen·môr′, -mōr′) See GREAT GLEN OF SCOTLAND.

Glenn (glen), **John H., Jr.,** born 1921, U.S. Marine Corps officer; first U.S. astronaut to orbit the earth, Feb. 20, 1962.

gle·noid (glē′noid) *adj.* Having a shallow, cuplike cavity serving as a socket, as the part of the shoulder blade into which the bone of the upper arm fits. [< Gk. *glēnoeidēs* like a socket < *glēnē* socket]

Glen plaid A plaid pattern of muted colors, used in materials for suits, etc. [after *Glen(urquhart)*, a Scottish clan]

gli·a·din (glī′ə-din) *n. Biochem.* Any of a group of simple proteins derived from the gluten of wheat, rye, or other grains. [< F *gliadine* < Gk. *glia* glue]

glib (glib) *adj.* **glib·ber, glib·best 1.** Speaking fluently without much thought or sincerity: a *glib* talker. **2.** More facile than sincere: a *glib* compliment. **3.** Characterized by smoothness or ease, as of manner. [Cf. obs. *glibbery* < MLG *glibberich* slippery] — **glib′ly** *adv.* — **glib′ness** *n.*

glide (glīd) *v.* **glid·ed, glid·ing** *v.i.* **1.** To move, slip, or flow smoothly or effortlessly. **2.** To pass unnoticed or imperceptibly, as time: often with *by.* **3.** *Aeron.* To descend along an oblique line gradually and without the use of motor power; also, to operate or fly in a glider. **4.** *Music & Phonet.* To produce a glide. — *v.t.* **5.** To cause to glide. — *n.* **1.** The act of gliding; a gliding motion. **2.** *Phonet.* **a** A transitional sound made in passing from the position of one speech sound to that of another, as the (w) heard between (ōō) and (a) in *bivouac.* **b** A semivowel. **3.** A gliding step, as in dancing; also, a dance in which this step is used. **4.** *Music Rare* A slur, glissando, or portamento. [OE *glīdan*]

glide path *Aeron.* **1.** The path followed by an aircraft or winged missile as it descends from horizontal flight to the surface. **2.** The line to be followed in descending to a landing, marked out by radio signals. Also **glide slope.**

glid·er (glī′dər) *n.* **1.** One who or that which glides. **2.** *Aeron.* An airplane without an engine, constructed so as to soar on rising air currents or to be towed behind a powered airplane and released. **3.** A swing made of an upholstered couch hung in a metal frame so as to glide back and forth. **4.** *Austral.* A flying phalanger: also **gliding possum.**

glid·ing (glī′ding) *adj.* That glides: a *gliding* step. — **glid′ing·ly** *adv.*

gliding angle See under ANGLE².

gliding range *Aeron.* The greatest distance that can be traveled by an aircraft from a given height under normal gliding conditions. Also **gliding distance.**

gliff (glif) *n. Scot.* **1.** A brief moment. **2.** A quick glimpse. **3.** A sudden scare.

glim (glim) *n. Slang* **1.** An electric light or other source of light. **2.** An eye. [Akin to GLEAM]

glim·mer (glim′ər) *v.i.* **1.** To shine with a faint, unsteady light; flicker. **2.** To appear fitfully or faintly. — **Syn.** See SHINE. — *n.* **1.** A faint, unsteady light. **2.** A faint perception or trace; inkling: a *glimmer* of the truth. [ME *glimeren* to shine. Akin to GLEAM.]

glim·mer·ing (glim′ər·ing) *n.* A glimmer. — *adj.* That glimmers. — **glim′mer·ing·ly** *adv.*

glimpse (glimps) *n.* **1.** A momentary view or look. **2.** A faint intimation; inkling. **3.** *Archaic* A sudden passing gleam or flash, as of light. — *v.* **glimpsed, glimps·ing** *v.t.* **1.** To see for an instant; catch a glimpse of. — *v.i.* **2.** To look for an instant: with *at.* [ME *glimsen* to shine faintly. Akin to GLEAM.]

Glin·ka (gling′kə), **Mikhail Ivanovich,** 1803–57, Russian composer.

glint (glint) *v.i.* **1.** To gleam; glitter. **2.** To move quickly and obliquely; dart. — *v.t.* **3.** To reflect; shine. — **Syn.** See SHINE. — *n.* **1.** A gleam; flash. **2.** A gloss or luster, as of metal. **3.** *Scot.* A glimpse. [ME *glinten*, var. of *glenten* to shine < Scand. Cf. dial. Sw. *glänta* to shine.]

gli·o·ma (glī·ō′mə) *n. pl.* **-ma·ta** (-mə·tə), **-mas** *Pathol.* A tumor consisting of tissue formed from neuroglia cells in various stages of development. [< NL < Gk. *glia* glue + -ōma tumor] — **gli·o·ma·tous** (glī·ō′mə·təs, -om′ə-) *adj.*

glis·sade (gli-säd′, -sād′) *n.* **1.** The act of skillfully sliding down a slope of ice, snow, etc., as in mountain-climbing. **2.** A gliding dance step. — *v.i.* **-sad·ed, -sad·ing** To execute a glissade. [< F < *glisser* to slip]

glis·san·do (gli-sän′dō) *Music n. pl.* **-di** (-dē) or **-dos 1.** A passing from one tone to another by a continuous change of pitch; also, the imitation of this by a rapid succession of tones on keyboard instruments, etc. **2.** A passage so written or performed. — *adj.* Of or pertaining to a glissando. — *adv.* In the manner of a glissando. Abbr. *gliss.* [< F *glissant*, ppr. of *glisser* to slip + Ital. *-ando*, ppr. suffix]

glis·ten (glis′ən) *v.i.* To shine or sparkle, as the reflected light from a wet surface: streets *glistening* after a rain. — **Syn.** See SHINE. — *n.* Brightness; sparkle. [OE *glisnian* to shine]

glis·ter (glis′tər) *Archaic & Poetic v.i.* To glisten. — *n.* Sparkle; glisten. [< MDu. *glisteren*]

glit·ter (glit′ər) *v.i.* **1.** To sparkle brightly or brilliantly, as a diamond. **2.** To display striking magnificence, opulence, or colorfulness; be brilliantly showy, attractive, or outstanding. — **Syn.** See SHINE. — *n.* Sparkling magnificence; brilliance. [< ON *glitra*]

glitter ice *Canadian* Ice from a freezing rain.

glit·ter·ing (glit′ər·ing) *adj.* Brilliantly sparkling; magnificent. **— glit′ter·ing·ly** *adv.*

glit·ter·y (glit′ər·ē) *adj.* Radiating bright rays of light, as a jewel; sparkling; glittering.

gloam·ing (glō′ming) *n.* The dusk of early evening; twilight. Also *Archaic & Poetic* **gloam** (glōm). [OE *glōmung*]

gloat (glōt) *v.i.* To give oneself up to an intense, prolonged, often malicious or evil delight: usually with *over*: to *gloat* over another's bad luck. [Cf. ON *glotta* to grin]

gloat·ing (glō′ting) *adj.* Triumphantly rejoicing, especially with malicious or evil satisfaction. **— gloat′ing·ly** *adv.*

glob (glob) *n.* **1.** A small drop or ball of something. **2.** A rounded, often large mass of something. **3.** A daub or spot, as of color. [Prob. < GLOBE; infl. in form by *blob*]

glob·al (glō′bəl) *adj.* **1.** Pertaining to or involving the whole world: *global* war. **2.** Spherical. **— glob′al·ly** *adv.*

glo·bate (glō′bāt) *adj.* Formed like a globe; spherical. Also **glo′bat·ed.**

globe (glōb) *n.* **1.** A perfectly round body; ball; sphere; also, anything with a more or less spherical shape, as a fishbowl. **2.** The earth: usually with *the;* also, any planet. **3.** A sphere on which is drawn a map of the earth or of the heavens. **4.** A ball, usually of gold, borne as an emblem of authority. **— *v.t. & v.i.* globed, glob·ing** To form into a globe. [< F < L *globus* ball]

globe amaranth A cultivated plant (*Gomphrena globosa*), an immortelle, of the amaranth family.

globe·fish (glōb′fish) *n. pl.* **·fish** or **·fish·es** Any of various spiny-finned plectognath fishes (family *Tetraodontidae*) of tropical seas, capable when disturbed of inflating their bodies into a globular form: also called *blowfish, porcupine fish, puffer, swellfish.*

globe·flow·er (glōb′flou′ər) *n.* Any of a genus (*Trollius*) of plants of the crowfoot family, having globular, yellow flowers.

globe·trot·ter (glōb′trot′ər) *n.* One who travels all over the world, especially for sightseeing. **— globe′trot′ting** *n.*

GLOBEFISH
a Normal. *b* Inflated. (About 7 inches long)

glo·big·er·i·na (glō·bij′ə·rī′nə) *n.* One of a genus (*Globigerina*) of small marine foraminifers whose calcareous shells accumulate in vast quantities on the sea bottoms, forming deposits called **globigerina ooze.** [< NL < L *globus* ball + *gerere* to bear]

glo·bin (glō′bin) *n. Biochem.* The protein constituent of hemoglobin. [< L *globus* ball + -IN]

glo·boid (glō′boid) *adj.* Having an approximately spherical or globular shape. **— *n.* Any globate body or mass.

glo·bose (glō′bōs, glō·bōs′) *adj.* Spherical. Also **glo′bous** (-bəs) [< L *globosus < globus* ball] **— glo·bose′ness** *n.* **— glo·bos·i·ty** (glō·bos′ə·tē) *n.*

glob·u·lar (glob′yə·lər) *adj.* **1.** Spherical. **2.** Formed of globules.

glob·ule (glob′yōōl) *n.* A tiny sphere of matter or drop of liquid. [< F < L *globulus,* dim. of *globus* ball]

glob·u·lif·er·ous (glob′yə·lif′ər·əs) *adj.* Producing or containing globules.

glob·u·lin (glob′yə·lin) *n. Biochem.* Any one of a group of simple plant and animal proteins, insoluble in water but soluble in dilute saline solutions. [< GLOBULE]

glob·u·lous (glob′yə·ləs) *adj.* **1.** Containing or consisting of globules. **2.** Spherical; globular. Also **glob′u·lose** (-lōs).

glo·chid·i·ate (glō·kid′ē·āt) *adj. Biol.* Barbed, as hairs and bristles. [< NL *glochidium* barbed hair, dim. of Gk. *glōchis* point of an arrow]

glock·en·spiel (glok′ən·spēl) *n.* A portable musical instrument consisting of a series of chromatically tuned metal bars and played by striking with small, light hammers. [< G < *glocken* bells + *spiel* play]

glom·er·ate (glom′ər·āt, -it) *adj.* Gathered or wound into a rounded mass; tightly clustered. [< L *glomeratus,* pp. of *glomerare* to collect < *glomus, -eris* mass]

glom·er·a·tion (glom′ə·rā′shən) *n.* **1.** Something made into a rounded, cohering mass. **2.** A jumbled mass; conglomeration.

GLOCKENSPIEL

glom·er·ule (glom′ər·ōōl) *n. Bot.* A cymose flower cluster condensed into a headlike form. [< F < NL *glomerulus,* dim. of L *glomus, -eris* mass]

glo·mer·u·lus (glə·mer′yə·ləs) *n. pl.* **·li** (-lī) *Anat.* A coil of blood vessels forming a small tuft at the expanded end of each uriniferous tubule. [< NL. See GLOMERULE.]

gloom (glōōm) *n.* **1.** Partial or total darkness; heavy shadow. **2.** Darkness or depression of the mind or spirits. **3.** A dark or gloomy place. **4.** *Scot.* A sulky look; frown. **— *v.i.* 1.** To look sullen, displeased, or dejected. **2.** To be or become dark or threatening. **— *v.t.* 3.** To make dark, sad, or sullen. [ME *glom(b)en* to look sad]

gloom·ing (glōō′ming) *n. Poetic* Gloaming

gloom·y (glōō′mē) *adj.* **gloom·i·er, gloom·i·est** **1.** Dark; dismal. **2.** Affected with melancholy; morose. **3.** Producing gloom or melancholy. **— gloom′i·ly** *adv.* **— gloom′i·ness** *n.*

glo·ri·a (glôr′ē·ə, glō′rē·ə) *n.* **1.** A halo or nimbus. **2.** A material of wool and silk, wool and cotton, etc., used in covering umbrellas and in dressmaking.

Glo·ri·a (glôr′ē·ə, glō′rē·ə) *n.* **1.** *Eccl.* One of several Latin hymns of praise to God beginning with the word *Gloria.* **2.** *Eccl.* The section of the Mass consisting of the recitation or singing of the *Gloria in excelsis Deo.* **3.** *Music* A musical setting of the *Gloria in excelsis Deo.* [< L, glory]

Gloria in ex·cel·sis De·o (in ek·sel′sis dē′ō, dā′ō) A Latin doxology beginning *Gloria in excelsis Deo* ("Glory to God in the highest"): also called the *greater doxology.*

Gloria Pa·tri (pat′rē, pä′trē) A short Latin doxology beginning with the words *Gloria Patri* ("Glory be to the Father"): also called the *lesser doxology.*

glo·ri·fi·ca·tion (glôr′ə·fə·kā′shən, glō′rə-) *n.* **1.** The act of glorifying or exalting. **2.** The state of being invested with glory. **3.** *Informal* A glorified form of something.

glo·ri·fy (glôr′ə·fī, glō′rə-) *v.t.* **·fied, ·fy·ing** **1.** To make glorious. **2.** To honor or exalt; worship. **3.** To give great praise to; laud. **4.** To make seem more splendid or glorious than is actually so. [< OF *glorifier* < LL *glorificare* < L *gloria* glory + *facere* to make] **— glo′ri·fi′er** *n.*

glo·ri·ole (glôr′ē·ōl, glō′rē-) *n.* A halo or aureole. [< F < L *gloriola,* dim. of *gloria* glory]

glo·ri·ous (glôr′ē·əs, glō′rē-) *adj.* **1.** Full of or deserving glory; renowned; illustrious. **2.** Bringing glory or honor: a *glorious* victory. **3.** Resplendent; beautiful: a *glorious* sunset. **4.** *Informal* Very pleasant; delightful. [< L *gloriosus < gloria* glory] **— glo′ri·ous·ly** *adv.* **— glo′ri·ous·ness** *n.*

glo·ry (glôr′ē, glō′rē) *n. pl.* **·ries** **1.** Distinguished honor or praise; exalted reputation. **2.** Something bringing praise or renown; an object of special distinction. **3.** Worshipful praise; adoration: to give *glory* to God. **4.** Magnificence; splendor: the *glory* of Rome. **5.** The bliss of heaven: to go to *glory.* **6.** A state of exaltation, extreme well-being, prosperity, etc.: to be in one's *glory.* **7.** A nimbus; halo. **— *v.i.* ·ried, ·ry·ing** **1.** To rejoice proudly or triumphantly; take pride: with *in.* **2.** To boast; brag. [< OF *glorie* < L *gloria*]

Glos. Gloucestershire.

gloss[1] (glôs, glos) *n.* **1.** The luster or sheen of a polished surface. Abbr. *gl.* **2.** A deceptive or superficial appearance. **— *v.t.* 1.** To make smooth or lustrous, as by polishing or buffing. **2.** To hide or attempt to hide (errors, defects, etc.) by falsehood or equivocation: usually with *over.* **— *v.i.* 3.** To become shiny. **— Syn.** see PALLIATE. [< Scand. Cf. ON *glossi* blaze, spark.] **— gloss′er** *n.*

gloss[2] (glôs, glos) *n.* **1.** An explanatory note; especially, a marginal or interlinear note. **2.** A commentary; also, sometimes, a translation. **3.** A glossary. **4.** An artful or deceptive explanation designed to cover up a fault, defect, etc. **— *v.t.* 1.** To write glosses for (a text, word, etc.); annotate. **2.** To excuse or change by false explanations: often with *over:* to *gloss* over the truth. **— *v.i.* 3.** To make glosses. [< OF *glose* note < L *glossa* a difficult word (in a text) < Gk. *glōssa* foreign word; orig., tongue] **— gloss′er** *n.*

gloss. Glossary.

Glos·sa (glôs′ə), Cape See (Cape) LINGUETTA.

glos·sal (glôs′əl, glos′-) *adj.* Of or pertaining to the tongue.

glos·sa·ry (glôs′ə·rē, glos′-) *n. pl.* **·ries** A lexicon of the technical, obscure, or foreign words of a work or field. [< L *glossarium < glossa.* See GLOSS[2].] **— glos·sar·i·al** (glo·sâr′ē·əl, glô-) *adj.* **— glos·sar′i·al·ly** *adv.* **— glos·sa·rist** (glos′ə·rist, glôs′-) *n.*

glos·sec·to·my (glos·sek′tə·mē, glô-) *n. pl.* **·mies** *Surg.* Total or partial removal of the tongue.

glos·si·tis (glo·sī′tis, glô-) *n. Pathol.* Inflammation of the tongue. **— glos·sit·ic** (-sit′ik) *adj.*

glosso- *combining form* The tongue; speech; language. Also, before vowels, **gloss-.** [< Gk. *glōssa* tongue]

glos·sog·ra·phy (glo·sog′rə·fē, glô-) *n.* The making of glosses or of glossaries. **— glos·sog′ra·pher** *n.*

glos·so·la·li·a (glos′ə·lā′lē·ə, glôs′-) *n.* **1.** Unintelligible speech or sounds. **2.** Speech in an unknown or imaginary language. [< NL < GLOSSO- + Gk. *lalia* speech]

glos·sol·o·gy (glo·sol′ə·jē, glô-) *n.* Linguistics. Also **glot·tol·o·gy** (glo·tol′ə·jē).

gloss·y (glôs′ē, glos′ē) *adj.* **gloss·i·er, gloss·i·est** **1.** Having a bright sheen; lustrous. **2.** Made superficially attractive. **3.** Specious. **— *n. pl.* ·ies** A glossy photographic print. **— gloss′i·ly** *adv.* **— gloss′i·ness** *n.*

glost (glôst, glost) *n.* Lead glaze used in making pottery; also, glazed pottery. [Var. of GLOSS[1]]

-glot *combining form* Using or able to use (a specified number of) languages: *polyglot.* [< Gk. *glōtta,* var. of *glōssa* tongue, language]

glot·tal (glot′l) *adj.* **1.** Of, pertaining to, or situated in the glottis. **2.** *Phonet.* Articulated in the glottis: also *laryngeal.*

glottal stop *Phonet.* A sound produced in the larynx by closing the glottis and then releasing the impounded breath with a coughlike explosion.

glot·tic (glot'ik) *adj.* **1.** Glottal. **2.** Linguistic.

glot·tis (glot'is) *n. pl.* **glot·ti·des** (glot'ə-dēz) or **glot·tis·es** *Anat.* The cleft between the vocal cords at the upper orifice of the larynx. [< NL < Gk. *glōttis* < *glōtta* tongue]

glotto- *combining form* Language: glottology. [< Gk. *glōtta*, var. of *glōssa* language]

glot·to·chro·nol·o·gy (glot'ō-krə-nol'ə-jē) *n. pl.* **·gies** *Ling.* **1.** A technique for inferring, by statistical comparison of selected vocabulary items, the probable dates when the various members of a language family separated from one another, from their parent language, etc.: also called *lexicostatistics.* **2.** The study of the time during which a separation process in language took place. [< GLOTTO- + CHRONOLOGY]

Glouces·ter (glos'tər, glôs'-) **1.** The county seat of Gloucestershire, England, a county borough in the central part of the county; pop. 91,000 (1976). **2.** A port and resort city in NE Massachusetts; pop. 25,789. **3.** Gloucestershire, England.

Glouces·ter (glos'tər, glôs'-), **Duke of** See HUMPHREY or RICHARD III.

Glouces·ter·shire (glos'tər-shir, glôs'-) A county in west central England; 1,258 sq. mi.; pop. 485,400 (1976); county seat, Gloucester.

Gloucs. Gloucestershire.

glove (gluv) *n.* **1.** A covering for the hand, having a separate sheath for each finger. **2.** In baseball, a large leather covering for the hand, with a separate sheath for each finger, used for catching the ball. **3.** A boxing glove (which see). **— to be hand in glove** (with) To be in close, harmonious relationship (with). **— to handle with kid gloves** To use great care and tact in dealing with. **— to put on the gloves** *Informal* To box or spar. **—** *v.t.* **gloved, glov·ing 1.** To put gloves on. **2.** To furnish with gloves. **3.** To serve as a glove for. [OE *glōf*]

glov·er (gluv'ər) *n.* A maker of or dealer in gloves.

glow (glō) *v.i.* **1.** To give off light and heat, especially without flame; be incandescent. **2.** To shine as if greatly heated. **3.** To show a strong, bright color; be red, as from heat; flush. **4.** To be animated, as with health, emotion, etc. **5.** To be very hot; burn. **— Syn.** See SHINE. **—** *n.* **1.** The incandescence given off by a heated substance. **2.** Vividness or brilliance of color. **3.** Ruddiness, as from health or emotion. **4.** Strong emotion; ardor. **5.** Bodily warmth, as from exercise, etc. [OE *glōwan*]

glow·er (glou'ər) *v.i.* **1.** To stare with an angry frown; scowl sullenly. **2.** *Scot.* To stare intently. **—** *n.* The act of glowering; a fierce or threatening stare. [? Freq. of obs. *glow* to stare] **— glow'er·ing·ly** *adv.*

glow·fly (glō'flī') *n. pl.* **·flies** A firefly.

glow·ing (glō'ing) *adj.* **1.** Incandescent; burning. **2.** Intense and bright; vivid: said of colors. **3.** Ardent; enthusiastic; fervid: *glowing* admiration. **4.** Having a glow of good health, excitement, etc. **— glow'ing·ly** *adv.*

glow·worm (glō'wûrm') *n.* **1.** A European beetle (genus *Lampyris*), the larva and wingless female of which display phosphorescent light. **2.** The firefly or its larvae.

glox·in·i·a (glok-sin'ē-ə) *n.* A plant (genus *Sinningia*) with large, bell-shaped flowers of red, white, purple, or intermediate shades. [after B. P. *Gloxin,* 18th c. German physician]

gloze¹ (glōz) *v.* **glozed, gloz·ing** *v.t.* **1.** To explain away; palliate: usually with *over.* **2.** *Obs.* To explain by notes or glosses. **—** *v.i.* **3.** *Obs.* To flatter. **4.** *Obs.* To make notes or glosses. **—** *n.* **1.** *Rare* Specious show or pretense. **2.** *Rare* Flattery. **3.** *Archaic* A gloss or comment. [< OF *gloser* to explain < *glose* note < L *glossa.* See GLOSS².]

gloze² (glōz) *v.t. & v.i.* **glozed, gloz·ing** *Rare* To shine; gleam. [Cf. GLOSS¹]

glt. Gilt (bookbinding).

glu·ci·num (gloo-sī'nəm) *n.* Beryllium: a former name. Also **glu·cin'i·um** (-sin'ē-əm) Abbr. *Gl.* [< NL < Gk. *glykys* sweet; because some of its salts are sweet to taste]

Gluck (glook), **Alma,** 1884–1938, U.S. soprano born in Rumania: original name **Reba Fier·sohn** (fēr'sōn). **— Christoph Willibald,** 1714–87, German composer.

glu·co·pro·tein (gloo'kō-prō'tē·in, -tēn) See GLYCOPROTEIN.

glu·cose (gloo'kōs) *n.* **1.** *Chem.* A monosaccharide carbohydrate, $C_6H_{12}O_6$, less sweet than cane sugar. It is widely distributed in the form of dextrose in plants and animals and is obtained by the hydrolysis of starch and other carbohydrates. **2.** A thick yellowish syrup containing dextrose, maltose, and dextrin, obtained by incomplete hydrolysis of starch and used in confectionery, baking, etc. [< F < Gk. *glykys* sweet] **— glu·cos'ic** (-kos'ik) *adj.*

glu·co·side (gloo'kə-sīd) *n. Chem.* **1.** Any of a large class of glycosides of which the carbohydrate portion is glucose. **2.** Any glycoside. [< GLUCOSE + -IDE]

glu·co·su·ri·a (gloo'kō-soor'ē-ə) *n.* Glycosuria.

glue (gloo) *n.* **1.** An adhesive in the form of an impure gelatine made from certain animal substances, as skin, bones, and cartilage: also called *animal glue.* **2.** An adhesive or cement made of casein, synthetic resin, rubber, blood, plastic, or some other material. **3.** Any sticky substance used as an adhesive. **—** *v.t.* **glued, glu·ing** To stick or fasten with or as with glue. [< OF *glu* birdlime < LL *glus, glutis*]

glue·y (gloo'ē) *adj.* **glu·i·er, glu·i·est 1.** Having the nature of glue; sticky; viscous. **2.** Covered or spread with glue.

glum (glum) *adj.* **glum·mer, glum·mest** Moody and silent; sullen. [Akin to GLOOM] **— glum'ly** *adv.* **— glum'ness** *n.*

glu·ma·ceous (gloo-mā'shəs) *adj.* **1.** Having glumes. **2.** Suggestive of glumes.

glume (gloom) *n. Bot.* One of the two lowest bracts on the spikelet of certain grassy plants. [< L *gluma* husk]

glunch (gloonsh, glunsh) *Scot. v.i.* To frown; look sullen. **—** *adj.* Sullen. **—** *n.* A sulky look.

glut (glut) *v.* **glut·ted, glut·ting** *v.t.* **1.** To feed or supply to excess; satiate; gorge. **2.** To supply (the market) with an excessive quantity of certain goods so that the price falls. **—** *v.i.* To eat to excess. **—** *n.* **1.** An excessive supply of something. **2.** The act of glutting, or the state of being glutted. [< obs. *glut* glutton < OF *gloutir* to swallow < L *glutire*]

glu·tam·ic acid (gloo-tam'ik) *Biochem.* A white crystalline amino acid, $C_5H_9O_4N$, obtained by acid hydrolysis of animal and vegetable proteins.

glu·ta·mine (gloo'tə-mēn, -min) *n. Biochem.* An amine derived from glutamic acid, $C_5H_{11}O_3N_2$, found in the roots and leaves of certain plants. [< GLUT(EN) + -AMINE]

glu·ta·thi·one (gloo'tə-thī'ōn) *n. Biochem.* A peptide of glutamic acid, cysteine, and glycine, $C_{10}H_{17}O_6N_3S$, obtained from yeast and occurring also in muscle tissue, blood, and plants. [< GLUTA(MIC) + THI- + -ONE]

glu·te·al (gloo-tē'əl, gloo'tē-əl) *adj. Anat.* Of or pertaining to the muscles of the buttocks. [< GLUTEUS]

glu·te·lin (gloo'tə-lin) *n. Biochem.* A plant protein found in cereal grains. [< GLUTEN + -lin, an arbitrary ending]

glu·ten (gloot'n) *n.* A tough, sticky mixture of plant proteins obtained by washing out the starch from wheat or other cereal flour and used as an adhesive and thickener. [< L, glue] **— glu·te·nous** (gloot'n·əs) *adj.*

gluten bread Bread made from flour rich in gluten and containing little starch.

glu·te·us (gloo-tē'əs) *n. pl.* **·te·i** (-tē'ī) *Anat.* Any of three muscles of the buttocks. [< NL < Gk. *gloutos* rump]

glu·ti·nous (gloot'n-əs) *adj.* Resembling glue; sticky. **— glu'ti·nous·ly** *adv.* **— glu'ti·nous·ness** *n.*

glut·ton¹ (glut'n) *n.* **1.** One who eats to excess. **2.** One who has a great appetite or capacity for something. **— Syn.** See GOURMET. [< OF *glouton* < L *gluto, -onis* glutton]

glut·ton² (glut'n) *n.* A wolverine, especially of Asia or Europe. [Trans. of G *vielfrass* great eater]

glut·ton·ize (glut'n-īz) *v.t. & v.i.* **·ized, ·iz·ing** To eat like a glutton.

glut·ton·ous (glut'n-əs) *adj.* **1.** Given to excess in eating; voracious. **2.** Desiring or indulging in anything excessively. **— glut'ton·ous·ly** *adv.*

glut·ton·y (glut'n-ē) *n. pl.* **·ton·ies** The act or habit of eating to excess.

gly·cer·ic (gli-ser'ik, glis'ər-) *adj.* Of or derived from glycerol.

glyceric acid *Chem.* A colorless, syrupy compound, $C_3H_6O_4$, formed during alcoholic fermentation and by oxidizing glycerol with nitric acid.

glyc·er·ide (glis'ər-īd, -id) *n. Chem.* An ether or ester of glycerol with a fatty acid.

glyc·er·in (glis'ər-in) *n.* Glycerol. Also **glyc'er·ine** (-in, -ēn).

glyc·er·ol (glis'ər-ōl, -ol) *n. Chem.* A sweet, oily, colorless alcohol, $C_3H_8O_3$, formed by decomposition of natural fats with alkalis or superheated steam, used in medicine, industry, and the arts. [< Gk. *glykeros* sweet + -OL²]

glyc·er·yl (glis'ər-il) *n. Chem.* The trivalent glycerol radical C_3H_5. [< GLYCER(IN) + -YL]

glyceryl stearate Stearin (def. 1).

gly·cine (glī'sēn, glī-sēn') *n. Biochem.* A sweet, colorless amino acid, $C_2H_5O_2N$, obtained by the hydrolysis of various proteins. [< Gk. *glykys* sweet + -INE²]

glyco- *combining form* Sweet: glycogen. [< Gk. *glykys* sweet]

gly·co·gen (glī'kə-jən) *n. Biochem.* A white, mealy, amorphous polysaccharide, $(C_6H_{10}O_5)_x$, contained principally in the liver and hydrolized into glucose: also called *animal starch.* [< GLYCO- + -GEN]

gly·co·gen·ic (glī'kə-jen'ik) *adj.* **1.** Relating to the formation of glycogen. **2.** Caused by glycogen.

gly·col (glī'kōl, -kol) *n. Chem.* **1.** One of several alcohols containing two hydroxyl radicals, having the general formula $C_nH_{2n}(OH)_2$. **2.** Ethylene glycol. [< GLYC(ERIN) + -OL¹]

gly·col·ic acid (glī-kol'ik) *Chem.* An acid, $C_2H_4O_3$, found in the juice of cane sugar and unripe grapes and also made synthetically.

gly·co·pro·te·in (glī'kō-prō'tē-in, -tēn) *n. Biochem.* Any of a group of proteins containing a carbohydrate group other than nucleic acid, as mucin: also spelled *glucoprotein.* [< GLYCO- + PROTEIN]

gly·co·side (glī'kə-sīd) *n. Chem.* Any of a group of carbohydrates combined with a sugar and a nonsugar, that when decomposed yield glucose or some other sugar and a principle, as digitalin, quercetin, salicin, etc. [Var. of GLUCOSIDE]

gly·co·su·ri·a (glī/kə·soōr/ē·ə) *n. Pathol.* A condition, as diabetes mellitus, in which the urine contains glucose: also *glucosuria.* [< NL < F *glycose* glucose + Gk. *ouron* urine] — **gly/co·su/ric** *adj.*

Glyn (glin), **Elinor,** 1864?–1943, *née* Sutherland, English novelist active in the United States.

gly·ox·a·line (glī·ok/sə·lin) *n. Chem.* Imidazole. [< GLY-(COL) + OXAL(IC) + -INE²]

glyph (glif) *n.* **1.** *Archit.* A vertical groove or channel, as in a Doric frieze. Compare TRIGLYPH. **2.** *Archeol.* An incised or raised figure or form that represents a word, idea, etc.; pictograph; hieroglyph. **3.** Any incised or raised figure. [< Gk. *glyphē* a carving < *glyphein* to carve] — **glyph/ic** *adj.*

-glyph *combining form* Carving: hieroglyph. [< Gk. *glyphē* a carving]

glyph·og·ra·phy (glif·og/rə·fē) *n.* A process for making plates for printing by engraving on a copperplate covered with a wax film. [< Gk. *glyphē* a carving + -GRAPHY] — **gly·phog/ra·pher** *n.* — **glyph·o·graph·ic** (glif/ə·graf/ik) or **·i·cal** *adj.*

glyp·tic (glip/tik) *adj.* Pertaining to carving or engraving, especially on gems. [< Gk. *glyptikos* < *glyphē* a carving] **glyp·tics** (glip/tiks) *n.pl.* (construed as sing.) The art of engraving or cutting designs, especially on precious stones.

glypto- *combining form* Carved: *glyptography.* [< Gk. *glyptos* carved]

glyp·to·dont (glip/tə·dont) *n. Paleontol.* Any of a genus (*Glyptodon*) of extinct American armadillos. [< NL *Glyptodon* < Gk. *glyptos* carved + *odous, odontos* tooth]

glyp·to·graph (glip/tə·graf, -gräf) *n.* A design cut on a gem.

glyp·tog·ra·phy (glip·tog/rə·fē) *n. pl.* **·phies 1.** The art or operation of engraving on gems. **2.** The study of engraved gems. [< GLYPTO- + -GRAPHY] — **glyp·tog/ra·pher** *n.* — **glyp·to·graph·ic** (glip/tə·graf/ik) or **·i·cal** *adj.*

gm. Gram(s).

G.M. 1. General manager. **2.** *Brit.* George Medal. **3.** Grand Master.

G-man (jē/man/) *n. pl.* **-men** (-men/) An agent of the Federal Bureau of Investigation. [< G(OVERNMENT) MAN]

G.m.a.t. Greenwich mean astronomical time.

Gmc. Germanic.

GMT or **G.M.T.** or **G.m.t.** Greenwich mean time.

gnar (när) *v.i.* **gnarred, gnar·ring** *Obs.* To snarl or growl. Also **gnarr.** [Imit.]

gnarl[1] (närl) *v.i. Obs.* To snarl; growl. [Freq. of GNAR]

gnarl[2] (närl) *n.* A protuberance on a tree; a tough knot. — *v.t.* To make knotty and twisted like an old tree. [Back formation < GNARLED]

gnarled (närld) *adj.* **1.** Having gnarls. **2.** Weather-beaten and rugged. **3.** Of the hands, having the prominent knuckles and tendons and somewhat twisted fingers typically produced by hard work. Also **gnarl/y.** [Var. of KNURLED]

gnash (nash) *v.t.* **1.** To grind or snap (the teeth) together, as in rage. **2.** To bite or chew by grinding the teeth. — *v.i.* **3.** To grind the teeth. — *n.* A snap or bite of the teeth. [Var. of obs. *gnast* < Scand. Cf. ON *gnista* to gnash.]

gnat (nat) *n.* **1.** Any of various small stinging or biting flies, as the buffalo gnats, punkies, and midges. **2.** *Brit.* A mosquito. — **to strain at a gnat** To object to or fuss about something of little importance. [OE *gnæt*]

gnat·catch·er (nat/kach/ər) *n.* Any of several small American birds (genus *Polioptila*); especially, the **blue-gray gnatcatcher** (*P. caerulea*), having a black tail and short wings.

gnath·ic (nath/ik) *adj.* Of or pertaining to the jaw. [< Gk. *gnathos* jaw]

gnathic index A measure of the relative prominence of the jaw, expressed as the ratio of the distance from nasion to basion taken as 100, to the distance from the basion to the alveolar point.

gna·thi·on (nā/thē·on, nath/ē·on) *n. Anat.* The lowest point of the symphysis of the jaw; the point of the chin. [< NL, dim. of Gk. *gnathos* the jaw]

gnatho- *combining form* Jaw. [< Gk. *gnathos* jaw]

gna·thon·ic (na·thon/ik) *adj. Rare* Given to deceitful flattery. [after *Gnatho*, a sycophant in Terence's *Eunuchus*]

gna·tho·stome (na/thə·stōm) *n. Zool.* Any vertebrate having true jaws.

-gnathous *combining form* Having a jaw of an indicated kind: *prognathous.* [< Gk. *gnathos* jaw + -OUS]

gnaw (nô) *v.t.* **gnawed, gnawed** or sometimes **gnawn, gnaw·ing 1.** To bite or eat away little by little with or as with the teeth. **2.** To make by gnawing: to *gnaw* a hole. **3.** To bite on repeatedly. **4.** To torment or oppress with fear, pain, etc. — *v.i.* **5.** To bite, chew, or corrode persistently or continually. **6.** To cause constant worry, pain, etc. [OE *gnagan*] — **gnaw/er** *n.* — **gnaw/ing·ly** *adv.*

gnaw·ing (nô/ing) *n.* **1.** A dull, persistent sensation of discomfort or distress. **2.** *pl.* Pangs of hunger.

gneiss (nīs) *n.* **1.** A coarse-grained, banded metamorphic rock consisting essentially of the same components as granite but displaying a foliated arrangement of components. **2.** Any of a number of highly metamorphosed, banded rocks containing feldspar. [< G] — **gneiss/ic** *adj.*

gneiss·oid (nīs/oid) *adj.* Resembling gneiss.

gnome[1] (nōm) *n.* In folklore, one of a group of dwarfish beings typically resembling little old men and living in caves where they guard precious metals, buried treasure, etc. [< F < NL *gnomus*] — **gnom/ish** *adj.*

gnome[2] (nōm) *n.* A pithy proverbial saying or general truth; maxim. [< Gk. *gnōmē* thought, maxim]

gno·mic (nō/mik, nom/ik) *adj.* **1.** Consisting of or resembling gnomes or maxims; aphoristic. **2.** Of or denoting a writer of maxims, as certain Greek poets. Also **gno/mi·cal.** — **gno/mi·cal·ly** *adv.*

gno·mol·o·gy (nə·mol/ə·jē) *n.* A compilation of or a treatise on gnomic sayings.

gno·mon (nō/mon) *n.* **1.** A pointer or similar device used to indicate time by the shadow it casts, as on a sundial. For illustration see SUNDIAL. **2.** *Geom.* The figure that remains after a parallelogram has been removed from the corner of a similar but larger parallelogram. [< Gk. *gnōmōn* indicator < *gnō-*, stem of *gignōskein* to know] — **gno·mon·ic** (nō·mon/ik) or **·i·cal** *adj.*

-gnomy *combining form* Knowledge or art of judging: *physiognomy.* [< Gk. *gnōmē* judgment]

gno·si·ol·o·gy (nō/sē·ol/ə·jē, nō/zē-) *n. Rare* Epistemology.

gno·sis (nō/sis) *n.* A special knowledge of spiritual mysteries; especially, such knowledge as the Gnostics claimed to possess. [< NL < Gk. *gnōsis* knowledge < *gignōskein* to know]

-gnosis *combining form Med.* Knowledge; recognition: *prognosis.* [< Gk. *gnōsis* knowledge]

gnos·tic (nos/tik) *adj.* Of, pertaining to, or possessing knowledge, especially spiritual knowledge or insight. Also **gnos/·ti·cal.** [< Gk. *gnōstikos* knowing < *gnōsis.* See GNOSIS.] — **gnos/ti·cal·ly** *adv.*

Gnos·tic (nos/tik) *adj.* Of or pertaining to the Gnostics or Gnosticism. — *n.* An adherent or advocate of Gnosticism.

Gnos·ti·cism (nos/tə·siz/əm) *n.* A hybrid system of ancient Greek and Oriental philosophy, modified by an attempted synthesis with Christian doctrine, marked especially by the asserted possession of a superior spiritual knowledge, and denounced as heretical by the Church.

gno·thi se·au·ton (gnō/thē se/ou·ton/) *Greek* Know thyself: an ancient maxim.

GNP or **G.N.P.** Gross national product.

gnu (noō, nyoō) *n. pl.* **gnus** or **gnu** A South African antelope (genus *Connochaetes*) having an oxlike head with curved horns, a mane, and a long tail: also called *wildebeest.* [< Xhosa *nqu*]

GNU
(To 4 feet high
at shoulder)

go[1] (gō) *v.* **went, gone, go·ing;** *3rd person sing. present* **goes** *v.i.* **1.** To proceed or pass along; move. **2.** To move from a place; leave; depart: often used as a command or signal, as in a race: *Go!* **3.** To have a regularly scheduled route or specific destination: This train *goes* to Chicago daily. **4.** To move or proceed toward for some specific purpose or goal: She *went* to dress for dinner. **5.** To be in motion or operation: The motor is *going.* **6.** To work or function properly: This watch won't *go.* **7.** To extend or reach: This pipe *goes* to the basement. **8.** To move or act in a specified way: The motor *went* fast. **9.** To emit or produce a specified sound or signal: The chain *goes* "clank." **10.** To fail, give way, or collapse: His hearing *went.* **11.** To have a specific place or position; belong: The plates *go* on that shelf. **12.** To pass into someone's possession; be awarded or given: The cake *goes* to John. **13.** To be allotted or applied: This *goes* for rent. **14.** To pass from one person to another: Measles *went* through the entire school. **15.** To pass into a state or condition; become: to *go* insane. **16.** To be, continue, or appear in a specified state or condition: to *go* unpunished; to *go* without a hat. **17.** To proceed, happen, or end in a specific or stated manner: The election *went* badly for him. **18.** To be considered or ranked: a good lunch as lunches *go.* **19.** To be suitable; harmonize; fit: These colors *go* well together. **20.** To be phrased or expressed; have a certain form or sequence: How does the tune *go?* **21.** To have recourse; make appeal; resort: to *go* to court. **22.** To die. **23.** To pass: said of time. **24.** To pass away; disappear; end: My headache has *gone.* **25.** To be abolished, relinquished, or given up: These extra expenses must *go.* **26.** To serve, contribute, or help: This *goes* to prove my point. **27.** To serve to make up a certain amount or quantity: Two ounces of butter *go* to each serving. **28.** To be sold or bid for: with *at* or *for:* These shoes will *go* at a high price. **29.** To subject oneself; put oneself: He *went* to great pains to do it. **30.** To continue one's actions to or beyond certain limits: He *goes* too far in his criticism. **31.** To endure or bear up; last: Can he *go* two more rounds? **32.** To be about to do something indicated:

used in the progressive form and followed by the present infinitive: They are *going* to protest. — *v.t.* **33.** *Informal* To furnish or provide (bail). **34.** *Informal* To risk or bet; wager: I'll *go* a dollar on that race. **35.** *Informal* To put up with; tolerate: I cannot *go* that music. — **to go** *Informal* **1.** Remaining: ten pages *to go.* **2.** Prepared for taking outside: a chocolate milkshake *to go.* — **to go about 1.** To be occupied or busy with. **2.** To move about; circulate. **3.** *Naut.* To change to another tack; turn. — **to go after 1.** To attempt to catch; chase. **2.** To follow in sequence or in turn. — **to go against** To be opposed to; act contrary to. — **to go along 1.** To continue; carry on. **2.** To be in accord; agree to cooperate: often with *with.* **3.** To escort; accompany: with *with.* — **to go around 1.** To move about or circulate. **2.** To enclose; encircle. **3.** To be enough for all to have some. — **to go at 1.** To attack. **2.** To work at. — **to go back on 1.** To be disloyal to; forsake. **2.** To fail to fulfill or abide by. — **to go behind** To inquire or investigate so as to test the validity of. — **to go beyond** To surpass; exceed. — **to go by 1.** To pass. **2.** To conform to or be guided by: to *go by* a decision, rules, etc. **3.** To be known by: What name does she *go by?* — **to go down 1.** To sink or descend. **2.** To experience defeat. **3.** To attain lasting remembrance as (something specified): to *go down* in history as a dictator. **4.** To decrease, as prices or values. — **to go for 1.** To reach for; try to get. **2.** To advocate. **3.** *Informal* To attack. **4.** *Informal* To be strongly attracted by; like. — **to go halves (or shares)** *Informal* To share on an equal basis. — **to go hard with** To bring trouble and unhappiness to. — **to go in for** *Informal* **1.** To strive for; advocate. **2.** To like or participate in. — **to go into 1.** To investigate. **2.** To take up, as an occupation. **3.** To be contained in: 4 *goes into* 12 three times. — **to go in with** To unite or join forces with. — **to go off 1.** To explode or be discharged, as a gun or dynamite. **2.** To depart; leave. **3.** *Informal* To come to pass or occur in some specified manner: The concert *went off* well. — **to go on 1.** To act; behave. **2.** To happen: What's *going on* here? **3.** To persevere; endure. **4.** To approach (a particular age or time); near: He is *going on* 40. **5.** *Informal* To chatter. **6.** To enter or appear on stage. **7.** To continue. — **to go one better than** *Informal* To surpass (someone) by a single degree or quality. — **to go out 1.** To go to social gatherings, places of entertainment, etc. **2.** To be extinguished, as a light. **3.** To become obsolete or outdated, as fashions in dress. **4.** To strike: The union *went out* for higher wages. **5.** To be drawn forth in sympathy: My heart *goes out* to him. — **to go over 1.** To rehearse; repeat. **2.** To examine carefully. **3.** *Informal* To succeed. **4.** To be changed into another form: Ice *goes over* to water quickly. **5.** To change sides or allegiance. — **to go through 1.** To search or inspect thoroughly. **2.** To undergo; suffer; endure. **3.** To run over, as a part or role. **4.** To spend or use up completely. **5.** To be accepted or approved, as a plan, application, etc. — **to go through with** To perform to the finish; complete. — **to go together 1.** To be suitable; harmonize. **2.** To keep company, as sweethearts. — **to go under 1.** To be overwhelmed or conquered. **2.** To fail, as a business. — **to go up** To increase, as prices or values. — **to go with 1.** To be suitable to; harmonize with. **2.** To accompany. **3.** *Informal* To keep company, as sweethearts. — **to go without** To do or be without. — **to go without saying** To be taken for granted; be self-evident. — **to let go 1.** To release one's hold; set free. **2.** To abandon one's interest or share in. — **to let oneself go** To be or become uninhibited in actions, expression of feelings, etc. — *n.* **1.** The act of going. **2.** *Informal* The capacity for energetic action; vigor: He has plenty of *go.* **3.** *Informal* A try; attempt: to have a *go* at something. **4.** *Informal* A success: He made a *go* of it. **5.** *Informal* An agreement; bargain: It's a *go.* — **no go** *Informal* Useless; hopeless; also, something that is useless or hopeless. — **on the go** *Informal* In constant motion; very busy. [OE *gān*]
go² (gō) *n.* A Japanese game resembling chess or checkers, played with round black and white counters on a board marked in squares. [< Japanese]
GO *Mil.* General Order.
go·a (gō′ə) *n.* A black-tailed gazelle (*Procapra picticaudata*) of the mountains of Tibet. [< Tibetan *dgoba*]
Go·a (gō′ə) A district of the former Portuguese India, on the west coast of India; annexed by India in 1961; 1,394 sq. mi.; pop. 551,064 (est. 1956); capital, New Goa. Portuguese **Gô′a.** See map of INDIA.
goad (gōd) *n.* **1.** A pointed stick for urging on oxen or other beasts. **2.** Something that spurs or drives. — *v.t.* To prick or drive with or as with a goad; incite. [OE *gād*]
go·a·head (gō′ə·hed′) *n.* A signal or permission to move ahead or proceed: to get the *go-ahead.* — *adj.* **1.** Moving forward; advancing. **2.** Aggressively pushing forward.
goal (gōl) *n.* **1.** Something toward which effort or movement is directed; an end or objective. **2.** The terminal point of a journey or race. **3.** In some games, as football or hockey, the point or structure to which the players try to bring the ball, puck, etc., so as to score; also, the advancement of the ball, puck, etc., to this point; also, the score made by doing this. — **Syn.** See PURPOSE. [ME *gol*; origin uncertain]

goal·ie (gō′lē) *n.* *Informal* A goalkeeper.
goal·keep·er (gōl′kē′pər) *n.* In hockey, soccer, etc., a player whose special function is to prevent the ball or puck from passing over, into, or through the goal for a score. Also **goal/tend′er.** Abbr. *g*, *g.*
goal line A line, as at either end of a football field, that marks the goal.
goal post One of two posts joined by a crosspiece and set at each end of a football or soccer field to form the goal.
goat (gōt) *n.* **1.** A hollow-horned ruminant (genus *Capra*) related to the sheep and found wild or domesticated in all parts of the world. ♦ Collateral adjectives: *hircine; capric.* **2.** The Rocky Mountain goat. **3.** A lecherous man. **4.** *Slang* One who is the butt of a joke or on whom blame is placed; scapegoat. — **to get one's goat** *Slang* To move one to anger or annoyance. [OE *gāt*]
Goat (gōt) *n.* The constellation and sign of the zodiac Capricorn.
goat antelope Any of certain ruminant mammals related to the goats, as the chamois or Rocky Mountain goat.
goat·ee (gō·tē′) *n.* A man's beard trimmed short to a pointed end below the chin.
goat·fish (gōt′fish′) *n.* *pl.* **·fish** or **·fish·es** Any tropical marine fish (family *Mullidae*), usually red or golden in color, with two barbels hanging from the chin: also called *red mullet, surmullet.*
goat-god (gōt′god′) *n.* The god Pan.
goat·herd (gōt′hûrd′) *n.* One who tends goats.
goat·ish (gō′tish) *adj.* **1.** Pertaining to or suggestive of a goat. **2.** Lustful. — **goat′ish·ly** *adv.* — **goat′ish·ness** *n.*
Goat Island An island in the Niagara River, dividing Niagara Falls into American Falls and Horseshoe Falls.
goats·beard (gōts′bird′) *n.* **1.** A European salsify (*Tragopogon pratensis*) having long, feathery pappus, naturalized in the United States: also called *Joseph flower.* **2.** A perennial herb of the rose family (*Aruncus sylvester*) with long compound panicles of whitish flowers in slender spikes and slender, toothed leaves. Also **goat′beard′, goat's′-beard′.**
goat·skin (gōt′skin′) *n.* **1.** The hide of a goat. **2.** Leather made from the hide of a goat. **3.** Something made from this leather, as a container for wine or an article of apparel.
goat's-rue (gōts′rōō′) *n.* **1.** A hardy perennial herb (*Galega officinalis*) of the Old World. **2.** An American herb (*Tephrosia virginiana*) of the pea family.
goat·suck·er (gōt′suk′ər) *n.* **1.** Any of numerous nocturnal, insectivorous birds (family *Caprimulgidae*) with flattened heads and wide mouths, as the whippoorwill or nighthawk. **2.** The frogmouth (def. 1).
gob¹ (gob) *n.* *Informal* **1.** A piece, mass, or lump, as of a soft or viscous substance. **2.** *pl.* Great quantities; lots: *gobs* of money. [< OF *gobe* mouthful, lump, ? < Celtic]
gob² (gob) *n.* *Slang* A sailor of the U.S. Navy. [Origin uncertain]
gob·bet (gob′it) *n.* **1.** A piece or hunk of raw meat. **2.** *Archaic* A large lump or mass of food. **3.** *Obs.* Any lump, piece, or fragment. [< F *gobet*, dim. of *gobe.* See GOB¹.]
gob·ble¹ (gob′əl) *v.* **·bled, ·bling** *v.t.* **1.** To swallow (food) greedily and in gulps. **2.** *U.S. Slang* To seize or acquire in a grasping manner. — *v.i.* **3.** To eat greedily and quickly. [< F *gover* to bolt, devour]
gob·ble² (gob′əl) *v.i.* **·bled, ·bling** To make the throaty sound of a male turkey. — *n.* This sound. [Var. of GABBLE.]
gob·ble·dy·gook (gob′əl·dē·gōōk′) *n.* *Informal* Pedantic, repetitious, and pompous jargon. Also **gob′ble·de·gook′.** [Coined by M. Maverick, U.S. Congressman, about 1940]
gob·bler (gob′lər) *n.* A male turkey.
Gob·e·lin (gob′ə·lin, gō′bə-; *Fr.* gô·blaň′) *n.* A rich tapestry typically having a colorful, pictorial design, made in Paris or Beauvais, France. [after *Gobelin*, name of the family that began producing the tapestry in the 15th century]
go-be·tween (gō′bə·twēn′) *n.* One who acts as an agent or mediator between other persons in business matters, intrigue, etc.; intermediary.
Go·bi (gō′bē) A desert in central Asia; 500,000 sq. mi.: Chinese *Ham Hai.* Also **Gobi Desert.**
go·bi·oid (gō′bē·oid) *adj.* Of, like, or related to the gobies. *n.* A gobioid fish.
gob·let (gob′lit) *n.* **1.** A drinking vessel, typically of glass, with a base and stem and usually no handles. **2.** A large, shallow drinking cup formerly used on festive occasions. [< OF *gobelet*, dim. of *gobel* a drinking cup < Celtic]
gob·lin (gob′lin) *n.* In folklore, a misshapen, ugly, elflike being regarded as malevolent or mischievous. [< OF *gobelin* < Med.L *gobelinus*, ? < Gk. *kobalos* rogue]
go·bo (gō′bō) *n.* *pl.* **·bos 1.** A portable shield placed around a microphone to keep out extraneous sounds. **2.** A screen for shielding the lens of a television camera from the direct rays of light. [Origin uncertain]
go·by (gō′bē) *n.* *pl.* **·by** or **·bies** Any of a widely distributed family (*Gobiidae*) of spiny-rayed, fresh-water and tropical marine fishes having ventral fins united into a funnel-shaped suction disk. [< L *gobius* < Gk. *kōbios*, a small fish]
go-by (gō′bī′) *n.* *Informal* An intentional ignoring, disregard, or slight.

go-cart (gō′kärt′) *n.* **1.** A small wagon or similar vehicle designed for young children to ride in or pull. **2.** A light framework with rollers or small wheels, designed to support babies learning to walk. **3.** A handcart. **4.** A light carriage. **5.** See GO-KART.

god (god) *n.* **1.** One of various beings, usually male, in mythology, primitive religions, etc., conceived of as immortal, as embodying a particular quality or principle, as personifying or controlling a particular element or phenomenon of nature, or as having special powers or influence over some phase of life. **2.** A statue, image, or symbol of such a being. **3.** Any person or thing made the chief object of one's love, interest, or aspiration: Money is his *god*. [OE]

God (god) *n.* **1.** In monotheism, the self-existent and eternal creator, sustainer, and ruler of life and the universe. **2.** This Being regarded as the source or embodiment of some specific attribute, principle, virtue, etc.: *God* of justice. **3.** In Christian Science, the divine, creative Principle; Life, Truth, and Love; Mind; Spirit.

Go·da·va·ri (gō-dä′və-rē) A river in central India, flowing about 900 miles, generally SE, to the Bay of Bengal.

god·child (god′chīld′) *n. pl.* **·chil·dren** One whom a person sponsors at baptism, circumcision, etc.

god·damn (god′dam′) *interj.* A strong oath used to express anger, annoyance, surprise, etc. Also **God damn.** — *adj. & adv.* Goddamned: also **god·dam** (god′dam′, -dam′).

god·damned (god′damd′) *adj.* Utterly detestable or outrageous. — *adv. Informal* To an extreme degree; very: *goddamned* wonderful.

God·dard (god′ərd), **Henry Herbert,** 1866–1957, U.S. psychologist.

god·daugh·ter (god′dô′tər) *n.* A female godchild.

god·dess (god′is) **1.** A female deity. **2.** A woman or girl of extraordinary beauty.

Go·des·berg (gō′dəs-berkh) A resort town in West Germany, on the Rhine; pop. 65,600 (est. 1960). Also **Bad Godesberg** (bät).

go·dev·il (gō′dev′əl) *n. U.S.* **1.** A dray sled for hauling rocks, logs, etc. **2.** A pointed iron weight dropped into the bore of an oil well to explode the charge of dynamite. **3.** A railroad handcar used by work gangs. **4.** A jointed, flexible device for cleaning a pipeline of obstructions.

god·fa·ther (god′fä′thər) *n.* A man who sponsors a child at its baptism. — *v.t.* To act as a godfather to.

god-fear·ing (god′fir′ing) *adj.* **1.** *Often cap.* Having reverence for God. **2.** Pious; devout.

god·for·sak·en (god′fər-sā′kən) *adj.* **1.** *Often cap.* Abandoned by God. **2.** Totally wicked or depraved: *godforsaken* murderers. **3.** Wretched; desolate: a *godforsaken* town.

God·frey of Bouil·lon (god′frē; bōō-yôṅ′), 1061?–1100, duke of Lower Lorraine, a leader of the first crusade 1096–1100. Also **Godefroy de Bouillon.**

god·head (god′hed′) *n.* Godhood; divinity.

God·head (god′hed′) *n.* The essential nature of God; the Deity.

god·hood (god′hŏŏd) *n.* The state or quality of being divine.

Go·di·va (gə-dī′və) A legendary eleventh-century English lady, wife of the Earl of Mercia, who fulfilled an agreement with her husband to ride naked through Coventry if he would remove oppressive taxes.

god·less (god′lis) *adj.* **1.** Having or believing in no god. **2.** Wicked. — **god′less·ly** *adv.* — **god′less·ness** *n.*

god·like (god′līk′) *adj.* **1.** Befitting or like God or a god. **2.** Being of supreme excellence, beauty, etc. — **god′like′ness** *n.*

god·ling (god′ling) *n.* A minor deity.

god·ly (god′lē) *adj.* **·li·er, ·li·est** **1.** Filled with reverence and love for God; pious. **2.** *Archaic* Belonging to or emanating from God. — **god′li·ly** *adv.* — **god′li·ness** *n.*

god·moth·er (god′muth′ər) *n.* A woman who sponsors a child at its baptism. — *v.t.* To act as a godmother to.

Go·dol·phin (gō-dol′fin), **Sidney,** 1645–1712, first Earl of Godolphin, English statesman.

go·down (gō-doun′) *n.* In China and the East Indies, a warehouse. [< Malay *godong* warehouse]

Go·doy (gō-thoi′), **Manuel de,** 1767–1851, Spanish statesman.

god·par·ent (god′pâr′ənt) *n.* A godfather or godmother.

go·droon (gə-drōōn′) See GADROON.

God's acre A burying ground.

God's country *U.S.* Any healthful, beautiful region.

god·send (god′send′) *n.* **1.** Something received or acquired unexpectedly that is just what one needed or wanted. **2.** Something most welcome that happens by a stroke of good luck. [Earlier *God's send* < GOD + ME *sande* message]

god·ship (god′ship) *n.* The rank or character of a god.

god·son (god′sun′) *n.* A male godchild.

God·speed (god′spēd′) *n.* An expression of one's best wishes for someone's quick and successful termination of a journey or venture. [Shortened form of *God speed you*]

Go·du·nov (gô-dōō-nôf′), **Boris Fyodorovich,** 1552?–1605, czar of Russia 1598–1605.

God·ward (god′wərd) *adv.* Toward or in reference to God. — *adj.* Directed toward or having reference to God. Also **God′wards.**

Godwin (god′win), **Mary Wollstonecraft,** 1759–97, English writer; wife of William Godwin and mother of Mary Wollstonecraft Shelley. — **William,** 1756–1836, English political philosopher and writer.

God·win Aus·ten (god′win ôs′tin) See K2.

god·wit (god′wit) *n.* A shore bird (genus *Limosa*) resembling a curlew, with long legs and a long bill that tilts up.

Goeb·bels (gœb′əls), **Joseph Paul,** 1897–1945, German Nazi politician and minister of propaganda 1933–45.

go·er (gō′ər) *n.* A person or thing that goes or attends: often used in combination, as in *partygoer, filmgoer*.

Goe·ring (gœ′ring), **Hermann Wilhelm,** 1893–1946, German Nazi politician and head of the Luftwaffe. Also **Göring.**

Goe·thals (gō′thəlz), **George Washington,** 1858–1928, U.S. army engineer; builder of the Panama Canal.

Goethe (gœ′tə), **Johann Wolfgang von,** 1749–1832, German poet, dramatist, and novelist.

goe·thite (gō′thīt, gœ′tīt) *n.* An imperfect, adamantine, reddish or blackish brown ferric hydroxide, crystallizing in the orthorhombic system: also spelled *göthite*. [after *Goethe*]

gof·fer (gof′ər, gôf′-) *n.* **1.** A fluted or crimped ornamentation, as along the edge of a fabric. Also **gof′fer·ing.** **2.** An iron or press used in fluting or crimping. — *v.t.* To make fluted or crimped ornamentations in. Also spelled *gauffer*. [< F *gaufrer* to crimp cloth < *gaufre* honeycomb]

Gog (gog) **and Magog** (mā′gog) In Biblical prophecy, the nations, led by Satan, that will war against the kingdom of God. *Rev.* xx 8.

go-get·ter (gō′get′ər) *n. U.S. Informal* A hustling, energetic, aggressive person.

gog·gle (gog′əl) *n.* **1.** *pl.* Spectacles designed to protect the eyes against dust, sparks, wind, etc. **2.** An erratically circular or sidewise movement of the eyes; fixed staring or apparent bulging of the eyeballs. — *v.* **·gled, ·gling** *v.i.* **1.** To roll the eyes erratically. **2.** Of the eyes, to move erratically, bulge, or be fixed in a stare. — *v.t.* **3.** To cause (the eyes) to goggle. — *adj.* Of the eyes, rolling erratically, staring, or bulging. [ME *gogelen* to look aside]

gog·gle-eyed (gog′əl-īd′) *adj.* Having eyes that goggle.

Gogh (gō, gôk; *Du.* khôkh), **Vincent van** See VAN GOGH.

gog·let (gog′lit) *n.* A long-necked jar of porous earthenware used to keep water cool by evaporation: also called *gurglet*. [< Pg. *gorgoleta*]

go-go girl (gō′gō′) A scantily clad girl who performs provocative variations of the twist in a discothèque, cabaret, etc., usually alone on a stage or platform. Also **go-go dancer.**

Go·gol (gō′gəl, *Russian* gô′gôl), **Nikolai Vasilievich,** 1809–1852, Russian novelist, short-story writer, and dramatist.

Goi·del·ic (goi-del′ik) *n.* The branch of the Celtic languages including Irish, the Gaelic of the Scottish Highlands, and Manx; Gaelic: distinguished from *Brythonic.* — *adj.* Of or pertaining to the Gaels or their languages. Also **Goi·dhel′ic.** [< OIrish *Góidel* Gael]

go·ing (gō′ing) *n.* **1.** The act of departing or moving; leaving. **2.** The condition of ground or roads as affecting walking, riding, racing, etc.: It's bad *going*. **3.** *Informal* A particular condition influencing progress or activity: Adolescence is often rough *going*. — **goings on** *Informal* Actions or behavior: used chiefly to express disapproval. — *adj.* **1.** That goes, moves, or works. **2.** Continuing to function: a *going* concern. **3.** Resulting from continued operation: the *going* value of a business. **4.** In existence. **5.** Departing.

goi·ter (goi′tər) *n. Pathol.* Any of various abnormal enlargements of the thyroid gland, visible as a swelling in the front of the neck: also called *struma.* Also **goi′tre.** [< F, back formation < *goitreux*, ult. < L *guttur* throat]

goi·trous (goi′trəs) *adj.* **1.** Pertaining to, of the nature of, or affected with goiter. **2.** Denoting a locality where goiter is prevalent.

go-kart (gō′kärt′) *n. U.S.* A racing vehicle consisting of a bare chassis on small wheels and driven by a low-powered gasoline engine: also spelled *go-cart.*

Gol·con·da (gol-kon′də) *n.* A mine or other source of wealth. Also **gol·con′da.** [after *Golconda*, India]

Gol·con·da (gol-kon′də) A ruined city near Hyderabad, India.

gold (gōld) *n.* **1.** A precious, yellow, metallic element (symbol Au) that is highly ductile, malleable, and resistant to oxidation: also called *aurum*. See ELEMENT. **2.** Coin made of this metal. **3.** Wealth; riches. **4.** A bright yellow color. **5.** Something having the value, beauty, etc., of gold: a heart of *gold*. — *adj.* **1.** Pertaining to, made of, or containing gold. **2.** Producing gold: a *gold* mine. **3.** Resembling gold, as in color. **4.** Based on or redeemable in gold. [OE]

gold basis The gold standard (which see).

gold·beat·er's skin (gōld′bēt′ərz) The outer membrane of the large intestine of an ox, used by goldbeaters to separate sheets of gold while beating them into gold leaf.

gold·beat·ing (gōld'bē'ting) n. The act or operation of hammering sheets of gold into gold leaf. — **gold'beat'er** n.

gold beetle Any of certain beetles (family *Chrysomelidae*) having a metallic luster; especially, a leaf beetle (*Coptocycla bicolor*) found on the sweet potato.

Gold·berg (gōld'bûrg), **Arthur Joseph**, born 1908, U.S. Secretary of Labor 1961–62; associate justice of the Supreme Court 1962–65; U.S. ambassador to the UN 1965–68.

gold·brick (gōld'brik') U.S. *Slang* n. One who shirks work: said especially of soldiers. Also **gold'brick'er**. — v.t. & v.i. 1. To shirk (work or duty). 2. To cheat or swindle.

gold brick *Informal* 1. A brick or bar of cheap metal gilded to resemble gold, as for purposes of swindling. 2. Anything deceitfully substituted for an object of value.

gold·bug (gōld'bug') n. A gold beetle.

gold certificate 1. A piece of U.S. paper currency used only within the Federal Reserve System to transfer balances. 2. Formerly, a U.S. Treasury note, redeemable in gold.

Gold Coast 1. A section of the African shoreline on the Gulf of Guinea between the Ivory Coast and the Slave Coast. 2. *Informal* A residential or resort district frequented by rich people.

Gold Coast Colony A former British colony on the Gold Coast. See GHANA.

gold digger 1. One who or that which digs for gold. 2. *U.S. Slang* A woman who uses feminine wiles to get money and gifts from men.

gold dust Gold in the form of powder or fine particles.

gold·en (gōl'dən) adj. 1. Made of or containing gold. 2. Having the color or luster of gold; bright yellow. 3. Resembling gold, as in value. 4. Characterized by happiness, prosperity, etc. — **gold'en·ly** adv. — **gold'en·ness** n.

golden age 1. In Greek and Roman legend, an early period of civilization marked by perfect innocence, peace, and happiness. 2. A period of prosperity or excellence, as in a nation's history, art, literature, etc.

golden anniversary A 50th anniversary.

golden aster A North American perennial (genus *Chrysopsis*) of the composite family, with yellow-rayed flowers.

golden bantam corn A type of sweet corn with tender, plump, yellow kernels.

golden bough In the folklore and mythology of many cultures, the mistletoe.

golden buck Welsh rabbit served with a poached egg.

golden calf 1. A molten image made by Aaron and worshiped by the Israelites. *Ex.* xxxii. 2. Riches, as unduly prized; mammon: preceded by *the*.

golden eagle See under EAGLE.

gold·en·eye (gōl'dən·ī') n. A large diving duck (*Bucephala clangula*) of America and Europe having a blackish green back, white breast, and bright yellow eyes.

Golden Fleece In Greek legend, the fleece of gold guarded by a dragon in the sacred grove of Colchis, recovered by Jason and the Argonauts with Medea's help. See PHRIXUS.

Golden Gate A strait, about 2 miles wide, leading from the Pacific Ocean to San Francisco Bay.

golden glow A common garden plant (*Rudbeckia laciniata*) of the composite family, having tall stems and many-rayed yellow flowers.

golden goose In folklore, a goose that each day laid a golden egg and was finally killed by its owner who wanted all the gold at once.

Golden Horde A fierce and powerful Mongol horde who laid waste to eastern Europe in the 13th century: named from the golden tent of their leader, Batu Khan.

Golden Horn The crescent-shaped inlet of the Bosporus that forms the harbor of Istanbul, Turkey.

Golden Legend The name given by Caxton to his English translation, published in 1483, of a collection of lives of saints written originally in Latin by Jacobus de Voragine: also called *Legenda Aurea*.

golden mean Moderation, as in eating or drinking; avoidance of extremes. [Trans. of L *aurea mediocritas*]

golden pheasant A vividly colored pheasant (*Chrysolophus pictus*) of China and Tibet.

golden plover See under PLOVER.

golden robin The Baltimore oriole.

gold·en·rod (gōl'dən·rod') n. A widely distributed North American herb (genus *Solidago*) of the composite family, having small, usually yellow flowers: the State flower of Alabama, Kentucky, and Nebraska.

golden rule The rule or principle of treating others as one wants to be treated. *Matt.* vii 12.

gold·en·seal (gōl'dən·sēl') n. 1. An herb (*Hydrastis canadensis*) of the United States, with a yellow rootstock, a single radical leaf, a hairy stem, and a single greenish white flower. 2. The rootstock of this plant, the source of hydrastine.

golden section In esthetics, the division of a line or figure so that the smaller length is to the larger as the larger is to the whole, roughly a ratio of 3 to 5.

Golden State Nickname of CALIFORNIA.

golden wattle A plant (genus *Acacia*) related to the mimosa and having yellow flowers; especially, *A. pycantha*, widely distributed in Australia.

golden wedding The 50th anniversary of a marriage.

gold·en-winged warbler (gōl'dən-wingd') A North American warbler with yellow wings (*Vermivora chrysoptera*).

golden-winged woodpecker Flicker[2].

gold-ex·change standard (gōld'iks-chānj') A monetary system by which the currency of one country is kept at par with the currency of another country that maintains a gold standard.

gold·eye (gōld'dī) n. A small fresh-water fish (*Amphiodon alosoides*) of western and northern North America: also called *Winnipeg goldeye*.

gold-filled (gōld'fild') adj. Filled with a base metal over which a thick covering of gold is laid.

gold·finch (gōld'finch') n. 1. A European finch (genus *Carduelis*) having a crimson face, a black hood, and a yellow patch on each wing: also called *redcap*. 2. An American finch (*Spinus tristis*) of which the male, in the summer, has a yellow body with black tail.

gold·fin·ny (gōld'fin'ē) n. pl. ·nies A bright-colored European wrasse (genus *Centrolabrus*).

gold·fish (gōld'fish') n. pl. ·fish or ·fish·es A small carp (genus *Carassius*), usually golden in color, originally of China, now cultivated as an ornamental aquarium fish.

gold foil Thin sheets of gold, thicker than gold leaf.

gold·i·locks (gōl'dē-loks') n. 1. A European herb (*Linosyrus vulgaris*) of the composite family, with yellow flower heads. 2. A person with light blond hair.

gold leaf Sheets of gold hammered to extreme thinness.

Gold·mark (gōld'märk), **Karl**, 1830–1915, Hungarian composer.

gold mine 1. A mine producing gold ore. 2. *Informal* Any source of great profit, riches, etc.

gold note A gold certificate (def. 2).

gold-of-pleas·ure (gōld'əv-plezh'ər) n. An erect annual herb (*Camelina sativa*) of the mustard family, with long, lanceolate leaves, small, numerous flowers, and pear-shaped pods, naturalized from Europe: also called *false flax*.

Gol·do·ni (gōl-dō'nē), **Carlo**, 1707–93, Italian dramatist.

gold plate Vessels and utensils of gold, collectively.

gold point 1. *Econ.* That point in the rate of foreign exchange at which bullion can be shipped in payment of accounts without entailing a loss. 2. *Physics* The melting point of gold, 1063° C.: used as a reference temperature.

gold reserve 1. Gold held in reserve by the U.S. Treasury to protect and formerly to redeem U.S. notes. 2. The gold bullion or coin owned by the central bank of a country.

gold rush A mass movement of people to an area where gold has been discovered, as that to California in 1849.

Golds·bo·ro (gōldz'bûr'ō, -bûr'ə) A city in east central North Carolina; pop. 31,111.

gold·smith (gōld'smith') n. One who makes or deals in articles of gold.

Gold·smith (gōld'smith'), **Oliver**, 1728–74, British poet, novelist, and dramatist.

goldsmith beetle 1. A large European scarabaeid beetle (*Cetonia aurata*) of a brilliant golden color. 2. A bright yellow American beetle (*Cotalpa lanigera*).

gold standard A monetary system based on gold of a specified weight and fineness as the unit of value.

gold-star mother (gōld'stär') A mother of a member of the U.S. armed forces killed in action during wartime.

gold stick An official of the British royal household who attends the sovereign on state occasions; also, the gilt rod he carries as an emblem of office.

gold·stone (gōld'stōn') n. Aventurine glass having numerous gold specks that give it a jeweled appearance.

gold·thread (gōld'thred') n. 1. A North American evergreen herb (*Coptis groenlandica*) of the crowfoot family, with long, bright yellow, fibrous roots. 2. The roots of this plant, sometimes used in medicine.

Gold·wyn (gōld'win), **Samuel**, born 1882, U.S. motion-picture producer born in Poland.

go·lem (gō'lem, -ləm) n. In medieval Jewish legend, an automaton made to resemble a human being and given life by a magic incantation. [< Hebrew, embryo, monster]

golf (golf, gôlf) n. An outdoor game played on a large course with a small resilient ball and a set of clubs, the object being to direct the ball into a series of variously distributed holes (usually nine or eighteen) in as few strokes as possible. — v.i. 1. To play golf. — v.t. 2. To hit into the air, as if with a golf club. [Cf. dial. E (Scot.) *gowf* strike] — **golf'er** n.

golf club 1. One of several slender clubs with wooden or metal heads, used in playing golf. 2. An organization of golfers; also, the building and grounds used by them.

golf course The course over which a game of golf is played. Also **golf links**.

Gol·fo de Ca·li·for·nia (gôl'fō thä kä'lē-fôr'nyä) The Spanish name for the (Gulf of) CALIFORNIA.

GOLDEN SECTION
Square *ABIG* is constructed on line *AB*; *AG* is bisected at *C*, whereby *CB* = *CD*, and square *DEFA* is constructed. Thus $DA:AG::AG:DG$.

Gol·gi body (gôl′jē) *Biol.* A netlike structure of rod-shaped elements found in the cytoplasm of animal cells. Also **Golgi apparatus.** [after Camillo *Golgi*, 1844–1926, Italian pathologist, who discovered it]

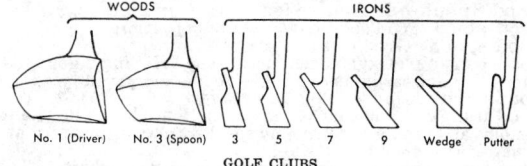

GOLF CLUBS

gol·go·tha (gol′gə-thə) *n.* **1.** A burial place. **2.** Any place of torment or sacrifice. [after *Golgotha*]

Gol·go·tha (gol′gə-thə) A place near Jerusalem where Jesus was crucified; Calvary. *Matt.* xxvii 33. [< LL < Gk. < Aramaic *gogolthā* skull < Hebrew *gulgōleth*]

gol·iard (gōl′yərd) *n.* One of a class of wandering students of the late Middle Ages in Europe who wrote and sang Latin satirical verses and songs. [< OF, glutton < *gole* gluttony < L *gula* throat] — **gol·iar·dic** (gōl·yär′dik) *adj.*

gol·iar·der·y (gōl·yär′dər-ē) *n.* The poetry of the goliards.

Go·li·ath (gə-lī′əth) In the Bible, a giant Philistine slain by David with a sling. I *Sam.* xvii 4.

goliath beetle Any of a genus (*Goliathus*) of very large African beetles; especially, *G. goliathus*, the male of which may attain a length of five and a wingspread of eight inches.

gol·li·wog (gol′ē-wog) *n.* **1.** A grotesque black doll. **2.** A grotesque person. Also **gol′li·wogg.** [after illustrations by Florence Upton (1895) for a series of children's books]

gol·ly (gol′ē) *interj.* An exclamation of mild surprise, impatience, etc. [Euphemistic alter. of GOD]

go·losh (gə-losh′) See GALOSH.

Goltz (gôlts), **Baron Kolmar von der**, 1843–1916, German field marshal in World War I.

gom·bo (gum′bō) See GUMBO.

gom·broon (gom·broon′) *n.* A Persian pottery of semi-transparent white. [after a town on the Persian Gulf]

gom·er·al (gom′ər-əl) *n. Scot.* A fool; dolt. Also **gom′er·el, gom′er·il.**

Gó·mez (gō′mes), **Juan Vicente**, 1857?–1935, Venezuelan general; chief of state 1908–35.

Go·mor·rah (gə-môr′ə, -mor′ə), **Go·mor·rha** See SODOM.

Gom·pers (gom′pərz), **Samuel**, 1850–1924, U.S. labor leader.

gom·pho·sis (gom-fō′sis) *n. Anat.* An articulation or union made by the firm implantation of a hard part, as bone, into a socket or cavity, as the setting of teeth in the jaw. [< NL < Gk. < *gomphos* bolt]

go·mu·ti (gō-moō′tē) *n.* **1.** A feather palm (*Arenga pinnata*) of Malaya, a source of palm sugar. **2.** A durable, black, hairlike fiber obtained from this palm, valuable as water-resistant cordage. [< Malay *gumuti*]

Go·myel (gō′myily′) A city in the SE Byelorussian S.S.R.; pop. 272,000 (est. 1970). Also **Go′mel.**

gon- Var. of GONO-.

-gon *combining form* Having (an indicated number of) angles: *pentagon*. [< Gk. *gōnia* angle]

gon·ad (gō′nad, gon′ad) *n. Anat.* A male or female sex gland, in which the reproductive cells develop; an ovary or testis. [< GON- + -AD[1]] — **gon′a·dal, go·na·di·al** (gō-nā′dē-əl), **go·nad·ic** (gō-nad′ik) *adj.*

gon·a·do·trop·ic (gon′ə-dō-trop′ik, gə-nad′ə-) *adj. Biochem.* Pertaining to or designating certain substances, especially one derived from the pituitary gland, that stimulate or nourish the gonads. Also **go·na·do·troph′ic** (-trof′ik).

Gon·court (gôⁿ·koor′), **Edmond Louis Antoine Huot de**, 1822–96, and his brother, **Jules Alfred Huot de**, 1830–70, French novelists.

Gond (gond) *n.* A Dravidian of central India.

Gon·dar (gon′dər) A city in NW Ethiopia; pop. about 13,000.

Gon·di (gon′dē) *n.* The Dravidian language of the Gonds.

gon·do·la (gon′də-lə, gon-dō′lə) *n.* **1.** A long, narrow, flat-bottomed Venetian boat having high points at the ends, propelled by one man with an oar or pole at the stern. **2.** *U.S.* A large, flat-bottomed, river boat; also, a gondola car. **3.** *Canadian Informal* A broadcasting booth commanding a view of an arena, stadium, etc. **4.** *Aeron.* The car attached below a dirigible balloon. [< Ital *gondola* to rock]

gondola car *U.S.* A long, shallow, open freight car.

gon·do·lier (gon′də-lir′) *n.* The boatman of a gondola.

Gond·wa·na (gond·wä′nə) *Geol.* A hypothetical land mass

GONDOLAS

a Venetian. *b* Railroad. *c* Dirigible.

of the Paleozoic and early Mesozoic eras, believed to have extended eastward from South America to Africa and thence across the Indian Ocean to India and Australia. Also **Gond·wa′na·land′.** [after a region in central India]

gone (gôn, gon) Past participle of GO. — *adj.* **1.** Moved away; left. **2.** Beyond hope; ruined; lost. **3.** Dead; departed. **4.** Ended; past. **5.** Marked by faintness or weakness. **6.** Consumed; spent. **7.** *U.S. Slang* Causing, feeling, or expressing intense satisfaction; ecstatic. — **far gone 1.** Exhausted; wearied. **2.** Greatly involved. **3.** Almost ended or dead. — **gone on** *Informal* In love with.

gone·ness (gôn′nis, gon′-) *n.* A state or feeling of weakness or exhaustion.

gon·er (gôn′ər, gon′-) *n. Informal* A person or thing that is close to death, ruined, or beyond all hope of saving.

Gon·er·il (gon′ər-əl) In Shakespeare's *King Lear*, one of the two ungrateful daughters of Lear.

gon·fa·lon (gon′fə-lən) *n.* A banner or ensign fixed to a crosspiece rather than to a pole, usually cut so as to end in streamers; especially, such a banner used by medieval Italian republics. Also **gon·fa·non** (gon′fə-nən). [< Ital. *gonfalone* < OHG *gundfano* war banner]

gon·fa·lon·ier (gon′fə-lə-nir′) *n.* **1.** One who carries a gonfalon. **2.** The title of a magistrate or other high official in several Italian medieval and Renaissance republics.

gong (gông, gong) *n.* **1.** A heavy metal disk giving a deep, resonant tone when struck. **2.** A flat, saucerlike bell struck with a small mechanical hammer. [< Malay]

Gon·gor·ism (gong′gə-riz′əm) *n.* **1.** An artificially elegant style of speech or writing; especially, an ornate literary style cultivated by imitators of the Spanish poet **Luis de Góngo·ra y Ar·go·te** (gông′gō-rä ē är-gō′tä), 1561–1627. **2.** An instance of the use of this style. Compare EUPHUISM.

go·nid·i·um (gō-nid′ē-əm) *n. pl.* **-nid·i·a** (-nid′ē-ə) *Bot.* **1.** In algae, a naked or membranous-coated propagative cell produced asexually. **2.** In mosses, a cell filled with green granules. **3.** In lichens, one of the green algal cells of a thallus. [< NL, dim. of Gk. *gonos* seed] — **go·nid′i·al** *adj.*

gonio- *combining form* Angle; corner: *goniometry.* [< Gk. *gōnia* angle, corner]

go·ni·om·e·ter (gō′nē-om′ə-tər) *n.* **1.** An instrument for measuring angles, either by direct contact or by utilizing beams of light. **2.** A device used in aeronautical navigation systems to change the directional characteristics of a radio antenna. — **go·ni·o·met·ric** (gō′nē-ə-met′rik) or **-ri·cal** *adj.*

go·ni·om·e·try (gō′nē-om′ə-trē) *n.* The measurement of angles.

go·ni·on (gō′nē-on) *n. pl.* **-ni·a** (-nē-ə) *Anat.* The tip of the angle on either side of the lower jaw. [< NL < Gk. *gōnia* angle]

-gonium *combining form* Reproductive cell; seed: *sporogonium.* [< Gk. *gonos* seed]

gono- *combining form* Procreative; sexual: *gonophore.* Also, before vowels, **gon-.** [< Gk. *gonos* seed]

gon·o·coc·cus (gon′ə-kok′əs) *n. pl.* **-coc·ci** (-kok′sī) The parasitic bacterium (*Neisseria gonorrheae*) that causes gonorrhea. [< NL. See GONO-, COCCUS.]

gon·o·cyte (gon′ə-sīt) *n. Biol.* An oocyte or spermatocyte.

gon·of (gon′əf), **gon·oph** See GANEF.

gon·o·phore (gon′ə-fôr, -fōr) *n.* **1.** *Bot.* An elongation of the axis of a flower, lifting the stamens and pistil high above the floral envelopes. **2.** *Zool.* A reproductive bud that gives rise to a medusa.

gon·or·rhe·a (gon′ə-rē′ə) *n. Pathol.* A contagious venereal infection, caused by the gonococcus, in which there is a purulent inflammation of the mucous membranes of the genitourinary tract. Also **gon′or·rhoe′a.** [< LL < Gk. *gonorrhoia* < *gonos* seed + *rheein* to flow] — **gon′or·rhe′al** *adj.*

-gony *combining form* Production of; generation: *cosmogony.* [< L *-gonia* < Gk. *< gonos* seed, reproduction. Cf. -GENY.]

Gon·za·ga (gon-tsä′gä) An Italian noble family of Mantua, notably **Federigo**, 1500–40, and his brothers, **Ercole**, 1505–1563, and **Ferrante**, 1507–57, dukes of Mantua; **Luigi**, 1568–1591, Jesuit philosopher, canonized as **Saint Aloysius**.

Gon·za·lez-Vi·de·la (gōn-sä′läs-bē-thä′lä), **Gabriel**, born 1898, Chilean statesman; president 1946–52.

goo (goō) *n. U.S. Slang* Any sticky substance. [? < BURGOO]

goo·ber (goō′bər) *n. U.S.* A peanut. Also **goober pea.** [? < Bantu *nguba*]

good (good) *adj.* **bet·ter, best 1.** Morally excellent; virtuous; righteous. **2.** Honorable; worthy: a *good* reputation; in *good* standing. **3.** Generous; loving; kind: a *good* father. **4.** Well-behaved; tractable: a *good* child **5.** Proper; desirable: *good* manners. **6.** Favorable; approving: a *good* opinion. **7.** Pleasant; agreeable: *good* company; a *good* time. **8.** Having beneficial effects; salutary; helpful: *good* for business; *good* advice. **9.** Reliable; safe: a *good* investment. **10.** Suitable; qualified: a *good* man for the job. **11.** Skillful; expert: He is *good* at sports. **12.** Genuine; valid: a *good* excuse. **13.** Backed by sufficient funds: a *good* check. **14.** Excellent in quality, degree, or kind: *good* literature; *good* food. **15.** Orthodox; conforming: a *good* Republican. **16.** Of sufficient quantity or extent; ample: a *good* rest. **17.** Unspoiled; fresh: *good* meat. **18.** Being in sound condition; healthy: *good* lungs; *good* eyes. **19.** Satisfactory or appropriate for a specific action, purpose, etc.: *good* weather for flying. **20.** Attractive or striking in appearance: She looks *good* in that hat. **21.** Great or fairly great in amount, extent, etc.: a *good* share. **22.** Maximum in amount, extent, etc.; full: a *good* two miles away. **— as good as** Practically; virtually: as *good as* done. **— good and** *Informal* Altogether; completely; very: *good and* hot. **— good for 1.** Capable of lasting, surviving, or remaining valid or in operation for (an indicated period of time). **2.** *Informal* Able or willing to pay, give, or produce (something indicated). **3.** Entitling one to or acceptable for: a ticket *good* for ten trips. **4.** Used to show approval: *Good* for him! **— no good 1.** Worthless. **2.** Futile. **—** *n.* **1.** That which is desirable, serviceable, fitting, etc. **2.** Benefit; advantage; profit: for the *good* of mankind. **3.** That which is morally or ethically desirable. **— for good (and all)** For the last time; permanently; forever. **— to come to no good** To end in failure or disgrace. **— to make good 1.** To be successful. **2.** To compensate for; replace; repay. **3.** To fulfill (a promise, agreement, etc.). **4.** To prove; substantiate. **— to the good** To the credit, profit, or advantage of someone or something. **—** *interj.* Well. An exclamation of satisfaction or assent. **—** *adv. Informal* Well. ◆ *Good* is gaining acceptance in informal usage as a substitute for the adverb *well* when reference is made to the functioning of a machine or the like, as in *The car runs good*. In other contexts it is usually nonstandard. [OE *gōd*] **— Syn.** (adj.) **1.** upright. **4.** dutiful, obedient. **8.** advantageous, profitable. **9.** secure. **10.** able, competent. **16.** adequate. **17.** wholesome.

good afternoon A salutation made in the afternoon.
good book The Bible. Also **Good Book**.
good-by (good/bī/) *adj., n. & interj. pl.* **-bys** (-bīz/) Farewell. Also **good/-bye/**. [Contraction of *God be with you*]
good cheer 1. Feasting; revelry. **2.** Choice food and drink, as served on festive occasions. **3.** A mood or spirit of joy, optimism, courage, etc.: to be of *good cheer*.
Good Conduct Medal A medal awarded by the U.S. military to enlisted personnel for exemplary behavior, efficiency, and fidelity.
good day A salutation made during the day.
good evening A salutation made in the evening.
good fellow A jovial, companionable person.
good-fel·low·ship (good/fel/ō-ship) *n.* Warm, jovial companionship.
good-for-noth·ing (good/fər-nuth/ing) *n.* A worthless person. **—** *adj.* Having no use or worth.
Good Friday The Friday before Easter, a day observed by Christians as a commemoration of the crucifixion of Jesus.
good·heart·ed (good/här/tid) *adj.* Kind; charitable; generous. **— good/heart/ed·ly** *adv.* **— good/heart/ed·ness** *n.*
Good Hope, Cape of A promontory in SW Cape Province, South Africa, on the Atlantic.
good humor A cheerful, kindly mood or temper.
good-hu·mored (good/hyoo/mərd, -yoo/-) *adj.* Having, marked by, or indicating a cheerful, kindly temper or mood. **— good/-hu/mored·ly** *adv.*
good·ish (good/ish) *adj.* **1.** Somewhat good; rather good. **2.** Rather big; considerable.
good-look·ing (good/look/ing) *adj.* Having an attractive appearance; handsome.
good looks Attractive or handsome appearance.
good·ly (good/lē) *adj.* **·li·er, ·li·est 1.** Having a pleasing appearance. **2.** Being of fine quality. **3.** Large; sizable: a *goodly* amount. **— good/li·ness** *n.*
good·man (good/mən) *n. pl.* **·men** (-mən) *Archaic* **1.** A title of civility, similar to *Mr.*, used for a man below the rank of gentleman. **2.** The male head of a family or household.
good morning A salutation made in the morning.
good nature A pleasant, mild disposition or temperament.
good-na·tured (good/nā/chərd) *adj.* Having or revealing a pleasant disposition: *good-natured* banter. **— good/-na/-tured·ly** *adv.* **— good/-na/tured·ness** *n.*
Good Neighbor Policy A policy of the U.S. government for promoting political and economic amity with Latin-American countries, first enunciated in 1933 by President Franklin D. Roosevelt.
good·ness (good/nis) *n.* **1.** The state or quality of being good; especially: **a** Excellence of character, morals, etc.; virtue. **b** Generous and kindly feelings; benevolence: *goodness* of heart. **2.** The best or most nourishing part of anything; essence; strength. **3.** God: used alone or with other words in various exclamatory or exclamatory utterances: *Goodness* knows; for *goodness*' sake. **— Syn.** See VIRTUE.
good night A salutation made at night.
goods (goodz) *n.pl.* **1.** Merchandise; wares. **2.** Fabric; material. **3.** Property, especially when personal and movable. **4.** *U.S. Slang* The necessary qualifications or abilities for a specific purpose, act, etc. **5.** *Brit.* Freight. Abbr. *gds.* **— to deliver the goods** *U.S. Informal* To produce what is specified, promised, or expected. **— to get** (or **have**) **the**

goods on *U.S. Slang* To get (or have) incriminating evidence against.
Good Samaritan 1. In a New Testament parable, the only one of several passers-by to aid a man who had been injured and robbed. *Luke* x 30–37. **2.** Any humane person.
Good Shepherd A name for Jesus. *John* x 11, 12.
good-sized (good/sīzd/) *adj.* Quite big or large.
good speed Good luck; success; Godspeed.
good-tem·pered (good/tem/pərd) *adj.* Having a good disposition; not easily angered. **— good/-tem/pered·ly** *adv.*
good turn A kind, helpful act; favor.
good usage Standard use: said of diction, phraseology, and idioms acceptable to cultivated speakers and writers of a language. Also **good use**.
good·wife (good/wīf/) *n. pl.* **·wives** (-wīvz/) *Archaic* **1.** The female head of a family or household; mistress. **2.** A title of respect for a woman: the correlative of *goodman*.
good will 1. A desire for the well-being of others; benevolence. **2.** Cheerful, ready consent or willingness. **3.** In commerce, the intangible assets of a business in terms of its prestige and friendly relations with customers, etc. Also **good·will** (good/wil/).
good-will ambassador (good/wil/) Any official or unofficial representative of one country traveling abroad to promote friendly relations and understanding.
Good·win Sands (good/win) A ten-mile stretch of dangerous shoals in the Straits of Dover.
good·y[1] (good/ē) *n. pl.* **good·ies** *Informal* **1.** Usually *pl.* Something tasty, as a piece of candy or a cooky. **2.** A prissy, mawkish, or sanctimonious person: also **good/y-good/y.** **—** *adj.* Good or pious in a weak, sentimental way: also **good/y-good/y. —** *interj.* A child's cry of pleasure.
good·y[2] (good/ē) *n. pl.* **good·ies** *Archaic* A married woman of low social rank: used as a term of address or reference with the surname. [< GOODWIFE]
Good·year (good/yir) **Charles,** 1800–60, U.S. industrialist and inventor; originated rubber vulcanization process.
goo·ey (goo/ē) *adj.* **goo·i·er, goo·i·est** *U.S. Slang* Sticky or viscous. [< GOO]
goof (goof) *Slang n.* **1.** A dull-witted or incapable individual; dope. **2.** A mistake or blunder. **—** *v.i.* **1.** To make a mistake; blunder. **—** *v.t.* **2.** To make a mess of; botch: usually with *up.* **3.** To act like a goof. **— to goof off** *U.S. Slang* **1.** To waste time; loaf. **2.** To shirk duty or work. [Cf. obs. *goff* a stupid person < F *goffe*]
goof·y (goo/fē) *adj.* **goof·i·er, goof·i·est** *Slang* Typical of a goof; stupid; dopy. **— goof/i·ly** *adv.* **— goof/i·ness** *n.*
goo·gly (goo/glē) *n. pl.* **·glies** In cricket, a deceptive ball which appears from the position and movement of the bowler's hand to be likely to break in one direction, but in fact breaks in the other. [Cf. dial. E *goggle* to roll or sway]
goo·gol (goo/gol) *n. Math.* The number 10 raised to the hundredth power (10^{100}), or 1 followed by 100 zeros. [Adopted by Edward Kasner, 1878–1955, U.S. mathematician, from a child's word for any enormous number]
goo·gol·plex (goo/gol-pleks/) *n. Math.* The number 10 multiplied by itself 10^{100} times; 10 raised to the googol power.
gook (gook, gook) **1.** *U.S. Slang* Any dirty or slimy substance, as sludge or sediment. **2.** *U.S. Slang* A sticky, thick fluid or syrup. **3.** *Mil. Slang* A native inhabitant of a foreign country who is considered to be inferior in intelligence, culture, etc., by the troops stationed there: an offensive term. [? < GOO]
goon (goon) *n. U.S. Slang* **1.** A thug or hoodlum; especially, a roughneck hired to break strikes, intimidate workers during labor disputes, etc. **2.** A stupid person; dolt. **3.** A young person who is unattractive or unpopular. [after a character created by E. C. Segar, 1894–1938, U.S. cartoonist]
goo·ney (goo/nē) *n.* An albatross (*Diomedea nigripes*) of Pacific waters, having a wingspread up to 7 feet. [Cf. dial. E *gawney* fool]
goop (goop) *n. U.S. Slang* A rude, boorish person. [after a group of characters created by Gelett Burgess]
goo·ral (goo/rəl) *n.* A goral (which see).
goos·an·der (goos-an/dər) *n.* The merganser, a bird. [Origin uncertain]
goose[1] (goos) *n. pl.* **geese** (gēs) or **goos·es** *for def. 4.* **1.** Any of a subfamily (*Anserinae*) of wild or domesticated web-footed birds larger than ducks and smaller than swans. ◆ Collateral adjective: *anserine.* **2.** The female of this bird: distinguished from *gander.* **3.** The flesh of the goose, used as food. **4.** A tailor's pressing iron with a long, curved handle. **5.** A silly or ridiculous person. **— to cook one's goose** *Informal* To spoil or ruin one's chances, plans, etc. [OE *gōs*]
goose[2] (goos) *U.S. Slang v.t.* **goosed, goos·ing 1.** To give a quick, playful prod or poke to the backside of. **2.** To accelerate (a gasoline engine) in spurts. **—** *n. pl.* **goos·es** A sudden poke in the backside. [? Special use of GOOSE]
goose·ber·ry (goos/ber/ē, -bər-ē, gooz/-) *n. pl.* **·ries 1.** The tart berry of a spiny shrub (genus *Ribes*) of the saxifrage family, used for jams, pies, etc. **2.** The shrub itself.
goose egg *Slang* **1.** The figure zero used to indicate that no points have been scored, as in a game. **2.** A score of nothing.
goose flesh A taut, prickling sensation in the skin induced

typically by cold or fear and marked by a roughening of the skin's surface through erection of the papillae and tiny hairs of the skin. Also **goose bumps, goose pimples, goose skin.**

goose·foot (gōōs/fŏŏt/) *n. pl.* **·foots** Any plant of a widely distributed genus (*Chenopodium*) of shrubs and herbs with small green flowers, typical of a family (*Chenopodiaceae*) that includes several food plants, as beets and spinach.

goose·grass (gōōs/gras/, -gräs/) *n.* Any of various herbs and grasses, as cleavers or silverweed.

goose·herd (gōōs/hûrd/) *n.* One who tends a flock of geese.

goose·neck (gōōs/nek/) *n.* Any of various mechanical devices curved like a goose's neck, as a bent joint for pipes or a flexible shaft between the base and bulb of a desk lamp.

goose-step (gōōs/step/) *v.i.* **-stepped, -step·ping** To march along or mark time in a step consisting of the alternate kicking forward of each leg stiffly and sharply.

goose step 1. The action of goose-stepping. **2.** The manner of moving the legs in goose-stepping.

goos·y (gōō/sē) *adj.* **goos·i·er, goos·i·est 1.** Typical of a goose; scatter-brained; flighty. **2.** Producing or exhibiting the condition of goose flesh. Also **goos/ey.** — **goos/i·ness** *n.*

GOP or **G.O.P.** Grand Old Party: the Republican Party.

go·pher (gō/fər) *n. U.S. & Canadian* **1.** A burrowing American rodent (family *Geomyidae*), with large cheek pouches, as the **pocket gopher** (genera *Thomomys* and *Geomys*). **2.** One of various western North American ground squirrels. **3.** A large, nocturnal, burrowing land tortoise (*Gopherus polyphemus*) of the southern United States. [< F *gaufre* honeycomb]

Go·pher (gō/fər) *n.* A Minnesotan: a nickname.

gopher snake A large, nonpoisonous, burrowing snake (*Drymarchon corais couperi*) of the southern United States: also called *bull snake, indigo snake.*

Gopher State Nickname of MINNESOTA.

go·pher·wood (gō/fər-wŏŏd/) *n.* **1.** Yellowwood (def. 1). **2.** The wood, perhaps pine or fir, used by Noah in building the ark. *Gen.* vi 14. [< Hebrew *gōfer, gōpher*]

go·ral (gō/rəl) *n. pl.* **·rals** or **·ral** A Himalayan goat antelope (genus *Naemorhedus*) having very small horns and a grayish coat: also *gooral.* [< native name]

gor·bel·ly (gôr/bel/ē) *n. pl.* **·lies** *Archaic* **1.** A potbelly. **2.** A fat or big-bellied person. [OE *gor* dirt + BELLY]

gor·cock (gôr/kok/) *n.* A moor cock (which see). [Origin uncertain]

Gor·di·an knot (gôr/dē-ən) **1.** A knot supposed to have been tied by **Gor·di·us** (gôr/dē-əs), legendary king of Phrygia, and declared by an oracle to be capable of being undone only by the man who should rule Asia. Alexander the Great cut the knot in two with his sword. **2.** Any difficulty that can be solved only by drastic measures. — **to cut the Gordian knot** To solve a problem or difficulty by drastic measures.

Gor·don (gôr/dən), **Charles George,** 1833–85, British army officer; killed during a revolt in the Egyptian Sudan: called **Chinese Gordon.** — **Lord George,** 1751–93, English religious agitator against Roman Catholicism.

Gordon setter A variety of setter having a black coat marked with tan, chestnut, or red.

gore¹ (gôr, gōr) *n.* Blood that has been shed; especially, a copious amount of thickened, clotted, or dried blood. [OE *gor* dirt, filth]

gore² (gôr, gōr) *v.t.* **gored, gor·ing 1.** Of a bull, boar, etc., to pierce or wound with the horns or tusks. **2.** *Obs.* To pierce or run through with a spear, etc. [ME *goren*; prob. akin to OE *gār* spear]

gore³ (gôr, gōr) *n.* **1.** A triangular or tapering section of cloth set into a garment, sail, etc., to provide greater fullness. **2.** *Dial.* A wedge-shaped section of land. — *v.t.* **gored, gor·ing 1.** To cut into gore-shaped pieces. **2.** To furnish with gores. [OE *gāra* triangular piece of land]

Gor·gas (gôr/gəs), **William Crawford,** 1854–1920, U.S. surgeon general of the army 1914–19; chief sanitation expert at the building of the Panama Canal.

gorge (gôrj) *n.* **1.** A narrow, deep ravine; especially, a ravine with a stream flowing through it. **2.** The act of gorging. **3.** That which is gorged, as a greedily swallowed meal. **4.** Deep or violent disgust, resentment, etc.: Such brutality makes one's *gorge* rise. **5.** A mass clogging or obstructing a passage: an ice *gorge.* **6.** An entrance into the rear of a bastion or into a similar part of a fortification. **7.** *Archaic* In falconry, the crop of a hawk. **8.** *Archaic* The throat; gullet. — *v.* **gorged, gorg·ing** *v.t.* **1.** To stuff with food; glut. **2.** To swallow gluttonously; gulp down. — *v.i.* **3.** To stuff oneself with food. [< OF < L *gurges* whirlpool] — **gorg/er** *n.*

gor·geous (gôr/jəs) *adj.* **1.** Dazzlingly colorful; brilliant; resplendent. **2.** *Informal* Extremely beautiful, pleasant, etc.. [< OF *gorgias* elegant; ult. origin uncertain] — **gor/geous·ly** *adv.* — **gor/geous·ness** *n.*

gor·ger·in (gôr/jər·in) *n. Archit.* The part of a column forming the juncture between the shaft and the capital: also called *neckina.* [< Fr. < *gorge* throat]

gor·get (gôr/jit) *n.* **1.** A piece of armor protecting the

throat. **2.** An article of dress covering the neck and breast, as a wimple, formerly worn by women. **3.** *Zool.* On a bird or animal, a throat patch having a distinctive color or texture. [< OF *gorgete,* dim. of *gorge* throat]

gor·gon (gôr/gən) *n.* A terrifying or hideously ugly woman. [< GORGON]

Gor·gon (gôr/gən) In Greek mythology, one of three sisters (Stheno, Euryale, and Medusa) with serpents for hair, so terrifying that the sight of them turned the beholder to stone. [< L *Gorgo, -onis* < Gk. *Gorgō* < *gorgos* terrible] — **Gor·go·ni·an** (gôr·gō/nē·ən) *adj.*

gor·go·nei·on (gôr/gə·nē/ən) *n. pl.* **·nei·a** (-nē/ə) A depiction of the head of Medusa. [< Gk., neut. of *gorgoneios* of a Gorgon]

Gor·gon·zo·la (gôr/gən·zō/lə) *n.* A strongly flavored,white Italian cheese n ade from pressed milk and somewhat resembling Roquefort. [after *Gorgonzola,* a town in Italy]

gor·hen (gôr/hen/) *n.* A moor hen (def. 1). [Origin uncertain]

go·ril·la (gə·ril/ə) *n.* **1.** An African jungle ape (*Gorilla gorilla*), the largest and most powerful of the anthropoids, having a massive body, long arms, and tusklike canine teeth. **2.** *Slang* A brutal criminal; thug. **3.** *Slang* A powerful, brutish man. [< NL < Gk., appar. < native name]

Gö·ring (gœ/ring), **Hermann Wilhelm** See GOERING.

Go·ri·zia (gō·rē/tsyä) A commune in NE Italy, on the Yugoslav border; pop. 41,854 (1961). *Slovenian* **Go·ri·ca** (gō·rē/tsä).

Gor·ki (gôr/kē, *Russ.* gôry/kyi), **Maxim** Pseudonym of **Alexei Maximovich Pyesh·kov** (pyesh/kôf), 1868–1936, Russian author. Also **Gor/ky.**

GORILLA
(To 6 feet tall; weight to 600 pounds)

Gor·kiy (gôr/kē, *Russ.* gôry/kyi) A city in west central R.S.F.S.R., on the Volga; pop. 1,170,000 (1970): formerly *Nyizhniy Novgorod.* Also **Gor/ki, Gor/ky.**

Gör·litz (gœr/lits) A city in East Germany, on the Neisse; pop. 88,632 (est. 1966).

Gor·lov·ka (gor·lôf/kə) A city in the eastern Ukrainian S.S.R., in the Donbas; pop. 335,000 (est. 1970).

gor·mand (gôr/mənd) See GOURMAND.

gor·mand·ize (gôr/mən·diz; *for n., also* -dēz) *v.t. & v.i.* **·ized, ·iz·ing** To eat voraciously or gluttonously. — *n. Rare* Gourmandise. — **gor/mand·iz/er** *n.*

gorse (gôrs) *n. Brit.* Furze, a plant. [OE *gors(t)*] — **gors/y** *adj.*

go·ry (gôr/ē, gō/rē) *adj.* **·ri·er, ·ri·est 1.** Covered or stained with gore. **2.** Resembling gore. **3.** Characterized by bloodshed or violence: a *gory* battle. — **Syn.** See BLOODY. [< GORE¹] — **gor/i·ly** *adv.* — **go/ri·ness** *n.*

gosh (gosh) *interj.* An exclamation expressing surprise, awe, etc. [Euphemistic alter. of GOD]

gos·hawk (gos/hôk/, gôs/-) *n.* Any of various large, short-winged hawks (genus *Accipiter*) formerly used in falconry; especially, *A. gentilis* of Europe and North America. Also *dove hawk.* [OE *gōshafoc* < *gōs* goose + *hafoc* hawk]

Go·shen (gō/shən) **1.** The region in Egypt inhabited by the Israelites. *Gen.* xlv 10. **2.** Any place of peace or plenty.

gos·ling (goz/ling) *n.* A young goose. [< ON *gǣslingr*]

gos·pel (gos/pəl) *n.* **1.** The teachings of the Christian church as originally preached by Jesus Christ and the apostles. **2.** A narrative of Christ's life and teachings, as exemplified by any of the first four books of the New Testament. **3.** Any statement or information accepted as unquestionably true. **4.** A doctrine, principle, or course of action considered to be of major importance. [OE *godspell* good news, trans. of Gk. *euangelion.* See EVANGEL.]

Gos·pel (gos/pəl) *n.* **1.** Any of the first four books of the New Testament, attributed to Matthew, Mark, Luke, and John. **2.** A passage from one of the four Gospels, read as part of the Eucharistic service in certain churches.

gos·pel·er (gos/pəl·ər) *n.* **1.** One who reads the Gospel in a religious service. **2.** One who maintains that his sect alone imparts the truth of the gospel: a derisive term formerly applied to Puritans, Protestants, etc. Also **gos/pel·ler.**

Gos·plan (gos·plän/) *n.* In the Soviet Union, an official planning commission concerned with agriculture, industry, health, etc. [< Russian *gos(udar)* national + *plan* plan]

gos·po·din (gos·po·dyēn/) *n. pl.* **·da** (-dä) *Russian* A form of address equivalent to "Mister," used in the Soviet Union as a courtesy title for non-Russians.

gos·sa·mer (gos/ə·mər) *n.* **1.** Fine strands of spider's silk, especially when floating in the air or suspended from grass or shrubbery. **2.** Any flimsy, delicate substance. **3.** A filmy, gauzelike fabric. **4.** Formerly, a thin, waterproof outer garment. — *adj.* Resembling gossamer; flimsy; unsubstantial: also **gos/sa·mer·y** (-mər-ē). [< ME *gossomer* Indian summer, lit., goose summer; appar. so called because often seen in autumn when geese are in season]

Gosse (gôs, gos), **Sir Edmund William,** 1849–1928, English poet and critic.

gos·sip (gos′əp) *n.* **1.** Idle, often malicious talk, especially about others. **2.** Informal, chatty talk or writing, as of personages, social events, etc. **3.** A person, especially a woman, who indulges in idle or malicious talk. **4.** *Archaic* A close friend, especially a woman. **5.** *Archaic* A godparent. — *v.* **·siped** or **·sipped, ·sip·ing** or **·sip·ping** *v.i.* **1.** To talk idly, usually about the affairs of others; chat. — *v.t.* **2.** To repeat or impart as gossip. [OE *godsibb* baptismal sponsor < *god* + *sibb* a relative] — **gos′sip·er** *n.*

gos·sip·mong·er (gos′əp·mung′gər, -mong′-) *n.* One who spreads gossip.

gos·sip·ry (gos′əp·rē) *n. Rare* Gossip or gossips collectively.

gos·sip·y (gos′əp·ē) *adj.* **1.** Indulging in gossip. **2.** Marked by or full of gossip; chatty.

gos·soon (go·sōon′) *n. Irish* **1.** A lad. **2.** A serving boy. [Alter. of F *garçon* boy]

got (got) Past tense and past participle of GET. ◆ **have got** In the sense of "must" or "possess," *have got* is in wide informal use: *I* have (or *I've*) *got* to leave; *We* have got (or *We've got*) plenty and intend to keep it. See note under GOTTEN.

Go·ta·ma (gō′tə·mə) See BUDDHA.

Gö·te·borg (yœ′tə·bôr′y′) A port city in SW Sweden; pop. 444,131 (1969). Also **Goth·en·burg** (got′n·bûrg, goth′-).

Goth (goth, gôth) *n.* **1.** A member of a Germanic people that invaded the Roman Empire in the third, fourth, and fifth centuries: divided into the Ostrogoths (**East Goths**) and Visigoths (**West Goths**). **2.** A rude or uncouth person; barbarian. [< LL *Gothi* the Goths < Gk. *Gothoi* < Gothic]

Goth. or **goth.** Gothic.

Go·tha (gō′tä) A city in SW East Germany; pop. 56,470 (est. 1959).

Goth·am (goth′əm, gō′thəm; *Brit.* got′əm) **1.** A village near Nottingham, England, noted in legend for the foolishness of its inhabitants. **2.** A nickname for New York City. — **Goth′am·ite** (-īt) *n.*

Goth·ic (goth′ik) *adj.* **1.** Of or pertaining to the Goths or to their language. **2.** Of or pertaining to a style of architecture much used in Europe, from about 1200 to 1500, characterized by pointed arches, ribbed vaulting, flying buttresses, etc. **3.** Denoting a type of literature usually having a medieval setting, and emphasizing the grotesque and the supernatural. **4.** Belonging to or characteristic of the Middle Ages; medieval. **5.** Barbarous; rude. — *n.* **1.** The extinct East Germanic language of the Goths, known chiefly from fragments of a translation of the Bible made by Ulfilas in the fourth century. **2.** Gothic architecture or art. Also *(for adj. defs. 3–5)* **goth′ic.** — **Goth′i·cal·ly** *adv.*

goth·ic (goth′ik) *n. Sometimes cap. Printing* **a** *U.S.* Sans serif. **b** *Brit.* Black letter.

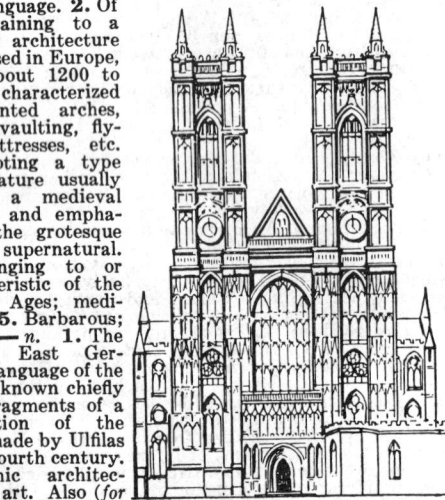

GOTHIC ARCHITECTURE
Westminster Abbey, London,
13th–15th century.

Goth·i·cism (goth′ə·siz′əm) *n.* **1.** The style or characteristics of Gothic architecture, art, literature, etc. **2.** Imitation of or enthusiasm for this style. **3.** Crudeness of manners or style. **4.** A Gothic idiom.

Goth·i·cize (goth′ə·sīz) *v.t.* **·cized, ·ciz·ing** To make Gothic.

gö·thite (gō′thīt, gœ′-) See GOETHITE.

Got·land (got′lənd, *Sw.* gôt′länd) An island of SE Sweden, in the Baltic Sea; 1,167 sq. mi. Formerly **Gott′land, Goth′land.**

got·ten (got′n) Past participle of GET. ◆ *Gotten,* obsolete in British, is current in American English along with *got.* In the informal senses of obligation and possession only *got* is used: *I've got to go; He's got a fine library.*

Göt·ter·däm·mer·ung (gœt′ər·dem′ər·ŏŏngk), **Die** *German* Twilight of the gods: title of a music drama by Richard Wagner. See RING OF THE NIBELUNG.

Göt·ting·en (gœt′ing·ən) A city in Lower Saxony, West Germany; pop. 77,800 (1960).

Götz von Ber·lich·ing·en (gœts fən ber′liKH·ing′ən) See BERLICHINGEN.

gouache (gwosh) *n.* **1.** A method of painting using opaque colors mixed with water and gum. **2.** The opaque pigment so used. **3.** A painting done in this medium. [< F < Ital. *guazzo* a spray < L *aquatio* a watering < *aqua* water]

Gou·da cheese (gou′də, gōō′-) A mild, yellow cheese similar to Edam cheese. [after *Gouda,* town in the Netherlands where first made]

Gou·dy (gou′dē), **Frederic William,** 1865–1947, U.S. printer and type designer.

gouge (gouj) *n.* **1.** A chisel having a scoop-shaped blade, used chiefly for cutting or carving wood. **2.** A groove or cavity made by or as by a gouge. **3.** *U.S. Informal* The action of cutting or scooping with or as with a gouge. **4.** *U.S. Informal* The act of cheating or defrauding. **5.** *U.S Slang* A swindler. — *v.t.* **gouged, goug·ing** **1.** To cut or carve with or as with a gouge. **2.** To scoop, force, or tear out: to *gouge* out an eye. **3.** *U.S. Informal* To cheat in a bargain; especially, to charge exorbitant prices; swindle. [< LL *gulbia,* prob. < Celtic] — **goug′er** *n.*

gou·lash (gōō′läsh, -lash) *n.* A stew made with beef or veal and vegetables, seasoned with paprika, etc.: also called *Hungarian goulash.* [< Hung. *gulyas (hus)* shepherd's (meat)]

Gould (gōōld), **Jay,** 1836–92, U.S. financier.

Gou·nod (gōō·nō′), **Charles François,** 1818–93, French composer.

gou·ra·mi (gōō·rä′mē, gŏŏr′ə·mē) *n.* **1.** A large, freshwater fish (*Osphromenus olfax*) of SE Asia, highly esteemed as food. **2.** Any of various related fishes frequently kept in home aquariums, as the **banded gourami** (*Colisa fasciata*), the **dwarf gourami** (*C. lalia*), and the **three-spot gourami** (*Trichogaster trichopterus*). [< Malay *gurami*]

gourd (gôrd, gōrd, gōōrd) *n.* **1.** The fruit of any of various plants (family *Cucurbitaceae*), having hard, durable shells; especially, the dried, ornamental fruit of an American variety (*Cucurbita pepo ovifera*). **2.** The fruit of the calabash tree. **3.** A utensil, as a ladle or drinking cup, made from the dried shell of one of these fruits. **4.** Any cucurbitaceous plant. [< F *gourde* < L *cucurbita* gourd]

gourde (gōōrd) *n.* The monetary unit of Haiti. Abbr. *g., G., gde.* [< Fr., fem. of *gourd* < Sp. *gordo* fat, heavy]

gour·mand (gŏŏr′mənd, *Fr.* gōōr·män′) *n.* **1.** One who takes hearty pleasure in eating. **2.** Formerly, a glutton. Also spelled *gormand.* — **Syn.** See GOURMET. [< F, glutton]

gour·mand·ise (gŏŏr′mən·dēz) *n.* The state of being a gourmand; also, the tastes or habits of a gourmand: also *gormandize.* [ME *gromandise* < MF *gourmandise*]

gour·met (gŏŏr·mā′, *Fr.* gōōr·me′) *n.* A fastidious devotee of good food and drink. [< F < OF, winetaster]

— **Syn.** *Gourmet, gourmand, glutton,* and *epicure* denote one who finds special pleasure in eating and drinking. *Gourmet* is applied to one who savors every mouthful and has a discriminating taste in dishes, wines, etc. *Gourmand* is applied to one of less fastidious taste who finds hearty enjoyment in eating, but is not a *glutton,* one who has an inordinate appetite. An *epicure* is primarily one of very refined taste in the pleasures of the table, but the word is extended to one of refined taste in any field of sensuous or esthetic pleasure.

Gour·mont (gōōr·môn′), **Remy de,** 1858–1915, French novelist and critic.

gout (gout) *n.* **1.** *Pathol.* A disease arising from a defect in metabolism and characterized by recurrent attacks of painful inflammation of the joints, especially in the great toe, and by an excess of uric acid in the blood. **2.** A drop or clot, especially of blood. [< F *goutte* drop < L *gutta*]

goût (gōō) *n. French* Taste.

gout·y (gou′tē) *adj.* **gout·i·er, gout·i·est** **1.** Pertaining to, characteristic of, or like gout. **2.** Causing or resulting from gout. **3.** Affected with gout. **4.** Enlarged or swollen, as from gout. — **gout′i·ly** *adv.* — **gout′i·ness** *n.*

gou·ver·nante (gōō·ver·nänt′) *n. French* **1.** A chaperon. **2.** A governess.

Gov. or **gov.** Governor.

gov·ern (guv′ərn) *v.t.* **1.** To rule or direct by right or authority: to *govern* a nation. **2.** To guide or control the course or action of; influence. **3.** To serve as a rule or deciding factor for: This decision *governed* the case. **4.** To keep in check; curb. **5.** *Gram.* **a** To regulate (a word) as to form: In "Take me home," the verb *governs* the pronoun. **b** To require (a particular case, mood, or form): In English, a transitive verb *governs* the objective case. — *v.i.* **6.** To exercise authority; rule. [< OF *governer* < L *gubernare* to steer < Gk. *kybernaein*] — **gov′ern·a·ble** *adj.*

— **Syn. 1.** command, administer, manage, lead. **3.** decide, determine. **4.** restrain, inhibit. **6.** reign.

gov·ern·ance (guv′ər·nəns) *n.* Exercise of authority; direction; control.

gov·ern·ess (guv′ər·nis) *n.* **1.** A woman employed in a private household to train and instruct children. **2.** *Archaic* A female governor.

gov·ern·ment (guv′ərn·mənt, -ər-) *n.* **1.** The authoritative administration of the affairs of a nation, state, city, etc.; the jurisdiction or control exercised over people in a political community; rule. **2.** The officially constituted governing body of a nation, community, etc. **3.** The system or established form of rule by which a nation, community, etc., is controlled: democratic *government*. **4.** Any governed territory, district, etc. **5.** Management; regulation; control: the *government* of one's behavior. **6.** *Gram.* A syntactical relationship in which one word determines the case or mood of another. Abbr. *govt.*, *Govt.* — **gov·ern·men·tal** (guv'ərn·men'təl, -ər-) *adj.* — **gov'ern·men'tal·ly** *adv.*

Government Issue *U.S.* Something furnished by a governmental agency, as uniforms to Army personnel. Abbr. *GI, G.I.*

gov·er·nor (guv'ər·nər) *n.* **1.** One who governs; as: **a** The elected chief executive of any State in the U.S. **b** An official appointed to administer a province, territory, etc. **c** *Brit.* The manager or head of a prison, bank, society, etc. Abbr. *gov.*, *Gov.* **2.** *Mech.* A device for controlling the speed of an engine, motor, compressor, etc., by regulating its fuel supply or motive force. **3.** *Brit. Informal* One's father. **4.** *Brit. Informal* Boss.

governor general *pl.* **governors general 1.** *Often cap. Brit.* The chief representative of the Crown in a dominion or colony. **2.** A governor of governors under his jurisdiction. Also *Brit.* **gov'er·nor-gen'er·al.** — **gov'er·nor-gen'er·al·ship** *n.*

gov·er·nor·ship (guv'ər·nər·ship) *n.* The position, jurisdiction, or term of office of a governor.

Governors Island A small island in New York Harbor; site of Fort Jay, a U.S. military post.

Govt. or **govt.** Government.

gow·an (gou'ən) *n.* *Scot.* Any of various white or yellow wildflowers; especially, the English daisy.

gowd (goud) *n.* *Scot.* Gold.

Gow·er (gou'ər, gōr), **John**, 1325?–1408, English poet.

gowk (gouk) *n.* *Scot.* **1.** The cuckoo. **2.** A fool; simpleton.

gown (goun) *n.* **1.** A woman's dress, especially one for formal occasions: evening *gown*. **2.** Any long, loose garment or wrapper: dressing *gown*. **3.** A long and loose outer robe worn as a distinctive habit of certain officials, scholars, clergymen, etc. See GENEVA GOWN. **4.** The students and faculty members of a college or university collectively, as distinguished from the townspeople: now used only in the expression **town and gown.** — *v.t. & v.i.* To dress in a gown. [< OF *goune* < Med.L *gunna* a loose robe]

gowns·man (gounz'mən) *n.* *pl.* **·men** (-mən) One who wears a gown as a mark of his profession, office, or status.

goy (goi) *n.* *pl.* **goy·im** (goi'im) *Yiddish* A non-Jew; Gentile: often a contemptuous term.

Go·ya (gô'yə), **Francisco José de,** 1746–1828, Spanish painter: full surname **Goya y Lu·cien·tes** (ē lōō·thyen'tās).

G.P. 1. General practitioner. **2.** Graduate in Pharmacy.

GPM or **gpm** or **g.p.m.** Gallons per minute.

GPO or **G.P.O. 1.** General Post Office. **2.** Government Printing Office.

G.P.U. The OGPU. (Russ. *Gosudarstvennoye politicheskoye upravleniye*).

GQ or **G.Q.** or **g.q.** *Mil.* General quarters.

gr. 1. Grade. **2.** Grain(s). **3.** Gram(s). **4.** Grammar. **5.** Great. **6.** Gross. **7.** Group.

Gr. 1. Grecian; Greece. **2.** Greek.

G.R. King George (L *Georgius Rex*).

Graaf·i·an follicle (grä'fē·ən) *Anat.* One of the numerous, small, round sacs embedded in the cortex of the ovary, each of which contains a single ovum: also called *ovisac.* Also **Graafian vesicle.** [after Regnier de *Graaf*, 1641–73, Dutch physician and anatomist]

graal (grāl) See GRAIL.

grab[1] (grab) *v.* **grabbed, grab·bing** *v.t.* **1.** To grasp or seize suddenly or forcibly. **2.** To take possession of by force or by dishonest means. **3.** *Informal* To get hurriedly, in what little time is available: Let's *grab* a bite before the show. — *v.i.* **4.** To make a sudden grasp. — **Syn.** See GRASP. — *n.* **1.** The act of grabbing. **2.** That which is grabbed. **3.** A dishonest or unlawful acquisition. **4.** A mechanical apparatus used to grasp and lift heavy objects. [Cf. MDu. *grabben* to grip] — **grab'ber** *n.*

grab[2] (grab) *n.* A coasting vessel of the East Indies, having two or three masts and triangular sails. [< Arabic *ghurāb*]

grab bag *U.S.* A bag or other receptacle filled with miscellaneous unidentified articles, from which one draws an object at random.

grab·ble (grab'əl) *v.i.* **·bled, ·bling 1.** To feel about with the hands; grope. **2.** To flounder; sprawl. [Cf. Du. *grab·belen*, freq. of *grabben* to grab]

gra·ben (grä'bən) *n.* *Geol.* A generally elongate depression of the land caused by the downward faulting of a portion of the earth's crust. [< G, ditch]

grab rope *Naut.* Any of various ropes used for grasping or for steadying oneself, as one strung along a gangplank.

Grac·chus (grak'əs), **Gaius Sempronius,** 153?–121 B.C., and his brother, **Tiberius Sempronius,** 163?–133 B.C., Roman political reformers: called **the Grac·chi** (grak'ī).

grace (grās) *n.* **1.** Beauty or harmony of motion, form, manner, or proportion. **2.** Any attractive or excellent quality or endowment. **3.** Favor or service freely rendered; good will. **4.** The act of showing or granting such favor. **5.** Clemency; mercy. **6.** The perception of what is appropriate and right: He had the *grace* to go. **7.** An extension of time granted after a date previously set, as for fulfilling an obligation or paying a debt. **8.** A short prayer giving thanks or asking a blessing before or after a meal. **9.** *Theol.* **a** The unmerited but freely given love and favor of God toward man. **b** The divine influence operating in man to regenerate, sanctify, or strengthen him. **c** The state or condition of being pleasing and acceptable to God. **d** Any divinely inspired spiritual virtue or excellence. **10.** *Music* A note or notes added to a melody as an embellishment; ornament. — **to be in the good** (or **bad**) **graces of** To be regarded with favor (or disfavor) by. — **with good** (or **bad**) **grace** In a cheerfully willing (or grudgingly reluctant) manner. — *v.t.* **graced, grac·ing 1.** To add grace and beauty to; adorn. **2.** To dignify; honor. **3.** *Music* To ornament with grace notes or other embellishments. [< OF < L *gratia* favor]

Grace (grās) *n.* A title or form of address for a duke, duchess, archbishop, or bishop: preceded by *Your, His, Her,* etc.

grace cup A cup used at the end of a meal for the drinking of the final toast; also, the toast itself.

grace·ful (grās'fəl) *adj.* Characterized by grace, elegance, or beauty of form, movement, language, etc. — **grace'ful·ly** *adv.* — **grace'ful·ness** *n.*

— **Syn.** *Graceful* and *beautiful* are compared as they mean possessed of pleasing qualities. In their narrowest sense, *graceful* refers to movement, *beautiful* to appearance. When used more broadly, *graceful* may refer to a person who displays any admirable qualities, one of which may be beauty; *beautiful* retains the sense of the pictorial, though we may apply it to what can be perceived only by the mind's eye.

grace·less (grās'lis) *adj.* **1.** Lacking grace, charm, or elegance. **2.** Having no sense of what is right or decent. — **grace'less·ly** *adv.* — **grace'less·ness** *n.*

grace note *Music* A note written smaller than those of the main text, played or sung as an embellishment and regarded as having no time value or harmonic value.

Grac·es (grā'siz) In Greek mythology, three sister goddesses —Aglaia (splendor), Euphrosyne (mirth), and Thalia (abundance)—who confer grace, beauty, charm, and joy upon human beings and on nature. Also **the three Graces.**

grac·ile (gras'il) *adj.* Gracefully slender; slight. [< L *gracilis* slender] — **gra·cil·i·ty** (grə·sil'ə·tē) *n.*

gra·ci·o·so (grä'shē·ō'sō, *Sp.* grä·thyō'sō) *n.* *pl.* **·sos 1.** A clown in Spanish comedy; a buffoon. **2.** *Obs.* A favorite. [< Sp., graceful]

gra·cious (grā'shəs) *adj.* **1.** Characterized by or showing kindness, affability, politeness, etc. **2.** Condescendingly polite or indulgent, as to inferiors. **3.** Full of compassion; merciful. **4.** Loosely, elegant; refined: *gracious* living. **5.** *Obs.* Happy; fortunate; prosperous. — *interj.* An exclamation of mild surprise. [< OF < L *gratiosus* < *gratia* favor] — **gra'cious·ly** *adv.* — **gra'cious·ness** *n.*

grack·le (grak'əl) *n.* **1.** Any of various New World blackbirds (family *Icteridae*) having long tails and dark plumage; especially, the **common grackle** (*Quiscalus quiscula*), with iridescent plumage, and the large, crowlike **boat-tailed grackle** (*Cassidix mexicana*): also called *crow blackbird.* **2.** Any of various Old World birds (family *Sturnidae*) allied to the starlings, as the myna. [< NL *Gracula*, name of a genus < L *graculus* jackdaw]

grad (grad) *n.* *U.S. Informal* A graduate.

grad. Graduate; graduated.

gra·date (grā'dāt) *v.t. & v.i.* **·dat·ed, ·dat·ing 1.** To pass or cause to pass imperceptibly from one shade or degree of intensity to another, as color or light. **2.** To arrange or be arranged in grades.

gra·da·tion (grā·dā'shən) *n.* **1.** An orderly and gradual progression or arrangement according to size, quality, rank, degree, etc. **2.** *Usually pl.* A step, degree, or relative position in such a progression or arrangement. **3.** The act or process of arranging in steps or grades. **4.** In art, etc., a passing by imperceptible degrees from one shade of color or kind of surface to another. **5.** *Ling.* Ablaut. [< F < L *gradatio, -onis* a going by steps < *gradus* step] — **gra·da'·tion·al** *adj.* — **gra·da'tion·al·ly** *adv.*

grade (grād) *n.* **1.** A degree or step in any scale, as of quality, merit, rank, etc. **2.** A stage or degree in an orderly progression, classification, or process. **3.** A group or category of persons or things of the same class or quality. **4.** *U.S.* In education: **a** One of the levels of progress, each generally constituting a year's work, into which an elementary or

secondary school is divided. **b** The pupils in such a division. **c** *pl.* Elementary school: preceded by *the*: children in *the grades*. **5.** *U.S.* A rating or mark indicating the quality of work done, as in a school subject or examination. **6.** In the U.S. armed forces, rank or rating. See below. **7.** The degree of inclination of a road, track, or other surface as compared with the horizontal. **8.** A rise or elevation in a road, track, etc. **9.** In animal husbandry, an animal produced by crossbreeding ordinary stock with purebred stock. Abbr. *gr.* — **at grade** At the same level or degree of inclination. — **to make the grade** *Informal* To succeed in any project or undertaking. — **up to grade** In accordance with an established standard of quality, progress, etc. — *v.* **grad·ed, grad·ing** *v.t.* **1.** To arrange or classify by grades or degrees; sort according to size, quality, type, etc. **2.** In education, to determine the grade of. **3.** To level or reduce (a road, ground, etc.) to a desirable gradient. **4.** To gradate. **5.** To improve (livestock) by crossbreeding with superior stock: often with *up.* — *v.i.* **6.** To be of a specific grade or rank. **7.** To change by degrees. [< F < L *gradus* step]
-grade *combining form* **1.** Progressing or moving: *retrograde.* **2.** *Zool.* Walking in a specified manner: *plantigrade.* [< L *-gradus* < *gradi* to walk]

grade crossing An intersection of rights of way, as roads or railroads, at the same level: also called *level crossing.*
grad·er (grā′dər) *n.* **1.** One who or that which grades. **2.** *U.S.* A pupil in a specified school grade: a third *grader.*
grade school An elementary school (which see).
gra·di·ent (grā′dē·ənt) *n.* **1.** Degree of inclination, as in a slope; grade. **2.** An incline; ramp. **3.** *Physics* A rate of change in certain variable factors, as pressure, temperature, etc.; also, a diagram or scale showing such a rate of change. — *adj.* **1.** Rising or descending gradually or by uniform degrees. **2.** *Zool.* Adapted for or capable of walking or running; gressorial. [< L *gradiens, -entis,* ppr. of *gradi* to walk]
gra·din (grā′din, *Fr.* grȧ·daṅ′) *n.* **1.** One of a series of rising seats or steps. **2.** *Eccl.* A ledge or shelf above and at the back of an altar. Also **gra·dine** (grə·dēn′). [< F < Ital. *gradino,* dim. of *grado* < L *gradus* a step]
grad·u·al (graj′ōō·əl) *adj.* **1.** Moving, changing, proceeding, etc., slowly and by degrees. **2.** Having a slight degree of inclination; not abrupt or steep, as a slope. — *n. Eccl.* **1.** An antiphon sung after the Epistle and before the Gospel in the Eucharistic service. **2.** A book containing the parts of the Mass sung by the choir. [< Med.L *gradualis* < L *gradus* a step] — **grad′u·al·ly** *adv.* — **grad′u·al·ness** *n.*

TABLE OF COMPARATIVE GRADES
(UNITED STATES ARMED SERVICES)

Grade	Army	Air Force	Marine Corps	Navy	Coast Guard
O–11	General of the Army	General of the Air Force	(no equivalent)	Admiral of the Fleet	(no equivalent)
O–10	General	General	General	Admiral	Admiral
O–9	Lieutenant General	Lieutenant General	Lieutenant General	Vice Admiral	Vice Admiral
O–8	Major General	Major General	Major General	Rear Admiral (upper half)	Rear Admiral (upper half)
O–7	Brigadier General	Brigadier General	Brigadier General	Rear Admiral (lower half)	Rear Admiral (lower half)
O–6	Colonel	Colonel	Colonel	Captain	Captain
O–5	Lieutenant Colonel	Lieutenant Colonel	Lieutenant Colonel	Commander	Commander
O–4	Major	Major	Major	Lieutenant Commander	Lieutenant Commander
O–3	Captain	Captain	Captain	Lieutenant	Lieutenant
O–2	1st Lieutenant	1st Lieutenant	1st Lieutenant	Lieutenant (Junior Grade)	Lieutenant (Junior Grade)
O–1	2nd Lieutenant	2nd Lieutenant	2nd Lieutenant	Ensign	Ensign
W–4	Chief Warrant Officer				
W–3	Chief Warrant Officer	SAME	SAME	SAME	SAME
W–2	Chief Warrant Officer				
W–1	Warrant Officer				
E–9	Sergeant Major Specialist 9	Chief Master Sergeant	Master Gunnery Sergeant Sergeant Major	Master Chief Petty Officer	Master Chief Petty Officer
E–8	Master Sergeant First Sergeant Specialist 8	Senior Master Sergeant	Master Sergeant First Sergeant	Senior Chief Petty Officer	Senior Chief Petty Officer
E–7	Sergeant First Class Platoon Sergeant Specialist 7	Master Sergeant	Gunnery Sergeant	Chief Petty Officer	Chief Petty Officer
E–6	Staff Sergeant Specialist 6	Technical Sergeant	Staff Sergeant	Petty Officer First Class	Petty Officer First Class
E–5	Sergeant Specialist 5	Staff Sergeant	Sergeant	Petty Officer Second Class	Petty Officer Second Class
E–4	Corporal Specialist 4	Airman First Class	Corporal	Petty Officer Third Class	Petty Officer Third Class
E–3	Private First Class	Airman Second Class	Lance Corporal	Seaman	Seaman
E–2	Private	Airman Third Class	Private First Class	Seaman Apprentice	Seaman Apprentice
E–1	Recruit	Recruit	Private	Seaman Recruit	Seaman Recruit

TABLE OF GRADES
(CANADIAN ARMED FORCES)

The Canadian Forces Reorganization Act, which came into effect on February 1, 1968, unified the Royal Canadian Navy, the Canadian Army, and the Royal Canadian Air Force into a single service called the Canadian Armed Forces. Following are the new rank designations.

Officers	Men
General	Chief Warrant Officer
Lieutenant-General	Master Warrant Officer
Major-General	Warrant Officer
Brigadier-General	Sergeant
Colonel	Master Corporal
Lieutenant-Colonel	Corporal
Major	Private (Career Status)
Captain	Private
Lieutenant	
2nd Lieutenant	
Officer Cadet	

grad·u·al·ism (graj′oo-əl-iz′əm) *n.* The principle or practice of proceeding slowly, especially in regard to political or social change. **— grad′u·al·ist** *n.* **— grad′u·al·ist′ic** *adj.*

grad·u·and (graj′oo-ənd) *n. Canadian* A student who is about to graduate.

grad·u·ate (*v.* graj′oo-āt; *n. & adj.* graj′oo-it) *v.* ·at·ed, ·at·ing *v.i.* **1.** To receive a diploma or degree upon completion of a course of study. ◆ He *graduated from college* is now more widely used than the older form, He *was graduated from college.* He *graduated college* is considered nonstandard. **2.** To change gradually or by degrees. *— v.t.* **3.** Of an educational institution, to grant a diploma or degree to (someone) upon completion of a course of study. **4.** To arrange or sort according to size, degree, etc. **5.** To mark (a thermometer, scale, etc.) in units or degrees; calibrate. *— n.* **1.** One who has been granted a diploma or degree by an educational institution upon completion of a course of study. **2.** A beaker or similar vessel marked in units or degrees, used for measuring liquids, etc. *— adj.* **1.** Denoting a graduate student. **2.** Pertaining to or intended for such a student: *graduate* school. Abbr. *grad.* [< Med.L *graduatus,* pp. of *graduare* < L *gradus* step, degree]

graduate nurse A nurse (def. 2).

graduate student A student who has received a college or university degree and is working toward earning a more advanced degree.

grad·u·a·tion (graj′oo-ā′shən) *n.* **1.** The act of graduating or the state of being graduated. **2.** The ceremony of granting diplomas or degrees; commencement. **3.** A mark or division in a graduated scale; also, such divisions collectively.

gra·dus (grā′dəs) *n.* **1.** A dictionary of prosody used as an aid in writing Latin or Greek verse. **2.** *Music* A collection of studies or exercises arranged in order of difficulty. [< L *Gradus (ad Parnassum)* step (to Parnassus), title of a Latin dictionary, 1702]

Grae·ae (grē′ē) In Greek mythology, the three daughters of the sea god Phorcus, who, sharing the use of a single eye and a single tooth, guarded the habitation of the Gorgons: also spelled *Graiae.*

Grae·cia Mag·na (grē′shə mag′nə) In classical geography, the Greek colonies in southern Italy: also *Magna Graecia.*

Grae·cism (grē′siz-əm) *n.* A Grecism.

Grae·cize (grē′sīz) *v.t. & v.i.* ·cized, ·ciz·ing To Grecize.

Graeco- See GRECO-.

Graf (gräf) *n. pl.* **Graf·en** (gräf′ən) Count: a German, Austrian, or Swedish title of nobility equivalent to the English earl or French count. **Gräf·in** (gref′ēn) *n.fem.*

graf·fi·to (grə-fē′tō) *n. pl.* ·ti (-tē) *Archeol.* An inscription or drawing scratched on a rock, wall, etc. [< Ital. < *graffio* a scratch, ult. < Gk. *graphein* to write, draw]

graft[1] (graft, gräft) *n.* **1.** In horticulture: **a** A shoot (the cion) inserted into a prepared slit in a tree or plant (the stock) so as to become a living part of it. **b** The point of union of the cion and the stock. **2.** A plant, fruit, etc., obtained as a result of this operation. **2.** *Surg.* A piece of viable tissue transplanted to another part of the body or to the body of another individual. *— v.t.* **1.** In horticulture: **a** To insert (a cion) into a tree or plant. **b** To obtain (a plant, fruit, etc.) by grafting. **2.** *Surg.* To transplant (a piece of viable tissue) as a graft. **3.** To attach or incorporate, as by grafting: to *graft* new ideas on outworn concepts. *— v.i.* **4.** To insert or transplant grafts. **5.** To be or become grafted. [Earlier *graff* < OF *grafe* < LL *graphium* stylus < Gk. *grapheion* < *graphein* to write] **— graft′er** *n.*

graft[2] (graft, gräft) *U.S. n.* **1.** The act of getting personal advantage or profit by dishonest or unfair means, especially through one's political or official connections. **2.** Anything thus gained. *— v.t.* **1.** To acquire by graft. *— v.i.* **2.** To practice graft. [Cf. dial. E *graft* work, livelihood] **— graft′er** *n.*

graft·age (graf′tij, gräf′-) *n.* In horticulture, the process or technique of making grafts.

gra·ham (grā′əm) *adj.* Made of unsifted whole-wheat flour. [after Sylvester *Graham,* 1794–1851, U.S. vegetarian]

Gra·ham (grā′əm), **Martha,** born 1893?, U.S. dancer and choreographer. **— Thomas,** 1805–69, Scottish chemist.

graham cracker *U.S.* A cracker made of graham flour. Also *Canadian* **graham wafer.**

Gra·hame (grā′əm), **Kenneth,** 1859–1932, English author.

Graham Land See PALMER PENINSULA.

Grai·ae (grā′ē, grī′ē) See GRAEAE.

grail (grāl) *n.* In medieval legend, the cup or dish used at the Last Supper by Jesus Christ, in which Joseph of Arimathea caught some of the blood shed at the Crucifixion. It later became a symbol of religious perfection, visible only to those who were morally and spiritually worthy. Also called *Holy Grail, Sangreal:* also spelled *graal.* [< OF *graal* < Med.L *gradalis;* ult. origin uncertain]

grain (grān) *n.* **1.** A hard seed or kernel; especially, that of any of the cereal plants, as wheat, oats, barley, corn, etc. **2.** The harvested seeds of these plants. **3.** These plants collectively. **4.** Any very small, hard mass. **5.** The smallest possible quantity of anything: a *grain* of truth. **6.** The smallest unit of weight used in several systems in the U.S. and Great Britain, first fixed by the weight of a grain of wheat. Abbr. *g., G., gr.* See table inside back cover. **7.** The direction or arrangement of the fibers or fibrous particles in various kinds of wood; also, the markings or pattern resulting from such an arrangement. **8.** The side of a piece of leather from which the hair has been removed; also, the characteristic texture or patterned markings of this side. **9.** A paint, stamp, or pattern used to imitate the characteristic markings of leather, wood, etc. **10.** The comparative size or texture of the particles composing a substance, surface, or pattern: marble of fine *grain.* **11.** The yarn or fibers that make up a textile, as distinguished from the textile itself. **12.** The direction of cleavage of a mineral substance, as diamond, coal, etc. **13.** A state of crystallization: to boil syrup to the *grain.* **14.** Natural disposition or temperament. **15.** *Obs.* The color, usually red, produced by a fast dye; also, the source, as cochineal or kermes, of such a dye. **— against the grain** Contrary to one's natural temperament or inclinations. *— v.t.* **1.** To form into grains; granulate. **2.** To paint or stain in imitation of the grain of wood, marble, etc. **3.** To give a roughened or granular appearance or texture to. **4.** In leathermaking: **a** To scrape the hair from. **b** To soften or raise the grain or pattern of. *— v.i.* **5.** To form grains. [Fusion of OF *grain* seed and *graine* seed, grain, both < L *granum* seed] **— grain′er** *n.* **— grain′less** *adj.*

grain alcohol Ethanol, especially when made from grain.

grain elevator *U.S.* A building especially designed for the storage of grain.

Grain·ger (grān′jər), **Percy Aldridge,** 1882–1961, U.S. composer and pianist born in Australia.

grains of paradise The seeds of a West African plant (*Aframomum melegueta*) of the ginger family, used as a diuretic and stimulant: also called *guinea grains.*

grain·y (grā′nē) *adj.* **grain·i·er, grain·i·est 1.** Full of or consisting of grains or kernels. **2.** Having a granular texture. **3.** Resembling the grain in wood. **4.** Rough in tone and showing details poorly: said of photographs. **— grain′·i·ness** *n.*

gral·la·to·ri·al (gral′ə-tôr′ē-əl, -tō′rē-) *adj.* Of or pertaining to a former order (*Grallatores*) of long-legged wading birds, including the herons and snipes. [< L *grallator* one who walks on stilts < *grallae* stilts]

gram[1] (gram) *n.* The basic unit of mass or weight in the metric system, equivalent to 15.432 grains, or one thousandth of a kilogram. Also spelled *gramme.* Abbr. *g, g., gm., gr.* See table inside back cover. [< F *gramme* < LL *gramma* small weight < Gk. *gramma*]

gram[2] (gram) *n.* **1.** The chickpea of India and the East Indies, used as food or fodder. **2.** Any of various leguminous plants, as **black gram** (*Phaseolus mungo*). [< Pg. *grão* < L *granum* seed]

gram. Grammar; grammarian; grammatical.

-gram[1] *combining form* Something written or drawn: *telegram.* [< Gk. *gramma* letter, writing < *graphein* to write]

-gram[2] *combining form* A gram: used in the metric system: *kilogram.* [< GRAM[1]]

gra·ma (grä′mə) *n.* Any of various pasture grasses (genus *Bouteloua*) of the western and SW United States; especially, **blue grama** (*B. gracilis*). Also **grama grass.** [< Sp. < L *gramen* grass]

gram·a·rye (gram′ə-rē) *n. Archaic* Occult lore; magic. Also **gram′a·ry.** [< OF *gramaire* grammar; in later use, learning, lore, magical skill. See GRAMMAR.]

gram atom *Chem.* The quantity of an element, expressed in grams, that is equal to the atomic weight of that element. Also **gram′-a·tom′ic weight** (-ə-tom′ik).

gram calorie See under CALORIE.

gram equivalent *Chem.* That quantity of a substance, expressed in grams, that will combine with or displace 1.008 grams of hydrogen or 8 grams of oxygen. Also **gram′-e·quiv′·a·lent weight** (gram′i-kwiv′ə-lənt).

gra·mer·cy (grə-mûr′sē, gram′ər-sē) *interj. Archaic* **1.** Many thanks. **2.** An exclamation of surprise. [< OF *grand merci* great thanks]

gra·min·e·ous (grə-min′ē-əs) *adj.* **1.** Pertaining to or like grass. **2.** Belonging to the grass family (*Gramineae*).

gram·i·niv·o·rous (gram′ə-niv′ər-əs) *adj.* **1.** Feeding on grains or grasses. **2.** Adapted for feeding on grains, as the jaws of some rodents.

gram·mar (gram′ər) *n.* **1.** In modern usage, the scientific study of the morphology and syntax of a language or dialect; also, a description of the morphologic and syntactic structure of a language or dialect: often called *descriptive grammar.* **2.** Formerly, the study of all aspects of language, as phonology, orthography, syntax, etymology, semantics, and prosody. **3.** A system of morphologic and syntactic rules and principles for the regulation of a given language: often called *prescriptive* or *normative grammar.* **4.** A treatise or book dealing with grammatical matters, whether descriptive or prescriptive. **5.** Speech or writing considered with regard to current standards of correctness: His *grammar* is excellent. **6.** The elements of any science or art, or a book or treatise dealing with them. Abbr. *gr., gram.* [< OF *gramaire* < L *grammatica* < Gk. *grammatikē* (*technē*) literary (art) < *grammata* literature, orig. pl. of *gramma* letter < *graphein* to write. Related to GLAMOUR.]

gram·mar·i·an (grə-mâr/ē-ən) *n.* A specialist in grammar.

grammar school 1. An elementary school (which see). **2.** *Brit.* A secondary school, especially one in which Latin and Greek are taught.

gram·mat·i·cal (grə-mat/i-kəl) *adj.* **1.** Of or pertaining to grammar. **2.** Conforming to the usage of standard speech or writing. — **gram·mat/i·cal·ly** *adv.* — **gram·mat/i·cal·ness** *n.*

grammatical gender See under GENDER.

gramme (gram) See GRAM[1].

gram molecule *Chem.* The quantity of a compound, expressed in grams, that is equal to the molecular weight of that compound: also called *mole.* Also **gram/-mo·lec/u·lar weight** (-mə-lek/yə-lər).

Gram-neg·a·tive (gram/neg/ə-tiv) *adj.* Designating bacteria that are decolorized by alcohol in Gram's method.

Gra·mont (grà-môn/), **Comte Philibert de,** 1621?–1707, French courtier and adventurer.

gram·o·phone (gram/ə-fōn) *n.* *Chiefly Brit.* A record player. [< *Gramophone,* a trade name]

Gram·pi·ans (gram/pē-ənz) A mountain chain in Scotland dividing the Highlands from the Lowlands; highest peak, Ben Nevis, 4,406 ft. Also **Grampian Hills, Grampian Mountains.**

Gram-pos·i·tive (gram/poz/ə-tiv) *adj.* Designating bacteria that retain the violet dye in Gram's method.

gram·pus (gram/pəs) *n. pl.* **·pus·es 1.** A large, dolphin-like cetacean (*Grampidelphis griseus*) of Atlantic and Pacific waters: also called *springer.* **2.** The killer whale. [Alter. of obs. *grapeys* < OF *grapois, graspeis* < Med.L *crassus piscis* fat fish]

Gram's method (gramz) *Bacteriol.* A method for differentiating and classifying bacteria by staining them first with aniline gentian violet, then with an iodine solution, followed by immersion in alcohol. Those bacteria decolorized by the alcohol are **Gram-negative,** and those retaining the purple dye are **Gram-positive.** [after Hans C. J. *Gram,* 1855–1938, Danish physician.]

Gra·na·da (grə-nä/də, *Sp.* grä-nä/thä) **1.** A Province of southern Spain; 4,438 sq. mi.; pop. 769,403 (1960). **2.** The capital of Granada in the central part of the Province; site of the Alhambra and former capital of a Moorish kingdom; pop. 157,178 (1960).

gran·a·dil·la (gran/ə-dil/ə) *n.* **1.** The edible fruit of various species of passionflower; especially, the **giant granadilla** (*Passiflora quadrangularis*), with a soft pulp of a sweet, acid flavor. **2.** Any plant yielding this fruit. [< Sp., dim. of *granada* pomegranate]

gran·a·dil·lo (gran/ə-dil/ō) *n.* **1.** Any of various tropical American trees, especially a West Indian tree (*Brya ebenus*) yielding a hard, durable wood used in making flutes, clarinets, recorders, etc. **2.** Rosewood (def. 1). [< Sp.]

gran·a·ry (gran/ər·ē, grā/nər-) *n. pl.* **·ries 1.** A storehouse for threshed grain. **2.** A region where grain grows in abundance. [< L *granarium* < *granum* grain]

Gran Cha·co (grän chä/kō) A large lowland plain of central South America, extending into Paraguay, Bolivia, and Argentina: also **El Chaco.**

grand (grand) *adj.* **1.** Impressive because of great size, extent, or splendor; imposing; magnificent. **2.** In literature and the arts, lofty or sublime in subject or treatment; conceived or executed on a large or impressive scale. **3.** Noble or dignified in character, manner, or bearing; majestic; stately. **4.** Worthy of respect because of age, experience, or dignity: often with *old:* the *grand* old man of politics. **5.** Of high or highest rank or official position: a *grand* duke; the *grand* jury. **6.** First in size or importance; principal; main: the *grand* ballroom. **7.** Characterized by pomp or luxury; sumptuous. **8.** Conscious of one's wealth or importance; haughty. **9.** Comprehensive; all-inclusive: the *grand* total. **10.** Having a family relationship one degree more distant than: used in combination: *grandson; grandaunt.* **11.** *Informal* Highly satisfactory; admirable; excellent. — *n.* **1.** A grand piano. **2.** *U.S. Slang* A thousand dollars. [< OF < L *grandis*] — **grand/ly** *adv.* — **grand/ness** *n.*
— **Syn.** (adj.) *Grand* and *great* as applied to persons mean outstanding in character or achievement. *Grand* is used only in a good sense, *great* in good or bad: a *grand* humanitarian, a *great* architect, a *great* (but not a *grand*) rascal.

gran·dam (gran/dam, -dəm) *n.* *Archaic* A grandmother; an old woman. Also **gran/dame** (-dām, -dəm). [< AF *graund dame*]

Grand Army of the Republic An organization of Union army and navy veterans of the Civil War in the United States, founded in 1866. Abbr. *GAR, G.A.R.*

grand-aunt (grand/ant/, -änt/) *n.* An aunt of one's father or mother; great-aunt.

Grand Banks (bangks) A submarine shoal in the North Atlantic east and south of Newfoundland; about 420 by 350 mi.; a major fishing ground. Also **Grand Bank.**

Grand Canal 1. A large canal in Venice, Italy, constituting the city's main thoroughfare. **2.** The longest canal of China, constituting the main north-south waterway of north China; length, about 1,000 mi.

Grand Canary The most populous and important of the Canary Islands; 592 sq. mi.; chief city, Las Palmas. *Spanish* **Gran Ca·na·ri·a** (gräng kä·nä/ryä).

Grand Canyon A gorge formed by the Colorado River in NW Arizona; length, about 250 mi.; width, 4–18 mi.; depth, about one mile.

Grand Canyon National Park A national park on the Colorado River in NW Arizona, including a large section of Grand Canyon; 1,008 sq. mi.; established 1919.

Grand Canyon State Nickname of ARIZONA.

grand·child (grand/chīld/) *n. pl.* **·chil·dren** (-chil/drən) A child of one's son or daughter.

grand climacteric The sixty-third year of life. See CLIMACTERIC (n. def. 1).

Grand Cou·lee (kōō/lē) A valley in east central Washington through which the Columbia River formerly flowed; site of **Grand Coulee Dam,** 550 ft. high, 4,300 ft. long, forming Franklin D. Roosevelt Lake.

grand·dad (gran/dad/) *n.* *Informal* Grandfather. Also **grand/dad/dy.**

grand·daugh·ter (gran/dô/tər, grand/-) *n.* A daughter of one's son or daughter.

grand duchess 1. The wife or widow of a grand duke. **2.** A woman who is sovereign of a grand duchy. **3.** Formerly, in Russia, a daughter of a czar, or a daughter of any of his descendants in the male line. Abbr. *G.D.*

grand duchy The territory under the rule of a grand duke or grand duchess. Abbr. *G.D.*

grand duke 1. The sovereign of a grand duchy, holding a rank just below king. **2.** Formerly, in Russia, a ruler of a principality; later, a son or grandson of a czar. Abbr. *G.D.*

grande dame (gränd däm/) *French* A great lady.

gran·dee (gran-dē/) *n.* **1.** A Spanish or Portuguese nobleman of the highest rank. **2.** Any person of high rank or great importance. [< Sp. *grande* great]

Grande-Terre (gränd-târ/), **Grande Terre** See GUADALOUPE.

gran·deur (gran/jər, -jŏor) *n.* **1.** The quality or condition of being grand; magnificence; splendor. **2.** Greatness or nobility of character. [< F < *grand* great]

Grand Falls A waterfall on the upper Hamilton River in Labrador; 245 ft. high; 200 ft. wide.

grand·fa·ther (grand/fä/thər) *n.* **1.** The father of one's father or mother. **2.** An ancestor.

grandfather clause *U.S.* In some Southern States, a constitutional clause intended to deprive Negroes of the right to vote. Such clauses were declared unconstitutional in 1915.

grandfather clock A clock having a pendulum and enclosed in a tall cabinet. Also **grandfather's clock.**

grand·fa·ther·ly (grand/fä/thər·lē) *adj.* **1.** Resembling or characteristic of a grandfather. **2.** Having qualities considered suitable to a grandfather; benevolent; kindly.

Grand Forks A city in eastern North Dakota on the Red River; pop. 39,008.

gran·dil·o·quence (gran·dil/ə·kwəns) *n.* The quality of being grandiloquent; pompous or bombastic speech or style.

gran·dil·o·quent (gran·dil/ə·kwənt) *adj.* Speaking in or characterized by a pompous or bombastic style. — **Syn.** See RHETORICAL. [< L *grandiloquus* < *grandis* great + *loqui* to speak; infl. in form by ELOQUENT] — **gran·dil/o·quent·ly** *adv.*

gran·di·ose (gran/dē·ōs, gran/dē·ōs/) *adj.* **1.** Producing an effect of grandeur; imposing. **2.** Pretentiously grand; pompous; bombastic. [< F < Ital. *grandioso* < L *grandis* great] — **gran/di·ose/ly** *adv.* — **gran·di·os·i·ty** (gran/dē·os/ə·tē) *n.*

gran·di·o·so (grän·dē·ō/sō) *Music adj.* Grand or imposing. — *adv.* In a grand or imposing manner. [< Ital.]

Grand Island A city in SE central Nebraska; pop. 31,269.

grand jury A body of persons, consisting of not fewer than twelve nor more than twenty-four, called to hear complaints of the commission of offenses and to ascertain whether there is prima-facie evidence for an indictment.

Grand Lac (grän läk/) The French name for TONLE SAP.

Grand Lama The Dalai Lama (which see).

grand larceny See under LARCENY.

grand·ma (grand/mä/, gran/mä/, gram/mä, gram/ə) *n.* *Informal* Grandmother. Also **grand·ma·ma** (grand/mə·mä/, -mä/mə), **grand/mam·ma/.**

grand mal (grän mäl/) *Pathol.* A type of epilepsy characterized by severe convulsions and loss of consciousness: distinguished from *petit mal.* [< F, lit., great sickness]

Grand Ma·nan (mə·nan/) An island in the Bay of Fundy, SW New Brunswick, Canada; 57 sq. mi.

Grand Mogul See under MOGUL.

grand monde (grän mônd/) *French* Fashionable society.

grand·moth·er (grand/muth/ər) *n.* **1.** The mother of one's father or mother. **2.** A female ancestor.

grand·moth·er·ly (grand/muth/ər·lē) *adj.* **1.** Resembling or characteristic of a grandmother. **2.** Having qualities typical of a grandmother; overly protective or solicitous.

Grand Mufti The titular head of the Moslem community in Jerusalem.

grand·neph·ew (grand'nef'yōo, -nev'-, gran'-) *n.* A son of one's nephew or niece.

grand·niece (grand'nēs', gran'-) *n.* A daughter of one's nephew or niece.

Grand Old Party In U.S. politics, the Republican Party. Abbr. *GOP, G.O.P.*

grand opera A form of opera, usually having a serious and dramatically complex plot, in which the entire text is set to music. Compare OPÉRA COMIQUE.

grand·pa (grand'pä', gram'pä', gram'pə) *n. Informal* Grandfather. Also **grand·pa·pa** (grand'pə·pä', grand'pä'· pə).

grand·par·ent (grand'pâr'ənt, gran'-) *n.* A grandmother or grandfather.

grand piano A large piano having strings arranged horizontally in a curved, wooden case. Grand pianos range in size from the large **concert grand**, used in public performances, to the **baby grand**, intended for home use.

Grand Prairie A city in northern Texas, a suburb of Dallas; pop. 50,904.

Grand Pré (grän prā') A village in central Nova Scotia; home of the Acadians in Longfellow's poem *Evangeline.*

grand prix (grän prē') *French* Grand prize.

Grand Prix Any of an international group of automobile road races at the highest level of speed, power, and skill.

Grand Rapids A city in western Michigan; pop. 197,649.

Grand River **1.** The former name of the Colorado River NE of its confluence with the Green River in SE Utah. **2.** A river in southern Iowa and NW Missouri, flowing about 215 miles SE to the Missouri. **3.** A river in southern and western Michigan, flowing north and west about 260 miles to Lake Michigan.

grand·sire (grand'sīr', -sər) *n. Archaic* **1.** A grandfather. **2.** An ancestor. **3.** Any venerable old man.

grand slam **1.** In bridge, the winning, by the declarer, of all thirteen tricks in a round of play; also, a bid to do so. **2.** *U.S. Informal* In baseball, a home run hit when there is a runner on every base.

grand·son (grand'sun', gran'-) *n.* A son of one's son or daughter.

grand·stand (grand'stand', gran'-) *n.* A raised platform or series of seats for spectators at a racetrack, sports stadium, public event, etc.

grandstand play *U.S. Informal* Any sports play or similar action performed to win applause or approval.

Grand Teton National Park A mountainous region of NW Wyoming including part of the Teton range; 465 sq. mi.; established 1929.

grand tour **1.** Formerly, an extended journey through the chief cities of continental Europe, undertaken as part of the education of sons of wealthy or aristocratic families. **2.** Any extended sightseeing trip, circuit, etc.

grand·un·cle (grand'ung'kəl) *n.* An uncle of one's father or mother; great-uncle.

grand vizier See under VIZIER.

grange (grānj) *n.* **1.** *Often cap. U.S.* Any subsidiary lodge or branch of the Grange. **2.** *Brit.* A farm, with its dwelling house, barns, etc.; especially, the residence of a gentleman farmer. **3.** Formerly, a farm establishment belonging to a feudal manor or monastery, serving as a storage place for the grain paid as rent or tithes. **4.** *Obs.* A granary. [< AF *graunge,* OF *grange* < Med.L *granea* < L *granum* grain]

Grange (grānj) *n.* The order of Patrons of Husbandry, an association of U.S. farmers founded in 1867 to promote agricultural interests.

grang·er (grān'jər) *n.* **1.** *Often cap. U.S.* A member of a grange. **2.** A farmer.

grang·er·ize (grān'jə·rīz') *v.t.* **·ized, ·iz·ing** **1.** To illustrate (a book already in print) with prints, engravings, etc., taken from other books. **2.** To mutilate (a book) by cutting out the illustrations. [after Rev. James *Granger,* 1723–76, whose *Biographical History of England* (1769) was designed to be so illustrated] — **grang'er·ism, grang'er·i·za'tion** *n.* — **grang'er·iz'er** *n.*

grani- *combining form* Grain: *graniform.* [< L *granum* grain]

Gra·ni·cus (grə·nī'kəs) A river in NW Turkey, flowing 45 miles NE to the Sea of Marmara; scene of Alexander the Great's defeat of the Persians in 334 B.C.: Turkish *Kocabas.*

gra·nif·er·ous (grə·nif'ər·əs) *adj. Bot.* Bearing grain.

gran·i·form (gran'ə·fôrm') *adj.* Formed like a grain.

gran·ite (gran'it) *n.* **1.** A hard, coarse-grained, igneous rock composed principally of quartz, feldspar, and mica, much used as a building material, in sculpture, etc. **2.** Great hardness, firmness, endurance, etc. [< Ital. *granito,* orig. pp. of *granire* to make seeds < *grano* seed < L *granum* grain] — **gra·nit·ic** (grə·nit'ik) *adj.*

Granite City A city in SW Illinois, near St. Louis; pop. 40,440.

Granite State Nickname of NEW HAMPSHIRE.

gran·ite·ware (gran'it·wâr') *n.* **1.** A variety of ironware coated with hard enamel. **2.** A type of fine, hard pottery.

gran·it·ite (gran'it·īt) *n.* Granite containing biotite.

gran·it·oid (gran'it·oid) *adj.* Designating any igneous rock having the structure or appearance of granite.

gra·niv·o·rous (grə·niv'ər·əs) *adj.* Feeding chiefly on grain or seeds.

gran·ny (gran'ē) *n. pl.* **·nies** **1.** Grandmother: used familiarly. **2.** An old woman. **3.** *Informal* A fussy, interfering person. **4.** *Southern U.S.* A nurse or midwife. **5.** A granny knot. Also **gran'nie.**

granny knot A knot resembling the square knot but having the second tie crossed in such a way as to form an insecure yet easily jammed fastening For illustration see KNOT. Also **granny's knot** (gran'ēz), **granny's bend.**

grano- *combining form* Granitic: *granolith.* [< L *granum* grain]

gran·o·lith (gran'ə·lith) *n.* Pulverized granite cement used as stone for paving. — **gran·o·lith·ic** (gran'ə·lith'ik) *adj.*

gran·o·phyre (gran'ə·fīr) *n.* A fine-grained, porphyritic rock consisting of a groundmass of closely interpenetrating quartz and feldspar crystals. [< GRANO- + (POR)PHYRY] — **gran·o·phy·ric** (gran'ə·fī'rik) *adj.*

grant (grant, gränt) *v.t.* **1.** To confer or bestow, as a privilege, charter, etc. **2.** To allow (someone) to have; give, as permission. **3.** To accede to; yield to, as a request. **4.** To admit as true, as for the sake of argument; concede. **5.** To transfer (property), especially by deed. — *n.* **1.** The act of granting. **2.** That which is granted, as a piece of property, a sum of money, or a special power or privilege. **3.** One of certain tracts of land in Maine, New Hampshire, or Vermont, originally granted by patent to an individual or individuals. **4.** *Law* A transfer of real property by deed. [< AF *graunter, granter,* ult. < L *credens, -entis,* ppr. of *credere* to believe] — **grant'a·ble** *adj.* — **grant'er** *n.*
— **Syn.** (verb) *Grant, accord, award,* and *concede* are compared in the sense of giving. We *grant* out of generosity, often in response to supplication: to *grant* liberty to a captive. We *accord* what is due, *award* what is deserved or earned, and *concede* what is justly claimed. Compare GIVE. — (noun) **2.** See SUBSIDY.

Grant (grant), Ulysses S(impson), 1822–85, U.S. general in the Civil War, 18th president of the United States 1869–77: original name **Hiram Ulysses Grant.**

grant·ed (gran'tid, grän'-) *Past participle of* GRANT. — **to take for granted** **1.** To assume to be true; believe unquestioningly. **2.** To accept as one's due; be complacently neglectful of: *to take one's friends for granted.*

gran·tee (gran·tē', grän-) *n. Law* The person to whom a grant is made.

grant-in-aid (grant'in·ād', gränt'-) *n. pl.* **grants-in-aid** (grantz'in·ād, gräntz'-) **1.** A grant of funds by a central government to a local government or agency for assistance in a civic undertaking. **2.** A similar grant made by a private organization in support of any worthy enterprise. **3.** A grant of money for needy students.

grant·or (gran'tər, gran·tôr') *n. Law* The person by whom a grant is made.

gran·u·lar (gran'yə·lər) *adj.* **1.** Composed of, like, or containing grains or granules. **2.** Having a granulated surface. — **gran·u·lar·i·ty** (-lar'ə·tē) *n.* — **gran'u·lar·ly** *adv.*

gran·u·late (gran'yə·lāt) *v.t. & v.i.* **·lat·ed, ·lat·ing** **1.** To make or become granular; form into grains. **2.** To become or cause to become roughened, as by the formation of granules. **3.** *Physiol.* To produce or develop granulations. — **gran'u·la'tive** *adj.* — **gran'u·la'tor** *n.*

granulated sugar Sugar in the form of small grains.

gran·u·la·tion (gran'yə·lā'shən) *n.* **1.** The act or process of granulating or of becoming granulated. **2.** A granulated surface, or one of the elevations in such surface. **3.** *Physiol.* **a** The process of forming new tissue, as in the healing of wounds, ulcers, and the like. **b** The minute, flesh-colored, beadlike projections so formed. **4.** *Astron.* An evanescent mottled appearance observed in the photosphere of the sun, attributed to gaseous convection currents in the outer layers.

gran·ule (gran'yōol) *n.* **1.** A small grain or particle; tiny pellet. **2.** *Biol.* One of the small bodies in the cytoplasm of cells. [< LL *granulum,* dim. of L *granum* grain]

gran·u·lite (gran'yə·līt) *n.* A uniformly granular metamorphic rock composed mainly of quartz and feldspar, and often containing garnet. — **gran·u·lit·ic** (gran'yə·lit'ik) *adj.*

gran·u·lose (gran'yə·lōs) *n.* That portion of starch granules capable of being changed into sugar by certain ferments. [< GRANUL(E) + -OSE²]

Gran·ville-Bark·er (gran'vil·bär'kər), Harley, 1877–1946, English playwright, critic, producer, and actor.

grape (grāp) *n.* **1.** One of the smooth-skinned, juicy, edible berries borne in clusters by various climbing vines or small shrubs (genus *Vitis*), cultivated in many species as a fruit and for making wine. **2.** Any of the vines bearing these berries; especially, the wine grape and the fox grape. **3.** A dark, purplish blue color. **4.** Grapeshot. [< OF, bunch of grapes < *graper* to gather grapes < *grape* hook < Gmc.]

grape·fruit (grāp′frōōt′) *n.* **1.** A large, round citrus fruit having a pale yellow rind and tart, juicy pulp. **2.** The tree (*Citrus paradisi*) bearing this fruit, native to tropical regions and cultivated in the southern United States. Also called *pomelo.*

grape hyacinth A plant (genus *Muscari*) of the lily family, having spikes of small, usually blue, globular flowers.

grape rot A widespread and malignant disease of grapes, caused by a parasitic fungus (*Plasmopara viticola*) and characterized by the formation of a milky coating on the leaves: also called *downy mildew.* Also **grape blight.**

grap·er·y (grā′pər·ē) *n. pl.* **·er·ies** A building or enclosure where grapes are grown; vinery.

grape·shot (grāp′shot′) *n.* A kind of shot consisting of a cluster of iron balls, formerly fired from cannons.

grape·stone (grāp′stōn′) *n.* A seed of a grape.

grape sugar Dextrose.

grape·vine (grāp′vīn′) *n.* **1.** Any of the climbing vines that bear grapes. **2.** *U.S.* A secret or unofficial means of relaying information, usually from person to person: also **grapevine telegraph.**

graph (graf, gräf) *n.* **1.** A diagram representing variations in the relationship between two or more factors by means of a series of connected points, or by bars, curves, lines, etc. **2.** *Math.* The locus of a point moving in relation to coordinates so that all of the values involved satisfy the functions of an equation. — *v.t.* To express or represent in the form of a graph. [Short for *graphic formula*]

-graph *combining form* **1.** That which writes or records: *seismograph.* **2.** A writing or record: *autograph.* [< F -*graphe* < L -*graphus* < Gk. -*graphos* < *graphein* to write]

-grapher *combining form* Forming nouns of agency corresponding to words in -*graph* or -*graphy*: *photographer.*

graph·ic (graf′ik) *adj.* **1.** Presenting an exact picture; describing in full detail; vivid. **2.** Of, pertaining to, or illustrated by graphs or diagrams. **3.** Pertaining to, consisting of, or expressed by writing or inscribed representation: *graphic* signs. **4.** Of, pertaining to, or characteristic of the graphic arts. **5.** *Math.* Pertaining to or denoting a process, solution, etc., based on the use of graphs. **6.** *Geol.* Denoting a rock or mineral having crystals arranged so as to produce an appearance of written or printed signs on exposed or cut surfaces: *graphic* granite; *graphic* gold. Also **graph′i·cal.** [< L *graphicus* < Gk. *graphikos* of writing < *graphē* writing] — **graph′i·cal·ly** or **graph′ic·ly** *adv.*

— **Syn. 1.** *Graphic, pictorial,* and *picturesque* are compared as they mean vivid like a picture. A written or spoken description is *graphic* if it conjures up a mental image as precise as a picture. *Pictorial* is applied to the form or content of a description rather than to the result; a *pictorial* description attempts to show what is seen by the eye, with or without success. Something seen is *picturesque* if we think that it would make a striking picture: a *picturesque* mountain inn. Compare VIVID.

-graphic *combining form* Forming adjectives corresponding to nouns ending in -*graph*: *photographic.* Also **-graphical.**

graphic accent A mark over a letter, used to indicate stress, as in Spanish *lección.*

graphic arts 1. Those visual arts involving the use of lines or strokes on a flat surface, as painting, drawing, engraving, etc. **2.** In recent usage, those arts that involve impressions or reproductions taken from blocks, plates, type, or the like, as in printing, etching, wood engraving, lithography, etc.

graph·ics (graf′iks) *n.pl.* (construed as *sing.*) **1.** The science or art of making drawings or diagrams that conform with mathematical rules, as in engineering, architecture, etc.; mechanical drawing. **2.** Calculation, as of structural stresses, by means of such drawings or diagrams.

graph·ite (graf′īt) *n.* A soft, black, chemically inert variety of carbon having a metallic luster and a slippery texture, used as a lubricant and in making pencils, electrodes, crucibles, etc. Also called *black lead, plumbago.* [< G *graphit* < Gk. *graphein* to write + -*it* -ITE¹] — **gra·phit′ic** (-fit′ik) *adj.*

graph·i·tize (graf′ə·tīz) *v.t.* **·tized, ·tiz·ing 1.** To coat or impregnate with graphite. **2.** To make into graphite by a heating process. — **graph′i·ti·za′tion** *n.*

grapho- *combining form* Of or pertaining to writing: *graphology.* Also, before vowels, **graph-.** [< Gk. *graphē* writing < *graphein* to write]

graph·ol·o·gy (gra·fol′ə·jē) *n.* The study of handwriting, especially as a method of estimating the writer's character. — **graph·o·log′i·cal** (graf′ə·loj′i·kal) *adj.* — **graph·ol′o·gist** *n.*

graph·o·mo·tor (graf′ə·mō′tər) *adj. Med.* Pertaining to or influencing the muscular movements made in writing.

graph·o·phone (graf′ə·fōn) *n.* An early type of record player. [< *Graphophone,* a trade name]

graph·o·spasm (graf′ə·spaz′əm) *n.* Writer's cramp.

graph paper Paper marked by intersecting lines, usually into small, equal squares, and used for drawing graphs, curves, mechanical diagrams, etc.: also called *plotting paper.*

-graphy *combining form* **1.** A writing, recording, or process

of representation: *biography, photography.* **2.** A descriptive science: *petrography.* [< Gk. -*graphia* < *graphein* to write]

grap·lin (grap′lin) *n. Archaic* A grapnel. Also **grap′line** (-lin). [Alter. of GRAPNEL]

grap·nel (grap′nəl) *n.* **1.** A small anchor with several flukes at the end of the shank. For illustration see ANCHOR. **2.** Any of various devices consisting of a clamp, hook, or arrangement of hooked parts, used to seize and hold objects. [ME *grapenel,* dim. of OF *grapin* hook]

grap·ple (grap′əl) *v.* **·pled, ·pling** *v.t.* **1.** To seize or take hold of with or as with a grapnel; grip tightly. — *v.i.* **2.** To struggle in close combat; come to grips with one another, as in wrestling. **3.** To struggle or contend: with *with*: to *grapple* with a problem. **4.** To use a grapnel. — *n.* **1.** A grapnel. **2.** The act of grappling. **3.** A grip or close hold, as in wrestling. [< OF *grappil* grapnel] — **grap′pler** *n.*

grap·pling (grap′ling) *n.* **1.** The act of seizing, grasping, or struggling in close combat. **2.** A grapnel.

grappling iron A grapnel. Also **grappling hook.**

grap·y (grā′pē) *adj.* **grap·i·er, grap·i·est** Of or like grapes.

Gras·mere (gras′mir, gräs′-) A lake in Westmorland, England; length, one mile.

grasp (grasp, gräsp) *v.t.* **1.** To seize firmly with or as with the hand; take hold of firmly; grip. **2.** To seize greedily or eagerly; grab. **3.** To take hold of with the mind; comprehend. — *v.i.* **4.** To make the motion of grasping or clutching. — **to grasp at 1.** To try to seize. **2.** To accept eagerly, as an offer or suggestion. — *n.* **1.** The act of grasping; also, a grip of the hand. **2.** The power or ability to seize; reach: Victory was within his *grasp.* **3.** Absolute possession or control; domination: the tyrant's *grasp.* **4.** Intellectual comprehension or mastery: matters beyond one's *grasp*; a thorough *grasp* of the subject. [ME *graspen,* metathetic var. of *grapsen* < LG] — **grasp′a·ble** *adj.* — **grasp′er** *n.*

— **Syn.** (verb) *Grasp, grip, grab, embrace, clasp, clutch,* and *snatch* mean to lay hold of with the arm or hands, usually forcibly. *Grasp* is to seize, and *grip* to hold tightly, with the fingers or hand; both imply determination but not urgency. *Grab* is akin to *grasp,* but suggests roughness or violence in seizing. *Embrace* is to encircle with the arms, and most frequently refers to a gesture of affection or regard. *Clasp* is to hold by grasping or embracing, so as to prevent escape or removal: the child *clasped* her doll in her arms. *Clutch* combines the meanings of *grasp* and *grip,* but implies eagerness or urgency in seizing, and often further implies an insecure hold: she *clutched* at my arm as she fell. *Snatch* is akin to *grab,* and refers to any sudden or jerky seizure. Compare CATCH.

grasp·ing (gras′ping, gräs′-) *adj.* **1.** Greedy. **2.** That grasps. — **grasp′ing·ly** *adv.* — **grasp′ing·ness** *n.*

grass (gras, gräs) *n.* **1.** Any plant of a large family (*Gramineae,* formerly *Poaceae*) characterized by rounded and hollow jointed stems, narrow, sheathing leaves, flowers borne in spikes or panicles, and hard, grainlike seeds; also, such plants collectively. **2.** Herbage generally; especially, the herbaceous plants eaten by grazing animals. **3.** Any of numerous plants with grasslike foliage: often used in descriptive plant names: blue-eyed *grass.* **4.** Ground on which grass is growing; lawn. **5.** Grazing ground; pasture. **6.** *pl.* Stalks or sprays of grass. **7.** *Slang* Green vegetables; salad. — **to let the grass grow under one's feet** To let opportunity go by; waste time. — *v.t.* **1.** To cover with grass or turf. **2.** To feed with grass; pasture. **3.** To spread (cloth, etc.) on the grass, for bleaching by the sun. **4.** In sports, to fell or bring down, as by a punch or shot; also, to land (a fish). — *v.i.* **5.** To graze. **6.** To produce grass; become covered with grass. [OE *græs.* Akin to GREEN, GROW.]

Grasse (gräs), **François Joseph Paul, Comte de,** 1722–88, French admiral in the American Revolution.

grass cloth Cloth woven from grass or from various tough vegetable fibers, as ramie.

grass hockey *Canadian* Field hockey (which see).

grass·hop·per (gras′hop′ər, gräs′-) *n.* **1.** Any of several orthopterous insects, as the locust and katydid, with powerful hind legs adapted for leaping, many species of which are destructive to crops and vegetation. For illustration see INSECTS (injurious). **2.** *U.S. Slang* Any small, light airplane, used for dusting crops, military observation, etc.

grass·land (gras′land′, gräs′-) *n.* **1.** Land reserved for pasturage or mowing. **2.** Land in which grasses are the predominant vegetation, as the American prairies.

grass-of-Par·nas·sus (gras′əv·pär·nas′əs, gräs′-) *n.* Any of a genus (*Parnassia*) of smooth, perennial herbs of the saxifrage family, bearing white flowers.

grass·plot (gras′plot′, gräs′-) *n.* A piece of ground planted with grass; lawn.

grass·quit (gras′kwit, gräs′-) *n.* Any of various small, fringilline birds (genus *Tiaris*) of the warmer parts of America. [< GRASS + *quit,* local Jamaican name for a finch]

grass·roots (gras′rōōts′, -rŏŏts′, gräs′-) *n.pl. U.S. Informal* Those people, often living in rural areas, thought of as having fundamental, practical, and highly independent views or interests. — *adj. U.S. Informal* **1.** Coming from, pertaining to, or directed toward such people: a *grassroots* political campaign. **2.** Basic; fundamental. Also **grass′-roots′.**

grass snipe The pectoral sandpiper.

grass tree 1. Any of various Australian plants (genus *Xan-*

thorrhoea) having a thick trunk crowned with long, wiry, grasslike leaves and yielding acaroid gum: also called *black-boy*. **2.** Any of various similar plants of Australasia.

grass widow A woman who is divorced, separated, or lives apart from her husband. [Origin uncertain]

grass widower A man who is divorced, separated, or lives apart from his wife.

grass·y (gras′ē, gräs′ē) *adj.* **grass·i·er, grass·i·est 1.** Covered with or abounding in grass. **2.** Consisting of or containing grass. **3.** Resembling or characteristic of grass. — **grass′i·ly** *adv.* — **grass′i·ness** *n.*

grate[1] (grāt) *v.* **grat·ed, grat·ing** *v.t.* **1.** To reduce to fine pieces, shreds, or powder by rubbing against a rough or sharply perforated surface: to *grate* cheese. **2.** To rub or grind together so as to produce a harsh, scraping sound: to *grate* the teeth. **3.** *Rare* To cause annoyance to; irritate. **4.** *Archaic* To wear or scrape away; abrade. — *v.i.* **5.** To have an annoying or irritating effect: with *on* or *upon*. **6.** To produce a harsh, scratching, or creaking sound, as by friction against a rough surface. [< OF *grater* < Gmc.]

grate[2] (grāt) *n.* **1.** A framework of crossed or parallel bars placed over an opening, as a window, door, drain, etc. **2.** A metal framework used to hold the burning fuel in a furnace or fireplace. **3.** A fireplace. **4.** *Mining* A perforated metal screen through which crushed ores are sifted for grading. — *v.t.* **grat·ed, grat·ing** To fit with a grate or grates. [< Med.L *grata* < Ital. < L *cratis* lattice. Doublet of CRATE.]

grate·ful (grāt′fəl) *adj.* **1.** Thankful for benefits or kindnesses received; appreciative. **2.** Expressing thanks or gratitude: a *grateful* look. **3.** Giving pleasure; welcome; agreeable: a *grateful* breeze. [< obs. *grate* pleasing (< L *gratus*) + -FUL] — **grate′ful·ly** *adv.* — **grate′ful·ness** *n.*
— **Syn. 1.** *Grateful* and *thankful* are close in meaning, but one distinction is commonly observed, in that *grateful* refers to our feelings of gratitude to another person, and *thankful* refers to similar feelings toward divine providence, fate, or some less immediate agency. We are *grateful* for a kind word or an expression of sympathy, but *thankful* for good health or fair weather. — **Ant.** ungrateful.

grat·er (grā′tər) *n.* **1.** One who or that which grates. **2.** A kitchen utensil with sharp-edged perforations, used to grate vegetables, cheese, etc.

Gra·ti·an (grā′shē·ən, -shən) Anglicized name of **Flavius Gra·ti·a·nus** (grā-shē·ā′nəs), 359–83, Roman emperor 375–83.

grat·i·fi·ca·tion (grat′ə·fə·kā′shən) *n.* **1.** The act of gratifying, or the state of being gratified. **2.** That which gratifies or pleases. **3.** *Obs.* A recompense or reward, as one given for services performed; gratuity.

grat·i·fy (grat′ə·fī) *v.t.* **·fied, ·fy·ing 1.** To give pleasure or satisfaction to. **2.** To satisfy, humor, or indulge, as a desire or need. **3.** *Obs.* To reward. — **Syn.** See SATISFY. [< MF *gratifier* < L *gratificari* < *gratus* pleasing + *facere* to make] — **grat′i·fi′er** *n.*

grat·i·fy·ing (grat′ə·fī′ing) *adj.* Giving pleasure or satisfaction; agreeable. — **grat′i·fy′ing·ly** *adv.*

gra·tin (grät′n, grat′n; *Fr.* grȧ·tan′) See AU GRATIN.

grat·ing[1] (grā′ting) *n.* **1.** An arrangement of parallel, crossing, or interlaced bars or slats serving as a partition, cover, or screen; grate; lattice. **2.** *Physics* A diffraction grating (which see).

grat·ing[2] (grā′ting) *adj.* **1.** Harsh or disagreeable in sound; rasping. **2.** Irritating; annoying. — **grat′ing·ly** *adv.*

gra·tis (grā′tis, grat′is) *adv.* Without requiring payment. — *adj.* Free of charge; gratuitous. [< L, var. of *gratiis* out of kindness, orig. ablative plural of *gratia* favor]

grat·i·tude (grat′ə·tōōd, -tyōōd) *n.* Appreciation or thankfulness for having received any favor, kindness, good fortune, etc. [< F < LL *gratitudo* < L *gratus* pleasing]

Grat·tan (grat′n), **Henry,** 1746–1820, Irish statesman and orator.

gra·tu·i·tous (grə·tōō′ə·təs, -tyōō′-) *adj.* **1.** Given or obtained without requirement of payment or return; free. **2.** Lacking cause or justification; uncalled-for; unwarranted: a *gratuitous* snub. **3.** *Law* Involving no compensation or benefit in return. [< L *gratuitus*] — **gra·tu′i·tous·ly** *adv.* — **gra·tu′i·tous·ness** *n.*

gra·tu·i·ty (grə·tōō′ə·tē, -tyōō′-) *n.* *pl.* **·ties 1.** A gift, usually of money, given in return for services rendered; tip. **2.** *Brit.* A sum of money given to members of the armed forces upon retirement from service, reenlistment, etc.

grat·u·lant (grach′ōō·lənt) *adj.* Expressing joy or congratulation. [< L *gratulans, -antis,* ppr. of *gratulari.* See GRATULATE.]

grat·u·late (grach′ōō·lāt) *Archaic v.t.* **·lat·ed, ·lat·ing 1.** To greet or welcome with joy. **2.** To congratulate. [< L *gratulatus,* pp. of *gratulari* to rejoice < *gratus* pleasing] — **grat′u·la′tion** *n.* — **grat′u·la·to·ry** (-lə·tôr′ē, -tō′rē) *adj.*

Grau·bün·den (grou·bün′dən) A canton in eastern Switzerland; 2,745 sq. mi.; pop. 145,600 (1960); capital, Chur: French *Grisons.*

grau·pel (grou′pəl) *n. Meteorol.* Small, compact pellets of snow. [< G, hailstone]

gra·va·men (grə·vā′men) *n. pl.* **·vam·i·na** (-vam′ə·nə) **1.** *Law* The part of an accusation bearing most seriously against the accused; the burden or gist of a charge. **2.** A grievance. **3.** Essential part; gist. [< LL, trouble < L *gravare* to burden < *gravis* heavy]

grave[1] (grāv) *adj.* **1.** Of great importance or concern; weighty: a *grave* responsibility. **2.** Filled with or indicative of danger; critical: a *grave* situation. **3.** Solemn and dignified; sober; sedate: a *grave* manner. **4.** Somber: said of colors. **5.** *Phonet.* **a** Having the tonal quality indicated by the grave accent; also, marked with this accent, as the vowel *è.* **b** Unaccented, as a syllable. — **Syn.** See SEDATE. — *n.* A mark (ˋ) used in French to indicate the open quality of *e,* or to make a distinction in writing between two homographs, as in *ou, où;* in English prosody, to indicate the pronunciation of a final *ed,* as in preparèd; in classical Greek, to indicate a lowering of the tone from a higher pitch: also **grave accent.** [< F < L *gravis* heavy] — **grave′ly** *adv.* — **grave′ness** *n.*

grave[2] (grāv) *n.* **1.** A burial place for a dead body, usually an excavation in the earth. **2.** A sepulcher; tomb. **3.** Death; often preceded by *the.* **4.** Any place or state regarded as an end, extinction, or final loss. — **to have one foot in the grave 1.** To be very old or frail. **2.** To be dangerously ill; be near death. — **to turn (over) in one's grave** To be presumably disturbed or uneasy after one's death because of the behavior of the living. [OE *græf.* Akin to GRAVE[3].] — **grave′less** *adj.*

grave[3] (grāv) *v.t.* **graved, grav·en, grav·ing 1.** To form by carving; sculpture. **2.** To engrave upon a hard surface; incise. **3.** To impress firmly; fix indelibly, as on the memory. [OE *grafan* to dig. Akin to GRAVE[2].]

grave[4] (grāv) *v.t.* **graved, grav·ing** *Naut.* To clean (a ship's bottom) by scraping or burning off barnacles, seaweed, etc., and coating with pitch. [? < OF, beach]

gra·ve[5] (grä′vā) *Music adj.* Slow and solemn. — *adv.* Slowly and solemnly. — *n.* A movement, passage, etc. performed in such a manner. [< Ital.]

grave-clothes (grāv′klōz′, -klōthz′) *n.pl.* The clothes or wrappings in which a corpse is interred.

grave-dig·ger (grāv′dig′ər) *n.* One whose occupation is digging graves.

grav·el (grav′əl) *n.* **1.** A mixture of small, rounded pebbles or fragments of stone, often combined with coarse sand. **2.** *Pathol.* **a** Aggregations of sandlike crystals formed in the kidneys. **b** The disease of which these are characteristic. **3.** *Obs.* Sand. — *v.t.* **grav·eled** or **·elled, grav·el·ing** or **·el·ling 1.** To cover or pave with gravel. **2.** To confound; baffle. **3.** *U.S. Informal* To irritate; annoy. **4.** *Obs.* To run (a vessel) aground. [< OF *gravele,* dim. of *grave* beach]

grav·el-blind (grav′əl·blīnd′) *adj.* Almost blind: intermediate between *sandblind* and *stone-blind.*

grav·el·ly (grav′əl·ē) *adj.* **1.** Consisting of or containing gravel. **2.** Like gravel. **3.** Harsh, as a voice.

grav·en (grā′vən) Past participle of GRAVE[3].

graven image A carved or sculptured idol.

Grav·en·stein (grav′ən·stēn, -stīn, grä′vən-) *n.* A variety of large, yellowish red eating apple. [after *Gravenstein,* village in southern Denmark]

grav·er (grā′vər) *n.* **1.** An engraver's tool used for cutting, incising, or chasing. **2.** An engraver or a stonecarver.

Graves (grävz, *Fr.* gräv) *n.* A moderately dry, usually white wine produced in a district of Bordeaux, SW France.

Graves (grāvz), **Robert (Ranke),** born 1895, English poet and author.

Graves' disease *Pathol.* Exophthalmic goiter. [after Robert J. *Graves,* 1797–1853, Irish physician]

Graves·end (grāvz′end′) A municipal borough and port in NW Kent, England, on the Thames; pop. 51,388 (1961).

grave·stone (grāv′stōn′) *n.* A stone marking a grave.

Gra·vet·ti·an (grə·vet′ē·ən) *adj. Anthropol.* Denoting a cultural stage of the Upper Paleolithic perod. [after *La-Gravette,* rock shelter in Couze valley, SW France]

grave·yard (grāv′yärd′) *n.* A burial place; cemetery.

graveyard shift *U.S. Informal* A work shift scheduled during the late hours of the night, generally beginning at midnight.

grav·id (grav′id) *adj.* Pregnant. [< L *gravidus* < *gravis* heavy] — **grav′id·ly** *adv.* — **grav′id·ness, gra·vid·i·ty** (grə·vid′ə·tē) *n.*

gra·vim·e·ter (grə·vim′ə·tər) *n.* A type of hydrometer used to determine specific gravity. [< L *gravis* heavy + -METER]

grav·i·met·ric (grav′ə·met′rik) *adj. Chem.* **1.** Determined by weight, as the constituents of a compound: distinguished from *volumetric.* **2.** Pertaining to measurement by weight. Also **grav′i·met′ri·cal.** — **grav′i·met′ri·cal·ly** *adv.*

gra·vim·e·try (grə·vim′ə·trē) *n.* The measurement of weight, density, or specific gravity.

grav·ing dock (grā′ving) A dry dock in which a ship's bottom may be examined, cleaned, and repaired.

---

grav·i·pause (grav′ə-pôz) *n.* The region in space where the gravitational field of one celestial body ends, or is neutralized by that of another. [< GRAVI(TY) + PAUSE]

grav·i·sphere (grav′ə-sfir) *n.* The spherical area within which the gravitational field of a body is dominant. [< GRAVI(TY) + SPHERE] — **grav′i·spher′ic** (-sfir′ik, -sfer′-) *adj.*

grav·i·tate (grav′ə-tāt) *v.i.* **·tat·ed, ·tat·ing** **1.** To move or tend to move as a result of the force of gravity. **2.** To move or be attracted as though influenced by a powerful force or natural impulse. **3.** To sink or settle to a lower level. [< NL *gravitatus,* pp. of *gravitare* to press down < L *gravis* heavy] — **grav′i·tat′er** *n.*

grav·i·ta·tion (grav′ə-tā′shən) *n.* **1.** *Physics* The force whereby any two bodies attract each other directly in proportion to the product of their masses and inversely as the square of the distance between them. **2.** The act or process of gravitating. **3.** A movement, tendency, or inclination, as toward a source of attraction or influence. — **grav′i·ta′tion·al** *adj.* — **grav′i·ta′tion·al·ly** *adv.*

grav·i·ta·tive (grav′ə-tā′tiv) *adj.* **1.** Pertaining to or produced by gravitation. **2.** Tending or causing to gravitate.

grav·i·ty (grav′ə-tē) *n. pl.* **·ties 1.** *Physics* Gravitation as manifested by the tendency of material bodies to fall toward the center of the earth. **2.** Gravitation in general. **3.** Weight; heaviness: the center of *gravity.* **4.** Great importance or significance; seriousness: the *gravity* of this condition. **5.** Solemnity of manner or behavior; dignified reserve: the *gravity* of a judge. **6.** Lowness of pitch, as of musical tones. [< F *gravité* < L *gravitas, -tatis* heaviness < *gravis* heavy]

gravity cell *Electr.* A primary cell in which the two electrolytes are kept separate by differences in specific gravity.

gravity fault *Geol.* A fault in which the upper portion, or hanging wall, has slipped downward in relation to the lower portion, or footwall.

gra·vure (grə-vyo͝or′, grāv′yər) *n.* **1.** A process of printing or engraving by means of photographically prepared plates. **2.** A plate, usually of copper or wood, used in this process; also, a print made from such a plate. [< F < *graver* to engrave]

gra·vy (grā′vē) *n. pl.* **·vies 1.** The juice, melted fat, etc. exuded by cooked or cooking meat; also, a sauce made from or resembling such a liquid. **2.** *U.S. Slang* Money or profit easily acquired. [ME *gravey;* origin uncertain]

gravy boat A pointed or elongated dish for serving gravy.

gravy train *U.S. Slang* A job or situation giving considerable rewards for little effort: usually in the expression **to ride the gravy train,** to enjoy a sinecure.

gray (grā) *adj.* **1.** Of a color produced by a mixture of black and white. **2.** Dark or dull, as from obscured or insufficient light; dismal; gloomy: a *gray* day. **3.** Having gray hair. **4.** Characteristic of old age; venerable. **5.** Ancient; old. — *n.* **1.** Any achromatic color consisting of a mixture of black and white. **2.** Something gray, as an animal. **3.** Gray material, clothing, etc. **4.** The state of being unbleached or undyed: said of fabrics. — *v.t. & v.i.* To make or become gray. Also, *esp. Brit.,* **grey.** [OE *græg*] — **gray′ly** *adv.* — **gray′ness** *n.*

Gray (grā). **Asa,** 1810–88, U.S. botanist. — **Thomas,** 1716–1771, English poet.

gray·back (grā′bak′) *n.* **1.** Any of various birds or animals having gray or grayish coloration, as the gray whale, hooded crow, etc. **2.** *U.S. Informal* A Confederate soldier during the American Civil War.

gray·beard (grā′bird′) *n.* An old man; also, one having the wisdom or experience of old age.

gray·fish (grā′fish′) *n. pl.* **·fish** or **·fish·es** A dogfish (which see).

gray fox See under FOX.

Gray Friar A Franciscan friar.

gray goods Fabric in an unbleached, undyed, or unfinished state: also called *greige.*

gray-head·ed (grā′hed′id) *adj.* **1.** Having gray hair. **2.** Old; aged. **3.** Of or characteristic of old age.

gray·hound (grā′hound′) *n. Rare* A greyhound.

gray·ish (grā′ish) *adj.* Somewhat gray: also, *esp. Brit.,* **greyish.**

gray·lag (grā′lag′) *n. pl.* **·lag** or **·lags** The common wild gray goose (*Anser anser*) of Europe. [< GRAY + LAG; so called because it migrates late.]

gray·ling (grā′ling) *n. pl.* **·ling** or **·lings 1.** A troutlike fish (genus *Thymallus*) having a large, colorful dorsal fin: sometimes called *umber.* **2.** Any of several North American butterflies (family *Satyridae*) having gray and brown markings.

gray matter 1. *Anat.* The reddish gray nervous tissue of the brain and spinal cord, composed largely of nerve cell bodies and nonmyelinic nerve fibers: distinguished from *white matter.* **2.** *Informal* Brains; intelligence.

gray·out (grā′out′) *n.* A temporary loss or blurring of vision caused by oxygen deficiency, experienced especially by aviators subjected to rapid acceleration.

Gray's Inn A London legal society, or the set of buildings occupied by it. See INNS OF COURT.

Grays Peak The highest peak of the Front Range in Colorado; 14,274 ft.

Gray·son (grā′sən), **David** See (Ray Stannard) BAKER.

gray squirrel See under SQUIRREL.

gray·wacke (grā′wak, -wak·ə) *n. Geol.* A dark-colored, sedimentary rock composed of fragments of quartz, feldspar, or other rocks firmly cemented together: also, *esp. Brit.,* **greywacke.** [< G *grauwacke* gray wacke. See WACKE.]

gray whale A medium-sized whale (*Rhachianectes glaucus*) of the northern Pacific.

gray wolf The timber wolf (which see).

Graz (gräts) The capital of Styria Province, SE Austria; pop. 237,041 (1961).

graze[1] (grāz) *v.* **grazed, graz·ing** *v.i.* **1.** To feed upon growing grass or herbage. — *v.t.* **2.** To put (livestock) to feed on growing grass, pasturage, etc. **3.** To tend (livestock) at pasture. **4.** To cause (a field, etc.) to be fed on, as by livestock. **5.** To feed on or eat, as herbage. [OE *grasian* < *græs* grass] — **graz′er** *n.*

graze[2] (grāz) *v.* **grazed, graz·ing** *v.t.* **1.** To brush against lightly in passing. **2.** To scrape or abrade slightly in passing: The bullet *grazed* his arm. — *v.i.* **3.** To move so as to brush or scrape lightly against something. — *n.* **1.** A grazing; a light contact made in passing. **2.** A scrape or abrasion made by such a contact. [? < GRAZE[1]] — **graz′ing·ly** *adv.*

gra·zier (grā′zhər) *n. Brit.* **1.** One who grazes cattle for market. **2.** *Austral.* One who occupies grazing land for sheep farming under a lease or license.

graz·ing (grā′zing) *n.* Pasturage.

gra·zi·o·so (grä·tsyō′sō) *Music adj.* Graceful; elegant. — *adv.* Gracefully; elegantly. [< Ital.]

Gr.Br. or **Gr.Brit.** Great Britain.

grease (*n.* grēs; *v.* grēs, grēz) *n.* **1.** Animal fat in a soft state, as after melting or rendering. **2.** Any thick fatty or oily substance, as a lubricant. **3.** Wool that has been shorn but not yet cleansed: also **grease wool. 4.** The condition of wool or fur before being cleansed: wool in the *grease.* — *v.t.* **greased, greas·ing** To smear or lubricate with grease or fat. — **to grease the hand** (or **palm**) of *Slang* To bribe with money or gifts. [< OF *graisse,* ult. < L *crassus* fat]

grease cup In machinery, a receptacle supplying a lubricant to the part or bearing to which it is attached.

grease monkey *U.S. Slang* A garage attendant or mechanic.

grease paint A waxy or greasy substance of various colors, used for theatrical make-up.

greas·er (grē′sər; *esp. for def. 2* grē′zər) *n.* **1.** One who or that which oils or greases. **2.** *U.S. Slang* A Mexican or Spanish-American: an offensive term.

grease·wood (grēs′wo͝od′) *n.* Any of various stunted and prickly shrubs (genus *Sarcobatus*) of the goosefoot family, growing on the alkaline plains of the western United States: also called *chico.* Also **grease′bush′.**

greas·y (grē′sē, -zē) *adj.* **greas·i·er, greas·i·est 1.** Smeared or spotted with grease. **2.** Containing much grease or fat; oily. **3.** Appearing or feeling like grease; smooth; slick; slippery. — **greas′i·ly** *adv.* — **greas′i·ness** *n.*

greasy spoon *U.S. Slang* A cheap, crudely maintained restaurant, considered unappetizing or unsanitary.

great (grāt) *adj.* **great·er, great·est 1.** Very large in bulk, volume, expanse, etc.; immense; big. **2.** Large in quantity or number: a *great* army. **3.** Prolonged in duration or extent; a *great* distance. **4.** More than ordinary; considerable; extreme: *great* pain. **5.** Being larger or more important than others of the same kind: the *great* auk. **6.** Of unusual importance or consequence; momentous; significant: a *great* victory. **7.** Marked by or possessing loftiness or nobility of thought, action, etc.: *great* deeds. **8.** Unusual in ability or achievement; highly gifted: a *great* composer. **9.** Distinguished; renowned; illustrious: a *great* family. **10.** Impressive; remarkable: a *great* display of fireworks. **11.** Much favored; popular: a *great* slogan at that time. **12.** Characterized by or manifesting constant and absorbed interest; enthusiastic: a *great* hiker. **13.** Proficient; skillful. **14.** Being of a degree of relationship more remote by a single generation: used in combination: *great-uncle; great-grandson.* **15.** *Informal* Excellent; first-rate: He's a *great* fellow. **16.** *Archaic* Pregnant: often followed by *with.* — **to be great on** *Informal* To be well informed or enthusiastic about; excel in. — **Syn.** See GRAND. — *n.* **1.** Those who are eminent, powerful, etc.: preceded by *the.* **2.** *Usually pl. Informal* An outstanding or distinguished person: one of baseball's *greats.* — *adv. Informal* Very well; splendidly. Abbr. *gr., gt.* [OE *grēat*] — **great′ness** *n.*

Great Appalachian Valley A longitudinal chain of lowlands of the Appalachian Mountains extending from Canada to Alabama: also *Great Valley.*

Great Artesian Basin A huge artesian basin in Australia; about 680,000 sq. mi. Also **Great Australian Basin.**

great auk See under AUK.

great-aunt (grāt′ant′, -änt′) *n.* An aunt of either of one's parents; grandaunt.

Great Australian Bight A wide bay of the Indian Ocean in the coast of southern Australia.

Great Barrier Reef The world's largest chain of coral reefs, off the eastern coast of Queensland, Australia; length, about 1,260 mi.: also *Barrier Reef.*

Great Basin An inland drainage region in the western United States, between the Wasatch and the Sierra Nevada mountains; over 200,000 sq. mi.

Great Bear The constellation Ursa Major.

Great Bear Lake A lake in the western Northwest Territories, Canada; 12,000 sq. mi.; drained by the **Great Bear River,** that flows 100 miles west to the Mackenzie River.

Great Britain 1. The principal island of the United Kingdom, comprising England, Scotland, and Wales; 88,748 sq. mi.; pop. 53,827,545 (1971); capital, London. **2.** Since the Act of Union, 1707, the political name for England, Scotland, and Wales: also *Britain*. Abbr. *G.B., Gr. Br., Gr. Brit.*

great calorie See under CALORIE.

Great Charter The Magna Carta.

great circle *Geom.* A circle formed on the surface of a sphere by a plane that passes through the center of the sphere.

great-cir·cle course (grāt/sûr/kəl) A course, as of a ship or aircraft, plotted along a great circle of the earth, and constituting the shortest distance between two points.

great·coat (grāt/kōt/) *n.* A heavy overcoat.

Great Dane One of a breed of smooth-haired dogs of large size and great strength.

Great Divide 1. The Continental Divide (which see); also, any similar large mountain ridge. **2.** The figurative boundary between life and death. **3.** A major crisis.

great·en (grāt/n) *v.t. & v.i. Archaic* To make or become great or greater.

great·er (grāt/ər) Comparative of GREAT. — *adj. Usually cap.* Comprising a (specified) city and its suburbs.

Greater Antilles See under ANTILLES.

Greater Caucasus See CAUCASUS (def. 1).

Greater Dog The constellation Canis Major.

greater doxology The Gloria in Excelsis Deo.

Greater London See LONDON.

Greater Manchester A metropolitan county in NW England; 692 sq. mi.; pop. 2,730,000 (1976).

Greater New York The five boroughs of New York City collectively; also, loosely, New York City and its suburbs.

Greater Sunda Islands Formerly, Borneo, Celebes, Java, Sumatra, and the Molucca Islands.

Great Falls A city in west central Montana; pop. 60,091.

Great Glen of Scotland A depression extending 60 miles across Scotland, dividing the central from the NW Highlands: also *Glen More.*

great go *Brit. Informal* The final examination for a bachelor's degree at Cambridge University.

great-grand·child (grāt/grand/chīld/) *n.* A child of a grandchild.

great-grand·daughter (grāt/gran/dô/tər) *n.* A daughter of a grandchild.

great-grand·father (grāt/grand/fä/thər) *n.* The father of a grandparent.

great-grand·mother (grāt/grand/muth/ər) *n.* The mother of a grandparent.

great-grand·parent (grāt/grand/pâr/ənt) *n.* The father or mother of a grandparent.

great-grand·son (grāt/grand/sun/) *n.* A son of a grandchild.

great gross Twelve gross, a unit of quantity. Abbr. *g.gr.*

great-heart·ed (grāt/här/tid) *adj.* **1.** Noble or generous in spirit; magnanimous. **2.** High-spirited; courageous.

great horned owl A large owl (*Bubo virginianus*) having earlike tufts of feathers that resemble horns, found chiefly in North America: also called *cat owl.* For illustration see HORNED OWL.

Great Kar·roo (kə·rōō/) A plateau region of south central Cape Province, South Africa: also *Central Karroo.*

Great Lakes A chain of five lakes in central North America on the Canada-United States border, comprising Lakes Superior, Michigan, Huron, Erie, and Ontario; total, 94,710 sq. mi.; the largest group of fresh-water lakes in the world; drained by the St. Lawrence River.

great laurel The great or rosebay rhododendron. See under RHODODENDRON.

great·ly (grāt/lē) *adv.* **1.** In or to a great degree; exceedingly; very much. **2.** In a manner or style characteristic of or befitting greatness.

Great Mogul See under MOGUL.

Great Mother Cybele.

great-neph·ew (grāt/nef/yōō, -nev/-) *n.* The son of one's nephew or niece; grandnephew.

great-niece (grāt/nēs/) *n.* The daughter of one's nephew or niece; grandniece.

great northern diver See under LOON[1].

great panda Panda (def. 2).

Great Plains A sloping plateau in western North America, bordering the eastern base of the Rocky Mountains from Canada to New Mexico and Texas.

great primer See under PRIMER[1].

Great Rebellion The Civil War in England. See table under WAR.

Great Rift Valley A great depression of the Near East and eastern Africa, extending from Syria to Mozambique: also *Rift Valley.*

Great Russia The central and northwestern regions of the U.S.S.R.

Great Russian *adj.* Of or pertaining to Great Russia, its people, or their language. — *n.* **1.** A native or inhabitant of Great Russia. **2.** The East Slavic language of the Great Russians, used as the standard literary language.

Greats (grāts) *n.pl. Brit. Informal* The studies or final examination for an honors degree in the humanities at Oxford University. [< GREAT GO]

Great Salt Lake A salt lake in NW Utah having no outlet; about 2,000 sq. mi.: also *Salt Lake.*

Great Sandy Desert The northern belt of the desert region of Western Australia, north of the Gibson Desert.

Great Schism The division in the Roman Catholic Church, 1378–1417, when rival popes ruled at Rome and Avignon.

great seal *Often cap.* The chief seal of a government, used to authenticate important official documents.

Great Seal The Lord Chancellor of England; also, his office.

Great Slave Lake A lake in southern Northwest Territories, Canada; 11,170 sq. mi.

Great Smoky Mountains A mountain range in North Carolina and Tennessee; highest point Clingmans Dome, 6,642 ft.; site of **Great Smoky Mountains National Park,** 789 sq. mi., established 1930. Also **Great Smok/ies** (-ēz).

Great St. Bernard Pass See under ST. BERNARD PASS.

great-un·cle (grāt/ung/kəl) *n.* An uncle of either of one's parents; granduncle.

Great Valley See CENTRAL VALLEY, GREAT APPALACHIAN VALLEY.

Great Victoria Desert See VICTORIA DESERT.

Great Wall of China A monumental defensive wall in northern China, extending approximately 1,500 miles between the ancient Chinese empire and Mongolia; originally constructed 246–209 B.C.: also *Chinese Wall.*

Great War World War I. See table under WAR.

Great Week In the Eastern Orthodox Church, the week before Easter.

great white heron 1. A large white heron (*Ardea occidentalis*) of southern North America. **2.** The common egret. See under EGRET.

great white trillium A trillium (*Trillium grandiflorum*) of the NE United States, noted for its large flowers that change from white to rosy pink.

Great White Way The brightly lighted theater district of New York City near Broadway and Times Square.

great willow herb The willow herb.

Great Yarmouth A county borough and port in SE Norfolk, England, on the North Sea; pop. 50,760 (est. 1969): also *Yarmouth.*

great year See under PRECESSION OF THE EQUINOXES.

greave (grēv) *n. Usually pl.* Armor serving to protect the leg from knee to ankle. [< OF *greve*; ult. origin unknown]

greaves (grēvz) *n.pl.* Scraps remaining after tallow or animal fat has been rendered; cracklings. [Akin to LG *greven*]

grebe (grēb) *n.* Any of a family (*Podicipedidae*) of swimming and diving birds having lobed toes and very short tails; especially, the **horned grebe** (*Podiceps auritus*) and the **pied-billed grebe** (*Podilymbus podiceps*), or dabchick. [< F *grèbe*; ult. origin uncertain]

Gre·cian (grē/shən) *adj.* Greek. — *n.* **1.** A Greek. **2.** One learned in the language or literature of Greece. Abbr. *Gr.*

Grecian bend A posture in which the pelvis and buttocks are thrust backward, affected by fashionable women during the late 19th century, and often emphasized with a bustle.

Gre·cism (grē/siz·əm) *n.* **1.** A Greek idiom. **2.** The style or spirit of Greek art, culture, etc. Also spelled *Graecism.*

Gre·cize (grē/sīz) *v. ·cized, ·ciz·ing v.t.* **1.** To make Greek in form, character, etc.; Hellenize. **2.** To translate into Greek. — *v.i.* **3.** To adopt or imitate Greek customs, speech, etc. Also spelled *Graecize.* [< F *gréciser* < L *graecizare* < *Graecus* a Greek]

Greco- *combining form* Greek: *Greco-Roman.* Also spelled *Graeco-.* [< L *Graecus* Greek]

Grec·o (grek/ō, grā/kō), **El,** 1548?–1614, Spanish painter born in Crete: original name **Domenicos The·o·to·co·pou·los** (thā/ô·tô·kō/pōō·lôs). [< Sp., the Greek]

Greco-Persian Wars See table for WAR.

Gre·co-Ro·man (grē/kō·rō/mən) *adj.* Of or pertaining to Greece and Rome together: *Greco-Roman art:* also *Graeco-Roman.*

gree[1] (grē) *v.t. & v.i. Scot. & Brit. Dial.* To bring or come to agreement.

gree[2] (grē) *n. Obs.* **1.** Satisfaction; legal redress. **2.** Good will; favor. [< OF *gre*, ult. < L *gratus* pleasing]

gree[3] (grē) *n. Scot. & Archaic* **1.** Superiority; victory. **2.** The prize of victory.

Greece (grēs) A kingdom of SE Europe; 50,547 sq. mi.; pop. 8,838,000 (est. 1969); capital, Athens: Greek *Ellas*.

greed (grēd) *n.* Selfish and grasping desire for possession, especially of wealth; avarice; covetousness. [Back formation < GREEDY]

greed·y (grē'dē) *adj.* **greed·i·er, greed·i·est 1.** Excessively eager for acquisition or gain; covetous; grasping. **2.** Having an excessive appetite for food and drink; voracious; gluttonous. [OE *grǣdig*] — **greed'i·ly** *adv.* — **greed'i·ness** *n.*

gree-gree (grē'grē) *n.* A grigri.

Greek (grēk) *adj.* **1.** Of or pertaining to Greece, or its people, language, or culture. **2.** Of or pertaining to the Greek Church. — *n.* **1.** One of the people of ancient Greece; especially, a member of one of the four major tribes: Achaean, Aeolian, Dorian, and Ionian. **2.** One of the people of modern Greece, descended, with admixture, from the ancient Greeks. **3.** The Indo-European language of ancient or modern Greece. Ancient, or classical, Greek, from Homer to about A.D. 200, is divided into four linguistic dialects: Aeolic, Attic, Doric, and Ionic. Abbr. *Gk., Gr.* — **Late Greek** The Greek language from about A.D. 200 to 600, including the patristic writings. Abbr. *LGk., L.Gk.* — **Medieval Greek** The Greek language of the Byzantine period, from 600 to 1500. Abbr. *Med. Gk.* — **Modern Greek** The language of Greece since 1500, in its literary form retaining many classical features: also called *Romaic*, especially in its spoken form. Abbr. *Mod. Gr.* **4.** Language or information that is unintelligible or beyond one's comprehension; gibberish: It's all *Greek* to me. **5.** A member of the Greek Church. **6.** *U.S. Slang* A member of a fraternity designated by Greek letters. [< L *Graecus* < Gk. *Graikos* Greek]

Greek Catholic 1. A member of the Eastern Orthodox Church. **2.** A member of a Uniat church.

Greek Church 1. The Eastern Church. **2.** Loosely, the Eastern Orthodox Church.

Greek cross A cross formed by an upright crossing the middle of a beam of equal length. See GAMMADION. For illustration see CROSS.

Greek fire An incendiary substance first used by the Byzantine Greeks in naval warfare.

Greek Orthodox Church The established church of Greece, an autonomous branch of the Eastern Orthodox Church.

Greek Revival A style of architecture of the 18th and early 19th centuries, using modified Greek structural elements.

Gree·ley (grē'lē) A city in northern Colorado; pop. 26,314.

Gree·ley (grē'lē), **Horace,** 1811–72, U.S. editor and politician.

Gree·ly (grē'lē), **Adolphus Washington,** 1844–1935, U.S. general and Arctic explorer.

green (grēn) *adj.* **1.** Of the color between blue and yellow in the spectrum, as the foliage of growing plants. **2.** Covered with or abounding in grass, growing plants, etc.; verdant. **3.** Consisting of edible green leaves or plant parts: a *green* salad. **4.** Not fully developed; immature; unripe: *green* fruit. **5.** Not cured or ready for use; unseasoned: *green* lumber. **6.** Lacking training or skill; inexperienced. **7.** Easily duped; credulous; gullible. **8.** Pale or unhealthy in appearance; wan. **9.** Full of vitality; flourishing; vigorous. **10.** Untreated or unprocessed; fresh; raw. **11.** Characterized by unusually mild weather; snowless: a *green* season. — *n.* **1.** The color between blue and yellow in the spectrum, characteristic of the foliage of growing plants. **2.** A green pigment, dye, or substance. **3.** Green material, clothing, etc.; also, something green worn as an emblem, distinctive garb, etc. **4.** A smooth, usually level, grassy area or plot: the village *green*. **5.** In golf, the area of smooth, clipped grass surrounding the hole. **6.** *pl.* Freshly cut leaves, branches, vines, etc., used as decoration. **7.** *pl.* The edible leaves and stems of certain plants, as spinach, beets, etc. — *v.t. & v.i.* To make or become green. [OE *grēne.* Akin to GRASS, GROW.] — **green'ly** *adv.* — **green'ness** *n.*

Green (grēn), **Anna Katherine,** 1846–1935, U.S. writer. — **Henrietta Howland,** 1834–1916, *née* Robinson, U.S. financier: called **Hetty Green.** — **John Richard,** 1837–83, English historian. — **Julian,** born 1900, French novelist of American parentage. — **William,** 1873–1952, U.S. labor leader; president of the American Federation of Labor 1924–1952.

green algae A class (*Chlorophyceae*) of algae in which the cells containing chlorophyll are dominant.

Green·a·way (grē'nə-wā), **Kate,** 1846–1901, English painter and illustrator whose drawings popularized a style of children's clothes.

green·back (grēn'bak') *n.* One of a class of United States notes used as legal tender, so called because the back is printed in green.

Greenback Party A former U.S. political party founded in 1874, advocating the use of money issued by the government as the only legal tender. — **Green'back'er** *n.*

Green Bay 1. An inlet of Lake Michigan extending about 95 miles into NE Wisconsin. **2.** A city in Wisconsin at the southern tip of this inlet; pop. 87,809.

green bean A string bean (which see).

green·belt (grēn'belt') *n.* An area of parks or undeveloped land surrounding a planned community.

green·bri·er (grēn'brī'ər) *n.* Any of various plants of the genus *Smilax,* especially *S. rotundifolia,* a thorny vine having small, greenish flowers: also called *cat brier.*

green corn Sweet corn (def. 2).

green dragon An American herbaceous plant (*Arisaema dracontium*) related to the jack-in-the-pulpit.

Greene (grēn), **Graham,** born 1904, English novelist. — **Nathanael,** 1742–86, American Revolutionary general. — **Robert,** 1560?–92, English dramatist and poet.

green·er·y (grē'nər·ē) *n. pl.* **·er·ies 1.** Green plants; verdure. **2.** A place where plants are grown or kept.

green-eyed (grēn'īd') *adj.* **1.** Having green eyes. **2.** Jealous.

green·finch (grēn'finch') *n.* **1.** An Old World finch (*Chloris chloris*), the male of which has green and yellow plumage. **2.** The Texas sparrow.

green·gage (grēn'gāj') *n.* A variety of sweet plum having green skin and flesh. [< GREEN + GAGE[3]]

green gland *Zool.* One of two excretory organs near the head in decapod crustaceans.

green glass Ordinary, inexpensive glass of a green color, used for bottles, etc.

green·gro·cer (grēn'grō'sər) *n. Brit.* A shopkeeper dealing in fresh vegetables, fruit, etc. — **green'gro'cer·y** (-sər-ē) *n.*

green·head (grēn'hed') *n. pl.* **·heads** or **·head** The male mallard, a duck.

green·heart (grēn'härt') *n.* **1.** A large hardwood tree (*Ocotea rodiaei*) of British Guiana and the U.S. Pacific coast; also, its tough, durable wood: also called *bebeeru.* **2.** Any of several other tropical American trees or their wood.

green heron A small, New World heron (*Butorides virescens*) having dark, bluish green back plumage.

green·horn (grēn'hôrn') *n.* **1.** An inexperienced person; beginner. **2.** One easily imposed on or duped. **3.** *U.S. Informal* A newly arrived immigrant: a disparaging term. [< GREEN immature + HORN; ref. to a young animal]

green·house (grēn'hous') *n.* A heated shed or building constructed chiefly of glass, in which tender or exotic plants are grown or sheltered; hothouse.

green·ing (grē'ning) *n.* One of several varieties of apples having a green skin when ripe.

green·ish (grē'nish) *adj.* Somewhat green.

Green·land (grēn'lənd) An island belonging to Denmark, off NE North America, the largest island in the world (excluding Australia); 840,154 sq. mi.; pop. 47,000 (UN est. 1969): Danish *Grønland.*

GREENLAND

green lead ore Pyromorphite.

green·let (grēn'lit) *n.* A vireo.

green light 1. A green signal light indicating that vehicles, pedestrians, etc., may proceed. **2.** *Informal* Approval or authorization to proceed with some project or activity.

green·ling (grēn'ling) *n.* Any of a genus (*Hexagrammos*) of large, carnivorous food fishes living in North Pacific waters.

green manure 1. A crop, as of beans, clover, etc., plowed under while still green to improve the fertility of the soil. **2.** Undecomposed manure.

green mold Blue mold (def. 2).

green monkey A monkey (*Cercopithecus sabaeus*) of West Africa, having greenish fur and a long tail.

Green Mountain Boys The soldiers from Vermont who fought under Ethan Allen in the American Revolution.

Green Mountains A Vermont range of the Appalachians; highest peak, Mt. Mansfield, 4,393 ft.

Green Mountain State Nickname of VERMONT.

Green·ock (grē'nək, grin'ək, grēn'-) A burgh and port in Scotland, on the Firth of Clyde; pop. 74,578 (1961).

green·ock·ite (grē'nək-īt) *n.* A yellow, transparent cadmium sulfide, CdS, crystallizing in the hexagonal system. [after Lord *Greenock,* 1783–1859, its discoverer]

green onion A young onion, usually eaten raw and used in salads; scallion.

Green·ough (grē'nō), **Horatio,** 1805–52, U.S. sculptor.

green pepper 1. The unripe fruit of the sweet pepper. **2.** The unripe fruit of the red pepper, used in pickling.

green plover A bird, the lapwing.

Green River The largest tributary of the Colorado River, flowing 730 miles, generally south through Wyoming, Colorado, and Utah.

green·room (grēn'rōōm', -rŏŏm') *n.* The waiting room in a theater used by performers when they are off-stage.

green·sand (grēn'sand') *n. Geol.* **1.** A sedimentary deposit of dark green glauconite grains. **2.** A sandstone of the Cretaceous system, so called from the color imparted to it by the glauconite with which it is mingled.

Greens·bor·o (grēnz'bûr·ō) A city in north central North Carolina; pop. 144,076.

green·shank (grēn'shangk') *n.* A European sandpiper (*Tringa nebularia*) having greenish gray legs and feet.

green·sick·ness (grēn'sik'nis) *n.* Chlorosis (def. 1).

green soap A soft soap made from linseed oil and the hydroxides of potassium and sodium, used in the treatment of skin diseases.

green·stone (grēn'stōn') *n. Geol.* One of various kinds of compact, igneous rocks to which a green color has been imparted by the presence of chlorite, hornblende, or epidote.

green·sward (grēn'swôrd') *n.* Turf green with grass.

green tea Tea from tea leaves that have been heated, withered, and rolled without undergoing fermentation.

greenth (grēnth) *n. Rare* Verdure.

green thumb A special knack for making plants thrive.

Green·ville (grēn'vil) **1.** A city in NW South Carolina; pop. 66,188. **2.** A city in western Mississippi, on the Mississippi River; pop. 41,502.

green vitriol Copperas.

Green·wich (grĕn'ich, -ij, grin-) **1.** A metropolitan borough of SE London on the Thames, England; former site of the Royal Observatory; location of the prime meridian; pop. 228,030 (1969). **2.** A town in extreme SW Connecticut; pop. 59,755.

Greenwich mean time Time as reckoned from the meridian at Greenwich, England. Also **Greenwich time.** Compare TIME ZONE.

Green·wich Village (grĕn'ich) A section of New York City in lower Manhattan, traditionally frequented by artists, writers, and students.

green·wood (grēn'wŏŏd') *n.* A forest in leaf.

greet[1] (grēt) *v.t.* **1.** To express friendly recognition or courteous respect to, as upon meeting; address a salutation to; welcome. **2.** To meet or receive in a specified manner. **3.** To present itself to; be evident or perceptible to: The warmth of a fire *greeted* us. — *v.i.* **4.** To offer a salutation upon meeting. [OE *grētan*] — **greet'er** *n.*
— **Syn. 1.** *Greet, salute, hail, accost,* and *address* are compared as they mean to speak to. One *greets* another in the first moments of meeting by words of recognition, welcome, etc. *Salute* refers to ceremonious or formal expressions of respect; it is now chiefly used of a formal military greeting. *Hail* is to *greet* heartily, or to attract attention by calling out; it may be extremely informal, or business-like and impersonal: to *hail* a friend on the street, to *hail* a passing ship. *Accost* means to approach and begin to speak to; the word frequently implies that the speaker is unknown, and his greeting unwelcome or offensive. *Address* means simply to speak to, but in a formal way or in a planned discourse.

greet[2] (grēt) *v.i.* **grat, greet·ing** *Scot.* To weep. — *n.* Weeping.

greet·ing (grē'ting) *n.* **1.** The act of one who greets; salutation; welcome. **2.** A friendly or complimentary message.

greeting card An ornamental card with complimentary greetings celebrating birthdays, holidays, etc.

greg·a·rine (greg'ǝ·rēn, -rin) *n.* One of an order (*Gregarinida*) of sporozoans parasitic in insects, crustaceans, etc. — *adj.* Of, pertaining to, or characteristic of these sporozoans. [< NL *Gregarina*, generic name < L *gregarius* living together, communal]

gre·gar·i·ous (gri·gâr'ē·ǝs) *adj.* **1.** Habitually associating with others, as in flocks, herds, or groups. **2.** Enjoying or seeking the company of others; sociable. **3.** Of, pertaining to, or characteristic of a flock, crowd, or aggregation. **4.** *Bot.* Growing in compact groups, but not matted together, as certain mosses; clustered. [< L *gregarius* < *grex, gregis* flock] — **gre·gar'i·ous·ly** *adv.* — **gre·gar'i·ous·ness** *n.*

gre·go (grē'gō, grā'-) *n.* A short, hooded coat, originally worn in the Levant. [< Ital. *greco* Greek < L *Graecus*]

Gre·go·ri·an (gri·gôr'ē·ǝn, -gō'rē-) *adj.* Of, pertaining to, or associated with one named Gregory, especially Pope Gregory I or Pope Gregory XIII.

Gregorian calendar See under CALENDAR.

Gregorian Chant The system of plainsong associated with the liturgical reforms made by Pope Gregory I, and used in the services of the Roman Catholic and some other churches.

Greg·o·ry (greg'ǝr·ē), **Lady Augusta**, 1852–1932, *née* Persse, Irish playwright.

Gregory I, Saint, 540?–604, pope 590–604; reformed the church service: called **Gregory the Great.**

Gregory VII, Saint, 1020?–85, pope 1073–85; original name *Hildebrand.*

Gregory XIII, 1502–85, pope 1572–85; calendar reformer: original name **Ugo Buon·cam·pag·ni** (bwŏn'käm·pän'yē).

Gregory of Nys·sa (nis'ǝ), **Saint,** died 395?, early Christian theologian; bishop of Nyssa.

Gregory of Tours, Saint, 538?–594?, Frankish bishop and historian.

greige (grā, grāzh) *adj.* In an unbleached or unfinished state: said of woven fabrics before processed. — *n.* Gray goods. [< F *grège* raw, unfinished; infl. in form by *beige*]

grei·sen (grī'zǝn) *n.* A crystalline mixture of quartz and mica. [< G]

gre·mi·al (grē'mē·ǝl) *n.* A cloth laid on the lap of a bishop officiating at a mass or ordination. [< L *gremium* lap]

grem·lin (grem'lin) *n.* A mischievous, imaginary creature jokingly said to cause mechanical trouble in airplanes; also, any similar gnomelike troublemaker. [Origin uncertain]

Gre·na·da (gri·nā'dǝ) The southernmost of the Windward Islands; a self-governing member of the West Indies Associated States; 133 sq. mi., including dependencies; pop. 105,000 (1971); capital, St. George.

gre·nade (gri·nād') *n.* **1.** A small explosive or incendiary bomb designed either to be thrown by hand or projected from a rifle. **2.** A glass container that shatters and diffuses its volatile contents when thrown. [< F, pomegranate < Sp. *granada* < L *granatus* having seeds < *granum* seed]

gren·a·dier (gren'ǝ·dir') *n.* **1.** Formerly, a soldier assigned to throw grenades. **2.** A member of a specially constituted corps or regiment, as the British Grenadier Guards. **3.** Any of a family (*Macrouridae*) of deep-sea fishes having bodies tapering to a pointed tail. [< F < *grenade.* See GRENADE.]

gren·a·dine[1] (gren'ǝ·dēn', gren'ǝ·dēn) *n.* A silk, wool, or cotton fabric of loose, open weave. [< F, ? after *Granada*]

gren·a·dine[2] (gren'ǝ·dēn', gren'ǝ·dēn) *n.* A syrup made from pomegranates or red currants, used for flavoring beverages. [< F < *grenade* pomegranate. See GRENADE.]

Gren·a·dines (gren'ǝ·dēnz) A group of 600 islands in the Windward group, comprising dependencies of Grenada and St. Vincent; 30 sq. mi.; pop. 15,000.

Gren·del (gren'dǝl) See under BEOWULF.

Gren·fell (gren'fel), **Sir Wilfred (Thomason)**, 1865–1940, English physician and medical missionary.

Gre·no·ble (grǝ·nō'bǝl, *Fr.* grǝ·nô'bl') A city in SE France; pop. 161,230 (1968).

Gren·ville (gren'vil), **George**, 1712–70, English statesman; prime minister 1763–65. — **Sir Richard**, 1541?–91, English admiral: also *Greynville.*

Gresh·am (gresh'ǝm), **Sir Thomas**, 1519?–79, English merchant and financier.

Gresham's law *Econ.* The principle stating that of two forms of currency of equal face value but unequal exchange, the less valuable form tends to drive the other from circulation, owing to the hoarding of the preferred form. Also **Gresham's theorem.** [after Sir Thomas *Gresham*]

gres·so·ri·al (gre·sôr'ē·ǝl, -sō'rē-) *adj. Zool.* Adapted for walking, as the feet of certain birds or insects. Also **gres·so'ri·ous.** [< L *gressus,* pp. of *gradi* to walk]

Gret·na Green (gret'nǝ) A village in Dumfries, Scotland, near the English border; former scene of runaway marriages.

Greuze (grœz), **Jean Baptiste**, 1725–1805, French painter.

Grev·ille (grev'il), **Sir Fulke**, 1554–1628, English poet and statesman.

grew (grōō) Past tense of GROW.

grew·some (grōō'sǝm) See GRUESOME.

grey (grā) See GRAY.

Grey (grā), **Charles**, 1764–1845, second Earl Grey, English statesman; prime minister 1830–34. — **Sir Edward**, 1862–1933, first Viscount Grey of Fallodon, English statesman. — **Lady Jane**, 1537?–54, English pretender to the throne; proclaimed queen 1553; deposed and beheaded. — **Zane**, 1875–1939, U.S. novelist.

Grey Cup In Canada, the annual award symbolizing the national professional football championship.

grey·hound (grā'hound') *n.* **1.** One of a breed of tall, slender, smooth-coated dogs noted for their speed. **2.** A fast ocean vessel. Also, *Rare,* grayhound. [OE *grīghund*]

Grey·lock (grā'lok), **Mount** The highest point in Massachusetts, in the Berkshire Hills; 3,505 ft.

Greyn·ville (gren'vil), **Sir Richard.** See (Sir Richard) GRENVILLE.

grey·wacke (grā'wak, -wak·ǝ) See GRAYWACKE.

GREYHOUND
(28 inches high at shoulder)

grib·ble (grib'ǝl) *n.* A small marine isopod (genus *Limnoria*) that bores into and destroys submerged timber. [? Akin to GRUB]

grid (grid) *n.* **1.** An arrangement of regularly spaced parallel or intersecting bars, wires, etc.; grating; gridiron. **2.** A system of intersecting parallel lines dividing a map, chart, etc., into squares. **3.** A network of high-tension wires transmitting electric power over a wide area. **4.** *Electr.* A perforated or grooved metal plate in a storage cell or battery, serving to conduct electric current and to support active materials. **5.** *Electronics* An electrode, usually in the form of a wire screen, mounted between the cathode and anode of an electron tube that by its potential controls the flow of electrons. [Back formation < GRIDIRON]

grid bias *Electronics* Voltage applied to the grid of an electron tube to make it negative with respect to a cathode.

grid declination The angular difference, east or west, between true north and grid north in the grid system on a map.

grid·dle (grid′l) *n.* A flat, often rimless pan used for cooking pancakes, etc. — *v.t.* **·dled, ·dling** To cook on a griddle. [< AF *gredil*. Prob. akin to OF *greille*. See GRILLE.]

grid·dle·cake (grid′l-kāk′) *n.* A pancake baked on a griddle: also, *U.S.*, *flapjack.*

gride (grīd) *v.t.* & *v.i.* **grid·ed, grid·ing 1.** To grind or scrape harshly; grate. **2.** To cut; pierce. — *n.* A harsh grinding or scraping sound. [Metathetic var. of GIRD²]

grid·i·ron (grid′ī′ərn) *n.* **1.** A football field. **2.** A cooking utensil consisting of a metal grating set in a frame, used for broiling meat, fish, etc. **3.** Something resembling a cooking gridiron, as a network of beams or pipes. **4.** In the theater, a steel framework high above the stage, serving as support for curtains, backdrops, etc. [ME *gredire*, var. of *gredile* griddle; infl. in form by ME *ire* iron]

grid leak *Electronics* A resistor connected between the grid and cathode of an electron tube to allow escape of excess negative charges from the grid.

grid north The arbitrary northerly direction of the vertical grid lines on a map or chart.

grid road *Canadian* A road following a grid line of the original survey.

grid variation The angular difference, east or west, between grid north and magnetic north: also called *grivation.*

grief (grēf) *n.* **1.** Deep sorrow or mental distress caused by loss, remorse, affliction, etc. **2.** A cause of such sorrow. **3.** *Obs.* Physical pain or discomfort; also, a cause of pain. — **Syn.** See SORROW. — **to come to grief** To end badly; meet with disaster; fail. [< OF < *grever.* See GRIEVE.]

grief-strick·en (grēf′strik′ən) *adj.* Overwhelmed by grief; extremely sorrowful or remorseful.

Grieg (grēg, *Norw.* grig), **Edvard (Hagerup),** 1843–1907, Norwegian composer.

grie·shoch (grē′shəkh) *n. Scot.* Hot or glowing embers.

griev·ance (grē′vəns) *n.* **1.** A real or imaginary wrong regarded as cause for complaint or resentment. **2.** A feeling of resentment or hostility arising from a sense of having been wronged. **3.** *Obs.* Suffering; distress.

grieve (grēv) *v.* **grieved, griev·ing** *v.t.* **1.** To cause to feel sorrow or grief; sadden. **2.** *Obs.* To oppress, injure, or offend. — *v.i.* **3.** To feel sorrow or grief; mourn; lament. [< OF *grever* < L *gravare* to oppress < *gravis* heavy] — **griev′·er** *n.* — **griev′ing·ly** *adv.*

griev·ous (grē′vəs) *adj.* **1.** Causing grief, sorrow, or misfortune; distressing. **2.** Meriting severe punishment or censure; grave: a *grievous* sin. **3.** Expressing grief or sorrow; mournful. **4.** Causing pain or physical suffering: a *grievous* wound. — **griev′ous·ly** *adv.* — **griev′ous·ness** *n.*

griffe¹ (grif) *n. Archit.* A clawlike ornament projecting from the base of a column. [< F, claw < *griffer* to grasp]

griffe² (grif) *n. U.S. Dial.* **1.** A person having one Negro and one mulatto parent. **2.** A mulatto. **3.** A person of mixed Negro and American Indian descent. Also **griff.** [< F < Sp. *grifo*, orig., a griffin (mythical beast)]

grif·fin¹ (grif′ən) *n.* In Greek mythology, a creature with the head and wings of an eagle and the body of a lion: also *griffon, gryphon.* [< OF *grifoun* < L *gryphus* < Gk. *grýps*]

grif·fin² (grif′ən) *n.* A newcomer to India who is unfamiliar with Eastern customs. Also **griff.** [Origin uncertain]

Grif·fith (grif′ith) **D(avid Lewelyn) W(ark),** 1875–1948, U.S. motion-picture producer and director.

grif·fon (grif′ən) *n.* **1.** Griffin¹. **2.** One of a breed of dogs characterized by coarse, wiry hair. **3.** A large vulture (*Gyps fulvus*) of the Old World: also **griffon vulture.** [< F]

grift·er (grif′tər) *n. U.S. Slang* A petty swindler or confidence man; especially, one who operates a dishonest game of chance at a carnival or circus. [? < GRAFTER]

grig (grig) *n.* **1.** A very lively person. **2.** *Dial.* A cricket or grasshopper. **3.** *Dial.* A small eel. [Origin uncertain]

Gri·gnard (grē-nyär′), **(François Auguste) Victor,** 1871–1934, French chemist.

gri·gri (grē′grē) *n. Southern U.S.* A talisman, charm, or fetish of a kind originally used by African Negroes: also spelled *greegree, gris-gris.* [< African name]

grill (gril) *v.t.* **1.** To cook on a gridiron or similar utensil; broil. **2.** To subject to or torment with extreme heat. **3.** *U.S. Informal* To question or cross-examine persistently and searchingly. **4.** To emboss with a pattern of fine lines or dots, as postage stamps. — *v.i.* **5.** To undergo grilling. — *n.* **1.** A gridiron or similar cooking utensil. **2.** A meal or portion of grilled food. **3.** A grillroom. **4.** A grille. **5.** A rectangular pattern of fine lines or dots embossed on some postage stamps. [< F *gril*, var. of *grille* grating. See GRILLE.] — **grill′er** *n.*

gril·lage (gril′ij) *n.* A framework of crossed timbers or steel beams serving as a foundation, especially on soft or marshy ground. [< F < *grille.* See GRILLE.]

grille (gril) *n.* **1.** A grating, often of decorative, open metalwork, used as a screen, barrier, divider, etc. **2.** In court tennis, a square opening at the rear of the hazard side of the court. Also spelled *grill.* [< F < OF *greille* grating, gridiron, ult. < L *craticula*, dim. of *cratis* grating, lattice, hurdle. Akin to CRATE, GRATE.]

grilled (grild) *adj.* **1.** Broiled, as on a grill or gridiron. **2.** Having a grille.

Grill·par·zer (gril′pär·tsər), **Franz,** 1791–1872, Austrian dramatist.

grill·room (gril′rōōm′, -rŏŏm′) *n.* A restaurant or eating place where grilled foods are prepared and served.

grilse (grils) *n. pl.* **grilse** (*Rare* **grils·es**) A young salmon that has returned for the first time from the sea to fresh water. [Origin unknown]

grim (grim) *adj.* **grim·mer, grim·mest 1.** Stern or forbidding in appearance or character; formidable; terrifying. **2.** Unyielding; relentless; uncompromising. **3.** Repellent in nature or significance; sinisterly ironic; ghastly: a *grim* joke. **4.** Savagely destructive; fierce. [OE] — **grim′ly** *adv.* — **grim′ness** *n.*

— **Syn. 1.** harsh, dread, terrible. **2.** implacable. **3.** grisly¹.

gri·mace (gri-mās′) *n.* A distorted facial expression, usually indicative of pain, annoyance, disgust, etc. — *v.i.* **·maced, ·mac·ing** To distort the features; make faces. [< MF < Sp. *grimazo*, prob. < Gmc.] — **gri·mac′er** *n.*

Gri·mal·di man (gri-mäl′dē) *Anthropol.* A type of Paleolithic man represented by skeletons found in caves at Grimaldi, Italy, near Mentone, on the French border.

gri·mal·kin (gri-mal′kin, -môl′-) *n.* **1.** A cat, particularly an old female cat. **2.** A shrewish old woman. [< GRAY + *malkin* slattern, cat; dim. of *Matilda, Maud.*]

grime (grīm) *n.* Dirt, especially soot, rubbed into or coating a surface. — *v.t.* **grimed, grim·ing** To make dirty; begrime. [< Flemish *grijm*]

Grimes Golden (grīmz) A golden yellow eating apple. [after T. P. *Grimes*, who first grew it, c. 1790, in West Virginia]

Grimm (grim), **Jakob (Ludwig Karl),** 1785–1863, and his brother **Wilhelm (Karl),** 1786–1859, German philologists; noted for their collection of fairy tales.

Grimm's Law A statement by J. L. K. Grimm (earlier enunciated by Rasmus Rask) of the development of the consonants from Indo-European into Germanic. See VERNER'S LAW.

Grims·by (grimz′bē) A borough and port in Humberside, England, on the Humber; pop. 94,700 (1976).

grim·y (grī′mē) *adj.* **grim·i·er, grim·i·est** Full of or covered with grime; dirty. — **grim′i·ly** *adv.* — **grim′i·ness** *n.*

grin¹ (grin) *v.* **grinned, grin·ning** *v.i.* **1.** To smile broadly. **2.** To draw back the lips so as to show the teeth, as in a snarl or a grimace of pain, rage, etc. — *v.t.* **3.** To express by grinning. — *n.* **1.** The act of grinning. **2.** A facial expression produced by grinning, as a broad smile. — **Syn.** See SMILE. [OE *grennian*] — **grin′ner** *n.* — **grin′ning·ly** *adv.*

grin² (grin) *n. Dial.* A snare; trap. [OE]

grind (grīnd) *v.* **ground, grind·ing** *v.t.* **1.** To reduce to fine particles, as by crushing or friction; pulverize. **2.** To sharpen, polish, or wear down by friction or abrasion. **3.** To rub together or press down with a scraping or turning motion; grate: to *grind* the teeth. **4.** To oppress; crush. **5.** To operate by or as by turning a crank, as a coffee mill. **6.** To produce by or as by grinding. **7.** To produce mechanically or laboriously; followed by *out.* **8.** To teach or instill with great and constant effort: with *into*: to *grind* Latin into their heads. — *v.i.* **9.** To perform the operation or action of grinding. **10.** To undergo grinding; become ground. **11.** To scrape; grate. **12.** *Informal* To study or work steadily and laboriously. **13.** *U.S. Slang* To rotate the hips, as in the striptease. — *n.* **1.** The act of grinding. **2.** The sound made by grinding. **3.** A specified state of pulverization, as of coffee, produced by grinding. **4.** *Informal* Prolonged and laborious work or study. **5.** *U.S. Informal* A student who studies constantly. **6.** *U.S. Slang* A rotation of the hips performed by a stripteaser, etc. [OE *grindan*] — **grind′ing·ly** *adv.*

grin·de·li·a (grin-dē′lē·ə) *n.* **1.** Any of a genus (*Grindelia*) of coarse, herbaceous plants of the composite family, having stiff leaves and large, yellow flowers. **2.** The dried leaves and flowers of certain of these plants, used in medicine. [< NL, after D. H. *Grindel*, 1777–1836, Russian botanist]

grind·er (grīn′dər) *n.* **1.** One who grinds; especially, one who sharpens tools, etc. **2.** A device used for grinding, as a coffee mill, etc. **3.** A molar. **4.** *pl. Informal* The teeth. **5.** *Slang* A hero sandwich.

grind·er·y (grīn′dər·ē) *n. pl.* **·er·ies, 1.** A place where edged tools or other instruments are ground. **2.** *Brit.* Materials and tools used by leatherworkers.

grind·stone (grīnd′stōn′) *n.* **1.** A flat, circular stone rotated on an axle, used for sharpening tools, abrading, polishing, etc. **2.** A millstone. **— to keep** (or **have**) **one's nose to the grindstone** To work hard and continuously.

grin·go (gring′gō) *n. pl.* **·gos** In Latin America, a foreigner, particularly one from the United States or any other country where English is the official language: an offensive term. [< Am. Sp., gibberish < Sp. *griego* Greek, gibberish]

grip¹ (grip) *n.* **1.** The act of seizing and holding firmly; tight grasp; clutch. **2.** The ability to seize or maintain a hold; grasping power. **3.** Control; domination; mastery. **4.** Mental or intellectual grasp; understanding. **5.** The manner of grasping or holding something, as a tool or implement. **6.** A distinctive handclasp, as one used by members of a fraternal organization in greeting one another. **7.** That part of an object designed or adapted for grasping in the hand; handle. **8.** A device or mechanical part that seizes or holds something. **9.** The strength of the hand in grasping or squeezing. **10.** *U.S.* A suitcase or valise. **11.** *U.S.* A handy man on a theatrical set; stagehand. **— to come to grips 1.** To struggle in hand-to-hand combat. **2.** To deal decisively or energetically, as with a problem; grapple. — *v.* **gripped** or **gript, grip·ping** *v.t.* **1.** To seize; grasp firmly; hold onto tightly. **2.** To capture, as the mind or imagination; attract and hold the interest of. **3.** To join or attach securely with a grip or similar device. — *v.i.* **4.** To take firm hold. **5.** To capture the imagination or attention. — **Syn.** See GRASP. [Fusion of OE *gripe* grasp and *gripa* handful, both < *gripan* to seize. Akin to GROPE.] — **grip′per** *n.* — **grip′ping·ly** *adv.*

grip² (grip) *n.* Influenza

gripe (grīp) *v.* **griped, grip·ing** *v.t.* **1.** *U.S. Informal* To annoy; vex; anger. **2.** To cause sharp pain or cramps in the bowels of. **3.** *Archaic* To seize and hold firmly; clutch; grip. **4.** *Archaic* To oppress; afflict. — *v.i.* **5.** *U.S. Informal* To complain; grumble. **6.** To cause cramps or sharp pains in the bowels; also, to experience such pains. **7.** *Archaic* To clutch; grip. — *n.* **1.** *U.S. Informal* A complaint; grievance. **2.** *Usually pl.* Spasmodic pain in the bowels. **3.** *Archaic* The act of griping or clutching; firm grasp; clutch. **4.** *Archaic* Oppressive hold or control; power. [OE *gripan*] — **grip′er** *n.*

grippe (grip) *n.* Influenza. [< F < *gripper* to seize; ? infl. by Russ. *khrip* hoarseness] — **grip′py** *adj.*

grip·ple (grip′əl) *adj. Obs.* or *Dial.* Covetous; greedy. [OE *gripul* < *gripan* to seize]

grip·sack (grip′sak′) *n. U.S.* A traveling bag; valise.

Gri·qua (grē′kwə, grik′wə) *n.* In South Africa, a person of mixed Hottentot and Boer or European descent. [< Afrikaans]

Gris (grēs), **Juan,** 1887–1927, Spanish painter.

gri·saille (gri·zāl′, *Fr.* grē·zä′y′) *n.* **1.** A style of painting using shades of gray only, often in imitation of bas-relief. **2.** A work painted or decorated in this manner. [< F *gris* gray]

Gri·sel·da (gri·zel′də) In Boccaccio's *Decameron,* Chaucer's *Canterbury Tales,* etc., a heroine of unshakable patience, meekness, and virtue.

gris·e·ous (gris′ē·əs, griz′-) *adj.* Grayish, often with a mottled appearance. [< Med.L *griseus*]

gri·sette (gri·zet′) *n.* A French working girl; especially, one of flirtatious or free-and-easy manners. [< F, orig., a gray woolen fabric worn by workingwomen < *gris* gray]

gris·gris (grē′grē) See GRIGRI.

gris·kin (gris′kin) *n. Brit.* The lean part of a loin of pork. [< obs. *grice* pig + -KIN]

gris·ly¹ (griz′lē) *adj.* **·li·er, ·li·est 1.** Inspiring fear or horror; macabre; gruesome. **2.** Repellent; forbidding; grim. [OE *grislic*] — **gris′li·ness** *n.*

gris·ly² (griz′lē) See GRIZZLY.

gri·son (grī′sən, griz′ən) *n.* A weasellike, carnivorous mammal (*Grison vittata*) of South America. [< F *gris* gray]

Gri·sons (grē·zôN′) The French name for GRAUBÜNDEN.

GRISON
(About 12 to 14 inches long)

grist (grist) *n.* **1.** Grain that is to be ground; also, a portion or batch of such grain. **2.** Ground grain; meal. **— grist for one's mill** Something that can be used to one's profit or advantage. [OE < *grindan* to grind]

gris·tle (gris′əl) *n.* Cartilage, especially in meat. [OE]

gris·tly (gris′lē) *adj.* **1.** Pertaining to or resembling gristle. **2.** Consisting of or containing gristle. — **gris′tli·ness** *n.*

grist·mill (grist′mil′) *n.* A mill for grinding grain.

grit (grit) *n.* **1.** Small, rough, hard particles, as of sand, stone, etc. **2.** A hard, coarse-grained sandstone, often used for making grindstones. **3.** Specified texture or coarseness, as of a whetstone, sandpaper, etc. **4.** Resolute spirit; courageous determination; pluck. — *v.* **grit·ted, grit·ting** *v.t.* **1.** To grind or press together, as the teeth. **2.** To cover with grit. — *v.i.* **3.** To make a grating sound. [OE *grēot*]

Grit (grit) *Canadian n.* A member of the Liberal Party. — *adj.* Of or pertaining to the Liberal Party.

grith (grith) *n. Obs.* In early English law: **a** Protection or

security, as within the precincts of a church. **b** A place of sanctuary or refuge. Also, *esp. Scot., girth.* [OE < ON *gridh* home; in pl., asylum]

grits (grits) *n.pl.* **1.** Coarse meal made from hulled grain. **2.** *U.S.* Coarsely ground hominy: also called *hominy grits.* [OE *grytte*]

grit·ty (grit′ē) *adj.* **·ti·er, ·ti·est 1.** Like, containing, or consisting of grit. **2.** Courageously determined; plucky. — **grit′ti·ly** *adv.* — **grit′ti·ness** *n.*

gri·va·tion (gri·vā′shən) See GRID VARIATION.

griv·et (griv′it) *n.* A small monkey (*Cercopithecus aethiops*) of Abyssinia, having greenish gray fur and a black face. [Origin unknown]

griz·zle¹ (griz′əl) *v.t. & v.i.* **·zled, ·zling** To become or cause to become gray. — *n.* **1.** The color gray, especially when produced by intermixed hairs, specks, etc., of black and white. **2.** Gray or graying hair. **3.** A gray wig. — *adj.* Gray. [< OF *grisel* < *gris* gray]

griz·zle² (griz′əl) *v.i.* **·zled, ·zling** *Brit. Informal* To whine or grumble; fret. [Freq. of dial. E *grize* to grind the teeth]

griz·zled (griz′əld) *adj.* **1.** Streaked, flecked, or intermixed with gray. **2.** Having gray or graying hair.

griz·zly (griz′lē) *adj.* **·zli·er, ·zli·est** Grayish; grizzled. Also, *Obs., grisly.* — *n. pl.* **·zlies** A grizzly bear.

grizzly bear A large, brownish or grayish bear (*Ursus horribilis*) of western North America.

gro. Gross (unit of quantity).

groan (grōn) *v.i.* **1.** To utter a low, prolonged sound of or as of pain, anguish, disapproval, etc.; moan. **2.** To make a noise resembling such a sound; creak harshly. **3.** To suffer, as from cruel or unfair treatment; be oppressed: usually with *under* or *beneath.* **4.** To be heavily loaded; be overburdened. — *v.t.* **5.** To utter or express with or as with a groan. — *n.* **1.** A low moaning or murmuring sound uttered to express pain, derision, etc. **2.** A creaking or roaring sound. [OE *grānian*] — **groan′er** *n.* — **groan′ing·ly** *adv.*

groat (grōt) *n.* **1.** An English silver coin of the 14th–17th centuries, worth fourpence. **2.** An insignificant sum. [< MDu. *groot,* orig., great, large]

groats (grōts) *n.pl.* Hulled, usually coarsely crushed grain, as barley, oats, or wheat. [OE *grotan*]

gro·cer (grō′sər) *n.* One who deals in foodstuffs and various other household supplies. [OF *grossier* wholesaler < Med.L *grossarius* < LL *grossus* gross, great]

gro·cer·y (grō′sər·ē, grōs′rē) *n. pl.* **·cer·ies 1.** *U.S.* A store in which foodstuffs and household supplies are sold. **2.** *pl.* The merchandise sold by a grocer.

Grod·no (grôd′nô) A city in the western Byelorussian S.S.R., on the Nyeman; pop. 132,000 (est. 1970).

grog (grog) *n.* **1.** Alcoholic liquor, especially rum, mixed with water. **2.** Any intoxicating drink. [after Old *Grog,* nickname (with ref. to his grogram cloak) of Admiral E. Vernon, 1684–1757, who first rationed it to English sailors]

grog·ger·y (grog′ər·ē) *n. pl.* **·ger·ies** *U.S. Archaic* A barroom, especially one of disreputable character.

grog·gy (grog′ē) *adj.* **·gi·er, ·gi·est** *Informal* **1.** Dazed or not fully conscious, as from a blow or exhaustion. **2.** Drunk. [< GROG] — **grog′gi·ly** *adv.* — **grog′gi·ness** *n.*

grog·ram (grog′rəm) *n.* A loosely woven, sometimes stiffened, fabric of coarse silk, or silk mixed with mohair or wool. [< F *gros-grain* coarse grain]

grog·shop (grog′shop′) *n. Archaic* A small, squalid, or disreputable barroom or public house.

groin (groin) *n.* **1.** *Anat.* The fold or crease formed at the juncture of either of the thighs with the abdomen. **2.** *Archit.* The curve formed by the intersection of two vaults. For illustration see VAULT. — *v.t.* To build with or form into groins. [? OE *grynde* abyss, hollow]

groin rib *Archit.* A rib covering a groin.

Gro·li·er (grō′lē·ər, *Fr.* grō·lyä′) *adj.* Designating a bookbinding style or design characterized by gilded ornamental scrolls, geometrical figures, interlaced lines, etc. [after Jean *Grolier* de Servières]

Gro·lier de Ser·viè·res (grō·lyä′ də ser·vyâr′), **Jean,** 1479–1565, French bibliophile.

grom·met (grom′it) *n.* **1.** A reinforcing eyelet of metal or other durable material, through which a rope, cord, or fastening may be passed. **2.** *Naut.* A ring of rope or metal used to secure the edge of a sail. Also **grummet.** [< F *gromette* < *gourmer* to curb]

GROIN RIBS IN GROIN VAULTING

grom·well (grom′wəl) *n.* Any of a genus (*Lithospermum*) of herbs of the borage family, having hard, stony seeds. [< OF *gromil* < L *gruinum milium* < *gruinum* crane + *milium* millet]

Gro·my·ko (grō·mē′kō), **Andrei Andreevich,** born 1909, Soviet diplomat.

Gro·ning·en (grō′ning·ən, *Du.* khrō′ning·ən) A city in the northern Netherlands; pop. 144,485 (est. 1960).

Grøn·land (grœn′lån′) The Danish name for GREENLAND.

groom (grōōm, grŏŏm) *n.* **1.** A man or boy employed to tend horses; stableman. **2.** A bridegroom. **3.** One of several honorary functionaries in the British royal household. **4.** *Archaic* A male servant. — *v.t.* **1.** To attend to the neatness or appearance of; make tidy, smooth, or trim. **2.** To take care of (a horse) by cleaning, currying, etc. **3.** *U.S.* To prepare by giving special training or attention to, as for a political office. [ME *grom.* Cf. OF *gromet* servant.]

grooms·man (grōōmz′mən, grōōms′-) *n. pl.* ·**men** (-mən) The best man at a wedding.

Groot (grōt), **Gerhard,** 1340–84, Dutch religious reformer: called **Ge·rar·dus Mag·nus** (jə·rär′dəs mag′nəs).

groove (grōōv) *n.* **1.** A long, narrow indentation or furrow cut into a surface, especially by a tool. **2.** Any narrow depression, channel, or rut. **3.** A fixed, settled routine or habit of thought, conduct, etc. **4.** *Printing* The channel in the bottom of a piece of type. **5.** *Anat.* Any of various furrows or depressions in an organ or part of the body. — **in the groove** *U.S. Slang* Operating, working, or performing expertly or smoothly. — *v.t.* **grooved, groov·ing** To form a groove in; furrow. [< Du. *groeve.* Akin to GRAVE², GRAVE³.]

groov·y (grōō′vē) *adj.* **groov·i·er, groov·i·est** *Slang* Pleasing or agreeable.

grope (grōp) *v.* **groped, grop·ing** *v.i.* **1.** To feel about with or as with the hands, as in the dark; feel one's way. **2.** To search bewilderedly or uncertainly. — *v.t.* **3.** To seek out or find by or as by groping. — *n.* The act of groping. [OE *grāpian.* Akin to GRIP¹.] — **grop′er** *n.* — **grop′ing·ly** *adv.*

Gro·pi·us (grō′pē·əs), **Walter,** 1883–1969, German architect active in the United States from 1937; founder of Bauhaus.

Gros (grō), **Baron Antoine Jean,** 1771–1835, French painter.

gros·beak (grōs′bēk′) *n.* Any of various finchlike birds characterized by a short, stout beak, as the rose-breasted grosbeak. [< F *gros-bec* < *gros* large + *bec* beak]

gro·schen (grō′shən) *n. pl.* ·**schen** **1.** A bronze coin of Austria, equivalent to one hundredth of a schilling. **2.** Popularly, the ten-pfennig piece of Germany. **3.** Formerly, a minor silver coin of Germany.

gros de Londres (grō də lôn′dr′) A silk fabric having horizontal ribs. [< F, heavy (silk) of London]

gros·grain (grō′grān) *n.* A strong, horizontally corded silk or rayon fabric. [< F *gros-grain* coarse grain]

gross (grōs) *adj.* **1.** Undiminished by deductions; total; entire: distinguished from *net: gross* income. **2.** Conspicuously bad or wrong; flagrant: *gross* errors. **3.** Excessively or unattractively fat or large; hulking. **4.** Coarse in composition, structure, or texture. **5.** Coarse or obscene in character; vulgar. **6.** Lacking in perception or discrimination; insensitive; dull. **7.** Dense; compact; thick. **8.** *Anat.* or *Pathol.* Visible without the aid of a microscope: a *gross* lesion. — **Syn.** See FLAGRANT. — *n. pl.* **gross** for def. 1, **gross·es** for *def. 2* A unit of quantity comprising twelve dozen. Abbr. *gr., gro.* **2.** The entire amount; mass; bulk. — **in the gross 1.** In bulk; all together. **2.** Wholesale. — *v.t.* To earn or produce as total income or profit, before deductions for expenses, etc. [< OF *gros* < LL *grossus* thick] — **gross′ly** *adv.* — **gross′ness** *n.*

gross national product The total market value of a nation's goods and services, before any deductions or allowances are made. Abbr. *GNP, G.N.P.*

gross ton See under TON¹ (def. 1).

gros·su·lar·ite (gros′yə·lə·rīt′) *n.* A type of garnet containing calcium and aluminum. [< NL *grossularia* gooseberry + -ITE¹]

gross weight Total weight. Abbr. *gr. wt.*

grosz (grōsh) *n. pl.* **grosz·y** (grōsh′ē) A monetary denomination or small coin of Poland, the hundredth part of a zloty [< Polish]

Grosz (grōs), **George,** 1893–1959, German painter and illustrator active in the United States.

grot (grot) *n. Poetic* A grotto. [< F *grotte* < Ital. *grotta.* See GROTTO.]

Grote (grōt), **George,** 1794–1871, English historian.

gro·tesque (grō·tesk′) *adj.* **1.** Distorted, incongruous, or fantastically ugly in appearance or style; bizarre; outlandish. **2.** Characterized by fantastic combinations of human and animal figures with conventional design forms, as ornamental work. — **Syn.** See FANCIFUL. — *n.* **1.** One who or that which is grotesque. **2.** Grotesque style or quality. [< F < Ital. *grottesco* < *grotta* grotto, excavation; with ref. to works of art found in excavations of ancient houses] — **gro·tesque′ly** *adv.* — **gro·tesque′ness** *n.*

gro·tes·que·ry (grō·tes′kə·rē) *n. pl.* ·**ries 1.** Grotesque style, quality, character or behavior. **2.** A grotesque object, action, etc. Also **gro·tes′que·rie.**

Gro·ti·us (grō′shē·əs), **Hugo,** 1583–1645, Dutch jurist and statesman: original name **Huig de Groot** (də grōt′).

grot·to (grot′ō) *n. pl.* ·**toes** or ·**tos 1.** A cave. **2.** An artificial cavelike structure, as for a recreational retreat, shrine, etc. [< Ital. *grotta* < L *crypta.* Doublet of CRYPT.]

grouch (grouch) *U.S. Informal v.i.* To be discontented; grumble. — *n.* **1.** A grumbling person. **2.** A sulky mood. **3.** A complaint. [< OF *groucher* to murmur]

grouch·y (grou′chē) *adj.* **grouch·i·er, grouch·i·est** *U.S. Informal* Ill-humored; surly. — **grouch′i·ly** *adv.* — **grouch′i·ness** *n.*

Grou·chy (grōō·shē′), **Marquis Emmanuel de,** 1766–1847, French general.

ground¹ (ground) *n.* **1.** The layer of solid substances constituting the surface of the earth; land. **2.** Soil, sand, etc., at or near the earth's surface. **3.** *Sometimes pl.* An area or tract of land; especially, one reserved or used for a specific purpose: a burial *ground.* **4.** *pl.* Private land, as the surrounding premises of a dwelling, public institution, etc. **5.** *Usually pl.* The fundamental cause, reason, or motive for an action, belief, etc.: *grounds* for suspicion: when plural, often construed as singular. **6.** A matter for discussion or consideration; subject; topic. **7.** *Often pl.* A foundation or basis, as for a decision, argument, or relationship; footing: when plural, often construed as singular. **8.** *pl.* Sediment; dregs; especially, the particles remaining after a beverage has been brewed. **9.** The solid bottom of a body of water. **10.** In various arts and crafts, the basic working surface or background on or against which colors, forms, designs, etc., are placed. **11.** *Electr.* **a** The connection of an electrical current or circuit with the earth through a conductor. **b** A stake, water pipe, or other solid connection with the earth, to which a ground wire is attached. **c** The potential in a part of a circuit, as the chassis of a radio set, etc., that is zero with respect to other voltages and may or may not be at the potential of the earth. **12.** *Music* A ground bass. — **Syn.** See REASON. — **from the ground up** In every detail; thoroughly; completely. — **on home** (or **on one's own**) **ground 1.** In accustomed circumstances or surroundings. **2.** Dealing with a thoroughly familiar subject. — **to break ground 1.** To dig into or cut through the soil, as in plowing, excavating a building site, etc. **2.** To make a start in any undertaking. **3.** *Naut.* To be raised or loosened from the bottom, as an anchor. — **to cover ground 1.** To move or travel, especially over a considerable distance. **2.** To make progress. — **to gain ground 1.** To advance; make headway. **2.** To increase in favor, popularity, influence, etc. — **to give ground** To yield a position or advantage; retreat. — **to hold** (or **stand**) **one's ground** To maintain one's position; refuse to yield or retreat. — **to lose ground 1.** To fail to maintain an advantage or gain; fall behind. **2.** To decline in favor, popularity, influence, etc. — **to shift one's ground** To change one's point of view, as in an argument or discussion. — *adj.* **1.** Being on, near, or at a level with the ground. **2.** Living, growing, or active on or in the ground; terrestrial. — *v.t.* **1.** To put, place, or set on the ground. **2.** To base on or as on a foundation; establish; found. **3.** To train (someone) in basic principles or elements; teach fundamentals to. **4.** *Aeron.* To confine (an aircraft, pilot, etc.) to the ground. **5.** *Electr.* To place in connection with the earth or a ground, as a circuit. **6.** *Naut.* To run (a vessel) aground. **7.** To supply with a ground or background, as a painting. — *v.i.* **8.** To come or fall to the ground. **9.** In baseball, to hit a ground ball. **10.** *Naut.* To run aground. [OE *grund*]

ground² (ground) Past tense and past participle of GRIND.

ground·age (groun′dij) *n.* A fee charged for allowing a vessel to stop at a port.

ground alert *Mil.* A state of preparedness in which airplanes and their crews stand ready for a quick takeoff.

ground bait Fishing bait, sometimes weighted, that drops or settles to the bottom of the water.

ground ball In baseball, etc., a batted ball that rolls or bounces along the ground: also called *grounder.*

ground bass *Music* A short melodic phrase in the bass, repeated continually with varied melody and harmony.

ground beetle Any of various beetles of the family *Carabidae,* often found under logs, stones, etc. For illustration see INSECTS (beneficial).

ground cherry Any of various plants (genus *Physalis*) of the nightshade family, having round berries enclosed in ribbed, inflated husks.

ground cover Plants or shrubs characteristically forming an extensive, dense growth close to the earth.

ground crew *Aeron.* A group of workers responsible for the servicing and maintenance of aircraft on the ground.

ground·er (groun′dər) *n.* A ground ball.

ground floor In a building, the floor that is level or almost level with the ground. — **to get in on the ground floor** *U.S. Informal* To enter upon a project or undertaking at its beginning and thus be in a position of special advantage.

ground glass 1. Glass of which the surface has been treated so that it diffuses light and is not fully transparent. **2.** Finely powdered glass, used as an abrasive, etc.

ground hemlock A low, evergreen shrub (*Taxus canadensis*) of the yew family, native to the northern United States.

ground hog The woodchuck.

ground-hog day (ground′hŏg′, -hog′) The second day of February, on which, according to popular tradition, the ground hog emerges from hibernation and, if he sees his shadow, goes underground again for six more weeks of winter.

ground ivy A creeping herb (*Glecoma hederacea*) of the mint family, having bluish purple flowers.

ground·less (ground'lis) *adj.* Having no reason or cause; baseless. — **ground'less·ly** *adv.* — **ground'less·ness** *n.*

ground·ling (ground'ling) *n.* **1.** A plant or animal living, growing, or remaining on or close to the ground. **2.** A fish that keeps close to the bottom of the water. **3.** A person of crude or undiscriminating tastes, especially in regard to entertainment, literature, etc. **4.** Formerly, as in the Elizabethan theater, a spectator who stood in the pit.

ground loop *Aeron.* A violent turning of an aircraft during landing, takeoff, or taxiing.

ground·mass (ground'mas') *n.* *Geol.* A compact, fine-grained or glassy portion of igneous rock, as porphyry, in which larger, distinctly formed crystals are embedded.

ground·nut (ground'nut') *n.* **1.** A climbing, leguminous plant (*Apios americana*) of North America, having fragrant, brownish flowers and roots bearing edible tubers. **2.** Any of various plants bearing edible tubers or underground nutlike seed pods, as the peanut. **3.** An edible tuber, pod, or seed of any of these plants.

ground owl The burrowing owl (which see).

ground pine **1.** Any of various creeping, evergreen plants (genus *Lycopodium*) of the club moss family. **2.** A European herb (*Ajuga chamaepitys*) of the mint family having a characteristic resinous odor.

ground pink The moss pink (which see).

ground plan **1.** A diagrammatic plan of any floor of a building. **2.** Any preliminary plan or basic outline.

ground plate **1.** A groundsill. **2.** A bedplate supporting railroad ties. **3.** *Electr.* A metal plate in the ground, forming a connection between a circuit and the earth.

ground plum **1.** A leguminous plant (*Astragalus caryocarpus*) of the Midwestern United States. **2.** The thick, fleshy, plum-shaped pod of this plant.

ground rattlesnake The pygmy rattlesnake (which see).

ground rent Rent paid for the right to occupy, build on, or make improvements on a piece of land.

ground robin The towhee.

ground·sel¹ (ground'səl) *n.* A common herb (genus *Senecio*) of the composite family having numerous yellow flowers. [OE *gundæswelge*, lit., that swallows pus (with ref. to its use in poultices); infl. in form by OE *grund* ground]

ground·sel² (ground'səl) See GROUNDSILL.

ground·sill (ground'sil') *n.* The lowest horizontal timber in a frame building: also *groundsel*. [< GROUND¹ + SILL]

ground speed The speed of an aircraft measured according to the distance traveled over the earth's surface: distinguished from *air speed*.

ground squirrel **1.** One of several small, terrestrial rodents (genus *Citellus*) of the squirrel family, as the **thirteen-lined ground squirrel** (*C. tridecemlineatus*) of central and western North America. **2.** A chipmunk.

ground swell A billowing of the ocean in broad, deep waves caused by a prolonged storm, earthquake, etc., and often reaching areas remote from their source.

ground water Water beneath the earth's surface, accumulating as a result of seepage, and serving as the source of springs, wells, etc.

ground wave A radio wave that travels along the surface of the ground.

ground wire *Electr.* The wire connecting an electrical apparatus with the ground or with a grounded object.

ground·work (ground'wûrk') *n.* A foundation; basis.

ground zero The point on the ground vertically beneath or above the point of detonation of an atomic or thermonuclear bomb: also called *hypocenter.*

group (grōōp) *n.* **1.** A collection or assemblage of persons or things, considered as a unit; aggregation; cluster. **2.** A number of persons or things having in common certain characteristics, attitudes, interests, etc. **3.** *Biol.* A number of plants or animals considered to be related because of certain common characteristics. **4.** In painting or sculpture, two or more figures or objects forming all or part of a harmonious unit or design. **5.** *Mil.* An administrative and tactical or service unit composed of two or more battalions or squadrons. **6.** *Naval* A number of ships or aircraft assigned for a specific mission or purpose. **7.** In the U.S. Air Force, a subdivision of a wing, designated for a specific purpose. **8.** *Chem.* **a** An arrangement of atoms constituting part of a molecule; a radical: the hydroxyl *group* (OH). **b** A set of elements having similar properties, as in the periodic table. **9.** *Geol.* A rock formation consisting of two or more strata. **10.** *Ling.* A subdivision of a linguistic family, not as inclusive as a branch. **11.** *Math.* A set consisting of elements that, when subjected to some specified rule of combination, result in elements belonging to the set. Abbr. *gr.* — *Syn.* See COMPANY. — *v.t.* **1.** To arrange, gather, or classify in a group or groups. — *v.i.* **2.** To form or be part of a group. [< F *groupe* < Ital. *groppo* knot, lump < Gmc.]

group captain In the Royal, Royal Canadian, or other Commonwealth air forces, a commissioned officer ranking next below an Air Commodore. See table at GRADE.

group·er (grōō'pər) *n.* Any of certain serranoid food fishes (*Mycteroperca, Epinephelus,* and related genera); especially, the **red grouper** (*Epinephelus morio*) of the southern Atlantic and Gulf coasts. [< Pg. *garupa,* appar. < S. Am. Ind.]

group insurance Any of various systems of life, accident, or health insurance covering members of a group, as the employees of a business organization, under a single contract.

group·ie (grōō'pē) *n.* A girl who follows a pop singer or group on tours, usually for sexual reasons.

grouse¹ (grous) *n. pl.* **grouse** Any of a family (*Tetraonidae*) of game birds of the northern hemisphere, related to the pheasants and the domestic chicken, and characterized by rounded bodies and mottled plumage; especially, the **spruce grouse** (*Canachites canadensis*) of North America, the **red grouse** (*Lagopus scoticus*) of the British Isles, and the ruffed grouse (which see). [Origin uncertain]

grouse² (grous) *Informal v.i.* **groused, grous·ing** To grumble; grouch. — *n.* A complaint. [Orig. Brit. army slang; ? < OF *grousser* to murmur] — **grous'er** *n.*

grout (grout) *n.* **1.** A thin mortar used to fill crevices between stones, bricks, tiles, etc. **2.** A finishing coat, as of plaster, applied to walls or ceilings. **3.** Coarse meal or porridge. **4.** *pl.* Groats. **5.** *pl.* Dregs; grounds. — *v.t.* To fill, surround, or finish with grout. [OE *grūt* coarse meal] — **grout'er** *n.*

grout·y (grou'tē) *adj.* **grout·i·er, grout·i·est** *U.S. Archaic* Cross or surly; sulky.

grove (grōv) *n.* A small wood or group of trees, especially when cleared of underbrush. [OE *grāf*]

grov·el (gruv'əl, grov'-) *v.i.* **grov·eled** or **·elled, grov·el·ing** or **·el·ling** **1.** To lie prostrate or crawl face downward, as in abjection, fear, etc. **2.** To act with abject humility; abase oneself, as from fear or servility. **3.** To take pleasure in what is base or sensual. [Back formation < GROVELING] — **grov'el·er** or **grov'el·ler** *n.*

grov·el·ing (gruv'əl·ing, grov'-) *adj.* **1.** Lying or crawling in an abject, prostrate position. **2.** Abjectly humble; servile. **3.** Low; sordid Also **grov'el·ling.** [ME *grovelynge,* adv. < *on gruff* face down (< ON *ā grufu*) + -LING²]

grow (grō) *v.* **grew, grown, grow·ing** *v.i.* **1.** To increase in size by the assimilation of nutriment; undergo the process of development characteristic of living organisms or parts; progress toward maturity. **2.** To germinate and develop to maturity, as from a seed or spore; originate, as from a basic source or cause; arise. **3.** To be produced as vegetation; flourish; thrive: Weeds *grow* in gardens. **4.** To increase in size, amount, or degree: Our fears *grew.* **5.** To come to be gradually; become: She *grew* angry. **6.** To become joined or attached by or as by growth. — *v.t.* **7.** To cause to grow; cultivate: to *grow* roses. **8.** To produce by a natural process; develop: to *grow* hair. **9.** To cover with a growth: used in the passive: The lawn was *grown* with weeds. — **to grow on** To become increasingly acceptable, pleasing, or necessary to. — **to grow out of** **1.** To outgrow. **2.** To result from. — **to grow up** **1.** To become an adult; reach maturity or full growth. **2.** To come into being; arise. [OE *grōwan*]

grow·er (grō'ər) *n.* **1.** One who grows plants, produce, etc. **2.** A plant, etc., that grows in a specified way: a rapid *grower.*

growing pains **1.** Muscular discomfort experienced during rapid growth in childhood or early adolescence. **2.** Problems or difficulties arising in the early stages of an enterprise.

growl (groul) *v.i.* **1.** To utter a deep, guttural sound, as that made by a hostile or agitated animal. **2.** To speak gruffly and angrily; grumble. **3.** To rumble, as distant thunder. — *v.t.* **4.** To utter or express by growling. — *n.* **1.** A deep, sustained, guttural sound uttered by a hostile or agitated animal. **2.** Any sound resembling this. **3.** A gruff, angry utterance. [? < OF *grouler* to mumble < Gmc.]

growl·er (grou'lər) *n.* **1.** One who or that which growls. **2.** *U.S. Slang* A can, mug, pitcher, etc., used for carrying beer from a saloon, etc. **3.** *Canadian* In the Atlantic Provinces, a small iceberg. **4.** *Brit. Slang* A four-wheeled horse cab.

grown (grōn) Past participle of GROW. — *adj.* Arrived at full physical growth or stature; mature; adult.

grown-up (grōn'up') *n.* A mature person; adult.

grown-up (grōn'up') *adj.* **1.** Physically or mentally mature; adult. **2.** Characteristic of or appropriate to an adult.

growth (grōth) *n.* **1.** The act or process of growing; advancement toward or attainment of full size or maturity; development. **2.** A gradual increase in size, importance, influence, etc. **3.** Something grown or in the process of growing: a *growth* of timber. **4.** Origin; source: ideas of foreign *growth.* **5.** *Pathol.* An abnormal formation of tissue; tumor: a cancerous *growth.* — *Syn.* See PROGRESS.

growth stock In finance, stock in a company that is expected to increase its sales and profits relatively rapidly.

Groz·nyy (grōz'nē) A city in the SE R.S.F.S.R., east of the Caspian Sea; pop. 341,000 (est. 1970). Also **Groz'ny.**

grub (grub) *v.* **grubbed, grub·bing** *v.i.* **1.** To dig in the ground. **2.** To lead a dreary or miserable existence; toil unceasingly; drudge. **3.** To make careful or plodding search;

rummage. **4.** *Slang* To eat. — *v.t.* **5.** To dig from the ground; root out: often with *up* or *out*. **6.** To clear (ground) of roots, stumps, etc. **7.** *Slang* To provide with food. **8.** *U.S. Slang* To scrounge. — *n.* **1.** The wormlike larva of certain insects, as of the June beetle. **2.** A drudge. **3.** *Slang* Food. [ME *grubben*. Akin to GRAVE², GRAVE³.]

grub·ber (grub′ər) *n.* **1.** One who grubs. **2.** A machine or tool used in grubbing, as a grub hoe.

grub·by (grub′ē) *adj.* **·bi·er, ·bi·est** **1.** Dirty; unclean; sloppy. **2.** Full of or infested with grubs. — **grub′bi·ly** *adv.* — **grub′bi·ness** *n.*

grub hoe A heavy hoe used for grubbing out roots, etc. For illustration see HOE.

grub·stake (grub′stāk′) *U.S. Informal n.* **1.** Money, supplies, or equipment provided a prospector on condition that he share his finds with the donor. **2.** Money or assistance furnished to advance any venture. — *v.t.* **·staked, ·stak·ing** To supply with a grubstake.

grub·street (grub′strēt′) *adj.* Characteristic of literary hacks or their work. Also **Grub′street′.**

Grub Street **1.** The former name for Milton Street, London, once frequented by needy authors and literary hacks. **2.** Impoverished writers and literary hacks, as a class.

grudge (gruj) *n.* A feeling of ill will, rancor, or enmity, harbored for a remembered wrong, etc. — *v.* **grudged, grudg·ing** *v.t.* **1.** To be displeased or resentful because of the possessions, good fortune, etc. of (another): They *grudge* him his wealth. **2.** To give or allow unwillingly and resentfully; begrudge. — *v.i.* **3.** *Obs.* To be discontented. [< OF *grouch-er.* Cf. GROUCH.] — **grudg′er** *n.* — **grudg′ing·ly** *adv.*

gru·el (grōō′əl) *n.* **1.** A semiliquid food made by boiling meal in water or milk. **2.** *Brit. Informal* Severe punishment; beating. — *v.t.* **gru·eled** or **·elled, gru·el·ing** or **·el·ling** To disable or exhaust by hard work, punishment, relentless questioning, etc. [< OF, meal, ult. < Med.L *grutum* coarse meal < Gmc.] — **gru′el·er** or **gru′el·ler** *n.*

gru·el·ing (grōō′əl·ing) *adj.* Causing strain or exhaustion; severely trying. — *n.* Any grueling experience or treatment. Also **gru′el·ling.**

grue·some (grōō′səm) *adj.* Inspiring repugnance; frightful; also spelled **grewsome.** [< Scot. *grue* to shudder + -SOME¹] — **grue′some·ly** *adv.* — **grue′some·ness** *n.*

gruff (gruf) *adj.* **1.** Brusque and rough in manner or speech; surly: a *gruff* fellow. **2.** Hoarse and guttural; harsh. [< Du. *grof* rough] — **gruff′ly** *adv.* — **gruff′ness** *n.*

gru·gru (grōō′grōō′) *n.* **1.** Any of a genus (*Acrocomia*) of spiny palms of South America, some of which yield edible nuts. **2.** The edible larva of a weevil (*Rhynchophorus palmarum*) of South America, destructive to the grugru and other palms. [< Sp. *grugru* < Carib]

grum (grum) *adj.* **grum·mer, grum·mest** *Rare* Morose; sullen; surly. [Prob. blend of GRIM and GLUM]

grum·ble (grum′bəl) *v.* **·bled, ·bling** *v.i.* **1.** To complain in a surly manner; mutter discontentedly. **2.** To utter low, throaty sounds; growl. **3.** To rumble. — *v.t.* **4.** To utter or express by grumbling. — *n.* **1.** A low, muttered complaint. **2.** *pl.* A sullen, complaining mood: preceded by *the.* **3.** A rumble. [Cf. Du. *grommelen* < *grommen* to growl] — **grum′bler** *n.* — **grum′bling·ly** *adv.* — **grum′bly** *adj.*

Grum·ble·to·ni·an (grum′bəl·tō′nē·ən) *n.* A former nickname for a member of a political party that opposed the policies of William III of England.

grume (grōōm) *n. Rare* **1.** A thick, semifluid substance. **2.** A clot, as of blood. [< F < L *grumus* little pile]

grum·met (grum′it) *n.* A grommet (which see).

gru·mous (grōō′məs) *adj.* **1.** *Rare* Consisting of or resembling grume; clotted, as blood; lumpy. **2.** *Bot.* Consisting of clustered grains. Also **gru′mose** (-mōs).

grumph·ie (grum′fē) *n. Scot.* A pig; a sow. Also **grumph′y.**

grump·y (grum′pē) *adj.* **grump·i·er, grump·i·est** Ill-tempered; cranky; surly. Also **grump′ish.** [? Blend of GRUNT and DUMP] — **grump′i·ly** *adv.* — **grump′i·ness** *n.*

Grun·dy (grun′dē), **Mrs.** Conventional, prudish, or disapproving people collectively. [after *Mrs. Grundy,* a straitlaced, carping neighbor, often discussed but never appearing, in Thomas Morton's comedy *Speed the Plow* (1798)]

Grü·ne·wald (grü′nə·vält), **Mathias,** 1480?–1530?, German painter.

grun·ion (grun′yən, grōōn·yōn′) *n.* A small fish (*Leuresthes tenuis*) common off the coast of California, notable for its unusual breeding habits. [Prob. < Sp. *gruñón* grunter]

grunt (grunt) *v.i.* **1.** To make the deep, guttural sound of a hog. **2.** To make a similar sound, as in annoyance, assent, effort, etc. — *v.t.* **3.** To utter or express by grunting. — *n.* **1.** A short, deep, guttural sound, as of a hog. **2.** Any of various food fishes (*Haemulon* and allied genera) of warm American seas, characterized by the ability to make a grunting sound. [OE *grunnettan*]

grunt·er (grun′tər) *n.* **1.** An animal or person that grunts; especially, a hog. **2.** A grunt (def. 2).

Grus (grus) *n.* A constellation, the Crane. See CONSTELLATION. [< L]

grush·ie (grush′ē, grōōsh′ē) *adj. Scot.* Growing luxuriantly; thick.

grutch (gruch, grōōch) *Scot. & Brit. Dial. v.t. & v.i.* To grudge. — *n.* A grudge.

Gru·yère cheese (grē·yâr′, grōō-; *Fr.* grü·yâr′) *n.* A light yellow, whole-milk Swiss cheese having a firm texture and few or no holes. [after *Gruyère,* a town in Switzerland]

Gru·zyi·ya (grōō′zyi·yə) The Russian name for GEORGIA. Also **Gru′zi·ya.** Officially **Gru·zyin·ska·ya S.S.R.** (grōō·zyēn′skä·yä)

gr.wt. Gross weight.

gry·phon (grif′ən) See GRIFFIN¹.

GS **1.** *Mil.* General Staff. **2.** German silver.

G.S. **1.** General Secretary. **2.** Girl Scouts.

GSA General Services Administration.

GSC *Mil.* General Staff Corps.

G-string (jē′string′) *n.* **1.** A narrow loincloth supported by a waistband. **2.** A similar garment worn by stripteasers. **3.** On musical instruments, a string tuned to G.

G.S.U.S.A. Girl Scouts of the U.S.A.

gt. **1.** Gilt (bookbinding). **2.** Great. **3.** (*pl.* **gtt.**) Gutta (def. 1).

G.T.C. or **g.t.c.** Good till canceled (or countermanded).

gtd. Guaranteed.

g.u. *Anat.* Genitourinary.

gua·cha·ro (gwä′chä·rō) *n. pl.* **·ros** A fruit-eating, nocturnal bird (*Steatornis caripensis*) of South America, the fat of whose young provides a butterlike oil: also called *fatbird, oilbird.* [< Sp. *guácharo*]

gua·co (gwä′kō) *n. pl.* **·cos** **1.** A tropical American plant (*Mikania guaco*) of the composite family, used as an antidote for snakebite. **2.** One of certain plants (genus *Aristolochia*) of the birthwort family, also used in treating snakebite. [< Sp. < native name]

Gua·da·la·ja·ra (gwä′thä·lä·hä′rä) The capital of Jalisco, Mexico, in the central part of the State; pop. 1,196,218 (1970).

Gua·dal·ca·nal (gwä′dəl·kə·nal′) The largest island of the British Solomon Islands; 2,500 sq. mi.; scene of an Allied invasion in World War II, 1943.

Gua·dal·qui·vir (gwä′thäl·kē·vir′) A river in southern Spain, flowing about 360 miles SW to the Gulf of Cádiz.

Gua·da·lupe Hi·dal·go (gwä′thä·lōō′pä ē·thäl′gō) See GUSTAVO A. MADERO.

Gua·da·lupe Mountains (gô′də·lōōp′, gwä′də·lōōp′) A range in western Texas and southern New Mexico; highest point, **Guadalupe Peak,** Texas, 8,751 ft.

Gua·de·loupe (gwä′də·lōōp′) A French Overseas Department in the Lesser Antilles, comprising the islands Basse-Terre (also **Guadeloupe proper**) and Grande-Terre; with dependencies, 687 sq. mi.; pop. 324,000 (est. 1969); capital, Basse-Terre.

Gua·di·a·na (*Pg.* gwə·thyä′nə; *Sp.* gwä·thyä′nä) A river in SW Spain and SE Portugal, flowing west about 510 miles to the Gulf of Cádiz.

guai·a·col (gwī′ə·kōl, -kol) *n. Chem.* A colorless liquid or white crystalline compound, $C_7H_8O_2$, obtained from guaiacum, or wood tar, and also made synthetically and forming many compounds used in medicine. [< GUAIAC(UM) + -OL²]

guai·a·cum (gwī′ə·kəm) *n.* **1.** Any of a genus (*Guaiacum* or *Guajacum*) of tropical American trees or shrubs of the caltrop family, especially *G. officinale* and *G. sanctum.* **2.** The hard, durable, resinous wood of any of these trees or shrubs; lignum vitae (def. 2). **3.** A greenish brown resin obtained from certain of these trees, used in medicine, in making paints and varnishes, etc.: also **guai·ac** (gwī′ak). Also **guai′o·cum.** [< NL < Sp. *guayacán* < Taino]

Guai·ra (gwī′rə), **La** See LA GUAIRA.

Guam (gwäm) The largest island of the Marianas group, an Unincorporated Territory of the United States; 209 sq. mi.; pop. 86,900 (1970); capital, Agana. — **Gua·ma·ni·an** (gwə·mä′nē·ən) *adj. & n.*

guan (gwän) *n.* A large gallinaceous bird (subfamily *Penelopinae*) of Central and South America, related to the curassows. [< Sp. < Carib]

gua·na·co (gwä·nä′kō) *n. pl.* **·cos** An undomesticated ruminant (*Lama huanacus*) of South America, closely related to, but larger than, the domesticated llama. [< Sp. < Quechua *huanacu*]

GUANACO
(3½ to 4 feet high at shoulder)

Gua·na·jua·to (gwä′nä·hwä′tō) A State of central Mexico; 11,805 sq. mi.; pop. 2,285,249 (1970); capital **Guanajuato,** pop. about 25,000.

gua·nase (gwä′nās) *n. Biochem.* An enzyme found in the pancreas, thymus, and adrenal glands, capable of changing guanine into xanthine. [< GUAN(INE) + -ASE]

gua·ni·dine (gwä′nə·dēn, -din) *n. Chem.* A strongly basic, crystalline compound, CH_5N_3, found in certain plant and animal tissues and having many derivatives used in making plastics, resins, explosives, etc. Also **gua′ni·din** (-din). [< GUANINE]

gua·nine (gwä′nēn) *n. Biochem.* A white, amorphous compound, $C_5H_5N_5O$, contained in guano, fish scales, muscle tissue, the pancreas, etc., and also occurring as a decomposition product of nucleoproteins. Also **gua·nin** (-nin). [< GUAN(O) + -INE²]

gua·no (gwä'nō) *n. pl.* **·nos** **1.** The accumulated excrement of sea birds, found chiefly on rocks and islands of the Peruvian coast, and used as a fertilizer. **2.** Any similar fertilizer. [< Sp. < Quechua *huanu* dung]

Guan·tá·na·mo (gwän·tä'nə·mō) A city in SE Cuba, near **Guantánamo Bay,** a sheltered Caribbean inlet, site of a U.S. naval station; pop. 135,100 (est. 1967).

Gua·po·ré (gwä·pô·rä') A river of central South America, forming part of the Brazil-Bolivia border and flowing about 750 miles NW to the Mamoré: also *Iténez.*

guar. Guaranteed.

gua·ra·ni (gwä'rä·nē') *n.* The standard monetary unit of Paraguay, equivalent to 100 centimos.

Gua·ra·ni (gwä'rä·nē') *n. pl.* **·nis** or **·ni** **1.** A member of any of a group of South American Indian tribes, comprising the southern branch of the Tupian stock, and formerly occupying the valleys of the Paraná and the Uruguay. **2.** The Tupian language of these tribes. [< Tupi, *warrior*]

guar·an·tee (gar'ən·tē') *n.* **1.** A pledge, warrant, or formal promise that something will meet stated specifications or that a specified act will be performed or continued: also called *warranty.* **2.** A guaranty (def. 2). **3.** A guarantor. **4.** One who receives a guaranty. **5.** Something that assures or seems to assure a specified condition or outcome: Popularity is a *guarantee* of success. — *v.t.* **1.** To assume responsibility for the quality or performance of; certify; vouch for: We *guarantee* our work. **2.** To accept responsibility for; be answerable for: to *guarantee* payment of a debt. **3.** To give security to (a person or thing), as against loss, damage, injury, etc. **4.** To provide or promise assurance of; ensure: They *guaranteed* our safety. **5.** To affirm (something) with certainty; promise; swear. [Var. of GUARANTY]

guar·an·tor (gar'ən·tər, -tôr') *n.* One who makes or gives a guaranty.

guar·an·ty (gar'ən·tē) *n. pl.* **·ties** **1.** A pledge or promise to be responsible for the contract, debt, or duty of another person in case of his default or miscarriage. **2.** Something given or taken as security to insure that a guaranty, pledge, or promise will be carried out. **3.** A guarantor. — *v.t.* **·tied,** **·ty·ing** To guarantee. [< OF *guarantie* < *guarantir* to warrant < *guarant* warrant < Gmc. Doublet of WARRANTY.]

guard (gärd) *v.t.* **1.** To watch over or care for so as to keep from harm; protect. **2.** To keep vigilant watch over so as to prevent escape, insubordination, etc. **3.** To control or prevent exit or entry through; serve as sentinel at. **4.** To maintain cautious control over; keep in check: to *guard* one's speech. **5.** To furnish (something) with a protective device or shield. **6.** *Archaic* To escort. — *v.i.* **7.** To take precautions; be alert: followed by *against.* **8.** To serve as a guard. — *n.* **1.** One who guards or stands watch over something; as: **a** One who has charge of or restrains prisoners, etc.; warder; keeper. **b** One who keeps protective watch over something of value. **c** One who has supervisory control over a point of entry, exit, etc. **2.** A group of persons, as soldiers, policemen, etc., serving in any of these functions; also, such a group serving as a ceremonial escort. **3.** The act of guarding; watchful care; protective supervision. **4.** That which provides protection; defense; safeguard. **5.** Any device, contrivance, or attachment protecting against injury, damage, loss, etc. **6.** A defensive posture or stance, as in boxing or fencing. **7.** In football, one of two linemen (the **right** and **left guard**) whose position in the front line is usually between one of the tackles and the center; also, the position itself. **8.** In basketball, one of two players (the **right** and **left guard**) who direct the offense and are in the front line of defense; also, the position itself. **9.** *Brit.* A railway conductor, brakeman, or gatekeeper. — **off** (one's) **guard** Unprepared for attack or adverse circumstances; not vigilant or alert. — **on** (one's) **guard** Watchful, as against attack, danger, or untoward circumstances; cautious. — **to mount guard** To go on duty as a sentry. — **to stand guard 1.** To maintain a protective watch. **2.** To serve as a sentry. [< OF *guarder, garder* < Gmc. Akin to WARD.] — **guard'er** *n.*

Guar·da·fui (gwär'dä·fwē'), **Cape** A cape in extreme NE Somalia, on the Gulf of Aden and the Indian Ocean.

guar·dant (gär'dənt) See GARDANT.

guard cell *Bot.* One of a pair of specialized epidermal cells that surround and control the pores by which gases enter and leave the stomata of plants.

guard duty A military assignment imposing the responsibility of strict watch over a camp, building, prisoners, etc.

guard·ed (gär'did) *adj.* **1.** Cautious; prudent; reserved: *guarded* criticism. **2.** Closely defended or kept under surveillance by a guard. **3.** Needing close care: a patient in *guarded* condition. — **guard'ed·ly** *adv.* — **guard'ed·ness** *n.*

guard·house (gärd'hous') *n.* **1.** The quarters and headquarters for military guards. **2.** A jail confining military personnel convicted of minor offenses and those awaiting court-martial.

guard·i·an (gär'dē·ən) *n.* **1.** One who guards or watches over for safekeeping, preservation, confinement, etc.; protector; custodian; guard: the *guardians* of justice. **2.** One who is legally assigned care of the person, property, etc., of an individual not competent to act for himself, especially of an infant or minor. ◆ Collateral adjective: *custodial.* — *adj.* Keeping guard; protecting. [< OF *guarden* < *guarder* to guard. Doublet of WARDEN.] — **guard'i·an·ship** *n.*

guard·rail (gärd'rāl') *n.* **1.** A railing for support or protection, as on a stairway or around a monument. **2.** On railroads, a rail close alongside a main rail, used to keep the wheels from jumping the track at curves.

guard·room (gärd'rōōm', -rŏŏm') *n.* **1.** A room for the use and accommodation of military or other guards. **2.** A room where prisoners are kept under guard.

Guards (gärdz) *n.pl.* Any of various regiments of the household troops of Great Britain.

guards·man (gärdz'mən) *n. pl.* **·men** (-mən) **1.** A man who serves as a guard. **2.** *U.S.* A member of the National Guard. **3.** *Brit.* An officer or soldier of a Guards regiment.

Guar·ne·ri (gwär·nä'rē) A family of Italian violin makers in Cremona, notably **Giuseppe Antonio,** 1687?–1745. Also **Guar·nie'ri** (-nyä'rē).

Guar·ne·ri·us (gwär·ner'ē·əs) *n.* A violin made by a member of the Guarneri family.

Guat. Guatemala.

Gua·te·ma·la (gwä'tə·mä'lä) A Republic in northern Central America; 42,042 sq. mi.; pop. 5,200,000 (est. 1970); capital, **Guatemala** (also Guatemala City) in the central part; pop. 700,000 (est. 1970). — **Gua'te·ma'lan** *adj. & n.*

gua·va (gwä'və) *n.* **1.** A tree or shrub (genus *Psidium*) of the myrtle family, native to tropical America. **2.** Its small, pear-shaped edible fruit, from which conserves and jellies are made. [< Sp. *guayaba,* appar. < S. Am. Ind.]

Guay·a·quil (gwī'ä·kēl') A port city in western Ecuador, on the **Gulf of Guayaquil,** an inlet of the Pacific; pop. 738,591 (est. 1969).

gua·yu·le (gwä·yōō'lā) *n.* **1.** A perennial shrub (*Parthenium argentatum*) of the composite family, yielding rubber and grown in Mexico and in the SW United States. **2.** The rubber of this shrub: also **guayule rubber.** [< Sp. < Nahuatl]

gu·ber·na·to·ri·al (gōō'bər·nə·tôr'ē·əl, -tō'rē-, gyōō'-) *adj.* Of or pertaining to a governor. [< L *gubernator* steersman, governor < *gubernare* to steer, govern]

gu·ber·ni·ya (gōō·byer'nyē·yə) *n.* **1.** In the Soviet Union, an administrative division under a rural soviet. **2.** Prior to 1917, an administrative division equivalent to a province. Also **gu·byer'nyi·ya.** [< Russ. ult. < L *gubernare* to steer, govern]

guck (guk) *n. U.S. & Canadian Slang* Goo; muck.

gude (gūd) *adj. & n. Scot.* Good: also spelled *quid.*

gudg·eon¹ (guj'ən) *n.* **1.** A small, carplike, fresh-water fish (genus *Gobio*) of Europe, very easily caught, used for bait. **2.** A minnow. **3.** A bait, allurement, or enticement. **4.** *Archaic* A gullible person; dupe. — *v.t.* To cheat; dupe. [< OF *goujon* < L *gobio,* var. of *gobius.* See GOBY.]

gudg·eon² (guj'ən) *n.* **1.** A metal pivot or journal at the end of a shaft or axle, on which a wheel, etc., turns. **2.** The socket of a hinge that holds the pin. **3.** A metal pin joining two pieces of stone. [< OF *goujon* pivot]

Gud·run (gōōd'rōōn) **1.** A Danish princess, heroine of the **Gudrun Lied,** a 13th-century German epic. **2.** In the *Volsunga Saga,* the daughter of the king of the Nibelungs and wife of Sigurd, later married to Atli. Also spelled *Guthrun.*

Gue·dal·la (gwe·dal'ä), **Philip,** 1889–1944, English historian and biographer.

Guel·der·land (gel'dər·länt) See GELDERLAND.

guel·der-rose (gel'dər·rōz') *n.* A cultivated European variety of cranberry (*Viburnum opulus*) with ball-shaped clusters of white flowers: also called *bush cranberry, cranberry tree, marsh elder, snowball.* [< *Guelder*(land) *rose*]

Guel·ders (gel'dərz) See GELDERLAND.

Guelph (gwelf) *n.* **1.** A member of a medieval political faction in Italy that supported the papacy in its struggle against the Ghibellines, who favored the German emperors. **2.** A member of a German princely family, founded in the ninth century, from which the present line of British sovereigns is descended. Also **Guelf.** [< Ital. *Guelfo,* ult. after OHG *Welf,* a family name] — **Guelph'ic** or **Guelf'ic** *adj.*

Guen·e·ver (gwen'ə·vər), **Guen·e·vere** (-vir) See GUINEVERE.

gue·non (gə·nôn', *Fr.* gə·nôṅ') *n.* A long-tailed monkey (genus *Cercopithecus*), found in Africa, whose banded hairs give it a mottled appearance. [F; ult. origin unknown]

guer·don (gûr'dən) *Poetic n.* Reward; recompense. — *v.t.* To reward. [< OF < Med.L *widerdonum* < OHG *widarlōn* < *widar* in turn + *lōn* reward] — **guer'don·er** *n.*

Guer·ni·ca (ger·nē'kä) A town in northern Spain, object of a German bombing (1937). Also **Guernica y Lu·no** (ē lōō'nō).

guern·sey (gûrn'zē) *n. pl.* **·seys** A closely fitting knitted woolen shirt or sweater worn by seamen.

Guern·sey (gûrn′zē) *n.* *pl.* **·seys** One of a breed of dairy cattle, originally from the island of Guernsey, having fawn and white coloration.

Guern·sey (gûrn′zē) One of the Channel Islands; 25 sq. mi.

guer·ril·la (gə·ril′ə) *n.* One of an irregular combatant band often operating in rear of the enemy; a partisan. Of or pertaining to guerrillas or their warfare. Also **gue·ril′la.** [< Sp., dim. of *guerra* war]

guess (ges) *v.t.* **1.** To form a judgment or opinion of (some quantity, fact, etc.) on uncertain or incomplete knowledge; surmise; conjecture; estimate. **2.** To conjecture correctly: to *guess* the answer. **3.** *U.S.* To believe; think; suppose: I *guess* we'll be late. — *v.i.* **4.** To form a judgment or opinion on uncertain or incomplete knowledge: often with *at*. **5.** To conjecture correctly: How did you *guess?* — *n.* **1.** An opinion or conclusion arrived at by guessing; a supposition; surmise; conjecture. **2.** The act of guessing. [ME *gessen*, prob. < Scand. Cf. Sw. *gissa*, Dan. *gisse* guess] — **guess′er** *n.*

guess·ti·mate (ges′tə·mit) *n. Slang* An estimate that is little better than a guess. [Blend of GUESS and ESTIMATE]

guess·work (ges′wûrk′) *n.* **1.** The process of guessing. **2.** Something based on a guess or guesses, as an opinion.

guest (gest) *n.* **1.** One who is received and entertained by another or others, as at a party or meal, or for a visit, etc. **2.** One who pays for lodging, meals, or other accommodations at a hotel, boarding house, etc.; a patron. **3.** *Zool.* A commensal organism. **4.** *Obs.* A stranger. — *adj.* **1.** Intended for guests: a *guest* house. **2.** Acting or performing on invitation in some specified way: a *guest* speaker. — *v.t.* **1.** *Rare* To entertain as a guest. — *v.i.* **2.** To be a guest. [OE *giest*; infl. in form by ON *gestr* stranger. Akin to HOST[1], HOST[2].]

guest room A room used for the lodging of guests.

guest rope *Naut.* **1.** A rope attached to a ship's side and used to fasten or to steady any small boat, barge, etc., alongside. **2.** An extra line used to steady or lengthen the tow rope of a boat. Also **guess-rope** (ges′rōp′).

Gueux (gœ) *n.pl.* The Dutch nobles and burghers who, from 1566 on, resisted the Inquisition and Philip II in the Netherlands. [< F, beggars, ruffians]

guff (guf) *n. Slang* Empty talk; nonsense; baloney. [Imit.]

guf·faw (gə·fô′) *n.* A loud burst of boisterous laughter. — *v.i.* To utter such a laugh. [Imit.]

Gug·gen·heim (gŏŏg′ən·hīm), **Daniel,** 1856–1930, and his brother **John Simon,** 1867–1941, U.S. industrialists and philanthropists.

Guggenheim Fellowship Any of the grants of money given by the **John Simon Guggenheim Memorial Foundation** to support a wide range of work in research and the arts.

Gui. Guinea.

Gui·an·a (gē·an′ə, -ä′nə) A coastal region of NE South America, bounded by the Orinoco, Amazon, Casiquiare, and the Rio Negro.

guid (gŭd) See GUDE.

gui·dance (gīd′ns) *n.* **1.** The act, process, or result of guiding. **2.** Something that guides. **3.** *U.S.* In education, an advising service for pupils and their families.

guide (gīd) *v.* **guid·ed, guid·ing** *v.t.* **1.** To lead or direct, as to a destination; show the way to. **2.** To direct the motion or physical progress of, as a vehicle, tool, animal, etc. **3.** To lead or direct the affairs, standards, opinions, etc., of: Let these principles *guide* your life. — *v.i.* **4.** To act as a guide. — *n.* **1.** A person who guides; especially, one who conducts others on fishing trips, through museums, on sightseeing tours, etc., for pay. **2.** One who or that which is taken as a model or example. **3.** A guidebook. **4.** A book that explains, outlines, or gives practical instruction in some subject. **5.** A guidepost. **6.** *Mech.* Any device that regulates the operation or controls the movement of a part or object. **7.** *Mil.* A soldier stationed in the flank of a line to mark a pivot or regulate an alignment. [< OF *guider*] — **guid′a·ble** *adj.* — **guid′er** *n.*

guide·board (gīd′bôrd′, -bōrd′) *n.* A sign attached to a post, as at a crossroads, giving directions for travelers.

guide·book (gīd′bŏŏk′) *n.* A handbook containing directions and other information for tourists, visitors, etc.

guid·ed missile (gī′did) *Mil.* An unmanned aerial missile whose course can be altered during flight by mechanisms within the missile that are preset, self-reacting, or actuated by radio signals.

guide·line (gīd′līn′) *n.* **1.** A line, as a rope, for guiding. **2.** A word, phrase, etc., printed along the upper margin of printed copy, to guide readers. **3.** Any suggestion, rule, etc., that guides, directs, or sets a standard: government *guidelines* designed to regulate wage and price increases.

guide·post (gīd′pōst′) *n.* **1.** A post with an attached sign giving directions to travelers, as at a roadside. **2.** Anything that guides, directs, or limits; guideline.

guide rope **1.** *Aeron.* A long rope suspended from a balloon or dirigible and trailed along the ground, used as a brake or to regulate the altitude of the aircraft. **2.** A rope attached to another object to guide or steady it.

Gui·do d'A·rez·zo (gwē′dō dä·ret′tsō), 995?–1050?, Italian monk and musical theorist: called **Guido A·re·ti·no** (ä′re·tē′nō).

gui·don (gī′don, gīd′n) *n.* **1.** *Mil.* A small flag carried by troops for unit identification; also, the soldier who carries it. **2.** Formerly, a forked flag carried by mounted troops. [< F < Ital. *guidone*]

Gui·do Re·ni (gwē′dō rā′nē) See RENI.

Gui·enne (gē·yen′) A former province of SW France; formerly the kingdom of Aquitaine: also spelled *Guyenne.*

guild (gild) *n.* **1.** A corporation or association of persons having similar pursuits or interests, formed for mutual aid, protection, etc.; especially, such an association of artisans or merchants in medieval times. **2.** Any fellowship or sodality. **3.** *Ecol.* One of four groups of plants having characteristic modes of life, namely, the lianas, epiphytes, saprophytes, and parasites. Also spelled *gild.* [Fusion of OE *gild* payment, *gegyld* association, and ON *gildi* payment] — **guild′ship** *n.*

guil·der (gil′dər) *n.* **1.** The basic monetary unit of the Netherlands; also, a Dutch silver coin of this value. **2.** One of various gold and silver coins formerly current in Germany, Austria, and the Netherlands. Also called *gulden:* also spelled *gilder.* Abbr. *g., G., gld.* [Earlier *guldren,* alter. of Du. *gulden* golden]

guild·hall (gild′hôl′) *n. Brit.* **1.** The hall where a guild meets. **2.** A town hall.

Guild·hall (gild′hôl′) The hall of the Corporation of the City of London, England.

guilds·man (gildz′mən) *n.* *pl.* **·men** (-mən) A member of a guild.

guild socialism An English theory of socialism that advocates ownership of all industry by the state with guilds of workers exercising the powers of management and control.

guile (gīl) *n.* **1.** Treacherous cunning or craft; deceit: He is full of *guile.* **2.** *Obs.* A stratagem or trick. [< OF < Gmc.]

guile·ful (gīl′fəl) *adj.* Full of guile; treacherous; deceitful. — **guile′ful·ly** *adv.* — **guile′ful·ness** *n.*

guile·less (gīl′lis) *adj.* Free from guile; artless; candid; sincere. — **Syn.** See INGENUOUS. — **guile′less·ly** *adv.* — **guile′less·ness** *n.*

Guil·ford Courthouse (gil′fərd) A national military park in north central North Carolina, scene of an important Revolutionary War battle, 1781.

Guil·laume (gē·yōm′), **Charles Édouard,** 1861–1938, French physicist.

guil·le·mot (gil′ə·mot) *n.* Any of several narrow-billed auks (genera *Uria* and *Cepphus*), found in northern latitudes; especially, the **black guillemot** (*C. grylle*), and the **foolish guillemot** or common murre (*U. aalge*). [< F]

guil·loche (gi·lōsh′) *n.* An ornamental pattern or border composed of two or more curved bands or lines that intertwine. [< F *guillochis*; ult. origin unknown]

guil·lo·tine (*n.* gil′ə·tēn, gē′ə·tēn; *v.* gil′ə·tēn′, gil′ə·tēn) *n.* **1.** The instrument of capital punishment in France, consisting of a weighted blade that slides down between two vertical guides and beheads the victim. **2.** A similar machine for cutting paper, trimming the edges of books, etc. **3.** *Surg.* An instrument for removing the tonsils. **4.** *Brit.* A method of shortening debate on a bill in Parliament by fixing the time of voting. — *v.t.* **·tined, ·tin·ing** To behead with the guillotine. [< F, after J. I. *Guillotin,* 1738–1814, French physician who advocated a humane means of execution]

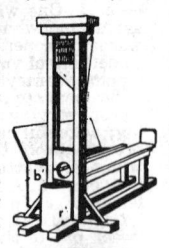

GUILLOTINE
b Basket for body.
r Receptacle for head.

guilt (gilt) *n.* **1.** The fact or condition of having committed an offense, especially a willful violation of a legal or moral code; culpability. **2.** A feeling of remorse arising from a real or imagined commission of an offense. **3.** Guilty conduct; sin; crime. [OE *gylt*]

— **Syn. 1.** blameworthiness, reprehensibility. **3.** delinquency, felony.

guilt by association The act of presuming a person to be guilty because of his known activities or associations.

guilt·less (gilt′lis) *adj.* **1.** Free from guilt; innocent. **2.** Lacking knowledge or experience: with *of.* — **guilt′less·ly** *adv.* — **guilt′less·ness** *n.*

guilt·y (gil′tē) *adj.* **guilt·i·er, guilt·i·est** **1.** Deserving of blame for some offense; culpable: often with *of:* He is *guilty* of theft. **2.** Convicted of some offense, as by a jury, court, etc. **3.** Involving, pertaining to, or characterized by guilt: *guilty* pleasures. **4.** Prompted by or showing guilt: a *guilty* fear. — **guilt′i·ly** *adv.* — **guilt′i·ness** *n.*

guimpe (gimp, gamp) *n.* **1.** A short blouse, usually having sleeves and worn with a jumper. **2.** A chemisette worn under a low-necked dress. [< F]

Guin. Guinea.

guin·ea (gin′ē) *n.* **1.** Formerly, an English gold coin, issued from 1663 to 1813, so called because the gold of which it was coined came from Guinea. **2.** A British money of account, equal to 21 shillings. **3.** The guinea fowl. **4.** *U.S. Slang* An Italian or person of Italian descent: an offensive term. Abbr. (def. 1, 2) *g. G.*

Guin·ea (gin′ē), **Republic of** A Republic in western Africa; 97,000 sq. mi.; pop. 3,890,000 (est. 1969); capital, Conakry: formerly *French Guinea*. French *République de Guinée*.

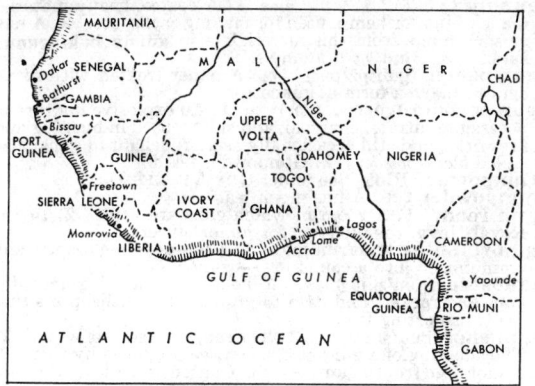

Guinea, Gulf of A large bay of the Atlantic on the western coast of Africa, south of the great bulge of the continent.

Guinea corn Durra.

guinea fowl A gallinaceous bird (*Numida meleagris*) of African origin, having dark gray plumage speckled with white spots, long domesticated in Europe and America. Also **guinea, guinea hen.**

guinea grains Grains of paradise (which see).

Guinea pepper A variety of cayenne pepper.

guinea pig 1. A small, domesticated cavy, usually white, variegated with red and black, having a short tail and short ears, and widely used in biological and medical experiments. 2. Any person used in experimentation.

Guinea worm A threadlike nematode worm (*Dracunculus medinensis*), common in streams and pools of tropical Africa and Asia, whose parasitic larvae infect the legs and lower trunk of men and animals.

Guin·e·vere (gwin′ə·vir) In Arthurian legend, Arthur's unfaithful queen and the mistress of Lancelot: also spelled *Guenever, Guenevere.* Also **Guin′e·ver** (-vər).

gui·pure (gi·pyŏŏr′, *Fr.* gē·pür′) *n.* 1. A lace in which the patterns are held in place by connecting threads rather than attached to a mesh or net ground. 2. A kind of gimp (the fabric). [< F < *guiper* to cover with silk < Gmc.]

guise (gīz) *n.* 1. External appearance or aspect; semblance. 2. Assumed or false appearance; pretense: under the *guise* of peace. 3. *Archaic* Style or condition of dress. 4. *Obs.* Usual manner or behavior. — *v.* **guised, guis·ing** *v.t.* 1. *Archaic* To dress; costume. 2. *Brit. Dial.* To disguise. — *v.i.* 3. *Brit. Dial.* To go about in disguise or costume. [< OF < Gmc. Akin to WISE².]

Guise (gēz; *Fr.* gēz, gü·ēz′) A French ducal family, notably **François de Lorraine,** 1519–63, second Duc de Guise, general and statesman, and his son, **Henri de Lorraine,** 1550–1588, third Duc de Guise, general who instigated the Massacre of St. Bartholomew.

gui·tar (gi·tär′) *n.* A musical instrument having a fretted fingerboard, a large sound box with indented sides, and strings, usually six, that are plucked with fingers or plectrum. [< Sp. *guitarra* < Gk. *kithara.* Doublet of CITHARA, ZITHER.] — **gui·tar′ist** *n.*

gui·tar·fish (gi·tär′fish′) *n.* *pl.* **·fish** or **·fish·es** An elongate sharklike ray (family *Rhinobatidae*) of warm seas, with a tough skin sometimes used for leather.

guit-guit (gwit′gwit′) *n.* The honey creeper, a bird. [Imit.]

Gui·try (gē·trē′), **Sacha,** 1885–1957, French playwright and actor.

Gui·zot (gē·zō′), **François Pierre Guillaume,** 1787–1874, French statesman and historian.

Gu·ja·rat (gŏŏj′ə·rät′) A State in western India, created in 1960 by the division of Bombay State; 72,137 sq. mi.; pop. 25,189,000 (est. 1971); capital, Ahmedabad.

Gu·ja·ra·ti (gŏŏj′ə·rä′tē) *n.* The Indic language of the natives of Gujarat and adjoining regions.

Gujarat States A group of former princely states in western India: now part of Gujarat State; 7,493 sq. mi.

gu·lar (gŏŏ′lər, gyŏŏ′-) *adj.* Of or pertaining to the throat; pharyngeal. [< L *gula* throat]

gulch (gulch) *n.* *U.S.* A deep, narrow ravine cut out by a rushing stream. [? < *dial. gulch* to swallow greedily]

gul·den (gŏŏl′dən) *n.* The guilder. [< Du., lit., golden]

Gü·lek Bo·ghaz (gü·lek′ bō·gäz′) A pass over the Taurus mountains in southern Turkey: ancient *Cilician Gates.*

gules (gyōōlz) *n.* 1. The color red. 2. *Heraldry* The tincture red: in a blazon without color, indicated by parallel vertical lines. [< OF *gueules* red-dyed ermine fur, ? < L *gula* throat]

gulf (gulf) *n.* 1. A large area of ocean or sea partially enclosed by an extended sweep of land. Abbr. *G.* 2. An abyss; chasm; gorge. 3. A wide or impassable separation, as in social or economic position, education, etc. 4. That which engulfs or devours. — *v.t.* To swallow up; engulf. [< OF *golfe* < Ital. *golfo* < LGk. *kolphos* < Gk. *kolpos* bay]

Gulf of, etc. See specific name, as (Gulf of) ADEN, (Gulf of) MEXICO, etc.

Gulf·port (gulf′pôrt) A port city in SE Mississippi, on Mississippi Sound; pop. 40,791.

Gulf States Florida, Alabama, Mississippi, Louisiana, and Texas; the States bordering on the Gulf of Mexico.

Gulf Stream A warm ocean current flowing NE along the eastern coast of North America; also, loosely, the great warm current system that includes it, flowing NE from the Caribbean and crossing the North Atlantic to NW Europe. For illustration see OCEAN CURRENT.

gulf·weed (gulf′wēd′) *n.* Sargasso.

gull¹ (gul) *n.* 1. A long-winged, web-footed sea bird (family *Laridae*), usually white and gray, and having the upper mandible hooked. 2. One of various related birds, as a tern or gannet. [ME < Celtic. Cf. Welsh *gwylan* gull]

gull² (gul) *n.* 1. *Archaic* A person easily tricked or cheated; a dupe. 2. *Obs.* A trick or deception. — *v.t.* *Archaic* To deceive; swindle; cheat. [? < obs. *gull* swallow; infl. by ME *goll* gosling]

Gul·lah (gul′ə) *n.* 1. One of a group of Negroes dwelling on a narrow coastal strip of South Carolina, Georgia, and NE Florida, or on islands lying off this coast. 2. The creolized (English and African) language of these people.

gul·let (gul′it) *n.* 1. The passage from the mouth to the stomach; esophagus. 2. The throat; pharynx; also, anything resembling a throat. 3. A channel for water, as a ravine or gully. [< OF *goulet,* dim. of *goule* throat < L *gula*]

gul·li·ble (gul′ə·bəl) *adj.* Easily cheated or fooled; credulous. — **gul′li·bil′i·ty** *n.* — **gul′li·bly** *adv.*

Gul·li·ver (gul′ə·vər), **Lemuel** The hero of Jonathan Swift's political and social satire **Gulliver's Travels** (1726), that describes his voyages to the wonderlands of Lilliput, Brobdingnag, Laputa, and the country of the Houyhnhnms.

gul·ly¹ (gul′ē) *n.* *pl.* **·lies** A channel, ravine, or ditch; especially, a ravine cut in the earth by running water. — *v.t.* **·lied, ·ly·ing** To cut or wear a gully in. [Var. of GULLET]

gul·ly² (gul′ē) *n.* *Scot.* A knife.

gulp (gulp) *v.t.* 1. To swallow greedily, hastily, or in large amounts: often with *down.* 2. To choke back or stifle, as if by swallowing. — *v.i.* 3. To swallow convulsively while drinking or as a sign of surprise, relief, etc. — *n.* 1. The act of gulping. 2. The amount swallowed in gulping. [< Du. *gulpen;* of imit. origin] — **gulp′er** *n.* — **gulp′ing·ly** *adv.*

gum¹ (gum) *n.* 1. A sticky, viscid substance exuded from various trees and plants, soluble in water and hardening on exposure to air. 2. Any similar substance exuded from plants or trees, as resin. 3. A preparation made from such substances and used in art, industry, etc. 4. Chewing gum (which see). 5. Mucilage; glue. 6. The gum tree. 7. Rubber. 8. The adhesive material on the reverse side of postage stamps. 9. *U.S. Dial.* **a** *pl.* Rubber overshoes. **b** A hollow section of a gum tree made into a barrel, watering trough, etc. — *v.* **gummed, gum·ming** *v.t.* 1. To smear, stiffen, or clog with gum or a gummy substance. 2. To glue or stick together with gum. — *v.i.* 3. To exude or form gum. 4. To become stiff, sticky, or clogged with gum or a gummy substance. — **to gum up** *Slang* To ruin or spoil in some way; bungle. [< OF *gomme* < L *gummi* < Gk. *kommi*]

gum² (gum) *n. Often pl.* The fleshy tissue that covers the alveolar arches of the jaws and surrounds the necks of the teeth. ◆ Collateral adjective: *gingival.* — *v.t.* & *v.i.* **gummed, gum·ming** *U.S. Dial.* To chew without teeth. [OE *goma* inside of the mouth]

gum ammoniac Ammoniac² (which see).

gum arabic The gum from various species of acacia, especially *A. arabica,* used in medicine, candy, ink, etc.

gum benzoin Benzoin (def. 1).

gum·bo (gum′bō) *n.* *pl.* **·bos** 1. The okra or its edible, slippery pods. 2. A thick soup or stew containing okra pods. 3. *U.S. & Canadian* In the West, a type of fine, silty soil forming a sticky mud when wet. Also **gumbo soil.** 4. A patois of French spoken by Negroes in Louisiana and the French West Indies: also spelled *gombo.* [< Bantu (Angola)]

gum·boil (gum′boil′) *n.* A small boil or abscess on the gum.

gum·drop (gum′drop′) *n.* *U.S.* A small, round piece of jellylike candy, made of sweetened and flavored gum arabic, gelatin, etc., usually colored and coated with sugar.

gum elastic Rubber.

gum·ma (gum′ə) *n.* *pl.* **gum·ma·ta** (gum′ə·tə) or **gum·mas** *Pathol.* A soft tumor having a rubberlike consistency, occurring in tertiary syphilis. [< NL < L *gummi* gum¹] — **gum′ma·tous** *adj.*

gum·mo·sis (gu·mō′sis)   *n. Bot.* A symptom of disease in certain plants, characterized by the formation of a gummy exudation and the disintegration of tissue.

gum·my (gum′ē)   *adj.* **·mi·er, ·mi·est 1.** Of or like gum; sticky; viscid. **2.** Covered or clogged with gum or a gum-like substance. **3.** Exuding gum or similar matter. Also **gum·mose** (gum′ōs). **—gum′mous** (-əs). **— gum′mi·ness** *n.*

gum plant Any of several composite plants (genus *Grindelia*) of the western United States, covered with a gummy substance. Also **gum weed.**

gump·tion (gump′shən)   *n. Informal* **1.** Bold, energetic initiative; courage to act. **2.** Shrewd common sense. [< dial. E (Scot.). Cf. ME *gome* care, heed]

gum resin A mixture of gum and resin that exudes as a milky juice from incisions in certain plants.

gum·shoe (gum′shōo′)   *n. U.S.* **1.** A rubber shoe or overshoe. **2.** *pl.* Sneakers. **3.** *Slang* A detective. **—** *v.i.* **·shoed, ·shoe·ing** *Slang* To go stealthily and noiselessly; sneak.

gum·tree (gum′trē′)   *n.* Any of various species of eucalyptus trees of Australia.

gum tree Any of various trees that produce gum.

gum water A solution of gum, especially gum arabic, in water, used in art, pharmacy, etc.

gum·wood (gum′wŏŏd′)   *n.* The wood of any gum tree.

gun (gun)   *n.* **1.** A weapon or projectile device from which a missile is thrown by the force of an explosive, by compressed air, by a spring, etc. **2.** Loosely, any portable firearm. **3.** *Mil.* **a** Any of various cannons with a flat trajectory, high muzzle velocity, and a barrel of over .25 caliber: anti-tank *gun.* **b** Any of various automatic weapons: machine *gun*; submachine *gun.* Abbr. *G* **4.** Any device resembling a gun in shape or operation: grease *gun.* **5.** The discharging of a firearm, especially a cannon, as in firing salutes or signaling. **6.** *U.S. Slang* The throttle controlling an engine, as in an automobile or airplane. **7.** *U.S. Slang* A gunman. **— big gun** *Slang* A person of influence or importance. **— to give it (or her) the gun** *Slang* **1.** To increase sharply the speed of a motor or machine. **2.** To give added speed, efficiency, intensity, etc., to some action. **— to go great guns** *U.S. Slang* To work or perform with great skill, speed, brilliancy, etc. **— to spike (someone's) guns** To destroy or make ineffective someone's plans, ideas, etc.; to frustrate. **— to stick to one's guns** To continue in one's actions, plans, opinions, etc., in spite of opposition. **—** *v.* **gunned, gun·ning** *v.i.* **1.** To go shooting or hunting with a gun. **—** *v.t. U.S. Slang* **2.** To open the throttle of (an engine). **3.** To shoot (a person) with a gun. **— to gun for (or after)** *U.S. Slang* **1.** To seek or pursue with intent to injure or kill. **2.** To seek out in order to win favor or support, settle a dispute, etc. [ME *gonne, gunne* < ON *gunna*, orig. nickname for *Gunnhildr*, fem. personal name]

gun·boat (gun′bōt′)   *n.* A small, armed naval vessel, used for patrolling rivers and coastal waters.

gun carriage The mechanical structure, often wheeled, upon which a cannon is mounted for firing or maneuvering.

gun·cot·ton (gun′kot′n)   *n.* A type of cellulose nitrate used as an explosive.

gun dog A dog trained to accompany and assist a hunter.

gun·fire (gun′fīr′)   *n.* **1.** The firing of a gun or guns. **2.** *Mil.* The use of artillery or small arms in warfare, as distinguished from the use of bayonets, mines, bombs, etc.

gun·flint (gun′flint′)   *n.* A piece of flint used to strike a spark and ignite the charge in a flintlock.

gung ho (gung′hō′)   **1.** *U.S. Slang* Eager; enthusiastic; zealous: to be *gung ho* about army life. **2.** Formerly, work together: motto of certain U.S. Marine units in World War II. [< Chinese]

gun·lock (gun′lok′)   *n.* The mechanism in certain guns by which the hammer is driven and the charge exploded.

gun·man (gun′mən)   *n. pl.* **·men** (-mən) **1.** A man armed with a gun; especially, an armed criminal. **2.** A gunsmith.

gun·met·al (gun′met′l)   *adj.* Of or pertaining to the color of dark gray having a bluish tinge.

gun metal 1. A bronze made of copper, tin, and zinc, used for castings, valves, gears, and the like. **2.** Any of various metal alloys of a dark bluish gray color, used for metal novelties and trinkets. **3.** A dark gray color with a bluish tinge: also **gun-metal gray.**

gun moll *U.S. Slang* **1.** A female associate or accomplice of criminals. **2.** A female thief.

Gun·nar (gŏŏn′är)   In the *Volsunga Saga*, the husband of Brynhild and brother of Gudrun. Compare GUNTHER.

gun·nel¹ (gun′əl)   See GUNWALE.

gun·nel² (gun′əl)   *n. pl.* **·nels** or **·nel** A fish (*Pholis gunnellus*) of the blenny family, found in North Atlantic waters.

gun·ner (gun′ər)   *n.* **1.** One who operates a gun. **2.** In the U.S. Navy and Marine Corps, a warrant officer whose duties were traditionally, but are not now necessarily, connected with ordnance. **3.** In the U.S. Army, a noncommissioned officer who does the actual aiming or operating of a gun. **4.** *Brit. Mil.* An artilleryman. **5.** One who hunts with a gun.

gun·ner·y (gun′ər·ē)   *n.* **1.** The science and art of constructing and operating guns. **2.** The use and firing of artillery. **3.** Guns collectively.

gun·ning (gun′ing)   *n.* The art or act of hunting with a gun.

Gun·ni·son River (gun′ə·sən) A river in west central Colorado, flowing about 180 miles NW to the Colorado River.

gun·ny (gun′ē)   *n. pl.* **·nies** A coarse, heavy material made of jute or hemp, used for making sacks, etc. **2.** A bag or sack made from this material: also **gunny bag, gunny sack.** [< Hind. *gonī* gunny sack]

gun·pa·per (gun′pā′pər)   *n.* A paper treated with nitric acid to make a form of guncotton.

gun·pow·der (gun′pou′dər)   *n.* **1.** An explosive mixture of potassium nitrate, charcoal, and sulfur, used in blasting and fireworks, and still occasionally as a propellant in guns: also called *black powder.* **2.** Gunpowder tea.

Gunpowder Plot See under GUY FAWKES DAY.

gunpowder tea A fine green tea.

gun room 1. A room in which guns are kept. **2.** In the Royal Navy, the quarters for junior officers.

gun·run·ning (gun′run′ing)   *n.* The smuggling of guns and ammunition into a country. **— gun′run′ner** *n.*

gun·ship (gun′ship′)   *n.* A helicopter carrying machine guns and rockets and used to protect other helicopters that are transporting troops.

gun·shot (gun′shot′)   *n.* **1.** The range or reach of a gun. **2.** The shooting of a gun; also, the noise produced by this. **3.** A shot fired from a gun. **—** *adj.* Caused or made by the shot of a gun: a *gunshot* wound.

gun·shy (gun′shī′)   *adj.* Afraid of a gun or of its sound.

gun·smith (gun′smith′)   *n.* One who makes or repairs firearms.

gun·stock (gun′stok′)   *n.* A stock (def. 20a).

Gun·ter (gun′tər), **Edmund,** 1581–1626 English mathematician; inventor of Gunter's chain, the sector, and the scale.

Gunter's chain See under CHAIN.

Gun·ther (gŏŏn′tər)   In the *Nibelungenlied*, the brother of Kriemhild and husband of Brunhild: identified with *Gunnar*.

gun·wale (gun′əl)   *n. Naut.* The upper edge of the side of a vessel or boat: also spelled *gunnel.* [< GUN + WALE¹ (plank)]

gup·py (gup′ē)   *n. pl.* **·pies** A small, tropical, fresh-water fish (genus *Lebistes*), valued as an aquarium fish because of its coloring. [after R. J. L. *Guppy*, British scientist]

gur·gi·ta·tion (gûr′jə·tā′shən)   *n.* A surging or whirling movement, as of liquid in a whirlpool or in a boiling state. [< L *gurgitatus*, pp. of *gurgitare* to engulf < *gurges* whirlpool]

gur·gle (gûr′gəl)   *v.i.* **·gled, ·gling** **1.** To flow irregularly, with a bubbling sound, as water issuing from a bottle. **2.** To make such a sound. **—** *v.t.* **3.** To utter with a gurgling sound. **—** *n.* **1.** The act of gurgling. **2.** The sound of gurgling. [Var. of GARGLE] **— gur′gling·ly** *adv.*

gur·glet (gûr′glit)   *n.* A goglet (which see).

Gur·kha (gŏŏr′kə)   *n.* One of a Rajput people of Hindu religion living in Nepal, well known as soldiers.

gur·nard (gûr′nərd)   *n. pl.* **·nards** or **·nard** Any of various marine fishes (family *Triglidae*), having a spiny head, mailed cheeks, large pectoral fins, and three fingerlike rays used for locomotion, probing for food, etc. Also **gur′net** (-nit). [< OF *grognard* grumbler < *grogner* to grunt < L *grunnire*]

gu·ru (gŏŏ′rōō)   *n.* **1.** In Hindu religion, a teacher or guide. **2.** Any wise leader, advisor, or guide. [< Hind. *gurū* venerable one, teacher]

gush (gush)   *v.i.* **1.** To pour out in volume and with sudden force, as a liquid: Blood *gushed* from the wound. **2.** To emit a sudden flow, as of blood, tears, etc.: Her eyes *gushed* with tears. **3.** *Informal* To give expression to one's emotions, enthusiasms, etc., in an excessive, often insincere manner: to be overly enthusiastic. **—** *v.t.* **4.** To pour forth (blood, tears, words, etc.). **—** *n.* **1.** A sudden flow or outburst, as of liquid or sound. **2.** That which gushes forth. **3.** *Informal* An extravagant and often insincere effusion of emotion, enthusiasm, praise, etc. [ME *guschen*, prob. < Scand. Cf. ON *gusa* to gush.] **— gush′ing·ly** *adv.*

gush·er (gush′ər)   *n.* **1.** One who gushes. **2.** An oil well that spurts oil without the need of pumps.

gush·y (gush′ē)   *adj.* **gush·i·er, gush·i·est 1.** Given to or exhibiting gush. **2.** *Informal* Effusive. **— gush′i·ness** *n.*

gus·set (gus′it)   *n.* **1.** A piece of material, usually triangular, inserted into a garment, glove, shoe, etc., for added strength or roomier fit. **2.** An angle iron or metal bracket used to strengthen a corner or angle of a structure. **3.** In a suit of armor, a piece of mail covering any gap occurring between two adjacent armor plates. **—** *v.t.* To furnish with a gusset. [< OF *gousset*, dim. of *gousse* pod, shell]

gust¹ (gust)   *n.* **1.** A sudden, violent rush of wind or air. **2.** A sudden burst or outpouring of fire, sound, water, etc. **3.** A brief outburst of emotion. [< ON *gustr*]

gust² (gust)   *n. Archaic* **1.** Appreciation or enjoyment; relish. **2.** Flavor or savor, as of food. **3.** The sense of taste. **—** *v.t. Scot.* To taste; relish. [< L *gustus* taste]

Gus·taf V (gŏŏs′täf), 1858–1950, king of Sweden 1907–50. Also **Gus·ta·vus V** (gŏŏs·tä′vəs).

Gustaf VI A·dolf (ä′dolf), born 1882, king of Sweden 1950–. Also **Gustavus VI.**

gus·ta·tion (gus·tā′shən)   *n.* The act of tasting, or the sense of taste; taste.

gus·ta·to·ry (gus'tə-tôr'ē, -tō'rē) *adj.* Of or pertaining to the sense of taste or the act of tasting. Also **gus·ta·tive** (gus'tə-tiv).

Gus·ta·vo A. Ma·de·ro (gōos-tä'vō ä mä-thä'rō) A city in the Federal District of Mexico; includes Guadalupe Hidalgo, site of a church containing a famous portrait of the Virgin Mary; pop. 92,947 (1960).

Gus·ta·vus I (gus-tä'vəs, -tā'-), 1496–1560, king of Sweden 1523–60; established Lutheranism in Sweden. Also called **Gustavus Va·sa** (vä'sä).

Gustavus II, 1594–1632, king of Sweden 1611–32; noted for his military skill: called **the Lion of the North**. Also **Gustavus A·dolph·us** (ä-dolf'əs).

gus·to (gus'tō) *n.* **1.** Keen enjoyment or enthusiasm; relish. **2.** Individual taste or preference. **3.** In art, a characteristic style or treatment. [< Ital. < L *gustus* taste]

gust·y (gus'tē) *adj.* **gust·i·er, gust·i·est** **1.** Characterized by fitful gusts of wind or rain. **2.** Given to sudden outbursts of feeling, action, etc. **3.** Emitting air, sound, etc., in sudden bursts or gusts. — **gust'i·ly** *adv.* — **gust'i·ness** *n.*

gut (gut) *n.* **1.** The alimentary canal or any part of it; especially, the stomach or intestine. **2.** *pl.* Bowels; entrails. **3.** The specially prepared intestines of certain animals, used as strings for musical instruments, surgical sutures, etc.; catgut. **4.** *pl.* The fundamental elements of something: *guts* of the motor. **5.** *pl. Slang* a Courage; stamina; grit. b Effrontery. **6.** A strong cord made from fiber drawn out of a silkworm when ready to spin its cocoon, used for snells in fishing tackle. **7.** A narrow passage, as a strait, or a gorge between mountains. — *adj.* Easy or simple: *gut* course in college. — *v.t.* **gut·ted, gut·ting** **1.** To take out the intestines of; eviscerate. **2.** To plunder. **3.** To destroy the contents of: Fire *gutted* the building. [OE *guttas*]

Gu·ten·berg (gōot'n-bûrg, *Ger.* gōo'tən-berkh), **Johann,** 1400?–68?, German printer; inventor of movable type: original name **Johannes Gens·fleisch** (gens'flīsh).

Gutenberg Bible An edition of the Vulgate printed in Mainz before 1456, generally ascribed to J. Gutenberg and regarded as the first large work printed from movable type.

Guth·run (gōoth'rōon) See GUDRUN.

Gu·tru·ne (gōo-trōo'nə) In Wagner's *Ring of the Nibelung*, the wife of Siegfried and sister of Gunther. Compare GUDRUN.

gut·sy (gut'sē) *adj.* **·si·er, ·si·est** *Slang* **1.** Tough, courageous, and bold: a *gutsy* reporter. **2.** Lusty.

gut·ta (gut'ə) *n. pl.* **gut·tae** (gut'ē) **1.** In pharmacy, a drop, as of liquid. Abbr. *gt.* (pl. *gtt.*). **2.** *Archit.* One of the small, droplike ornaments on the under part of mutules and regulae of the Doric entablature. [< L]

gut·ta-per·cha (gut'ə-pûr'chə) *n.* A coagulated, rubberlike material, usually grayish white in color, formed from the purified juice of various Malayan trees (genera *Palaquium* and *Payena*), used in electrical insulation, in the arts, as a dental plastic, etc. [< Malay *getah* gum + *percha* gum tree]

guttat. *Med.* By drops (L *guttatim*).

gut·tate (gut'āt) *adj.* **1.** Having or resembling drops. **2.** Spotted, as if by drops. Also **gut'tat·ed.** [< L *guttatus* speckled < *gutta* drop]

gut·ter (gut'ər) *n.* **1.** A channel or ditch constructed at the side or along the middle of a street, for carrying off surface water. **2.** A furrow or ditch formed by running water. **3.** A trough, fixed below or along the eaves of a house, for carrying off rain water from the roof: also called *eave trough*. **4.** A state or condition of life, marked by poverty, filth, immorality, etc. **5.** Any groove, trough, or channel, as that on the sides of a bowling alley. — *v.t.* **1.** To form channels or grooves in. **2.** To furnish with gutters, as a house. — *v.i.* **3.** To flow in channels, as water. **4.** To melt rapidly and flow down the sides in channels or gutters: said of lighted candles. [< OF *goutier* < *goute* drop < L *gutta*] — **gut'ter·y** *adj.*

gut·ter·snipe (gut'ər-snīp') *n.* A neglected child, usually of the slums, who spends much time in the streets.

gut·tur·al (gut'ər-əl) *adj.* **1.** Pertaining to the throat. **2.** Having a harsh, or muffled, grating quality, as sounds produced in the throat. **3.** *Phonet.* Velar. — *n. Phonet.* A velar sound. [< NL *gutturalis* < L *guttur* throat] — **gut'tur·al·i·ty** (gut'ə-ral'ə-tē), **gut'tur·al·ness** *n.* — **gut'tur·al·ly** *adv.*

gut·tur·al·ize (gut'ər-əl-īz') *v.t. & v.i.* **·ized, ·iz·ing** **1.** To speak or articulate gutturally. **2.** *Phonet.* To velarize. — **gut'tur·al·i·za'tion** *n.*

guy¹ (gī) *n.* **1.** *Informal* A man or boy; fellow. **2.** *Brit.* A person of grotesque appearance. **3.** *Brit.* An effigy of Guy Fawkes exhibited and burned on Guy Fawkes Day. — *v.t.* **guyed, guy·ing** *Informal* To ridicule. [after *Guy Fawkes*]

guy² (gī) *n.* A rope, cable, wire, etc., used to steady, guide, or secure something. — *v.t.* To secure, steady, or guide with a guy. [< OF *guie* < *guier*, var. of *guider* to guide]

Guy·a·na (gē-ä'nə, -an'ə) An independent member of the British Commonwealth of Nations on the NE coast of South America; 83,000 sq. mi.; pop. 763,000 (est. 1970); capital, Georgetown. — **Guy·a·nese** (gē'ə-nēz', -nēs') *adj. & n.*

Guy·enne (gē-yen') See GUIENNE.

Guy Fawkes Day (gī' fôks') A British celebration commemorating the Gunpowder Plot of November 5, 1605, an abortive conspiracy, led by Guy Fawkes (1570–1606), to assassinate King James I and the members of Parliament while in assembly in retaliation for the increased severity of penal laws against Roman Catholics.

guz·zle (guz'əl) *v.t. & v.i.* **·zled, ·zling** To drink greedily or to excess. [? < OF *gosiller* < *gosier* throat] — **guz'zler** *n.*

g.v. Gravimetric volume.

Gwa·li·or (gwä'lē-ôr) A former princely state in central India; 26,008 sq. mi.

gwe·duck (gōo'ē-duk') See GEODUCK.

Gwent (gwent) A county in SE Wales; 738 sq. mi.; pop. 440,500 (1976); county seat, Cwmbran.

Gwin·nett (gwi-net'), **Button,** 1735?–77, American patriot; signer of the Declaration of Independence.

Gwyn (gwin), **Nell,** 1650–87, English actress; mistress of Charles II: original name **Eleanor Gwyn** or **Gwinn.**

Gwy·nedd (gwi'neth) A county in NW Wales; 1,492 sq. mi.; pop. 223,500 (1976); county seat, Caernarvon.

gybe (jīb) See JIBE¹.

gym (jim) *n. U.S. Informal* **1.** A gymnasium. **2.** In a school or college, a course in physical training. [Short for GYMNASIUM]

gym. Gymnasium; gymnastics.

gym·kha·na (jim-kä'nə) *n.* **1.** *Brit.* A meet for various athletic contests, especially racing; also, the place where this is held. **2.** *U.S.* A contest of driving skill in sports cars. [< Hind. *gend-khana* racket court; infl. by *gymnastics*]

gym·na·si·ast (jim-nā'zē-ast) *n.* **1.** A student at a Gymnasium. **2.** A gymnast.

gym·na·si·um (jim-nā'zē-əm) *n. pl.* **·si·ums** or **·si·a** (-zē-ə) **1.** A building or room equipped for certain athletic activities or contests. **2.** A place where ancient Greek youths met for physical exercise and training, and for discussion. [< L < Gk. *gymnasion* < *gymnazein* to exercise < *gymnos* naked]

Gym·na·si·um (gim-nä'zē-ŏŏm) *n.* In continental Europe, especially Germany, a secondary school to prepare students for the universities.

gym·nast (jim'nast) *n.* One skilled in gymnastics. [< Gk. *gymnastēs* trainer < *gymnazein*. See GYMNASIUM.]

gym·nas·tic (jim-nas'tik) *adj.* Of or pertaining to gymnastics. Also **gym·nas'ti·cal.** — **gym·nas'ti·cal·ly** *adv.*

gym·nas·tics (jim-nas'tiks) *n.pl.* **1.** Physical exercises designed to improve strength, agility, and coordination. **2.** (*construed as sing.*) The art or practice of such exercises. Also **gymno-** *combining form* Naked; bare: *gymnosperm.* Also, before vowels, **gymn-.** [< Gk. *gymnos* naked]

gym·nos·o·phist (jim-nos'ə-fist) *n.* **1.** One of an ancient Hindu sect of ascetic philosophers who wore little clothing. **2.** A nudist. [< L *gymnosophistae*, pl. < Gk. *gymnosophistai* < *gymnos* naked + *sophistēs* sophist] — **gym·nos'o·phy** *n.*

gym·no·sperm (jim'nə-spûrm') *n.* One of a class of plants (*Gymnospermae*) whose ovules and seeds are not enclosed in an ovary or case, as certain evergreens: distinguished from *angiosperm.* — **gym'no·sper'mous** *adj.*

gyn- See GYNO-.

gyn. or **gynecol.** Gynecological; gynecology.

gy·nae·ce·um (jī'nə-sē'əm, jin'ə- *for def. 1;* jī·nē'sē·əm, ji- *for def. 2*) *n. pl.* **·ce·a** (-sē'ə) **1.** The quarters for women in ancient Greek and Roman houses. **2.** *Bot.* The gynoecium. Also **gy·nae·ci·um** (jī'nə-sī'əm, jin'ə- *for def. 1;* jī·nē'sē·əm, ji- *for def. 2*). [< L *gynaeceum* < Gk. *gynaikeion* < *gynē, gynaikos* woman]

gynaeco- See GYNECO-.

gy·nan·dro·mor·phism (jī-nan'drō-môr'fiz-əm, ji-, gī-) *n. Biol.* The occurrence of male and female characteristics in the same individual. — **gy·nan'dro·mor'phic, gy·nan'dro·mor'phous** *adj.*

gy·nan·drous (jī-nan'drəs, ji-, gī-) *adj.* **1.** *Bot.* Having the stamens united with or seemingly borne upon the pistil, as in orchids. **2.** Exhibiting gynandry. [< Gk. *gynandros* of doubtful sex < *gynē* woman + *anēr, andros* man]

gy·nan·dry (jī-nan'drē, ji-, gī-) *n.* Hermaphroditism.

gy·nar·chy (jī'när-kē, jin'är-) *n. pl.* **·chies** Government by a woman or by women. — **gy·nar·chic** (jī-när'kik, ji-) *adj.*

gyneco- *combining form* Female; pertaining to women: *gynecomorphous*: also spelled *gynaeco-*. Also, before vowels, **gynec-.** [< Gk. *gynē, gynaikos* woman]

gy·ne·coc·ra·cy (jī'nə-kok'rə-sē, jin'ə-) *n. pl.* **·cies** Government by a woman or by women; gynarchy. [< Gk. *gynaikokratia* < *gynē, gynaikos* woman + *krateein* to rule]

gy·ne·col·o·gy (gī'nə-kol'ə-jē, jī'nə-, jin'ə-) *n.* That branch of medicine dealing with the functions and diseases peculiar to women. [GYNECO- + -LOGY] — **gy·ne·co·log·i·cal** (gī'nə-kə-loj'i-kəl, jī'nə-, jin'ə-) *adj.* — **gy'ne·col'o·gist** *n.*

gy·ne·co·mor·phous (jī-nē'kō-môr'fəs, jin'ə-kō-, gī-) *adj.* Having the shape, appearance, or characteristics of a female.

gyno- *combining form* **1.** Woman; female. **2.** *Bot. & Med.* Female reproductive organ; ovary; pistil: *gynophore.* Also before vowels, **gyn-.** [< Gk. *gynē* woman]

gy·noe·ci·um (jĭ-nē′sē-ə-əm, jĭ-) *n. pl.* **·ci·a** (-sē-ə) *Bot.* The female parts of a flower collectively; the pistil or pistils taken as a unit: also spelled *gynaeceum, gynaecium.* Also **gy·ne·ci·um** (jĭ-nē′sē-əm, jĭ-). Compare ANDROECIUM. [< NL < L *gynaeceum.* See GYNAECEUM.]

gy·no·phore (jĭ′nə-fôr, -fōr, jĭn′ə-) *n. Bot.* A stalk supporting the gynoecium of certain plants.

-gynous *combining form* **1.** Female; of women: *philogynous.* **2.** *Biol.* Having or pertaining to female organs or pistils: *epigynous.* [< Gk. *gynē* woman]

Gyor (dyûr) A city in NW Hungary; pop. 68,000 (1960): German *Raab.*

gyp¹ (jip) *U.S. Informal v.t. & v.i.* **gypped, gyp·ping** To cheat, swindle, or defraud. — *n.* **1.** A fraud; swindle. **2.** One who cheats or swindles. Also spelled *gip.* [? < *gypsy*]

gyp² (jip) *n. Brit. Informal* A male servant at the universities of Cambridge or Durham. [? obs. *gippo* scullion < F *jupeau* tunic]

gyp·se·ous (jip′sē-əs) *adj.* Resembling, containing, or consisting of gypsum.

gyp·sif·er·ous (jip-sif′ər-əs) *adj.* Containing gypsum.

gyp·soph·i·la (jip-sof′ə-lə) *n.* Any of a large genus (*Gypsophila*) of hardy herbs having small, rosy or white flowers. [< NL < Gk. *gypsos* chalk + *phileein* to love]

gyp·sum (jip′səm) *n.* A mineral, hydrous calcium sulfate, CaSO₄·2H₂O, found in massive or granular form and used to make plaster of Paris, as a fertilizer, etc. Also called *parget.* [< L < Gk. *gypsos* chalk]

gyp·sy (jip′sē) *n. pl.* **·sies** A person who looks like, or leads the life of, a Gypsy. — *adj.* Of, pertaining to, or like a gypsy or the Gypsies. — *v.i.* **·sied, ·sy·ing** To live or wander like a gypsy or the Gypsies. Also spelled *gipsy.*

Gyp·sy (jip′sē) *n. pl.* **·sies** **1.** A member of a wandering, dark-haired, dark-skinned Caucasian people believed to have migrated to Europe from India in the 15th century, and known throughout the world as fortune tellers, musicians, etc.: also called *Romany.* **2.** Romany (def. 2). Also spelled *Gipsy.* [Earlier *gipcyan,* aphetic var. of *Egypcyan* Egyptian]

gypsy moth A moth (*Porthetria* or *Lymantria dispar*) of Europe, naturalized in the United States, having larvae destructive to foliage. The male is light brown, the larger female nearly white. For illustration see INSECTS (injurious).

gy·ral (jĭ′rəl) *adj.* **1.** Having a circular, revolving, or whirling motion; gyratory. **2.** Of a gyrus. — **gy′ral·ly** *adv.*

gy·rate (jĭ′rāt) *v.i.* **·rat·ed, ·rat·ing** **1.** To rotate or revolve, usually around a fixed point or axis. **2.** To turn in a spiral motion. — *adj.* Winding or coiled about; convolute. [< L *gyratus,* pp. of *gyrare* to gyrate < *gyrus* circle < Gk. *gyros*] — **gy·ra·tor** (jĭ′rā′tər, jĭ-rā′-) *n.*

gy·ra·tion (jĭ-rā′shən) *n.* **1.** The act of gyrating; a spiral or whirling motion. **2.** A single whorl of a spiral shell.

gy·ra·to·ry (jĭ′rə-tôr′ē, -tō′rē) *adj.* Having a circular or spiral motion.

gyre (jīr) *n. Poetic* **1.** A circular, gyrating motion or path.

2. A spiral or round form, as a ring or vortex. [< L *gyrus* < Gk. *gyros* circle]

gyr·fal·con (jûr′fal′kən, -fôl′-, -fô′-) See GERFALCON.

gy·ro (jĭ′rō) *n.* A gyroscope or gyrocompass.

gyro- *combining form* **1.** Rotating; gyrating: *gyroscope.* **2.** Spiral. **3.** Gyroscope: *gyrocompass.* Also, before vowels, **gyr-.** [< Gk. *gyros* circle]

gy·ro·com·pass (jĭ′rō-kum′pəs, -kom′-) *n.* A compass that employs, instead of a magnetic needle, a motor-driven gyroscope so mounted that its axis of rotation maintains a constant position with reference to the true or geographic north.

gy·ro·ho·ri·zon (jĭ′rō-hə-rī′zən) *n. Aeron.* Artificial horizon (which see).

gy·ro·mag·net·ic (jĭ′rō-mag-net′ik) *adj. Physics* Of or pertaining to any relationship between the magnetic properties of a body and its rotational motion.

gy·ron (jĭ′ron) *n. Heraldry* A charge formed by two lines drawn from the edge of an escutcheon and meeting in an acute angle at the center or fess point. [< F *giron* < OHG *gēro* gusset, triangular piece]

gyro pilot *Aeron.* An automatic pilot.

gy·ro·plane (jĭ′rə-plān′) *n.* An aircraft whose chief support in the air is obtained from the rapid rotation of airfoils about a vertical or nearly vertical axis, as a helicopter.

gy·ro·scope (jĭ′rə-skōp) *n.* Any of a class of devices consisting essentially of a heavy mass, usually a wheel, so mounted that when set to rotate at high speeds it resists all forces tending to change the angular position of its axis of rotation, used in stabilizing and navigational devices, as a toy, etc. [< F] — **gy·ro·scop·ic** (-skop′ik) *adj.*

gy·rose (jĭ′rōs) *adj. Bot.* Marked with wavy lines. [< GYRE + -OSE¹]

gy·ro·sta·bi·liz·er (jĭ′rō-stā′bə-li′zər) *n.* A gyroscopic device designed to reduce the rolling motion of ships.

gy·ro·stat (jĭ′rə-stat) *n.* An instrument consisting of a gyroscope set or fixed in a rigid case, used to illustrate the dynamics of rotating rigid bodies. [< GYRO(SCOPE) + -STAT]

GYROSCOPE
Showing possible directional movements.

gy·ro·stat·ic (jĭ′rə-stat′ik) *adj.* Pertaining to the gyrostat or to gyrostatics. — **gy·ro·stat′i·cal·ly** *adv.*

gy·ro·stat·ics (jĭ′rə-stat′iks) *n.pl.* (*construed as sing.*) The branch of physics that investigates the laws governing the rotation of solid bodies.

gy·rus (jĭ′rəs) *n. pl.* **·ri** (-rī) *Anat.* A rounded, serpentine ridge in the brain between two fissures or sulci; especially, a convolution of the cortex. [< NL < L *gyrus* circle]

gyve (jīv) *Archaic n. Usually pl.* A fetter or shackle for the limbs. — *v.t.* **gyved, gyv·ing** To bind with fetters; shackle. [ME *give, gyves;* origin uncertain]

H

h, H (āch) *n. pl.* **h's** or **hs, H's** or **Hs, aitch·es** (ā′chiz) **1.** The eighth letter of the English alphabet. The shape of the Phoenician consonant *hēth* was adopted by the Greeks as *eta* and became Roman *H.* Also *aitch.* **2.** The sound represented by the letter *h,* a voiceless, glottal fricative. In a few English words of French origin, as *heir, honor, hour,* etc., the letter *h* has no phonetic value; usage varies in certain other words, as *herb, homage,* etc., in which some persons pronounce an initial (*h*) and some do not. **3.** Anything shaped like an H. **4.** *U.S. Slang* Heroin. — *symbol* **1.** *Chem.* Hydrogen (symbol H). **2.** *Physics* Strength or intensity of magnetic field (symbol H). **3.** *Electr.* Henry (symbol H). **4.** The eighth in a series. **5.** The medieval Roman numeral for 200.

h. or **h** Hit(s) (baseball).

H. or **h.** **1.** Harbor. **2.** Hard; hardness. **3.** Heavy sea. **4.** Height. **5.** Hence. **6.** High. **7.** *Music* Horns. **8.** Hour(s). **9.** Hundred. **10.** Husband.

ha (hä) *n. & interj.* An exclamation or sound made by a quick expulsion of breath, expressing surprise, discovery, triumph, laughter, etc. Also spelled *hah.*

ha. Hectare(s).

haaf (häf) *n.* A deep-sea fishing ground off the coast of the Shetland or Orkney Islands. [< ON *haf* sea]

Haa·kon VII (hô′kŏŏn), 1872–1957, king of Norway 1905–1957.

haar (här) *n. Scot.* A mist or fog; especially, a chilly fog.

Haar·lem (här′ləm) A city in the western Netherlands, capital of North Holland province; pop. 172,235 (est. 1970): also *Harlem.*

Hab. Habakkuk.

Ha·bak·kuk (hə-bak′ək, hab′ə-kuk) Seventh-century B.C. Hebrew prophet. — *n.* A book of the Old Testament written by him. Also, in the Douai Bible, **Ha·bac′uc.**

ha·ba·ne·ra (ä′bä-nā′rä) *n.* **1.** A slow, Cuban dance of African origin. **2.** Music for or in the manner of this dance, in duple meter. [< Sp., of Havana]

Ha·ba·ne·ro (ä′vä-nā′rō) *n.* A native or inhabitant of Havana.

ha·be·as cor·pus (hā′bē-əs kôr′pəs) *Law* A writ commanding a person who detains another to produce the detained person before a court, especially in order to determine the lawfulness of the detention. [< L, (you) have the body]

Ha·ber (hä′bər), *Fritz,* 1868–1934, German chemist; developed the **Haber process** for the fixation of atmospheric nitrogen by reaction with hydrogen to form ammonia.

hab·er·dash·er (hab′ər-dash′ər) *n.* **1.** *U.S.* A shopkeeper who deals in men's furnishings, as neckties, shirts, hats, socks, etc. **2.** *Brit.* A dealer in or peddler of ribbons, trimmings, thread, needles, and other small wares. [Prob. < AF *hapertas,* kind of fabric]

hab·er·dash·er·y (hab′ər-dash′ər-ē) *n. pl.* **·er·ies** **1.** The goods sold by haberdashers. **2.** A haberdasher's shop.

hab·er·geon (hab′ər-jən) *n.* **1.** A short jacket of mail, usually sleeveless. **2.** A hauberk. Also spelled *haubergeon*. [< OF *haubergeon*, dim. of *hauberc*. See HAUBERK.]

hab·ile (hab′il) *adj. Rare* Able; skillful; clever; adroit. [Var. of ABLE; infl. in form by F *habile* able or L *habilis* apt]

ha·bil·i·ment (hə-bil′ə-mənt) *n. Usually pl.* Clothing; attire; garb. [< OF *habillement* < *habiller* to dress, make fit < L *habilis* fit, apt]

ha·bil·i·tate (hə-bil′ə-tāt) *v.t.* **·tat·ed, ·tat·ing 1.** *U.S.* In the West, to supply (a mine) with money, equipment, etc. **2.** *Rare To* dress; clothe. [< Med.L *habilitatus*, pp. of *habilitare* to enable < L *habilis* fit] **— ha·bil′i·ta′tion** *n.*

hab·it (hab′it) *n.* **1.** An act or practice so frequently repeated as to become relatively fixed in character and almost automatic in performance. **2.** A tendency or disposition to act consistently in a certain manner or to repeat frequently a certain action. **3.** An addiction: the drug *habit*. **4.** Mental or moral disposition or attitude: the scholar's *habit* of mind. **5.** A characteristic appearance or condition of the body or constitution. **6.** The clothing or garb associated with a particular profession, activity, religious order, etc.: a monk's *habit*; a riding *habit*. **7.** *Biol.* A characteristic action, aspect, or mode of growth of a plant or animal: a plant of trailing *habit*. **— v.t. 1.** To clothe; dress. **2.** *Archaic* To dwell in. **3.** *Obs.* To accustom. **— v.i. 4.** *Obs.* To dwell. [< OF < L *habitus* condition, dress < *habere* to have] **— Syn.** (noun) **1.** *Habit, habitude, custom, wont, practice, usage,* and *fashion* refer to a mode of behavior that has become usual through much repetition. *Habit* is a specific way of acting; *habitude* is a general tendency or attitude: the *habit* of putting the left leg into trousers first, the scientific *habitude* of skepticism. *Habit* and *habitude* properly refer to individual behavior; the corresponding word for group or mass behavior is *custom*: the American *custom* of using both knife and fork with the right hand. *Custom* may or may not be based on individual *habits*; shaking hands is a *custom*, but not an individual *habit*, while having coffee in midmorning may be both. *Wont* is a vague term for what is usual, applicable either to *habit* or *custom*: he arrived late, as was his *wont*. *Practice* is a usual way of acting, working, or behaving, and implies a voluntary choice: the whalers' *practice* of discarding the fins. *Usage* refers to a *practice* which is regarded as setting a standard: to avoid words not in polite *usage*. *Fashion* is a *custom* or *practice* in small matters, such as dress: crinolines came back into *fashion*.

hab·it·a·ble (hab′it·ə-bəl) *adj.* Suitable for habitation. [< L *habitabilis* < *habitare* to inhabit] **— hab′it·a·bil′i·ty, hab′·it·a·ble·ness** *n.* **— hab′it·a·bly** *adv.*

hab·i·tant (hab′ə-tənt, *Fr.* à·bē·tän′) *n.* **1.** An inhabitant. **2.** A French farmer in Canada or Louisiana, or his descendants: also **ha·bi·tan′.** [< F < L *habitans, -antis,* ppr. of *habitare* to dwell]

hab·i·tat (hab′ə-tat) *n.* **1.** The region or environment where a plant or animal is normally found, as salt water, desert, equatorial forest, etc. **2.** The place where a person or thing usually resides or is found. [< NL, it dwells]

hab·i·ta·tion (hab′ə-tā′shən) *n.* **1.** A place of abode; residence. **2.** The act or state of dwelling or inhabiting. **— Syn.** See HOME.

hab·it·ed (hab′it·id) *adj.* **1.** Clothed; arrayed. **2.** *Archaic* Dwelt in.

ha·bit·u·al (hə-bich′ōō-əl) *adj.* **1.** Practiced or recurring by habit or as if by habit; customary: *habitual* courtesy; also, occurring frequently or constantly; inveterate: His drunkenness is *habitual*. **2.** Given to or addicted to a specified practice: a *habitual* liar. **3.** Expected from habit or usage; usual: her *habitual* place. [< Med.L *habitualis* < L *habitus*. See HABIT.] **— ha·bit′u·al·ly** *adv.* **— ha·bit′u·al·ness** *n.*

hab·it-form·ing (hab′it-fôr′ming) *adj.* Producing or resulting in a habitual practice or addiction.

ha·bit·u·ate (hə-bich′ōō-āt) *v.t.* **·at·ed, at·ing** To accustom (oneself, a person, an animal, etc.) to a given condition or experience by repetition. [< LL *habituatus*, pp. of *habituare* to condition] **— ha·bit′u·a′tion** *n.*

hab·i·tude (hab′ə-tōōd, -tyōōd) *n.* **1.** Customary or characteristic state of mind or body. **2.** A usual course of action. **— Syn.** See HABIT. [< MF < L *habitudo* condition]

ha·bit·u·é (hə·bich′ōō-ā, hə·bich′ōō-ā′; *Fr.* à·bē·tü·ā′) *n.* One who frequents a specific restaurant, club, etc. [< F, pp. of *habituer* to accustom]

Habs·burg (häps′bōōrkh) See HAPSBURG.

ha·bu (hä′bōō) *n.* A very poisonous crotaline snake (genus *Trimeresurus*) of Okinawa and other Ryukyu Islands, related to the American rattlesnake. [< Japanese]

ha·chure (*n.* ha·shōōr′, hash′ōōr; *v.* ha·shōōr′) *n.* **1.** In art, one of the lines used in hatching. **2.** In mapmaking, one of the short, parallel lines used to show the direction and degree of slope in hills and other elevations. **— v.t. ·chured, ·chur·ing** To mark, shade, or indicate with hachures. [< F < *hacher*. See HATCH³.]

ha·ci·en·da (hä′sē·en′də, *Sp.* ä·syen′dä) *n.* In Spanish America: **a** A landed estate; a country house. **b** A farming, mining, or manufacturing establishment in the country. [< Am. Sp. < L *facienda* things to be done < *facere* to do, make]

hack¹ (hak) *v.t.* **1.** To cut or chop crudely or irregularly, as

with an ax, cleaver, sword etc. **2.** In basketball, to strike (an opposing player) on the arm. **3.** In Rugby football, to kick (an opposing player) in the shins. **4.** *Brit. Dial.* To break up, as clods of earth. **— v.i. 5.** To make cuts or notches with heavy, crude blows. **6.** To emit short, dry coughs. **— n. 1.** A gash, cut, or nick made by or as by a sharp instrument. **2.** An ax, hoe, or other tool for hacking. **3.** A kick on the shins, or the bruise or cut that results, as in Rugby football. **4.** A short, dry cough. [OE *haccian* to cut] **— hack′er** *n.*

hack² (hak) *n.* **1.** A horse for hire. **2.** A horse used for ordinary work or riding, as a saddle horse. **3.** An old, worn-out horse; jade. **4.** A person who hires himself out to do routine or tedious work, especially literary work; drudge. **5.** *U.S.* A hackney coach or carriage. **6.** *U.S. Informal* A taxicab. **— v.t. 1.** To let out for hire, as a horse. **2.** To use or employ as a hack. **3.** To make stale or trite by constant use; hackney. **— v.i. 4.** *U.S. Informal* To drive a taxicab. **5.** *Brit.* To ride on horseback at a jogging or ordinary pace. **— adj. 1.** Of or designated for a hack: a *hack* stand. **2.** For hire as a hack or drudge: a *hack* writer. **3.** Of a routine or mercenary nature: *hack* writing. **4.** Trite; hackneyed: a *hack* phrase. **— Syn.** See VENAL. [< HACKNEY]

hack³ (hak) *n.* **1.** A frame or rack on which to dry cheese, fish, bricks, etc. **2.** A row of bricks laid out to dry. **3.** A pile of bricks not yet fired. **— v.t.** To set (bricks, cheese, fish, etc.) on hacks to dry. [Var. of HATCH¹]

hack·a·more (hak′ə·môr, -mōr) *n. U.S.* A type of halter made of rawhide or rope, used in breaking foals to a bridle. [Alter. of Sp. *jaquima* halter]

hack·ber·ry (hak′ber′ē, -bər·ē) *n. pl.* **·ries 1.** An American tree (genus *Celtis*) resembling the elm and having small, sweet, edible fruit. **2.** The fruit or wood of this tree. Also called *hagberry, sugarberry*. [Var. of *hagberry* < ON *heggr* hedge + BERRY]

hack·but (hak′but) *n.* A harquebus. [< MF *hacquebut* < Du. *hakebus* < *hake* hook + *bus* gun]

hack·ee (hak′ē) *n.* A chipmunk. [Imit.]

Hack·en·sack (hak′ən·sak) A city in eastern New Jersey, on the **Hackensack River** that flows south about 45 miles from SE New York to Newark Bay; pop. 36,008.

hack·ham·mer (hak′ham′ər) *n.* A hammer shaped like an adz, used for dressing stone.

hack·ie (hak′ē) *n. U.S. Slang* The driver of a taxicab.

hack·le¹ (hak′əl) *n.* **1.** One of the long, narrow feathers on the neck or saddle of a rooster, pigeon, etc. **2.** The neck feathers collectively of a rooster, etc. For illustration see FOWL. **3.** In angling: **a** A tuft of feathers from the neck of a rooster, etc., used in trimming an artificial fly. **b** A hackle fly. For illustration see LURE. **4.** *pl.* The erectile hairs on the neck and back of a dog, that rise in anger, etc. **5.** A hatchel. **— v.t. ·led, ·ling 1.** To furnish (a fly) with a hackle. **2.** To hatchel. [Var. of HATCHEL] **— hack′ler** *n.*

hack·le² (hak′əl) *v.t. & v.i.* **·led, ·ling** *Rare* To cut or chop roughly or crudely; mangle; hack. [Freq. of HACK¹]

hackle fly An artificial fly for angling, trimmed with hackles.

hack·man (hak′mən) *n. pl.* **·men** (-mən) *U.S.* The driver of a hack or public carriage.

hack·ma·tack (hak′mə·tak) *n. U.S. & Canadian* **1.** The tamarack. **2.** The wood of this tree. [< N. Am. Ind.]

hack·ney (hak′nē) *n. pl.* **·neys 1.** A horse of medium size used for ordinary driving and riding. **2.** A carriage for hire. **3.** *Obs.* A horse kept for hire. **4.** One hired to do menial, tedious tasks; drudge. **— v.t.** *Rare* **1.** To make commonplace or trite by constant use. **2.** To hire out or use as a hackney. **— adj.** *Rare* **1.** Let out for hire. **2.** Much used; common; trite. [< OF *haquenee* horse; ult. origin unknown]

hack·neyed (hak′nēd) *adj.* Made commonplace by frequent use; trite. **— Syn.** See TRITE.

hack·saw (hak′sô′) *n.* A saw with a fine-toothed, narrow blade set in a frame, used for cutting metal. Also **hack saw.**

had (had) Past tense and past participle of HAVE.

HACKSAW

Had·ding·ton (had′ing·tən) **1.** The county seat of East Lothian, Scotland, in the central part of the country; pop. about 5,000. **2.** The former name for EAST LOTHIAN: also **Had·ding·ton·shire** (-shir).

had·dock (had′ək) *n. pl.* **·dock** or **·docks** A food fish (*Melanogrammus aeglefinus*) of the North Atlantic, allied to but smaller than the cod. [ME; origin unknown]

hade (hād) *Geol. n.* The inclination from the vertical of a fault plane or vein of ore. **— v.i. had·ed, had·ing** To incline from a vertical position, as a fault. [Cf. dial. E *hade* slope]

ha·des (hā′dēz) *n. Often cap. Informal* Hell: a euphemism.

Ha·des (hā′dēz) **1.** In Greek mythology: **a** The brother of Zeus, god of the underworld, identified with the Greek and Roman *Pluto* and the Roman *Dis*. **b** The underground kingdom of the dead, ruled by Hades. **2.** In the Revised Version of the New Testament, the condition or the abode of the dead. [< Gk. *Haidēs* < *a-* not + *idein* to see]

Had·field (had′fēld), **Sir Robert Abbott,** 1859–1940, English metallurgist.

Ha·dhra·maut (hä′drä·mout′, -môt′) A region on the southern coast of the Arabian Peninsula, in South Yemen. Also **Ha′dra·maut′.**

hadj (haj) *n.* The pilgrimage to Mecca required of every Moslem at least once in his life: also spelled *haj, hajj.* [< Turkish < Arabic *hājj* pilgrimage. Akin to HEGIRA.]

hadj·i (haj′ē) *n.* **1.** A Moslem who has made the pilgrimage to Mecca: used also before a name as a title. **2.** In the Near East, a Christian who has made a pilgrimage to the Holy Sepulcher at Jerusalem. Also spelled *haji, hajji:* also **hadj′ee.**

Had·ley (had′lē), **Henry Kimball,** 1871–1937, U.S. composer.

had·n′t (had′nt) Had not.

Ha·dri·an (hā′drē·ən) Anglicized name of **Publius Aelius Ha·dri·a·nus** (hā′drē·ā′nəs), 76–138, Roman emperor 117–138. Also **Adrian.**

Ha·dri·an·op·o·lis (hā′drē·ən·op′ə·lis) The ancient name for ADRIANOPLE.

Hadrian's Wall A wall extending from Solway Firth to the mouth of the Tyne, built by Hadrian about 122–128, to protect Roman Britain from the Picts and Scots.

hae (hā, ha) *v.t. Scot.* To have.

Haeck·el (hek′əl), **Ernst Heinrich,** 1834–1919, German naturalist and philosopher.

haem-, haemo- See HEMO-.

haema- See HEMA-.

hae·ma·chrome (hē′mə·krōm, hem′ə-), **hae·ma·gogue** (hē′mə·gôg, -gog, hem′ə-), etc. See HEMACHROME, HEMAGOGUE, etc.

haemat-, haemato- See HEMATO-.

hae·ma·tox·y·lon (hē′mə·tok′sə·lon, hem′ə-) *n.* **1.** Any of a genus (*Haematoxylon*) of tropical American trees, especially the bloodwood tree (*H. campechianum*), whose heartwood supplies a purple red coloring matter. **2.** The wood or the dyestuff of this tree. Also **hae′ma·tox′y·lin** (-lin). [< NL < Gk. *haima, -atos* blood + *xylon* wood]

-haemia See -EMIA.

hae·mo·flag·el·late (hē′mə·flaj′ə·lāt, hem′ə-), **hae·mo·glo·bin** (hē′mə·glō′bin, hem′ə-), etc. See HEMOFLAGELLATE, HEMOGLOBIN, etc.

hae·res (hē′rēz) See HERES.

ha·fiz (hä′fiz) *n.* One who has memorized the Koran: a Moslem title of respect. [< Arabic *hāfiz* one who remembers]

Ha·fiz (hä·fēz′) Pseudonym of **Shams ud-din Mohammed,** 14th-century Persian poet and philosopher.

haf·ni·um (haf′nē·əm) *n.* A quadrivalent metallic element (symbol Hf) found in zirconium minerals. See ELEMENT. [< NL, from L *Hafnia* Copenhagen]

haft (haft, häft) *n.* A handle; especially, the handle of a knife, sword, sickle, etc. — *v.t.* To supply with or set in a haft. [OE *hæft* handle < *habban* to hold, have]

hag¹ (hag) *n.* **1.** A repulsive and usually malicious old woman. **2.** A witch; sorceress. **3.** A hagfish. **4.** *Obs.* A female demon or ghost. [OE *hægtes* witch]

hag² (hag) *Scot. & Brit. Dial. v.t. & v.i.* To hack or hew. — *n.* **1.** A cutting or felling of wood; also, the wood so cut. **2.** A particularly soft place in a bog or marsh. **3.** A firm spot of ground in a bog. [< ON *höggva* to hew]

Hag. Haggai.

Ha·gar (hā′gər) Abraham's concubine; mother of Ishmael. *Gen.* xvi 1.

hag·ber·ry (hag′ber′ē, -bər·ē) *n. pl.* **·ries** The hackberry.

hag·bush (hag′boȯsh′) *n.* The azedarach. [? OE *haga* hedge + BUSH]

hag·but (hag′but) *n.* A harquebus. [Var. of HACKBUT]

hag·don (hag′dən) *n.* The shearwater, a bird. [? < HAG², v.]

Ha·gen (hä′gən) In the *Nibelungenlied* and in Wagner's *Ring of the Nibelung,* the murderer of Siegfried.

Ha·gen (hä′gən) A city in central North Rhine–Westphalia, West Germany; pop. 203,050 (est. 1970). Also **Ha·gen·in·West·fal·en** (in vest′fäl′ən).

Ha·gers·town (hā′gərz·toun) A city in western Maryland; pop 35,862.

hag·fish (hag′fish′) *n. pl.* **·fish** or **·fish·es** A primitive eel-like, marine cyclostome allied to the lamprey, that bores its way into the bodies of living fishes by means of a rasping, suctorial mouth: also called *hag.* [< HAG¹ + FISH]

Hag·ga·dah (hə·gä′də, *Hebrew* hä·gô′dô) *n. pl.* **·doth** (-dōth) **1.** The nonlegal elements of Talmudic literature, consisting of illustrative fables, proverbs, etc.: distinguished from *Halakah.* **2.** The story of the Exodus read at the Seder on the first two nights of Passover. **3.** A book containing this narrative and the accompanying ritual. Also **Ha·ga′dah, Hag·ga′da.** [< Hebrew < *higgid* to tell]

hag·gad·ic (hə·gad′ik, -gä′dik) *adj.* Of or pertaining to the Haggadah. Also **ha·gad′ic, hag·gad′i·cal.**

hag·ga·dist (hə·gä′dist) *n.* A haggadic writer or scholar. Also **ha·ga′dist.** — **hag·ga·dis·tic** (hag′ə·dis′tik), **hag′a·dis′tic** *adj.*

Hag·ga·i (hag′ē·ī, hag′ī) Sixth-century B.C. Hebrew prophet. — *n.* A book of the Old Testament written by him. Abbr. *Hag.* Also, in the Douai Bible, *Aggeus.*

hag·gard (hag′ərd) *adj.* **1.** Having a worn, gaunt, or wild look, as from fatigue, worry, hunger, etc. **2.** Wild or intractable: said especially of a hawk captured after having reached its adult state. — *n.* **1.** In falconry, a wild hawk captured after growing its adult plumage. **2.** *Obs.* A fierce, unmanageable person. [< OF *hagard* wild < MHG *hag* hedge] — **hag′gard·ly** *adv.* — **hag′gard·ness** *n.*

Hag·gard (hag′ərd), **Sir Henry (Rider),** 1856–1925, English novelist: called H. Rider Haggard.

hag·gis (hag′is) *n.* A Scottish dish made of a calf's or sheep's vitals (heart, lungs, liver, etc.) mixed with suet, oatmeal, and onions, then seasoned and boiled in the animal's stomach. [ME *hagas* < *haggen* to chop + *es* food]

hag·gish (hag′ish) *adj.* Characteristic of a hag; haglike. — **hag′gish·ly** *adv.* — **hag′gish·ness** *n.*

hag·gle (hag′əl) *v.* **·gled, ·gling** *v.i.* **1.** To argue or bargain in a petty, mean way, especially about price or terms. — *v.t.* **2.** To cut in an unskillful way; hack; mangle. **3.** To tire or harass, as by wrangling. — *n.* The act of haggling. [Freq. of HAG²] — **hag′gler** *n.*

hag·i·ar·chy (hag′ē·är′kē, hā′jē-) *n. pl.* **·chies** **1.** A government by holy men: also **hag·i·oc·ra·cy** (hag′ē·ok′rə·sē, hā′jē-). **2.** An order or hierarchy of saints.

hagio- *combining form* Sacred: *hagiography.* Also, before vowels, **hagi-.** [< Gk. *hagios* sacred]

Hag·i·og·ra·pha (hag′ē·og′rə·fə, hā′jē-) *n.pl.* The third of the three ancient divisions of the Old Testament, containing all those books not found in the Pentateuch or the Prophets. The Hagiographa consist of the following books (names in the Douai Bible, when different, are given in parentheses): I Chronicles (I Paralipomenon), II Chronicles (II Paralipomenon), Ruth, Ezra (I Esdras), Nehemiah (II Esdras), Esther, Job, Psalms, Proverbs, Ecclesiastes, Song of Solomon (Canticle of Canticles), Lamentations, Daniel. [< Gk. < *hagios* sacred + *graphein* to write]

hag·i·og·ra·pher (hag′ē·og′rə·fər, hā′jē-) *n.* **1.** A writer of or authority on the lives of saints. **2.** Any writer on sacred subjects; especially, one of the authors of the Hagiographa.

hag·i·og·ra·phy (hag′ē·og′rə·fē, hā′jē-) *n. pl.* **·phies** **1.** The writing or study of the lives of saints. **2.** A book or collection of such writings. — **hag·i·o·graph·ic** (hag′ē·ə·graf′ik, hā′jē-) or **·i·cal** *adj.*

hag·i·ol·a·try (hag′ē·ol′ə·trē, hā′jē-) *n.* The worship of saints. — **hag·i·o·la·ter** *n.* — **hag·i·o·la·trous** *adj.*

hag·i·ol·o·gy (hag′ē·ol′ə·jē, hā′jē-) *n. pl.* **·gies** **1.** That part of literature dealing with the lives of the saints. **2.** A book on saints' lives. **3.** A list of saints. — **hag·i·o·log·ic** (hag′ē·ə·loj′ik, hā′jē-) or **·i·cal** *adj.* — **hag·i·ol′o·gist** *n.*

hag·i·o·scope (hag′ē·ə·skōp′, hā′jē-) *n.* An opening cut in an interior wall of a church to allow those in a side aisle to see the main altar. — **hag′i·o·scop′ic** (-skop′ik) *adj.*

hag·rid·den (hag′rid′n) *adj.* Tormented or distressed, as by a witch.

Hague (hāg), **The** A city in the western Netherlands, the political capital of the country; seat of the Hague Tribunal, and of the first international peace conference held in 1899; pop. 550,613 (est. 1970): Dutch *Den Haag* or '*s Gravenhage.*

Hague Tribunal The Permanent Court of Arbitration.

hah (hä) See HA.

ha·ha¹ (hä′hä′, hä′hä′) *n. & interj.* A sound imitating laughter. — *v.i.* To laugh. Also spelled *haw-haw.* [Imit.]

ha·ha² (hä′hä′) *n.* A hedge or wall around a garden, etc., but set low in a ditch so as not to obstruct the view; a sunk fence: also spelled *haw-haw.* [< F *haha*]

Hahn (hän), **Otto,** 1879–1968, German physical chemist.

Hah·ne·mann (hä′nə·män), **(Christian Friedrich) Samuel,** 1755–1843, German physician; founder of homeopathy.

Hai·da (hī′də) *n.* **1.** A member of any of the tribes of North American Indians inhabiting the Queen Charlotte Islands, British Columbia, and Prince of Wales Island, Alaska. **2.** The family of languages spoken by these tribes.

Hai·dar·a·bad (hī′dər·ə·bad′) See HYDERABAD.

Hai·dar A·li (hī′dər ä′lē) See HYDER ALI.

Hai·duk (hī′dook) *n.* **1.** One of a body of Hungarian mercenary soldiers of the 16th century. **2.** One of the bandit mountaineers of the Balkans who fought against Turkish rule. **3.** Formerly in Europe, a male servant in Hungarian livery. Also spelled *Heiduc, Heyduc, Heyduck, Heyduke.* [< Hung. *hajduk* drover]

Hai·fa (hī′fə) A port city in NW Israel, on the Bay of Acre; pop. 209,900 (est. 1967).

Haig (hāg), **Douglas,** 1861–1928, first Earl Haig, British field marshal in World War I.

haik (hīk, hāk) *n.* An outer garment worn by Arabs, consisting of an oblong piece of cloth wrapped around the head and body. [< Arabic *hayk* < *hāk* to weave]

hai·ku (hī′koo) *n. pl.* **·ku** **1.** A Japanese verse form in three lines of five, seven, and five syllables respectively. **2.** An example of this form. Also called *hokku.* [< Japanese]

hail¹ (hāl) *n.* **1.** Small lumps or pellets of ice that fall from the sky during a storm; hailstones. **2.** A rapid or heavy showering: a hail of blows. **3.** *Rare* A hailstorm. — *v.i.* **1.** To pour down hail. **2.** To fall or shower like hail. — *v.t.* **3.** To hurl or pour like hail: to *hail* curses. [OE *hægel*]

hail² (hāl) *v.t.* **1.** To call loudly to in greeting; salute. **2.** To call to so as to attract attention: to *hail* a cab. **3.** To name as; designate: They *hailed* him captain. — *v.i.* **4.** To call out so as to attract attention or give greeting, especially between ships. — **Syn.** See GREET. — **to hail from** To come from, as a birthplace, residence, point of origin, etc. — *n.* **1.** The act of hailing. **2.** A shout, as of greeting or to attract attention. **3.** The distance a shout can be heard; earshot: within *hail*. — *interj.* An exclamation of greeting or tribute, usually respectful. [ME *hailen, heilen* < ON *heilla* < *heill* whole, hale. Akin to HALE².] — **hail'er** *n.*

hail Columbia *U.S. Slang* **1.** A severe punishment or reprimand. **2.** A noisy rumpus or commotion: to raise *hail Columbia*. [Euphemism for HELL]

Hai·le Se·las·sie (hī'lē sə·las'ē, -lä'sē), emperor of Ethiopia, 1930–; in exile 1936–41: original name **Taffari Ma·kon·nen** (mä·kô'nen).

hail fellow A pleasant companion. Also **hail fellow well met.**

hail-fel·low (hāl'fel'ō) *adj.* Very friendly or cordial in manner, often superficially so.

Hail Mary Ave Maria (which see).

hail·stone (hāl'stōn') *n.* A pellet of hail.

hail·storm (hāl'stôrm') *n.* A storm in which hail falls.

Hai·nan (hī'nän') An island of Kwangtung Province, SE China; 13,000 sq. mi.; separated from the mainland by **Hainan Strait,** a part of the South China Sea.

Hai·naut (e·nō') A Province of SW Belgium; 1,437 sq. mi.; pop. 1,331,810 (est. 1970); capital, Mons: Flemish *Henegouwen.*

hain't (hānt) *Illit. & Dial.* **1.** Have not. **2.** Has not.

Hai·phong (hī'fong') A port city in North Vietnam; pop. 182,496 (est. 1970).

hair (hâr) *n.* **1.** One of the fine, threadlike structures that grow from the skin of most mammals. ◆ Collateral adjectives: *capillary, pilar.* **2.** Such structures collectively; especially: **a** Those that grow on the human head. **b** The natural coat of most animals. **c** A similar mass growing on the body surfaces of insects, etc. **3.** *Bot.* A hairlike outgrowth of the epidermis in plants. **4.** Material or fabric woven of hair, as haircloth. **5.** Any exceedingly minute space, measure, degree, etc.: to miss by a *hair*. — **hair of the dog (that bit one)** *Informal* Alcoholic liquor drunk in the hope of relieving a hangover. — **not to turn a hair** To show or reveal no sign of embarrassment, fear, anger, etc. — **to a hair** With the utmost exactness or perfection; in minute detail. — **to get in one's hair** *Slang* To vex or annoy one. — **to let one's hair down** *U.S. Slang* To discard one's reserve. — **to make one's hair stand on end** To frighten or horrify one. — **to split hairs** To make trivial or oversubtle distinctions. — *adj.* **1.** Like, or made of, hair. **2.** Designated for the care of the hair: *hair* oil. [OE *hær*] — **hair'less** *adj.*

Hair may appear as a combining form or as the first element in two-word phrases; as in:

hairband	hair dye	hair restorer
hair bleach	hair dyer	hair ribbon
hair braid	hair dyeing	hair sorter
haircap	hairlock	hair straightener
hair carder	hair mattress	hair style
hair clipper	hairmonger	hair tonic
hair collecting	hairmongering	hair wash
hair collector	hair net	hair washer
hair crimper	hair oil	hair waver
hair curler	hair powder	hair-waving
hair drawer	hair remover	hairwork

hair·ball (hâr'bôl') *n.* A rounded mass of hair often found in the stomachs of animals, as cats, that groom themselves by licking.

hair·breadth (hâr'bredth', -bretth') *n.* An extremely small space or margin. — *adj.* Very narrow or close: *hairbreadth* escape. Also **hair's'-breadth'** (hârz'-), **hairs'·breadth'.**

hair·brush (hâr'brush') *n.* A brush for grooming the hair.

hair·cloth (hâr'klôth', -kloth') *n.* A stiff fabric of horsehair or camel's hair, with a cotton or linen warp, used for stiffening, upholstering, etc.

hair·cut (hâr'kut') *n.* The act of cutting the hair or the style in which it is cut.

hair·do (hâr'doō') *n. pl.* **·dos 1.** A style of dressing or arranging a woman's hair. **2.** The hair so arranged.

hair·dress·er (hâr'dres'ər) *n.* One who cuts or arranges the hair, especially women's hair; coiffeur or coiffeuse.

hair·dres·sing (hâr'dres'ing) *n.* **1.** The act of arranging or dressing the hair. **2.** A preparation used in dressing the hair.

Caption (illustration):
HAIR
(Section through the skin)
a Shaft. *b* Root. *c* Sebaceous gland. *d* Erector pili muscle. *e* Root sheath. *f* Follicle. *g* Bulb. *h* Papilla. *i* Fat cells.

haired (hârd) *adj.* Having or characterized by a (specified kind of) hair: used in combination: *gray-haired.*

hair·line (hâr'līn') *n.* **1.** The edge of the growth of hair on the head, especially in front. **2.** A very thin line. **3.** A narrow stripe in textiles. **4.** *Printing* **a** A very thin line on a type face. **b** A style of type using such lines.

hair·piece (hâr'pēs') *n.* A toupee or wig.

hair·pin (hâr'pin') *n.* A thin, U-shaped piece of metal, etc., used by women to hold the hair or a hat in place. For illustration see PIN. — *adj.* Bending in the shape of a U.

hair-rais·er (hâr'rā'zər) *n.* *Informal* Something that causes excitement or fear.

hair-rais·ing (hâr'rā'zing) *adj.* Causing fright or terror.

hair seal Any of various seals (family *Phocidae*) not valued for their fur.

hair shirt A girdle or shirt made of haircloth, worn next to the skin by religious ascetics as a penance or mortification.

hair space *Printing* The thinnest of the metal spaces for separating letters or words.

hair·split·ting (hâr'split'ing) *n.* Insistence upon minute or trivial distinctions. — *adj.* Characterized by petty or overly fine distinctions. — **hair'split'ter** *n.*

hair·spring (hâr'spring') *n.* The very fine, spiral spring that regulates the movement of the balance wheel in a watch or clock.

hair·streak (hâr'strēk') *n.* A small butterfly (family *Lycaenidae*) with narrow stripes on the underside of the wings.

hair stroke Any very fine line in printing or writing.

hair trigger A trigger so delicately adjusted that it discharges the firearm at the slightest pressure.

hair-trig·ger (hâr'trig'ər) *adj. Informal* Stimulated or set in operation by the slightest provocation.

hair·weaving (hâr'wē'ving) *n.* The act or process of sewing a toupee into the wearer's remaining hair. — **hair weaver** — **hair'weave'** *n.*

hair·worm (hâr'wûrm') *n.* Any of various nematode worms (families *Gordiidae* and *Mermithidae*) that inhabit running water and whose larvae are parasitic in insects: sometimes called *horsehair snake.*

hair·y (hâr'ē) *adj.* **hair·i·er, hair·i·est 1.** Covered with or having much hair; hirsute. **2.** Made of or resembling hair. **3.** *U.S. Slang* **a** Dangerous; menacing. **b** Superb; excellent. — **hair'i·ness** *n.*

Hai·ti (hā'tē) **1.** A Republic comprising the western portion of Hispaniola; 10,714 sq. mi.; pop. 5,000,000 (est. 1970); capital, Port-au-Prince. Officially **Republic of Haiti.** See map of CARIBBEAN. **2.** A former name for HISPANIOLA. *French* **Ha·i·ti** (à·ē·tē').

Hai·ti·an (hā'tē·ən, -shən) *adj.* Of or pertaining to Haiti, its people, or their culture. — *n.* **1.** A native or inhabitant of Haiti. **2.** A French patois spoken by the Haitians: also **Haitian Creole.** Also spelled *Haytian.*

haj (haj) *n.* See HADJ.

haj·i (haj'ē), **haj·ji** See HADJI.

hake (hāk) *n. pl.* **hake** or **hakes 1.** A marine food fish (genus *Merluccius*) related to the cod; especially, *M. smiridus* of Europe and the New England **silver hake** (*M. bilinearis*). **2.** The codling¹ (def. 2). [OE *hacod* pike < *haca* hook]

Ha·ken·kreuz (hä'kən·kroits') *n. German* Swastika, especially as the symbol of Nazism; literally, hooked cross.

ha·kim¹ (hä'kēm) *n.* In Moslem countries, a judge, ruler, or governor. [< Arabic *ḥākim* governor]

ha·kim² (hä·kēm') *n.* In Moslem countries, a physician. Also **ha·keem'.** [< Arabic *ḥakīm* wise]

Hak·luyt (hak'loōt), **Richard,** 1552?–1616, English historian and geographer.

Ha·ko·da·te (hä·kō·dä·tā) A port city on SW Hokkaido island, Japan; pop. 249,000 (est. 1968).

hal- Var. of HALO-.

Hal. *Chem.* Halogen.

Ha·la·kah (hä·lä·khä', *Hebrew* hä·lô'khô) *n. pl.* **·koth** (-khōth) The legal elements of Talmudic literature, consisting of those decrees, ordinances, usages, and customs that seek to interpret, but are not included in, the Scriptures: distinguished from *Haggadah.* Also **Ha·la·cha'.** [< Hebrew *halākhah* a rule to go by < *halākh* to walk, go] — **ha·lak·ic** (hə·lak'ik) *adj.*

ha·la·kist (hä'lə·kist, hə·lä'kist) *n.* One who frames halakic precepts from Biblical laws. Also **ha'la·chist.**

ha·la·tion (hä·lā'shən, ha-) *n. Photog.* A halolike light around brightly lit places in a photograph. [< HALO]

hal·berd (hal'bərd; *earlier* hôl'-, hô'-) *n.* A weapon used in the 15th and 16th centuries, an ax and a spear point combined, mounted on a long pole. Also **hal'bert** (-bərt). [< OF *halleberde* < MHG *helmbarte* < *helm* handle + *barte* broadax]

hal·ber·dier (hal'bər·dir') *n.* A soldier or attendant armed with a halberd.

hal·cy·on (hal'sē·ən) *n.* **1.** A legendary bird, identified with the kingfisher, supposedly able to charm the wind and sea into quiescence at the winter solstice so that it might breed in a nest on the water. **2.** Any kingfisher of the genus

Halcyon. — *adj.* **1.** Calm; peaceful. **2.** Of or pertaining to the halcyon. [< L, var. of *alcyon* < Gk. *alkyōn* kingfisher]

halcyon days **1.** The seven days before and the seven days after the winter solstice, when the halcyon was thought to breed and bring calm, peaceful weather. **2.** Any period of peace and quiet.

Hal·cy·o·ne (hal-sī′ə-nē) See ALCYONE.

Hal·dane (hôl′dān), **J(ohn) B(urdon) S(anderson)**, 1892–1964, English geneticist. — **John Scott**, 1860–1936, English scientist; father of the preceding. — **Richard Burdon**, 1856–1928, first Viscount Haldane of Cloan, English statesman; brother of John Scott.

hale¹ (hāl) *v.t.* **haled, hal·ing** **1.** To compel to go: to *hale* into court. **2.** *Archaic & Poetic* To haul; pull. [Var. of HAUL.] — **hale′er** *n.*

hale² (hāl) *adj.* **1.** Having sound and vigorous health; robust. **2.** *Scot. & Dial.* Free from defect or injury; whole. [OE *hāl.* Akin to WHOLE.] — **hale′ness** *n.*

Hale (hāl), **Edward Everett**, 1822–1909, U.S. clergyman and author. — **George Ellery**, 1868–1938, U.S. astronomer. — **Sir Matthew**, 1609–76, English jurist. — **Nathan**, 1755–76, American Revolutionary patriot; hanged as a spy by the British.

Ha·le·a·ka·la (hä′lä-ä-kä-lä′) The largest extinct volcanic crater in the world, on eastern Maui island, Hawaii; 10,032 ft. high; 19 sq. mi.; 2,000 ft. deep.

Ha·lé·vy (à-lā-vē′), **Jacques François Fromental Élie**, 1799–1862, French composer.

half (haf, häf) *n.* *pl.* **halves** (havz, hävz) **1.** Either of two equal or approximately equal parts into which a thing is or may be divided; also, a quantity equal to such a part. **2.** *U.S. Informal* A fifty-cent piece. **3.** In sports: **a** In basketball, football, etc., either of two equal periods into which a game is divided and between which play is suspended. **b** *Informal* In football, a halfback. **c** In golf, a score that is the same as an opponent's score on a hole or round. — **better half** *Informal* One's wife or husband. — *adj.* **1.** Being either of two equal, or nearly equal, parts of a thing, amount, value, etc. **2.** Not complete; imperfect; partial: *half* rhyme. — *adv.* **1.** To the extent of half or approximately half. **2.** To a considerable extent; very nearly: I was *half* inclined to go. **3.** *Informal* To any extent; at all: used with *not*: not *half* good enough. Abbr. (n. & adj.) *hf.* [OE *healf*]

Half frequently appears as the first element in hyphenated compounds, with the following meanings:

1. Exactly half; as in:

half-acre	half-dozen	half-minute	half-rod
half-barrel	half-foot	half-monthly	half-round
half-bushel	half-full	half-peck	half-second
half-century	half-gallon	half-pound	half-size
half-circle	half-inch	half-price	half-spoonful
half-day	half-liter	half-quarter	half-squadron
half-decade	half-mile	half-quire	half-weight

2. Not fully; partially; partly; as in:

half-admiring	half-buried	half-eaten	half-playful
half-admitted	half-civilized	half-educated	half-raw
half-afraid	half-clear	half-false	half-read
half-alive	half-conscious	half-frozen	half-right
half-altered	half-crazy	half-grown	half-ripe
half-angry	half-dead	half-hard	half-safe
half-ashamed	half-deserted	half-hidden	half-serious
half-asleep	half-digested	half-human	half-shut
half-awake	half-done	half-humorous	half-shy
half-begging	half-dressed	half-joking	half-spoiled
half-bent	half-drunk	half-mad	half-true
half-blind	half-earnest	half-open	half-wild

half-and-half (haf′ənd-haf′, häf′ənd-häf′) *n.* **1.** A mixture of half one thing and half another. **2.** *Brit.* A mixture of two malt liquors, especially of porter and ale. — *adj.* Half of one thing and half of another. — *adv.* In two equal parts.

half·back (haf′bak′, häf′-) *n.* **1.** In football, either of two players who along with the quarterback and fullback make up the backfield; also, the position played by this player. **2.** In other sports, as field hockey and soccer, any of several players whose position is primarily behind the forward line. Abbr. *hb, hb.*

half-baked (haf′bākt′, häf′-) *adj.* **1.** Incompletely baked; doughy. **2.** *Informal* Stupid; half-witted. **3.** *Informal* Imperfectly planned or conceived: a *half-baked* venture.

half·beak (haf′bēk′, häf′-) *n.* A marine fish (genus *Hyporhamphus*), having a flat, extended lower jaw.

half binding A style of bookbinding having leather or some other material on the spine and often on the corners, with cloth or paper on the sides; also, such a binding.

half blood **1.** The relationship between persons with one parent in common; also, a person in such a relationship. **2.** A half-breed (which see). **3.** A half-blooded animal. Also **half-blood** (haf′blud′, häf′-).

half-blood·ed (haf′blud′id, häf′-) *adj.* **1.** Related to another through only one parent. **2.** Having parents of different races. **3.** Produced by crossing an animal of known pedigree with one of different stock. Also **half′blood′.**

half boot A low boot extending somewhat above the ankle.

half-bound (haf′bound′, häf′-) *adj.* Having a half binding. Abbr. *hf.bd.*

half-breed (haf′brēd′, häf′-) *n.* One having parents of different racial stock; especially, the offspring of a white person and an American Indian. — *adj.* Hybrid; mongrel: also **half-bred** (-bred′).

half brother A brother related through only one parent.

half buck *U.S. Slang* A half dollar.

half-caste (haf′kast′, häf′käst′) *n.* **1.** A person having one Asian and one European parent; Eurasian. **2.** One having parents of different races; a half-breed. — *adj.* Of or pertaining to mixed racial stock.

half cock In a firearm, the position of the hammer when raised halfway and so locked as not to be released by a pull of the trigger.

half-cocked (haf′kokt′, häf′-) *adj.* Of firearms, having the hammer at half cock. — **to go off halfcocked** **1.** To discharge too soon, as a firearm. **2.** *U.S. Informal* To act or speak too impulsively or hastily.

half crown A British silver coin worth 2½ shillings.

half dollar A U.S. silver coin worth fifty cents, first minted in 1794.

half eagle A U.S. gold coin worth five dollars, withdrawn in 1934.

half gainer A dive in which one springs forward off the board, twists about, and plunges into the water head first with one's back toward the board.

half hatchet A hatchet whose blade is level with the top of the handle. For illustration see HATCHET.

half-heart·ed (haf′här′tid, häf′-) *adj.* Possessing or showing little interest, enthusiasm, etc. — **half′heart′ed·ly** *adv.* — **half′heart′ed·ness** *n.*

half hitch A knot made by passing the end of a rope once around the rope, then through the loop, and then drawing the end tight. For illustration see HITCH.

half hose Socks or short stockings.

half-hour (haf′our′, häf′-) *n.* **1.** A period of thirty minutes. **2.** The point thirty minutes past the beginning of an hour. — *adj.* **1.** Lasting for a half-hour. **2.** Occurring at or marking the half-hour.

half-hour·ly (haf′our′lē, häf′-) *adv.* At intervals of a half-hour; every half-hour. — *adj.* Occurring at intervals of a half-hour, or every half-hour.

half leather A half binding using leather in combination with another material.

half-length (haf′length′, häf′-) *adj.* **1.** Of half the full length. **2.** Of portraits, showing the person from the waist up. — *n.* A portrait showing only the upper half of the person.

half life *Physics* The period of time during which half the atoms of a radioactive element or isotope will undergo disintegration.

half-light (haf′līt′, häf′-) *n.* A dim light, as at dusk.

half-mast (haf′mast′, häf′mäst′) *n.* The position of a flag flown about halfway up the staff, used to show respect to the dead or as a signal of distress. — *v.t.* To put (a flag, etc.) at half-mast. Also **half-staff.**

half-moon (haf′mōōn′, häf′-) *n.* **1.** The moon when only half its disk is brightly illuminated. **2.** Something similar in shape to a half-moon or to a crescent. — *adj.* Shaped like a half-moon.

half mourning **1.** A second and less solemn period of mourning. **2.** Mourning attire of white, gray, lavender, or purple, worn during this period.

half nelson A wrestling hold in which one arm is passed under the opponent's armpit, usually from behind, and the hand pressed against the back of his neck.

half note *Music* A note having one half the time value of a whole note. Also, *esp. Brit.*, **minim.** For illustration see NOTE.

half pay **1.** Half of full salary. **2.** The reduced salary of an officer in the armed services when not in active service or when retired.

half·pen·ny (hā′pən-ē, hāp′nē) *n.* *pl.* **half·pence** (hā′pəns) or **half·pen·nies** (hā′pən-ēz, hāp′nēz). **1.** The sum of one half of a penny. **2.** A British bronze coin equivalent to such a sum. — *adj.* **1.** Costing a halfpenny. **2.** Of little value.

half pint **1.** A measure of capacity equal to one half of a pint. **2.** *U.S. Slang* A person of short stature.

half relief Mezzo-relievo (which see).

half rhyme Near rhyme (which see).

half sister A sister related through only one parent.

half-sole (haf′sōl′, häf′-) *v.t.* **soled, sol·ing** To repair (a shoe, boot, etc.) by attaching a half sole.

half sole The part of the sole of a boot or shoe extending from the shank or arch to the toe.

half sovereign A British gold coin worth ten shillings, no longer in circulation.

half-staff (haf′staf′, häf′stäf′) *n. & v.t.* Half-mast (which see).

half step **1.** *Music* A semitone. **2.** *Mil.* A step of fifteen inches at quick time; in double time, one of eighteen inches.

half tide The tide or the interval midway between high tide and low tide.

half-tim·bered (haf′tim′bərd, häf′-) *adj.* *Archit.* Having a framework of timbers, with the spaces between filled with masonry or plaster.

half title **1.** The title of a book, usually abridged, printed at the head of the first page of text or occupying a full page preceding the text. **2.** The title of any part or section of a book printed on the leaf preceding the section.

half·tone (haf′tōn′, häf′-) *n.* **1.** In photoengraving: **a** A picture whose lights and shadows are composed of minute dots obtained by photographing the original through a finely lined screen. **b** The process by which such pictures are made. **2.** In art, photography, etc., any tone or shading halfway between a highlight and a deep shadow. — *adj.* Consisting of, pertaining to, or made by a halftone.

half tone *Music* A semitone (which see).

half-track (haf′trak′, häf′-) *n.* A type of military vehicle propelled by caterpillar treads in the rear, and steered by a pair of wheels in front.

half-truth (haf′trōōth′, häf′-) *n.* A statement or assertion that is only partly true or part of the truth.

half volley In tennis, etc., a return in which the ball is struck almost immediately after it bounces off the ground.

half·way (haf′wā′, häf′-) *adv.* **1.** At or to a point in the middle; at or to half the distance. **2.** Incompletely; partially: only *halfway* prepared. — *adj.* **1.** Midway between two points. **2.** Partial; inadequate: *halfway* measures.

half-wit (haf′wit′, häf′-) *n.* A feeble-minded person.

half-wit·ted (haf′wit′id, häf′-) *adj.* **1.** Having or showing weak mentality; feeble-minded. **2.** Frivolous or silly; foolish. — **half′-wit′ted·ly** *adv.* — **half′-wit′ted·ness** *n.*

hal·i·but (hal′ə-bət, hol′-) *n. pl.* **·but** or **·buts 1.** Either of two large flatfishes (genus *Hippoglossus*) of northern seas, much esteemed as food; especially, the **Atlantic halibut** (*H. hippoglossus*), and the **Pacific halibut** (*H. stenolepis*). **2.** A related, smaller species, the **Greenland halibut** (*Reinhardtius hippoglossoides*), found chiefly in waters north of Maine. Also spelled *holibut*. [ME *halybutte*, OE *halig* holy + BUT²]

Hal·i·car·nas·sus (hal′ə-kär·nas′əs) An ancient Greek city in SW Asia Minor; site of the Mausoleum, one of the Seven Wonders of the Ancient World.

hal·ide (hal′īd, -id; hā′līd, -lid) *n. Chem.* Any compound of a halogen with an element or radical. — *adj.* Of, like, or derived from a halide; haloid. Also **hal·id** (hal′id, hā′lid).

hal·i·dom (hal′ə-dəm) *n. Archaic* **1.** Holiness. **2.** A holy relic. **3.** A sanctuary. [OE *hāligdōm* < *hālig* holy + -DOM]

Hal·i·fax (hal′ə-faks) **1.** The capital of Nova Scotia, Canada; the principal Atlantic port in Canada; pop. 121,086. **2.** A county borough in SW Yorkshire, England; pop. 93,570 (est. 1969). — **Hal·i·go·ni·an** (hal′i·gō′nē·ən) *adj. & n.*

Hal·i·fax (hal′ə-faks), **Earl of**, 1881–1959, Edward Frederick Lindley Wood, British statesman.

hal·ite (hal′īt, hā′līt) *n.* A massive or granular, white or variously colored sodium chloride: also called *rock salt.*

hal·i·to·sis (hal′ə-tō′sis) *n.* Offensive or foul-smelling breath. [< NL < L *halitus* breath + -OSIS]

hal·i·tus (hal′ə-təs) *n.* A breath or exhalation. [< L]

hall (hôl) *n.* **1.** A passage or corridor in a building. **2.** A room at the entry of a house or building; vestibule; lobby. **3.** A large building or room used for public business or entertainment: a dance *hall.* **4.** A meeting place for social, fraternal, religious, or other organizations. **5.** In a university or college, a large building used for various purposes, as for dormitories, classrooms, etc.; also, the body of students occupying such a building. **6.** In British universities: **a** A college dining room; also, the dinner served there. **b** A building where certain university students reside. **c** Formerly at Oxford or Cambridge, a minor college; also, the building housing it. **7.** The main house on the estate of a baron, squire, etc. **8.** In medieval times, the large main room of a castle or other great house, used for dining, entertaining, or sleeping. [OE *heall*]

Hall (hôl), **Charles Francis**, 1821–71, U.S. Arctic explorer. — **Charles Martin**, 1863–1914, U.S. chemist and metallurgist. — **G(ranville) Stanley**, 1844–1924, U.S. psychologist and educator.

hal·lah (khä′lə, hä′-) *n.* Bread, usually in the form of a braided loaf, traditionally eaten by Jews in celebration of the Sabbath: also spelled *chaleh, challah.* [< Hebrew, orig., a portion of dough set aside for priestly use]

Hal·lam (hal′əm), **Henry**, 1777–1859, English historian.

Hal·le (häl′ə) A city in SW East Germany; pop. 266,000 (est. 1967). Also **Hal·le-an-der-Saa·le** (häl′ə-än-dər-zä′lə).

Hal·leck (hal′ək), **Fitz-Greene**, 1790–1867, U.S. poet. — **Henry Wager**, 1815–72, Union general in the Civil War.

hal·lel (häl′el, hə·lal′) *n.* In Judaism, a song of praise, Psalms 113 to 118 inclusive. [< Hebrew *hallēl* to praise]

hal·le·lu·jah (hal′ə-lōō′yə) *interj.* Praise ye the Lord! — *n.* A musical composition whose theme is one of praise based on the word *hallelujah.* Also **hal′le·lu′iah.** [< Hebrew *hallelū* praise (imperative) + *yāh* Jehovah]

Hal·ley (hal′ē), **Edmund**, 1656–1742, English astronomer who predicted the reappearance of the comet later named for him. See COMET.

hal·liard (hal′yərd) See HALYARD.

hall·mark (hôl′märk′) *n.* **1.** An official mark stamped on gold and silver articles in England to guarantee their purity. **2.** Any mark or proof of genuineness or excellence. — *v.t.* To stamp with a hallmark. [< Goldsmiths′ *Hall*, London, where the assaying and stamping were formerly exclusively done + MARK]

hal·loo (hə-lōō′) *interj.* An exclamation or shout to attract attention, incite hounds to the chase, etc. — *n.* A cry of "halloo." — *v.i.* **1.** To shout "halloo"; cry out. — *v.t.* **2.** To incite or encourage with shouts. **3.** To shout to; hail. **4.** To shout (something). Also **hal·lo** (hə-lō′), **hal·loa** (hə-lō′): also spelled *holla, hollo, holloa, hillo, hilloa, hullo.* [< OF *halloer* to pursue noisily]

hal·low¹ (hal′ō) *v.t.* **1.** To make holy; consecrate. **2.** To look upon as holy; reverence. [OE *hālgian* < *hālig* holy]

hal·low² (hə·lō′) *interj., n. & v.t.* Halloo.

hal·lowed (hal′ōd, *in liturgical use* hal′ō·id) *adj.* **1.** Made holy; consecrated. **2.** Honored or regarded as holy. — **Syn.** See HOLY. — **hal′lowed·ness** *n.*

Hal·low·een (hal′ō-ēn′, hol′-) *n.* The evening of Oct. 31, vigil of All Saints′ Day, celebrated by children with masquerading. Also **Hal′low·e′en′.** [< (ALL)HALLOW(S) E(V)EN]

Hal·low·mas (hal′ō-məs) *n. Archaic* The feast of Allhallowmas or All Saints′ Day on Nov. 1. Also **Hal′low·mass** [< (ALL)HALLOWMAS]

Hall·statt (häl′shtät) *adj.* Pertaining to or denoting a period in central Europe extending from about the ninth to the fifth century B.C., and characterized by the use of bronze tools, the making of pottery, jewelry, etc., the introduction of iron, and the use of domesticated animals. Also **Hall·stat·ti·an** (häl-shtät′ē·ən). [after *Hallstatt*, village in central Austria, where the relics were discovered]

hall tree A clothes tree (which see).

hal·lu·ci·nate (hə-lōō′sə-nāt) *v.t.* **·nat·ed, ·nat·ing** To affect or afflict with hallucinations. [< L *hallucinatus*, pp. of *hallucinari, alucinari* to wander mentally]

hal·lu·ci·na·tion (hə-lōō′sə-nā′shən) *n.* **1.** *Psychol.* Any of numerous auditory, visual, or tactile perceptions that have no external cause or stimulus: distinguished from *illusion.* **2.** The seemingly real object of such a perception. **3.** A mistaken notion. — **Syn.** See DELUSION, DREAM.

hal·lu·ci·na·to·ry (hə-lōō′sə-nə-tôr′ē, -tō′rē) *adj.* Of, characterized by, or causing hallucination.

hal·lu·ci·no·gen (hə-lōō′sin·ə·jən) *n.* Any drug or chemical capable of inducing hallucinations.

hal·lu·ci·no·gen·ic (hə-lōō′sə-nə-jen′ik) *adj.* **1.** Causing or having to do with hallucinations or with a distortion of perception or consciousness: *hallucinogenic* drugs. **2.** Of or pertaining to hallucinogens.

hal·lu·ci·no·sis (hə-lōō′sə-nō′sis) *n. Psychiatry* A mental disorder characterized by persistent hallucinations.

hal·lux (hal′əks) *n. pl.* **hal·lu·ces** (hal′yōō-sēz) *Anat.* **1.** The first or innermost digit of the foot; the great toe. **2.** In a bird, the hind toe. [< NL < L *hallex*; infl. in form by *hallus* thumb]

hall·way (hôl′wā′) *n. U.S.* **1.** A hall or corridor. **2.** A passage or room leading into the main part of a building.

halm (hôm) See HAULM.

Hal·ma·he·ra (häl′mä·hā′rä) An island of Indonesia NE of Celebes; about 6,870 sq. mi.: also *Djailolo, Jailolo, Jilolo.* See map of INDONESIA.

ha·lo (hā′lō) *n. pl.* **·los** or **·loes 1.** In art, a disk or ring of light surrounding the head of a deity or holy person; nimbus. **2.** A splendor or glory investing a person or thing held in affection, reverence, etc. **3.** *Meteorol.* A luminous circle around the sun or moon, caused by the refraction of light passing through ice crystals floating in the atmosphere. — *v.t.* **1.** To enclose with a halo. — *v.i.* **2.** To form a halo. [< L < Gk. *halōs* circular threshing floor]

halo- *combining form* **1.** Of or relating to salt: *halophyte.* **2.** Of the sea. **3.** Related to or containing a halogen. Also, before vowels, **hal-.** [< Gk. *hals, halos* salt, the sea]

hal·o·gen (hal′ə·jən) *n. Chem.* Any of the nonmetallic elements belonging to the seventh group in the periodic table, as fluorine, chlorine, bromine, iodine, and astatine. [< Gk. *hals* sea, salt + -GEN] — **ha·log·e·nous** (hə·loj′ə·nəs) *adj.*

hal·o·ge·na·tion (hal′ə·jə·nā′shən) *n. Chem.* The introduction of a halogen into an organic compound.

hal·oid (hal′oid, hā′loid) *adj.* Of, like, or derived from a halogen. — *n.* A salt formed from a halogen and a metal.

hal·o·phyte (hal′ə·fīt) *n. Bot.* A plant that grows in saline soil, as in salt marshes. — **hal′o·phyt′ic** (-fit′ik) *adj.*

Hals (häls), **Frans**, 1580?–1666, Dutch painter.

Hal·sey (hôl′zē), **William Frederick**, 1882–1959, U.S. admiral in World War II.

Häl·sing·borg (hel′sing·bôr·y′) A port city in SW Sweden on the Öresund; pop. 76,183 (1960).

halt¹ (hôlt) *n.* A complete but temporary stop in any activity or movement. — **to call a halt** To demand that something be stopped; put a stop to. — *v.t. & v.i.* To bring or come to a halt. [< F *halte* < G *halt*, orig. imperative of *halten* to stop] — **halt′er** *n.*

halt² (hôlt) *v.i.* **1.** To be imperfect or defective in some way, as in logic, verse meter, etc. **2.** To be in doubt; waver. **3.** *Archaic* To walk with a limp; hobble. — *n. Archaic* A limp; lameness. — **the halt** Lame or crippled persons. [OE *healt* lame] — **halt'er** *n.*

hal·ter¹ (hôl'tər) *n.* **1.** A strap or rope, especially one with a headstall, by which to lead or secure a horse, cow, etc. **2.** A woman's upper garment designed to leave the arms and back bare, and held up by a band around the neck. **3.** A rope with a noose for hanging a person. **4.** Death by hanging. — *v.t.* **1.** To put a halter on; secure with a halter. **2.** To hang (someone). [OE *hælftre*]

hal·ter² (hal'tər) *n. pl.* **hal·te·res** (hal·tir'ēz) *Entomol.* One of a pair of small, knobbed appendages on each side of the thorax in dipterous insects, used to give balance in flight: also called *balancer*. [< NL < Gk. *haltēres* weights held in the hands of a jumper to give impetus]

halt·ing (hôlt'ing) *adj.* Marked by halts or hesitations: *halting* speech. — **halt'ing·ly** *adv.*

ha·lutz (khä·lōōts') *n. pl.* **ha·lu·tzim** (khä·lōō·tsēm') A pioneer Jewish farmer in Palestine or Israel: also spelled *chalutz*. [< Hebrew *hālūṣ* warrior, vanguard]

halve (hav, häv) *v.t.* **halved, halv·ing** **1.** To divide into two equal parts; share equally. **2.** To lessen by half; take away half of. **3.** In golf, to play (a match or hole) in the same number of strokes as one's opponent. [< HALF]

halves (havz, hävz) Plural of HALF. — **by halves** **1.** Imperfectly. **2.** Half-heartedly. — **to go halves** To share or divide equally.

hal·yard (hal'yərd) *n. Naut.* A rope for hoisting or lowering a sail, a yard, or a flag: also spelled *halliard, haulyard*. [< HALE¹ + YARD¹]

Ha·lys (hā'lis) The ancient name for KIZIL-IRMAK.

ham (ham) *n.* **1.** The thigh of an animal, as of the hog. **2.** The meat of a hog's thigh, smoked, salted, or otherwise prepared for food. **3.** *pl.* The back of the thigh together with the buttocks. **4.** That part of the leg behind the knee joint. **5.** *Slang* An actor who overacts or exaggerates; also, the overacting itself. **6.** *Informal* An amateur radio operator. — *v.t. & v.i.* **hammed, ham·ming** *Slang* To act in an overemotional or exaggerating manner; overact. [OE *hamm*] — **ham'my** *adj.*

Ham (ham) The second son of Noah. *Gen.* v 32, ix 24.

Ha·ma (hä'mä) A town in western Syria on the Orontes; pop. 196,225 (1968): *Old Testament* **Ha·math** (hä'mäth). Also **Ha'mah**.

Ha·ma·dan (hä'mä·dän') A city in western Iran; pop. 124,167 (1966): ancient *Ecbatana*.

ham·a·dry·ad (ham'ə·drī'əd, -ad) *n. pl.* **·ads** or **·a·des** (-ə·dēz) In mythology, a wood nymph fabled to live and die with the tree she inhabited. [< Gk. *hamadryas, -ados* < *hama* together with + *drys* oak tree]

ha·mal (hə·mäl', -môl') *n.* **1.** In Oriental countries, a porter. **2.** In India, a manservant. Also spelled *hammal*: also **ha·maul'**. [< Arabic *hammāl* < *hamala* to carry]

Ha·ma·mat·su (hä·mä·mät·sōō) A city on south central Honshu island, Japan; pop. 333,010 (1960).

ham·a·me·li·da·ceous (ham'ə·mē'lə·dā'shəs) *adj. Bot.* Pertaining or belonging to a family (*Hamamelidaceae*) of trees and shrubs of warm and temperate regions, including the witch hazel and liquidambar. [< NL < Gk. *hammamēlis* tree with pearlike fruit]

Ha·man (hā'mən) In the Bible, a Persian minister who was hanged when his plot to destroy the Jews was disclosed by Esther to King Ahasuerus (*Esth.* iii-vii).

Ham·ble·to·ni·an (ham'bəl·tō'nē·ən) *n.* **1.** One of a famous breed of American trotting horses. **2.** An annual harness race for three-year-old trotters. [after *Hambletonian,* 1849-76, American stud]

Ham·born (häm'bôrn) See DUISBURG-HAMBORN.

Ham·burg (ham'bûrg) *n.* **1.** A European variety of small, domestic fowl. **2.** A black, sweet, juicy grape of Europe. Also **Ham'burgh**. [after *Hamburg,* Germany]

Ham·burg (ham'bûrg, *Ger.* häm'bŏŏrkh) A State and city of northern West Germany, on the Elbe estuary; the chief port of Germany; 288 sq. mi.; pop. 1,832,600 (est. 1967).

ham·burg·er (ham'bûr'gər) *n.* **1.** Ground or chopped beef. **2.** Such meat fried, broiled, or baked in the form of a patty: also called *burger, Salisbury steak.* Also **hamburger steak**. **3.** A sandwich consisting of such meat placed between the halves of a round roll. Also **ham·burg** (ham'bûrg). [after *Hamburg,* Germany]

Ham·den (ham'dən) A town in southern Connecticut, near New Haven; pop. 49,357.

hame (hām) *n.* One of the two curved bars fitted to the collar of a draft horse and holding the traces of the harness. For illustration see HARNESS. [OE *hama* dress, covering]

Ha·meln (hä'meln) A city in Lower Saxony, West Germany, on the Weser; town of the Pied Piper of Hamelin; pop. 49,600 (est. 1960). Also **Ham·e·lin** (ham'ə·lin).

Ha·mil·car Bar·ca (hə·mil'kär bär'kə, ham'əl·kär), died 229? B.C., Carthaginian general; father of Hannibal.

Ham·il·ton (ham'əl·tən) **1.** The capital and chief port of Bermuda, on Bermuda island; pop. 3,000 (1966). **2.** A port

city in southern Ontario, Canada, on Lake Ontario; pop. 307,473. **3.** A burgh in northern Lanark, Scotland; pop. 41,928 (1961). **4.** A city in SW Ohio; pop. 67,865. **5.** A township in western New Jersey; pop. 79,609: also **Hamilton Square**.

Ham·il·ton (ham'əl·tən), **Alexander,** 1757-1804, American statesman born in the British West Indies; leader of the Federalists; killed by Aaron Burr. — **Lady Emma,** 1765?-1815, *née* Lyon, mistress of Lord Nelson. — **Sir William Rowan,** 1805-65, Irish mathematician and astronomer.

Ham·il·ton (ham'əl·tən), **Mount** A peak of the Coast Ranges in western California; 4,372 ft.; since 1888, site of the Lick Observatory, University of California.

Ham·il·to·ni·an (ham'əl·tō'nē·ən) *adj.* Pertaining to or resembling the political doctrines of Alexander Hamilton. — *n.* A supporter of Hamilton or his political beliefs.

Hamilton River A river in southern Labrador, flowing 600 miles, generally east, to **Hamilton Inlet,** a bay of the Atlantic.

Ham·ite (ham'īt) *n.* **1.** A descendant of Ham, one of the sons of Noah. **2.** A member of an ethnic group that includes the ancient Egyptians, inhabiting NE Africa.

Ha·mit·ic (ha·mit'ik) *adj.* **1.** Of or pertaining to Ham or the Hamites. **2.** Designating a group of languages spoken by the Hamites. — *n.* A North African subfamily of the Hamito-Semitic family of languages, including ancient Egyptian, the modern Berber dialects, etc.

Ham·i·to-Se·mit·ic (ham'ə·tō-sə·mit'ik) *n.* A large family of languages spoken in northern Africa and part of SW Asia, consisting of the subfamilies Hamitic and Semitic. — *adj.* Of the Hamito-Semitic languages or the people who speak them.

ham·let (ham'lit) *n.* **1.** A group of houses forming a small rural community; a little village. **2.** *Brit.* A village without a church of its own. [< OF *hamelet,* dim. of *hamel* < LL *hamellum* village < Gmc.]

Ham·let (ham'lit) In Shakespeare's play of this name, the hero, a Danish prince whose indecision conflicts with his efforts to avenge the murder of his father.

ham·mal (hə·mäl', -môl') See HAMAL.

Ham·mar·skjöld (häm'är·shuld), **Dag,** 1905-61, Swedish statesman; secretary general of the United Nations 1953-1961.

ham·mer (ham'ər) *n.* **1.** A tool usually consisting of a handle with a metal head set crosswise at one end, used for driving nails, pounding or flattening metal, breaking stone, etc. **2.** Any object, implement, or machine that serves the same function as or resembles such a tool. **3.** A mechanical part that operates by striking; as: **a** The part of a gunlock that strikes the primer or firing pin to detonate a firearm. **b** One of the padded levers that strike the strings of a piano to produce sound. **c** A piece that strikes a bell or gong. **4.** *Anat.* The malleus. For illustration see EAR. **5.** An auctioneer's mallet. **6.** A metal ball of specified weight attached to a flexible handle, thrown for distance in athletic contests. — **to go (or come) under the hammer** To be for sale at an auction. — *v.t.* **1.** To strike, beat, or drive with or as with a hammer. **2.** To produce or shape with or as with hammer blows: often with *out*. **3.** To join or fasten by hammering, as with nails. **4.** To force, impress, etc., by emphatic repetition: to *hammer* a lesson into their heads. — *v.i.* **5.** To strike blows with or as with a hammer. **6.** To have the sound or feeling of rapid pounding: My heart *hammers.* **7.** To work at persistently: often with *away*: to *hammer* away at a task. [OE *hamer*] — **ham'mer·er** *n.*

HAMMERS
a Bricklayer's.
b Tack (upholsterer's). *c* Machinist's straight-peen.
d Shoemaker's.
e Rawhide-faced.
f Machinist's ball-peen. *g* Riveting.
h Blacksmith's.
i Claw. *j* Tinner's.

hammer and sickle The Communist emblem, shown on the flag of the U.S.S.R., in which a crossed sickle and hammer symbolize the peasant and the worker.

hammer and tongs *Informal* With noisy vigor; energetically: to go at it *hammer and tongs.*

ham·mered work (ham'ərd) Metalwork hammered by hand, usually showing the marks of the hammer strokes.

Ham·mer·fest (häm'ər·fest) A port city in northern Norway; pop. 5,177 (est. 1959).

ham·mer·head (ham'ər·hed') *n.* **1.** A voracious shark (genus *Sphyrna*) of warm seas, having a transversely elongated head with the eyes at each end. **2.** The head of a hammer. **3.** The umbrette, a bird. **4.** A fruit-eating bat (family *Pteropidae*) of Africa.

ham·mer·less (ham'ər·lis) *adj.* Having no hammer visible, as certain firearms.

hammer lock A wrestling hold in which an opponent's arm is twisted behind his back and upward.

Ham·mer·stein (ham′ər-stīn), **Oscar**, 1847–1919, U.S. operatic manager born in Germany. — **Oscar**, 1895–1960, U.S. songwriter and librettist; grandson of the preceding.
ham·mer·toe (ham′ər-tō′) *n. Pathol.* 1. An abnormal condition of the toe in which it is bent permanently downward. 2. A toe thus deformed.
ham·mock¹ (ham′ək) *n.* A hanging bed or couch of sturdy cloth or netting, suspended from a support at each end. [< Sp. *hamaca* < native West Indian name]
ham·mock² (ham′ək) *n. Southern U.S.* A thickly wooded tract of fertile land, often elevated. [Var. of HUMMOCK]
Ham·mond (ham′ənd) A city in NW Indiana; pop. 107,790.
Ham·mu·ra·bi (hä′mŏŏ-rä′bē, ham′ə-) King of Babylonia in the first dynasty, about 2000 B.C.; promulgator of a system of laws called the **Code of Hammurabi**.
Hamp·den (ham′dən, hamp′dən), **John**, 1594–1643, English statesman; leader of parliamentary opposition to Charles I. — **Walter**, 1879–1955, U.S. actor: full name **Walter Hampden Dough·er·ty** (dok′ər-tē).
ham·per¹ (ham′pər) *v.t.* To interfere with the movements of; impede; restrain. — **Syn.** See HINDER¹. — *n. Naut.* Necessary but encumbering equipment of a ship, as the rigging. [ME *hampren*; origin uncertain]
ham·per² (ham′pər) *n.* 1. A large, usually covered basket. 2. A covered receptacle used to store soiled laundry. [< OF *hanapier* case to hold a cup or goblet < *hanap* cup < LG. Doublet of HANAPER.]
Hamp·shire (hamp′shir) *n.* A breed of large, hornless sheep.
Hamp·shire (hamp′shir) A county in southern England; 1,456 sq. mi.; pop. 1,434,700 (1976); county seat, Winchester: shortened form *Hants.*
Hamp·stead (hamp′sted, -stid) A borough of London, including **Hampstead Heath**, a public common once the resort of highwaymen; pop. 98,902 (1961).
Hamp·ton (hamp′tən) A port city in SE Virginia (pop. 120,779), on **Hampton Roads**, a channel through which the James, Nansemond, and Elizabeth rivers flow to Chesapeake Bay; scene of the Civil War engagement of the armored warships "Monitor" and "Merrimack," Mar. 9, 1862.
Hamp·ton (hamp′tən), **Wade**, 1752?–1835, American Revolutionary soldier. — **Wade**, 1818–1902, Confederate general in the Civil War; grandson of the preceding.
ham·ster (ham′stər) *n.* Any of various burrowing rodents of Europe and Asia, with large cheek pouches and short tails; especially, the **golden hamster** (*Cricetus auratus*), widely used as a laboratory animal. [< G < OHG *hamastro*]
ham·string (ham′string′) *n.* 1. One of the tendons at the back of the human knee. 2. The large sinew at the back of the hock of a quadruped. —*v.t.* **·strung**, **·string·ing** 1. To cripple or disable by or as by cutting the hamstring of. 2. To destroy the efficiency of; frustrate.
Ham·sun (häm′sŏŏn, ham′sən), **Knut**, 1859–1952, Norwegian novelist.
Ham·tramck (ham-tram′ik) A city in SE Michigan, an enclave in Detroit; pop. 27,245.
ham·u·lus (ham′yə-ləs) *n.* *pl.* **·li** (-lī) A little hook or hooklike part, as one of the barbicels of a feather. [< L]
ham·za (ham′zə) *n.* In Arabic orthography, the sign of the glottal stop, transliterated as an apostrophe.
Han (hän) A Chinese dynasty, 206 B.C.–A.D. 220, noted for the revival of culture and the introduction of Buddhism.
Han (hän) A river in east central China, flowing 800 miles SE to the Yangtze: Chinese *Han Shui*.
han·a·per (han′ə-pər) *n.* A wicker receptacle for documents or valuables. [< OF *hanapier*. Doublet of HAMPER².]
hance (hans) *n. Archit.* Haunch. [ME, aphetic var. of ENHANCE]
Han Cities (hän) See WUHAN.
Han·cock (han′kok), **John**, 1737–93, American patriot; signer of the Declaration of Independence. — **Winfield Scott**, 1824–86, Union general in the Civil War.
hand (hand) *n.* 1. In man and other primates, the end of the forearm beyond the wrist, especially adapted for grasping, and comprising the palm, fingers, and thumb. ◆ Collateral adjective: *manual.* 2. In other organisms, a part that serves a similar function; as: **a** The paw of an opossum. **b** The foot of a monkey. **c** The large claw of a lobster. **d** The foot of a hawk. 3. An action performed by the hand or as by the hand; agency: to die by one's own *hand.* 4. The use of the hand or hands as distinct from mechanical methods; manual means: to launder by *hand.* 5. A characteristic mark, or kind of work: The work shows the *hand* of a master. 6. A part or role in doing something: We all had a *hand* in it. 7. Assistance; cooperation: to give a *hand.* 8. *Usually pl.* Possession or control; supervisory care: in God's *hands.* 9. A pledge or promise, often of marriage: He won her *hand.* 10. A position or location to the side: The house is on the right *hand.* 11. One of two or more sides, aspects, or viewpoints: usually with *on:* on the one *hand;* on the other *hand.* 12. A source of knowledge, information, etc.: preceded by an ordinal number: a story at second *hand.* 13. A person, considered as producing something: a book written by several *hands.* 14. A person, considered with reference to his skill or ability: an old *hand* at checkers. 15. A manual laborer: a stage *hand;* field *hand.* 16. A member of a group, company, or crew: All *hands* cooperated. 17. Style of handwriting: a legible *hand.* 18. A person's signature. 19. Show of approval by clapping: Give her a *hand.* 20. Something that resembles a hand in function; as: **a** The sign ☞ used to call attention or show direction. **b** The pointer of a clock, gauge, etc. 21. Something that resembles a hand in appearance; as: **a** A cluster of bananas. **b** A bundle of tobacco leaves. 22. A unit of measurement four inches long, used to state the height of horses. 23. In card games: **a** The cards held by a player, or by all the players, in one round of a game. **b** The player holding such cards. **c** The complete playing of all the cards given out at one deal. *Abbr. hd.* — **at hand** 1. Near by; readily available. 2. About to occur. — **at the hand** (or **hands**) **of** By the action of; directly from. — **clean hands** Freedom from guilt; innocence. — **from hand to hand** Into the possession of one person after another. — **from hand to mouth** Using or spending immediately all of one's income, provisions, etc.; without thought for the future, or without possibility of saving or planning. — **hand and foot** 1. So as to satisfy all needs or wishes: wait on him *hand and foot.* 2. So as to be unable to move the hands and feet. — **hand in** (or **and**) **glove** In close alliance or connection. — **hand in hand** Each holding the hand of the other; in close association. — **hands down** With ease; effortlessly. — **Hands off!** A command not to touch or interfere. — **Hands up!** A command to raise the hands, intended to forestall resistance. — **in hand** 1. In one's immediate grasp or possession. 2. Under control. 3. In process of execution. — **off one's hands** Out of one's care or responsibility. — **on hand** 1. In one's possession; available for use. 2. *U.S.* Present. — **on one's hands** In one's care or responsibility. — **out of hand** 1. Unruly; uncontrollable. 2. Immediately; without delay. 3. Finished and done with. — **to hand** 1. Within reach; readily accessible. 2. In one's possession. — **to have one's hands full** To be engaged in a great or excessive amount of work. — **to keep one's hand in** To continue an activity or interest so as not to lose skill or knowledge. — **to lay hands on** 1. To seize violently; do physical harm to. 2. To bless, consecrate, ordain, etc. — **to show one's hand** To disclose one's involvement or intentions. — **to turn** (or **put**) **one's hand to** To engage in; undertake. — **to throw up one's hands** To give up; accede in despair. — **to wash one's hands of** To refuse further responsibility for; dismiss from consideration. — **upper hand** The controlling advantage. — **with a heavy hand** 1. In a clumsy manner or style. 2. In an overbearing, dictatorial manner. — **with a high hand** In an arrogant, tyrannical manner. —*v.t.* 1. To give, offer, or transmit with the hand or hands. 2. To assist or lead with the hand: He *handed* her to the car. 3. *Naut.* To roll up and make fast; furl, as a sail. — **to hand down** 1. To transmit to one's heirs, or from the members of one generation to another. 2. To deliver or announce the decision or verdict of a court. — **to hand in** To give to a person or persons in authority; submit. — **to hand it to** *Slang* To give deserved praise or recognition to. — **to hand on** To give to the next in succession. — **to hand out** To distribute or offer among individuals. — **to hand over** To give up possession of; surrender. — *adj.* Of or pertaining to the hand or hands; as: **a** Suitable for carrying in the hand. **b** Operated or controlled by hand: a hand loom. **c** Executed by hand: hand embroidery. [OE *hand*]
Hand (hand), **Learned**, 1872–1961, U.S. jurist.
hand ax *Anthropol.* A piece of hard stone crudely shaped to be held in the hand and used as an ax, characteristic of the Lower Paleolithic period. Also **hand axe.**
hand·bag (hand′bag′) *n.* 1. A woman's purse or other bag for carrying small articles. 2. A small suitcase.
hand·ball (hand′bôl′) *n.* 1. A game in which the players hit a ball against the wall of a court by striking it with their hands. 2. The small rubber ball used in this game.
hand·bar·row (hand′bar′ō) *n.* A flat framework for carrying loads, having handles at either end for the bearers.
hand·bill (hand′bil′) *n.* A printed advertisement or notice, usually distributed by hand.
hand·book (hand′bŏŏk′) *n.* 1. A small guidebook, reference book, or book of instructions; manual. *Abbr. hdbk.* 2. *U.S.* A place away from a racetrack where bets on the races are made; also, the book in which bets are recorded.
hand·breadth (hand′bredth′, -bretth′) *n.* A unit of measurement, usually 2½ to 4 inches, approximately equal to the width of the hand: also *hand's breadth.*
hand·car (hand′kär′) *n.* A small, open railroad car propelled by a hand pump or a motor.
hand·cart (hand′kärt′) *n.* A cart pushed or pulled by hand.
hand·clasp (hand′klasp′, -kläsp′) *n.* The act of clasping a person's hand, as in greeting, an introduction, etc.

hand·cuff (hand′kuf′) *n. Usually pl.* One of a pair of metal rings joined by a chain, designed to lock around the wrist or wrists; a manacle. — *v.t.* To fetter with handcuffs.

HANDCUFFS

hand·ed (han′did) *adj.* **1.** Characterized by the use of a (specified) hand, or designed for a person who uses a (specified) hand: used in combination: a *left-handed* batter; a *left-handed* golf club. **2.** Having or characterized by a (specified kind of) hand or (a specified number of) hands: used in combination: *four-handed; empty-handed.*

hand·ed·ness (han′did·nis) *n.* The tendency of an individual to prefer the use of either the right or the left hand.

Han·del (han′dəl), **George Frideric,** 1685–1759, German composer active in England and Italy: original name **Georg Friedrich Hän·del** (hen′dəl): called **George Frederick Handel.**

hand·fast (hand′fast′, -fäst′) *Archaic n.* **1.** A firm grasp or hold. **2.** A contract entered upon by clasping hands; especially, a betrothal or marriage contract. — *v.t.* **1.** To grasp with the hand. **2.** To betroth or marry by joining of hands.

hand·fast·ing (hand′fas′ting, -fäs′-) *Archaic n.* **1.** A betrothal. **2.** A form of private or unsolemnized marriage contracted by clasping hands.

hand·ful (hand′fŏŏl) *n. pl.* **·fuls 1.** As much or as many as a hand can hold at once. **2.** A small number or quantity. **3.** *Informal* Something or someone difficult to control.

hand glass 1. A small mirror with a handle. **2.** A magnifying glass designed to be held in the hand.

hand grenade A grenade designed to be thrown by hand.

hand·grip (hand′grip′) *n.* **1.** A grip or clasp of the hand, as in greeting. **2.** *pl.* Close combat; hand-to-hand struggle. **3.** A handle.

hand·gun (hand′gun′) *n.* A pistol.

hand·i·cap (han′dē·kap) *n.* **1.** A race or contest in which disadvantages are imposed on contestants of superior ability, or advantages given to those of inferior ability, so that each contestant may have an equal chance of winning. **2.** One of the conditions stipulated in such a contest; especially, a disadvantage imposed on a more able contestant. **3.** Any disadvantage that makes achievement or success difficult; especially, a physical disability. — *v.t.* **·capped, ·cap·ping 1.** To serve as a hindrance or disadvantage to. **2.** To determine or assign handicaps in a contest or race. [? < *hand in cap,* a lottery game] — **hand′i·cap·per** *n.*

hand·i·craft (han′dē·kraft′, -kräft′) *n.* **1.** Skill and expertness in working with the hands. **2.** A trade or occupation requiring such skill. **3.** *Obs.* A handicraftsman. Also *U.S.* **hand′craft′.** [OE *handcræft*]

hand·i·crafts·man (han′dē·krafts′mən, -kräfts′-) *n. pl.* **·men** (-mən) One who works at or is skilled in a handicraft.

hand·i·ly (han′də·lē) *adv.* **1.** In a handy manner; dexterously; easily. **2.** Conveniently.

hand·i·ness (han′dē·nis) *n.* **1.** Manual skill; expertness. **2.** Convenience. — **Syn.** See DEXTERITY.

hand·i·work (han′dē·wûrk′) *n.* **1.** Work done by the hands; any article or articles made by hand. **2.** The result or product of working or action. [OE *handgeweorc*]

hand·ker·chief (hang′kar·chif) *n.* A piece of cloth, usually square, used for wiping the nose or face, or worn or carried as an ornamental accessory. *Abbr. hdkf., hkf.*

hand·knit (hand′nit′) *adj.* Knitted by hand. Also **hand′-knit′ted.**

han·dle (han′dəl) *v.* **·dled; ·dling** *v.t.* **1.** To touch, hold, or move with the hand or hands. **2.** To use the hands upon or in the operation of; manipulate: to *handle* clay; to *handle* a tool. **3.** To have control over; manage; direct. **4.** To dispose of; deal with, as in the course of business: to *handle* an inquiry. **5.** To treat of or discuss: He *handles* the subject well. **6.** To act or behave toward: to *handle* someone courteously. **7.** To trade or deal in as a commodity. — *v.i.* **8.** To respond to manipulation or control: This car *handles* well. — *n.* **1.** That part of an object, tool, utensil, etc., designed to be grasped in the hand. **2.** Something that resembles or serves the same function as a handle. **3.** That which serves as an opportunity or advantage in achieving a desired end. **4.** *Informal* A title added to a person's name. — **to fly off the handle** To lose control over one's emotions; become suddenly and unreasonably angry. [OE *handlian* < *hand* hand]

han·dle·bar (han′dəl·bär′) *n. Usually pl.* **1.** The curved steering bar of a bicycle, etc. **2.** *U.S. Informal* A luxuriant mustache resembling handlebars: also **handlebar mustache.**

han·dler (hand′lər) *n.* **1.** One who handles. **2.** In sports: **a** One who trains or manages animals such as dogs or horses for contests, races, shows, etc. **b** The trainer, second, etc., of a boxer.

hand·load·ing (hand′lō′ding) *n.* The process of preparing small arms ammunition by hand; especially, loading the cartridges with powder and fitting the bullets and primers.

hand·made (hand′mād′) *adj.* Made by hand rather than by machine.

hand·maid·en (hand′mād′n) *n. Archaic* A female servant or attendant. Also **hand′maid′.**

hand-me-down (hand′mē·doun′) *n. Informal* **1.** A worn or outgrown garment that has been passed on to another person. **2.** Anything shabby or secondhand. — *adj.* Passed on to another or others; secondhand: *hand-me-down* ideas.

hand organ A large music box or similar mechanical instrument played by turning a hand crank, often carried or wheeled by street musicians: also called *barrel organ.*

hand·out (hand′out′) *n.* **1.** Any free ration of food, money, apparel, etc., as to a beggar or tramp. **2.** A prepared statement distributed as publicity or information.

hand-pick (hand′pik′) *v.t.* **1.** To gather by hand. **2.** To choose with care. **3.** To select for a particular purpose or job.

hand·rail (hand′rāl′) *n.* A railing of a convenient height for grasping in the hand, serving as support or protection at the edge of a staircase, balcony, etc.

hand·saw (hand′sô′) *n.* A saw used with one hand.

hand's breadth A handbreadth (which see).

hand·sel (hand′səl, han′-) *n.* **1.** A gift given at the start of a new year, enterprise, or situation in life as an expression of goodwill or in order to ensure good luck. **2.** A first use, example, or foretaste of something that is to come. **3.** Money given as a pledge of future payment. — *v.t.* **hand·seled** or **·selled, hand·sel·ing** or **·sel·ling 1.** To give a handsel to. **2.** To begin or launch with a ceremony; inaugurate. **3.** To do, use, or experience for the first time. Also spelled *hansel.* [OE *handselen* < *hand* hand + *selen* gift]

hand·set (hand′set′) *n.* A telephone receiver and transmitter combined in a unit that may be held in one hand.

hand·shake (hand′shāk′) *n.* The act of clasping and shaking a person's hand, as in greeting, agreement, parting, etc.

hand·some (han′səm) *adj.* **1.** Pleasing or well-proportioned in appearance, form, feature, etc.: generally implying a quality of stateliness, dignity, or masculinity: a *handsome* boy. **2.** Considerable in quantity or proportions; ample. **3.** Generous; gracious; chivalrous: a *handsome* gesture. — **Syn.** See BEAUTIFUL. [< HAND + -SOME, orig. with sense "easy to handle"] — **hand′some·ly** *adv.* — **hand′some·ness** *n.*

hand·spike (hand′spīk′) *n.* A bar used as a lever for moving heavy objects.

hand·spring (hand′spring′) *n.* An acrobatic turn in which the body is supported by one or both hands while the feet are quickly passed in an arc over the head.

hand-to-hand (han′tə·hand′) *adj.* At close quarters; in close contact: *hand-to-hand* fighting.

hand-to-mouth (han′tə·mouth′) *adj.* Consuming immediately what is obtained; improvident or impoverished.

hand·work (hand′wûrk′) *n.* Work done by hand rather than by machine.

hand·writ·ing (hand′rī′ting) *n.* **1.** Writing done by hand, as distinct from printing, typing, etc.; calligraphy. **2.** A characteristic style or form of writing: That is my *handwriting.* **3.** *Archaic* Something written by hand. — **to see the handwriting on the wall** To sense or be aware beforehand of impending misfortune, etc.

hand·y (han′dē) *adj.* **hand·i·er, hand·i·est 1.** Ready at hand; available; nearby. **2.** Skillful with the hands. **3.** Easy or convenient to use; useful: a *handy* tool.

hand·y·man (han′dē·man′) *n. pl.* **·men** (-men′) A man employed to perform, or one skillful at performing odd jobs; a jack-of-all-trades. Also **handy man.**

hang (hang) *v.* **hung** or (*esp. for defs. 3, 13*) **hanged, hang·ing** *v.t.* **1.** To fasten, attach, or support from above only; suspend. **2.** To attach by means of a hinge, etc., so as to allow the thing attached to swing, rotate, or move. **3.** To put to death on a gallows, cross, etc., especially by suspending the victim by the neck with a noose. **4.** To cause to bend downward; droop: to *hang* one's head in sorrow. **5.** To decorate or cover with things suspended or fastened: The wall was *hung* with paintings; also, to fasten (wallpaper) to a wall. **6.** To suspend (pictures, etc.) in a gallery for display; also, to display the pictures of (an artist). **7.** To fasten in position at the correct angle or in proper balance, as a scythe, etc. **8.** *U.S.* To cause (a jury, etc.) to be unable to reach a decision or verdict; deadlock. **9.** To damn: used as a mild oath. — *v.i.* **10.** To be suspended from above; dangle. **11.** To be attached so as to swing or move easily. **12.** To fall, drape, or fit: Her coat *hangs* well. **13.** To be put to death or to die by hanging. **14.** To bend or project downward or outward; droop. **15.** To keep one's hold; cling: with *on* or *onto*: to *hang* onto the railing. **16.** To be suspended without apparent support; hover; float in the air. **17.** To be imminent; threaten: with *over*: Danger *hangs* over us. **18.** To depend; be contingent: with *on* or *upon*: It all *hangs* upon his decision. **19.** To be in a state of uncertainty or indecision. **20.** To pay close attention; be solicitous: with *on* or *upon*: He *hung* on her words. — **to be hung up** *U.S. Slang* To be halted or impeded, usually temporarily. — **to hang around** (or **about**) *Informal* To loiter or linger about. — **to hang back** To be reluctant or unwilling. — **to hang in the balance** To be undecided or doubtful: His fate *hangs in the balance.* — **to hang on** To be tenacious; persist. — **to hang one on** *U.S. Slang* **1.** To get very drunk. **2.** To strike (someone) with the fist. — **to hang out 1.** To lean out, as through a window. **2.** *Slang* To spend one's time; dwell. — **to hang together 1.** To remain in close association. **2.** To be coherent or consistent. **— to hang up 1.** *Chiefly U.S.* To end a telephone conversation. **2.** To delay or suspend the progress of. *— n.* **1.** The way in which a thing hangs: the *hang* of a dress. **2.** *Informal* A bit; a rap: I don't give a *hang.* **— to get the hang of** *U.S. Informal* **1.** To acquire the knack of; master. **2.** To understand the basic idea of. [Fusion of ME *hangen* (OE *hangian* to hang down), OE *hon* to suspend, and ME *henge* to cause or condemn to hang (< ON *hengja*)]

han·gar (hang/ər) *n.* A shelter or workshop for aircraft.

hang·bird (hang/bûrd/) *n.* A bird that builds a hanging nest, as the Baltimore oriole.

Hang·chow (hang/chou/, *Chinese* häng/jō/) A port city in eastern China, capital of Chekiang province, at the head of **Hangchow Bay,** an inlet of the East China Sea; pop. 1,100,000 (est. 1970). Also **Hang/-chou/.**

hang·dog (hang/dôg/, -dog/) *adj.* Sneaky, furtive, or degraded in manner or appearance. *— n.* A low, skulking, or contemptible fellow; sneak.

hang·er (hang/ər) *n.* **1.** A device, as a loop, peg, etc., on or from which something may be hung; especially, a hooked frame of shoulder width for garments. **2.** One who hangs something. **3.** In automobiles, a hinged bracket that joins to the chassis the shackles holding the springs.

hang·er·on (hang/ər·on/, -ôn/) *n. pl.* **hang·ers-on** (hang/ərz-) A clinging or self-seeking follower; parasite.

hang·fire (hang/fīr/) *n.* A delay in the explosion of a propelling charge, igniter, or the like. Compare MISFIRE.

hang-gli·der (hang/glī/dər) *n.* A Rogallo-wing glider fitted to carry a person holding to a horizontal bar beneath.

hang·ing (hang/ing) *adj.* **1.** Suspended from something; dangling. **2.** Leaning or inclining downward; overhanging. **3.** Lying on a steep slope: a *hanging* meadow. **4.** Worthy of or involving capital punishment: a *hanging* offense; also, prone to inflict the death sentence: a *hanging* judge. **5.** Undecided: The matter was left *hanging.* **6.** Drooping; downcast: a *hanging* face. *— n.* **1.** The act of suspending, or the state of being suspended. **2.** Execution by being hanged from the neck. **3.** *Usually pl.* Something hung on a wall, window, etc., as adornment.

hanging figures *Printing* Arabic numerals used with Old Style type faces, of which the bottoms of the 3, 4, 5, 7, and 9 extend below the line and the 6 and 8 are taller than the other figures: distinguished from *lining figures*: also called *Old Style figures.*

hanging indention See under INDENTION.

hanging wall *Geol.* The layer of an inclined fault plane that overlies the footwall.

hang·man (hang/mən) *n. pl.* **·men** (-mən) A public executioner who hangs condemned persons.

hang·nail (hang/nāl/) *n.* Skin partially torn loose at the side or root of a fingernail. [Alter. of AGNAIL; infl. by HANG]

hang·out (hang/out/) *n. Slang* A habitual loitering or dwelling place of some person or group: a thieves' *hangout.*

hang·o·ver (hang/ō/vər) *n. U.S. Informal* **1.** The headache following overindulgence in alcoholic liquor. **2.** Something or someone remaining from a past era or regime.

hang·up (hang/up/) *n. Slang* An obsession.

Han Hai (hän/ hī/) A Chinese name for the GOBI.

hank (hangk) *n.* **1.** A skein of yarn or thread. **2.** A definite measure of yarn or thread. **3.** A loop or curl, as of hair. **4.** *Naut.* **a** A rope, string, coil, or tie. **b** A ring of rope or iron on the edge of a jib or staysail, used for fastening it. [ME < Scand. Cf. Icel. *hankar,* genitive of *hönk* skein, coil.]

han·ker (hang/kər) *v.i.* To yearn; have desire: with *after, for,* or an infinitive. [Cf. Flemish *hankeren* to long for]

hank·er·ing (hang/kər·ing) *n.* A yearning; craving. **— Syn** See DESIRE.

Han·kow (hang/kou/, *Chinese* häng/jō/), **Han-k'ou** See WUHAN.

han·ky-pan·ky (hang/kē-pang/kē) *n.* **1.** *Informal* Trickery; deceit. **2.** *U.S. Slang* Illicit sexual activity; adultery. [An arbitrary formation, ? < HAND]

Han·na (han/ə), **Mark,** 1837–1904, U.S. financier and politician: full name **Marcus Alonzo Hanna.**

Han·nah (han/ə) A Jewish prophetess; mother of Samuel. I *Sam.* i 2.

Han·ni·bal (han/ə·bəl), 247?–183? B.C., Carthaginian general: invaded Italy by crossing the Alps; son of Hamilcar Barca.

Ha·noi (hä·noi/) The capital of the Democratic Republic of Vietnam (North Vietnam), in the central part; pop. 414,620 (est. 1970).

Ha·no·taux (à·nō·tō/), **(Albert Auguste) Gabriel,** 1853–1944, French statesman and historian.

Han·o·ver (han/ō·vər) **1.** A former Prussian province included since 1945 in the State of Lower Saxony, West Germany. **2.** A city in West Germany; capital of Lower Saxony; 527,200 (est. 1967). *German* **Han·no·ver** (hä·nō/vər).

Han·o·ver (han/ō·vər) **1.** The name of a reigning family of Great Britain, founded by George I, who was elector of

Hanover, and ending with Victoria: also called **House of Hanover. 2.** A member of this family.

Han·o·ve·ri·an (han/ō·vir/ē·ən) *adj.* **1.** Of or pertaining to Hanover, Germany. **2.** Of or pertaining to the former ruling family of Hanover. *— n.* A supporter of the Hanovers.

Han·sard (han/sərd) *n. Brit. & Canadian* The printed record of the proceedings of Parliament. [after Luke *Hansard,* 1752–1828, its first publisher]

hanse (hans) *n.* **1.** A guild of medieval merchants. **2.** An entrance fee or other payment made to such a guild. [< OF < OHG *hansa* band]

Hanse (hans) *n.* The Hanseatic League.

Han·se·at·ic (han/sē·at/ik) *adj.* Pertaining to the Hanse towns.

Hanseatic League A medieval league of free towns in northern Germany and neighboring countries, called **Hanse towns,** that banded together for protection and trade.

han·sel (han/səl) See HANDSEL.

Han·sen's disease (han/sənz) Leprosy. [after Gerhart *Hansen,* 1841–1912, Norwegian physician]

Han Shui (hän/ shwä/) The Chinese name for the HAN.

han·som (han/səm) *n.* A low, two-wheeled, one-horse carriage, with the driver seated behind and above the cab: also **hansom cab.** [after J. A. *Hansom,* 1803–82, English inventor]

han·tle (han/təl) *n. Scot.* A good many; a good deal.

Hants (hants) Hampshire.

Ha·nuk·kah (khä/noo-kə, hä/-) *n.* A Jewish festival, lasting eight days from Kislev 25 (early December), in memory of the rededication of the temple at Jerusalem under the Maccabees in 165 B.C.: also called, among Christians, *Feast of Dedication:* also spelled *Chanukah.* Also **Ha/·nu·kah.** [< Hebrew *hanukkah* dedication]

HANSOM

han·u·man (hän/oo-mən) *n.* The entellus, a monkey. [< Hind., lit., the one with a jaw]

Han·u·man (hän/oo-mən) In Hindu mythology, a monkey god.

Han·yang (hän/yäng/) See WUHAN.

hap (hap) *Archaic n.* **1.** A casual occurrence; happening. **2.** Luck; chance. *— v.i.* **happed, hap·ping** To happen; chance. [< ON *happ*]

ha·pax le·go·me·non (hä/paks lə·gom/ə·non) *Greek* Occurring but once: said of nonce words or phrases.

hap·haz·ard (hap/haz/ərd) *adj.* Dependent upon or happening by chance; accidental; random. *— n.* Mere chance; hazard. *— adv.* By chance; at random. [< HAP + HAZARD] **— hap/haz/ard·ly** *adv.* **— hap/haz/ard·ness** *n.*

haph·ta·rah (häf/tä·rä/, -tō/rō) *n. pl.* **·roth** (-rōth/, -rōth) A selection from the Prophets read in the synagogue service after each lesson from the Pentateuch. [< Hebrew *haphtārāh* conclusion]

hap·less (hap/lis) *adj.* Having no luck; unfortunate; unlucky. **— hap/less·ly** *adv.* **— hap/less·ness** *n.*

hap·lite (hap/līt) See APLITE.

haplo- *combining form* Simple; single: also, before vowels, **hapl-.** [< Gk. *haploos* simple]

hap·loid (hap/loid) *adj. Biol.* Having only one set of unpaired chromosomes, as a germ cell, in contradistinction to the normal diploid number as found in somatic cells. Also **hap·loid/ic.** *— n.* A haploid organism or cell.

hap·lol·o·gy (hap·lol/ə·jē) *n. Gram.* The elimination of a syllable that is similar to the next syllable, as in *lab(o)ratory.*

hap·lo·sis (hap·lō/sis) *n. Biol.* The halving of the chromosome number during meiosis.

hap·ly (hap/lē) *adv. Archaic* By chance; perhaps.

hap·pen (hap/ən) *v.i.* **1.** To take place or occur; come to pass. **2.** To occur by chance rather than by design. **3.** To chance: We *happened* to hear him sing. **4.** To come by chance: with *on* or *upon.* **5.** To come or go by chance: with *in, along, by,* etc. **— to happen to 1.** To befall. **2.** To become of: What *happened to* your old friend? [< HAP]

— Syn. 1, 2. *Happen, chance, occur, befall,* and *betide* mean to take place. *Happen* may now be used in this sense without any other implication, though formerly it denoted the absence of any evident cause; to render this meaning we now say *chance. Occur* is close to *happen,* but the two are not always interchangeable. We may ask where an accident *happened* (or *occurred*), but we distinguish between "It did not *occur* to me" and "It did not *happen* to me." *Befall* and *betide* are both archaic; they differ from the other synonyms in that they may be used transitively: great fortune *befell* him, woe *betide* you.

hap·pen·ing (hap/ən·ing) *n.* **1.** Something that happens; an event. **2.** A staged but usually partly improvised event, often bizarre or spectacular, intended to engage the attention or elicit a response through shock or novelty.

hap·pen·stance (hap/ən·stans, -stəns) *n. U.S. Informal* **1.** A chance occurrence; accident. **2.** Chance: to occur by *happenstance.* [< HAPPEN + (CIRCUM)STANCE]

hap·pi·ly (hap′ə·lē) *adv.* **1.** In a happy manner; cheerfully. **2.** With good fortune; luckily. **3.** With skill; felicitously; aptly: The letter is *happily* phrased.

hap·pi·ness (hap′ē·nis) *n.* **1.** The state or quality of being pleased and content. **2.** Good fortune; prosperity; good luck. **3.** Aptness or skill; felicity, as of a remark.
—**Syn. 1.** *Happiness, felicity, gladness, bliss,* and *blessedness* denote a sustained feeling of pleasure or satisfaction. *Happiness* is a general term, often indicating little more than freedom from sadness, sorrow, etc. *Felicity* is more formal and colder, but refers to the same quality. *Gladness* is joyful, overflowing *happiness,* but falls short of *bliss,* which is ecstatic, perfected *happiness. Blessedness* is *happiness* so profound as to be attributed to divine favor. Compare PLEASURE, SATISFACTION.

hap·py (hap′ē) *adj.* **·pi·er, ·pi·est 1.** Enjoying, showing, or characterized by pleasure; joyous; contented. **2.** Attended with good fortune; lucky. **3.** Produced or uttered with skill and aptness; felicitous: a *happy* phrase. **4.** *U.S. Slang* Manifesting irrational or abnormal behavior for some (specified) reason or in some (specified) way; crazy; nutty: used in combination: *slap-happy; trigger-happy.* [< HAP]
—**Syn. 1.** glad, joyful, delighted, blissful, rapturous. Compare CHEERFUL. —**Ant.** unhappy, sad, unfortunate, inopportune.

hap·py-go-luck·y (hap′ē-gō·luk′ē) *adj.* Trusting habitually to luck; cheerful; unconcerned; easygoing.

Haps·burg (haps′bûrg, *Ger.* häps′boŏrkh) A German family prominent from about 1100, to which belonged rulers of Austria, Hungary, Bohemia, the Holy Roman Empire, and Spain; the male line ended in 1740: also spelled *Habsburg.*

Haps·burg-Lor·raine (haps′bûrg-lə·rān′, *Ger.* häps′boŏrkh· lō·rān′) The royal house of Austria, 1740–1918.

ha·ra·ki·ri (här′ə·kir′ē; hä′rä·kē′rē) *n.* Suicide by disembowelment, traditionally practiced by high-ranking Japanese when disgraced or in lieu of execution: also *hari-kari.* Also **ha′ra-ka′ri** (-kä′rē). [< Japanese *hara* belly + *kiri* cut]

ha·rangue (hə·rang′) *n.* A lengthy, loud, and vehement speech; tirade. —**Syn.** See SPEECH. —*v.* **·rangued, ·rangu· ing** *v.t.* **1.** To address in a harangue. —*v.i.* **2.** To deliver a harangue. [< F < Med.L *harenga* < OHG *hari* army, host + *hringa* ring] —**ha·rangu′er** *n.*

Ha·rar (hä′rər) A Province of east central Ethiopia; 156,000 sq. mi.; pop. about 2 million; capital, **Harar,** pop. about 40,000: formerly also *Harrar.*

har·ass (har′əs, hə·ras′) *v.t.* **1.** To trouble or pursue relentlessly with cares, annoyances, etc.; torment. **2.** *Mil.* To worry (an enemy) by raids and small attacks. [< OF *harasser* < *harer* to set dogs on, prob. < OHG *haren* to cry out] —**har′ass·er** *n.* —**har′ass·ment** *n.*

Har·bin (här′bin) The capital of Heilungkiang Province, NE China, on the Sungari; pop. 1,595,000 (est. 1958).

har·bin·ger (här′bin·jər) *n.* **1.** One who or that which goes before and announces the coming of something; herald. **2.** Formerly, a courier who rode in advance of a party to arrange for lodging. —*v.t.* To act as a harbinger to; presage; herald. [< OF *herbergeor* provider of shelter < *herberge* shelter < Gmc.]

har·bor (här′bər) *n.* **1.** A sheltered place, natural or artificial, on the coast of a sea, lake, etc., used to provide protection and anchorage for ships; port. *Abbr. h., H.* **2.** Any place of refuge or rest. —*v.t.* **1.** To give refuge to; shelter; especially, to conceal or be hospitable to harmful persons or things: to *harbor* thieves. **2.** To entertain in the mind; cherish: to *harbor* a grudge. —*v.i.* **3.** To take shelter in or as in a harbor. Also *Brit.* **har′bour.** [ME *herberwe* < OE *here* army + *beorg* refuge] —**har′bor·er** *n.* —**har′bor·less** *adj.*

har·bor·age (här′bər·ij) *n.* **1.** A port or place of anchorage for ships. **2.** Shelter; lodging; entertainment.

har·bor·mas·ter (här′bər·mas′tər, -mäs′-) *n.* An officer in charge of enforcing the regulations of a harbor.

harbor seal A hair seal (*Phoca vitulina*) common along the north Atlantic coast of the United States: also called *sea calf, sea dog.*

hard (härd) *adj.* **1.** Resisting indentation or compression; solid; firm; unyielding: opposed to *soft.* **2.** Requiring vigorous mental or physical effort to do, solve, understand, explain, etc.; difficult; arduous: a *hard* problem; a *hard* task. **3.** Difficult to manage, control, or deal with: a *hard* man at home. **4.** Energetic and steady; industrious: a *hard* worker. **5.** Showing little mercy or feeling; stern: a *hard* judge. **6.** Strict or exacting in terms: a *hard* bargain. **7.** Having force or intensity; severe; violent: a *hard* knock. **8.** Involving or inflicting sorrow, discomfort, pain, poverty, etc.: *hard* times. **9.** *U.S. Informal* Verified and specific: said of facts, information, etc. **10.** Given to shrewdness, practicality, and obstinacy: a *hard* head. **11.** Too harsh, brilliant, or penetrating to be esthetically pleasing: a *hard* light. **12.** *U.S. Informal* Menacing, cruel, or disreputable in character or appearance; tough: a *hard* face. **13.** Containing certain mineral salts that interfere with the cleansing action of soap: said of water. **14.** *U.S.* Containing much alcohol; strong: *hard* cider. **15.** *Econ.* **a** Metallic and not paper: said of money. **b** Fully backed by gold or silver and not by credit alone: said of money and currency. **c** Available only at high rates of interest: said of money or credit. **d** Having a relatively long useful life; durable: said of goods. **16.** *Agric.* High in gluten content: said of wheat. **17.** *Phonet.* **a** Denoting (c) or (g) when articulated as a stop, as in *cod* or *god,* and not as a fricative or affricate. **b** In Slavic languages, not palatalized. **18.** *Physics* Denoting radiant energy of great penetrating power, as gamma rays. *Abbr. h., H.* —**hard and fast** Fixed and unalterable. —**hard of hearing** Deaf or partially deaf. —**hard up** *Informal* **1.** Poor; broke. **2.** In need of (something): with *for.* —**to be hard on** To be severe, cruel, or damaging to. —*adv.* **1.** With great energy or force; vigorously: to work *hard.* **2.** Intently; earnestly: to look *hard* for something. **3.** With effort or difficulty: to breathe *hard.* **4.** With resistance; reluctantly: to die *hard.* **5.** Securely; tightly: to hold on *hard.* **6.** So as to become firm or solid: to freeze *hard.* **7.** In close proximity; near: with *after, by,* or *upon.* **8.** *Naut.* To the extreme limit; fully: *Hard* aport. —**to be hard put** To have great difficulty. [OE *heard*]
—**Syn.** (adj.) **1.** impenetrable, rigid. **2.** See DIFFICULT. **4.** assiduous, diligent. **5.** harsh, severe. —**Ant.** soft, penetrable, yielding, easy, lenient, mild.

hard-bit·ten (härd′bit′n) *adj.* Tough; unyielding.

hard-boiled (härd′boild′) *adj.* **1.** Boiled until cooked through: said of an egg. **2.** *Informal* Callous; tough.

hard cash Actual money; cash on hand.

hard cider Cider that has fermented.

hard coal Anthracite.

hard-core (härd′kôr′, -kōr′) *adj. U.S.* Unlikely to change; inflexible; rigid: a *hard-core* radical.

Har·de·ca·nute (här′də·kə·noŏt′, -nyoŏt′), 1019?–42, king of Denmark 1035–42; king of England 1040–42; son of Canute.

hard·en (här′dən) *v.t.* **1.** To make hard or harder; solidify. **2.** To make unyielding, pitiless, or indifferent. **3.** To strengthen or make firm in character, disposition, etc. **4.** To make tough or hardy; inure. —*v.i.* **5.** To become hard. **6.** In commerce: **a** To become higher, as prices. **b** To become stable.

Har·den (här′dən), **Sir Arthur,** 1865–1940, English biochemist.

hard·en·er (här′dən·ər) *n.* **1.** One who or that which hardens. **2.** One who hardens cutting tools. **3.** Any substance added to paint or varnish to give a resistant finish.

hard·en·ing (här′dən·ing) *n.* **1.** Any material that hardens another. **2.** The process of becoming hard or rigid.

hard-fist·ed (härd′fis′tid) *adj.* **1.** Stingy; miserly. **2.** Having hard hands, as a laborer. —**hard′-fist′ed·ness** *n.*

hard·hack (härd′hak′) *n.* The steeplebush.

hard-hand·ed (härd′han′did) *adj.* **1.** Having hard or calloused hands. **2.** Governing with severity; despotic.

hard-hat (härd′hat′) *n.* A construction worker, especially one who holds militantly conservative views. [from the protective helmets worn in construction work]

hard·head (härd′hed′) *n. pl.* **·heads** *for defs. 1, 2;* **·head** or **·heads** *for defs. 3, 4.* **1.** A shrewd and practical person. **2.** An obstinate person. **3.** The menhaden. **4.** The alewife.

hard-head·ed (härd′hed′id) *adj.* **1.** Having a shrewd and practical mind. **2.** Having a stubborn character; obstinate. —**hard′head′ed·ly** *adv.* —**hard′head′ed·ness** *n.*

hard-heart·ed (härd′här′tid) *adj.* Lacking pity; unfeeling. —**hard′heart′ed·ly** *adv.* —**hard′heart′ed·ness** *n.*

har·di·hood (här′dē·hoŏd) *n.* **1.** Resolute courage; boldness; daring. **2.** Audacity; impudence.

har·di·ly (här′də·lē) *adv.* With hardihood; boldly.

har·di·ness (här′dē·nis) *n.* **1.** The state of being hardy or strong; robustness. **2.** Hardihood; boldness.

Har·ding (här′ding), **Warren Gamaliel,** 1865–1923, 29th president of the United States 1921–23.

hard labor Compulsory physical labor imposed upon imprisoned criminals as part of their punishment.

hard landing The high-velocity landing of a space vehicle with the resultant destruction of most of its equipment.

hard·ly (härd′lē) *adv.* **1.** Scarcely; barely; only just: I *hardly* felt it. **2.** Not quite; not: That is *hardly* enough.
◆ **hardly, barely, scarcely** *Hardly, barely,* and *scarcely* are sometimes used to intensify a negative, as in *I can't hardly see him.* Such locutions are nonstandard in writing and in formal contexts, and should otherwise be avoided.

hard maple The sugar maple (which see).

hard·ness (härd′nis) *n.* **1.** The state or quality of being hard. **2.** *Mineral.* The resistance of a mineral to scratching: see MOHS SCALE. **3.** *Metall.* The resistance of a metal to cutting, abrasion, denting, etc. *Abbr. h., H.*

hard-nosed (härd′nōzd′) *adj. Slang* Hard-bitten or firmly businesslike. Also **hard-nose** (härd′nōz′).

hard·pan (härd′pan′) *n. U.S.* **1.** A layer of very hard, often claylike matter under soft soil. **2.** Solid, unbroken ground. **3.** The firm foundation of anything.

hard rubber Vulcanite.

hards (härdz) *n.pl.* The refuse or coarse part of flax or hemp: also called *hurds.* [OE *heordan*]

hard sauce Butter, sugar, and flavorings creamed together and eaten on puddings, etc.

hard sell *U.S. Informal* Loud, aggressive, and insistent selling or advertising: distinguished from *soft sell.*

hard·set (härd'set') *adj.* **1.** In a difficult situation; beset. **2.** Firmly fixed or set. **3.** Obstinate.

hard-shell (härd'shel') *adj.* **1.** Having a hard shell, as a lobster or crab before molting. **2.** *U.S. Informal* Rigidly orthodox; inflexible; hard-core.

hard-shelled clam (härd'sheld') The quahog.

hard-shelled crab A crab, especially the blue crab (*Callinectes sapidus*) of North America, before it has molted. After molting it is known as a *soft-shelled crab.*

hard·ship (härd'ship) *n.* **1.** A difficult, painful condition, as from privation, suffering, etc. **2.** An instance of this.

hard-spun (härd'spun') *adj.* Spun with a fine twist.

hard·stand (härd'stand') *n.* A paved or hard-surfaced area for the parking of aircraft or ground vehicles.

hard·tack (härd'tack') *n.* Hard, crackerlike biscuit for army and navy use: also called *pilot bread, sea biscuit, sea bread, ship biscuit.* [< HARD + TACK²]

hard·top (härd'top') *n.* An automobile with the body design of a convertible, but with a rigid top.

hard·ware (härd'wâr') *n.* **1.** Manufactured articles of metal, as utensils or tools. **2.** Weapons: military *hardware.* **3.** Mechanical, electronic, or other devices or materials, as distinguished from people, planning, operation l procedures, etc. **4.** Any of the machinery that makes up a digital computer installation: distinguished from *software.*

hard water Water containing in solution salts of calcium and magnesium, which inhibit soap lathering.

hard·wood (härd'wood') *n.* **1.** Wood from broad-leaved, deciduous trees, as oak, maple, etc., as distinguished from the wood of coniferous trees. **2.** Any hard, compact, heavy wood. **3.** A tree yielding such wood.

har·dy¹ (här'dē) *adj.* **·di·er, ·di·est** **1.** Able to endure hardship, fatigue, privation, etc.; robust; tough. **2.** Having courage and valor; bold; brave. **3.** Having audacity and daring; foolhardy; rash. **4.** Able to survive the winter outdoors: said of plants. [< OF *hardi,* pp. of *hardir* to embolden < OHG *hartjan* to make hard]

har·dy² (här'dē) *n.* *pl.* **·dies** A square-shanked chisel or fuller for insertion in a square hole (**hardy hole**) in a blacksmith's anvil. [HARD + -Y¹]

Har·dy (här'dē), **Thomas,** 1840–1928, English novelist and poet.

hare (hâr) *n.* *pl.* **hares** or **hare** **1.** Any of a genus (*Lepus*) of rodentlike mammals allied to but larger than rabbits, and having a cleft upper lip, long ears, and long hind legs adapted for leaping. ◆ Collateral adjective: *leporine.* **2.** The common American rabbit. **3.** In the game of hare and hounds, one of the players who are pursued. [OE *hara*]

Hare (hâr) *n.* The constellation Lepus.

hare and hounds A game in which some players (hounds) pursue others (hares) who trail bits of paper behind them.

hare·bell (hâr'bel') *n.* **1.** A perennial herb (*Campanula rotundifolia*) with blue, bell-shaped flowers. **2.** Any of several related plants, as the **western harebell** (*C. petiolata*) of the U.S. Also called *bluebell.*

hare·brained (hâr'brānd') *adj.* Foolish; flighty; giddy.

hare·lip (hâr'lip') *n.* A congenital fissure of the upper lip, resembling the cleft lip of a hare. — **hare'lipped'** *adj.*

har·em (hâr'əm, har'-) *n.* **1.** The apartments of a Moslem household reserved for females. **2.** The women occupying the harem. Also **ha·reem** (hä-rēm'). [< Arabic *harim* (something) forbidden, sacred < *harama* to forbid]

Har·gei·sa (här-gā'sə) A town in northern Somalia; former capital of British Somaliland; pop. about 40,000.

Har·greaves (här'grēvz), **James,** died 1778, English weaver; invented the spinning jenny.

har·i·cot (har'ə-kō) *n.* **1.** A stew of meat, especially mutton, and vegetables; ragout. **2.** The ripe seeds or green pods of the kidney bean and other string beans; also, the kidney bean. [< F; ult. origin uncertain]

ha·ri·ka·ri (har'ē-kar'ē; hä'rē-kä'rē) *n.* Hara-kiri.

hark (härk) *v.i.* **1.** To listen; harken: usually in the imperative. — *v.t.* **2.** *Archaic* To hear; listen to. — **Syn.** See LISTEN. — **to hark back** **1.** In hunting, to retrace the trail so as to find a lost scent: said of hounds. **2.** To return to some previous point; revert. — *n.* A cry used to urge on or guide hounds. [ME *herkien*]

hark·en (här'kən) *v.t.* **1.** *Archaic* To hear; listen to; heed. — *v.i.* **2.** *Poetic* To listen; give heed. Also spelled *hearken.* — **Syn.** See LISTEN. [OE *heorcnian*]

harl (härl) *n.* **1.** Filaments or fibers, especially of flax or hemp. **2.** A herl. [Prob. < MLG *herle*]

Har·lan (här'lən), **John Marshall,** 1899–1971, U.S. jurist; associate justice of the Supreme Court 1955–71.

Har·lei·an (här'lē-ən) *adj.* Of or pertaining to a collection of manuscripts and books in the British Museum, originally belonging to **Robert Harley** (här'lē), 1661–1724, and his son **Edward,** 1689–1741, earls of Oxford.

Har·lem (här'ləm) **1.** A section of northern Manhattan,

New York City, with a large, predominantly Negro population: formerly a village. **2.** Haarlem.

Harlem River A navigable tidal stream forming the NE boundary of Manhattan Island, connected with the Hudson River by a ship canal.

har·le·quin (här'lə·kwin, -kin) *n.* A buffoon. — *adj.* **1.** Parti-colored; motley, like the dress of a Harlequin. **2.** Designating eyeglasses with frames slanting upward like the eyes of a Harlequin's mask. [< MF < Ital. *arlecchino,* prob. akin to OF *Herlequin,* a devil in medieval legend]

Har·le·quin (här'lə·kwin, -kin) A pantomime character originally from old Italian comedy, the lover of Columbine, traditionally dressed in parti-colored tights, with shaved head, masked face, and bearing a wooden sword or wand.

har·le·quin·ade (här'lə·kwin·ād', -kin-) *n.* **1.** A pantomime; especially, a pantomime passage in which the Harlequin and clown play the leading parts. **2.** Fantastic antics.

harlequin bug A shiny black or blue bug (*Murgantia histrionica*) with red or yellow spots, feeding on cabbage and related plants: also called *cabbage bug, calicoback, fire bug.*

harlequin duck A northern sea duck (*Histrionicus histrionicus*) the male of which has variegated plumage.

har·le·quin·esque (här'lə·kwin·esk') *adj.* Having the style, dress, or colors of a harlequin.

harlequin snake A coral snake (which see).

Har·ley Street (här'lē) A street in the West End of London, occupied chiefly by physicians and surgeons.

Har·lin·gen (här'lin·jən) A city in extreme southern Texas; pop. 33,503.

har·lot (här'lət) *n.* **1.** An unchaste woman; whore; strumpet. **2.** *Obs.* A rogue. [< OF *herlot* fellow, rogue]

har·lot·ry (här'lət·rē) *n.* *pl.* **·ries** The trade or behavior of a harlot.

harm (härm) *n.* **1.** Injury; damage; hurt. **2.** Offense against morality; wrong; evil: What *harm* is there in that? — *v.t.* To do harm to; damage; hurt. — **Syn.** See INJURE. [OE *hearm* an insult]

har·mat·tan (här'mə·tan') *n.* *Meteorol.* A dry, sandy wind of the west coast of Africa, blowing from the interior. [< Sp. *harmatán* < native name]

harm·ful (härm'fəl) *adj.* Having power to injure or do harm: a *harmful* drug; a *harmful* influence. — **harm'ful·ly** *adv.* — **harm'ful·ness** *n.*

har·mine (här'mēn, -min) *n.* Banisterine (which see). Also **har'min** (-min). [< Gk. *harmala* wild rue + -INE²]

harm·less (härm'lis) *adj.* Inflicting no injury; not harmful; innocuous. — **harm'less·ly** *adv.* — **harm'less·ness** *n.*

har·mon·ic (här·mon'ik) *adj.* **1.** Producing, characterized by, or pertaining to harmony; consonant; harmonious. **2.** *Music* **a** Pertaining to harmony in musical sounds. **b** Pertaining to a tone whose rate of vibration is an integral multiple of a given primary tone. **3.** *Math.* Derived from or originally suggested by the numerical relations between the vibrations of the musical harmonics of a fundamental tone: *harmonic* functions. **4.** *Physics* Designating or characterized by a harmonic. — *n.* **1.** *Music* **a** A tone on a stringed instrument produced by touching a string lightly at a point. **b** A partial tone with a vibration rate that is an integral multiple of a given primary tone. **2.** *Physics* Any component of a periodic quantity that is an integral multiple of a given fundamental frequency. [< L *harmonicus* < Gk. *harmonikos* < *harmonia* harmony] — **har·mon'i·cal·ly** *adv.*

har·mon·i·ca (här·mon'i·kə) *n.* **1.** A musical instrument consisting of metal reeds fixed in slots in a small oblong frame, and played by blowing and inhaling through the slots: also called *mouth organ.* **2.** An instrument in which graduated nesting glass bowls revolve on a spindle and produce notes when their edges are touched: also spelled *armonica.* **3.** An instrument composed of glass or metal strips, struck by hammers. [< L, fem. of *harmonicus* harmonic]

har·mon·ics (här·mon'iks) *n.pl.* (construed as sing. in def. 1) **1.** The branch of acoustics dealing with musical sounds. **2.** *Music* **a** The overtones or partials of a fundamental. **b** Those notes produced on a violin, cello, etc., by lightly stopping the vibrating string at certain points.

har·mo·ni·ous (här·mō'nē·əs) *adj.* **1.** Made up of sounds, colors, or other elements that combine agreeably: a *harmonious* pattern. **2.** Manifesting agreement and concord in views, attitudes, feelings, etc.; free from dissension: a *harmonious* meeting. **3.** Pleasing to the ear; euphonious. — **har·mo'ni·ous·ly** *adv.* — **har·mo'ni·ous·ness** *n.*

har·mo·nist (här'mə·nist) *n.* **1.** One skilled in musical harmony. **2.** One who collates parallel passages in different writings, as the Gospels, in order to emphasize similarity of ideas, language, etc. — **har'mo·nis'tic** *adj.* — **har'mo·nis'ti·cal·ly** *adv.*

har·mo·ni·um (här·mō'nē·əm) *n.* A type of reed organ in which air is compressed in the bellows, then driven out through the reeds; melodeon. [< F < L *harmonia*]

har·mo·nize (här'mə·nīz) *v.t.* & *v.i.* **·nized, ·niz·ing** **1.** To make or become harmonious, suitable, or agreeable. **2.** To arrange or sing in musical harmony. **3.** To show the harmony or agreement of, as the Gospels. Also *Brit.* **har′mo·nise.** — **har′mo·ni·za′tion** *n.* — **har′mo·niz′er** *n.*

har·mo·ny (här′mə·nē) *n. pl.* **·nies 1.** Accord or agreement in feeling, manner, action, etc.: to live in *harmony*. **2.** A state of order, agreement, or esthetically pleasing relationships among the elements of a whole: the *harmony* of color in a painting. **3.** Pleasing sounds; music. **4.** *Music* **a** A simultaneous combination of tones or a group of melodic tones that suggest a simultaneous combination. **b** Musical structure in terms of the relations between successive harmonies. **c** The science or study of this structure. **5.** A scholarly work displaying the similarities, etc., of different books or passages: a *harmony* of the Gospels. [< OF *armonie* < L *harmonia* < Gk. *harmos* joint < *harmozein* to join] — **Syn. 1, 2.** *Harmony, concord, accord, consonance,* and *congruity* characterize unity among persons or things. *Harmony* and *concord* among persons is more than the absence of dissension; these words imply some mutual regard, goodwill, or cooperation: *harmony* reigned at the meeting, a *concord* of opinion. *Accord* is more often applied to things and may indicate mere similarity or consistency: a verdict in *accord* with the evidence. *Consonance* is the *accord* of things that are especially fit to be put together. *Congruity* is applied only to things, and implies a correspondence in form, style, etc.: the *congruity* of the Ionic capital with the fluted column. — **Ant.** discord, incongruity, inconsistency.

Harms·worth (härmz′wûrth) **Alfred Charles William** See NORTHCLIFFE.

har·ness (här′nis) *n.* **1.** The combination of traces, straps, etc., forming the gear of a draft animal and used to attach it to a wheeled vehicle or plow. **2.** Any similar arrangement of straps, cords, etc.; especially, one used for attaching something, as a parachute, to the body, or for raising a load. **3.** A device on a loom that alternately raises and lowers the warp threads. **4.** *Archaic* The armor of a knight, soldier, or horse. — **Syn.** See CAPARISON. — **in harness** Working at one's routine job. — *v.t.* **1.** To put harness on (a horse, etc.). **2.** To make use of the power or potential of: to *harness* a waterfall. **3.** *Archaic* To dress in or equip with armor. [< OF *harneis*; ult. origin unknown] — **har′ness·er** *n.*

HARNESS NOMENCLATURE
A Single harness. *B* Double harness.
a Runner. *b* Blinder. *c* Throatlatch. *d* Browband or front piece. *e* Bit. *f* Curb bit. *g* Nose piece. *h* Crown piece. *i* Curb chain. *k* Checkrein. *l* Breech stay. *m* Hame. *n* Collar showing afterwale. *o* Terrets. *p* Saddle. *q* Pole chain. *r* Bellyband strap. *s* Breeching strap. *t* Hipstrap. *u* Backstrap. *v* Crupper. *w* Breeching. *x* Traces. *y* Whiffletree or swingletree. *z* Martingale.

har·nessed antelope (här′nist) Any of several African antelopes with harnesslike markings; especially, the bushbuck.
harness hitch A type of knot that forms a loop having no free ends.
harness race A race for pacers or trotters harnessed to sulkies.
Har·ney Peak (här′nē) A mountain in the Black Hills, SW South Dakota; the highest point in the State; 7,242 ft.
Har·old I (har′əld), died 1040, king of England 1035–40: called **Harold Harefoot.**
Harold II, 1022?–66, king of England 1066; killed at the Battle of Hastings.
harp (härp) *n.* **1.** A stringed musical instrument that in its present form is upright and triangular in shape, and is played by plucking with the fingers and sometimes has foot pedals that change the pitch of the strings. **2.** A harplike object or device. **3.** *U.S. Slang* An Irishman: an offensive term. — *v.i.* **1.** To play on a harp. — *v.t.* **2.** *Rare* To utter; express. — **to harp on** (or **upon**) To talk or write about persistently and vexatiously. [OE *hearpe*] — **harp′er** *n.*
Harp (härp) *n.* The constellation Lyra.
Har·pers Ferry (här′pərz) A town in NE West Virginia; scene of John Brown's raid and arrest (1859); pop. 423.
harp·ings (här′pingz) *n.pl. Naut.* **1.** Strong wooden planks surrounding the bow of a ship. **2.** Extensions of the ribbands. Also **harp′ins.** [Prob. < F *harper* to grip]
harp·ist (här′pist) *n.* One who plays the harp.
har·poon (här·po͞on′) *n.* A barbed missile weapon, carrying a long cord, for striking whales or large fish. — *v.t.* To strike, take, or kill with or as with a harpoon. [< F *harpon* grappling iron < *harper* to grip < *harpe* claw] — **har·poon′er,** **har′poon·eer′** (-ir′) *n.*
harpoon gun A gun that fires a harpoon, used in whaling.
harp·si·chord (härp′sə·kôrd) *n.* A keyboard instrument

widely used from the 16th to the 18th century and revived in the 20th, similar in appearance to a grand piano, but having the strings plucked by quills or leather points instead of struck. [< MF *harpechorde* < Ital. *arpicordo* < LL *harpa* harp + L *chorda* string < Gk. *chordē*]
har·py (här′pē) *n. pl.* **·pies 1.** A rapacious, predatory person, especially a woman. **2.** A large, crested, voracious tropical American eagle (*Thrasaetus harpyia*): also **harpy eagle.** [< HARPY]
Har·py (här′pē) *n. pl.* **·pies** In Greek mythology, one of several filthy, winged monsters with the head of a woman and the tail, legs, and talons of a bird, who fouled or seized the food of their victims, carried off the souls of the dead, etc. [< F *Harpie* < L *Harpyia* < Gk. < *harpazein* to seize]
har·que·bus (här′kwə·bəs) *n.* An early portable firearm, in its later form having a matchlock and fired from a forked rest: also *arquebus,* *hackbut, hagbut.* Also **har′que·buse, har′que·buss.** [< F *harquebuse* < MLG *hakebusse* hooked gun]

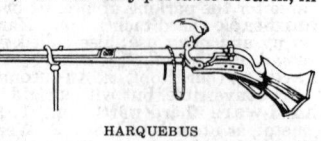

HARQUEBUS

Har·rar (ha′rər) See HARAR.
har·ri·dan (har′ə·dən) *n.* A hateful old woman; vicious hag. [< OF *haridelle* jade]
har·ri·er¹ (har′ē·ər) *n.* **1.** One who or that which harries. **2.** Any of several hawks of the genus *Circus,* especially the marsh hawk. [< HARRY + -ER¹]
har·ri·er² (har′ē·ər) *n.* **1.** A small hound used for hunting hares. **2.** *Brit. Usually pl.* A pack of such hounds and the persons engaged in the hunt. **3.** A cross-country runner. [< HARE + -IER]
Har·ri·man (har′i·mən), **Edward Henry,** 1848–1909, U.S. financier and railroad magnate. — (**William**) **Averell,** born 1891, U.S. diplomat and politician; son of the preceding.
Har·ris (har′is) See LEWIS WITH HARRIS.
Har·ris (har′is), **Joel Chandler,** 1848–1908, U.S. writer. — **Roy,** born 1898, U.S. composer.
Har·ris·burg (har′is·bûrg) The capital of Pennsylvania, in the south central part on the Susquehanna River; pop. 68,061.
Har·ri·son (har′ə·sən) A family prominent in American political history, notably **Benjamin,** 1726?–91, Revolutionary statesman; signer of the Declaration of Independence, and his son, **William Henry,** 1773–1841, military commander; ninth president of the United States for a month in 1841; **Benjamin,** 1833–1901, grandson of William Henry; 23rd president of the United States 1889–93.
Har·ro·vi·an (ha·rō′vē·ən, hə-) *adj.* Of or pertaining to **Harrow,** a boys' public school at Harrow-on-the-Hill, England. — *n.* A student at or alumnus of Harrow.
har·row (har′ō) *n.* A farm implement set with spikes or disks, for leveling plowed ground, breaking clods, etc. For illustration see DISK HARROW. — *v.t.* **1.** To draw a harrow over (a field, etc.). **2.** To disturb the mind or feelings of painfully; distress. — *v.i.* **3.** To undergo harrowing. [ME *harwe,* prob. < Scand. Cf. ON *herfi.*] — **har′row·er** *n.*
har·row·ing (har′ō·ing) *adj.* Lacerating or tormenting to the feelings. — **har′row·ing·ly** *adv.*
Har·row-on-the-Hill (har′ō·on·tha·hil′) An urban district in SE England, near London; site of a famous boys' public school· pop. 208,963 (1961). Also **Har′row.**
har·ry (har′ē) *v.* **·ried, ·ry·ing** *v.t.* **1.** To lay waste, as in war or invasion; pillage; sack. **2.** To harass in any way. — *v.i.* **3.** To make raids. [OE *hergian* to ravage]
harsh (härsh) *adj.* **1.** Grating, rough, or unpleasant to any of the senses: a *harsh* tone; a *harsh* light. **2.** Unpleasing to the mind or the artistic sense; ungraceful; crude. **3.** Manifesting severity and rigor; cruel; unfeeling: a *harsh* punishment. [ME *harsk,* prob. < Scand. Cf. Sw. *härsk,* Dan. *harsk* rancid.] — **harsh′ly** *adv.* — **harsh′ness** *n.*
hars·let (härs′lit) See HASLET.
hart (härt) *n.* The male of the red deer, especially after it has passed its fifth year. [OE *heort*]
Hart (härt), **Moss,** 1904–61; U.S. playwright and author.
har·tal (här·täl′) *n.* In India, a suspension of business as a form of mourning or of passive political resistance. [< Hind. *hartāl* < *hat* shop + *tālā* lock]
Harte (härt), **Bret,** 1836–1902, U.S. novelist and short-story writer: original name **Francis Brett Harte.**
harte·beest (här′bēst, härt·ə-) *n.* A large, grayish brown antelope (genus *Alcelaphus*) of Africa. Also **hart′beest.** [< Afrikaans < Du. *hert* hart + *beest* beast]
Hart·ford (härt′fərd) The capital of Connecticut, in the central part on the Connecticut River; pop. 158,017.
harts·horn (härts′hôrn) *n.* **1.** The antler of a hart, formerly a source of ammonia. **2.** Ammonium carbonate or a preparation made from it; sal volatile.
hart's-tongue (härts′tung′) *n.* A fern (*Phyllitis scolopendrium*) having long, narrow fronds. Also **hart′stongue′.**
har·um-scar·um (hâr′əm·skâr′əm) *adj.* Reckless and wild; harebrained; irresponsible. — *adv.* In a wild, unre-

strained manner. — *n.* 1. A reckless person. 2. Wild and heedless behavior. [prob. < obs. *hare* to frighten + SCARE]

Ha·run al-Ra·shid (hä·rōōn′ äl′ rä·shēd′), 763?–809, caliph of Baghdad; hero of the *Arabian Nights.*

ha·rus·pex (hə·rus′peks, har′əs·peks) *n.* *pl.* **ha·rus·pi·ces** (hə·rus′pə·sēz) A soothsayer of ancient Etruria or Rome who interpreted the will of the gods from inspection of the entrails of sacrificed animals: also spelled *aruspex.* [< L] — **ha·rus′pi·cal** (-pi·kəl) *adj.* — **ha·rus·pi·cy** (hə·rus′pə·sē) *n.*

Har·vard (här′vərd), **John**, 1607–38, English clergyman in America; endowed Harvard College.

har·vest (här′vist) *n.* 1. The act of gathering or collecting a ripened crop of grain, fruit, vegetables, etc. 2. The yield of such a crop; also, the crop itself. 3. The time of year when such crops are gathered. 4. The consequences or products of any effort, action, or event. — *v.t.* & *v.i.* 1. To gather (a crop). 2. To gather the crop of (a field, hive, etc.). 3. To reap or suffer (consequences, etc.). [OE *hærfest* autumn, harvest]

har·vest·er (här′vis·ter) *n.* 1. One who harvests. 2. A reaping machine.

harvest fly A large cicada (*Tibicen linnei*) of North America, that in late summer is noted for its shrill, noisy cry.

harvest home 1. An old English festival held as the last load of harvest is brought home. 2. A song sung at such festivals. 3. The season when harvesting ends.

har·vest·man (här′vist·mən) *n.* *pl.* **·men** (-mən) 1. One who labors in the harvest. 2. A daddy-longlegs (def. 1).

harvest moon The full moon that occurs near the autumnal equinox.

harvest tick A mite (genus *Trombicula*), mostly red, that attaches itself to the skin and is especially abundant about harvest time. Also **harvest bug.**

Har·vey (här′vē), **William**, 1578–1657, English physician; discovered the circulation of the blood.

Har·vey (här′vi) A city in NE Illinois; pop. 34,636.

Har·wich (har′ij, -ich) A municipal borough and port in NE Essex, England; pop. 13,569 (1961).

Harz Mountains (härts) A mountain range in central Germany between the Elbe and the Leine; highest peak, Brocken, 3,747 ft. Also **Hartz.**

has (haz) Present indicative, third person singular, of HAVE.

Ha·sa (hä′sə, has′ə) See EL HASA.

has-been (haz′bin) *n.* *Informal* One who or that which is no longer popular or effective.

Has·dru·bal (haz′drōō·bəl, haz·drōō′bəl), died 207 B.C., Carthaginian general; brother of Hannibal.

ha·sen·pfef·fer (hä′sən·fef′ər) *n.* A highly-seasoned dish made of marinated rabbit, braised and simmered. [< G < *hase* rabbit, hare + *pfeffer* pepper]

hash¹ (hash) *n.* 1. A dish of chopped meat and potatoes or other vegetables, usually sautéed, then baked or browned. 2. A mess; jumble; mishmash. 3. A new presentation of old material; reworking. — **to make a hash of** *Informal* 1. To bungle; spoil; mess up. 2. To destroy or overcome (an argument, adversary, etc.). — **to settle** (or **fix**) **one's hash** *Informal* To deal with punitively; to subdue. — *v.t.* 1. To cut or chop into small pieces; mince. 2. *U.S. Informal* To discuss at length and in detail: often with *over:* They *hashed* the plan over. 3. *U.S. Informal* To make a mess of things; bungle. [< OF *hacher* to chop. See HATCH³.]

hash² (hash) *n.* *Slang* Hashish.

hash house *U.S. Slang* A cheap restaurant.

hash·ish (hash′ēsh, -ish) *n.* 1. The tops and sprouts of hemp, used as a narcotic and intoxicant. 2. An intoxicating preparation of this plant. Also called *bhang, cannabis.* Also **hash′eesh.** [< Arabic *hashish* hemp]

hash mark *Mil. Slang* A service stripe.

hash slinger *U.S. Slang* A waiter or waitress in a cheap restaurant.

Has·i·dim (has′i·dim, *Hebrew* khä·sē′dim) See CHASSIDIM.

has·let (has′lit, hāz′-) *n.* The heart, liver, etc., of a hog or other animal, used as food: also spelled *harslet.* [< OF *haslet* broiled meat < *haste* spit < L *hasta* spear]

has·n't (haz′ənt) Has not.

hasp (hasp, häsp) *n.* A hinged fastening for a door, lid, etc., especially one that passes over a staple and is secured by a padlock or other device. — *v.t.* To shut or fasten with or as with a hasp. [OE *hæpse*]

HASP

Has·sam (has′əm), **Childe**, 1859–1935, U.S. painter.

has·sle (has′əl) *n.* *U.S. Slang* An argument; squabble; fight. Also **has′sel.** [? < HAGGLE + TUSSLE]

has·sock (has′ək) *n.* 1. An upholstered stool or cushion, used for kneeling or as a footstool. 2. A rank tuft of coarse or boggy grass. [OE *hassuc* coarse grass, ? < Celtic]

hast (hast) *Archaic* or *poetic* second person singular, present tense, of HAVE: used with *thou.*

has·tate (has′tāt) *adj. Bot.* Triangular or spear-shaped, with the base diverging on each side into an acute lobe: said of leaves. [< L *hasta* spear]

haste (hāst) *n.* 1. Swiftness of movement or action; rapidity; speediness; celerity. 2. Undue or reckless hurry; precipitancy: *Haste* makes waste. 3. The urge or necessity to act quickly; urgency. — **to make haste** To hurry. — *v.t.* & *v.i.* **hast·ed, hast·ing** *Poetic* To hasten. [< OF < Gmc.]

has·ten (hā′sən) *v.i.* 1. To move or act with speed; be quick; hurry. — *v.t.* 2. To cause to hurry or move quickly; expedite. — **Syn.** See QUICKEN. — **has′ten·er** *n.*

Has·tings (hās′tingz) A county borough on the coast of East Sussex, England; scene of Battle of Hastings, 1066, fought at Senlac Hill, where William of Normandy defeated Harold II of England; pop. 74,600 (1976).

Has·tings (hās′tingz), **Warren**, 1732–1818, British statesman; first governor general of India 1774–84.

hast·y (hās′tē) *adj.* **hast·i·er, hast·i·est** 1. Characterized by swiftness; speedy; quick; rapid. 2. Acting or made with excessive or reckless speed; precipitate; rash. 3. Manifesting impatience or anger: *hasty* words. 4. Easily excited to anger: a *hasty* temper. — **hast′i·ly** *adv.* — **hast′i·ness** *n.*

hasty pudding 1. A dish made of meal, seasoning, and boiling water or milk. 2. *U.S.* A mush made with cornmeal.

hat (hat) *n.* 1. A covering for the head, especially one with a crown and brim. 2. A cardinal's hat; also, the rank and dignity of a cardinal. — **to pass the hat** To solicit and collect contributions of money, as at a meeting. — **to talk through one's hat** *Informal* To talk nonsense; also, to bluff. — **to throw** (**toss**, etc.) **one's hat into the ring** To enter a contest or competition, especially a contest for political office. — **under one's hat** *U.S. Informal* Secret; private: Keep it *under your hat.* — *v.t.* **hat·ted, hat·ting** To provide or cover with a hat. [OE *hæt.* Akin to HOOD.]

Hat may appear as a combining form or as the first element in two-word phrases; as in:

hat brim	hatless	hat peg	hat-shaped
hat brush	hatmaker	hatpin	hat shop
hatful	hatmaking	hatrack	hat-wearing

hat·a·ble (hā′tə·bəl) *adj.* Deserving to be hated. Also **hate′·a·ble.**

hat·band (hat′band′) *n.* 1. A ribbon or band of cloth around a hat just above the brim. 2. Such a band in black, worn as a sign of mourning.

hat·box (hat′boks′) *n.* A box or piece of luggage for holding a hat or hats.

hatch¹ (hach) *n.* 1. An opening in a floor, deck, etc., giving access to spaces beneath; especially, such an opening in the deck of a ship: also called *hatchway.* 2. A cover or grating over such an opening: also **hatch cover.** 3. A door or gate with an opening above; also, the lower half of a door that is divided into two independently swinging parts. 4. A floodgate (def. 1). — **Down the hatch!** *U.S. Slang* Drink up!: a popular toast. [OE *hæcc* grating]

hatch² (hach) *v.t.* 1. To bring forth (young) from the egg by incubation. 2. To bring forth young from (the egg). 3. To devise, as a plan or plot. — *v.i.* 4. To emerge from the egg. — *n.* 1. The act of hatching. 2. The brood hatched at one time. 3. The result or outcome of any plan. — **Syn.** See FLOCK. [ME *hacchen*] — **hatch′er** *n.*

hatch³ (hach) *v.t.* To mark with close parallel or crossed lines in order to produce shading effects, etc. — *n.* Any of these lines. [< OF *hacher* to chop < *hache* an ax < Gmc.]

hatch·el (hach′əl) *n.* An implement for cleaning flax or hemp, consisting of a set of teeth fastened in a board: also *hackle, heckle.* — *v.t.* **hatch·eled** or **·elled, hatch·el·ing** or **·el·ling** 1. To comb or clean with a hatchel, as flax or hemp: also *hackle.* 2. *Rare* To irritate; heckle. [ME *hechele.* Related to HOOK] — **hatch′el·er** or **hatch′el·ler** *n.*

hatch·er·y (hach′ər·ē) *n.* *pl.* **·er·ies** A place for hatching eggs, especially those of poultry or fish.

hatch·et (hach′it) *n.* 1. A small, short-handled ax, for use with one hand. 2. A tomahawk. — **to bury the hatchet.** To cease from hostilities; make peace. — **to dig** (or **take**) **up the hatchet** To begin hostilities; declare war. [< F *hachette*, dim. of *hache* an ax < Gmc.]

hatchet face A thin, sharp-featured face. — **hatch′et-faced′** *adj.*

hatch·ing (hach′ing) *n.* 1. In drawing and engraving, close parallel or crossed lines, used to give shading effects, etc. 2. The use or the making of such lines.

hatch·ment (hach′mənt) *n. Heraldry* A square tablet set diagonally, displaying the arms of a deceased person outside his house or over his tomb. [Alter. of ACHIEVEMENT]

hatch·way (hach′wā′) *n.* Hatch¹ (def. 1).

hate (hāt) *v.* **hat·ed, hat·ing** *v.t.* 1. To regard with extreme aversion; have great dislike for; detest. 2. To be unwilling; dislike: I *hate* doing that. — *v.i.* 3. To feel hatred. — *n.* 1. An extreme feeling of dislike or animosity; hatred. 2. A person or thing detested. [OE *hatian*] — **hat′er** *n.*

HATCHETS
a Broad.
b Lathing.
c Half.
d Claw.

—Syn. (verb) **1.** *Hate, detest, loathe, abhor,* and *abominate* all refer to violent or extreme dislike. *Hate* frequently refers to a deep, personal feeling actuated by enmity or malice; Iago *hated* Othello. *Detest* is not as strong as *hate,* and suggests a violent antipathy, such as may arise between two persons of dissimilar tastes and interests. *Loathe* and *abhor* both suggest aversion or disgust; *loathe* pictures that which causes a nauseating repugnance, and *abhor,* that from which we turn or shrink away: to *loathe* weak coffee, to *abhor* quarreling. *Abominate* is used of things *hated* for moral reasons, and often indicates a righteous indignation: to *abominate* treachery and deceit. Compare DESPISE. **—Ant.** love.

hate·ful (hāt′fəl) *adj.* **1.** Arousing or worthy of hatred; detestable; loathsome; odious. **2.** *Rare* Feeling or manifesting hatred. **— hate′ful·ly** *adv.* **— hate′ful·ness** *n.*

hath (hath)   Archaic or poetic third person singular, present tense, of HAVE.

Hath·a·way (hath′ə-wā), **Anne,** 1556?–1623, wife of William Shakespeare.

Ha·thor (hä′thôr)   The Egyptian goddess of love and joy, often represented as having a cow's head or ears.

Ha·thor·ic (hə-thôr′ik, -thor′-) *adj.* **1.** *Archit.* Denoting columns with capitals representing the head of Hathor. **2.** Of or pertaining to Hathor.

hat·pin (hat′pin′) *n.* A long pin used to secure a woman's hat to her hair. For illustration see PIN.

ha·tred (hā′trid) *n.* Intense dislike or aversion; animosity; enmity.   [ME < *hate* + *-red* < OE *-ræden* state]
—Syn. detestation, loathing, abhorrence, abomination. Compare HATE, ENMITY, ANTIPATHY. **—Ant.** love.

Hat·shep·sut (ha-chep′sŏŏt)   Queen of Egypt 1501?–1481? B.C.

hat·ter (hat′ər) *n.* One who makes or deals in hats.

Hat·ter·as (hat′ər-əs), **Cape** A promontory on SE **Hatteras Island,** a narrow barrier beach between the Atlantic and Pamlico Sound off the eastern coast of North Carolina.

hat·te·ri·a (ha-tir′ē-ə) *n.* The sphenodon, a reptile.   [Origin uncertain]

Hat·ties·burg (hat′iz-bûrg)   A city in SE Mississippi; pop. 38,277.

hat tree   A frame with hooks or pegs on which to hang hats, coats, etc.

hau·ber·geon (hô′bər-jən)   See HABERGEON.

hau·berk (hô′bûrk) *n.* A long coat of chain mail.   [< OF *hauberc* < OHG *halsberc* protector for the neck]

haugh (häkh, häf) *n. Scot.* Low, flat land beside a river.

haugh·ty (hô′tē) *adj.* **·ti·er, ·ti·est** Exhibiting great satisfaction with oneself and disdain for others; arrogant; supercilious. **— Syn.** See ARROGANT.   [< OF *haut* high] **— haugh′ti·ly** *adv.* **— haugh′ti·ness** *n.*

haul (hôl) *v.t.* **1.** To pull or draw strongly; drag; tug. **2.** To transport or carry, as in a truck, car, etc. **3.** *Naut.* To change the course of (a ship), especially so as to sail closer to the wind. **— v.i. 4.** To pull or drag; tug. **5.** To change direction: said of the wind. **6.** To change one's views or course of action. **7.** *Naut.* To change course; especially, to steer nearer the wind. **— to haul off 1.** To draw back the arm so as to punch. **2.** *Naut.* To change course away from some object. **— to haul up 1.** To compel to go: I was *hauled up* before the court. **2.** To come to a stop. **3.** *Naut.* To sail nearer the wind. **— n. 1.** A strong pull; tug. **2.** That which is caught, won, taken, etc., at one time: a good *haul* of fish. **3.** The distance over which something is hauled. **4.** That which is hauled.   [< OF *haler* < Gmc.]

haul·age (hô′lij) *n.* **1.** The act or operation of hauling. **2.** A charge for hauling, as by a railroad. **3.** Force expended in hauling.

haul·er (hô′lər) *n.* One who or that which hauls. Also *Brit.* **haul·ier** (hô′lyər).

haulm (hôm) *n.* **1.** The stalks or stems of peas, beans, potatoes, etc., used for thatching or litter. **2.** Any plant stem. Also spelled *halm.*   [OE *healm*] **— haulm′y** *adj.*

haul·yard (hôl′yərd)   See HALYARD.

haunch (hônch, hänch) *n.* **1.** In man and animals, the part of the body comprising the upper thigh, including the hip and buttock. **2.** The third leg and loin of an animal, considered as meat. **3.** *Archit.* That part of an arch lying between the impost and the apex: also called *hance.*   [< OF *hanche* < Gmc.] **— haunched** *adj.*

haunch bone   The innominate bone (which see).

haunt (hônt, hänt; *for n. def. 2, also* hant) *v.t.* **1.** To visit or resort to (a person or place) repeatedly; especially, to do so supernaturally, as a ghost or spirit. **2.** To recur persistently to the mind or memory of: The tune *haunts* me. **3.** To linger about; pervade. **— v.i. 1.** To appear or recur often, especially as a ghost. **— n. 1.** A place often visited; resort; den; hangout; also, the habitat or feeding place of animals. **2.** *Dial.* A ghost.   [< OF *hanter*]

haunt·ed (hôn′tid, hän′-) *adj.* Often visited by ghosts or spirits: a *haunted* castle.

haunt·ing (hôn′ting, hän′-) *adj.* Persistently recurring to the mind; difficult to forget: a *haunting* tune. **— haunt′ing·ly** *adv*

Haupt·mann (houpt′män), **Gerhart,** 1862–1946, German poet and dramatist.

Hau·sa (hou′sə) *n. pl.* **Hau·sa 1.** One of a Negroid people

of Nigeria and Sudan. **2.** The language of these people, much used as a medium of commerce. Also **Haus′sa.**

hau·sen (hô′zən, *Ger.* hou′zən) *n.* The Russian sturgeon (genus *Acipenser*).   [< G]

Haus·frau (hous′frou′) *n. German* A housewife.

Haus·ho·fer (hous′hō′fər), **Karl,** 1869–1946, German geographer; exponent of geopolitics.

Hauss·mann (ōs-mán′), **Baron Georges,** 1809–91, French administrator and city planner.

haus·tel·lum (hôs-tel′əm) *n. pl.* **·tel·la** (-tel′ə) *Zool.* The proboscis or sucking organ of certain insects and crustaceans.   [< NL, dim. of L *haustrum* machine for drawing water < *haurire* to draw]

haus·to·ri·um (hôs-tôr′ē-əm, -tō′rē-) *n. pl.* **·to·ri·a** (-tôr′ē-ə, -tō′rē-ə) *Bot.* A root or sucker found in certain parasitic plants by which they absorb nutriment without damage to the host.   [< NL < L *haustor* drainer < *haurire* to draw]

haut·boy (hō′boi, ō′-) *n.* An oboe.   [< F *hautbois* < *haut* high (in tone) + *bois* wood]

hau·teur (hō-tûr′, *Fr.* ō-tœr′) *n.* Haughty manner or spirit; haughtiness; arrogance.   [< F]

haut monde (ō mônd′)   *French* High society.

Ha·van·a (hə-van′ə)   A Province of western Cuba; 3,173 sq. mi.; pop. 2,150,300 (1970); capital, **Havana,** capital of Cuba and largest port of the West Indies, pop. 990,000 (est. 1966): Spanish *La Habana.*

have (hav) *v.t.* Present indicative: I, you, we, they **have** (*Archaic* **thou hast**), he, she, it **has** (*Archaic* **hath**); past indicative **had** (*Archaic* **thou hadst**); present subjunctive **have**; past subjunctive **had**; *pp.* **had**; *ppr.* **hav·ing 1.** To be in actual material possession of; possess as property; own; control. **2.** To be connected with by some bond of relationship resembling possession; be possessed of: to *have* a good teacher; to *have* a corrupt government. **3.** To be characterized by; bear or possess as an attribute, quality, etc.: to *have* courage; to *have* three equal angles. **4.** To hold in the mind or among the feelings; find in oneself; entertain; cherish: to *have* an idea; to *have* a suspicion. **5.** To receive, take, or acquire: to *have* a drink. **6.** To achieve control or mastery of: Now I *have* it. **7.** To suffer from; be stricken with: to *have* boils. **8.** To take part in; engage in: to *have* a quarrel. **9.** To undergo or experience: to *have* a bad fright. **10.** To plan and execute; arrange and carry out; hold: to *have* a party; to *have* a trial. **11.** To give birth to; bring forth: to *have* twins. **12.** To manifest or exercise; act or behave with: to *have* patience. **13.** To cause to, or cause to be: *Have* her come in; *Have* it cleaned. **14.** To allow or permit; tolerate; brook: I'll *have* no complaining. **15.** To assert or announce; maintain; declare: So rumor *has* it. **16.** *Rare* To know (a subject, language, etc.): to *have* mathematics and Greek. **17.** *Informal* To catch (someone) at a disadvantage in a game, argument, etc.; prevail over. **18.** *Informal* To cheat; trick; defraud. **19.** *Informal* To perform the sexual act with. **20.** As an auxiliary, *have* is used: **a** With past participles to form perfect tenses expressing completed action: often with the addition of other auxiliary verbs: I *have* gone; I *have* been given; I shall *have* gone. **b** With the infinitive to express obligation or compulsion: I *have* to go. **— to have at** To attack. **— to have done** To stop; desist. **— to have it in for** *Informal* To hold a grudge against. **— to have it out** To continue a fight or discussion to a final settlement. **— to have on** To be dressed in. **— to let someone have it** *Informal* To attack or assault someone.   ◆ *Have* is used in the form *had* (past subjunctive) in certain phrases expressing obligation or preference: You *had* better hurry; I *had* rather die. **— n.** *Informal* A person or country with relatively much wealth: the *haves* and the *have-nots*.   [OE *habban*]
—Syn. (verb) **1.** *Have, hold, own,* and *possess* mean to keep as one's own. In modern usage, *have* retains little force in this sense, and may be ambiguous because of its many other idiomatic and auxiliary uses; if possible, one of the other words is better substituted. *Hold* is an emphatic word, meaning to retain firmly in one's grasp, custody, or control: to *hold* a fort against attack. *Own* refers to a natural or legal right to keep, use, occupy, and dispose of: to *own* a house, to *own* a rare painting. *Possess* is equivalent to *own,* but is preferred in legal usage.

have·lock (hav′lok) *n.* A cover for a military cap, made with a long rear flap, as a protection from the sun.   [after Sir Henry *Havelock*, 1795–1857, British general]

ha·ven (hā′vən) *n.* **1.** A place of anchorage for ships; harbor; port. **2.** A refuge; shelter; safe place. **— v.t.** To shelter in or as in a haven.   [OE *hæfen*]

have-not (hav′not′) *n.* *Informal* A person or country relatively lacking in wealth: the *haves* and *have-nots.*

have·n't (hav′ənt)   Have not.

hav·er[1] (hav′ər, häv′-, av′-, äv′-) *n. Scot.* Oats.

ha·ver[2] (hā′vər) *v.i. Scot.* To talk foolishly; babble.

ha·ver·el (hā′vər-əl, ä′-) *n. Scot.* A fool; babbler.

Hav·er·ford (hav′ər-fərd)   An urban township in SE Pennsylvania; pop. 55,132.

Ha·ver·hill (hā′vər-əl, -vril)   A city in NE Massachusetts; pop. 46,120.

hav·er·sack (hav′ər-sak) *n.* A bag for carrying rations, etc., on a march or hike.   [< F *havresac* < G *habersack* oat sack]

Ha·ver·sian canals (hə-vûr′shən) *Anat.* The numerous channels for capillary blood vessels in bone substance. [after C. *Havers*, 1650–1702, English anatomist]

hav·er·sine (hav′ər-sĭn) *n. Trig.* Half of a versed sine.

hav·iour (hăv′yər) *n. Obs.* Behavior. Also **hav′ior.**

hav·oc (hav′ək) *n.* General carnage or destruction; ruin. — **to cry havoc** To give the signal for pillage and destruction. — **to play havoc with** To ruin; destroy; devastate. — *v.t. & v.i.* **·ocked, ·ock·ing** *Rare* To lay waste; destroy. [< OF *havot* to plunder < Gmc.]

Ha·vre-de-Grâce (äv′r′də-gräs′) The former name for LE HAVRE.

haw[1] (hô) *v.i.* To hesitate in speaking; search for words: to hem and haw. — *n. & interj.* A sound made by a speaker when he hesitates: a conventional representation.

haw[2] (hô) *n.* The fruit of the hawthorn; also, the hawthorn. [OE *haga*]

haw[3] (hô) *n.* 1. The third eyelid or nictitating membrane of certain animals. 2. *pl.* A disease of this membrane. [Origin uncertain]

haw[4] (hô) *n. & interj.* An order to turn to the left or near side in driving horses: opposed to *gee.* — *v.t. & v.i.* To turn to the left. [Origin uncertain]

Ha·wai·i (hə-wä′ē, hə-wī′yə) 1. A State of the United States comprising the Hawaiian Islands; 6,435 sq. mi.; pop. 769,913; capital, Honolulu; entered the Union Aug. 21, 1959, as the 50th state: nickname *Aloha State.* 2. The largest of the Hawaiian Islands; 4,020 sq. mi. **Ha·wai·ian** (hə-wī′yən) *adj.* Of or pertaining to Hawaii, the Hawaiians, or their language. — *n.* 1. A native or naturalized inhabitant of Hawaii. 2. The aboriginal Polynesian language of Hawaii.

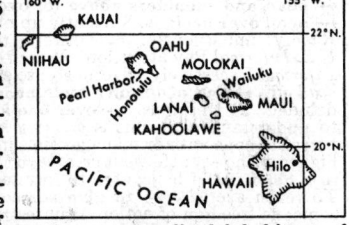

Hawaiian guitar A type of guitar played on the lap or on a horizontal stand, the pitches and chords being selected by sliding a metal bar up and down the strings.

Hawaiian Islands A group of islands in the North Pacific constituting the State of Hawaii: formerly *Sandwich Islands.*

Hawaii Volcanoes National Park Two areas containing Mauna Loa and Kilauea on the island of Hawaii and the extinct crater of Haleakala on Maui Island; 270.9 sq. mi.; established 1916: formerly **Hawaii National Park.**

haw·finch (hô′fĭnch′) *n.* A European grosbeak (genus *Coccothraustes*), having a very large beak.

haw-haw[1] (hô′hô′) See HA-HA[1].

haw-haw[2] (hô′hô′) See HA-HA[2].

hawk[1] (hôk) *n.* 1. Any of a large and widely distributed family (*Accipitridae*) of diurnal birds of prey, having broad, rounded wings, a long tail, and powerful talons, as the marsh hawk, goshawk, and the rough-legged hawk. ♦ Collateral adjective: *accipitrine.* 2. Any of various related birds of the same order (*Falconiformes*), as the gerfalcon, kestrel, sparrow hawk, and osprey. 3. One who seeks to resolve a war primarily by means of military force: opposed to *dove*[1] (def. 4). 4. A person who preys on others; swindler; shark. — *v.i.* 1. To hunt game with hawks; practice falconry. 2. To fly in search of prey; hunt on the wing, as a hawk. [OE *hafoc, hafuc*]

hawk[2] (hôk) *v.t. & v.i.* To cry (goods) for sale in the streets; peddle. [Back formation < HAWKER[2]]

hawk[3] (hôk) *v.t.* 1. To cough up (phlegm). — *v.i.* 2. To clear the throat with a coughing sound. — *n.* An effort to clear phlegm from the throat; also, the sound of this. [Imit.]

hawk[4] (hôk) *n.* A small, square board with a handle underneath, used to hold plaster or mortar. [Origin uncertain]

hawk·er[1] (hô′kər) *n.* One who hunts with hawks; a falconer.

hawk·er[2] (hô′kər) *n.* One who peddles goods in the street. [< MLG *hoker* peddler, huckster]

hawk·ey (hô′kē) *n. Scot.* A white-faced cow. Also **hawk′ie.**

Hawk·eye (hôk′ī′) *n.* A native or inhabitant of Iowa.

hawk-eyed (hôk′īd′) *adj.* Having very keen eyesight.

Hawkeye State Nickname of IOWA.

haw·king (hô′kĭng) *n.* Falconry.

Haw·kins (hô′kĭnz), *Sir* **Anthony Hope**, 1863–1933, English novelist: pseudonym *Anthony Hope.* — *Sir* **John**, 1532–1595, English naval officer: also **Haw′kyns.**

hawk·ish (hôk′ĭsh) *adj.* Being or characteristic of a hawk[1] (def. 3); disposed to rely on military force to resolve a war: opposed to *dovish.*

hawk moth A large, stout-bodied moth (family *Sphingidae*) that flies by twilight and sucks nectar from flowers: also called *hummingbird moth, sphinx moth.*

hawk·nose (hôk′nōz′) *n.* A large, beaklike nose. — **hawk′-nosed′** *adj.*

hawks·bill (hôks′bĭl′) *n.* A small, tropical marine turtle (*Eretmochelys imbricata*) that furnishes the best grade of tortoise shell used in commerce. Also **hawk·bill** (hôk′bĭl′), **hawk′s-·bill′, hawksbill turtle.**

hawk's-eye (hôks′ī′) *n.* A variety of tigereye, a gemstone.

hawk·shaw (hôk′shô) *n. Informal* A detective: a humorous term. [after a character in *The Ticket of Leave Man*, a play by Tom Taylor, 1817–80, English author]

hawk·weed (hôk′wēd′) *n.* Any species of a genus (*Hieracium*) of weedy perennial herbs of the composite family having small red, yellow, or orange flowers.

hawse (hôz) *n. Naut.* 1. The part of a ship's bow where the hawseholes are located. 2. *pl.* Hawseholes. 3. The position of the two cables in front of a ship moored with two anchors. 4. The space between the bow of a moored ship and the point directly above her anchor. [< ON *hals* neck, bow of a ship]

hawse·hole (hôz′hōl′) *n. Naut.* A hole in the bow of a ship, through which cables and hawsers pass.

haw·ser (hô′zər) *n. Naut.* A rope or cable used for mooring, towing, etc. [< OF *haucier* to lift]

haw·ser-laid (hô′zər-lād′) *adj.* Made of three small ropes laid up into one; cable-laid.

haw·thorn (hô′thôrn) *n.* A thorny ornamental shrub or small tree (genus *Crataegus*) of the rose family having a white or pink flower and a small pome fruit called *haw:* the State flower of Missouri. Also called *haw.* [OE *haguthorn*]

Haw·thorne (hô′thôrn) A city in southern California, a suburb of Los Angeles; pop. 33,035.

Haw·thorne (hô′thôrn), **Nathaniel,** 1804–64, U.S. novelist and short-story writer.

hay[1] (hā) *n.* Grass, clover, or the like, cut and dried for fodder. — **not hay** *U.S. Slang* Not a small sum of money. — **to hit the hay** *U.S. Slang* To go to bed. — **to make hay while the sun shines** To take full advantage of an opportunity. — *v.i.* 1. To mow, cure, gather, and store hay; prepare grass, etc., for use as fodder. — *v.t.* 2. To make (grass, etc.) into hay. 3. To feed with hay. 4. To sow (land, etc.) with hay plants. [OE *hēg*]

hay[2] (hā) *n.* A country-dance with a winding in and out movement. [< MF *haye*]

hay[3] (hā) *n. Obs.* A hedge, palisade, or fence. [OE *hege*]

Hay (hā), **Ian** See BEITH. — **John Milton,** 1838–1905, U.S. statesman and writer.

hay·cock (hā′kŏk′) *n.* A dome-shaped pile of hay in the field.

Hay·dn (hīd′n), **Franz Joseph,** 1732–1809, Austrian composer.

Hayes (hāz), **Helen,** born 1900, U.S. actress: original name Helen Hayes Brown. — **Roland,** 1887–1976, U.S. tenor. — **Rutherford Birchard,** 1822–93, 19th president of the United States 1877–81.

hay fever *Pathol.* An allergic reaction to the airborne pollen of certain plants, characterized by sneezing, running nose, inflamed eyes, headaches, etc.: also called *pollinosis.*

hay·fork (hā′fôrk′) *n.* 1. A long-handled fork for turning or pitching hay by hand. 2. A large power-driven fork for moving or lifting hay.

hay·ing (hā′ĭng) *n.* The act or process of cutting, curing, and storing hay.

hay·loft (hā′lôft′, -lŏft′) *n.* An open upper section of a barn or stable, used for storing hay.

hay·mak·er (hā′mā′kər) *n.* 1. One who makes hay, especially one who spreads it to dry. 2. *Slang* A wide, swinging blow of the fist, knockout. — **hay′mak′ing** *n.*

Hay·mar·ket (hā′mär′kĭt) 1. A street in London between Piccadilly Circus and Pall Mall, site of many theaters. 2. A square in Chicago; site of a labor riot and massacre, 1886.

hay·mow (hā′mou′) *n.* 1. A mass of hay, especially one stored in a loft or bay. 2. A hayloft.

hay·rack (hā′rak′) *n.* 1. An open frame or rack mounted on a wagon body, in which hay, straw, etc., are hauled; also, a wagon so equipped. 2. A framework for holding hay to feed livestock.

hay·ride (hā′rīd′) *n.* A ride taken for pleasure by a group of people in a wagon partly full of hay.

hay·seed (hā′sēd′) *n.* 1. Grass seed that has shaken loose from hay. 2. The chaff, seeds, etc., that fall from hay. 3. *U.S. Slang* A hick; rustic; yokel.

hay·stack (hā′stak′) *n.* A conical pile of hay stacked outdoors, sometimes covered. Also **hay·rick** (hā′rik′).

Hay·ti·an (hā′tē-ən, -shən) See HAITIAN.

hay·ward (hā′wôrd′, -wərd) *n. Obs.* 1. An officer whose duty is to inspect fences and enclosures for cattle, etc. 2. An officer who impounds stray animals. [< HAY[2] + WARD]

Hay·ward (hā′wərd) A city in western California; near San Francisco Bay; pop. 93,058.

hay·wire (hā′wīr′) *n.* Wire for baling hay. — *adj. U.S. Slang* 1. Broken; broken down; dilapidated. 2. Confused; messy. 3. Crazy; nutty. — **to go haywire** *Informal* To act or become crazy.

haz·ard (haz′ərd) *n.* 1. Danger of loss, injury, etc.; peril;

risk; jeopardy. **2.** Chance; accident; fortuitousness: The result depends on mere *hazard*; also, a single chance event. **3.** A gambling game played with two dice, an early form of craps. **4.** An obstacle or trap on a golf course. **5.** In English billiards, a stroke that pockets the object ball (**winning hazard**), or one that pockets the player's ball after contact with another ball (**losing hazard**). **6.** In court tennis: **a** The side of the court into which the ball is served (**hazard side**). **b** Any of the various openings into which the ball may be driven to score points for the driver. **7.** *Obs.* That which is risked or staked. — *v.t.* **1.** To put in danger; risk: to *hazard* one's life. **2.** To venture (a statement, opinion, etc.): to *hazard* a guess. **3.** To take a chance on; gamble on: to *hazard* an attempt. [< OF *hasard* < Arabic *al-zahr* a die] — **Syn.** (noun) 1. See DANGER. 2. See CHANCE.
haz·ard·ous (haz′ər·dəs) *adj.* **1.** Exposed to or involving danger, risk, loss, etc. **2.** Dependent on chance; fortuitous. — **haz′ard·ous·ly** *adv.* — **haz′ard·ous·ness** *n.*
haze¹ (hāz) *n.* **1.** A light suspension of water vapor, smoke, dust, or other particles in the air that cuts down visibility. **2.** A lack of clarity, as in perception or knowledge; mental confusion. [? Back formation < HAZY]
haze² (hāz) *v.t.* **hazed, haz·ing 1.** *U.S.* To subject (newcomers or initiates) to pranks and humiliating horseplay. **2.** *Naut.* To harass by imposing of heavy or disagreeable tasks. [< OF *haser* to irritate] — **haz′er** *n.*
ha·zel (hā′zəl) *n.* **1.** A bushy shrub or small tree of the birch family (genus *Corylus*); also, the wood of this tree. **2.** The hazelnut. **3.** The color of the hazelnut shell, a medium yellowish brown. — *adj.* **1.** Of or pertaining to the hazel. **2.** Of the color hazel. [OE *hæsel*]
ha·zel·ly (hā′zəl·ē) *adj.* Of the color of a hazelnut shell.
ha·zel·nut (hā′zəl·nut′) *n.* The hard-shelled edible nut of the hazel: also called *filbert*.
Hazel Park A city in SE Michigan, near Detroit; pop. 23,784.
haz·ing (hā′zing) *n.* The act or practice of one who hazes.
Ha·zle·ton (hāz′əlt·n, -əl·tən) A city of eastern Pennsylvania; pop. 30,426.
Haz·litt (haz′lit), **William,** 1778–1830, English critic and essayist.
haz·y (hā′zē) *adj.* **haz·i·er, haz·i·est 1.** Characterized or obscured by haze or vapor; misty. **2.** Lacking clarity in thought, idea, etc.; vague; confused; obscure. [Cf. OE *hasu* gray] — **haz′i·ly** *adv.* — **haz′i·ness** *n.*
haz·zan (khä·zän′, khä′zən) *n.* A cantor (def. 1): also spelled *chazan, khazen*. [< Hebrew *hazzān* prefect]
hb. or **hb** Halfback.
H-beam (āch′bēm′) *n.* A structural member having a cross section resembling an H: also called *H-girder.*
H.B.M. His (or Her) Britannic Majesty.
H-bomb (āch′bom′) *n.* A hydrogen bomb (which see).
H.C. House of Commons.
H.C.F. or **h.c.f.** or **hcf** Highest common factor.
h.c.l. *Informal* High cost of living.
hd. 1. Hand. **2.** Head.
H.D. See (Hilda) DOOLITTLE
hdbk. Handbook.
hdkf. Handkerchief.
he¹ (hē) *pron., possessive* **his,** *objective* **him;** *pl. nominative* **they,** *possessive* **their** or **theirs,** *objective* **them 1.** The nominative singular pronoun of the third person, used of the male person or being previously mentioned or understood. **2.** That person; anyone; one: *He* who hesitates is lost. — *n. pl.* **hes** A male person or animal. [OE *hē*]
he² (hā) *n.* The fifth letter of the Hebrew alphabet. See ALPHABET.
he- *combining form* Male; masculine: used in hyphenated compounds: *he-goat.* [< HE]
He *Chem.* Helium.
HE or **H.E.** High explosive.
H.E. 1. His Eminence. **2.** His Excellency.
head (hed) *n. pl.* **heads** or *for def. 15* **head 1.** The part of a vertebrate animal situated at the top or front of the spinal column, containing the brain, eyes, ears, nose, and mouth. ◆ Collateral adjective: *cephalic.* **2.** The analogous part of other animals and organisms. **3.** A part having the shape or situation of a head: the *head* of a pin. **4.** A representation of the head in drawing, sculpture, etc. **5.** A leader or chief person, as a president, boss, ruler, etc. **6.** The position or rank of a leader: the *head* of one's profession. **7.** The front, forward, or beginning part of something: the *head* of a parade. **8.** The highest or uppermost part of something: the *head* of the stairs. **9.** The superior part of something: the *head* of the class. **10.** The source, as of a river. **11.** The part of a bomb or other missile that contains the explosive. **12.** Mind; intelligence: Use your *head*; also, mental aptitude; a *head* for mathematics. **13.** Self-control; self-possession; sanity: Don't lose your *head.* **14.** A person: to charge two dollars a *head.* **15.** Of animals, a single specimen: four *head* of cattle. **16.** The length of a head: to win by a *head.* **17.** A newspaper headline; also, the headlines at the top of a newspaper story. **18.** A subject: He had much to say on that *head*; also, a divi-

sion of a subject: to treat the matter under four *heads.* **19.** The side of a coin on which a face is struck; obverse: opposed to *tail.* **20.** The tip or point of a boil, abscess, etc., where the pus may break through. **21.** Progress in the face of opposition; headway: to make *head* against a storm. **22.** A climax, culmination, or crisis: He brought matters to a *head.* **23.** A compact cluster of leaves or leaf stalks: a *head* of cabbage; also, a rounded, compact bud: a *head* of cauliflower. **24.** A cluster of cereal grain at the top of a stem. **25.** *Bot.* A capitulum. **26.** The foam on the surface of fermented liquid, as on beer or ale. **27.** An amount of stored-up pressure: a *head* of steam. **28.** The height of a column or source of fluid, determining the pressure at the point of use: water under a sixty-foot *head.* **29.** A projecting, usually high, piece of land on a coast, as a cape or promontory. **30.** The taut, sounding membrane of a drum, tambourine, etc. **31.** The part of a tape recorder that directly imparts magnetic patterns to the tape or removes them from it. **32.** *Naut.* **a** The upper edge or corner of a sail. For illustration see SAIL. **b** The front part or bow of a ship. **c** A toilet. **33.** *Mining* A heading. **34.** *Gram.* The part of an endocentric construction that functions in the same manner as the construction itself. In *the man holding the flag, man* is the *head*: also called *head word.* Abbr. *hd.* — **by** (or **down by**) **the head** *Naut.* Having the bow more deeply submerged than the stern. — **head and shoulders above** (or **over**) Much better than. — **head over heels 1.** Violently up-ended; end over end. **2.** Rashly; impetuously. **3.** Entirely; totally. — **Heads up!** *U.S. Informal* Pay attention!; Watch out! — **one's head off** *Informal* Excessively; vigorously; to exhaustion: to yell *one's head off.* — **out of** (or **off**) **one's head** *Informal* **1.** Crazy; deluded. **2.** Delirious. — **over one's head 1.** Too difficult to understand: Calculus is *over my head.* **2.** Beyond one's power to cope with or manage: He's in *over his head.* **3.** To a higher authority: He went *over the captain's head.* — **to come to a head 1.** Of boils, etc., to form a core or tip of pus. **2.** To reach a crisis. — **to give someone his head** To give someone freedom of action or unrestricted authority. — **to go to one's head 1.** To decrease one's stability, sobriety, etc. **2.** To make one conceited. — **to have a head** *Informal* To have a bad headache, especially one from a hangover. — **to have rocks** (or **holes**) **in the head** *U.S. Slang* **1.** To be crazy. **2.** To be stupid. — **to keep one's head** To maintain one's self-control or poise, as during a crisis. — **to keep one's head above water 1.** To keep afloat. **2.** To manage to exist, keep out of debt, etc. — **to lose one's head** To lose one's self-control; become excited. — **to make head or tail of** To understand: usually used in the negative. — **to take it into one's head 1.** To do or originate something on one's own initiative. **2.** To do something impulsive or capricious. — **to turn one's head** To spoil or make vain by praising. — **Syn.** See CHIEF. — *v.t.* **1.** to be first or most prominent on: to *head* the list. **2.** To be chief or leader of; command; preside over. **3.** To turn or direct the course of: to *head* a vessel toward shore. **4.** To furnish with a head. **5.** To cut off the head or top of: to *head* a tree. **6.** To pass around the head of, as a stream. **7.** In soccer, to bunt (the ball) with the head. — *v.i.* **8.** To move in a specified direction or toward a specified point: to *head* for home. **9.** To come to or form a head. **10.** To originate; rise: said of streams. — **to head off** To intercept the course of: We'll *head* them *off* at the pass. — *adj.* **1.** Principal; chief. **2.** Situated at the top or front. **3.** Bearing against the front: a *head* wind. [OE *hēafod*]
-head *suffix Rare* Condition; state; totality: *godhead*: same as *-hood.* [ME *-hede*]
head·ache (hed′āk′) *n.* **1.** A pain in the head. **2.** *U.S. Informal* A difficulty, trouble, or vexation. — **head′ach′y** (-ā′kē) *adj.*
head·band (hed′band′) *n.* **1.** A band worn about the head; fillet. **2.** A narrow band of cloth fastened to the inner back or spine of a book at both the top and bottom. **3.** A decorative band at the head of a page or chapter in a printed book.
head·board (hed′bôrd′, -bōrd′) *n.* A board at the head end of a bed, grave, etc.
head·cheese (hed′chēz′) *n.* *U.S.* A cooked, seasoned, and jellied cheeselike mass made of small pieces of the head and feet of a hog or calf.
head·dress (hed′dress′) *n.* **1.** A covering or ornament for the head. **2.** The style in which the hair is arranged; coiffure.
head·ed (hed′id) *adj.* **1.** Having a head or heading. **2.** Formed or grown into a head, as lettuce. **3.** Having or characterized (of a specified kind of) head or (a specified number of) heads: used in combination: *clear-headed; two-headed.*
head·er (hed′ər) *n.* **1.** One who or that which makes or puts on heads, as of nails, rivets, etc. **2.** *Agric.* A harvesting machine that cuts off the ripe ends of the grain. **3.** *Informal* A fall or plunge with the head leading: now only in the phrase **to take a header. 4.** In building: **a** A brick or stone placed with its end toward the face of a wall. **b** In a floor or roof, a timber placed between two trimmers and supporting the ends of the tailpieces. **5.** A pipe, as in plumbing, from which two or more tributary pipes run.
head·first (hed′fûrst′) *adv.* **1.** With the head first. **2.**

Without deliberation; recklessly. Also **head′fore′most′** (-fôr′mōst′, -məst, -fôr′-).

head gate 1. An upstream gate controlling the flow of water into a canal lock. **2.** A floodgate for any race, sluice, etc.

head·gear (hed′gir′) *n.* **1.** A hat, headdress, protective helmet, etc. **2.** The parts of the harness placed about the horse's head. **3.** *Mining* Hoisting apparatus at the top of a mine shaft. **4.** *Naut.* The running rigging of headsails.

head·hunt·ing (hed′hun′ting) *n.* Among certain savage tribes, the custom of decapitating slain enemies and preserving the heads as trophies. **— head′-hunt′er** *n.*

head·ing (hed′ing) *n.* **1.** A caption or title, as of a chapter. **2.** A section or division of a subject or discourse. **3.** Something serving as the front or top part of anything. **4.** Material from which the heads of barrels, etc., are made. **5.** *Mining* **a** A drift. **b** The end of a drift or gallery. **6.** *Naut. & Aeron.* Direction; course. **7.** *Aeron.* The horizontal direction in which the long axis of an aircraft is pointed.

head·land (hed′lənd *for def. 1;* hed′land′ *for def. 2*) *n.* **1.** A cliff projecting into the water. **2.** A strip of unplowed land at the ends of furrows or near a fence.

head·less (hed′lis) *adj.* **1.** Having no head; decapitated. **2.** Having no leader. **3.** Stupid; erratic; brainless.

head·light (hed′līt′) *n.* A powerful light, as at the front of a locomotive, motor vehicle, etc.

head·line (hed′līn′) *n.* **1.** A summarizing word or words set in bold type at the head of a newspaper column or story. **2.** A line at the head of a page, containing title, page number, etc. **— v.t. head·lined, head·lin·ing 1.** To provide with a headline, as a news story. **2.** To have top billing in a show.

head·lin·er (hed′lī′nər) *n.* One billed as the main attraction or star of a theatrical performance.

head·lock (hed′lok′) *n.* A hold in which a wrestler's head is gripped between his opponent's arm and body.

head·long (hed′lông′, -long′) *adv.* **1.** Headfirst. **2.** Without deliberation; recklessly; rashly. **3.** With unbridled speed or force. **— adj. 1.** Made with the head foremost. **2.** Advancing impetuously; rash. **3.** *Rare* Steep.

head·mas·ter (hed′mas′tər, -mäs′-) *n.* The principal of a school, especially a private school. Also **head master.**

head·mis·tress (hed′mis′tris) *n. fem.* The female principal of a school, especially one for girls. Also **head mistress.**

head money 1. A poll tax or other per capita tax. **2.** A bounty paid for the capture of prisoners, outlaws, etc.

head·most (hed′mōst′) *adj.* Most advanced; foremost.

head-on (hed′on′, -ôn′) *adj. & adv.* Front end to front end.

head·phone (hed′fōn′) *n.* An earphone.

head·piece (hed′pēs′) *n.* **1.** A hat, helmet, or other covering for the head. **2.** The head; intelligence. **3.** A headset. **4.** *Printing* A decorative design at the top of a page.

head pin In tenpins, the kingpin.

head·quar·ters (hed′kwôr′tərz) *n. pl.* (*construed as sing. or pl.*) **1.** The place from which a chief or leader directs the operations of a military unit, police force, political organization, etc. **2.** Any center of operations. **3.** The persons working in a center of operations. Abbr. *hq, h.q., HQ, H.Q.*

head·race (hed′rās′) *n.* The channel by which water is led to a water wheel, or to any machinery. [< HEAD + RACE²]

head·rest (hed′rest′) *n.* Any device to support the head.

head·room (hed′rōōm′, -rŏŏm′) *n.* Headway (def. 3).

head·sail (hed′sāl′, -səl) *n. Naut.* A sail set forward of the foremast, as a jib; also, one set on the foremast.

head·set (hed′set′) *n.* A pair of headphones.

head·ship (hed′ship) *n.* The position or function of a chief authority; command.

heads·man (hedz′mən) *n. pl.* **·men** (-mən) A public executioner who carries out the death sentence by decapitation.

head·spring (hed′spring′) *n.* **1.** A fountainhead; source. **2.** A gymnastic feat in which the performer springs from a supine position using his head as lever.

head·stall (hed′stôl′) *n.* The part of a bridle that fits over the horse's head.

head·stand (hed′stand′) *n.* The act of holding one's body upside-down in a vertical position, with its weight resting on the head and, usually, the hands or elbows.

head start An advance start; also, an advantage.

head·stock (hed′stok′) *n. Mech.* One of various machine parts that support or hold some revolving part, as the live spindle of a lathe.

head·stone (hed′stōn′) *n.* **1.** The memorial stone at the head of a grave. **2.** The cornerstone or keystone of a structure; also **head stone.**

head·strong (hed′strông′, -strong′) *adj.* **1.** Stubbornly bent on having one's own way; obstinate; determined. **2.** Proceeding from willfulness or obstinacy. **— Syn.** See OBSTINATE. **— head′strong′ness** *n.*

head voice Falsetto.

head·wait·er (hed′wā′tər) *n.* A restaurant employee who supervises waiters, seats guests, makes reservations, etc.

head·wa·ters (hed′wô′tərz, -wot′ərz) *n. pl.* The tributaries or other waters that form the source of a river.

head·way (hed′wā′) *n.* **1.** Forward motion; progress. **2.** The space or time interval between two trains, ships, etc., traveling over the same route. **3.** The clear distance in height under a bridge, archway, etc.: also *headroom.*

head wind A wind from ahead, blowing directly opposite to the course of a ship, aircraft, etc.

head word 1. A word or expression that introduces or begins, as a chapter, often printed in distinctive type. **2.** *Gram.* A head (*n.* def. 34).

head·work (hed′wûrk′) *n.* Mental labor. **— head′work′er** *n.*

head·y (hed′ē) *adj.* **head·i·er, head·i·est 1.** Tending to affect the senses; intoxicating: a *heady* fragrance. **2.** Headstrong; obstinate. **— head′i·ly** *adv.* **— head′i·ness** *n.*

heal (hēl) *v.t.* **1.** To restore to health or soundness; make healthy again; cure. **2.** To bring about the remedy or cure of, as a wound or disease. **3.** To remedy, repair, or mend (a quarrel, breach, etc.). **4.** To cleanse of sin, grief, worry, etc.; purify: to *heal* the spirit. **— v.i. 5.** To become well or sound; mend. **6.** To perform a cure or cures. [OE *hǣlan*] **— heal′a·ble** *adj.* **— heal′ing·ly** *adv.*

heal-all (hēl′ôl′) *n.* **1.** A remedy for all diseases; panacea. **2.** The selfheal (which see).

heal·er (hē′lər) *n.* **1.** One who or that which heals. **2.** One who undertakes to heal through prayer and faith.

health (helth) *n.* **1.** Soundness of any living organism; vigor of body and mind; freedom from defect or disease. **2.** General condition of body or mind; tone: good *health;* poor *health.* **3.** A toast wishing health or happiness. **— adj. 1.** Pertaining to, connected with, or engaged in public-health work: *health* education; *health* inspection. **2.** Conducive to good health: a *health* food. [OE *hǣlth < hāl* whole]

Health, Education and Welfare, Department of An executive department of the U.S. government (established 1953) headed by the Secretary of Health, Education and Welfare, administering Social Security and other welfare services and supervising public health and education programs.

health·ful (helth′fəl) *adj.* **1.** Promoting health; salubrious. **2.** Having or manifesting health; healthy. **— health′ful·ly** *adv.* **— health′ful·ness** *n.*

health·y (hel′thē) *adj.* **health·i·er, health·i·est 1.** Having good health; sound; well. **2.** Conducive to health; healthful; salutary: *healthy* recreation. **3.** Indicative or characteristic of sound condition: a *healthy* complexion; a *healthy* skepticism. **— health′i·ly** *adv.* **— health′i·ness** *n.* **—Syn. 1.** hale, robust, vigorous. **2.** salubrious, hygienic. **— Ant.** unhealthy, sick, ill, morbid.

heap (hēp) *n.* **1.** A collection of things piled up; a pile; mass; mound. **2.** *Informal* A large number; lot. **— v.t. 1.** To pile into a heap; make a mound or mass of. **2.** To fill or pile (a container) full or more than full. **3.** To strew with heaps: to *heap* a field with bodies. **4.** To bestow in great quantities: to *heap* insults on someone. **5.** To bestow great quantities upon: to *heap* someone with riches. **— v.i. 6.** To form or rise in a heap or pile. [OE *hēap* crowd]

heap·ing (hē′ping) *adj.* Having the contents raised above the top; heaped.

hear (hir) *v.* **heard** (hûrd), **hear·ing** *v.t.* **1.** To perceive by means of the ear. **2.** To listen to; give ear to. **3.** To learn by word of mouth; be informed of: to *hear* good news. **4.** To attend (an opera, concert, recitation, etc.) as part of the audience. **5.** To listen to officially or judicially: to *hear* a case in court. **6.** To respond or accede to: to *hear* a prayer. **— v.i. 7.** To perceive or be capable of perceiving sound by means of the ear. **8.** To be informed or made aware; receive information: with *of, about,* or *from.* **— Syn.** See LISTEN. **— to hear of** To approve of: usually in the negative: He won't *hear* of it. [OE *hēran*] **— hear′er** *n.*

hear·ing (hir′ing) *n.* **1** The special sense by which sounds are perceived; the capacity to hear. **2.** The act or process of perceiving sound. **3.** Reach or range within which sound may be heard; earshot. **4.** An opportunity to be heard, as in a court, investigative session, etc. **5.** *Law* **a** The examination of an accused person and of witnesses. **b** A judicial trial, especially without a jury, as in an equity suit.

hearing aid Any of various portable instruments for the improvement of hearing, especially by the use of microphones connected with transistors or electron tubes operated by small batteries.

heark·en (här′kən) See HARKEN.

hear·say (hir′sā′) *n.* Information received indirectly; common talk; report; rumor.

hearsay evidence *Law* Evidence of a declaration made out of court, typically the testimony of a witness as to what another person told him and generally not admissible.

hearse (hûrs) *n.* **1.** A vehicle for conveying a dead person to the place of burial. **2.** In Roman Catholic ritual, a triangular frame on which lighted candles are placed during the singing of Tenebrae in Holy Week. [< F *herse* harrow < L *hirpex, -icis;* so called because the frame about a coffin resembled a harrow]

Hearst (hûrst), **William Randolph**, 1863–1951, U.S. newspaper publisher.

heart (härt) *n.* **1.** *Anat.* The primary organ of the circulatory system of animals, a hollow muscular structure that maintains the circulation of the blood by alternate contraction or systole and dilatation or diastole. ◆ Collateral adjective: *cardiac.* **2.** The seat of emotion, especially of love and affection, as distinguished from the head, the center of intellect and reason. **3.** The part of the body containing the heart; bosom: to clasp a child to one's *heart.* **4.** Tenderness; affection; love: to win one's *heart.* **5.** The capacity for kindness and sympathy: a good *heart.* **6.** Firmness of will; courage: The men lost *heart.* **7.** One's inmost thoughts or feelings: to pour out one's *heart.* **8.** Enthusiasm; energy: to put one's whole *heart* into a task. **9.** State of mind; mood: a heavy *heart.* **10.** A person, especially a dear or courageous one: a brave *heart.* **11.** The central or inner part of anything; the core: the *heart* of the city. **12.** The vital or essential part; essence: the *heart* of the matter. **13.** Of plants, land, etc., the capacity to produce in abundance; fertility. **14.** Anything represented as or shaped like a heart; especially, a conventional rounded figure with a cusp and a point joining two lobes. **15.** A playing card bearing red, heart-shaped spots or pips. **16.** *pl.* The suit of such playing cards. **17.** *pl.* A game of cards played with a full pack, in which the object is to take no hearts or to take all of them. **— after one's own heart** Conforming to one's ideas; suiting one's taste. **— at heart** In one's deepest thoughts or feelings; essentially; basically. **— by heart** By rote; by memory. **— from (the bottom of) one's heart** With all sincerity; with deep feeling. **— heart and soul** With complete sincerity; entirely; wholly. **— one's heart of hearts** The deepest and most intimate part of one's being. **— to break the heart of** To cause deep disappointment and sorrow to. **— to eat one's heart out 1.** To endure great remorse or grief. **2.** To have a great longing. **— to have a heart** To be sympathetic and generous. **— to have a change of heart** To change one's opinions, attitudes, feelings, etc. **— to have one's heart in one's mouth** To be excessively excited or frightened. **— to have the heart** To be callous or cruel enough: usually in the negative: I don't *have the heart* to hurt him. **— to lose heart** To become discouraged. **— to lose one's heart (to)** To fall in love (with). **— to set one's heart on** To long for; crave. **— to take to heart 1.** To consider seriously. **2.** To be concerned or anxious about. **— to wear one's heart on one's sleeve** To show one's feelings openly. **— with all one's heart 1.** With great willingness. **2.** With great sincerity. **—** *v.t. Rare* **1.** To hearten. **2.** To place in the heart. [OE *heorte*]

Heart may appear as a combining form or as the first element in two-word phrases; as in:

heart action	heart-gripping	heart-sorrowing
heart-affecting	heart-happy	heart stimulant
heart attack	heart-hardened	heart strain
heart-burdened	heart-hardening	heart-swelling
heart-cheering	heartheaviness	heart-swollen
heart-chilling	heartheavy	heart-tearing
heart complaint	heart-ill	heart-thrilling
heart-corroding	heart-melting	heartthrob
heart-dulling	heart-moving	heart-throbbing
heart-fallen	heart murmur	heart-tickling
heart failure	heart-purifying	heart-warm
heart-fashioned	heart-ravishing	heart-warming
heart-flowered	heart-robbing	heart-weariness
heart-freezing	heart-shaking	heart-weary
heart-fretting	heartsickening	heart-wounded
heart-gnawing	heartsickness	heart-wringing

heart·ache (härt′āk′) *n.* Mental anguish; grief; sorrow.

heart·beat (härt′bēt′) *n. Physiol.* A pulsation of the heart consisting of one full systole and diastole.

heart·block (härt′blok′) *n. Pathol.* A condition in which the ventricular beats of the heart do not regularly follow the atrial: also called *Adams-Stokes disease.*

heart·break (härt′brāk′) *n.* Deep grief; overwhelming sorrow. **— heart′break′er** *n.* **— heart′break′ing** *adj. & n.* **— heart′break′ing·ly** *adv.*

heart·bro·ken (härt′brō′kən) *adj.* Overwhelmingly grieved. **— heart′bro′ken·ly** *adv.* **— heart′bro′ken·ness** *n.*

heart·burn (härt′bûrn′) *n.* **1.** *Pathol.* A burning sensation in the esophagus due to acidity in the stomach: also called *cardialgia, pyrosis, water brash.* **2.** Discontent; jealousy.

heart·burn·ing (härt′bûrn′ing) *n.* Gnawing discontent, as from envy or jealousy. **—** *adj.* Deeply felt; distressful.

heart cherry A variety of cherry having heart-shaped fruit.

heart disease Any abnormal condition of the heart.

heart·ed (här′tid) *adj.* Having or characterized by a (specified kind of) heart: used in combination: *lighthearted.*

heart·en (här′tən) *v.t.* To give heart or courage to.

heart·felt (härt′felt′) *adj.* Deeply felt; most sincere.

heart-free (härt′frē′) *adj.* Having the affections free; not in love.

hearth (härth) *n.* **1.** The floor of a fireplace, furnace, or the like. **2.** The fireside; home. **3.** *Metall.* **a** The part of a reverberatory furnace upon which the ore is laid to be subjected to the action of fire. **b** In a blast furnace, the lowest part, through which the melted metal flows. [OE *heorth*]

hearth money Peter's pence (def. 2).

hearth·stone (härth′stōn′) *n.* **1.** A stone forming a hearth. **2.** The fireside; home. **3.** A soft stone used for whitening floors, doorsteps, etc.

heart·i·ly (här′tə·lē) *adv.* **1.** With sincerity or cordiality; earnestly; enthusiastically. **2.** Abundantly and with good appetite: to eat *heartily.* **3.** Completely; thoroughly: to be *heartily* disgusted.

heart·land (härt′land′) *n.* In geopolitics, any geographic area supposed to give the nation controlling it power over surrounding areas and a strategic advantage in any struggle for world domination.

heart·less (härt′lis) *adj.* **1.** Having no sympathy or kindness; pitiless. **2.** Having little courage or enthusiasm; dispirited. **— heart′less·ly** *adv.* **— heart′less·ness** *n.*

heart-rend·ing (härt′ren′ding) *adj.* Causing great distress or emotional anguish; grievous.

hearts·ease (härts′ēz′) *n.* **1.** Freedom from sorrow or care. **2.** The pansy or various similar plants of the genus *Viola.* **3.** The common persicaria, a plant. Also **heart′s′-ease′.**

heart·seed (härt′sēd′) *n.* The balloon vine.

heart·sick (härt′sik′) *adj.* Deeply disappointed or despondent. Also **heart′sore′** (-sôr′, -sōr′).

heart·some (härt′səm) *adj. Brit. Dial.* Cheerful or animated; lively; merry; gay. **— heart′some·ly** *adv.*

heart-strick·en (härt′strik′ən) *adj.* Overwhelmed with grief or fear. Also **heart′-struck′** (-struk′).

heart·strings (härt′stringz′) *n.pl.* The strongest feelings or affections.

heart-to-heart (härt′tə-härt′) *adj.* Marked by frankness, intimacy, and sincerity.

heart-whole (härt′hōl′) *adj.* **1.** Having the affections free; not in love. **2.** Undaunted; sincere. **— heart′-whole′ness** *n.*

heart·wood (härt′wŏŏd′) *n.* The duramen. For illustration see EXOGEN.

heart·worm (härt′wûrm′) *n. Vet.* A nematode worm (genus *Filaria*) parasitic in the heart and blood stream of dogs.

heart·y (här′tē) *adj.* **heart·i·er, heart·i·est 1.** Full of affectionate warmth or cordiality; friendly: a *hearty* welcome. **2.** Strongly felt; unrestrained; vigorous: a *hearty* dislike. **3.** Healthy and strong. **4.** Supplying abundant nourishment: a *hearty* meal; also, enjoying or requiring abundant nourishment: a *hearty* appetite. **5.** Fertile: said of land. **—** *n. pl.* **heart·ies** A hearty fellow or sailor. **— heart′i·ness** *n.*

heat (hēt) *n.* **1.** The state or quality of being hot; hotness; also, degree of hotness; high temperature. **2.** That which raises the temperature of a body or substance; also, the rise in temperature itself. **3.** *Physics* A form of energy directly associated with and proportional to the random molecular motions of a substance or body as caused by combustion, friction, chemical action, radiation, etc., and convertible into other forms of energy. ◆ Collateral adjective: *thermal.* **4.** The sensation produced by a rise in temperature. **5.** Condition, appearance, or color indicating high temperature. **6.** Hot weather, or a hot climate. **7.** Warmth supplied for a building, room, etc., as by a heating device: The *heat* comes on at six o'clock. **8.** *Metall.* **a** A single heating, melting, or smelting operation, as in working iron or steel. **b** The material thus treated. **9.** A single effort or trial, especially a course in a race: to run several *heats.* **10.** Great intensity of feeling, especially of anger or irritation; excitement; passion: the *heat* of debate. **11.** The highest point of intensity; greatest excitement or fury: the *heat* of battle. **12.** *Zool.* **a** Sexual excitement. **b** The period of sexual excitement in females; estrus. **13.** *Physiol.* The sensation of warmth experienced when certain receptors in the skin are stimulated. **14.** *U.S. Slang* **a** Any vigorous activity. **b** In the underworld, pressure applied to obtain information by or as by torture. **c** In the underworld, intensive police action, as raids, etc. **—** *v.t. & v.i.* **1.** To make or become hot or warm. **2.** To excite or become excited. Abbr. (n. defs. 3, 8, 9) *ht.* [OE *hǣtu*] **— heat′ed** *adj.* **— heat′ed·ly** *adv.*

heat capacity The amount of heat required to raise the temperature of a given mass by one degree.

heat content *Physics* Enthalpy.

heat death *Physics* The state of complete thermodynamic equilibrium in a material system: also called *thermal death.*

heat engine An engine for the conversion of heat into mechanical energy, as an internal combustion engine.

heat·er (hē′tər) *n.* **1.** An apparatus or device for producing heat or warmth, as a stove, furnace, etc. **2.** A workman whose job is to heat something: a rivet *heater.* **3.** *Electronics* An element in an electron tube that heats the cathode to the temperature of emission. **4.** *U.S. Slang* A pistol.

heat exhaustion A mild form of heat stroke: also called *heat prostration.*

heath (hēth) *n.* **1.** A low, hardy, evergreen shrub of a large genus (*Erica*), with narrow, usually whorled leaves and small tubular or globose, rose, white, or yellow flowers, typical of a widely distributed family (*Ericaceae*) of hardwood shrubs and small trees, including the arbutus, azalea, and rhododendron. **2.** The common heather. **3.** *Brit.* An area of open land overgrown with heath or coarse herbage. **4.** In Coverdale's and later versions of the Old Testament, a desert plant, tamarisk or savin. *Jer.* xvii 6; xlviii 6. [OE *hǣth*]

heath aster A common aster (*Aster ericoides*) of the eastern United States, having thick clusters of small white or pink flowers: also called *dogfennel*.

heath·ber·ry (hēth′ber′ē, -bər-ē) *n. pl.* **·ries** Any of various plants bearing berries and growing on heaths.

hea·then (hē′thən) *n. pl.* **·thens** or **·then 1.** A member of a tribe or people that has not adopted Christianity, Judaism, or Islam, especially a person worshiping many gods; idolater. **2.** In the Old Testament, a non-Jew; Gentile. **3.** Any irreligious or uncultivated person. — *adj.* **1.** Unbelieving; irreligious. **2.** Of or pertaining to heathen peoples. [OE *hǣthen.* Akin to HEATH.] — **hea′then·ism, hea′then·ry** (-rē). — **Syn.** (noun) **1.** *Heathen, pagan,* and *Gentile* originally designated a person who had not been converted to a dominant religion. *Heathen* has now become restricted to members of aboriginal peoples, usually those having polytheistic religions. *Pagan* is used of ancient peoples, as the Greeks and Romans, and *Gentile,* a Biblical word, refers to any non-Jew.

hea·then·dom (hē′thən-dəm) *n.* **1.** Heathen beliefs and practices. **2.** The countries or regions inhabited by heathen peoples; also, heathen peoples collectively.

hea·then·ish (hē′thən-ish) *adj.* **1.** Of or pertaining to the heathen. **2.** Suitable to or resembling the heathen; barbarous. — **hea′then·ish·ly** *adv.* — **hea′then·ish·ness** *n.*

hea·then·ize (hē′thən-īz) *v.t. & v.i.* **·ized, ·iz·ing** To make or become heathenish or heathen.

heath·er (heth′ər) *n.* **1.** A hardy evergreen shrub (genus *Calluna*) related to the heath; especially, the **common** or **Scotch heather** (*C. vulgaris*), having spikelike racemes of pinkish flowers: also called *ling.* **2.** A dull, grayish red color. [ME *hadder;* origin unknown; infl. in form by HEATH]

heath·er·y (heth′ər-ē) *adj.* **1.** Resembling heather. **2.** Abounding in heather.

heath grass A perennial grass (*Sieglingia decumbens*) found on heaths and moors in Europe. Also **heather grass.**

heath grouse A European grouse (*Lyrurus tetrix*) found in the heath country of Great Britain, the male of which is mostly black, with a lyre-shaped tail: also called *black grouse.* Also **heath·bird** (hēth′bûrd′), **heath cock.**

heath hen An extinct American grouse (*Tympanuchus cupido cupido*) of western North America.

heath·y (hē′thē) *adj.* **heath·i·er, heath·i·est 1.** Of or resembling heath. **2.** Covered by or abounding in heath.

heat lightning *Meteorol.* A fitful play of lightning without thunder, sometimes seen near the horizon on hot evenings.

heat of fusion *Physics* The latent heat required to melt a given mass of a solid that is at the melting point.

heat of vaporization *Physics* The latent heat needed to vaporize a mass of a liquid without raising its temperature.

heat prostration Heat exhaustion (which see).

heat pump A device resembling a refrigerating machine, used for transferring heat between some large body like the atmosphere, the earth, a lake, etc., and a smaller space like a room, house, etc., for heating or cooling the latter.

heat rash Prickly heat, a skin inflammation.

heat shield *Aerospace* A covering at the front of a space vehicle to protect it from heat generated on reentry.

heat stroke A state of exhaustion or collapse, usually accompanied by fever, caused by excessive or prolonged exposure to great heat.

heat wave A period of very hot weather.

heaume (hōm) *n.* In medieval armor, a large helmet sometimes fitting over an inner one and resting on the shoulders; casque. [< F < OF *helme.* Akin to HELM².]

heave (hēv) *v.* **heaved** or (*esp. Naut.*) **hove, heav·ing** *v.t.* **1.** To throw or hurl, especially with great effort. **2.** To raise with effort; lift; hoist. **3.** To cause to rise or bulge: to *heave* one's chest. **4.** To utter painfully: to *heave* a sigh. **5.** *Naut.* **a** To pull up (an anchor, net, etc.). **b** To pull or haul on (a rope, cable, etc.). **c** To cause (a ship) to move in a specified direction by or as by hauling on cables or ropes. **6.** *Geol.* To fracture or displace (a vein or stratum) horizontally. — *v.i.* **7.** To rise or swell up; bulge. **8.** To rise and fall repeatedly: The stormy sea *heaves.* **9.** To vomit; retch. **10.** *Naut.* **a** To move or proceed: said of ships. **b** To haul or pull, as on a rope; push, as on a capstan bar. — **heave, ho!** *Naut.* Pull (or push) hard together! — **to heave in** (or **into**) **sight** To appear to rise into view, as a ship on the horizon. — **to heave to 1.** To bring (a ship) to a standstill by heading into the wind with the sails hauled in or shortened. **2.** To cause a ship to lie to, as in a storm. — *n.* **1.** The act or exertion of heaving. **2.** *Geol.* The horizontal displacement of the parts of a fractured mineral vein or stratum, measured at right angles to the strike of the fault. [OE *hebban* to lift]

heav·en (hev′ən) *n.* **1.** *Theol.* The abode of God and his angels, where virtuous souls receive eternal reward after death, especially in the Christian and Islamic religions; celestial paradise. **2.** In various religious systems, any supernatural region inhabited by a deity or deities, slain heroes, etc., as Valhalla or Elysium. **3.** *Usually pl.* The regions around and above the earth; firmament; sky. **4.** Any condition of great happiness. **5.** Any place resembling heaven in beauty or happiness. [OE *heofon*] — **heav′en·li·ness** *n.*

Heav·en (hev′ən) God, or the Supreme Being; the celestial powers: *Heaven* keep thee.

heav·en·ly (hev′ən-lē) *adj.* **1.** Of or belonging to the heaven of God. **2.** Of or pertaining to the natural sky: *heavenly* bodies. **3.** Full of the beauty and peace befitting heaven: often a general expression of approval. — **heav′en·li·ness** *n.*

heav·en·ward (hev′ən-wərd) *adv.* Toward heaven. Also **heav′en·wards.** — *adj.* Directed toward heaven.

heav·er (hē′vər) *n.* **1.** One who heaves or lifts. **2.** A short bar or stick used as a lever for twisting rope; handspike.

heaves (hēvz) *n.pl.* (*construed as sing.*) *Vet.* An asthmatic disease of horses: also called *broken wind.*

heav·i·er-than-air (hev′ē-ər-than-âr′) *adj.* Having a weight greater than that of the air it displaces: said of airplanes, etc.

heav·i·ly (hev′ə-lē) *adv.* **1.** With great weight or burden: *heavily* loaded. **2.** With affliction and pain; sorely; grievously: His woes press *heavily.* **3.** With power and intensity; severely: to be *heavily* attacked. **4.** Densely; thickly: *heavily* populated. **5.** In a ponderous and clumsy way.

heav·i·ness (hev′ē-nis) *n.* **1.** The quality of being heavy; weight; ponderousness. **2.** Sadness; grief.

Heav·i·side layer (hev′i·sīd) The lower region of the ionosphere, about 60 miles above the earth, that reflects radio waves of relatively low frequency back to the earth: also called *E layer, Kennelly-Heaviside layer.* [after O. *Heaviside,* 1850–1925, English physicist]

heav·y (hev′ē) *adj.* **heav·i·er, heav·i·est 1.** Having great weight; hard to lift or move. **2.** Having relatively great weight in relation to size; having high specific gravity: the *heavy* metals. **3.** Having more than usual quantity, volume, etc.: a *heavy* vote; a *heavy* snowfall. **4.** Practicing or indulging on a large scale: a *heavy* smoker; a *heavy* buyer. **5.** Having force and severity: a *heavy* blow; a *heavy* sea. **6.** Exceeding the usual weight: *heavy* woolens. **7.** Having great importance; grave; serious: a *heavy* responsibility. **8.** Much; considerable: *heavy* emphasis. **9.** Hard to do or accomplish; difficult; arduous: *heavy* labor; *heavy* going. **10.** Dark or threatening: *heavy* skies. **11.** Hard to endure or bear; oppressive. **12.** Sorrowful; mournful: a *heavy* duty. **13.** Feeling or expressing grief; despondent: a *heavy* heart. **14.** Giving an impression of weight or ponderousness; thick; massive: *heavy* features; *heavy* lines. **15.** Lacking animation and grace; ponderous: a *heavy* prose style; a *heavy* step. **16.** Lacking precision and delicacy; clumsy: a *heavy* hand. **17.** Of food, not easily digested; rich, coarse, fatty, etc. **18.** Of bread, pastry, etc., dense in texture; poorly leavened. **19.** Permeating and strong: a *heavy* odor. **20.** Profound; unbroken: a *heavy* silence. **21.** Showing fatigue; needing rest: *heavy* eyes. **22.** Lacking vigor or alertness; thick; dull: to awake with a *heavy* head. **23.** Producing basic, often massive goods, as steel, used in other industries: *heavy* industry. **24.** Weighed down; burdened: a tree *heavy* with fruit; eyes *heavy* with sleep. **25.** Pregnant: *heavy* with young. **26.** In the theater, designating a serious or tragic role, or the role of a villain. **27.** Describing the strongest of three levels of stress used in utterances. **28.** *Physics* **a** Designating an isotope having a mass greater than that of others occurring in the same element: *heavy* hydrogen. **b** Designating an atomic particle intermediate in mass between pi-mesons and protons. **29.** *Mil.* **a** Designating the more massive types of weapons: *heavy* tank. **b** Formerly, designating troops or units with relatively massive equipment: *heavy* cavalry. — *adv.* Heavily. — **to hang heavy** To pass very slowly; drag by tediously, as time. — *n. pl.* **heav·ies 1.** In the theater, the role or the actor of a serious or tragic personage; also, the villain or the actor portraying him. **2.** *U.S. Informal* In sports, a heavyweight boxer, wrestler, etc. **3.** *pl.* Heavy artillery or cavalry. [OE *hefig*]

heav·y-du·ty (hev′ē-dōō′tē, -dyōō′-) *adj.* **1.** Strongly constructed for long strain, hard use, etc. **2.** Subject to a high import or export tax rate.

heavy earth Baryta.

heav·y-hand·ed (hev′ē-han′did) *adj.* **1.** Bungling; clumsy. **2.** Oppressive; domineering; cruel. — **heav′y-hand′ed·ly** *adv.* — **heav′y-hand′ed·ness** *n.*

heav·y-heart·ed (hev′ē-här′tid) *adj.* Melancholy; depressed; sad. — **heav′y-heart′ed·ly** *adv.* — **heav′y-heart′ed·ness** *n.*

heavy hydrogen Deuterium.

heav·y·set (hev′ē·set′) *adj.* Solidly built; stocky.
heavy spar Barite.
heavy water Deuterium oxide, D_2O, the compound of oxygen and the heavy isotope of hydrogen.
heav·y·weight (hev′ē·wāt′) *n.* **1.** A person or animal of much more than average weight. **2.** A boxer or wrestler over 175 pounds in weight. **3.** *U.S. Informal* A person of great influence, importance, or intelligence. — *adj.* Of more than average weight or thickness.
Heb. or **Hebr.** Hebrew(s).
Heb·bel (heb′əl), **Friedrich,** 1813–63, German dramatist.
heb·do·mad (heb′də·mad) *n.* **1.** The number seven. **2.** A period of seven days; week. [< L *hebdomas, -adis* < Gk. *hebdomas* < *hepta* seven]
heb·dom·a·dal (heb·dom′ə·dəl) *adj.* Occurring or appearing every seven days; weekly. Also **heb·dom′a·dar′y** (-der′ē). — **heb·dom′a·dal·ly** *adv.*
He·be (hē′bē) In Greek mythology, the goddess of youth and spring, cupbearer to the gods.
he·be·phre·ni·a (hē′bə·frē′nē·ə) *n. Psychiatry* A form of schizophrenia, usually associated with puberty, characterized by shallow, unsystematic behavior, inappropriate emotions, and other exaggerated mannerisms. [< NL < Gk. *hēbē* youth + *phrēn* mind] — **he′be·phren′ic** (-fren′ik) *adj.*
heb·e·tate (heb′ə·tāt) *v.i. & v.t.* **·tat·ed, ·tat·ing** To make or become blunt or dull. — *adj. Bot.* Having a blunt, soft point, as in certain plants. [< L *hebetatus,* pp. of *hebetare* to be dull < *hebes* dull] — **heb′e·ta′tion** *n.* — **heb′e·ta′tive** *adj.*
heb·e·tude (heb′ə·tōōd, -tyōōd) *n.* The state of being dull or obtuse; lethargy. [< LL *hebetudo* < L *hebes, -etis* dull]
He·bra·ic (hi·brā′ik) *adj.* Relating to or characteristic of the Hebrew people and their culture and language. Also **He·bra′i·cal.** [< LL *Hebraicus* < Gk. *Hebraikos* < *Hebraios* a Hebrew] — **He·bra′i·cal·ly** *adv.*
He·bra·ism (hē′brā·iz′əm, -brə-) *n.* **1.** A Hebrew idiom. **2.** Hebrew thought, character, practice, etc. **3.** The religion of the Hebrews; Judaism.
He·bra·ist (hē′brā·ist, -brə-) *n.* **1.** One proficient in or a student of the Hebrew language. **2.** One who conforms to and upholds Hebraic thought and traditions. Also **He′brew·ist.** — **He′bra·is′tic** or **·ti·cal** *adj.*
He·bra·ize (hē′brā·īz, -brə-) *v.* **·ized, ·iz·ing** *v.t.* **1.** To make Hebrew. — *v.i.* **2.** To adopt Hebrew customs, language, etc.
He·brew (hē′brōō) *n.* **1.** A member of that group of Semitic peoples claiming descent from the house of Abraham; Israelite; Jew. **2.** The ancient Semitic language of the Israelites as used in much of the Old Testament: now retained as a scholarly and religious language. **3.** The modern Hebrew language: official language of the republic of Israel. — **Epistle to the Hebrews** A book of the New Testament of uncertain authorship, addressed to Hebrew Christians: also **Hebrews.** — *adj.* Hebraic; Jewish. *Abbr.* **Heb., Hebr.** [< OF *Hebreu* < L *Hebraeus* < Gk. *Hebraios* < Hebrew *'ibhri,* lit., one from beyond (Jordan)]
Hebrew calendar See (Hebrew) CALENDAR.
Heb·ri·des (heb′rə·dēz) The islands off the western coast of Scotland, divided into two groups, the **Inner Hebrides** and the **Outer Hebrides;** about 3,000 sq. mi.: also *Western Islands.* — **Heb′ri·de·an** (-dē′ən) or **He·brid·i·an** (hə·brid′ē·ən) *adj. & n.*
He·bron (hē′brən) A town in western Jordan, near Jerusalem; since 1967, occupied by Israel; pop. about 36,000: ancient *Kirjath-Arba;* Arabic *El Khalil.*
Hec·a·te (hek′ə·tē) In Greek mythology, a goddess of earth, moon, and underworld, later associated with sorcery: also spelled *Hekate.*
hec·a·tomb (hek′ə·tōm, -tōōm) *n.* **1.** In ancient Greece, a great sacrifice to the gods, originally of a hundred oxen. **2.** Any great slaughter or sacrifice. [< L *hecatombe* < Gk. *hekatombē* < *hekaton* hundred + *bous* ox]
heck (hek) *interj. Slang* Hell: a euphemism.
heck·le (hek′əl) *v.t.* **·led, ·ling 1.** To try to confuse or annoy with taunts, questions, etc. **2.** To hatchel (flax, etc.). — *n.* A hatchel. [ME *hechelen* < *hechele.* See HATCHEL.] — **heck′ler** *n.*
hec·tare (hek′tar) *n.* A unit of area in the metric system, equal to 10,000 square meters or 2.471 acres: also spelled *hektare. Abbr.* **ha.** See table inside back cover.
hec·tic (hek′tik) *adj.* **1.** Characterized by great excitement, turmoil, haste, etc.: a *hectic* trip. **2.** Denoting a particular condition or habit of body, as in wasting diseases. **3.** Pertaining to or affected with hectic fever. Also **hec′ti·cal.** [< F *hectique* < LL *hecticus* < Gk. *hektikos* consumptive < *hexis* state of the body < *echein* to have] — **hec′ti·cal·ly** *adv.*
hectic fever *Pathol.* A daily rise in body temperature occurring in a wasting disease, as in pulmonary tuberculosis.
hectic flush The flush on the cheeks in hectic fever.
hecto- *combining form* In the metric system and in technical usage, a hundred times (a specified unit): *hectogram.* Also spelled *hekto-.* Also, before vowels, **hect-.** [< F < Gk. *hekaton* hundred]
hec·to·cot·y·lus (hek′tə·kot′ə·ləs) *n. pl.* **·li** (-lī) *Zool.* One of the arms in a male cephalopod, modified to serve as a reproductive organ. [< HECTO- + Gk. *kotylē* cup]

hec·to·gram (hek′tə·gram) *n.* In the metric system, a measure of weight equal to 100 grams or 3.527 ounces avoirdupois: also spelled *hektogram.* Also **hec′to·gramme.** *Abbr.* **hg.** See table inside back cover.
hec·to·graph (hek′tə·graf, -gräf) *n.* A gelatin pad for making multiple copies of a writing or drawing: also called *copygraph.* — *v.t.* To copy by hectograph. — **hec′to·graph′ic** *adj.* — **hec′to·graph′i·cal·ly** *adv.*
hec·to·li·ter (hek′tə·lē′tər) *n.* In the metric system, a measure of capacity equal to 100 liters or 2.838 U.S. bushels. Also *esp. Brit.* **hec′to·li′tre.** *Abbr.* **hl, hl.** See table inside back cover.
hec·to·me·ter (hek′tə·mē′tər, hek·tom′ə·tər) *n.* In the metric system, a measure of length equal to 100 meters or 328.08 feet. Also *esp. Brit.* **hec′to·me′tre.** *Abbr.* **hm., hm** See table inside back cover.
hec·tor (hek′tər) *v.t. & v.i.* **1.** To bully; bluster; rant. **2.** To tease; torment. — *n.* A quarrelsome, domineering fellow; bully. [after *Hector*]
Hec·tor (hek′tər) In the *Iliad,* a Trojan hero, son of Priam and Hecuba: killed by Achilles to avenge Patroclus.
hec·to·stere (hek′tə·stir) *n.* In the metric system, a measure of volume equal to 100 cubic meters.
Hec·u·ba (hek′yōō·bə) In the *Iliad,* the wife of Priam and mother of Hector, Troilus, Paris, Cassandra, and others.
he'd (hēd) **1.** He had. **2.** He would.
hed·dle (hed′l) *n.* One of the sets of vertical cords or wires in a loom used to separate adjacent warp threads and make a channel for the shuttle. [OE *hefeld* thread for weaving]
he·der (hē′dər) *n. Brit. Dial.* A young male sheep.
hedge (hej) *n.* **1.** A fence or barrier formed of privet or other bushes set close together; also, any boundary or barrier. **2.** The act of hedging a bet, risk, etc.; also, that which is used to hedge. — *v.* **hedged, hedg·ing** *v.t.* **1.** To surround or border with a hedge; separate with a hedge. **2.** To set barriers and restrictions to, so as to hinder freedom of movement or action; hem: often with *in* or *about:* to *hedge* a person in. **3.** To guard against undue loss from (a bet, investment, etc.) by making compensatory bets, investments, etc. — *v.i.* **4.** To make compensatory bets, etc., in order to restrict losses. **5.** To avoid forthright statement or action; temporize; tergiversate. **6.** To work on hedges or fences. [OE *hegg*] — **hedg′er** *n.* — **hedg′y** *adj.*
hedge apple The Osage orange.
hedge bill A bill[3] (def. 1). Also **hedging bill.**
hedge garlic A tall weed (*Sisymbrium alliaria*) of the mustard family, with heart-shaped leaves, white flowers, erect pods, and a garlicky odor.
hedge·hog (hej′hôg′, -hog′) *n.* **1.** A small, nocturnal, insectivorous mammal (family *Erinaceidae*) of Europe, having stout spines on the back and sides. **2.** *U.S.* The porcupine. **3.** *Mil.* An obstacle made of barbed wire on frames.

EUROPEAN HEDGEHOG
(About 10 inches long)

hedge·hop (hej′hop′) *v.i.* **·hopped, ·hopping** To fly close to the ground in an airplane, rising over houses, trees, etc., as in spraying insecticide or bombing. — **hedge′hop′per** *n.*
hedge hyssop A European perennial herb (*Gratiola officinalis*) of the figwort family, once used medicinally.
hedge parson *Brit.* Formerly, one of a class of vagabond and illiterate clergy. Also **hedge priest.**
hedge·row (hej′rō′) *n.* A dense row of bushes, trees, etc., planted as a hedge.
hedge sparrow A small brownish European warbler (*Prunella modularis*) that frequents hedges.
He·din (he·dēn′), **Sven,** 1865–1952, Swedish explorer.
He·djaz (hē·jaz′, he-) See HEJAZ.
he·don·ic (hē·don′ik) *adj.* **1.** Of or pertaining to pleasure. **2.** Of or pertaining to hedonism or hedonics. [< Gk. *hēdonikos* < *hēdonē* pleasure < *hēdys* sweet]
he·don·ics (hē·don′iks) *n.pl.* (construed as sing.) **1.** *Psychol.* The study of pleasurable and unpleasurable states. **2.** *Philos.* The part of ethics that treats of pleasure.
he·don·ism (hēd′n·iz′əm) *n.* **1.** *Philos.* The doctrine that pleasure is the only good and proper goal of moral endeavor. **2.** The self-indulgent pursuit of pleasure.
he·don·ist (hēd′n·ist) *n.* One who regards the pursuit of pleasure as the chief activity of life; also, a believer in hedonism. — **he′don·is′tic** *adj.* — **he′don·is′ti·cal·ly** *adv.*
-hedral *combining form* Having (a specified number of) sides or faces: *octahedral.* [< -HEDR(ON) + -AL]
-hedron *combining form* A figure having (a specified number of) sides or faces: *octahedron.* [< Gk. *hedra* surface]
hee·bie-jee·bies (hē′bē·jē′bēz) *n.pl. Slang* A fit of nervousness. [Coined by Billy de Beck, died 1942, U.S. cartoonist]
heed (hēd) *v.t.* **1.** To pay attention to; take more than casual notice of; listen to. — *v.i.* **2.** To pay attention; listen. — *n.* Careful attention or consideration. [OE *hēdan*] — **heed′er** *n.*
heed·ful (hēd′fəl) *adj.* Giving heed; attentive; mindful. — **heed′ful·ly** *adv.* — **heed′ful·ness** *n.*
heed·less (hēd′lis) *adj.* Not showing any heed or attention; careless; reckless. — **heed′less·ly** *adv.*

heed·less·ness (hēd′lis·nis) *n.* The state or quality of being heedless. — *Syn.* See TEMERITY.

hee·haw (hē′hô′) *n.* **1.** The braying sound of a donkey. **2.** Loud, rude laughter. — *v.i.* **1.** To bray. **2.** To laugh in a loud, rude manner. [Imit.]

heel[1] (hēl) *n.* **1.** In man, the rounded posterior part of the foot under and in back of the ankle; also, the rounded part of the palm of the hand nearest the wrist. **2.** The analogous part of the hind foot of an animal. **3.** That part of a shoe, stocking, or other article of footwear covering the heel. **4.** In a shoe or boot, the built-up portion on which the rear of the foot rests. For illustration see SHOE. **5.** Something that is like the human heel in appearance or location, as the rounded end of a loaf of bread, or the lower rear part of the head of a golf club. **6.** *Naut.* **a** The lower end of a mast, spar, frame, etc. **b** The lower part of the stern. **7.** *Slang* A habitually dishonorable person; contemptible chiseler; crumb. **8.** *Rare* The entire foot. — **at heel** Right at one's heels; close behind. — **down at the heel** **1.** Having the heels of one's shoes worn down. **2.** Shabby; slovenly; run-down. — **on** (or **upon**) **the heels of** **1.** Right behind. **2.** Close after; quickly following. — **to cool one's heels** To be kept waiting. — **to drag one's heels** To act or agree reluctantly. — **to heel** **1.** To an attendant position close behind one. **2.** To submission; under control. — **to kick up one's heels** **1.** To have a good time. **2.** To let oneself go. — **to lay by the heels** To put in prison; capture. — **to take to one's heels** To run away; flee. — *v.t.* **1.** To supply with a heel, as a shoe. **2.** To follow on the heels of; pursue closely. **3.** *U.S. Slang* To supply with something, especially with money or a weapon. **4.** In golf, to strike (the ball) with the heel of the club. **5.** In cockfighting, to arm (a cock) with steel spurs. — *v.i.* **6.** To move the heels, as in dancing. **7.** To follow at one's heels. [OE *hēla*] — **heel′less** *adj.*

heel[2] (hēl) *Naut. v.t. & v.i.* To lean or cause to lean to one side; cant, as a ship. — *Syn.* See TIP. — *n.* The act of heeling or inclining laterally from an upright position; a cant; list: also **heel′ing.** [Earlier *heeld,* OE *hieldan*]

heel-and-toe (hēl′ən·tō′) *adj.* Designating a manner of walking in which the heel of one foot touches the ground before the toes of the other foot leave it.

heel bone The calcaneus.

heeled (hēld) *adj.* **1.** Having heels; fitted with heels: often used in combination: *high-heeled.* **2.** *U.S. Slang* **a** Supplied with money. **b** Armed, as with a gun.

heel·er (hēl′ər) *n.* **1.** One who heels shoes. **2.** *U.S. Slang* A ward heeler (which see).

heel·piece (hēl′pēs′) *n.* **1.** A piece fastened to or forming the heel of a stocking or shoe. **2.** The bar of iron connecting the soft iron cores in an electromagnet.

heel·post (hēl′pōst′) *n.* A post serving as or supporting the heel or end of something, as a door or gate.

heel·tap (hēl′tap′) *n.* **1.** A thickness of leather on the heel of a shoe. **2.** A small quantity of liquor left in a glass.

Heep (hēp), **Uriah** See URIAH HEEP.

heeze (hēz) *v.t.* **heezed, heez·ing** *Scot.* To hoist. [Akin to LG *hiesen*]

Hef·ner lamp (hef′nər) See under STANDARD LAMP.

heft (heft) *Informal v.t.* **1.** To test or gauge the weight of by lifting. **2.** To lift up; heave. — *v.i.* **3.** To weigh. — *n.* **1.** Weight. **2.** *U.S.* The bulk or gist. [Akin to HEAVE]

heft·y (hef′tē) *adj.* **heft·i·er, heft·i·est** *Informal* **1.** Heavy; weighty: a *hefty* package. **2.** Large and bulky, and usually powerful. **3.** Forceful; powerful: a *hefty* blow.

He·gel (hā′gəl), **Georg Wilhelm Friedrich,** 1770–1831, German philosopher. — **He·ge·li·an** (hə·gā′lē·ən) *n. & adj.*

He·ge·li·an·ism (hə·gā′lē·ən·iz′əm) *n.* The philosophical system of Hegel. Its central assumption is that the real is the rational, so that all things are logically related, and anything short of the absolute totality is a distortion of reality. It maintains that dialectic reasoning, a process whereby thought passes repeatedly in ascending stages from thesis to antithesis to synthesis, can unravel the necessary order of development in which human consciousness and reality participate. Also **He·gel·ism** (hā′gəl·iz′əm).

he·gem·o·ny (hə·jem′ə·nē, hej′ə·mō′nē, hē′jə-) *n. pl.* **·nies** Domination or leadership; especially, the predominant influence of one state over others. [< Gk. *hēgemonia* < *hēgeesthai* to lead] — **heg·e·mon·ic** (hej′ə·mon′ik) *adj.*

he·gi·ra (hi·jī′rə, hej′ə·rə) *n.* Any precipitate flight or departure: also spelled *hejira.* [< Med.L < Arabic *hijrah* departure < *hajara* to go away]

He·gi·ra (hi·jī′rə, hej′ə·rə) *n.* **1.** The flight of Mohammed from Mecca to Medina in 622, now taken as the beginning of the Moslem era. **2.** The Moslem era. Also spelled *Hejira.*

he·gu·men (hi·gyōō′men) *n.* In the Eastern Orthodox Church, the head or the second in charge of a monastery, corresponding to an abbot or a prior in the Roman Catholic Church. See ARCHIMANDRITE. Also **he·gu′me·nos** (-nos), **he·gou′me·nos.** [< Med.L *hegumenus* < Gk. *hēgoumenos,* var. of *hēgeomenos,* ppr. of *hēgeesthai* to lead]

he·gu·me·ne (hi·gyōō′mə·nē) *n.* In the Eastern Orthodox Church, the head of a nunnery, corresponding to an abbess in the Roman Catholic Church. [< Gk. *hegoumenē,* fem. var. of *hēgeomenos.* See HEGUMEN.]

he·gu·me·ny (hi·gyōō′mə·nē) *n. pl.* **·nies** The office or position of a hegumen.

Hei·del·berg (hīd′l·bûrg, *Ger.* hī′dəl·berkh) A university city in Baden-Württemberg, West Germany; pop. 121,929(1970).

Heidelberg man *Anthropol.* A type of primitive man (*Homo heidelbergensis*) known only by a massive lower jawbone discovered in 1907 in a sandpit near Heidelberg.

Hei·duc (hī′dŏŏk) See HAIDUK.

heif·er (hef′ər) *n.* A young cow that has not produced a calf. [OE *heahfore*]

Hei·fetz (hī′fits), **Ja·scha** (yä′shə), born 1901, U.S. violinist born in Lithuania.

heigh (hā, hī) *interj. Archaic* An exclamation to attract attention, give encouragement, indicate pleasure, etc.

heigh-ho (hī′hō′, hā′-) *interj. Archaic* An exclamation of weariness, disappointment, surprise, etc.

height (hīt) *n.* **1.** The state or quality of being high or relatively high. **2.** The distance from the base to the top; altitude; stature. **3.** The distance above a given level, as the sea or horizon. **4.** *Often pl.* A lofty or high place; eminence; elevation. **5.** The highest part of anything; summit; apex. **6.** The highest degree; culmination: the *height* of quality. *Abbr.* (defs. 2, 3) *h., H., hgt., ht.* (def. 4) *Hts.* [OE *htehtho*]

height·en (hīt′n) *v.t. & v.i.* **1.** To make or become high or higher; raise or lift. **2.** To make or become more in degree, amount, size, etc.; intensify. — **height′en·er** *n.* — *Syn.* **1.** elevate, exalt. **2.** aggravate. See INCREASE.

height of land *Canadian* A watershed.

height-to-pa·per (hīt′tə·pā′pər) *n. Printing* The standard height of type: in the United States, 0.9186 inch; in England, 0.9175 inch. See TYPE-HIGH.

heil (hīl) *German interj.* Hail! — *v.t.* To salute with "heil."

Heil·bronn (hīl′brôn) A city in Baden-Württemberg, West Germany; pop. 99,440 (est. 1970).

Hei·lung·kiang (hā′lŏŏng·jyäng′) A Province of NE China; 108,880 sq. mi.; pop. 14,860,000 (est. 1957); capital, Harbin. Also **Hei′-lung′-chiang/.**

Heim·dall (hām′däl) In Norse mythology, the guardian of Bifrost, the rainbow bridge that leads to Asgard. Also **Heim′dal, Heim′dallr** (-däl·r′).

Hei·ne (hī′nə), **Heinrich,** 1797–1856, German lyric poet.

Hei·nie (hī′nē) *n. Slang* A German soldier; kraut; krauthead: a contemptuous term. [< G *Heine,* dim. of *Heinrich*]

hei·nous (hā′nəs) *adj.* Extremely wicked; atrocious; odious. [< OF *hainos* < *haine* hatred < *hair* to hate] — **hei′nous·ly** *adv.* — **hei′nous·ness** *n.*

heir (âr) *n.* **1.** Anyone inheriting rank or property from a deceased person; inheritor; also, anyone likely to inherit upon the death of an incumbent or holder. **2.** One who or that which takes over or displays the qualities of some forerunner. **3.** *Law* **a** In the common law, one who on the death of another becomes entitled by operation of law to succeed to the deceased person's estate as an estate of inheritance: also **heir at law. b** In the civil law, one of various persons who may succeed to the rights of a deceased person either by his act or by the operation of law. **4.** *Archaic* An offspring. [< OF < L *heres*] — **heir′ess** *n. fem.* — **heir′less** *adj.*

heir apparent *pl.* **heirs apparent** *Law* One who must by course of law become the heir if he survives his ancestor.

heir·dom (âr′dəm) *n.* Heirship; inheritance.

heir·loom (âr′lōōm) *n.* **1.** Anything that has been handed down in a family for generations. **2.** *Law* Those chattels and articles that descend to an heir along with the estate. [< HEIR + LOOM, in obs. sense "tool"]

heir presumptive *pl.* **heirs presumptive** *Law* An heir whose claim to an estate may become void by the birth of a nearer relative.

heir·ship (âr′ship) *n.* **1.** The state or condition of being an heir. **2.** The right to inheritance.

Hei·sen·berg (hī′zən·berkh), **Werner,** 1901–1976, German physicist.

heist (hīst) *U.S. Slang v.t.* To steal. — *n.* A robbery. [Var. of HOIST]

He·jaz (hē·jaz′, he-) A division of western Saudi Arabia having its own constitution and legally constituting a separate kingdom; about 150,000 sq. mi.; pop. about 2 million; capital, Mecca: also *Hedjaz.*

he·ji·ra (hi·jī′rə, hej′ə·rə) See HEGIRA.

He·ji·ra (hi·jī′rə, hej′ə·rə) See HEGIRA.

Hek·a·te (hek′ə·tē) See HECATE.

Hek·la (hek′lə) An active volcano in SW Iceland; 4,747 ft.

hek·tare (hek′târ), **hek·to·gram** (hek′tə·gram), etc. See HECTARE, etc.

hekto- See HECTO-.

Hel (hel) In Norse mythology: **a** The goddess of those who died of old age or disease. **b** The kingdom of the dead not killed in battle: compare VALHALLA. Also **Hel·a** (hel′ə).

held (held) Past tense of HOLD.

Helen of Troy In Greek mythology, the beautiful daughter of Zeus and Leda, and the wife of Menelaus, king of Sparta. Her elopement to Troy with Paris caused the Trojan War.

Hel·e·na (hel′ə-nə) The capital of Montana, in the west central part; pop. 22,730.

Hel·e·na (hel′ə-nə), **Saint**, 247?–327?, mother of Constantine the Great.

Hel·e·nus (hel′ə-nəs) In Greek legend, a son of Priam and Hecuba, endowed with the gift of prophecy.

Hel·go·land (hel′gō-land′, *Ger.* hel′gə-länt′) A small island in the North Sea off NW Germany, near which the British defeated the Germans, Aug. 28, 1914, in the naval battle of **Helgoland Bight** (bīt). Also **Hel′i·go·land′**.

heli- See HELIO-.

he·li·a·cal (hi-lī′ə-kəl) *adj.* **1.** Pertaining to the sun; solar. **2.** Occurring near the sun, as those visible risings and settings of certain stars that are almost simultaneous with those of the sun. Also **he·li·ac** (hē′lē-ak). [< LL *heliacus* < Gk. *hēliakos* < *hēlios* the sun] **— he·li′a·cal·ly** *adv.*

he·li·an·thus (hē′lē-an′thəs) *n.* A sunflower. [< NL < Gk. *hēlios* sun + *anthos* flower]

he·li·ast (hē′lē-ast) *n.* A dicast, an Athenian judge. [< Gk. *heliastēs* < *heliazesthai* to sit in court]

hel·i·cal (hel′i-kəl) *adj.* Pertaining to or shaped like a helix. **— hel′i·cal·ly** *adv.*

hel·i·ces (hel′ə-sēz) Alternative plural of HELIX.

hel·i·cline (hel′ə-klīn) *n.* A ramp with a curving or spiral passageway. [< HELI(X) + (IN)CLINE]

helico- *combining form* Spiral; helical: *helicodromic.* Also, before vowels, **helic-.** [< Gk. *helix* spiral]

hel·i·co·dro·mic (hel′i-kō-drō′mik, -drom′ik) *adj. Aerospace* Having a flight path curving like a corkscrew. [< HELICO- + -DROM(OUS) + -IC]

hel·i·coid (hel′ə-koid) *adj.* Coiled spirally, as certain univalve shells. Also **hel′i·coi′dal.** **—** *n. Geom.* A surface generated by a straight line moving along a fixed helix in such a way as to maintain a constant angle with its axis. [< Gk. *helikoeidēs* spiral-shaped] **— hel′i·coi′dal·ly** *adv.*

hel·i·con (hel′i-kon, -kən) *n. Music* A large, roughly circular tuba. [< HELICON; infl. by HELIX]

Hel·i·con (hel′i-kon, -kən) A mountain range in Boeotia, east central Greece; highest point, 5,736 ft.; legendary home of the Muses; site of the fountain of Hippocrene. **— Hel·i·co·ni·an** (hel′i-kō′nē-ən) *adj.*

hel·i·cop·ter (hel′ə-kop′tər, hē′lə-) *n. Aeron.* A type of aircraft whose aerodynamic support is obtained from engine-driven airfoil blades rotating around a vertical axis, and that is capable of rising and descending vertically. [< F *hélicoptère* < Gk. *helix, ikos* spiral + *pteron* wing]

helio- *combining form* Sun; of the sun: *heliotropic.* Also, before vowels, **heli-.** [< Gk. *hēlios* the sun]

he·li·o·cen·tric (hē′lē-ə-sen′trik) *adj.* Having or regarding the sun as the center: the *heliocentric* universe. Also **he′li·o·cen′tri·cal.** **— he′li·o·cen·tric′i·ty** (-tris′ə-tē) *n.*

heliocentric parallax See under PARALLAX.

He·li·o·gab·a·lus (hē′lē-ə-gab′ə-ləs), 204–222, Marcus Aurelius Antoninus, Roman emperor 218–222. Also spelled *Elagabalus.* Compare AURELIUS.

he·li·o·gram (hē′lē-ə-gram′) *n.* A message sent by means of a heliograph. Also **he′li·o** (-lē-ō). Abbr. *hg.*

he·li·o·graph (hē′lē-ə-graf′, -gräf′) *n.* **1.** *Astron.* An instrument for taking photographs of the sun. **2.** A mirror for signaling by flashes of light. Also **he′li·o** (-lē-ō). **—** *v.t. & v.i.* To signal with a heliograph. **— he′li·og·ra·pher** (hē′lē-og′rə-fər) *n.* **— he′li·og′ra·phy** *n.*

he·li·o·la·try (hē′lē-ol′ə-trē) *n.* Worship of the sun. **— he′li·ol′a·ter** *n.* **— he′li·ol′a·trous** *adj.*

he·li·om·e·ter (hē′lē-om′ə-tər) *n. Astron.* An instrument for measuring angles between celestial bodies. **— he·li·o·met·ric** (hē′lē-ə-met′rik) or **·ri·cal** *adj.* **— he′li·om′e·try** *n.*

He·li·op·o·lis (hē′lē-op′ə-lis) **1.** An ancient city at the apex of the Nile delta in lower Egypt: Egyptian *On.* **2.** The Ancient Greek name for BAALBEK.

He·li·os (hē′lē-os) In Greek mythology, the sun god, son of Hyperion: also called *Hyperion, Titan.*

he·li·o·scope (hē′lē-ə-skōp′) *n. Astron.* A device within a telescope by which the eyes are protected from pain or injury while observing the sun.

he·li·o·stat (hē′lē-ə-stat′) *n. Astron.* An instrument consisting of a mirror moved by clockwork so that the rays of the sun are reflected from it in a constant direction.

he·li·o·tax·is (hē′lē-ə-tak′sis) *n.* Phototaxis resulting from the light of the sun. [< HELIO- + (PHOTO)TAXIS] **— he′li·o·tac′tic** (tak′tik) *adj.*

he·li·o·ther·a·py (hē′lē-ō-ther′ə-pē) *n. Med.* Exposure to the sun for purposes of treatment.

he·li·o·trope (hē′lē-ə-trōp′, hēl′yə-) *n.* **1.** An herb (genus *Heliotropium*), of the borage family, with white or purplish fragrant flowers. **2.** Any plant that turns toward the sun. **3.** The garden heliotrope or common valerian (*Valeriana officinalis*). **4.** The bloodstone. **5.** A soft, rosy purple, the color of heliotrope flowers. [< F *héliotrope* < L *heliotropium* < Gk. *hēliotropion* < *hēlios* sun + *trepein* to turn]

he·li·o·trop·ic (hē′lē-ə-trop′ik, -trō′pik, hēl′yə-) *adj.* Characterized by or pertaining to heliotropism. **— he′li·o·trop′i·cal·ly** *adv.*

he·li·ot·ro·pism (hē′lē-ot′rə-piz′əm) *n. Biol.* The tendency of some organisms to move or turn toward the sunlight (**positive heliotropism**) or away from it (**negative heliotropism**). Also **he′li·ot′ro·py.**

he·li·o·type (hē′lē-ə-tīp′) *n.* A photomechanical printing surface consisting of a gelatin film from which, after exposure under a negative and hardening with chrome alum, an impression may be taken in an ordinary press. Also **he′li·o·typ′ic** (-tip′ik). **— he′li·o·typ′y** (-tī′pē) *n.*

he·li·o·zo·an (hē′lē-ə-zō′ən) *n. Zool.* Any of an order (*Heliozoa*) of protozoan aquatic organisms with filamentous pseudopodia radiating from a spherical body. [< NL *Heliozoa* < Gk. *hēlios* sun + *zōion* animal]

hel·i·port (hel′ə-pôrt′, -pōrt′, hē′lə-) *n.* An airport for helicopters. [< HELI(COPTER) + (AIR)PORT]

he·li·um (hē′lē-əm) *n.* An odorless, nonflammable, gaseous element (symbol He) that is found chiefly in certain natural gas deposits, used to inflate balloons, dirigibles, etc. See ELEMENT. [< NL < Gk. *hēlios* sun]

he·lix (hē′liks) *n. pl.* **he·lix·es** or **hel·i·ces** (hel′ə-sēz) **1.** *Geom.* A line, thread, wire, or the like, curved into a shape such as it would assume if wound in a single layer round a cylinder; a form like a screw thread. **2.** Any spiral. **3.** *Anat.* The recurved border of the external ear. **4.** *Archit.* A small volute. **— Syn.** See SPIRAL. [< L, spiral < Gk.]

hell (hel) *n.* **1.** *Sometimes cap.* In various religions, the abode of the dead or the place of punishment for the wicked after death; the abode of evil spirits. Compare GEHENNA, HADES, INFERNO, TARTARUS. **2.** Any condition of great mental or physical suffering; agony; also, anything causing such suffering. **3.** A gambling house. **4.** A hellbox. **5.** In Christian Science, mortal belief; error; death; suffering and destruction. **— a** (or **one**) **hell of a** *Slang* A remarkably bad, good, difficult, etc. (thing): an intensive usage: *a hell of a* pain. **— like hell** *Slang* **1.** Very much, very fast, very bad, very loud, etc.: an intensive usage: He ran *like hell.* **2.** Not at all; never: an emphatic negative usage: *Like hell* he will! **— to be hell on** *Slang* **1.** To be damaging or harmful to. **2.** To be unpleasant or difficult for. **3.** To be very harsh or strict with. **— to catch** (or **get**) **hell** *U.S. Slang* To be roundly scolded or punished, as for a misdeed. **— to give** (**someone**) **hell** *Slang* To upbraid or punish (someone) severely. **— to raise hell** *Slang* To create a disturbance; make an uproar. **— interj.** An exclamation used as an imprecation or as an expression of anger or impatience. [OE *hel*]

he'll (hēl) He will.

Hel·lad·ic (he-lad′ik) *adj.* Of or pertaining to the pre-Greek civilization of the Aegean.

Hel·las (hel′əs) **1.** Ancient or modern Greece. **2.** Originally, a small district and town in Thessaly; later, all lands inhabited by Greek-speaking peoples. [< Gk.]

hell·bend·er (hel′ben′dər) *n. U.S.* **1.** A large and voracious aquatic salamander (*Cryptobranchus alleganiensis*), very tenacious of life, common to the Ohio River Valley: also called *land pike.* **2.** *Slang* An extended drunken spree. **3.** *Slang* A drunken, disorderly person.

hell·bent (hel′bent′) *adj. U.S. Slang* Determined to have or do; recklessly eager: *hell-bent* for home.

hell·box (hel′boks′) *n. Printing* A receptacle for broken or battered type.

hell·broth (hel′brôth′, -broth′) *n.* A magical mixture prepared for evil purposes.

hell·cat (hel′kat′) *n.* **1.** A furious or shrewish woman. **2.** A witch; hag.

hell·div·er (hel′dī′vər) *n.* The dabchick.

Hel·le (hel′ē) In Greek legend, the daughter of Nephele and Athamas who was drowned in the strait thereafter called *Hellespont,* or "sea of Helle."

hel·le·bore (hel′ə-bôr, -bōr) *n.* **1.** A perennial herb (genus *Helleborus*) of the crowfoot family, having serrated leaves and large flowers; especially, the **green hellebore** (*H. viridis*) of America and the **black hellebore** (*H. niger*) of Europe, the root of which is a powerful cathartic. **2.** The false hellebore. [< L *helleborus* < Gk. *helleboros*]

Hel·len (hel′ən) In Greek legend, son of Deucalion and the eponymous ancestor of the Hellenes or Greeks.

Hel·lene (hel′ēn) *n.* A Greek. Also **Hel·le′ni·an.** [< Gk. *Hellēn*]

Hel·len·ic (he-len′ik, -lē′nik) *adj.* Greek; Grecian. **—** *n.* A subfamily of the Indo-European languages, consisting of the Greek language and its dialects, ancient and modern.

Hel·len·ism (hel′ə-niz′əm) *n.* **1.** Ancient Greek character, ideals, or civilization. **2.** An idiom or turn of phrase peculiar to Greek. **3.** Assimilation of Greek speech, ideas, and culture, as by the Romans or the Jews of the Diaspora.

Hel·len·ist (hel′ə-nist) *n.* **1.** An adopter of Greek language, ideas, etc., especially a Jew of the Diaspora. **2.** A scholar or specialist in Greek language and literature. **3.** Any of the Byzantine Greeks of the 15th century who contributed to the revival of classical learning in Europe.

Hel·le·nis·tic (hel′ə-nis′tik) *adj.* **1.** Pertaining to, resembling, or characteristic of the Hellenists or Hellenism. **2.** Of or pertaining to the Hellenistic Age. Also **Hel'le·nis'ti·cal.**

Hellenistic Age The period that began with the conquests of Alexander the Great and ended about 300 years later, characterized by the spread of Greek language and culture throughout the Near East.

Hellenistic Greek Koine.

Hel·le·nize (hel'ə·nīz) *v.t.* & *v.i.* **·nized, ·niz·ing** To make or become Greek. — **Hel'le·ni·za'tion** *n.* — **Hel'le·niz'er** *n.*

hel·ler¹ (hel'ər) *n.* **1.** In Czechoslovakia, the hundredth part of a koruna. **2.** Any of several small coins formerly current in Germany and Austria. [< G, after *Hall*, a Swabian town where first minted]

hel·ler² (hel'ər) *n.* *Slang* A formidably rough and mischievous person. [< HELL]

hel·le·ry (hel'ə·rē) *n.* *Canadian Slang* Roughhouse.

Hel·les (hel'əs), **Cape** The southern extremity of the Gallipoli Peninsula, Turkey.

Hel·les·pont (hel'əs·pont) The ancient name for the DARDANELLES. See HELLE.

hell·fire (hel'fīr') *n.* The flames or the punishment of hell.

Hell Gate A narrow channel of the East River in New York City.

hell·gram·mite (hel'grə·mīt) *n.* The aquatic larva of the dobson fly, much used as bait: also called *crawler, dobson.*

hell·hound (hel'hound') *n.* **1.** A hound of hell, as Cerberus. **2.** A cruel and fiendish person.

hel·lion (hel'yən) *n.* *Informal* A person who delights in deviltry; a mischief-maker. [< HELL]

hell·ish (hel'ish) *adj.* **1.** Of, like, or pertaining to hell. **2.** Malignant. — **hell'ish·ly** *adv.* — **hell'ish·ness** *n.*

hell·kite (hel'kīt') *n.* A wantonly cruel or pitiless person.

hel·lo (hə·lō') *interj.* **1.** An exclamation of greeting, especially over the telephone. **2.** An exclamation used to gain attention. **3.** An exclamation of surprise. — *n.* *pl.* **·loes** The saying or calling of "hello." — *v.t.* & *v.i.* **·loed, ·lo·ing** To call or say "hello" to.

Hell's Angels A youth organization composed of various motorcycle clubs whose members generally wear leather jackets, boots, etc., and are noted for their pugnacity.

helm¹ (helm) *n.* **1.** *Naut.* The steering apparatus of a vessel. **2.** Any place of control or responsibility. — *v.t.* To manage the helm of. [OE *helma* rudder]

helm² (helm) *n.* *Archaic* & *Poetic* A helmet; covering. — *v.t.* To cover or supply with a helmet. [OE *helm* covering]

Hel·mand (hel'mənd) A river in Afghanistan, flowing 700 miles, generally SW, to the Seistan depression: also *Hilmand.*

hel·met (hel'mit) *n.* **1.** Any of a number of protective coverings for the head; as: **a** The topmost piece of a suit of medieval or ancient armor. **b** The metal headguard worn by modern soldiers. **c** The leather or plastic headgear used by football players. **d** In various hazardous occupations, a head protector, as worn by firemen, welders, divers, etc. **e** A pith sun hat worn in hot countries. **2.** Something resembling a helmet in appearance or position. [< OF, dim. of *helme* helmet < Gmc.] — **hel'met·ed** *adj.*

helmet liner A fiber or plastic helmet worn under the metal shell of a military helmet.

HELMETS

a Greek warrior's.
b German, World War II.
c 16th-cent. knight's.
d Football.

Helm·holtz (helm'hōlts), **Hermann Ludwig Ferdinand von,** 1821–94, German physiologist and physicist.

hel·minth (hel'minth) *n.* A worm; especially, a parasitic intestinal worm. [< Gk. *helmins, -inthos* worm]

hel·min·thi·a·sis (hel'min·thī'ə·sis) *n.* *Pathol.* Any disorder caused by infestation with worms. [< Gk. *helmins, -inthos* worm + -IASIS]

hel·min·thic (hel·min'thik) *adj.* **1.** Tending to expel worms; anthelmintic. **2.** Pertaining to helminths. — *n.* A vermifuge; an anthelmintic.

hel·min·thol·o·gy (hel'min·thol'ə·jē) *n.* **1.** The study of intestinal worms and their effects. **2.** The branch of zoology that treats of worms, especially of parasitic worms. [< Gk. *helmins, -inthos* worm + -LOGY]

helms·man (helmz'mən) *n.* *pl.* **·men** (-mən) A steersman; one who guides a ship. — **Syn.** See PILOT.

Hé·lo·ise (ā·lō·ēz'), died 1164?, French abbess, mistress and then wife of Abelard.

hel·ot (hel'ət, hē'lət) *n.* **1.** A slave; serf; bondsman. **2.** *Usually cap.* One of a class of serfs in ancient Sparta. [< L *helotes* < Gk. *heilōs, heilōtos*; appar. < *Helos*, a Laconian town enslaved by Sparta]

hel·ot·ry (hel'ət·rē, hē'lət-) *n.* **1.** Serfdom. Also **hel'ot·ism.** **2.** Helots as a class.

help (help) *v.* **helped** (*Archaic* **holp**), **helped** (*Archaic* **holp·en**), **help·ing** *v.t.* **1.** To assist in doing something; be of service to; cooperate with. **2.** To assist (someone or something) in some action, motion, change, etc.: with *onto, into, out of, up, down,* etc. **3.** To provide aid or relief to; succor: to *help* the sick. **4.** To be, or be considered, responsible for: He can't *help* being lame. **5.** To avoid; refrain from: I couldn't *help* laughing. **6.** To remedy; alleviate; cure: Rest *helps* a cold. **7.** To promote the effectiveness or operation of; contribute to: Curiosity *helps* learning. **8.** To serve; wait on, as a salesclerk or waiter. — *v.i.* **9.** To give assistance; be of service. **10.** To give remedy or relief. — **cannot help but** Cannot avoid; be obliged to. — **to help oneself 1.** To serve oneself, as with food. **2.** To take without requesting or being offered; to appropriate. — *n.* **1.** The act of helping; assistance; aid. **2.** Remedy; relief. **3.** One who or that which gives assistance. **4.** *U.S.* A farm laborer or a domestic servant. **5.** Any hired worker or helper. [OE *helpan*]
— **Syn.** (verb) **1.** *Help, aid,* and *assist* mean to join with another person in accomplishing something, whether by doing work, giving encouragement, supplying means, or removing obstacles. *Help* is the strongest term, implying response to a known or expressed need; we *help* those in trouble or danger. We *aid* a person by adding our effort to his own, and *assist* him by assuming a subordinate capacity and doing what he bids. — **Ant.** hinder.

help·er (hel'pər) *n.* One who or that which helps.

help·ful (help'fəl) *adj.* Affording help; giving service; beneficial. — **help'ful·ly** *adv.* — **help'ful·ness** *n.*

help·ing (hel'ping) *n.* **1.** The act of assisting or aiding. **2.** A single portion of food served at table.

helping verb An auxiliary verb. See AUXILIARY (*n.,* def. 3a).

help·less (help'lis) *adj.* **1.** Unable to help oneself; dependent; feeble. **2.** Incompetent; incapable. **3.** Without recourse to help. — **help'less·ly** *adv.* — **help'less·ness** *n.*

help·mate (help'māt') *n.* **1.** A helper; partner. **2.** A wife. Also **help·meet** (help'mēt').

Hel·sing·ør (hel'sing·œr') A port city on northern Zeeland, Denmark; pop. 29,755 (1965). English *Elsinore.*

Hel·sin·ki (hel'sing·kē) The capital of Finland, in the southern part on the Gulf of Finland; pop. 519,200 (est. 1966). *Swedish* **Hel·sing·fors** (hel'sing·fôrs').

hel·ter-skel·ter (hel'tər·skel'tər) *adv.* In a hurried and confused manner. — *adj.* Hurried and confused. — *n.* Disorderly hurry; confused and hasty action. [Imit.]

helve (helv) *n.* The handle, as of an ax.

Hel·ve·tia (hel·vē'shə) **1.** A European country of Roman times including a large part of what is now Switzerland. **2.** The Latin name for SWITZERLAND.

Hel·ve·tian (hel·vē'shən) *adj.* **1.** Of or pertaining to the Helvetii or to Helvetia. **2.** Swiss. — *n.* **1.** An inhabitant of Helvetia. **2.** A Swiss.

Hel·vet·ic (hel·vet'ik) *adj.* Helvetian; Swiss. — *n.* A Swiss Protestant follower of Zwingli and other Swiss reformers.

Hel·ve·ti·i (hel·vē'shē·ī) *n. pl.* An ancient Germano-Celtic tribe living in Helvetia at the time of Julius Caesar.

Hel·vé·tius (hel·vē'shəs, *Fr.* el·vā·syüs'), **Claude Adrien,** 1715–71, French philosopher.

hem¹ (hem) *n.* **1.** A finished edge made on a piece of fabric or a garment by turning the raw edge under and sewing it down. **2.** Any similar border or edging. — *v.t.* **hemmed, hem·ming 1.** To provide with a hem. **2.** To shut in; enclose; restrict: usually with *in, about,* etc. [OE] — **hem'mer** *n.*

hem² (hem) *interj.* A sound made as in clearing the throat to attract attention, cover embarrassment, etc.; ahem. — *v.i.* **hemmed, hem·ming 1.** To make the sound "hem." **2.** To hesitate in speaking. — **to hem and haw** To hesitate in speaking so as to keep from being explicit. [Imit.]

hem- See also words beginning HAEM-.

hem- See HEMO-.

hema- *combining form* Blood: *hemapoiesis.* Also spelled *haema-.* [< Gk. *haima* blood]

he·ma·chrome (hē'mə·krōm, hem'ə-) *n.* *Biochem.* The red coloring matter of the blood: also spelled *haemachrome.*

he·ma·gogue (hē'mə·gôg, -gog, hem'ə-) *n.* *Med.* An agent that promotes or favors the discharge of blood, as in menstruation: also spelled *haemogogue.* Also **he'ma·gog.** [< HEM- + -AGOG] — **he'ma·gog'ic** (-goj'ik) *adj.*

he·mal (hē'məl) *adj.* **1.** Pertaining to blood or the vascular system; of the nature of blood. **2.** Pertaining to or situated on the side of the body that contains the heart. Also spelled *haemal.* [< Gk. *haima* blood + AL]

he·man (hē'man') *n. pl.* **·men** (-men') *Informal* A virile, muscular man.

Hem·ans (hem'ənz, hē'mənz), **Felicia Dorothea,** 1793–1835, *née* Browne, English poet.

he·ma·poi·e·sis (hē'mə·poi·ē'sis, hem'ə-) *n.* Hematopoiesis (which see): also spelled *haemapoiesis.*

he·ma·tal (hē'mə·təl, hem'ə-) *adj.* Of or pertaining to the blood or blood vessels: also spelled *haematal.*

he·ma·te·in (hē'mə·tē'in, hem'ə-) *n.* *Chem.* A reddish brown, crystalline substance, $C_{16}H_{12}O_6$, extracted from hematoxylin: also spelled *haematein.* [< HEMAT + EIN]

he·mat·ic (hi·mat/ik) *adj.* **1.** Of, pertaining to, or contained in blood. **2.** Effecting a change in the blood. — *n.* A medicine that acts upon the blood. Also spelled *haematic.*

hem·a·tin (hem/ə·tin, hē/mə-) *n. Biochem.* Heme. Also spelled *haematin.*

hem·a·tin·ic (hem/ə·tin/ik, hē/mə-) *n. Med.* Any agent that increases the amount of hemoglobin and the number of red corpuscles in the blood. — *adj.* Of or pertaining to heme. Also spelled *haematinic.*

hem·a·tite (hem/ə·tit, hē/mə-) *n.* Red ferric oxide, Fe_2O_3, an ore of iron, occurring in masses and crystallizing in the hexagonal system: also called *ferric oxide.* Also spelled *haematite.* [< L *haematites* < Gk. *haimatites* bloodlike < *haima* blood] — **hem·a·tit·ic** (hem/ə·tit/ik, hē/mə-) *adj.*

hemato- *combining form* Blood: *hematocele:* also, before vowels, **hemat-.** Also spelled *haemato-.* [< Gk. *haima, haimatos* blood]

hem·a·to·cele (hem/ə·tō·sēl/, hē/mə-) *n. Pathol.* A hemorrhage within a membranous cavity: also spelled *haematocele.*

hem·a·toc·ry·al (hem/ə·tok/rē·əl, hē/mə-) *adj. Zool.* Cold-blooded, as fishes and reptiles: also spelled *haematocryal.* [< HEMATO- + Gk. *kryos* cold]

hem·a·to·gen·e·sis (hem/ə·tō·jen/ə·sis, hē/mə-) *n.* The formation of blood: also spelled *haematogenesis.* — **hem/a·to·gen/ic, hem/a·to·ge·net/ic** (-jə·net/ik) *adj.*

he·ma·tog·e·nous (hē/mə·toj/ə·nəs, hem/ə-) *adj.* **1.** Producing blood. **2.** Originating in the blood. Also spelled *haematogenous.*

he·ma·toid (hē/mə·toid, hem/ə-) *adj.* Bloody, or resembling blood: also spelled *haematoid.*

he·ma·tol·o·gy (hē/mə·tol/ə·jē, hem/ə-) *n.* The study of the blood and its diseases: also spelled *haematology.* Also **he/ma·to·lo/gi·a** (-tə·lō/jē·ə). — **he·ma·tol·o·gist** *n.*

he·ma·tol·y·sis (hē/mə·tol/ə·sis, hem/ə-) *n.* Hemolysis.

he·ma·to·ma (hē/mə·tō/mə, hem/ə-) *n. pl.* **·to·ma·ta** (-tō/mə·tə) *Pathol.* A tumor or swelling formed by the effusion of blood: also spelled *haematoma.* [< HEMAT- + -OMA]

hem·a·to·poi·e·sis (hē/mə·tō/poi·ē/sis, hem/ə-) *n.* The formation or development of blood: also spelled *haematopoiesis.* Also called *hemapoiesis.* [< HEMATO- + Gk. *poiēsis* a making < *poieein* to make] — **he/ma·to/poi·et/ic** (-et/ik) *adj.*

he·ma·to·sis (hē/mə·tō/sis, hem/ə-) *n. Physiol.* The formation of blood; also, the conversion of venous blood into arterial blood by aeration in the lungs: also spelled *haematosis.* [< NL < Gk. *haimatōsis* < *haimatoein* to make into blood]

he·ma·to·ther·mal (hē/mə·tō·thûr/məl, hem/ə-) *adj. Zool.* Warm-blooded, as mammals and birds: also spelled *haematothermal.*

hem·a·tox·y·lin (hem/ə·tok/sə·lin, hē/mə-) *n. Chem.* A colorless crystalline compound, $C_{16}H_{14}O_6 \cdot 3H_2O$, containing the coloring matter of logwood, used as a dye and indicator: also spelled *haematoxylin.* [< HEMATO- + XYL- + -IN]

hem·a·to·zo·on (hem/ə·tō·zō/on, hē/mə-) *n. pl.* **·zo·a** (-zō/ə) An animal parasite living in the blood: also spelled *haematozoon.* [< HEMATO- + Gk. *zōion* animal]

hem·a·tu·ri·a (hem/ə·tŏŏr/ē·ə, -tyŏŏr/-, hē/mə-) *n. Pathol.* Bloody urine. [< HEMAT- + -URIA]

heme (hēm) *n. Biochem.* The insoluble, protein-free, iron-bearing constituent of hemoglobin, $C_{34}H_{32}FeN_4O_4$: also called *hematin.*

hem·e·ly·tron (hem·el/ə·tron) *n. pl.* **·tra** (-trə) *Entomol.* One of the partially thickened and hardened forewings of certain insects: also called *hemielytron.* [< HEMI- + ELYTRON] — **hem·el/y·tral** *adj.*

hem·er·a·lo·pi·a (hem/ər·ə·lō/pē·ə) *n. Pathol.* A physical defect in which sight is less distinct by daylight than by night or by artificial light: distinguished from *nyctalopia.* Also called *day blindness.* [< NL < Gk. *hēmera* day + *alaos* blind + *ōps* eye] — **hem/er·a·lo/pic** *adj.*

hemi- *prefix* Half: *hemisphere.* Also, before vowels, **hem-.** [< Gk., half]

-hemia See -EMIA.

hem·i·al·gi·a (hem/ē·al/jē·ə) *n. Pathol.* Pain or neuralgia confined to one side of the body or head. [< HEMI- on one side + -ALGIA]

he·mic (hē/mik, hem/ik) *adj.* Of or pertaining to blood: also spelled *haemic.*

hem·i·cel·lu·lose (hem/i·sel/yə·lōs) *n. Biochem.* Any of a class of polysaccharide carbohydrates occurring mainly in plants, more readily hydrolyzed than cellulose.

hem·i·chor·date (hem/i·kôr/dāt) *Zool. adj.* Of, pertaining to, or belonging to a division of chordates (*Hemichordata*) characterized by paired gill slits and a primitive notochord, including many small marine forms. — *n.* A member of this division. [< NL < Gk. *hēmi-* half + *chordata* chordate]

hem·i·cra·ni·a (hem/i·krā/nē·ə) *n. Pathol.* Migraine. [< F *hemicraine* < LL *hemicrania* < Gk. *hēmikrania* < *hēmi-* half + *kranion* skull]

hem·i·cy·cle (hem/i·si/kəl) *n.* **1.** A semicircle. **2.** A semicircular building, arena, wall, etc.

hem·i·dem·i·sem·i·qua·ver (hem/ē·dem/ē·sem/ē·kwā/vər) *n. Music Chiefly Brit.* A sixty-fourth note.

hem·i·el·y·tron (hem/ē·el/ə·tron) See HEMELYTRON.

hem·i·he·dral (hem/i·hē/drəl) *adj. Mineral.* Pertaining to

crystals that possess only half the planes required for complete symmetry in their class. [< HEMI- + Gk. *hedra* seat, surface] — **hem/i·he/dral·ly** *adv.*

hem·i·mor·phic (hem/i·môr/fik) *adj. Mineral.* Pertaining to crystals that are unsymmetrical with reference to the opposite ends of an axis. — **hem/i·mor/phism** (-fiz-əm) *n.*

hem·i·mor·phite (hem/i·môr/fīt) *n.* A white to yellowish or brown hydrous zinc silicate, $Zn_2SiO_4 \cdot H_2O$, an important ore of zinc: sometimes called *calamine.*

he·min (hē/min) *n. Biochem.* A brownish red, crystalline compound, $C_{34}H_{32}O_4N_4FeCl$, formed by the action of sodium chloride and glacial acetic acid on hemoglobin: also spelled *haemin.* [< Gk. *haima* blood]

Hem·ing·way (hem/ing·wā), **Ernest,** 1899–1961, U.S. novelist and short-story writer.

hem·i·ple·gi·a (hem/i·plē/jē·ə) *n. Pathol.* Paralysis of one side of the body. Also **hem/i·ple/gy.** [< HEMI- + -PLEGIA] — **hem/i·ple/gic** (-plē/jik, -plej/ik) *adj.*

he·mip·ter·ous (hi·mip/tər·əs) *adj.* Pertaining or belonging to an order (*Hemiptera*) of insects generally having suctorial mouth parts and four wings that are thick at the base and membranous at the free end, including the cicadas, crickets, plant lice, etc. [< NL < Gk. *hēmi-* half + *pteron* wing] — **he·mip/ter** *n.* — **he·mip/ter·al** *adj.* — **he·mip/-ter·an** *adj. & n.*

hem·i·sphere (hem/ə·sfir) *n.* **1.** A half-sphere, formed by a plane passing through the center of the sphere. **2.** A half of the terrestrial or celestial globe, or a map or projection of either of these. The world is usually considered as divided either at the equator into the **Northern Hemisphere** and **Southern Hemisphere,** or at some meridian between Europe and America into the **Eastern Hemisphere** and **Western Hemisphere. 3.** *Anat.* One of two large convoluted masses forming the bulk of the cerebrum. [< F *hémisphère* < L *hemisphaerium* < Gk. *hēmisphairion* < *hēmi-* half + *sphaira* sphere] — **hem/i·spher·ic** (hem/ə·sfir/ik, -sfer-) or **·i·cal** *adj.*

hem·i·sphe·roid (hem/ə·sfir/oid) *n.* A half of a spheroid. — **hem/i·sphe·roi/dal** (-sfi·roid/l) *adj.*

hem·i·stich (hem/i·stik) *n.* **1.** Half of a line of verse, especially when divided by a caesura. **2.** A line of verse shorter than the normal line of a given meter or poem.

hem·i·ter·pene (hem/i·tûr/pēn) *n. Chem.* Any of a group of isomeric hydrocarbons related to the terpenes, and having the general formula C_5H_8.

hem·i·trope (hem/i·trōp) *Crystall. n.* A twin crystal. — *adj.* **1.** Having one part in reverse position with reference to the other: said of a crystal form. **2.** Turned halfway. Also **hem/i·trop/ic** (-trop/ik, -trō/pik) *adj.* [< F *hémitrope* < Gk. *hēmi-* half + *tropē* a turning < *trepein* to turn]

he·mit·ro·pous (hi·mit/rə·pəs) *adj.* **1.** *Bot.* Half anatropous: said of a half-inverted ovule. **2.** *Entomol.* Adapted for pollinating certain kinds of flowers: said of some insects, as bees. **3.** Hemitropic.

hem·line (hem/lin/) *n.* The line formed by the lower edge of a garment, as a dress or coat.

hem·lock (hem/lok) *n.* **1.** One of several North American or Asian evergreen trees (genus *Tsuga*) of the pine family; especially, *T. canadensis* of North America, having coarse, nonresinous wood used for paper pulp, and yielding an important tanning material. Also **hemlock spruce. 2.** A large, biennial herb (*Conium maculatum*) of the parsley or carrot family, yielding coniine: also **poison hemlock. 3.** A poison made from this herb. **4.** Any of several related herbs, as the water hemlock. [OE *hymlice*]

hemo- *combining form* Blood: *hemoglobin:* also, before vowels, **hem-.** Also spelled *haemo-.* [< Gk. *haima* blood]

he·mo·flag·el·late (hē/mə·flaj/ə·lāt, hem/ə-) *n.* A flagellate protozoan parasite of the blood, as a trypanosome or leishmania: also spelled *haemoflagellate.*

he·mo·glo·bin (hē/mə·glō/bin, hem/ə-) *n. Biochem.* The complex respiratory pigment in red corpuscles, composed of globin in union with heme, and serving as a carrier of oxygen: also spelled *haemoglobin.*

he·moid (hē/moid) *adj.* Resembling blood; hematoid: also spelled *haemoid.*

he·mo·leu·co·cyte (hē/mə·lōō/kə·sit, hem/ə-) *n.* A leucocyte: also spelled *haemoleukocyte.* Also **he/mo·leu/co·cyte.**

he·mo·ly·sin (hē/mə·li/sin, hem/ə-, hi·mol/ə·sin) *n. Biochem.* A substance contained or formed in the blood and having the power to liberate hemoglobin from the red blood corpuscles: also spelled *haemolysin.*

he·mol·y·sis (hi·mol/ə·sis) *n.* Dissolution or breakdown of red blood corpuscles with liberation of their hemoglobin: also called *hematolysis:* also spelled *haemolysis.* — **he·mo·lyt·ic** (hē/mə·lit/ik, hem/ə-) *adj.*

he·mo·phil·i·a (hē/mə·fil/ē·ə, -fil/yə, hem/ə-) *n. Pathol.* A disorder characterized by immoderate bleeding even from slight injuries, typically affecting males, who inherit it through the mother: also spelled *haemophilia.* [< NL < Gk. *haima* blood + *philia* fondness]

he·mo·phil·i·ac (hē/mə·fil/ē·ak, hem/ə-) *n.* One afflicted with hemophilia; a bleeder: also spelled *haemophiliac.* Also **he/mo·phile** (-fil).

he·mo·phil·ic (hē/mə·fil/ik, hem/ə-) *adj.* **1.** Pertaining to hemophilia. **2.** Thriving in blood, as certain bacteria. Also spelled *haemophilic.*

hem·op·ty·sis (hem·op'tə·sis) *n. Pathol.* The spitting up of blood or of bloody sputum, especially from the lungs or bronchial tubes: also spelled *haemoptysis.* [< HEMO- + *ptysis* spitting < Gk. *ptyein* to spit]

hem·or·rhage (hem'ər·ij, hem'rij) *n.* Copious discharge of blood from a ruptured blood vessel. — *v.i.* **·rhaged, ·rhag· ing** To bleed copiously. Also, *Brit., haemorrhage.* [< L *haemorrhagia* < Gk. *haimorrhagia* < *haima* blood + *-rhagia* < *rhēgnynai* to burst] — **hem·or·rhag·ic** (hem/ə·raj'ik) *adj.*

hem·or·rhoid (hem'ə·roid) *n. Pathol.* A tumor or dilation of a vein in the anal region, usually painful: also, in the plural, *piles:* also spelled *haemorrhoid.* [< F *hémorrhoides, pl.* < L *haemorrhoidae* < Gk. *haimorrhoides (phlebes)* bleeding (veins) < *haima* blood + *rheein* to flow] — **hem·or·rhoi· dal** (hem'ə·roid'l) *adj.*

hem·or·rhoid·ec·to·my (hem'ə·roid·ek'tə·mē) *n. pl.* **·mies** *Surg.* The removal of hemorrhoids: also spelled *haemor· rhoidectomy.*

he·mo·sta·sia (hē'mə·stā'zhə, -zhē·ə, hem'ə-) *n. Med.* **1.** Congestion of blood in a part. **2.** The checking of hemorrhage: also spelled *haemostasia.* Also **he·mos·ta·sis** (hi·mos'· tə·sis). [< NL < Gk. *haima* blood + *stasis* a standing]

he·mo·stat (hē'mə·stat, hem'ə-) *n. Med.* A device or drug for checking the flow of blood from a ruptured vessel: also spelled *haemostat.*

he·mo·stat·ic (hē'mə·stat'ik, hem'ə-) *Med. adj.* **1.** Stopping the flow of blood. **2.** Preventive of bleeding. — *n.* A hemostat. Also spelled *haemostatic.*

hemp (hemp) *n.* **1.** A tall, annual herb (*Cannabis sativa*) of the mulberry family, native in Asia but cultivated elsewhere, with small green flowers and a tough bark: also called *bhang, cannabis, Indian hemp, marihuana.* **2.** The tough, strong fiber obtained from this plant, used for cloth and cordage. **3.** A narcotic prepared from the plant, as bhang or hashish. **4.** *Informal* The hangman's rope. [OE *henep*]

hemp agrimony A coarse European herb (*Eupatorium can· nabinum*) resembling the boneset of the United States.

hemp dogbane Indian hemp (def. 2).

hemp·en (hem'pən) *adj.* **1.** Made of hemp. **2.** Of, pertaining to, or resembling hemp.

Hemp·field (hemp'fēld) An urban township in SW Pennsylvania; pop. 39,196.

hemp nettle A common prickly weed (*Galeopsis tetrahit*) of the mint family.

hemp·seed (hemp'sēd') *n.* The seed of hemp.

Hemp·stead (hemp'sted) A village in SE New York, on Long Island; pop. 39,411.

hemp·y (hem'pē) *adj.* **hemp·i·er, hemp·i·est** *Scot. & Brit. Dial.* Worthy of hanging: used humorously. Also **hemp'ie.**

hem·stitch (hem'stich') *n.* The ornamental finishing of a hem, made by pulling out several threads adjoining it and drawing the cross threads together in groups. — *v.t.* To embroider with a hemstitch. — **hem'stitch'er** *n.*

hen (hen) *n.* **1.** The mature female of the domestic fowl. **2.** The remale of other birds, especially gallinaceous birds. **3.** The female of the lobster and certain fishes. **4.** *Slang* A woman; especially, an unpleasant old woman. [OE *henn*]

hen-and-chickens (hen'ən·chik'· ənz) *n.* A plant that propagates by means of offshoots, runners, and other ground parts, as the ground ivy and the houseleek.

HEMSTITCH
A Threads pulled. *B* Cross threads drawn together at one edge. *C* Cross threads drawn together at both edges.

hen·bane (hen'bān') *n.* A poisonous Old World herb (*Hy· oscyamus niger*) of the nightshade family, with sticky, malodorous foliage and reddish brown flowers, the source of hyoscyamine: also called *hyoscyamus.*

hen·bit (hen'bit') *n.* A low herb (*Lamium amplexicaule*) of the mint family. [Trans. of MLG *hoenderbeet*]

hence (hens) *adv.* **1.** As a consequence; therefore; thus: The apples are green, *hence* you must not eat them. Abbr. *h., H.* **2.** From this time or date: a week *hence;* also, ever afterwards; from now on; henceforth. **3.** Away from this place; from here: to go *hence.* **4.** *Rare* From this cause or source: *Hence* he has his courage. — **Syn.** See THEREFORE. — *interj. Archaic & Poetic* Go! Depart! [ME *hennes < henne* (OE *heonan* from here) + *-s*, adverbial suffix]

hence·forth (hens'fôrth', -fôrth'; hens'fôrth', -fôrth') *adv.* From this time on. Also **hence'for'ward** (-fôr'wərd).

hench·man (hench'mən) *n. pl.* **·men** (-mən) **1.** A faithful follower. **2.** *U.S.* A political supporter or subordinate who works chiefly for personal gain. **3.** *Obs.* A page or groom. [ME *henxstman < OE hengst* horse + *man* groom]

hen·coop (hen'kōōp', -kōōp) *n.* A cage or coop for hens.

hen·dec·a·gon (hen·dek'ə·gon) *n.* A polygon with eleven sides and eleven angles. [< Gk. *hendeka* eleven + -GON] — **hen·de·cag·o·nal** (hen'də·kag'ə·nəl) *adj.*

hen·dec·a·syl·lab·ic (hen'dek·ə·si·lab'ik) *adj.* Containing eleven syllables. — *n.* A metrical line containing eleven syllables: also **hen'dec·a·syl'la·ble.** [< L *hendecasyllabus* < Gk. *hendekasyllabos* + -IC]

hen·di·a·dys (hen·dī'ə·dis) *n.* The use of two nouns connected by a conjunction to express the same idea as a noun with a modifier, as, with *might and main* instead of by *main strength.* [< LL < Gk. *hen dia dyoin* one through two]

Hen·don (hen'dən) A municipal borough in Middlesex, England; site of Royal Air Force airfield; pop. 151,500 (1961).

He·ne·gou·wen (hā'nə·gou'wən) The Flemish name for HAINAUT.

hen·e·quen (hen'ə·kin) *n.* **1.** A tough fiber obtained from the leaves of the Mexican plant *Agave fourcroydes.* **2.** The plant from which this fiber is obtained. Also **hen'e·quin.** [< Sp. < Taino]

Hen·gist (heng'gist, hen'jist), died 488, and his brother **Hor· sa** (hôr'sə), died 455, Jute chieftains; reputed first Germanic invaders of England.

Hen·ley (hen'lē) A municipal borough in Oxfordshire, England; site of an annual rowing regatta since 1839; pop. 9,131 (1961). Also **Hen'ley-on-Thames'** (-temz').

Hen·ley (hen'lē), **William Ernest,** 1849–1903, English author, critic, and editor.

hen·na (hen'ə) *n.* **1.** An Oriental shrub or small tree (*Law· sonia inermis*) with lance-shaped leaves and small white flowers. **2.** A cosmetic made from the leaves of this plant, used for dyeing the hair, fingernails, etc. **3.** A color varying from reddish orange to coppery brown. — *v.* **hen·naed, hen· na·ing** *v.t.* To dye with henna. [< Arabic *henna*]

Hen·ne·pin (hen'ə·pin, *Fr.* en·pan'), **Louis,** 1640–1706?, French missionary and explorer; active in North America.

hen·ner·y (hen'ər·ē) *n. pl.* **·ner·ies** A place where hens are kept.

hen·o·the·ism (hen'ō·thē·iz'əm) *n.* Belief in one god without denying the existence of others. [< Gk. *hen* one + THE· ISM] — **hen'o·the·is'tic** *adj.*

hen party *Slang* A social gathering for women only.

hen·peck (hen'pek') *v.t.* To domineer over or harass (one's husband) by nagging, ill temper, and petty annoyances.

hen·pecked (hen'pekt') *adj.* Dominated by one's wife.

hen·ry (hen'rē) *n. pl.* **·ries** or **·rys** *Electr.* The unit of inductance, equal to the inductance of a circuit in which the variation of a current at the rate of one ampere per second induces an electromotive force of one volt. Symbol *H.* [after Joseph *Henry,* 1797–1878, U.S. physicist]

Hen·ry (hen'rē), **Cape** A cape in southern Virginia at the southern entrance of Chesapeake Bay.

Hen·ry (hen'rē), **O.** See O. HENRY. — **Patrick,** 1736–99, American Revolutionary statesman and orator.

Henry I, 1068–1135, king of England 1100–35, son of William the Conqueror: called *Beauclerc.*

Henry II, 1133–89, king of England 1154–89, first Plantagenet king: called **Henry Plantagenet.**

Henry III, 1207–72, king of England 1216–72, held captive by the barons.

Henry III, 1551–89, king of France 1574–89, plotted the Massacre of St. Bartholomew's Day, 1572.

Henry IV, 1050–1106, Holy Roman Emperor 1056–1106, excommunicated by Pope Gregory VII.

Henry IV, 1367–1413, king of England 1399–1413, first Lancastrian king: called *Bolingbroke.*

Henry IV, 1553–1610, king of France 1589–1610, first Bourbon king: called **Henry of Navarre.**

Henry V, 1387–1422, king of England 1413–22, conquered Normandy; heir to the French throne.

Henry VI, 1421–71, king of England 1422–61, 1470–71.

Henry VII, 1457–1509, king of England 1485–1509, first Tudor king: called **the Huckster King.**

Henry VIII, 1491–1547, king of England 1509–47, asserted royal supremacy over the Catholic Church in England.

Henry the Navigator, 1394–1460, Portuguese prince; patron of explorers and sea expeditions.

Hens·lowe (henz'lō), **Philip,** died 1616, English theatrical manager.

hent (hent) *v.t. Archaic* To seize; catch. — *n. Obs.* A catch or grasp; also, that which is seized in the mind. [OE *hentan*]

Hen·ty (hen'tē), **George Alfred,** 1832–1902, English novelist.

hep (hep) *adj. U.S. Slang* Hip⁴. [Origin unknown]

hep·a·rin (hep'ə·rin) *n. Biochem.* A polysaccharide found in liver and other animal tissues and having the power to prevent the coagulation of blood, used in medicine and surgery. [< Gk. *hēpar* liver + -IN]

he·pat·ic (hi·pat'ik) *adj.* **1.** Of, pertaining to, or resembling the liver. **2.** Occurring in, affecting, or acting upon the liver. **3.** *Bot.* Pertaining to or resembling a class of plants, the liverworts. **4.** Liver-colored. — *n.* **1.** A drug acting on the liver. **2.** A liverwort. Also **he·pat'i·cal.** [< L *he· paticus* < Gk. *hēpatikos* < *hēpar* liver]

he·pat·i·ca (hi·pat′ə·kə) *n. pl.* **·cas** or **·cae** (-sē) Any of a genus (*Hepatica*) of small perennial herbs with three-lobed leaves and delicate, variously colored flowers: also called *liverleaf, liverwort.* [< NL < L *hepaticus* of the liver]

hepatico- *combining form* Hepato-.

hep·a·ti·tis (hep′ə·tī′tis) *n. Pathol.* Inflammation of the liver.

hep·a·tize (hep′ə·tīz) *v.t.* **·tized, ·tiz·ing** *Pathol.* To convert (tissue) through congestion into a firm mass resembling liver, as the lungs during pneumonia. — **hep′a·ti·za′tion** *n.*

hepato- *combining form* Pertaining to the liver: *hepatogenic.* Also, before vowels, **hepat-.** [< Gk. *hēpar, hēpatos* the liver]

hep·a·to·gen·ic (hep′ə·tō·jen′ik) *adj.* Produced or originating in the liver. Also **hep·a·tog·e·nous** (hep′ə·toj′ə·nəs).

He·phaes·tus (hi·fes′təs) In Greek mythology, the god of fire and metallurgy, son of Zeus and Hera: identified with the Roman *Vulcan.* Also *Greek* **He·phais·tos** (hi·fīs′tos).

Hep·ple·white (hep′əl·hwīt) *adj.* Denoting an English style of furniture characterized by graceful curves and light, slender woodwork, developed in the reign of George III. [after G. *Hepplewhite,* died 1786, the designer]

hepta- *combining form* Seven: *heptachord.* Also, before vowels, **hept-.** [< Gk. *hepta-* < *hepta* seven]

hep·tad (hep′tad) *n.* **1.** The number seven; also, seven things. **2.** *Chem.* An atom, radical, or element that has a valence of seven. [< Gk. *heptas, -ados* a group of seven]

hep·ta·gon (hep′tə·gon) *n.* A polygon having seven sides and seven angles. — **hep·tag·o·nal** (hep·tag′ə·nəl) *adj.*

HEPPLEWHITE CHAIR

hep·ta·he·dron (hep′tə·hē′drən) *n. pl.* **·drons** or **·dra** (-drə) A polyhedron bounded by seven plane faces. — **hep′ta·he′dral** (-drəl) *adj.*

hep·tam·er·ous (hep·tam′ər·əs) *adj.* **1.** Having seven parts. **2.** *Bot.* Having seven members in each whorl: said of flowers: often written **7-merous.** [< HEPTA- + -MEROUS]

hep·tam·e·ter (hep·tam′ə·tər) *n.* In prosody, a line of verse consisting of seven metrical feet.

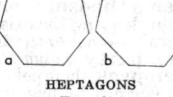

HEPTAGONS
a Regular.
b Irregular.

hep·tane (hep′tān) *n. Chem.* A colorless flammable liquid hydrocarbon of the methane series, C_7H_{16}, used as a solvent and in the determination of the octane number of motor fuels. [< HEPT(A)- + -ANE²]

hep·tan·gu·lar (hep·tang′gyə·lər) *adj.* Having seven angles.

hep·tar·chy (hep′tär·kē) *n. pl.* **·chies 1.** A group of seven kingdoms or governments, each with its own ruler; especially, the seven Anglo-Saxon kingdoms of England from the fifth to the ninth century (Essex, Wessex, Sussex, Kent, East Anglia, Northumbria, and Mercia). **2.** Government by a group of seven rulers.

hep·ta·stich (hep′tə·stik) *n.* A poem, stanza, or strophe consisting of seven lines.

Hep·ta·teuch (hep′tə·tōōk, -tyōōk) *n.* The first seven books of the Old Testament. [< HEPTA- + Gk. *teuchos* book]

her (hûr) *pron.* The objective case of the pronoun *she.* — *pronominal adj.* The possessive case of the pronoun *she,* used attributively: *her* garden. [OE *hire*]

her. Heraldic; heraldry.

He·ra (hir′ə, hē′rə) In Greek mythology, the queen of the gods and goddess of women and marriage, sister and wife of Zeus: identified with the Roman *Juno.* Also spelled *Here.*

Her·a·cle·a (her′ə·klē′ə) An ancient city of southern Italy; scene of a Roman defeat by Pyrrhus of Epirus, 280 B.C.

Her·a·cles (her′ə·klēz) Hercules. Also **Her′a·kles.** — **Her·a·cle·an** (her′ə·klē′ən) *adj.*

Her·a·clid (her′ə·klid) *n. pl.* **Her·a·cli·dae** (her′ə·klī′dē) A descendant of Hercules, especially one of the ancient Spartan royalty, who claimed such descent. [< Gk. *Herakleidēs*] — **Her·a·cli·dan** (her′ə·klī′dən) *adj.*

Her·a·cli·tus (her′ə·klī′təs), 535?–475? B.C., Greek philosopher.

He·ra·klei·on (ē·rä′klē·ôn) The Greek name for CANDIA: also *Iraklion.*

her·ald (her′əld) *n.* **1.** Any bearer of important news; messenger: often used in the title of a newspaper. **2.** One who or that which announces or shows what is to follow; harbinger. **3.** *Brit.* An official whose duty and profession is to grant or record arms, trace genealogies, record the creation of peers, etc. **4.** Formerly, an officer whose business it was to carry messages and challenges, arrange tournaments, etc. — *v.t.* To announce or proclaim publicly; to usher in. [< OF *heralt,* ? < OHG *heren* to call]

he·ral·dic (hi·ral′dik) *adj.* Of or pertaining to heraldry or heralds.

her·ald·ry (her′əl·drē) *n. pl.* **·ries 1.** The art or science that treats of armorial bearings, genealogies, etc. **2.** A heraldic device; also, a collection of such devices. **3.** The symbolism of heraldic bearings. **4.** The office or function of a herald. **5.** The ceremony attendant upon heraldry.

Heralds' College (her′əldz) In England, a corporate body of officials instituted in 1484 to determine all questions concerning heraldry. Also **College of Heralds.**

He·rat (hə·rät′) A Province of NW Afghanistan; 50,000 sq. mi.; pop. about 1,150,000; capital, **Herat,** pop. 75,000 (est. 1970).

herb (ûrb, hûrb) *n.* **1.** A plant without woody tissue, that withers and dies away after flowering. **2.** Any such plant valued as a medicine, seasoning, scent, etc. **3.** *Rare* Herbage. [< L *herba* grass, herbage]

her·ba·ceous (hûr·bā′shəs) *adj.* **1.** Pertaining to, having the character of, or similar to herbs. **2.** Having the semblance, color, or structure of an ordinary leaf.

herb·age (ûr′bij, hûr′-) *n.* **1.** Herbs collectively, especially the vegetation used for pasturage. **2.** The leaves, stems, and other succulent parts of herbaceous plants.

herb·al (hûr′bəl, ûr′-) *adj.* Of or pertaining to herbs. — *n.* Formerly, a treatise on herbs or plants.

herb·al·ist (hûr′bəl·ist, ûr′-) *n.* **1.** A dealer in herbs, especially medicinal herbs. **2.** Formerly, one skilled in the study of herbs or plants.

her·bar·i·um (hûr·bâr′ē·əm) *n. pl.* **·bar·i·ums** or **·bar·i·a** (-bâr′ē·ə) **1.** A collection of dried plants scientifically arranged. **2.** A room or building containing such a collection.

Her·bart (hûr′bärt, *Ger.* her′bärt), **Johann Friedrich,** 1776–1841, German philosopher. — **Her·bar·ti·an** (hûr·bär′tē·ən) *adj.* — **Her·bar′ti·an·ism** *n.*

herb bennet See under AVENS. [< OF *herbe beneite* < Med.L *herba benedicta,* lit., blessed herb]

Her·bert (hûr′bərt), **George,** 1593–1633, English clergyman and poet. — **Victor,** 1859–1924, U.S. composer born in Ireland.

her·bi·cide (hûr′bə·sīd) *n.* A weed killer.

her·bif·er·ous (hûr·bif′ər·əs) *adj.* Producing herbs or vegetation. [< L *herbifer* < *herba* grass + *ferre* to bear]

her·bi·vore (hûr′bə·vôr, -vōr) *n.* A herbivorous animal.

her·biv·o·rous (hûr·biv′ər·əs) *adj.* **1.** Feeding on vegetable matter; plant-eating. **2.** Belonging to a group or division of mammals (now generally called *Ungulata*) that feed mainly on herbage, as cows, horses, camels, etc. [< L *herba* grass + -VOROUS] — **her·biv′o·rous·ly** *adv.*

herb Paris A European herb of the lily family (*Paris quadrifolia*): also called *paris, truelove.*

herb Robert A species of geranium (*Geranium robertianum*).

herb·y (ûr′bē, hûr′-) *adj.* **1.** Of the nature of herbs; herbaceous. **2.** Relating to or abounding with herbs; grassy.

Her·ce·go·vi·na (her′tsə·gō′vi·nä) See HERZEGOVINA.

Her·cu·la·ne·um (hûr′kyə·lā′nē·əm) An ancient city near Naples, buried by an eruption of Vesuvius in A.D. 79.

her·cu·le·an (hûr·kyōō′lē·ən, hûr′kyə·lē′ən) *adj.* **1.** Having great strength; prodigious in power; gigantic. **2.** Requiring great strength; extremely laborious: a *herculean* task.

Her·cu·le·an (hûr·kyōō′lē·ən, hûr′kyə·lē′ən) *adj.* Of or pertaining to Hercules (Heracles); Heraclean.

Her·cu·les (hûr′kyə·lēz) In classical mythology, the son of Alcmene and Zeus, renowned for his great strength and endurance, and for his performance of the twelve gigantic labors imposed upon him by Eurystheus through the enmity of Hera: also called *Heracles, Alcides.* — *n.* **1.** Any man of great size and strength. **2.** A constellation. See CONSTELLATION.

Her·cu·les'-club (hûr′kyə·lēz·klub′) *n.* **1.** A prickly shrub or small tree (*Zanthoxylum Clava-Herculis*) of the rue family, with pungent and aromatic bark: also called *prickly ash.* **2.** A prickly shrub or tree (*Aralia spinosa*) of the ginseng family: also called *angelica tree, prickly ash.*

herd¹ (hûrd) *n.* **1.** A number of cattle or other animals feeding, moving about, or kept together. **2.** A large crowd of people. — **the herd** The common people; the masses. — *v.t. & v.i.* To bring or group together in or as in a herd. — *Syn.* See FLOCK. [OE *heord*] — **herd′er** *n.*

herd² (hûrd) *n. Scot. & Brit. Dial.* A herdsman; shepherd. — *v.t.* To care for or drive (sheep, cattle, etc.).

-herd *combining form* Herdsman: *swineherd, cowherd, etc.* [OE *hierde* herdsman]

Her·der (hûr′dər, *Ger.* her′dər), **Johann Gottfried von,** 1744–1803, German poet, critic, and philosopher.

her·dic (hûr′dik) *n.* A carriage, usually two-wheeled, with low-hung body, back entrance, and side seats. [after Peter *Herdic,* 1824–88, U.S. inventor]

herd's-grass (hûrdz′gras′, -gräs′) *n.* **1.** Redtop. **2.** Timothy. Also **herd′-grass′.** [after John *Herd,* early New Hampshire farmer]

herds·man (hûrdz′mən) *n. pl.* **·men** (-mən) *Brit.* One who owns or tends a herd. Also **herd′er, herd′man.**

Herds·man (hûrdz′mən) *n.* The constellation Boötes. See CONSTELLATION.

here (hir) *adv.* **1.** In, at, or about this place: opposed to *there.* Also used to indicate or emphasize: George *here* is a good swimmer; This paper *here.* **2.** To this place; hither. **3.** At this point in time, in an action, etc.: *Here* you begin; also, now to be seen; now following: *Here* are my reasons. **4.** In the present life: distinguished from *hereafter.* — *interj.* An exclamation used to answer a roll call, attract attention, call

an animal, etc. **— here and there** **1.** In one place or another; so as to be irregularly scattered. **2.** Hither and thither. **— here goes!** For better or worse, I start now! **— neither here nor there** Foreign to the matter under consideration; irrelevant. **— n. 1.** This place. **2.** This time; this life: the *here* and now. ◆ The adverb *here* cannot, in standard English, appear in the adjective position, as this *here* book. This book *here* is the accepted order. [OE *hēr*]
He·re (hir'ē) See HERA.
here·a·bout (hir'ə·bout') *adv.* About this place; in this vicinity. Also **here'a·bouts'**.
here·af·ter (hir·af'tər, -äf'-) *adv.* **1.** At some future time. **2.** From this time forth. **3.** In the state of life after death. **— n.** A future state or existence. [OE *hēræfter*]
here·at (hir·at') *adv.* **1.** At this time. **2.** By reason of this; because of this.
here·by (hir·bī') *adv.* **1.** By means or by virtue of this. **2.** *Obs.* Near this.
he·red·i·ta·ble (hə·red'i·tə·bəl) *adj.* Heritable. [< MF *héréditable*] **— he·red'i·ta·bil'i·ty** *n.* **— he·red'i·ta·bly** *adv.*
her·e·dit·a·ment (her'ə·dit'ə·mənt) *n. Law* Every kind of property capable of being inherited. **— corporeal hereditament** Visible and tangible objects corresponding to and embraced by the term "lands," such as houses, trees, crops, water, etc. **— incorporeal hereditament** Invisible and intangible rights related to lands.
he·red·i·tar·y (hə·red'ə·ter'ē) *adj.* **1.** Derived from ancestors; inherited. **2.** Of or pertaining to heredity or inheritance. **3.** *Biol.* Transmitted or transmissible directly from an animal or plant to its offspring: distinguished from *congenital.* **4.** *Law* **a** Passing, capable of passing, or necessarily passing by inheritance from an ancestor to an heir. **b** Holding possession or title through inheritance. **— Syn.** See INNATE. [< L *hereditarius* < *hereditas.* See HEREDITY.] **— he·red'i·tar'i·ly** *adv.* **— he·red'i·tar'i·ness** *n.*
he·red·i·tist (hə·red'ə·tist) *n.* An adherent of the theory that personality is determined by heredity.
he·red·i·ty (hə·red'ə·tē) *n. pl.* **·ties** *Biol.* **1.** Transmission of genetically determined characteristics from parents to offspring. **2.** The tendency manifested by an organism to develop in the likeness of a progenitor. **3.** The sum total of an individual's inherited characteristics. [< F *hérédité* < L *hereditas, -tatis* inheritance < *heres, -edis* heir]
Heref. or **Herefs.** Herefordshire.
Her·e·ford (her'ə·fərd, *U.S.* hûr'fərd) *n.* One of a breed of beef cattle originating in Herefordshire, and having a white face and a red coat with white markings.
Hereford and Worcester A county in western England; 1,515 sq. mi.; pop. 585,900 (1976); county town, Worcester.
Her·e·ford·shire (her'ə·fərd·shir', -shər) A former county in SW England; 842 sq. mi.; pop. 138,425 (1971); county seat, Hereford, pop. 40,431. Also **Her'e·ford.**
here·in (hir·in') *adv.* **1.** In or into this place; in this. **2.** In this case, circumstance, matter, etc. [OE *hērinne*]
here·in·af·ter (hir'in·af'tər, -äf'-) *adv.* In a subsequent part of this document, deed, contract, etc.
here·in·be·fore (hir'in·bi·fôr', -fōr') *adv.* In a preceding part of this document, deed, contract, etc.
here·in·to (hir·in'tōō) *adv.* **1.** Into this place. **2.** Into this case, circumstance, matter, etc.
here·of (hir·uv', -ov) *adv.* **1.** Of this. **2.** In regard to this.
here·on (hir·on', -ôn') *adv.* On this: hereupon.
he·res (hir'ēz) *n. pl.* **he·re·des** (hi·rē'dēz) *Law* An heir.
he·re·si·arch (hi·rē'sē·ärk, her'ə·sē·ärk') *n.* The chief exponent of a heresy; founder of a heretical sect. **— Syn.** See HERETIC. [< LL *haeresiarcha* < Gk. *hairesiarches* < *hairesis* sect + *archēs* leader < *archein* to rule.]
her·e·sy (her'ə·sē) *n. pl.* **·sies** **1.** A belief or opinion contrary to the established doctrines of a church or religious system. **2.** Any belief or opinion that is contrary to established doctrine: a political *heresy.* **3.** The holding of such a belief or opinion. [< OF *heresie,* ult. < Gk. *hairesis* sect, lit., a choosing < *hairesthai* to choose]
her·e·tic (her'ə·tik) *n.* **1.** One who holds beliefs or opinions contrary to the established doctrines of his religion. **2.** One who maintains unorthodox or controversial opinions on any subject. [< OF *heretique* < LL *haereticus* < Gk. *hairetikos* able to choose < *haireesthai* to choose]
— Syn. *Heretic, schismatic, heresiarch, dissenter,* and *nonconformist* denote a person who advocates a doctrine at variance with that accepted by a church or religious system. A *heretic* formulates or chooses views that the church officially opposes and condemns as false; a *schismatic* holds views that create sharp division of opinion within the church, leading frequently to the creation of a separate sect. A *heresiarch* is the author of a heresy or the leader of a heretical party, and thus is at once a *heretic* and a *schismatic.* *Dissenter* and *nonconformist* are applied to English subjects who held aloof from the Church of England. Much of the odium has been stripped from these words; *heretic* is now applied, without reproach, to one who contradicts the orthodox view in any field.
he·ret·i·cal (hə·ret'i·kəl) *adj.* Of, pertaining to, or characterized by heresy. **— he·ret'i·cal·ly** *adv.*

here·to (hir·tōō') *adv.* To this thing, matter, etc.
here·to·fore (hir'tə·fôr', -fōr') *adv.* Before now; previously.
here·un·der (hir·un'dər) *adv.* **1.** Under or beneath this heading, statement, etc. **2.** Under the terms of this statement, provision, etc.
here·un·to (hir'un·tōō') *adv.* To this; hereto.
here·up·on (hir'ə·pon', -pôn') *adv.* Immediately resulting from or following this; upon this.
here·with (hir·with', -with') *adv.* **1.** Along with this. **2.** By means of or through this.
Her·ges·hei·mer (hûr'gəs·hī'mər), **Joseph,** 1880–1954, U.S. novelist.
her·i·ot (her'ē·ət) *n.* In feudal law, a tribute or payment rendered to a lord from the goods of a deceased tenant. [OE *heregeatwa* < *here* army + *geatwa* equipment]
her·i·ta·ble (her'ə·tə·bəl) *adj.* **1.** That can be inherited. **2.** *Rare* Capable of inheriting. [< OF < *heriter* to inherit] **— her'i·ta·bil'i·ty** *n.* **— her'i·ta·bly** *adv.*
her·i·tage (her'ə·tij) *n.* **1.** That which is inherited, as possessions, characteristics, conditions, etc. **2.** A cultural tradition, body of knowledge, etc., handed down from past times. **3.** *Law* Property that is or can be inherited by descendants. **4.** In the Bible: **a** The Israelites as the chosen people of God. **b** The Christian Church. [< OF < *heriter* to inherit < L *hereditare* < *heres, -edis* heir]
her·i·tor (her'ə·tər) *n.* An inheritor. [< AF *heriter,* OF *heritier* < L *hereditarius.* See HEREDITARY.] **— her'e·trix** or **her'i·trix** (-triks) or **her'i·tress** (-tris) *n.fem.*
Her·ki·mer (hûr'kə·mər), **Nicholas,** 1728–77, American Revolutionary general.
herl (hûrl) *n.* **1.** A barb of a feather, used in making artificial flies for angling. **2.** A fly so made. Also called *harl.*
her·ma (hûr'mə) *n. pl.* **·mae** (-mē) or **·mai** (-mī) In ancient Greece, a rough stone post surmounted by a sculptured head, often of Hermes, used as a sign post, boundary marker, etc. Also **herm.** [< L < Gk. *Hermēs* Hermes]
Her·mann (hûr'mən) See ARMINIUS.
Her·mann·stadt (her'män·shtät) The German name for SIBIU.
her·maph·ro·dite (hûr·maf'rə·dīt) *n.* **1.** An individual having both male and female sexual characteristics in marked degree. **2.** *Biol.* **a** An organism having both male and female reproductive organs, as the earthworm. **b** A monoclinous plant or flower. **3.** *Naut.* A hermaphrodite brig (which see). **— adj.** Hermaphroditic. [< L *hermaphroditus* < Gk. *hermaphroditos,* after *Hermaphroditus*]
hermaphrodite brig *Naut.* A brigantine.
her·maph·ro·dit·ic (hûr·maf'rə·dit'ik) *adj.* Of, pertaining to, or characteristic of a hermaphrodite. Also **her·maph'ro·dit'i·cal.** **— her·maph'ro·dit'i·cal·ly** *adv.*
her·maph·ro·dit·ism (hûr·maf'rə·dit·iz'əm) *n.* The state or condition of being a hermaphrodite.
Her·maph·ro·di·tus (hûr·maf'rə·dī'təs) In Greek mythology, the son of Hermes and Aphrodite, who became united with the nymph Salmacis in a single body.
her·me·neu·tic (hûr'mə·nōō'tik, -nyōō'-) *adj.* Of or pertaining to hermeneutics; interpretive; explanatory. Also **her'me·neu'ti·cal.** **— her'me·neu'ti·cal·ly** *adv.*
her·me·neu·tics (hûr'mə·nōō'tiks, -nyōō'-) *n.pl.* (*construed as sing.*) The science or art of interpretation, especially of the Scriptures. [< Gk. *hermēneutikē* (*technē*) interpretive (art) < *hermēneulēs* interpreter]
Her·mes (hûr'mēz) In Greek mythology, the messenger of the gods, conductor of the dead to Hades, and also the god of science, commerce, travel, eloquence, and cunning, usually depicted with winged sandals, a hat, and a caduceus: identified with the Roman *Mercury.*
Hermes Tris·me·gis·tus (tris'mə·jis'təs) The Greek name for the Egyptian god Thoth regarded as the founder of alchemy, astrology, and other occult sciences.
her·met·ic (hûr·met'ik) *adj.* **1.** Made impervious to air and liquids, as by fusion; airtight. **2.** *Usually cap.* Of or pertaining to Hermes Trismegistus, or to the writings attributed to him. **3.** Of or relating to alchemy; occult; magical. Also **her·met'i·cal.** [< Med.L *hermeticus* < *Hermes* (*Trismegistus*); with ref. to alchemy] **— her·met'i·cal·ly** *adv.*
Her·mi·o·ne (hûr·mī'ə·nē) In Greek legend, the daughter of Menelaus and Helen of Troy.
her·mit (hûr'mit) *n.* **1.** One who abandons society and lives in seclusion, often for religious reasons; anchorite; recluse. **2.** A molasses cooky containing spice and sometimes raisins. **3.** *Obs.* A beadsman. [< OF *hermite* < LL *eremita* < Gk. *erēmitēs* < *erēmia* desert < *erēmos* deserted] **— her·mit'ic** or **·i·cal** *adj.* **— her·mit'i·cal·ly** *adv.*
her·mit·age (hûr'mə·tij) *n.* **1.** The retreat or dwelling of a hermit. **2.** Any secluded dwelling place. **— Syn.** See CLOISTER.
Her·mit·age (hûr'mə·tij, *Fr.* âr·mē·tázh') A rich, flavorful wine produced near Valence, in SE France.
hermit crab Any of various decapod crustaceans (genus *Pagurus*) having a soft abdomen and occupying the empty shell of a univalve mollusk.

hermit thrush A thrush (*Hylocichla guttata*) of North America, having a spotted breast and reddish tail, and noted for its beautiful song.

hermit warbler A brilliantly colored songbird (*Dendroica occidentalis*) of western North America.

Her·mon (hûr′mən), **Mount** A mountain on the Syria-Lebanon border; 9,232 ft.

hern (hûrn) *n. Archaic & Dial.* A heron. [Var. of HERON]

her·ni·a (hûr′nē·ə) *n. pl.* **·ni·as** or **·ni·ae** (nĭ·ē) *Pathol.* The protrusion of an organ or part of an organ, as of the intestine, through an opening in the wall surrounding it; rupture. [< L] — **her′ni·al** *adj.*

hernio- *combining form* Hernia: *herniotomy.*

her·ni·o·plas·ty (hûr′nē·ə·plas′tē) *n. pl.* **·ties** *Surg.* An operation for the complete repair and cure of hernia. — **her′ni·o·plas′tic** *adj.*

her·ni·ot·o·my (hûr′nē·ot′ə·mē) *n. pl.* **·mies** *Surg.* An operation for the relief of hernia.

he·ro (hir′ō, hē′rō) *n. pl.* **·roes 1.** A man distinguished for exceptional courage, fortitude, or bold enterprise, especially in time of war or danger. **2.** One idealized or held in esteem for superior qualities or deeds of any kind. **3.** The principal male character in a drama, fictional work, etc. **4.** In classical mythology and legend: **a** The son of a god or goddess and a mortal. **b** A man of great nobility or physical prowess who was often worshiped as a demigod after death. **5.** *U.S.* A sandwich made with a loaf of bread cut lengthwise: also **hero sandwich.** [< L *heros* < Gk. *hērōs*]

He·ro (hir′ō) In Greek legend, a priestess of Aphrodite at Sestos, whose lover, Leander, nightly swam the Hellespont from Abydos to join her. Finding him drowned one night, she cast herself into the sea.

Her·od I (her′əd), 73?–4 B.C., king of Judea 37–4 B.C.: called **Herod the Great.**

Herod A·grip·pa I (ə·grip′ə), 10? B.C.–A.D. 44, king of Judea 41–44.

Herod An·ti·pas (an′ti·pas), died A.D. 39?, tetrarch of Galilee 4 B.C.–A.D. 39; the Herod of the Gospels; son of Herod the Great.

He·ro·di·an (hi·rō′dē·ən) *adj.* Of or pertaining to Herod the Great, his dynasty, or his followers. — *n.* One of the followers of Herod Antipas.

He·ro·di·as (hi·rō′dē·əs) The second wife of Herod Antipas. *Mark* vi 17–28. See SALOME.

He·rod·o·tus (hi·rod′ə·təs), Fifth-century B.C. Greek historian: called the **Father of History.**

he·ro·ic (hi·rō′ik) *adj.* **1.** Characteristic of or befitting a hero; noble; brave: *heroic deeds.* **2.** Resembling or of the nature of a hero: a *heroic* warrior. **3.** Showing great daring or boldness; extreme in action or effect: a *heroic* attempt; *heroic* measures. **4.** Of or pertaining to the heroes of antiquity: the *heroic* age. **5.** Relating to or describing a hero or heroic deeds; epic: *heroic* poetry. **6.** Grandiose or high-flown in style or language. **7.** Of sculpture, considerably larger than life size. Also **he·ro′i·cal.** — *n.* **1.** *Often pl.* Heroic verse. **2.** *pl.* Melodramatic or extravagant language, action, or ideas. — **he·ro′i·cal·ly** *adv.*

heroic age 1. The age when demigods and heroes are supposed to have been on earth. **2.** The age that produced epic poetry.

heroic couplet An English verse form consisting of two rhyming lines of iambic pentameter.

heroic verse One of several verse forms used especially in epic and dramatic poetry, as the Greek and Latin dactylic hexameter, the Italian ottava rima, the French Alexandrine, and the iambic pentameter of the English heroic couplet and blank verse.

her·o·in (her′ō·in) *n.* A white, odorless, crystalline derivative of morphine, $C_{21}H_{23}O_5N$, a powerful, habit-forming narcotic, the manufacture of which is prohibited in the United States: also called *diacetylmorphine.* [< G]

her·o·ine (her′ō·in) *n.fem.* **1.** A girl or woman of heroic character; the female counterpart of a hero. **2.** The principal female character of a drama, fictional work, etc. [< L *heroina* < Gk. *hērōinē*, fem. of *hērōs* hero]

her·o·ism (her′ō·iz′əm) *n.* **1.** The character or qualities of a hero or heroine. **2.** Heroic behavior.

her·on (her′ən) *n.* **1.** Any of several wading birds (family *Ardeidae*), having a long neck, a long, slender bill, and long legs, as the **gray heron** (*Ardea cinerea*) of Europe, and the **great blue heron** (*A. herodias*) of America. **2.** Any of various similar or related birds, as the egret or the bittern. [< OF *hairon*, ult. < Gmc.]

Her·on (hir′on) Third-century A.D. Greek mathematician and physicist. Also **Hero of Alexandria.**

her·on·bill (her′ən·bil′) *n.* The stork's-bill (which see). Also **her′on's-bill′, her′ons·bill′.**

her·on·ry (her′ən·rē) *n. pl.* **·ries** A place where herons congregate and breed.

hero worship Enthusiastic or extravagant admiration for heroes or other persons. — **hero worshiper**

herp. or **herpet.** or **herpetol.** Herpetology.

GREAT
BLUE
HERON

(About 4 feet high)

her·pes (hûr′pēz) *n. Pathol.* Any of various infections of the skin and mucous membranes, characterized by the eruption of vesicles, with inflammation and sometimes acute neuralgia. [< L < Gk. *herpes* < *herpein* to creep]

herpes la·bi·a·lis (lā′bē·ā′lis) *Pathol.* A cold sore. [L, herpes of the lips]

herpes sim·plex (sim′pleks) *Pathol.* A form of herpes affecting various parts of the body, especially the face and lips. [L, simple herpes]

herpes zos·ter (zos′tər) *Pathol.* Shingles. [< L, herpes + *zoster* (< Gk., girdle, belt)]

her·pet·ic (hûr·pet′ik) *adj.* Affected by, relating to, or characteristic of herpes. Also **her·pet′i·cal.**

her·pe·tol·o·gy (hûr′pə·tol′ə·jē) *n.* The branch of zoology that treats of reptiles and amphibians. [< Gk. *herpeton* reptile < *herpein* to creep + -LOGY] — **her·pe·to·log·i·cal** (hûr′pə·tə·loj′i·kəl) *adj.* — **her′pe·tol′o·gist** *n.*

Herr (her) *n. pl.* **Her·ren** (her′ən) *German* A title of address equivalent to the English *Mister.* Abbr. *Hr.*

Herr·en·volk (her′ən·fōlk′) *n. German* The master race.

Her·re·ra (er·rä′rä), **Francisco de,** 1576–1656, Spanish painter and architect.

Her·rick (her′ik), **Robert,** 1591–1674, English lyric poet.

her·ring (her′ing) *n. pl.* **·rings** or **·ring 1.** A small food fish (*Clupea harengus*) frequenting the North Atlantic in great numbers, the young of which are canned as sardines, and the adults smoked, pickled, or salted. **2.** Any of various fish allied to the herring, especially *Clupea pallasii* of Pacific waters, and the shad, sardine, etc. [OE *hæring*]

her·ring·bone (her′ing·bōn′) *n.* **1.** A pattern utilizing a design, often repeated, resembling the spinal structure of a herring, in which the ribs form slanting parallel lines on either side of the spine. **2.** Something made in or consisting of such a pattern, as an embroidery stitch, textile weave, or arrangement of masonry. **3.** In skiing, a method of walking up an incline with the tips of the skis pointed outward so as to make tracks in a herringbone pattern. — *adj.* Having or forming the pattern of a herringbone. — *v.* **·boned, ·bon·ing** *v.t.* **1.** To ornament with or arrange in a herringbone pattern. — *v.i.* **2.** To produce a herringbone pattern. **3.** In skiing, to walk up an incline with the tips of the skis pointed outward.

herring choker *Canadian Slang* A Maritimer.

herring gull A large, common, widely distributed gull (*Larus argentatus*) that feeds on herring and floating refuse.

Her·riot (e·ryō′), **Édouard,** 1872–1957, French statesman; premier 1924–25, 1932.

her·ry (her′ē) *v.t. Scot.* To harry. — **her′ri·ment** or **her′ry·ment** *n.*

hers (hûrz) *pron.* **1.** The possessive case of the pronoun *she,* used predicatively: That book is *hers.* **2.** The one or ones belonging to or relating to her: John's story is funnier than *hers.* — **of hers** Belonging or relating to her: a double possessive. [OE *hire* + -s (after *his*)]

Her·schel (hûr′shəl), **Sir John Frederick William,** 1792–1871, English astronomer. — **Sir William,** 1738–1822, English astronomer born in Germany; father of the preceding: original name **Friedrich Wilhelm Herschel.**

her·self (hər·self′) *pron.* A form of the third person singular feminine pronoun, used: **1.** As a reflexive or as object of a preposition in a reflexive sense: She excused *herself* from the table; She often talks to *herself.* **2.** As an emphatic or intensive form of *she*: She *herself* called the police. **3.** As a designation of a normal, proper, or usual state: After her illness, she was *herself* again. **4.** *Irish* As a pronoun in the nominative case meaning *she*: How is *herself* these days?

Herst·mon·ceux (hûrst′mən·sōō, hûrs′-) A village in SE Sussex, England, to which the British meteorological station, time clocks, and the Royal Observatory were moved from Greenwich: also *Hurstmonceux.*

Her·ter (hûr′tər), **Christian Archibald,** 1895–1966, U.S. diplomat; Secretary of State 1959–61.

Hert·ford·shire (här′fərd·shir, härt′-, -shər) A county in SE England; 632 sq. mi.; pop. 941,700 (1976); county seat, Hertford, pop. 15,734. Also **Hert′ford.** Shortened form **Herts** (härts, hûrts).

Her·to·gen·bosch, 's (ser′tō·khən·bôs′) See 's HERTOGEN-BOSCH.

hertz (hûrts) *n. Physics* A unit of electromagnetic wave frequency, equal to one cycle per second. [after H. R. *Hertz*]

Hertz (herts), **Heinrich Rudolph,** 1857–94, German physicist. — **Hertz′i·an** (hert′sē·ən, hûrt′-) *adi.*

Hertzian wave An electromagnetic wave in the radio and radar range, artificially produced. [after H. R. *Hertz*]

Hertz·og (her′tsokh), **James Barry Munnik,** 1866–1942, South African general and statesman; prime minister of South Africa 1924–39.

Hertz·sprung-Rus·sell diagram (herts′sprung·rus′əl) *Astron.* A classification of stars plotted on a chart in which the luminosity increases on a vertical scale from bottom to top and the color or spectral type changes from blue or white to red on a horizontal scale from left to right: also called *Russell diagram.* See MAIN SEQUENCE. [after Ejnar *Hertz-*

sprung, born 1873, Dutch astronomer, and Henry Norris *Russell,* 1877–1957, U.S. astronomer]

Her·ze·go·vi·na (hûr′tsə·gō·vē′nə) See under BOSNIA AND HERZEGOVINA. Serbo-Croatian *Hercegovina.* **— Her′ze·go·vin′i·an** (-vin′ē·ən) *adj. & n.*

Herzl (her′tsəl), **Theodor,** 1860–1904, Austro-Hungarian journalist; founded the Zionist movement. See ZIONISM.

he's (hēz) **1.** He is. **2.** He has.

Hesh·wan (hesh·vän′, hesh′vän) *n.* The second month of the Hebrew year: also called *Marchesvan* or *Bul.* Also **Heshvan′.** See (Hebrew) CALENDAR.

He·si·od (hē′sē·əd, hes′ē·əd) Eighth-century B.C. Greek poet. **— He·si·od·ic** (hē′sē·od′ik, hes′ē-) *adj.*

He·si·o·ne (hi·sī′ə·nē) In Greek legend, Laomedon's daughter, rescued from a sea monster by Hercules.

hes·i·tan·cy (hez′ə·tən·sē) *n. pl.* **·cies** The act or condition of hesitating; hesitation; uncertainty. Also **hes′i·tance.**

hes·i·tant (hes′ə·tənt) *adj.* Lacking certainty or decisiveness; hesitating; irresolute. [< L *haesitans, -antis,* ppr. of *haesitare.* See HESITATE.] **— hes′i·tant·ly** *adv.*

hes·i·tate (hez′ə·tāt) *v.i.* **·tat·ed, ·tat·ing** **1.** To be slow or doubtful in acting, making a decision, etc.; be uncertain; waver. **2.** To be reluctant; scruple: I *hesitate* to ask. **3.** To pause or falter. **4.** To falter or stammer in speech. [< L *haesitatus,* pp. of *haesitare,* freq. of *haerere* to stick]

hes·i·ta·tion (hez′ə·tā′shən) *n.* **1.** The act of hesitating. **2.** A pause or delay caused by indecision or uncertainty. **3.** A state of doubt. **4.** A pause or faltering in speech.

hes·i·ta·tive (hez′ə·tā′tiv) *adj.* Manifesting or characterized by hesitation; hesitating. **— hes′i·ta·tive·ly** *adv.*

Hes·pe·ri·a (hes·pir′ē·ə) Land of the West: an ancient Greek name for Italy and a Latin name for Iberia.

Hes·pe·ri·an (hes·pir′ē·ən) *adj.* **1.** *Poetic* In or of the west; western. **2.** Of or pertaining to the Hesperides. [< L *hesperius* < Gk. *hesperios* western]

Hes·per·i·des (hes·per′ə·dēz) *n.pl.* **1.** In Greek mythology, the daughters of Atlas who, together with a dragon, guarded the golden apples given to Hera by Gaea. **2.** The garden where these apples grew. [< Gk. *hesperis* western] **— Hes·per·id·i·an** (hes′pə·rid′ē·ən) or **Hes′per·id′e·an** *adj.*

hes·per·i·din (hes·per′ə·din) *n.* A white, tasteless, odorless, crystalline glycoside bioflavonoid, $C_{28}H_{34}O_{15}$, obtained from citrus fruits. [< HESPERID(IUM) + -IN]

hes·per·i·di·um (hes′pə·rid′ē·əm) *n. pl.* **·id·i·a** (-id′ē·ə) *Bot.* The fruit of a citrus plant, as the orange. [< NL < Gk. *Hesperides* the Hesperides; with ref. to the golden apples]

Hes·pe·rus (hes′pər·əs) *n.* The evening star, especially Venus. Also *Poetic* **Hes′per.** [< L < Gk. *Hesperos*]

Hess (hess), **Myra,** 1890–1965, English pianist. **— Rudolf,** born 1894, German Nazi leader; sentenced to life imprisonment in 1946. **— Victor Francis,** 1883–1965, Austrian physicist active in the United States.

Hesse (hes) A State of western West Germany; 8,150 sq. mi.; pop. 5,422,600 (est. 1970); capital, Wiesbaden. *German* **Hes·sen** (hes′ən).

Hes·se (hes′ə), **Hermann,** 1877–1962, German novelist.

Hesse-Nas·sau (hes′nas′ô) A former province of Prussia in western Germany. *German* **Hes·sen-Nas·sau** (hes′ən-näs′ou).

hes·sian (hesh′ən) *n.* A coarse hempen cloth. [after *Hesse*]

Hes·sian (hesh′ən) *n.* **1.** A native or citizen of Hesse. **2.** A soldier from Hesse hired by the British to fight in the American Revolution. **3.** A mercenary. **4.** *pl.* Hessian boots. **— adj.** Of or pertaining to Hesse or its inhabitants.

Hessian boots High, tasseled men's boots, worn in England early in the 19th century.

Hessian fly A small, blackish fly (*Phytophaga destructor*), whose larvae are very destructive to wheat, barley, and rye.

hess·ite (hes′īt) *n.* A metallic, lead-gray, silver telluride, Ag_2Te, crystallizing in the isometric system. [after G. H. *Hess,* 1802–50, Swiss chemist]

hes·son·ite (hes′ən·īt) *n.* Essonite, a mineral.

hest (hest) *n. Archaic* Behest.

Hes·ti·a (hes′tē·ə) In Greek mythology, the goddess of the hearth: identified with the Roman *Vesta.*

Hes·y·chast (hes′i·kast) *n.* One of a sect of mystics that originated among the monks of Mt. Athos in the 14th century. [< Med.L *hesychasta* < Gk. *hēsychastēs* < *hēsychazein* to be still < *hēsychos* quiet] **— Hes′y·chas′tic** *adj.*

het (het) *Dial.* Past tense and past participle of HEAT. **— het up** Excited; angry

he·tae·ra (hi·tir′ə, -tī′rə) *n. pl.* **·tae·rae** (-tir′ē, -tī′rē) In ancient Greece, a professional courtesan or concubine, often an educated slave or freedwoman. Also **he·tai·ra** (hi·tī′rə). [< Gk. *hetaira,* fem. of *hetairos* companion]

he·tae·rism (hi·tir′iz·əm, -tī′riz·əm) *n.* **1.** Concubinage. **2.** The practice of communal marriage, said to have characterized primitive society. Also **he·tai·rism** (hi·tī′riz′əm).

hetero- *combining form* Other; different: *heterogeneous:* opposed to *homo-.* Also, before vowels, **heter-.** [< Gk. *hetero-* < *heteros* other]

het·er·o·cer·cal (het′ər·ə·sûr′kəl) *adj. Zool.* Of, having, or denoting a tail fin with lobes of unequal size and an extension of the backbone into the larger, upper lobe, as in sharks, sturgeons, etc. [< HETERO- + Gk. *kerkos* tail]

het·er·o·chro·mat·ic (het′ər·ə·krō·mat′ik) *adj.* Of, characterized by, or consisting of different colors; having a pattern of different colors: distinguished from *homochromatic.* Also **het′er·o·chrome′** (-krōm′).

het·er·o·chro·ma·tin (het′ər·ə·krō′mə·tin) *n. Biol.* The part of chromatin that contains few or no genes and is not significantly altered during mitosis.

het·er·o·chro·mo·some (het′ər·ə·krō′mə·sōm) *n. Biol.* A sex chromosome (which see).

het·er·o·chro·mous (het′ər·ə·krō′məs) *adj. Bot.* Having different colors, as the ray and disk florets of a compound flower: distinguished from *homochromous.* [< HETERO- + Gk. *chrōma* color]

het·er·o·clite (het′ər·ə·klīt′) *n.* **1.** *Gram.* A word that is irregular in inflection, particularly a noun. **2.** *Rare* An anomaly. **— adj.** **1.** *Gram.* Having an irregular inflection. **2.** *Rare* Anomalous. Also **het′er·o·clit′ic** (-klit′ik) or **·i·cal.** [< F *hétéroclite* < L *heteroclitus* < Gk. *heteroklitos* irregular < *hetero-* other + *klinein* to bend]

het·er·o·cy·clic (het′ər·ə·sī′klik, -sik′lik) *adj. Chem.* Pertaining to or designating an organic ring compound containing atoms of one or more elements other than carbon.

het·er·o·dox (het′ər·ə·doks′) *adj.* **1.** At variance with accepted or established doctrines or beliefs, especially in religion. **2.** Holding unorthodox beliefs or opinions. [< Gk. *heterodoxos* < *hetero-* other + *doxa* opinion]

het·er·o·dox·y (het′ər·ə·dok′sē) *n. pl.* **·dox·ies** **1.** The state or quality of being heterodox. **2.** A heterodox doctrine or belief.

het·er·o·dyne (het′ər·ə·dīn′) *adj. Telecom.* Denoting a radio circuit, receiver, etc., in which the incoming signal is combined with a signal of fixed frequency and the signal resulting from their beats is used as the amplifier input. **— v.i.** **·dyned, ·dyn·ing** To modify a signal in this manner.

het·er·oe·cious (het′ə·rē′shəs) *adj. Biol.* Of, pertaining to, or exhibiting heteroecism.

het·er·oe·cism (het′ə·rē′siz·əm) *n. Biol.* A type of parasitism characterized by the development of different stages on different hosts. [< HETER(O)- + Gk. *oikos* house]

het·er·o·gam·ete (het′ər·ə·gam′ēt, -gə·mēt′) *n. Biol.* Either of two gametes sexually or otherwise differentiated from each other: opposed to *isogamete.*

het·er·og·a·mous (het′ə·rog′ə·məs) *adj.* **1.** *Biol.* **a** Having a union of unlike gametes: opposed to *isogamous.* **b** Having a sexual generation alternating with an asexual one. **2.** *Bot.* **a** Bearing flowers that are sexually of two kinds: opposed to *homogamous* (def. 1). **b** Pertaining to or characterized by indirect pollination.

het·er·og·a·my (het′ə·rog′ə·mē) *n. pl.* **·mies** The state or condition of being heterogamous. **— het·er·o·gam·ic** (het′-ər·ə·gam′ik) *adj.*

het·er·o·ge·ne·i·ty (het′ər·ə·jə·nē′ə·tē) *n. pl.* **·ties** The state or condition of being heterogeneous; dissimilarity.

het·er·o·ge·ne·ous (het′ər·ə·jē′nē·əs) *adj.* **1.** Consisting of parts or elements that are dissimilar or unrelated; not homogeneous. **2.** Differing in nature or kind; unlike. [< Med.L *heterogeneus* < Gk. *heterogenēs* < *hetero-* other + *genos* kind] **— het′er·o·ge′ne·ous·ly** *adv.* **— het′er·o·ge′ne·ous·ness** *n.* **— Syn.** *Heterogeneous, miscellaneous, various,* and *mixed* characterize a collection or group of things that are not all alike. *Heterogeneous* emphasizes difference most strongly. *Miscellaneous* suggests diversity arising from lack of any unifying principle in selection; whatever is left over after a collection has been assorted by categories is called *miscellaneous: miscellaneous* undated ancient coins. *Various* means different within a category; garnet, turquoise, and zircon are *various* gemstones. *Mixed* is most frequently applied to that which is composed of a few clearly defined different kinds; a *mixed* party consists of men and women. **— Ant.** homogeneous.

het·er·o·gen·e·sis (het′ər·ə·jen′ə·sis) *n. Biol.* **1.** Metagenesis (which see). **2.** Abiogenesis (which see). **— het·er·o·ge·net·ic** (het′ər·ə·jə·net′ik) *adj.*

het·er·og·e·nous (het′ə·roj′ə·nəs) *adj. Biol.* Originating outside the organism.

het·er·og·o·nous (het′ə·rog′ə·nəs) *adj.* Pertaining to or characterized by heterogony. **— het·er·og′o·nous·ly** *adv.*

het·er·og·o·ny (het′ə·rog′ə·nē) *n. pl.* **·nies** *Bot.* **1.** The condition of having, in the same species, flowers that differ in kind, especially in the length of stamens and pistils: opposed to *homogony.* **2.** *Biol.* Reproduction in which a sexual generation alternates with an asexual one.

het·er·og·ra·phy (het′ə·rog′rə·fē) *n. pl.* **·phies** **1.** Spelling in which the same letter represents different sounds in different words or syllables, as *c* in *camp* and *cent.* **2.** Spelling that varies from the accepted standard usage. **— het·er·o·graph·ic** (het′ər·ə·graf′ik) or **·i·cal** *adj.*

het·er·og·y·nous (het′ə·roj′ə·nəs) *adj. Zool.* Denoting organisms having two different kinds of females, one of which is fully developed sexually and the other incapable of reproduction, as bees or ants.

het·er·ol·o·gous (het′ə·rol′ə·gəs) *adj. Biol.* Pertaining to or characterized by heterology.

het·er·ol·o·gy (het′ə·rol′ə·jē) *n. pl.* **·gies** *Biol.* **1.** The lack of correspondence between structures owing to differences in origin. **2.** Abnormality of structure.

het·er·ol·y·sis (het′ə·rol′ə·sis) *n. Biochem.* Dissolution effected by an outside agent; especially, the destruction of a cell by external enzymes or lysins: opposed to *autolysis.* — **het·er·o·lyt·ic** (het′ə·rə·lit′ik) *adj.*

het·er·om·er·ous (het′ə·rom′ər·əs) *adj. Bot.* Having parts that differ in number, form, or composition, as a whorl of flowers: opposed to *isomerous.*

het·er·o·mor·phic (het′ə·rə·môr′fik) *adj.* **1.** *Biol.* Deviating from the normal in form, structure, or size. **2.** *Entomol.* Varying in form at different stages of development; undergoing complete metamorphosis. Also **het′er·o·mor′phous** (-fəs). — **het′er·o·mor′phism** *n.*

het·er·on·o·mous (het′ə·ron′ə·məs) *adj.* **1.** Subject to the law or rule of another: opposed to *autonomous.* **2.** *Biol.* Subject to or characterized by different laws of growth or specialization, as the segments of certain arthropods. [< HETERO- + Gk. *nomos* law, rule]

het·er·on·o·my (het′ə·ron′ə·mē) *n.* The state or condition of being subject to the rule or authority of another: opposed to *autonomy.*

het·er·o·nym (het′ər·ə·nim′) *n.* A word spelled like another, but having a different sound and meaning, as *bass,* a male voice, and *bass,* a fish. Compare HOMOGRAPH. [< HETER(O)- + Gk. *onyma* name; on analogy with *synonym*]

het·er·on·y·mous (het′ə·ron′ə·məs) *adj.* **1.** Relating to or of the nature of a heteronym. **2.** Having different names, as a pair showing a corresponding relationship: *nephew* and *niece* are *heteronymous* terms. **3.** *Pathol.* Designating a form of diplopia in which the image seen by the right eye is on the left side and vice versa.

Het·er·ou·si·an (het′ər·ō·ōō′sē·ən, -ou′sē-) *n. Theol.* A member of the Arian faction that believed the nature of Christ to be essentially different from that of God the Father. — *adj.* Of or pertaining to the Heterousians or their beliefs. Also *Heterousian.* Compare HOMOIOUSIAN, HOMOOUSIAN. [< LGk. *heteroousia* < *heteroousios* of different essence < Gk. *hetero-* other + *ousia* being]

het·er·o·phyl·lous (het′ər·ə·fil′əs) *adj. Bot.* Having leaves differing in size, form, or function on the same plant. — **het′·er·o·phyl′ly** (-fil′ē) *n.*

het·er·o·plas·ty (het′ər·ə·plas′tē) *n. pl.* **·ties** *Surg.* A plastic operation in which the grafted tissue is taken from an organism or person other than the patient.

het·er·o·po·lar (het′ər·ə·pō′lər) *adj. Chem.* Designating a valence linkage characterized by an unsymmetrical distribution of electric charge: distinguished from *homopolar.* — **het′er·o·po·lar′i·ty** (-lar′ə·tē) *n.*

het·er·op·ter·ous (het′ə·rop′tər·əs) *adj.* Designating a suborder (*Heteroptera*) of hemipterous insects that includes the true bugs. [< NL < Gk. *hetero-* other + *pteron* wing]

het·er·o·sex·u·al (het′ər·ə·sek′shōō·əl) *adj.* **1.** Pertaining to or characterized by heterosexuality. **2.** *Biol.* Of or pertaining to the opposite sex or to both sexes. — *n.* A heterosexual individual. Opposed to *homosexual.*

het·er·o·sex·u·al·i·ty (het′ər·ə·sek′shōō·al′ə·tē) *n.* **1.** The condition of being sexually attracted to persons of the opposite sex. **2.** Sexual relations between those of opposite sexes. Opposed to *homosexuality.*

het·er·o·sis (het′ə·rō′sis) *n. Biol.* Exceptional vigor of growth, etc., in plant or animal organisms, resulting from crossbreeding between two different types: also called *hybrid vigor.* [< NL < Gk. *heterōsis* alteration < *heteros* other]

het·er·o·sphere (het′ər·ə·sfir′) *n.* The outer portion of the earth's atmosphere, in which varying proportions of the component gases are mixed with radioactive particles and meteoritic debris. — **het′er·o·spher′ic** (-sfir′ik, -sfer′-) *adj.*

het·er·os·po·rous (het′ə·ros′pər·əs, het′ə·rə·spôr′əs, -spō′rəs) *adj. Bot.* Having or producing both microspores and megaspores. — **het′er·os′po·ry** (-pər·ē) *n.*

het·er·o·tax·is (het′ər·ə·tak′sis) *n.* Any irregular or abnormal arrangement of parts, as of parts of the body, rock strata, geographic features, etc. Also **het′er·o·tax′i·a** (-tak′sē·ə), **het′er·o·tax′y** (-tak′sē). [< NL < Gk. *hetero-* other + *taxis* arrangement] — **het′er·o·tac′tic** (-tak′tik), — **het′er·o·tac′tous** (-tak′təs), **het′er·o·tax′ic** (-tak′sik) *adj.*

het·er·o·thal·lic (het′ər·ə·thal′ik) *adj. Bot.* Having or designating two dissimilar types of mycelia that participate as opposite sexes in the reproductive process: distinguished from *homothallic.* [< HETERO- + Gk. *thallos* sprout]

het·er·o·to·pi·a (het′ər·ə·tō′pē·ə) *n. Pathol.* **1.** The misplacement of an organ or part in the body. **2.** The formation or presence of tissue in a part of the body where it is not normally found. Also **het′er·ot′o·py** (-ot′ə·pē). [< NL < Gk. *hetero-* other + *topos* place] — **het′er·o·top′ic** (-top′ik), **het′er·ot′o·pous** (-ot′ə·pəs) *adj.*

het·er·o·troph·ic (het′ər·ə·trof′ik) *adj. Biol.* Obtaining nourishment chiefly or entirely from complex organic substances: distinguished from *autotrophic:* also *holozoic.* [< HETERO- + Gk. *trophē* nurture < *trephein* to feed]

het·er·o·typ·ic (het′ər·ə·tip′ik) *adj. Biol.* Designating the first stage in meiotic division, in which the chromosomes split at an early period. Also **het′er·o·typ′i·cal.**

Het·er·ou·si·an (het′ə·rōō′sē·ən, -rou′sē-) *adj. & n.* Heterousian.

het·er·o·zy·gote (het′ər·ə·zī′gōt, -zig′ōt) *n. Biol.* A hybrid that carries different alleles of the same character and that does not breed true. — **het′er·o·zy′gous** (-zī′gəs) *adj.*

heth (kheth) *n.* The eighth letter in the Hebrew alphabet: also spelled *cheth.* See ALPHABET.

het·man (het′mən) *n. pl.* **·mans** (-mənz) A Cossack chieftain; ataman. [< Polish < G *hauptmann* captain]

heugh (hyōōkh) *n. Scot.* **1.** A precipice or crag. **2.** A steep-sided ravine or pit. Also **heuch.**

heu·land·ite (hyōō′lən·dīt) *n.* A hydrous silicate of aluminum and calcium belonging to the group of zeolites. [after H. *Heuland,* 19th c. English mineralogist]

heu·ris·tic (hyōō·ris′tik) *adj.* **1.** Aiding or guiding in discovery. **2.** Designating an educational method by which a pupil is stimulated to make his own investigations and discoveries. [< Gk. *heuriskein* to find out]

hew (hyōō) *v.* **hewed, hewn** or **hewed, hew·ing** *v.t.* **1.** To make or shape with or as with blows of an ax or other cutting tool: often with *out.* **2.** To cut or strike with an ax, sword, etc.; chop; hack. **3.** To fell with or as with ax blows: usually with *down.* — *v.i.* **4.** To make cutting and repeated blows, as with an ax or sword. **5.** To conform or adhere, as to a principle or line of conduct. [OE *hēawan*] — **hew′er** *n.*

hex (heks) *U.S. Dial.* or *Informal n.* **1.** An evil spell. **2.** A witch. — *v.t.* To bewitch. [< G *hexe* witch]

hexa- *combining form* Six: hexagon. Also, before vowels, **hex-.** [< Gk. *hexa-* < *hex* six]

hex·a·chord (hek′sə·kôrd) *n. Music* A series of six tones with a half step between the third and fourth tones, and whole steps between the others.

hex·ad (hek′sad) *n.* A group or series of six. [< LL *hexas, hexadis* the number six < Gk. *hexas, hexados* < *hex* six] — **hex·ad′ic** *adj.*

hex·a·em·er·on (hek′sə·em′ə·ron) *n.* **1.** The six days of the Creation. **2.** A treatise dealing with the Creation. Also **hex′a·hem′er·on** (-hem′-). [< LL < Gk. *hexaēmeros,* lit., of six days < *hex* six + *hēmera* day] — **hex′a·em′er·ic** *adj.*

hex·a·gon (hek′sə·gon) *n. Geom.* A polygon having six sides and six angles. [< L *hexagonum* < Gk. *hexagonos* six-cornered < *hex* six + *gonia* angle]

hex·ag·o·nal (hek·sag′ə·nəl) *adj.* **1.** Having the form of a hexagon. **2.** Of solid figures, having the form of a hexagon as a base; six-sided. **3.** *Crystall.* Denoting a crystal system characterized by three equal axes intersecting in one plane at 60° and one axis of different length intersecting the others at right angles, as in calcite. — **hex·ag′o·nal·ly** *adv.*

HEXAGON

hex·a·gram (hek′sə·gram) *n.* **1.** A six-pointed star made by or as by completing the equilateral triangles based on the sides of a regular hexagon. **2.** Any of various figures formed by six intersecting lines.

hex·a·he·dron (hek′sə·hē′drən) *n. pl.* **·drons** or **·dra** (-drə) A polyhedron bounded by six plane faces. [< NL] — **hex′a·he′dral** *adj.*

HEXAGRAM

hex·am·er·ous (hek·sam′ər·əs) *adj.* **1.** *Bot.* Having a floral whorl divided into six parts: often written **6-merous. 2.** *Zool.* Having parts arranged radially in six divisions or in multiples of six. Also **hex·am′er·al.** [< HEXA- + -MEROUS]

hex·am·e·ter (hek·sam′ə·tər) *n.* **1.** In prosody, a line of verse consisting of six metrical feet. **2.** The dactylic verse of Greek and Latin epics, consisting of four dactyls or spondees followed usually by a dactyl and ending with a spondee or trochee. — *adj.* Having six metrical feet in a line of verse. [< L < Gk. *hexametros*] — **hex·a·met·ric** (hek′sə·met′rik), **hex·am′e·tral** (-ə·trəl), **hex′a·met′ri·cal** *adj.*

hex·a·meth·yl·ene·tet·ra·mine (hek′sə·meth′ə·lēn·tet′rə·mēn) *n.* Methenamine (which see). Also **hex′a·mine** (-mēn).

hex·ane (hek′sān) *n. Chem.* Any of the five volatile, colorless isomers, C_6H_{14}, of the methane series of saturated hydrocarbon compounds. [< HEX(A)- + -ANE]

hex·an·gu·lar (hek·sang′gyə·lər) *adj.* Having six angles.

hex·a·pla (hek′sə·plə) *n. Often cap.* An edition of a work in which six versions of the text are set in parallel columns, as the one made by Origen of the Old Testament. [< Gk., pl. of *hexaploos* < *hex* six + *-ploos* -fold] — **hex′a·plar** *adj.*

hex·a·pod (hek′sə·pod) *n.* One of the class (*Hexapoda*) comprising the true or six-legged insects. — *adj.* Having six feet. [< Gk. *hexapous, -podos* six-footed] — **hex·ap·o·dous** (hek·sap′ə·dəs) *adj.*

hex·ap·o·dy (hek·sap′ə·dē) *n. pl.* **·dies** A line of verse consisting of six metrical feet.

hex·ar·chy (hek′sär·kē) *n. pl.* **·ar·chies** A group of six states or governments, each having a separate ruler. [< HEX(A)- + -ARCHY]

hex·a·stich (hek′sə-stik) *n.* In prosody, a poem or stanza of six lines. Also **hex·as·ti·chon** (heks-as′tə-kon). [< L *hexastichus* < Gk. *hexastichos* < *hex* six + *stichos* line] — **hex′a·stich′ic** *adj.*

Hex·a·teuch (hek′sə-tōōk, -tyōōk) *n.* The first six books of the Old Testament. [< HEXA- + Gk. *teuchos* tool, book] — **Hex′a·teu′chal** *adj.*

hex·en·be·sen (hek′sən-bā′zən) *n.* Witches′-broom, an abnormal plant growth. [< G, witches′-broom]

hex·one (hek′sōn) *n.* A colorless liquid ketone, $C_6H_{12}O$, used as a solvent for gums and resins. — *adj.* Designating any of a group of amino acids containing six carbon atoms in the molecule, as lysine. [< HEX(A)- + -ONE]

hex·o·san (hek′sə-san) *n.* *Biochem.* Any of a group of polysaccharides forming a hexose when hydrolized. [< HEXOSE + -AN]

hex·ose (hek′sōs) *n.* *Biochem.* Any simple sugar, as glucose or fructose, containing six carbon atoms to the molecule. [< HEX(A)- + -OSE]

hex·yl (hek′səl) *n.* *Chem.* The univalent hydrocarbon radical, C_6H_{13}, of hexane and its derivatives. [< HEX(A)- + -YL]

hex·yl·re·sor·ci·nol (hek′səl-rə-zôr′sə-nōl) *n.* A yellowish white compound, $C_{12}H_{18}O_2$, with a pungent odor and sharp taste, used as a germicide and antiseptic.

hey (hā) *interj.* An exclamation calling for attention or expressing surprise, pleasure, inquiry, etc. [ME *hei*]

hey·day[1] (hā′dā′) *n.* **1.** Period of greatest vigor; height, as of power. **2.** Exuberance; ardor. [Prob. < HIGH DAY]

hey·day[2] (hā′dā′) *interj.* *Archaic* An exclamation of gaiety, astonishment, etc. [< Du. *heida!* hey there!]

Hey·drich (hī′drikh), **Reinhard,** 1904–42, German Gestapo leader; assassinated: called **the Hangman.**

Hey·duck (hī′dōōk), **Hey·duc, Hey·duke.** See HAIDUK.

Hey·se (hī′zə), **Paul von,** 1830–1914, German dramatist and novelist.

Hey·ward (hā′wərd), **Du·Bose** (də-bōz′), 1885–1940, U.S. novelist and playwright.

Hey·wood (hā′wōōd), **John,** 1497?–1580?, English playwright and wit. — **Thomas,** 1575?–1641, English playwright and actor.

Hez·e·ki·ah (hez′ə-kī′ə) Eighth-century B.C. king of Judah. II *Kings* xviii–xx.

hf. Half.

Hf *Chem.* Hafnium.

HF or **H.F., hf** or **h.f.** High frequency.

hf.bd. Half-bound (bookbinding).

hf.mor. Half-morocco (bookbinding).

hg. 1. Hectogram(s). **2.** Heliogram.

Hg *Chem.* Mercury (L *hydrargyrum*).

HG High German.

H.G. 1. His (or Her) Grace. **2.** *Brit.* Home Guard.

H-gird·er (āch′gûr′dər) *n.* An H-beam (which see).

hgt. Height.

H.H. 1. His (or Her) Highness. **2.** His Holiness.

hhd. Hogshead.

H-hour (āch′our′) *n.* The hour appointed for a military operation to begin: also called *zero hour.*

hi (hī) *interj.* **1.** *U.S.* An exclamation of greeting. **2.** *Brit.* A call to attract attention. [Var. of HEY]

H.I. Hawaiian Islands (unofficial).

Hi·a·le·ah (hī′ə-lē′ə) A city in SE Florida, near Miami; noted for its racetrack; pop. 102,452.

hi·a·tus (hī-ā′təs) *n.* *pl.* **·tus·es** or **·tus 1.** A gap or space from which something is missing, as in a manuscript; lacuna. **2.** Any opening, break, or interruption of continuity. **3.** A pause or break due to the coming together in a word or successive words of two separately pronounced vowels without an intervening consonant, as between the two o′s in *coordinate.* **4.** *Anat.* Any natural cleft or opening. [< L]

Hi·a·wath·a (hī′ə-woth′ə, -wô′thə, hē′ə-). **1.** A Mohawk chief credited with organizing the Five Nations. **2.** The hero of Longfellow′s poem *The Song of Hiawatha* (1855).

hi·ba·chi (hi-bä′chē) *n.* *pl.* **·chis** A deep container or brazier to hold burning coals, covered with a grill and used for heating and cooking. [< Japanese]

hi·ber·nac·u·lum (hī′bər-nak′yə-ləm) *n.* *pl.* **·la** (lə) **1.** A shelter or structure in which an animal hibernates. Also **hi·ber·na·cle** (hī′bər-nak′əl). **2.** *Biol.* A bud or case formed as winter protection for a plant or animal part. [< NL < L, winter residence < *hibernare* to pass the winter]

hi·ber·nal (hī-bûr′nəl) *adj.* Of or pertaining to winter; wintry. [< L *hibernalis* < *hibernus* wintry]

hi·ber·nate (hī′bər-nāt) *v.i.* **·nat·ed, ·nat·ing 1.** To pass the winter in a dormant state, as certain animals. Compare ESTIVATE. **2.** To remain inactive or secluded. [< L *hibernatus*, pp. of *hibernare* < *hiems* winter] — **hi′ber·na′tion** *n.*

Hi·ber·ni·a (hī-bûr′nē-ə) Latin and poetic name for Ireland. [< L, alter. of *Iverna* < Celtic. Related to ERIN.]

Hi·ber·ni·an (hī-bûr′nē-ən) *adj.* Irish. — *n.* A native or citizen of Ireland.

Hi·ber·ni·an·ism (hī-bûr′nē-ən-iz′əm) *n.* **1.** An idiom or turn of phrase peculiar to the Irish. **2.** An Irish custom, trait, etc. Also **Hi·ber′ni·cism** (-nə-siz′əm).

hi·bis·cus (hī-bis′kəs, hi-) *n.* A plant of a genus (*Hibiscus*) of herbs, shrubs, or trees of the mallow family, having large, showy, variously colored flowers: the state flower of Hawaii: sometimes called *rose mallow.* [< L < Gk. *hibiskos* mallow]

hic·cup (hik′əp) *n.* **1.** An involuntary contraction of the diaphragm, causing a sudden, audible inspiration of breath checked by a spasmodic closure of the glottis. **2.** *pl.* A condition characterized by repetition of such spasms. — *v.* **·cuped** or **·cupped, ·cup·ing** or **·cup·ping** — *v.i.* **1.** To make a sound of or as of a hiccup. **2.** To have the hiccups. — *v.t.* **3.** To utter with hiccups. Also **hic·cough** (hik′əp). [Imit.]

hic ja·cet (hik jā′set) *Latin* Here lies: often inscribed on tombstones. Abbr. *H.J.*

hick (hik) *n.* *Informal* One having the clumsy, unsophisticated manners, speech, or dress supposedly typical of rural areas; bumpkin; yokel. — *adj.* Of, pertaining to, or typical of hicks. [Alter. of *Richard*, a personal name]

hick·ey (hik′ē) *n.* *pl.* **·eys** *U.S. Informal* **1.** Any gadget or contrivance. **2.** A pimple or blemish. **3.** *Mech.* A device used for bending a pipe or conduit. **4.** *Electr.* A fitting used to connect a fixture to an outlet box. [Origin unknown]

Hick·ok (hik′ok), **James Butler,** 1837–76, U.S. frontier scout and marshal: called **Wild Bill Hickok.**

hick·o·ry (hik′ər-ē, hik′rē) *n.* *pl.* **·ries 1.** Any of several North American deciduous trees (genus *Carya*) of the walnut family, having hard, durable wood and yielding edible nuts, as the shagbark and the pecan. **2.** The wood of any of these trees. **3.** A walking stick or switch made of this wood. — *adj.* Denoting a strong cotton fabric formerly used for men′s work clothes, etc. [< Algonquian *pawcohiccoro*]

Hicks·ville (hiks′vil) A village in SE New York, on Long Island; pop. 49,820.

hid (hid) Past tense and alternative past participle of HIDE[1].

hi·dal·go (hi-dal′gō, *Sp.* ē-ᴛᴛᴀl′gō) *n.* *pl.* **·gos** (-gōz, *Sp.* -gōs) A Spanish nobleman of lower rank than a grandee. [< *Sp.* < *hijo de algo* son of something]

Hi·dal·go (hi-dal′gō, *Sp.* ē-ᴛᴛᴀl′gō) A State in central Mexico; 8,058 sq. mi.; pop. 1,156,177 (1970); capital, Pachuca.

hid·den (hid′n) Past participle of HIDE[1]. — *adj.* Not seen or known; concealed; obscure; mysterious.

hid·den·ite (hid′n-īt) *n.* A transparent, yellow to green variety of spodumene, used as a gemstone. [after W. E. *Hidden,* 1853–1918, U.S. mineralogist]

Hidden Peak See GASHERBRUM.

hide[1] (hīd) *v.* **hid, hid·den** or **hid, hid·ing** *v.t.* **1.** To put or keep out of sight; conceal. **2.** To keep secret; withhold from knowledge: to *hide* one′s fears. **3.** To block or obstruct the sight of; keep from view: The smoke *hid* the buildings. **4.** To turn away as from shame or so as to ignore: *Hide* not thy face from me. — *v.i.* **5.** To keep oneself out of sight; remain concealed. — **to hide out** *U.S. Informal* To remain in concealment, especially as a fugitive. [OE *hȳdan*] — **hid′er** *n.*
— **Syn. 1.** *Hide, conceal,* and *secrete* mean to put or keep out of sight. We may *hide* without intention, but we *conceal* intentionally. An object is *hidden* or *concealed* when covered from view, when disguised as something else, or when buried out of reach. It is *secreted* when put into some private place where others would not think of looking. — **Ant.** display, show, disclose, reveal.

hide[2] (hīd) *n.* **1.** The skin of an animal, especially when stripped from the carcass or made into leather. **2.** *Informal* The human skin. — *v.t.* **hid·ed, hid·ing** *Informal* To flog severely; whip. [OE *hȳd* skin]

hide[3] (hīd) *n.* In Old English law, a measure of land, originally about 120 acres, considered enough to support a family. [OE *hīd, hīgid*]

hide-and-seek (hīd′n-sēk′) *n.* A children′s game in which those who hide are sought by one who is "it." Also **hide-and-go-seek′.**

hide·a·way (hīd′ə-wā′) *n.* A place of concealment; hidden retreat.

hide·bound (hīd′bound′) *adj.* **1.** Obstinately fixed in opinion; narrow-minded; bigoted. **2.** Having the skin too tightly adhering to the back and ribs: said of cattle, etc. **3.** Having bark that adheres so tightly as to impede growth.

hid·e·ous (hid′ē-əs) *adj.* **1.** Extremely ugly: a *hideous* sight. **2.** Morally odious or detestable; shocking: a *hideous* murder. [< AF *hidous,* OF *hideus* < *hisde, hide* fright; ult. origin unknown] — **hid′e·ous·ly** *adv.* — **hid′e·ous·ness** *n.*

hide-out (hīd′out′) *n.* *Informal* A place of concealment or refuge, especially from legal authority. Also **hide′out′.**

hid·ing[1] (hī′ding) *n.* **1.** The act of one who or that which hides. **2.** A state or place of concealment.

hid·ing[2] (hī′ding) *n.* *Informal* A flogging; whipping.

hi·dro·sis (hi-drō′sis) *n.* *Pathol.* **1.** Any skin disease characterized by sweating. **2.** Excessive sweating. [< NL < Gk. *hidroein* to sweat < *hidros* sweat] — **hi·drot·ic** (hi-drot′ik) *adj.*

hie (hī) *v.t.* & *v.i.* **hied, hie·ing** or **hy·ing** To hasten; hurry: often reflexive: I *hied* myself home. [OE *hīgian*]

hi·e·mal (hī′ə·məl) *adj.* Of or pertaining to winter; wintry. [< L *hiemalis* < *hiems* winter]

hi·er·a·co·sphinx (hī′ər·ā′kō·sfingks′) *n.* In ancient Egyptian art, a hawk-headed sphinx. [< Gk. *hierax* hawk + SPHINX]

hi·er·arch (hī′ə·rärk) *n.* A leader of a religious group; a high priest or prelate. [< Med.L *hierarcha* < Gk. *hierarchēs* sacred + *hieros* ruler < *archein* to rule]

hi·er·ar·chi·cal (hī′ə·rär′ki·kəl) *adj.* Of, belonging to, or characteristic of a hierarchy. Also **hi′er·ar′chic, hi′er·ar′·chal.** — **hi′er·ar′chi·cal·ly** *adv.*

hi·er·ar·chism (hī′ə·rär′kiz·əm) *n.* The principles, character, or rule of a hierarchy. — **hi′er·ar′chist** *n.*

hi·er·ar·chy (hī′ə·rär′kē) *n.* *pl.* **·chies** 1. Any group of persons or things arranged in successive orders or classes, each of which is subject to or dependent on the one above it. 2. A body of ecclesiastics so arranged. 3. Government or rule by such a body of ecclesiastics. 4. In science and logic, a series of systematic groupings in graded order, as the kingdoms, phyla, classes, orders, families, genera, and species of biology. 5. *Theol.* **a** Any of the three ranks of angels, each of which is divided into three orders. **b** The body of angels collectively. [< LL *hierarchia* < Gk., rule of a hierarch]

hi·er·at·ic (hī′ə·rat′ik) *adj.* 1. Of or pertaining to priests or priestly usage; sacerdotal. 2. Denoting or pertaining to a cursive and shortened form of hieroglyphic writing used by priests in ancient Egypt. 3. Denoting or characteristic of a style of art using forms or methods fixed by religious tradition. Also **hi′er·at′i·cal.** [< L *hieraticus* < Gk. *hieratikos* of a priest's office < *hieros* sacred] — **hi′er·at′i·cal·ly** *adv.*

hiero- *combining form* Sacred; divine: *hierocracy.* Also, before vowels, **hier-.** [< Gk. *hieros* sacred]

Hi·er·o I (hī′ər·ō), died 467 B.C., tyrant of Syracuse 478?–467 B.C.; patron of literature. Also **Hi′er·on** (-on).

hi·er·oc·ra·cy (hī′ə·rok′rə·sē) *n.* *pl.* **·cies** Government by priests or members of the clergy. [< HIERO- + -CRACY] — **hi·er·o·crat·ic** (hī′ər·ə·krat′ik) *or* **·i·cal** *adj.*

hi·er·o·dule (hī′ər·ə·dyool′) *n.* In ancient Greece, a temple slave consecrated to the service of a particular deity. [< Gk. *hierodoulos* < *hieron* temple + *doulos* slave]

hi·er·o·glyph·ic (hī′ər·ə·glif′ik, hī′rə·glif′ik) *n.* 1. *Usually pl.* A picture or symbol representing an object, idea, or sound, as in the writing system of the ancient Egyptians. 2. *pl.* A system of writing using such pictures or symbols. 3. Any symbol or character having an obscure or hidden meaning. 4. *pl.* Illegible writing. Also **hi·er·o·glyph** (hī′ər·ə·glif′, hī′rə·glif). — *adj.* 1. Pertaining to, consisting of, or resembling hieroglyphics. 2. Written in or inscribed with hieroglyphics. 3. Difficult to decipher. Also **hi′er·o·glyph′i·cal.** [< LL *hieroglyphicus* < Gk. *hieroglyphikos* hieroglyphic < *hieros* sacred + *glyphein* to carve] — **hi·er·o·glyph′i·cal·ly** *adv.* — **hi·er·og·ly·phist** (hī′ər·og′lə·fist, hī·rog′-) *n.*

Hieroglyphic Hittite See under HITTITE.

hi·er·ol·o·gy (hī′ə·rol′ə·jē, hī·rol′-) *n.* *pl.* **·gies** The religious literature, traditions, etc., of a people or culture.

Hi·er·on·y·mite (hī′ə·ron′ə·mīt) *n.* A member of one of several religious orders of hermits named for St. Jerome: also called *Jeronymite.* [< Med.L *Hieronymita* < LL *Hieronymus* Jerome]

hi·er·o·phant (hī′ər·ə·fant′, hī·er′-) *n.* 1. In ancient Greece, a high priest or official interpreter of religious rites. 2. One who explains or interprets any esoteric cult or doctrine. [< LL *hierophanta* < Gk. *hierophantēs* < *hieros* sacred + *phainein* to show] — **hi′er·o·phan′tic** *adj.*

hi·fa·lu·tin (hī′fə·loot′n) See HIGHFALUTIN.

hi-fi (hī′fī′) *n.* 1. High fidelity (which see). 2. Radio, phonograph, or recording equipment capable of reproducing sound with high fidelity. — *adj.* Of or pertaining to high fidelity.

Hig·gin·son (hig′in·sən), **Thomas Wentworth,** 1823–1911, U.S. author and social reformer.

hig·gle (hig′əl) *v.i.* **·gled, ·gling** To argue over terms, prices, etc.; haggle. [Var. of HAGGLE]

hig·gle·dy-pig·gle·dy (hig′əl·dē·pig′əl·dē) *adj.* Disordered or confused; jumbled; topsy-turvy. — *adv.* In chaotic confusion or disorder. — *n.* Great confusion; muddle. [< obs. *higle-pigle*, a varied reduplication, ? < PIG]

hig·gler (hig′lər) *n.* 1. One who higgles. 2. A peddler.

high (hī) *adj.* 1. Reaching or extending upward to some great or considerable distance; lofty; tall. 2. Having a specified elevation: ten feet *high.* 3. Located at some distance above the ground or other horizontal. 4. Reaching to the height of: used in combination: *knee-high.* 5. Produced or extending to or from a height: a *high* jump; a *high* dive. 6. Greater or more than is usual or normal in degree, amount, intensity, force, etc.: *high* fever; *high* speed. 7. Superior, lofty, or exalted in quality, character, rank, kind, etc.: *high* office; a *high* official. 8. Most important; principal; main: the *high* street. 9. Having serious consequences; grave: *high* treason. 10. Elated; joyful: *high* spirits. 11. *Informal*

Feeling the effects of liquor, drugs, etc.; intoxicated. 12. Expensive; costly: *high* rent. 13. Luxurious or fashionable: *high* living. 14. Advanced to the fullest extent or degree: *high* noon; *high* tide. 15. Complex; advanced: usually in the comparative degree: *higher* mathematics; *higher* mammals. 16. Strict or extreme in opinion, doctrine, etc.: *high* Tory. 17. Arrogant; haughty. 18. Remote: *high* and far-off times. 19. Of or pertaining to an elevated or inland district: *High* German. 20. Slightly decomposed; gamy: said of meat. 21. Of sounds, having relatively short wavelengths; shrill. 22. *Music* **a** Having relatively short wavelengths: said of vocal or instrumental tones. **b** Being above the proper or indicated pitch; sharp. 23. *Mech.* Denoting a gear arrangement, as in a transmission, yielding the most rapid output speed. 24. *Phonet.* Of vowel sounds, produced with the tongue raised close to the roof of the mouth, as (ē) in *bead:* opposed to *low.* — **high and dry** 1. Completely above water level. 2. Stranded; helpless. — **high and mighty** *Informal* Overbearing; haughty. — *adv.* 1. To or at a high level, position, degree, price, rank, etc. 2. In a high manner. — **high and low** Everywhere. — *n.* 1. A high level, position, etc.: The stock market reached a new *high.* 2. *Mech.* A gear arrangement yielding the most rapid output speed. 3. *Meteorol.* An area of high barometric pressure; anticyclone. 4. *U.S. Informal* High school. — **on high** 1. In or at a high place. 2. In heaven. Abbr. *h., H.* [OE *hēah*] — **Syn.** (adj.) 1. *High, tall, elevated,* and *lofty* refer to things that in some way stand over or above their surroundings. A *high* mountain extends far upward from a valley; a *high* mountain pass lies at a great distance above it. *High* may thus refer either to extent or to position. *Tall* applies only to extent, and refers chiefly to growing things: a *tall* man, a *tall* tree. *Elevated* is *high* in position: an *elevated* plateau. *Lofty* is *high* in either sense, but in addition implies imposing majesty or stateliness: a *lofty* castle. *High* and *lofty* are frequently used in extended sense to describe rank, position, character, motives, etc. — **Ant.** low, short, base.

high·ball[1] (hī′bôl′) *n.* *U.S.* A drink of whisky or other liquor mixed with soda, ginger ale, etc., and served with ice in a tall glass. [Prob. < HIGH + *ball*, obs., a drink of whisky]

high·ball[2] (hī′bôl′) *n.* A railroad signal to go ahead. — *v.i. U.S. Slang* To go at great speed. [From a large ball that could be raised or lowered, once used as a semaphore]

high·bind·er (hī′bīn′dər) *n.* *U.S. Slang* 1. A gangster; criminal. 2. Formerly, one of the members of a Chinese secret society who hired out as assassins. [? < HELLBENDER]

high·born (hī′bôrn′) *adj.* Of noble birth or ancestry.

high·boy (hī′boi′) *n.* A tall chest of drawers, usually in two sections, the lower one mounted on legs: also, *Brit., tallboy.* Compare LOWBOY. [Origin unknown]

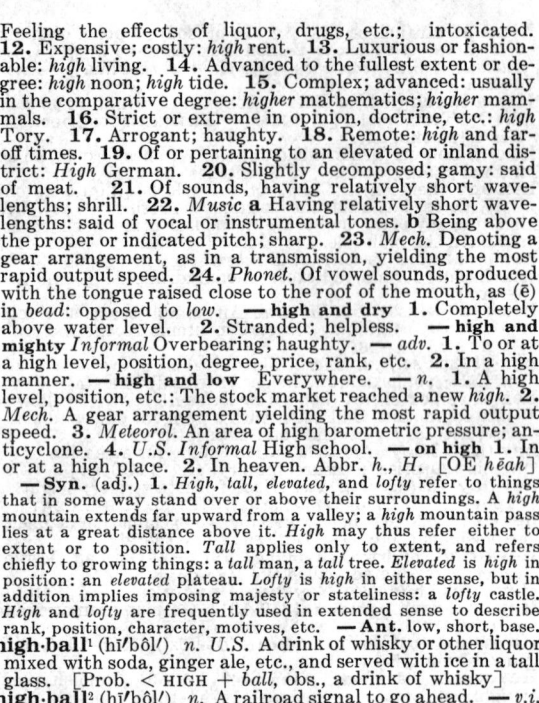

HIGHBOY

high·bred (hī′bred′) *adj.* 1. Descended from fine stock; well-born. 2. Characteristic of or indicating good breeding.

high·brow (hī′brou′) *Informal n.* One who has or claims to have intellectually superior tastes: sometimes a term of derision. — *adj.* Of, pertaining to, or suitable for a highbrow: also **high′browed′.** — **high′brow′ism** *n.*

high·chair (hī′châr′) *n.* A baby's chair standing on tall legs and equipped with an eating tray. Also **high chair.**

High-Church (hī′chûrch′) *adj.* Of or pertaining to a group (**High Church**) in the Anglican Church that stresses the authority of the church and emphasizes ritual. Compare LOW-CHURCH, BROAD-CHURCH. — **High′-Church′man** *n.*

high-class (hī′klas′, -kläs′) *adj. Slang* High or superior in quality, condition, status, etc.

high-col·ored (hī′kul′ərd) *adj.* 1. Deep or brilliant in color. 2. Florid; ruddy. 3. Vivid or exaggerated.

high comedy Comedy dealing with the world of polite society and relying chiefly on witty dialogue for its effect.

high command Those in supreme authority, as of a military force, political party, business organization, etc.

high day A holyday; feast day.

high·er criticism (hī′ər) Critical investigation that makes use of historical and scientific techniques in determining the authorship, historical accuracy, credibility, etc., of the Bible. Compare LOWER CRITICISM.

higher education Education beyond secondary schooling; especially, college or university education.

high·er-up (hī′ər·up′) *n. Informal* A person of superior rank or position.

high explosive Any of a class of explosives that detonate with extreme force and rapidity, often used as the bursting charge in bombs, etc. Abbr. *HE, H.E.*

high-fa·lu·tin (hī′fə·loot′n) *adj. Informal* Extravagant, pompous, or high-flown in manner, speech, etc.: also spelled *hifalutin.* Also **high′fa·lu′ting.** [? < HIGH-FLOWN]

high fashion A style of dress that is different from and newer than that worn by the majority, and is characterized by great elegance or flamboyance of design, material, etc.: also called *high style.*

high fidelity *Electronics* The reproduction of a signal or

HIERO-
GLYPHICS

sound with a minimum of distortion, especially by phonographic equipment: also called *hi-fi.*

high·fli·er (hī′flī/ər) *n.* **1.** One who or that which flies high. **2.** *Informal* One having extravagantly pretentious or unrealistic ambitions, opinions, tastes, etc. Also **high′fly′er.**

high-flown (hī′flōn/) *adj.* **1.** Extravagant or bombastic in style, language, etc. **2.** Pretentious: *high-flown* tastes.

high·fly·ing (hī′flī/ing) *adj.* **1.** Flying high. **2.** Having extravagant, pretentious aims, ideas, etc.

high frequency *Telecom.* A radio frequency in the band from 3 to 30 megacycles. Abbr. *hf, HF, h.f., H.F.*

High German See under GERMAN.

high-grade (hī′grād/) *adj.* Of superior quality.

high-hand·ed (hī′han/did) *adj.* Arbitrary and overbearing. — **high′hand′ed·ly** *adv.* — **high′hand′ed·ness** *n.*

high hat A top hat (which see).

high-hat (hī′hat/) *Informal v.t.* **-hat·ted, -hat·ting** To treat snobbishly; snub. — *adj.* **1.** Snobbish; condescending; patronizing. **2.** Elegant; fashionable. — *n.* A snob.

high-hole (hī′hōl/) *n. U.S. Dial.* The flicker, a bird. Also **high′-hold′er** (-hōl′dər).

high·jack (hī′jak/), etc. See HIJACK.

high jinks Boisterous fun or roughhousing.

high jump In athletics, a jump or jumping contest for height: distinguished from *broad jump.*

high·land (hī′lənd) *n.* **1.** Elevated land, as a plateau or promontory. **2.** *Usually pl.* A hilly or mountainous region. — *adj.* Of, pertaining to, or of the nature of a highland.

high·land·er (hī′lən-dər) *n.* A native or inhabitant of a highland region.

High·land·er (hī′lən-dər) *n.* **1.** A native or inhabitant of the Highlands. **2.** A soldier of a Highlands regiment.

Highland fling A lively Scottish dance.

Highland Park **1.** A city in SE Michigan, an enclave in Detroit; pop. 35,444. **2.** A city in NE Illinois, a suburb of Chicago; pop. 32,263.

High·lands (hī′ləndz) The mountainous parts of northern and western Scotland in and north of the Grampians.

high·light (hī′līt/) *n.* **1.** An area or point in a painting, photograph, etc., showing or representing a brightly lighted part. **2.** An event, scene, detail, etc., of special importance or vividness. — *v.t.* **1.** *Informal* To give special emphasis or importance to; feature. **2.** To provide or emphasize with a highlight or highlights.

high·lin·er (hī′lī/nər) *n. Canadian* In the Maritimes, the boat or captain making the largest fishing haul.

high·ly (hī′lē) *adv.* **1.** In or to a high degree; greatly; extremely: *highly* agreeable. **2.** With great approval or appreciation: to think *highly* of someone. **3.** In a high position or rank: *highly* placed in his firm. **4.** At a high price or rate.

High Mass *Eccl.* A Mass celebrated with full ceremony, music, incense, etc., at which the celebrant is assisted by a deacon and subdeacon.

high-mind·ed (hī′mīn/did) *adj.* **1.** Possessing or manifesting noble thoughts or sentiments. **2.** *Archaic* Haughty; arrogant. — **high′-mind′ed·ly** *adv.* — **high′-mind′ed·ness** *n.*

high-muck-a-muck (hī′muk/ə-muk) *n. U.S. Slang* A person of high position or considerable influence, especially one conscious of his own importance. [< Chinook jargon *hiu muck-amuck* plenty of food]

high-necked (hī′nekt/) *adj.* Having a high neckline.

high·ness (hī′nis) *n.* The condition of being high; loftiness.

High·ness (hī′nis) *n.* A title or form of address for persons of royal rank: often preceded by *His, Her, Your,* etc.

high-oc·tane (hī′ok/tān) *adj.* Designating gasoline having antiknock properties and a high octane number.

high-pitched (hī′picht/) *adj.* **1.** High in pitch, as a voice, tone, etc. **2.** Of a roof, having a steep slope. **3.** Lofty or exalted. **4.** High-strung; overwrought. **5.** *Music* Built for a pitch higher than standard pitch: said of instruments.

high place In early Semitic religions, an altar or place of worship, usually on a bare, lofty hill or mountain.

High Point A city in central North Carolina; pop. 63,204.

high-pres·sure (hī′presh/ər) *adj.* **1.** Using or sustaining high steam pressure, as an engine. **2.** Having or showing high barometric pressure. **3.** *Informal* Exerting vigorously persuasive methods or tactics: *high-pressure* salesmanship. — *v.t.* **·sured, ·sur·ing** *Informal* To persuade or influence by aggressive or insistent methods.

high priest A chief priest.

high-proof (hī′prⁿf/) *adj.* Containing a large percentage of alcohol: *high-proof* whisky.

high relief Alto-relievo (which see).

high-rise (hī′rīz/) *adj.* Describing a relatively tall building or structure. — *n.* A tall building, as a many-storied apartment house: also **high rise.**

high·road (hī′rōd/) *n.* **1.** A main road. **2.** An easy or sure method or course: the *highroad* to fame. — **Syn.** See ROAD.

high school A school following elementary school or junior high school, in the United States typically comprising grades 9, 10, 11, and 12. Abbr. *h.s., H.S.*

high seas The open waters of an ocean or sea that are beyond the territorial jurisdiction of any one nation.

high sign *U.S. Informal* A sign, gesture, etc., used as a signal or warning.

high-sound·ing (hī′soun/ding) *adj.* Pretentious or imposing in sound or implication: *high-sounding* praise.

high-spir·it·ed (hī′spir/it-id) *adj.* Having a courageous, vigorous, or fiery spirit; mettlesome.

high·stick (hī′stik/) *v.t. & v.i.* In hockey, to check illegally by hitting the puck-carrier high on the body with the stick.

high-strung (hī′strung/) *adj.* Very nervous; excitable.

high style High fashion (which see).

hight (hīt) *adj. Archaic* Called or named. [OE *heht,* pt. of *hātan* to call]

high tea *Brit.* A fairly substantial late afternoon or early evening meal at which meat is usually served.

high-ten·sion (hī′ten/shən) *adj. Electr.* Pertaining to, characterized by, or operating under very high voltage, usually in excess of 1,000 volts.

high-test (hī′test/) *adj.* **1.** Designating a substance or product that has passed severe tests for fitness, quality, etc. **2.** Denoting a grade of gasoline with a low boiling point.

high tide **1.** The maximum level reached by the incoming tide. **2.** The time that this occurs. **3.** A culminating point.

high time **1.** So late as to be almost past the proper time: It's *high time* he paid his bills. **2.** *Informal* A hilarious and enjoyable time.

high-toned (hī′tōnd/) *adj.* **1.** *U.S. Informal* Of superior quality, or having pretensions to superiority. **2.** Characterized by or having a lofty character, high principles, etc.: often used ironically. **3.** High in tone or pitch.

high treason Treason against the sovereign or state.

high-ty-tigh·ty (hī′tē-tī/tē) *adj. & interj.* Hoity-toity.

high-up (hī′up/) *Informal adj.* Of high rank or position. — *n.* One who is in a high rank or position.

high water **1.** High tide. **2.** The condition of a body of water at its time of highest elevation, as during a flood.

high-wa·ter mark (hī′wô/tər, -wot′ər) **1.** The highest point reached by a body of water, as during high tide, a flood, etc. **2.** A mark left by such waters after receding. **3.** A point of highest achievement or development.

high·way (hī′wā/) *n.* **1.** A road or thoroughfare; especially, a main or principal road of some length that is open to the public. **2.** A main route on land or water. **3.** An ordinary, natural, or direct course of action, progress, etc.

high·way·man (hī′wā/mən) *n. pl.* **·men** (-mən) Formerly, a robber, usually mounted on horseback, who waylaid travelers on highways.

H.I.H. His (or Her) Imperial Highness.

Hii·u·ma (hē′ⁿⁿ·mä) An island of Estonia, in the Baltic Sea off the mainland; 373 sq. mi.: Russian *Dago.* Also *Khiuma.*

hi·jack (hī′jak/) *v.t. U.S. Slang* **1.** To seize illegally while in transit, as cargo, vehicles, etc.: to *hijack* an airliner. **2.** To hold up and rob (a truck, etc.). **3.** To seize or steal valuables from (a person). **4.** To coerce or compel (someone). Also spelled *highjack.* [Orig. from hoboes who hailed their victim with "Hi Jack" and proceeded to rob him]

hi·jack·er (hī′jak/ər) *n. U.S. Slang* One who engages in hijacking: also spelled *highjacker.*

hike (hīk) *v.* **hiked, hik·ing** *v.i.* **1.** To walk for a considerable distance, especially through rugged terrain, woods, etc. **2.** To rise or be uneven, as part of a garment: often with *up.* — *v.t.* **3.** *Informal* To raise or lift: usually with *up.* **4.** *Informal* To increase (prices, etc.): usually with *up.* — *n.* **1.** A long walk or march. **2.** *Informal* An increase: a price *hike.* [? Var. of HITCH] — **hik′er** *n.*

hi·lar·i·ous (hi-lâr′ē-əs, hī-) *adj.* Boisterously gay or cheerful. — **hi·lar′i·ous·ly** *adv.* — **hi·lar′i·ous·ness** *n.*

hi·lar·i·ty (hi-lar′ə-tē, hī-) *n. pl.* **·ties** Noisy, exuberant gaiety; boisterous merriment. [< OF *hilarite* < L *hilaritas, -tatis* < *hilaris* < Gk. *hilaros* cheerful]

Hil·a·ry of Poitiers (hil′ər-ē), **Saint,** 300?–367, French bishop and theologian.

Hil·de·brand (hil′də-brand) See GREGORY VII.

Hil·des·heim (hil′dəs-hīm) A city in SW Lower Saxony, West Germany; pop. 92,500 (1960).

hil·ding (hil′ding) *Archaic n.* A base or contemptible person; wretch. — *adj.* Mean; contemptible; base.

hill (hil) *n.* **1.** A conspicuous, usually rounded, elevation of the earth's surface, not as high as a mountain. **2.** A heap or pile: often used in combination: a *molehill.* **3.** A small mound of earth placed over or around certain plants and tubers. **4.** A plant or group of plants thus covered. — *v.t.* **1.** To surround or cover with hills, as potatoes. **2.** To form a hill or heap of. [OE *hyll*] — **hill′er** *n.*

Hill (hil), **Ambrose Powell,** 1825–65, Confederate general in the Civil War. — **Archibald Vivian,** born 1886, English physiologist. — **James Jerome,** 1838–1916, U.S. railroad magnate and financier.

Hil·la·ry (hil′ər-ē), **Sir Edmund,** born 1919, British mountaineer and Antarctic explorer born in New Zealand.

hill·bil·ly (hil′bil′ē) *n. pl.* **·lies** *U.S. Informal* A person coming from or living in the mountains or a backwoods area, especially of the southern United States: originally a disparaging term. [< HILL + BILLY²]

Hill·man (hil′mən), **Sidney**, 1887–1946, U.S. labor leader born in Lithuania.

hill myna See under MYNA.

hil·lo (hil′ō, hi·lō′), **hil·loa** See HALLOO.

hill·ock (hil′ək) *n.* A small hill or mound. — **hill′ock·y** *adj.*

hill·side (hil′sīd′) *n.* The side or slope of a hill.

hill station In India, a town or resort in the foothills or mountains, often serving as a refuge from the heat.

hill·top (hil′top′) *n.* The summit of a hill.

hill·y (hil′ē) *adj.* **hill·i·er, hill·i·est** 1. Having many hills. 2. Resembling a hill; steep. — **hill′i·ness** *n.*

Hil·mand (hel′mund) See HELMAND.

Hi·lo (hē′lō) A port city on the eastern part of the island of Hawaii; pop. 26,353.

hilt (hilt) *n.* The handle of a sword, dagger, etc. — **to the hilt** Thoroughly; fully. — *v.t.* To provide with a hilt. [OE]

hi·lum (hī′ləm) *n. pl.* **·la** (-lə) 1. *Bot.* **a** The scar on a seed at the point where it was attached to the funiculus or placenta: also called *umbilicum.* **b** The nucleus of a starch grain. 2. *Anat.* The small opening where ducts, vessels, and nerves enter or leave an organ: also **hi·lus** (hī′ləs) *pl.* **·li** (-lī). [< L, a trifle]

him (him) *pron.* The objective case of the pronoun *he.*

H.I.M. His (or Her) Imperial Majesty.

Hi·ma·chal Pra·desh (hi·mä′chəl prə·dāsh′) A centrally administered territory of NE central India, bordering on Tibet; 10,880 sq. mi.; pop. 3,432,000 (est. 1971); capital, Simla.

Hi·ma·la·yas (hi·mäl′yəz, -mä′lə·yəz; him′ə·lā′əz) A mountain chain between Tibet and India and in Nepal, including Mount Everest (29,- 028 ft.), the world's highest recorded point. Also **The Hi·ma′la·ya.** — **Hi·ma·la·yan** (hi·mäl′yən, him′ə·lā′ən) *adj.*

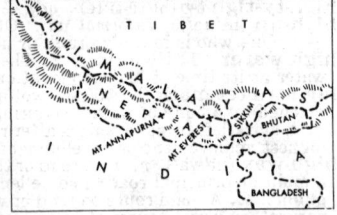

him·a·ti·on (hi·mat′ē·on) *n. pl.* **·mat·i·a** (-mat′ē·ə) A large mantle or oblong piece of cloth worn as a mantle in ancient Greece. [< Gk.]

Hi·me·ji (hē·me·jē′) A city on southern Honshu island, Japan; pop. 403,000 (est. 1968).

Himm·ler (him′lər), **Heinrich**, 1900–45, German Nazi official; chief of the Gestapo 1934–45.

him·self (him·self′) *pron.* A form of the third person singular masculine pronoun, used: 1. As a reflexive or object of a preposition in a reflexive sense: He cut *himself*; A child learns to do things for *himself.* 2. As an intensive form of *he*: He *himself* will do it. 3. As a designation of a normal, proper, or usual state: He is not *himself.* 4. *Irish* As a pronoun in the nominative case meaning *he*: *Himself* has said so.

Him·yar·ite (him′yə·rīt) *n.* 1. One of an ancient Arab tribe of SW Arabia. 2. An Arab descendant of this tribe. 3. An Arabic dialect akin to Ethiopic. [after Arabic *Himyar*, a legendary king of Yemen + -ITE¹] — **Him·yar·it·ic** (him′yə·rit′ik) *adj.*

hind¹ (hīnd) *adj.* **hind·er, hind·most** or **hind·er·most** Situated at or toward the rear part; posterior. [OE *hindan*]

hind² (hīnd) *n.* 1. The female of the red deer, especially when fully grown. 2. Any of various fishes (genus *Epinephelus*) of southern Atlantic waters, related to the groupers and sea basses. [OE]

hind³ (hīnd) *n.* 1. In Scotland and some parts of northern England, a hired farm laborer. 2. *Archaic* A peasant. [OE *hīna, hīgna*, genitive pl. of *hīgan* domestics]

Hind. 1. Hindi. 2. Hindu. 3. Hindustan. 4. Hindustani.

hind·brain (hīnd′brān′) *n. Anat.* The rhombencephalon.

Hin·de·mith (hin′də·mit), **Paul**, 1895–1963, German composer.

Hin·den·burg (hin′dən·bûrg, *Ger.* hin′dən·bŏŏrkh) The German name for ZABRZE.

Hin·den·burg (hin′dən·bûrg, *Ger.* hin′dən·bŏŏrkh), **Paul von**, 1847–1934, German general and statesman; last president of the German Weimar Republic 1925–34: full name **Paul Ludwig Hans Anton von Beneckendorf und von Hindenburg.**

hin·der¹ (hin′dər) *v.t.* 1. To interfere with the progress of; delay; retard; check. 2. To prevent from acting or occurring; deter; thwart. — *v.i.* 3. To be an impediment or obstacle. [OE *hindrian* < *hinder* behind] — **hin′der·er** *n.*

— **Syn.** 1. *Hinder, retard, impede,* and *hamper* mean to put difficulties in the way or progress of. *Hinder* and *retard* mean to slow down or delay, but *hinder* also implies active interference: heavy traffic *hindered* snow removal, the coming of spring was *retarded. Impede* retains much of its original meaning of fettering the feet, and *hamper* its original meaning of weighing down with

encumbrances: mud holes *impede* a hiker, a shopper is *hampered* by parcels. 2. balk, bar, block, stop. Compare BAFFLE, PREVENT.

hind·er² (hīn′dər) Comparative of HIND¹. — *adj.* Pertaining to or situated at the rear or posterior end. [OE]

hind·gut (hīnd′gut′) *n. Anat.* The embryonic structure from which the colon develops.

Hin·di (hin′dē) *n.* 1. The principal language of northern India, belonging to the Indic branch of the Indo-Iranian languages, usually divided into **Western Hindi**, of which Hindustani is the major dialect, and **Eastern Hindi.** 2. A form of literary Hindustani used by Hindus, usually written in the Devanagari script. *Abbr.* **Hind.** [< Hind. *hindī* < *Hind* India < Persian < OPersian *Hindu* land on the Indus < Skt. *sindhu* river, the Indus]

hind·most (hīnd′mōst′) Superlative of HIND¹. Also **hind′·er·most** (hīn′dər-).

Hin·doo (hin′dōō), **Hin·doo·ism** (-iz′əm) See HINDU, etc.

hind·quar·ter (hīnd′kwôr′tər) *n.* 1. One of the two back quarters of a carcass of beef, lamb, etc., usually cut between the 12th and 13th ribs and including a hind leg. 2. *pl.* The posterior parts; rump.

hin·drance (hin′drəns) *n.* 1. The act of hindering. 2. One who or that which hinders. — **Syn.** See IMPEDIMENT.

hind·sight (hīnd′sīt′) *n.* 1. The understanding of an event after it has happened. 2. The rear sight of a gun, rifle, etc.

Hin·du (hin′dōō) *n.* 1. A native of India who speaks one of the Indic languages. 2. One whose religion is Hinduism. 3. Loosely, a native of Hindustan. — *adj.* Of, pertaining to, or characteristic of the Hindus or Hinduism. Also spelled **Hindoo.** *Abbr.* **Hind.** [< Persian *Hindū* < *Hind.* See HINDI.]

Hin·du·ism (hin′dōō·iz′əm) *n.* The religion of the Hindus of India, characterized by worship of Brahma, conceived of as the single supreme being, and by the observance of a now illegal caste system. Also spelled *Hindooism.*

Hindu Kush (kōōsh) A mountain range in central Asia, on the Afghanistan-Pakistan border; highest point, Tirich Mir, 25,263 ft.: ancient *Caucasus Indicus.*

Hin·du·stan (hin′dōō·stan′, -stän′) 1. The Persian name for the land east of the Indus. 2. Loosely, the region of the Ganges plain where Hindi is largely spoken. 3. Loosely, the Republic of India as opposed to Pakistan. Also **Hin′do·stan′** (-dō-). *Abbr.* **Hind.** [< Persian < *Hindu* + *-stan* country]

Hin·du·sta·ni (hin′dōō·stä′nē, -stan′ē) *n.* The major dialect of Hindi, the official language and general medium of communication in India. See URDU. — *adj.* 1. Of or pertaining to Hindustan or its people. 2. Of or pertaining to Hindustani. *Abbr.* **Hind.**

hinge (hinj) *n.* 1. A device consisting of two parts, usually metal plates, connected by a pin inserted into interlocking grooves, and constituting a movable joint on which a door, gate, lid, etc., swings or turns. 2. A natural movable joint connecting two parts, as the shells of a bivalve. 3. That on which something turns or depends; pivotal point; governing principle. — *v.* **hinged, hing·ing** *v.t.* 1. To attach by or equip with a hinge or hinges. — *v.i.* 2. To hang or turn on or as on a hinge. 3. To depend or be contingent: with *on* or *upon*: The outcome *hinges* on his decision. [ME *hengen*, prob. < ON *hengja* to hang. Akin to HANG.]

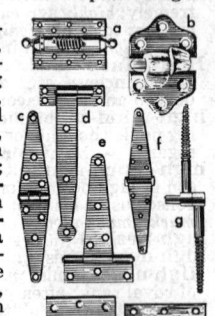

hin·ny¹ (hin′ē) *n. pl.* **·nies** The hybrid offspring of a stallion and a she-ass. Compare MULE¹. [< L *hinnus* < Gk. *ginnos*]

hin·ny² (hin′ē) *v.i.* **·nied, ·ny·ing** *Rare* To whinny; neigh. [Var. of WHINNY]

hint (hint) *n.* 1. An indirect suggestion or implication; subtle or covert allusion. 2. A slight indication or trace. 3. *Obs.* An opportunity; occasion. — *v.t.* 1. To suggest indirectly; intimate; imply. — *v.i.* 2. To show one's wishes, intentions, etc., by a hint or hints. 3. To give a slight indication or suggestion: with *at.* — **Syn.** See IMPLY. [OE *hentan*]

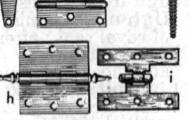

HINGES

a Spring. b Blind.
c Strap. d Plate.
e T-hinge. f Link.
g Gate. h Butt.
i H-hinge.

hin·ter·land (hin′tər·land′) *n.* 1. An inland region immediately adjacent to a coastal area. 2. A region remote from urban areas; back country. 3. An area adjacent to and dependent upon a port or other urban center. [< G]

hip¹ (hip) *n.* 1. The part of the human body projecting below the waist on either side, formed by the edge of the pelvis and the upper part of the femur, together with the flesh that covers them. 2. An analogous part in animals. 3. The hip joint. 4. *Archit.* The angle at the juncture of adjacent sloping sides of a roof. — **hip and thigh** Mercilessly; unsparingly: to smite *hip and thigh.* — **on** (or **upon**) **the hip** In a position not favorable to success; at a disadvantage: an allusion to wrestling. — *v.t.* **hipped, hip·ping** *Archit.* To build (a roof) with a hip or hips. [OE *hype*]

hip² (hip)   *n.* The ripened fruit of a rose. [OE *hēope*]

hip³ (hip)   *interj.* An exclamation used to introduce or signal for a cheer. [Origin unknown]

hip⁴ (hip)   *adj. U.S. Slang* Aware; informed; not square: often followed by *to*. [? Alter. of HEP]

hip bath A sitz bath (which see).

hip·bone (hip′bōn′)   *n.* The innominate bone (which see).

hip joint *Anat.* The joint between the hipbone and the thighbone.

hip·parch (hip′ärk)   *n.* In ancient Greece, a cavalry commander. [< Gk. *hipparchos* < *hippos* horse + *archein* to rule]

Hip·par·chus (hi·pär′kəs)   Second-century B.C. Greek astronomer.

hipped¹ (hipt)   *adj.* **1.** Having or characterized by (a specified kind of) hips: used in combination: *slim-hipped.* **2.** *Archit.* Having a hip or hips, as a roof.

hipped² (hipt)   *adj.* **1.** *U.S. Slang* Fanatically interested or concerned; obsessed: followed by *on: hipped* on modern art. **2.** *Brit. Informal* Low in spirits; depressed: also **hip′pish.** [< HYP(OCHONDRIA) + -ED]

hip·pet·y-hop (hip′ə·tē·hop′)   *adv. Informal* With a jerky gait or motion. Also **hip·pet·y-hop·pet·y** (-hop′ə·tē).

hip·pie (hip′ē)   *n.* One of a group of people, typically young people, whose strikingly unconventional dress and behavior, marked especially by the use of psychedelic drugs, express withdrawal from or nonparticipation in conventional, middle-class life and indifference to its values. [Var. of HIPSTER]

hip·po (hip′ō)   *n. pl.* **·pos** *Informal* A hippopotamus.

Hip·po (hip′ō)   An ancient ruined city just south of Bône, Algeria; a center of early Christianity: also *Hippo Regius.*

hippo- *combining form* Horse: *hippodrome.* Also, before vowels, **hipp-.** [< Gk. *hippos* horse]

hip·po·cam·pus (hip′ə·kam′pəs)   *n. pl.* **·pi** (-pī) *Anat.* One of two curved ridges on the floor of each of the lateral ventricles of the brain. [< L < Gk. *hippos* horse + *kampos* sea monster] — **hip′po·cam′pal** *adj.*

hip·po·cras (hip′ə·kras)   *n.* An old medicinal cordial made of spiced wine. [< OF *ypocras,* after *Hippocrates*]

Hip·poc·ra·tes (hi·pok′rə·tēz), 460?–377? B.C., Greek physician: called **the Father of Medicine.** — **Hip·po·crat·ic** (hip′-ə·krat′ik) *adj.*

Hippocratic oath An oath, attributed to Hippocrates, incorporating a code of ethics for physicians and administered to those about to receive a medical degree.

Hip·po·crene (hip′ə·krēn, hip′ə·krē′nē)   A fountain on Mount Helicon, Greece, said to have sprung from a stroke of the foot of Pegasus, and traditionally sacred to the Muses. [< L < Gk. *hippokrēnē* < *hippos* horse + *krēnē* fountain]

hip·po·drome (hip′ə·drōm)   *n.* **1.** An arena or similar structure for horse shows, circuses, etc. **2.** In ancient Greece and Rome, a course or track for horse races and chariot races. [< F < L *hippodromos* < Gk. < *hippos* horse + *dromos* running, course < *dramein* to run]

hip·po·griff (hip′ə·grif)   *n.* A mythological beast with the wings, head, and claws of a griffin, and the hindquarters of a horse. Also **hip′po·gryph.** [< F *hippogriffe* < Ital. *ippogrifo* < Gk. *hippos* horse + LL *gryphus* griffin]

HIPPOGRIFF

Hip·pol·y·ta (hi·pol′ə·tə)   In Greek mythology, a queen of the Amazons whose girdle Hercules obtained as one of his labors: also called *Antiope.*

Hip·pol·y·tus (hi·pol′ə·təs)   In Greek mythology, the son of Theseus and Hippolyta who, having spurned the advances of his stepmother Phaedra, was unjustly accused of ravishing her and was killed when his horses were frightened by a sea monster sent by Poseidon, on whom Theseus had called.

Hip·pom·e·don (hi·pom′ə·don)   An ancient Greek hero. See SEVEN AGAINST THEBES.

Hip·pom·e·nes (hi·pom′ə·nēz)   In Greek legend, the youth who won the hand of Atalanta by defeating her in a race.

hip·po·pot·a·mus (hip′ə·pot′ə·məs)   *n. pl.* **·mus·es** or **·mi** (-mī) A large, chiefly aquatic, herbivorous mammal (*Hippopotamus amphibius*), native to Africa, and having short legs, a massive, thick-skinned, hairless body, and a very broad muzzle: also called *river horse.* [< L < Gk. *hippopotamos* < *hippos* horse + *potamos* river]

HIPPOPOTAMUS
(About 5 feet high at shoulder; to 14 feet long)

Hip·po Re·gi·us (hip′ō rē′jē·əs)   See HIPPO.

-hippus *combining form Paleontol.* Horse: *eohippus.* [< Gk. *hippos* horse]

hip roof *Archit.* A roof having sloping ends and sides.

hip·ster (hip′stər)   *n. U.S. Slang* One who is hip; especially, one versed in jazz music. [< HIP⁴ + -STER]

hi·ra·ga·na (hi′rə·gä′nə)   *n.* One of two sets of Japanese syl-labic symbols, used with the basic Chinese ideographs to show case forms and parts of speech, and also to indicate pronunciation. See KANA. Compare KATAKANA.

Hi·ram (hī′rəm)   Tenth-century B.C. king of Tyre. I *Kings* v.

hir·cine (hûr′sin, -sīn)   *adj.* **1.** Resembling or characteristic of a goat; especially, having a goatlike smell. **2.** Lustful. [< L *hircinus* < *hircus* goat]

hire (hīr)   *v.t.* **hired, hir·ing** **1.** To obtain the services of (a person) for compensation; employ. **2.** To acquire the use of (a thing) for a fee; rent. **3.** To grant the use or services of (someone or something) in return for payment: often with *out.* — **to hire out** To provide one's services in return for compensation: She *hires out* as a domestic. — *n.* **1.** Compensation paid for labor, services, etc. **2.** The act of hiring, or the condition of being hired. — **for hire** Procurable for use or service in return for compensation. [OE *hýr*] — **hir′-able** or **hire′a·ble** *adj.* — **hir′er** *n.*

hired girl A woman hired to do household or farm chores.

hired hand A person employed on a farm.

hired man A man hired to do odd jobs, especially on a farm.

hire·ling (hīr′ling)   *n.* One who serves for hire; especially, one who does something unpleasant or reprehensible for mercenary motives: usually a contemptuous term. — *adj.* Of, pertaining to, or characteristic of a hireling; mercenary.

Hi·ro·hi·to (hir·ō·hē·tō), born 1901, emperor of Japan 1926–.

Hi·ro·shi·ge (hir·ō·shē·ge), **Ando,** 1797–1858, Japanese painter.

Hi·ro·shi·ma (hir′ə·shē′mə, hi·rō′shi·mə)   A port city in SW Honshu island, Japan; devastated by the first atomic bomb used in warfare, August 6, 1945; pop. 542,000 (est. 1968).

hir·ple (hûr′pəl)   *v.i.* **hir·pled, hir·pling** *Scot.* To walk lamely; hobble. — *n.* A limp.

hir·sel¹ (hûr′səl)   *Scot. v.t.* **hir·seled** or **hir·selled, hir·sel·ing** or **hir·sel·ling** To arrange in flocks, as sheep. — *n.* A flock of sheep.

hir·sel² (hûr′səl)   *v.i.* **hir·seled** or **hir·sel·led, hir·sel·ing** or **hir·sel·ling** *Scot.* To move along with a sliding, slipping, or scraping motion. Also **hir′sle.**

hir·sute (hûr′sōōt, hûr·sōōt′)   *adj.* **1.** Covered with hair; hairy. **2.** Pertaining to or consisting of hair. **3.** *Biol.* Covered with hairlike processes; bristly. [< L *hirsutus* rough] — **hir′sute·ness** *n.*

hi·ru·di·noid (hi·rōō′də·noid)   *adj.* Pertaining to or resembling a leech. [< L *hirudo, -dinis* leech + -OID]

hi·run·dine (hi·run′din, -dīn)   *adj.* Of, pertaining to, or resembling the swallow. [< L *hirundo, -dinis* a swallow]

his (hiz)   *pron.* **1.** The possessive case of the pronoun *he,* used predicatively: This room is *his.* **2.** The one or ones belonging or pertaining to him: Her book is better than *his;* He protects himself and *his.* — **of his** Belonging or pertaining to him: a double possessive. — *pronominal adj.* The possessive case of the pronoun *he,* used attributively: *his* book. [OE]

his'n (hiz′ən)   *pron. Dial.* His. Also **hisn.**

His·pa·ni·a (his·pā′nē·ə, -nyə, -pä′-)   **1.** The Latin name for the region comprising modern Spain and Portugal. **2.** *Poetic* Spain.

His·pan·ic (his·pan′ik)   *adj.* **1.** Pertaining to the people, language, or culture of Spain, or of the area comprising Spain and Portugal. **2.** Characterized by a culture having its origins in Spain or Portugal.

His·pan·i·cism (his·pan′ə·siz′əm)   *n.* An idiom or turn of phrase peculiar to Spanish.

His·pa·ni·o·la (his′pə·nyō′lə)   An island of the West Indies; about 30,000 sq. mi.; divided into Haiti and the Dominican Republic: formerly *Haiti.*

his·pid (his′pid)   *adj. Biol.* Covered with stiff hairs or small spines. [< L *hispidus* hairy] — **his·pid·i·ty** (his·pid′ə·tē) *n.*

hiss (his)   *v.i.* **1.** To utter or produce a prolonged, sibilant sound, as that of *ss,* of air or steam escaping under pressure, etc. **2.** To utter such a sound as an expression of disapproval or derision, especially toward a speaker, performer, etc. — *v.t.* **3.** To utter or express with a hiss. **4.** To express disapproval of or contempt for by hissing. **5.** To rout or silence by hissing: with *off, down,* etc. — *n.* The sound produced by hissing. [ME *hissen,* imit.] — **hiss′er** *n.*

hiss·ing (his′ing)   *n.* **1.** The act of one who or that which hisses. **2.** A hiss. **3.** *Archaic* An object of scorn or contempt.

hist¹ (hist)   *interj.* An exclamation calling for attention, silence, etc. [Imit.]

hist² (hist)   *Dial. vt.* To hoist. — *n.* A hoist.

hist. **1.** Histology. **2.** Historian; historical; history.

his·tam·i·nase (his·tam′ə·nās)   *n. Biochem.* An enzyme capable of inactivating histamine, used in the treatment of allergic conditions. [< HISTAMIN(E) + -ASE]

his·ta·mine (his′tə·mēn, -min)   *n. Biochem.* A white, crystalline substance, $C_5H_9N_3$, found in plant and animal tissues. It reduces blood pressure, has a contracting action on the uterus, and is released in allergic reactions. [< HIST(IDINE) + AMINE] — **his·ta·min·ic** (his′tə·min′ik) *adj.*

his·ti·dine (his′tə·dēn, -din)   *n. Biochem.* A natural amino acid, $C_6H_9O_2N_3$, obtained from protamines and from the action of sulfuric acid on ptomaines. [< Gk. *histion* tissue + -ID(E) + -INE²]

histo -*combining form* Tissue: *histology.* Also, before vowels, **hist-.** [< Gk. *histos* web]

his·to·gen·e·sis (his'tə·jen'ə·sis) *n. Biol.* The formation and development of tissues. Also **his·tog·e·ny** (his·toj'ə·nē). — **his'to·gen'ic** *adj.*

his·to·gram (his'tə·gram) *n. Stat.* A graph of frequency distribution in the form of a series of rectangles, each proportional in width to the range of values within a class and proportional in height to the number of items falling in the class.

his·toid (his'toid) *adj. Pathol.* Resembling or composed of connective tissue: a *histoid* tumor.

his·tol·o·gy (his·tol'ə·jē) *n. pl.* **·gies** 1. The branch of biology that treats of the microscopic structure of the tissues of plants and animals. 2. The tissue structure of an organism, part, etc. Abbr. *hist.* [< HISTO- + -LOGY] — **his·to·log·i·cal** (his'tə·loj'i·kəl) *adj.* — **his·tol'o·gist** *n.*

his·tol·y·sis (his·tol'ə·sis) *n. Biol.* The degeneration and dissolution of organic tissue. [< HISTO- + -LYSIS]

his·tone (his'tōn) *n. Biochem.* One of a group of simple proteins having basic properties and yielding amino acids on hydrolysis.

his·to·ri·an (his·tôr'ē·ən, -tō'rē-) *n.* 1. A writer of or authority on history. 2. A compiler of a record, especially for a specific group or purpose: the class *historian.* Abbr. *hist.*

his·tor·ic (his·tôr'ik, -tor'-) *adj.* 1. Important or famous in history. 2. Memorable; significant. 3. Historical.

his·tor·i·cal (his·tôr'i·kəl, -tor'-) *adj.* 1. Constituting, belonging to, or of the nature of history: *historical* events. 2. Pertaining to, concerned with, or treating of events of history: a *historical* account. 3. Of, pertaining to, or based on known facts as distinct from legendary or fictitious accounts: *historical* evidence. 4. Based on or representing facts, personages, or events of history: a *historical* novel. 5. Recording or revealing facts of history; serving as a source for knowledge of the past. 6. Following or dealing with the chronological order of events or development. 7. Historic. Abbr. *hist.* — **his·tor'i·cal·ly** *adv.* — **his·tor'i·cal·ness** *n.*

historical linguistics The study of a language or languages in chronological development with emphasis on coherent lines of evolution: also called *diachronic linguistics.*

historical method The practice of basing conclusions and general principles upon a study of historical facts.

historical present *Gram.* The present tense used to narrate a past event.

historical school Any of various schools of thought, as in economics, law, etc., having principles based on or derived from the study of historical facts.

his·to·ric·i·ty (his'tə·ris'ə·tē) *n. pl.* **·ties** Authenticity based on historical fact.

his·to·ri·og·ra·pher (his·tôr'ē·og'rə·fər, -tō'rē-) *n.* A historian or chronicler, especially one officially associated with a group or public institution.

his·to·ri·og·ra·phy (his·tôr'ē·og'rə·fē, -tō'rē-) *n.* 1. The writing of history. 2. Written history.

his·to·ry (his'tə·rē, his'trē) *n. pl.* **·ries** 1. That branch of knowledge concerned with past events, especially those involving human affairs. 2. A record or account, usually written and in chronological order, of past events, especially those concerning a particular nation, people, field of knowledge or activity, etc. 3. A connected or related series of facts, events, etc., especially those concerning a specific group or subject: the *history* of a political party. 4. Past events in general. 5. Something in the past. 6. An unusual or noteworthy past: That house has a *history.* 7. A drama depicting historical events. 8. A long narrative or story. Abbr. (for defs. 1, 2) *hist.* [< L *historia* < Gk., knowledge, narrative < *histōr* knowing. Doublet of STORY.]
— **Syn.** *History, chronicle,* and *annals* denote a systematic record of past events. A *history* is a narrative that recounts events with attention to their importance, their mutual relations, causes, and consequences; it is therefore highly selective. A *chronicle* is a record of events in order of time; *annals* are similar but are divided year by year. Neither *chronicles* nor *annals* attempt to interpret events. Compare NARRATIVE, RECORD.

his·tri·on·ic (his'trē·on'ik) *adj.* 1. Of or pertaining to actors or acting. 2. Overly dramatic; theatrical; affectedly emotional. Also **his'tri·on'i·cal.** [< L *histrionicus* < *histrio,* -onis actor] — **his'tri·on'i·cal·ly** *adv.*

his·tri·on·ics (his'trē·on'iks) *n.pl.* (construed as *sing.* in *def.* 1) 1. Theatrical art or representation; dramatics. 2. Feigned emotional display; affectation in manner, speech, etc.

hit (hit) *v.* **hit, hit·ting** *v.t.* 1. To give a blow to; strike forcibly: I *hit* him. 2. To reach or strike with or as with a missile, hurled or falling object, etc.: to *hit* a target. 3. To come forcibly in contact with; meet with impact; collide with. 4. To cause (something) to make forcible contact; bump; bang: often with *on, against,* etc.: to *hit* one's head against. 5. To inflict (a blow, etc.) on: I *hit* him a tremendous blow. 6. To set in motion or propel by striking. 7. To arrive at, achieve, or discover, either by intention or inadvertently. 8. To accord with; suit. 9. To affect adversely; cause to suffer. 10. To attack; beset. 11. In baseball, to succeed in making (a specified kind of base hit): to *hit* a triple. 12. *U.S. Informal* To begin to journey on: to *hit* the road. 13. *U.S. Informal* To arrive in or reach (a place). 14. *U.S. Slang* To make use of or indulge in to excess: to *hit* the bottle. 15. *U.S. Slang* To request or obtain (a loan, sum of money, etc.) from: usually with *for:* I *hit* him for a raise. — *v.i.* 16. To deliver a blow; strike. 17. To make forcible contact; collide; bump: often with *against, on,* etc. 18. To come or light; happen: followed by *on* or *upon:* to *hit* on the right answer. — **Syn.** See STRIKE. — **to hit it off** To be friendly; get along well. — **to hit (someone or something) off** To depict, characterize, or satirize cleverly and accurately. — *n.* 1. A blow, stroke, shot, etc., that reaches the objective aimed at. 2. A forceful impact; collision. 3. A popular or obvious success. 4. A fortunate chance or circumstance. 5. An apt or telling remark, witticism, piece of sarcasm, etc. 6. In baseball, a base hit (which see). Abbr. *h., h* 7. In backgammon, a game won by a player whose opponent has removed one or more men from the board. [OE *hittan* < ON *hitta* to come upon] — **hit'ter** *n.*

hit-and-run (hit'n·run') *adj.* 1. Designating, characteristic of, or caused by the driver of a vehicle who illegally continues on his way after hitting a pedestrian or another vehicle. 2. In baseball, pertaining to or designating a prearranged play in which the runner or runners advance during the pitch and the batter tries to hit the ball.

hitch (hich) *v.t.* 1. To fasten or tie, especially temporarily, with a knotted rope, strap, etc. 2. To harness to a vehicle: sometimes with *up:* to *hitch* a horse to a buggy. 3. To move, pull, raise, etc., with a jerk: often with *up:* He *hitched* his pants up. 4. *Informal* To marry: We were *hitched* yesterday. 5. *U.S. Slang* To obtain (a ride) by hitchhiking. — *v.i.* 6. To move with a jerk or limp: to *hitch* forward. 7. To become fastened, caught, or entangled. 8. To strike the feet together, as in running: said of horses. 9. *Informal* To get on together; agree. 10. *U.S. Slang* To travel by hitchhiking. — *n.* 1. An obstacle; halt; delay: a *hitch* in the program. 2. A sudden, jerking movement; tug. 3. A limp or hobble. 4. A fastening or device used to fasten. 5. Any of various knots used for quick, temporary fastening. 6. *U.S. Informal* A period of enlistment in military service, especially in the navy. 7. *U.S. Slang* In hitchhiking, a ride. [ME *hicchen;* origin uncertain]

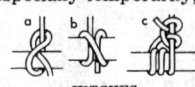

HITCHES
a Half-hitch.
b Clove-hitch.
c Rolling-hitch.

hitch·hike (hich'hīk') *v.i.* **·hiked, ·hik·ing** To travel by signaling for and receiving rides in passing vehicles. — **hitch'hik'er** *n.*

hitch·ing post (hich'ing) A post to which a horse, etc., may be hitched.

hith·er (hith'ər) *adv.* To or toward this place: Come *hither.* — *adj.* Situated toward this side; nearer. [OE *hider*]

hith·er·most (hith'ər·mōst') *adj.* Nearest to this place. —

hith·er·to (hith'ər·tōō', hith'ər·tōō') *adv.* 1. Until this time; up to now. 2. *Archaic* Thus far.

hith·er·ward (hith'ər·wərd) *adv.* Hither. Also **hith'er·wards.**

Hit·ler (hit'lər), **Adolf,** 1889–1945, German dictator born in Austria; leader of the Nazi party and chancellor 1933–45: called **der Führer** (the Leader). — **Hit·ler·i·an** (hit·lir'ē·ən) *adj.*

Hit·ler·ism (hit'lər·iz'əm) *n.* The policies and practices of the Nazis under the leadership of Adolf Hitler.

hit or miss Without regard for the outcome; at random.

hit-or-miss (hit'ər·mis') *adj.* Haphazard; careless.

Hit·tite (hit'īt) *n.* 1. One of an ancient people who established a powerful empire in Asia Minor and northern Syria about 2000–1200 B.C. 2. A language of the Hittites, in the Anatolian family of languages, known from cuneiform inscriptions found in Asia Minor that date from about 1400 B.C. (**Cuneiform Hittite**). 3. A language attributed to the Hittites, known from hieroglyphic inscriptions found in Asia Minor and northern Syria that date from about 1000 B.C. (**Hieroglyphic Hittite**). See INDO-HITTITE. — *adj.* Of or relating to the Hittites or their language. [< Hebrew *Hittīm*]

hive (hīv) *n.* 1. An artificial structure serving as a habitation for honeybees; beehive. 2. A colony of bees inhabiting a hive; swarm. 3. A place astir with industrious activity. 4. A teeming multitude; throng. — *v.* **hived, hiv·ing** *v.t.* 1. To induce (bees) to enter into or collect in a hive. 2. To house or shelter in or as in a hive. 3. To store (honey) in a hive. 4. To store or hoard for future use. — *v.i.* 5. To enter a hive. 6. To dwell in or as in a hive. [OE *hȳf*]

hives (hīvz) *n.* Any of various skin disorders characterized by swellings, itching, etc., as urticaria. [Origin unknown]

H.J. Here lies (L *hic jacet*).

H.J.S. Here lies buried (L *hic jacet sepultus*).

hkf. Handkerchief.

hl. or **hl** Hectoliter(s).

H.L. House of Lords.

hm. or **hm** Hectometer(s).

h'm *interj.* Ahem; hem²; hum².

H.M. His (or Her) Majesty.

H.M.S. **1.** His (or Her) Majesty's Ship (or Steamer). **2.** His (or Her) Majesty's Service.

ho (hō) *interj.* **1.** An exclamation, often repeated, expressing exultation, derision, etc. **2.** A call to attract attention. **3.** An exclamation calling attention to a place, direction, or destination: used after the specified term: Land *ho*; [Imit.]

ho. House.

Ho *Chem.* Holmium.

ho.ac.tzin (hō-ak'tsin) See HOATZIN.

Hoang Ho (hwäng'hō') See HWANG HO. Also **Hoang'ho'.**

hoar (hôr, hōr) *adj.* **1.** Having hair that is white or gray with age. **2.** Ancient; venerable. **3.** White or grayish white in color; whitened, as with frost. — *n.* **1.** Hoariness. **2.** Hoarfrost. [OE *hār* gray-haired]

hoard (hôrd, hōrd) *n.* An accumulation of something stored away for safekeeping or future use. — *v.t.* **1.** To amass and store away or hide (money, valuables, etc.). — *v.i.* **2.** To amass and store away scarce, valuable, or desirable things. [OE *hord* treasure] — **hoard'er** *n.*

hoard.ing[1] (hôr'ding, hōr'-) *n.* **1.** The act of one who hoards. **2.** *Usually pl.* That which is hoarded.

hoard.ing[2] (hôr'ding, hōr'-) *n. Brit.* **1.** A temporary fence, as one surrounding a construction site. **2.** A billboard. [< OF *hourd* palisade < Gmc.]

hoar.frost (hôr'frôst', -frost', hōr'-) *n.* Frost whitening the surface on which it is formed: also called *white frost.*

hoar.hound (hôr'hound', hōr'-) See HOREHOUND.

hoarse (hôrs, hōrs) *adj.* **1.** Deep, harsh, and grating in sound, as the voice of a person with a cold, the croaking of frogs or crows, etc. **2.** Having a husky, gruff, or croaking voice. [OE *hā(r)s*] — **hoarse'ly** *adv.* — **hoarse'ness** *n.*

hoars.en (hôr'sən, hōr'-) *v.t. & v.i.* To make or become hoarse.

hoar.y (hôr'ē, hō'rē) *adj.* **hoar.i.er, hoar.i.est** **1.** Ancient; aged; venerable. **2.** Gray or white with age. **3.** White or whitish in color. — **hoar'i.ness** *n.*

hoary marmot See under MARMOT.

ho.at.zin (hō-at'sin) *n.* A bird (genus *Opisthocomus*) of South America, having mostly olive plumage and a yellowish crest, and, in the young, a pair of hooked claws on each wing: also spelled *hoactzin.* [< Am.Sp. < Nahuatl *uatzin*]

hoax (hōks) *n.* A trick or deception, usually perpetrated as a practical joke on the public. — *v.t.* To deceive by a hoax. [< HOCUS(-POCUS)] — **hoax'er** *n.*

hob[1] (hob) *n.* **1.** A projection at the back or side of the interior of a fireplace, serving as a shelf on which to keep things warm. **2.** Any of several games in which rings, etc., are tossed at a stake; also, the stake or peg used. [? Var. of HUB]

hob[2] (hob) *n.* **1.** A hobgoblin or elf. **2.** *Brit. Dial.* A rustic or clown. — **to play (or raise) hob** To cause mischief or confusion; make trouble: often with *with.* [Orig. a nickname for *Robert, Robin*]

Ho.bart (hō'bərt, -bärt) The capital of Tasmania, in the SE part on the Derwent river; pop. 53,257 (est. 1966).

Hob.be.ma (hob'ə-mä), **Meindert,** 1638?–1709, Dutch landscape painter.

Hobbes (hobz), **Thomas,** 1588–1679, English philosopher.

Hobb.ism (hob'iz-əm) *n.* The philosophy of Thomas Hobbes, who believed that an absolute monarch is necessary to control the antagonisms of individual interests.

hob.ble (hob'əl) *v.* **.bled, .bling** *v.i.* **1.** To walk with or as with a limp; go lamely. **2.** To progress clumsily or irregularly. — *v.t.* **3.** To hamper the free movement of (a horse, etc.) by fettering the legs. **4.** To cause to move lamely or awkwardly. **5.** To impede the progress of; hamper. — *n.* **1.** An awkward or limping gait. **2.** A rope, strap, pair of linked rings, etc., used to hobble the legs of an animal. **3.** A difficult or embarrassing situation. [? Freq. of HOP. Cf. G *hoppeln* to hobble.] — **hob'bler** *n.*

hob.ble.bush (hob'əl-boosh') *n.* A shrub (*Viburnum alnifolium*) of the honeysuckle family, having clusters of white flowers and berries that turn black when ripe.

hob.ble.de.hoy (hob'əl-dē-hoi') *n.* An adolescent boy, especially when awkward and gawky. [Origin uncertain]

hobble skirt A woman's long skirt so narrow at or below the knees as to impede the wearer's natural stride.

Hobbs (hobz) A city in SE New Mexico; pop. 26,275.

hob.by[1] (hob'ē) *n. pl.* **.bies** A subject or pursuit of absorbing interest, undertaken primarily for pleasure during one's leisure time; avocation. [after *Robin,* a personal name]

hob.by[2] (hob'ē) *n. pl.* **.bies** A small falcon (*Falco subbuteo*) of the Old World, formerly used for hawking. [< OF *hobet,* dim. of *hobe* falcon, ? < *hober* to move]

hob.by.horse (hob'ē-hôrs') *n.* **1.** A rocking horse (which see). **2.** A toy consisting of a stick surmounted by a likeness of a horse's head. **3.** A figure of a horse attached to a person's waist so that he appears to be riding it, used in morris dances, pantomimes, etc.; also, the person so equipped. **4.** A topic or idea in which one has an obsessive interest.

hob.gob.lin (hob'gob'lin) *n.* **1.** An imaginary cause of terror or unreasonable dread; bugbear. **2.** A mischievous imp or goblin. [< HOB[2] + GOBLIN]

hob.nail (hob'nāl') *n.* **1.** A short, large-headed nail used to stud the soles of heavy shoes or boots for protection against wear or slipping. **2.** One of the regularly spaced knobs or tufts forming a design on glassware, bedspreads, etc.

hob.nailed (hob'nāld') *adj.* **1.** Provided or studded with hobnails. **2.** Rustic; loutish.

hob.nob (hob'nob') *v.i.* **.nobbed, .nob.bing** **1.** To associate in a friendly manner; be on intimate terms: He *hobnobs* with the best people. **2.** To drink together convivially. [OE *habban* to have + *nabban* to have not]

ho.bo (hō'bō) *n. pl.* **.boes** or **.bos** *U.S.* **1.** A tramp; vagrant. **2.** An itinerant, usually unskilled worker. [< *Hey, Bo,* a vagabond's greeting] — **ho'bo.ism** *n.*

Ho.bo.ken (hō'bō-kən) A port city in NE New Jersey, on the Hudson; pop. 45,380.

Hob.son-Job.son (hob'sən-job'sən) *n.* Anglo-Indian (*n.* def. 3).

Hob.son's choice (hob'sənz) A choice in which one must take what is offered or nothing. [after Thomas *Hobson,* 1544?–1631, English liveryman, who required each customer to take the horse nearest the door]

Ho Chi Minh (hō'chē' min'), 1890?–1969, Vietnamese Communist leader; president of North Vietnam 1945–69: original name **Ngyen-Ai-Quoc.**

hock[1] (hok) *n.* **1.** The joint of the hind leg in the horse, ox, etc., corresponding to the ankle in man. For illustration see HORSE, SHEEP. **2.** The corresponding joint in a fowl. For illustration see FOWL. — *v.t.* To disable by cutting the tendons of the hock; hamstring. [OE *hōh* heel]

hock[2] (hok) *n.* Any white Rhine wine: originally **Hoch.hei.mer** (hok'hī-mər) < G *Hochheimer* < *Hochheim,* a German town where first produced]

hock[3] (hok) *U.S. Informal v.t.* To pawn. — *n.* The state of being in pawn. — **in hock** *Informal* **1.** In pawn. **2.** In prison. **3.** In debt. [< Du. *hok* prison, debt]

hock.ey (hok'ē) *n.* **1.** A game played on ice (*ice hockey*), in which players on opposing teams, wearing skates and wielding sticks curved at one end, try to drive a small disk (puck) into the opponent's goal. **2.** A similar game played on a field (*field hockey*), in which a small ball is used instead of a puck. **3.** A hockey stick. [< *hock* bent stick, var. of HOOK]

hockey stick A stick having a characteristic curve or bend at one end, used to move the ball or puck in hockey.

hock.shop (hok'shop') *n. U.S. Informal* A pawnshop (which see). Also **hock shop.**

ho.cus (hō'kəs) *v.t.* **.cused** or **.cussed, .cus.ing** or **.cus.sing** **1.** To deceive by a trick; dupe; cheat. **2.** To drug. **3.** To add drugs to, as a drink. [Abbreviation of HOCUS-POCUS]

ho.cus-po.cus (hō'kəs-pō'kəs) *n.* **1.** A verbal formula used in conjuring or sleight of hand. **2.** The deceptive skill of a conjurer or juggler. **3.** Meaningless language, gestures, etc., intended to mislead or deceive. **4.** Any trickery or deception. — *v.t. & v.k.* **.po.cused** or **.cussed, .po.cus.ing** or **.cus.sing** To trick; cheat. [A sham Latin phrase, ? alter. of *hoc est corpus* this is my body, a Eucharistic formula]

hod (hod) *n.* **1.** An open, troughlike receptacle with a long handle that is rested on the bearer's shoulder, used to carry bricks, mortar, etc. **2.** A coalscuttle. [< obs. *hot* < OF *hotte* pannier < Gmc. Cf. MDu. *hodde.*]

hod.den (hod'n) *n.* A coarse, heavy woolen cloth, which, when woven from naturally black or gray and white wool, is called **hodden gray.** [Origin unknown]

Ho.dei.da (hō-dā'də, -dī'-) A port city in western Yemen, on the Red Sea; pop. about 30,000: also *Hudaida.* Also **Ho.dei'dah.**

hodge.podge (hoj'poj') *n.* **1.** A jumbled mixture or collection; conglomeration. **2.** A stew of mixed meats and vegetables. Also *hotchpotch.* [Var. of HOTCHPOTCH]

Hodg.kin's disease (hoj'kinz) *Pathol.* A generally fatal disease characterized by progressive enlargement of the lymph nodes, lymphoid tissue, and spleen. [after Dr. Thomas *Hodgkin,* 1798–1866, English physician, who described it]

ho.di.er.nal (hō'dē-ûr'nəl) *adj.* Of or pertaining to the present day. [< L *hodiernus* < *hoc die* (on) this day]

ho.do.scope (hō'də-skōp) *n. Physics* A series of Geiger counters arranged for the detection of cosmic rays. [< Gk. *hodos* way + -SCOPE]

hoe (hō) *n.* An implement for removing weeds, etc., having a flat, thin blade attached at an angle to a long handle. — *v.t. & v.i.* **hoed, hoe.ing** To dig, scrape, or till with a hoe. [< OF *houe* < OHG *houwa* < *houwan* to cut] — **ho'er** *n.*

Hoe (hō) An American family prominent in the manufacture and improvement of printing equipment, notably **Robert,** 1784–1833, and his son **Richard March,** 1812–86.

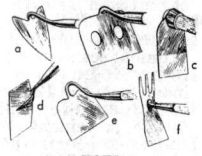

HOES

a Warren. *b* Mortar. *c* Grub. *d* Scuffle. *e* Garden. *f* Weeding.

hoe·cake (hō′kāk′) n. Southern U.S. A thin, flat cake made from cornmeal, originally baked on a hoe.

hoe·down (hō′doun′) n. U.S. Informal A lively, boisterous country dance or square dance; also, the music for such a dance. [Origin uncertain]

Hoek van Hol·land (hōōk vän hôl′änt) The Dutch name for HOOK OF HOLLAND.

Ho·fer (hō′fər), **Andreas**, 1767–1810, Tyrolese patriot; executed.

Hoff·man (hof′mən), **Malvina**, 1887–1966, U.S. sculptor.

Hoff·mann (hôf′män), **Ernst Theodor Amadeus**, 1776–1822, German writer and composer.

Hof·mann (hôf′män), **August Wilhelm von**, 1818–92, German chemist. — **Josef**, 1876–1957, U.S. pianist and composer born in Poland.

Hof·manns·thal (hôf′mäns·täl), **Hugo von**, 1874–1929, Austrian poet and dramatist.

hog (hog, hôg) n. 1. A pig; especially one weighing more than 120 pounds and raised for the market. 2. An animal related to the pig, as the peccary, warthog, etc. 3. Informal A gluttonous, greedy, or filthy person. 4. Scot. & Brit. Dial. A young sheep before its first shearing. 5. Informal A pig (def. 7). — v. **hogged**, **hog·ging** v.t. 1. Slang To take more than one's share of; grab selfishly. 2. To arch (the back) like a hog's. 3. To cut short, as a horse's mane. — v.i. 4. To sag at both ends: said of a ship. [OE hog]

ho·gan (hō′gôn, -gən) n. A Navaho Indian dwelling, typically a hut made of rough timbers and branches covered with earth. [< Navaho qoghan house]

Ho·garth (hō′gärth), **William**, 1697–1764, English painter and engraver.

hog·back (hog′bak′, hôg′-) n. Geol. A sandy or rocky ridge caused by unequal erosion on the edges of tilted strata.

Hog·ben (hog′bən), **Lancelot**, 1895–1975, English scientist and writer.

hog cholera Vet. A highly infectious, contagious, and often fatal disease of swine caused by a filterable virus and characterized by loss of appetite, fever, and exhaustion.

hog·fish (hog′fish′, hôg′-) n. pl. **·fish** or **·fish·es** 1. A labroid food fish (Lachnolaemus maximus) of Florida and the West Indies. 2. The pigfish.

Hogg (hog), **James**, 1770–1835, Scottish poet: called the Ettrick Shepherd.

hog·gish (hog′ish, hôg′-) adj. 1. Of or like a hog. 2. Greedy or very dirty; piggish. — **hog′gish·ly** adv. — **hog′gish·ness** n.

HOGFISH (def. 1) (About 14 inches long)

hog·ma·nay (hog′mə·nā′) n. Scot. & Brit. Dial. The day before New Year's Day, when children, often masked, traditionally go about soliciting gifts and refreshments.

hog·nose (hog′nōz′, hôg′-) n. Any of several American nonvenomous snakes (genus Heterodon) with flattened heads and prominent snouts: also called sand viper. Also **hog′-nosed snake.**

hog·nosed skunk (hog′nōzd′, hôg′-) A white-backed skunk (Conepatus mesoleucus) of South and Central America: also called conepate.

hog·nut (hog′nut′, hôg′-) n. 1. The nut of the pignut hickory. 2. The earthnut (def. 3).

hog peanut A leguminous vine (Amphicarpa bracteata) bearing pods with a single seed: also called earthpea.

hogs·head (hogz′hed′, hôgz′-) n. 1. A large cask; especially, one with a capacity of 63 to 140 gallons. 2. A liquid measure of varying capacity; especially, one equal to 63 gallons, or 8.42 cubic feet. Abbr. hhd.

hog·suck·er (hog′suk′ər, hôg′-) n. A fresh-water fish (Hypentelium nigricans) of the eastern United States.

hog·tie (hog′tī′, hôg′-) v.t. **·tied**, **·ty·ing** or **·tie·ing** 1. To tie together all four feet, or the hands and feet of. 2. Informal To render (a person) powerless or ineffective, as if by tying up in this manner. Also **hog′tie′.**

Hog·town (hog′toun, hôg′-) Canadian Slang Toronto. — **Hog′town′er** n.

hog·wash (hog′wosh′, -wôsh′, hôg′-) n. 1. Kitchen refuse, swill, etc., fed to hogs. 2. Any worthless nonsense; especially, insincere or misleading talk, writing, etc.

hog·weed (hog′wēd′, hôg′-) n. Any of numerous weeds of persistent growth, as the ragweeds, knotweed, etc.

hog wild U.S. Slang Wildly excited.

Ho·hen·lin·den (hō′ən·lin′dən) A village in Bavaria east of Munich; scene of French victory over the Austrians, 1800.

Ho·hen·lo·he (hō′ən·lō′ə) A German princely family, prominent from the 12th to the 19th centuries.

Ho·hen·stau·fen (hō′ən·shtou′fən) A German princely family, prominent especially in the 12th and 13th centuries.

Ho·hen·zol·lern (hō′ən·tsôl′ərn) A family of Prussian kings 1701–1918 and German emperors 1871–1918.

Ho·hen·zol·lern (hō′ən·tsôl′ərn) A former Prussian province in southern Germany.

hoick (hoik) Informal v.t. 1. To throw (an aircraft) into sharp, sudden changes of direction, as in making a steep climb. — v.i. 2. To engage in this kind of maneuver or operation: usually with about or around. [Origin unknown]

hoicks (hoiks) interj. A cry used to stir up the hounds in hunting. Also **yoicks.**

hoi·den (hoid′n) See HOYDEN.

hoi pol·loi (hoi′ pə·loi′) The common people; the masses; the herd: usually used contemptuously, and preceded by a redundant the. [< Gk., the many]

hoist (hoist) v.t. To raise, lift, or heave up, especially by some mechanical means. — **Syn.** See ELEVATE. — n. 1. Any machine designed for raising large or heavy objects; a lift. 2. The act of hoisting; a boost. 3. Naut. **a** The height of a flag as measured along the edge next to the pole or halyard. **b** The vertical dimension of any square sail other than a course. **c** A group of flags raised together for display or signaling. [? < Du. hijschen] — **hoist′er** n.

hoi·ty-toi·ty (hoi′tē·toi′tē) interj. An exclamation of disapproval or contemptuous astonishment. — adj. 1. Self-important; haughty. 2. Flighty; giddy. 3. Easily offended; petulant. — n. pl. **·ties** 1. Arrogance. 2. Flighty behavior. Also (for interj. and adj.) **highty-tighty.** [Reduplication of obs. hoit to romp; infl. in meaning by HIGH]

Ho·kan (hō′kən) n. A family of North American Indian languages spoken primarily in California and Mexico.

ho·key-po·key (hō′kē·pō′kē) n. 1. Hocus-pocus. 2. Cheap ice cream sold by street vendors. Also **ho′ky-po′ky.**

Hok·kai·do (hok·kī·dō) One of the main islands of Japan, north of Honshu; about 29,000 sq. mi.: formerly Yezo: also Ezo. Also **Ho·ku·shu** (hō·kō·shōō).

hok·ku (hôk′kōō) See HAIKU.

ho·kum (hō′kəm) n. U.S. Slang 1. The devices or mannerisms used by a performer, speaker, etc., to get a response from an audience. 2. Meaningless claptrap; bunk. 3. Insincere flattery. — **Syn.** See JEST. [Alter. of HOCUS]

Ho·ku·sai (hō·kōō·sī), **Katsuhika**, 1760–1849, Japanese painter and engraver.

hol- Var. of HOLO-.

Hol·arc·tic (hol·ärk′tik, -är′tik, hōl-) adj. Pertaining to or designating a large zoogeographical realm, commonly subdivided into the Nearctic and Palearctic realms. See under ZOOGEOGRAPHIC REALM.

ho·lard (hō′lərd) n. The total quantity of water found in the soil. Compare CHRESARD, ECHARD. [< HOL- + Gk. ardeia irrigation]

Hol·bein (hōl′bīn, Ger. hōl′bīn), **Hans**, 1465?–1524, **the Elder**, and his son **Hans**, 1497?–1543, **the Younger**, German painters.

HOLC or **H.O.L.C.** Home Owners' Loan Corporation.

hold[1] (hōld) v. **held**, **held** (Archaic **hold·en**), **hold·ing** v.t. 1. To take and keep in the hand, arms, etc.; clasp; grip. 2. To sustain or keep in position; support. 3. To keep in a specified state, posture, etc.: to hold one's head high. 4. To contain or enclose; have the space or capacity for: The barrel holds ten gallons. 5. To keep under control; restrain; check. 6. To retain possession or control of; keep under one's power or influence. 7. To keep in reserve; designate for future use or disposition. 8. To have the use, benefit, or responsibilities of: to hold office. 9. To regard or consider in a specified manner: to hold someone dear. 10. To bind by contract or sense of duty: Hold him to his agreement. 11. Music To prolong or sustain (a tone). 12. Law **a** To adjudge; decide. **b** To have title to. 13. To maintain in the mind; harbor: to hold a grudge. 14. To conduct or engage in; carry on: to hold a conference. — v.i. 15. To maintain a grip or grasp. 16. To withstand strain or pressure; remain firm or unbroken: Will the rope hold? 17. To remain or continue in a specified state, position, etc.: The breeze held all day. 18. To remain relevant or true: This decision holds for all such cases. 19. To adhere resolutely, as to a principle, belief or purpose; cling. 20. To forbear; stop: usually in the imperative. — **Syn.** See HAVE, RETAIN. — **to hold back** 1. To keep in check; restrain. 2. To refrain. 3. To keep apart or aside; retain, as for an undisclosed purpose. — **to hold down** 1. To suppress; keep under control. 2. Informal To be employed at (a job). — **to hold forth** To preach or speak at great length. — **to hold in** 1. To keep in check; curb. 2. To restrain or conceal (one's feelings, etc.). — **to hold off** 1. To keep at a distance, as from attacking, approaching, etc. 2. To refrain from doing something. — **to hold on** 1. To maintain a grip or hold. 2. To persist or continue. 3. Informal To stop or wait: usually in the imperative. — **to hold one's own** To maintain one's position, as in a contest; lose no ground. — **to hold out** 1. To stretch forth; offer. 2. To last; endure: Our supplies held out. 3. To continue resistance. 4. Slang To give something anticipated or due. — **to hold out for** Informal To insist upon as a condition of an agreement. — **to hold over** 1. To put off to a later time; defer action on. 2. To remain or retain beyond the expected time or limit, as in office. 3. To keep or use as a means of intimidating or controlling. — **to hold up** 1. To support; prop. 2. To exhibit to view. 3. To delay; stop. 4. Informal To endure; remain firm or unbroken. 5. Informal To stop by force so as to rob. 6. Informal To charge too high a price. — **to hold water** 1. To contain water without leaking. 2. Informal To be credible, valid, or sound, as an argument, account, etc. — **to hold with** To approve of.

— *n.* **1.** The act or method of grasping, as with the hands, arms, etc.; grip. **2.** Something grasped, held, or seized for support. **3.** A controlling force or influence. **4.** A cell in a jail or prison. **5.** An object or device used to hold or secure something; receptacle. **6.** *Law* A holding or tenure: used in combination: *copyhold; freehold.* **7.** *Music* **a** The holding of a note or rest beyond its written time value. **b** The symbol (⌒) indicating this: also called *fermata, pause.* **8.** *Archaic* A fortification; stronghold. [OE *haldan*]
hold² (hōld) *n.* *Naut.* The space below the decks of a vessel, where cargo is stowed. [< HOLE or < MDu. *hol*]
hold·back (hōld′bak′) *n.* **1.** That which restrains or holds something back; a check. **2.** A strap enabling a horse to push back or hold back a carriage, etc.
hold·en (hōld′n) Archaic past participle of HOLD.
hold·er (hōl′dər) *n.* **1.** One who or that which holds. **2.** An object used as an aid in holding. **3.** An owner; possessor: chiefly in compounds: *householder.* **4.** *Law* One who has legal possession of a bill of exchange, check, or promissory note for which he is entitled to receive payment.
hold·fast (hōld′fast′, -fäst′) *n.* **1.** A strong or firm grasp. **2.** Any of various devices, as a nail, clamp, hook, etc., for fastening or keeping something securely in place. **3.** *Bot.* A specialized organ of attachment at the base of certain algae.
hold·ing (hōl′ding) *n.* **1.** The act of one who or that which holds. **2.** A piece of land rented from another or occupied under another's authority. **3.** *Often pl.* Property held by legal right, especially stocks or bonds. **4.** In some sports, illegally obstructing an opponent's freedom of movement.
holding company A company that invests in the stocks of one or more other corporations, which it may thus control.
hold·o·ver (hōld′ō′vər) *n.* *Informal* **1.** One who or that which remains from a previous time or situation. **2.** An incumbent continuing in office after his term has expired. **3.** An entertainer kept on from one engagement to the next.
hold·up (hōld′up′) *n.* **1.** Stoppage or delay of some activity. **2.** *Informal* A waylaying and robbing of a person. **3.** *Informal* An overcharge; extortion. — **Syn.** See THEFT.
hole (hōl) *n.* **1.** A cavity extending into any solid mass or body; hollow; pit. **2.** An opening made through or in anything; perforation; aperture; tear. **3.** An animal's burrow or enclosed hiding place. **4.** Any small, crowded, squalid place, especially a dwelling. **5.** A prison cell or dungeon. **6.** A defect; fault: to point out the *holes* in an argument. **7.** *Informal* An awkward or painful situation; predicament. **8.** In golf: **a** A small cavity into which the ball is played. **b** A division of the course, usually one of nine or eighteen, containing a tee, fairway, and the green in which such a hole is located. **9.** *U.S.* A small harbor or cove. **10.** *U.S.* A deep, wide place in a creek, stream, etc. — **hole in one** In golf, the act of sinking the ball into a hole with one drive from the tee. — **in the hole** *Informal* In debt. — *v.* **holed, hol·ing** *v.t.* **1.** To make a hole or holes in; perforate. **2.** To drive, push, or propel (a ball, etc.) into a hole. **3.** To dig (a shaft, tunnel, etc.) — *v.i.* **4.** To make a hole or holes. — **to hole out** In golf, to hit the ball into a hole. — **to hole up** **1.** To hibernate, as in a cave or hole. **2.** To hide oneself away; isolate oneself. [OE *hol.* Appar. related to HOLLOW.]
— **Syn.** (noun) **1.** *Hole, cavity, hollow, cave, pit,* and *excavation* are compared as they denote an unfilled space within a solid body. *Hole* is the most general word, and also the most ambiguous; a *hole* in a stocking goes through it, a *hole* in a piece of timber may or may not go through, a *hole* in the ground does not go through the earth, but may be narrow or wide, shallow or very deep. *Hollow* and *cavity* refer to an empty space within something otherwise solid or filled; of the two, *cavity* is somewhat more learned or formal: the pleural *cavity.* *Hollow* is frequently used of any depression or concavity in a surface: the *hollows* of the sea. *Cave* and *pit* denote primarily certain large natural *cavities;* a *cave* is in rock, and a *pit* in the ground. An *excavation* is a man-made *cavity* or *pit,* as for the foundations of a building. Compare BREACH.
hole-and-cor·ner (hōl′ən-kôr′nər) *adj.* *Informal* Concealed from public view; clandestine; furtive.
hole-high (hōl′hī′) *adj.* In golf, even with the hole with respect to distance from the tee.
hol·ey (hō′lē) *adj.* Having a hole or holes.
hol·i·but (hol′ə-bət) See HALIBUT.
hol·i·day (hol′ə-dā) *n.* **1.** A day appointed by law or custom for the suspension of general business in commemoration of some event. ◆ Collateral adjective: *ferial.* **2.** Any day of rest. **3.** A day for special religious observance. **4.** *pl.* *Chiefly Brit.* A vacation. — *adj.* Pertaining to or befitting a holiday; festive. — *v.i.* *Chiefly Brit.* To spend a holiday or vacation. [OE *hālig dæg* holy day]
ho·li·er-than-thou (hō′lē-ər-thən-thou′) *adj.* *Informal* Affecting an attitude of superior goodness or virtue.
ho·li·ly (hō′lə-lē) *adv.* In a holy manner; piously; sacredly.
ho·li·ness (hō′lē-nis) *n.* The state or quality of being holy.
Ho·li·ness (hō′lē-nis) *n.* A title or form of address for the Pope: preceded by *His* or *Your.*
Hol·ins·hed (hol′inz-hed, -in-shed), **Raphael,** died 1580?, English chronicler. Also **Hol·lings·head** (hol′ingz-hed).

ho·lism (hō′liz-əm) *n.* *Philos.* The theory that a material object, especially a living organism, has a reality other and greater than the sum of its constituent parts. [< HOL- + -ISM] — **ho·lis·tic** (hō-lis′tik) *adj.* — **ho·lis·ti·cal·ly** *adv.*
holk (hōk) See HOWK.
hol·la (hol′ə, hə-lä′), **hol·lo** (hol′ō, hə-lō′), **hol·loa** (hol′ō, hə-lō′) See HALLOO.
hol·land (hol′ənd) *n.* A cotton or linen fabric, often glazed, used for making window shades, upholstery, etc.
Hol·land (hol′ənd) See NETHERLANDS.
hol·lan·daise sauce (hol′ən-dāz′) A creamy sauce made of butter, egg yolks, lemon juice or vinegar, and seasonings, and served with vegetables, seafood, etc. [< F, fem. of *hollandais* of Holland]
Hol·land·er (hol′ən-dər) *n.* A native or citizen of the Netherlands; a Dutchman.
Hol·lan·di·a (hô-län′dē-ä) The former name for KOTABARU.
Hol·lands (hol′əndz) *n.* Gin in which the juniper is added directly to the mash instead of to the distilled spirits, originally made in Holland. Also **Holland gin.**
hol·ler (hol′ər) *U.S. Informal v.t. & v.i.* To call out loudly; shout; yell. — *n.* A loud shout; yell. [Var. of HALLOO]
hol·low (hol′ō) *adj.* **1.** Having a cavity within; enclosing an empty space; not solid: a *hollow* sphere. **2.** Having a deep opening or depression formed by or as by scooping out; concave. **3.** Sunken; fallen: *hollow* cheeks. **4.** Deep or muffled in tone, as if reverberating from an empty vessel: a *hollow* groan. **5.** Not genuine or significant; meaningless; empty: a *hollow* triumph. **6.** Hungry. — *n.* **1.** A cavity or empty space within or in the surface of anything; depression; hole. **2.** A valley; basin. — **Syn.** See HOLE. — *v.t. & v.i.* To make or become hollow: usually with *out.* — *adv. Informal* Completely; thoroughly: used chiefly in the phrase **to beat (all) hollow.** [OE *holh*] — **hol′low·ly** *adv.* — **hol′low·ness** *n.*
hol·low-eyed (hol′ō-īd′) *adj.* Having sunken eyes surrounded by dark areas, as from illness or fatigue.
hol·low-heart·ed (hol′ō-här′tid) *adj.* Insincere; deceitful. — **hol′low-heart′ed·ly** *adv.* — **hol′low-heart′ed·ness** *n.*
hol·low·ware (hol′ō-wâr′) *n.* Utensils, serving dishes, etc., especially of silver, that are more or less hollow, taken collectively: distinguished from *flatware.*
hol·lus·chick (hol′əs-chik) *n. pl.* **·chick·ie** (-chik′ē) A male fur seal six years old or younger; a bachelor (def. 5). [? < Russ. *golyshka* childless < *golyī* naked]
hol·ly (hol′ē) *n. pl.* **·lies** Any of a genus (*Ilex*) of trees or shrubs characteristically having glossy, dark green leaves edged with spines, and scarlet berries, especially *I. aquifolium,* whose foliage is widely used as a Christmas decoration. [OE *holen*]
hol·ly·hock (hol′ē-hok) *n.* A tall, cultivated plant (*Althaea rosea*) of the mallow family, having spikes of showy flowers of various colors. Also called *rose mallow.* [ME *holihoc* < *holi* holy + *hoc* mallow]

HOLLYHOCK

a Single.
b Double.

holly oak The holm oak (which see).
Hol·ly·wood (hol′ē-wood) *n.* **1.** A section of NW Los Angeles, California, considered the center of the motion-picture industry in the United States. **2.** The American motion-picture industry or its characteristic atmosphere. **3.** A city in SE Florida; pop. 106,873.
Hollywood bed A bed, with or without a headboard, consisting of a mattress and box spring supported by legs.
holm¹ (hōm) *n.* **1.** An island in a river. **2.** *Brit.* Low, flat land near a stream. [OE; infl. in meaning by ON *holmr* land by water, island]
holm² (hōm) *n.* **1.** The holm oak. **2.** *Brit. Dial.* Holly. [OE *holen* holly. Doublet of HOLLY.]
Holmes (hōmz), **Oliver Wendell,** 1809–94, U.S. physician, poet, and essayist. — **Oliver Wendell,** 1841–1935, U.S. jurist; associate justice of the Supreme Court 1902–32; son of the preceding.
Holmes (hōmz), **Sherlock** See SHERLOCK HOLMES.
hol·mic (hōl′mik) *adj. Chem.* Pertaining to or containing holmium, especially in its higher valence.
hol·mi·um (hōl′mē-əm) *n.* A metallic element (symbol Ho) of the lanthanide series, found in gadolinite. See ELEMENT. [after *Holmia,* Latinized name of Stockholm, Sweden]
holm oak (hōm) An oak (*Quercus ilex*) of southern Europe, whose foliage resembles holly: also called *holly oak, ilex.*
holo- *combining form* Whole; wholly: *holograph.* Also, before vowels, *hol-.* [< Gk. *holos* whole]
hol·o·blas·tic (hol′ə-blas′tik) *adj. Biol.* Undergoing segmentation throughout the entire mass, as the ova of all mammals except the monotremes: opposed to *meroblastic.*
hol·o·caust (hol′ə-kôst) *n.* **1.** Wholesale destruction and loss of life, especially by fire. **2.** A sacrificial offering that is wholly consumed by fire. — **the Holocaust** The genocidal destruction of Jews by Nazi Germany and its allies. [< F *holocauste* < LL *holocaustum* < Gk. *holokauston,* neut. of

holokaustos < *holos* whole + *kaustos* burnt] — **hol'o·caus'tal, hol'o·caus'tic** *adj.*

Hol·o·cene (hŏl'ə·sēn) *adj. Geol.* Designating the Recent epoch in geological time. [< HOLO- + Gk. *kainos* recent]

Hol·o·fer·nes (hŏl'ə·fûr'nēz) In the book of Judith in the Apocrypha, an Assyrian general slain by Judith.

hol·o·gram (hŏl'ə·gram', hō'lə-) *n.* **1.** A negative produced by means of holography; also, the image patterns on such a negative. **2.** The image projected from such a negative.

hol·o·graph (hŏl'ə·graf, -gräf) *adj.* Denoting a document, as a will, letter, etc., wholly in the handwriting of the person whose signature it bears. — *n.* A document so written. [< F *holographe* < Gk. *holographos* < *holos* entire + *graphein* to write] — **hol'o·graph'ic** or **·i·cal** *adj.*

ho·log·ra·phy (hə·lŏg'ra·fē) *n.* A form of lensless photography using a split coherent wave source, such as a laser beam, to record an interference pattern on film which can be projected as a three-dimensional image. [< HOLO- + -GRAPHY] — **hol'o·graph'ic** *adj.*

hol·o·he·dral (hŏl'ə·hē'drəl) *adj. Crystall.* Having the maximum number of symmetrically arranged planes possible in a given crystal system.

hol·o·mor·phic (hŏl'ə·môr'fik) *adj. Crystall.* Completely symmetrical in form, as the opposite ends of certain crystals.

hol·o·phote (hŏl'ə·fōt) *n.* A lamp, as in a lighthouse, so arranged that all light is thrown in the desired direction. [< HOLO- + Gk. *phōs, phōtos* light] — **hol'o·pho'tal** *adj.*

hol·o·phras·tic (hŏl'ə·fras'tik) *adj. Ling.* Polysynthetic. [< HOLO- + Gk. *phrastikos* expressive < *phrazein* to tell]

hol·o·phyt·ic (hŏl'ə·fit'ik) *adj.* Autotrophic.

hol·o·thu·ri·an (hŏl'ə·thoōr'ē·ən) *n. Zool.* Any of a class (*Holothuroidea*) of echinoderms, as the sea cucumbers, etc., having a generally wormlike shape, and tentacles about the mouth. — *adj.* Of or pertaining to the *Holothuroidea.* [< L *holothurium,* a kind of zoophyte < Gk. *holothurion*]

hol·o·type (hŏl'ə·tīp') *n.* In taxonomy, a specimen selected to represent a new species. — **hol'o·typ'ic** (-tip'ik) *adj.*

hol·o·zo·ic (hŏl'ə·zō'ik) *adj.* Heterotrophic.

holp (hōlp), **holp·en** (hōl'pən) Archaic past tense and past participle of HELP.

Hol·stein (hōl'stīn, -stēn) *n.* One of a breed of large, black-and-white dairy and beef cattle, originally developed in Friesland: also **Hol'stein-Frie'sian** (-frē'zhən).

Hol·stein (hōl'stīn, *Ger.* hōl'shtīn) A former Danish duchy, now part of Schleswig-Holstein, northern West Germany.

hol·ster (hōl'stər) *n.* A leather case for a pistol. [< Du.]

ho·lus-bo·lus (hō'ləs-bō'ləs) *adv. Informal* In a single mass or quantity; all at one time. [dog Latin < WHOLE + BOLUS]

ho·ly (hō'lē) *adj.* **·li·er, ·li·est** **1.** Regarded with reverence because associated with or derived from God; having a divine nature or origin; sacred: *holy* Scripture. **2.** Completely devoted to the service of God or religion; having great spiritual and moral worth; saintly: a *holy* martyr. **3.** Designated or set apart for religious worship or observance; consecrated: a *holy* place; *holy* day. **4.** Characterized by religious exaltation, reverence, etc.; spiritually pure: *holy* love. **5.** Evoking or meriting reverence or awe: *holy* mysteries. — *n. pl.* **·lies** A sacred or holy place. [OE *hālig*]

— **Syn.** (adj.) **1.** *Holy, sacred, consecrated, blessed,* and *hallowed* are applied to things regarded with great reverence in religious worship. *Holy* is the strongest word, being applied only to things that have the most immediate connection with God. *Sacred* is applied to that which is inviolate on any account, and thus has less force than *holy: Holy* Scripture, a *sacred* altar. Things formally dedicated to religious use are *consecrated; blessed* originally meant the same thing, but now means especially favored by God; we speak of the *consecrated* ground of a graveyard, or of a *consecrated* church building, or the *blessed* life of a saint. *Hallowed* refers to that which has been made *sacred* by long-continued worship: a hymn *hallowed* by years of use. — **Ant.** unholy.

Holy Alliance A treaty concluded by Russia, Austria, and Prussia at Paris (1815) binding the rulers in brotherhood.

Holy Bible The Bible.

Holy City A city considered sacred by a religion.

Holy Communion The Eucharist.

Holy Cross, Mount of the A peak in west central Colorado, having snow-filled ravines in the shape of a cross; 13,986 ft.: formerly **Holy Cross National Monument.**

ho·ly·day (hō'lē·dā') *n.* A day designated as a religious festival: sometimes called *holiday.* Also **holy day.**

Holy Father A title of the Pope.

Holy Ghost The third person of the Trinity: also called *Holy Spirit.*

Holy Grail The Grail (which see).

Holy Innocents' Day December 28, a church festival commemorating Herod's slaughter of the children of Bethlehem. *Matt.* ii 16: also called *Childermas.*

Holy Land Palestine.

Holy Office **1.** A tribunal of the Roman Catholic Church for the detection and suppression of heresy, the supervision and protection of faith and morals, etc.: officially called *Congregation of the Holy Office.* **2.** Formerly, the Inquisition.

holy of holies **1.** The innermost shrine of the Jewish tabernacle and temple, in which the ark of the covenant was kept. **2.** Any sacred place. Also called *sanctum sanctorum.*

Hol·yoke (hōl'yōk) A city in west central Massachusetts; pop. 50,112.

holy orders *Eccl.* **1.** The sacramental rite of admission to the priesthood or ministry; ordination. **2.** The rank or position of an ordained minister; clerical status. **3.** The grades or degrees of the ministry: **a** In the Anglican Church, bishops, priests, and deacons. **b** In the Eastern Orthodox Church, bishops, priests, deacons, subdeacons, and readers. **c** In the Roman Catholic Church, priests, deacons, subdeacons (the **major orders**), acolytes, exorcists, readers, and doorkeepers (the **minor orders**). — **to take holy orders** To be ordained.

Holy Roller One belonging to a religious sect whose members express religious emotion by violent bodily movements and shouting: a humorous or derogatory term.

Holy Roman Empire An empire in central and western Europe, formally established in 962 and ended in 1806. It was regarded as the reestablishment and extension of the Western Roman Empire as a universal political power under the ecclesiastical rule of the Pope.

HOLY ROMAN EMPIRE
ca. A.D. 1000

holy rood A cross or crucifix; especially, one above the rood screen or the entrance to the chancel in a church or cathedral.

Holy Rood The cross on which Jesus Christ was crucified.

Holy Saturday The Saturday before Easter.

Holy Scripture The Bible.

Holy See See under SEE².

Holy Sepulcher See under SEPULCHER.

Holy Spirit The Holy Ghost.

ho·ly·stone (hō'lē·stōn') *n.* A flat piece of soft sandstone used to scour the wooden decks of a ship. — *v.t.* **·stoned, ·ston·ing** To scrub with a holystone. [Said to be so called because used to clean decks for Sunday]

Holy Synod The supreme governing body in any of the Eastern Orthodox churches.

holy terror *Slang* A formidable or unruly person.

Holy Thursday **1.** In the Roman Catholic Church, the Thursday of Holy Week; Maundy Thursday. **2.** In the Anglican Church, Ascension Day.

ho·ly·tide (hō'lē·tīd') *n.* A day or period of religious observance.

holy water *Eccl.* Water blessed by a priest.

Holy Week The week before Easter Sunday.

Holy Writ The Scriptures.

hom·age (hom'ij, om'-) *n.* **1.** Respect or honor given or shown, especially by outward action; obeisance: usually with *pay* or *do:* to pay *homage* to a hero. **2.** In feudal law, the formal acknowledgment of allegiance by a vassal to his lord. **3.** An act, payment, etc., indicating such allegiance. — *v.t.* **·aged, ·ag·ing** *Obs.* To pay respect or allegiance to. [< OF < LL *hominaticum* < *homo, -inis* vassal, client, man]

hom·ag·er (hom'ə·jər, om'-) *n.* A vassal (def. 1).

hom·bre¹ (om'brā, om'brē) *n. U.S. Slang* Man; fellow. [< Sp.]

hom·bre² (om'bər) See OMBER.

Hom·burg (hom'bûrg) *n.* A felt hat having a brim slightly turned up at the sides, and the crown indented lengthwise. Also *Homburg.* [after *Homburg,* Germany]

home (hōm) *n.* **1.** A house, apartment, or other dwelling serving as the abode of a person, family, or household; residence. **2.** A family or other group dwelling together; household: a happy *home.* **3.** The country, region, city, etc., where one lives. **4.** One's birthplace or place of residence during one's formative years. **5.** A place or environment natural or dear to one because of personal relationships or feelings of comfort and security. **6.** A peaceful or restful place; refuge; haven. **7.** The habitation or natural environment of an animal. **8.** The place in which something originates, develops, or is typically found: New Orleans is the *home* of jazz. **9.** An establishment for the shelter and care of the orphaned, needy, infirm, etc. **10.** In some games, especially baseball, the goal or base that must be reached in order to win or score. — **at home 1.** In one's own residence, town, country, etc. **2.** At one's ease, as if in one's residence; unconstrained. **3.** Having a thorough knowledge of or familiarity with; conversant: *at home* in the sciences. **4.** Prepared to receive callers. **5.** An informal social gathering at one's home. — *adj.* **1.** Of or pertaining to one's home, country, etc.; domestic. **2.** Being at the base of operations or place of origin: the *home* office. **3.** Going straight to the point; effective: a *home* thrust. — *adv.* **1.** To or at one's home. **2.** To the place or point intended; to the mark: to thrust a dagger *home.* **3.** Deeply and intimately; to the heart: Her words struck *home.* **4.** *Naut.* Toward or into a vessel: to pull the hawsers *home.* ◆ *Home* is frequently used without the preposition *at* after verbs such as *stay* and *remain,* which do not imply motion (He stayed *home* last night), although some authorities prefer *at home* in these expressions. A preposition is never required where motion is implied (He went *home* last night). — *v.* **homed, hom·ing** *v.t.* **1.** To cause (an aircraft or guided missile) to proceed toward a specified spot or target by means of radio waves, radar, or automatic timing devices. **2.** To furnish with a home. **3.** *Rare* To send home. — *v.i.* **4.** To go home; return home, as a homing pigeon. **5.** To be directed toward a target by means of automatic, built-in devices responsive to heat radiations, radio waves, echoes, etc., proceeding from the target: said of guided missiles: usually followed by *in* or *in on.* **6.** To have residence. [OE *hām*] — **Syn.** (noun) **1.** *Home, habitation, abode, dwelling, residence,* and *domicile* denote the place where one lives. A *home* is more than a house. The word embraces the personal ties that hold one to a particular place; thus we may say that a man's *home* is a certain house or town or region or country. *Habitation* is equally wide, but is chiefly used in contrasting those who have settled *homes* with nomads, who do not. An *abode* is a place where one stays, temporarily or permanently. A *dwelling* is a house, in legal usage, and so is a *residence:* the latter term distinguishes a building used for living quarters from one used for business. *Residence* is also used as a more formal synonym for *home. Domicile* is rarely used outside of law; it denotes a *dwelling,* the owner of which has certain rights and responsibilities. Compare HOUSE.

Home may appear as a combining form or as the first element in two-word phrases; as in:

home address	**home-cooked**	**home-lover**	**home-owning**
home-baked	**home defense**	**home-loving**	**home-raised**
home base	**home-folks**	**home market**	**home site**
home builder	**home-grown**	**home office**	**home town**
home-built	**home life**	**homeowner**	**home-woven**

Home (hyo̅o̅m), **Earl of** See DOUGLAS-HOME.
home·bod·y (hōm′bod′ē) *n. pl.* **·ies** One who prefers to stay at home or whose main interest is in the home.
home·bred (hōm′bred′) *adj.* **1.** Bred at home. **2.** Uncultivated; unsophisticated. **3.** *Canadian Slang* A home-brew.
home·brew (hōm′bro̅o̅′) *n.* **1.** An alcoholic beverage, especially beer, made at home, as for home use. **2.** *Canadian Slang* An athlete native to the country he plays in or place he represents. — **home′-brewed′** *adj.*
home·com·ing (hōm′kum′ing) *n.* **1.** A return to one's home. **2.** *U.S.* In colleges, universities, etc., an annual celebration for visiting alumni.
home economics The science of home management, as of food, clothing, children, budgets, etc.
home·land (hōm′land′) *n.* The country of one's birth or allegiance.
home·less (hōm′lis) *adj.* Having no home. — **home′less·ness** *n.*
home·like (hōm′līk′) *adj.* Typical or reminiscent of home; comfortably familiar. — **home′like′ness** *n.*
home·ly (hōm′lē) *adj.* **·li·er, ·li·est 1.** Having a familiar, everyday character; belonging to ordinary domestic life; unpretentious: *homely* truths. **2.** Having plain or ugly features; not good-looking. **3.** Lacking in refinement or elegance; commonplace. — **home′li·ness** *n.*
home·made (hōm′mād′) *adj.* **1.** Made at home: opposed to (*Dial.*) **boughten.** **2.** Simply or crudely fashioned.
home·mak·er (hōm′mā′kər) *n.* **1.** One in charge of managing her own home; housewife. **2.** In social work, a woman assigned by a social agency to a household in which the mother is absent or incapacitated. — **home′mak′ing** *n.*
homeo- *combining form* Like; similar: *homeomorphism:* also spelled **homoeo-, homoio-.** [< Gk. *homoios* similar]
Home Office In the British government, the department concerned with domestic affairs, as the police, elections, etc.
ho·me·o·mor·phism (hō′mē·ə·môr′fiz·əm, hom′ē-) *n.* Similarity in the crystalline forms of unlike chemical compounds: also spelled *homoeomorphism.* — **ho′me·o·mor′phous** *adj.*
ho·me·op·a·thist (hō′mē·op′ə·thist, hom′ē-) *n.* One who advocates or practices homeopathy: also spelled *homoeopathist.* Also **ho·me·o·path** (hō′mē·ə·path′, hom′ē-).
ho·me·op·a·thy (hō′mē·op′ə·thē, hom′ē-) *n.* A system of therapy using minute doses of medicines that produce the symptoms of the disease treated: opposed to *allopathy:* also spelled *homoeopathy.* [< HOMEO- + -PATHY] — **ho′me·o·path′ic** *adj.* — **ho′me·o·path′i·cal·ly** *adv.*
ho·me·o·sta·sis (hō′mē·ə·stā′sis, hom′ē-) *n. Biol.* The tendency of an organism to maintain a uniform and beneficial physiological stability within and between its parts; organic equilibrium. — **ho′me·o·stat′ic** (-stat′ik) *adj.*
home plate In baseball, the five-sided marker at which a player stands when batting, and to which he must return in scoring a run. For illustration see BASEBALL.

hom·er[1] (hō′mər) *n. U.S. Informal* **1.** In baseball, a home run. **2.** A homing pigeon.
ho·mer[2] (hō′mər) *n.* Either of two ancient Hebrew measures of quantity: **a** A dry measure of ten ephahs. **b** A liquid measure of ten baths. See BATH[2]. Also called *kor.* [< Hebrew *hōmer* < *hāmar* to swell up]
Ho·mer (hō′mər) Ninth-century B.C. Greek epic poet; traditional author of the *Iliad* and the *Odyssey.*
Ho·mer (hō′mər), **Winslow,** 1836–1910, U.S. painter.
Ho·mer·ic (hō·mer′ik) *adj.* Of, pertaining to, or suggestive of Homer, his epic poetry, or the legendary age he describes. Also **Ho·me·ri·an** (hō·mir′ē·ən), **Ho·mer′i·cal.**
Homeric laughter Uproarious and irrepressible laughter.
home room 1. The school room in which a class meets daily for the checking of attendance, hearing of bulletins, etc. **2.** The group of students in a home room.
home rule Self-government in local affairs within the framework of state or national laws. Abbr. *H.R.*
home ruler One who favors home rule.
home run In baseball, a hit, usually of great distance or power, that cannot be fielded so as to prevent the batter from touching all the bases and scoring a run. Abbr. *hr, h.r.*
home·sick (hōm′sik′) *adj.* Unhappy or ill through longing for home; nostalgic. — **home′sick′ness** *n.*
home·spun (hōm′spun′) *adj.* **1.** Spun or woven at home. **2.** Plain and simple in character; unsophisticated: *homespun* humor. **3.** Made of homespun fabric, as a garment. — *n.* **1.** Fabric woven at home or by hand. **2.** A rough, loosely woven fabric similar to this.
home·stead (hōm′sted) *n.* **1.** A house and its land, etc., occupied as a home. **2.** *Law* Such an establishment protected by statute from seizure by creditors. **3.** *U.S.* A tract of land occupied under the Homestead Act. — *v.i.* **1.** *U.S.* To occupy or acquire land under the Homestead Act. — *v.t.* **2.** *U.S.* To settle on (land) under the Homestead Act.
Homestead Act *U.S.* A Congressional enactment of 1862, later revised and extended, that provided a settler with 160 acres of free public land for cultivation and improvement and for eventual ownership.
home·stead·er (hōm′sted′ər) *n.* **1.** One who has a homestead. **2.** *U.S.* One who holds land acquired under the Homestead Act.
homestead law *U.S.* A law in many States exempting up to a certain amount a dwelling and the land upon which it is situated from certain liabilities incurred by the owner. Also **homestead exemption law.**
home·stretch (hōm′strech′) *n.* **1.** The straight portion of a racetrack forming the final approach to the finish. **2.** The last stage of any journey or endeavor.
home·ward (hōm′wərd) *adv.* Toward home. Also **home′wards** (-wərdz). — *adj.* Directed toward home.
home·work (hōm′wûrk′) *n.* Work done at home, especially school work.
home·y (hō′mē) *adj.* **hom·i·er, hom·i·est** Suggesting the comforts of home; homelike: also spelled *homy.* — **home′y·ness** or **hom′i·ness** *n.*
hom·i·ci·dal (hom′ə·sīd′l, hō′mə-) *adj.* **1.** Of or relating to homicide. **2.** Tending to homicide; murderous. — **hom′i·ci′dal·ly** *adv.*
hom·i·cide (hom′ə·sīd, hō′mə-) *n.* **1.** The killing of any human being by another. **2.** A person who has killed another. [< F < L *homicidium* < *homicida* murderer < *homo* man + *-cidere* < *caedere* to cut, kill]
hom·i·let·ic (hom′ə·let′ik) *adj.* **1.** Pertaining to or having the nature of a sermon or homily. **2.** Of or pertaining to homiletics. Also **hom′i·let′i·cal.** — **hom′i·let′i·cal·ly** *adv.*
hom·i·let·ics (hom′ə·let′iks) *n.pl.* (construed as sing.) The branch of theological study that treats of the art of writing and delivering sermons. [< Gk. *homilētikos* sociable < *homilein* to be in company with < *homilos* assembly]
hom·i·ly (hom′ə·lē) *n. pl.* **·lies 1.** A sermon, especially one based on a Biblical text. **2.** A solemn discourse or reproof, especially on morals or conduct. — **Syn.** See SPEECH. [< OF *omelie* < LL *homilia* < Gk. *homilia* < *homilos* assembly < *homos* the same + *ilē* crowd] — **hom′i·list** *n.*
hom·ing (hō′ming) *adj.* **1.** Returning home. **2.** Helping or causing an aircraft, missile, etc., to home.
homing device Any of various mechanisms, either airborne or on the ground, used for directing or guiding an aircraft, guided missile, or the like.
homing pigeon A pigeon capable of making its way home from great distances, often used for conveying messages: also called *carrier pigeon.*
hom·i·nid (hom′ə·nid, hō′mə-) *n. Zool.* Any of a family (*Hominidae*) of the primate order, of which only man survives. — *adj.* Of or pertaining to any member of this family. [< NL < L *homo, hominis* man]
hom·i·nine (hom′ə·nīn) *adj.* Belonging to that branch of the family *Hominidae* that includes modern man.
hom·i·noid (hom′ə·noid, hō′mə-) *adj.* **1.** Manlike. **2.** *Zool.* Pertaining to or describing any member of a superfamily or

group (*Hominoidea*) of the primate order, including the gibbons, orangutans, gorillas, chimpanzees, and modern man. — *n.* **1.** An animal resembling man. **2.** Any primate of the superfamily *Hominoidea*. [< NL < L *homo, hominis* man]

hom·i·ny (hom′ə·nē) *n.* Kernels of dried, hulled white maize, sometimes coarsely ground, prepared as a food by boiling in milk or water. [< Algonquian *rockahominie* parched corn]

hominy grits Grits (def. 2).

Ho·mo (hō′mō) *n. pl.* **Hom·i·nes** (hom′ə·nēz) *Zool.* The generic name of various species of erect, large-brained primates (family *Hominidae*), now represented only by modern man (*H. sapiens*). [< L, man]

homo- *combining form* Same; like: *homogeneous*: opposed to *hetero-*. [< Gk. *homo-* < *homos* same]

ho·mo·cen·tric (hō′mə·sen′trik, hom′ə-) *adj.* Having the same center.

ho·mo·cer·cal (hō′mə·sûr′kəl, hom′ə-) *adj.* Of, having, or denoting a tail fin with lobes of equal size. [< HOMO- + Gk. *kerkos* tail]

ho·mo·chro·mat·ic (hō′mə·krō·mat′ik, hom′ə-) *adj.* Pertaining to, characterized by, or consisting of one color; monochromatic: distinguished from *heterochromatic*. — **ho·mo·chro·ma·tism** (hō′mə·krō′mə·tiz′əm, hom′ə-) *n.*

ho·mo·chro·mous (hō′mə·krō′məs, hom′ə-) *adj. Bot.* Having one color, as a compound flower: distinguished from *heterochromous*. [< HOMO- + Gk. *chrōma* color]

ho·mo·cy·clic (hō′mə·sī′klik, -sik′lik, hom′ə-) *adj. Chem.* Pertaining to or designating a cyclic compound having only carbon atoms in the ring, as benzene.

homoeo- See HOMEO-.

ho·moe·o·mor·phism (hō′mē·ə·môr′fiz·əm, hom′ē-), **ho·moe·o·path·ist** (hō′mē·ə·path′ist, hom′ē-), etc. See HOMEOMORPHISM, etc.

ho·mo·er·o·tism (hō′mō·er′ə·tiz′əm) *n.* Sexual desire for a member of the same sex. — **ho′mo·e·rot′ic** (-i·rot′ik) *adj.*

ho·mog·a·mous (hō·mog′ə·məs) *adj. Bot.* **1.** Bearing flowers that are all sexually alike: opposed to *heterogamous*. **2.** Having pistils and stamens that mature simultaneously: opposed to *dichogamous*. [< HOMO- + -GAMOUS]

ho·mog·a·my (hō·mog′ə·mē) *n.* **1.** *Bot.* The state of being homogamous. **2.** *Biol.* Interbreeding of individuals having similar characteristics. [< HOMO- + -GAMY]

ho·mo·ge·ne·ous (hō′mə·jē′nē·əs, hom′ə-) *adj.* **1.** Having the same composition, structure, or character throughout; uniform: a *homogeneous* mass. **2.** Similar or identical in nature or form; like. **3.** *Math.* **a** Having a common property. **b** Having all terms of the same degree, as an algebraic equation. **c** Having no unknown term undifferentiated: said of a differential equation. [< Med.L *homogeneus* < Gk. *homogenēs* of the same race < *homos* same + *genos* race] — **ho′·mo·ge·ne·ous·ly** *adv.* — **ho′mo·ge·ne·ous·ness, ho′mo·ge·ne′i·ty** (hō′mə·jə·nē′ə·tē, hom′ə-) *n.*

ho·mog·en·ize (hə·moj′ə·nīz, hō′mə·jə·nīz′) *v.t.* **·ized, ·iz·ing** **1.** To make or render homogeneous. **2.** To process, as milk, by subjecting to high temperature and pressure so as to break up fat globules and disperse them uniformly; emulsify. — **ho·mog′en·i·za′tion** *n.* — **ho·mog′en·iz′er** *n.*

ho·mog·e·ny (hə·moj′ə·nē) *n. Biol.* Similarity of structures as a result of descent from a common ancestor. [< Gk. *homogeneia* community of birth < *homos* same + *genos* race] — **ho·mog′e·nous** (-ə·nəs) *adj.*

ho·mog·o·ny (hə·mog′ə·nē) *n. Bot.* The condition of having stamens and pistils of uniform respective length in all flowers of the same species: opposed to *heterogony*. [< HOMO- + -GONY] — **ho·mog′o·nous** (-ə·nəs) *adj.*

ho·mo·graft (hō′mə·graft′, hom′ə-) *n.* A tissue or organ transplanted from one individual to another of the same species.

hom·o·graph (hom′ə·graf, -gräf, hō′mə-) *n.* A word identical with another in spelling, but differing from it in origin and meaning and sometimes in pronunciation, as *wind*, an air current, and *wind*, to coil: also called *homonym*. Compare HETERONYM. [< Gk. *homographos* having the same letters < *homos* same + *graphein* to write] — **hom′o·graph′ic** *adj.*

homoio- See HOMEO-.

ho·moi·o·ther·mal (hə·moi′ə·thûr′məl) *adj. Zool.* Preserving a uniform body temperature: distinguished from *poikilothermal*: also *homothermal, warm-blooded*.

Ho·moi·ou·si·an (hō′moi·ōō′sē·ən, -ou′sē-) *n. Theol.* In the fourth century, a member of the Arian faction that maintained that the nature of Christ is similar to but not identical with that of God the Father. — *adj.* Of or pertaining to the Homoiousians or their beliefs. Compare HOMOOUSIAN, HETEROOUSIAN. [< Gk. *homoios* like + *ousia* being]

ho·mol·o·gate (hō·mol′ə·gāt) *v.* **·gat·ed, ·gat·ing** *v.t.* **1.** In Scottish law, to ratify. — *v.i.* **2.** To agree. [< Med.L *homologatus*, pp. of *homologare* < Gk. *homologein* to agree]

ho·mo·log·i·cal (hō′mə·loj′i·kəl, hom′ə-) *adj.* Homologous. Also **ho′mo·log′ic.** — **ho′mo·log′i·cal·ly** *adv.*

ho·mol·o·gize (hō·mol′ə·jīz) *v.* **·gized, ·giz·ing** *v.t.* **1.** To make homologous. — *v.i.* **2.** To be homologous.

ho·mol·o·gous (hō·mol′ə·gəs) *adj.* **1.** Similar or related in structure, position, proportion, value, etc.; corresponding in nature or relationship. **2.** *Biol.* Corresponding in structure

or origin, as an organ or part of one animal to a similar organ or part of another: The foreleg of a horse and the wing of a bird are *homologous*: distinguished from *analogous*. **3.** *Genetics* Denoting either of a pair of sexually differentiated chromosomes, one maternal and one paternal, that come together in synapsis during mitosis and become separated in the gametes. **4.** *Chem.* Designating a series of organic compounds having the same structure, but in which each differs from the preceding one by a constant increment, as the methane series. **5.** *Med.* Pertaining to or designating a serum protecting against the same bacterium from which it is prepared. [< Gk. *homologos* agreeing < *homos* same + *logos* measure, proportion < *legein* to speak]

hom·o·lo·graph·ic (hom′ə·lə·graf′ik) *adj.* Designating an equal-area map or map projection in which the parallels are straight lines and the equator is twice the length of the prime meridian. [< Gk. *homalos* even + *graphein* to write]

hom·o·logue (hom′ə·lôg, -log) *n.* That which is homologous; especially, a homologous part, organ, etc. Also **hom′o·log.**

ho·mol·o·gy (hō·mol′ə·jē) *n. pl.* **·gies** **1.** The state or quality of being homologous; correspondence in structure or properties. **2.** A homologous relationship, as of organs, etc.

ho·mol·o·sine (hə·mol′ə·sīn, -sin) *adj.* Designating a map using homolographic projection and sinusoidal projection in combination. [< HOMOLO(GRAPHIC) + SINE]

ho·mo·mor·phism (hō′mə·môr′fiz·əm, hom′ə-) *n.* **1.** *Biol.* **a** Resemblance between unrelated parts or organisms. **b** Adaptive mimicry without structural similarity. **2.** *Entomol.* Resemblance between larva and adult insect as a result of undergoing incomplete metamorphosis. **3.** *Bot.* The possession of perfect flowers of only one kind. Also **ho′mo·mor′phy.** — **ho′mo·mor′phic, ho′mo·mor′phous** *adj.*

hom·o·nym (hom′ə·nim, hō′məs-) *n.* **1.** A homophone. **2.** A homograph. **3.** A word identical with another in spelling and pronunciation, but differing from it in origin and meaning, as *butter*, the food, and *butter*, one who butts. **4.** One who has the same name as another; namesake. **5.** *Biol.* A generic or specific name that must be rejected because of previous application to another animal or plant. [< Gk. *homos* same + *onyma* name] — **hom·o·nym·ic** (hom′ə·nim′ik, hō′mə-) *adj.* ◆*Homonym* is unfortunately used with a variety of meanings: one of two words that sound alike but otherwise differ, as *fair* and *fare*, more precisely called *homophones*; one of two words that are spelled alike but otherwise differ, as *bear* (the animal) and *bear* (to carry), more precisely called *homographs*; and finally, and most precisely, with the sense of definition 3 above.

ho·mon·y·mous (hō·mon′ə·məs) *adj.* Having the nature of a homonym; indicated by the same name.

ho·mon·y·my (hō·mon′ə·mē) *n.* The state or character of being homonymous.

Ho·mo·ou·si·an (hō′mō·ōō′sē·ən, -ou′sē-, hom′ō-) *n. Theol.* In the fourth century, any of the Christians who believed that the nature of Christ was identical and consubstantial with that of God the Father. — *adj.* Of or pertaining to the Homoousians and their beliefs. Compare HOMOIOUSIAN, HETEROOUSIAN. [< Gk. *homos* same + *ousia* being]

hom·o·phone (hom′ə·fōn, hō′mə-) *n.* A word identical with another in pronunciation but differing from it in origin, spelling, and meaning, as *fair* and *fare, read* and *reed*: also called *homonym*. Compare HOMOGRAPH. [< Gk. *homophōnos* of the same sound < *homos* same + *phōnē* sound]

hom·o·phon·ic (hom′ə·fon′ik, hō′mə-) *adj.* **1.** Of, pertaining to, or having the same sound. **2.** *Music* Having one predominant part carrying the melody, with the other parts used for harmonic effect: opposed to *polyphonic*. Also **ho·moph·o·nous** (hō·mof′ə·nəs).

ho·moph·o·ny (hō·mof′ə·nē) *n.* **1.** The state or quality of being homophonic. **2.** Homophonic music.

ho·mo·po·lar (hō′mə·pō′lər) *adj. Chem.* Designating a covalent linkage characterized by a symmetrical distribution of electric charge: distinguished from *heteropolar*. — **ho′mo·po·lar′i·ty** (-lär′ə·tē) *n.*

ho·mop·ter·ous (hō·mop′tər·əs) *adj.* Of or pertaining to a suborder (*Homoptera*) of hemipterous insects with sucking mouth parts and usually two pairs of wings, including the cicadas, aphids, etc. [< NL *Homoptera* < Gk. *homos* same + *pteron* wing] — **ho·mop′ter·an** *adj. & n.*

ho·mor·gan·ic (hō′môr·gan′ik) *adj. Phonet.* Describing speech sounds, especially consonants, that are produced with the same organs or in the same area, as (b), (p), and (m).

Homo sa·pi·ens (sā′pē·enz) The scientific name for the only surviving species of the genus *Homo*; modern man. [< NL < L *homo* man + *sapiens* wise]

ho·mo·sex·u·al (hō′mə·sek′shōō·əl, hom′ə-) *adj.* Pertaining to, characterized by, or practicing homosexuality. — *n.* A homosexual individual. Opposed to *heterosexual*.

ho·mo·sex·u·al·i·ty (hō′mə·sek′shōō·al′ə·tē, hom′ə-) *n.* **1.** The condition of being sexually attracted to persons of the same sex. **2.** Sexual relations between those of the same sex. Opposed to *heterosexuality*.

ho·mos·po·rous (hō·mos′pər·əs, hō′mə·spôr′əs, -spō′rəs) *adj. Bot.* Having or producing spores of one kind only. — **ho·mos′po·ry** (-pər·ē) *n.*

ho·mo·tax·is (hō′mə·tak′sis, hom′ə-) *n. Geol.* Similarity of arrangement of groups of rock strata containing generally similar organic remains, however widely separated from one another geographically. **— ho′mo·tax′ic** *adj.*

ho·mo·thal·lic (hō′mə·thal′ik, hom′ə-) *adj. Bot.* Having or designating a single mycelium that performs the functions of both sexes in the reproductive process: distinguished from *heterothallic.* [< Gk. *homos* same + *thallos* branch]

ho·mo·ther·mal (hō′mə·thûr′məl, hom′ə-) See HOMOIO-THERMAL.

ho·mo·zy·go·sis (hō′mə·zī·gō′sis, -zi-, hom′ə-) *n. Biol.* The formation of a homozygote by the union of like gametes.

ho·mo·zy·gote (hō′mə·zī′gōt, -zig′ōt, hom′ə-) *n. Biol.* A zygote formed by the conjugation of two gametes having the same allele of a specific genetic character. [< HOMO- + ZY-GOTE] **— ho·mo·zy·gous** (hō′mə·zī′gəs, hom′ə-) *adj.*

Homs (hôms) A city in western Syria, on the Orontes; pop. 231,875 (est. 1968): ancient *Emesa.* Also *Hums.*

ho·mun·cu·lus (hō·mung′kyə·ləs) *n. pl.* ·li (-lī) **1.** A very small man; midget; dwarf. **2.** A minute human body formerly believed to have been contained in the spermatozoon or ovum. [< L, dim. of *homo* man] **— ho·mun′cu·lar** *adj.*

ho·my (hō′mē) See HOMEY.

hon. Honorably; honorary.

Hon. Honorable.

ho·nan (hō·nän′). *n.* A fine Chinese silk woven from thread produced by wild silkworms. Also **Ho′nan′.** [after *Honan*]

Ho·nan (hō′nän′) A Province of north central China; 64,479 sq. mi.; pop. 48,670,000 (est. 1957); capital, Kaifeng.

Hond. Honduras.

Hon·do (hon·dō) See HONSHU.

Hon·du·ras (hon·dŏŏr′əs, -dyŏŏr′-) A Republic of NE Central America; 43,277 sq. mi.; pop. 2,495,000 (est. 1969); capital, Tegucigalpa. **— Hon·du′ran** *adj. & n.*

Honduras, British See BRITISH HONDURAS.

Honduras, Gulf of An inlet of the Caribbean Sea in Honduras, British Honduras, and Guatemala. Also **Bay of Honduras.**

hone¹ (hōn) *n.* A fine, compact whetstone used for sharpening edged tools, razors, etc. **— v.t. honed, hon·ing** To sharpen, as a razor, on a hone. [OE *hān* stone]

hone² (hōn) *v.i.* **honed, hon·ing** *Dial.* **1.** To pine; hanker. **2.** To moan; grumble. [< F *hogner* to mutter]

Ho·neg·ger (hō′neg·ər, *Fr.* ô·ne·gâr′), Arthur, 1892–1955, French composer.

hon·est (on′ist) *adj.* **1.** Not given to lying, cheating, stealing, etc.; acting honorably and justly; trustworthy: an *honest* man. **2.** Not characterized by falsehood or intent to mislead; meriting belief; truthful: an *honest* statement. **3.** Giving or having full worth or value; genuine; fair: *honest* weight. **4.** Performed or earned in a reliable and conscientious manner: *honest* toil; *honest* wages. **5.** Characterized by openness and sincerity; frank: an *honest* opinion. **6.** *Archaic* Chaste; virtuous. [< OF *honeste* < L *honestus* < *honos* honor]

hon·est·ly (on′ist·lē) *adv.* **1.** In an honest manner. **2.** Really; truly; indeed: used for emphasis: *Honestly,* I'll go.

hon·es·ty (on′is·tē) *n.* **1.** The state or quality of being honest; uprightness of character, conduct, etc.; integrity. **2.** Truthfulness; sincerity; fairness. **3.** *Archaic* Chastity; virtue. **4.** A garden plant (*Lunaria annua*) of the mustard family, having broad leaves, ornamental, translucent pods, and white or purple flowers: also called *moonwort, satinflower.*

hone·wort (hōn′wûrt′) *n.* Any of a number of plants of the parsley family, especially *Cryptotaenia canadensis,* having small whitish flowers, and the stone parsley.

hon·ey (hun′ē) *n. pl.* **hon·eys 1.** A sweet, viscous substance made by bees from nectar gathered from flowers. **2.** Anything resembling or suggestive of honey. **3.** Sweetness. **4.** Sweet one; darling: a term of endearment. **5.** *U.S. Slang* Something regarded as a superior example of its kind: a *honey* of a car. **— v. hon·eyed** or **hon·ied, hon·ey·ing — v.t. 1.** To sweeten with or as with honey. **2.** To talk in a loving or flattering manner to. **— v.i. 3.** *Rare* To talk fondly or in a coaxing manner. **— adj.** Of or resembling honey; sweet. [OE *hunig*]

honey ant A small ant (genus *Myrmecocystus*) of tropical America, having one form of worker that receives and stores in its abdomen the honey gathered by the other workers.

honey bag The receptacle or dilatation of the esophagus in which the bee produces honey. Also called *honey sac.*

honey bear 1. A small, bandy-legged bear (*Helarctos malayanus*) of Malaya, having a smooth coat and feeding largely on fruits and honey: also called *Malayan bear, sun bear.* **2.** The sloth bear (which see). **3.** The kinkajou.

hon·ey·bee (hun′ē·bē′) *n.* A bee that produces honey; especially, the common species *Apis mellifera.*

hon·ey·comb (hun′ē·kōm′) *n.* **1.** A wax structure consisting of series of hexagonal cells, made by bees for the storage of honey, pollen, or their eggs. **2.** Anything full of small holes or cells like those of a honeycomb. **— v.t. 1.** To fill with small holes, cells, or cavities; riddle. **2.** To penetrate

or pervade so as to undermine or weaken: a nation *honeycombed* with discontent. **— adj.** Having the characteristic structure or design of a honeycomb. [OE *hunigcamb*]

honeycomb moth A moth (*Galleria melonella*) that infests beehives: also called *bee moth, waxworm.*

honey creeper A small, brightly colored bird (family *Coeribidae*) of the warmer parts of America: also called *quit-quit.*

hon·ey·dew (hun′ē·dŏŏ′, -dyŏŏ′) *n.* **1.** A sweet fluid exuded by the leaves of various plants during warm weather. **2.** A sweetish substance secreted by certain insects, as aphids.

honeydew melon A variety of melon having a smooth, white skin and sweet, greenish pulp.

honey eater Any of several oscine birds (family *Meliphagidae*) of Australia, that extract nectar from flowers: also called *bellbird, honeysucker.*

hon·eyed (hun′ēd) *adj.* **1.** Full of, consisting of, or resembling honey. **2.** Sweet, soothing, or flattering; dulcet: *honeyed* tones. Also spelled *honied.*

honey guide Any of numerous small birds (genera *Indicator* and *Prodotiscus*) of Africa, Asia, and the East Indies, said to lead persons to the nests of wild bees.

honey locust A large, thorny, leguminous North American tree (*Gleditsia triacanthos*) bearing long pods.

honey mesquite Mesquite (def. 1).

hon·ey·moon (hun′ē·mōōn′) *n.* **1.** A vacation spent by a newly-married couple. **2.** The first, happy period of a marriage. **3.** *U.S. Informal* The early and easy period of any relationship. **— v.i.** To spend one's honeymoon.

honey mouse A small phalanger (*Tarsipes spenserae*) feeding on nectar and small insects. Also **honey possum.**

honey plant Any of numerous plants important for producing nectar for honeybees.

honey sac A honey bag (which see).

hon·ey·stone (hun′ē·stōn′) *n.* A soft, yellowish or reddish aluminum mineral having a resinous appearance.

hon·ey·suck·er (hun′ē·suk′ər) *n.* The honey eater.

hon·ey·suck·le (hun′ē·suk′əl) *n.* **1.** Any of a large genus (*Lonicera*) of ornamental erect or climbing shrubs having tubular white, buff, or crimson flowers. **2.** Any of a number of similar fragrant plants. [OE *hunisūce*]

honeysuckle ornament The anthemion.

hong (hong, hông) *n.* **1.** In China, a warehouse or factory consisting of a series of connected rooms or buildings. **2.** Formerly, any one of the foreign factories operated at Canton. [< Chinese *hang* row of houses, mercantile association]

Hong Kong (hong′ kong′, hông′ kông′) A British Crown Colony in SE China comprising **Hong Kong Island,** Kowloon peninsula, and the New Territories; 398 sq. mi.; pop. 3,-988,000 (est. 1969); capital, Victoria.

Ho·ni·a·ra (hō′nē·ä′rä) The capital of the British Solomon Islands Protectorate, on the NW coast of Guadalcanal; pop. about 7,500.

hon·ied (hun′ēd) See HONEYED.

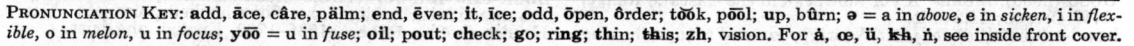

ho·ni soit qui mal y pense (ô·nē′ swä′ kē mál′ ē päṅs′) *French* Shamed be he who thinks evil of it: motto of the Order of the Garter.

honk (hôngk, hongk) *n.* **1.** The sound made by a goose. **2.** A sound resembling this, as that of an automobile horn. **— v.i. 1.** To make the sound of the goose. **2.** To make the sound of an automobile horn. **— v.t. 3.** To cause (an automobile horn) to sound. [Imit.] **— honk′er** *n.*

hon·ky (hông′kē, hong′kē) *n. pl.* ·kies *U.S. Slang* A white man: an offensive term. Also **hon′kie.** [? < HUNKY]

hon·ky-tonk (hông′kē·tôngk′, hong′kē·tongk′) *n. U.S. Slang* A noisy, squalid barroom or tavern; also, the jangling music associated with such places. [Prob. imit.]

Hon·o·lu·lu (hon′ə·lōō′lōō) The capital of Hawaii, a port on SE Oahu; pop. 324,871.

hon·or (on′ər) *n.* **1.** High regard, respect, or esteem: Give *honor* to the dead. **2.** Glory; fame; credit: The *honor* goes entirely to him. **3.** *Usually pl.* An outward token, sign, act, etc., that manifests high regard or esteem: He has received many *honors.* **4.** A strong sense of what is right; keen moral judgment: to act with *honor.* **5.** A reputation for high standards of conduct: Our *honor* is at stake. **6.** A cause or source of esteem or pride: to be an *honor* to one's profession. **7.** High rank or position; dignity: the *honor* of being governor. **8.** A privilege or pleasure: May I have the *honor* of this dance? **9.** *Usually pl.* Special recognition given to a student by an educational institution for superior scholarship or excellence in some field of study, etc. **10.** Chastity in women; also, a reputation for chastity. **11.** In bridge, one of the five highest cards of a suit; in whist, one of the four highest cards of a suit. **12.** In golf, the privilege of playing first from the tee. **— on** (or **upon**) **one's honor** Pledging one's word on the truth of something stated or on the keeping of a promise. **— to do honor to 1.** To show esteem for; pay homage to. **2.** To bring respect or credit to. **— to do the honors 1.** To act as a host or hostess. **2.** To perform any of various social courtesies, as proposing toasts, etc. **— v.t. 1.** To regard with honor or respect. **2.** To treat with courtesy. **3.** To worship or venerate, as a deity. **4.** To confer an honor upon; dignify. **5.** To accept or pay, as a check or draft. Also *Brit.* **hon′our.** [< OF < L] **— hon′or·er** *n.*

Hon·or (on′ər) *n.* A title or form of address for a judge mayor, etc.: preceded by *Your, His,* or *Her.*

hon·or·a·ble (on′ər·ə·bəl) *adj.* **1.** Worthy of honor or respect: an *honorable* man. **2.** Conferring honor or credit: *honorable* work. **3.** Having eminence or high rank; illustrious. **4.** Possessing or according with high moral principles; upright: an *honorable* act. **5.** Accompanied by marks or tokens of honor: *honorable* burial. Also *Brit.* **hon′our·a·ble.** — **hon′or·a·ble·ness** *n.* — **hon′or·a·bly** *adv.*

Hon·or·a·ble (on′ər·ə·bəl) *adj.* A formal epithet or title of courtesy for certain important officials, as cabinet members, justices of the Supreme Court, governors, etc.: preceded by *The.* Also *Brit.* **Hon′our·a·ble.** Abbr. *Hon.*

honorable mention The distinction of being named with honor, especially in the announcement of the results of a competition in which one was not a winner.

hon·o·rar·i·um (on′ə·râr′ē·əm) *n. pl.* **·rar·i·ums** or **·rar·i·a** (-râr′ē·ə) A payment given, as to a professional man, for services rendered when law, custom, or propriety forbids a set fee. **— Syn.** See SALARY. [< L *honorarium* (*donum*) honorary (gift), neut. of *honorarius* honorary]

hon·or·ar·y (on′ə·rer′ē) *adj.* **1.** Designating an office, title, etc., bestowed as an honor, without the customary powers, duties, or salaries. **2.** Having such a title, office, etc.: an *honorary* chairman. **3.** Bringing, conferred in, or denoting honor: an *honorary* membership. **4.** Depending on one's honor for discharge; not legally binding: said of certain debts or obligations. Abbr. *hon.* [< L *honorarius*]

hon·or·if·ic (on′ə·rif′ik) *adj.* **1.** Conferring or implying honor or respect. **2.** Denoting certain phrases, words, or word elements, as in Oriental languages, used in respectful address. **— n.** Any honorific title, word, phrase, etc. [< L *honorificus* < *honor* honor + *facere* to make] **— hon′or·if′i·cal·ly** *adv.*

Ho·no·ri·us (hə·nôr′ē·əs, -nō′rē-), **Flavius,** 384–423, Roman emperor of the West 395–423.

honor point *Heraldry* The point just above the fess point. For illustration see ESCUTCHEON.

honors of war Marks of respect or concessions granted to a capitulating force, such as permission to retain arms.

honors system In some colleges and universities, a plan for selected students of superior ability to undertake individual, specialized work in place of the classroom routine.

honor system In some colleges, schools, and correctional institutions, a system of government by which persons are trusted to obey regulations, carry out assignments, etc., without immediate supervision.

Hon·shu (hon·shōō) The largest island of Japan; 88,745 sq. mi. (including outlying islands): also *Hondo.*

hooch (hōōch) *n. U.S. Slang* **1.** Alcoholic liquor, especially cheap whisky. **2.** Illegally distilled spirits; bootleg liquor. Also spelled *hootch.* [< *hoochinoo,* alter. of *Hutanuwu,* name of Alaskan Indian tribe that made liquor]

Hooch (hōkh), **Pieter de,** 1629?–77?, Dutch painter: also *Hoogh.*

hood[1] (hōod) *n.* **1.** A covering for the head and back of the neck, sometimes forming part of a robe or other garment. **2.** Anything resembling a hood in form or use; as: **a** *U.S.* The movable metal cover protecting the engine of an automobile. **b** A projecting cover for a hearth, ventilator, etc. **c** An ornamental fold attached to the back of an academic gown to designate the degree held and the university affiliation of the wearer. **d** The collapsible cover of a carriage. **3.** In falconry, a cover for the head and eyes of a hawk when it is not hunting. **4.** *Bot.* A concave expansion, as in the petals of certain flowers. **5.** *Zool.* **a** A bird's crest. **b** In certain animals, as the cobra, the folds of skin near the head, capable of voluntary expansion. **— v.t.** To cover or furnish with or as with a hood. [OE *hōd*]

hood[2] (hōod) *n. U.S. Slang* A hoodlum. [< HOODLUM]

-hood *suffix of nouns* **1.** Condition or quality of; state of being: *babyhood, falsehood.* **2.** Class or totality of those having a certain character: *priesthood.* [OE *hād* state, condition]

Hood (hōod), **John Bell,** 1831–79, Confederate general in the Civil War. **— Robin** See ROBIN HOOD. **— Thomas,** 1799–1845, English poet and humorist.

⸺ood (hōod), **Mount** A volcanic peak in the Cascade Range, W Oregon; 11,245 ft.

⸺ed (hōod′id) *adj.* **1.** Wearing, covered with, or having

a hood. **2.** Shaped like a hood. **3.** *Zool.* Having a part or formation resembling a hood. **4.** *Bot.* Cucullate.

hooded crow The gray crow (*Corvus cornix*) of Europe, with a black head, wings, and tail, closely related to the carrion crow: also called *grayback.*

hooded seal A large seal (*Cystophora cristata*) of the North Atlantic, the male of which has an inflatable sac over the fore part of the head and the muzzle: also called *bladdernose.*

hood·ie (hōod′ē) *n. Scot.* The hooded crow of Europe.

hood·lum (hōod′ləm) *n. U.S.* **1.** A young street rowdy or tough. **2.** A thug or ruffian. [? < dial. G *hodalum* rowdy] **— hood′lum·ism** *n.*

hoo·doo (hōō′dōō) *n.* **1.** Voodoo. **2.** *Informal* One who or that which brings bad luck; a jinx. **3.** *Informal* Bad luck. **— v.t.** *Informal* To bring bad luck to. [Var. of VOODOO] **— hoo′doo·ism** *n.*

hood·wink (hōod′wingk′) *v.t.* **1.** To blindfold. **2.** To deceive as if by blindfolding; trick; cheat. **3.** To conceal or hide. [< HOOD + WINK] **— hood′wink′er** *n.*

hoo·ey (hōō′ē) *n. & interj. U.S. Slang* Nonsense.

hoof (hōof, hōof) *n. pl.* **hoofs** or, sometimes, **hooves 1.** The horny sheath incasing the foot in various mammals, as horses, cattle, swine, etc. ◆ Collateral adjective: *ungular.* For illustration see HORSE. **2.** The entire foot of such an animal. **3.** An animal with hoofs, especially as a unit of a herd. **4.** The human foot: a humorous usage. **— on the hoof** Alive; not butchered: said of cattle. **— v.t. & v.i. 1.** To trample with the hoofs. **2.** *Informal* To walk or dance: usually with *it.* [OE *hōf*]

hoof·beat (hōof′bēt′, hōof′-) *n.* The sound made by a hoofed animal in walking, trotting, etc.

hoof·bound (hōof′bound′, hōof′-) *adj. Vet.* Having a contraction and dryness of the hoofs that causes lameness.

hoofed (hōoft, hōoft) *adj.* Having hoofs; ungulate.

hoof·er (hōof′ər, hōof′ər) *n. U.S. Slang* A professional dancer, especially a tap dancer.

hoof·print (hōof′print′, hōof′-) *n.* One of the tracks left by a hoofed animal.

Hoogh (hōkh), **Pieter de** See HOOCH.

Hoogh·ly (hōog′lē) A branch of the Ganges in West Bengal, flowing about 160 miles south to the Bay of Bengal: also *Hugli.*

hook (hōok) *n.* **1.** A curved or bent piece of metal, wood, bone, etc., having one free end that serves to hold up, fasten, or drag something. **2.** A fishhook. **3.** A curved cutting tool, especially a sickle. **4.** The fixed half of a hinge from which a door, gate, etc., swings. **5.** Something that catches or ensnares; trap. **6.** Something resembling or suggesting a hook in shape or contour; as: **a** A recurved organ or part of an animal or plant. **b** A curved point of land. **c** A bend in a river. **d** A hook-shaped part of a letter or other written symbol. **7.** In baseball, a curve. **8.** In boxing, a short, swinging blow, with the elbow bent. **9.** In golf, a stroke made by a player that sends the ball curving to his left. **10.** *Music* One of the lines at the end of the stem of a note, used to indicate the note's value. **11.** *Naut. Slang* An anchor. **— by hook or by crook** In one way or another; by any possible means. **— hook, line, and sinker** *Informal* Entirely; unreservedly. **— off the hook** *Slang* Free from a troublesome situation, obligation, etc. **— on one's own hook** *Informal* **1.** By one's own efforts. **2.** On one's own initiative or responsibility. **— v.t. 1.** To fasten, attach, or take hold of with or as with a hook. **2.** To catch on or with a hook, as fish. **3.** To make or bend into the shape of a hook. **4.** To catch on or wound with the horns, as those of a bull. **5.** To make (a rug, mat, etc.) by looping yarn through a backing of canvas or burlap. **6.** In baseball, to pitch (the ball) in a curve. **7.** In boxing, to strike with a short, swinging blow. **8.** In golf, to drive (the ball) to one's left instead of in a straight line. **9.** In hockey, to check illegally by catching at the puck-carrier from side or rear with the stick. **10.** *Informal* To trick; dupe. **11.** *Slang* To pilfer; steal. **— v.i. 12.** To curve like a hook; bend. **13.** To be fastened or caught with or as with a hook or hooks: The blouse *hooks* in back. **— to hook it** *Slang* To run away; escape. **— to hook up 1.** To fasten or attach with a hook or hooks. **2.** To put together or connect, as parts of a mechanism. **— to hook up to** To connect (apparatus) to a source of power. **— to hook up with** *Slang* **1.** To become a companion or adherent of; join. **2.** To marry. [OE *hōc*]

hook·ah (hōok′ə) *n.* An Oriental tobacco pipe having a long, flexible tube that passes through a vessel of water, thus cooling the smoke: also called *hubblebubble, kalian, narghile, water pipe.* Also **hook′a.** [< Arabic *huqqah*]

hook and eye A fastening for clothes, consisting of a small hook of wire with a blunt end doubled over that passes through a loop of metal or thread.

hook-and-lad·der truck (hōok′ən·lad′ər) A fire engine equipped with ladders, axes, long hooked poles, etc.

Hooke (hōok), **Robert,** 1635–1703, English physicist.

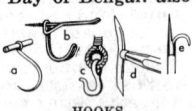

HOOKS
a Box or longshoreman's. *b* Coat hook. *c* Eyehook. *d* Ice hook. *e* Boat hook.

hooked (hŏŏkt) *adj.* **1.** Curved like a hook. **2.** Supplied with a hook or hooks. **3.** Made by means of a hook, as a rug. **4.** *Slang* Married. **5.** *Slang* Addicted to a habit or practice, especially a harmful one. **— hook·ed·ness** (hŏŏk′id·nis) *n.*

hooked rug A rug made by looping yarn or strips of cloth with a hooked tool through a backing of burlap or canvas.

hook·er[1] (hŏŏk′ər) *n.* **1.** A fishing smack, usually with one mast, used on the English and Irish coasts. **2.** Any old, badly rigged, or clumsy vessel. **3.** Formerly, a two-masted Dutch vessel. [< Du. *hoeker* < *hoek* hook]

hook·er[2] (hŏŏk′ər) *n.* **1.** One who or that which hooks. **2.** *Slang* A drink of straight liquor, especially of whisky. **3.** *U.S. Slang* A prostitute. [< HOOK + -ER[1]]

Hook·er (hŏŏk′ər), **Joseph**, 1814–79, U.S. general in the Civil War: called **Fighting Joe.** **— Sir Joseph Dalton,** 1817–1911, English botanist. **— Richard,** 1554?–1600, English theologian. **— Thomas,** 1586?–1647, English clergyman in America.

hook·nose (hŏŏk′nōz′) *n.* A nose with a downward curve; aquiline nose. **— hook′-nosed′** (-nōzd′) *adj.*

Hook of Holland A headland and harbor of SW Netherlands: Dutch *Hoek van Holland.*

hook·up (hŏŏk′up′) *n.* **1.** *Telecom.* **a** A diagram showing the apparatus and connections used for a radio broadcast or other electrical transmission. **b** The apparatus itself. **2.** *Aeron.* The contact of an aircraft in flight with the refueling hose of a tanker aircraft. **3.** *Informal* A relationship or connection, as between countries, persons, etc.

hook·worm (hŏŏk′wûrm′) *n.* Any of various bloodsucking nematode worms (family *Ancylostomatidae*), with hooked mouth parts, parasitic in the intestines of man and certain other mammals; especially, the **American hookworm** (*Necator americanus*), causing ancylostomiasis in man.

hookworm disease Ancylostomiasis.

hook·y[1] (hŏŏk′ē) *adj.* **hook·i·er, hook·i·est 1.** Full of hooks. **2.** Pertaining to or like a hook.

hook·y[2] (hŏŏk′ē) *n. U.S. Informal* Absence without leave, as from school: now only in the phrase **to play hooky,** to be a truant. [< HOOK, in dial. sense of "make off"]

hoo·lie (hŏŏl′lē) *adj. & adv. Scot.* Easy; slow. Also **hoo′ly.**

hoo·li·gan (hŏŏl′lə·gən) *n. Slang* A young hoodlum; petty gangster. [after *Hooligan,* name of an Irish family in London] **— hoo′li·gan·ism** *n.*

hoop (hŏŏp, hŏŏp) *n.* **1.** A circular band of metal, wood, etc.; especially, such a band used to confine the staves of a barrel, cask, or the like. **2.** A child's toy in the shape of a large ring, used to roll along the ground or twirl around the body. **3.** One of the rings of flexible metal, whalebone, etc., used to make a woman's skirt stand out from her body. **4.** The encircling band of a finger ring. **5.** *Usually Brit.* In croquet, a wire wicket. **—** *v.t.* **1.** To surround or fasten with a hoop or hoops. **2.** To encircle. [OE *hōp*]

hoop·er (hŏŏ′pər, hŏŏp′ər) *n.* A cooper.

hoop·la (hŏŏp′lä) *n. U.S. Slang* Boisterous noise; excitement. [Orig. a coach driver's exclamation]

hoo·poe (hŏŏ′pōō) *n.* An Old World bird (family *Upupidae*), having a long, pointed bill and an erectile crest. Also **hoo′poo.** [< F *huppe* < L *upupa*]

hoop skirt 1. A bell-shaped structure made from several hoops of graduated sizes, used to expand a woman's skirt. **2.** The skirt worn over this.

hoop snake A snake traditionally believed to take its tail in its mouth and roll like a hoop, as the mud snake.

hoo·ray (hŏŏ·rā′, hə-, hŏŏ-) See HURRAH.

hoose·gow (hŏŏs′gou) *n. U.S. Slang* Jail or prison. Also **hoos′gow.** [< Sp. *juzgado* tribunal]

Hoo·sier (hŏŏ′zhər) *n. U.S.* A native or resident of Indiana. [Prob. < dial. *hoosier* mountaineer, in ref. to Kentucky settlers in southern part of the State]

Hoosier State A nickname of INDIANA.

hoot[1] (hŏŏt) *n.* **1.** The cry of an owl. **2.** A sound similar to this, as of a train whistle. **3.** A loud outcry, especially one uttered in derision. **—** *v.i.* **1.** To make the sound of an owl. **2.** To make a sound similar to this. **3.** To jeer or call out, as in contempt or disapproval. **—** *v.t.* **4.** To jeer at or mock with derisive cries. **5.** To drive off with hoots: They *hooted* him off the stage. **6.** To express (disapproval, scorn, etc.) by hooting. [< Scand. Cf. Sw. *huta.*]

hoot[2] (hŏŏt) *n. U.S. Informal* An insignificant amount; bit: commonly in the expression **I don't give a hoot,** I don't care a bit. [Earlier *hooter,* ? alter. of *iota.* Cf. JOT.]

hootch (hŏŏch) See HOOCH.

hootch·y-cootch·y (hŏŏ′chē-kŏŏ′chē) *n. pl.* **·chies** *U.S. Slang* An erotic dance in which a woman sways or rotates her hips. Also **hoot′chie-coot′chie.** [Origin unknown]

hoot·en·an·ny (hŏŏt′n·an′ē) *n. pl.* **·nies 1.** *U.S.* A gathering of folk singers, especially for a public performance. **2.**

Informal A gadget; thingamajig. Also **hoot·nan·ny** (hŏŏt′·nan′ē). [Origin unknown]

Hoo·ton (hŏŏt′n), **Earnest Albert,** 1887–1954, U.S. anthropologist and author.

hoot owl An owl that hoots, as the barred owl.

hoots (hŏŏts, ōots) *interj. Scot.* Fie! Pshaw!

Hoo·ver (hŏŏ′vər), **Herbert Clark,** 1874–1964, U.S. mining engineer and statesman; 31st president of the United States, 1929–33. **— J**(ohn) **Edgar,** 1895–1972, U.S. lawyer; director of the Federal Bureau of Investigation 1924–72.

Hoover Dam A dam in the Colorado River on the Arizona-Nevada border, forming Lake Mead; 727 ft. high; 1,282 ft. long: formerly *Boulder Dam.*

Hoo·ver·ville (hŏŏ′vər·vil) *n.* Any group of ramshackle huts, usually on the outskirts of a town, in which the jobless camped during the depression of the early 1930's. [after Herbert *Hoover* + -*ville* city, town]

hooves (hŏŏvz, hŏŏvz) Alternative plural of HOOF.

hop[1] (hop) *v.* **hopped, hop·ping** *v.i.* **1.** To move by making short leaps on one foot. **2.** To move in short leaps on both feet or on all four feet, as a bird, rabbit, etc. **3.** To limp. **4.** *Informal* To dance. **5.** *Informal* To go, especially by airplane. **—** *v.t.* **6.** To jump over, as a fence. **7.** *Informal* To get on or board, by or as by hopping: to *hop* a train. **— to hop off** To leave the ground in flight, as an airplane. **— to hop it** *Brit. Slang* To go away; beat it. **—** *n.* **1.** The act of hopping. **2.** *Informal* A dance or dancing party. **3.** *Informal* A trip in an airplane. [OE *hoppian*]

hop[2] (hop) *n.* **1.** A perennial climbing herb (*Humulus lupulus*) with opposite lobed leaves and scaly fruit. **2.** *pl.* The dried ripe cones of the female hop vine, used medicinally, and as an aromatic, bitter flavoring in beer and other drinks. [< MDu. *hoppe*]

hop·cal·ite (hop′kəl·īt) *n.* A granular mixture of the oxides of copper, cobalt, manganese, and silver, effective as a protection against carbon monoxide. [< (*Johns*) *Hop*(*kins University*) + (*University of*) *Cal*(*ifornia*) + -ITE[1]]

hop clover 1. A yellow clover (*Trifolium procumbens*) whose dried flowers resemble hops. **2.** Black medic.

hope (hōp) *v.* **hoped, hop·ing** *v.t.* **1.** To desire with expectation of fulfillment: I *hope* to join you later. **2.** To wish; want: I *hope* that you will be happy. **—** *v.i.* **3.** To have desire or expectation: usually with *for:* to *hope* for the best. **4.** *Archaic* To place confidence; rely. **— to hope against hope** To continue hoping even when it may be in vain. **—** *n.* **1.** Desire accompanied by expectation of fulfillment. **2.** Confident expectation. **3.** That which is desired or anticipated: Our *hope* is to succeed. **4.** One who or that which is a cause of hopeful expectation or confidence: to be the *hope* of a team. **5.** *Archaic* Confidence; trust. [OE *hopa*]

Hope (hōp), **Anthony** See (Sir Anthony Hope) HAWKINS.

hope chest A box or chest used by young women to hold linen, clothing, etc., in anticipation of marriage.

Hope diamond A large and famous colored (blue) diamond, 44.5 carats.

hope·ful (hōp′fəl) *adj.* **1.** Full of or manifesting hope: a *hopeful* attitude. **2.** Affording grounds for hope; promising: a *hopeful* situation. **—** *n.* A young person who seems likely to succeed: often a humorous usage. **— hope′ful·ness** *n.*

hope·ful·ly (hōp′fəl·ē) *adv.* **1.** With hope. **2.** I (or we, you, they, etc.) hope: in function like an adverbial clause modifying a whole sentence: *Hopefully,* I'll finish next week.

Ho·peh (hō′pā′) A Province in NE China; 81,479 sq. mi.; pop. 44,720,000 (est. 1957); capital, Paoting. Also **Ho′pei′.**

hope·less (hōp′lis) *adj.* **1.** Without hope; despairing: a *hopeless* feeling. **2.** Affording no ground for hope: a *hopeless* predicament. **— hope′less·ly** *adv.* **— hope′less·ness** *n.*

Ho·pi (hō′pē) *n.* **1.** One of a group of North American Pueblo Indians of Shoshonean stock, now on a reservation in NE Arizona: also called *Moqui* or *Moki.* **2.** Their Shoshonean language. [< Hopi *hópitu,* lit., peaceful ones]

Hop·kins (hop′kinz), **Sir Frederick Gowland,** 1861–1947, English biochemist. **— Gerard Manley,** 1844–89, English Roman Catholic priest and poet. **— Harry** (Lloyd), 1890–1946, U.S. social worker and administrator; adviser to President F. D. Roosevelt. **— Johns,** 1795–1873, U.S. financier and philanthropist. **— Mark,** 1802–87, U.S. educator and theologian.

Hop·kin·son (hop′kin·sən), **Francis,** 1737–91, American patriot; signer of the Declaration of Independence.

hop·lite (hop′līt) *n.* In ancient Greece, a heavily armed foot soldier. [< Gk. *hoplitēs* < *hoplon* shield]

hop-o'-my-thumb (hop′ə·mǐ·thum′) *n.* A tiny person. [after *Hop-o'-my-thumb,* hero of a fairy tale by Perrault]

hopped-up (hopt′up′) *adj. U.S. Slang* **1.** Stimulated by narcotics; drugged. **2.** Exhilarated; excited. **3.** Supercharged: said of an automobile engine. [? < HOP[2]]

hop·per (hop′ər) *n.* **1.** One who or that which hops. **2.** A jumping insect or larva. **3.** Any of various funnel-shaped receptacles in which coal, sand, grain, etc., may be kept until ready for discharge through the bottom.

(About 12 inches long; bill 2½ inches)

HOOPOE

Hop·per (hop′ər), **Edward**, 1882–1967, U.S. painter.
hopper car A freight car, open at the top, for coal, gravel, etc., with a device at the bottom for rapid unloading.
hop·ple (hop′əl) v.t. **·pled**, **·pling** To hobble (a horse). — n. A fetter or hobble for the legs of a horse. [Var. of HOBBLE]
hop·sack·ing (hop′sak′ing) n. **1.** A coarse fabric of hemp or jute, used for bags, etc. **2.** A rough, loosely woven dress fabric, used in sportswear, coats, etc. [< HOP² + SACK]
hop·scotch (hop′skoch′) n. A children's game in which the player hops on one foot over the lines of a diagram marked on the ground, sidewalk, etc., to recover a block or pebble previously tossed into successive sections of the diagram.
hor. Horizon; horizontal.
ho·ra (hô′rə, hôr′ə) n. An Israeli or Rumanian round dance, or the music for it. [< Hebrew and Rumanian]
Hor·ace (hôr′is, hor′-) Anglicized name of **Quintus Horatius Flac·cus** (flak′əs), 65–8 B.C., Roman poet.
Ho·rae (hô′rē) In Greek mythology, the three goddesses of the seasons and of orderliness: also called *the Hours*.
ho·ral (hô′rəl) adj. Of or pertaining to an hour or hours; hourly. [< L *hora* hour]
ho·ra·ry (hô′rə-rē) adj. **1.** Pertaining to or designating the hours. **2.** Occurring hourly. **3.** Continuing for an hour. **4.** Referring to propitious or specific times. [< L *hora* hour]
Ho·ra·tian (hə-rā′shən) adj. **1.** Of or pertaining to Horace. **2.** Of, resembling, or characteristic of the writings of Horace.
Horatian ode An ode characterized by the repetition of a uniform stanzaic form: also called *Lesbian ode, Sapphic ode*.
Ho·ra·ti·i (hə-rā′shē-ī) In Roman legend, three Roman brothers who fought and killed the Curiatii, three brothers from Alba Longa.
Ho·ra·tius Co·cles (hə-rā′shəs kō′klēz) In Roman legend, a hero who with two comrades held the bridge over the Tiber against the Etruscan army.
horde (hôrd, hōrd) n. **1.** A multitude, pack, or swarm, as of people, animals, insects, etc. **2.** A tribe or clan of nomadic Mongols. **3.** Any nomadic tribe or group. — v.i. **hord·ed, hord·ing** To gather in or live in a horde. [< F < G < Polish *horda* < Turkish *ordū* camp. Akin to URDU.]
Ho·reb (hô′reb) The mountain where the law was given to Moses, generally identified with Mount Sinai. *Ex.* iii 1.
hore·hound (hôr′hound′, hōr′-) n. **1.** A whitish, bitter, perennial herb (genus *Marrubium*) of the mint family. **2.** The juice or extract of this plant. **3.** A candy or cough remedy flavored with this extract. **4.** One of various allied plants. Also spelled *hoarhound*. [OE *hārhūne*]
ho·ri·zon (hə-rī′zən) n. **1.** The line of the apparent meeting of the sky with the earth or sea (**visible** or **apparent horizon**). **2.** The bounds or limits of one's observation, knowledge, or experience. **3.** *Astron.* **a** The plane tangent to the earth's surface at the point where the observer stands and at right angles to the line of gravity (**sensible horizon**). **b** The great circle of the celestial sphere whose plane, parallel to the sensible horizon, cuts the center of the earth midway between the zenith and nadir (**celestial** or **rational horizon**). **4.** *Geol.* **a** A layer or level of rock stratum or strata characterized by the presence of one or more distinctive fossils and therefore identified with a particular time. **b** One of the layers in a cross section of soil. Abbr. **hor.** [< OF *orizonte* < L *horizon* < Gk. *horizōn (kyklos)* bounding (circle), ppr. of *horizein* to bound < *horos* limit, bound]
hor·i·zon·tal (hôr′ə-zon′təl, hor′-) adj. **1.** Of, pertaining to, or close to the horizon. **2.** Parallel to the horizon; level: opposed to *vertical*. **3.** Included or measured in a plane of the horizon: *horizontal* distance. **4.** Equal and uniform: a *horizontal* tariff. — n. A line, plane, member, etc., assumed to be parallel with the horizon. — **Syn.** See LEVEL. Abbr. **hor.** — **hor′i·zon′tal·ly** adv.
horizontal bar In gymnastics, a metal or wooden bar fixed in a horizontal position a few feet above the ground or floor, used for chinning and other exercises.
horizontal union A craft union (which see).
hor·mone (hôr′mōn) n. **1.** *Physiol.* An internal secretion produced in and by one of the endocrine glands, as the pituitary, thyroid, adrenals, etc., and carried by the blood stream or body fluids to other parts of the body where it has a specific physiological effect. **2.** *Bot.* A similar substance in plants; auxin. [< Gk. *hormōn*, ppr. of *hormaein* to excite] — **hor·mo·nal** (hôr-mō′nəl), **hor·mon·ic** (hôr-mon′ik) adj.
Hor·muz (hôr′muz) A small island of SE Iran in the **Strait of Hormuz**, a channel connecting the Persian Gulf and the Gulf of Oman: also *Ormuz*.
horn (hôrn) n. **1.** A hard, bonelike, permanent, often curved growth of epidermal tissue, usually occurring in pairs and projecting from the head in various hoofed animals, as in oxen, sheep, cattle, etc. **2.** Either of the two antlers of a deer, shed annually. **3.** Any outgrowth projecting naturally from the head of an animal, as a feeler of an insect, a tentacle of a snail, the feather tuft in certain owls, etc. **4.** The substance of which animal horn is made; also, any similar substance. **5.** The appendage like an animal's horn attributed to demons, deities, etc. **6.** In the Bible, a symbol of glory and power. **7.** *Usually pl. Obs.* The imaginary projections on the forehead of a cuckold. **8.** A vessel or implement

formed from or shaped like a horn: a powder *horn*. **9.** One of the extremities of the crescent moon. **10.** The pommel of a saddle. For illustration see SADDLE. **11.** A device for sounding warning signals: an automobile *horn*. **12.** A cornucopia. **13.** Any pointed or tapering projection, as the point of an anvil. **14.** One of the two or more alternatives of a dilemma. **15.** *Music* **a** Any of the various brass instruments, formerly made from animal horns, in the shape of a long, coiled tube widening out into a bell at one end. **b** The French horn (which see). Abbr. **h., H. 16.** *Informal* Any musical wind instrument. **17.** *Electronics* A hollow, tubular device terminating in a cone of varying cross section, for collecting sound waves, as in a loudspeaker. **18.** *Geog.* **a** One of the branches forming the delta of a stream or river. **b** A cape or peninsula. **19.** *Aeron.* Any of several levers operating a cable connected to a control surface of an aircraft. — **to blow one's own horn** To extol oneself; brag. — **to haul (or pull or draw) in one's horns 1.** To check one's anger, zeal, etc.; restrain oneself. **2.** To retract or withdraw, as a previous statement. — adj. Of or like horn: a *horn* spoon. — v.t. **1.** To provide with horns. **2.** To shape like a horn. **3.** To attack with the horns; gore. **4.** *Obs.* To cuckold. — **to horn in** *Slang* To intrude or enter without being invited. [OE. Akin to CORN².] — **horn′less** adj.
Horn, Cape The southern extremity of South America, on the last island of the Fuegian archipelago. Also **the Horn.** See map of (Strait of) MAGELLAN.
horn·beam (hôrn′bēm′) n. A small tree of the birch family (genus *Carpinus*), with white, hard wood.
horn·bill (hôrn′bil′) n. Any of a family (*Bucerotidae*) of tropical Asian and African birds, having a large bill surmounted by a hornlike extension.
horn·blende (hôrn′blend) n. A common variety of amphibole, greenish black or black, containing iron and silicate of magnesium, calcium, and aluminum. — **horn′blend′ic** adj.
hornblende schist A schistose rock consisting essentially of hornblende in parallel layers.
horn·book (hôrn′book′) n. **1.** A leaf or page containing a printed alphabet, etc., covered with transparent horn and framed, formerly used in teaching reading to children. **2.** A primer or book of rudimentary knowledge.
horned (hôrnd, *Poetic* hôr′nid) adj. **1.** Having a horn or horns. **2.** Having a projection or process resembling a horn: the *horned* moon; *horned* snail. **3.** *Obs.* Cuckolded.
horned owl Any of various American owls with conspicuous ear tufts; especially, the great horned owl or the screech owl.
horned pout A species (*Ictalurus nebulosus*) of bullhead, a type of fish. Also **horn pout.**
horned toad A harmless, flat-bodied, spiny lizard (*Phrynosoma cornutum*) with a very short tail and toadlike appearance, common in semiarid regions of the western United States. Also **horn toad.**
horned viper A venomous African or Indian viper (*Cerastes cornutus*) with a hornlike growth over each eye: also called *sand viper*.
hor·net (hôr′nit) n. Any of various social wasps (family *Vespidae*) capable of inflicting a severe sting; especially, the baldfaced hornet (*Dolichovespula maculata*) of America, and the **giant hornet** (*Vespa crabo*) of Europe. [OE *hyrnet*]
Horn·ie (hôr′nē) *Scot.* The devil.
horn·mad (hôrn′mad′) adj. **1.** Furious enough to gore: said of horned animals. **2.** Furiously angry; maddened.
horn of plenty A cornucopia.
horn·pipe (hôrn′pīp′) n. **1.** An obsolete musical instrument resembling the clarinet. **2.** A lively English dance for one or more performers, originally danced by sailors to the music of a hornpipe. **3.** The music for such a dance.
horn silver Cerargyrite.
horn·stone (hôrn′stōn′) n. Chert.
horn·swog·gle (hôrn′swog′əl) v.t. **·gled, ·gling** *Slang* To deceive; bamboozle; cheat.
horn·tail (hôrn′tāl′) n. Any of various large, wasplike insects (family *Siricidae*), the female of which has a sharp, horn-shaped ovipositor and the larvae of which are wood borers. For illustration see INSECTS (injurious).
horn·worm (hôrn′wûrm′) n. A caterpillar with a hornlike hind appendage, the larva of a hawk moth.
horn·wort (hôrn′wûrt′) n. An aquatic herb (*Ceratophyllum demersum*) common in ponds, and slow streams.
horn·y (hôr′nē) adj. **horn·i·er, horn·i·est 1.** Made of horn or a similar substance. **2.** Having horns or projections resembling horns. **3.** Hard as horn; calloused; tough. **4.** *Slang* Lecherous. — **horn′i·ness** n.

GREAT
HORNED OWL
(Nearly 2 feet long)

horn·y-hand·ed (hôr′nē-han′did) *adj.* Having hard or calloused hands, as from hard labor.

horol. Horology.

hor·o·loge (hôr′ə-lōj, hor′-) *n.* A timepiece, as a watch, clock, sundial, etc. [< OF *horloge* < L *horologium* < Gk. *hōrologion* < *hōra* time + *legein* to tell]

ho·rol·o·ger (hô·rol′ə·jər, hō-) *n.* One skilled in horology; also, one who makes or sells timepieces. Also **ho·rol′o·gist.**

hor·o·log·ic (hôr′ə-loj′ik, hor′-) *adj.* 1. Pertaining to horology or to a horologe. 2. *Bot.* Opening and closing at certain hours, as some flowers. Also **hor′o·log′i·cal.**

Hor·o·lo·gi·um (hôr′ə-lō′jē-əm, hor′-) *n.* A constellation, the Clock. See CONSTELLATION. [< L < Gk. *hōrologion*]

ho·rol·o·gy (hô-rol′ə-jē, hō-) *n.* The science of the measurement of time or of the construction of timepieces.

hor·o·scope (hôr′ə-skōp, hor′-) *n.* 1. In astrology, the aspect of the heavens, with special reference to the positions of the planets at any specific instant, especially at a person's birth. 2. The diagram of the twelve divisions or houses of the heavens, used in predicting the future. [< L *horoscopus* < Gk. *hōroskopos* observer of hour of nativity < *hōra* hour + *skopos* watcher < *skopeein* to watch]

ho·ros·co·py (hō·ros′kə·pē, hō-) *n.* 1. The art of casting horoscopes. 2. The position of the heavenly bodies at any specific moment, especially at a person's birth; horoscope.

Ho·ro·witz (hôr′ə-wits, hor′-), **Vladimir,** born 1904, U.S. pianist born in Russia.

hor·ren·dous (hô-ren′dəs, ho-) *adj.* Horrible; frightful. [< L *horrendus* < *horrere* to bristle] **— hor·ren′dous·ly** *adv.*

hor·rent (hôr′ənt, hor′-) *adj. Rare* 1. Bristling. 2. Horrified. [< L *horrens, -entis,* ppr. of *horrere* to bristle]

hor·ri·ble (hôr′ə-bəl, hor′-) *adj.* 1. Exciting or tending to excite horror; frightful; shocking. 2. *Informal* Inordinate; excessive: a *horrible* liar. 3. *Informal* Unpleasant; ugly: a *horrible* day. [< F < L *horribilis* < *horrere* to bristle] **— hor′ri·ble·ness** *n.* **— hor′ri·bly** *adv.*

hor·rid (hôr′id, hor′-) *adj.* 1. Causing great aversion or horror; dreadful. 2. *Informal* Very objectionable; offensive. 3. *Archaic* Bristling. [< L *horridus* bristling < *horrere* to bristle] **— hor′rid·ly** *adv.* **— hor′rid·ness** *n.*

hor·rif·ic (hô-rif′ik, ho-) *adj.* Causing horror; horrible.

hor·ri·fy (hôr′ə-fī, hor′-) *v.t.* **·fied, ·fy·ing** 1. To affect or fill with horror. 2. *Informal* To shock or surprise painfully; startle. **— hor′ri·fi·ca′tion** *n.*

hor·rip·i·la·tion (hô-rip′ə-lā′shən, ho-) *n.* Goose flesh. [< L *horripilare* < *horrere* to bristle + *pilus* hair]

hor·ror (hôr′ər, hor′-) *n.* 1. A painful, strong emotion caused by extreme fear, dread, repugnance, etc. 2. One who or that which excites such an emotion. 3. *Often pl.* A quality that excites horror: the *horrors* of crime. 4. Great aversion; loathing: a *horror* of cats. 5. *Informal* Something disagreeable, ugly, etc.: The rug was a *horror.* 6. *Obs.* A shuddering or bristling. **— Syn.** See FEAR. **— the horrors** *Informal* 1. The blues. 2. Delirium tremens. [< L]

Hor·sa (hôr′sə) See under HENGIST.

hors de com·bat (ôr də kôn̄·bà′) *French* Out of the fight; out of action.

hors d'oeuvre (ôr dûrv′, *Fr.* ôr dœ′vr′) An appetizer, as olives, celery, etc., generally served before a meal. ♦ This form is both singular and plural in French. An English plural, **hors d'oeuvres,** is also seen. [< F]

horse (hôrs) *n. pl.* **hors·es** or **horse** 1. A large, strong, herbivorous mammal (*Equus caballus*) with solid hoofs and a long mane and tail, employed in the domestic state as a draft or pack animal or for riding. ♦ Collateral adjective: *equine.* 2. The full-grown male horse as contrasted with the mare; a gelding or stallion. 3. *Zool.* Any of various animals belonging to the horse family (*Equidae*), as the ass, zebra, etc. 4. Any of various extinct mammals (family *Equidae*) related to or of the ancestral line of the horse, as the eohippus. 5. Mounted soldiers; cavalry: a regiment of *horse.* 6. A contrivance upon which a person may sit, ride, etc., as if on horseback. 7. A device, generally having four legs, for holding or supporting something: often in combination: *clotheshorse.* 8. In gymnastics, a wooden leather-covered block on four legs, used for vaulting and other exercises. 9. A man: a friendly, joking, or opprobrious term. 10. *Mining* A mass of rock, similar to the wall rock, found in a vein of ore. 11. *Informal* In chess, a knight. 12. *U.S. Slang* In schools, a translation or other similar aid used illicitly by students in working out lessons; pony. 13. *U.S. Slang* Heroin. **— a horse of another** (or **a different**) **color** A completely different matter. **— out of** (or **straight from**) **the horse's mouth** From the most direct and reliable source. **— to back the wrong horse** 1. To make a bet on a horse that loses a race. 2. To support a cause already lost. **— to be** (or **get**) **on one's high horse** *Informal* To act haughtily or scornfully. **— to hold one's horses** *Informal* To restrain one's impetuosity or impatience. **— To horse!** A command for cavalry troops to mount. **— *v.* horsed, hors·ing** *v.t.* 1. To furnish with a horse or horses. 2. To put on horseback. 3.

To place on another's back or on a sawhorse for flogging; also, to flog. 4. *U.S. Slang* To subject to horseplay or ridicule. **— *v.i.* 5.** To mount or ride on a horse. 6. *Slang* To engage in horseplay: often with *around.* **— *adj.* 1.** Of or pertaining to a horse or horses. 2. Mounted on horses. 3. Large for its kind: *horse* chestnut. [OE *hors*]

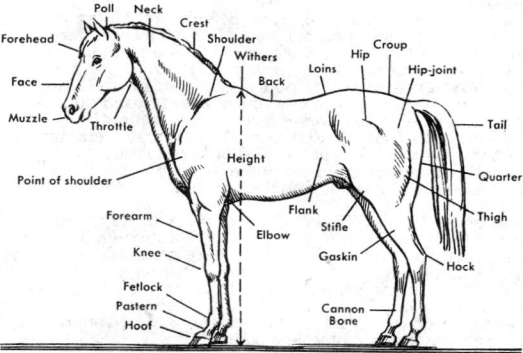

HORSE (Anatomical nomenclature)

[Labels: Poll, Neck, Crest, Shoulder, Withers, Loins, Hip, Croup, Hip-joint, Forehead, Back, Tail, Face, Quarter, Muzzle, Throttle, Height, Thigh, Point of shoulder, Forearm, Flank, Stifle, Elbow, Gaskin, Knee, Hock, Fetlock, Cannon Bone, Pastern, Hoof]

horse·back (hôrs′bak′) *n.* 1. A horse's back. 2. A ridge of earth or rock; hogback. **— *adv.*** On a horse's back.

horse·block (hôrs′blok′) *n.* A block or platform used in mounting or dismounting from a horse.

horse·car (hôrs′kär′) 1. A tramcar drawn by horses. 2. A car for transporting horses.

horse chestnut 1. Any of various trees (genus *Aesculus*) of Asian origin, having digitate leaves, clusters of flowers, and large chestnutlike fruits: also called, especially in the United States, *buckeye.* 2. The fruit of this tree.

horse·cloth (hôrs′klôth′, -kloth′) *n.* A cloth or blanket to cover the back of a horse, either for warmth or as a trapping.

horse·draw·ing (hôrs′drô′ing) *n. Canadian* A contest in which horses or teams pull a loaded stoneboat.

horse·fish (hôrs′fish′) *n. pl.* **·fish** or **·fish·es** The moonfish.

horse·flesh (hôrs′flesh′) *n.* 1. The flesh of a horse, especially as used for food. 2. Horses collectively.

horse·fly (hôrs′flī′) *n. pl.* **·flies** 1. Any of various large, robust flies (family *Tabanidae*), the female of which sucks the blood of horses, cattle, etc. 2. Any of various other flies that pester horses, as the botfly.

horse gentian Any of several perennial, weedy herbs (genus *Triosteum*) of the honeysuckle family, especially the feverwort.

Horse Guards 1. A body of cavalry serving as house guards; especially, the personal escort of the British sovereign. 2. *Informal* A building opposite Whitehall, London, serving as the headquarters of the Horse Guards.

horse·hair (hôrs′hâr′) *n.* 1. The hair of horses, especially that of their manes and tails. 2. A fabric made of such hair; haircloth. **— *adj.* 1.** Of, pertaining to, or made of horsehair. 2. Covered with haircloth, as furniture. 3. Stuffed with horsehair, as furniture, mattresses, etc.

horsehair snake A hairworm.

horse·hide (hôrs′hīd′) *n.* 1. The hide of a horse. 2. Leather made from a horse's hide.

horse latitudes *Naut.* A belt of high pressure at about 35° north or south latitude, characterized by calms and light variable winds, with diminishing to prevailing westerlies toward the poles and trade winds toward the equator.

horse·laugh (hôrs′laf′, -läf′) *n.* A loud, scornful laugh.

horse·leech (hôrs′lēch′) *n.* 1. A large leech (genus *Haemopis*), said to enter the nostrils of horses, etc., that drink from ponds. 2. *Archaic* A veterinarian. Also **horse′leach′.**

horse·less (hôrs′lis) *adj.* 1. Not possessing a horse. 2. Formerly, not requiring a horse to provide motive power.

horse mackerel 1. A carangoid fish (*Trachurus symmetricus*) of Pacific waters. 2. A tuna (*Thunnus thynnus*).

horse·man (hôrs′mən) *n. pl.* **·men** (-mən) 1. A man who rides a horse. 2. A cavalryman. 3. A man who is skilled in riding or handling horses.

horse·man·ship (hôrs′mən·ship) *n.* The art of riding and managing horses; equestrian skill.

horse marine 1. A member of an imaginary corps of mounted marines. 2. One who is as awkward and out of place as a mounted marine on shipboard; misfit. 3. A mounted marine or sailor on duty ashore.

horse·mint (hôrs′mint′) *n.* 1. An erect American herb (*Monarda punctata*) of the mint family: also called *wild bergamot.* 2. Either of two European woodland mints (*Mentha longifolia* and *M. aquatica*), both naturalized in America.

horse nettle A rough roadside weed (*Solanum carolinense*) with straw-colored prickles, white flowers, and yellow berries, found in the central and southern United States.

horse opera *U.S. Slang* A motion picture dealing with cowboys, Indians, cattle thieves, etc.

horse pistol A large pistol formerly carried in a holster by horsemen.

horse·play (hôrs′plā′) *n.* Rough, boisterous play or fun.

horse·pow·er (hôrs′pou′ər) *n. Mech.* The standard theoretical unit of the rate of work, equal to 550 pounds lifted one foot in one second. Abbr. **hp, h.p., HP, H.P.**

horse·pow·er-hour (hôrs′pou′ər·our′) *n. Mech.* A measure of work performed or the amount of energy used up in working at the rate of one horsepower in one hour.

horse·rad·ish (hôrs′rad′ish) *n.* **1.** A coarse, common garden herb (*Armoracia lapathifolia*) of the mustard family. **2.** A condiment made from its pungent root.

horse sense *Informal* Innate practical intelligence; common sense.

horse·shoe (hôrs′shōō′, hôrs′-) *n.* **1.** A piece of metal, U-shaped to fit the edge of a horse's hoof, to which it is nailed as a protective device. **2.** Something resembling a horseshoe in shape. **3.** *pl.* A game similar to quoits, in which the object is to throw horseshoes over or near a stake. — *v.t.* **·shoed, ·shoe·ing** To furnish with horseshoes.

horseshoe crab A large marine arthropod (*Limulus polyphemus*) having a horseshoe-shaped carapace, a posterior shield composed of the abdominal segments, and a long telson: also called *king crab*.

horse·tail (hôrs′tāl′) *n.* **1.** The tail of a horse. **2.** Formerly, in Turkey, a horsetail used singly or in two's or three's as a symbol of a pasha's rank. **3.** A perennial, pteridophytic plant (genus *Equisetum*) of wide distribution, and having jointed, hollow stems; the scouring rush.

HORSESHOE CRAB
A Carapace seen from above. B Under side:
1. Carapace.
2. Cephalothorax.
3. Oral appendages.
4. Ambulatory legs.
5. Operculum.
6. Abdomen.
7. Telson.

horse·weed (hôrs′wēd′) *n.* A common North American weed (*Erigeron canadensis*) of the composite family: also called *butterweed*.

horse·whip (hôrs′hwip′) *n.* A whip for managing horses. — *v.t.* **·whipped**, **·whip·ping** To flog with a horsewhip.

horse·wom·an (hôrs′wŏŏm′ən) *n. pl.* **·wom·en** (-wim′in) **1.** A woman who rides on horseback. **2.** A woman who is skilled in riding or managing horses.

horst (hôrst) *n. Geol.* A portion of the earth's crust that has been elevated and separated from the surrounding land by faults. Also **horste.** [< G]

hors·y (hôr′sē) *adj.* **hors·i·er, hors·i·est** **1.** Pertaining to, suggestive of, or having the nature of a horse or horses. **2.** Associated with or devoted to horses, horseracing, fox hunting, etc. **3.** *Slang* Gross or coarse in appearance, manner, etc. Also **hors′ey.** — **hors′i·ly** *adv.* — **hors′i·ness** *n.*

hort. Horticulture; horticultural.

hor·ta·tive (hôr′tə·tiv) *adj.* Hortatory. [< L *hortativus*, pp. of *hortari* to urge] — **hor′ta·tive·ly** *adv.*

hor·ta·to·ry (hôr′tə·tôr′ē, -tō′rē) *adj.* **1.** Of, characterized by, or giving exhortation or encouragement. **2.** *Gram.* Pertaining to a mood used in some languages to express exhortation, encouragement, etc., or to the imperative or subjunctive moods when used in this manner. [< L *hortatorius*]

Hor·thy von Nagy·bá·nya (hôr′tē fôn nod′y′·bä′nyä), **Nicolaus**, Hungarian admiral and statesman, regent of Hungary 1920–44: called **Admiral Horthy.**

hor·ti·cul·ture (hôr′tə·kul′chər) *n.* **1.** The cultivation of a garden. **2.** The art or science of growing garden vegetables, fruits, flowers, ornamental shrubs, etc. Abbr. **hort.** [< L *hortus* garden + *cultura* cultivation] — **hor′ti·cul′tur·al** *adj.* — **hor′ti·cul′tur·ist** *n.*

hor·tus sic·cus (hôr′təs sik′əs) *Latin* Literally, a dry garden; a herbarium.

Ho·rus (hō′rəs) In Egyptian mythology, the hawk-headed god of the sun.

Hos. Hosea.

ho·san·na (hō-zan′ə) *interj.* Praised be the Lord. — *n.* **1.** A cry of "hosanna." **2.** Any exultant expression of adoration or praise. [< LL < Gk. *hōsanna* < Hebrew *hōshi ähnnā* save, we pray]

hose (hōz) *n. pl.* **hose** (*Archaic* **hos·en**) *for defs. 1, 2;* **hos·es** *for def. 3* **1.** *pl.* Stockings or socks. **2.** *pl.* Formerly, a garment worn by men for covering the legs and lower part of the body like tight trousers. **3.** A flexible tube of rubber, plastic, etc., for conveying water and other fluids. — *v.t.* **hosed, hos·ing 1.** To water, drench, or douse with a hose. **2.** *Canadian Slang* To cheat or defeat. [OE *hosa*]

Ho·se·a (hō-zē′ə, -zā′ə) Eighth-century B.C. Hebrew prophet. — *n.* A book of the Old Testament bearing his name: also, in the Douai Bible, *Osee.*

ho·sier (hō′zhər) *n. Brit.* A dealer in or manufacturer of hose or material similar to that used in hose.

ho·sier·y (hō′zhər·ē) *n.* **1.** Stockings and socks of all types. **2.** *Brit.* The hosier's business.

hosp. Hospital.

hos·pice (hos′pis) *n.* A place of rest or shelter, usually maintained by a religious order for pilgrims, travelers, etc. [< F < L *hospitium* inn, hospitality < *hospes* host, guest]

hos·pi·ta·ble (hos′pi·tə·bəl, hos·pit′ə·bəl) *adj.* **1.** Behaving in a kind and generous manner toward guests; fond of entertaining guests. **2.** Affording or expressing welcome and generosity toward guests: a *hospitable* gesture. **3.** Receptive in mind: *hospitable* to new points of view. [< OF < L *hospitare* to entertain] — **hos′pi·ta·ble·ness** *n.* — **hos′pi·ta·bly** *adv.*

hos·pi·tal (hos′pi·tal) *n.* **1.** An institution that provides medical, surgical, or psychiatric treatment and nursing care for the ill or injured temporarily lodged there; also, the building used for this purpose. **2.** Formerly, a charitable institution for those in need of shelter and maintenance: a foundling *hospital.* **3.** Formerly, an inn or hospice for pilgrims and other travelers. [< OF < L *hospitalis* relating to a guest < *hospes* guest. Doublet of HOTEL, HOSTEL.]

hos·pi·tal·er (hos′pi·tal·ər) *n.* **1.** *Brit.* In certain London hospitals, originally religious establishments, the title of the chief religious officer or chaplain. **2.** Formerly, a member of a religious order devoting its services to the sick and needy. **3.** *Rare* One cared for in a hospital. Also **hos′pi·tal·ler.**

Hos·pi·tal·er (hos′pi·tal·ər) *n.* A member of a military religious order known as the **Knights of St. John of Jerusalem**, that originated in the early 11th century in a hospital built at Jerusalem to care for crusaders and pilgrims: also called *Knights Hospitaller.* Also **Hos′pi·tal·ler.**

hos·pi·tal·i·ty (hos′pə·tal′ə·tē) *n. pl.* **·ties** The spirit, practice, or act of being hospitable.

hos·pi·tal·ize (hos′pi·tal·īz′) *v.t.* **·ized, ·iz·ing** To put in a hospital for treatment and care.

hos·pi·tal·i·za·tion (hos′pi·təl·ə·zā′shən, -ī·zā′shən) *n.* **1.** The act of hospitalizing. **2.** *U.S.* A form of insurance that guarantees all or partial payment of hospital expenses: also **hospital insurance.**

hos·pi·ti·um (hos·pish′ē·əm) *n. pl.* **·ti·a** (-ē·ə) *Archaic* An inn; hospice. [< L < *hospes* guest]

hos·po·dar (hos′pə·där) *n.* Formerly, a title of dignity given to the princes or governors of Moldavia and Wallachia. [< Rumanian, ult. < Slavic]

host¹ (hōst) *n.* **1.** A man who extends hospitality to others, usually to guests in his own home. **2.** *Biol.* Any living plant or animal from which a parasite obtains nourishment and protection. **3.** The landlord of an inn. — *v.t. Informal* To conduct or entertain in the role of a host: to *host* the VIPs around town. [< OF *hoste* < L *hospes* guest, host. Akin to GUEST, HOST².]

host² (hōst) *n.* **1.** A large number of men or things; a multitude. **2.** An army. — *Syn.* See ARMY. [< OF < L *hostis* enemy. Akin to GUEST, HOST¹.]

host³ (hōst) *n. Eccl. Sometimes cap.* The Eucharistic bread or wafer. [< OF *hoiste* < L *hostia* sacrificial victim]

hos·tage (hos′tij) *n.* **1.** A person given or held as a pledge until specified conditions are met, as in war. **2.** The state of any person so treated. **3.** A pledge or security. [< OF]

hos·tel (hos′təl) *n.* **1.** One of a chain of supervised lodging houses for young people on bicycle or hiking trips. **2.** *Archaic* An inn. [< OF < LL *hospitale* inn < *hospes* guest. Doublet of HOTEL, HOSPITAL.]

hos·tel·er (hos′təl·ər) *n. Archaic* An innkeeper.

hos·tel·ry (hos′təl·rē) *n. pl.* **·ries** *Archaic* An inn; hotel.

hostel school *Canadian* A federal boarding school for Eskimos and Indians, usually in the North.

host·ess (hōs′tis) *n.* **1.** A woman who performs the duties of a host. **2.** A woman employed in a restaurant, etc., to greet and serve guests. **3.** A woman paid to dance with the patrons of a public dance hall. **4.** A female innkeeper.

hos·tile (hos′təl, *esp. Brit.* -tīl) *adj.* **1.** Having or expressing enmity or opposition; antagonistic; unfriendly. **2.** Of, pertaining to, or characteristic of an enemy: *hostile* acts; *hostile* forces. [< F < L *hostilis*] — **hos′tile·ly** *adv.*

hos·til·i·ty (hos·til′ə·tē) *n. pl.* **·ties 1.** The state of being hostile. **2.** A hostile act. **3.** *pl.* War or acts of war. — **Syn.** See ENMITY.

hos·tler (hos′lər, os′-) *n.* A stableman; groom: also spelled *ostler.* [< OF *hostelier* innkeeper]

hot (hot) *adj.* **hot·ter, hot·test 1.** Having or giving off great heat; having a high temperature: a *hot* oven. **2.** Having a relatively high degree of heat; very warm: a *hot* day. **3.** Feeling or showing abnormal bodily warmth: a *hot* forehead. **4.** Giving the sensation of heat or burning to the tongue or skin: *hot* pepper. **5.** Carrying an electric current, especially one of high voltage. **6.** Dangerously radioactive. **7.** Constantly in action or use: War news kept the wires *hot.* **8.** In hunting, strong or fresh, as a scent. **9.** Not far behind; close: in *hot* pursuit. **10.** In some games, close to the hidden object or the solution sought. **11.** Marked by or showing strong or violent emotion; excited; passionate: *hot* words. **12.** Marked by intense activity; raging; violent: a *hot* battle. **13.** *Slang* Exciting; lively: a *hot* town tonight. **14.** *Slang* Lustful; sexy. **15.** *Slang* Strongly disposed toward; eager;

enthusiastic: often with *for: hot* for jazz. **16.** *Informal* Controversial: a *hot* issue. **17.** *Informal* So new as to not have lost its freshness, currency, excitement, etc.: a *hot* item. **18.** *Slang* Excellent, skillful, lucky, etc.: He is not so *hot* tonight. **19.** *U.S. Slang* Recently stolen or illegally procured: a *hot* car; also, wanted by the police: the *hottest* criminal in town. **20.** *Slang* Dangerous or uncomfortable: This town got too *hot* for him. **21.** *Music Slang* **a** Designating jazz marked by a fast tempo, heavily accented beat, exciting improvisations, etc. **b** Playing or performing such jazz: a *hot* trumpet. — **in hot water** *Informal* In trouble. — **to make it hot for** *Informal* To make the situation extremely uncomfortable for. — *adv.* In a hot manner. [OE *hāt*] — **hot′ly** *adv.* — **hot′· ness** *n.*

hot air *Slang* Empty or pretentious talk; exaggeration.
hot·bed (hot′bed′) *n.* **1.** A bed of rich earth, protected by glass and warmed usually by fermenting manure, used to promote the growth of plants in advance of their season. **2.** A place or condition favoring rapid growth or great activity: a *hotbed* of corruption.
hot-blood·ed (hot′blud′id) *adj.* Easily moved or excited; passionate; amorous; impulsive.
hot·box (hot′boks′) *n.* The journal box of a railroad car or other wheeled vehicle when overheated by friction.
hot cake A pancake or griddlecake. — **to go** (or **sell**) **like hot cakes** *Informal* To be disposed of quickly.
hotch (hoch) *v.t. & v.i. Scot. & Brit. Dial.* To shake; fidget.
hotch·pot (hoch′pot) *n. Law* A bringing together and mixing of property of different persons in order to divide it equally. [< OF *hochepot.* Cf. MDu. *hutspot.*]
hotch·potch (hoch′poch) *n.* **1.** A hodgepodge. **2.** *Law* A hotchpot. [Var. of HOTCHPOT]
hot cross bun A circular cake or bun marked with a cross of frosting, eaten especially during Lent.
hot dog *Informal* A cooked frankfurter, usually grilled, served in a split roll, and garnished with mustard, relish, etc.
ho·tel (hō·tel′) *n.* **1.** An establishment or building providing lodging, food, and other services to travelers and long-term residents. **2.** In France, an official residence or private mansion in a city or town. **3.** *Canadian* Beer parlor. [< F *hôtel* < OF *hostel* inn. Doublet of HOSTEL, HOSPITAL.]
hô·tel de ville (ō·tel′ de vēl′) *French* A town hall.
hô·tel Dieu (ō·tel′ dyœ′) *French* A hospital.
hot·foot (hot′fŏŏt′) *Informal n.* The practical joke of furtively wedging a match between the upper and sole of a victim's shoe, lighting it, and letting it burn down. — *v.i.* To hurry; go quickly: often with *it.* — *adv.* In all haste.
hot·head (hot′hed′) *n.* A hotheaded person.
hot·head·ed (hot′hed′id) *adj.* **1.** Quick-tempered. **2.** Impetuous. — **hot′head′ed·ly** *adv.* — **hot′head′ed·ness** *n.*
hot·house (hot′hous′) *n.* A greenhouse kept warm artificially for the growth of out-of-season or delicate plants.
Ho·tien (hō′tyen′) The Chinese name for KHOTAN.
hot line A direct means of communication; especially, a telephone line for emergency use by heads of state of nuclear powers, or for immediate communication between an official and his chief subordinates.
hot plate **1.** A heated metal plate for maintaining at a uniform temperature anything set upon it. **2.** A small portable gas or electric stove.
hot pot *Chiefly Brit.* A dish of meat stewed with potatoes in a covered pot.
hot-press (hot′pres′) *v.t.* To subject to heat and mechanical pressure, as for giving a gloss to paper or cloth, for extracting oil, etc. — *n.* A machine for hotpressing.
hot rod *U.S. Slang* An automobile, usually an older model, modified for high speeds.
hot seat *U.S. Slang* The electric chair.
hot spring A natural spring emitting waters with a temperature of 98° F. or above: also called *thermal spring.*
Hot Springs A city in central Arkansas (pop. 35,631), near Hot Springs National Park, a resort area, containing mineral and thermal springs.
hot·spur (hot′spûr′) *n.* An impetuous, headstrong person; a hothead. [after nickname of Sir Henry Percy]
Hot·ten·tot (hot′ən·tot) *n.* **1.** A member of a South African people believed to be related to both the Bantus and the Bushmen. **2.** The language of this people, related to and having some of the clicks of Bushman. — *adj.* Of or pertaining to the Hottentots or their language.
Hottentot bread The elephant's-foot, a plant.
hou·dah (hou′də) See HOWDAH.
Hou·dan (hōō′dan) *n.* A breed of domestic fowl originating in France, having mottled black and white plumage and a V-shaped comb. [after *Houdan*, a town in France]
Hou·di·ni (hōō·dē′nē), **Harry**, 1874–1926, U.S. magician and author: original name **Ehrich Weiss** (wīs).
Hou·don (ōō·dôn′), **Jean Antoine**, 1741?–1828, French sculptor.
hound[1] (hound) *n.* **1.** A dog of any of several breeds kept for hunting, especially one that hunts by scent and in a pack.

2. A dog of any breed. **3.** A mean, detestable man. **4.** In the game of hare and hounds, one who acts the part of a hound. **5.** *U.S. Slang* One fond of a specific pastime, activity, food, etc.: a bridge *hound.* — **to follow** (or **ride to**) **the hounds** To engage in hunting (a fox, etc.) on horseback and with a pack of hounds. — *v.t.* **1.** To hunt with or as with hounds; pursue relentlessly. **2.** To incite to pursue. **3.** *Informal* To nag persistently; pester. [OE *hund* dog]
hound[2] (hound) *n.* **1.** *Naut.* One of the projections at the head of a mast that supports the top trestletrees and lower rigging. **2.** A brace used to strengthen the running gear of a vehicle. [ME *houn* < ON *hūnn* knob]
hound's-tongue (houndz′tung′) *n.* **1.** A coarse weed (*Cynoglossum officinale*) of the borage family, with reddish flowers, prickly nutlets, and hairy leaves shaped like a dog's tongue: also called *dog's tongue.* **2.** Any of various other plants of the same genus.
hound's-tooth check (houndz′tōōth′) A design of small, broken checks in cloth, especially worsteds.
hour (our) *n.* **1.** A space of time equal to 1/24 of a civil day; sixty minutes. ◆ Collateral adjective: *horal.* **2.** Any one of the twelve points on a timepiece indicating such a space of time: The train leaves on the *hour.* **3.** A definite time of day as shown in hours and minutes by a timepiece: The *hour* is 6:15. **4.** An indefinite, but usually short, period of time: The happiest *hour* of one's life. **5.** A particular or regularly fixed time for some activity: the cocktail *hour.* **6.** *pl.* A set period of time for work or other regular pursuits: office *hours*; school *hours.* **7.** *pl.* One's usual time of rising and of going to bed: to keep regular *hours.* **8.** The present time or current situation: the topic of the *hour.* **9.** Distance calculated by the time ordinarily required to cover it: an *hour* away from home. **10.** In education: **a** A single class session or period, usually 50 minutes long. **b** A unit of credit in college and university study, one credit usually given each semester for a class meeting one hour weekly. **11.** *Eccl.* **a** The canonical hours (which see). **b** The office or prayers recited or sung at these hours. **12.** *Astron.* **a** A sidereal hour (which see). **b** An angular measure of right ascension or longitude, being 15 degrees or the 24th part of a great circle of the sphere. Abbr. *h., H., hr.* — **after hours** After the prescribed hours of work, school, etc. — **one's hour** The time of one's death. — **the small** (or **wee**) **hours** The early hours of the morning. [< L *hora* < Gk. *hōra* time, period]
hour circle *Astron.* Any great circle that passes through the poles of the celestial sphere and intersects the celestial equator at right angles.
hour·glass (our′glas′, -gläs′) *n.* An old device for measuring time, consisting of two globular glass vessels connected by a narrow neck through which a quantity of sand, mercury, or water runs from the upper vessel to the lower during a stated interval of time, usually an hour.

HOURGLASS

hour hand The hand that indicates the hour on a clock or similar timepiece.
hou·ri (hōō′rē, hour′ē) *n.* In Moslem belief, one of the beautiful virgins allotted to those who attain Paradise. [< F < Persian *hūri* < Arabic *hūrīyah* black-eyed woman]
hour·ly (our′lē) *adj.* **1.** Of, happening, or performed every hour. **2.** Occurring or accomplished in the course of an hour: an *hourly* production rate. **3.** Frequent. — *adv.* **1.** At intervals of an hour; every hour. **2.** Hour by hour: to hope *hourly* for something. **3.** Frequently; often.
Hours (ourz) *n.pl.* In Greek mythology, the Horae.
house (*n.* hous; *v.* houz) *n. pl.* **hous·es** (hou′zəz) **1.** A building intended as a dwelling for human beings, especially one used as the residence of a family or single tenant. **2.** A household; family. **3.** The abode of a fraternity, religious community, or other group living together as a unit. **4.** A dormitory or resident hall, especially in a college or university; also, the group of students residing there. **5.** *Brit.* A college in a university. **6.** Anything providing shelter or protection to an animal, as the shell of a snail. **7.** A structure for storing or sheltering something, as goods, plants, animals, etc. **8.** A building used for any of various purposes: a *house* of correction. **9.** A place of worship, as a church or synagogue. **10.** A theater or other place of entertainment. **11.** The audience in such a place of entertainment. **12.** *Govt.* **a** A legislative or deliberative body: *House* of Representatives. **b** A quorum of such a body. **c** The chamber or building such a body occupies. **13.** An advisory or legislative group, especially in academic or ecclesiastical matters: the *house* of bishops. **14.** *Often cap.* A line of ancestors and descendants regarded as forming a single family: the *House* of Stuart. **15.** A business firm or establishment: a publishing *house.* **16.** In astrology: **a** One of the twelve divisions of the heavens, made by projecting great circles through the north and south points of the horizon, used in casting horoscopes. **b** A sign of the zodiac considered as the seat of greatest influence of a particular planet. **17.** *Slang*

A brothel. *Abbr.* ho. **— like a house on fire** Very quickly and vigorously. **— on the house** At the expense of the proprietor; free of charge. **— to bring down the house** To receive loud and enthusiastic applause. **— to clean house** *U.S. Slang* To get rid of undesirable conditions or persons, as in an organization. **— to keep house** To manage the affairs or work of a home **— to put** (or **set**) **one's house in order** To tidy up one's personal or business affairs. **—** *v.* **housed, hous·ing** *v.t.* **1.** To take or put into a house; furnish with a house; lodge. **2.** To store in a house or building. **3.** In carpentry, to fit into a mortise, joint, etc. **4.** *Naut.* To place in a secure or safe position, as in time of storms. **—** *v.i.* **5.** To take lodgings; dwell. [OE *hūs*] **— house′ful** *n.*

House (hous), **Edward Mandell**, 1858–1938, U.S. diplomat; adviser to President Wilson: called **Colonel House**.

house arrest Legal detention in one's own house.

house·boat (hous′bōt′) *n.* A barge or flat-bottomed boat fitted out as a dwelling and used in quiet waters.

house·boy (hous′boi′) *n.* A houseman.

house·break·ing (hous′brā′king) *n.* **1.** The act of breaking into and entering another's home with intent to commit theft or some other felony. **2.** *Brit.* The act of demolishing or razing old buildings. **— house′break′er** *n.*

house·bro·ken (hous′brō′kən) *adj.* Trained to urinate and defecate outdoors or in a specific place, as a dog.

house·carl (hous′kärl) *n.* A member of the bodyguard or household troops of a Danish or early English king or noble. [OE *hūscarl* < ON *hūskarl* < *hūs* house + *karl* churl, man]

house·coat (hous′kōt′) *n.* A woman's garment, usually long with a loose skirt, for informal wear within the house.

house·dress (hous′dres′) *n.* A dress, usually of printed cotton fabric, worn especially during household chores.

house finch A small, red-breasted finch (*Carpodacus mexicanus*) of western North America: also called *linnet*.

house·fly (hous′flī′) *n.* *pl.* **·flies** The common fly (*Musca domestica*), found in nearly all parts of the world, often an agent in transmitting certain diseases. For illustration see INSECTS (injurious).

house guest A guest invited to stay one or more nights.

house·hold (hous′hōld′) *n.* **1.** A number of persons dwelling as a unit under one roof; especially, a family living together, including servants, etc. **2.** A home or the various domestic affairs of a home. **—** *adj.* Of or pertaining to the home; domestic. [< HOUSE + HOLD, n.]

house·hold·er (hous′hōl′dər) *n.* **1.** One who owns a house, or occupies a house as if it were his own. **2.** The head of a family. **3.** *Law* In Great Britain, one who occupies a house so as to qualify him for the exercise of the franchise.

household troops A special body of soldiers assigned to protect a sovereign, his family, and his residence.

household word A person, product, place, etc., that is known or familiar to many people. Also **household name.**

house·keep·er (hous′kē′pər) *n.* **1.** One who performs the tasks of maintaining a home, as a housewife. **2.** A paid employee who manages the various domestic affairs of a home.

house·keep·ing (hous′kē′ping) *n.* The performance or management of household tasks or affairs.

hou·sel (hou′zəl) *Obs. n.* The Eucharist. **—** *v.t.* **hou·seled** or **·selled, hou·sel·ing** or **·sel·ling** To administer the Eucharist to. [OE *hūsl*]

house·leek (hous′lēk′) *n.* An Old World garden plant (*Sempervivum tectorum*), having pink flowers and thick, fleshy leaves, and usually found growing on walls and roofs.

house·line (hous′līn′) *n.* *Naut.* A small three-stranded line of fine-dressed hemp, used for seizings, etc.

house·maid (hous′mād′) *n.* A girl or woman employed to do housework.

housemaid's knee *Pathol.* A chronic inflammation of the bursa in front of the knee.

house·man (hous′mən) *n.* *pl.* **·men** (-mən) A handyman employed to do heavy work about a house, hotel, etc.: also called *houseboy.*

house·mas·ter (hous′mas′tər, -mäs′-) *n.* *Chiefly Brit.* A teacher in charge of one of the houses of a boys' school.

house·moth·er (hous′muth′ər) *n.* A woman acting as a supervisor or housekeeper for a group of people living together, as in a dormitory, fraternity house, etc.

House of Burgesses In colonial times, the lower house of the legislature of Virginia.

house of cards A weak, unstable organization, plan, etc.

House of Commons 1. The lower house of the British Parliament, the members of which are elected. **2.** The lower house of the Canadian Parliament. *Abbr.* H.C.

house of correction An institution confining those given short-term sentences for minor offenses and considered to be capable of rehabilitation.

House of Delegates The lower house of the legislature in Maryland, Virginia, and West Virginia.

House of Keys See under KEYS.

House of Lords The upper and nonelective house of the British Parliament, made up of the peerage and the highest ranking clergy. *Abbr.* H.L.

House of Representatives 1. The lower, larger branch of the United States Congress, and of many State legislatures,

composed of members elected on the basis of population. **2.** A similar legislative body, as in Australia, Mexico, etc.

house organ A publication regularly issued by a business organization for its employees and customers.

house party An entertainment of a group of guests for several days, usually in a country or beach house or a college fraternity; also, the guests.

house physician A physician resident by appointment in a hospital, hotel, or other institution.

house-rais·ing (hous′rā′zing) In rural communities, a social gathering of neighbors to help erect a new house.

house·room (hous′rōōm′, -rōōm′) *n.* Room or lodging in a house; accommodation.

house sparrow A sparrow (def. 1).

house·top (hous′top′) *n.* The roof of a house. **— to shout** (or **proclaim, cry,** etc.) **from the housetops** To give wide publicity to; publish abroad.

house·wares (hous′wârz′) *n.* Kitchen utensils, dishes, glassware, and other wares used in the home.

house·warm·ing (hous′wôr′ming) *n.* A party held by or for those who have just moved into new living quarters.

house·wife (hous′wīf′ for def. 1, huz′if for def. 2) *n.* *pl.* **house·wives** (hous′wīvz′) for def. 1; **house·wives** (huz′ifs) or **house·wives** (huz′ivz) for def. 2 **1.** A married woman who manages the affairs of her own household as a full-time occupation; homemaker. **2.** *Chiefly Brit.* A small kit holding sewing articles: also called *hussy*; also spelled *huswife.*

house·wife·ly (hous′wīf′lē) *adj.* Characteristic of or pertaining to a housewife who is orderly, thrifty, etc. **—** *adv.* In the manner of a good housewife.

house·wife·ry (hous′wī′fər·ē, -wīf′rē) *n.* The duties of a housewife; housekeeping.

house·work (hous′wûrk′) *n.* The chores involved in keeping house, washing, cooking, etc.

house wren See under WREN.

hous·ing[1] (hou′zing) *n.* **1.** The act of providing shelter or lodging: the *housing* of war victims; also, the shelter or lodging so provided. **2.** The providing of houses on a large scale: the *housing* of low-income families. **3.** Houses or dwellings collectively. **4.** That which serves as a shelter, cover, etc.: a bamboo *housing* for plants. **5.** A slot, groove, notch, or the like cut in a piece of wood, etc., for the reception of another piece. **6.** A niche, as for a statue. **7.** *Mech.* **a** Something that holds part of a machine in place, as a frame or set of brackets. **b** A casing or cover for a machine or part of a machine. **8.** *Naut.* The part of a mast below the decks.

hous·ing[2] (hou′zing) *n.* **1.** An ornamental cover for a horse. **2.** *Usually pl.* Trappings. [< OF *houce*, prob. < Gmc.]

housing project An institutionally owned residential complex, usually comprising a group of apartment buildings.

Hous·man (hous′mən), **A(lfred) E(dward)**, 1859–1936, English poet and classical scholar.

Hous·ton (hyōōs′tən), **Sam**, 1793–1863, U.S. general and politician; first president of the Republic of Texas 1836–38, 1841–44.

Hous·ton (hyōōs′tən) A city in SE Texas; pop. 1,232,802.

hous·to·ni·a (hōōs·tō′nē·ə) *n.* Any of various low, slender North American plants (genus *Houstonia*) of the madder family, especially the common bluet (*H. caerulea*). [after Dr. William *Houston*, 1695–1733, English naturalist]

Hou·yhn·hnm (hōō·in′əm, hwin′əm) In Swift's *Gulliver's Travels*, one of a race of horses possessing reason and all the noble qualities of ideal man and ruling over the Yahoos. See YAHOO. [Imit. of the whinny of a horse]

hove (hōv) Past tense of HEAVE.

hov·el (huv′əl, hov′-) *n.* **1.** A small, wretched dwelling. **2.** A low, open shed for sheltering cattle, tools, etc. **— Syn.** See HUT. **—** *v.t.* **hov·eled** or **·elled, hov·el·ing** or **·el·ling** To shelter or lodge in a hovel. [? Dim. of OE *hof* building]

hov·er (huv′ər, hov′-) *v.i.* **1.** To remain suspended in or near one place in the air. **2.** To linger or remain nearby, as if watching: with *around, near,* etc. **3.** To remain in an uncertain or irresolute state: with *between:* to *hover* between sleeping and waking. **— Syn.** See FLY[1]. **—** *n.* The act or state of hovering. [< obs. *hove* to float] **— hov′er·er** *n.*

Hov·er·craft (huv′ər·kraft′, hov′-, -kräft′) *n.* A vehicle designed to travel just above the surface of land or water on a cushion of air generated by powerful fans: a trade name. Also **hov′er·craft.**

how[1] (hou) *adv.* **1.** In what way or manner: *How* was it done? **2.** To what degree, extent, or amount: I saw *how* courageously he acted. **3.** In what state, or condition: *How* do you feel? **4.** For what reason or purpose: I can't see *how* he came to do it. **5.** At what price; for what sum: *How* is the stock selling today? **6.** To what effect; with what meaning: *How* did he intend that remark to be taken? **7.** By what name or designation: *How* about having lunch? **8.** *Informal* What: *How* about having lunch? **—** *n.* A manner, method, or means of doing. **— how come?** or **how so?** *Informal* How does it happen to be so?; Why? [OE *hū*]

how[2] (hou) *interj.* An expression of greeting attributed to and used humorously in imitation of American Indians.

How·ard (hou′ərd), **Catherine**, died 1542, fifth wife of Henry VIII of England; executed.

how·be·it (hou·bē′it) *adv. Archaic* Nevertheless; be that as it may. — *conj. Obs.* Although.

how·dah (hou′də) *n.* A seat for riders on an elephant or camel, often fitted with a canopy. [< Hind. *haudah*]

how·die (hou′dē, ou′-, hō′-, ŏ′-) *n. Scot.* A midwife.

how-do-you-do (hou′də-yə-dŏŏ′) *n. Informal* An embarrassing or difficult situation: usually preceded by *fine, pretty, nice,* etc. Also **how-d'ye-do** (hou′dyə-dŏŏ′).

How do you do? What is the state of your health?: a conventional phrase used as a formal greeting when being introduced to or meeting a person.

how·dy (hou′dē) *interj. Informal* An expression of greeting. [Contr. of HOW DO YOU (DO)?]

Howe (hou), **Elias,** 1819–67, U.S. machinist; invented the sewing machine. — **Julia Ward,** 1819–1910, U.S. poet and reformer. — **Richard,** 1725–99, Earl Howe, British admiral in the American Revolution. — **William,** 1729–1814, fifth Viscount Howe, British general in the American Revolution; brother of Richard Howe.

How·ells (hou′əlz), **William Dean,** 1837–1920, U.S. novelist and editor.

how·ev·er (hou·ev′ər) *adv.* **1.** In whatever manner; by whatever means. **2.** To whatever degree or extent: Spend *however* much it costs. — *conj.* Nevertheless; in spite of; still; yet. — **Syn.** See BUT[1]. Also **how·e′er** (-âr′).

how·it·zer (hou′it·sər) *n.* A cannon with a barrel of medium length using shells of low muzzle velocity and operating at a relatively high angle of fire. [< Du. *houwitzer,* ult. < Czechoslovakian *houfnice* catapult]

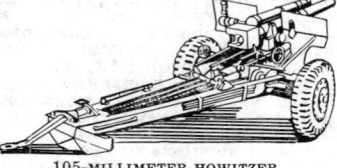

105-MILLIMETER HOWITZER

howk (hōk) *v.t. & v.i. Brit. Dial.* To dig: also spelled **holk.**

howl (houl) *v.i.* **1.** To utter the loud, mournful wail of a dog, wolf, or other animal. **2.** To utter such a cry in pain, grief, or rage. **3.** To make a sound similar to this: The storm *howled* all night. **4.** To laugh loudly: The audience *howled.* — *v.t.* **5.** To utter or express with howling: to *howl* one's disapproval. **6.** To condemn, suppress, or drive away by howling: often with *down.* — *n.* **1.** The wailing cry of a wolf, dog, or other animal. **2.** Any howling sound. [ME *houlen.* Cf. G *heulen.*]

How·land Island An island in the central Pacific; 1 sq. mi.; site of a U.S. aerological station.

howl·er (hou′lər) *n.* **1.** One who or that which howls. **2.** Any of a group of monkeys (genus *Alouatta*) found in Central and South America, having a long, grasping tail and making loud howling sounds; as, the **ursine howler** (*A. seniculus*): also called **howling monkey. 3.** *Informal* An absurd blunder in speaking or writing.

how·let (hou′lit) *n. Archaic* An owl. [< F *hulotte*]

howl·ing (hou′ling) *adj.* **1.** Producing or uttering howls. **2.** Characterized by or filled with howls: the *howling* wilderness. **3.** *Slang* Very great; tremendous: a *howling* success.

How·rah (hou′rə) A city in NE India, on the Hooghly near Calcutta; pop. 613,757 (1965).

how·so·ev·er (hou′sō·ev′ər) *adv.* **1.** In whatever manner. **2.** To whatever degree or extent.

hoy[1] (hoi) *n.* **1.** A heavy barge or scow. **2.** An obsolete type of sailing barge, having one mast and used as a tender or as a vessel to sail along the coast. [< MDu. *hoei*]

hoy[2] (hoi) *interj.* Ho; hallo: a cry to attract attention. Compare AHOY. [Imit. Cf. Du. *hui!*]

hoy·den (hoid′n) *n.* A boisterous or ill-mannered girl; tomboy. — *adj.* Boisterous. — *v.i.* To act like a hoyden. Also spelled **hoiden.** [Origin uncertain] — **hoy′den·ish** *adj.* — **hoy′den·ish·ness** *n.*

Hoyle (hoil) *n.* A book of rules and instructions for indoor games, especially card games. — **according to Hoyle** Following the prescribed rules and regulations; acting fairly or correctly in any matter. [after Sir Edmund *Hoyle,* 1672–1769, English writer on whist and other card games]

HP or **hp, H.P.** or **h.p. 1.** High pressure. **2.** Horsepower.

HQ or **hq, H.Q.** or **h.q.** Headquarters.

hr. (*pl.* **hrs.**) Hour.

h.r. or **hr** Home run(s).

Hr. Mister (G *Herr*).

H.R. 1. Home Rule. **2.** House of Representatives.

Hr·dlič·ka (hûrd′lich·kə), **Aleš,** 1869–1943, U.S. anthropologist born in Bohemia.

H.R.H. His (or Her) Royal Highness.

H.R.I.P. Here rests in peace (L *hic requiescit in pace*).

Hrolf (rolf) See ROLLO.

Hr·vat·ska (hûr′vät·skä) The Serbo-Croatian name for CROATIA.

h.s. 1. Here is buried (L *hic sepultus* or *situs*). **2.** High school. **3.** In this sense (L *hoc sensu*).

H.S. 1. High School. **2.** *Brit.* Home Secretary. **3.** Hydrofoil ship.

H.S.H. His (or Her) Serene Highness.

Hsin·king (shin′jing′) A former name for CHANGCHUN. Also **Hsin′ching′.**

H.S.M. His (or Her) Serene Majesty.

ht. 1. Heat. **2.** Height.

Hts. Heights.

Huam·bo (wäm′bō) The former name for NOVA LISBOA.

hua·ra·che (wä·rä′chä, hŏŏ·rä′chē) *n.* A Mexican sandal woven of strips of leather and having leather heel straps. Also **hua·ra·cho** (-chō). [< Am. Sp., ? < Tarascan]

Huás·car (wäs′kär), 1495?–1533, Incan ruler of Peru; murdered by his brother Atahualpa.

Huas·ca·rán (wäs′kä·rän′) An extinct Andean volcano; the highest point in Peru; 22,205 ft.

hub (hub) *n.* **1.** The center part of a wheel into which the axle is inserted. **2.** Any center of great activity or interest. — **the Hub** A nickname for Boston. [Prob. var. of HOB]

Hub·bard (hub′ərd), **Elbert (Green),** 1856–1915, U.S. writer and publisher.

hub·ble-bub·ble (hub′əl·bub′əl) *n.* **1.** A bubbling or gargling sound. **2.** A hubbub; uproar. **3.** A hookah or water pipe. [Reduplication of BUBBLE]

hub·bub (hub′ub) *n.* **1.** A loud, confused noise, as of many voices shouting or talking. **2.** Uproar. [Origin unknown]

hub·cap (hub′kap′) *n.* A circular metal plate that clamps over the hub of a wheel of a motor vehicle.

hu·bris (hyŏŏ′bris) *n.* Wanton arrogance arising from overbearing pride or from passion. [< Gk. *hybris*]

huck·a·back (huk′ə·bak) *n.* A durable linen or cotton cloth with a coarse, uneven surface, much used for towels. Also **huck.** [Origin unknown]

huck·le (huk′əl) *n. Rare* The hip; also, a hump resembling the hip. [Dim. of obs. *huck* hip. Akin to ON *hūka* to crouch.]

huck·le·ber·ry (huk′əl·ber′ē) *n. pl.* **·ries 1.** The edible black or dark blue berry of any of various North American shrubs (genus *Gaylussacia*) of the heath family, similar to the blueberry. **2.** Any of the shrubs yielding this berry. Also called *hurtleberry.* [Prob. alter. of HURTLEBERRY]

huck·le·bone (huk′əl·bōn′) *n.* **1.** The innominate bone (which see). **2.** The talus.

huck·ster (huk′stər) *n.* **1.** A peddler of small wares or provisions, especially fresh fruits and vegetables. **2.** A petty, greedy tradesman. **3.** *U.S. Slang* One engaged in the advertising business. — *v.t.* **1.** To sell; peddle. **2.** To haggle over. — *v.i.* To retail. [< MDu. *hoekster* < *heuken* to retail]

Hu·dai·da (hō·dä′də, -dī′-) See HODEIDA.

Hud·ders·field (hud′ərz·fēld) A county borough in SW Yorkshire, England; pop. 130,600 (est. 1969).

hud·dle (hud′l) *v.* **·dled, ·dling** *v.i.* **1.** To crowd or nestle together closely, as from fear or cold. **2.** To draw or hunch oneself together, as from cold. **3.** In football, to gather in a huddle. — *v.t.* **4.** To bring, push, or crowd together closely. **5.** To draw or hunch (oneself) together: often with *up.* **6.** To make or do hurriedly or confusedly. **7.** To put on (one's clothes) hastily or carelessly. — *n.* **1.** A number of persons or things crowded or jumbled together. **2.** A state of confusion or disorder. **3.** In football, the grouping of a team behind its line of scrimmage before each play in order to receive signals and instructions. **4.** *U.S. Informal* Any small, private conference. [Origin uncertain]

Hu·di·bras·tic (hyŏŏ′di·bras′tik) *adj.* Pertaining to or in the style of Samuel Butler's *Hudibras,* a mock-heroic poem published in 1663–1678, written in tetrameter couplets.

Hud·son (hud′sən), **Henry,** died 1611?, English navigator and explorer; discovered the Hudson River for the Dutch, 1609, and Hudson Bay for the English, 1610. — **W(illiam) H(enry),** 1841–1922, English author and naturalist born in Argentina.

Hudson Bay An inland sea in north central Canada; 850 mi. long; 650 mi. wide, connected with the Atlantic by **Hudson Strait;** 450 mi. long.

Hudson River A river in eastern New York State, flowing 306 miles south to New York Bay, forming part of the New York–New Jersey border.

Hudson's Bay blanket *Canadian* A heavy woolen blanket having one or more broad bright stripes at each end: also called *point blanket.*

Hudson's Bay Company A joint-stock company chartered in England in 1670 in order to carry on the fur trade in what is now Canada.

Hudson seal Muskrat fur dyed black and plucked and sheared to simulate Alaskan sealskin.

hue¹ (hyōō) *n.* **1.** The attribute of a color that determines its position in the spectrum and differentiates it from an achromatic color of the same brightness. Compare COLOR. **2.** Color: the autumnal *hues.* **3.** A particular tint or shade of color. **4.** *Obs.* Appearance; form. [OE *hiw* appearance]

hue² (hyōō) *n.* A loud outcry or clamor; shouting: now only in the phrase **hue and cry,** meaning: **a** Any great public stir or clamor. **b** Formerly, the pursuit of a felon with loud shouts and cries, all who heard being legally obliged to join the search. [< OF *hu* cry < *huer* to shout after]

Hué (hwā, hyōō·āʹ) A port city in northern South Vietnam; pop. 170,884 (est. 1969). Also **Hue.**

Huel·va (welʹvä) A Province of SW Spain; 3,894 sq. mi.; pop. 399,934 (1960); capital, **Huelva,** pop. 74,384.

huff (huf) *n.* A fit of sudden anger or irritation: to be in a *huff.* — *v.t.* **1.** To offend; make angry. **2.** To treat insolently or arrogantly; bully; hector. **3.** In checkers, to remove (an opponent's piece) from the board as a forfeit for his neglecting to capture an opposing piece. — *v.i.* **4.** To take offense. **5.** To puff; blow. **6.** *Obs.* To puff or swell with anger or pride; bluster. [Imit.]

huf·fish (hufʹish) *adj.* **1.** Petulant; sulky. **2.** *Obs.* Arrogant. — **hufʹfish·ly** *adv.* — **hufʹfish·ness** *n.*

huf·fy (hufʹē) *adj.* **huff·i·er, huff·i·est 1.** Taking offense easily; touchy. **2.** Petulant; sulky. — **huffʹi·ly** *adv.* — **huffʹi·ness** *n.*

hug (hug) *v.* **hugged, hug·ging** *v.t.* **1.** To take and clasp affectionately within the arms; press in close embrace. **2.** To grasp and squeeze between the forepaws, as a bear. **3.** To cherish or cling to, as a belief or principle. **4.** To keep close to: The ship *hugged* the shore. — *v.i.* **5.** To lie or crowd closely together; snuggle. — *n.* **1.** A close, affectionate embrace. **2.** A tight clasp with the arms, as in wrestling. **3.** A bear's grip. [Prob. < ON *hugga* to console]

huge (hyōōj) *adj.* Very great in size, quantity, extent, etc. [< OF *ahuge* high] — **hugeʹly** *adv.* — **hugeʹness** *n.*

hug·ger·mug·ger (hugʹər·mugʹər) *n.* **1.** Disorder; confusion. **2.** *Archaic* Secrecy; concealment. — *adj.* **1.** Secret; sly. **2.** Disorderly; slovenly. — *v.t.* **1.** To keep secret; suppress. — *v.i.* **2.** To act or proceed furtively. [< obs. *hoker-moker,* prob. reduplication of ME *mokern* to conceal]

Hugh Ca·pet (hyōō kāʹpit, kapʹit; *Fr.* ka·peʹ), 938?–996, king of France 987–996, founder of the Capetian dynasty.

Hughes (hyōōz), **Charles Evans,** 1862–1948, U.S. statesman and jurist; chief justice of the Supreme Court 1930–41. — **(James) Langston,** 1902–1967, U.S. poet and author. — **Thomas,** 1822–96, English author and social reformer.

Hug·li (hōōgʹlē) See HOOGHLY.

hug-me-tight (hugʹmē·tītʹ) *n. U.S.* A woman's short, snug, knitted jacket or shoulder piece, often without sleeves.

Hu·go (hyōōʹgō, *Fr.* ü·gōʹ), **Victor (Marie),** 1802–85, French poet, novelist, and dramatist.

Hu·gue·not (hyōōʹgə·not) *n.* Any French Protestant of the 16th and 17th centuries. [< F < G *eidgenoss* confederate]

huh (hu) *interj.* An exclamation of inquiry, surprise, contempt, etc. [Origin unknown]

hu·la (hōōʹlə) *n.* A Hawaiian dance performed by both men and women, either alone or together, and characterized by sinuous arm movements that tell a story in pantomime. Also **hu·la-hu·la.** [< Hawaiian]

hulk (hulk) *n.* **1.** The body of an old, wrecked, or dismantled ship. **2.** *Often pl.* An old ship used for a prison or for purposes other than seagoing. **3.** Any bulky, unwieldy object or person. **4.** *Archaic* A heavy, clumsy ship. — *v.i.* **1.** To rise or loom bulkily: usually with *up.* **2.** *Brit. Dial.* To lounge or slouch about. [OE *hulc* ship, prob. Med.L *hultus* < Gk. *holkas* towed vessel < *helkein* to drag]

hulk·ing (hulʹking) *adj.* Big and unwieldy, bulky, or clumsy; a great *hulking* fellow. Also **hulkʹy.**

hull (hul) *n.* **1.** The outer, relatively smooth covering of certain fruits or seeds. **2.** The calyx of some fruits, as the strawberry or raspberry. **3.** Any outer covering. **4.** *Naut.* The body of a ship, exclusive of the masts, sails, yards, and rigging. **5.** *Aeron.* **a** The main, covered structure or framework of a rigid dirigible. **b** The part of the fuselage of a flying boat that rests upon the water. — *v.t.* **1.** To remove the hull of. **2.** To strike or pierce the hull of (a ship). [OE *hulu*]

Hull (hul), **Cordell,** 1871–1955, U.S. diplomat; secretary of state 1933–44.

Hull (hul) See KINGSTON-UPON-HULL.

hul·la·ba·loo (hulʹə·bə·lōōʹ) *n.* A loud, confused noise; uproar. Also **hulʹla·bal·looʹ.** [Imit. reduplication of HULLO]

hull down *Naut.* Of a ship, so far away as to have the hull hidden below the horizon.

hul·lo (hə·lōʹ) See HALLOO.

hum¹ (hum) *v.* **hummed, hum·ming** *v.i.* **1.** To make a low, murmuring or droning sound, as a bee on the wing. **2.** To sing with the lips closed, not articulating the words. **3.** To give forth a confused, indistinct sound: The streets *hummed*

with traffic. **4.** To mumble or murmur indistinctly, as from confusion or embarrassment; hem. **5.** *Informal* To be very busy or active: The office *hummed.* — *v.t.* **6.** To sing, as a tune, with closed lips and without articulation of words. **7.** To put into a specified state or condition by humming: to *hum* a child to sleep. — *n.* The act of humming, or the sound made by humming. [ME *hummer*] — **humʹmer** *n.*

hum² *interj.* A nasal, murmuring sound made to express mental concentration, deliberation, hesitation, etc.

hu·man (hyōōʹmən) *adj.* **1.** Of, belonging to, or characteristic of man. **2.** Having or showing the nature, qualities, or attributes of a man; that is a man. **3.** Consisting of a man or men: *human* sacrifice; *human* race. — *n.* A human being. [< OF *humain* < L *humanus*] — **huʹman·ness** *n.*

human being A man, woman, or child; a person.

hu·mane (hyōō·mānʹ) *adj.* **1.** Having or characterized by kindness, sympathy, tenderness, etc.; compassionate; benevolent. **2.** Tending to refine or civilize: *humane* learning. [Var. of HUMAN] — **hu·maneʹly** *adv.* — **hu·maneʹness** *n.*

hu·man·ism (hyōōʹmən·iz′əm) *n.* **1.** The character or quality of being human. **2.** A system or attitude in thought, religion, etc., in which human ideals and the perfection of human personality are made central, so that cultural and practical interests rather than theology and metaphysics are at the focus of attention. **3.** The study of the humanities.

Hu·man·ism (hyōōʹmən·iz′əm) *n.* The intellectual and literary movement during the Renaissance, characterized by the rediscovery and study of the Greek and Roman classics and by an emphasis on human interests rather than on religion or the world of nature. Compare SCHOLASTICISM.

hu·man·ist (hyōōʹmən·ist) *n.* **1.** One learned in or devoted to the study of the humanities; especially, a classical scholar. **2.** One who subscribes to a humanism (def. 2). — **hu·manʹis·tic** *adj.* — **hu·man·isʹti·cal·ly** *adv.*

Hu·man·ist (hyōōʹmən·ist) *n.* One of the Renaissance scholars and writers who devoted themselves to Humanism.

hu·man·i·tar·i·an (hyōō·manʹə·târʹē·ən) *n.* **1.** One who seeks to promote the welfare of mankind by eliminating pain and suffering; philanthropist. **2.** An adherent of theological or ethical humanitarianism. — *adj.* Of or pertaining to humanitarianism or the humanitarians.

hu·man·i·tar·i·an·ism (hyōō·manʹə·târʹē·ən·iz′əm) *n.* **1.** Philanthropy. **2.** *Theol.* The doctrine that Jesus Christ was merely a man and not divine. **3.** In ethics: **a** The doctrine that man's chief duty is to work for the welfare of the human race. **b** The doctrine that human perfectibility is attainable through man's own efforts without divine aid.

hu·man·i·ty (hyōō·manʹə·tē) *n.* *pl.* **·ties 1.** The human race; mankind collectively. **2.** The state or quality of being human; human nature. **3.** The state or quality of being humane; benevolence; also, a humane act. — **the humanities 1.** The study of classical Greek and Latin literature. **2.** The area of learning that includes literature, philosophy, history, the fine arts, etc., as distinguished from the sciences. [< OF *humanite* < L *humanitas, -tatis* < *humanus* human]

hu·man·ize (hyōōʹmən·īz) *v.* **·ized, ·iz·ing** *v.t.* **1.** To make human; give human characteristics or qualities to. **2.** To make humane; make gentle, kindly, etc. — *v.i.* **3.** To become human or humane. — **hu·man·i·zaʹtion** (-ə·zāʹshən, -ī·zāʹ-) *n.* — **huʹman·izʹer** *n.*

hu·man·kind (hyōōʹmən·kīndʹ) *n.* The human race; people.

hu·man·ly (hyōōʹmən·lē) *adv.* **1.** In a human manner. **2.** Within human power or ability: Is this *humanly* possible? **3.** In accordance with man's experience or knowledge.

human potentials movement The various methods of heightening sensitivity and creativity, of achieving wholeness and tranquility, of raising consciousness, and the like, regarded collectively as a late 20th-century phenomenon.

Hum·ber (humʹbər) The estuary of the Ouse and Trent rivers, flowing into the North Sea from NE England.

Hum·ber·side (humʹbər·sīdʹ) A county in NE England; 1,355 sq. mi.; pop. 848,800 (1976); county seat, Kingston-upon-Hull.

Hum·bert I (humʹbərt), 1844–1900, king of Italy 1878–1900; assassinated.

Humbert II, born 1904, king of Italy May to June 1946; abdicated; became the **Count di Sarre.**

hum·ble (humʹbəl) *adj.* **·bler, ·blest 1.** Free from pride or vanity; modest; meek; unassuming. **2.** Lowly in station, rank, condition, etc.; unpretentious; modest. **3.** Servile; fawning. **4.** Respectful. — *v.t.* **bled, bling 1.** To reduce the pride of; make meek. **2.** To lower in rank or dignity. — Syn. See ABASE. [< F < L *humilis* low < *humus* ground] — **humʹble·ness** *n.* — **humʹbler** *n.* — **humʹbly** *adv.*

hum·ble·bee (humʹbəl·bēʹ) *n.* A bumblebee. [ME *humbylbee* < *humbler,* freq. of HUM + BEE]

humble pie Formerly, a pie containing the inner and less choice parts (*humbles*) of a deer: also spelled *umble pie.* — **to eat humble pie** To be forced to make humble apologies or admit that one is in error; be humiliated. [< OF *numbles* < LL *lumbulus,* dim. of L *lumbus* loin + PIE]

Hum·boldt (humʹbōlt, *Ger.* hōōmʹbōlt), Baron **(Friedrich Heinrich) Alexander von,** 1769–1859, German scientist and explorer. — Baron **(Karl) Wilhelm von,** 1767–1835, German philologist and statesman; brother of the preceding.

Humboldt Current A part of the South Equatorial Current flowing generally north along the west coast of South America and then westward. Also *Peru Current*.

hum·bug (hum′bug) *n.* 1. Anything intended or used to delude or deceive; fraud; sham. 2. One who seeks to cheat or deceive others; charlatan; cheat. 3. The quality or practice of deceiving. 4. *Brit. & Canadian* A hard candy, usually brown with white stripes. — *v.* **·bugged, ·bug·ging** *v.t.* 1. To delude; trick. — *v.i.* 2. To practice deception. [Origin unknown] — **hum′bug·ger** *n.* — **hum′bug·ger·y** *n.*

hum·ding·er (hum-ding′ər) *n.* *Slang* One who or that which is remarkable or out of the ordinary.

hum·drum (hum′drum′) *adj.* Lacking interest, variety, or excitement; tedious; dull: a *humdrum* routine. — *n.* 1. That which is tedious or dull, as talk, daily life, etc. 2. A dull, tiresome person; bore. [Reduplication of HUM]

Hume (hyōōm), **David**, 1711–76, Scottish historian and philosopher.

hu·mer·al (hyōō′mər·əl) *adj.* 1. Of or pertaining to the humerus. 2. Of or pertaining to the shoulder or shoulders. [< L *humerus* shoulder]

hu·mer·us (hyōō′mər·əs) *n.* *pl.* **·mer·i** (-mər·ī) 1. *Anat.* **a** The bone of the upper part of the arm, extending from the shoulder to the elbow. For illustration see SKELETON. **b** The part of the arm containing this bone; brachium. 2. *Zool.* A corresponding bone in the upper part of the forelimb of most vertebrates. [< L, shoulder]

hu·mic (hyōō′mik) *adj.* Of, pertaining to, or derived from humus: *humic* acid. [< L *humus* ground, soil]

hu·mid (hyōō′mid) *adj.* Containing vapor or water; moist; damp. [< L *humidus* < *humere, umere* to be moist] — **hu′·mid·ly** *adv.*

hu·mid·i·fy (hyōō·mid′ə·fī) *v.t.* **·fied, ·fy·ing** To make moist or humid, as the atmosphere of a room. — **hu·mid′i·fi·ca′tion** *n.* — **hu·mid′i·fi′er** *n.*

hu·mid·i·ty (hyōō·mid′ə·tē) *n.* Moisture; dampness, especially of the atmosphere. — **relative humidity** The ratio, expressed as a percentage, of the amount of water vapor actually in the air to the total amount present during saturation at the same temperature. Abbr *r.h.*

hu·mi·dor (hyōō′mə·dôr) *n.* 1. A jar, container, etc., in which moisture is retained, used for storing cigars and tobacco. 2. An apparatus, as a tube containing a damp sponge, placed in such a container to keep the air moist.

hu·mil·i·ate (hyōō·mil′ē·āt) *v.t.* **·at·ed, ·at·ing** To lower the pride or self-esteem of; subject to feelings of inferiority, worthlessness, etc.; mortify. — **Syn.** See ABASE. [< L *humiliatus*, pp. of *humiliare* < *humilis* lowly] — **hu·mil′i·a·to′ry** (-ə·tôr′ē, -ə·tō′rē) *adj.*

hu·mil·i·a·tion (hyōō·mil′ē·ā′shən) *n.* The act of humiliating, or the state of being humiliated. — **Syn.** See CHAGRIN.

hu·mil·i·ty (hyōō·mil′ə·tē) *n.* *pl.* **·ties** 1. The state or quality of being humble; a modest sense of one's own merit. 2. An act of submission or deference. [< L *humilitas* lowness]

hum·ming (hum′ing) *adj.* 1. Making a low, murmuring or buzzing sound. 2. *Informal* Unusually active or intense; spirited; brisk. — **hum′ming·ly** *adv.*

hum·ming·bird (hum′ing·bûrd′) *n.* Any of a large family (*Trochilidae*) of very small birds of the New World, having brilliant plumage, a long, slender bill for sipping nectar from flowers, and rapidly vibrating wings that produce a humming sound during flight, especially the **ruby-throated hummingbird** (*Archilochus colubris*) and the **rufous hummingbird** (*Selasphorus rufus*).

hummingbird moth The hawk moth (which see).

hum·mock (hum′ək) *n.* 1. A low mound of earth or rock; hillock. 2. A wooded tract of land rising above an adjacent marsh or swamp. 3. A ridge or pile of ice in an ice field. [Origin unknown] — **hum′mock·y** *adj.*

hu·mor (hyōō′mər, yōō′-) *n.* 1. The quality of anything that is or seems to be funny or appeals to the comic sense. 2. The ability to apprehend, appreciate, or express what is amusing, comic, etc. 3. Speech, writing, or actions that are amusing or comic. 4. A temporary state of mind or feeling; mood: to be in a good *humor.* 5. Temperament; disposition: a man of sanguine *humor.* 6. A sudden or unpredictable liking, inclination, etc.; whim; caprice. 7. *Physiol.* **a** Any functioning liquid or semiliquid substance of the body, as blood, bile, lymph, etc. **b** The aqueous humor of the eye. 8. A chronic skin eruption supposed to be due to a disorder of the blood. 9. In ancient physiology, one of the four principal bodily fluids (**cardinal humors**), blood, phlegm, choler (yellow bile). and melancholy (black bile), which, according to their proportions in the body, were believed to influence health and temperament. — **out of humor** Out of sorts; irritable; cross. — *v.t.* 1. To comply with the moods or caprices of; indulge. 2. To adapt oneself to the nature or requirements of (something). Also *Brit.* **hu′mour.** [< OF < L *umor* < *umere* to be moist]

hu·mor·al (hyōō′mər·əl, yōō′-) *adj.* Relating to or arising from the humors of the body

hu·mor·esque (hyōō′mə·resk′, yōō′-) *n.* A playful, lively musical composition; caprice. [< G *humoreske*]

hu·mor·ist (hyōō′mər·ist, yōō′-) *n.* 1. One who displays or exercises a sense of humor; joker; wag. 2. A professional writer, entertainer, etc., proficient in the writing or telling of humorous stories or jokes. — **hu′mor·is′tic** *adj.*

hu·mor·ous (hyōō′mər·əs, yōō′-) *adj.* 1. Full of or characterized by humor; laughable; funny: a *humorous* situation. 2. Displaying or using humor: a *humorous* writer 3. *Archaic* Capricious; whimsical. 4. *Obs.* Humoral. 5. *Obs.* Moist; humid — **hu′mor·ous·ly** *adv* — **hu′mor·ous·ness** *n.* — **Syn.** 1. *Humorous, comical, droll, witty, facetious, jocular, jocose,* and *waggish* describe that which is intended to provoke, or actually does provoke, laughter. *Humorous* is the general term applied both to the intention and the effect. Something *comical* is intrinsically funny; *droll* is applied to that which is *comical* because odd or queer. A *witty* remark appeals to the intellect, deriving its humor from its expression in words or picture; a *facetious* remark is intended to provoke amusement, though it may not always succeed. *Jocular* and *jocose* are close synonyms of *facetious*, but also imply a hearty good nature. *Waggish* is often used to describe the temperament of the inveterate joker, the man who is always inclined to turn aside from the serious to the *humorous*. — **Ant.** serious, solemn, sober.

hump (hump) *n.* 1. A rounded protuberance, especially on the back, as the normal mass of tissue in the camel, bison, etc., or the deformity produced in man by a curvature of the spine. 2. A low mound of earth; hummock. 3. *Brit. Slang* A fit of depression; the blues. — **over the hump** Beyond the most critical or halfway point; over the worst. — **the Hump** The Himalayas between China and India or Burma: name used by airmen in World War II. — *v.t.* 1. To bend or round into a hump; hunch; arch. 2. *U.S. Informal* To hurry or exert (oneself). [Akin to LG *hump*, Du. *homp*]

hump·back (hump′bak′) *n.* 1. A back with a hump. 2. A person having a back with a hump; hunchback. 3. A large whalebone whale (genus *Megaptera*) with a low, humplike dorsal fin and long flippers. — **hump′backed′** *adj.*

Hum·per·dinck (hoom′pər·dingk), **Engelbert**, 1854–1921, German composer.

humph (humf) *interj.* An exclamation of doubt, dissatisfaction, etc. [< HUM¹]

Hum·phrey (hum′frē), 1391–1447, Duke of Gloucester, son of Henry IV of England; Protector during minority of Henry VI: called **the Good Duke Humphrey.**

Humphreys Peak See SAN FRANCISCO MOUNTAIN.

Hump·ty Dump·ty (hump′tē dump′tē) A character in a nursery rhyme and riddle, personifying an egg that fell from a wall and could not be pieced together again.

hump·y (hum′pē) *adj.* **hump·i·er, hump·i·est** 1. Covered with or full of humps. 2. Like a hump.

Hums (hoomz) See HOMS.

hu·mus (hyōō′məs) *n.* The black or brown substance of the soil, formed by the decay of animal and vegetable matter, and providing nutrition for plant life. [< L, ground]

Hun (hun) *n.* 1. One of a barbarous, nomadic Asian people who invaded Europe in the fourth and fifth centuries, led by Attila. 2. Any barbarous or destructive person. 3. A German: an opprobrious term applied in World War I. [OE *Hune* < LL *Hunnus*] — **Hun′nish** *adj.* — **Hun′nish·ness** *n.*

Hu·nan (hoō′nän′) A Province of south central China; 80,-000 sq. mi.; pop. 36,220,000 (est. 1957); capital, Changsha.

hunch (hunch) *n.* 1. *U.S. Informal* A premonition of some coming event. 2. A hump. 3. A lump or hunk. — *v.t.* 1. To bend or draw up so as to form a hump: to *hunch* one's shoulders. — *v.i.* 2. To move or thrust oneself forward jerkily. [Origin unknown]

hunch·back (hunch′bak′) *n.* 1. A deformed back with a hump. 2. A person having such a back

hunch·backed (hunch′bakt′) *adj.* Having a hunchback.

hun·dred (hun′drid) *n.* 1. The sum of ninety and ten, written as 100, c, or C: a cardinal number. Abbr. *h., H.* 2. Anything consisting of or representing a hundred units, as an organization, bill, etc. 3. An ancient subdivision of a county, common in England and Ireland and still used in Delaware. — *adj.* Being ten more than ninety. [OE]

Hundred Days The last period of Napoleon's rule, from his return to Paris from Elba on March 20, 1815, until his defeat at Waterloo and his abdication on June 28, 1815.

hun·dred·fold (hun′drid·fōld′) *n.* An amount or number a hundred times as great as a given unit. — *adv* So as to be a hundred times as many or as great. — *adj.* 1. Consisting of one hundred parts. 2. One hundred times as many or as great.

hun·dredth (hun′dridth) *adj.* 1. Having the number one hundred: the ordinal of *one hundred.* 2. Being one of a hundred equal parts. — *n.* 1. One of a hundred equal parts. 2. That which is numbered one hundred.

hun·dred·weight (hun′drid·wāt′) *n.* A unit of weight commonly reckoned in the United States at 100 pounds avoirdupois, in England at 112 pounds. Abbreviated *c., C., cwt.*

Hundred Years' War A long series of wars, 1337–1453,

between England and France, during which England ceased to be a continental power and lost all her French possessions except Calais. See table for WAR.

Hun·e·ker (hun′ə·kər), **James Gibbons**, 1860–1921, U.S. author and music and drama critic.

hung (hung) Past tense and past participle of HANG.

Hung. Hungarian; Hungary.

Hun·gar·i·an (hung·gâr′ē·ən) *adj.* Of or pertaining to Hungary, its people, or their language. — *n.* **1.** A native or citizen of Hungary; especially, a Magyar. **2.** The Finno-Ugric language of the Hungarians: also called *Magyar.* [< Med.L *Hungarus*]

Hungarian goulash Goulash (which see).

Hungarian partridge See under PARTRIDGE.

Hun·ga·ry (hung′gə·rē) A Republic in central Europe; 35,912 sq. mi.; pop. 10,440,000 (est. 1973); capital, Budapest: Hungarian *Magyarország.* Officially **Hungarian People's Republic.**

hun ger (hung′gər) *n.* **1.** The state of discomfort, queasiness, or weakness caused by lack of food: to be faint with *hunger.* **2.** A desire or need for food. **3.** Any strong desire or craving. — *v.i.* **1.** To feel or suffer from hunger; be hungry. **2.** To have a desire or craving: with *for* or *after.* — *v.t.* **3.** To cause to undergo hunger; starve. [OE *hungor*]

hunger strike A self-imposed fast, as by a prisoner, political or religious leader, etc., as a means of protest.

hun·gry (hung′grē) *adj.* **·gri·er, ·gri·est 1.** Desiring or in need of food. **2.** Eagerly desirous; craving: *hungry* for applause. **3.** Indicating or characterized by hunger or craving: a *hungry* look. **4.** Not fertile; poor or barren: *hungry* soil. [OE *hungrig* < *hungor*] — **hun′gri·ly** *adv.* — **hun′gri·ness** *n.*

hunk (hungk) *n. Informal* A large piece or lump; chunk: a *hunk* of meat. [Prob. < Flemish *hunke*]

hun·kers (hung′kərz) *n. pl. Scot. & Dial.* Haunches. — **on one's hunkers** In a squatting position.

hunks (hungks) *n. sing. & pl.* **1.** A surly, crusty old person. **2.** A stingy man; miser. [Origin unknown]

hunk·y (hung′kē) *n. U.S. Slang* Bohunk (which see).

hun·ky-do·ry (hung′kē·dôr′ē, -dō′rē) *adj. U.S. Slang* Fully satisfactory; all right. Also **hunk′y.** [Fanciful extension of slang *hunky* safe, satisfactory]

hunt (hunt) *v.t.* **1.** To pursue (game) for the purpose of killing or catching. **2.** To range over (an area) in search of game. **3.** To use or direct in the chase, as hounds, a horse, etc. **4.** To chase, drive away, or pursue with hostility, violence, etc. **5.** To search for eagerly; seek: to *hunt* the truth. **6.** To search (a place) thoroughly: to *hunt* the woods. **7.** In bell ringing, to shift the order of (a bell) in its set during a hunt. — *v.i.* **8.** To seek or pursue game. **9.** To search or seek: often with *for* or *after.* **10.** In bell ringing, to shift the order of a bell in its set during a hunt. — **to hunt down 1.** To pursue until caught or killed. **2.** To search for until found. — **to hunt up 1.** To go in search of. **2.** To find after a search. — *n.* **1.** The act of hunting game; chase. **2.** A group of huntsmen taking part in a chase. **3.** A search; pursuit. **4.** An area used for hunting. **5.** In bell ringing, a regular series of changes successively performed on a set of from five to twelve bells. [OE *huntian*]

Hunt (hunt), **(James Henry) Leigh,** 1784–1859, English poet and essayist. — **William Holman,** 1827–1910, English painter.

hunt·er (hun′tər) *n.* **1.** One who hunts game; huntsman. **2.** One who hunts or seeks anything. **3.** An animal used in hunting, as a dog or horse. **4.** A hunting watch.

Hun·ter (hun′tər), **John,** 1728–93, British surgeon.

hunter's moon The full moon after the harvest moon.

hunt·ing (hun′ting) *n.* **1.** The act of one who or that which hunts. **2.** *Electr.* A form of instability in an electromechanical system, especially as indicated by a needle that swings back and forth about a mean position. — *adj.* Of, pertaining to, or used for hunting.

hunting case The case of a hunting watch.

Hunt·ing·don·shire (hun′ting·dən·shir) A former county in east central England; 366 sq. mi.; pop. 202,337 (1971); county seat, Huntingdon; pop. 111,300 (1976). Also **Hunt′ing·don.** Shortened form **Hunts.**

hunting knife A long, sharp, single- or double-edged knife used by hunters to skin and cut up game.

hunting leopard The cheetah.

Hunt·ing·ton (hun′ting·tən), **Collis P(otter),** 1821–1900, U.S. railroad magnate. — **Ellsworth,** 1876–1947, U.S. geographer and explorer. — **Samuel,** 1731–96 American patriot; signer of the Declaration of Independence.

Hunt·ing·ton (hun′ting·tən) A city in western West Virginia, on the Ohio River; pop. 74,315.

Huntington Park A city in SW California, a suburb of Los Angeles; pop. 33,744.

hunting watch A watch having the dial protected by a metal cap or lid: also called *hunter.*

hunt·ress (hun′tris) *n.* **1.** A woman who hunts. **2** A mare used in hunting.

hunts·man (hunts′mən) *n. pl.* **·men** (-mən) **1.** One who hunts game; hunter. **2.** One who directs a hunt, hounds, etc.

hunts·man's-cup (hunts′mənz·kup′) *n.* Pitcher plant.

hunt's-up (hunts′up′) *n.* **1.** A lively tune played on a horn to awaken huntsmen in the morning. **2.** Any rousing tune.

Hunts·ville (hunts′vil) A city in northern Alabama; pop. 137,802.

Hun·ya·dy (hōōn′yô·dē), **Já·nos,** 1387–1456, Hungarian general and hero; defeated the Turks. Also **Hun′ya·di.**

Hu·on pine (hyōō′on) A large, coniferous tree (*Dacrydium franklini*) with close-grained timber, growing in Tasmania. [after *Huon* River, Tasmania]

Hu·pa (hōō′pə) *n.* **1.** One of a tribe of North American Indians living in NW California. **2.** The Athapascan language of this tribe.

Hu·peh (hōō′pe′) A Province in east central China; 72,394 sq. mi.; pop. 30,790,000 (est. 1957); capital, Wuhan. Also **Hu′pei′.**

hur·dle (hûr′dəl) *n.* **1.** A light, portable barrier for horses or runners to leap over in races. **2.** *pl.* A race in which such barriers are used: often with *the.* **3.** An obstacle or difficulty to be surmounted. **4.** *Chiefly Brit.* A movable framework, as of interlaced twigs or branches, used for temporary fencing, animal pens, etc. **5.** *Brit.* Formerly, a sledge on which condemned persons were dragged to the place of execution. — *v.* **·dled, ·dling** *v.t.* **1.** To leap over (a barrier) in a race. **2.** To make, cover, or enclose with hurdles. **3.** To surmount or overcome (a difficulty, problem, etc.). — *v.i.* **4.** To leap over hurdles, obstacles, etc. [OE *hyrdel*] — **hur′dler** *n.*

hurds (hûrdz) *n.pl.* Hards.

hur·dy-gur·dy (hûr′dē·gûr′dē) *n. pl.* **·dies 1.** Any of various mechanized musical instruments played by turning a crank, as the barrel organ. **2.** Formerly, a stringed instrument shaped like a lute or guitar whose strings were set vibrating by a resined wheel turned by a crank at one end. [Appar. imit. of the instrument]

hurl (hûrl) *v.t.* **1.** To throw, fling, or send with force. **2.** To throw down; overthrow. **3.** To utter with vehemence: to *hurl* insults. — *v.i.* **4.** To throw something at a person or thing. **5.** In baseball, to pitch. — *n.* The act of hurling; also, a forceful throw or pitch. [ME *hurlen,* ? < Scand. Cf. Dan. *hurle* to whirr, Norw. *hurla* to buzz.] — **hurl′er** *n.*

hurl·ing (hûr′ling) *n.* An Irish game resembling field hockey. Also **hur′ley.** [< HURL]

hur·ly (hûr′lē) *n. pl.* **·lies** Confusion; noise; uproar.

hur·ly-bur·ly (hûr′lē·bûr′lē) *n. pl.* **·lies** Tumult; confusion; turmoil. — *adj.* Full of turmoil and confusion; tumultuous. [< earlier *hurling and burling*]

Hu·ron (hyŏŏr′ən, -on) *n.* A member of any one of four confederated tribes of North American Indians of Iroquoian stock, formerly occupying the territory between Lake Huron and Lake Ontario. [< F, ruffian]

Hu·ron (hyŏŏr′ən), **Lake** The second largest of the Great Lakes, between Michigan and Ontario; 23,010 sq. mi.

hur·rah (hŏŏ·rô′, hə·rä′) *n. & interj.* An exclamation expressing triumph, joy, encouragement, etc. — *v.i.* **1.** To shout a hurrah or hurrahs. — *v.t.* **2.** To cheer with hurrahs. Also spelled **hooray.** Also **hur·ray′** (-rā′). [? < G *hurra*]

hur·ri·cane (hûr′ə·kān) *n.* **1.** *Meteorol.* A tropical cyclone, especially one originating in the West Indies and often covering a wide area; having a wind velocity exceeding 75 miles per hour. See BEAUFORT SCALE. **2.** Anything suggesting a hurricane in violence or speed. [< Sp. *huracán* < Carib]

hurricane deck A light, upper deck on a passenger vessel, especially on river steamers in the United States.

hurricane lamp 1. A lamp so constructed that high winds will not extinguish its flame: also called *tornado lamp.* **2.** A lamp consisting of a candle covered by a glass chimney.

hur·ried (hûr′ēd) *adj.* **1.** Urged or forced to move, act, etc., in haste. **2.** Done or carried on in great or too great haste: a *hurried* decision. — **hur′ried·ly** *adv.* — **hur′ried·ness** *n.*

hur·ry (hûr′ē) *v.* **·ried, ·ry·ing** *v.i.* **1.** To act or move rapidly or in haste; hasten. — *v.t.* **2.** To cause or urge to act or move more rapidly: often with *up.* **3.** To cause to act or move too hastily: to *hurry* a man into marriage. **4.** To hasten the progress, completion, etc., of, often unduly. — *n. pl.* **·ries 1.** The act of hurrying; haste. **2.** Eagerness to move, act, etc. [ME *horyen.* Cf. G *hurren* to move quickly.]

hur·ry-scur·ry (hûr′ē·skûr′ē) *n. pl.* **·ries** A hasty, confused bustling about; agitated, impatient haste. — *v.i.* **·ried, ·ry·ing** To act in haste and confusion; rush pell-mell. — *adv.* In disorderly haste; confusedly. — *adj.* Hurried; confused. Also **hur′ry-skur′ry.**

Hurst·mon·ceux (hûrst′mən·sōō′, hûrs′-) See HERSTMONCEUX.

hurt (hûrt) *v.* **hurt, hurt·ing** *v.t.* **1.** To cause physical harm or pain to; injure. **2.** To damage, injure, or impair in some way; do harm to: to *hurt* one's reputation. **3.** To grieve or distress; cause mental suffering to. — *v.i.* **4.** To cause discomfort, suffering, or damage. **5.** To give out a feeling of pain: My head *hurts.* **6.** *Informal* To feel pain, soreness, etc.: I *hurt* all over. — *n.* **1.** Any injury, wound, ache, etc. **2.** Damage; impairment: What *hurt* did it do? **3.** An injury to the feelings; affront. [< OF *hurter* to hit] — **hurt′er** *n.* — **Syn.** (verb) **1.** wound, damage, mar.

hurt·ful (hûrt′fəl) *adj.* Causing hurt; injurious. — **hurt′ful·ly** *adv.* — **hurt′ful·ness** *n.*

hur·tle (hûr′təl) v. ·tled, ·tling v.i. 1. To collide or strike violently with a loud sound; clash: with *against* or *together*. 2. To rush headlong or impetuously: to *hurtle* across a room. 3. To make a rushing or crashing sound, as in moving or colliding. — v.t. 4. To hurl, throw, or drive violently. 5. *Archaic* To strike against; collide with. — n. *Rare* A hurtling; colliding. [Freq. of ME *hurten* to hit, hurt]

hur·tle·ber·ry (hûr′təl·ber′ē) n. pl. ·ries 1. The whortleberry. 2. The huckleberry. [Appar. < ME *hurtil-* < OE *horta* whortleberry + BERRY]

hurt·less (hûrt′lis) adj. 1. Harmless. 2. Unharmed.

Hus (hus, *Czech* hŏŏs), **Jan** See HUSS.

hus·band (huz′bənd) n. 1. A man joined to a woman in lawful wedlock. Abbr. h., H. 2. *Archaic* A manager or steward of an estate, household, etc. — v.t. 1. To manage prudently; use or spend wisely; conserve: to *husband* one's forces. 2. *Rare* To be a husband to; marry. 3. *Archaic* To match with a husband; mate. 4. *Obs.* To cultivate or till. [OE *hūsbonda* < *hūs* house + *bonda* freeholder; infl. by ON *hūsbōndi*] — **hus′band·less** adj.

hus·band·man (huz′bənd·mən) n. pl. ·men (-mən) *Archaic* One who tills the soil; farmer.

hus·band·ry (huz′bən·drē) n. 1. The occupation or business of farming. 2. Careful management; economy; thrift. 3. Management of household affairs, expenditures, etc.

Hu·sein ibn-A·li (hŏŏ·sīn′ ib′n·ä′lē), 1856–1931, Arab ruler; first king of Hejaz 1916–24.

hush (hush) v.t. 1. To make silent; cause to be quiet. 2. To suppress mention of; keep hidden or secret: usually with *up.* 3. To soothe or allay, as fears. — v.i. 4. To be or become quiet or still. — n. Deep silence; quiet. — adj. *Archaic* Quiet. — interj. Be quiet! [Back formation < ME *hussht* quiet]

hush·a·by (hush′ə·bī′) interj. Go to sleep.

hush-hush (hush′hush′) adj. *Informal* Conducted or done in secrecy.

Hu Shih (hŏŏ′shir′), 1891–1962, Chinese philosopher, statesman, and author.

hush money A bribe to secure silence or secrecy.

hush·pup·py (hush′pup′ē) n. pl. ·pies *Southern U.S.* A small fried ball of cornmeal dough.

husk (husk) n. 1. The outer coating of certain fruits or seeds, especially of an ear of corn. 2. Any outer covering, especially when comparatively worthless. — v.t. To remove the husk or outer covering of. [ME *huske*, prob. < Du. *huuskijn*, dim. of *huus* house] — **husk′er** n.

husk·ing bee (hus′king) *U.S.* A cornhusking. Also **husk′·ing.**

husk·y[1] (hus′kē) adj. **husk·i·er, husk·i·est** 1. Dry, rough, or coarse in vocal quality; hoarse: a *husky* whisper. 2. Full of, containing, or made of husks. 3. Like a husk. [< HUSK] — **husk′i·ly** adv. — **husk′i·ness** n.

husk·y[2] (hus′kē) *U.S. Informal* adj. **husk·i·er, husk·i·est** Physically strong; burly. — n. pl. **husk·ies** A strong or powerfully built person. [Special use of HUSKY[1], with ref. to toughness of husks]

Husk·y (hus′kē) n. pl. **Husk·ies** *U.S. & Canadian* 1. A heavily furred Eskimo dog. Also **husk′y.** 2. An Eskimo. 3. The Eskimo language. [? Alter. of ESKIMO]

Huss (hus), **John**, 1369?–1415, Bohemian religious reformer; burned as a heretic. Also **Jan Hus.**

hus·sar (hŏŏ·zär′) n. 1. A member of any light-armed cavalry regiment found in some European armies and usually distinguished by brilliant dress uniforms. 2. Formerly, one of a body of light-armed horse troopers organized in the Hungarian army. [< Hungarian *huszár* < Serbian *gusar* < Ital. *corsaro* < Med.L *corsarius*. Doublet of CORSAIR.]

Hus·sein A·li (hŏŏ·sīn′ ä′lē) Original name of BAHAULLAH.

Huss·ite (hus′īt) n. A follower of John Huss. — adj. Of or pertaining to John Huss or his religious doctrines. — **Huss′·ism, Huss·it·ism** (hus′īt·iz′əm) n.

hus·sy (huz′ē, hus′ē) n. pl. ·sies 1. A woman of questionable behavior or reputation. 2. A pert or forward girl; minx: a playful or derogatory term. 3. *Brit. Dial.* A small case for needles, thread, etc. [Alter. of HOUSEWIFE]

hust·ings (hus′tingz) n.pl. (*usually construed as sing.*) 1. *Brit.* A court formerly held in the larger cities and still surviving in London. 2. *Brit.* Formerly, the temporary platform on which candidates for Parliament were nominated and addressed the electors. 3. The proceedings at an election. 4. Any place where political speeches are made. [OE *hūsting* council < ON *hūsthing* < *hūs* house + *thing* assembly]

hus·tle (hus′əl) v. ·tled, ·tling v.t. 1. To push about or crowd roughly or rudely; jostle. 2. To force, push, or thrust hurriedly: to *hustle* an intruder outside. 3. *U.S. Informal* To cause to proceed rapidly or too rapidly; hurry: to *hustle* a bill through a legislature. 4. *U.S. Informal* To obtain or prepare quickly: often with *up*: to *hustle* up a sandwich. 5. *U.S. Slang* To sell or solicit (something) in an aggressive or unethical manner. — v.i. 6. To push or shove roughly; elbow. 7. *U.S. Informal* To move or work with great energy or speed; bustle. 8. *U.S. Slang* To make money by clever or often unscrupulous means. 9. *U.S. Slang* To engage in prostitution. — n. 1. The act of hustling; a pushing or shoving. 2. *Informal* Energetic activity; drive; push. [< Du. *hutselen* to shake, toss] — **hus′tler** n.

hus·wife (huz′if) n. A housewife (def. 2).

hut (hut) n. 1. A small, rude house or cabin; hovel. 2. *Mil.* A movable structure, often of metal, used as a temporary shelter or storehouse. — v.t. & v.i. **hut·ted, hut·ting** To shelter or live in a hut. [< OF *hutte* < OHG *hutta*]
— **Syn.** (noun) *Hut, cabin, shed, lean-to, shack, shanty,* and *hovel* denote various types of small buildings. A *hut* is usually a small and primitive dwelling, though the word is applied to some commodious and elaborate structures, as a Quonset *hut.* A *cabin* is a small building devoted to a particular purpose; it is less primitive than a *hut*, and is usually to be found in a rural or forest setting: a hunting *cabin,* a seashore *cabin.* A simple building consisting mostly of a roof to provide shelter from the rain is a *shed;* a rude *shed* made by setting planks, boughs, etc., against a bar fixed horizontally above the ground is a *lean-to. Sheds* are more often used for storage than as dwellings: a tool *shed;* a *lean-to* serves to provide temporary shelter against the weather for men in the open. *Shack* and *shanty* suggest makeshift or ramshackle construction; a *hovel* is an even more wretched dwelling, with an implication of dirt and squalor. — **Ant.** mansion, palace.

hutch (huch) n. 1. A coop or pen for confining small animals: rabbit *hutch.* 2. A cupboard for dishes, etc., set on a sideboard. 3. A chest, locker, or bin in which to store things. 4. A small hut or cabin. 5. *Mining* A truck or small wagon used to transport coal or ore. 6. A trough, as used by bakers for kneading dough or by miners for washing ore. — v.t. To store up or hoard, as in a chest. [< F *huche* < LL *hutica*]

Hutch·ins (huch′inz), **Robert Maynard,** born 1899, U.S. educator.

Hutch·in·son (huch′in·sən) A city in central Kansas, on the Arkansas River; pop. 37,574.

Hutch·in·son (huch′in·sən), **Anne,** 1591–1643, *née* Marbury, English preacher in America; banished from Massachusetts Colony. — **Thomas,** 1711–80, American colonial governor.

hut·ment (hut′mənt) n. A group of huts, as in a camp.

Hut·ter·ite (hut′ər·īt) n. One of an Anabaptist sect now living in communistic rural settlements in Alberta, Saskatchewan, and adjacent United States. Also **Hut·ter′i·an Brethren** (hut·tir′ē·ən). [after Jakob Hutter, died 1536, Moravian reformer]

hutz·pah (hŏŏts′pə, khŏŏts′-) See CHUTZPAH.

Hux·ley (huks′lē) An English family prominent in science and literature, notably **T**(**homas**) **H**(**enry**), 1825–95, biologist and Darwinian; **Julian** (**Sorell**), 1887–1975, biologist, and his brother, **Aldous** (**Leonard**), 1894–1963, novelist and critic, grandsons of Thomas Henry.

Huy·gens (hī′gənz), **Christiaan,** 1629–95, Dutch mathematician, physicist, and astronomer. Also **Huy′ghens.**

Huys·mans (wēs·mäns′), **Joris Karl,** 1848–1907, French novelist.

huz·za (hə·zä′) *Archaic* n. & interj. An exclamation of joy, encouragement, triumph, etc. — v. ·zaed, ·za·ing v.i. 1. To shout a huzza or huzzas. — v.t. 2. To cheer or applaud with huzzas. [Origin uncertain. Cf. G *hussa.*]

H.V. or **h.v.** or **hv** High voltage.

h.w. High water.

Hwai·ning (hwī′ning′) A former name for ANKING.

hwan (hwän) n. pl. **hwan** The monetary unit of South Korea: in 1960 worth about ⅗₀ of a U.S. cent.

Hwang Hai (hwäng′ hī′) The Chinese name for the YELLOW SEA.

Hwang Ho (hwäng′ hō′) A river in China, flowing 2,900 miles east from the Tibetan highlands across northern China to the Gulf of Chihli: also *Yellow River, Hoang Ho, Hoangho.*

hy·a·cinth (hī′ə·sinth) n. 1. Any of various plants (genus *Hyacinthus*) of the lily family, cultivated for their spikelike clusters of fragrant, bell-shaped flowers. 2. The bulb or flower of this plant. 3. In Greek mythology, a plant, perhaps the iris, larkspur, or gladiolus, supposed to have sprung from the blood of the slain Hyacinthus. 4. A brownish, reddish, or orange zircon: also called *jacinth.* 5. In ancient times, a bluish or purplish gem, probably the sapphire or amethyst. 6. Blue or purplish blue. [Var. of older *jacynth* < OF *jacincte* < L *hyacinthus* < Gk. *hyakinthos.* Doublet of JACINTH.] — **hy′a·cin′thine** (-thin, -thīn) adj.

HYACINTH (def. 1)

Hy·a·cin·thus (hī′ə·sin′thəs) In Greek mythology, a youth whom Apollo loved and accidentally killed and from whose blood sprang a flower bearing the words of grief, *AI, AI.*

Hy·a·des (hī′ə·dēz) n.pl. 1. In Greek mythology, five daughters of Atlas whom Zeus set among the stars. 2. *Astron.* A cluster of five stars in the constellation Taurus, shaped like the letter V and considered by ancient astronomers to be a sign of rain when they rose with the sun. Also **Hy·ads** (hī′adz). [< L < Gk., ? < *hyein* to rain]

hy·ae·na (hī·ē′nə) See HYENA.

hy·a·line (hī'ə·lin, -līn) *n.* **1.** *Biochem.* A horny, nitrogenous substance, similar to chitin, that forms the walls of hydatid cysts. **2.** *Anat.* The hyaloid membrane. **3.** *Poetic* A glassy, transparent surface, as that of the sea. Also **hy'a·lin** (-lin). — *adj.* Resembling glass; transparent: the *hyaline* substance of a cell. [< L *hyalinus* < Gk. *hyalos* glass]

hyaline cartilage *Anat.* A form of cartilage that contains little fibrous tissue and in which the cells are embedded in a homogeneous translucent matrix.

hy·a·lite (hī'ə·līt) *n.* A colorless and transparent, or sometimes milky, variety of opal.

hyalo- *combining form* Glass; of or resembling glass: *hyaloplasm.* Also, before vowels, **hyal-.** [< Gk. *hyalos* glass]

hy·al·o·gen (hī·al'ə·jən) *n.* *Biochem.* Any of various insoluble substances found in animal tissues, relating to mucin, and yielding hyaline on hydrolysis.

hy·a·loid (hī'ə·loid) *adj.* Transparent as glass; hyaline. — *n.* *Anat.* The hyaloid membrane. [< Gk. *hyaloeidēs* glassy]

hyaloid membrane *Anat.* The delicate, transparent membrane enveloping the vitreous humor of the eye.

hy·a·lo·plasm (hī'ə·lō·plaz'əm) *n.* *Biol.* The clear fluid substance of the protoplasm of a cell, as distinguished from the granular substance. — **hy·a·lo·plas'mic** *adj.*

hy·brid (hī'brid) *n.* **1.** An animal or plant produced by a male and female of different species, varieties, or breeds. **2.** A mongrel or half-breed. **3.** Anything of mixed origin or of incongruous or different elements. **4.** *Ling.* A word composed of elements from more than one language, as *genocide.* — *adj.* Of, pertaining to, or having the nature of a hybrid. [< L *hybrida* offspring of tame sow and wild boar]

hy·brid·ism (hī'brid·iz'əm) *n.* **1.** The state, quality, or fact of being hybrid. Also **hy·brid·i·ty** (hī·brid'ə·tē). **2.** The producing of hybrids; interbreeding. **3.** *Ling.* The mingling in one word of elements from more than one language.

hy·brid·ize (hī'brid·īz) *v.t. & v.i.* **·ized, ·iz·ing** To produce or cause to produce hybrids. Also *Brit.* **hy'brid·ise.** — **hy·brid·i·za·tion** (hī'brid·ə·zā'shən, -ī·zā'-) *n.* — **hy'brid·iz'er** *n.*

hybrid vigor *Biol.* Heterosis.

hy·bris (hī'bras) *n.* Hubris. [< Gk.]

hyd. Hydrostatics.

hy·dan·to·in (hī·dan'tō·in) *n.* *Chem.* A white crystalline compound, $C_3H_4N_2O_2$, synthesized from methanol, used in organic synthesis. [< HYD(ROGEN) + (ALL)ANTO(IS) + -IN]

hy·da·tid (hī'də·tid) *n.* **1.** *Pathol.* A cyst containing a watery fluid, formed in man and animals by the larvae of a tapeworm. **2.** *Zool.* The encysted larval stage of a tapeworm; a cysticercus. — *adj.* Of or pertaining to such a cyst. [< Gk. *hydatis* drop of water]

Hyde (hīd), **Douglas,** 1860-1949, Irish poet and patriot; first president of Ireland 1938-45. — **Edward,** 1609-74, first Earl of Clarendon, English historian and statesman.

Hyde (hīd), **Mr.** See JEKYLL.

Hyde Park 1. A public park in the West End of London, England; noted as a meeting place of soapbox orators. **2.** A village in southern New York, on the Hudson; site of the estate and grave of Franklin D. Roosevelt; pop. 2,805.

Hy·der·a·bad (hī'dər·ə·bad', -bäd') **1.** A former State of south central India, merged, November 1, 1956, into the States of Andhra Pradesh, Bombay, and Mysore: formerly *Nizam's Dominions*: also *Haidarabad.* **2.** The capital of Andhra Pradesh, India, in the NW part of the State; pop. 1,294,800 (est. 1971). **3.** A city in SE West Pakistan, on the Indus; pop. 434,537 (est. 1969).

Hy·der A·li (hī'dər ä'lē) died 1782, maharaja of Mysore, fought against the British 1767–82. Also *Haidar Ali.*

hyd·no·car·pate (hid'nə·kär'pāt) *n.* *Chem.* A salt or ester of hydnocarpic acid.

hyd·no·car·pic acid (hid'nə·kär'pik) *Biochem.* A crystalline fatty acid, $C_{16}H_{28}O_2$, extracted from the oil of the seeds of the chaulmoogra. [< Gk. *hydnon* truffle + *karpos* fruit]

hydr- Var. of HYDRO-.

hy·dra (hī'drə) *n. pl.* **·dras** or **·drae** (-drē) **1.** Any of various small, fresh-water polyps (genus *Hydra*) characterized by a long, slender body and tentacles about the mouth. **2.** An evil that tends to reappear despite all efforts to eradicate it. [< Gk. *hydra* water serpent]

Hy·dra (hī'drə) *n.* **1.** In Greek mythology, a nine-headed serpent that grew two heads for each one that was cut off, slain by Hercules with a firebrand. **2.** A constellation, the Hydra: see CONSTELLATION. [< L < Gk.]

hy·drac·id (hī·dras'id) *n.* *Chem.* An acid that contains no oxygen, as hydrochloric acid.

hy·dra·gogue (hī'drə·gog, -gog) *n.* Any purgative that causes abundant watery discharges. — *adj.* Causing watery discharges. Also **hy'dra·gog.** [< F < L *hydragogus* < Gk. *hydragōgos* < *hydōr* water + *agein* to lead]

hy·dran·ge·a (hī·drān'jē·ə, -jə) *n.* Any of various trees and shrubs (genus *Hydrangea*) of the saxifrage family, with opposite, usually serrate leaves and large clusters of white, blue, or pink flowers. [< NL < Gk. *hydōr* water + *angeion* vessel]

hy·drant (hī'drənt) *n.* A large, upright pipe connected to a water main and equipped with one or more outlets from which water can be drawn for firefighting, watering the street, etc.; fireplug. [< Gk. *hydōr* water + -ANT]

hy·dranth (hī'dranth) *n.* *Zool.* The nutritive and terminal part of a hydroid polyp, containing the mouth, tentacles, and digestive cavity. [< HYDRA + Gk. *anthos* flower]

Hy·dra·o·tes (hī·drä·ō'tēz) The ancient name for the RAVI.

hy·drar·gy·rism (hī·drär'jə·riz'əm) *n.* *Pathol.* Mercury poisoning. Also **hy·drar·gy·ri·a·sis** (hī·drär'jə·rī'ə·sis).

hy·drar·gy·rum (hī·drär'jə·rəm) *n.* *Chem.* Mercury. [< NL < L *hydrargyrus* < Gk. *hydrargyros* < *hydōr* water + *argyros* silver] — **hy'drar·gy'ric** (-jir'ik) *adj.*

hy·dras·tine (hī·dras'tēn, -tin) *n.* *Chem.* A bitter, crystalline alkaloid, $C_{21}H_{21}NO_6$, derived from the roots of goldenseal, formerly used as a stomachic. [< NL *Hydrastis*, botanical genus name < Gk. *hydōr* water]

hy·drate (hī'drāt) *Chem. n.* Any of a class of compounds associated with water in definite molecular proportions, as chloral. — *v.t.* **·drat·ed, ·drat·ing** To combine with water or its elements to form a hydrate. [< HYDR- + -ATE³] — **hy·dra·tion** (hī·drā'shən) *n.*

hy·drat·ed (hī'drāt·əd) *adj.* Chemically combined with water, as in the formation of a hydrate.

hydraul. Hydraulics.

hy·drau·lic (hī·drô'lik) *adj.* **1.** Of or pertaining to hydraulics. **2.** Operated by means of water or other liquid under pressure: a *hydraulic* elevator, crane, etc. **3.** Hardening under water: *hydraulic* cement. [< L *hydraulicus* < Gk. *hydraulikos* of a water organ < *hydraulos* water organ < *hydōr* water + *aulos* pipe] — **hy·drau'li·cal·ly** *adv.*

hydraulic brake *Mech.* A brake actuated by fluids under pressure in cylinders and tubular connecting lines.

hydraulic press *Mech.* A machine operating by means of a fluid that, under pressure, converts a small force into a larger force acting over an extended area.

hydraulic ram *Mech.* A device by which the fall of a comparatively large quantity of water furnishes the power to raise a smaller quantity to a height above that of the source.

hy·drau·lics (hī·drô'liks) *n.pl.* (construed as sing.) The science of the laws governing the motion of water and other liquids and of their practical applications in engineering.

hy·dra·zine (hī'drə·zēn, -zin) *n.* *Chem.* **1.** A colorless fuming liquid, N_2H_4, derived from a diazo acid, used as a reducing agent in organic synthesis and as a rocket or jet fuel. **2.** One of a group of hydrazine derivatives formed by the replacement of one or more hydrogen atoms by an organic radical: phenyl *hydrazine.* [< HYDR- + AZ(O) + -INE²]

hy·dra·zo·ic acid (hī'drə·zō'ik) *Chem.* A colorless, very toxic acid, HN_3, whose salts, **hy·dra·zo·ates** (hī'drə·zō'āts), explode violently when heated: also called *triazoic acid.*

hy·dric (hī'drik) *adj.* Of, pertaining to, or containing hydrogen.

hy·dride (hī'drīd, -drid) *n.* *Chem.* **1.** A compound of hydrogen with another element or radical. **2.** Formerly, a hydroxide. Also **hy'drid** (-drid).

hy·dri·od·ic acid (hī'drē·od'ik) *Chem.* An aqueous solution of hydrogen iodide, used in medicine.

hy·dro (hī'drō) *Canadian adj.* Hydroelectric. — *n.* **1.** Hydroelectricity. **2.** *Informal* Electricity.

hydro- *combining form* **1.** Water; of, related to, or resembling water: *hydrophone.* **2.** *Chem.* Denoting a compound of hydrogen: *hydrochloric.* Also, before vowels, **hydr-.** [< Gk. *hydro- < hydōr* water]

hy·dro·bro·mic acid (hī'drə·brō'mik) *Chem.* An aqueous solution of hydrogen bromide, sometimes used as a sedative.

hy·dro·car·bon (hī'drə·kär'bən) *n.* *Chem.* Any of a large and important group of organic compounds that contain hydrogen and carbon only, as benzene, ethylene, methane, etc.

hy·dro·cele (hī'drə·sēl) *n.* *Pathol.* A localized accumulation of serous fluid in a body cavity, especially in the testicles or along the spermatic cord. [< L < Gk. *hydrokēlē < hydōr* water + *kēlē* tumor]

hy·dro·ceph·a·lus (hī'drə·sef'ə·ləs) *n.* *Pathol.* A condition characterized by the accumulation of fluid within the ventricles or between the membranes of the brain, especially in very young children, causing abnormal enlargement of the head. Also **hy·dro·ceph'a·ly.** [< HYDRO- + Gk. *kephalē* head] — **hy'dro·ceph'a·loid** (-loid), **hy'dro·ceph'a·lous** *adj.*

hy·dro·chlo·ric acid (hī'drə·klôr'ik, -klō'rik) *Chem.* An aqueous solution of hydrogen chloride, widely used in industry, medicine, and the arts: also called *muriatic acid.*

hy·dro·chlo·ride (hī'drə·klôr'īd, -klō'rīd) *n.* *Chem.* A salt produced by the union of hydrochloric acid with an organic base.

hy·dro·cy·an·ic acid (hī'drō·sī·an'ik) *Chem.* An aqueous solution of hydrogen cyanide, a colorless, volatile, very poisonous liquid with a bitter odor: also called *prussic acid.*

hy·dro·dy·nam·ic (hī'drō·dī·nam'ik) *adj.* **1.** Of or pertaining to the force or motion of water and other fluids. **2.** Of or pertaining to hydrodynamics. Also **hy'dro·dy·nam'i·cal.**

hy·dro·dy·nam·ics (hī'drō·dī·nam'iks) *n.pl.* (construed as sing.) The branch of dynamics that treats of the motions and forces of liquids, especially water.

hy·dro·e·lec·tric (hī'drō·i·lek'trik) *adj.* Of or pertaining to electricity generated by the energy of water. — **hy·dro·e·lec·tric·i·ty** (hī'drō·i·lek'tris'ə·tē, -ē'lek-) *n.*

hy·dro·flu·or·ic acid (hī'drə·flŏŏ·ôr'ik, -or'-, -flŏor'ik) *Chem.*

An aqueous solution of hydrogen fluoride, used for etching glass, treating metals, etc.

hy·dro·foil (hī′drə·foil) *n.* **1.** A streamlined surface designed to provide support in or reduce the resistance of the water through which it moves, as an attachment to a boat or to a hydroplane. **2.** A horizontal rudder used in raising or submerging a submarine. **3.** A hydrofoil boat.

hydrofoil boat A boat that travels with the hull above the water surface, supported by hydrofoils.

hy·dro·gel (hī′drə·jel) *n. Chem.* A colloid that has assumed a jellylike form in the presence of water.

hy·dro·gen (hī′drə·jən) *n.* The lightest of the elements (symbol H), an odorless, colorless, flammable gas, occurring chiefly in combination with oxygen as water and uniting chemically with many elements to form hydrocarbons, carbohydrates, and other important compounds. See ELEMENT. [< F *hydrogène* < Gk. *hydōr* water + -GEN] — **hy·drog·e·nous** (hī·droj′ə·nəs) *adj.*

hy·dro·gen·ate (hī′drə·jə·nāt′, hī·droj′ə·nāt) *v.t.* **·at·ed, ·at·ing** *Chem.* To combine with, treat with, or expose to the chemical action of hydrogen. Also **hy′dro·gen·ize′** (-īz′). — **hy·dro·gen·a·tion** (hī′drə·jə·nā′shən) *n.*

hydrogen bomb A very destructive thermonuclear bomb having no theoretical limit in size and power, releasing energy by the fusion, under extremely high temperatures, of light elements, as hydrogen isotopes: also called *H-bomb.*

hydrogen bromide *Chem.* A colorless, corrosive, acrid, gaseous compound of hydrogen and bromine, HBr, used as a catalyst and in the manufacture of hydrobromic acid.

hydrogen chloride *Chem.* A corrosive, pungent, gaseous compound of hydrogen and chlorine, HCl, used in organic synthesis and in the manufacture of hydrochloric acid.

hydrogen cyanide *Chem.* An unstable, colorless, intensely poisonous gas, HCN, used chiefly as an extermination agent of rodents, insects, and other vermin.

hydrogen fluoride *Chem.* A colorless, fuming, highly corrosive gaseous compound of hydrogen and fluorine, HF, used as a catalyst and reagent in many chemical processes.

hydrogen iodide *Chem.* A colorless, suffocating gas, HI, used in the manufacture of hydriodic acid.

hydrogen ion The positively charged ion (H+) present in all acid solutions. Compare *p*H.

hydrogen peroxide *Chem.* An unstable, colorless, syrupy liquid, H_2O_2, whose aqueous solutions are important as antiseptics and bleaching agents: also called *peroxide.*

hydrogen sulfide *Chem.* A colorless, gaseous, poisonous compound, H_2S, having a characteristic odor of rotten eggs.

hy·drog·ra·phy (hī·drog′rə·fē) *n.* **1.** The science of surveying, describing, and mapping seas, lakes, rivers, etc., especially to determine their use for navigation. **2.** Surface waters as represented on a map. — **hy·drog′ra·pher** *n.* — **hy′dro·graph′ic** or **·i·cal** *adj.* — **hy′dro·graph′i·cal·ly** *adv.*

hy·droid (hī′droid) *Zool. adj.* **1.** Pertaining or belonging to a group of hydrozoans that includes the hydra. **2.** Designating an asexual stage in the development of certain hydrozoans, characterized by the budding of polyps to form colonies. — *n.* A hydroid coelenterate, especially a polyp.

hy·dro·ki·net·ic (hī′drō·ki·net′ik) *adj.* **1.** Relating to the motion and kinetic energy of fluids. **2.** Of or pertaining to hydrokinetics. Also **hy′dro·ki·net′i·cal.**

hy·dro·ki·net·ics (hī′drō·ki·net′iks) *n.pl.* (construed as *sing.*) The branch of hydrodynamics dealing with the laws governing fluids in motion.

hy·drol·o·gy (hī·drol′ə·jē) *n.* The branch of physical geography that deals with the waters of the earth, their distribution, characteristics, and effects in relation to human activities. [< HYDRO- + -LOGY] — **hy·dro·log·ic** (hī′drə·loj′ik) or **·i·cal** *adj.* — **hy′dro·log′i·cal·ly** *adv.* — **hy·drol′o·gist** *n.*

hy·drol·y·sis (hī·drol′ə·sis) *n. pl.* **·ses** (-sēz) *Chem.* **1.** Action between the ions of water (H+ and OH−) and those of a salt to form an acid and a base, changing the *p*H of the solution when the acid and base are sufficiently different in strength. **2.** The decomposition of a compound by water, with each of the resultant compounds containing part of the water. [< HYDRO- + -LYSIS]

hy·dro·lyt·ic (hī′drə·lit′ik) *adj.* Of, pertaining to, or causing hydrolysis.

hy·dro·lyte (hī′drə·līt) *n.* Any substance affected by hydrolysis.

hy·dro·lyze (hī′drə·līz) *v.t. & v.i.* **·lyzed, ·lyz·ing** To undergo or cause to undergo hydrolysis. — **hy′dro·lyz′a·ble** *adj.* — **hy·dro·ly·za·tion** (hī′drə·lə·zā′shən, -lī·zā′-) *n.*

hy·dro·man·cy (hī′drō·man′sē) *n.* Divination by means of signs observed in water. — **hy′dro·manc′er** *n.* — **hy′dro·man′tic** (-tik) *adj.*

hy·dro·me·chan·ics (hī′drō·mə·kan′iks) *n.pl.* (construed as *sing.*) That branch of physics dealing with the way in which various forces act on liquids. — **hy′dro·me·chan′i·cal** *adj.*

hy·dro·me·du·sa (hī′drō·mə·dōō′sə, -dyōō′-) *n. pl.* **·sae** (-sē) *Zool.* A free-swimming medusa in the sexual stage of the life cycle of certain hydrozoans.

hy·dro·mel (hī′drə·mel) *n.* A liquor consisting of honey diluted with water, which, when fermented, becomes mead. [< OF < L < Gk. *hydromeli* < *hydōr* water + *meli* honey]

hy·dro·met·al·lur·gy (hī′drō·met′əl·ûr′jē) *n.* The process utilizing chemical reactions in various aqueous solutions to extract metal from ores. — **hy′dro·met′al·lur′gi·cal** *adj.*

hy·dro·me·te·or (hī′drō·mē′tē·ər) *n. Meteorol.* A condition produced by water in the atmosphere, as rain, snow, hail, etc. — **hy·dro·me·te·or·ol·o·gy** (hī′drō·mē′tē·ə·rol′ə·jē) *n.*

hy·drom·e·ter (hī·drom′ə·tər) *n.* A sealed tube marked with a graduated scale and weighted at one end, that determines the specific gravity or density of a liquid by the level to which the tube sinks while floating vertically. — **hy·dro·met·ric** (hī′drə·met′rik) or **·ri·cal** *adj.* — **hy·drom′e·try** *n.*

hy·dro·path·y (hī·drop′ə·thē) *n.* A treatment that professes to cure all diseases by the use of water both internally and externally: also called *water cure.* — **hy·dro·path·ic** (hī′drə·path′ik) or **·i·cal** *adj.* — **hy·drop′a·thist, hy′dro·path** *n.*

hy·dro·phane (hī′drə·fān) *n.* A whitish or light-colored opal, partly translucent when dry, but almost transparent when wet. — **hy·droph·a·nous** (hī·drof′ə·nəs) *adj.*

hy·dro·phil·ic (hī·drə·fil′ik) *adj. Chem.* Designating a colloid system in which the solid particles strongly attract and hold molecules of water.

hy·dro·pho·bi·a (hī′drə·fō′bē·ə) *n.* **1.** Rabies. **2.** Any morbid fear of water. [< L < Gk., < *hydōr* water + *phobos* fear] — **hy′dro·pho′bic** (hī′drə·fō′bik, -fob′ik) *adj.*

hy·dro·phone (hī′drə·fōn) *n.* **1.** An electrical instrument for detecting underwater sounds, especially of enemy submarines. **2.** A device for detecting leaks in water pipes. **3.** *Med.* An instrument for the detection of sounds transmitted through a column of liquid, used in auscultation.

hy·dro·phyte (hī′drə·fīt) *n. Bot.* A plant growing in water or in wet ground. — **hy·dro·phyt·ic** (hī′drə·fit′ik) *adj.*

hy·drop·ic (hī·drop′ik) *adj.* Dropsical. Also **hy·drop′i·cal.** [< OF *idropique* < L *hydropicus* < Gk. *hydrōpikos* < *hydrōps* dropsy < *hydōr* water] — **hy·drop′i·cal·ly** *adv.*

hy·dro·plane (hī′drə·plān) *n.* **1.** A seaplane (which see). **2.** A type of motor boat designed so that its hull is raised partially out of the water when driven at high speeds. **3.** A hydrofoil (def. 2). — *v.i.* **·planed, ·plan·ing** To drive or ride in or as if in a hydroplane (boat).

hydro pole *Canadian* A pole for power lines.

hy·dro·pon·ics (hī′drə·pon′iks) *n.pl.* (construed as *sing.*) The science of growing plants with their roots in nutrient mineral solutions rather than in soil: also called *aquiculture, tank farming, water culture.* [< HYDRO- + Gk. *ponos* labor] — **hy′dro·pon′ic** *adj.*

hy·drop·sy (hī′drop′sē) *n.* Dropsy. Also **hy·drops** (hī′drops′). [< L *hydrōps* < Gk. *hydrōps*]

hy·dro·qui·none (hī′drō·kwi·nōn′, -kwin′ōn) *n. Chem.* A white crystalline compound, $C_6H_4(OH)_2$, derived from quinone, used as an antiseptic and as a photographic developer. Also **hy·dro·quin′ol** (-kwin′ōl, -ol).

hydros. Hydrostatics.

hy·dro·scope (hī′drə·skōp) *n.* An instrument enabling one to see far below the surface of the water. — **hy′dro·scop′ic** (-skop′ik) or **·i·cal** *adj.*

hy·dro·sol (hī′drə·sol, -sōl) *n. Chem.* An aqueous solution of a colloid. [< HYDRO- + SOL(UTION)]

hy·dro·some (hī′drə·sōm) *n. Zool.* The whole attached colony of a compound hydrozoan. Also **hy′dro·so′ma** (-sō′mə). [< HYDRO- + -SOME²]

hy·dro·sphere (hī′drə·sfir) *n.* **1.** The total water, both salt and fresh, on the surface of the earth. **2.** The moisture in the atmosphere enveloping the earth. — **hy′dro·spher′ic** (-sfir′ik, -sfer′-) *adj.*

hy·dro·stat (hī′drə·stat) *n.* **1.** A device for preventing the explosion of a steam boiler due to lack of water. **2.** An electrical device for detecting the presence of water, as a protection against leakage, overflow, etc.

hy·dro·stat·ic (hī′drə·stat′ik) *adj.* Of or relating to hydrostatics. Also **hy·dro·stat′i·cal.** — **hy′dro·stat′i·cal·ly** *adv.*

hy·dro·stat·ics (hī′drə·stat′iks) *n.pl.* (construed as *sing.*) The science that deals with the pressure and equilibrium of fluids, especially of liquids. Abbr. *hyd., hydros.*

hy·dro·sul·fate (hī′drə·sul′fāt) *n. Chem.* A compound of sulfuric acid and an alkaloid or other organic base.

hy·dro·sul·fide (hī′drə·sul′fīd) *n. Chem.* A compound derived from hydrogen sulfide by replacing one of the hydrogen atoms with a basic radical or a base.

hy·dro·sul·fu·rous acid (hī′drō·sul·fyŏŏr′əs, hī′drə·sul′fər·əs) Hyposulfurous acid (which see).

hy·dro·tax·is (hī′drə·tak′sis) *n. Biol.* The response of organisms toward or away from water. — **hy′dro·tac′tic** *adj.*

hy·dro·ther·a·peu·tics (hī′drō·ther′ə·pyōō′tiks) *n.pl.* (construed as *sing.*) Hydrotherapy. — **hy′dro·ther′a·peu′tic** *adj.*

hy·dro·ther·a·py (hī′drō·ther′ə·pē) *n. Med.* The scientific use of water in the treatment of various diseases. — **hy·dro·ther·a·pic** (hī′drō·thə·rap′ik) *adj.*

hy·dro·ther·mal (hī′drə·thûr′məl) *adj. Geol.* Of or pertaining to hot water, especially as an agent in dissolving, transporting, or redepositing minerals in the earth's crust.

hy·dro·tho·rax (hī′drə·thôr′aks, -thō′raks)   *n. Pathol.* An accumulation of effused serous fluid in the pleural cavity. — **hy·dro·tho·rac·ic** (hī′drō-thə-ras′ik) *adj.*

hy·drot·ro·pism (hī·drŏt′rə·piz′əm)   *n. Biol.* A tropism in response to water. — **hy·dro·trop·ic** (hī′drə-trop′ik) *adj.*

hy·drous (hī′drəs)   *adj.* **1.** Watery. **2.** *Chem.* Containing water of crystallization or hydration.

hy·drox·ide (hī·drok′sīd)   *n. Chem.* A compound containing the hydroxyl ion.

hy·drox·y acid (hī·drok′sē)   *Chem.* Any of a class of organic acids containing the hydroxyl group.

hy·drox·yl·a·mine (hī·drok′sil·ə·mēn′, -am′in)   *n. Chem.* A colorless crystalline organic compound, NH_2OH, weakly basic and unstable, used as a reducing agent and intermediate.

hy·drox·yl group (hī·drok′sil)   *Chem.* The univalent group or radical OH, found in bases, acids, alcohols, phenols, and amphoteric compounds, forming acid, basic, or neutral compounds, depending on the relative electronegative or electropositive character of the atom or group with which it is combined.

hydroxyl ion   An anion consisting of one atom each of hydrogen and oxygen and bearing a charge of -1, characteristic of bases.

hy·dro·zo·an (hī′drə-zō′ən)   *adj. Zool.* Pertaining to or belonging to a widely distributed class (*Hydrozoa*) of freshwater and marine coelenterates, both solitary and colonial, including the hydra, certain jellyfishes and corals, and the Portuguese man-of-war. — *n.* A hydrozoan organism.

Hy·drus (hī′drəs)   A constellation, the Water Snake. See CONSTELLATION. [< L < Gk.]

hy·e·na (hī·ē′nə)   *n.* Any of a group of wolflike, carnivorous mammals (family *Hyaenidae*), feeding chiefly on carrion, with short hind legs, a bristly mane, and strong teeth, as the **striped laughing hyena** (*Hyaena hyaena*) of Africa and Asia, the **spotted hyena** (*Crocuta crocuta*) of Africa south of the Sahara, and the **brown hyena** (*H. brunnea*) of southern Africa. Also **hyaena.** [< L *hyæna* < Gk. *hyaina* sow]

hy·e·tal (hī′ə-təl)   *adj.* Of or pertaining to rain.

hyeto- *combining form* Rain: *hyetograph*. Also, before vowels, **hyet-.** [< Gk. *hyetos* rain < *hyein* to rain]

hy·e·to·graph (hī′i·tə·graf′, -gräf′)   *n. Meteorol.* A chart showing the distribution of rainfall during a stated period of time, usually a year.

hy·e·tog·ra·phy (hī′i·tog′rə·fē)   *n. Meteorol.* The scientific study concerned with the geographic distribution and mapping of rainfall. — **hy·e·to·graph·ic** (hī′i·tə·graf′ik) or **·i·cal** *adj.* — **hy′e·to·graph′i·cal·ly** *adv.*

Hy·ge·ia (hī·jē′ə)   In Greek mythology, the goddess of health, daughter of Aesculapius, the god of medicine. [< Gk. *hygieia* health]

hy·giene (hī′jēn, -ji·ēn)   *n.* The science of health. [< F *hygiène* < Gk. *hygieinos* healthful]

hy·gi·en·ic (hī′jē·en′ik, hī·jē′nik, -jen′ik)   *adj.* **1.** Of or pertaining to hygiene. **2.** Sanitary. — **hy′gi·en′i·cal·ly** *adv.*

hy·gi·en·ics (hī′jē·en′iks, hī·jē′niks)   *n.pl.* (*construed as sing.*) The science of preserving or promoting health; hygiene.

hy·gi·en·ist (hī′jē·ən·ist)   *n.* One who studies or is versed in the principles of hygiene. Also **hy′gie·ist** (-jē·ist), **hy′gie·ist.**

hygro- *combining form* Wet; moist: *hygrometer*. Also, before vowels, **hygr-.** [< Gk. *hygros* wet, moist]

hy·gro·graph (hī′grə·graf, -gräf)   *n.* A self-recording hygrometer.

hy·grom·e·ter (hī·grom′ə·tər)   *n.* An instrument for measuring the humidity or moisture in the atmosphere. [< HYGRO- + -METER] — **hy′gro·met′ric** (hī′grə·met′rik) *adj.*

hy·grom·e·try (hī·grom′ə·trē)   *n.* The branch of physics that deals with the measurement of moisture in the air.

hy·gro·scope (hī′grə·skōp)   *n.* A device for indicating the approximate humidity of the air.

hy·gro·scop·ic (hī′grə·skop′ik)   *adj.* **1.** Pertaining to the hygroscope, or capable of being detected only by it. **2.** Able to absorb or condense moisture from the atmosphere.

Hyk·sos (hik′sōs, -sos)   A dynasty of kings of Egypt, probably of Syro-Semitic origin, who ruled at Memphis 1685–1580 B.C.: often called *Shepherd Kings.*

hy·la (hī′lə)   *n.* Any of a genus (*Hyla*) of frogs, especially the tree frog. [< NL < Gk. *hylē* wood]

hylo- *combining form* **1.** Matter; of or pertaining to matter: *hylozoism.* **2.** Wood; of or pertaining to wood. Also, before vowels, **hyl-.** [< Gk. *hylē* wood]

hy·loph·a·gous (hī·lof′ə·gəs)   *adj. Biol.* Wood-eating.

hy·lo·zo·ism (hī′lə·zō′iz·əm)   *n.* The doctrine that all matter is endowed with life, or that life and matter are inseparable. [< HYLO- + Gk. *zōē* life] — **hy′lo·zo′ic** *adj.* — **hy′lo·zo′ist** *n.* — **hy′lo·zo·is′tic** *adj.* — **hy′lo·zo·is′ti·cal·ly** *adv.*

hy·men (hī′mən)   *n.* **1.** *Anat.* A thin mucous membrane partially covering the external entrance of the vagina in a virgin. **2.** Marriage; also, a wedding song or poem. [< Gk. *hymēn* skin, membrane]

Hy·men (hī′mən)   In Greek mythology, the god of marriage.

hy·me·ne·al (hī′mə·nē′əl)   *adj.* Of or pertaining to marriage or a wedding. — *n.* A wedding song or poem.

hymeno- *combining form* Membrane: *hymenopterous.* Also, before vowels, **hymen-.** [< Gk. *hymēn* skin, membrane]

hy·men·op·ter·on (hī′mən·op′tər·on)   *n. pl.* **·ter·a** (-tər·ə) A hymenopterous insect. Also **hy′men·op′ter.**

hy·men·op·ter·ous (hī′mən·op′tər·əs)   *adj. Entomol.* Of, pertaining to, or belonging to an extensive and highly developed order of insects (*Hymenoptera*), typically having four membranous wings, of which the front pair are larger, including bees, wasps, sawflies, etc. [< NL < Gk. *hymēn* membrane + *ptera*, pl. of *pteron* wing] — **hy·men·op·ter·an** (hī′mən·op′tər·ən) *adj. & n.*

Hy·met·tus (hī·met′əs)   A mountain range in east central Greece; highest point, 3,367 ft. *Greek* **Hy·met·tos** (ē·mē·tôs′).

hymn (him)   *n.* A song of praise, adoration, thanksgiving, etc., especially one sung at a religious service. — *v.t.* **1.** To praise or worship with a hymn or hymns. **2.** To express in a hymn, song, etc.: to *hymn* praises. — *v.i.* **3.** To sing hymns. [Fusion of OE *hymen* and OF *ymne*, both < LL *ymnus*, *hymnus* < Gk. *hymnos* song, ode] — **hym′nic** (-nik) *adj.*

hym·nal (him′nəl)   *n.* A book of hymns. Also *Canadian* **hym′na·ry** (-nə·rē), **hymn′book** (-bŏŏk′). — *adj.* Of or relating to a hymn or hymns.

hym·nist (him′nist)   *n.* A writer of hymns. Also **hym′no·dist** (-nə·dist).

hym·no·dy (him′nə·dē)   *n. pl.* **·dies** **1.** The composing or singing of hymns. **2.** Hymns collectively. [< LL *hymnodia* < Gk. *hymnoidia* < *hymnos* hymn + *ōidē* singing]

hym·nol·o·gy (him·nol′ə·jē)   *n.* **1.** The study of hymns, their use, classification, history, etc. **2.** The writing of hymns. **3.** Hymns collectively. [< HYMN + -(O)LOGY] — **hy·mno·log·ic** (him′nə·loj′ik) or **·i·cal** *adj.* — **hym·nol′o·gist** *n.*

hy·oid (hī′oid)   *n. Anat.* In man, a U-shaped bone, or in other vertebrates, a series of bones, at the base of the tongue, for the attachment of the swallowing muscles. Also **hyoid bone.** For illustration see LARYNX, MOUTH. — *adj.* Pertaining to the hyoid bone. [< F *hyoïde* < Gk. *hyoeidēs* < Υ upsilon + *eidos* form]

hy·os·cine (hī′ə·sēn)   *n.* Scopolamine. [< HYOSC(YAMUS) + -INE]

hy·os·cy·a·mine (hī′ə·sī′ə·mēn, -min)   *n. Chem.* A white, crystalline, poisonous alkaloid, $C_{17}H_{23}NO_3$, extracted from henbane, deadly nightshade, and other plants and used as a sedative, mydriatic, etc. Also **hy′os·cy·a·min** (-min).

hy·os·cy·a·mus (hī′ə·sī′ə·məs)   *n.* The henbane. [< Gk. *hyoskyamos* henbane < *hys* hog + *kyamos* bean]

hyp- Var. of HYPO-.

hyp. **1.** Hypotenuse. **2.** Hypothesis; hypothetical.

hyp·a·bys·sal (hip′ə·bis′əl)   *adj. Geol.* Pertaining to or designating minor igneous intrusions, that, in the molten state, have risen near the surface. [< HYP- + ABYSSAL]

hyp·aes·the·si·a (hip′is·thē′zhə, -zhē·ə)   See HYPESTHESIA.

hy·pae·thral (hī·pē′thrəl)   See HYPETHRAL.

hype (hīp)   *n. Slang* Blatant promotion or publicity.

hyper- *prefix* **1.** Over; above; excessive: *hypercritical.* **2.** *Med.* Denoting an abnormal state of excess: *hypertension;* opposed to *hypo-.* **3.** *Chem.* Denoting the highest in a series of compounds. [< Gk. *hyper- < hyper* above]

In the following self-explanatory compounds, *hyper-* appears in sense 1:

hyperactive	hyperobtrusive
hyperacute	hyperorthodoxy
hyperbrutal	hyperpathetic
hypercarnal	hyperpatriotic
hypercivilized	hyperpersonal
hyperclassical	hyperpolysyllabic
hyperconfident	hyperproduction
hyperconscientious	hyperpurist
hyperdemocratic	hyperrational
hyperdiabolical	hyperresonance
hyperelegant	hyperreverential
hyperemphasize	hypersaintly
hyperenthusiasm	hypersensual
hyperexcitement	hypersentimental
hypergrammatical	hyperskeptical
hyperidealistic	hypersophisticated
hyperintellectual	hypersubtlety
hypermetaphorical	hypertechnical
hypermodest	hypertragically
hypermystical	hypervigilant

hy·per·a·cid·i·ty (hī′pər·ə·sid′ə·tē)   *n. Med.* An excess of acidity, as of the gastric juice.

hy·per·a·cu·si·a (hī′pər·ə·kyōō′zhē·ə)   *Pathol.* Abnormal acuteness of hearing. Also **hy′per·a·cu′sis** (-sis). [< HYPER- + Gk. *akousis* hearing]

hy·per·ae·mi·a (hī′pər·ē′mē·ə)   See HYPEREMIA.

hy·per·aes·the·si·a (hī′pər·es·thē′zhə, -zhē·ə)   See HYPERESTHESIA.

hy·per·al·ge·si·a (hī′pər·al·jē′zē·ə, -sē·ə)   *n. Pathol.* An excessive sensitivity to pain. Also **hy′per·al′ge·sis** (-sis). [< HYPER- + Gk. *algēsis* sense of pain < *algos* pain] — **hy′per·al·ge′sic** (-zik, -sik) *adj.*

hy·per·bar·ism (hī′pər·bar′iz·əm)   *n. Med.* A disturbed condition caused by atmospheric pressure greater than the pressure within the body: opposed to *hypobarism.* [< HYPER- + Gk. *baros* weight] — **hy′per·bar′ic** (-bar′ik) *adj.*

hy·per·bo·la (hī·pûr′bə·lə) *n. Math.* A curve traced by a point moving so that the difference between its distances from two fixed points or foci remains constant; the curve produced by the intersection of a plane with the surface of a cone, the plane intersecting both nappes. [< NL < Gk. *hyperbolē* a throwing beyond, excess. See HYPERBOLE.]

hy·per·bo·le (hī·pûr′bə·lē) *n.* An exaggeration or overstatement intended to produce an effect without being taken literally, as: *He was centuries old; She wept gallons of tears.* [< L < Gk. *hyperbolē* a throwing beyond, excess < *hyper-* over + *ballein* to throw]

hy·per·bol·ic (hī′pər·bol′ik) *adj.* **1.** Of, pertaining to, or using hyperbole. **2.** *Math.* Of or pertaining to the hyperbola. Also **hy′per·bol′i·cal.** — **hy′per·bol′i·cal·ly** *adv.*

hy·per·bo·lism (hī·pûr′bə·liz′əm) *n.* **1.** The use of hyperbole. **2.** An example of hyperbole.

hy·per·bo·lize (hī·pûr′bə·līz) *v.t. & v.i.* **·lized, ·liz·ing** To express in or use hyperbole; exaggerate.

hy·per·bo·loid (hī·pûr′bə·loid) *n. Math.* A quadratic surface generated by rotating a hyperbola about an axis of symmetry. If the rotation is about the axis passing through the foci, a **hyperboloid of two sheets** results, if about the other axis, a **hyperboloid of one sheet.**

HYPERBOLOID OF
TWO SHEETS
O Origin. *x, y, z* Axes.

hy·per·bo·re·an (hī′pər·bôr′ē·ən, -bō′rē-) *adj.* Of or pertaining to the far north; frigid; arctic.

Hy·per·bo·re·an (hī′pər·bôr′ē·ən, -bō′rē-) *n.* In Greek mythology, one of the people who lived in the far north in a land of everlasting peace and sunshine and who worshiped Apollo. — *adj.* Of or pertaining to the Hyperboreans. [< L *hyperboreus* < Gk. *hyperboreos* < *hyper-* beyond + *Boreas* north wind.]

hy·per·cor·rect (hī′pər·kə·rekt′) *adj.* **1.** Excessively correct; finicky. **2.** *Ling.* Of, pertaining to, or showing hypercorrection. — **hy′per·cor·rect′ly** *adv.*

hy·per·cor·rec·tion (hī′pər·kə·rek′shən) *n. Ling.* The adoption of a spelling, usage, etc., to replace one mistakenly supposed to be erroneous, as *between you and I.*

hy·per·cor·rect·ness (hī′pər·kə·rekt′nis) *n.* The state or quality of being hypercorrect (def. 1).

hy·per·crit·ic (hī′pər·krit′ik) *n.* A hypercritical person.

hy·per·crit·i·cal (hī′pər·krit′i·kəl) *adj.* Excessively critical or carping; faultfinding. — **hy′per·crit′i·cal·ly** *adv.* — **hy′per·crit′i·cism** (-siz′əm) *n.*

hy·per·cube (hī′pər·kyo͞ob) *n. Math.* A tesseract.

hy·per·du·li·a (hī′pər·do͞o·lī′ə, -dyo͞o-) *n.* In the Roman Catholic Church, the veneration given to the Virgin Mary as the most sacred of mortal creatures: distinguished from *dulia, latria.* [< Med.L < *hyper-* beyond + *dulia* service]

hy·per·e·mi·a (hī′pər·ē′mē·ə) *n. Pathol.* An excessive accumulation or flow of blood in any part of the body: also spelled *hyperaemia.* — **hy′per·e′mic** *adj.*

hy·per·es·the·sia (hī′pər·is·thē′zhə, -zhē·ə) *n.* Exaggerated sensitiveness to touch, heat, pain, etc.: also spelled *hyperaesthesia.* — **hy′per·es·thet′ic** (-thet′ik) *adj.*

hy·per·eu·tec·tic (hī′pər·yo͞o·tek′tik) *adj. Chem.* Having the minor component in a proportion greater than that of the corresponding eutectic mixture.

hy·per·ex·ten·sion (hī′pər·ik·sten′shən) *n. Physiol.* Excessive extension, as of an arm or leg.

hy·per·gly·ce·mi·a (hī′pər·glī·sē′mē·ə) *n. Pathol.* An excessively high level of glucose in the blood. [< HYPER- + Gk. *glykys* sweet + -EMIA] — **hy′per·gly·ce′mic** *adj.*

hy·per·gol·ic (hī′pər·gol′ik) *adj. Aerospace* Denoting a type of rocket propellant that ignites spontaneously on contact with an oxidizer. [< HYPER- + G *gola,* a code word used in German rocketry]

Hy·pe·ri·on (hī·pir′ē·ən) In Greek mythology: **a** A Titan, the son of Uranus and Gaea and father of Helios, Selene, and Eos. **b** Helios. **c** In later use, Apollo.

hy·per·ki·ne·sia (hī′pər·ki·nē′zhə, -zhē·ə) *n. Pathol.* Excessive muscular motion; spasm. Also **hy′per·ki·ne′sis** (-nē′sis). — **hy′per·ki·net′ic** (-net′ik) *adj.*

hy·per·me·ter (hī·pûr′mə·tər) *n.* A line of verse containing one or more syllables in excess of those required by the meter. — **hy·per·met·ric** (hī′pər·met′rik) or **·ri·cal** *adj.*

hy·per·me·tro·pi·a (hī′pər·mə·trō′pē·ə) *n. Pathol.* An abnormal condition of the eye in which objects at a distance are seen more plainly than those near at hand; farsightedness. Also **hy′per·met′ro·py** (-met′rə·pē). Also called *hyperopia.* [< NL < Gk. *hypermetros* excessive + *ōps* eye] — **hy′per·me·trop′ic** (-mə·trop′ik, -trō′pik) *adj.*

Hy·perm·nes·tra (hī′pərm·nes′trə) In Greek mythology, the only one of the Danaides who did not kill her husband on her wedding night.

hy·per·on (hī′pər·on) *n. Physics* Any of a class of atomic particles having a mass intermediate between that of a neu-

tron and a deuteron: formerly called *V-particle.* [< HYPER- + -ON]

hy·per·o·pi·a (hī′pər·ō′pē·ə) *n. Pathol.* Hypermetropia. — **hy′per·op′ic** (-op′ik) *adj.*

hy·per·os·to·sis (hī′pər·os·tō′sis) *n. pl.* **·ses** (-sēz) *Pathol.* An abnormal increase in or outgrowth of bony tissue. — **hy′per·os·tot′ic** (-tot′ik) *adj.*

hy·per·phys·i·cal (hī′pər·fiz′i·kəl) *adj.* Beyond the realm of the physical; supernatural. — **hy′per·phys′i·cal·ly** *adv.*

hy·per·pi·e·sia (hī′pər·pī·ē′zhə, -zhē·ə) *n. Pathol.* Hypertension. Also **hy′per·pi·e′sis** (-sis). [< NL < Gk. *hyper-* beyond + *piesis* pressure < *piezein* to press]

hy·per·pi·tu·i·ta·rism (hī′pər·pi·to͞o′i·tə·riz′əm, -tyo͞o′-) *n. Pathol.* **1.** Excessive activity of the pituitary gland. **2.** The condition or disorders resulting from this.

hy·per·pla·sia (hī′pər·plā′zhə, -zhē·ə) *n. Pathol.* **1.** An abnormal increase in the number of cells in a part or organ. **2.** Enlargement resulting from such an increase. — **hy′per·plas′ic** (-plas′ik), **hy′per·plas′tic** (-plas′tik) *adj.*

hy·per·ploid (hī′pər·ploid) *adj. Biol.* Pertaining to or designating a chromosome number greater than the diploid number but not an exact multiple of it. — **hy′per·ploid′y** *n.*

hy·perp·ne·a (hī′pərp·nē′ə) *n. Pathol.* Unusually rapid or labored breathing. Also **hy′perp·noe′a.** [< NL < Gk. *hyper-* above + *pnoē* breathing < *pneein* to breathe]

hy·per·py·rex·i·a (hī′pər·pī·rek′sē·ə) *n. Pathol.* Very high fever. — **hy′per·py·ret′ic** (-ret′ik), **hy′per·py·rex′i·al** *adj.*

hy·per·sen·si·tive (hī′pər·sen′sə·tiv) *adj.* **1.** Excessively sensitive. **2.** Allergic. — **hy′per·sen′si·tive·ness, hy′per·sen′si·tiv′i·ty** (-sen′sə·tiv′ə·tē) *n.*

hy·per·sen·si·tize (hī′pər·sen′sə·tīz) *v.t.* **·tized, ·tiz·ing** *Photog.* To increase the sensitiveness or speed of, as a plate or film, usually by immersion in a suitable solution or by exposure to mercury vapor. — **hy′per·sen′si·ti·za′tion** *n.*

hy·per·son·ic (hī′pər·son′ik) *adj.* Of, pertaining to, or characterized by supersonic speeds of mach 5 or greater.

hy·per·son·ics (hī′pər·son′iks) *n.pl.* (construed as sing.) The branch of dynamics concerned with the design, characteristics, and performance of objects moving at hypersonic speeds, as guided missiles, rockets, etc.

hy·per·space (hī′pər·spās′) *n.* Space regarded as having more than three dimensions.

hy·per·sthene (hī′pər·sthēn) *n.* A pearly, dark-colored, ferrous magnesium silicate of the pyroxene group, found massive in igneous rocks. [< HYPER- + Gk. *sthenos* strength]

hy·per·sthe·ni·a (hī′pər·sthē′nē·ə) *n.* Excessive physical vigor and tone. [< HYPER- + Gk. *sthenos* strength] — **hy′·per·sthen′ic** (-sthen′ik) *adj.*

hy·per·ten·sion (hī′pər·ten′shən) *n. Pathol.* High blood pressure: also *hyperpiesia.* — **hy′per·ten′sive** (-siv) *adj.*

hy·per·ther·mi·a (hī′pər·thûr′mē·ə) *n. Med.* Therapy by artificially induced fever. Also **hy′per·ther′my.** [< HYPER- + Gk. *thermē* heat] — **hy′per·ther′mal** *adj.*

hy·per·thy·roid·ism (hī′pər·thī′roid·iz′əm) *n. Pathol.* **1.** Excessive activity of the thyroid gland. **2.** Any disorder caused by this. — **hy′per·thy′roid** *adj. & n.*

hy·per·ton·ic (hī′pər·ton′ik) *adj.* **1.** *Pathol.* Pertaining to or designating an excess of tone or tension. **2.** *Chem.* Designating a solution having an osmotic pressure greater than that of another with which it is compared. — **hy′per·to·nic′i·ty** (-tō·nis′ə·tē) *n.*

hy·per·tro·phy (hī·pûr′trə·fē) *n. Pathol.* **1.** The excessive development of an organ or part. **2.** The enlargement resulting from such a condition. — *v.i. & v.t.* **·phied, ·phy·ing** To grow or cause to grow excessively. — **hy·per·troph·ic** (hī′pər·trof′ik, -trō′fik) or **·i·cal** *adj.*

hy·per·ven·ti·la·tion (hī′pər·ven′tə·lā′shən) *n.* **1.** An excess supply of air to the lungs, often resulting in a lowered carbon dioxide content of the blood. **2.** Physical therapy by exposure of the body to drafts of air.

hy·per·vi·ta·min·o·sis (hī′pər·vī′tə·min·ō′sis) *n. Pathol.* A condition due to an excess of vitamins.

hyp·es·the·sia (hip′is·thē′zhə, -zhē·ə) *n. Pathol.* Diminished sensitiveness; partial loss of sensation: also spelled *hypaesthesia.* — **hyp′es·the′sic** (-sik) or **·thet′ic** (-thet′ik) *adj.*

hy·pe·thral (hi·pē′thrəl, hī-) *adj.* Open to the sky; unroofed: also spelled *hypaethral.* [< L *hypaethrus* < Gk. *hypaithros* < *hypo-* under + *aithēr* ether, clear sky]

hy·pha (hī′fə) *n. pl.* **·phae** (-fē) *Bot.* One of the long, threadlike, branching bodies that constitute the mycelium of a fungus. [< NL < Gk. *hyphē* web] — **hy′phal** *adj.*

hy·phe·mi·a (hī·fē′mē·ə) *n. Pathol.* **1.** Deficiency of blood, or a lack of supply of the red corpuscles in the blood. **2.** Extravasation of the blood into a surrounding tissue, especially in the eye. Also **hy·phae′mi·a.** [< HYPO- + -HEMIA]

hy·phen (hī′fən) *n.* A mark (- or - or =) used to connect the elements of certain compound words or to show division of a word at the end of a line. — *v.t.* To hyphenate. [< LL < Gk. *hyph′ hen* under one, together < *hypo-* under + *hen* one]

hy·phen·ate (hī′fən·āt) *v.t.* **·at·ed, ·at·ing** **1.** To connect by a hyphen. **2.** To write with a hyphen. — **hy′phen·a′tion** *n.*

hy·phen·at·ed (hī'fən·ā'tid) *adj. U.S.* Pertaining to or designating a person whose country of birth, parental nationality, ancestry, etc., is indicated by a hyphenated compound, as *Anglo-American*; *Italo-American*: often an opprobrious term.

hy·phen·ize (hī·fə·nīz) *v.t.* **·ized**, **·iz·ing** To hyphenate. — **hy'phen·i·za'tion** *n.*

hyp·na·gog·ic (hip'nə·goj'ik) *adj.* **1.** Inducing or promoting sleep, as by a drug or by hypnosis. **2.** *Psychol.* Of or pertaining to the mental condition occurring just before sleep; dreamlike; visionary. [< HYPN(O)- + -AGOGUE]

hyp·na·pa·gog·ic (hip'nə·pə·goj'ik) *adj.* Preventing or inhibiting sleep. [< HYPN(O)- + AP(O)- + -AGOGUE]

hyp·nic (hip'nik) *adj.* Pertaining to or inducing sleep.

hypno- *combining form* Sleep; of or related to sleep: *hypnology*. Also, before vowels, **hypn-**. [< Gk. *hypnos* sleep]

hyp·no·a·nal·y·sis (hip'nō·ə·nal'ə·sis) *n. Psychoanal.* A technique that utilizes analytic data obtained through hypnosis. — **hyp'no·an'a·lyt'ic** (-an'ə·lit'ik) *adj.*

hyp·noi·dal (hip·noid'l) *adj. Psychiatry* Characterizing a condition resembling light hypnosis, with heightened suggestibility, partial somnolence, etc. Also **hyp·noid'.**

hyp·nol·o·gy (hip·nol'ə·jē) *n.* The science of sleep. — **hyp·no·log·ic** (hip'nə·loj'ik) or **·i·cal** *adj.* — **hyp·nol'o·gist** *n.*

hyp·no·pae·di·a (hip'nō·pē'dē·ə) *n.* Training and instruction during sleep: a word used by Aldous Huxley in his novel *Brave New World* (1932), now applied to a technique in actual use. [< HYPNO- + Gk. *paideia* education (< *pais, paidos* child)] — **hyp'no·pae'dic** (-pē'dik) *adj.*

Hyp·nos (hip'nos) In Greek mythology, the god of sleep: identified with the Roman *Somnus.* Also **Hyp'nus** (-nəs).

hyp·no·sis (hip·nō'sis) *n. pl.* **·ses** (-sēz) *Psychol.* **1.** A trancelike condition that can be artificially induced, characterized by an altered consciousness, diminished will power, and an increased responsiveness to suggestion. **2.** The causing of such a condition.

hyp·no·ther·a·py (hip'nō·ther'ə·pē) *n. Med.* The use of hypnotism in treating disease, especially mental disease.

hyp·not·ic (hip·not'ik) *adj.* **1.** Pertaining to hypnosis or hypnotism. **2.** Readily hypnotized. **3.** Tending to produce sleep. — *n.* **1.** A drug or other agent producing sleep. **2.** A hypnotized person. **3.** A person susceptible to hypnosis. [< Gk. *hypnōtikos* < *hypnos* sleep] — **hyp·not'i·cal·ly** *adv.*

hyp·no·tism (hip'nə·tiz'əm) *n.* **1.** The act or practice of inducing hypnosis. **2.** The study of the techniques and phenomena of hypnosis. **3.** Hypnosis.

hyp·no·tist (hip'nə·tist) *n.* One who hypnotizes.

hyp·no·tize (hip'nə·tīz) *v.t.* **·tized**, **·tiz·ing** **1.** To produce hypnosis in. **2.** To fascinate; charm. Also *Brit.* **hyp'no·tise.** — **hyp'no·tiz'a·ble** *adj.* — **hyp'no·ti·za'tion** (-tə·zā'-shən, -tī·zā'-) *n.* — **hyp'no·tiz'er** *n.*

hy·po¹ (hī'pō) *n. Photog.* Sodium thiosulfate (formerly called *sodium hyposulfite*), used as a fixing agent.

hy·po² (hī'pō) *n. pl.* **·pos** *Informal* A hypodermic injection or syringe.

hy·po³ (hī'pō) *n. pl.* **·pos** *Slang* A hypochondriac.

hypo- *prefix* **1.** Under; beneath: *hypodermic.* **2.** Less than: *hypomania.* **3.** *Med.* Denoting a lack of or deficiency in: *hypothyroidism*: opposed to *hyper-.* **4.** *Chem.* Indicating the lowest member in a series of compounds (that is, the lowest degree of oxidation): *hypochlorous acid.* Also, before vowels, **hyp-.** [< Gk. < *hypo* under]

In the following self-explanatory compounds, *hypo-* appears in senses 2 and 3:

hypoactive	hypocartharsis	hypokinesia
hypoactivity	hypocathartic	hypokinesis
hypoalimentation	hypodynamic	hypokinetic
hypoalkaline	hypoendocrinism	hypomotility
hypoalkalinity	hypofunction	hyposecretion

hy·po·a·cid·i·ty (hī'pō·ə·sid'ə·tē) *n. Med.* Deficient or subnormal acidity, as of the gastric juices.

hy·po·bar·ism (hī'pə·bär'iz·əm) *n. Med.* A condition brought about when the atmospheric pressure is less than that of the gases within the body: opposed to *hyperbarism.* [< HYPO- + Gk. *baros* weight] — **hy'po·bar'ic** *adj.*

hy·po·blast (hī'pə·blast) *n. Biol.* The innermost layer of the gastrula, from which is derived the epithelium of the embryonic digestive tract. — **hy'po·blas'tic** *adj.*

hy·po·caust (hī'pə·kôst) *n.* In ancient Roman buildings, the space, usually beneath the floor, in which heated air was accumulated for distribution through a heating system. [< L *hypocaustum* < Gk. *hypokauston* < *hypo-* beneath + *kaiein* to burn]

hy·po·cen·ter (hī'pə·sen'tər) *n.* Ground zero.

hy·po·chlo·rite (hī'pə·klôr'īt, -klō'rīt) *n. Chem.* A salt of hypochlorous acid.

hy·po·chlo·rous acid (hī'pə·klôr'əs, -klō'rəs) *Chem.* An acid, HClO, obtained by the action of chlorine on mercurous oxide and water, and used as an oxidizer and bleach.

hy·po·chon·dri·a (hī'pə·kon'drē·ə, hip'ə-) *n.* **1.** A persistent anxiety about one's health, usually associated with some one or another part of the body and imagined symptoms of illness. **2.** A morbid melancholy and depression of mind or spirits. Also **hy·po·chon·dri·a·sis** (hī'pō·kən·drī'ə·sis). [<

L, abdomen (once taken to be the seat of this condition) < Gk. *hypochondria*, neut. pl. < *hypochondrios* under the cartilage < *hypo-* under + *chondros* cartilage]

hy·po·chon·dri·ac (hī'pə·kon'drē·ak, hip'ə-) *adj.* **1.** Pertaining to or affected with hypochondria. **2.** Of, pertaining to, or situated in the hypochondrium. See illustration at ABDOMEN. Also **hy·po·chon·dri·a·cal** (hī'pō·kən·drī'ə·kəl). — *n.* A person subject to or affected with hypochondria. — **hy'po·chon·dri'a·cal·ly** *adv.*

hy·po·chon·dri·um (hī'pə·kon'drē·əm, hip'ə-) *n. pl.* **·dri·a** (-drē·ə) *Anat.* The region of the abdomen situated on either side of the epigastrium, under the costal cartilages and short ribs. [< NL < Gk. *hypochondrion.* See HYPOCHONDRIA.]

hy·po·co·ris·tic (hī'pō·kə·ris'tik) *adj.* Of, pertaining to, or making use of an endearing diminutive or pet name. [< Gk. *hypokoristikos* < *hypo-* under + *korizesthai* to caress < *koros* child] — **hy·po·cor·ism** (hī'pō·kôr'iz·əm) *n.*

hy·po·cot·yl (hī'pə·kot'l) *n. Bot.* The part of the axis of a seedling below the seed leaves or cotyledons. [< HYPO- + COTYL(EDON)] — **hy'po·cot'y·lous** *adj.*

hy·poc·ri·sy (hi·pok'rə·sē) *n. pl.* **·sies** The pretense of having feelings or characteristics one does not possess; especially, the deceitful assumption of praiseworthy qualities; insincerity. [< OF *ypocrisie* < L *hypocrisis* < Gk. *hypokrisis* pretense < *hypokrinesthai* to play a part, act]

— **Syn.** *Hypocrisy, dissimulation, pretense, sanctimony, sanctimoniousness, pharisaism,* and *cant* denote a false show of qualities not actually possessed. *Hypocrisy* is the most extreme word; it denotes the feigning of admirable qualities, as goodness, sincerity, honesty, etc., by those who actually have the opposite qualities of badness, insincerity, dishonesty, etc. *Dissimulation* is less extreme; it denotes the masking or disguise of one's true nature, which may be either good or bad. *Pretense* is even milder, and may be worthy: to make a *pretense* of not hearing a slur. *Sanctimony,* originally a worthy holiness or nobility of nature, has become the hypocritical pretense of piety; this pejorative sense is even stronger in *sanctimoniousness. Pharisaism* is the hypocritical observance of the letter of a law, especially a moral law, while actually disregarding its spirit. *Cant,* in the sense here compared, refers to the pious utterances of the sanctimonious.

hyp·o·crite (hip'ə·krit) *n.* One who practices hypocrisy. [< Gk. *hypokritēs* actor. See HYPOCRISY.] — **hyp'o·crit'i·cal** *adj.* — **hyp'o·crit'i·cal·ly** *adv.*

hy·po·cy·cloid (hī'pə·sī'kloid, hip'ə-) *n. Math.* A curve generated by a point on the circumference of a circle that rolls around the inner circumference of another circle.

hy·po·derm (hī'pə·dûrm) *n. Zool.* The layer that secretes the outer skin of an arthropod: also called *hypodermis.*

hy·po·der·ma (hī'pə·dûr'mə) *n.* **1.** *Bot.* The distinct sheath of tissue beneath the epidermis of stems in plants. **2.** *Zool.* The hypoderm. [< NL < Gk. *hypo-* under + *derma* skin]

hy·po·der·mal (hī'pə·dûr'məl) *adj.* **1.** *Bot.* **a** Pertaining to the hypoderma. **b** Below the epidermis. **2.** Hypodermic.

hy·po·der·mic (hī'pə·dûr'mik) *adj.* **1.** Of or pertaining to the area under the skin. **2.** *Zool.* Pertaining to the hypoderm. — *n.* A hypodermic injection or syringe.

hypodermic needle The needle of a hypodermic syringe.

hypodermic syringe A syringe having a sharp, hollow needle for injection of substances beneath the skin.

hy·po·der·mis (hī'pə·dûr'mis) *n. Zool.* The hypoderm.

hy·po·eu·tec·tic (hī'pō·yōō·tek'tik, hip'ō-) *adj. Chem.* Having the minor component in a proportion less than that in the corresponding eutectic mixture, as a steel alloy with less than 0.85 percent carbon.

hy·po·gas·tric (hī'pə·gas'trik) *adj.* Pertaining to or situated in the hypogastrium. See illustration at ABDOMEN.

hy·po·gas·tri·um (hī'pə·gas'trē·əm) *n. pl.* **·tri·a** (-trē·ə) *Anat.* The region at the lower part of the abdomen on the middle line. [< NL < Gk. *hypogastrion* < *hypo-* below + *gastēr* belly]

hy·po·ge·al (hī'pə·jē'əl, hip'ə-) *adj.* **1.** Situated beneath the surface of the earth; underground. **2.** *Geol.* Underlying the superficial outcropping strata. **3.** Hypogeous.

hyp·o·gene (hip'ə·jēn) *adj. Geol.* **1.** Formed beneath the earth's surface, as granite: opposed to *epigene.* **2.** Denoting ore deposits formed by ascending waters.

hy·pog·e·nous (hī·poj'ə·nəs, hip·oj'-) *adj. Bot.* Growing beneath, as fungi on the under surface of a leaf. Compare EPIGENOUS. [< HYPO- + -GENOUS]

hy·po·ge·ous (hī'pə·jē'əs, hip'ə-) *adj.* **1.** Underground; subterranean. **2.** *Bot.* Growing or fruiting underground. [< L *hypogeus* < Gk. *hypogeios* < *hypo-* under + *gē* earth]

hyp·o·ge·um (hip'ə·jē'əm, hī'pə-) *n. pl.* **·ge·a** (-jē'ə) **1.** *Archit.* The part of a building below the ground. **2.** Any manmade underground structure or vault. [< L < Gk. *hypogeios* subterranean]

hy·po·glos·sal (hī'pə·glos'əl, hip'ə-) *adj. Biol.* Situated beneath the tongue. — *n.* The hypoglossal nerve. [< HYPO- + Gk. *glōssa* tongue]

hypoglossal nerve *Anat.* The twelfth cranial nerve, concerned in the motor and sensory functions of the tongue.

hy·po·gly·ce·mi·a (hī'pə·glī·sē'mē·ə) *n. Pathol.* An excessively low level of glucose in the blood. [< HYPO- + Gk. *glykys* sweet + -EMIA] — **hy'po·gly·ce'mic** *adj.*

hy·pog·y·nous (hī·poj'ə·nəs, hi-) *adj. Bot.* **1.** Situated on or growing from the receptacle of the flower beneath the ovary or pistil. **2.** Designating a flower having parts thus situated. [< HYPO- + GYNOUS] — **hy·pog′y·ny** n.

hy·po·ma·ni·a (hī′pə-mā′nē-ə, -mān′yə, hip′ə-) n. A mild form of mania, characterized by a condition of moderate elation and overactivity.

hyp·o·nas·ty (hip′ə-nas′tē, hī′pə-) n. Bot. Upward growth of a plant member, resulting from a more active growth on its lower side: distinguished from epinasty. [< HYPO- + Gk. nastos compact] — **hyp′o·nas′tic** adj. — **hyp′o·nas′·ti·cal·ly** adv.

hy·po·ni·trite (hī′pə-nī′trīt) n. Chem. A salt of hyponitrous acid.

hy·po·ni·trous acid (hī′pə-nī′trəs) Chem. An unstable white crystalline acid, $(HNO)_2$, formed by the union of hydroxylamine and nitrous acid, and in other ways.

hy·po·phos·phate (hī′pə-fos′fāt) n. Chem. A salt of hypophosphoric acid.

hy·po·phos·phite (hī′pə-fos′fīt) n. Chem. A salt of hypophosphorous acid.

hy·po·phos·phor·ic acid (hī′pō-fos-fôr′ik, -for′ik) Chem. A crystalline tetrabasic acid, $H_4P_2O_6$, formed from moist phosphorus by oxidation.

hy·po·phos·pho·rous acid (hī′pə-fos′fər-əs) Chem. A monobasic acid, H_3PO_2, derived from phosphorus and acting as a powerful reducing agent.

hy·poph·y·ge (hī-pof′ə-jē, hi-) n. Archit. A horizontal rounded groove under a structural member, as in archaic Doric capitals. [< Gk. hypophygē refuge, recess < hypo- under + pheugein to flee]

hy·poph·y·sis (hī-pof′ə-sis, hi-) n. pl. ·ses (-sēz) Anat. A process or outgrowth. [< NL < Gk., undergrowth < hypo- under + physis nature < phyein to grow]

hypophysis cer·e·bri (ser′ə-brī) Anat. The pituitary gland. [< NL, outgrowth of the brain]

hy·po·pi·tu·i·ta·rism (hī′pō-pi-tōō′i·tə-riz′əm, -tyōō′-) n. Pathol. **1.** Diminished activity of the pituitary gland. **2.** The abnormal condition produced by this, marked by excessive fat and persistent adolescent traits.

hy·po·pla·sia (hī′pə-plā′zhə, -zhē-ə, hip′-) n. **1.** Pathol. The condition of arrested development in an organ or part. **2.** Bot. A deficiency of cells, leading to a cessation of growth in plants. — **hy′po·plas′tic** (-plas′tik) adj.

hy·po·ploid (hī′pə-ploid, hip′ə-) adj. Biol. Denoting a chromosome number less than an exact multiple of the basic haploid number. — **hy′po·ploid′y** n.

hy·po·pne·a (hī′pə-nē′ə, hip′ə-) n. Med. Abnormal rapidity and shallowness of breathing. Also **hy′po·pnoe′a**. [< NL < Gk. hypo- under + pnoē breathing < pneein to breathe]

hy·po·po·di·um (hī′pə-pō′dē-əm, hip′ə-) n. pl. ·di·a (-dē-ə) Bot. The basal portion of a leaf, including the stalk; a supporting structure in plants. [< NL < Gk. hypo- under + podion, dim. of pous, podos foot]

hy·po·py·on (hī-pō′pē-on, hi-) n. Pathol. An accumulation of pus in the cavity of the eye that contains the aqueous humor. [< NL < Gk., a kind of ulcer < hypo- under + pyon pus]

hy·pos·ta·sis (hī-pos′tə-sis, hi-) n. pl. ·ses (-sēz) **1.** Fundamental principle; basis. **2.** Philos. A logical distinction or entity conceived as a self-subsisting object. **3.** Theol. **a** Any one of the persons of the Trinity. **b** The separate personal subsistence of each of the three persons of the Trinity in one divine substance. **4.** Pathol. **a** A settling down of a fluid of the body. **b** A morbid deposition of sedimentary matter within the body. [< L Gk. hypostasis substance, subsistence < hypo- under + histhastai to stand, middle voice of histanai to cause to stand]

hy·po·stat·ic (hī′pə-stat′ik, hip′ə-) adj. **1.** Pertaining to hypostasis; elemental. **2.** Theol. Pertaining to or existing as essential substance or personality, especially as regards the nature or concept of God. **3.** Pathol. Resulting from downward pressure or deposition of sediment in the body: hypostatic congestion. **4.** Genetics Denoting a factor hidden or masked by another that is not an allelomorph. Also **hy′po·stat′i·cal**. [< Gk. hypostatikos] — **hy′po·stat′i·cal·ly** adv.

hypostatic union Theol. The union of two natures, human and divine, in the one person or hypostasis of Christ.

hy·pos·ta·tize (hī-pos′tə-tīz, hi-) v.t. ·tized, ·tiz·ing To ascribe substantial or distinct existence to; consider as real. — **hy·pos′ta·ti·za′tion** n.

hy·po·sthe·ni·a (hī′pə-sthē′nē-ə) n. Pathol. Deficient vitality. [< HYPO- + Gk. sthenos strength] — **hy′po·sthen′ic** (-sthen′ik) adj.

hyp·o·style (hip′ə-stīl, hī′pə-) adj. Archit. Having a roof or ceiling resting upon rows of columns; especially, denoting one of the pillared halls characteristic of ancient Egyptian architecture. — n. A hypostyle building or hall. [< HYPO- + Gk. stylos pillar]

hy·po·sul·fite (hī′pə-sul′fīt) n. Chem. **1.** Sodium thiosulfate. **2.** A salt of hyposulfurous acid.

hy·po·sul·fu·rous acid (hī′pō-sul-fyŏŏr′əs, hī′pə-sul′fər-əs)

Chem. An unstable acid, $H_2S_2O_4$, of strong reducing and bleaching properties: also called hydrosulfurous acid.

hy·po·tax·is (hī′pə-tak′sis, hip′ə-) n. Gram. Subordinate or dependent arrangement or relationship of clauses, phrases, etc.: opposed to parataxis. — **hy′po·tac′tic** (-tak′tik) adj.

hy·pot·e·nuse (hī·pot′ə-nōōs, -nyōōs, hi-) n. Geom. The side of a right triangle opposite the right angle. Also **hy·poth′e·nuse** (-poth′-). Abbr. hyp. [< L hypotenusa < Gk. hypoteinousa (gramme) a subtending (line) < hypo- under + teinein to stretch]

hypoth. Hypothesis; hypothetical.

hy·po·thal·a·mus (hī′pə-thal′ə-məs, hip′ə-) n. pl. ·mi Anat. A group of structures forming part of the diencephalon, controlling visceral activities, regulating body temperature and many metabolic processes, and influencing certain emotional states. — **hy·po·tha·lam·ic** (hī′pə-thə-lam′ik) adj.

hy·poth·ec (hī-poth′ik, hi-) n. Law A pledge or mortgage of lands or goods as security for debt where the property pledged remains in possession of the debtor. [< F hypothèque < LL hypotheca < Gk. hypothēkē pledge < hypotithenai to deposit as a pledge < hypo- under + tithenai to put]

hy·poth·e·car·y (hī-poth′ə-ker′ē, hi-) adj. Law Of, pertaining to, or secured by a hypothec.

hy·poth·e·cate (hī-poth′ə-kāt, hi-) v.t. ·cat·ed, ·cat·ing Law To pledge (personal property) as security for debt without transfer of possession. [< Med.L hypothecatus, pp. of hypothecare < LL hypotheca pledge] — **hy·poth′e·ca′tion** n. — **hy·poth′e·ca′tor** n.

hy·po·ther·mi·a (hī′pō-thûr′mē-ə, hip′ō-) n. **1.** Pathol. An abnormally low body temperature. **2.** Med. Therapeutic anesthesia produced by gradually reducing body temperature. Also **hy′po·ther′my**. [< HYPO- + Gk. thermē heat] — **hy′po·ther′mal** adj.

hy·poth·e·sis (hī-poth′ə-sis, hi-) n. pl. ·ses (-sēz) **1.** An unproved scientific conclusion drawn from known facts and used as a basis for further investigation or experimentation. **2.** An assumption or set of assumptions provisionally accepted as a basis for reasoning or argument. **3.** Logic A conditional proposition. Abbr. hyp., hypoth. [< NL < Gk., foundation, supposition < hypotithenai to put under < hypo- under + tithenia to put]

— Syn. Hypothesis, theory, supposition, assumption, and conjecture are compared as they denote an unproved assertion about reality. In science, a hypothesis is a proposition advanced as possibly true, and consistent with known data, but requiring further investigation; a theory is a hypothesis so well substantiated as to be generally accepted: the nebular hypothesis of the origin of the solar system, the atomic theory of Dalton. Supposition and assumption are propositions accepted with less assurance than a hypothesis; their acceptance facilitates investigation, but the investigation may quickly show them to be untrue. A conjecture is a conclusion drawn from admittedly insufficient data; it differs from a guess only in not being wholly random and uninformed. Compare GUESS.

hy·poth·e·size (hī-poth′ə-sīz, hi-) v. ·sized, ·siz·ing v.t. **1.** To offer or assume as a hypothesis. — v.i. **2.** To make a hypothesis; theorize.

hy·po·thet·i·cal (hī′pə-thet′i·kəl) adj. **1.** Pertaining to or of the nature of a hypothesis. **2.** Based on hypothesis; theoretical. **3.** Based on supposition; imaginary: a hypothetical situation. **4.** Characterized by the use of hypotheses. **5.** Logic Denoting a proposition based on another proposition; conditional. Also **hy′po·thet′ic**. Abbr. hyp., hypoth. [< L hypotheticus < Gk. hypothetikos] — **hy·po·thet′i·cal·ly** adv.

hy·po·thy·roid·ism (hī′pō-thī′roid·iz′əm) n. Pathol. **1.** Deficient functioning of the thyroid gland. **2.** A disorder resulting from this, as goiter. — **hy′po·thy′roid** adj. & n.

hy·po·ton·ic (hī′pə-ton′ik) adj. **1.** Pathol. Deficient in body tone. **2.** Chem. Having less osmotic pressure than an isotonic fluid. — **hy′po·to·nic′i·ty** (-tō-nis′ə-tē) n.

hy·po·xan·thine (hī′pə-zan′thēn, -thin) n. Biochem. A crystalline alkaloid, $C_5H_4N_4O$, found especially in the muscular tissue of animals, and in certain seeds. Also **hy′po·xan′thin** (-thin). [< Gk. hypoxanthos yellowish brown < hypo- under + xanthos yellow] — **hy′po·xan′thic** adj.

hypso- combining form Height: hypsometer. [< Gk. hypsos height]

hyp·sog·ra·phy (hip-sog′rə-fē) n. **1.** The science that deals with the topographic features of the earth's surface above sea level. **2.** A representation or description of such features, as on a map or in an atlas. **4.** Hypsometry. [< HYPSO- + -GRAPHY] — **hyp·so·graph·ic** (hip′sə-graf′ik) or ·i·cal adj.

hyp·som·e·ter (hip-som′ə-tər) n. An instrument that measures heights above sea level by indicating the boiling point of water at a given altitude. [< HYPSO- + -METER]

hyp·som·e·try (hip-som′ə-trē) n. In geodesy, the process of determining the altitudes of points upon the earth's surface above sea level. — **hyp·so·met·ric** (hip′sə-met′rik) or ·ri·cal adj. — **hyp·so·met′ri·cal·ly** adv. — **hyp·som′e·trist** n.

hy·ra·coid (hī′rə-koid) n. A hyrax. — adj. Of or pertaining to a hyrax or to the order Hyracoidea. Also **hy′ra·coi′de·an**. [< NL Hyracoidea, genus name]

---

hy·rax (hī′raks) *n. pl.* **hy·rax·es** or **hy·ra·ces** (hī′rə·sēz) Any of various small, harelike, ungulate mammals (order *Hyracoidea*) of Africa and SW Asia; especially, the **rock hyrax** (genus *Procavia*) that lives in crevices, and the arboreal **tree hyrax** (genus *Dendrohyrax*): in the Bible called *cony*. [Gk., shrewmouse]

Hyr·ca·ni·a (hûr·kā′nē·ə) A province of the ancient Persian Empire, on the SE shore of the Caspian Sea. — **Hyr·ca′ni·an** *adj. & n.*

hy·son (hī′sən) *n.* A green tea from China, the early crop of which is known as **young hyson,** and the inferior leaves are **hyson skin.** [< Chinese *hsi-ch'un,* lit., blooming spring]

hys·sop (his′əp) *n.* **1.** A bushy, medicinal herb (*Hyssopus officinalis*) of the mint family, with small clusters of blue flowers. **2.** In the Bible, an unidentified plant furnishing the twigs used in the Mosaic purificatory and sacrificial rites, etc. **3.** One of various other plants, as the **giant hyssop** (genus *Agastache*). [OE and OF *ysope* < L *hyssopus* < Gk. *hyssōpos* < Hebrew *ēzōb*]

hyster- Var. of HYSTERO-.

hys·ter·ec·to·my (his′tə·rek′tə·mē) *n. pl.* **·mies** *Surg.* Complete removal of the uterus. [< HYSTER- + -ECTOMY]

hys·ter·e·sis (his′tə·rē′sis) *n.* **1.** *Physics* **a** The tendency of a magnetic substance to persist in any state of magnetization. **b** The property of a medium, by virtue of which work is done in changing the direction or intensity of magnetic force among its parts. **c** Some analogous phenomenon, as in dielectrics. **2.** Any state of a material or substance that can be adequately described only in terms of its previous history and condition. [< Gk. *hysterēsis* deficiency < *hystereein* to lag] — **hys·ter·et·ic** (his′tə·ret′ik) *adj.*

hys·te·ri·a (his·tir′ē·ə, -ter′-) *n.* **1.** Abnormal excitement; wild emotionalism; frenzy. **2.** *Psychiatry* A psychoneurotic condition characterized by violent emotional paroxysms and disturbances in the sensory and motor functions, and by changes in consciousness that are symbolically or psychically determined. — **Syn.** See FRENZY. [< NL < Gk. *hystera* the womb; because the condition was thought to affect women more than men]

hys·ter·ic (his·ter′ik) *adj.* Hysterical. — *n.* One who is subject to hysteria.

hys·ter·i·cal (his·ter′i·kəl) *adj.* **1.** Resembling a symptom of hysteria; uncontrolled; violent: *hysterical* laughter. **2.** Characterized or caused by hysteria: *hysterical* paralysis. **3.** Inclined to or suffering from hysteria. — **hys·ter′i·cal·ly** *adv.*

hys·ter·ics (his·ter′iks) *n.pl.* A hysterical fit, as wild outbursts of alternate laughing and crying.

hys·ter·i·tis (his′tə·rī′tis) *n. Pathol.* Inflammation of the womb.

hystero- *combining form* **1.** The womb; uterine: *hysterotomy.* **2.** Hysteria: *hysterogenic.* Also, before vowels, *hyster-.* [< Gk. *hystera* the womb]

hys·ter·o·gen·ic (his′tər·ə·jen′ik) *adj.* Producing or involved in the production of hysteria.

hys·ter·oid (his′tər·oid) *adj.* Resembling hysteria. Also **hys′ter·oid·al.**

hys·ter·on prot·er·on (his′tə·ron prot′ə·ron) **1.** A figure of speech in which the normal order of things or events is reversed. Example: "Is your father well? Is he yet alive?" **2.** *Logic* A fallacy in which one asserts a consequent and then infers the antecedent. [< LL < Gk., the latter (put) first]

hys·ter·ot·o·my (his′tə·rot′ə·mē) *n. pl.* **·mies** *Surg.* **1.** The operation of cutting into the womb. **2.** Cesarean section. [< HYSTERO- + -TOMY]

hys·tri·co·mor·phic (his′tri·kō·môr′fik) *adj.* Of or pertaining to a suborder of rodents (*Hystricomorpha*), including porcupines, cavies, etc. [< Gk. *hystrix* porcupine + -MORPHIC]

hyte (hīt) *adj. Scot.* Crazy; mad.

I

i, I (ī) *n. pl.* **i's** or **is,** or **I's** or **Is, eyes** (īz) **1.** The ninth letter of the English alphabet. The shape of the Phoenician consonant *yod* was adopted by the Greeks as *iota* and became Roman *I.* **2.** Any sound represented by the letter *i.* **3.** Anything shaped like the letter *i.* — *symbol* **1.** The Roman numeral for 1: written I or i. **2.** *Chem.* Iodine (symbol I).

i′ (i) *prep. Scot. & Archaic* In.

i-[1] Reduced var. of IN-[1].

i-[2] See Y-.

i. 1. Incisor. **2.** Interest. **3.** Intransitive. **4.** Island.

I (ī) *pron., possessive* **my** or **mine,** *objective* **me;** *pl. nominative* **we,** *possessive* **our** or **ours,** *objective* **us** The nominative singular pronoun of the first person, used by a speaker or writer in referring to himself. — *n. pl.* **I's 1.** The pronoun *I* used as a noun: His talk was full of *I's.* **2.** *Philos.* The ego. [OE *ic*]

◆ When the pronoun *I* is the object of a preposition or of a verb, the objective form *me* is used no matter how many other such objects precede. Thus, *between you and me* is the proper form, not *between you and I.*

I. 1. Island(s); Isle(s). **2.** Iowa (unofficial).

-ia[1] *suffix of nouns* Occurring in: **1.** *Geog.* Names of countries: *Australia.* **2.** *Pathol.* Names of diseases and related terms: *hysteria.* **3.** *Bot.* Names of genera: *Lobelia.* **4.** Words borrowed directly from Latin or Greek: *militia.* [< L and Gk. *-ia,* suffix of fem. nouns]

-ia[2] *suffix of nouns* Occurring in: **1.** *Biol.* Names of classes: *Mammalia.* **2.** Names of classical festivals: *Bacchanalia.* **3.** Words, usually collectives, borrowed directly from Latin or Greek: *regalia.* [< L and Gk. *-ia,* plural suffix of neut. nouns]

Ia. Iowa (unofficial).

IADB Inter-American Defense Board.

IAEA International Atomic Energy Agency (of the United Nations).

I·a·go (ē·ä′gō) The treacherous, scheming villain of Shakespeare's *Othello.*

-ial *suffix of adjectives* Var. of -AL[1], with connective *-i-*, as in *filial, nuptial.*

i·amb (ī′amb) *n.* **1.** In prosody, a metrical foot consisting of an unaccented syllable followed by an accented one, as in English verse, or a short syllable followed by a long one, as in Latin or Greek verse (˘ -). **2.** A line of verse made up of or characterized by such feet: Thĕ bīrd | wăs grēen | ănd gōld | ĕn īn | thĕ sūn. [< L *iambus* < Gk. *iambos* < *iambein* to assail verbally; because orig. used by satiric poets]

i·am·bic (ī·am′bik) *adj.* **1.** Consisting of or characterized by the use of iambs. **2.** Pertaining to or resembling an iamb or iambs. — *n.* **1.** A foot, line, or stanza consisting of an iamb or iambs. **2.** A piece of verse written in iambs. [< L *iambicus* < Gk. *iambikos*]

i·am·bus (ī·am′bəs) *n. pl.* **·bi** (-bī) or **·bus·es** An iamb.

-ian *suffix of adjectives and nouns* Var. of -AN, with *-i-* of the stem or as a connective: *amphibian, Bostonian.*

-iana See -ANA.

IAS Indicated air speed.

Ia·și (yä′shē, yäsh) The Rumanian name for JASSY.

-iasis *suffix Med.* Denoting a process and its results, especially in diseased conditions: *psoriasis.* [Var. of -OSIS]

i·at·ric (ī·at′rik) *adj.* Pertaining to physicians or the medical art. Also **i·at′ri·cal.** [< Gk. *iatrikos* healing < *iatros* physician < *iasthai* to heal]

-iatrics *combining form* Medical treatment: *pediatrics.* [< Gk. *iatrikos* pertaining to the art of healing]

iatro- *combining form* Medicine and: [< Gk. *iatros* physician]

i·at·ro·gen·ic (ī·at′rə·jen′ik) *adj. Med.* Generated or induced by the physician, as physical or mental ailments resulting from the treatment or from an alarming diagnosis.

-iatry *combining form* Medical or curative treatment: *psychiatry.* [< Gk. *iatreia* healing]

IATSE or **I.A.T.S.E.** International Alliance of Theatrical Stage Employees.

ib. or **ibid.** In the same place (L *ibidem*).

I·ba·dan (ē·bä′dän) A city in SW Nigeria; pop. about 600,-000.

I·bá·ñez (ē·vä′nyeth), Vicente Blasco See BLASCO-IBÁÑEZ.

I-beam (ī′bēm′) *n.* A beam or joist that in cross section has the shape of the letter I.

I·be·ri·a (ī·bir′ē·ə) **1.** The part of SW Europe comprising Spain and Portugal: also **Iberian Peninsula.** **2.** An ancient region in Asia, between the Caucasus and Armenia, corresponding to Soviet Georgia.

I·be·ri·an (ī·bir′ē·ən) *adj.* **1.** Of, pertaining to, or characteristic of the Iberian Peninsula, its people, or their culture. **2.** Of or pertaining to the members or language of an ancient ethnological group that inhabited the Iberian Peninsula probably as early as the Neolithic era. **3.** Of or pertaining to ancient Iberia in Asia or its people. — *n.* **1.** One of the ancient or modern inhabitants of the Iberian Peninsula. **2.** The unclassified language of the ancient inhabitants of the Iberian Peninsula, of which Basque may be a modern survival. **3.** One of the inhabitants of ancient Iberia in Asia. [< L *Iberus* < Gk. *Iberes* Spaniards]

I·ber·ville (dē′bər·vil, *Fr.* dē-ber-vēl′), **Sieur d'**, 1661–1706, Pierre Le Moyne, French-Canadian explorer in America.

i·bex (ī′beks) *n. pl.* **i·bex·es** or **i·bi·ces** (ī′bə-sēz, ib′ə-) One of various wild goats of Europe and Asia, with long, recurved horns; especially, the **Alpine ibex** (*Capra ibex*) and the **Cretan ibex** (*C. hircus*). [< L]

i·bi·dem (i-bī′dem) *adv. Latin* In the same place; in the work, chapter, etc., just mentioned. Abbr. *ib., ibid.*

i·bis (ī′bis) *n. pl.* **i·bis·es** or **i·bis** 1. One of various wading birds (family *Threskiornithidae*), related to the heron; especially, the **sacred ibis** (*Threskiornis aethiopica*), venerated by the ancient Egyptians. 2. The wood ibis (which see). [< L < Gk. < Egyptian]

-ible See -ABLE.

Ib·lees (ib′lēs) See EBLIS.

ibn-Sa·ud (ib′n sä-ōōd′), **Abdul Aziz**, 1880?–1953, king of Saudi Arabia 1932–53. See SAUD.

I·bo (ē′bō) *n. pl.* **I·bo** 1. A member of a group of Negro tribes of western Africa. 2. The Sudanic language of these tribes. [< native name]

Ib·ra·him Pa·sha (ib-rä-hēm′ pä′shə), 1789–1848, Egyptian general and viceroy.

IBRN International Bank for Reconstruction and Development.

Ib·sen (ib′sən), **Henrik**, 1828–1906, Norwegian dramatist.

IBT International Brotherhood of Teamsters.

-ic *suffix* 1. Forming adjectives with the meanings: **a** Of, pertaining to, or connected with: *cosmic, volcanic.* **b** Of the nature of; resembling: *angelic.* **c** Produced by or in the manner of: *Homeric.* **d** Consisting of; containing: *alcoholic.* **e** *Chem.* Having a higher valence than that indicated by *-ous*: said of elements in compounds: *cupric* oxide, *sulfuric* acid. 2. Forming nouns by the substantive use of adjectives in *-ic: classic, lunatic.* 3. Occurring in nouns derived from Latin and Greek nouns formed from adjectives: *stoic, music.* See note under *-ICS.* [< F *-ique* or L *-icus* or Gk. *-ikos*]

◆ **-ically, -icly** A few adjectives in *-ic* form adverbs by adding *-ly* directly, as *publicly*, but in most cases the adverb is formed by adding *-ly* to the adjective in *-ical*, as *musically*, or by adding *-ally* when the adjective exists only in the *-ic* form, as *athletically*.

IC Immediate constituent.

I·çá (ē-sä′) The Portuguese (Brazilian) name for the PUTUMAYO.

ICA International Cooperation Administration.

-ical *suffix* 1. Forming parallel adjectives from adjectives in *-ic*, often in the same sense, as *alphabetic, alphabetical*, but sometimes with extended or special senses, as *economic, economical.* 2. Forming adjectives from nouns in *-ic* or *-ics: musical, mathematical.* [< LL *-icalis* < L *-icus* + *-alis*]

ICAO International Civil Aviation Organization.

Icarian Sea In ancient times, the Aegean Sea off the coast of Asia Minor, where Icarus was supposed to have drowned.

Ic·a·rus (ik′ə-rəs, ī′kə-) In Greek mythology, the son of Daedalus, who, escaping with his father from Crete by means of artificial wings, flew so high that the sun melted the wax that fastened the wings and he fell into the sea and drowned. — **I·car·i·an** (i-kâr′ē·ən, ī-) *adj.*

ICBM The intercontinental ballistic missile, having a range of at least 5,000 miles. Compare *IRBM.*

ICC or **I.C.C.** Interstate Commerce Commission.

ice (īs) *n.* 1. Congealed or frozen water; the solid condition assumed by water at or below freezing point. ◆ Collateral adjective: *glacial.* 2. The frozen surface of a body of water. 3. Something resembling ice in appearance: camphor *ice.* 4. A frozen dessert made without cream, usually flavored with fruit juice. 5. Icing for cake. 6. *Slang* A diamond or diamonds. 7. The frozen surface of a hockey rink. — **to break the ice** 1. To dispel reserve or formality, especially at a social gathering. 2. To do something for the first time; make a start. — **to cut no ice** *U.S. Informal* To have no influence; be of no account. — **on ice** *U.S. Slang* 1. Set aside; in reserve. 2. Certain to be achieved or won. 3. Incommunicado. — *v.* **iced, ic·ing** *v.t.* 1. To cause to turn to ice; freeze. 2. To cover or surround with ice. 3. To chill with or as with ice. 4. To cover or decorate with icing. 5. In hockey, to put (a team) on the ice. — *v.i.* 6. To turn to ice; become frozen: often with *over* or *up.* 7. In hockey, to shoot the puck from the defensive zone to beyond the red line at the other end of the rink. [OE *īs*]

-ice *suffix of nouns* Condition, quality, or act: *cowardice, notice.* [< OF *-ice* < L *-itius, -itia, -itium*]

Ice. Iceland; Icelandic.

ice age The glacial epoch.

ice ax An ax used by mountaineers for cutting steps in the ice, usually having a spiked butt. For illustration see AX.

ice bag A flexible, waterproof container designed to hold ice, applied to parts of the body: also called *ice pack.*

ice·berg (īs′bûrg′) *n.* A thick mass of ice separated from a glacier and floating in the ocean. [Prob. < Du. *ijsberg*]

ice·blink (īs′blingk′) *n.* A shining whiteness on the horizon produced by the reflection of light from distant masses of ice. [Cf. Du. *ijsblin*, Dan. *iisblink*]

ice·boat (īs′bōt′) *n.* 1. A framework with skatelike runners and sails for sailing over ice. 2. An icebreaker (def. 1).

ice boulder A boulder deposited through glacial action.

ice·bound (īs′bound′) *adj.* Surrounded or obstructed by ice; frozen in: an *icebound* ship; an *icebound* harbor.

ice·box (īs′boks′) *n. U.S.* A cabinet for holding ice, in which food or other perishables are stored.

ice·break·er (īs′brā′kər) *n.* 1. A vessel having a strong prow and powerful engines, used to break up ice in icebound waterways and harbors. 2. A structure for deflecting floating ice from the base of a bridge, a pier, etc.: also **ice apron.**

ice bridge *Canadian* A winter road on the ice of a river or lake.

ice·cap (īs′kap′) *n.* A covering of ice and snow permanently overlying an extensive tract of land and moving in all directions from a center.

ice-cold (īs′kōld′) *adj.* Cold as ice.

ice cream A mixture of cream, butterfat, or milk, flavoring, sweetening, and often egg whites, beaten to a uniform consistency and frozen. [Orig., *iced cream*]

iced (īst) *adj.* 1. Coated or covered with ice or sleet. 2. Made cold with ice. 3. Covered with icing, as a cake.

ice·fall (īs′fôl′) *n.* The steepest part of a glacier, resembling a frozen waterfall.

ice field A large, flat expanse of floating ice. Also **ice floe.**

ice foot A ledge of ice formed in polar regions by sea water and snow frozen along the shore. [Trans. of Dan. *isfod*]

ice hockey Hockey played by skaters on ice.

ice hook A hook attached to a pole, used in handling large blocks of ice. For illustration see HOOK.

ice·house (īs′hous′) *n.* A building in which ice is stored.

I·çel (ē·chel′) A city in southern Turkey; pop. 68,574 (1960): also *Mersin.*

Icel. Iceland; Icelandic.

Ice·land (īs′lənd) An island in the North Atlantic comprising a Republic; 39,758 sq. mi.; pop. 202,000 (est. 1968); capital, Reykjavik: Icelandic *Island.*

Ice·land·er (īs′lan′dər) *n.* A native or citizen of Iceland.

Ice·land·ic (īs·lan′dik) *adj.* Of or pertaining to Iceland, its inhabitants, or their language. — *n.* The North Germanic language of Iceland; especially, this language since the 16th century. Abbr. *Ice., Icel.* — **Old Icelandic** The language of Iceland before the 16th century, exemplified in the Eddas: sometimes called *Old Norse.*

Iceland moss An edible and medicinal lichen (*Cetraria islandica*) of the arctic regions.

Iceland spar *Mineral.* A transparent variety of calcite exhibiting double refraction and having the property of polarizing light.

ice·man (īs′man′, -mən) *n. pl.* **·men** (men′, -mən) One who supplies or delivers ice to consumers.

ice needle *Meteorol.* One of a type of thin, airborne ice crystals forming the chief component of cirrus clouds, sometimes visible in sunlight.

I·ce·ni (ī·sē′nī) *n.pl.* An ancient British tribe led by their queen, Boadicea, against the Romans and defeated by Suetonius Paulinus, A.D. 61. [< L]

ice pack 1. A large expanse of floating ice cakes jammed together and frozen into a single mass. 2. An ice bag.

ice pick An awllike tool for breaking ice into small pieces.

ice plant 1. A fig marigold (*Mesembryanthemum crystallinum*) of southern Africa, the Mediterranean region, and southern California, having leaves covered with glistening frostlike protuberances. 2. A factory where ice is made.

ice point *Physics* The melting point of ice at standard atmospheric pressure 0.0° C: one of the fixed points of the international temperature scale.

ice rain 1. A rain that freezes quickly into a coating of ice. 2. Frozen rain; sleet.

ice sheet A very large icecap, especially one sufficiently extensive to cover the major part of a continent.

ice-skate (īs′skāt′) *v.i.* **-skat·ed, -skat·ing** To skate on ice.

ice skate A skate for use on ice, usually consisting of a shoe with a metal runner attached to the sole.

ice water 1. *U.S.* Water chilled by ice. 2. Melted ice.

Ich·a·bod Crane (ik′ə·bod krān′) An oafish schoolteacher in Washington Irving's *Legend of Sleepy Hollow.*

I·chang (ē′chäng′) A port city in south central China, on the Yangtze; pop. about 100,000. Also **I′-ch'ang′.**

Ich dien (ikh dēn) *German* I serve: motto of the Prince of Wales.

ich·neu·mon (ik·nōō′mən, -nyōō′-) *n.* 1. An Old World carnivore (genus *Herpestes*) of somewhat weasellike aspect, as the mongoose, feeding on mice, eggs, snakes, etc. 2. An

IBEX
(About 3 feet high at shoulder)

ichneumon fly. [< L < Gk. *ichneumōn*, lit., tracker < *ichneuein* to track down < *ichnos* footstep, trace; because it was believed to hunt for and eat crocodiles' eggs]

ichneumon fly A hymenopterous insect (family *Ichneumonidae*) whose larvae feed upon caterpillars or other insect larvae. For illustration see INSECTS (beneficial).

ich·nite (ik′nīt) *n.* Paleontol. A fossil footprint. Also **ich·no·lite** (ik′nə·līt). [< Gk. *ichnos* footprint]

ich·nog·ra·phy (ik·nog′rə·fē) *n. pl.* **·phies** **1.** A ground plan of a building or other structure. **2.** The art of drawing ground plans. [< LL *ichnographia* < Gk. < *ichnos* trace + *graphein* to write] — **ich·no·graph·ic** (ik′nə·graf′ik) or **·i·cal** *adj.*

i·chor (ī′kôr, ī′kər) *n.* **1.** In classical mythology, the ethereal fluid supposed to flow in the veins of the gods. **2.** Pathol. A watery, acrid fluid discharged from sores. [< Gk. *ichōr*] — **i·chor·ous** (ī′kər·əs) *adj.*

ichth. Ichthyology.

ich·thy·ic (ik′thē·ik) *adj.* Pertaining to or typical of fishes.

ichthyo- *combining form* Fish: *ichthyology*. Also, before vowels, **ichthy-**. [< Gk. *ichthys* fish]

ich·thy·o·cen·taur (ik′thē·ō·sen′tôr) *n.* A fabulous monster, combining the form of man and fish.

ich·thy·oid (ik′thē·oid) *adj.* Like a fish: also **ich′thy·oi′dal**. — *n.* A fishlike vertebrate.

Ich·thy·ol (ik′thē·ōl, -ol) *n.* Proprietary name for a compound of sulfonated hydrocarbons obtained by the distillation of certain shales, used especially to treat skin diseases.

ich·thy·o·lite (ik′thē·ə·līt) *n.* Paleontol. A fossil fish.

ich·thy·ol·o·gy (ik′thē·ol′ə·jē) *n.* The branch of zoology that treats of fishes. [< ICHTHYO- + -LOGY] — **ich·thy·o·log·ic** (ik′thē·ə·loj′ik) or **·i·cal** *adj.* — **ich′thy·ol′o·gist** *n.*

ich·thy·oph·a·gous (ik′thē·of′ə·gəs) *adj.* That feeds on fish.

ich·thy·oph·a·gy (ik′thē·of′ə·jē) *n.* The practice of feeding on fish. [< ICHTHYO- + -PHAGY]

ich·thy·or·nis (ik′thē·ôr′nis) *n.* Paleontol. One of a genus (*Ichthyornis*) of extinct sea birds of the Cretaceous period, having primitive vertebrae. [< ICHTHY- + Gk. *ornis* bird]

ich·thy·o·saur (ik′thē·ə·sôr′) *n.* Paleontol. Any of an order (*Ichthyosauria*) of extinct marine reptiles of the Mesozoic era, having a porpoiselike form with four paddlelike limbs, dorsal and caudal fins, and fishlike vertebrae. [< ICHTHYO- + Gk. *sauros* lizard]

ich·thy·o·sau·rus (ik′thē·ə·sôr′əs) *n. pl.* **·sau·ri** (-sôr′ī) An ichthyosaur.

ich·thy·o·sis (ik′thē·ō′sis) *n.* Pathol. A congenital skin disease characterized by dry, scaly, or horny formations. — **ich′thy·ot′ic** (-ot′ik) *adj.*

ICTHYOSAURUS
(To about 30 feet long)

-ician *suffix of nouns* One skilled in or engaged in some specified field: *logician, mathematician*: originally used with names of arts and sciences ending in *-ic* or *-ics*, but now, by analogy, with any stem, as in *beautician, mortician*. [< F *-icien*]

i·ci·cle (ī′si·kəl) *n.* A hanging, tapering mass or rod of ice formed by the freezing of drops of dripping water. [OE *īsgicel* < *īs* ice + *gicel* piece of ice, icicle] — **i′ci·cled** *adj.*

i·ci·ly (ī′sə·lē) *adv.* In an icy manner.

i·ci·ness (ī′sē·nis) *n.* **1.** The state or quality of being frozen or extremely cold. **2.** Marked aloofness of manner.

ic·ing (ī′sing) *n.* **1.** A glazing or coating made of sugar, usually mixed with egg whites or cream, used to cover or decorate cakes, pastry, etc. **2.** The formation of ice on the surface of an aircraft by the freezing of atmospheric moisture. **3.** In hockey, the act of one who ices (def. 7).

i·ci on parle fran·çais (ē·sē′ ôṅ pȧrl′ fräṅ·se′) *French* French is spoken here.

ICJ International Court of Justice.

ick·er (ik′ər) *n.* Scot. A head of grain; an ear of corn.

Ick·es (ik′əs, -ēz), **Harold (Le Claire)**, 1874–1952, U.S. government administrator and writer.

i·con (ī′kon) *n. pl.* **i·cons** or **i·co·nes** (ī′kə·nēz) **1.** In the Eastern Orthodox Church, a pictorial representation of Jesus Christ, the Virgin Mary, or some other sacred figure, to which veneration is offered. **2.** An image; likeness; picture. **3.** Philos. A sign or symbol that resembles the thing it represents. Also spelled **eikon, ikon**. [< Gk. *eikōn* image]

i·con·ic (ī·kon′ik) *adj.* **1.** Pertaining to or of the nature of an icon. **2.** In art, stylized; conventional: applied originally to the commemorative portrait statues of antiquity, and later to memorial busts, portraits, etc. Also **i·con′i·cal**.

I·co·ni·um (ī·kō′nē·əm) The ancient name for KONYA.

icono- *combining form* Image: *iconography*. Also, before vowels, **icon-**. [< Gk. *eikōn* image]

i·con·o·clasm (ī·kon′ə·klaz′əm) *n.* The attitudes or behavior of an iconoclast.

i·con·o·clast (ī·kon′ə·klast) *n.* **1.** One who attacks conventional or cherished beliefs and institutions as being false or harmful. **2.** One who seeks to destroy, or opposes the use of, images used in religious worship; especially, one who formerly opposed the use of images in the Christian Church. [< LL *iconoclastes* < Gk. *eikonoklastēs* < *eikōn* image + *-klastēs* breaker < *klaein* to break, destroy]

i·con·o·clas·tic (ī·kon′ə·klas′tik) *adj.* Of or characteristic of iconoclasts or iconoclasm.

i·co·nog·ra·phy (ī′kə·nog′rə·fē) *n. pl.* **·phies 1.** The art of illustration by means of pictures, images, or symbols. **2.** In the study of art, the description and classification of images in order to establish the thematic significance of the subject matter depicted; also, the subject matter itself. **3.** Obs. A pictorial representation; diagram. [< Med.L *iconographia* < Gk. *eikonographia* < *eikōn* icon + *graphein* to write] — **i·con·o·graph·ic** (ī·kon′ə·graf′ik) or **·i·cal** *adj.*

i·co·nol·a·try (ī′kə·nol′ə·trē) *n.* The worship or veneration of images. [< ICONO- + -LATRY] — **i′co·nol′a·ter** *n.*

i·co·nol·o·gy (ī′kə·nol′ə·jē) *n.* **1.** The study of icons. **2.** The study and analysis of images in art employed as a method of determining the meaning of works of art when viewed in historical perspective. [< ICONO- + -LOGY] — **i·con·o·log·i·cal** (ī·kon′ə·loj′i·kəl) *adj.*

i·con·o·scope (ī·kon′ə·skōp) *n.* Telecom. The part of a television camera that, by means of an electron beam, converts the image to be transmitted into electrical impulses. [< ICONO- + -SCOPE]

i·co·nos·ta·sis (ī′kə·nos′tə·sis) *n.* In the Eastern Orthodox Church, a screen on which icons are displayed and that separates the main part of the church from the sanctuary. Also called **i·con·o·stas** (ī·kon′ə·stas). [< NL < Modern Gk. *eikonostasis* < Gk. *eikōn* icon + *stasis* standing]

i·co·sa·he·dron (ī′kə·sə·hē′drən) *n. pl.* **·dra** (-drə) or **·drons** Geom. A polyhedron bounded by twenty plane faces. [< Gk. *eikosaedron*] — **i′co·sa·he′dral** (-drəl) *adj.*

icosi- *combining form* Twenty. [< Gk. *eikosi* twenty]

-ics *suffix of nouns* **1.** An art, science, or field of study: *mathematics*. **2.** Methods, practices, or activities: *athletics*. [See -IC]

◆ **-ic, -ics** Nouns ending in *-ics* are construed as singular when they strictly denote an art, science, or system (as, mathematics is difficult; politics offers an uncertain future); they are construed as plural if they denote personal attributes (as, his mathematics are poor; his politics are suspect), if they denote inherent qualities (as, the acoustics are bad), or if they denote specific activities (as, athletics are compulsory; hysterics are unseemly; our tactics are superior to the enemy's).

ic·ter·us (ik′tər·əs) *n.* **1.** Pathol. Jaundice. **2.** Bot. Yellowness of leaves, caused by protracted wet or cold. [< LL < Gk. *ikteros* jaundice] — **ic·ter′ic** (ik·ter′ik) *adj.*

Ic·ti·nus (ik·tī′nəs) Fifth-century B.C. Greek architect; designer of the Parthenon.

ic·tus (ik′təs) *n. pl.* **·tus·es** or **·tus 1.** In prosody, the accenting of a word or syllable; metrical stress. **2.** Pathol. A sudden attack or stroke. [< L, pp. of *icere* to strike]

i.c.w. Interrupted continuous wave.

i·cy (ī′sē) *adj.* **i·ci·er, i·ci·est 1.** Consisting of, containing, or covered with ice: *icy* particles; an *icy* sidewalk. **2.** Resembling or having the characteristics of ice: *icy* green; an *icy* corpse. **3.** Extremely cold; freezing: an *icy* gale. **4.** Forbiddingly aloof; coldly hostile: an *icy* greeting. [OE *īsig*]

id (id) *n.* Psychoanal. The unconscious part of the psyche, independent of a sense of reality, logic, and morality, but actuated by fundamental impulses toward fulfilling instinctual needs; the reservoir of psychic energy or libido. See EGO (def. 3). [< NL < L *id* it, trans. of G *es*]

id. The same (L *idem*).

-id¹ *suffix of nouns* **1.** Offspring of: often occurring in names from classical mythology: *Danaid, Nereid*. **2.** An epic about a specified person or subject: *Aeneid*. **3.** Zool. **a** A member of a family: *leporid*. **b** A member of a class: *arachnid*. **4.** Astron. A meteor seeming to originate in a specified constellation: *Perseid*. [< L *-is, -idis* < Gk. *-is, -idos*, suffix of patronymics]

-id² *suffix of adjectives* Having a particular quality, or existing in a particular state: *humid, fluid*. [< F *-ide* < L *-idus*; or directly < L]

-id³ Chem. Var. of -IDE.

Id. Idaho (unofficial).

I'd (īd) **1.** I would. **2.** I should. **3.** I had.

ID card (īdē′) An identification card.

ID or **I.D.** or **i.d.** Inside diameter.

Ida. Idaho (unofficial).

I·da (ī′də), **Mount 1.** A mountain in central Crete, the highest on the island; 8,058 ft.: also *Psilitori*. **2.** A mountain range in NW Turkey; highest peak, Mt. Gagarus, 5,797 ft.: also **Ida Mountains**.

-idae *suffix* Zool. Forming the names of families: *Canidae*. [< NL *-idae* < L < Gk. *-idai*, plural patronymic suffix]

I·dae·an (ī·dē′ən) *adj.* Of or pertaining to Mount Ida.

I·da·ho (ī′də·hō) A NW State of the United States; 83,557 sq. mi.; pop. 713,008; capital, Boise; entered the Union July 3, 1890; nickname, *Gem State*. — **I′da·ho′an** *adj. & n.*

Idaho Falls A city in SE Idaho, on the Snake River; pop. 35,776.

-ide *suffix* Chem. Used in the names of compounds, usually binary, and attached to the electronegative or nonmetallic element or radical: sodium *chloride*. Also spelled **-id**. [< F *-ide*. See -ID².]

i·de·a (ī·dē′ə) *n.* **1.** That which is conceived in the mind as a

result of conscious thinking or creative imagination; a thought. **2.** That which is established in the mind as a result of passive perception; an impression or notion. **3.** A conviction; opinion; belief: He has strong *ideas* on the subject. **4.** An intention; aim; plan: He has the *idea* of becoming a writer. **5.** Vague knowledge; indication; inkling: I had an *idea* you might come. **6.** A fleeting thought; passing fancy; whim: It was just an *idea* of mine. **7.** *Informal* Significance; meaning; purpose: Do you get the *idea?* **8.** *Philos.* **a** The Platonic concept of an archetype or fundamental example, of which an existing thing is but an imperfect representation. **b** That which is immediately perceived by the mind or the senses. **c** The concept of absolute truth or reason. **9.** *Music* A phrase or theme. **10.** *Obs.* The concept of anything in its highest or most desirable state. **11.** *Obs.* A remembered image of a real person or thing. [< L < Gk. < *ideein* to see]
— **Syn.** *Idea, concept, conception, thought, notion, image,* and *impression* denote something that exists in the mind during the processes of perceiving, thinking, or willing. *Idea* is the most general term, applicable to almost any part or aspect of mental activity: I have no *idea* of going to the party, he has some *idea* of the cost of this painting. A *concept* is an *idea* of a category or kind generalized from particular instances; the *concept* of "horse" arises from the many horses we see. A *conception* is the result of a creative act of the mind: the *conception* of the steam engine, our *conception* of life on Mars. *Thought* suggests an *idea* elaborated in the mind, and not directly attributable to a sense impression: he has many sound *thoughts* on the matter. A *notion* is a vague or capricious *idea,* often without any sound basis: to have a *notion* the stock market will rise. An *image* is a mental representation of something which has been seen: the *image* of her face. An *impression,* like an *image,* arises from something external, but need not be pictorial: my *impression* is that he was lying.

i·de·al (ī·dē′əl, ī·dēl′)   *n.* **1.** A concept or standard of supreme perfection; a thing conceived as an ultimate object of attainment. **2.** A person or thing taken as a standard of perfection; a model of the highest excellence. **3.** A high principle; lofty aim: to live up to one's *ideals.* **4.** That which exists only as a concept of the mind. — *adj.* **1.** Conforming to an absolute standard of excellence; embodying or exemplifying perfection. **2.** Representing the best of its kind; of great worth or excellence: an *ideal* monarch. **3.** Completely satisfactory; greatly to be desired: an *ideal* situation. **4.** Capable of existing as a mental concept only, by virtue of unattainable perfection; utopian; imaginary: the *ideal* society. **5.** Pertaining to or existing in the form of an idea or ideas. **6.** *Philos.* **a** Pertaining to or existing as a Platonic idea. **b** Pertaining to or characteristic of the concepts or theories of idealism. [< F *idéal* < L *idealis*]
— **Syn.** (noun) **1.** *Ideal, archetype,* and *prototype* are compared as they denote a model to be followed. An *ideal* can exist only in the mind, since it is intended to be perfect: the *ideal* of perfect brotherhood among all men. An *archetype* is a pattern more or less rigidly imitated; it may exist in the mind or in actuality: Alexander the Great was the *archetype* of military adventurers. A *prototype* is an early or the earliest model of a thing, later copies of which show progressive improvement: Faraday constructed the *prototype* of the generator. Compare EXAMPLE. — (adj.) **1.** perfect, consummate, transcendent, superlative, peerless. **4.** visionary, utopian, fanciful, imaginary, unreal.

i·de·al·ism (ī·dē′əl·iz′əm)   *n.* **1.** The characteristic or practice of idealizing; the envisioning of things as they should be or are wished to be rather than as they are. **2.** Pursuit of an ideal. **3.** That which is idealized. **4.** In literature and art, the imaginative treatment of subject matter in accordance with preconceived standards of perfection: opposed to *realism.* **5.** *Philos.* Any of several theories that there is no reality, no world of objects or thing in itself apart from a reacting mind or consciousness, that only the mental is knowable, and therefore that reality is essentially spiritual or mental, variously developed by Berkeley, Kant, Hegel, and others: opposed to *realism.*

i·de·al·ist (ī·dē′əl·ist)   *n.* **1.** One who formulates, strives after, or attempts to live in accordance with, ideals. **2.** An impractical dreamer; romantic. **3.** An exponent of idealism in literature or art. **4.** One who holds the beliefs of any philosophic idealism. — *adj.* Idealistic.

i·de·al·is·tic (ī′dē·əl·is′tik, ī·dē′əl-)   *adj.* Of, pertaining to, or characteristic of idealists or idealism. Also **i′de·al·is′ti·cal.** — **i′de·al·is′ti·cal·ly** *adv.*

i·de·al·i·ty (ī′dē·al′ə·tē)   *n. pl.* **·ties** **1.** The state or quality of being ideal. **2.** Existence in the mind only; also, that which exists in the mind only. **3.** The ability to formulate ideals; creative imagination.

i·de·al·ize (ī·dē′əl·īz)   *v.* **·ized, ·iz·ing** *v.t.* **1.** To regard as conforming to some standard of perfection; consider to be ideal; hold in high esteem. **2.** To make or portray as ideal; glorify. — *v.i.* **3.** To form an ideal or ideals. **4.** To consider or represent things in their ideal form. Also *Brit.* **i·de·al·ise.** — **i·de′al·i·za′tion** *n.* — **i·de′al·iz′er** *n.*

i·de·al·ly (ī·dē′əl·ē, ī·dēl′ē)   *adv.* **1.** In conformance with an ideal; in the best possible manner or situation; perfectly. **2.** As conceived in the mind; in the abstract.

i·de·ate (ī·dē′āt; *for n., also* ī·dē′it)   *v.* **·at·ed, ·at·ing** *v.t.* **1.** To form an idea of; frame in the mind; conceive. — *v.i.* **2.** To form mental concepts; think. — *n. Philos.* The object corresponding to an idea.

i·de·a·tion (ī′dē·ā′shən)   *n.* The mental process of forming ideas. — **i′de·a′tion·al** *adj.*

i·dée fixe (ē·dā′ fēks′)   *French* A fixed idea.

i·dem (ī′dem)   *pron. & adj. Latin* The same: used as a reference to what has been previously mentioned. Abbr. *id.*

idem quod (ī′dem kwod)   *Latin* The same as. Abbr. *i.q.*

i·den·tic (ī·den′tik)   *adj.* **1.** Identical. **2.** In diplomacy, identical in form, as notes sent by two governments.

i·den·ti·cal (ī·den′ti·kəl)   *adj.* **1.** One and the same; the very same. **2.** Alike or equal in every respect. **3.** *Genetics* Designating either of a pair of human twins that develop from a single fertilized ovum and are thus invariably of the same sex and genetic constitution: distinguished from *fraternal.* [< Med.L *identicus* < *idem* the same] — **i·den′ti·cal·ly** *adv.* — **i·den′ti·cal·ness** *n.*
— **Syn.** *Identical, same,* and *selfsame* are applied to two or more specified objects, meaning that they are actually one: The virus of chickenpox is *identical* with that of shingles. Carbolic acid is the *same* substance as phenol. *Identical* and *same* may be used loosely, however, to mean closely alike or equivalent: *identical* twins, cowry shells had the *same* value as gold or silver. The strict sense is clearest in *selfsame:* hydrogen chloride and hydrochloric acid are not the *selfsame* thing. — **Ant.** other, different, distinct, diverse.

i·den·ti·fi·ca·tion (ī·den′tə·fə·kā′shən)   *n.* **1.** The act of identifying, or the state of being identified. **2.** Anything by which identity can be established.

identification card   A card bearing the owner's name, employment, and other credentials: also called *ID card.*

identification tag   Either of two metal disks worn by a soldier on a cord or chain about the neck, bearing his name, serial number, and other personal data: also called *dog tag.*

i·den·ti·fy (ī·den′tə·fī)   *v.* **·fied, ·fy·ing** *v.t.* **1.** To establish as being a particular person or thing; prove to be as supposed or claimed; recognize. **2.** *Biol.* To determine the genus and species of. **3.** To regard as the same; consider to be equivalent: to *identify* money with happiness. **4.** To serve as a means of recognizing; be characteristic of: Black and white stripes *identify* the zebra. **5.** To associate closely: One *identifies* her with good food. **6.** To consider (oneself) as one in character, fate, etc., with another person, a character in fiction, or the like: to *identify* oneself with Hamlet. **7.** *Psychol.* To imagine (oneself) to be thinking or behaving like a person with whom one has formed a strong emotional tie. — *v.i.* **8.** To put oneself in the place of another. [< LL *identificare*] — **i·den′ti·fi′a·ble** *adj.* — **i·den′ti·fi′er** *n.*

I·den·ti·kit (ī·den′tə·kit′)   *n.* A set of drawings of separate facial features that can be superimposed to create the likeness of someone, especially someone sought by the police: a trade name. [< IDENTI(FICATION) + KIT[1]]

i·den·ti·ty (ī·den′tə·tē)   *n. pl.* **·ties** **1.** The state of being identical; sameness or oneness: an *identity* of interests. **2.** The state of being a specific person or thing and no other: His *identity* is in doubt. **3.** The distinctive character belonging to an individual; individuality: to lose one's *identity.* [< F *identité* < LL *identitas, -tatis* < L *idem* the same]

ideo-   *combining form* Idea: *ideograph.* [< Gk. *idea* form, idea]

id·e·o·graph (id′ē·ə·graf′, -gräf′, ī′dē-)   *n.* **1.** A pictorial symbol of an object, or the graphic representation of a thought, as distinguished from a representation of the sound of a word in the given language. **2.** A graphic symbol, as +, =, ¶, 4, $. Also **id·e·o·gram** (id′ē·ə·gram′, ī′dē-). — **id′e·o·graph′ic** or **·i·cal** *adj.* — **id′e·o·graph′i·cal·ly** *adv.*

id·e·og·ra·phy (id′ē·og′rə·fē, ī′dē-)   *n.* The graphic representation of ideas by symbolic characters; use of ideographs.

i·de·ol·o·gy (ī′dē·ol′ə·jē, id′ē-)   *n. pl.* **·gies** **1.** The ideas or manner of thinking characteristic of an individual or group; especially, the ideas and objectives that influence a whole group or national culture, shaping especially their political and social procedure. **2.** The science that treats of the origin, evolution, and expression of human ideas. **3.** Fanciful or visionary speculation. [< IDEO- + -LOGY] — **i·de·o·log·ic** (ī′dē·ə·loj′ik, id′ē) or **·i·cal** *adj.* — **i′de·o·log′i·cal·ly** *adv.* — **i′de·ol′o·gist** *n.*

i·de·o·mo·tor (ī′dē·ə·mō′tər, id′ē-)   *adj. Physiol.* Of or pertaining to involuntary muscular or neural movements that are induced by an idea: distinguished from *sensorimotor.* — **i′de·o·mo′tion** (-mō′shən) *n.*

ides (īdz)   *n.pl.* In the ancient Roman calendar, the 15th of March, May, July, and October, and the 13th of the other months. [< OF < L *idus*]

id est (id est)   *Latin* That is. Abbr. *i.e.*

Id·fu (id′fōo)   A town in southern Egypt, on the Nile; site of a famous ancient temple; pop. about 20,000: also *Edfu.*

idio-   *combining form* One's own; peculiar to a person or thing; individual: *idiosyncrasy.* [< Gk. *idios* own, private]

id·i·o·blast (id′ē·ə·blast′)   *n.* **1.** *Biol.* One of the hypothetical structural units that are thought to make up animal and vegetable cells. **2.** *Bot.* A plant cell differing markedly in contents, etc., from those of surrounding tissues.

id·i·o·cy (id′ē·ə·sē) *n. pl.* **·cies 1.** The condition of being an idiot. **2.** Extreme stupidity or foolishness. **3.** A stupid or senseless act or utterance. [< IDIOT]

id·i·o·graph·ic (id′ē·ə·graf′ik) *adj. Psychol.* Pertaining to the close study of an individual case.

id·i·o·lect (id′ē·ə·lekt) *n. Ling.* The language or speech of an individual. [< IDIO- + (DIA)LECT]

id·i·om (id′ē·əm) *n.* **1.** An expression peculiar to a language, not readily understandable from its grammatical construction or from the meaning of its component parts, as *to put up with* (tolerate, endure). **2.** The language or dialect of a region or people. **3.** The special terminology or mode of expression of a class, occupational group, etc.: *legal idiom.* **4.** The distinctive character of a specific language. **5.** Typical style, form, or character, as in art, literature, or music. [< F < L *idioma* < Gk. *idiōma* peculiarity, property < *idioein* to appropriate < *idios* one's own]

id·i·o·mat·ic (id′ē·ə·mat′ik) *adj.* **1.** Peculiar to or characteristic of a specific language. **2.** Of the nature of an idiom. **3.** Employing many idioms. Also **id·i·o·mat′i·cal.** [< Gk. *idiōmatikos* characteristic < *idiōma.* See IDIOM.] — **id′i·o·mat′i·cal·ly** *adv.* — **id′i·o·mat′i·cal·ness** *n.*

id·i·o·mor·phic (id′ē·ō·môr′fik) *adj.* **1.** Having its own distinctive form. **2.** *Mineral.* Possessing characteristic crystallographic faces. — **id′i·o·mor′phi·cal·ly** *adv.*

id·i·op·a·thy (id′ē·op′ə·thē) *n. pl.* **·thies** *Pathol.* **1.** A disease of indeterminate cause; a spontaneous or primary disease. **2.** A disease generated by an allergy. [< IDIO- + -PATHY] — **id·i·o·path·ic** (id′ē·ō·path′ik) or **·i·cal** *adj.*

id·i·o·plasm (id′ē·ō·plaz′əm) *n. Biol.* Germ plasm (which see). — **id′i·o·plas′mic** (-plaz′mik), **id′i·o·plas·mat′ic** (-plaz·mat′ik) *adj.*

id·i·o·syn·cra·sy (id′ē·ō·sing′krə·sē) *n. pl.* **·sies 1.** A habit, mannerism, mode of expression, etc., peculiar to an individual; personal oddity; quirk. **2.** The distinctive physical or psychological constitution of an individual. Also *Obs.* **id·i·oc·ra·sy** (id′ē·ok′rə·sē). [< Gk. *idiosynkrasia* < *idios* peculiar + *synkrasis* a mixing together < *syn* together + *krasis* mixing] — **id′i·o·syn·crat′ic** (-sin·krat′ik) *adj.* — **id′i·o·syn·crat′i·cal·ly** *adv.*

id·i·ot (id′ē·ət) *n.* **1.** A person exhibiting mental deficiency in its most severe form and requiring constant care. **2.** An extremely foolish or stupid person. [< OF *idiot* < L *idiota* < Gk. *idiōtēs* private person < *idios* one's own]
— **Syn. 1.** *Idiot, imbecile,* and *moron* denote a person who is mentally deficient. The *idiot* is incapable of learning and understanding, and is completely helpless. An *imbecile* may learn to communicate with others, but is incapable of earning his own living. A *moron* may take a normal place in society, but needs constant supervision. **2.** dullard, simpleton. Compare FOOL.

idiot board *U.S. Slang* A placard containing a script and used to prompt a television performer.

idiot box *U.S. Slang* A television set.

id·i·ot·ic (id′ē·ot′ik) *adj.* Of or characteristic of an idiot; senseless; stupid. Also **id′i·ot′i·cal.** — **id′i·ot′i·cal·ly** *adv.*

id·i·ot·ism (id′ē·ət·iz′əm) *n.* **1.** Senseless or idiotic behavior. **2.** Idiocy. **3.** *Obs.* An idiom. [< F *idiotisme*]

i·dle (īd′l) *adj.* **i·dler** (īd′lər), **i·dlest** (īd′list) **1.** Not engaged in work; not occupied. **2.** Not in the process of being used; not operating: The factory was *idle* during the strike. **3.** Unwilling to work; avoiding effort; lazy: an *idle* rogue. **4.** Spent in inactivity; reserved for or providing leisure: *idle* moments. **5.** Having no power or effectiveness; fruitless; vain: *idle* threats. **6.** Of little value or significance; frivolous; trifling: *idle* chatter. **7.** Having no basis in fact; unfounded: *idle* reports. — *v.* **i·dled, i·dling** *v.i.* **1.** To spend time in inactivity; be engaged in wasteful, useless, or trivial activities; loaf. **2.** To move or progress lazily or aimlessly; linger without purpose. **3.** *Mech.* To operate without transmitting power, usually at reduced speed: said of motors or machines. — *v.t.* **4.** To spend (time) wastefully or unprofitably; fritter: often with *away.* **5.** *U.S. Informal* To cause to be idle, as a person or an industry. **6.** To cause to idle, as a motor. [OE *īdel* empty, useless] — **i′dle·ness** *n.*

idle pulley *Mech.* A pulley used to guide a driving belt, increase its tension, or increase its arc of contact on one of the working pulleys.

i·dler (īd′lər) *n.* **1.** One who idles; a lazy person; a loafer. **2.** An idle wheel or pulley. **3.** One of a ship's crew who stands no night watches. **4.** An empty railroad car.

idle wheel *Mech.* **1.** A gearwheel that conveys motion from one wheel to another without change in the direction of rotation. **2.** An idle pulley.

i·dly (īd′lē) *adv.* **1.** In an idle manner. **2.** Without effect or purpose; uselessly; vainly.

I·do (ē′dō) *n.* A simplified form of Esperanto, introduced in 1907. [< Esperanto *ido* offspring]

IDLE WHEEL

id·o·crase (id′ō·krās, ī′dō-) *n.* Vesuvianite, a mineral. [< IDIO- + Gk. *krasis* mixture]

i·dol (īd′l) *n.* **1.** An image or object representing or con-

sidered as a god, and worshiped as having divine powers. **2.** In the Christian and Jewish religions, a false or nonexistent god; object of heathen worship. **3.** One who is loved or admired to an excessive degree; object of infatuation. **4.** *Obs.* An unsubstantial image; apparition; phantom. **5.** A false or misleading idea; a fallacy. [< OF *idele* < L *idolum* < Gk. *eidōlon* image, phantom < *eidos* form, shape]

i·dol·a·ter (ī·dol′ə·tər) *n.* **1.** One who worships an idol or idols. **2.** A blindly devoted admirer. [< OF *idolatre* < LL *idolatres* < Gk. *eidōlatrēs*] — **i·dol′a·tress** (-tris) *n. fem.*

i·dol·a·trize (ī·dol′ə·trīz) *v.* **·trized, ·triz·ing** *v.t.* **1.** To make an idol of; idolize. — *v.i.* **2.** To worship idols.

i·dol·a·trous (ī·dol′ə·trəs) *adj.* **1.** Pertaining to, characterized by, or practicing the worship of idols. **2.** Blindly devoted. — **i·dol′a·trous·ly** *adv.* — **i·dol′a·trous·ness** *n.*

i·dol·a·try (ī·dol′ə·trē) *n. pl.* **·tries 1.** The worship of idols. **2.** Excessive or undiscerning admiration or veneration; blind infatuation. [< OF *idolatrie* < LL *idololatria* < Gk. *eidōlatreia* < *eidolon* idol + *latreia* worship]

i·dol·ism (īd′l·iz′əm) *n.* **1.** A false idea. **2.** Idol worship.

i·dol·ize (īd′l·īz) *v.* **·ized, ·iz·ing** *v.t.* **1.** To love or admire blindly or to excess; adore. **2.** To worship as an idol. — *v.i.* **3.** To worship idols. Also *Brit.* **i′dol·ise.** — **i′dol·i·za′tion** *n.* — **i′dol·iz′er** *n.*

i·dol·o·clast (ī·dol′ə·klast) *n.* A breaker of images; iconoclast. [< IDOL + (ICON)OCLAST] — **i·dol′o·clas′tic** *adj.*

I·dom·e·neus (ī·dom′ə·nōōs, -nyōōs) In Greek legend, a king of Crete and ally of the Greeks in the Trojan War.

I·du·mae·a (ī′dyōō·mē′ə, id′yōō-) See EDOM. Also **I′du·me′a.** — **I′du·mae′an** *adj. & n.*

I·dun (ē′dōōn) See ITHUNN.

i·dyl (īd′l) *n.* **1.** A short poem or prose piece depicting simple scenes of pastoral, domestic, or country life. **2.** An extended descriptive or narrative poem. **3.** Any event, scene, etc., of a kind suitable for or reminiscent of an idyl. **4.** *Music* A composition of simple or pastoral character. Also *Brit.* **i′dyll.** [< L *idyllium* < Gk. *eidyllion,* dim. of *eidos* form]

i·dyl·ist (īd′l·ist) *n.* A writer of idyls Also **i′dyll·ist.**

i·dyl·lic (ī·dil′ik) *adj.* **1.** Of, pertaining to, or having the essential qualities of an idyl. **2.** Charmingly simple or picturesque. Also **i·dyl′li·cal.** — **i·dyl′li·cal·ly** *adv.*

i.e. That is (L *id est*).

-ie *suffix* Little; dear: used in nicknames or affectionately, as in *Annie, birdie.* [Var. of -Y³]

IE or **I.E.** Indo-European.

-ier *suffix of nouns* One who is concerned with or works with: *cashier.* Also, after *w,* **-yer,** as in *lawyer.* [< F. See -EER.]

I·e·ya·su (ē·yä·yä·sōō) See IYEYASU.

if (if) *conj.* **1.** In the event that; in case: We shall turn back *if* it rains. **2.** On condition that; provided that: He will come by plane *if* the weather permits. **3.** Allowing the possibility that; granting that: *If* I am wrong, I'm sorry. ◆ In the preceding senses, *if* is often used in elliptical constructions: I'll do it *if* possible; He's sixty, *if* a day. **4.** Whether: See *if* the mail has come. **5.** Even though; although: Her clothes are neat, *if* not stylish. ◆ *If* is also used in exclamatory clauses to express (**a**) a wish: *If* I had only thought of that!; and (**b**) surprise or irritation: *If* he hasn't done it again! — *n.* A possibility or condition. [OE *gif*]

If (ēf) An islet SW of Marseilles, France: site of the **Château d'If,** formerly a state prison.

IF or **I.F., i.f.** or **i-f** Intermediate frequency.

IFC International Finance Corporation.

if·fy (if′ē) *adj. Informal* Doubtful as to outcome; uncertain.

If·ni (ēf′nē) A Spanish Overseas Province in SW Morocco; 741 sq. mi.; pop. 49,889 (1960); capital, Sidi Ifni.

I.F.S. Irish Free State.

I.G. **1.** Amalgamation (G *Interessengemeinschaft*). **2.** Indo-Germanic. **3.** Inspector General: also **IG**

Ig·dra·sil (ig′drə·sil) See YGDRASIL.

ig·loo (ig′lōō) *n. pl.* **·loos 1.** A dome-shaped house or hut used by Eskimos, usually built of blocks of solidified snow. **2.** A small cavity in the snow made by a seal to cover its breathing hole in the ice. [< Eskimo *igdlu* house]

ign. 1. Ignites; ignition. **2.** Unknown (L *ignotus*).

ig·na·ti·a (ig·nā′shē·ə, -shə) *n.* The dried seed of a small tree (*Strychnos ignatia*) native to the Philippines, used like nux vomica. [< NL (*faba*) *ignatia* (bean) of Ignatius]

Ig·na·ti·us Loyola (ig·nā′shē·əs, -shəs), **Saint** See LOYOLA.

Ignatius of Antioch, Saint, died 107?, bishop of Antioch; martyred: called **The·oph·o·rus** (thē·of′ə·rəs).

Ignatius of Constantinople, Saint, 799?–877, patriarch of Constantinople.

ig·ne·ous (ig′nē·əs) *adj.* **1.** *Geol.* Formed by the action of great heat within the earth, as rocks consolidated from a molten state: sometimes *pyrogenic.* **2.** Pertaining to, characteristic of, or resembling fire. [< L *igneus < ignis* fire]

ig·nes·cent (ig·nes′ənt) *adj.* **1.** Emitting sparks when struck, as certain stones. **2.** Flaming up; flaring. — *n.* An ignescent substance. [< L *ignescens, -entis,* ppr. of *ignescere* to catch fire < *ignis* fire]

igni- *combining form* Fire: *ignite.* [< L *ignis* fire]

ig·ni·fy (ig′nə·fī) *v.t.* **·fied, ·fy·ing** *Rare* **1.** To set on fire; burn. **2.** To fuse or melt. [Cf. LL *ignifacere* to set on fire]

ig·nis fat·u·us (ig'nis fach'ōō-əs) *pl.* **ig·nes fat·u·i** (ig'nēz fach'ōō-ī) **1.** A flickering, phosphorescent light sometimes seen over marshes or swamps, thought to be caused by the spontaneous combustion of marsh gas: also called *friar's lantern, will-o'-the-wisp.* **2.** A deceptive attraction; misleading objective or expectation. [< Med.L, foolish fire]

ig·nite (ig·nīt') *v.* **·nit·ed, ·nit·ing** *v.t.* **1.** To set on fire; make burn. **2.** To enkindle; arouse. **3.** *Chem.* To cause to glow with intense heat; bring to the point of combustion. — *v.i.* **4.** To start to burn; catch fire. [< L *ignitus,* pp. of *ignire* to burn] — **ig·nit/a·ble** or **ig·nit/i·ble** *adj.* — **ig·nit/a·bil/i·ty** or **ig·nit/i·bil/i·ty** *n.*

ig·nit·er (ig·nī'tər) *n.* **1.** One who or that which ignites. **2.** A detonator (def. 1). **3.** *Electronics* An electrode used to initiate the action of an ignitron: also **ig·ni/tor.**

ig·ni·tion (ig·nish'ən) *n.* **1.** The act of igniting, or the state of being ignited. **2.** The process of igniting the explosive mixture of fuel and air in a cylinder of an internal-combustion engine. **3.** A device for igniting; especially, the device or system that fires the mixture in an internal-combustion engine. *Abbr.* **ign.** [< Med.L *ignitio, -onis* burning < L *ignire* to burn]

ig·ni·tron (ig·nī'tron, ig'nə·tron) *n.* *Electronics* A rectifier tube having a mercury pool as its cathode and an igniter inserted therein as an auxiliary electrode, used to control the starting of a unidirectional current flow. [< IGNI(TE) + (ELEC)TRON]

ig·no·ble (ig·nō'bəl) *adj.* **1.** Dishonorable in purpose or character; degraded; base. **2.** Not of noble rank; of humble ancestry. **3.** Of low quality; inferior. — **Syn.** See MEAN². [< F < L *ignobilis* < *in-* not + *gnobilis* known] — **ig·no·bil·i·ty** (ig'nō·bil'ə·tē), **ig·no/ble·ness** *n.* — **ig·no/bly** *adv.*

ig·no·min·i·ous (ig'nə·min'ē·əs) *adj.* **1.** Marked by or involving dishonor or disgrace; shameful. **2.** Meriting disgrace; despicable. **3.** Tending to dimish one's self-respect; humiliating. [< L *ignominiosus* < *ignominia.* See IGNOMINY.] — **ig'no·min'i·ous·ly** *adv.* — **ig'no·min'i·ous·ness** *n.*

ig·no·min·y (ig'nə·min'ē) *n.* *pl.* **·min·ies** **1.** Disgrace or dishonor. **2.** That which causes or merits disgrace; dishonorable quality or conduct. [< L *ignominia* < *in-* not + *gnomen* name, reputation]

ig·no·ra·mus (ig'nə·rā'məs, -ram'əs) *n.* An ignorant person. [< L, we do not know]

ig·no·rance (ig'nər·əns) *n.* The state of being ignorant; lack of knowledge, information, or awareness. Also *Obs.* **ig'no·ran·cy.** [< F < L *ignorantia*]

ig·no·rant (ig'nər·ənt) *adj.* **1.** Having no learning or education; unenlightened; uneducated. **2.** Lacking awareness; unaware: with *of: ignorant* of the facts. **3.** Lacking information or experience; uninformed; inexperienced: with *in: ignorant* in diplomacy. **4.** Resulting from or indicating lack of knowledge: an *ignorant* remark. [< OF < L *ignorans, -antis,* ppr. of *ignorare.* See IGNORE.] — **ig'no·rant·ly** *adv.*
— **Syn.** *Ignorant, illiterate, unlettered, uneducated, untaught, untutored,* and *unlearned* mean having little or no knowledge. *Ignorant* is a very wide term; infants are *ignorant,* as are savages; a person may have much knowledge but be *ignorant* of a particular fact. *Illiterate* originally meant not versed in literature; it now means unable to read and write, and is sometimes used to mean stupid. *Unlettered* refers to those whose book learning is small. *Uneducated, untaught, untutored,* and *unlearned* are applied with little discrimination to those who have had little schooling. — **Ant.** aware, cognizant, learned, educated, well-informed.

ig·nore (ig·nôr', -nōr') *v.t.* **·nored, ·nor·ing** **1.** To refuse to notice or recognize; disregard intentionally. **2.** *Law* To reject (a bill of indictment) for insufficient evidence. — **Syn.** See NEGLECT. [< F *ignorer* < L *ignorare* to have no knowledge of, ignore < *in-* not + *gno-,* stem of *gnoscere* to know] — **ig·nor/er** *n.* — **ig·nor/a·ble** (-ə·bəl) *adj.*

I·go·rot (ig'ə·rōt', ē'gə-) *n.* *pl.* **·rot** or **·rots** **1.** A member of any one of several Malay tribes of northern Luzon, Philippines, some of whom are head-hunters. **2.** The Indonesian language of these tribes. Also **I·gor·ro·te** (ē'gôr·rō'tā). [< Sp. *Igorrote,* prob. < Tagalog]

I·graine (i·grān') In Arthurian legend, the mother of King Arthur: also *Ygerne.*

i·gua·na (i·gwä'nə) *n.* **1.** Any of several tropical American lizards (family *Iguanidae,* < especially *Iguana iguana,* which sometimes attains a length of 6 feet. **2.** A lizard of a related genus. [< Sp. < Carib] — **i·gua·ni·an** (i·gwä'nē·ən) *adj. & n.*

IGUANA
(To 6 feet long)

i·guan·o·don (i·gwän'ə·don) *n.* *Paleontol.* Any of a genus (*Iguanodon*) of large, powerfully built, herbivorous, bipedal dinosaurs (order *Ornithischia*), found in Jurassic and Cretaceous rocks in Europe. [< NL < IGUANA + Gk. *odōn* tooth]

I·guas·sú (ē'gwä·sōō') A river in SE Brazil, flowing about 820 miles west to the Paraná; near its mouth are **Iguassú Falls;** height, 210 ft. Also **I'gua·çu'.** *Spanish* **I'gua·zú'.**

IGY or **I.G.Y.** International Geophysical Year.

IHP or **ihp, I.H.P.** or **i.h.p.** Indicated horsepower.

ih·ram (ē·räm') *n.* **1.** The garb worn by Moslem pilgrims to Mecca, consisting of a white cotton cloth around the waist and loins, and another over the left shoulder. **2.** The restrictions and regulations imposed on one wearing this garb. [< Arabic *ihram* interdiction < *harama* to forbid]

IHS A monogram of the name Jesus, derived from the Greek IΗ(ΣΟΤ)Σ, Jesus.

Ijs·sel (ī'səl) A branch of the lower Rhine in the Netherlands, flowing 72 miles north to Lake Ijssel: also *Yssel. Dutch* **IJs/sel.**

Ijs·sel (ī'səl), **Lake** A fresh-water lake in the central Netherlands, created by diking of the Zuider Zee: *Dutch* **IJs/sel·meer/** (-mār').

Ikh·na·ton (ik·nä'tən) Fourteenth-century B.C. Egyptian king, Amenhotep IV; monotheist religious reformer. Also *Akhenaten.*

i·kon (ī'kon) See ICON.

i·lang-i·lang (ē'läng·ē'läng) See YLANG-YLANG.

il– Assimilated var of IN-¹ and IN-².

ILA International Longshoremen's Association.

-ile *suffix* Found in many adjectives derived from French and Latin, and in nouns based on or patterned after such adjectives: *docile, agile, juvenile, missile.* Also, sometimes, **-il,** as in *civil, fossil.* [< F *-il, -ile* < L *-ilis,* suffix of adjectives; or directly < L]

il·e·ac (il'ē·ak) *adj.* **1.** Of or pertaining to the ileum. **2.** Relating to ileus. Also **il'e·al** (-əl). [< ILEUM + -AC]

Île de France (ēl də fräns') A former province of north central France including Paris and the surrounding region.

Île du Dia·ble (ēl dü dyä'bl') The French name for DEVIL'S ISLAND.

il·e·i·tis (il'ē·ī'tis) *n.* *Pathol.* Inflammation of the ileum.

ileo– *combining form* Ileum: *ileostomy.* [< L *ileum* the groin, small intestine]

il·e·os·to·my (il'ē·os'tə·mē) *n.* *pl.* **·mies** *Surg.* The operation of creating an artificial opening into the ileum. [< ILEO- + -STOMY]

I·ler·da (i·lûr'də) The ancient name for LÉRIDA.

Îles Co·mores (ēl kô·môr') A French name for the COMORO ISLANDS.

il·e·um (il'ē·əm) *n.* *pl.* **il·e·a** (il'ē·ə) *Anat.* The lowest of the three divisions of the small intestine, extending from the jejunum to the cecum. For illustration see INTESTINE. [< LL < L *ileum* groin, small intestine]

il·e·us (il'ē·əs) *n.* *Pathol.* Obstruction of the intestines, with resultant severe colic. [< L *ileus, ileos* colic < Gk. *eileos, ileos* < *eilein* to twist]

i·lex (ī'leks) *n.* **1.** Any of a genus (*Ilex*) of trees or shrubs with small white flowers and red berries; a holly. **2.** The holm oak. [< L, holm oak]

Il·ford (il'fərd) A municipal borough in SW Essex, England; pop. 178,210 (1961).

I·lí·a (ē·lyē·ä) The Greek name for ELIS.

Il·i·ac (il'ē·ak) *adj.* Pertaining to Ilium (Troy); also, pertaining to the Trojan War. Also **Il'i·an.**

Il·i·ad (il'ē·əd) An ancient Greek epic poem in twenty-four books, traditionally ascribed to Homer, describing events connected with the siege of Troy. — *n.* **1.** Any similar long narrative poem. **2.** A lengthy account or series of misfortunes. [< L *Ilias, -adis* < Gk. *Ilias, -ados* < *Ilios, Ilion* Ilium (Troy)]

il·i·um (il'ē·əm) *n.* *pl.* **il·i·a** (il'ē·ə) *Anat.* The large upper portion of either of the innominate bones of the pelvis. For illustration see PELVIS. [< NL < L *ilium,* usually in pl. *ilia* loins, belly] — **il'i·ac** (-ak) *adj.*

Il·i·um (il'ē·əm) See TROY. Also **Il'i·on** (-ən).

ilk¹ (ilk) *n.* Breed; sort; class: Smith and others of his *ilk:* a usage still objected to by some authorities because it arose from a misunderstanding of the phrase *of that ilk.* — *adj. Obs.* Same. — *pron. Obs.* The same. — **of that ilk** *Scot. & Brit. Dial.* Of the same name, place, or estate: Kent *of that ilk*—that is, Kent of Kent. [OE *ilca* same]

ilk² (ilk) *adj. Scot. & Brit. Dial.* Each; every. Also **il'ka** (-kə). [Var. of EACH]

ill (il) *adj.* **worse, worst** **1.** Not in good health; suffering from a physical disorder; sick. **2.** Destructive in effect; harmful: an *ill* wind. **3.** Hostile or malevolent in attitude or intent; unfriendly; spiteful; bitter: *ill* will. **4.** Portending danger or disaster; unfavorable: an *ill* omen. **5.** Morally bad; evil; unsavory; *ill* repute. **6.** Contrary to accepted standards or good practice; improper; incorrect: *ill* behavior. **7.** Not proficient; unskillful. — **Syn.** See SICK¹. — *n.* **1.** Evil; wrong: Do good in return for *ill.* **2.** Injury; harm: I wish him no *ill.* **3.** A cause of unhappiness, misfortune, injustice, etc. **4.** Disaster; trouble: to bode *ill.* **5.** A malady; sickness. — *adv.* **1.** Not well; badly. **2.** With difficulty; hardly: I can *ill* afford the expense. **3.** Unsuitably; poorly: Such conduct *ill* befits the occasion. — **ill at ease** Uncomfortable; nervous; fidgety. [ME < ON *illr*]

Ill may be used in combination, as in the following list. Such combinations are hyphenated when they appear before the words they modify, as in *ill-concealed* envy, but are not hyphenated when used predicatively, as in: His envy was *ill concealed*.

ill-accoutered	ill-contrived	ill-kept	ill-pleased
ill-assorted	ill-equipped	ill-matched	ill-suited
ill-concealed	ill-housed	ill-mated	ill-tongued
ill-conceived	ill-informed	ill-placed	ill-trained

ill. Illustrated; illustration; illustrator.
Ill. Illinois.
I'll (il) **1.** I will. **2.** I shall.
ill-ad·vised (il′ad·vīzd′) *adj.* Undertaken or acting in accordance with poor or insufficient advice; injudicious; rash.
Il·lam·pu (ē·yäm′pōō) A peak of the Andes in western Bolivia; 21,490 ft.: also *Sorata*.
il·la·tion (i·lā′shən) *n.* **1.** The act of inferring. **2.** That which is inferred; an inference or deduction. [< L *illatio, -onis* < *illatus,* pp. of *inferre* to bring in, infer]
il·la·tive (il′ə·tiv) *adj.* **1.** Of or pertaining to inference. **2.** Expressing inference, as the word *therefore*.
ill-be·ing (il′bē′ing) *n.* Ill condition.
ill-bod·ing (il′bō′ding) *adj.* Portending evil or disaster.
ill-bred (il′bred′) *adj.* Showing the effects of poor breeding; unmannerly; impolite; rude.
ill-con·sid·ered (il′kən·sid′ərd) *adj.* Done with insufficient deliberation or forethought; thoughtless; unwise.
ill-de·fined (il′di·fīnd′) *adj.* Not well defined; unclear.
ill-dis·posed (il′dis·pōzd′) *adj.* **1.** Having an unpleasant disposition; unfriendly. **2.** Disinclined; averse. **3.** Badly arranged. — **ill′-dis·pos′ed·ly** (-əd·lē) *adv.* — **ill′-dis·pos′-ed·ness** *n.*
il·le·gal (i·lē′gəl) *adj.* **1.** Not legal; contrary to law; unlawful. **2.** Violating official rules, as in sports. — **Syn.** See CRIMINAL. — **il·le′gal·ly** *adv.*
il·le·gal·i·ty (il′ē·gal′ə·tē) *n. pl.* **·ties 1.** The state or quality of being illegal; unlawfulness. **2.** An illegal act.
il·le·gal·ize (i·lē′gəl·īz) *v.t.* **·ized, ·iz·ing** To make illegal.
il·leg·i·ble (i·lej′ə·bəl) *adj.* Not legible; incapable of being read; difficult or impossible to decipher. — **il·leg′i·bil′i·ty, il·leg′i·ble·ness** *n.* — **il·leg′i·bly** *adv.*
il·le·git·i·ma·cy (il′i·jit′ə·mə·sē) *n. pl.* **·cies** The state or quality of being illegitimate; especially, the status or condition of a person born out of wedlock; bastardy.
il·le·git·i·mate (il′i·jit′ə·mit) *adj.* **1.** Born out of wedlock. **2.** Not according to law; unlawful. **3.** Contrary to good usage; incorrect. **4.** Contrary to logic; illogical; unsound. [< L *illegitimus* < *in-* not + *legitimus.* See LEGITIMATE.] — **il·le·git′i·mate·ly** *adv.*
ill fame Bad repute. — **house of ill fame** A brothel.
ill-fat·ed (il′fā′tid) *adj.* **1.** Destined for or having had an unhappy fate; doomed. **2.** Characterized by or resulting in misfortune; unlucky: an *ill-fated* day.
ill-fa·vored (il′fā′vərd) *adj.* **1.** Unpleasant in appearance; ugly. **2.** Objectionable; disagreeable. — **ill′-fa′vored·ly** *adv.* — **ill′-fa′vored·ness** *n.*
ill-found·ed (il′foun′did) *adj.* Based on weak or incorrect evidence or premises; unsupported.
ill-got·ten (il′got′n) *adj.* Obtained illegally or evilly.
ill humor A disagreeable mood; ill temper; sullenness.
ill-hu·mored (il′hyōō′mərd) *adj.* Characterized by ill humor; irritable; cross. — **ill′-hu′mored·ly** *adv.* — **ill′-hu′mored·ness** *n.*
il·lib·er·al (i·lib′ər·əl) *adj.* **1.** Not generous in giving; stingy. **2.** Narrow-minded; intolerant. **3.** Lacking breadth of culture; provincial. — **il·lib′er·al·ly** *adv.* — **il·lib′er·al·ness** *n.*
il·lib·er·al·i·ty (i·lib′ə·ral′ə·tē) *n. pl.* **·ties 1.** The state or quality of being illiberal. **2.** An illiberal act or circumstance.
il·lic·it (i·lis′it) *adj.* Not permitted; unlawful; unauthorized. [< F *illicite* < L *illicitus* < *in-* not + *licitus.* See LICIT.] — **il·lic′it·ly** *adv.* — **il·lic′it·ness** *n.*
Il·li·ma·ni (ē′yē·mä′nē) A peak of the Andes in western Bolivia; 21,185 ft.
il·lim·it·a·ble (i·lim′it·ə·bəl) *adj.* Incapable of being limited; limitless; boundless. — **Syn.** See INFINITE. — **il·lim′it·a·bil′i·ty, il·lim′it·a·ble·ness** *n.* — **il·lim′it·a·bly** *adv.*
il·lin·i·um (i·lin′ē·əm) *n.* Promethium, an element: the former name. [< NL, after *Illinois*]
Il·li·nois (il′ə·noi′, -noiz′) *n. pl.* **·nois** A North American Indian of a tribe belonging to the Illinois Confederacy. [< F < N.Am.Ind.]
Il·li·nois (il′ə·noi′, -noiz′) A north central State of the United States; 56,400 sq. mi.; pop. 11,113,976; capital, Springfield; entered the Union Dec. 3, 1818; nickname, *Prairie State*. Abbr. *Ill.* — **Il′li·nois′an** (-noi′ən, -noi′zən) *adj. & n.*
Illinois Confederacy A confederacy of Algonquian tribes of North American Indians whose territory included Illinois and parts of Wisconsin and Iowa.
Illinois River A river in central and western Illinois, flowing 273 miles SW to the Mississippi.
illit. Illiterate.
il·lit·er·a·cy (i·lit′ər·ə·sē) *n. pl.* **·cies 1.** The state of being illiterate; lack of education; especially, inability to read and write. **2.** An error in speaking or writing indicative of lack of education.

il·lit·er·ate (i·lit′ər·it) *adj.* **1.** Lacking education; untaught; especially, unable to read and write. **2.** Of language, characteristic of the least educated. — **Syn.** See IGNORANT. — *n.* An illiterate person; especially, one who cannot read and write. [< L *illitteratus* < *in-* not + *litteratus.* See LITERATE.] — **il·lit′er·ate·ly** *adv.* — **il·lit′er·ate·ness** *n.*
ill-judged (il′jujd′) *adj.* Indicating lack of judgment; imprudent.
ill-look·ing (il′lŏŏk′ing) *adj.* **1.** Homely; ugly. **2.** Of evil appearance.
ill-man·nered (il′man′ərd) *adj.* Characterized by bad manners; discourteous; rude. — **ill′man·nered·ly** *adv.*
ill nature Unpleasant or spiteful disposition; surliness.
ill-na·tured (il′nā′chərd) *adj.* Surly; cross. — **ill′-na′tured·ly** *adv.* — **ill′-na′tured·ness** *n.*
ill·ness (il′nis) *n.* **1.** The state of being in poor health; sickness. **2.** An ailment; disease. **3.** *Obs.* Badness; evil.
il·log·ic (i·loj′ik) *n.* Absence of logic.
il·log·i·cal (i·loj′i·kəl) *adj.* Not logical; neglectful of the rules of logic or reason. — **il·log′i·cal′i·ty, il·log′i·cal·ness** *n.* — **il·log′i·cal·ly** *adv.*
ill-o·mened (il′ō′mənd) *adj.* Attended by or associated with bad omens; ill-starred; unfortunate.
ill repute Evil reputation. — **house of ill repute** Brothel.
ill-sort·ed (il′sôr′tid) *adj.* Badly arranged or matched.
ill-spent (il′spent′) *adj.* Wasted; misspent.
ill-starred (il′stärd′) *adj.* Unlucky, as if under the influence of an evil star.
ill temper Cross disposition; irritable mood.
ill-tem·pered (il′tem′pərd) *adj.* Displaying ill temper; cross; surly. — **ill′-tem′pered·ly** *adv.* — **ill′-tem′pered·ness** *n.*
ill-timed (il′tīmd′) *adj.* Occurring at an unsuitable time; untimely; inopportune.
ill-treat (il′trēt′) *v.t.* To act cruelly toward; maltreat. — **Syn.** See ABUSE. — **ill′-treat′ment** *n.*
il·lume (i·lōōm′) *v.t.* **·lumed, ·lum·ing** *Poetic* To illuminate. [< ILLUMINE, prob. infl. by F *rallumer* to light]
il·lu·mi·nance (i·lōō′mə·nəns) *n. Physics* The luminous flux per unit area of a uniformly illuminated surface.
il·lu·mi·nant (i·lōō′mə·nənt) *n.* Something that gives light. [< L *illuminans, -antis,* ppr. of *illuminare* to give light]
il·lu·mi·nate (*v.* i·lōō′mə·nāt; *adj. & n.* i·lōō′mə·nit, -nāt) *v.* **·nat·ed, ·nat·ing** *v.t.* **1.** To give light to; light up. **2.** To shed light upon; clarify. **3.** To enlighten, as the mind. **4.** To make illustrious; glorify. **5.** To decorate with lights. **6.** To decorate (an initial letter, page, manuscript, etc.) with embellishments, ornamental borders, figures, etc., of gold or other colors. — *v.i.* **7.** To shed light; become lighted. — *adj.* **1.** *Archaic* Lighted up. **2.** *Obs.* Enlightened. — *n.* One who is or claims to be especially enlightened in spiritual or intellectual matters. [< L *illuminatus,* pp. of *illuminare* < *in-* thoroughly + *luminare* to light < *lumen* light]
il·lu·mi·na·ti (i·lōō′mə·nä′tē, -nä′tī) *n. pl. of* **il·lu·mi·na·to** (i·lōō′mə·nä′tō, -nä′tō) **1.** *Often cap.* Those who have or profess to have special intellectual or spiritual enlightenment. **2.** In early church usage, baptized persons, to whom a lighted taper was given as a symbol of spiritual enlightenment. [< L, pl. of *illuminatus,* pp. of *illuminare* to light up]
il·lu·mi·na·tion (i·lōō′mə·nā′shən) *n.* **1.** The act of illuminating, or the state of being illuminated. **2.** An amount or source of light: inadequate *illumination*. **3.** Decoration by means of lighting. **4.** Mental or spiritual enlightenment. **5.** Embellishment, as of a page, manuscript, etc., by means of gold or colored decorations, letters, etc.; also, a letter, ornament, etc., used in such decoration. **6.** *Physics* Illuminance. [< L *illuminatio, -ionis*]
il·lu·mi·na·tive (i·lōō′mə·nā′tiv) *adj.* Capable of illuminating; serving to illuminate.
il·lu·mi·na·tor (i·lōō′mə·nā′tər) *n.* One who or that which illuminates; as: **a** A device for casting or concentrating light. **b** One who illuminates manuscripts, books, etc.
il·lu·mine (i·lōō′min) *v.t. & v.i.* **·mined, ·min·ing** To illuminate or be illuminated. [< F *illuminer* < L *illuminare* to illuminate] — **il·lu′mi·na·ble** *adj.*
Il·lu·mi·nism (i·lōō′mə·niz′əm) *n.* The beliefs or teachings of the Illuminati (def. 1). — **Il·lu′mi·nist** *n.*
illus. Illustrated; illustration; illustrator.
ill-use (*v.* il′yōōz′; *n.* il′yōōs′) *v.t.* **·used, ·us·ing** To treat cruelly, neglectfully, or unjustly; abuse. — *n.* Bad, cruel, or unjust treatment: also **ill′-us′age** (-yōō′sij, -yōō′zij) *n.*
il·lu·sion (i·lōō′zhən) *n.* **1.** A false, misleading, or overly optimistic idea; misconception; delusion: to outgrow one's youthful *illusions*. **2.** A general impression not consistent with fact: Red gives an *illusion* of heat. **3.** *Psychol.* A sensory impression that results in misinterpretation of the true character of an actual object: an optical *illusion*: distinguished from *hallucination*. **4.** A delicate, transparent, netted fabric used as veiling, trimming, etc. **5.** *Obs.* The act of deceiving or misleading by false appearances. — **Syn.** See DELUSION. [< OF < L *illusio, -onis* mocking, deceit < *illudere* to make sport of < *in-* toward, against + *ludere* to play] — **il·lu′sion·al** (-əl), **il·lu′sion·ar·y** (-er-ē) *adj.*
il·lu·sion·ism (i·lōō′zhən·iz′əm) *n.* A belief or theory that the material world is an illusion.

il·lu·sion·ist (i·lōō′zhən·ist) *n.* **1.** One given to illusions; a visionary; dreamer. **2.** A performer who creates illusions; magician. **3.** A believer in illusionism.

il·lu·sive (i·lōō′siv) *adj.* Deceptive; unreal; illusory. — **il·lu′sive·ly** *adv.* — **il·lu′sive·ness** *n.*

il·lu·so·ry (i·lōō′sər·ē) *adj.* Of the nature of illusion; tending to mislead or delude; deceptive; unreal. — **il·lu′so·ri·ly** *adv.* — **il·lu′so·ri·ness** *n.*

illust. Illustrated; illustration; illustrator.

il·lus·trate (il′ə·strāt, i·lus′trāt) *v.t.* **·trat·ed, ·trat·ing** **1.** To explain or make clear by means of examples, comparisons, etc.; exemplify. **2.** To supply or accompany (a book, article, lecture, etc.) with pictures intended as explanation. **3.** To decorate (a book, etc.) with drawings, photographs, or the like. **4.** *Obs.* To enlighten. **5.** *Obs.* To make illustrious; give distinction to. [< L *illustratus*, pp. of *illustrare* to light up < *in-* thoroughly + *lustrare* to illuminate]

il·lus·tra·tion (il′ə·strā′shən) *n.* **1.** That which illustrates; as: **a** An example, comparison, anecdote, etc., by which a subject or statement is elucidated or explained. **b** A print, drawing, or picture of any kind inserted in written or printed text to elucidate or adorn it. Abbr. *ill., illus., illust.* **2.** The act or art of illustrating. [< L *illustratio, -onis*]

il·lus·tra·tive (i·lus′trə·tiv, il′ə·strā′tiv) *adj.* Serving to illustrate. — **il·lus·tra′tive·ly** *adv.*

il·lus·tra·tor (il′ə·strā′tər, i·lus′trā·tər) *n.* One who or that which illustrates; especially, an artist who executes illustrations for books, etc. Abbr. *ill., illus., illust.*

il·lus·tri·ous (i·lus′trē·əs) *adj.* **1.** Greatly distinguished; renowned. **2.** Conferring greatness or glory: *illustrious deeds.* **3.** *Obs.* Luminous. [< L *illustris < in-* in + *lustrum* light] — **il·lus′tri·ous·ly** *adv.* — **il·lus′tri·ous·ness** *n.*

— **Syn. 1.** *Illustrious, distinguished,* and *eminent* mean widely known for some superior ability or achievement. *Illustrious* implies a special glory in that for which a person is noted: an *illustrious* statesman. *Distinguished* and *eminent* are less emphatic but still imply a degree of excellence and renown that marks one as different from others or *distinguished,* or that raises him above his fellows and makes him *eminent.* Compare FAMOUS.

il·lu·vi·a·tion (i·lōō′vē·ā′shən) *n.* The process, mechanical or chemical, by which material is added to the topsoil of an area: distinguished from *eluviation.* [< L *illuvies* inundation, flood + -ATION] — **il·lu′vi·al** *adj.*

ill will Hostile feeling; malevolence.

ill-wish·er (il′wish′ər) *n.* One who wishes evil to another.

il·ly (il′lē) *adv.* Not well; badly; ill. ◆ While *illy* is regularly formed from the adjective *ill,* the form *ill* is preferred for the adverb as well.

Il·lyr·i·a (i·lir′ē·ə) An ancient country bordering the east coast of the Adriatic.

Il·lyr·i·an (i·lir′ē·ən) *n.* **1.** One of the inhabitants of ancient Illyria. **2.** The Indo-European language of the Illyrians, of which few traces remain, regarded by some linguists as the ancestor of modern Albanian. — *adj.* Of or pertaining to ancient Illyria, its inhabitants, or their language.

Il·lyr·i·cum (i·lir′i·kəm) A Roman colony in Illyria.

Il·men (il′mən, *Russ.* ēly′/myiny′), Lake A lake in the NW R.S.F.S.R.; 425–850 sq. mi. Also **Il′myen′.**

il·men·ite (il′mən·īt) *n.* A black, opaque oxide of iron and titanium, $FeTiO_3$, crystallizing in the hexagonal system. [after the *Ilmen* Mountains, a range in the Urals]

I·lo·ca·no (ē′lō·kä′nō) *n.* **1.** One of a Malay people inhabiting western and NW Luzon in the Philippines. **2.** The Indonesian language of this people. Also **I′lo·ka′no.** [< Philippine Sp. *Ilocano,* lit., river man < Tagalog *ilog* river]

ILO or **I.L.O.** International Labor Organization (of the United Nations).

I·lo·i·lo (ē′lō·ē′lō) A port city on SE Panay island, Philippines; pop. 150,976 (1960).

I.L.P. *Brit.* Independent Labour Party.

ILS Instrument landing system.

I·lus (ī′ləs) In Greek mythology, the father of Laomedon and grandfather of Priam; founder of Troy. [< Gk. *Ilos*]

im-[1] Var. of EM-[1].

im-[2] Assimilated var. of IN-[1] and IN-[2].

I'm (īm) I am.

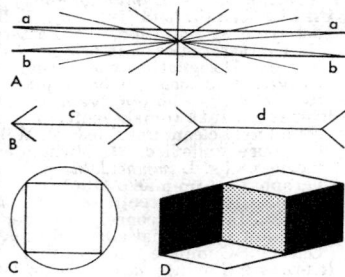

OPTICAL ILLUSIONS
A Parallel lines *aa* and *bb* appear warped because of adjacent lines.
B Branching lines make *d* seem longer, but lines *c* and *d* are equal.
C True circle seems to dip in at corners of square.
D Orientation of figure changes when viewed steadily.

I.M. Isle of Man.

im·age (im′ij) *n.* **1.** A representation or likeness of a real or imaginary person, creature, or object. **2.** A mental representation of something not perceived at the moment through the senses; mental picture; impression: a false *image* of oneself. **3.** The way in which a person or thing is popularly perceived or regarded, especially through the agency of the mass media, as television, magazines, etc.; public impression: a politician striving to improve his *image.* **4.** A person or thing that closely resembles another; counterpart. **5.** A sculptured likeness; a statue, especially one regarded as an object of religious veneration; icon. **6.** A representative example; embodiment. **7.** A rhetorical or literary device that evokes a mental picture; a figure of speech or a vivid description or comparison. **8.** *Optics* The counterpart of an object produced by reflection, refraction, or the passage of rays through a small aperture. **9.** The optical replica of a scene reproduced by a television camera. **10.** *Psychoanal.* An imago. **11.** *Obs.* An apparition. — *v.t.* **·aged, ·ag·ing** **1.** To form a mental picture of; imagine. **2.** To make a visible representation of; portray; delineate. **3.** To mirror; reflect. **4.** To describe effectively in speech or writing, as with vivid comparisons or descriptions, figures of speech, etc. **5.** To symbolize. [< OF < L *imago* < the base of *imitari* to imitate]

image orthicon Orthicon (which see).

image point A point beneath the surface of the earth at ground zero equal in depth to the height of the airburst of an atomic or hydrogen bomb, considered as a source of radiating reflected shock.

im·age·ry (im′ij·rē) *n. pl.* **·ries 1.** Mental images collectively, as created by imagination or memory. **2.** The act or process of forming mental images. **3.** The use of vivid descriptions or figures of speech in speaking or writing. **4.** Images used in art or decoration.

im·ag·i·na·ble (i·maj′ə·na·bəl) *adj.* Capable of being imagined; conceivable. [< LL *imaginabilis*] — **im·ag′i·na·bly** *adv.*

im·ag·i·nal (i·maj′ə·nəl) *adj. Entomol.* Of or pertaining to an imago.

im·ag·i·nar·y (i·maj′ə·ner′ē) *adj.* **1.** Existing in the imagination only; unreal. **2.** *Math.* Of, pertaining to, or involving imaginary numbers or systems of imaginary numbers. — *n. pl.* **·nar·ies** *Math.* An imaginary number. — **im·ag′i·nar′i·ly** *adv.* — **im·ag′i·nar′i·ness** *n.*

— **Syn. 1.** fancied, fantastic, illusory, chimerical, quixotic. Compare IDEAL. — **Ant.** real, actual.

imaginary number *Math.* A number of the form $a + bi,$ where a and b are real numbers, i is equal to $\sqrt{-1},$ and b is not zero. If a equals zero, the result is a **pure imaginary number.** Compare COMPLEX NUMBER.

im·ag·i·na·tion (i·maj′ə·nā′shən) *n.* **1.** The process of forming mental images of the objects of perception or thought in the absence of the concrete external stimuli; the picturing process of the mind. **2.** The mental ability to reproduce the images of memory; the reproductive faculty of the mind. **3.** The mental ability to create original and striking images and concepts by recombining the products of past experience; the creative or constructive faculty of the mind. **4.** A creation of the mind; mental image or concept. **5.** An absurd fancy; erroneous idea. **6.** *Archaic* A fantastic or unrealistic plan or scheme. [< L *imaginatio, -onis < imaginatus,* pp. of *imaginari.* See IMAGINE.] — **im·ag′i·na′tion·al** *adj.*

— **Syn.** *Imagination, fancy,* and *fantasy* refer to the mind's ability to elaborate images. *Imagination* is the exercise of this faculty in useful and creative ways. *Fancy* is more superficial, and *fantasy* suggests that the images are erratic or bizarre.

im·ag·i·na·tive (i·maj′ə·na·tiv, -nā′tiv) *adj.* **1.** Endowed with great creative imagination. **2.** Given to flights of fancy. **3.** Of, produced by, or characterized by the creative imagination: *imaginative* poetry. — **im·ag′i·na·tive·ly** *adv.* — **im·ag′i·na·tive·ness** *n.*

im·ag·ine (i·maj′in) *v.* **·ined, ·in·ing** *v.t.* **1.** To form a mental picture or idea of; conceive or create in the mind. **2.** To suppose; conjecture; guess: I hardly *imagine* that he will be elected. **3.** *Archaic* To plot: to *imagine* the death of the king. — *v.i.* **4.** To use the imagination. **5.** To suppose; conjecture; guess. [< L *imaginari* to imagine < *imago* image]

im·a·gism (im′ə·jiz′əm) *n.* A movement in poetry originating around 1910, characterized by the use of precise, concrete images and freedom in versification and form. [< F *Des Imagistes,* the title of the first anthology of imagist poetry] — **im′a·gist** *n. & adj.* — **im′a·gis′tic** *adj.*

i·ma·go (i·mā′gō) *n. pl.* **i·ma·goes** or **i·mag·i·nes** (i·maj′ə·nēz) **1.** *Entomol.* An insect in its adult, sexually mature stage. Compare LARVA, PUPA. **2.** *Psychoanal.* An infantile, unconscious concept of a parent or other loved one persisting in the adult. [< L]

i·mam (i·mäm′) *n.* A Moslem priest who recites prayers and leads devotions. Also **i·maum** (i·mäm′, i·môm′). [< Arabic *imām* leader < *amma* to lead]

I·mam (i·mäm′) *n.* **1.** A title of Mohammed and his four immediate successors. **2.** A title of a Moslem religious leader. **3.** The title of the leaders of the Shiahs, or heterodox Persian sect of Moslems; Ali and his ten successors: ascribed also to the Mahdi. Also **I·maum** (i·mäm′, i·môm′).

i·mam·ate (i·mäm′āt) *n.* **1.** The office or rank of an Imam. **2.** The territory under the jurisdiction of an Imam.

i·ma·ret (i·mä′ret) *n.* In Turkey, an inn or hostel. [< Turkish 'imâret < Arabic 'imârah building]

im·bal·ance (im·bal′əns) *n.* **1.** The state or condition of lacking balance or being out of balance. **2.** *Physiol.* Any defective coordination of the muscles, endocrine glands, etc.

im·balm (im·bäm′) See EMBALM.

im·bark (im·bärk′) See EMBARK.

im·be·cile (im·bə·sil, -səl) *adj.* **1.** Mentally deficient. **2.** Stupid; senseless. Also **im·be·cil·ic** (im′bə·sil′ik). — *n.* **1.** A person exhibiting a degree of mental deficiency between that of the idiot and the moron. **2.** Any very foolish or stupid person. — **Syn.** See IDIOT. [< F *imbécile* < L *imbecillus* weak, feeble] — **im′be·cile·ly** *adv.*

im·be·cil·i·ty (im′bə·sil′ə·tē) *n.* *pl.* **·ties** **1.** The condition of being an imbecile (def. 1). **2.** Foolishness; stupidity. **3.** A foolish or stupid action. [< F *imbécillité* < L *imbecillitas, -tatis* feebleness]

im·bed (im·bed′) See EMBED.

im·bibe (im·bīb′) *v.* **·bibed, ·bib·ing** *v.t.* **1.** To drink in; drink. **2.** To take in as if drinking; suck up; absorb. **3.** To take in and retain mentally: to *imbibe* learning. **4.** *Obs.* To saturate; imbue. — *v.i.* **5.** To drink. [< F *imbiber* < L *imbibere* < *in-* in + *bibere* to drink] — **im·bib′er** *n.*

im·bi·bi·tion (im′bi·bish′ən) *n.* The act of imbibing.

im·bit·ter (im·bit′ər) See EMBITTER.

im·blaze (im·blāz′) See EMBLAZE.

im·bod·y (im·bod′ē) See EMBODY.

im·bold·en (im·bōl′dən) See EMBOLDEN.

im·bos·om (im·bŏŏz′əm, -bŏŏ′zəm) See EMBOSOM.

im·bow·er (im·bou′ər) See EMBOWER.

im·bri·cate (*adj.* im′brə·kit; *v.* im′brə·kāt) *adj.* **1.** Arranged in a regular pattern with overlapping edges, as tiles or shingles on a roof. **2.** Covered or decorated with a design resembling overlapping scales, leaves, etc. **3.** *Biol.* Having or consisting of overlapping parts, as the scales of fishes, the buds or bracts of certain plants, etc. Also **im·bri·ca·tive** (-kā′tiv). — *v.t. & v.i.* **·cat·ed, ·cat·ing** To overlap in a regular arrangement. [< L *imbricatus*, pp. of *imbricare* to cover with gutter tiles < *imbrex* gutter tile < *imber* rain]

im·bri·ca·tion (im′brə·kā′shən) *n.* **1.** An overlapping of the edges, as of shingles or tiles. **2.** A decoration resembling overlapping leaves, scales, etc.

im·bro·glio (im·brōl′yō) *n.* *pl.* **·glios** **1.** A confused state of affairs; complicated misunderstanding; troublesome situation. **2.** A confused heap or tangle. [< Ital.]

Im·bros (im′brəs) An island of Turkey, in the Aegean off the Gallipoli Peninsula; 108 sq. mi.: Turkish *Imroz.*

im·brown (im·broun′) See EMBROWN.

im·brue (im·brōō′) *v.t.* **·brued, ·bru·ing** To stain or drench, especially with blood: also spelled *embrue.* [< OF *embreuver* < L *imbibere.* See IMBIBE.]

im·brute (im·brōōt′) *v.t. & v.i.* **·brut·ed, ·brut·ing** To make or become brutal or bestial; brutalize.

im·bue (im·byōō′) *v.t.* **·bued, ·bu·ing** **1.** To pervade or permeate (with emotions, ideals, etc.). **2.** To wet thoroughly; saturate, as with color. [< L *imbuere* to wet, soak]

im·id·az·ole (im′id·az′ōl, -ə·zōl′) *n.* *Chem.* A crystalline, organic base, $C_3H_4N_2$: also called *glyoxaline.* [< IMID(O) + AZOLE]

im·ide (im′īd, -id) *n.* *Chem.* A compound containing the bivalent NH group united to a bivalent organic acid radical. Also **im′id** (-id). [< AMIDE]

imido- combining form *Chem.* Indicating the presence of an imide in a compound. Also, before vowels, **imid-.** [< IMIDE]

i·mine (i·mēn′, im′in) *n.* *Chem.* An organic compound in which a nonacid organic radical is united with the bivalent NH radical. [< AMINE]

imino- combining form *Chem.* Indicating the presence of an imine in a compound. Also, before vowels, **imin-.** [< IMINE]

imit. Imitation; imitative.

im·i·ta·ble (im′ə·tə·bəl) *adj.* Capable of being imitated. — **im′i·ta·bil′i·ty** *n.*

im·i·tate (im′ə·tāt) *v.t.* **·tat·ed, ·tat·ing** **1.** To behave or attempt to behave in the same way as; follow the example of. **2.** To mimic or impersonate. **3.** To make a copy or reproduction of; use as a model; duplicate. **4.** To have or take on the appearance of; look like; counterfeit. [< L *imitatus*, pp. of *imitari* to imitate] — **im′i·ta·tor** *n.* — **Syn.** copy, simulate, ape. Compare DUPLICATE.

im·i·ta·tion (im′ə·tā′shən) *n.* **1.** The act of imitating. **2.** That which is done by or results from imitating; a likeness; copy. **3.** An artificial, often inferior, copy or reproduction; a counterfeit. **4.** *Biol.* Mimicry. **5.** *Music* The repetition of musical material in another voice soon after its original statement. **6.** A literary work in which the writer consciously makes use of the subject material or style of another. — **Syn.** See DUPLICATE. — *adj.* Resembling or made to re-

semble something superior; not genuine: *imitation* diamonds. Abbr. *imit.* [< L *imitatio, -onis*]

im·i·ta·tive (im′ə·tā′tiv) *adj.* **1.** Tending to imitate; characterized by imitation. **2.** Patterned after or reproducing the characteristics of an original. **3.** Not genuine; spurious. **4.** *Ling.* Designating words that resemble natural sounds, as *buzz, clink, swish*; onomatopoeic. Abbr. *imit.* — **im′i·ta′tive·ly** *adv.* — **im′i·ta′tive·ness** *n.*

im·mac·u·late (i·mak′yə·lit) *adj.* **1.** Without spot or stain; completely clean; unsullied. **2.** Without sin; morally blameless; pure; undefiled. **3.** Without error or blemish; faultless; flawless. [< L *immaculatus* < *in-* not + *maculatus* < *macula* spot] — **im·mac′u·late·ly** *adv.* — **im·mac′u·late·ness** *n.*

Immaculate Conception *Theol.* The doctrine that the Virgin Mary was conceived in her mother's womb without the taint of original sin: a dogma in the Roman Catholic Church. Compare VIRGIN BIRTH.

im·mane (i·man′) *adj.* *Archaic* Of vast size; gigantic; also, monstrous; cruel. [< L *immanis*]

im·ma·nence (im′ə·nəns) *n.* **1.** A permanent abiding within; an indwelling. **2.** The presence of God pervading all creation. Also **im′ma·nen·cy.**

im·ma·nent (im′ə·nənt) *adj.* **1.** Existing or remaining within; indwelling. **2.** Of God, pervading all creation. [< L *immanens, -entis*, ppr. of *immanere* < *in-* in + *manere* to stay] — **im′ma·nent·ly** *adv.*

Im·man·u·el (i·man′yōō·əl) A name of the Messiah. *Isa.* vii 14; *Matt.* i 23. Also *Emmanuel.* [< Hebrew, God with us]

im·ma·te·ri·al (im′ə·tir′ē·əl) *adj.* **1.** Of little or no importance; inconsequential; irrelevant. **2.** Not consisting of material substance; insubstantial. [< Med.L *immaterialis* < *in-* not + *materialis* < *materia* matter] — **im′ma·te′ri·al·ly** *adv.* — **im′ma·te′ri·al·ness** *n.*

im·ma·te·ri·al·ism (im′ə·tir′ē·əl·iz′əm) *n.* The doctrine that the material world has no existence apart from its perception by the mind. — **im′ma·te′ri·al·ist** *n.*

im·ma·te·ri·al·i·ty (im′ə·tir′ē·al′ə·tē) *n.* *pl.* **·ties** **1.** The state or quality of being immaterial. **2.** That which has no material existence.

im·ma·te·ri·al·ize (im′ə·tir′ē·əl·īz′) *v.t.* **·ized, ·iz·ing** To make immaterial or incorporeal.

im·ma·ture (im′ə·chŏŏr′, -tyŏŏr′, -tŏŏr′) *adj.* **1.** Not mature or ripe; not fully grown; in an incomplete or imperfect state. **2.** *Geog.* In an early stage of development; young. **3.** *Archaic* Premature. [< L *immaturus* < *in-* not + *maturus* mature] — **im′ma·ture′ly** *adv.* — **im′ma·ture′ness** *n.*

im·ma·tu·ri·ty (im′ə·chŏŏr′ə·tē, -tyŏŏr′-, -tŏŏr′-) *n.* *pl.* **·ties** The state or quality of being immature.

im·meas·ur·a·ble (i·mezh′ər·ə·bəl) *adj.* Not capable of being measured; without limit; immense. — **im·meas′ur·a·bly** *adv.* — **im·meas′ur·a·bil′i·ty, im·meas′ur·a·ble·ness** *n.*

im·me·di·a·cy (i·mē′dē·ə·sē) *n.* **1.** The state or quality of being immediate; especially, freedom from the intervention of any intermediate person or thing; direct relationship. **2.** *Philos.* **a** Consciousness or direct awareness, apart from memory or reasoning. **b** Intuitive knowledge as distinguished from that arrived at by proof or reasoning.

im·me·di·ate (i·mē′dē·it) *adj.* **1.** Done or occurring without delay or lapse of time; instant. **2.** Pertaining to the present moment: We have no *immediate* vacancies. **3.** Separated by no appreciable interval of time or space: the *immediate* future; the *immediate* neighborhood. **4.** Very close in rank or relationship: the *immediate* family. **5.** Occurring or acting without an intervening agency or cause; direct. **6.** Directly related or having a direct bearing: an *immediate* effect. **7.** Pertaining to or characterized by direct knowledge or perception; intuitive. [< Med.L *immediatus* < *in-* not + *mediatus*. See MEDIATE.] — **im·me′di·ate·ness** *n.*

immediate constituent *Gram.* See under CONSTITUENT.

im·me·di·ate·ly (i·mē′dē·it·lē) *adv.* **1.** Without lapse of time; instantly; at once. **2.** In direct or close succession. **3.** Without an intervening agency or cause; directly. — *conj.* As soon as; at the instant that.

— **Syn.** 1. *Immediately, instantly, at once, promptly, directly, forthwith,* and *presently* mean with little or no lapse of time. *Immediately* and *instantly* are the most forceful, indicating no delay whatever: he answered *immediately*, she recognized her lost jewels *instantly*. *Immediately*, however, may also be used when a very short delay is expected or implied; it is then interchangeable with *at once, promptly*, and *directly*: please ship this order *immediately* (or *at once*, or *promptly*), hearing the signal, he came *immediately* (or *directly*). *Forthwith* and *presently* suggest the passage of a small, but noticeable, interval of time. *Forthwith* often means as soon as possible or convenient; *presently* emphasizes delay and the lapse of time: he set out for the colonies *forthwith*; I knocked, and *presently* the door was opened.

im·med·i·ca·ble (i·med′i·kə·bəl) *adj.* Incapable of responding to medical treatment; incurable. [< L *immedicabilis* < *in-* not + *medicabilis* curable < *medicare* to heal]

Im·mel·mann turn (im′əl·män, -mən) *Aeron.* An airplane maneuver consisting of a partial loop followed by a half-roll, used to gain altitude while reversing the direction of flight. [after Max *Immelmann*, 1890–1916, German aviator]

im·me·mo·ri·al (im′ə·môr′ē·əl, -mō′rē-) *adj.* Reaching back beyond memory; originating in the distant past; ancient. [< Med.L *immemorialis* < *in-* not + L *memorialis* < *memoria*] — **im·me·mo'ri·al·ly** *adv.*

im·mense (i·mens') *adj.* 1. Of great size, degree, or extent; huge; enormous. 2. Having no limits; boundless; infinite. 3. *Slang* Excellent; admirable. [< F < L *immensus* < *in-* not + *mensus*, pp. of *metiri* to measure] — **im·mense'ly** *adv.* — **im·mense'ness** *n.*
— **Syn.** 1. vast, prodigious, stupendous, gigantic.

im·men·si·ty (i·men'sə·tē) *n.* *pl.* **·ties** 1. The condition or quality of being immense; hugeness; vastness. 2. Boundless space; infinity. [< MF *immensité* < L *immensitas* < *immensus*. See IMMENSE.]

im·men·sur·a·ble (i·men'shŏor·ə·bəl, -sə·rə-) *adj.* Immeasurable. [< MF < L *immensurabilis* < *in-* not + *mensurabilis*. See MENSURABLE.] — **im·men'sur·a·bil'i·ty** *n.*

im·merge (i·mûrj') *v.* **·merged**, **·merg·ing** *v.t.* 1. To immerse. — *v.i.* 2. To plunge or sink into a liquid. [< L *immergere* < *in-* + *mergere* to dip] — **im·mer'gence** *n.*

im·merse (i·mûrs') *v.t.* **·mersed**, **·mers·ing** 1. To plunge or dip into water or other fluid so as to cover completely. 2. To involve deeply; engross. 3. To baptize by immersion. [< L *immersus*, pp. of *immergere* to dip]

im·mersed (i·mûrst') *adj.* 1. *Bot.* Growing entirely under water. 2. *Biol.* Embedded in a surrounding part or parts, as an organ. 3. Baptized by immersion.

im·mer·sion (i·mûr'shən, -zhən) *n.* 1. The act of immersing, or the state of being immersed. 2. Baptism by plunging the entire body under water. 3. *Astron.* The disappearance of a heavenly body by passing behind or entering into the shadow of another. [< LL *immersio*, *-onis*. See IMMERSE.]

im·mer·sion·ism (i·mûr'shən·iz'əm, -zhən-) *n.* 1. The doctrine that immersion is essential in baptism. 2. The custom of baptizing by immersion. — **im·mer'sion·ist** *n.*

im·mesh (i·mesh') *v.t.* To enmesh.

im·me·thod·i·cal (im/ə·thod'i·kəl) *adj.* Not methodical; disordered. — **im/me·thod'i·cal·ly** *adv.* — **im/me·thod'i·cal·ness** *n.*

im·mi·grant (im/ə·grənt) *adj.* Coming into a country or region of which one is not a native in order to settle there. Compare EMIGRANT. — *n.* A person who immigrates.

im·mi·grate (im/ə·grāt) *v.* **·grat·ed**, **·grat·ing** *v.i.* 1. To come into a country or region of which one is not a native in order to settle there. — *v.t.* 2. To bring in as immigrants or settlers. — **Syn.** See MIGRATE. [< L *immigratus*, pp. of *immigrare* to go into < *in-* in + *migrare* to migrate]

im·mi·gra·tion (im/ə·grā'shən) *n.* 1. The act of immigrating; entrance of a settler or settlers from a foreign country. 2. The total number of aliens entering a country for permanent residence during a stated period. 3. Immigrants collectively. — **im·mi·gra·to·ry** (im/ə·grə·tôr/ē, -tō/rē) *adj.*

im·mi·nence (im/ə·nəns) *n.* 1. The state or quality of being imminent. 2. That which is imminent; especially, impending disaster. Also **im/mi·nen·cy.** [< LL *imminentia*]

im·mi·nent (im/ə·nənt) *adj.* About to happen; impending; threatening: said especially of danger or catastrophe. [< L *imminens*, *-entis* < *imminere* to lean over, impend < *in-* on + *-minere* to project] — **im/mi·nent·ly** *adv.*
— **Syn.** *Imminent* and *impending* both derive from the idea of something hanging and about to fall, and refer to events that are about to happen. *Imminent* is less emphatic and points to an indefinite time in the future; *impending* indicates that which is expected in the near future. — **Ant.** remote.

im·min·gle (i·ming/gəl) *v.t.* & *v.i.* **·gled**, **·gling** To blend thoroughly; intermix.

im·mis·ci·ble (i·mis/ə·bəl) *adj.* Not capable of being mixed, as oil and water. [< L *in-* not + *miscere* to mix] — **im·mis/ci·bil/i·ty** *n.* — **im·mis/ci·bly** *adv.*

im·mit·i·ga·ble (i·mit/ə·gə·bəl) *adj.* Incapable of being mitigated. [< L *immitigabilis* < *in-* not + *mitigare*. See MITIGATE.] — **im·mit/i·ga·bly** *adv.*

im·mix (i·miks') *v.t.* To mix in; commingle. [< L *immixtus*, pp. of *immiscere* < *in-* in + *miscere* to mix]

im·mix·ture (i·miks'chər) *n.* The act of immixing, or the state of being immixed.

im·mo·bile (i·mō/bəl, -bēl) *adj.* 1. Incapable of being moved; immovable. 2. Not moving; motionless. [< OF < LL *immobilis* < L *in-* not + *movere* to move. See MOBILE.]

im·mo·bil·i·ty (im/ō·bil/ə·tē) *n.* The state or quality of being immobile; motionlessness.

im·mo·bi·lize (i·mō/bə·līz) *v.t.* **·lized**, **·liz·ing** 1. To make immovable; fix in place. 2. To make unable to move or mobilize, as a body of troops. 3. To withdraw (specie) from circulation and hold as security or reserve; replace (circulating capital) with fixed capital. [< F *immobiliser* < LL *immobilis*. See IMMOBILE.] — **im·mo/bi·li·za/tion** *n.*

im·mod·er·ate (i·mod/ər·it) *adj.* Not moderate; exceeding reasonable or proper bounds; unrestrained. [< L *immoderatus* < *in-* not + *moderatus*. See MODERATE.] — **im·mod/er·ate·ly** *adv.* — **im·mod/er·ate·ness** *n.*
— **Syn.** excessive, extravagant, inordinate, intemperate.

im·mod·er·a·tion (i·mod/ə·rā/shən) *n.* Lack of moderation; excess. Also **im·mod/er·a·cy** (-ər·ə·sē). [< L *immoderatio*, *-onis*]

im·mod·est (i·mod/ist) *adj.* 1. Without sense of decency; indecent; improper. 2. Lacking humility; self-assertive; bold. [< L *immodestus* < *in-* not + *modestus*. See MODEST.] — **im·mod/est·ly** *adv.* — **im·mod/es·ty** *n.*
— **Syn.** 1. shameless, wanton, lewd, obscene. 2. forward, brazen. — **Ant.** modest, decent, decorous, chaste.

im·mo·late (im/ə·lāt) *v.t.* **·lat·ed**, **·lat·ing** To sacrifice; especially, to kill as a sacrificial victim. [< L *immolatus*, pp. of *immolare* to sprinkle with sacrificial meal < *in-* on + *mola* meal] — **im/mo·la/tor** *n.*

im·mo·la·tion (im/ə·lā/shən) *n.* 1. The act of immolating, or the state of being immolated. 2. A sacrificial victim. [< L *immolatio*, *-onis*]

im·mor·al (i·môr/əl, i·mor/-) *adj.* 1. Violating the moral law; contrary to conscience or public morality. 2. Sexually impure; licentious. — **im·mor/al·ly** *adv.*
— **Syn.** 1. *Immoral*, *amoral*, *unmoral*, and *nonmoral* agree in meaning not moral. The *immoral* person violates moral principles knowingly; he is consciously wicked, dissolute, evil, etc. The *amoral* person lacks the sense of right and wrong, and thus may violate morality without evil intent. *Unmoral* and *nonmoral* mean not within the realm of morality; a baby is *unmoral*, meteorology is a *nonmoral* study. — **Ant.** moral, virtuous, righteous.

im·mo·ral·i·ty (im/ə·ral/ə·tē, -ôr·al/-) *n.* *pl.* **·ties** 1. The state or quality of being immoral; wickedness; dissoluteness. 2. Sexual impurity or misconduct. 3. An immoral act.

im·mor·tal (i·môr/təl) *adj.* 1. Not subject to death; living forever; deathless: opposed to *mortal*. 2. Having unending existence; everlasting; eternal. 3. Pertaining to immortality or to beings or concepts that are immortal; divine. 4. Of enduring fame; remembered through the ages; memorable. — *n.* 1. An immortal being. 2. *pl.* The gods of classical mythology. 3. A person who has gained enduring fame. — **the Immortals** The forty members of the French Academy: also **the Forty Immortals**. [< L *immortalis* < *in-* not + *mortalis*. See MORTAL.] — **im·mor/tal·ly** *adv.*
— **Syn.** (adj.) undying, unfading, imperishable, indestructible. — **Ant.** mortal, transient, transitory, ephemeral.

im·mor·tal·i·ty (im/ôr·tal/ə·tē) *n.* 1. Unending existence; eternal life. 2. Eternal fame. [< OF *immortalité* < L *immortalitas*]

im·mor·tal·ize (i·môr/təl·īz) *v.t.* **·ized**, **·iz·ing** To make immortal; endow with perpetual life or fame. Also *Brit.* **im·mor/tal·ise**. — **im·mor/tal·iz/er** *n.* — **im·mor/tal·i·za/tion** *n.*

im·mor·telle (im/ôr·tel') *n.* An everlasting (def. 2).

im·mo·tile (i·mō/til) *adj.* Not motile.

im·mov·a·ble (i·mōō/və·bəl) *adj.* 1. Incapable of being moved; firmly fixed; stable. 2. Unable to move; motionless; stationary. 3. Firm of purpose or opinion; steadfast; unyielding. 4. Not easily aroused emotionally; impassive; stolid. 5. *Law* Pertaining to real property as distinguished from personal property: opposed to *movable*. — *n.pl. Law* Real property. — **im·mov/a·bil/i·ty, im·mov/a·ble·ness** *n.* — **im·mov/a·bly** *adv.*

immovable feast A church feast celebrated on the same date each year.

im·mune (i·myōōn') *adj.* 1. Protected against a disease, poison, or the like, as by inoculation. 2. Not susceptible to harmful influence: *immune* to corruption. 3. Not subject to obligation, penalty, etc. — *n.* One who is immune, especially to a disease. [< OF < L *immunis*]

immune response *Physiol.* The complex defensive reaction in organisms that causes, among other things, the rejection of a skin or organ graft from another. Also **immune reaction.**

im·mu·ni·ty (i·myōō/nə·tē) *n.* *pl.* **·ties** 1. Protection against or lack of susceptibility to a disease, poison, infection, or the like. 2. Resistance to harmful influence. 3. Exemption from obligation, penalty, etc.; as: **a** The exemption of ecclesiastical persons or institutions from civil obligations or jurisdiction. **b** Diplomatic immunity (which see) [< OF *immunité* < L *immunitas* < *immunis* exempt < *in-* not + *munis* serviceable < *munus* service, duty]

im·mu·nize (im/yə·nīz) *v.t.* **·nized**, **·niz·ing** To make immune; especially, to protect against a disease by inoculation. — **im/mu·ni·za/tion** *n.*

immuno- *combining form* Immune; immunity: *immunology*. [< IMMUNE]

im·mu·no·gen·ic (i·myōō/nō·jen/ik) *adj.* Producing or conferring immunity to a specified disease.

im·mu·no·ge·net·ics (i·myōō/nō·jə·net/iks) *n.* The study of the interrelationship of immunity to disease and specific genetic factors.

im·mu·nol·o·gy (im/yə·nol/ə·jē) *n.* The branch of medical science that deals with immunity to disease. [< IMMUNO- + -LOGY] — **im·mu·no·log·i·cal** (i·myōō/nə·loj/i·kəl) *adj.* — **im/mu·nol/o·gist** *n.*

im·mu·no·re·ac·tion (i·myōō/nō·rē·ak/shən) *n.* The reaction between antigen and antibody to produce immunity.

im·mure (i·myŏŏr′) *v.t.* **·mured, ·mur·ing 1.** To enclose within walls; imprison. **2.** To place in seclusion; confine. **3.** To entomb within a wall. **4.** *Obs.* To fortify by surrounding with a wall or walls. [< Med.L *immurare* < *in-* in + LL *murare* to wall < *murus* wall] — **im·mure′ment** *n.*

im·mu·ta·ble (i·myōō′tə·bəl) *adj.* Not mutable; unchanging; unalterable. [< L *immutabilis.* See MUTABLE.] — **im·mu′ta·bil′i·ty, im·mu′ta·ble·ness** *n.* — **im·mu′ta·bly** *adv.*

Im·o·gen (im′ə·jən) In Shakespeare's *Cymbeline,* the heroine, a model of conjugal fidelity.

imp (imp) *n.* **1.** An evil spirit; a young, small, or minor demon. **2.** A mischievous or unruly child. **3.** *Obs.* An offspring. **4.** *Obs.* A shoot of a plant. — *v.t.* **1.** In falconry, to graft feathers into or onto (a wing) to improve or restore the power of flight. **2.** *Obs.* To engraft. [OE *impa* a graft < *impian* to ingraft. Cf. LL *impotus* a shoot < Gk. *emphytos* < *emphyein* to implant < *en-* in + *phyein* to produce]

imp. 1. Imperative. **2.** Imperfect. **3.** Imperial. **4.** Impersonal. **5.** Import; imported; importer. **6.** Important. **7.** Imprimatur. **8.** Improper.

Imp. Imperator.

im·pact (*n.* im′pakt; *v.* im·pakt′) *n.* **1.** A striking together; collision. **2.** The forcible momentary contact of a moving body with another either moving or at rest: the *impact* of a bullet. **3.** Strong influence; powerful effect: the *impact* of science on culture. — *v.t.* To press or drive firmly into something; pack. [< L *impactus,* pp. of *impingere.* See IMPINGE.]

im·pact·ed (im·pak′tid) *adj.* **1.** Packed or wedged firmly. **2.** *Dent.* Denoting a tooth remaining in the jawbone and unable to emerge through the gum.

im·pac·tion (im·pak′shən) *n.* **1.** The act of impacting, or the state of being impacted. **2.** *Dent.* An impacted tooth. [< L *impactio, -onis* a striking]

im·paint (im·pānt′) *v.t. Obs.* To paint or depict.

im·pair (im·pâr′) *v.t.* To cause to become less in quality, power, or value; make worse. — *n. Archaic* Impairment. [< OF *empeirer* < LL *in-* thoroughly + *pejorare* to make worse < L *pejor* worse]
— **Syn.** harm, weaken, enfeeble, deteriorate, spoil. Compare HURT. — **Ant.** improve, repair.

im·paired (im·pârd′) *adj. Canadian* Incapable of adequately controlling a vehicle because of excessive use of alcohol or drugs; chiefly legal use.

im·pair·ment (im·pâr′mənt) *n.* The act of impairing, or the state of being impaired; deterioration.

im·pa·la (im·pä′lə) *n.* A dark red antelope (*Aepyceros melampus*) of South Africa, with spreading horns in the male. [< native name, possibly Swazi or Zulu]

im·pale (im·pāl′) *v.t.* **·paled, ·pal·ing 1.** To fix upon a pale or sharp stake. **2.** To torture or put to death by thrusting a sharp stake through the body. **3.** To make helpless as if by fixing upon a stake. **4.** *Heraldry* To place (two coats of arms) side by side on an escutcheon. **5.** *Rare* To enclose with or as with stakes or palings; fence in. Also spelled *empale.* [< OF *empaler* < LL *impalare* < *in-* + *palus* stake] — **im·pale′ment** *n.* — **im·pal′er** *n.*

im·pal·pa·ble (im·pal′pə·bəl) *adj.* **1.** Not capable of being perceived by the sense of touch. **2.** Not capable of being distinguished by the mind; intangible. **3.** Consisting of very fine particles that give no sensation of grittiness when rubbed between the fingers. [< Med.L *impalpabilis.* See PALPABLE.] — **im·pal′pa·bil′i·ty** *n.* — **im·pal′pa·bly** *adv.*

im·pal·u·dism (im·pal′yə·diz′əm) *n. Pathol.* Chronic malarial infection. [< L *in-* in + *palus, paludis* swamp]

im·pa·na·tion (im′pə·nā′shən) *n. Theol.* The doctrine that the body and blood of Christ are united into one substance with the consecrated bread and wine of the Eucharist: distinguished from *consubstantiation, transubstantiation.* [< Med.L *impanatus,* pp. of *impanare* to embody in bread < *in-* in + *panis* bread]

im·pan·el (im·pan′əl) *v.t.* **·pan·eled** or **·elled, ·pan·el·ing** or **·el·ling 1.** To enroll upon a panel or list, as for jury duty. **2.** To choose (members of a jury, etc.) from such a list. Also spelled *empanel.* — **im·pan′el·ment** *n.*

im·par·a·dise (im·par′ə·dīs) *v.t.* **·dised, ·dis·ing** To place in or as in paradise; make supremely happy.

im·par·i·pin·nate (im·par′ə·pin′āt) *adj. Bot.* Pinnate with an odd terminal leaflet. [< L *impar* unequal + PINNATE]

im·par·i·ty (im·par′ə·tē) *n. pl.* **·ties** Lack of correspondence; inequality; disparity. [< LL *imparitas, -tatis* < L *in-* not + *par* equal]

im·park (im·pärk′) *v.t.* **1.** To enclose (land) as a park. **2.** To confine in or as in a park. [< AF *enparker,* OF *emparquer* < F *parc*] — **im·par·ka·tion** (im′pär·kā′shən) *n.*

im·part (im·pärt′) *v.t.* **1.** To make known; disclose: to *impart* information. **2.** To bestow a measure or quantity of: to *impart* happiness. [< OF *empartir* < L *impartire* < *in-* in + *partire* to share < *pars, partis* part, share] — **im·par·ta·tion** (im′pär·tā′shən) *n.* — **im·part′ment** *n.* — **im·part′er** *n.*

im·par·tial (im·pär′shəl) *adj.* Not favoring one above another; free from bias; disinterested. [< *in-* not + PARTIAL] — **im·par′tial·ly** *adv.* — **im·par′tial·ness** *n.*

im·par·ti·al·i·ty (im′pär·shē·al′ə·tē, im·pär′-) *n.* Freedom from bias; fairness. — **Syn.** See JUSTICE.

im·part·i·ble¹ (im·pär′tə·bəl) *adj.* Not subject to partition; not divisible. [< LL *impartibilis* < *in-* not + *partibilis.* See PARTIBLE.] — **im·part′i·bil′i·ty** *n.* — **im·part′i·bly** *adv.*

im·part·i·ble² (im·pär′tə·bəl) *adj.* Capable of being imparted.

im·pass·a·ble (im·pas′ə·bəl, -päs′-) *adj.* That cannot be traveled over or through: an *impassable* jungle. — **im·pass′a·bil′i·ty, im·pass′a·ble·ness** *n.* — **im·pass′a·bly** *adv.*

im·passe (im′pas, im·pas′; *Fr.* añ·päs′) *n.* **1.** A situation that has become so difficult or complicated that no further progress is possible; deadlock; stalemate. **2.** A way or passage open at one end only; blind alley; dead end. [< F]

im·pas·si·ble (im·pas′ə·bəl) *adj.* **1.** Incapable of emotion; unfeeling. **2.** Incapable of suffering pain. **3.** Not subject to harm; invulnerable. [< OF *impassible* < Med.L *impassibilis* < *in-* not + *passibilis.* See PASSIBLE.] — **im·pas′si·bil′i·ty, im·pas′si·ble·ness** *n.* — **im·pas′si·bly** *adv.*

im·pas·sion (im·pash′ən) *v.t.* To fill with passion; inflame. [< Ital. *impassionare*]

im·pas·sion·ate (im·pash′ən·it) *adj. Rare* Without passion; dispassionate.

im·pas·sioned (im·pash′ənd) *adj.* Filled with passion or strong feeling; fervent. — **im·pas′sioned·ly** *adv.* — **im·pas′sioned·ness** *n.*

im·pas·sive (im·pas′iv) *adj.* **1.** Not feeling emotion; unmoved. **2.** Calm; serene. **3.** Unconscious. [< *in-* not + PASSIVE] — **im·pas′sive·ly** *adv.* — **im·pas′sive·ness, im·pas·siv·i·ty** (im′pa·siv′ə·tē) *n.*

im·paste (im·pāst′) *v.t.* **·past·ed, ·past·ing 1.** To enclose in or as in a paste. **2.** To make into a paste or crust. **3.** To apply paint, etc., thickly to. [< Ital. *impastare*] — **im·pas·ta·tion** (im′pas·tā′shən) *n.*

im·pas·to (im·päs′tō) *n.* **1.** A technique of painting in which pigment is applied thickly to a surface. **2.** The pigment so applied. [< Ital.]

im·pa·tience (im·pā′shəns) *n.* **1.** Lack of patience; inability to tolerate delay, discomfort, or opposition. **2.** Eagerness for change or new experience; restlessness. [< OF *impacience* < L *impatientia.* See IMPATIENT.]

im·pa·ti·ens (im·pā′shē·enz) *n.* Any of a large genus (*Impatiens*) of herbs with stems enlarged at the joints, opposite leaves, and irregular flowers, as the jewelweed: also called *touch-me-not.* [< L, impatient; because the ripe seed pods burst open at a touch.]

im·pa·tient (im·pā′shənt) *adj.* **1.** Lacking patience; easily annoyed at delay, discomfort, etc.; irritable. **2.** Unwilling to tolerate with *of*: *impatient* of delay. **3.** Restlessly eager: *impatient* for success. **4.** Exhibiting lack of patience: an *impatient* gesture. [< OF *impacient* < L *impatiens, -entis* < *in-* not + *patiens.* See PATIENT.] — **im·pa′tient·ly** *adv.*

im·pav·id (im·pav′id) *adj.* Fearless; intrepid; bold. [< L *impavidus* < *in-* not + *pavidus* timid] — **im·pa·vid·i·ty** (im′pə·vid′ə·tē) *n.* — **im·pav′id·ly** *adv.*

im·pawn (im·pôn′) *v.t.* To pledge as security; pawn.

im·peach (im·pēch′) *v.t.* **1.** To charge (a high public official) before a legally constituted tribunal with crime or misdemeanor in office. **2.** To challenge or bring discredit upon the honesty or validity of. — **Syn.** See ACCUSE. [< OF *empescher* to hinder < LL *impedicare* to entangle < *in-* in + *pedica* fetter < *pes, pedis* foot] — **im·peach′er** *n.*

im·peach·a·ble (im·pē′chə·bəl) *adj.* **1.** Liable to be impeached. **2.** Making liable to impeachment: an *impeachable* offense. — **im·peach′a·bil′i·ty** *n.*

im·peach·ment (im·pēch′mənt) *n.* **1.** The act of impeaching, or the state of being impeached. **2.** Arraignment of a high public official before a proper tribunal. **3.** In the United States, the presentation of formal charges against an official of the federal government by the House of Representatives, the trial to be held before the Senate. [< OF *empeschement* obstruction]

im·pearl (im·pûrl′) *v.t.* **1.** *Poetic* To adorn with pearls or pearllike objects. **2.** To form into drops resembling pearls. **3.** To make pearly. [< F *emperler*]

im·pec·ca·ble (im·pek′ə·bəl) *adj.* **1.** Free from error, fault, or flaw. **2.** Incapable of doing wrong; unerring. — **n.** An impeccable person. [< LL *impeccabilis* < L *in-* not + *peccare* to sin] — **im·pec′ca·bil′i·ty** *n.* — **im·pec′ca·bly** *adv.*

im·pec·cant (im·pek′ənt) *adj.* Free from sin or error. [< L *in-* not + ppr. of *peccare* to sin] — **im·pec′cance, im·pec′can·cy** *n.*

im·pe·cu·ni·ous (im′pə·kyōō′nē·əs) *adj.* Having no money; poor; penniless. Also **im·pe·cu·ni·ar·y** (im′pə·kyōō′nē·er′ē). [< F *impécunieux* < L *in-* not + *pecuniosus* < *pecunia* money] — **im′pe·cu′ni·ous·ly** *adv.* — **im′pe·cu′ni·ous·ness, im′pe·cu·ni·os′i·ty** (-os′ə·tē) *n.*

im·ped·ance (im·pēd′ns) *n.* **1.** *Electr.* The total opposition to an alternating current presented by a circuit, equal to the square root of $[R^2 + (X_L - X_C)^2]$, where R is the true resistance, X_L the inductive reactance, and X_C the capacitive reactance: sometimes called *resistance.* **2.** *Physics* In a sound-transmitting medium, the ratio of the pressure per unit area of a given surface on a wave front to the volume velocity or flux through the surface. [< IMPEDE + -ANCE]

im·pede (im·pēd′) *v.t.* **·ped·ed, ·ped·ing** To retard or hinder in progress or action; put obstacles in the way of. — **Syn.**

See HINDER[1]. [< L *impedire*, lit., to shackle the feet < *in-* in + *pes, pedis* foot] — **im·ped′er** n.

im·pe·di·ent (im·pē′dē·ənt) *adj.* That impedes. — n. That which impedes. [< L *impediens, -entis*, ppr. of *impedire*. See IMPEDE.]

im·ped·i·ment (im·ped′ə·mənt) n. **1.** That which hinders or obstructs; an obstacle. **2.** A physical handicap, especially a speech defect. **3.** *Law* A A disability that prevents the making of a valid contract, as infancy, insanity, etc. **b** A disability that affects the validity of a marriage. — **absolute impediment** *Law* A disability that makes it impossible for a person to contract a valid marriage. — **prohibitive impediment** *Law* A disability that does not make a marriage null and void but subjects the parties to a punishment. — **relative impediment** *Law* That which bars persons within specified degrees of consanguinity, as a brother and sister, from contracting a valid marriage with each other. See also DIRIMENT IMPEDIMENT OF MARRIAGE. [< L *impedimentum* < *impedire*. See IMPEDE.] — **im·ped′i·men′tal** (-men′təl), **im·ped′i·men′ta·ry** (-men′tər·ē) *adj.*

— **Syn. 1.** *Impediment, hindrance, encumbrance,* and *obstacle* denote something that checks or halts progress. *Impediment* suggests something that entangles the feet and interferes with freedom of action or movement. *Hindrance* is used of that which holds one back and makes him fall short of his goal, while an *encumbrance* weighs him down and makes progress difficult. An *obstacle* is something one must remove or go around before proceeding.

im·ped·i·men·ta (im·ped′ə·men′tə) *n.pl.* **1.** The baggage, supplies, and equipment carried by an army. **2.** Any cumbersome baggage or equipment; also, any drawbacks or burdens. **3.** *Law* Impediments. [< L]

im·ped·i·tive (im·ped′ə·tiv) *adj.* Acting as an impediment.

im·pel (im·pel′) *v.t.* **pelled, pel·ling 1.** To force or drive to an action; move by an impulse; urge on. **2.** To drive or push forward; propel. — **Syn.** See ACTUATE. [< L *impellere* < *in-* on + *pellere* to drive]

im·pel·lent (im·pel′ənt) *adj.* Tending to impel. — n. An impelling person, thing, or force. [< L *impellens, -entis*, ppr. of *impellere*. See IMPEL.]

im·pel·ler (im·pel′ər) n. **1.** One who or that which impels. **2.** *Mech.* **a** The rotor of a pump or blower. **b** The centrifugal compressor of a jet engine.

im·pend (im·pend′) *v.i.* **1.** To be about to occur; be imminent. **2.** To be suspended; hang: with *over.* [< L *impendere* to overhang < *in-* on + *pendere* to hang]

im·pen·dent (im·pen′dənt) *adj.* Impending. [< L *impendens, -entis*, ppr. of *impendere*. See IMPEND.] — **im·pen′dence, im·pen′den·cy** n.

im·pend·ing (im·pen′ding) *adj.* **1.** About to occur; imminent; threatening. **2.** Overhanging. — **Syn.** See IMMINENT.

im·pen·e·tra·bil·i·ty (im·pen′ə·trə·bil′ə·tē) n. **1.** The state or quality of being impenetrable. **2.** *Physics* The property of matter that makes impossible the occupation of the same space by two bodies at the same time.

im·pen·e·tra·ble (im·pen′ə·trə·bəl) *adj.* **1.** Incapable of being penetrated; that cannot be pierced, entered, seen through, etc.; impervious; dense. **2.** Incapable of being understood; incomprehensible. **3.** Inaccessible to intellectual or moral influences. **4.** *Physics* Possessing impenetrability. [< OF *impenetrable* < L *impenetrabilis* < *in-* not + *penetrabilis* < *penetrare*. See PENETRATE.] — **im·pen′e·tra·bil′i·ty, im·pen′e·tra·ble·ness** n. — **im·pen′e·tra·bly** *adv.*

im·pen·i·tence (im·pen′ə·təns) n. The state or quality of being impenitent. Also **im·pen′i·ten·cy.** [< LL *impaenitentia*]

im·pen·i·tent (im·pen′ə·tənt) *adj.* Not penitent; obdurate. [< LL *impaenitens, -entis* < L *in-* not + *paenitens.* See PENITENCE.] — **im·pen′i·tent·ly** *adv.* — **im·pen′i·tent·ness** n.

im·pen·nate (im·pen′āt) *adj. Ornithol.* Lacking true wings or feathers. [< *in-* not + PENNATE]

imper. Imperative.

im·per·a·tive (im·per′ə·tiv) *adj.* **1.** Urgently necessary; obligatory; unavoidable. **2.** Having the nature of or expressing a command; peremptory; authoritative. **3.** *Gram.* Designating the mood used to express commands, requests, exhortations, etc. — n. **1.** That which is imperative. **2.** *Gram.* The mood used to express command, exhortation, etc., or a verb or verb form in this mood. Abbr. *imp., imper., impv.* [< LL *imperativus* < *imperare* to command] — **im·per′a·tive·ly** *adv.* — **im·per′a·tive·ness** n.

im·pe·ra·tor (im′pə·rā′tər, -tôr) n. **1.** The official designation of the Roman emperors; also, a title of honor for a victorious Roman general. Abbr. *Imp.* **2.** Any emperor or absolute ruler. [< L, commander, emperor] — **im·per·a·to·ri·al** (im·per′ə·tôr′ē·əl, -tō′rē-) *adj.*

im·pe·ra·trice (im′pə·rā′tris) n. *Obs.* An empress. Also **im′pe·ra′trix** (-triks). [< F *impératrice* < L *imperatrix, -icis*]

im·per·cep·ti·ble (im′pər·sep′tə·bəl) *adj.* **1.** That can be barely perceived, as by reason of smallness, extreme delicacy, subtlety, gradualness, etc.: an *imperceptible* improvement. **2.** Not discernible by the mind or senses. [< F < L *imperceptibilis.* See PERCEIVE.] — **im′per·cep′ti·ble·ness, im′per·cep′ti·bil′i·ty** n. — **im′per·cep′ti·bly** *adv.*

im·per·cep·tion (im′pər·sep′shən) n. Lack of perception.

im·per·cep·tive (im′pər·sep′tiv) *adj.* Not perceptive; lacking the power of perception. — **im·per·cep·tiv·i·ty** (im′pər·sep·tiv′ə·tē), **im′per·cep′tive·ness** n.

imperf. 1. Imperfect. **2.** Imperforate.

im·per·fect (im·pûr′fikt) *adj.* **1.** Falling short of perfection; faulty; defective: an *imperfect* performance; *imperfect* knowledge. **2.** Wanting in completeness; not fully or adequately formed or made; unfinished; deficient. **3.** Denoting a tense that indicates action, usually past action, as uncompleted, continuing, or synchronous with some other action. **4.** *Bot.* Lacking certain parts normally present. **5.** *Law* Without binding force; not legally enforceable. — n. *Gram.* The imperfect tense, or a verb or verb form in this tense, as *was speaking* in *He was speaking when I entered.* Abbr. *imp., imperf., impf.* [< L *imperfectus.* See PERFECT.] — **im·per′fect·ly** *adv.* — **im·per′fect·ness** n.

im·per·fec·tion (im′pər·fek′shən) n. **1.** The state or quality of being imperfect. **2.** A defect; flaw. [< OF < LL *imperfectio, -onis* < L *imperfectus* incomplete. See PERFECT.]

im·per·fec·tive (im′pər·fek′tiv) *Gram. adj.* Denoting an aspect of the verb, as in the Slavic languages, that describes present, past, or future action without regard for the completion of such actions. — n. The imperfective aspect, or a verb in this aspect. — **im·per′fec·tive·ly** *adv.*

im·per·fo·ra·ble (im·pûr′fər·ə·bəl) *adj.* That cannot be perforated.

im·per·fo·rate (im·pûr′fər·it) *adj.* **1.** Without perforations; not perforated. **2.** Not separated by lines of perforations: said of stamps. Also **im·per′fo·rat′ed** (-rā′tid). — n. An unperforated stamp. Abbr. *imperf.*

im·per·fo·ra·tion (im·pûr′fə·rā′shən) n. The state of being imperforate.

im·pe·ri·al (im·pir′ē·əl) *adj.* **1.** Of or pertaining to an empire. **2.** Designating a nation having sovereign power over colonies or dependencies. **3.** Pertaining to or suitable to the rank of an emperor or supreme ruler. **4.** Possessing commanding power or dignity; majestic; magnificent. **5.** Exercising the authority of or having the manner of a supreme ruler or commander; imperious; overbearing. **6.** Superior in size or quality. **7.** Designating or conforming to the legal standards of weights and measures of the United Kingdom. — **Syn.** See KINGLY. — n. **1.** A pointed tuft of hair on the chin: from the emperor Napoleon III, who wore such a beard. **2.** An article of more than usual size or of superior excellence. **3.** A size of paper: in the United States, 23 x 31 inches; in Great Britain, 22 x 30 inches. **4.** A gold coin of Russia prior to 1917. **5.** The top of a stagecoach or other carriage. Abbr. *imp.* [< OF < L *imperialis* < *imperium* rule, power] — **im·pe′ri·al·ly** *adv.* — **im·pe′ri·al·ness** n.

Im·pe·ri·al (im·pir′ē·əl) n. An adherent or soldier of the emperor of the Holy Roman Empire.

Imperial City The capital city of an empire; especially, Rome in the ancient Roman or Holy Roman empires.

imperial eagle See under EAGLE.

imperial gallon See under GALLON.

im·pe·ri·al·ism (im·pir′ē·əl·iz′əm) n. **1.** The creation, maintenance, or extension of an empire, comprising many nations and areas, all controlled by a central government. **2.** The development of foreign trade and exploitation of raw materials of backward countries through the use of political and military pressures, without necessarily assuming direct political control of the nations affected. **3.** A system of imperial government. **4.** Imperial character, authority, or spirit. — **im·pe′ri·al·is′tic** *adj.* — **im·pe′ri·al·is′ti·cal·ly** *adv.*

im·pe·ri·al·ist (im·pir′ē·əl·ist) n. **1.** One who advocates or upholds imperialism. **2.** A partisan or supporter of an emperor. — *adj.* Of or pertaining to imperialism; imperialistic.

imperial jade 1. A variety of jadeite valued for its rich emerald-green color. **2.** A green-tinted aventurine quartz, used as a gem.

imperial moth A large American moth (*Eacles* or *Basilona imperialis*) having yellow wings sprinkled and barred with lavender, with a wingspread often of 5 inches.

IMPERIAL MOTH

Imperial Valley An agricultural region of SE California and northern Lower California, mostly below sea level, reclaimed from the Colorado Desert.

im·per·il (im·per′il) *v.t.* **per·iled** or **·illed, ·per·il·ing** or **·il·ling** To place in peril; endanger.

im·pe·ri·ous (im·pir′ē·əs) *adj.* **1.** Characterized by an attitude of command; domineering; arrogant. **2.** Urgent; imperative. **3.** *Obs.* Imperial; lordly. [< L *imperiosus* < *imperium*] — **im·pe′ri·ous·ly** *adv.* — **im·pe′ri·ous·ness** n.

— **Syn. 1.** dictatorial, peremptory, overbearing, haughty, despotic. — **Ant.** meek, humble.

im·per·ish·a·ble (im·per′ish·ə·bəl) *adj.* Not perishable; not subject to decay; enduring; everlasting. **—im·per′ish·a·bil′i·ty, im·per′ish·a·ble·ness** n. **—im·per′ish·a·bly** adv.

im·pe·ri·um (im·pir′ē·əm) n. pl. **·pe·ri·a** (-pir′ē·ə) **1.** Absolute power or authority; supreme command. **2.** Law The right to command; authority to use the force of the state to enforce its laws. [< L. See EMPIRE.]

im·per·ma·nent (im·pûr′mə·nənt) adj. Not permanent; fleeting. **—im·per′ma·nence, im·per′ma·nen·cy** n.

im·per·me·a·ble (im·pûr′mē·ə·bəl) adj. **1.** Not permitting passage or penetration. **2.** Impervious to moisture. [< LL impermeabilis. See PERMEABLE.] **—im·per′me·a·bil′i·ty, im·per′me·a·ble·ness** n. **—im·per′me·a·bly** adv.

im·per·mis·si·ble (im′pər·mis′ə·bəl) adj. Not to be permitted. **—im′per·mis′si·bil′i·ty** n. **—im′per·mis′si·bly** adv.

impers. Impersonal.

im·per·son·al (im·pûr′sən·əl) adj. **1.** Not personal; without direct reference to a person or persons; objective: an impersonal observation. **2.** Not having the characteristics of a person: an impersonal deity. **3.** Gram. **a** Of a verb, having no specific subject: in English the word it is usually used with such verbs, as in It snows in winter. **b** Of a pronoun, having no definite reference, as French on in Ici on parle français. —n. Gram. An impersonal verb or pronoun. Abbr. imp., impers. [< LL impersonalis. See PERSONAL.] **—im·per′son·al′i·ty** (-al′ə·tē) n. **—im·per′son·al·ly** adv.

im·per·son·al·ize (im·pûr′sən·əl·īz′) v.t. **·ized, ·iz·ing** To make impersonal.

im·per·son·ate (v. im·pûr′sən·āt; adj. im·pûr′sən·it) v.t. **·at·ed, ·at·ing 1.** To adopt or mimic the appearance, mannerisms, etc., of. **2.** To act or play the part of. **3.** Archaic To represent in human form; personify. —adj. Embodied in one person. [< IN-² + PERSONATE] **—im·per′son·a′tion** n. **—im·per′son·a·tor** n.

im·per·ti·nence (im·pûr′tə·nəns) n. **1.** Deliberate disrespectfulness; unwarranted boldness; insolence; rudeness. **2.** Lack of pertinence; irrelevancy. **3.** Unsuitability; inappropriateness; incongruity. **4.** An impertinent remark, act, etc. Also **im·per′ti·nen·cy.** **—Syn.** See IMPUDENCE.

im·per·ti·nent (im·pûr′tə·nənt) adj. **1.** Deliberately disrespectful or unmannerly; unwarrantedly bold; impudent. **2.** Not pertinent; irrelevant. **3.** Not suitable; inappropriate; incongruous. [< OF < LL impertinens, -entis < in- not + pertinens. See PERTINENT.] **—im·per′ti·nent·ly** adv.

im·per·turb·a·ble (im′pər·tûr′bə·bəl) adj. Incapable of being disturbed or agitated; unruffled; calm. [< LL imperturbabilis. See PERTURB.] **—im′per·turb′a·bil′i·ty, im′per·turb′a·ble·ness** n. **—im′per·turb′a·bly** adv.

im·per·tur·ba·tion (im·pûr′tər·bā′shən) n. Freedom from agitation; calmness.

im·per·vi·a·ble (im·pûr′vē·ə·bəl) adj. Impervious.

im·per·vi·ous (im·pûr′vē·əs) adj. **1.** Incapable of being passed through, as by moisture or light rays; impenetrable; impermeable. **2.** Not open; unreceptive: a mind impervious to reason. [< L impervius < in- not + per- through + via way, road] **—im·per′vi·ous·ly** adv. **—im·per′vi·ous·ness** n.

im·pe·ti·go (im′pə·tī′gō) n. Pathol. A contagious skin disease marked by pustules. [< L < impetere to attack. See IMPETUS.] **—im·pe·tig·i·nous** (im′pə·tij′ə·nəs) adj.

im·pe·trate (im′pə·trāt) v.t. **·trat·ed, ·trat·ing 1.** To obtain by entreaty. **2.** Rare To beseech; supplicate. [< L impetratus, pp. of impetrare to obtain by request < in- to + patrare to bring to pass] **—im′pe·tra′tion** n. **—im′pe·tra′tor** n.

im·pe·tra·tive (im′pə·trā′tiv) adj. Of the nature of entreaty; tending to obtain by entreaty. [< L impetrativus < impetrare. See IMPETRATE.]

im·pet·u·os·i·ty (im·pech′ōō·os′ə·tē) n. pl. **·ties 1.** The quality of being impetuous. **2.** An impetuous action.

im·pet·u·ous (im·pech′ōō·əs) adj. **1.** Tending to act on sudden impulse and without forethought. **2.** Resulting from sudden impulse; rashly hasty: an impetuous decision. **3.** Moving with violent force; furious; rushing: an impetuous wind. [< MF impétueux < L impetuosus < impetus. See IMPETUS.] **—im·pet′u·ous·ly** adv. **—im·pet′u·ous·ness** n.

—Syn. 1. impulsive, reckless, rash. **2.** sudden, spontaneous, precipitate, swift, headlong. **—Ant.** deliberate.

im·pe·tus (im′pə·təs) n. **1.** The force that sets a body in motion; also, the energy with which a body moves or is driven. **2.** Any motivating force; stimulus; incentive. [< L < impetere to attack < in- upon + petere to seek]

impf. Imperfect.

imp. gal. Imperial gallon.

Imp·hal (imp′hul) The capital of Manipur, India, in the central part of the Territory; pop. about 103,000.

im·phee (im′fē) n. An African cereal grass (Sorghum vulgare). [< Zulu imfe]

im·pi (im′pē) n. pl. A body of armed warriors. [< Zulu]

im·pi·e·ty (im·pī′ə·tē) n. pl. **·ties 1.** Lack of reverence for God; ungodliness. **2.** Lack of respect for those to whom respect is due; undutifulness. **3.** An impious act. [< OF impieté < L impietas, -tatis. See IMPIOUS.]

im·pig·no·rate (im·pig′nə·rāt) v.t. **·rat·ed, ·rat·ing** To put in pledge; pawn; mortgage. [< Med. L impignoratus, pp. of impignorare to pawn < L in- in, on + pignus, -oris pledge]

imp·ing (imp′ing) n. **1.** The process of grafting. **2.** A graft, as of feathers on a hawk's wing. [See IMP]

im·pinge (im·pinj′) v.i. **·pinged, ·ping·ing 1.** To strike; fall: with on, upon, or against: sound waves impinging on the ear drum. **2.** To encroach; infringe: with on or upon: to impinge upon someone's authority. [< L impingere < in- against + pangere to strike] **—im·pinge′ment** n. **—im·ping′er** n.

im·pi·ous (im′pē·əs) adj. **1.** Lacking in reverence for God; ungodly; blasphemous. **2.** Lacking in due respect, as for one's parents. [< L impius < in- not + pius reverent] **—im′pi·ous·ly** adv. **—im′pi·ous·ness** n.

imp·ish (imp′ish) adj. Characteristic of or resembling an imp; mischievous. **—imp′ish·ly** adv. **—imp′ish·ness** n.

im·pla·ca·ble (im·plā′kə·bəl, -plak′ə-) adj. That cannot be appeased or pacified; inexorable. [< F < L implacabilis < in- not + placere to please] **—im·pla′ca·bil′i·ty, im·pla′ca·ble·ness** n. **—im·pla′ca·bly** adv.

—Syn. unrelenting, unforgiving, unappeasable, relentless, merciless. **—Ant.** placable, lenient, clement, yielding.

im·pla·cen·tal (im′plə·sen′təl) Zool. adj. Having no placenta, as the monotremes and marsupials. Also **im·pla·cen·tate** (-tāt). —n. An implacental mammal. [< IN-¹ + PLACENTAL]

im·plant (v. im·plant′, -plänt′; n. im′plant′, -plänt′) v.t. **1.** To fix firmly, as in the ground; plant; embed. **2.** To instill in the mind: to implant new ideas; inculcate. **3.** Med. **a** To insert (living tissue), as in grafting. **b** To embed in (living tissue). —n. Med. **1.** A tissue implanted in the body. **2.** A small tube containing radioactive material, embedded in tissue for therapeutic or remedial purposes. [< F implanter]

im·plan·ta·tion (im′plan·tā′shən) n. **1.** The act of implanting, or the state of being implanted. **2.** Med. **a** The insertion of living tissue into another part of the body, as in skin grafting. **b** The introduction of a solid drug under the skin. **c** The inoculation of bacteria into body fluids as a test of virulence. **3.** Pathol. The lodging in an organ or part of tumor cells that have metastasized through the body fluids. **4.** Dent. The setting of a natural or false tooth into the jaw.

im·plau·si·ble (im·plô′zə·bəl) adj. Not plausible; lacking the appearance of truth or trustworthiness. **—im·plau′si·bil′i·ty, im·plau′si·ble·ness** n. **—im·plau′si·bly** adv.

im·plead (im·plēd′) v.t. Law **1.** To sue in a court of justice. **2.** To accuse; arraign. **3.** To plead, as a cause. [< AF enpleder, OF empleidier < LL empleidiare. See PLEAD.] **—im·plead′a·ble** adj.

im·plead·er (im·plē′dər) n. A complainant or prosecutor.

im·pledge (im·plej′) v.t. **·pledged, ·pledg·ing** To put in pledge; pawn.

im·ple·ment (n. im′plə·mənt; v. im′plə·ment) n. **1.** A piece of equipment used in some form of work or activity; tool; instrument; utensil. **2.** Any means or agent for the accomplishment of a purpose. **—Syn.** See TOOL. —v.t. **1.** To provide what is necessary for the accomplishment or carrying into effect of: to implement a relief program. **2.** To satisfy the conditions or requirements of; fulfill. **3.** To supply what is lacking in; supplement. **4.** To furnish with implements. [< L implementum a filling up < implere to fill up < in- in + plere to fill] **—im′ple·men′tal** adj.

im·ple·men·ta·tion (im′plə·men·tā′shən) n. A putting into effect, fulfillment or carrying through, as of ideas, etc.

im·ple·tion (im·plē′shən) n. **1.** The act of filling, or the state of being full. **2.** That which fills. [< LL implementum < L implere. See IMPLEMENT.]

im·pli·cate (im′plə·kāt) v.t. **·cat·ed, ·cat·ing 1.** To show to be involved or concerned, as in a plot or crime. **2.** To indicate as something to be inferred; imply. **3.** To fold or twist together; entangle; intertwine. [< L implicatus, pp. of implicare to involve < in- in + plicare to fold]

im·pli·ca·tion (im′plə·kā′shən) n. **1.** The act of involving, or the state of being involved, as in a crime. **2.** The act of implying, or the state of being implied. **3.** That which is implied; an inference. **4.** The act of entangling, or the state of being entangled.

im·pli·ca·tive (im′plə·kā′tiv) adj. Tending to implicate. Also **im·pli·ca·to·ry** (im′pli·kə·tôr′ē, -tō′rē). **—im′pli·ca′tive·ly** adv.

im·plic·it (im·plis′it) adj. **1.** Unreserved; absolute: implicit confidence. **2.** Implied or understood, but not specifically expressed: implicit agreement. **3.** Essentially contained, but not apparent; inherent: with in: The man is implicit in the child. **4.** Obs. Intertwined. [< F implicite < L implicitus, later form of implicatus, pp. of implicare to involve. See IMPLICATE.] **—im·plic′it·ly** adv. **—im·plic′it·ness** n.

im·plied (im·plīd′) adj. Understood, suggested, or included without being specifically expressed: an implied obligation.

im·pli·ed·ly (im·plī′id·lē) adv. By implication.

im·plode (im·plōd′) v.i. **·plod·ed, ·plod·ing 1.** To collapse inward violently. —v.t. **2.** Phonet. To articulate by implosion. [< IM- + (EX)PLODE]

im·plore (im·plôr′, -plōr′) v. **·plored, ·plor·ing** v.t. **1.** To call upon in humble or urgent entreaty; beseech; entreat: He implored his gods to save him. **2.** To beg for urgently: I implore your mercy. —v.i. **3.** To make urgent supplication. **—Syn.** See ENTREAT. [< L implorare < in- thoroughly +

plorare to cry out] **— im·plo·ra·tion** (im/plə·rā/shən) *n*. **— im·plor/er** *n*. **— im·plor/ing·ly** *adv*. **— im·plor/ing·ness** *n*.

im·plo·sion (im·plō/zhən) *n*. **1.** A violent inward collapse, as from external pressure. **2.** *Phonet*. The initial, sudden blockage of the breath stream in the production of a stop consonant: distinguished from *plosion*. [< IMPLODE, on analogy with *explosion*]

im·plo·sive (im·plō/siv) *Phonet. adj*. Produced by implosion. **—** *n*. An implosive consonant.

im·ply (im·plī/) *v.t.* **·plied, ·ply·ing 1.** To involve necessarily as a circumstance, condition, effect, etc.: An action *implies* an agent. **2.** To indicate or suggest without stating; hint at; intimate. **3.** To have the meaning of; signify. **4.** *Obs*. To entangle; infold. **— Syn.** See INFER. [< OF *emplier* < L *implicare* to involve < *in-* in + *plicare* to fold. Doublet of EMPLOY.]
— Syn. 1. *Imply* and *involve* mean to have some necessary connection. *Imply* states that the connection is causal or inherent, while *involve* is vaguer, and does not define the connection. **2.** *Imply, hint, intimate, insinuate* mean to convey a meaning indirectly or covertly. *Imply* is the general term for signifying something beyond what the words obviously say: his advice *implied* confidence in the stock market. *Hint* suggests indirection in speech or action: our host's repeated glances at his watch *hinted* that it was time to go. *Intimate* suggests a process more elaborate and veiled than hint: she *intimated* that his attentions were unwelcome. *Insinuate* suggests slyness and a derogatory import: in his remarks, he *insinuated* that the Senator was a fool.

im·pol·i·cy (im·pol/ə·sē) *n. pl.* **·cies** Poor policy; inexpediency. [< IMPOLITIC, on analogy with *policy*]

im·po·lite (im/pə·līt/) *adj*. Lacking in politeness; discourteous; rude. [< L *impolitus* < *in-* not + *politus*. See POLITE.] **— im/po·lite/ly** *adv*. **— im/po·lite/ness** *n*.

im·pol·i·tic (im·pol/ə·tik) *adj*. Not in keeping with good policy; not prudent; inexpedient; injudicious. [< IN-[1] + POLITIC] **— im·pol/i·tic·ly** *adv*. **— im·pol/i·tic·ness** *n*.

im·pon·der·a·ble (im·pon/dər·ə·bəl) *adj*. Incapable of being estimated, calculated, or valued. **—** *n*. An imponderable factor or circumstance. **— im·pon/der·a·bil/i·ty, im·pon/der·a·ble·ness** *n*. **— im·pon/der·a·bly** *adv*.

im·pone (im·pōn/) *v.t.* **·poned, ·pon·ing** *Obs*. To wager; stake. [< L *imponere* to place upon < *in-* on + *ponere* to place]

im·po·rous (im·pôr/əs, -pō/rəs) *adj. Obs*. Very close or compact in texture; solid. **— im·po·ros·i·ty** (im/pə·ros/ə·tē) *n*.

im·port[1] (*v.* im·pôrt/, -pōrt/, im/pôrt, -pōrt; *n.* im/pôrt, -pōrt) *v.t.* **1.** To bring or cause to be brought into a country from abroad for commercial purposes, as merchandise. **2.** To bring in from an outside source or another relationship; introduce. **3.** To have as its meaning; signify. **—** *n.* **1.** An imported commodity. Abbr. *imp*. **2.** The act of importing; importation. **3.** That which is implied; meaning; significance. **4.** *Canadian Slang* A professional athlete; especially, a U.S. football player brought to Canada to play. [< F *importer* < L *importare* to bring in < *in-* + *portare* to carry] **— im·port/a·ble** *adj*. **— im·port/a·bil/i·ty** *n*.

im·port[2] (*n.* im/pôrt, -pōrt; *v.* im·pôrt/, -pōrt/) *n.* Importance: a matter of no *import*. **—** *v.i.* **1.** To be of consequence; be important; matter. **—** *v.t.* **2.** *Archaic* To be of importance or significance to; concern. [< F *importere* < Ital. *importare* < Med.L *importare* to be important]

im·por·tance (im·pôr/təns) *n.* **1.** The quality of being important; consequence; significance. **2.** Worthiness of esteem; standing: a man of *importance*. **3.** Excessive dignity of manner; pretentiousness. **4.** *Obs*. Meaning. **5.** *Obs*. Urgency. [< F < Med.L *importantia*]

im·por·tant (im·pôr/tənt) *adj*. **1.** Having much significance, value, or influence; outstanding; great. **2.** Deserving of special notice or attention; noteworthy; memorable: an *important* date in history. **3.** Having special relevance; mattering greatly: with *to*: evidence *important* to the case. **4.** Considering oneself worthy of high esteem or special attention; pretentious; pompous. **5.** *Obs*. Pressing; importunate. Abbr. *imp*. [< F < L *importans, -antis*, ppr. of *importare*. See IMPORT[2].] **— im·por/tant·ly** *adv*.
— Syn. 1. significant, momentous, weighty, grave[1], serious. **3.** relevant, material, influential. **— Ant.** unimportant, insignificant, trivial, irrelevant, immaterial.

im·por·ta·tion (im/pôr·tā/shən, -pōr-) *n.* **1.** The act of importing. **2.** That which is imported.

im·port·er (im·pôr/tər, -pōr/-) *n.* One who is in the business of importing merchandise. Abbr. *imp*.

im·por·tu·na·cy (im·pôr/chə·nə·sē) *n.* The quality of being importunate; importunity.

im·por·tu·nate (im·pôr/chə·nit) *adj*. **1.** Urgently or stubbornly persistent in demand; insistent: an *importunate* creditor. **2.** Of a demand or request, repeatedly made; pressing. **3.** *Obs*. Troublesome; vexatious. [< Med.L *importunatus*, pp. of *importunari*. See IMPORTUNE.] **— im·por/tu·nate·ly** *adv*. **— im·por/tu·nate·ness** *n*.

im·por·tune (im/pôr·tōōn/, -tyōōn/, im·pôr/chən) *v.* **·tuned, ·tun·ing** *v.t.* **1.** To harass with persistent demands or requests. **2.** To ask or beg for persistently or urgently. **3.** *Obs*. To annoy. **4.** *Obs*. To impel; urge. **—** *v.i.* **5.** To make persistent requests or demands. **— *adj*. Importunate. [< F < L *importunus* not blowing towards port (of a wind), hence unfavorable. See OPPORTUNE.] **— im/por·tune/ly** *adv*. **— im/por·tun/er** *n*.

im·por·tu·ni·ty (im/pôr·tōō/nə·tē, -tyōō/-) *n. pl.* **·ties 1.** Persistence in making demands or requests. **2.** *pl*. Repeated demands or requests. [< F *importunité* < L *importunitas, -tatis*]

im·pose (im·pōz/) *v.t.* **·posed, ·pos·ing 1.** To establish by authority as an obligation, penalty, etc.; exact: to *impose* a fine. **2.** To inflict or enforce in an arbitrary or authoritarian manner: to *impose* one's will. **3.** To force (oneself, one's company, etc.) upon others; intrude. **4.** To palm off as true or genuine; foist. **5.** *Eccl*. To lay on (hands), as in confirmation or ordination. **6.** *Printing* To arrange in correct order in a form, as pages of type. **7.** *Obs*. To place; lay down; deposit **— to impose on** (or **upon**) **1.** To take advantage of; make unwarranted or unfair use of. **2.** To deceive by trickery or false representation; cheat. **3.** *Rare* To exert an influence on. [< F *imposer* < *im-* on + *poser*. See POSE[1].] **— im·pos/a·ble** *adj*. **— im·pos/er** *n*.

im·pos·ing (im·pō/zing) *adj*. Impressive in appearance or manner; grand; stately.

imposing stone *Printing* A flat, level slab on which forms of type are imposed for adjustment, correction, etc. Also **imposing table**.

im·po·si·tion (im/pə·zish/ən) *n.* **1.** The act of imposing or imposing on. **2.** That which is imposed, as a tax, duty, or the like, or an undue or excessive requirement. **3.** An act of trickery or deception. **4.** The laying on of hands, as in the religious ceremonies of confirmation or ordination. **5.** *Printing* The act or process of imposing pages of type. [< L *impositio, -onis* < *impositus*. See IMPOST[1].]

im·pos·si·bil·i·ty (im·pos/ə·bil/ə·tē) *n. pl.* **·ties 1.** The quality of being impossible. **2.** Something impossible. [< F *impossibilité* < L *impossibilitas, -tatis*]

im·pos·si·ble (im·pos/ə·bəl) *adj*. **1.** Incapable of existing or taking place. **2.** Incapable of being done or put into practice; impracticable. **3.** Contrary to fact or reality; inconceivable; absurd. **4.** Incapable of being considered or fulfilled; hopeless; vain. **5.** Not acceptable; objectionable; intolerable. [< F. See POSSIBLE.] **— im·pos/si·bly** *adv*.

im·post[1] (im/pōst) *n.* **1.** A tax or duty; especially, a customs duty. **2.** In horse racing, the designated weight carried by a horse in a handicap race. **—** *v.t.* To classify (imported goods) for the purpose of determining customs duties. [< OF < Med.L *impostum* < L *impositus*, pp. of *imponere* to lay or place upon < *in-* on + *ponere* to lay, place]

im·post[2] (im/pōst) *n. Archit*. The top or uppermost section of a pillar, column, or wall, serving as support for an arch. For illustration see ARCH. [< MF *imposte* < Ital. *imposta*, ult. < L *imponere*. See IMPOST[1].]

im·pos·tor (im·pos/tər) *n.* One who deceives; especially, one who assumes the name or character of another. [< F *imposteur* < LL *impostor* < L *impositus*. See IMPOST[1].]

im·pos·tume (im·pos/chōōm, -tyōōm) *n. Archaic* An abscess. Also **im·pos/thume**. [Earlier *empostume* < OF, alter. of L *apostema* ulcer < Gk. *apostēma*]

im·pos·ture (im·pos/chər) *n.* Deception by means of false pretenses; especially, the act of posing under a false name or character. [< F < LL *impostura* < *impostor* < L *impositus*. See IMPOST[1].]

im·po·tence (im/pə·təns) *n.* **1.** The condition or quality of being impotent; especially: **a** Helplessness; ineffectiveness. **b** Physical weakness. **c** Incapacity for sexual intercourse: said of males. **2.** *Obs*. Lack of self-control. Also **im/po·ten·cy**. [< OF < L *impotentia*]

im·po·tent (im/pə·tent) *adj*. **1.** Powerless to act or to accomplish anything; helpless. **2.** Physically weak. **3.** Incapable of sexual intercourse: said of males. **4.** *Obs*. Lacking self-control; unrestrained. [< OF < L *impotens, -entis* < *in-* not + *potens*. See POTENT.] **— im/po·tent·ly** *adv*.

im·pound (im·pound/) *v.t.* **1.** To shut up in a pound, as a stray dog. **2.** To seize and place in custody of a court of law. **3.** To collect (water) in a pond, reservoir, etc., as for irrigation. **— im·pound/age** (-poun/dij) *n.* **— im·pound/er** *n*.

im·pov·er·ish (im·pov/ər·ish) *v.t.* **1.** To reduce to poverty. **2.** To exhaust the fertility of, as soil. Also spelled *empoverish*. [< OF *empovrir* < *em-* thoroughly + L *pauperare* to impoverish < *pauper* poor] **— im·pov/er·ish·ment** *n*.

im·pow·er (im·pou/ər) See EMPOWER.

im·prac·ti·ca·ble (im·prak/ti·kə·bəl) *adj*. **1.** Incapable of being carried out or put into effect; not feasible. **2.** Incapable of being used for an intended or desired purpose; unserviceable. **3.** Hard to get on with; intractable; obstinate. [< *in-* not + PRACTICABLE] **— im·prac/ti·ca·bil/i·ty, im·prac/ti·ca·ble·ness** *n.* **— im·prac/ti·ca·bly** *adv*.

im·prac·ti·cal (im·prak/ti·kəl) *adj*. Not practical. [< *in-* not + PRACTICAL] **— im·prac/ti·cal/i·ty** (-kal/ə·tē) *n.*

im·pre·cate (im′prə·kāt) *v.t.* ·cat·ed, ·cat·ing To invoke or call down (some curse or calamity): to *imprecate* evil upon a person. [< L *imprecatus*, pp. of *imprecari* to pray to < *in-* to + *precari* to pray < *prex, precis* prayer] — **im′pre·ca′tor** *n.* — **im′pre·ca·to′ry** (-kə·tôr′ē, -tō′rē) *adj.*

im·pre·ca·tion (im′prə·kā′shən) *n.* **1.** The act of imprecating. **2.** A malediction; curse. — **Syn.** See CURSE.

im·pre·cise (im′pri·sīs′) *adj.* Not precise; inexact. — **im′·pre·cise′ly** *adv.* — **im′pre·ci′sion** (-sizh′ən) *n.*

im·pregn (im·prēn′) *v.t. Obs.* To impregnate. [< LL *im-praegnare* to make pregnant]

im·preg·na·ble[1] (im·preg′nə·bəl) *adj.* **1.** Incapable of being taken by force; proof against attack: an *impregnable* fortress. **2.** Incapable of being overcome; firmly resistant; unyielding: *impregnable* moral strength. [< OF *imprenable* < *im-* not (< L *in-*) + *prenable* < *prendre* to take < L *prehendere*] — **im·preg′na·bil′i·ty** *n.* — **im·preg′na·bly** *adv.*

im·preg·na·ble[2] (im·preg′nə·bəl) *adj.* Capable of being impregnated.

im·preg·nate (im·preg′nāt) *v.t.* ·nat·ed, ·nat·ing **1.** To make pregnant; cause to conceive. **2.** To fertilize, as an ovum. **3.** To saturate or permeate, as with another substance. **4.** To fill or imbue, as with ideas, etc. — **Syn.** See PERMEATE. — *adj.* Made pregnant. [< LL *impraegna-tus*, pp. of *impraegnare* to impregnate < L *in-* + *praegnans* pregnant. See PREGNANT.] — **im·preg′na·tor** *n.*

im·preg·na·tion (im′preg·nā′shən) *n.* **1.** The act of impregnating, or the state of being impregnated. **2.** That with which anything is impregnated.

im·pre·sa (im·prā′zə) *n. Obs.* An emblem or motto for a shield, bookplate, etc. Also **im·prese** (im·prēz′). [< Ital., enterprise, device, emblem]

im·pre·sa·ri·o (im′prə·sä′rē·ō) *n.* *pl.* ·sa·ri·os or ·sa·ri (-sä′rē) One who manages or sponsors performers or performances for entertainment; especially, the organizer or director of an opera company or similar group that offers musical performances. [< Ital. < *impresa* enterprise]

im·pre·scrip·ti·ble (im′pri·skrip′tə·bəl) *adj.* Not subject to withdrawal or revocation; inalienable. [< F] — **im′pre·scrip′ti·bil′i·ty** *n.* — **im′pre·scrip′ti·bly** *adv.*

im·press[1] (*v.* im·pres′; *n.* im′pres) *v.t.* **1.** To produce a marked effect upon the mind or feelings of; influence. **2.** To establish firmly in the mind, as ideas, beliefs, etc.: to *impress* a fact on the memory. **3.** To form or make (an imprint or mark) by pressure; stamp: to *impress* a design on metal. **4.** To form or make an imprint or mark upon. **5.** To exert pressure with; press. **6.** *Electr.* To establish (a voltage) in a conductor or circuit by means of a dynamo, battery, or other source of electrical energy. — *n.* **1.** The act or process of impressing. **2.** A mark, indentation, or design produced by pressure. **3.** Distinctive character or mark; stamp. [< L *impressus*, pp. of *imprimere* to impress < *in-* on + *premere* to press] — **im·press′er** *n.*

im·press[2] (*v.* im·pres′; *n.* im′pres) *v.t.* **1.** To force to enter public service, especially naval service. **2.** To seize (property) for public use. — *n.* The act of impressing; impressment. [< IM-[2] + PRESS[2]] — **im·press′er** *n.*

im·press·i·ble (im·pres′ə·bəl) *adj.* Capable of being impressed or of receiving an impression; susceptible. — **im·press′i·bil′i·ty, im·press′i·ble·ness** *n.* — **im·press′i·bly** *adv.*

im·pres·sion (im·presh′ən) *n.* **1.** An effect, especially a profound effect, produced on the mind, the senses, or the feelings. **2.** A generalized effect or feeling: an *impression* of strength. **3.** A vague remembrance or uncertain belief: He had the *impression* that they had met. **4.** A material change produced by any agency: The enemy's efforts made no *impression* on the fort. **5.** A mark, design, or imprint made by pressure. **6.** The act or process of impressing. **7.** *Printing* **a** The act or result of pressing type or plates to paper. **b** The total number of copies of a publication printed at one time from type or plates; especially, a reprint made from unaltered type or plates; also, a single copy belonging to this printing: distinguished from *edition.* **8.** *Dent.* An imprint in plaster, wax, etc., of a tooth or of the teeth and surrounding parts. **9.** *Psychol.* The process, effect, or result of stimulating a nerve or sensory organ. — **Syn.** See IDEA, OPINION. — **to be under the impression** (**that**) To have a vague notion (that); think. [< OF < L *impressio, -onis*]

im·pres·sion·a·ble (im·presh′ən·ə·bəl) *adj.* Highly receptive to impressions; readily influenced or molded; sensitive. [< F] — **im·pres′sion·a·bil′i·ty, im·pres′sion·a·ble·ness** *n.*

im·pres·sion·ism (im·presh′ən·iz′əm) *n.* **1.** In art, a theory and school of painting, developed in the third quarter of the 19th century by Manet, Monet, Pissarro, Renoir, and others, that attempted to produce the flat, purely visual impression of the subject with the color values of light, shade, and air as actually apprehended, and whose paintings often seem misty and out of focus. **2.** In literature, a theory and practice of presenting the most immediate and arresting aspects of character, emotion, scene, or situation with relatively little explicit or realistic detail. **3.** In music, a style of composition, developed in the late 19th and early 20th centuries, as by Debussy and Ravel, that attempted to create impressions, moods, and atmospheric qualities by

means of new tonal effects and other characteristic devices. — **im·pres′sion·ist** *n. & adj.* — **im·pres′sion·is′tic** *adj.*

im·pres·sive (im·pres′iv) *adj.* Producing or tending to produce an impression; exciting emotion or admiration. [< IM-PRESS[1]] — **im·pres′sive·ly** *adv.* — **im·pres′sive·ness** *n.*

im·press·ment (im·pres′mənt) *n.* The act of impressing men into public service, especially naval service, or of seizing property for public use. [< IMPRESS[2]]

im·pres·sure (im·presh′ər) *n. Archaic* Impression.

im·prest[1] (im′prest) *n.* A loan or prepayment of money from public funds, especially for the purpose of carrying on some government business or service. [< obs. *in prest* on loan < OF *prest* loan; infl. in form by Ital. *impresto*, pp. of *imprestare* to lend; ult. < L *praestare* to furnish, supply]

im·prest[2] (im·prest′) Archaic past tense and past participle of IMPRESS.

im·pri·ma·tur (im′pri·mā′tər, -mä′-) *n.* **1.** Official license or approval for publication of a literary work, especially that granted by a censor or board of censors or by the Roman Catholic Church. *Abbr. imp.* **2.** Authorization in general; sanction. [< L, let it be printed < *imprimere.* See IMPRESS[1].]

im·pri·mis (im·prī′mis) *adv.* In the first place; firstly. [< L]

im·print (*v.* im·print′; *n.* im′print) *v.t.* **1.** To produce or reproduce (a figure, mark, etc.) by pressure: to *imprint* a design on wax. **2.** To mark or produce a mark on, as with a stamp or seal. **3.** To fix firmly in the heart, mind, etc. — *n.* **1.** A mark or indentation made by printing, stamping, or pressing. **2.** Characteristic effect; impression; stamp. **3.** The name of the publisher, place of publication, date of issue, etc., printed in a book or other publication, usually at the foot of the title page; also, the name of the printer on any printed matter. [< OF *empreinte*, fem. sing. of pp. of *empreindre* < L *imprimere* < *in-* in + *premere* to press]

im·pris·on (im·priz′ən) *v.t.* **1.** To put into a prison; hold in confinement. **2.** To confine or restrain forcibly, as in a small space, close grasp, tight garment, etc. [< OF *emprisoner* < *em-* in + *prison.* See PRISON.] — **im·pris′on·ment** *n.*

im·prob·a·bil·i·ty (im/prob·ə·bil′ə·tē, im·prob/-) *n.* *pl.* ·ties **1.** The quality of being improbable; unlikelihood. **2.** An unlikely circumstance, event, or result.

im·prob·a·ble (im·prob′ə·bəl) *adj.* Not probable; not likely to be true or not reasonably to be expected. [< L *improbabilis.* See PROBABLE.] — **im·prob′a·ble·ness** *n.* — **im·prob′a·bly** *adv.*

im·pro·bi·ty (im·prō′bə·tē) *n.* Lack of integrity or honesty; unscrupulousness; dishonesty. [< F *improbité* < L *improbitas, -talis* < *improbus* wicked < *in-* not + *probus* honest]

im·promp·tu (im·promp′tōō, -tyōō) *adj.* Made, done, or uttered on the spur of the moment; extempore; offhand. — **Syn.** See EXTEMPORANEOUS. — *n.* Anything produced on the impulse of the moment. — *adv.* Without preparation. [< F < L *in promptu* in readiness]

im·prop·er (im·prop′ər) *adj.* **1.** Deviating from fact, truth, or established usage; erroneous. **2.** Not conforming to accepted standards of conduct or good taste; indecorous; unseemly. **3.** Unsuitable for the intended occasion or use. **4.** Inconsistent with its type or class; irregular. *Abbr. imp.* [< OF *improprie* < L *improprius* < *in-* not + *proprius* one's own] — **im·prop′er·ly** *adv.* — **im·prop′er·ness** *n.*

improper fraction *Math.* A fraction in which the numerator exceeds the denominator.

im·pro·pri·ate (*v.* im·prō′prē·āt; *adj.* im·prō′prē·it) *v.t.* ·at·ed, ·at·ing **1.** To transfer (ecclesiastical property or revenue) to laymen. **2.** *Obs.* To appropriate. — *adj.* **1.** Placed in the hands of laymen. **2.** *Obs.* Appropriated. [< Med.L *impropriatus*, pp. of *impropriare* to make as one's own < L *in-* on + *proprius* one's own] — **im·pro′pri·a′tion** *n.*

im·pro·pri·a·tor (im·prō′prē·ā′tər) *n.* A layman to whom ecclesiastical property or revenue has been transferred.

im·pro·pri·e·ty (im′prə·prī′ə·tē) *n.* *pl.* ·ties **1.** The quality of being improper. **2.** An improper action. **3.** An improper usage in speech or writing. [< L *improprietas, -tatis*]

im·prove (im·prōōv′) *v.* ·proved, ·prov·ing *v.t.* **1.** To raise to a higher or more desirable quality, value, or condition; make better. **2.** *U.S.* To increase the value or profit of, as land by cultivation or the construction of buildings. **3.** To use to good advantage; utilize: to *improve* one's leisure time. — *v.i.* **4.** To become better. — **to improve on** (or **upon**) To do or produce something better than: to *improve* on one's earlier work. [< AF *empromver* < OF *en-* into + *prou* profit] — **im·prov′a·bil′i·ty, im·prov′a·ble·ness** *n.* — **im·prov′a·ble** *adj.* — **im·prov′a·bly** *adv.* — **im·prov′er** *n.*

im·prove·ment (im·prōōv′mənt) *n.* **1.** The act of making better, or the state of becoming better; betterment; amelioration. **2.** A modification or addition by means of which a thing's excellence or value is increased; a change for the better. **3.** A person, thing, or process that constitutes an advance in progress or an increase in excellence over another. **4.** *U.S.* A valuable or useful addition to, or modification of, real property, as buildings, fences, etc. **5.** Advantageous use: *improvement* of one's free hours.

im·prov·i·dence (im·prov′ə·dəns) *n.* The quality of being improvident; lack of foresight or thrift.

im·prov·i·dent (im·prov′ə·dənt) *adj.* **1.** Lacking foresight;

incautious; rash. **2.** Taking no thought of future needs; thriftless. **— im·prov′i·dent·ly** *adv.*
— Syn. 1. short-sighted, reckless, careless, imprudent. **— Ant.** thrifty, economical, cautious.

im·pro·vi·sa·tion (im′prə·vī·zā′shən, im′prov·ə-) *n.* **1.** The act of improvising. **2.** Something improvised. **— im′pro·vi·sa′tion·al** *adj.*

im·pro·vi·sa·to·ry (im′prə·vī′zə·tôr′ē, -tō′rē) *adj.* **1.** Of or pertaining to an improviser. **2.** Of the nature of improvisation. Also **im·prov·i·sa·to·ri·al** (im·prov′ə·zə·tôr′ē·əl, -tō′rē-).

im·pro·vise (im′prə·vīz) *v.* **·vised, ·vis·ing** *v.t.* **1.** To produce without previous thought or preparation; especially, to perform or invent (music, verse, drama, etc.) without notes, text, or prepared material. **2.** To contrive or construct from whatever comes to hand: to *improvise* a raft out of driftwood. **— v.i. 3.** To produce anything extemporaneously or from whatever is on hand. [< F *improviser* < Ital. *improvvisare* < *improvviso* unforeseen < L *improvisus* < *in-* not + *provisus* pp. of *providere* to foresee] **— im′pro·vis′er, im·prov′i·sa·tor** (im·prov′ə·zā′tər, im′prə·vī-) *n.*

im·prov·vi·sa·to·re (ēm′prôv·vē·zä·tō′rā) *n.* *pl.* **·ri** (-rē) *Italian* An improviser of poems and songs.

im·pru·dence (im·prōōd′ns) *n.* **1.** The quality of being imprudent. **2.** An imprudent act or course of behavior.

im·pru·dent (im·prōōd′nt) *adj.* Not prudent; lacking discretion; unwise. [< L *imprudens, -entis* < *in-* not + *prudens*. See PRUDENT.]
— Syn. indiscreet, injudicious, impolitic, ill-advised, heedless, thoughtless, rash[1], foolhardy, improvident. **— Ant.** prudent, discreet, judicious, well-advised, thoughtful, careful.

im·pu·dence (im′pyə·dəns) *n.* **1.** The quality of being impudent; offensive boldness. **2.** Impudent speech or conduct. **3.** *Obs.* Immodesty. Also **im′pu·den·cy.** [< L *impudentia*]
— Syn. 1. Impudence, impertinence, insolence, and *effrontery* are offensive rudeness in speech or manner. *Impudence* and *impertinence* are close synonyms; *impudence* is the stronger term, and stresses a lack of shame, while *impertinence* emphasizes that the character of an action is not befitting an occasion or a person. *Insolence* is rudeness stemming from an unwarranted assumption of authority or importance. *Effrontery* is both shameless and bold, and openly insulting. **— Ant.** courtesy, civility.

im·pu·dent (im′pyə·dənt) *adj.* **1.** Offensively bold; insolently assured; saucy; brazen. **2.** *Obs.* Immodest; shameless. [< OF < L *impudens, -entis* < *in-* not + *pudens* modest, orig. ppr. of *pudere* to feel shame] **— im′pu·dent·ly** *adv.*

im·pu·dic·i·ty (im′pyōō·dis′ə·tē) *n.* Immodesty. [< F *impudicité* < L *impudicitia* < *impudicus* shameless < *in-* not + *pudicus* modest < *pudere* to feel shame]

im·pugn (im·pyōōn′) *v.t.* To attack (a statement, motives, etc.) with criticism or arguments; dispute the truth, validity, or trustworthiness of; challenge. [< OF *impugner* < L *impugnare* < *in-* against + *pugnare* to strike, fight < *pugnus* fist] **— im·pugn·a·ble** *adj.* **— im·pug·na·tion** (im′pəg·nā′shən), **im·pugn′ment** *n.* **— im·pugn′er** (im·pyōō′nər) *n.*

im·pu·is·sance (im·pyōō′ə·səns, im′pyōō·is′əns, im·pwis′əns) *n.* Lack of power or ability; impotence. [< F]

im·pu·is·sant (im·pyōō′ə·sənt, im′pyōō·is′ənt, im·pwis′ənt) *adj.* Powerless; impotent. [< F < *im-* not + *puissant*. See PUISSANT.]

im·pulse (im′puls) *n.* **1.** A brief and vigorous exertion or communication of force tending to produce motion; motivating power. **2.** The motion produced by an impelling force; impetus. **3.** A sudden, unreasoned inclination to action; involuntary reaction or response: to act on *impulse*. **4.** A sudden incitement to action induced by a particular mental state or emotion: an *impulse* of generosity. **5.** *Physiol.* The transference of a stimulus through a nerve fiber. **6.** *Physics* **a** A force acting for a short time. **b** The change in momentum due to a force. **7.** *Electr.* A surge of current flowing in one direction. [< L *impulsus*, pp. of *impellere*. See IMPEL.]

im·pul·sion (im·pul′shən) *n.* **1.** The act of impelling, or the state of being impelled. **2.** An impelling force. **3.** The motion produced by an impelling force; impetus. **4.** Sudden inclination or incitement to action; impulse.

im·pul·sive (im·pul′siv) *adj.* **1.** Actuated by impulse rather than by reflection; prone to act suddenly and without forethought. **2.** Prompted by impulse; spontaneous; unpremeditated. **3.** Having the power of impelling or inciting to action; exerting force or influence. **4.** *Physics* Acting by instantaneous or intermittent force or impulse. **— Syn.** See SPONTANEOUS. [< OF *impulsif* < Med.L *impulsivus*] **— im·pul′sive·ly** *adv.* **— im·pul′sive·ness** *n.*

im·pu·ni·ty (im·pyōō′nə·tē) *n.* *pl.* **·ties** Freedom or exemption from punishment, harm, or unpleasant consequence. [< L *impunitas, -tatis* < *impunis* unpunished < *in-* not + *poena* punishment]

im·pure (im·pyōōr′) *adj.* **1.** Containing something offensive or contaminating; tainted. **2.** Mixed with an inferior or worthless substance; adulterated. **3.** Contrary to moral purity; sinful. **4.** Not purified according to ceremonial law; unfit for religious use. **5.** Having the characteristics of more than one style or period; mixed: said of a work of art, literature, etc. **6.** Containing elements not properly belonging; especially, of language, containing foreign idioms or grammatical or rhetorical errors. **7.** Of a color, mixed with white, black, or another color. [< L *impurus* < *in-* not + *purus* pure] **— im·pure′ly** *adv.* **— im·pure′ness** *n.*

im·pu·ri·ty (im·pyōōr′ə·tē) *n.* *pl.* **·ties 1.** The state or quality of being impure. **2.** That which is impure or makes impure. [< OF *impurite* < L *impuritas*]

im·put·a·ble (im·pyōō′tə·bəl) *adj.* Capable of being imputed; ascribable; chargeable. **— im·put′a·bil′i·ty, im·put′·a·ble·ness** *n.* **— im·put′a·bly** *adv.*

im·pu·ta·tion (im′pyōō·tā′shən) *n.* **1.** The act of imputing; especially, the charging of a wrongdoing or fault to someone; accusation. **2.** That which is imputed or charged. [< LL *imputatio, -onis* < L *imputare*. See IMPUTE.]

im·pu·ta·tive (im·pyōō′tə·tiv) *adj.* **1.** Transferred or transmitted by imputation; imputed. **2.** Tending to impute. [< LL *imputativus*] **— im·pu′ta·tive·ly** *adv.*

im·pute (im·pyōōt′) *v.t.* **·put·ed, ·put·ing 1.** To attribute (a fault, crime, etc.) to a person; charge. **2.** To consider as the cause or source of; ascribe: with *to*: to *impute* one's happiness to one's own virtues. **3.** *Theol.* To ascribe (a good or evil quality or condition) indirectly, or as coming through the agency of another. **— Syn.** See ATTRIBUTE. [< OF *emputer* < L *imputare* to enter into the account < *in-* in + *putare* to reckon] **— im·put′er** *n.*

im·pu·tres·ci·ble (im′pyōō·tres′ə·bəl) *adj.* Not subject to putrefaction.

impv. Imperative.

Im·roz (im·rôz′) The Turkish name for IMBROS.

in (in) *prep.* **1.** Held by or within the confines of; enclosed by: apples *in* a bag; a child *in* her arms. **2.** Surrounded by; amidst: buried *in* the mud; walking *in* the rain. **3.** Within the limits or boundaries of: sightseeing *in* Paris. **4.** Within the range or scope of: He said it *in* my hearing; The child is *in* my care. **5.** Within the category, class, or number of; included as a member of; belonging to: twelve inches *in* a foot; a violinist *in* the orchestra; *in* the best society. **6.** Existing as a part, characteristic, or property of: *in* the works of Shaw; *in* the natural state; It is not *in* his nature to be unkind. **7.** Having as a location or area of influence; affecting: dust *in* one's eye; a cold *in* the head. **8.** Wearing; covered by; decorated with: a man *in* a straw hat; a room *in* flowered chintz. **9.** Made of a specified color, style, or material: a dress *in* green; a watch *in* gold. **10.** Arranged, disposed, or proceeding so as to form: trees *in* a row; hair *in* ringlets; to go *in* circles. **11.** Engaged at; occupied by; while performing the act of: *in* business; *in* pursuit of happiness. **12.** For the purpose of: to run *in* pursuit. **13.** By means of; by the use of: speaking *in* whispers; painted *in* water colors. **14.** According to; as estimated by: *In* my opinion, you are wrong. **15.** With regard or respect to: Students vary *in* talent; I have faith *in* his ability. **16.** Affected by; under the influence of: *in* doubt as to the outcome; to shout *in* rage. **17.** Throughout the course of; during: a concert given *in* the evening. **18.** *U.S.* At or before the end or expiration of: a note due *in* three days. **— Syn.** See AT. **— in that** For the reason that; because; since: *In that* you have already done the work, you may be excused. **— adv. 1.** To or toward the inside from the outside: Please come *in*. **2.** In one's home, place of business, etc.: We stayed *in* all day. **3.** In or into some activity or office: to join *in*; He got *in* by one vote. **4.** Into some place, condition, or position: We moved *in* yesterday; Tuck the baby *in*. **5.** Into some understood substance, object, etc.: Blend *in* the oil. **— to be in for** *Informal* To be certain to experience (usually something unpleasant): He's *in for* trouble. **— to have it in for** *Informal* To hold a grudge against. **— adj. 1.** That is in or remains within. **2.** That has gained power or control: the *in* group. **3.** Coming or leading in: the *in* door; the *in* train. **— n. 1.** A member of the group in power or at an advantage. **2.** *Informal* A means of entrance or access, especially to a desirable condition or situation. **3.** *Informal* A position of favor or influence: to have an *in* with the boss. **— ins and outs 1.** Twistings and turnings, as of a road, passageway, etc. **2.** The full complexities or particulars; intricacies: the *ins and outs* of a business. **— v.t.** **inned, in·ning** *Dial.* **1.** To gather, as hay or crops. **2.** To enclose, as land. [OE]

in-¹ *prefix* Not; without; un-; non-. Also: *i-* before *gn*, as in *ignore*; *il-* before *l*, as in *illiterate*; *im-* before *b, m, p*, as in *imbalance, immiscible, impecunious; ir-* before *r*, as in *irresistible.* ◆ See note under UN-². [< L]
Following is a list of self-explanatory words containing the prefix in-¹:

inacceptable	inassignable	incohesive
inacquaintance	inassimilate	incompassionate
inacquiescent	inauthentic	incomplex
inaidable	incapacious	incomposite
inappealable	incelebrity	inconcealable
inapplication	incertain	inconsecutive
inarable	incognoscible	incontiguous

inconversion	infeminine	insubmergible
incooperative	infrugal	insubmissive
incorrodible	inhomogeneity	insubvertible
indeficiency	inhomogeneous	intranquillity
indetectable	inirritability	intranscalent
indevotion	inobservable	intransferable
indevout	inobtrusive	intransformable
indiscussible	inoppressive	intransfusible
indivertible	inoppugnable	intranslatable
individable	inopulent	intransmissible
indivinity	inostensible	intransmutable
indivision	insagacity	intransparent
indocibility	insalutary	inutilized
indocible	insalvable	inutterable
ineffulgent	insapient	invalorous
inequable	insaturable	inverisimilitude
inerudite	insensuous	inverity
inexcitable	inseverable	invirile
inexhausted	insolidity	invirility
inextension	insonorous	inviscid
infelonious	insubduable	invital

in-² *prefix* In; into; on; within; toward: *include, incur, invade*: also used intensively, as in *inflame*, or without perceptible force. Also *il-* before *l*, as in *illuminate*; *im-* before *b, m, p,* as in *imbibe, immigrate, impress*; *ir-* before *r,* as in *irradiate.* [< OE *in;* sometimes < L *in-,* prep.]

in. Inch(es).

-in *suffix Chem.* Occasionally used to denote neutral compounds, as fats, proteins, and glycerides: *stearin, albumin, lecithin.* Also *-ein.* [Var. of -INE²]

In *Chem.* Indium.

in·a·bil·i·ty (in′ə·bil′ə·tē) *n.* The state or quality of being unable; lack of the necessary power or means.

in ab·sen·ti·a (in ab·sen′shē·ə, -shə) *Latin* In absence (of the person concerned).

in·ac·ces·si·ble (in′ak·ses′ə·bəl) *adj.* Not accessible; incapable of being reached or closely approached. **— in′ac·ces′si·bil′i·ty, in′ac·ces′i·ble·ness** *n.* **— in′ac·ces′si·bly** *adv.*

in·ac·cu·ra·cy (in·ak′yər·ə·sē) *n. pl.* **·cies 1.** The state or quality of being inaccurate. **2.** An error; mistake.

in·ac·cu·rate (in·ak′yər·it) *adj.* Not accurate; inexact; incorrect. **— in·ac′cu·rate·ly** *adv.* **— in·ac′cu·rate·ness** *n.*

In·a·chus (in′ə·kəs) In Greek mythology, a river god who became the first king of Argos; father of Io.

in·ac·tion (in·ak′shən) *n.* Absence of action; idleness.

in·ac·ti·vate (in·ak′tə·vāt) *v.t.* **·vat·ed, ·vat·ing 1.** To make inactive. **2.** *Med.* To stop the activity of (a serum or its complement) by heat or other means. **— in·ac′ti·va′tion** *n.*

in·ac·tive (in·ak′tiv) *adj.* **1.** Characterized by inaction; not engaging in activity; idle; inert. **2.** Marked by absence of effort or desire for action; indolent. **3.** *Mil.* Not immediately available for active service; not mobilized. **4.** *Chem.* Incapable of rotating the plane of polarized light, as certain compounds. **5.** *Physics* Not radioactive. **— in·ac′tive·ly** *adv.* **— in·ac·tiv′i·ty** (in·ak·tiv′ə·tē), **in·ac′tive·ness** *n.*

in ac·tu (ak′tōō) *Latin* In reality.

in·a·dapt·a·ble (in′ə·dap′tə·bəl) *adj.* Incapable of adaptation. **— in′a·dap′ta·bil′i·ty** *n.*

in·ad·e·qua·cy (in·ad′ə·kwə·sē) *n. pl.* **·cies 1.** The state or quality of being inadequate; insufficiency. **2.** A defect.

in·ad·e·quate (in·ad′ə·kwit) *adj.* Not adequate; not equal to that which is required; insufficient. **— in·ad′e·quate·ly** *adv.* **— in·ad′e·quate·ness** *n.*

in·ad·mis·si·ble (in′əd·mis′ə·bəl) *adj.* Not admissible; not to be considered, approved, or allowed. **— in′ad·mis′si·bil′i·ty** *n.* **— in′ad·mis′si·bly** *adv.*

in·ad·ver·tence (in′əd·vûr′təns) *n.* **1.** The fact or quality of being inadvertent; lack of due care or attention. **2.** A result of inattention; oversight. Also **in′ad·ver′ten·cy.** [< Med.L *inadvertentia*]

in·ad·ver·tent (in′əd·vûr′tənt) *adj.* **1.** Not exercising due care or consideration; negligent. **2.** Resulting from inattention or oversight; unintentional. **— in′ad·ver′tent·ly** *adv.*

in·ad·vis·a·ble (in′əd·vī′zə·bəl) *adj.* Not advisable; injudicious; unwise. **— in′ad·vis′a·bil′i·ty** *n.*

-inae *suffix Zool.* Used in the names of subfamilies: *Cervinae* (see CERVINE). [< NL < L, fem. pl. of *-inus,* adj. suffix]

in ae·ter·num (ē·tûr′nəm) *Latin* Forever; everlastingly.

in·af·fa·ble (in·af′ə·bəl) *adj.* Not affable; austere; disagreeable. **— in·af′fa·bil′i·ty** *n.* **— in·af′fa·bly** *adv.*

in·al·ien·a·ble (in·āl′yən·ə·bəl) *adj.* Not transferable; that cannot be rightfully taken away. **— in·al′ien·a·bil′i·ty** *n.* **— in·al′ien·a·bly** *adv.*

in·al·ter·a·ble (in·ôl′tər·ə·bəl) *adj.* Not alterable. **— in·al′ter·a·bil′i·ty** *n.* **— in·al′ter·a·bly** *adv.*

in·am·o·ra·ta (in·am′ə·rä′tə, in′am-) *n. pl.* **·tas** A woman who is loved or in love. [< Ital. *innamorata,* fem. pp. of *innamorare < in-* in + *amore* love]

in·am·o·ra·to (in·am′ə·rä′tō, in′am-) *n. pl.* **·tos** A male lover.

in-and-in (in′and·in′) *adv.* Repeatedly within successive generations of the same or closely related parentage: to breed stock *in-and-in.*

in·ane (in·ān′) *adj.* **1.** Lacking in sense; empty-headed; silly: an *inane* person. **2.** Empty of meaning; pointless;

foolish: an *inane* remark. **3.** Having no contents or inner substance; void; empty. **— n.** That which is void; especially, infinite space. [< L *inanis* empty] **— in·ane′ly** *adv.*

in·an·i·mate (in·an′ə·mit) *adj.* **1.** Lacking the essential qualities inherent in living animals: an *inanimate* object. **2.** Showing no signs of life; unconscious. **3.** Lacking animation; torpid; spiritless. **— Syn.** See LIFELESS. [< LL *inanimatus*] **— in·an′i·mate·ly** *adv.* **— in·an′i·mate·ness** *n.*

in·a·ni·tion (in′ə·nish′ən) *n.* **1.** Exhaustion caused by lack of nourishment or inability to assimilate food. **2.** Emptiness. [< F < LL *inanitio, -onis* < L *inanitus,* pp. of *inanire* to empty < *inanis* empty]

in·an·i·ty (in·an′ə·tē) *n. pl.* **·ties 1.** Lack of sense or meaning; silliness; foolishness. **2.** Something inane; a foolish remark, action, etc. **3.** Emptiness. [< OF *inanite* < L *inanitas < inanis* empty]

in·ap·peas·a·ble (in′ə·pē′zə·bəl) *adj.* Incapable of being appeased; insatiable; unrelenting.

in·ap·pe·tence (in·ap′ə·təns) *n.* Lack of appetite or desire; indifference. **— in·ap′pe·tent** *adj.*

in·ap·pli·ca·ble (in·ap′li·kə·bəl) *adj.* Not applicable; irrelevant; unsuitable. **— in·ap′pli·ca·bil′i·ty, in·ap′pli·ca·ble·ness** *n.* **— in·ap′pli·ca·bly** *adv.*

in·ap·po·site (in·ap′ə·zit) *adj.* Not pertinent or suitable. **— in·ap′po·site·ly** *adv.*

in·ap·pre·ci·a·ble (in′ə·prē′shē·ə·bəl, -shə·bəl) *adj.* Imperceptible; unnoticeable. **— in′ap·pre′ci·a·bly** *adv.*

in·ap·pre·ci·a·tive (in′ə·prē′shē·ā′tiv, -shə·tiv) *adj.* Failing to express or show appreciation. **— in′ap·pre′ci·a·tive·ly** *adv.* **— in′ap·pre′ci·a·tive·ness** *n.*

in·ap·pre·hen·si·ble (in′ap·ri·hen′sə·bəl) *adj.* Incapable of being perceived by the mind or senses.

in·ap·pre·hen·sion (in′ap·ri·hen′shən) *n.* Lack of apprehension; failure or inability to understand.

in·ap·pre·hen·sive (in′ap·ri·hen′siv) *adj.* **1.** Not fearful or anxious; unaware of or untroubled by danger. **2.** Lacking the ability to perceive or understand.

in·ap·proach·a·ble (in′ə·prō′chə·bəl) *adj.* **1.** Incapable of being reached or approached. **2.** Unrivaled. **— in′ap·proach′a·bil′i·ty** *n.* **— in′ap·proach′a·bly** *adv.*

in·ap·pro·pri·ate (in′ə·prō′prē·it) *adj.* Not appropriate; unsuitable; unfitting. **— in′ap·pro′pri·ate·ly** *adv.* **— in′ap·pro′pri·ate·ness** *n.*

in·apt (in·apt′) *adj.* **1.** Not apt or fit. **2.** Lacking skill or aptitude; inept; clumsy. **— in·apt′ly** *adv.* **— in·apt′ness** *n.*

in·ap·ti·tude (in·ap′tə·tōōd, -tyōōd) *n.* **1.** Lack of skill. **2.** Unsuitability.

in·arch (in·ärch′) *v.t. Bot.* To graft by joining a branch to new stock without severing it from the parent stock. [< IN-² + ARCH¹]

in·arm (in·ärm′) *v.t.* To encircle with or as with the arms.

in·ar·tic·u·late (in′är·tik′yə·lit) *adj.* **1.** Uttered without the distinct sounds of spoken language: *inarticulate* cries. **2.** Incapable of speech; dumb. **3.** Unable to speak coherently or to express oneself fully. **4.** Unspoken; unexpressed: *inarticulate* grief. **5.** *Zool.* Not segmented, as certain worms. **— in·ar′tic·u·late·ly** *adv.* **— in·ar′tic·u·late·ness** *n.*

in ar·ti·cu·lo mor·tis (in är·tik′yōō·lō môr′tis) *Latin* At the moment of death.

in·ar·ti·fi·cial (in·är′tə·fish′əl) *adj.* **1.** Not artificial; natural; simple; unaffected. **2.** Inartistic; inept. **— in·ar′ti·fi′ci·al′i·ty** (-fish′ē·al′ə·tē) *n.* **— in·ar′ti·fi′cial·ly** *adv.*

in·ar·tis·tic (in′är·tis′tik) *adj.* **1.** Contrary to the principles of art; made or done without skill or taste. **2.** Lacking in artistic ability or appreciation. Also **in·ar′tis·ti·cal.** **— in′ar·tis′ti·cal·ly** *adv.*

in·as·much as (in′əz·much′) **1.** Considering the fact that; seeing that; because. **2.** Insofar as; according as.

in·at·ten·tion (in′ə·ten′shən) *n.* Lack of attention; heedlessness; negligence.

in·at·ten·tive (in′ə·ten′tiv) *adj.* Not attentive; heedless; negligent. **— Syn.** See ABSTRACTED. **— in′at·ten′tive·ly** *adv.* **— in′at·ten′tive·ness** *n.*

in·au·di·ble (in·ô′də·bəl) *adj.* Incapable of being heard. **— in·au′di·bil′i·ty, in·au′di·ble·ness** *n.* **— in·au′di·bly** *adv.*

in·au·gu·ral (in·ô′gyər·əl) *adj.* Of or pertaining to an inauguration. **— n.** A speech made at an inauguration; especially, an address delivered by a president.

in·au·gu·rate (in·ô′gyə·rāt) *v.t.* **·rat·ed, ·rat·ing 1.** To begin or commence upon formally; initiate: to *inaugurate* a reform. **2.** To induct into office with formal ceremony. **3.** To celebrate the public opening or first use of: to *inaugurate* a bridge. [< L *inauguratus,* pp. of *inaugurare* to take omens, consecrate, install. See AUGUR.] **— in·au′gu·ra′tor** *n.*

in·au·gu·ra·tion (in·ô′gyə·rā′shən) *n.* **1.** The act of inaugurating. **2.** A ceremony of formal induction into office. **— Syn.** See BEGINNING. [< L *inauguratio, -onis*]

Inauguration Day The day on which the inauguration of the president of the United States takes place, established as January 20th by the Twentieth Amendment to the Constitution, but prior to 1937 occurring on March 4th.

in·aus·pi·cious (in′ô·spish′əs) *adj.* Not auspicious; ill-omened; unfavorable. **— in′aus·pi′cious·ly** *adv.* **— in′aus·pi′cious·ness** *n.*

inbd. Inboard.

in·be·ing (in'bē'ing) *n.* **1.** Inherent existence. **2.** Essential nature. [< IN-² + BEING]

in·board (in'bôrd', -bōrd') *adj. & adv.* **1.** *Naut.* **a** Inside the hull. **b** Toward the center line of a vessel. **2.** *Aeron.* Inward from the tip of an airfoil; close to the fuselage. **3.** *Mech.* Toward the inside of a machine; close to the main bearing.

in·born (in'bôrn') *adj.* Implanted by nature; existing from birth; natural; inherent. — **Syn.** See INNATE.

in·bound (in'bound') *adj.* Bound inward; approaching a destination: an *inbound* ship.

in·breathe (in·brēth') *v.t.* ·**breathed**, ·**breath·ing** **1.** To draw in, as breath; inhale. **2.** To inspire.

in·bred (in'bred'; *for def. 2, also* in'bred') *adj.* **1.** Inborn; innate. **2.** Produced by inbreeding; also, bred in-and-in.

in·breed (in'brēd', in'brēd') *v.t.* ·**bred**, ·**breed·ing** **1.** To breed by continual mating of closely related stock; breed in-and-in. **2.** *Rare* To develop or produce within; engender.

in·breed·ing (in'brē'ding) *n. Biol.* The mating of closely related individuals, both plant and animal, resulting in the perpetuation of certain genetic characteristics.

in·burst (in'bûrst') *n.* **1.** A bursting inward. **2.** That which bursts in: an *inburst* of water.

in·by (in'bī') *Scot. adv.* Toward the interior or center; inward. — *adj.* Nearby. Also **in'bye**. [< IN-² + BY]

inc. **1.** Inclosure. **2.** Including. **3.** Inclusive. **4.** Income. **5.** Incorporated. **6.** Increase.

In·ca (ing'kə) *n.* **1.** A member of a group of Quechuan Indian tribes dominant in Peru at the time of the Spanish conquest. **2.** An emperor or chief of the Incas. [< Sp. < Quechua *ynca* royal prince]

in·cage (in·kāj') See ENCAGE.

in·cal·cu·la·ble (in·kal'kyə·lə·bəl) *adj.* **1.** Incapable of being calculated; too great or numerous to be determined. **2.** Not predictable; uncertain. — **in·cal'cu·la·bil'i·ty** *n.* — **in·cal'cu·la·bly** *adv.*

in·ca·les·cent (in'kə·les'ənt) *adj.* Growing warm; increasing in heat. [< L *incalescens, -entis,* ppr. of *incalescere* to grow hot < *in-* thoroughly + *calescens.* See CALESCENT.] — **in'ca·les'cence** *n.*

in cam·er·a (in kam'ər·ə) **1.** In closed or secret session; privately. **2.** *Law* In a judge's chambers, or in the presence of a judge alone, rather than in open court. [< L, in a room]

In·can (ing'kən) *adj.* Of or pertaining to the Incas, their culture, or their empire. — *n.* **1.** An Inca. **2.** The language of the Incas; Quechua.

in·can·desce (in'kən·des') *v.t. & v.i.* ·**desced**, ·**desc·ing** To be or become, or cause to become, luminous with heat. [< L *incandescere* to grow hot < *in-* in + *candescere,* inceptive of *candere* to glow white]

in·can·des·cence (in'kən·des'əns) *n.* **1.** The state of being incandescent. **2.** The light emitted by something incandescent. Also **in'can·des'cen·cy.**

in·can·des·cent (in'kən·des'ənt) *adj.* **1.** Luminous or glowing with intense heat. **2.** Shining with intense brilliance. [< L *incandescens, -entis,* ppr. of *incandescere.* See INCANDESCE.] — **in'can·des'cent·ly** *adv.*

incandescent lamp A lamp having as its source of light a filament that is heated to incandescence when an electric current is passed through it.

in·can·ta·tion (in'kan·tā'shən) *n.* **1.** The uttering or intoning of words or syllables supposed to produce magical results. **2.** The magic words or formula so uttered. **3.** The practice of magic or sorcery. [< F < L *incantatio, -onis* < *incantare* to make an incantation. See ENCHANT.]

in·ca·pa·ble (in·kā'pə·bəl) *adj.* **1.** Lacking in natural ability, power, or capacity; incompetent. **2.** *Law* Not legally qualified or eligible. — **incapable of** **1.** Lacking the necessary ability or fitness for: *incapable of* learning. **2.** Morally or intellectually restrained from: *incapable of* deceit. **3.** Of such a nature or condition as not to allow or admit of: *incapable of* being achieved. **4.** *Archaic* Insensible to. — *n.* A totally incompetent person. — **in·ca'pa·bil'i·ty, in·ca'pa·ble·ness** *n.* — **in·ca'pa·bly** *adv.*

in·ca·pac·i·tate (in'kə·pas'ə·tāt) *v.t.* ·**tat·ed**, ·**tat·ing** **1.** To deprive of capability or capacity, especially for normal physical activity; disable. **2.** *Law* To deprive of legal capacity; disqualify. — **in'ca·pac'i·ta'tion** *n.*

in·ca·pac·i·ty (in'kə·pas'ə·tē) *n. pl.* ·**ties** **1.** Lack of ability, power, or fitness; disability. **2.** *Law* A condition or circumstance that legally disqualifies.

in·cap·su·late (in·kap'sə·lāt, -syōō-) *v.t.* ·**lat·ed**, ·**lat·ing** To enclose as in a capsule. [< IN- + CAPSUL(E) + -ATE¹]

in·car·cer·ate (*v.* in·kär'sə·rāt; *adj.* in·kär'sər·it, -sə·rāt) *v.t.* ·**at·ed**, ·**at·ing** **1.** To put in prison; imprison. **2.** To confine;

enclose. — *adj.* Imprisoned. [< Med.L *incarceratus,* pp. of *incarcerare* to imprison < L *in-* in + *carcer* jail] — **in·car'·cer·a'tion** *n.* — **in·car'cer·a'tor** *n.*

in·car·di·nate (in·kär'də·nāt) *v.t.* ·**nat·ed**, ·**nat·ing** In the Roman Catholic Church: **a** To establish in a particular church, diocese, or place as principal priest, deacon, etc. **b** To make (someone) a cardinal. [< Med.L *incardinatus,* pp. of *incardinare* to install a priest < *in-* in + *cardinalis* a chief priest] — **in·car'di·na'tion** *n.*

in·car·na·dine (in·kär'nə·dīn, -din) *adj.* **1.** Flesh-colored; pale red; pink. **2.** Blood-red; crimson. — *n.* An incarnadine color. — *v.t.* ·**dined**, ·**din·ing** To color deep red or flesh-color. [< F *incarnadin* < Ital. *incarnatino,* dim. of *incarnato* flesh-colored, pp. of *incarnare.* See INCARNATE.]

in·car·nate (*adj.* in·kär'nit; *v.* in·kär'nāt) *adj.* **1.** Embodied in flesh, especially in human form: a fiend *incarnate.* **2.** Personified; exemplified: cruelty *incarnate.* **3.** *Bot.* Flesh-colored or roseate. — *v.t.* ·**nat·ed**, ·**nat·ing** **1.** To embody in flesh; give bodily form to. **2.** To invest with or present in concrete shape or form. **3.** To represent in living form; typify. [< LL *incarnatus,* pp. of *incarnare* to embody in flesh < L *in-* in + *caro, carnis* flesh]

in·car·na·tion (in'kär·nā'shən) *n.* **1.** The assumption of bodily form, especially human form. **2.** *Often cap.* The assumption by Jesus Christ of the human form and condition. **3.** The bodily form assumed by a deity or supernatural being. **4.** A person, animal, or thing in which some ideal, quality, or other abstract idea, is incarnated. [< AF *incarnaciun* < LL *incarnatio, -onis*]

in·case (in·kās') *v.t.* ·**cased**, ·**cas·ing** To enclose in or as in a case: also spelled *encase.*

in·case·ment (in·kās'mənt) *n.* **1.** The act of incasing, or the state of being incased. **2.** That which incases.

in·cau·tion (in·kô'shən) *n.* Lack of caution; carelessness.

in·cau·tious (in·kô'shəs) *adj.* Lacking in caution; heedless; imprudent. — **in·cau'tious·ly** *adv.* — **in·cau'tious·ness** *n.*

in·ca·va·tion (in'kə·vā'shən) *n.* **1.** The act of making hollow. **2.** A hollow. [< L *incavatus,* pp. of *incavare* < *in-* in + *cavare* to make hollow < *cavus* hollow. Cf. EXCAVATE.]

in·cen·di·ar·y (in·sen'dē·er'ē) *adj.* **1.** Of or pertaining to the malicious burning of property. **2.** Tending to inflame mob passion; inciting to riot, rebellion, etc.; inflammatory. **3.** Capable of generating intense heat, as any of various substances such as magnesium, thermit, or white phosphorus. — *n. pl.* ·**ar·ies** **1.** One who maliciously sets fire to property; one who commits arson. **2.** One who stirs up mob violence, political strife, etc.; an agitator. **3.** An incendiary bomb. [< L *incendiarius* < *incendium* fire < *incendere* to set on fire. See INCENSE¹.] — **in·cen'di·a·rism** (-ə·riz·əm) *n.*

incendiary bomb A bomb designed to start a fire.

in·cense¹ (in·sens') *v.t.* ·**censed**, ·**cens·ing** To inflame with anger; enrage. [< OF *incenser* < L *incendere* to set on fire < *in-* in + *candere* to glow] — **in·cense'ment** *n.*

in·cense² (in'sens) *n.* **1.** An aromatic substance that gives off an agreeable odor when burned; especially, certain gums and spices burned in religious ceremonies. **2.** The odor or smoke produced in burning such a substance. **3.** Any pleasant fragrance or aroma. **4.** *Rare* Pleasing flattery; homage. — *v.* ·**censed**, ·**cens·ing** *v.t.* **1.** To perfume with incense. **2.** To burn incense to. — *v.i.* **3.** To burn incense. [< OF *encens* < L *incensus,* pp. of *incendere* to set on fire]

in·cen·tive (in·sen'tiv) *n.* That which incites, or tends to incite, to action; motivating force; stimulus. — *adj.* Serving to incite to action. [< L *incentivus* < *incentus,* pp. of *incinere* to set the tune < *in-* in + *canere* to sing]

in·cept (in·sept') *v.t.* **1.** *Biol.* To take or receive within itself; engulf. **2.** *Obs.* To begin; undertake. — *v.i.* **3.** *Brit.* To complete the taking of the degree of doctor or master: now used only at Cambridge University. [< L *inceptus,* pp. of *incipere* to begin < *in-* in + *capere* to take]

in·cep·tion (in·sep'shən) *n.* Beginning, as of an undertaking; start. [< L *inceptio, -onis* < *inceptus.* See INCEPT.]

in·cep·tive (in·sep'tiv) *adj.* **1.** Beginning; incipient; initial. **2.** *Gram.* Of a class of verbs or the aspect of a verb, denoting the beginning of an action. In Latin, for example, such verbs are formed by the addition of *-scere* to the present stem, as *cale(scere),* to grow warm, from *cale(re),* to be hot. — *n. Gram.* An inceptive word or construction, or the inceptive aspect. [< L *inceptus,* pp. of *incipere.* See INCEPT.] — **in·cep'tive·ly** *adv.*

in·cer·ti·tude (in·sûr'tə·tōōd, -tyōōd) *n.* **1.** Uncertainty; doubtfulness; indecisiveness. **2.** Insecurity. [< F < Med.L *incertitudo* < L *incertus* < *in-* not + *certus* certain]

in·ces·san·cy (in·ses'ən·sē) *n.* The state or quality of being incessant; the *incessancy* of their chatter.

in·ces·sant (in·ses'ənt) *adj.* Continuing without interruption; never ceasing. — **Syn.** See CONTINUAL. [< LL *incessans, -antis* < L *in-* not + *cessare* to cease] — **in·ces'sant·ly** *adv.*

in·cest (in'sest) *n.* Sexual intercourse between persons so closely related that marriage between them is forbidden by law or taboo. **— spiritual incest** *Eccl.* Sexual intercourse between persons forbidden to marry because of a spiritual relationship, as between godparent and godchild. [< L *incestum* < *incestus* unchaste < *in-* not + *castus* chaste]

in·ces·tu·ous (in·ses′chŏŏ·əs) *adj.* **1.** Guilty of incest. **2.** Pertaining to or involving incest. [< L *incestuosus*] **— in·ces′tu·ous·ly** *adv.*

inch[1] (inch) *n.* **1.** A measure of length equal to the twelfth part of a foot or 2.54 centimeters: symbol ″. Abbr. *in.* See table inside back cover. **2.** *Meteorol.* **a** The amount of rainfall or snowfall capable of covering a level surface to the depth of one inch. **b** A unit of atmospheric pressure expressed by an inch of the mercury column of a barometer suspended vertically at any point on or above the earth's surface. **3.** A very small distance, quantity, or degree. — **by inches** Gradually; very slowly. Also **inch by inch.** — **every inch** In every way; completely: *every inch* a lady. — *v.t.* & *v.i.* To move or advance by inches or small degrees. [OE *ynce* < L *uncia* the twelfth part, inch, ounce, orig., unit < *unus* one. Doublet of OUNCE.]

inch[2] (inch) *n. Scot. & Irish* A small island. [< Gaelic *innis* island]

inch. or **incho.** Inchoative.

inch·meal (inch′mēl′) *adv.* Inch by inch. [< INCH + -MEAL]

in·cho·ate (in·kō′it) *adj.* **1.** In an early or rudimentary stage; barely begun; incipient. **2.** Lacking order, form, coherence, etc. [< L *inchoatus, incohatus,* pp. of *incohare* to begin] **— in·cho′ate·ly** *adv.* **— in·cho′ate·ness** *n.*

in·cho·a·tion (in′kō·ā′shən) *n.* Initial stage; beginning.

in·cho·a·tive (in·kō′ə·tiv) *adj.* **1.** *Gram.* Inceptive. **2.** *Rare* Inchoate. — *n. Gram.* An inceptive. Abbr. *inch, incho.*

In·chon (in·chon′) A port city in NE South Korea, on the Yellow Sea; pop. 318,363 (est. 1959): also *Chemulpo, Chemulpho.* Japanese *Jinsen.*

inch·worm (inch′wûrm′) *n.* A measuring worm.

in·ci·dence (in′sə·dəns) *n.* **1.** The degree of occurrence or effect: a high *incidence* of illiteracy. **2.** The act or manner of falling on, impinging upon, or affecting something. **3.** *Physics* The striking of a surface by a body, by radiation, etc.; also, the direction or angle of falling. **4.** *Geom.* Partial coincidence of similar elements in two configurations or figures, as of a point and a line containing it.

in·ci·dent (in′sə·dənt) *n.* **1.** A distinct event or piece of action. **2.** An event or action subordinate to some other; a minor episode or casual occurrence. **3.** Something that is characteristically or legally dependent upon or connected with another thing. **4.** An occurrence capable of precipitating a crisis, especially in international affairs; contretemps. **— Syn.** See EVENT. — *adj.* **1.** Naturally or usually appertaining or attending: with *to:* the dangers *incident* to travel. **2.** Attached as a subsidiary; appurtenant: The right of alienation is *incident* to a title. **3.** Falling or striking: *incident* rays of light. [< F < L *incidens, -entis,* ppr. of *incidere* to fall upon < *in-* on + *cadere* to fall]

in·ci·den·tal (in′sə·den′təl) *adj.* **1.** Occurring in the course of or as a result or adjunct of something: an *incidental* remark. **2.** Naturally or usually attending: with *to:* problems *incidental* to adolescence. **3.** Occurring without design or regularity; casual; also, minor; secondary: *incidental* expenses. — *n.* **1.** An incidental circumstance or event. **2.** *pl.* Minor or casual expenses or items.

in·ci·den·tal·ly (in′sə·den′təl·ē; *for def. 2, also* in′sə·dent′lē) *adv.* **1.** As a subordinate, casual, or chance occurrence along with something else: The book *incidentally* contains some valuable references. **2.** By the by; by the way: used parenthetically to introduce a new or related subject, a passing observation, or the like.

in·cin·er·ate (in·sin′ə·rāt) *v.t.* **·at·ed, ·at·ing** To consume with fire; reduce to ashes; cremate. [< Med.L *incineratus,* pp. of *incinerare* < *in-* in + *cinis, cineris* ashes] **— in·cin′er·a′tion** *n.*

in·cin·er·a·tor (in·sin′ə·rā′tər) *n.* An apparatus for burning refuse or for cremating.

in·cip·i·ence (in·sip′ē·əns) *n.* Early stage; beginning; inception. Also **in·cip′i·en·cy.**

in·cip·i·ent (in·sip′ē·ənt) *adj.* Coming into existence; just beginning to appear. [< L *incipiens, -entis,* ppr. of *incipere.* See INCEPT.] **— in·cip′i·ent·ly** *adv.*

in·ci·pit (in′si·pit) *Latin* Here begins: a term often found at the beginning of medieval manuscripts.

in·cise (in·sīz′) *v.t.* **·cised, ·cis·ing** **1.** To cut into, or cut marks upon, with a sharp instrument. **2.** To produce (designs, marks, etc.) by cutting; engrave; carve. [< OF *inciser* < L *incidere* to cut into < *in-* in + *caedere* to cut]

in·cised (in·sīzd′) *adj.* **1.** Cut in or into; engraved; carved. **2.** Having the margin or margins deeply notched, as a leaf.

in·ci·sion (in·sizh′ən) *n.* **1.** The act of incising. **2.** A cut; gash. **3.** *Surg.* A cut made in soft tissue. **4.** A notch, as in the margin of a leaf, a butterfly's wing, etc. **5.** Incisive quality; acuteness. [< OF < L *incisio, -onis*]

in·ci·sive (in·sī′siv) *adj.* **1.** Sharp; keen; penetrating; trenchant: an *incisive* mind. **2.** Cutting; biting; sarcastic: *incisive* wit. [< Med.L *incisivus*] **— in·ci′sive·ly** *adv.* **— in·ci′sive·ness** *n.*

in·ci·sor (in·sī′zər) *n.* A front tooth adapted for cutting; in man, one of eight such teeth, four in each jaw. For illustration see TOOTH. Abbr. *i.* [< NL]

in·ci·so·ry (in·sī′zər·ē) *adj.* Adapted for cutting.

in·ci·sure (in·sizh′ər) *n. Anat.* A notch or cut.

in·cite (in·sīt′) *v.t.* **·cit·ed, ·cit·ing** To spur to action; urge on; stir up; instigate. [< OF *inciter* < L *incitare* < *in-* thoroughly + *citare* to rouse, freq. of *ciere* to set in motion] **— in′ci·ta′tion** *n.* **— in·cit′er** *n.*

in·cite·ment (in·sīt′mənt) *n.* **1.** The act of inciting. **2.** That which incites; an incentive; stimulus.

in·ci·vil·i·ty (in′si·vil′ə·tē) *n. pl.* **·ties 1.** The state or quality of being uncivil; discourteous or rude manner or behavior. **2.** An uncivil or rude act.

incl. 1. Inclosure. **2.** Including.

in·clasp (in·klasp′, -kläsp′) See ENCLASP.

in·clem·ent (in·klem′ənt) *adj.* **1.** Of the weather, severe; stormy. **2.** Without mercy; harsh. [< L *inclemens, -entis*] **— in·clem′en·cy** (-ən·sē) *n.* **— in·clem′ent·ly** *adv.*

in·clin·a·ble (in·klī′nə·bəl) *adj.* **1.** Having a particular inclination or tendency; also, well-disposed. **2.** Capable of being inclined.

in·cli·na·tion (in′klə·nā′shən) *n.* **1.** A personal leaning or bent; propensity; liking. **2.** A tendency toward a state or condition; trend. **3.** An activity, condition, etc., toward which one is inclined. **4.** The act of inclining, or the state of being inclined. **5.** Deviation or degree of deviation from the vertical or horizontal; slant; slope. **6.** A slanting or sloping surface. **7.** *Geom.* The angle formed between two intersecting lines, planes, etc. **8.** *Astron.* The angle formed between the orbital plane of a planet and the ecliptic or other suitable plane. [< OF < L *inclinatio, -onis*] **— in′cli·na′tion·al, in·cli·na·to·ry** (in·klī′nə·tôr′ē, -tō′rē) *adj.*

in·cline (*v.* in·klīn′; *n.* in′klīn, in·klīn′) *v.* **·clined, ·clin·ing** *v.i.* **1.** To diverge from the horizontal or vertical; lean; slant; slope. **2.** To have a bent or preference; be disposed. **3.** To tend in some quality or degree: purple *inclining* toward blue. **4.** To bend the head or body, as in courtesy; bow. — *v.t.* **5.** To cause to bend, lean, or slope. **6.** To impart a tendency or leaning to (a person); dispose; influence. **7.** To bow or nod, as the head. **— to incline one's ear** To hear with favor; heed. — *n.* An inclined plane or surface; gradient; slope. [< OF *encliner* < L *inclinare* < *in-* on + *clinare* to lean] **— in·clin′er** *n.*

in·clined (in·klīnd′) *adj.* **1.** Having a tendency or inclination; disposed; willing: *inclined* to work hard. **2.** Sloping; leaning; bent. **3.** Bending or intersecting so as to form an angle with another line, plane, etc.

inclined plane A plane forming any but a right angle with a horizontal plane; also, a simple machine consisting of an inclined track or ramp.

INCLINED PLANE *ab* Base. *bc* height. *ac* Inclined plane. *bac* Angle formed by plane.

in·cli·nom·e·ter (in′klə·nom′ə·tər) *n.* **1.** An instrument for measuring the attitude or tilt of an aircraft, ship, etc., with relation to the horizontal. **2.** A dip needle. [< INCLIN(E) + -METER]

in·close (in·klōz′), **in·clo·sure** (in·klō′zhər) See ENCLOSE, etc.

in·clude (in·klōōd′) *v.t.* **·clud·ed, ·clud·ing** **1.** To have as a component part or parts; comprise; contain: This volume *includes* all his works. **2.** To place in a general category, group, etc.; consider in a reckoning: I *include* your last purchase in this bill. **3.** To have or involve as a subordinate part, quality, etc.; imply: Religion *includes* morality. **4.** *Archaic* To enclose. [< L *includere* < *in-* in + *claudere* to shut] **— in·clud′a·ble** or **in·clud′i·ble** *adj.*

in·clud·ed (in·klōō′did) *adj.* **1.** Taken in as a part; covered: all expenses *included.* **2.** *Bot.* Not protruding beyond its associated organ, as stamens within the corolla.

in·clu·sion (in·klōō′zhən) *n.* **1.** The act of including, or the state of being included. **2.** That which is included. **3.** *Mineral.* A gaseous, liquid, or solid substance enclosed in a mineral mass or crystal. **4.** *Biol.* An inactive particle contained within a living cell. [< L *inclusio, -onis* < *includere.* See INCLUDE.]

inclusion body *Pathol.* A stainable particle found in the cytoplasm or nucleus of cells infected with a filterable virus.

in·clu·sive (in·klōō′siv) *adj.* **1.** Including: with *of:* income *inclusive* of dividends. **2.** Including the limits specified: from 1959 to 1964 *inclusive.* **3.** Comprehensive: an *inclusive* report. Abbr. *inc.* [< Med.L *inclusivus*] **— in·clu′sive·ly** *adv.* **— in·clu′sive·ness** *n.*

in·co·er·ci·ble (in′kō·ûr′sə·bəl) *adj.* **1.** Incapable of being coerced. **2.** Resistant to forces that tend to change the form or properties of a substance or material.

in·cog (in·kog′) *adj., adv.,* & *n. Informal* Incognito.

incog. Incognito.

in·cog·i·ta·ble (in·koj′ə·tə·bəl) *adj.* Unthinkable; inconceivable. [< LL *incogitabilis*] **— in·cog′i·ta·bil′i·ty** *n.*

in·cog·i·tant (in·koj′ə·tənt) *adj.* Unthinking; thoughtless. [< L *incogitans, -antis* < *in-* not + *cogitare.* See COGITATE.]

in·cog·ni·to (in·kog′nə·tō, in′kog·nē′tō) *adj.* & *adv.* Under an assumed name or identity, especially so as to avoid recognition or attention; in disguise. — *n. pl.* **-tos** (-tōz) **1.** The state of being incognito. **2.** The name or disguise assumed by one who is incognito. **3.** One who takes on an assumed name or identity. [< Ital. < L *incognitus* unknown < *in-* not + *cognitus*, pp. of *cognoscere* to know. See COGNITION.] — **in·cog'ni·ta** (-tə) *n. & adj. fem.*

in·cog·ni·zant (in-kog'nə-zənt) *adj.* Not cognizant; unaware: with *of.* — **in·cog'ni·zance** *n.*

in·co·her·ence (in'kō-hir'əns) *n.* **1.** The state or quality of being incoherent. **2.** That which is incoherent. Also **in'co·her'en·cy.**

in·co·her·ent (in'kō-hir'ənt) *adj.* **1.** Lacking in logical connection; disjointed; confused: an *incoherent* speech. **2.** Unable to think clearly or express oneself logically. **3.** Consisting of parts or ingredients that do not stick together; not cohesive; loose: an *incoherent* mass. **4.** Lacking in agreement or harmony; inconsistent; disorganized. — **in'co·her'ent·ly** *adv.* — **in'co·her'ent·ness** *n.*

in·com·bus·ti·ble (in'kəm-bus'tə-bəl) *adj.* Incapable of being burned; not flammable; fireproof. — *n.* An incombustible substance or material. — **in'com·bus'ti·bil'i·ty, in'·com·bus'ti·ble·ness** *n.* — **in'com·bus'ti·bly** *adv.*

in·come (in'kum) *n.* **1.** An amount of money, or sometimes its equivalent, received periodically (when unqualified, annually) by an individual, a corporation, etc., in return for labor or services rendered, or as the proceeds from property, investments, commercial activities, etc. Abbr. *inc.* **2.** Something that comes in. **3.** *Rare* A coming in; influx; arrival. — **earned income** Income from labor, business transactions, or other activities in which the personal effort of the recipient is involved. — **unearned income** Income received as rent, interest, dividends, or the like.

in·com·er (in'kum'ər) *n.* One who or that which comes in.

income tax A tax levied on annual income over a specified amount and with certain legally permitted deductions: distinguished from *capital levy.*

in·com·ing (in'kum'ing) *adj.* Coming in or about to come in: *incoming* profits; the *incoming* year. — *n.* **1.** The act of coming in, entrance or arrival. **2.** *Usually pl. Rare* Income.

in·com·men·su·ra·ble (in'kə-men'shər-ə-bəl, -sər-ə-) *adj.* **1.** Lacking a common measure or standard of comparison. **2.** *Math.* Not expressible in terms of a common factor or divisor: 4 and √7 are *incommensurable* numbers. **3.** Greatly out of proportion; not in accordance: conclusions *incommensurable* with the facts. — *n.* That which is incommensurable. — **in'com·men'su·ra·bil'i·ty, in'com·men'su·ra·ble·ness** *n.* — **in'com·men'su·ra·bly** *adv.*

in·com·men·su·rate (in'kə-men'shər-it) *adj.* **1.** Inadequate; disproportionate: a salary *incommensurate* with the position. **2.** Incommensurable. — **in'com·men'su·rate·ly** *adv.* — **in'com·men'su·rate·ness** *n.*

in·com·mode (in'kə-mōd') *v.t.* **·mod·ed, ·mod·ing** To cause inconvenience to; disturb; bother. [< MF *incommoder* < L *incommodare* < *incommodus* inconvenient < *in-* not + *commodus* convenient]

in·com·mo·di·ous (in'kə-mō'dē-əs) *adj.* **1.** Not affording sufficient accommodation; uncomfortably small; cramped. **2.** Causing discomfort or annoyance; inconvenient. — **in'·com·mo'di·ous·ly** *adv.* — **in'com·mo'di·ous·ness** *n.*

in·com·mod·i·ty (in'kə-mod'ə-tē) *n. pl.* **·ties** Inconvenience; annoyance.

in·com·mu·ni·ca·ble (in'kə-myōō'ni·kə-bəl) *adj.* **1.** Incapable of being communicated. **2.** *Obs.* Incommunicative. — **in'com·mu'ni·ca·bil'i·ty** *n.*

in·com·mu·ni·ca·do (in'kə-myōō'nə-kä'dō) *adj. & adv.* Confined without means of communication. [< Sp., pp. of *incommunicar* < L *in-* not + *communicare* to share]

in·com·mu·ni·ca·tive (in'kə-myōō'nə-kā'tiv, -kā'tiv) *adj.* Not communicative; taciturn; reserved. — **in'com·mu'ni·ca'tive·ly** *adv.* — **in'com·mu'ni·ca'tive·ness** *n.*

in·com·mut·a·ble (in'kə-myōō'tə-bəl) *adj.* Incapable of being changed or exchanged; unalterable. — **in'com·mut'a·bil'i·ty, in'com·mut'a·ble·ness** *n.* — **in'com·mut'a·bly** *adv.*

in·com·pact (in'kəm-pakt') *adj.* Not compact; loosely put together. — **in'com·pact'ly** *adv.* — **in'com·pact'ness** *n.*

in·com·pa·ra·ble (in-kom'pər-ə-bəl) *adj.* **1.** Incapable of being equaled or surpassed; matchless. **2.** Not comparable; lacking in qualities or characteristics that can be compared. [< F < L *incomparabilis*] — **in·com'pa·ra·bil'i·ty, in·com'·pa·ra·ble·ness** *n.* — **in·com'pa·ra·bly** *adv.*

in·com·pat·i·bil·i·ty (in'kəm-pat'ə-bil'ə-tē) *n. pl.* **·ties 1.** The state or quality of being incompatible. **2.** That which is incompatible.

in·com·pat·i·ble (in'kəm-pat'ə-bəl) *adj.* **1.** Incapable of coexisting harmoniously; discordant; mismated. **2.** Disagreeing in nature; irreconcilable; conflicting. **3.** Incapable of being held or occupied by one person at the same time, as more than one rank or office. **4.** *Med.* Having a harmful or undesirable effect when combined or used together. **5.** *Logic* Incapable of being true simultaneously: said of two or more propositions. — **Syn.** See INCONGRUOUS. — *n.pl.* Incom-

patible persons, drugs, etc. [< Med.L *incompatibilis*] — **in·com·pat'i·ble·ness** *n.* — **in'com·pat'i·bly** *adv.*

incompatible equations Inconsistent equations (which see).

in·com·pe·tence (in-kom'pə-təns) *n.* **1.** The state, quality, or fact of being incompetent. **2.** *Law* Lack of legal qualification. Also **in·com'pe·ten·cy.**

in·com·pe·tent (in-kom'pə-tənt) *adj.* **1.** Lacking in ability or skill; inadequate to the task; incapable; unfit: an *incompetent* teacher. **2.** Reflecting a lack of ability or skill. **3.** *Law* Not legally qualified. — *n.* One who is incompetent. [< F *incompétent* < L *incompetentem*] — **in·com'pe·tent·ly** *adv.*

in·com·plete (in'kəm-plēt') *adj.* **1.** Not having all essential elements or parts; unfinished. **2.** Not fully developed; defective; imperfect: *incomplete* growth. — **in'com·plete'ly** *adv.* — **in'com·plete'ness, in'com·ple'tion** *n.*

in·com·pli·ant (in'kəm-plī'ənt) *adj.* Not compliant; unyielding; inflexible. — **in'com·pli'ance, in'com·pli'an·cy** *n.* — **in'com·pli'ant·ly** *adv.*

in·com·pre·hen·si·ble (in'kəm-pri-hen'sə-bəl, in-kom'-) *adj.* **1.** Incapable of being understood; unintelligible. **2.** *Archaic* That cannot be confined within limits; boundless. [< L *incomprehensibilis*] — **in'com·pre·hen'si·bil'i·ty, in'·com·pre·hen'si·ble·ness** *n.* — **in'com·pre·hen'si·bly** *adv.*

in·com·pre·hen·sion (in'kom-pri-hen'shən, in-kom'-) *n.* Lack of understanding.

in·com·pre·hen·sive (in'kom-pri-hen'siv, in-kom'-) *adj.* Not comprehensive; limited in scope.

in·com·press·i·ble (in'kəm-pres'ə-bəl) *adj.* Incapable of being compressed. — **in'com·press'i·bil'i·ty** *n.*

in·com·put·a·ble (in'kəm-pyōō'tə-bəl) *adj.* Incapable of being computed; incalculable. — **in'com·put'a·bil'i·ty** *n.*

in·con·ceiv·a·ble (in'kən-sē'və-bəl) *adj.* Incapable of being conceived by the mind; unbelievable. — **in'con·ceiv'a·bil'i·ty, in'con·ceiv'a·ble·ness** *n.* — **in'con·ceiv'a·bly** *adv.*

in·con·clu·sive (in'kən-klōō'siv) *adj.* **1.** Not leading to an ultimate conclusion; not finally settling a point in question; indeterminate; indecisive: *inconclusive* evidence. **2.** Not achieving a definite result; ineffective: *inconclusive* efforts. — **in'con·clu'sive·ly** *adv.* — **in'con·clu'sive·ness** *n.*

in·con·den·sa·ble (in'kən-den'sə-bəl) *adj.* Incapable of being condensed. Also **in'con·den'si·ble** — **in'con·den'sa·bil'·i·ty** *n.*

in·con·dite (in-kon'dit) *adj. Rare* **1.** Poorly composed. **2.** Unpolished; rough; crude. [< L *inconditus* < *in-* not + *conditus*, pp. of *condere* to put together] — **in·con'dite·ly** *adv.*

in·con·form·i·ty (in'kən-fôr'mə-tē) *n.* Lack of conformity.

in·con·gru·ent (in·kon'grōō-ənt) *adj.* Not congruent; incongruous. — **in·con'gru·ence** *n.* — **in·con'gru·ent·ly** *adv.*

in·con·gru·i·ty (in'kong-grōō'ə-tē, in'kən-) *n. pl.* **·ties 1.** The state or quality of being incongruous; unsuitableness; inappropriateness. **2.** That which is incongruous. [< F *incongruité* < Med.L *incongruitas,-tatis*]

in·con·gru·ous (in·kong'grōō-əs) *adj.* **1.** Inconsistent with what is suitable, reasonable, or proper; not suited to the circumstances; out of place; inappropriate. **2.** Not corresponding or conforming; at odds: with *with* or *to*: a plan *incongruous* with reason; a costume *incongruous* to the occasion. **3.** Consisting of elements or qualities not properly belonging together; lacking harmony or consistency; incompatible. [< L *incongruus* < *in-* not + *congruus* agreeing] — **in·con'gru·ous·ly** *adv.* — **in·con'gru·ous·ness** *n.*

— **Syn. 1.** *Incongruous, incompatible,* and *inconsistent* characterize things that do not go well together. Different styles, as in art or dress, are *incongruous.* Conflicting beliefs, doctrines, or personalities are *incompatible.* Human actions not in keeping with one another or propositions based on opposing principles are *inconsistent.*

in·con·nu (in'kə-nōō', -nyōō'; *Fr.* aṅ-kô-nü') *n.* A large, salmonoid, fresh-water fish (*Stenodus leucichthys*) of NW Canada and Alaska. [F. lit., unknown]

in·con·se·quent (in-kon'sə-kwənt) *adj.* **1.** Not following from the premises; contrary to logical inference. **2.** Not proceeding according to the usual course; irrelevant; disconnected. **3.** Illogical in thought or action; eccentric. — **in·con'se·quence** *n.* — **in·con'se·quent·ly** *adv.*

inconsequent drainage In physical geography, drainage established prior to the deformation of the drained section, and continuing after such a change in the earth's surface.

in·con·se·quen·tial (in'kon-sə-kwen'shəl, in-kon'-) *adj.* **1.** Having little or no consequence; unimportant; trivial. **2.** Inconsequent. — *n.* A thing of no importance. — **in'con·se·quen'ti·al'i·ty** (-kwen'shē-al'ə-tē), **in'con·se·quen'tial·ness** *n.* — **in'con·se·quen'tial·ly** *adv.*

in·con·sid·er·a·ble (in'kən-sid'ər-ə-bəl) *adj.* **1.** Small in quantity, size, or value. **2.** Not worth considering; trivial. — **in'con·sid'er·a·ble·ness** *n.* — **in'con·sid'er·a·bly** *adv.*

in·con·sid·er·ate (in'kən-sid'ər-it) *adj.* **1.** Lacking in concern for the rights or needs of others; thoughtless. **2.** Not carefully considered or thought out. — **in'con·sid'er·ate·ly** *adv.* — **in'con·sid'er·ate·ness, in'con·sid·er·a'tion** *n.*

in·con·sis·ten·cy (in'kən-sis'tən-sē) *n. pl.* **·cies 1.** Lack of congruity, uniformity, or agreement; discrepancy. **2.** Something that is inconsistent. Also **in′con·sis′tence.**

in·con·sis·tent (in′kən·sis′tənt) *adj.* **1.** Lacking in agreement or compatibility; inconsonant; at variance. **2.** Containing contradictory elements or parts; lacking internal conformity: an *inconsistent* policy. **3.** Lacking uniformity in behavior or thought; erratic; changeable. — **Syn.** See INCONGRUOUS. — **in′con·sis′tent·ly** *adv.*

inconsistent equations *Math.* Two or more equations such that no possible set of values for the variables in one equation will satisfy the values of any other: $x + y = 5$ and $x + y = 6$ are *inconsistent equations*: also called *incompatible equations.*

in·con·sol·a·ble (in′kən·sō′lə·bəl) *adj.* Not to be consoled; disconsolate; dejected. — **in′con·sol′a·bil′i·ty, in′con·sol′a·ble·ness** *n.* — **in′con·sol′a·bly** *adv.*

in·con·so·nance (in·kon′sə·nəns) *n.* The quality or condition of being inconsonant; lack of accord, harmony, etc.

in·con·so·nant (in·kon′sə·nənt) *adj.* Not consonant; not in accord. — **in·con′so·nant·ly** *adv.*

in·con·spic·u·ous (in′kən·spik′yōō·əs) *adj.* **1.** Not conspicuous; not readily or easily seen; not prominent or striking. **2.** Not attracting attention to oneself; shrinking from or not meriting notice. — **in′con·spic′u·ous·ly** *adv.* — **in′con·spic′u·ous·ness** *n.*

in·con·stan·cy (in·kon′stən·sē) *n.* *pl.* **·cies 1.** The state or quality of being inconstant; variability. **2.** Lack of constancy; fickleness. **3.** An instance of inconstant behavior.

in·con·stant (in·kon′stənt) *adj.* Not constant; variable; fickle. — *n.* One who or that which is inconstant. [< F < L *inconstans, -antis*] — **in·con′stant·ly** *adv.*

in·con·stru·a·ble (in′kən·strōō′ə·bəl) *adj.* Incapable of being construed.

in·con·sum·a·ble (in′kən·sōō′mə·bəl) *adj.* **1.** Incapable of being consumed; not consumable. **2.** *Econ.* Used without being consumed, as machinery, currency, etc. — **in′con·sum′a·bly** *adv.*

in·con·tam·i·na·ble (in′kən·tam′ə·nə·bəl) *adj.* Incapable of being contaminated.

in·con·tam·i·nate (in′kən·tam′ə·nit) *adj.* Not contaminated; unsullied; undefiled. [< L *incontaminatus* < *in-* not + *contaminatus.* See CONTAMINATE.]

in·con·test·a·ble (in′kən·tes′tə·bəl) *adj.* Not admitting of question; unassailable: *incontestable* evidence. [< F] — **in′con·test′a·bil′i·ty, in′con·test′a·ble·ness** *n.*

incontestable clause A provision in a life insurance policy, stating a condition or conditions under which the insurer may not contest the terms of the policy.

incontestable right The unquestioned right of the registrant of a trademark to the ownership of that trademark after five consecutive years of its use.

in·con·test·a·bly (in′kən·tes′tə·blē) *adv.* In a degree, manner, etc., not to be contested or disputed; unquestionably; indubitably.

in·con·ti·nence (in·kon′tə·nəns) *n.* **1.** The quality or condition of being incontinent. **2.** An instance of incontinence. Also **in·con′ti·nen·cy.**

in·con·ti·nent[1] (in·kon′tə·nənt) *adj.* **1.** Exercising little control or restraint, especially in sexual desires. **2.** Incapable of keeping back: often *with of.* **3.** Unrestrained; unchecked: an *incontinent* flow of abuse. **4.** *Pathol.* Unable to control bodily discharges, as urine. [< OF < L *incontinens, -entis.* See CONTINENT.]

in·con·ti·nent[2] (in·kon′tə·nənt) *adv.* *Obs.* Immediately; forthwith. [< OF < LL *in continenti (tempore)* in continuous (time)]

in·con·ti·nent·ly[1] (in·kon′tə·nənt·lē) *adv.* In an incontinent manner; without control or restraint.

in·con·ti·nent·ly[2] (in·kon′tə·nənt·lē) *adv.* *Obs.* Incontinent[2].

in·con·ti·nu·i·ty (in′kon·tə·nōō′ə·tē, -nyōō′-) *n.* *pl.* **·ties** Lack of or break in continuity.

in·con·tin·u·ous (in·kon·tin′yōō·əs) *adj.* Not continuous; broken or interrupted.

in·con·trac·tile (in′kən·trak′təl) *adj.* Incapable of contracting or being contracted, as a muscle, part, or organ; not contractile.

in·con·trol·la·ble (in′kən·trō′lə·bəl) *adj.* Incapable of being controlled; uncontrollable. — **in′con·trol′la·bly** *adv.*

in·con·tro·vert·i·ble (in′kən·trə·vûr′tə·bəl) *adj.* Not admitting of controversy; undeniable. — **in′con·tro·vert′i·bil′i·ty, in′con·tro·vert′i·ble·ness** *n.* — **in′con·tro·vert′i·bly** *adv.*

in·con·ven·ience (in′kən·vēn′yəns) *n.* **1.** The state or quality of being inconvenient. **2.** Something that is inconvenient; a hindrance; trouble. — *v.t.* **·ienced, ·ienc·ing** To cause inconvenience to; to incommode; to trouble. [< OF < LL *inconvenientia*]

in·con·ven·ien·cy (in′kən·vēn′yən·sē) *n.* *pl.* **·cies** Inconvenience.

in·con·ven·ient (in′kən·vēn′yənt) *adj.* Causing or lending itself to discomfort and difficulty; troublesome; awkward. [< OF *inconvenient* < L *inconveniens, -entis.* See CONVENIENT.] — **in′con·ven′ient·ly** *adv.*

in·con·vers·a·ble (in′kən·vûr′sə·bəl) *adj.* *Rare* Not inclined to conversation; uncommunicative; taciturn.

in·con·ver·sant (in·kon′vər·sənt, in′kən·vûr′sənt) *adj.* Not conversant or familiar: with *in* or *with*: *inconversant* in mathematics; *inconversant* with the laws.

in·con·vert·i·ble (in′kən·vûr′tə·bəl) *adj.* Incapable of being changed, exchanged, or converted; especially, of paper money, not exchangeable for specie. — **in′con·vert′i·bil′i·ty, in′con·vert′i·ble·ness** *n.* — **in′con·vert′i·bly** *adv.*

in·con·vin·ci·ble (in′kən·vin′sə·bəl) *adj.* Not to be convinced; not convincible. — **in′con·vin′ci·bil′i·ty, in′con·vin′ci·ble·ness** *n.* — **in′con·vin′ci·bly** *adv.*

in·co·ny (in·kun′ē) *adj.* *Obs.* Pretty; fine; delicate. [Origin uncertain]

in·co·or·di·nate (in′kō·ôr′də·nit, -nāt) *adj.* Not coordinated. Also **in′co·or′di·nat′ed** (-nā′tid).

in·co·or·di·na·tion (in′kō·ôr′də·nā′shən) *n.* **1.** Lack of coordination. **2.** *Physiol.* Inability to effect voluntary muscular actions in proper order and at adequate speed.

in·co·pre·sent·a·ble (in′kō·prē·zen′tə·bəl) *adj.* Not presentable to the senses or intellect at the same time. [< IN-[1] + CO-[1] + PRESENTABLE] — **in′co·pre·sent′a·bil′i·ty** *n.*

incor. or **incorp.** Incorporated.

in·cor·o·nate (in·kôr′ə·nāt, -nit; -kor′-) *adj.* Wearing a crown; crowned. Also **in·cor′o·nat′ed** (-nā′tid). [< ML *incoronatus,* pp. of *incoronare* to crown]

in·cor·o·na·tion (in·kôr′ə·nā′shən, -kor′-) *n.* *Rare* Coronation.

in·cor·po·ra·ble (in·kôr′pə·rə·bəl) *adj.* Capable of being incorporated.

in·cor·po·ral (in·kôr′pə·rəl) *adj.* Not having material existence; incorporeal. [< L *incorporalis* < *in-* not + *corporalis.* See CORPORAL[1].] — **in·cor′po·ral′i·ty** (-ral′ə·tē), **in·cor′po·ral·ness** *n.* — **in·cor′po·ral·ly** *adv.*

in·cor·po·rate[1] (*v.* in·kôr′pə·rāt; *adj.* in·kôr′pə·rit) *v.* **·rat·ed, ·rat·ing** *v.i.* **1.** To form a legal corporation or other association capable of acting as an individual. **2.** To become combined or merged as one body or whole. — *v.t.* **3.** To take in or include as part of a whole: His philosophy *incorporates* some of Nietzsche's ideas. **4.** To add or inject (an ingredient, certain elements, etc.): He *incorporated* Nietzsche's ideas into his philosophy. **5.** To form (persons, groups, etc.) into a legal corporation or other association. **6.** To combine or merge into a whole; mix; blend. **7.** *Rare* To give material form to; embody. — **Syn.** See ENROLL, MIX, UNITE. — *adj.* **1.** Joined or combined into a single unit or whole; closely blended. **2.** Legally incorporated. [< LL *incorporatus,* pp. of *incorporare* to embody < *in-* in + *corporare.* See CORPORATE.]

in·cor·po·rate[2] (in·kôr′pər·it) *adj.* **1.** Not consisting of matter; incorporeal. **2.** Not formed into a corporation. [< L *incorporatus*]

in·cor·po·rat·ed (in·kôr′pə·rā′tid) *adj.* **1.** Forming one body or whole; combined. **2.** Organized into a legal corporation. Abbr. (def. 2) *inc., incor., incorp.*

incorporated territory A territory considered to be a part of the United States, in which the inhabitants have almost all the rights and privileges provided by the Constitution, as Alaska and Hawaii before their admission as States.

in·cor·po·rat·ing (in·kôr′pə·rā′ting) *adj.* *Ling.* Polysynthetic.

in·cor·po·ra·tion (in·kôr′pə·rā′shən) *n.* **1.** The act or process of incorporating. **2.** A corporation.

in·cor·po·ra·tive (in·kôr′pə·rā′tiv) *adj.* **1.** Tending to incorporate. **2.** Of a language, polysynthetic or agglutinative.

in·cor·po·ra·tor (in·kôr′pə·rā′tər) *n.* **1.** One who incorporates. **2.** One who forms a corporation. **3.** One of the members of a corporation named in the incorporating charter.

in·cor·po·re·al (in′kôr·pôr′ē·əl, -pō′rē-) *adj.* **1.** Not consisting of matter; immaterial; insubstantial. **2.** Of or pertaining to nonmaterial things; spiritual. **3.** *Law* Having no material existence, but regarded as existing by the law; intangible: *incorporeal* rights. Also *Obs.* **in·cor·po·re·ous** (in′kôr·pôr′ē·əs, -pō′rē·əs). [< L *incorporeus* < *in-* not + *corpus, -oris* body] — **in′cor·po′re·al′i·ty** (-al′ə·tē) *n.* — **in′cor·po′re·al·ly** *adv.*

in·cor·po·re·i·ty (in·kôr′pə·rē′ə·tē) *n.* *pl.* **·ties 1.** The quality or being immaterial; incorporeality. **2.** An incorporeal entity.

in·corpse (in·kôrps′) *v.t.* **·corpsed, ·corps·ing** *Archaic* To become combined or embodied with; incorporate.

in·cor·rect (in′kə·rekt′) *adj.* **1.** Inaccurate or untrue as to fact or usage; wrong: an *incorrect* answer. **2.** Not proper or fitting; unsuitable: *incorrect* behavior. **3.** Not conforming to known or accepted standards; erroneous; faulty: an *incorrect* idea. [< L *incorrectus*] — **in′cor·rect′ly** *adv.* — **in′cor·rect′ness** *n.*

in·cor·re·spon·dence (in·kôr′ə·spon′dəns, -kor′-) *n.* Lack of correspondence, agreement, similarity, etc. Also **in·cor′·re·spon′den·cy.**

in·cor·re·spon·dent (in·kôr′ə·spon′dənt, -kor′-) *adj.* Not correspondent; not correlated or conforming.

in·cor·ri·gi·ble (in-kôr′ə·jə-bəl, -kor′-) *adj.* **1.** Incapable of being reformed or chastened; irreclaimable. **2.** Firmly implanted; ineradicable, as a bad habit. **3.** Incapable of being corrected or amended. — *n.* One who is incorrigible. [< MF < *in-* not + *corrigible.* See CORRIGIBLE.] — **in·cor′ri·gi·bil′i·ty, in·cor′ri·gi·ble·ness** *n.* — **in·cor′ri·gi·bly** *adv.*

in·cor·rupt (in′kə·rupt′) *adj.* **1.** Not morally corrupt; especially, not susceptible to bribery; honest; upright. **2.** Not marred by decay or spoilage; untainted; fresh. **3.** Free from errors or alterations, as language, a literary text, etc. Also **in′cor·rupt′ed.** [< L *incorruptus* < *in-* not + *corruptus.* See CORRUPT.] — **in′cor·rupt′ly** *adv.* — **in′cor·rupt′ness** *n.*

in·cor·rupt·i·ble (in′kə·rup′tə·bəl) *adj.* **1.** Not accessible to bribery; steadfastly honest. **2.** Incapable of corruption; not subject to decay or spoilage. — **in′cor·rupt′i·bil′i·ty, in′cor·rupt′i·ble·ness** *n.* — **in′cor·rupt′i·bly** *adv.*

incr. Increased; increasing.

in·cras·sate (in·kras′āt) *v.t. & v.i.* **·sat·ed, ·sat·ing 1.** To make or become thick or thicker. **2.** To thicken (a fluid). — *adj. Biol.* Thickened: also **in·cras′sat·ed.** [< L *incrassatus,* pp. of *incrassare* < *in-* in + *crassus* thick] — **in′cras·sa′tion** *n.* — **in·cras′sa·tive** (-kras′ə·tiv) *adj.*

in·crease (*v.* in·krēs′, *n.* in′krēs) *v.* **·creased, ·creas·ing** *v.i.* **1.** To become greater, as in amount, size, degree, etc.; grow. **2.** To grow in numbers, especially by reproduction; multiply: May your tribe *increase.* — *v.t.* **3.** To make greater, as in amount, size, degree, etc.; augment; enlarge. — *n.* **1.** A growing or becoming greater, as in size, quantity, etc. **2.** The amount of growth or augmentation; that which is added; increment. Abbr. *inc.* [< OF *encreistre* < L *increscere* < *in-* + *crescere* to grow. Akin to *creare* to create.] — **in·creas′a·ble** *adj.* — **in·creas′er** *n.* — **in·creas′ing·ly** *adv.* — **Syn.** (verb) *Increase, augment, enlarge, extend, multiply, prolong, heighten, enhance,* and *magnify* agree in the general sense of making greater. Chiefly we *increase* in quantity, *augment* in amount or intensity, *enlarge* in size, *extend* in dimension, *multiply* in number, *prolong* in time or space, *heighten* in degree, and *enhance* or *magnify* in force or influence. Compare ADD, FASTEN. — **Ant.** decrease, reduce, diminish, lessen, curtail.

in·cre·ate (in′krē·āt′) *adj. Rare* Not created; existing through all time, as divine beings.

in·cred·i·ble (in·kred′ə·bəl) *adj.* **1.** Not credible; impossible to believe; unbelievable. **2.** Hard to believe; amazing; wonderful: an *incredible* mistake; an *incredible* person. — **in·cred′i·bil′i·ty, in·cred′i·ble·ness** *n.* — **in·cred′i·bly** *adv.*

in·cre·du·li·ty (in′krə·dōō′lə·tē, -dyōō′-) *n.* The quality or state of being incredulous; disbelief; skepticism. — **Syn.** See DOUBT. Also **in·cred·u·lous·ness** (in·krej′ə·ləs·nis). [< OF *incredulite* < L *incredulitatem*]

in·cred·u·lous (in·krej′ə·ləs) *adj.* **1.** Not willing or not disposed to believe; skeptical. **2.** Characterized by or showing disbelief: an *incredulous* laugh. [< L *incredulus* < *in-* not + *credulus.* See CREDULOUS.] — **in·cred′u·lous·ly** *adv.*

in·cre·ment (in′krə·mənt) *n.* **1.** The act of increasing or growing larger, more valuable, more numerous, etc. **2.** Something added or gained; increase; addition. **3.** *Math.* Any positive or negative change in a variable. — **unearned increment** *Econ.* Any increase of value produced by forces independent of the person who receives it; especially, increase of value in land that springs from the increase of population or other cause independent of the land itself and of its owner. [< L *incrementum* < *increscere.* See INCREASE.] — **in′cre·men′tal** (-men′təl) *adj.*

in·cres·cent (in·kres′ənt) *adj.* Becoming larger; growing; waxing: said especially of the moon. [< L *increscens, -entis,* ppr. of *increscere.* See INCREASE.]

in·cre·tion (in·krē′shən) *n. Physiol.* **1.** An internal secretion, as a hormone. **2.** The secreting of such a substance. [< IN-² + (SE)CRETION]

in·crim·i·nate (in·krim′ə·nāt) *v.t.* **·nat·ed, ·nat·ing 1.** To imply the wrongdoing or guilt of (a person, etc.). **2.** To charge with a crime or fault. — **Syn.** See ACCUSE. [< Med.L *incriminatus,* pp. of *incriminare* < *in-* in + *criminare* to accuse one of a crime] — **in·crim′i·na′tion** *n.* — **in·crim′i·na·to′ry** (-nə·tôr′ē, -tō′rē) *adj.*

in·crust (in·krust′) *v.t.* **1.** To cover with or as with a crust or hard coating; form a crust on. **2.** To decorate lavishly, as with jewels. Also spelled *encrust.* [< OF *encrouster* < L *incrustare* < *in-* on + *crustare* to form a crust]

in·crus·ta·tion (in′krus·tā′shən) *n.* **1.** A crust, coating, or scale; especially, a coating of lavish ornament. **2.** The act of incrusting, or the state of being incrusted. Also spelled *encrustation.*

in·cu·bate (in′kyə·bāt, ing′-) *v.* **·bat·ed, ·bat·ing** *v.t.* **1.** To sit upon (eggs) in order to hatch them; brood. **2.** To hatch (eggs) in this manner or by artificial heat. **3.** To maintain under conditions favoring optimum growth or development, as bacterial cultures. — *v.i.* **4.** To sit on eggs; brood. **5.** To undergo incubation. [< L *incubatus,* pp. of *incubare* < *in-* on + *cubare* to lie] — **in′cu·ba′tive** *adj.*

in·cu·ba·tion (in′kyə·bā′shən, ing′-) *n.* **1.** The act of incu-

bating, or the state of being incubated. **2.** *Med.* The period between the time of exposure to an infectious disease and the appearance of the symptoms. [< L *incubatio, -onis*]

in·cu·ba·tor (in′kyə·bā′tər, ing′-) *n.* **1.** An apparatus kept at a uniform warmth, as by a lamp, for artificial hatching of eggs. **2.** *Bacteriol.* A device for the artificial development of microorganisms, especially one in which the temperature may be regulated. **3.** An apparatus for keeping warm a prematurely born baby. **4.** One who or that which incubates. [< L, a hatcher]

in·cu·bus (in′kyə·bəs, ing′-) *n. pl.* **·bus·es** or **·bi** (-bī) **1.** Anything that tends to oppress or discourage. **2.** A nightmare. **3.** In folklore, a male demon that has sexual intercourse with sleeping women. Compare SUCCUBUS. [< Med. L, a demon that causes nightmares < LL, nightmare < L *incubare* to lie on]

in·cu·des (in·kyōō′dēz) Plural of INCUS.

in·cul·cate (in·kul′kāt, in′kul-) *v.t.* **·cat·ed, ·cat·ing** To impress upon the mind by frequent repetition or forceful admonition; instill. [< L *inculcatus,* pp. of *inculcare* to tread on < *in-* on + *calcare* to tread < *calx, calcis* heel] — **in′cul·ca′tion** *n.* — **in′cul·ca′tor** *n.*

in·cul·pa·ble (in·kul′pə·bəl) *adj.* Free from blame or guilt.

in·cul·pate (in·kul′pāt, in′kul-) *v.t.* **·pat·ed, ·pat·ing 1.** To charge with fault; blame. **2.** To involve in an accusation; incriminate. [< Med.L *inculpatus,* pp. of *inculpare* to blame < *in-* in + *culpa* fault] — **in′cul·pa′tion** *n.* — **in·cul′pa·to′ry** (-pə·tôr′ē, -tō′rē) *adj.*

in·cult (in·kult′) *adj. Rare* Uncultivated. [< L < *in-* not + *cultus,* pp. of *colere* to cultivate]

in·cum·ben·cy (in·kum′bən·sē) *n. pl.* **·cies 1.** The state or quality of being incumbent. **2.** That which is incumbent. **3.** The holding of an office or benefice and the discharging of its duties. **4.** The period during which such an office is held.

in·cum·bent (in·kum′bənt) *adj.* **1.** Resting upon one as a moral obligation, or as necessary under the circumstances; obligatory. **2.** Resting, leaning, or weighing wholly or partly upon something. — *n.* One who holds an office or performs official duties. [< L *incumbens, -entis,* ppr. of *incumbere* to rest on < *in-* on + *cubare* to lie] — **in·cum′bent·ly** *adv.*

in·cum·ber (in·kum′bər), **in·cum·brance** (in·kum′brəns), etc. See ENCUMBER, etc.

in·cu·nab·u·la (in′kyōō·nab′yə·lə) *n. pl.* of **in·cu·nab·u·lum** (-ləm) **1.** Specimens of early European printing from movable type; especially, books printed before A.D. 1500. **2.** The earliest stages of development; beginnings. [< L < *in-* in + *cunabula,* dim. of *cunae* cradle] — **in′cu·nab′u·lar** *adj.*

in·cur (in·kûr′) *v.t.* **·curred, ·cur·ring** To become subject to (unpleasant consequences); bring on oneself. [< L *incurrere* to run into < *in-* in + *currere* to run] — **in·cur′rence** *n.*

in·cur·a·ble (in·kyŏŏr′ə·bəl) *adj.* Not curable or remediable. — *n.* One suffering from an incurable disease. — **in·cur′a·bil′i·ty, in·cur′a·ble·ness** *n.* — **in·cur′a·bly** *adv.*

in·cu·ri·ous (in·kyŏŏr′ē·əs) *adj.* Not curious; indifferent. — **in·cu′ri·os′i·ty** *n.* — **in·cu′ri·ous·ly** *adv.*

in·cur·rent (in·kûr′ənt) *adj.* Characterized by an inward flowing. [< L *incurrens, -entis,* ppr. of *incurrere.* See INCUR.]

in·cur·sion (in·kûr′zhən, -shən) *n.* **1.** A hostile, often sudden entrance into a territory; an invasion; raid. **2.** A running in or running against; encroachment. [< L *incursio, -onis* < *in-* + *currere.* See INCUR.] — **in·cur′sive** *adj.*

in·cur·vate (in·kûr′vāt) *v.t. & v.i.* **·vat·ed, ·vat·ing** To curve or cause to curve, especially inwards. — *adj.* Curved, especially inwards. [< L *incurvatus,* pp. of *incurvare* to curve inward < *in-* in + *curvare* to curve] — **in′cur·va′tion** *n.*

in·curve (*v.* in·kûrv′; *n.* in′kûrv) *v.i. & v.t.* **·curved, ·curv·ing** To curve inward. — *n.* In baseball, a pitch that curves toward the batter.

in·cus (ing′kəs) *n. pl.* **in·cu·des** (in·kyōō′dēz) **1.** *Anat.* The anvil-shaped central bone of the group of three small bones in the middle ear of mammals: also called *anvil.* **2.** *Meteorol.* An anviltop. [< L, anvil] — **in′cu·dal** (-kyə·dəl) *adj.*

in·cuse (in·kyōōz′) *adj.* Formed by hammering or stamping, as the figure or design on a coin. — *n.* A figure or design made in this way. [< L *incusus,* pp. of *incudere* to forge with a hammer < *in-* on + *cudere* to beat]

ind. **1.** Independent. **2.** Index. **3.** Indicated; indicative. **4.** Indigo **5.** Indirect. **6.** Industrial.

Ind (ind) **1.** *Poetic* India. **2.** *Obs.* The Indies.

Ind. **1.** India; Indian. **2.** Indiana. **3.** Indies.

I.N.D. In the name of God (L *in nomine Dei*).

In·da (in′də) See INDRA.

in·da·ba (in·dä′bä) *n.* A great meeting of South African tribes; council. [< Zulu *in-daba* subject, matter]

in·da·mine (in′də·mēn, -min) *Chem.* Any of a class of unstable organic bases forming bluish and greenish salts, used as dyes. Also **in′da·min** (-min). [< IND(IGO) + AMINE]

in·debt·ed (in·det′id) *adj.* **1.** Legally obligated to pay for value received; in debt. **2.** Morally obligated to acknowledge benefits or favors; beholden. [< OF *endette,* pp. of *endetter* < *en-* in + *dette* debt. See DEBT.]

in·debt·ed·ness (in·det′id·nis) *n.* **1.** The state of being indebted. **2.** The amount of one's debts.

in·de·cen·cy (in·dē′sən·sē) *n. pl.* **·cies 1.** The quality or condition of being indecent. **2.** An indecent act, speech, etc.

in·de·cent (in·dē′sənt) *adj.* **1.** Offensive to one's moral sense or modesty; immodest. **2.** Contrary to propriety or good taste; indelicate; vulgar. **— in·de′cent·ly** *adv.*
— **Syn. 1.** lewd, obscene. **2.** improper, indecorous, unseemly.

in·de·cid·u·ous (in′di·sij′ōō·əs) *adj. Bot.* **1.** Not deciduous; not dropping off at maturity, as leaves. **2.** Evergreen.

in·de·ci·pher·a·ble (in′di·sī′fər·ə·bəl) *adj.* Not decipherable; unreadable. **— in′de·ci′pher·a·bil′i·ty** *n.*

in·de·ci·sion (in′di·sizh′ən) *n.* Inability to make decisions; vacillation.

in·de·ci·sive (in′di·sī′siv) *adj.* **1.** Not decisive; not bringing about a definite conclusion, solution, etc. **2.** Incapable of making decisions; hesitant; irresolute. **— in′de·ci′sive·ness** *n.* **— in′de·ci′sive·ly** *adv.*

indecl. *Gram.* Indeclinable.

in·de·clin·a·ble (in′di·clī′nə·bəl) *adj. Gram.* Not declinable; having no set of inflected forms.

in·de·com·pos·a·ble (in′dē·kəm·pō′zə·bəl) *adj.* Not decomposable; incapable of being split into parts.

in·dec·o·rous (in·dek′ər·əs, in′di·kôr′əs) *adj.* Not decorous; not fitting or proper; unseemly. **— in·dec′o·rous·ly** *adv.* **— in·dec′o·rous·ness** *n.*

in·de·cor·um (in′di·kôr′əm, -kō′rəm) *n.* Lack or absence of propriety; unseemliness.

in·deed (in·dēd′) *adv.* In fact; in truth: used to emphasize an affirmation, to mark a qualifying word or clause, to denote a concession, or interrogatively to elicit confirmation of a fact stated. **—** *interj.* Is that true? [< IN-² + DEED]

indef. Indefinite.

in·de·fat·i·ga·ble (in′də·fat′ə·gə·bəl) *adj.* Not yielding readily to fatigue; tireless; unflagging. [< MF *indéfatigable* < L *indefatigabilis* < *in-* not + *de-* intens. + *fatigare* to tire out. See FATIGUE.] **— in′de·fat′i·ga·bil′i·ty, in′de·fat′i·ga·ble·ness** *n.* **— in′de·fat′i·ga·bly** *adv.*

in·de·fea·si·ble (in′də·fē′zə·bəl) *adj.* Not defeasible; incapable of being annulled, set aside, or made void. **— in′de·fea′si·bil′i·ty** *n.* **— in′de·fea′si·bly** *adv.*

in·de·fec·ti·ble (in′di·fek′tə·bəl) *adj.* Not subject to defect or decay. **— in′de·fec′ti·bil′i·ty** *n.* **— in′de·fec′ti·bly** *adv.*

in·de·fen·si·ble (in′di·fen′sə·bəl) *adj.* **1.** Incapable of being justified, proved, excused, etc. **2.** Incapable of being defended or protected against armed attack. **— in′de·fen′si·bil′i·ty, in′de·fen′si·ble·ness** *n.* **— in′de·fen′si·bly** *adv.*

in·de·fin·a·ble (in′di·fī′nə·bəl) *adj.* Incapable of being defined or described; vague; subtle; ineffable. **— in′de·fin′a·ble·ness** *n.* **— in′de·fin′a·bly** *adv.*

in·def·i·nite (in·def′ə·nit) *adj.* **1.** Not definite or precise; undetermined; vague. **2.** Without a fixed number; indeterminate; unlimited. **3.** *Bot.* **a** Having no fixed number, as stamens when too numerous to be counted easily. **b** Indeterminate, as an inflorescence. **4.** *Gram.* Not definite or determining, as the *indefinite* articles *a* and *an.* **— in·def′i·nite·ly** *adv.* **— in·def′i·nite·ness** *n.*

indefinite article See under ARTICLE.

indefinite pronoun *Gram.* A pronoun that represents an object indefinitely or generally, as *each, none, another.*

in·de·his·cent (in′də·his′ənt) *adj. Bot.* Not opening spontaneously when ripe, as certain grains and fruits. [*in-* not + *dehiscent.* See DEHISCE.] **— in′de·his′cence** *n.*

in·del·i·ble (in·del′ə·bəl) *adj.* **1.** Incapable of being blotted out or effaced: *indelible* recollections. **2.** Leaving a mark or stain not easily erased: *indelible* ink. [< L *indelibilis* < *in-* not + *delibilis* perishable < *delere* to destroy] **— in·del′i·bil′i·ty, in·del′i·ble·ness** *n.* **— in·del′i·bly** *adv.*

in·del·i·ca·cy (in·del′ə·kə·sē) *n. pl.* **·cies 1.** The quality of being indelicate; coarseness. **2.** An indelicate thing, act, etc.

in·del·i·cate (in·del′ə·kit) *adj.* **1.** Lacking or offending a sense of delicacy or good taste; crude. **2.** Unconcerned about the feelings of others; tactless. **— in·del′i·cate·ly** *adv.*

in·dem·ni·fy (in·dem′nə·fī) *v.t.* **·fied, ·fy·ing 1.** To compensate (a person, etc.) for loss or damage sustained. **2.** To make good (a loss). **3.** To give security against future loss or punishment. [< L *indemnis* unhurt (< *in-* not + *damnum* harm) + -FY] **— in·dem′ni·fi·ca′tion** *n.*

in·dem·ni·tee (in·dem′nə·tē′) *n.* One who is indemnified.

in·dem·ni·tor (in·dem′nə·tər) *n.* One who indemnifies.

in·dem·ni·ty (in·dem′nə·tē) *n. pl.* **·ties 1.** That which is given as compensation for a loss or for damage. **2.** An agreement to remunerate another for loss or protect him against liability. **3.** Exemption from penalties or liabilities. [< F *indemnité* < L *indemnitas* < *indemnis.* See INDEMNIFY.]

in·de·mon·stra·ble (in′di·mon′strə·bəl, in·dem′ən·strə·bəl) *adj.* Incapable of being proved or demonstrated. **— in′de·mon′stra·ble·ness, in·dem′on·stra·bil′i·ty** *n.* **— in′de·mon′stra·bly** *adv.*

in·dene (in′dēn) *n. Chem.* A colorless, oily hydrocarbon, C_9H_8, obtained from coal tar. [< IND(OLE) + -ENE]

in·dent¹ (in·dent′; *for n., also* in′dent) *v.t.* **1.** To set in from the margin, as the first line of a paragraph. **2.** To cut or mark the edge or border of with toothlike notches; serrate.

3. To make an order for goods from; draw upon (a supply). **4.** To make an order for (goods). **5.** To draw up (a document, contract, etc.) in duplicate. **6.** To cut or tear (a document and its copies) along an irregular line so as to identify the halves when fitted together. **7.** To cut or tear (a document and its copies) at the edges or top in an irregular line. **8.** To indenture, as an apprentice. **—** *v.i.* **9.** To be notched or cut; form a recess. **10.** To set a line, paragraph, etc., in from the margin. **11.** To write out an order or requisition in duplicate. **12.** *Archaic* To enter into a bargain or contract for something. **—** *n.* **1.** A cut or notch on the edge of a thing. **2.** A space before the first word of a paragraph; indention. **3.** An indenture. **4.** In commerce, a foreign order for the exportation of goods, usually at a stated price. **5.** A certificate issued at the close of the American Revolution by the government for principal or interest due on the public debt. **6.** *Brit.* An official order for supplies. [< OF *endenter* < Med.L *indentare* < *in-* + *dens, dentis* tooth]

in·dent² (in·dent′; *for n., also* in′dent) *v.t.* **1.** To press or push in so as to form a dent or depression; impress. **2.** To make a dent in. **—** *n.* A dent or depression; indentation. [< IN-² + DENT¹]

indent. *Printing* Indention.

in·den·ta·tion (in′den·tā′shən) *n.* **1.** A notch or series of notches in an edge or border. **2.** The act of notching, or the condition of being notched. **3.** A dent. **4.** An indention.

in·den·tion (in·den′shən) *n.* **1.** *Printing* **a** The setting in of a line or body of type at the left side. **b** The space thus left blank. **2.** A dent; indentation. **— hanging indention** *Printing* Equal indention of all lines of a paragraph except the first, which is not indented.

in·den·ture (in·den′chər) *n.* **1.** *Law* A deed or contract made between two or more parties. **2.** *Usually pl.* Such a contract between master and apprentice. **3.** An official or validated inventory or list. **4.** The act of indenting, or the state of being indented. **5.** Indentation. **—** *v.t.* **·tured, ·tur·ing 1.** To bind by indenture. **2.** To make an indentation in. [< OF *endenture* < Med.L *indentare.* See INDENT¹.]

in·de·pen·dence (in′di·pen′dəns) *n.* **1.** The quality or condition of being independent. **2.** Sufficient income for one's needs; a competency.

In·de·pen·dence (in′di·pen′dəns) A city in western Missouri, near Kansas City; pop. 111,630.

Independence Day July 4, a holiday in the United States commemorating the adoption of the Declaration of Independence, July 4, 1776.

in·de·pen·den·cy (in′di·pen′dən·sē) *n. pl.* **·cies 1.** Independence. **2.** An independent state or territory.

In·de·pen·den·cy (in′di·pen′dən·sē) *n. Eccl.* The doctrine that each congregation of the Christian church is an entity independent of central ecclesiastical control.

in·de·pen·dent (in′di·pen′dənt) *adj.* **1.** Not subject to the authority of another; autonomous; self-determining; free. **2.** Not dependent on or part of some larger group, system, etc.; separate; disconnected: an *independent* arrangement; an *independent* union. **3.** Not an adherent of a party or faction: an *independent* voter. **4.** Not affected or influenced in action, opinion, etc., by others: an *independent* stand; also, not guided by others: *independent* research. **5.** Acting so as to manage one's own affairs; self-sufficient; self-reliant. **6.** Not needing financial support or help; self-supporting. **7.** Having a competence; also, constituting a competence: *independent* means. **8.** *Gram.* Constituting or capable of constituting a complete sentence; not subordinate: said of clauses. **9.** *Math.* **a** Capable of taking any value without regard to the variation of other quantities. **b** Denoting two or more quantities or functions such that the value of none of them depends upon that of the others. **—** *n.* **1.** One who or that which is independent. **2.** One who is not an adherent of a party or faction. Abbr. *ind.* **— in′de·pen′dent·ly** *adv.*

In·de·pen·dent (in′di·pen′dənt) *n.* **1.** A believer in Independency. **2.** In England, a Congregationalist. **—** *adj.* Of or pertaining to Independents or Independency.

independent clause *Gram.* A clause constituting or capable of constituting a sentence.

in·de·scrib·a·ble (in′di·skrī′bə·bəl) *adj.* Incapable of being described; especially, too complex, extreme, etc., to be described; ineffable. **— in′de·scrib′a·bil′i·ty, in′de·scrib′a·ble·ness** *n.* **— in′de·scrib′a·bly** *adv.*

in·de·struc·ti·ble (in′di·struk′tə·bəl) *adj.* Incapable of being destroyed; very tough and durable. **— in′de·struc′ti·bil′i·ty, in′de·struc′ti·ble·ness** *n.* **— in′de·struc′ti·bly** *adv.*

in·de·ter·mi·na·ble (in′di·tûr′mi·nə·bəl) *adj.* **1.** Not determinable; incapable of being ascertained, measured, etc. **2.** Incapable of being decided or settled. **— in′de·ter′mi·na·ble·ness** *n.* **— in′de·ter′mi·na·bly** *adv.*

in·de·ter·mi·na·cy (in′di·tûr′mə·nə·sē) *n.* The state or quality of being indeterminate.

indeterminacy principle The uncertainty principle (which see).

in·de·ter·mi·nate (in′di·tûr′mə·nit) *adj.* **1.** Not definite in extent, amount, or nature. **2.** Not clear or precise; vague. **3.** Not decided; unsettled. **4.** Not fixed; inconclusive. **5.** *Bot.* Not definitely terminated, as the axis of a raceme. **6.**

Math. Designating any of a class of undefined expressions, as infinity minus infinity, zero divided by infinity, etc. — **in′·de·ter′mi·nate·ly** *adv.* — **in′·de·ter′mi·nate·ness** *n.*

in·de·ter·mi·na·tion (in′di·tûr′mə·nā′shən) *n.* **1.** Lack of determination. **2.** The quality or condition of being indeterminate.

in·de·ter·min·ism (in′di·tûr′mə·niz′əm) *n. Philos.* The doctrine that the human will, though it may be influenced by certain conditions external to it, is not absolutely determined by them, but does retain some degree of freedom to act or to choose motives that will influence action. — **in·de·ter′min·ist** *n. & adj.* — **in′de·ter′min·is′tic** *adj.*

in·dex (in′deks) *n.* *pl.* **·dex·es** or **·di·ces** (-də·sēz) **1.** An alphabetical list, as at the end of a book or similar publication, of topics, names, etc., and the numbers of the pages where they occur in the text. **2.** A descriptive list, as of items in a collection; catalogue. **3.** Anything that serves as an indicator, as the needle on the dial of scientific instruments; the pointer on a sign post, etc. **4.** The index finger. **5.** Anything that indicates or gives evidence of; sign: *Alertness is an index of intelligence.* **6.** *Printing* A mark (☞) used to direct attention to a specific word, passage, etc.: also called *fist, hand.* **7.** A numerical expression of the ratio between one dimension or magnitude and another: *the cephalic index.* **8.** *Math.* A subscript or superscript. *Abbr. ind.* — *v.t.* **1.** To provide with an index, as a book. **2.** To enter in an index, as a subject. **3.** To indicate. [< L, forefinger, sign. See INDICATE.] — **in′dex·er** *n.* — **in·dex′i·cal** *adj.*

In·dex (in′deks) *n.* A list of books the Roman Catholic Church condemns as dangerous to faith and morals, and forbids its members to read except with special permission. Also **Index Lib·ro·rum Pro·hib·i·to·rum** (li·brō′rəm prō·hib′i·tō′rəm).

index finger The finger next to the thumb: also called *forefinger.*

index number *Stat.* A figure indicating the relative changes, if any, in costs, production, etc., at a given period of time, as compared with those of a specific period in the past represented by the number 100 and used as an arbitrary base.

index of refraction *Optics* Refractive index (which see).

In·di·a (in′dē·ə) **1.** A Republic of the Commonwealth of Nations in southern Asia; 1,259,797 sq. mi.; pop. 546,955,-945 (est. 1971); capital, New Delhi: Hindi *Bharat.* Officially **Republic of India. 2.** The large peninsula of southern Asia, comprising India, Pakistan, and several smaller states. [< L < Gk. < *Indos* the Indus river < O.Persian *Hindu* land on the Indus < Skt. *Sindhu* river, the Indus. Cf. HINDI.]

India ink 1. A black pigment composed of lampblack mixed with a binding material, originally made in India, China, and Japan and molded in sticks or cakes. **2.** A liquid ink made from this pigment. **3.** Any of various heavy drawing inks. Also called *Chinese ink.*

In·di·a·man (in′dē·ə·mən) *n. pl.* **·men** (-mən) A merchant ship in the India trade, especially one in the service of the East India Company.

In·di·an (in′dē·ən) *n.* **1.** A citizen of the Republic of India. **2.** A native of India or the East Indies. **3.** A member of the aboriginal races of North America, South America, and the West Indies. **4.** Loosely, any of the languages of the American Indian. **5.** The constellation Indus. — *adj.* **1.** Of or pertaining to India and the East Indies and their peoples. **2.** Of or pertaining to the aborigines of North America, South America, and the West Indies. **3.** Made by or used by Indians. *Abbr. Ind.* [< LL *Indianus* < L *India.*]

In·di·an·a (in′dē·an′ə) A north central State of the United States; 36,291 sq. mi.; pop. 5,193,669; capital, Indianapolis; entered the Union Dec. 11, 1816; nickname, *Hoosier State. Abbr. Ind.* — **In′di·an′i·an** *adj. & n.*

Indian agent *U.S. & Canadian* A federal representative in Indian affairs, often on a reservation.

In·di·an·ap·o·lis (in′dē·ə·nap′ə·lis) The capital of Indiana, in the central part on the West Fork of the White River; pop. 744,624.

Indian bean The catalpa tree.

Indian bread Tuckahoe, a fungus.

Indian buffalo The water buffalo (which see).

Indian club A bottle-shaped wooden club used in gymnastics, usually in pairs.

Indian corn Corn (def. 1).

Indian Desert See THAR DESERT.

Indian Empire Formerly, British India and a number of associated Indian states.

Indian file Single file, the usual order of the American Indians when walking a trail.

Indian giver *U.S. Informal* One who gives a present and then wants it back.

Indian hemp 1. Hemp (def. 1). **2.** A perennial American herb (*Apocynum cannabinum*) of the dogbane family, having milky juice and roots with medicinal properties: also called *Canada hemp, hemp dogbane.* Also **Indian physic.**

Indian licorice Jequirity, a plant.

Indian mallow A tall weed (*Abutilon incanum*) of the mal-

low family, with large velvety leaves and small yellow flowers: also called *butterweed.*

Indian meal Cornmeal (which see).

Indian millet The tall grass (*Sorghum vulgare*) of which sorgo, broomcorn, and durra are varieties.

Indian mulberry Aal, a plant.

Indian Mutiny An uprising of native soldiers in India (1857–58) occasioned by resentment against British colonial policies: also called *Sepoy Mutiny.*

Indian Ocean An ocean, bounded by Africa, Asia, Australia, and Antarctica; 28,357,000 sq. mi.

Indian paintbrush The painted cup, a flower.

Indian pipe A saprophytic herb (*Monotropa uniflora*) with one pipe-shaped white flower and no leaves, common in moist woodlands of North America and Asia.

Indian pudding A pudding made with cornmeal, milk, and molasses.

Indian red An iron oxide, especially that from Hormuz, used as a paint and cosmetic pigment; rouge.

Indian rice Wild rice.

Indian River A lagoon of ea tern Florida, extending about 120 miles between the mainland and a coastal strip.

Indian States Formerly, the semi-independent states of India ruled by native princes: also *Native States.*

Indian summer 1. A period of mild, warm weather occurring in late autumn, often after the first frost. **2.** The last years of life, thought of as peaceful and serene.

Indian Territory Formerly, a territory of the United States set aside for Indians; now part of Oklahoma.

Indian turnip The jack-in-the-pulpit or its root.

In·di·an-wres·tle (in′dē-ən-res′əl) *v.i.* **·tled, ·tling** To engage in any of various contests of strength and agility in which two people grasp hands, lock legs, etc., and attempt to force each other into an inferior position.

India paper 1. A thin, yellowish, absorbent printing paper, made in China and Japan from vegetable fiber, and used in taking the finest proofs from engraved plates. **2.** Bible paper (which see).

India print Lightweight cotton fabric, usually handblocked in Oriental patterns and rich colors.

India proof A proof taken on India paper.

India rubber Rubber (def. 1).

In·dic (in′dik) *adj.* Pertaining to India, its peoples, languages, and culture; Indian. — *n.* A branch of the Indo-Iranian subfamily of Indo-European languages, including many of the ancient and modern languages of India, as Sanskrit, Gujarati, Hindi, Bengali, Romany, etc. [< L *Indicus* < Gk. *Indikos* < *India.* See INDIA.]

indic. Indicating; indicative; indicator.

in·di·can (in′də·kən) *n.* **1.** *Chem.* A colorless, crystalline, toxic glycoside, $C_{14}H_{17}O_6N$, contained in several species of indigo plants. **2.** *Biochem.* An indoxyl compound containing potassium sulfate, $C_8H_6NSO_4K$, found in the urine and other body fluids of certain animals, including man: also called *uroxanthin.* [< L *indicum* indigo + -AN]

in·di·cant (in′də·kənt) *adj. Obs.* Indicating. — *n.* An indicator.

in·di·cate (in′də·kāt) *v.t.* **·cat·ed, ·cat·ing 1.** To be or give a sign of; signify: *Storm clouds indicate rain; The scrawled handwriting indicated great haste.* **2.** To direct attention to; point out: *to indicate the right page; The witness indicated the accused.* **3.** To express or make known; especially, to express briefly or generally: *The union indicated its acceptance of the wage offer; The gauge indicates wind velocity.* **4.** *Med.* To show or suggest a disease or a treatment: said of symptoms. [< L *indicatus,* pp. of *indicare* < *in-* in + *dicare* to point out, proclaim] — **in′di·ca·to′ry** (-kə·tôr′ē, -tō′rē) *adj.*

in·di·ca·tion (in′də·kā′shən) *n.* **1.** The act of indicating; manifestation. **2.** That which indicates or suggests; a token; sign: *to give some indication of one's opinion; no indication that the insult was deliberate.* **3.** A degree or quantity shown on a measuring instrument. **4.** *Med.* A sign showing the cause, progress, most effective treatment, etc., of a disease. [< F]

in·dic·a·tive (in·dik′ə·tiv) *adj.* **1.** Suggestive of; pointing out: *indicative of immaturity; indicative of a fine education.* **2.** *Gram.* Pertaining to or denoting a mood in which an act or condition is stated or questioned as an actual fact, rather than as a potentiality or an unrealized condition. — *n. Gram.* **a** The indicative mood. **b** A verb in this mood. *Abbr. ind., indic.* — **in·dic′a·tive·ly** *adv.* [< F *indicatif* < L *indicatus.* See INDICATE.]

in·di·ca·tor (in′də·kā′tər) *n.* **1.** One who or that which indicates or points out. **2.** An instrument or device that measures or shows position or condition; as: **a** A speedometer on a motor vehicle. **b** A gauge showing the pressure of fluids, as in an engine, steam boiler, etc. **c** A device showing the position of an elevator. **d** A water gauge. **3.** The pointer, needle, or the like on such a measuring instrument. **4.** *Chem.* A substance that by color change, or in some other visible way, shows the condition of or some change in a system, as an acid-base or oxidation-reduction reaction. Abbr. *indic.* [< LL]

in·di·ces (in′də-sēz) Alternative plural of INDEX.

in·di·cia (in-dish′ə) *n.* *pl. of* **in·di·cium** (-dish′əm) **1.** Discriminating marks; indications; signs. **2.** *U.S.* Markings on envelopes used in place of stamps or cancellations when mail is sent in bulk. [< L, pl. of *indicium* sign]

in·dict (in-dīt′) *v.t.* *Law* To prefer an indictment against: said of the action of grand juries. **2.** To charge with a crime or offense; accuse. — **Syn.** See ACCUSE. [< AF *enditer* to make known, inform; later infl. in form by Med.L *dictare* to accuse. Akin to INDITE.] — **in·dict′a·ble** *adj.* — **in·dict·ee** (in-dī-tē′) *n.* — **in·dict′er**, **in·dict′or** *n.*

in·dic·tion (in-dik′shən) *n.* **1.** A fiscal period of fifteen years, introduced by Constantine, at the beginning of which property was assessed for taxation. **2.** The tax based on this assessment. **3.** A cycle of fifteen years used in Roman times to date ordinary happenings. **4.** Any particular year in such a cycle; also, the number designating it. [< L *indictio, -onis* < *indicere* to announce < *in-* in + *dicere* to say, tell]

in·dict·ment (in-dīt′mənt) *n.* **1.** The act of indicting, or the state of being indicted. **2.** *Law* A formal written charge of crime, preferred at the suit of the government and presented by a grand jury on oath to the court, as the basis for trial of the accused. [< AF *enditement*]

In·dies (in′dēz) **1.** The East Indies. **2.** The East Indies, India, and Indochina. **3.** The West Indies.

in·dif·fer·ence (in-dif′ər-əns) *n.* **1.** The state or quality of being indifferent; lack of concern; apathy. **2.** Unimportance; insignificance: It is a matter of *indifference* to me. **3.** Mediocrity. — **Syn.** See APATHY. Also **in·dif′fer·en·cy.**

in·dif·fer·ent (in-dif′ər-ənt) *adj.* **1.** Having no interest or feeling; unconcerned; apathetic. **2.** Lacking in distinction; mediocre: an *indifferent* performance. **3.** Only average in size, amount, etc. **4.** Having little importance or significance. **5.** Showing no preference; unbiased. **6.** Not active; inert: said of chemical compounds, electrical or magnetic properties, etc. **7.** *Biol.* Undifferentiated; not specialized, as some sorts of body tissue. [< OF *indifferent* < L *indifferens*. See IN-[1], DIFFERENT.] — **in·dif′fer·ent·ly** *adv.*

in·dif·fer·ent·ism (in-dif′ər-ən-tiz′əm) *n.* **1.** Systematic indifference. **2.** The doctrine that the differences in religious faiths are of no importance. — **in·dif′fer·ent·ist** *n.*

in·di·gence (in′də-jəns) *n.* The state of being indigent; poverty. Also **in′di·gen·cy.**

in·di·gene (in′də-jēn) *n.* A person, animal, or thing native to the soil or region; autochthon. Also **in′di·gen** (-jən, -jen). [< F *indigène.*]

in·dig·e·nous (in-dij′ə-nəs) *adj.* **1.** Originating or occurring naturally in the place or country specified; native; not exotic; autochthonous. **2.** Innate; inherent. — **Syn.** See NATIVE. Also **in·dig′e·nal.** [< LL *indigenus* < L *indigena* native < *indu-* within + *gen-*, root of *gignere* to be born] — **in·dig′e·nous·ly** *adv.* — **in·dig′e·nous·ness** *n.*

in·di·gent (in′də-jənt) *adj.* **1.** Lacking means of subsistence; needy; poor. **2.** *Archaic* Lacking; deficient: often with *of.* [< F < L *indigens, -entis,* ppr. of *indigere* to lack, want < *indu-* within + *egere* to need] — **in′di·gent·ly** *adv.*

in·di·gest·ed (in′də-jes′tid) *adj.* **1.** Not carefully thought over or considered. **2.** Disordered; confused. **3.** Unformed; shapeless. **4.** Not digested; undigested.

in·di·gest·i·ble (in′də-jes′tə-bəl) *adj.* Difficult to digest; not digestible. — **in′di·gest′i·bil′i·ty, in′di·gest′i·ble·ness** *n.* — **in′di·gest′i·bly** *adv.*

in·di·ges·tion (in′də-jes′chən) *n.* Difficulty in digesting food; dyspepsia. [< F]

in·dign (in-dīn′) *adj.* *Obs. & Poetic* **1.** Unworthy. **2.** Shameful; unseemly. **3.** Undeserved, as punishment. [< MF *indigne* < L *indignus* < *in-* not + *dignus* worthy]

in·dig·nant (in-dig′nənt) *adj.* Feeling or showing indignation. [< L *indignans, -antis,* ppr. of *indignari* to think unworthy < *indignus* unworthy] — **in·dig′nant·ly** *adv.*

in·dig·na·tion (in′dig-nā′shən) *n.* Anger aroused by injustice or baseness; righteous anger. — **Syn.** See ANGER. [< OF < L *indignatio, -onis* < pp. of *indignari* to think unworthy < *in-* not + *dignus* worthy]

in·dig·ni·ty (in-dig′nə-tē) *n.* *pl.* **·ties** **1.** An act that humiliates, degrades, or injures self-respect; affront; insult. **2.** *Obs.* Base character or conduct. **3.** *Obs.* Unworthiness. [< L *indignitas, -tatis* < *indignus* < *in-* not + *dignus* worthy]

in·di·go (in′də-gō) *n.* *pl.* **·gos** or **·goes** **1.** A blue coloring substance obtained especially from certain leguminous plants (genus *Indigofera*) or synthesized from various hydrocarbons. **2.** A deep violet blue. **3.** Any of various plants yielding a blue dyestuff; especially, the **indigo plant** (*I. tinctoria*), an important source of commercial indigo, and the **false** or **wild indigo** (genus *Baptisia*), having yellow or bluish flowers. — *adj.* Deep violet blue. Abbr. *ind.* [< Sp. < L *indicum* < Gk. *Indikon* (*pharmakon*) Indian (dye)]

indigo blue 1. Indigotin. **2.** The color indigo.

indigo bunting A finch (*Passerina cyanea*) of North America, the male of which is a brilliant indigo and the female brownish. Also **indigo bird.**

in·di·goid (in′də-goid) *adj.* Pertaining to or designating a class of vat dyes resembling indigo. — *n.* A dye of this type. [< INDIG(O) + -OID]

indigo snake The gopher snake (which see).

in·dig·o·tin (in-dig′ə-tin, in′də-gō′tin) *n.* A dark blue crystalline compound, $C_{16}H_{10}N_2O_2$, extracted from indican or made synthetically; indigo blue. [< INDIGO + *t* + -IN]

in·di·rect (in′də-rekt′) *adj.* **1.** Not following a direct line or path; roundabout: an *indirect* route. **2.** Not straightforward or open; underhand: *indirect* manipulation. **3.** Not coming as an immediate result, effect, etc.: *indirect* benefits. **4.** Not aimed directly, as a matter under consideration or a person involved: an *indirect* proof. **5.** Not proceeding through a direct line of succession, as an inheritance. **6.** *Mil.* Designating gunfire aimed at a target blocked from view, by sighting at a known aiming point. **7.** *Gram.* Not expressed in the exact words of the source: an *indirect* question. Abbr. *ind.* — **in′di·rect′ly** *adv.* — **in′di·rect′ness** *n.*

indirect discourse See under DISCOURSE.

in·di·rec·tion (in′də-rek′shən) *n.* **1.** Indirect method or practice. **2.** Dishonest dealing; deceit.

indirect lighting Lighting that is reflected, as from a white ceiling, or diffused to give a minimum of glare and shadow.

indirect object See under OBJECT.

indirect tax A tax, such as a customs duty, the burden of which is ultimately passed on to another, as in the form of higher market prices: distinguished from *direct tax.*

in·dis·cern·i·ble (in′di-sûr′nə-bəl, -zûr′-) *adj.* Incapable of being discerned; imperceptible. — **in′dis·cern′i·ble·ness** *n.* — **in′dis·cern′i·bly** *adv.*

in·dis·cov·er·a·ble (in′dis-kuv′ər-ə-bəl) *adj.* Incapable of being discovered. — **in′dis·cov′er·a·bil′i·ty** *n.*

in·dis·creet (in′dis-krēt′) *adj.* Lacking discretion; imprudent. — **in′dis·creet′ly** *adv.* — **in′dis·creet′ness** *n.*

in·dis·crete (in′dis-krēt′) *adj.* Not discrete; not separated; unified. — **in′dis·crete′ly** *adv.* — **in′dis·crete′ness** *n.*

in·dis·cre·tion (in′dis-kresh′ən) *n.* **1.** The state or quality of being indiscreet. **2.** An indiscreet act, speech, etc.

in·dis·crim·i·nate (in′dis-krim′ə-nit) *adj.* **1.** Showing no discrimination; not perceiving differences. **2.** Confused; chaotic. — **in′dis·crim′i·nate·ly** *adv.* — **in′dis·crim′i·nate·ness** *n.* — **in′dis·crim′i·nat′ing** *adj.* — **in′dis·crim′i·na′tion** *n.* — **in′dis·crim′i·na′tive** *adj.*

in·dis·pen·sa·ble (in′dis·pen′sə-bəl) *adj.* **1.** Not to be dispensed with; essential. **2.** Not to be set aside or ignored: an *indispensable* responsibility. — **Syn.** See NECESSARY. — *n.* An indispensable person or thing. — **in′dis·pen′sa·bil′i·ty, in′dis·pen′sa·ble·ness** *n.* — **in′dis·pen′sa·bly** *adv.*

in·dis·pose (in′dis-pōz′) *v.t.* **·posed, ·pos·ing 1.** To render unwilling or averse; disincline. **2.** To render unfit; disqualify. **3.** To make slightly ill or ailing.

in·dis·posed (in′dis-pōzd′) *adj.* **1.** Mildly ill; unwell. **2.** Disinclined; not willing. — **Syn.** See SICK[1].

in·dis·po·si·tion (in′dis-pə-zish′ən) *n.* **1.** Slight illness. **2.** The state of being disinclined; unwillingness.

in·dis·put·a·ble (in′dis-pyōō′tə-bəl, in-dis′pyōō-tə-bəl) *adj.* Incapable of being disputed; unquestionable. [< LL *indisputabilis*] — **in′dis·put′a·bil′i·ty, in′dis·put′a·ble·ness** *n.* — **in′dis·put′a·bly** *adv.*

in·dis·sol·u·ble (in′di-sol′yə-bəl, in-dis′ə-lyə-bəl) *adj.* **1.** Incapable of being dissolved, separated into its elements, or destroyed; extremely stable. **2.** Binding; extremely durable: an *indissoluble* link. [< L *indissolubilis*] — **in′dis·sol′u·bil′i·ty, in′dis·sol′u·ble·ness** *n.* — **in′dis·sol′u·bly** *adv.*

in·dis·tinct (in′dis-tingkt′) *adj.* **1.** Not clearly perceptible to the senses or mind; blurred; faint. **2.** Not readily distinguishable from something else; confused; vague. **3.** Not producing clear and well-defined impressions, images, etc.: *indistinct* eyesight. **4.** *Obs.* Indiscriminate. [< L *indistinctus*] — **in′dis·tinct′ly** *adv.* — **in′dis·tinct′ness** *n.*

in·dis·tinc·tive (in′dis-tingk′tiv) *adj.* **1.** Having no distinguishing qualities or characteristics; not distinctive. **2.** Incapable of distinguishing; undiscriminating. — **in′dis·tinc′tive·ly** *adv.* — **in′dis·tinc′tive·ness** *n.*

in·dis·tin·guish·a·ble (in′di-sting′gwish-ə-bəl) *adj.* Incapable of being perceived or distinguished. — **in′dis·tin′guish·a·ble·ness, in′dis·tin′guish·a·bil′i·ty** *n.* — **in′dis·tin′guish·a·bly** *adv.*

in·dite (in-dīt′) *v.t.* **·dit·ed, ·dit·ing 1.** *Archaic* To put into written words; compose; write. **2.** *Obs.* To direct (a person) to do something; enjoin. [< AF *enditer* to make known, inform < L *in-* in + *dictare* to declare. Akin to INDICT.] — **in·dite′ment** *n.* — **in·dit′er** *n.*

in·di·um (in′dē-əm) *n.* A soft, malleable, silver-white metallic element (symbol In), found in very small quantities in sphalerite and many other ores. See ELEMENT. [< NL < *indium* indigo + -IUM; with ref. to its spectrum color]

individ. Individual.

in·di·vid·u·al (in′də-vij′ōō-əl) *adj.* **1.** Existing as a unit; single. **2.** Separate, as distinguished from others of the same kind; particular: *individual* voters. **3.** Pertaining to or meant for a single person, animal, etc.: an *individual* serving. **4.** Differentiated from others by peculiar or distinctive characteristics: an *individual* style. **5.** *Obs.* Incapable of being divided; inseparable. — *n.* **1.** A single human being as distinct from others. **2.** A person. **3.** *Biol.* **a** A plant or animal existing and functioning independently. **b** A single member of a compound organism, especially one forming part of a hydrozoan colony. ◆ Although *individual* is often used as a synonym for *person,* many careful writers use it only when there is emphasis upon individuality or when a single person is in contrast with a body: The members of **a** group are also *individuals.* [< Med.L *individualis* < L *individuus* indivisible < *in-* not + *dividere* to divide] — **in/di·vid/u·al·ly** *adv.*

in·di·vid·u·al·ism (in/də·vij/ōō·əl·iz/əm) *n.* **1.** Personal independence in action, thought, interests, etc. **2.** The state of being separate or individual. **3.** Self-interest without regard for others. **4.** The social theory that emphasizes the importance of the individual, his rights, and independence of action. **5.** *Econ.* Laissez-faire. **6.** *Philos.* Egoism.

in·di·vid·u·al·ist (in/də·vij/ōō·əl·ist) *n.* **1.** One who is independent in character, action, thought, etc. **2.** One who advocates individualism. — **in/di·vid/u·al·is/tic** *adj.*

in·di·vid·u·al·i·ty (in/də·vij/ōō·al/ə·tē) *n.* *pl.* **·ties 1.** A quality or trait that distinguishes one person or thing from others; also, the sum or aggregate of such traits in one person or thing. **2.** Strikingly distinctive character or personality. **3.** The state of having separate, independent existence. **4.** *Archaic* The quality of indivisibility.

in·di·vid·u·al·ize (in/də·vij/ōō·əl·īz/) *v.t.* **·ized, ·iz·ing 1.** To make individual; give individual characteristics to; distinguish. **2.** To treat, mention, or consider individually; particularize. — **in/di·vid/u·al·i·za/tion** *n.*

in·di·vid·u·ate (in/də·vij/ōō·āt) *v.t.* **·at·ed, ·at·ing 1.** To distinguish from others; individualize. **2.** *Archaic* To give individuality to. [< Med.L *individuatus,* pp. of *individuare* < *individuus.* See INDIVIDUAL.]

in·di·vid·u·a·tion (in/də·vij/ōō·ā/shən) *n.* **1.** The action or process of making or becoming individual. **2.** The state of being an individual; individuality. **3.** *Zool.* The development of separate units of a compound organism, as in a colony of hydrozoans. **4.** *Philos.* The differentiation of the individual from the species and from every other individual. [< Med.L *individuatio, -onis*]

in·di·vis·i·ble (in/də·viz/ə·bəl) *adj.* Not divisible; incapable of being divided. — *n.* Something that is indivisible. — **in/di·vis/i·ble·ness, in/di·vis/i·bil/i·ty** *n.* — **in/di·vis/i·bly** *adv.*

Indo- *combining form* Indian: *Indonesia.* [< Gk. *Indos* Indian]

In·do-Ar·y·an (in/dō-âr/ē·ən) *adj.* Of or pertaining to the Indic branch of the Indo-Iranian subfamily of languages. — *n.* An Aryan of India. See ARYAN.

In·do·chi·na (in/dō-chī/na) **1.** The SE peninsula of Asia, comprising the Union of Burma, Cambodia, Laos, the Malay Peninsula, Thailand, North Vietnam and South Vietnam: sometimes *Farther India.* **2.** The states of Cambodia, Laos, North Vietnam and South Vietnam: formerly *French Indochina.* Also **Indo-China.**

In·do·chi·nese (in/dō-chī·nēz/, -nēs/) *adj.* Of or pertaining to Indochina, its inhabitants, or their language. — *n.* *pl.* **·nese 1.** A member of one of the Mongoloid peoples of Indochina. **2.** The Sino-Tibetan family of languages.

in·doc·ile (in·dos/əl) *adj.* Not docile; not submissive to discipline or instruction. — **in·do·cil·i·ty** (in/do·sil/ə·tē, -dō-) *n.*

in·doc·tri·nate (in·dok/trə·nāt) *v.t.* **·nat·ed, ·nat·ing** To instruct in doctrines, principles, or systems of belief; especially, to teach (a person or persons) partisan or sectarian dogmas. [< Med.L *in-* into + *doctrinare* to teach < L *doctrina* teaching < *docere* to teach] — **in·doc/tri·na/tion** *n.*

In·do-Eu·ro·pe·an (in/dō-yoŏr/ə·pē/ən) *n.* **1.** The largest family of languages in the world, comprising most of the languages of Europe and many languages of India and SW Asia. These languages are conventionally divided into two classifications. *centum* and *satem* (from the Latin and Avestan words for 'hundred'), primarily according to the representation of the proto-Indo-European palatalized velar (k) as velar stops in the *centum* (mainly western) division, and as sibilants in the *satem* (mainly eastern) division. The principal *centum* subfamilies are Hellenic, Italic, Celtic, and Germanic. The principal *satem* subfamilies are Indo-Iranian, Armenian, Albanian, and Balto-Slavic. A lesser-known, extinct language in the Indo-European family is Tocharian, generally classed with the *centum* languages. Among those scholars who consider the Hittite languages as Indo-European, Cuneiform Hittite is grouped with the *centum* languages, while Hieroglyphic Hittite is thought by some to be a *satem* language. See also THRACIAN, PHRYGIAN, LIGURIAN, ILLYRIAN, MESSAPIAN, and VENETIC. **2.** The assumed prehistoric parent language of this family of languages, now fairly well reconstructed by linguists. See also INDO HITTITE. — *adj.* Of or pertaining to the Indo-European family of languages, or to the peoples speaking them. Also *Aryan, Indo-Germanic.* Abbr. *IE, I.E.*

In·do-Ger·man·ic (in/dō-jər·man/ik) *n. & adj.* Indo-European: English form of a German term. Abbr. *I.G.*

In·do-Hit·tite (in/dō·hit/īt) *n.* A language hypothesized by some as the parent of both the Indo-European and Anatolian families. According to this theory, Hittite (or at least Cuneiform Hittite, the most prominent member of the Anatolian family) is a sister language to Indo-European, rather than an offspring of it.

In·do-I·ra·ni·an (in/dō·i·rā/nē·ən) *n.* A subfamily of the Indo-European family of languages, consisting of Indic and Iranian branches. — *adj.* Of or pertaining to this subfamily.

in·dole (in/dōl) *n. Chem.* A white, crystalline, malodorous compound, C_8H_7N, found in jasmine flowers, decomposing animal proteins, and certain albuminous compounds, and used in perfumery. Also **in/dol** (-dōl, -dol). [< IND(IGO) + -OLE]

in·do·lence (in/də·ləns) *n.* The state of being indolent. Also **in/do·len·cy.** [< L *indolentia* freedom from pain]

in·do·lent (in/də·lənt) *adj.* **1.** Averse to exertion or work; lazy; idle. **2.** *Pathol.* Attended by little or no pain: an *indolent* ulcer. [< LL *indolens, -entis* < *in-* not + *dolens,* ppr. of *dolere* to feel pain] — **in/do·lent·ly** *adv.*

in·dom·i·ta·ble (in·dom/i·tə·bəl) *adj.* Not easily defeated or subdued; persevering; stubborn: *indomitable* courage. [< LL *indomitabilis* < L < *in-* not + *domitare* to tame, intens. of *domare* to subdue] — **in·dom/i·ta·bly** *adv.*

In·do·ne·sia (in/də·nē/zhə, -shə) A Republic of SE Asia, comprising over 100 large and small islands of the Malay Archipelago and West New Guinea; 735,268 sq. mi.; pop. 119,572,-000 (1970); capital, Jakarta; formerly *Netherlands East Indies.* Officially **Republic of Indonesia.**

In·do·ne·sian (in/dō-nē/zhən, -shən) *n.* **1.** A citizen of the Republic of Indonesia. **2.** One of a small, light-brown-skinned people native throughout the Malay Peninsula and Archipelago, the Philippines, Sumatra, Java, etc., believed to be an admixture of Polynesian and Mongoloid stocks. **3.** A subfamily of the Austronesian family of languages spoken by these people, including Formosan, Igorot, Javanese, Malagasy, Malay, Tagalog, etc.: also called *Malayan.* — *adj.* Of or pertaining to Indonesia, its peoples, or their languages.

Indonesian Borneo See under BORNEO.

Indonesian Timor See under TIMOR.

in·door (in/dôr/, -dōr/) *adj.* **1.** Pertaining to or meant for the interior of a house or building. **2.** Located or performed within a house or building. [Earlier *within-door*]

in·doors (in/dôrz/, -dōrz/) *adv.* Inside or toward the inside of a building. [< INDOOR + -S[3]]

in·do·phe·nol (in/dō-fē/nōl) *n. Chem.* One of a series of quinone derivatives resembling indigo, used as a blue dye for cotton and wool. [< IND(IG)O + PHENOL]

In·dore (in·dôr/, -dōr/) **1.** A former princely state in west central India; 9,934 sq. mi. **2.** A city in western Madhya Pradesh; former capital of the state of Indore; pop. 395,035 (1961).

in·dorse (in·dôrs/), etc. See ENDORSE, etc.

in·dow (in·dou/), etc. See ENDOW, etc.

in·dox·yl (in·dok/sil) *n. Chem.* A crystalline compound, C_8H_7NO, formed from indican and used as an intermediate in the synthesis of indigo. [< IND(IGO) + (HYDR)OXYL]

In·dra (in/drə) In the early Hindu religion, the principal god of the firmament, thunder, and rain, who later is regarded as a god of the second rank: also called *Inda.*

in·draft (in/draft/, -dräft/) *n.* **1.** The act of drawing in; a pulling inwards. **2.** That which is drawn in; an inward flow, as of air. Also **in/draught/.**

in·drawn (in/drôn/) *adj.* **1.** Drawn in: *indrawn* breath. **2.** Abstracted; preoccupied.

in·dri (in/drē) *n.* A lemur of Madagascar; especially, a short-tailed species (*Indris brevicaudata*) about two feet long, having fur prevailingly black in color. [< F < Malagasy *indry* See there; mistaken for the name of the animal]

in·du·bi·ta·ble (in·dōō/bə·tə·bəl, -dyōō/-) *adj.* Not to be doubted; unquestionable; certain. [< MF] — **in·du/bi·ta·ble·ness** *n.* — **in·du/bi·ta·bly** *adv.*

induc. Induction.

in·duce (in·dōōs/, -dyōōs/) *v.t.* **·duced, ·duc·ing 1.** To cause to act, speak, etc., by convincing or other influence; persuade; prevail on: They *induced* him to accept. **2.** To bring on; produce; cause: a sickness *induced* by fatigue. **3.** To reach, as a conclusion, by an inductive process of reasoning. **4.** *Physics* To produce by induction, as an electric current or magnetic effect. [< L *inducere* to introduce < *in-* in + *ducere* to lead] — **in·duc/er** *n.* — **in·duc/i·ble** *adj.*

in·duce·ment (in·dōōs/mənt, -dyōōs/-) *n.* **1.** That which induces or is used for inducing; incentive. **2.** The act of inducing. **3.** *Law* **a** In a pleading, the allegations that introduce and explain the issue in dispute. **b** In the law of defamation, a bringing forth of the defamatory meaning of an utterance by proving facts not apparent on its face.

in·duct (in·dukt′) *v.t.* **1.** *U.S.* To bring (a draftee) into military service. **2.** To install formally in an office, benefice, etc.; inaugurate; invest. **3.** To initiate in knowledge, experience, etc.: with *to.* **4.** *Physics* To produce by induction; induce. [< L *inductus*, pp. of *inducere.* See INDUCE.]

in·duc·tance (in·duk′təns) *n. Electr.* **1.** The ability of a circuit to produce induction; the ratio of the increase in the magnetic flux of a circuit to the increase in the current producing it: expressed in henrys. **2.** Inductive reactance.

in·duc·tee (in′duk·tē′) *n.* One inducted or being inducted, as into military service.

in·duc·tile (in·duk′təl, -til) *adj.* **1.** Not ductile; not malleable. **2.** Not submissive; unyielding. **— in·duc·til′i·ty** *n.*

in·duc·tion (in·duk′shən) *n.* **1.** The act of inducting or state of being inducted; installation. **2.** The act of inducing or causing; a producing. **3.** The bringing forward of separate facts as evidence in order to prove a general statement. **4.** *Electr.* The production of magnetization or electrification in a body by the mere proximity of a magnetic field or electric charge, or of an electric current in a conductor by the variation of the magnetic field in its vicinity. **5.** *Logic* **a** The process of inferring or aiming at a general principle or law from observation of particular instances. **b** A conclusion reached by this process. Compare DEDUCTION. **6.** *Physiol.* The stimulating effect of one tissue upon the growth or alteration of another. **7.** *Archaic* A preface. **— Syn.** See INFERENCE. [< OF < L *inductio, -onis*] **— in·duc′tion·al** *adj.*

induction coil *Electr.* A device, consisting of two concentric coils and an interrupter, that changes a low steady voltage into a high intermittent alternating voltage by electromagnetic induction, and is most often used as a spark coil.

in·duc·tive (in·duk′tiv) *adj.* **1.** Pertaining to, proceeding by, or resulting from induction: *inductive* reasoning. **2.** *Electr.* Produced by or causing induction or inductance. **3.** *Rare* Introductory. [< LL *inductivus*] **— in·duc′tive·ly** *adv.* **— in·duc′tive·ness** *n.*

inductive reactance *Electr.* That element of reactance in a circuit caused by self-induction, equal to $2\pi fl$, where *f* is the frequency of the current and *l* is the inductance, and expressed in ohms. See IMPEDANCE.

in·duc·tiv·i·ty (in′duk·tiv′ə·tē) *n. Electr.* **1.** Specific capability for induction. **2.** Inductance (def. 1).

in·duc·tor (in·duk′tər) *n.* **1.** One who or that which inducts. **2.** *Electr.* Any part of an electrical apparatus that acts inductively upon another. [< L]

in·due (in·dōō′, -dyōō′) See ENDUE.

in·dulge (in·dulj′) *v.* ·dulged, ·dulg·ing *v.t.* **1.** To yield to or gratify, as desires or whims: to *indulge* a love of good food. **2.** To yield to or gratify the desires, whims, etc., of; humor: to *indulge* a child. **3.** In business, to grant more time (to someone) for payment of a bill. **4.** *Eccl.* To grant an indulgence to. **5.** *Obs.* To grant as a privilege or favor. **— v.i. 6.** To gratify one's own desire; indulge oneself: with *in.* **— Syn.** See PAMPER. [< L *indulgere* to be kind to, ? < *in-*, intens. + *-dulgere*, akin to Gk. *dolichos* long] **— in·dulg′er** *n.*

in·dul·gence (in·dul′jəns) *n.* **1.** The act of indulging or state of being indulgent. **2.** That which is indulged in. **3.** Something granted as a favor. **4.** In business, permission to defer paying a bill, fulfilling a contract, etc. **5.** In the Roman Catholic Church, remission of temporal punishment due for a sin after it has been forgiven through sacramental absolution. **6.** In English history, the granting through royal proclamation (**Declaration of Indulgence**) of a larger measure of religious freedom to Nonconformists, especially during the reigns of Charles II and James II. Also **in·dul′gen·cy.** [< OF < L *indulgentia*]

in·dul·gent (in·dul′jənt) *adj.* Prone to indulge; lenient. [< L *indulgens, -entis*, ppr. of *indulgere* to concede. See INDULGE.] **— in·dul′gent·ly** *adv.*

in·du·line (in′dyə·lēn, -lin) *n. Chem.* Any one of an extensive group of coal-tar dyestuffs yielding a deep indigo color. Also **in′du·lin** (-lin). [< IND(IGO) + -UL(E) + -INE²]

in·dult (in·dult′) *n.* In the Roman Catholic Church, an indulgence or privilege granted by the Pope as exemption from some canonical or ecclesiastical duty. [< LL *indultum* < *indultus*, pp. of *indulgere* to concede. See INDULGE.]

in·du·pli·cate (in·dōō′plə·kit, -dyōō′-) *adj. Bot.* Having the edges turned or folded inward without overlapping: said of calyx or corolla in a flower bud, or of leaves in a leaf bud. Also **in·du′pli·ca·tive.** **— in·du′pli·ca′tion** *n.*

in·du·rate (*v.* in′dōō·rāt, -dyōō-; *adj.* in′dōō·rit, -dyōō-) *v.t. & v.i.* ·rat·ed, ·rat·ing **1.** To make or become hard or unfeeling. **2.** To make or become hardy; inure. **— adj.** Hard or hardened; unfeeling: also **in′du·rat′ed.** [< L *induratus*, pp. of *indurare* to make hard. See ENDURE.] **— in′du·ra′tion** *n.* **— in′du·ra′tive** *adj.*

In·dus (in′dəs) A river flowing about 1,900 miles, NW through western Tibet and Kashmir and generally SW through West Pakistan, to the Arabian Sea.

In·dus (in′dəs) *n.* A constellation, the Indian. See CONSTELLATION. [< L]

in·du·si·um (in·dōō′zē·əm, -zhē-, -dyōō′-) *n. pl.* **·si·a** (-zē·ə, -zhē·ə) **1.** *Bot.* An outgrowth of a fern leaf covering the immature sori or fruit clusters. **2.** *Biol.* Any membranous envelope, as the larval case of an insect, the amnion, etc. [< L, tunic < *induere* to put on; infl. in form by Gk. *endysis* dress, garment < *endyein* to put on] **— in·du′si·al** *adj.*

in·dus·tri·al (in·dus′trē·əl) *adj.* **1.** Of, characteristic of, or resulting from industry or industrial products. **2.** Engaged in industry: an *industrial* worker. **3.** Having many industries: an *industrial* area. **4.** Intended for use in industry. **5.** Relating to, affecting, or benefiting workers in industry. **— n. 1.** *pl.* Stocks or securities of enterprises in industry. **2.** *Rare* A person engaged in industry. Abbr. *ind.* [< F *industriel* and Med.L *industrialis*] **— in·dus′tri·al·ly** *adv.*

industrial arts The technical skills used in industry, especially as subjects of study in schools.

industrial design The esthetic and practical design of industrial products; also, the study of such design.

industrial disease A disease or disabling condition affecting workers in a particular industry.

industrial engineer An engineer who supervises production in factories, lays out machinery, determines work flow by time and motion studies, etc.

in·dus·tri·al·ism (in·dus′trē·əl·iz′əm) *n.* An economic system based chiefly on large-scale industries and production of goods rather than on agriculture, foreign trade, etc.

in·dus·tri·al·ist (in·dus′trē·əl·ist) *n.* A person important in the ownership or management of industry.

in·dus·tri·al·ize (in·dus′trē·əl·īz′) *v.t.* ·ized, ·iz·ing **1.** To establish large-scale industries in; render industrial: to *industrialize* an area. **2.** To make or form into an industry. Also *Brit.* **in·dus′tri·a·lise′.** **— in·dus′tri·al·i·za′tion** *n.*

industrial relations The relations between management and employees in industrial concerns; also, the administration and conduct of such relations.

industrial revolution 1. The changes resulting from the replacement of handicraft production by machine and factory production. **2.** *Often cap.* The period of the change to industrial production, beginning in the mid-18th century in England, and later in other countries.

industrial school 1. A school for teaching manual and industrial arts. **2.** An institution to which delinquent or neglected young persons are committed by the court for education and training.

industrial union A labor union to which all workers in a particular industry may belong: also called *vertical union.* Compare CRAFT UNION.

Industrial Workers of the World A syndicalistic labor organization founded at Chicago in 1905 and continuing until the early 1920's. Abbr. *IWW, I.W.W.*

in·dus·tri·ous (in·dus′trē·əs) *adj.* **1.** Characterized by or showing assiduity in work or effort; hard-working; diligent. **2.** *Obs.* Skillful; clever. **— Syn.** See BUSY. [< F *industrieux* < L *industrius.* See INDUSTRY.] **— in·dus′tri·ous·ly** *adv.* **— in·dus′tri·ous·ness** *n.*

in·dus·try (in′dəs·trē) *n. pl.* **·tries 1.** Any specific branch of production or manufacture: the automobile *industry.* **2.** Manufacturing and productive interests collectively, as distinguished from agriculture and from labor. **3.** Diligent and regular application to work or tasks; assiduity. **4.** *Obs.* Ingenuity; skill. [< MF *industrie* < L *industria* diligence < *industrius* diligent, ? ult. < *struere* to construct, pile up]

in·dwell (in′dwel′) *v.* ·dwelt, ·dwel·ling *v.t.* **1.** To dwell in; inhabit. **— v.i. 2.** To dwell; abide: with *in.* **— in′dwell′er** *n.* **— in′dwell′ing** *n.*

In·dy (dan′·dē′), **d'** See D'INDY.

-ine¹ *suffix* Like; pertaining to; of the nature of: *marine, canine.* [< F *-in, -ine* < L *-inus*, adj. suffix]

-ine² *suffix* **1.** *Chem.* **a** Used in the names of halogens: *bromine, fluorine.* **b** Used to indicate an alkaloid or basic substance: *morphine, aniline.* **c** Var. of -IN. **2.** Used in names of commercial products: *brilliantine.* [Special use of -INE¹]

-ine³ *suffix* **1.** Used to form feminine words, names, and titles: *heroine, Josephine.* **2.** Used to form originally feminine abstract nouns: *medicine, doctrine.* [< F < L *-ina*, suffix of fem. nouns < Gk. *-inē*; or directly < L or < Gk.]

-ine⁴ *suffix* Like; resembling: *crystalline.* [< L *-inus* < Gk. *-inos*]

in·earth (in·ûrth′) *v.t. Poetic* To place in the earth; bury.

in·e·bri·ant (in·ē′brē·ənt) *adj.* Intoxicating. **— n.** Anything that intoxicates.

in·e·bri·ate (*v.* in·ē′brē·āt; *n. & adj.* in·ē′brē·it, -āt) *v.t.* ·at·ed, ·at·ing **1.** To make drunk; intoxicate. **2.** To exhilarate; excite. **— n.** A habitual drunkard. **— adj.** Intoxicated. [< L *inebriatus*, pp. of *inebriare* to intoxicate < *in-* thoroughly + *ebriare* to make drunk < *ebrius* drunk]

in·e·bri·at·ed (in·ē′brē·ā′tid) *adj.* Intoxicated; drunk.

in·e·bri·a·tion (in·ē′brē·ā′shən) *n.* The act of inebriating or the state of being inebriated; intoxication; drunkenness. Also **in·e·bri·e·ty** (in′ē·brī′ə·tē). [< L *inebriatio, -onis*]

in·ed·i·ble (in·ed′ə·bəl) *adj.* Not edible; uneatable; unsuitable as food. **— in·ed′i·bil′i·ty** *n.*

in·ed·i·ted (in·ed/it·id) *adj.* **1.** Not published. **2.** Not edited.

in·ef·fa·ble (in·ef/ə·bəl) *adj.* **1.** Too overpowering to be expressed in words; unutterable: *ineffable* joy. **2.** Too lofty or sacred to be uttered: the *ineffable* name of Jehovah. **3.** Indescribable; indefinable. [< MF < L *ineffabilis* < *in-* not + *effabilis* utterable < *effari* < *ex-* out + *fari* to speak] — **in·ef/fa·bil/i·ty, in·ef/fa·ble·ness** *n.* — **in·ef/fa·bly** *adv.*

in·ef·face·a·ble (in/i·fā/sə·bəl) *adj.* Not effaceable; ineradicable. — **in·ef·face/a·bil/i·ty** *n.* — **in·ef·face/a·bly** *adv.*

in·ef·fec·tive (in/i·fek/tiv) *adj.* **1.** Not effective; not producing the effect expected. **2.** Incompetent: an *ineffective* teacher. — **in·ef·fec/tive·ly** *adv.* — **in·ef·fec/tive·ness** *n.*

in·ef·fec·tu·al (in/i·fek/chōō·əl) *adj.* **1.** Not effectual; not able to produce a proper or intended effect. **2.** Unsuccessful; fruitless: an *ineffectual* attempt. — **in·ef·fec/tu·al/i·ty, in·ef·fec/tu·al·ness** *n.* — **in·ef·fec/tu·al·ly** *adv.*

in·ef·fi·ca·cious (in·ef/ə·kā/shəs) *adj.* Not efficacious; not producing the effect desired or intended, as a medicine. — **in·ef/fi·ca/cious·ly** *adv.* — **in·ef/fi·ca/cious·ness** *n.*

in·ef·fi·ca·cy (in·ef/ə·kə·sē) *n.* The state or quality of being inefficacious.

in·ef·fi·cien·cy (in/i·fish/ən·sē) *n.* The state or quality of being inefficient.

in·ef·fi·cient (in/i·fish/ənt) *adj.* **1.** Not efficient; not performing a function directly and economically; wasteful. **2.** Lacking in capability; incompetent. — **in·ef/fi/cient·ly** *adv.*

in·e·las·tic (in/i·las/tik) *adj.* Not elastic; inflexible; unadaptable. — **in·e·las·tic·i·ty** (in/i·las·tis/ə·tē) *n.*

in·el·e·gance (in·el/ə·gəns) *n.* **1.** The quality of being inelegant. **2.** Something inelegant. — **in·el/e·gant·ly** *adv.*

in·el·e·gan·cy (in·el/ə·gən·sē) *n., pl.* **·cies** Inelegance.

in·el·e·gant (in·el/ə·gənt) *adj.* **1.** Not elegant; lacking in beauty, polish, grace, refinement, etc. **2.** Coarse; crude; vulgar. — **in·el/e·gant·ly** *adv.*

in·el·i·gi·ble (in·el/ə·jə·bəl) *adj.* Not eligible; not qualified or suitable for some position, function, etc. — *n.* One who is not eligible. — **in·el/i·gi·bil/i·ty** *n.* — **in·el/i·gi·bly** *adv.*

in·el·o·quent (in·el/ə·kwənt) *adj.* Not eloquent; not persuasive. — **in·el/o·quence** *n.* — **in·el/o·quent/ly** *adv.*

in·e·luc·ta·ble (in/i·luk/tə·bəl) *adj.* Not to be escaped from or avoided; inevitable. [< L *ineluctabilis* < *in-* not + *eluctabilis* resistible < *eluctari* to struggle out < *luctari* to struggle] — **in/e·luc/ta·bil/i·ty** *n.* — **in/e·luc/ta·bly** *adv.*

in·e·lud·i·ble (in/i·lōōd/ə·bəl) *adj.* Not to be eluded; inescapable. — **in/e·lud/i·bil/i·ty** *n.* — **in/e·lud/i·bly** *adv.*

in·ept (in·ept/) *adj.* **1.** Not suitable or appropriate; out of place. **2.** Clumsy; awkward; incompetent. [< L *ineptus* < *in-* not + *aptus* fit] — **in·ept/ly** *adv.* — **in·ept/ness** *n.*

in·ep·ti·tude (in·ep/tə·tōōd, -tyōōd) *n.* **1.** The state or quality of being inept. **2.** An inept act or remark.

in·e·qual·i·ty (in/i·kwol/ə·tē) *n., pl.* **·ties** **1.** The state or quality of being unequal. **2.** An instance of this. **3.** Lack of evenness of proportion; variableness: *inequalities* of climate. **4.** Disparity of social position, opportunity, justice, etc. **5.** *Math.* A statement that two quantities are not equal, made by placing the sign ≠ between them, or by the sign > or <, the angle being toward smaller quantity. — *Syn.* See DISPARITY. [< OF *inequalite* < L *inaequalitas*]

in·eq·ui·ta·ble (in·ek/wə·tə·bəl) *adj.* Not equitable; unfair. — **in·eq/ui·ta·bly** *adv.*

in·eq·ui·ty (in·ek/wə·tē) *n., pl.* **·ties** **1.** Lack of equity; injustice. **2.** An unfair act or course of action.

in·e·rad·i·ca·ble (in/i·rad/ə·kə·bəl) *adj.* Not eradicable; impossible to remove or root out. — **in/e·rad/i·ca·bly** *adv.*

in·e·ras·a·ble (in/i·rā/sə·bəl) *adj.* Not erasable; impossible to erase or rub out. — **in/e·ras/a·bly** *adv.*

in·er·ra·ble (in·er/ə·bəl, -ûr/-) *adj.* Incapable of error; infallible. [< LL *inerrabilis* < *in-* not + *errare* to err] — **in·er/ra·bil/i·ty, in·er/ra·ble·ness** *n.* — **in·er/ra·bly** *adv.*

in·er·rant (in·er/ənt, -ûr/-) *adj.* Free from error; unerring. — **in·er/ran·cy** *n.*

in·er·rat·ic (in/i·rat/ik) *adj.* Not erratic; following a fixed course.

in·ert (in·ûrt/) *adj.* **1.** Lacking independent power to move or to resist applied force. **2.** Disinclined to move or act; sluggish. **3.** *Chem.* Devoid of active properties; unable or unlikely to form compounds: an *inert* gas. [< L *iners, inertis* < *in-* not + *ars, artis* art] — **in·ert/ly** *adv.* — **in·ert/ness** *n.*

in·er·tia (in·ûr/shə) *n.* **1.** The state of being inert; inactivity; sluggishness. **2.** *Physics* The property of matter by virtue of which any physical body persists in its state of rest or of uniform motion until acted upon by some external force. [< L, idleness] — **in·er/tial** *adj.*

inertial guidance The determination of the course or position of a ship, aircraft, missile, etc., by a built-in gyroscopic or other device that detects any change in direction or speed. Also **inertial navigation.**

in·es·cap·a·ble (in/ə·skā/pə·bəl) *adj.* Impossible to escape; unavoidable; ineluctable. — **in/es·cap/a·bly** *adv.*

in es·se (in es/ē) *Latin* In being; actually existing: distinguished from *in posse.*

in·es·sen·tial (in/i·sen/shəl) *adj.* **1.** Not essential; unessential. **2.** *Rare* Without substance; immaterial. — *n.* Something inessential. — **in/es·sen/ti·al/i·ty** *n.*

in·es·ti·ma·ble (in·es/tə·mə·bəl) *adj.* **1.** Not to be estimated or computed; immeasurable. **2.** Having great value; priceless. — **in·es/ti·ma·bly** *adv.*

in·ev·i·ta·ble (in·ev/ə·tə·bəl) *adj.* That cannot be avoided or prevented from happening; unavoidable; certain. — *n.* Something inevitable. [< L *inevitabilis* < *in-* not + *evitare* to avoid < *ex-* out of + *vitare* to avoid] — **in·ev/i·ta·bil/i·ty, in·ev/i·ta·ble·ness** *n.* — **in·ev/i·ta·bly** *adv.*

in·ex·act (in/ig·zakt/) *adj.* Not exact; not completely accurate or true. — **in/ex·act/ly** *adv.* — **in/ex·act/ness** *n.*

in·ex·act·i·tude (in/ig·zak/tə·tōōd, -tyōōd) *n.* Condition or quality of being inexact; inexactness.

in·ex·cus·a·ble (in/ik·skyōō/zə·bəl) *adj.* Not excusable; impossible to excuse or justify. — **in·ex·cus/a·bil/i·ty, in·ex·cus/a·ble·ness** *n.* — **in·ex·cus/a·bly** *adv.*

in·ex·e·cu·tion (in/ek·sə·kyōō/shən) *n.* Lack or failure of execution; nonperformance.

in·ex·er·tion (in/ig·zûr/shən) *n.* Lack of exertion; failure to exert oneself.

in·ex·haust·i·ble (in/ig·zôs/tə·bəl) *adj.* **1.** Incapable of being exhausted or used up; unending. **2.** Incapable of fatigue; tireless: an *inexhaustible* talker. — **in·ex·haust/i·bil/i·ty, in/ex·haust/i·ble·ness** *n.* — **in·ex·haust/i·bly** *adv.*

in·ex·is·tent (in/ig·zis/tənt) *adj.* Not existing; nonexistent. — **in/ex·ist/ence, in/ex·ist/en·cy** *n.*

in·ex·o·ra·ble (in·ek/sər·ə·bəl) *adj.* **1.** Not to be moved by entreaty or persuasion; unyielding. **2.** Unalterable; relentless. [< L *inexorabilis.* See IN-[1], EXORABLE.] — **in·ex/o·ra·bil/i·ty, in·ex/o·ra·ble·ness** *n.* — **in·ex/o·ra·bly** *adv.*

in·ex·pe·di·ent (in/ik·spē/dē·ənt) *adj.* Not expedient; unsuited to a particular purpose; inadvisable. — **in/ex·pe/di·ence, in/ex·pe/di·en·cy** *n.* — **in/ex·pe/di·ent·ly** *adv.*

in·ex·pen·sive (in/ik·spen/siv) *adj.* Not expensive; costing little. — **in/ex·pen/sive·ly** *adv.* — **in/ex·pen/sive·ness** *n.*

in·ex·pe·ri·ence (in/ik·spir/ē·əns) *n.* Lack of experience or of the knowledge derived from experience.

in·ex·pe·ri·enced (in/ik·spir/ē·ənst) *adj.* Not experienced; lacking in the skill and knowledge derived from experience.

in·ex·pert (in·ek/spûrt) *adj.* Not expert; unskilled; inept. — **in·ex/pert·ly** *adv.* — **in·ex/pert·ness** *n.*

in·ex·pi·a·ble (in·ek/spē·ə·bəl) *adj.* **1.** Incapable of being expiated or atoned for; unpardonable. **2.** *Archaic* Unappeasable; implacable: *inexpiable* wrath.

in·ex·plain·a·ble (in/ik·splān/ə·bəl) *adj.* Not explainable; incapable of explanation; inexplicable.

in·ex·pli·ca·ble (in·eks/pli·kə·bəl, in/iks·plik/ə·bəl) *adj.* Not explicable; impossible to explain; inexplainable. — **in·ex/pli·ca·bil/i·ty, in·ex/pli·ca·ble·ness** *n.* — **in·ex/pli·ca·bly** *adv.*

in·ex·plic·it (in/ik·splis/it) *adj.* Not explicit; not clearly set forth; vague. — **in/ex·plic/it·ly** *adv.* — **in/ex·plic/it·ness** *n.*

in·ex·press·i·ble (in/ik·spres/ə·bəl) *adj.* Incapable of being expressed or put into words. — **in/ex·press/i·bil/i·ty, in/ex·press/i·ble·ness** *n.* — **in/ex·press/i·bly** *adv.*

in·ex·pres·sive (in/ik·spres/iv) *adj.* **1.** Not expressive; lacking expression; expressionless. **2.** *Archaic* Inexpressible. — **in/ex·pres/sive·ly** *adv.* — **in/ex·pres/sive·ness** *n.*

in·ex·pug·na·ble (in/iks·pug/nə·bəl) *adj.* Not to be taken by force; impregnable. [< OF < L *inexpugnabilis* < *in-* not + *ex-* intens. + *pugnare* to fight] — **in/ex·pug/na·bil/i·ty, in/ex·pug/na·ble·ness** *n.* — **in/ex·pug/na·bly** *adv.*

in·ex·ten·si·ble (in/ik·stens/ə·bəl) *adj.* Not extensible; incapable of being extended. — **in/ex·ten/si·bil/i·ty** *n.*

in ex·ten·so (in ik·sten/sō) *Latin* At full length; fully.

in·ex·tin·guish·a·ble (in/ik·sting/gwish·ə·bəl) *adj.* Incapable of being extinguished; unquenchable. — **in/ex·tin/guish·a·ble·ness** *n.* — **in/ex·tin/guish·a·bly** *adv.*

in·ex·tir·pa·ble (in/ik·stûr/pə·bəl) *adj.* Impossible to extirpate or root out; ineradicable. [< L *inextirpabilis*]

in ex·tre·mis (in ik·trē/mis) *Latin* At the point of death.

in·ex·tri·ca·ble (in·eks/tri·kə·bəl) *adj.* **1.** Impossible to extricate oneself from: an *inextricable* set of circumstances. **2.** Impossible to disentangle or undo, as a knot. **3.** Too intricate to be solved or made clear. [< L *inextricabilis* < *in-* not + *extricare*. See EXTRICATE.] — **in·ex/tri·ca·bil/i·ty, in·ex/tri·ca·ble·ness** *n.* — **in·ex/tri·ca·bly** *adv.*

inf. 1. Below (L *infra*). **2.** Inferior. **3.** Infinitive. **4.** Information.

Inf. or **inf.** Infantry.

in·fal·li·ble (in·fal/ə·bəl) *adj.* **1.** Exempt from fallacy or error of judgment, as in opinion or statement. **2.** Not liable to fail; unfailing; sure: an *infallible* remedy. **3.** In Roman Catholic doctrine, incapable of error in matters of faith and morals: said especially of the Pope speaking ex cathedra. — *n.* One who or that which is infallible. — **in·fal/li·bil/i·ty, in·fal/li·ble·ness** *n.* — **in·fal/li·bly** *adv.*

in·fa·mous (in/fə·məs) *adj.* **1.** Having a vile reputation; notoriously bad. **2.** Deserving or producing infamy; odious: an *infamous* act. **3.** *Law* a Denoting a crime, such as treason, felony, perjury, etc., punishable by imprisonment in a penitentiary. **b** Convicted of an infamous crime. [< Med.L *infamosus* < L *infamis* < *in-* not + *fama* fame < *fari* to speak] — **in·fa·mous·ly** *adv.* — **in·fa·mous·ness** *n.*

in·fa·my (in′fə-mē) *n. pl.* **·mies 1.** Lack of honor or good reputation; public disgrace; evil notoriety. **2.** The state or quality of being infamous. **3.** An infamous act. **4.** *Law* The impaired legal and civil status of a person convicted of an infamous crime.

in·fan·cy (in′fən-sē) *n. pl.* **·cies 1.** The state or period of being an infant; babyhood. **2.** The earliest beginnings of anything. **3.** The period of being a minor.

in·fant (in′fənt) *n.* **1.** A child in the earliest stages of life; a baby. **2.** *Law* One who has not attained the age of legal majority, usually 21; a minor. — *adj.* **1.** Of or typical of infancy or infants. **2.** Beginning to exist or develop; nascent. [< OF *enfant* < L *infans, -antis* not speaking < *in-* not + *fans, fantis,* ppr. of *fari* to speak] — **in′fant·hood** *n.*

in·fan·ta (in-fan′tə) *n.* **·** A daughter of a Spanish or Portuguese king. [< Sp., infant (fem.) < L *infans.* See INFANT.]

in·fan·te (in-fan′tā) *n.* A son, except the eldest, of a Spanish or Portuguese king. [< Sp., infant (masc.) < L *infans.* See INFANT.]

in·fan·ti·cide (in-fan′tə-sīd) *n.* **1.** The killing of an infant, especially at birth. **2.** One who has killed an infant. [< F < LL *infanticidium* < L *infans, -antis* child + *caedere* to kill]

in·fan·tile (in′fən-til, -til) *adj.* **1.** Of or pertaining to infancy or infants: an *infantile* disease. **2.** Like or characteristic of infancy or infants; babyish. **3.** Being at the earliest stage of development. **4.** *Psychoanal.* Characterized by infantilism. Also **in′fan·tine** (-tīn, -tin). — **Syn.** See CHILDISH. [< L *infantilis*]

infantile paralysis Poliomyelitis.

infantile scurvy *Pathol.* A deficiency disease of young children characterized by foul breath, diarrhea, anemia, hemorrhages, etc.: also called *Barlow's disease.*

in·fan·til·ism (in-fan′tə-liz-əm) *n.* **1.** Abnormal persistence of infantile mental and physical characteristics into adult life, together with a lack of sexual development. **2.** Behavior in an adult indicating a lack of emotional maturity.

in·fan·try (in′fən-trē) *n. pl.* **·tries** Soldiers, units, or a branch of an army trained and equipped to fight on foot, with relatively light weapons. *Abbr. inf., Inf.* [< F *infanterie* < Ital. *infanteria* < *infante* boy, page, foot soldier < L *infans, infantis* child]

in·fan·try·man (in′fən-trē-mən) *n. pl.* **·men** (-mən) A soldier of the infantry.

in·farct (in′färkt) *n. Pathol.* A portion of tissue that has been completely deprived of its blood supply by an embolus and is consequently undergoing necrosis. [< Med.L *infarctus* < L *infartus,* pp. of *infarcire* < *in-* in + *farcire* to stuff]

in·farc·tion (in-färk′shən) *Pathol.* **1.** The forming of an infarct. **2.** An infarct.

in·fat·u·ate (*v.* in-fach′ōō-āt; *for adj., also* in-fach′ōō-it) *v.t.* **·at·ed, ·at·ing 1.** To inspire with a foolish and unreasoning love or passion. **2.** To make foolish or fatuous. — *adj.* Infatuated. [< L *infatuatus,* pp. of *infatuare* to make a fool of < *in-* intens. + *fatuus* foolish] — **in·fat′u·a′tion** *n.*

in·fat·u·at·ed (in-fach′ōō-ā-tid) *adj.* **1.** Possessed by a foolish passion, especially one for another person. **2.** Made fatuous; possessed by folly. — **in·fat′u·at·ed·ly** *adv.*

in·fea·si·ble (in-fē′zə-bəl) *adj.* Not feasible; impracticable. — **in·fea′si·bil′i·ty, in·fea′si·ble·ness** *n.*

in·fect (in-fekt′) *v.t.* **1.** To affect or infuse with disease-producing organisms, as a wound or part of the body. **2.** To cause (a person, etc.) to contract a communicable disease. **3.** To contaminate with impurities or harmful properties; pollute. **4.** To affect or inspire, as with attitudes or beliefs, especially harmfully; to exert an influence upon. — **Syn.** See POLLUTE. [< L *infectus,* pp. of *inficere* to dip into, stain < *in-* in + *facere* to do, make] — **in·fec′tor** or **in·fect′er** *n.*

in·fec·tion (in-fek′shən) *n.* **1.** An injurious invasion of body tissue by disease-producing organisms. **2.** A disease or other harmful condition resulting from an invasion of body tissue by injurious organisms; also, the region affected by such a condition; festering. **3.** The communication or transference of a disease, idea, mood, etc.: *infection* by airborne bacteria; *infection* by propaganda. **4.** *Rare* An agency that infects, as a microbe, mood, principle, etc.: to clear the air of *infections.* — **Syn.** See CONTAGION. [< OF]

in·fec·tious (in-fek′shəs) *adj.* **1.** Liable to produce infection; carrying disease-producing organisms. **2.** Denoting diseases communicable by infection. **3.** Tending to excite similar reactions in others: *infectious* laughter. **4.** *Law* Tainting with illegality; rendering liable to confiscation. **5.** *Obs.* Infected. — **in·fec′tious·ly** *adv.* — **in·fec′tious·ness** *n.*

infectious disease Any disease that is due to the growth and action of microorganisms or parasites in the body, and that may or may not be contagious.

infectious hepatitis See HEPATITIS.

infectious mononucleosis *Pathol.* An acute communicable disease marked by fever, sore throat, a swelling of the lymph nodes, especially in the neck, and an increase in mononuclear cells: also called *glandular fever.*

in·fec·tive (in-fek′tiv) *adj.* Liable to produce infection; infectious. [< L *infectivus*]

in·fe·cund (in-fē′kənd, -fek′ənd) *adj.* Not fecund; not fruitful; barren. — **in·fe·cun·di·ty** (in′fi-kun′də-tē) *n.*

in·fe·lic·i·tous (in′fə-lis′ə-təs) *adj.* Not felicitous, happy, or suitable in application, condition, or result. — **in′fe·lic′i·tous·ly** *adv.* — **in′fe·lic′i·tous·ness** *n.*

in·fe·lic·i·ty (in′fə-lis′ə-tē) *n. pl.* **·ties 1.** The state or quality of being infelicitous. **2.** That which is infelicitous, as an inappropriate remark, etc. [< L *infelicitas, -tatis*]

in·feoff (in-fēf′), **in·feoff·ment** (in-fēf′mənt) See ENFEOFF, etc.

in·fer (in-fûr′) *v.* **·ferred, ·fer·ring** *v.t.* **1.** To derive by reasoning; conclude or accept from evidence or premises; deduce. **2.** To involve or imply as a conclusion; give evidence of: said of facts, statements, etc. **3.** Loosely, to imply; hint. — *v.i.* **4.** To draw an inference. [< L *inferre* to bring into < *in-* in + *ferre* to bring, carry] — **in·fer′a·ble** *adj.* — **in·fer′a·bly** *adv.*

◆ **infer, imply** *Infer* and *imply* both mean to involve as a necessary consequence, and in this sense they are often used interchangeably: An effect *infers* a cause; an effect *implies* a cause. In other senses the two words differ. *Infer* also means to derive or conclude by reasoning: I *inferred* from the noise that you were at home. *Imply,* on the other hand, means to suggest implicitly something that might be *inferred* by an observer: The noise *implied* that you were at home. *Infer* stresses the use of reason in reaching a conclusion, whereas *imply,* the more general term, may be applied also to conclusions that are suggested or presumed.

in·fer·ence (in′fər-əns) *n.* **1.** That which is inferred; a deduction or conclusion. **2.** The act or process of inferring. **3.** Loosely, a conjecture. [< Med.L *inferentia* < L *inferens, -entis,* ppr. of *inferre.* See INFER.]

— Syn. 1. *Inference, induction,* and *deduction* are processes of reasoning. *Inference* is the comprehensive term for the formal drawing of conclusions; it includes both *induction* and *deduction.* *Induction* is the *inferring* of a universal or general rule from particular instances. *Deduction* is the reverse process of drawing a conclusion as to a particular instance from general premises.

in·fer·en·tial (in′fə-ren′shəl) *adj.* Deducible by inference. — **in′fer·en′tial·ly** *adv.*

in·fe·ri·or (in-fir′ē-ər) *adj.* **1.** Lower in quality, worth, or adequacy. **2.** Lower in rank or importance. **3.** Mediocre; ordinary: an *inferior* wine. **4.** *Biol.* Situated below or downward, as an organ or part. **5.** *Bot.* Growing below some other organ. **6.** *Astron.* **a** Between the earth and the sun: an *inferior* planet. **b** Below the horizon; below the celestial pole. **7.** *Printing* Set below the line. — *n.* **1.** A person inferior in rank or in attainments. **2.** *Printing* An inferior character. *Abbr. inf.* [< L, lower, compar. of *inferus* low] — **in·fe·ri·or·i·ty** (in-fir′ē-ôr′ə-tē, -or′-) *n. pl.* **·ties** The state or quality of being inferior.

inferiority complex 1. In Adlerian psychology, a neurotic condition arising from the child's repressed anger and fear at being inferior, especially in some physical aspect. **2.** Loosely, an exaggerated sense of one's own limitations and incapacities, sometimes compensated for by aggressive behavior.

in·fer·nal (in-fûr′nəl) *adj.* **1.** Of or pertaining to the mythological world of the dead, or to hell. **2.** Diabolical; hellish. **3.** *Informal* Damnable; hateful. [< OF < L *infernalis* < *infernus* situated below < *inferus* low] — **in·fer′nal·ly** *adv.*

infernal machine An insidious explosive device.

in·fer·no (in-fûr′nō) *n. pl.* **·nos 1.** The infernal regions; hell. **2.** Any place comparable to hell. [< Ital.]

In·fer·no (in-fûr′nō) The first of the three parts of Dante's *Divine Comedy,* describing the poet's journey through Hell.

infero- *combining form Anat. & Zool.* On the under side; below. [< L *inferus* low]

in·fer·tile (in-fûr′til) *adj.* Not fertile or productive; infecund; sterile. — **in′fer·til′i·ty** *n.*

in·fest (in-fest′) *v.t.* **1.** To overrun or occur in large numbers so as to be annoying or dangerous. **2.** Of lice and other parasites, to invade (a region of the body). [< MF *infester* or L *infestare* to assail < *infestus* hostile] — **in·fest′er** *n.*

in·fes·ta·tion (in′fes-tā′shən) *n.* The act of infesting, or the state of being infested. [< LL *infestatio, -onis*]

in·feu·da·tion (in′fyōō-dā′shən) *n.* **1.** In feudal law, the granting of an estate in fee; enfeoffment. **2.** The granting of tithes to laymen. [< Med.L *infeudatio, -onis* < *infeudare* to enfeoff < *in-* in + *feudum.* See FEUD².]

in·fi·del (in′fi-dəl) *n.* **1.** One who rejects all religious belief; unbeliever. **2.** Among Christians, one who is not a Christian. **3.** Among Moslems, one who is not a Moslem. — *adj.* **1.** Having no religious belief. **2.** Rejecting a particular faith, especially Christianity or Islam. **3.** Of, relating to, or characteristic of an infidel. [< MF *infidèle* < L *infidelis* unfaithful < *in-* not + *fidelis* faithful]

in·fi·del·i·ty (in′fi-del′ə-tē) *n. pl.* **·ties 1.** Lack of fidelity; disloyalty. **2.** A disloyal or treacherous act. **3.** Unfaithfulness of a marriage partner; adultery. **4.** Lack of belief in a particular religion, especially Christianity or Islam.

in·field (in′fēld′) *n.* **1.** In baseball: **a** The space within the base lines of the field, and some adjacent space beyond the second and third base lines. **b** The infielders collectively. Distinguished from *outfield*. **2.** The area enclosed by a race-track, running track, etc.

in·field·er (in′fēld′ər) *n.* In baseball, either the first base-man, second baseman, shortstop, or third baseman, or the pitcher or catcher considered as a fielder.

in·fight·ing (in′fī′ting) *n.* **1.** Fighting done at close quar-ters. **2.** Internal competition or conflict within an organi-zation or among similar rival groups.

in·fil·trate (in·fil′trāt, in′fil·trāt) *v.* **·trat·ed, ·trat·ing** *v.t.* **1.** Of a faction or political group, to gain or seek control of (an organization, government, etc.) by secretly occupying posi-tions of power. **2.** To cause (a liquid or gas) to pass into or through pores or interstices. **3.** To filter or move through or into; permeate. — *v.i.* **4.** To pass into or through a sub-stance. — *n.* **1.** That which infiltrates or has infiltrated. **2.** *Pathol.* A substance that abnormally seeps into or per-meates the tissues.

in·fil·tra·tion (in′fil·trā′shən) *n.* **1.** The act of infiltrating, or the state of being infiltrated. **2.** That which infiltrates. — **in·fil·tra·tive** (in·fil′trə·tiv) *adj.*

infin. Infinitive.

in·fi·nite (in′fə·nit) *adj.* **1.** Having no boundaries or limits; extending without end: *infinite* space. **2.** Very numerous or great; vast: an *infinite* supply. **3.** All-embracing; absolute; perfect: *infinite* wisdom. **4.** *Math.* Of, pertaining to, or des-ignating a quantity conceived as always exceeding any other quantity in value. — *n.* **1.** That which is infinite. **2.** *Math.* An infinite quantity. — **the Infinite** God. [< OF < L *infin-itus* unlimited < *in-* not + *finitus* finite < *finis* limit] — **in′-fi·nite·ly** *adv.* — **in′fi·nite·ness** *n.*

— **Syn.** (adj.) **1.** *Infinite, limitless, boundless, illimitable, mea-sureless, numberless, countless, innumerable,* and *eternal* mean con-tinuing forever in space or time. *Infinite* includes the senses of all the others, and more; it is applied to those things which we believe to have no bounds. *Limitless, boundless,* and *illimitable* formally include this sense, but they are chiefly used of things whose limits we have not yet discovered or cannot formulate: the *boundless* seas, *limitless* space. *Measureless, numberless, countless,* and *in-numerable* often mean merely vast in dimension or number. *Eternal* means *infinite* in time, but it is also used to mean continued for a very long time. Compare EVERLASTING. — **Ant.** finite, limited, circumscribed, transitory.

in·fin·i·tes·i·mal (in′fin·ə·tes′ə·məl) *adj.* **1.** Infinitely small. **2.** So small as to be incalculable and insignificant for all practical purposes. **3.** *Math.* Denoting a quantity conceived as continually diminishing toward zero as a limit. — *n.* An infinitesimal quantity. [< NL *infinitesimus* < *infinitus* in-finite + *-esimus* (after *centesimus* hundredth). See INFIN-ITE.] — **in′fin·i·tes′i·mal·ly** *adv.*

infinitesimal calculus Differential and integral cal-culus.

in·fin·i·ti·val (in·fin′ə·tī′vəl) *adj.* *Gram.* Of or pertaining to the infinitive. — **in·fin′i·ti′val·ly** *adv.*

in·fin·i·tive (in·fin′ə·tiv) *Gram. adj.* **1.** Without limitation of person or number: opposed to *finite*. **2.** Of, pertaining to, or using the infinitive. — *n.* A verb form generally used either as the principal verb of a verb phrase, most often with-out its sign *to*, or as a noun, most often with its sign and re-taining its verbal capability of having subject and comple-ment. Abbr. *inf., infin.* [< Med.L *infinitivus*]

in·fin·i·tude (in·fin′ə·tōod, ·tyōod) *n.* **1.** The quality of be-ing infinite or boundless. **2.** An unlimited quantity.

in·fin·i·ty (in·fin′ə·tē) *n. pl.* **·ties 1.** The quality or state of being infinite. **2.** Something considered infinite, as space or time. **3.** A very large amount or number. **4.** *Math.* **a** An infinite number or quantity, denoted by the symbol ∞. **b** The point or series of points in space that by supposition lie at an infinite distance from the point in question. [< OF *infinite* < L *infinitas, -tatis* < *infinitus*. See INFINITE.]

in·firm (in·fûrm′) *adj.* **1.** Feeble or weak, as from old age or illness. **2.** Lacking resolution, stability, or firmness of pur-pose. **3.** Not legally secure. [< OF *enferm* < L *infirmus* < *in-* not + *firmus* firm] — **in·firm′ly** *adv.* — **in·firm′ness** *n.*

in·fir·ma·ry (in·fûr′mər·ē) *n. pl.* **·ries 1.** A place for the treatment of the sick, especially in a school, factory, etc.; dispensary. **2.** A small hospital. [< Med.L *infirmaria* < L *infirmus* infirm, indisposed. See INFIRM.]

in·fir·mi·ty (in·fûr′mə·tē) *n. pl.* **·ties 1.** The state or quality of being infirm; debility; weakness. **2.** A physical or mental defect or ailment. **3.** A moral failing or flaw. [< F *infir-mité* < L *infirmitas, -atis*]

in·fix (in·fiks′) *v.t.* **1.** To set firmly or insert in, as by thrust-ing. **2.** To implant (an idea, fact, etc.) in the mind; incul-cate. **3.** *Gram.* To insert (an infix) within a word. — *n. Gram.* A modifying addition inserted in the body of a word. Compare PREFIX, SUFFIX. — **in·fix′ion** *n.*

infl. Influence(d).

in fla·gran·te de·lic·to (in flə·gran′tē di·lik′tō) *Latin* In the very act of committing a crime; literally, while the crime is blazing: also *flagrante delicto*.

in·flame (in·flām′) *v.* **·flamed, ·flam·ing** *v.t.* **1.** To set on

fire; kindle. **2.** To excite to violent emotion or activity. **3.** To increase or make more intense, as anger, passion, etc. **4.** To produce heat, swelling, and soreness in; to cause inflam-mation in. — *v.i.* **5.** To catch fire; burst into flame. **6.** To become excited or aroused. **7.** To become inflamed, as by infection, irritation, etc. [< OF *enflammer* < L *inflam-mare* < *in-* in + *flamma* flame] — **in·flam′er** *n.*

in·flam·ma·bil·i·ty (in·flam′ə·bil′ə·tē) *n.* The state or con-dition of being inflammable. Also **in·flam′ma·ble·ness.**

in·flam·ma·ble (in·flam′ə·bəl) *adj.* **1.** Flammable. **2.** Easily excited or aroused. — *n.* A flammable thing or sub-stance. [< F < L *inflammare*. See INFLAME.] — **in·flam′-ma·bly** *adv.*

in·flam·ma·tion (in′flə·mā′shən) *n.* **1.** The act of inflam-ing, or the state of being inflamed. **2.** *Pathol.* A diseased condition produced in a tissue, organ, or part by an infec-tion, injury, or irritant, and characterized by heat, redness, swelling, and pain. [< L *inflammatio, -onis*]

in·flam·ma·to·ry (in·flam′ə·tôr′ē, -tō′rē) *adj.* **1.** Tending to produce or arouse excitement, violence, anger, etc. **2.** *Med.* Characterized by, pertaining to, or causing inflamma-tion. [< F *inflammatoire* < L *inflammare*. See INFLAME.]

in·flate (in·flāt′) *v.* **·flat·ed, ·flat·ing** *v.t.* **1.** To cause to ex-pand by filling with gas or air; distend; swell. **2.** To enlarge excessively; increase unduly; puff up: to *inflate* one's self-esteem. **3.** *Econ.* To increase (prices, credit, available cur-rency, etc.) far in excess of usual or prior levels. — *v.i.* **4.** To become inflated. [< L *inflatus,* pp. of *inflare* to blow into < *in-* in + *flare* to blow] — **in·fla′ta·ble** *adj.* — **in·flat′er,** **in·fla′tor** *n.*

in·flat·ed (in·flā′tid) *adj.* **1.** Distended or puffed out, as by air or gas. **2.** Bombastic; high-flown: *inflated* rhetoric. **3.** Raised above a normal or proper level, as prices. **4.** Puffed up with conceit. **5.** *Bot.* Hollowed or puffed out; bulbous.

in·fla·tion (in·flā′shən) *n.* **1.** The act of inflating, or the state of being inflated. **2.** *Econ.* **a** An unstable rise in price levels resulting from an increase in circulating currency and a mounting demand for available commodities and services. **b** An overissue of a country's currency, especially paper cur-rency not redeemable in specie. [< L *inflatio, -onis*] — **in·fla′tion·ar′y** *adj.*

inflationary spiral A continuously accelerating rise in income and prices that results in a lowering of the value of money and is due to the purchasing power's being ahead of the output of goods and services.

in·fla·tion·ist (in·flā′shən·ist) *n.* A believer in the issuing of a large amount of currency. — **in·fla′tion·ism** *n.*

in·flect (in·flekt′) *v.t.* **1.** To vary the tone or pitch of (the voice); modulate. **2.** To turn from a straight or usual course; bend. **3.** *Gram.* **a** To give or recite the inflections of (a word) by conjugating or declining. **b** To alter the form of (a word) by inflection. — *v.i.* **4.** *Gram.* To have grammati-cal inflection. [< L *inflectere* < *in-* in + *flectere* to bend]

in·flec·tion (in·flek′shən) *n.* **1.** The act of inflecting, or the state of being inflected. **2.** An angle or bend. **3.** Modula-tion of the voice. **4.** *Geom.* A change in a plane curve from convex to concave. **5.** *Gram.* **a** A pattern of change in form undergone by words to express grammatical and syntactical relations, as of case, number, gender, person, tense, etc. The inflection of nouns, pronouns, and adjectives is called *declen-sion;* that of verbs, *conjugation.* **b** An affix denoting the grammatical function of a word, as the *'s* in *boy's,* denoting the possessive case. **c** An inflected form. Sometimes called *flection:* also *Brit.* **in·flex′ion.**

◆ The few inflections surviving in English include: *s* for the regular plural of nouns, and for the third person singular present indicative of verbs; *'s* for the possessive; *-er* for the comparative, and *-est* for the superlative of many adjectives and adverbs; *-ed* for the past tense and the past participle of regular verbs, and *-ing* for the present participle.

in·flec·tion·al (in·flek′shən·əl) *adj. Ling.* **1.** Belonging to, relating to, or showing grammatical inflection. **2.** Synthetic (def. 5). Also *Brit.* **in·flex′ion·al.** — **in·flec′tion·al·ly** *adv.*

in·flexed (in·flekst′) *adj. Bot.* Abruptly turned or bent in-ward, as the petals of a flower.

in·flex·i·ble (in·flek′sə·bəl) *adj.* **1.** Incapable of being bent; rigid. **2.** Unyielding in disposition or purpose; pertinacious; stubborn. **3.** That cannot be altered; unchangeable; fixed: the *inflexible* laws of nature. [< L *inflexibilis*] — **in·flex′i-bil′i·ty, in·flex′i·ble·ness** *n.* — **in·flex′i·bly** *adv.*

in·flict (in·flikt′) *v.t.* **1.** To deal; lay on: to *inflict* a blow. **2.** To impose (something disagreeable): to *inflict* punish-ment. **3.** To cause (another) to suffer or endure. [< L *inflictus,* pp. of *infligere* to strike on < *in-* on + *fligere* to strike] — **in·flict′er** or **in·flic′tor** *n.* — **in·flic′tive** *adj.*

in·flic·tion (in·flik′shən) *n.* **1.** The act of inflicting. **2.** That which is inflicted, as pain, punishment, etc.

in·flo·res·cence (in′flə·res′əns) *n.* **1.** A flowering; flourish-ing. **2.** *Bot.* **a** The mode of arrangement of flowers in rela-tion to the stem or axis. **b** A cluster of flowers. **c** All the flow-ers growing on a single plant. **d** A single flower. [< NL *in-*

florescentia < LL *inflorescens,* ppr. of *inflorescere* to come into flower. See IN-², FLORESCENCE.] — **in′flo·res′cent** *adj.*

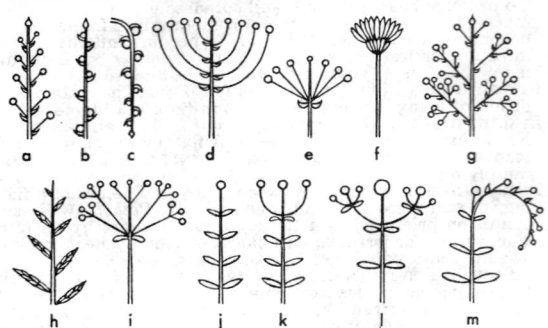

TYPES OF INFLORESCENCE

Simple racemose: *a* Raceme, *b* Spike, *c* Catkin, *d* Corymb, *e* Umbel, *f* Head.
Compound racemose: *g* Panicle, *h* Compound spike, *i* Compound umbel.
Cymose: *j* Simple terminal flower, *k* Simple cyme, *l* Compound cyme, *m* Scorpioid cyme.

in·flow (in′flō′) *n.* **1.** The act of flowing in. **2.** That which flows in.

in·flu·ence (in′floo-əns) *n.* **1.** The power of persons or things to produce effects on others, especially by imperceptible or indirect means. **2.** Power or indirect sway resulting from social position, wealth, authority, etc. **3.** One who or that which possesses the power to affect others, especially indirectly. **4.** In astrology, an ethereal fluid or occult force supposedly flowing from the stars to affect the destiny of men. — **under the influence** *Informal* Drunk; tipsy. — *v.t.* **·enced, ·enc·ing 1.** To produce an effect upon the actions or thought of; persuade; mold. **2.** To have an effect upon; affect; modify. Abbr. *infl.* [< OF < LL *influentia* < L *influens, -entis,* ppr. of *influere* < *in-* + *fluere* to flow. Doublet of INFLUENZA.] — **in′flu·enc·er** *n.*
— **Syn.** (verb) **1.** *Influence, affect, move, sway, persuade,* and *mold* agree in meaning to have an effect upon a person's behavior. We *influence* another's actions or thoughts, but *affect* his emotions. *Influence* implies a greater degree of control than *affect,* and is often more permanent in its results. We *move* or *sway* a person to make a decision, or to go in a certain direction, *persuade* him to adopt a view or begin an action, and *mold* his character.

in·flu·ent (in′floo-ənt) *adj.* Flowing in. — *n.* That which flows in, as in a tributary. [< L *influens, -entis,* ppr. of *influere.* See INFLUENCE.]

in·flu·en·tial (in′floo-en′shəl) *adj.* **1.** Having or exercising influence. **2.** Wielding great influence or power; effective. [< LL *influentia.* See INFLUENCE.] — **in′flu·en′tial·ly** *adv.*

in·flu·en·za (in′floo-en′zə) *n.* **1.** *Pathol.* A contagious, infectious virus disease characterized by respiratory inflammation, headache, fever, muscular pains, and often irritation of the intestinal tract: also called *flu, grip, grippe.* **2.** *Vet.* A similar disease of horses, swine, etc. [< Ital., (illness due to) the influence (of the stars) < LL *influentia* < L *influere* to flow in. Doublet of INFLUENCE.] — **in·flu·en′zal** *adj.*

in·flux (in′fluks′) *n.* **1.** A flowing in, as of a liquid or gas. **2.** A continuous coming, as of people or things. **3.** The place at which a river flows into another body of water; mouth. [< MF < LL *influxus,* pp. of *influere* to flow in]

in·fold (in·fōld′) *v.t.* **1.** To wrap in folds; envelop. **2.** To embrace. **3.** To turn or fold inward; make a fold in. Also spelled *enfold.* — **in·fold′er** *n.*

in·form (in·fôrm′) *v.t.* **1.** To acquaint (someone) with facts, data, opinion, etc.; make something known to; notify. **2.** To pervade or animate; give quality or character to: with *with* or *by.* **3.** *Rare* To shape or form (the mind, character, etc.). — *v.i.* **4.** To disclose information. **5.** To give incriminating information: with *on* or *against.* [< OF *enformer* < L *informare* to give form to < *in-* in + *forma* form]

in·form² (in·fôrm′) *adj.* *Archaic* Shapeless; unformed. [< MF < *informe* < L *informis* < *in-* not + *forma* form]

in·for·mal (in·fôr′məl) *adj.* **1.** Not in the usual or prescribed form; unofficial: an *informal* treaty. **2.** Without ceremony or formality; relaxed; casual: *informal* manners. **3.** Not requiring formal attire: an *informal* dinner. **4.** Characteristic of or suitable to the language of ordinary conversation or familiar writing, but inappropriate for use in formal discourse. ◆ *Informal* language is widely used by educated people and is not to be confused with nonstandard usage or slang. — **in·for′mal·ly** *adv.*

in·for·mal·i·ty (in′fôr-mal′ə-tē) *n. pl.* **·ties 1.** The state or quality of being informal. **2.** An informal act or proceeding.

in·form·ant (in·fôr′mənt) *n.* **1.** One who imparts information. **2.** *Ling.* A native speaker of a language or dialect

whose speech is used by linguists in recording and studying linguistic forms, sounds, etc. [< L *informans, -antis,* ppr. of *informare.* See INFORM¹.]

in·for·ma·tion (in′fər-mā′shən) *n.* **1.** Knowledge acquired or derived; facts; data. **2.** Timely or specific knowledge; news. **3.** The act of informing, or the state of being informed. **4.** A service or facility for providing facts: Call *information.* **5.** *Law* An accusation or complaint made without the intervention of a grand jury. **6.** In communication theory, that property of a signal or message whereby it conveys something unpredictable by and meaningful to the recipient, usually measured in bits. Abbr. *inf.* — **Syn.** See KNOWLEDGE. [< F < L *informatio, -onis*] — **in′for·ma′tion·al** *adj.*

information theory The statistical and mathematical study of the coding, transmission, storage and retrieval, etc., of information, and of the computers, telecommunication channels, and other systems that process information.

in·form·a·tive (in·fôr′mə-tiv) *adj.* Affording information; instructive. Also **in·form′a·to·ry** (-tôr′ē, -tō′rē).

in·formed (in·fôrmd′) *adj.* Educated or knowledgeable.

in·form·er (in·fôr′mər) *n.* **1.** One who informs against others; stool pigeon; tattletale. **2.** An informant.

infra- *prefix* Below; beneath; on the lower part: *infracostal.* Compare SUPRA-. [< L]

in·fra·cos·tal (in′frə-kos′təl) *adj. Anat.* Situated below the ribs. [< INFRA- + L *costa* rib]

in·fract (in·frakt′) *v.t.* To break; infringe; violate (a law, pledge, etc.). [< L *infractus,* pp. of *infringere.* See INFRINGE.] — **in·frac′tor** *n.*

in·frac·tion (in·frak′shən) *n.* The act of breaking or violating (a pledge, law, etc.); infringement. [< L *infractio, -onis*]

in·fra dig·ni·ta·tem (in′frə dig′nə-tā′təm) *Latin* Beneath one's dignity. Also *Brit. Informal* **in′fra dig′.**

in·fra·lap·sar·i·an·ism (in′frə-lap-sâr′ē-ən-iz′əm) *n. Theol.* The doctrine that God, foreseeing the fall of man, elected some to eternal salvation. See SUBLAPSARIANISM, SUPRALAPSARIANISM. [< INFRA- + L *lapsus* fall + -ARIAN + -ISM] — **in′fra·lap·sar′i·an** *adj. & n.*

in·fran·gi·ble (in·fran′jə-bəl) *adj.* **1.** Not breakable or capable of being broken into parts. **2.** Inviolable. — **in·fran′gi·bil′i·ty, in·fran′gi·ble·ness** *n.* — **in·fran′gi·bly** *adv.*

in·fra·red (in′frə-red′) *adj. Physics* Having a wavelength greater than that of visible red light and shorter than that of a microwave: said of electromagnetic waves.

in·fra·son·ic (in′frə-son′ik) *adj.* Subsonic (def. 1).

in·fra·struc·ture (in′frə-struk′chər) *n.* The foundations or framework of something, especially the transportation system, communications network, etc., of a nation or organization: opposed to *superstructure.* [< INFRA- + STRUCTURE.] — **in′fra·struc′tur·al** *adj.*

in·fre·quen·cy (in·frē′kwən-sē) *n.* The quality or state of being infrequent; rareness. Also **in·fre′quence.**

in·fre·quent (in·frē′kwənt) *adj.* Present or occurring at widely separated intervals; rare. — **in·fre′quent·ly** *adv.*

in·fringe (in·frinj′) *v.t.* **·fringed, ·fring·ing** To break or disregard the terms or requirements of, as an oath or law; violate. — **to infringe on** (or **upon**) To transgress or trespass on rights or privileges; encroach on. [< L *infringere* < *in-* in + *frangere* to break] — **in·fring′er** *n.*

in·fringe·ment (in·frinj′mənt) *n.* **1.** The act of infringing. **2.** Any violation of a right, privilege, regulation, etc.

in·fun·dib·u·li·form (in′fən-dib′yə-lə-fôrm′) *adj. Bot.* Funnel-shaped. [< NL *infundibuliformis*]

in·fun·dib·u·lum (in′fən-dib′yə-ləm) *n. pl.* **·la** *Anat.* Any of various funnel-shaped structures or organs; especially, the passage connecting the third ventricle of the brain with the pituitary body. [< L *infundibulum,* a funnel < *infundere* to pour into. See INFUSE.] — **in·fun·dib′u·lar, in·fun·dib′u·late** (-lāt, -lit) *adj.*

in·fu·ri·ate (*v.* in·fyoor′ē-āt; *adj.* in·fyoor′ē-it) *v.t.* **·at·ed, ·at·ing** To make furious or very angry; enrage. — *adj. Rare* Enraged; furious. [< Med.L *infuriatus,* pp. of *infuriare* to madden < *in-* in + *furia* rage] — **in·fu′ri·ate·ly** *adv.* — **in·fu′ri·at′ing·ly** *adv.* — **in·fu′ri·a′tion** *n.*

in·fus·cate (in·fus′kit) *adj. Entomol.* Tinged or darkened with brown, as part of an insect's wing. Also **in·fus′cat·ed** (-kā′təd). [< L *infuscatus,* pp. of *infuscare* to make dark < *in-* in + *fuscare* to darken < *fuscus* dark]

in·fuse (in·fyooz′) *v.t.* **·fused, ·fus·ing 1.** To instill or inculcate, as principles or qualities. **2.** To inspire; imbue: with *with.* **3.** To pour in. **3.** To steep, so as to make an extract or infusion. [< L *infusus,* pp. of *infundere* to pour in < *in-* in + *fundere* to pour] — **in·fus′er** *n.*

in·fus·i·ble¹ (in·fyoo′zə-bəl) *adj.* Incapable of fusion. [< IN-¹ + FUSIBLE] — **in·fus′i·bil′i·ty, in·fus′i·ble·ness** *n.*

in·fus·i·ble² (in·fyoo′zə-bəl) *adj.* Capable of being infused or poured in. [< INFUSE + -IBLE] — **in·fus′i·bil′i·ty, in·fus′i·ble·ness** *n.*

in·fu·sion (in·fyoo′zhən) *n.* **1.** The act of infusing. **2.** That which is infused. **3.** A liquid extract obtained by infusing or soaking a substance in water. **4.** *Med.* The operation of introducing saline or other solutions into the veins. [< OF or < L *infusio, -onis*]

in·fu·sion·ism (in·fyoo′zhən-iz′əm) *n. Theol.* The doctrine that the human soul is of divine origin and is infused into the body at conception or birth: distinguished from *creationism* and *traducianism.* **— in·fu'sion·ist** *n.*

in·fu·sive (in·fyōō'siv) *adj.* Having the power of infusing.

in·fu·so·ri·al (in'fyōō·sôr'ē·əl, -sō'rē-) *adj.* 1. Of or pertaining to infusorians. 2. Containing or composed of infusorians: *infusorial earth.*

in·fu·so·ri·an (in'fyōō·sôr'ē·ən, -sō'rē-) *n.* 1. Any of a former division (*Infusoria*) of the animal kingdom, including especially those microscopic protozoans found in infusions of decaying matter. 2. Any of a class (*Infusoria,* now *Ciliata*) of protozoans characterized by ciliated bodies and free-living aquatic habits, including paramecia and stentors. [< NL *infusoria* < L *infusus,* pp. of *infundere* to pour into]

in fu·tu·ro (in fyōō·tyoor'ō) *Latin* In the future.

-ing[1] *suffix* 1. The act or art of doing the action expressed in the root verb: *hunting.* 2. The product or result of an action: a *painting.* 3. Material for: *flooring.* 4. That which performs the action of the root verb: a *covering.* ◆ In formal writing when the *-ing* form of the verb (see *gerund*) is modified by a noun or pronoun the modifier appears in the possessive. Thus, "We objected to *his* (or *John's*) *leaving*" is preferred to "We objected to *him* (or *John*) *leaving*," although the latter is common in speech. [OE, *-ung, -ing*]

-ing[2] *suffix* Used in the present participle of verbs and in participial adjectives: He is *talking*; an *eating* apple. [ME *-inde* < OE *-ende*; infl. by ME *-inge* -ING[1]]

-ing[3] *suffix of nouns* 1. Related or belonging to; having the quality of: *sweeting.* 2. Descendant of: *Browning.* 3. Small; little: *atheling.* [OE]

in·gath·er (in·gath'ər) *v.t. & v.i.* To gather in; harvest; assemble. **— in·gath'er·er** *n.*

Inge (ing), **William Ralph,** 1860–1954, English churchman and author: called **the Gloomy Dean.**

in·gem·i·nate (in·jem'ə·nāt) *v.t.* **·nat·ed, ·nat·ing** To repeat or reiterate. [< L *ingeminatus,* pp. of *ingeminare* to double. See IN-[2], GEMINATE.] **— in·gem'i·na'tion** *n.*

in·gen·er·ate[1] (v. in·jen'ər·āt; adj. in·jen'ər·it) *Rare v.t.* **·at·ed, ·at·ing** To produce within; engender. **—** *adj.* Inborn. [< L *ingeneratus,* pp. of *ingenerare* to engender < *in-* in + *generare.* See GENERATE.]

in·gen·er·ate[2] (in·jen'ər·it) *adj.* Not brought into being by generation. [< LL *ingeneratus* self-existent < *in-* not + *generatus.* See GENERATE.]

in·gen·ious (in·jēn'yəs) *adj.* 1. Showing ingenuity; cleverly conceived; skillful. 2. Having inventive and adaptive ability; clever. 3. *Obs.* Displaying genius or great intellectual power. [< MF *ingénieux* < L *ingeniosus* talented < *ingenium* natural quality, ability < *in-* in + *gignere* to beget] **— in·gen'ious·ly** *adv.* **— in·gen'ious·ness** *n.*

in·gé·nue (an'zhə·nōō', Fr. aṅ·zhā·nü') *n. pl.* **·nues** (-nōōz', Fr. -nü') 1. A young woman or girl of guileless simplicity and innocence. 2. The role of a young girl in a play, film, etc.; also, an actress who plays such roles. [< F, fem. of *ingénu* < L *ingenuus,* See INGENUOUS.]

in·ge·nu·i·ty (in'jə·nōō'ə·tē, -nyōō'-) *n. pl.* **·ties** 1. Imaginative resources; inventiveness. 2. Originality of design or execution; cleverness. 3. A cleverly conceived act, device, etc. 4. *Rare* Candor. [< L *ingenuitas, -atis* < *ingenuus*]

in·gen·u·ous (in·jen'yoo·əs) *adj.* 1. Straightforward; candid; frank. 2. Innocent and simple; naive. [< L *ingenuus* inborn, natural, frank < *in-* in + *genus* birth, origin] **— in·gen'u·ous·ly** *adv.* **— in·gen'u·ous·ness** *n.*

— Syn. 1. *Ingenuous, artless, guileless, naive, unsophisticated,* and *simple* characterize persons free from pretense or calculation. *Ingenuous* persons are frank, confiding, and do not conceal their feelings. *Artless* describes a childlike lack of affectation, and is akin to *guileless,* which suggests absence of ulterior motives or of any attempt to gain favor by a complaisant manner. A *naive* man is trustful of others, and unsuspicious, sometimes to the point of credulity; the *unsophisticated* person lacks worldly wisdom; one who is *simple* is straightforward in his desires, motives, and dealings. The last four synonyms are often deprecatory in force, suggesting a lack of common sense.

In·ger·soll (ing'gər·səl, -sôl), **Robert Green,** 1833–99, U.S. lawyer, lecturer, and politician: called **the Great Agnostic.**

in·gest (in·jest') *v.t.* To take or put (food, etc.) into the body by or as by swallowing. [< L *ingestus* pp. of *ingerere* to carry in < *in-* in + *gerere* to carry] **— in·ges'tion** *n.* **— in·ges'tive** *adj.*

in·ges·ta (in·jes'tə) *n.pl.* Things that are ingested, as food, etc.: opposed to *egesta.* [< L neut. pl. of *ingestus,* pp. of *ingerere* to carry in]

in·gle (ing'gəl) *n. Scot.* A fire or fireplace. [< Scottish Gaelic *aingeal* fire]

in·gle·nook (ing'gəl·nook') *n. Chiefly Brit.* A corner by the fire.

In·gle·wood (ing'gəl·wood) 1. A city in SW California, near Los Angeles; pop. 89,985. 2. An unincorporated place in north central Tennessee, near Nashville; pop. 26,527.

in·glo·ri·ous (in·glôr'ē·əs, -glō'rē-) *adj.* 1. Not reflecting honor or courage; disgraceful; ignominious. 2. *Rare* Ob-

scure; humble. [< L *ingloriosus*] **— in·glo'ri·ous·ly** *adv.* **— in·glo'ri·ous·ness** *n.*

in·go·ing (in'gō'ing) *adj.* Entering; going in.

in·got (ing'gət) *n.* 1. A mass of cast metal from the crucible or mold. 2. *Obs.* A mold in which an ingot may be cast. [? ME < OE *in-* in + *goten,* pp. of *geotan* to pour]

ingot iron *Metall.* 1. Extremely pure iron of high ductility and rust resistance, widely used as a construction material and base for special steels. 2. *Brit.* Mild steel.

in·graft (in·graft', -gräft') See ENGRAFT.

in·grain (v. in·grān'; n. & adj. in'grān') *v.t.* 1. To impress firmly on the mind or character; fix deeply. 2. *Archaic* To dye in fast colors. Also spelled *engrain.* **—** *adj.* 1. Dyed in the yarn before manufacture or weaving, as a rug. 2. Thoroughly inwrought; deeply instilled. **—** *n.* A carpet made of ingrained worsted; also, the yarn from which it is made. [Var. of ENGRAIN]

in·grained (in·grānd') *adj.* 1. Worked into the inmost texture; deep-rooted; firmly established: *ingrained* virtue. 2. Thorough; inveterate: an *ingrained* braggart.

in·grate (in'grāt) *n.* An ungrateful person. **—** *adj. Archaic* Ungrateful. [< OF *ingrat* < L *ingratus* unpleasant, ungrateful < *in-* not + *gratus* pleasing]

in·gra·ti·ate (in·grā'shē·āt) *v.t.* **·at·ed, ·at·ing** To bring (oneself) deliberately into the favor or confidence of others. **— in·gra'ti·at'ing·ly** *adv.* **— in·gra'ti·a'tion** *n.* **— in·gra'ti·a·to'ry** (-ə·tôr'ē, -tō'rē) *adj.* [< L *in-* into + *gratia* favor]

in·grat·i·tude (in·grat'ə·tōōd, -tyōōd) *n.* Lack of gratitude; insensibility to kindness; thanklessness.

in·gra·ves·cent (in'grə·ves'ənt) *adj. Pathol.* Increasing in severity or gravity, as a disease. [< L *ingravescens, -entis,* ppr. of *ingravescere* to grow heavier or worse < *in-* in + *gravis* heavy] **— in'gra·ves'cence** *n.*

in·gre·di·ent (in·grē'dē·ənt) *n.* 1. Anything that enters into the composition of a mixture: the *ingredients* of a stew. 2. A component of anything. [< F *ingrédient* < L *ingrediens, -entis,* ppr. of *ingredi* to enter < *in-* in + *gradi* to walk]

In·gres (aṅ'gr'), **Jean Auguste Dominique,** 1780–1867, French painter.

in·gress (in'gres) *n.* 1. A going in, as into a building; entrance; also, the right of going in. Also **in·gres·sion** (in·gresh'ən). 2. A place of entrance. [< L *ingressus,* pp. of *ingredi* to enter]

in·gres·sive (in·gres'iv) *adj.* 1. Pertaining to entrance; entering. 2. *Gram.* Inceptive. **— in·gres'sive·ness** *n.*

in-group (in'grōōp') *n. Sociol.* Any group with strong feelings of mutual cohesiveness and identification to the degree of excluding nonmembers. Compare OUT-GROUP.

in·grow·ing (in'grō'ing) *adj.* 1. Growing into the flesh: an *ingrowing* hair. 2. Growing within or into.

in·grown (in'grōn') *adj.* 1. Grown into the flesh, as a toenail. 2. Grown within; innate: *ingrown* vice.

in·growth (in'grōth') *n.* 1. A growing inward. 2. A thing that grows inward; inward growth.

in·gui·nal (ing'gwə·nəl) *adj. Anat.* Of, pertaining to, or located in the groin. [< L *inguinalis* < *inguen, -inis* groin]

inguino- *combining form* In, affecting, or related to the groin. Also, before vowels, **inguin-.** [< L *inguen, -inis* groin]

in·gulf (in·gulf') See ENGULF.

in·gur·gi·tate (in·gûr'jə·tāt) *v.t. & v.i.* **·tat·ed, ·tat·ing** To eat or drink greedily or to excess; gorge; swill. [< L *ingurgitatus,* pp. of *ingurgitare* to pour in, gorge oneself < *in-* in + *gurges, -itis* whirlpool] **— in·gur'gi·ta'tion** *n.*

in·hab·it (in·hab'it) *v.t.* 1. To live or reside in; occupy as a home. **—** *v.i.* 2. *Archaic* To dwell; abide. [< OF *enhabiter* < L *inhabitare* < *in-* in + *habitare* to dwell, freq. of *habere* to have] **— in·hab'it·a·bil'i·ty** *n.* **— in·hab'it·a·ble** *adj.* **— in·hab'it·er** *n.* **— in·hab'i·ta'tion** *n.*

in·hab·i·tan·cy (in·hab'ə·tən·si) *n. pl.* **·cies** 1. The act of inhabiting, or the state of being inhabited. 2. Place of residence; dwelling.

in·hab·i·tant (in·hab'ə·tənt) *n.* One who or that which dwells permanently in a fixed place, as distinguished from a lodger or visitor; resident. [< AF < L *inhabitans, -antis,* ppr. of *inhabitare.* See INHABIT.]

in·hab·it·ed (in·hab'it·id) *adj.* Lived in; populated.

in·ha·lant (in·hā'lənt) *adj.* 1. Inhaling. 2. Used for inhaling. **—** *n.* A medicinal preparation to be inhaled. [< L *inhalans, -antis,* ppr. of *inhalare.* See INHALE.]

in·ha·la·tion (in'hə·lā'shən) *n.* 1. The act of inhaling. 2. That which is inhaled; an inhalant.

in·ha·la·tor (in'hə·lā'tər) *n.* A device for enabling one to inhale air, medicinal vapors, anesthetics, etc.

in·hale (in·hāl') *v.t.* **·haled, ·hal·ing** 1. To draw into the lungs, as breath, tobacco smoke, etc.; breathe in. **—** *v.i.* 2. To draw breath, tobacco smoke, etc., into the lungs. Opposed to *exhale.* [< L *inhalare* < *in-* in + *halare* to breathe]

in·hal·er (in·hāl'ər) *n.* 1. One who inhales. 2. *Med.* An inhalator. 3. A respirator.

in·har·mo·ni·ous (in'här·mō'nē·əs) *adj.* Lacking harmony;

discordant. Also **in·har·mon·ic** (-mon′ik), **in·har·mon·i·cal.** — **in·har·mo′ni·ous·ly** *adv.* — **in·har·mo′ni·ous·ness** *n.*

in·haul (in′hôl′) *n. Naut.* A line for bringing in a sail.

in·here (in·hir′) *v.i.* **-hered, ·her·ing** To be a permanent or essential part; be inseparably associated, as rights, qualities, etc.: with *in.* [< L *inhaerere* < *in-* to + *haerere* to stick] — **in·her′ence, in·her′en·cy** *n.*

in·her·ent (in·hir′ənt, -her′-) *adj.* Forming a permanent and essential element or quality of something; intrinsic; inborn. [< L *inhaerens, -entis,* ppr. of *inhaerere.* See INHERE.] — **in·her′ent·ly** *adv.*
— **Syn.** *Inherent, intrinsic,* and *essential* mean belonging to the very nature of a person or thing. *Inherent* stresses the inseparability of a part, element, or quality: the *inherent* will to live. *Intrinsic* denotes that which is a property of a thing itself, in contrast with the qualities it derives from its external relations; we speak of the *intrinsic* beauty of the Parthenon. *Essential* refers to the essence or stuff of which a thing is composed: the *essential* difference between steam and water vapor.

in·her·it (in·her′it) *v.t.* **1.** To receive (property, rank, title, etc.) by legal succession or will; fall heir to. **2.** To derive (traits, qualities, etc.) from one's parents or ancestors. **3.** To receive from one's predecessors. **4.** *Rare* To succeed as heir. **5.** *Rare* To obtain as one's portion. **6.** *Obs.* To place (an heir) in possession of: usually with *of.* — *v.i.* **7.** To take possession of an inheritance. **8.** To derive traits, qualities, etc.: with *from.* [< OF *enheriter* < LL *inhereditare* to appoint an heir < *in-* in + *heres, -edis* heir]

in·her·it·a·ble (in·her′ə·tə·bəl) *adj.* **1.** Capable of being inherited; heritable. **2.** Capable of inheriting; entitled to inherit. [< AF *enheritable*] — **in·her′it·a·bil′i·ty, in·her′it·a·ble·ness** *n.* — **in·her′it·a·bly** *adv.*

in·her·i·tance (in·her′ə·təns) *n.* **1.** The act or fact of inheriting. **2.** That which is legally transmissible or transmitted to an heir; legacy. **3.** Derivation of qualities from one's forebears. **4.** A property, quality, attitude, or combination of these derived from predecessors; heritage. **5.** Hereditary right: an earl by *inheritance.* [< OF *enheritance*]

inheritance tax A tax imposed on an inherited estate.

in·her·i·tor (in·her′ə·tər) *n.* An heir. — **in·her′i·tress** (-tris), **in·her′i·trix** (-triks) *n. fem.*

in·he·sion (in·hē′zhən) *n.* The condition of inhering or being fixed in something; inherence. [< LL *inhaesio, -onis,* pp. of *inhaerere.* See INHERE.]

in·hib·it (in·hib′it) *v.t.* **1.** To restrain or check (an impulse, action, process, etc.). **2.** *Rare* To prohibit or forbid. [< L *inhibitus,* pp. of *inhibere* to check < *in-* in + *habere* to have, hold] — **in·hib′i·ter** *n.* — **in·hib′it·a·ble** *adj.* — **in·hib′i·tive,** *and* **in·hib′i·to·ry** (-tôr′ē, -tō′rē) *adj.*

in·hi·bi·tion (in′hi·bish′ən, in′i-) *n.* **1.** A checking or restraining; arrestation; especially, a self-imposed restriction on one's behavior. **2.** The act or process of checking, retarding, slowing down, etc. **3.** *Psychol.* **a** The blocking of one impulse or process by another. **b** Any mental or emotional block. [< OF < L *inhibitio, -onis* < *inhibere.* See INHIBIT.]

in·hib·i·tor (in·hib′ə·tər) *n.* **1.** Anything that inhibits. **2.** *Chem.* A substance that retards or stops a chemical reaction, usually when added in small quantity. Compare CATALYST. **3.** *Med.* An agent that checks organic activity. [< Med.L]

in hoc sig·no vin·ces (in hok sig′nō vin′sēz) *Latin* By this sign (i.e., of the cross) thou wilt conquer: motto of the emperor Constantine.

in·hos·pi·ta·ble (in·hos′pi·tə·bəl, in′hos·pit′ə·bəl) *adj.* **1.** Not hospitable. **2.** Not affording shelter, comfort, etc.: *inhospitable* climate. — **in·hos·pi·ta·ble·ness** (in·hos′pi·tə·bəl·nis, in′hos·pit′-) *n.* — **in·hos·pi·ta·bly** (in·hos′pi·tə·blē, in′hos·pit′-) *adv.* — **in·hos′pi·tal′i·ty** (-tal′ə·tē) *n.*

in·hu·man (in·hyoo′mən) *adj.* **1.** Not befitting human nature; brutal; bestial. **2.** Not of the ordinary human type; monstrous: *inhuman* shapes. [< MF *inhumain* < L *inhumanus*] — **in·hu′man·ly** *adv.* — **in·hu′man·ness** *n.*

in·hu·mane (in′hyoo·mān′) *adj.* Not humane; cruel; brutal. — **in·hu·mane′ly** *adv.*

in·hu·man·i·ty (in′hyoo·man′ə·tē) *n. pl.* **·ties** **1.** Lack of human or humane qualities; ferocious cruelty. **2.** A cruel act, word, etc. [< OF *inhumanite* < L *inhumanitas*]

in·hu·ma·tion (in′hyoo·mā′shən) *n.* Burial; interment.

in·hume (in·hyoom′) *v.t.* **·humed, ·hum·ing** To place in the earth, as a dead body; bury; inter. [< L *inhumare* < *in-* in + *humus* soil, earth] — **in·hum′er** *n.*

in·im·i·cal (in·im′i·kəl) *adj.* **1.** Characterized by harmful opposition; antagonistic: a trend *inimical* to learning. **2.** Behaving as an enemy; unfriendly; hostile. [< LL *inimicalis* < L *inimicus* unfriendly < *in-* not + *amicus* friend] — **in·im′i·cal′i·ty** (-kal′ə·tē) *n.* — **in·im′i·cal·ly** *adv.*

in·im·i·ta·ble (in·im′ə·tə·bəl) *adj.* Defying imitation; matchless. [< L *inimitabilis*] — **in·im′i·ta·bil′i·ty, in·im′i·ta·ble·ness** *n.* — **in·im′i·ta·bly** *adv.*

in·i·on (in′ē·ən) *n. pl.* **in·i·a** (in′ē·ə) *Anat.* The occipital protuberance at the rear of the skull. [< NL < Gk., nape of the neck < *is, inos* sinew, tendon]

in·iq·ui·tous (in·ik′wə·təs) *adj.* Characterized by iniquity; unjust. — **in·iq′ui·tous·ly** *adv.* — **in·iq′ui·tous·ness** *n.*

in·iq·ui·ty (in·ik′wə·tē) *n. pl.* **·ties** **1.** Grievous violation of

right or justice; wickedness. **2.** A wrongful act; unjust thing or deed; sin. [< OF *iniquite* < L *iniquitas* < *iniquus* unequal < *in-* not + *aequus* equal]

init. **1.** Initial. **2.** In the beginning (L *initio*).

in·i·tial (in·ish′əl) *adj.* **1.** Standing at the beginning. **2.** Of or pertaining to the beginning; first. — *n.* **1.** *pl.* The first letters of one's proper name, used as identification and signature. **2.** The first letter of a word, name, etc. **3.** A large capital or elaborately decorated letter set at the beginning of a verse, chapter, etc. — *v.t.* **·tialed** or **·tialled, ·tial·ing** or **·tial·ling** To mark or sign with initials. Abbr. *init.* [< L *initialis* < *initium* beginning < *inire* to enter upon < *in-* in + *ire* to go] — **in·i′tial·ly** *adv.*

Initial Teaching Alphabet An alphabet of 43 characters representing the sounds of English: also called Augmented Roman. For illustration see ALPHABET. Abbr. *I.T.A.*

in·i·ti·ate (in·ish′ē·āt; *for adj. & n.,* in·ish′ē·it) *v.t.* **·at·ed, ·at·ing** **1.** To begin; commence; originate. **2.** To admit to membership in an organization, fraternity, cult, etc., usually with special rites and the imparting of secret knowledge. **3.** To instruct in fundamentals or rudiments. **4.** In government, to exercise the initiative. — *adj.* Initiated. — *n.* One who has been ritually admitted to an organization, fraternity, cult, etc.; especially, one who has been initiated recently. [< L *initiatus,* pp. of *initiare* to begin < *initium* beginning. See INITIAL.] — **in·i′ti·a·tor** *n.*

in·i·ti·a·tion (in·ish′ē·ā′shən) *n.* **1.** The act of initiating, or the state of being initiated. **2.** The special instruction or ceremonial rites admitting one to some position, society, knowledge, etc. — **Syn.** See BEGINNING.

in·i·ti·a·tive (in·ish′ē·ə·tiv, -ē·ā′tiv, -ish′ə·tiv) *n.* **1.** The power or right to take the first step or the next step in some action: to have the *initiative.* **2.** The action of commencing or originating: to take the *initiative.* **3.** The spirit needed to originate action: a man of *initiative.* **4.** In government: **a** The right or power to propose legislative measures. **b** The process by which the electorate acts to originate legislation. Compare REFERENDUM. — **on one's own initiative** Without instruction or compulsion; freely. — *adj.* **1.** Of or pertaining to initiation. **2.** Initiatory. — **in·i′ti·a·tive·ly** *adv.*

in·i·ti·a·to·ry (in·ish′ē·ə·tôr′ē, -tō′rē) *adj.* **1.** Introductory; initial. **2.** Serving to initiate.

in·ject (in·jekt′) *v.t.* **1.** To force or shoot in by mechanical or physical means; especially, to drive (a fluid, drug, etc.) into a bodily cavity, blood vessel, or tissue by means of a syringe or hypodermic needle. **2.** To introduce (some new element): with *into.* **3.** To throw in or introduce abruptly (a comment, suggestion, etc.); interject. [< L *injectus,* pp. of *injicere* to throw in < *in-* in + *jacere* to throw]

in·jec·tion (in·jek′shən) *n.* **1.** The act or process of injecting. **2.** That which is injected. **3.** The state of being bloodshot or hyperemic. [< L *injectio, -onis*]

in·jec·tor (in·jek′tər) *n.* One who or that which injects.

in·ju·di·cious (in′jōō·dish′əs) *adj.* Not judicious; imprudent. — **in′ju·di′cious·ly** *adv.* — **in′ju·di′cious·ness** *n.*

in·junc·tion (in·jungk′shən) *n.* **1.** The act of enjoining. **2.** An authoritative order or direction. **3.** *Law* A judicial order requiring the party enjoined to take, or more commonly to refrain from taking, some specified action. [< LL *injunctio, -onis* < *injunctum,* pp. of *injungere* to join to, enjoin. See IN-², JUNCTION.] — **in·junc′tive** *adj.*

in·jure (in′jər) *v.t.* **·jured, ·jur·ing** **1.** To harm, damage, or impair, especially physically; hurt. **2.** To wrong or offend. [Back formation < INJURY] — **in′jur·er** *n.*
— **Syn.** **1.** *Injure, harm, wound, damage, mar,* and *spoil* mean to affect in such a way as to lessen health, strength, value, beauty, etc. *Injure* is the general term for any kind of impairment, especially in legal usage; it is also specifically applied to impairment of the body. *Harm* is close to one sense of *injure,* and *wound* to another: a reputation may be *injured* or *harmed;* a person is *injured* or *wounded* in a battle. To *damage* is to impair in value, and the word is chiefly applied to property loss: the gale *damaged* several houses. To *mar* is to *injure* in appearance or well-being: scenery *marred* by billboards; to *spoil* is to render unfit for use or service: too much pepper *spoiled* the stew. Compare HURT, IMPAIR.

in·ju·ri·ous (in·joor′ē·əs) *adj.* **1.** Causing damage or hurt; harmful. **2.** Slanderous; abusive. [< OF *injurieux* < L *injurius*] — **in·ju′ri·ous·ly** *adv.* — **in·ju′ri·ous·ness** *n.*

in·ju·ry (in′jər·ē) *n. pl.* **·ries** **1.** Harm, damage, or grievous distress inflicted or suffered. **2.** A particular instance of such harm: an internal *injury.* **3.** *Law* Any wrong or damage done to another person, his reputation or property; also, a wrongful violation of another's legal rights. **4.** *Obs.* An insult. — **Syn.** See INJUSTICE. [< OF *injurie* < L *injuria* < *injurius* unjust < *in-* not + *jus, juris* right, law]

in·jus·tice (in·jus′tis) *n.* **1.** The fact or quality of being unjust; a violation or denial of justice. **2.** An unjust act; wrong. [< OF < L *injustitia* < *injustus* unjust]
— **Syn.** *Injustice, injury, tort,* and *wrong* are compared as they denote an act that inflicts undeserved hardship. *Injustice* is a violation of fair play or equal treatment. It may inflict a positive hurt, or it may deny to some a privilege accorded to others: the *injustice* of a severe punishment for a minor offense, the *injustice* of a property requirement for voting. *Injustice* may affect one person or many; an *injury* does positive harm to an individual,

or to several individuals considered separately. An *injured* person may gain redress at law by a civil suit; *tort* is the legal term for an *injury* (excluding a breach of contract). A *wrong* is an act regarded as reprehensible in itself, whether it injures the community or a single person; criminal acts, as well as *torts*, are *wrongs*. —**Ant.** justice, fairness, impartiality, equity.

ink (ingk) *n.* **1.** Any of various colored substances used in a fluid or viscous consistency for writing, drawing, and printing. **2.** The dark fluid ejected by cuttlefish and other cephalopods to darken the water and conceal themselves. —*v.t.* To spread ink upon; stain or color with ink. [< OF *enque* < LL *encaustum* purple ink < Gk. *enkauston*, neut. of *enkaustos*. See ENCAUSTIC.] —**ink′er** *n.*

ink·ber·ry (ingk′ber′ē) *n. pl.* **·ries** **1.** A small shrub (*Ilex glabra*) of the holly family, with oblong leaves and roundish, black, shining berries. **2.** Pokeweed. **3.** The berry of either of these plants.

Ink·er·man (ing′kər·mən, *Russian* in·kyir·män′) An eastern suburb of Sevastopol; site of a Russian defeat in the Crimean War, 1854.

ink·horn (ingk′hôrn′) *n.* A small container for ink, originally made of horn.

inkhorn term A bookish, pedantic word.

in·kle (ing′kəl) *n.* A kind of linen tape; also, the thread or yarn from which it is made. [? < Du. *enkel* a single narrow tape]

ink·ling (ingk′ling) *n.* **1.** A slight suggestion; intimation; hint. **2.** A vague idea or notion. [ME *inklen* to hint at, ? < OE *inca* suspicion]

ink sac *Zool.* A pear-shaped, glandular organ in the mantle of the cuttlefish and other cephalopods, from which an inky substance is ejected as a protective concealment.

ink·stand (ingk′stand′) *n.* **1.** A rack or device for holding ink, pens, etc. **2.** An inkwell.

Ink·ster (ingk′stər) A village in SE Michigan, near Detroit; pop. 38,595.

ink·well (ingk′wel′) *n.* A container for ink.

ink·wood (ingk′wŏŏd′) *n.* An evergreen tree (*Exothea paniculata*) of southern Florida, the West Indies, and Guatemala, having reddish brown, hard, heavy wood: also called *butterbough*.

ink·y (ing′kē) *adj.* **ink·i·er, ink·i·est** **1.** Resembling ink in color; dark; black. **2.** Of, pertaining to, or containing ink. **3.** Smeared or stained with ink. —**ink′i·ness** *n.*

inky cap A mushroom (genus *Coprinus*) whose gills dissolve into a black liquid after the spores have matured.

in·lace (in·lās′) See ENLACE.

in·laid (in′lād, in·lād′) *adj.* **1.** Decorated with wood, ivory, or other contrasting material embedded flush with the surface: an *inlaid* panel. **2.** Inserted to form a flush embedded pattern: *inlaid* ivory.

in·land (in′lənd; *for n. and adv., also* in′land′) *adj.* **1.** Remote from the sea or the border. **2.** Pertaining to or located in the interior of a country: *inland* population. **3.** Operating within a country or region; not foreign; domestic: *inland* trade. —*n.* The interior of a country. —*adv.* In or towards the interior of a land.

in·land·er (in′lən·der, -land′ər) *n.* One who lives inland.

Inland Sea A sea between Honshu and Shikoku and Kyushu islands, Japan.

in-law (in′lô′) *n. Informal* A close relative by marriage, as a son-in-law, mother-in-law, etc.

in·lay (*v.* in·lā′, in′lā′; *n.* in′lā′) *v.t.* **·laid, ·lay·ing** **1.** To set or embed (ivory, gold, etc.) flush into a surface so as to form a decorative pattern. **2.** To decorate, as a piece of furniture, by inserting such designs. **3.** To insert (a page, illustration, etc.) in a larger or heavier sheet cut to serve as a mat or frame for it; also, to fit (a book) with inlaid illustrations. —*n.* **1.** That which is inlaid. **2.** A pattern or design so produced. **3.** *Dent.* A filling for a tooth, made of gold, porcelain, etc., to fit a prepared cavity. —**in′lay′er** *n.*

inlay graft *Bot.* A graft made by inserting a cion at a place in the stock from which a closely matching piece of bark has been removed.

in.-lb. Inch-pound.

in·let (*n.* in′let, -lit; *v.* in·let′) *n.* **1.** A relatively narrow channel of water; as: **a** A stream or bay leading into the land from a larger body of water. **b** A passage between nearby islands, floes, etc. **c** An entry from one body of water into another, as from the sea into a lagoon. **2.** An entrance or opening, as to a culvert. **3.** The passage through which something is fed or filled: the *inlet* of the pond. **4.** Something set in or inserted. —*v.t.* **·let, ·let·ting** To insert; inlay.

in·li·er (in′lī′ər) *Geol.* An outcrop of older rock surrounded by later strata.

in loc. cit. In the place cited (L *in loco citato*).

in lo·co (in lō′kō) *Latin* In place; in the right or proper spot.

in lo·co pa·ren·tis (in lō′kō pə·ren′tis) *Latin* In the place

INKBERRY (def. 1)
a Flowers.
b Fruit.

in·ly (in′lē) *adv. Poetic* **1.** Inwardly. **2.** Intimately; deeply. —*adj. Obs.* Inward; heartfelt. [ME *inliche* < OE *inlice* inwardly < *inlic* inward]

in·mate (in′māt′) *n.* **1.** One who is lodged or confined in a prison, asylum, hospital, etc. **2.** An inhabitant. **3.** One who dwells with another or others. [? < INN + MATE]

in me·di·as res (in mē′dē·əs rēz′) *Latin* In the midst of things: used especially of narratives, as most epics, that open in the middle of events and not at the beginning.

in me·mo·ri·am (in mə·môr′ē·əm, -mō′rē-) *Latin* In memory (of); as a memorial (to).

in·mesh (in·mesh′) See ENMESH.

in·most (in′mōst′, -məst) *adj.* **1.** Located farthest from the outside; innermost. **2.** Most intimate. [OE *innemest*]

inn (in) *n.* **1.** A public house where travelers may obtain meals or lodging; a roadside hotel or restaurant. **2.** *Brit.* A house of residence for students: now only in the names of such residences, as *Inns* of Court. **3.** *Obs.* A dwelling place; abode. [OE *inn* room, house < *inne* indoors]

Inn (in) A river in eastern Switzerland, western Austria, and southern Bavaria, flowing 320 miles NE to the Danube.

in·nards (in′ərdz) *n.pl. Dial. & Informal* The internal organs or parts; insides. [Alter. of INWARDS]

in·nate (i·nāt′, in′āt) *adj.* **1.** Inherent in one's nature; inborn: an *innate* love of music. **2.** Originating from the constitution of the mind or intellect; not acquired: *innate* knowledge. [< LL *innatus*, pp. of *innasci* to be born in < L *in-* in + *nasci* to be born] —**in·nate′ly** *adv.* —**in·nate′ness** *n.*
—**Syn. 1.** *Innate*, *inborn*, *congenital*, and *hereditary* characterize qualities regarded as belonging to a person from birth. *Innate*, which is closely synonymous with inherent, is applied to things as well as persons: the *innate* weakness of despotism. *Inborn* is akin to *innate* but is applied only to living beings: the *inborn* placidity of a cow. *Congenital* is chiefly applied to bodily structure, defects, diseases, etc.: *congenital* deafness. *Hereditary* traces a quality to genetic factors in the parents or ancestors.

in·ner (in′ər) *adj.* **1.** Located or occurring farther inside; inward; interior: *inner* layers. **2.** Located or occurring within; internal: *inner* movements. **3.** Pertaining to the mind or spirit; subjective: a rich *inner* life. **4.** More obscure; hidden; esoteric: *inner* significance. [OE *innerra*, compar. of *inne* in (adv.)] —**in′ner·ly** *adv.* —**in′ner·ness** *n.*

inner city *U.S.* The central area of a large city, usually including the business and entertainment sections.

Inner Light In Quakerism, the Divine presence in man, source of guidance and certainty: also **Inner Word.**

Inner Mongolia See under MONGOLIA.

in·ner·most (in′ər·mōst′) *adj.* Inmost; farthest within. —*n.* The inmost part, thing, or place.

Inner Temple A London legal society, or the set of buildings occupied by it See INNS OF COURT.

inner tube A flexible, inflatable tube, usually of rubber, used inside a pneumatic tire.

in·ner·vate (i·nûr′vāt, in′ər·vāt) *v.t.* **·vat·ed, ·vat·ing** *Physiol.* **1.** To supply with nerves or nervous filaments. **2.** To give stimulus to (a nerve); innerve. [< INNERVE]

in·ner·va·tion (in′ər·vā′shən) *n.* **1.** *Physiol.* The supply of nervous energy to any part of the nervous system. **2.** *Anat.* The arrangement of nerve filaments in any part of the body.

in·nerve (i·nûrv′) *v.t.* **·nerved, ·nerv·ing** To impart nervous energy to; animate; stimulate. [< IN-² + NERVE]

In·ness (in′is), **George,** 1825–94, U.S. painter.

in·ning (in′ing) *n.* **1.** In baseball, a division of the game during which each team has a turn to bat. **2.** *pl.* In cricket, the period during which one side bats. **3.** *Often pl.* A chance for action; opportunity; turn: now the Democrats have their *innings*. **4.** *Archaic* The reclamation of marsh or flooded land; also, *pl.*, land so reclaimed. [OE *innung*, gerund of *innian* to put in]

inn·keep·er (in′kē′pər) *n.* The proprietor or host of an inn.

in·no·cence (in′ə·səns) *n.* **1.** The quality or fact of being innocent. **2.** A flower, the bluet (def. 2). **3.** A slender-stemmed, erect herb (*Collinsia verna*) with a blue and white corolla; also, a related California herb (*C. bicolor*). [< OF < L *innocentia* < *innocens*. See INNOCENT.]

in·no·cen·cy (in′ə·sən·sē) *n. pl.* **·cies** Innocence (def. 1); also, an instance of innocence.

in·no·cent (in′ə·sənt) *adj.* **1.** Not tainted with sin, evil, or moral wrong; pure: an *innocent* babe. **2.** Free from blame or guilt, especially legally; guiltless. **3.** Not tending to harm or injure; innocuous: *innocent* pastimes. **4.** Not maliciously intended: an *innocent* lie. **5.** Lacking in worldly knowledge; naive: an *innocent* girl. **6.** Deficient in sense or intelligence; simple; half-witted. **7.** Devoid of; entirely lacking in: with *of*: *innocent* of grammar. **8.** Not contraband; lawful. **9.** Spotless; clean: the *innocent* snow. —*n.* **1.** One who is free from evil or sin; especially, a young child. **2.** A simple or unsuspecting person lacking guile; also, a simpleton. **3.** *pl.* The bluet, a flower. [< OF < L *innocens, -entis* < *in-* not + *nocens*, ppr. of *nocere* to harm] —**in′no·cent·ly** *adv.*
—**Syn.** (adj.) **1.** chaste, virtuous, sinless, immaculate. **2.** un-

offending. **5.** unsophisticated, guileless. Compare INGENUOUS. — **Ant.** sinful, unchaste; guilty, culpable, criminal.

In·no·cent I (in′ə·sənt), Saint, died 417, pope 402–17, condemned Pelagianism.

Innocent II, died 1143, pope 1130–43, condemned Abelard: original name **Gregorio Pa·pa·re·schi** (pä′pä·räs′kē).

Innocent III, 1161?–1216, pope 1198–1216, raised the papal power to the highest point: original name **Lotario de' Con·ti** (dā kōn′tē).

Innocent IV, died 1254, pope 1243–54, warred against Frederick II: original name **Sinibaldo de' Fie·schi** (dā fyes′kē).

Innocent XI, 1611–89, pope 1676–89, quarreled with Louis XIV on the limitation of papal powers in France: original name **Benedetto O·de·scal·chi** (ō′dā·skäl′kē).

in·noc·u·ous (i·nok′yŏō·əs) *adj.* Having no harmful qualities or effects; harmless. [< L *innocuus* < *in-* not + *nocuus* harmful < *nocere* to harm] — **in·noc′u·ous·ly** *adv.* — **in·noc′u·ous·ness** *n.*

in·nom·i·nate (i·nom′ə·nit) *adj.* **1.** Having no specific name. **2.** Anonymous. [< LL *innominatus* < *in-* not + *nominatus,* pp. of *nominare* to name. See NOMINATE.]

innominate bone *Anat.* One of two large, irregular bones resulting from the consolidation of the ilium, ischium, and pubis to form the sides of the pelvis: also called *haunch bone, hipbone, hucklebone.* For illustration see PELVIS.

in·no·vate (in′ə·vāt) *v.* **·vat·ed, ·vat·ing** *v.t.* **1.** To introduce or bring in (something new). — *v.i.* **2.** To make changes; bring in new ideas, methods, etc.: often with *in, on,* or *upon.* [< L *innovatus,* pp. of *innovare* to renew < *in-* in + *novare* to make new, alter < *novus* new] — **in′no·va·tive** *adj.* — **in′no·va·tor** *n.*

in·no·va·tion (in′ə·vā′shən) *n.* **1.** Something newly introduced; a new method, device, etc. **2.** The act of introducing a change or something new. — **in′no·va′tion·al** *adj.* — **in′no·va′tion·ist** *n.* [< L *innovatio, -onis*]

in·nox·ious (i·nok′shəs) *adj.* Not noxious; harmless. [< L *innoxius* < *in-* not + *noxius.* See NOXIOUS.]

Inns·bruck (inz′brŏŏk, *Ger.* ins′brŏŏk) The capital of Tyrol, Austria, on the Inn; pop. 100,699 (1961).

Inns of Court The four legal societies of London, the Inner Temple, Middle Temple, Lincoln's Inn, and Gray's Inn, that have the exclusive right of admitting to the English bar; also, the buildings occupied by these societies.

in·nu·en·do (in′yŏō·en′dō) *n. pl.* **·does 1.** An oblique comment, hint, or suggestion, usually derogatory; a subtle aspersion; insinuation. **2.** *Law* In pleading, an explanatory phrase employed to make a previous phrase more explicit. [< L, by nodding at, intimating, ablative gerund of *innuere* to nod to, signify < *in-* to + *-nuere* to nod]

in·nu·mer·a·ble (i·nŏō′mər·ə·bəl, i·nyŏō′-) *adj.* Too numerous to be counted; very numerous; numberless. Also **in·nu′mer·ous.** — **Syn.** See INFINITE. [< L *innumerabilis*] — **in·nu′mer·a·bil′i·ty, in·nu′mer·a·ble·ness** *n.* — **in·nu′mer·a·bly** *adv.*

in·nu·tri·tion (in′nŏō·trish′ən, -yŏō-) *n.* Lack of nutrition; failure of nourishment. — **in′nu·tri′tious** *adj.*

in·ob·serv·ance (in′əb·zur′vəns) *n.* **1.** Failure to notice or heed; inattention. **2.** Nonobservance, as of a law, custom, promise, etc.; disregard. — **in′ob·serv′ant** *adj.* [< MF < L *inobservantia*]

in·oc·u·la·ble (in·ok′yə·lə·bəl) *adj.* Capable of being inoculated. — **in·oc′u·la·bil′i·ty** *n.*

in·oc·u·late (in·ok′yə·lāt) *v.* **·lat·ed, ·lat·ing** *v.t.* **1.** To communicate a mild form of a disease to (a person, animal, etc.) by implanting its bacteria or virus, usually as a means of producing immunity; also, to implant (a disease, bacteria, etc.). **2.** To inject immunizing serums, vaccines, or other antigenic materials into. **3.** To implant ideas, opinions, etc., in the mind of. — *v.i.* **4.** To perform inoculation. [< L *inoculatus,* pp. of *inoculare* to put an eye or bud into < *in-* in + *oculus* eye, bud] — **in·oc′u·la·tive** (-lā′tiv) *adj.* — **in·oc′u·la·tor** (-lā′tər) *n.*

in·oc·u·la·tion (in·ok′yə·lā′shən) *n.* The act of inoculating; especially, the introduction of disease-producing organisms into the body to produce immunity. [< L *inoculatio, -onis* < *inoculatus.* See INOCULATE.]

in·oc·u·lum (in·ok′yə·ləm) *n.* The prepared material, as bacteria, viruses, spores, etc., used in making an inoculation. Also **in·oc′u·lant** (-lənt). [< NL. See INOCULATE.]

in·o·dor·ous (in·ō′dər·əs) *adj.* Having no odor.

in·of·fen·sive (in′ə·fen′siv) *adj.* Giving no offense; causing no harm or annoyance; innocuous. — **in′of·fen′sive·ly** *adv.* — **in′of·fen′sive·ness** *n.*

in·of·fi·cious (in′ə·fish′əs) *adj. Law* Negligent of duty; forgetful of moral obligations; especially, designating a will in which the testator fails to provide for his nearest relatives and dependents. — **in′of·fi′cious·ly** *adv.*

in om·ni·a pa·ra·tus (in om′nē·ə pə·rā′təs) *Latin* Prepared for anything.

I·nö·nü (ē·nœ·nü′), Ismet, born 1884, Turkish military commander and statesman; president 1938–50; prime minister 1961–; earlier name **Ismet Pa·za** (pä·zä′)

in·op·er·a·ble (in·op′ər·ə·bəl) *adj.* **1.** Incapable of being

cured or improved by surgical operation: *inoperable* cancer. **2.** Not practicable; unworkable. — **in·op′er·a·bil′i·ty, in·op′er·a·ble·ness** *n.* — **in·op′er·a·bly** *adv.*

in·op·er·a·tive (in·op′ər·ə·tiv) *adj.* **1.** Not functioning. **2.** Not effectual or in effect. — **in·op′er·a·tive·ness** *n.*

in·op·por·tune (in·op′ər·tōōn′, -tyōōn′) *adj.* Untimely or inappropriate; unsuitable, especially with respect to time: an *inopportune* request. [< LL *inopportunus*] — **in·op′por·tune′ly** *adv.* — **in·op′por·tune′ness** *n.*

in·or·di·nate (in·ôr′də·nit) *adj.* **1.** Exceeding proper limits; immoderate; excessive: *inordinate* pride. **2.** Unrestrained, as in conduct, feeling, etc.; intemperate: *inordinate* passion. **3.** Lacking order or regularity; disorderly. — **in·or′di·na·cy** (-nə·sē), **in·or′di·nate·ness** *n.* — **in·or′di·nate·ly** *adv.*

inorg. Inorganic.

in·or·gan·ic (in′ôr·gan′ik) *adj.* **1.** Not having the organized anatomical structure of animal or vegetable life; inanimate: *inorganic* nature. **2.** Not characterized by life processes. **3.** Not essential; extraneous. **4.** *Chem.* Of, pertaining to, or designating those compounds lacking carbon, but including the carbonates and cyanides. **4.** *Ling.* Not belonging to the normal development of a word; extraneous, as the final *t* in *against.* — **in′or·gan′i·cal·ly** *adv.*

inorganic chemistry The branch of chemistry dealing with compounds lacking carbon or containing it only in the form of carbonates, carbides, and most cyanides.

in·os·cu·late (in·os′kyə·lāt) *v.t. & v.i.* **·lat·ed, ·lat·ing 1.** To unite or join by running together, as blood vessels or nerve fibers. **2.** To join so as to become continuous; blend. — **in·os·cu·la′tion** (-lā′shən) *n.*

in·o·si·tol (in·ō′sə·tōl, -tol) *n. Biochem.* A crystalline, water-soluble, polyhydric alcohol, $C_6H_6(OH)_6$, regarded as forming part of the vitamin B complex, widely distributed in plant and animal tissue. Also **in·o·site** (in′ə·sīt). [< Gk. *is, inos* sinew, tendon + *-IT(E)¹* + *-OL¹*]

in·pa·tient (in′pā′shənt) *n.* A patient who is lodged and fed as well as medically treated in a hospital, clinic, or the like: distinguished from *outpatient.*

in per·pet·u·um (in pər·pech′ŏō·əm) *Latin* Forever.

in per·so·nam (in pər·sō′nəm) *Latin* Against the person, rather than against specific things.

in pet·to (ēn pet′tō) *Italian* In the breast; secretly: said of Roman Catholic cardinals appointed by the Pope but not officially named in consistory.

in phase *Physics* A condition in which two or more waves having the same frequency reach their maximum, minimum, and all other corresponding values at the same instant. Also **in·phase** (in′fāz′).

in pos·se (in pos′ē) *Latin* Having a possible but not an actual existence; potential: distinguished from *in esse.*

in pro·pri·a per·so·na (in prō′prē·ə pər·sō′nə) *Latin* In one's own person.

in·put (in′pŏŏt′) *n.* **1.** The amount of energy delivered to a machine, storage battery, etc. **2.** *Electr.* The voltage, current, power, etc., delivered to a circuit or other device; also, the terminals where these are applied. **3.** *Physiol.* The amount of food taken into the body. **4.** *Electronics* Information derived from external sources and placed in the storage compartments of an electronic computer; also, loosely, information fed into a computer or other system.

in·quest (in′kwest) *n.* **1.** A judicial or legal investigation into a special matter; especially, one undertaken before a jury or by a coroner. **2.** The body of men chosen to make such an inquiry, especially a coroner's jury; also, its findings. **3.** An inquiry; questioning. [< OF *enqueste* < L *inquisitus, inquestus,* pp. of *inquirere.* See INQUIRE.]

in·qui·e·tude (in·kwī′ə·tŏōd, -tyŏōd) *n.* **1.** A state of restlessness; uneasiness. **2.** *pl.* Anxieties; disquieting thoughts. [< OF *inquietude* < LL *inquietudo*] — **in·qui′et** *adj.* — **in·qui′et·ly** *adv.*

in·qui·line (in′kwə·līn, -lin) *n. Zool.* Any of various animals living, sometimes commensally, in the abode of another and sharing its food. — *adj. Zool.* Living as an inquiline. [< L *inquilinus* lodger < *in-* in + *colere* to dwell]

in·quire (in·kwīr′) *v.* **·quired, ·quir·ing** *v.i.* **1.** To seek information by asking questions; ask: to *inquire* about one's health. **2.** To make an investigation, search, or inquiry: with *into.* — *v.t.* **3.** To ask information about: They *inquired* the way. Also spelled *enquire.* — **Syn.** See ASK. [< OF *enquerre;* infl. by L *inquirere* to inquire into < *in-* into + *quaerere* to seek] — **in·quir′er** *n.* — **in·quir′ing·ly** *adv.*

in·quir·y (in·kwīr′ē, in′kwər·ē) *n. pl.* **·quir·ies 1.** The act of inquiring or seeking, as for facts, truth, etc. **2.** Investigation; research, especially by questioning. **3.** A question; query. Also spelled *enquiry.* [ME *enquery* < *enquere*]

in·qui·si·tion (in′kwə·zish′ən) *n.* **1.** An official investigation of the beliefs and activities of individuals, political groups, etc., for the ultimate purpose of enforcing social and political orthodoxy. **2.** The act of inquiring or searching out. **3.** An inquest. [< OF < L *inquisitio, -onis* < *inquisitus.* See INQUEST.] — **in′qui·si′tion·ist, in·quis·i·tor** (in·kwiz′ə·tər) *n.*

In·qui·si·tion (in′kwə·zish′ən) *n.* A judicial system of the Roman Catholic Church for the discovery, examination, and punishment of heretics, active in central and southern Europe from the 13th to the 19th centuries, succeeded by the Congregation of the Holy Office: also called *Holy Office*. — **the Spanish Inquisition** An independent court of the Roman Catholic Church founded in Spain in 1481, notorious for its severities under the inquisitor-general Torquemada.

in·qui·si·tion·al (in′kwə·zish′ən·əl) *adj.* **1.** Of or pertaining to an inquisition or the Inquisition. **2.** Characterized by questioning, prying, etc., or by harsh severities like those of the Inquisition. — **in′qui·si′tion·al·ly** *adv.*

in·quis·i·tive (in·kwiz′ə·tiv) *adj.* **1.** Somewhat too curious, especially about another's affairs; unduly questioning; prying. **2.** Eager for knowledge or learning: an *inquisitive* mind. [< OF *inquisitif* < LL *inquisitivus*] — **in·quis′i·tive·ly** *adv.* — **in·quis′i·tive·ness** *n.*

— **Syn.** *Inquisitive, curious, prying,* and *snoopy* characterize persons who try to find out matters private to others. The *inquisitive* person asks questions, as does the *curious* person, but different motives may be implied. *Inquisitive* implies a conscious desire to learn the secrets of others, while *curious* often indicates an interested desire to know something which is properly one's concern, but of which one is ignorant. The *prying* person is both *inquisitive* and meddlesome, and is persistent in asking impertinent questions. The informal *snoopy* describes the person who seeks to gain information by spying and other underhand means.

in·quis·i·tor (in·kwiz′ə·tər) *n.* **1.** One who inquires, investigates, or examines. **2.** A member of the Inquisition. [< OF < L *inquisitor*]

in·quis·i·to·ri·al (in·kwiz′ə·tôr′ē·əl, -tō′rē-, in′kwiz-) *adj.* **1.** Of, pertaining to, or resembling an inquisitor or inquisition; offensively curious. **2.** Acting in the capacity of an inquisitor. **3.** *Law* Pertaining to a system of criminal procedure in which the proceedings are conducted secretly and the judge acts as prosecutor. [< MF < Med.L *inquisitorius*] — **in·quis′i·to′ri·al·ly** *adv.* — **in·quis′i·to′ri·al·ness** *n.*

in re (in rē′) *Law* In the thing; in the case or matter (of); concerning: *in re* Smith vs. Jones. [< L]

in rem (in rem′) *Law* Against the thing; not directed against any specific person. [< L]

I.N.R.I. Jesus of Nazareth, King of the Jews (L *Iesus Nazarenus, Rex Iudaeorum*).

in·road (in′rōd′) *n.* **1.** *Usually pl.* A serious encroachment; harmful trespass: with *on* or *upon*: *inroads* on one's happiness. **2.** A hostile raid or foray. [< IN-² + obs. *road* riding]

in·rush (in′rush′) *n.* A sudden rushing in; invasion.

ins. **1.** Inches. **2.** Inspector. **3.** Insular. **4.** Insulated; insulation. **5.** Insurance.

in·sal·i·vate (in·sal′ə·vāt) *v.t.* **·vat·ed, ·vat·ing** To mix (food) with saliva in chewing. — **in·sal′i·va′tion** *n.*

in·sa·lu·bri·ous (in′sə·lōō′brē·əs) *adj.* Not wholesome; not healthful. [< L *insalubris*] — **in′sa·lu′bri·ous·ly** *adv.* — **in′sa·lu′bri·ty** *n.*

in·sane (in·sān′) *adj.* **1.** Not sane; mentally deranged or unsound; crazy; demented. **2.** Characteristic of one who is not sane: an *insane* stare. **3.** Extremely foolish or eccentric; hare-brained: *insane* schemes. **4.** Set apart for or used by demented persons: *insane* asylum. [< L *insanus* < *in-* not + *sanus* whole] — **in·sane′ly** *adv.* — **in·sane′ness** *n.*

in·san·i·tar·y (in·san′ə·ter·ē) *adj.* Not sanitary; dangerous to health; unhygienic: *insanitary* drains. — **in·san′i·ta′tion** *n.*

in·san·i·ty (in·san′ə·tē) *n.* *pl.* **·ties 1.** The state of being insane; mental derangement; madness: not a technical term in medicine or psychiatry. **2.** *Law* A defect or weakness of mind that makes a person incapable of understanding the nature of particular acts or legal actions and consequently releases him from legal responsibility. **3.** Extreme folly.

— **Syn. 1.** *Insanity, lunacy, madness, dementia,* and *psychosis* denote unsoundness of mind. *Insanity* is the most general popular term for a pronounced and continuing mental derangement; *lunacy* denotes a periodic or intermittent *insanity*. *Madness* is an older popular term for *insanity*, suggesting its violent manifestations. In medical and psychiatric usage, other terms are used for *insanity*, as *dementia* for mental deterioration, and *psychosis* for severe and prolonged mental disorders. Compare MANIA. — **Ant.** sanity, rationality.

in·sa·tia·ble (in·sā′shə·bəl, -shē·ə·bəl) *adj.* Incapable of being sated or satisfied; extremely greedy; inappeasable: *insatiable* ambition. Also **in·sa·ti·ate** (in·sā′shē·it). [< OF *insaciable* < LL *insatiabilis* < L *in-* not + *satiare*. See SATIATE.] — **in·sa′ti·a·bil′i·ty, in·sa′tia·ble·ness** *n.* — **in·sa′tia·bly, in·sa′ti·ate·ly** *adv.* — **in·sa′ti·ate·ness** *n.*

in·scribe (in·skrīb′) *v.t.* **·scribed, ·scrib·ing 1.** To write, mark, or engrave (words, names, characters, etc.), especially for some solemn or public purpose. **2.** To mark (a document, tablet, etc.) conspicuously and durably with writing or engraving. **3.** To enter (a name) on a formal or official list. **4.** To sign or dedicate (a book, photograph, etc.) for presentation. **5.** *Geom.* To draw (one figure) in another so that the latter circumscribes the former. [< L *inscribere* < *in-* on, in + *scribere* to write] — **in·scrib′er** *n.*

in·scrip·tion (in·skrip′shən) *n.* **1.** That which is inscribed; also, the act of inscribing. **2.** A durable marking or engrav-

ing on a solid object; especially, such markings on ancient artifacts and monuments. **3.** An informal written dedication, as of a book or work of art. [< L *inscriptio, -onis* < *inscriptus*, pp. of *inscribere*. See INSCRIBE.] — **in·scrip′tion·al, in·scrip′tive** *adj.*

in·scroll (in·skrōl′) *v.t.* To record upon a scroll.

in·scru·ta·ble (in·skrōō′tə·bəl) *adj.* That cannot be searched into or understood; incomprehensible; impenetrable. — **Syn.** See MYSTERIOUS. [< LL *inscrutabilis* < *in-* not + *scrutare* to explore] — **in·scru′ta·bil′i·ty, in·scru′ta·ble·ness** *n.* — **in·scru′ta·bly** *adv.*

in·sect (in′sekt) *n.* **1.** *Zool.* Any of a large, cosmopolitan class (*Insecta*) of small to minute air-breathing arthropods, usually passing through a metamorphosis, and having six legs, a body divided into a head, thorax, and abdomen, and one or two pairs of wings or none. **2.** Loosely, any small, air-breathing invertebrate resembling or suggesting an insect, as spiders, centipedes, ticks, etc. **3.** An insignificant or contemptible person. [< L (*animal*) *insectum* (animal) notched or cut into < *insectus*, pp. of *insecare* < *in-* in + *secare* to cut; alluding to their segmented bodies]

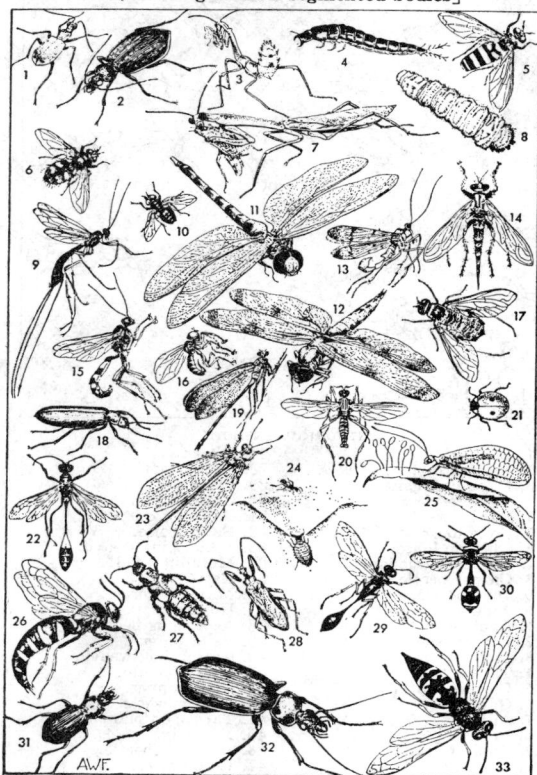

BENEFICIAL INSECTS
(For illustration of INJURIOUS INSECTS see p. 698)

1. Tiger beetle.	16. Big-headed fly.
2. Fiery hunter.	17. Bee fly.
3. Praying mantis nymph.	18. Spanish fly.
4. Ground beetle larva.	19. Damsel fly.
5. Syrphus or hover fly.	20. Dance fly.
6. Tachina fly, genus	21. Ladybug.
Winthemia.	22. Digger wasp, genus
7. Praying mantis.	*Ammophila*.
8. Syrphus fly larva.	23. Ant lion.
9. Ichneumon fly, genus	24. Ant lion larva and pit.
Ephialtes.	25. Lacewing.
10. Tachina fly, genus	26. Digger wasp, genus
Alophora.	*Bembidula*.
11. Darning needle.	27. Rove beetle.
12. Dragonfly.	28. Assassin bug.
13. Scorpion fly.	29. Mud dauber.
14. Assassin fly.	30. Potter wasp.
15. Ichneumon fly, genus	31. Ground beetle.
Amblyteles.	32. Caterpillar hunter.
	33. Cicada killer.

in·sec·tar·i·um (in′sek·târ′ē·əm) *n.* *pl.* **·i·ums** or **·i·a** (-ē·ə) A place for keeping living insects and breeding them. Also **in·sec·tar·y** (in′sek·ter·ē). [< NL]

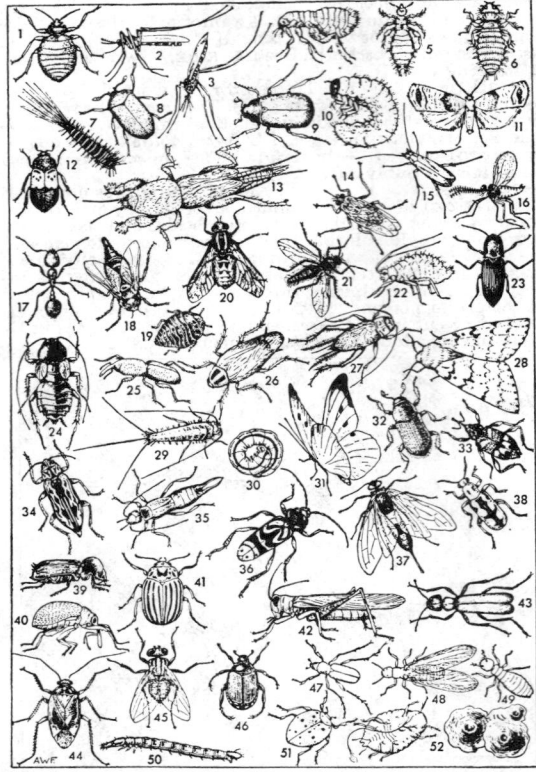

INJURIOUS INSECTS

1. Bedbug.
2. Mosquito, genus *Culex*.
3. Mosquito, genus *Anopheles*.
4. Flea.
5. Body louse.
6. Chicken louse.
7. Carpet beetle larva.
8. Carpet beetle.
9. June beetle.
10. June beetle grub.
11. Codling moth.
12. Larder beetle.
13. Mole cricket.
14. Tsetse fly.
15. Clothes moth.
16. Gall midge.
17. Ant.
18. Botfly.
19. Phylloxera.
20. Deer fly.
21. Midge.
22. Plant louse; aphid.
23. Click beetle.
24. Oriental roach.
25. Rice weevil.
26. Cockroach.
27. Cricket.
28. Gypsy moth.
29. Firebrat.
30. Cutworm larva.
31. Cabbage butterfly.
32. Bark beetle.
33. White pine weevil.
34. Metallic woodborer.
35. Earwig.
36. Maple borer.
37. Horntail.
38. Asparagus beetle.
39. Palm borer.
40. Cotton boll weevil.
41. Potato beetle.
42. Grasshopper.
43. Blister beetle.
44. Tarnished plant bug.
45. Housefly.
46. Japanese beetle.
47. Rose chafer.
48. Termite, winged form.
49. Termite, wingless form.
50. Wireworm.
51. Mexican bean beetle.
52. San José scale, showing scales.

in·sec·ti·cide (in-sek′tə-sīd) *n.* A substance used or prepared for killing insects. [< INSECT + -CIDE]

in·sec·ti·val (in′sek-tī′vəl, in-sek′tə-) *adj.* Of, pertaining to, or resembling an insect.

in·sec·ti·vore (in-sek′tə-vôr, -vōr) *n.* 1. Any of an order (*Insectivora*) of insect-eating mammals, as shrews, moles, etc. 2. An animal or plant that feeds on insects. [< F < L *insectum* insect + -*vorus* devouring < *vorare* to devour]

in·sec·tiv·o·rous (in′sek-tiv′ər-əs) *adj.* Feeding upon or subsisting upon insects, as shrews, moles, hedgehogs, etc.

in·se·cure (in′sə-kyŏor′) *adj.* 1. Liable to break, fail, collapse, etc.; unsafe. 2. Troubled by anxiety and apprehensiveness; threatened. [< Med.L *insecurus*] — **in′se·cure′·ly** *adv.* — **in′se·cure′ness** *n.*

in·se·cu·ri·ty (in′sə-kyŏor′ə-tē) *n. pl.* **·ties** 1. The state or quality of being unsafe or liable to injury, failure, loss, etc. 2. A condition of anxiety and apprehensiveness; sense of being unsafe and threatened. 3. *Often pl.* An instance of insecurity. [< Med.L *insecuritas*]

in·sem·i·nate (in-sem′ə-nāt) *v.t.* **·nat·ed, ·nat·ing** 1. To make pregnant; inject semen into the vagina of. 2. To sow (seed); also, to implant (ideas, etc.). 3. To sow seed in; implant in. [< L *inseminatus*, pp. of *inseminare* < *in-* in + *seminare* to sow < *semen, -inis* seed]

in·sem·i·na·tion (in-sem′ə-nā′shən) *n.* The act of inseminating, or the state of being inseminated.

in·sen·sate (in sen′sāt, -sit) *adj.* 1. Showing a lack of humane feeling; unmoved; brutish: *insensate* cruelty. 2. Without sense or reason; stupid; foolish. 3. Lacking physical sensation; inanimate: *insensate* stone. [< LL *insensatus*] — **in·sen′sate·ly** *adv.* — **in·sen′sate·ness** *n.*

in·sen·si·ble (in-sen′sə-bəl) *adj.* 1. Deprived of consciousness; unconscious. 2. Incapable of feeling or perceiving; indifferent: with *to*: *insensible* to pain; *insensible* to ridicule. 3. So slight or gradual as to escape notice; imperceptible: *insensible* stages. 4. Unaware; incognizant: with *of*: *insensible* of peril. 5. Lacking all emotion; apathetic. [< LL *insensibilis*] — **in·sen′si·bil′i·ty** *n.* — **in·sen′si·bly** *adv.*

in·sen·si·tive (in-sen′sə-tiv) *adj.* 1. Not keenly responsive in feeling or reaction: an *insensitive* nature. 2. Without physical feeling or sensation. 3. Not affected by physical agencies: with *to*: *insensitive* to light. — **in·sen′si·tiv′i·ty, in·sen′si·tive·ness** *n.* — **in·sen′si·tive·ly** *adv.*

in·sen·ti·ent (in-sen′shē-ənt, -shənt) *adj.* Lacking senses or consciousness; inanimate. — **in·sen′ti·ence** *n.*

in·sep·a·ra·ble (in-sep′ər-ə-bəl) *adj.* Incapable of being separated: *inseparable* friends. — *n. Usually pl.* Persons or things that are always together. — **in·sep′a·ra·bil′i·ty, in·sep′a·ra·ble·ness** *n.* — **in·sep′a·ra·bly** *adv.*

in·sert (*v.* in·sûrt′; *n.* in′sûrt) *v.t.* 1. To put in; place; set; introduce. 2. To introduce into a body of printed matter: to *insert* a clause in a contract. — *n.* 1. That which is inserted. 2. In bookbinding, illustrations, maps, etc., not part of the printed text, bound into the finished book: also called *inset.* 3. *U.S.* A circular, pamphlet, etc., set within a newspaper, magazine, or book for mailing. 4. In motion pictures, a cut-in. [< L *insertus*, pp. of *inserere* < *in-* in + *serere* to sow, plant] — **in·sert′er** *n.*

in·sert·ed (in-sûr′tid) *adj.* 1. *Anat.* Attached, as the tendon of a muscle to a bone. 2. *Bot.* Growing from a part.

in·ser·tion (in-sûr′shən) *n.* 1. The act of inserting. 2. That which is inserted; as: **a** A word, sentence, etc., introduced into written or printed matter. **b** A strip of lace or embroidery sewn into plain cloth for ornament. **c** Each appearance of an advertisement, as in a newspaper. 3. *Bot.* Place or mode of attachment, as of a leaf to a branch. 4. *Anat.* The end of a muscle that is attached to the bone or part that it moves: distinguished from *origin.*

in·ses·so·ri·al (in′sə-sôr′ē-əl, -sō′rē-) *adj.* Perching, or fitted for perching: said of birds. [< L *insessor* sitter < *insessum*, pp. of *insidere* < *in-* on + *sedere* to sit]

in·set (*v.* in·set′; *n.* in′set) *v.t.* **·set, ·set·ting** To set in; insert; implant. — *n.* 1. In bookbinding, an insert. 2. A small diagram, map, etc., inserted in the border of a larger one. 3. A piece of material let or set into a garment. 4. Influx, as of the tide.

in·sheathe (in-shēth′) *v.t.* **·sheathed, ·sheath·ing** To place in or as in a sheath.

in·shore (in′shôr′, -shōr′) *adj.* 1. Near the shore: *inshore* fishing. 2. Coming toward the shore: an *inshore* wind. — *adv.* Toward the shore.

in·shrine (in-shrīn′) See ENSHRINE.

in·side (*n. & adj.* in′sīd′, -sīd′; *adv. & prep.* in·sīd′) *n.* 1. The part, surface, space, etc., that lies within; side away from the edge or periphery; interior. 2. The internal nature or workings that are concealed: the *inside* of the affair; the *inside* of one's mind. 3. *pl. Informal* The inner parts of the body or a machine; innards. — **inside out** Reversed so that the inside is exposed. — *adj.* 1. Situated within; inner; internal; interior. 2. Restricted to a few; confidential; private: *inside* information. 3. Involving those within an organization: an *inside* problem. 4. In baseball, passing too close to the batter: said of pitches. 5. Suitable for, used, or working indoors; indoor. — *adv.* 1. In or into the interior; within. 2. Indoors. — *prep.* In or into the interior of; within: *inside* the tank. — **inside of** *Informal* 1. Within; enclosed by: *inside of* a larger box. 2. Within the time or distance specified: It can't be done *inside of* a year.

inside job *Informal* A crime committed by, or with the help of, a person(s) close to or employed by the victim.

in·sid·er (in′sī′der) *n.* 1. A member of a given group, club, etc. 2. One close to a source, as of knowledge or influence.

inside track 1. The shortest path around a race track, next to the inside rail. 2. *Informal* A special advantage.

in·sid·i·ous (in-sid′ē-əs) *adj.* 1. Subtly cunning or deceitful; treacherous; wily. 2. Progressing imperceptibly but harmfully: *insidious* disease. [< L *insidiosus* < *insidiae* ambush < *insidere* to sit in, lie in wait < *in-* on + *sedere* to sit] — **in·sid′i·ous·ly** *adv.* — **in·sid′i·ous·ness** *n.*

in·sight (in′sīt) *n.* 1. Perception into the inner nature or real character of a thing; penetrating discernment and understanding. 2. *Psychol.* **a** Discernment and evaluation of one's own mental processes, powers, etc.; self-knowledge. **b** The ability of one who is mentally ill to recognize the nature of his disorder. — **Syn.** See ACUMEN.

in·sight·ful (in′sīt′ful) *adj.* Having or manifesting insight.

in·sig·ni·a (in·sig′nē-ə) *n. pl. of* **in·sig·ne** (in·sig′nē) **1.** Badges, emblems, brassards, and the like, used as significant marks of membership, office, or honor: the royal *insignia.* **2.** (*construed as sing.*) A badge or emblem of rank, membership, etc. ◆ This sense of *insignia* now has a regular English plural *insignias:* the various *insignias* of royalty. **3.** Marks betokening anything, especially a particular condition: the *insignia* of grief. [< L, neut. pl. of *insignis* eminent < *in-* in + *signum* sign, emblem, badge]

in·sig·nif·i·cance (in′sig·nif′ə·kəns) *n.* The quality or state of being insignificant; unimportance.

in·sig·nif·i·can·cy (in′sig·nif′ə·kən·sē) *n. pl.* **·cies 1.** Insignificance. **2.** An insignificant person or thing.

in·sig·nif·i·cant (in′sig·nif′ə·kənt) *adj.* **1.** Having no importance; trivial; trifling. **2.** Having no meaning; meaningless; negligible: an *insignificant* difference. **3.** Lacking size or quantity; petty: an *insignificant* fee. **4.** Of persons, lacking distinction, character, etc. — **in′sig·nif′i·cant·ly** *adv.* — **Syn.** See TRIVIAL. **Ant.** significant, meaningful, important.

in·sin·cere (in′sin·sir′) *adj.* Not sincere; not expressing true feelings; hypocritical. — **in′sin·cere′ly** *adv.* — **in′sin·cer′i·ty** (-ser′ə·tē) *n.* [< LL *insincerus*]

in·sin·u·ate (in·sin′yoō-āt) *v.* **·at·ed, ·at·ing** *v.t.* **1.** To suggest by innuendo; give sly or indirect intimations of; hint. **2.** To introduce subtly and gradually by devious means: to *insinuate* mistrust. — *v.i.* **3.** To give sly and indirect intimations [< L *insinuatus,* pp. of *insinuare* to arrive at < *in-* in + *sinuare* to curve < *sinus* curve] — **in·sin′u·at′ing·ly** *adv.* — **in·sin′u·a′tive** *adj.* — **in·sin′u·a′tor** *n.*

in·sin·u·a·tion (in·sin′yoō-ā′shən) *n.* **1.** That which is insinuated; a sly hint. **2.** The act of insinuating.

in·sip·id (in·sip′id) *adj.* **1.** Lacking spirit and vivacity; vapid; dull: an *insipid* recital. **2.** Lacking flavor or savor; tasteless; flat; bland. [< L *insipidus* < *in-* not + *sapidus* savory < *sapere* to savor, taste] — **in·si·pid′i·ty** (in′si·pid′ə·tē), **in·sip′id·ness** *n.* — **in·sip′id·ly** *adv.* — **Syn.** **1.** spiritless, lifeless, jejune. **2.** flavorless, savorless.

in·sip·i·ence (in·sip′ē·əns) *n.* Lack of wisdom; foolishness. [< MF < L *insipientia* < *insipiens, -entis* unwise < *in-* not + *sapiens* wise] — **in·sip′i·ent** *adj.*

in·sist (in·sist′) *v.i.* **1.** To demand or advocate flatly and forcefully: with *on* or *upon:* to *insist* on adjournment. **2.** To assert firmly and steadfastly: with *on* or *upon.* **3.** To dwell on or repeatedly emphasize something: with *on* or *upon:* to *insist* on the main point. — *v.t.* **4.** To demand forcefully: with a noun clause as object: He *insisted* that the gate be opened. **5.** To maintain positively: with a noun clause as object: He *insisted* that he was right. [< OF *insister* < L *insistere* to stand on, tread on < *in-* on + *sistere* to cause to stand < *stare* to stand] — **in·sis′tence, in·sis′ten·cy** *n.*

in·sis·tent (in·sis′tənt) *adj.* **1.** Insisting; persistent. **2.** Compelling: *insistent* colors. — **in·sis′tent·ly** *adv.*

in si·tu (in sī′tyoō) *Latin* In its original site or position.

in·snare (in·snâr′) See ENSNARE.

in·so·bri·e·ty (in′sə·brī′ə·tē) *n. pl.* **·ties** Lack of sobriety; intemperance, especially in drinking.

in·so·far (in′sō·fär′) *adv.* To such an extent; in such measure: followed by *as.* Also **in so far.**

insol. Insoluble.

in·so·late (in′sō-lāt) *v.t.* **·lat·ed, ·lat·ing** To expose to the rays of the sun, as for bleaching, drying, etc. [< L *insolatus,* pp. of *insolare* to expose to the sun < *in-* in + *sol* sun]

in·so·la·tion (in′sō·lā′shən) *n.* **1.** Exposure to the rays of the sun. **2.** *Med.* **a** Sunstroke. **b** A method of treating disease by exposure to the rays of the sun. **3.** *Meteorol.* **a** Solar radiation received by the earth or other planets. **b** The rate of delivery of such radiant energy per unit of area.

in·sole (in′sōl′) *n.* **1.** The fixed inner sole of a shoe or boot. For illustration see SHOE. **2.** A removable inner sole placed in a shoe to improve its fit or to protect against dampness.

in·so·lence (in′sə·ləns) *n.* **1.** The character or quality of being insolent. **2.** An insult. — **Syn.** See IMPUDENCE. [< L *insolentia* < *insolens, -entis* unwonted. See INSOLENT.]

in·so·lent (in′sə·lənt) *adj.* Overbearing or offensively impertinent in conduct or speech; insulting; disrespectful. — *n.* An insolent person. — **Syn.** See ARROGANT. [< L *insolens, -entis* unusual, haughty < *in-* not + *solens, -entis,* ppr. of *solere* to be wont, accustomed] — **in′so·lent·ly** *adv.*

in·sol·u·ble (in·sol′yə·bəl) *adj.* **1.** Not soluble; incapable of being dissolved. **2.** Not solvable; incapable of being solved or explained. [< L *insolubilis*] — **in·sol′u·bil′i·ty, in·sol′u·ble·ness** *n.* — **in·sol′u·bly** *adv.*

in·solv·a·ble (in·sol′və·bəl) *adj.* Incapable of being explained or solved; insoluble.

in·sol·ven·cy (in·sol′vən·sē) *n. pl.* **·cies** The state of being insolvent; bankruptcy.

in·sol·vent (in·sol′vənt) *adj. Law* **1.** Unable to meet the claims of creditors; not solvent; bankrupt. **2.** Insufficient for the payment of debts: an *insolvent* estate. **3.** Pertaining to insolvency. — *n.* A debtor who is not solvent.

in·som·ni·a (in·som′nē-ə) *n.* Chronic inability to sleep. [< L < *insomnis* sleepless < *in-* without + *somnus* sleep] — **in·som′ni·ous** *adj.*

in·som·ni·ac (in·som′nē·ak) *n.* One who suffers from insomnia.

in·so·much (in′sō·much′) *adv.* **1.** To such a degree: with *that* or *as.* **2.** Inasmuch: with *as.*

in·sou·ci·ance (in·soō′sē·əns, *Fr.* aṅ·soō·syäṅs′) *n.* The quality or state of being insouciant; unconcern. [< F]

in·sou·ci·ant (in·soō′sē·ənt, *Fr.* aṅ·soō·syäṅ′) *adj.* Lighthearted; carefree; unconcerned. [< F < *in-* not + *souciant,* ppr. of *soucier* to disturb < L *sollicitare* to disturb, move] — **in·sou·ci·ant·ly** (in·soō′sē·ənt·lē) *adv.*

in·soul (in·sōl′) See ENSOLE.

insp. Inspected; inspector.

in·span (in·span′) *v.t.* **·spanned, ·span·ning** To harness or yoke to a vehicle. [< Afrikaans < Du. *inspannen*]

in·spect (in·spekt′) *v.t.* **1.** To look at or examine carefully; especially, to examine for faults or defects. **2.** To examine or review officially and with ceremony, as troops. [< L *inspectus,* pp. of *inspicere* to look into < *in-* into + *specere* to look]

in·spec·tion (in·spek′shən) *n.* **1.** The act of inspecting; careful or critical examination. **2.** An official examination, check, or review, as of troops. [< OF < L *inspectio, -onis*] — **in·spec′tion·al** *adj.*

in·spec·tive (in·spek′tiv) *adj.* **1.** Of or pertaining to inspection. **2.** Tending to inspect.

in·spec·tor (in·spek′tər) *n.* **1.** One who inspects. **2.** An official examiner or checker. **3.** An officer of police usually ranking next below the superintendent. *Abbr. ins., insp.* [< L] — **in·spec′tor·al, in·spec·to·ri·al** (-tôr′ē·əl, -tō′rē·əl) *adj.*

in·spec·tor·ate (in·spek′tər·it) *n.* **1.** The office or duties of an inspector. Also **in·spec′tor·ship** (-ship). **2.** A staff of inspectors. **3.** A district administered by an inspector.

Inspector General A high staff officer of the military, air, or naval service, responsible for conducting inspections; also, an officer of his department on the staff of a service unit, as a division, etc. *Abbr. IG, I.G.*

in·sphere (in·sfir′) See ENSPHERE.

in·spir·a·ble (in·spīr′ə·bəl) *adj.* Capable of being inspired.

in·spi·ra·tion (in′spə·rā′shən) *n.* **1.** The infusion or arousal within the mind of some idea, feeling, or impulse, especially one that leads to creative action. **2.** The state or quality of being inspired. **3.** One who or that which acts as an inspiring influence. **4.** Something that results from being inspired, as an especially effective idea, etc. **5.** *Theol.* Divine influence exerted upon the mind or spirit; especially, the divine influence underlying prophetic or scriptural revelation. **6.** The act of drawing in the breath; inhalation: opposed to *expiration.* [< OF < L *inspiratio, -onis*]

in·spi·ra·tion·al (in′spə·rā′shən·əl) *adj.* **1.** Of or pertaining to inspiration. **2.** Tending to inspire; inspiring. **3.** Derived from inspiration; inspired. — **in′spi·ra′tion·al·ly** *adv.*

in·spir·a·to·ry (in·spīr′ə·tôr′ē, -tō′rē) *adj.* Of or pertaining to inspiration or inhalation. [< L *inspiratus* + -ORY]

in·spire (in·spīr′) *v.* **·spired, ·spir·ing** *v.t.* **1.** To exert an invigorative influence upon (a person); animate; stir: His words *inspired* the crowd. **2.** To move (a person) to a particular feeling, idea, etc.: It *inspires* me with hope. **3.** To arouse or create (a feeling, idea, principle, etc.); generate: to *inspire* fear. **4.** To impart or suggest by divine intervention: hymns divinely *inspired.* **5.** To direct or guide, as by special divine influence: Let God's will *inspire* you. **6.** To breathe in; inhale: opposed to *expire.* **7.** *Obs.* To breathe or blow upon or into. — *v.i.* **8.** To inhale. **9.** To give or provide inspiration. [< OF *inspirer* < L *inspirare* to breathe into < *in-* into + *spirare* to breathe] — **in·spir′er** *n.*

in·spir·it (in·spir′it) *v.t.* To fill with renewed spirit or life; animate; exhilarate; enliven. — **in·spir′it·ing·ly** *adv.*

in·spis·sate (in·spis′āt) *v.t. & v.i.* **·sat·ed, ·sat·ing** To thicken, as by evaporation. [< L *inspissatus,* pp. of *inspissare* to thicken < *in-* thoroughly + *spissare* to thicken < *spissus* thick] — **in·spis·sa·tion** (in′spi·sā′shən) *n.* — **in·spis·sa·tor** (in′spi·sā′tər) *n.*

inst. 1. *Archaic* Instant (this month). **2.** Instantaneous. **3.** Instrument(al).

Inst. Institute; Institution.

in·sta·bil·i·ty (in′stə·bil′ə·tē) *n. pl.* **·ties 1.** Lack of stability or steadiness. **2.** Unsteadiness of character; unreliability; irresolution. [< MF *instabilité.* See STABILITY.]

in·sta·ble (in·stā′bəl) *adj.* Unstable.

in·stall (in·stôl′) *v.t.* **1.** To fix in position and adjust for service or use: to *install* a hot-water system. **2.** To place in any office, position, rank, etc. **3.** To establish in a place or position; settle: He *installed* himself in the easy chair. Also *Chiefly Brit.* **in·stal′.** [< MF *installer* < Med.L *installare* < *in-* in + *stallum* seat < OHG *stal* seat] — **in·stall′er** *n.*

in·stal·la·tion (in′stə·lā′shən) *n.* **1.** Any device or system, especially mechanical, set in place and readied for use. **2.** The act of installing, or the state of being installed. **3.** *Mil.* Any large, fixed base or facility of the armed service.

in·stall·ment¹ (in·stôl′mənt) *n.* **1.** A portion of a debt or sum of money made payable in specified amounts at specified intervals. **2.** One of several parts of anything supplied or presented at fixed intervals, as a serial in a newspaper or magazine. Also *Brit.* **in·stal′ment.** [< obs. *estall* to arrange payments < OF *estaler* to stop < OHG *stal* seat, place]

in·stall·ment² (in·stôl′mənt) *n.* Installation. Also *Brit.* **in·stal′ment.**

installment plan A system of paying for goods or services by fixed, periodic amounts.

in·stance (in′stəns) *n.* **1.** A case or example: to cite an *instance* of his honesty. **2.** A step in proceedings: in the first *instance*. **3.** *Law* A process or proceeding in a court; suit. **4.** *Archaic* Urgency. **— at the instance of** At the request or urging of. **— for instance** For example. **—** *v.t.* **·stanced, ·stanc·ing 1.** To cite as an example; adduce. **2.** *Rare* To show by an instance; exemplify. [< OF < L *instantia* presence, urgent pleading < *instans, -antis*. See INSTANT.]

in·stan·cy (in′stən·sē) *n.* *pl.* **·cies 1.** The quality of being instant or pressing; urgency. **2.** *Rare* Immediateness. **3.** *Rare* Imminence. [< L *instantia*. See INSTANCE.]

in·stant (in′stənt) *n.* **1.** A very short time; moment; twinkling. **2.** A specific point in time: at the same *instant*. **—** *adj.* **1.** Happening with no delay; instantaneous; immediate: *instant* recognition. **2.** Pressing; urgent: an *instant* need. **3.** Prepared quickly by the addition of water, milk, etc.: *instant* coffee; *instant* cocoa. **4.** *Archaic* Of or pertaining to the current month: the 10th *instant*: distinguished from *proximo, ultimo*. Abbr. (def. 4) *inst.* **—** *adv. Poetic* Instantaneously; instantly. [< OF < L *instans, -antis*, ppr. of *instare* to stand near, urge < *in-* upon + *stare* to stand]

in·stan·ta·ne·ous (in′stən·tā′nē·əs) *adj.* **1.** Happening with no delay; immediate. **2.** Acting or completed within a moment: an *instantaneous* flash. **3.** *Math.* Associated with a particular value of a variable; especially, pertaining to the average value of one variable within an infinitesimal interval of another variable: see CALCULUS. Abbr. *inst.* [< INSTANT, on analogy with *simultaneous*] **— in′stan·ta′ne·ous·ly** *adv.* **— in′stan·ta′ne·ous·ness** *n.*

in·stant·er (in·stan′tər) *adv.* Immediately; at once. [< L]

in·stant·ly (in′stənt·lē) *adv.* **1.** Without delay; at once. **2.** *Archaic* With urgency; insistently. **— Syn.** See IMMEDIATELY. **—** *conj.* As soon as.

in·star¹ (in·stär′) *n. Entomol.* An insect or arthropod in any stage during metamorphosis between successive molts; also, the stage itself. [< L, form, likeness]

in·star² (in·stär′) *v.t.* **·starred, ·star·ring 1.** To adorn with or as with stars. **2.** To make a star of. [< IN² + STAR]

in·state (in·stāt′) *v.t.* **·stat·ed, ·stat·ing 1.** *Rare* To place or establish in a certain condition, office, or position; place; install. **2.** *Obs.* To endow.

in sta·tu quo (in stā′tyōō kwō′, stach′ōō) *Latin* In the present or in the original condition.

in·stau·ra·tion (in′stô·rā′shən) *n. Archaic* Restoration; renewal; repair. [< L *instauratio, -onis* < *instauratus*, pp. of *instaurare* to renew]

in·stead (in·sted′) *adv.* **1.** In place or lieu; rather than: with *of*: a friend *instead* of an enemy. **2.** In the place of that just mentioned: to look for silver and find gold *instead*.

in·step (in′step′) *n. Anat.* The arched upper part of the human foot, extending from the toes to the ankle. ◆ Collateral adjective: *tarsal*. **2.** The part of a shoe or stocking covering the upper part of the foot. **3.** The front part of the hind leg of a horse, from the hock to the pastern joint.

in·sti·gate (in′stə·gāt) *v.t.* **·gat·ed, ·gat·ing 1.** To spur on or goad to some drastic course or deed; incite: to *instigate* one to murder. **2.** To bring about by inciting; foment; provoke: to *instigate* treason. [< L *instigatus*, pp. of *instigare* < *in-* against + the root *-stig-* to prick, goad] **— in′sti·ga′tive** *adj.* **— in′sti·ga′tor** *n.*

in·sti·ga·tion (in′stə·gā′shən) *n.* **1.** The act of instigating. **2.** An incentive; stimulus. [< L *instigatio, -onis*]

in·still (in·stil′) *v.t.* **1.** To introduce (a quality, feeling, idea, etc.) gradually or by degrees; infuse slowly: to *instill* courage. **2.** To pour in gradually by drops. Also *esp. Brit.* **in·stil′.** [< L *instillare* to put in by drops < *in-* + *stillare* to drop < *stilla* drop] **— in·stil·la·tion** (in′stə·lā′shən) *n.* **— in·still′er** *n.* **— in·still′ment** or **in·stil′ment** *n.*

in·stinct (*n.* in′stingkt; *adj.* in·stingkt′) *n.* **1.** *Biol. & Psychol.* An innate tendency or response of a given species to act in ways that are essential to its existence, development, and preservation. **2.** A natural aptitude; talent; knack. **—** *adj.* Animated from within; filled; alive: usually with *with*. [< L *instinctus*, pp. of *instinguere* to impel < root *-stig-*. See INSTIGATE.] **— in·stinc′tu·al** (-chōō·əl) *adj.*

in·stinc·tive (in·stingk′tiv) *adj.* **1.** Arising from or as from instinct: an *instinctive* fear. **2.** Of or pertaining to instinct. **— Syn.** See SPONTANEOUS. **— in·stinc′tive·ly** *adv.*

in·sti·tute (in′stə·tōōt, -tyōōt) *v.t.* **·tut·ed, ·tut·ing 1.** To set up or establish; found. **2.** To set in operation; initiate; start. **3.** *Eccl.* To place (a clergyman) in spiritual charge of a parish: with *in* or *into*. **—** *n.* **1.** A group or society devoted to the promotion of some particular field, often of a learned nature: an art *institute*; also, the building or buildings housing such a society. **2.** In education: **a** A short, intensive series of lectures, discussions, etc., designed for a particular occupational group. **b** *Usually cap.* A college for specialized instruction, often technical. **c** A center for postgraduate study and research in a highly specialized field, usually connected with a university. **3.** Something instituted, as an established principle, rule, or order. **4.** *Usually pl. & cap.* An elementary treatise on the principles of law: Coke's *Institutes*. Abbr. (for *n.* defs. 1, 2) *Inst.* [< L *institutus*, pp. of *instituere* to establish < *in-* in, on + *statuere* to set up]

in·sti·tu·tion (in′stə·tōō′shən, -tyōō′-) *n.* **1.** A principle, custom, system, etc., that forms part of a society or civilization: the *institution* of slavery. **2.** A corporate body organized to perform some particular function, often in education, research, charity, etc.: an *institution* of learning; a financial *institution*; also, the building or buildings housing such a body. Abbr. *Inst.* **3.** A mental hospital, prison, or other place of confinement: a euphemistic use. **4.** *Informal* A familiar and characteristic object, custom, or person: The grumpy postman was a local *institution*. **5.** The act of instituting, establishing, or setting in operation. **6.** *Eccl.* **a** The investment of a clergyman with the spiritual care of a parish. **b** The establishment of a sacrament, especially of the Eucharist, by Jesus Christ. [< OF < L *institutio, -onis*]

in·sti·tu·tion·al (in′stə·tōō′shən·əl, -tyōō′-) *adj.* **1.** Of, pertaining to, or characteristic of an institution. **2.** Of or relating to an organized society or the building where it operates. **3.** Designating a form of advertising intended to promote good will and prestige rather than to get immediate sales. **4.** Dealing with the fundamentals of a subject, especially of law. **— in′sti·tu′tion·al·ly** *adv.*

in·sti·tu·tion·al·ism (in′stə·tōō′shən·əl·iz′əm, -tyōō′-) *n.* **1.** The system of institutions. **2.** The belief in the authority of established institutions, especially of religion.

in·sti·tu·tion·al·ize (in′stə·tōō′shən·əl·īz′, -tyōō′-) *v.t.* **·ized, ·iz·ing 1.** To make institutional. **2.** To turn into or regard as an institution. **3.** *U.S. Informal* To put (someone) in an institution, as for the aged. **— in′sti·tu′tion·al·i·za′tion** *n.*

in·sti·tu·tion·ar·y (in′stə·tōō′shən·er′ē, -tyōō′-) *adj.* **1.** Of or pertaining to legal institutes. **2.** Relating to social, political, or ecclesiastical institutions.

in·sti·tu·tive (in′stə·tōō′tiv, -tyōō′-) *adj.* **1.** Tending or intended to institute or establish; having power to ordain. **2.** Established by authority; instituted. **— in′sti·tu′tive·ly** *adv.*

in·sti·tu·tor (in′stə·tōō′tər, -tyōō′-) *n.* **1.** One who establishes, organizes, or sets in operation; a founder. **2.** *U.S.* In the Protestant Episcopal Church, one who institutes a clergyman into a church or parish. Also **in′sti·tut′er.** [< L]

instr. 1. Instructor. **2.** Instrument(al).

in·struct (in·strukt′) *v.t.* **1.** To impart knowledge or skill to, especially by systematic method; educate; teach. **2.** To give specific orders or directions to; order: He *instructed* his men to break camp. **3.** To give information or explanation to; inform; apprise. **— Syn.** See TEACH. [< L *instructus*, pp. of *instruere* < *in-* in + *struere* to build]

in·struc·tion (in·struk′shən) *n.* **1.** The act of instructing or teaching. **2.** Knowledge or factual matter imparted; also, an item of such knowledge taught, as a rule, precept, or lesson. **3.** *pl.* Directions; orders. **— Syn.** See EDUCATION. [< OF < L *instructio, -onis*] **— in·struc′tion·al** *adj.*

in·struc·tive (in·struk′tiv) *adj.* Serving to instruct; conveying knowledge; informative. **— in·struc′tive·ly** *adv.* **— in·struc′tive·ness** *n.*

in·struc·tor (in·struk′tər) *n.* **1.** One who instructs; teacher. **2.** *U.S.* A college teacher ranking next below an assistant professor. Abbr. *instr.* [< L] **— in·struc′tress** *n. fem.*

in·struc·tor·ship (in·struk′tər·ship) *n.* The position or office of an instructor.

in·stru·ment (*n.* in′strə·mənt; *v.* in′strə·ment) *n.* **1.** A tool or implement, especially one used for exacting work: a surgical *instrument*. **2.** A device for producing musical sounds: a stringed *instrument*. Abbr. *inst., instr.* **3.** An apparatus for measuring or recording; as: **a** A gauge or device for indicating engine performance, etc., in automobiles, aircraft, refineries, and other complex systems. **b** A device used for precise measurement or control in scientific experimentation. **c** A system or device used for navigation and control in aircraft, ships, rockets, etc. **4.** Anything serving to accomplish a purpose; means; agency: an *instrument* of government. **5.** A person doing the will of another; cat's-paw; dupe. **6.** *Law* A formal legal document, as a contract, deed, etc. **— on instruments** *Aeron.* Flying, landing, or navigating by means of instruments rather than by visual observation of the horizon, ground objects, etc. **— Syn.** See TOOL. **—** *v.t.* To provide instrumentation for (an aircraft, missile, or other apparatus). [< L *instrumentum* < *instruere*. See INSTRUCT.]

in·stru·men·tal (in′strə·men′təl) *adj.* **1.** Serving as a means or instrument; useful; helpful; also, serving as the decisive or effective means: Einstein was *instrumental* in shaping modern physics. **2.** Of or pertaining to an instrument or tool. **3.** Of, pertaining to, composed for, or performed on musical instruments. **4.** *Gram.* Pertaining to a case of the noun, as in some inflected languages, indicating the means or instrument by or with which something is done. **—** *n. Gram.* **1.**

The instrumental case. **2.** A word in this case. *Abbr.* (for adj. defs. 3, 4; for n. defs. 1, 2) *inst., instr.* — **in·stru·men·tal·ly** *adv.* [< Med.L *instrumentalis* < *instrumentum*]

in·stru·men·tal·ism (in′strə·men′təl·iz′əm) *n. Philos.* The doctrine that reflective thought is an instrument to successful action, and that ideas are true or valid to the extent that they are useful in guiding action.

in·stru·men·tal·ist (in′strə·men′təl·ist) *n.* **1.** One who plays a musical instrument. **2.** *Philos.* An adherent of instrumentalism.

in·stru·men·tal·i·ty (in′strə·men·tal′ə·tē) *n. pl.* **·ties 1.** Anything serving to accomplish a purpose; means; agency. **2.** The condition of being instrumental.

in·stru·men·ta·tion (in′strə·men·tā′shən) *n.* **1.** The use of instruments; work performed with instruments, as in medicine. **2.** *Music* **a** The study of the characteristics of instruments and groupings of instruments. **b** Loosely, orchestration. **3.** A branch of engineering concerned with the use of instruments in military, technical, and scientific operations; also, an assembly of instruments, considered as a unit. **4.** Instrumentality; agency. [< F < L *instrumentum*]

in·stru·ment·ed (in′strə·men′tid) *adj.* Equipped with, employing, controlled or operated by, instruments: an *instrumented* rocket.

instrument flying Navigation of an aircraft by instruments alone.

instrument panel The panel holding the gauges and other indicators of performance in an automobile, airplane, engine room, etc. Also **instrument board.**

in·sub·or·di·nate (in′sə·bôr′də·nit) *adj.* Not subordinate or obedient; not submitting to authority; rebellious. — *n.* An insubordinate person. — **in′sub·or′di·nate·ly** *adv.*

in·sub·or·di·na·tion (in′sə·bôr′də·nā′shən) *n.* The state, quality, or fact of being insubordinate; disobedience.

in·sub·stan·tial (in′səb·stan′shəl) *adj.* **1.** Not real; imaginary; illusive. **2.** Not substantial, solid, or firm; flimsy. — **in′sub·stan′ti·al′i·ty** (-shē·al′ə·tē) *n.*

in·suf·fer·a·ble (in·suf′ər·ə·bəl) *adj.* Not to be endured; intolerable. — **in·suf′fer·a·ble·ness** *n.* — **in·suf′fer·a·bly** *adv.*

in·suf·fi·cien·cy (in′sə·fish′ən·sē) *n. pl.* **·cies** Lack of adequate effectiveness, amount, quality, etc.; inadequacy; deficiency. [< LL *insufficientia* < *insufficiens, -entis*]

in·suf·fi·cient (in′sə·fish′ənt) *adj.* Not enough; inadequate; deficient. — **in·suf·fi′cient·ly** *adv.*

in·suf·flate (in·suf′lāt, in′sə·flāt) *v.t.* **·flat·ed, ·flat·ing 1.** To breathe or blow into or upon. **2.** *Med.* To blow (air, gas, vapor, or powder) into the lungs or any body cavity. **3.** *Eccl.* To breathe upon, as at baptism. [< L *insufflatus*, pp. of *insufflare* to blow or breathe into < *in-* in + *sufflare* to blow up. See SUFFLATE.] — **in·suf·fla·tion** (in′sə·flā′shən) *n.* — **in·suf′fla·tor** *n.*

in·su·lar (in′sə·lər, -syə-) *adj.* **1.** Of, like, or pertaining to an island. **2.** Dwelling or situated on an island. **3.** Composing or forming an island. **4.** Separated; isolated. **5.** Narrow or limited in customs, opinions, etc.; provincial. **6.** *Anat.* Pertaining to an island of tissue, especially to the islands of Langerhans in the pancreas. — *n.* An islander. *Abbr. ins.* [< L *insularis* < *insula* island] — **in′su·lar·ism, in·su·lar·i·ty** (in′sə·lar′ə·tē, -syə-) *n.*

in·su·late (in′sə·lāt, -syə-) *v.t.* **·lat·ed, ·lat·ing 1.** To surround or separate with nonconducting material in order to prevent or lessen the leakage of electricity, heat, sound, radiation, etc. **2.** To place in a detached state or situation; isolate. [< L *insulatus* < *insula* island]

in·su·la·tion (in′sə·lā′shən, -syə-) *n.* **1.** Nonconducting material used for insulating. **2.** The act of insulating, or the state of being insulated. *Abbr. ins.*

in·su·la·tor (in′sə·lā′tər, -syə-) *n.* **1.** *Electr.* A device made of dielectric material, as glass or porcelain, and used to insulate and support a conductor. **2.** One who or that which insulates.

in·su·lin (in′sə·lin, -syə-) *n. Biochem.* **1.** A protein hormone secreted in the pancreas of man and other vertebrates, essential in regulating the metabolism of sugar. **2.** Any of various therapeutic preparations of this hormone, used in treating diabetes. [< L *insula* island (of Langerhans) + -IN]

In·sull (in′sul), **Samuel,** 1859–1938, U.S. utilities promoter born in England.

in·sult (*v.* in·sult′; *n.* in′sult) *v.t.* To treat with insolence or contempt; disparage; abuse; affront. — **Syn.** See OFFEND. — *n.* An act, remark, etc., that offends or affronts. [< MF *insulter* < L *insultare* to leap at, insult, freq. of *insilire* to leap upon < *in-* on + *salire* to leap] — **in·sult′er** *n.*

in·sult·ing (in·sul′ting) *adj.* Conveying or inflicting insult; deliberately abusive or scornful. — **in·sult′ing·ly** *adv.*

in·su·per·a·ble (in·soo′pər·ə·bəl) *adj.* Not to be surmounted or overcome. [< L *insuperabilis*] — **in·su′per·a·bil′i·ty, in·su′per·a·ble·ness** *n.* — **in·su′per·a·bly** *adv.*

in·sup·port·a·ble (in′sə·pôr′tə·bəl, -pôr′-) *adj.* **1.** Not bearable; insufferable. **2.** Having no grounds; unjustifiable. — **in′sup·port′a·ble·ness** *n.* — **in′sup·port′a·bly** *adv.*

in·sup·press·i·ble (in′sə·pres′ə·bəl) *adj.* Incapable of being suppressed; irrepressible. — **in′sup·press′i·bly** *adv.*

in·sur·ance (in·shoor′əns) *n.* **1.** Protection against risk, loss, or ruin, by a contract in which an insurer or underwriter guarantees to pay a sum of money to the insured or the beneficiary in the event of some contingency, as death, accident, fire, etc., in return for the payment of premiums; also, the business of providing this protection. **2.** A contract guaranteeing such protection; policy. Also **insurance policy. 3.** The payment made by the insured party; premium. **4.** The amount for which anything is insured. **5.** Any safeguard against risk or harm. *Abbr. ins.*

in·sur·ant (in·shoor′ənt) *n.* One to whom an insurance policy is issued.

in·sure (in·shoor′) *v.* **·sured, ·sur·ing** *v.t.* **1.** To guarantee against risk or loss of (life, property, etc.) with insurance; cover with insurance. **2.** To ensure. — *v.i.* **3.** To issue or buy insurance. [ME *ensuren*, infl. by AF *enseurer* < *en-* in + *seur* sure] — **in·sur′a·bil′i·ty** *n.* — **in·sur′a·ble** *adj.*

in·sured (in·shoord′) *n.* The person or persons protected by insurance.

in·sur·er (in·shoor′ər) *n.* **1.** One who or that which insures. **2.** A person or company contracting, upon payment of premiums, to protect one against specified loss or damage.

in·sur·gence (in·sûr′jəns) *n.* The act of rising in insurrection; revolt; uprising.

in·sur·gen·cy (in·sûr′jən·sē) *n.* **1.** The state of being insurgent. **2.** In international law, the status of insurrectionists not strong enough to be recognized as belligerents.

in·sur·gent (in·sûr′jənt) *adj.* Rising in revolt against established authority; rebellious. — *n.* **1.** One who takes part in forcible resistance or opposition to an existing government; especially, a rebel not recognized as a belligerent. **2.** *U.S.* A member of a political party who rebels against party leadership. [< L *insurgens, -entis,* ppr. of *insurgere* to rise up against < *in-* against + *surgere* to rise]

in·sur·mount·a·ble (in′sər·moun′tə·bəl) *adj.* Incapable of being surmounted, passed over, or overcome; insuperable. — **in′sur·mount′a·bly** *adv.*

in·sur·rec·tion (in′sə·rek′shən) *n.* An organized resistance to established government. [< F < LL *insurrectio, -onis* < L *insurrectus*, pp. of *insurgere* to rise up against. See INSURGENT.] — **in′sur·rec′tion·al** *adj.* — **in′sur·rec′tion·ar′y** *adj. & n.* — **in′sur·rec′tion·ism** *n.* — **in′sur·rec′tion·ist** *n.*

in·sus·cep·ti·ble (in′sə·sep′tə·bəl) *adj.* Incapable of being affected or infected; resistant; immune: often with *to* or *of.* — **in′sus·cep′ti·bil′i·ty** *n.*

in·swathe (in·swāth′) See ENSWATHE.

in·swept (in′swept′) *adj.* Narrowed or tapering in front.

int. 1. Intelligence. **2.** Interest. **3.** Interior. **4.** Interjection. **5.** Internal. **6.** International. **7.** Interval. **8.** Intransitive.

in·tact (in·takt′) *adj.* Remaining whole, unchanged, and undamaged; unimpaired. [< L *intactus* untouched < *in-* not + *tactus,* pp. of *tangere* to touch] — **in·tact′ness** *n.*

in·ta·glio (in·tal′yō, *Ital.* ēn·tä′lyō) *n. pl.* **·glios** or **·gli** (-lyē) **1.** Incised carving; a sunken design. **2.** The art of making such designs. **3.** A work, especially a gem, with incised carving. **4.** A countersunk die for producing a relief design. [< *Ital.* < *intagliare* to engrave < *in-* in + *tagliare* to cut]

intaglio printing A method of printing from sunken or incised plates: also called *copperplate* or *steel-die printing.*

in·take (in′tāk′) *n.* **1.** The act of taking in or absorbing. **2.** That which is taken in: the annual *intake.* **3.** The amount or quantity absorbed: the *intake* of air. **4.** The place where water is drawn into a pipe, channel, or conduit. **5.** The amount of energy or power taken into a machine or system. **6.** The air shaft of a mine. **7.** A narrowing or contraction, as in the width of a tube, knitted garment, etc.

in·tan·gi·ble (in·tan′jə·bəl) *adj.* **1.** Incapable of being perceived by touch; lacking physical substance; impalpable. **2.** Indefinite or vague to the mind. — *n.* That which is intangible; especially, any incorporeal asset or benefit, as a trademark, franchise, or good will. [< Med.L *intangibilis*] — **in·tan′gi·bil′i·ty, in·tan′gi·ble·ness** *n.* — **in·tan′gi·bly** *adv.*

in·tar·si·a (in·tär′sē·ə) *n.* A style of mosaic woodwork, popular in Renaissance Italy. [< *Ital. intarsio* < *intarsiare* to inlay, encrust < *in-* in + Arabic *tarsi* incrustation]

in·te·ger (in′tə·jər) *n.* **1.** *Math.* Any of the numbers ± 1, ± 2, ± 3, etc., as distinguished from a fraction or mixed number: also called *whole number.* **2.** A whole entity. [< L, untouched < *in-* not + root *tag-*, of *tangere* to touch. Doublet of ENTIRE.]

in·te·ger vi·tae (in′tə·jər vī′tē) *Latin* Innocent; pure: literally, blameless in life. Horace, *Odes* I:22.

in·te·gra·ble (in′tə·grə·bəl) *adj.* Capable of being integrated, as a mathematical function or differential equation. [< L *integrare* to make whole. See INTEGRATE.]

in·te·gral (in′tə·grəl) *adj.* **1.** Being an indispensable part of a whole; essential; constituent. **2.** Formed of parts that together constitute a unity: an *integral* whole. **3.** Whole;

entire; complete. **4.** *Math.* **a** Pertaining to an integer. **b** Produced by integration. — *n.* **1.** An entire thing; a whole. **2.** *Math.* The result of integration. [< LL *integralis*] — **in'te·gral'i·ty** (-gral/ə·tē) *n.* — **in'te·gral·ly** *adv.*

integral calculus See under CALCULUS.

in·te·grand (in/tə·grand) *n. Math.* An expression to be integrated. [< L *integrandus*, gerundive of *integrare* to make whole]

in·te·grant (in/tə·grənt) *adj.* Contributing to or essential to composing a whole; integral. — *n.* A component. [< L *integrans, -antis,* ppr. of *integrare* to make whole]

in·te·grate (in/tə·grāt) *v.* **·grat·ed, ·grat·ing** *v.t.* **1.** To bring together into a whole; fit together; unify. **2.** *U.S.* To make the use or occupancy of (a school, park, neighborhood, etc.) available to persons of all races. **3.** To make whole or complete by the addition of necessary parts. **4.** *Rare* To give the total or mean value of. **5.** *Math.* To find the integral value of. **6.** *Psychol.* To effect the integration of. — *v.i.* **7.** *U.S.* To become available to persons of all races, as a school, etc. [< L *integratus,* pp. of *integrare* to make whole, renew < *integer.* See INTEGER.] — **in'te·gra'tive** *adj.*

in·te·gra·tion (in/tə·grā'shən) *n.* **1.** The act or operation of integrating; the bringing or fitting together of parts into a whole. **2.** *U.S.* The act or process of making public facilities, as schools, restaurants, parks, etc., available to persons of all races, national groups, etc. **3.** *Math.* The process of determining a function from its derivatives. **4.** *Physiol.* The interaction of different cellular and nervous processes in such a way as to secure maximum unity in the performance of bodily functions. **5.** *Psychoanal.* The orderly balancing of the physical, emotional, or mental components of the personality into a more or less stable pattern of behavior. — **sign of integration** A sign ($\int$) prefixed to the differential whose integral is to be taken: originally a long *S* (for Latin *summa* sum). [< L *integratio, -onis*]

in·te·gra·tor (in/tə·grā'tər) *n.* **1.** One who or that which integrates. **2.** Any mechanical device for obtaining the numerical value of an integral, especially the area of an irregular figure, as a planimeter. [< L]

in·teg·ri·ty (in·teg/rə·tē) *n.* **1.** Uprightness of character; probity; honesty. **2.** The condition or quality of being unimpaired or sound. **3.** The state of being complete or undivided: the *integrity* of the kingdom. [< L *integritas, -tatis < integer* untouched. See INTEGER.]

in·teg·u·ment (in·teg/yə·mənt) *n.* A covering or outer coating; especially, a natural covering or envelope, as the skin of an animal, coat of a seed, etc. [< L *integumentum* covering < *integere* to cover < *in-* thoroughly + *tegere* to cover] — **in·teg/u·men/ta·ry** *adj.*

in·tel·lect (in/tə·lekt) *n.* **1.** The power of the mind to grasp ideas and relations, and to exercise dispassionate reason and rational judgment; reason; understanding. **2.** A mind or intelligence, especially a strong or brilliant one. **3.** An intelligent person. **4.** Mental power collectively: the *intellect* of the nation. [< L *intellectus* perception, understanding, sense, pp. of < *intelligere.* See INTELLIGENT.]
— **Syn. 1.** *Intellect, mind, reason, intelligence, wits,* and *brains* are compared as they denote the human power of thinking. *Intellect,* reflecting an older psychological use that has been abandoned, refers specifically to the powers of knowing and thinking, as distinguished from those of feeling and willing, while *mind* is the sum of all these powers or faculties. *Reason* is the ability to think, or at its simplest the ability to elaborate sense impressions into concepts; we speak of *reason* as distinguishing man from the lower animals. *Intelligence* is chiefly used to mean the capacity to learn or to deal with new situations; this power can be tested and measured. *Wits* and *brains* are popular words for *intelligence* as it is applied to specific situations; *wits* suggests inborn *intelligence,* and *brains,* the competence and resourcefulness that are achieved through effort.

in·tel·lec·tion (in/tə·lek/shən) *n.* **1.** Exercise of the intellect. **2.** A specific act of the intellect; notion; idea. [< Med.L *intellectio, -onis*]

in·tel·lec·tive (in/tə·lek/tiv) *adj.* Of or pertaining to the intellect; intellectual. [< OF *intellectif* < LL *intellectivus*] — **in'tel·lec/tive·ly** *adv.*

in·tel·lec·tu·al (in/tə·lek/chŏŏ·əl) *adj.* **1.** Of or pertaining to the intellect; noetic; mental. **2.** Engaging, or requiring the use of, the intellect: *intellectual* work. **3.** Possessing or showing intellect, especially of a high order. — *n.* **1.** One who pursues and enjoys matters of the intellect and of refined taste. **2.** One whose work requires primarily the use of the intellect. **3.** One who possessess high intelligence. **4.** *pl. Archaic* Mental powers or faculties. [< L *intellectualis*] — **in'tel·lec/tu·al·ly** *adv.*

in·tel·lec·tu·al·ism (in/tə·lek/chŏŏ·əl·iz/əm) *n.* **1.** Devotion to intellectual interests. **2.** The exercise of the intellect. **3.** *Philos.* **a** The doctrine that pure reason is wholly or largely the source of knowledge. **b** The doctrine that the ultimate principle of all reality is intellect or reason. — **in'tel·lec/tu·al·ist** *n.* — **in'tel·lec/tu·al·is/tic** *adj.*

in·tel·lec·tu·al·i·ty (in/tə·lek/chŏŏ·al/ə·tē) *n. pl.* **·ties 1.** The quality of being intellectual. **2.** Intellectual force, ability, or endowment.

in·tel·lec·tu·al·ize (in/tə·lek/chŏŏ·əl·īz) *v.* **·ized, ·iz·ing** *v.t.*

1. To make intellectual; view or express intellectually. — *v.i.* **2.** To think; reason.

in·tel·li·gence (in·tel/ə·jəns) *n.* **1.** The faculty of perceiving and comprehending meaning; mental quickness; active intellect; understanding. **2.** The ability to adapt to new situations, and to learn from experience. **3.** The inherent ability to seize the essential factors of a complex matter. **4.** The quality or ability measured by an intelligence test. **5.** The collection of secret information, as by police or military authorities. **6.** Information that has been so collected; also, the staff of persons occupied with this process. **7.** *Often cap.* An intelligent or rational being, especially one that is not embodied. **8.** *Archaic* Any informative report received or relayed; news; tidings. **9.** In Christian Science, the primal and eternal quality of infinite Mind; God. Abbr. *int.* — **Syn.** See INTELLECT. [< OF < L *intelligens, -entis,* ppr. of *intelligere.* See INTELLIGENT.]

intelligence quotient *Psychol.* A number indicating the level of a person's mental development, obtained by multiplying his mental age by 100, and dividing the result by his chronological age, the latter generally not exceeding 16. Abbr. *IQ, I.Q.*

in·tel·li·genc·er (in·tel/ə·jən·sər) *n. Archaic* A sender or conveyor of intelligence or news; a messenger; spy.

intelligence test *Psychol.* Any standardized test, or series of tests, designed to determine relative mental capacity.

in·tel·li·gent (in·tel/ə·jənt) *adj.* **1.** Having an active, discerning mind; mentally perceptive; acute: an *intelligent* reader. **2.** Marked or characterized by intelligence. **3.** Endowed with intellect or understanding; reasoning: an *intelligent* creature. **4.** *Rare* Cognizant: with *of.* [< L *intelligens, -entis,* ppr. of *intelligere* to understand, perceive < *inter-* between + *legere* to choose] — **in·tel/li·gent·ly** *adv.* — **Syn. 1.** quick-witted, sharp-witted, knowing, alert. Compare BRIGHT, CLEVER. — **Ant.** unintelligent, slow-witted, stupid.

in·tel·li·gen·tial (in·tel/ə·jen/shəl) *adj.* **1.** Exercising or characterized by intelligence; rational. **2.** Conveying intelligence or information.

in·tel·li·gent·si·a (in·tel/ə·jent/sē·ə, -gent/-) *n.pl.* Intellectual or educated people collectively, especially those with a broad and informed point of view. [< Russian *intelligentsiya, ?* < Ital. *intelligenza* intelligence < L *intelligentia*]

in·tel·li·gi·bil·i·ty (in·tel/ə·jə·bil/ə·tē) *n. pl.* **·ties** The quality or state of being readily understood; clarity.

in·tel·li·gi·ble (in·tel/ə·jə·bəl) *adj.* **1.** Capable of being understood. **2.** *Philos.* Capable of being apprehended only by the intellect, not by the senses. — **Syn.** See CLEAR. [< L *intelligibilis*] — **in·tel/li·gi·bly** *adv.*

in·tem·er·ate (in·tem/ər·it) *adj. Rare* Undefiled; pure. [< L *intemeratus* < *in-* not + *temeratus,* pp. of *temerare* to violate < *temere* rashly, by chance]

in·tem·per·ance (in·tem/pər·əns) *n.* Lack of temperance or moderation; especially, excessive use of alcoholic drinks. [< OF < L *intemperantia*]

in·tem·per·ate (in·tem/pər·it) *adj.* **1.** Lacking moderation, as in speech or action; unrestrained. **2.** Given to or characterized by excessive use of alcoholic drinks: *intemperate* habits. **3.** Excessive or extreme, as climate or the weather. — **in·tem/per·ate·ly** *adv.* — **in·tem/per·ate·ness** *n.*

in·tend (in·tend/) *v.t.* **1.** To have as a specific aim or purpose; plan; propose: He *intends* to speak up. **2.** To make, design, or destine for a purpose, use, etc.: a dress *intended* for summer. **3.** To mean or signify; indicate: a gesture *intending* dismissal. **4.** *Archaic* To direct or aim. — *v.i.* **5.** To have a purpose or plan. [< OF *entendre* < L *intendere* to stretch out (for) < *in-* in, at + *tendere* to stretch]

in·ten·dance (in·ten/dəns) *n.* **1.** Management or superintendence. **2.** An intendancy. [< F]

in·ten·dan·cy (in·ten/dən·sē) *n. pl.* **·cies 1.** The office or work of an intendant; intendants collectively. **2.** An administrative district in Spanish America.

in·ten·dant (in·ten/dənt) *n.* **1.** A superintendent; provincial administrator, as under the Bourbons in France. **2.** A Spanish or Mexican district administrator. [< F]

in·tend·ed (in·ten/did) *adj.* **1.** Planned; proposed: the *intended* results. **2.** Prospective: one's *intended* wife. — *n. Informal* Prospective husband or wife.

in·tend·ment (in·tend/mənt) *n.* **1.** *Law* True meaning as fixed by law. **2.** *Obs.* Intention. [< OF *entendement*]

in·ten·er·ate (in·ten/ər·āt) *v.t.* **·at·ed, ·at·ing** *Rare* To make tender; soften. [< L *in-* very + *tener* tender + -ATE[1]] — **in·ten/er·a/tion** *n.*

intens. Intensive.

in·tense (in·tens/) *adj.* **1.** Having great or extreme force; present in a very high degree; very strong; overpowering: *intense* light; *intense* feelings. **2.** Performed strenuously and steadily; ardent; diligent; hard: *intense* study. **3.** Expressing strong emotion, as determination, deep inquiry, etc.: an *intense* look; also, characterized by strong and earnest feelings: an *intense* person. **4.** Having its quality strongly concentrated. **5.** *Photog.* Having extreme contrast: said of negatives and prints. [< OF < L *intensus,* pp. of *intendere* to stretch out] — **in·tense/ly** *adv.* — **in·tense/ness** *n.*

in·ten·si·fy (in·ten/sə·fī) *v.* **·fied, ·fy·ing** *v.t.* **1.** To make more intense or acute; aggravate; increase; also, to make intense. **2.** *Photog.* To increase the contrast of (a negative or print). **—v.i. 3.** To become more intense; become intense. **— in·ten′si·fi·ca′tion, in·ten′si·fi′er** *n.*

in·ten·sion (in-ten′shən) *n.* **1.** *Rare* Resolution; determination. **2.** *Archaic* Intensification. **3.** *Rare* Depth; force. **4.** *Logic* All the implications in a concept or term; connotation: distinguished from *extension.* [< L *intensio, -onis*]

in·ten·si·ty (in-ten′sə-tē) *n. pl.* **·ties 1.** The state or quality of being intense; extreme force, brightness, concentration, etc. **2.** The strength or degree of some action, quality, feeling, etc.: pain of low *intensity.* **3.** Power and vehemence of thought or feeling; also, extreme effort and concentration. **4.** *Physics* The measured force, energy, or quantity of action of any physical agent per unit of volume, area, mass, etc.: *intensity* of radiation. **5.** *Electr.* **a** The strength of an electric or magnetic field. **b** Current strength in amperes. **c** Electromotive force; potential. **6.** *Photog.* Strong contrast between light and dark in a negative or print.

in·ten·sive (in-ten′siv) *adj.* **1.** Of, pertaining to, or marked by intensity. **2.** Intensifying. **3.** *Agric.* Pertaining to a method of farming whereby much capital and labor are expended upon making a small area highly productive. Compare EXTENSIVE. **4.** *Med.* Increasing in strength or degree, as successive injections, drug dosages, or other measures in treating an illness. **5.** *Gram.* Adding emphasis or force. **6.** *Logic* Of or relating to intension. **— n. 1.** That which gives intensity or emphasis. **2.** *Gram.* An intensive particle, word, or phrase. [< F *intensif* < Med.L *intensivus*] **— in·ten′sive·ly** *adv.* **— in·ten′sive·ness** *n.*

intensive particle *Gram.* A particle or prefix expressing heightened meanings: as *be-* in *besmirch*; *for-* in *forlorn*; *de-* in *desiccate*; *per-* in *perjure.* Also **intensive prefix.**

in·tent (in-tent′) *n.* **1.** Purpose; aim; goal; design. **2.** The act of intending. **3.** *Law* The state of mind in which or the purpose with which one does an act; also, the character that the law imputes to an act. **— Syn.** See PURPOSE. **— adj. 1.** Firmly directed or fixed; unwavering; steadfast: an *intent* stare. **2.** Directing one's mind or efforts steadfastly; earnestly attentive: with *on* or *upon*: *intent* on mischief. [< OF *entent, entente* < L *intentus*, pp. of *intendere* to stretch out, endeavor] **— in·tent′ly** *adv.* **— in·tent′ness** *n.*

in·ten·tion (in-ten′shən) *n.* **1.** Purpose, either ultimate or immediate; aim; goal. **2.** The act of intending. **3.** *pl. Informal* Purpose with regard to marriage. **4.** *Law* The will, design, or resolve to do or refrain from doing an act. **5.** *Med.* Natural course, operation, or process, as in the healing of a wound. **6.** *Logic* The general concept or notion of a thing. **— Syn.** See PURPOSE. [< OF *entencion* < L *intentio, -onis*]

in·ten·tion·al (in-ten′shən-əl) *adj.* **1.** Resulting from purpose; deliberate; intended. **2.** *Rare* Of or pertaining to intention. [< Med.L *intentionalis*] **— in·ten′tion·al·ly** *adv.*

in·ten·tioned (in-ten′shənd) *adj.* Having or characterized by (a specified kind of) intention or intentions: used in combination: *well-intentioned.*

in·ter (in-tûr′) *v.t.* **·terred, ·ter·ring** To place in a grave; bury. [< OF *enterrer* < LL *interrare* < *in-* in + *terra* earth]

inter- *prefix* **1.** With each other; together: *intertwine.* **2.** Mutual; mutually: *intercommunity.* **3.** Between (the units signified): *intercollegiate.* **4.** Occurring or situated between: *interlinear.* [< L *inter-* < *inter* between, among]

Following is a list of self-explanatory words containing the prefix *inter-*:

interacademic	intercranial	intermundane
interagency	intercross	intermural
interagent	intercrust	interocular
interallied	intercultural	interoffice
interanimate	interdiffuse	interparental
interarmy	interdiffusion	interparty
interatomic	interdigital	interpersonal
interatrial	interfaith	interplace
interbank	interfibrous	interpolar
interborough	interfraternity	interreact
interbrachial	interfriction	interreceive
intercapillary	interglandular	interregional
intercardinal	interglobular	interrule
intercarotid	intergroup	interscapular
intercarpal	interinsular	interscene
intercaste	interionic	interschool
interchain	interisland	intersocial
interchurch	interjoin	intersonant
intercirculate	interjunction	intertangle
intercity	interknot	interterritorial
interclasp	interlap	intertraffic
interclass	interlibrary	intertubular
interclub	interligamentous	interunion
intercolonial	interlink	interuniversity
intercommunion	interlobate	intervarietal
intercompany	interlocal	intervertebral
intercomplexity	interlocated	interwind
interconversion	intermammary	interwork
interconvertible	intermigration	interwreathe

inter. Intermediate.

in·ter·act (in′tər-akt′) *v.i.* To act on each other. **— in′·ter·ac′tive** *adj.* **— in′ter·ac·tiv′i·ty** *n.*

in·ter·ac·tion (in′tər-ak′shən) *n.* Action on each other.

in·ter a·li·a (in′tər ā′lē-ə) *Latin* Among other things.

in·ter a·li·os (in′tər ā′lē-ōs) *Latin* Among other persons.

in·ter-A·mer·i·can (in′tər-ə-mer′ə-kən) *adj.* Of or involving two or more nations of North, Central, or South America.

in·ter·bed·ded (in′tər-bed′id) *adj. Geol.* Occurring between beds or strata of rocks.

in·ter·blend (in′tər-blend′) *v.t. & v.i.* **·blend·ed** or **·blent, ·blend·ing** To blend or be blended together thoroughly.

in·ter·brain (in′tər-brān′) *n. Anat.* The diencephalon.

in·ter·breed (in′tər-brēd′) *v.* **·bred, ·breed·ing** *v.t.* **1.** To breed (different stocks) together; hybridize; crossbreed. **2.** To produce (offspring) by crossbreeding. **—v.i. 3.** To breed with each other: said of genetically dissimilar stocks or individuals; also, to cause or practice such breeding.

in·ter·ca·lar·y (in-tûr′kə-ler′ē) *adj.* **1.** Added to the calendar. **2.** Having an added day or month. **3.** Interpolated; intervening. [< L *intercalarius*]

in·ter·ca·late (in-tûr′kə-lāt) *v.t.* **·lat·ed, ·lat·ing 1.** To insert or interpolate. **2.** To insert, as an additional day or month, into the calendar. [< L *intercalatus*, pp. of *intercalare* to insert < *inter-* between + *calare* to proclaim, call]

in·ter·ca·la·tion (in-tûr′kə-lā′shən) *n.* **1.** The act of intercalating. **2.** That which is intercalated, as a day.

in·ter·cede (in′tər-sēd′) *v.i.* **·ced·ed, ·ced·ing 1.** To plead or petition in behalf of another or others: I *interceded* for him with the police. **2.** To come between parties in a dispute; mediate. [< L *intercedere* to come between < *inter-* between + *cedere* to pass, go] **— in′ter·ced′er** *n.*

in·ter·cel·lu·lar (in′tər-sel′yə-lər) *adj. Biol.* Situated between or among cells.

in·ter·cept (*v.* in′tər-sept′; *n.* in′tər-sept) *v.t.* **1.** To seize or stop on the way; prevent from reaching the destination. **2.** To meet, as a moving person, ship, airplane, etc. **3.** To interrupt the course of; obstruct: to *intercept* the light. **4.** *Math.* To mark off or bound a line, plane, surface, or solid. **— n. 1.** In the U.S. Air Force, an act or instance of interception. **2.** *Math.* **a** An intercepted part. **b** A point of interception. [< L *interceptus*, pp. of *intercipere* < *inter-* between + *capere* to seize] **— in′ter·cep′tive** *adj.*

in·ter·cep·tion (in′tər-sep′shən) *n.* The act of intercepting, or the state of being intercepted.

in·ter·cep·tor (in′tər-sep′tər) *n.* **1.** One who or that which intercepts. **2.** An airplane designed for the pursuit and interception of enemy aircraft. Also **in′ter·cept′er.** [< L]

in·ter·ces·sion (in′tər-sesh′ən) *n.* **1.** The act of interceding between persons; entreaty in behalf of others. **2.** Prayer on behalf of others. [< L *intercessio, -onis* < *intercessus*, pp. of *intercedere.* See INTERCEDE.] **— in′ter·ces′sion·al** *adj.*

in·ter·ces·sor (in′tər-ses′ər) *n.* One who intercedes; a mediator. [< L] **— in′ter·ces′so·ry** *adj.*

in·ter·change (*v.* in′tər-chānj′, *n.* in′tər-chānj′) *v.* **·changed, ·chang·ing** *v.t.* **1.** To put each of (two things) in the place of the other. **2.** To cause to alternate. **3.** To give and receive in return, as gifts. **—v.i. 4.** To change places one with the other. **— n. 1.** A reciprocal giving in exchange. **2.** An exchanging of places. **3.** Alternation. **4.** An intersection of a superhighway with another highway or road, so designed that vehicles may enter or turn off without obstructing traffic. [< OF *entrechangier* < *entre-* between (< L *inter-*) + *changier* < LL *cambiare* to exchange] **— in′ter·chang′er** *n.*

in·ter·change·a·ble (in′tər-chān′jə-bəl) *adj.* Capable of being interchanged or substituted one for the other; permitting transposition. [< OF *entrechangeable*] **— in′ter·change′a·bil′i·ty, in′ter·change′a·ble·ness** *n.* **— in′ter·change′a·bly** *adv.*

in·ter·clav·i·cle (in′tər-klav′i-kəl) *n. Anat.* A median ventral bone between the clavicles or in front of the sternum in some vertebrates. **— in′ter·cla·vic′u·lar** (-klə-vik′yə-lər) *adj.*

in·ter·col·le·giate (in′tər-kə-lē′jit, -jē-it) *adj.* Pertaining to or involving two or more colleges: *intercollegiate* sports.

in·ter·col·um·ni·a·tion (in′tər-kə-lum′nē-ā′shən) *n. Archit.* **1.** The method of spacing between columns. **2.** The space between two consecutive columns. [< L *intercolumnium* space between columns + -ATION] **— in′ter·co·lum′nar** *adj.*

in·ter·com (in′tər-kom′) *n. Informal* A telephone or radio system for intercommunication.

in·ter·com·mu·ni·cate (in′tər-kə-myoo′nə-kāt) *v.i.* **·cat·ed, ·cat·ing** To communicate with one another; especially, to talk between offices, buildings, etc., by means of a telephone or radio system. **— in′ter·com·mu′ni·ca′tion** *n.* **— in′ter·com·mu′ni·ca′tive** *adj.* **— in′ter·com·mun′i·ca·tor** *n.*

in·ter·com·mu·ni·ty (in′tər-kə-myoo′nə-tē) *n. pl.* **·ties** The condition of being common to two or more; mutuality.

in·ter·con·nect (in′tər-kə-nekt′) *v.t. & v.i.* To connect or be connected one with the other. **— in′ter·con·nec′tion** *n.*

in·ter·con·ti·nen·tal (in′tər-kon′tə-nen′təl) *adj.* Reaching or capable of reaching from one continent to another; also, pertaining to or involving two or more continents.

intercontinental ballistic missile The ICBM.

in·ter·cos·tal (in′tər·kos′təl) *adj.* *Anat.* Situated or occurring between the ribs. [< NL *intercostalis* < L *inter-* between + *costa* rib] — **in′ter·cos′tal·ly** *adv.*

in·ter·course (in′tər·kôrs, -kōrs) *n.* **1.** Mutual exchange; commerce; communication. **2.** The interchange of ideas. **3.** Sexual connection; coitus. [< OF *entrecours* < L *intercursus*, pp. of *intercurrere* to run between < *inter-* between + *currere* to run]

in·ter·crop (*v.* in′tər·krop′; *n.* in′tər·krop′) *Agric.* *v.t.* & *v.i.* **·cropped, ·crop·ping** To cultivate between rows of a crop. — *n.* A crop cultivated between rows of another crop.

in·ter·cross (in′tər·krôs′, -kros′) *v.t.* **1.** To cross (each other). **2.** To cross by interbreeding. — *v.i.* **3.** To cross each other. **4.** To interbreed. — *n.* A hybrid.

in·ter·cur·rent (in′tər·kur′ənt) *adj.* **1.** Occurring in between; intervening. **2.** *Pathol.* Taking place during and altering the course of a previously existing disease. [< L *intercurrens, -entis*, ppr. of *intercurrere* to run between]

in·ter·de·nom·i·na·tion·al (in′tər·di·nom′ə·nā′shən·əl) *adj.* Of or pertaining to two or more religious denominations.

in·ter·den·tal (in′tər·den′təl) *adj.* **1.** Situated between the teeth. **2.** *Phonet.* Produced with the tip of the tongue between the teeth, as (*th*) in *thing*: also *dentilingual*. — *n.* *Phonet.* An interdental consonant: also called *dentilingual*.

in·ter·de·pen·dent (in′tər·di·pen′dənt) *adj.* Dependent one on another; reciprocally dependent. — **in′ter·de·pend′ence, in′ter·de·pend′en·cy** *n.* — **in′ter·de·pend′ent·ly** *adv.*

in·ter·dict (*v.* in′tər·dikt′, *n.* in′tər·dikt′) *v.t.* **1.** To prohibit or debar (some action, right of use, etc.) authoritatively; also, to forbid (a person or persons) to have or do something. **2.** *Eccl.* To exclude (a place or certain persons) from participation in rites and services. — **Syn.** See PROHIBIT. — *n.* **1.** In the Roman Catholic Church, a ban forbidding the sacraments and solemn services to a place or to certain church members, but not imposing excommunication. **2.** In Scottish law, an injunction. **3.** In ancient Roman law, a prohibitory edict of the praetor. [< OF *entredit* < L *interdictum*, pp. of *interdicere* to forbid < *inter-* between + *dicere* to say; refashioned after L] — **in′ter·dic′tive, in′ter·dic′to·ry** (-tə·rē) *adj.* — **in′ter·dic′tive·ly** *adv.* — **in′ter·dic′tor** *n.*

in·ter·dic·tion (in′tər·dik′shən) *n.* **1.** The act of interdicting, or the state of being interdicted. **2.** An interdict.

in·ter·dis·ci·pli·nar·y (in′tər·dis′ə·plə·ner′ē) *adj.* Pertaining to or involving two or more branches of knowledge.

in·ter·est (in′tər·ist, -trist) *n.* **1.** A feeling of curiosity or attentiveness. **2.** The power to arouse curiosity or attentiveness: the subject has *interest*; also, something that has such power: Tennis is his chief *interest*. **3.** That which is of advantage; profit; benefit. **4.** Involvement or concern in something: an *interest* in good government; also, selfish concern: to be guided by *interest* alone. **5.** Payment for the use of money or credit, usually expressed as a percentage of the amount owed or used, and depending also on the duration of the debt. See COMPOUND INTEREST, SIMPLE INTEREST. *Abbr.* *i., int.* **6.** Something added in making a return; something more than is due: to give back a blow with *interest*. **7.** Legal or financial right, claim, or share, as in a business or estate; also, that in which one has such a right, claim, or share. **8.** *Usually pl.* A group of persons involved in a particular business, industry, cause, etc.: the dairy *interests*. — **in the interest (or interests) of** For the promotion or furthering of; in behalf of. — *v.t.* **1.** To excite or hold the curiosity or attention of. **2.** To cause to be concerned in; involve: with *in*. **3.** *Obs.* To relate to; concern; affect. [< OF < L *interest* it is of concern or advantage; 3rd person sing. of *interesse* to lie between, be important < *inter-* between + *esse* to be]

in·ter·est·ed (in′tər·is·tid, -tris-, -tə·res′) *adj.* **1.** Having or displaying curiosity; having the attention involved. **2.** Having a concern or wish for something: to be *interested* in finding a job. **3.** Having a right or share in; being part owner. **4.** Seeking personal advantage; not impartial; biased. — **in′ter·est·ed·ly** *adv.* — **in′ter·est·ed·ness** *n.*

in·ter·est·ing (in′tər·is·ting, -tris-, -tə·res′/-) *adj.* Exciting interest, attention, or curiosity; attractive. — **in′ter·est·ing·ly** *adv.* — **in′ter·est·ing·ness** *n.*

in·ter·face (in′tər·fās) *n.* A surface forming the common boundary between adjacent solids, spaces, etc.

in·ter·fa·cial (in′tər·fā′shəl) *adj.* **1.** Formed by two faces: *interfacial* angle. **2.** Of or pertaining to an interface.

in·ter·fere (in′tər·fir′) *v.i.* **·fered, ·fer·ing** **1.** To get in the way; be an obstacle or obstruction; impede: often with *with*: Feeling *interferes* with reason. **2.** To intervene and take part in the affairs of others; especially, to interpose oneself without invitation or warrant; meddle. **3.** In sports, to obstruct the play of an opponent illegally. **4.** *Rare* To come into opposition; clash. **5.** *Rare* To strike one foot against another in walking or running: said of horses. **6.** *Physics* To cause interference. [< OF (*s'*)*entreferir* to strike each other < L *inter-* between + *ferire* to strike] — **in′ter·fer′er** *n.* — **in′ter·fer′ing·ly** *adv.*

in·ter·fer·ence (in′tər·fir′əns) *n.* **1.** The act of interfering; obstruction; meddling. **2.** In sports, illegal obstruction of the play of an opponent. **3.** In football: **a** The protecting of the ball carrier from opposing tacklers. **b** The players providing this protection. **4.** In patent law, the conflict created by an application for a patent covering, wholly or partly, another pending application or an unexpired patent. **5.** *Physics* The effect produced by two or more wave trains, as of light, sound, or other forms of radiant energy, that on meeting tend to neutralize or to augment each other by a combination of dissimilar or like phases. **6.** *Telecom.* A disturbance in the reception of radio and other electromagnetic signals due to conflict with undesired signals.

in·ter·fe·ren·tial (in′tər·fə·ren′shəl) *adj.* Of or pertaining to interference.

in·ter·fe·rom·e·ter (in′tər·fə·rom′ə·tər) *n.* *Physics* Any of various instruments that use the interference of light or sound waves for the comparison of wavelengths and the measurement of very small distances. [< INTERFER(E) + -(O)METER] — **in′ter·fe·rom′e·try** *n.*

in·ter·fer·on (in′tər·fir′on) *n.* *Biochem.* A protein produced by virus-infected cells that halts the multiplication of the virus. [< INTERFER(E) + -ON]

in·ter·fer·tile (in′tər·fûr′til) *adj.* *Biol.* Having the power to interbreed.

in·ter·flu·ent (in·tûr′floo·ənt) *adj.* Flowing into each other; blending. Also **in·ter′flu·ous** (-əs). [< L *interfluens, -entis*, ppr. of *interfluere* to flow between] — **in·ter′flu·ence** *n.*

in·ter·fold (in′tər·fōld′) *v.t.* & *v.i.* To fold together or one within another.

in·ter·fuse (in′tər·fyōōz′) *v.* **·fused, ·fus·ing** *v.t.* **1.** To cause to permeate or spread throughout, as a fluid between or among parts, tissues, etc. **2.** To spread through or permeate with something. **3.** To intermix or combine. — *v.i.* **4.** To become intermixed or combined. — **in′ter·fu′sion** *n.*

in·ter·ga·lac·tic (in′tər·gə·lak′tik) *adj.* *Astron.* Between or among galaxies: *intergalactic* space.

in·ter·gla·cial (in′tər·glā′shəl) *adj.* *Geol.* Pertaining to or occurring in the interval between two glacial periods.

in·ter·grade (*v.* in′tər·grād′; *n.* in′tər·grād′) *v.i.* **·grad·ed, ·grad·ing** To merge gradually one into another. — *n.* A transitional or intermediate form. — **in′ter·gra·da′tion** *n.* — **in′ter·gra′di·ent** (-grā′dē·ənt) *adj.*

in·ter·growth (in′tər·grōth′) *n.* A growing together.

in·ter·im (in′tər·im) *n.* A time between periods or events; an intervening time; the meantime. — *adj.* For or during an intervening period of time; temporary: an *interim* appointment. — *adv.* *Rare* Meantime. [< L, meanwhile]

in·te·ri·or (in·tir′ē·ər) *adj.* **1.** Of, pertaining to, or situated on the inside; internal; inner. **2.** Remote from the coast or border; inland. **3.** Pertaining to the internal affairs of a country; domestic: *interior* trade. **4.** Not exposed to view; private, as one's inner mental and spiritual life. — *n.* **1.** The internal part; the inside. **2.** The inland region of a country, continent, etc. **3.** The domestic affairs of a country. **4.** The inner character or nature of a person or thing. **5.** A representation of the inside of a building or room, as in a picture, stage set, etc. *Abbr.* *int.* — **Department of the Interior** An executive department of the U.S. government (established 1849), headed by the Secretary of the Interior, that controls Indian affairs and conservation of natural resources and supervises power projects. [< OF *interieur* < L *interior*, compar. of *inter* within] — **in·te′ri·or′i·ty** (-ôr′ə·tē, -or′-) *n.* — **in·te′ri·or·ly** *adv.*

interior angle *Geom.* **1.** Any of four angles formed between two straight lines cut by a third line. **2.** The angle formed in the interior of a polygon by two adjacent sides.

interior decoration The decorating and furnishing of interiors, as homes, offices, etc.; also, this occupation.

interj. Interjection.

in·ter·ject (in′tər·jekt′) *v.t.* To throw in between other things; introduce abruptly; interpose: to *interject* a comment. [< L *interjectus*, pp. of *interjicere* < *inter-* between + *jacere* to throw]

in·ter·jec·tion (in′tər·jek′shən) *n.* **1.** The act of interjecting. **2.** That which is interjected, as an exclamation, sudden remark, etc. **3.** *Gram.* A word expressing emotion or simple exclamation, as *Oh! Alas! Look!*: one of the eight traditional parts of speech. *Abbr.* *int., interj.* [< OF < L *interjectio, -onis*] — **in′ter·jec′tion·al** *adj.* — **in′ter·jec′tion·al·ly** *adv.*

in·ter·jec·to·ry (in′tər·jek′tər·ē) *adj.* Interjectional; interruptive. — **in′ter·jec′to·ri·ly** *adv.*

in·ter·knit (in′tər·nit′) *v.t.* & *v.i.* **·knit·ted** or **·knit, ·knit·ting** To knit or be knitted, one with the other.

in·ter·lace (in′tər·lās′) *v.* **·laced, ·lac·ing** *v.t.* **1.** To join by or as by weaving together; intertwine. **2.** To blend; combine: to *interlace* speech and song. **3.** To vary or relieve the sameness of; intersperse: with *with*: to *interlace* a lecture with quips. — *v.i.* **4.** To interlock or alternate with one another. [< OF *entrelacier*] — **in′ter·lac′ment** *n.*

In·ter·la·ken (in′tər·lä′kən) A resort town in central Switzerland between the lakes of Brienz and Thun; pop. about 4,000.

in·ter·lam·i·nate (in′tər·lam′ə·nāt) *v.t.* **·nat·ed, ·nat·ing**

To lay or insert between laminae; arrange in layers. **— in′·ter·lam′i·na′tion** *n.* **— in′ter·lam′i·nar** (-nər) *adj.*

in·ter·lard (in′tər·lärd′) *v.t.* **1.** To vary and diversify by interjecting something different; intersperse: with *with*: to *interlard* discourse with profanity. **2.** To occur frequently in: Pieties *interlard* his speech. [< MF *entrelarder* to lard]

in·ter·lay (in′tər·lā′) *v.t.* **·laid, ·lay·ing 1.** To lay or place among or between; interpose. **2.** To decorate or give variety to with something put or laid between.

in·ter·leaf (in′tər·lēf′) *n. pl.* **·leaves** (-lēvz′) **1.** An extra leaf, usually left blank for notes, inserted or bound between the regular leaves of a book. **2.** The matter written on a leaf so inserted.

in·ter·leave (in′tər·lēv′) *v.t.* **·leaved, ·leav·ing 1.** To insert interleaves into (a book). **2.** To insert an interleaf or interleaves between (printed leaves).

in·ter·line¹ (in′tər·līn′) *v.t.* **·lined, ·lin·ing 1.** To insert (words, phrases, etc.) between written or printed lines. **2.** To annotate (a text, document, etc.) between the lines. [< OF *entreligner* < Med.L *interlineare* < L *inter-* between + *linea* line] **— in′ter·lin′er** *n.*

in·ter·line² (in′tər·līn′) *v.t.* **·lined, ·lin·ing** To put a lining between the usual lining and the outer fabric of (a garment). [< INTER- + LINE²]

in·ter·lin·e·ar (in′tər·lin′ē·ər) *adj.* **1.** Situated or written between the lines. **2.** Having lines inserted between the lines. Also **in′ter·lin′e·al.** [< Med.L *interlinearis*]

in·ter·lin·e·ate (in′tər·lin′ē·āt) *v.t.* **·at·ed, ·at·ing** To interline (a book, etc.) [< Med.L *interlineatus,* pp. of *interlineare.* See INTERLINE¹.] **— in′ter·lin′e·a′tion** *n.*

in·ter·lin·ing¹ (in′tər·lī′ning) *n.* Interlineation.

in·ter·lin·ing² (in′tər·lī′ning) *n.* **1.** An intermediate lining placed between the usual lining and the outer fabric of a garment. **2.** The material of which such a lining is made.

in·ter·lock (*v.* in·tər·lok′; *n.* in′tər·lok′) *v.t. & v.i.* **1.** To join firmly, especially by hooking, dovetailing, or twisting. **2.** *Mech. & Electr.* To interconnect so that the operation of one part depends upon the operation of another, often for reasons of safety. **— n. 1.** The act of interlocking, or the state of being interlocked. **2.** *Mech. & Electr.* A connection, switch, etc., that causes the operation of one part to depend on the operation of another. **— in′ter·lock′er** *n.*

interlocking directorates *Econ.* Boards of directors that control two or more separate corporations through overlapping membership.

in·ter·lo·cu·tion (in′tər·lō·kyoo′shən, -lə-) *n.* Interchange of speech between two or more people; dialogue. [< L *interlocutio, -onis* < *interlocutus,* pp. of *interloqui* to speak between < *inter-* between + *loqui* to speak]

in·ter·loc·u·tor (in′tər·lok′yə·tər) *n.* **1.** One who takes part in a conversation. **2.** *U.S.* The center man in a minstrel troupe who asks questions of the end man: also called *middleman.* [< L *interlocutus,* pp. of *interloqui* to speak between, converse] **— in′ter·loc′u·tress** (-tris) *n.fem.*

in·ter·loc·u·to·ry (in′tər·lok′yə·tôr′ē, -tō′rē) *adj.* **1.** Pertaining to or having the nature of dialogue. **2.** Interposed, as in a conversation, narrative, etc.: *interlocutory* humor. **3.** *Law* **a** Pronounced during the pendency of a suit, as a decision; provisional. **b** Of or pertaining to such a decision.

in·ter·lope (in′tər·lōp′) *v.i.* **1.** To intrude in the affairs of others; meddle. **2.** Originally, to engage in a commerce, trade, etc., legally belonging to others. [< INTER- + *lope* < Du. *loopen* to run] **— in′ter·lo′per** *n.*

in·ter·lude (in′tər·lood) *n.* **1.** A period that occurs in and divides some longer or periodic process: noise with *interludes* of quiet; also, a feature that breaks up a sameness of appearance, impression, etc.: grass plains with *interludes* of settlement. **2.** In English drama: **a** A separate episode, usually light or humorous, introduced between the acts or parts of a longer performance. **b** A short dramatic allegory or farce of the sort written by John Heywood and others and forming the earliest examples of modern drama. **3.** A short passage of instrumental music played between the stanzas of a hymn, acts of a play, etc. [< Med.L *interludium* < L *inter-* between + *ludus* game, play < *ludere* to play]

in·ter·lu·nar (in′tər·loo′nər) *adj. Astron.* Pertaining to the period between old and new moon, during which the moon is invisible. Also **in′ter·lu′na·ry.**

in·ter·mar·riage (in′tər·mar′ij) *n.* The act of intermarrying, or the state of having intermarried.

in·ter·mar·ry (in′tər·mar′ē) *v.i.* **·ried, ·ry·ing 1.** To marry someone not a member of one's own religion, race, class, etc. **2.** To become connected through the marriage of members: said of different families, tribes, castes, etc. **3.** To marry each other: said of members of the same family, clan, etc.

in·ter·med·dle (in′tər·med′l) *v.i.* **·dled, ·dling** To interfere unduly in the affairs of others; meddle. [< AF *entremedler*] **— in′ter·med′dler** *n.*

in·ter·me·di·a·cy (in′tər·mē′dē·ə·sē) *n.* The state or character of being intermediate.

in·ter·me·di·ar·y (in′tər·mē′dē·er′ē) *adj.* **1.** Situated, act-

ing, or coming between; intermediate. **2.** Acting as a mediator. **— n. pl. ·ar·ies 1.** One who acts as an agent or mediator between persons, parties, etc.; go-between. **2.** An intermediate form, stage, or product. **3.** Something acting between persons or things; means. [< F *intermédiaire* < L *intermedius.* See INTERMEDIATE¹.]

in·ter·me·di·ate¹ (in′tər·mē′dē·it) *adj.* Situated or occurring between two points, places, levels, etc., or on the way from one to another. **— n. 1.** Something intermediate. **2.** *Chem.* A substance formed at a stage between the raw material and the finished product. Abbr. *inter.* [< Med.L *intermediatus* < L *intermedius* < *inter-* between + *medius* middle] **— in′ter·me′di·ate·ly** *adv.* **— in′ter·me′di·ate·ness** *n.*

in·ter·me·di·ate² (in′tər·mē′dē·āt) *v.i.* **·at·ed, ·at·ing** To act as an intermediary; mediate. [< INTER- + MEDIATE]

intermediate range ballistic missile The IRBM (which see).

in·ter·me·di·a·tion (in′tər·mē′dē·ā′shən) *n.* The act of intermediating; intervention.

in·ter·me·di·a·tor (in′tər·mē′dē·ā′tər) *n.* One who adjusts differences; a mediator; also, an intervening agent; intermediary. **— in′ter·me′di·a·to′ry** (-tôr′ē, -tō′rē) *adj.*

in·ter·ment (in·tûr′mənt) *n.* The act of interring; burial.

in·ter·mez·zo (in′tər·met′sō, -med′zō) *n. pl.* **·zos** or **·zi** (-sē, -zē) **1.** A short musical, dramatic, or ballet offering given between the acts of a play or opera. **2.** *Music* **a** A short movement connecting the main divisions of a large musical composition. **b** A similar piece of instrumental music. [< Ital. < L *intermedius* intermediate]

in·ter·mi·na·ble (in·tûr′mə·nə·bəl) *adj.* Having no apparent end or limit; continuing for a very long time; endless. **— Syn.** See EVERLASTING. [< OF] **— in·ter′mi·na·bly** *adv.*

in·ter·min·gle (in′tər·ming′gəl) *v.t. & v.i.* **·gled, ·gling** To mingle together; mix.

in·ter·mis·sion (in′tər·mish′ən) *n.* **1.** An interval of time between events or activities; recess. **2.** The act of intermitting, or the state of being intermitted. **3.** *U.S.* The time between acts of a play, opera, etc.; entr'acte. [< L *intermissio, -onis* < *intermissus,* pp. of *intermittere.* See INTERMIT.] **— in′ter·mis′siev** *adj.*

in·ter·mit (in′tər·mit′) *v.t. & v.i.* **·mit·ed, ·mit·ting** To stop temporarily or at intervals; pause. [< L *intermittere* < *inter-* between + *mittere* to send, put] **— in′ter·mit′tence** *n.*

in·ter·mit·tent (in′tər·mit′ənt) *adj.* **1.** Ceasing from time to time; coming at intervals. **2.** Having periods of intermission or temporary cessation. **— in′ter·mit′tent·ly** *adv.*

intermittent fever *Pathol.* A fever in which the acute stages occur periodically, as in malaria.

in·ter·mix (in′tər·miks′) *v.t. & v.i.* To mix together.

in·ter·mix·ture (in′tər·miks′chər) *n.* **1.** The act of intermixing, or the state of being intermixed. **2.** A mass of mixed ingredients. **3.** An additional ingredient; admixture.

in·ter·mo·lec·u·lar (in′tər·mə·lek′yə·lər) *adj.* Between or among molecules.

in·tern (*n.* in′tûrn; *v.* in·tûrn′) *n.* **1.** A medical graduate serving in and living at a hospital for clinical training before being licensed to practice medicine; also, an advanced student in a field other than medicine who is undergoing supervised practical training. **2.** One who is interned; internee. Also spelled *interne.* **— v.t. 1.** To confine or detain (belligerent or enemy nationals, ships, etc.) during wartime. **2.** To confine or detain (combatant soldiers, airmen, etc.) during wartime: said of neutral countries. **— v.i. 3.** To serve as an intern in professional training. **— n. 4.** *Archaic* Internal. [< F *interne* resident within < L *internus* internal]

in·ter·nal (in·tûr′nəl) *adj.* **1.** Of, pertaining to, or situated on the inside; interior; inner. **2.** Belonging to or derived from the inside; based on the thing itself; intrinsic: *internal* evidence. **3.** Pertaining to the inner self or the mind; subjective. **4.** Pertaining to the domestic affairs of a country: *internal* revenue. **5.** Relating to or affecting the inside of the body. **6.** Intended to be taken or applied inwardly: *internal* medication. **7.** *Anat.* Situated relatively nearer to the axis of the body or farther from the surface. Abbr. *int.* **— n. 1. pl.** The internal bodily organs; entrails. **2.** *Usually pl. Rare* An essential quality or attribute. [< LL *internalis* < *internus*] **— in·ter′nal·ly** *adv.*

in·ter·nal-com·bus·tion (in·tûr′nəl·kəm·bus′chən) *adj.* Designating a heat engine in which the fuel burns inside the engine itself, most often in a cylinder.

in·ter·nal·i·ty (in′tər·nal′ə·tē) *n. pl.* **·ties 1.** The quality or state of being internal. **2.** An internal object or characteristic. **3.** Devotion to or concern with matters of the mind, spirit, etc.; subjectivity.

internal medicine The branch of medicine that is concerned with the diseases of the internal organs.

internal revenue Revenue (def. 1).

internal rhyme Rhyme that occurs between words in the same line of poetry.

internal secretion *Physiol.* A secretion of any of the endocrine glands.

internat. International.

in·ter·na·tion·al (in′tər·nash′ən·əl) *adj.* **1.** Existing or conducted between or among nations. **2.** Of, pertaining to, or affecting various nations and their peoples: news of *international* interest. **3.** Of or pertaining to the relations between nations. Abbr. *int., internat.* — *n.* A person having ties with more than one nation, as a naturalized citizen or foreign-born resident. — **in′ter·na′tion·al·ly** *adv.*

In·ter·na·tion·al (in′tər·nash′ən·əl) *n.* **1.** Any one of several international socialistic organizations of the latter half of the 19th and early part of the 20th centuries. — **First International** A federation of trade unions, founded in London, 1864, by Karl Marx and Friedrich Engels, for the political organization of workers; disbanded in Philadelphia, 1876: full title, **International Workingmen's Association.** — **Second International** An organization formed at Paris, 1889, to unite Socialist Party groups in various countries; dissolved at the beginning of World War I and revived in 1919: also called **Socialist International.** — **Third International** The Comintern. — **Vienna International** A socialist society organized in Vienna in 1921: also called the **Two-and-a-half International.** — **Labor and Socialist International** An organization formed at Hamburg, 1923, by combining the Second International and the Vienna International. — **Fourth International** A political group made up of intellectual radicals, formed in 1936 by Leon Trotsky, in opposition to Stalinist communism: also called **Trotskyist International. 2.** The Internationale. — *adj.* Of or pertaining to any organization called an International.

international candle *Physics* An international unit of luminous intensity, defined by the use of carbon filament lamps built and operated under specified conditions, that was the standard from 1921 to 1940. See CANDLE (def. 4).

International Court of Justice The principal judicial organ of the United Nations, established in 1945 to decide disputes between nations on the basis of international law. All members of the United Nations are parties *ipso facto,* and certain other nations are admitted with special conditions. Also called *World Court.* Abbr. *ICJ.*

International Date Line See DATE LINE (def. 2).

In·ter·na·tio·nale (in′tər·nash′ən·ăl, *Fr.* aṅ·ter·nȧ·syô·nȧl′) The revolutionary anthem of the working class movement, especially of the Third International, first sung in France in 1871: usually written *L'Internationale.* [< F]

International Geophysical Year The period of 18 months from July 1, 1957 to Dec. 31, 1958, devoted to intensive geophysical investigation by scientists of many countries. Abbr. *IGY, I.G.Y.*

in·ter·na·tion·al·ism (in′tər·nash′ən·əl·iz′əm) *n.* **1.** The belief that mutual understanding and cooperation among nations will advance the common welfare: distinguished from *nationalism.* **2.** The state or quality of being international. — **in′ter·na′tion·al·ist** *n.* — **in′ter·na′tion·al′i·ty** *n.*

In·ter·na·tion·al·ism (in′tər·nash′ən·əl·iz′əm) *n.* The principles and program of action supported by any organization called an International.

in·ter·na·tion·al·ize (in′tər·nash′ən·əl·īz′) *v.t.* **·ized, ·iz·ing** To place under international control; make international.

International Labor Organization An organization founded in 1919 under the provisions of the Versailles Treaty and now a specialized agency of the United Nations, established for the improvement of international labor practices. Abbr. *ILO, I.L.O.*

international law The system of rules that nations commonly abide by and acknowledge as obligatory in their mutual relations: also called *law of nations.*

International Morse Code A variation, differing in eleven letters, of the telegraphic code devised by S. F. B. Morse: also called *continental Morse code.*

international nautical mile See under MILE.

International Phonetic Alphabet The alphabet of the **International Phonetic Association,** a society founded in France in 1886 to promote the study of phonetics, in which the phones, phonemes, and allophones of a language can be transcribed. Each symbol represents a specific sound defined as to place and manner of articulation. Abbr. *IPA, I.P.A.* See chart on page 42.

international pitch See under PITCH.

in·terne (in′tûrn) See INTERN.

in·ter·ne·cine (in′tər·nē′sin, -sīn) *adj.* **1.** Destructive to both sides; mutually deadly. **2.** Involving great slaughter; sanguinary. [< L *internecinus* < *internecare* to kill, slaughter < *inter-* among + *necare* to kill]

in·tern·ee (in′tûr·nē′) *n.* An interned person. [< INTERN + -EE]

in·ter·neu·ron (in′tər·nŏŏr′on, -nyŏŏr′-) *n. Anat.* A neuron within the central nervous system that relays the nerve impulse from an afferent to an efferent neuron.

in·tern·ist (in·tûr′nist) *n.* A specialist in internal medicine. [< INTERN(AL) + -IST]

in·tern·ment (in·tûrn′mənt) *n.* The act of interning, or the state of being interned.

internment camp A military station for the detention of prisoners of war, enemy aliens, etc.

in·ter·node (in′tər·nōd′) *n.* A part or a region between two nodes or joints. [< L *internodium* < *inter-* between + *nodus* node] — **in′ter·no′dal** (-nōd′l) *n. & adj.*

in·ter nos (in′tər nōs′) *Latin* Between or among ourselves.

in·tern·ship (in′tûrn·ship) *n.* The position and status of an intern in professional training; also, the period of an intern's training. Also **in′terne·ship.**

in·ter·nun·cial (in′tər·nun′shəl) *adj.* **1.** *Anat.* Designating a nerve cell serving to link nerve fibers in the spinal cord or brain. **2.** Of or pertaining to an internuncio.

in·ter·nun·ci·o (in′tər·nun′shē·ō, -sē·ō) *n. pl.* **·ci·os 1.** A diplomatic representative of the Pope ranking just below a nuncio: also called *papal delegate.* **2.** A go-between. [< Ital. < L *inter-* between + *nuntius* messenger]

in·ter·o·ce·an·ic (in′tər·ō′shē·an′ik) *adj.* Situated between or connecting two oceans.

in·ter·o·cep·tor (in′tər·ə·sep′tər) *n. Physiol.* A sensory nerve ending specialized to respond to stimuli originating in the viscera and other internal organs: also called *enteroceptor.* Compare EXTEROCEPTOR, PROPRIOCEPTOR. [< *entero-* < INTERNAL + (*re*)*ceptor*] — **in′ter·o·cep′tive** *adj.*

in·ter·os·cu·late (in′tər·os′kyə·lāt) *v.i.* **1.** To form a connecting link; osculate. **2.** To inosculate with each other; interpenetrate. — **in′ter·os′cu·la′tion** *n.*

in·ter·pel·lant (in′tər·pel′ənt) *adj.* Causing interpellation. — *n.* One who interpellates: also **in·ter·pel·la·tor** (in′tər·pə·lā′tər, in·tûr′pə·lā′tər). [< L *interpellans, -antis,* ppr. of *interpellare.* See INTERPELLATE.]

in·ter·pel·late (in′tər·pel′āt, in·tûr′pə·lāt) *v.t.* **·lat·ed, ·lat·ing** To subject to an interpellation. [< L *interpellatus,* pp. of *interpellare* to interrupt by speaking < *inter-* between + *pellere* to drive]

in·ter·pel·la·tion (in′tər·pə·lā′shən, in·tûr′-) *n.* In various parliaments, a demand that a member of the government explain some official act or policy. [< L *interpellatio, -onis*]

in·ter·pen·e·trate (in′tər·pen′ə·trāt) *v.* **·trat·ed, ·trat·ing** *v.t.* **1.** To penetrate thoroughly; pervade; permeate. **2.** To penetrate mutually. — *v.i.* **3.** To penetrate each other. **4.** To penetrate between or among parts or things. — **in′ter·pen′e·tra′tion** *n.* — **in′ter·pen′e·tra′tive** *adj.*

in·ter·phase (in′tər·fāz′) *n. Biol.* The stage of a living cell just before the commencement of mitosis.

in·ter·phone (in′tər·fōn′) *n.* A telephone system between various parts of a building, office, ship, airplane, etc.

in·ter·plan·e·tar·y (in′tər·plan′ə·ter′ē) *adj.* **1.** Between or among planets. **2.** Situated or occurring in the solar system, but not within the atmosphere of the sun or any planet.

in·ter·play (in′tər·plā′) *n.* Reciprocal action, movement, or influence. — *v.i.* To act on each other; interact.

in·ter·plead (in′tər·plēd′) *v.i. Law* To litigate adverse claims by bill of interpleader. [< AF *entrepleder*]

in·ter·plead·er (in′tər·plē′dər) *n. Law* A proceeding in which one who has money or goods claimed by two or more persons may ask that the claimants be required to litigate the title between themselves.

Interpol International Police Organization.

in·ter·po·late (in·tûr′pə·lāt) *v.* **·lat·ed, ·lat·ing** *v.t.* **1.** To introduce (additions, comments, interruptions, etc.) into a discourse, process, or series; also, to insert (unacknowledged additions) in order to falsify a text. **2.** To interrupt (a discourse, process, or series) with additions; also, to falsify (a text) with unacknowledged additions. **3.** *Math.* **a** To compute intermediate values in (a series): distinguished from *extrapolate.* **b** To insert (intermediate values) into a series. — *v.i.* **4.** To make additions, insertions, interruptions, etc., in a discourse, process, or series. [< L *interpolatus,* pp. of *interpolare* to polish, form anew < *interpolis* refurbished < *inter-* between + root of *polire* to polish] — **in·ter′po·la′tive** *adj.* — **in·ter′po·la′ter, in·ter′po·la′tor** *n.*

in·ter·po·la·tion (in·tûr′pə·lā′shən) *n.* **1.** The act of interpolating, or the state of being interpolated. **2.** That which is inserted by interpolating.

in·ter·pose (in′tər·pōz′) *v.* **·posed, ·pos·ing** *v.t.* **1.** To put between other things; cause to come between, especially as a separation or barrier: to *interpose* a moment of calm. **2.** To put in or inject (a comment, digression, etc.) in the course of speech or argument. **3.** To introduce or exercise (authority, action, etc.) in order to intervene or interfere: to *interpose* a prohibition. — *v.i.* **4.** To come between; intervene. **5.** To put in a remark; interrupt. [< F *interposer* to place between < *inter-* between (< L) + *poser.* See POSE[1].] — **in′ter·po′sal** *n.* — **in′ter·pos′er** *n.* — **in′ter·pos′ing·ly** *adv.*

in·ter·po·si·tion (in′tər·pə·zish′ən) *n.* **1.** The act of interposing, or the state of being interposed. **2.** That which is interposed. **3.** *U.S.* The opposition of a State to any Federal action believed to trespass on its sovereignty. [< OF]

in·ter·pret (in·tûr′prit) *v.* **·pret·ed, ·pret·ing** *v.t.* **1.** To give the meaning of; explain or make clear; especially, to restate in clear language; construe. **2.** To judge (persons, events, etc.) in a personal or particular way. **3.** To convey the meaning of (an experience, a song, play, etc.) by artistic representation or performance. — *v.i.* **4.** To explain or construe. **5.** To restate orally in one language what is said in another. [< F *interpréter* < L *interpretatus,* pp. of *interpre-*

tari < *interpres* agent, interpreter] **—in·ter′pret·a·ble** *adj.* **— in·ter′pret·a·bil′i·ty, in·ter′pret·a·ble·ness** *n.*

in·ter·pre·ta·tion (in·tûr′prə·tā′shən) *n.* **1.** The act or process of interpreting; elucidation; explanation. **2.** The sense arrived at in interpreting; the explanation given; meaning. **3.** The meaning assigned to actions, intentions, etc. **4.** One's concept of a work of art or subject as expressed in performance, criticism, or artistic representation. [< F] **— in·ter′pre·ta′tion·al** *adj.*

in·ter·pre·ta·tive (in·tûr′prə·tā′tiv) *adj.* **1.** Of or pertaining to interpretation. **2.** Providing an interpretation; explanatory. Also **in·ter′pre·tive. — in′ter′pre·ta′tive·ly** *adv.*

in·ter·pret·er (in·tûr′prit·ər) *n.* One who interprets or translates; especially, one who serves as oral translator between people speaking different languages. [< OF *interpreteur* < LL *interpretator*]

in·ter·ra·cial (in′tər·rā′shəl) *adj.* **1.** Of, pertaining to, or for members of different races. **2.** Between, among, or affecting different races, or persons of different races.

in·ter·ra·di·al (in′tər·rā′dē·əl) *adj.* Situated between rays or radii.

in·ter·reg·num (in′tər·reg′nəm) *n.* **1.** An interval between the end of a sovereign's reign and the accession of his lawful successor. **2.** Any suspension of the usual ruling powers of a state. **3.** Any break in continuity or in a series; interruption. [< L *interregnum* < *inter-* between + *regnum* reign]

in·ter·re·late (in′tər·ri·lāt′) *v.t. & v.i.* **·lat·ed, ·lat·ing** To bring or come into reciprocal relation.

in·ter·re·lat·ed (in′tər·ri·lā′tid) *adj.* Reciprocally related.

in·ter·re·la·tion (in′tər·ri·lā′shən) *n.* Mutual or reciprocal relation. **— in′ter·re·la′tion·ship** *n.*

in·ter·rex (in′tər·reks) *n.* *pl.* **in·ter·re·ges** (in′tər·rē′jēz) One who governs during an interregnum; especially, in Roman history, one of the magistrates appointed to govern during a vacancy on the throne or in the consulate. [< L *interrex* < *inter-* between + *rex* king]

interrog. Interrogative.

in·ter·ro·gate (in·ter′ə·gāt) *v.* **·gat·ed, ·gat·ing** *v.t.* **1.** To examine formally by questioning; put questions to. **—v.i.** **2.** To ask questions. **— Syn.** See ASK. [< L *interrogatus,* pp. of *interrogare* < *inter-* between + *rogare* to ask]

in·ter·ro·ga·tion (in·ter′ə·gā′shən) *n.* **1.** The act of interrogating or questioning. **2.** A question; query. **3.** An interrogation point. **4.** *Telecom.* The transmission of a signal pulse or combination of such pulses by an interrogator.

interrogation point A question mark (?). Also **interrogation mark.**

in·ter·rog·a·tive (in′tə·rog′ə·tiv) *adj.* **1.** Asking or having the nature of a question. **2.** *Gram.* Of or pertaining to a word, phrase, or construction used to ask or indicate a question. **— n.** *Gram.* An interrogative word, phrase, or construction. [< L *interrogativus*] **— in′ter·rog′a·tive·ly** *adv.*

interrogative pronoun *Gram.* A pronoun that is used to introduce a question, as *which, whose, what.*

in·ter·ro·ga·tor (in·ter′ə·gā′tər) *n.* **1.** One who interrogates; questioner; examiner. **2.** *Telecom.* A radio or radar transmitter that sends triggering pulses to a transponder.

in·ter·rog·a·to·ry (in′tə·rog′ə·tôr′ē, ·tō′rē) *adj.* Pertaining to, expressing, or implying a question. **— n.** *pl.* **·tor·ies** **1.** A question; interrogation. **2.** *Law* A formal set or series of questions. **— in′ter·rog′a·to′ri·ly** (·tôr′ə·lē, ·tō′rə·) *adv.*

in·ter·rupt (in′tə·rupt′) *v.t.* **1.** To break the continuity or regularity of; intrude upon the course of. **2.** To hinder or stop (someone talking, working, etc.) by intervening. **— v.i.** **3.** To intervene abruptly in an action, speech, etc. [< L *interruptus,* pp. of *interrumpere* < *inter-* between + *rumpere* to break] **— in′ter·rup′tive** *adj.* **— in′ter·rup′tive·ly** *adv.*

in·ter·rupt·ed (in′tə·rup′tid) *adj.* **1.** Broken in upon; lacking continuity. **2.** *Bot.* Exhibiting an abrupt change in the course of development, as the alternation of leaflets with larger leaves. **— in′ter·rupt′ed·ly** *adv.*

interrupted screw *Mil.* A screw placed in the breech of certain guns, permitting the block to be engaged or released by turning through a small arc.

in·ter·rupt·er (in′tə·rup′tər) *n.* **1.** One who or that which interrupts. **2.** *Electr.* A device, usually automatic, for rapidly breaking and making an electric circuit, as in an induction coil. **3.** *Mil.* **a** A device that prevents the firing of a movable gun when it is pointed so that it would damage the vehicle on which it is mounted. **b** A device that prevents an artillery fuse from functioning until the projectile has left the gun. Also **in′ter·rup′tor.**

in·ter·rup·tion (in′tə·rup′shən) *n.* **1.** The act of interrupting, or the state of being interrupted. **2.** That which interrupts. **3.** A temporary cessation; intermission; interval.

in·ter·scho·las·tic (in′tər·skə·las′tik) *adj.* Between or among schools, especially elementary and secondary schools.

in·ter se (in′tər sē′) *Latin* Between (or among) themselves.

in·ter·sect (in′tər·sekt′) *v.t.* **1.** To divide by cutting or passing across. **— v.i.** **2.** To cross each other. [< L *intersectus,* pp. of *intersecare* < *inter-* between + *secare* to cut]

in·ter·sec·tion (in′tər·sek′shən) *n.* **1.** A place of crossing; especially, a place where streets or roads meet and cross. **2.** The act of intersecting, or the state of being intersected. [< L *intersectio, -onis*]

in·ter·sec·tion·al[1] (in′tər·sek′shən·əl) *adj.* Of or pertaining to an intersection or intersections.

in·ter·sec·tion·al[2] (in′tər·sek′shən·əl) *adj.* Pertaining to or involving two or more sections or regions.

in·ter·ses·sion (in′tər·sesh′ən) *n.* A period between sessions; also, a brief period of instruction between academic semesters or sessions. **— in′ter·ses′sion·al** *adj.*

in·ter·sex (in′tər·seks′) *n.* *Biol.* An individual, usually sterile, showing biological characteristics of both sexes. **— in′ter·sex′u·al** *adj.* **— in′ter·sex′u·al′i·ty** *n.*

in·ter·space (*v.* in′tər·spās′; *n.* in′tər·spās′) *v.t.* **·spaced, ·spac·ing** **1.** To make a space or spaces between. **2.** To occupy a space between. **— n.** Space between. **— in′ter·spa′tial** (·shəl) *adj.* **— in′ter·spa′tial·ly** *adv.*

in·ter·sperse (in′tər·spûrs′) *v.t.* **·spersed, ·spers·ing** **1.** To scatter among other things; set here and there. **2.** To diversify or adorn with other things scattered here and there; interlard. [< L *interspersus,* pp. of *interspergere* < *inter-* among + *spargere* to scatter] **— in′ter·spers′ed·ly** *adv.* **— in′ter·sper′sion** (-spûr′zhən) *n.*

in·ter·state (in′tər·stāt′) *adj.* Between, among, or involving different States of the United States, or their citizens.

Interstate Commerce Commission A commission, now consisting of eleven members appointed by the President, established in 1884 to systematize and control commerce across state lines in the United States. Abbr. *ICC, I.C.C.*

in·ter·stel·lar (in′tər·stel′ər) *adj.* Between or among the stars.

in·ter·stice (in·tûr′stis) *n.* *pl.* **·stic·es** (-stə·sēz) **1.** A narrow opening between adjoining parts or things; small space; crack. **2.** *Rare* An interval of time. [< F < L *interstitium* < *interstitius,* pp. of *intersistere* to stand between < *inter-* between + *sistere* to cause to stand < *stare* to stand]

in·ter·sti·tial (in′tər·stish′əl) *adj.* **1.** Pertaining to, existing in, or forming an interstice. **2.** *Biol.* Situated within or between the tissues of an organ or part: *interstitial* fluid. [< L *interstitius*] **— in′ter·sti′tial·ly** *adv.*

in·ter·strat·i·fy (in′tər·strat′ə·fī′) *v.i. & v.t.* **·fied, ·fy·ing** *Geol.* To be or cause to be formed or arranged as strata between other strata. **— in′ter·strat′i·fi·ca′tion** *n.*

in·ter·tex·ture (in′tər·teks′chər) *n.* **1.** The act of interweaving, or the state of being interwoven. **2.** That which is interwoven, as a web, tissue, etc.

in·ter·tri·bal (in′tər·trī′bəl) *adj.* Pertaining to or involving two or more tribes. **— in′ter·tri′bal·ly** *adv.*

in·ter·trop·i·cal (in′tər·trop′i·kəl) *adj.* *Geog.* Of, pertaining to, or situated within or between the tropics (of Cancer and Capricorn). Also **in′ter·trop′ic. — in′ter·trop′i·cal·ly** *adv.*

in·ter·twine (in′tər·twīn′) *v.t. & v.i.* **·twined, ·twin·ing** To unite by twisting together or interlacing; intertwist. **— in′·ter·twine′ment** *n.* **— in′ter·twin′ing·ly** *adv.*

in·ter·twist (in′tər·twist′) *v.t.* **1.** To join by twisting together; intertwine. **— in′ter·twist′ing·ly** *adv.*

in·ter·ur·ban (in′tər·ûr′bən) *adj.* Between or among cities. **— n.** An interurban railroad, electric trolley line, etc.; also, the train or cars operating on such a line.

in·ter·val (in′tər·vəl) *n.* **1.** The time coming between two events, periods, points in time, etc. **2.** A space between two objects or distance between two points. **3.** A break in the continuity or course of something; interlude; pause: *intervals* of calm during a battle. **4.** *Brit.* An intermission, as in a play or concert. **5.** *Mil.* The space kept between units or soldiers standing abreast. **6.** *Music* The difference in pitch between two tones sounded either simultaneously (**harmonic interval**) or in succession (**melodic interval**); also, the two tones or their collective sound. Abbr. *int.* **— at intervals 1.** From time to time; intermittently. **2.** At some distance from one another, with spaces intervening. [< OF *entreval, in-*

INTERVALS (def. 6)
1. Unison or prime. 2. Minor second (augmented unison). 3. Major second. 4. Minor third (augmented second). 5. Major third. 6. Perfect fourth. 7. Augmented fourth; tritone (diminished fifth). 8. Perfect fifth. 9. Minor sixth (augmented fifth). 10. Major sixth. 11. Minor seventh. 12. Major seventh. 13. Octave.
The intervals shown in parenthesis are virtually identical with their counterparts. They are actually identical on keyboard instruments, but may vary slightly on others.

tervalle < L *intervallum* between the ramparts < *inter*- between + *vallum* rampart] — **in'ter·val'lic** (-val'ik) *adj.*

in·ter·vale (in'tər·vāl') *n. U.S. & Canadian* A low tract of land between hills, especially along a river. Also **in'ter·val·land'** (-vəl·land'). [Fusion of INTERVAL + VALE[1]]

in·ter·vene (in'tər·vēn') *v.i.* **·vened, ·ven·ing** **1.** To interfere or take a decisive role, especially with a view to correction, solution, or settlement. **2.** To occur so as to modify an action, expectation, etc.: unless death *intervenes.* **3.** To be located between. **4.** To take place between other events or times; happen in the meantime: Many years *intervened.* **5.** *Law* To interpose in a lawsuit so as to become a party to it. [< L *intervenire* < *inter*- between + *venire* to come] — **in'ter·ven'er** *n.*

in·ter·ven·ient (-vēn'yənt) *adj. & n.*

in·ter·ven·tion (in'tər·ven'shən) *n.* **1.** The act of intervening. **2.** Interference with the acts of others; especially, interference in the affairs of one country by another. [< LL *interventio, -onis* < *interventus,* pp. of *intervenire* to intervene] — **in'ter·ven'tion·al** *adj.*

in·ter·ven·tion·ist (in'tər·ven'shən·ist) *n.* One who intervenes or who advocates intervention, as in the affairs of another state. — *adj.* **1.** Of or concerned with intervention or interventionists. **2.** Advocating or bringing about intervention.

in·ter·view (in'tər·vyōō) *n.* **1.** A conversation conducted by a reporter, writer, radio or television commentator, etc., with a person from whom information is sought; also, the record of such a conversation. **2.** A meeting of several persons for formal discussion; especially, a meeting with a person applying for a job. — *v.t.* To have an interview with. [< MF *entrevue* < *entrevoir* to glimpse < L *inter*- between + *videre* to see] — **in'ter·view'er** *n.*

in·ter·vo·cal·ic (in'tər·vō·kal'ik) *adj. Phonet.* Situated between two vowels.

in·ter·volve (in'tər·volv') *v.t. & v.i.* **·volved, ·volv·ing** To wind or coil one within another; involve or be involved with each other. [< INTER- + L *volvere* to roll]

in·ter·weave (in'tər·wēv') *v.t. & v.i.* **·wove** or **·weaved, ·wo·ven** or *less frequently* **·wove, ·weav·ing** To weave together; intermingle or connect closely; interlace; blend.

in·tes·tate (in·tes'tāt, -tit) *adj.* **1.** Not having made a will or a valid will before death. **2.** Not legally devised or disposed of by will. — *n.* One who dies intestate. [< L *intestatus* < *in*- not + *testatus,* pp. of *testari* to make a will < *testis* witness] — **in·tes'ta·cy** (-tə·sē) *n.*

in·tes·ti·nal (in·tes'tə·nəl) *adj.* Of, found in, or affecting the intestine. — **in·tes'ti·nal·ly** *adv.*

intestinal fortitude Courageous perseverance; pluck.

in·tes·tine (in·tes'tin) *n. Anat.* **1.** *Often pl.* The section of the alimentary canal extending from the pylorus to the anus. **2.** One of the two parts of the intestine: the **small intestine,** consisting of the duodenum, jejunum, and ileum; and the **large intestine,** consisting of the cecum and vermiform appendix, the colon, and the rectum. ◆ Collateral adjective: *alvine.* — *adj.* Domestic; civil. [< L *intestinus* internal < *intus* within < *in* in]

INTESTINES

a Duodenum. *b* Small intestine. *c* Large intestine. *d* Appendix. *e* Jejunum. *f* Ileum. *g* Cecum. *h* Rectum. *A* Ascending colon. *B* Transverse colon. *C* Descending colon.

in·thrall (in·thrôl') See ENTHRALL.

in·throne (in·thrōn') See ENTHRONE.

in·ti·ma (in'tə·mə) *n. pl.* **·mae** (-mē) **1.** *Anat.* The innermost coat of an organ or part, especially of a lymphatic, blood vessel, or artery. **2.** *Entomol.* The lining membrane of the trachea of an insect. [< NL < L *intimus* innermost. See INTIMATE.] — **in'ti·mal** *adj.*

in·ti·ma·cy (in'tə·mə·sē) *n. pl.* **·cies** **1.** The state of being intimate; confidential friendship; close association. **2.** An instance of this. **3.** *Usually pl.* Sexual relations, especially when illicit.

in·ti·mate[1] (in'tə·mit) *adj.* **1.** Characterized by pronounced closeness of friendship, relationship, or association. **2.** Deeply personal; private: *intimate* thoughts. **3.** Having illicit sexual relations: with *with:* a euphemism. **4.** Resulting from close study of or familiarity with a matter: *intimate* knowledge of a crime. **5.** Pertaining to the inmost nature or being; essential; intrinsic: the *intimate* structure of matter. — *n.* A close or confidential friend. — **Syn.** See FRIEND. [< F *intime* < L *intimus,* superl. of *intus* within] — **in'ti·mate·ly** *adv.* — **in'ti·mate·ness** *n.*

in·ti·mate[2] (in'tə·māt) *v.t.* **·mat·ed, ·mat·ing** **1.** To make known without direct statement; hint; imply. **2.** *Rare* To make known formally; declare. — **Syn.** See IMPLY. [< L *intimatus,* pp. of *intimare* to announce < *intimus,* superl. of *intus* within]

in·ti·ma·tion (in'tə·mā'shən) *n.* **1.** Information given indirectly; a hint. **2.** A declaration or notification. [< F]

in·tim·i·date (in·tim'ə·dāt) *v.t.* **·dat·ed, ·dat·ing** **1.** To make timid; cause fear in; scare. **2.** To discourage or restrain from acting by threats or violence: to *intimidate* a witness. [<

Med.L *intimidatus,* pp. of *intimidare* < L *in*- very + *timidus* afraid] — **in·tim'i·da'tor** *n.*

— **Syn. 1.** *Intimidate, daunt, dismay, cow, bully, browbeat,* and *bulldoze* mean to make fearful or compliant. *Intimidate* is literally to make timid, by whatever means. *Daunt* and *dismay* mean to frighten or terrorize, but have been greatly weakened in usage; *daunt* now implies reluctance to act, and *dismay* points to a loss of courage or spirit. *Cow* suggests the use of superior strength or force which breaks the spirit of another; *bully* refers to the use of threats to keep another person in submission. *Browbeat* and *bulldoze* imply violent methods of coercion.

in·tim·i·da·tion (in·tim'ə·dā'shən) *n.* **1.** The act of intimidating. **2.** The state or fact of being intimidated.

in·tinc·tion (in·tingk'shən) *n. Eccl.* The action and practice of dipping the bread or wafer of the Eucharist into the wine. [< LL *intinctio, -onis* < *intinctus,* pp. of *intingere* to dip in < *in*- in + *tingere* to tinge]

in·ti·tle (in·tīt'l) See ENTITLE.

in·tit·ule (in·tit'yōōl) *v.t.* **·uled, ·ul·ing** To give a title to. [< F *intituler* < LL *intitulare* < L *in*- in + *titulus* title]

in·to (in'tōō) *prep.* **1.** To or toward the inside of from outside; past or through the outer boundary or limit of: to go *into* the forest; to cut *into* a melon. **2.** To a time in; until a time within: on *into* the night. **3.** To the form, state, or condition of: to change water *into* steam. **4.** Dividing: Two *into* six is three. **5.** *Rare & Dial.* Contained in; in. [OE]

in·tol·er·a·ble (in·tol'ər·ə·bəl) *adj.* **1.** Not tolerable; that cannot be borne or endured; insufferable. **2.** More than usual or normal; excessive. — **in·tol'er·a·bil'i·ty, in·tol'er·a·ble·ness** *n.* — **in·tol'er·a·bly** *adv.*

in·tol·er·ance (in·tol'ər·əns) *n.* **1.** The state or quality of being intolerant; bigotry. **2.** Incapacity or unwillingness to tolerate or endure. Also **in·tol'er·an·cy.**

in·tol·er·ant (in·tol'ər·ənt) *adj.* **1.** Not tolerant; not disposed to tolerate beliefs, practices, racial or social types, etc., different from one's own; bigoted. **2.** Unable or unwilling to bear or endure: with *of: intolerant* of bright light. — *n.* One who is intolerant; a bigot. — **in·tol'er·ant·ly** *adv*

in·tomb (in·tōōm'), **in·tomb·ment** (in·tōōm'mənt), etc. See ENTOMB, etc.

in·to·nate (in'tō·nāt) *v.t.* **·nat·ed, ·nat·ing 1.** To intone. **2.** *Phonet.* To voice. [< Med.L *intonatus,* pp. of *intonare* to intone, thunder < L *in*- in + *tonus* tone]

in·to·na·tion (in'tō·nā'shən) *n.* **1.** Way of speaking a language or utterance; accent: an American *intonation*; especially, the meaning and melody given to speech by higher and lower levels of pitch. **2.** The act of intoning or intonating. **3.** *Ling.* The significant speech pattern or patterns resulting from pitch sequences and pauses. **4.** *Music* **a** The production of or capacity to produce musical tones of accurate pitch. **b** Pitch or the accuracy of pitch. **c** The opening notes of a plainsong, usually sung by one voice.

in·tone (in·tōn') *v.* **·toned, ·ton·ing** *v.t.* **1.** To utter or recite in a musical monotone; chant. **2.** To give particular tones or intonation to. **3.** To sing the opening notes of (a plainsong, psalm, etc.). — *v.i.* **4.** To speak or sing in a monotone; chant. **5.** To emit a slow, protracted sound. [< MF *entonner* < Med.L *intonare.* See INTONATE.] — **in·ton'er** *n.*

in to·to (in tō'tō) *Latin* In the whole; altogether; entirely.

in·tox·i·cant (in·tok'sə·kənt) *n.* That which intoxicates. — *adj.* Intoxicating.

in·tox·i·cate (in·tok'sə·kāt) *v.* **·cat·ed, ·cat·ing** *v.t.* **1.** To make drunk; inebriate. **2.** To elate or excite to a degree of frenzy. **3.** *Med.* To poison, as by bacterial or internal body toxins, serum injections, drugs, etc. — *v.i.* **4.** To possess intoxicating properties. [< Med.L *intoxicatus,* pp. of *intoxicare* to poison, drug < L *toxicum* poison] — **in·tox'i·ca'tive** *adj.* — **in·tox'i·ca'tor** *n.*

in·tox·i·cat·ed (in·tok'sə·kā'tid) *adj.* **1.** Drunk; inebriated. **2.** Unduly elated or excited.

in·tox·i·ca·tion (in·tok'sə·kā'shən) *n.* **1.** Inebriation; drunkenness. **2.** A state of great excitement or elation. **3.** The act of intoxicating. **4.** *Med.* The process or condition of being poisoned.

intr. Intransitive.

intra- *prefix* Within; inside of. [< L *intra*- < *intra* within] *Intra*- may appear as a prefix with the meaning *situated* or *occurring within*; as in:

intra-abdominal	intracephalic	intraecclesiastical
intra-abdominally	intracerebellar	intraepiphyseal
intra-acinous	intracerebral	intraepithelial
intra-alveolar	intracervical	intrafilamentary
intra-arachnoid	intracloacal	intrafistular
intra-arterial	intracolic	intragastric
intra-articular	intracollegiate	intraglandular
intra-aural	intracontinental	intraglobular
intra-auricular	intracorporeal	intragyral
intrabranchial	intracorpuscular	intrahepatic
intrabronchial	intracortical	intrahyoid
intrabuccal	intracutaneous	intra-imperial
intracanalicular	intracystic	intrajugular
intracapsular	intradermal	intralamellar
intracarpal	intradermic	intralaryngeal
intracarpellary	intradivisional	intraligamentary
intracartilaginous	intraduodenal	intraligamentous

intralingual
intralobar
intralobular
intralocular
intralumbar
intramammary
intramandibular
intramarginal
intramastoid
intramedullary
intramembranous
intrameningeal
intrametropolitan
intramontane
intramundane
intramyocardial
intranasal
intranational
intraneural
intraocular
intraoral
intraorbital
intraosseous

intraosteal
intraovarian
intraovular
intraparochial
intrapelvic
intrapericardiac
intrapericardial
intraperineal
intraperiosteal
intraperitoneal
intraphilosophic
intraplacental
intrapleural
intrapolar
intrapontine
intraprostatic
intrapulmonary
intrarectal
intrarenal
intraretinal
intrascrotal
intrasegmental
intraseptal

intraserous
intraspinal
intraspinally
intrastation
intrastation'
intraterritorial
intrathecal
intrathoracic
intratracheal
intratropical
intratubal
intratubular
intratympanic
intra-umbilical
intra-urban
intra-urethral
intra-uterine
intravalvular
intravascular
intraventricular
intravertebral
intravesical

in·tra·car·di·ac (in'trə·kar'dē·ak) *adj.* Occurring or situated within the heart; endocardial.

in·tra·cel·lu·lar (in'trə·sel'yə·lər) *adj.* Occurring or situated within a cell or cells.

in·tra·cos·tal (in'trə·cos'təl) *adj.* On the inner rib.

in·trac·ta·ble (in·trak'tə·bəl) *adj.* **1.** Not tractable; not easily controlled or guided; stubborn; unruly. **2.** Difficult to manipulate, treat, or work; lacking plasticity. — **in·trac'·ta·bil'i·ty, in·trac'ta·ble·ness** *n.* — **in·trac'ta·bly** *adv.*

in·tra·dos (in·trā'dos) *n.* The interior curved surface of an arch or vault. For illustration see ARCH. [< F *intrados* < L *intra-* within + F *dos* back < L *dorsum*]

in·tra·mo·lec·u·lar (in'trə·mə·lek'yə·lər) *adj.* Occurring or situated within a molecule.

in·tra·mu·ral (in'trə·myōō'rəl) *adj.* **1.** Taking place within a school, college, etc.: *intramural* football: opposed to *extramural*. **2.** Situated or occurring within the walls or limits of a city, building, organization, etc. **3.** *Anat.* Situated or taking place within the tissues forming the walls of a hollow organ or part. — **in'tra·mu'ral·ly** *adv.*

in·tra mu·ros (in'trə myōō'rōs) *Latin* Within the walls.

in·tra·mus·cu·lar (in'trə·mus'kyə·lər) *adj.* Situated in or affecting the inside of a muscle: an *intramuscular* injection. — **in'tra·mus'cu·lar·ly** *adv.*

intrans. Intransitive.

in·tran·si·gent (in·tran'sə·jənt) *adj.* Refusing to compromise or come to terms, especially in politics; unbending. — *n.* One who is intransigent, especially in politics: also **in·tran'si·gent·ist.** Also *French* **in·tran·si·geant** (aṅ·trän·sē·zhäṅ'). [< F *intransigeant* < Sp. *intransigente* < L *in-* not + *transigens, -entis,* ppr. of *transigere* to agree. See TRANSACT.] — **in·tran'si·gence, in·tran'si·gen·cy** *n.* — **in·tran'·si·gent·ly** *adv.*

in·tran·si·tive (in·tran'sə·tiv) *Gram. adj.* Of or pertaining to intransitive verbs. — *n.* An intransitive verb (which see). Abbr. *i., int., intr., intrans.* — **in·tran'si·tive·ly** *adv.*

intransitive verb *Gram.* A verb that has or needs no complement to complete its meaning.

in·tra·state (in'trə·stāt') *adj.* Confined within or pertaining to a single state, especially of the United States.

in·tra·tel·lu·ric (in'trə·tə·lōōr'ik) *adj. Geol.* **1.** Formed or occurring within the earth. **2.** Pertaining to the constituents of an effusive rock that crystallized before reaching the surface, or to the phenocrysts that formed prior to solidification of the groundmass.

in·tra·u·ter·ine (in'trə·yōō'tər·in, -īn) *adj.* Within the uterus.

intrauterine device Any loop, coil, or other device of plastic or stainless steel that is inserted in the uterus as a continuous contraceptive. *Abbr. IUD.*

in·tra·va·sa·tion (in·trav'ə·sā'shən) *n.* Entrance of foreign matter or fluid into a blood vessel or lymphatic.

in·tra·ve·nous (in'trə·vē'nəs) *adj.* Situated in or affecting the inside of a vein: an *intravenous* injection.

in·treat (in·trēt') See ENTREAT.

in·trench (in·trench'), **in·trench·ment** (in·trench'mənt) See ENTRENCH, etc.

in·trep·id (in·trep'id) *adj.* Unshaken by fear; dauntless; bold. — **Syn.** See BRAVE. [< L *intrepidus* < *in-* not + *trepidus* agitated] — **in·tre·pid·i·ty** (in·trə·pid'ə·tē) *n.* — **in·trep'id·ly** *adv.*

in·tri·ca·cy (in'tri·kə·sē) *n. pl.* **·cies** **1.** The state or quality of being intricate. **2.** That which is intricate.

in·tri·cate (in'tri·kit) *adj.* **1.** Perplexingly entangled, complicated, or involved: an *intricate* knot. **2.** Difficult to follow or understand; puzzling. — **Syn.** See COMPLEX. [< L *intricatus,* pp. of *intricare* to entangle < *in-* in + *tricae* difficulties] — **in'tri·cate·ly** *adv.* — **in'tri·cate·ness** *n.*

in·tri·gant (in'trə·gənt, *Fr.* aṅ·trē·gäṅ') *n. pl.* **·gants** (-gənts,

Fr. -gäṅ') Intriguer. [< F < Ital *intrigante,* ppr. of *intrigare* to intrigue < L *intricare* to entangle. See INTRICATE.]

in·tri·gante (in'trə·gant', -gänt'; *Fr.* aṅ·trē·gäṅt') *n. pl.* **·gantes** (-gants', -gänts'; *Fr.* -gäṅt') A woman intriguer.

in·trigue (in·trēg'; *for n., also* in'trēg) *v.* **·trigued, ·tri·guing** *v.t.* **1.** To arouse the interest or curiosity of; fascinate; beguile. — *v.i.* **2.** To use secret or underhand means; plot; conspire. **3.** To carry on a secret or illicit love affair. — *n.* **1.** A plotting or scheming by secret or underhand means. **2.** A plot or scheme. **3.** A secret or illicit love affair. **4.** The quality or power of arousing curiosity or interest. **5.** The events and situations that complicate the plot of a drama. [< F *intriguer* < Ital. *intrigare* < L *intricare.* See INTRICATE.] — **in·tri'guer** *n.*

in·trin·sic (in·trin'sik) *adj.* **1.** Belonging to or arising from the true or fundamental nature of a thing; essential; inherent. **2.** *Anat.* Located within, or belonging exclusively to, a part of the body, as certain muscles and nerves. Also **in·trin'si·cal.** — **Syn.** See INHERENT. [< OF *intrinseque* < Med.L < L *intrinsecus* internally] — **in·trin'si·cal·ly** *adv.* — **in·trin'si·cal·ness** *n.*

intro- *prefix* In; into; within: *introvert.* [< L *intro-* < *intro* inwardly]

introd. Introduction; introductory.

in·tro·duce (in'trə·dōōs', -dyōōs') *v.t.* **·duced, ·duc·ing** **1.** To make (a person or persons) acquainted face to face, usually in a formal manner: often with *to.* **2.** To bring into use or notice first; institute; launch: to *introduce* a new technique. **3.** To broach or propose: to *introduce* an idea. **4.** To bring in as something added; establish as a new element: The rabbit was *introduced* into Australia. **5.** To present (a person, product, etc.) to an audience, a specific group, or the general public. **6.** To bring (a person or persons) to first knowledge of something: with *to:* to *introduce* a class to algebra; also, to bring (something new) to the attention of someone: with *to.* **7.** To put in; insert: to *introduce* a feeding tube. **8.** To bring forward for official notice or action: to *introduce* a resolution. **9.** To begin; start; open: to *introduce* a talk with a joke. [< L *introducere* < *intro-* within + *ducere* to lead] — **in'tro·duc'er** *n.* — **in'tro·duc'i·ble** *adj.*

in·tro·duc·tion (in'trə·duk'shən) *n.* **1.** The act of introducing. **2.** First knowledge or acquaintance; initiation: one's *introduction* to politics. **3.** The presentation of a person to another, to a group, etc.; also, a means of acquainting persons, as a letter, etc. **4.** Something that leads up to what follows, as the first part of a book, the opening of a musical work, etc. **5.** An elementary treatise in any branch of study. **6.** Something introduced. Abbr. *introd.* [< OF]

in·tro·duc·to·ry (in'trə·duk'tər·ē) *adj.* Serving as an introduction; prefatory; preliminary. Also **in'tro·duc'tive.** Abbr. *introd.* [< LL *introductorius*] — **in'tro·duc'to·ri·ly** *adv.*

in·tro·fy (in'trə·fī) *v.t.* **·fied, ·fy·ing** *Chem.* To increase the wetting or penetrating properties of (a liquid). [< INTRO- + -FY] — **in'tro·fac'tion** *n.* — **in'tro·fi·er** *n.*

in·tro·it (in·trō'it, in'troit) *n. Eccl.* **1.** In the Roman Catholic Church, the opening act of worship in the Mass, consisting usually of a psalm or part of a psalm followed by the Gloria Patri. **2.** In the Anglican Church, an anthem or hymn sung at the beginning of public worship. [< F < L *introitus* an entrance < *introire* < *intro-* in + *ire* to go] — **in·tro'i·tal** (-təl) *adj.*

in·tro·jec·tion (in'trə·jek'shən) *n.* **1.** *Psychoanal.* Identifying oneself with other persons or objects. **2.** *Psychol.* The attribution of sentient qualities to inanimate objects; personification. [< INTRO- + (PRO)JECTION] — **in'tro·jec'tive** *adj.*

in·tro·mis·sion (in'trə·mish'ən) *n.* The insertion of one thing into another. [< L *intromissus,* pp. of *intromittere* < *intro-* within + *mittere* to send] — **in'tro·mis'sive** *adj.*

in·trorse (in·trôrs') *adj. Bot.* Turned inward or toward the axis, as an anther that faces the axis of a flower: opposed to *extrorse.* [< L *introrsus* inward, contraction of *introversus* < *intro-* within + *versus* turned] — **in·trorse'ly** *adv.*

in·tro·spect (in'trə·spekt') *v.i.* To practice introspection or self-examination. [< L *i·trospectus,* pp. of *introspicere, intro-* within + *specere* to look']

in·tro·spec·tion (in'trə·spek'shən) *n.* The observation and analysis of one's own mental processes and emotional states.

in·tro·spec·tive (in'trə·spek'tiv) *adj.* Pertaining to or given to introspection. — **in'tro·spec'tive·ly** *adv.* — **in'tro·spec'·tive·ness** *n.*

in·tro·sus·cept (in'trə·sə·sept') *v.t.* To intussuscept.

in·tro·ver·sion (in'trə·vûr'zhən, -shən) *n.* **1.** The act of introverting, or the state of being introverted. **2.** *Psychol.* The turning of one's interest inward upon the self rather than toward external objects and actions: opposed to *extroversion.* **3.** *Med.* The turning inward upon itself of an organ or part. [< NL *introversio, -onis* < L *intro-* within + *versio, -onis* a turning] — **in·tro·ver'sive** (-vûr'siv) *adj.*

in·tro·vert (in'trə·vûrt) *n.* **1.** *Psychol.* A person whose interest is directed primarily toward the self. **2.** Loosely, one who is sober, reserved, etc. Opposed to *extrovert.* **3.** *Bio'.*

An organ or part that is introverted or capable of being introverted. — *v.t.* **1.** To turn inward; cause to bend in an inward direction. **2.** To turn (the mind or thoughts) toward the self. **3.** *Biol.* To turn (a tubular organ) inward upon itself; invaginate. — *adj.* Characterized by or tending to introversion. [< INTRO- + L *vertere* to turn]

in·trude (in-trōōd′) *v.* **·trud·ed, ·trud·ing** *v.t.* **1.** To thrust or force in: to *intrude* one's views. **2.** *Geol.* To cause to enter by intrusion. — *v.i.* **3.** To come in without leave or invitation; thrust oneself in: often with *upon.* [< L *intrudere* < *in-* in + *trudere* to thrust] — **in·trud′er** *n.*

in·tru·sion (in-trōō′zhən) *n.* **1.** The act or condition of intruding; encroachment. **2.** That which intrudes. **3.** *Geol.* **a** The movement of molten rock into an earlier solid rock formation. **b** An intrusive rock. **4.** *Law* Illegal entry upon or seizure of property after an estate is determined and before entry by the remainderman or reversioner.

in·tru·sive (in-trōō′siv) *adj.* **1.** Coming or thrusting in without warrant; obtrusive. **2.** Prone to intrude; given to intrusion. **3.** *Geol.* Denoting igneous rock that has solidified in fissures or cavities of other rock. **4.** *Phonet.* Denoting speech sounds that result from the adjustment of the vocal organs to the sounds preceding and following and have no etymological basis, as the (d) in *spindle* (Old English *spinel*); epenthetic: also *excrescent.* — **intrusive r** An (r) sometimes added to a word ending in a vowel, usually just before another word beginning with a vowel, as in "lawr and order". [< L *intrusus*, pp. of *intrudere.* See INTRUDE.] — **in·tru′sive·ly** *adv.* — **in·tru′sive·ness** *n.*

in·trust (in-trust′) See ENTRUST.

in·tu·bate (in′tyōō-bāt, -tōō-) *v.t.* **·bat·ed, ·bat·ing** *Med.* To treat by intubation. [< IN-² + L *tuba* tube + -ATE²]

in·tu·ba·tion (in′tyōō-bā′shən, -tōō-) *n. Med.* The insertion of a tube into an orifice or breathing organ, especially, into the larynx in cases of diphtheria to facilitate breathing.

in·tu·it (in-tyōō′it, -tōō′-) *v.t. & v.i.* **·it·ed, ·it·ing** To know or discover by intuition. [< L *intuitus* < *intueri* to look upon < *in-* on + *tueri* to look]

in·tu·i·tion (in′tōō-ish′ən, -tyōō-) *n.* **1.** A direct knowledge or awareness of something without conscious attention or reasoning; nonintellectual perception or apprehension. **2.** Anything perceived or learned without conscious attention, reasoning, concentration, etc. **3.** The ability or quality of perceiving without conscious attention or reasoning: woman's *intuition.* [< Med.L *intuitio, -onis* < *intuitus*, pp. of *intueri* to look upon. See INTUIT.]

in·tu·i·tion·al (in′tōō-ish′ən-əl, -tyōō-) *adj.* **1.** Pertaining to or resulting from intuition. **2.** Marked by or possessing intuition. — **in·tu·i′tion·al·ly** *adv.*

in·tu·i·tion·al·ism (in′tōō-ish′ən-əl-iz′əm, -tyōō-) *n.* Intuitionism. — **in·tu·i′tion·al·ist** *n.*

in·tu·i·tion·ism (in′tōō-ish′ən-iz-əm, -tyōō-) *n.* **1.** *Philos.* **a** The doctrine that intuition rather than intellect demonstrates certain truths to be fundamental. **b** The doctrine that objects perceived by the senses are intuitively known to be real. **2.** In ethics, the doctrine holding that man has an intuitive apprehension and an intrinsically valid judgment of moral values. — **in·tu·i′tion·ist** *n.*

in·tu·i·tive (in-tōō′ə-tiv, -tyōō′-) *adj.* **1.** Perceived or learned by intuition; proceeding from intuition. **2.** Characterized by, possessing, or knowing through intuition. **3.** Of or pertaining to intuition: the *intuitive* faculty. — **in·tu′i·tive·ly** *adv.* — **in·tu′i·tive·ness** *n.*

in·tu·i·tiv·ism (in-tōō′ə-tiv-iz′əm, -tyōō′-) *n.* **1.** Intuitionism (def. 2). **2.** Intuitive faculty. — **in·tu′i·tiv·ist** *n.*

in·tu·mesce (in′tōō-mes′, -tyōō-) *v.i.* **·mesced, ·mesc·ing** **1.** To swell; become tumid. **2.** To bubble up. [< L *intumescere*, intens. of *tumescere*, inceptive of *tumere* to swell]

in·tu·mes·cence (in′tōō-mes′əns, -tyōō-) *n.* **1.** The process or act of swelling or becoming tumid. **2.** State of being swollen; tumidity. **3.** A swollen organ, part, or mass. Also **in′tu·mes′cen·cy.** — **in′tu·mes′cent** *adj.*

in·turn (in′turn′) *n.* A turning inward, as of the toes.

in·tus·sus·cept (in′təs-sə-sept′) *v.t.* To receive within itself or within another part; invaginate: also **introsuscept.** [< L *intus* within + *susceptus*, pp. of *suscipere* to take up < *sub-* under + *capere* to take] — **in′tus·sus·cep′tive** *adj.*

in·tus·sus·cep·tion (in′təs-sə-sep′shən) *n.* **1.** A receiving within. **2.** *Pathol.* The infolding of one portion of an intestine into the portion adjoining it. **3.** *Physiol.* The reception into an organism of foreign matter, such as food, and its conversion into living tissue.

in·twine (in-twīn′), **in·twist** (in-twist′) See ENTWINE, etc.

in·uk·shuk (in′ōŏk-shōŏk) *n.* A cairn having the rough shape of a man, erected by Eskimos as a landmark. [< Eskimo]

in·u·lin (in′yə-lin) *n. Biochem.* A polysaccharide, (C₆H₁₀O₅)ₙ, occurring in the roots of some composite plants, as the dahlia and the elecampane, and yielding a fructose on hydrolysis. [< L *inula* elecampane + -IN]

in·unc·tion (in-ungk′shən) *n.* **1.** The act of anointing. **2.** An ointment, unguent, etc. **3.** *Med.* The process of rubbing (an ointment or other medicament) into the skin. [< L *inunctio, -onis* < *inunctus*, pp. of *inungere* to anoint]

in·un·date (in′un-dāt) *v.t.* **·dat·ed, ·dat·ing** **1.** To cover by overflowing; flood. **2.** To overwhelm with abundance or excess. [< L *inundatus*, pp. of *inundare* < *in-* in, on + *undare* to overflow < *unda* wave] — **in′un·da·tor** *n.* — **in·un·da·to·ry** (in-un′də-tôr′ē, -tō′rē) *adj.*

in·un·da·tion (in′un-dā′shən) *n.* **1.** A flood. **2.** A condition of superabundance.

in·ur·bane (in′ûr-bān′) *adj.* Not urbane; lacking in courtesy or polish; crude. — **in′ur·ban′i·ty** *n.*

in·ure (in-yoŏr′) *v.* **·ured, ·ur·ing** *v.t.* **1.** To cause to accept or tolerate by use or exercise; accustom; habituate. — *v.i.* **2.** *Rare* To have or take effect. Also spelled *enure.* [< IN-² + obs. *ure* work < OF *eure* < L *opera* work] — **in·ure′ment** *n.*

in·urn (in-ûrn′) *v.t.* **1.** To put (the ashes of a cremated person) into an urn. **2.** To entomb or bury. — **in·urn′ment** *n.*

in·u·tile (in-yōō′təl, -til) *adj.* Having no use; useless. [< F < L *inutilis*] — **in·u′tile·ly** *adv.* — **in′u·til′i·ty** (-til′ə-tē) *n.*

inv. **1.** Invented; invention; inventor. **2.** Invoice.

Inv. Inverness.

in va·cu·o (in vak′yōō-ō) *Latin* In a vacuum.

in·vade (in-vād′) *v.* **·vad·ed, ·vad·ing** *v.t.* **1.** To enter by force with the intent of conquering or plundering. **2.** To rush or swarm into as if to occupy or overrun: Crowds *invaded* the bargain basement. **3.** To trespass upon; intrude upon: to *invade* privacy. **4.** To penetrate and spread through injuriously. — *v.i.* **5.** To make an invasion. [< L *invadere* < *in-* in + *vadere* to go] — **in·vad′er** *n.*

in·vag·i·nate (in-vaj′ə-nāt) *v.* **·nat·ed, ·nat·ing** *v.t.* **1.** To put into or as into a sheath; ensheathe. **2.** To infold so as to form a depression or pouch. **3.** To intussuscept. — *v.i.* **4.** To undergo invagination. [< L *in-* in + *vagina* sheath + -ATE²] — **in·vag′i·na·ble** (-nə-bəl) *adj.*

in·vag·i·na·tion (in-vaj′ə-nā′shən) *n.* **1.** The process of invaginating. **2.** An invaginated organ or part. **3.** *Biol.* In the embryo, the formation of the gastrula by an infolding of the blastula. **4.** *Surg.* An operation for hernia. **5.** *Pathol.* Intussusception.

in·va·lid¹ (in′və-lid) *n.* A sickly or bedridden person; one disabled by injury or chronic disease. — *adj.* **1.** Enfeebled by ill health. **2.** Of or pertaining to disabled persons. — *v.t.* **1.** To cause to become an invalid; disable. **2.** *Chiefly Brit.* To release or classify (a soldier, sailor, etc.) as unfit for duty because of ill health. — *v.i.* **3.** To become an invalid. **4.** *Rare* To retire from active duty because of ill health. [< F *invalide* < L *invalidus* not strong]

in·val·id² (in-val′id) *adj.* Not valid; having no force, weight, or cogency; null; void. [< L *invalidus*] — **in·val′id·ly** *adv.*

in·val·i·date (in-val′ə-dāt) *v.t.* **·dat·ed, ·dat·ing** To weaken or destroy the validity of; render invalid; annul. [< INVALID² + -ATE¹] — **in·val′i·da′tion** *n.* — **in·val′i·da′tor** *n.*

in·val·id·ism (in′və-lid-iz′əm) *n.* The condition of being an invalid; prolonged or chronic ill health.

in·va·lid·i·ty (in′və-lid′ə-tē) *n.* Lack of validity.

in·val·u·a·ble (in-val′yōō-ə-bəl, -yōō-bəl) *adj.* Having a value beyond estimation; priceless. — **in·val′u·a·bly** *adv.*

In·var (in-vär′) *n.* A steel alloy containing 35.5 percent nickel and having a very low coefficient of expansion at temperatures up to about 245° F: a trade name. Also **in·var′.** [< INVAR(IABLE)]

in·var·i·a·ble (in-vâr′ē-ə-bəl) *adj.* Not variable; not subject to alteration; unchangeable; constant. — **in·var′i·a·bil′i·ty, in·var′i·a·ble·ness** *n.* — **in·var′i·a·bly** *adv.*

in·var·i·ant (in-vâr′ē-ənt) *adj.* Not subject to change or variation; constant. — *n. Math.* A quantity that remains unchanged; constant. — **in·var′i·ance, in·var′i·an·cy** *n.*

in·va·sion (in-vā′zhən) *n.* **1.** The act of invading with hostile armed forces; a military inroad. **2.** Any attack or onset of something injurious or disagreeable, as a disease. **3.** Encroachment by intrusion or trespass. **4.** Entrance with intent to overrun or occupy. [< LL *invasio, -onis* < *invasum*, pp. of *invadere.* See INVADE.] — **in·va′sive** *adj.*

in·vec·tive (in-vek′tiv) *n.* Violent accusation or denunciation; vituperation; abuse. — *adj.* Using or characterized by vituperation or abuse; bitterly censorious. [< OF *invectif* < LL *invectivus* < L *invectus*, pp. of *invehere.* See INVEIGH.] — **in·vec′tive·ly** *adv.* — **in·vec′tive·ness** *n.*

in·veigh (in-vā′) *v.i.* To utter vehement censure or invective: with *against.* [< L *invehere* to carry into < *in-* into + *vehere* to carry] — **in·veigh′er** *n.*

in·vei·gle (in-vē′gəl, -vā-) *v.t.* **·gled, ·gling** To entice or induce by guile or flattery; draw; cajole: often with *into.* [< F *aveugler* to blind, deceive < *aveugle* blind, ult. < L *ab-* without + *oculus* eye] — **in·vei′gle·ment** *n.* — **in·vei′gler** *n.*

in·vent (in-vent′) *v.t.* **1.** To devise or create by original effort; especially, to conceive or make originally (some mechanical, electrical, or other device). **2.** To fabricate in the mind; make up, as something untrue or contrary to fact: to *invent* an excuse. **3.** *Obs.* To come or chance upon; find. [< L *inventus*, pp. of *invenire* to come upon, discover < *in-* on + *venire* to come] — **in·vent′i·ble** *adj.*

in·ven·tion (in-ven′shən) *n.* **1.** The act or process of inventing. **2.** A device or useful contrivance conceived or made by original effort: to patent an *invention.* **3.** The skill or ingenuity needed for inventing or contriving; inventive powers. **4.** A mental fabrication or concoction. **5.** The use of the imagination in producing literary or artistic creations. **6.** In classical rhetoric, the choosing or finding of topics suitable for discussion or argument. **7.** *Music* A type of short composition based on one or more simple themes treated contrapuntally. **8.** *Archaic* A finding; discovery. Abbr. *inv.* [< OF *invencion*] **— in·ven'tion·al** *adj.*

in·ven·tive (in·ven'tiv) *adj.* **1.** Skillful at invention or contrivance; ingenious. **2.** Characterized by or created by invention. **3.** Pertaining to invention. **— in·ven'tive·ly** *adv.* **— in·ven'tive·ness** *n.*

in·ven·tor (in·ven'tər) *n.* One who invents; especially, one who has originated some method, process, or mechanical device. Also **in·vent'er.** Abbr. *inv.* [< L]

in·ven·to·ry (in'vən·tôr'ē, -tō'rē) *n. pl.* **·ries** **1.** A list of articles, with the description and quantity of each. **2.** A list of all finished goods in stock, goods in the process of manufacture, and the raw materials or supplies used, made annually by a business concern. **3.** The things entered or to be entered in a detailed stock list. **4.** The process of making a list of stock or items. **5.** The value of the goods or stock of a business. **— v.t. ·ried, ·ry·ing** **1.** To make an inventory of; to list in detail. **2.** To insert in an inventory. [< Med.L *inventarium,* L *inventorium.* See INVENT.] **— in'ven·to'ri·al** (-tôr'ē·əl, -tō'rē-) *adj.* **— in'ven·to'ri·al·ly** *adv.*

in·ve·rac·i·ty (in'və·ras'ə·tē) *n. pl.* **·ties** **1.** Lack of veracity; untruthfulness. **2.** An untruth; lie.

in·ver·ness (in'vər·nes') *n.* Often *cap.* **1.** A type of overcoat having a detachable cape. **2.** The cape itself: also called **Inverness cape.** [from *Inverness,* Scotland]

In·ver·ness (in'vər·nes') A county in NW Scotland; 4,211 sq. mi.; pop. 83,425 (1961); county seat, **Inverness;** pop. about 28,300. Also **In·ver·ness'shire** (-shir).

in·verse (in·vûrs', in'vûrs) *adj.* **1.** Reversed or opposite in order, effect, etc. **2.** Turned upside down; inverted. **3.** *Math.* Having an opposite direction of change in variables. **— n. 1.** That which is in direct contrast or opposition; the reverse; opposite. **2.** *Math.* **a** The performance or results of an inversion. **b** A reciprocal. **— in·verse'ly** *adv.*

inverse correlation Negative correlation (which see).

inverse proportion *Math.* The relationship between two variables whose product is a constant.

in·ver·sion (in·vûr'zhən, -shən) *n.* **1.** The act of inverting, or the state of being inverted. **2.** That which is inverted. **3.** In grammar and rhetoric, a reversing of the usual word order in a phrase, clause, or sentence. **4.** *Chem.* A rearrangement of the molecular structure of compounds, with the forming of two new isomers whose effects on the plane of polarization are opposed to each other. **5.** *Math.* The operation of canceling the effect of another operation: division is the *inversion* of multiplication. **6.** *Meteorol.* An increase of temperature with altitude, often caused by a warm air mass overlying a colder one. **7.** *Music* The modification of arrangements of tones by changing simultaneous thirds to sixths, seconds to sevenths, etc. (**harmonic inversion**), or by changing melodic intervals to symmetric though identical forms (**melodic inversion**); also, the arrangement so produced. **8.** *Pathol.* Any reversal in the normal position or relation of an organ or part. **9.** *Phonet.* A tongue position in which the tip is turned up and back; retroflexion. **10.** *Psychiatry* Homosexuality. [< L *inversio, -onis* < *inversus,* pp. of *invertere.* See INVERT.] **— in·ver'sive** *adj.*

in·vert (*v.* in·vûrt'; *adj. & n.* in'vûrt) *v.t.* **1.** To turn upside down; turn completely over. **2.** To reverse the order, effect, or operation of. **3.** To alter by inversion, as in chemistry, music, etc. **4.** *Phonet.* To articulate with inversion of the tongue. **— v.i. 5.** To undergo inversion. **— adj.** *Chem.* Inverted. **— n. 1.** One who or that which is inverted. **2.** *Psychiatry* A homosexual. [< L *invertere* < *in-* in + *vertere* to turn] **— in·vert'i·ble** *adj.*

in·ver·tase (in·vûr'tās) *n. Biochem.* An enzyme found in certain plants and animals, that inverts cane sugar into fructose and glucose. [< INVERT + -ASE]

in·ver·te·brate (in·vûr'tə·brit, -brāt) *adj.* **1.** *Zool.* Not vertebrate; lacking a backbone or spinal column. **2.** Lacking firmness or character; morally or intellectually flabby; irresolute. Also **in·ver'te·bral** (-brəl). **— n. 1.** An invertebrate animal. **2.** One who lacks firmness of character.

inverted arch *Archit.* An arch having its crown downward, used in foundations.

inverted commas *Brit.* Quotation marks.

inverted mordent See under MORDENT.

in·vert·er (in·vûr'tər) *n.* **1.** One who or that which inverts. **2.** *Electr.* A converter (which see).

invert soap A synthetic detergent with positive ions in its molecular structure instead of the negative ions of ordinary soap, and having good bactericidal and wetting properties.

invert sugar A mixture of fructose and glucose occurring naturally in some fruits and artificially produced by the hydrolysis of cane sugar.

in·vest (in·vest') *v.t.* **1.** To commit or use (money, capital,

etc.) for the purchase of property, securities, a business, etc., with the expectation of profit. **2.** To spend or use (money, time, effort, etc.) for: often with *in.* **3.** To place in office formally; install. **4.** To give power, authority, or rank to. **5.** To cover or surround as if with a garment; shroud. **6.** To provide or endow with qualities or traits: to *invest* a hero with glory. **7.** *Mil.* To surround or hem in; besiege. **8.** *Rare* To confer or settle (a right, power, etc.): with *in.* **9.** *Obs.* To don. **— v.i. 10.** To make an investment·or investments. [< L *investire* to clothe, enshroud < *in-* on + *vestire* to clothe < *vestis* clothing; infl. in meaning by Ital. *investire* to invest] **— in·ves'tor** *n.*

in·ves·ti·gate (in·ves'tə·gāt) *v.* **·gat·ed, ·gat·ing** *v.t.* **1.** To search or inquire into; make a formal or official examination of. **— v.i. 2.** To make an investigation. [< L *investigatus,* pp. of *investigare* < *in-* in + *vestigare* to track, trace < *vestigium* track] **— in·ves'ti·ga·ble** (-gə·bəl) *adj.* **— in·ves'ti·ga'tive** *adj.* **— in·ves'ti·ga·to·ry** (-gə·tôr'ē, -tō'rē) *adj.*

in·ves·ti·ga·tion (in·ves'tə·gā'shən) *n.* **1.** A formal or official examination or study, as by the police or a governmental body. **2.** The act of investigating. [< F]

in·ves·ti·ga·tor (in·ves'tə·gā'tər) *n.* **1.** A detective, especially a private detective. **2.** One who investigates. **— in·ves'ti·ga·to'ri·al** (-tôr'ē·əl, -tō'rē·əl) *adj.*

in·ves·ti·tive (in·ves'tə·tiv) *adj.* **1.** Of or pertaining to investiture. **2.** Having the function of investing; serving to invest. [< L *investitus,* pp. of *investire.* See INVEST.]

in·ves·ti·ture (in·ves'tə·chər) *n.* **1.** The act or ceremony of investing with an office, authority, or right. **2.** An investing or clothing, as with a quality, garment, etc. **3.** In feudal law, the formal delivery of possession of lands. **4.** *Archaic* That which invests. [< Med.L *investitura*]

in·vest·ment (in·vest'mənt) *n.* **1.** The investing of money or capital to gain interest or income. **2.** Money or capital so invested. **3.** The form of property in which one invests. **4.** The act of investing, or the state of being invested. **5.** Investiture. **6.** *Biol.* An outer covering of an animal, plant, organ, or part. **7.** *Mil.* The surrounding of a fort or town to create a state of siege; blockade. **8.** *Archaic* Clothing.

investment company An organization that manages the pooled capital of its investors or stockholders. **— closed-end investment company** An investment company that has a set amount of capital stock and issues no new shares. **— open-end investment company** An investment company that issues shares according to demand: also called *mutual fund.* Also **investment trust.**

in·vet·er·a·cy (in·vet'ər·ə·sē) *n.* The condition or quality of being inveterate.

in·vet·er·ate (in·vet'ər·it) *adj.* **1.** Firmly established by long continuance; deep-rooted: an *inveterate* custom. **2.** Confirmed or hardened in a particular character, habit, or opinion: an *inveterate* bigot. [< L *inveteratus,* pp. of *inveterare* to make old < *in-* very + *vetus* old] **— in·vet'er·ate·ly** *adv.* **— in·vet'er·ate·ness** *n.*

in·vi·a·ble (in·vī'ə·bəl) *adj.* Not viable; unable to survive. **— in·vi'a·bil'i·ty, in·vi'a·ble·ness** *n.* **— in·vi'a·bly** *adv.*

in·vid·i·ous (in·vid'ē·əs) *adj.* **1.** Exciting or creating ill will or dislike; offensive: *invidious* remarks. **2.** Provoking anger or resentment by being unjustly discriminating: *invidious* distinctions. **3.** *Obs.* Showing envy. [< L *invidiosus* < *invidia* envy. Doublet of ENVIOUS.] **— in·vid'i·ous·ly** *adv.* **— in·vid'i·ous·ness** *n.*

in·vig·i·late (in·vij'ə·lāt) *v.t.* **·lat·ed, ·lat·ing** *Brit.* To keep watch over or proctor students at examination. [< L *invigilatus,* pp. of *invigilare* < *in-* thoroughly + *vigilare* to watch] **— in·vig'i·la'tion** *n.* **— in·vig'i·la'tor** *n.*

in·vig·or·ate (in·vig'ər·āt) *v.t.* **·at·ed, ·at·ing** To give vigor and energy to; animate. [< L *in-* in + *vigor* vigor + -ATE²] **— in·vig'or·at'ing·ly** *adv.* **— in·vig'or·a'tion** *n.* **— in·vig'or·a'tive** *adj.* **— in·vig'or·a'tive·ly** *adv.* **— in·vig'or·a'tor** *n.*

in·vin·ci·ble (in·vin'sə·bəl) *adj.* Not to be overcome; unconquerable. [< F < L *invincibilis.* See IN¹-, VINCIBLE.] **— in·vin'ci·bil'i·ty, in·vin'ci·ble·ness** *n.* **— in·vin'ci·bly** *adv.*

Invincible Armada See under ARMADA.

in vi·no ver·i·tas (in vī'nō ver'i·tas) *Latin* In wine (there is) truth.

in·vi·o·la·ble (in·vī'ə·lə·bəl) *adj.* **1.** Not to be profaned, defiled, etc.; sacrosanct. **2.** Not to be violated or broken: an *inviolable* law. [< L *inviolabilis*] **— in·vi'o·la·bil'i·ty, in·vi'o·la·ble·ness** *n.* **— in·vi'o·la·bly** *adv.*

in·vi·o·late (in·vī'ə·lit) *adj.* **1.** Not violated; not profaned or broken; intact. **2.** Inviolable. **— in·vi'o·la·cy** *n.* **— in·vi'o·late·ly** *adv.* **— in·vi'o·late·ness** *n.*

in·vis·i·ble (in·viz'ə·bəl) *adj.* **1.** Not visible; not capable of being seen. **2.** Not in sight; concealed. **3.** Too indistinct or minute to be seen; imperceptible. **4.** Not apparent to the mind; not readily grasped: *invisible* shades of meaning. **5.** Not publicly or openly acknowledged: an *invisible* organization. **6.** *Econ.* Not appearing in regular processes or financial statements: *invisible* assets. **7.** Producing invisibility: an *invisible* cloak. **— n.** One who or that which is invisible.

— the Invisible The Supreme Being; God. [< OF] **— in·vis′i·bil′i·ty, in·vis′i·ble·ness** *n.* **— in·vis′i·bly** *adv.*

in·vis·i·ble An ink that is colorless and invisible until made to take on color by heat, light, or chemical action: also called *sympathetic ink.*

in·vi·ta·tion (in′və·tā′shən) *n.* **1.** The act of inviting. **2.** The means or words by which one invites or is invited: a written *invitation.* **3.** The act of alluring or inducing; enticement. [< L *invitatio, -onis*] **— in′vi·ta′tion·al** *adj.*

in·vi·ta·to·ry (in·vī′tə·tôr′ē, -tō′rē) *adj.* Containing or offering an invitation. **—** *n. pl.* **·ries** *Eccl.* A form of invitation to worship or prayer. [< Med.L *invitatorius*]

in·vite (*v.* in·vīt′; *n.* in′vīt) *v.* **·vit·ed, ·vit·ing** *v.t.* **1.** To ask (someone) courteously to be present in some place, to attend some event, or to perform some action. **2.** To make formal or polite request for: to *invite* suggestions. **3.** To present opportunity or inducement for; attract: his opinions *invite* criticism. **4.** To tend to cause or make likely; court: Speeding *invites* accidents. **5.** To tempt; entice. **—** *v.i.* **6.** To give invitation; entice. **—** *n. Slang* An invitation. [< F *inviter* < L *invitare* to entertain] **— in·vit′er** *n.*

in·vit·ing (in·vī′ting) *adj.* That invites or allures; attractive. **— in·vit′ing·ly** *adv.* **— in·vit′ing·ness** *n.*

in vi·vo (in vī′vō) *Latin* Within the living organism.

in·vo·ca·tion (in′və·kā′shən, -vō-) *n.* **1.** The act of invoking or appealing to a deity, or other agent for help, inspiration, witness, etc. **2.** A prayer, as at the opening of a banquet, ceremony, etc. **3.** An appeal for assistance to the Muses or some divine being at the beginning of an epic or other poem. **4.** The act of conjuring an evil spirit; also, the words or incantation used. **5.** *Law* An order from a judge during the course of a trial asking that the evidence or documents from another case be presented in court. [< OF < L *invocatio, -onis* < *invocare.* See INVOKE.] **— in·voc·a·tive** (in·vok′ə·tiv), **in·voc·a·to·ry** (in·vok′ə·tôr′ē, -tō′rē) *adj.*

in·voice (in′vois) *n.* **1.** A descriptive list of merchandise sent or services rendered to a purchaser, including quantities, prices, shipping and other costs, etc. **2.** The merchandise or services so itemized. *Abbr. inv.* **—** *v.t.* **·voiced, ·voic·ing** To make an invoice of; list on an invoice. [< F *envois,* pl. of *envoi* a thing sent < *envoyer* to send. See ENVOY[1].]

in·voke (in·vōk′) *v.t.* **·voked, ·vok·ing** **1.** To call upon for aid, protection, witness, etc.: to *invoke* the Muses. **2.** To declare relevant and operative, as a law, power, right, etc.: to *invoke* the Fifth Amendment. **3.** To appeal to for confirmation; quote as an authority. **4.** To summon or conjure by incantation. **5.** To call or petition for; make supplication for: to *invoke* a blessing. [< F *invoquer* < L *invocare* to call upon < *in-* on + *vocare* to call] **— in·vok′er** *n.*

in·vol·u·cel (in·vol′yə·sel) *n. Bot.* A secondary involucre, as at the base of one of the individual flowers or clusters forming a compound umbel. Also **in·vol·u·cel′lum** (-sel′əm). [< NL *involucellum,* dim. of L *involucrum* covering]

in·vo·lu·crate (in′və·lōō′krit, -krāt) *adj.* Provided with or forming an involucre. Also **in·vo·lu′crat·ed.**

in·vo·lu·cre (in′və·lōō′kər) *n. Bot.* A ring or rosette of bracts, somewhat resembling a calyx, surrounding the base of a compound umbel. [< F < L *involucrum* covering < *involvere.* See INVOLVE.] **— in′vo·lu′cral** (-krəl) *adj.*

in·vo·lu·crum (in′və·lōō′krəm) *n. pl.* **·cra** (-krə) An enveloping or saclike membrane.

in·vol·un·tar·y (in·vol′ən·ter′ē) *adj.* **1.** Done or occurring contrary to one's wish or will or without one's consent or choice; unintentional. **2.** *Physiol.* Functioning or acting independently and without conscious control: *involuntary* muscles. **— in·vol′un·tar′i·ly** *adv.* **— in·vol′un·tar′i·ness** *n.*

in·vo·lute (in′və·lōōt) *adj.* **1.** Having complications and intricacies; involved. **2.** *Bot.* Having the edges rolled inward, as a leaf. **3.** *Zool.* Having the whorls nearly or entirely concealing the axis, as a shell. Also **in′vo·lut′ed.** **—** *n. Math.* The curve traced by a point on a line as the line unrolls from a fixed curve called the *evolute.* [< L *involutus,* pp. of *involvere* to involve]

in·vo·lu·tion (in′və·lōō′shən) **1.** A complicating or intertwining; entanglement. **2.** Something involved or complicated. **3.** *Biol.* Arrest and reversal of development; degeneration. **4.** *Physiol.* **a** The return of the uterus to its normal condition after childbirth. **b** Change, characterized by diminishing physical vigor and organic functioning, usually commencing in late middle age. **5.** *Math.* The multiplication of a quantity by itself any number of times; the raising of a quantity to any power: opposed to *evolution.* **6.** In rhetoric, complicated or cumbrous arrangement of words, clauses, or phrases. **— in′vo·lu′tion·al** *adj.*

involutional melancholia *Psychiatry* A psychotic re-

INVOLUTE

Involute *AC* is formed by the locus of point *P* (*P*[1], *P*[2], *P*[3], *P*[4], etc.) as line *BC* unrolls from curve *BA*. The length of the tangent to the curve (*P*[1]*Q*[1], *P*[2]*Q*[2], etc.) from any point on the involute is equal to the length of the curve to the point of tangency (*AQ*[1] = *P*[1]*Q*[1]; *AQ*[2] = *P*[2]*Q*[2]; etc.).

action associated with psychotic involution and characterized by depression, anxiety, guilt, and other disturbances.

in·volve (in·volv′) *v.t.* **·volved, ·volv·ing** **1.** To include as a relevant or necessary aspect: The job *involves* long hours. **2.** To have effect on; affect by drawing in or spreading. **3.** To implicate; associate significantly: usually with *in* or *with:* He is *involved* in the scandal. **4.** To absorb or engross: usually with *in:* to be *involved* in one's work. **5.** To make intricate or tangled. **6.** To wrap up or envelop: to *involve* an issue in obscurity. **7.** *Math.* To raise (a number) to a given power. **— Syn.** See IMPLY. [< L *involvere* to roll into or up < *in-* in + *volvere* to roll] **— in·volve′ment** *n.*

in·volved (in·volvd′) *adj.* Not easily comprehended; complicated; intricate. **— Syn.** See COMPLEX. **— in·volv′ed·ness** (in·vol′vid·nis) *n.*

in·vul·ner·a·ble (in·vul′nər·ə·bəl) *adj.* **1.** Not capable of being wounded or physically injured. **2.** Not to be overcome or damaged by attack; unconquerable. **— in·vul′ner·a·bil′i·ty, in·vul′ner·a·ble·ness** *n.* **— in·vul′ner·a·bly** *adv.*

in·wall (*n.* in·wôl′; *v.* in·wôl′) *n.* An inner wall or lining, as of a blast furnace. **—** *v.t.* To enclose with a wall.

in·ward (in′wərd) *adv.* **1.** Toward the inside, center, or interior. **2.** In or into the mind or thoughts. **3.** *Rare* In or on the inside. Also *inwards.* **—** *adj.* **1.** Situated within, especially with reference to the body; internal. **2.** Pertaining to the mind or spirit. **3.** Proceeding toward the inside: an *inward* thrust. **4.** Inland. **5.** Inherent; intrinsic. **—** *n.* The inner part; inside. [OE *inweard*]

in·ward·ly (in′wərd·lē) *adv.* **1.** Within the mind or heart; secretly: *inwardly* anxious. **2.** On the inside; within. **3.** Toward the center or interior. **4.** Essentially; intrinsically. [OE *inweardlice*]

in·ward·ness (in′wərd·nis) *n.* **1.** The state of being inward; existence within. **2.** Inner quality or meaning; true nature; essence. **3.** Intensity of feeling; deep emotion. **4.** Spiritual quality; unworldliness. **5.** *Obs.* Close relationship.

in·wards (in′wərdz; *for n., also* in′ərdz) *adv.* Inward. **—** *n.pl.* The internal organs of the body; entrails.

in·weave (in·wēv′) *v.t.* **·wove** or **·weaved, ·wo·ven** or *less frequently* **·wove, ·weav·ing** To weave in or together; include as a component or pattern in or as in a fabric.

in·wind (in·wīnd′) See ENWIND.

in·wrap (in·rap′) See ENWRAP.

in·wreathe (in·rēth′) See ENWREATHE.

in·wrought (in·rôt′) *adj.* **1.** Worked into a fabric, metal, etc., as a pattern. **2.** Decorated with such a pattern or design. **3.** Closely combined with something; blended in. [< IN- in + WROUGHT]

I·o (ī′ō) In Greek mythology, the daughter of Inachus, beloved by Zeus and changed into a heifer because of the jealousy of Hera, who set the giant Argus to watch over her and later sent a gadfly to torment her.

Io Ionium.

Io. Iowa (unofficial).

Io·an·ni·na (yô·ä′nē·nä) A city in NW Greece; pop. about 33,000. Also *Janina, Yanina.*

I.O.B.B. Independent Order of B'nai B'rith.

i·o·date (ī′ə·dāt) *v.t.* **·dat·ed, ·dat·ing** To iodize. **—** *n.* A salt of iodic acid. [< IOD- + -ATE[3]] **— i′o·da′tion** *n.*

i·od·ic (ī·od′ik) *adj. Chem.* Of, pertaining to, or containing iodine, especially in its pentavalent state.

i·o·dide (ī′ə·dīd) *n. Chem.* A compound of iodine and one other element; especially, a salt of hydriodic acid: potassium *iodide.* Also **i′o·did** (-did). [< IOD- + -IDE]

i·o·dine (ī′ə·dīn, -din; *in technical usage* ī′ə·dēn) *n.* **1.** A grayish black crystalline element (symbol I) of the halogen group, having a metallic luster and yielding, when heated, corrosive fumes of a rich violet color, used in medicine as an antiseptic and also in photography and organic synthesis. See ELEMENT. **2.** *Informal* A solution of iodine used as an antiseptic. Also **i·o·din** (ī′ə·din). [< F *iode* < Gk. *iōdēs* violetlike (< *ion* a violet + *eidos* form) + -INE[2] (as in *chlorine*); from its violet-colored vapor]

i·o·dism (ī′ə·diz′əm) *n. Pathol.* An abnormal condition resulting from the excessive or improper use of iodine or its compounds. [< IOD- + -ISM]

i·o·dize (ī′ə·dīz) *v.t.* **·dized, ·diz·ing** To treat with, combine with, or expose to the vapor of iodine. [< IOD- + -IZE] **— i′o·diz′er** *n.*

iodo- *combining form* Iodine: *iodoform.* Also, before vowels, **iod-.**

i·o·do·form (ī·ō′də·fôrm) *n. Chem.* A light yellow crystalline compound, CHI[3], used in medicine as an antiseptic. [< IODO- + FORM(YL)]

i·o·dol (ī′ə·dōl, -dol) *n. Chem.* A yellowish brown crystalline compound, C[4]I[4]NH, used like iodoform. [< IOD- + -OL]

i·o·dom·e·try (ī′ə·dom′ə·trē) *n. Chem.* The method of making quantitative determinations of certain chemicals by the use of standard solutions of iodine, or by the liberation of free iodine. Also **i·o·dim·e·try** (ī′ə·dim′ə·trē). [< IODO- + -METRY] **— i·o·do·met·ric** (ī′ə·dō·met′rik) or **·ri·cal** *adj.*

i·o·dous (ī′ə·dəs) *adj. Chem.* **1.** Of, pertaining to, or like iodine. **2.** Containing iodine in its lower valence. [< IOD- + -OUS]

I·ol·cus (ī·ol′kəs) An ancient city in Thessaly, NE Greece.
i·o·lite (ī′ə·līt) n. Cordierite. [< Gk. *ion* violet + -LITE]
I·o moth (ī′ō) A large American moth (*Automeris io*) having conspicuous eyelike spots on the hind wings.
i·on (ī′ən, ī′on) n. *Physics* An electrically charged atom, radical, or molecule, produced by the dissolution of an electrolyte, or by the action of electric fields, high temperatures, various forms of radiation, etc., in adding or removing electrons. [< Gk. *ion*, neut. of *iōn*, ppr. of *ienai* to go]
-ion suffix of nouns 1. Action, state, quality, or process of: *communion*. 2. State or result of being: *union*. Also -*ation*, -*tion*. [< F -*ion* < L -*io*, -*ionis*]
I·o·na (ī·ō′nə) A small island of the Inner Hebrides, Scotland; site of a monastery established by St. Columba in 563.
ion engine A reaction engine producing a small but sustained thrust by emission of positive ions accelerated in an electrical field. Compare PLASMA ENGINE.
Io·nes·co (yə·nes′kō, ē·ə-), **Eugene,** born 1912, French playwright, born in Rumania.
ion exchange *Chem.* A process whereby ions may be reversibly interchanged at the boundary of a liquid and solid in contact, the composition of the solid not being altered.
I·o·ni·a (ī·ō′nē·ə) The coastal region and adjacent islands of western Asia Minor, colonized by the ancient Greeks.
I·o·ni·an (ī·ō′nē·ən) adj. Pertaining to Ionia, its inhabitants, or their culture. — n. One of an ancient Hellenic people who settled in eastern Greece and Ionia about 1100 B.C.
Ionian Islands An island group in the Ionian Sea comprising a geographical division of Greece; 864 sq. mi.
Ionian Sea A part of the Mediterranean between Greece and Sicily and the foot of the Italian peninsula.
i·on·ic (ī·on′ik) adj. *Chem.* Of or consisting of ions.
I·on·ic (ī·on′ik) adj. 1. Ionian. 2. *Archit.* Of or pertaining to an order of Greek architecture characterized by a capital having typical scroll-like ornaments. For illustration see CAPITAL². 3. In Greek and Latin prosody, designating either of two metrical feet: the **greater Ionic,** consisting of two long syllables followed by two short ones (— — ◡◡), or the **lesser Ionic,** consisting of two short syllables followed by two long ones (◡◡ — —). — n. 1. In prosody: a An Ionic foot. b A verse consisting of Ionic feet. 2. A dialect of ancient Greek including the language of the Homeric poems. 3. *Printing* A style of type with a heavy, easily read face. [< L *Ionicus* < Gk. *Iōnikos*]
i·o·ni·um (ī·ō′nē·əm) n. A radioactive isotope of thorium, of mass 230 and a half life of about 80,000 years. Abbr. *Io*. [< ION + (URAN)IUM; from its ionizing action]
i·on·ize (ī′ən·īz) v.t. & v.i. ·ized, ·iz·ing To convert or become converted, totally or in part, into ions. [< ION + -IZE] — **i′on·i·za′tion** n. — **i′on·iz′er** n.
i·on·o·gen·ic (ī′ən·ə·jen′ik) adj. *Chem.* Forming or supplying ions, as an electrolyte.
i·o·none (ī′ə·nōn) n. *Chem.* Either of two isomeric ketones, $C_{13}H_{20}O$, containing the aromatic principle of violet and orrisroot. [< Gk. *ion* violet + -ONE]
i·on·o·pause (ī·on′ə·pôz) n. *Meteorol.* The zone of transition between the ionosphere and exosphere, beginning at about 400 miles above the earth's surface. [< ION + PAUSE]
i·on·o·sphere (ī·on′ə·sfir) n. A region of the earth's atmosphere above the mesosphere, consisting of several layers subject to ionization, with seasonal variations. See HEAVISIDE LAYER. [< ION + SPHERE] — **i·on′o·spher′ic** (-sfir′ik, -sfer′-) adj.
I.O.O.F. Independent Order of Odd Fellows.
i·o·ta (ī·ō′tə) n. 1. The ninth letter and fourth vowel in the Greek alphabet (I, ι), corresponding to English *i*. See ALPHABET. 2. A very small or insignificant amount. [< L < Gk. *iōta*. Doublet of JOT.]
i·o·ta·cism (ī·ō′tə·siz′əm) n. Overfrequent use of the letter iota or of the sound (ē) that it represents. [< LL *iotacismus* < Gk. *iōtakismos* < *iōta*]
IOU A written acknowledgment of indebtedness having on it these letters (meaning *I owe you*). Also **I.O.U.**
-ious suffix of adjectives Characterized by; full of: occurring especially in adjectives formed from nouns ending in -*ion*: *suspicious, cautious*. [< L -*iosus* full of]
I.O.W. Isle of Wight.
I·o·wa (ī′ə·wə) n. pl. ·was or ·wa 1. One of a North American tribe of Siouan Indians formerly living in Minnesota, now on reservations in Oklahoma and Kansas. 2. The Siouan language of this tribe.
I·o·wa (ī′ə·wə, ī′ə·wä) A north central State of the United States; 56,280 sq. mi.; pop. 2,825,041; capital, Des Moines; entered the Union Dec. 28, 1846: nickname *Hawkeye State*. — **I′o·wan** adj. & n.
Iowa City A city in eastern Iowa; pop. 46,850.
Iowa River A river in Iowa, flowing about 300 miles from the north central part SE to the Mississippi.
i.p. 1. Innings pitched: also **ip** 2. In passing (chess).
IPA or **I.P.A.** International Phonetic Alphabet (or Association).

ip·e·cac (ip′ə·kak) n. 1. Either of two creeping or shrubby plants (*Cephaelis ipecacuanha* and *C. acuminata*) of the madder family, yielding the medicinal alkaloid emetine. 2. The dried root of either of these plants. 3. An extract of this root, used as an emetic or cathartic. Also **ip·e·cac·u·an·ha** (ip′ə·kak′yōō·ä′nə). [< Pg. *ipecacuanha* < Tupi *ipe-kaa-guéne* < *ipe* little + *kaa* tree, herb + *guéne* causing sickness]
Iph·i·ge·ni·a (if′ə·jə·nī′ə) In Greek legend, the daughter of Agamemnon and Clytemnestra and sister of Orestes and Electra, who was offered as a sacrifice to Artemis at Aulis so that the Greek fleet might sail on to Troy.
ip·o·moe·a (ip′ə·mē′ə) n. 1. Any of a large genus (*Ipomoea*) of plants having trumpet-shaped flowers, including the morning-glory and sweet potato. 2. The dried root of a Mexican species (*I. orizabensis*), used as a cathartic. [< NL < Gk. *ips, ipos* a type of worm + *homoios* like]
Ip·po·li·tov-I·va·nov (ē·pô·lē′tôf·ē·vä′nôf), **Mikhail,** 1859–1935, Russian composer.
ip·se dix·it (ip′sē dik′sit) *Latin* 1. Literally, he himself said (it). 2. An unproved or dogmatic assertion.
ip·sis·si·ma ver·ba (ip·sis′ə·mə vûr′bə) *Latin* The very words; the exact language. In a different grammatical case, **ip·sis·si·mis ver·bis** (ip·sis′ə·mis vûr′bis), the phrase means "in the very words."
ip·so fac·to (ip′sō fak′tō) *Latin* By the fact itself; by that very fact or act: called *ipso facto*.
ip·so ju·re (ip′sō jŏŏr′ē) *Latin* By the law itself.
Ip·sus (ip′səs) An ancient town in southern Phrygia, Asia Minor; scene of a battle, 301 B.C.
Ips·wich (ips′wich) The county seat of Suffolk, England, a county borough in the SE part; pop. 122,500 (1976).
i.q. The same as (L *idem quod*).
IQ or **I.Q.** Intelligence quotient.
ir- Assimilated var. of IN-¹ and IN-².
Ir *Chem.* Iridium.
Ir. Ireland; Irish.
I.R.A. Irish Republican Army.
i·ra·cund (ī′rə·kund) adj. *Rare* Easily angered; choleric. [< L *iracundus* < *ira* anger] — **i·ra·cun′di·ty** n.
i·ra·de (i·rä′dē) n. Formerly, a written decree of a Moslem ruler, as of the Sultan of Turkey. [< Turkish < Arabic *irādah* will, desire]
I·ra·kli·on (ē·rä′klē·ôn) The Greek name for CANDIA: also *Herakleion*.
I·ran (i·ran′, ē·rän′) A kingdom of SW Asia; about 630,000 sq. mi.; pop. 31,597,000 (est. 1973); capital, Teheran: formerly and now unofficially *Persia*.
Iran. Iranian.
I·ra·ni·an (i·rä′nē·ən) adj. Of or pertaining to Iran, its people, or their language. — n. 1. A native or inhabitant of Iran; a Persian. 2. A branch of the Indo-Iranian subfamily of Indo-European languages, including Modern Persian, Kurdish, and Pashto, and such ancient languages as Avestan, Old Persian, and Scythian. 3. Modern Persian.
I·raq (i·rak′, ē·räk′) A Republic in SW Asia, approximately coextensive with ancient Mesopotamia; 171,599 sq. mi.; pop. 10.384.000 (est. 1973); capital, Baghdad. Also *Rare* **I·rak′**. See map of SAUDI ARABIA.
I·ra·qi (ē·rä′kē) adj. Of or pertaining to Iraq, its people, or their language. — n. 1. A native or inhabitant of Iraq. 2. The dialect of Arabic spoken in Iraq.
i·ras·ci·ble (i·ras′ə·bəl, ī·ras′-) adj. 1. Easily provoked to anger; irritable; quick-tempered. 2. Resulting from or characterized by anger or irritability. [< OF < L *irascibilis* < *irasci* to be angry < *ira* anger] — **i·ras′ci·bil′i·ty, i·ras′ci·ble·ness** n. — **i·ras′ci·bly** adv.
i·rate (ī′rāt, ī·rāt′) adj. Angry; enraged. [< L *iratus*, pp. of *irasci* to be angry] — **i′rate·ly** adv.
IRBM The intermediate range ballistic missile, having a range between 200 and 1500 miles. Compare *ICBM*.
ire (īr) n. Wrath; anger. [< OF < L *ira* anger]
Ire. Ireland.
ire·ful (īr′fəl) adj. Full of ire; wrathful; angry. — **ire′ful·ly** adv. — **ire′ful·ness** n.
Ire·land (īr′lənd) 1. The westernmost of the British Isles, divided into Ireland (the Republic) and Northern Ireland; 31,838 sq. mi. 2. A Republic occupying the southern part of Ireland; 26,600 sq. mi.; pop. 2,944,000 (est. 1970); capital, Dublin: Irish Gaelic *Eire*. Formerly *Irish Free State* (Irish Gaelic *Saorstat Eireann*). Also *Irish Republic*. Also **Republic of Ireland**.
Ireland, Northern See NORTHERN IRELAND.
I·re·ne (ī·rē′nē) In Greek mythology, the goddess of peace, daughter of Zeus and Themis: identified with the Roman *Pax*.
i·ren·ic (ī·ren′ik, ī·rē′nik) adj. Peaceful in purpose; conciliatory. Also **i·ren′i·cal.** [< Gk. *eirēnikos* < *eirēnē* peace]
i·ren·ics (ī·ren′iks, ī·rē′niks) n.pl. (construed as sing.) Theology concerned with promoting Christian unity.
Ire·ton (īr′tən), **Henry,** 1611–51, English Roundhead general.

i·ri·da·ceous (ĭ′rə·dā′shəs, ĭr′ə-) *adj. Bot.* Belonging or pertaining to the iris family (*Iridaceae*) of perennial herbs. [< Gk. *iris, iridos* iris + -ACEOUS]

ir·i·dec·to·my (ĭr′ə·dek′tə·mē, ī′rə-) *n. pl.* **·mies** *Surg.* The removal of part of the iris. [< IRID(O)- + -ECTOMY]

ir·i·des·cence (ĭr′ə·des′əns) *n.* The quality of being iridescent; sheen of varied and shifting colors.

ir·i·des·cent (ĭr′ə·des′ənt) *adj.* Displaying the colors of the rainbow in shifting hues and patterns, as soap bubbles, mother-of-pearl, etc. [< Gk. *iris, iridos* rainbow + -ES-CENT] **— ir′i·des′cent·ly** *adv.*

i·rid·ic (ĭ·rid′ik, ī·rid′-) *adj. Chem.* Of or containing iridium in its higher valence. [< IRID(IUM) + -IC]

i·rid·i·um (ĭ·rid′ē·əm, ī·rid′-) *n.* A hard, brittle, silver-gray metallic element (symbol Ir) of the platinum group, used in certain alloys for making penpoints, jewelry, etc. See ELEMENT. [< NL < L *iris, iridis* rainbow < Gk. *iris* + -IUM; from the iridescence of some of its salts]

irido- *combining form* The iris of the eye: *iridotomy.* Also, before vowels, **irid-.** [< Gk. *iris, iridos* iris]

ir·i·dos·mine (ĭr′ə·dos′mĭn, -dos′-, ī′rə-) *n.* Osmiridium. Also **ir′i·dos′mi·um** (-mē·əm). [< IRID(IUM) + OSMIUM]

ir·i·dot·o·my (ĭr′ə·dot′ə·mē, ī′rə-) *n. pl.* **·mies** *Surg.* Any incision into the iris. [< IRIDO- + -TOMY]

i·ris (ī′ris) *n. pl.* **i·ris·es** or **i·ri·des** (ĭr′ə·dēz, ī′rə-) **1.** *Anat.* The colored, circular, contractile membrane between the cornea and the lens of the eye, having the pupil as its central aperture. For illustration see EYE. **2.** *Bot.* Any of a genus (*Iris*) of plants with sword-shaped leaves and large handsome flowers, typical of a family (*Iridaceae*) of herbaceous plants including the crocus, gladiolus, etc.: also called *fleur-de-lis, flower-de-luce.* **3.** The rainbow. **4.** Iridescence. [< L *iris* rainbow, iris < Gk. *iris*]

I·ris (ī′ris) In Greek mythology, the goddess of the rainbow, attendant of Zeus and Hera, and in Homer's *Iliad,* the messenger of the gods.

iris diaphragm *Optics* An adjustable diaphragm for regulating the amount of light passed by a lens, as in a camera.

I·rish (ī′rish) *adj.* Of or pertaining to Ireland, its people, or their language. **—** *n.* **1.** The people of Ireland collectively; also, those of Irish ancestry: preceded by *the.* **2.** The ancient or modern language of Ireland, belonging to the Goidelic branch of the Celtic languages: also called *Irish Gaelic:* sometimes called *Erse.* Historically, the language is divided into **Old Irish,** from approximately 700 to 1100; **Middle Irish,** from 1100 to 1600; and **Modern Irish,** after 1600. **3.** The dialect of English spoken in Ireland: also called *Irish English.* **4.** Irish whisky. [ME *Irisc* < OE *Ir-* + -*isc* < OIrish *Eiru* Ireland < *Eire.* Cf. EIRE.]

Irish English Irish (def. 3).

Irish Free State A former name for IRELAND (def. 2).

Irish Gaelic Irish (def. 2).

I·rish·ism (ī′rish·iz′əm) *n.* An idiom or usage characteristic of the Irish.

Irish·man (ī′rish·mən) *n. pl.* **·men** (-mən) A man of Irish birth or ancestry.

Irish moss Carrageen, a seaweed.

Irish potato The common or white potato.

Irish Republic See IRELAND (def. 2).

Irish Republican Army A secret organization originally formed to obtain Irish independence from the British, outlawed by the Irish government in 1936. Abbr. *I.R.A.*

Irish Sea The part of the Atlantic separating Ireland from England, Scotland, and Wales; 130 mi. long, 130 mi. wide.

Irish setter A reddish brown variety of setter.

Irish stew A stew of meat, potatoes, onions, carrots, etc.

Irish terrier A small terrier having a wiry, reddish coat.

Irish wolfhound A large, powerful hunting dog of an ancient breed, characterized by straight, heavy forelegs and a hard, rough coat.

I·rish·wom·an (ī′rish·wŏŏ′mən) *n. pl.* **·wom·en** (-wĭm′ən) A woman of Irish birth or ancestry.

i·ri·tis (ĭ·rī′tĭs) *n. Pathol.* Inflammation of the iris. [< NL < L *iris* iris + -ITIS] **— i·rit·ic** (ĭ·rit′ik) *adj.*

irk (ûrk) *v.t.* To annoy or weary; vex. [ME *irken*; origin uncertain]

irk·some (ûrk′səm) *adj.* Troublesome; tiresome; tedious. **— irk′some·ly** *adv.* **irk′some·ness** *n.*

Ir·kutsk Region (ĭr·kŏŏtsk′) An administrative division of the southern Siberian R.S.F.S.R., near Lake Baikal; 296,486 sq. mi.; pop. 1,976,453 (1959); center, Irkutsk, pop. 365,000. Also **Irkutsk Oblast.** *Russian* **Ir·kut′ska·ya** (-skä′yä) **Oblast.**

IRO International Refugee Organization.

i·ron (ī′ərn) *n.* **1.** A tough, abundant, malleable, easily oxi-

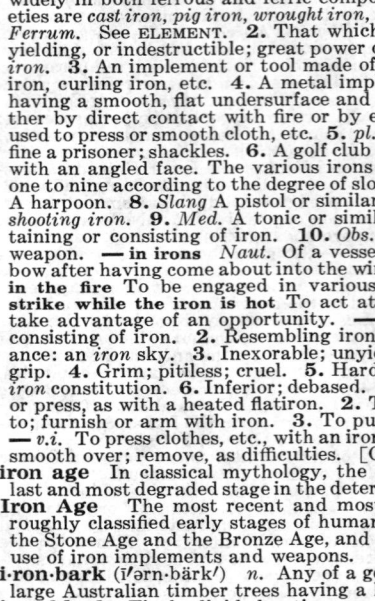

IRIS

a Bearded.
b Japanese.
c Siberian.

IRISH
WOLFHOUND
(32 inches high
at shoulder)

dized and strongly magnetic metallic element (symbol Fe), seldom obtained in its pure, silver-white form but occurring widely in both ferrous and ferric compounds. Typical varieties are *cast iron, pig iron, wrought iron,* and *steel:* also called *Ferrum.* See ELEMENT. **2.** That which is firm, harsh, unyielding, or indestructible; great power or strength: a will of *iron.* **3.** An implement or tool made of iron, as a branding iron, curling iron, etc. **4.** A metal implement or appliance having a smooth, flat undersurface and a handle, heated either by direct contact with fire or by electric current, and used to press or smooth cloth, etc. **5.** *pl.* Chains used to confine a prisoner; shackles. **6.** A golf club having a metal head with an angled face. The various irons are numbered from one to nine according to the degree of slope for each face. **7.** A harpoon. **8.** *Slang* A pistol or similar firearm: also called *shooting iron.* **9.** *Med.* A tonic or similar preparation containing or consisting of iron. **10.** *Obs.* A sword or similar weapon. **— in irons** *Naut.* Of a vessel, unable to turn its bow after having come about into the wind. **— to have irons in the fire** To be engaged in various enterprises. **— to strike while the iron is hot** To act at the right moment; take advantage of an opportunity. **—** *adj.* **1.** Made of or consisting of iron. **2.** Resembling iron in color or appearance: an *iron* sky. **3.** Inexorable; unyielding; firm: an *iron* grip. **4.** Grim; pitiless; cruel. **5.** Hardy; indefatigable: an *iron* constitution. **6.** Inferior; debased. **—** *v.t.* **1.** To smooth or press, as with a heated flatiron. **2.** To add or apply iron to; furnish or arm with iron. **3.** To put in chains; shackle. **—** *v.i.* To press clothes, etc., with an iron. **— to iron out** To smooth over; remove, as difficulties. [OE *īren, īsen, īsern*]

iron age In classical mythology, the era constituting the last and most degraded stage in the deterioration of mankind.

Iron Age The most recent and most advanced of three roughly classified early stages of human progress, following the Stone Age and the Bronze Age, and characterized by the use of iron implements and weapons.

i·ron·bark (ī′ərn·bärk′) *n.* Any of a genus (*Eucalyptus*) of large Australian timber trees having a hard, solid bark.

iron black Finely divided antimony.

i·ron·bound (ī′ərn·bound′) *adj.* **1.** Bound with iron. **2.** Faced or surrounded with rocks, as a seacoast; rugged. **3.** Unalterable; inflexible; unyielding.

i·ron·clad (ī′ərn·klad′) *adj.* **1.** Covered by or encased in iron or steel armor. **2.** Strict; unbreakable, as a rule, etc. **—** *n.* Formerly, a warship sheathed with armor.

Iron Cross A German military decoration in the form of a Maltese cross, awarded for conspicuous bravery.

iron curtain An impenetrable barrier of censorship and secrecy: a term coined by Winston Churchill to describe the demarcation imposed by the Soviet Union between its sphere of influence and the rest of the world.

Iron Duke See (Duke of) WELLINGTON.

i·rone (ī·rōn′) *n. Chem.* A colorless, volatile, aromatic oil, $C_{14}H_{22}O$, extracted from orrisroot and used in perfumery. [< IR(IS) + -ONE]

i·ron·er (ī′ərn·ər) *n.* One who or that which irons.

iron froth A spongy variety of hematite.

Iron Gate A narrow gorge in the valley of the Danube, SW Rumania, on the Yugoslav border: German *Eisernes Tor.* Rumanian *Portile de Fier.* Also **Iron Gates.**

iron glance A crystallized variety of hematite.

iron gray The color of freshly cut or broken iron. **— i′ron·gray′** *adj.*

Iron Guard A fascist organization active in Rumania prior to World War II.

i·ron·hand·ed (ī′ərn·han′did) *adj.* Exerting severe discipline or rigorous control; despotic.

iron horse *U.S. Informal* A locomotive.

i·ron·ic (ī·ron′ik) *adj.* **1.** Of the nature of or characterized by irony. **2.** Given to the use of irony. Also **i·ron′ic·al.** **— i·ron′i·cal·ly** *adv.* **— i·ron′i·cal·ness** *n.*

i·ron·ing (ī′ərn·ing) *n.* **1.** The act or process of pressing clothes, etc., with a heated iron. **2.** Articles to be ironed.

ironing board A board or folding table, usually padded, on which articles of clothing, etc., are ironed.

iron lung A cabinetlike enclosure fitted with automatically operated bellows, in which the respiration of a patient is artificially maintained, as in cases of poliomyelitis.

i·ron·mas·ter (ī′ərn·mas′ter, -mäs′-) *n. Brit.* The proprietor of an ironworks.

i·ron·mon·ger (ī′ərn·mung′gər, -mong′-) *n. Brit.* One who sells iron articles; a hardware dealer.

i·ron·mon·ger·y (ī′ərn·mung′gər·ē, -mong′-) *n. pl.* **·ger·ies** *Brit.* **1.** Iron articles collectively; hardware. **2.** Trade in such articles. **3.** An ironmonger's place of business.

iron pyrites Pyrite (which see).

I·ron·sides (ī′ərn·sīdz′) Nickname of Oliver Cromwell. **—** *n.pl.* Any of Cromwell's soldiers. **— Old Ironsides** See CONSTITUTION.

i·ron·smith (ī′ərn·smith′) *n.* A worker in iron; a blacksmith.

i·ron·stone (ī′ərn·stōn′) *n.* **1.** Any mineral or rock containing iron; iron ore. **2.** A kind of glazed, usually white pottery.

i·ron·ware (ī′ərn·wâr′) *n.* Articles made of iron; hardware.

i·ron·weed (ī′ərn·wēd′) *n.* An herb or shrub (genus *Verno-*

nia) of the composite family, having alternate leaves, and heads of tubular, mostly purple or reddish flowers.

i·ron·wood (ī'ərn·wŏŏd') *n.* **1.** Any of various trees having unusually hard, heavy, or strong wood; especially, the **Catalina ironwood** (*Lyonothamnus floribundus*) of southern California. **2.** The wood of any of these trees.

i·ron·work (ī'ərn·wûrk') *n.* **1.** Parts or objects made of iron, as structural or ornamental parts of a building. **2.** The act of working in iron.

i·ron·work·er (ī'ərn·wûr'kər) *n.* **1.** One who works in iron. **2.** One engaged in the erection or repair of metal structures.

i·ron·works (ī'ərn·wûrks') *n.pl.* (*often construed as sing.*) An establishment where iron is produced or heavy ironwork is manufactured.

i·ro·ny (ī'rə·nē) *n. pl.* **·nies 1.** A sarcastic or humorous manner of discourse in which what is literally said is meant to express its opposite, as when "That's very good" means "That's very bad"; also, an instance of this. **2.** A result, ending, etc., the reverse of what was expected. **3.** A situation, event, pairing, etc., in which main elements are rationally or emotionally incompatible because of contrast, conflict, or surprise, but are nevertheless undeniable; also, the quality inherent in such a situation, event, etc. **4.** The use of irony or ironic contrast in literature, art, etc. **5.** The feigning of ignorance as a technique in argument; Socratic irony. **— Syn.** See SARCASM. **— dramatic irony** An effect achieved by making the audience aware of something a character or participant does not know. [< L *ironia* < Gk. *eirōneis* < *eirōn* dissembler < *eirein* to speak]

i·ron·y² (ī'ər·nē) *adj.* Consisting of, containing, or resembling iron.

Ir·o·quoi·an (ir'ə·kwoi'ən) *n.* **1.** A family of North American Indian languages, including Cayuga, Cherokee, Conestoga, Erie, Mohawk, Oneida, Onondaga, Seneca, Tuscarora, Wyandot, and certain other languages. **2.** A member of a tribe speaking any of these languages. **— adj.** Of or pertaining to the Iroquois Indians or to their languages.

Ir·o·quois (ir'ə·kwoi, -kwoiz) *n. pl.* **·quois 1.** A member of any of the powerful North American Indian tribes comprising the confederacy known as the Five Nations; also, these tribes collectively. See FIVE NATIONS. **2.** A member of a tribe speaking an Iroquoian language. **— adj.** Of or pertaining to the Iroquois. [< F < Algonquian *Irinakoiw*, lit., real adders]

ir·ra·di·ant (i·rā'dē·ənt) *adj.* Sending forth light; shining. [< L *irradians, -antis,* ppr. of *irradiare* to shine] **— ir·ra'di·ance, ir·ra'di·an·cy** *n.*

ir·ra·di·ate (v. i·rā'dē·āt; *adj.* i·rā'dē·it, -āt) *v.* **·at·ed, ·at·ing** *v.t.* **1.** To direct light upon; light up; illuminate. **2.** To make clear or understandable; enlighten, as with intellectual or spiritual insight. **3.** To make radiant; suffuse, as with emotion. **4.** To send forth in or as in rays of light; diffuse; radiate. **5.** To treat with or subject to X-rays, ultraviolet light, or similar rays. **6.** To expose to or heat with radiant energy. **— v.i. 7.** To be radiant; shine. **— adj.** Made bright; illuminated. [< L *irradiatus*, pp. of *irradiare* < *in-* thoroughly + *radiare* to shine < *radius* ray] **— ir·ra'di·a'tive** *adj.* **— ir·ra'di·a'tor** *n.*

ir·ra·di·a·tion (i·rā'dē·ā'shən) *n.* **1.** The act of irradiating, or the state of being irradiated. **2.** Light emitted; ray; beam. **3.** Enlightenment, as of the mind or spirit. **4.** Treatment with any form of radiant energy, as for therapeutic or preservative purposes. **5.** Exposure to radiation. **6.** The amount or intensity of radiation falling on a surface at a given time. **7.** *Optics* An apparent enlargement of a bright object when seen against a dark background.

ir·ra·tion·al (i·rash'ən·əl) *adj.* **1.** Not possessed of or incapable of exercising the power of reason. **2.** Contrary to reason; absurd; senseless. **3.** *Math.* **a** Denoting a number that cannot be expressed as an integer or a quotient of integers. **b** Denoting an algebraic function that has at least one variable irreducibly under a radical sign, as $\sqrt{x} + xy = z$. **4.** In Greek and Latin prosody: **a** Denoting a syllable that distorts the normal meter of a line. **b** Denoting a foot containing such a syllable. [< L *irrationalis*] **— ir·ra'tion·al·ly** *adv.* **— ir·ra'tion·al·ness** *n.*

ir·ra·tion·al·ism (i·rash'ən·əl·iz'əm) *n.* Irrational thought or behavior.

ir·ra·tion·al·i·ty (i·rash'ən·al'ə·tē) *n. pl.* **·ties 1.** The state or quality of being irrational. **2.** That which is irrational; absurd or senseless thought or behavior.

irrational number *Math.* A number that cannot be expressed as an integer or quotient of integers, as $\sqrt{2}$, $\sqrt{5}$, etc.

Ir·ra·wad·dy (ir'ə·wä'dē) A river rising in Tibet, flowing about 1,200 miles south through Burma to the Bay of Bengal.

ir·re·cip·ro·cal (ir'i·sip'rə·kəl) *adj.* Not reciprocal.

ir·re·claim·a·ble (ir'i·klā'mə·bəl) *adj.* Incapable of being reclaimed. **— ir're·claim'a·bil'i·ty, ir·re·claim'a·ble·ness** *n.* **— ir're·claim'a·bly** *adv.*

ir·rec·on·cil·a·ble (i·rek'ən·sī'lə·bəl, i·rek'ən·sī'lə·bəl) *adj.* **1.** Not able or willing to be reconciled; unyieldingly hostile: *irreconcilable* enemies. **2.** Having differences that cannot be brought into accord; incompatible: *irreconcilable* theories. **— n. 1.** One who refuses to yield or compromise. **2.** *pl.* Incompatible or contradictory ideas. **— ir·rec'on·cil'a·bil'i·ty, ir·rec'on·cil'a·ble·ness** *n.* **— ir·rec'on·cil'a·bly** *adv.*

ir·re·cov·er·a·ble (ir'i·kuv'ər·ə·bəl) *adj.* **1.** Incapable of being recovered or regained; lost beyond recall. **2.** Incapable of being remedied or set right. **— ir're·cov'er·a·ble·ness** *n.* **— ir're·cov'er·a·bly** *adv.*

ir·re·cu·sa·ble (ir'i·kyōō'zə·bəl) *adj.* Incapable of being rejected: *irrecusable* proof. [< F *irrécusable* < LL *irrecusabilis* < *in-* not + *recusare* to reject] **— ir're·cu'sa·bly** *adv.*

ir·re·deem·a·ble (ir'i·dē'mə·bəl) *adj.* **1.** Incapable of being recovered, bought back, or paid off. **2.** Not to be converted into coin: said of some types of paper money. **3.** Beyond redemption; incorrigible. **4.** Affording no change or relief; irremediable; hopeless. **— ir're·deem'a·bly** *adv.*

ir·re·den·tist (ir'i·den'tist) *n.* **1.** *Usually cap.* A member of a party formed in Italy about 1878, that had as its aim the acquisition of certain regions subject to other governments but having an Italian-speaking population. **2.** One who advocates the acquisition by his country of a region considered as belonging to it for reasons of common language, culture, or former association. **— adj.** Of or pertaining to the irredentists or their policies. [< Ital. *irredentista* < (*Italia*) *ir·redenta* unredeemed (Italy) < L *in-* not + *redemptus* redeemed. See REDEEM.] **— ir·re'den'tism** (-tiz·əm) *n.*

ir·re·duc·i·ble (ir'i·dōō'sə·bəl, -dyōō'-) *adj.* **1.** Incapable of being decreased or diminished. **2.** Incapable of being converted to a simpler or more basic form. **— ir're·duc'i·bil'i·ty** *n.* **— ir're·duc'i·bly** *adv.*

ir·ref·ra·ga·ble (i·ref'rə·gə·bəl) *adj.* That cannot be refuted or disproved; incontrovertible. [< LL *irrefragabilis* < L *in-* not + *refragari* to oppose < *frangere* to break] **— ir·ref'ra·ga·bil'i·ty** *n.* **— ir·ref'ra·ga·bly** *adv.*

ir·re·fran·gi·ble (ir'i·fran'jə·bəl) *adj.* **1.** That cannot be broken or violated: an *irrefrangible* law. **2.** Incapable of being refracted, as certain light rays. [< IN- not + REFRANGIBLE] **— ir're·fran'gi·bly** *adv.*

ir·ref·u·ta·ble (i·ref'yə·tə·bəl, ir'i·fyōō'tə·bəl) *adj.* Incapable of being disproved. **— ir·ref'u·ta·bil'i·ty** (i·ref'yə·tə·bil'ə·tē, ir'i·fyōō'-) *n.* **— ir·ref'u·ta·bly** (i·ref'yə·tə·blē, ir'i·fyōō'-) *adv.*

irreg. Irregular(ly).

ir·re·gard·less (ir'i·gärd'lis) *adv.* Regardless: a nonstandard or humorous usage.

ir·reg·u·lar (i·reg'yə·lər) *adj.* **1.** Lacking symmetry or uniformity; unevenly shaped or arranged. **2.** Occurring at an uneven rate or at unequal intervals: an *irregular* pulse. **3.** Not according to established rules or usual procedure; unconventional. **4.** Not conforming to accepted standards of responsibility or conduct; disorderly; improper: *irregular* habits. **5.** *Gram.* Not conforming to the usual pattern of inflection or conjugation: said especially of strong verbs. **6.** *Mil.* Of troops, not belonging to a regularly organized military force. **7.** *Bot.* Lacking symmetry, as flowers in whorls of which the members differ in size or shape. **— n.** One who exercises a calling without belonging to its regular organization, as a soldier not in a regular military force. [< OF *irreguler* < Med.L *irregularis*] **— ir·reg'u·lar·ly** *adv.*

ir·reg·u·lar·i·ty (i·reg'yə·lar'ə·tē) *n. pl.* **·ties 1.** The state or quality of being irregular. **2.** That which is irregular.

irregular ode A pseudo-Pindaric ode (which see).

ir·rel·a·tive (i·rel'ə·tiv) *adj.* **1.** Not relative; having no relationship. **2.** Irrelevant. **— ir·rel'a·tive·ly** *adv.* **— ir·rel'a·tive·ness** *n.*

ir·rel·e·vance (i·rel'ə·vəns) *n.* **1.** The state or quality of being irrelevant. **2.** That which is irrelevant.

ir·rel·e·van·cy (i·rel'ə·vən·sē) *n. pl.* **·cies** Irrelevance.

ir·rel·e·vant (i·rel'ə·vənt) *adj.* Not relevant; not pertinent; inapplicable. **— ir·rel'e·vant·ly** *adv.*

ir·re·liev·a·ble (ir'i·lē'və·bəl) *adj.* Not relievable.

ir·re·lig·ion (ir'i·lij'ən) *n.* **1.** Lack of religious faith. **2.** Indifference or hostility toward religion. **— ir're·lig'ion·ist** *n.*

ir·re·lig·ious (ir'i·lij'əs) *adj.* **1.** Lacking in religious faith or piety. **2.** Profane. **— ir're·lig'ious·ly** *adv.*

ir·rem·e·a·ble (i·rem'ē·ə·bəl, i·rē'mē-) *adj.* *Poetic* Affording no return. [< L *irremeabilis*] **— ir·rem'e·a·bly** *adv.*

ir·re·me·di·a·ble (ir'i·mē'dē·ə·bəl) *adj.* Incapable of being remedied; incurable; irreparable. [< L *irremediabilis*] **— ir're·me'di·a·ble·ness** *n.* **— ir're·me'di·a·bly** *adv.*

ir·re·mis·si·ble (ir'i·mis'ə·bəl) *adj.* **1.** Not remissible; unexpiable; unpardonable, as a sin. **2.** Required by duty or obligation; obligatory. **— ir're·mis'si·bil'i·ty, ir're·mis'si·ble·ness** *n.* **— ir're·mis'si·bly** *adv.*

ir·re·mov·a·ble (ir'i·mōō'və·bəl) *adj.* Not removable; permanent. **— ir're·mov'a·bil'i·ty** *n.* **— ir're·mov'a·bly** *adv.*

ir·rep·a·ra·ble (i·rep'ər·ə·bəl) *adj.* Incapable of being repaired, rectified, remedied, or made good. **— ir·rep'a·ra·bil'i·ty, ir·rep'a·ra·ble·ness** *n.* **— ir·rep'a·ra·bly** *adv.*

ir·re·peal·a·ble (ir/i·pē/lə·bəl) *adj.* Not repealable.

ir·re·place·a·ble (ir/i·plā/sə·bəl) *adj.* Not replaceable; having no equivalent or substitute.

ir·re·plev·i·sa·ble (ir/i·plev/ə·sə·bəl) *adj. Law* Not repleviable. Also **ir·re·plev·i·a·ble** (-plev/ē·ə·bəl). [< IR- + AF *replevisable* < OF *replevir* to replevy. See REPLEVIN.]

ir·re·pres·si·ble (ir/i·pres/ə·bəl) *adj.* Not repressible; incapable of being controlled or restrained. — **ir/re·pres/si·bil/i·ty, ir/re·pres/si·ble·ness** *n.* — **ir/re·pres/si·bly** *adv.*

ir·re·proach·a·ble (ir/i·prō/chə·bəl) *adj.* Not meriting reproach; blameless. [< F *irréprochable*] — **ir/re·proach/a·ble·ness** *n.* — **ir/re·proach/a·bly** *adv.*

ir·re·sis·ti·ble (ir/i·zis/tə·bəl) *adj.* **1.** Not resistible; incapable of being withstood or opposed. **2.** Completely fascinating or enchanting. — **ir/re·sis/ti·bil/i·ty, ir/re·sis/ti·ble·ness** *n.* — **ir/re·sis/ti·bly** *adv.*

ir·res·o·lu·ble (i·rez/ə·lyoo·bəl) *adj.* **1.** Incapable of being resolved. **2.** Incapable of being relieved or dispelled.

ir·res·o·lute (i·rez/ə·loot) *adj.* Not resolute or resolved; lacking firmness of purpose; wavering; hesitating. — **ir·res/o·lute·ly** *adv.* — **ir·res/o·lute·ness** *n.*
— **Syn.** vacillating, indecisive, undecided, faint-hearted, doubtful. — **Ant.** resolute, decisive, determined.

ir·res·o·lu·tion (i·rez/ə·loo/shən) *n.* Lack of resolution; infirmity of purpose; indecision.

ir·re·solv·a·ble (ir/i·zol/və·bəl) *adj.* **1.** Incapable of being resolved or disentangled; inextricably complicated. **2.** Not separable into elements; incapable of being analyzed.

ir·re·spec·tive (ir/i·spek/tiv) *adj.* Existing without regard or relationship to something else: now chiefly in the adverbial phrase **irrespective of,** regardless of; independent of. — **ir/re·spec/tive·ly** *adv.*

ir·re·spir·a·ble (ir/i·spīr/ə·bəl, i·res/pi·rə·bəl) *adj.* Not respirable; unsuitable for breathing.

ir·re·spon·si·ble (ir/i·spon/sə·bəl) *adj.* **1.** Lacking in responsibility; unreliable. **2.** Free from or incapable of responsibility. — *n.* One who is irresponsible. — **ir/re·spon/si·bil/i·ty, ir/re·spon/si·ble·ness** *n.* — **ir/re·spon/si·bly** *adv.*

ir·re·spon·sive (ir/i·spon/siv) *adj.* **1.** Not responsive; not reacting to stimuli. **2.** Not answering; unresponding. — **ir/re·spon/sive·ness** *n.*

ir·re·ten·tive (ir/i·ten/tiv) *adj.* Not retentive; lacking the ability to retain or remember. — **ir/re·ten/tive·ness** *n.*

ir·re·trace·a·ble (ir/i·trā/sə·bəl) *adj.* Incapable of being retraced; as a path, footsteps, etc.

ir·re·triev·a·ble (ir/i·trē/və·bəl) *adj.* Not retrievable; irrecoverable; irreparable. — **ir/re·triev/a·bil/i·ty, ir/re·triev/a·ble·ness** *n.* — **ir/re·triev/a·bly** *adv.*

ir·rev·er·ence (i·rev/ər·əns) *n.* **1.** Lack of awe, veneration, or respect. **2.** Behavior or utterance indicative of this. **3.** The condition of not being held in reverence.

ir·rev·er·ent (i·rev/ər·ənt) *adj.* Characterized by or showing irreverence. — **ir·rev/er·ent·ly** *adv.*

ir·re·vers·i·ble (ir/i·vûr/sə·bəl) *adj.* **1.** Incapable of being turned in the opposite direction. **2.** Incapable of being annulled, repealed, or undone. — **ir/re·vers/i·bil/i·ty, ir/re·vers/i·ble·ness** *n.* — **ir/re·vers/i·bly** *adv.*

ir·rev·o·ca·ble (i·rev/ə·kə·bəl) *adj.* **1.** Incapable of being revoked or repealed: an *irrevocable* decision. **2.** Incapable of being brought back: the *irrevocable* past. — **ir·rev/o·ca·bil/i·ty, ir·rev/o·ca·ble·ness** *n.* — **ir·rev/o·ca·bly** *adv.*

ir·ri·ga·ble (ir/ə·gə·bəl) *adj.* Capable of being irrigated.

ir·ri·gate (ir/ə·gāt) *v.t.* **·gat·ed, ·gat·ing 1.** To supply (land) with water, as by means of ditches or other artificial channels. **2.** To revitalize or refresh by or as if by watering. **3.** *Med.* To moisten or wash out, as a wound, with water applied in a stream, spray, etc. **4.** *Rare* To moisten; wet. [< L *irrigatus,* pp. of *irrigare* to bring water to < *in-* to + *rigare* to water] — **ir/ri·ga/tor** *n.*

ir·ri·ga·tion (ir/ə·gā/shən) *n.* The act of irrigating, or the state of being irrigated. — **ir/ri·ga/tion·al** *adj.*

ir·ri·ga·tion·ist (ir/ə·gā/shən·ist) *n.* One who is an authority on land irrigation.

ir·ri·ga·tive (ir/ə·gā/tiv) *adj.* **1.** Of or pertaining to irrigation. **2.** Serving to irrigate.

ir·rig·u·ous (i·rig/yoo·əs) *adj. Rare* **1.** Well-watered. **2.** Irrigative.

ir·ri·ta·bil·i·ty (ir/ə·tə·bil/ə·tē) *n. pl.* **·ties** The state or quality of being irritable.

ir·ri·ta·ble (ir/ə·tə·bəl) *adj.* **1.** Easily annoyed or angered; peevish; irascible. **2.** *Biol.* Responding readily to the action of stimuli or of the environment. **3.** *Pathol.* Influenced to an abnormal degree by the action of stimulants or irritants. — **ir/ri·ta·ble·ness** *n.* — **ir/ri·ta·bly** *adv.*

ir·ri·tan·cy (ir/ə·tən·sē) *n.* Irritating quality; irritation.

ir·ri·tant (ir/ə·tənt) *n.* **1.** That which irritates or causes irritation. **2.** *Med.* An agent of inflammation, pain, etc. — *adj.* **1.** Causing irritation. **2.** *Med.* Irritating the eyes, nose, or digestive system: an *irritant* gas.

ir·ri·tate (ir/ə·tāt) *v.t.* **·tat·ed, ·tat·ing 1.** To excite annoyance, impatience, or ill temper in; vex. **2.** To make sore or inflamed. **3.** *Biol.* To excite (a cell, tissue, or organ) to a characteristic function or action. [< L *irritatus,* pp. of *irritare* to irritate] — **ir/ri·ta/tor** *n.*

— **Syn. 1.** *Irritate, fret, provoke, exasperate,* and *aggravate* mean to annoy and anger to a degree less than rage or fury. That which is contrary to our wishes, expectations, or habits may *irritate* us by making us impatient. *Fret* is to *irritate* persistently, and *provoke* is to *irritate* to the point of anger. *Exasperate* is a stronger word, and indicates that the limit of patience has been reached; it is applied to that which is extremely *provoking. Aggravate,* in its informal sense, is a close synonym of *provoke.* Compare ANGER, PIQUE. — **Ant.** soothe, calm, mollify.

ir·ri·tat·ing (ir/ə·tā/ting) *adj.* Causing irritation. — **ir/ri·tat/ing·ly** *adv.*

ir·ri·ta·tion (ir/ə·tā/shən) *n.* **1.** The act of irritating, or the state of being irritated; annoyance. **2.** *Pathol.* A condition of abnormal excitability or sensitivity in an organ or part.

ir·ri·ta·tive (ir/ə·tā/tiv) *adj.* **1.** Causing irritation. **2.** Accompanied or produced by irritation.

ir·rup·tion (i·rup/shən) *n.* **1.** A breaking or rushing in. **2.** A violent incursion; sudden invasion. [< L *irruptio, -onis* < *irruptus,* pp. of *irrumpere* to burst in < *in-* in + *rumpere* to break]

ir·rup·tive (i·rup/tiv) *adj.* **1.** Characterized by or tending to irruption. **2.** *Geol.* Intrusive.

IRS Internal Revenue Service.

Ir·tish (ir·tish/) A river in the NE Kazakh S.S.R and the central R.S.F.S.R., flowing 1,844 miles NW to the Ob. Also **Ir·tysh/.**

Ir·ving (ûr/ving) A town in north central Texas, a suburb of Dallas; pop. 97,260.

Ir·ving (ûr/ving), **Sir Henry,** 1838–1905, English actor: original name **John Henry Brod·ribb** (brôd/rib/). — **Washington,** 1783–1859, U.S. writer, historian, and humorist.

Ir·ving·ton (ûr/ving·tən) A town in NE New Jersey, a suburb of Newark; pop. 59,743.

is (iz) Present indicative, third person singular of BE. [OE]

is- Var. of ISO-.

Is. 1. Isaiah. **2.** Island(s); isle: also **is.**

Isa. Isaiah.

I·saac (ī/zək) A Hebrew patriarch, son of Abraham and Sarah, and father of Esau and Jacob. *Gen.* xxi 3. [< Hebrew *yishaq* < *sahaq* to laugh]

I·saacs (ī/zəks), **Rufus Daniel** See (Marquis of) READING.

Is·a·bel·la I (iz/ə·bel/ə), 1451–1504, queen of Castile; wife of Ferdinand V of Aragon; aided Christopher Columbus: called **Isabella the Catholic.**

i·sa·cou·stic (ī/sə·koos/tik) *adj. Physics* **1.** Of or pertaining to equality in the clearness or intensity of sound. **2.** Denoting a line, curve, or surface connecting all points within an enclosed space having the same acoustic characteristics. [< IS- + ACOUSTIC]

i·sa·go·ge (ī/sə·gō/jē) *n.* An introduction, as to a field of study. [< L < Gk. *eisagōgē* < *eisagein* to introduce < *eis-* into + *agein* to lead] — **i/sa·gog/ic** (-goj/ik) *adj.*

i·sa·gog·ics (ī/sə·goj/iks) *n.pl. (construed as sing.)* The part of exegetical theology that has to do with the literary history of the books of the Bible, their authorship, time and place of composition, etc.; Biblical introduction.

I·sa·iah (ī·zā/ə, ī·zī/ə) Eighth-century B.C. Hebrew prophet. — *n.* A book of the Old Testament attributed to him. See DEUTERO-ISAIAH. Also, in the Douai Bible, **I·sai/as** (-əs). Abbr. *Is., Isa.* [< Hebrew *yesha'yāhu* Salvation of God]

i·sal·lo·bar (ī·sal/ō·bär) *n. Meteorol.* A line on a weather map connecting places that show equal changes in barometric pressure. [< IS- + ALLO- + Gk. *baros* weight]

I·sar (ē/zär) A river in Western Austria and SW West Germany, flowing 163 miles NE to the Danube.

i·sa·tin (ī/sə·tin) *n. Chem.* A yellowish or brownish red crystalline compound, $C_8H_5NO_2$, obtained by oxidizing indigo, and used in the making of dyes. Also **i/sa·tine** (-tēn, -tin). [< L *isatis* woad < Gk. + -IN] — **i/sa·tin/ic** *adj.*

I·sau·ri·a (ī·sô/rē·ə) An ancient district of SE Asia Minor between Cilicia and Pisidia. — **I·sau/ri·an** *adj. & n.*

is·ba (ēs/bä) *n. Russian* A log hut.

Is·car·i·ot (is·kar/ē·ət) See JUDAS.

is·che·mi·a (is·kē/mē·ə) *n. Pathol.* A localized anemia, due chiefly to a contracted blood vessel. Also **is·chae/mi·a.** [< NL < Gk. *ischaimos* stopping blood < *ischein* to hold + *haima* blood] — **is·che/mic** *adj.*

Is·chia (ēs/kyä) An island in the Tyrrhenian Sea, near Naples; 18 sq. mi.

is·chi·at·ic (is/kē·at/ik) *adj.* Of or pertaining to the ischium. Also **is·chi·ad/ic** (-ad/ik), **is·chi·al** (is/kē·əl).

is·chi·um (is/kē·əm) *n. pl.* **·chi·a** (-kē·ə) **1.** *Anat.* The lowest of the three sections composing either of the innominate bones of the pelvis, constituting in man the part of the hip bone on which the body rests when sitting. For illustration see PELVIS. **2.** *Zool.* The third joint of any limb in crustaceans. [< L < Gk. *ischion* hip, hip joint]

-ise Var. of -IZE.

is·en·trop·ic (īs/en·trop/ik, -trō/pik) *adj. Physics* Being or occurring without change in entropy.

I·sère (ē·zâr/) A river in SE France, flowing 150 miles SW to the Rhone.

I·seult (i·soolt/) In medieval romance: **a** Iseult the Beautiful of Ireland, married to King Mark and beloved of Tristan.

b Iseult of the White Hand of Brittany, married to Tristan. See TRISTAN. Also called *Isolde, Isolt, Isoude, Yseult.*

Is·fa·han (is/fä·hän′) A city in west central Iran; former capital of Persia; pop. 424,045 (1966): formerly *Ispahan.*

-ish[1] *suffix of adjectives* **1.** Of or belonging to (a specified national group): *Danish; Polish.* **2.** Of the nature of; like: *boyish; roguish.* **3.** Having the bad qualities of: *babyish; selfish.* **4.** Tending toward; inclined to: *bookish.* **5.** Somewhat; rather: *bluish; tallish.* **6.** *Informal* Approximately: *fortyish.* [OE *-isc,* adjectival suffix]

-ish[2] *suffix of verbs* Appearing chiefly in verbs of French origin: *brandish, establish.* [< OF *-iss-,* stem ending of *-ir* verbs < L *-isc-,* stem ending of inceptives]

Ish·er·wood (ish/ər·wood), **Christopher,** born 1904, British author and playwright.

Ish·ma·el (ish/mē·əl) In the Bible, the son of Abraham and Hagar, banished with his mother, and considered to be the progenitor of the Arabs. *Gen.* xxi 9–21. — *n.* An outcast. [< Hebrew *Yishmā′ēl* God heareth]

Ish·ma·el·ite (ish/mē·əl·īt′) *n.* **1.** A descendant of Ishmael. **2.** A wanderer. — **Ish/ma·el·it·ish** (-ī′tish) *adj.*

Ish·tar (ish/tär) In Babylonian and Assyrian mythology, the goddess of love and fertility: identified with the Phoenician *Astarte* or *Ashtoreth.*

Is·i·dore of Seville, (iz/ə·dôr, -dōr; *Fr.* ē·zē·dôr′), **Saint,** 560?–636, Spanish theologian and scholar; bishop of Seville.

i·sin·glass (ī/zing·glas′, -gläs′, ī/zən-) *n.* **1.** A preparation of nearly pure gelatin made from the swim bladders of certain fishes. **2.** Mica, chiefly in the form of thin sheets. [Prob. < MDu. *huysenblas* sturgeon bladder < *huysen* sturgeon + *blas* bladder; infl. in form by GLASS]

I·sis (ī/sis) In Egyptian mythology, the goddess of fertility, sister and wife of Osiris, usually depicted as crowned with cow's horns enclosing a solar disk.

is·ken·de·run (is·ken/de·rōōn′) A port city in southern Turkey, at the NE end of the Mediterranean; pop. about 64,000; formerly *Alexandretta.* Also **Is·kan/der·un′, Is·ken/·der·on′.**

isl. Island(s).

Is·la de Pas·cu·a (ēs/lä dä päs/kōō·ä) The Spanish name for EASTER ISLAND.

Is·la de Pi·nos (ēs/lä tħä pē/nōs) Spanish name for (Isle of) PINES.

Is·lam (is·läm′, is/ləm, iz/-) *n.* **1.** The religion of the Muslims, that maintains that there is but one God, Allah, and that Mohammed is his prophet: also called *Mohammedanism, Moslemism, Muslimism.* Also **Is·lam·ism** (is/ləm·iz/əm, iz/ləm-). **2.** Muslims collectively. **3.** The areas of the world where Islam is the main religion. [< Arabic *islām* submission < *salama* to be resigned]

Is·lam·a·bad (is·läm/ə·bäd) City and administrative capital of Pakistan since 1967; construction begun in 1961; pop. 70,000 (est. 1968).

Is·lam·ic (is·lam/ik, -läm/-, iz-) *adj.* Moslem. Also **Is/lam·it/ic** (-it/ik).

Is·lam·ite (is/ləm·īt, iz/-) *n.* A Moslem.

Is·lam·ize (is/ləm·īz, iz/-) *v.t. & v.i.* **·ized, ·i·zing** To convert or adapt to Islam.

is·land (ī/lənd) *n.* **1.** A tract of land entirely surrounded by water. The major continental land masses are not usually considered islands. Abbr. *i., I., is., Is.,* isl. **2.** Something resembling an island and set apart from its surroundings, as a piece of elevated woodland in a prairie or a section of a thoroughfare kept free of traffic for the safety of pedestrians. **3.** *Anat.* Any of various isolated structures of the body, consisting of cells differentiated from those of the surrounding tissues. — *v.t.* **1.** To cause to become or resemble an island; set apart; isolate. **2.** To intersperse with or as with islands. [OE *īgland* < *īg, īeg* island + *land;* the *s* was added in the 15th c. because of a mistaken association with *isle*]

Is·land (ī/länt) The Icelandic name for ICELAND.

is·land·er (ī/lən·dər) *n.* A native or inhabitant of an island.

islands of Lang·er·hans (läng/ər·häns) *Anat.* Clusters of cells dispersed through the tissues of the pancreas and involved in the secretion of insulin. Also **islets of Langerhans.** [after Paul *Langerhans,* 1847–88, German histologist]

Islands of the Blessed In Greek mythology, islands in the Western Ocean, the abode of favorites of the gods after death.

island universe *Astron.* A galaxy.

Is·las Ca·na·rias (ēz/läs kä·nä/ryäs) The Spanish name for the CANARY ISLANDS.

isle (īl) *n.* An island, especially one of comparatively small size: used in place names, as the British *Isles,* or poetically. Abbr. *I., is., Is.* — *v.* **isled, isl·ing** *v.t.* **1.** To enisle. — *v.i.* **2.** To live on an isle or island. [< OF < L *insula*]

Isle of, etc. See specific name, as (Isle of) MAN, (Isle of) PINES, etc.

Isle Roy·ale (īl roi/əl) An island in NW Lake Superior, part of Michigan; included in **Isle Royale National Park;** 209 sq. mi.; established 1940.

is·let (ī/lit) *n.* A small island. [< OF *islette,* dim. of *isle*]

Is·ling·ton (iz/ling·tən) A metropolitan borough of northern London; pop. 228,833 (1961).

ism (iz/əm) *n.* A distinctive theory, doctrine, or system: usually used disparagingly. [< -ISM]

-ism *suffix of nouns* **1.** The act, process, or result of: *ostracism.* **2.** The condition of being: *skepticism.* **3.** The characteristic action or behavior of: *heroism.* **4.** The beliefs, teachings, or system of: *Calvinism.* **5.** Devotion to; adherence to the teachings of: *nationalism.* **6.** A characteristic or peculiarity of: said especially of a language or idio n: *Americanism.* **7.** *Med.* An abnormal condition resulting from an excess of: *alcoholism.* [< L *-ismus* < Gk. *-ismos*]

Is·ma·il·i·a (is/mä·ē/lē·ə) A town in NE Egypt at the midpoint of the Suez Canal; pop. 115,200 (est. 1959). Also **Is/·ma·i/li·ya.**

Is·ma·il·i·an (is/mə·il/ē·ən) *n.* A member of a sect of the Shiah branch of Islam. Also **Is/ma·e/li·an** (-ē/lē·ən). [after *Ismail,* son of the sixth imam of the Moslems]

Is·ma·il Pa·sha (is/mä·ēl/ pä/shə), 1830–95, viceroy of Egypt 1863–67 and khedive 1867–79.

is·n't (iz/ənt) Is not.

iso- *combining form* **1.** Equal; the same; identical: *isocline.* **2.** *Chem.* Isomeric with, or an isomer of: *isopropyl.* Also, before vowels, *is-.* [< Gk. *isos* equal]

iso. Isotropic.

i·so·ag·glu·ti·na·tion (ī/sō·ə·glōō/tə·nā/shən) *n. Med.* The agglutination of the red blood corpuscles of an individual by a serum taken from another individual of the same species.

i·so·ag·glu·tin·in (ī/sō·ə·glōō/tə·nin) *n. Biochem.* A substance capable of effecting isoagglutination.

i·so·am·yl acetate (ī/sō·am/il) *Chem.* A sweet-smelling, colorless, liquid ester, C$_7$H$_{14}$O$_2$, widely used as a solvent and in artificial fruit flavors, cosmetics, etc.: also called *banana oil, pear oil.*

i·so·bar (ī/sə·bär) *n.* **1.** *Meteorol.* A line drawn on a weather map or chart such that all points on it have the sa ne barometric pressure for a given time or period. **2.** *Physics* Any of two or more atoms having the same mass number but different atomic numbers. [< Gk. *isobarēs* of equal weight < *isos* equal + *baros* weight]

i·so·bar·ic (ī/sə·bar/ik) *adj.* **1.** Of or pertaining to isobars. **2.** Indicating or characterized by equal barometric pressure.

i·so·bath (ī/sə·bath) *n.* A contour line drawn on a map such that all points on it have the sa ne depth beneath the surface of the ocean; also, a similar line indicating depth beneath the surface of the earth. [< ISO- + Gk. *bathys* deep] — **i/so·bath/ic** *adj.*

i·so·cheim (ī/sə·kīm) *n. Meteorol.* A line drawn on a weather map or chart such that all points on it have the same mean winter temperature. Also **i/so·chime.** [< ISO- + Gk. *cheima* winter] — **i/so·chei/mal** *adj.*

i·so·chore (ī/sə·kôr) *n. Physics* A curve plotted to show the relation between pressure and temperature of a substance or fluid maintained at constant volume. Also **i/so·chor.** [< ISO- + Gk. *chōra* space] — **i/so·chor/ic** *adj.*

i·so·chro·mat·ic (ī/sō·krō·mat/ik) *adj.* **1.** *Optics* Having or denoting identity of color, as the interference patterns of light waves in biaxial crystals. **2.** *Photog.* Orthochromatic.

i·soch·ro·nal (ī·sok/rə·nəl) *adj.* **1.** Of equal duration. **2.** Occurring in or characterized by equal intervals of time. Also **i·soch·ron·ic** (ī/sə·kron/ik), **i·soch/ro·nous.** [< ISO- + Gk. *chronos* time] — **i·soch/ro·nal·ly** *adv.*

i·soch·ro·nism (ī·sok/rə·niz/əm) *n.* The condition or property of being isochronal.

i·soch·ro·nize (ī·sok/rə·nīz) *v.t.* **nized, ·niz·ing** To make isochronal.

i·soch·ro·ous (ī·sok/rō·əs) *adj.* Having the same color or tint throughout. [< ISO- + -CHROOUS]

i·so·cli·nal (ī/sə·klī/nəl) *adj.* **1.** Dipping at the same angle and in the same direction. **2.** Designating a line on the earth's surface such that at all points on it the declination of a magnetic needle with respect to the vertical is constant. **3.** *Geol.* Pertaining to an isocline. — *n.* An isoclinal line. Also **i/so·clin/ic** (-klin/ik).

i·so·cline (ī/sə·klīn) *n. Geol.* An anticline or syncline in which the strata are so closely folded that they have the same dip. [< ISO- + Gk. *klinein* to bend]

i·so·cra·cy (ī·sok/rə·sē) *n. pl.* **·cies** A form of government in which all have equal political power. [< Gk. *isokratia* < *isos* same + *kratos* power] — **i·so·crat·ic** (ī/sə·krat/ik) *adj.*

I·soc·ra·tes (ī·sok/rə·tēz), 436–338 B.C., Athenian orator and rhetorician.

i·so·cy·a·nine (ī/sō·sī/ə·nēn, -nin) *n. Chem.* Any of a group of cyanine derivatives used in sensitizing photographic plates. Also **i/so·cy/a·nin** (-nin).

i·so·di·a·met·ric (ī/sō·dī/ə·met/rik) *adj.* **1.** Having axes or diameters of equal length. **2.** Equal in the three dimen-

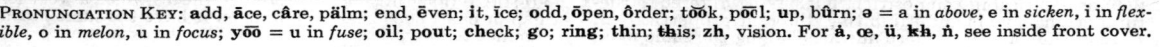

ISOCLINE
Vertical iso-
clinal folds.

sions. **3.** *Crystall.* Having only the lateral axes equal, as crystals of the tetragonal and hexagonal systems.

i·so·di·mor·phism (ī'sō-dī-môr'fiz-əm) *n. Crystall.* The phenomenon in which two or more crystals are both isomorphous and dimorphous. — **i'so·di·mor'phous** *adj.*

i·so·dy·nam·ic (ī'sō-dī-nam'ik, -di-) *adj.* **1.** Relating to or characterized by equality of force. **2.** Designating any line on the earth's surface at all points of which the intensity of terrestrial magnetism is the same. Also **i'so·dy·nam'i·cal.**

i·so·e·lec·tric (ī'sō-i-lek'trik) *adj.* **1.** Exhibiting the same electric potential. **2.** *Chem.* Designating the pH value at which a colloidal suspension is electrically neutral or at its minimum ionization.

i·so·e·lec·tron·ic (ī'sō-i-lek-tron'ik) *adj. Physics* Of or denoting atoms having a similar configuration of electrons.

i·so·gam·ete (ī'sō-gam'ēt, -gə-mēt') *n. Biol.* One of a pair of uniting gametes sexually and morphologically undifferentiated: opposed to *heterogamete.*

i·sog·a·mous (ī'sog'ə-məs) *adj. Biol.* Pertaining to or characterized by isogamy: opposed to *heterogamous.*

i·sog·a·my (ī'sog'ə-mē) *n. Biol.* The union of two isogametes, as in certain seaweeds. [< ISO- + Gk. *gamos* marriage]

i·sog·e·nous (ī·soj'ə-nəs) *adj. Biol.* Of similar origin, as organs or parts developed from the same cells or tissues. [< ISO- + Gk. *genos* offspring]

i·so·ge·o·therm (ī'sə-jē'ə-thûrm) *n. Geol.* A line or surface below the earth's crust such that all points on it have the same mean temperature. [< ISO- + GEO- + Gk. *thermē* heat] — **i'so·ge'o·ther'mal, i'so·ge'o·ther'mic** *adj.*

i·so·gloss (ī'sə-glôs, -glos) *n. Ling.* A line on a map, as in a dialect atlas, delimiting an area or areas in which a certain linguistic feature, as pronunciation, vocabulary, or syntax, is found. [< ISO- + Gk. *glōssa* language]

i·so·gon (ī'sə-gon) *n.* A polygon having equal angles. [< Gk. *isogōnios* equiangular]

i·so·gon·ic (ī'sə-gon'ik) *adj.* **1.** Having equal angles. **2.** Denoting a line on the earth's surface such that all points on it have equal magnetic declination. Also **i·sog·o·nal** (ī·sog'ə-nəl). — *n.* An isogonic line. [< Gk. *isogōnios* equiangular]

i·so·gram (ī'sə-gram) *n.* A line on a map, chart, diagram, etc., such that all points on it have equal value with respect to a given geographical feature, physical condition, etc.

i·so·griv (ī'sə-griv) *n.* A line drawn on a map or chart such that all points on it have equal grid variation. [< ISO- + GRIV(ATION)]

i·so·hel (ī'sə-hel) *n. Meteorol.* A line drawn on a map such that all points on it have equal amounts of sunshine. [< ISO- + Gk. *hēlios* sun]

i·so·hy·et (ī'sə-hī'et) *n. Meteorol.* A line drawn on a map such that all points on it have equal rainfall. [< ISO- + Gk. *hyetos* rain]

i·so·la·ble (ī'sə-lə-bəl, is'ə-) *adj.* Capable of being isolated.

i·so·late (ī'sə-lāt, is'ə-) *v.t.* **·lat·ed, ·lat·ing** **1.** To set apart, as from a mass, group, or situation; cause to be alone. **2.** *Med.* To place away from others, as a person with a communicable disease. **3.** *Chem.* To obtain (an element or substance) in a free or uncombined state. **4.** *Bacteriol.* To obtain (specified bacteria or organisms of disease) as a pure culture. **5.** *Electr.* To insulate. [Back formation from *isolated* < Ital. *isolato,* pp. of *isolare* to isolate < *isola* island < L *insula* island] — **i'so·la'tor** *n.*

i·so·lat·ing (ī'sə-lā'ting, is'ə-) *adj. Ling.* Denoting a language, as Chinese, in which there is no distinction in form between the parts of speech, and in which meaning is determined primarily by word order.

i·so·la·tion (ī'sə-lā'shən, is'ə-) *n.* **1.** The act of isolating. **2.** The state of being isolated; aloneness; solitude.

i·so·la·tion·ism (ī'sə-lā'shən-iz'əm, is'ə-) *n.* A policy advocating national self-sufficiency and freedom from foreign political and economic alliances.

i·so·la·tion·ist (ī'sə-lā'shən-ist, is'ə-) *n.* One who favors isolationism. — *adj.* Of or pertaining to isolationism.

I·solde (i-sōld', *Ger.* i-zôl'də) See ISEULT. Also **I·solt'** (i-sōlt').

i·so·lead (ī'sə-lēd) *n. Mil.* A curved line on a chart indicating the required lead of a gun in relation to a moving target.

i·so·leu·cine (ī'sə-lōō'sēn) *n. Biochem.* An amino acid, $C_6H_{13}NO_2$, found in body tissues and believed to be essential in nutrition. [< ISO- + LEUCINE]

i·so·logue (ī'sə-lôg, -log) *n. Chem.* An isologous compound. Also **i'so·log.** [< ISOLOGOUS]

i·sol·o·gous (ī-sol'ə-gəs) *adj. Chem.* Having similar molecular structure but different atoms of the same valence: applied especially to those groups of hydrocarbon compounds having a constant difference of two hydrogen atoms in their composition. [< ISO- + Gk. *logos* proportion]

isom. Isometric.

i·so·mag·net·ic (ī'sō-mag-net'ik) *adj.* Designating or connecting points at which specified properties of the earth's magnetic field remain constant. — *n.* An isomagnetic line.

i·so·mer (ī'sə-mər) *n.* **1.** *Chem.* One of two or more compounds identical in composition, but having different structural arrangements and exhibiting different properties. **2.** *Physics* One or more nuclides having the same mass

number and atomic number but differing in energy characteristics. [< Gk. *isomerēs* equally divided < *isos* equal + *meros* part] — **i·so·mer'ic** (-mer'ik) *adj.*

i·som·er·ism (ī-som'ə-riz'əm) *n. Chem.* The condition of having different chemical or physical properties, or both, but identical molecular compositions.

i·som·er·ous (ī-som'ər-əs) *adj.* **1.** Having an equal number of parts, organs, markings, etc. **2.** *Bot.* Equal in number, as the members of successive whorls of flowers: opposed to *heteromerous.*

i·so·met·ric (ī'sə-met'rik) *adj.* **1.** Pertaining to or characterized by equality in dimensions or measurements. **2.** *Crystall.* Pertaining to that system of crystallization in which the three axes are equal in length and at right angles to one another: also *cubic.* **3.** *Physics* Designating a line on a chart or diagram indicating changes in the temperature or pressure of a gas kept at constant volume. Also **i'so·met'ri·cal.** **4.** Based upon the forceful contraction of muscles against immovable resistance without shortening muscle fibers, a means of strengthening muscles: *isometric* exercises. — *n. Physics* An isometric line. — **i'so·met'ri·cal·ly** *adv.*

i·so·me·tro·pi·a (ī'sō-mə-trō'pē-ə) *n. Optics* Equality of refraction in both eyes. [< Gk. *isos* same + *metron* measure + -OPIA]

i·som·e·try (ī-som'ə-trē) *n.* **1.** Equality in measured parts or proportions. **2.** *Geog.* Equality of elevation above sea level. [< Gk. *isometria* equality of measure < *isos* same + *metron* measure]

i·so·morph (ī'sə-môrf) *n.* An organism or substance exhibiting isomorphism. [< ISO- + Gk. *morphē* form]

i·so·mor·phic (ī'sə-môr'fik) *adj.* **1.** Having similar form or appearance but of different ancestry or genetic constitution. **2.** *Chem.* Isomorphous.

i·so·mor·phism (ī'sə-môr'fiz-əm) *n.* **1.** *Chem.* A similarity in crystalline form shown by substances of different composition, or by different elements combined with identical atoms of other elements: distinguished from *polymorphism.* **2.** *Biol.* A similarity of characteristics and appearance in organisms belonging to different groups.

i·so·mor·phous (ī'sə-môr'fəs) *adj. Chem.* Similar in form but differing in composition: *isomorphous* crystals.

i·so·ni·a·zid (ī'sō-nī'ə-zid) *n. Chem.* A white, crystalline compound, $C_6H_5NO_2$, used as an anti-tuberculosis drug.

i·son·o·my (ī-son'ə-mē) *n.* Equality of civil rights. [< Ital. *isonomia* < Gk. < *isos* same + *nomos* law] — **i·so·nom·ic** (ī'sō-nom'ik) *adj.*

I·son·zo (ē-zōn'tsō) A river in NW Yugoslavia and NE Italy, flowing 84 miles south to the Gulf of Trieste.

i·so·oc·tane (ī'sō-ok'tān) *n. Chem.* Trimethylpentane. [< ISO- + OCTANE]

i·so·pi·es·tic (ī'sō-pī-es'tik) *adj.* Showing equal pressure; isobaric. — *n.* An isobar (def. 1). [< ISO- + Gk. *piestos* compressible < *piezein* to press]

i·so·pleth (ī'sə-pleth) *n. Meteorol.* An isogram showing the variations of a climatic element with respect to two coordinates, temporal and spatial. [< Gk. *isoplēthēs* equal in number or quantity < *isos* equal + *plēthos* number, quantity]

i·so·pod (ī'sə-pod) *n.* Any of an order (*Isopoda*) of terrestrial and aquatic crustaceans having flattened bodies lacking a carapace, and seven pairs of legs. — *adj.* Of or pertaining to isopods. [< NL < Gk. *isos* equal + *pous, podos* foot] — **i·sop·o·dan** (ī-sop'ə-dən) *n. & adj.* — **i·sop'o·dous** *adj.*

i·so·prene (ī'sə-prēn) *n. Chem.* A volatile liquid hydrocarbon, C_5H_8, of the terpene group, obtained when crude rubber is subjected to pyrolysis. [Appar. an arbitrary coinage]

i·so·pro·pyl (ī'sə-prō'pil) *n. Chem.* The univalent radical $(CH_3)_2CH$, an important constituent of many organic compounds. [< ISO- + PROPYL]

i·sop·ter·ous (ī-sop'tər-əs) *adj. Entomol.* Of or pertaining to an order (*Isoptera*) of social insects having soft bodies, strong mandibles, and well-developed claws, including the termites. [< ISO- + -PTEROUS]

i·so·rhy·thm (ī'sə-rith'əm) *n. Music* A device in which a rhythm is continually reiterated independently of the melody. [< ISO- + RHYTHM] — **i'so·rhyth'mic** *adj.*

i·sos·ce·les (ī-sos'ə-lēz) *adj. Geom.* Of a triangle, having two sides of equal length. [< LL < Gk. *isoskelēs* equal-legged < *isos* equal + *skelos* leg]

i·so·seis·mic (ī'sə-sīz'mik, -sīs'-) *adj.* Pertaining to or designating equal intensities of earthquake shocks. — *n.* A line on a map drawn such that all points on it receive equal shocks from a given earthquake. [< ISO- + SEISMIC] Also **i'so·seis'mal.**

i·sos·ta·sy (ī-sos'tə-sē) *n.* **1.** *Geol.* The equilibrium of earth's crust as a result of the action of terrestrial gravitation upon rock masses of unequal specific gravity. **2.** Equilibrium resulting from equal pressure on all sides. [< ISO- + Gk. *stasis* standing] — **i·so·stat·ic** (ī'sə-stat'ik) *adj.*

isoth. Isothermal.

i·so·there (ī'sə-thir) *n. Meteorol.* A line drawn on a weather map or chart such that all points on it have the same mean summer temperature. [< ISO- + Gk. *theros* summer]

ISOSCELES TRIANGLE
$AB = CB$

i·so·therm (ī'sə·thûrm) *n. Meteorol.* A line drawn on a weather map or chart such that all points on it have the same mean temperature. [< ISO- + Gk. *thermē* heat]

i·so·ther·mal (ī'sə·thûr'məl) *adj.* **1.** Pertaining to, indicating, or having equal temperatures. **2.** *Physics* Designating a relationship between variables characterized by constant temperature. **3.** *Meteorol.* Of or pertaining to an isotherm. — *n. Meteorol.* An isotherm.

isothermal layer *Meteorol.* The stratosphere.

i·so·tone (ī'sə·tōn) *n. Physics* One of two or more atomic nuclei having the same number of neutrons. [< ISOTONIC]

i·so·ton·ic (ī'sə·ton'ik) *adj.* **1.** *Physiol.* **a** Having the same osmotic pressure on opposite sides of a membrane: said of solutions, especially blood or plasma. **b** Denoting the contraction of a muscle under a small but uniform tension, or the curve showing such a contraction. **2.** *Music* Pertaining to or having equal tones. [< Gk. *isotonos* having equal accent or tone < *isos* equal + *tonos* accent, tone] — **i·so·to·nic·i·ty** (ī'sə·tō·nis'ə·tē) *n.*

i·so·tope (ī'sə·tōp) *n. Physics* Any of two or more forms of an element having the same atomic number and similar chemical properties but differing in mass number and radioactive behavior. [< ISO- + Gk. *topos* place] — **i·so·top·ic** (ī'sə·top'ik) *adj.*

i·sot·o·py (ī·sot'ə·pē) *n.* The nature or relationship of isotopes.

i·so·trop·ic (ī'sə·trop'ik, -trō'pik) *adj.* **1.** *Physics* Exhibiting the same physical properties in every direction. **2.** *Biol.* Lacking clearly determined axes, as certain eggs. Also **i·sot·ro·pous** (ī·sot'rə·pəs). Abbr. *iso.* [< ISO- + -TROPIC]

i·sot·ro·py (ī·sot'rə·pē) *n.* The state or quality of being isotropic. Also **i·sot'ro·pism** (-piz'əm). [< ISO- + -TROPY]

I·soude (i·sōōd') See ISEULT.

Is·pa·han (is'pä·hän') See ISFAHAN.

Isr. Israel.

Is·ra·el (iz'rē·əl) The patriarch Jacob. *Gen.* xxxii 28. — *n.* **1.** The Jewish people, traditionally regarded as descended from Jacob. **2.** In the Judeo-Christian tradition, the members of any religious group considered to be the chosen people of God. [< Hebrew *Yisrā'ēl* God persevereth]

Is·ra·el (iz'rē·əl) **1.** A Republic comprising parts of Palestine, proclaimed as a Jewish national state in 1948; 7,993 sq. mi.; pop. 2,911,000 (est. 1970.) capital, Jerusalem. **2.** An ancient Jewish kingdom in the northern part of Palestine.

[map: MEDITERRANEAN SEA, Beirut, LEBANON, SYRIA, Damascus, Haifa, Tel Aviv, Amman, Jerusalem, Gaza, DEAD SEA, ISRAEL, JORDAN, SAUDI ARABIA, UNITED ARAB REPUBLIC (EGYPT), Aqaba — Before June, 1967]

Is·rae·li (iz·rā'lē) *adj.* Of or pertaining to modern Israel, its people, or their culture. — *n. pl.* **·lis** A native or inhabitant of Israel.

Is·ra·el·ite (iz'rē·əl·īt') *n.* **1.** Any of the people of Israel or their descendants; a Hebrew; a Jew. **2.** A person considered to be one of God's chosen people. — *adj.* Of or pertaining to the Hebrews; Jewish: also **Is'ra·el·it'ish** (-ī'tish), **Is'ra·el·it'ic** (-it'ik).

Is·ra·fel (iz'rə·fel) In the Koran, the angel who is to sound the resurrection trumpet. Also **Is'ra·feel, Is'ra·fil** (-fēl).

Is·sa·char (is'ə·kär) In the Old Testament, a son of Jacob and Leah. *Gen.* xxx 18. — *n.* The tribe of Israel descended from him.

Is·sei (ēs·sā) *n. pl.* **·sei** or **·seis** Formerly, a Japanese who emigrated to the United States after the Oriental exclusion proclamation of 1907, and was not legally eligible to become an American citizen. Compare NISEI, KIBEI. [< Japanese *is* first + *sei* generation]

is·su·a·ble (ish'ōō·ə·bəl, -yōō-) *adj.* **1.** That can issue or be issued. **2.** *Law* That can be established as an issue.

is·su·ance (ish'ōō·əns, -yōō-) *n.* The act or procedure of issuing; promulgation.

is·su·ant (ish'ōō·ənt, -yōō-) *adj.* **1.** Issuing; emerging. **2.** *Heraldry* Having only the upper half shown.

is·sue (ish'ōō, -yōō) *n.* **1.** The act or procedure of giving out, supplying, or publishing, especially from an official source. **2.** An item or set of items, as stamps, magazines, etc., thus issued; especially, those issued at a single time. **3.** A result; consequence; outcome. **4.** A matter of importance depending on a result or decision. **5.** A subject of discussion or interest. **6.** A going out; outflow; discharge. **7.** A point of outflow or egress; outlet; exit. **8.** Offspring; progeny. **9.** *Law* **a** A point in question between parties to an action. **b** Profits; proceeds, as from property. **10.** *Med.* **a** A discharge, as of blood or pus. **b** An incision or artificially induced sore permitting the outflow of such a discharge. **11.** *Obs.* A deed; action. **— at issue a** Under discussion; in question. **b** In controversy or disagreement. **— to join issue** To enter into a debate or controversy. **— to take issue** To disagree. — *v.* **·sued, ·su·ing** *v.i.* **1.** To come forth; flow out; emerge. **2.** To be derived; originate; proceed. **3.** To come or occur as a consequence; result. **4.** To come to an end; terminate: often followed by *in.* **5.** To be sent out, circulated, or published; appear. **6.** To be produced as profit; accrue. **7.** *Rare* or *Law* To be born or descended. — *v.t.* **8.** To give or send forth, as from an official or authoritative source; put into circulation; publish. **9.** To make known; announce; utter: to *issue* commands. **10.** To give out; distribute, as supplies. **11.** To allow or cause to come out; emit; exude. [< OF *issue* < *issir, eissir* < L *exire* < *ex-* out + *ire* to go] — **is'su·er** *n.*

Is·sus (is'əs) An ancient port town in Cilicia, NE Asia Minor; scene of the victory of Alexander the Great over Darius III, 333 B.C.

Is·syk Kul (ē'sik kōōl', *Russ.* ē·sik' kōōly') The second largest mountain lake in the world, eastern Kirghiz S.S.R.; 2,395 sq. mi. Also **Issyk Kul'.**

-ist *suffix of nouns* **1.** One who or that which does or has to do with: often used with verbs in *-ize: catechist.* **2.** One whose profession is; one who practices: *pharmacist.* **3.** A student or devotee of: *genealogist.* **4.** One who advocates or adheres to: in extension from nouns ending in *-ism: socialist.* [< F *-iste* (< Gk. *-istēs*) or L *-ista* or Gk. *-istēs*]

Is·tan·bul (is'tan·bōōl', -tän-; *Turkish* is·täm'bōōl) The largest city of Turkey, a port on the Bosporus at its entrance into the Sea of Marmara; pop. 1,742,978 (1965); ancient *Byzantium;* formerly, as *Constantinople,* capital of Turkey until 1923: also *Stambul.* Also **Is'tan·boul', Is·tan'bul.**

isth. Isthmus.

isth·mi·an (is'mē·ən, isth'-) *adj.* **1.** Of or pertaining to an isthmus. **2.** *Usually cap.* Pertaining to, situated on, or inhabiting a specified isthmus, as the Isthmus of Corinth or the Isthmus of Panama. — *n.* An inhabitant of an isthmus.

Isthmian games A religious festival celebrated every two years in ancient Greece on the Isthmus of Corinth.

isth·mus (is'məs, isth'-) *n. pl.* **·mus·es** or **·mi** (-mī) **1.** A narrow piece of land extending into a body of water and connecting two larger land masses. **2.** *Biol.* A contracted structure connecting two larger organs, parts, or cavities in a plant or animal. [< L < Gk. *isthmos* narrow passage]

-istic *Suffix of adjectives* Having the qualities of: formed from nouns ending in *-ist* or *-ism: communistic.*

is·tle (is'lē, ist'lē) *n.* A fiber derived principally from a tropical American plant (*Agave fourcroydes* or *A. lophantha*), used for carpets, cordage, etc.: also called *pita, Tampico fiber:* also spelled *ixtle.* [< Am. Sp. *ixtle* < Nahuatl]

Is·tri·a (is'trē·ə) A peninsula, mostly in Yugoslavia, in the north Adriatic Sea; 1,908 sq. mi. *Serbo-Croatian* (ēs'trä). Also **Istrian Peninsula.** — **Is'tri·an** *adj. & n.*

it (it) *pron., possessive* **its**; *pl. nominative* **they**, *possessive* **their** or **theirs,** *objective* **them** The nominative and objective singular neuter pronoun of the third person, used: **1.** As a substitute for a specific noun or name when referring to things or places, or when referring to infants or animals of unspecified sex. **2.** To represent some implied idea, condition, action, or situation: How was it?; I'm opposed to *it.* **3.** As the subject or predicate nominative of a verb whose logical subject is indefinite: Who is it? It is John. **4.** As the subject of an impersonal verb: *It* rained yesterday. **5.** As the indefinite subject of a verb introducing a clause or a phrase: *It* seems that he knew. **6.** As the indefinite object after certain verbs in idiomatic expressions: to brazen it out. — *n.* In certain children's games, the player required to perform some specified act. [OE *hit*]

I.T.A. Initial Teaching Alphabet.

it·a·col·u·mite (it'ə·kol'yə·mīt) *n.* A variety of sandstone that is flexible in thin slabs. [after *Itacolumi,* a mountain in eastern Brazil]

ital. or **it.** Italic(s).

Ital. or **It.** Italian; Italy.

I·tal·ia (ē·tä'lyä) The Italian name for ITALY.

Italia ir·re·den·ta (ē're·den'tä) See IRREDENTIST.

I·tal·ian (i·tal'yən) *adj.* Of or pertaining to Italy, its people, or their language. — *n.* **1.** A native or naturalized inhabitant of Italy. **2.** The Romance language of Italy. Abbr. *It., Ital.* [< L *Italianus* < *Italia* Italy < Gk.]

I·tal·ian·ate (*adj.* i·tal'yən·āt, -it; *v.* i·tal'yən·āt) *adj.* Italian in manner, style, etc. — *v.t.* **·at·ed, ·at·ing** To Italianize. [< Ital. *italianato* made Italian] — **I·tal·ian·a'tion** *n.*

Italian East Africa Formerly, Eritrea, Italian Somaliland, and Ethiopia.

Italian hand A flowing script that originated in Italy in the 15th century and developed into a modern style of type face. **— fine Italian hand** Intrigue; subtlety; cunning.

I·tal·ian·ism (i·tal′yən·iz′əm) *n.* **1.** An Italian idiom, custom, or manner. **2.** Italian manner or spirit.

I·tal·ian·ize (i·tal′yən·īz) *v.t. & v.i.* **·ized, ·iz·ing** To make or become Italian in manner, customs, language, etc. — **I·tal·ian·i·za′tion** *n.*

Italian millet See under MILLET.

Italian Somaliland A former UN Trust Territory in eastern Africa; about 194,000 sq. mi. See SOMALIA.

Italian squash Zucchini.

Italian sonnet The Petrarchan sonnet (which see).

i·tal·ic (i·tal′ik) *n. Usually pl.* A style of type in which the letters slant, usually used to denote emphasis or to distinguish titles, foreign expressions, etc., within a body of printed matter: *These words are printed in italics.* — *adj.* Designating or printed in italics. Compare ROMAN. *Abbr. it., ital.* [< ITALIC]

I·tal·ic (i·tal′ik) *adj.* Relating to any of the peoples of ancient Italy. — *n.* A subfamily of the Indo-European languages, comprising three branches, Falisco-Latinian (including Latin and the Romance languages), Osco-Umbrian, and Sabellian. [< L *Italicus* < Gk. *Italikos*]

I·tal·i·cism (i·tal′ə·siz′əm) *n.* An Italianism (def. 1).

i·tal·i·cize (i·tal′ə·sīz) *v.* **·cized, ·ciz·ing** *v.t.* **1.** To print in italics. **2.** To underscore (written words or phrases) with a single line to indicate italics. — *v.i.* **3.** To use or indicate the use of italics. — **i·tal·i·ci·za′tion** *n.*

It·a·ly (it′ə·lē) A Republic in southern Europe; 116,286 sq. mi.; pop. 54,504,000 (1970); capital, Rome. Italian *Italia.*

I·tas·ca (ī·tas′kə), **Lake** A lake in northern Minnesota, considered to be the source of the Mississippi River.

itch (ich) *v.i.* **1.** To experience or produce an irritation that causes a desire to scratch or rub the affected area or part. **2.** To have a restless or unsatisfied desire to do or acquire something; hanker. — *n.* **1.** An itching sensation or irritation. **2.** Any of various usually contagious skin diseases accompanied by itching, as scabies: often preceded by *the.* **3.** A restless desire or yearning. [ME *yitchen, yicchen, icchen* < OE *giccan*]

itching palm A greedy or unscrupulous desire for gain.

itch mite Any of various mites (*Sarcoptes* and related genera) that cause scabies and mange.

itch·y (ich′ē) *adj.* **itch·i·er, itch·i·est** Having or producing an itching sensation. — **itch′i·ness** *n.*

-ite¹ *suffix of nouns* **1.** A native or inhabitant of: *Gothamite.* **2.** A follower of or sympathizer with: *Luddite, Pre-Raphaelite.* **3.** A descendant of: *Ishmaelite.* **4.** Resembling or related to: often used in the names of commercial products: *dynamite, vulcanite.* **5.** *Mineral.* A rock or mineral: *graphite, hematite.* **6.** *Paleontol.* A fossil or fossilized substance: *lignite, trilobite.* **7.** *Zool.* A part of the body or of an organ: *dendrite, somite.* [< F *-ite* < L *-ita* < Gk. *-ītēs*]

-ite² *suffix Chem.* A salt or ester of an acid having a name that ends in *-ous: sulfite.* [< F *-ite*; arbitrarily coined (1787) from *-ate.* See *-ATE*³.]

-ite³ *suffix* Derived from the past participial form of certain Latin verbs and occurring in: **1.** Adjectives: *infinite, polite.* **2.** Verbs: *unite.* **3.** Nouns: *appetite.* [< L *-itus*]

i·tem (ī′təm) *n.* **1.** A single unit or article included in a category, series, or enumeration. **2.** An entry in an account or list of particulars. **3.** A brief article or paragraph consisting of a single piece of news, information, etc., as in a newspaper. **4.** *Obs.* An admonition; intimation; hint. — *v.t.* To record or take note of as an item; list or enter by items. — *adv.* Likewise; also: used to introduce a statement or entry in a list, enumeration, or series. [< L, thus, like it]

i·tem·ize (ī′təm·īz) *v.t.* **·ized, ·iz·ing** To set down or specify by items. — **i′tem·i·za′tion** *n.* — **i′tem·iz′er** *n.*

item veto The power or action of a government executive to veto parts of a bill without vetoing the entire bill.

I·té·nez (ē·tā′nes) See GUAPORÉ.

it·er·ance (it′ər·əns) *n.* Repetition; iteration.

it·er·ant (it′ər·ənt) *adj.* Repeating.

it·er·ate (it′ə·rāt) *v.t.* **·at·ed, ·at·ing** **1.** To state or utter again or repeatedly; repeat. **2.** *Rare* To do another time or repeatedly. [< L *iteratus*, pp. of *iterare* to repeat < *iterum* again. Akin to ITEM.] — **it′er·a′tion** *n.*

it·er·a·tive (it′ə·rā′tiv, it′ər·ə·tiv) *adj.* **1.** Characterized by repetition; repeated. **2.** *Gram.* Frequentative.

i·te·rum (it′ər·əm) *adv. Latin* Again; once more.

Ith·a·ca (ith′ə·kə) **1.** An island of Greece, in the Ionian group; 36 sq. mi.: legendary home of Odysseus. *Greek* **I·thá·ki, I·tha·ki** (ē·thä′kē). **2.** A city in south central New York, on the southern end of Cayuga Lake; pop. 26,226. — **Ith′a·can** *adj. & n.*

ith·er (ith′ər) *adj. & pron. Scot.* Other.

I·thunn (ē′th̷ŏŏn) In Norse mythology, the wife of Bragi and keeper of the golden apples of youth: also called *Idun.* Also **I′thun.**

I·thu·ri·el (i·thyŏŏr′ē·əl) In Milton's *Paradise Lost,* an angel sent by Gabriel to search for Satan.

ith·y·phal·lic (ith′i·fal′ik) *adj.* **1.** Characterized by a large phallus, as certain primitive art works. **2.** Denoting the phallus carried in festivals of Bacchus. **3.** Grossly ribald. **4.** In classical prosody, pertaining to the characteristic meter used in hymns to Bacchus. — *n.* **1.** A poem in ithyphallic meter. **2.** A piece of indecent or obscene verse. [< L *ithyphallicus* < Gk. *ithyphallikos* < *ithyphallos* < *ithys* erect, rigid + *phallos* phallus]

i·tin·er·an·cy (ī·tin′ər·ən·sē, i·tin′-) *n.* **1.** The state of being itinerant. **2.** The act of traveling from place to place in order to perform official duties or transact business. **3.** In the Methodist Church, the system whereby a minister is assigned to a circuit of duties for a stated period. **4.** Itinerants collectively. Also **i·tin′er·a·cy** (-ə·sē).

i·tin·er·ant (ī·tin′ər·ənt, i·tin′-) *adj.* **1.** Going from place to place; wandering, as in search of employment. **2.** Traveling to a series of places in order to fulfill official duties: an *itinerant* judge. — *n.* One who travels from place to place. [< LL *itinerans, -antis,* ppr. of *itinerari* to make a journey < *iter, itineris* journey, route] — **i·tin′er·ant·ly** *adv.*

i·tin·er·ar·y (ī·tin′ə·rer′ē, i·tin′-) *n. pl.* **·ar·ies** **1.** A route followed in traveling. **2.** A plan for or graphic representation of a journey. **3.** A detailed account or record of a journey. **4.** A guidebook for travelers. — *adj.* Pertaining to travel or routes of travel.

i·tin·er·ate (ī·tin′ə·rāt, i·tin′-) *v.i.* **·at·ed, ·at·ing** To journey from place to place. — **i·tin′er·a′tion** *n.*

-ition *suffix of nouns* **1.** Condition, state, or quality: *ambition.* **2.** Act or process, or the result of an act or process: *audition.* [< L *-itio, -onis*]

-itious *suffix of adjectives* Characterized by; having the quality of: *ambitious.* [< L *-icius, -itius*]

-itis *suffix Pathol.* Inflammation of: *peritonitis.* [< Gk.]

it'll (it′l) **1.** It will. **2.** It shall.

I·to (ē′tō) **Hirobumi,** 1841–1909, Japanese statesman.

ITO International Trade Organization.

-itol *suffix Chem.* Denoting a class of alcohols containing two or more hydroxyl radicals. [<-ITE + -OL]

its (its) *pronominal adjective* The possessive case of the pronoun *it,* used attributively: *its* leaves; *its* appearance. [< IT + 's, possessive case ending; written *it's* until the 19th century]

it's (its) **1.** It is. **2.** It has.

it·self (it·self′) *pron.* A form of the third person singular neuter pronoun, used: **a** As a reflexive or as object of a preposition in a reflexive sense: The situation will right *itself;* The motor started by *itself.* **b** As an intensifier or to give emphasis: simplicity *itself.* **c** As a designation for a normal or usual state: The house isn't *itself* with the children gone.

it's me See note under ME.

-ity *suffix of nouns* State, condition, or quality: *maternity, superiority.* [< F *-ité* < L *-itas*]

I·tys (ī′tis) In Greek mythology, the son of Tereus and Procne, slain by Procne and Philomela. See PHILOMELA.

IU or **I.U.** *Biochem.* International unit(s).

IUD Intrauterine device (which see).

I·u·lus (ī·yōō′ləs) See ASCANIUS.

-ium *suffix Chem.* Denoting certain elements or compounds: *ammonium, titanium.* [< L]

I·van III (ī′vən, *Russian* i·vän′), 1440–1505, grand duke of Muscovy 1462–1505: called **the Great.**

Ivan IV, 1530–84, first czar of Russia 1547–84: called **the Terrible.**

I·van·hoe (ī′vən·hō) A historical romance by Sir Walter Scott, set in England at the time of Richard I.

I·va·no·vo (ē·vä′nə·və) A city in the R.S.F.S.R., near Moscow; pop. 407,000 (est. 1967).

I've (īv) I have.

-ive *suffix of adjectives* **1.** Having a tendency or predisposition to: *disruptive.* **2.** Having the nature, character, or quality of: *massive.* Also *-ative.* [< F *-if* < L *-ivus*]

Ives (īvz), **Charles,** 1874–1954, U.S. composer. — **Frederic Eugene,** 1856–1937, U.S. inventor; pioneer in photography. — **James Merritt** See CURRIER AND IVES.

i·vied (ī′vēd) *adj.* Covered or overgrown with ivy.

i·vo·ry (ī′vər·ē) *n. pl.* **·ries** **1.** The hard, white, smooth-textured dentine constituting the chief substance of the tusks of elephants, walruses, etc. **2.** Any substance resembling ivory. **3.** The creamy white color of ivory. **4.** *Usually pl.* Articles made of ivory. **5.** Any form of dentine. **6.** A tusk, especially that of an elephant. **7.** *pl. Slang* **a** The teeth. **b** The keys of a piano. **c** Dice. — *adj.* **1.** Made of or resembling ivory. **2.** Of the color ivory. [< OF *ivurie* < L *eboreus* of ivory < *ebur, -oris* ivory]

i·vo·ry-bill (ī′vər·ē·bil′) *n.* A large, nearly extinct North American woodpecker (*Campephilus principalis*) having an ivorylike bill. Also **i′vo·ry-billed′ woodpecker.**

ivory black A black pigment made by charring ivory.

Ivory Coast The coastal region of western Africa along the Gulf of Guinea. See map of (Gulf of) GUINEA.

Ivory Coast, Republic of the An independent Republic in western Africa; 128,364 sq. mi.; pop. 4,195,000 (est. 1969); capital, Abidjan: French *République de la Côte d'Ivoire.*

ivory gull A white arctic gull (*Pagophila eburnea*).

ivory nut The hard, ivorylike seed of the ivory palm, used in making small carvings, buttons, etc.: also called *jarina, tagua nut, vegetable ivory.*

ivory palm A South American palm (*Phytelephas macro-carpa*).

ivory tower A condition or attitude of withdrawal from the world and reality.

i·vo·ry·type (ī'vər·ē·tīp') *n. Photog.* A picture made by fixing a translucent photograph over another.

i·vy (ī'vē) *n. pl.* **i·vies 1.** A widely cultivated climbing or spreading plant (*Hedera helix*), having glossy, evergreen leaves, small yellowish flowers, and black berries: also **English ivy. 2.** One of various other climbing plants, as the **Japanese** or **Boston ivy** (*Parthenocissus tricuspidata*), and the **ground ivy** (*Nepeta hederacea*). [OE *ifig*]

Ivy League An association of colleges in the NE United States, comprising Brown, Columbia, Cornell Dartmouth, Harvard, Princeton, the University of Pennsylvania, and Yale: often used attributively to denote the fashions or manners considered characteristic of students in these colleges: *Ivy League* clothes.

ivy vine An American vitaceous plant (*Ampelopsis cordata*), having heart-shaped leaves.

i·wis (i·wis') *adv. Archaic* Certainly; indeed: in later use written mistakenly *I wis*, through confusion with the verb *wit*. Also spelled *ywis*. [OE *gewis*]

I·wo Ji·ma (ē'wō jē'mä, ē'wə jē'mə) The largest of the Volcano Islands in the North Pacific; scene of an American victory over the Japanese (1945).

IWW or **I.W.W.** Industrial Workers of the World.

Ix·elles (ēk·sel') A commune in central Belgium, a suburb of Brussels; pop. 92,532 (est. 1960).

ix·i·a (ik'sē·ə) *n.* Any of a genus (*Ixia*) of South African bulbous plants of the iris family, having spikes of showy flowers: also called *corn lily*. [< NL < Gk. *ixos* birdlime;

from the viscid substance exuded by some of their species]

Ix·i·on (ik·sī'ən) In Greek mythology, a Thessalian king whom Zeus punished for his love for Hera by having him tied to a perpetually revolving wheel in Hades.

Ix·ta·ci·hua·tl (ēs'tä·sē'wät·l) A dormant volcano in central Mexico; 17,342 ft.; last eruption, 1868. Also **Iz·tac·ci·hua·tl** (ēs'täk·sē'wät·l).

ix·tle (iks'tlē, ist'lē, is'lē) See ISTLE.

I·ye·ya·su (ē·yä·yä·sōō), 1542–1616; Japanese shogun and statesman. Also *Ieyasu*.

Iy·yar (ē·yär', ē'yär) *n.* The eighth month of the Hebrew year. Also **I·yar'.** See (Hebrew) CALENDAR.

-ization *suffix* Used to form nouns from verbs in *-ize*, and denoting a condition, act, process, or result: *civilization, ionization.* [< -IZE + -ATION]

-ize *suffix of verbs* **1.** To cause to become or resemble; make into: *Christianize.* **2.** To subject to the action of; affect with: *oxidize.* **3.** To change into; become: *mineralize.* **4.** To act in the manner of; practice: *sympathize.* Also *-ise.* [< F *-iser* < LL *-izare* < Gk. *-izein*]
◆ The spelling of this suffix varies in British and American usage; *-ize* is the preferred spelling in the United States, while *-ise* is preferred in England. However, certain words, as *advise*, are always spelled with *-ise*, whereas others, as *baptize*, are always spelled with *-ize*.

I·zhevsk (ē'zhifsk) The capital of the Udmurt A.S.S.R., in the southern part of the Republic; pop. 422,000 (est. 1970).

Iz·mir (ēz·mir') A port in western Turkey; pop. 411,626 (1965): formerly, *Smyrna.*

iz·zard (iz'ərd) *n. Archaic* The letter Z. **— from A to iz-zard** From beginning to end. [< earlier *ezed*, var. of ZED]

J

j, J (jā) *n. pl.* **j's** or **js, J's** or **Js, jays** (jāz) **1.** The tenth letter of the English alphabet. The shape of the Phoenician consonant *yod* was adopted by the Greeks as *iota* and became Roman *I*. In the 17th century, the calligraphic practice of carrying initial *I* (which usually had consonantal value) both above and below the line gradually developed into a graphic distinction between *i* the vowel and *i* or *j* the consonant. Also *jay.* **2.** The sound represented by the letter *j*, usually a voiced affricate, as in *judge* (juj) or, in borrowings from Modern French, often (zh), as in *jabot.* **— symbol** In Roman numerals, one: used as a variant of *i* at the end of a number, as *vij*, especially in medical prescriptions.

J *Physics* Joule.

J. 1. Journal. **2.** Judge. **3.** Justice.

ja (yä) *interj. & adv. German* Yes.

Ja. January.

JA Judge Advocate.

jab (jab) *v.t. & v.i.* **jabbed, jab·bing 1.** To poke or thrust sharply. **2.** To punch or strike with short blows. **—** *n.* **1.** A sharp thrust. **2.** A rapid punch. [Var. of JOB²]

Jab·al·pur (jub'əl·pôr, -pōr) See JUBBULPORE.

jab·ber (jab'ər) *v.t. & v.i.* To speak rapidly, unintelligibly, or without making sense; chatter. **— Syn.** See BABBLE. **—** *n.* Rapid, nonsensical, or unintelligible talk; chatter. [Prob. imit.] **— jab'ber·er** *n.*

Jab·ber·wock·y (jab'ər·wok'ē) A nonsense poem from Lewis Carroll's *Through the Looking-Glass.*

jab·i·ru (jab'ə·rōō) *n.* **1.** A large tropical American wading bird (*Jabiru mycteria*) of the stork family, with white plumage. **2.** The wood ibis. [< Pg. < Tupi]

jab·o·ran·di (jab'ə·ran'dē) *n.* **1.** Any of a genus (*Pilocarpus*) of numerous South American shrubs of the rue family, especially *P. jaborandi.* **2.** The dried leaves of this and allied plants yielding pilocarpine. [< Pg. < Tupi]

ja·bot (zha·bō', *Fr.* zhà·bō') *n. pl.* **·bots** (-bōz', *Fr.* -bō') A ruffle or similar decoration falling from the neckline or at the front of a blouse, shirt, or bodice. [< F, lit., gizzard]

ja·bot·i·ca·ba (jə·bot'ə·kä'bə) *n.* A semitropical evergreen tree (*Myrciaria cauliflora*) of the myrtle family, cultivated in Florida and California, and having edible, grapelike fruit. [< Tupi *jabuti* tortoise + *caba* fat]

jac·a·mar (jak'ə·mär) *n.* A tropical American insect-eating bird (family *Galbulidae*) of various genera, having metallic green or coppery plumage. [< F < Tupi *jacamaciri*]

ja·ça·na (zhä'sə·nä') Any of a family (*Jacanidae*) of small tropical wading birds with long, straight toes adapted for walking over floating leaves of aquatic plants. [< Tupi]

jac·a·ran·da (jak'ə·ran'də) *n.* **1.** Any of a genus (*Jacaranda*) of tropical American trees and shrubs of the bignonia family. **2.** The hard, fine-textured wood of any of these trees. [< Pg. < Tupi]

ja·cinth (jā'sinth, jas'inth) *n.* Hyacinth (def. 4). [< OF *iacinte* < L *hyacinthus.* Doublet of HYACINTH.]

jack¹ (jak) *n.* **1.** *Sometimes cap.* A man or boy; fellow; especially: **a** A man employed at manual labor or odd jobs: usually used in combination: *jack-of-all-trades; lumberjack.* **b** A sailor. **2.** Any of various devices, as a mechanism for turning a spit, that perform or aid in an operation formerly done by a man or boy: often used in combinations denoting a specific use: *bootjack.* **3.** Any of various devices or appliances operating by means of a lever, screw, or other mechanical force, used for raising heavy weights through short distances. **4.** In names or designations of animals: **a** A male: sometimes used in combination: *jackass.* **b** Any of various kinds of animals, birds, or fish: often in combination: *jackdaw; jack* rabbit. **5.** A playing card showing the picture of a young man, being in most card games the lowest face card; the knave. **6.** A flag, usually consisting of the union or canton of a national flag, flown at the bow of a ship as a signal, or as an indication of nationality when in port. **7.** *U.S. Slang* Money. **8.** *U.S. & Canadian* A jacklight. **9.** A jackstone. **10.** In some games of bowling, a small ball or pin serving as a mark at which the players aim. **11.** In a harpsichord, one of the pieces of wood holding a quill or leather point that plucks a string. **12.** *Electr.* A metallic connecting device provided with spring clips to which the wires of a circuit may be attached, and into which a plug may be inserted. **13.** *Naut.* An iron crosstree at the topgallant masthead: also **jack crosstree. — every man jack** Each individual of a specified group. **—** *v.t.* **1.** To raise or lift with or as with a jack: usually with *up.* **2.** *Informal* To increase, as a price or charge: with *up.* **3.** *U.S.* To jacklight. [after *Jack*, a nickname for John, a personal name]

jack² (jak) *n.* **1.** A SE Asian tree (*Artocarpus heterophyllus*) of the mulberry family, resembling the breadfruit tree. **2.** The yellow wood of this tree, furnishing valuable lumber. **3.** The large fruit, resembling the breadfruit, produced by this tree. [< Pg. *jaca* < Malayalam *chakka*]

jack³ (jak) *n.* **1.** A medieval protective garment, usually made of quilted or padded leather. **2.** *Archaic* A leather jug or drinking vessel. [< F *jaque* peasant's short jacket < *Jaques, Jacques,* French personal name used to signify a peasant. See JACQUERIE.]

jack-a-dan·dy (jak'ə·dan'dē) *n. pl.* **·dies** A fop.

jack·al (jak′əl, -ôl) *n.* **1.** Any of various African or Asian doglike carnivorous mammals (family *Canidae*), that hunt in packs and feed on small animals and carrion. **2.** One who does menial work to serve another's purpose. [< Turkish *chakal* < Persian *shaghal*]

jack·a·napes (jak′ə·nāps) *n.* **1.** An impertinent fellow; an upstart. **2.** *Archaic* A monkey; ape. [< *Jack Napes*, nickname of William de la Pole, 15th c. Duke of Suffolk]

jack·ass (jak′as′) *n.* **1.** A male ass. **2.** A doltish or foolish person; blockhead. [< JACK¹ (def. 4a) + ASS¹]

jackass brig *Naut.* A brigantine.

jack bean A three-leaved climber (*Canavalia ensiformis*) of the bean family, having purple flowers and long pods, grown for stock feed: also called *overlook.*

jack·boot (jak′bōōt′) *n.* A heavy topboot reaching above the knee.

jack·daw (jak′dô′) *n.* A glossy, black, crowlike bird (*Corvus monedula*) of Europe, sometimes tamed as a pet: also called *daw.* [< JACK¹ (def. 4b) + DAW]

jack·e·roo (jak′ə·rōō′) *n. pl.* **·roos** *Austral. Informal* A station employe being trained for managerial status. Also **jack′a·roo′.** [< JACK¹ + (KANGA)ROO]

jack·et (jak′it) *n.* **1.** A short coat, usually not extending below the hips. **2.** Anything resembling a jacket; an outer covering or case; as: **a** The skin of a cooked potato. **b** The metal covering encasing a bullet or shell. **c** A removable paper cover for a bound book. **d** An insulating cover or layer surrounding a pipe, boiler, etc. **e** *U.S.* An open envelope or folder used for filing letters, documents, etc. — *v.t.* To cover or surround with or as with a jacket. [< OF *jaquet*, dim. of *jaque* short jacket. See JACK³.]

jack·fish (jak′fish′) *n. pl.* **·fish** or **·fish·es** *Canadian* A pike.

Jack Frost A personification of frost or winter weather.

jack·ham·mer (jak′ham′ər) A rock drill operated by compressed air.

jack-in-the-box (jak′in·thə·boks′) *n.* A toy consisting of a box containing a grotesque figure that springs up when the lid is unfastened: also **jack′-in-a-box′.**

jack-in-the-pul·pit (jak′in·thə·pōōl′pit) *n.* A common American herb (*Arisaema triphyllum*) of the arum family, growing from a turnip-shaped bulb, and having a clublike spadix in a leaflike spathe: also called *Indian turnip.*

Jack Ketch (kech) *Brit.* A public executioner or hangman. [after *John Ketch*, died 1686, executioner under James II]

jack·knife (jak′nīf′) *n. pl.* **·knives** (-nīvz′) **1.** A large pocketknife. **2.** A dive in which the body is doubled forward with the knees unbent and the hands touching the ankles, and then straightened before entering the water. — *v.t. & v.i.* **·knifed**, **·knif·ing** To double up in the manner of a jackknife.

JACK-IN-THE-PULPIT
a Flower.
b Fruit.

jack·light (jak′līt′) *U.S. & Canadian n.* A torch or light used in hunting or fishing at night to attract and dazzle game or fish. — *v.t. & v.i.* To hunt with a jacklight.

jack oak A black-barked oak (*Quercus marilandica*) of the eastern United States.

jack-of-all-trades (jak′əv·ôl′trādz′) *n.* One who is able to do many kinds of work.

jack-o'-lan·tern (jak′ə·lan′tərn) *n.* **1.** A lantern made of a pumpkin hollowed and carved into a grotesque face. **2.** A will-o'-the-wisp.

jack pine A pine (*Pinus banksiana*), growing chiefly on barren tracts of North America.

jack·plane (jak′plān′) *n.* A carpenter's roughing plane.

jack·pot (jak′pot′) *n.* **1.** In poker, a pot that accumulates until one of the players is dealt a pair of jacks or cards of higher value with which he may open the betting. **2.** Any pot, pool, or prize in which the amount won is cumulative. — **to hit the jackpot** *U.S. Informal* **1.** To win the biggest possible prize. **2.** To achieve a major success.

jack rabbit One of a genus (*Lepus*) of large American hares with long hind legs and long ears.

jacks (jaks) *n.pl.* (construed as *sing.*) The game of jackstones.

jack·screw (jak′skrōō′) *n.* A mechanical jack in which force is transmitted by the action of a screw.

jack·shaft (jak′shaft′, -shäft′) *n.* **1.** A shaft sunk in a mine **2.** A bar or crosspiece for supporting a mechanical drill, held in place by jackscrews.

jack·snipe (jak′snīp′) *n.* **1.** A small European snipe (*Limnocryptes minimus*). **2.** The pectoral sandpiper.

Jack·son (jak′sən) **1.** The capital of Mississippi, in the south central part, on the Pearl River; pop. 153,698. **2.** A city in southern Michigan, on the Grand River; pop. 45,484. **3.** A city in western Tennessee, on the South Fork of the Forked Deer River; pop. 39,996.

Jack·son (jak′sən), **Andrew,** 1767–1845, U.S. general; seventh president of the United States 1829–37: called *Old Hickory.* — **Helen Hunt,** 1830–85, *née* Fiske, U.S. poet and novelist: pseudonym **H.H.** — **Robert Houghwout,** 1892–

1954, U.S. author and jurist; associate justice of the Supreme Court 1941–54. — **Thomas Jonathan,** 1824–63, Confederate general in the Civil War: called *Stonewall Jackson.*

Jackson Day January 8th, the anniversary of Andrew Jackson's victory at New Orleans in 1815.

Jack·so·ni·an (jak·sō′nē·ən) *adj.* Of or pertaining to Andrew Jackson or his policies. — *n.* A supporter of Andrew Jackson or his policies.

Jack·son·ville (jak′sən·vil) A port city in NE Florida, near the mouth of the St. Johns River; pop. 528,865.

jack·stay (jak′stā′) *n. Naut.* **1.** A rope or rod along the upper surface of a yard, to which a sail is fastened. **2.** A rope or rod running up and down on the forward side of a mast, on which a yard travels.

jack·stone (jak′stōn′) *n.* **1.** One of a set of stones or knobbed metal pieces used in a children's game in which the pieces are tossed and picked up in a variety of ways: also called *jack.* **2.** *pl.* (construed as *sing.*) The game itself: also called *jacks.* [Var. of earlier *checkstone*]

jack·straw (jak′strô′) *n.* **1.** One of a set of thin strips of wood, bone, etc. used in a game in which the players attempt to pick up each strip without moving any of the others: also called *spilikin.* **2.** *pl.* (construed as *sing.*) The game itself. **3.** A man unworthy of consideration or lacking in influence; a puppet. **4.** Anything insignificant or worthless.

jack·tar (jak′tär′) *n. Informal* A sailor. Also **Jack Tar.**

jack towel A roller towel (which see).

jack·y (jak′ē) *n. Brit. Slang* Gin. [Dim. of *Jack,* a personal name]

Ja·cob (jā′kəb) A Hebrew patriarch, second son of Isaac and father of the founders of the twelve Hebrew tribes. Also *Israel.* [< Hebrew *Ya'aqob* he grasps the heel. Cf. *Gen.* xxv 26.]

Jac·o·be·an (jak′ə·bē′ən) *adj.* **1.** Of or pertaining to James I of England or the period in which he reigned. **2.** Of or pertaining to an English architectural and furniture style of the early 17th century. — *n.* A notable person of the Jacobean era. [< LL *Jacobaeus* < *Jacobus* James]

jac·o·bin (jak′ə·bin) *n.* One of a breed of pigeons having neck feathers ruffed so as to form a hood. [< JACOBIN (def. 3), because their feathers resemble a friar's hood]

Jac·o·bin (jak′ə·bin) *n.* **1.** During the French Revolution, a member of a French political society that inaugurated the Reign of Terror. **2.** A sympathizer with the policies of the Jacobins; an extreme radical. **3.** A Dominican friar. [< OF *Jacobin* of St. James < Med.L *Jacobinus* < LL *Jacobus* James; with ref. to the church of St. James, in Paris, where they first met]

Jac·o·bin·i·cal (jak′ə·bin′i·kəl) *adj.* Pertaining to or characteristic of the French Jacobins; politically radical. Also **Jac·o·bin′ic.** — **Jac·o·bin′i·cal·ly** *adv.*

Jac·o·bin·ism (jak′ə·bin·iz′əm) *n.* The political philosophy, practices, or characteristics of the Jacobins; extreme radicalism in politics.

Jac·o·bin·ize (jak′ə·bin·īz′) *v.t.* **·ized, ·iz·ing** To affect with or convert to Jacobinism.

Jac·o·bite (jak′ə·bīt) *n.* An adherent of James II of England after his abdication in 1688, or a supporter of one of his descendants. — *adj.* Of or pertaining to the Jacobites: also **Jac·o·bit·ic** (jak′ə·bit′ik), **Jac·o·bit′i·cal.** [< L *Jacobus* James + -ITE¹]

Jac·o·bit·ism (jak′ə·bīt′iz·əm) *n.* The beliefs or sympathies of the Jacobites.

Ja·cob's-lad·der (jā′kəbz·lad′ər) *n.* **1.** A common ornamental herb (*Polemonium caeruleum*), having an arrangement of its leaves and leaflets suggestive of a ladder. **2.** Any of several related species.

Jacob's ladder 1. A ladder from earth to heaven that Jacob saw in a dream. *Gen.* xxviii 12. **2.** *Naut.* A rope ladder, often with wooden rungs.

ja·co·bus (jə·kō′bəs) *n.* An English gold coin of the reign of James I. [< L *Jacobus* James]

Ja·co·bus de Vo·ra·gi·ne (jə·kō′bəs də vo·rä′ji·nā), 1230?–1298, archbishop of Genoa; author of the *Golden Legend.*

jac·o·net (jak′ə·net) *n.* **1.** A soft, thin, white cotton cloth. **2.** A cotton fabric having one side glazed. [after *Jaganath* (now Puri) in India, where first made]

jac·quard (jə·kärd′, *Fr.* zhȧ·kȧr′) *adj.* Of or pertaining to a textile or pattern produced on a Jacquard loom.

Jacquard loom A loom specially equipped for weaving figured textiles, as brocades or damasks, and controlled by a punched paper strip. [after J. M. *Jacquard,* 1752–1834, French weaver and inventor]

Jacque·mi·not (jak′mi·nō, *Fr.* zhȧk·mē·nō′) *n.* A variety of deep red hybrid rose. [after J. F. *Jacqueminot,* 1787–1865, French general]

Jacque·rie (zhȧk·rē′) *n.* **1.** The revolt of French peasants in 1358. **2.** Any peasant revolt: also **jacque·rie′.** [after *Jacques Bonhomme,* a scornful nickname given by the nobles to the French peasantry]

jac·ta·tion (jak·tā′shən) *n.* **1.** Boasting. **2.** *Pathol.* Jactitation. [< L *jactatio, -onis* < *jactare,* freq. of *jacere* to throw]

jac·ti·ta·tion (jak′tə·tā′shən) *n.* **1.** An act of public or ostentatious boasting. **2.** *Pathol.* Abnormal tossing or twitching, as in acute disease. **3.** *Law* A false boast or assertion repeated to the injury of another. [< Med.L *jactitatio, -onis* < L *jactitare* to say publicly, freq. of *jactare* to hurl]

jade[1] (jād) *n.* **1.** Either of two hard, translucent minerals, jadeite or nephrite, usually green but sometimes white or variously colored, used as a gemstone. [< F *jade,* var. of *ejade* < Sp. *(piedra de) ijada* (stone of) the side; because supposed to cure pain in the side]

jade[2] (jād) *n.* **1.** An old, worthless, or unmanageable horse. **2.** A disreputable, ill-tempered, or perverse woman; hussy. — *v.t.* & *v.i.* **jad·ed, jad·ing** To weary or become weary through hard work or overuse; tire. [Origin uncertain]

jad·ed (jā′did) *adj.* **1.** Worn-out; exhausted. **2.** Dulled, as from overindulgence; sated. — **jad′ed·ly** *adv.* — **jad′ed·ness** *n.*

jade green Any shade of green characteristic of jade.

jade·ite (jā′dīt) *n.* A translucent sodium-aluminum silicate of the pyroxene group, a variety of jade. [< JADE[1] + -ITE[1]]

jad·ish (jā′dish) *adj.* Having the nature or characteristics of a jade. — **jad′ish·ly** *adv.* — **jad′ish·ness** *n.*

jae·ger (yā′gər; *for def. 1, also* jā′gər) *n.* **1.** Any of a genus (*Stercorarius*) of sea birds that pursue and harass gulls and terns until they drop or disgorge their prey. **2.** A huntsman or hunting attendant. **3.** Formerly, a soldier of the German or Austrian army especially trained in scouting, sharpshooting, and forestry. Also spelled *yager.* Also **jä′ger.** [< G, hunter < *jagen* to hunt]

Ja·el (jā′əl) In the Bible, the Israelite heroine who killed the sleeping Sisera by driving a nail through his head. *Judg.* iv 21. [< Hebrew *yā'el,* lit., goat]

Ja·én (hä·ān′) A Province of southern Spain; 5,209 sq. mi.; pop. 763,391 (1960); capital, **Jaén,** pop. 64,917.

Jaf·fa (jaf′ə, yaf′ə) A port in western Israel; included in Tel Aviv since 1950: Old Testament *Joppa.*

Jaff·na (jäf′nə) A port city on the NW **Jaffna Peninsula,** the northernmost part of Ceylon; pop. 94,248 (1963).

jag[1] (jag) *n.* **1.** A sharp, projecting point; notch; tooth. **2.** *Dial.* A stab or jab, as with a sharp point. — *v.t.* **1.** To cut notches or jags in. **2.** To cut unevenly or with slashing strokes. **3.** *Dial.* To jab or stick with something sharp. Also **jagg.** [ME *jagge;* origin unknown]

jag[2] (jag) *n.* **1.** *Slang* A bout or period of unrestrained activity: a crying *jag;* a spending *jag.* **2.** *Slang* Sufficient liquor or drugs to cause intoxication: to have a *jag* on. **3.** *Slang* A drunken spree. **4.** *Dial.* A small load, as of hay.

JAG Judge Advocate General.

Jag·a·nath (jug′ə·nät, -nôt) See JUGGERNAUT. Also **Jag·a·na·tha** (jug′ə·nä′tə), **Jag·gur·nath** (jug′ər·nät).

jag·ged (jag′id) *adj.* Having jags or notches; serrate. — **Syn.** See ROUGH. — **jag′ged·ly** *adv.* — **jag′ged·ness** *n.*

jag·ger·y (jag′ər·ē) *n.* A coarse, dark sugar made from the sap of the East Indian date palm. Also **jag′gar·y, jag′gher·y, jag·ra** (jag′rə). [< Hind. *jāgrī* < Skt. *çarkara* sugar]

jag·gy (jag′ē) *adj.* **·gi·er, ·gi·est** Jagged.

jag·uar (jag′wär, jag′yōō·är) *n.* A large, tawny, spotted feline (*Panthera onca*) of Central and South America. [< Pg. < Tupi *jaguara*]

ja·gua·run·di (jä′gwə·run′dē) *n.* A carnivorous wildcat (genus *Felis*) of tropical America, having grayish brown fur: also called *eyra, yaguarundi.* Also **ja′gua·ron′·di.** [< Tupi]

JAGUAR
(To about 7 feet long; tail about 2 feet)

Jah (jä, yä) *Hebrew* Jehovah. *Ps.* lxviii 4.

Jah·ve, Jah·veh, Jah·we, Jah·weh (yä′ve), **Jah·vism, Jah·wism** (yä′viz·əm), etc. See YAHWEH, etc.

jai a·lai (hī ə·lī′) A Spanish and Basque game now popular in Latin America, somewhat similar to handball, but played with a long, curved, wicker basket strapped to the arm: also *pelota.* [< Sp. < Basque, jolly festival]

Jai·hun (jī·hōōn′) The Arabic name for the AMU DARYA.

jail (jāl) *n.* **1.** A building or place of confinement for those guilty of minor offenses or those awaiting trial. **2.** Loosely, any prison. — *v.t.* To put or hold in jail; imprison. Also, *Brit., gaol.* [< OF *jaiole,* ult. < L *cavea* cave]

jail·bird (jāl′bûrd′) *n. Informal* **1.** A prisoner. **2.** A former prisoner, especially a habitual offender.

jail delivery **1.** In British law, the clearing of a jail by the trial and disposition of all prisoners, as at the assizes. **2.** The escape or forcible liberation of prisoners from jail.

jail·er (jā′lər) *n.* The officer in charge of a jail: also, *Brit., gaoler.* Also **jail′or.**

Jai·lo·lo (jī·lō′lō) See HALMAHERA.

Jain (jīn) *n.* An adherent of Jainism. — *adj.* Of or pertaining to the Jains or to Jainism. Also **Jai·na** (jī′nə). [< Hind. *Jaina < jina* victorious]

Jain·ism (jī′niz·əm) *n.* A religion of India, founded about 500 B.C., that has elements of Brahmanism and Buddhism, its principal distinctive features being the worship of sages or saints and an extreme respect for the lives of animals.

Jai·pur (jī·pōōr′) **1.** A former princely state in the Rajpu-

tana States, India. **2.** The capital of Rajasthan, formerly the capital of Jaipur; pop. 533,151 (est. 1971).

Ja·kar·ta (jä·kär′tä) The capital of the Republic of Indonesia, a port on NW Java; pop. 2,922,000 (1961): formerly *Batavia.* Also *Djakarta.*

jake (jāk) *adj. Slang* All right; fine.

jakes (jāks) *n.pl.* (*construed as sing.*) *Archaic & Dial.* A privy. [? after *Jake* or *Jacques,* personal names]

jal·ap (jal′əp) *n.* **1.** The dried root of any of several Mexican plants of the morning-glory family, especially *Exogonium purga,* used as a purgative. **2.** Any allied plant yielding a similar drug. Also *Obs.* **jal′op.** [< Sp. *(purga de) Jalapa* (medicine from) Jalapa] — **ja·lap·ic** (jə·lap′ik) *adj.*

Ja·la·pa En·rí·quez (hä·lä′pä en·rē′käs) The capital of Veracruz, Mexico, in the central part of the State; pop. 66,509 (1960). Also **Ja·la′pa.**

jal·a·pin (jal′ə·pin) *n.* A resinous glycoside contained in jalap, used in medicine as a cathartic. [< JALAP + -IN]

Ja·lis·co (hä·lēs′kō) A State in west central Mexico; 31,296 sq. mi.; pop. 3,322,750 (1970); capital, Guadalajara.

ja·lop·y (jə·lop′ē) *n. pl.* **·lop·ies** *U.S. Informal* A decrepit automobile. Also **ja·lop′py.** [Origin uncertain]

ja·lou·sie (jal′ōō·sē, zhal′ōō·sē′) *n.* A screen or shutter consisting of overlapping horizontal slats, often of glazed glass, that can be tilted to keep out sun and rain while admitting air and light. Compare VENETIAN BLIND. [< F, lit. jealousy]

Jal·u·it (jal′ōō·it) The largest atoll and administrative center of the Marshall Islands; 4 sq. mi.

jam[1] (jam) *v.* **jammed, jam·ming** *v.t.* **1.** To force or ram into or against something; wedge. **2.** To pack and block up by crowding. **3.** To cause (a machine, door, part, etc.) to become wedged or stuck. **4.** To interfere electronically with (a radio broadcast, radar transmission, etc.). **5.** To bruise or crush by violent pressure. — *v.i.* **6.** To become wedged; stick fast. **7.** To cease operation, as a machine, gun, etc., because parts have stuck or wedged together. **8.** To improvise jazz music; also, to take part in a jam session. — *n.* **1.** A crowding together, as of people, cars, etc. **2.** The act of jamming. **3.** *Informal* An embarrassing or dangerous predicament. — **Syn.** See PREDICAMENT. [Akin to CHAMP[1]]

jam[2] (jam) *n.* A pulpy, sweet conserve of whole fruit boiled with sugar. [? < JAM[1], v.]

Jam. Jamaica.

Ja·mai·ca (jə·mā′kə) **1.** An island of the Greater Antilles comprising an independent member of the British Commonwealth; 4,411 sq. mi.; pop. 1,972,000 (1970); capital, Kingston. **2.** A district of Queens borough, New York City.

Ja·mai·can (jə·mā′kən) *adj.* Of or pertaining to the island of Jamaica and its people. — *n.* A native or inhabitant of Jamaica.

jamb (jam) *n.* **1.** A side post or side of a doorway, window, etc. **2.** A jambeau. [< OF *jambe* leg, support < LL *gamba* hoof, leg]

jam·beau (jam·bō′) *n. pl.* **·beaux** (-bōz′) A piece of armor for the leg. Also **jambe** (jam). [< OF *jambe* leg]

jam·bo·ree (jam′bə·rē′) *n.* **1.** *Informal* A boisterous frolic or spree. **2.** A large, especially international, assembly of Boy Scouts. [Origin unknown]

James (jāmz) **1.** One of the twelve apostles, son of Zebedee and brother of John, called **James the Greater.** **2.** One of the twelve apostles, son of Alphaeus, called **James the Less.** **3.** A brother of Jesus (*Gal.* 1, 19). — *n.* A book of the New Testament consisting of the epistle attributed to James the Less.

James (jāmz), **Henry,** 1843–1916, U.S. novelist, playwright, and critic active in England. — **Jesse (Woodson),** 1847–82, U.S. outlaw. — **William,** 1842–1910, U.S. philosopher and psychologist; brother of Henry.

James I, 1566–1625, first Stuart king of England 1603–25; as **James VI,** king of Scotland 1567–1625.

James II, 1633–1701, king of England 1685–88; deposed.

James Bay The southern projection of Hudson Bay, Canada.

James Edward See (James Edward) STUART.

James·i·an (jām′zē·ən) *adj.* Of, pertaining to, or characteristic of the writings or ideas of William or Henry James. Also **James′e·an.**

Jame·son (jā′n′sən), **Sir Leander Starr,** 1853–1917, British administrator in South Africa; leader of the unsuccessful **Jameson's raid** into the Transvaal, Dec. 29, 1895: called **Dr. Jameson.**

James River **1.** A river in central Virginia, flowing generally SE 340 miles to Hampton Roads. **2.** A river in North and South Dakota, flowing 710 miles SE to the Missouri: also *Dakota River.*

James the Greater See JAMES.

James the Less See JAMES.

James·town (jāmz′toun) **1.** A restored village in eastern Virginia, site of the first permanent English settlement within the present limits of the United States; founded 1607. **2.**

A city in SW New York; pop. 39,795. **3.** The capital of St. Helena, a port on the NW coast; pop. 1,475 (1971).

Jam·mu and Kashmir (jum′ōō) A State of northern India; 86,024 sq. mi.; pop. 4,615,025 (est. 1971); capitals, Srinagar (summer) and Jammu (winter); pop. 102,738 (1971). A dispute over the State between India and Pakistan, which occupies part of the State, was submitted to the United Nations in 1948 and is still pending. See map of TIBET.

jam-packed (jam′pakt′) *adj. Informal* Crowded to capacity; as tightly packed as possible.

jam session An informal gathering of jazz musicians performing improvisations on various themes.

Jam·shed·pur (jäm′shed-pōōr′) A city in SE Bihar, India; pop. 402,460 (est. 1971).

Jam·shid (jam′shid) In Iranian mythology, an early king, said to have reigned 700 years. Also **Jam′shyd.**

Jan. January.

Ja·ná·ček (yä′nä-chek), **Leoš,** 1854–1928, Czech composer.

Jane·ite (jān′īt) *n.* An enthusiastic admirer of the works of Jane Austen.

Janes·ville (jānz′vil) A city in southern Wisconsin, near Beloit; pop. 46,426.

Ja·net (zha·ne′), **Pierre Marie Félix,** 1859–1947, French psychologist.

jan·gle (jang′gəl) *v.* **·gled, ·gling** *v.i.* **1.** To make harsh, unmusical sounds. **2.** To wrangle; bicker. — *v.t.* **3.** To cause to sound discordantly. — *n.* **1.** A discordant sound. **2.** A quarrel; wrangling. [< OF *jangler*] — **jan′gler** *n.*

Ja·nic·u·lum (jə-nik′yə-ləm) A hill in Rome, on the Tiber.

Ja·ni·na (yä′nē-nä) See IOANNINA.

jan·i·tor (jan′i-tər) *n.* **1.** One who is employed to clean and care for a building, etc. **2.** A doorkeeper; porter. [< L *janua* door] — **jan′i·to′ri·al** (-tôr′ē-əl, -tō′rē-) *adj.* — **jan′i·tress** *n.fem.*

jan·i·zar·y (jan′ə-zer′ē) *n. pl.* **·zar·ies** *Often cap.* **1.** A soldier in the Turkish sultan's army, originally composed of slaves, organized in the 14th century and suppressed in 1826. **2.** Any Turkish soldier. Also **jan′i·sar·y, jan′is·sar·y** (-ser′-ē). [< F *janissaire* < Turkish *yenicheri* new army]

Jan May·en (yän′ mī′ən) An island of Norway in the Greenland Sea; 144 sq. mi.

Jan·sen (jan′sən, *Du.* yän′sən), **Cornelis,** 1585–1638, Dutch Roman Catholic theologian; founder of Jansenism. Also **Jan·se·ni·us** (jan-sē′nē-əs).

Jan·sen·ism (jan′sən-iz′əm) *n. Theol.* The doctrines taught by Cornelis Jansen, emphasizing predestination and the irresistibility of God's grace, and denying free will. — **Jan′sen·ist** *n.* — **Jan′sen·is′tic** or **·ti·cal** *adj.*

jan·ty (jōn′tē, jän′-) *adj. Archaic* Jaunty.

Jan·u·ar·y (jan′yōō-er′ē) *n. pl.* **·ar·ies** or **·ar·ys** The first month of the year, containing 31 days. Abbr. *Ja., Jan.* [< L *Januarius* < *Janus* Janus]

Ja·nus (jā′nəs) In Roman mythology, the god of portals and of beginnings and endings, usually depicted as having two faces looking in opposite directions.

Ja·nus-faced (jā′nəs-fāst′) *adj.* Two-faced; deceitful.

Jap (jap) *adj. & n. Slang* Japanese: an offensive term.

Jap. Japan; Japanese.

ja·pan (jə-pan′) *n.* **1.** Any of various glossy black lacquers or varnishes, originally from Japan, used for coating objects. **2.** A glossy, black, vitreous enamel baked onto machine parts, etc. **3.** Ornamental objects decorated or lacquered in the Japanese manner. — *adj.* Pertaining to, enameled with, or lacquered with japan. — *v.t.* **·panned, ·pan·ning** To enamel or lacquer with or as with japan. [< JAPAN]

Ja·pan (jə-pan′) A constitutional empire of eastern Asia, comprising the four main islands of Honshu, Hokkaido, Kyushu, and Shikoku with many adjacent smaller islands; 142 720 sq. mi.; pop. 103,540,000 (1970); capital, Tokyo; Japanese *Nihon, Nippon, Dai Nippon.*

Japan, Sea of The part of the Pacific Ocean between Japan and the Asian mainland.

Japan clover A perennial, cloverlike herb (*Lespedeza striata*) of the bean family, from eastern Asia, cultivated in the United States and used for feeding horses, etc.

Japan Current A warm ocean current originating in the Philippine Sea, flowing NE past the SE coast of Japan and into the North Pacific. Also **Japan Stream.**

Jap·a·nese (jap′ə-nēz′, -nēs′) *adj.* Of or pertaining to Japan, its people, or their language. — *n. pl.* **·nese 1.** A native of Japan, or a person of Japanese ancestry. **2.** The language of Japan, generally considered to be unrelated to any other language. Abbr. *Jap.*

Japanese barberry A dwarfed variety of barberry (*Berberis thunbergi*), used for hedges, etc.

Japanese beetle A destructive beetle (*Popillia japonica*) introduced to the United States from Japan. The adults eat the leaves and fruits of various plants, and the larvae feed on grass roots. For illustration see INSECTS (injurious).

Japanese ivy A climbing shrub (*Parthenocissus tricuspidata*) native to the Orient and related to the Virginia creeper.

Japanese persimmon 1. A tree (*Diaspyros kaki*) native to Asia, having edible orange or yellow fruit. **2.** The fruit. Also called *kaki.*

Japanese river fever Tsutsugamushi disease.

Jap·a·nesque (jap′ə-nesk′) *adj.* Japanese in style.

jape (jāp) *Archaic v.* **japed, jap·ing** *v.i.* **1.** To joke; make jests. — *v.t.* **2.** To mock; jibe at. — *n.* A jest; jibe. [ME *jappen*; origin uncertain] — **jap′er** *n.* — **jap′er·y** *n.*

Ja·pheth (jā′fith) Third and youngest son of Noah. *Gen.* v 32. Also **Ja′phet** (-fit). [< Hebrew *Yepheth*, lit., extension]

Ja·phet·ic (jə-fet′ik) *adj.* **1.** Pertaining to or descended from Japheth. **2.** Formerly, Indo-European or Ural-Altaic.

ja·pon·i·ca (jə-pon′i-kə) *n.* **1.** An Asian shrub (*Chaenomeles lagenaria*) with bright scarlet flowers: also **Japanese quince. 2.** The camellia. [< NL, Japanese]

Jap·o·nism (jap′ə-niz′əm) *n.* A Japanese trait, as in art.

Ja·pu·rá (zhä′pōō-rä′) A river flowing from the Andes of SW Colombia SE about 1,150 miles to the Amazon. Also *Yapurá.*

jar[1] (jär) *n.* **1.** A wide-mouthed vessel of glass or earthenware, usually deep and cylindrical. **2.** The quantity a jar contains: also **jar′ful** (-fōōl′). [< F *jarre* < Arabic *jarrah*]

jar[2] (jär) *v.* **jarred, jar·ring** *v.t.* **1.** To strike against or bump so as to cause shaking, movement, etc.; jolt. **2.** To affect (one's nerves, feelings, etc.) unpleasantly or painfully. — *v.i.* **3.** To have an unpleasant or painful effect: with *on* or *upon*: Her manner *jars* on my nerves. **4.** To disagree or conflict; clash. **5.** To bump or jolt: with *against*. **6.** To make or have a disagreeable sound. — *n.* **1.** A shaking, shock, or jolt: the *jar* of a sudden stop. **2.** A disagreeable sound or jumble of sounds; discord. **3.** A painful or irritating shock to the feelings; wrench. [Imit.]

jar[3] (jär) *n.* A swinging, as of a door on its hinges: now only in the phrases **on a jar** and **on the jar**, slightly opened. [OE *cerr.* See AJAR[1].]

jar·di·nière (jär′də-nir′, *Fr.* zhàr-dē-nyâr′) *n.* A pot or stand for flowers or plants. [< F, fem. of *jardinier* gardener]

jar·gon[1] (jär′gən) *n.* **1.** Confused, unintelligible speech; gibberish. **2.** A language, dialect, or form of speech regarded as meaningless or confusing. **3.** The technical or specialized vocabulary or phraseology used among themselves by the members of a particular profession, sect, or similarly restricted group; cant; lingo: legal *jargon.* **4.** A mixture of two or more dissimilar languages, often serving as a lingua franca; pidgin. — **Syn.** See DIALECT. — *v.i.* To speak in jargon; talk incomprehensibly. [< OF, a chattering]

jar·gon[2] (jär′gon) *n.* A colorless, yellowish, leaf-green, or smoky variety of zircon, esteemed as a gemstone. Also **jar·goon′** (-gōōn′). [< F, ult. < Persian *zargūn* gold-colored]

jar·go·nelle (jär′gə-nel′) *n.* A variety of early pear. Also **jar′go·nel, jar′go·nelle′.** [< F, dim. of *jargon* jargon[2]]

jar·gon·ize (jär′gon-īz) *v.* **·ized, ·iz·ing** *v.t.* **1.** To translate into jargon. — *v.i.* **2.** To express oneself in jargon.

ja·ri·na (jə-rē′nə) *n.* The ivory nut. [< Pg.]

jarl (yärl) *n.* Formerly, a Scandinavian nobleman or chieftain; an earl. [< ON. Akin to EARL.]

jar·o·site (jar′ə-sīt, jə-rō′-) *n.* A hydrous sulfate of iron and potassium, occurring massive or in brown or yellow crystals. [after Barranco *Jarosa*, in Spain]

jar·o·vize (yär′ə-vīz) *v.t.* **·vized, ·viz·ing** To vernalize (a plant, crop, etc.). [< Russian *yar′ovizirovaty′* < *yarovoi* spring (adj.)] — **jar′o·vi·za′tion** *n.*

Jar·row (jar′ō) A municipal borough and port in NE Durham, England, on the Tyne; pop. 29,370 (est. 1969).

jar·vey (jär′vē) *n. Brit. Informal* The driver of a hackney coach. [after *Jarvis*, a personal name]

Jas. James.

jas·mine (jas′min jaz′-) *n.* **1.** An ornamental plant (genus *Jasminum*) of the olive family, with fragrant, generally white flowers. **2.** Any of various other plants, as the **Cape Jasmine** (*Gardenia jasminoides*), the **Carolina** or **yellow jasmine** (*Gelsemium sempervirens*), etc. Also called *jessamine.* [< F *jasmin* < Persian *yāsmin*]

Ja·son (jā′sən) In Greek legend, a prince of Iolcus who led the Argonauts in search of the Golden Fleece, and who married Medea. [< Gk., healer]

jas·per (jas′pər) *n.* **1.** An opaque, usually red, brown, or yellow variety of quartz, admitting of a high polish: also **jas′per·ite. 2.** In the Bible, one of the twelve stones in the breastplate of the high priest. *Ex.* xxviii 20. [< MF *jaspre*, var. of *jaspe* < L *jaspis* < Gk. < Semitic. Cf. Hebrew *yashpeh.*] — **jas·pid′e·an** (-pid′ē·ən), **jas·pid′e·ous** (-pid′ē·əs) *adj.*

Jasper National Park A park in the eastern Rockies, western Alberta, Canada; 4,200 sq. mi.; established 1907.

Jas·pers (yäs′pərz), **Karl,** 1883–1969, German philosopher.

Jas·sy (yä′sē) A city in NE Rumania; pop. 173,570 (est. 1968): Rumanian *Iaşi*.

Jat (jät, jŏt) *n. Hindi* One of a numerous Indian people in the Punjab, Rajputana, and Uttar Pradesh.

JATO (jā′tō) *n. Aeron.* An airplane takeoff assisted by a jet-propulsion unit or a rocket; also, the unit or rocket used. Also **ja′to.** [< J(ET) A(SSISTED) T(AKE)O(FF)]

jaun·dice (jôn′dis, jän′-) *n.* 1. *Pathol.* A diseased condition of the liver due to the presence of bile pigments in the blood and characterized by yellowness of the skin and eyeballs. 2. A state of mind, feeling, perception, etc., that distorts the judgment. — *v.t.* **·diced, ·dic·ing** 1. To affect with jaundice. 2. To alter or influence (the mind, feelings, etc.) so as to affect the judgment. [< OF *jaunisse* < *jaune* yellow < L *galbinus* yellowish < *galbus* yellow]

jaunt (jônt, jänt) *n.* A short journey, especially for pleasure. — *v.i.* To make such a journey. [Origin unknown]

jaunt·ing car (jôn′ting, jän′-) In Ireland, a horse-drawn, two-wheeled vehicle having seats placed back to back lengthwise over the wheels: also called *sidecar.* Also **jaunty car.**

jaunt·y (jôn′tē, jän′-) *adj.* **jaunt·i·er, jaunt·i·est** 1. Having a lively and self-confident air or manner; cheerfully brisk. 2. Trim; dashing; a *jaunty* hat. 3. *Obs.* Genteel. [< F *gentil.* See GENTLE.] — **jaunt′i·ly** *adv.* — **jaunt′i·ness** *n.*

jaup (jôp, jäp) *Scot. & Brit. Dial. v.t. & v.i.* To splash. — *n.* A splash, as of mud.

Jau·rès (zhō·res′), **Jean Léon,** 1859–1914, French socialist leader; assassinated.

Jav. Javanese.

ja·va (jav′ə, jä′və) *n. Sometimes cap. U.S. Slang* Coffee.

Ja·va (jav′ə, jä′və) *n.* 1. A type of coffee. 2. A type of domestic chicken with black or black-and-white feathers. [after *Java*, where first grown]

Ja·va (jä′və, jav′ə) An island of Indonesia SE of Sumatra; 48,842 sq. mi. See map of INDONESIA.

Java man Pithecanthropus.

Jav·a·nese (jav′ə·nēz′, -nēs′) *adj.* Of or pertaining to Java, its language, or its people. — *n. pl.* **·nese** 1. A native or naturalized inhabitant of Java. 2. The Indonesian language of central Java, closely related to Malay, and containing some elements of Sanskrit. Abbr. *Jav.*

Ja·va·ri (zhä′vä·rē′) A river forming part of the Brazil-Peru boundary and flowing about 600 miles NE to the Amazon: Spanish *Yavarí.* Also **Ja′va·ry′.**

Java Sea The part of the Pacific between Borneo and Java.

Javanese sparrow A finchlike bird (*Munia oryzivora*) of Java, kept as a cage bird: also called *waxbill, ricebird.*

jave·lin (jav′lin, jav′ə·lin) *n.* 1. A light spear thrown as a weapon. 2. A long spear with a wooden shaft, thrown for distance in an athletic contest. [< F, prob. < Celtic]

Ja·velle water (zhə·vel′) A solution of potassium or sodium hypochlorite, used as an antiseptic and bleaching agent. Also **Ja·vel′ water.** [after *Javel*, place near Paris where made]

jaw (jô) *n.* 1. *Anat.* **a** Either of the two bony structures forming the framework of the mouth and holding the teeth, consisting of the **upper jaw** or maxilla, and the **lower jaw** or mandible. **b** *pl.* The mouth and its associated parts. 2. One of a pair of gripping parts capable of opening and closing, as of a tool: the *jaws* of a vise. 3. Anything suggesting the action of the jaws: the *jaws* of death. 4. *pl.* The narrow entrance of a gorge, canyon, etc. 5. *Informal* A talk; chat. 6. *Informal* Impudent talk. — *v.i.* 1. *Informal* To talk; jabber. — *v.t.* 2. *Informal* To scold or abuse. [ME *lowe, jowe* < F *joue* cheek]

HUMAN JAW

jaw·bone (jô′bōn′) *n.* 1. One of the bones of the jaw, especially that of the lower jaw. 2. *Slang* Credit.

jaw·break·er (jô′brā′kər) *n.* 1. *U.S. Informal* A type of very hard candy. 2. A machine that crushes ore: also **jaw′crush′er** (-krush′ər). 3. *Informal* A word hard to pronounce.

Jax·ar·tes (jak·sär′tēz) The ancient name for the SYR DARYA.

jay[1] (jā) *n.* 1. Any of various corvine birds, usually of brilliant coloring, as the **European jay** (*Garrulus glandarius*), the Canada jay, and the blue jay (which see). 2. *Obs. Slang* A stupid, gullible person; greenhorn. [< OF < Med.L *gaius*]

jay[2] (jā) *n.* The letter J.

Jay (jā), **John,** 1745–1829, American statesman, diplomat, and jurist; first chief justice of the Supreme Court, 1789–95.

jay·hawk·er (jā′hô′kər) *n.* 1. A guerrilla raider of the Civil War period in Kansas; also, any freebooting guerrilla. 2. *Usually cap.* A Kansan. [Origin uncertain]

jay·vee (jā′vē′) *U.S. Informal n.* 1. The junior varsity. 2. *Often pl.* A member of the junior varsity.

jay·walk (jā′wôk′) *v.i. Informal* To cross a street recklessly, violating traffic regulations or signals. [< JAY[1] (def. 2) + WALK] — **jay′walk′er** *n.* — **jay′walk′ing** *n.*

jazz (jaz) *n.* 1. A kind of music, chiefly extemporaneous but sometimes arranged, characterized by melodic, harmonic, and rhythmic variation, syncopation, flatted thirds and sevenths, and a melody played against various chord patterns, as in Dixieland, ragtime, boogie-woogie, swing, and bop. 2. Loosely, any contemporary popular dance music. 3. *U.S. Slang* Lying and exaggerated talk; also, idle and foolish talk. 4. *U.S. Slang* Liveliness and animation. 5. *U.S. Slang* Copulation. — *adj.* Of or pertaining to jazz. — *v.t.* 1. *U.S. Slang* To quicken the tempo of; speed up. 2. *U.S. Slang* To copulate with. 3. *U.S. Slang* To address with lies, exaggeration, etc. 4. To play or arrange (music) as jazz. — *v.i.* 5. *U.S. Slang* To utter lies, exaggeration, etc. 6. *U.S. Slang* To copulate. — **to jazz up** *U.S. Slang* To make more lively and exciting. [< Creole *jass* coition; from its origin in the brothels of New Orleans] — **jazz′er** *n.*

jazz band A group or company of musicians who play jazz.

jazz·y (jaz′ē) *adj.* **jazz·i·er, jazz·i·est** Resembling or characteristic of jazz. — **jazz′i·ly** *adv.*

J.C.D. 1. Doctor of Canon Law (L *Juris Canonici Doctor*). 2. Doctor of Civil Law (L *Juris Civilis Doctor*).

JCS Joint Chiefs of Staff.

jct. or **jctn.** Junction.

J.D. Doctor of Laws (L *Juris Doctor*).

Je. June.

jeal·ous (jel′əs) *adj.* 1. Fearful or suspicious of being displaced by a rival in affection or favors. 2. Vindictive toward another because of supposed or actual rivalry. 3. Vigilant in guarding; closely watchful: to be *jealous* of a privilege. 4. Resulting or arising from jealousy: *jealous* fears. 5. Demanding exclusive worship and love: a *jealous* God. 6. *Obs.* Zealous. — Syn. See ENVIOUS. [< OF *gelos* < Med.L *zelosus* < LL *zelus* < Gk. *zēlos* zeal. Doublet of ZEALOUS.] — **jeal′ous·ly** *adv.* — **jeal′ous·ness** *n.*

jeal·ous·y (jel′əs·ē) *n. pl.* **·ous·ies** 1. The state or quality of being jealous. 2. The fact of being jealous.

jean (jēn, jān) *n.* 1. A sturdy, twilled cotton cloth used in workclothes. 2. *pl.* Trousers or overalls made of this material. 3. *pl. U.S. Informal* Trousers. [after F *Gênes* Genoa, where it was made; orig. *jene fustian*]

Jeanne d'Arc (zhän dark) See JOAN OF ARC.

Jeans (jēnz), **Sir James (Hopwood),** 1877–1946, English astronomer, physicist, and philosopher.

Jebb (jeb), **Sir Richard Claverhouse,** 1841–1905, British classical scholar.

jeb·el (jeb′əl) *n. Arabic* A mountain: also French *djebel.*

Je·bel Mu·sa (jeb′əl mōō′sə) A mountain in northern Morocco on the Strait of Gibraltar; one of the Pillars of Hercules; 2,790 ft.

Jed·burgh (jed′bûr·ə) The county seat of Roxburghshire, Scotland; pop. about 4,000. Also **Jed′dart.**

Jed·da (jed′ə) See JIDDA.

jee (jē) See GEE[2].

jeep (jēp) *n.* A motor vehicle equipped with four-wheel drive and having a quarter-ton carrying capacity, used for military reconnaissance and the transportation of passengers and light cargo. [< G(ENERAL) P(URPOSE) (VEHICLE); infl. by "*jeep*," cry and name of a small creature in comic strip *Popeye* by E. C. Segar]

jeer[1] (jir) *v.i.* 1. To speak or shout in a derisive, mocking manner; scoff. — *v.t.* 2. To treat with derision or mockery; scoff at. — *n.* A derisive and flouting word or remark. [Origin unknown] — **jeer′er** *n.* — **jeer′ing·ly** *adv.*

jeer[2] (jir) *n. Naut. Usually pl.* A tackle for raising or lowering a lower yard of a sailing ship. [? < GEE[2] + -ER[1]]

je·fe (hā′fā) *n. Spanish* Chief; leader; head; commander.

Jef·fers (jef′ərz), **(John) Robinson,** 1887–1962, U.S. poet.

Jef·fer·son (jef′ər·sən), **Joseph,** 1829–1905, U.S. actor. — **Thomas,** 1743–1826, American statesman, diplomat, and writer; drafted the Declaration of Independence; third president of the United States 1801–09.

Jefferson, Mount 1. A peak in the Cascade Range, NW central Oregon; 10,495 ft. 2. A peak in the White Mountains, New Hampshire, 5,725 ft.

Jefferson City The capital of Missouri, in the central part, on the Missouri River; pop. 32,407.

Jef·fer·so·ni·an (jef′ər·sō′nē·ən) *adj.* Of, pertaining to, or characteristic of Thomas Jefferson or his political ideas and beliefs. — *n.* An adherent of Jefferson or his school of thought. — **Jef′fer·so′ni·an·ism** *n.*

Jef·frey (jef′rē), **Francis,** 1773–1850, Lord Jeffrey, Scottish literary critic, essayist, and jurist.

Jef·freys (jef′rēz), **George,** 1648–89, first Baron Jeffreys of Wem, British jurist infamous for his severity.

je·had (ji·häd′) See JIHAD.

Jeh·lam (jā′lum) See JHELUM.

Je·hol (jə·hol′, -hōl′; *Chinese* ru′hu′) 1. A former province of NE China; 74,000 sq. mi. 2. See CHENGTEH.

Je·hosh·a·phat (ji·hosh′ə·fat, -hos′-) Ninth-century B.C. king of Judah. *I Kings* 22.41.

Je·ho·vah (ji·hō′və) In the Old Testament, God; the Lord: the common English rendering of the Tetragrammaton. See YAHWEH. [< Hebrew *JHVH* Yahweh, either Creator or

Eternal < *hayāh* to be, with the substitution of vowels from *adhonay* my Lord] — **Je·ho′vi·an, Je·ho′vic** *adj.*

Jehovah's Witnesses A Christian sect strongly opposed to war and denying the authority of the government in matters of conscience.

Je·ho·vism (ji·hō′viz·əm), **Je·ho·vist** (ji·hō′vist), etc. See YAHWISM, etc.

Je·hu (jē′hyōō) Ninth-century B.C. king of Israel; son of Jehoshaphat, and a furious charioteer. II *Kings* ix 20.

je·june (jə·jōōn′) *adj.* 1. Lacking in substance or nourishment; barren. 2. Lacking interest; insipid; dry. 3. Loosely, lacking sophistication; naive. [< L *jejunus* hungry] — **je·june′ly** *adv.* — **je·june′ness** *n.*

je·ju·num (jə·jōō′nəm) *n. pl.* **·na** (-nə) *Anat.* That portion of the small intestine that extends from the duodenum to the ileum. [< NL < L *jejunus* hungry]

Je·kyll (jē′kəl, jek′əl), **Doctor** In Robert Louis Stevenson's *The Strange Case of Dr. Jekyll and Mr. Hyde*, the physician who is able periodically to transform his own personality into that of his other self, the viciously criminal Mr. Hyde.

jell (jel) *v.t. & v.i. U.S. Informal* 1. To jelly; congeal. 2. To assume or cause to assume definite form: His ideas haven't *jelled.* — *n. U.S. Dial. Jelly.* [Back formation < JELLY]

Jel·li·coe (jel′i·kō), **John Rushworth**, 1859–1935, first Earl Jellicoe, British admiral; governor general of New Zealand 1920–24.

jel·lied (jel′ēd) *adj.* 1. Made gelatinous, as by chilling: *jellied consommé.* 2. Covered with or prepared in jelly.

jel·li·fy (jel′ə·fī) *v.t. & v.i.* **·fied, ·fy·ing** To make into or become a jelly. — **jel′li·fi·ca′tion** *n.*

Jel·lo (jel′ō) *n.* A fruit-flavored gelatin dessert. [< Jell-O, a trade name]

jel·ly (jel′ē) *n. pl.* **·lies** 1. Any food preparation made with gelatin, etc., and having a consistency such that it quivers when shaken but will not flow; especially, such a food made of boiled and sweetened fruit juice and used as a spread or filler. 2. Any gelatinous substance. — *v.* **·lied, ·ly·ing** *v.t.* 1. To make into a jelly. 2. To cover or fill with jelly. — *v.i.* 3. To become jelly. [< OF *gelee* < L *gelata*, pp. of *gelare* to freeze]

jel·ly·bean (jel′ē·bēn′) *n. U.S.* A bean-shaped candy having a hard, colored coating over a gelatinous center.

jel·ly·fish (jel′ē·fish′) *n. pl.* **·fish** or **·fish·es** 1. Any of a number of marine coelenterates (classes *Hydrozoa* and *Scyphozoa*) of jellylike substance, often having umbrella-shaped bodies with trailing tentacles, as the medusa. 2. *Informal* One lacking determination or stamina; weakling.

jem·a·dar (jem′ə·där′) *n. Anglo-Indian* 1. An Indian army lieutenant. 2. A police or customs officer. Also **jem′i·dar′.** [< Hindi < Persian *jamā′at* body of men]

Je·mappes (zhə·mâp′) A town in SW Belgium; scene of a French victory over the Austrians, 1792; pop. about 13,000.

jem·my (jem′ē) *n. pl.* **·mies** *Brit.* 1. A short crowbar; jimmy. 2. A baked sheep's head. [Var. of JIMMY]

Jen·a (yā′nə) A city in southern East Germany; site of Napoleon's defeat of the Prussians, 1806; pop. about 83,000.

je ne sais quoi (zhən sə kwȧ′) *French* An indefinable something; literally, I know not what.

Jen·ghiz Khan (jen′giz kän) See GENGHIS KHAN.

Jen·ner (jen′ər), **Edward**, 1749–1823, English physician; discovered vaccination. — **Sir William**, 1815–98, English physician and pathologist.

jen·net (jen′it) *n.* 1. A small Spanish horse, a cross of Arabian and native stock. 2. A female donkey. Also spelled *genet.* [< OF *genet* < Sp. *jinete* a light horseman < Arabic *Zenāta*, a Barbary tribe]

jen·ny (jen′ē) *n. pl.* **·nies** 1. A spinning jenny (which see). 2. The female of some birds and animals: *jenny wren; jenny ass.* [after *Jenny*, a personal name]

jeop·ard·ize (jep′ər·dīz) *v.t.* **·ized, ·iz·ing** To put in jeopardy; expose to loss or injury; imperil. Also **jeop′ard.**

jeop·ard·y (jep′ər·dē) *n.* 1. Danger of death, loss, or injury; peril. 2. *Law* The peril in which a defendant is put when placed on trial for a crime. — **Syn.** See DANGER. [< OF *jeu parti* even chance < L *jocus partitus* divided play]

Jeph·thah (jef′thə, jep′-) A judge in Israel; sacrificed his daughter. *Judg.* xi. [Hebrew, lit., He (God) openeth]

je·quir·i·ty (ji·kwir′ə·tē) *n. pl.* **·ties** 1. A twining, tropical shrub (*Abrus praecatorius*) of India, Brazil, and Florida: also called *Indian licorice, wild licorice.* 2. The seeds (**jequirity beans**) of this plant, used as beads and in medicine: also called *jumble-beads.* Also **je·quer′i·ty.** [< F *jequirity* < Tupi]

Jer. Jeremiah.

jer·bo·a (jər·bō′ə) *n.* Any of various nocturnal rodents (family *Dipodidae*) of Asia and North Africa, with very long hind legs adapted for leaping, especially *Jaculus jaculus.* [< NL < Arabic *yarbu*]

je·reed (je·rēd′) *n.* 1. A wooden javelin used in military games by horsemen in Moslem countries: also spelled *jerreed, jerrid.* Also **je·rid′.** [< Arabic *jerīd*]

JERBOA
(About 6 inches long; tail 9 inches)

jer·e·mi·ad (jer′ə·mī′ad) *n.* A lament or tale of woe; complaint. [< F *jérémiade* < *Jérémie* Jeremiah]

Jer·e·mi·ah (jer′ə·mī′ə) Seventh-century B.C. Hebrew prophet. — *n.* The Old Testament book containing his prophecies. Also, in the Douai Bible, **Jer′e·mi′as** (-əs) [< Hebrew *Yirmĕyāhū*, lit., God looseneth (from the womb)]

Je·rez (hā·rāth′, -rās′) A city in SW Spain; pop. 127,194 (est. 1959); formerly *Xeres.* Also **Je·rez de la Fron·te·ra** (thə lä frōn·tā′rä).

Jer·i·cho (jer′i·kō) A village in western Jordan, north of the Dead Sea; site of an ancient city of the same name. *Josh.* vi.

Jericho rose Rose of Jericho (which see).

jerk¹ (jûrk) *v.t.* 1. To give a sharp, sudden pull, tug, or twist to. 2. To throw, move, or thrust with a sharp, suddenly arrested motion. 3. To utter in a gasping or broken manner: with *out.* — *v.i.* 4. To give a jerk or jerks. 5. To move with sharp, sudden motions; twitch. — *n.* 1. A sudden sharp pull, twist, or thrust. 2. *Physiol.* An involuntary contraction of a muscle caused by reflex action. 3. *Slang* A stupid, ineffectual, dull man. 4. *pl. U.S. Informal* Spasms or shakes, as from delirium tremens, excitement, etc. 5. *pl. Brit. Slang* Physical training. [? Var. of archaic *yerk*]

jerk² (jûrk) *v.t.* To cure (meat) by cutting into strips and drying. — *n.* Jerked meat, especially beef. [Alter. of Sp. *charquear* < *charqui.* See CHARQUI.]

jer·kin (jûr′kin) *n.* 1. A close-fitting jacket or vest, usually sleeveless. 2. Formerly, such a garment, often of leather, worn in the 16th and 17th centuries. [Origin unknown]

jerk·wa·ter (jûrk′wô′tər, -wot′ər) *U.S. Informal adj.* 1. Not on the main line: a *jerkwater* town. 2. Insignificant; small: a *jerkwater* college. — *n.* A train serving a branch line. [< JERK¹, v. + WATER]

jerk·y¹ (jûr′kē) *adj.* **jerk·i·er, jerk·i·est** 1. Characterized by or moving with jerks or with fits and starts: a *jerky* train. 2. Not smooth or flowing; rough or abrupt in style, transitions, etc.: a *jerky* sentence structure. 3. Foolish. — **jerk′i·ly** *adv.* — **jerk′i·ness** *n.*

jerk·y² (jûr′kē) *n.* Meat cured by being cut into strips and dried: also called *charqui.* Also **jerked beef** (jûrkt). [Alter. of CHARQUI]

jer·o·bo·am (jer′ə·bō′əm) *n.* An oversized champagne bottle holding about 4/5 gallon. [after *Jeroboam*]

Jer·o·bo·am I (jer′ə·bō′əm) Tenth-century B.C. Hebrew king; led revolt against Rehoboam, founded the kingdom of Israel, as distinguished from Judah. I *Kings* xi, xii. [< Hebrew *Yārobh′ām*, lit., the people increases]

Jeroboam II Eighth-century B.C. king of Israel; son of Joash. II *Kings* xiv.

Je·rome (jə·rōm′, *Brit.* jer′əm), **Saint**, 340?–420, one of the Latin church fathers; prepared the Vulgate: original name Eusebius Hi·er·on·y·mus (hī′ə·ron′ə·məs).

Je·ron·y·mite (jə·ron′ə·mīt) *n.* A Hieronymite (which see).

jer·ry (jer′ē) *n. pl.* **·ries** *Chiefly Brit. Slang.* 1. Often *cap.* A German; especially, a German soldier. 2. A chamber pot. [from resemblance of the German helmet to a chamber pot]

jer·ry·build (jer′ē·bild′) *v.t.* **·built, ·build·ing** To build flimsily and with inferior materials. [Origin unknown]

jer·sey (jûr′zē) *n. pl.* **·seys** 1. A ribbed, somewhat elastic fabric of wool, cotton, silk, etc., used for clothing. 2. A dress made of jersey. 3. A close-fitting, knit shirt, usually worn by athletes. [< Jersey, a Channel Island]

Jer·sey (jûr′zē) *n. pl.* **·seys** One of a breed of small cattle, usually fawn-colored, originating in the island of Jersey and noted for milk rich in butterfat. — *adj.* Of or pertaining to the island of Jersey or to the State of New Jersey.

Jer·sey (jûr′zē) The largest of the Channel Islands; 45 sq. mi.; pop. 57,296 (1961); capital St. Helier.

Jersey City A port city in NE New Jersey, on the Hudson River; pop. 260,545.

Je·ru·sa·lem (ji·rōō′sə·ləm, -lem) The principal city of Palestine and the ancient and modern capital of Israel· identified with ancient *Salem*; divided in 1948 into an Israeli Sector and a Jordanian Sector and reunited by Israeli occupation in 1967; regarded as holy by Jews, Christians, and Muslims; pop. about 280,000 (1970). [< Hebrew *Yerūshālayim* Possession, or City of Peace (*Shālōm*)]

Jerusalem artichoke 1. A tall sunflower (*Helianthus tuberosus*) having an edible tuber. 2. The tuber itself. [Alter. of Ital. *girasole* sunflower + ARTICHOKE]

Jerusalem cross A cross having four arms each ending in a crossbar. For illustration see CROSS.

Jerusalem oak An annual shrubby plant (*Chenopodium botrys*) of the goosefoot family, having a pungent odor and sometimes cultivated for ornament.

Jes·per·sen (yes′pər·sən), (**Jens**) **Otto** (**Harry**), 1860–1943, Danish philologist and grammarian.

jess (jes) *n.* In falconry, a short strap on each leg of a hawk, used for attaching a leash. — *v.t.* To fasten a jess or jesses on. [< OF *ges* < L *jactus* a throw < *jacere* to throw]

jes·sa·mine (jes′ə·min) *n.* Jasmine, a plant.

jes·sant (jes′ant) *adj. Heraldry* 1. Shooting forth, as a plant. 2. Issuing, as an animal, from the middle of an ordinary. [< OF *issant*, ppr. of *isser* to spring forth]

Jes·se (jes′ē) The father of David. I *Sam.* xvi 1.

Jes·sel·ton (jes′əl·tən) The former name of *Kota Kinabalu*, in Sabah, Borneo.

jest (jest) *n.* **1.** Something said or done to provoke laughter; joke. **2.** Playfulness; fun: to speak in *jest*. **3.** An object of laughter; laughingstock. **4.** *Obs.* An exploit; also, a tale of an exploit. — *v.i.* **1.** To make amusing remarks; tell jokes; quip. **2.** To speak or act in a playful way; trifle. [< OF *geste, jeste* < L *gesta* deeds < *gerere* to do]
— **Syn.** (noun) **1.** *Jest, joke, witticism, quip, wisecrack, gag, wheeze,* and *hokum* denote something said or done to excite laughter. A *jest* is usually oral, but may also be a playful act. *Joke* is also a general term, but specifically it refers to a brief narrative or anecdote with a funny ending. A practical *joke* is an act designed to surprise or embarrass another. A *witticism* is a witty retort or remark; *quip* and the slang *wisecrack* are *witticisms* in a mocking or satirical vein. A *quip* is a theatrical interpolation, a *witticism*, or comic business. A familiar or hackneyed *gag* is a *wheeze* or *hokum*, but the latter term includes all hackneyed theatrical devices for evoking tears, laughter, or any other emotional reaction.
jest·er (jes′tər) *n.* One who jests; especially, a medieval court fool.
jest·ing (jes′ting) *n.* The action of one who jokes. — *adj.* Of the nature of a jest; prone to jest. — **jest′ing·ly** *adv.*
Je·su (jē′zōō, -sōō) *Poetic* Jesus.
Jes·u·it (jezh′ōō·it, jez′yōō-) *n.* **1.** A member of the Society of Jesus, a religious order founded in 1534 by Ignatius Loyola to combat the Reformation and propagate the faith among the heathen. **2.** A scheming person; a casuist; an equivocator: a derogatory term. [< NL *Jesuita* < L *Jesus* Jesus] — **Jes′u·it′ic** or **·i·cal** *adj.* — **Jes′u·it′i·cal·ly** *adv.*
Jes·u·it·ism (jezh′ōō·it·iz′əm, jez′yōō-) *n.* **1.** The doctrines, system, principles, and methods of the Jesuits. **2.** Deceptive practices, subtle distinctions, or political duplicity: a derogatory term. Also **Jes′u·i·try.**
Jes·u·it·ize (jezh′ōō·it·īz′, jez′yōō-) *v.t. & v.i.* **·ized, ·iz·ing** To be or make Jesuitic.
Jesuits' bark Cinchona (def. 2).
Je·sus (jē′zəs) **1.** Founder of Christianity, 6? B.C.–29? A.D., son of Mary; regarded in the Christian faith as Christ, the Messiah. **2.** In Christian Science, the highest human concept of the divine. Also **Jesus Christ, Jesus of Nazareth.**
Je·sus (jē′zəs) The son of Sirach, lived about the third or fourth century B.C.; author of *Ecclesiasticus.*
Jesus freak *Slang* A person fanatically devoted to Jesus Christ; especially, a young person of this sort in a communal group of radically evangelistic Protestants.
jet[1] (jet) *n.* **1.** A hard black lignite, taking a high polish, used for jewelry, buttons, etc. **2.** A deep, glossy black. **3.** *Obs.* Black marble. — *adj.* **1.** Made of or resembling jet. **2.** Black as jet; jet-black. [< OF *jaiet* < L *gagates* < Gk. *gagatēs,* after *Gagai,* a Lycian town where it was mined]
jet[2] (jet) *n.* **1.** A sudden spurt or gush of liquid or gas emitted from a narrow orifice. **2.** Liquid or gas that spurts from an orifice. **3.** A spout or nozzle. **4.** A jet-propelled aircraft. — *v.t. & v.i.* **jet·ted, jet·ting** To spurt or emit in a stream; spout. [< F *jeter* to throw, ult. < L *jacere* to throw]
Jet, meaning operating by, of, or relating to jet propulsion, may appear as a combining form or as the first element in two-word phrases; as in:

jet aircraft	jet bomber	jet pilot
jet airplane	jet fighter	jet plane
jet aviation	jetliner	jet-propelled

jet deflection Directional control of the blast in a jet aircraft in order to change speed or direction.
jet engine A reaction and heat engine that takes in outside air to oxidize fuel that it converts into the energy of a powerful jet of heated gas expelled to the rear under high pressure.
Jeth·ro (jeth′rō) Moses' father-in-law. *Exod.* xviii.
jet lag *n.* The fatigue, confusion, and other symptoms of disruption of biological rhythms due to long jet flights across time zones. Also **jet fatigue, jet syndrome.**
jet motor A reaction and heat engine that contains its own oxidizer and produces thrust by projecting a jet of gas.
jet·port (jet′pôrt′, -pōrt′) *n.* An airport designed to accommodate jet aircraft.
jet propulsion **1.** Propulsion by means of a jet of gas or other fluid. **2.** *Aeron.* Propulsion by means of jet engines.
jet rotor The jet-powered rotor unit of a helicopter.
jet·sam (jet′səm) *n.* **1.** Goods thrown into the sea to lighten an imperiled vessel. Compare FLOTSAM, LAGAN. **2.** Such goods washed ashore. [Earlier *jetson,* short for JETTISON]
jet set A wealthy social set of frivolous persons who travel abroad or to distant places, especially via jet aircraft, solely for pleasure and usually on a whim.
jet stream **1.** The strong flow of gas or other fluid expelled from a jet engine, rocket motor, and the like. **2.** *Meteorol.* A high-velocity circumpolar wind circulating, usually from west to east, near the base of the stratosphere.
jet·ti·son (jet′ə·sən) *v.t.* **1.** To throw overboard (goods or cargo). **2.** To discard (something that hampers). — *n.* **1.** The act of jettisoning. **2.** Jetsam. [< AF *getteson* < L *jactatio, -onis* a throwing < *jactare.* See JET².]
jet·ty (jet′ē) *n. pl.* **·ties 1.** A structure of piling, rocks, etc.,

extending out into a body of water to divert a current or to protect a harbor or shoreline. **2.** A wharf or pier. [< OF *jetee,* orig. pp. of *jeter* to throw. See JET²]
jet·ty[2] (jet′ē) *adj. Poetic* Like or made of jet; black as jet. — **jet′ti·ness** *n.*
jet vane *Aeron.* A fixed or adjustable vane of heat-resistant material placed in a jet stream for stability and control.
jet wash *Aeron.* The backwash caused by a jet engine, rocket, guided missile, etc.
jeu (zhœ) *n. pl.* **jeux** (zhœ) *French* Play; pastime; game.
jeu de mots (zhœ də mō′) *pl.* **jeux de mots** (zhœ) *French* Play on words; pun.
jeu d'es·prit (zhœ des·prē′) *pl.* **jeux d'esprit** (zhœ) A witticism. [< F]
jeune fille (zhœn fē′y′) *French* Young girl.
jew (jōō) *v.t. Informal* To get the better of in a bargain: usually with *down:* an offensive term.
Jew (jōō) *n.* **1.** A member or descendant of the Hebrew people. **2.** Any person professing Judaism. **3.** Originally, a member of the tribe or the kingdom of Judah. — *adj.* Jewish: an offensive usage. [< OF *giu, juieu* < L *Judaeus* < Gk. *Ioudaios* < Hebrew *y'hudi* descendant of Judah] — **Jew′ess** *n.fem.*
Jew-bait·ing (jōō′bā′ting) *n.* The act of harassing, harrying, or otherwise persecuting the Jews. — **Jew′bait′er** *n.*
jew·el (jōō′əl) *n.* **1.** A precious stone; gem. **2.** An article for personal adornment, especially one made of cut gems and precious metal. **3.** A person or thing of rare excellence or value. **4.** A bit of gem, crystal, glass, etc., used to form a durable bearing, as in a watch. — *v.t.* **jew·eled** or **·elled, jew·el·ing** or **·el·ling** To adorn with jewels; set jewels in. [< OF *jouel,* ult. < L *jocus* a joke, sport]
jew·el·er (jōō′əl·ər) *n.* A dealer in or maker of jewelry. Also **jew′el·ler.**
jew·el·ry (jōō′əl·rē) *n.* **1.** Jewels collectively. **2.** The art of mounting precious stones, making small items of personal adornment, etc.; the trade of a jeweler. Also *Brit.* **jew′el·ler·y.**
jew·el·weed (jōō′əl·wēd′) *n.* A species of touch-me-not, especially the North American spotted jewelweed (*Impatiens biflora*) having deep yellow flowers.
Jew·ett (jōō′it), **Sarah Orne,** 1849–1909, U.S. novelist.
jew·fish (jōō′fish′) *n. pl.* **·fish** or **·fish·es** One of various large fish of the sea bass family, especially *Epinephelus itajara* of the Florida coast.
Jew·ish (jōō′ish) *adj.* Of, pertaining to, or resembling the Jews, their customs, religion, etc. — *n.* Loosely, Yiddish.
Jewish calendar The Hebrew calendar. See under CALENDAR.
Jewish holidays See HANUKKAH, PASSOVER, ROSH HASHANA, SUKKOTH, and YOM KIPPUR for the principal holidays of Judaism.
Jew·ry (jōō′rē) *n. pl.* **·ries 1.** The Jewish people. **2.** *Obs.* Judea. **3.** *Obs.* A ghetto.
jew's-harp (jōōz′härp′) *n.* A small musical instrument that is held between the teeth when played and consists of a lyre-shaped frame with a flexible steel tongue that is plucked with the finger. Also **jews'-harp.**
jew's-pitch (jōōz′pich′) *n.* Bitumen. Also **jews'-pitch'.**
je·zail (jə·zīl′) *n. Afghan* A long and heavy Afghan musket.
Jez·e·bel (jez′ə·bel) The wife of Ahab, notorious for her evil actions. I *Kings* xvi 31. — *n.* A bold, vicious woman.
Jez·re·el (jez′rē·əl, jez·rēl′), **Plain of** A plain in northern Israel between the Jordan valley and Mount Carmel. *Judg.* vi 33. Also *Esdraelon.*
j.g. or **jg** Junior grade.
Jhe·lum (jā′ləm) A river in Kashmir and West Pakistan, flowing about 480 miles to the Chenab: also *Jehlam.*
jib[1] (jib) *n. Naut.* A triangular sail, set on a stay and extending from the foretopmast head to the jib boom or the bowsprit. For illustrations see SCHOONER, SHIP. **2.** The boom of a crane or derrick. — **the cut of one's jib** *Informal* One's appearance. — *v.t. & v.i.* **jibbed, jib·bing** *Naut.* To jibe. [? Short for GIBBET]
jib[2] (jib) *v.i.* **jibbed, jib·bing 1.** To move restively sidewise or backward; refuse to go forward, as a horse. **2.** To balk. — *n.* A horse that jibs: also **jib′ber.** [Cf. OF *giber* kick]
jib boom *Naut.* A spar forming a continuation of the bowsprit and holding a jib.
jibe[1] (jīb) *v.* **jibed, jib·ing** *v.i.* **1.** *Naut.* To swing from one side of a vessel to the other: said of a fore-and-aft sail or its boom. **2.** To change course so that the sails shift in this manner. — *v.t.* **3.** To cause to swing from one side of a vessel to the other. Also spelled *gibe, gybe, jib.* [< Du. *gijben*]
jibe[2] (jīb) See GIBE¹.
jibe[3] (jīb) *v.i.* **jibed, jib·ing** *U.S. Informal* To agree; be in accordance. [Origin uncertain]
Ji·bu·ti (ji·bōō′tē) See DJIBOUTI.
Jid·da (jid′ə) A port in Saudi Arabia, on the Red Sea, near Mecca; pop. about 160,000: also *Jedda.* Also **Jid′dah.**

jif·fy (jif′ē) *n. pl.* **·fies** *Informal* An instant; moment. Also **jiff**. [Origin unknown]

jig (jig) *n.* **1.** A fast, lively dance; also, the music for such a dance. Compare GIGUE. **2.** *Mech.* A device for holding the material being worked or for guiding a tool. **3.** In fishing, any of various combinations of hooks, spoons, etc., that are agitated in the water to attract and catch fish. **4.** *Mining* A wire sieve or other device for separating or cleaning coal by jolting and shaking in water. **— the jig is up** *Slang* All hope of success is gone. **—** *v.* **jigged, jig·ging** *v.i.* **1.** To dance or play a jig. **2.** To move jerkily, especially up and down; bob. **3.** To use or operate a jig in working. **4.** To fish with a jig. **—** *v.t.* **5.** To jerk up and down or to and fro; jiggle. **6.** To hold, form, process, etc., with a jig. **7.** To catch (fish) with a jig. [Cf. OF *gigue* a fiddle]

JIG (def. 2)
a Drill jig.
b Material being drilled. c Support block.

jig·ger[1] (jig′ər) *n.* **1.** One who or that which jigs. **2.** A small glass or cup for measuring liquor, holding about one and one half ounces; also, the amount of liquor so measured. **3.** In billiards, a bridge. **4.** In golf, a short club with an iron head used in making an approach. **5.** A jig used in catching fish. **6.** *Mech.* A jig. **7.** Any of various types of jolting mechanisms or devices, as an apparatus for separating ores, a potter's wheel, etc. **8.** *Naut.* **a** A small sail set in the stern of a sailing craft, as a yawl. **b** A light tackle used on board ship. **c** A jigger mast. **9.** *Informal* Any small device or thing one is unable to name definitely.

jig·ger[2] (jig′ər) *n.* A chigger or chigoe. Also **jigger flea**. [Alter. of CHIGGER]

jig·gered (jig′ərd) *adj. Informal* Confounded; damned.

jigger mast *Naut.* **1.** The aftermost mast of a four- or five-masted vessel. **2.** A mast in the stern of a yawl, etc., and holding the jigger.

jig·gle (jig′əl) *v.t. & v.i.* **·gled, ·gling** To move unsteadily up and down or backwards and forwards with slight, quick jerks. **—** *n.* A jerky, unsteady movement. [Freq. of JIG, v.]

jig·saw (jig′sô′) *n.* A saw having a slim blade set vertically in a frame and operated with a reciprocating motion, used for cutting curved or irregular lines.

jigsaw puzzle A puzzle consisting of a picture mounted on wood or cardboard and then cut or stamped into irregular interlocking pieces for reassembly.

ji·had (ji·häd′) *n.* **1.** A religious war of Moslems against enemies of their faith. **2.** Any crusade for or against a belief or faith. Also spelled *jehad*. [< Arabic *jihād*]

jill (jil) See GILL[2].

Ji·lo·lo (ji·lō′lō) See HALMAHERA.

jilt (jilt) *v.t.* To cast off or discard (a previously favored lover or sweetheart). **—** *n.* A woman or girl who discards a lover. [Cf. dial. E (Scottish) *jillet* giddy girl] **— jilt′er** *n.*

jim-crow (jim′krō′) *U.S. Slang adj.* Serving to segregate Negroes: *jim-crow* laws. **—** *v.t.* To subject (Negroes) to segregation or discrimination. Also **Jim′-Crow′.**

Jim Crow *U.S. Slang* **1.** A Negro: an offensive term. **2.** The segregation of Negroes. **— Jim-Crow·ism** (jim′krō′iz·əm) *n.*

Ji·mé·nez de Cis·ne·ros (hē·mā′näth thā thes·nā′rōs), **Francisco,** 1436–1517, Spanish cardinal and statesman.

jim·my (jim′ē) *n. pl.* **·mies** A burglar's crowbar. **—** *v.t.* **·mied, ·my·ing** To break or pry open with or as with a jimmy. Also, *Brit.,* **jemmy.** [after *Jimmy,* dim. of *James,* a personal name]

jimp (jimp) *Scot. adj.* **1.** Natty. **2.** Scanty; scarce. Also **jimp′y.** **—** *adv.* **1.** Neatly. **2.** Barely; scarcely. Also **jimp′ly, jimp′y.**

jim·son·weed (jim′sən·wēd′) A tall, coarse, evil-smelling, very poisonous annual weed (*Datura stramonium*) of the nightshade family, yielding the alkaloids atropine and scopolamine: also called **stramonium**. Also **Jimson weed.** [Alter. of *Jamestown* weed, so called because first observed in Jamestown, Va.]

jin·gal (jing·gôl′) *n.* A heavy musket mounted on a swivel rest, formerly used in China and Burma: often spelled **gingal,** **gingall.** Also **jin′gall.** [< Hind. *jangāl* large musket]

jing·ko (jing′kō) See GINKGO.

jin·gle (jing′gəl) *v.* **·gled, ·gling** *v.i.* **1.** To make light ringing or tinkling sounds. **2.** To have an intrusive rhyme or rhythm: said of writing or music, often in deprecation. **—** *v.t.* **3.** To cause to make ringing or tinkling sounds. **—** *n.* **1.** A tinkling, clinking, or rapidly ringing sound; also, *Rare,* that which makes such a sound. **2.** A catchy short song or poem, especially one used for advertising. **3.** Rapid repetition in rhyme, rhythm, alliteration, etc. [Imit.] **— jin′gly** *adj.*

jin·go (jing′gō) *n. pl.* **·goes** One who boasts of his patriotism and favors an aggressive foreign policy. **— by jingo!** *Informal* An exclamation expressing strong conviction, surprise, etc. **—** *adj.* Of, pertaining to, or characteristic of the jingoes. [Originally a nonsense word from magician's jargon; origin uncertain] **— jin′go·ish** *adj.* **— jin′go·ism** *n.* **— jin′go·ist** *n.* **— jin′go·is′tic** *adj.*

jink (jingk) *v.i. Scot.* To move quickly; dodge. **—** *n.* **1.** *pl.* Frolics; pranks: high jinks. **2.** *Scot.* A dodging turn.

jink·er (jing′kər) *n.* **1.** *Canadian* In Newfoundland, a jinx or a gremlin. **2.** *Scot.* One who jinks.

Jin·nah (jin·sen′), **Mohammed Ali,** 1876–1948, Indian Moslem statesman; first governor general of Pakistan 1947–48.

jin·ni (jin′ē, ji·nē′) *n. pl.* **jinn** (jin) In Moslem mythology, one of the supernatural beings able to assume human or animal form and often at the call and service of men: sometimes spelled *djinni, genie.* Also **jin·nee′.** [< Arabic *jinnī*]

jin·rik·sha (jin·rik′shə, -shō) *n.* A small oriental two-wheeled carriage drawn by one or two men: also called *rickshaw, ricksha.* Also **jin·rick′sha, jin·rik′i·sha.** [< Japanese *jin* man + *riki* power + *sha* carriage]

Jin·sen (jin·sen) The Japanese name for INCHON.

jinx (jingks) *Slang n.* A person or thing supposed to bring bad luck. **—** *v.t.* To bring bad luck to. [< earlier *jynx* < Gk. *iynx* the wryneck (a bird anciently used in witchcraft)]

ji·pi·ja·pa (hē′pē·hä′pä) *n.* **1.** A shrubby, stemless, palm-like plant (*Carludovica palmata*) native to South America. **2.** A panama hat made from the fiber of the leaves of this plant. [after *Jipijapa,* town in Ecuador]

jit·ney (jit′nē) *n.* **1.** *U.S.* A motor vehicle that carries passengers for a small fare. **2.** *Obs. Slang* A small coin; a nickel. [Origin unknown]

jit·ter (jit′ər) *v.i. U.S. Slang* To be nervous or anxious; fidget. **— the jitters** *Slang* **1.** Intense nervousness. **2.** Nervous fear or apprehension. **— jit′ter·y** *adj.*

jit·ter·bug (jit′ər·bug′) *U.S. Slang n.* One who dances rapidly and spasmodically to jazz. **—** *v.i.* **·bugged, ·bug·ging** To dance to jazz in a fast, violent way.

jiu·jit·su (jōō·jit′sōō), **jiu·jut·su** (jōō·jut′sōō, -jōōt′sōō) See JUJITSU.

jive (jīv) *n. Slang* **1.** The jargon of jazz music and musicians. **2.** Jazz music. [Origin unknown]

Jl. July.

jo (jō) *n. Scot.* A sweetheart of either sex: also spelled *joe.*

Jo·ab (jō′ab) David's nephew. II *Sam.* xviii 2.

Jo·a·chim (yō′ä·kim, *Ger.* yo′ä·khim), **Joseph,** 1831–1907, Hungarian violinist and composer.

Joan of Arc (jōn), 1412?–31, French heroine and martyr; compelled the English to raise the siege of Orléans in 1429; captured and burned as a heretic; canonized 1920: also called *the Maid of Orléans.* Also, *French, Jeanne d'Arc.*

jo·an·nes (jō·an′əs) See JOHANNES.

job[1] (job) *n.* **1.** Anything that is to be done; undertaking; task. **2.** A definite single piece of work, especially one done in one's profession or occupation. **3.** A position or situation of employment: a full-time *job.* **4.** A specific piece of work done for a set fee; also, the thing or material worked on. **5.** Something done ostensibly for the public good, but actually for private or partisan profit. **6.** *Informal* An affair; circumstance. **7.** *Slang* A robbery or other criminal act. **— odd job** A piece of occasional or miscellaneous work. **— on the job** *Informal* **1.** During working hours. **2.** Attending strictly to the matter at hand. **— to lie (or lay) down on the job** *Informal* To evade work or responsibility. **—** *v.* **jobbed, job·bing** *v.i.* **1.** To work by the job or piece. **2.** To be a jobber or middleman. **3.** To use a position of public trust for private advantage. **—** *v.t.* **4.** To buy in bulk and resell in lots to dealers. **5.** To sublet (work) among separate contractors. **—** *adj.* Done by the job or piece. [Origin uncertain]

job[2] (job) *Archaic v.t. & v.i.* **jobbed, job·bing** To jab. **—** *n.* A jab. [ME *jobben*]

Job (jōb) In the Bible, the chief character in the Book of Job, who, despite great suffering and adversity, kept his faith in God. **—** *n.* The book itself.

job action A slowdown, deliberate enforcement of all rules, or other disruptive action short of an employees' strike.

job·ber (job′ər) *n.* **1.** One who buys goods in bulk from the manufacturer or importer and sells to the retailer; wholesaler. **2.** Formerly, one who purchased goods in job lots. **3.** One who works by the job, or on small jobs; pieceworker. **4.** In politics, one who gains private advantage from a position of public trust. **5.** *Brit.* A middleman who deals in stocks and securities among stockbrokers.

job·ber·y (job′ər·ē) *n. pl.* **·ber·ies** Corrupt use of a public office or trust for private or partisan gain.

job·hold·er (job′hol′dər) *n.* One who has a steady job.

job·less (job′lis) *adj.* Without a job. **— job′less·ness** *n.*

job lot **1.** A collection of miscellaneous goods sold to a retailer. **2.** Any collection of things inferior in quality.

job printer A printer who does miscellaneous printing, such as circulars, cards, letterheads, etc. **— job printing**

Job's comforter One who discourages and disheartens under the guise of offering sympathy and consolation.

Job's-tears (jōbz′tirz′) *n.* **1.** A hardy, annual, tropical grass (*Coix lacryma-jobi*). **2.** The white, pearly seeds of this plant, sometimes used as beads.

Jo·cas·ta (jō·kas′tə) In Greek legend, the queen who unwittingly marries her own son Oedipus.

Jock (jok) *n. Slang* A Scotsman: nickname for *John.*

jock·ey (jok′ē) *n. pl.* **·eys** One employed to ride horses in races. **—** *v.i.* **1.** To maneuver for an advantage: to *jockey* for position. **2.** To act fraudulently; be tricky. **3.** To ride as a jockey. —*v.t.* **4.** To ride (a horse) in a race. **5.** To place or guide by skillful handling or control. **6.** To trick; cheat. [Dim. of JOCK] —**jock′ey·ing** *n.* —**jock′ey·ism** *n.*

jock·o (jok′ō) *n. pl.* **-os** Any ape or monkey, especially the chimpanzee.

jock·strap (jok′strap′) *n.* An athletic supporter. Also **jock strap**. [< cant *jock* the male genitals + STRAP]

jo·cose (jō·kōs′) *adj.* **1.** Disposed to jesting or joking. **2.** Characterized by or having the nature of jokes; playful: *jo-cose* conversation. [< L *jocosus* < *jocus* joke] —**jo·cose′ly** *adv.* —**jo·cose′ness, jo·cos′i·ty** (-kos′ə·tē) *n.* —**Syn.** jocular, facetious, sportive, waggish. See HUMOROUS. —**Ant.** serious.

joc·u·lar (jok′yə·lər) *adj.* **1.** Making jokes; given to joking. **2.** Having the nature of a joke; intended as a joke. Also **joc′u·la·to·ry** (-tôr′ē, -tō′rē). —**Syn.** See HUMOROUS. [< L *jocularis* < *joculus*, dim. of *jocus* joke] —**joc′u·lar′i·ty** (-lâr′ə·tē) *n.* —**joc′u·lar·ly** *adv.*

jo·cund (jok′ənd, jō′kənd) *adj.* Having a cheerful, gay disposition or appearance; jovial; glad. [< OF *jocund* < LL *jocundus*, alter. of L *jucundus* pleasant < *juvare* to delight] —**joc′und·ly** *adv.* —**joc′und·ness** *n.*

jo·cun·di·ty (jō·kun′də·tē) *n. pl.* **·ties 1.** The state or quality of being jocund. **2.** A jocund action, remark, etc.

Jodh·pur (jōd·pŏŏr′, jōd′pŏŏr) **1.** A former princely state in the Rajputana States, India: also *Marwar*. **2.** A city in central Rajasthan; formerly the capital of Jodhpur state; pop. 270,404 (est. 1971).

jodh·purs (jod′pərz) *n.pl.* Wide riding breeches, close-fitting from knee to ankle, often having a strap passing under the foot. Also **jodhpur breeches**. [after *Jodhpur*, India]

joe (jō) *n.* See JO.

Joe (jō) *n. U.S. Slang* A man: a good *Joe*.

Jo·el (jō′əl) A Hebrew prophet. —*n.* A book of the Old Testament by this prophet. [< Hebrew, the Lord is God]

joe-pye weed (jō′pī′) Either of several tall American herbs, as *Eupatorium purpureum* or *E. maculatum*, with whorled leaves and pale purple flowers: also called *trumpetweed*.

jo·ey (jō′ē) *n.* In Australia, a young animal, especially a young kangaroo.

Jof·fre (zhôf′r′), **Joseph Jacques Césaire**, 1852–1931, French marshal; commander in chief of French army in World War I, 1914–16: called **Papa**.

jog (jog) *v.* **jogged, jog·ging** *v.i.* **1.** To proceed slowly or monotonously: with *on* or *along*. **2.** To move with a slow, jolting pace, trot, etc. —*v.t.* **3.** To push or touch with a slight jar; shake lightly; especially, to nudge (someone) so as to get his attention. **4.** To give a slight reminder to; stimulate: to *jog* the memory. **5.** *Printing* To align (edges of paper) by jolting. —*n.* **1.** The act of jogging. **2.** A nudge. **3.** A slow, jolting motion or pace. **4.** *U.S.* An angle or projection in a surface, as in a wall; jag. **5.** *U.S.* A sudden temporary turning or veering in a road, course, etc. [Prob. imit. Akin to SHOG.] —**jog′ger** *n.*

jog·gle (jog′əl) *v.* **·gled, ·gling** *v.t.* **1.** To shake slightly; jog. **2.** To fasten or join together by a joggle or joggles. **3.** To fasten or join together with a dowel or dowels. —*v.i.* **4.** To move with an irregular or jolting motion; shake. —*n.* **1.** The act of joggling. **2.** An irregular shaking or jolting. **3.** A projection formed on a piece, as of stone, timber, etc., that serves to fit it firmly to an adjoining piece having a corresponding notch. **4.** A dowel. **5.** A shoulder to receive the thrust of a brace or strut. [Freq. of JOG, *v.*]

joggle post **1.** A vertical post having one or more shoulders, or joggles, to receive the feet of struts; kingpost. **2.** A post or beam built of timbers jogged together.

Jog·ja·kar·ta (jog′yə·kär′tə) A city in southern Java; former capital of Indonesia; pop. 308,530 (1961): also *Djokjakarta, Jokjakarta.*

jog trot **1.** A slow, easy trot, as of a horse. **2.** A slow, humdrum habit of living or doing the daily tasks.

jo·han·nes (jō·han′ēz) *n.* A former gold coin of Portugal: also *joannes.* [after *Joannes* V of Portugal]

Jo·han·nes·burg (jō·han′is·bûrg, yō·hän′is-) A city in southern Transvaal, South Africa; pop. 1,294,800 (1967).

Jo·hans·son gauge (vo·hän′sən) One of a series of metallurgically perfect steel blocks made in specified sizes, used in precision measurements. Also **Jo·hans′son block**. [after C. E. *Johansson*, Swedish engineer]

john (jon) *n. Slang* A toilet.

John (jon) One of the twelve apostles, son of Zebedee and brother of James: called **Saint John the Evangelist, Saint John the Divine.** —*n.* **1.** The fourth Gospel of the New Testament, attributed to him. **2.** One of the three New Testament epistles that bear his name.

John, 1167?–1216, king of England 1199–1216, signed the Magna Carta 1215: called **John Lack·land** (lak′land).

John, **Augustus Edwin**, 1879–1961, British portrait painter.

John I, 1357–1433, king of Portugal 1385–1433: called **the Great.**

John III, 1624–96, king of Poland 1674–96, fought against Turks: original name **John So·bi·es·ki** (sō·byes′kē).

John IV, 1605?–56, king of Portugal 1640–56, founded the Braganza dynasty: called **the Fortunate.**

John XXIII, 1881–1963, pope 1958–1963: original name **Angelo Giuseppe Ron·cal·li** (rōn·käl′lē).

John Barleycorn A humorous personification of malt and corn liquor, or of intoxicating liquors in general.

John Birch Society (bûrch) An ultraconservative organization founded in 1958 in the U.S. to resist alleged communist infiltration and activities. [after *John Birch,* U.S. Air Force captain]

John Bull 1. The English people. **2.** A typical Englishman. Also **Johnny Bull.** [after a character in a satire (1712) by Dr. John Arbuthnot] —**John-Bul·lism** (jon′bŏŏl′iz·əm).

John Doe (dō) A name to designate a fictitious or real personage in any legal transaction or proceeding.

John Do·ry (dôr′ē, dō′rē) A small food fish (family *Zeidae*) of the Atlantic coast of Europe, the Mediterranean and Australian seas: also called *dory.* Also **john do′ry, John Do′ree.**

John Hancock *U.S. Informal* A person's autograph. [after *John Hancock,* whose large signature is the first on the Declaration of Independence]

John·ny (jon′ē) *n. pl.* **·nies** *U.S.* A Confederate soldier: also **Johnny Reb.** Also **John′nie.**

Johnny Appleseed See (John) CHAPMAN.

john·ny·cake (jon′ē·kāk′) *n. U.S.* A flat cake of cornmeal, baked on a griddle: also called *corncake.* [? < obs. *jonikin,* a type of bread (< N. Am. Ind.) + CAKE]

John·ny-come-late·ly (jon′ē·kum′·lāt′lē) *n. U.S. Informal* One who has recently arrived, joined, etc.

john·ny-jump-up (jon′ē·jump′up′) *n.* **1.** Any of various American spring violets. **2.** The bird's-foot violet. **3.** The wild pansy. Also **john′ny jump′er.**

John·ny-on-the-spot (jon′ē·on·thə·spot′) *n. U.S. Informal* One who is always on hand when needed or when opportunity presents itself.

John of Austria, Don, 1547–78, Spanish general and admiral; defeated Turks at Lepanto, 1571.

John of Damascus, Saint, 676?–749, Greek theologian: called **John Dam·a·scene** (dam′ə·sēn).

John of Gaunt, 1340–99, Duke of Lancaster; son of Edward III of England, patron of Chaucer; supporter of Wyclif.

John of Lancaster See (Duke of) BEDFORD.

John of Leyden, 1510–36, Dutch Anabaptist active in Germany; executed: original name **Jan Bock·el·son** (bōk′əl·sən).

John of Salisbury, died 1180, English theologian.

John of the Cross, Saint, 1542–91, Spanish Carmelite mystic and reformer. Also, *Spanish, San Juan de la Cruz.*

John o′ Groats (ə grōts′) A locality of northern Scotland, often erroneously regarded as the northernmost point of Britain. Also **John o′ Groats House.**

John·son (jon′sən), **Andrew**, 1808–75, 17th president of the United States 1865–69; impeached, 1868. — **James Weldon**, 1871–1938, U.S. lawyer, author, leader. — **Lyndon Baines**, born 1908, 36th president of the United States 1963–1969. — **Samuel**, 1709–1784, English lexicographer, poet, and man of letters: called **Dr. Johnson.** — **Sir William**, 1715–74, British colonial administrator in America.

Johnson City A city in NE Tennessee; pop. 33,770.

Johnson grass A perennial pasture grass (*Sorghum hale-′pense*) valued for hay, but considered a weed in cultivated land. [after Wm. *Johnson,* 19th c. Alabama planter]

John·so·ni·an (jon·sō′nē·ən) *adj.* Pertaining to or resembling Samuel Johnson or his work. —*n.* An admirer of Dr. Johnson, especially a student of his life and work.

John·ston (jon′stən), **Albert Sidney**, 1803–62, Confederate general in the Civil War. — **Joseph Eggleston**, 1807–91, Confederate general in the Civil War.

Johnston Island A small island in the central Pacific SW of Honolulu; U.S. possession since 1858.

Johns·town (jonz′toun′) A city in SW central Pennsylvania; site of a disastrous flood in 1889; pop. 42,476.

John the Baptist, 6? B.C.–A.D. 30?, forerunner and baptizer of Jesus; beheaded by Herod Antipas.

Jo·hore (jə·hôr′, -hōr′) A state in Malaysia, on the Malay Peninsula; 7,330 sq. mi.; pop. 1,236,412 (1966); capital, **Johore Bah·ru** (bä′rōō).

joie de vi·vre (zhwä də vēv′r′) *French* Joy of living.

join (join) *v.t.* **1.** To become a member of, as a club, party, staff, etc. **2.** To come to as a companion or participant; meet and accompany: to *join* friends for dinner. **3.** To unite in act or purpose: to *join*′orces. **4.** To come to a junction with; become part of: The path *joins* the road. **5.** To set or bring together; connect: to *join* two wires. **6.** To put together in close contact; make contiguous: to *join* hands. **7.** To unite in marriage. **8.** To take a place with, in, or among: This book *joins* others of its type. **9.** *Informal* To adjoin. **10.** *Geom.* To connect (two points) by drawing a straight or curved line. —*v.i.* **11.** To enter into association or agreement: often with *with.* **12.** To take part: usually with *in*. **13.** To come together; connect; unite. — **to join battle** To engage in a battle or conflict. — **to join up** *Informal* To enlist. — *n*. A joint or seam. [< OF *joign-*, stem of *joindre* < L *jungere* to join]

join·der (join′dər) *n.* **1.** The act of joining. **2.** *Law* a A joining of causes of action or defense in a complaint. b A joining of parties as plaintiffs or as defendants in an action. **c** The formal acceptance of an issue tendered.

join·er (joi′nər) *n.* **1.** One who or that which joins. **2.** *U.S. Informal* one who joins many clubs, lodges, etc. **3.** *Brit.* A carpenter or cabinetmaker.

join·er·y (joi′nər·ē) *n.* **1.** The art or skill of a joiner. **2.** The articles constructed by a joiner.

joint (joint) *n.* **1.** A place or point at which two or more things or parts of the same thing are joined or fitted together, either solidly or so as to be movable; junction. **2.** *Anat.* A place of union between two separate bones; especially, one permitting some freedom of movement; articulation. **3.** *Biol.* A junction uniting two portions or segments of an animal body; especially, that of an insect, crustacean, or other arthropod. **4.** *Bot.* The portion of the stem of a plant from which branches grow; a node. **5.** *Geol.* One of a series of approximately parallel or cross-cutting fractures that interrupts the physical continuity of a rock mass. **6.** A portion or part between two nodes or joints. **7.** One of the pieces into which a carcass is divided by the butcher; especially, a large cut from the shoulder or leg containing the bone, as for the table. **8.** *Slang* a A place of low repute, as for drinking, gambling, etc. b Any place of dwelling or gathering; any establishment. — **out of joint 1.** Dislocated. **2.** Disordered; disorganized. — *adj.* **1.** Belonging to or used by two or more; held or shared in common: *joint* bank account. **2.** Sharing with another: *joint* owner. **3.** Produced by combined action: a *joint* literary effort. **4.** *Govt.* Of or relating to both branches of a legislature. **5.** *Law* Joined together in unity of interest or liability; regarded as a legal entity. — *v.t.* **1.** To fasten by means of a joint or joints. **2.** To form or shape with a joint or joints, as a board. **3.** To cut at the joints, as meat. [< OF < L *junctus*, pp. of *jungere* to join]

joint account A bank account in the name of two or more persons, each of whom may deposit and withdraw funds.

Joint Chiefs of Staff *U.S.* A body within the Department of Defense, consisting of a military chairman, the Chief of Staff of the Army, the Chief of Naval Operations, and the Chief of Staff of the Air Force.

joint committee A committee composed of representatives from houses of a legislature.

joint·ed (join′tid) *adj.* **1.** Having a joint or joints. **2.** Having a (specified kind of) joint: *short-jointed*.

joint·er (join′tər) *n.* **1.** A tool used for smoothing wood to make joints. **2.** A trying plane. **3.** A sharp triangular part attached to the beam of a plow. **4.** One who joints.

joint·ly (joint′lē) *adv.* In a joint manner; unitedly.

joint resolution *U.S.* A resolution passed by both houses of Congress and having the force of law if signed by the President.

joint stock Capital or stock that is held as a common fund.

joint-stock company (joint′stok′) An unincorporated business association of many persons, each of whom owns shares of stock which he may sell or transfer at will.

join·ture (join′chər) *n.* **1.** *Law* A settlement of property made to a woman by her husband for her use after his death; also, the property. **2.** *Obs.* A joining together. — *v.t.* **·tured**, **·tur·ing** To settle a jointure on. [< F < L *junctura* < *jungere* to join]

joint·weed (joint′wēd′) *n.* A slender, erect American annual herb (*Polygonella articulata*) with small, white or pink flowers on jointed stems.

joint·worm (joint′wûrm′) *n.* The larva of a plant-feeding fly (genus *Harmolita*), especially *H. tritici*, which damages wheat, barley, etc., by causing a gall-like excrescence at the joints of the stalk.

Join·ville (zhwaṅ·vēl′), **Jean de**, 1224?–1317, French crusader and chronicler.

joist (joist) *n.* Any of the parallel beams placed horizontally from wall to wall, to which the boards of a floor or the laths of a ceiling are fastened. — *v.t.* To furnish with joists. [< OF *giste* < *gesir* to lie < L *jacere* to lie]

JOISTS
a Joist.
b Floorboards.

Jó·kai (yō′koi), **Maurus**, 1825–1904, Hungarian novelist and nationalist. Also **Mór Jó′kai.**

joke (jōk) *n.* **1.** Something said or done to amuse; especially, a funny story. **2.** Something said or done in fun rather than in earnest. **3.** One who or that which excites mirth; laughing-stock; butt. **4.** A matter of little importance; trifle: Poverty is no *joke*. — **Syn.** See JEST. — *v.* **joked, jok·ing** *v.i.* **1.** To tell or make jokes; jest. **2.** To say something in fun and not in earnest. [< L *jocus*] — **jok′ing·ly** *adv.*

jok·er (jō′kər) *n.* **1.** One who jokes. **2.** In a deck of cards, an extra card that in certain games counts as the highest trump or as any card the holder wishes. **3.** *U.S.* An unobtrusive clause in a legislative bill, etc., that undermines or

nullifies its original purpose. **4.** Any hidden or unknown factor causing difficulty. **5.** *Slang* An ineffectual person.

Jok·ja·kar·ta (jōk′yə·kär′tə) See JOGJAKARTA.

jole (jōl) See JOWL.

Jo·li·et (jol′ē·et) A city in NE Illinois; pop. 80,378.

Jo·liot-Cu·rie (zhô·lyô′kü·rē′), **Frédéric**, 1900–58, and his wife **Irene**, 1896–1956, *née* Curie, French physicists.

Jol·li·et (jol′ē·et, *Fr.* zhô·lye′), **Louis**, 1645–1700, French-Canadian explorer in America. Also **Jo′li·et.**

jol·li·fi·ca·tion (jol′ə·fə·kā′shən) *n.* Jollity; merrymaking.

jol·li·fy (jol′ə·fī) *v.t. & v.i.* **·fied, ·fy·ing** *Informal* To be or cause to be merry or jolly.

jol·li·ty (jol′ə·tē) *n. pl.* **·ties** **1.** The state or quality of being jolly; gaiety. **2.** *Brit.* A festive occasion or gathering.

jol·ly (jol′ē) *adj.* **·li·er, ·li·est** **1.** Full of good humor and high spirits; cheerful; jovial. **2.** Characterized by or exciting gaiety; festive; merry. **3.** *Brit. Informal* Very pleasant; delightful. **4.** *Brit. Informal* Extraordinary; remarkable: a *jolly* bore. — *v.t.* **·lied, ·ly·ing** *Informal* **1.** To attempt to put or keep in good humor by agreeable or flattering attentions: often with *along* or *up*. **2.** To make fun of in a good-natured manner; chaff. — *n. pl.* **·lies** **1.** *Brit. Informal* A merry or festive gathering. **2.** *Brit. Slang* A sailor. — *adv. Brit. Informal* Uncommonly; extremely; very: *jolly* ugly. [< OF *joli*] — **jol′li·ly** *adv.* — **jol′li·ness** *n.*

jolly boat A small boat belonging to a ship. [< Dan. *jolle* yawl + BOAT]

Jolly Roger The pirate flag bearing the skull and crossbones.

Jo·lo (hō′lō, hō·lō′) **1.** The chief island in the Sulu archipelago, Philippines; 345 sq. mi. **2.** The capital of Sulu Province, on the NW coast of Jolo; pop. about 18,000.

jolt (jōlt) *v.t.* **1.** To strike or knock against with or as with a jarring blow or bump; jar; jostle. **2.** To shake up or about with such a blow or bump; joggle. — *v.i.* **3.** To move with a series of irregular bumps or jars, as over a rough road. — *n.* **1.** A sudden bump or jar as from a blow. **2.** An unexpected surprise or emotional shock. [? Blend of ME *jot* bump and *joll* bump] — **jolt′er** *n.* — **jolt′y** *adj.*

Jo·ma·da (jō·mä′dä) *n.* Either of two months of the Moslem year. See (Moslem) CALENDAR.

Jon. Jonah.

Jo·nah (jō′nə) Eighth- or ninth-century B.C. Hebrew prophet, who, cast overboard during a storm because he had disobeyed God, was swallowed by a great fish and then cast up on the shore alive three days later. — *n.* **1.** A book of the Old Testament containing his story: also, in the Douai Bible, **Jo′nas** (-nəs). **2.** Any person whose presence is looked upon as bringing bad luck. [< Hebrew *Yōnāh*, lit., dove]

Jon·a·than (jon′ə·thən) Son of Saul and close friend of David. I *Sam.* xviii. [< Hebrew *Yōnāthān*, lit., the Lord has given]

Jon·a·than (jon′ə·thən) *n.* A yellowish red variety of late autumn apple.

Jones (jōnz), **Casey** See CASEY JONES. — **Daniel**, 1881–1967, English phonetician. — **Ernest**, 1879–1958, British psychoanalyst and biographer of Sigmund Freud. — **Henry Arthur**, 1851–1929, English playwright. — **In·i·go** (in′i·gō), 1573–1652, English architect and stage designer. — **John Paul**, 1747–92, American Revolutionary naval officer born in Scotland: original name **John Paul**. — **Rufus Matthew**, 1863–1948, U.S. Quaker leader, philosopher, and writer.

jon·gleur (jong′glər, *Fr.* zhôṅ·glœr′) *n.* A wandering minstrel of medieval England and France who entertained by singing songs, telling tales, and composing ballads. — **Syn.** See MINSTREL. [< OF < L *joculator.* See JUGGLER.]

jon·quil (jon′kwil, jong′-) *n.* **1.** A species of narcissus (*Narcissus jonquilla*) related to the daffodil, having long, linear leaves and fragrant, white or yellow flowers. **2.** The bulb or flower of this plant. [< F *jonquille*, ult. < L *juncus* a rush]

Jon·son (jon′sən), **Ben**, 1573?–1637, English dramatist, poet, and actor.

Jop·lin (jop′lən) A city in SW Missouri; pop. 39,256.

Jop·pa (jop′ə) The Old Testament name for JAFFA. *Jonah* i 3.

jor·dan (jôr′dən) *n. Obs.* or *Dial.* A chamber pot.

Jor·dan (jôr′dən) The chief river of Palestine, flowing over 200 miles south to the Dead Sea. [< Hebrew *Yardēn* flowing downward < *Yāradh* to descend]

Jor·dan (jôr′dən), **David Starr**, 1851–1931, U.S. zoologist.

Jordan, Hashemite Kingdom of A constitutional monarchy comprising the territories of Transjordan and Arab Palestine; about 37,300 sq. mi.; pop. 2,160,000 (est. 1969); capital, Amman: formerly *Trans-Jordan*, *Transjordania*. Also **Jordan.** See maps of ISRAEL, SAUDI ARABIA. — **Jor·da·ni·an** (jôr·dā′nē·on) *adj. & n.*

Jordan almond A large Spanish almond, frequently sugar-coated as a confection. [ME *jardyne almaunde* < OF *jardin almande* garden almond]

jo·rum (jôr′əm, jō′rəm) *n.* A drinking bowl or its contents. Also **jo′ram.** [? after *Joram*, a Biblical character who brought vessels of silver and gold to David. II *Sam.* viii 10]

jo·seph (jō′zəf) *n.* A long coat buttoned down the front and having a small cape, worn chiefly by women in the 18th century as a riding habit. [In allusion to the coat of *Joseph* (*Gen.* xxxvii 3)]

Jo·seph (jō′zəf) In the Old Testament, a son of Jacob and Rachel, sold into slavery in Egypt by his brothers. *Gen.* xxx 24. — *n.* The tribe descended from him. [< Hebrew *Yōsēph*, lit., He will add]

Joseph Husband of Mary, the mother of Jesus. *Matt.* i 18.

Joseph II, 1741–90, Holy Roman Emperor, 1765–90.

Joseph flower The goatsbeard (def. 1). Also **Joseph's flower.**

Jo·seph·ine (jō′zə·fēn, *Fr.* zhô-zā-fēn′), **Empress**, 1763–1814, widow of Vicomte Alexandre de Beauharnais, married Napoleon Bonaparte 1796, divorced 1809.

Joseph of Arimathea A wealthy disciple of Christ who provided a tomb for his burial. *Matt.* xxvii 57–60. See GRAIL.

Jo·se·phus (jō·sē′fəs), **Flavius**, 37–100?, Jewish soldier, statesman, and historian.

josh (josh) *U.S. Slang* *v.t.* & *v.i.* To make good-humored fun of (someone); tease; banter. — *n.* A good-natured joke. [Blend of JOKE and BOSH] — **josh′er** *n.*

Josh. Joshua.

Josh Bil·lings (josh bil′ingz) See (Henry Wheeler) SHAW.

Josh·u·a (josh′ōō·ə) Israelite leader and successor of Moses. — *n.* The book of the Old Testament bearing his name. [< Hebrew *Yehōshua'* God is salvation]

Joshua tree A tall, treelike desert plant (*Yucca brevifolia*) with forking branches that end in a cluster of leaves.

Jo·si·ah (jō·sī′ə) Seventh-century B.C. king of Judah. II *Kings* xxii 1.

Jos·quin des Prés (zhôs·kaň′ dā prā′), 1445?–1521, Flemish composer.

joss (jos) *n.* A Chinese god. [Pidgin English < Pg. *deos* God]

joss house A Chinese temple or place for religious images.

joss paper Gold or silver paper burnt by the Chinese at funerals, etc.

joss stick A stick of perfumed paste burnt by the Chinese as incense.

jos·tle (jos′əl) *v.t.* & *v.i.* **·tled, ·tling** To push or crowd roughly so as to shake up; elbow; shove. — *n.* A shoving or colliding against; jostling. [Freq. of JOUST] — **jos′tler** *n.*

jot (jot) *v.t.* **jot·ted, jot·ting** To make a hasty and brief note of: usually with *down.* — *n.* The least bit; iota. [< IOTA]

jot·ting (jot′ing) *n.* That which is jotted down; short note.

Jo·tun (yō′tōōn, yō′-) In Norse mythology, a giant. Also **Jö·tun** (yœ′tōōn).

Jo·tun·heim (yō′tōōn·hām, yō′-) In Norse mythology, the abode of the giants. Also **Jö·tun·heim** (yœ′tōōn·hām), **Jö·tun·heim·er** (-hām·ər).

Jou·bert (zhōō·bâr′), **Joseph**, 1754–1824, French moralist and man of letters. — **Petrus Jacobus**, 1831–1900, Boer general and statesman.

jouk (jōōk) *v.i. Scot.* To dodge; also, to bow.

joule (joul, jōōl) *n. Physics* The mks unit of work equivalent to a force of 1 newton acting through a distance of 1 meter and equal to 10,000,000 ergs or 0.737324 foot-pounds. Abbr. *J* [after J. P. *Joule*]

Joule (joul, jōōl), **James Prescott**, 1818–89, English physicist.

jounce (jouns) *v.t.* & *v.i.* **jounced, jounc·ing** To shake or move roughly up and down; bounce; jolt. — *n.* A shake; a bump. [Origin unknown]

jour. 1. Journal. 2. Journeyman.

Jour·dan (zhōōr·däн′), **Comte Jean Baptiste**, 1762–1833, French marshal.

jour·nal (jûr′nəl) *n.* 1. A diary or record of daily occurrences; especially, a ship's log or logbook. 2. A newspaper, especially one published daily. 3. Any periodical or magazine: a learned *journal.* 4. An official record of the daily proceedings of a legislature or other deliberative body. 5. In bookkeeping: **a** A daybook. **b** In double entry, a book in which daily transactions are entered to facilitate later posting in the ledger. 6. *Mech.* The part of a shaft or axle that rotates in or against a bearing. Abbr. *J., jour.* [< OF < L *diurnalis.* Doublet of DIURNAL.]

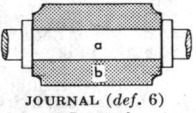

JOURNAL (def. 6)
a Journal.
b Bearing.

journal box *Mech.* The box or bearing for a rotating axle or shaft.

jour·nal·ese (jûr′nəl·ēz′, -ēs′) *n.* The style of writing supposedly characteristic of newspapers, magazines, etc.: a derogatory term.

jour·nal·ism (jûr′nəl·iz′əm) *n.* The occupation, practice, and academic field concerned with writing, editing, and publishing newspapers and other periodicals.

jour·nal·ist (jûr′nəl·ist) *n.* One whose occupation is journalism.

jour·nal·is·tic (jûr′nəl·is′tik) *adj.* Pertaining to or like journalism or journalists. — **jour′nal·is′ti·cal·ly** *adv.*

jour·nal·ize (jûr′nəl·īz) *v.* **·ized, ·iz·ing** *v.t.* 1. To enter (daily transactions) in a journal. 2. To write or describe in,

or as in, a journal or diary. — *v.i.* 3. To keep a journal or diary. Also *Brit.* **jour′nal·ise.**

jour·ney (jûr′nē) *n.* 1. Travel from one place to another, especially by land; trip. 2. The distance traveled, or traversable, in a specified time. — *v.i.* To make a trip; travel. [< OF *journee* a day's travel < L *diurnum*, orig. neut. sing. of *diurnus* daily < *dies* day] — **jour′ney·er** *n.*

— **Syn.** (noun) 1. *Journey, voyage, tour, trip, excursion,* and *pilgrimage* denote a going from one place to another. *Journey* is the general term, implying no particular distance nor means of locomotion, but the tendency is to restrict it to travel by land; *voyage* is commonly reserved for travel by sea. A *tour* is a *journey* to a number of different places by a circuitous route. A *trip* is a short *journey.* Both *tour* and *trip* imply a return to the starting point; this is made explicit in *excursion,* which describes a temporary departure from a place. A *pilgrimage* is a *journey* to a destination held in reverence or honor.

jour·ney·man (jûr′nē·mən) *n. pl.* **·men** (-mən) A worker who has completed his apprenticeship in a skilled trade or craft. Abbr. *jour.*

jour·ney·work (jûr′nē·wûrk′) *n.* Work of a journeyman.

joust (just, joust, jōōst) *n.* 1. A formal combat between two mounted knights armed with lances; tilt. 2. *pl.* Tournament. — *v.i.* To engage in a joust. Also spelled *just.* [< OF *jouste* < *jouster* < LL *juxtare* to approach < *juxta* nearby] — **joust′er** *n.*

Jove (jōv) Jupiter. — **by Jove!** A mild oath expressing surprise, emphasis, etc.

jo·vi·al (jō′vē·əl) *adj.* Possessing or expressive of good-natured mirth or gaiety; convivial; jolly. [< F < LL *Jovialis* born under the influence of Jupiter] — **jo′vi·al·ly** *adv.* — **jo′vi·al·ness** *n.*

jo·vi·al·i·ty (jō′vē·al′ə·tē) *n.* The quality or state of being jovial; conviviality; merriment. Also **jo·vi·al·ty** (jō′vē·əl·tē).

Jo·vi·an (jō′vē·ən) *adj.* Of, pertaining to, or like Jove or Jupiter.

Jo·vi·an (jō′vē·ən), 332?–364, Roman emperor 363–364: full name **Flavius Claudius Jo·vi·a·nus** (jō′vē·ā′nəs).

jow (jou, jō) *Scot. v.t.* & *v.i.* To ring; toll. — *n.* The stroke or sound of a bell.

Jow·ett (jou′it), **Benjamin**, 1817–93, English classical scholar and translator.

jowl[1] (joul, jōl) *n.* 1. The fleshy part under the lower jaw, especially when fat and pendulous; double chin. 2. The wattle of fowls. 3. The dewlap of cattle. Also spelled *jole.* [ME *cholle* < OE *ceolu* throat]

jowl[2] (joul, jōl) *n.* 1. The jaw, especially the lower jaw. 2. The cheek. Also spelled *jole.* [ME *chavel* < OE *ceafl*]

joy (joi) *n.* 1. A strong feeling of happiness arising from the expectation of some good, or from its realization; gladness; delight. 2. A state of contentment or satisfaction: to have *joy* in one's work. 3. Anything that causes delight or gladness. 4. An expression or manifestation of this feeling. — **Syn.** See PLEASURE. — *v.i.* 1. To be glad; rejoice. — *v.t.* 2. *Obs.* To gladden. [< OF *joie* < L *gaudium* < *gaudere* to rejoice]

joy·ance (joi′əns) *n. Poetic* Enjoyment; delight.

Joyce (jois), **James (Augustine Aloysius)**, 1882–1941, Irish novelist, poet, and short-story writer active in Switzerland.

joy·ful (joi′fəl) *adj.* 1. Full of joy. 2. Showing or causing joy. — **joy′ful·ly** *adv.* — **joy′ful·ness** *n.*

joy·less (joi′lis) *adj.* Completely lacking in joy; causing no joy; dreary; sad. — **joy′less·ly** *adv.* — **joy′less·ness** *n.*

joy·ous (joi′əs) *adj.* Joyful. — **joy′ous·ly** *adv.* — **joy′ous·ness** *n.*

joy ride *Informal* 1. A ride taken for pleasure, especially in an automobile. 2. A reckless ride in a stolen vehicle. 3. Something resembling a joy ride in its recklessness, danger, etc. — **joy rider** — **joy riding**

joy stick *Informal* The control stick of an airplane.

J.P. Justice of the Peace.

Jr. or **jr.** Junior.

Ju. Judges.

Juan de Fu·ca Strait (hwän′ də fōō′kə) An inlet of the Pacific between Vancouver Island and the Washington mainland.

Ju·an Fer·nan·dez (jōō′ən fər·nan′dēz, *Sp.* hwän fer·nän′däs) A Chilean island group in the South Pacific; about 70 sq. mi. See (Alexander) SELKIRK.

Juá·rez (hwä′rās), **Benito Pablo**, 1806–72, Mexican patriot and statesman; president 1857–61, 1861–65, 1867–71, 1871–1872.

Juárez See CIUDAD JUÁREZ.

ju·ba (jōō′bə) *n.* A lively Southern Negro dance. [Of African origin]

Ju·ba (jōō′bä) A river in southern Somalia, flowing about 550 miles south to the Indian Ocean.

Ju·bal (jōō′bəl) A descendant of Cain; a musician or inventor of musical instruments. *Gen.* iv 21.

jub·bah (jōōb′ə) *n.* A long, loose outer garment worn in some Moslem countries. [< Arabic *jubbah*] Also **jub′hah.**

Jub·bul·pore (jub′əl·pôr′) A city in northern Madhya Pradesh, India; pop. 406,214 (est. 1971): also *Jabalpur*.

ju·be (jōō′bē) *n.* **1.** A rood loft. **2.** *Obs.* An ambo. [< L *jube* imperative of *jubere* to bid; from the first word of a prayer anciently recited from this gallery]

ju·bi·lant (jōō′bə·lənt) *adj.* Exultingly joyful or triumphant. [< L *jubilans, -antis*, ppr. of *jubilare* to exult] — **ju′bi·lance, ju′bi·lan·cy** *n.* — **ju′bi·lant·ly** *adv.*

ju·bi·late (jōō′bə·lāt) *v.t. & v.i.* **·lat·ed, ·lat·ing** To rejoice; exult. [< L *jubilatus*, pp. of *jubilare* to exult]

Ju·bi·la·te (jōō′bə·lā′tē, -lä′-) *n.* **1.** The 100th Psalm (in the Vulgate and Douai versions, the 99th): from the opening word of the Latin version. **2.** The music to which this psalm may be set. **3.** The third Sunday after Easter (**Jubilate Sunday**), the introit of which begins *Jubilate*. [< L, imperative of *jubilare* to exult, to be joyful]

ju·bi·la·tion (jōō′bə·lā′shən) *n.* Rejoicing; exultation.

ju·bi·lee (jōō′bə·lē) *n.* **1.** In Jewish history, an institution of the Levitical Law (*Lev.* xxv 8–17) to be observed during every fiftieth year, at which time Hebrew slaves were to be freed, alienated lands returned, and the fields left uncultivated. **2.** In the Roman Catholic Church, a year of special indulgence occurring every twenty-fifth year (**ordinary jubilee**) or a special period (**extraordinary jubilee**) decreed by the Pope, during which certain religious acts will secure remission from the penal consequences of sin: also called *Annus Sanctus*. **3.** A special anniversary of an event; especially, the fiftieth (**golden jubilee**), the twenty-fifth (**silver jubilee**), or the sixtieth or seventy-fifth (**diamond jubilee**). **4.** Any season or time of rejoicing. **5.** Jubilation. Also **ju′·bi·le.** [< OF *jubile* < LL *jubilaeus* (infl. by *jubilum* shout of joy) < Gk. *iōbēlaios* < Hebrew *yōbēl* ram's horn, trumpet, with which the beginning of the jubilee year was announced]

Judaeo- See JUDEO-.

Judah (jōō′də) In the Old Testament, a son of Jacob and Leah. *Gen.* xxix 35. — *n.* **1.** The tribe of Israel descended from him. **2.** The kingdom comprising the tribes of Judah and Benjamin, ruled over by the descendants of Solomon. I *Kings* xi-xii. [< Hebrew *Yehūdhāh* praised]

Ju·da·ic (jōō·dā′ik) *adj.* Of or pertaining to the Jews. Also **Ju·da′i·cal.** [< L *Judaicus* < Gk. *Ioudaikos* < *Ioudaios*. See JEW.] — **Ju·da′i·cal·ly** *adv.*

Ju·da·ism (jōō′dē·iz′əm) *n.* **1.** The religious beliefs or practices of the Jews. **2.** The observance of Jewish rites or practices. See CONSERVATIVE JUDAISM, ORTHODOX JUDAISM, REFORM JUDAISM. — **Ju′da·ist** *n.* — **Ju′da·is′tic** *adj.*

Ju·da·ize (jōō′dē·īz) *v.* **·ized, ·iz·ing** *v.t.* **1.** To bring into conformity with Judaism. — *v.i.* **2.** To accept Judaism; follow Jewish rites or customs. Also *Brit.* **Ju′da·ise.**

Ju·das (jōō′dəs) **1.** The disciple of Jesus who betrayed him with a kiss: also **Judas Is·car·i·ot** (is·kar′ē·ət). **2.** Jude. — *n.* One who betrays another under the guise of friendship.

Judas Maccabeus See under MACCABEES.

Judas tree Any of a genus (*Cercis*) of leguminous trees, as *C. siliquastrum*, a European species, with reddish purple flowers: also called *redbud*. [From a tradition that Judas hanged himself upon a tree of this kind]

Jude (jōōd) **1.** One of the twelve apostles: called *Judas* (not Iscariot). *Luke* vi 16, *Acts* i 13, *John* xiv 22. **2.** The author of a book of the New Testament, possibly the brother of James and Jesus: called *Judas*. *Matt.* xiii 55, *Mark* vi 3. — *n.* A book of the New Testament, the Epistle of Jude, by this author.

Ju·de·a (jōō·dē′ə) The southern part of ancient Palestine under Persian, Greek, and Roman dominion: also **Ju·dae′a.**

Ju·de·an (jōō·dē′ən) *adj.* **1.** Of or pertaining to Judea or its inhabitants. **2.** Jewish. — *n.* **1.** A native of Judea. **2.** A Jew. Also spelled *Judaean*.

Judeo- *combining form* Jewish: *Judeo-Christian*. Also spelled *Judaeo-* [< L *Judaeus* < Gk. *Ioudaios* Judean. See JEW.]

Judg. Judges.

judge (juj) *n.* **1.** A public officer invested with the power to administer justice by hearing and deciding cases in a court of law. Abbr. *J.* **2.** One appointed to make decisions, as in a contest or controversy; arbitrator. **3.** One considered competent to decide upon the merits of a thing or to make critical evaluations: a *judge* of music. **4.** In Jewish history, one of the rulers of Israel during the period between the death of Joshua and the anointing of Saul. — *v.* **judged, judg·ing** *v.t.* **1.** To hear and decide in an official capacity the merits of (a case) or the guilt of (a person); try. **2.** To decide authoritatively, as a contest or controversy. **3.** To hold as judgment or opinion; consider; suppose. **4.** To form an opinion or judgment concerning. **5.** To govern: said of the ancient Hebrew judges. — *v.i.* **6.** To act as a judge; sit in judgment. **7.** To form a judgment or estimate. **8.** To make a judgment or decision. [< OF *juge* < L *judex, -icis* < *ius* right + *dic-*, root of *dicere* to speak] — **judg′er** *n.*

— **Syn.** (noun) **1, 2.** *Judge, referee, umpire, arbitrator,* and *arbiter* denote a person who makes decisions in a conflict of views.

Judge, apart from its use as the title of a government official, characterizes a person who has the requisite knowledge, experience, and impartiality to make decisions. A *referee* or *umpire* is one having authority to settle disputes between parties; both terms are applied to the officials in sports contests. A court of law may appoint a *referee* to settle a dispute between litigants. An *arbitrator* is a *referee* who derives his authority from the consent of the disputing parties, having been chosen by them to settle their quarrel. *Arbiter* is usually applied to one who, without official authority or standing, has the prestige to make decisions acceptable to others.

judge advocate *Mil.* **1.** A commissioned officer in the U.S. Army belonging to the Judge Advocate General's Corps. **2.** The legal staff officer for a commander: in full **staff judge advocate**. **3.** The prosecutor in a general or special court-martial: in full **trial judge advocate**.

Judge Advocate General A major general in the U.S. Army or the U.S. Air Force, serving as head of the Judge Advocate General's Department and supervising military justice and other legal matters. Abbr. *JAG*

judge-made (juj′mād′) *adj.* Made by judicial decision.

Judg·es (juj′iz) *n.pl. (construed as sing.)* A book of the Old Testament, containing a history of the Jewish people during the time of the judges. Abbr. *Ju., Judg.*

judge·ship (juj′ship) *n.* The office, functions, or period in office of a judge.

judg·mat·ic (juj·mat′ik) *adj. Informal* Showing good judgment; judicious. Also **judg·mat′i·cal.** [< JUDGE; on analogy with DOGMATIC] — **judg·mat′i·cal·ly** *adv.*

judg·ment (juj′mənt) *n.* **1.** The act of judging. **2.** The result of judging; the decision or opinion reached through judging. **3.** The faculty of judging; ability to judge wisely; discernment; discrimination. **4.** *Law* **a** The sentence or final order of a court in a civil or criminal proceeding; decision. **b** A debt or other obligation resulting from such a decision. **c** The document drawn up as a record of such a decision. **5.** A disaster or misfortune regarded as inflicted by God as a punishment for sin. **6.** *Often cap. Theol.* The Last Judgment. **7.** *Logic* **a** The form of thought in which two terms are compared and their fitness to be joined under a given relation is affirmed or denied. **b** The verbal expression of this, usually called a *proposition*. **8.** *Obs.* Uprightness; rectitude. Also **judge′ment.** — **Syn.** See SENSE.

Judgment Day *Theol.* The day or time of the Last Judgment: also *Day of Judgment*.

ju·di·ca·ble (jōō′di·kə·bəl) *adj.* **1.** Capable of being tried or judged. **2.** Subject to being judged. Also **ju·di·ci·a·ble** (jōō·dish′ē·ə·bəl).

ju·di·ca·tive (jōō′də·kā′tiv, -kə-) *adj.* Competent to judge; judging. [< L *judicatus*, pp. of *judicare* to judge]

ju·di·ca·tor (jōō′də·kā′tər) *n.* One who acts as judge.

ju·di·ca·to·ry (jōō′di·kə·tôr′ē, -tō′rē) *adj.* Pertaining to the administration of justice. — *n. pl.* **·ries** **1.** Any body of persons with judicial authority; tribunal. **2.** The administration of justice; judicial process.

ju·di·ca·ture (jōō′də·kə·chŏŏr) *n.* **1.** The action or function of administering justice, as in courts of law. **2.** The right, power, or authority of administering justice; jurisdiction. **3.** A court of law; also, judges collectively.

ju·di·cial (jōō·dish′əl) *adj.* **1.** Of or pertaining to the administering of justice or to the making of judgments in courts of justice: the *judicial* branch of a government: distinguished from *executive, legislative*. **2.** Of or pertaining to courts of law or to judges: *judicial* powers. **3.** Decreed or enforced by a court of law: *judicial* separation. **4.** Of or befitting a judge: *judicial* gravity; *judicial* robes. **5.** Serving to decide or determine; judging: *judicial* duels. **6.** Inclined to make judgments; discriminating; critical. **7.** *Theol.* Proceeding from God, as a judgment or penalty. [< L *judicialis* < *judex, -icis* judge] — **ju·di′cial·ly** *adv.*

judicial separation *Law* Partial dissolution of a marriage, obtained by legal decree and involving cessation of cohabitation between husband and wife: also called *legal separation*.

ju·di·ci·ar·y (jōō·dish′ē·er′ē, -dish′ə·rē) *adj.* Of or pertaining to courts, judges, or the judgments made in courts of law. — *n. pl.* **·ar·ies** **1.** The department of government that administers the law. **2.** The system of courts set up to carry out this function. **3.** The judges collectively.

ju·di·cious (jōō·dish′əs) *adj.* **1.** Having, showing, or exercising good judgment; prudent. **2.** Proceeding from or done with good judgment. [< F *judicieux* < L *judicium* judgment] — **ju·di′cious·ly** *adv.* — **ju·di′cious·ness** *n.*

Ju·dith (jōō′dith) **1.** A book in the Old Testament Apocrypha and the Douai Bible. **2.** A Jewish woman, heroine of this book, who rescued her countrymen by slaying the Assyrian general, Holofernes. [< Hebrew *Jehūdhīth*, woman of Judah. See JUDAH.]

ju·do (jōō′dō) *n.* **1.** Jujitsu, or a system of physical conditioning based upon it and usually practiced as a sport. **2.** An outgrowth of jujitsu developed during World War II and intended to kill or maim one's opponent. [< Japanese *ju* gentle, pliant + *do* way of life]

Ju·dy (jōō′dē) A puppet, the wife of Punch.

jug¹ (jug) *n.* **1.** A pitcher or similar vessel for holding liquids. **2.** *U.S.* A bulging vessel of earthenware, metal, or glass, with a handle and a narrow neck stopped by a cork or screw cap. **3.** *Slang* A prison or jail. — *v.t.* **jugged, jug· ging 1.** To put into a jug. **2.** To cook in a jug. **3.** *Slang* To imprison; jail. [after *Jug*, a nickname for *Joan*]

jug² (jug) *n.* The sound of a nightingale's note; also, a sound made to mimic this. — *v.i.* **jugged, jug·ging** To make the sound of the nightingale.

ju·gal (jōō′gəl) *adj. Anat.* Of or pertaining to the zygoma. [< L *jugalis* < *jugum* yoke]

ju·gate (jōō′git, -gāt) *adj.* **1.** *Biol.* Occurring in pairs. **2.** *Bot.* Having paired leaflets. [< L *jugatus*, pp. of *jugare* to bind together < *jugum* yoke]

jugged hare *Brit.* Hare stewed in a jug or jar.

jug·ger·naut (jug′ər·nôt) *n.* **1.** Any slow and irresistible destructive force. **2.** A belief or an institution requiring blind self-sacrifice. [after JUGGERNAUT]

Jug·ger·naut (jug′ər·nôt) The eighth avatar of Vishnu whose idol at Puri, India, is annually drawn on a heavy car under the wheels of which devotees are said to have thrown themselves. Also spelled *Jaganath, Jaganatha, Jaggurnath.* [< Hind. *jagannāth* < Skt. *jagannātha* lord of the universe < *jagat* world + *nātha* lord]

jug·gle (jug′əl) *v.* **·gled, ·gling** *v.t.* **1.** To keep (two or more balls or other objects) continuously moving from the hand into the air by skillfully tossing and catching. **2.** To manipulate for the purpose of deception or fraud: to *juggle* financial accounts. — *v.i.* **3.** To perform as a juggler. **4.** To practice deception or fraud. — *n.* **1.** An act of juggling. **2.** A trick or deception. [< OF *jogler* < L *joculari* to jest]

jug·gler (jug′lər) *n.* **1.** One who performs juggling tricks. **2.** One who practices deception or fraud. [< OF *joglere* < L *joculator* < *joculari* to jest]

jug·gler·y (jug′lər·ē) *n. pl.* **·gler·ies 1.** The juggler's art; legerdemain. **2.** Deception; fraud.

jug·gling (jug′ling) *n.* Jugglery.

ju·glan·da·ceous (jōō′glan·dā′shəs) *adj. Bot.* Designating a family (*Juglandaceae*), the walnut family, of trees with odd-pinnate leaves and monoecious flowers. [< NL *Juglandaceae*, the walnut family < L *juglans, -andis* walnut]

Ju·go·slav (yōō′gō·släv′, -slav′), **Ju·go·sla·vi·a** (yōō′gō· slä′vē·ə) See YUGOSLAV, YUGOSLAVIA.

Ju·go·sla·vi·ja (yōō′gō·slä′vē·yä) The Serbo-Croatian name for YUGOSLAVIA.

jug·u·lar (jug′yə·lər, jōō′gyə-) *adj.* **1.** *Anat.* Of or pertaining to the throat or the jugular vein. **2.** *Biol.* Of a fish, having the ventral fins at the throat, in front of the pectoral fins. — *n. Anat.* A jugular vein. [< NL *jugularis* < L *jugulum* collar bone]

jugular vein *Anat.* One of the large veins on either side of the neck that returns blood from the brain, face, and neck.

ju·gu·late (jōō′gyə·lāt) *v.t.* **·lat·ed, ·lat·ing 1.** *Med.* To arrest the course of (a disease) by drastic measures. **2.** *Obs.* To cut the throat of. [< L *jugulatus*, pp. of *jugulare* to slay, cut the throat of < *jugulum* collar bone] — **ju′gu·la′tion** *n.*

Ju·gur·tha (jōō·gûr′thə), died 104 B.C., Numidian king.

juice (jōōs) *n.* **1.** The liquid part of a vegetable, fruit, or animal. **2.** *Usually pl.* The fluids of the body. **3.** The liquid contained in anything. **4.** The essence of anything. **5.** *U.S. Slang* Electricity. **6.** *U.S. Slang* Gasoline, oil, or other liquid fuel. **7.** *U.S. Slang* Vital force; strength. [< OF *jus* < L]

juic·er (jōō′sər) *n.* A device for extracting juice.

juic·y (jōō′sē) *adj.* **juic·i·er, juic·i·est 1.** Abounding with juice; moist. **2.** Full of interest; colorful; spicy. — **juic′i·ly** *adv.* — **juic′i·ness** *n.*

ju·jit·su (jōō·jit′sōō) *n.* A Japanese system of hand-to-hand fighting in which surprise and a knowledge of anatomy and leverage are used to overcome the weight and strength of one's opponent: also spelled *jiujitsu, jiujutsu.* Also **ju·jut·su** (jōō·jit′sōō, -jōōt′sōō). Compare JUDO. [< Japanese *jujutsu* the yielding art < *ju* pliant + *jutsu* art]

ju·ju (jōō′jōō) *n.* **1.** A West African fetish or talismanic object. **2.** The power ascribed to a juju. **3.** The rituals connected with jujus. **4.** A taboo worked by a juju. [< West African, ? ult. < F *joujou* toy]

ju·jube (jōō′jōōb; *for def. 1, also* jōō′jōō·bē) *n.* **1.** A gelatinous candy lozenge. **2.** Any of a genus (*Zizyphus*) of Old World trees or shrubs of the buckthorn family; especially, *Z. jujuba*: also called *Christ's-thorn, lotus, lotus tree.* **3.** The edible fruit of *Zizyphus.* [< F or < Med.L *jujuba*, alter. of L *zizyphum* < Gk. *zizyphon* < Persian *zīzafūn*]

Juke (jōōk) Fictitious name for a New York family whose history, as investigated through several generations by late 19th century sociologists, showed a high degree of crime, alcoholism, disease, and pauperism. Compare KALLIKAK.

juke box A large automatic phonograph, usually coin-operated and permitting selection of the records to be played.

juke joint *U.S. Slang* A roadhouse or barroom for drinking and dancing. [< Gullah *jook* disorderly, wicked; (*juke house* brothel) < W African]

Jul. July.

ju·lep (jōō′lip) *n.* **1.** A mint julep (which see). **2.** A sweetened, syrupy drink used as a vehicle for medicine. **3.** A cool drink made with herbs. [< OF < Persian *gulāb* rose water < *gul* rose + *āb* water]

Jul·ian (jōōl′yən) Anglicized name of **Flavius Claudius Ju·li·a·nus** (jōō·lē·ā′nəs), 331–363, Roman emperor 361–363; renounced Christianity: called **Julian the Apostate**.

Jul·ian (jōōl′yən) *adj.* Of, pertaining to, or named after, Julius Caesar.

Ju·li·an·a (jōō′lē·an′ə), born 1909, queen of the Netherlands 1948–: full name **Juliana Louise Emma Marie Wilhelmina**.

Julian Alps A division of the eastern Alps in NW Yugoslavia and eastern Italy; highest peak, Triglav, 9,394 ft.

Julian calendar See under CALENDAR.

ju·li·enne (jōō′lē·en′, *Fr.* zhü·lyen′) *n.* A clear meat soup containing vegetables chopped or cut into thin strips. — *adj.* Cut into thin strips: *julienne* potatoes. [< F, after *Julienne* or *Julien*, (a cook?) a personal name]

Ju·li·et (jōō′lē·et, jōōl′yit) The heroine of Shakespeare's *Romeo and Juliet.*

Jul·ius II (jōōl′yəs), 1443–1513, pope 1503–13, patron of Raphel and Michelangelo: original name **Giuliano del·la Ro·ve·re** (del′lä rō·vā′rä).

Julius Caesar See (Gaius Julius) CAESAR.

Jul·lun·dur (jul′ən·dər) A city in central Punjab, India; pop. 281,623 (est. 1971).

Ju·ly (jōō·lī′, jōō-) *pl.* **·lys** The seventh month of the calendar year, having 31 days. Abbr. *Jl., Jul., Jy.* [< AF *Julie* < L (*mensis*) *Julius* (month) of Julius; because inserted in the calendar by Julius Caesar]

Ju·ma·da (jōō·mä′də) See JOMADA.

jum·ble (jum′bəl) *v.* **·bled, ·bling** *v.t.* **1.** To mix in a confused mass; put or throw together without order. **2.** To mix up in the mind; muddle. — *v.i.* **3.** To meet or unite confusedly. — *n.* **1.** A confused mixture or collection; hodgepodge: also **jum′ble·ment. 2.** A thin sweet cake. [Imit.]

jum·ble-beads (jum′bəl·bēdz′) *n.pl.* The seeds of the jequirity.

jum·bo (jum′bō) *n. pl.* **·bos** A very large person, animal, or thing. — *adj.* Very large. [after *Jumbo*, an unusually large elephant exhibited by P. T. Barnum < ? W African]

jumbo jet The Boeing 747, a large jet airliner capable of carrying up to 490 passengers.

Jum·na (jum′nə) A river in northern India, flowing about 860 miles SW to the Ganges.

jump (jump) *v.i.* **1.** To spring from the ground, floor, etc., by a propulsive effort, as of the foot and leg muscles; leap; bound. **2.** To move or be moved jerkily; bob; bounce; jiggle. **3.** To rise or change abruptly: Prices *jumped.* **4.** To pass suddenly, as if by leaping: to *jump* to a conclusion. **5.** To start in astonishment. **6.** To spring down from or out of a window, ladder, airplane, etc. **7.** *Informal* To set about one's business at once. **8.** In checkers, to capture a piece by passing another over it to a vacant square beyond. **9.** In bridge, to bid so as to exceed the preceding bid by more than the minimum. — *v.t.* **10.** To leap over or across. **11.** To cause to leap over or across some obstacle: to *jump* a horse. **12.** To raise or increase (prices, demands, etc.). **13.** To pass over; skip; omit. **14.** In bridge, to cause (a bid) to exceed the preceding bid by more than the minimum. **15.** *U.S.* To leave or quit abruptly: to *jump* town. **16.** *Informal* To get onto; board: to *jump* a train. **17.** *Informal* To attack suddenly or by surprise. **18.** *U.S.* In hunting, to cause (game) to leave cover; flush. **19.** *U.S.* To elevate in rank; also, to pass above (someone) by promotion. — **to jump a claim** To take possession of another's mining or land claim by force and fraud. — **to jump at** To accept hastily. — **to jump bail** *U.S.* To forfeit one's bail bond by failing to appear when legally summoned. — **to jump off** *Mil.* To begin an attack. — **to jump on** (or **all over**) *Informal* To assail with abuse; scold. — **to jump ship** *Naut.* To end one's service in a ship's crew by desertion. — **to jump the gun** *Slang* **1.** To begin before the starting signal is given. **2.** To start prematurely. — **to jump the track** Of a train, etc., to leave the rails. — *n.* **1.** The act of jumping; a leap; spring; bound. **2.** An abrupt movement upward or outward; a jerk; bob: The lid took a little *jump.* **3.** A sudden rise or transition: a *jump* in prices. **4.** The length or height of a leap. **5.** Something that is jumped over or across, as a hurdle, obstacle, or fence. **6.** A leap by parachute from an airplane. **7.** In sports, a competition in jumping: broad *jump.* **8.** *pl. Informal* The nervous twitches of St. Vitus's dance, delirium tremens, etc. — **on the jump** *Informal* Working or moving about at top speed; very busy. — **to get** (or **have**) **the jump on** *U.S. Slang* To get or have a head start on or an advantage over. — *adj.* **1.** *Mil.* Of or pertaining to paratroops: *jump* boots; *jump* area. **2.** *U.S. Slang* Of popular music, having a fast, excited tempo. [Cf. Scand. *gumpa* to jump]

jump ball In basketball, a ball tossed up between two opposing players by the referee.

jump bid In bridge, a bid that exceeds the preceding bid by more than the minimum.

jump·er[1] (jum′pər) *n.* **1.** One who or that which jumps. **2.** A piece of mechanism or a tool having a jumping motion. **3.** A type of sled. **4.** *Electr.* A wire used to cut out part of a circuit, or to close a temporary gap in it.

jum·per[2] (jum′pər) *n.* **1.** A sleeveless dress, usually worn over a blouse or sweater. **2.** A loose jacket or smock worn over other clothes. **3.** A hooded fur jacket. [Prob. alter. of OF *juppe* jacket, ult. < Arabic *jubbah* short coat]

jump·ing bean (jump′ing) The seed of certain Mexican shrubs (genera *Sebastiania* and *Sapium*) of the spurge family, that jumps about owing to the movements of a small moth larva (*Laspeyrescia saltitans*) inside.

jumping jack A toy figure of a man, whose jointed limbs are moved by strings.

jumping mouse Any of a family (*Zapodidae*) of small, hibernating mice of North America, having long hind legs and tail and able to leap 9 to 15 feet.

jump·ing-off place (jump′ing-ôf′, -of′) **1.** The utmost limit or extent. **2.** A point from which to make a start.

jump-off (jump′ôf′, -of′) *n.* The commencement of a planned attack by ground forces.

jump shot In basketball, a shot made by a player from the highest point of his jump from the floor.

jump·y (jum′pē) *adj.* **jump·i·er**, **jump·i·est** **1.** Subject to sudden changes; fluctuating. **2.** Given to startled movements; nervous; apprehensive. — **jump′i·ness** *n.*

Jun. or **jun.** Junior.

Junc. or **junc.** Junction.

jun·ca·ceous (jung-kā′shəs) *adj. Bot.* Of or pertaining to the rush family (*Juncaceae*), mostly growing in moist places. [< NL *Juncaceae*, the rush family < L *juncus* rush]

jun·co (jung′kō) *n. pl.* **·cos** Any of various small birds (genus *Junco*) of North America, commonly seen in flocks during winter; especially, the widely distributed **slate-colored junco** (*J. hyemalis*): also called *snowbird.* [< Sp. < L *juncus* rush]

junc·tion (jungk′shən) *n.* **1.** The act of joining, or the state of being joined. **2.** The place where lines or routes, as roads, railways, streams, etc., come together or cross. [< L *junctio, -onis* < *jungere* to join] — **junc′tion·al** *adj.*

junc·ture (jungk′chər) *n.* **1.** The act of joining, or the state of being joined; junction. **2.** A point or line of junction, as of two bodies; an articulation, joint, or seam. **3.** A point in time, especially one at which a critical decision must be made. **4.** A crisis; emergency. **5.** *Ling.* The passage from one sound to the next in the stream of speech. [< L *junctura* < *jungere* to join]

June (jōōn) The sixth month of the calendar year, having 30 days. *Abbr. Je.* [OE < L, or ME < OF *Juin* < L (*mensis*) *Junius* (month) of the Junii, a Roman gens]

Ju·neau (jōō′nō) The capital of Alaska, a port in the SE part; pop. 6,050.

June·ber·ry (jōōn′ber′ē) *n. pl.* **·ries** The serviceberry (which see).

June bug **1.** A large, brightly colored scarabaeid beetle (genus *Polyphylla*) that begins to fly early in June. Also **June beetle.** For illustration see INSECTS (injurious). **2.** The figeater (def. 1).

Jung (yoong) **Carl Gustav,** 1875–1961, Swiss psychologist, psychiatrist, and author.

Jung·frau (yoong′frou) A mountain peak in the Bernese Alps, Switzerland; 13,653 ft.

jun·gle (jung′gəl) *n.* **1.** A dense tropical thicket of high grass, reeds, vines, brush, or trees choked with undergrowth, and usually inhabited by wild animals. **2.** Any similar tangled growth. **3.** *U.S. Slang* A gathering place for hoboes. [< Hind. *jangal* desert, forest < Skt. *jangala* dry, desert]

jungle fever A malarial or intermittent fever characteristic of the East Indian jungles.

jungle fowl One of a genus (*Gallus*) of East Indian gallinaceous birds, of which one species (*G. gallus*) is held to be the original of the domestic fowl.

jun·gly (jung′glē) *adj.* **·gli·er**, **·gli·est** Like or overgrown with jungle.

jun·ior (jōōn′yər) *adj.* **1.** Younger in years or lower in rank. **2.** Denoting the younger of two: opposed to *senior.* **3.** Belonging to youth or earlier life. **4.** Later in effect or tenure. **5.** Pertaining to the third year of a high-school or collegiate course of four years. — *n.* **1.** The younger of two. **2.** One later or lower in service or standing. **3.** A student in the third or junior year. *Abbr. jr., Jr., jun., Jun.* [< L *junior,* compar. of *juvenis* young]

junior college A school giving college courses up to and including the sophomore year.

junior high school A school intermediate between elementary school and high school, in the United States typically comprising grades 7 and 8, and sometimes grade 9.

jun·ior·i·ty (jōōn-yôr′ə-tē, -yor′-) *n.* The state or rank of being a junior.

Junior League A local branch of the Association of the Junior Leagues of America, Inc., composed of young society women engaged in volunteer welfare work.

junior varsity In school and college sports, a team of upperclassmen who represent the school in competition below the varsity level: also called *jayvee.*

ju·ni·per (jōō′nə·pər) *n.* **1.** Any of a genus (*Juniperus*) of evergreen pinaceous shrubs; especially, the common juniper (*J. communis*) of Europe and America. **2.** The dark blue berry of this shrub, used in making gin and as a diuretic. **3.** Retem, a leafless shrub mentioned in the Old Testament. [< L *juniperus*]

Jun·ius (jōōn′yəs, jōō′nē·əs) Pseudonym of an unknown English political writer, 1768–72.

junk[1] (jungk) *n.* **1.** Castoff material of any sort that can be put to some use; odds and ends, as scrap iron, old bottles, or paper. **2.** *Informal* Worthless matter; rubbish; trash. **3.** *Slang* Narcotics; dope. **4.** *Naut.* **a** Old cable or cordage used for making gaskets, oakum, etc. **b** Salt meat used on ships. — *v.t. Informal* To discard as trash; scrap. [ME *jonke*; origin uncertain]

junk[2] (jungk) *n.* A large Chinese vessel with high poop, prominent stem, and battened lug sails. [< Sp. and Pg. *junco* < Malay *djong* ship]

junk mail Unsolicited mail, such as advertisements, sent at other than first-class rates and usually addressed to *occupant* (of a given address).

Jun·ker (yoong′kər) *n.* **1.** One of the landed aristocracy of Prussia. **2.** Loosely, a German military man or official who is arrogant, narrow-minded, and despotic. **3.** A younger member of a German noble family. [< G < *jung* young + *herr* master] — **Jun′ker·dom** *n.* — **Jun′ker·ism** *n.*

Jun·kers (yoong′kərs), **Hugo,** 1859–1935, German airplane engineer and builder.

jun·ket (jung′kit) *n.* **1.** A feast, banquet, picnic, or pleasure trip. **2.** *U.S.* A trip taken by a public official with all expenses paid, usually from public funds. **3.** A delicacy made of curds or of sweetened milk and rennet. — *v.i.* **1.** To have a feast; banquet. **2.** *U.S.* Of a public official, to go on a trip, especially at public expense. — *v.t.* **3.** To entertain by feasting; regale. [< It. *giuncata* cream cheese served in a reed basket < *giunco* < L *juncus* rush] — **jun′ket·er** *n.*

junk·ie (jung′kē) *n. Slang* A dope addict. Also **junk′y.**

junk·man (jungk′man′) *n. pl.* **·men** (-men′) One who purchases, collects, and sells junk. Also **junk′deal′er** (-dē′lər).

junk·yard (jungk′yärd′) *n.* A place where junk is stored that may be used or sold again.

Ju·no (jōō′nō) In Roman mythology, the wife of Jupiter, queen of the gods and goddess of marriage: identified with the Greek *Hera.* — *n.* A woman of queenly beauty.

Ju·no·esque (jōō′nō·esk′) *adj.* Resembling the stately beauty of Juno.

Ju·not (zhü·nō′), **Andoche,** 1771–1813, Duc d'Abrantès, French general under Napoleon.

jun·ta (jun′tə, *Sp.* hōōn′tä) *n.* **1.** A Central or South American legislative council. **2.** A body of men gathered together for some secret purpose, especially for political intrigue; faction; cabal: also **jun′to** (-tō). — **Syn.** See CABAL. [< Sp. < L *juncta,* pp. fem. of *jungere* to join]

Ju·pi·ter (jōō′pə·tər) In Roman mythology, the god ruling over all other gods and all men: identified with the Greek *Zeus:* also called *Jove.* — *n.* The largest planet of the solar system, fifth in order from the sun. See PLANET.

Ju·pi·ter-Am·mon (jōō′pə·tər·am′ən) A Roman name for the Egyptian god Amen. Also **Ju′pi·ter-A′men, Ju′pi·ter-A′mon** (ä′mən).

Jupiter Plu·vi·us (plōō′vē·əs) *Latin* Jupiter considered as the sky god and the giver of rain.

ju·pon (jōō′pon, jōō·pon′; *Fr.* zhü·pôn′) *n.* **1.** A medieval doublet or tunic, especially one worn under armor. **2.** A sleeveless surcoat emblazoned with heraldic insignia. Also spelled *gipon.* [< F < *jupe* < OF *juppe.* See JUPE.]

Ju·ra (jōōr′ə) Plural of JUS.

Ju·ra (jōōr′ə, *Fr.* zhü·rä′) A mountain range in eastern France and western Switzerland; highest peak, Crêt de la Neige, 5,652 ft. Also **Jura Mountains.**

ju·ral (jōōr′əl) *adj.* **1.** Of or pertaining to law; legal. **2.** Relating to rights and obligations as subjects of jurisprudence. [< L *jus, juris* law]

ju·rant (jōōr′ənt) *adj.* Taking oath. — *n.* One who takes an oath. [< L *jurans, -antis,* ppr. of *jurare* to swear < *jus, juris* law]

Ju·ras·sic (jōō·ras′ik) *Geol. adj.* Of or pertaining to a period of the Mesozoic era succeeding the Triassic and followed by the Cretaceous. See chart for GEOLOGY. — *n.* The Jurassic period or corresponding rock system. [< F *jurassique,* after *Jura*]

ju·rat (jōōr′at) *n.* **1.** *Law* The statement at the foot of an affidavit, stating the names of the persons swearing to it, and where, when, and before whom it was sworn. **2.** In the Cinque Ports, the Channel Islands, and certain French towns, an officer with duties similar to those of a magistrate or alderman. [< L *juratus,* pp. of *jurare* to swear]

CHINESE JUNK

ju·ra·to·ry (jŏŏr′ə·tôr′ē, -tō′rē) *adj.* *Law* Of or pertaining to an oath.

Jur.D. Doctor of Law (L *Juris Doctor*).

ju·re di·vi·no (jōō′rē di·vī′nō) *Latin* By divine law.

ju·re hu·ma·no (jōō′rē hyōō·man′ō) *Latin* By human law.

ju·rel (hōō·rel′) *n.* One of various carangoid fishes (genus *Caranx*), especially *C. crysos* and *C. latus*, found along the southern Atlantic coast of the United States. [< Sp.]

ju·rid·i·cal (jŏŏ·rid′i·kəl) *adj.* Pertaining to the law and to the administration of justice by courts and judges. Also **ju·rid′ic.** [< L *juridicus* < *jus, juris* law + *dicere* to say, speak] — **ju·rid′i·cal·ly** *adv.*

juridical days Days when the courts are in session.

ju·ris·con·sult (jŏŏr′is·kən·sult′, -kon′sult) *n.* One learned in the law; a jurist. [< L *jurisconsultus* < *jus, juris* law + *consultus* skilled]

ju·ris·dic·tion (jŏŏr′is·dik′shən) *n.* **1.** Lawful right to exercise official authority, whether executive, legislative, or judicial. **2.** The territory within or the matter over which such authority may be lawfully exercised. **3.** Power of those in authority; control. [< OF *juridiction* < L *jurisdictio, -onis* < *jus, juris* law + *dicere* to say, speak] — **ju′ris·dic′tion·al** *adj.* — **ju′ris·dic′tion·al·ly** *adv.*

jurisp. Jurisprudence.

ju·ris·pru·dence (jŏŏr′is·prōōd′ns) *n.* **1.** The philosophy or science of law and its administration. **2.** A system of laws. [< L *jurisprudentia* < *jus, juris* law + *prudentia* knowledge] — **ju′ris·pru·den′tial** (-prōō·den/shəl) *adj.*

ju·ris·pru·dent (jŏŏr′is·prōōd′nt) *adj.* Skilled in the law. — *n.* One skilled in the law.

ju·rist (jŏŏr′ist) *n.* One versed in the law. [< F *juriste* < Med.L *jurista* < L *jus, juris* law]

ju·ris·tic (jŏŏ·ris′tik) *adj.* Of or pertaining to a jurist or the profession of law. Also **ju·ris′ti·cal.** — **ju·ris′ti·cal·ly** *adv.*

juristic act A proceeding intended to have a legal result and having the necessary qualifications.

ju·ror (jŏŏr′ər) *n.* **1.** One who serves on a jury or is sworn in for jury duty. **2.** One who takes an oath; jurant. [< AF *jurour* < L *jurator* < *jurare* to swear]

Ju·ruá (zhōō·rwä′) A river rising in western Peru and flowing about 1,200 miles, generally NE, across Brazil to the Amazon.

ju·ry¹ (jŏŏr′ē) *n.* *pl.* **·ries 1.** A body of legally qualified persons summoned to serve on a judicial tribunal, there sworn to try well and truly a cause and give a verdict according to the evidence. See GRAND JURY, PETIT JURY. **2.** A committee of award in a competition. [< AF *juree* oath < Med. L *jurata*, orig. pp. of L *jurare* to swear < *jus, juris* law]

ju·ry² (jŏŏr′ē) *adj.* *Naut.* Rigged up temporarily, for relief, replacement, or emergency use: a *jury* mast. [Prob. < OF *ajurie* aid < L *adjutare* to help. See ADJUTANT.]

ju·ry·man (jŏŏr′ē·mən) *n.* *pl.* **·men** (-mən) A juror.

ju·ry·rigged (jŏŏr′ē·rigd′) *adj.* *Naut.* Rigged for temporary use.

jus (jus) *n.* *pl.* **ju·ra** (jŏŏr′ə) **1.** Law in its abstract sense, as distinguished from statute law; right; justice. **2.** Any right that is enforceable by law. [< L, law]

jus. or **just.** Justice.

jus ca·no·ni·cum (jus kə·non′i·kəm) *Latin* Canon law.

jus ci·vi·le (jus si·vī′lē) *Latin* Civil law.

jus di·vi·num (jus di·vī′nəm) *Latin* Divine law.

jus gen·ti·um (jus jen′shē·əm) *Latin* The law of nations.

jus na·tu·ra·le (jus nach′ə·rā′lē) *Latin* Natural law; the law of nature. Also **jus na·tu·rae** (nə·tyōō′rē).

Jus·se·rand (zhüs·rän′), **Jean** (**Adrien Antoine**) **Jules,** 1855–1932, French diplomat and author.

jus·sive (jus′iv) *Gram. adj.* Expressing mild command. — *n.* A jussive mood, word, or construction. [< L *jussus,* pp. of *jubere* to order]

jussive subjunctive *Gram.* The subjunctive used to express mild command, as in Latin *dicat,* let him speak.

just¹ (just) *adj.* **1.** Fair, evenhanded, and impartial in acting or judging. **2.** Adhering to high moral standards; upright; honest. **3.** Morally right; equitable. **4.** Legally valid; legitimate: a *just* title. **5.** Rightly given; merited; deserved: a *just* reward. **6.** Well-founded; substantial: a *just* criticism. **7.** True; correct; accurate: a *just* picture of affairs. **8.** Fitting; proper; decorous: *just* proportions. **9.** *Archaic* Righteous in the sight of God. — *adv.* **1.** To the exact point; precisely: *just* right. **2.** Exactly now: He is *just* leaving. **3.** A moment ago; very recently: He *just* left. **4.** By very little; barely: It *just* missed. **5.** Only; merely: *just* a layman. **6.** *Informal* Simply; really; very: It's *just* lovely. [< OF < L *justus* < *jus* law] — **just′ly** *adv.* — **just′ness** *n.*

just² (just) See JOUST.

juste mi·lieu (zhüst mē·lyœ′) *French* Golden mean.

jus·tice (jus′tis) *n.* **1.** The quality of being just. **2.** The rendering of what is due or merited; also, that which is due or merited. **3.** Conformity to the law; legal validity: a code of *justice.* **4.** The administration of law; also, the means by which law is applied: a court of *justice.* **5.** A judge, espe-cially of a Supreme Court. Abbr. *J., jus., just.* **6.** *Theol.* An attribute of God, and of his laws and judgments. **7.** The abstract principle by which right and wrong are defined. — **Department of Justice** An executive department of the U.S. government (established 1870), headed by the Attorney General, that represents the government in legal matters, enforces antitrust laws, civil rights laws, etc., and supervises internal security and immigration. — **to bring to justice** To arrest and try (a wrongdoer). — **to do justice** To display fairly or well: The hat didn't *do* her *justice.* — **to do justice** To To treat fittingly; appreciate: He *did justice to* the meal. [< OF < L *justitia* < *justus.* See JUST¹.]

— **Syn.** *Justice, equity, fairness,* and *impartiality* are compared as they mean conformity to principles of right judging. *Justice* is the most general term, applicable to verdicts, decisions, actions, causes, claims, and persons. *Justice* also implies a strict rendering of deserts. More narrowly, to administer *justice* means to apply the law of the land. *Equity* means equal treatment, *fairness,* and *impartiality,* but is often a technical term of law denoting a system of *justice,* distinct from the common law, that aims to achieve equal treatment rather than strict *justice.* — **Ant.** injustice, inequity, unfairness, bias, partiality.

justice of the peace A local magistrate of limited jurisdiction elected or appointed to prevent breaches of the peace, having authority to fine and imprison in minor cases, commit to a higher court, perform marriages, etc. Abbr. *J.P.*

jus·tice·ship (jus′tis·ship) *n.* The office of a justice.

jus·ti·ci·a·ble (jus·tish′ə·bəl) *adj.* Proper to be tried in a court. — *n.* A person subject to the jurisdiction of another. [< AF < *justicier* to punish]

jus·ti·ci·a·ry (jus·tish′ē·er′ē) *adj.* Of or pertaining to law or the administration of justice. — *n.* *pl.* **·ar·ies 1.** A high judicial officer; judge. **2.** In Norman and early Plantagenet England, the chief deputy of the king in matters of state and of justice: also **jus·ti′ci·ar** (-ər), **jus·ti′ci·er.** [< Med. L *justiciarius* judge < *justitia.* See JUSTICE.]

jus·ti·fi·a·ble (jus′tə·fī′ə·bəl) *adj.* Capable of being justified; defensible. — **jus′ti·fi′a·bil′i·ty, jus′ti·fi′a·ble·ness** *n.* — **jus′ti·fi′a·bly** *adv.* [< OF < *justifier.* See JUSTIFY.]

jus·ti·fi·ca·tion (jus′tə·fə·kā′shən) *n.* **1.** The act of justifying, or the state of being justified. **2.** The ground of justifying, or that which justifies. [< LL *justificatio, -onis* < *justificare.* See JUSTIFY.]

jus·ti·fi·ca·tive (jus′tə·fə·kā′tiv) *adj.* Tending to justify, or capable of justifying; vindicatory. Also **jus·tif·i·ca·to·ry** (jus·tif′ə·kə·tôr′ē, -tō′rē).

jus·ti·fi·er (jus′tə·fī′ər) *n.* One who justifies.

jus·ti·fy (jus′tə·fī) *v.* **·fied, ·fy·ing** *v.t.* **1.** To show to be just, right, or reasonable; vindicate. **2.** To declare or prove guiltless or blameless; absolve; excuse. **3.** To provide adequate grounds for; substantiate; warrant: His behavior *justifies* mistrust. **4.** *Law* **a** To show sufficient reason for (an action charged against one). **b** To establish as a qualified bondsman. **5.** *Printing* To adjust (lines) to the proper length by spacing. **6.** *Theol.* To cause to be free of grievous sin, and reconciled with God. — *v.i.* **7.** *Printing* To be properly spaced; fit. [< OF *justifier* < LL *justificare* to pardon < L *justus* just + *facere* to make]

Jus·tin (jus′tin), **Saint,** 105?–165?, Greek ecclesiastic; probably beheaded at Rome: called **Justin Martyr.**

Jus·tin·i·an I (jus·tin′ē·ən) Anglicized name of **Flavius Anicius Jus·tin·i·a·nus** (jus·tin′ē·ā′nus) 483–565, Byzantine emperor 527–565; codified Roman laws: called **the Great.**

Justinian Code Roman law as codified under Justinian I.

jus·ti·ti·a om·ni·bus (jus·tish′ē·ə om′nə·bəs) *Latin* Justice for all: motto of the District of Columbia.

jus·tle (jus′əl) See JOSTLE.

jut (jut) *v.i.* **jut·ted, jut·ting** To extend beyond the main portion; protrude; project: often with *out.* — *n.* Anything that juts; a projection. [Var. of JET²]

jute (jōōt) *n.* **1.** A tall annual Asian herb (*Corchorus capsularis* of *C. olitorius*) of the linden family. **2.** The tough fiber obtained from the inner bark of this plant, used for bags, cordage, etc. [< Bengali *jhuto* < Skt. *jūta* braid of hair]

Jute (jōōt) *n.* A member of a Germanic tribe from Jutland, some of whom invaded Britain in the fifth century. [< LL *Jutae* the Jutes. Akin to OE *Ēotas.*] — **Jut·ish** (jōō′tish) *adj.*

Jut·land (jut′lənd) A peninsula of northern Europe comprising continental Denmark and Germany north of the Eider; 11,411 sq. mi.; the **Battle of Jutland,** only major engagement of British and German fleets, was fought 70 miles to the west in 1916: Danish *Jylland.*

jut·ty (jut′ē) *n.* *Obs.* A jetty¹.

juv. Juvenile.

ju·ve·nal (jōō′və·nəl) *n.* *Ornithol.* The plumage acquired by a bird after leaving the nest. [< L *juvenalis* < *juvens* young person]

Ju·ve·nal (jōō′və·nəl) Anglicized name of **Decimus Junius Ju·ve·na·lis** (jōō′və·nā′lis), 60?–140?, Roman satirical poet.

ju·ve·nes·cence (jōō′və·nes′əns) *n.* The state of being or becoming young.

ju·ve·nes·cent (jōō/və·nes/ənt) *adj.* **1.** Becoming young; growing young again. **2.** Making young; rejuvenating. [< L *juvenescens, -entis,* ppr. of *juvenescere* to grow younger < *juvenis* young person]

ju·ve·nile (jōō/və·nəl, -nīl) *adj.* **1.** Young; youthful; also, immature. **2.** Designed for or proper to young persons: *juvenile books.* — *n.* **1.** A young person; youth. **2.** An actor who interprets youthful roles. **3.** A book for young persons. Abbr. *juv.* [< L *juvenilis* < *juvenis* young person] — **ju/ve·nile·ly** *adv.* — **ju/ve·nile·ness** *n.*

juvenile court A court that has jurisdiction in cases involving dependent, neglected, and delinquent children, usually under the age of 18, and is concerned more with reform and guidance than with punishment.

juvenile delinquent One who is guilty of antisocial behavior or of violations of the law, but is too young to be punished as an adult criminal. — **juvenile delinquency**

ju·ve·nil·i·a (jōō/və·nil/ē·ə, -nil/yə) *n.pl.* Works produced in youth, especially writings or paintings. [< L, orig. neut. pl. of *juvenilis* young < *juvenis* young person]

ju·ve·nil·i·ty (jōō/və·nil/ə·tē) *n. pl.* **·ties 1.** A youthful or immature act or manner. **2.** The state of being juvenile; youthfulness; youth. **3.** Youths collectively.

juxta- *prefix* Near; next to: *juxtamarine,* bordering on the sea. [< L *juxta* near]

jux·ta·pose (juks/tə·pōz/) *v.t.* **·posed, ·pos·ing** To place close together; put side by side. [< F *juxtaposer* < L *juxta* near + *poser.* See POSE[1].]

jux·ta·po·si·tion (juks/tə·pə·zish/ən) *n.* The act of placing side by side, or the state of being side by side or contiguous.

j.v. Junior varsity.

J.W.V. or **JWV** Jewish War Veterans.

Jy. July.

Jyl·land (yül/län) The Danish name for JUTLAND.

K

k, K (kā) *n. pl.* **k's** or **ks, K's** or **Ks, kays** (kāz) **1.** The eleventh letter of the English alphabet. The shape of the Phoenician letter *kaph* was adopted by the Greeks as *kappa* and became Roman *K.* Also **kay. 2.** The sound represented by the letter *k,* a voiceless plosive that varies from velar to alveolar position according to the place of articulation of the accompanying vowel, as in *coop* and *keep.* It normally has no phonetic value when initial before *n,* as in *knee, knight, know,* etc. — *symbol Chem.* Potassium (K for *kalium*).

k Kilo.

k. **1.** *Electr.* Capacity. **2.** Carat or karat. **3.** *Math.* Constant.

K **1.** *Physics* Kelvin (temperature scale). **2.** King (chess). **3.** Koruna.

K. Köchel listing.

K. or k. **1.** Calends (L *kalendae*). **2.** Kilogram. **3.** King. **4.** Knight. **5.** Kopeck(s). **6.** Krone.

K2 (kā/tōō/) The world's second highest mountain peak, in the Karakoram range, northern Kashmir, India; 28,250 ft.; also *Dapsang, Godwin Austen.*

ka (kä) *n.* In Egyptian religion, the genius or spiritual self, believed to dwell in man and images and to survive in the tomb. [< Egyptian]

ka. Cathode or kathode.

Ka·a·ba (kä/ə·bə, kä/bə) *n.* The Moslem shrine at Mecca enclosing a sacred black stone, supposedly given to Abraham by the angel Gabriel, toward which worshipers face when praying: also spelled *Caaba.* [< Arabic *ka'ba* square building < *ka'b* cube]

Kaap·land (käp/länt) The Afrikaans name for CAPE OF GOOD HOPE PROVINCE.

kaas (käs) See KAS.

kab (kab) See CAB[2].

ka·ba·ka (kə·bä/kə) *n. Often cap.* Emperor: Ugandan title.

kab·a·la (kab/ə·lə, kə·bä/lə), **kab·ba·la** See CABALA.

ka·bar (kä/bär) See CABER.

ka·ba·ra·go·ya (kä·bä/rä·gō/yä) *n.* A carnivorous lizard (*Varanus salvator*) of the East Indies, one of the monitors, often reaching a length of seven feet. [? < Tagalog]

ka·ba·ya (kä·bä/yä) *n.* A white cotton jacket, often lace-trimmed or embroidered, worn with the sarong in the Malay Peninsula. [< Malay < Pers.]

ka·bel·jou (kä/bəl·you) *n.* A large sciaenoid food fish (*Johnius hololepidotus*) found in African and Australian waters. [< Afrikaans ; Du. *kabeljauw* cod]

ka·bi·ki (kə·bē/kē) *n.* An ornamental tropical tree (*Mimusops elenchi*) having thick, entire leaves and clusters of small white fragrant flowers from which a perfume is distilled.

ka·bob (kə·bob/) *n.* **1.** Shish kebab (which see). **2.** In India, any roast meat. [< Arabic *kabāb*]

ka·bu·ki (kä·bōō/kē) *n.* A form of Japanese play on popular or comic themes, employing elaborate costume, stylized gesture, music, and dancing. [< Japanese]

Ka·bul (kä/bəl) **1.** A river in eastern Afghanistan and western Pakistan, flowing 320 miles east to the Indus. **2.** The capital of Afghanistan, in the east central part on the Kabul river; pop. 299,800 (est. 1969).

Ka·byle (kə·bīl/) *n.* **1.** One of the Berbers living in Algeria or Tunisia. **2.** The Berber dialect spoken by these people.

ka·chi·na (kə·chē/nə) *n.* Among the Hopi and other Pueblo Indians, one of a host of mythical spirit ancestors; also, a small, painted wooden doll representing one of these spirits [< Hopi *gačina* supernatural]

Kad·dish (kä/dish) *n.* In Judaism, a prayer beginning with a doxology, especially recited by mourners and part of the regular daily synagogue service. [< Aramaic, holy]

ka·di (kä/dē) See CADI.

Ka·di·ak (kä/dē·ak, *Russ.* kə·dyäk/) See KODIAK ISLAND.

Kadiak bear See KODIAK BEAR.

kae (kā) *n. Scot.* A jackdaw.

kaf·fee·klatsch (kôf/ē·kläch/, *Ger.* käf/ä·kläch/) *n. Sometimes cap.* An informal conversational gathering where coffee is drunk. Also spelled **coffee klatch, coffee klatsch.** [< G < *kaffee* coffee + *klatsch* chitchat]

kaf·fir (kaf/ər) *n.* A variety of sorghum grown in dry regions as a grain and forage plant: also spelled *kafir.* Also **kaffir corn.** [after *Kaffir*]

Kaf·fir (kaf/ər) *n.* **1.** A member of a powerful group of South African Bantu tribes. **2.** Xhosa, the language of these tribes. **3.** A non-Moslem: term used contemptuously by Arab Moslems. Also **Kaf/ir.** [< Arabic *kāfir* unbeliever]

Kaffir cat A wildcat (*Felis ocreata*) of Africa and Asia Minor, having yellowish striped fur and believed to be an ancestor of the domestic cat.

kaf·fi·yeh (kə·fē/ye) *n.* A large, square kerchief worn by Arabs over the head and shoulders. [< Arabic *kaffīyah*]

Kaf·fra·ri·a (kə·frā/rē·ə) A region in eastern Cape of Good Hope Province, South Africa.

kaf·ir (kaf/ər) See KAFFIR.

Ka·fir (kä/fər, kaf/ər) *n.* One of the people of Kafiristan. Also **Kaf/ir.**

Ka·fi·ri (kä·fir/ē) *n.* The Indic language of the Kafirs.

Ka·fi·ri·stan (kə·fir/i·stan, kä-, -stän) Former name of NURISTAN.

Kaf·ka (käf/kä), **Franz,** 1883–1924, Austrian novelist and short-story writer, born in Prague.

kaf·tan (kaf/tən, käf·tän/) See CAFTAN.

Ka·ga·no·vich (kä/gä·nô/vich), **Lazar (Moiseevich),** born 1893, Soviet politician and administrator.

Ka·ga·wa (kä·gä·wä), **Toyohiko,** 1888–1960, Japanese Christian social reformer and evangelist.

Ka·ge·ra (kä·gā/rä) A river in east central Africa, flowing about 250 miles, generally NE, to Lake Victoria.

Ka·go·shi·ma (kä·gō·shē/mä) A port city on southern Kyushu island, Japan; pop. 295,964 (1960). Also **Ka·go·si·ma.**

ka·gu (kä/gōō) *n.* A crested flightless bird (*Rhynochetos jubatus*) of New Caledonia, having a bright red bill and gray plumage. [< native New Caledonian name]

kai·ak (kī/ak) See KAYAK.

Kai·bab Plateau (kī/bab) A large tableland 7,500 to 9,300 feet high, in northern Arizona and southern Utah.

Kai·e·teur Falls (kī/ə·tōōr/) A waterfall in central Guyana in the Potaro River; 741 ft. high.

Kai·feng (kī/fung/) The capital of Honan Province, China, in the northern part of the Province; pop. 330,000, (est. 1970). Also **Kai·feng/.**

kail (kāl), **kail·yard** (kāl/yärd/) See KALE, KALEYARD.

Ka·i·lu·a-La·ni·kai (kä/ē·lōō/ə·lä/nē·kī/) A village on eastern Oahu, Hawaii; pop. 33,783.

kain (kān) *n.* Rental or tax paid in produce, livestock, eggs, etc.: also spelled *cain, kane.* [< OIrish *cāin* law]

kai·nite (kī/nīt, kā/ə·nīt) *n.* A mineral salt containing potassium sulfate, magnesium sulfate, and magnesium chloride, used as a fertilizer. [< G *kainit* < Gk. *kainos* recent]

Kair·ouan (kīr·wän′, *Fr.* ker·wän′) A city in NE Tunisia; a holy city of the Moslems; pop. 46,200 (1961): also *Qairwan*. Also **Kair·wan′.**

kai·ser (kī′zər) *n.* Emperor. [< G < L *Caesar* Caesar]

Kai·ser (kī′zər) Title of the emperors of the Holy Roman Empire, 962–1806; the Austrian emperors, 1804–1918; and the German emperors, 1871–1918.

Kaiser (kī′zər), **Georg,** 1878–1945, German dramatist. — **Henry J**(ohn), 1882–1967, U.S. industrialist.

Kai·sers·lau·tern (kī′zərs·lou′tərn) A city in Rhineland-Palatinate, SW West Germany; pop. 99,850 (est. 1970).

kaj·e·put (kaj′ə·pət) See CAJUPUT.

ka·ka (kä′kə) *n.* A New Zealand parrot (genus *Nestor*), typically with olive-green body, gray crown, and red face, neck, abdomen, and rump. [< Maori]

ka·ka·po (kä′kə·pō′) *n. pl.* **·pos** A nocturnal, flightless, greenish brown New Zealand parrot (*Strigops habroptilus*). [< Maori *kaka* parrot + *po* night]

ka·ke·mo·no (kä′ke·mō′nō) *n. pl.* **·nos** A picture on paper or silk attached to a roller and used as a wall hanging. [< Japanese < *kake* to hang + *mono* thing]

ka·ki (kä′kē) *n.* The Japanese persimmon. [< Japanese, persimmon]

ka la-a·zar (kä′lä·ä·zär′, -az′ər) *n. Pathol.* An infectious fever of India, China, and Egypt, caused by a protozoan parasite (*Leishmania donovani*): also called *visceral leishmaniasis.* [< Hind. *kālā-āzār* black disease]

kal. Calends (L *kalendae*).

Ka·la·ha·ri Desert (kä′lä·hä′rē) An arid plateau region in southern Africa, largely in Botswana.

Kal·a·ma·zoo (kal′ə·mə·zoō′) A city in SW Michigan; pop. 85,555.

ka·lam·ka·ri (kä′läm·kä′rē) *n.* An East Indian cotton fabric having designs drawn and colored by hand. [< Hind.]

Ka·lat (kə·lät′) A former princely state of eastern Baluchistan, West Pakistan; 30,799 sq. mi.; capital, **Kalat:** also *Khelat.*

Kalb (kalb, *Ger.* kälp), **Baron de** See DE KALB.

kale (kāl) *n.* **1.** A variety of headless cabbage. **2.** *Scot.* Cabbage of any kind; also, broth of kale; broth. **3.** *U.S. Slang* Money. Also spelled *kail.* [Var. of COLE]

ka·lei·do·scope (kə·lī′də·skōp) *n.* **1.** A tube-shaped optical toy that shows constantly changing symmetrical patterns as loose bits of colored glass are moved about under a set of mirrors. **2.** A swiftly changing scene, pattern, etc. [< Gk. *kalos* beautiful + *eidos* form + -SCOPE]

ka·lei·do·scop·ic (kə·lī′də·skop′ik) *adj.* **1.** Of or pertaining to a kaleidoscope. **2.** Rapidly changing and intricate. Also **ka·lei′do·scop′i·cal,** — **ka·lei′do·scop′i·cal·ly** *adv.*

kal·ends (kal′əndz) See CALENDS.

Ka·le·va·la (kä′lə·vä′lä) *n.* A collection of ancient poems embodying the myths and hero legends of Finland: the national epic of Finland. [< Finnish, land of heroes]

kale·wife (kāl′wīf′) *n. pl.* **·wives** (-wīvz′) *Scot.* A woman who sells vegetables.

kale·yard (kāl′yärd′) *n. Scot.* A kitchen garden: also spelled *kailyard.*

kaleyard school A late 19th-century school of writers, including J. M. Barrie and Ian Maclaren, who described Scottish life with much use of dialect.

Kal·gan (käl′gän′) A city in Hopeh Province, China; pop. 1,000,000 (est. 1970).

Ka·li (kä′lē) In Hinduism, the four-armed black goddess of generation and destruction; an aspect of Devi. [< Skt., black]

kal·ian (käl·yän′) *n.* The hookah of Persia; Persian version of the hubblebubble. [< Persian *kaliān*]

Ka·li·da·sa (kä′lē·dä′sä) Fifth-century Hindu poet and dramatist; author of *Sakuntala.*

ka·lif (kā′lif, kal′if), **ka·liph** See CALIPH.

Ka·li·man·tan (kä′lē·män′tän) The Indonesian name for (Indonesian) BORNEO.

Ka·li·nin (kä·lē′nin, *Russ.* kə·lyē′nyin) A city in the western R.S.F.S.R., on the Volga; pop. 345,000 (est. 1970): formerly *Tver, Tver′.*

Ka·li·nin (kə·lyē′nyin), **Mikhail Ivanovich,** 1875–1946, Soviet political leader; president 1923–46.

Ka·li·nin·grad (kä·lē′nin·grad, *Russ.* kə·lyē′nyin·grät) A port city in the extreme western R.S.F.S.R., on the Pregel river; pop. 202,000 (1959); formerly the capital of East Prussia as German *Königsberg.*

Ka·lisz (kä′lēsh) A city in west central Poland; pop. about 66,000. German **Ka·lisch** (kä′lish).

ka·li·um (kā′lē·əm) *n.* Potassium. [< KALI]

Kal·li·kak (kal′ə·kak) Fictitious name for a New Jersey family whose history showed one branch with a high incidence of crime, disease, and pauperism, while another branch did not deviate in these respects. Compare JUKE. [< Gk. *kalli-* beautiful + *kakos* evil]

Kal·mar (käl′mär) A port city in SE Sweden on **Kalmar Sound,** an inlet of the Baltic between Sweden and Öland island; pop. 30,446 (1960).

kal·mi·a (kal′mē·ə) Any plant of a genus (*Kalmia*) of North American shrubs of the heath family, with evergreen leaves and umbellate clusters of rose, purple, or white flowers. [< NL, after Peter *Kalm,* 1716–79, Swedish botanist]

Kal·muck (kal′muk) *n.* **1.** A member of one of the Buddhistic Mongol tribes inhabiting a region extending from western China to the Volga river. **2.** The Mongolian language of these tribes. Also **Kal′muk, Kal·myk** (kal′mik).

ka·long (kä′lông) *n.* A fruit-eating bat (family *Pteropodidae*) of Africa, Asia, and Australia. [< Malay *kālong*]

kal·pak (kal′pak) See CALPAC.

kal·so·mine (kal′sə·mīn) See CALCIMINE.

Ka·lu·ga (kə·loō′gə) A city in western R.S.F.S.R. on the Oka river; pop. 211,000 (est. 1970).

ka·lyp·tra (kə·lip′trə) *n.* A thin veil worn by women of ancient Greece, either over the face or as a headdress. [< Gk. < *kalyptein* to hide]

Ka·ma (kä′mə) In Hinduism, the god of love and desire. [< Skt. *Kāma* desire]

Ka·ma (kä′mə) A river in the SW central R.S.F.S.R., flowing 1,262 miles, generally SW, to the Volga.

kam·a·cite (kam′ə·sīt) *n.* A type of meteoric iron containing nickel. [< G *kamacit* < Gk. *kamax, -akos* vine pole]

Ka·ma·ku·ra (kä·mä·koōr·ä) A city on Honshu island, Japan; site of a 42-foot image of Buddha; pop. about 91,000.

ka·ma·la (kə·mä′lə, ka·n′ə·lə) *n.* **1.** An East Indian tree (*Mallotus philippinensis*) of the spurge family. **2.** The fine orange-red powder from the capsular fruit of this tree, used as a purgative and in dyeing. [< Skt.]

Kam·chat·ka (ka·n·chat′kə, *Russ.* kə·n·chät′kə) A peninsula in the eastern R.S.F.S.R., extending 750 miles southward between the Bering and Okhotsk seas; 104,200 sq. mi.

kame (kām) *n.* **1.** *Geol.* A conical hill or short ridge of stratified sand and gravel deposited by a retreating glacier. **2.** *Scot.* A comb. [See COOMB]

Ka·me·ha·me·ha I (kä·mā′hä·mä′hä), 1753?–1819, first king of Hawaii 1810–19.

Ka·me·rad (kä′mə·rät′) *n. pl.* **·rad·en** (-rä′dən) *German* Comrade: said by German soldiers ready to surrender.

Kam·er·lingh On·nes (kä′mər·ling ôn′əs), **Heike,** 1853–1926, Dutch physicist.

Ka·me·run (kä′mə·roōn) The German name for CAMEROONS.

Ka·met (kä′met) A mountain on the Tibetan border of Uttar Pradesh state, India; 25,447 ft.

ka·mi (kä′mē) *n.* **1.** The gods collectively of the first and second mythological dynasties of Japan; also, their descendants, the mikados. **2.** The deified spirits of the heroes and famous men of Japan. [< Japanese]

Ka·mien·sko·ye (kä′myin·sko·yə) The former name for DNIEPRODZERZHINSK. Also **Ka′men·sko·e.**

kam·ik (kam′ik) *n. Canadian* A mukluklike skin boot.

ka·mi·ka·ze (kä′mi·kä′zē) *n.* **1.** In World War II, the suicidal Japanese tactic of ramming with a piloted airplane or boat carrying explosives. **2.** A suicidal attack; also, the craft used in such an attack, or the pilot. [< Japanese, lit., divine wind < *kami* god + *kaze* wind]

Kam·pa·la (käm·pä′lä) The capital of Uganda, in the southern part; pop. 330,000 (est. 1970).

kam·pong (käm·pong′, käm′pong) *n.* An enclosed space; a compound. [< Malay]

kam·sin (kam′sin), **kam′seen** (-sēn) See KHAMSIN.

Kan. Kansas (unofficial).

ka·na (kä′nə) *n.* Japanese syllabic writing, consisting of two systems of 48 characters each, hiragana and katakana, used in addition to the Chinese ideographs. [< Japanese]

Ka·nak·a (kə·nak′ə, kan′ə·kə) *n.* **1.** A native of Hawaii. **2.** Any South Sea islander. [< Polynesian, man]

Ka·na·ra (kä′nə·rə, kə·nä′rə) A region of the southern Deccan Plateau, India; about 60,000 sq. mi.: also *Canara.* **Ka·narese Kar′na·tak.**

Ka·na·rese (kä′nə·rēz′, -rēs′) *adj.* Of or pertaining to Kanara. — *n. pl.* **·rese 1.** A native or inhabitant of Kanara. **2.** The Dravidian language of Kanara. Also spelled *Canarese.*

Ka·na·za·wa (kä·nä·zä·wä) A port city of western Honshu island, Japan; pop. 298,967 (1960).

Kan·chen·jun·ga (kun′chən·joōng′gə) The third highest mountain in the world, in the eastern Nepal Himalayas; 28,146 ft.: formerly *Kinchinjunga.*

Kan·da·har (kän′də·här′) A city in southern Afghanistan; pop. 127,000 (est. 1969): also *Qandahar.*

Kan·din·ski (kän·din′skē, *Russ.* kän·dyēn′skē), **Vasili,** 1866–1944, Russian painter active in Germany and France.

Kan·dy (kan′dē, kän′dē) A city in central Ceylon; site of a temple of Buddha; pop. about 57,000: formerly *Candy.*

kane (kān) See KAIN.

Kane (kān), **Elisha Kent,** 1820–57, U.S. Arctic explorer.

kan·ga·roo (kang′gə·rōō′) *n. pl.* **·roos** Any of a large family (*Macropodidae*) of herbivorous marsupials of the Australian region, having weak forelimbs, strong hind limbs, and a stout tail, moving by leaping bounds and ranging in size from nine feet long to about the size of a rat. [< Australian]

KANGAROO
(To 6 feet high)

kangaroo court *U.S.* An unauthorized and irregular court in which the law is disregarded or willfully misinterpreted.

kangaroo rat 1. Any of a genus (*dipodomys*) of pouched rodents of the SW United States and Mexico having elongated hind limbs and tail. **2.** Any of several Australian rodents (genus *Notomys*) noted for their leaping habits.

Kan·ka·kee (kang′kə·kē′) A city in NE Illinois, on the **Kankakee River** that flows generally west about 135 miles from northern Indiana to the Illinois River; pop. 30,944.

Kan·nap·o·lis (kə·nap′ə·lis) An unincorporated place in south central North Carolina, near Concord; pop. 36,293.

Ka·no (kä′nō) A city in northern Nigeria; pop. about 130,000.

Kans. Kansas.

Kan·sas (kan′zəs) A central State of the United States; 82,276 sq. mi.; pop. 2,249,071; capital, Topeka; entered the Union Jan. 29, 1861; nickname *Sunflower State.* — **Kan′san** (-zən) *adj. & n.*

Kansas City 1. A city in western Missouri, on the Missouri River; pop. 507,330. **2.** A city in NE Kansas, on the Missouri River; pop. 168,213.

Kan·su (kän′sōō′, *Chinese* gän′sōō′) A Province in NW China; 150,000 sq. mi.; pop. 12,800,000 (1958); capital, Lanchow.

Kant (kant, *Ger.* känt), **Immanuel**, 1724–1804, German philosopher.

Kant·i·an (kan′tē·ən) *adj.* Of or pertaining to Kant or his philosophy. — *n.* A follower of Kantianism.

Kant·i·an·ism (kan′tē·ən·iz′əm) *n.* The transcendental philosophy of Immanuel Kant, a doctrine of a priori knowledge stating that man experiences the material world through sense perception, but its reality is determined by purely mental forms and categories. Also **Kant′ism**.

Kao·hsiung (gou′shyoong′) A port city in SW Taiwan; pop. 469,000 (est. 1965).

Kao·lan (gou′län′) A former name for LANCHOW.

ka·o·li·ang (kä′ō·lē·ang′) *n.* Any of a variety of sorghums native to eastern Asia. [< Chinese < *kao* tall + *liang* grain]

ka·o·lin (kā′ə·lin) *n.* A claylike and friable hydrous aluminum silicate used in making porcelain. Also **ka′o·line** (-lin). [< F < Chinese *Kao-ling* mountain where first mined < *kao* tall + *ling* hill]

ka·o·lin·ite (kā′ə·lin·īt′) *n.* A very pure form of kaolin.

ka·pa (kap′ə) *n. pl.* **kap·a-kap·a** Tapa (def. 2). [< Hawaiian]

Ka·pell·meis·ter (kä·pel′mīs′tər) *n. pl.* **·ter** German The musical director of a choir, orchestra, etc., originally in a nobleman's court or chapel: also *chapelmaster.*

kaph (käf) *n.* The eleventh letter in the Hebrew alphabet: also spelled *caph.* See ALPHABET.

Ka·pı·da·ğı Peninsula (kä′pi·dä·i′) An extension of NW Turkey into the Sea of Marmara: ancient *Cyzicus.*

Ka·pi·tal (kä′pi·täl′), **Das** A treatise on economics and politics by Karl Marx, in which he elaborates his doctrine of the class struggle, concentrating on the materialistic conception of history and the theory of surplus value.

ka·pok (kā′pok) *n.* A cottony or silky fiber covering the seeds of the kapok tree, used for mattresses, life preservers, insulation material, etc. [< Malay *kāpoq*]

kapok tree A tropical tree (*Ceiba pentandra*) having seeds covered with silky fiber. Also called *silk-cotton tree.*

kap·pa (kap′ə) *n.* The tenth letter in the Greek alphabet (Κ, κ), corresponding to the English k. See ALPHABET.

ka·put (kä·pōōt′) *adj. Slang* Ruined; done for. [< G]

Ka·ra (kä′rə) A river in the NW R.S.F.S.R., flowing 130 miles north to **Kara Bay,** an inlet of Baidarata Bay.

kar·a·bi·ner (kar′ə·bē′nər) *n.* In mountaineering, a steel loop or ring that is snapped into a piton and through which a rope is passed to hold the climber. [Short for G *karabinerhaken* carbine clasp]

KARABINER
a Closed.
b Open.

Ka·ra·chi (kə·rä′chē) A port city on the Arabian Sea NW of the Indus delta; former capital of Pakistan; pop. 2,886,000 (1968).

Ka·ra·den·iz Bo·ğa·zi (kä′rä·deng·ēz′ bō′ä·zi′) The Turkish name for BOSPORUS.

Ka·ra·fu·to (kä·rä·fōō·tō) The Japanese name for the southern part of SAKHALIN.

Ka·ra·gan·da (kä′rä·gän·dä′) A city in the central Kazakh S.S.R.; pop. 522,000 (est. 1970).

Kar·a·george (kar′ə·jôrj), 1776?–1817, Serbian patriot; founder of a royal dynasty.

Kar·a·ko·ram (kar′ə·kôr′əm, -kō′rəm) A mountain range in NE Kashmir; highest peak, K2, 28,250 ft.: traversed by **Karakoram Pass** at 18,290 ft. on the China-Kashmir trade route: also *Mustagh.* Also **Kar′a·ko′rum.**

kar·a·kul (kar′ə·kəl) *n.* **1.** A breed of sheep raised in the Soviet Union, Iran, Iraq, etc. **2.** The black or gray, loosely curled fur made from the pelt of the karakul lamb. Also spelled *caracul.* [after *Kara Kul*, a lake in Bukhara]

Ka·ra Kum (kä′rä kōōm′) A desert in the central Turkmen S.S.R., extending from the Caspian Sea to Amu Darya.

Ka·ra Sea (kä′rə) An inlet of the Arctic Ocean between Novaya Zemlya and the northern Soviet Union.

kar·at (kar′ət) *n.* **1.** The twenty-fourth part by weight of gold in an article: 18-*karat* gold has ¹⁸⁄₂₄ or ¾ gold by weight. **2.** Loosely, a carat. Abbr. *k.*, *kt.* [Var. of CARAT]

ka·ra·te (kä·rä′tä, -tē) *n.* An Oriental method of hand-to-hand combat utilizing a variety of sudden, forceful blows, as with the side of the hand or the fingertips. [< Japanese]

Kar·ba·la (kär′bə·lə) A city in central Iraq; a Moslem pilgrimage center; pop. about 61,000. Also **Kar′be·la.**

Ka·re·li·an A.S.S.R. (kə·rē′lē·ən, -rēl′yən) An administrative division of the NW R.S.F.S.R.; 66,560 sq. mi.; pop. 714,000 (1970); capital, Petrozavodsk. Also **Ka·re′li·a** (-le·ə, -rel′yə). *Russian* **Ka·rel·ska·ya A.S.S.R.** (kä·ryely′skä·yä). Also **Ka·rel′ska·ya.**

Karelian Isthmus A land bridge between the Gulf of Finland and Lake Ladoga in the R.S.F.S.R.

Ka·re·lo-Fin·nish S.S.R. (kə·rē′lō·fin′ish) A former constituent republic of the Soviet Union, reduced (1956) to an autonomous republic. See KARELIAN A.S.S.R.

Karl-Marx-Stadt (kärl′märks′shtät′) A city in southern East Germany; pop. 286,226 (1959): formerly *Chemnitz.*

Kar·lov·ci (kär′lôv·tsē) A town in NE Yugoslavia; by a treaty signed here (1699), Turkey ceded most of her European territories to Poland, Venice, and Austria. *German* **Kar·lo·witz** (kär′lō·vitz).

Kar·lo·vy Va·ry (kär′lô·vē vär′ē) A town in NW Bohemia, Czechoslovakia; pop. 45,000 (est. 1966). *German* **Karls·bad** (kärls′bät): also *Carlsbad.*

Karls·ruh·e (kärls′rōō·ə) A city in Baden-Württemberg, SW West Germany; pop. 253,300 (1967): also *Carlsruhe.*

kar·ma (kär′mə, kûr′-) *n.* **1.** In Buddhism and Hinduism, the doctrine of responsibility for all one's acts in all incarnations, that explains and justifies good and evil fortune. **2.** Loosely, fate or destiny. [< Skt., deed]

karn (kärn) *n. Brit.* A cairn.

Kar·nak (kär′nak) A village in Upper Egypt, on the Nile; near the site of ancient Thebes.

Kärn·ten (kern′tən) The German name for CARINTHIA.

Ká·rol·yi (kä′rō·yē), **Count Mihály**, 1875–1955, Hungarian politician.

ka·ross (kə·ros′) *n. Afrikaans* **1.** An African garment made of skins sewed together in a square. **2.** A rug of skins.

Kar·rer (kär′ər), **Paul**, 1889–1971, Swiss chemist.

kar·roo (kə·rōō′, ka-) *n. pl.* **·roos** A dry plateau or tableland of South Africa. Also **ka·roo′.** See GREAT KARROO, SOUTHERN KARROO, NORTHERN KARROO. [< Hottentot]

Kar·roo (kə·rōō′, ka-) *adj. Geol.* Belonging to or designating a period or rock system of the late Paleozoic and early Mesozoic eras, well developed in South Africa. Also **Ka·roo′.**

karyo- *combining form Biol.* Nucleus: *karyoplasm:* also spelled *caryo-.* Also, before vowels, **kary-.** [< Gk. *karyon* nut]

kar·y·og·a·my (kar′ē·og′ə·mē) *n. Biol.* Cell conjugation with fusion of nuclei. [< KARYO- + -GAMY]

kar·y·o·ki·ne·sis (kar′ē·ō·ki·nē′sis) *n. Biol.* Mitosis. [< KARYO- + Gk. *kinēsis* movement] — **kar′y·o·ki·net′ic** (-net′ik) *adj.*

kar·y·o·lymph (kar′ē·ə·limf′) *n. Biol.* The clear protoplasmic fluid surrounding the structures of the cell nucleus.

kar·y·o·plasm (kar′ē·ə·plaz′əm) *n. Biol.* Nucleoplasm. — **kar′y·o·plas′mic** *adj.*

kar·y·o·some (kar′ē·ə·sōm′) *n. Biol.* **1.** A mass of chromatin in the resting nucleus of the cell. **2.** The cell nucleus itself. Also **kar′y·o·so′ma** (-sō′mə).

kar·y·o·tin (kar′ē·ō′tin) *n. Biol.* Chromatin: also spelled *caryotin.* [< KARYO- + (CHROMA)TIN]

kas (käs) *n.* A massive cupboard used by the early Dutch settlers in America: also spelled *kaas.* [< Du.]

Kas. Kansas (unofficial).

Kas·bah (käz′bä) See CASBAH.

ka·sher (kä′shər) See KOSHER.

Kash·gar (käsh′gär′) A town in the western Sinkiang-Uighur Autonomous Region, China; pop. 175,000 (est. 1970): Chinese *Shufu.*

Kash·gar·i·a (käsh·gär′i·ə) See (Chinese) TURKESTAN.

kash·mir (kash′mir, kazh′-) See CASHMERE.

Kash·mir (kash·mir′, kash′mir) See JAMMU AND KASHMIR. Formerly *Cashmere.*

Kash·mi·ri (kash·mir′ē) *n.* The Indic language of the Kashmirians.

Kash·mi·ri·an (kash·mir′ē·ən) *adj.* Of or pertaining to Kashmir or its people. — *n.* A native of Kashmir. Also spelled *Cashmerian.*

Kas·sa (kôsh′shô) The Hungarian name for KOŠICE.

Kas·sa·la (kas′ə·lə) A city in NE Sudan; pop. 40,000 (1965).

Kas·sel (käs′əl) A city in Hesse, eastern West Germany; pop. 211,600 (est. 1967). Also *Cassel.*

Kas·sim (kä·sēm′), **Abdul Karim**, 1914–63, Iraqi general; premier 1958–63; executed. Also **Kas·sem** (kä·sem′).

Kas·tro (käs′trô) A former name for MYTILENE. Also **Kas′. tron** (-trən).

kata- See CATA-.

ka·tab·a·sis (kə·tab′ə·sis) *n.* *pl.* **·ses** (-sēz) **1.** The march back to the sea of the Greek mercenaries who followed Cyrus against Artaxerxes. See ANABASIS. **2.** Any retreat. [< Gk., a going down < *katabainein* to go down]

kat·a·bat·ic (kat′ə·bat′ik) *adj.* *Meteorol.* Pertaining to or designating a down-flowing wind cooled by radiation.

ka·tab·o·lism (kə·tab′ə·liz′əm) See CATABOLISM.

Ka·tah·din (kə·tä′din) *Mount* A peak in central Maine, the highest point in the state; 5,268 ft.

ka·ta·ka·na (kä′tə·kä′nə) *n.* One of two sets of Japanese syllabic symbols, used chiefly in formal documents. See KANA. Compare HIRAGANA. [< Japanese]

ka·tal·y·sis (kə·tal′ə·sis) See CATALYSIS.

kat·a·mor·phism (kat′ə·môr′fiz·əm) *n.* Metamorphism.

Ka·tan·ga (kə·tang′gə) A Province of the SE Republic of Zaire; 191,878 sq. mi.; pop. 2,753,714 (1970); capital, Lubumbashi. — **Ka·tan·gese′** (-gēz′, -gēs′) *adj.* & *n.*

ka·thar·sis (kə·thär′sis) See CATHARSIS.

Ka·thi·a·war (kä′tē·ə·wär′) A peninsula of western India.

kath·ode (kath′ōd) See CATHODE.

kat·i·on (kat′ī′ən) See CATION.

Kat·mai National Monument (kat′mī) A region of the NE Alaska Peninsula, southern Alaska; 14,214 sq. mi.; contains **Katmai Volcano**; 7,000 ft.; last eruption, 1912.

Kat·man·du (kät′män·dōō′) The capital of Nepal, in the central part; pop. 121,019 (1961). Also **Kath′man·du′**.

Ka·to·wi·ce (kä′tô·vē′tse) A city in southern Poland; pop. 291,600 (est. 1968). *German* **Kat·to·witz** (kät′ō·vits).

Kat·rine (kat′rin), **Loch** A lake in SW Perthshire, Scotland.

Kat·te·gat (kat′ə·gat) A strait between Sweden and Jutland: also *Categat′*. Also **Kat·te·gott** (kät′ə·got).

ka·ty·did (kā′tē·did) *n.* A green, arboreal insect (family *Tettigonidae*) allied to the grasshoppers and crickets. [Imit., from sound produced by the males]

katz·en·jam·mer (kat′sin·jam′ər, kät′sən·yä′mər) *n.* **1.** A farcical or bewildering situation. **2.** A harsh, loud noise. **3.** A hangover. [< G *katzen*, *pl.* of *katze* cat + *jammer* misery]

Kau·ai (kou′ī) One of the Hawaiian Islands; 551 sq. mi.

Kauf·man (kôf′mən), **George S.**, 1889–1961, U.S. playwright.

Kau·nas (kou′näs) A city in the south central Lithuanian S.S.R., on the Nemen; pop. 214,000 (1959): Russian *Kovno*.

kau·ri (kou′rē) *n.* **1.** A large timber tree (*Agathis australis*) of New Zealand. **2.** Its wood. **3.** Any tree of the genus *Agathis*. **4.** Kauri gum. Also **kau′ry**. [< Maori]

kauri gum A resinous exudation of the kauri tree, used in varnishes, for linoleum, etc. Also **kauri copal**, **kauri resin**.

ka·va (kä′vä) *n.* **1.** A shrub (*Piper methysticum*) of the pepper family. **2.** An intoxicating and narcotic beverage made from the roots of this plant by the Polynesians: also **ka′va-ka′va**. [< Polynesian *kawa* bitter]

ka·vass (kə·väs′) *n.* A guard or military courier attending Turkish dignitaries: also, a Turkish police officer. [< Turkish < Arabic *qawwās* a maker of bows < *qaws* bow]

Ka·ve·ri (kä′vûr·ē) See CAUVERY.

Ka·vir (kä·vēr′) See DASHT-I-KAVIR.

Ka·wa·gu·chi (kä·wä·gōō·chē) A city on central Honshu island, Japan; pop. 284,000 (est. 1968).

Ka·wa·sa·ki (kä·wä·sä·kē) A port city on central Honshu island, Japan, on Tokyo Bay; pop. 910,000 (est. 1968).

kav (kā) *n.* The letter K.

Kav (kā), **Sir** A boastful knight of the Round Table.

kay·ak (kī′ak) *n.* *U.S.* & *Canadian* The hunting canoe of arctic America, made of sealskins stretched over a pointed frame, with a hole amidships where the user sits, fastening the deck covering around him to keep out water: also spelled *kaiak*. [< Eskimo]

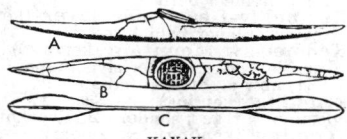
KAYAK
A Side view. B Top view. C Paddle.

kayles (kālz) *n.pl.* *Brit. Dial.* **1.** A game of ninepins or skittles. **2.** The pins used in this game. [Cf. G or Du. *kegel*]

kay·o (kā′ō) *Slang* *v.t.* **kay·oed**, **kay·o·ing** In boxing, to knock out. — *n.* In boxing, a knockout. Also **K.O.**, **KO**, **k.o.** [< *k(nock) o(ut)*]

Kay·se·ri (kī′sə·rē′) A city in central Turkey; pop. 102,795 (1960): ancient *Caesarea Mazaca*.

Ka·zakh (kä·zäk′, *Russ.* kə·zäkh′) *n.* One of a Turkic people, formerly largely nomadic, dwelling in the Kazakh S.S.R.

Kazakh S.S.R. A constituent Republic of the south central Soviet Union; 1,064,000 sq. mi.; pop. 12,850,000 (1970);

capital, Alma-Ata. Also **Ka·zakh·stan** (kä′zäk·stän′, *Russ.* kə·zəkh·stän′) *Russian* **Ka·zakh′ska·ya S.S.R.** (-skä·yä).

Ka·zan (kə·zän′y′) The capital of the Tatar A.S.S.R. on the Volga; pop. 869,000 (est. 1970). Also **Ka·zan′′**.

ka·zoo (kə·zōō′) *n.* A toy musical instrument consisting of a small tube with a paper diaphragm that vibrates when one hums into the tube. [Origin uncertain, ? imit.]

KB King's bishop (chess).

K.B. **1.** King's Bench. **2.** Knight Bachelor.

KBP King's bishop's pawn (chess).

kc. or **kc** Kilocycle(s).

Kč. or **Kčs.** Koruna.

K.C. **1.** King's Counsel. **2.** Knights of Columbus.

kcal. Kilocalorie.

K.C.B. Knight Commander (of the Order) of the Bath.

K.C.V.O. Knight Commander of the (Royal) Victorian Order.

K.D. Knocked down.

ke·a (kā′ə, kē′ə) *n.* A large New Zealand parrot (*Nestor notabilis*), olive brown variegated with blue and green, that feeds on carrion and fruit. [< Maori]

Kean (kēn), **Edmund**, 1787–1833, English actor.

Kear·ny (kär′nē) A town in NE New Jersey, near Newark; pop. 37,585.

Kear·ny (kär′nē), **Philip**, 1814–62, U.S. general; killed in the Civil War.

Keats (kēts), **John**, 1795–1821, English poet.

ke·bar (kē′bär) See CABER.

keb·bie (keb′ē) *n.* *Scot.* A cudgel, or rude walking stick.

keb·bock (keb′ək) *n.* *Scot.* A cheese. Also **keb′buck.**

Ke·ble (kē′bəl), **John**, 1792–1866, English divine and poet; founder of the Oxford movement.

Kech·ua (kech′wä), **Kech·uan** (kech′wən) See QUECHUA, QUECHUAN.

keck¹ (kek) *v.i.* **1.** To heave as in vomiting; retch. **2.** To show or feel great disgust. [Imit.]

keck² (kek) *n.* A hollow stalk of a plant. [Back formation < KEX, mistaken as a plural]

keck·le (kek′əl) *v.t.* **·led**, **·ling** *Naut.* To wrap (a cable, etc.) with canvas, rope, etc., as protection against chafing. [Origin unknown]

Kecs·ke·mét (kech′ka·māt) A city in central Hungary; pop. 66,819 (1960).

Ke·dah (kā′dä) A State in Malaysia; on the Malay Peninsula; 3,660 sq. mi.; pop. 885,775 (est. 1966): capital, Alor Star.

ked·dah (ked′ə) *n.* An enclosure or corral for the capture of wild elephants: also spelled *khedah*. [< Hind. *khedā*]

kedge (kej) *Naut.* *n.* A light anchor used in warping, freeing a vessel from shoals, etc.: also **kedge anchor.** — *v.* **kedged, kedg·ing** *v.i.* **1.** To move a vessel by hauling up to a kedge that has been dropped at a distance. **2.** Of a vessel, to be moved in this way. — *v.t.* **3.** To move (a vessel) in this way. [Origin uncertain]

Ke·dron (kē′drən) A valley east of Jerusalem. *John* xviii 1. Also *Kidron*.

ke·ef (kē·ef′) See KEF.

keek (kēk) *v.i.* *Scot.* To peep; pry. [ME < MDu.]

keel¹ (kēl) *n.* **1.** *Naut.* a The main structural member of a vessel, running fore and aft along the bottom, to which all the crosswise members are solidly fixed; the backbone of a ship. **b** A fin keel (which see). **2.** A ship. **3.** Any part or object resembling a keel in shape or function. **4.** *Aeron.* **a** A vertical fin extending longitudinally at the bottom of an airship. **b** The center bottom of an airplane fuselage. **5.** *Biol.* A median longitudinal ridge or process, as of the breastbone of a fowl; carina. — **on an even keel** In equilibrium; steady. — *v.t.* & *v.i.* To turn over with the keel uppermost; capsize. — **to keel over 1.** To turn bottom up; capsize. **2.** To fall over or be felled, as from an injury. [< ON *kjölr* or OHG *kiol*. Akin to Du. *kiel*.]

keel² (kēl) *n.* **1.** A coal barge used on the Tyne in England. **2.** The quantity of coal in a barge load. **3.** A former British unit of weight for coal, equal to 21.2 long tons. [< MDu. *kiel* ship. Akin to OE *cēol* and ON *kjöll*.]

keel³ (kēl) *v.t.* *Obs.* To cool. [OE *cēlan*]

keel⁴ (kēl) *n.* *Scot.* Red chalk or ocher; ruddle.

Keel (kēl) *n.* The constellation Carina.

keel·age (kē′lij) *n.* *Naut.* The sum paid for anchoring a vessel in a harbor.

keel·boat (kēl′bōt′) *n.* A shallow, decked freight boat having a keel but no sails, usually propelled by poles or by the current, and used on rivers in the western United States.

keel·haul (kēl′hôl′) *v.t.* **1.** *Naut.* To haul (a man) underwater from one side of a ship to the other or from stem to stern as a torture or punishment. **2.** To reprove severely; castigate. Also **keel·hale** (kēl′hāl′). [< Du. *kielhalen*]

Kee·ling Islands (kē′ling) See COCOS ISLANDS.

keel·son (kēl′sən) *n.* *Naut.* A beam running above the keel of a ship: also spelled *kelson*. [Akin to KEEL¹]

Kee·lung (kē′lōōng′) A port city on northern Taiwan; pop. 304,740 (est. 1965): also *Kilung*, *Chilung*.

keen[1] (kēn) *adj.* **1.** Able to cut or penetrate readily; very sharp: a *keen* knife. **2.** Having mental acuteness, penetration, refined perception, etc. **3.** Manifesting intense absorption or eagerness: a *keen* interest. **4.** Of senses or sense organs, having great acuity and sensitivity: *keen* eyes. **5.** Having a piercing, intense quality or impact: a *keen* wind. **6.** Eager; enthusiastic: with *about*, *for*, *on*, or an infinitive. **7.** *U.S. Slang* Fine; excellent. **— Syn.** See ASTUTE. [ME *kene* < OE *cēne*] **— keen'ly** *adv.* **— keen'ness** *n.*

keen[2] (kēn) *n.* A wailing lamentation for the dead. **—** *v.i.* To wail loudly over the dead. [< Irish *caoine* < *caoinim* I wail] **— keen'er** *n.*

keep (kēp) *v.* **kept, keep·ing** *v.t.* **1.** To retain possession or control of; hold to or for oneself; avoid releasing or giving away: to *keep* one's earnings; to *keep* a secret. **2.** To hold or continue to hold in some specified state, condition, relation, place, etc.: *Keep* your hands off; *Keep* the car in repair; *Keep* dogs and cats apart. **3.** To store or hold in a regular place: He *keeps* his money in the bank; Where have you been *keeping* yourself? **4.** To continue or cause to continue; maintain: to *keep* step; to *keep* the peace. **5.** To be faithful to or abide by (a promise, vow, one's word, etc.). **6.** To do the required work of; manage; conduct: to *keep* a shop; to *keep* house. **7.** To defend from harm: May God *keep* you. **8.** To care for; be in charge of; tend: to *keep* the flocks. **9.** To detain: What's *keeping* him? **10.** To prevent: with *from*: What *keeps* it from falling? **11.** To confine: The prisoners are *kept* in cells. **12.** To observe, as with rites or ceremony; celebrate: to *keep* the Sabbath. **13.** To be the support of; maintain in food, clothing, etc. **14.** To write down and preserve in good order: to *keep* accounts; to *keep* a diary. **15.** To stay in or on: *Keep* your seat; *Keep* the path. **16.** To have regularly for sale; stock. **17.** To maintain for use or employ for service: to *keep* chickens; to *keep* a butler. **18.** To preserve in good condition, as foods. **—** *v.i.* **19.** To persist; continue: often with *on*: to *keep* talking; to *keep* on working. **20.** To remain; stay: *Keep* down; *Keep* away; *Keep* indoors. **21.** To stay in good condition: It will *keep* on ice. **22.** To remain good for a later time: The news will *keep.* **— Syn.** See RETAIN, CELEBRATE. **— to keep back 1.** To restrain. **2.** To withhold. **— to keep in with** *Informal* To remain in the good graces of. **— to keep to oneself 1.** To remain solitary. **2.** To avoid revealing. **— to keep track of** (or **tabs on**) To continue to be informed about. **— to keep up 1.** To hold the pace. **2.** To maintain in good condition. **3.** To cause to continue: *Keep up* the good work. **4.** To cause to stay awake or out of bed. **— to keep up with** To stay abreast of (someone or something). **—** *n.* **1.** Means of subsistence: to earn one's *keep*. **2.** Guard or custody; care: They are in my *keep*. **3.** The donjon or strongest building of a castle; also, a castle or fortress. **— for keeps 1.** Very seriously; not for mere amusement: to play *for keeps*. **2.** Permanently: It's yours *for keeps*. [OE *cēpan* to observe]

keep·er (kē'pər) *n.* **1.** One who keeps or guards; especially: **a** A guardian or protector. **b** The attendant of an insane person. **c** The overseer of a prison. **d** The caretaker of a wild animal. **2.** One in charge of (a specified place, thing, etc.): used in combination: *gatekeeper.* **3.** A device for keeping something in place, as a lock nut. **4.** Something that keeps without spoiling.

keep·ing (kē'ping) *n.* **1.** The act of one who keeps. **2.** Custody, charge, or possession. **3.** Maintenance; support. **— in keeping (with)** In right relation or proportion (to).

keep·sake (kēp'sāk') *n.* Anything kept, or given to be kept, for the sake of the giver; a memento.

kees·hond (kās'hond, kēs'-) *n. pl.* **·hond·en** (-hon'dən) A breed of dog, originally Arctic or sub-Arctic, with a short, closely knit body, thick, feathery coat, and curly tail. [< Du. *Kees*, nickname for Cornelius + *hond* dog; so called from the first breeder]

keeve (kēv) *n.* A large vat or tub. [OE *cýf*]

Kee·wa·tin (kē·wä'tin) A district of the Northwest Territories, Canada; 228,160 sq. mi.; pop. 2,413.

kef (kāf) *n.* **1.** A dreamy and languorous repose. **2.** Indian hemp or similar narcotic smoked to produce this state: also spelled *keef, kief.* [< Arabic *kaif* good humor]

keg (keg) *n.* A small, strong barrel, usually holding 5 to 10 gallons, or 100 pounds when used for nails. Abbr. *kg, kg.* [ME *cag*, prob. < ON *kaggi*]

keg·ler (keg'lər) *n. Informal* A bowler. [< G *kegel* ninepin]

Kei·jo (kā·jō) The Japanese name for SEOUL.

keir (kir) See KIER.

keis·ter (kēs'tər) *n. U.S. Slang* **1.** The buttocks. **2.** A box, trunk, suitcase, or the like. Also spelled *keyster, kiester*: also **keest'er.** [? < Yiddish < G *kiste* box]

Kei·tel (kī'tl), **Wilhelm,** 1882–1946, German field marshal in World War II; executed.

Keith (kēth), **Sir Arthur,** 1866–1955, British anthropologist.

keit·lo·a (kīt'lō·ə, kāt'-) *n.* A South African two-horned rhinoceros. [< Sechuana *kgetlwa*]

KEESHOND
(18 inches high
at shoulder)

Ke·ku·lé von Stra·do·nitz (kā'kōō·lā fôn shträ'dō·nits), **Friedrich August,** 1829–96, German chemist.

Ke·lan·tan (kə·län·tän') A State in northern Malaya; 5,750 sq. mi.; pop. 545,620 (est. 1959); capital, Kota Bharu.

Kel·ler (kel'ər), **Helen Adams,** 1880–1968, U.S. writer and lecturer; blind and deaf from infancy.

ke·loid (kē'loid) *n. Pathol.* A fibrous tumor in the connective tissue of the skin: also spelled *cheloid.* [< F *chéloïde, kéloïde* < Gk. *chēlē* crab's claw + -OID]

kelp (kelp) *n.* **1.** Any of various large, coarse, brown algae (family *Laminariaceae*); especially, the **giant kelp** (*Macrocystis pyrifera*) found mainly on the Pacific coast of the United States. **2.** The ashes of such algae, a source of iodine. [ME *culp*; origin uncertain]

kel·pie (kel'pē) *n. Scot.* A water sprite in the form of a horse, supposed to be an omen of drowning. Also **kel'py.**

kel·son (kel'sən) See KEELSON.

Kelt (kelt), **Kelt·ic** (kel'tik) See CELT, CELTIC.

kel·ter (kel'tər) *n. Brit. Dial.* Working order; kilter.

Kel·vin scale (kel'vin) *Physics* The absolute scale of temperature, based on the average kinetic energy per molecule of a perfect gas. Zero is equal to −273° Celsius or −459.4° Fahrenheit. [after William Thompson, 1824–1907, Lord *Kelvin*, English physicist]

Ke·mal A·ta·türk (ke·mäl' ä·tä·türk'), 1881–1938, Turkish general and statesman; founder of modern Turkey; first president 1923–38. Also *Mustafa Kemal.*

Kem·ble (kem'bəl), **Frances Anne,** 1809–93, English actress active in the United States: called **Fanny Kemble.** — **John Philip,** 1757–1823, English actor and theatrical manager; uncle of the preceding.

Ke·me·ro·vo (ke'mə·rō·vō, *Russ.* kye'myir·ə·və) A city in the south central Siberian R.S.F.S.R.; pop. 277,000 (1959).

Kem·pis (kem'pis), **Thomas à** See THOMAS À KEMPIS.

ken (ken) *v.* **kenned** or **kent, ken·ning** *v.t.* **1.** *Scot.* To know. **2.** *Scot. Law* To recognize as heir. **3.** *Archaic* To see. **—** *v.i.* **4.** *Scot. & Brit. Dial.* To have knowledge or understanding. **—** *n.* Range of sight or knowledge; cognizance. [OE *cennan*, infl. by ON *kenna*]

Ken. Kentucky (unofficial).

kench (kench) *n. U.S.* A bin for salting fish or skins. [? Var. of dial. E *canch* trench]

Ken·dal (ken'dal) *n.* **1.** A green woolen cloth made at Kendal, England. **2.** The color of this cloth. Also **Kendal green.**

Ken·il·worth (ken'əl·wûrth) An urban district in central Warwickshire, England; site of the ruins of **Kenilworth Castle** where Leicester entertained Queen Elizabeth I, 1575; pop. 14,427 (1961).

Ken·nan (ken'ən), **George Frost,** born 1904, U.S. diplomat and writer.

Ken·ne·bec River (ken'ə·bek) A river in central Maine, flowing about 150 miles south to the Atlantic.

Ken·ne·dy (ken'ə·dē), **Cape** A cape of eastern Florida, site of U.S. testing and launching center for rockets, missiles, and artificial satellites; formerly *Cape Canaveral.*

Ken·ne·dy (ken'ə·dē), **John Fitzgerald,** 1917–63, 35th president of the United States 1961–63; assassinated. — **Robert Francis,** 1925–68, U.S. Senator and political leader; brother of the preceding; assassinated.

ken·nel[1] (ken'əl) *n.* **1.** A house for a dog or for a pack of hounds. **2.** *Often pl.* An establishment where dogs are bred for sale, boarded, trained, etc. **3.** A pack of hounds. **4.** The hole or lair of a fox or like beast. **5.** A vile lodging. **—** *v.* **ken·neled** or **·nelled, ken·nel·ing** or **·nel·ling** **—** *v.t.* **1.** To keep or confine in or as in a kennel. **—** *v.i.* **2.** To lodge or take shelter in a kennel. [< MF *chenil* < L *canis* dog]

ken·nel[2] (ken'əl) *n.* The gutter of a street; channel; puddle. [ME *canel* < OF < L *canalem* channel]

Ken·nel·ly (ken'əl·ē), **Arthur Edwin,** 1861–1939, U.S. electrical engineer born in India.

Ken·nel·ly-Heav·i·side layer (ken'əl·ē·hev'ē·sīd) The Heaviside layer (which see).

Ken·ne·saw Mountain (ken'ə·sô) Two summits in NW Georgia; scene of a decisive Union victory in the Civil War, 1864; now a national monument.

ken·ning[1] (ken'ing) *n. Scot.* **1.** The smallest recognizable portion; a trace; shade. **2.** Recognition.

ken·ning[2] (ken'ing) *n.* In early Germanic poetry, a metaphor used instead of the name of a thing, as "oar-steed" for "ship." [< ON *kennungar* symbols]

Ken·ny (ken'ē), **Elizabeth,** 1886–1952, Australian nurse; developed a treatment for poliomyelitis: called **Sister Kenny.**

ke·no (kē'nō) *n.* A gambling game resembling lotto, in which balls are generally used as counters. Compare LOTTO, BINGO, BEANO. [? *Prob.* < F *quine* five winners < L *quini* five each < *quinque* five]

ke·no·gen·e·sis (kē'nə·jen'ə·sis, ken'ə-) *n.* Cenogenesis.

Ke·no·sha (kə·nō'shə) A city in SE Wisconsin, on Lake Michigan; pop. 117,917.

ke·no·sis (kə·nō'sis) *n. Theol.* The action of Christ in putting aside his divinity in the Incarnation. *Phil.* ii 5–8. [< Gk. *kenōsis* an emptying < *kenoein* to empty < *kenos* empty]

— ke·not·ic (kə·not'ik) *adj.*

ken·o·tron (ken'ə·tron) *n. Electronics* A two-electrode electron tube used as a rectifier. [< Gk. *kenōsis* an emptying + (ELEC)TRON]

Ken·sing·ton (ken'zing·tən) A metropolitan borough of western London; pop. 170,891 (1961).

Kent (kent) *n.* 1. A county in SE England; 1,525 sq. mi.; pop. 1,440,800 (1976); county seat, Maidstone. 2. An ancient kingdom of SE England.

Kent (kent), **James**, 1763–1847, U.S. jurist. — **Rockwell**, 1882–1971, U.S. artist and illustrator.

Kent·ish (ken'tish) *adj.* Of or pertaining to Kent. — *n.* The Old English and Middle English dialects of Kent.

kent·ledge (kent'lij) *n. Naut.* Permanent pig-iron ballast. [? < QUINTAL + -AGE]

Ken·tuck·y (kən·tuk'ē) An east central State of the United States; 40,395 sq. mi.; pop. 3,219,311; capital, Frankfort; entered the Union June 1, 1792; nickname *Bluegrass State.* Abbr. *Ky.* — **Ken·tuck'i·an** *adj. & n.*

Kentucky bluegrass See under BLUEGRASS.

Kentucky boat A large flat-bottomed river boat, usually towed or propelled by oars, formerly used for transporting freight. Also **Kentucky ark, Kentucky flat.**

Kentucky coffee 1. A tall tree (*Gymnocladus dioicus*) whose seeds were used as a substitute for coffee. 2. One of these seeds: also **Kentucky coffee bean.** Also called *coffee nut.*

Kentucky Derby A famous American horse race, run annually at Churchill Downs, Louisville, Ky., since 1875.

Kentucky River A river in Kentucky, flowing generally NW, 259 miles to the Ohio River.

Ken·ya (kēn'yə, ken'-) A republic of the Commonwealth of Nations in eastern Africa; 224,960 sq. mi.; pop. 12,430,000 (est. 1973); capital, Nairobi: formerly *East African Protectorate.* See map of ETHIOPIA.

Kenya, Mount An extinct volcano in central Kenya; 17,040 ft.

Ke·os (kē'os) An island of Greece in the Cyclades; ancient *Ceos, Cea:* medieval *Zea.*

kep (kep) *v.t. Scot.* To catch; stop. [Var. of KEEP, v.]

Ke·phal·le·ni·a (ke'fä·li·nē'ä) The Greek name for CEPHALONIA.

kep·i (kep'ē) *n.* A flat-topped military cap with vizor. [< F *képi* < dial. G (Swiss) *käppi,* dim. of *kappe* cap]

Kep·ler (kep'lər), **Johann**, 1571–1630, German astronomer; formulated **Kepler's laws** of planetary motion.

kept (kept) Past tense and past participle of KEEP.

Ke·ra·la (kā'rä lu) A State of extreme SW India; 15,003 sq. mi.; pop. 20,296,000 (est. 1971); capital, Trivandrum.

ke·ram·ic (kə·ram'ik), **ke·ram·ics** See CERAMIC, CERAMICS.

ker·a·tin (ker'ə·tin) *n. Biochem.* A highly insoluble albuminous compound that forms the essential ingredient of horny tissue, as of horns, claws, and nails. — **ke·rat·i·nous** (kə·rat'ə·nəs) *adj.* [< Gk. *keras, -atos* horn + -IN]

ker·a·ti·tis (ker'ə·tī'tis) *n. Pathol.* Inflammation of the cornea.

kerato- *combining form* 1. Horn: *keratogenous.* 2. Cornea of the eye: *keratoplasty.* Also, before vowels, **kerat-.** [< Gk. *keras, -atos* horn]

ker·a·to·con·junc·ti·vi·tis (ker'ə·tō·kən·jungk'tə·vī'tis) *n. Pathol.* Inflammation of the cornea and conjunctiva.

ker·a·tog·e·nous (ker'ə·toj'ə·nəs) *adj.* Promoting the growth of horn or horny tissue.

ker·a·toid (ker'ə·toid) *adj.* Resembling keratin or horn; horny. [< Gk. *keratoeidēs* hornlike]

ker·a·to·plas·ty (ker'ə·tō·plas'tē) *n. pl.* **·ties** *Surg.* The operation of transplanting corneal tissue; plastic surgery of the cornea. — **ker'a·to·plas'tic** *adj.*

ker·a·tose (ker'ə·tōs) *adj.* Of or like horny tissue.

kerb (kûrb) *n. Brit.* Curb (def. 2).

kerb·stone (kûrb'stōn') *n. Brit.* A curbstone (which see).

Kerch (kûrch, *Russ.* kyerch) A port city at the end of the **Kerch Peninsula,** an eastern extension of the Crimea; pop. 99,000 (1959). Also **Kerch'.**

ker·chief (kûr'chif) *n.* A square of fabric used to cover the head or neck, or as a handkerchief. [ME *keverchef, kerchef* < OF *couvrechef* < *covrir* to cover + *chef* head]

Ke·ren·sky (kə·ren'skē), **Alexander Feodorovich,** 1881–1970, Russian revolutionary leader; prime minister, July–Nov. 1917; removed by Bolsheviks.

Ke·res (kēr'ēz) *n. pl.* of Ker (kûr) In Greek mythology, malignant spirits and bringers of evil. [< Gk. *Kēres*]

kerf (kûrf) *n.* 1. The cut or notch made by a saw, ax, etc. 2. The piece or amount cut off. [OE *cyrf* a cutting]

Ker·gue·len Islands (kûr'gə·lən) An archipelago in the southern Indian Ocean, constituting a part of the French Southern and Antarctic Territories; 2,700 sq. mi.

Ker·ky·ra (ker'kē·rä) The Greek name for CORFU.

Ker·man (ker·män') A city in SE Iran; pop. 62,157 (1956).

Ker·man·shah (ker'män·shä') A city in western Iran; pop. 186,930 (1966). Also **Ker'man·sha·han'** (-hän').

ker·mes (kûr'mēz) *n.* 1. The dried bodies of the females of a scale insect (genus *Kermes*), used as a red dyestuff. 2. The kermes oak. [< Arabic *qirmiz.* Related to CRIMSON.]

kermes oak A small evergreen oak (*Quercus coccifera*) of the Mediterranean region, infested by the kermes insect.

ker·mis (kûr'mis) *n.* 1. In Flanders, etc., a periodical outdoor festival. 2. An indoor or outdoor festival imitative of this. Also spelled *kirmess:* also **ker·mess** (kûr'mis) [< Du. *kermis* < *kerk* church + *miss* mass]

kern¹ (kûrn) *Printing n.* The part of the face of a type that projects beyond the shaft or shank. — *v.t.* To form (type) with a kern. [< F *carne* corner < L *cardo, -inis* hinge]

kern² (kûrn) *n.* Formerly, especially in medieval times, a light-armed Irish foot soldier; also, a band of such soldiers. Also **kerne.** [ME < Irish *ceithern*]

Kern (kûrn), **Jerome (David)**, 1885–1945, U.S. composer.

ker·nel (kûr'nəl) *n.* 1. The entire contents of a seed or grain within its coating. 2. The edible part of a nut. 3. The central part of anything; nucleus; gist. — *v.i.* **ker·neled** or **·nelled, ker·nel·ing** or **·nel·ling** To envelop as a kernel. [OE *cyrnel,* dim. of *corn* seed]

ker·o·sene (ker'ə·sēn, ker'ə·sēn') *n.* A mixture of hydrocarbons distilled from crude petroleum and used for burning in lamps, stoves, and some engines: also called *coal oil.* Also **ker·o·sine** (ker'ə·sēn, ker'ə·sēn'). [< Gk. *kēros* wax + -ENE]

Ker·ry (ker'ē) *n. pl.* **·ries** One of an Irish breed of cattle raised in County Kerry.

Ker·ry (ker'ē) A county of Munster, SW Ireland; 1,815 sq. mi.; pop. 116,450 (est. 1969); county seat, Tralee.

Kerry blue terrier A terrier of a breed originating in Ireland, having a long head and soft, bluish gray coat.

ker·sey (kûr'zē) *n.* A coarse, ribbed, closely napped woolen cloth. [after *Kersey,* village in Suffolk, England]

ker·sey·mere (kûr'zē·mir) *n.* Cassimere.

Kes·sel·ring (kes'əl·ring), **Albert**, 1887–1960, German field marshal in World War II.

kes·trel (kes'trəl) *n.* A European falcon (*Falco tinnunculus*) resembling the American sparrow hawk, noted for its hovering habits. [ME *castrel* < OF *cresserelle*]

ketch (kech) *n.* A fore-and-aft rigged, two-masted vessel similar to a yawl but having the mizzen or jiggermast forward of the rudder post. [ME *cache,* prob. < CATCH, v., because used as a pursuit vessel]

KERRY BLUE TERRIER (18½ inches high at shoulder)

Ketch·i·kan (kech'i·kan) A port town in SE Alaska; pop. 6,994.

ketch·up (kech'əp) *n.* A spicy sauce or condiment for meat, fish, etc., of which the base is tomatoes, or sometimes mushrooms or walnuts: also spelled *catchup, catsup.* [< Malay *kēchap,* ? ult. < Chinese *ke-tsiap* brine of pickled fish]

GAFF-RIGGED KETCH

ke·tene (kē'tēn) *n. Chem.* 1. A pungent, colorless gas, $H_2C:CO$, obtained by decomposing acetone or acetic anhydride with intense heat. 2. Any of a group of organic compounds of the form $R_2C:CO$. [< KET(ONE) + -ENE]

keto- *combining form Chem.* Containing or characteristic of ketone. Also, before vowels, **ket-,** as in *ketosis.* [< KETONE]

ke·to·e·nol tautomerism (kē'tō·ē'nol, -ē'nol) *Chem.* Tautomerism in which certain organic compounds may occur in the ketone and enol forms.

ke·tone (kē'tōn) *n. Chem.* One of a class of organic compounds in which the carbonyl radical unites with two hydrocarbon radicals. The simplest member is acetone. [< G *keton,* var. of F *acétone* acetone] — **ke·ton·ic** (ki·ton'ik) *adj.*

ke·tose (kē'tōs) *n. Chem.* Any of a class of monosaccharides containing a ketone group.

ke·to·sis (ki·tō'sis) *n. Pathol.* Excessive formation of ketones in the body, as in acidosis and diabetes.

Ket·ter·ing (ket'ər·ing), **Charles Franklin,** 1876–1958, U.S. electrical engineer and inventor.

Ket·ter·ing (ket'ər·ing) A city in SW Ohio, near Dayton; pop. 71,864.

ket·tle (ket'l) *n.* 1. A metallic vessel for boiling or stewing. 2. A teakettle. 3. A kettle-shaped cavity, as in rock or glacial drift: also **kettle hole.** 4. A kettledrum. — **kettle of fish** A trying or difficult situation. [OE *cetel* < L *catillus,* dim. of *catinus* a deep vessel]

ket·tle·drum (ket'l·drum') *n.* A large drum having a copper or brass hemispherical shell and a parchment head that can be tuned through a small range of definite pitches; timpano.

Keu·ka Lake (kyoō'kə, kə·yoō'-) One of the Finger Lakes in west central New York.

kev·el (kev'əl) *n. Naut.* A belaying cleat or peg, usually used in pairs. [< OF (Norman) *keville* pin, peg < L *clavicula* bar of a door, dim. of L *clavis* key]

Kew (kyoō) A district of Richmond and suburb of London, in Surrey, England; pop. about 4,000.

Ke·wee·naw Peninsula (kē'wə·nô) A Michigan headland

PRONUNCIATION KEY: add, āce, câre, pälm; end, ēven; it, īce; odd, ōpen, ôrder; tŏŏk, pōōl; up, bûrn; ə = a in *above,* e in *sicken,* i in *flexible,* o in *melon,* u in *focus;* yōō = u in *fuse;* oil; pout; check; go; ring; thin; this; zh, vision. For å, œ, ü, kh, ń, see inside front cover.

extending 60 miles NE into Lake Superior to form **Kewee-naw Bay.**

Kew·pie (kyōō′pē) *n.* A chubby, cherubic doll, made of plastic, etc.: a trade name. Also **kew′pie doll.**

kex (keks) *n. Brit. Dial.* A dry, hollow stalk. [ME]

key[1] (kē) *n. pl.* **keys** 1. An instrument for moving the bolt or tumblers of a lock in order to lock or unlock. 2. An instrument for holding and turning a screw, nut, valve, or the like, as for winding a clock. 3. Anything serving to disclose, open, or solve something: the *key* to the puzzle. 4. Something that opens or prepares a way: the *key* to the situation. 5. A gloss, table, or group of notes interpreting certain symbols, ciphers, problems, etc. 6. Any one of the finger levers in typewriters, typesetting machines, computers, etc. 7. *Telecom.* A circuit breaker or opener operated by the fingers, as in a telegraph or radiotelegraph sending apparatus. 8. *Music* **a** In musical instruments, a lever to be pressed by the finger or thumb. **b** A system of tones in which a piece of music is written or performed, where all the tones bear a definite relationship to some specific tone (the keynote or tonic): the *key* of C. 9. The tone or pitch of the voice: to speak in a low *key.* 10. Level of intensity of expression, feeling, or artistic execution: He writes in a high *key.* 11. A characteristic tone or style: Keats's *key.* 12. *Mech.* **a** A wedge, cotter, bolt, or pin used to secure various parts. **b** One of various instruments for fixing a collar to a shaft. 13. *Archit.* A keystone. 14. In building, any special surfacing or surface for holding plaster in place. 15. In woodwork, the roughness on the unfinished face of a veneer giving stronger adherence to the glue. 16. *Bot.* A key fruit. — *v.t.* **keyed, key·ing** 1. To fasten with or as with a key. 2. To wedge tightly or support firmly with a key, wedge, etc. 3. To complete (an arch) by adding the keystone. 4. To provide with a key or keys. 5. To provide with a cross-reference or a system of cross-references. 6. To provide with a solution. 7. *Music* To regulate the pitch or tone of. — **to key up** 1. To raise the pitch or intensity of. 2. To cause excitement, expectancy, etc., in. — *adj.* Of chief and decisive importance: a *key* figure. [OE *cǣg*]

key[2] (kē) *n. pl.* **keys** A low island, especially one of coral, along a coast; cay. [< Sp. *cayo* < Taino, islet]

Key (kē), **Francis Scott**, 1779–1843, American lawyer and poet; wrote *The Star-Spangled Banner.*

key·board (kē′bôrd′, -bōrd′) *n.* A row or rows of keys as in a piano or typewriter; also, the range or arrangement of the keys, as of an organ, piano, etc.

key club *U.S.* A night club reserved for members who pay a fee to obtain a key.

keyed (kēd) *adj.* 1. Having keys, as a musical instrument, machine, etc. 2. In building, secured by a key or keystone. 3. Provided with cross-references or solutions.

key fruit *Bot.* A samara.

key·hole (kē′hōl′) *n.* A hole for a key, as in a door or lock.

key log The log caught or wedged in a log jam that must be released to break the jam.

Keynes (kānz), **John Maynard**, 1883–1946, first Baron of Tilton, English economist.

key·note (kē′nōt′) *n.* 1. The basic idea or principle of a philosophy, political platform, literary work, etc. 2. *Music* The tonic of a key, from which it is named: also **key tone.** — *v.t.* **·not·ed, ·not·ing** To sound the keynote of.

keynote address *U.S.* An opening address, especially at a political convention, presenting the basic issues and partisan principles. Also **keynote speech.**

key·not·er (kē′nō′tər) *n. U.S.* One who delivers a keynote address.

Key of the Mediterranean See GIBRALTAR.

key plug The part of a cylinder lock that receives the key. For illustration see LOCK.

key punch A keyboard machine for punching the cards or tape used in data-processing systems.

Keys (kēz) *n.pl.* The 24 members of the **House of Keys,** the elective branch of the legislature of the Isle of Man.

Key·ser·ling (kī′zər·ling), **Count Hermann Alexander,** 1880–1946, German philosopher born in Russia.

key signature *Music* The sharps or flats following the clef sign at the beginning of each staff, placed so as to apply to specific tones whenever they occur.

keyst·er (kēs′tər) See KEISTER.

key·stone (kē′stōn′) *n.* 1. *Archit.* The uppermost and last-set stone of an arch, that completes it and locks its members together. 2. The fundamental element, as of a science.

Keystone State Nickname of PENNSYLVANIA.

key·way (kē′wā′) *n.* 1. *Mech.* The groove or recess in a shaft or wheel hub for the insertion of a key: also called **key bed.** 2. The keyhole of a cylinder lock.

Key West A port city on **Key West Island,** westernmost of the Florida Keys; pop. 29,312.

kg. or **kg** 1. Keg(s). 2. Kilogram(s).

K.G. Knight (of the Order) of the Garter.

K.G.B. In the Soviet Union, the Commission of State Security, an agency charged with detecting and countering security threats from abroad. [< Russian *K(omissia) G(osudarstvennoy) B(ezopasnosti)*]

Kha·ba·rovsk Territory (khä·bä′rəfsk) An administrative division of the eastern R.S.F.S.R.; 318,400 sq. mi.; pop. 1,142,535 (1959); capital, **Khabarovsk,** pop. 437,000 (1967). *Russian* **Kha·ba·rov·skiy Kray** (khə·bə·rôf′skyē krī).

khad·dar (kud′ər) *n.* Homespun cotton cloth made in India. Also **kha·di** (kä′dē). [< Hind. *khǎdar*]

khak·i (kak′ē, kä′kē; *in Canada, often* kär′kē) *n. pl.* **khak·is** 1. A color ranging from light sand to medium brown. 2. A stout cotton cloth of this color used for uniforms. 3. *pl.* A uniform made of khaki; sun tans. — *adj.* Of the color khaki. [< Hind. *khākī* dusty < Persian *khāk* dust]

kha·lif (kā′lif, kal′if) See CALIPH.

Khal·ki·di·ki (khäl′kē·thē·kē′) A Greek name for CHALCIDICE.

kham·sin (kam′sin, kam·sēn′) *n.* A hot wind from the Sahara that prevails in Egypt and the Levant before the vernal equinox; simoom: also spelled *kamseen, kamsin.* Also **kham·seen** (kam·sēn′). [< Arabic *khamsīn* < *khamsūn* fifty; so called because it occurs for a period of 50 days]

khan[1] (kän, kan) *n.* 1. The title of the imperial successors to the Mongol conqueror Genghis Khan. 2. A title for rulers, officials, or dignitaries in Central Asia, Afghanistan, Iran, etc. [< Turkic *khān* lord, prince]

khan[2] (kän, kan) *n.* An Oriental inn surrounding a courtyard. [< Arabic *khān* inn < Persian]

khan·ate (kän′āt, kan′-) *n.* The realm of a khan.

Kha·nia (khä·nyä′) The Greek name for CANEA.

Khar·kov (kär′kôf, *Russ.* khäry′kəf) A city in the NE Ukrainian S.S.R.; pop. 1,223,000 (1970). Also **Khar′·kov.**

Khar·toum (kär·tōōm′) The capital of the Sudan, in the central part at the junction of the White and Blue Nile rivers; pop. 261,840 (est. 1971). Also **Khar·tum′.**

Khay·yám (kī·äm′), **Omar.** See OMAR KHAYYÁM.

kha·zen (khä′zən) See HAZZAN.

khed·ah (ked′ə) See KEDDAH.

khe·dive (kə·dēv′) *n.* The title of the Turkish viceroy of Egypt from 1867 to 1914. [< F *khédive* < Turkish *khedīv* < Persian]

Khe·lat (kə·lät′) See KALAT.

Kher·son (khyir·sôn′) A city in the southern Ukrainian S.S.R., near the mouth of the Dnieper; pop. 157,000 (1959).

khid·mut·gar (kid′mət·gär) *n. Hindi* A waiter.

Khi·os (khē′ôs) See CHIOS.

khir·kah (kir′kə) *n.* A garment made of patches and shreds, worn by dervishes. [< Arabic < *kharka* to tear, rend]

Khi·u·ma (khē′ōō·mä) See HIIUMA.

Khi·va (kē′və, *Russ.* khyē·və) A city in the Uzbek S.S.R.; former capital of an independent khanate; pop. about 15,000.

Khmer (kmer) *n.* 1. One of the native inhabitants of Cambodia, who developed a great civilization that reached its height in the 9th to 14th centuries. 2. The Austro-Asiatic language of the Khmers, related to Mon.

Khmer Republic The official name of CAMBODIA.

Khoi·san (koi′sän) *n.* A family of languages spoken by Negroid tribes in SW Africa, including the Bushman and Hottentot subfamilies.

Kholm (khôlm) The Russian name for CHELM.

Khond (kond) *n.* 1. A member of an aboriginal hill people of India, of Dravidian stock. 2. Their Dravidian language.

Kho·tan (kō′tän′) A town and oasis in the SW Sinkiang-Uighur Autonomous Region, China; pop. about 50,000: Chinese *Hotien.*

Khrush·chev (krōōsh·chôf′, *Russ.* khrōō·shchôf′), **Nikita Sergeyevich,** 1894–1971, Soviet statesman; first secretary of the Communist Party 1953–1964; chairman of the Council of Ministers (premier) 1958–1964.

Khu·fu (kōō′fōō) See CHEOPS.

Khu·zi·stan (khōō′zē·stän′) A region of SW Iran, corresponding to ancient Elam.

Khy·ber Pass (kī′bər) The chief pass on the Afghanistan-Pakistan border; over 30 miles long: also *Khaiber Pass.*

kHz Kilohertz.

KIA *Mil.* Killed in action.

Kiang·ling (jyäng′ling′) A city in southern Hupeh Province, China; pop. about 16,000: formerly *Kingchow.*

Kiang·si (jyäng′shē′) A Province in SE China; 63,629 sq. mi.; pop. 18,610,000 (est. 1957); capital, Nanchang.

Kiang·su (jyäng′sōō′) A Province in eastern China; 40,927 sq. mi.; pop. 45,230,000 (est. 1957); capital, Nanking.

Kiao·chow (jyou′chou′) A former German leased territory on the SE coast of Shantung, China; 400 sq. mi.

kib·butz (ki·bōōts′) *n. pl.* **·but·zim** (-bōōt·sēm′) A cooperative or collective farm in Israel. [< Hebrew, gathering]

kibe (kib) *n.* An ulcerated chilblain, especially one on the heel. [ME. Cf. Welsh *cibi* a chilblain.]

Ki·bei (kē′bā′) *n. pl.* **·bei** or **·beis** A U.S. citizen of Japanese parentage, born in the United States but educated in Japan. Compare ISSEI, NISEI. [< Japanese]

kib·itz (kib′its) *v.i. Informal* To act as a kibitzer. [Back formation < KIBITZER]

kib·itz·er (kib′it·sər) *n. Informal* One who meddles in the affairs of others; especially, a spectator who gives gratuitous advice to card players. [< Yiddish < G *kiebitzen* to look on < *kiebitz* peewit, perh. imit.]

kib·lah (kib′lä) *n.* The direction toward which Moslems kneel and bow in prayer, indicated by a niche on the wall in each mosque in Islam. See KAABA. [< Arabic *giblah* something placed opposite < *qabala* to be opposite]

ki·bosh (kī′bosh) *n. Archaic Slang* Nonsense; humbug. — **to put the kibosh on** To put a stop to; squelch. [Prob. < Yiddish]

kick (kik) *v.i.* **1.** To strike out with the foot or feet, as in swimming, propelling a ball, etc. **2.** To strike out habitually with the foot, hooves, etc.: This horse *kicks.* **3.** Of firearms, to recoil. **4.** In football, to punt, try for an extra point or field goal by kicking, etc. **5.** *U.S. Informal* To object or complain. — *v.t.* **6.** To strike with the foot. **7.** To drive or impel by striking with the foot. **8.** In football, to score (an extra point or a field goal) by kicking the ball. **9.** Of firearms, to strike in recoiling. — **to kick around** *U.S. Informal* **1.** To abuse; neglect. **2.** To roam from place to place. **3.** To be neglected; go unnoticed. **4.** To give thought or consideration to; discuss. — **to kick back 1.** To recoil violently or unexpectedly, as a gun. **2.** *U.S. Slang* To pay back (part of a commission, salary, fee, etc.) to someone in a position to grant favors, usually as a bribe. — **to kick in** *U.S. Informal* To contribute or participate by contributing. — **to kick off 1.** In football, to put the ball in play by kicking it toward the opposing team. **2.** *U.S. Slang* To die. — **to kick out** *U.S. Informal* To exclude or eject violently or suddenly, as with a kick. — **to kick the bucket** *Slang* To die. — **to kick the habit** *U.S. Slang* To free oneself of narcotic addiction. — **to kick up** *U.S. Slang* To make or stir up (trouble, confusion, etc.). — **to kick upstairs** *Informal* To give an apparent promotion to (someone) in order to remove from a position of actual power. — *n.* **1.** A blow or thrust with the foot. **2.** *U.S. Informal* An objection or complaint. **3.** *U.S. Slang* Power to stimulate, excite, or intoxicate: whisky with a *kick.* **4.** *U.S. Slang* A pleasant and exciting sensation; thrill. **5.** *U.S. Slang* Energy; vigor; pep. **6.** *U.S. Slang* An intense temporary interest. **7.** The recoil of a firearm. **8.** In football: **a** A kicking of the ball; especially, a punt. **b** A turn at kicking the ball. **c** The distance a kicked ball travels. **9.** The depression in the bottom of a molded bottle. [ME *kike*; origin unknown]

Kick·a·poo (kik′ə·po͞o) *n.* **1.** A member of a tribe of Algonquian Indians formerly of northern Illinois and SW Wisconsin. **2.** The Algonquian language of this tribe.

kick·back (kik′bak′) *n.* **1.** *Informal* A strong reaction; recoil; repercussion. **2.** *U.S. Slang* A paying back of part of a salary, fee, etc., also, the money so paid.

kick·er (kik′ər) *n.* **1.** One who or that which kicks. **2.** *U.S. Informal* A complainer. **3.** *U.S. Slang* Some concealed point that will affect the case or argument. **4.** *U.S. & Canadian Informal* An outboard motor or motorboat.

kick·off (kik′ôf′, -of′) *n.* **1.** In football, the kick with which play is begun. **2.** Any beginning.

kick plate A metal plate affixed to the bottom portion of a door to protect its surface. Also **kick·ing plate** (kik′ing).

kick·shaw (kik′shô) *n.* **1.** A trifle or trinket. **2.** Any unsubstantial, fancy, or unrecognizable dish of food. Also **kick′shaws** (-shôz). [Alter. of F *quelque chose* something]

kid[1] (kid) *n.* **1.** A young goat. **2.** Leather made from the skin of a kid. **3.** *pl.* Gloves or shoes made of kidskin. **4.** The meat of a young goat. **5.** *Informal* A child; youngster. — *adj. Informal* Younger: my *kid* brother. — *v.t. & v.i.* **kid·ded, kid·ding 1.** *Slang* To make fun of (someone); to tease. **2.** *Slang* To deceive or try to deceive (someone); fool. **3.** Of a goat, to give birth. [ME < ON *kith*] — **kid′der** *n.*

kid[2] (kid) *n.* **1.** A small tub for sailors' rations. **2.** On fishing vessels, a small wooden tub to hold fish. [? Var. of KIT[1]]

Kid (kid), **Thomas** See KYD.

Kidd (kid), **William**, 1645?–1701, British sea captain and pirate; hanged: called **Captain Kidd.**

Kid·der·min·ster (kid′ər·min′stər) *n.* A two-ply ingrain carpet, showing warp and filling on each side. [after *Kidderminster*, England, where first made]

kid·dy (kid′ē) *n. pl.* **·dies** *Slang* A small child. Also **kid′die.**

kid glove A glove made of kidskin or similar material. — **to handle with kid gloves** To treat tactfully or gingerly.

kid·nap (kid′nap) *v.t.* **kid·naped** or **·napped, kid·nap·ing** or **nap·ping 1.** To seize and carry off (someone) by force or fraud, usually so as to demand a ransom. **2.** To steal (a child). [< KID[1] (def. 5) + *nap,* dial. var. of NAB] — **kid′nap·er** or **kid′nap·per** *n.*

kid·ney (kid′nē) *n. pl.* **·neys 1.** *Anat.* Either of two glandular organs situated at the back of the abdominal cavity close to the spinal column in vertebrates, serving to separate waste products from the blood and to excrete them as urine. ◆ Collateral adjective: *renal.* **2.** The meat of the kidney of certain animals, used as food. **3.** Temperament, nature, or type: a man of my own *kidney.* [Origin unknown]

kidney bean 1. The edible kidney-shaped seed of a common plant (*Phaseolus vulgaris*) of the bean family. **2.** The plant itself. **3.** The bean of the scarlet runner.

kidney ore A variety of hematite found in compact, kidney-shaped masses.

kidney stone 1. *Pathol.* A hard mineral concretion formed in the kidney; renal calculus. **2.** A nephrite.

kidney vetch A European herb (*Anthyllis vulneraria*) of the pea family with clover-like red or yellow flower heads, formerly used in treating kidney diseases.

Ki·dron (kē′drən, kid′rən) See KEDRON.

kid·skin (kid′skin′) *n.* Leather tanned from the skin of a young goat, used for gloves, shoes, etc.

kief (kēf) See KEF.

Kiel (kēl) The capital of Schleswig-Holstein, West Germany, a port on the Baltic; pop. 270,700 (est. 1960).

Kiel Canal A ship canal from Kiel to the mouth of the Elbe; about 61 miles long.

Kiel·ce (kyel′tse) A city in SE central Poland; pop. about 74,000.

kier (kir) *n.* A vat in which fabrics are boiled, cleaned, and bleached: also spelled *keir.* [Prob. < ON *ker* tub]

Kier·ke·gaard (kir′kə·gôr), **Søren Aabye,** 1813–55, Danish philosopher and theologian.

kie·sel·guhr (kē′zəl·go͞or) *n.* Diatomaceous earth. [< G *kiesel* flint + *guhr* sediment]

kiest·er (kēs′tər) See KEISTER.

Ki·ev (kē·ev′, kē′ev; *Russ.* kyē′yif) The capital of the Ukrainian S.S.R., in the north central part on the Dnieper; pop. 1,632,000 (est. 1970).

kike (kīk) *n. Slang* A Jew: a vulgar and offensive term. [? < *-ki* or *-ky* ending of names of Russian Jewish immigrants]

Ki·kla·dhes (kē·klä′thes) The Greek name for CYCLADES: also *Kyklades.*

Ki·ku·yu (ki·ko͞o′yo͞o) *n. pl.* **·yu 1.** A member of a Bantu tribe of British East Africa in the area of Mount Kenya. **2.** The Bantu language of this tribe.

Ki·lau·e·a (kē′lou·ā′ə) An active crater on Mauna Loa volcano, on the island of Hawaii.

Kild. Kildare.

Kil·dare (kil·dâr′) A county in central Leinster Province, Ireland; 654 sq. mi.; pop. 64,402 (est. 1969); county seat, **Kildare.**

kil·der·kin (kil′dər·kin) *n.* **1.** A cask with the capacity of half a barrel. **2.** Formerly, an English measure equivalent to 18 U.S. gallons. [ME < MDu. *kinderkin, kindeken* little child; infl. by Med.L *quintale* quintal]

Kil·i·man·ja·ro (kil′i·män·jä′rō) The highest mountain in Africa, in NE Tanganyika; 19,565 ft.

Kilk. Kilkenny.

Kil·ken·ny (kil·ken′ē) A county in southern Leinster Province, Ireland; 796 sq. mi.; pop. 61,668 (est. 1969); county seat, **Kilkenny;** pop. 10,159 (est. 1969).

Kilkenny cats In Irish legend, two cats said to have fought until only their tails remained.

kill[1] (kil) *v.t.* **1.** To deprive of life; cause the death of. **2.** To slaughter for food; butcher. **3.** To bring to an end; destroy; ruin. **4.** *U.S. Slang* To make a very strong emotional impression upon, as of amusement, embarrassment, etc. **5.** To destroy the active qualities of; neutralize. **6.** To spoil the effect of; cancel by contrast, as a color. **7.** In printing, to expunge or delete. **8.** To turn off or stop (a motor, live circuit, etc.). **9.** To pass (time) aimlessly. **10.** In tennis, to hit (a ball) to an opponent so hard that it cannot be returned. **11.** To veto or quash (legislation). — *v.i.* **12.** To cause death; put an end to life. **13.** To murder; slay. **14.** To undergo death; die. — *n.* **1.** The act of killing, especially in hunting. **2.** An animal or animals killed as prey or quarry. — **in at the kill** Present at the climax. [ME *cullen, killen*; origin uncertain]
— **Syn.** (verb) **1.** *Kill, slay, dispatch, murder, assassinate,* and *execute* mean to put to death. *Kill* is the general term applicable to all organisms, and frequently extended to inanimate things: frost *killed* the buds, to *kill* a story. *Slay,* now chiefly a literary word, means to *kill* violently and intentionally. *Dispatch* is largely a euphemism, and suggests haste or casualness. *Murder, assassinate,* and *execute* are said only of persons. *Murder* refers to a deliberate, often premeditated, killing; *assassinate* means to *murder* stealthily, and is often applied to political killings. *Execute* refers to the carrying out of a legal sentence of death.

kill[2] (kil) *n.* A creek, stream, or channel: an element in many U.S. geographical names: *Schuylkill.* [< Du. *kil* < MDu. *kille*]

Kil·lar·ney (ki·lär′nē) An urban district of central County Kerry in SW Ireland near the three **Lakes of Killarney;** pop. about 6,300.

kill·deer (kil′dir) *n. pl.* **·deers** or **·deer** A North American wading bird (*Charadrius vociferus*) of the plover family, having a loud cry. Also **kill′dee** (-dē). [Imit., from its cry]

HUMAN KIDNEY
a Pyramid.
b Papillae.
c Cortex. *d* Ureter. *e* Pelvis.

kill·er (kil′ər) *n.* **1.** One who or that which kills. **2.** The killer whale. **3.** *U.S. Slang* A very attractive person.

killer whale Any of a genus (*Orcinus*) of cetaceans related to the dolphins and noted for their voracity; especially, the **Atlantic killer** (*O. orca*) and the **Pacific killer** (*O. rectipinna*). Also called *grampus*.

KILLER WHALE
(20 to 30 feet long)

kil·lick (kil′ək) *n. Naut.* A small anchor; especially, a heavy stone in a wooden frame used as an anchor for small boats. Also **kil′lock.** [Origin unknown]

Kil·lie·cran·kie (kil′ē·krang′kē) A mountain pass in the Grampians, Scotland; scene of a battle in 1689.

kil·li·fish (kil′i·fish′) *n. pl.* **·fish** or **·fish·es** Any of a family (*Cyprinodontidae*) of widely distributed small fishes (*Fundulus* and related genera), found in fresh or brackish waters of North America. [Appar. < KILL² + FISH]

kil·li·kin·ick (kil′ē·ki·nik′) *n.* Kinnikinic (which see).

kill·ing (kil′ing) *n.* **1.** Homicide. **2.** The act of one who or that which kills. — **to make a killing** To get or win an extraordinarily large amount of money. — *adj.* **1.** Used to kill. **2.** Likely to kill. **3.** Resulting in death; fatal.

kill·joy (kil′joi′) *n.* One who spoils pleasure for others.

Kil·mar·nock (kil·mär′nək) A burgh in northern Ayr, Scotland; pop. 47,509 (1961).

Kil·mer (kil′mər), (**Alfred**) **Joyce**, 1886–1918, U.S. poet and editor; killed in World War I.

kiln (kil, kiln) *n.* An oven or furnace for baking, burning, or drying bricks, lime, pottery, cement, etc. [OE *cylne* < L *culina* kitchen]

kiln-dry (kil′drī′, kiln′-) *v.t.* **-dried, -dry·ing** To dry in a kiln.

kil·o (kil′ō, kē′lō) *n. pl.* **kil·os** **1.** A kilogram. **2.** A kilometer. Abbr. *k*

kilo- *prefix* In the metric system, a thousand times (a specified unit): *kilogram.* [< F < Gk. *chilioi* a thousand]

kilo. **1.** Kilogram(s): also **kilog.** **2.** Kilometer(s): also **kilom.**

kil·o·cal·o·rie (kil′ə·kal′ə·rē) *n.* A kilogram calorie. See under CALORIE. Abbr. *kcal.*

kil·o·cy·cle (kil′ə·sī′kəl) *n.* **1.** *Telecom.* A unit of electromagnetic wave frequency of 1,000 cycles per second. **2.** One thousand cycles. Abbr. *kc, kc.*

kil·o·gram (kil′ə·gram) *n.* In the metric system, a thousand grams. Also **kil′o·gramme.** [< F *kilogramme*] Abbr. *k., K.; kg, kg., kilo., kilog.* See table inside back cover.

kilogram calorie See under CALORIE.

kil·o·gram-me·ter (kil′ə·gram-mē′tər) *n.* A unit of work, the equivalent of the force expended in raising a mass of one kilogram one meter against gravity, about 7.2 foot-pounds. Also *esp. Brit,* **kil′o·gram-me′tre.**

kil·o·hertz (kil′ə·hurts′) *n.* A kilocycle. Abbr. *kHz.*

kilol. Kiloliter.

kil·o·li·ter (kil′ə·lē′tər) *n.* In the metric system, a thousand liters. Also *esp. Brit.* **kil′o·li·tre.** Abbr. *kl, kl., kilol.* See table inside back cover.

kil·o·me·ter (kil′ə·mē′tər, ki·lom′ə·tər) *n.* In the metric system, a thousand meters. Also *esp. Brit.* **kil′o·me′tre.** Abbr. *km, km., kilo., kilom.* See table inside back cover. — **kil·o·met·ric** (kil′ə·met′rik) or **·ri·cal** *adj.* [< F *kilomètre*]

kil·o·ton (kil′ə·tun′) *n.* **1.** A weight of 1,000 tons. **2.** A unit equivalent to the explosive power of 1,000 tons of TNT; used in expressing the energy of thermonuclear weapons.

kil·o·watt (kil′ə·wät) *n. Electr.* A unit of power equal to 1,000 watts. Abbr. *kw, kw.*

kil·o·watt-hour (kil′ə·wät·our′) *n.* The work done or the energy resulting from one kilowatt acting for one hour, equal to approximately 1.34 horsepower-hours. Abbr. *K.W.H., kw-h, kwh, kw-hr, kw.-hr.*

kilt (kilt) *n.* A short pleated skirt worn by Scottish Highland men and Irishmen. — *v.t.* **1.** To make broad, vertical pleats in; pleat. **2.** *Scot.* To tuck up, as a skirt. [ME; prob. < Scand. Cf. Dan. *kilte* to tuck up.] — **kilt′ing** *n.*

kilt·ed (kil′tid) *adj.* **1.** Attired in a kilt. **2.** Gathered in pleats; pleated. **3.** Tucked up.

kil·ter (kil′tər) *n. Informal* Proper or working order: now only in the phrase **out of kilter,** out of order. Also, *Brit. Dial.,* **kelter.** [Origin uncertain]

kil·tie (kil′tē) *n. Scot.* One who wears a kilt, especially a regimental kilt. Also **kilt′y.**

kilt·ing (kil′ting) *n.* A series of flat overlapping pleats.

Ki·lung (kē′lŏŏng′) See KEELUNG.

kim·ber·lite (kim′bər·līt) *n.* A variety of peridotite occurring in South Africa, and decomposing into a clay rich in deposits of diamonds: also called *blue ground.*

Kim·ber·ley (kim′bər·lē) A city in northern Cape of Good Hope Province, South Africa; pop. 77,180 (1960).

ki·mo·no (kə·mō′nə, ki·mō′nō) *n. pl.* **·nos** **1.** A loose robe fastened with a wide sash, worn in Japan as an outer garment. **2.** A woman's negligee. [< Japanese]

kin (kin) *n.* One's relatives by blood, collectively; one's family; one's kinsfolk. — **next of kin** In law, one's nearest relative or relatives. — *adj.* **1.** Related by blood; consanguineous. **2.** Similar in one or more ways; kindred; alike. [OE *cyn.* Akin to KIND². Cf. L *genus,* Gk. *genos* race.]

-kin *suffix* Little; small: *lambkin.* [< MDu. *-kijn, -ken*]

ki·na (kē′nä) *n.* The monetary unit of Papua New Guinea, equivalent to 100 toea.

kin·aes·the·sia (kin′is·thē′zhə, -zhē·ə), **kin·aes·the·sis** (kin′is·thē′sis) See KINESTHESIA, etc.

kin·ase (kin′ās, kī′nās) *n. Biochem.* An enzyme capable of activating another enzyme. [< KIN(ETIC) + -ASE]

Kin·car·dine (kin·kär′din) A county in eastern Scotland; 382 sq. mi.; pop. 48,810 (1961), excluding Aberdeen; county seat, Stonehaven: also *The Mearns.* Also **Kin·car′dine·shire** (-shir).

Kin·chin·jun·ga (kin′chin·jung′gə) See KANCHENJUNGA.

kind¹ (kīnd) *adj.* **1.** Gentle and considerate in behavior; goodhearted; benign. **2.** Proceeding from or manifesting goodheartedness: a *kind* act. **3.** *Archaic* Affectionate; loving. **4.** *Obs.* Natural; appropriate; lawful. [OE *gecynde*] — **Syn.** 1. sympathetic, kindly, gracious, compassionate, benevolent. Compare CHARITABLE, HUMANE.

kind² (kīnd) *n.* **1.** A class or grouping; type; variety. **2.** The distinguishing nature or character of something: They differ in *kind.* **3.** *Obs.* Nature in general; the ordained and proper course of things. — **in kind** **1.** With a thing of the same sort: to return an insult *in kind.* **2.** In produce instead of money: to pay taxes *in kind.* — **kind of** *Informal* In a way; somewhat: This is *kind of* foolish. — **of a kind** Inferior in quality; of sorts. [OE *gecynd.* Akin to KIN.]

◆ Although the construction used in *these kind* (or *sort*) *of books are,* where *kind of* (or *sort of*) is sensed as an adjective qualifying the following substantive, is not regularly accepted in formal writing, it has a long literary history and is considered correct by some authorities.

kin·der·gar·ten (kin′dər·gär′tən) *n.* A school or class for young children, usually from the ages of four to six, in which the development of basic skills and socialization is furthered through games, music, handcrafts, group play, etc. [< G]

kin·der·gart·ner (kin′dər·gärt′nər) *n.* A kindergarten pupil or teacher. Also **kin′der·gar·ten·er** (-gär′tən·ər). [< G]

kind·heart·ed (kīnd′här′tid) *adj.* Having or showing a kind and sympathetic nature. — **kind′heart′ed·ly** *adv.* — **kind′heart′ed·ness** *n.*

kin·dle (kin′dəl) *v.* **·dled, ·dling** *v.t.* **1.** To cause to burn; set fire to; ignite. **2.** To excite or inflame, as the feelings or passions. **3.** To make bright or glowing as if with flame. — *v.i.* **4.** To take fire; start burning. **5.** To become excited or inflamed. **6.** To become bright or glowing. [ME < ON *kynda*] — **kin·dler** *n.*

kind·less (kīnd′lis) *adj.* **1.** *Poetic* Heartless; unkind. **2.** *Obs.* Unnatural; degenerate. — **kind′less·ly** *adv.*

kin·dling (kind′ling) *n.* **1.** Sticks, small pieces of wood, or other material with which a fire is started or kindled. **2.** The act of one who or that which kindles.

kind·ly (kīnd′lē) *adj.* **·li·er, ·li·est** **1.** Having or showing kindness; sympathetic; kind. **2.** Having a favorable effect; beneficial: a *kindly* sun. **3.** *Obs.* Proper to its kind; natural. — *adv.* **1.** In a kind manner or spirit; good-naturedly. **2.** Enthusiastically; heartily: I thank you *kindly.* — **to take kindly to** **1.** To accept with liking or interest: to *take kindly to* new ideas. **2.** To be naturally attracted to: A duck *takes kindly* to water. — **kind′li·ness** *n.*

kind·ness (kīnd′nis) *n.* **1.** The quality of being kind; good will; kindly disposition. **2.** A kind act or service; a favor. **3.** A kindly feeling. — **Syn.** See BENEVOLENCE.

kin·dred (kin′drid) *adj.* **1.** Belonging to the same family; related by blood; akin. **2.** Having a like nature or character; similar; cognate; related. — *n.* **1.** One's relatives by blood. **2.** A family, clan, or other group related by blood. — **Syn.** Compare RELATIONSHIP. [ME *kynrede* < OE *cynn* kin + *rǣden* condition]

kine (kīn) *n. Archaic* Cattle: plural of COW¹.

kin·e·mat·ics (kin′ə·mat′iks) *n.pl. (construed as sing.)* The branch of physics treating of motion without reference to particular forces or bodies. [< Gk. *kinēma, -atos* movement < *kineein* to move] — **kin′e·mat′ic** or **·i·cal** *adj.* — **kin′e·mat′i·cal·ly** *adv.*

kin·e·mat·o·graph (kin′ə·mat′ə·graf, -gräf) See CINEMATOGRAPH.

kin·e·scope (kin′ə·skōp) *n.* **1.** The cathode-ray tube of a television set, which reproduces by the action of an electron beam upon a fluorescent or phosphorescent screen: also called *picture tube.* **2.** A filmed record of a television program: also **kin·e** (kin′ē). [< KINE(MATOGRAPH) + -SCOPE]

kinesi- *combining form* A movement: *kinesimeter.* [< Gk. *kinēsis* motion]

ki·ne·sim·e·ter (ki·nə·sim′ə·tər) *n.* An instrument for measuring the motion of a part of the body. Also **ki·ne·si·om·e·ter** (ki·nē′sē·om′ə·tər).

-kinesis *combining form* **1.** Movement; activation: *telekinesis.* **2.** Division: *karyokinesis.* [< Gk. *kinēsis* motion]

kin·es·the·si·a (kin′is·thē′zhə, -zhē·ə) *n. Physiol.* The perception of muscular movement, tension, etc., derived from the functioning of afferent nerves connected with muscle tissue, skin, joints, and tendons: also called *muscle sense*: also spelled *kinaesthesia*. Also **kin·es·the·sis** (-thē′sis). [< NL < Gk. *kineein* to move + *aisthēsis* perception] — **kin′es·thet′ic** (-thet′ik) *adj.*

ki·net·ic (ki·net′ik) *adj.* **1.** Of or pertaining to motion. **2.** Producing or caused by motion: *kinetic* energy. [< Gk. *kinētikos* < *kineein* to move]

ki·ne·tics (ki·net′iks) *n.pl.* (*construed as sing.*) The branch of physics dealing with the effect of forces in the production or modification of motion in bodies.

kinetic theory *Physics* **1.** The theory that matter in all its forms is composed of small particles in constant random motion. **2.** The theory of the direct relation between the temperature of a gas, liquid, or solid and the average velocity of the particles composing it.

kineto- *combining form* A movement. [< Gk. *kinētos* moving]

kin·folk (kin′fōk′) *n.pl.* One's relatives or family; kin: also *kinsfolk.* Also **kin′folks′** (-fōks′).

king (king) *n.* **1.** The sovereign male ruler of a kingdom; monarch. ◆ Collateral adjective: *regal.* **2.** One who is preeminent among others of the same kind or class: a cattle *king.* **3.** Any one of the four playing cards in a deck bearing the likeness of a king. **4.** In chess, the principal piece, for whose defense all the moves of the other pieces are made. Abbr. *K.* **5.** In checkers, a piece that, having reached the opponent's last rank of squares, is then crowned and may move in any direction. Abbr. *k., K.* [OE *cyng, cyning*]

King (king), **Charles Glen,** 1878–1956, U.S. chemist. — **Ernest Joseph,** 1878–1956, U.S. admiral; Chief of Naval Operations in World War II. — **Martin Luther, Jr.,** 1929–68, U.S. leader of nonviolent civil rights movement for Negroes; winner of Nobel peace prize in 1964; assassinated. — **Rufus,** 1755–1827, American statesman and diplomat. — **William Lyon Mackenzie,** 1874–1950, Canadian statesman; prime minister 1921–26, 1926–30, 1935–48: called **Mackenzie King.**

king apple A kind of winter apple with red stripes.

King Arthur See ARTHUR.

king·bird (king′bûrd′) *n.* Any of various North American flycatchers (genus *Tyrannus*); especially, the **Eastern kingbird** (*T. tyrannus*), or bee martin.

king·bolt (king′bōlt′) *n.* A vertical central bolt attaching the body of a wagon or similar vehicle to the fore axle, or a railroad car to a truck, and serving as a pivot in turning: also called *kingpin.*

King Charles spaniel A black-and-tan breed of toy spaniel, originating in the Far East and having a rounded head, short, turned-up nose, and long, silky coat.

King·chow (king′jō′) A former name for KIANGLING.

king crab **1.** The horseshoe crab (which see). **2.** Any of a genus (*Paralithodes*) of usually large crablike crustaceans (family *Lithodidae*), common in the north Pacific, with a small, triangular body and very long legs; especially, the **Alaskan king crab** (*P. camtschatica*), used as food.

king·craft (king′kraft′, -kräft′) *n.* The craft or calling of kings; kingly statesmanship.

king·cup (king′kup′) *n. Chiefly Brit.* **1.** Any of several common buttercups. **2.** The common marsh marigold.

king·dom (king′dəm) *n.* **1.** The territory, people, state, or realm ruled by a king or a queen; monarchy. **2.** Any place or area of concern thought of as a sovereign domain; sphere. **3.** Any one of the three primary divisions of natural objects known as the *animal, vegetable,* and *mineral kingdoms.* **4.** The spiritual dominion of God. **5.** *Archaic* The authority or rule of a king or queen; kingship. [OE *cyningdom*]

king·fish (king′fish′) *n. pl.* **·fish** or **·fish·es** **1.** Any of various American food fishes (genus *Menticirrhus*), especially one species (*M. saxatilis*) common on the northern Atlantic coast. **2.** The cero. **3.** The king mackerel. **4.** *U.S. Informal* A leader who exercises uncontested power.

king·fish·er (king′fish′ər) *n.* Any of several nonpasserine birds (family *Alcedinidae*) of world-wide distribution, generally crested, with straight, deeply cleft bills, that feed on fish; especially, the **eastern belted kingfisher** (*Megaceryle alcyon*) of the United States.

King Horn The hero of certain medieval English and French romances.

King James Bible An English translation of the Bible from Hebrew and Greek, proposed by James I and completed by Anglican scholars in 1611, the version used by most English-speaking Protestants. Also **Authorized Version.** Abbr. *Auth. Ver., A.V.* Complete revisions were published in England in 1885 (**Revised Version**), abbr. *E.R.V., E.V.,* and in the United States in 1901 (**American Standard Version** or **American Revised Version**), abbr. *A.R.V.,* and in 1952 (**Revised Standard Version**), abbr. *RSV, R.S.V.*

King Lear See LEAR.

king·let (king′lit) *n.* **1.** A young or insignificant king. **2.**

Any of several small birds, resembling the warblers; especially, the American **golden-crowned kinglet** (*Regulus satrapa*) and the **ruby-crowned kinglet** (*R. calendula*).

king·ly (king′lē) *adj.* **·li·er, ·li·est** Pertaining to or worthy of a king; regal; kinglike. — *adv.* In a regal or kingly way; royally. — **king′li·ness** *n.*
— **Syn.** (adj.) *Kingly, royal, regal, princely,* and *imperial* mean of or like a monarch. All may be applied to a king's office or power. In addition, *kingly* is used chiefly of personal qualities, *royal* asserts direct connection with a reigning house, and *regal* is applied to the character of a *royal* court: *kingly* forbearance, a *royal* palace, *regal* robes. *Princely,* in extended use, suggests opulence or generosity: a *princely* gift; *imperial,* referring to an emperor, suggests greater power, grandeur, etc., than *kingly*: *imperial* armies, an *imperial* crown.

king mackerel A large food fish (*Scomberomorus cavalla*) of warm American waters: also called *cavalla, cero, kingfish.*

king-of-arms (king′uv·ärmz′) *n.* In Great Britain, one of a body of officials instituted in 1484 to examine and inquire concerning rights and titles in heraldry. Also **king of arms.**

king·pin (king′pin′) *n.* **1.** In bowling or tenpins, the foremost pin of a set arranged in order for playing: also called *head pin.* **2.** In ninepins, the center pin. **3.** A kingbolt. **4.** *Informal* The person of central importance in a group, etc.

king post In carpentry, a single vertical strut supporting the apex of a triangular truss and resting on a crossbeam. For illustration see ROOF. Also **king·post** (king′pōst′).

Kings (kingz) *n.pl.* (*construed as sing.*) **1.** Either of two books, I Kings and II Kings, of the Old Testament, recounting the histories of the Hebrew kings after David. **2.** In the Douai version of the Old Testament, a group of four books, comprising I Samuel, II Samuel, I Kings, and II Kings.

king salmon The chinook salmon (which see).

King's Bench See COURT OF KING'S BENCH.

King's Counsel In Great Britain and Canada, barristers who are designated as counsel of the crown: in the reign of a queen called **Queen's Counsel.** Abbr. *K.C., Q.C.*

king's English Standard English considered as set by official authority: also called *queen's English.*

king's evidence *Brit. Law* State's evidence: in the reign of a queen called **queen's evidence.**

king's evil Scrofula: formerly supposed to be curable by a monarch's touch.

king's highway In Canada, a main road maintained by a provincial government: in the reign of a queen called **queen's highway.**

king·ship (king′ship) *n.* **1.** The state, power, office, or dignity of a king. **2.** The monarchical type of government, and the realm so governed; monarchy; kingdom. **3.** As a title, the person of a king: his royal *kingship.*

king-size (king′sīz′) *adj. Informal* Greater in length or size than is usual. Also **king′-sized′** (-sīzd′).

Kings·ley (kingz′lē), **Charles,** 1819–75, English clergyman and novelist. — **Sidney,** born 1906, U.S. playwright.

King's Lynn A municipal borough of western Norfolk, England; pop. 26,173 (1951): also *Lynn, Lynn Regis.*

Kings Mountain A ridge in Northern South Carolina; scene of an American victory in the Revolutionary War, 1780.

king snake A large, harmless, colubrine snake (*Lampropeltis getulus*) of the southern United States that kills other snakes and feeds largely on rats and mice.

Kings·port (kingz′pôrt, -pōrt) A city in NE Tennessee, on the Holston River; pop. 31,938.

King's Scout In Great Britain and Canada, a Boy Scout of the highest rank: in the reign of a queen called **Queen's Scout.**

king's silver A soft, very pure silver formerly used for costly dishes and plate.

King·ston (king′stən, kingz′tən) **1.** The capital of Jamaica, a port on the SE coast; pop. 125,526 (est. 1961, including Port Royal). **2.** A city in SE New York, on the Hudson River; pop. 25,544. **3.** A city in SE Ontario, Canada; pop. 53,526.

King·ston-on-Thames (king′stən·on′temz′, kingz′tən-) A municipal borough in NE Surrey, England; site of the **King's Stone** on which the West Saxon kings were crowned and of the last battle of the Civil War, 1648; pop. 36,450 (1961). Also **King′ston-up·on′-Thames/.**

King·ston-up·on-Hull (king′stən·ə·pon′hul′, kingz′tən-) The county seat of Humberside, England; pop. 278,800 (1976): also *Hull.*

Kings·town (king′stən, kingz′toun) The capital of St. Vincent in the Windward Islands; a port on the southwestern coast; pop. 21,000 (est. 1969).

Kings·ville (kingz′vil) A city in southern Texas; pop. 28,915.

king truss A truss, as in roofing, having a king post.

king·wood (king′wŏŏd′) *n.* **1.** The wood of a Brazilian tree (*Dalbergia cearensis*) prized in cabinetwork for its fine texture and violet stripings. **2.** The tree producing this wood.

kin·in (kī′nin) *n. Biochem.* **1.** Any of a group of peptide compounds produced in blood and other animal tissues and believed to have a hormonelike effect on the blood and smooth animal tissue. **2.** Loosely, phytokinin (which see). [< Gk. *kinēma* motion < *kinein* to move + -IN]

kink (kingk)　　*n.*　**1.** An abrupt bend, curl, or tangle in a line, hair, etc. **2.** A mental quirk. **3.** A painful cramp. **4.** A slight defect in a plan, process, system, etc. — *v.i. & v.t.* To form or cause to form a kink or kinks. [< Du., twist, curl]

kink·a·jou (king′kə·jōō)　*n.* An arboreal, carnivorous mammal (*Potos flavus*), related to the raccoon, of the warmer parts of Central and South America, having large eyes, soft woolly fur, and a long prehensile tail: also called *honey bear.* [< F *quincajou* < Tupi]

kink·y (kingk′ē)　*adj.* **kink·i·er, kink·i·est** **1.** Kinked; frizzy. **2.** *U.S. Slang* Weird; perverse. — **kink′i·ness** *n.*

kin·ni·ki·nic (kin′ē·kə·nik′)　*n.* A mixture of ground leaves and bark of certain plants, smoked by some American Indians: sometimes called *killikinnic.* Also **kin′ni·kin·nic′, kin′ni·kin·nick′.** [< Algonquian, lit., that which is mixed]

KINKAJOU
(About 3 feet long)

ki·no (kē′no)　*n.* The dried, red, astringent juice or gum of certain tropical plants, used in medicine and tanning. Also **kino gum.** [< native W. African name]

Kin·ross (kin·rôs′)　A county of east central Scotland: 82 sq. mi.; pop. 6,704 (1961); county seat, **Kinross;** pop. about 2,500. Also **Kin·ross′shire** (-shir).

Kin·sey (kin′zē), **Alfred Charles,** 1894–1956, U.S. zoologist; published statistical reports on U.S. sexual behavior.

kins·folk (kinz′fōk′)　*n.pl.* Kinfolk.

Kin·sha·sa (kēn·shä′sä)　The capital of the Republic of Zaire, in the western part; formerly *Léopoldville;* pop. 1,323,039 (1970).

kin·ship (kin′ship)　*n.* Relationship, especially by blood. — Syn. See RELATIONSHIP.

kins·man (kinz′mən)　*n.* *pl.* **·men** (-mən) A male blood relation. — **kins′wom·an** (-wŏŏm′ən) *n.fem.*

ki·osk (kē·osk′, kē′osk, kī′-)　*n.* **1.** In Turkey, a lightly constructed, open summerhouse or pavilion. **2.** A similar structure, used as a booth, newsstand, bandstand, etc. [< F *kiosque* < Turkish *kiûshk* < Persian *kûshk* palace]

Kio·to (kyō·tō)　See KYOTO.

Ki·o·wa (kī′ə·wä, -wə)　*n.* A member of a tribe of Plains Indians formerly inhabiting parts of Nebraska and Wyoming.

kip[1] (kip)　*n.* **1.** The untanned skin of a calf, a lamb, or an adult of any small breed of cattle. **2.** A collection of such skins. Also **kip′skin** (-skin′). [ME < Du.]

kip[2] (kip)　*n. Slang* **1.** A lodging house. **2.** A bed in a lodging house. **3.** *Obs.* A brothel. [Cf. Dan. *horekippe* brothel]

kip[3] (kip)　*n. pl.* **kip** The monetary unit of Laos.

Kip·ling (kip′ling), (**Joseph**) **Rudyard,** 1865–1936, English author and poet.

kip·per (kip′ər)　*n.* **1.** A salmon or herring cured by kippering. **2.** The male salmon during the spawning season. — *v.t.* To cure (fish) by splitting, salting, and drying or smoking. [? OE *cypera* spawning salmon]

Kir·by-Smith (kûr′bē·smith′), **Edmund** See (Edmund Kirby) SMITH.

Kirch·hoff (kirkh′hôf), **Gustav Robert,** 1824–87, German physicist.

Kir·ghiz (kir·gēz′)　*n.* *pl.* **·ghiz** or **·ghiz·es** **1.** One of a Turkic people of Mongoloid stock, largely nomadic, dwelling in the region between the Volga and the Irtish rivers. **2.** The Turkic language of the Kirghiz. Also **Kir·giz′.**

Kir·ghiz S.S.R. (kir·gēz′, *Russ.* kyir·gyēz′)　A constituent republic of the southern Soviet Union; 76,640 sq. mi.; pop. 2,933,000 (1970); capital, Frunze. Also **Kir·ghi·zi·a** (kir·gē′zhē·ə, -zhə). *Russian* **Kir·ghiz′ska·ya S.S.R.** (-skä·yä).

Kirghiz Steppe A vast steppe region in the central Kazakh S.S.R.: also (the) *Steppes.*

Ki·rin (kē′rin′)　A Province of NE China; 72,201 sq. mi.; pop. 12,550,000 (est. 1957); capital, Changchun.

Kir·jath-Ar·ba (kûr′jath·är′bə)　The ancient name for HEBRON.

kirk (kûrk)　*n. Scot. & Brit. Dial.* A church.

Kirk (kûrk), **The** In Scotland, the established Presbyterian Church, as distinguished from the Church of England or the Episcopal Church in Scotland.

Kirk·cud·bright (kər·kōō′brē)　A county in SW Scotland; 900 sq. mi.; pop. 28,877 (1961); county seat, **Kircudbright,** pop. about 2,500. Also **Kirk·cud′bright·shire** (-shir).

Kirk·la·re·li (kərk·lä′rə·lē)　A town in NE Turkey; scene of a Bulgarian victory over the Turks, 1912; pop. about 14,000. Formerly **Kirk·ki·lis·sa** (kirk′kē·lē·sä).

Kirk·man (kûrk′mən)　*n.* *pl.* **·men** (-mən) A member of the established Church of Scotland.

Kir·kuk (kir·kŏŏk′)　A city in NE Iraq; pop. 120,593 (1960).

Kirk·wood (kûrk′wŏŏd)　A city in eastern Missouri, near St. Louis; pop. 31,769.

Kir·man (kir·män′)　*n.* A type of Persian rug having naturalistic floral patterns and soft, rich coloring. [after *Kerman,* Iran, where originally made]

kir·mess (kûr′mis)　See KERMIS.

kirn[1] (kûrn, kirn)　*n. Scot.* **1.** The last sheaf gathered at the harvest. **2.** A festival celebrating the end of the harvest. [Origin uncertain]

kirn[2] (kûrn, kirn)　*n. & v. Scot.* Churn.

Ki·rov (kyē′rəf)　A city in the western R.S.F.S.R., on the Vyatka river; pop. 332,000 (est. 1970): formerly *Vyatka.*

Ki·ro·va·bad (kyi·rə·vä·bät′)　A city in the west central Azerbaijan S.S.R.; pop. 116,000 (1959): formerly *Yelizavetpol, Gandzha.*

Ki·ro·vo·grad (kyi·rə·vo·grät′)　A city in the central Ukrainian S.S.R.; pop. 189,000 (est. 1970).

kirsch (kirsh)　*n.* A brandy distilled from the fermented juice of cherries and their pits, originally from Germany and Alsace. Also **kirsch′was′ser** (-väs′ər). [< G *kirsche* cherry]

kir·tle (kûrt′l)　*n. Archaic* **1.** A woman's skirt or petticoat. **2.** A man's short outer garment; tunic. [OE *cyrtel,* prob. ult. < L *curtus* short] — **kir′tled** *adj.*

Ki·shi·nev (kish′i·nef, *Russ.* kyi·shi·nyôf′)　The capital of the Moldavian S.S.R., in the central part; pop. 357,000 (est. 1970): Rumanian *Chisinău.*

Kis·ka (kis′kə)　An island in the Rat Island group of the Aleutian Islands, SW Alaska.

Kis·lew (kis·lef′, kis′lef)　*n.* The third month of the Hebrew year: also *Chisleu.* Also **Kish′lev, Kis′lev.** See (Hebrew) CALENDAR.

kis·met (kiz′met, kis′-)　*n.* Appointed lot; fate. [< Turkish < Arabic *qisma* < *qasama* to divide]

Kis·pest (kish′pesht)　A city in north central Hungary, near Budapest; pop. about 66,550 (est. 1967).

kiss (kis)　*v.t. & v.i.* **1.** To touch or caress with the lips as a sign of greeting or parting, love, desire, reverence, etc. **2.** To meet or touch lightly: the billiard balls just *kissed.* — *n.* **1.** A touch or caress with the lips; osculation. **2.** A light meeting or touching. **3.** A small candy. [OE *cyssan*]

kiss·er (kis′ər)　*n.* **1.** One who kisses. **2.** *Slang* The face.

kissing bug **1.** An assassin bug (*Reduvius personatus*) that occasionally bites man on the lips or cheeks: also called *masked hunter.* **2.** One of several other bloodsucking insects.

Kissinger (kis′ing·ər), **Henry Alfred,** born 1923, German-born U.S. public official; secretary of state 1973–77.

kist[1] (kist)　*n. Scot.* A chest, box, or coffin. — **kist′ful** *n.*

kist[2] (kist)　See CIST[2].

Kist·na (kist′nə)　A river in southern India, flowing 800 miles eastward to the Bay of Bengal: also *Krishna.*

kit[1] (kit)　*n.* **1.** A collection of articles, tools, etc., for a special purpose. **2.** A set of parts, materials, etc., from which something is to be made or assembled. **3.** One's effects or outfit, especially for traveling. **4.** A box, bag, knapsack, or other container. **5.** *Informal* A collection of persons or things; the whole lot: the whole *kit* and caboodle of them: compare CABOODLE. [ME < MDu. *kitte* jug, vessel]

kit[2] (kit)　*n.* A kitten.

kit[3] (kit)　*n.* A small, three-stringed violin, used from the 16th to the 18th century: also *kit violin.* [Origin uncertain]

kitch·en (kich′ən)　*n.* **1.** A room specially set apart and equipped for cooking food. **2.** The equipment used for cooking and serving food. **3.** A culinary department; cuisine [OE *cycene,* ult. < L *coquina* < *coquere* to cook]

kitchen cabinet **1.** A cupboard or cabinet in a kitchen. **2.** *U.S.* A group of unofficial members of the Cabinet of a U.S. President.

kitch·en·er (kich′ən·ər)　*n.* **1.** One employed to manage or work in a kitchen. **2.** *Brit.* A large cooking stove.

Kitch·en·er (kich′ən·ər), **Horatio Herbert,** 1850–1916, first Earl Kitchener of Khartoum; English statesman and field marshal.

kitch·en·ette (kich′ən·et′)　*n.* A small, compactly arranged kitchen. Also **kitch′en·et′.**

kitchen garden A home vegetable garden.

kitchen midden *Anthropol.* A prehistoric refuse heap or mound containing shells, human and animal bones, rude stone implements, etc.: also called *shellheap, shellmound.* [< Dan. *køkken* kitchen + *mødding* dunghill. See MIDDEN.]

kitchen police *Mil.* Enlisted men detailed to perform routine kitchen chores; also, such duty. Abbr. *KP, K.P.*

kitch·en·ware (kich′ən·wâr′)　*n.* Kitchen utensils.

kite (kīt)　*n.* **1.** A lightweight structure, usually of wood and paper, made to be flown in the wind at the end of a long string. **2.** Any of several predatory birds of the hawk family (*Falconidae*) with long, pointed wings and a forked tail, some species of which are carrion birds. **3.** *Naut.* One of several light sails for use in a very light wind. **4.** In commerce, any negotiable paper not representing a genuine transaction, but so employed, as to obtain money, sustain credit, etc.; also, a bank check drawn with insufficient funds on deposit. — *v.* **kit·ed, kit·ing** *v.i.* **1.** To soar or fly like a kite; move along swiftly. **2.** In commerce, to obtain money or credit by the use of kites. — *v.t.* **3.** In commerce, to issue as a kite: to *kite* a check. [OE *cȳta*]

kite balloon See under BALLOON.

kith (kith)　*n. Archaic* One's friends, acquaintances, or associates: now only in phrase **kith and kin.** [OE *cȳth* native land < *cūth* known]

kith·a·ra (kith′ə·rə) *n.* A cithara.

kithe (kīth) *v.t. & v.i. Scot.* To make or become known; show: also spelled *kythe.* [OE *cȳthan < cūth* known]

kitsch (kich) *n.* Art or literature of a cheap, popular, or sentimental quality. [< G, rubbish, trash]

kit·ten (kit′ən) *n.* A young cat. **— to have kittens** *U.S. Slang* To express one's emotions violently, especially anger; explode. *— v.t. & v.i.* To give birth (to kittens). [ME *kitoun < OF chitoun*, var. of *chaton* kitten]

kit·ten·ish (kit′ən·ish) *adj.* Playfully coy. **— kit′ten·ish·ly** *adv.* **— kit′ten·ish·ness** *n.*

kit·ti·wake (kit′ē·wāk) *n.* A gull (genus *Rissa*) of northern seas, having a rudimentary hind toe. [Imit.]

kit·tle (kit′l) *Scot. v.t.* **1.** To puzzle or perplex. **2.** To make sprightly; tickle. *— adj.* Skittish; ticklish. [ME *kytellen < OE kitelung*]

Kitt·redge (kit′rij), **George Lyman,** 1860–1941, U.S. educator, Shakespearean scholar, and folklorist.

kit·ty¹ (kit′ē) *n.*, *pl.* **·ties 1.** In certain card games, the pool to which each player contributes a percentage of his winnings, used to cover expenses, the cost of refreshments, etc. **2.** Money pooled for any specific purpose. **3.** In certain card games, a hand or part of a hand left over after a deal, which may be used by the highest bidder: also called *widow.* [Origin uncertain]

kit·ty² (kit′ē) *n.*, *pl.* **·ties 1.** A kitten or cat. **2.** A pet name for a cat.

kit·ty-cor·nered (kit′ē·kôr′nərd) *adj.* Cater-cornered.

Kitty Hawk A village in NE North Carolina, on Albemarle Sound, site of the first sustained airplane flight, made by Wilbur and Orville Wright in December, 1903.

kit violin Kit³.

Kiung·shan (kyōōng′shän′, *Chinese* jyōōng′shän′) A city in northern Hainan, Kwangtung Province, China. Former name **Kiung′chow′** (-chou′, *Chinese* -jō′).

Kiu·shu (kyōō-shōō) See KYUSHU.

ki·va (kē′və) *n.* In Pueblo culture, a room devoted to secret religious ceremonies, tribal councils, etc., entered by an opening in the roof. [< Hopi]

Ki·vu (kē′vōō), **Lake** A lake in east central Africa just north of Lake Tanganyika; about 1,100 sq. mi.

Ki·wa·ni·an (kə·wä′nē·ən, -wô′-) *n.* A member of Kiwanis. *— adj.* Of or pertaining to Kiwanis.

Ki·wa·nis (kə·wä′nis, -wô′-) A chain of men's clubs organized in 1915 to promote higher standards in business and professional relations. Also **Kiwanis Clubs.** [< N. Am. Ind. *keewanis* to make oneself known]

ki·wi (kē′wē) *n.*, *pl.* **·wis 1.** A New Zealand bird (genus *Apteryx*) with undeveloped wings, now nearly extinct: also called *apteryx.* **2.** *Mil. Slang* An air force officer who does not make flights. **3.** *Austral.* A New Zealander. [< Maori]

Kiz·il-Ir·mak (ki·zil′ir·mäk′) A river in central Turkey, flowing 715 miles north to the Black Sea: ancient *Halys.*

Kjö·len (kyœ′lən) A range of mountains between Norway and Sweden: highest peak, Kebnekaise, 6,963 ft.

KKK or **K.K.K.** Ku Klux Klan.

KKt King's knight (chess).

KKtP King's knight's pawn (chess).

kl. or **kl** Kiloliter(s).

Kla·gen·furt (klä′gən·fŏŏrt) The capital of Carinthia, southern Austria; pop. 62,782 (1961).

Klai·pe·da (klī′pe·dä, *Russ.* -pyi·də) A port city in the western Lithuanian S.S.R., on the Baltic; pop. about 89,000: also *Memel.*

Klam·ath Falls (klam′əth) A city in southern Oregon, at the south end of Upper Klamath Lake; pop. 15,775.

Klamath Lakes Two connected lakes, **Lower Klamath Lake** in northern California, now dry, and **Upper Klamath Lake** in southern Oregon, the source of the **Klamath River** that flows 263 miles through California, to the Pacific.

Klan (klan) See KU KLUX KLAN.

Klans·man (klanz′mən) *n.*, *pl.* **·men** (-mən) A member of the Ku Klux Klan.

Klau·sen·burg (klou′zen·bŏŏrkh) The German name for CLUJ.

klax·on (klak′sən) *n.* **1.** An early type of automobile horn. **2.** A low-pitched horn, especially one used on ships to signal alarms. Also spelled *claxon*: also **klaxon horn.** [< *Klaxon* a trade name < Gk. *klazein* to make a harsh sound]

Klea·gle (klē′gəl) *n.* An official in the Ku Klux Klan.

Klé·ber (klā·bâr′), **Jean Baptiste,** 1753–1800, French Revolutionary general: assassinated.

Klebs-Löff·ler bacillus (klebz′lœf′lər) The diphtheria bacillus. [after Edwin *Klebs*, 1834–1913, and Friedrich H. J. *Löffler*, 1852–1915, German bacteriologists]

Klee (klā, klē), **Paul,** 1879–1940, Swiss painter and etcher.

Kleen·ex (klē′neks) *n.* A soft paper tissue, used as a handkerchief, etc.: a trade name. Also **kleen′ex.**

Klein (klīn) **Felix,** 1849–1925, German mathematician.

Klein bottle *Math.* A one-sided figure forming an enclosure continuous with its outer surface, theoretically constructed by twisting a tube through the fourth dimension and joining the ends. [after Felix *Klein*]

klep·to·ma·ni·a (klep′tə·mā′nē·ə) *n.* An obsessive impulse to steal, often to steal articles for which the affected person has no need or desire: also spelled *cleptomania.* [< Gk. *kleptēs* thief + -MANIA] **— klep′to·ma′ni·ac** (-mā′nē·ak) *n.*

klieg light (klēg) A powerful arc floodlight, used in making motion pictures. [after Anton *Kliegl*, 1872–1927, and his brother John, 1869–1959, lighting pioneers born in Germany]

klip·spring·er (klip′spring·ər) *n.* A small, agile African antelope (*Oreotragus oreotragus*) inhabiting mountainous regions from Ethiopia to the Cape of Good Hope. [< Afrikaans < Du., lit., cliff-springer]

Klon·dike (klon′dīk) A region in NW Canada in the basin of the **Klondike River,** a tributary of the Yukon River.

kloof (klōōf) *n.* In South Africa, a mountain pass or cleft; gorge. [< Afrikaans < Du. < *klooven* to cleave]

Klop·stock (klôp′shtôk), **Friedrich Gottlieb,** 1724–1803, German poet.

klys·tron (klis′tron, -trən, klī′stron, -strən) *n. Electronics* An electron tube for generating and amplifying ultrahigh frequency currents by means of a flow of electrons between cavities within which they are rhythmically accelerated and retarded by electrical oscillations. [< Gk. *kleistos* closed + (ELEC)TRON]

km. or **km** Kilometer(s).

kn. Kronen.

knack (nak) *n.* **1.** The ability to do something readily and well. **2.** Cleverness; adroitness. *— v.t. & v.i. Rare* To strike or snap sharply. [ME *knak, knekke.* Cf. Du. *knakken.*]

knack·er (nak′ər) *n. Brit.* **1.** One whose trade is buying and slaughtering old or disabled horses for their hides, meat, etc. **2.** One who buys and dismantles old houses, ships, etc., for the material. [Origin uncertain]

knack·wurst (näk′wûrst) *n.* A short, thick sausage seasoned with garlic: also spelled *knockwurst.* [< G < *knacken* to sputter, crackle + *wurst* sausage]

knap¹ (nap) *v.t. & v.i.* **knapped, knap·ping** *Dial.* **1.** To break in pieces; snap. **2.** To bite sharply; nibble. *— n. Dial.* A sharp cracking noise. [Imit.]

knap² (nap) *n. Chiefly Dial.* The top of a hill or knoll; crest. [OE *cnæp*]

knap·sack (nap′sak′) *n.* A case or bag worn strapped across the shoulders, for carrying equipment or supplies; rucksack. [< Du. *knapzak < knappen* to bite, eat + *zak* sack]

knap·weed (nap′wēd′) *n.* **1.** A common European meadow plant (*Centaurea nigra*) naturalized in the United States, with heads of purple flowers: also called *bullweed.* **2.** Any of various other species of *Centaurea.* [ME *knopweed* < obs. *knop* knob + WEED]

knar (när) *n.* A knot on a tree or in wood. [ME *knarre* < Du. *knar* stump, knot] **— knar′ry** *adj.*

knave (nāv) *n.* **1.** A dishonest person; rogue; rascal. **2.** A playing card, the jack. **3.** *Archaic* A male servant. **— Syn.** See SCOUNDREL. [OE *cnafa* youth. Cf. Du. *knaap.*]

knav·er·y (nā′vər·ē) *n.*, *pl.* **·er·ies 1.** Deceitfulness; trickery; rascality. **2.** An act of trickery or deceit. **3.** *Archaic* Mischievousness; waggishness.

knav·ish (nā′vish) *adj.* Of, pertaining to, or characteristic of a knave. **— knav′ish·ly** *adv.* **— knav′ish·ness** *n.*

knead (nēd) *v.t.* **1.** To mix and work (dough, clay, etc.) into a uniform mass, usually by pressing, turning, and pulling with the hands. **2.** To work upon by thumps or squeezes of the hands; massage. **3.** To make by or as by kneading. [OE *cnedan*] **— knead′er** *n.*

knee (nē) *n.* **1.** *Anat.* The joint of the human leg that articulates the femur with the tibia and fibula and includes the patella; also, the region about this joint. **2.** *Zool.* **a** A part homologous to the human knee, as the stifle joint in horses, dogs, etc. **b** A part corresponding or similar to the human knee, as the carpal joint in hoofed animals, or the joint at the top of the tarsus in birds. **3.** Something like or suggesting a bent knee, as a bent piece of metal or wood used in carpentry, construction, etc. **4.** The part of a garment covering the knee. *— v.t.* **1.** To touch or strike with the knee. *— v.i.* **2.** *Obs.* or *Poetic* To kneel. [OE *cnēow*]

knee action A method of suspending the front wheels of a vehicle, permitting independent vertical motion.

knee breeches Breeches extending from the waist to a point just below the knee.

knee·cap (nē′kap′) *n.* **1.** The patella. Also **knee′pan′.** **2.** A protective pad for the knee: also **knee′pad′.**

knee-deep (nē′dēp′) *adj.* **1.** Rising to the knee: a *knee-deep* flood. **2.** Sunk to the knees: *knee-deep* in mud.

knee-high (nē′hī′) *adj.* Reaching as high as the knees.

knee-hole (nē′hōl′) *n.* A space for the knees, as in a desk.

knee jerk *Physiol.* A reflex kick of the lower leg caused by a sudden, brisk tapping of the tendon just below the kneecap; the patellar reflex.

kneel (nēl) *v.i.* **knelt** or **kneeled, kneel·ing** To fall or rest on the bent knee or knees. [OE *cnēowlian*] **— kneel′er** *n.*

knee·piece (nē′pēs′) *n.* In medieval armor, a protective covering for the knee and adjacent parts.

knell (nel) *n.* **1.** The tolling of a bell, especially one announcing a death. **2.** An omen of death, extinction, or failure. **3.** Any sad or doleful sound. —*v.i.* **1.** To sound a knell; toll mournfully. **2.** To sound like a doleful bell. —*v.t.* **3.** To summon or proclaim by or as by a knell. [OE *cnyll* < *cnyllan* to knell]

Knel·ler (nel′ər), Sir Godfrey, 1646–1723, English painter born in Germany: original name **Gottfried Knil·ler** (knil′ər).

knelt (nelt) Past tense and past participle of KNEEL.

Knes·set (knes′et) *n.* The unicameral Constituent Assembly of the Republic of Israel. [< Hebrew, gathering]

knew (nōō, nyōō) Past tense of KNOW.

Knick·er·bock·er (nik′ər·bok′ər) *n.* **1.** A descendant of one of the early Dutch settlers in New York State. **2.** A New Yorker. [after Diedrich *Knickerbocker*, fictitious Dutch author of Washington Irving's *History of New York*]

knick·er·bock·ers (nik′ər·bok′erz) *n.pl.* Wide short breeches gathered below the knee: also called *knickers*. [< KNICKERBOCKER; from resemblance to Dutch breeches]

knick·ers (nik′ərz) *n.pl.* **1.** Knickerbockers. **2.** *Chiefly Brit.* A woman's or girl's undergarment, similar to bloomers.

knick·knack (nik′nak) *n.* A trifling article; trinket; trifle: also spelled *nicknack.* [Reduplication of KNACK]

knife (nīf) *n.* *pl.* **knives** (nīvz) **1.** An instrument for cutting, piercing, or spreading, with one or more sharp-edged, often pointed, blades, commonly set in a handle. **2.** A blade forming a part of an implement or machine. **3.** A weapon, such as a dagger, dirk, poniard, etc. —*v.t.* **knifed, knif·ing 1.** To stab or cut with a knife. **2.** *U.S. Slang* To discredit or betray behind one's back. [OE *cnif*]

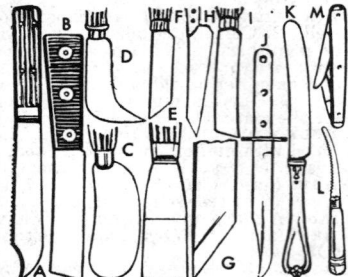

KNIVES

A Saw-back fish. *B* Hacking. *C* Paperhanger's. *D* Oilcloth. *E* Putty. *F* Woodcarver's. *G* Blade of mat knife. *H* Felt. *I* Paring. *J* Hunting. *K* Table. *L* Paring or fruit. *M* Folding pocket knife or penknife.

knife-edge (nīf′ej′) *n.* **1.** The sharpened cutting side of a knife. **2.** Anything as sharp as a knife. **3.** A sharp wedge of steel, serving as fulcrum for a balance beam or a pendulum.

knife switch *Electr.* A switch in which one or more knife-like blades, pivoted at one end, complete the circuit when pressed between upright flat springs.

knight (nīt) *n.* **1.** In medieval times: **a** A feudal tenant serving his superior as a mounted soldier. **b** A gentleman, usually of the nobility, trained for mounted combat and raised with special ceremonies to honorable military rank and the order of chivalry. **2.** In Great Britain, since the 16th century, the holder of a nonhereditary dignity below the rank of baronet, conferred by the sovereign as a reward for personal merit or for service to the country. The holder is entitled to use *Sir* before his given name. **3.** A champion or devoted follower; any man devoted to the service of a woman, principle, etc. **4.** In chess, a piece having a horse's head and moving in an L-shaped pattern either three squares on one arm and two on the other or vice versa, capturing only on the square where it lands, and able to overleap intervening pieces. Abbr. *k.*, *K.*; (for def. 4) *Knt, Kt* —*v.t.* To make (a man) a knight. [OE *cniht* boy, military attendant]

knight bachelor *pl.* **knights bachelors** In England, a member of the most ancient but lowest order of knighthood. Abbr. *K.B.*

knight banneret *pl.* **knights bannerets** Banneret[2].

knight errant *pl.* **knights errant** A wandering knight who went forth to redress wrongs or seek adventures.

knight-er·rant·ry (nīt′er′ən·trē) *n.* *pl.* **·ries 1.** The customs and practices of the knights errant; chivalry. **2.** Quixotic behavior or action.

knight-head (nīt′hed′) *n.* *Naut.* One of two timbers rising from the keel of a vessel and supporting the bowsprit between them, originally carved to represent knights.

knight·hood (nīt′hŏŏd) *n.* **1.** The character, rank, or vocation of a knight. **2.** Knights collectively. **3.** Chivalry.

Knight Hospitaler *pl.* **Knights Hospitalers** A Hospitaler (which see).

knight·ly (nīt′lē) *adj.* **1.** Pertaining to a knight; chivalrous. **2.** Composed of knights; chivalric; a *knightly* order. —**knight′li·ness** *n.*

Knights of Columbus A fraternal society of American Roman Catholic men, founded 1882. Abbr. *K.C., K. of C.*

Knights of Labor A national organization of laboring men in the United States, organized for mutual benefit and protection, and active between 1869 and 1917.

Knights of Pythias A secret philanthropic order founded in Washington, D.C., in 1864. Abbr. *K. of P., K.P.*

Knights of St. John of Jerusalem See under HOSPITALER.

Knights of the Garter Knights of the **Order of the Garter**, the highest order of knighthood in Great Britain. Abbr. *K.G.*

Knights of the Round Table The body of knights comprising King Arthur's court. See ROUND TABLE.

Knight Templar *pl.* **Knights Templars** for def. 1, **Knights Templar** for def. 2. **1.** In medieval history, a member of a military and religious order founded in 1119 by the Crusaders for the defense of the Latin Kingdom of Jerusalem and the protection of pilgrims, taking its name from its headquarters next to the Temple of Solomon. It was suppressed in 1312. **2.** A Freemason of an order claiming descent from the medieval order of Knights Templars. Abbr. *K.T.*

knit (nit) *v.* **knit** or **knit·ted, knit·ting** *v.t.* **1.** To form (a fabric or garment) by interlocking loops of a single yarn or thread by means of needles. **2.** To fasten or unite closely and firmly; reunite; mend. **3.** To draw (the brows) together into wrinkles; contract. —*v.i.* **4.** To make a fabric by interlocking loops of yarn or thread. **5.** To become closely and firmly united; grow together, as broken bones. **6.** To come together in wrinkles; contract. —*n.* The fabric made by knitting. [OE *cnyttan*. Akin to KNOT.] —**knit′ter** *n.*

knit·ting (nit′ing) *n.* **1.** The act of one who or that which knits. **2.** The fabric produced by knitting.

knitting needle A straight, slender rod, pointed at one or both ends, used in hand knitting.

knives (nīvz) Plural of KNIFE.

knob (nob) *n.* **1.** A rounded protuberance, bunch, or lump. **2.** A rounded handle, as of a door. **3.** A rounded mountain; knoll. [ME *knobbe*, prob. < MLG *knobbe*. Cf. Flemish *knobbe*, Du. *knop.*] —**knobbed** *adj.* —**knob′like** *adj.*

knob·by (nob′ē) *adj.* **·bi·er, ·bi·est 1.** Full of knobs. **2.** Knoblike.

knob·ker·rie (nob′ker·ē) *n.* A knobbed stick used as a club or a missile by certain South African tribes. Also **knob′stick′** (-stik′). [< Afrikaans *knopkirie* < Du. *knobbe* + Hottentot *kirri* stick]

knock (nok) *v.t.* **1.** To deal a blow to; hit. **2.** To strike together; bring into collision: to *knock* heads. **3.** To drive or move by hitting: to *knock* a ball over the fence. **4.** To make by striking or pounding: to *knock* a hole in the wall. **5.** To strike or push so as to make fall: with *down, over, off,* etc. **6.** *U.S. Slang* To find fault with; disparage. —*v.i.* **7.** To strike a blow or blows, especially with the knuckles; rap: with *at* or *on:* to *knock* at a door. **8.** To come into collision; bump. **9.** To make a pounding or clanking noise, as an engine with faulty combustion. —**to knock around** (or **about**) **1.** *Informal* To wander from place to place. **2.** To treat roughly; abuse. —**to knock down 1.** To take apart for shipping or storing. **2.** At auctions, to sell to the highest bidder. **3.** *U.S. Slang* To embezzle (a part of money passing through one's hands). **4.** *U.S. Slang* To earn, as wages or salary: How much do you *knock down* every week? —**to knock off 1.** *Informal* To stop or leave off (work, talking, etc.). **2.** To deduct. **3.** *Informal* To do or make quickly or easily: to *knock off* an assignment in ten minutes. **4.** *U.S. Slang* To kill; also, to overwhelm or defeat. **5.** *U.S. Slang* To rob (a place); burglarize. —**to knock (oneself) out** *U.S. Slang* **1.** To make a great effort; work very hard. **2.** To become exhausted. —**to knock out 1.** In boxing, to defeat (an opponent) by knocking to the canvas for a count of ten. **2.** To make unconscious. **3.** To defeat. **4.** *U.S. Slang* To tire greatly; exhaust. **5.** *U.S. Slang* To make a strong emotional impression upon, especially one of great amusement. —**to knock out of the box** In baseball, to hit the pitches of (an opposing pitcher) so well as to cause (his) removal from the game. —**to knock together** To build or make roughly or hurriedly. —**to knock up 1.** *U.S. Slang* To make pregnant. **2.** *Brit.* To rouse by knocking at the door. **3.** *Brit.* To exhaust or become exhausted. —*n.* **1.** A sharp blow; rap; also, a knocking. **2.** A noise made by an engine in faulty condition or by defective combustion. **3.** A misfortune or reversal: a hard *knock.* **4.** *U.S. Slang* Hostile criticism; disparagement. [OE *cnocian*]

knock·a·bout (nok′ə·bout′) *n.* *Naut.* A small sailboat rigged like a sloop. Compare RACEABOUT. —*adj.* **1.** Marked by roughness. **2.** Suitable for rough or casual occasions.

knock·down (nok′doun′) *adj.* **1.** Powerful enough to upset or overthrow; overwhelming: a *knockdown* blow. **2.** Made so as to be easily taken apart or put together: a *knockdown* chair. —*n.* **1.** A felling or upsetting, especially by a blow. **2.** An article made for easy assembly and disassembly. **3.** *U.S. Slang* An introduction, as to a person.

knock·er (nok′ər) *n.* **1.** One who or that which knocks. **2.** A hinged metal hammer fastened to a door as a means of knocking. **3.** *U.S. Slang* A faultfinder.

knock-knee (nok′nē′) *n.* **1.** An inward curvature of the legs that causes the knees to knock or rub together in walking. **2.** *pl.* Legs so curved.

knock·kneed (nok′nēd′) *adj.* Having knock-knees.

knock·out (nok′out′) *adj.* Forcible enough and so placed as to render unconscious; overpowering; stunning. — *n.* **1.** A knocking unconscious or a knocking out of action. **2.** A knockout blow. **3.** In boxing, a flooring of one fighter for a count of ten; a kayo. Compare TECHNICAL KNOCKOUT. *Abbr.* KO, k.o., K.O. **3.** *Slang* A remarkably impressive person or thing. **4.** *Electr.* A punched disk, as in a connection box, that can easily be knocked out to form a circular hole.

knockout drops Drops of some powerful hypnotic, often chloral hydrate, put into a drink to produce unconsciousness.

knock·wurst (näk′wûrst) See KNACKWURST.

knoll¹ (nōl) *n.* A small round hill; a mound. [OE *cnoll* hill]

knoll² (nōl) *Archaic & Dial.* *v.i. & v.t.* To knell. — *n.* A knell. [Prob. var. of KNELL]

knop (nop) *n.* A rounded protuberance; an ornamental boss or stud; knob. [ME *knop* < OE *cnopa* tuft. Cf. MD *cnop*.]

knosp (nosp) *n.* A budlike knob. [< G *knospe* bud]

Knos·sos (nos′əs, knos′əs) An ancient city of Crete, its capital during the Minoan period: also *Cnossus*.

knot¹ (not) *n.* **1.** An intertwining of rope, string, etc., one free end being passed through a loop and drawn tight; also, the lump thus made. **2.** An ornamental bow of silk, lace, braid, etc. **3.** A hard, gnarled portion of the trunk of a tree at the insertion of a branch. **4.** The rounded, crossgrained mark on sawed lumber left by this. **5.** A cluster or group of persons or things. **6.** A bond or union: the marriage *knot*. **7.** An enlargement in a muscle, of a gland, etc., resembling a knot. **8.** Something not easily solved; a difficulty; problem. **9.** *Naut.* **a** A division of a log line, marked by pieces of cloth or knotted string at equal distances, and used to determine the rate of a ship's motion. **b** A speed of a nautical mile in an hour, equivalent to 1.1516 statute miles per hour. **c** A nautical mile. ◆ Since a knot is a measure of speed per hour, a ship is properly said to be moving at *twenty knots* rather than at *twenty knots an hour*. **10.** *Bot.* **a** A node or joint in a stem; also, a protuberance or swelling. **b** *pl.* Any of several diseases of trees, characterized by such swellings. — *v.* **knot·ted,** **knot·ting** *v.t.* **1.** To tie in a knot; form a knot or knots in. **2.** To secure or fasten by a knot. **3.** To form knobs, bosses, etc., in. — *v.i.* **4.** To form a knot or knots. **5.** To become knotted or tangled. [OE *cnotta*]

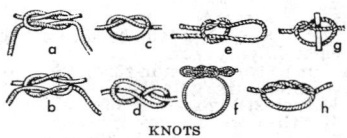

KNOTS
a Square or reef. *b* Granny. *c* Overhand. *d* Figure-eight. *e* Slipknot. *f* Double bowknot. *g* Boat. *h* Surgeon's.

knot² (not) *n.* A sandpiper (*Calidris canutus*) of northern regions, having a reddish breast. [Origin unknown]

knot·grass (not′gras′, -gräs′) *n.* **1.** A widely distributed herb (*Polygonum aviculare*) of the buckwheat family, with jointed stems and small greenish flowers. **2.** A short, creeping grass (*Paspalum distichum*).

knot·hole (not′hōl′) *n.* A hole in a plank or board left by the falling out of a knot.

knot·ted (not′id) *adj.* **1.** Tied with a knot or into knots. **2.** Having knots; knotty. **3.** Having knobs, bosses, etc.; bumpy; lumpy. **4.** Tangled up; snarled. **5.** Hard to solve; puzzling. **6.** Ornamented with knots.

knot·ty (not′ē) *adj.* **·ti·er, ·ti·est** **1.** Full of or tied in knots. **2.** Difficult or intricate; puzzling. — **knot′ti·ness** *n.*

knot·weed (not′wēd′) *n.* Any of various prostrate plants (genus *Polygonum*) of the buckwheat family.

knout (nout) *n.* A whip or scourge used formerly for flogging in Russia. — *v.t.* To flog with the knout. [< Russian *knut* < ON *knútr, knúta* knot]

know (nō) *v.* **knew, known, know·ing** *v.t.* **1.** To be cognizant of; have a concept of in the mind through seeing, reading, hearing, etc. **2.** To be certain of; apprehend as true or factual. **3.** To be acquainted with through previous encounter, report, etc.; be familiar with. **4.** To be sure about the identity of; recognize: I *know* that voice. **5.** To have a practical and operative grasp of through instruction, study, exercise, etc.: to *know* French. **6.** To be able: with *how* and an infinitive: to *know* how to swim. **7.** To distinguish between; discriminate: with *from*: to *know* good from bad. **8.** To have learned by rote; have memorized: The actor *knows* his lines. **9.** To have experienced; have come to grips with: We *know* poverty. **10.** *Archaic* To have sexual intercourse with. — *v.i.* **11.** To have cognizance or awareness; apprehend. **12.** To have understanding or certainty; be sure. — **to know better** To be aware of something truer or more correct than what one says or does. — **to know by** To recognize or be sure of through some sign: to *know* her *by* her walk. — **to know of** To be cognizant of somebody or some-

thing, but not familiar by personal experience: with stress on *of*: I don't know him, but I *know of* him. — *n. Informal* The fact of knowing: now only in the phrase **to be in the know,** to have inside or secret information. [OE *cnāwan*] — **know′·a·ble** *adj.* — **know′er** *n.*

know-how (nō′hou′) *n. Informal* Mastery of a complicated operation or procedure; technical skill.

know·ing (nō′ing) *adj.* **1.** Perceptive; astute; shrewd; also, hinting at having sly or secret knowledge concerning something: a *knowing* manner. **2.** Conscious; intentional. **3.** Having knowledge or information. — **know′ing·ly** *adv.* — **know′ing·ness** *n.*

know-it-all (nō′it-ôl′) *n. Informal* A person claiming knowledge in many subjects. Also **know-all** (nō′ôl′).

knowl·edge (nol′ij) *n.* **1.** A result or product of knowing; information or understanding acquired through experience; practical ability, or skill. **2.** Deep and extensive learning; erudition. **3.** The cumulative culture of the human race. **4.** A sure conviction; certainty. **5.** The act, process, or state of knowing; cognition. **6.** Any object of knowing or mental apprehension; that which is or may be known; also, actual or possible range of information. **7.** Specific information; notification; notice. **8.** *Archaic* Sexual intercourse: often preceded by *carnal.* **9.** In Christian Science, evidence obtained from the five corporeal senses, the opposite of spiritual Truth. [ME *knowlechen, knowlegen* to admit, recognize < OE *cnāwlǣc* acknowledgement] — **Syn.** *Knowledge, information, learning, erudition,* and *lore* are compared as they refer to a store of facts in the mind. *Knowledge* is more than this store; the word also includes the contribution of the mind in understanding data, perceiving relations, elaborating concepts, formulating principles, and making evaluations. The raw data taken into the mind is *information. Learning* is the *knowledge* gained by study and experience; *erudition* is very extensive *learning;* both words are applied to the humanities rather than to science and technology. *Lore* is *knowledge* of a particular, usually uncommon, subject. *Knowledge, cognition, perception, apprehension,* and *comprehension* are compared as they refer to the process of learning. *Knowledge* is a general term embracing all the others. *Cognition* is that activity of the mind which receives sense impressions and elaborates concepts from them. *Perception* is primarily the reception of sense impressions, but is extended to include the ability to understand that which the senses receive. *Apprehension* and *comprehension* are the act of taking into the mind. *Apprehension* stresses the seizure of new information; *comprehension,* the understanding of data. — **Ant.** ignorance.

knowl·edge·a·ble (nol′ij-ə-bəl) *adj.* Having knowledge.

known (nōn) Past participle of KNOW. — *adj.* Recognized by all as the truth; understood; axiomatic: *known* facts.

know-noth·ing (nō′nuth′ing) *n.* **1.** An uneducated or ignorant person; ignoramus. **2.** An agnostic.

Know-noth·ing (nō′nuth′ing) *n.* A member of a nativist party in U.S. politics (1853–56), so called because its early members professed to "know nothing" about it when questioned. — **Know′noth′ing·ism** *n.*

known quantity *Math.* A quantity whose value is given, generally denoted in algebra by *a, b, c,* etc.

Knox (noks), **Henry,** 1750–1806, American Revolutionary general. — **John,** 1505?–72, Scottish Calvinist reformer, theologian, and historian. — **(William) Frank(lin),** 1874–1944, U.S. publisher and public official; secretary of the navy, 1940–1944.

Knox·ville (noks′vil) A city in eastern Tennessee, on the Tennessee River; pop. 174,587.

Knt Knight (chess).

knuck·le (nuk′əl) *n.* **1.** One of the joints of the fingers, or the region about it; especially, one of the joints connecting the fingers to the hand. **2.** The protuberance formed by one of these joints when the finger is bent. **3.** The carpal joint of the pig, calf, etc., the flesh of which is used as food. **4.** *pl.* Brass knuckles (which see). **5.** The projecting tubular part of a hinge, through which the pin passes. **6.** In shipbuilding, an angular fitting of timbers. — *v.* **knuck·led, knuck·ling** — *v.t.* **1.** To rub, press, or hit with the knuckles. — *v.i.* **2.** To hold the knuckles on the ground in shooting a marble. — **to knuckle down** To apply oneself seriously and assiduously. — **to knuckle under** To yield; submit; give in. [ME *knokel.* Akin to Du. *knokkel,* dim. of *knok* bone. Cf. OE *cnycled* bent.]

knuckle ball In baseball, a slow, irregularly spinning pitch delivered by pressing the ball between the thumb and the first knuckles before releasing it. Also **knuck′ler.**

knuck·le·bone (nuk′əl·bōn′) *n.* **1.** In man, one of the bones forming a knuckle. **2.** In certain animals, as sheep, a leg bone with a knob at the end; also, this knob. **3.** *pl.* (*construed as sing.*) An old game played with the knucklebones of sheep.

knuck·le·dusters (nuk′əl·dus′tərz) *n.pl.* Brass knuckles.

knur (nûr) *n.* A knot or knob. [ME *knorre.* Akin to Du. *knor,* G *knorre.*]

knurl (nûrl) *n.* **1.** A protuberance; lump. **2.** One of a series of small ridges on the edge of a metal object, as a coin, thumbscrew, etc. **3.** *Scot.* A solidly built person. — *v.t.* To

ridge or mill, as the edge of a coin. [? Dim. of KNUR] —
knurl·y *adj.*

Knut (knōōt) See CANUTE.

KO or **K.O.** or **k.o.** Knockout (boxing).

ko·a·la (ko-ä'lə) An arboreal marsupial (*Phascolarctos cinereus*) having large ears, gray, woolly fur, and no tail, and feeding on the leaves and buds of the eucalyptus: also called *native bear*. [< native Australian name]

Ko·ba·rid (kō'bä-rēd) The Serbo-Croatian name for CAPORETTO.

Ko·be (kō-be) A port city on southern Honshu, Japan; pop. 1,086,000 (est. 1959).

Kø·ben·havn (kœ'pən-houn') The Danish name for COPENHAGEN.

KOALAS
(28 to 32 inches long)

Ko·blenz (kō'blents) A city in the northern Rhineland Palatinate, West Germany; pop. 97,500 (1960). Also *Coblenz*.

ko·bold (kō'bold, -bōld) *n.* In German folklore: **a** A household sprite, by turns helpful or mischievous. **b** An elf or gnome of mines, caves, etc. [< G; ult. origin unknown]

Ko·ca·baş (kô-jä-bäsh') The Turkish name for GRANICUS.

Koch (kokh), **Robert,** 1843–1910, German physician; one of the founders of modern medical bacteriology.

Kö·chel listing (kœ'shəl, -khəl) The chronological serial number applied to an opus of Mozart. Also **Köchel number.** Abbr. *K., K.V.* [after L. von *Köchel,* 1800–77, Austrian botanist, mineralogist, and music editor]

Ko·chi (kō-chē) A city on central Shikoku island, Japan; pop. 242,000 (est. 1968).

ko·dak (kō'dak) *v.t. & v.i.* **·daked** or **·dakked, ·dak·ing** or **·dak·king** To photograph with a Kodak.

Ko·dak (kō'dak) *n.* A small portable camera carrying a roll of sensitized film: a trade name. Also **ko'dak.**

Ko·di·ak bear (kō'dē-ak) A very large brown bear (*Ursus middendorffi*) found on Kodiak Island and adjacent islands off the Alaskan coast: also *Kadiak bear.*

Ko·di·ak Island (kō'dē-ak) An island in the Gulf of Alaska SE of Alaska Peninsula: also *Kadiak.* See map of BERING SEA.

Ko·dok (kō'dok) A town in the south central Sudan: formerly *Fashoda.*

ko·el (kō'əl) *n.* A cuckoo (*Eudanamys orientalis*) native to India, the East Indies, and Australia: also called *cooee bird.* [< Hind. < Skt. *kokila*]

Koest·ler (kest'lər), **Arthur,** born 1905, Hungarian novelist and journalist active in England.

K. of C. Knight(s) of Columbus.

Koff·ka (kôf'kä), **Kurt,** 1886–1941, U.S. psychologist born in Germany.

K. of P. Knight(s) of Pythias.

Ko·hel·eth (kō-hel'ith) The preacher in the book of Ecclesiastes, often identified with Solomon. — *n.* The Hebrew name for the book of Ecclesiastes. [< Hebrew *qōheleth*]

Koh·i·noor (kō'i-nōōr') *n.* A famous Indian diamond weighing when cut about 106 carats, a British crown jewel since 1849. Also **Koh'i·nor', Koh'i·nur'.** For illustration see DIAMOND. [< Persian *kōhinūr,* lit., mountain of light]

kohl (kōl) *n.* In Eastern countries, a powder of antimony used to darken the eyelids. [< Arabic *kuhl.* Cf. ALCOHOL.]

Köh·ler (kœ'lər), **Wolfgang,** 1887–1959, German psychologist active in the United States.

kohl·ra·bi (kōl'rä-bē, kōl-rä'-) *n. pl.* **·bies** A variety of cabbage with an edible turnip-shaped stem. [< G < Ital. *cavoli rape* (pl.) < L *caulis* cabbage + *rapa* turnip]

Koi·ne (koi-nā') *n.* The modified Attic dialect of Greek used during the Hellenistic Age and in the Septuagint and the New Testament. Its spoken form is the parent of modern Greek. Also called *Hellenistic Greek.* [< Gk. *koinē* (*dialektos*) common (language)]

koi·ne (koi-nā') *n.* Any mixed dialect that becomes the lingua franca of a region.

Ko·kand (kō-känt') A city in the eastern Uzbek S.S.R.; pop. 105,000 (1959).

ko·ka·nee (kō-kan'ē) *n.* The sockeye, a salmon.

Ko·ko·mo (kō'kə-mō) A city in north central Indiana; pop. 44,042.

Ko·ko Nor (kō'kō' nôr') A salt lake in NE Tsinghai Province, China; 2,300 sq. mi.: also *Kuku Nor.*

Ko·ku·ra (kō-kōō-rä) A port city on northern Kyushu island, Japan; pop. 276,000 (est. 1959).

ko·la (kō'lə), **kola nut tree** See COLA².

kola nut See COLA NUT.

Ko·la Peninsula (kō'lə) A projection of the NW Soviet Union between the Barents Sea and the White Sea; 50,000 sq. mi.; 250 mi. long. *Russian* **Kol·u·os·trov** (kôly'/-skyē pol-ōō-ô'strəf). Also **Kol'·skiy.**

Ko·lar Gold Fields (kō-lär') A city in eastern Mysore, India; pop. 146,200 (1961).

ko·lin·sky (kə-lin'skē, kō-) *n. pl.* **·skies 1.** Any of several minks (genus *Mustela*) of Asia and Russia. **2.** The fur of any of these animals, often dyed to resemble sable. Also called *Tartar mink.* [< Russian *kolinski* of Kola.]

Kol·khi·da (kol-khyē'də) The Russian name for COLCHIS.

kol·khoz (kol-khôz') *n.* A collective farm in the Soviet Union. Also **kol·hoz', kol·khos'.** [< Russian *kol(lektivnoe) collective* + *khoz(yaistvo)* farm, household]

Koll·witz (kôl'vits), **Käthe,** 1867–1945, *née* Schmidt, German painter, lithographer, and etcher.

Kol·mar (kôl'mär) See COLMAR.

Köln (kœln) The German name for COLOGNE.

Kol Ni·dre (kōl nid·rä', nid'rə) In Judaism: **a** The solemn annulment of vows intoned at the beginning of the service on the eve of Yom Kippur. **b** The melody to which this is chanted. [< Aramaic, all vows; from the first words]

Ko·lozs·vár (kō'lōzh-vär) The Hungarian name for CLUJ.

Ko·lusch·an (kə-lush'ən) *n.* A North American Indian stock of SE Alaska, the Tlingit tribes. [< Russian *kalyuschka* piece of wood (inserted in the lower lip), ? < Aleut]

Ko·ly·ma (kə-li-mä') A river in NE Siberia, flowing 1,335 miles north to the East Siberian Sea. Also **Ko·li·ma'.**

Kom·an·dor·ski Islands (kom'ən-dôr'skē) An island group of the eastern R.S.F.S.R. in the Bering Sea; 850 sq. mi.: also *Commander Islands. Russian* **Kom·an·dor·ski·ye Os·tro·va** (kəm-ən-dôr'skyē-yə os-trə-vä').

ko·mat·ik (kō-mad'ik) *n. Canadian* An Eskimo sled: also spelled *comatik.*

Ko·mi A.S.S.R. (kô'myi) An administrative division of NE R.S.F.S.R.; 160,600 sq. mi.; pop. 965,000 (est. 1970); capital Syktyvkar.

Kom·in·tern (kô'min-tûrn) See COMINTERN.

Ko·mo·do dragon (kə-mō'dō) A monitor lizard (*Varanus komodensis*) inhabiting a few of the Sunda Islands near Java. It is the world's largest lizard, sometimes reaching a length of 10 feet and a weight of 300 pounds.

Kom·so·mol (kom'so-mōl') *n.* The Young Communist League in the Soviet Union. [< Russian *Kom(munisticheskii)* Communist + *So(yuz)* League + *Mol(odezhi)* of Youth]

Kon·a·kri (kon'ə-krē) See CONAKRY.

Kon·go (kong'gō) The German name for the CONGO.

Kö·nigs·berg (kœ'nikhs-berkh) The former German name for KALININGRAD.

ko·ni·ol·o·gy (kō'nē-ol'ə-jē) See CONIOLOGY.

Kon·stanz (kôn'stänts) The German name for CONSTANCE.

Kon·ya (kôn'yä) A city in SW central Turkey; pop. 122,704 (1960): ancient *Iconium.* Also **Kon'ia.**

Koo (kōō), **V. K.** Wellington, born 1887, Chinese diplomat.

Kooch Be·har (kōōch' bi-här') See COOCH BEHAR.

koo·doo (kōō'dōō) *n. pl.* **·doos** Either of two large African antelopes (genus *Strepciseros*) with spiral horns in the male, the **greater koodoo** (S. *strepciseros*), and the **lesser koodoo** (S. *imberbis*): also spelled *kudu.* [< Hottentot]

kook (kōōk) *n. U.S. Slang* A silly or peculiar person. [? Alter. of *cuckoo*]

kook·a·bur·ra (kōōk'ə-bûr'ə) A large Australian bird (*Dacelo gigas*) allied to the kingfisher, noted for its harsh, laughing cry: also called *laughing jackass.* [< native Australian name]

kook·y (kōō'kē) *adj.* **kook·i·er, kook·i·est** *U.S. Slang* **1.** Of or pertaining to a kook. **2.** Of or pertaining to a peculiar or unusual situation or happening. Also **kook·ie. — kook'i·ness** *n.*

KOODOO
(About 4 feet high at shoulder)

koo·ra·jong (kōō'rə·jong) See KURRAJONG.

Koo·te·nay (kōō'tə-nā) A river rising in Kootenay National Park, SE British Columbia (543 sq. mi., established 1920); flowing through northern Montana and Idaho, and through **Kootenay Lake,** British Columbia (75 mi. long), to the Columbia River; length 450 mi. Also **Koo'·te·nai.**

kop (kop) *n.* In South Africa, a hill. [< Afrikaans, head]

ko·peck (kō'pek) *n.* A Russian bronze coin, the hundredth part of a ruble: also spelled *copeck.* Also **ko'pek.** Abbr. *k., K., kop.* [< Russian *kopeika < kopye* lance]

koph (kôf) *n.* The nineteenth letter in the Hebrew alphabet. See ALPHABET.

kop·je (kop'ē) *n.* In South Africa, a hillock. [< Afrikaans, dim. of Du. *kop* hill]

kor (kôr, kōr) *n.* A homer, the Hebrew measure.

Ko·ran (kō-rän', -ran') *n.* The sacred book of the Moslems, recording in Arabic the revelations of Allah (God) to Mohammed: also *Alcoran, Alkoran.* [< Arabic *Qur'ān,* lit., recitation < *qar'ā* to read]

Kor·do·fan (kôr'dō-fän') A Province of central Sudan; 146,930 sq. mi.; pop. 2,022,200 (1964); capital, El Obeid.

Ko·re·a (kō-rē'ə, kō-) A peninsula of eastern Asia; 85,266 sq. mi.; 1910–45 Japanese *Chosen*; divided (1948) into the **Republic of Korea (South Korea)**; 38,031 sq. mi.; pop. 32,100,000 (est. 1970); capital, Seoul, and the **Democratic People's Republic of Korea (North Korea)**; 47,255 sq. mi.; pop. 13,300,000 (est. 1969); capital, Pyongyang. See map of JAPAN.

Ko·re·an (kō-rē'ən, kō-) *adj.* Of or pertaining to Korea, its inhabitants, or their language. — *n.* **1.** A native of Korea, or a person of Korean ancestry. **2.** The language of Korea, generally considered to be unrelated to any other language.

Korean War See table for WAR.

Korea Strait The passage from the Sea of Japan to the East China Sea between Korea and Japan.

Kort·rijk (kôrt′rĭk) The Flemish name for COURTRAI.

ko·ru·na (kô′rŏŏ·nä) *n. pl.* **ko·ru·ny** (kô′rŏŏ·nē) or **ko·run** (kô′rŏŏn) The monetary unit of Czechoslovakia, equivalent to 100 hellers. Also called *crown.* Abbr. *K, Kč.* [< Czechoslovakian < L *corona* crown]

Kor·zyb·ski (kôr·zĭb′skē), **Alfred** (**Habdanl**), 1879–1950, U.S. scientist born in Poland; originator of general semantics.

kos (kos) *n. pl.* **kos** In India, a land measure varying from 1½ to 3 miles according to locality. Also **koss.** [< Hind. < Skt. *krósa,* lit., a shout]

Kos (kos, kôs) An island of the Dodecanese group; 114 sq. mi.: Italian *Coo:* also *Cos.*

Kos·ci·us·ko (kos′ē·us′kō), **Thaddeus,** 1746–1817, Polish patriot and general born in Lithuania; fought in the American Revolution. *Polish* **Koś·ciusz·ko** (kôsh·chōōsh′kô).

Kos·ci·us·ko (kos′ē·us′kō), **Mount** A mountain in SE New South Wales; highest peak in Australia; 7,305 ft.

ko·sher (*adj., n.* kō′shər; *v.* kosh′ər) *adj.* **1.** Permitted by or conforming to Jewish (ceremonial) law; ritually clean or proper: most often said of food and its preparation. **2.** *Slang* Legitimate; proper. — *n.* Kosher food. — *v.t.* To make kosher. Also spelled *kasher.* [< Hebrew *kāshēr* fit, proper]

Ko·ši·ce (kō′shē·tse) A city in SE Slovakia, Czechoslovakia; pop. 136,400 (est. 1968): Hungarian *Kassa.*

Kos·suth (kos′ōōth, ko·sōōth′; *Hungarian* kô′shōōt), **Ferenc,** 1841–1914, Hungarian politician. — **Louis,** 1802–94, Hungarian patriot, orator, and revolutionist; led revolt of 1848; father of the preceding. Also, *Hungarian,* **Lajos Kossuth.**

Kos·tro·ma (kə·stro·mä′) A city in the western R.S.F.S.R. on the Volga; pop. 171,000 (1959).

Ko·sy·gin (ko·sig′in), **Alexei Nikolayevich,** born 1904, Soviet statesman; chairman of the Council of Ministers (premier) 1964–.

Ko·ta·bar·u (kō·tä·bar′ōō) The capital of West Irian, a port in the NE part; pop. 16,735 (1959): formerly *Hollandia.*

Ko·ta Kin·a·ba·lu (kō′tə kin′ə·bə·lōō) A seaport and the capital of Sabah, Malaysia, on the NW coast of Borneo; pop. 21,704 (1960): formerly, **Jesselton.**

ko·to (kō′tō) *n. pl.* ·**tos** A Japanese musical instrument somewhat like a psaltery, with 13 strings stretched over a long, narrow sounding box. [< Japanese]

Kot·ze·bue (kôt′sə·bōō), **August Friedrich Ferdinand von,** 1761–1819, German dramatist.

kou·miss (kōō′mis), **kou·mys** See KUMISS.

Kous·se·vitz·ky (kōō′sə·vit′skē), **Serge,** 1874–1951, U.S. orchestral conductor born in Russia. Also, *Russian,* **Sergei Aleksandrovich Koussevitzky.**

kous·so (kōōs′ō) See CUSSO.

Kov·no (kôv′nō) The Russian name for KAUNAS.

Ko·weit (kō·wāt′) See KUWAIT.

Kow·loon (kou′lōōn′) The chief port city of Hong Kong on the Kowloon Peninsula (3 sq. mi.) NE of Hong Kong Island; pop. 692,800 (est. 1966).

kow·tow (kou′tou, kō′-) *v.i.* **1.** To behave in an obsequious, servile manner. **2.** To strike the forehead on the ground as a sign of obeisance, reverence, etc. — *n.* The act of kowtowing. Also **ko·tow** (kō′tou′). [< Chinese *k'o-t'ou,* lit., to knock the head] — **kow′tow′er** *n.*

Ko·zhi·kode (kō′zhə·kōd′) A port city in SW India; pop. about 159,000: also *Calicut.*

KP King's pawn (chess).

KP or **K.P.** Kitchen police.

K.P. 1. Knight (of the Order of St.) Patrick. **2.** Knights of Pythias.

kr 1. Kreutzer. **2.** Krone.

Kr *Chem.* Krypton.

KR King's rook (chess).

Kra (krä), **Isthmus of** A neck of land, about 40 miles wide at its narrowest point, connecting the Malay Peninsula with Burma and Thailand.

kraal (kräl) *n.* **1.** In South Africa, a village or group of native huts, usually surrounded by a stockade. **2.** The social unit such a community comprises. **3.** A fenced enclosure for cattle or sheep, especially in South or central Africa. — *v.t.* To confine in a kraal. Also spelled *craal.* [< Afrikaans, village, pen < Pg *curral* pen for cattle. Akin to CORRAL.]

Krae·pe·lin (krä′pə·lĭn), **Emil,** 1856–1926, German psychiatrist.

Krafft-E·bing (kräft′ä′bing), **Baron Richard von,** 1840–1902, German neurologist and psychiatrist.

kraft (kraft, kräft) *n.* A tough, usually dark brown paper, made from high-grade sulfate wood pulp and used for wrapping and in making bags. [< G, strength]

Krag-Jör·gen·sen rifle (krag′jûr′gən·sən) A breechloading rifle used in the U.S. Army 1892–98. Also **Krag.** [after O. *Krag* and E. *Jörgensen,* Norwegian inventors]

Krain (krīn) The German name for CARNIOLA.

krait (krīt) *n.* Any of several venomous snakes (genus *Bungarus*) of Asia. [< Hind. *karait*]

Kra·ka·to·a (krä′kə·tō′ä) A volcanic island between Java and Sumatra; major eruption, 1883. Also **Kra′ka·tau′** (-tou).

kra·ken (krä′kən, krä′-) *n.* A legendary sea monster believed to inhabit the waters off Norway. [< Norw.]

Kra·ków (krä′kōōf) The Polish name for CRACOW. *Russian* **Kra·kov** (krä′kəf).

Kra·nach (krä′näkh), **Lucas** See CRANACH.

Kranj (kräny′) The Slovenian name for CARNIOLA.

Krapp (krap), **George Philip,** 1872–1934, U.S. educator, grammarian, and linguistic scholar.

Kras·no·dar Territory (kraz′nə·där, kras′-, *Russ.* krəs·no·där′) An administrative division of the SW R.S.F.S.R.; 32,500 sq. mi.; pop. 3,762,499 (1959); capital, **Krasnodar** (formerly *Yekaterinodar*), pop. 312,000. *Russian* **Kras·no·dar′skiy Kray′** (-skyē krī′).

Kras·no·yarsk Territory (kraz′nə·yärsk, kras′-, *Russ.* krəs·no·yärsk′) An administrative division of the central R.S.F.S.R.; 930,700 sq. mi.; pop 2,615,098 (1959); capital, **Krasnoyarsk,** pop. 648,000 (est. 1970). *Russian* **Kras·no·yar′skiy Kray′** (-skyē krī′).

K ration A highly condensed, packaged emergency ration provided for soldiers of the U.S. Army in World War II.

kraut (krout) *n.* **1.** Sauerkraut. **2.** *Slang* A German; especially, a German soldier: an offensive term: also **kraut′·head′** (-hed′). [< G *kraut* cabbage]

Kre·feld (krä′felt) A city in North Rhine Westphalia, West Germany; pop. 223,900 (est. 1967).

Kreis·ler (krīs′lər), **Fritz,** 1875–1962, Austrian violinist and composer active in the United States.

Kre·men·chug (kryi·myin·chōōk′) A city in the central Ukrainian S.S.R. on the Dnieper; pop. 86,000 (1959).

Krem·lin (krem′lin) **1.** The walled citadel of Moscow containing the government offices of the Soviet Union. **2.** The government of the Soviet Union. [< Russian *kreml'* citadel]

Krem·lin·ol·o·gy (krem′lin·ol′ə·jē) *n. Informal* The study of the motives, inner workings, etc., of Soviet leadership. — **Krem·lin·ol′o·gist** *n.*

Kre·te (krē′tē) The Greek name for CRETE. Also **Kri′ti**

kreut·zer (kroit′sər) *n.* Any of several small silver or copper coins formerly current in Austria and Germany. Also **kreu′zer.** Abbr. *kr* [< G < *kreuz* cross]

Krieg (krēk) *n.* German War.

krieg·spiel (krēg′spēl, -shpēl) *n.* An instructive game in which figures representing troops, guns, etc., are moved about a terrain model or map in simulation of actual military maneuvers. [< G *kriegsspiel* < *krieg* war + *spiel* game]

Kriem·hild (krēm′hild, *Ger.* krēm′hilt) In the *Nibelungenlied,* the wife of Siegfried and sister of King Gunther; rival of Brunhild. Also **Kriem·hil·de** (krēm′hil·də).

krill (kril) *n.* Tiny marine crustaceans, eaten by whales. [< Norw. *kril* young fry of fish]

krim·mer (krim′ər) *n.* The loosely curled, usually gray fur made from the pelts of lambs raised in the Crimean Peninsula: also spelled *crimmer.* [< G < *Krim* Crimea]

kris (krēs) *n.* A Malay dagger or short sword with a wavy-edged blade: also spelled *crease, creese.* [< Malay]

Krish·na (krish′nə) **1.** A widely worshiped Hindu god, the eighth avatar of Vishnu. He is the narrator and hero of the *Bhagavad-Gita.* **2.** See KISTNA. — **Krish′na·ism** *n.*

Kriss Krin·gle (kris kring′gəl) St. Nicholas; Santa Claus. [< G *Christkindl,* dim. of *Christkind* Christ child]

Kris·ti·a·ni·a (kris′chē·a′nē·ə) The former name for OSLO.

Kri·voi Rog (kryi·voi′ rôk′) A city in the SE Ukrainian S.S.R.; pop. 573,000 (est. 1970).

Krk (kûrk) An island of Yugoslavia in the northern Adriatic; 165 sq. mi.: Italian *Veglia.*

Kró·lew·ska Hu·ta (krōō·lef′skä hōō′tä) A former name for CHORZÓW.

kró·na¹ (krō′nə) *n. pl.* ·**nur** (-nər) The monetary unit of Iceland, equivalent to 100 aurar. Also called *crown.* ·Abbr. *k., K., kn., kr.* [< Icel.]

kro·na² (krō′nə, *Sw.* krōō′nə) *n. pl.* ·**nor** (-nôr) The monetary unit of Sweden, containing 100 öre; also, a Swedish silver coin of this value. Also called *crown.* Abbr. *k., K., kn., kr.* [< Sw.]

kro·ne¹ (krō′ne) *n. pl.* ·**ner** (-ner) **1.** The monetary unit of Denmark, containing 100 öre. **2.** The monetary unit of Norway, containing 100 øre. **3.** A Danish or Norwegian silver coin of this denomination. Also called *crown.* Abbr. *k., K., kn., kr.* [< Dan.]

kro·ne² (krō′uə) *n. pl.* ·**nen** (-nən) Any of several gold and silver coins formerly current in Germany, Austria, and Austria-Hungary: also called *crown.* Abbr. *k., K., kn., kr.* [< G]

Kro·nos (krō′nos) See CRONUS.

Kron·stadt (krōn′shtät) A Soviet port and naval base on an island in the Gulf of Finland; pop. 59,000 (1959). *Russian* **Kron·shtadt** (krən·shtät′).

Kro·pot·kin (krə·pot′kin, *Russ.* kro·pôt′kyin), **Peter,** 1842–1921, Russian scientist and anarchist. Also, *Russian,* **Pëtr Alekseevich Kropotkin.**

KRP King's rook's pawn (chess).
kru·bi (krōō′bē) *n. pl.* **·bis** A plant (*Amorphophallus titanum*) of the arum family native in Sumatra, having a huge malodorous, vaselike spathe. Also **kru′but** (-but). [< native Sumatran name]
Kru·ger (krōō′gər, *Afrikaans* krü′gər), **Stephanus Johannes Paulus**, 1825–1904, Boer leader; president of the Transvaal Republic 1883–1900: called **Oom Paul** (ōm pô′ōōl).
Kru·gers·dorp (krōō′gərz·dôrp, *Afrikaans* krü′gərs·dôrp) A town in southern Transvaal, South Africa; pop. 89,493 (1960).
krul·ler (krul′ər)· See CRULLER.
Krupp (krup, *Ger.* krōōp) A German family prominent in the manufacture of steel and munitions, notably **Alfred**, 1812–87; and his son, **Friedrich Alfred**, 1854–1902.
Krym (krim) The Russian name for the CRIMEA. Also **Krym′ska·ya Oblast** (-skä·yä).
kry·o·lite (krī′ə-līt), **kry·o·lith** (-lith) See CRYOLITE.
kryp·ton (krip′ton) *n.* A colorless gaseous element (symbol Kr), present in minute amounts in the atmosphere, used as a filler in incandescent and fluorescent electric lamps. See ELEMENT. [< Gk., neut. of *kryptos* hidden]
kt. Karat or carat.
Kt Knight (chess).
K.T. **1.** Knight Templar. **2.** *Brit.* Knight (of the Order) of the Thistle.
Kua·la Lum·pur (kwä′lə lōōm′pōōr) The capital of Malaysia and Selangor State, in the central part of Malaya; pop. 451,728 (1970).
Ku·ban (kōō·bäny′′) A river in the Georgian S.S.R. and the R.S.F.S.R., flowing 584 miles, generally NW, to the Black Sea. Also **Ku·ban′**.
Ku·blai Khan (kōō′blī kän′), 1216?–94, Mongol emperor, founder of the Mongol dynasty of China. Also **Kub·la Khan** (kōō′blə).
ku·chen (kōō′khən) *n.* A yeast-dough coffee cake usually containing fruits and nuts, and covered with sugar. [< G]
Ku·ching (kōō′ching) The capital of Sarawak, Malaysia; pop. 56,000 (1960).
ku·dos (kyōō′dos, kōō-) *n.* Glory; credit; praise: used only in the singular. [< Gk. *kydos* glory]
ku·du (kōō′dōō) See KOODOO.
Kuen·lun (kōōn′lōōn′) See KUNLUN.
Ku·fic (kyōō′fik) *adj.* Relating to **Kufa**, an ancient Arabian city on the Euphrates, or to the primitive Arabic characters used by its writers. — *n.* The Arabic alphabet as written at Kufa. Also spelled *Cufic*.
Ku·fra (kōō′frä) A group of five oases in the center of the Libyan Desert: Italian *Cufra*. Also **Ku′fa·ra** (-fə·rə).
Kui·by·shev (kōō′ē·bi·shif) A city in the SW R.S.F.S.R., on the Volga; pop. 1,016,000 (est. 1968): formerly *Samara*. Also **Ku′y·by·shev**.
Ku Klux Klan (kōō′ kluks′ klan′, kyōō′) **1.** A secret society formed in the South after the Civil War to prevent Negro equality. **2.** An anti-Negro, anti-Catholic, and anti-Jewish secret society founded in Georgia in 1915 and most active during the 1920's in both the South and other parts of the United States. Abbr. *KKK, K.K.K.* [Alter. of Gk. *kyklos* circle + *clan*] — **Ku′ Klux′ Klan′ner**
Ku·ku Nor (kōō′kōō′ nôr′) See KOKO NOR.
ku·lak (kōō·läk′) *n.* In Russia, a wealthy peasant who employed labor, and opposed the Soviet collectivization of farms. [< Russian, lit., fist, tight-fisted man]
Kul·tur (kōōl·tōōr′) *n.* **1.** Civilization, culture, and social organization. **2.** The undemocratic and pompous aspects of the German imperial and Nazi regimes: an ironical usage. **3.** In Nazi jargon, the racial and historic superiorities of Germany and the Germans. [< G]
Kul·tur·kampf (kōōl·tōōr′kämpf) *n.* The political struggle from 1872 to 1887 between the German imperial government and the Roman Catholic Church over the state's attempts to control educational and ecclesiastical appointments. [< G < KULTUR + *kampf* struggle]
Ku·lun (kōō′lōōn′) The Chinese name for ULAN BATOR.
Ku·ma·mo·to (kōō·mä·mō·tō) A port city on the west coast of Kyushu island, Japan; pop. 383,000 (est. 1959).
Ku·ma·si (kōō·mä′sē) A city in south central Ghana, the capital of Ashanti; pop. 190,362 (1960): formerly *Coomassie*.
ku·miss (kōō′mis) *n.* **1.** Fermented mare's or camel's milk, used as a beverage by the nomads of central Asia. **2.** A similar drink made from cow's milk. Also spelled *koumiss, koumys*. Also **ku′mys**. [< Russian *kumys* < Tatar *kumiz*]
küm·mel (kim′əl, *Ger.* kü′məl) *n.* A liqueur flavored with aniseed, cumin, or caraway, made chiefly in Germany and Russia. [< G, caraway seed < L *cuminum*. See CUMIN.]
kum·mer·bund (kum′ər·bund) See CUMMERBUND.
kum·quat (kum′kwot) *n.* **1.** A small, round or ovoid orange fruit with a sour pulp and edible rind, borne by any of several trees (genus *Fortunella*) and cultivated in China, Japan, and the United States for making preserves or confections. **2.** The tree bearing this fruit. Also spelled *cumquat*. [Cantonese alter. of Pekinese *chin-chü*, lit., golden orange]
Kun (kōōn), **Béla**, born 1886, Hungarian Communist leader; premier 1919; disappeared 1937.

Kung (kōōng), **Hsiang-hsi**, 1881,–1967, Chinese statesman.
K'ung Fu·tse (kōōng′ fōō′tse′) See CONFUCIUS.
Ku·ni·yo·shi (kōō·nē·yō·shē), **Yasuo**, 1893–1953, U.S. painter born in Japan.
Kun·lun (kōōn′lōōn′) Mountain ranges in northern Tibet and the southern Sinkiang-Uighur Autonomous Region; highest peak, Ulugh Muztagh, 25,340 ft.: also *Kuenlun*.
Kun·ming (kōōn′ming′) The capital of Yünnan Province, China; pop. 1,700,000 (est. 1970): formerly *Yunnan*. Also **K'un′ming′**.
kunz·ite (kōōnts′īt) *n.* A lilac variety of spodumene, used as a gemstone. [after G. F.*Kunz*, 1856–1932, U.S. mineralogist]
Kuo·min·tang (kwō′min′tang′) *n.* The nationalist party of China, founded in 1912 by Sun Yat-sen and led after 1927 by Chiang Kai-shek. [< Chinese *kuo* nationalist + *min* people's + *tang* party]
Ku·ra (kōō·rä′) A river in Transcaucasia, flowing 940 miles NE to the Caspian Sea: ancient *Cyrus*. Also **Kur** (kōōr).
kur·bash (kōōr′bash) *n.* A whip of heavy hide. — *v.t.* To whip with the kurbash. [< Turkish *qirbach*]
Kurd (kûrd, kōōrd) *n.* A member of a nomadic Moslem people dwelling chiefly in Kurdistan.
Kurd·ish (kûr′dish, kōōr′-) *adj.* Of or pertaining to the Kurds, their culture, or their language. — *n.* The Iranian language of the Kurds.
Kur·di·stan (kûr′di·stan, kōōr′di·stän) A region in NW Iran, NE Iraq, and SE Turkey, peopled largely by Kurds.
Ku·re (kōō·re) A port city on SW Honshu island, Japan; pop. 209,000 (est. 1959).
Ku·rile Islands (kōō′ril, kōō·rēl′) An island chain of the R.S.F.S.R. between the southern tip of Kamchatka and the main islands of Japan; 5,700 sq. mi.: Japanese *Chishima Retto*. Also **Ku′rile Islands**, **Ku′riles**. *Russian* **Ku·ril·ski·ye Os·tro·va** (kōō·ryē′l′skyi·yə əs·tro·vä′). Also **Ku·ril′′ski·ye**.
Ku·ril·i·an (kōō·ril′ē·ən) *adj.* Of or pertaining to the Kurile Islands or their inhabitants. — *n.* A Kurile native.
Kur·land (kōōr′lənd) See COURLAND.
kur·ra·jong (kûr′ə·jong) *n.* Any of various Australian trees, as the **black kurrajong** (*Brachychiton populneum*), having a bark that yields a durable, tough fiber: also spelled *currajong, koorajong*. [< native Australian name]
Kursk (kōōrsk) A city in the SW R.S.F.S.R.; pop. 284,000 (est. 1970).
kur·to·sis (kər·tō′sis) *n. Stat.* The relative degree of curvature near the mode of a frequency curve, as compared with that of a normal curve of the same variance. [< Gk. *kyrtos* curved + -OSIS]
ku·ruş (kōō·rōōsh′) *n. pl.* **·ruş** Piaster (def. 2). [< Turkish]
Ku·ru·su (kōō·rōō·sōō), **Saburo**, 1888?–1954, Japanese diplomat.
Kush (kush), **Kush·it·ic** (kōōsh·it′ik) See CUSH, etc.
kus·so (kus′ō) See CUSSO.
Ku·tu·zov (kōō·tōō′zôf), **Mikhail Ilarionovich**, 1745–1813, Russian field marshal; defeated Napoleon at Smolensk 1812.
Ku·wait (kōō·wīt′) An independent shiekdom in NE Arabia; about 5,000 sq. mi.; pop. 733,196 (1970); capital, **Kuwait**. pop. 99,609 (1965): also *Koweit*. See map of SAUDI ARABIA. — **Ku·wait′i** *adj.* & *n.*
Kuyp (koip), **Albert** See CUYP.
Kuz·netsk Basin (kōōz·nyetsk′) The richest coal basin in the Soviet Union, a region along the Tom in the south central R.S.F.S.R. *Russian* **Kuz·net′skiy Bas·sein** (-skyē bə·syän′). Also **Kuz·bas** (kōōz·bäs′).
kv. or **kv** Kilovolt(s).
K.V. Köchel listing (G *Köchel Verzeichnis*).
kva or **kv.-a.** Kilovolt-ampere.
kvass (kväs, kvas) *n.* A Russian fermented drink resembling sour beer, made from rye, barley, etc.: also spelled *quass*. Also **kvas**. [< Russian *kvas*]
kw. or **kw** Kilowatt(s).
kwa·cha (kwä′chä) *n.* The monetary unit of Malawi, equivalent to 100 tambala, and of Zambia, equivalent to 100 ngwee.
Kwang·chow (kwäng′chō′, *Chinese* gwäng′jō′) The Chinese name for CANTON.
Kwang·si-Chuang Autonomous Region (kwang′sē′ chwang′, *Chinese* gwäng′sē′jwäng′) An administrative division of SE China; 85,000 sq. mi.; pop. 19,390,000 (est. 1958); capital, Nanning.
Kwang·tung (kwang′tōōng′, *Chinese* gwän′dōōng′) A Province of SE China; 85,000 sq. mi.; pop. 37,960,000 (est. 1957); capital, Canton.
Kwan·tung Leased Territory (kwan′tōōng′, *Chinese* gwän′dōōng′) A region on the southern tip of Liaotung Peninsula, leased, 1905–45, by Japan; 1,337 sq. mi.
kwash·i·or·kor (kwäsh′ē·ôr′kôr) *n. Pathol.* A nutritional disease, usually associated with a maize diet, prevalent among young children in South Africa and elsewhere, characterized by swelling of the hands, feet, and face and by the discolored blotches on the body. [< native African name]
Kwei·chow (kwā′chou′, *Chinese* gwä′jō′) A Province of southern China; 65,000 sq. mi.; pop. 16,890,000 (est. 1957); capital, Kweiyang.

Kwei·yang (kwā′yang′, *Chinese* gwä′yäng′) The capital of Kweichow Province, China; pop. 1,500,000 (est. 1970).
K.W.H., kw-h, kwh, kw.-hr., kw-hr Kilowatt-hour(s).
Ky. Kentucky.
ky·a·nite (kī′ə·nīt) See CYANITE.
ky·an·ize (kī′ən·īz) *v.t.* **·ized, ·iz·ing** To impregnate (wood) with mercuric chloride to prevent decay. Also *Brit.* **ky′an·ise.** [after J. H. *Kyan*, 1774–1850, Irish inventor] — **ky′·an·i·za′tion** (-ə·zā′shən, -ī·zā′-) *n.*
kyar (kyär) Coir.
kyat (kyät) *n.* A monetary unit of Burma, equivalent to 100 pyas. [< Burmese]
Kyd (kid), **Thomas,** 1558–94, English dramatist. Also *Kid.*
Ky·kla·des (kē·klä′thes) See KIKLADHES.
ky·lix (kī′liks) *n.* *pl.* **ky·li·kes** (kī′li·kēz) In ancient Greece, a shallow earthenware drinking cup with a stem and small handles, used chiefly at banquets: also *cylix.* [< Gk., cup]
ky·mo·graph (kī′mə·graf, -gräf) *n.* **1.** *Med.* A device for recording variations in the pulse, respiration, etc., on a continuous graph. **2.** *Aeron.* An instrument for graphing the deviations of an air-

KYLIX

plane from straight and level flight. Also *cymograph.* [< Gk. *kyma* wave + -GRAPH] — **ky′mo·graph′ic** *adj.*
Kym·ric (kim′rik), **Kym·ry** (kim′rē) See CYMRIC, etc.
Kyn·e·wulf (kin′ə·woolf, kün′-) See CYNEWULF.
Kyong·song (kyông·sông) See SEOUL.
Kyo·to (kyō·tō) A city on SW Honshu island, Japan; the capital of the Japanese Empire until 1868; pop. 1,418,933 (est. 1970): also *Kioto.*
ky·pho·sis (kī·fō′sis) *n. Pathol.* Backward curvature of the spine; humpback. [< NL < Gk. *kyphōsis* < *kyphos* humpbacked] — **ky·phot·ic** (kī·fot′ik) *adj.*
Kyr·i·e e·le·i·son (kir′i·ē i·lā′i·sən) **1.** In the Roman Catholic and Eastern Orthodox churches, an ancient liturgical petition for mercy beginning with the words *Kyrie eleison* ("Lord, have mercy"). **2.** A musical setting of *Kyrie eleison.* [< LL < Gk. *Kyrie eleēson*]
kyte (kīt) *n. Scot.* The belly; stomach. [Cf. Du. *kijte.*]
kythe (kīth) See KITHE.
Ky·the·ra (kē′thē·rä) An island of Greece south of the Peloponnesus; 108 sq. mi. Latin *Cythera,* Italian *Cerigo.*
Kyu·shu (kyoō·shoō) The southernmost of the five principal islands of Japan; 16,247 sq. mi.: also *Kiushu.*

L

l, L (el) *n.* *pl.* **l's** or **ls, L's** or **Ls, ells** (elz) **1.** The twelfth letter of the English alphabet. The shape of the Phoenician letter *lamed* was adopted by the Greeks as *lambda* and became Roman *L.* Also *ell.* **2.** The sound represented by the letter *l,* normally a voiced alveolar continuant. **3.** Anything shaped like the letter L. — *symbol* The Roman numeral 50.
l- or l *Chem.* Levo-.
l. or l Liter.
L 1. Latin. **2.** *Physics* Length. **3.** Longitude.
L or l *Electr.* Coefficient of inductance.
L or £ or l Pound (sterling) (L *libra*).
L. 1. Latin. **2.** Licentiate. **3.** Linnaeus. **4.** Lodge (fraternal).
L. or l. 1. Book (L *liber*). **2.** Lake. **3.** Latitude. **4.** Law. **5.** Leaf. **6.** Left. **7.** Length. **8.** Line. **9.** Link. **10.** Lira; lire. **11.** Low.
la¹ (lä) *n. Music* The sixth syllable used in solmization; the sixth degree of a major scale; also, the tone A.
la² (lä, lò) *interj.* An exclamation expressing surprise, emphasis, etc.: also spelled *law.* [OE *lä.* Doublet of LO.]
La *Chem.* Lanthanum.
La. Louisiana.
L.A. 1. Legislative Assembly. **2.** Library Association. **3.** Local Agent. **4.** Los Angeles.
laa·ger (lä′gər) *n.* In South Africa, a defensive enclosure or camp, especially one formed by a group of wagons. — *v.t.* & *v.i.* To camp in or form into a laager. Also spelled *lager.* [< Afrikaans < Du. *leger* camp]
Laa·land (lô′län) An island of Denmark in the Baltic Sea; 479 sq. mi.; chief city, Maribo: also *Lolland.*
lab (lab) *n. U.S. Informal* Laboratory.
lab. Laboratory.
Lab. Labrador.
La·ban (lā′bən) In the Old Testament, the father of Rachel and Leah. *Gen.* xxix 10–30. [< Hebrew *lābhān,* lit. white]
lab·a·rum (lab′ə·rəm) *n.* *pl.* **·ra** (-rə) **1.** A standard bearing the monogram of Christ, used by Constantine and later Roman emperors. **2.** An ecclesiastical banner borne in processions. [< LL < Gk. *labaron;* ult. origin unknown]
lab·da·num (lab′də·nəm) *n.* A resin derived from various species of the rockrose (genus *Cistus*), used in perfumery and in medicine: also *ladanum.* [< L *ladanum, ledanum* < Gk. *ladanon, lēdanon* < *lēdon* mastic < Arabic < Persian]
La·be (lä′be) The Czech name for the ELBE.
lab·e·fac·tion (lab′ə·fak′shən) *n. Rare* A weakening or deterioration. Also **lab′e·fac′ta′tion** (-fak′tā′shən). [< LL ˌ*labefactio, -onis* < L *labefactus,* pp. of *labefacere* to cause to totter < *labare* to totter, fall to pieces + *facere* to make]
la·bel (lā′bəl) *n.* **1.** A slip of paper, strip of cloth, printed legend, etc., on a container or article showing its nature, producer, destination, etc. **2.** A term or phrase used to classify or describe persons, schools of thought, etc. **3.** *Archit.* A projecting molding over a wall opening; dripstone. **4.** A strip of cloth or other material attached to a document to hold a seal. **5.** *Heraldry* A band with several dependent

points, drawn across the upper part of a shield to denote an eldest son. — *v.t.* **la·beled** or **·belled, la·bel·ing** or **·bel·ling 1.** To mark with a label; attach a label to. **2.** To classify; designate. [< OF, ribbon, ? < OHG *lappa* rag] — **la′·bel·er** or **la′bel·ler** *n.*
la·bel·lum (lə·bel′əm) *n.* *pl.* **·bel·la** (-bel′ə) *Bot.* The lip or lower petal of an orchid, often enlarged or conspicuous by its shape. [< NL < L, dim. of *labrum* lip]
la·bi·a (lā′bē·ə) Plural of LABIUM.
la·bi·al (lā′bē·əl) *adj.* **1.** Of or pertaining to a labium. **2.** *Phonet.* Articulated or modified by the lips, as are (p), (b), (m), (w), or the rounded vowels (ō) and (oō). **3.** *Music* Producing tones by the action of an air current upon liplike edges, as in the flute or the flue pipes of an organ. — *n.* **1.** A labial sound. **2.** An organ pipe with lips; flue pipe [< Med.L *labialis* < L *labium* lip]
la·bi·al·ize (lā′bē·əl·īz′) *v.t.* **·ized, ·iz·ing** *Phonet.* **1.** To make labial; give a labial sound to. **2.** To round (a vowel). — **la′bi·al·ism, la′bi·al·i·za′tion** *n.*
la·bi·ate (lā′bē·āt, -it) *adj.* **1.** Having lips or liplike parts. **2.** *Bot.* **a** Bilabiate. **b** Belonging to or designating a family of plants (*Labiatae*), the mint family, typically having bilabiate corollas and square stems. Also **la′bi·at′ed.** — *n.* A labiate plant. [< NL *labiatus* < L *labium* lip]
La·biche (là·bēsh′), **Eugene Marin,** 1815–88, French dramatist.
la·bile (lā′bil) *adj.* **1.** Liable to lapse or change; unstable. **2.** *Med.* In electrotherapy, pertaining to the method of application in which an electrode is moved over the part being treated. [< L *labilis* < *labi* to slip, fall] — **la·bil′i·ty** *n.*
labio- *combining form* Related to, or formed by the lips and (another organ): *labiodental.* [< L *labium* lip]
la·bi·o·den·tal (lā′bē·ō·den′təl) *Phonet. adj.* Formed with the lower lip and the upper front teeth, as (f) and (v) in English. — *n.* A sound so formed. Also *dentilabial.*
la·bi·o·na·sal (lā′bē·ō·nā′zəl) *Phonet.* adj. Produced with the lips closed and the voiced breath passing through the nose, as (m). — *n.* A sound so formed.
la·bi·o·ve·lar (lā′bē·ō·vē′lər) *Phonet. adj.* Produced with the lips rounded and partially closed and the back of the tongue near or against the velum, as (w). — *n.* A sound so formed.
la·bi·um (lā′bē·əm) *n.* *pl.* **·bi·a** (-bē·ə) **1.** *Anat.* **a** A lip or liplike part. **b** One of the four folds of the vulva, comprising the two outer folds of skin (**labia majora**) and the two inner folds of mucous membrane (**labia minora**). **2.** *Entomol.* A movable sclerite between the maxillae of an insect, forming the lower surface of the mouth; the lower lip. **3.** *Bot.* The lower lip of a bilabiate flower. [< L, lip]
la·bor (lā′bər) *n.* **1.** Physical or manual work done for hire in economic production. **2.** Arduous physical or mental exertion; toil. **3.** The working class collectively, especially as organized into labor unions. **4.** A piece of work; task: a rewarding *labor.* **5.** *Med.* The pain and stress of childbirth; especially, the uterine contractions just prior to giving birth. **6.** *Naut.* Heavy rolling and pitching of a vessel. — **Depart-**

ment of Labor An executive department of the U.S. government (established 1913), headed by the Secretary of Labor, that carries out policies regarding wages, working conditions, unemployment, etc. — *v.i.* **1.** To work hard physically or mentally; exert oneself for a cause or purpose; toil; strive. **2.** To progress with great effort or painful exertion: the lame man *labored* past. **3.** To suffer the pangs of childbirth; travail. **4.** To be oppressed or hampered: to *labor* under difficulties. **5.** *Naut.* To roll and pitch in a heavy sea. — *v.t.* **6.** To work out laboriously; overwork; overelaborate: to *labor* an argument. **7.** *Archaic* or *Poetic* To till; plow; cultivate. Also, *Brit.*, **labour.** [< OF *labor, labour* < L *labor* toil, distress]

lab·o·ra·to·ry (lab′rə·tôr′ē, -tō′rē; *Brit.* lə·bor′ə·trē) *n. pl.* **·ries 1.** A building or room equipped for conducting scientific experiments, analyses, tissue and blood examinations, etc. **2.** A department, as in a factory, for research, testing, and experimental technical work. Also, *Informal,* **lab.** [< Med.L *laboratorium* < L *laborare* to labor < *labor* toil]

laboratory school A school for educational experimentation.

Labor Day In most States of the United States and in Canada, a legal holiday, usually the first Monday in September, originally set aside as a holiday in honor of labor.

la·bored (lā′bərd) *adj.* **1.** Performed laboriously; difficult; painful: *labored* breathing. **2.** Overelaborate; strained: *labored* prose.

la·bor·er (lā′bər·ər) *n.* One who performs physical or manual labor, especially unskilled labor.

la·bo·ri·ous (lə·bôr′ē·əs, -bō′rē-) *adj.* **1.** Requiring much labor; toilsome. **2.** Diligent; industrious. — **Syn.** see DIFFICULT. — **la·bo′ri·ous·ly** *adv.* — **la·bo′ri·ous·ness** *n.* [< OF *laborieux* < L *laboriosus* < *labor* labor, toil]

la·bor·ite (lā′bər·īt) *n.* One who supports labor interests, especially in politics. Also, *Brit.* **la′bour·ite.**

la·bor om·ni·a vin·cit (lā′bôr om′nē·ə vin′sit) *Latin* Labor conquers all things: the motto of Oklahoma.

labor relations The relations between management and working force in business and industry, especially in matters of wages, hours, pensions, etc.; also, the administration and conduct of such relations.

la·bor-sav·ing (lā′bər·sā′ving) *adj.* Doing away with, or diminishing the need for, manual work: *laborsaving* devices.

labor union An association of workers organized to improve working conditions and advance mutual interests: also called *trade union.*

la·bour (lā′bər), **la·bour·er** (lā′bər·ər), etc. British spelling of LABOR, etc.

La·bour·ite (lā′bər·īt) *n.* A member of a Labour party in Great Britain or in one of the nations belonging to the British Commonwealth.

Labour Party 1. In Great Britain, a large political party drawing its chief support from labor and trade unions and committed to socialist reforms. **2.** A similar party in other members of the British Commonwealth of Nations.

Lab·ra·dor (lab′rə·dôr′) **1.** The northernmost district of Newfoundland, Canada; about 110,000 sq. mi.; pop. 21,157. **2.** The peninsula of NE North America between the Saint Lawrence River and Hudson Bay; about 530,000 sq. mi. See map of GREENLAND.

lab·ra·dor·ite (lab′rə·dôr′īt) *n.* A triclinic lime-soda feldspar exhibiting a brilliant play of colors. [after *Labrador,* where originally found + -ITE¹]

la·bret (lā′bret) *n.* A stud or plug of wood, stone, etc., worn in a hole pierced through the lip by various primitive peoples. [Dim. of LABRUM]

la·broid (lā′broid) *adj.* Of or pertaining to a family (*Labridae*) of fishes including the wrasses, tautog, etc. — *n.* A labroid fish. [< NL *Labroidea* < *Labrus* a genus of the family *Labridae* < L *labrus* a kind of fish < *labrum* lip]

la·brum (lā′brəm, -rəm) *n. pl.* **·bra** (-brə) **1.** A lip, especially an outer lip, or liplike part. **2.** *Anat.* A ring of cartilage surrounding the rim of the socket in a ball and socket joint. **3.** *Zool.* **a** A liplike projection in front of the mouth parts of insects and other arthropods. **b** The outer edge of the univalve shell of a gastropod. [< L, lip]

La Bru·yère (là brü·yâr′), **Jean de,** 1645–96, French writer and moralist.

La·bu·an (lā′boo·än′) An island off the NW coast of Borneo, administered together with Sabah; 30 sq. mi.; chief town, Victoria.

la·bur·num (lə·bûr′nəm) *n.* Any of a genus (*Laburnum*) of leguminous Old World trees yielding a poisonous alkaloid, especially the **golden-chain laburnum** (*L. anagyroides*), with pendulous racemes of yellow flowers and hard, dark wood. [< NL < L; ult. origin unknown]

lab·y·rinth (lab′ə·rinth) *n.* **1.** An arrangement or system of winding, intricate passages or paths, as in a building, enclosed garden, park, etc., designed to confuse whoever tries to go through and find the exit; maze. **2.** Anything resembling a labyrinth, as a confusing network of streets or passageways. **3.** Any intricate or perplexing set of difficulties, state of affairs, etc. **4.** *Anat.* The winding passages of the inner ear, including the cochlea, the vestibule, and the semicircular canals. [< LABYRINTH]

Lab·y·rinth (lab′ə·rinth) In Greek mythology, the maze used to confine the Minotaur, constructed by Daedalus for Minos of Crete. [< L *labyrinthus* < Gk. *labyrinthos*; ult. origin unknown, prob. non-Hellenic]

lab·y·rin·thine (lab′ə·rin′thin, -thēn) *adj.* **1.** Of, pertaining to, or in the form of a labyrinth. **2.** Like a labyrinth; intricate; perplexing. Also **lab′y·rin′thi·an, lab′y·rin′thic, lab′y·rin′thi·cal.** — **lab′y·rin′thi·cal·ly** *adv.*

lac¹ (lak) *n.* A resinous deposit left on certain trees by the Indian lac insect and used in making varnishes, paints, etc. [< Hind. *lākh* < Prakrit *lakkha* < Skt. *lākshā*]

lac² (lak) *n.* **1.** In India, the sum of 100,000: said especially of rupees. **2.** Any very great number. Also spelled *lakh.* [< Hind. *lākh* < Skt. *laksha* 100,000]

CRETAN
LABYRINTH
(Reverse of a
coin of Cnossus, circa
2 B.C.)

Lac·ca·dive, Min·i·coy, and A·min·di·vi Islands (lak′ə·div. min′i·koi and um′in·dē′vi) A group of 19 islands off the Malabar Coast, a centrally administered territory of India; 10.76 sq. mi.; pop. 21,195 (1951); headquarters at Kozhikode in Kerala, India.

lac·co·lith (lak′ə·lith) *n. Geol.* A mass of intrusive lava, generally with a flat base, that has spread out between strata and forced up the overlying rocks to form domes. Also **lac′co·lite** (-līt). [< Gk. *lakkos* reservoir + -LITH¹] — **lac′·co·lith′ic, lac′co·lit′ic** (-lit′ik) *adj.*

lace (lās) *n.* **1.** A cord or string passed through eyelets or over hooks for fastening together the edges of a shoe, garment, etc. For illustration see SHOE. **2.** A delicate openwork fabric or network, made by hand or on a machine, of linen, silk, cotton, etc. **3.** A silver or gold braid used to decorate uniforms, hats, etc. **4.** A dash of alcoholic liquor added to coffee or tea. — *v.* **laced, lac·ing** *v.t.* **1.** To fasten or draw together by tying the lace or laces of. **2.** To pass (a cord or string) through eyelets or over hooks as a lace. **3.** To trim with or as with lace. **4.** To compress the waist of (a person) by tightening laces of a corset. **5.** To intertwine or interlace. **6.** To streak with lines or colors. **7.** To add a dash of alcoholic liquor to. **8.** *Informal* To beat; thrash. — *v.i.* **9.** To be fastened by means of a lace or laces: These shoes *lace.* — **to lace into** *Informal* **1.** To strike or attack with a heavy blow or blows. **2.** To scold; berate. [< OF *laz, las,* orig. noose < L *laqueus* noose, trap. Akin to LASH, LATCH.]

Lac·e·dae·mon (las′ə·dē′mən) See SPARTA.

Lac·e·dae·mo·ni·an (las′ə·di·mō′nē·ən) *adj. & n.* Spartan.

lac·er·ate (las′ər·āt) *v.t.* **·at·ed, ·at·ing 1.** To tear raggedly; rend; mangle; especially, to wound the flesh by tearing. **2.** To injure; harrow: to *lacerate* one's feelings. — *adj.* **1.** Jagged; torn. **2.** Harrowed; distressed. **3.** *Biol.* Having the edges jagged or irregularly cleft. [< L *laceratus,* pp. of *lacerare* to tear < *lacer* mangled] — **lac′er·a·ble** *adj.*

lac·er·a·tion (las′ər·ā′shən) *n.* **1.** The act of lacerating. **2.** The wound or jagged tear resulting from lacerating.

La·cer·ta (lə·sûr′tə) *n.* A constellation, the Lizard. See CONSTELLATION. [< L, lizard]

lac·er·til·i·an (las′ər·til′ē·ən) *adj.* Of or pertaining to an order or suborder (*Lacertilia*) of reptiles, including lizards, chameleons, and related limbless forms. — *n.* A lacertilian reptile. Also **la·cer·ti·an** (lə·sûr′shē·ən, -shən). [< NL *Lacertilia* < L *lacertus, lacerta* lizard]

lace·wing (lās′wing′) *n.* Any of various neuropterous insects with four lacy wings and shiny eyes, as the **brown lacewing** (genus *Hemerobius*) and the **green lacewing** (genus *Chrysopa*), the larvae of which destroy aphids and other insects. For illustration see INSECTS (beneficial).

lace·wood (lās′wood′) *n.* **1.** A tree (*Cardwellia sublimis*) of Queensland, Australia: also called *silky oak.* **2.** The wood of the lacewood, used for furniture, veneering, etc.

lace·work (lās′wûrk′) *n.* **1.** Lace. **2.** Any decorative openwork resembling lace.

lach·es (lach′iz) *n. Law* Unreasonable and inexcusable delay in asserting a right, so that the court is warranted in refusing relief. [< AF *laches, lachesse,* OF *laschesse* < *lasche* negligent < *laschier* to slacken < L *laxare* < *laxus* lax]

Lach·e·sis (lak′ə·sis) One of the three Fates or Moirai. [< L < Gk., lit., a lot < *lanchanein* to obtain by lot or fate]

lach·ry·mal (lak′rə·məl) *adj.* Of, pertaining to, or producing tears. — *n.* **1.** *pl.* The organs secreting tears: also **lachrymal glands. 2.** A lachrymatory. Also spelled *lacrimal.* [< Med.L *lacrimalis, lacrymalis* < L *lacrima* tear]

lach·ry·ma·tor (lak′rə·mā′tər) *n.* A tear gas: also spelled *lacrimator.* [< L *lacrima* tear + -ATOR]

lach·ry·ma·to·ry (lak′rə·mə·tôr′ē, -tō′rē) *n. pl.* **·ries** A small bottle of glass, alabaster, etc., with a narrow neck, found in ancient tombs, and formerly supposed to have held the tears of mourners. — *adj.* Of, pertaining to, or producing tears. Also spelled *lacrimatory.* [< Med.L *lacrimatorium* < L, neut. of *lacrimatorius* of tears < *lacrima* tear]

lach·ry·mose (lak′rə·mōs) *adj.* **1.** Shedding, or given to shedding, tears; tearful. **2.** Provoking tears; sad: a *lachry-*

mose tale. Also spelled *lacrimose.* [< L *lacrimosus* < *lacrima* tear] — **lach·ri·mose·ly** *adv.*

lac·ing (lā′sing) *n.* **1.** The act of one who or that which laces. **2.** A cord or string for holding together opposite parts of a shoe, garment, etc.; lace. **3.** A fastening made with lacing. **4.** *Informal* A thrashing; beating. **5.** An ornamental braid, especially of gold or silver.

la·cin·i·ate (lə·sin′ē·āt, -it) *adj.* **1.** Fringed. **2.** *Bot.* Slashed or cut irregularly into narrow lobes or segments; incised. Also **la·cin′i·at′ed.** [< NL *lacinia* a slash in a leaf or petal, (< L, a flap) + -ATE¹]

lac insect Any of a family (*Lacciferidae*) of hemipterous insects, especially an Indian species (*Laccifer lacca*), the females of which exude lac.

lack (lak) *n.* **1.** Deficiency or complete absence of something needed or desired. **2.** That which is absent or deficient; shortage; need. — *v.t.* **1.** To be without; have none or too little of. **2.** To be short by: He *lacks* two months of his majority. — *v.i.* **3.** To be wanting or deficient; be missing. [ME *lac*, prob. < MLG *lak* deficiency]

lack·a·dai·si·cal (lak′ə·dā′zi·kəl) *adj.* Affectedly pensive or melancholy; languishing; listless. — **Syn.** See LANGUID. [< *lackadaisy*, alter. of LACKADAY] — **lack′a·dai′si·cal·ly** *adv.* — **lack′a·dai′si·cal·ness** *n.*

lack·a·day (lak′ə·dā′) *interj. Archaic* An exclamation of grief or regret. [Aphetic var. of ALACKADAY. See ALACK.]

Lack·a·wan·na (lak′ə·won′ə) A city in western New York, on Lake Erie, near Buffalo; pop. 28,657.

lack·ey (lak′ē) *n. pl.* **·eys** **1.** A male servant of low status, usually in livery; footman. **2.** Any servile follower or attendant; lickspittle. — *v.t. & v.i.* To attend or act as a lackey. Also *lacquey.* [< OF *laquay* < Sp. *lacayo*]

lack·lus·ter (lak′lus′tər) *adj.* Lacking sheen and brightness; dull. — *n.* A lack of brightness or luster; also, that which lacks brightness. Also **lack′lus′tre.**

La·co·ni·a (lə·kō′nē·ə) An ancient country in the SE Peloponnesus, Greece; capital Sparta: Greek *Lakonia.* Also **La·con′i·ca** (lə·kon′i·kə). See map of ATTICA. — **La·co′ni·an** *adj. & n.*

la·con·ic (lə·kon′ik) *adj.* Brief and concise in expression; pithy. Also **la·con′i·cal.** — **Syn.** See TERSE. [< L *Laconicus* < Gk. *Lakonikos* < *Lakōn* a Spartan; with ref. to the habitual terseness of Spartan speech] — **la·con′i·cal·ly** *adv.*

lac·o·nism (lak′ə·niz′əm) *n.* **1.** Brevity and pithiness of utterance. **2.** A terse, pointed phrase; laconic expression. Also **la·con·i·cism** (lə·kon′ə·siz′əm).

La Co·ru·ña (lä kō·rōō′nyä) A port commune in NW Spain, on the Atlantic; pop. 177,502 (1960): also *Coruña.*

lac·quer (lak′ər) *n.* **1.** A transparent varnish made from various resins, sometimes containing nitrocellulose, dissolved in volatile solvent. **2.** A resinous varnish obtained from the lacquer tree (*Toxicodendron vernicifluum*) of China and Japan, and used to impart a high polish to wood. **3.** Decorative woodwork or articles of wood painted with this lacquer: also **lac′quer·work′** (-wûrk′). — *v.t.* To coat with or as with lacquer. Also *Obs.* **lack′er.** [< MF *lacre* a kind of sealing wax < Pg. < *lacca* gum lac < Hind. *lākh.* See LAC¹; infl. in form by F *lacque* lac¹.] — **lac′quer·er** *n.*

lac·quey (lak′ē) See LACKEY.

lac·ri·mal (lak′rə·məl), **lac·ri·ma·tor** (lak′rə·mā′tər), etc. See LACHRYMAL, LACHRYMATOR, etc.

la·crosse (lə·krôs′, -kros′) *n. U.S. & Canadian* A ball game of American Indian origin, played with long, racketlike implements by two teams of ten men each, the object being to advance the ball down the field and into the opponents' goal. [< dial. F (Canadian) *la crosse,* lit., the crozier, hooked stick]

La Crosse (lə krôs′, -kros′) A city in western Wisconsin, on the Mississippi River; pop. 51,153.

lact- Var. of LACTO-.

lac·tam (lak′tam) *n. Chem.* Any of a series of organic ring compounds containing the CO·NH group and formed by the elimination of water from the carboxyl and amino groups. [< LACT- + AM(INO)]

lac·ta·ry (lak′tər·ē) *adj.* Of or pertaining to milk. [< L *lactarius* < *lac, lactis* milk]

lac·tate (lak′tāt) *v.i.* **·tat·ed, ·tat·ing** **1.** To form or secrete milk. **2.** To suckle young. — *n.* A salt or ester of lactic acid. [< L *lactatus,* pp. of *lactare* to suckle]

lac·ta·tion (lak·tā′shən) *n.* **1.** The mammalian formation or secretion of milk. **2.** The period during which milk is produced. **3.** The act of suckling young.

lac·te·al (lak′tē·əl) *adj.* **1.** Of, pertaining to, or resembling milk; milky. **2.** Carrying chyle. Also **lac′te·an, lac′te·ous.** — *n. Anat.* Any of the lymphatic vessels that carry chyle from the small intestine to the thoracic duct. [< L *lacteus* < *lac, lactis* milk]

lac·tes·cent (lak·tes′ənt) *adj.* **1.** Becoming milky; milklike. **2.** *Biol.* Having or secreting a milky juice, as certain plants and insects. [< L *lactescens, -entis,* ppr. of *lactescere,* inceptive of *lactere* to be milky < *lac, lactis* milk]

lac·tic (lak′tik) *adj.* Of, pertaining to, or derived from milk.

lactic acid *Chem.* A limpid, syrupy acid, $C_3H_6O_3$, with a bitter taste, present in sour milk.

lac·tif·er·ous (lak·tif′ər·əs) *adj.* Producing, secreting, or conveying milk or a milky fluid. [< LL *lactifer* milk-bearing (< L *lac, lactis* milk) + -OUS]

lacto- *combining form* Milk: *lactogenic.* Also, before vowels, **lact-.** [< L *lac, lactis* milk]

lac·to·ba·cil·lus (lak′tō·bə·sil′əs) *n. pl.* **·cil·li** (-sil′ī) Any of a group of rod-shaped, aerobic bacteria (genus *Lactobacillus*) that form lactic acid, especially *L. acidophilus,* used to ferment milk. [< NL < L *lac, lactis* milk + BACILLUS]

lac·to·fla·vin (lak′tō·flā′vin) *n.* Riboflavin (which see).

lac·to·gen·ic (lak′tō·jen′ik) *adj.* Stimulating the milk glands.

lac·tom·e·ter (lak·tom′ə·tər) *n.* A hydrometer for determining the specific gravity of milk: also *galactometer.*

lac·tone (lak′tōn) *n. Chem.* One of a class of cyclical esters formed by dehydration of acids containing a hydroxyl and a carboxyl group. [< LACT- + -ONE] — **lac·ton·ic** (lak·ton′ik) *adj.*

lac·to·pro·te·in (lak′tō·prō′tē·in, -tēn) *n.* A protein derived from milk.

lac·to·scope (lak′tə·skōp) *n.* An instrument for determining the proportion of cream in milk.

lac·tose (lak′tōs) *n. Biochem.* A white, odorless, crystalline disaccharide, $C_{12}H_{22}O_{11}$, present in milk: also called *milk sugar, sugar of milk.* [< LACT(O)- + -OSE²]

la·cu·na (lə·kyōō′nə) *n. pl.* **·nas** or **·nae** (-nē) **1.** A space from which something is missing or has been omitted, especially in a manuscript; blank; hiatus. **2.** A small pit, hollow, or depression. **3.** *Anat.* Any of the minute cavities in bone containing the osteoblasts, or bone cells. **4.** *Biol.* An intercellular space or passage in animal or plant tissue. Also **la·cune′** (-kyōōn′). [< L, hole, pool < *lacus* basin, pond]

la·cu·nar (lə·kyōō′nər) *adj.* **1.** Of or pertaining to a lacuna or lacunas. **2.** Containing or characterized by lacunas. Also **la·cu′nal, la·cu·nar·y** (lak′yōō·ner′ē). — *n. pl.* **la·cu·nars** or **lac·u·nar·i·a** (lak′yōō·nâr′ē·ə) *Archit.* A ceiling or undersurface made up of sunken panels or compartments; also, any one of the panels or compartments.

la·cu·nose (lə·kyōō′nōs) *adj.* Marked by shallow depressions. [< L *lacunosus* < *lacuna.* See LACUNA.]

la·cus·trine (lə·kus′trin) *adj.* **1.** Of or pertaining to a lake or lakes; limnetic. **2.** Found in or growing in lakes, as certain plants. **3.** Formed in or near lakes, as geological deposits. Also **la·cus′tral, la·cus′tri·an.** [< L *lacus* lake]

lac·y (lā′sē) *adj.* **lac·i·er, lac·i·est** Made of or resembling lace. — **lac′i·ly** *adv.* — **lac′i·ness** *n.*

lad (lad) *n.* **1.** A boy or youth; stripling. **2.** Familiarly, any male. [< ME *ladde,* ? ult. < ON]

lad·a·num (lad′ə·nəm) See LABDANUM.

lad·der (lad′ər) *n.* A device of wood, metal, rope, etc., for climbing and descending, usually consisting of two parallel side pieces connected by a series of rungs, or rounds, placed at regular intervals to serve as footholds. [OE *hlǣd(d)er*]

lad·der·back (lad′ər·bak′) *n.* A chair back having two posts connected by horizontal slats: also, such a chair.

ladder stitch An embroidery stitch having parallel crossbars between rows of stitching, producing a ladderlike effect.

lad·die (lad′ē) *n.* A lad.

lade (lād) *v.* **lad·ed, lad·ed** or **lad·en, lad·ing** *v.t.* **1.** To load with a cargo or burden; also, to load as a cargo. **2.** To dip or lift (a liquid) in or out, as with a ladle. — *v.i.* **3.** To receive cargo. **4.** To dip or lift a liquid. [OE *hladan* to load]

lad·en¹ (lād′n) Alternative past participle of LADE. — *adj.* **1.** Burdened; oppressed. **2.** Weighed down; loaded.

lad·en² (lād′n) *v.t. & v.i.* **lad·ened, lad·en·ing** To lade. [Var. of LADE]

la·di·da (lä′dē·dä′) *adj.* Pretentious or affected. — *n.* **1.** A pretentious person. **2.** Affected behavior — *interj.* An exclamation expressing ridicule at pretentions, affectations, etc. [Imit. of affected speech]

ladies' auxiliary *U.S.* A woman's group forming part of a men's lodge, club, etc.

La·din (lä·dēn′) *n.* **1.** A Rhaeto-Romanic dialect spoken in the Engadine and Friuli regions of Switzerland and northern Italy. **2.** One who speaks Ladin. [< L *Latinus* Latin]

lad·ing (lā′ding) *n.* **1.** The act of one who or that which lades. **2.** A load or cargo.

La·di·no (lä·dē′nō) *n.* **1.** A Spanish dialect, with many Hebrew elements, spoken by the Sephardim living in Turkey and other countries. **2.** In Latin America, a mestizo. [< Sp., wise, learned, cunning < L *Latinus* Latin]

Lad·is·laus I (lad′is·lôs), 1040–95, king of Hungary 1077–1095, canonized 1192. Also **Lad·is·las** (lad′is·ləs, -läs). Also **Saint Ladislaus.**

la·dle (lād′l) *n.* A cup-shaped vessel with a long handle, for dipping or conveying liquids. — *v.t.* **dled, dling** To dip up or carry in a ladle. [OE *hlædel* < *hladan* to lade] — **la′dler** *n.*

La·do·ga (lä′də·gə), **Lake** A lake in the NW R.S.F.S.R., the largest in Europe; 7,100 sq. mi. *Russian* **La·dozh·sko·ye O·ze·ro** (lä′dəsh·skə·yə ô′zyi·rə).

la·drone (lə·drōn′) *n.* In Spain, Latin America, etc., a robber or highwayman; freebooter. [< Sp. *ladron* < L *latro*, *-onis* robber] **— la·dro′nism** *n.*

La·drone Islands (lə·dron′) The former name for the MARIANAS ISLANDS. Also **La·drones′**.

la·dy (lā′dē) *n. pl.* **·dies** 1. A woman showing the refinement, gentility, and tact associated with the upper ranks of society. 2. A woman of superior position in society. 3. A term of reference or address for any woman. 4. A woman at the head of a domestic establishment: now only in the phrase **the lady of the house.** 5. The woman a man loves; beloved. 6. A wife or consort, especially when the husband has a high position. 7. The grinding organ in the stomach of a lobster. **— adj.** 1. Of or pertaining to a lady; ladylike. 2. Denoting a female: a *lady* doctor. ◆ *Woman* doctor is preferable here. The use of *lady* for its connotations of gentility is often mistaken politeness. [OE *hlǣfdīge*, lit., bread-kneader < *hlāf* bread, loaf + *-dige*, a stem akin to *dah* dough]

La·dy (lā′dē) 1. In Great Britain: **a** A title of reference or address used with the surname or territorial name of a marchioness, countess, viscountess, or baroness. **b** A title used with the given names of the daughters of dukes, marquises, and earls. **c** A title used, with the husband's given name, for the wives of men holding the courtesy title *Lord*. **d** A title used with the surname of the wife of a baronet or other knight. 2. The Virgin Mary: usually with *Our*.

la·dy·bug (lā′dē·bug′) *n.* Any of a family (*Coccinellidae*) of brightly colored beetles; especially, the **two-spotted ladybug** (*Adalia bipunctata*), usually red spotted with black, that feeds on aphids and other insects. Also **lady beetle, la′dy·bird.** For illustration see INSECTS (beneficial).

Lady chapel *Chiefly Brit.* A chapel of the Virgin, usually situated behind the high altar of a larger church.

Lady Day 1. March 25, the church festival of the Annunciation, in Great Britain serving as the spring quarter day. 2. Formerly, any of various days observed in honor of the Virgin Mary.

la·dy·fin·ger (lā′dē·fing′gər) *n.* A small sponge cake of about the size and shape of a finger. Also **la′dys·fin′ger** (lā′dēz-).

lady in waiting *pl.* **ladies in waiting** A lady appointed to attend upon a queen or princess.

la·dy-kill·er (lā′dē·kil′ər) *n. Slang* A man supposed to be unusually fascinating to women. **— la′dy·kill′ing** *adj. & n.*

la·dy·kin (lā′di·kin) *n.* A little lady. [Dim. of LADY]

la·dy·like (lā′dē·līk′) *adj.* 1. Like or suitable to a lady; gentle; delicate. 2. Effeminate.

la·dy·love (lā′dē·luv′) *n.* A woman beloved; sweetheart.

Lady of the Lake See VIVIAN.

la·dy·palm (lā′dē·päm′) *n.* A low, reedlike fan palm (genus *Rhapis*) with broad leaves and yellowish flowers, native to southern China and cultivated in Florida and California.

la·dy·ship (lā′dē·ship) *n.* The rank or condition of a lady: used as a title, with *Her* or *Your*.

lady's man A man attentive to and fond of the company of women. Also **ladies′ man.**

La·dy·smith (lā′dē·smith) A town in western Natal, South Africa; besieged by Boers 1899–1900; pop. about 16,000.

la·dy′s-slip·per (lā′dēz-slip′ər) *n.* Any plant of a genus (*Cypripedium*) of the orchid family, having a flower that suggests a slipper in shape. Also **la·dy′s-slip′per** (lā′dē-).

LADY'S-SLIPPER (About 2 feet high)

la·dy′s-smock (lā′dēz-smok′) *n.* The cuckoo flower. Also **lady smock.**

la·dy′s-thumb (lā′dēz-thum′) *n.* A plant (*Polygonum persicaria*) of the buckwheat family, having deep pink or purple flowers: also called *persicaria*.

la·dy′s-tress·es (lā′dēz-tres′iz) *n.* Any of various orchids (genus *Spiranthes*), having small flowers in more or less twisted spikes. Also **la′dy′s-trac′es** (-träs′iz), **lady tresses.**

Laën·nec (lä·nek′), **René Théophile Hyacinthe**, 1781–1826, French physician: invented the stethoscope.

La·er·tes (lā·ûr′tēz) 1. In the *Odyssey*, a king of Ithaca, father of Odysseus. 2. In Shakespeare's *Hamlet*, brother of Ophelia and son of Polonius.

Lae·ta·re Sunday (lē·târ′ē) *n.* The fourth Sunday in Lent: so called from the first word in the Mass of that day. [< L, imperative sing. of *laetari* to rejoice < *laetus* joyful]

laevo- See LEVO-.

lae·vo·gy·rate (lē′vō·jī′rāt), etc. See LEVOGYRATE.

La Farge (lə färj′), **John**, 1835–1910, U.S. painter.

La·fay·ette (lä′fē·et′, laf′ē·et′) 1. A city in west central Indiana, on the Wabash River; pop. 44,955. 2. A city in southern Louisiana; pop. 68,908.

La·fay·ette (lä′fē·et′, laf′ē·et′; *Fr.* lȧ·fà·yet′), **Marquis de,** 1757–1834, French general, revolutionist, and statesman; fought in the American Revolution: full name **Marie Joseph Paul Yves Roch Gilbert du Motier de Lafayette.** Also **La Fay·ette′.**

La Fol·lette (lə fol′it), **Robert Marion,** 1855–1925, U.S. political leader, legislator, and reformer.

La Fon·taine (lä fon·tān′, *Fr.* lȧ fôṅ·ten′), **Jean de,** 1621–95, French writer, noted for his fables.

lag¹ (lag) *v.i.* **lagged, lag·ging** 1. To move slowly; stay or fall behind; straggle: sometimes followed by *behind*. 2. In billiards, to shoot one's cue ball to the end rail so that it will rebound to the head rail, the player whose ball stops nearest the head rail winning first place in the order of play. 3. In marbles, to throw one's taw as near as possible to a line on the ground to decide the order of play. **— n.** 1. The condition or act of retardation or falling behind. 2. The amount or period of retardation. 3. In billiards and marbles, an act of lagging. [? < Scand. Cf. Norw. *lagga* to go slowly.]

lag² (lag) *n.* 1. A stave of a barrel, cask, drum, etc. 2. A part of a lagging. **— v.t.** **lagged, lag·ging** To provide or cover with lags or lagging. [Prob. < ON *lögg* rim of a barrel]

lag³ (lag) *Slang v.t.* **lagged, lag·ging** 1. To arrest. 2. To send to penal servitude. **— n.** 1. A convict. 2. A period of penal servitude. [Origin unknown]

lag·an (lag′ən) *n.* In maritime law, goods cast from a vessel in peril, but to which a buoy or float is attached as evidence of ownership: also called *ligan*. Compare FLOTSAM, JETSAM. [< AF < Gmc. Prob. akin to ON *lögn* net laid in the sea.]

Lag b'O·mer (läg′ bō′mər) A Jewish festival, the 18th day of Iyyar. [< Hebrew, lit., 33rd of the 49 days from the second day of Passover to the first of Pentecost]

la·ger (lä′gər) *n.* 1. A beer stored for sedimentation before use. Also **lager beer.** 2. Laager. [< G *lager-bier*, lit., store beer < *lager* storehouse + *bier* beer]

La·ger·kvist (lä′yər·kvist), **Pär Fabian,** born 1891, Swedish novelist and dramatist.

La·ger·löf (lä′yər·lœf), **Selma (Ottiliana Lovisa),** 1858–1940, Swedish novelist.

lag·gard (lag′ərd) *n.* One who lags; loiterer; straggler. **— adj.** Falling behind; loitering; slow. **— Syn.** See DILATORY. [< LAG¹ + -ARD] **— lag′gard·ly** *adv.* **— lag′gard·ness** *n.*

lag·ger (lag′ər) *n.* One who or that which lags.

lag·ging (lag′ing) *n.* 1. Strips of wood or other insulating material used to form a jacketing for a steam boiler, cylinder, etc. 2. A frame, usually of wood, used to support an arch during construction. 3. The act of covering with lagging. [< LAG²]

La Gio·con·da (lä jō·kôn′dä) See MONA LISA.

la·gniappe (lan·yap′, lan′yap) *n.* 1. *Southern U.S.* A small present given to the purchaser of an article by a merchant or storekeeper. 2. *Informal* Anything given beyond strict obligation; an extra. Also **la·gnappe′.** [< dial. F (Creole) < F *la* the + Sp. *ñapa* lagniappe < Quechua *yapa*]

La·go di Be·na·co (lä′gō dē be·nä′kō) See (Lake) GARDA.

La·go di Co·mo (lä′gō dē kō′mō) See (Lake) COMO.

La·go di Gar·da (lä′gō dē gär′dä) See (Lake) GARDA.

La·go Mag·gio·re (lä′gō mä·jō′rä) A lake in northern Italy and Switzerland; 82 sq. mi.

lag·o·morph (lag′ə·môrf) *n.* Any of an order (*Lagomorpha*) of gnawing mammals differing from the rodents in dentition and jaw structure, including rabbits, hares, and pikas. [< NL *Lagomorpha* < Gk. *lagōs* hare + *morphē* form]

la·goon (lə·gōōn′) *n. Geog.* A body of shallow water, as a bay, inlet, pond, or lake, usually connecting with a river, larger lake or the sea; especially, the water within a coral atoll. Also **la·gune′.** [< F *lagune* < Ital. *laguna* < L *lacuna*. See LACUNA.]

Lagoon Islands A former name for the ELLICE ISLANDS.

La·gos (lä′gōs, lā′gos) The capital of Nigeria, in the SW part on the Gulf of Guinea; pop. 665,246 (1963).

La·grange (lə·gränj′, *Fr.* lȧ·gräṅzh′), **Comte Joseph Louis,** 1736–1813, French mathematician.

lag screw A heavy screw with a square head and no slot: also called *coach screw*. For illustration see SCREW. [< LAG²]

Lag·ting (läg′ting) *n.* The upper house of the Norwegian parliament. [< Norw. *lag* society, law + *ting* parliament]

La Guai·ra (lä gwī′rä) A port city in northern Venezuela, the port for Caracas; pop. about 16,000. Also **La Guay′ra.**

La Guar·di·a (lə gwär′dē·ə), **Fiorello H(enry),** 1882–1947, U.S. lawyer, politician, and public administrator.

La Ha·ba·na (lä hä·vä′nä) The Spanish name for HAVANA.

La Ha·bra (lə hä′brə) A city in SW California, near Los Angeles; pop. 41,350.

La Hogue (lȧ ōg′) See SAINT-VAAST-LA-HOGUE. Also **La Hogue′.**

La·hore (lə·hōr′) The capital of West Pakistan, in the eastern part; pop. 1,296,400 (est. 1969).

Lai·bach (lī′bäkh) The German name for LJUBLJANA.

la·ic (lā′ik) *adj.* Lay². **— n.** A layman. [< LL *laicus* < Gk. *laikos* < *laos* the people] **— la′i·cal·ly** *adv.*

la·i·cize (lā′ə·sīz) *v.t.* **·cized, ·ciz·ing** To remove from ecclesiastical control; secularize. **— la′i·ci·za′tion** *n.*

laid (lād) Past tense and past participle of LAY¹.

laid paper Paper watermarked with fine parallel lines.

laigh (lākh) *Scot. adj. & adv.* Low. **— n.** A hollow or lowland. Also **laich.**

l'Aiglon (lä·glôn′) François Charles Joseph Bonaparte. See under BONAPARTE. [< F, lit., the eaglet]

Lai·ka (lī′kə) *n.* 1. A breed of Siberian dog of medium size and white or gray coloring. **2.** A dog of this breed sent aloft in the second Soviet earth satellite, November, 1957.

lain (lān) Past participle of LIE[1].

lair[1] (lâr) *n.* A resting place or den, especially that of a wild animal. — *v.i.* **1.** To live or rest in a lair. — *v.t.* **2.** To place in a lair. **3.** To serve as a lair for. [OE *leger* bed. Akin to LIE[1].]

lair[2] (lâr) *n. Scot.* Lore; learning. [OE *lār*]

laird (lârd) *n. Scot.* The proprietor of a landed estate. [Northern ME *laverd, lard*] — **laird′ly** *adj.* — **laird′ship** *n.*

lais·sez faire (les′ā-fâr′) **1.** In economics, the theory that the state should exercise as little control as possible in trade and industrial affairs, especially in conditions of labor, restrictions on individual competition, etc.; policy of noninterference. **2.** Noninterference or indifference. Also **lais′ser faire′.** [< F, lit., let do < *laissez*, imperative of *laisser* to let + *faire* to do, make]

laith (lāth) *adj. Scot.* Loath. [OE *lāth*] — **laith′ly** *adv.*

la·i·ty (lā′ə-tē) *n. pl.* **·ties** **1.** The people collectively; laymen: distinguished from *clergy.* **2.** All of those outside a specific profession or occupation. [< LAY[2] + -ITY]

La·i·us (lā′yəs) In Greek legend, a king of Thebes, husband of Jocasta, who was unwittingly killed by his son Oedipus.

lake[1] (lāk) *n.* **1.** A sizable inland body of either salt or fresh water. Abbr. *l., L.* ◆ Collateral adjective *lacustrine.* **2.** A large pool of any liquid: a *lake* of pitch. [Fusion of OE *lacu* stream, pool and OF *lac* basin, pond, lake < L *lacus.* Akin to LEACH, LEAK.]

lake[2] (lāk) *n.* **1.** A deep red pigment made by combining cochineal with a metallic oxide. **2.** The color of this pigment. **3.** Any insoluble metallic compound yielding variously colored pigments by the chemical interaction of mordant and dye. [Var. of LAC[1]]

Lake, Lake of, etc. See specific name, as (Lake of) GENEVA, (Lake) MICHIGAN, etc.

Lake (lāk), **Simon,** 1866–1945, U.S. engineer and naval architect; pioneer in submarine design.

Lake Charles A city in SW Louisiana, on the Calcasieu River; pop. 77,998.

Lake District A region in Cumberland, Lancashire, and Westmoreland counties, England, containing 15 lakes. Also **Lake Country, Lake Land.**

lake dweller An inhabitant of a lake dwelling.

lake dwelling A habitation built on piles over the shallow waters of a lake, especially in prehistoric times.

Lake·head (lāk′hed′) *Canadian* The region around Port Arthur and Fort William on Lake Superior.

lake herring A whitefish (*Leucichthys artedi*) of the Great Lakes: also called *cisco.*

Lake·hurst (lāk′hûrst) A borough in east central New Jersey; former site of a naval air station; pop. 2,641.

Lake·land (lāk′lənd) A resort city in central Florida; pop. 41,350.

Lake Poets The English poets Coleridge, Wordsworth, and Southey, who lived for a while in the Lake District.

lak·er (lā′kər) *n. U.S. & Canadian* **1.** A lake fish; especially, the lake trout. **2.** A vessel engaged in lake trade.

Lake Success A village in SE New York, on Long Island; headquarters of the UN Security Council, 1946–50; pop. 3,254.

lake trout A salmonoid fish (*Salvelinus namaycush*) of the Great Lakes region of North America, somewhat resembling the brook trout but having red or pale spots on the sides: also called *laker, namaycush, salmon trout, togue, tuladi.*

Lake·wood (lāk′wŏŏd) **1.** A city in northern Ohio, on Lake Erie; a suburb of Cleveland; pop. 70,173. **2.** A city in SW California, near Los Angeles; pop. 82,973.

lakh (lak) See LAC[2].

lak·ing (lā′king) *n. Med.* The reddening of blood plasma by the escape of hemoglobin from the red corpuscles. [< LAKE[2] + -ING] — **laked, lak′y** *adj.*

La·ko·ni·a (lā·kō′nyē′ä) The modern Greek name for LACONIA.

lak·y[1] (lā′kē) *adj.* **lak·i·er, lak·i·est** Pertaining to or like a lake. [< LAKE[1]]

lak·y[2] (lā′kē) *adj.* **lak·i·er, lak·i·est** Of or pertaining to the pigment or color lake. [< LAKE[2]]

la·la·pa·loo·za (lol′ə·pə·lōō′zə) See LOLLAPALOOZA. Also **lal′la·pa·loo′za.**

lall (lal) *v.i.* To articulate (r) as (l).

Lal·lan (lal′ən) *Scot. adj.* Of or pertaining to the Lowlands of Scotland; Lowland. — *n.* The dialect of the Scottish Lowlands: also called *Lowland.* Also **Lal′land.**

lal·la·tion (la·lā′shən) *n.* **1.** An imperfect articulation of (r) that makes it sound like (l). **2.** Any unintelligible speech; babbling. [< L *lallatus*, pp. of *lallare* to sing "la la"]

La·lo (lä·lō′), **Edouard Victor Antoine,** 1823–92, French composer.

lam (lam) *Slang v.* **lammed, lam·ming** *v.i.* **1.** To run away, especially to avoid arrest; flee. — *v.t.* **2.** To beat; thrash. — *n.* Sudden flight or escape. — **on the lam** In flight; flee-

ing. — **to take it on the lam** To flee hastily; run away. [? < ON *lemja* to thrash. Akin to LAME.]

lam. Laminated.

Lam. Lamentations.

L.A.M. Master of Liberal Arts (L *Liberalium Artium Magister*).

la·ma (lä′mə) *n.* A priest or monk of Lamaism. See DALAI LAMA. [< Tibetan *blama*]

La·ma·ism (lä′mə·iz′əm) *n.* The form of Buddhism practiced in Tibet and Mongolia, characterized by a complex hierarchy and Shamanistic beliefs and practices. [< LAMA[1] + -ISM] — **La′ma·ist** *n.* — **La·ma·is′tic** *adj.*

La Man·cha (lä män′chä) A region of south central Spain.

La Manche (là mänsh′) The French name for the ENGLISH CHANNEL.

La·marck (là·márk′), **Chevalier de,** 1744–1829; French naturalist; founder of Lamarckism: original name **Jean Baptiste Pierre Antoine de Mo·net** (də mō·ne′) — **La·marck·i·an** (lə·märk′ē·ən) *adj. & n.*

La·marck·ism (lə·märk′iz·əm) *n. Biol.* The theory of organic evolution holding that species have developed through the inheritance of characteristics acquired by the individual in response to environmental influences.

La·mar·tine (là·mȧr·tēn′), **Alphonse Marie Louis de Prat de,** 1790–1869, French poet.

la·ma·ser·y (lä′mə·ser′ē) *n. pl.* **·ser·ies** A Lamaist monastery. [< F *lamaserie* < *lama* lama]

lamb (lam) *n.* **1.** A young sheep. **2.** The meat of a lamb used as food. **3.** Lambskin. **4.** Any gentle or innocent person, especially a child. **5.** A gullible person. — **the Lamb** Christ. — *v.i.* To give birth: said of a ewe. [OE]

Lamb (lam), **Charles,** 1775–1834, English essayist and critic: pseudonym *Elia.* — **William** See (Viscount) MELBOURNE.

lam·baste (lam·bāst′) *v.t.* **·bast·ed, ·bast·ing** *Slang* **1.** To beat or thrash. **2.** To scold; castigate. [< LAM[1] + BASTE[3]] — **lam·bast′ing** *n.*

lamb·da (lam′də) *n.* The eleventh letter in the Greek alphabet (Λ, λ), corresponding to the English *l.* See ALPHABET. [< Gk. < Phoenician *lamed*]

lamb·da·cism (lam′də·siz′əm) *n.* An inability to articulate (l) correctly. [< L *lambdacismus* < Gk. *lambdakismos* < *lambdakizein* to utter the sound represented by lambda imperfectly < *lambda* lambda]

lamb·doid (lam′doid) *adj.* **1.** Resembling in form the Greek letter lambda (Λ). **2.** *Anat.* Denoting the suture between the occipital and the two parietal bones of the skull. Also **lamb·doi′dal.**

lam·bent (lam′bənt) *adj.* **1.** Playing over a surface with a soft, undulatory movement; flickering; licking: a *lambent* flame. **2.** Softly radiant. **3.** Lightly and playfully brilliant: *lambent* wit. [< L *lambens, -entis*, ppr. of *lambere* to lick] — **lam·ben·cy** *n.* — **lam·bent·ly** *adv.*

lam·bert (lam′bərt) *n. Physics* The cgs unit of brightness, equal to that of a perfectly diffusing surface emitting or reflecting light at the rate of one lumen per square centimeter. [after J. H. *Lambert*, 1728–77, German physicist]

Lam·beth (lam′bəth) A metropolitan borough of SW London; pop. 325,070 (est. 1969).

Lambeth Palace The official London residence of the archbishop of Canterbury.

lamb·kill (lam′kil′) *n.* A North American shrub (*Kalmia angustifolia*) with deep pink flowers and narrow leaves said to be poisonous to animals: also called *sheep laurel.*

lamb·kin (lam′kin) *n.* **1.** A little lamb. **2.** A small child: a term of affection. Also **lamb′ie.** [Dim. of LAMB]

Lamb of God Christ, as the paschal lamb. *John* i 29.

lam·bre·quin (lam′bər·kin, -brə-) *n.* **1.** *U.S.* A draped strip of cloth, leather, etc., hanging from the casing above a window or doorway, and covering the upper half of the opening. **2.** In medieval times, an ornamental, protective covering of heavy fabric for a helmet. [< F < Du. *lamperkin*, dim. of *lamper* veil]

lamb·skin (lam′skin) *n.* **1.** The dressed hide of a lamb with the wool preserved. **2.** Dressed leather made from a lamb's hide.

lamb's lettuce Corn salad.

lame[1] (lām) *adj.* **lam·er, lam·est** **1.** Crippled or disabled, especially in the legs or feet. **2.** Sore; painful: a *lame* back. **3.** Weak; ineffective: a *lame* effort. — *v.t.* **lamed, lam·ing** To make lame; cripple. [OE *lama.* Akin to LAM.] — **lame′ly** *adv.* — **lame′ness** *n.*

lame[2] (lām) *n.* A thin plate of metal, especially in the flexible parts of armor. [< F < L *lamina* lamina]

la·mé (la·mā′) *n.* A fabric woven of flat gold or silver thread, sometimes mixed with silk or other fiber. [< F, orig. pp. of *lamer* to laminate < *lame* lame[2]]

la·med (lä′med) *n.* The twelfth letter in the Hebrew alphabet. Also **la′medh.** See ALPHABET.

lame duck *Informal* **1.** *U.S.* An officeholder, especially a member of a legislative body, whose term continues for a time after his defeat for reelection. **2.** On the stock exchange, one who cannot fulfill his contracts. **3.** An ineffectual or disabled person.

la·mel·la (lə·mel′ə) *n. pl.* **·mel·lae** (-mel′ē) **1.** A thin plate, scale, or layer, as in bone or the gills of bivalves. **2.** *Bot.* **a** One of the thin plates or gills attached to the under side of a mushroom. **b** The membrane, composed largely of pectin, occurring between any two plant cells. [< NL < L, dim. of *lamina* plate, leaf]

lam·el·lar (lə·mel′ər, lam′ə·lər) *adj.* Lamellate.

lam·el·late (lam′ə·lāt, lə·mel′āt) *adj.* **1.** Composed of or arranged in thin layers or lamellae. **2.** Resembling a lamella; scalelike; flat. Also **lam·el·lat′ed.** — **lam′el·la′tion** *n.*

lamelli- *combining form* Lamellae; resembling lamellae: *lamellibranch.* [< L *lamella* plate]

la·mel·li·branch (lə·mel′i·brangk) *n. Zool.* One of a class (*Pelecypoda*, formerly *Lammelibranchiata*) of bivalves including clams, mussels, and oysters, having platelike gills and a mantle enclosing a laterally compressed body. — *adj.* Of or pertaining to the class of lamellibranchs. [< NL *lamellibranchia*, name of this class < L *lamella* (See LAMELLA) + Gk. *branchia* gills, pl. of *branchion* fin] — **la·mel′li·bran′chi·ate** (-brang′kē·āt, -it) *adj. & n.*

la·mel·li·corn (lə·mel′i·kôrn) *adj. Entomol.* **1.** Having a lateral, leaflike expansion on the last segment of each antenna, as a group of beetles (*Lamellicornia*) including the stag beetle and the scarabs. **2.** Terminating in a leaflike part, as an antenna. — *n.* A lamellicorn beetle. [< NL *lamellicornis* < L *lamella* (See LAMELLA) + *cornu* horn]

la·mel·li·form (lə·mel′i·fôrm) *adj.* Having the form of a thin plate, scale, or lamella; scalelike.

la·mel·li·ros·tral (lə·mel′i·ros′trəl) *adj. Ornithol.* Of or belonging to a group of birds having ridges of lamellae on the edges of the bill and tongue, as ducks, swans, and geese. Also **la·mel′li·ros′trate** (-trāt). [< NL *lamellirostris* < L *lamella* (See LAMELLA) + *rostrum* beak]

la·mel·lose (lə·mel′ōs, lam′ə·lōs) *adj.* Lamellate. [< LAMELL(A) + -OSE¹]

la·ment (lə·ment′) *v.t.* To feel or express sorrow over; feel remorse or regret over. — *v.i.* To feel or express sorrow, grief, or regret. — *n.* **1.** An expression of grief; lamentation. **2.** An elegiac melody or writing. [< L *lamentari* < *lamentum* wailing, weeping] — **la·ment′er** *n.*

lam·en·ta·ble (lam′ən·tə·bəl, lə·ment′ə-) *adj.* **1.** That warrants lamenting; deplorable; regrettable; distressing: a *lamentable* failure. **2.** *Archaic* Expressing grief; mournful. — **lam′en·ta·ble·ness** *n.* — **lam′en·ta·bly** *adv.*

lam·en·ta·tion (lam′ən·tā′shən) *n.* **1.** The act of lamenting or bewailing. **2.** A lament; wail; moan.

Lam·en·ta·tions (lam′ən·tā′shənz) *n.pl. (construed as sing.)* **1.** A lyrical poetic book of the Old Testament, attributed to Jeremiah the prophet. *Abbr.* **Lam. 2.** *Eccl.* Any music to which a portion of Lamentations is sung at Tenebrae.

lam·ent·ed (lə·ment′əd) *adj.* Mourned for; grieved over: usually said of one who has died.

La Me·sa (lä mā′sä) A city in SW California, near San Diego; pop. 39,178.

la·mi·a (lā′mē·ə) *n. pl.* **·mi·as** or **·mi·ae** (-mē·ē) In ancient Greek and Roman belief, one of a group of female monsters who lived on the flesh and blood of children and youths. [< L < Gk.]

La·mi·a (lā′mē·ə) In Greek mythology, a queen of Libya, beloved of Zeus, who was robbed of her children by Hera and took revenge by killing the children of others.

lam·i·na (lam′ə·nə) *n. pl.* **·nae** (-nē) or **·nas 1.** A thin scale or sheet. **2.** A layer or coat lying over another, as in bone, minerals, armor, etc. **3.** *Bot.* The blade or flat expanded portion of a leaf, or the blade of a petal. [< L]

lam·i·nar·i·a·ceous (lam′ə·nâr′ē·ā′shəs) *adj.* Of or belonging to a genus (*Laminaria*) of brown algae, including the giant kelp. [< NL *Laminaria(a)* + -ACEOUS]

lam·i·nate (lam′ə·nāt) *v.* **·nat·ed, ·nat·ing** *v.t.* **1.** To beat, roll, or press (metal) into thin sheets. **2.** To separate or cut into thin sheets. **3.** To make of layers united by the action of heat and pressure. **4.** To cover with thin sheets or laminae. — *v.i.* **5.** To separate into sheets or laminae: slate *laminates* easily. — *adj.* Laminated. [< NL *laminatus* < *lamina* leaf]

lam·i·nat·ed (lam′ə·nā′təd) *adj.* Made up of or arranged in thin sheets; laminate. *Abbr.* **lam.**

lam·i·na·tion (lam′ə·nā′shən) *n.* **1.** The act of laminating, or the state of being laminated. **2.** Something composed of thin sheets or laminae. **3.** A lamina.

lam·i·ni·tis (lam′ə·nī′tis) *n. Vet.* Founder.

lam·i·nose (lam′ə·nōs) *adj.* Laminate; laminar. [< LAMIN(A) + -OSE¹]

Lam·mas (lam′əs) *n.* **1.** *Eccl.* In the Roman Catholic and Anglican churches, August 1, the feast commemorating the deliverance of St. Peter from prison. **2.** In the early English church, a festival celebrated August 1, when bread from the first grain was blessed at Mass. **3.** Formerly, in Scotland, a quarter day, falling on August 1. Also **Lammas day.** [OE *hlāfmæsse* bread feast < *hlāf* bread, loaf + *mæsse* mass]

Lam·mas·tide (lam′əs·tīd′) *n.* The season of Lammas. [< LAMMAS + TIDE¹ (def. 4)]

lam·mer·gei·er (lam′ər·gī′ər) *n.* The largest European bird of prey (*Gypaëtus barbatus*) of the vulture family, dwelling in the mountains: also called *ossifrage.* Also **lam′mer·geir** (-gīr), **lam′mer·gey′er**, lit., lamb-vulture < *lämmer*, pl. of *lamm* lamb + *geier* vulture]

La·mont (lə·mont′), **Thomas W(illiam)**, 1870–1948, U.S. banker.

La·motte-Fou·qué (lä·môt′foō·kā′) See FOUQUÉ.

lamp (lamp) *n.* **1.** A device for holding one or more electric light bulbs and directing their light; also, an electric light bulb. **2.** Any of various devices for producing light by combustion, incandescence, electric arc, or fluorescence. **3.** A vessel in which oil or alcohol is burned through a wick to produce light or heat. **4.** Any of several devices for producing therapeutic heat or rays: sun *lamp.* **5.** *Slang pl.* The eyes. — *v.t. Slang* To look at. [< OF *lampe* < L *lampas* < Gk. < *lampein* to shine]

lam·pad (lam′pad) *n.* A lamp or torch; candlestick. [< Gk. *lampas, lampados* < *lampein* to shine]

lam·pas¹ (lam′pəs) *n. Vet.* Inflammation of the roof of a horse's mouth. Also **lam′pers** (-pərs). [< F < OF, throat]

lam·pas² (lam′pəs) *n.* Any patterned, damasklike fabric, used as furniture covering. [< F; origin uncertain]

lamp·black (lamp′blak′) *n.* A black pigment consisting of fine carbon deposited from the smoke of burning oil or gas, used in printer's ink, etc.: also called *carbon black.*

Lam·pe·du·sa (läm′pe·dōō′zä) The largest of the Pelagic Islands; 8 sq. mi.: ancient *Lopadusa.*

lam·per eel (lam′pər) A lamprey.

lam·pi·on (lam′pē·ən) *n.* A small, oil-burning lamp. [< F < Ital. *lampione* carriage or street lamp < L *lampas.* See LAMP.]

lamp·light (lamp′līt′) *n.* Light from lamps; artificial light.

lamp·light·er (lamp′lī′tər) *n.* **1.** One whose work is lighting lamps, especially street lamps. **2.** Anything by which a lamp is lighted, as a torch, electric device, etc.

lam·poon (lam·poōn′) *n.* A scurrilous, but often humorous, attack in prose or verse directed against a person; pasquinade. — *v.t.* To abuse or satirize in a lampoon. [< MF *lampon* < *lampons* let's drink (a song refrain) < *lamper* to guzzle] — **lam·poon′er, lam·poon′ist** *n.* — **lam·poon′er·y** *n.*

— **Syn.** (noun) *Lampoon, pasquinade,* and *squib* denote written satire or ridicule. A *lampoon* typically uses coarse humor to provoke derision or contempt; it is called a *pasquinade* if abusive or anonymous, or if posted in a public place. A *squib* is a mild *lampoon,* such as might be interpolated in some serious composition. Compare CARICATURE.

lamp·post (lamp′pōst′) *n.* A post supporting a lamp in a street, park, etc.

lam·prey (lam′prē) *n. pl.* **·preys** An eellike, carnivorous cyclostome (*Petromyzon* and related genera) having in the adult stages a circular suctorial mouth with sharp rasping teeth on its inner surface. [< OF *lampreie* < Med.L *lampreda, lampetra;* ult. origin uncertain. Cf. OE *lamprede.*]

lamp shell *Zool.* A brachiopod.

la·nai (lä·nä′ē) *n. pl.* **·is** *Hawaiian* A veranda or porch.

La·na·i (lä·nä′ē) An island in the central Hawaiian Islands; 141 sq. mi.

Lan·ark (lan′ərk) A county in south central Scotland; 879 sq. mi.; pop. 1,541,455 (est. 1969); county seat, **Lanark,** pop. about 8,407 (est. 1969). Also **Lan′ark·shire** (-shir).

la·nate (lā′nāt) *adj.* **1.** Resembling wool; woolly. **2.** *Bot.* Provided or covered with long, fine, woollike hairs. Also **la′nat·ed.** [< L *lanatus* < *lana* wool]

Lan·ca·shire (lang′kə·shir) A county in NW England; 1,173 sq. mi.; pop. 1,370,100 (1976); county seat, Preston, pop. 132,000 (1976).

Lan·cas·ter (lang′kəs·tər; *for defs. 1, 2, & 3, also* lang′·kas′tər, lan′-) **1.** A city in SE Pennsylvania; pop. 57,690. **2.** A city in south central Ohio; pop. 32,911. **3.** An unincorporated place in SW California; pop. 30,948. **4.** Lancashire or its county seat.

Lan·cas·ter (lang′kəs·tər), **House of** A royal house of England, reigning from 1399 to 1461, the three kings of which were Henry IV, Henry V, and Henry VI. See YORK, also WARS OF THE ROSES in table for WAR.

Lan·cas·tri·an (lang·kas′trē·ən) *adj.* Belonging or relating to the House of Lancaster. — *n.* **1.** An adherent of the House of Lancaster, as opposed to the Yorkists. **2.** A native or inhabitant of Lancashire.

lance (lans, läns) *n.* **1.** A spearlike weapon used by mounted soldiers or knights. **2.** One who is armed with a lance; lancer. **3.** Any of various long, slender weapons resembling a lance, as a whaler's spear, a fish spear, etc. **4.** A lancet. **5.** The sand lance (which see). — *v.t.* **lanced, lanc·ing 1.** To pierce with a lance. **2.** To cut or open with a lancet. [ME *launce* < OF < L *lancea* light spear < Celtic]

lance corporal 1. *Mil.* In the U.S. Marine Corps, an enlisted man ranking next below a corporal. See table at GRADE. **2.** *Brit. Mil.* A private acting as a corporal, usually without increased pay.

lance·let (lans′lit, läns′-) *n.* Any of several species of small, fishlike, translucent animals (genus *Branchiostoma*) having a notochord and other vertebrate characteristics, that burrow in the sand of warm sea beaches: also called *amphioxus*. [Dim. of LANCE]

Lan·ce·lot of the Lake (lan′sə·lot, län′-)   In Arthurian romance, the bravest and ablest of the knights of the Round Table, lover of Guinevere and father of Galahad: also spelled *Launcelot*. Also **Lancelot du Lac** (dü làk). [< F, servant]

lan·ce·o·late (lan′sē·ə·lit, -lāt) *adj.* **1.** Shaped like the head of a lance. **2.** *Bot.* Narrowing to a point; tapering, as certain leaves. See illustration of LEAF. [< LL *lanceolatus* < *lanceola* small lance, dim. of *lancea*. See LANCE.]

lanc·er (lan′sər, län′-) *n.* A cavalryman armed with a lance.

lanc·ers (lan′sərz, län′-) *n.pl.* (*construed as sing.*) A type of quadrille; also, the music for it. Also **lan′ciers** (-sərz).

lance sergeant *Brit. Mil.* A corporal acting temporarily as a sergeant, usually without increased pay.

lan·cet (lan′sit, län′-) *n.* **1.** A small, two-edged, usually pointed surgical knife, used to open abscesses, boils, etc. **2.** *Archit.* **a** A lancet arch. **b** A lancet window. [< F *lancette*, dim. of *lance* < OF. See LANCE.]

lancet arch *Archit.* A narrow, acutely pointed arch.

lan·cet·ed (lan′sit·id, län′-) *adj.* Having lancet windows or arches.

lancet fish An ocean fish (genus *Alepisaurus*) with large, lancetlike teeth.

lancet window A narrow, acutely pointed window.

lance·wood (lans′wood′, läns′-) *n.* **1.** A tough, elastic wood from Cuba, Guiana, or Brazil, used for carriage shafts, fishing rods, billiard cues, etc. **2.** Any of various trees (genus *Oxandra*) yielding this wood.

Lan·chow (lan′chou′, *Chinese* län′jō′) The capital of Kansu Province, NW China; pop. 1,500,000 (est. 1970): formerly *Kaolan*. Also **Lan′-chou′**.

lan·ci·nate (lan′sə·nāt) *v.t.* **·nat·ed**, **·nat·ing** To stab or pierce, as with pain; tear. [< L *lancinatus*, pp. of *lancinare* to tear to pieces] — **lan′ci·na′tion** *n.*

Lancs. or **Lancs** Lancashire.

land (land) *n.* **1.** The solid, exposed surface of the earth as distinguished from the oceans, lakes, etc. **2.** A country or region, especially considered as a place of human habitation. **3.** The people of such a country or region: The whole *land* mourns him. **4.** Ground considered with reference to its uses, location, character, etc.: pasture *land*; arable *land*. **5.** *Law* **a** Any tract of ground whatever that may be owned as goods together with all its appurtenances, as water, forests, buildings, etc. **b** A share or interest in land, tenements, or any hereditament, both corporeal and incorporeal. ◆ Collateral adjective *praedial*. **6.** Rural places as distinguished from cities or towns: a return to the *land*. **7.** *Econ.* Natural resources as used in production. **8.** An unindented part of a surface marked by indentations; especially, one of the helical ridges inside a rifle barrel. — **Syn.** See NATION. — *v.t.* **1.** To transfer from a vessel to the shore; put ashore. **2.** To bring (something in flight) down to rest: to *land* a plane. **3.** To bring to some point, condition, or state: His words *landed* him in trouble. **4.** In fishing, to pull (a fish) out of the water; catch. **5.** *Informal* To obtain; win: to *land* a job. **6.** *Informal* To deliver (a blow). — *v.i.* **7.** To go or come ashore from a ship or boat. **8.** To touch at a port; come to land. **9.** To descend and come to rest after a flight or jump; come down. **10.** To come to some place, condition, or state; end up: to *land* in jail. [OE]

-land *combining form* **1.** A region of a certain kind: *woodland*. **2.** The country of; *Scotland*. **3.** A specified place or realm: *cloudland*. [< LAND]

lan·dau (lan′dô, -dou) *n.* **1.** A former type of closed sedan having a back seat with a collapsible top. **2.** A four-wheeled carriage with a collapsible top. [after *Landau*, a Bavarian city where it was first made]

lan·dau·let (lan′dô·let′) *n.* **1.** A former type of coupe with a collapsible top over the rear section. **2.** A small landau. Also **lan′dau·lette′**. [Dim. of LANDAU]

land bank *U.S.* **1.** A bank making mortgage loans on land or other real property. **2.** In colonial United States, a bank taking mortgages on land in exchange for a currency note.

LANDAUS
a Closed-top. *b* Open.

land·ed (lan′did) *adj.* **1.** Having an estate in land: *landed* gentry. **2.** Consisting in land: *landed* property.

landed immigrant *Canadian* A person admitted to Canada as a settler and potential citizen.

-landed *combining form* From or of a land. [< LAND]

land·fall (land′fôl′) *n.* A sighting of or coming to land; also. the land so sighted or reached.

land grant Government land granted to a railroad, educational institution, etc.

land-grant (land′grant) *adj.* Denoting a State agricultural or mechanical college, or a State university of which such a college forms a part, that received grants of land from the Federal government under the Morrill Act of 1862.

land·grave (land′grāv′) *n.* **1.** In medieval and Renaissance Germany, a count having jurisdiction over a specified territory. **2.** Later, the title of any of various German princes. [< MHG *lantgrave* < *lant*, *land* land + *grave*, *graf* count]

land·gra·vi·ate (land′grā′vē·it, -āt) *n.* The territory, office, authority, or jurisdiction of a landgrave. Also **land′gra′vate** (-grā·vāt). [< Med.L *landgraviatus* < *landgravio* count < MLG *landgrave*. See LANDGRAVE.]

land·gra·vine (land′grə·vēn) *n.* The wife of a landgrave. [< G *landgräfin*, fem. of *landgraf*. See LANDGRAVE.]

land·hold·er (land′hōl′dər) *n.* An owner or occupant of land.

land·ing (lan′ding) *n.* **1.** The act of going or placing ashore from any kind of craft or vessel. **2.** The place where a craft or vessel lands; wharf; pier. **3.** The act of descending and settling on the ground after a flight, leap, etc. **4.** *Archit.* The platform or floor at the top of a flight of stairs, between flights of stairs, or interrupting a flight of stairs.

landing beam *Aeron.* A directional radio beam marking the glide path in an instrument landing system.

landing craft A type of military vessel designed for landing men and materiel in amphibious operations.

landing field A tract of ground selected or prepared for the landing and takeoff of aircraft.

landing gear *Aeron.* The understructure of an aircraft, designed to carry the load when alighting, resting, or taxiing.

landing strip An unimproved, or only slightly improved, surface used for the takeoff, landing, servicing, storage, etc., of aircraft under rugged or emergency conditions; airstrip.

Lan·dis (lan′dis), **Kenesaw Mountain**, 1866–1944, U.S. jurist; professional baseball commissioner 1920–44.

land·la·dy (land′lā′dē) *n.* *pl.* **·dies** **1.** A woman who owns and rents out real estate. **2.** The wife of a landlord. **3.** A woman who keeps an inn.

länd·ler (lent′lər) *n.* **1.** A slow Austrian country dance, probably the precursor of the waltz. **2.** Music for or in the manner of this dance, in triple meter. [< G < dial. G *Landl* upper Austria, dim. of *land* land]

land·less (land′lis) *adj.* Owning no land.

land·locked (land′lokt′) *adj.* **1.** Surrounded by land; having no seacoast. **2.** Living in landlocked water: said especially of a normally anadromous fish: *landlocked* salmon.

land·lord (land′lôrd′) *n.* **1.** A man who owns and rents out real estate. **2.** An innkeeper. **3.** *Brit.* The lord of a manor. [OE *landhláford* < *land* land + *hláford* lord]

land·lord·ism (land′lôrd·iz·əm) *n.* **1.** Actions, conduct, or opinions peculiar to landlords as a group; also, the point of view that landed interests should be paramount. **2.** The system under which land is owned by persons to whom tenants pay a fixed rent.

land·lub·ber (land′lub′ər) *n.* An awkward or inexperienced person on board a ship. [< LAND + LUBBER]

land·man (land′mən) *n.* *pl.* **·men** (-mən) Landsman.

land·mark (land′märk′) *n.* **1.** A fixed object serving as a boundary mark to a tract of land, or as a guide to travelers, etc. **2.** A prominent or memorable object in the landscape. **3.** A distinguishing fact, event, etc. [OE *landmearc* < *land* land + *mearc* boundary]

land mass A very large area of land, especially one of continental size or larger: the Eurasian *land mass*.

land mine *Mil.* An explosive bomb placed in the ground.

land office A government office for the transaction of business pertaining to the public lands.

land-of·fice business (land′ô′fis, -of′is) *U.S. Informal* Business conducted at a rapid pace.

Land of Enchantment Nickname of NEW MEXICO.

Land of Opportunity Nickname of ARKANSAS.

Land of Promise See PROMISED LAND.

Land of the Little Sticks *Canadian* The region of stunted trees bordering the Barren Lands.

Land of the Midnight Sun Any country, such as Norway, Sweden, or Finland, which has land within the Arctic Circle, where the midnight sun is visible.

Land of the Rising Sun Japan.

Lan·dor (lan′dər, -dôr), **Walter Savage**, 1775–1864, English poet, essayist, and critic.

land·own·er (land′ō′nər) *n.* One who owns real estate. — **land′own′er·ship** *n.* — **land′own′ing** *n. & adj.*

land pike *U.S.* The hellbender (def. 1).

land-poor (land′poor′) *adj.* *Informal* Owning much land that yields an income insufficient to meet its expenses.

land power **1.** A nation having military strength on land. **2.** The military strength of a nation.

land·scape (land′skāp) *n.* **1.** A stretch of inland natural scenery as seen from a single point. **2.** A picture representing such scenery. **3.** The branch of painting, photography, etc., that deals with inland natural scenery. Also *Obs.* **land′**

skip (-skip). — *v.* **·scaped, ·scap·ing** *v.t.* **1.** To improve or change the features or appearance of a park, lawn, garden, etc. — *v.i.* **2.** To be a landscape gardener. [< Du. *landschap* < *land* land + *-schap* -ship. Akin to OE *landscipe*.]

landscape architect One whose profession is to plan the decorative arrangement of outdoor features, especially at or around building sites. — **landscape architecture**

landscape gardener One who plans and carries out the arrangement of plants, trees, etc. — **landscape gardening**

land·scap·ist (land'skā·pist) *n.* A painter of landscapes.

Land·seer (land'sir), **Sir Edwin Henry**, 1802–73, English painter.

Land's End A cape on the SW coast of Cornwall, the westernmost point of England. Also **Lands End.**

land·side (land'sīd') *n.* The flat side of a plowshare, away from the furrow.

land·slide (land'slīd') *n.* **1.** The slipping down of a mass of soil, rock, and debris on a mountain side or other steep slope. **2.** The mass of soil, rock, etc., slipping down. Also *Chiefly Brit.* **land·slip'** (-slip'). **3.** An overwhelming plurality of votes for one political party or candidate in an election.

Lands·mål (läns'môl) *n.* One of the two official forms of Norwegian, based on consolidation of various Norwegian dialects: also called *New Norwegian.* Compare RIKSMÅL. [< Norw., lit., land's language < *land* land + *mål* speech]

lands·man (landz'mən) *n. pl.* **·men** (-mən) One who lives and works on land: distinguished from *seaman*

Lands·ting (läns'ting) *n.* The senate or upper house of the Danish Rigsdag, or parliament. Also **Lands'thing.** [< Dan., lit., land's parliament < *land* + *t(h)ing* parliament]

Land·sturm (länt'shtoorm) *n.* **1.** A general levy in time of war, as made in certain European countries. **2.** The final reserve forces of a nation, called out in cases of great emergency or for home defense. [< G, lit., landstorm < dial. G (Swiss), trans. of F *levée en masse* general levy of troops]

Land·tag (länt'täk) *n.* Formerly, the general legislative assembly in a German state, especially Prussia. [< G < MHG *lanttac*, lit., land-day < *land*, *lant* land + *tag*, *tac* day]

land·ward (land'wərd) *adj. & adv.* Being, facing, or going toward the land. Also **land'wards** (-wərdz).

Land·wehr (länt'vâr) *n.* A trained militia. [< G < *land* land + *wehr* defense < *wehren* to defend]

lane[1] (lān) *n.* **1.** A narrow rural path or way, confined between fences, walls, hedges, or similar boundaries; also, a narrow city street. **2.** Any narrow way, passage, or similar course: a *lane* through a crowd of people. **3.** A prescribed route for transoceanic shipping or for aircraft. **4.** A marked division of a highway or road for traffic moving in the same direction. **5.** In sports, any of a set of parallel courses for contestants in races. — **Syn.** See ROAD. [OE *lanu*]

lane[2] (lān) *Scot. adj.* Alone. — **his lane, my lane, their lane,** etc. Himself alone, myself alone, themselves alone, etc. — **lane'ly** *adj.*

Lan·franc (lan'frangk), 1005?–89, Lombard theologian and scholar; archbishop of Canterbury 1070–89.

lang (lang) *adj. Scot.* Long.

lang. Language.

Lang (lang), **Andrew**, 1844–1912, Scottish poet, biographer, and man of letters. — **Cosmo Gordon,** 1864–1945, first Baron Lang of Lambeth, British prelate; archbishop of Canterbury 1928–42.

Lang·er·hans (läng'ər·häns), **islands of** See ISLANDS OF LANGERHANS.

Lang·land (lang'lənd), **William,** 1332?–1400?, English poet. Also **Lang'ley** (-lē).

lang·lauf (läng'louf) *n.* A cross-country ski run. [< G < *lang* long + *lauf* course < *laufen* to run]

lang·läuf·er (läng'loi·fər) *n.* A cross-country skier. [< G < *langlauf.* See LANGLAUF.]

Lang·ley (lang'lē), **Samuel Pierpont,** 1834–1906, U.S. scientist, astronomer, and inventor; pioneer in aerodynamics.

Lang·muir (lang'myoor), **Irving,** 1881–1957, U.S. chemist.

Lan·go·bard (lang'gō·bärd') *n.* A Lombard (def. 1). [< LL, prob. < OHG *lang* long + *bart* beard] — **Lan'go·bar'dic** *adj.*

lan·grage (lang'grij) *n.* A type of shot formerly used in naval warfare to destroy an enemy's rigging and sails. Also **lan'grel** (-grəl), **lan'gridge.** [Origin unknown]

lang·shan (lang'shan) *n.* A breed of large domestic fowl from China. [after *Langshan,* China, near Shanghai]

lang·syne (lang'sīn', -zīn') *adv. Scot,* Long since; long ago: used also as a noun. See AULD LANG SYNE.

Lang·ton (lang'tən), **Stephen,** died 1228?, English prelate, statesman, and scholar; archbishop of Canterbury 1207–28?.

Lang·try (lang'trē), **Lily,** 1852–1929, *née* Emily Charlotte Le Breton, English actress: called **the Jersey Lily.**

lan·guage (lang'gwij) *n.* **1.** The expression and communication of emotions or ideas between human beings by means of speech and hearing, the sounds spoken or heard being systematized and confirmed by usage among a given people over a period of time. **2.** Transmission of emotions or ideas between any living creatures by any means. **3.** The words forming the means of communication among members of a single nation or group at a given period: tongue: the French

language. **4.** The impulses, capacities, and powers that induce and make possible the creation and use of all forms of human communication by speech and hearing. **5.** The vocabulary or technical expressions used in a specific business, science, etc.: the *language* of mathematics. **6.** One's characteristic manner of expression or use of speech. Abbr. *lang.* [< OF *langage* < *langue* tongue < L *lingua* tongue, language. Akin to TONGUE.]

language arts Those elementary-school subjects, especially reading, spelling, literature, and composition, both written and oral, that deal with the acquisition of facility in one's native language.

langue d'oc (läng dôk') The dialects of Old French spoken south of the Loire in the Middle Ages, surviving in modern Provençal: so called from the use of the word *oc* for "yes." [< OF, lit., language of *oc* < Provençal *oc* yes < L *hoc* this]

Langue·doc (läng·dôk') A region and former province in southern France.

langue d'o·ïl (läng dô·ēl') The dialects of Old French spoken north of the Loire during the Middle Ages, from which modern French developed: so called from the use of the word *oïl* or *oui* for "yes." [< OF, lit., language of *oïl* < L *hoc illi* this for that < *hoc* this + *ille* that]

lan·guet (lang'gwet) *n.* Anything resembling a tongue in shape or function. [< F *languette,* dim. of *langue* tongue]

lan·guid (lang'gwid) *adj.* **1.** Indisposed toward physical exertion; affected by weakness or fatigue. **2.** Feeling little interest in or inclination toward anything; lacking animation; listless. **3.** Lacking in activity or quickness of movement: a *languid* attempt. [< L *languidus* faint, weak < *languere* to languish] — **lan'guid·ly** *adv.* — **lan'guid·ness** *n.*
— **Syn. 1.** *Languid, languorous, listless,* and *lackadaisical* mean lacking in energy or vigor. *Languid* most clearly attributes this condition to weariness or weakness. *Languorous* has come to suggest indolence and dreaminess, rather than debility. A *listless* person is inattentive, uninterested, or even bored, as the result of disease or fatigue. *Lackadaisical* implies more censure than *listless,* and refers to half-heartedness, laziness, or lack of proper concern. — **Ant.** energetic, vivacious.

lan·guish (lang'gwish) *v.i.* **1.** To become weak or feeble; fail in health or vitality; grow listless. **2.** To droop gradually from restless longing; pine. **3.** To pass through a period of external discomfort and mental anguish: to *languish* in prison. **4.** To adopt a look of sentimental longing or melancholy. [< OF *languiss-,* stem of *languir* < L *languescere.* inceptive of *languere* to be weary, languish] — **lan'guish·er** *n.*

lan·guish·ing (lang'gwish·ing) *adj.* **1.** Lacking alertness or force. **2.** Sentimentally pensive or melancholy. **3.** Becoming weak or listless. — **lan'guish·ing·ly** *adv.*

lan·guor (lang'gər) *n.* **1.** Lassitude of body; weakness; fatigue. **2.** A lack of energy or enthusiasm; spiritlessness. **3.** A mood of tenderness or sentimental dreaminess. **4.** The absence of activity; dullness; stagnation. **5.** Oppressiveness; stillness. [< OF < L < *languere* to languish]

lan·guor·ous (lang'gər·əs) *adj* **1.** Languid. **2.** Producing languor. — **Syn.** See LANGUID. — **lan'guor·ous·ly** *adv.* — **lan'guor·ous·ness** *n.*

lan·gur (lung·goor') *n.* Any of a subfamily (*Colobinae*) of slender, long-tailed Asian monkeys, as the entellus. [< Hind. *langūr* < Skt. *lāngūlin,* lit., having a tail]

lan·iard (lan'yərd) See LANYARD.

la·ni·ar·y (lā'nē·er'ē, lan'ē-) *adj.* Pertaining to the canine teeth. — *n. pl.* **·ar·ies** A canine tooth. [< L *laniarius* pertaining to a butcher < *lanius* butcher < *laniare* to tear]

La·nier (lə·nir'), **Sidney,** 1842–81, U.S. poet.

la·nif·er·ous (lə·nif'ər·əs) *adj.* Bearing wool or hair resembling wool. Also **la·nig'er·ous** (-nij'-). [< L *lanifer* < *lana* wool) + -OUS]

lan·i·tal (lan'ə·tal) *n.* A fiber originally produced in Italy from casein, similar to wool in chemical composition and function. [< *Lanital,* a trade name]

lank (langk) *adj.* **1.** Lean; shrunken. **2.** Long, flat, and straight; not curly: *lank* hair. — **Syn.** See LEAN[2]. [OE *hlanc* flexible] — **lank'ly** *adv.* — **lank'ness** *n.*

Lan·kes·ter (lang'kəs·tər), **Sir Edwin Ray,** 1847–1929, English zoologist and anatomist.

lank·y (lang'kē) *adj.* **lank·i·er, lank·i·est** Ungracefully tall and thin; loose-jointed. — **Syn.** See LEAN[2]. [< LANK + -Y[1]] — **lank'i·ly** *adv.* — **lank'i·ness** *n.*

lan·ner (lan'ər) *n.* **1.** A falcon (*Falco biarmicus*) of southern Europe and Asia. **2.** In falconry, the female of this falcon. [< OF *lanier,* ? ult. < L *laniarius.* See LANIARY.]

lan·ner·et (lan'ər·et) *n.* In falconry, the male of the lanner. [< OF *laneret,* dim. of *lanier.* See LANNER.]

lan·o·lin (lan'ə·lin) *n.* A fatty substance obtained from the wool of sheep and used in ointments, cosmetics, soaps, etc.; also called *wool fat.* Also **lan'o·line** (-lin, -lēn). [< L *lan(a)* wool + *ol(eum)* oil + -IN]

la·nose (lā'nōs) *adj.* Woolly; lanate. [< L *lanosus* < *lana* wool] — **la·nos'i·ty** (lā·nos'ə·tē) *n.*

lans·downe (lanz'doun) *n.* A closely woven fabric made of silk, or similar fiber, mixed with wool. [Origin unknown]

Lan·sing (lan'sing) The capital of Michigan, in the south central part; pop. 131,546.

lans·que·net (lans′kə·net) *n.* **1.** A card game. **2.** A mercenary soldier of the 15th to the 17th century, especially in France or Germany. [< F < G *landsknecht* a (mercenary) foot soldier < *land* country + *knecht* servant]

lan·ta·na (lan·tā′nə, -tä′-) *n.* Any of a genus (*Lantana*) of mainly tropical American shrubs of the verbena family bearing spikes or umbels of red, orange, lilac, or white flowers. [< NL, viburnum]

lan·tern (lan′tərn) *n.*
1. A protective, usually portable, case with transparent or translucent sides for enclosing a light. **2.** *Archit.* A structure with open or glazed sides, built above the main part of a building or on top of a tower to admit light and air. **3.** A lighthouse, especially the structure on top that protects the light. **4.** *Archaic* A magic lantern; slide projector. [< F *lanterne* < L *lanterna* < Gk. *lamptēr* < *lampein* to shine]

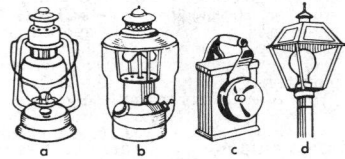

LANTERNS
a Kerosene. *b* Gasoline. *c* Battery-powered. *d* Electric post.

lantern fish Any of various small, large-eyed marine fishes (family *Myctophidae*), bearing rows of phosphorescent organs along the under parts of their bodies.

lantern fly Any of various homopterous insects (family *Fulgoridae*), usually tropical, formerly supposed to produce light from a large protuberant snout.

lantern jaws Long, sunken jaws that make the face appear thin. — **lan·tern-jawed** (lan′tərn-jôd′) *adj.*

lantern wheel *Mech.* A pinion in which a circle of bars inserted into two parallel disks mesh with the teeth of another wheel: sometimes called *trundle.* Also **lantern pinion.**

lan·tha·nide series (lan′thə·nīd) *Physics* The rare-earth elements beginning with lanthanum (according to some authorities, with cerium) and ending with lutetium, characterized by closely related properties and great difficulty of separation. [< LANTHAN(UM) + *-ide,* var. of *-ID²*]

lan·tha·non (lan′thə·non) *n.* Any element belonging to the lanthanide series.

lan·tha·num (lan′thə·nəm) *n.* A dark lead gray metallic element (symbol La) chemically related to aluminum. See ELEMENT. [< NL < Gk. *lanthanein* to lie concealed]

lant·horn (lant′hôrn, lan′tərn) *n. Brit.* A lantern.

Lan·tsang (län′tsäng′) The Chinese name for the MEKONG.

la·nu·gi·nous (lə·nōō′jə·nəs, -nyōō′-) *adj.* Covered with fine soft hair or down; downy. Also **la·nu′gi·nose** (-nōs) [< L *lanuginosus* < *lanugo, -inis* down < *lana* wool]

la·nu·go (lə·nōō′gō, -nyōō′-) *n. pl.* **·gos** *Biol.* A downy growth; especially, the soft, rudimentary hair on the body of the human fetus. [< L, down < *lana* wool]

lan·yard (lan′yərd) *n.* **1.** *Naut.* A small, usually four-stranded hemp rope used on a ship, especially one rove through deadeyes and used in setting up riggings. **2.** A cord used in firing certain types of cannon. **3.** A stout cord worn around the neck, used by sailors for attaching a knife (**knife lanyard**), or by soldiers for attaching a side arm. Also spelled *laniard.* [Alter. of obs. *lanyer* < OF *lasniere* thong < *lasne* noose; infl. in form by YARD¹ (spar)]

La·o (lä′ō) *n. pl.* **La·o** **1.** A Buddhistic people living in Laos and northern and eastern Thailand. **2.** Their Thai language.

La·oag (lä·wäg′) A port city on NW Luzon, Philippines; pop. about 22,000.

La·oc·o·on (lä·ok′ə·won, -ō·won) **1.** In Greek legend, a Trojan priest of Apollo who warned against the wooden horse of the Greeks, and was destroyed with his two sons by two large serpents. **2.** An antique sculpture in the Vatican, representing the slaughter of Laocoön and his sons.

La·od·i·ce·a (lä·od′ə·sē′ə) **1.** Any of several ancient Greek cities in Asia and Asia Minor, especially that in Phrygia, seat of one of the seven Christian churches mentioned in the book of Revelations. **2.** The ancient name for LATAKIA.

La·od·i·ce·an (lä·od′ə·sē′ən) *adj.* **1.** Of or pertaining to Laodicea. **2.** Indifferent or lukewarm, especially as to religion, as the early Christians of Laodicea. — *n.* **1.** An inhabitant of ancient Laodicea. **2.** An indifferent or lukewarm person.

La·oighis (lä′ish) A county of western Leinster Province, Ireland; 664 sq. mi.; pop. 45,069 (est: 1969); county seat, Maryborough: also *Leix.*

La·om·e·don (lä·om′ə·don) In Greek legend, the founder of Troy and father of Priam.

La·os (lous, lä′os, lä′ōs) A Republic in NW Indochina; 91,428 sq. mi.; pop. 2,300,000 (est. 1975); capital Vientiane. See map of THAILAND. — **La·o′tian** (lou′shən, lä·ō′shən, lä-ō′shən) *adj.*

Lao·tse (lou′dzu′), 604?–531? B.C., Chinese philosopher and mystic, founder of Taoism. Also **Lao-tze, Lao-tzu.**

lap¹ (lap) *n.* **1.** The chairlike place formed by the lower torso and thighs of a person seated. **2.** The clothing that covers the lower torso and thighs when one sits. **3.** The front part of a skirt when lifted up so as to hold or carry something. **4.** A place of nurture or fostering: fortune's *lap.* **5.** Control, care, or custody: in the *lap* of the gods. — **to throw into someone's lap** To give over the responsibility or control of something to someone else. [OE *laeppa.* Akin to Du. *lap* patch and L *labi* to slip.]

lap² (lap) *n.* **1.** The state of overlapping. **2.** A rotating disk used with an abrasive for grinding and polishing gems, metal, or glass. **3.** One circuit of a race course that consists of several circuits. **4.** The part of one thing, especially something thin and flat, that lies over another; also, the amount by which it lies over. — *v.* **lapped, lap·ping** *v.t.* **1.** To fold about something; wrap around something. **2.** To lay (one thing) partly over or beyond another: to *lap* weatherboards. **3.** To reach or extend partly over or beyond; overlap. **4.** To grind or polish (gems, metal, etc.) with a lap. **5.** To surround with love, comfort, etc.: now only in the passive: to be *lapped* in maternal tenderness. — *v.i.* **6.** To be folded. **7.** To lie partly upon or beside something else; overlap. **8.** To project beyond or into something else. [ME *lappen* to fold]

lap³ (lap) *v.t. & v.i.* **lapped, lap·ping** **1.** To drink as an animal does by taking up (a liquid) into the mouth with the tongue. **2.** To wash against (the shore, etc.) with a sound resembling that of lapping. — *n.* **1.** The act of one who or that which laps. **2.** The sound of lapping, or a similar sound. — **to lap up** **1.** To drink by lapping. **2.** *Informal* To eat or drink gluttonously. **3.** To listen to or take in with eagerness: to *lap up* flattery, knowledge, etc. [OE *lapian* to lap, prob. infl. by OF *laper* to lick < Gmc.] — **lap′per** *n.*

Lap. Lapland.

La Palma (lä päl′mä) See PALMA (def. 2).

laparo- *combining form Med.* The flanks or loins; abdominal wall. Also, before vowels, **lapar-.** [< Gk. *lapara* flank]

lap·a·rot·o·my (lap′ə·rot′ə·mē) *n. pl.* **·mies** *Surg.* The operation of opening the abdomen by incision in the flanks; also, loosely, any abdominal incision. [< LAPARO- + -TOMY]

La Paz (lä päz′, *Sp.* lä päs′) The de facto capital of Bolivia, in the western part; pop. 525,000 (est. 1969). See SUCRE.

lap·board (lap′bôrd′, -bōrd′) *n.* A flat wide board held on the lap and used as a desk or table.

lap dissolve In motion pictures and television, the slow emergence of one scene out of another, caused by the lapping of a fade-in over a fade-out.

lap dog A dog small enough to be held on the lap.

la·pel (lə·pel′) *n.* The part of a front of a coat, jacket, etc., that is folded back to form a downward extension of the collar. [Dim. of LAP¹]

La Pé·rouse (lä pā·rōōz′), **Comte de,** 1741–88, Jean François de Galaup, French navigator.

lap·ful (lap′fŏŏl′) *n.* As much as the lap can hold.

lap·i·dar·y (lap′ə·der′ē) *n. pl.* **·dar·ies** **1.** One whose work is to cut, engrave, or polish precious stones. **2.** A connoisseur, collector, or dealer in precious stones. — *adj.* **1.** Pertaining to the art of cutting or engraving precious stones. **2.** Inscribed upon or cut in stone. [< L *lapidarius* of stone]

lap·i·date (lap′ə·dāt) *v.t.* **·dat·ed, ·dat·ing** **1.** To hurl stones at. **2.** To stone to death. [< L *lapidatus,* pp. of *lapidare* < *lapis, -idis* stone] — **lap′i·da′tion** *n.*

la·pid·i·fy (lə·pid′ə·fī) *v.t. & v.i.* **·fied, ·fy·ing** To turn to stone; petrify. [< F *lapidifier* < Med.L *lapidificare* < L *lapis, -idis* stone + *facere* to make] — **la·pid′i·dif·ic** (lap′ə·dif′ik) or **·i·cal** *adj.* — **la·pid′i·fi·ca′tion** *n.*

la·pil·lus (lə·pil′əs) *n. pl.* **·li** (-lī) **1.** A small stone. **2.** *Usually pl.* A small, rounded fragment of igneous rock, generally less than one inch in diameter, that solidifies after being ejected from a volcano. [< L, dim. of *lapis* stone]

lap·in (lap′in, *Fr.* lä·pan′) *n.* **1.** A rabbit. **2.** Rabbit fur, usually dyed to resemble more expensive furs. [< F]

lap·is laz·u·li (lap′is laz′yōō·lī) **1.** A bluish violet variety of lazurite containing small amounts of calcite and other minerals, valued as a gemstone. **2.** The color of lapis lazuli. Also **lap′is.** [< NL < L *lapis* stone + Med.L *lazuli,* genitive of *lazulus* azure < Arabic *lāzaward.* See AZURE.]

Lap·i·thae (lap′ə·thē) *n.pl.* of **Lap·ith** (lap′ith) In Greek mythology, a wild tribe of Thessaly who, at the wedding of their king Pirithous, fought and overcame the centaurs.

lap-joint (lap′joint′) *v.t.* To join together by a lap joint.

lap joint A joint in which a layer of material laps over another, as in shingling. For illustration see FLASHING. — **lap·joint·ed** (lap′joint′tid) *adj.*

La·place (lä·pläs′), **Marquis de,** 1749–1827, Pierre Simon, French astronomer and mathematician.

Lap·land (lap′land) A region of northern Norway, Sweden, and Finland, and the NW Soviet Union inhabited by Lapps.

La Pla·ta (lä plä′tä) A port city in eastern Argentina; pop. 337,060 (1960). See also RÍO DE LA PLATA.

Lapp (lap) *n.* **1.** A member of a formerly nomadic Mongoloid people of Lapland, of short stature and marked brachycephaly, now settled largely in Sweden and Norway. Also **Lap·land·er** (lap′lan-dər). **2.** The Finno-Ugric language of the Lapps: also **Lap′pish.** [< Sw.]

Lapp. Lappish.

lap·per[1] (lap′ər) *n.* One who or that which laps.

lap·per[2] (lap′ər) *v.t. & v.i.* Scot. Lopper[2].

lap·pet (lap′it) *n.* **1.** A hanging flap or fold on a headdress or garment. **2.** A loose or pendent flap or fold of flesh, as the lobe of the ear, the wattle of a bird, etc. [Dim. of LAP[1]]

lapse (laps) *n.* **1.** A gradual passing away; imperceptible slipping downward or onward. **2.** A pronounced fall into ruin, decay, or disuse. **3.** A slip or mistake, usually trivial: a *lapse* of the tongue. **4.** A failure or miscarriage through fault or negligence: a *lapse* of justice. **5.** Law A forfeiture brought about by the failure to perform some necessary act. **6.** Apostasy or backsliding. — *v.i.* **lapsed, laps·ing 1.** To pass gradually or by degrees; sink slowly; slip: to *lapse* into a coma. **2.** To fall into ruin or a state of neglect. **3.** To deviate from one's principles or beliefs; backslide. **4.** To become void, usually by failure to meet obligations: the insurance policy *lapsed.* **5.** Law To pass or be forfeited to another because of negligence, failure, or death of the holder. **6.** To pass away, as time; elapse. [< L *lapsus* slip < *labi* to glide, slip] — **laps′a·ble, laps′i·ble** *adj.* — **laps′er** *n.*

lapse rate *Meteorol.* The rate of decrease of atmospheric pressure with the increase of altitude.

lap·strake (lap′strāk′) *Naut. adj.* Built with planks overlapping and riveted together; clinkerbuilt: said of a boat. — *n.* A boat so built; also, this method of building. Also **lap′streak′** (-strēk′). [< LAP[1] + STRAKE]

lap·sus (lap′səs) *n. Latin* A slip; a mistake.

lapsus cal·a·mi (kal′ə-mī) *Latin* A slip of the pen.

lapsus lin·guae (ling′gwē) *Latin* A slip of the tongue.

lapsus me·mo·ri·ae (mə-mô′ri-ē) *Latin* A memory slip.

Lap·tev Sea (läp′tyif) A part of the Arctic Ocean north of the Yakut S.S.R.: formerly *Nordenskjöld Sea.* *Russian* **Mor·e Lap·te·vykh** (môr′yə läp′tyi-vikh)

La·pu·ta (lə-pyōō′tə) In Swift's *Gulliver's Travels,* a flying island peopled by philosophers engaged in absurd undertakings.

lap·wing (lap′wing′) *n.* A crested, ploverlike bird (*Vanellus vanellus*) of the Old World, noted for its flopping, awkward flight and its shrill cry: also called *green plover, pewit, weep.* [OE *hlēapwince* < *hleapan* to leap + *wince,* prob. < *wancol* unsteady; infl. in form by LAP[1] and WING]

lar (lär) *Often cap.* The singular of LARES.

lar·board (lär′bôrd, -bôrd′, -bōrd′) *Naut. adj.* Being on or toward the left side of a ship as one faces the bow. — *n.* The left-hand side of a ship: now replaced by *port.* Opposed to *starboard.* [ME *laddebord,* lit., prob., lading side < OE *hladan* to lade + *bord* side; infl. in form by STARBOARD]

lar·ce·ner (lär′sə-nər) *n.* One who commits larceny; thief. Also **lar′ce·nist.**

lar·ce·ny (lär′sə-nē) *n. pl.* **·nies** Law The unlawful removal, without claim of right, of the personal goods of another with intent to defraud the owner; theft. The distinction between **grand larceny** and **petty** (or **petit**) **larceny,** based on the value of the stolen property, has been abolished in England and in some parts of the United States. — **Syn.** See THEFT. [< AF *larcin,* OF *larrecin* < L *latrocinium* theft < *latrocinari* to rob < *latro* robber] — **lar′ce·nous** *adj.* — **lar′ce·nous·ly** *adv.*

larch (lärch) *n.* **1.** Any one of several coniferous, deciduous trees (genus *Larix*) of the pine family, especially the tamarack. **2.** The strong, durable wood of this tree. [< G *lärche* < MHG *lerche* < L *larix, laricis*]

lard (lärd) *n.* The semisolid fat of a hog after rendering. — *v.t.* **1.** To cover or smear with lard; grease. **2.** To prepare (lean meat or poultry) by inserting strips of bacon or fat before cooking. **3.** To intersperse or furnish (speech or writing) with embellishments, quotations, etc. [< OF, bacon < L *lardum* lard] — **lard′y** *adj.*

lar·da·ceous (lär-dā′shəs) *adj.* Of or like lard; fatty.

lar·der (lär′dər) *n.* **1.** A room or cupboard where articles of food are stored. **2.** The provisions of a household. [< AF *larder,* OF *lardier* < Med.L *lardarium,* orig., a storehouse for bacon < *lardum* lard]

larder beetle A small, blackish beetle (*Dermestes lardarius*) about ⅓ inch long, whose larva feeds on dried meats, cheese, etc. For illustration see INSECTS (injurious).

Lard·ner (lärd′nər), **Ring,** 1885–1933, U.S. journalist and short-story writer: full name **Ringgold Wilmer Lardner.**

lard oil An oil expressed from lard, used as a lubricant, etc.

lar·don (lär′dən) *n.* A thin slice of bacon or pork for larding meat. Also **lar·doon** (lär-dōōn′). [< F < *lard.* See LARD.]

La·re·do (lə-rā′dō) A port city in southern Texas, on the Rio Grande; pop. 69,024.

lar·es (lâr′ēz, lā′rēz) *n.pl. of* **lar** (lär) *Often cap.* In ancient Rome, tutelary deities, especially the spirits of departed ancestors presiding over the household: associated with the *penates.*

lares and pe·na·tes (pə-nā′tēz) **1.** The household gods. **2.** The cherished belongings of one's household.

large (lärj) *adj.* **larg·er, larg·est 1.** Having considerable size, quantity, capacity, extent, etc.; big. **2.** Having a greater size, quantity, capacity, extent, etc., than another; bigger: Give me the *large* size. **3.** Having considerable breadth of sympathy or comprehension: Take *large* views. **4.** *Obs.* Free and openhanded in giving; generous. **5.** *Naut.* Of a wind, on the quarter or aft of the beam; favorable. *Abbr. lg., lge.* — *adv.* **1.** In a size greater than usual: Print *large.* **2.** *Naut.* Before the wind, or with the wind on the quarter: to sail *large.* — **at large 1.** Free; at liberty: The maniac is *at large.* **2.** In general; not divided or classified: the people *at large.* **3.** Elected from the whole State, not from a particular district: congressman *at large.* **4.** Exhaustively; fully: He spoke *at large* of his specialty. — **in** (**the**) **large** Fully; completely; on a sizable scale. [< OF < L *larga,* fem. of *largus* abundant] — **large′ness** *n.* — **Syn.** (adj.). **1.** vast, grand, massive, bulky, spacious.

large calorie See under CALORIE.

large·heart·ed (lärj′här′tid) *adj.* Generous; openhanded. — **large′heart′ed·ness** *n.*

large intestine See under INTESTINE.

large·ly (lärj′lē) *adv.* **1.** To a great extent; mainly; chiefly. **2.** On a big scale; extensively; abundantly.

large·mind·ed (lärj′mīn′did) *adj.* Liberal in ideas; not narrow-minded; tolerant. — **large′-mind′ed·ness** *n.*

large-scale (lärj′skāl′) *adj.* **1.** Of large size or scope. **2.** Made according to a large scale: said of maps.

lar·gess (lär-jes′; lär′jis, -jes) *n.* Liberal giving; also, something liberally given. Also **lar′gesse.** [< F *largesse* < L *largus* abundant]

lar·ghet·to (lär-get′ō) *Music adj.* Moderately slow. — *adv.* In a moderately slow tempo: a direction to the performer. — *n. pl.* **·tos** A moderately slow movement or passage. [< Ital., dim. of *largo.* See LARGO.]

lar·ghis·si·mo (lär-gis′i-mō) *Music adj.* Very slow. — *adv.* In a very slow tempo: a direction to the performer. — *n. pl.* **·mos** A very slow passage or movement. [< Ital., superl. of *largo.* See LARGO.]

larg·ish (lär′jish) *adj.* Somewhat large.

lar·go (lär′gō) *Music adj.* Slow; broad. — *adv.* In a slow tempo: a direction to the performer. — *n. pl.* **·gos** A slow movement or passage. [< Ital., slow, large < L *largus* abundant]

lar·i·at (lar′ē-ət) *n.* **1.** A rope for tethering animals. **2.** A lasso. — *v.t.* To fasten or catch with a lariat. [< Sp. *la reata* < *la* the + *reata* rope < *reatar* to tie]

la·rine (lar′in, lā′rin) *adj.* **1.** Denoting a subfamily (*Larinae*) of birds comprising the gulls, having the upper mandible as long as the lower. **2.** Of or resembling birds of this subfamily; gull-like. [< NL < LL *larus* gull < Gk. *laros*]

La·ri·sa (lä′rē-sä) A city in eastern Thessaly, Greece; pop. 55,391 (1961). Also **La·ris·sa** (lə-ris′ə).

lark[1] (lärk) *n.* **1.** Any of numerous small singing birds (family *Alaudidae*), chiefly of the Old World, as the skylark. **2.** Any of various similar but unrelated birds, as the titlark or meadowlark. [ME *laverke* < OE *lāferce, læwerce*]

lark[2] (lärk) *n. Informal* A hilarious time; frivolous adventure; prank. — *v.t.* **1.** To jump (a fence) on horseback. — *v.i.* **2.** To play pranks; frolic. [Origin uncertain] — **lark′-er** *n.* — **lark′some** *adj.*

lark·spur (lärk′spûr) *n.* Any of several showy herbs (genus *Delphinium*) of the crowfoot family with loose, terminal clusters of white, pink, blue, or red flowers, as the **scarlet larkspur** (*D. cardinale*). [< LARK[1] + SPUR]

La Roche·fou·cauld (lä rôsh-fōō-kō′), **Duc François de,** 1613–80, Prince de Marcillac, French moralist and writer.

La Ro·chelle (lä rō-shel′) A port city in western France, on the Bay of Biscay; Huguenot stronghold, besieged and taken by Cardinal Richelieu, 1627–28; pop. 72,075 (1968).

La·rousse (lä·rōōs′), **Pierre Athanase,** 1817–1875, French grammarian, lexicographer, and encyclopedist.

lar·ri·gan (lar′ə-gən) *n. Canadian* A high moccasin made of prepared oiled leather, worn chiefly by lumbermen, trappers, etc. [< dial. E (Canadian); origin unknown]

lar·ri·kin (lar′ə-kin) *Austral. Slang n.* A rough, disorderly fellow. — *adj.* Rowdy. [< dial. E (Australian), prob. < *Larry,* nickname for *Lawrence,* a personal name]

lar·rup (lar′əp) *Informal v.t.* To beat; thrash. — *n.* A blow. [< dial. E, ? < Du. *larpen* to thrash]

lar·um (lar′əm) *n. Archaic* An alarm. [Aphetic var. of ALARUM]

lar·va (lär′və) *n. pl.* **·vae** (-vē) **1.** *Entomol.* The first stage of an insect after leaving the egg, as the caterpillar, grub, or maggot. **2.** *Zool.* The immature form of any animal that is unlike the adult and must undergo metamorphosis. [< L, ghost, mask] — **lar′val** *adj.*

la·ryn·ge·al (lə-rin′jē-əl, -jəl) *adj.* **1.** Of, pertaining to, or near the larynx. **2.** *Phonet.* Glottal. Also **la·ryn·gal** (lə-ring′gəl). [< NL *laryngeus* < Gk. *larynx, laryngos* larynx]

lar·yn·gis·mus (lar′ən-jiz′məs) *n. Pathol.* Spasm of the muscles of the glottis. [< NL < Gk. *laryngismos* shouting < *laryngizein* to shout < *larynx, laryngos* larynx] — **lar′-yn·gis′mal** *adj.*

lar·yn·gi·tis (lar′ən-jī′tis) *n. Pathol.* Inflammation of the larynx. — **lar′yn·git′ic** (-jit′ik) *adj.*

laryngo- *combining form* The larynx; pertaining to the larynx: *laryngoscope.* Also, before vowels, **laryng-.** [< Gk. *larynx, laryngos* larynx]

lar·yn·gol·o·gy (lar'ing·gol'ə·jē) *n.* Scientific knowledge of the larynx, its functions, and its pathology. — **la·ryn·go·log·i·cal** (lə·ring'gō·loj'i·kəl) *adj.* — **lar'yn·gol'o·gist** *n.*

la·ryn·go·scope (lə·ring'gə·skōp) *n.* An instrument for examining the larynx. — **la·ryn'go·scop'ic** (-skop'ik) *adj.*

lar·yn·gos·co·py (lar'ing·gos'kə·pē) *n.* Examination of the larynx by means of the laryngoscope.

lar·yn·got·o·my (lar'ing·got'ə·mē) *n.* *Surg.* The operation of cutting into the larynx. [< Gk. *laryngotomia* < *larynx, laryngos* larynx + *tomē* a cutting < *temnein* to cut]

lar·ynx (lar'ingks) *n. pl.* **la·ryn·ges** (lə·rin'jēz) or **lar·ynx·es** *Anat.* A constituent organ of the respiratory tract in mammals and most other vertebrates, situated at the upper part of the trachea, and consisting of a cartilaginous box containing the valvelike vocal cords. Compare illustrations under LUNG, THROAT. [< NL < Gk. *larynx, laryngos* larynx]

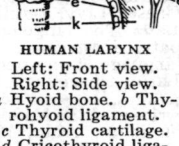

HUMAN LARYNX
Left: Front view.
Right: Side view.
a Hyoid bone. *b* Thyrohyoid ligament. *c* Thyroid cartilage. *d* Cricothyroid ligament. *e* Cricoid cartilage. *f* Epiglottis. *g* Thyrohyoid membrane. *h, i* Vocal cords. *j* Laryngeal ventricle. *k* Trachea.

La·sa (lä'sä') The Chinese name for LHASA.

la·sa·gna (lə·zän'yə) *n.* Broad, flat noodles, often served baked in a meat and tomato sauce. Also **la·sa'gne.** [< Ital.]

La Salle (lä säl'), **Sieur Robert Cavelier de,** 1643–87, French explorer in America.

La Scala (lä skäl'ä) An opera house and opera company in Milan, Italy.

las·car (las'kər) *n.* A native East Indian sailor. [< Hind. *lashkar* army (used for *lashkari* belonging to the army, a soldier) < Persian < Arabic *al-'askar* the army]

Las Ca·sas (läs kä'säs), **Bartolome de,** 1474–1566, Spanish Dominican missionary: called **Apostle of the Indians.**

las·civ·i·ous (lə·siv'ē·əs) *adj.* 1. Having or manifesting wanton desires; lustful. 2. Arousing sensual desires. [< LL *lasciviosus* < L *lascivia* wantonness < *lascivus* sportive, lustful] — **las·civ'i·ous·ly** *adv.* — **las·civ'i·ous·ness** *n.*

Las Cru·ces (läs krōō'sis) A city in southern New Mexico, near the Rio Grande; pop. 37,857.

la·ser (lā'zər) *n. Physics* A maser that can generate or amplify light waves: also called *optical maser.* [< l(ight) a(mplification by) s(timulated) e(mission of) r(adiation)]

lash[1] (lash) *n.* 1. A whip or scourge, especially the flexible cord or its tip. 2. A single whip stroke. 3. Anything that wounds the feelings as a whip stroke wounds the flesh. 4. An eyelash. 5. A heavy blow of wind, rain, waves, etc., against something. — *v.t.* 1. To strike, punish, or command with or as with a whip; flog. 2. To switch spasmodically or in a whiplike manner: The lion *lashes* his tail. 3. To beat or dash against violently. 4. To censure violently; assail sharply in speech or writing; castigate. 5. To incite: He *lashed* the mob into a fury. — *v.i.* 6. To deliver a whip stroke or strokes. 7. To switch or wriggle rapidly. — **to lash out** 1. To hit out suddenly and violently. 2. To break into angry verbal abuse. [< Prob. fusion of MLG *lasch* flap and OF *laz* cord; infl. in form and sense by OF *lachier* to fasten. Akin to LACE, LATCH.] — **lash'er** *n.*

lash[2] (lash) *v.t.* To bind or tie; especially, to bind one thing to another with rope or cord. [< OF *lacier, lachier* < L *laqueus* noose. Akin to LACE.] — **lash'er** *n.*

lashed (lasht) *adj.* Having lashes or eyelashes.

lash·ing[1] (lash'ing) *n.* 1. The act of one who or that which lashes. 2. A flogging; whipping. 3. A berating; scolding.

lash·ing[2] (lash'ing) *n.* The passing of a rope, cord, or the like, around two or more objects to fasten them together; also, the rope used to do this.

Lash·io (läsh'yō) The capital of Shan State and Northern Shan States, Upper Burma; the southern terminus of the Burma Road; pop. about 5,000.

Las·ki (las'kē), **Harold J(oseph),** 1893–1950, English political scientist.

Las Pal·mas (läs päl'mäs) A port city on Grand Canary in the Canary Islands; pop. 193,862 (1960). Officially **Las Pal'mas de Gran Ca·na·ria.** (thä grän' cä·nä'ryä).

La Spe·zia (lä spā'tsyä) See SPEZIA.

lass (las) *n.* 1. A young woman; girl. 2. A sweetheart. 3. *Scot.* A servant girl; maid. [< Scand. Cf. OSw. *lösk kona* an unmarried woman]

Las·salle (lä·säl'), **Ferdinand (Johann Gottlieb),** 1825–64, German socialist.

Las·sen Volcanic National Park (las'ən) An area of lava formations in northern California containing **Lassen Peak,** 10,453 ft., active volcano; 161 sq. mi.; established, 1916.

las·sie (las'ē) *n.* A little girl; lass. [Dim. of LASS]

las·si·tude (las'ə·tōōd, -tyōōd) *n.* A state of weariness or fatigue; languor. [< F < L *lassitudo* < *lassus* faint]

las·so (las'ō) *n. pl.* **·sos** or **·soes** A long rope or leather thong with a running noose, used for catching horses and cattle. — *v.t.* To catch with or as with a lasso. [< Sp. *lazo* < L *laqueus* snare] — **las'so·er** *n.*

last[1] (last, läst) *adj.* 1. Coming after all others; final in order, sequence, or time: the *last* page; the *last* day of summer. 2. Being the only one remaining of several or many: his *last* dime. 3. Next before the present or current; most recent: *last* year. 4. Least probable or least suitable: the *last* man I'd choose for the job. 5. Newest; most fashionable. 6. Conclusive; final: the *last* word in science. 7. *Rare* Standing beneath all others in estimation; least: the *last* of nations. 8. *Rare* Standing above or beyond all others; ultimate; utmost: to the *last* degree. — *adv.* 1. After all others in time or order. 2. At a time next preceding the present: He was *last* seen going west. 3. In conclusion; finally. — *n.* 1. The end; final part or portion. 2. The final appearance, experience, or mention: We'll never hear the *last* of this. — **at last** At length; at the end; finally. — **to breathe one's last** To die. [OE *latost*, superl. of *lǣt*, late, slow]

last[2] (last, läst) *v.i.* 1. To remain in existence; continue to be; endure. 2. To continue unimpaired or unaltered; to suffer no diminution: He *lasted* through six rounds of the fight. 3. To be as much as or more than needed; hold out: Will our supplies *last* through the winter? [OE *lǣstan*, to follow a track, continue, accomplish. Akin to LAST[3].] — **last'er** *n.*

last[3] (last, läst) *n.* A shaped form, usually of wood, on which to make a shoe or boot. — *v.t.* To fit to or form on a last. — **to stick to one's last** To attend only to one's proper business. [OE *lǣste* boot, shoemaker's last < *lǣst* footstep, track. Akin to LAST[2].] — **last'er** *n.*

last[4] (last, läst) *n.* Any of various large units of weight or measure, the amount of which varies for different commodities and in different places; especially, a unit of 4,000 pounds. [OE *hlæst* load < *hladan* to lade]

last ditch A final defensive situation; ultimate extremity. — **last-ditch** (last'dich') *adj.*

Las·tex (las'teks) *n.* Rubber manufactured in fine strands and wound with rayon, cotton, silk, or wool: a trade name. Also **las'tex.** [< (E)LAS(TIC) + TEX(TILE)]

last·ing[1] (las'ting, läs'-) *adj.* Continuing; durable; permanent. — **Syn.** See PERMANENT. — *n.* Endurance; continuance. [< LAST[2]] — **last'ing·ly** *adv.* — **last'ing·ness** *n.*

last·ing[2] (las'ting, läs'-) *n.* A strong twilled fabric used for the uppers of shoes and for covering buttons. [< LAST[3]]

Last Judgment *Theol.* **a** The final trial and sentencing by God of all mankind. **b** The time of this.

last·ly (last'lē, läst'-) *adv.* In the last place; in conclusion.

last rites 1. Observances appropriate to death or funerals. 2. *Eccl.* Sacraments administered to persons in peril of death, usually penance, the Eucharist, and extreme unction.

Last Supper 1. The last meal of Jesus Christ and his disciples before the Crucifixion and on the night of Judas' betrayal: also called *Lord's Supper.* 2. The celebrated wall painting of this scene by Leonardo da Vinci.

last word 1. The final word. 2. The definitive and most authoritative utterance. 3. *Informal* The most fashionable and desirable thing.

Las Ve·gas (läs vā'gəs) The largest city of Nevada, in the SE part; famous for its gambling casinos; pop. 125,787.

lat. Latitude.

Lat. 1. Latin. 2. Latvia.

Lat·a·ki·a (lat'ə·kē'ä) *n.* A fine grade of tobacco developed in Turkey. [after *Latakia*, because produced near there]

La·ta·ki·a (lä'tä·kē'ä) A Province of western Syria; 1,753 sq. mi.; pop. 625,475 (est. 1962); capital, Latakia (ancient *Laodicea*), pop. 72,378 (est. 1962).

latch (lach) *n.* 1. A fastening for a door or gate, usually consisting of a movable bar that falls or slides into a notch and is raised or pulled from either side by means of a string or lever. 2. Any similar fastening or catch for a door, window, etc. — **Syn.** See LOCK[1]. — *v.t. & v.i.* To fasten by means of a latch; close. — **to latch on to** *U.S. Slang* 1. To obtain, especially something highly desirable. 2. To comprehend. [OE *laeccan* to seize. Akin to LACE, LASH.]

latch·et (lach'it) *n. Archaic* A lace, thong, or strap that fastens a shoe or sandal to the foot. Also **shoe latchet.** [< OF *lachet*, dial. var. of *lacet*, dim. of *las, laz.* See LACE.]

latch·key (lach'kē') *n.* A key for releasing a latch, especially on an outside or front door: also called *passkey.*

latch·string (lach'string') *n.* A string fastened to a latch and passed through a hole above it to the outside of the door so that the latch may be lifted.

late (lāt) *adj.* **lat·er** or **lat·ter, lat·est** or **last** 1. Appearing or coming after the expected time; tardy. 2. Occurring at an unusually advanced time: a *late* hour; a *late* marriage. 3. Beginning at or continuing to an advanced hour: a *late* session. 4. Recent or comparatively recent: often implying something completed: the *late* war. 5. Deceased; especially, recently deceased: the *late* king. **6.** Far advanced toward the end or close: *late* antiquity. — **Syn.** See MODERN. — *adv.* **1.** After the expected time; tardily. **2.** At or until an advanced time of the day, month, year, etc.: *late* last year; to sleep *late*. **3.** *Archaic* Not long ago; recently: I have *late* loved. — **of late** Recently; lately: Where has he been *of late?* [OE *læt*] — **late/ness** *n.*

late·com·er (lāt/kum'ər) *n.* **1.** A person who arrives late, as at a party. **2.** A person who has only recently achieved a certain goal, condition, success, etc.

lat·ed (lā'tid) *adj. Poetic* Belated.

la·teen (la·tēn') *adj. Naut.* Designating a rig common in the Mediterranean, having a triangular sail (**lateen sail**) suspended from a long yard set obliquely to the mast. [< F (*voile*) *latine* Latin (sail), fem. of *latin* < L *Latinus*]

la·teen-rigged (la·tēn'rigd') *adj. Naut.* Having a lateen sail or sails.

Late Greek See under GREEK.

Late Latin See under LATIN.

late·ly (lāt/lē) *adv.* Not long ago; recently; of late.

la·ten·cy (lā'tən·sē) *n.* The state of being latent.

la·tent (lā'tənt) *adj.* **1.** Not visible or apparent, but capable of developing or being expressed; dormant. **2.** *Bot.* Undeveloped, as a concealed bud. [< L *latens, -entis*, ppr. of *latere* to be hidden] — **la/tent·ly** *adv.*

latent heat *Physics* The amount of additional heat required to change the state of a unit mass of a body from solid to liquid or from liquid to vapor after the melting point or boiling point has been reached.

latent period 1. *Pathol.* The incubation period of a disease before symptoms appear. **2.** *Physiol.* The time lapse between a stimulus and its response.

lat·er (lā'tər) *adv.* At a subsequent time; after some time.

lat·er·al (lat'ər·əl) *adj.* **1.** Pertaining to the side or sides; situated at, occurring, or coming from the side. **2.** *Phonet.* Produced with the breath passing over one or both sides of the tongue, as (l). — *n.* **1.** Something occurring at or on, or otherwise pertaining to, the side or sides of a main entity. **2.** In football, a lateral pass. **3.** *Phonet.* A lateral sound. [< L *lateralis* < *latus, lateris* side] — **lat/er·al·ly** *adv.*

lateral pass In football, a pass that travels across the field or toward the passer's goal line, rather than forward.

Lat·er·an (lat'ər·ən) **1.** The basilica of St. John Lateran, the cathedral church of the pope as bishop of Rome. **2.** The palace, now a museum, adjacent to the basilica. [< L *Lateranus*, name of a Roman family]

lat·er·ite (lat'ər·īt) *n.* **1.** A reddish, porous clay consisting principally of aluminum and iron hydroxide, formed in tropical regions by the disintegration of underlying rocks. **2.** A type of soil produced by such disintegration.

la·tes·cent (lə·tes'ənt) *adj.* Becoming obscure, latent, or hidden. [< L *latescens, -entis*, ppr. of *latescere*, inceptive of *latere* to be hidden] — **la·tes/cence** *n.*

la·tex (lā'teks) *n. pl.* **lat·i·ces** (lat'ə·sēz) or **la·tex·es** The viscid, milky emulsion secreted by certain plants, as the rubber tree, milkweed, euphorbia, poppies, etc., that coagulates on exposure to air and is the basis of natural rubber and various other commercial products. [< L, liquid]

lath (lath, läth) *n.* **1.** A thin strip of wood or metal, especially one of a number nailed to studs or joists to support a coat of plaster, or on rafters to support shingles or slates. **2.** Metal mesh sheets, fiber boards, or other materials used to support plaster, tiles, etc. **3.** Laths collectively: also **lath/work'** (-wûrk'). — *v.t.* To cover or line with laths. [Prob. fusion of OE *laett* and OE *laethth* (assumed); infl. in form by Welsh *llath*] — **lath/er** *n.*

lathe (lāth) *n.* **1.** A machine that holds and spins pieces of wood, metal, plastic, etc., so that they are cut and shaped when the operator holds abrading tools against them. **2.** A potter's wheel. — *v.t.* **lathed, lath·ing** To form or shape on a lathe; turn. [Prob. < MDu. *lade* or Dan. *lad*]

lath·er (lath'ər) *n.* **1.** The suds or foam formed by soap or detergents moistened with water. The foam of profuse sweating, as of a horse. — **in a lather** *U.S. Slang* In a state of intense excitement or agitation. — *v.t.* **1.** To cover with lather. **2.** *Informal* To flog; thrash. — *v.i.* **3.** To form lather. **4.** To become covered with lather, as a horse. [OE *lēathor* washing soda, soap. Akin to LAVE.] — **lath/er·er** *n.* — **lath/er·y** *adj.*

lath·ing (lath/ing, läth/-) *n.* **1.** The act or process of covering with laths. **2.** Laths collectively. **3.** Any work with laths or like material.

lathing hatchet A hatchet with a narrow blade for cutting and attaching wooden laths. For illustration see HATCHET.

lath·y (lath/ē, läth/ē) *adj.* **lath·i·er, lath·i·est** Like a lath; long and slender.

lati- *combining form* Broad: *latifolius*. [< L *latus* broad, wide]

lat·i·ces (lat'ə·sēz) Plural of LATEX.

lat·i·cif·er·ous (lat'ə·sif'ər·əs) *adj. Bot.* Containing or producing latex. [< L *latex, laticis* liquid + -FERROUS]

lat·i·fo·li·ate (lat'ə·fō'lē·it, -āt) *adj. Bot.* Having broad leaves. Also **lat'i·fo'li·ous.** [< NL *latifoliatus* < L *latus* broad + *folia* leaf]

lat·i·fun·di·um (lat'ə·fun'dē·əm) *n. pl.* **·di·a** (-dē·ə) A large landed property. [< L < *latus* wide + *fundus* estate]

Lat·i·mer (lat'ə·mər), **Hugh,** 1485?–1555, English Protestant prelate; burned at the stake.

Lat·in (lat'n) *adj.* **1.** Pertaining to ancient Latium, its inhabitants, culture, or language. **2.** Pertaining to or denoting the peoples or countries, such as France, Italy, and Spain, whose languages and cultures are derived from the ancient Roman civilization. **3.** Of or belonging to the Western or Roman Catholic Church as distinguished from the Eastern Orthodox Church. — *n.* **1.** The Indo-European, Italic language of ancient Latium and Rome, extensively used in western Europe until modern times as the language of learning, and still the official language of the Roman Catholic Church. **2.** A member of one of the modern Latin peoples. **3.** A member of the Western or Roman Catholic Church: a term used especially in the Eastern Orthodox Church. **4.** One of the people of ancient Latium. *Abbr. L, L., Lat.* — **Old Latin** The language before the first century B.C., as preserved in inscriptions and the comedies of Plautus. — **Classical Latin** The literary and rhetorical language of the period 80 B.C. to A.D. 200, standardized in such writers as Cicero, Caesar, Livy, Vergil, Tacitus, Horace, and Juvenal. — **Late Latin** The language from 200–600, including that of the patristic writings. *Abbr. LL, LL., L.L.* — **Low Latin** The language of any period after the classical, such as Medieval Latin, especially as modified by other languages. *Abbr. LL, LL., L.L.* — **Medieval Latin** The language used by the writers of the Middle Ages, from 600–1500: also called *Middle Latin. Abbr. Med.L, Med.L., ML, ML., M.L.* — **New** (or **Neo-**) **Latin** A form of the language based on Latin and Greek elements, developed since the Renaissance and used chiefly for scientific and taxonomic terms. *Abbr. NL, NL., N.L.* — **Vulgar Latin** The popular speech of the Romans from about A.D. 200 through the medieval period, and the chief source of the Romance languages. *Abbr. VL, V.L.* [< L *Latinus* of Latium, Latin]

Latin alphabet The Roman alphabet based upon the Etruscan and Greek alphabets, comprising in its full form twenty-three characters, and the parent of the modern alphabets of western Europe: also called *Roman alphabet.*

Latin America The countries of the western hemisphere south of the Rio Grande, in which the official languages are derived from Latin. See SPANISH AMERICA. — **Lat·in-A·mer·i·can** (lat'n·ə·mer'ə·kən) *adj.*

Latin American A native or inhabitant of Latin America.

Latin American Free Trade Association A customs union of Argentina, Brazil, Chile, Mexico, Paraguay, Peru, and Uruguay. Also **Latin American Common Market.**

Lat·in·ate (lat'ən·āt) *adj.* Designating a style or diction in English heavily dependent upon words and sentence patterns derived from Latin.

Latin Church The Roman Catholic Church. Compare UNIAT CHURCH.

Latin cross A cross in which the upright is longer than the beam that crosses it near the top. For illustration see CROSS.

La·tin·ic (lə·tin'ik) *adj.* Of Latin.

Lat·in·ism (lat'ən·iz'əm) *n.* An idiom in another language taken from or imitating Latin.

Lat·in·ist (lat'ən·ist) *n.* One versed or learned in Latin.

La·tin·i·ty (lə·tin'ə·tē) *n.* The use of Latin; also, the style or idiom of Latin.

Lat·in·ize (lat'ən·īz) *v.* **·ized, ·iz·ing** *v.t.* **1.** To translate into Latin. **2.** To make Latin in customs, thought, etc. **3.** To cause to resemble the Roman Catholic Church, as in dogma or ritual. **4.** To transliterate into Latin characters. — *v.i.* **5.** To use Latin words, forms, etc. [< L *latinizare* < *Latinus* Latin] — **Lat/in·i·za/tion** *n.* — **Lat/in·iz/er** *n.*

Latin Quarter A section of Paris on the south bank of the Seine, known for its many artists and students.

lat·ish (lā'tish) *adj.* Rather late.

lat·i·tude (lat'ə·tōōd, -tyōōd) *n.* **1.** *Geog.* Angular distance on the earth's surface northward or southward of the equator, measured in degrees along a meridian. **2.** *Often pl.* A region or place considered with reference to its distance north or south of the equator: The winters are mild in those *latitudes.* **3.** Freedom from narrow restrictions or customary limitations; independence or breadth of scope in thought, conduct, etc. **4.** *Astron.* The angular distance of a heavenly body from the ecliptic (**celestial latitude**). **5.** *Photog.* The range of exposure to which a film may be subjected without losing the ability to produce a good image. *Abbr. l., L., lat.* [< L *latitudo* < *latus* broad] — **lat·i·tu·di·nal** (lat'ə·tōō'də·nəl, -tyōō'-) *adj.* Of or pertaining to latitude. — **lat'i·tu'di·nal·ly** *adv.*

lat·i·tu·di·nar·i·an (lat'ə·tōō'də·nâr'ē·ən, -tyōō'-) *adj.* Characterized by or tolerant of liberal or unorthodox attitudes, beliefs, etc., especially in matters of religion. — *n.* **1.** One who is latitudinarian, especially in religion. **2.** *Often cap.* In the Anglican Church, one of a party of 17th-century churchmen who considered adherence to established doctrines relatively unimportant. [< L *latitudo, -inis* (see LATITUDE) + -ARIAN] — **lat'i·tu'di·nar'i·an·ism** *n.*

La·ti·um (lā'shē·əm) An ancient country in central Italy.

La·to·na (lə·tō′nə)   In Roman mythology, the mother of Diana and Apollo: identified with the Greek *Leto*.

la·tri·a (lə·trī′ə)   *n.* In the Roman Catholic Church, the supreme worship that can properly be given to God only: distinguished from *dulia* and *hyperdulia*. [< LL *latria* < Gk. *latreia* service, worship < *latreuein* to work for hire, worship < *latris* hired servant]

la·trine (lə·trēn′)   *n.* A privy or public toilet, especially in a camp, barracks, etc. [< F < LL *latrina* bath, privy < *lavatrina* < *lavare* to wash]

La·trobe (lə·trōb′), **Benjamin Henry,** 1764–1820, U.S. architect born in England.

-latry   *combining form* Worship of; excessive devotion to: *bibliolatry*. [< Gk. *latreia* worship]

lat·ten (lat′n)   *n.* **1.** Thin sheet metal. **2.** An alloy containing or resembling brass, formerly hammered thin and used to make church ornaments, etc. [< OF *laton, leiton,* ? < MHG *latta* thin plate, lath. Akin to LATH.]

lat·ter (lat′ər)   *adj.* **1.** Being the second of two persons or things referred to: often preceded by *the* and used absolutely: opposed to *former*: The *latter* statement is truer than the former. **2.** Later or nearer to the end: His *latter* years were happy. [OE *lætra*, compar. of *læt* late]

lat·ter-day (lat′ər-dā′)   *adj.* Belonging to the present or recent times; modern: a *latter-day* martyr.

Latter-day Saint   A Mormon.

lat·ter·ly (lat′ər-lē)   *adv.* **1.** Recently; lately. **2.** At a later time; toward the end.

lat·ter·most (lat′ər-mōst′)   *adj.* Last; latest.

lat·tice (lat′is)   *n.* **1.** A structure consisting of strips of metal, wood, etc., crossed or interlaced to form regularly spaced openings. **2.** A window, screen, gate, etc., made from or consisting of such a structure. **3.** *Physics* **a** A space lattice (which see). **b** The geometric arrangement of fissionable and nonfissionable material composing the moderator of a nuclear reactor. — *v.t.* **·ticed, ·tic·ing**   **1.** To furnish or enclose with a lattice. **2.** To form into or arrange like a lattice. [< OF *lattis* < *latte* lath < MHG. Akin to LATH.]

LATTICE

lat·tice·work (lat′is·wûrk′)   *n.* Openwork made from, consisting of, or resembling a lattice or lattices.

lat·tic·ing (lat′is·ing)   *n.* **1.** The process of forming or providing with a lattice. **2.** Latticework.

Latv.   Latvia.

Lat·vi·a (lat′vē·ə)   A constituent Republic of the Soviet Union, in the NE part on the Baltic Sea; 24,600 sq. mi.; pop. 2,365,000 (1970); capital, Riga. Officially **Latvian S.S.R.** *Russian* **Lat·viy·ska·ya S.S.R.** (lät·vyē′skä·yä).

Lat·vi·an (lat′vē·ən)   *adj.* Of or pertaining to Latvia, its people, or their language; Lettish. — *n.* **1.** A native or inhabitant of Latvia; a Lett. **2.** The Lettish language.

laud (lôd)   *v.t.* To praise highly; extol. — **Syn.** See PRAISE. — *n.* **1.** *pl. Eccl.* The prescribed prayers immediately following matins, the two offices together constituting the first of the seven canonical hours. **2.** A hymn of praise or honor. [< OF *laude* < L *laus, laudis* praise] — **laud′er** *n.*

Laud (lôd), **William,** 1573–1645, English prelate; archbishop of Canterbury 1633–45; beheaded.

laud·a·ble (lô′də·bəl)   *adj.* **1.** Deserving approbation; praiseworthy. **2.** *Archaic Med.* Indicative of healing: said of pus, etc. — **laud′a·bil′i·ty, laud′a·ble·ness** *n.* — **laud′a·bly** *adv.*

lau·da·num (lô′də·nəm)   *n.* **1.** Tincture of opium. **2.** Formerly, any preparation in which opium predominated. [< NL < Med.L, var. of L *ladanum* labdanum]

laud·a·tion (lô·dā′shən)   *n.* The act of lauding; praise.

laud·a·to·ry (lô′də·tôr′ē, -tō′rē)   *adj.* Expressing or containing praise; complimentary. Also **laud′a·tive.** [< L *lauditorius* < *laudare* to praise, celebrate]

Lau·der (lô′dər), **Sir Harry (MacLennan),** 1870–1950, Scottish singer, songwriter, and comedian.

Lau·e (lou′ə), **Max von,** 1879–1960, German physicist.

laugh (laf, läf)   *v.i.* **1.** To produce the characteristic explosive or inarticulate sounds, facial expressions, and other physical manifestations expressive of merriment, elation, derision, discomposure, etc. **2.** To express or experience amusement, satisfaction, etc. **3.** To produce an effect of happy animation, gaiety, etc.; be bright and sparkling. — *v.t.* **4.** To express or utter with laughter. **5.** To induce, persuade, or bring about a specified result by or as by laughing: I *laughed* myself sick. — **to laugh at 1.** To express amusement at. **2.** To ridicule; mock. **3.** To make light of; belittle. — **to laugh away** To dispel or minimize with laughter. — **to laugh down** To rout, silence, or cause to seem ridiculous by laughing. — **to laugh off** To rid one's self of or dismiss laughingly. — **to laugh on (or out of) the other (or wrong) side of one's mouth (or face)** To feel annoyance or regret after boasting, exulting, or seeming to triumph. — **to laugh up (or in) one's sleeve** To be covertly amused or exultant, especially over another's discomfiture. — *n.* **1.** An act or sound of laughing. **2.** Manner of laughing. **3.** *Infor-*

mal A cause for or provocation to laughter. — **to have the last laugh** To triumph or succeed after seeming at a disadvantage. [OE *hliehhan, hlæhhan*] — **laugh′er** *n.* — **Syn.** (verb) **1.** guffaw, giggle, titter, snicker, snigger, chuckle, chortle, cackle.

laugh·a·ble (laf′ə·bəl, läf′-)   *adj.* Provoking or likely to provoke laughter; ridiculous; funny. — **laugh′a·ble·ness** *n.* — **laugh′a·bly** *adv.*

laugh·ing (laf′ing, läf′-)   *adj.* **1.** Uttering or expressing laughter; seeming to laugh. **2.** Resembling or suggestive of laughter. **3.** Constituting cause for laughter: a *laughing* matter. — *n.* Laughter. — **laugh′ing·ly** *adv.*

laughing gas   Nitrous oxide.

laughing gull   A gull (*Larus atricilla*) of the Atlantic coast of North America, having a black head and strident voice.

laughing jackass   The kookaburra, a bird.

laugh·ing·stock (laf′ing·stok′, läf′-)   *n.* One who or that which provokes ridicule; a butt.

laugh·ter (laf′tər, läf′-)   *n.* **1.** The characteristic sound, facial expression, or action of laughing. **2.** A manifestation or reaction of amusement, merriment, hilarity, etc. [OE *hleahtor* < root of *hliehhan* to laugh]

launce (lôns)   *n.* The sand lance (which see).

Laun·ce·lot (lôn′sə·lot, län′-)   See LANCELOT.

launch¹ (lônch, länch)   *v.t.* **1.** To move or push (a vessel, etc.) into the water, especially for the first time on its completion. **2.** To set forcibly in flight or motion, as a rocket, missile, etc. **3.** To start (a person, organization, enterprise, etc.) on a career or course of action. **4.** To put into action or operation; initiate; open: to *launch* a campaign. **5.** To hurl; fling. — *v.i.* **6.** To make a beginning; start; venture: usually with *out* or *forth*. **7.** To begin (an action, speech, etc.) vehemently or impetuously; plunge; burst: usually with *into*. **8.** To begin to move, as a ship; sail: usually with *into, on, out,* etc. — *n.* The action or procedure of launching a vessel, missile, etc. [< AF *lancher,* OF *lancier* < *lance*. See LANCE.]

launch² (lônch, länch)   *n.* **1.** An open or half-decked motor boat, used as a pleasure craft, patrol boat, etc. **2.** Formerly, the largest of the boats carried by a ship, used for transporting men and supplies. [< Sp. *lancha,* prob. < Malay *lanca* three-masted boat < *lancār* speedy]

launch·er (lôn′chər, län′-)   *n.* **1.** A device used for setting projectiles in motion, as: **a** An installation for launching rockets, guided missiles, etc. **b** A rifle attachment for firing grenades. **2.** One who or that which launches.

launch·ing (lôn′ching, län′-)   *n.* **1.** The procedure or ceremony of moving a vessel into water for the first time on its completion. **2.** The action or procedure of setting a rocket, missile, etc., into flight. **3.** An introducing or bringing to public notice of a project, enterprise, etc.

launching pad   *Aerospace* The platform from which a rocket or guided missile is fired. Also **launch pad.**

laun·der (lôn′dər, län′-)   *v.t.* **1.** To wash (clothing, linens, etc.). **2.** To wash and prepare for use by or as by ironing. — *v.i.* **3.** To do the work of washing and ironing. **4.** To undergo washing: Nylon *launders* easily. — *n.* A trough or gutter for conveying water, washing ore, etc. [Contraction of ME *lavender* laundress < OF *lavandier* launderer < LL *lavandarius,* ult. < L *lavare* to wash] — **laun′der·er** *n.*

laun·dress (lôn′dris, län′-)   *n.* A woman paid or employed to do laundry; washerwoman.

laun·dro·mat (lôn′drə·mat, län′-)   *n. U.S.* A commercial establishment where the customer brings laundry to be washed and dried in coin-operated automatic machines. Also **laun′der·ette′** (-dər·et′). [< *Laundromat,* a trade name]

laun·dry (lôn′drē, län′-)   *n. pl.* **·dries**   **1.** A room, commercial establishment, etc., where laundering is done. **2.** Articles to be laundered or that have been laundered. **3.** The work of laundering. [Alter. of obs. *lavendry* < OF *lavenderie* < *launder*. See LAUNDER.]

laun·dry·man (lôn′drē·mən, län′-)   *n. pl.* **·men** (-mən)   **1.** A man who works in or manages a commercial laundry. **2.** A man who calls for and delivers laundry.

laun·dry·wom·an (lôn′drē·wŏŏm′ən, län′-)   *n. pl.* **·wom·en** (-wim′ən)   A laundress.

lau·ra (lôr′ə)   *n. pl.* **·ras** or **·rae** (-rē)   In early monasticism, a community of anchorites. [< Gk., lane, alley]

Lau·ra (lôr′ə)   The idealized lady to whom Petrarch's sonnets were addressed: identified with **Laure de Noves** (də nôv′), 1308–1348, of Avignon.

lau·ra·ceous (lô·rā′shəs)   *adj. Bot.* Of or belonging to the laurel family (*Lauraceae*). [< NL < L *laurus* laurel]

lau·re·ate (*adj., n.* lô′rē·it; *v.* -āt)   *adj.* **1.** Singled out for special honor because of excellence in one's achievements; especially, designating a poet thus honored. **2.** Crowned or decked with laurel as a mark of honor. **3.** *Obs.* or *Poetic* Made of or in imitation of laurel. — *n.* **1.** A person honored with a noteworthy prize or award. **2.** A poet laureate (which see). — *v.t.* **·at·ed, ·at·ing**   **1.** To crown with or as with laurel. **2.** To confer the title of poet laureate upon. [< L *laureatus* crowned with laurel < *laurea* laurel tree or crown, orig. fem. of *laureus* made of laurel < *laurus* laurel] **— lau're·ate·ship** *n.*

lau·rel (lôr'əl, lor'-) *n.* **1.** An evergreen tree or shrub (genus *Laurus*) typifying a family (*Lauraceae*) of trees and shrubs that includes cinnamon, sassafras, etc.; especially, the true or **Grecian laurel** (*L. nobilis*) of Mediterranean regions: also called **bay, bay tree, sweet bay. 2.** Any of various similar or related trees and shrubs, as the mountain laurel (which see). **3.** *Often pl.* A crown or wreath of laurel leaves, conferred or worn as a symbol of honor, achievement, etc. **4.** *pl.* Honor or distinction gained by outstanding achievement. **— to look to one's laurels** To be on guard against losing a position of eminence, honor, etc. **— to rest on one's laurels** To be content with what one has already achieved or accomplished. **—** *v.t.* **lau·reled** or **·relled, lau·rel·ing** or **·rel·ling 1.** To honor by or as by crowning with laurel. **2.** To adorn with laurel. [< OF *laurier, lorier* < *lor* < L *laurus*]

Lau·rel (lôr'əl, lor'-) A city in SE Mississippi; pop. 24,145.

Lau·rence (lôr'əns, lor'-), **Saint** See (Saint) LAWRENCE.

Lau·ren·cin (lô·rän·saṅ'), **Marie,** 1885–1956, French painter.

Lau·ren·tian (lô·ren'shən) *adj.* **1.** Of, pertaining to, or situated near the St. Lawrence River. **2.** *Geol.* Pertaining to or denoting the most ancient Archean rocks, conspicuous in North America.

Laurentian Mountains A mountain range in eastern Canada, extending from the St. Lawrence River to the Arctic Ocean; highest peak, 3,905 ft. Also *French* **Lau·ren·tides** (lô·rän·tēd')

Laurentian Plateau A horseshoe-shaped Pre-Cambrian plateau covering about half of Canada, from the Labrador coast, around Hudson Bay, and west to the Arctic near the mouth of the Mackenzie River: also called *Canadian Shield.* Also **Laurentian Shield.**

Lau·ri·er (lô·ryā'), **Sir Wilfrid,** 1841–1919, Canadian statesman; premier 1896–1911.

lau·rus·tine (lô'rəs·tin) *n.* A shrub (*Viburnum tinus*) of the honeysuckle family, having fragrant pink or white flowers. Also **lau·rus·ti·nus** (lô'rəs·tī'nəs). [< NL *laurustinus* < L *laurus tinus* < *laurus* laurel + *tinus* plant]

Lau·sanne (lō·zän') A city in western Switzerland, on the northern shore of Lake Geneva; pop. 138,300 (est. 1969).

laus De·o (lôs dē'ō, lous dā'ō) *Latin* Praise be to God.

Lau·trec (lō·trek') See TOULOUSE-LAUTREC.

lau·wine (lô'win) *n.* *Rare* An avalanche: also spelled *lawine.* [< G *Lawine* < LL *labina*]

la·va (lä'və, lav'ə) *n.* **1.** Molten rock that issues from an active volcano or through a fissure in the earth's crust. **2.** Rock formed by the solidifying of this substance. [< Ital., orig., a stream formed by rain < *lavare* to wash < L]

la·va·bo (lə·vä'bō, -vä'-) *n. pl.* **·boes 1.** *Often cap.* In the Anglican and Roman Catholic churches: **a** The ritual washing of the hands performed by the celebrant during the Eucharist. **b** The portion of the 26th Psalm (in the Vulgate and Douai versions the 25th) recited during this ceremony: from the opening word of the Latin version. **c** A small towel used in this rite. **d** The basin used in this rite. **2.** A washbasin with a container for water equipped with a spigot or spout, formerly used in medieval monasteries, etc. [< L, I shall wash < *lavare* to wash]

lav·age (lav'ij, *Fr.* lȧ·väzh') *n. Med.* A washing out of an organ, as the stomach. [< F < *laver* to wash < L *lavare*]

La·val (lȧ·vȧl'), **Pierre,** 1883–1945, French lawyer and politician; premier 1931–32, 1935–36; premier of the Vichy government 1942–44; executed.

la·va-la·va (lä'və·lä'və) *n.* A loincloth or waistcloth of printed calico worn by natives of Samoa and other islands of the Pacific. [< Samoan]

lav·a·liere (lav'ə·lir') *n.* An ornamental pendant worn on a thin chain around the neck. Also **lav'a·lier', French la·va·lière** (lȧ·vȧ·lyâr'). [< F *la vallière* a type of necktie, ? after Louise de La Vallière, 1644–1710, mistress of Louis XIV]

la·va·tion (lə·vā'shən) *n.* A washing. [< L *lavatio, -onis* < *lavare* to wash] **— la·va'tion·al** *adj.*

lav·a·to·ry (lav'ə·tôr'ē, -tō'rē) *n. pl.* **·ries 1.** A room equipped with washing and, usually, toilet facilities. **2.** A basin, small sink, or similar receptacle used for washing. **3.** *Eccl.* A ritual washing of the hands, as during the Eucharist. [< LL *lavatorium* a place for washing < L *lavare* to wash]

lave[1] (lāv) *v.t.* & *v.i.* **laved, lav·ing** *Chiefly Poetic* **1.** To wash; bathe. **2.** To flow along or lap, as a stream against its banks. [Fusion of OE *lafian* to wash, pour and OF *laver* to wash, both < L *lavare* to wash. Akin to LATHER.]

lave[2] (lāv) *n. Scot.* & *Brit. Dial.* The remainder. [OE *lāf*]

lav·en·der (lav'ən·dər) *n.* **1.** Any of various aromatic Old World plants (genus *Lavandula*) of the mint family, having spikes of fragrant, pale violet flowers; especially, the **true lavender** (*L. officinalis*), of which the dried flowers and aromatic oil (**oil of lavender**) are much used in perfumery, and the **spike lavender** (*L. latifolia*) yielding a similar oil (**oil of spike**) having various commercial uses. **2.** The dried flowers and foliage of this plant, used to scent linen, clothing, etc. **3.** The pale, reddish violet color characteristic of the flowers of this plant. **—** *adj.* Pale reddish violet. **—** *v.t.*

To perfume with lavender. [< AF *lavendre* < Med.L *lavendula, livendula,* ? < L *livere* to be bluish < *lividus* blue; infl. in form by *lavare* to wash, because used as a perfume in baths]

la·ver[1] (lā'vər) *n.* **1.** In the ancient Jewish Temple, a large ceremonial vessel in which the priests washed before offering sacrifices. **2.** *Archaic* A large basin or similar receptacle used for washing. **3.** *Archaic* A means or agency of spiritual cleansing, as the water of baptism. [< OF *laveoir* < LL *lavatorium.* See LAVATORY.]

la·ver[2] (lā'vər) *n.* Any of various edible seaweeds (genus *Porphyra*). [< L, a water plant]

La·ve·ran (lȧ·vrän'), **Charles Louis Alphonse,** 1845–1922, French pathologist.

lav·er·ock (lav'ər·ək, läv'rək) *n. Scot.* The lark. Also **lav·rock** (lav'rək).

lav·ish (lav'ish) *adj.* **1.** Generous and unrestrained in giving, spending, using, etc.; prodigal. **2.** Provided or expended in great abundance; profuse; unstinted. **—** *v.t.* To give or bestow generously or profusely. [< OF *lavasse, lavache* downpour of rain < *lavaci* < L *lavatio* a washing] **— lav'ish·er** *n.* **— lav'ish·ly** *adv.* **— lav'ish·ness** *n.*

La·voi·sier (lȧ·vwȧ·zyā'), **Antoine Laurent,** 1743–94, French chemist; identified and named oxygen; guillotined.

law[1] (lô) *n.* **1.** A rule of conduct, recognized by custom or decreed by formal enactment, considered by a community, nation, or other authoritatively constituted group as binding upon its members. **2.** A system or body of such rules. See CIVIL LAW, COMMON LAW, STATUTE LAW. **3.** The condition of society when such rules are observed: to establish *law* and order. **4.** The body of authoritatively established rules relating to a specified subject, area, or activity subject to legal control: criminal *law.* **5.** Remedial justice as administered by the courts or legal authorities: to resort to the *law.* **6.** The branch of knowledge concerned with jurisprudence. **7.** The vocation of an attorney, solicitor, etc.; the legal profession: to practice *law.* **8.** The rules and principles of common law and statute law, as distinguished from equity **9.** An authoritative rule or command; governing force: His will is *law.* **10.** *Often cap.* Divine will, command, or precept, especially as expressed in the Scriptures; also, a body or system of rules having such divine origin. **11.** A rule of conduct, moral principle, etc., derived from a generally recognized concept of universal justice. **12.** Any generally accepted rule, procedure, or principle governing a specified area of conduct, field of activity, body of knowledge, etc. **13.** In science and philosophy, a formal statement of the manner or order in which a set of natural phenomena occur under certain conditions. **14.** *Math.* A rule or formula governing a function or operation. **15.** *Chiefly Brit.* A start given to a weaker competitor. Abbr. **L.** or *l.* **— the law 1.** The legal authorities; the police. **2.** *Informal* A policeman. **— the Law 1.** The Mosaic Law (which see). **2.** The Torah. **— to go to law** To engage in litigation. **— to lay down the law** To utter one's wishes, instructions, etc., in an authoritative manner. **—** *v.t.* & *v.i. Informal* or *Dial.* To take legal action (against someone); go to law. [OE *lagu* < ON *lag* something laid or fixed, in pl., law. Akin to LAY[1].]

— Syn. (noun) *Law, statute, ordinance, regulation,* and *canon* denote a rule of conduct imposed by some authority. *Law* is the general term, but often it refers specifically to the rules laid down by the sovereign power in a nation. A *statute* is a written *law* enacted by a legislative body. In the United States, a *statute* enacted by a municipal body is called an *ordinance.* Rules or *laws* laid down by an administrative body, manager, etc., are *regulations.* A *canon* was originally a church *law;* it has since been extended to mean any principle which is regarded as established by common practice or by eminent authority. **13.** See AXIOM.

law[2] (lô) *adj. Scot.* Low.

law[3] (lô) *interj. Dial.* An exclamation expressing astonishment, admiration, etc. [Fusion of *law,* var. of LA[2] and *law,* alter. of LORD, used as an exclamation]

Law (lô), **(Andrew) Bonar,** 1858–1923, British statesman. **— John,** 1671–1729, Scottish financier and promoter.

law·a·bid·ing (lô'ə·bī'ding) *adj.* Obedient to the law.

law·break·er (lô'brā'kər) *n.* One who violates the law. **— law'break'ing** *n.* & *adj.*

Lawes (lôz), **Henry,** 1595–1662, English composer.

law·ful (lô'fəl) *adj.* **1.** Permitted or not forbidden by law. **2.** Recognized by or admitted under the law: *lawful* debts. **3.** Valid, authentic, etc., according to law: *lawful* marriage. **— law'ful·ly** *adv.* **— law'ful·ness** *n.*

— Syn. 1. *Lawful, legal, licit,* and *legitimate* agree in the sense of sanctioned by law. *Lawful* may be used of statute, canon, or any other kind of law, but *legal* is restricted to statute law only: *lawful* pleasures, *legal* restrictions. *Licit* may refer to regulations as well as laws; it implies strict conformity to the letter of the law. *Legitimate,* as formerly used, described children born of a *legal* marriage; it has now been greatly widened in sense to imply sanction of custom, public opinion, justice, etc.: a *legitimate* business profit, a *legitimate* conclusion.

law·giv·er (lô'giv'ər) *n.* One who originates or institutes a law or system of laws. **— law'giv'ing** *n.* & *adj.*

law·ine (lô′win, *Ger.* lä·vē′nə) See LAUWINE.

law·ing (lô′ing) *n. Scot.* A bill or reckoning in a tavern.

law·less (lô′lis) *adj.* **1.** Not controlled by law, authority, discipline, etc. **2.** Not in conformity with law; contrary to rules, regulations, etc. **3.** Having no law or restrictive regulations. — **law′less·ly** *adv.* — **law′less·ness** *n.*

law·mak·er (lô′mā′kər) *n.* One who enacts or helps to enact laws; a legislator. — **law′mak′ing** *n. & adj.*

Law·man (lô′mən) See LAYAMON.

law merchant The body of rules or usages regulating commercial transactions; commercial or mercantile law.

lawn[1] (lôn) *n.* **1.** A stretch of grassy land; especially, an area of closely mown grass near a house, in a park, etc. **2.** *Archaic* A glade in or bordering on a wood. [Obs. *laund* < OF *launde* heath < Breton *lann* < Celtic] — **lawn′y** *adj.*

lawn[2] (lôn) *n.* **1.** A fine, thin linen or cotton fabric. **2.** A fine sieve used to strain clay, cement, etc. [Earlier *laune* (*lynen*) Laon (linen), after *Laon*, France, where it was formerly made] — **lawn′y** *adj.*

lawn mower A machine operated by a motor or propelled by hand, used to cut the grass of lawns.

lawn tennis See under TENNIS.

Law of Moses The Mosaic Law (which see).

law of nations International law (which see).

law of parsimony *Philos.* A regulative principle in the interpretation of natural phenomena or scientific data, requiring that the simplest and least cumbersome assumption be preferred. Compare OCKHAM'S RAZOR.

Law·rence (lôr′əns, lor′-) **1.** A city in NE Massachusetts, on the Merrimac River; pop. 66,915. **2.** A city in eastern Kansas, on the Kansas River; pop. 45,683.

Law·rence (lôr′əns, lor′-), **D**(avid) **H**(erbert), 1885–1930, English novelist and poet. — **Ernest Orlando**, 1901–58, U.S. physicist.

Law·rence (lôr′əns, lor-), **Saint** Third-century Christian martyr. Also *Laurence.*

Law·rence (lôr′əns, lor′-), **Sir Thomas**, 1769–1830, English painter. — **T**(homas) **E**(dward), 1885–1935, English archeologist, soldier, and writer; led Arab revolt against Turkey in World War I; after 1927 changed his name to **Thomas Edward Shaw** (shô): called **Lawrence of Arabia.**

law·ren·ci·um (lô·ren′sē·əm) *n.* A very short-lived radioactive element (symbol Lw), originally produced by bombarding californium with the nuclei of a boron isotope. See ELEMENT. [after E. O. *Lawrence*]

law·suit (lô′sōōt′) *n.* A case, action, or proceeding brought to a court of law for settlement.

Law·ton (lôt′n) A city in SW Oklahoma; pop. 74,470.

law·yer (lô′yər) *n.* **1.** A member of any branch of the legal profession; especially, one who advises and acts for clients or pleads in court. **2.** The burbot, a fish. **3.** *Brit. Dial.* A long stem of a brier or bramble. [< LAW[1] + -YER]

— **Syn 1.** *Lawyer, counselor, counsel, barrister, solicitor, attorney,* and *advocate* are names for persons qualified to practice law. *Lawyer* is the general term for one versed in law and duly admitted to the bar. *Counselor,* as one who gives advice, is the common term of address of a judge to a trial *lawyer; counsel* is used in the same way, and also to denote a number of persons acting together as a legal staff: the *counsel* for the defence. In Britain, a *lawyer* qualified to conduct court cases is a *barrister;* a *solicitor* may give legal advice and may prepare court cases, but usually may not conduct them. *Attorney* is often used as a synonym for *lawyer,* but strictly denotes a legal agent: John Smith is an *attorney* (better, *lawyer*); Smith is Robinson's *attorney. Advocate* is used of a trial *lawyer* in Scotland and France; this term is seldom used in the United States except in *judge advocate* and other military usages.

lax (laks) *adj.* **1.** Lacking strictness, authoritative force, or disciplinary control; negligent. **2.** Lacking precision or exactness; vague: a *lax* interpretation of the law. **3.** Lacking tautness, firmness, or rigidity; slack. **4.** Of the bowels or bowel movements, not easily controlled or retained; loose. **5.** *Bot.* Having parts loosely arranged, as a flower cluster. **6.** *Phonet.* Produced with the tongue and jaw relatively relaxed, as (i) and (ōō): also *wide:* opposed to *tense.* [< L *laxus* loose] — **lax′ly** *adv.* — **lax′ness** *n.*

lax·a·tion (lak·sā′shən) *n.* **1.** The act of loosening, or the state of being loosened; relaxation. **2.** *Med.* Defecation. [< L *laxatio, -onis* < *laxare* to loosen < *laxus* loose]

lax·a·tive (lak′sə·tiv) *n.* A medicine taken to produce evacuation of the bowels; a gentle purgative. — *adj.* **1.** Loosening or producing evacuation of the bowels; gently purgative. **2.** Characterized by or having loose bowel movements. [< F, fem. of *laxatif* < L *laxativus* < *laxare.* See LAXATION.]

lax·i·ty (lak′sə·tē) *n.* The state or quality of being lax. [< F *laxité* < L *laxitas* < *laxus* loose]

lay[1] (lā) *v.* **laid, lay·ing** *v.t.* **1.** To cause to lie; deposit; especially, to place in a horizontal, reclining, or low position. **2.** To put or place; especially, to cause to be in a specified place, state, or condition. **3.** To construct, produce, or establish as a basis or support: to *lay* the groundwork. **4.** To place or arrange in regular order or proper position: to *lay*

bricks. **5.** To produce internally and deposit (an egg or eggs). **6.** To think out; prearrange; devise: to *lay* plans. **7.** To attribute or ascribe: to *lay* the blame. **8.** To impose as a penalty, assessment, obligation, etc.: to *lay* a fine. **9.** To set forth; advance; present: to *lay* one's claim before a court. **10.** To cause to fall; knock down; level: often with *low,* etc. **11.** To cause to settle, subside, or lie level: to *lay* the dust. **12.** To render ineffective; quell; quiet: to *lay* a ghost; to *lay* a rumor. **13.** To bury, as in a grave; inter. **14.** To apply in or as in a layer; spread, as paint. **15.** To set or prepare (a trap, etc.). **16.** To prepare (a table, etc.) for use by setting out the necessary equipment. **17.** To set or locate (a scene, action, etc.). **18.** To strike or inflict blows with: to *lay* a whip across someone's back. **19.** To offer or stake as a wager; bet. **20.** To twist strands so as to produce (rope, cable, etc.). **21.** *Mil.* **a** To aim (a cannon). **b** To drop (bombs). **22.** *U.S. Slang* To have sexual intercourse with. — *v.i.* **23.** To produce and deposit eggs. **24.** To make a bet or bets. **25.** *Naut.* To move to a specified place or position: to *lay* aloft. **26.** *Dial.* or *Illit.* To lie; recline. — **to lay about** (one) **1.** To strike out or deal blows on all sides. **2.** To exert or bestir oneself (to do something). — **to lay aside 1.** To place or set apart; put down. **2.** To save or reserve for future use. **3.** To remove; doff. — **to lay away 1.** To store up; save. **2.** To bury in or as in a grave. — **to lay by 1.** To save or reserve. **2.** To put aside; discard. **3.** *Naut.* To lay to. — **to lay down 1.** To place or put aside, in a low position, etc. **2.** To give up or relinquish; sacrifice: to *lay* down one's life. **3.** To state or proclaim authoritatively or dogmatically: to *lay* down the rules. **4.** To wager or bet. — **to lay for** *U.S. Informal* To await an opportunity to attack or harm (someone). — **to lay hold of** To seize; grasp. — **to lay in** To procure and store. — **to lay into** To attack vigorously. — **to lay it on** *Informal* To be extravagant, lavish, or exorbitant, especially in praise or flattery. — **to lay low 1.** To strike down; prostrate. **2.** *U.S. Slang* To go into hiding. — **to lay off 1.** To mark out; chart; plan. **2.** *U.S.* To dismiss from a job, usually temporarily. **3.** *U.S. Informal* To stop working; take a rest. **4.** *U.S. Slang* To stop or cease; especially, to stop annoying, teasing, etc. **5.** *Archaic* To doff, as a garment. — **to lay on 1.** To apply or spread, as pigment. **2.** To strike or attack vigorously. **3.** *Brit.* To install or supply, as a utility: to *lay on* electricity. — **to lay open 1.** To produce or cut an opening in. **2.** To reveal; expose. — **to lay out 1.** To arrange or display for use, inspection, etc. **2.** To arrange according to a plan; map. **3.** To spend or supply (a sum of money). **4.** To prepare (a corpse) for burial. **5.** *Informal* To strike down; prostrate. — **to lay over 1.** To overlay. **2.** *U.S. Informal* To stop for a time in the course of a journey. — **to lay to 1.** To work vigorously at. **2.** *Naut.* To maintain a vessel facing into the wind in a stationary or nearly stationary position. — **to lay up 1.** To make a store of. **2.** To incapacitate or confine, as by illness, injury, etc. — *n.* **1.** The manner in which something lies or is placed; relative arrangement: the *lay* of the land. **2.** An individual's share of the profits of the catch taken on a whaling or fishing voyage. **3.** The direction or twist given to the strands of a rope. **4.** *Chiefly Brit. Slang* A line of work or activity, especially of a dishonest nature. **5.** *U.S. Slang* A partner in sexual intercourse; also, an act of sexual intercourse. [OE *lecgan* to cause to lie < pt. of *licyan* to lie, recline. Akin to LAW[1]]

◆ **lay, lie** Formal writing demands a distinction between these two words, although in informal or uneducated speech *lay* has taken over many of the functions of *lie. Lay* takes an object: We *lay* the papers on his desk every morning. *Lie,* meaning recline or be situated, does not take an object: The papers *lie* on the desk until Mr. Smith arrives. The past tenses of these verbs are particularly liable to misuse and should be handled carefully: We *laid* the papers on his desk, and they *lay* there until he arrived.

lay[2] (lā) *adj.* **1.** Of, pertaining to, or belonging to the laity; secular. **2.** Not belonging to or endorsed by a learned profession; nonprofessional: a *lay* opinion. [< OF *lai* < Med.L *laicus* < Gk. *laïkos* < *laos* the people]

lay[3] (lā) Past tense of LIE[1].

lay[4] (lā) *n.* **1.** A song, ballad, or narrative poem. **2.** A melody. [< OF *lai,* prob. < Gmc.]

Lay·a·mon (lā′ə·mən, lä′yə-) Thirteenth-century English priest and poet, author of *Brut,* a long chronicle covering the history of Britain to A.D. 689: also called *Lawman.*

lay brother A brother in a monastery who is under the vows and wears the habit of the order but has not taken holy orders, and who usually does manual work.

lay day In commerce, one of the stipulated number of days allowed a ship's lessee for loading or discharging cargo without having to pay extra charges.

lay·er (lā′ər) *n.* **1.** A single thickness, coating, covering, etc., especially when applied to a surface or constituting one of the levels of a series; stratum. **2.** One who or that which lays; especially, a hen considered as an egg producer. **3.** A shoot or twig constituting part of a growing plant, of which a part is placed in the ground for rooting. — *v.t. & v.i.* **1.** To form a layer or layers. **2.** To propagate (a plant) by means of a layer or layers. [< LAY¹ + -ER¹]

lay·er·age (lā′ər·ij) *n.* In horticulture, the propagation of plants by means of layers.

layer cake A cake, usually frosted, made in layers having a sweetened filling between them.

lay·ette (lā·et′) *n.* The supply of clothing, bedding, etc., provided for a newborn infant. [< F, dim. of *laie* packing box, drawer < Flemish *laeye* < MDu. < *lade* chest, trunk]

lay figure **1.** A jointed model of the human body, used by artists in place of a living model, especially to show the arrangement of drapery. **2.** A mere puppet; a tool of the interests of others. [Earlier *layman* (< Du. *leeman* < *led* limb, joint + *man* man)]

lay·man (lā′mən) *n.* *pl.* **·men** (mən) **1.** One without training or skill in a learned profession or specialized branch of knowledge. **2.** A man belonging to the laity, as distinguished from the clergy. [< LAY² + MAN]

lay·off (lā′ôf′, -of′) *n.* *U.S.* **1.** The temporary dismissal of employees. **2.** A period of enforced unemployment.

lay·out (lā′out′) *n.* **1.** A planned arrangement, as: **a** The relative positions of streets, rooms, furnishings, etc. **b** Written matter, illustrations, etc., arranged and prepared for printing. **2.** That which is laid out or provided, as equipment. **3.** *U.S. Informal* An establishment; dwelling. **4.** *U.S. Informal* An organization; situation; setup.

lay·o·ver (lā′ō′vər) *n.* A break or interruption in a journey, as between trains; a stopover.

lay reader In the Anglican Church, a layman licensed to conduct certain services, as Evening Prayer.

lay·wom·an (lā′wŏŏm′ən) *n.* *pl.* **·wom·en** (-wim′ən) A woman who is not ordained or a member of a religious order. [< LAY² + WOMAN]

la·zar (lā′zər, laz′ər) *n.* *Archaic* A beggar or pauper afflicted with a loathsome disease; especially, a leper. [< Med.L *lazarus*, after *Lazarus* (*Luke* xvi 20)]

laz·a·ret·to (laz′ə·ret′ō) *n.* *pl.* **·tos** **1.** A hospital for the treatment of contagious diseases, as leprosy or plague; a pesthouse. Also **lazar house. 2.** A ship or building used as a place of quarantine. '**3.** *Naut.* A storage space between decks in the stern of a vessel: also **laz′a·ret′, laz′a·rette′** (-ret′). [< Ital. dial. (Venetian) *lazareto, nazareto* (Santa Madonna di) *Nazaret*, Venetian church formerly used as a hospital; infl. by *lazzaro* leper. See LAZAR.]

Laz·a·rus (laz′ə·rəs) In the New Testament: **a** A brother of Martha and Mary, raised from the dead by Christ. *John* xi 1. **b** A sick beggar in the parable of the rich and the poor man. *Luke* xvi 20.

Laz·a·rus (laz′ə·rəs), **Emma,** 1849–87, U.S. poet.

laze (lāz) *v.* **lazed, laz·ing** *v.i.* **1.** To be lazy; loaf; idle. — *v.t.* **2.** To pass (time) in idleness. — *n.* Time spent in idleness or relaxation. [Back formation < LAZY]

laz·u·li (laz′yŏŏ·lī) *n.* *Rare* Lapis lazuli (which see).

laz·u·lite (laz′yŏŏ·līt) *n.* An azure blue, brittle phosphate of aluminum and magnesium, crystallizing in the monoclinic system. [< Med.L *lazulum* lapis lazuli + -ITE¹]

laz·u·rite (laz′yŏŏ·rīt) *n.* A deep blue silicate of sodium and aluminum containing sulfur, the principal constituent of lapis lazuli. [< Med.L *lazur* azure + -ITE¹]

la·zy (lā′zē) *adj.* **·zi·er, ·zi·est 1.** Unwilling to work or engage in energetic activity; indolent; slothful. **2.** Moving or acting slowly or heavily; sluggish. **3.** Conducive to or characterized by idleness or languor. **4.** Shown lying on one side, as a symbol used as a brand for livestock. [Prob. < MLG *lasich* loose, feeble] — **la′zi·ly** *adv.* — **la′zi·ness** *n.*

la·zy·bones (lā′zē·bōnz′) *n. Informal* A lazy person.

Lazy Susan A revolving tray, often divided into compartments, used to hold condiments, etc. Also **lazy Susan.**

lazy tongs Tongs consisting of a connected series of extensible, pivoted joints operated by a scissorslike handle, enabling the user to pick up objects at a distance.

laz·za·ro·ne (laz′ə·rō′nä, *Ital.* läd′dzä·rō′nä) *n.* *pl.* **·ni** (-nē) A homeless Neapolitan beggar or casual worker. [< Ital., aug. of *lazzaro* leper < Med.L *lazarus*. See LAZAR.]

lb. Pound(s) [L *libra, librae*).

L.B. 1. Bachelor of Letters (L *Litterarum Baccalaureus*). **2.** Local Board.

lbs. Pounds.

l.c. 1. Left center. **2.** In the place cited (L *loco citato*). **3.** *Printing* Lower case.

L/C or **l/c** Letter of credit.

L.C. Library of Congress.

L.C.D. or **l.c.d.** or **lcd** Least (or lowest) common denominator.

L.C.L. or **l.c.l.** Less than carload lot.

L.C.M. or **l.c.m.** or **lcm** Least (or lowest) common multiple.

LCT or **L.C.T.** Local civil time.

ld. *Printing* Lead.

Ld. 1. Limited. **2.** Lord.

L.D. or **LD** Low Dutch.

L.D.S. Licentiate in Dental Surgery.

l.e. or **le** Left end.

-le *suffix* Repeatedly: used to form frequentative verbs, often without appreciable force: *sparkle.* [OE *-lian*]

lea¹ (lē) *n.* *Chiefly Poetic* A grassy field or tract; meadow. [OE *léah*, orig., open ground in a wood]

lea² (lē) *n.* A measure of yarn varying in length, equaling 80 yards for worsted, 120 yards for cotton or silk, and 300 yards for linen. [Back formation < earlier *leas*, prob. < F *lier* < L *ligare* to bind]

lea. 1. League. **2.** Leather.

leach (lēch) *v.t.* **1.** To cause (a liquid) to percolate or filter through something. **2.** To subject to the filtering action of a liquid. **3.** To remove or dissolve by or as by the filtering action of a liquid. — *v.i.* **4.** To be removed or dissolved by percolation or filtration. **5.** To lose soluble material by percolation or filtration. — *n.* **1.** The act or process of leaching. **2.** A solution obtained from leaching. **3.** A vessel in which something is subjected to leaching. [OE *leccan* to wet, irrigate. Akin to LAKE¹, LEAK.] — **leach′er** *n.*

leach·y (lē′chē) *adj.* **leach·i·er, leach·i·est** Coarsely porous, as soil.

Lea·cock (lē′kok), **Stephen Butler,** 1869–1944, Canadian economist and humorist.

lead¹ (lēd) *v.* **led, lead·ing** *v.t.* **1.** To go with or ahead of so as to show the way; guide; conduct. **2.** To cause to progress by or as by pulling or holding; draw along: to *lead* a child by the hand. **3.** To serve as or indicate a route for: The path *led* him to the hut. **4.** To be in command of; control the actions or affairs of; direct. **5.** To influence or determine the ideas, conduct, or actions of; induce; motivate. **6.** To be first among; be at the head of or ahead of. **7.** To begin or inaugurate the action or proceedings of; be the principal participant in: to *lead* a discussion. **8.** To conduct the performance of (musicians or music). **9.** To experience or live; also, to cause to experience or go through: to *lead* a merry life; They *led* him a wild chase. **10.** To direct or effect the course of (water, conduits, cable, etc.). **11.** In card games, to begin a round by playing (a specified card or type of card). **12.** In marksmanship, to aim ahead of (a moving target). — *v.i.* **13.** To act as guide; conduct. **14.** To be led; yield readily to being pulled or guided. **15.** To afford a way or passage; extend: The road *leads* through a swamp. **16.** To be conducive; tend: followed by *to:* Delinquency *leads* to crime. **17.** To have control or command; be most important or influential. **18.** To be first or in advance. **19.** In card games, to make the first play in a game or round. **20.** In boxing, to strike the first of a succession of blows. — **to lead off 1.** To make a start; begin. **2.** In baseball, to be the first batter in a line-up or inning. — **to lead on 1.** To entice or tempt, especially to wrongdoing. **2.** To go first or in advance. — **to lead the way 1.** To act as a guide. **2.** To take the initiative; set an example. — **to lead up to 1.** To be preliminary to; result in. **2.** To approach or arrive at (a subject, outcome, etc.) gradually or cautiously. — *n.* **1.** Position in advance or at the head. **2.** The distance or interval by which someone or something leads or precedes. **3.** Position of primary importance, responsibility, etc. **4.** Guidance; leadership; example: Follow his *lead.* **5.** Indication; clue: Give me a *lead.* **6.** In dramatic presentations: **a** A starring role. **b** A performer having such a role. **7.** In journalism, the introductory portion or paragraph of a news story, usually consisting of a brief summary of its contents. **8.** In card games: **a** The right or obligation to play first in a game or round. **b** The card, suit, etc., thus played. **9.** In boxing, the first of a succession of blows. **10.** In baseball, a position taken by a runner part of the way between the base he has attained and the next base. **11.** *Electr.* A short wire or conductor, as on a transformer, used as a connection to a source of current. **12.** A cord, leash, etc., for leading an animal. **13.** *Naut.* The course or direction of a rope. **14.** *Mining* **a** A lode or vein of ore. **b** A deposit of gold along the course of an old river bed. **15.** In marksmanship, the act of aiming ahead of a moving target. [OE *lǣden* to cause to go]
— **Syn.** (verb) **1.** precede, escort, usher. **4.** command, head, run. **6.** excel, outstrip. — **Ant.** follow.

lead² (led) *n.* **1.** A soft, heavy, malleable, dull gray metallic element (symbol Pb), occurring most commonly in the sulfide mineral galena: also called *plumbum.* See ELEMENT. **2.** Any of various objects made of lead or similar metal; especially, a weight suspended from a line, used in sounding, etc. **3.** Graphite, especially in the form of thin rods or cylinders used as the writing material in pencils. **4.** Bullets, shot, etc. **5.** White lead (which see). **6.** *pl.* Strips of lead used to secure and separate small window panes, pieces of stained glass, etc. **7.** *pl. Brit.* A flat roof covered with sheets of lead; also, the sheets so used. **8.** *Printing* A thin strip of type metal used to provide space between printed lines. Abbr. *ld.* — *v.t.* **1.** To cover, weight, fasten, treat, or fill with lead. **2.** *Printing* To separate or space (lines of type) with leads. **3.** To join (window panes, stained glass, etc.) with leads. — *v.i.* **4.** To become filled or clogged with lead, as a rifle groove. [OE *léad*; ult. origin prob. < Celtic. Akin to Du. *lood*, G *lot*.] — **lead′y** *adj.*

lead acetate *Chem.* A white, soluble, poisonous, crystalline salt, $Pb(C_2H_3O_2)_2 \cdot 3H_2O$, having a sweet taste, made by the action of acetic acid on litharge: also called *sugar of lead.*

lead arsenate *Chem.* A white, poisonous crystalline compound, $Pb_3(AsO_4)_2$, used in insecticides.

Lead·beat·er's possum (led′bē′tər) An arboreal marsupial (*Gymnobelideus leadbeateri*) of Australia, related to the flying phalangers; thought to be extinct until rediscovered in 1961.

lead dioxide *Chem.* The compound PbO_2, a dark brown powder used in the manufacture of storage batteries.

lead·en (led′n) *adj.* **1.** Dull gray, as lead. **2.** Made of lead. **3.** Weighty; inert: a *leaden* mass. **4.** Heavy or labored in movement, style, spirit, etc., sluggish. **5.** Oppressive; gloomy. **— lead′en·ly** *adv.* **— lead′en·ness** *n.*

lead·er (lē′dər) *n.* **1.** One who or that which goes ahead or in advance. **2.** One who acts as a guiding force, commander, etc. **3.** *Music* **a** A conductor or director of an orchestra, choral group, etc. **b** The principal performer in a section of an orchestra, chorus, etc. **4.** The foremost horse, etc., of a harnessed team. **5.** An article of merchandise offered at a special low price to attract customers. **6.** A pipe for draining or carrying a liquid, as rainwater. **7.** *Brit.* The chief editorial article in a newspaper. **8.** In fishing, a length of gut, etc., used for attaching a hook or lure to the line. **9.** *pl. Printing* Dots or hyphens in a horizontal row, serving to guide the eye across a page, column, etc. **— Syn.** See CHIEF.

lead·er·ship (lē′dər·ship) *n.* **1.** The office, position, or capacity of a leader; authoritative control; guidance. **2.** Ability to lead, exert authority, etc. **3.** A group of leaders.

lead glass (led) Flint glass (which see).

lead-in (led′in′) *n. Telecom.* A wire connecting a radio receiving set with its antenna: also, *Brit., down-lead.*

lead·ing[1] (lē′ding) *adj.* **1.** Having the capacity or effect of controlling, influencing, guiding, etc. **2.** Most important; chief; principal. **3.** Situated or going at the head; first. **—** *n.* The act of one who or that which leads; guidance.

lead·ing[2] (led′ing) *n.* **1.** The act or process of filling, covering, or separating with lead. **2.** A border of lead, as for window panes. **3.** *Printing* Spacing between lines.

lead·ing article (lē′ding) **1.** *Brit.* A leader. **2.** The first or main editorial or article in a newspaper, magazine, etc.

leading edge (lē′ding) *Aeron.* The forward edge of an airfoil or propeller blade.

leading question (lē′ding) A question having the intention or effect of eliciting the reply desired by the questioner.

leading strings (lē′ding) **1.** Strings by which young children are supported when learning to walk. **2.** A condition of restrictive guidance, restraint, or control.

leading tone (lē′ding) *Music* The note a semitone below the tonic, as the seventh step of a major scale; also, any tone tending to resolve to a note a semitone away.

lead line (led) A line used for taking soundings.

lead-off (led′ôf′, -of′) *n.* **1.** A beginning action, move, etc., as the opening play in a competitive game. **2.** A player or participant who begins the action in a game or competition, as the first batter in a baseball line-up: also **leadoff man.**

lead pencil (led) A pencil having a thin stick of graphite as its writing material.

lead·plant (led′plant′, -plänt) A low shrub (*Amorpha canescens*) of the southwestern United States, having grayish leaves and stems. Also **lead plant.**

lead poisoning (led) *Pathol.* Poisoning caused by the absorption of lead by the tissues, characterized by anemia, muscular paralysis, etc.: also called *plumbism, saturnism.*

leads·man (ledz′mən) *n. pl.* **·men** (-mən) *Naut.* A man who takes soundings with a lead line.

lead tetraethyl Tetraethyl lead (which see).

lead·wort (led′wûrt′) *n.* Plumbago (def. 3).

leaf (lēf) *n. pl.* **leaves** (lēvz) **1.** One of the lateral expanded appendages of the stem of a plant, commonly flat, thin, and green in color, and functioning as the principal area of photosynthesis. **2.** Foliage collectively; leafage. **3.** Loosely, a petal. **4.** A product, as tobacco, tea, etc., in the form of gathered leaves. **5.** One of the sheets of paper in a book, etc., each side being a single page. **6.** A flat piece, hinged or otherwise movable, constituting part of a table, gate, screen, etc. **7.** Metal in a very thin sheet or plate: gold *leaf.* **8.** A thin layer or sheet of flexible or separable material. **9.** One of the plates or strips of metal forming a leaf spring. Abbr. *l., L.* **— in leaf** Covered with or having sprouted leaves. **— to turn over a new leaf** To begin anew, especially with the intention of improving one's ways. **—** *v.i.* To put forth or produce leaves. **— to leaf through** To turn, riffle, or glance at the pages of (a book, etc.). [OE *lēaf*]

leaf·age (lē′fij) *n.* Leaves collectively; foliage.

leaf beet Chard, a vegetable.

leaf curl A plant disease caused by various fungi, characterized by deformation of the leaves. Also **leaf blister.**

leaf fat A layer of fat surrounding the kidneys of a hog, from which leaf lard is obtained.

leaf·hop·per (lēf′hop′ər) *n.* Any of a family (*Cicadellidae*) of homopterous leaping insects that suck the juices of plants.

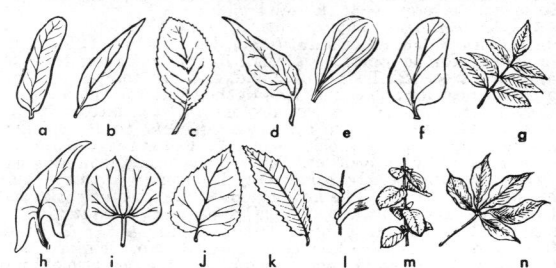

TYPES OF LEAVES
a Oblong. *b* Lanceolate. *c* Ovate with acute tip. *d* Acuminate. *e* Spatulate. *f* Obtuse. *g* Pinnately compound. *h* Sagittate. *i* Binate. *j* Cordate. *k* Serrate. *l* Amplexicaul. *m* Decussate. *n* Digitately compound.

leaf insect Any of a genus (*Phyllium*) of insects having flattened legs and wing covers, and resembling leaves.

leaf lard Lard made from leaf fat.

leaf·less (lēf′lis) *adj.* Having or bearing no leaves.

leaf·let (lēf′lit) *n.* **1.** One of the divisions of a compound leaf. **2.** A small printed sheet or circular, often folded. **3.** A little leaf. **4.** A small, leaflike part. [< LEAF + -LET]

leaf miner Any of certain moths (family *Gracilariidae*) or flies (family *Trypetidae*) whose larvae feed upon and are destructive to the leaves of plants and trees.

leaf mold **1.** A rich, earthy material composed chiefly of decayed or decaying leaves. **2.** A fungous growth forming discolored patches on the leaves of plants.

leaf spot A disease of fruit trees caused by a fungus (*Physalospora malorum*), resulting in widespread damage: also called *black rot, fruit rot.*

leaf spring *Mech.* A spring made of superimposed metal plates or strips.

leaf·stalk (lēf′stôk′) *n.* A petiole (def. 1).

leaf·y (lē′fē) *adj.* **leaf·i·er, leaf·i·est 1.** Bearing, covered with, or characterized by a profusion of leaves. **2.** Consisting of leaves. **3.** Resembling or of the nature of a leaf or leaves. **— leaf′i·ness** *n.*

LEAF SPRING

league[1] (lēg) *n.* **1.** A measure of distance varying from about 2.42 to 4.6 statute miles, but usually reckoned as approximately 3 miles. **2.** A square league; especially, an old Spanish land measure equaling about 4,438 acres. Abbr. *lea.* [< OF *legue* < LL *leuga, leuca* Gaulish mile < Celtic]

league[2] (lēg) *n.* **1.** An association or confederation of persons, organizations, or states, formed for stated reasons and purposes. **2.** A compact or covenant binding such a union. **3.** An association of athletic teams competing primarily among themselves. **— Syn.** See ALLIANCE. **— in league** In close alliance; working or acting in cooperation. **—** *v.t.* & *v.i.* **leagued, lea·guing** To form or unite in a league. [< OF *ligue* < Ital. *liga, lega* < *legare* to bind < L *ligare*]

League of Nations An international organization established in 1920, primarily for the preservation of world peace, and formally dissolved in 1946, when many of its functions were taken over by the United Nations.

lea·guer[1] (lē′gər) *Archaic n.* **1.** A siege. **2.** A military camp, especially of a besieging force. **—** *v.t.* To beleaguer; besiege. [< Du. *leger* camp]

lea·guer[2] (lē′gər) *n.* A member of a league.

Le·ah (lē′ə) In the Old Testament, Laban's elder daughter, who became the first wife of Jacob. *Gen.* xxix 16.

Lea·hy (lā′hē), **William Daniel**, 1875–1959, U.S. admiral and diplomat.

leak (lēk) *n.* **1.** An opening, as a crack, hole, or faulty closure, permitting an undesirable escape or entrance of fluid, light, etc. **2.** Any condition or agency by which something is let through or escapes: a *leak* in the security system. **3.** *Electr.* A failure or defect in insulation permitting an unwanted flow of electric current. **4.** An act or instance of leaking; leakage. **— to spring a leak** To develop or acquire an opening permitting leakage. **—** *v.i.* **1.** To let a fluid, etc., pass or escape through a hole, crack, or similar opening. **2.** To pass, flow, or escape through a hole, crack, etc. **3.** To be divulged despite efforts at or pretenses of secrecy: usually with *out:* The plans *leaked* out. **—** *v.t.* **4.** To let (a liquid, etc.) escape. **5.** To disclose (information, etc.) with or without authorization. [< ON *leka* to drip. Akin to LEACH, LAKE[1].]

leak·age (lē′kij) *n.* **1.** The act or circumstance of leaking. **2.** That which escapes or passes through by leaking. **3.** An allowance for loss by leaking.

leak·y (lē′kē) *adj.* **leak·i·er, leak·i·est** **1.** Having a leak; permitting leakage. **2.** *Archaic* Tending to divulge secrets, information, etc. — **leak′i·ness** *n.*

leal (lēl) *adj. Scot.* Loyal; faithful. — **leal′ly** *adv.*

lean¹ (lēn) *v.* **leaned** or **leant** (lent), **lean·ing** *v.i.* **1.** To rest or incline for support: usually with *against* or *on*: to *lean* against a tree. **2.** To incline, bend, or slant from or as from an erect position: The trees *lean* in the wind. **3.** To have or show a tendency, inclination, preference, etc.: often with *to* or *toward*: to *lean* toward conservatism. **4.** To depend for support, comfort, etc.; rely. — *v.t.* **5.** To cause to incline or bend from an erect position. **6.** To place or rest (something) so as to be supported by something else: usually with *against*, *on*, or *upon*. — *n.* The act or condition of leaning; deviation from the vertical; slant. [OE *hleonian, hlinian*]

lean² (lēn) *adj.* **1.** Not fat or plump; thin; spare. **2.** Free from or not containing fat: *lean* meat. **3.** Not rich, productive, plentiful, or satisfying; meager. **4.** Of a mixture of fuel and air, containing a relatively low proportion of fuel and a high proportion of air. — *n.* Meat or flesh having little or no fat. [OE *hlǣne* thin] — **lean′ly** *adv.* — **lean′ness** *n.*
— **Syn.** (adj.) **1.** *Lean, spare, lank, lanky, skinny,* and *gaunt* mean thin in body and having little flesh. *Lean* and *spare* stress the absence of fatty tissue, but are consistent with muscular strength and vigor. *Lank* suggests emaciation, and *lanky* describes one who is both tall and *lank*. *Skinny* implies underdevelopment, with consequent lack of strength and vigor, and *gaunt* is used of extreme emaciation, such as results from prolonged illness or old age. — **Ant.** fat, stout, plump.

Le·an·der (lē·an′dər) In Greek legend, the lover of Hero.

lean·ing (lē′ning) *n.* **1.** An inclination; tendency; predisposition. **2.** The act of one who or that which leans. — *adj.* Inclining or deviating from the vertical: a *leaning* tower.

lean-to (lēn′tōō′) *n. pl.* **-tos** (-tōōz′) **1.** A crude hut or shelter consisting of branches, planks, etc., sloping to the ground from a raised support. **2.** A shed or extension of a building having a roof sloping in one direction and supported by an adjoining wall or structure. — **Syn.** See HUT. — *adj.* Designating a roof that slopes only in one direction.

leap (lēp) *v.* **leaped** or **leapt** (lept, lēpt), **leap·ing** *v.i.* **1.** To rise or project oneself by or as by a sudden thrust from the ground or similar supporting surface, surroundings, etc.; jump; spring. **2.** To move, react, etc., suddenly or impulsively. **3.** To make an abrupt transition: to *leap* to a conclusion. — *v.t.* **4.** To traverse or clear by or as by a jump: to *leap* a barrier. **5.** To cause to jump: to *leap* a horse over a hedge. — *n.* **1.** The act of leaping; a bound. **2.** The space traversed or to be traversed by leaping. **3.** A place from which a leap has been or may be made. **4.** An abrupt transition. [OE *hlēapan*] — **leap′er** *n.*

leap·frog (lēp′frôg′, -frog′) *n.* A game in which each player puts his hands on the back of another, who is bending over, and leaps over him in a straddling position. — *v.* **-frogged**, **·frog·ging** *v.t.* **1.** To jump over as in the game of leapfrog. **2.** *Mil.* To bypass (an enemy position) in order to gain a more important objective. — *v.i.* **3.** To jump or advance as in the game of leapfrog.

leap year A year of 366 days, in which a 29th day is added to February to compensate for the difference between the length of the common and astronomical years. Every year divisible by 4 (as 1964) is a leap year, except those completing a century, which must be divisible by 400 (as 2000).

lear¹ (lir) *n. Scot.* Learning; knowledge; lore.

lear² (lir, lâr) See LEHR.

Lear (lir) A legendary king of Britain mentioned in early chronicles, hero of Shakespeare's tragedy *King Lear.*

Lear (lir), **Edward,** 1812–88, English humorist and painter.

lea·rig (lē′rig′, lā′-) *n. Scot.* A grassy ridge left unturned at the edge of a plowed field. [< OE *lǣg* lea + *hrycg* ridge]

learn (lûrn) *v.* **learned** or **learnt, learn·ing** *v.t.* **1.** To acquire knowledge of or skill in by study, instruction, practice, etc. **2.** To find out; become aware of: to *learn* the facts. **3.** To commit to memory; memorize. **4.** To acquire by experience or example: to *learn* bad habits. — *v.i.* **5.** To gain knowledge or acquire skill. **6.** To become informed; know: with *of* or *about.* ◆ *Learn* as a synonym for *teach,* as in *I'll learn you,* was once acceptable English but is now nonstandard. [OE *leornian.* Akin to LORE¹.] — **learn′er** *n.*

learn·ed (lûr′nid; *for def. 3* lûrnd, lûrnt) *adj.* **1.** Having profound, extensive, or specialized knowledge, education, etc.; erudite: *learned* men. **2.** Characterized by or devoted to scholarship: *learned* pursuits. **3.** Acquired by learning, repetition, etc.: a *learned* response.

learn·ing (lûr′ning) *n.* **1.** Knowledge obtained by study, extensive education, etc.; scholarship; erudition. **2.** The act of acquiring knowledge or skill. **3.** *Psychol.* Modification of behavior, mental processes, etc., as a result of previous experience. — **Syn.** See KNOWLEDGE.

lear·y (lir′ē) See LEERY.

lease¹ (lēs) *n.* A system of crossing warp threads in weaving. [Appar. var. of LEASH]

lease² (lēs) *n.* **1.** A contract for the temporary occupation or use of premises, property, etc., in exchange for payment of rent. **2.** The period of such occupation or use. **3.** Property held or used under such a contract. **4.** Opportunity to make use of or enjoy: a *lease* on life. — *v.t.* **leased, leas·ing** **1.** To grant possession or use of under a lease. **2.** To hold or use under a lease. [< AF *les,* OF *lais* a letting < *laissier* to let, leave < L *laxare* to loosen < *laxus* loose] — **leas′a·ble** *adj.*

lease·back (lēs′bak′) *n.* A transaction whereby a buyer of real property leases it to the seller. [< (*sale and) lease back*]

lease·hold (lēs′hōld′) *n.* **1.** Tenure by lease. **2.** Land held by lease. — *adj.* Held by lease. — **lease′hold′er** *n.*

leash (lēsh) *n.* **1.** A thong, cord, etc., by which a dog or other animal is led or restrained. **2.** Restraint; control. **3.** In hunting, etc., three of the same kind; a brace and a half. — *v.t.* To hold or secure by a leash. [< OF *lesse, laisse* < L *laxa,* fem. of *laxus* loose]

leas·ing (lē′sing) *n. Archaic* A lie; lying; falsehood. [OE *lēasung* < *lēasian* to tell lies < *lēas* without, false]

least (lēst) Alternative superlative of LITTLE. — *adj.* **1.** Smallest in degree, quantity, value, size, etc. **2.** Most inconsiderable or insignificant; slightest. — *n.* That which is smallest, slightest, or most insignificant. — **at least 1.** By the lowest possible estimate: She is *at least* forty years old. **2.** At any rate; in any event. — **in the least** In the slightest degree; at all. — *adv.* In the lowest or smallest degree. [OE *lǣst, lǣsest,* superl. of *lǣssa* less]

least bittern See under BITTERN.

least common denominator The least common multiple of all the denominators of a given group of fractions: 24 is the *least common denominator* of ¾, ⅛, and 1/12: also called *lowest common denominator.* Abbr. *lcd, l.c.d., L.C.D.*

least common multiple The smallest number evenly divisible by each of a given set of numbers: 12 is the *least common multiple* of 2, 3, 4, and 6: also called *lowest common multiple.* Abbr. *lcm, l.c.m., L.C.M.*

least flycatcher See under FLYCATCHER.

least sandpiper See under SANDPIPER.

least squares *Math.* A method of deducing the most probable value of a quantity from a set of observations or measurements, in accordance with the principle that the sum of the squares of all deviations from this value is at a minimum.

least·wise (lēst′wīz′) *adv. Informal* At least; at any rate. Also *Dial.* **least′ways** (-wāz′).

leath·er (leth′ər) *n.* **1.** Animal skin or hide, usually with the hair or fur removed, prepared for use by tanning or a similar process. **2.** An article or part made of leather. Abbr. *lea.* — *v.t.* **1.** To cover or equip with leather. **2.** *Informal* To flog with or as with a leather strap. [OE *lether*]

leath·er·back (leth′ər·bak′) *n.* A very large turtle (*Dermochelys coriacea*), having a flexible, leathery carapace.

leath·er·board (leth′ər·bôrd′, -bōrd′) *n.* Hard imitation leather made from pulped scrap leather or other materials.

leath·er·ette (leth′ər·et′) *n.* Imitation leather, used in bookbinding, upholstery, etc. [< LEATHER + -ETTE]

leath·er·head (leth′ər·hed′) *n. Slang* A stupid person.

leath·ern (leth′ərn) *adj. Archaic* **1.** Made of leather. **2.** Resembling leather; leathery. [OE *letheren* < *lether* leather]

leath·er·neck (leth′ər·nek′) *n. U.S. Slang* A marine. [< LEATHER + NECK; from the leather neckband formerly part of the uniform]

leath·er·oid (leth′ər·oid) *n.* A leatherlike material made of vegetable fiber treated chemically. [< LEATHER + -OID]

leath·er·wood (leth′ər·wŏŏd′) *n.* A North American shrub (*Dirca palustris*), with white, soft wood and tough, fibrous bark: also called *wicopy.*

leath·er·y (leth′ər·ē) *adj.* Resembling leather in texture or appearance; tough. — **leath′er·i·ness** *n.*

leave¹ (lēv) *v.* **left, leav·ing** *v.t.* **1.** To go or depart from; quit. **2.** To allow to remain behind or in a specified place, condition, etc.: to *leave* books on one's desk. **3.** To have or cause as an aftermath; result in: Oil *leaves* stains. **4.** To cause to be placed, given, or made available in one's absence: *Leave* your name at the desk. **5.** To commit for action, decision, etc.; entrust: *Leave* it to me. **6.** To terminate one's connection or association with; withdraw from. **7.** To abandon; forsake. **8.** To have remaining after one's death: to *leave* a large family. **9.** To transmit as a legacy; bequeath: He *left* his fortune to charity. **10.** To have as a remainder as the result of an arithmetic operation: Twelve minus eight *leaves* four. **11.** *Slang* or *Illit.* To let; permit. — *v.i.* **12.** To depart or go away; set out. — **to leave alone 1.** To refrain or desist from harassing, interfering with, etc. **2.** To allow to remain solitary or unattended. — **to leave off 1.** To stop; cease. **2.** To omit or refrain from using. — **to leave out 1.** To omit. **2.** To exclude. Abbr. (defs. 1, 12) *lv.* [OE *lǣfan,* lit., to let remain] — **leav′er** *n.*
◆ **leave, let** *Leave* and *let,* often confused, are not synonyms. *Leave* means to depart or to permit to remain (*He left the room; He left the book on the table*), as distinguished from *let,* which means simply to permit (*Let him stay*). *Let* can be followed by the infinitive without *to; leave* cannot. *Leave it to him to decide* and *Let him decide* are standard, but *Leave him decide* is nonstandard. *Leave* may be substituted for *let* only when followed by an object plus *alone. Leave me alone* is an acceptable substitute for *Let me alone.*

leave² (lēv) *n.* **1.** Permission to do something. **2.** Permission to be absent; especially: **a** Official permission granted to a member of the armed forces to be absent from duty. **b** The period covered by such permission: also **leave of absence**. **3.** Departure: formal farewell: usually in the phrase **to take (one's) leave**. **— on leave** Absent from work or duty with permission. [OE *lēaf* permission]

leave³ (lēv) *v.i.* **leaved, leav·ing** To put forth leaves; leaf.

leaved (lēvd) *adj.* **1.** Having a leaf or leaves. **2.** Having or characterized by (a specified kind or number of) leaves: used in combination: *four-leaved* clover.

leav·en (lev'ən) *n.* **1.** An agent of fermentation, as yeast, added to dough or batter to produce a light texture. **2.** A portion of fermented dough used for this purpose. **3.** Any component, addition, or pervasive influence that produces a significant change. Also **leav'en·ing.** *— v.t.* **1.** To cause fermentation in. **2.** To affect in character; temper. [< OF *levain* < L *levamen* alleviation < *levare* to raise]

Leav·en·worth (lev'ən-wûrth) A city in NE Kansas, on the Missouri River; site of a Federal prison; pop. 25,147.

leaves (lēvz) Plural of LEAF.

leave-tak·ing (lēv'tā'king) *n.* An act or ceremony of departure; farewell.

leav·ings (lē'vingz) *n.pl.* Unused or unconsumed portion; remains; remnants.

leav·y (lē'vē) *adj.* **·i·er, ·i·est** *Poetic* Leafy.

Leb·a·nese (leb'ə-nēz', -nēs') *adj.* Of or pertaining to Lebanon (def. 1) or its people. *— n.* A native or citizen of Lebanon (def. 1).

Leb·a·non (leb'ə-nən) **1.** A Republic of SW Asia, at the eastern end of the Mediterranean; about 3,400 sq. mi.; pop. 3,042,000 (est. 1973); capital, Beirut. See map of ISRAEL. **2.** A city in SE Pennsylvania; pop. 28,572.

Lebanon Mountains A range extending through Lebanon; highest peak, Dahr el Quadib, 10,031 ft.

Le·bens·raum (lā'bəns-roum') *n.* *German* Territory claimed by a nation as necessary for its economic independence or growth; literally, space for living.

Le·brun (lə-brœn'), **Albert,** 1871–1950, French statesman; president 1932–40. **— Charles,** 1619–90, French painter: also **Le Brun.** **— Marie Anne Elisabeth Vigee-** See VIGEE-LEBRUN.

Le Cap (lə kap') See CAP HAÏTIEN.

lech·er (lech'ər) *n.* A man inordinately disposed to sexual indulgence; a lewd and prurient man. [< OF *lecheor* < *lechier* to live in debauchery, lick < OHG *leccōn* to lick]

lech·er·ous (lech'ər-əs) *adj.* **1.** Given to or characterized by immoderate sexual indulgence or lewdness. **2.** Inciting to lust; lewd. **— lech'er·ous·ly** *adv.* **— lech'er·ous·ness** *n.*

lech·er·y (lech'ərē) *n. pl.* **·ries** Unconstrained sexual indulgence. [< OF *lecherie, licherie* < *lecheor.* See LECHER.]

lec·i·thin (les'ə·thin) *n.* *Biochem.* Any of a class of phospholipids contained in plant and animal tissues, as egg yolk, brain tissue, etc., used in the processing of foods, textiles, cosmetics, and drugs. [< Gk. *lekithos* egg yolk + -IN]

Leck·y (lek'ē), **W(illiam) E(dward) H(artpole),** 1838–1903, Irish historian and essayist.

Le·conte de Lisle (lə-kônt' də lēl'), **Charles Marie René,** 1818–94, French poet.

Le Cor·bu·sier (lə kôr·bü·zyā'), 1887–1965, Swiss architect: original name **Charles Edouard Jean·ne·ret** (zhän·re').

Le Creu·sot (lə krœ·zō') A commune in east central France; pop. about 34,102 (1968).

lect. Lecture; lecturer.

lec·tern (lek'tərn) *n.* **1.** A stand having an inclined, shelflike surface on which a speaker, instructor, etc., may place books or papers. **2.** In some churches, a reading desk from which certain parts of the service are read. [< OF *lettrun* < LL *lectrum* < L *lectus,* pp. of *legere* to read]

lec·tion (lek'shən) *n.* **1.** A passage of Scripture read as part of a religious service. **2.** A variant reading in a text. [< OF *lectiun* < L *lectio, -onis* < *lectus,* pp. of *legere* to read]

lec·tion·ar·y (lek'shən·er'ē) *n. pl.* **·ar·ies** A book or list of lessons for church service. [< Med.L *lectionarium* < L *lectio.* See LECTION.]

lec·tor (lek'tər) *n.* **1.** *Eccl.* A person assigned to read portions of the service. **2.** In certain foreign universities, a lecturer. [< L, reader < *lectus,* pp. of *legere* to read]

lec·ture (lek'chər) *n.* **1.** A discourse on a specific subject, delivered to an audience for instruction or information. Abbr. *lect.* **2.** A formal reproof or lengthy reprimand. **— Syn.** See SPEECH. *— v.* **·tured, ·tur·ing** *v.i.* **1.** To deliver a lecture or lectures. *— v.t.* **2.** To deliver a lecture to; instruct by means of lectures. **3.** To rebuke sternly or at length. [< L *lectura* act of reading < *lectus,* pp. of *legere* to read]

lec·tur·er (lek'chər·ər) *n.* **1.** One who lectures. **2.** A position in certain colleges and universities, as: **a** In the United States, one who lectures but does not hold standard academic rank. **b** In Great Britain, an instructor who lectures but does not have professorial rank; a reader. Abbr. *lect.*

lec·ture·ship (lek'chər·ship) *n.* The position of lecturer.

led (led) Past tense and past participle of LEAD¹.

Le·da (lē'də) In Greek mythology, the wife of Tyndareus and mother of Clytemnestra, Castor, Pollux, and Helen, of which the latter three, according to many legends, were fathered by Zeus in the form of a swan.

ledge (lej) *n.* **1.** A narrow, shelflike projection along the side of a mountain, cliff, or other rocky formation. **2.** A shelf, sill, or similar surface projecting from or forming the top of a wall, etc. **3.** An underwater or coastal reef or ridge. **4.** *Mining* A metal-bearing rock stratum; vein. [ME *legge,* prob. < root of *leggen.* See LAY¹.] **— ledg'y** *adj.*

led·ger (lej'ər) *n.* **1.** An account book in which all final entries of the transactions of a business concern are recorded. **2.** A horizontal stone slab placed over a grave or tomb. **3.** A horizontal supporting timber fastened to the uprights of a scaffolding. **4.** Ledger bait or ledge tackle: also spelled *leger.* *— adj.* Remaining or lying in one place: now obsolete except in certain expressions: also spelled *leger.* [ME *legger,* prob. < *leggen* (see LAY¹); infl. by MDu. *legger* to lay]

ledger bait Fishing bait made to lie at the bottom: also spelled *leger bait.*

ledger board The horizontal board forming the top rail of a fence, the handrail of a staircase, etc.

ledger line 1. *Music* A short line added above or below the musical staff, used for the placement of a note beyond the range of the staff. **2.** A fishing line used with ledger tackle. Also spelled *leger line.*

ledger tackle Fishing tackle of which the bait or sinker lies on the bottom: also spelled *leger tackle.*

lee (lē) *n.* **1.** Shelter or protection, especially from the wind, provided by any object, barrier, etc. **2.** *Chiefly Naut.* **a** A place or side sheltered from the wind. **b** The direction opposite that from which the wind is blowing. *— adj. Chiefly Naut.* Pertaining to or being on the lee: opposed to *weather.* [OE *hlēo* shelter]

Lee (lē) A prominent Virginia family, including **Richard Henry,** 1732–94, and his brother **Francis Lightfoot,** 1734–97, Revolutionary statesmen and signers of the Declaration of Independence; **Henry,** 1756–1818, Revolutionary soldier and statesman: called **Light-Horse Harry;** his son **Robert E(dward),** 1807–70, Confederate commander in chief in the Civil War; **Fitzhugh,** 1835–1905, Confederate general, nephew of Robert Edward.
— Ann, 1736–84, English mystic active in America; founder of the Shakers: called **Mother Ann.**
— Charles, 1731–82, American Revolutionary general.
— Sir Sidney, 1859–1926, English editor and scholar.
— T(sung) D(ao), born 1926, U.S. physicist born in China.

lee·board (lē'bōrd', -bôrd') *n.* *Naut.* A board, framework of planks, etc., lowered on the lee side of a flat-bottomed vessel to prevent it from drifting to leeward.

leech¹ (lēch) *n.* **1.** Any of a class (*Hirudinea*) of carnivorous or bloodsucking, chiefly aquatic annelid worms; especially, the **medicinal leech** (*Hirudo medicinalis*), formerly used for bloodletting. **2.** One who clings to or preys upon another for gain; a parasite. **3.** *Archaic* A physician. *— v.t.* *Archaic* **1.** To bleed or treat with leeches. **2.** To treat medically; cure. [OE *læce,* orig., physician]

leech² (lēch) *n.* *Naut.* **1.** Either of the side edges of a square sail. For illustration see SAIL. **2.** The after edge of a fore-and-aft sail. [ME *leche.* Akin to Du. *lijk,* ON *lik* boltrope.]

Leeds (lēdz) A city and borough in West Yorkshire, England; pop. 748,300 (1976).

leek (lēk) *n.* **1.** A culinary herb (*Allium porrum*) of the lily family, closely allied to the onion but having a narrow bulb and broader, dark green leaves: the national emblem of Wales. **2.** Any of various related plants. [OE *lēac*]

leer¹ (lir) *n.* A sly look or sidewise glance expressing salacious desire, malicious intent, knowing complicity, etc. *— v.i.* To look with a leer. [OE *hlēor* cheek, face]

leer² (lir, lâr) See LEHR.

leer·ing (lir'ing) *adj.* Having or looking with a lecherous, malicious, or sly expression. **— leer'ing·ly** *adv.*

leer·y (lir'ē) *adj.* **leer·i·er, leer·i·est** *Informal* **1.** Suspicious; wary. **2.** Sly; knowing. Also spelled *leary.* [< LEER¹ + -Y]

lees (lēz) *n.pl.* Sediment, especially in wine or liquor; dregs. [Pl. of obs. *lee* < OF *lie* < Med.L *lia,* prob. < Celtic]

lee shore The shore on the lee side of a vessel, constituting a source of danger because the vessel is blown toward it.

leet (lēt) *n.* In England, a former court for petty offenses: also called *court-leet.* [< AF *lete;* ult. origin uncertain]

lee tide A tide running in the same direction as the wind.

Leeu·war·den (lā'vär·dən) The capital of Friesland Province, northern Netherlands; pop. 82,649 (1960).

Leeu·wen·hoek (lā'vən·hōōk), **Anton van,** 1632–1723, Dutch naturalist; pioneer in microscopy.

lee·ward (lē'wərd, *Naut.* lōō'ərd) *adj.* **1.** Of or pertaining to the direction toward which the wind is blowing. **2.** Being on or toward the side sheltered from the wind. *— n.* The side or direction toward which the wind is blowing. — *adv.* Toward the lee. Opposed to *windward.*

Leeward Islands (lē′wərd) **1.** A northern group of West Indian islands in the Lesser Antilles, extending SE from Puerto Rico to the Windward Islands. **2.** A former British colony in this group, consisting of Antigua, St. Christopher, Nevis and Anguilla, Montserrat, and the British Virgin Islands. **3.** See under SOCIETY ISLANDS.

lee·way (lē′wā′) *n.* **1.** Additional space, time, range, etc., providing greater freedom of motion or action; latitude. **2.** Deviation from a set course. **3.** *Naut.* The lateral drift to leeward of a vessel in motion.

left[1] (left) Past tense and past participle of LEAVE[1].

left[2] (left) *adj.* **1.** Pertaining to, designating, or being on the side of the body that is toward the north when one faces east, and usually having the weaker and less dominant hand, etc. **2.** Pertaining to, designating, or situated on the corresponding side of anything moving, facing, or capable of facing in a specified direction. **3.** Nearest to or tending in the direction of the left side. **4.** Worn on a left hand, foot, etc. **5.** *Sometimes cap.* Designating a person, party, faction, etc., having absolutely or relatively liberal, democratic, socialistic, or laborite views and policies. — *n.* **1.** Any part, area, etc., on or toward the left side. **2.** *Often cap.* A group, party, etc., whose views and policies are left (*adj.* def. 5); especially, in Europe, such parties whose members sit to the presiding officer's left in a deliberative assembly. **3.** In boxing: **a** A blow with the left hand. **b** The left hand. — *adv.* On, to, or toward the left. Abbr. *l., L.* [ME (Kentish) variant of presumed OE *lyft* weak, infirm]

Left Bank A district of Paris along the south bank of the Seine, traditionally frequented by artists, students, etc.

left face In military drill, a 90-degree pivot to the left, using the ball of the right foot and the heel of the left.

left-hand (left′hand′) *adj.* **1.** Of, for, pertaining to, or situated on the left side or the left hand. **2.** Turning, opening, or swinging to the left.

left-hand·ed (left′han′did) *adj.* **1.** Using the left hand habitually and more easily than the right. **2.** Done with the left hand. **3.** Adapted or intended for use by the left hand. **4.** Turning or moving from right to left, or counterclockwise. **5.** Ironical, insincere, or ambiguous in intent or effect: a *left-handed* compliment. **6.** Clumsy; awkward. **7.** Morganatic: from the bridegroom's giving his left hand rather than his right to the bride. — *adv.* With the left hand. — **left′-hand′ed·ly** *adv.* — **left′-hand′ed·ness** *n.*

left-hand·er (left′han′dər) *n.* **1.** One who is left-handed. **2.** A left-handed blow.

left·ist (lef′tist) *n.* One whose views and policies are left (*adj.* def. 5). — *adj.* Left (*adj.* def. 5). — **left′ism** *n.*

left·o·ver (left′ō′vər) *n. Usually pl.* An unused or unconsumed part or remnant, especially of cooked or prepared food. — *adj.* Left as a remnant.

left wing 1. *Sometimes cap.* A party, group, faction, etc., having leftist policies. **2.** The wing, part, etc., on the left side. — **left-wing** (left′wing′) *adj.* — **left′-wing′er** *n.*

left·y (lef′tē) *n. Slang* A left-handed or leftist person.

leg (leg) *n.* **1.** One of the limbs or appendages serving as a means of support and locomotion in animals and man. ◆ Collateral adjective: *crural.* **2.** *Anat.* **a** A lower limb of the human body, extending from the hip to the ankle. **b** The part of the lower limb between the knee and the ankle. **3.** A support resembling a leg in shape, position, or function. **4.** The portion of an article of clothing, as hose, trousers, etc., designed to cover a leg. **5.** A division or section of a course or journey. **6.** One of the divisions of an angled or forked object, as a pair of compasses. **7.** *Math.* Either of the sides of a triangle adjacent to the base or the hypotenuse. **8.** *Naut.* The distance traveled by a vessel in a single direction while tacking. **9.** In bridge, sports, etc., the first game of a rubber or series won by either side. **10.** In cricket, the sector of the field lying to the left of and behind a right-handed batsman. **11.** *Archaic* An obeisance; bow: used chiefly in the expression **to make a leg** — **on one's last legs** On the verge of collapse or death. — **to give (someone) a leg up** To assist by boosting or providing support. — **to have not a leg to stand on.** To have no sound or logical basis, as for argument, justification, etc. — **to pull one's leg** *Informal* To make fun of; tease; fool. — **to shake a leg** *Slang* **1.** To make haste; hurry. **2.** To dance. — *v.i.* **legged, leg·ging** *Informal* To walk or run: usually followed by *it.* [< ON *leggr*]

leg. 1. Legal. **2.** Legate. **3.** Legato. **4.** Legislation; legislature.

leg·a·cy (leg′ə·sē) *n. pl.* **·cies 1.** Personal property, money, etc., bequeathed by will; a bequest. **2.** Anything received

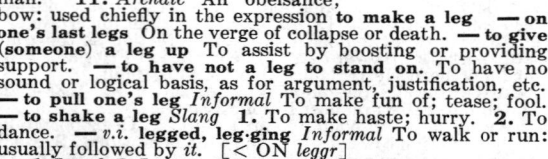

PERIOD STYLES IN
CHAIR LEGS
a Louis XIII. *b* Louis
XIV. *c* Louis XV.
d Louis XVI.

from or passed on by an ancestor, predecessor, or earlier era. [< OF *legacie,* orig. legateship < Med.L *legatia* the district of a legate. See LEGATE.]

le·gal (lē′gəl) *adj.* **1.** Of, pertaining to, or concerned with law; juristic: *legal* documents. **2.** Established or authorized by law; based upon law: *legal* power. **3.** Conforming with or permitted by law; lawful. **4.** According to, determined by, or coming under the jurisdiction of statute law, rather than equity. **5.** Characteristic of or appropriate to those who practice law. **6.** *Theol.* **a** Relating to or based on the Mosaic law. **b** Pertaining to the doctrine of salvation by works rather than grace. Abbr. *leg.* — **Syn.** See LAWFUL. — *n. Usually pl.* A bond issue, etc., legally approved for investment of funds by savings banks, trustees, etc. [< OF < L *legalis* < *lex, legis* law. Doublet of LOYAL.] — **le′gal·ly** *adv.*

legal age Age (*n.* def. 3).

legal cap A type of white writing paper generally used by lawyers, having a ruled margin and usually measuring about 8½ x 13 inches.

legal holiday *U.S.* A day, usually commemorative, on which banks are closed and official business is suspended or limited by law.

le·gal·ism (lē′gəl·iz′əm) *n.* **1.** Strict conformity to law; especially, the stressing of the letter and forms of the law rather than the spirit of justice. **2.** *Theol.* The doctrine of salvation by works or strict adherence to a religious code rather than by grace. — **le′gal·ist** *n.* — **le′gal·is′tic** *adj.*

le·gal·i·ty (li·gal′ə·tē) *n. pl.* **·ties 1.** The condition or quality of being legal; lawfulness. **2.** Adherence to law.

le·gal·ize (lē′gəl·īz) *v.t.* **·ized, ·iz·ing** To make legal. Also *Brit.* **le′gal·ise.** — **le′gal·i·za′tion** (-ə·zā′shən, -ī·zā-) *n.*

Le Gal·lienne (lə gal′yən, gal·yen′), **Eva,** born 1899, U.S. actress born in England. — **Richard,** 1866–1947, English journalist and author; father of the preceding.

legal medicine Medical jurisprudence (which see).

legal reserve The amount of money that a bank or insurance company is required by law to set aside as security.

legal separation A judicial separation (which see).

legal tender Coin or other money that may be legally offered in payment of a debt, and that a creditor must accept.

legal year A calendar year (which see).

leg·ate (leg′it) *n.* **1.** An ecclesiastic appointed as an official representative of the Pope. **2.** An official envoy, usually acting as a diplomatic representative of a government. **3.** In ancient Rome: **a** An adviser or deputy of a general or commander in chief. **b** Under the empire, a governor of a province. Abbr. *leg.* — **Syn.** See AMBASSADOR. [< OF *legat* < L *legatus,* pp. of *legare* to send as a deputy, bequeath] — **leg·a·tine** (leg′ə·tin, -tīn) *adj.* — **leg′ate·ship** *n.*

leg·a·tee (leg′ə·tē′) *n.* One to whom a legacy is bequeathed. [< L *legatus* (see LEGATE) + -EE]

le·ga·tion (li·gā′shən) *n.* **1.** The official residence or business premises of a diplomatic minister or envoy of lower rank than an ambassador. **2.** The official staff of a foreign envoy or diplomatic mission. **3.** The position or rank of a legate. **4.** The sending of an official representative or delegation; also, the mission of such a representative or delegation. Abbr. *leg.* [< F < L *legatio, -onis,* pp. of *legare* to send]

le·ga·to (li·gä′tō) *Music adj.* Smooth and flowing, with unbroken transition between successive notes. — *adv.* In a smooth, connected style or manner. — *n. pl.* **·tos** A smooth, connected style, performance, or passage. [< Ital., lit., bound, pp. of *legare* to bind < L *ligare*]

le·ga·tor (li·gā′tər, leg′ə·tôr′) *n.* One who makes a will; a testator. [< L < *legatus,* pp. of *legare* to bequeath]

leg bye In cricket, a run scored on a ball that glances off a part of the batsman's body other than his hand.

leg·end (lej′ənd) *n.* **1.** An unauthenticated story from earlier times, preserved by tradition and popularly thought to be historical. **2.** A body or accumulation of such stories, as those connected with a people or culture. **3.** A romanticized or popularized concept of a well-known person. **4.** An inscription or motto, as on a coin, monument, banner, etc. **5.** A caption or explanatory description accompanying an illustration, chart, map, etc. **6.** *Obs.* An account of the life of a saint; also, a collection of such accounts. — **Syn.** See FICTION. [< OF *legende* < Med.L *legenda* things read, neut. pl. of L *legendus* to be read, gerundive of *legere* to read]

Le·gen·da Au·re·a (li·jen′də ô′rē·ə) The Golden Legend.

leg·en·dar·y (lej′ən·der′ē) *adj.* **1.** Of, pertaining to, constituting, or of the nature of a legend. **2.** Famous in or as in legend or tradition; fabled.

Le·gen·dre (lə·zhän′dr′), **Adrien Marie,** 1752–1833, French mathematician.

leg·end·ry (lej′ən·drē) *n.* Legends collectively; legend.

leg·er (lej′ər) See LEDGER (*n.* def. 4 and *adj.*).

Lé·ger (lā·zhā′), **Fernand,** 1881–1955, French painter.

leger bait or **line** or **tackle** See LEDGER BAIT, etc.

leg·er·de·main (lej′ər·də·mān′) *n.* **1.** Sleight of hand. **2.** Any artful trickery or deception; hocus-pocus. [ME *ly-garde de mayne* < MF *léger de main,* lit., light of hand < *léger* light + *de* of + *main* hand] — **leg′er·de·main′ist** *n.*

le·ges (lē′jēz) Plural of LEX.

leg·ged (leg′id, legd) *adj.* Having or characterized by (a specified kind or number of) legs: used in combination: *bow-legged; two-legged.*

leg·ging (leg′ing) *n.* A gaiter or similar covering for the leg, usually extending from the knee to the instep.

leg·gy (leg′ē) *adj.* **·gi·er, ·gi·est 1.** Having disproportionately long legs. **2.** *Informal* Having or displaying attractive, shapely legs. **3.** Of plants, having long, often bare, stems or stalks; spindly. — **leg′gi·ness** *n.*

leg·horn (leg′hôrn, -ərn) *n.* **1.** Finely plaited straw made from a bleached and dried variety of wheat. **2.** A hat or bonnet made from this straw. **3.** *Usually cap.* One of a breed of small, hardy domestic fowl originally developed in Italy, and producing eggs prolifically. [after *Leghorn*]

Leg·horn (leg′hôrn) A port city in NW Italy, on the Ligurian Sea; pop. 159,973 (1961): Italian *Livorno.*

leg·i·ble (lej′ə-bəl) *adj.* **1.** Capable of being read or deciphered; easy to read. **2.** Readily perceived or discovered from apparent signs or evidence. [< LL *legibilis* < L *legere* to read] — **leg′i·bil′i·ty, leg′i·ble·ness** *n.* — **leg′i·bly** *adv.*

le·gion (lē′jən) *n.* **1.** In ancient Rome, a major military unit consisting primarily of infantry troops with an auxiliary force of cavalry, altogether comprising between 4,200 and 6,000 men. **2.** *Usually pl.* Any large military force; army. **3.** A great number; multitude. ◆ Sometimes used predicatively with the adjectival sense *innumerable,* as in Their members are *legion.* **4.** *Usually cap.* Any of various military or honorary organizations, usually national in character. See AMERICAN LEGION, FOREIGN LEGION, LEGION OF HONOR, LEGION OF MERIT. — **Syn.** See ARMY. [< OF *legium* < L *legio, -onis* < *legere* to choose, levy troops]

le·gion·ar·y (lē′jən·er′ē) *adj.* **1.** Of or pertaining to a legion. **2.** Constituting a legion or multitude. — *n. pl.* **·ar·ies** A soldier or member of a legion.

legionary ant A driver ant (which see).

le·gion·naire (lē′jən·âr′) *n. Often cap.* A member of a legion (def. 4). [< F *légionnaire*]

Legion of Honor A French order of merit instituted by Napoleon Bonaparte in 1802 for civil or military services.

Legion of Merit *U.S.* A military decoration awarded for exceptionally meritorious conduct in the performance of outstanding services. See DECORATION. Abbr. *LM*

legis. Legislation; legislature.

leg·is·late (lej′is·lāt) *v.* **·lat·ed, ·lat·ing** *v.i.* **1.** To make a law or laws. — *v.t.* **2.** To cause to be in a specified state by legislation: often with *into* or *out of:* to attempt to *legislate* crime out of existence. [Back formation < LEGISLATOR]

leg·is·la·tion (lej′is·lā′shən) *n.* **1.** The act or procedures of making and enacting laws. **2.** An officially enacted law or laws. Abbr. *leg., legis.* [< LL *legislatio, -onis* < *legis,* genitive of *lex* law + *latio, -onis* a bringing, proposing < *latus,* pp. of *ferre* to bring]

leg·is·la·tive (lej′is·lā′tiv) *adj.* **1.** Of, pertaining to, or involved in legislation: *legislative* functions. **2.** Having the power to legislate; making and enacting laws: the *legislative* branch of the government: distinguished from *executive, judicial.* **3.** Of or pertaining to a legislature. **4.** Enacted by or resulting from legislation. — *n.* The legislative branch of a government. — **leg′is·la′tive·ly** *adv.*

Legislative Assembly In Canada, the legislature of a Province.

Legislative Council In Quebec, the appointive upper chamber of the Legislative Assembly.

leg·is·la·tor (lej′is·lā′tər) *n.* **1.** One active in the formation and enactment of laws; a lawmaker. **2.** A member of a legislature. [< L, proposer of a law < *lex, legis* law + *lator* bearer, proposer < *latus,* pp. of *ferre* to bring] — **leg′is·la′tress** (-tris), **leg′is·la′trix** (-triks) *n.fem.*

leg·is·la·to·ri·al (lej′is·lə·tôr′ē·əl, -tō′rē-) *adj.* Of, pertaining to, or concerned with legislation or legislators.

leg·is·la·ture (lej′is·lā′chər) *n.* A body of persons officially constituted and empowered to make and enact the laws of a nation or state; especially, in the United States, the law-making body of a State, Territory, etc., as distinguished from Congress. Abbr. *leg., legis.*

le·gist (lē′jist) *n.* One learned or skilled in the law. [< OF *legiste* < Med.L *legista* < L *lex, legis* law]

le·git (lə·jit′) *Slang n.* Legitimate drama, theatrical productions, etc. — *adj.* Legitimate.

le·git·i·ma·cy (lə·jit′ə·mə·sē) *n.* The state or condition of being legitimate.

le·git·i·mate (*adj.* lə·jit′ə·mit; *v.* lə·jit′ə·māt) *adj.* **1.** In accordance with law; authorized or sanctioned by law; lawful. **2.** Conforming to established rules or standards; regular in form, style, etc. **3.** Based on or resulting from orderly, rational deduction or inference; logical; reasonable. **4.** Authentic; valid. **5.** Born in wedlock. **6.** According to or based on strict hereditary right: *legitimate* sovereignty. **7.** In the theater: **a** Denoting drama performed by living actors before an audience actually present, as distinguished from motion pictures, television, etc. **b** Of or pertaining to a theater, stage, etc., devoted to such performances. **c** Origi-

nally, denoting drama considered to have literary or artistic merit, as distinguished from burlesque, vaudeville, etc. — **Syn.** See LAWFUL. — *v.t.* **·mat·ed, ·mat·ing 1.** To make or establish as legitimate. **2.** To show reason or authorization for; justify. [< Med.L *legitimatus,* pp. of *legitimare* to declare to be lawful < L *legitimus* lawful < *lex, legis* law] — **le·git′i·mate·ly** *adv.* — **le·git′i·mate·ness** *n.* — **le·git′i·ma′tion** (-mā′shən) *n.*

le·git·i·mist (lə·jit′ə·mist) *n.* A supporter or advocate of rule or authority based on hereditary right; especially, in France, a supporter of the claims of the elder line of the Bourbon family. [< F *légitimiste*] — **le·git′i·mism** *n.* — **le·git′i·mis′tic** *adj.*

le·git·i·mize (lə·jit′ə·mīz) *v.t.* **·mized, ·miz·ing** To legitimate. Also **le·git′i·ma·tize** (-mə·tīz). — **le·git′i·mi·za′tion** *n.*

leg·less (leg′lis) *adj.* Having no legs.

leg·man (leg′man′, -mən) *n. pl.* **-men** (-men′, -mən) *U.S.* **1.** On a newspaper, a reporter who covers news events in person or visits news sources. **2.** One who runs errands or collects information, especially for an office.

Leg·ni·ca (leg·nē′tsä) A city in SW Poland; pop. 73,400 (1968): German *Liegnitz.*

leg-of-mut·ton (leg′ə·mut′n) *adj.* Having the characteristically triangular or tapering shape of a haunch of mutton: **leg-of-mutton** sleeve.

Le·gree (lə·grē′), **Simon** See SIMON LEGREE.

leg·ume (leg′yōōm, lə·gyōōm′) *n.* **1.** The fruit or seed of any leguminous plant, especially when used as food or fodder. **2.** Any leguminous plant. **3.** *Bot.* The characteristic, sutured seed vessel of such a plant; a pod. For illustration see FRUIT. [< F *légume* < L *legumen,* lit., something gathered < *legere* to gather]

leg·u·min (lə·gyōō′min) *n. Biochem.* A protein present in the seeds of leguminous plants. [< LEGUM(E) + -IN]

le·gu·mi·nous (lə·gyōō′mə·nəs) *adj.* **1.** Of or belonging to a large, widely distributed family (*Leguminosae*) of plants, of which peas, beans, etc., are typical members. **2.** Pertaining to, characteristic of, or consisting of legumes. [< L *legumen, -inis* legume + -OUS]

leg·work (leg′wûrk′) *n. Informal* Chores, errands, etc., accomplished by or as by going about on foot.

Le·hár (lā′här), **Franz,** 1870–1948, Hungarian composer.

Le Ha·vre (lə hä′vər, -vrə; *Fr.* lə à′vr′) A port city in northern France, at the mouth of the Seine; pop. 199,509 (1968): formerly *Havre-de-Grâce.*

Le·high River (lē′hī) A river in eastern Pennsylvania, flowing about 100 miles south and east to the Delaware River.

Leh·man (lē′mən, lā′-), **Herbert H(enry),** 1878–1963, U.S. banker and statesman.

Leh·mann (lā′mən, *Ger.* lā′män), **Lotte,** 1888–1976, German soprano.

lehr (lir, lâr) A long oven in which glass is annealed: also spelled *lear, leer.* [? < G *lehr* model, pattern]

le·hu·a (lā·hōō′ä) *n.* **1.** A tree (*Metrosideros tremuloides*) of the myrtle family, native in the islands of the Pacific, and having vivid red flowers and hard wood. **2.** The blossom of this tree. [< Hawaiian]

lei[1] (lā, lā′ē) *n. pl.* **leis** A festival garland of blossoms, feathers, etc., as worn in Hawaii. [< Hawaiian]

lei[2] (lā) Plural of LEU.

Leib·nitz (līb′nits, *Ger.* līp′nits), **Baron Gottfried Wilhelm von,** 1646–1716, German philosopher and mathematician. Also **Leib′niz.** — **Leib·nitz′i·an** *adj. & n.*

Leices·ter (les′tər) *n.* One of a breed of sheep having long wool, originally developed in Leicestershire.

Leices·ter (les′tər), **Earl of,** 1532?–88, Robert Dudley, English courtier, favorite of Elizabeth I.

Leices·ter·shire (les′tər·shir) A county in central England; 832 sq. mi.; pop. 829,800 (1976); county seat, **Leices′ter,** pop. 287,300 (1976). Also **Leices′ter.**

Leics. Leicestershire.

Lei·den (līd′n) A city in the western Netherlands; pop. 96,440 (1960): also *Leyden.*

Leif Er·ic·son (lēf er′ik·sən) See ERICSON.

Leigh·ton (lā′tən), **Frederick,** 1830–96, Baron Leighton of Stretton, English painter.

Lein·ster (len′stər) A Province in SE Ireland, on the Irish Sea; 7,580 sq. mi.; pop. 1,332,149 (est. 1969).

Leip·zig (līp′sik, -sig; *Ger.* līp′tsikh) A city in south central East Germany; pop. 591,500 (est. 1967).

leish·man·i·a (lēsh·man′ē·ə) *n.* Any of a genus (*Leishmania*) of protozoans parasitic in the cells of various organs, and transmitted chiefly by various insects. [after Sir William *Leishman,* 1865–1926, English army surgeon]

leish·man·i·a·sis (lēsh′mən·ī′ə·sis) *n. Pathol.* A disease caused by leishmania, as kala-azar. Also **leish′man·i′o·sis.**

leis·ter (lēs′tər) *n.* A fishing spear having three or more prongs. — *v.t.* To spear with a leister. [< ON *liōstr* < *liōsta* to strike]

lei·sure (lē′zhər, lezh′ər) *n.* **1.** Freedom from the demands of work or duty. **2.** Time available for recreation or relaxation; spare time. **— at leisure 1.** Free from pressing necessity or obligation; having time to spare. **2.** Unoccupied; not employed. **3.** When one has time or opportunity; at one's convenience: also at **one's leisure.** *— adj.* **1.** Not spent in work or necessary activity; free: *leisure* time. **2.** Having considerable leisure: the *leisure* classes. [< OF *leisir* to be permitted < L *licere*]

lei·sure·ly (lē′zhər-lē, lezh′ər-) *adj.* Free from exertion or pressure; relaxed and unhurried. Also **lei′sured** (-zhərd). *— adv.* In a leisurely manner. **— lei′sure·li·ness** *n.*

Leith (lēth) A former port city on the Firth of Forth in SE Scotland, now part of Edinburgh.

leit·mo·tif (līt′mō·tēf′) *n. Music* A theme used to indicate a certain person, event, attribute, or idea throughout an opera, etc. Also **leit′mo·tiv′** (-tēf′). [< G *leitmotiv* < *leiten* to lead + *motiv* motive < Med.L *motivus.* See MOTIVE.]

Leix (lāks) See LAOIGHIS.

lek (lek) *n.* The standard monetary unit of Albania, equivalent to 100 qindarka. [< Albanian]

Lek (lek) The northern branch of the Rhine delta in the central Netherlands.

Le·ly (lē′lē), **Sir Peter,** 1618–80, Dutch painter active in England: original name **Pieter Van der Faes** (vän dər fäs′).

LEM (lem) Lunar excursion module (which see). Also **L.E.M., LM, L.M.**

Le·maî·tre (lə·me′tr′), **François Élie Jules,** 1853–1914, French poet and critic. **— Abbé Georges Édouard,** 1894–1966, Belgian physicist and astronomer.

lem·an (lem′ən, lē′mən) *n. Archaic* **1.** A sweetheart or lover of either sex. **2.** A mistress; paramour. [ME *lemman,* *leofmon* < OE *lēof* beloved + *mann* man]

Le·man (lē′mən), **Lake** See (Lake of) GENEVA.

Le Mans (lə män′) A city in NW France; pop. 140,520 (1968).

Lem·berg (lem′berkh) The German name for Lvov.

lem·ma[1] (lem′ə) *n. pl.* **lem·mas** or **lem·ma·ta** (lem′ə·tə) **1.** *Logic* **a** A subsidiary proposition employed as auxiliary in demonstrating another one. **b** A proposition assumed to be true. **2.** A theme or title. [< L < Gk. *lēmma* something taken, a premise < *lēmm-,* stem of *lambanein* to take]

lem·ma[2] (lem′ə) *n. Bot.* A small, chaffy bract enclosing the palea and flower in a spikelet of grass. [< Gk. *lemma* husk < *lepein* to peel]

lem·ming (lem′ing) *n.* Any of several small arctic rodents (genera *Lemmus, Dicrostonyx,* and *Myopus*), having a short tail and furry feet; especially, a European species (*Lemmus lemmus*), noted for recurrent mass migrations often terminated by drowning in the ocean. [< Norw.]

LEMMING
(To 6 inches
long)

lem·nis·cus (lem·nis′kəs) *n. pl.* **·nis·ci** (-nis′ī) *Anat.* A band or fillet of nerve fibers in the medulla or the pons. [< NL < L, ribbon < Gk. *lēmniskos*]

Lem·nos (lem′nəs) An island of Greece in the Aegean Sea; 186 sq. mi. **— Lem·ni·an** (lem′nē·ən) *adj. & n.*

lem·on (lem′ən) *n.* **1.** The oval, citrus fruit of an evergreen tree (*Citrus limon*), having juicy, acid pulp and a yellow rind yielding an essential oil (**lemon oil**) used as a flavoring and perfuming agent. **2.** The tree bearing this fruit. **3.** The bright, clear yellow of the rind of a lemon. **4.** *Slang* Something or someone disappointing, unsatisfactory, or unattractive. *— adj.* Bright, clear yellow. [< OF *limon* < Sp. *limón* < Arabic *laimūn* < Persian *limūn.* Akin to LIME[2].]

lem·on·ade (lem′ən·ād′) *n.* A drink made of lemon juice, water, and sugar. [< F *limonade* < *limon* lemon]

lemon geranium A cultivated plant (*Pelargonium limoneum*) with foliage having the odor of lemons.

lem·on·grass (lem′ən·gras′) *n.* Any of various tropical grasses (genus *Cymbopogon*) yielding an oil (**lemongrass oil**) having the odor of lemons, used as a flavor, in perfume, etc.

lemon squash *Brit.* Lemonade.

lemon verbena A tropical American shrub (*Lippia citriodora*) with flowers and leaves having an odor of lemon.

lem·on·wood (lem′ən·wŏŏd′) *n.* **1.** A tree (*Calycophyllum candidissimum*) of Central America, having tough, flexible wood. **2.** The wood of this tree. Also called *degame.*

lem·on·y (lem′ə·nē) *adj.* Suggestive of lemon.

lem·pi·ra (lem·pē′rä) *n.* The standard monetary unit of Honduras, equivalent to 100 centavos. [< Am. Sp., after *Lempira,* an Indian chief who fought the Spanish]

le·mur (lē′mər) *n.* Any of various small, arboreal, mostly nocturnal mammals (class or suborder *Lemuroidea*) related to the monkeys, as the loris, potto, etc.; especially, any of a genus (*Lemur*) having a foxlike face and soft fur, found chiefly in Madagascar. [< NL < L *lemures* ghosts; with ref. to their nocturnal habits]

lem·u·res (lem′yŏŏ·rēz) *n.pl.* In ancient Roman religion, the shades or spirits of the dead; ghosts; specters. [< L]

Le·na (lē′nə, *Russ.* lyen′ə) A river in the eastern R.S.F.S.R., flowing 2,648 miles, generally north, to the Laptev Sea.

Len·a·pe (len′ə·pē) *n.* The generic name of the Delawares, an Algonquian people; also, their language: also called *Leni-Lenape, Lenni-Lenape.* [Short for Algonquian (Lenape) *Leni-lenape,* lit., real man < *leni* real + *lenape* man]

Le·nard rays (lā′närt) *Physics* Cathode rays from a type of vacuum tube known as a **Lenard tube.** [after Philipp Eduard Anton **Lenard,** 1862–1947, German physicist]

Len·clos (län·klō′), **Ninon de,** 1620–1705, French courtesan and wit: original name **Anne Lenclos** or **L'En·clos′.**

lend (lend) *v.* **lent, lend·ing** *v.t.* **1.** To grant the use or possession of with the understanding that the thing or its equivalent will be returned. **2.** To grant the use of (money) at a stipulated rate of interest. **3.** To impart, as an abstract quality. **4.** To make available, as for aid or support; give. **5.** To adapt or suit (itself or oneself) to a specific use or purpose. *— v.i.* **6.** To make a loan or loans. [OE *lǣnan* < *lǣn* a loan. Akin to LOAN[1].] **— lend′er** *n.*

lending library A circulating library (which see).

lend-lease (lend′lēs′) *n.* In World War II, the furnishing of goods and services to any country whose defense was deemed vital to the defense of the United States, under the terms of the **Lend-Lease Act** passed by Congress March 11, 1941. *— v.t.* **-leased, -leas·ing** To supply by lend-lease.

le·nes (lē′nēz) Plural of LENIS.

L'En·fant (län·fän′), **Pierre Charles,** 1754–1825, French engineer and architect; planned the city of Washington, D.C.

length (lengkth, length) *n.* **1.** Linear extent from end to end; usually, the longest dimension of a thing, as distinguished from its width and thickness. Abbr. *L, l., L.* **2.** Extent from beginning to end, as of a period of time, series, book, word, etc. **3.** The state or quality of being long or prolonged, either in time or space. **4.** Duration or continuance, especially in respect to time. **5.** The measurement along, extent of, or distance equivalent to something specified: arm's *length.* **6.** A piece or standard unit of something, measured longitudinally: a *length* of pipe. **7.** *Often pl.* The limit of one's efforts, ability, etc.: to go to great *lengths.* **8.** In racing, the extent from front to back of a competing horse, boat, etc., used as a unit of estimating position. **9.** *Phonet.* **a** The duration of a sound; quantity of a vowel. **b** Loosely, the quality of a vowel. **10.** In prosody, quantity. **— at length 1.** After a while; finally. **2.** Without omission or abridgment; fully. [OE *lengthu < lang* long]

length·en (lengk′thən, leng′-) *v.t. & v.i.* To make or become longer.

length·wise (lengkth′wīz′, length′-) *adv.* In the direction or dimension of length; longitudinally. Also **length′ways′** (-wāz′). *— adj.* According to length; longitudinal.

length·y (lengk′thē, leng′-) *adj.* **length·i·er, length·i·est** Unusually or unduly long. **— length′i·ly** *adv.* **— length′i·ness** *n.*

le·ni·en·cy (lē′nē·ən·sē, lēn′yən·sē) *n.* The state or quality of being lenient. Also **le′ni·ence.** **— Syn.** See MERCY.

le·ni·ent (lē′nē·ənt, lēn′yənt) *adj.* **1.** Gentle or merciful in disposition, effect, etc.; not stern or severe; mild. **2.** *Archaic* Soothing; emollient. [< L *leniens, -entis,* ppr. of *lenire* to soothe < *lenis* soft, mild] **— le′ni·ent·ly** *adv.*

Len·i-Len·a·pe (len′ē·len′ə·pē) *n.* Lenape (which see). Also **Len′ni·Len·a·pe.**

Le·nin (len′in, *Russ.* lyi′nyin), **Vladimir Ilyich,** 1870–1924, Russian revolutionist and statesman; chief leader and theorist of the Bolshevik Revolution; head of the U.S.S.R. 1917–1924: original name **Vladimir Ilyich Ul·ya·nof** (ŏŏl′ya′nəf). Also, erroneously, **Nikolai Lenin.**

Le·ni·na·kan (le′ni·nä·kän′, *Russ.* lyi·nyi·nä·kän′) A city in the NW Armenian S.S.R.; pop. 164,000 (est. 1970).

Le·nin·grad (len′in·grad, *Russ.* lyi·nyin·grät′) A city in the NW R.S.F.S.R., on the Neva; capital of the Russian Empire 1712–1917; pop. 3,950,000 (1970, including suburbs): formerly *St. Petersburg.* From 1914–24 *Petrograd.*

Len·in·ism (len′in·iz′əm) A modification of Marxism constituting the doctrine and practice of the Bolsheviks and the Communist Party in the Soviet Union under Lenin. **— Len′in·ist, Len′in·ite** *n. & adj.*

Lenin Peak A mountain on the Kirghiz-Tadzhik S.S.R. border, the second highest in the Soviet Union; 23,382 ft.

le·nis (lē′nis) *adj. Phonet.* Weakly articulated, with little or no aspiration: opposed to *fortis.* *— n. pl.* **le·nes** (lē′nēz) **1.** A lenis consonant. **2.** Smooth breathing (which see). [< L, smooth, soft]

len·i·tive (len′ə·tiv) *adj.* Having the power or tendency to allay pain or distress; soothing. *— n.* That which soothes or mitigates; a palliative. [< Med.L *lenitivus < L lenitus,* pp. of *lenire* to soothe]

len·i·ty (len′ə·tē) *n.* The state or quality of being lenient. **— Syn.** See MERCY. [< OF *lenité < L lenitas, -tatis* softness < *lenis* soft]

Len·nox (len′əks) An unincorporated place in SW California, near Los Angeles; pop. 16,121.

le·no (lē′nō) *n.* **1.** A weave having paired and twisted warp yarns. For illustration see WEAVE. **2.** A loose, open fabric of such a weave. [< F *linon < lin* flax < L *linum*]

lens (lenz) *n.* **1.** *Optics* A piece of glass or other transparent substance, bounded by two curved surfaces or by one curved and one plane surface, by which rays of light are made to converge or diverge. Compare illustration for FOCUS. **2.** Two or more such pieces in combination. **3.** Any device that concentrates or disperses radiation, etc., other than light by action similar to that of an optical lens. **4.** *Anat.* A transparent, biconvex body situated behind the iris of the eye and serving to focus an image on the retina: also called *crystalline lens*. For illustration see EYE. [< L *lens, lentis* lentil; so called from the similarity in form]

a Biconvex. b Plano-convex. c Convexo-concave. d Biconcave. e Plano-concave. f Concavo-convex.

LENSES

lent (lent) Past tense and past participle of LEND.

Lent (lent) *n.* **1.** *Eccl.* The period of forty days, excluding Sundays, from Ash Wednesday to Easter, observed annually as a season of fasting, penitence, and self-denial. **2.** *Obs.* Any period of fasting. [Short for *Lenten* < OE *lencten, lengten* the spring]

len·ta·men·te (len′tä·men′tä) *adv. Music* Slowly. [< Ital. < *lento* slow. See LENTO.]

lent·en (len′tən) *adj.* **1.** Plain; meager; spare. **2.** Somber; dismal. [OE *lencten* spring, Lent]

Lent·en (len′tən) *adj.* Of, pertaining to, suitable for, or characteristic of Lent. [< LENT]

len·ti·cel (len′tə·sel) *n. Bot.* A loose, lenticular mass of cells in a plant stem, constituting an opening that permits an interchange of gases between the plant and the air. [< NL *lenticella*, dim. of L *lens, lentis* lentil]

len·tic·u·lar (len·tik′yə·lər) *adj.* **1.** Having the characteristic form of a biconvex lens; lentil-shaped. Also **len·ti·form** (len′tə·fôrm). **2.** Of or pertaining to a lens. [< LL *lenticularis* < *lenticula*, dim. of L *lens, lentis* lentil]

len·ti·go (len·tī′gō) *n. pl.* **·tig·i·nes** (-tij′ə·nēz) *Med.* **a** A freckle. **b** Freckles, or a similar pigmented condition of the skin. [< L < *lens, lentis* lentil] — **len·tig·i·nous** (len·tij′ə·nəs), **len·tig′i·nose** (-nōs) *adj.*

len·til (len′təl) *n.* **1.** A leguminous plant (*Lens culinaris*) native to the Old World, having broad pods containing flattish, edible seeds. **2.** The seed of this plant. [< F *lentille* < L *lenticula*, dim. of *lens, lentis* lentil]

len·tis·si·mo (len·tis′i·mō) *Music adj.* Very slow. — *adv.* Very slowly. [< Ital., superl. of *lento* slow. See LENTO.]

len·to (len′tō) *Music adj.* Slow. — *adv.* Slowly: a direction to the performer. — *n. pl.* **·tos** A slow movement or passage. [< Ital. < L *lentus*]

len·toid (len′toid) *adj.* Lens shaped; lenticular.

l'en·voi (len′voi, *Fr.* län·vwä′) See ENVOY². Also **l'en′voy.**

Le·o (lē′ō) *n.* A constellation, the Lion, containing the bright star Regulus; also, the fifth sign of the zodiac. See CONSTELLATION, ZODIAC. [< NL < L]

Le·o I (lē′ō), Saint, died 461, pope 440–461: called **the Great.**

Leo III, 680?–741, Byzantine emperor 717–741: called **the Isaurian.**

Leo III, Saint, died 816, pope 795–816.

Leo X, 1475–1521, pope 1513–21: original name *Giovanni de' Medici.*

Leo XIII, 1810–1903, pope 1878–1903.

Le·o Mi·nor (lē′ō mī′nər) A constellation, the Lesser Lion. See CONSTELLATION. [< L]

Le·om·in·ster (lem′in·stər) A city in north central Massachusetts; pop. 32,939.

Le·ón (lā·ôn′) **1.** A region and former kingdom in NW Spain; 20,504 sq. mi. **2.** A Province in NW Spain; 5,432 sq. mi.; pop. 600,935 (1965); capital, León; pop. 95,000. **3.** A city in central Mexico; pop. 453,976 (1970).

Le·o·nar·do da Vin·ci (lē′ə·när′dō də vin′chē, *Ital.* lā′ō·när′dō dä vēn′chē) See DA VINCI.

Le·on·ca·val·lo (lā·ôn′kä·väl′lō), Ruggiero, 1858–1919, Italian operatic composer.

le·o·ne (lē·ōn′) *n.* The monetary unit of Sierra Leone, equivalent to 100 cents.

Le·o·nid (lē′ə·nid) *n. pl.* **Le·o·nids** or **Le·o·ni·des** (lē·on′ə·dēz) *Astron.* One of the meteors of a meteor shower having its radiant point in the constellation Leo, and appearing annually about November 14. [< F < NL *Leo, Leonis* the constellation Leo + -ID¹]

Le·on·i·das (lē·on′ə·dəs), died 480 B.C., king of Sparta; killed in defense of Thermopylae.

le·o·nine (lē′ə·nīn, -nin) *adj.* Pertaining to, resembling, or characteristic of a lion. [< L *leoninus* < *leo, leonis* lion]

Le·o·nine (lē′ə·nīn, -nin) *adj.* Of or pertaining to any of the thirteen popes named Leo. [< L *leoninus*]

le·on·ti·a·sis (lē′on·tī′ə·sis) *n. Pathol.* A thickening of the facial bones or tissue, resulting in a leonine appearance, and characteristic of certain forms of leprosy. [< NL < Gk. < *leōn, leontos* lion + -IASIS]

leop·ard (lep′ərd) *n.* **1.** A ferocious, carnivorous mammal (*Panthera pardus*) of the cat family, native to Asia and Africa, and having a tawny coat with dark brown or black spots grouped in rounded clusters. A black variety having faintly discernible spots also occurs: also called *panther.* **2.** Any of various similar felines, as the cheetah, jaguar, or snow leopard (which see).

LEOPARD
(About 2½ feet high at shoulder)

3. The fur of a leopard. **4.** *Heraldry* A lion shown in side view, with the right front paw raised, and the head facing the observer. [< OF < LL *leopardus* < Gk. *leopardos* < *leōn* lion + *pardos* panther] — **leop′ard·ess** *n.fem.*

Le·o·par·di (lā′ō·pär′dē), Count Giacomo, 1798–1837, Italian poet and philologist.

leopard lily Any of various lilies having spotted flowers; especially, *Lilium pardalinum* of the western United States.

leopard moth A European moth (*Zeuzera pyrina*) introduced into the United States, and having larvae destructive to trees and shrubs.

leop·ard's-bane (lep′ərdz·bān′) *n.* A plant (*Arnica acaulis*) of the composite family, having yellow flowers.

Le·o·pold I (lē′ə·pōld), 1640–1705, Holy Roman Emperor 1658–1705.

Leopold I, 1790–1865, king of Belgium 1831–65.

Leopold II, 1747–92, Holy Roman Emperor 1790–92.

Leopold II, 1835–1909, king of Belgium 1865–1909.

Leopold III, born 1901, king of Belgium 1934–51; abdicated.

Le·o·pold·ville (lē′ə·pōld·vil′) A former name for KINSHASA.

le·o·tard (lē′ə·tärd) *n. Often pl.* A close-fitting, stretchable garment worn by dancers, acrobats, etc. [after Jules *Léotard,* 19th c. French aerialist]

Le·pan·to (le·pän′tō) The Italian name for NAUPAKTOS; scene of a European naval victory over the Turks, 1571.

Le·panto, Gulf of See Gulf of) CORINTH.

Le·pa·ya (lye′pə·yə) See LIEPAJA.

lep·er (lep′ər) *n.* One afflicted with leprosy. [< obs. *leper* leprosy < OF *lepre, liepre* < L *lepra* < Gk., orig. fem. of *lepros* scaly < *lepos* scale < *lepein* to peel]

lepido- *combining form* Scale (as of fish): *lepidolite.* Also, before vowels, **lepid-.** [< Gk. *lepis, -idos* scale]

le·pid·o·lite (li·pid′ə·līt, lep′ə·də·līt′) *n.* A variety of mica containing lithium. [< Gk. *lepis, -idos* scale + -LITE]

lep·i·dop·ter·an (lep′ə·dop′tər·ən) *n.* A lepidopteron. — *adj.* Lepidopterous.

lep·i·dop·ter·on (lep′ə·dop′tər·on) *n. pl.* **·ter·a** (-tər·ə) Any lepidopterous insect; a moth or butterfly. [< NL < Gk. *lepis, -idos* scale + *pteron* wing]

lep·i·dop·ter·ous (lep′ə·dop′tər·əs) *adj.* Belonging or pertaining to an order (*Lepidoptera*) of insects comprising the butterflies and moths, characterized by four wings covered with minute scales, and undergoing complete metamorphosis. Also **lep′i·dop′ter·al.**

lep·i·do·si·ren (lep′ə·dō·sī′rən) *n.* One of a genus (*Lepidosiren*) of primitive, eellike lungfishes, as *L. paradoxa* of South America. [< LEPIDO- + SIREN (def. 4)]

lep·i·dote (lep′ə·dōt) *adj. Bot.* Covered with tiny scales; scurfy. [< NL *lepidotus* < Gk. *lepidōtos* < *lepis, -idos* scale]

Lep·i·dus (lep′ə·dəs), Marcus Aemilius, died 13 B.C., Roman politician; triumvir with Antony and Octavian.

Le·pon·tine Alps (li·pon′tin) The central part of the Alps, in southern Switzerland and northern Italy.

lep·o·rid (lep′ə·rid) *n.* One of a family (*Leporidae*) of gnawing mammals comprising the rabbits and hares. — *adj.* Of or pertaining to this family. [< NL *Leporidae*, family name < L *lepus, leporis* hare]

lep·o·rine (lep′ə·rīn, -rin) *adj.* Pertaining to or characteristic of hares. [< L *leporinus* < *lepus, leporis* hare]

lep·re·chaun (lep′rə·kôn) *n.* In Irish folklore, a tiny elfin cobbler supposed to own hidden treasure. [< Irish *lupracán* < OIrish *luchorpan* < *lu* little + *corpán,* dim. of *corp* body < L *corpus, -oris*]

lep·ro·sar·i·um (lep′rə·sâr′ē·əm) *n. pl.* **·i·ums** or **·i·a** (-ē·ə) A hospital or similar institution for the treatment of leprosy. [< NL < LEPROS(Y) + (SANIT)ARIUM]

lep·rose (lep′rōs) *adj. Bot.* Scurfy or scalelike, as certain lichens. [< L *leprosus* < *lepra.* See LEPER.]

lep·ro·sy (lep′rə·sē) *n. Pathol.* A chronic, communicable disease caused by a microorganism (*Mycobacterium leprae*) and characterized by nodular skin lesions, nerve paralysis, and physical mutilation: also called *Hansen's disease.* [< OF *leprosie,* prob. < LL *leprosus* < L *lepra.* See LEPER.]

lep·rous (lep′rəs) *adj.* **1.** Affected with leprosy. **2.** Of or resembling leprosy. **3.** Leprose. [< OF *lepros, leprous* < LL *leprosus* < L *lepra.* See LEPER.] — **lep′rous·ly** *adv.*

-lepsy *combining form* Seizure; attack: *epilepsy, catalepsy.* Also **-lepsia.** [< Gk. *lepsis* seizure < *lambanein* to seize]

lepto- *combining form* Fine; slender; small: *leptophyllous.* Also, before vowels, **lept-.** [< Gk. *leptos* slender]

lep·ton¹ (lep′ton) *n. pl.* **·ta** (-tə) A monetary denomination of modern Greece, one hundredth of a drachma. [< Gk. *lepton (nomisma),* lit., small coin, neut. of *leptos* small, fine]

lep·ton² (lep′ton) *n. pl.* **·tons** *Physics* Any of a class of atomic particles comprising the electron, the muon, and the neutrino. [< Gk., neut. of *leptos* fine]

lep·to·phyl·lous (lep′tō·fil′əs) *adj. Bot.* Having slender, elongated leaves.

lep·tor·rhine (lep′tə·rīn, -rin) *adj.* Catarrhine (def. 1).

PRONUNCIATION KEY: add, āce, câre, pälm; end, ēven; it, īce; odd, ōpen, ôrder; tŏŏk, pōōl; up, bûrn; ə = a in *above,* e in *sicken,* i in *flexible,* o in *melon,* u in *focus;* yōō = u in *fuse;* oil; pout; check; go; ring; thin; this; zh, vision. For à, œ, ü, kh, ń, see inside front cover.

Le·pus (lē′pəs) n. A constellation, the Hare. See CONSTEL-
LATION. [< L]
Lé·ri·da (lā′rē·thä) A city in NE Spain; pop. 63,850 (1960):
ancient *Ilerda.*
Ler·mon·tov (lyer′mən·tôf), **Mikhail Yurevich,** 1814–41,
Russian poet and novelist.
Le·sage (lə·sàzh′), **Alain René,** 1668–1747, French novelist
and dramatist.
les·bi·an (lez′bē·ən) *Sometimes cap. n.* A homosexual woman. — *adj.* Pertaining to or characteristic of homosexual
women. [< LESBIAN]
Les·bi·an (lez′bē·ən) n. **1.** A native or inhabitant of Lesbos. **2.** Sappho or one of her followers, alleged to have been
homosexuals. — *adj.* **1.** Of or pertaining to Lesbos or its
inhabitants. **2.** Of, pertaining to, or characteristic of
Sappho or her poetry. **3.** *Rare* Erotic. [< L *Lesbius* < Gk.
Lesbios < *Lesbos* Lesbos, the home of Sappho]
les·bi·an·ism (lez′bē·ən·iz′əm) n. *Sometimes cap.* Homosexuality among women.
Lesbian Ode Horatian ode (which see).
Les·bos (lez′bəs, -bos) An island of Greece off NW Turkey;
623 sq. mi.: also *Mytilene.*
Les Cayes (lā kā′) A port city in SW Haiti; pop. 95,446
(est. 1969, with suburbs): also *Aux Cayes, Cayes.*
lese maj·es·ty (lēz′ maj′is·tē) An offense against sovereign
authority or a sovereign; treason. Also *Fr.* **lèse-ma·jes·té**
(lez′mà·zhes·tā′). [< F < L *laesa majestas* < *laesa,* fem. of
laesus, pp. of *laedere* to injure + *majestas* majesty]
le·sion (lē′zhən) n. **1.** *Pathol.* Any abnormal or harmful
change in the structure of an organ or tissue. **2.** An injury;
damage. [< F *lésion* < L *laesio, -onis* < *laesus,* pp. of *laedere* to injure]
Le·so·tho (le·sōō′tōō, -sō′thō) A constitutional monarchy
consisting of an enclave in the eastern part of South Africa;
11,716 sq. mi.; pop. 930,000 (est. 1969); capital, Maseru:
formerly *Basutoland.* See map of (Republic of) SOUTH
AFRICA. Officially **Kingdom of Lesotho.**
less (les) Alternative comparative of LITTLE. — *adj.* **1.**
Not as great in quantity or degree; not as much. ◆ Although *less* is widely used in place of *fewer,* especially in
speech and in informal writing, the distinction between
them remains a useful one. *Less* denotes things or amounts
that are not counted or measured in separate units; *fewer*
denotes things or units that can be counted or enumerated.
Thus, we speak of *less* coffee but *fewer* cups of coffee, *less*
time but *fewer* hours. **2.** Inferior in degree; smaller; lower:
with *than.* — *adv.* To a smaller degree or extent; not as:
followed by an adjective or adverb. — *n.* A smaller amount
or part. — *prep* With the subtraction of; minus. [OE *lǣs*]
-less *suffix of adjectives* **1.** Devoid of; without: *blameless,
harmless.* **2.** Deprived of; lacking: *motherless, stemless.* **3.**
Not able to (do something): *restless;* not susceptible of (some
action): *countless.* [OE *-leas* < *leas* free from]
L. ès S. Licentiate in Sciences (F *licencié ès sciences*).
les·see (les·ē′) n. One to whom a lease is granted; a tenant
holding property by lease. [< AF *lessee,* OF *lesse,* pp. of *lesser, laissier.* See LEASE²]
less·en¹ (les′ən) *v.t.* **1.** To make less; decrease. **2.** To make
little of; disparage. — *v.i.* **3.** To become less. — **Syn.** See
DECREASE.
less·en² (les′ən) *conj. U.S. Dial.* Unless. Also **less′n.**
Les·seps (les′əps, *Fr.* le·seps′), **Vicomte Ferdinand Marie
de,** 1805–94, French engineer and diplomat; supervised
building of the Suez Canal.
less·er (les′ər) *adj.* Not as large or important; minor.
Lesser Antilles See under ANTILLES.
Lesser Bear The constellation Ursa Minor.
Lesser Dog The constellation Canis Minor.
lesser doxology The Gloria Patri.
Lesser Lion The constellation Leo Minor.
lesser panda The panda (def. 1).
Lesser Slave Lake A lake in Alberta, Canada; 461 sq. mi.
Lesser Sunda Islands The former name for NUSA TENG-
GARA.
Les·sing (les′ing), **Gotthold Ephraim,** 1729–81, German
dramatist and critic.
les·son (les′ən) n. **1.** An instance or experience from which
useful knowledge may be gained; instructive or corrective
example. **2.** A division or portion of a course of study; period of instruction. **3.** An assignment to be studied or
learned, as by a student. **4.** A reprimand; reproof. **5.** A
portion of the Bible read or designated to be read at a religious service. — *v.t. Rare* **1.** To give a lesson or lessons
to; instruct. **2.** To admonish; rebuke. [< OF *lecon* < L
lectio, -ionis a reading. Doublet of LECTION.]
les·sor (les′ôr, les·ôr′) n. One who grants a lease; a landlord letting property under a lease. [< AF < *lesser, laissier.*
See LESSEE.]
lest (lest) *conj.* **1.** In order to prevent the chance that
(something might happen); for fear that: We hid it *lest* he
should see it. **2.** That: after expressions denoting anxiety:
We worried *lest* the money should not last. [OE (*thȳ) lǣs the*
(by the) less that]
let¹ (let) *v.* **let, let·ting** *v.t.* **1.** To allow; permit: to *let* her do

it. **2.** To permit to pass, come, go, etc.: followed by a preposition: *Let* him by. **3.** To cause; make: with *know* or *hear:
Let* me know when you arrive. **4.** To grant or assign, as a
contract for work to be performed. **5.** An auxiliary verb,
usually in the imperative, signifying: **a** An exhortation or
command: *Let's* go! **b** Willingness; acquiescence; inability to
prevent the inevitable: *Let* it rain. **c** An assumption or suggestion: *Let* x equal the sum of two numbers. **6.** *Chiefly
Brit.* To rent (a house, room, etc.) to a tenant. **7.** To cause
to flow, as blood. — *v.i.* **8.** *Chiefly Brit.* To be rented:
rooms to *let.* — **Syn.** See ALLOW. — **let alone** *Informal*
And surely not; not to say: He can't even float, *let alone*
swim. — **to let alone** (or **be**) To leave unmolested; refrain
from disturbing or tampering with. — **to let down 1.** To
cause to fall or descend; lower; loosen, as hair. **2.** To fail to
fulfill the hopes or expectations of; disappoint. — **to let in**
To insert into the substance, material, or body of something.
— **to let loose** To set free; release. — **to let off 1.** To emit;
release, as from pressure or tension. **2.** To discharge, dismiss, or excuse, as from work or obligation. **3.** To allow to
escape a punishment or penalty. — **to let on** *Informal* **1.**
To make it known; reveal. **2.** To pretend. — **to let out 1.**
To give vent to; emit. **2.** To release or unfasten in order to
make a garment, etc., wider or longer: to *let out* a hem. — **to
let up 1.** To grow less; abate. **2.** To reduce tension; relax.
— **to let up on** *Informal* To cease to subject to force or severe treatment; deal more gently with. ◆ When used with
another verb, as in senses 1, 3, and 5, *let* is followed by the
infinitive without *to.* See note under LEAVE¹. [OE *lǣtan*]
let² (let) n. **1.** In tennis or similar games, a service, point,
etc., that must be repeated because of some interruption or
hindrance of standard playing conditions. **2.** *Archaic* An
obstruction; obstacle. — *v.t.* **let** or **let·ted, let·ting** *Archaic*
To hinder; impede. [OE *lettan,* lit., to make late]
-let *suffix of nouns* **1.** Small; little: *booklet.* **2.** A band or ornament for (a specified part of the body): *anklet.* [< OF
-let, -lette < *-el* (< L *-ellus*) + *-et,* dim. suffixes]
let·down (let′doun′) n. **1.** A decrease; slackening, as of
speed, force, or energy. **2.** *Informal* Disappointment. **3.**
The descent of an airplane preparatory to landing.
le·thal (lē′thəl) *adj.* **1.** Causing death; deadly; fatal. **2.**
Pertaining to or characteristic of death. [< L *lethalis* < *le-
thum, letum* death] — **le·thal·i·ty** (lē·thal′ə·tē) n.
le·thar·gic (li·thär′jik) *adj.* **1.** Affected with or characterized by lethargy; drowsy; apathetic. **2.** Pertaining to or
causing lethargy. Also **le·thar′gi·cal.** — **le·thar′gi·cal·ly** *adv.*
leth·ar·gize (leth′ər·jīz) *v.t.* **-gized, -giz·ing** To make lethargic.
leth·ar·gy (leth′ər·jē) n. *pl.* **-gies 1.** A state of sluggish inaction, indifference, or dullness; apathy. **2.** *Pathol.* An abnormal condition characterized by excessive drowsiness or
deep and prolonged sleep. — **Syn.** See STUPOR. [< OF *le-
thargie* < LL *lethargia* < Gk. *lēthargia* < *lēthargos* forgetful
< *lēthē* oblivion]
Le·the (lē′thē) n. **1.** In Greek mythology, a river in the
realm of Hades a drink from which produced oblivion. **2.**
Oblivion; forgetfulness. [< Gk. *lēthē* oblivion] — **Le·the·
an** (lē·thē′ən) *adj.*
Le·to (lē′tō) In Greek mythology, the mother of Apollo and
Artemis by Zeus: identified with the Roman *Latona.*
Lett (let) n. **1.** One of a people inhabiting Latvia and adjacent Baltic regions. **2.** Lettish.
let·ter (let′ər) n. **1.** A standardized sign or character used
in writing or printing to represent a speech sound; character
in an alphabet. **2.** A written or printed message, usually of
a personal nature or concerning a specific subject, directed to
a specified person, group, or category of persons. **3.** An official document granting certain rights or privileges to a specified person: a *letter* of credit. **4.** Literal meaning as distinct
from implication or general interpretation; precise denotation; exact wording: the *letter* of the law. Compare SPIRIT
(def. 11). **5.** *pl.* Literature in general; literary culture; the
literary profession: a man of *letters.* **6.** *Printing* **a** A piece of
type producing the imprint of a single letter. **b** Such pieces
collectively. **c** A style of type. **7.** *U.S.* An emblem in the
form of the initial letter of a college, school, etc., conferred as
an award for outstanding performance in athletics. — **to
the letter** In accordance with the exact words or literal meaning; fully and precisely. — *v.t.* **1.** To inscribe letters on;
mark with letters. **2.** To print or inscribe by means of
letters. — *v.i.* **3.** To form letters, as by hand. [< OF *lettre* <
L *littera* letter of the alphabet, in pl., epistle] — **let′ter·er** n.
letter box *Chiefly Brit.* A mailbox (def. 1).
letter carrier A mailman.
let·tered (let′ərd) *adj.* **1.** Versed in letters; learned; literary; educated. **2.** Inscribed or marked with letters.
let·ter·head (let′ər·hed′) n. A printed heading, as a name
and address, on a sheet of writing paper; also, a sheet of paper bearing such a heading.
let·ter-high (let′ər·hī′) *adj.* **1.** In baseball, designating a
pitch that reaches the batter at chest height. **2.** *Printing*
Type-high (which see).
let·ter·ing (let′ər·ing) n. **1.** The act or art of forming letters; process of marking or stamping with letters. **2.** Let-

ters collectively, especially those of a single example of writing, printing, etc.

let·ter·man (let′ər·man′) *n. pl.* **·men** (-men′) *U.S. Informal* An athlete to whom a letter has been awarded.

letter of advice In commerce, a letter giving special information, as from a consignor to a consignee, from an agent to a principal, or from drawer to drawee of a bill of exchange.

letter of credence An official document accrediting an envoy to a foreign power. Also **letters of credence.**

letter of credit In banking and commerce: **a** A letter or statement issued by a bank and authorizing the bearer to draw a specified amount of money from that bank or its branches or agents. **b** A similar letter or statement establishing credit up to a specified amount at certain affiliated banks for a person who has paid or guaranteed that amount to the issuing bank. Abbr. *l/c, L/C*

letter of marque Formerly, a commission issued by a government authorizing a private person to arm a vessel for the purpose of seizing enemy ships and cargo. Also **letter of marque and reprisal, letters of marque.**

let·ter-per·fect (let′ər·pûr′fikt) *adj.* **1.** Memorized perfectly, as a speech. **2.** Perfect in memorization, as an actor. **3.** Correct in all details, as a piece of writing. — *adv.* Perfectly: said of memorizing or writing.

let·ter·press (let′ər·pres′) *n. Printing* **1.** The text of any printed matter, as distinguished from illustrations, decorations, etc. **2.** Printing produced from type or similar raised surfaces, as distinct from lithography, offset printing, etc.

letters of administration *Law* A document issued by a court authorizing a specified person to administer or settle the estate of one who has died.

letters patent *Law* The instrument granting a patent.

letters testamentary *Law* A document issued by a court officer authorizing the executor of a will to act as such.

Let·tic (let′ik) *adj. & n.* Lettish.

Let·tish (let′ish) *adj.* Of or pertaining to the Letts or their language. — *n.* The Balto-Slavic language of the Letts: also called *Latvian, Lett.*

let·tre de ca·chet (let′r′ də kà·she′) *French* Letter under seal; before the French Revolution, a royal order for the arbitrary imprisonment of some person.

let·tuce (let′is) *n.* **1.** Any plant of the genus *Lactuca;* especially, a cultivated herb (*L. sativa*) having crisp, edible leaves. **2.** The leaves of this plant served as or combined in a salad or a sandwich. **3.** *Slang* Paper money; greenbacks. [< OF *laituës,* pl. of *laituë* < L *lactuca* < *lac, lactis* milk; with ref. to the milky juice of some species]

let·up (let′up′) *n. Informal* **1.** A lessening or relaxation, as of force or intensity; lull. **2.** A respite; pause; interlude.

le·u (lā′ōō) *n. pl.* **lei** (lā) **1.** The standard monetary unit of Rumania, equivalent to 100 bani. **2.** A coin of this denomination. Also called *ley.* [< Rumanian, lit., lion < L *leo*]

Leu·cas (lōō′kəs) An ancient name for LEVKAS. Also **Leu·ca′di·a** (lōō·kā′dē·ə).

leu·cine (lōō′sin, -sēn) *n. Biochem.* A white, crystalline amino acid, $C_6H_{13}NO_2$, produced by the decomposition of proteins. Also **leu′cin** (-sin). [< Gk. *leukos* white + -INE²]

leu·cite (lōō′sīt) *n.* A whitish silicate of potassium and aluminum, $KAl(SiO_3)_2$, found in igneous rocks. [< Gk. *leukos* white + -ITE¹] — **leu·cit′ic** (-sit′ik) *adj.*

leuco- *combining form* White; lacking color: *leucocyte:* also, before vowels, **leuc-.** Also spelled **leuko-, leuk-.** ◆ *Leuco-* and *leuko-* are often used interchangeably, although *leuko-* is preferred for most medical terms. [< Gk. *leukos* white]

leu·co·crat·ic (lōō′kō·krat′ik) *adj. Geol.* Characterized by the predominance of light-colored minerals, as certain igneous rocks. [< LEUCO- + Gk. *krat(ein)* to rule + -IC]

leu·co·cyte (lōō′kə·sīt) *n. Physiol.* A white or colorless blood corpuscle, constituting an important agent in protection against infectious diseases. Also spelled *leukocyte:* also called *hemoleucocyte.* [< LEUCO- + -CYTE]

leu·co·cyt·ic (lōō′kə·sit′ik) *adj.* **1.** Of or pertaining to leucocytes. **2.** Characterized by an excess of leucocytes.

leu·co·cy·to·sis (lōō′kō·sī·tō′sis) See LEUKOCYTOSIS.

leu·co·der·ma (lōō′kō·dûr′mə) See LEUKODERMA.

leu·co·ma (lōō·kō′mə) See LEUKOMA.

leu·co·ma·ine (lōō·kō′mə-ēn, -in) *n. Biochem.* One of various, sometimes toxic, nitrogen compounds normally present in animal tissues as products of metabolism. [< LEUCO- + (PTO)MAINE]

leu·co·mel·a·nous (lōō′kō·mel′ə·nəs) *adj.* Having a light or fair complexion and dark eyes and hair. Also **leu·co·me·lan′ic** (-mə·lan′ik). [< LEUCO- + Gk. *melas, melanos* black]

leu·co·pe·ni·a (lōō′kō·pē′nē·ə) See LEUKOPENIA.

leu·co·plast (lōō′kə·plast) *n. Bot.* One of the colorless granules embedded in the protoplasmic mass of active vegetable cells, forming points about which starch accumulates. Also **leu′co·plas′tid** (-tid). [< LEUCO- + -PLAST]

leu·co·poi·e·sis (lōō′kō·poi·ē′sis) *n. Physiol.* The production of leucocytes. [< NL < LEUCO- + Gk. *poiesis* a making < *poieein* to make] — **leu′co·poi·et′ic** (-et′ik) *adj.*

leu·cor·rhe·a (lōō′kə·rē′ə), **leu·cor·rhoe·a** See LEUKORRHEA.

Leuc·tra (lōōk′trə) An ancient village of Boeotia, Greece; scene of the Theban defeat of the Spartans, 371 B.C.

leud (lōōd) *n. pl.* **leuds** or **leu·des** (lōō′dēz) A feudal vassal. [< Med.L *leudes* < OHG *liudi, liuti.* Akin to OE *lēod.*]

leuk- Var. of LEUCO-.

Leu·kas (lōō′kəs) See LEVKAS.

leu·ke·mi·a (lōō·kē′mē·ə) *n. Pathol.* A generally fatal disease of the blood and bloodmaking tissues, characterized by a marked increase in the number of leucocytes, accompanied by hyperactivity of the lymph glands, anemia, and exhaustion; cancer of the blood. Also **leu·kae′mi·a.** [< LEUK- + Gk. *haima* blood]

leuko- See LEUCO-.

leu·ko·cyte (lōō′kə·sīt) See LEUCOCYTE.

leu·ko·cy·to·sis (lōō′kō·sī·tō′sis) *n. Physiol.* An increase in the number of leucocytes in the blood, especially during pregnancy and infection and not as a symptom of leukemia. Also spelled *leucocytosis.* — **leu′ko·cy·tot′ic** (-tot′ik) *adj.*

leu·ko·der·ma (lōō′kō·dûr′mə) *n. Pathol.* A deficiency in skin pigmentation characterized by white patches: also called *vitiligo.* Also spelled *leucoderma.* [< LEUKO- + Gk. *derma* skin] — **leu′ko·der′mic** *adj.*

leu·ko·ma (lōō·kō′mə) *n. Pathol.* An abnormal condition of the eye, characterized by a whitish opacity of the cornea. Also spelled *leucoma.* [< NL < Gk. *leukos* white]

leu·ko·pe·ni·a (lōō′kō·pē′nē·ə) *n. Physiol.* A reduction in the number of leucocytes in the blood. Also spelled *leucopenia.* [< NL < Gk. *leukos* white + *penia* poverty < *penesthai* to be poor] — **leu′ko·pe′nic** *adj.*

leu·kor·rhe·a (lōō′kə·rē′ə) *n. Pathol.* A whitish discharge from the vagina and uterus, usually symptomatic of congestion: also spelled *leucorrhea, leucorrhoea.* Also **leu′kor·rhoe′a.** [< NL < Gk. *leukos* white + *rheein* to flow]

lev (lef) *n. pl.* **lev·a** (lev′ə) **1.** The monetary unit of Bulgaria, equivalent to 100 stotinki. **2.** A coin of this denomination. [< Bulgarian, lit., lion < OSlavic *livu,* ult. < Gk. *leon*]

Lev. Leviticus.

Lev·al·loi·si·an (lev′ə·loi′zē·ən) *adj. Anthropol.* Denoting a technological stage of the Lower Paleolithic, beginning in the Acheulean period. [after the *Levallois* flake, a type of flint tool first found near Levallois-Perret]

Le·val·lois-Per·ret (lə·và·lwà′pe·re′) A commune in northern France, a suburb of Paris; pop. 58,890 (1968).

le·vant (lə·vant′) *n.* A kind of morocco leather having an irregularly grained surface. Also **Levant morocco.**

Le·vant (lə·vant′) *n.* The regions bordering the eastern Mediterranean, between western Greece and western Egypt: usually preceded by *the.* [< F < L *levans, -antis,* pp. of *levare* to raise]

Levant dollar See under DOLLAR.

le·vant·er (lə·van′tər) *n.* A strong, easterly wind of the Mediterranean regions.

Le·van·ter (lə·van′tər) *n.* A Levantine.

le·van·tine (lə·van′tin, lev′ən·tīn, -tēn) *n.* A heavy, twilled silk fabric.

Le·van·tine (lə·van′tin, lev′ən·tīn, -tēn) *adj.* Of, pertaining to, or characteristic of the Levant. — *n.* A native or inhabitant of the Levant.

le·va·tor (lə·vā′tər) *n. pl.* **le·va·to·res** (lev′ə·tôr′ēz, -tō′rēz) or **le·va·tors** **1.** *Anat.* A muscle that raises an organ or part. **2.** *Surg.* An instrument used to raise the depressed part in a fracture of the skull. [< LL, raiser < L *levare* to raise]

lev·ee¹ (lev′ē) *n. U.S.* **1.** An embankment, especially along the shore of a river, built for protection against floods. **2.** A terrace or ridge constructed to control the flow of water in irrigation. **3.** A landing place; wharf. [< F *levée,* pp. fem. of *lever* to raise < L *levare*]

lev·ee² (lev′ē, lə·vē′) *n.* **1.** A reception or formal gathering of visitors, usually held early in the day by a person of rank or distinction. **2.** *Canadian Mil.* A formal reception held on New Year's Day by an officer's mess. **3.** Formerly: **a** An official audience held by a person of high rank before or upon rising from bed. **b** In Great Britain, a court reception held early in the day and attended by men only. **c** An official reception held by the president of the United States. [< F *levé* an arising, var. of *lever* < *se lever* to arise < L *levare* to raise]

lev·el (lev′əl) *n.* **1.** Relative place, degree, or stage; plane: a high *level* of development. **2.** Position in the vertical dimension: the *level* of the lower branches. **3.** A horizontal line or surface; also, the height or depth of such a line or surface: sea *level.* **4.** A flat expanse, as of land. **5.** Any of various devices used to find the conformity of a line or surface with the horizontal plane, as a spirit level (which see). **6.** A level of usage. — **on the level** *Informal* Without equivocation or deception; fair and square. — **to find one's** (or its) **level** To come to the appropriate place on a vertical scale of distances, values, etc. — *adj.* **1.** Having a surface with no irregularities in height; even; flat. **2.** Conforming to a horizontal plane; not sloping. **3.** Being in the same plane with or at the

same height as something else. **4.** Measured so as to have a surface even with the edge of the container: said especially of quantities specified in recipes. **5.** Equal to something or someone else, as in importance, degree of ability or development, etc. **6.** Even, as in quality or tone; uniform; unvarying. — **a level head** A calm and sensible mind. — **one's level best** *Informal* The best one can possibly do; one's utmost. — *v.* **lev·eled** or **·elled, lev·el·ing** or **·el·ling** *v.t.* **1.** To give an even or horizontal surface to; make flat. **2.** To destroy by or as by smashing to the ground; demolish; raze. **3.** To knock down; fell, as with a blow. **4.** To bring to a common state or condition; remove inequalities, as of rank or importance. **5.** To aim or point in a horizontal plane, as a weapon. **6.** To aim or direct (something) with force of emphasis: to *level* an accusation. **7.** In surveying, to measure or determine (differences in elevation) with a level. **8.** To make even or uniform, as colors. — *v.i.* **9.** To bring persons or things to a common state or condition. **10.** To take measurements with a level. **11.** To aim a weapon at a target. **12.** *U.S. Slang* To be straightforward or honest. — **to level off** To move or fly horizontally after gaining or losing altitude: said especially of an aircraft. — *adv.* In an even line or plane. [< OF *livel, nivel* < L *libella,* dim. of *libra* a balance] — **lev'el·ly** *adv.* — **lev'el·ness** *n.*
 — **Syn.** (adj.) **1.** *Level, flat, plane, plain,* and *smooth* characterize a surface wholly or relatively free of local elevations and depressions. *Level* primarily means horizontal; a tract of land may be *level,* though the ground itself is bumpy. *Flat* means free of small irregularities, or even, like the surface of still water; it does not necessarily mean the same as *level*: a *flat* (or *level*) roof, the *flat* side of a cliff. *Plane* means perfectly *flat*; this is a mathematical ideal rather than a reality found in nature; *plain,* originally the same word, is sometimes applied to notably *flat* terrain. A *smooth* surface has no small irregularities perceptible to sight or touch; it suggests something that has been polished; the surface of a sphere is *smooth,* though not *plane, flat,* or *level.* **3.** flush, even.
level crossing A grade crossing (which see).
lev·el·er (lev'əl·ər) *n.* One who or that which levels; especially, one who advocates social and political equality. Also *Brit.* **lev'el·ler.**
lev·el·head·ed (lev'əl·hed'id) *adj.* Characterized by common sense and cool judgment. — **lev'el·head'ed·ness** *n.*
leveling rod A graduated pole bearing a marker, used by surveyors in measuring differences in elevation. Also **leveling staff, leveling pole.**
Lev·el·ler (lev'əl·ər) *n.* A member of an egalitarian political party active in England in the middle of the 17th century.
level of usage *Ling.* A distinguishable variety of vocabulary, grammar, pronunciation, etc., of a language that is considered appropriate for a class within the speech community; standard or nonstandard English. Compare STYLE (def. 11).
Le·ven (lē'vən), **Loch** A lake in east central Scotland; 8 sq. mi.; site of an island on which there are the ruins of a castle where Mary Queen of Scots was imprisoned.
lev·er (lev'ər, lē'vər) *n.* **1.** *Mech.* A device consisting of a rigid structure, often a straight bar, pivoting on a fixed support (the fulcrum), and serving to impart pressure or motion from a force or effort applied at one point to a resisting force at another point. For illustration see MACHINE. **2.** Any of various tools, devices or parts operating on the above principle, as a crowbar, a starting bar for an engine, etc. **3.** Any means of exerting effective power. — *v.t. & v.i.* To move or pry with or as with a lever. [< OF *leveour,* lit., lifter < *lever* to raise < L *levare*]
Le·ver (lē'vər), **Charles James,** 1806–72, Irish novelist. — **William Hesketh,** 1851–1925, first Viscount Leverhulme, English industrialist.
lev·er·age (lev'ər·ij, lē'vər-) *n.* **1.** The use of a lever. **2.** The mechanical advantage gained by use of a lever.
lev·er·et (lev'ər·it) *n.* A young hare less than a year old. [< AF, OF *levrete,* dim. of *levre* hare < L *lepus, leporis*]
Le·ver·rier (lə·ve·ryā'), **Urbain Jean Joseph,** 1811–77, French astronomer.
Le·vi (lē'vī) In the Old Testament, a son of Jacob and Leah. *Gen.* xxix 34. — *n.* The tribe of Israel descended from him.
lev·i·a·ble (lev'ē·ə·bəl) *adj.* **1.** Subject to being levied upon. **2.** That can be levied, as a tax. [< LEVY + -ABLE]
le·vi·a·than (lə·vī'ə·thən) *n.* **1.** A gigantic unidentified water beast mentioned several times in the Bible. **2.** Any enormous creature or thing, as a whale or a large ship.
lev·i·gate (lev'ə·gāt; *for adj., also* lev'ə·git) *v.t.* **·gat·ed, ·gat·ing** **1.** To reduce to a fine powder. **2.** To mix with liquid to form a smooth paste. — *adj. Bot.* Smooth; glabrous. [< L *levigatus,* pp. of *levigare* to polish < *levis* smooth + *agere* to make] — **lev'i·ga'tion** *n.*
lev·in (lev'in) *n. Archaic* Lightning. [ME *levene,* prob. < Gmc.]
lev·i·rate (lev'ə·rāt, lē'və·rit) *n.* An ancient Jewish law

(*Deut.* xxv 5) requiring a man to marry the widow of his deceased brother under certain circumstances. [< L *levir* a husband's brother + -ATE[1]] — **lev/i·rat/ic** (-rat'ik) or **·i·cal** *adj.*
Le·vis (lē'vīz) *n.pl.* Close-fitting, heavy denim trousers having rivets to reinforce points of greatest strain: a registered trade mark. [after *Levi* Strauss, U.S. manufacturer]
Levit. Leviticus.
lev·i·tate (lev'ə·tāt) *v.* **·tat·ed, ·tat·ing** *v.i.* **1.** To rise and float in the air, as through buoyancy or supposed supernatural power. — *v.t.* **2.** To cause to rise and float in the air. [< L *levis* light, on analogy with *gravitate*] — **lev'i·ta'tor** *n.*
lev·i·ta·tion (lev'ə·tā'shən) *n.* **1.** The act of levitating, or the state of being levitated. **2.** The illusion of suspending a heavy object or the human body in the air without support. **3.** The illusion of floating in the air, as in dreams.
Le·vite (lē'vīt) *n.* In Jewish history, one of the tribe of Levi, from among whom those who assisted the priests in the Temple were traditionally chosen.
Le·vit·i·cal (lə·vit'i·kəl) *adj.* **1.** Of or pertaining to the Levites. **2.** Of or pertaining to the book of Leviticus or its laws. Also **Le·vit/ic.**
Le·vit·i·cus (lə·vit'i·kəs) The third book of the Old Testament, consisting chiefly of a compilation of ceremonial laws. Abbr. *Lev., Levit.* [< L *Leviticus* (*liber*) < Gk. *Leuitikon* (*biblion*), lit., Levitical (book)]
Lev·it·town (lev'it·toun') A village in SE New York, on Long Island; pop. 65,440.
lev·i·ty (lev'ə·tē) *n. pl.* **·ties** **1.** Conduct or attitude characterized by lack of seriousness; inappropriate gaiety; frivolity. **2.** Fickleness; inconstancy. **3.** The property of having relatively little weight; lightness. [< L *levitas, -tatis* < *levis* light]
Lev·kas (lef·käs') An island of Greece in the Ionian chain; 114 sq. mi.: Italian *Santa Maura*: ancient *Leucadia, Leucas.* Also *Leukas.*
levo- *combining form* Turned or turning to the left: used especially in chemistry and physics: *levorotatory.* Also spelled *laevo-.* Abbr. *l, l-* [< L *laevus* left]
le·vo·gy·rate (lē'vō·jī'rāt) *adj.* Levorotatory. Also spelled *laevogyrate.*
le·vo·ro·ta·tion (lē'vō·rō·tā'shən) *n. Optics* Counterclockwise rotation of the plane of polarized light. Also spelled *laevorotation.*
le·vo·ro·ta·to·ry (lē'vō·rō'tə·tôr'ē, -tō'rē) *adj. Optics* Causing the plane of polarization of light to rotate to the left, or counterclockwise: said of certain crystals, etc.: opposed to *dextrorotatory.* Also spelled *laevorotatory*: also *levogyrate.*
lev·u·lin (lev'yə·lin) *n. Biochem.* A colorless, amorphous compound resembling starch, and hydrolyzing readily into levulose. [< LEVUL(OSE) + -IN]
lev·u·lin·ic acid (lev'yə·lin'ik) *Chem.* An odorless, colorless acid, $C_5H_8O_3$, extracted from the nucleic acid of the thymus gland or made by boiling certain sugars with hydrochloric acid, and used as a disinfectant.
lev·u·lose (lev'yə·lōs) *n. Biochem.* Fructose. [< L *laevus* left + -UL(E) + -OSE[2]]
lev·y (lev'ē) *v.* **lev·ied, lev·y·ing** *v.t.* **1.** To impose and collect by authority or force, as a tax, fine, etc. **2.** To enlist or call up (troops, etc.) for military service. **3.** To prepare for, begin, or wage (war). — *v.i.* **4.** To make a levy. **5.** *Law* To seize property by judicial writ in order to fulfill a judgment: usually with *on.* — *n. pl.* **lev·ies** **1.** The act of levying. **2.** That which is levied, as money or troops. [< OF *levee,* pp. fem. of *lever* to raise < L *levare*] — **lev'i·er** *n.*
levy en masse A spontaneous arming for defense by civilians in times of military emergency.
lewd (lood) *adj.* **1.** Characterized by or inciting to lust or debauchery. **2.** Obscene; ribald; bawdy. **3.** *Obs.* Unprincipled; worthless. [OE *lǣwede* lay[2], unlearned, ? fusion of L *laicus* lay[2] and OE *lǣwan* to betray] — **lewd'ly** *adv.* — **lewd'ness** *n.*
Lew·es (loo'is), **George Henry,** 1817–78, English philosopher and critic.
lew·is (loo'is) *n.* A metal device that locks into a prepared hole in a heavy stone and to which hoisting gear is attached. Also **lew'is·son.** [? < the name *Lewis*]
Lew·is (loo'is). **Cecil Day** See DAY-LEWIS. — **C(live) S(taples),** 1898–1963, British critic and novelist. — **John L(lewellyn),** 1880–1969, U.S. labor leader. — **Matthew Gregory,** 1775–1818, English novelist and dramatist: called **Monk Lewis.** — **Meriwether,** 1774–1809, U.S. explorer. See (William) CLARK. — **(Percy) Wyndham,** 1884–1957, English painter and writer. — **Sinclair,** 1885–1951, U.S. novelist.
Lewis gun An obsolete gas-operated machine gun. [after Col. Isaac N. *Lewis,* 1858–1931, U.S. inventor]
lew·is·ite (loo'is·īt) *n. Chem.* An oily liquid, $C_2H_2Cl_3As$, used in chemical warfare as a blistering agent. [after W. L. *Lewis,* 1878–1943, U.S. chemist]
Lew·i·sohn (loo'i·sən), **Ludwig,** 1883–1955, U.S. novelist and critic born in Germany.
Lew·is·ton (loo'is·tən) A city in SW Maine, on the Androscoggin River; pop. 41,779.

LEVERS
A First class.
B Second class.
C Third class.
f Fulcrum.
p Force.
w Weight.

Lewis with Harris The northernmost island of the Outer Hebrides, Scotland; 825 sq. mi.

lex (leks) *n. pl.* **le·ges** (lē′jēz) *Latin* Law.

lex. Lexicon.

lex·i·cal (lek′sə-kəl) *adj.* **1.** Pertaining to words or morphemes as separate definable items in a vocabulary and not as elements in a linguistic or grammatical structure; semantic. **2.** Of or pertaining to a lexicon. [< Gk. *lexikos* pertaining to words < *lexikon* lexicon]

lexical meaning *Ling.* The meaning of a word or morpheme considered apart from the modifications of grammatical inflection, syntactic position, etc.

lexicog. Lexicographer; lexicographical; lexicography.

lex·i·cog·ra·pher (lek′sə-kog′rə-fər) *n.* One who works at writing or compiling a dictionary. *Abbr. lexicog.*

lex·i·cog·ra·phy (lek′sə-kog′rə-fē) *n.* The practice or profession of compiling dictionaries. *Abbr. lexicog.* [< NL *lexicografia* < Gk. *lexikographos* one who writes a lexicon < *lexikon* lexicon + *graphein* to write] — **lex′i·co·graph′ic** (-kō-graf′ik) or **·i·cal** *adj.* — **lex′i·co·graph′i·cal·ly** *adv.*

lex·i·con (lek′sə-kon) *n.* **1.** A dictionary; especially, a dictionary of Latin, Greek, or Hebrew. **2.** A vocabulary or list of words relating to a particular subject, occupation, or activity. **3.** *Ling.* All the morphemes of a language. [< Gk. *lexikon*, neut. of *lexikos* pertaining to words < *lexis* way of speaking < *legein* to say, speak]

lex·i·co·sta·tis·tics (lek′sə-kō-stə-tis′tiks) *n.pl.* (construed as *sing.*) *Ling.* Glottochronology (def. 1). [< Gk. *lexikos* pertaining to words + STATISTICS]

Lex·ing·ton (lek′sing-tən) **1.** A city in north central Kentucky; pop. 108,137. **2.** A town in NE Massachusetts; scene of the first battle of the American Revolution, April 19, 1775; pop. 31,886.

lex lo·ci (leks′ lō′sī) *Latin* The law of the place.

lex non scrip·ta (leks′ non skrip′tə) *Latin* Unwritten law; the common law.

lex scrip·ta (leks′ skrip′tə) *Latin* Written or statute law.

lex ta·li·o·nis (leks′ tal′ē-ō′nis) *Latin* The law of retaliation.

ley (lā) See LEU.

Ley·den (līd′n) See LEIDEN.

Leyden jar *Electr.* A device for accumulating a charge of static electricity, consisting principally of a glass jar coated with tinfoil inside and out nearly to the top. [after *Leyden*, earlier name of Leiden, where it was invented]

Ley·te (lā′tā) An island in the Visayan Islands, Philippines; 2,785 sq. mi.

Leyte Gulf An inlet of the Pacific between Leyte and Samar, Philippines; scene of a U.S. naval victory in World War II.

Ley·ton (lāt′n) A municipal borough in SW Essex, England; pop. 93,857 (1961).

l.f. or lf **1.** Left field(er). **2.** Left forward.

l.f. or lf. *Printing* Lightface.

L.F. or LF, l.f. or l-f Low frequency.

lg. or lge. Large.

l.g. or lg Left guard.

LG or LG or L.G. Low German.

LGk. or L.Gk. Late Greek.

l.h. or L.H. or LH Left hand.

LHA Local hour angle.

Lha·sa (lä′sä) The capital of Tibet, in the southern part; traditional seat of the Dalai Lama; pop. about 50,000: Chinese *Lasa.*

l.h.b. or lhb Left halfback.

L.H.D. Doctor of Humanities (L *Litterarum Humaniorum Doctor*).

Lhé·vinne (lā-vēn′), **Josef**, 1874–1944, and his wife **Rosina**, *née* Bessie, 1880–1976, Russian pianists active in the United States.

li (lē) *n. pl.* **li** A Chinese unit of distance, approximately one third of a mile.

li. Link(s) (unit of measurement).

Li *Chem.* Lithium.

L.I. Long Island.

li·a·bil·i·ty (lī′ə-bil′ə-tē) *n. pl.* **·ties 1.** The state or condition of being liable. **2.** That for which one is liable, as a financial obligation or debt. **3.** *pl.* In accounting, the entries on a balance sheet showing the debts or obligations of a business to its creditors, customers, etc.: opposed to *assets.* **4.** An obstacle or hindrance to success; disadvantage.

li·a·ble (lī′ə-bəl) *adj.* **1.** Justly or legally responsible, as for damages; answerable. **2.** Subject or susceptible, as to injury, illness, or other undesirable possibility: *liable* to colds, *liable* to be hurt. **3.** Officially obligated to be available, as for service or duty: *liable* for jury duty. **4.** *U.S. Informal* Likely: It's *liable* to fall. [< F *lier* < L *ligare* to bind]

li·ai·son (lē′ā-zon′, lē-ā′zon, lē′ə-zon; *Fr.* lē-e-zôṅ′) *n.* **1.** A means or agency for maintaining or furthering communication or unity, as between parts of an armed force or departments of a government. **2.** A relationship or connection, as between governments. **3.** An intimate relationship between a man and woman not married to each other; love affair. **4.** In spoken French and in many other languages, the carrying over of a final consonant to the initial vowel of a succeeding word, so that the consonant begins the spoken syllable, as in *il est arrivé* (ē le tȧ-rē-vā′). **5.** In cooking, a mixture of cream and egg yolks to thicken sauces, soups, etc. [< F < L *ligatio, -onis* < *ligare* to bind]

li·an·a (lē-an′ə, -ä′nə) *n.* Any of various twining or climbing plants of tropical forests, with ropelike, woody stems. Also **li·ane** (lē-än′). [< F *liane* < *lier* to bind < L *ligare*]

liang (lyang) *n. pl.* **liang** A Chinese unit of weight, equivalent to ¹⁄₁₆ of a catty, or about 1⅓ ounces.

Liao (lyou) A river in NE China, flowing 900 miles, generally SE, to the Gulf of Liaotung. *Chinese* **Liao Ho**.

Liao·ning (lyou′ning′) A Province of NE China; 58,301 sq. mi.; pop. 24,090,000 (est. 1957); capital Shenyang.

Liao·tung Peninsula (lyou′doong′) A peninsula in NE China, extending into the northern Yellow Sea and forming the eastern side of the Gulf of Liaotung.

Liao·yang (lyou′yäng′) A city in western Liaoning Province, China; pop. 250,000 (est. 1970).

li·ar (lī′ər) *n.* One who lies or utters falsehoods. [OE *lēogere*]

Li·as (lī′əs) *n. Geol.* The lowest of the rock series composing the Jurassic system of Europe. [< F *liais* kind of limestone; ult. origin unknown] — **Li·as·sic** (lī-as′ik) *adj.*

lib. **1.** Book (L *liber*). **2.** Librarian; library.

Lib. **1.** Liberal. **2.** Liberia.

li·ba·tion (lī-bā′shən) *n.* **1.** A liquid ceremonially poured out, as in honor of a deity; also, the act of pouring such a liquid. **2.** Humorously, a drink. [< F < L *libatio, -onis* < *libare* to pour out (as an offering)]

Li·bau (lē′bou) The German name for LIEPAJA.

li·bel (lī′bəl) *n.* **1.** *Law* **a** A written statement or graphic representation, especially in published form, that damages a person's reputation or exposes him to public ridicule. **b** The act or crime of making or publishing such a statement or representation. Distinguished from *slander.* **2.** Any defamatory or grossly unflattering statement or representation. **3.** *Law* The written statement of the claims of a plaintiff in a lawsuit, as in a church or admiralty court. **4.** *Obs.* A short treatise. — *v.t.* **beled** or **belled, bel·ing** or **bel·ling 1.** To publish or perpetrate a libel against. **2.** To defame or discredit, as by false or malicious statements. **3.** *Law* To bring suit against by presenting a libel (def. 3). — **Syn.** See ASPERSE. [< OF < L *libellus*, dim. of *liber* book]

li·bel·ant (lī′bəl-ənt) *n. Law* One who institutes a lawsuit by presenting a libel (def. 3). Also, *esp. Brit.*, **li′bel·lant**.

li·bel·ee (lī′bəl-ē′) *n. Law* The defendant in a lawsuit in which a libel (def. 3) is presented. Also, *esp. Brit.*, **li′bel·lee′**.

li·bel·er (lī′bəl-ər) *n.* One who libels or publishes a libel against another. Also, *esp. Brit.*, **li′bel·ler**.

li·bel·ous (lī′bəl-əs) *adj.* Constituting, containing, or of the nature of a libel; defamatory. Also, *esp. Brit.*, **li′bel·lous**. — **li′bel·ous·ly** *adv.*

li·ber (lī′bər) *n. Bot.* Phloem. [< L]

lib·er·al (lib′ər-əl, lib′rəl) *adj.* **1.** Characterized by or inclining toward opinions or policies favoring progress or reform, as in politics or religion. **2.** Not intolerant or prejudiced; broad-minded. **3.** Characterized by generosity or lavishness in giving; bountiful. **4.** Given or yielded freely or in large quantity; bounteous; plentiful; ample. **5.** Not literal or strict: a *liberal* interpretation of the law. **6.** Suitable for persons of broad cultural interests: *liberal* education; *liberal* arts. **7.** *Obs.* Appropriate to a person of free or gentle birth. **8.** *Obs.* Overly free or unrestrained; unbridled. — *n.* One having liberal opinions or convictions, especially in politics or religion. [< OF < L *liberalis* pertaining to a freeman < *liber* free] — **lib′er·al·ly** *adv.*

— **Syn.** (adj.) **1.** *Liberal, progressive,* and *radical* are antonyms of *conservative.* Their positive meanings are greatly influenced by the political and social views of those who use them. The *liberal* person is one who advocates the modification of laws and institutions in accordance with changing conditions. The *progressive* elements in a community are most strongly contrasted with the conservative or reactionary elements, advocating the abandonment of practices and ideas which are felt to be outworn. *Radical* describes those who seek to go to the roots of matters; often *radical* implies advocacy of abrupt or violent change. In the United States, *radical* tends to be a term of opprobrium. **3.** See GENEROUS. — **Ant.** conservative, reactionary, authoritarian.

Lib·er·al (lib′ər-əl, lib′rəl) *adj.* Designating or belonging to one of various political parties, as the Liberal Party of Canada, Great Britain, or Australia. — *n.* A member of such a party, especially of the Liberal Party of Canada, Great Britain, or Australia. *Abbr. Lib.*

liberal arts A group of subjects or college courses including literature, philosophy, languages, history, etc., and distinguished from scientific, technical, professional, or purely practical subjects; the arts, as in Bachelor of *Arts*; the humanities. [< L *artes liberales* arts suitable for a freeman]

lib·er·al·ism (lib′ər·əl·iz′əm) *n.* **1.** Liberal beliefs or policies, especially in regard to politics, social changes, etc. **2.** In religion: **a** A Protestant church movement advocating considerable latitude in Scriptural interpretation and in doctrine: compare FUNDAMENTALISM. **b** A movement or tendency verging on secular humanism and rejecting much orthodox theology. **3.** *Sometimes cap.* The policies or principles of the Liberal Party.

lib·er·al·i·ty (lib′ə·ral′ə·tē) *n. pl.* **·ties 1.** The quality of being liberal in giving; magnanimity; generosity. **2.** Liberal attitude or beliefs; broad-mindedness. **3.** *Rare* A liberal gift; bounty. **4.** *Rare* A donation.

lib·er·al·ize (lib′ər·əl·īz′) *v.t. & v.i.* **·ized, ·iz·ing** To make or become liberal. **—lib·er·al·i·za·tion** (lib′ər·əl·ə·zā′shən, -ī·zā′-, lib′rəl-) *n.* **—lib·er·al·iz′er** *n.*

Liberal Party 1. One of the principal political parties of Canada and Australia. **2.** In Great Britain, a Whiggish political party formed in the 1830's and the major opponent of the Conservative Party until after World War I. **3.** Any of various other political parties of liberal principles.

lib·er·ate (lib′ə·rāt) *v.t.* **·at·ed, ·at·ing 1.** To set free; release, as from bondage or confinement. **2.** To disengage; extricate, as from entanglement. **3.** To release from chemical combination, as a gas. [< L *liberatus,* pp. of *liberare* to free < *liber* free] **—lib·er·a′tion** *n.*

lib·er·a·tor (lib′ər·ā′tər) *n.* One who liberates; especially, one who emancipates a nation, people, etc.

Li·be·ri·a (lī·bir′ē·ə) A Republic on the west coast of Africa, founded in 1847 by freed U.S. slaves; about 43,000 sq. mi.; pop. 1,150,000 (est. 1969); capital, Monrovia. See map of (Gulf of) GUINEA. **—Li·be′ri·an** *adj. & n.*

lib·er·tar·i·an (lib′ər·târ′ē·ən) *n.* **1.** One who advocates liberty of thought or conduct, especially in politics or civil affairs. **2.** One who believes in the doctrine of free will. — *adj.* Pertaining to or characteristic of the beliefs of libertarians. **—lib·er·tar′i·an·ism** *n.*

li·ber·ti·cide (li·bûr′tə·sīd) *n.* A destroyer of liberty. [< L *libertas* liberty + -CIDE] **—li·ber′ti·ci′dal** *adj.*

lib·er·tine (lib′ər·tēn) *n.* **1.** One completely lacking in moral restraint; especially, a habitually unchaste or profligate man; a rake. **2.** *Rare* One who has unconventional or unorthodox religious opinions: a derogatory term. **3.** In ancient Rome, a freed slave, or the offspring of such a person. — *adj.* Characteristic of a libertine; morally unrestrained; profligate. [< L *libertinus* < *libertus* freedman < *liber* free]

lib·er·tin·ism (lib′ər·tēn·iz′əm, -tin-) *n.* **1.** The behavior of a libertine; licentiousness. **2.** Opposition to or rejection of authority in religious matters. Also **lib′er·tin·age** (-ij).

lib·er·ty (lib′ər·tē) *n. pl.* **·ties 1.** Freedom from oppression, tyranny, or the domination of a government not freely chosen; political independence. **2.** The state or condition of being free, as from confinement; release, as from bondage or slavery. **3.** Freedom of thought or action, or exemption from forms of compulsion or indignity, regarded as a human right. **4.** The ability or opportunity to act in accordance with one's own wishes or without repression or restraint by authority. **5.** Permission to perform an action, make a choice, etc.; privilege. **6.** An overly free, familiar, or disrespectful act or manner; impertinence. **7.** Permission to be present in and make free use of a specified place: followed by *of.* **8.** In the U.S. Navy and other maritime services, official permission to be absent from one's ship or place of duty, usually for a period not exceeding 48 hours. **—Syn.** See FREEDOM. **—at liberty 1.** Free; authorized or permitted (to do something). **2.** Not engaged in an activity or occupation; unemployed. **3.** Able to move about freely; unconfined. **—to take liberties or a liberty** To behave with unwarranted freedom or undue familiarity. [< F *liberté* < L *libertas, -tatis* < *liber* free]

Liberty Bell The bell in Independence Hall, Philadelphia, rung July 4, 1776, to celebrate the adoption of the Declaration of Independence, and cracked in 1835.

liberty cap A close-fitting, soft, brimless cap with the crown loosely folded over, worn by freedmen in ancient Rome and adopted as a symbol of liberty in the French Revolution: also called *Phrygian cap.*

Liberty Island A small island in Upper New York Bay; site of the Statue of Liberty: formerly *Bedloe's Island.*

Liberty Ship A type of U.S. cargo ship built in large numbers during World War II.

LIBERTY
CAP

Lib·i·a (lē′bē·ä) The Italian name for LIBYA.

li·bid·i·nous (li·bid′ə·nəs) *adj.* Characterized by or inclining toward excesses of sexual desire; lustful. [< F *libidineux* < L *libidinosus* < *libido, -inis* lust < *libet, lubet* it pleases] **—li·bid′i·nous·ly** *adv.* **—li·bid′i·nous·ness** *n.*

li·bi·do (li·bē′dō, -bī-′) *n.* **1.** Sexual desire or impulse. **2.** *Psychoanal.* The instinctual craving or drive behind all human activities. [< L, lust] **—li·bid′i·nal** (-bid′ə·nəl) *adj.*

li·bra (lī′brə *for def.* 1; lē′brä *for def.* 2) *n. pl.* **·brae** (-brē)

for def. 1; **·bras** (-bräs) *for def. 2* **1.** The ancient Roman pound, equivalent to 327 grams. **2.** A former gold coin of Peru. [< L, pound, balance]

Li·bra (lī′brə, lē′-) *n.* A constellation, the Balance or Scales; also, the seventh sign of the zodiac. See CONSTELLATION, ZODIAC. [< L]

li·brar·i·an (lī·brâr′ē·ən) *n.* **1.** One who has charge of a library. **2.** A person qualified by training for library service. Abbr. *lib.* **—li·brar′i·an·ship′** *n.*

li·brar·y (lī′brer·ē, -brə·rē) *n. pl.* **·brar·ies 1.** A collection of books, pamphlets, etc.; especially, such a collection arranged to facilitate reference. **2.** A building, room, or series of rooms housing such a collection. **3.** An institution or organization owning or administering such a collection. **4.** A commercial establishment that rents books. **5.** A series of similar books issued by a single publisher. Abbr. *lib.* [< OF *librarie* < L *librarium* < *liber, libri* book]

library science The science of managing a library and organizing the files, ordering books, etc.

Library of Congress The national library of the United States in Washington, D.C., established in 1800.

li·brate (lī′brāt) *v.i.* **·brat·ed, ·brat·ing 1.** To move back and forth; oscillate. **2.** To be poised; hover. [< L *libratus,* ppr. of *librare* to balance < *libra* balance]

li·bra·tion (lī·brā′shən) *n.* **1.** The act or state of balancing or librating. **2.** *Astron.* A real or apparent slow, swinging motion of a celestial body on each side of its mean position.

li·bra·to·ry (lī′brə·tôr′ē, -tō′rē) *adj.* Oscillating.

li·bret·tist (li·bret′ist) *n.* The writer of a libretto.

li·bret·to (li·bret′ō) *n. pl.* **·tos** or **·ti** (-tē) **1.** The verbal text of an opera or other large-scale vocal work. **2.** A book or pamphlet containing such a text. [< Ital., little book, dim. of *libro* < L *liber*]

Li·bre·ville (lē·brə·vēl′) The capital of the Republic of Gabon, a port on the western coast; pop. 57,000 (1967).

li·bri·form (lī′brə·fôrm) *adj. Bot.* Characteristic of or having the form of liber or bast. [< L *liber* inner bark + -FORM]

Lib·y·a (lib′ē·ə) **1.** A Republic in northern Africa; 679,358 sq. mi.; pop. 1,900,000 (est. 1970); capitals, Tripoli and Bengasi: Italian *Libia;* officially **Libyan Arab Republic. 2.** The ancient Greek and Roman name for North Africa, excluding Egypt.

Lib·y·an (lib′ē·ən) *adj.* Of or pertaining to Libya, its inhabitants, or their language. — *n.* **1.** A native or inhabitant of Libya. **2.** The extinct language of ancient Libya.

Libyan Desert A part of the Sahara Desert extending through eastern Libya, western Egypt, and NW Sudan.

Lib·y·co-Ber·ber (lib′i·kō-bûr′bər) *n.* A branch of the Hamitic subfamily of the Hamito-Semitic language family, consisting of ancient Libyan and the modern Berber dialects.

lice (līs) Plural of LOUSE.

li·cense (lī′sens) *n.* **1.** An official document giving permission to engage in a specified activity, perform a specified act, etc.; especially, the yearly metal tax tag of a car or the printed driver's permit. **2.** Unrestrained liberty of action; unlimited freedom. **3.** Abuse of freedom or privilege; laxity. **4.** Deviation from or relaxation of established rules or standards, especially for artistic effect: poetic *license.* **—Syn.** See FREEDOM. — *v.t.* **·censed, ·cens·ing** To grant a license to or for; give permission to; authorize. Also, *esp. Brit.,* **li′cence.** [< OF *licence* < L *licentia* < *licens, -entis,* ppr. of *licere* to be permitted] **—li′cens·a·ble** *adj.* **—li′cen·ser** or **li′cenc·er** or *Law* **li′cen·sor** *n.*

li·cen·see (lī′sen·sē′) *n.* One to whom a license has been granted. Also **li·cen·cee′.**

li·cen·ti·ate (lī·sen′shē·it, -āt) *n.* **1.** A person licensed, as by a university or official examining body, to practice a certain profession: a *licentiate* in dental surgery. **2.** In some Continental universities, a person holding a degree intermediate between bachelor and doctor. Abbr. (def. 2) *L.* [< Med.L *licentiatus,* pp. of *licentiare* to allow, license < L *licentia.* See LICENSE.]

li·cen·tious (lī·sen′shəs) *adj.* **1.** Lacking in moral restraint; sexually abandoned; lewd. **2.** *Rare* Disregarding or not conforming to established rules or limits. [< L *licentiosus* < *licentia*] **—li·cen′tious·ly** *adv.* **—li·cen′tious·ness** *n.*

li·chee (lē′chē) *n.* **1.** The edible fruit of a tree (*Litchi chinensis*) of the soapberry family, native to China: also **lichee nut. 2.** The tree itself. Also spelled *litchi, lychee.* [< Chinese *li-chih*]

li·chen (lī′kən) *n.* **1.** Any of various flowerless plants (class or group *Lichenes*) composed of fungi and algae in symbiotic union, commonly growing in flat greenish gray, brown, yellow, or blackish patches on rocks, trees, etc. **2.** *Pathol.* Any of several skin diseases characterized by an eruption of pimples. — *v.t.* To cover with lichens. [< L < Gk. *leichēn,* prob. < *leichein* to lick] **—li′chen·ous, li′chen·ose** (-ōs) *adj.*

li·chen·in (lī′kən·in) *n. Biochem.* A white, gelatinous carbohydrate, $C_6H_{10}O_5$, obtained from Iceland moss and other lichens. [< LICHEN + -IN]

li·chen·ol·o·gy (lī′kən·ol′ə·jē) *n.* The science or study of lichens. **—li′chen·ol′o·gist** *n.*

Lich·field (lich′fēld) A borough in SE Staffordshire, England: birthplace of Samuel Johnson: pop. 22,930 (1969).

lich gate (lich) A roofed gateway to a churchyard, originally used as a resting place for a bier. Also spelled *lych gate*. [OE *lic* corpse + GATE]

licht (likht) *Scot. n. & adj.* Light (in all senses). — *v.t. & v.i.* To light.

lic·it (lis′it) *adj.* Lawful. — **Syn.** See LAWFUL. [< F *licite*, ult. < L *licere* to be allowed] — **lic′it·ly** *adv.* — **lic′it·ness** *n.*

lick (lik) *v.t.* 1. To pass the tongue over the surface of. 2. To remove or consume by taking with the tongue: often followed by *up, off,* etc. 3. To move or pass lightly over or about: The flames *licked* the coals. 4. *Informal* To defeat; get the better of. 5. *Informal* To thrash; beat. — *v.i.* 6. To move quickly or lightly; flicker: The flames *licked* among the coals. — **to lick into shape** To put in proper form or condition. — **to lick one's chops** To show pleased anticipation. — **to lick (something) clean** 1. To eat up every morsel from (a dish, platter, etc.). 2. To clean by licking. — *n.* 1. A stroke of the tongue in licking. 2. A small amount, as that taken up by a stroke of the tongue. 3. A hasty application, as of a wet substance; a dab. 4. *U.S.* A salt lick (which see). 5. *Informal* A blow; whack. 6. *Often pl. Informal* An opportunity to do something; a turn. 7. *Informal* A stroke; spell, as of work. 8. *Slang* In jazz, a short, improvised interpolation. — **a lick and a promise** *Informal* Hasty and careless treatment, as in washing oneself or doing housework. — **last licks** *Informal* A final turn or inning, as in a game. [OE *liccian*]

lick·er·ish (lik′ər·ish) *adj. Archaic* 1. Lecherous; lustful. 2. Craving delicious food or drink; greedy. Also spelled *liquorish*. [Var. of LECHEROUS] — **lick′er·ish·ly** *adv.* — **lick′er·ish·ness** *n.*

lick·e·ty-split (lik′ə·tē·split′) *adv. U.S. Informal* At full speed.

lick·ing (lik′ing) *n.* 1. The act of one who or that which licks. 2. *Informal* A whipping; beating.

lick·spit·tle (lik′spit′l) *n.* A servile admirer or flatterer.

lic·o·rice (lik′ə·ris, -rish) *n.* 1. A perennial leguminous herb (*Glycyrrhiza glabra*) of southern and central Europe. 2. The dried root of this plant, or an extract made from it, used in medicine and confections. 3. A confection flavored with such a preparation. 4. Any of various plants having sweetish roots, as the jequirity. Also, *esp. Brit., liquorice.* [< AF *licorys*, OF *licoresse* < LL *liquirita*, alter. of Gk. *glycyrrhiza* < *glykys* sweet + *rhiza* root]

lic·tor (lik′tər) *n.* In ancient Rome, one of the officers or guards who attended the chief magistrates, and who bore the fasces as a symbol of office. [< L, prob. < *ligare* to tie]

lid (lid) *n.* 1. A hinged or removable cover placed at the top of a receptacle or an opening into the interior of something. 2. An eyelid. 3. *Bot.* A top, as of a pyxis or the capsule of a moss, separating at a transverse dividing line; an operculum. 4. *Informal* Restriction or restraint, as of vice or crime. 5. *Slang* A hat. — **to blow the lid off** *Slang* To expose a scandalous situation. — **to flip one's lid** *Slang* To lose one's temper, sanity, etc. [OE *hlid*] — **lid′ded** *adj.*

Lid·dell Hart (lid′əl härt′), **Basil Henry**, 1895–1970, English military authority and writer.

Li·di·ce (lē′di·tse, *Czech* li′dyi·tse) A village in west central Bohemia, Czechoslovakia, destroyed 1942 by the Nazis.

lid·less (lid′lis) *adj.* 1. Having no lid. 2. Without eyelids. 3. *Poetic* Always watchful; vigilant.

Li·do (lē′dō) An island of Italy on the Adriatic, near Venice; fashionable bathing resort.

lie[1] (lī) *v.i.* **lay, lain, ly·ing** 1. To be in a recumbent or prostrate position. 2. To place oneself in a recumbent position; rest at full length: often followed by *down*. 3. To be placed upon or rest against a surface, especially in a horizontal position. 4. To be buried, as in a grave or tomb. 5. To be or remain in a specified condition or state: to lie *dormant*. 6. To exist; be inherent: often followed by *in* or *within*: Our strength *lies* in our numbers. 7. To occupy a location; be situated: New York *lies* north of Philadelphia. 8. To continue or extend: The future *lies* before us. 9. *Law* To be admissible, as a charge or claim. 10. *Archaic* To reside temporarily; pass the night. ◆ See note under LAY[1]. — **to lie in** To be confined for or engaged in the process of childbirth. — **to lie in wait (for)** To wait in concealment so as to attack by surprise. — **to lie low** *Informal* To remain in concealment; conceal one's intentions. — **to lie to** *Naut.* To maintain a vessel in a stationary or nearly stationary position without anchoring. — **to lie with** 1. To rest with; be up to: The choice *lies* with him. 2. *Archaic* To have sexual intercourse with. — *n.* 1. The position, manner, or situation in which something lies; aspect. 2. In golf, the position of a ball that has come to rest. 3. The resting place or haunt of an animal, bird, or fish. [OE *licgan*]

lie[2] (lī) *n.* 1. An untrue statement made with the intent of deceiving; a falsehood. 2. That which creates or is intended to produce a false impression. — **to give the lie (to)** 1. To accuse (someone) of lying. 2. To expose as false; belie. — **white lie** A false statement made knowingly but with the intent of being polite or kind; a minor or trivial untruth. — *v.* **lied, ly·ing** *v.i.* 1. To make an untrue statement or statements, especially with intent to deceive. 2. To give an erroneous or misleading impression; deceive: Figures don't *lie*. — *v.t.* 3. To put or promote (oneself or someone) into a specified situation by telling lies: to *lie* oneself into power. — **to lie in one's teeth** or **throat** To lie outrageously. [OE *lyge*] — **Syn.** (noun) 1. *Lie, falsehood, untruth, fabrication, fib,* and *story* denote a statement that is not true. A *lie* is such a statement, known to be untrue, and made with the intent to deceive. A *falsehood* leaves open the question of intent to deceive, and *untruth* often implies error rather than malice; both *falsehood* and *untruth* are also used euphemistically for *lie. Fabrication* is applied to elaborate *lies* and *stories* that distort without actually contravening the truth. *Fib* and *story* are almost exclusively used of *falsehoods* told by young children, and both are generally regarded as trivial or not serious. Compare DECEPTION. — **Ant.** truth, fact.

Lie (lē), **Jonas,** 1880–1940, U.S. painter born in Norway. — **Trygve Halvdan,** 1896–1968, Norwegian statesman; first secretary general of the United Nations, 1946–53.

Lie·big (lē′bik), **Baron Justus von,** 1803–73, German chemist.

Lieb·knecht (lēp′knekht), **Karl,** 1871–1919, German socialist leader; assassinated.

Liech·ten·stein (lik′tən·stīn, *Ger.* lēkh′tən·shtīn) A sovereign Principality of central Europe, situated between Switzerland and Austria; 61 sq. mi.; pop. 21,000 (est. 1969); capital, Vaduz.

lied (lēd, *Ger.* lēt) *n. pl.* **lied·er** (lē′dər) A German song; especially, a ballad or lyric poem set to music. [< G]

Lie·der·kranz (lē′dər·kränts) *n.* 1. A soft cheese similar to but milder than Limburger: a trade name. 2. A German singing society; especially, a men's choral group. Also **lie′·der·kranz.** [< G, lit., garland of songs]

lie detector A polygraph (def. 3) used by criminologists in attempting to establish the truth or falsity of a subject's statements under questioning.

lief (lēf) *adv.* Willingly; readily: used chiefly in the phrase **would as lief:** also, *Obs., lieve.* ◆ The comparative form **lief′er** (*Obs., liever*) has been for the most part replaced by *rather.* — *adj. Archaic* 1. Dear; beloved. 2. Willing; inclined: used chiefly in antithesis to *loath.* [OE *lēof* dear]

liege (lēj) *n.* 1. A lord or sovereign to whom allegiance or feudal service is due. 2. A vassal or subject owing allegiance to a lord or sovereign. — *adj.* 1. Entitled to feudal allegiance, as of a vassal: now used chiefly in the phrase **liege lord.** 2. Bound in vassalage or owing allegiance to a lord or sovereign. 3. Pertaining to or characteristic of the relationship between vassal and lord. [< OF < Med.L *ligius* free < *laeticus* free < *letus* freedman < OHG *ledig* free]

Li·ège (lyezh) A city in eastern Belgium; pop. 150,127 (est. 1969). Formerly **Li·ége.** Flemish *Luik.*

liege·man (lēj′mən) *n. pl.* **·men** (-mən) 1. A feudal vassal. 2. A loyal follower or subject.

Lieg·nitz (lēg′nits) The German name for LEGNICA.

lien (lēn, lē′ən) *n.* A legal right to claim or dispose of property in payment of or as security for a debt or charge. [< F, band < L *ligamen* < *ligare* to tie]

li·en·ter·y (lī′ən·ter′ē) *n. Pathol.* Diarrhea characterized by the discharge of undigested or incompletely digested food. [< F *lienterie* < Med.L *lienteria* < Gk. *leienteria* < *leios* smooth + *enteron* intestine] — **li·en·ter′ic** *adj.*

Lie·pa·ja (lye′pä·yä) A port city in SW Latvia, on the Baltic; pop. 71,464 (1967): German *Libau.* Also *Lepaya.*

li·erne (lē·ûrn′) *n. Archit.* In Gothic vaulting, a connecting rib branching from a main rib. [< F *lier* to bind, tie]

lieu (lōō) *n.* Place; stead: now only in the phrase **in lieu of** In place of or instead of. [< F < L *locus* place]

Lieut. Lieutenant.

lieu·ten·an·cy (lōō·ten′ən·sē, *Brit.* lef·ten′ən·sē, or *Brit. Naval* lə·ten′-) *n.* The office, rank, or authority of a lieutenant.

lieu·ten·ant (lōō·ten′ənt, *Brit.* lef·ten′ənt, or *Brit. Naval* lə·ten′-) *n.* 1. *Mil.* A commissioned officer holding either of two ranks, **first** or **second lieutenant,** the former ranking next below a captain. See tables at GRADE. 2. *Naval* a *U.S.* A commissioned officer holding either of two ranks, **lieutenant** or **lieutenant (junior grade),** the former ranking next below a lieutenant commander and the latter next above an ensign. b *Brit. & Canadian* A commissioned officer ranking next below a lieutenant-commander. See tables at GRADE. 3. One deputized to perform the duties of a superior, either in the latter's absence or under his direction; deputy. Abbr. (for defs. 1, 2) Lieut., LT, lt. [< F < *lieu* place + *tenant,* ppr. of *tenir* to hold]

lieutenant colonel *Mil.* An officer ranking next above a major and next below a colonel. Also *Brit. & Canadian* **lieu·ten·ant-col·on·el** (lef·ten′ənt·ker′nəl). See tables at GRADE. Abbr. Lt. Col., LtCol.

lieutenant commander *Naval* An officer ranking next above a lieutenant and next below a commander. Also

Brit. & Canadian **lieu·ten·ant-com·man·der** (lə·ten′ənt·kə·man′dər). See tables at GRADE. Abbr. *LCDR, LCdr*

lieutenant general *Mil.* An officer ranking next above a major general and next below a general. Also *Brit. & Canadian* **lieu·ten·ant-gen·er·al** (lef·ten′ənt·gen′ər·əl). See tables at GRADE. Abbr. *Lt. Gen., LtGen*

lieutenant governor 1. *U.S.* An elected official who performs the duties of the governor of a State during his absence or disability or who replaces him in case of death or resignation. 2. In the British Empire, a deputy governor of a territory under the jurisdiction of a governor general.

lieve (lēv), **liev·er** (lē′vər) *adv. Obs.* Lief, liefer.

life (līf) *n. pl.* **lives** (līvz) 1. The form of existence that distinguishes animals and plants from inorganic substances and dead organisms, characterized by the properties and functions of protoplasm as manifested in metabolism, growth, reproduction, irritability, and internally initiated adaptations of individual organisms to the environment. 2. The characteristic state or condition of an organism that has not died. 3. Existence regarded as a desirable condition: *life*, liberty, and the pursuit of happiness. 4. A spiritual state regarded as a continuation or perfection of animate existence after death: eternal *life*. 5. Living organisms collectively: *life* on Mars. 6. A living being; person: to save a *life*. 7. The period of an individual's existence between birth and death; also, a specified portion or the previous or remaining portion of this period. 8. A narrative relating the events of a person's lifetime; a biography. 9. The period during which something continues to be effective, useful, etc.: the *life* of an engine. 10. Human affairs or relationships: daily *life*. 11. Manner of existence; characteristic activities, as of a specified group, locality, etc.: city *life*. 12. A source or support of existence; essential necessity. 13. Energetic force; vitality; animation: full of *life*. 14. A source of liveliness; animating spirit: the *life* of the party. 15. A living model; also, a representation of such a model: as large as *life*. 16. *Usually cap.* In Christian Science, the divine Principle; God. **—for dear life** As though to save one's life; with urgent effort, speed, etc. **—for life** For the remainder of one's existence; until death. **—for the life of me** (**him,** etc.) Under any circumstances; at all: usually with the negative. **—not on your life** *Informal* Under no circumstances; definitely not. **—the life of Riley** *U.S. Informal* An easy and happy life; the sweet life. **—to bring to life** 1. To make vital; animate. 2. To recall vividly to the mind or senses. **—to come to life** 1. To regain consciousness. 2. To become animated. 3. To seem to be real or alive. **—to take (someone's) life** To kill (someone). [OE *līf*]

life belt A life preserver in the form of a belt.

life·blood (līf′blud′) *n.* 1. The blood necessary to life. 2. Anything indispensable to existence; vital force.

life·boat (līf′bōt′) *n.* A boat constructed and equipped for saving lives at sea in the event of shipwreck, storm, etc.; especially, such a boat carried on board a larger vessel.

life buoy A life preserver, often in the form of a ring, thrown into the water to assist a person in danger of drowning.

life class An art class using living models.

life cycle *Biol.* The entire series of processes constituting the life history of an organism.

life expectancy The probable length of life of an individual, especially as predicted statistically in terms of age, sex, physical condition, occupation, and prevailing environmental factors: distinguished from *life span*.

life·guard (līf′gärd′) *n. U.S.* An expert swimmer employed at a beach, etc., to protect the safety of bathers.

Life Guards *Brit.* Two cavalry regiments that act as a personal guard for the British sovereign. [Appar. partial trans. of G *leibgarde* < *leib* body + *garde* guard]

life history *Biol.* 1. The complete series of phenomena characterizing the existence and development of an organism from its earliest stages to its death as a mature adult. 2. An individual instance of these phenomena.

life insurance Insurance on the life of an individual, usually requiring the insured to pay regular premiums during his lifetime or for a specified period thereof, and providing payment to the beneficiary or beneficiaries named in the policy upon the death of the insured or to the insured upon reaching a certain age. Also *Brit.* **life assurance.**

life jacket A life preserver in the form of a jacket or vest.

life·less (līf′lis) *adj.* 1. Not possessing the characteristics of living organisms; inanimate. 2. Deprived of life; dead. 3. Not inhabited by or incapable of sustaining living organisms: a *lifeless* desert. 4. Lacking animation or vitality; spiritless; dull. 5. Exhibiting no signs of life; apparently dead. **—life′less·ly** *adv.* **—life′less·ness** *n.*

— Syn. *Lifeless, inanimate, dead, deceased, departed, defunct,* and *extinct* are compared as they mean without life. Something *lifeless* may never have had life, or it may have lost life; these two senses are more strictly denoted by *inanimate* and *dead* respectively. Any organism may be *dead,* but *deceased* is used only of human beings. *Departed* and *defunct* are common euphemisms for *dead,* but *defunct* is also applied to inorganic things, as social institutions. Anything that once existed but no longer does is *extinct*: an *extinct* species. **— Ant.** living, alive, animate, vigorous, active.

life·like (līf′līk′) *adj.* 1. Resembling one who or that which is alive. 2. Accurately representing actual events or circumstances. **— life′like·ness** *n.*

life line 1. A rope affording support to those in precarious situations, as bathers in surf, sailors aboard ship, etc. 2. The line used to lower or raise an underwater diver. 3. A rope shot to or across a ship in distress, to which a heavier line, breeches buoy, etc., may be attached. 4. Any route used for transporting vital supplies. 5. In palmistry, a curved line crossing the palm of the hand diagonally, allegedly indicative of the duration or events of one's life.

life·long (līf′lông′, -long′) *adj.* Lasting through life.

life mask A cast, as in plaster, of the face of a living person.

life net A strong net designed to rescue those who jump or fall from great heights, used by firemen, etc.

life preserver 1. A buoyant device, either inflatable or filled with cork, kapok, etc., and made as a belt, jacket, or ring, used to keep afloat those in danger of drowning. 2. *Brit.* A blackjack, bludgeon, or similar weapon.

lif·er (līf′ər) *n. Slang* One sentenced to prison for life.

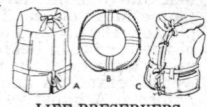

LIFE PRESERVERS
A Solid block cork.
B Cork ring buoy.
C Collar-type jacket.

life raft A raftlike structure used as a rescue craft; especially, an inflatable rubber boat equipped with oars.

life·sav·er (līf′sā′vər) *n.* 1. One who saves a life. 2. A person trained to rescue those in danger of drowning. 3. A life preserver in the form of a ring. 4. *Informal* One who or that which provides emergency aid. **— life′sav′ing** *n. & adj.*

life-size (līf′sīz′) *adj.* Having the same size as the thing or person portrayed. Also **life′-sized′.**

life span The extreme length of life regarded as biologically possible in an individual person or organism.

life style The manner in which a person or group lives, usually expressed by interests, possessions, etc.

life·time (līf′tīm′) *n.* The period of animate existence; also, the period of effective functioning: the *lifetime* of the car.

life·work (līf′wûrk′) *n.* The work of a productive lifetime.

lift (lift) *v.t.* 1. To take hold of and raise to a higher place or position; hoist. 2. To move, direct, or cause to rise to a higher position or level; elevate. 3. To hold up; support or display in the air. 4. To bring to a higher or more desirable degree or condition; cause to increase in quality, estimation, etc.; exalt. 5. To emit in loud or clearly audible tones, as the voice: to *lift* a cry. 6. To subject (the face) to surgery in order to remove signs of age: She had her face *lifted.* 7. *Informal* To take surreptitiously; steal; also, to plagiarize. 8. To take up from the ground, as seedlings. 9. *U.S.* To pay off, as a mortgage. 10. To cancel or revoke: to *lift* a ban. 11. To move or transport (goods, etc.). 12. In golf, to pick up (the ball), as from an unfavorable position. **—** *v.i.* 13. To exert effort in attempting to raise something. 14. To rise. 15. To become dispersed, cease temporarily, or move away by or as by rising: The fog *lifted.* 16. To come to a better or more desirable condition: Our spirits *lifted.* **—** *n.* 1. The act of lifting, raising, or rising; also, an instance of this. 2. The power or ability to lift. 3. The height, distance, or degree to which something rises or is raised. 4. Assistance given by or as by raising; aid in accomplishing an end. 5. A ride given to a traveler to or in the direction of his destination. 6. A feeling of exhilaration or well-being. 7. Elevated or erect position, bearing, etc.: the *lift* of her chin. 8. A machine or device used in lifting or hoisting: a ski *lift.* 9. An amount lifted or capable of being lifted; load. 10. *Brit.* A passenger or freight elevator. 11. Any of the layers of leather, etc., constituting the heel of a shoe. 12. *Informal* A theft. 13. *Aeron.* The component of aerodynamic forces acting on an aircraft, exerted at right angles to the relative wind and generally opposing the pull of gravity. 14. *Mining* **a** A vertical slice of ore removed in one set of operations. **b** A set of pumps. [ME *liften* < ON *lypta* to raise in the air. Akin to LOFT.] **— lift′er** *n.*

— Syn. (verb) 1. See ELEVATE. 7. See STEAL.

lift·off (lift′ôf′, -of′) *n. Aerospace* The vertical ascent of a rocket or spacecraft from its launching pad.

lift pump A pump that raises rather than forces a liquid to the point of ejection: distinguished from *force pump.*

lig·a·ment (lig′ə·mənt) *n.* 1. *Anat.* A band of firm, fibrous tissue forming a connection between bones, or serving to support an organ. 2. A bond or connecting tie. [< L *ligamentum* band < *ligare* to bind]

lig·a·men·tous (lig′ə·men′təs) *adj.* Pertaining to or of the nature of a ligament. Also **lig′a·men′tal, lig′a·men′ta·ry** *adj.*

li·gan (lī′gən) *n.* Lagan (which see).

li·gand (lig′ənd, lī′gənd) *n. Chem.* The molecule, ion, or group that binds the metal ion in the process of chelation.

li·gate (lī′gāt) *v.t.* **·gat·ed, ·gat·ing** To bind or constrict with a ligature. [< L *ligatus,* pp. of *ligare,* to bind, tie]

lig·a·ture (lig′ə·chŏŏr, -chər) *n.* 1. The act of tying up or constricting by binding. Also **li·ga·tion** (lī·gā′shən). 2. A band, strip, etc., used to tie, bind, or constrict. 3. *Surg.*

A thread or wire tied around a blood vessel to prevent bleeding, or around a tumor to be removed by strangulation. **4.** In printing and writing: **a** A character consisting of two or more connected letters, as æ, fi, ffi. **b** The symbol (⁀) used to indicate such a connection. **5.** *Music* A slur indicating a group of notes sung or played as a connected phrase; also, the group of notes thus indicated. — *v.t.* To ligate. [< F < L *ligatura* < *ligatus*, pp. of *ligare* to bind]

light¹ (līt) *n.* **1.** *Physics* **a** The form of radiant energy that stimulates the organs of sight, having for normal human vision wavelengths ranging from about 3900 to 7700 angstroms and traveling at a speed of about 186,300 miles a second. **b** A closely related form of radiant energy not stimulating human vision; ultraviolet or infrared light. Also called *luminous energy.* **2.** The condition or medium that makes vision possible; illumination. **3.** The sensation produced by stimulation of the organs of vision and visual centers of the brain. **4.** Any source of brightness, as a lamp, torch, the sun, etc. **5.** An emission of brightness, especially from a particular source or direction: The *light* falls obliquely. **6.** The daily illumination shed on the earth by the sun; daylight; also the period during which this illumination is visible. **7.** Mental or spiritual understanding or insight; enlightenment. **8.** The state of being unhidden and observable: to come to *light*. **9.** Way of being regarded; aspect: to see things in a new *light*. **10.** *pl.* Ability and understanding: to live according to one's own *lights*. **11.** A lively or intense expression on the face, especially in the eyes. **12.** An instance of kindling; ignition: a *light* for his cigarette. **13.** An opening admitting illumination, as a window, pane, etc. **14.** In graphic arts: **a** The representation of light or atmosphere. **b** A part of a picture showing an illuminated area. **15.** A person of authority or eminence; luminary: a lesser *light*. **16.** *Cap.* In Quakerism, the Inner Light (which see). **17.** *Archaic or Poetic* Eyesight. — **in the light of** In view of; considering. — **to see the light 1.** To come into being. **2.** To be presented to public notice. **3.** To acquire insight or understanding; become enlightened. — **to strike a light** To ignite something, as a match, by friction. — *adj.* **1.** Full of light; not dark; bright. **2.** Diluted or combined with white, as a color; pale. — *v.* **light·ed** or **lit, light·ing** *v.t.* **1.** To set burning, as wood, a fire, etc.; ignite; kindle. **2.** To cause to illuminate; set alight: *Light* the lamps. **3.** To make light; illuminate: A single lamp *lights* the room. **4.** To make bright, cheerful, animated, etc. **5.** To guide or conduct with light: The fires *lighted* him home. — *v.i.* **6.** To become ignited; start to burn. **7.** To become luminous, radiant, or bright: often with *up*. [OE *lēoht*]

light² (līt) *adj.* **1.** Having little weight; not heavy. **2.** Having little weight in proportion to bulk or size; low in specific gravity. **3.** Not in accordance with standard or correct weight; insufficiently heavy. **4.** Not burdensome or oppressive; easily borne. **5.** Not difficult or arduous; easily done. **6.** Having comparatively little effect; not intense, severe, etc. **7.** Not great in degree or concentration; thin: a *light* fog. **8.** Exerting little force or pressure; gentle: a *light* tap. **9.** Characterized by buoyancy or ease in motion; graceful. **10.** Moving or working swiftly and skillfully; agile; deft. **11.** Not clumsy, coarse, or massive in form or appearance; delicate; airy. **12.** Intended or enjoyed as entertainment; not lofty or heroic: *light* verse. **13.** Slight in importance or consequence; insignificant. **14.** Characterized by levity; frivolous; trivial. **15.** Easily distracted or diverted; flighty; fickle. **16.** Morally unrestrained; wanton. **17.** Slightly faint or delirious; dizzy; giddy. **18.** Easily eaten or digested; not rich, heavy, or fatty: *light* meals. **19.** Comparatively low in alcoholic content: *light* wines. **20.** Well-leavened; spongy or airy in texture: *light* biscuits. **21.** Crumbly in texture; friable; porous: *light* soil. **22.** Relatively swift and maneuverable; not cumbersome: a *light* cruiser. **23.** *Mil.* **a** Designating the less massive types of weapons or equipment: a *light* tank. **b** Formerly, designating troops or units with relatively less massive equipment: *light* cavalry. **24.** Producing goods relatively simple to manufacture and, when finished, ready for direct, immediate consumption: *light* industry. **25.** *Meteorol.* **a** Designating the relative velocity of air moving at a rate just beyond calm. **b** Designating a breeze moving at 4 to 7 miles per hour. See BEAUFORT SCALE. **26.** In phonetics, prosody, etc., designating an unaccented or unstressed syllable or vowel. **27.** Describing the least strong of three levels of stress used in utterances. — **to make light of** To treat or consider as trifling. — *v.i.* **light·ed** or **lit, light·ing 1.** To descend and settle down after flight, as a bird; land. **2.** To happen or come, as by chance or accident: with *on* or *upon*. **3.** To get down, as from a horse or carriage; dismount. **4.** To fall; strike, as a blow. — **to light into** *U.S. Informal* To attack; assail. — **to light out** *U.S. Informal* To depart in haste. — *adv.* **1.** Lightly. **2.** Without encumbrance or excess equipment: to travel *light*. [OE *lēoht, līht*]

light·en¹ (līt'n) *v.t.* **1.** To make light or bright; illuminate.

2. *Archaic* To enlighten. **3.** *Rare* To emit in a lightninglike flash. — *v.i.* **4.** To become light; grow brighter. **5.** To glow with light; gleam. **6.** To emit or display lightning.

light·en² (līt'n) *v.t.* **1.** To reduce the weight or load of; make less heavy. **2.** To make less oppressive, troublesome, etc.; diminish the severity of. **3.** To relieve, as of distress, uneasiness, etc.; ease. — *v.i.* **4.** To become less heavy.

light·er¹ (lī'tər) *n.* One who or that which lights; especially, a device used to light cigarettes, cigars, etc.

light·er² (lī'tər) *Naut.* *n.* A bargelike vessel used in loading or unloading ships, or in transporting loads for short distances. — *v.t. & v.i.* To transport (goods) by lighter. [< Du. *lichter* < *lichten* to make light, unload < *licht* light]

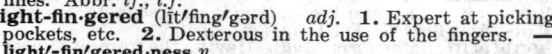

light·er·age (lī'tər·ij) *n.* **1.** The removal or conveying of cargo by lighter. **2.** A price charged for this service.

light·er-than-air (lī'tər·thən·âr') *adj.* *Aeron.* Designating aircraft, as balloons, dirigibles, etc., that depend for flight on a specific gravity less than that of air.

light·face (līt'fās') *n.* *Printing* Type having characters formed of light, thin lines. Abbr. *lf., l.f.*

LIGHTER²

light-fin·gered (līt'fing'gərd) *adj.* **1.** Expert at picking pockets, etc. **2.** Dexterous in the use of the fingers. — **light'-fin'gered·ness** *n.*

light-foot·ed (līt'foot'id) *adj.* **1.** Stepping with buoyancy and grace. **2.** Running lightly and swiftly. Also *Poetic* **light'foot'.** — **light'-foot'ed·ly** *adv.* — **light'-foot'ed·ness** *n.*

light-head·ed (līt'hed'id) *adj.* **1.** Frivolous in attitude or behavior; giddy. **2.** Slightly faint or delirious; dizzy. — **light'head'ed·ly** *adv.* — **light'head'ed·ness** *n.*

light-heart·ed (līt'här'tid) *adj.* Free from care; blithe; gay. — **light'heart'ed·ly** *adv.* — **light'heart'ed·ness** *n.*

light heavyweight A boxer or wrestler weighing between 161 and 175 pounds.

light·house (līt'hous') *n.* A tower or similar structure equipped with a powerful beacon, erected at or near a dangerous place to serve as a warning or guide for ships.

light·ing (līt'ing) *n.* **1.** The providing of light or the state of being lighted; illumination. **2.** A system or apparatus supplying illumination, as in a public building, theater, etc. **3.** The arrangement or effect of lighted areas contrasted with darker ones, as in a painting, photograph, etc.

light·ish (līt'ish) *adj.* Somewhat light.

light·less (līt'lis) *adj.* **1.** Unilluminated; dark. **2.** Providing no light.

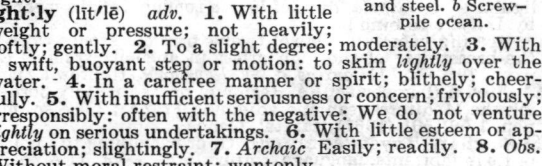

LIGHTHOUSES
a Stone or concrete and steel. *b* Screw-pile ocean.

light·ly (līt'lē) *adv.* **1.** With little weight or pressure; not heavily; softly; gently. **2.** To a slight degree; moderately. **3.** With a swift, buoyant step or motion: to skim *lightly* over the water. **4.** In a carefree manner or spirit; blithely; cheerfully. **5.** With insufficient seriousness or concern; frivolously; irresponsibly: often with the negative: We do not venture *lightly* on serious undertakings. **6.** With little esteem or appreciation; slightingly. **7.** *Archaic* Easily; readily. **8.** *Obs.* Without moral restraint; wantonly.

light meter *Photog.* An exposure meter (which see).

light-mind·ed (līt'mīn'did) *adj.* Characterized by levity or inanity; frivolous. — **light'-mind'ed·ly** *adv.*

light·ness¹ (līt'nis) *n.* **1.** The state or quality of being illuminated or bright. **2.** Paleness of color.

light·ness² (līt'nis) *n.* **1.** The condition or quality of having relatively little weight, heaviness, force, pressure, etc. **2.** Buoyancy or ease of motion; agility; grace. **3.** Freedom from sorrow or care; blitheness. **4.** Lack of seriousness.

light·ning (līt'ning) *n.* **1.** A sudden flash of light caused by the discharge of atmospheric electricity between electrified regions of cloud, or between a cloud and the earth. **2.** The discharge itself. [ME *lightening* < *lighten* to flash]

lightning arrester A device that protects electrical equipment against damage from lightning.

lightning bug *U.S.* A firefly.

lightning rod A pointed metal rod that protects buildings from lightning by grounding it harmlessly through a cable.

light opera Operetta (which see).

light quantum *Physics* A photon.

light ratio *Astron.* The factor 2.512, by which stars of successive apparent magnitudes differ in brightness.

lights (līts) *n.pl.* The lungs, especially of animals used as food. [ME *lihtes*; so called from their light weight]

light·ship (līt'ship') *n.* A vessel equipped with warning

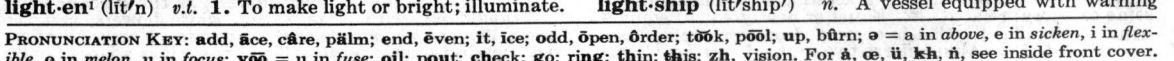

lights, signals, etc., and moored in dangerous waters as a guide to ships.

light·some[1] (līt′səm) *adj.* **1.** Giving forth light; luminous; radiant. **2.** Full of light; brightly lit.

light·some[2] (līt′səm) *adj.* **1.** Untroubled by care; cheerful; gay. **2.** Buoyant, airy, or graceful. **3.** Frivolous; flighty. — **light′some·ly** *adv.* — **light′some·ness** *n.*

light-struck (līt′struk′) *adj. Photog.* Fogged or damaged by exposure to light: said of a print, film, etc.

light·weight (līt′wāt′) *n.* **1.** A person or animal of much less than average weight. **2.** A boxer or wrestler weighing between 127 and 135 pounds. **3.** *U.S. Informal* An unimportant, incompetent, or inadequate person. — *adj.* Of less than average or required weight.

light·wood (līt′wo͝od′) *n.* Wood that burns readily, used as kindling; especially, *Southern U.S.*, the dried, resinous wood of the yellow pine.

light-year (līt′yir′) *n. Astron.* A unit of interstellar space measurement equal to the distance traversed by light in one year, approximately six trillion miles. Compare PARSEC.

lign·al·oes (līn·al′ōz, lig·nal′-) *n.* Agalloch, a wood. [< OF < L *lignum aloes* wood of aloes]

lig·ne·ous (lig′nē·əs) *adj.* Having the composition, texture, or appearance of wood. [< L *ligneus* < *lignum* wood]

ligni- *combining form* Wood: *ligniform.* Also, before vowels, **lign-.** Also **ligno-.** [< L *lignum* wood]

lig·ni·form (lig′nə·fôrm) *adj.* Having the form or appearance of wood.

lig·ni·fy (lig′nə·fī) *v.* **·fied, ·fy·ing** *v.t.* **1.** To convert into wood. — *v.i.* **2.** To be converted into wood through the formation of lignin. [< LIGNI- + -FY] — **lig′ni·fi·ca′tion** *n.*

lig·nin (lig′nin) *n. Bot.* An organic substance that, together with cellulose, constitutes the essential part of woody tissue.

lig·nite (lig′nīt) *n.* A compact, carbonized, brownish vegetable substance often retaining a woodlike structure, forming a fuel intermediate between peat and bituminous coal: also called *brown coal.* [< F] — **lig·nit′ic** (-nit′ik) *adj.*

lig·no·cel·lu·lose (lig′nō·sel′yə·lōs) *n. Bot.* A substance consisting of lignin combined with cellulose, of which the woody and fibrous parts of plants are constituted.

lig·num vi·tae (lig′nəm vī′tē) **1.** A tree (*Guaiacum* or *Guajacum officinale*) of tropical America, having hard, greenish brown, heavy wood. **2.** The wood of this tree: also called *guaiacum.* **3.** Any of various related or similar trees, as the **bastard lignum vitae** (*G. sanctum*) of tropical America. [< NL < L, wood of life]

lig·ro·in (lig′rō·in) *n. Chem.* Petroleum ether. [Origin unknown]

lig·u·la (lig′yə·lə) *n.* **1.** *Zool.* A strap-shaped organ or part: also *ligule.* **2.** *Bot.* A ligule.

lig·u·late (lig′yə·lit, -lāt) *adj.* **1.** Strap-shaped. **2.** Having a ligule or ligules.

lig·ule (lig′yo͞ol) *n.* **1.** *Bot.* **a** One of the strap-shaped ray flowers of various plants of the composite family. **b** A scale-like projection at the summit of the sheath formed by the leaf stalk around the stem in grasses: also *ligula.* **2.** *Zool.* A ligula. [< L *ligula*, dim. of *lingua* tongue; infl. in meaning by L *ligare* to bind]

lig·ure (lig′yo͝or) *n.* One of twelve precious stones worn in the breastplate of the high priest in ancient Israel. *Ex.* xxviii 19. [< LL *ligurius* < Gk. *ligyrion* < Hebrew *leshem*]

Li·gu·ri·a (li·gyo͝or′ē·ə) *n.* A Region of northern Italy bordering the Mediterranean and adjoining France; 2,088 sq. mi.; pop. 1,001,501 (1961); capital, Genoa.

Li·gu·ri·an (li·gyo͝or′ē·ən) *adj.* Of or pertaining to Liguria, or its inhabitants, language, culture, etc. — *n.* **1.** A native or inhabitant of Liguria. **2.** The Italian dialect spoken in Liguria. **3.** A member of an ancient people who inhabited northern and central Italy and adjoining regions. **4.** The extinct language of these people.

Ligurian Sea The part of the Mediterranean Sea along the coast of NW Italy.

lik·a·ble (lī′kə·bəl) *adj.* Of a nature to be liked; attractive; pleasing. Also **like′a·ble.** — **lik′a·ble·ness** *n.*

like[1] (līk) *v.* **liked, lik·ing** *v.t.* **1.** To take pleasure in; enjoy: I *like* swimming. **2.** To feel warmly or affectionately toward; be fond of: I *like* him. **3.** To wish or desire; prefer: I *like* that one. — *v.i.* **4.** To feel disposed; choose: Do as you *like.* **5.** *Archaic* To be pleasing to: with the dative: It *likes* me not. — *n. Usually pl.* Preference; inclination: chiefly in the phrase **likes and dislikes.** [OE *lician*]

like[2] (līk) *prep.* **1.** Having a close resemblance to; similar to: She is *like* her mother. **2.** With the characteristics or qualities of; in the manner of: to smell *like* a rose. **3.** Characteristic or typical of: How *like* him to behave that way! **4.** Indicative of; likely to result in: It looks *like* rain. **5.** As though having the need for; desirous of: preceded by *feel*: to feel *like* resting. **6.** Such as: cities *like* London, Rome, New York. — **like anything** (or **blazes, mad, hell,** etc.) *Informal* With great intensity, force, effort, etc. — *adj.* **1.** Having the same or similar characteristics; belonging in the same category; related. **2.** Equal or nearly equal; equivalent. **3.** Similar to what is portrayed or represented, as a portrait. **4.** *Rare* Alike: *like* as two peas. **5.** *Archaic* Bear-

ing a resemblance; similar: followed by *to* or *unto*: a sleep *like* unto death. — **like . . . , like . . .** As (the one is), so (is the other): *Like* father, *like* son. — *adv.* **1.** Dial. or *Informal* Probably: *Like* enough he'll go. **2.** Dial. or *Illit.* To a certain degree; somewhat: I'm hungry *like.* **3.** *U.S. Slang* or *Illit.* A meaningless interpolation, as before adjectives, etc.: It's *like* cool. — *n.* **1.** Anything similar or in the same category: preceded by *the*: physics, chemistry, and the *like.* **2.** One of equal value, standing, etc.: We will not see his *like* again. — **the like** (or **likes**) **of** *Informal* Anything or any-one resembling: not for *the likes* of you. — *conj.* **1.** *Informal* or *Illit.* As; in the manner that: It turned out *like* you said. **2.** *Informal* As if: It looks *like* it's going to rain. [OE *gelīc*]

♦ **like, as, as if** In formal American English, *like* is not considered acceptable as a conjunction (that is, when followed by a clause containing a verb), although this use has been defended or permitted by some grammarians. The preferred forms are: **a** *As* to introduce factual clauses of comparison: He sings *as* (not *like*) Caruso sang. **b** *As if* with the subjunctive to introduce contrary-to-fact clauses: He sings *as if* (not *like*) he were Caruso. **c** *As if* with the indicative in noncomparative factual clauses: It looks *as if* (not *like*) he means to stay. When no verb is expressed, however, *like* functions in its accepted role as a preposition: He sings *like* Caruso. *Like* is acceptable in place of *as if* when followed by a short verbless expression: It looks *like* new.

-like *suffix of adjectives* **1.** Resembling or similar to: *wave-like.* **2.** Having the characteristics of: *childlike.* [< LIKE[2]]

♦ Compounds in *-like* are usually solid, but are hyphenated when three *l*'s occur together, as in *shell-like.*

like·li·hood (līk′lē·ho͝od) *n.* **1.** The state or quality of being probable. **2.** Something probable.

like·ly (līk′lē) *adj.* **·li·er, ·li·est** **1.** Having or showing an apparent tendency or possibility; apt: followed by an infinitive: He is *likely* to go. **2.** Seemingly about to happen; imminent; probable: His promotion is *likely.* **3.** Apparently true; plausible; believable. **4.** Suitable, as for a purpose, activity, etc.; appropriate: a *likely* spot for a picnic. **5.** Capable of pleasing, being successful, etc.; promising: a *likely* lad. — Syn. See PROBABLE. — *adv.* Probably.

like-mind·ed (līk′mīn′did) *adj.* Having similar opinions, purposes, tastes, etc.

lik·en (lī′kən) *v.t.* To represent as similar; compare.

like·ness (līk′nis) *n.* **1.** The state or quality of being like; resemblance. **2.** A pictorial representation; portrait; image. **3.** Imitative form; guise.

like·wise (līk′wīz′) *adv.* **1.** Moreover; also; too. **2.** In like manner; similarly. [< LIKE[2] + -WISE]

lik·ing (lī′king) *n.* **1.** Feeling of attraction or affection; fondness. **2.** Preference; taste.

li·lac (lī′lak, -lək, -lok) *n.* **1.** A flowering shrub (genus *Syringa*) of the olive family, having panicles of numerous, fragrant purplish or white flowers; especially, the **common lilac** (*S. vulgaris*), the State flower of New Hampshire. **2.** The light pinkish purple color characteristic of the flowers of the common lilac. — *adj.* Having the characteristic purplish color of lilac blossoms. [< F < Sp. < Arabic *līlak, laylak* < Persian *līlak* bluish, var. of *nīlak*, dim. of *nīl* blue]

lil·an·geni (lil·än′gä·nē) *n.* The monetary unit of Swaziland, equivalent to 100 cents.

lil·i·a·ceous (lil′ē·ā′shəs) *adj.* Belonging to or characteristic of the lily family. [< LL *liliaceus* < L *lilium* lily]

lil·ied (lil′ēd) *adj.* Covered with or resembling lilies.

Lil·i·en·thal (lē′lē·ən·täl′), **Otto,** 1848–98, German aeronautical inventor.

Lil·ith (lil′ith) **1.** In Hebrew folklore, Adam's wife before Eve, later conceived of as a demon who stole children. **2.** In Babylonian and Assyrian legend, a female demon who haunted desolate places. [< Hebrew *Lilīth* < Assyrian-Babylonian *līlītu* of the night]

Li·li·u·o·ka·la·ni (lē·lē′ o͞o·ō·kä·lä′nē), **Lydia Kamehameha,** 1838–1917, queen of the Hawaiian Islands 1891–93.

Lille (lēl) A city in northern France; pop. 190,546 (1968).

Lil·li·bul·le·ro (lil′ē·bə·lâr′ō) A song ridiculing the Irish Catholics, popular in England at the time of the Revolution of 1688. Also **Lil′li·bur·le′ro.** [from the nonsense syllables of the refrain]

Lil·li·put (lil′ə·put, -pət) In Swift's *Gulliver's Travels* (1726), a country inhabited by a race of tiny people.

Lil·li·pu·tian (lil′ə·pyo͞o′shən) *adj.* **1.** Pertaining to Lilliput or its inhabitants. **2.** Very small; diminutive; dwarfed. — *n.* **1.** An inhabitant of Lilliput. **2.** A very small person. **3.** A petty or insignificant person.

lilt (lilt) *n.* **1.** A lively quality of speech, voice, song, etc., with pronounced variations of pitch. **2.** A light, buoyant motion or manner, as in walking. **3.** A cheerful tune. — *v.i. & v.t.* To speak, sing, move, etc., in a cheerful rhythmic manner. [ME *lulte.* Cf. Du. *lul* pipe.]

lil·y (lil′ē) *n. pl.* **·ies** **1.** Any of numerous wild or cultivated plants (genus *Lilium*) having bulbous rootstocks and showy, usually funnel-shaped flowers, as the **Madonna lily** (*L. candidum*), with large, satiny white flowers, and the **wood lily** (*L. philadelphicum*) of eastern North America, with reddish orange flowers. The lily typifies a large family

(*Liliaceae*) of perennial herbs, including the onion, hyacinth, and yucca. **2.** Any of various other plants having flowers resembling or thought to resemble those of a lily, as the calla or the water lily. **3.** The flower of any of these plants. **4.** A fleur-de-lis (defs. 1 & 2). — *adj.* Resembling a lily in whiteness, delicacy, beauty, etc.: the *lily* maid of Astolat. [OE *lilie* < L *lilium*, prob. < Gk. *leirion*]

lily iron A harpoon with a detachable head.

lil·y-liv·ered (lil'ē-liv'ərd) *adj.* Cowardly; fainthearted.

lil·y-of-the-val·ley (lil'ē-əv-thə-val'ē) *n. pl.* **lil·ies-of-the-valley** A perennial herb (*Convallaria majalis*) of the lily family, having small, fragrant white flowers borne in a one-sided raceme. Also **lily of the valley.**

lily pad One of the large, floating leaves of the water lily.

lil·y-white (lil'ē-hwīt') *adj.* **1.** White as a lily. **2.** *U.S.* Pertaining to or denoting organizations, political groups, etc., practicing discrimination against Negroes. Also **lily white.**

Lim. Limerick.

Li·ma (lē'mə, *Sp.* lē'mä *for def. 1*; lī'mə *for def. 2*) **1.** The capital of Peru, in the western part; pop. 2,541,300 (est. 1970). **2.** A city in western Ohio; pop. 53,734.

li·ma bean (lī'mə) **1.** A species (*Phaseolus limensis*) of the common bean, cultivated in many varieties, and having large, flat, edible seeds. **2.** The seed of this plant, commonly eaten as a vegetable. Also **Lima bean.** [after *Lima*, Peru]

lim·a·cine (lim'ə-sin, -sīn, lī'mə-) *adj. Zool.* Of, pertaining to, or characteristic of slugs (genus *Limax*) or similar, closely related gastropods. [< L *limax, -acis* slug]

limb¹ (lim) *n.* **1.** A part of the animal or human body attached to but distinct from the torso, and used in locomotion, holding, etc., as an arm, leg, or wing. **2.** One of the major divisions of a tree trunk; a large branch. **3.** An extended or branching part, division, etc. **4.** A person or thing regarded as a part, member, or representative of a larger body, group, etc. **5.** *Archaic Informal* A mischievous child; young rascal. — **limb of the law** **1.** A policeman. **2.** A lawyer. — **out on a limb** *U.S. Informal* In a risky, vulnerable, or questionable position. — *v.t. Rare* To dismember. [OE *lim*] — **limb'less** *adj.*

limb² (lim) *n.* **1.** *Astron.* The edge of the disk of the sun, moon, or other heavenly body. **2.** The graduated, curved edge of a quadrant or similar device. **3.** *Bot.* The spreading or expanded portion of a corolla, petal, leaf, or leaflike part. [< F *limbe* < L *limbus* edge, border] — **lim'bic** *adj.*

lim·bate (lim'bāt) *adj. Bot.* Bordered, as with a different color: a *limbate* leaf. [< LL *limbatus* < *limbus* border]

limbed (limd) *adj.* **1.** Having limbs. **2.** Having or characterized by a (specified kind of) limb or (a specified number of) limbs: used in combination: *strong-limbed; four-limbed.*

lim·ber¹ (lim'bər) *adj.* **1.** Bending or flexing easily; pliant; flexible. **2.** Able to bend or move easily; lithe and agile; supple. — *v.t.* **1.** To make pliant: often with *up.* — *v.i.* **2.** To exercise so as to become limber: with *up.* [Origin uncertain] — **lim'ber·ly** *adv.* — **lim'ber·ness** *n.*

lim·ber² (lim'bər) *n. Mil.* A two-wheeled, detachable vehicle at the forepart of a gun carriage, formerly used to transport ammunition. — *v.t. & v.i.* To attach a limber to (a gun): often with *up.* [Origin uncertain. Cf. F *limonière* < *limon* shaft.]

LIMBER²

lim·ber³ (lim'bər) *n. Often pl. Naut.* A lengthwise gutter or series of holes on each side of the keelson, permitting water to pass into the pump well. [? < F *lumière* hole, opening, lit., light]

lim·bo¹ (lim'bō) *n. pl.* **-bos** **1.** *Theol.* A region on the edge of hell for the souls of the righteous who died before the coming of Christ, and those of infants who die before baptism. **2.** A place or condition for the relegation of unwanted or forgotten persons, things, etc. **3.** A prison. [< L *limbus* border, *in limbo* on the border]

lim·bo² (lim'bō) *n. pl.* **-bos** A dance popular in the West Indies, in which dancers pass under a bar placed at successively lower levels. [Origin uncertain]

Lim·bourg (lim'bûrg, *Fr.* laṅ-bōōr') A Province of NE Belgium; 930 sq. mi.; pop. 563,645 (est. 1959); capital, Hasselt: Flemish *Limburg.*

Lim·burg (lim'bûrg, *Du.*, Flemish lim'bûrkh) **1.** A Province of the SE Netherlands; 857 sq. mi.; pop. 882,386 (est. 1959); capital, Maastricht. **2.** The Flemish name for LIMBOURG.

Lim·burg·er cheese (lim'bûr·gər) A soft, white cheese having a strong odor and flavor. Also **Lim'burg cheese.** **Lim'burg·er.** Also **lim'burg·er.** [after *Limburg*, Belgium]

lim·bus (lim'bəs) *n. pl.* **-bi** (-bī) A border or contrasting edge. [< L, border]

lime¹ (līm) *n.* **1.** A white, earthy substance, calcium oxide, CaO, prepared by calcining limestone or other forms of calcium carbonate, and extensively used in mortars and cements. When dry it is called **quicklime** or **unslaked lime,** becoming **slaked lime** (calcium hydroxide) upon the addition of water. **2.** *Archaic* Birdlime (which see). — *v.t.* **limed, lim·ing** **1.** To treat, mix, or spread with lime. **2.** *Archaic* To daub with birdlime. **3.** *Archaic* To catch or ensnare with or as with birdlime. **4.** *Archaic* To cement. [OE *līm*]

lime² (līm) *n.* **1.** A small, green, lemonlike citrus fruit whose aromatic juice is used for flavoring, in beverages, etc. **2.** The tropical tree (*Citrus aurantifolia*) yielding this fruit. [< F < Sp. *lima* < Arabic *limah.* Akin to LEMON.]

lime³ (līm) *n.* The European linden. See under LINDEN. Also **lime tree.** [Earlier *line* < OE *lind* linden]

Lime·house (līm'hous') A slum district of Stepney, east London, on the Thames.

lime·kiln (līm'kil', -kiln') *n.* A kiln in which limestone, seashells, etc., are burned to produce lime.

lime·light (līm'līt') *n.* **1.** Public attention or notice; conspicuousness: usually in the phrase **in the limelight. 2.** A bright light used to illuminate a performer, stage area, etc., and originally produced by heating lime to incandescence.

li·men (lī'mən) *n. pl.* **li·mens** or **lim·i·na** (lim'ə-nə) A threshold (def. 3). [< L, threshold]

lim·er·ick (lim'rik, -ə·rik) *n.* A humorous verse of five anapestic lines, of which the first, second, and fifth have three accents and rhyme with each other, and the third and fourth have two accents and rhyme with each other. Also **Lim'er·ick.** [? from the line "Will you come up to *Limerick*," sung after recitation of witty verse]

Lim·er·ick (lim'rik, -ə·rik) *n.* A county in central Munster province, Ireland; 1,037 sq. mi.; pop. 133,350 (1969), capital, Limerick; pop. 50,786.

Li·mes (lī'mēz, lē'mes) *n.* A Roman boundary fortified against the Germans. Also **Li'mes Ger·man·i·cus** (jər·man'i·kəs). [< L *limes* border]

lime·stone (līm'stōn') *n.* A sedimentary rock composed wholly or in part of calcium carbonate.

lime·wa·ter (līm'wô'tər, -wot'ər) *n.* An aqueous solution of calcium hydroxide, used in medicine.

lime·y (lī'mē) *n. pl.* **lime·ys** *U.S. Slang* **1.** A British sailor. **2.** Any Englishman. [from the former British maritime practice of drinking *lime* juice to prevent scurvy]

li·mi·co·line (li-mik'ə·līn, -lin) *adj.* Dwelling on shores. [< LL *limicola* dweller in mud < *limus* mud + *colere* to dwell]

li·mi·co·lous (li-mik'ə·ləs) *adj.* Living in mud, as certain worms.

lim·i·nal (lim'ə·nəl) *adj.* Of, relating to, or occurring at the limen or threshold (def. 3).

lim·it (lim'it) *n.* **1.** The furthest or utmost extent, range, demarcation, degree, etc., beyond which an activity, power, or function cannot or may not proceed: one's *limit* of endurance; the *limit* of jurisdiction. **2.** *Usually pl.* The boundaries or extent of a specified area: city *limits.* **3.** An amount or quantity established as the greatest permissible, as for a hunter's or fisherman's take, for individual expenses, etc. **4.** *Math.* A definite quantity or value that a series is conceived or proved to approach but never reach. **5.** In certain games, as poker, the largest amount that may be bet at one time. **6.** *Obs* A region or area enclosed within or as within boundaries. — **Syn.** See BOUNDARY. — **off limits** Forbidden to military personnel except on official business. — **the limit** *Informal* **1.** One who or that which tries one's patience, credulity, etc., to the utmost. **2.** To the utmost or most outrageous extent: usually with *go.* — *v.t.* To set a bound or bounds to; keep within a limit; confine; restrict. [< L *limes, limites*] — **lim'it·a·ble** *adj.* — **lim'i·ta·tive** (lim'ə·tā'tiv) *adj.* — **lim'it·er** *n.*

lim·i·tar·y (lim'ə·ter'ē) *adj.* **1.** Situated at a boundary. **2.** Restricted by or as by a limit; limited.

lim·i·ta·tion (lim'ə·tā'shən) *n.* **1.** That which limits; restriction; especially, something that restricts short of a normal or desired range; shortcoming: His temper is a *limitation.* **2.** The act of limiting, or the state of being limited. **3.** *Law* **a** A restrictive condition or stipulation. **b** A legally fixed period within which certain acts must be performed if they are to be valid. [< L *limitatio, -onis*]

lim·it·ed (lim'it·id) *adj.* **1.** Confined within, defined by, or specified according to a limit or limits; restricted: a *limited* area. **2.** Falling short of fullness or impressiveness: a *limited* success. **3.** Having powers restricted or modified by constitutional law or authority, as a government. **4.** Of a train, bus, etc., making few stops and carrying no more than a specified number of passengers, usually at a higher fare. **5.** *Chiefly Brit. & Canadian* Restricted in liability to the amount invested by shareholders in its stock: a *limited* company. — *n.* A limited train, bus, etc. Abbr. *Ld., ltd., Ltd.* — **lim'it·ed·ly** *adv.* — **lim'it·ed·ness** *n.*

limited edition An edition of a book, often specially printed and bound, of which only a set number are published.

limited monarchy See under MONARCHY.

lim·it·ing (lim'it·ing) *adj. Gram.* Denoting adjectives that designate, restrict, or indicate the number or quantity of the nouns they modify, rather than describe them, as *these* words, *another* example, *seven* swans.

lim·it·less (lim′it·lis) *adj.* Having no limit; boundless; immeasurable.

limn (lim) *v.t.* **1.** *Archaic* To draw or paint; also, to describe in words. **2.** *Obs.* To illuminate, as manuscripts. [ME *limnen* < *luminen* < OF *enluminer* < L *illuminare*] — **lim·ner** (lim′nər) *n.*

lim·net·ic (lim·net′ik) *adj. Ecol.* Pertaining to or dwelling in marshes, lakes, or ponds, as certain plants and animals. [< Gk. *limnētes* marsh-dwelling < *limnē* lake, marsh]

lim·nol·o·gy (lim·nol′ə·jē) *n.* The scientific study of bodies of fresh water, as lakes and ponds, with special reference to plant and animal life. [< Gk. *limnē* lake + -LOGY] — **lim′no·log′i·cal** *adj.* — **lim·nol′o·gist** *n.*

Li·moges (lē·mōzh′, *Fr.* lē·môzh′) *n.* A type of fine porcelain manufactured at Limoges, France. Also **Limoges ware.**

Li·moges (lē·mōzh′, *Fr.* lē·môzh′) A city in west central France; pop. 127,605 (1968).

lim·o·nene (lim′ə·nēn) *n. Chem.* One of two optically different aromatic terpenes, $C_{10}H_{16}$, occurring in various essential oils, as of oranges, lemons, etc. [< NL *Limonum* lemon (generic name) + -ENE]

li·mo·nite (lī′mə·nīt) *n.* An amorphous, brown or yellowish hydrous ferric oxide, $FeO(OH) \cdot H_2O$, occurring extensively in soil and rocks. [< Gk. *leimōn* meadow + -ITE²] — **li′mo·nit′ic** (-nit′ik) *adj.*

Li·mou·sin (lē·mōō·zaṅ′) A region and former province of central France.

lim·ou·sine (lim′ə·zēn′, lim′ə·zēn) *n.* **1.** A large automobile, originally having a closed compartment for passengers and an open driver's seat under a projecting roof. **2.** A large automobile used commercially as a passenger vehicle. [< F, a hood worn in *Limousin*]

limp¹ (limp) *v.i.* **1.** To walk with a halting or irregular step, as with an injured leg or foot. **2.** To progress in an irregular, defective, or labored manner. — *n.* The manner of walking of one who is lame; halting or irregular gait or progress. [Verbal development from OE *lemphealt* lame.] — **limp′er** *n.*

limp² (limp) *adj.* **1.** Lacking stiffness or firmness; flabby. **2.** Lacking force or vigor; weak. [Origin uncertain. Cf. ON *limpa* weakness.] — **limp′ly** *adv.* — **limp′ness** *n.*

lim·pet (lim′pit) *n.* Any of various small marine gastropods (*Acmaea* and related genera) with conical shells, noted for the tenacity with which they cling to rocks. [OE *lempedu* < LL *lampreda* limpet, lamprey]

lim·pid (lim′pid) *adj.* **1.** Characterized by liquid or crystalline clearness; transparent. **2.** Characterized by clarity, lucidity, or purity, as of style. — **Syn.** See CLEAR. [< L *limpidus* clear] — **lim·pid·i·ty** (lim·pid′ə·tē), **lim′pid·ness** *n.* — **lim′pid·ly** *adv.*

limp·kin (limp′kin) *n.* A wading bird (*Aramus guarauna*) of semitropical and tropical America, having a strident voice: also called *courlan.* [< LIMP¹ + KIN; from its walk]

Lim·po·po (lim·pō′pō) A river in South Africa, Bechuanaland, and Mozambique, flowing about 1,000 miles, generally east, to the Indian Ocean: also *Crocodile.*

lim·u·loid (lim′yə·loid) *adj.* Pertaining to or resembling the horseshoe crab. — *n.* A horseshoe crab. [< LIMULUS]

lim·u·lus (lim′yə·ləs) *n. pl.* **·li** (-lī) A horseshoe crab. [< L, dim. of *limus* sidelong, askance]

lim·y (lī′mē) *adj.* **lim·i·er, lim·i·est** Containing or resembling lime.

lin. **1.** Lineal. **2.** Linear.

lin·age (lī′nij) *n.* **1.** The number of lines in a piece of written or printed matter. **2.** Alignment. Also *lineage.*

lin·a·lo·ol (lin·al′ō·ōl, lin′ə·lōōl′) *n. Chem.* An unsaturated alcohol, $C_{10}H_{17}OH$, found in the essential oils of certain plants, as the bergamot. [< *linaloa*, a scented Mexican wood < Sp. *linaloe.* Cf. LIGNALOES.]

Linc. or **Lincs.** or **Lincs** Lincolnshire.

linch·pin (linch′pin′) *n.* A pin placed through the end of an axle in order to keep a wheel from sliding off. [OE *lynis* linchpin + PIN]

Lin·coln (ling′kən) *n.* A breed of sheep similar to the Leicester. [after *Lincoln*, England]

Lin·coln (ling′kən) **1.** The capital of Nebraska, in the SE part; pop. 149,518. **2.** Lincolnshire.

Lin·coln (ling′kən), **Abraham**, 1809–65, U.S. statesman; 16th president of the United States 1861–65; assassinated. — **Benjamin**, 1733–1810, American Revolutionary general. — **Mary**, 1818–82, *née* Todd, wife of Abraham Lincoln.

Lincoln green A green cloth. [after *Lincoln*, England]

Lincoln Park A city in SE Michigan, near Detroit; pop. 52,984.

Lin·coln's Birthday (ling′kənz) February 12, the anniversary of Abraham Lincoln's birth, a holiday in many States of the United States.

Lin·coln·shire (ling′kən·shir) A county in NE England; 2,663 sq. mi.; pop. 519,500 (1976); county seat, Lincoln, pop. 73,100. Also **Lincs.** Shortened form **Lincs** (lingks).

Lincoln's Inn A London legal society, or the set of buildings occupied by it. See INNS OF COURT.

Lind (lind), **Jenny**, 1820–87, Swedish soprano: called **the Swedish Nightingale.**

Lind·bergh (lind′bûrg), **Charles Augustus**, 1902–74. U.S. aviator; made the first solo transatlantic flight, 1927.

lin·den (lin′dən) *n.* Any of various shade trees (genus *Tilia*) having soft, white wood, heart-shaped leaves, and fragrant, cream-colored flowers; especially, the **American linden** (*T. americana*), also called *basswood, wicopy,* and the **European linden** (*T. europaea*), also called *lime, lime tree.* [OE, orig. adj. < *lind* linden, lime tree]

Lin·den (lin′dən) A city in NE New Jersey; pop. 41,409.

Lind·say (lin′zē), **(Nicholas) Vachel**, 1879–1931, U.S. poet.

line¹ (līn) *n.* **1.** A slender, continuous mark or indentation, as that drawn by a pen, pencil, or pointed tool. **2.** Any narrow band or strip resembling such a mark, as a streak, seam, or furrow. **3.** A wrinkle or crease in the skin, especially on the face or palm of the hand. **4.** Contour or profile, as of the edge of an area or outline of a mass. **5.** A division or boundary marked or conceived to exist between adjoining areas; border: the county *line.* **6.** A demarcation or limit separating contrasting concepts, kinds of behavior, etc.: the *line* between good and evil. **7.** A number of persons or things aligned so as to form a continuous, connected series; row. **8.** A chronological succession of persons related by or as by direct descent: the royal *line.* **9.** A row of written or printed words, as those across the width of a page or a column. **10.** A short letter; note. **11.** A single row of words forming a verse, as of a stanza. **12.** Course of movement or progress in or as in a line; path; route: *line* of march. **13.** Course of action, thought, or performance; method: a *line* of thought. **14.** *Often pl.* General plan or concept, as of form, content, etc.: a work on heroic *lines.* **15.** Alignment; agreement; accord: to bring discrepancies into *line.* **16.** Scope or field of activity, ability, etc.: that work is not in my *line.* **17.** Kind of work; occupation; business. **18.** Merchandise of a particular sort, as that sold by a manufacturer or dealer. **19.** *pl.* The words of an actor's or performer's part. **20.** *pl. Brit.* A certificate of marriage. **21.** *pl.* Lot in life; luck: used chiefly in the expression **hard lines.** **22.** *Biol.* A selectively bred strain of plants and animals. **23.** *U.S. Slang* A glib manner of speech intended to ingratiate or persuade. **24.** A pipe, conduit, or system of channels serving to convey liquids, gas, electricity, etc., to another place. **25.** In telephonic communication, etc.: **a** A wire or cable carrying power signals between stations. **b** A system of such connections. **c** A connection or channel of communication provided by such a system: to keep a *line* open. **26.** Any system of public transportation consisting of conveyances traveling over an established route or routes. **27.** The roadbed, track, or system of tracks of a railroad. **28.** A rope, string, cord, or the like; as: a *Naut.* Any rope, cable, etc., used for a specific purpose. **b** A wire, tape, etc., used for taking measurements, as in surveying. **c** A cord or string used for catching fish. **29.** *Math.* **a** The theoretical trace or course of a moving point, conceived of as having length, but no other dimension. **b** A line such that, when any part of it is superimposed on any other part, there will be no divergence between the parts: also **straight line.** **30.** *Geog.* **a** Any circle or arc conceived as plotted on the earth's surface for purposes of measurement or computation. **b** The equator. **31.** In the arts: **a** The representation of form by the use of strokes, rather than by shading or coloring. **b** The distinctive form or contours of any artistic creation. **32.** *Music* One of the parallel horizontal strokes that form the musical staff. **33.** *Telecom.* One of the narrow bands produced by the process of scanning. **34.** In advertising, an agate line (which see). **35.** *Mil.* **a** A trench or rampart. **b** A system of fortifications presenting an extended front. **c** *Often pl.* The disposition of troops in relation to enemy positions: the front *lines.* **d** An arrangement of soldiers, tanks, etc., aligned abreast rather than one behind the other. **e** The combatant forces, as distinguished from the supporting services and the staff. **36.** In the naval services, those officers in charge of combat operations. **37.** In football: **a** The line of scrimmage. See under SCRIMMAGE. **b** The linemen collectively. **38.** In bridge, a horizontal division of the score, separating points counting toward game, written below it, and bonus points, written above it. **39.** *Canadian* In Ontario, a concession road. *Abbr.* **l., L.** — **in line 1.** So as to form a line or row. **2.** In accordance with accepted standards or limitations: to keep prices *in line.* — **in line for** Next in order for; in the running for: *in line for* a promotion. — **on a line** At the same level; evenly aligned. — **on the line** Paid directly and promptly: cash *on the line.* — **out of line 1.** Not in conformity with accepted standards or practices. **2.** Insubordinate; unruly. — **to get a line on** *U.S. Informal* To acquire information about. — **to hold the line 1.** To maintain a defense or opposition; take a firm stand: *to hold the line* against high prices. **2.** To wait while maintaining an open telephone connection. **3.** In football, to prevent the opposing team from gaining ground. — *v.* **lined, lin·ing** *v.t.* **1.** To mark with lines; put lines upon. **2.** To place in a line; bring into alignment. **3.** To form a row or line along; border; edge: Statues *lined* the walk. **4.** To indicate by or as by lines; sketch: often with *in*: to *line* in the details. **5.** In baseball, to bat (a ball, hit, etc.) in an approximately horizontal trajectory: to *line* a single to center field. — *v.i.* **6.** To form a line; assume positions in a line: usually with *up*. — **to line out 1.** In baseball, to be retired by hitting a line drive that is caught. **2.** *U.S. Informal* To sing (a song). — **to line up 1.** To form a line. **2.** To bring into alignment. **3.** To rally, as in support of or opposition to an individual, issue, etc.; take a stand. **4.** To gather; marshal: to *line up* the facts. **5.** To compare, as for evaluation: How do the candidates *line up*? [OE *līne* cord; infl. by F *ligne* < L *linea* linen thread < *linum* flax]

line² (līn) *v.t.* **lined, lin·ing 1.** To put a covering or facing, usually of a different material, on the inner surface of. **2.** To constitute an inner covering or surface for: Tapestries *lined* the room. **3.** To fill or encrust, as with money, food, etc. **4.** To reinforce the back of (a sewed book) with fabric, paper, etc. — *n. Obs.* Flax fiber or thread. [OE *līn* flax]

lin·e·age¹ (lin′ē·ij) *n.* **1.** Line of descent from a progenitor; ancestry; pedigree. **2.** Those descended from the same ancestor; family; stock. [< OF *lignage* < L *linea* line]

line·age² (lī′nij) See LINAGE.

lin·e·al (lin′ē·əl) *adj.* **1.** Being or occurring in the direct line of descent or ancestry: a *lineal* descendant. **2.** Pertaining to or based upon direct descent or ancestry: a *lineal* prerogative. **3.** Consisting of lines; linear. Abbr. *lin.* [< L *linealis* < *linea* line] — **lin′e·al·ly** *adv.*

lin·e·a·ment (lin′ē·ə·mənt) *n.* **1.** A facial contour or feature. **2.** A distinguishing characteristic. [< L *lineamentum* < *linea* line]

lin·e·ar (lin′ē·ər) *adj.* **1.** Of or pertaining to a line or lines. **2.** Characterized by extension, direction, or motion along a line: *linear* perspective. **3.** Involving extension in one dimension only; pertaining to length. **4.** Composed of or using lines. **5.** Resembling a line or narrow strip. **6.** *Bot.* Narrow and elongated with parallel margins, as leaves. Abbr. *lin.* [< L *linearis* < *linea* line] — **lin′e·ar·ly** *adv.*

Linear A, Linear B See under MINOAN.

linear accelerator *Physics* An accelerator that drives electrons and other charged particles through a long vacuum tube by pulsed electric fields of very high frequency.

linear equation *Math.* An equation in which all variables are in the first degree only, and which takes the form of a straight line when plotted on the Cartesian coordinate system, as $5x + 8y - 3 = 0$.

linear measure 1. Measurement by length. **2.** A unit or system of units for measuring length. See table inside back cover.

linear perspective In painting, drawing, etc., a perspective in which the appearance of distance is achieved by means of converging lines.

lin·e·ate (lin′ē·it, -āt) *adj.* Marked with lines; striated; striped. Also **lin′e·at′ed** (-āt′id). [< L *lineatus*, pp. of *lineare* to make into a straight line]

lin·e·a·tion (lin′ē·ā′shən) *n.* **1.** A marking or pattern of lines. **2.** A contour or outline. **3.** Division into lines.

line·back·er (līn′bak′ər) *n.* In football, a defensive player stationed just behind the linemen. — **line′back′ing** *n.*

line-breed (līn′brēd′) *v.t.* **-bred, -breed·ing** *Biol.* To subject to line breeding.

line breeding *Biol.* Inbreeding to develop selected characteristics in a given line of stock.

line drive In baseball, a batted ball that travels in an approximately horizontal trajectory: also called *liner*.

line engraving 1. An engraving made from a metal plate on which the design to be reproduced is formed by incised lines. **2.** The process of making such engravings.

Line Islands (līn) A Pacific island group south of Hawaii, divided between the United States and Great Britain: also *Equatorial Islands.*

line·man (līn′mən) *n. pl.* **·men** (-mən) **1.** A man who installs, maintains, or repairs telephone lines or electric power lines: also *linesman.* **2.** A man employed by a railroad to inspect and maintain the track. **3.** In football, a center, guard, tackle, or end. **4.** In surveying, a man who holds the line, tape, or chain.

lin·en (lin′ən) *n.* **1.** A fabric woven from the fibers of flax. **2.** Articles or garments made of linen, or formerly made of linen but now often of cotton: bed *linen*; table *linen*. — *adj.* **1.** Made of the textile fiber of flax. **2.** Made of linen. [OE *līnen* made of flax < *līn* flax]

linen draper *Brit.* A retail dealer in dry goods.

linen paper Paper made from linen rags; also, paper similar to or imitating this.

line officer An officer of a combat branch of the service.

line of force *Physics* A hypothetical line in a field of force, coinciding at every point with the direction and intensity of the field.

line of vision The hypothetical straight line extending between the central fovea of the retina and the point to which vision is directed. Also **line of sight.**

lin·e·o·late (lin′ē·ə·lāt) *adj. Biol.* Marked with fine lines or striations. [< L *lineola*, dim. of *linea* line + -ATE¹]

lin·er¹ (lī′nər) *n.* **1.** A ship or airplane operated by a transportation line; especially, a transoceanic passenger ship. **2.** In baseball, a line drive. **3.** One who or that which marks or produces lines.

lin·er² (lī′nər) *n.* **1.** One who makes or fits linings. **2.** Something used as a lining, as a removable shell made to fit inside a helmet, ornamental container, etc.

lines·man (līnz′mən) *n. pl.* **·men** (-mən) **1.** In certain games, as tennis, an official making decisions on play at the lines of the court. **2.** In football, the official supervising the sidelines and marking the distances gained or lost in each play. **3.** A lineman (def. 1).

line squall *Meteorol.* A squall or series of squalls occurring along a cold front and usually marked by sudden changes in wind direction.

line storm *U.S. Dial.* An equinoctial (def. 1).

line-up (līn′up′) *n.* **1.** An arrangement of persons or things in a line. **2.** In sports: **a** The formation of players in a team game, as football or hockey, when drawn up for action. **b** The players in such a formation. **c** A list of the team members playing at the start of a game. **3.** In police work, a row of possible criminal suspects displayed for purposes of identification. **4.** A group of persons, organizations, etc., having a common purpose or occupation. Also **line′up′.**

lin·ey (lī′nē) See LINY.

ling¹ (ling) *n. pl.* **ling** or **lings 1.** A codlike food fish (*Molva molva*) of the North Atlantic. **2.** Any of various related or similar fishes, especially the burbot. [? < Du. *leng* or OE *lengu* length]

ling² (ling) *n.* The heather (def. 1). [< ON *lyng*] — **ling′y** *adj.*

-ling¹ *suffix of nouns* **1.** Little; young: *duckling*. **2.** Minor; petty: often used contemptuously: *princeling*. **3.** A person or thing related to or characterized by: *worldling*. [OE]

-ling² *suffix* Forming adverbs and adjectives: **1.** (from nouns) Toward: *sideling*. **2.** (from adjectives) Being; becoming: *darkling*. Also **-lings.** [OE -*ling*, -*linga*]

ling. Linguistics.

lin·gam (ling′gəm) *n.* A phallus or phallic symbol, used extensively in the cult worship of Siva. Also **lin′ga** (-gə). [< Skt. *lingam*, lit., symbol]

Lin·ga·yen Gulf (ling′gä·yen′) An inlet of the South China Sea in western Luzon, Philippines.

lin·ger (ling′gər) *v.i.* **1.** To stay on as if reluctant to leave; delay going; tarry. **2.** To proceed in a slow or dilatory manner; dawdle; loiter: to *linger* on the way. **3.** To continue to exist; endure; persist: often with *on*: The melody *lingers* on. **4.** To continue to live although ill, weak, suffering, etc. **5.** To pause or dwell with interest, pleasure, etc.: usually with *over*. **6.** To be tardy or hesitant in acting: procrastinate. — *v.t.* **7.** To spend or waste (time, one's life, etc.) idly or wearisomely: with *away* or *out*. **8.** *Rare* To prolong: protract: with *out*. — **Syn.** See ABIDE. [Northern ME *lenger*, freq. of OE *lengan* to delay. Akin to LONG.] — **lin′ger·er** *n.*

lin·ge·rie (län′zhə·rē, län′zhə·rā′, *Fr.* laṅ·zhrē′) *n.* Women's light undergarments, nightgowns, etc., originally of linen, now of silk, rayon, nylon, etc. [< F; collective noun formed from *linge* linen]

lin·ger·ing (ling′gər·ing) *adj.* **1.** Protracted; drawn out. **2.** Long-lasting; enduring. **3.** Slow. — **lin′ger·ing·ly** *adv.*

lin·go (ling′gō) *n. pl.* **·goes 1.** Language: used contemptuously or humorously of a tongue one does not understand. **2.** The specialized vocabulary and idiom of a profession, class, etc.: medical *lingo*. [< Pg. < L *lingua* tongue] — **Syn. 2.** cant, jargon, argot.

lin·gua (ling′gwə) *n. pl.* **·guae** (-gwē) The tongue, or a tonguelike part. [< L]

lingua fran·ca (ling′gwə frang′kə) **1.** Any jargon or pidgin used as a commercial or trade language, as pidgin English and Chinook jargon. **2.** A mixture of French, Spanish, Italian, Greek, and Arabic, spoken in Mediterranean ports: also called *sabir*. [< Ital., lit., language of the Franks; prob. infl. by *franco* rough and ready]

lin·gual (ling′gwəl) *adj.* **1.** Pertaining to the tongue or a tonguelike part. **2.** Pertaining to or characterized by the use of the tongue in utterance. — *n. Phonet.* A sound articulated chiefly with the tongue, as (t), (d), and (l). [< Med.L *lingualis* < L *lingua* tongue]

Lin·guet·ta (lēng·gwet′tä), **Cape** A promontory in SW Albania: also *Cape Glossa.*

lin·gui·form (ling′gwi·fôrm) *adj.* Tongue-shaped. [< L *lingua* tongue + -FORM]

lin·guist (ling′gwist) *n.* **1.** One who is fluent in several languages; a polyglot. **2.** A student of or specialist in linguistics. [< L *lingua* tongue, language + -IST]

lin·guis·tic (ling·gwis′tik) *adj.* **1.** Of or pertaining to language. **2.** Pertaining to linguistics. Also **lin·guis′ti·cal.** — **lin·guis′ti·cal·ly** *adv.*

linguistic atlas A dialect atlas (which see).

linguistic form Any unit of speech that has meaning, as an affix, word, phrase, sentence, etc. Compare MORPHEME.

---

linguistic geography The study of the distribution of languages and dialects among areas and peoples, with emphasis on the boundaries between distinctive features: also called *dialect geography*.

lin·guis·tics (ling-gwis'tiks) *n.pl.* (*construed as sing.*) The scientific study of language. Abbr. *ling.*

linguistic stock A family of languages, including a parent language together with all the languages and dialects derived from it.

lin·gu·late (ling'gyǝ·lāt) *adj.* 1. Having the shape of a tongue; linguiform. 2. Ligulate. [< L *lingulatus* < *lingula,* dim. of *lingua* tongue]

lin·i·ment (lin'ǝ·mǝnt) *n.* A liquid preparation rubbed on the skin to relieve pain and stiffness, as of sprains, etc. [< LL *linimentum* < L *linire* to anoint]

li·nin (lī'nin) *n. Biol.* An achromatic, filamentous substance in the nucleus of the cell, serving as a netlike framework for the chromatin. [< L *linum* flax + -IN]

lin·ing (lī'ning) *n.* 1. An inner surface, layer, or facing attached to or inserted in a garment, container, etc., as for protection, reinforcement, or warmth. 2. Any material used or adapted for such a purpose. 3. The act or process of providing an inner facing or layer. 4. Filling; contents.

lining figures *Printing* Arabic numerals aligned at their bases and uniform in height: distinguished from *hanging* or *Old Style figures.* Also, *Brit., ranging figures.*

link¹ (lingk) *n.* 1. One of the loops, rings, or interlocking parts constituting a chain. 2. A single constituent of an interrelated series, sequence, or set forming an entity: a weak *link* in his argument. 3. That which joins or connects separate parts, concepts, etc.: the *link* between science and philosophy. 4. A single sausage forming part of a connected length or string. 5. *Mech.* A movable rod connected to another part and transmitting power or motion. 6. In surveying, etc., the hundredth part of a chain, equal to 7.92 inches. Abbr. *l., L., li.* 7. *Chem.* A bond. — *v.t. & v.i.* To join or connect by or as by links; interlock; couple; unite. [ME *linke* < Scand. Cf. Icel. *hlekkr,* Sw. *länk* a link. Akin to OE *hlencan* to twist.]

link² (lingk) *n. Archaic* A torch. [Origin uncertain]

link³ (lingk) *v.i. Scot.* To walk lightly and quickly; trip.

link·age (ling'kij) *n.* 1. The act of linking, or the state of being linked. 2. A system of links; especially, a system of connected rods that transmit power or motion. 3. *Electr.* A relation between the magnetic flux through a coil and the number of turns in the coil. 4. *Genetics* Transmission of two or more traits together in inheritance as a result of the action of genes from the same chromosome. 5. A pantograph or similar device used for tracing lines.

link·boy (lingk'boi') *n.* A man or boy formerly employed to carry a torch to light the way along dark streets. Also **link·man** (-mǝn). [< LINK² + BOY]

linked (lingkt) *adj.* 1. Interlocked; connected; joined. 2. *Biol.* Exhibiting linkage.

linking verb (ling'king) *Gram.* A verb that merely connects the subject and predicate of a sentence without asserting action, especially the verbs *be, appear, become, feel, look, seem, smell, sound,* and *taste:* also called *copula.*

link motion *Mech.* A device controlling the valve of a steam engine, and operating chiefly by means of a slotted bar connected with one or two eccentric shafts. For illustration see MACHINE.

Lin·ko·ping (lin·shœ'ping) A city in SE Sweden; pop. 77,881 (1965).

links (lingks) *n.pl.* 1. A golf course. 2. *Scot.* A stretch of sandy, level ground. [OE *hlinc* slope]

link·work (lingk'wûrk') *n.* 1. A fabric, chain, etc., consisting of joined links. 2. A mechanical system consisting of links.

Lin·lith·gow (lin·lith'gō) The former name for WEST LOTHIAN. Also **Lin·lith'gow·shire** (-shir).

linn (lin) *n. Scot.* 1. A waterfall. 2. A pool, especially one into which a waterfall empties. 3. A steep ravine.

Lin·nae·us (li·nē'ǝs), **Carolus** Latinized name of **Karl von Lin·né** (lē·nā'), 1707–78, Swedish botanist and taxonomist.

Lin·ne·an (li·nē'ǝn) *adj.* 1. Pertaining to Linnaeus or his binomial system of classifying plants and animals according to genus and species. 2. Designating an obsolete system of botanical classification according to number of stamens or pistils. Also **Lin·nae'an.**

lin·net (lin'it) *n.* 1. A common fringilline songbird (*Carduelis cannabina*) of Europe, the male of which has a crimson breast and crown. 2. Any of various related or similar birds; especially, the house finch of western North America. [< OF *linette* < L *linum* flax; from its feeding on flax seeds]

lin·o·le·ic acid (lin'ǝ·lē'ik, li·nō'lē·ik) *Chem.* A fatty acid, $C_{18}H_{32}O_2$, found in linseed oil and other vegetable oils.

li·no·le·um (li·nō'lē·ǝm) *n.* A tough, durable material used as a floor covering, etc., made from a preparation of oxidized linseed oil and ground cork pressed upon canvas or burlap. [< L *linum* flax + *oleum* oil]

Li·no·type (lī'nǝ·tīp) *n.* A typesetting machine operated by a keyboard, and casting a complete line of type on a single metal piece: a trade name. Also **li'no·type.**

li·no·typ·er (lī'nǝ·tīp'ǝr) *n.* One who operates a Linotype. Also **li'no·typ·ist.**

lin·sang (lin'sang) *n.* Any of various long-tailed, carnivorous mammals (genera *Prionodon, Pardictis,* and *Poiana*) of Africa, Asia, and the East Indies. [< Javanese]

lin·seed (lin'sēd') *n.* Flaxseed (which see). [OE *linsǣd*]

linseed oil A yellowish oil made from flaxseed and used as a drying agent in the preparation of oil paints, linoleum, etc.

lin·sey-wool·sey (lin'zē·wōōl'zē) *n. pl.* **-wool·seys** 1. A coarse cloth woven of linen and wool or cotton and wool threads. 2. *Archaic* Confused nonsense; balderdash. [ME *lynsy-wolsye* < *lynsy* (? < *lin* linen + *saye* cloth) + WOOL]

lin·stock (lin'stok) *n.* A stick having one end divided to hold a match, formerly used in firing a cannon. [< Du. *lontstok* < *lont* match + *stok* stick]

lint (lint) *n.* 1. Bits of thread, fluff, etc. 2. A downy substance used as a surgical dressing. 3. *U.S.* The fibers clinging to the seeds of unginned cotton. [ME *linnet* lint < L *linteum* linen cloth < *linum* flax]

lin·tel (lin'tǝl) *n.* A horizontal part above the opening of a door or window, supporting the structure above it. [< OF < LL *lintellus, limitellus,* dim. of *limes, limitis* limit]

lint·er (lin'tǝr) *n. U.S.* A machine for removing the fibers clinging to cotton seeds after ginning.

lint·ers (lin'tǝrz) *n.pl. U.S.* The short fibers adhering to cotton seeds after ginning.

lint·white (lint'hwīt') *n. Scot.* or *Archaic* The linnet. [OE *linetwige,* lit., flaxplucker]

lint·y (lin'tē) *adj.* **lint·i·er, lint·i·est** Of, resembling, or full of lint.

lin·y (lī'nē) *adj.* **lin·i·er, lin·i·est** 1. Resembling a line; narrow. 2. Marked with lines or streaks. Also *liney.*

Lin Yu·tang (lin' yōō'täng'), 1895–1976, Chinese writer active in the United States.

Linz (lints) The capital of Upper Austria, on the Danube; pop. 205,700 (est. 1968).

li·on (lī'ǝn) *n.* 1. A large, tawny or brownish gray carnivorous mammal (*Panthera leo*) of the cat family, native to Africa and SW Asia, the adult male having a shaggy mane. ◆ Collateral adjective: *leonine.* 2. Any of various animals related or considered similar to the lion, as the mountain lion, sea lion, etc. 3. A representation of a lion as a heraldic or national symbol, especially as the national emblem of Great Britain. 4. One having qualities considered characteristic of a lion; especially, a man of noble courage, great strength, etc. 5. A prominent or notable person, especially one much sought after socially; celebrity. 6. *pl. Brit.* Places or things of interest; sights. — **the lion's share** The largest portion; an unduly large part. [< F < L *leo* < Gk. *leōn*] — **li'on·ess** (-is) *n.fem.*

LION
(About 3 feet high at shoulder and 7 feet long)

Li·on (lī'ǝn) *n.* The constellation and sign of the zodiac Leo.

Lion, Gulf of the A wide bay of the Mediterranean Sea in the southern coast of France. Also **Gulf of Lions.** French **Golfe du Lion** (gôlf dü lē·ôn').

li·on·heart·ed (lī'ǝn·här'tid) *adj.* Admirably brave.

li·on·ize (lī'ǝ·nīz) *v.* **·ized, ·iz·ing** — *v.t.* 1. To treat or regard as a celebrity. 2. *Brit.* To visit or exhibit as a place or object of interest. — *v.i.* 3. *Brit.* To go sightseeing. — **li'on·iz·a'tion** *n.* — **li'on·iz'er** *n.*

lip (lip) *n.* 1. One of the two folds of flesh that bound the mouth and serve in man as important organs of speech. ◆ Collateral adjective: *labial.* 2. A marginal part or structure resembling this, as at the opening of certain shells. 3. The rim or edge of any opening or cavity, as a wound, crater, chasm, etc. 4. The flared edge of a container, bell, etc. 5. *Slang* Brash and impudent talk; sass. 6. *Music* The shaping and control of the mouth in playing a wind instrument; embouchure. 7. *Anat.* A labium. 8. *Bot.* **a** Either of the two divisions, upper or lower, of a bilabiate corolla or calyx. **b** In orchids, a labellum. — **to button one's lip** *Slang* To stop talking; shut up. — **to hang on (someone's) lips** To listen to with rapt attention. — **to keep a stiff upper lip** To maintain one's fortitude, especially in adverse circumstances. — **to smack one's lips** To express anticipatory or remembered gusto; gloat. — *v.t.* **lipped, lip·ping** 1. To touch with the lips; apply the lips to. 2. *Rare* To utter or murmur. 3. *Music* In playing a wind instrument, to produce the correct pitch of (a tone) by adjusting the position of the lips. 4. In golf, to hit the ball just to or around the edge of (the hole). — *adj.* 1. Of, pertaining to, or applied to the lips. 2. Made or formed by the lips or a lip; labial. 3. Merely spoken; insincere; hypocritical: *lip* service. [OE *lippa*]

Lip·a·ri Islands (lip'ǝ·rē, *Ital.* lē'pä·rē) A group of volcanic islands off the NE coast of Sicily; 45 sq. mi.

lip·ase (lip'ās, lī'pās) *n. Biochem.* An enzyme that splits fats into fatty acids and glycerol. [< LIP(O)- + -ASE]

lip·id (lip'id, lī'pid) *n. Biochem.* Any of a large class of organic substances, insoluble in water and typically greasy to the touch, including the fats, waxes, and sterols. Also **lip·ide'** (lip'īd, lī'pīd). [< LIP(O)- + -ID(E)]

Li Po (lē′ bō′), 700?–762, Chinese poet. Also *Li T'ai-po.*
lipo- *combining form* Fat; fatty: *lipocyte.* Also, before vowels, **lip-.** [< Gk. *lipos* fat]
lip·o·cyte (lip′ō-sīt) *n. Biol.* A fat-bearing cell. [< LIPO- + -CYTE]
lip·oid (lip′oid) *adj.* Resembling fat. — *n. Biochem.* A fatlike substance.
li·pol·y·sis (li-pol′ə-sis) *n.* The breakdown and decomposition of fat. [< LIPO- + -LYSIS] — **lip·o·lyt·ic** (lip′ō-lit′ik) *adj.*
li·po·ma (li-pō′mə) *n. pl.* **·ma·ta** (-mə·tə) *or* **·mas** *Pathol.* A tumor, generally benign, consisting of fat cells. [< LIP(O)- + -OMA] — **li·pom·a·tous** (li-pom′ə-təs) *adj.*
lip·o·pro·te·in (lip′ō-prō′tē-in, -tēn) *n. Biochem.* Any of a class of proteins found in combination with lipids, as in blood, egg yolk, milk, etc.
Lip·pe (lip′ə) A former state of NW Germany, after 1945 in North Rhine-Westphalia.
lipped (lipt) *adj.* 1. Having a lip or lips. 2. Having or characterized by (a specified kind or number of) lips: used in combination: *tight-lipped; two-lipped.* 3. *Bot.* Labiate.
lip·pen (lip′ən) *v.t. & v.i. Scot.* To trust. [Origin uncertain]
lip·per (lip′ər) *n. Naut.* A slight rippling of the sea; also, light spray from such ripples. — *v.i.* To ripple. [? < LAP²]
Lip·pi (lip′ē, *Ital.* lēp′pē), **Filippino,** 1457–1504?, Florentine painter. — **Fra Filippo,** 1406?–69, Florentine painter and monk; father of the preceding: called **Fra Lippo Lippi.**
Lip·pi·zan·er (lip′it·sä′nər) *n.* One of a breed of horses developed in Austria, much used in exhibitions.
Lipp·mann (lip′mən), **Walter,** 1889–1974, U.S. journalist and author.
lip·py (lip′ē) *adj.* **·pi·er, ·pi·est** *Slang* Impudent; sassy.
lip-read (lip′rēd′) *v.t. & v.i.* **-read** (red), **-read·ing** (rēd′ing) To interpret (speech) by watching the movements of someone's lips.
lip reading The interpretation of speech by watching the movement of the lips, as by the deaf. — **lip reader**
lip service Devotion, homage, etc., expressed in words only; insincere tribute.
lip·stick (lip′stik′) *n.* A pastelike cosmetic, usually in the form of a small cylinder, used to color the lips.
liq. 1. Liquid. 2. Liquor.
li·quate (lī′kwāt) *v.t.* **·quat·ed, ·quat·ing** *Metall.* To heat (a metal) to melting point in order to purify it or separate it from material of higher melting points. [< L *liquatus,* pp. of *liquare* to melt] — **li·qua′tion** (li-kwā′shən) *n.*
liq·ue·fac·tion (lik′wə-fak′shən) *n.* The process of liquefying, or the state of being liquid.
liq·ue·fy (lik′wə-fī) *v.t. & v.i.* **·fied, ·fy·ing** To convert into or become liquid. Also **liq′ui·fy.** — **Syn.** See MELT. [< L *liquefacere* < *liquere* to be liquid + *facere* to make] — **liq′ue·fi′a·ble** *adj.* — **liq′ue·fi′er** *n.*
li·ques·cent (li-kwes′ənt) *adj.* Becoming or likely to become liquid; melting. [< L *liquescens, -entis,* ppr. of *liquescere,* incept. of *liquere* to become liquid] — **li·ques′cence** *n.*
li·queur (li-kûr′) *n.* A strong, usually sweetened alcoholic beverage made by infusing and distilling spirits with an aromatic fruit, seed, herb, peel, or crème flavoring: also called *cordial.* [< F < OF *licur.* Doublet of LIQUOR.]
liq·uid (lik′wid) *adj.* 1. Capable of flowing or of being poured; resembling oil, water, etc., in physical state. 2. Clear and flowing, as sounds; dulcet: *liquid* notes. 3. Clear and bright; limpid: the *liquid* gleam of her eyes. 4. Free and facile, as movement; fluent: *liquid* motion. 5. Consisting of or readily converted into cash: *liquid* assets. 6. *Physics* Consisting of molecules having free movement among themselves, but not tending to become widely separated; not gaseous or solid. 7. *Phonet.* Of consonants, produced without friction; vowellike, as (l) and (r). — *n.* 1. A substance in that state in which the molecules move freely among themselves but remain in one mass; a fluid that is not a gas. 2. *Phonet.* The sound (l) or (r), or sometimes other sonorants. Abbr. *liq.* [< F *liquide* < L *liquidus* < *liquere* to be liquid] — **liq·uid·i·ty** (li-kwid′ə-tē), **liq′uid·ness** *n.* — **liq′uid·ly** *adv.*
liquid air An extremely cold, liquid mixture of nitrogen and oxygen, obtained by subjecting air to reduced temperature and increased pressure, and used chiefly as a refrigerant.
liq·uid·am·bar (lik′wid-am′bər) *n.* 1. Any of a genus (*Liquidambar*) of trees of eastern Asia and Atlantic North America; especially, the sweet gum of eastern North America. 2. The fragrant balsam yielded by such trees. [< NL]
liq·ui·date (lik′wə-dāt) *v.* **·dat·ed, ·dat·ing** *v.t.* 1. To pay off or settle, as an obligation or debt. 2. To wind up the affairs of (a business firm, etc.) by determining the liabilities and using the assets to settle debts or obligations. 3. To convert into cash, as securities. 4. To do away with; wipe out. 5. *Slang* To kill or murder. — *v.i.* 6. To settle one's debts; go into liquidation. [< Med.L *liquidatus,* pp. of *liquidare* to make liquid or clear < L *liquidus* liquid]
liq·ui·da·tion (lik′wə-dā′shən) *n.* The act or procedure of liquidating, or the state of being liquidated. — **to go into**

liquidation Of a business firm, to settle affairs by ceasing to transact business and by realizing assets to settle debts.
liq·ui·da·tor (lik′wə-dā′tər) *n.* One who is assigned to settle the affairs of a business firm or estate undergoing liquidation.
liquid crystal A substance intermediate between liquid and solid, having the fluidity of a liquid and the optical anisotropy of a crystalline solid.
liquid fire A flammable liquid used in flamethrowers.
liq·uid·ize (lik′wi-dīz′) *v.t.* **·ized, ·iz·ing** To make liquid.
liquid measure A unit or system of units for measuring liquids. See table inside back cover.
liquid oxygen Oxygen liquefied by a reduction of temperature and an increase of pressure, used extensively to oxidize other components of rocket fuels: also called *lox.*
liq·uor (lik′ər) *n.* 1. Any alcoholic beverage; especially, distilled spirits, as whisky, brandy, rum, etc. 2. A liquid such as broth, juice, etc. 3. In pharmacy, etc., a solution, especially of a nonvolatile substance in water. Abbr. *liq.* — *v.t.* 1. *Slang* To ply or intoxicate with alcoholic drink: usually with *up.* — *v.i.* 2. To drink liquor, especially in large amounts: usually with *up.* [< OF *licor, licur* < L *liquor.* Doublet of LIQUEUR.]
liq·uo·rice (lik′ə-ris, -rish) See LICORICE.
liq·uor·ish (lik′ə-rish) See LICKERISH.
li·ra (lir′ə, *Ital.* lē′rä) *n. pl.* **li·re** (lir′ə, *Ital.* lē′rā) *or* **li·ras** (lir′əz) 1. The monetary unit of Italy, equivalent to 100 centesimi; also, a coin of this value. 2. The Turkish pound, the basic monetary unit of Turkey. See POUND¹ (def. 5c). Abbr. *l., L.* [< Ital. < L *libra* pound]
lir·i·o·den·dron (lir′ē-ō-den′drən) *n. pl.* **·dra** (-drə) One of a genus (*Liriodendron*) of Asian and North American trees of the magnolia family; especially, the tulip tree of the United States. [< NL < Gk. *leirion* lily + *dendron* tree]
lir·i·pipe (lir′ə-pīp) *n.* In medieval dress, the long tail of a clerical hood; also, any similar long streamer attached to a headdress. [< Med.L *liripipium;* ult. origin uncertain]
Lis·bon (liz′bən) The capital of Portugal, a port in the SW part on the Tagus estuary; pop. 828,000 (est. 1968). *Portuguese* **Lis·bo·a** (lēzh·bō′ə).
lisle (līl) *n.* 1. A fine twisted cotton thread used in knitting hosiery, etc. Also **lisle thread.** 2. A fabric, usually knitted, made from such thread. [after *Lisle,* now Lille, France]
Lisle (lēl) See LILLE.
lisp (lisp) *n.* 1. A speech defect or affectation in which the sibilants (s) and (z) are articulated with the tongue tip between the teeth so that the sounds produced are like (th) in *thank* and (th) in *this.* 2. The act or habit of speaking with a lisp. 3. A sound resembling a lisp. — *v.t. & v.i.* 1. To pronounce or speak with a lisp. 2. To speak in a childlike manner. [OE *āwlyspian*] — **lisp′er** *n.*
lis pen·dens (lis pen′denz) *Law* The doctrine giving a court control over the property involved in a suit until a judgment is rendered. [< L, a suit pending]
lis·some (lis′əm) *adj.* 1. Flexible; pliant; supple. 2. Moving with ease and grace; agile; lithe. Also **lis′som.** [Alter. of LITHESOME] — **lis′some·ly** *adv.* — **lis′some·ness** *n.*
list¹ (list) *n.* 1. An itemized series of names, words, etc., usually recorded in a set order. 2. A classification of persons or things belonging in the same category: usually with *on:* to be on the sick *list.* — *v.t.* 1. To place or record on or in a list; itemize. 2. To include in a register, catalogue, etc.; enter. [< OF *liste* < OHG *lista*] — **list′a·ble** *adj.*
list² (list) *n.* 1. A strip, edging, or selvage, as of cloth. 2. Fabric consisting of or woven like a selvage. 3. *U.S.* A ridge or furrow made with a lister in plowing. — *v.t.* 1. To edge with list. 2. To plow with or as with a lister. [OE *līste*]
list³ (list) *v.t. & v.i. Naut.* To lean or tilt to one side. — **Syn.** See TIP¹. — *n.* A leaning or inclination to one side. [Origin unknown]
list⁴ (list) *Poetic v.t.* 1. To listen to; hear. — *v.i.* 2. To listen — **Syn.** See LISTEN. [OE *hlystan* < *hlyst* hearing]
list⁵ (list) *Archaic v.t.* 1. Be pleasing or expedient to; suit. — *v.i.* 2. To desire; wish; choose. — *n.* Liking; desire. [OE *lystan* < *lust* desire]
list·ed security (lis′tid) A stock or bond that is listed on the roster of approved securities by a stock exchange.
lis·tel (lis′təl) *n. Archit.* A narrow molding; fillet. [< F < Ital. *listello,* dim. of *lista* list²]
lis·ten (lis′ən) *v.i.* 1. To make conscious use of the sense of hearing; be attentive in order to hear. 2. To pay attention; give heed. 3. To be influenced or persuaded. — *n. Rare* The act or state of listening. — **to listen in** 1. To participate in hearing (a broadcast, etc.). 2. To eavesdrop. [OE *hlysnan;* infl. by LIST⁴] — **lis′ten·er** *n.*
— **Syn.** (verb) 1. *Listen, list, hark, harken,* and *hear* mean to perceive sounds by ear. *Listen* and its poetic equivalent *list* imply conscious attention; *hark* and *harken,* both somewhat archaic or poetic, are usually used in the imperative, and stress attentive effort to hear or heed. *Hear* means merely to perceive sound, and may refer to a completely unconscious or involuntary act.
lis·ten·ing post (lis′ən·ing) 1. *Mil.* A position near enemy

lines from which an observer may detect hostile action. **2.** Any location where information is gathered for a specific purpose.

list·er (lis′tər) *n. U.S.* A plow with a double moldboard that produces a ridged furrow, often equipped with a drill for planting and covering the seed. [< LIST² + -ER¹]

Lis·ter (lis′tər), **Joseph,** 1827–1912, first Baron Lister of Lyme Regis, English surgeon; founder of antiseptic surgery.

Lis·ter·ism (lis′tə·riz′əm) *n.* The antiseptic method of surgery first practiced by Lister.

list·ing (lis′ting) *n.* **1.** The act of one who or that which lists. **2.** An entry in a list. **3.** A list.

list·less (list′lis) *adj.* Characterized by or exhibiting lack of energy or interest; languidly indifferent; apathetic; lackadaisical. — **Syn.** See LANGUID. [< LIST⁵ + -LESS] — **list′less·ly** *adv.* — **list′less·ness** *n.*

list price The price of merchandise as published in a catalogue or marked for retail sale, from which a discount is sometimes made.

lists (lists) *n.pl.* **1.** The barriers enclosing the jousting field of a medieval tournament. **2.** The field thus enclosed. **3.** Any arena, battleground, or scene of conflict or competition. — **to enter the lists** To engage in a contest or controversy. [OE *liste* border, infl. by OF *lisse* palisade]

Liszt (list), **Franz,** 1811–86, Hungarian composer and pianist.

lit¹ (lit) Alternative past tense and past participle of LIGHT¹ and LIGHT².

lit² (lit) *n.* The litas.

lit. 1. Liter. **2.** Literal(ly). **3.** Literary; literature.

Li T'ai-po (lē′ tī′bō′) See Li Po.

lit·a·ny (lit′ə·nē) *n. pl.* **·nies 1.** *Eccl.* A liturgical form of prayer consisting of a series of supplications said by the clergy, to which the choir or the congregation repeat a fixed response. — **the Litany** In the Book of Common Prayer, a set of prayers in this form. **2.** Any prayer or utterance resembling a litany, especially in length or repetition. [OE *lētanīa* < LL *litania* < Gk. *litaneia* < *lītaneuein* to pray]

li·tas (lē′täs) *n. pl.* **·tai** (-tä) or **·tu** (-tōō). The former monetary unit of Lithuania: also called *lit*.

Lit.B. Bachelor of Letters (or Literature) (L *Lit(t)erarum Baccalaureus*).

li·tchi (lē′chē) See LICHEE.

Lit.D. Doctor of Letters (or Literature) (L *Lit(t)erarum Doctor*).

lit de jus·tice (lē də zhü·stēs′) *French* Literally, bed of justice; the seat occupied by the king of France when holding a formal session of parliament; also, the session itself.

-lite *combining form Mineral.* Stone; stonelike: *actinolite.* [< F, var. of *-lithe* < Gk. *lithos* stone]

li·ter (lē′tər) *n.* In the metric system, a measure of capacity equal to the volume of one kilogram of water at 4° C. and normal atmospheric pressure, or to 1.0567 liquid quarts. Also, *esp. Brit., litre.* Abbr. *l, l., lit.* See table inside back cover.

lit·er·a·cy (lit′ər·ə·sē) *n.* The state or condition of being literate.

lit·er·al (lit′ər·əl) *adj.* **1.** Conforming or restricted to the exact, stated meaning; not figurative or inferred: the *literal* sense of the Scriptures. **2.** Following the exact words and order of an original; verbatim: a *literal* translation. **3.** Tending to recognize or accept stated meanings only; matter-of-fact; unimaginative. **4.** Free from figurative language, embellishments, etc., as a literary style; factual; unadorned. **5.** Pertaining to, consisting of, or expressed by letters: *literal* notation. Abbr. *lit.* [< OF < LL *literalis, litteralis* < *littera* letter] — **lit·er·al·i·ty** (lit′ər·al′ə·tē), **lit′er·al·ness** *n.*

lit·er·al·ism (lit′ər·əl·iz′əm) *n.* **1.** Close adherence to the exact word or sense, often to the point of unimaginativeness. **2.** In the fine arts and literature, representation without idealizing; realism. — **lit′er·al·ist** *n.* — **lit′er·al·is′tic** *adj*

lit·er·al·ize (lit′ər·əl·īz′) *v.t.* **·ized, ·iz·ing** To render or interpret according to literal meaning.

lit·er·al·ly (lit′ər·əl·ē) *adv.* **1.** In a literal manner; according to the letter; in the strictest sense. **2.** Actually; really. **3.** In effect; virtually: used loosely for emphasis. Abbr. *lit.*

lit·er·ar·y (lit′ə·rer′ē) *adj.* **1.** Of, pertaining to, or treating of literature: a *literary* journal. **2.** Characteristic of or appropriate to literature, especially to belles-lettres. **3.** Versed in or devoted to literature. **4.** Professionally engaged in the field of literature. Abbr. *lit.* [< L *litterarius*]

lit·er·ate (lit′ər·it) *adj.* **1.** Able to read and write. **2.** Having knowledge or learning; educated; cultured. **3.** Literary. — *n.* **1.** One able to read and write. **2.** An educated or well-informed person. [< L *litteratus* < *littera* letter]

lit·e·ra·ti (lit′ə·rä′tē, -rä′tī) *n.pl.* Men of letters; scholars. **2.** Literate or educated persons collectively. [< L]

lit·e·ra·tim (lit′ə·rā′tim, -rä′-) *adv.* Letter for letter; literally. [< L]

lit·er·a·ture (lit′ər·ə·chŏōr, -chər, lit′rə·chər) *n.* **1.** Written works collectively, especially those of enduring importance, exhibiting creative imagination and artistic skill. **2.** Poetry, fiction, essays, etc., as distinguished from factual, expository or journalistic writing; belles-lettres. **3.** The writings

of a particular period, language, country, etc.: Elizabethan *literature.* **4.** The writings pertaining to a particular subject or area: medical *literature*; technical *literature.* **5.** The occupation of a professional writer **6.** *Music* The total number of compositions for a particular voice, instrument, or combination of performers. **7.** *Informal* Any printed matter used or distributed for advertising, political purposes, etc.: campaign *literature.* **8.** *Rare* Knowledge of written works; learning. Abbr. *lit.* [< L *litteratura* < *littera* letter]

lith- Var. of LITHO-.

lith. Lithograph; lithography.

-lith *combining form* Stone; rock: *monolith.* [< Gk. *lithos* stone]

Lith. Lithuania; Lithuanian.

lith·arge (lith′ärj, li·thärj′) *n.* A yellowish monoxide of lead, PbO, made by heating lead in air, and used in glassmaking, as a pigment, etc. [< F *litarge* < L *lithargyrus* < Gk. *lithargyros* silver scum < *lithos* stone + *argyros* silver]

lithe (līth) *adj.* Bending easily or gracefully; supple; pliant; limber. [OE, soft] — **lithe′ly** *adv.* — **lithe′ness** *n.*

li·the·mi·a (li·thē′mē·ə) *n. Pathol.* An excess of urates and uric acid in the blood. Also **li·thae′mi·a.** [< *lith(ic acid),* obs. name for uric acid + -EMIA] — **li·the′mic** *adj.*

lithe·some (līth′səm) *adj.* Lithe. [< LITHE + -SOME¹]

lith·i·a (lith′ē·ə) *n.* Lithium oxide, Li₂O, a white, caustic compound. [< NL < Gk. *lithos* stone]

li·thi·a·sis (li·thī′ə·sis) *n. Pathol.* The formation of stone-like masses in the body. [< NL < Gk. *lithos* stone]

lithia water A mineral water containing lithium salts.

lith·ic (lith′ik) *adj.* **1.** Of or pertaining to stone. **2.** *Pathol.* Of or pertaining to calculi, especially in the bladder. **3.** *Chem.* Of or pertaining to lithium. [< Gk. *lithikos* of stone]

-lithic *combining form* Pertaining to a (specified) anthropological stage in the use of stone implements: *Neolithic.*

lith·i·um (lith′ē·əm) *n.* A soft, silver-white element (symbol Li), the lightest of the metals, found only in combination. See ELEMENT. [< NL < Gk. *lithos* stone]

litho- *combining form* Stone: *lithotomy.* Also, before vowels, *lith-.* [< Gk. *lithos* stone]

litho. or **lithog.** Lithograph; lithography.

lith·o·graph (lith′ə·graf, -gräf) *n.* A print produced by the process of lithography. Abbr. *lith., litho., lithog.* — *v.t.* To produce or reproduce by lithography. [< LITHO- + -GRAPH] — **li·thog·ra·pher** (li·thog′rə·fər) *n.* — **lith′o·graph′ic** or **·i·cal** *adj.* — **lith′o·graph′i·cal·ly** *adv.*

li·thog·ra·phy (li·thog′rə·fē) *n.* The art or process of producing printed matter from a flat stone or zinc or aluminum plate on which a drawing or design has been made in a greasy or water-repellent material. Abbr. *lith., litho., lithog.*

lith·oid (lith′oid) *adj.* Of or resembling stone; having stony structure or texture. Also **li·thoi·dal** (li·thoid′l).

lithol. Lithology

li·thol·o·gy (li·thol′ə·jē) *n.* **1.** The science that treats of the general structure and composition of rocks. **2.** The branch of medicine that treats of calculi. [< LITHO- + -LOGY] — **lith·o·log·ic** (lith′ə·loj′ik) or **·i·cal** *adj.* — **li·thol′o·gist** *n.*

lith·o·marge (lith′ə·märj) *n.* A variety of kaolin occurring in compact masses. [< LITHO- + L *marga* marl]

lith·o·phyte (lith′ə·fīt) *n.* **1.** *Zool.* A plantlike organism having a stony structure, as a coral. **2.** *Bot.* A plant that grows on rocky surfaces. — **lith′o·phyt′ic** (-fit′ik) *adj.*

lith·o·pone (lith′ə·pōn) *n.* A mixture of barium sulfate and zinc sulfide, used in the manufacture of paint, rubber, linoleum, etc. [< LITHO- + *pone,* ? < L *ponere* to place]

lith·o·sphere (lith′ə·sfir) *n.* The solid crust of the earth, as distinguished from the atmosphere and the hydrosphere.

li·thot·o·my (li·thot′ə·mē) *n. pl.* **·mies** *Surg.* The operation of removing calculi from the bladder by incision. [< LL *lithotomia* < Gk. *lithos* stone + -TOMY] — **lith·o·tom·ic** (lith′ə·tom′ik) or **·i·cal** *adj.* — **li·thot′o·mist** *n.*

li·thot·ri·ty (li·thot′rə·tē) *n. pl.* **·ties** *Surg.* The operation of pulverizing a calculus in the bladder to fine, easily voided fragments. Also **li·thot′ri·o·sy** (-rip·sē). [< LITHO- + L *tritus,* pp. of *terere* to rub, grind]

Lith·u·a·ni·a (lith′ōō·ā′nē·ə) A constituent Republic of the Soviet Union, in the NW part on the Baltic; 25,200 sq. mi.; pop. 3,129,000 (1971); capital, Vilna. Officially **Lithuanian S.S.R.** *Russian* **Li·tov·ska·ya S.S.R.** (lyi·tôf′skä·yä).

Lith·u·a·ni·an (lith′ōō·ā′nē·ən) *adj.* Of or pertaining to Lithuania, its people, or their language — *n.* **1.** A native or inhabitant of Lithuania. **2.** The Balto-Slavic language of the Lithuanians. Abbr. *Lith.*

lit·i·ga·ble (lit′ə·gə·bəl) *adj.* Subject to legal dispute.

lit·i·gant (lit′ə·gənt) *n.* A participant in a lawsuit. — *adj.* Engaged in litigation. [< F < L *litigans, -gantis,* ppr. of *litigare* to litigate]

lit·i·gate (lit′ə·gāt) *v.* **·gat·ed, ·gat·ing** *v.t.* **1.** To bring (a dispute, claim, etc.) before a court of law for decision or settlement; contest at law. — *v.i.* **2.** To engage in or bring action by a lawsuit. [< L *litigatus,* pp. of *litigare < lis, litis* lawsuit + *agere* to do. act] — **lit′i·ga′tor** *n.*

lit·i·ga·tion (lit′ə·gā′shən) *n.* **1.** The act or process of engaging in legal action. **2.** A judicial contest; lawsuit. **3.** *Rare* Dispute; controversy.

li·tig·ious (li·tij′əs) *adj.* **1.** Inclined to litigation; disputatious; quarrelsome. **2.** Subject to litigation. **3.** Of or pertaining to litigation. [< F *litigieux* < L *litigiosus* < *litigium* litigation] — **li·tig′ious·ly** *adv.* — **li·tig′ious·ness** *n.*

lit·mus (lit′məs) *n.* A blue dyestuff made from certain lichens. It is turned red by acids and remains, or changes back to, blue when treated with an alkali. [< AF *lytemoise* < ON *litmose* lichen used in dyeing < *litr* color + *mosi* moss]

litmus paper Paper dyed with litmus, used to test solutions for acidity.

li·to·tes (lī′tə·tēz, -tō-, lit′ə-) *n.* A figure of speech in which an assertion is made by the negation of its opposite. Example: *A fact of no small importance.* [< NL < Gk. *litotēs* < *litos* simple, spare]

li·tre (lē′tər) See LITER.

Litt.B. Bachelor of Letters (or Literature) (L *Lit(t)erarum Baccalaureus*)

Litt.D. Doctor of Letters (or Literature) (L *Lit(t)erarum Doctor*)

lit·ter (lit′ər) *n.* **1.** Waste materials, scraps, or carelessly dropped objects strewn about; clutter. **2.** Untidy or chaotic condition; mess. **3.** The young brought forth at one birth by any mammal normally having several offspring at one time. **4.** A stretcher used for carrying sick or wounded persons. **5.** A vehicle consisting of a couch carried between shafts by men or beasts of burden. **6.** Straw, hay, etc., spread in animal pens, or over plants as protection. **7.** The uppermost layer of a forest floor, consisting of slightly decomposed leaves, twigs, etc. — **Syn.** See FLOCK. — *v.t.* **1.** To make untidy or unsightly by strewing or carelessly discarding trash, etc. **2.** To drop or scatter carelessly. **3.** To provide with litter, as for bedding, covering, etc. **4.** To give birth to (pups, kittens, whelps, etc.) — *v.i.* **5.** To give birth to a litter of young. **6.** To drop or scatter refuse, especially in public places. [< OF *litiere* < Med.L *lectaria* < L *lectus* bed]

lit·te·rae hu·ma·ni·o·res (lit′ə·rē hyōō·mā′nē·ô′rēz) *Latin* Classical literature, history, and philosophy.

lit·té·ra·teur (lit′ər·ə·tûr′, *Fr.* lē·tā·ra·tœr′) *n.* One engaged in literature; man of letters. Also **lit′ter·a·teur′**. [< F]

lit·ter·bug (lit′ər·bug′) *n. U.S. Slang* One who litters public places, roads, etc., with trash.

lit·ter·y (lit′ər·ē) *adj.* Covered with litter; untidy; messy.

lit·tle (lit′l) *adj.* **lit·tler** or (for defs. 2 and 3) **less**, **lit·tlest** or (for defs. 2 and 3) **least** **1.** Small, or smaller compared to others, in physical size; not big; diminutive: *a little house.* **2.** Not long in duration or extent; short; brief: *a little time; a little distance away.* **3.** Small or relatively small in quantity or degree; not much; scant: *little wealth; little probability.* **4.** Having small force or effectiveness; weak: *a little effort; a little blow.* **5.** Not having great influence, wealth, or power; of minor status: *little businessmen.* **6.** Not important or significant; inconsiderable; trivial: *little details.* **7.** Narrow or limited in viewpoint; petty; mean: *little minds.* **8.** Appealing, endearing, or amusing because of affectionate association, familiarity, etc.: *a sweet little woman.* — *adv.* **less**, **least** **1.** Only slightly; not much; scarcely: *He sleeps little.* **2.** Not at all: used before a verb: *She little suspects.* — *n.* **1.** A small amount or quantity: usually preceded by *a*: *Give me just a little.* **2.** A negligible or insignificant amount: *Little can be done about it.* **3.** A short while or distance. — **in little** On a miniature scale. — **little by little** By small degrees; gradually. — **to make little of** To treat or regard as inconsequential. [OE *lȳtel* < *lȳt* small] — **lit′tle·ness** *n.* — **Syn.** See SMALL. — **Ant.** big, great, much.

Little America A U.S. base in Antarctica, on the Ross Shelf Ice; established by Richard E. Byrd, 1929.

Little Bear The constellation Ursa Minor.

Little Big·horn River (big′hôrn′) A river in Wyoming and Montana, flowing about 90 miles north to the Bighorn River. At a site on this river Custer and his forces were defeated by Indians, 1876: Also **Little Horn.**

little chief hare A pika (*Ochotona princeps*) of the Rocky Mountains: also called *cony.*

Little Colorado River A river flowing 315 miles generally NW through Arizona to the Colorado River in the Grand Canyon.

Little Corporal A nickname for Napoleon Bonaparte.

Little Dipper The constellation Ursa Minor.

Little Dog The constellation Canis Minor.

Little Englander In the 19th century, one opposed to the territorial expansion of the British Empire.

Little Fox The constellation Vulpecula.

little hours In the Roman Catholic Church, the offices of prime, tierce, sext, and nones.

Little John In medieval legend, one of Robin Hood's associates, notable for his great size and strength.

little magazine A literary magazine, often avant-garde, having a small readership and often a small page size.

lit·tle·neck (lit′l·nek′) *n. U.S.* A young, small quahog, often eaten raw. Also **littleneck clam.** [after *Little Neck*, community on Long Island, New York]

little office In the Roman Catholic church, an office of lessons and hymns in honor of the Virgin Mary.

Little Rho·dy (rō′dē) Nickname of RHODE ISLAND.

Little Rock The capital of Arkansas, in the central part, on the Arkansas River; pop. 132,483.

Little Russia A name formerly applied to the Ukraine, and often adjacent areas in Poland and Rumania.

Little Russian Ukrainian.

little slam See under SLAM².

Little St. Bernard Pass See under ST. BERNARD PASS.

little theater **1.** An amateur or community theater group; also, the theater used for their performances. **2.** Experimental or avant-garde drama, originating in a movement of the 1920's, and usually having a limited audience.

Lit·tle·ton (lit′l·tən), **Sir Thomas**, 1407?–81, English jurist.

lit·to·ral (lit′ər·əl) *adj.* Of or pertaining to a shore or coastal region. — *n.* A shore and its adjacent areas. [< L *littoralis* < *lit(t)us, -oris* seashore]

li·tur·gi·cal (li·tûr′ji·kəl) *adj.* Of, pertaining to, or associated with public worship, ecclesiastic ritual, etc. Also **li·tur′gic.** — **li·tur′gi·cal·ly** *adv.*

li·tur·gics (li·tûr′jiks) *n.pl.* (construed as sing.) **1.** The skills or procedures of conducting public worship. **2.** The study of liturgies.

lit·ur·gist (lit′ər·jist) *n.* **1.** A scholar specializing in the study or compiling of liturgies. **2.** One who uses or advocates liturgical forms of worship.

lit·ur·gy (lit′ər·jē) *n. pl.* **·gies** **1.** In various religions, the prescribed form for public worship; religious ritual. **2.** In the Roman Catholic Church, the Mass. **3.** The rite of the Eucharist, especially in the Eastern Orthodox Church: also **Divine Liturgy.** [< Med.L *liturgia* < Gk. *leitourgia* public duty, ult. < *laos* people + *ergon* work]

Lit·vi·nov (lit·vē′nôf), **Maxim Maximovich**, 1876–1951, Soviet statesman and diplomat. Original name **Maxim Maximovich Wal·lach** (väl′läkh).

Liu Shao-chi (lyōō′ shou′chē′), born 1898?, Chinese Communist leader; chairman of the People's Republic of China 1959–66.

liv·a·ble (liv′ə·bəl) *adj.* **1.** Suitable or agreeable for living in; habitable. **2.** Worth living; capable of being endured; tolerable. **3.** Agreeable or comfortable, as for association or companionship: followed by *with.* Also **live′a·ble.**

live¹ (liv) *v.* **lived, liv·ing** *v.i.* **1.** To function as an animate organism; be alive; have life. **2.** To continue in existence; remain alive: *as long as you live.* **3.** To remain or persist, as in the mind; be remembered: often with *on*: *The dead live on.* **4.** To remain valid or operative; endure; last: often with *on*: *The old customs live on.* **5.** To have as one's home; dwell; reside: with *in* or *at.* **6.** To use something as one's sole or customary nourishment; subsist: with *on*: *to live on air.* **7.** To maintain or support oneself; depend for livelihood: with *on* or *by*: *to live on one's income; to live by one's wits.* **8.** To pass life in a specified manner: *to live in peace.* **9.** To lead or regulate one's life, as in accordance with rules, principles, etc.: often with *by*: *to live by a strict code.* **10.** To enjoy a varied or satisfying life; be joyously or enthusiastically alive. **11.** To escape destruction; stay afloat or in flight despite danger, as a vessel or aircraft. — *v.t.* **12.** To spend or pass (life, time, etc.). **13.** To exemplify or put into practice in one's life: *to live one's religion.* — **to live and let live** To be forbearing or unprejudiced in regard to the conduct characteristics, etc., of others. — **to live down** To live or behave so as to expiate or expunge the memory of (an error, crime, etc.). — **to live in** To reside, as a domestic servant, at one's place of employment. — **to live it up** *U.S. Slang* To have fun. — **to live out** **1.** To live or exist to the end of. **2.** To reside, as a domestic servant, away from one's place of employment. — **to live through** To survive or withstand (an experience). — **to live up to** **1.** To satisfy (an ideal, expectations, etc.). **2.** To fulfill (a bargain, obligation, etc.). — **to live with** **1.** To reside with. **2.** To cohabit with. **3.** To put up with; endure. [OE *libban, lifian*]

— **Syn.** **5.** *Live, dwell, reside, abide, sojourn, lodge,* and *stay* agree in meaning to make one's home temporarily or permanently in one place. *Live* is the broadest of these words. A man may *live* in a house, a city, a region, or a country; he may *live* in a certain place for a month or for his entire life. *Dwell, reside,* and *abide* are all close synonyms of *live,* but are somewhat more restricted in usage. *Dwell* occurs frequently in poetry and lofty prose, while *reside* is a legal or formal word, and often is used to suggest an elegant or imposing home. *Abide* is archaic; unless limited by the context, it implies long continuance in one place. *Sojourn, lodge,* and *stay* all refer to a temporary home. One may *sojourn* in a place for several years, but always with the feeling that one may someday return to a permanent home elsewhere. *Lodge* is used of temporary shelter, such as a traveler seeks for the night, and *stay* is commonly used of guests: *to stay with friends.* — **Ant.** die.

live² (līv) *adj.* **1.** Functioning as an animate organism; alive. **2.** Pertaining to, characteristic of, or abounding in life; typical of the living state. **3.** Of present interest and importance;

currently valid: a *live* issue. **4.** Effectively forceful and energetic; dynamic: a *live* personality. **5.** Burning or glowing: a *live* coal. **6.** Vivid or brilliant, as color, tone, etc. **7.** Charged with electricity; transmitting voltage: a *live* wire. **8.** Capable of being detonated because of explosive contents, as a bomb. **9.** Being in the native or unwrought state, as rock. **10.** In television, radio, etc., consisting of or performed by persons present at the time of transmission: a *live* show; a *live* audience. **11.** In technical or mechanical use, having motion or the power to impart motion or force: *live* steam. **12.** In printing, publishing, etc., ready or retained for use; not to be destroyed or discarded: *live* copy. **13.** In sports or games, being or capable of being in play, as a ball. [Shortened form of ALIVE.]

live-bear·er (līv′bâr′ər)   *n.* An ovoviviparous fish, as a guppy. **— live′-bear′ing** *adj.*

live center *Mech.* The center of a rotating spindle, turning with the work, as on a lathe.

lived (līvd) *adj.* Having a (specified kind of) life or life span: used in combination: *long-lived.* [< LIFE + -ED³]

live-for·ev·er (līv′fər-ĕv′ər)   *n.* Any of several herbs (genus *Sedum*) of the orpine family; especially, *S. purpureum*, having succulent leaves and flat clusters of purplish flowers.

live·li·hood (līv′lē-hŏŏd)   *n.* Means of supporting or maintaining one's existence; subsistence; living. [ME *livelode* < OE *līflād* < *līf* life + *lād* way]

live load *Engin.* Moving or intermittent weight added to the fixed weight of a structure, as traffic crossing a bridge.

live·long (līv′lông′, -lŏng′)   *adj.* Long or seemingly long in passing; whole; entire: the *livelong* day. [ME *lefe longe*, lit., lief long; *lief*, here orig. intens., was later confused with *live*]

live·ly (līv′lē) *adj.* **·li·er, ·li·est 1.** Full of vigor or motion; energetic; active: a *lively* step. **2.** Arousing activity or excitement; rousing: a *lively* tune. **3.** Animated; vivacious: a *lively* lass. **4.** Characterized by or suggesting mental activity or emotional intensity; vivid; keen: a *lively* imagination. **5.** Striking and forceful to the mind or senses: a *lively* impression. **6.** Filled with activity; eventful; busy: a *lively* day. **7.** Invigorating; fresh; brisk: a *lively* breeze. **8.** Responsive to impact or bouncing readily, as a ball; resilient. **9.** Moving easily on water, as a vessel. *— adv.* In a lively manner; briskly: now usually in the expression **to step lively,** to hurry up. [OE *līflīce*] **— live′li·ly** *adv.* **— live′li·ness** *n.*

liv·en (līv′ən) *v.t.* & *v.i.* To make or become lively or cheerful: often with *up.* **— liv′en·er** *n.*

live oak Any of several evergreen trees (genus *Quercus*) having hard, durable wood; especially, *Q. virginiana* of the SE United States.

liv·er¹ (līv′ər)   *n.* **1.** *Anat.* The largest glandular organ of vertebrates, secreting bile and active in metabolism, in man situated just under the diaphragm and on the right side. ◆ Collateral adjective: *hepatic.* **2.** A similar digestive gland in invertebrates. **3.** Food consisting of or prepared from the liver of certain animals. [OE *lifer*]

liv·er² (līv′ər)   *n.* **1.** One who lives in a specified manner: a luxurious *liver.* **2.** A dweller.

liver extract A concentrated extract of mammalian liver, used in the treatment of anemia.

liver fluke Any of various trematode worms parasitic in the bile ducts of sheep, cows, pigs, and sometimes man, especially *Fasciola hepatica.*

liv·er·ied (līv′ər-ēd) *adj.* Dressed in livery, as a servant.

liv·er·ish (līv′ər-ish) *adj. Informal* Feeling or exhibiting supposed symptoms of disordered liver; bilious; irritable.

liv·er·leaf (līv′ər-lēf′)   *n.* The hepatica, a plant.

Liv·er·pool (līv′ər-pōōl) A port city in Merseyside, England, on the Mersey estuary; pop. 574,560 (1973). **— Liv·er·pud·li·an** (līv′ər-pŭd′lē-ən) *adj.* & *n.*

liv·er·wort (līv′ər-wûrt′)   *n.* **1.** Any mosslike cryptogam of the class *Hepaticae*, forming mats in damp, shady places: also called *scale moss.* **2.** A hepatica.

liv·er·wurst (līv′ər-wûrst′)   *n.* A sausage made of or containing ground liver. [< G *leberwurst*]

liv·er·y (līv′ər-ē) *n.* *pl.* **·er·ies 1.** The distinctive clothing or uniform worn by male household servants or other employees. **2.** The distinguishing dress of an organization or group. **3.** Formerly, the identifying dress, badge, etc., worn by the retainers of a feudal lord. **4.** Characteristic garb or outward appearance. **5.** The stabling and care of horses for pay. **6.** *U.S.* A livery stable. **7.** *Law* Delivery, as of lands. [< OF *livree* gift of clothes by a master to a servant < *livrer* to deliver, free < L *liberare* to free < *liber* free]

livery company A trade association of London, England, having its origin in one of the medieval guilds.

liv·er·y·man (līv′ər-ē-mən) *n.* *pl.* **·men** (-mən) **1.** A man who keeps or works in a livery stable. **2.** A member of a London guild or livery company. **3.** *Archaic* A servant or retainer wearing livery.

livery stable A stable where horses and vehicles are cared for or kept for hire.

lives (līvz) Plural of LIFE.

live steam Steam supplied direct from a boiler, having full power to do work: distinguished from *exhaust steam.*

live·stock (līv′stok′)   *n.* Domestic farm animals, as cattle, horses, and sheep, especially when raised for profit.

live wire 1. A wire carrying an electric current or potential. **2.** *Informal* An energetic, enterprising person; a go-getter.

liv·id (līv′id) *adj.* **1.** Having the skin abnormally discolored, as: **a** Flushed, purplish, etc., as from intense emotion, disease, or congestion. **b** Black-and-blue, as from contusion. **2.** Having a leaden pallor; dull or bluish gray. **3.** *Informal* Furious; enraged. **— Syn.** See PALE². [< F *livide* < L *lividus* < *livere* to be livid] **— liv′id·ly** *adv.* **— liv′id·ness** *n.* **— li·vid·i·ty** (li·vid′ə·tē) *n.*

liv·ing (līv′ing) *adj.* **1.** Alive; animate; not dead. **2.** Of, pertaining to, or characteristic of everyday life: *living* conditions. **3.** Used or intended for maintaining existence: a *living* wage. **4.** Having contemporary value, force, or application; currently valid or in use: a *living* institution; *living* languages. **5.** Of or pertaining to those who are alive: within *living* memory. **6.** Lifelike; real: the *living* image of his father. **7.** Being in the natural or typical state, as of force, activity, ruggedness, etc.: *living* rock. *— n.* **1.** The state or condition of one who or that which lives; animate existence. **2.** Those that are alive: preceded by *the.* **3.** Manner or conduct of life: virtuous *living.* **4.** Means of supporting existence; livelihood: to earn a *living.* **5.** In the Church of England, a benefice or the revenue derived from it.

living death A prolonged painful experience.

living picture A tableau vivant.

living room A room designed and furnished for the general use, social activities, etc., of a household; sitting room.

Liv·ing·ston (līv′ing·stən), **Robert R.,** 1746–1813, American statesman; helped draft the Declaration of Independence.

Liv·ing·stone (līv′ing·stən) A town in southern Zambia, on the Zambezi; pop. 43,000 (est. 1969).

Liv·ing·stone (līv′ing·stən), **David,** 1813–73, Scottish explorer and medical missionary in Africa.

living wage A wage that will enable a person to support himself and his family in reasonable security.

Li·vo·ni·a (li·vō′nē·ə) **1.** A region in the Latvian and Estonian S.S.R., formerly a province of Russia. **2.** A city in SE Michigan, near Detroit; pop. 110,109. **— Li·vo′ni·an** *adj.* & *n.*

Li·vor·no (li·vôr′nō) The Italian name for LEGHORN.

li·vre (lē′vər, *Fr.* lēv′r′)   *n.* An old French money of account, originally equal in value to a pound of silver. Abbr. *lv.* [< F < L *libra* pound]

Liv·y (līv′ē) Anglicized name of **Titus Liv·i·us** (līv′ē-əs), 59 B.C.–A.D. 17, Roman historian.

liv·yer (līv′yər) *n. Canadian* A permanent resident of Newfoundland. Also **liv′ier.**

lix·iv·i·ate (lik·siv′ē·āt) *v.t.* **·at·ed, ·at·ing** To leach. [< L *lixivius* made into lye < *lix* ashes, lye] **— lix·iv′i·al** *adj.* **— lix·iv′i·a′tion** *n.*

lix·iv·i·um (lik·siv′ē·əm) *n.* *pl.* **·i·ums** or **·i·a 1.** A solution of alkaline salts, as lye. **2.** A solution obtained by leaching. [< L < *lix* ashes, lye]

liz·ard (liz′ərd)   *n.* **1.** Any of various reptiles (suborder *Sauria*) typically having elongate, scaly bodies, long tails, and four legs, as the chameleon, iguana, skink, etc. **2.** Loosely, any similar reptile or amphibian. **3.** Leather made from the skin of a lizard. [< OF *laisard* < L *lacerta*]

Liz·ard (liz′ərd) *n.* The constellation Lacerta.

Lizard, the A promontory in SW Cornwall, England. Its extremity, **Lizard Head** or **Lizard Point,** is the southernmost point of Great Britain.

lizard fish Any of various elongate marine fishes (family *Synodontidae*), having lizardlike heads.

Lju·blja·na (lyōō′blyä·nä) The capital of Slovenia, Yugoslavia; pop. 183,-000 (est. 1968): German *Laibach.*

LIZARDS
a Wall. *b* Chameleon. *c* Monitor.

-'ll Contracted form of SHALL or WILL (*v.*) or of TILL (*prep.*).

ll. Lines.

LL or **LL.** or **L.L. 1.** Late Latin. **2.** Legal Latin. **3.** Low Latin.

lla·ma (lä′mə)   *n.* **1.** A camellike, humpless ruminant (genus *Auchenia* or *Lama*) of South America, having white or brownish thick, woolly hair, and frequently used as a beast of burden in the Andes. **2.** A textile made of llama wool, or the wool itself. [< Sp. < Quechua]

Lla·nel·ly (la·nel′ē) A municipal borough and resort in SE Dyfed, Wales; pop. 76,800 (1976).

lla·no (lä′nō, *Sp.* lyä′nō) *n.* *pl.* **·nos** (-nōz, *Sp.* -nōs) A flat, treeless plain, as those of the SW United States and northern Latin America. [< Sp., plain, flat < L *planus*]

LLAMA
(3½ feet high at shoulder)

Lla·no Es·ta·ca·do (lä′nō es′tə·kä′dō, *Sp.* lyä′nō es′tä·kä′-

thō) A treeless plateau region in western Texas and SE New Mexico south of the Great Plains: also *Staked Plain.* [< Sp., staked plain]

LL.B. Bachelor of Laws (L *Legum Baccalaureus*).

LL.D. Doctor of Laws (L *Legum Doctor*).

LL.M. Master of Laws (L *Legum Magister*).

Lloyd George (loid jôrj), **David**, 1863–1945, first Earl of Dwyfor, British statesman; prime minister 1916–22.

Lloyd's (loidz) *n.* A corporation of English marine and general underwriters and shipping men, founded at Lloyd's Coffee House in 1688 for the transaction of marine and risk insurance, the gathering and distribution of shipping data, etc., and publishing **Lloyd's Register,** an annual information list of the seagoing vessels of all nations.

LM *Mil.* Legion of Merit.

L.M. Licentiate in Medicine (or Midwifery).

LMT Local mean time.

ln Natural logarithm.

lo (lō) *interj.* See! observe!: now chiefly in the expression *Lo and behold!* [OE *lā*]

loach (lōch) *n.* Any of various fresh-water fishes (family *Cobitidae*), related to the carp and minnow. [< F *loche*]

load (lōd) *n.* **1.** The weight or quantity placed upon and sustained by a vehicle, bearer, surface, etc. **2.** A quantity borne or conveyed, measured by the capacity of the vehicle or bearer: often used in combination: *carload.* **3.** That which weighs down or is borne with difficulty; burden. **4.** That which oppresses; cause of mental or emotional strain. **5.** The charge or ammunition for a firearm, projectile, etc. **6.** The hours or amount of work required of an employee. **7.** *pl. Informal* An ample amount or quantity; lots: *loads* of time. **8.** *Engin.* Weight or pressure borne by a structure. See DEAD LOAD, LIVE LOAD. **9.** *Electr.* **a** The power delivered by a generating system. **b** A device or connected group of devices consuming electrical power. **10.** *Mech.* The resistance overcome by a motor or engine in driving machinery. **11.** *U.S. Slang* Enough liquor consumed to cause drunkenness: usually followed by *on.* **— to get a load of** *U.S. Slang* To take notice of; listen to or look at. **— v.t. 1.** To place a large quantity, burden, cargo, etc., upon; fill or cover, as with objects or a substance: to *load* a ship with ore. **2.** To place or take (material, cargo, objects, people, etc.) as on a conveyance: to *load* one on a ship. **3.** To burden, encumber, or oppress: often with *down.* **4.** To provide abundantly or in excess; heap: He was *loaded* with honors. **5.** To charge (a firearm, etc.) with explosive or ammunition. **6.** To put film or a photographic plate into (a camera). **7.** To tamper with, especially by adding weight to: to *load* dice. **8.** To make prejudicial; fill with special implication: to *load* the evidence in favor of the defendant. **9.** In insurance, to increase (a premium) by adding charges, as for expenses. **10.** *Electr.* To increase the power requirements of (a circuit or generating system). **— v.i. 11.** To put on or receive a load or cargo. **12.** To charge a firearm, cartridge, etc., with ammunition or explosive. **13.** To be charged with ammunition: The gun *loads* at the breech. **— to load the dice 1.** To add weight to dice for a fraudulent advantage. **2.** To prearrange or predetermine some outcome, either favorably or unfavorably. [OE *lād* way, journey, act of carrying goods. Doublet of LODE.] **— load′er** *n.*

load displacement *Naut.* The displacement of a ship loaded to full capacity.

load·ed (lō′did) *adj.* **1.** Filled or laden. **2.** Weighted, as fraudulent dice. **3.** Charged with ammunition. **4.** Charged with prejudicial implication; intended to trick or trap: a *loaded* question. **5.** *Slang* Intoxicated. **6.** *Slang* Wealthy.

load factor *Electr.* The ratio of the average load of a generating system to the maximum or peak load.

load·ing (lō′ding) *n.* **1.** The act or process of furnishing with a load. **2.** A load; burden. **3.** Something added to a substance to give it weight, body, etc. **4.** In insurance, an addition to the premium to cover expenses, fluctuations in the death rate, etc. **5.** *Aeron.* Wing loading (which see).

loading coil *Electr.* An inductance coil connected in a circuit to increase its period of oscillation.

load line *Naut.* A line, as the Plimsoll mark, on the side of a ship, indicating the depth to which it may be submerged by the weight of its cargo or under various conditions.

load·star (lōd′stär′), **load·stone** (lōd′stōn′) See LODESTAR, LODESTONE.

loaf¹ (lōf) *v.i.* **1.** To loiter lazily or aimlessly; spend time idly. **2.** To shirk or dawdle over one's work. **— v.t. 3.** To spend (time) idly: with *away.* [Back formation < LOAFER]

loaf² (lōf) *n. pl.* **loaves** (lōvz) **1.** A rounded or elongated mass of bread baked in a single piece. **2.** Any shaped mass of food, as of cake, chopped meat, etc. [OE *hlāf* bread]

loaf·er (lō′fər) *n.* **1.** One who loafs; an idler or slacker. **2.** A casual shoe resembling a moccasin. [Cf. G *landläufer* idler, loiterer, Du. *landloper* vagrant.]

loam (lōm) *n.* **1.** Loose-textured soil consisting of a mixture of sand and clay containing organic matter. **2.** A moistened mixture of clay and sand combined with straw, used in plastering, making foundry molds, etc. **3.** *Obs.* Earth or clay. **— v.t.** To coat or fill with loam. [OE *lām*] **— loam′y** *adj.*

loan¹ (lōn) *n.* **1.** Something lent; especially, a sum of money lent at interest. **2.** The act of lending: the *loan* of a knife. **3.** A loan-word (which see). **— on loan 1.** Borrowed. **2.** Temporarily transferred to work or duty away from one's regular post: *on loan* from the university. **— v.t. & v.i.** To lend. ◆ *Loan* as a verb is standard English, especially business English, in the United States but not in England. [ME < ON *lān.* Akin to OE *læn.*] **— loan′a·ble** *adj.*

loan² (lōn) *n. Scot.* **1.** A lane. **2.** A field or yard where cows are milked. Also **loan′ing** (lō′ning).

Lo·an·da (lō-än′dä) See LUANDA.

loan shark *U.S. Informal* One who lends money at an excessively high or illegal rate of interest.

loan-trans·la·tion (lōn′trans-lā′shən, -tranz-) *n.* **1.** The borrowing of expressions or complex words from other languages by direct translation of the construction. **2.** An instance of this, as English *superman* from German *Übermensch.* Also **loan translation.**

loan-word (lōn′wûrd′) *n.* A word adopted from another language and partly or completely naturalized, as the English word *chauffeur,* taken from the French: also called *loan.* Also **loan word, loan′word′.** [< G *lehnwort*]

loath (lōth) *adj.* Strongly disinclined; reluctant; unwilling: often followed by *to.* Also spelled *loth.* [OE *lāth* hateful]

loathe (lōth) *v.t.* **loathed, loath·ing** To feel great hatred or disgust for; abhor; detest. **— Syn.** See HATE. [OE *lāthian* to be hateful] **— loath′er** *n.*

loath·ful (lōth′fəl) *adj. Rare* Loathsome. **— loath′ful·ly** *adv.* **— loath′ful·ness** *n.*

loath·ing (lō′thing) *n.* Extreme dislike or disgust; abhorrence. **— loath′ing·ly** *adv.*

loath·ly (lōth′lē) *adj.* Loathsome; repulsive. **— adv.** Unwillingly. [OE *lāthlīc, lāthlīce*]

loath·some (lōth′səm) *adj.* Causing revulsion or disgust; repulsive. **— loath′some·ly** *adv.* **— loath′some·ness** *n.*

loaves (lōvz) Plural of LOAF.

lob (lob) *v.* **lobbed, lob·bing** *v.t.* **1.** To pitch or strike (a ball, etc.) in a high, arching curve. **— v.i. 2.** To move clumsily or heavily. **3.** To lob a ball. **— n. 1.** In tennis, a stroke that sends the ball high into the air. **2.** In cricket, a slow, underhand ball. [ME, prob. < LG or ON]

Lo·ba·chev·ski (lō′bä-chef′skē), **Nikolai Ivanovich**, 1793–1856, Russian mathematician.

lo·bar (lō′bər, -bär) *adj.* **1.** Of or pertaining to a lobe. **2.** Affecting one or more lobes of the lungs. [< NL *lobaris*]

lo·bate (lō′bāt) *adj.* **1.** Having or consisting of lobes. **2.** Resembling a lobe. Also **lo′bat·ed.** [< NL *lobatus*]

lo·ba·tion (lō-bā′shən) *n.* **1.** The condition of having or forming lobes. **2.** A lobe or lobelike part.

lob·by (lob′ē) *n. pl.* **·bies 1.** An entrance hall, vestibule, or public lounge in an apartment house, hotel, theater, etc. **2.** A public anteroom adjacent to the meeting chamber of a legislative body. **3** *U.S.* A group representing persons or organizations with a common interest, who attempt to influence the votes of legislators. **— v. ·bied, ·by·ing** *U.S. v.i.* **1.** To attempt to influence legislators in favor of some special interest. **— v.t. 2.** To attempt to influence (legislators or a legislative body). **3.** To exert influence for the passage of (a bill or other measure): often with *through.* [< Med.L *lobia.* Doublet of LODGE, *n.* LOGE, LOGGIA.]

lob·by·ism (lob′ē-iz′əm) *n. U.S.* The practice of lobbying. **— lob′by·ist** *n.*

lobe (lōb) *n.* **1.** A rounded division, protuberance, or part, as of a leaf. **2.** The soft lower part of the human ear. **3.** *Anat.* Any of several well-defined, often symmetrical portions of an organ or part of the body, as of the brain, lungs, liver, etc. **4.** *Ornithol.* One of the rounded projections on the toes of certain aquatic birds. [< F < L *lobus* < Gk. *lobos*]

lobed (lōbd) *adj.* **1.** Having lobes; lobate. **2.** *Bot.* Of leaves, having rounded divisions that extend not more than halfway from the margin to the midrib.

lo·be·li·a (lō-bē′lē-ə, -bēl′yə) *n.* Any of a large genus (*Lobelia*) of herbaceous plants having flowers of various colors, usually borne in racemes. [< NL, after Matthias de *Lobel,* 1538–1616, Flemish botanist]

Lo·ben·gu·la (lō′beng-gyōō′lə, lō-beng′gyə-lə), 1833?–94, king of the Matabele; defeated by the British, 1893.

lob·lol·ly (lob′lol-ē) *n. pl.* **·lies** *U.S.* **1.** *Informal* A mudhole; oozy mire. **2.** A loblolly bay or pine. [< dial. E *lob* bubble + *lolly* broth]

loblolly bay A tree (*Gordonia lasianthus*) of the SE United States, having glossy leaves and showy white flowers.

loblolly pine 1. A pine (*Pinus taeda*) of the southern United States, having scaly bark and wood valuable as lumber: also called *slash pine.* **2.** The wood of this tree.

lo·bo (lō′bō) *n. pl.* **·bos** The timber wolf of the western United States. [< Sp., wolf < L *lupus*]

lo·bot·o·my (lō-bot′ə-mē) *n. pl.* **·mies** *Surg.* The operation of cutting into or across a lobe of the brain, especially in order to modify or eliminate some function associated with a mental disorder. [< Gk. *lobos* lobe + -TOMY]

lob·scouse (lob′skous) *n.* A sailors' stew consisting of meat, vegetables, and hardtack. [Origin unknown]

lob·ster (lob′stər) *n.* 1. Any of various decapod marine crustaceans (genus *Homarus*) having the first pair of legs modified as claws, and compound eyes on flexible stalks. 2. Any of various similar or related crustaceans, as the spiny lobster. 3. The flesh of any of these crustaceans eaten as food. [OE *loppestre* < L *locusta* lobster, locust; infl. in form by OE *loppe* spider. Doublet of LOCUST.]

lobster pot A cagelike trap used for catching lobsters. Also **lobster trap.**

lobster shift *U.S. Informal* In newspaper work, the shift beginning work during the late hours of the night; graveyard shift. Also **lobster trick.**

lobster ther·mi·dor (thûr′mə-dôr) A dish made from lobster meat, mushrooms, etc., in a seasoned sauce, baked and served in a lobster shell.

lob·stick (lob′stik′) *n. Canadian* A spruce with all but the uppermost branches trimmed.

lob·ule (lob′yōōl) *n.* 1. A small lobe. 2. A subdivision of a lobe. [< NL *lobulus,* dim. of *lobus* lobe] — **lob′u·lar, lob′u·lose** *adj.*

lob·worm (lob′wûrm′) *n.* The lugworm (which see).

lo·cal (lō′kəl) *adj.* 1. Pertaining to, characteristic of, or confined to a relatively small area, region, or neighborhood. 2. Restricted, as by environmental influences, lack of general knowledge, etc.; limited. 3. Of or pertaining to a particular place or position in space: *local* time. 4. Stopping at all stations along its run, as a train. 5. *Med.* Relating to or affecting a specific part of the body; not general: a *local* anesthetic. — *n.* 1. A branch or chapter of an organization, as a trade union. 2. A bus, train, etc., that stops at all stations on its run. 3. A news item of local interest. [< F < L *localis* < *locus* place] — **lo′cal·ly** *adv.*

local color The characteristic appearance, mannerisms, speech, dress, etc., of a place or period, especially as presented in literature and the arts. — **local colorist**

lo·cale (lō-kal′) *n.* 1. A place or locality, especially with reference to some event or circumstance. 2. The setting of a literary, dramatic, or artistic work; scene. [< F]

local government 1. Independent government in local affairs by the political entity of a limited region. 2. The governing head or body of such a locality.

local government district *Canadian* A district administered by the provincial government because it lacks the population for a municipality. Also **local improvement district.**

lo·cal·ism (lō′kəl-iz′əm) *n.* 1. A manner of acting or speaking characteristic of a particular place; local custom or idiom. 2. A word, meaning of a word, pronunciation, etc., peculiar to a locality. 3. Narrowness; provincialism.

lo·cal·i·ty (lō-kal′ə-tē) *n. pl.* **·ties** 1. A place, region, neighborhood, etc. 2. Position, especially in relation to surroundings, other objects, etc. 3. The state or condition of being local. [< F *localité* < LL *localitas, -tatis*]

lo·cal·ize (lō′kəl-īz) *v.t.* **·ized, ·iz·ing** 1. To make local; confine or assign to a specific area. 2. To determine the place of origin of. — **lo′cal·iz′a·ble** *adj.* — **lo′cal·i·za′tion** *n.*

local option The right of a county or town, etc., to restrict or prohibit certain activities, as the sale of liquor.

Lo·car·no (lō-kär′nō) A town in SE central Switzerland, on Lago Maggiore; scene of an international conference, 1925; pop. about 8,000.

lo·cate (lō′kāt, lō-kāt′) *v.* **·cat·ed, ·cat·ing** *v.t.* 1. To discover the position or place of; find. 2. To establish or place at a particular site, position, etc.; situate: The store is *located* on the corner. 3. To place hypothetically as to setting, a relative position, etc. 4. *U.S.* To survey and fix the site or boundaries of (property, a mining claim, etc.). — *v.i.* 5. *U.S. Informal* To make one's residence; settle. [< L *locatus,* pp. of *locare* < *locus* place] — **lo′cat′a·ble** *adj.* — **lo′ca·ter** *n.*

lo·ca·tion (lō-kā′shən) *n.* 1. The act of locating, or the state of being located. 2. A site or situation, especially considered in regard to its surroundings. 3. Exact position or place occupied: *location* in a series. 4. A motion picture or television locale away from the studio: usually in the phrase **to be on location.** 5. *U.S.* A tract of land having established boundaries. 6. *Law* A renting or letting. [< L *locatio, -onis*]

loc·a·tive (lok′ə-tiv) *adj. Gram.* In certain inflected languages, as Latin, Greek, and Sanskrit, designating a noun case denoting place where or at which. — *n. Gram.* 1. The locative case. 2. A word in this case. [< L *locatus,* pp. of *locare* to locate; on analogy with L *vocativus* vocative]

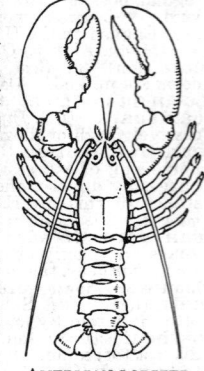

AMERICAN LOBSTER
(To 20 inches long)

lo·ca·tor (lō′kā-tər) *n.* 1. *U.S.* One who locates land, as by fixing boundaries of a claim. 2. A radar or other device for locating aircraft in flight. 3. *Mil.* One of a set of filing cards recording essential facts about personnel and equipment in supply depots, etc.: also **locator card.**

loc. cit. In the place cited (L *loco citato*).

loch (lokh, lok) *n. Scot.* 1. A lake. 2. A bay or arm of the sea.

lo·chi·a (lō′kē-ə, lok′ē-ə) *n.pl. Med.* The discharge from the vaginal passages after childbirth. [< NL < Gk. *lochia* < *lochos* childbirth] — **lo′chi·al** *adj.*

Loch·in·var (lokh′in-vär, lokh-in-vär′) The hero of a ballad in Scott's *Marmion,* who carries off his sweetheart from a celebration at which she is about to be married to another.

lo·ci (lō′sī) Plural of LOCUS.

lock[1] (lok) *n.* 1. A mechanical closing or fastening device having a bolt or combination of bolts secured or released by a key, dial, etc., and used to prevent unauthorized entry, access, or operation. 2. Any part or device that fastens, secures, or holds something firmly in place. 3. A section of a canal, etc., enclosed by gates at either end, within which the water depth may be varied to raise or lower boats from level to level. 4. The mechanism that explodes the charge of a gun: often used in combination: *flintlock.* 5. An interlocking, fastening, or jamming together of parts or elements. 6. A wrestling grip or hold: sometimes used in combination: hammer *lock;* head*lock.* 7. An air lock (which see). — **lock, stock, and barrel** Altogether; completely. — *v.t.* 1. To shut, fasten, or secure by means of a lock. 2. To keep, confine, imprison, etc., in or as in a locked enclosure: with *in, up,* or *away.* 3. To fit together securely; interlock; link. 4. To clasp or grip in or as in a firm hold: They were *locked* in a close embrace. 5. To make immovable by or as by jamming or fastening together. 6. To move (a vessel) through a waterway by means of locks. 7. To supply or divide (a canal, river, etc.) with locks. 8. *Printing* To secure (set type) in position in a chase by tightening the quoins: followed by *up.* — *v.i.* 9. To become locked or securely fastened. 10. To become firmly joined, linked, or interlocked. 11. To pass through locks, as of a canal. 12. To build locks, as in canals. — **to lock out 1.** To prevent (employees) from working by closing a factory, shop, etc. 2. To keep out by locking. [OE *loc* fastening, enclosure] — **lock′a·ble** *adj.*

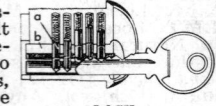

LOCK
Insertion of key raises tumblers (*a*), thus releasing key plug (*b*) and permitting key to turn.

lock[2] (lok) *n.* 1. Strands of hair forming a cluster or curl; tress; ringlet. 2. *pl.* The hair of the head. 3. A small tuft or wisp of cotton, wool, etc. [OE *locc*]

lock·age (lok′ij) *n.* 1. The construction and operation of canal locks. 2. Passage of a vessel through a lock. 3. The toll charged for passing through a lock. 4. The total height of the locks in a canal.

Locke (lok), **John,** 1632–1704, English philosopher.

lock·er (lok′ər) *n.* 1. A closet, cabinet, storage space, etc., fastened with a lock; as: **a** One of a series of metal cabinets, as in a school, gymnasium, or sports club, in which clothes, equipment, etc., are kept. **b** A cabinet or storage space in which frozen foods are kept. 2. A chest, trunk, etc., as on a ship or in a barracks, in which equipment or personal belongings are kept. 3. One who or that which locks.

locker room A room, especially in a gymnasium or clubhouse, having lockers for clothing and equipment.

lock·et (lok′it) *n.* A small ornamental case for enclosing a picture or keepsake, usually worn on a chain, ribbon, etc., around the neck. [< OF *locquet,* dim. of *loc* latch < Gmc.]

lock·jaw (lok′jô′) *n. Pathol.* A form of tetanus causing rigid closure of the jaws: also called *trismus.* Also **locked jaw** (lokt).

lock·nut (lok′nut′) *n. Mech.* **a** An auxiliary nut used to prevent the loosening of another. **b** A nut that automatically locks when screwed tight. Also **lock nut.**

lock·out (lok′out′) *n.* The closing of a factory or other place of business by an employer in order to make employees agree to terms.

Lock·port (lok′pôrt, -pōrt) A city in NW New York; pop. 25,399.

lock·smith (lok′smith′) *n.* A maker or repairer of locks. — **lock′smith′er·y, lock′smith′ing** *n.*

lock step A marching style in which each marcher follows as closely as possible the one in front of him.

lock stitch A stitch made by two interlocking threads, as on some sewing machines.

lock·up (lok′up′) *n.* 1. A jail or prison cell. 2. The act of locking up, or the condition of being locked up.

Lock·yer (lok′yər), **Sir Joseph Norman,** 1836–1920, English astronomer.

lo·co (lō′kō) *adj. U.S. Informal* Crazy; insane. — *n. pl.* **·cos** Locoweed. — *v.t.* **·coed, ·co·ing** 1. To poison with locoweed. 2. *U.S. Slang* To make insane. [< Sp., insane]

lo·co ci·ta·to (lō′kō sī-tā′tō) *Latin* In the place cited. Abbr. *l.c., loc. cit.*

Lo·co·fo·co (lō′kō·fō′kō) *n. pl.* **·cos** *U.S.* **1.** A radical section of the Democratic party in about 1835. **2.** A member of this group. [< *locofoco*, a type of friction match supposedly used to light one of their early meetings]

lo·co·mo·tion (lō′kə·mō′shən) *n.* The act or power of moving from one place to another. — *Syn.* See MOTION. [< L *loco* from a place + *motio*, *-onis* movement]

lo·co·mo·tive (lō′kə·mō′tiv) *n.* An engine that moves by its own power, used to pull passenger or freight trains on a railroad. — *adj.* **1.** Of, pertaining to, or used in locomotion. **2.** Moving or able to move from one place to another. **3.** Capable of moving by its own power, as an engine. [< L *loco* from a place + MOTIVE (adj.)]

lo·co·mo·tor ataxia (lō′kə·mō′tər) *Pathol.* A disease of the spinal cord usually caused by syphilis and characterized by inability to coordinate voluntary movements, especially in walking: also called *tabes dorsalis.*

lo·co·weed (lō′kō·wēd′) *n.* Any of several leguminous plants (genera *Astragalus* and *Oxytropis*) of the SW United States, often poisonous to livestock: also called *crazyweed.*

Lo·cris (lō′kris, lok′ris) An ancient state of central Greece, divided into **Eastern Locris**, NW of Boeotia, and **Western Locris**, north of the Gulf of Corinth. — **Lo′cri·an** *adj. & n.*

loc·u·lar (lok′yə·lər) *adj. Biol.* Having, consisting of, or divided into cells or cell-like parts: often used in combination: *bilocular.* Also **loc′u·late** (-lāt, -lit), **loc′u·lat′ed** (-lā′tid).

loc·u·lus (lok′yə·ləs) *n. pl.* **·li** (-lī) *Biol.* A small, cell-like compartment or division, as of an ovary or antler. Also **loc·ule** (lok′yōol). [< L, dim. of *locus* place]

lo·cum te·nens (lō′kəm tē′nenz) *Chiefly Brit.* One who temporarily replaces or substitutes for another, especially a physician or clergyman. Also *Informal* **locum.** [< L, holding the place < *locus* place + *tenens*, ppr. of *tenere* to hold]

lo·cus (lō′kəs) *n. pl.* **·ci** (-sī) **1.** A place; locality; area. **2.** *Math.* **a** A surface or curve regarded as traced by a line or point moving under specified conditions. **b** Any figure made up wholly of points or lines that satisfy given conditions. **3.** *Genetics* The linear position of a gene on a chromosome. [< L. Doublet of LIEU.]

lo·cus clas·si·cus (lō′kəs klas′ə·kəs) *Latin* An illustrative or authoritative passage from a standard work.

lo·cus si·gil·li (lō′kəs si·jil′ī) *Latin* The place of the seal, as in legal documents. Abbr. *L. S.*

lo·cust¹ (lō′kəst) *n.* **1.** Any of a family (*Locustidae*) of widely distributed orthopterous insects resembling grasshoppers but having short antennae, including those of migratory habits (*Locusta*, *Melanoplus*, and related genera), that destroy grain and vegetation in many parts of the world. **2.** A cicada. [< OF *locuste* < L *locusta.* Doublet of LOBSTER.]

lo·cust² (lō′kəst) *n.* **1.** A leguminous tree (*Robinia pseudoacacia*) of North America, having compound leaves and clusters of fragrant white flowers. **2.** The durable wood of this tree. **3.** Any of various related or similar trees, as the acacia, carob, and honey locust. [< L *locusta*; orig. applied to the carob pod from its fancied resemblance to the insect]

lo·cu·tion (lō·kyōō′shən) *n.* **1.** A verbal expression or phrase. **2.** Manner of speech or expression; phraseology. [< L *locutio*, *-onis* a speaking < *loqui* to speak]

loc·u·to·ry (lok′yə·tôr′ē, -tō′rē) *n. pl.* **·ries** A room used for conversation with visitors in a monastery or convent. [< Med.L *locutorium* < L *locutor* speaker < *loqui* to talk]

lode (lōd) *n. Mining* **1.** A deposit of metallic ore filling a fissure or series of fissures in native rock. **2.** Any deposit of ore located between definite boundaries of associated rock. Also called *vein.* [OE *lād* way, journey. Doublet of LOAD.]

lo·den cloth (lō′dən) A thick woolen, waterproof cloth of Tirolean origin, used for outer garments. Also **lo′den.** [< G < OHG *lodo*, *ludo* coarse cloth]

loden coat A short, warm coat, often with a hood, made of loden cloth.

lode·star (lōd′stär′) *n.* **1.** A star used as a guide in navigation or travel; especially, the polestar. **2.** A guiding principle, example, etc. Also spelled *loadstar.* [ME *lode* course, journey + STAR]

lode·stone (lōd′stōn′) *n.* **1.** A variety of magnetite exhibiting polarity and acting as a magnet when freely suspended. **2.** Something that attracts by or as by magnetism. Also spelled *loadstone.* [ME *lode* course + STONE; because formerly used in compasses]

lodge (loj) *n.* **1.** A local branch of a secret or fraternal society; also, the meeting place of such a society. Abbr. *L.* **2.** A small or rustic hut, cabin, etc., especially one used for vacations or as a base for outdoor activity: skiing *lodge.* **3.** A small house on the grounds of an estate, institution, etc., usually serving as quarters for an employee. **4.** A North American Indian dwelling, as a tepee, wigwam, or hogan; also, a family or group living in such a dwelling. **5.** The characteristic shelter or den of certain animals, as beavers. — *v.* **lodged**, **lodg·ing** *v.t.* **1.** To furnish with temporary quarters; house. **2.** To rent a room or rooms to; take as a paying guest. **3.** To serve as a shelter or dwelling for. **4.** To place or implant firmly, as by thrusting or inserting. **5.** To deposit for safekeeping or storage. **6.** To submit or enter (a complaint information, etc.) formally. **7.** To confer or invest (power, etc.): usually with *in* or *with.* **8.** To beat down (crops, etc.): said of wind or rain. — *v.i.* **9.** To take temporary shelter or quarters. **10.** To live in a rented room or rooms. **11.** To become or remain fixed or embedded. — *Syn.* See LIVE¹. [< OF *loge* summerhouse, hut < Med.L *lobia*, *laubia* porch, gallery < OHG *louba* < *loub* foliage; *n.*, doublet of LOBBY, LOGE, LOGGIA]

Lodge (loj), **Henry Cabot**, 1850–1924, U.S. statesman and historian. — **Henry Cabot**, born 1902, U.S. statesman and diplomat; grandson of the preceding. — **Sir Oliver (Joseph)**, 1851–1940, English physicist and writer. — **Thomas**, 1558?–1625, English dramatist and novelist.

lodge·pole (loj′pōl′) *n.* A pole used in building an American Indian lodge.

lodgepole pine A tall, slender pine (*Pinus contortus latifolia*) of western North America.

lodg·er (loj′ər) *n.* **1.** One who lives in a rented room or rooms in another's residence. **2.** Something fixed in place.

lodg·ing (loj′ing) *n.* **1.** A temporary dwelling place. **2.** *pl.* Living quarters consisting of a rented room or rooms in another's house. **3.** Accommodation for living and sleeping.

lodging house A rooming house (which see).

lodg·ment (loj′mənt) *n.* **1.** The act of lodging, or the state of being lodged. **2.** *Mil.* An established position or foothold gained in newly invaded territory. **3.** *Rare* Lodgings.

Lo·di (lō′dē) A commune in northern Italy; scene of Napoleon's defeat of Austrian forces, 1796; pop. about 37,000.

Łódź (wōoj) A city in central Poland; pop. 746,500 (est. 1966). *Russian* **Lodz, Lodz'** (lôtsy').

Loeb (lōb, *Ger.* lœp), **Jacques**, 1859–1924, U.S. physiologist born in Germany. — **James**, 1867–1933, U.S. banker and philanthropist active in Germany.

Loe·gres (lō′grēz) See LOGRES.

loess (lō′is, lœs) *n. Geol.* A pale, yellowish silt or clay forming finely powdered, usually wind-borne deposits along river valleys in Asia, Europe, and North America. [< G *löss* < *lösen* to pour, dissolve] — **loes′si·al** *adj.*

Loe·wi (lœ′vē), **Otto**, 1873–1961, U.S. pharmacologist born in Germany.

Lo·fo·ten Islands (lō·fō′tən) A group of islands off the NW coast of Norway; 475 sq. mi.

loft (lôft, loft) *n.* **1.** A floored space or low story directly under a roof; attic. **2.** *U.S.* A large, open workroom or storeroom on an upper story of a commercial building. **3.** A hayloft (which see). **4.** An upper section or gallery, as in a church: the choir *loft.* **5.** In golf: **a** The slope of the club face away from the vertical line of the shaft, intended to make a struck ball rise sharply in the air. **b** A stroke that causes the ball to rise sharply when struck. **c** The upward travel of a struck ball. **6.** A pigeon coop; also, a flock of pigeons kept in a single coop. **7.** *Naut.* A large, open room where parts of a vessel are drawn at full scale or assembled: a sail *loft.* — *v.t.* **1.** In sports: **a** To strike (a ball) so that it travels in a high arc. **b** To give loft to (a golf club). **2.** To keep or store in a loft. **3.** *Obs.* To provide with a loft. — *v.i.* **4.** In golf, to strike a ball so that it rises in a high arc. [Late OE < ON, air, sky, upper room. Akin to LIFT.]

loft·er (lôf′tər, lof′-) *n.* In golf, an iron with a widely sloping face, used for lofting the ball. Also **lofting iron.** For illustration see GOLF CLUB.

loft·y (lôf′tē, lof′-) *adj.* **loft·i·er**, **loft·i·est** **1.** Having great or imposing height; towering. **2.** Elevated in character, quality, style, etc.; noble. **3.** Exalted in rank or position; eminent. **4.** Showing contemptuous pride; arrogant; haughty. — *Syn.* See HIGH. — **loft′i·ly** *adv.* — **loft′i·ness** *n.*

log¹ (log, lôg) *n.* **1.** A full length or cut section of a felled tree trunk, limb, etc., stripped of branches. **2.** Something or someone inert, stupefied, etc. **3.** *Naut.* **a** A record of the daily progress of a vessel and of the events of a voyage. **b** Any of various devices for measuring the speed and mileage of a vessel. Compare LOG CHIP, LOG LINE, PATENT LOG. **4.** A record of operation or progress, as of an aircraft in flight. — *v.* **logged**, **log·ging** *v.t.* **1.** To cut down the trees of (a forest, region, etc.) for timber. **2.** To convert (timber) into logs. **3.** *Naut. & Aeron.* **a** To enter in a logbook. **b** To travel (a specified distance, number of hours, etc.). **c** To travel at (a specified speed). — *v.i.* **4.** To engage in the operation of cutting and transporting timber. [ME *logge*, prob. < Scand. Cf. ON *lāg*, Dan. *laag* felled tree.]

log² (log, lôg) A logarithm.

log- Var. of LOGO-.

-log (log) Var. of -LOGUE.

Lo·gan (lō′gən), **Mount** A peak in the SW Yukon Territory, Canada, second highest in North America; 19,850 ft.

lo·gan·ber·ry (lō′gən·ber′ē) *n. pl.* **·ries** **1.** A hybrid plant (*Rubus loganobaccus*), obtained by crossing the red raspberry with the blackberry. **2.** The edible fruit of this plant. [after J. H. Logan, 1841–1928, U.S. horticulturist]

---

lo·ga·ni·a·ceous (lō-gā/nē-ā/shəs) *adj. Bot.* Belonging to a family (*Loganiaceae*) of chiefly tropical and subtropical plants, many of which are poisonous. [< NL, after James *Logan*, 1674–1751, Irish botanist in America]

log·an stone (log/ən, lôg-) A rocking stone (which see). Also **lo'gan, log/gan stone.** [< dial. E *logan* rocking, moving to and fro + STONE]

log·a·oe·dic (log/ə-ē/dik, lôg/-) *adj.* In classical prosody, denoting several meters in which trochees and dactyls, or anapests and iambs, are combined to produce an effect resembling prose. — *n.* A logaoedic verse. [< LL *logaoedicus* < Gk. *logaoidikos* < *logos* speech + *aoidē* song]

log·a·rithm (log/ə-rith/əm, lôg/-) *n. Math.* The power to which a fixed number, called the base, must be raised in order to produce a given number, the antilogarithm. Also, in shortened form, *log.* [< NL < Gk. *logos* word, ratio + *arithmos* number]

log·a·rith·mic (log/ə-rith/mik, lôg/-) *adj.* Of, pertaining to, or involving a logarithm or logarithms. Also **log/a·rith/mi·cal.** — **log/a·rith/mi·cal·ly** *adv.*

log·book (log/bŏŏk/, lôg/-) *n.* The book in which the official record of a ship, aircraft, etc., is entered. Also **log book.**

log chip *Naut.* A quadrant-shaped board weighted on the curved edge and suspended in the water from a moving vessel in order to measure its speed. Also called *log ship.*

loge (lōzh) *n.* A box or upper section in a theater. [< F < OF. Doublet of LOBBY, LODGE, *n.*, LOGGIA.]

log·ger (log/ər, lôg/-) *n.* 1. A person engaged in logging; lumberjack. 2. A machine for hauling and loading logs.

log·ger·head (log/ər·hed, lôg/-) *n.* 1. A large marine turtle (genus *Caretta*) of tropical Atlantic waters. Also **loggerhead turtle.** 2. The loggerhead shrike. See under SHRIKE. 3. A post on a whaleboat, around which the line is turned to retard the motion of a harpooned whale. 4. A metal instrument having a long handle terminating in a ball that is heated and used to melt tar, heat liquids, etc. 5. *Archaic* or *Dial.* A blockhead; dunce. — **at loggerheads** Engaged in a quarrel; unable to agree. [< dial. E *logger* log tied to a horse's leg to impede movement + HEAD]

log·gi·a (loj/ē-ə, loj/ə; *Ital.* lôd/jä) *n.* A roofed gallery or portico that is open and supported by columns on one or more sides. [< Ital. < OF *loge.* Doublet of LOBBY, LODGE, *n.*, LOGE.]

LOGGIA

log·ging (lôg/ing, log/-) *n.* The business or occupation of felling timber and transporting logs to a mill or market.

log·i·a (log/ē-ə) *n. pl.* of **log·i·on** (log/ē-on) *Usually cap.* Collections of sayings attributed to a religious leader; especially, the maxims, doctrines, or truths ascribed to Jesus in the Bible. [< Gk., pl. of *logos* word]

log·ic (loj/ik) *n.* 1. The science concerned with the principles of valid reasoning and correct inference, either deductive or inductive. See FORMAL LOGIC, SYMBOLIC LOGIC. 2. Method of reasoning, inference, argument, etc.; especially, correct or sound reasoning. 3. Effective or convincing force, influence, etc.: the *logic* of his argument. 4. The causal relationships or apparently inevitable chain of events involved in an outcome, action, set of circumstances, etc. 5. The basic principles of reasoning developed by and applicable to any field of knowledge. 6. A system of or treatise on logic. — **to chop logic** To use oversubtle logic. [< F *logique* < L *logica* < Gk. *logikē* (*technē*) logical (art) < *logikos* of speaking or reason < *logos* word, speech, thought]

log·i·cal (loj/i-kəl) *adj.* 1. Relating to or of the nature of logic. 2. Conforming to the laws of logic; consistent in point of reasoning: a *logical* conclusion. 3. Capable of or characterized by clear reasoning: a *logical* writer. — **log/i·cal·i·ty** (-kal/ə·tē), **log/i·cal·ness** *n.* — **log/i·cal·ly** *adv.*

-logical *combining form* Of or related to a (specified) science or study: *biological, geological, zoological.* Also **-logic.** [< -LOG(Y) + -ICAL]

logical positivism A movement in philosophy that stresses sensory observation as the basis for assessing claims to knowledge about matters of fact, as well as the use of modern techniques of logical analysis in clarifying the meaning of statements. Also **logical empiricism.**

lo·gi·cian (lō-jish/ən) *n.* One versed in logic.

lo·gis·tic¹ (lō-jis/tik) *Rare adj.* Of or pertaining to arithmetical calculation. — *n. Often pl.* Arithmetical calculation. [< Med.L *logisticus* < Gk. *logistikos* < *logizesthai* to reckon < *logos* word, calculation] — **lo/gis·ti/cian** *n.*

lo·gis·tic² (lō-jis/tik) *adj.* Of or pertaining to logistics.

lo·gis·tics (lō-jis/tiks) *n.pl.* (*construed as sing.*) The branch of military science that deals with all aspects of procurement, movement, maintenance, and disposition of supplies, equipment, facilities, and personnel, and the provision of services. [< F *logistique* < *logis* quarters, lodging < *loger* to house, quarter < OF *logier.* See LODGE.]

log·jam (log/jam/, lôg/-) *n.* 1. A mass of floating logs that have become jammed together in a stream. 2. An obstruction or deadlock in the course of some procedure. Also **log jam, log/-jam/.**

logo- *combining form* Word; speech: *logomachy.* Also, before vowels, *log-.* [< Gk. *logos* word, speech]

log·o·gram (log/ə-gram, lôg/-) *n.* An abbreviation or other sign representing a word, as $ for *dollar.* — **log/o·gram·mat/ic** *adj.* — **log/o·gram·mat/i·cal·ly** *adv.*

log·o·graph (log/ə-graf, -gräf, lôg/-) *n.* A character or combination of characters used to represent a word. — **log/·o·graph/ic** or **·i·cal** *adj.* — **log/o·graph/i·cal·ly** *adv.*

lo·gog·ra·phy (lō-gog/rə-fē) *n.* 1. *Printing* The use of logotypes: also **log·o·typ·y** (log/ə-tīp/ē, lôg/-). 2. The reporting of speeches in longhand by several reporters, each taking down a few words in succession.

log·o·griph (log/ə-grif, lôg/-) *n.* 1. A word puzzle requiring the solver to discover some word by a recombination of the letters or elements of various other words. 2. Any anagram or puzzle involving an anagram. [< LOGO- + Gk. *griphos* riddle] — **log/o·griph/ic** *adj.*

lo·gom·a·chy (lō-gom/ə-kē) *n. pl.* **·chies** 1. Strife over mere words; verbal contention. 2. Any of various games in which letters are arranged into words. [< Gk. *logomachia* < *logos* word + *machē* battle] — **lo·gom/a·chist** (-kist) *n.*

log·or·rhea (log/ə-rē/ə, lôg/-) *n.* Abnormal talkativeness. Also **log/or·rhoe/a.** [< NL < LOGO- + -RRHEA]

log·os (log/os, lôg/-, lō/gos) *n. Often cap.* In Greek and Hellenistic philosophy, the cosmic reason giving order, purpose, and intelligibility to the world. [< Gk., word]

Log·os (log/os, lôg/-, lō/gos) *n. Theol.* 1. The creative Word of God, identified with the cosmic reason. 2. In the Christian religion, God, the second person of the Trinity, incarnate as Jesus Christ. *John* i 1–14.

log·o·type (log/ə-tīp, lôg/-) *n.* 1. *Printing* A piece of type bearing a syllable, word, or words. 2. A distinctive commercial design or style of type used to represent a company name, trademark, etc. Also **lo·go** (lō/gō).

Lo·gres (lō/grēz) In Arthurian legend, a name for England: also spelled *Loegres.*

log·roll (log/rōl/, lôg/-) *U.S. v.t.* To obtain passage of (a bill) by logrolling. — *v.i.* To engage in logrolling. Also **log/-roll/.** [Back formation < LOGROLLING]

log·roll·ing (log/rō/ling, lôg/-) *n. U.S.* 1. The trading of votes and influence between politicians; also, any such trading of help or approval for one's own benefit. 2. Birling. 3. The handling and removing of logs, as in clearing land. Also **log/-roll/ing.** — **log/roll/er** *n.*

-logue *combining form* Discourse; recitation: *monologue, prologue.* Also *-log.* [< OF *-logue* < L *-logus* < Gk. *logos* word, speech < *legein* to speak]

log ship A log chip (which see).

log·wood (log/wood/, lôg/-) *n.* 1. The heavy, reddish wood of a Central American tree (*Haematoxylon campechianum*), used as a dyestuff. 2. The tree itself.

lo·gy (lō/gē) *adj.* **·gi·er, ·gi·est** *U.S. Informal* Dull; heavy; lethargic. [Prob. < Du. *log* dull, heavy]

-logy *combining form* 1. The science or study of: *biology, conchology.* 2. Speech; discourse: *eulogy.* [< Gk. *-logia* < *logos* word, study < *legein* to speak]

Lo·hen·grin (lō/ən-grin) In medieval German legend, a knight of the Holy Grail and son of Parsifal, subject of an opera by Richard Wagner.

loin (loin) *n. Usually pl.* 1. The part of the back and flanks between the lower ribs and the hipbone. ◆ Collateral adjective: *lumbar.* 2. *pl. Chiefly Poetic* The lower back, thighs, and groin regarded as the seat of strength and procreative power, and as a zone to be clothed. 3. The forepart of the hindquarters of beef, lamb, veal, etc., with the flank removed. For illustration see MEAT. — **to gird (up) one's loins** To prepare for action. [< OF *loigne, logne* < L *lumbus*]

loin·cloth (loin/klôth/, -kloth/) *n.* A garment consisting of a piece or strip of cloth worn about the loins and hips.

Loire (lwär) The longest river in France, in the SE part, flowing 620 miles NW to the Bay of Biscay.

loi·ter (loi/tər) *v.i.* 1. To linger idly or aimlessly; loaf. 2. To proceed in a dilatory or aimless manner; dawdle. — *v.t.* 3. To pass (time) idly: with *away.* [ME *lotere*, freq. of *lote* to lurk. Cf. OE *lūtian* to lurk.] — **loi/ter·er** *n.*

Lo·ki (lō/kē) In Norse mythology, a god who created disorder and mischief, figuring occasionally as a helper but mostly as an enemy of the gods. [< ON]

loll (lol) *v.i.* 1. To lie or lean in a relaxed or languid manner; lounge. 2. To hang loosely; droop. — *v.t.* 3. To permit to droop or hang, as the tongue. — *n.* The act of lolling. [Cf. ME *lull*, MDu. *lollen* to sleep] — **loll/er** *n.*

Loll·and (lôl/än) See LAALAND.

lol·la·pa·loo·za (lol/ə-pə-loo/zə) *n. U.S. Slang* Something excellent or extraordinary: also spelled *lalapalooza, lallapalooza.* Also **lol/la·pa·loo/sa.** [Origin unknown]

Lol·lard (lol/ərd) *n.* A follower of John Wycliffe, 14th-century English religious reformer. Also **Lol/ler.** [< MDu. *lollaerd*, lit., grumbler, mumbler (of prayers) < *lollen* to mumble, doze]

lol·li·pop (lol/ē-pop/) *n.* A lump or piece of candy on the end of a stick: also called *sucker.* Also **lol/ly·pop/.** [Prob. < dial. E *lolly* tongue + POP¹]

Lo·max (lō′maks), **Alan**, born 1915, U.S. folklorist. — **John Avery**, 1872?–1948, U.S. folklorist, father of the preceding.

Lom·bard (lom′bərd, -bärd, lum′-) *n.* **1.** One of a Germanic tribe that established a kingdom in northern Italy in the sixth century: also called *Langobard, Longobard.* **2.** A native or inhabitant of Lombardy. [< OF < Ital. *Lombardo* < LL *Longobardus*, ? < OHG *lang* long + *bart* beard] — **Lom·bar′dic** *adj.*

Lom·bard (lom′bärd, -bərd, lum′-), **Peter**, 1100?–60?, Italian theologian. Also called **Peter the Lombard, Pe·trus Lom·bar·dus** (pē′trəs lom·bär′dəs).

Lombard Street 1. A street in London where many banks and financial offices are located. **2.** The world of London finance and financiers.

Lom·bar·dy (lom′bər·dē, lum′-) A Region of northern Italy; 9,190 sq. mi.; pop. 7,390,492 (1961); capital, Milan; formerly an independent kingdom, 568–774. *Italian* **Lom·bar·di·a** (lôm·bär′dē·ä).

Lombardy poplar A tall, graceful type of poplar (*Populus nigra*) originally imported from Europe.

Lom·bok (lom·bok′) An island of Indonesia, east of Bali; 1,825 sq. mi.

Lom·bro·si·an (lom·brō′zē·ən, -zhən) *adj.* Of or pertaining to the doctrines of Cesare Lombroso, especially to his theory that the criminal is a definite, atavistic type of man.

Lom·bro·so (lôm·brō′sō), **Cesare**, 1836–1909, Italian criminologist.

Lo·mé (lō·mā′) The capital of Togo, a port on the Gulf of Guinea; pop. 86,400 (1966).

lo·ment (lō′ment) *n. Bot.* The fruit of certain leguminous plants, having constrictions between the seeds and separating when ripe into sections, each containing a single seed. Also **lo·men·tum** (lō·men′təm). [< L *lomentum* bean meal < *lotum*, pp. of *lavare* to wash; because used as a cosmetic wash in antiquity] — **lo′men·ta′ceous** (-tā′shəs) *adj.*

Lo·mond (lō′mənd), **Loch** A lake in Dumbarton and Stirling counties, Scotland; 23 mi. long.

Lon·don (lun′dən) **1.** A city on the Thames, England, capital and chief city of the United Kingdom. The **City of London** represents London within its ancient boundaries and is the financial center: often called the **City**; 1 sq. mi.; pop. 4,234 (1971). **Greater London**, a metropolitan county, administered by the Greater London Council, comprises the former London and Middlesex counties, and parts of Surrey, Hertfordshire, Essex, and Kent; 848 sq. mi.; pop. 7,167,600 (1976). *Ancient* **Lon·din·i·um** (lən·din′ē·əm). **2.** A city in SW Ontario, Canada, on the Thames; pop. 221,430. — **Lon′don·er** *n.*

Lon·don (lun′dən), **Jack**, 1876–1916, U.S. author: original name **John Griffith London**.

London broil Broiled flank steak that is sliced thin for serving.

Lon·don·der·ry (lun′dən·der′ē) A county of Ulster, Northern Ireland; 801 sq. mi.; pop. 130,296 (1971); county seat, **Londonderry**, a seaport and a county borough; pop. 51,850: also *Derry.*

lone (lōn) *adj.* **1.** Being without companions; unaccompanied; solitary. **2.** Having no nearby counterparts or neighbors; isolated. **3.** Unfrequented; deserted; lonely. **4.** Lacking companionship; lonesome. **5.** Having no spouse; single or widowed. [Aphetic var. of ALONE]

lone hand In certain card games, as euchre: **a** A person playing without a partner. **b** A hand thus played.

lone·ly (lōn′lē) *adj.* **·li·er, ·li·est 1.** Unfrequented by human beings; deserted; desolate. **2.** Sad from lack of companionship or sympathy; lonesome. **3.** Characterized by or inducing the sadness of solitude: a *lonely* city. **4.** Having no companions or associates; habitually or frequently alone; solitary. — **lone′li·ly** *adv.* — **lone′li·ness** *n.*

lon·er (lōn′ər) *n. Informal* One who prefers to work, live, etc., by himself. Also *lone wolf.*

lone·some (lōn′səm) *adj.* **1.** Depressed or uneasy because of being alone; lonely; forlorn. **2.** Inducing a feeling of loneliness. **3.** Unfrequented; secluded: a *lonesome* retreat. — **(all) by one's lonesome** *Informal* By oneself; alone. — **lone′some·ly** *adv.* — **lone′some·ness** *n.*

Lone Star State Nickname of TEXAS.

lone wolf *U.S. Informal* A loner (which see).

long¹ (lông, long) *adj.* **1.** Characterized by or denoting extent, dimension, or measurement relatively great in proportion to breadth or width; not short. **2.** Having relatively great continuation or duration in time; prolonged; lasting. **3.** Having relatively great extension from beginning to end: a *long* tunnel. **4.** Being of a specified measurement or amount in extent or duration: ten miles *long*; three hours *long*. **5.** Having more than the standard quantity, extent, or duration: a *long* tone. **6.** Containing or consisting of many items or entries, as a list. **7.** Continuing beyond the usual or desirable extent or duration; lengthy. **8.** Slow or seemingly slow in passing, occurring, etc.; tedious. **9.** Ex-

tending far into time or space; having considerable range. **10.** Having a plentiful or excessive quantity of: with *on*: *long* on supplies. **11.** Tall: used chiefly with personal names: *Long* John Silver. **12.** In gambling: **a** Denoting odds indicating little likelihood of winning. **b** Denoting a bet, chance, guess, etc., characterized by such odds. **13.** In finance, holding considerable amounts of a stock, commodity, etc., in anticipation of a rise in its price. **14.** *Phonet.* **a** Denoting the vowel sounds of *Dane, dean, dine, dome, dune* as contrasted with those of *Dan, den, din, don, duck.* **b** Relatively more prolonged in sound, as the sound (ē) in *seed* compared with that in *seat.* **15.** In prosody: **a** Denoting syllables that have relatively more duration or quantity, as in classical verse. **b** Stressed, as in English verse. — **in the long run** As the ultimate result of inevitable consequences; eventually. — *adv.* **1.** For or during an extensive period of time: Will he stay *long*? **2.** For a time or period (to be specified): How *long* will he stay? **3.** For the whole extent or duration (of a specified period): It rained all day *long*. **4.** At a considerably distant time: *long* after midnight. — **as** (or **so**) **long as 1.** For or during the time that. **2.** Inasmuch as; since. — **long ago** A long time ago: also **long since.** — *n.* **1.** Something relatively long. **2.** A long syllable or sound, as in phonetics, prosody, etc. **3.** *pl.* In finance, those who have bought large amounts of a stock or commodity in anticipation of a rise in prices. **4.** *Music* In medieval notation, the note next longer than the breve. — **before long** Soon. — **the long and the short** The entire sum and substance; the whole. [OE *long, lang*]

◆ *Long*, meaning "for a long time," may appear as a combining form in hyphenated words, as in:

long-accustomed	long-enduring	long-neglected
long-awaited	long-established	long-past
long-borne	long-expected	long-planned
long-breathed	long-felt	long-projected
long-buried	long-forgotten	long-settled
long-cherished	long-held	long-sought
long-contented	long-hidden	long-threatened
long-continued	long-kept	long-wedded
long-delayed	long-lasting	long-wished
long-desired	long-lost	long-withheld

long² (lông, long) *v.i.* To have a strong or eager desire; wish earnestly; yearn. [OE *langian* to grow long]

Long (lông, long), **Crawford Williamson**, 1815–78, U.S. surgeon; pioneer in use of ether anesthesia in surgery. — **Huey Pierce**, 1893–1935, U.S. politician; assassinated.

long. Longitude.

long·an (lông′gən) *n.* **1.** The small, edible fruit of a tree (*Euphoria longan*) of the soapberry family, native to China and the East Indies. **2.** The tree itself. [< NL *longanum* < Chinese *lung-yen* dragon's eye]

lon·ga·nim·i·ty (lông′gə·nim′ə·tē) *n. pl.* **·ties** *Rare* Patient endurance of trials and sufferings. [< LL *longanimitas*] — **lon·gan·i·mous** (lông·gan′ə·məs) *adj.*

Long Beach 1. A resort city in SW California, on San Pedro Bay; pop. 358,633. **2.** A resort city in SE New York, on an island in the Atlantic south of Long Island; pop. 33,127.

long·boat (lông′bōt′, long′-) *n. Naut.* The largest boat carried by a sailing vessel.

long·bow (lông′bō′, long′-) *n.* A large bow drawn by hand and projecting long, feathered arrows. — **to draw** (or **pull**) **the longbow** To exaggerate, as in a narrative.

Long Branch A resort city in eastern New Jersey, on the Atlantic; pop. 31,774.

long·cloth (lông′klôth′, long′kloth′) *n.* A fine, soft, cotton cloth used for making children's garments.

long·dis·tance (lông′dis′təns, long′-) *adj.* **1.** Connecting distant places. **2.** Covering a relatively long distance. **3.** Existing at or operating from a distance. — *adv.* **1.** By long-distance telephone. **2.** At a distance.

long distance The telephone exchange, operator, or service that handles calls outside the immediate locality.

long division Arithmetical division, usually with large numbers in which all the steps of the process are shown.

long·drawn (lông′drôn′, long′-) *adj.* Prolonged; protracted. Also **long′-drawn′-out′** (-out′).

longe (lunj) See LUNGE².

lon·ge·ron (lon′jər·ən, *Fr.* lônzh·rôn′) *n. Aeron.* A main longitudinal member of the body of an airplane. [< F]

lon·gev·i·ty (lon·jev′ə·tē) *n.* **1.** Great age or length of life. **2.** The tendency to live long. [< L *longaevitas, -tatis* < *longaevus* long-lived < *longus* long + *aevum* age] — **lon·ge·vous** (lon·jē′vəs) *adj.*

long face An exaggeratedly solemn facial expression.

Long·fel·low (lông′fel·ō, long′-), **Henry Wadsworth**, 1807–1882, U.S. poet.

long·hair (lông′hâr′, long′-) *U.S. Slang adj.* **1.** Of or pertaining to intellectuals or their tastes. **2.** Of or pertaining to serious rather than popular music. — *n.* **1.** A longhair person; intellectual. **2.** Longhair music. Also **long′-hair′.**

long·hand (lông′hand′, long′-) *n.* Ordinary handwriting with the words spelled out in full: distinguished from *shorthand*.

long·head (lông′hed′, long′-) *n.* A dolichocephalic person.

long head *Informal* Shrewdness; foresight; common sense: chiefly in the phrase *to have a long head.*

long·head·ed (lông′hed′id, long′-) *adj.* 1. Dolichocephalic. 2. Characterized by or possessing shrewdness, foresight, etc.; astute. Also **long′-head′ed.** — **long′head′ed·ly** *adv.* — **long′head′ed·ness** *n.*

long·horn (lông′hôrn′, long′-) *n.* One of a breed of domestic cattle with long horns. Also **Texas longhorn.**

long house Among North American Indians, especially the Iroquois, a council house or community dwelling.

longi- *combining form* Long: *longicorn.* [< L *longus* long]

lon·gi·corn (lon′ji·kôrn) *adj.* 1. Having long antennae. 2. Of, pertaining to, or belonging to a family of beetles (*Cerambycidae*), usually having long, threadlike antennae. — *n.* A beetle belonging to this family. [< LONGI- + L *cornu* horn]

long·ing (lông′ing, long′-) *n.* A strong, earnest, persistent craving; desire. — *adj.* Having or showing such a craving. — **Syn.** See APPETITE. — **long′ing·ly** *adv.*

Lon·gi·nus (lon·ji′nəs), **Dionysius Cassius,** died 273 A.D., Greek Platonic philosopher. — **Lon·gi·ni·an** (lon·jin′ē·ən) *adj.*

long·ish (lông′ish, long′-) *adj.* Rather long.

Long Island An island of SE New York; 1,723 sq. mi.; separated from Connecticut by **Long Island Sound,** a sheltered arm of the Atlantic 90 miles long. Abbr. *L.I.*

lon·gi·tude (lon′jə·tood, -tyood, long′gə-) *n.* 1. *Geog.* Distance east or west on the earth's surface, usually measured by the angle that the meridian through a particular place makes with the prime meridian that runs through Greenwich, England. Longitude may be expressed either in hours and minutes (**longitude in time**) or in degrees (**longitude in arc**). 2. *Astron.* The angular distance eastward from the vernal equinox to the intersection with the ecliptic of the perpendicular from a heavenly body (**celestial longitude**). Abbr. *L, long.* [< F *L* < *longitudo* < *longus* long]

lon·gi·tu·di·nal (lon′jə·tood′ə·nəl, -tyood′-, long′gə-) *adj.* 1. Of or pertaining to longitude or length. 2. Running lengthwise. 3. *Biol.* Of, pertaining to, or extending along that axis of a body running from front to back or from head to tail (or crotch). — **lon′gi·tu′di·nal·ly** *adv.*

long johns (jonz) *U.S. Informal* Ankle-length, fitted underdrawers of knitted fabric.

long jump The broad jump (which see).

long·leaf pine (lông′lēf′, long′-) A pine (*Pinus palustris*) of the southern United States, having tough, resinous wood valuable as lumber and as a source of turpentine: also called *Georgia pine, pitch pine.* Also **long′leaf′, long′-leaf′, long′leaf′ pine, long′leaved′ pine.**

long·lin·er (lông′lī′nər, long′-) *n. Canadian* A type of fishing vessel.

long·lin·er·man (lông′lī′nər·mən, long′-) *n. pl.* **·men** (-mən) *Canadian* A fisherman on a longliner.

long-lived (lông′līvd′, -livd′, long′-) *adj.* Having a long life or period of existence. — **long′-lived′ness** *n.*

long measure Linear measure (which see).

long moss Spanish moss (which see).

Lon·go·bard (lông′gō·bärd) *n. pl.* **·bards** or **Lon·go·bar·di** (lông′gō·bär′dē) A Lombard (def. 1). [< LL] — **Lon′go·bar′di·an, Lon′go·bar′dic** *adj.*

Long Parliament See under PARLIAMENT.

long pig Human flesh as prepared for a feast by cannibals: so called from Maori and Polynesian term.

long-play·ing (lông′plā′ing, long′-) *adj.* LP (which see).

long-range (lông′rānj′, long′-) *adj.* 1. Designed to shoot or move over distances. 2. Taking account of, or extending over, a long span of future time: *long-range* plans.

long s *Printing* An early form of s (ſ, italic *ʃ*), generally used in England until the printing of John Bell's edition of Shakespeare in the late 18th century.

long·shore (lông′shôr′, -shōr′, long′-) *adj.* Belonging, living, or working along a shore or waterside. — *adv.* Along the shore. [Apheticvar. of ALONGSHORE]

long·shore·man (lông′shôr′mən, -shōr′-, long′-) *n. pl.* **·men** (-mən) A man employed on the waterfront to load and unload vessels; stevedore. [< LONGSHORE + MAN]

long shot *Informal* 1. In betting, a race horse or other gambling choice, backed at great odds and having little chance of winning. 2. Any venture, scheme, etc., with poor chances of success, but promising great rewards if realized. 3. In motion pictures, a shot in which the camera is placed some distance away from the scene to be photographed. — **not by a long shot** *Informal* Decidedly not; not at all.

long-sight·ed (lông′sī′tid, long′-) *adj.* 1. Hypermetropic; far-sighted. 2. Characterized by or having foresight; sagacious. — **long′-sight′ed·ly** *adv.* — **long′-sight′ed·ness** *n.*

Longs Peak (lôngz, longz) A mountain in Rocky Mountain National Park, north central Colorado; 14,255 ft.

long·spur (lông′spûr′, long′-) *n.* Any of a group of birds of the finch family (genera *Calcarius* and *Rhynchophanes*) with elongated hind claws, found in the arctic regions and Great Plains of North America.

long-stand·ing (lông′stan′ding, long′-) *adj.* Having existed over a long period: a *long-standing* debt.

long-sta·ple (lông′stā′pəl, long′-) *adj.* Having a long fiber: said of fabrics, especially cotton.

Long·street (lông′strēt, long′-), **James,** 1821–1904, Confederate general in the Civil War.

long-suf·fer·ing (lông′suf′ər·ing, long′-) *adj.* Patiently enduring injuries, misfortune, etc., for a long time. — *n.* Patient endurance of injuries, etc.: also **long′-suf′fer·ance.**

long-term (lông′tûrm′, long′-) *adj.* Involving or extending over a relatively long period of time: a *long-term* contract.

long-term bond In finance, a bond whose maturity will not be reached until several years after issue.

long-time (lông′tīm′, long′-) *adj.* Being such for a considerable period of time: a *long-time* friend.

Long Tom 1. A long swivel gun mounted on the decks of old sailing vessels. 2. A long-range coastal gun. 3. *Slang* Cannon. [< *long Tom Turk*; 19th-century naval slang]

long ton See under TON[1].

Long·view (lông′vyoo, long′-) A city in NE Texas; pop. 45,547.

long-wind·ed (lông′win′did, long′-) *adj.* 1. Continuing for a long time in speaking or writing: a *long-winded* lecturer. 2. Tediously long; lacking conciseness. 3. Capable of vigorous activity without becoming short of breath: a *long-winded* swimmer. — **long′-wind′ed·ly** *adv.* — **long′-wind′ed·ness** *n.*

long·wise (lông′wīz′, long′-) *adv.* Lengthwise. Also **long′ways′** (-wāz′).

loo (loo) *n. pl.* **loos** 1. A game of cards in which each player deposits a forfeit in a pool. 2. The forfeit so deposited. — *v.t.* To subject to a forfeit at loo. [Short for *lanterloo* < F *lanturelu*, name of the game; orig. a vaudeville refrain]

loo·by (loo′bē) *n. pl.* **·bies** *Informal* A big, clumsy person; a lout. [? Akin to LOB, LUBBER]

loof[1] (loof) *n. Scot.* The palm of the hand.

loof[2] (loof) *n.* Luff.

loo·fah (loo′fə) *n.* Any of a genus (*Luffa*) of the gourd family with conspicuous yellow or whitish flowers and a fibrous fruit used as a filter or as a sponge: also called *dishcloth gourd, vegetable sponge*: also *luffa.* Also **loo′fa.** [< Arabic *lūfah*]

look (look) *v.i.* 1. To use one's sense of sight. 2. To turn the eyes in a specified direction in order to see. 3. To glance or gaze in such a way as to convey a specific feeling or meaning: to *look* pleadingly. 4. To use one's eyes in order to examine, repair, explain, improve, etc.: Let's *look* at the engine. 5. To turn one's attention or notice; consider: *Look* at his fine record. 6. To appear to the sight or mind; seem: He *looks* reliable. 7. To face in a specified direction: The house *looks* on the park. 8. To expect: with an infinitive: I *look* to hear from you soon. — *v.t.* 9. To express by a glance or gaze: to *look* one's anger. 10. *Rare* To affect or influence by a stare or glance: to *look* someone into silence. — **it looks like** 1. It promises or suggests the coming of: *It looks like* snow. 2. *Informal* It seems as if: *It looks like* I'll have to move. — **to look after** 1. To take care of. 2. To watch or follow with the eye, as someone or something moving away. — **to look alive** *Informal* To be alert or attentive; move quickly: usually in the imperative. — **to look back** To reflect on the past; recall. — **to look down on** (or **upon**) To regard with condescension or contempt. Also **to look down one's nose on** (or **upon**). — **to look for** 1. To search for. 2. To anticipate; expect. — **to look forward to** To anticipate, especially with pleasure. — **to look in** (or **in on**) To make a short visit to. — **to look into** 1. To examine closely. 2. To make inquiries about. — **to look on.** 1. To be a spectator. 2. To consider; regard. — **to look oneself** To appear to be in a normal, usual, or healthy condition, state of mind, etc. — **to look out for** 1. To take close care of; protect: to *look out for* one's own interests. 2. To be watchful; be on guard: *Look out for* the icy steps. — **to look over** To examine; scrutinize. — **to look the other way** To ignore or avoid an unpleasant or unfavorable situation, sight, etc. — **to look to** 1. To attend to. 2. To turn to, as for help, advice, etc. 3. To anticipate; expect. — **to look up** 1. To search for and find, as in a file, book, etc. 2. *Informal* To discover the whereabouts of and make a visit to. 3. *Informal* To improve; become better: Things are *looking up.* — **to look up and down** 1. To inspect critically or appraisingly. 2. To search everywhere. — **to look up to** To have respect for. — *n.* 1. The act of looking. 2. A search, examination, etc., by or as by means of one's eyes. 3. Aspect or expression: a saintly *look.* 4. *Often pl. Informal* General appearance: I like the *looks* of this place. 5. *pl. Informal* Personal appearance: the *looks* of a model. — *interj.* 1. See! 2. Listen! Pay attention! [OE *lōcian*] — **Syn.** (verb) 1. *Look, gaze, stare, peer,* and *glance* mean to make an effort to see something. To *look* is merely to direct the eyes; to *gaze* is to *look* long and steadily, often with the implication of wonder, admiration, fascination, etc. *Stare* is to *gaze* intently, especially with wide-open eyes, as in amazement. *Peer* implies difficulty in seeing, and suggests a narrowing of the eyes or movement of the head, while *glance* refers to the act of *looking* briefly or hurriedly. 4., 5. scrutinize, inspect, regard, watch. Compare SEE[1], EXAMINE. — (noun) See AIR.

look·er (lŏŏk′ər) *n.* **1** One who looks or watches. **2.** *U.S. Slang* A handsome or good looking person.

look·er-on (lŏŏk′ər·on′, -ôn′) *n. pl.* **look·ers-on** A spectator; onlooker.

look-in (lŏŏk′in′) *n.* **1.** A hasty glance. **2.** A brief visit.

look·ing glass (lŏŏk′ing) A glass mirror.

look·out (lŏŏk′out′) *n.* **1.** The act of watching for someone or something. **2** A place where such a watch is kept. **3.** The person or persons watching. **4.** *Naut.* A crow's-nest. **5.** *Informal* Concern; worry: It's your *lookout*. **6.** *Chiefly Brit.* Prospect; outlook.

Look·out Mountain (lŏŏk′out′) A ridge in SE Tennessee, near Chattanooga; scene of a Civil War battle, 1863.

look-see (lŏŏk′sē′) *n. Slang* A brief inspection or survey: Have a *look-see*. [Orig. Pidgin English]

loom¹ (lōōm) *v.i.* **1.** To appear or come into view indistinctly, as through a mist, especially so as to seem large or ominous: often with *up*. **2.** To appear to the mind as large or threatening: Great difficulties *loom* ahead. — *n.* A looming appearance of something, as of a ship in the fog. [Origin uncertain. Cf. Sw. *loma* to move slowly (toward).]

loom² (lōōm) *n.* **1.** Any of various contrivances or machines on which thread or yarn is woven into fabric. **2.** Weaving. **3.** *Naut.* The shaft of an oar. [OE *gelōma* tool]

loom³ (lōōm) *n.* Any of various aquatic birds, as the auk, guillemot, puffin, or loon. [< ON *lomr*]

L.O.O.M. Loyal Order of Moose.

loon¹ (lōōn) *n.* Any of various diving, fish-eating waterfowl (genus *Gavia*), with short tail feathers and webbed feet, having a weird, laughing cry; especially, the **common loon** or **great northern diver** (*Gavia immer*). [See LOOM³]

LOON
(About 32 inches long)

loon² (lōōn) *n.* **1.** A stupid or crazy person. **2.** A worthless person; idler. **3.** *Archaic* A menial. **4.** *Scot.* A boy. [Cf. Du. *loen* stupid fellow, G *lümmel* lout]

loon·y (lōō′nē) *Informal adj.* **loon·i·er, loon·i·est 1.** Lunatic or demented. **2.** Foolish; erratic; silly. — *n. pl.* **·ies** A demented or insane person. Also spelled *luny.* [< LUNATIC]

loop¹ (lōōp) *n.* **1.** A folding or doubling over of one end of a piece of thread, rope, wire, etc., so as to form a circular or oval opening through which something may be passed. **2.** A ring or bent piece of metal, wood, thread, etc., serving as a fastener, staple, eyelet, or the like. **3.** Something having or suggesting the shape of a loop, as the closed part of a letter or other written symbol, a U-shaped curve or bend in a road or railroad track, etc. **4.** *Electr.* A complete magnetic or electrical circuit. **5.** *Aeron.* A complete circular turn made by an aircraft flying in a vertical plane. **6.** *Physics* The part of a vibrating string, column of air, or standing wave system that is between two nodes; an antinode. — *v.t.* **1.** To form a loop in or of. **2.** To fasten, connect, or encircle by means of a loop. **3.** *Aeron.* To fly (an aircraft) in a loop or loops. — *v.i.* **4.** To make a loop or loops. **5.** To move forward by forming loops, as a measuring worm. — **to loop the loop** To make a vertical circular turn in the air, especially in an aircraft. [ME *loupe*; ult. origin uncertain]

loop² (lōōp) *n. Metall.* A puddleball. [< F *loupe*]

loop³ (lōōp) *n. Archaic* A small window or aperture; loophole. [Cf. MDu. *lupen* to lie in wait, peer]

Loop, the The principal business, financial, hotel, and theatrical district of Chicago, near the lake front.

loop·er (lōō′pər) *n.* **1.** One who or that which loops or forms loops. **2.** A measuring worm.

loop·hole (lōōp′hōl′) *n.* **1.** A narrow slit in a wall, especially, one in a fortification through which small arms may be fired. **2.** An opportunity for escaping or evading something, especially a law; a basis of excuse. — *v.t.* **holed, hol·ing** To furnish with loopholes. [< LOOP³ + HOLE]

loop stitch Any of several sewing stitches, as the picot stitch, composed of a series of connected loops.

loop·y (lōō′pē) *adj.* **loop·i·er, loop·i·est 1.** Full of or having loops. **2.** *Scot.* Shrewd; sly. **3.** *Slang* Crazy; foolish.

loose (lōōs) *adj.* **loos·er, loos·est 1.** Not fastened or confined; unbound; unattached: *loose* hair; a *loose* end. **2.** Not drawn tight; not taut; slack: a *loose* rein; *loose* knot. **3.** Freed from bonds or restraint; at liberty: The prisoners are *loose*. **4.** Not firmly fitted or embedded in its place; tending to shake or shift about: a *loose* tooth; *loose* window. **5.** Not closely fitted; providing ample room, as clothing. **6.** Not bound or fastened together: *loose* sheets of paper. **7.** Not compact, firm, or dense in construction or construction: *loose* soil; a fabric of *loose* weave. **8.** Not packaged or put up in a container: *loose* butter. **9.** *Chem.* Uncombined, as an element. **10.** Not constricted; open: said of lax bowels or a cough attended with expectoration. **11.** Not properly controlled; lacking in restraint: a *loose* tongue. **12.** Dissolute; unchaste. **13.** Lacking in exactness or precision; not strictly accurate: a *loose* translation. **14.** *Informal* Not set aside for a specific use; available: *loose* funds. — **on the loose 1.** Not confined; at large. **2.** *Informal* Behaving in a free, unin-

hibited, and usually dissolute manner. — *adv.* **1.** In a loose manner· loosely. **2.** So as to be or become loose: to break *loose*. — **to cut loose** *Informal* To behave in a free, uninhibited manner. — *v.* **loosed, loos·ing** *v.t.* **1.** To set free, as from bondage, penalty, obligation, etc. **2.** To untie or undo. **3.** To make less tight, firm, or compact; loosen. **4.** To make less strict; relax. **5.** *Naut.* To cast off; release, as a boat from its moorings. **6.** To let fly; shoot, as an arrow. — *v.i.* **7.** To become loose. **8.** To loose something. [< ON *lauss*] — **loose′ly** *adv.* — **loose′ness** *n.*

loose end Something left undecided or undone, as a task, decision, etc. — **at loose ends 1.** In an unsettled or confused state; not certain of what to do next. **2.** Without a job.

loose-joint·ed (lōōs′join′tid) *adj.* **1.** Having joints not tightly articulated. **2.** Limber or flexible in movement.

loose-leaf (lōōs′lēf′) *adj.* Designed for or having pages that are easily inserted or removed: a *loose-leaf* notebook.

loos·en (lōō′sən) *v.t.* **1.** To untie or undo, as bonds or other restraints. **2.** To set free; release. **3.** To make less tight, firm, or compact: to *loosen* soil; to *loosen* one's hold. **4.** To effect laxity in the action of (the bowels). **5.** To relax the strictness of, as discipline. — *v.i.* **6.** To become loose or looser. — **to loosen up** *Informal* **1.** To become less tense; relax. **2.** To talk with ease; talk freely. **3.** To give more generously, as money. — **loos′en·er** *n.*

loose sentence A sentence that is grammatically complete before its end; especially, one that makes a full statement and then adds details: distinguished from *periodic sentence*.

loose·strife (lōōs′strīf′) *n.* **1.** Any of various plants (genus *Lysimachia*) of the primrose family, as the yellow-flowered **common loosestrife** (*L. vulgaris*). **2.** Any plant of the loosestrife family (*Lyraceae*), as the **purple loosestrife** (*Lythrum salicaria*). [< LOOSE + STRIFE; direct trans. of L *lysimachia* < Gk. *lysimachion* < *lyein* to loose + *machē* battle]

loot¹ (lōōt) *n.* **1** Goods taken as booty by a victorious army from a sacked city, enemy forces, etc. **2.** Anything unlawfully taken or seized, as by a burglar, etc. **3.** *U.S. Slang* Money. — *v.t.* **1.** To plunder, as a conquered city; pillage. **2.** To carry off as plunder. — *v.i.* **3.** To engage in plundering. [< Hind. *lūt* < Skt. *lunt*] — **loot′er** *n.*

loot² (lōōt) *Scot.* Past tense of LET¹.

lop¹ (lop) *v.t.* **lopped, lop·ping 1.** To cut or trim the branches, twigs, etc., from; as from a tree. **2.** To cut off, as branches, twigs, superfluous parts, etc.: usually with *off.* — *n.* A part or parts lopped off. [Origin unknown]

lop² (lop) *v.* **lopped, lop·ping** *v.i.* **1.** To droop or hang down loosely. **2.** To move about in an awkward or slouching manner. **3.** To move with short bounds or leaps. — *v.t.* **4.** To permit to droop or hang down loosely. — *adj.* Pendulous; drooping. [Origin unknown]

Lo·pa·du·sa (lō′pə·dōō′sə, -dyōō′-) The ancient name for LAMPEDUSA.

lope (lōp) *v.t. & v.i.* **loped, lop·ing** To run or cause to run with a steady, swinging stride or gallop. — *n.* A slow, easy stride or gallop. [< ON *hlaupa* to leap, run] — **lop′er** *n.*

lop-eared (lop′ird′) *adj.* Having drooping or pendulous ears.

Lo·pe de Ve·ga (lō′pā thā vā′gä) See (Lope de) VEGA.

lo·pho·branch (lō′fō·brangk, lof′ō-) *adj.* Of or pertaining to a division of carnivorous teleost fishes (*Lophobranchii*) having small tail fins and tuftlike gill elements, including pipefishes and sea horses. — *n.* One of the lophobranch fishes. [< Gk. *lophos* crest + *branchion* gill] — **lo′pho·bran′chi·ate** (-kē-it, -āt) *adj. & n.*

lop·per¹ (lop′ər) *n.* One who or that which lops.

lop·per² (lop′ər) *v.t. & v.i. Scot.* To curdle: also *lapper.*

lop·py (lop′ē) *adj.* **·pi·er, ·pi·est** Pendulous; limp.

lop·sid·ed (lop′sī′did) *adj.* Heavier, larger, or sagging on one side; lacking in symmetry. — **lop′sid′ed·ly** *adv.* — **lop′sid′ed·ness** *n.*

lop·stick (lop′stik′) *n. Canadian* A lobstick (which see).

loq. He (she, it) speaks (L *loquitur*).

lo·qua·cious (lō·kwā′shəs) *adj.* Characterized by or revealing a tendency toward continuous talking. — **Syn.** See TALKATIVE. [< L *loquax, loquacis* < *loqui* to speak] — **lo·qua′cious·ly** *adv.* — **lo·qua′cious·ness** *n.*

lo·quac·i·ty (lō·kwas′ə·tē) *n. pl.* **·ties** Talkativeness.

lo·quat (lō′kwot, -kwat) *n.* **1.** A low, pomaceous tree (*Eriobotrya japonica*) of the rose family, native to China and Japan, but cultivated in other countries for its fruit. **2.** The fruit. [Cantonese alter. of Chinese *luchü* rush orange]

Lo·rain (lō·rān′) A port city in northern Ohio, on Lake Erie; pop. 78,185.

lo·ran (lôr′an, lō′ran) *n.* A system of long-range navigation in which the position of a ship or aircraft is determined by recording the time intervals between radio signals transmitted from a network of synchronized ground stations. [< LO(NG) RA(NGE) N(AVIGATION)]

Lor·ca (lôr′kä) A city in SE Spain; pop. 21,000 (1967).

Lor·ca (lôr′kä), Federico Garcia See GARCIA LORCA.

---

lord (lôrd) *n.* **1.** One possessing great power and authority; ruler; master. **2.** In Great Britain: **a** Any one of the noblemen or peers (**lords temporal**) having the title of marquis, earl, viscount, or baron and having seats in the House of Lords. **b** Any of the higher churchmen (**lords spiritual**), as archbishops and bishops, who are members of the House of Lords. **3.** In feudal law, the owner of a manor under grant from the crown; a landlord. **4.** Formerly, a husband: now a humorous term. — *v.t.* To invest with the title of lord; make a lord of. — **to lord it** (**over**) To act in a domineering or arrogant manner (toward). [OE *hlāford, hlāf-weard,* lit., bread keeper < *hlāf* loaf + *weard* keeper, ward]

Lord (lôrd) **1.** God: preceded by *the* except in direct address. **2.** Jesus Christ: also *Our Lord.* **3.** In Great Britain: **a** A title of honor or nobility given generally to men noble by birth or ennobled by patent. The formal titles are as follows: *Baron* X, the *Marquis* of X, the *Earl* of X, *Viscount* X; informally all are addressed *Lord* X. **b** A ceremonious title given to any of the higher churchmen, as bishops or archbishops, or to certain high officials, as the *Lord* Mayor of London. Abbr. (for def. 3) *Ld.*

Lord Chancellor In Great Britain, the highest ranking official of state, the presiding officer of the House of Lords, Keeper of the Great Seal, and usually a member of the cabinet. Compare PRIME MINISTER. Also **Lord High Chancellor.**

Lord Chief Justice In Great Britain, the highest judicial officer of the government.

lord·ing (lôr′ding) *n.* **1.** A lordling. **2.** *Archaic* A lord. **3.** *Usually pl. Archaic* Masters; sirs: a form of address.

Lord Lieutenant 1. In Great Britain, the title of various high officials appointed by the sovereign; especially, the chief executive officer of a county. **2.** Formerly, the British viceroy in Ireland.

lord·ling (lôrd′ling) *n.* A young or unimportant lord; petty chieftain: often a contemptuous usage.

lord·ly (lôrd′lē) *adj.* **·li·er, ·li·est 1.** Befitting the rank and position of a lord; sumptuous; splendid. **2.** Of, pertaining to, or like a lord; noble; dignified. **3.** Arrogant; haughty: a *lordly* air. — *adv.* In a lordly manner. — **lord′li·ness** *n.*

Lord of Hosts Jehovah; God.

Lord of Misrule Formerly, a person chosen to preside over the festivities and games at Christmas in English royal or aristocratic households.

lor·do·sis (lôr·dō′sis) *n. Pathol.* Inward curvature of the spinal column resulting in an abnormal hollow in the back. Also **lor·do′ma** (-mə). [< NL < Gk. *lordōsis* < *lordos* bent backward] — **lor·dot′ic** (-dot′ik) *adj.*

Lord's Day Sunday; the Sabbath. — **Syn.** See SABBATH.

Lord's Day Act *Canadian* A federal regulatory statute intended to preserve Sunday as a day of rest.

lord·ship (lôrd′ship) *n.* **1.** The dominion, power, or authority of a lord. **2.** Sovereignty in general; supremacy. **3.** *Often cap.* In Great Britain, the title by which noblemen (excluding dukes), bishops, and judges are addressed or spoken of: preceded by *Your* or *His.* [OE *hlāfordscipe.* See LORD.]

Lord's Prayer The prayer beginning *Our Father,* taught by Christ to his disciples. *Matt.* vi 9–13.

Lord's Supper, the 1. The Last Supper (which see). **2.** The Eucharist; Holy Communion.

Lord's table, the *Eccl.* The Communion table; altar.

lore[1] (lôr, lōr) *n.* **1.** The body of traditional, popular, often anecdotal knowledge about a particular subject: the *lore* of the woods. **2.** Learning or erudition. **3.** *Archaic* The act of teaching. — **Syn.** See KNOWLEDGE. [OE *lār*]

lore[2] (lôr, lōr) *n. Zool.* The portion of a bird's head between the eyes and the beak, or a corresponding part in fishes and reptiles. [< L *lorum* strap, thong]

Lo·re·lei (lôr′ə·lī, *Ger.* lō′rə·lī) In German romantic literature, a siren on a rock in the Rhine who lured boatmen to shipwreck by her singing: also *Lurlei.* [< G]

Lo·rentz (lō′rents), **Hendrik Antoon,** 1853–1928, Dutch physicist.

lor·gnette (lôr·nyet′) *n.* **1.** A pair of eyeglasses with an ornamental handle into which they may be folded when not in use. **2.** An opera glass with a long handle. [< F < *longner* to spy, peer < OF *lorgne* squinting]

lor·gnon (lôr·nyôṅ′) *n. French* **1.** A monocle or lorgnette. **2.** An opera glass.

lo·ri·ca (lō·rī′kə) *n. pl.* **·cae** (-sē) **1.** *Zool.* A protective covering or shell, as in certain infusorians. **2.** In ancient Rome, a cuirass or corselet. [< L < *lorum* thong]

lor·i·cate (lôr′ə·kāt, lor′-) *adj.* Covered with, possessing, or resembling a lorica. [< L *loricatus,* pp. of *loricare* to clothe in mail, harness < *lorica* corselet]

Lo·rient (lô·ryäṅ′) A port city in NW France, on the Bay of Biscay; pop. about 47,000.

lor·i·keet (lôr′ə·kēt, lor′-) *n.* Any of certain small Polynesian parrots resembling the lory. [< LORY + (PARA)KEET]

lo·ris (lôr′is, lō′ris) *n. pl.* **·ris** or **·ris·es** A small, slow-moving, arboreal and nocturnal Asian lemur, as the **slender loris** (*Loris gracilis*) of southern India and Ceylon, and the **slow** or **East Indian loris** (*Nycticebus tardigradus*). [< F < Du. *loeres* booby]

lorn (lôrn) *adj.* **1.** *Archaic & Poetic* Abandoned; lonely; wretched; forlorn. **2.** *Obs.* Lost; doomed; ruined. [OE *loren,* pp. of *lēosan* to lose. Akin to FORLORN.]

Lor·rain (lô·raṅ′), **Claude,** 1600–82, French painter: original name *Claude Gelée* or *Gellée.*

Lor·raine (lô·rān′, lō-, lə-; *Fr.* lô·ren′) A region and former province of eastern France; after the Franco-Prussian War part of Alsace-Lorraine; restored to France, 1919: German *Lothringen.* See ALSACE–LORRAINE.

Lorraine cross A cross having two horizontal arms, the lower one longer than the other: also **cross of Lorraine.** For illustration see CROSS.

lor·ry (lôr′ē, lor′ē) *n. pl.* **·ries 1.** A low, four-wheeled wagon without sides. **2.** Any of various flat vehicles equipped to run on rails. **3.** *Brit.* A truck (def. 1). [Prob. dial. E *lurry* to pull]

lo·ry (lō′rē, lôr′ē) *n. pl.* **·ries** Any of a number of small parrots (genera *Lorius, Apnosmictus,* and others) of Australia and the neighboring islands, with brilliant plumage, long bill, and a tongue having a brushlike tip. [< Malay *lūrī*]

los·a·ble (lōō′zə·bəl) *adj.* Capable of being lost.

Los Al·a·mos (lôs al′ə·mōs, los) A town in north central New Mexico; site of the development of the atomic bomb; pop. 11,310.

Los An·ge·les (lôs an′jə·lēz, an′jə·ləs, ang′gə·ləs, ang′glis, los) A port in southern California, the third largest city in the United States; pop. 2,816,061: also, *Informal,* L.A.

lose (lōōz) *v.* **lost, los·ing** *v.t.* **1.** To part with, as by accident or negligence, and be unable to find; mislay. **2.** To fail to keep, control, or maintain: to *lose* one's footing. **3.** To be deprived of; suffer the loss of, as by accident, death, removal, etc.: to *lose* a leg; to *lose* one's parents. **4.** To fail to gain or win: to *lose* a prize. **5.** To fail to utilize or take advantage of; miss: to *lose* a chance. **6.** To fail to see or hear; miss: I *lost* not a word of the speech. **7.** To fail to keep in sight, memory, etc.: We *lost* him in the crowd. **8.** To occupy or absorb wholly; engross: usually in the passive: They were *lost* in the sound of the music. **9.** To cease to have: to *lose* one's courage. **10.** To squander; waste: to *lose* time. **11.** To wander from so as to be unable to find: to *lose* the path. **12.** To cause (someone or something) to be or become lost: You cannot *lose* him in these woods. **13.** To disappear: used reflexively: The river *loses* itself in the swamp. **14.** To outdistance or elude, as runners or pursuers. **15.** To cause the loss of: His rashness *lost* him the election. **16.** To bring to destruction or death; ruin: usually in the passive: All hands were *lost.* — *v.i.* **17.** To suffer loss: to *lose* on a transaction. **18.** To be defeated, as in battle or a contest. — **to lose oneself 1.** To lose one's way. **2.** To disappear or hide: He *lost himself* in the crowd. **3.** To become engrossed or absorbed: to *lose oneself* in thought. — **to lose out** *Informal* To fail or be defeated. — **to lose out on** *Informal* To fail to secure; miss: to *lose out on* a bargain. [Fusion of OE *losian* to be lost and *lēosan* to lose]

lo·sel (lō′zəl, lōō′zəl, loz′əl) *Archaic* or *Dial. adj.* Worthless. — *n.* A worthless fellow. [ME]

los·er (lōō′zər) *n.* **1.** One who loses, especially with reference to the manner in which one accepts defeat: a bad *loser.* **2.** Something that loses, as a race horse.

los·ing (lōō′zing) *n.* **1.** The act of one who or that which loses. **2.** *pl.* Money lost, especially in gambling. — *adj.* **1.** Incurring loss: a *losing* business. **2.** Not winning.

losing hazard See under HAZARD (def. 5).

loss (lôs, los) *n.* **1.** The act of losing; also, a specific instance of this. **2.** The state of being lost. **3.** One who or that which is lost. **4.** The number or amount lost. **5.** The harm, inconvenience, deprivation, etc., caused by losing something or someone. **6.** *pl. Mil.* **a** Casualties. **b** The number of casualties. **7.** *Physics* The part of electrical or mechanical energy that is dissipated in friction, excess heat, etc., and from which no productive work is obtained. **8.** In insurance: **a** Death, injury, property damage, etc., sustained by an insured. **b** The sum payable by the insurer on that account. — **at a loss** In a state of confusion or perplexity. [ME]

loss leader An article that a retail store sells below or near cost to promote sales of other merchandise.

loss ratio The ratio between the premiums paid to an insurance company and the losses sustained.

lost (lôst, lost) *adj.* **1.** Not to be found or recovered; missing: a *lost* umbrella. **2.** No longer possessed, seen, or known: *lost* friends; *lost* youth. **3.** Not won, gained, or secured: a *lost* fight. **4.** Having gone astray: a *lost* child. **5.** Bewildered; perplexed. **6.** Helpless: He is *lost* without his cane. **7.** Not used or taken advantage of; wasted: a *lost* opportunity. **8.** Destroyed; ruined: a *lost* reputation. **9.** No longer known or practiced: a *lost* art. — **to be lost in** To be absorbed or engrossed in: *lost in* thought. — **to be lost to 1.** To no longer belong to; to have been taken from. **2.** To be impervious or insensible to: to be *lost to* all sense of justice. **3.** To be no longer available to. — **to be lost upon** (or **on**) To have no effect upon: His wit was *lost upon* the class.

lost cause Any cause that has failed or cannot succeed.

Lost Generation A group of U.S. writers, including Ernest Hemingway, active in Paris after World War I; also, their contemporaries collectively. [Coined by Gertrude Stein]

Lost Pleiade Merope.

lost tribes Those members of the ten northern tribes of ancient Israel that were taken into Assyrian captivity (II *Kings* xvii 6) and are believed never to have returned.

lot (lot) *n.* **1.** That which is used in determining something by chance, as objects drawn at random from a container. **2.** The fact or process of deciding something by this method. **3.** The decisions or choices arrived at by such means. **4.** The share or portion that comes to one as a result of drawing lots. **5.** One's portion in life as ascribed to chance, fate, custom, etc.: A soldier's *lot* is a hard one. **6.** A number of things or persons considered as a single group or unit. **7.** A job lot (def. 1). **8.** A plot or quantity of land, as surveyed and apportioned for sale or for other special purpose: a city *lot*; a parking lot. **9.** *Informal* A (specified) type of person: usually in a derogatory sense: He's a bad *lot*. **10.** In motion pictures, a studio and the adjacent area belonging to it. **11.** *Often pl. Informal* A great deal: a *lot* of money; lots of trouble. **12.** *Chiefly Brit.* A tax or duty. — **Syn.** See DESTINY. — **a lot** (or **lots**) *Informal* Very much: He is *a lot* better; lots better. — **the lot** The whole of a certain number, quantity, or collection: He bought *the lot*. — **to cast** (or **draw**) **lots** To come to a decision or solution by the use of lots. — **to cast** (or **throw**) **in one's lot with** To join with and share the fortunes of. — *v.* **lot·ted**, **lot·ting** *v.t.* **1.** To apportion by lots; allot. **2.** To draw lots for. **3.** To divide, as land, into lots. — *v.i.* **4.** To cast lots. [OE *hlot*]

Lot (lôt) A river in south central France, flowing 300 miles west to the Garonne.

Lot (lot) In the Old Testament, a nephew of Abraham, whose wife, disobeying a warning, was turned into a pillar of salt when she looked back upon the destruction of Sodom from which they were fleeing. *Gen.* xi 27, xix.

lo·tah (lō′tə) *n. Anglo-Indian* A small, round, brass or copper pot, used in India for water, storing food, etc. Also **lo′ta.**

loth (lōth) See LOATH.

Lo·thair I (lō-thâr′), 795?–855, Holy Roman Emperor 840–855.

Lothair II, 1070?–1137, Holy Roman Emperor 1125–37: called **the Saxon.**

Lo·thar·i·o (lō-thâr′ē-ō) *n. pl.* **·os** A seducer; libertine. [after *Lothario*, name of a rake in Nicholas Rowe's play *The Fair Penitent*, 1703]

Loth·ring·en (lōth′ring-ən) The German name for LORRAINE.

Lo·thi·ans (lō′thē-ənz), **The** A region of SE Scotland comprising East Lothian, Midlothian, and West Lothian counties.

Lo·ti (lô-tē′), **Pierre** Pseudonym of **Louis Marie Julien Viaud** (vyō), 1850–1923, French novelist.

lo·tion (lō′shən) *n.* A liquid preparation, often medicated and used for external cleansing or soothing, as of the skin, eyes, etc. [< L *lotio, -onis* washing < *lavare* to wash]

lot·ter·y (lot′ər-ē) *n. pl.* **·ter·ies 1.** A method of distributing prizes, usually for fund-raising purposes, in which chances are sold in the form of numbered tickets, the winning tickets being selected by lot. **2.** Any matter in which the likelihood of success is uncertain: Marriage is a *lottery*. [< Ital. *lotteria* < *lotto* lottery, lot < F *lot* < Gmc.]

lot·to (lot′ō) *n.* A game of chance played by drawing numbers from a container and covering with counters the corresponding numbers on cards, the winner being the first to cover a row of numbers. Compare BEANO, BINGO, KENO. [< Ital. See LOTTERY.]

lo·tus (lō′təs) *n.* **1.** Any of various tropical plants of the water-lily family, noted for their large floating leaves and showy flowers; especially, the **white lotus** (*Nymphaea lotus*) and the **blue lotus** (*N. caerulea*) of Egypt, the **sacred lotus** (*Nelumbium nelumbo*) of India, with fragrant pink flowers, and the water chinquapin. **2.** A representation of any of these plants in art, architecture, sculpture, etc. **3.** Any of a genus (*Lotus*) of herbs or shrubs of the bean family. **4.** The jujube (def. 2). Also **lo′tos.** [< L < Gk. *lōtos*]

LOTUS
a Bud and leaf.
b Flower and leaf. *c* Stylized lotus in Egyptian architecture.

lo·tus-eat·er (lō′təs-ē′tər) *n.* **1.** In the *Odyssey*, one of a people living on the northern coast of Africa, who lived a life of indolence and forgetfulness induced by eating the fruit of the lotus tree. **2.** Anyone considered to be living an indolent, irresponsible existence.

lotus tree The jujube (def. 2).

Loua·la·ba (lwä·lä·bä′) The French spelling of LUALABA.

loud (loud) *adj.* **1.** Striking the auditory nerves with great force; having great volume or intensity of sound: *loud* thunder. **2.** Making or uttering a great noise or sound: a *loud* trumpet. **3.** Emphatic or urgent; insistent; clamorous: *loud* demands. **4.** *Informal* Crudely unrefined; vulgar, as manners, persons, etc. **5.** *Informal* Excessively showy; flashy:

a *loud* shirt. **6.** *Informal* Having a strong or disagreeable odor: *loud* cheese. — *adv.* In a loud manner. [OE *hlūd*] — **loud′ly** *adv.* — **loud′ness** *n.*

loud·en (loud′n) *v.t. & v.i.* To make or become louder.

loud·ish (lou′dish) *adj.* Rather loud.

loud-mouthed (loud′mouthd′, -mouth′) *adj.* Possessed of a loud voice; offensively clamorous or talkative.

loud-speak·er (loud′spē′kər) *n.* Any of various devices for converting an electric current into sound, as in a public-address system, radio, etc.: also called *speaker*.

lough (lokh) *n. Irish* A lake, loch, or arm of the sea.

lou·is (lōō′ē) *n. pl.* **lou·is** (lōō′ēz) A louis d'or (which see).

Lou·is (lōō′is, lōō′is; *Fr.* lwē), 778–840, Holy Roman Emperor 814–840; son and successor of Charlemagne: called **le Dé·bon·naire** (lə dā-bô-nâr′) (the Gracious), **le Pieux** (lə pyœ) (the Pious).

Louis IX, 1214–70; king of France 1226–70; defeated and captured while on a crusade in Egypt 1250; canonized 1297 as **Saint Louis.**

Louis XI, 1423–83, king of France 1461–83; laid the foundation for an absolute monarchy.

Louis XIII, 1601–43, king of France 1610–43, son of Henry IV.

Louis XIV, 1638–1715, king of France 1643–1715; son of Louis XIII: called **le Grand Mo·narque** (lə grän mō-nárk′) (the Great Monarch), *le Roi Soleil* (the Sun King).

Louis XV, 1710–74, king of France 1715–74, lost Canada to the English: called **le Bien-Ai·mé** (lə byaṅ ne-mā′) (the Well-Beloved).

Louis XVI, 1754–93, king of France 1774–92, grandson of Louis XV, dethroned by the French Revolution; guillotined.

Louis XVIII, 1755–1824, king of France 1814–24; brother of Louis XVI; ascended the throne after the fall of Napoleon: called **le Dé·si·ré** (lə dā-zē-rā′) (the Desired).

Lou·is (lōō′is), **Joe,** born 1914, U.S. prize fighter; heavyweight champion 1937–49: original name **Joseph Louis Bar·row** (bar′ō).

Lou·is·burg (lōō′is-bûrg) A town on the eastern coast of Cape Breton Island, Canada; captured from the French by the British, 1745 and 1758; pop. 1,314. Also **Lou′is·bourg.**

lou·is d'or (lōō′is dôr) **1.** A former French gold coin worth twenty francs. **2.** An old French coin, fluctuating in value, first minted in 1640 during the reign of Louis XIII and used through the reign of Louis XVI. Also called *louis*.

Lou·ise (lōō-ēz′), **Lake** A lake in Banff National Park, SW Alberta, Canada; 1.5 mi. long.

Lou·i·si·an·a (lōō-ē′zē-an′ə) A southern State of the United States, on the Gulf of Mexico; 48,523 sq. mi.; pop. 3,643,180; capital, Baton Rouge; entered the Union April 8, 1812: nickname, *Pelican* or *Creole State*. Abbr. *La.* — **Lou·i′si·an′i·an,** **Lou·i′si·an′an** *adj. & n.*

Louisiana Purchase The French colonial territory purchased by the United States in 1803 for $15,000,000. It lay between the Mississippi River and the Rocky Mountains and was bounded by Canada and the Gulf of Mexico.

Louis Napoleon See (Louis Napoleon) BONAPARTE.

Louis Phi·lippe (fē-lēp′), 1773–1850, king of France 1830–48; abdicated: called **le Roi Ci·toy·en** (lə rwä sē·twà·yaṅ′) (the Citizen King).

Louis Qua·torze (kȧ·tôrz′) Of or designating the style of architecture, decoration, and furniture characteristic of the period of Louis XIV in France (1643–1715), marked by baroque forms and ornate decoration employing animal and mythological figures richly carved. [< F]

Louis Quinze (kaṅz) Of or designating the style of architecture, decoration, and furniture characteristic of the period of Louis XV in France (1715–74), marked by the culmination of the rococo as expressed in flowing lines, rounded forms, and graceful shell, flower, and other ornaments. [< F]

Louis Seize (sez) Of or designating the style of architecture, decoration, and furniture that characterized the period of Louis XVI of France (1774–92), marked by a reversion to simple, rectilinear forms, graceful, delicate proportion, and the use of classical motifs as decorative details. [< F]

Louis Treize (trez) Of or designating the style of architecture, decoration, and furniture that characterized the period of Louis XIII of France (1610–43), marked by heavy, square forms, richly inlaid ornaments, and deep moldings or carvings. [< F]

Lou·is·ville (lōō′ē·vil) A city in northern Kentucky, on the Ohio River; pop. 361,958.

lounge (lounj) *v.* **lounged, loung·ing** *v.i.* **1.** To recline or lean in a relaxed, lazy manner. **2.** To move or walk slowly or leisurely; saunter. **3.** To pass time in doing nothing. — *v.t.* **4.** To spend or pass in idleness, as time. — *n.* **1.** A couch or sofa, especially one with little or no back and a headrest at one end. **2.** A room in a hotel, club, train, etc., containing furniture suitable for lounging and often having facilities for drinking or light refreshments. **3.** A lounging pace or gait. **4.** The act of lounging; also, a period of lounging. [Origin unknown] — **loung′er** *n.*

lounge lizard *Informal* A foppish idler who frequents places where wealthy or prominent people gather socially.

loup[1] (loup, loop) *v.t. & v.i.* **lap** or **loup·en, loup·ing** *Scot. & Brit. Dial.* To leap. [< ON *hlaupa*]

loup[2] (loo) *n.* A half-mask made of silk or velvet. [< F]

loup-cer·vier (loo·sâr·vyā′) *n.* *pl.* **-cer·viers** (-vyā′) or **-cer·vier** *Canadian* The Canada lynx. See under LYNX. [< dial. F (Canadian)]

loupe (loop) *n.* A small magnifying glass, especially one adapted as an eyepiece for jewelers or watchmakers. [< F]

loup-ga·rou (loo·gà·roo′) *n.* *pl.* **loups-ga·rous** (loo·gà·roo′) A werewolf. [< F *loup* wolf (< L *lupus*) + *garou* werewolf < Gmc.]

loup·ing ill (lou′ping, lō′-) *Vet.* A virus disease of sheep and sometimes of man, that attacks the nervous system and is transmitted by the bite of the tick. Also **loup ill.**

lour (lour), **lour·ing** (lour′ing), etc. See LOWER[1], etc.

Lourdes (loord) A town in SW France; shrine and grotto of the Virgin (*Our Lady of Lourdes*); pop. 17,627 (1968).

Lou·ren·ço Mar·ques (lō·ren′sō mär′kəs, *Pg.* lō·rān′sŏŏ mär′kish) The capital of Mozambique; a port in the southern part on Delgoa Bay; pop. 177,929 (1960).

louse (lous) *n.* *pl.* **lice** (līs) **1.** A small, flat-bodied, wingless insect (order *Anoplura*) living as an external parasite on man and some animals; especially, the **crab louse** (*Phthirus pubis*), the **body louse** (*Pediculus corporis*), and the **head louse** (*Pediculus capitis*). **2.** Any of various other insects parasitic on animals or plants, as the **biting bird louse** (order *Malophaga*) and the **plant louse** (family *Aphididae*). For illustration see INSECTS (injurious). **3.** *Slang* A contemptible or mean person; stinker; rat. — *v.t. & v.i.* **loused, lous·ing** *Slang* To ruin; bungle: with *up*. [OE *lūs*]

louse·wort (lous′wûrt′) *n.* Wood betony (def. 1).

lous·y (lou′zē) *adj.* **lous·i·er, lous·i·est** **1.** Infested with lice. **2.** *Slang* Contemptible; foul; mean. **3.** *Slang* Worthless; inferior. **4.** *Slang* Having plenty or too much (of): with *with*: *lousy* with money.

lout (lout) *n.* An awkward fellow; clown; boor. [? < ON *lutr* bent, stooped]

lout·ish (lou′tish) *adj.* Clumsy; awkward; boorish. — **lout′ish·ly** *adv.* — **lout′ish·ness** *n.*

Lou·vain (loo·vān′, *Fr.* loo·van′) A city in central Belgium; pop. 32,125 (est. 1967).

lou·ver (loo′vər) *n.* **1.** A window or opening, as in a gable, belfry, etc., provided with louver boards; also, a louver board. **2.** In medieval architecture, a cupola or turret shaped like a lantern for admitting light or permitting the escape of smoke. **3.** One of several narrow openings, as in the hood of an automobile, serving as an outlet for heated air. [< OF *lover*]

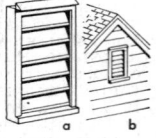

LOUVER
a Construction.
b Set in gable.

louver board One of a series of horizontal, overlapping slats in a window or opening, sloped downward to shed rain while admitting light and air. Also **louver boarding.**

Lou·vre (loo′vr′) A royal palace in Paris, begun in 1554 and made into an art museum in the late 18th century.

Lou·ÿs (loo·ē′, *Fr.* lwē), **Pierre** Pseudonym of **Pierre Louis** (lwē) 1870–1925, French novelist and poet born in Belgium.

lov·a·ble (luv′ə-bəl) *adj.* Worthy of love; amiable; also, evoking love. Also **love′a·ble.** — **lov′a·bil′i·ty, lov′a·ble·ness** *n.* — **lov′a·bly** *adv.*

lov·age (luv′ij) *n.* A European herb (*Levisticum officinale*) of the parsley family, formerly used as a home remedy. [< OF *luvesche* < LL *levisticum*, alter. of L *ligusticum* Ligurian]

love (luv) *n.* **1.** A deep devotion or affection for another person or persons: *love* for one's children. **2.** A strong sexual passion for another person. **3.** Sexual passion in general, or the gratification of it. **4.** One who is beloved. **5.** A term of endearment. **6.** A very great interest in, or enjoyment of, something; also, the thing so enjoyed. **7.** *Theol.* **a** The benevolence and mercifulness of God toward mankind. **b** The adoration or devout affection of man toward God. **c** The kindness and charitableness man should show toward others. **8.** *Often cap.* In Christian Science, God. **9.** In tennis, a score of nothing. — **for love** As a favor; without compensation. — **for love or money** For any consideration; under any circumstances. — **for the love of** For the sake of; in loving consideration of. — **in love** Experiencing love for someone or something. — **no love lost between** No affection or liking between; dislike between. — **to fall in love** To conceive a strong and passionate feeling for someone or something. — **to make love** To kiss, embrace, etc., as lovers. — *v.* **loved, lov·ing** *v.t.* **1.** To feel love or affection for. **2.** To take pleasure or delight in; like very much: to *love* good food. **3.** To show love for by kissing or caressing. — *v.i.* **4.** To feel love; be in love. [OE *lufu*]

— Syn. (*noun*) **1.** *Love, affection, devotion, attachment,* and *fondness* denote a warm feeling of regard, usually between persons. *Love* is the strongest term, describing the warmest, most intense regard of one person for another; it frequently includes sexual desire, and often implies a spiritual quality: conjugal *love, love* of poetry, *love* of God. *Affection* is a degree short of *love*; it is always felt for persons, and suggests a strong liking or sympathy characterized by kindness and tenderness: the *affection* between brother and sister. *Devotion* is steadfast loyalty and service, which may be rendered to a cause or to a person; *attachment* is weaker than *devotion*, often denoting no more than the wish to play an active part in another's life or in the activities of a group. We speak of a man's *devotion* to his king, but his *attachment* to a political party. *Fondness* originally meant silliness or sentimentality, but now refers to a strong liking or preference which is often demonstrative: *fondness* for little children, a *fondness* for chocolates. — **Ant.** hate, aversion, antipathy.

Love (luv) Cupid or Eros.

love affair An amorous attachment or liaison between two people not married to each other.

love apple A former name for the tomato.

love beads Colorful beads worn in long strands as a necklace, especially by hippies or young people.

love·bird (luv′bûrd′) *n.* One of several small parrots (genera *Agapornis* and *Psitta*) often kept as cage birds: so called from the affection they appear to show for their mates.

love child An illegitimate child; bastard.

love feast **1.** In early Christianity, a meal taken in common with others as a symbol of brotherly love; agape. **2.** A similar celebration observed in some modern religious sects or denominations. **3.** Any feast or banquet characterized by or promoting friendliness and feelings of good will.

love game In tennis, a game in which the losing player or players have won no points.

love-in (luv′in′) *n.* A gathering, usually of young people, to promote mutual love and understanding.

love-in-a-mist (luv′in·ə·mist′) *n.* A European garden plant (*Nigella damascena*) of the crowfoot or buttercup family, with blue flowers.

love-in-i·dle·ness (luv′in·īd′l·nis) *n.* The wild pansy.

love knot A knot tied in pledge of love and constancy; also, a representation of it, as in jewelry.

Love·lace (luv′lās), **Richard,** 1618–58, English poet.

love·less (luv′lis) *adj.* **1.** Having no love for anyone or anything; unloving. **2.** Receiving no love; unloved. — **love′less·ly** *adv.* — **love′less·ness** *n.*

love-lies-bleed·ing (luv′līz′blē′ding) *n.* Any of several species of amaranth; especially, *Amaranthus caudatus*, having crimson flowers.

love·lock (luv′lok′) *n.* A separate lock of hair hanging down or apart from the rest of the hair; especially, such a lock curled and tied with ribbons, as worn formerly by courtiers.

love·lorn (luv′lôrn) *adj.* Pining for one's lover.

love·ly (luv′lē) *adj.* **·li·er, ·li·est** **1.** Possessing mental or physical qualities that inspire admiration or love. **2.** Beautiful: a *lovely* rose. **3.** *Informal* Delightful; pleasing: a *lovely* visit. **4.** *Obs.* Affectionate. [OE *luflīc*] — **love′li·ness** *n.*

love·mak·ing (luv′mā′king) *n.* The act of making love; also, wooing; courtship.

love potion A magic draft or drink designed to arouse love toward a certain person in the one who drinks.

lov·er (luv′ər) *n.* **1.** One who loves: a *lover* of humanity. **2.** One in love with or making love to a person of the opposite sex. **3.** *pl.* Two persons having a love affair. **4.** One who enjoys or is strongly attracted to some object, diversion, pursuit, etc.: a *lover* of golf. — **lov′er·ly** *adj. & adv.*

Lov·er (luv′ər), **Samuel,** 1797–1868, Irish novelist.

love seat A double chair or small sofa for two persons.

love set A tennis set in which the winner wins every game.

love·sick (luv′sik′) *adj.* **1.** Languishing with love. **2.** Indicating or expressing such a condition: a *lovesick* serenade. — **love′sick′ness** *n.*

love·vine (luv′vīn′) *n.* The dodder.

lov·ing (luv′ing) *adj.* **1.** Affectionate; devoted; kind: *loving* friends or brothers. **2.** Indicative of love: *loving* looks and words. — **lov′ing·ly** *adv.* — **lov′ing·ness** *n.*

loving cup **1.** A wine cup formerly passed around by friends at a banquet. **2.** A similar cup presented as a trophy.

lov·ing-kind·ness (luv′ing·kīnd′nis) *n.* Kindness that comes from or indicates personal affection or regard.

low[1] (lō) *adj.* **1.** Having relatively little upward extension; not high or tall. **2.** Situated or placed below the normal or regular height: a *low* lamp. **3.** Located or lying below the normal or usual level; depressed: a *low* marsh; *low* country. **4.** Near the horizon: a *low* moon. **5.** Pertaining to latitudes nearest the equator. **6.** Less than normal in depth, height, quantity, degree, etc. **7.** Relatively small in amount, degree, value, intensity, etc. **8.** *Music* Of, pertaining to, or producing sounds of relatively long wavelengths: a *low* pitch. **9.** Not loud; faint: a *low* rustle. **10.** Dead or prostrate. **11.** Extending far downward; deep: a *low* bow. **12.** Cut so as to expose part of the wearer's shoulders, back, or chest; décolleté: a *low* blouse. **13.** Melancholy or sad; depressed: *low* spirits. **14.** Lacking in physical vigor or energy; feeble: to be in *low* health. **15.** Not nourishing or rich; simple:

plain: a *low* diet. **16.** Not adequately provided with; short of: to be *low* on groceries. **17.** *Informal* Having little or no ready cash; broke. **18.** Inexpensive; cheap: a *low* price. **19.** Poor, unfavorable, or disparaging: to have a *low* estimate of one's abilities. **20.** Humble or inferior, as in origin, rank, position, etc. **21.** Inferior in quality: a *low* grade of tobacco. **22.** Lacking in refinement; coarse; vulgar: *low* companions; *low* tastes. **23.** Morally base or mean: a *low* deed. **24.** Relatively recent, as a date. **25.** Relatively simple in structure, function, or organization: a *low* form of animal life. **26.** In the Anglican Church, of or pertaining to the Low Church or its doctrines or practices. **27.** *Mech.* Denoting a gear arrangement, as in transmissions, yielding a slow or the slowest output speed. **28.** *Phonet.* Of vowel sounds, produced with the tongue depressed and flat, as (ä) in *large*: opposed to *high*. **— adv. 1.** In or to a low level, position, degree, etc. **2.** In a low manner. **3.** Softly; quietly. **4.** With a low pitch. **5.** At a low price; cheaply. **6.** In or to a humble, poor, or degraded condition: brought *low*. **— n. 1.** A low level, position, degree, etc.: Prices reached a new *low*. **2.** *Meteorol.* An area of low barometric pressure. **3.** *Mech.* An arrangement of gears that yields a slow or the slowest output speed. **4.** In certain card games, the lowest trump card. **5.** In some sports and games, the lowest number or score. Abbr. *l., L.* [Early ME *lah* < ON *lagr*] **— low′ness** *n.*

low² (lō) *v.i.* **1.** To make the hollow, bellowing sound of cattle; moo. **— v.t. 2.** To utter by lowing. **— n.** The vocal sound made by cattle: also **low′ing.** [OE *hlōwan*]

low³ (lō) *n. Scot.* A glowing fire; blaze. Also **lowe.**

Low (lō), **David,** 1891–1963, British cartoonist.

Low Archipelago See TUAMOTU ARCHIPELAGO.

low area *Meteorol.* A low (n. def. 2).

low-born (lō′bôrn′) *adj.* Of humble birth.

low-boy (lō′boi′) *n.* A short-legged chest of drawers of about table height, similar to the lower part of a highboy.

low-bred (lō′bred′) *adj.* **1.** Of humble or inferior origin or birth. **2.** Vulgar; coarse.

low-brow (lō′brou′) *n. Informal* A person of uncultivated or vulgar tastes. **— adj.** Of or suitable for such a person: also **low′browed′.** **— low′brow′ism** *n.*

Low-Church (lō′chûrch′) *adj.* Of or belonging to a group (**Low Church**) in the Anglican Church that stresses evangelical doctrine and is, in general, opposed to extreme ritualism. Compare HIGH-CHURCH, BROAD-CHURCH. **— Low′-Church′man** (-mən) *n.*

low comedy Comedy that is characterized by slapstick and lively physical action rather than by witty dialogue.

Low Countries The region of NW Europe comprising the Netherlands, Belgium, and Luxembourg.

low-down¹ (lō′doun′) *n. Slang* The truth.

low-down² (lō′doun′) *adj. Informal* **1.** Immoral, unethical, or mean: a *low-down* trick. **2.** In jazz, slow, sad, or sensuous, as the blues.

Low-ell (lō′əl) A Massachusetts family prominent in American culture, notably **John,** 1743–1802, jurist and legislator; his grandson, **James Russell,** 1819–91, poet, essayist, and diplomat; **Percival,** 1855–1916, astronomer; brother of Abbot and Amy; **Abbot Lawrence,** 1856–1943, educator; **Amy,** 1874–1925, poet and critic; **Robert,** born 1917, poet; great grandnephew of James Russell and distant cousin of Amy.

Low-ell (lō′əl) A city in NE Massachusetts, on the Merrimack River; pop. 94,239.

low-er¹ (lou′ər) *v.i.* **1.** To look angry or sullen; scowl. **2.** To appear dark and threatening, as the weather. **— n. 1.** A sullen or gloomy look; a scowl. **2.** A dark, threatening look, as of the weather. Also spelled **lour.** [Cf. G *lauern* to lurk]

low-er² (lō′ər) Comparative of LOW. **— adj. 1.** Inferior in rank, value, condition, etc. **2.** Situated below something else: a *lower* shelf. **3.** *Often cap. Geol.* Older; designating strata normally beneath the newer (and upper) rock formations. **— n.** That which is beneath something else; especially, a lower berth. **— v.t. 1.** To bring to a lower position or level; let down, as a window. **2.** To reduce in degree, quality, amount, etc.: to *lower* prices. **3.** To undermine or weaken: Fatigue *lowers* the body's resistance. **4.** To bring down in estimation, rank, etc. **5.** To change (a sound) to a lower pitch or volume. **— v.i. 6.** To become lose; decrease; sink.

Lower Austria A Province of NE Austria; 7,402 sq. mi.; pop. 1,371,911 (1961); capital, Vienna: German *Niederösterreich.*

Lower Burma See under BURMA.

Lower California A peninsula of NW Mexico separating the Gulf of California from the Pacific; about 760 mi. long; 55,634 sq. mi.; divided into the **State of Lower California** (Spanish *Baja California*) in the north; 27,655 sq. mi.; pop. 856,773 (1970); capital, Mexicali, and the **Territory of Lower California** (Spanish *Baja California Sur*) in the south; 27,979 sq. mi.; pop. 123,786 (1970); capital, La Paz.

Lower Canada 1. The name of the province of Quebec before 1841, when Lower and Upper Canada made up the Province of Canada. **2.** *Rare* The province of Quebec.

low-er-case (lō′ər-kās′) *Printing adj.* Of, in, or indicating small letters, as distinguished from capitals. **— v.t. -cased, -cas-ing** To set as or change to lower-case letters.

lower case *Printing* **1.** In type cases, the lower tray, containing the small letters of the alphabet. See CASE². **2.** The small letters of the alphabet. Abbr. *l.c.*

lower class The socially or economically inferior group in society. **— low-er-class** (lō′ər-klas′, -kläs′) *adj.*

low-er-class-man (lō′ər-klas′mən, -kläs′-) *n. pl. -men* (-mən) A freshman or sophomore, or the equivalent.

lower criticism Critical investigation that seeks to ascertain the original wording of a text, especially of the Bible: also called *textual criticism.* Compare HIGHER CRITICISM.

Lower Egypt See under EGYPT.

Lower House The larger and more widely representative branch of a bicameral legislative body, as the House of Representatives of the Congress of the United States or the House of Commons in Ottawa. Also **Lower Chamber.**

low-er-ing (lou′ər-ing) *adj.* **1.** Frowning or sullen. **2.** Overcast and threatening, as the sky. Also spelled *louring.* **— low′er-ing-ly** *adv.*

Lower Lakes *U.S. & Canadian* Lakes Erie and Ontario.

Lower Mer-i-on (mer′ē-ən) An urban township in SE Pennsylvania, near Philadelphia; pop. 59,420.

low-er-most (lō′ər-mōst′) *adj.* Lowest.

Lower Paleolithic See under PALEOLITHIC.

Lower Saxony A State of north central West Germany; 18,295 sq. mi.; pop. 7,100,400 (est. 1970); capital, Hanover: German *Niedersachsen.*

Lower Silurian *Geol.* The Ordovician.

lower world 1. The abode of the dead; hell; Hades; Sheol. Also **lower regions. 2.** The earth.

low-er-y (lou′ər-ē) *adj.* Cloudy or overcast; threatening: also spelled *loury.*

Lowes (lōz), **John Livingston,** 1867–1945, U.S. scholar and educator.

lowest common denominator Least common denominator (which see).

lowest common multiple Least common multiple (which see).

Lowes-toft (lōs′tôft, -təft) *n.* A variety of porcelain originally made at Lowestoft, England.

Lowes-toft (lōs′tôft, -təft) A municipal borough and port in eastern Suffolk, England; pop. 45,687 (1961).

low frequency *Telecom.* Radio waves having a frequency of from 30 to 300 kilocycles. Abbr. *l-f, LF, l.f., L.F.*

Low German See under GERMAN.

low-key (lō′kē′) *adj.* Having a low degree of intensity; relatively pale or quiet; understated. Also **low-keyed** (lō′kēd′).

low-land (lō′lənd, -land′) *n. Usually pl.* Land lying lower than the adjacent country. **— adj.** Of, pertaining to, or characteristic of a low or level country.

Low-land (lō′lənd, -land′) *n.* The speech or dialect of the Scottish Lowlands; Lallan. **— adj.** Pertaining or belonging to the Scottish Lowlands.

Low-lands (lō′ləndz, -landz′) The less elevated districts in southern and eastern Scotland. **— Low′land′er** *n.*

Low Latin See under LATIN.

low-ly (lō′lē) *adj.* **-li-er, -li-est 1.** Humble or low in rank, origin, nature, etc. **2.** Full of humility; meek. **3.** Situated or lying low. **— adv. 1.** In a low condition, manner, position, etc. **2.** Modestly; humbly. **— low′li-ness** *n.*

Low Mass A form of Mass celebrated without music and by one priest usually assisted by a server or altar boy.

low-mind-ed (lō′mīn′did) *adj.* Having low, vulgar, or mean thoughts, sentiments, or motives. **— low′-mind′ed-ly** *adv.* **— low′-mind′ed-ness** *n.*

low-necked (lō′nekt′) *adj.* Having a low neckline.

low-pitched (lō′picht′) *adj.* **1.** Low in tone or range of tone. **2.** Having little slope, as a roof. **3.** *Music* Built for a pitch lower than standard pitch: said of instruments.

low-pres-sure (lō′presh′ər) *adj.* **1.** Having or operating under a low degree of pressure. **2.** *Meteorol.* Designating atmospheric pressure below that normal at sea level.

low relief Bas-relief (which see).

lowse (lōz) *adj. Scot.* Loose.

low-spir-it-ed (lō′spir′it-id) *adj.* Despondent; melancholy. **— low′-spir′it-ed-ly** *adv.* **— low′-spir′it-ed-ness** *n.*

Low Sunday The Sunday following Easter.

low-ten-sion (lō′ten′shən) *adj. Electr.* Pertaining to, characterized by, or operating under, a current of low voltage.

low-test (lō′test′) *adj.* Possessing a relatively high boiling point: said of gasoline.

low tide 1. The ebb tide at its lowest stage. **2.** The time this lowest stage occurs. **3.** The lowest point or level reached.

low water A very low level of water in a stream, etc.

low-wa-ter mark (lō′wô′tər, -wot′ər) *n.* **1.** The mark indicating the point reached at low water or tide. **2.** The point of greatest decline or failure of something.

lox¹ (loks) *n.* Salty smoked salmon, often eaten with cream cheese, bagels, etc. [< Yiddish < G *lachs* salmon]

---

lox² (loks) *n.* Liquid oxygen.

lox·o·drom·ic (lok'sə·drom'ik) *adj. Naut.* Pertaining to oblique sailing on the rhumb line. Also **lox'o·drom'i·cal.** [< Gk. *loxos* oblique + *dromos* a running]

loxodromic curve A rhumb line.

lox·o·drom·ics (lok'sə·drom'iks) *n.pl.* (construed as sing.) *Naut.* The art of oblique sailing. Also **lox·od·ro·my** (lok·sod'rə·mē).

loy·al (loi'əl) *adj.* **1.** Bearing true allegiance to a constituted authority, as to one's sovereign, government, etc. **2.** Constant and faithful in any relation or obligation implying trust, confidence, etc. **3.** Indicating or professing loyalty. — **Syn.** See FAITHFUL. [< OF *loial, leial* < L *legalis.* Doublet of LEGAL.] — **loy'al·ism** *n.* — **loy'al·ly** *adv.*

loy·al·ist (loi'əl·ist) *n.* One who supports and defends his government, especially in times of crisis or war.

Loy·al·ist (loi'əl·ist) *n.* **1.** In the American Revolution, a colonist who remained loyal to the British crown. **2.** *Canadian* A United Empire Loyalist (which see). **3.** In the Spanish Civil War, one who supported the government of the Republic against the uprising of Franco.

loy·al·ty (loi'əl·tē) *n. pl.* **·ties** The state, quality, or fact of being loyal; fidelity; allegiance. [< OF *loialte*]

loyalty oath *U.S.* An oath affirming loyalty to a government, party, etc.; especially, one stipulating that the signer has never been a member of any group, especially the Communist Party, considered subversive.

Lo·yo·la (loi·ō'lä, *Sp.* lō·yō'lä), **Saint Ignatius,** 1491–1556, Spanish soldier, priest, and mystic; founder of the Society of Jesus: original name **Inigo de Oñez y Loyola.** See JESUIT.

loz·enge (loz'inj) *n.* **1.** A small sweetened tablet or candy, now usually medicated and originally shaped like a diamond. **2.** *Math.* A rhombus having two oblique and two acute angles; diamond. [< OF *losenge,* ? < L *lapis, -idis* stone]

LP (el'pē') *adj.* Designating a phonograph record pressed with microgrooves and played at a speed of 33⅓ revolutions per minute: also *long-playing.* — *n.* An LP record: a trade mark. [L(ONG)-P(LAYING)]

L.P.S. *Brit.* Lord Privy Seal.

L.S. **1.** Licentiate in Surgery. **2.** Place of the seal (L *locus sigilli*).

LSD (el'es'dē') *n.* A drug that produces states similar to those of schizophrenia, used in medicine and illicitly as a hallucinogen. See LYSERGIC ACID. Also **LSD-25.** [< *l(y)s(ergic acid) d(iethylamide)*]

LSS or **L.S.S.** Lifesaving Service.

l.t. **1.** Left tackle: also **lt** **2.** Long ton: also **l.tn.**

LT or **Lt.** *Mil.* Lieutenant.

Lt.Col. or **LtCol** *Mil.* Lieutenant Colonel.

ltd. or **Ltd.** Limited.

Lt.Gen. or **LtGen** *Mil.* Lieutenant General.

L.Th. Licentiate in Theology.

Ltjg *Mil.* Lieutenant, Junior Grade.

Lu *Chem.* Lutetium.

Lu·a·la·ba (loo·ä·lä'bä) The upper Congo river.

Lu·an·da (loo·än'də) The capital of Angola, a port in the NW part; pop. 400,000 (est. 1968): formerly *Loanda, São Paulo de Loanda.*

Luang Pra·bang (lwäng prä·bäng') A city in north central Laos; site of the royal residence: pop. 22,200 (est. 1966).

lu·au (loo·ou') *n.* A Hawaiian feast with entertainment. [< *Hawaiian*]

lub·ber (lub'ər) *n.* **1.** An awkward, ungainly fellow. **2.** A landlubber (which see). [Origin uncertain. Cf. ON *lubba* short.] — **lub'ber·li·ness** *n.* — **lub'ber·ly** *adj. & adv.*

lubber line A fixed line in a compass, gyro, direction finder, etc., representing the heading of a ship or aircraft.

lubber's hole *Naut.* A hole through the floor of a top, by which sailors can go aloft without climbing over the rim.

Lub·bock (lub'ək) A city in NW Texas; pop. 149,101.

Lü·beck (loo'bek, *Ger.* lü'bek) A port city in NE West Germany; pop. 242,700 (est. 1967).

Lu·blin (loo'blin, *Polish* loo'blēn) A city in eastern Poland; pop. 173,300 (est. 1959): Russian *Lyublin.*

lu·bri·cant (loo'brə·kənt) *n.* A substance, as oil, grease, graphite, etc., used to coat moving parts in order to reduce friction and wear. — *adj.* Lubricating.

lu·bri·cate (loo'brə·kāt) *v.t.* **·cat·ed, ·cat·ing** **1.** To apply a lubricant to. **2.** To make slippery or smooth. [< L *lubricatus,* pp. of *lubricare* to make slippery < *lubricus* slippery] — **lu'bri·ca'tion** *n.* — **lu'bri·ca'tive** *adj.*

lu·bri·ca·tor (loo'brə·kā'tər) *n.* **1.** One who applies a lubricant. **2.** A lubricant. **3.** A device for applying a lubricant to machinery.

lu·bric·i·ty (loo·bris'ə·tē) *n. pl.* **·ties** **1.** Lewdness; lasciviousness. **2.** Shiftiness; elusiveness. **3.** Slipperiness; also, the property of or capacity for being slippery, as in a lubricant. [< F *lubricité* < L *lubricitas* < *lubricus* slippery]

lu·bri·cous (loo'brə·kəs) *adj.* **1.** Smooth and slippery. **2.** Shifty; elusive. **3.** Lewd; lascivious. Also **lu·bric** (loo'brik), **lu·bri·cious** (loo·brish'əs). [< L *lubricus*]

Lu·bum·ba·shi (loo·boom'bä·shē) The capital of Katanga Province, Republic of Zaire, in the SE part of the Province; pop. 318,000 (1970); formerly, Elisabethville.

Lu·can (loo'kən), A.D. 39–65, Roman epic poet: full name **Marcus Annaeus Lu·ca·nus** (loo·kā'nəs).

lu·carne (loo·kärn') *n.* A dormer window; also, a small window in a spire. [< F; ult. origin uncertain]

Luc·ca (look'kä) A city in Tuscany, north central Italy; pop. 89,940 (1961).

luce (loos) *n.* The pike, a fish: so called especially when fully grown. [< OF *lus* < L *lucius*]

lu·cent (loo'sənt) *adj.* **1.** Showing or giving off radiance. **2.** Transparent or semitransparent. [< L *lucens, -entis,* ppr. of *lucere* to shine] — **lu'cen·cy** *n.* — **lu'cent·ly** *adv.*

lu·cerne (loo·sûrn') *Brit.* Alfalfa. [< F *luzerne,* ? < L *lucerna* lamp]

Lu·cerne (loo·sûrn', *Fr.* lü·sern') A Canton of central Switzerland; 577 sq. mi.; pop. 253,100 (1960); capital, **Lucerne,** pop. 66,900: German *Luzern.*

Lucerne, Lake of A lake in central Switzerland; 44 sq. mi.: also *Lake of the Four Forest Cantons.*

lu·ces (loo'sēz) Plural of LUX.

Lu·cian (loo'shən) Second-century Greek satiric writer.

lu·cid (loo'sid) *adj.* **1.** Easily understood; rational; clear: a *lucid* explanation. **2.** Mentally sound, clear, or rational; sane: a *lucid* interval. **3.** Shining; bright. — **Syn.** See CLEAR. [< L *lucidus* < *lucere* to shine] — **lu·cid·i·ty** (loo·sid'ə·tē), **lu'cid·ness** *n.* — **lu'cid·ly** *adv.*

lu·ci·fer (loo'sə·fər) *n. Archaic* A friction match. Also **lucifer match.** [after *Lucifer*]

Lu·ci·fer (loo'sə·fər) *n.* **1.** The archangel who led the revolt of the angels and fell from Heaven: identified with *Satan.* **2.** The planet Venus when it appears as the morning star. [< L, light-bearer < *lux, lucis* light + *ferre* to bear]

lu·cif·er·ase (loo·sif'ə·rās) *n. Biochem.* An enzyme present in fireflies, etc., that oxidizes luciferin to produce light. [< L *lucifer* light-bearing + -ASE]

lu·cif·er·in (loo·sif'ər·in) *n. Biochem.* A protein that when acted upon by luciferase produces light in fireflies, etc. [< L *lucifer* light-bearing + -IN]

lu·cif·er·ous (loo·sif'ər·əs) *adj.* Bringing or emitting light. [< L *lucifer* light-bearing + -OUS]

Lu·ci·na (loo·sī'nə) In Roman mythology, the goddess presiding over childbirth. [< L *lucina,* fem. of *lucinus* bringing to the light < *lux, lucis* light]

Lu·cite (loo'sīt) *n.* A thermoplastic, transparent acrylic resin, easily machined into various shapes: a trade name.

luck (luk) *n.* **1.** That which happens by chance; fortune; lot. **2.** Good fortune; success. **3.** Any object regarded as bringing good fortune. — **to be down on one's luck** To suffer failure, poverty, etc. — **to be in luck** To meet with success or good fortune. — **to be out of luck** To be unlucky. — **to try one's luck** To attempt to do something without any certainty of success. [Prob. < MDu. *luk, geluk.*]

luck·i·ly (luk'ə·lē) *adv.* With or by good fortune; happily.

luck·less (luk'lis) *adj.* Having bad luck; unlucky. — **luck'less·ly** *adv.* — **luck'less·ness** *n.*

Luck·now (luk'nou) The capital of Uttar Pradesh, India; British forces were besieged here during the Sepoy Rebellion, 1857; pop. 763,600 (est. 1971).

luck·y¹ (luk'ē) *adj.* **luck·i·er, luck·i·est** **1.** Accompanied by or having good fortune; fortunate. **2.** Bringing or resulting in good fortune: a *lucky* break. **3.** Believed to bring good fortune: a *lucky* charm. — **Syn.** See FORTUNATE. — **luck'i·ness** *n.*

luck·y² (luk'ē) *n. pl.* **luck·ies** *Scot.* A grandam or aged woman; goody. Also **luck'ie.**

lu·cra·tive (loo'krə·tiv) *adj.* Producing or yielding gain, profit, or wealth; profitable; remunerative. [< L *lucrativus* < *lucratus,* pp. of *lucrari* to gain < *lucrum* wealth] — **lu'cra·tive·ly** *adv.* — **lu'cra·tive·ness** *n.*

lu·cre (loo'kər) *n.* Money or riches: now chiefly in the humorous phrase: **filthy lucre.** [< F < L *lucrum* gain]

Lu·cre·tius (loo·krē'shəs, -shē·əs), 96?–55 B.C., Roman poet: full name **Titus Lucretius Car·us** (kâr'əs).

lu·cu·brate (loo'kyoo·brāt) *v.i.* **·brat·ed, ·brat·ing** **1.** To study or write laboriously, especially at night. **2.** To write in a learned manner. [< L *lucubratus,* pp. of *lucubrare* to work by artificial light < *lux, lucis* light]

lu·cu·bra·tion (loo'kyoo·brā'shən) *n.* **1.** Earnest and labored study. **2.** The product of such study, especially a pedantic literary effort. [< L *lucubratio, -onis*] — **lu'cu·bra'tor** *n.* — **lu·cu·bra·to·ry** (-brə·tôr'ē, -tō'rē) *adj.*

lu·cu·lent (loo'kyoo·lənt) *adj. Rare* **1.** Lucid. **2.** Full of light; brilliant. [< L *luculentus* < *lux, lucis* light]

Lu·cul·lan (loo·kul'ən) *adj.* Of or like Lucius Licinius **Lucullus** (loo·kul'əs), died 57?B.C., wealthy Roman general and consul, famous for his extravagant banquets. Also **Lu·cul·le·an** (loo·kə·lē'ən), **Lu·cul'li·an.**

Lu·cy Sto·ner (loo'sē stō'nər) An advocate of women's rights. [after *Lucy Stone,* 1818–93, U.S. woman suffragist]

Lud·dite (lud'īt) In English industrial history, any of a band of workmen who joined in riots (1811–16) to wreck new textile machinery in the belief that its introduction reduced wages and increased unemployment. [after *Ned Lud,* a feeble-minded worker who, thirty years earlier, had destroyed his employer's stocking frames]

Lu·den·dorff (lŏŏ′dən·dôrf), **Erich von**, 1865–1937, German general; commander in chief in World War I.

Lü·der·itz (lü′dər·its) A port city in SW South-West Africa; pop. about 4,000.

Lu·dhi·a·na (lŏŏ′dē·ä′nə) A city in central Punjab, India; pop. 363,400 (est. 1969).

lu·di·crous (lŏŏ′də·krəs) *adj.* Exciting laughter or ridicule; ridiculous; absurd. [< L *ludicrus* < *ludere* to play] — **lu′di·crous·ly** *adv.* — **lu′di·crous·ness** *n.*

Lud·low (lud′lō) *n. Printing* A machine that casts type from brass matrices set by hand in a special stick, used in setting the large type for headings, advertisements, etc.: a trade name. Also **Ludlow ty·po·graph** (tī′pə·graf, -gräf).

Lud·wig II (lŏŏd′vikh), 1845–86, king of Bavaria, 1864–1886; patron of Richard Wagner; committed suicide.

Lud·wigs·ha·fen (lŏŏd′viks·hä′fən) A city in the Rhineland Palatinate, West Germany; pop. 173,000 (est. 1967). Also **Lud′wigs·ha·fen-am-Rhein′** (-äm-rīn′).

lu·es (lŏŏ′ēz) *n.* Syphilis. [< L, plague, discharge, ? < *luere* to flow] — **lu·et·ic** (lŏŏ·et′ik) *adj. & n.*

luff (luf) *Naut. n.* **1.** The sailing of a ship close to the wind. **2.** The rounded and fullest part of a vessel's bow. **3.** The foremost edge of a fore-and-aft sail. For illustration see SAIL. — *v.i.* **1.** To bring the head of a vessel nearer the wind. **2.** To bring the head of a vessel into the wind, with the sails shaking. Also **loof**. [ME *lof, loven.* Cf. OF *lof*, Du. *loeven.*]

luf·fa (luf′ə) *n.* A loofah (which see).

Luft·waf·fe (lŏŏft′väf′ə) *n. German* The German air force during World War II.

lug[1] (lug) *n.* **1.** An earlike projection for holding or supporting something: the *lugs* of a kettle. **2.** *Mech.* A nut, usually closed at one end. **3.** A loop at the side of a harness through which the shafts of a cart, etc., pass. **4.** *Scot.* The ear. **5.** *Slang* A fellow, especially a clumsy or stupid one. [Origin uncertain. Cf. Sw. *lugg* forelock.]

lug[2] (lug) *v.* **lugged, lug·ging** *v.t.* **1.** To carry or pull with effort; drag laboriously. **2.** *Informal* To bring, as irrelevant topics, into a conversation, discussion, etc.; introduce unreasonably. — *v.i.* **3.** To pull or drag with effort; tug. — *n.* **1.** The act or exertion of lugging; also, that which is lugged. **2.** *Naut.* A lugsail. [Prob. Scand. Cf. Sw. *lugga* to pull by the hair.]

lug[3] (lug) *n.* A lugworm (which see). [Origin uncertain]

Lu·gansk (lŏŏ·gänsk′) A city in the eastern Ukrainian S.S.R.; pop. 382,000 (1970): from 1935–58 *Voroshilovgrad*.

Lu·ger (lŏŏ′gər) *n.* A German automatic pistol. [after Georg *Luger*, 19th c. German engineer]

lug·gage (lug′ij) *n.* Suitcases, trunks, etc., used for traveling; baggage. [< LUG[2]]

lug·ger (lug′ər) *n. Naut.* A one-, two-, or three-masted vessel having lugsails only. [< LUG(SAIL) + -ER[2]]

LUGGER

lug·gie (lug′ē, lŏŏg′ē, lŏŏ′gē) *n. Scot.* A small wooden dish or pail having a luglike projection as a handle.

lug·sail (lug′səl, -sāl′) *n. Naut.* A four-cornered sail having no boom and bent to a yard that hangs obliquely on the mast: also called *lug.*

lu·gu·bri·ous (lŏŏ·gŏŏ′brē·əs, -gyŏŏ′-) *adj.* Very sad, or mournful, especially in a ludicrous manner. [< L *lugubris* < *lugere* to mourn] — **lu·gu′bri·ous·ly** *adv.* — **lu·gu′bri·ous·ness** *n.*

lug·worm (lug′wûrm′) *n.* An annelid worm (genus *Arenicola*) with two rows of tufted gills on the back, living in the sand of seashores and much used for bait: also called *lobworm.* [< LUG[3] + WORM]

lug wrench A wrench used for removing and replacing the nuts that attach the wheels to an automobile.

Lu·ian (lŏŏ′ē·ən, lŏŏ′yən) See LUWIAN.

Luik (loik) The Flemish name for LIÈGE.

Luke (lŏŏk) Physician and companion of St. Paul; traditionally thought to be the author of the third Gospel and of *The Acts of the Apostles*: called **Saint Luke**. — *n.* The third Gospel of the New Testament, attributed to Luke.

luke·warm (lŏŏk′wôrm′) *adj.* **1.** Moderately warm; tepid. **2.** Lacking in ardor, enthusiasm, or conviction; indifferent: a *lukewarm* greeting. [Prob. OE *hlēow* warm. Cf. LG *luk* tepid] — **luke′warm′ly** *adv.* — **luke′warm′ness** *n.*

lull (lul) *v.t.* **1.** To quiet or put to sleep by soothing sounds or motions. **2.** To calm or allay, especially by deception: to *lull* someone's suspicions. — *v.i.* **3.** To become calm or quiet. — *n.* **1.** A brief interval of calm or quiet during noise or confusion: a *lull* in a storm. **2.** A period of diminished activity, prosperity, etc.: a *lull* in business. [Prob. imit. Cf. Sw. *lulla* to sing to sleep.]

Lull (lŏŏl), **Raymond**, 1235?–1315, Spanish theologian and missionary. Also **Lul·ly** (lŏŏ′lē).

lull·a·by (lul′ə·bī) *n. pl.* **·bies** **1.** A song to lull a child to sleep; a cradlesong. **2.** A piece of instrumental music in the manner of a lullaby. **3.** *Obs.* A goodnight or farewell. — *v.t.* **·bied, ·by·ing** *Rare* To soothe with a lullaby. [< LULL]

Lul·ly (lü·lē′), **Jean Baptiste**, 1633?–87, French composer born in Italy: original name **Giovanni Battista Lul·li** (lŏŏl′lē).

lu·lu (lŏŏ′lŏŏ) *n. Slang* Anything exceptional or outstanding, as in beauty, size, difficulty, etc. [< *Lulu*, a nickname]

lum (lum) *n. Brit. Dial. & Scot.* A chimney.

lum·ba·go (lum·bā′gō) *n.* Pain in the lumbar region of the back; backache, especially in the small of the back. [< L < *lumbus* loin]

lum·bar (lum′bər, -bär) *adj.* Pertaining to or situated near the loins. — *n.* A lumbar vertebra, nerve, artery, etc. [< NL *lumbaris* < L *lumbus* loin]

lum·ber[1] (lum′bər) *n.* **1.** *U.S. & Canadian* Timber sawed into boards, planks, etc., of specified lengths. **2.** *Chiefly Brit.* Household articles no longer used and usually stored away. **3.** Anything useless or cumbersome. — *adj.* Made of, pertaining to, or dealing in lumber. — *v.t.* **1.** *U.S. & Canadian* To cut down (timber); also, to cut down the timber of (an area). **2.** *Chiefly Brit.* To fill or obstruct with useless articles. — *v.i.* **3.** *U.S. & Canadian* To cut down or saw timber for marketing. [Var. of *Lombard* in obs. sense of "money-lender, pawnshop," hence, stored articles] — **lum′ber·er** *n.*

lum·ber[2] (lum′bər) *v.i.* **1.** To move or proceed in a heavy or awkward manner. **2.** To move with a rumbling noise. — *n.* A rumbling noise. [ME *lomerer.* Cf. Sw. *lomra* to resound, *loma* to walk heavily.]

lum·ber·ing[1] (lum′bər·ing) *n. U.S. & Canadian* The business of felling, shaping, or selling lumber or timber.

lum·ber·ing[2] (lum′bər·ing) *adj.* **1.** Awkward, clumsy, or heavy in appearance, style, etc. **2.** Moving heavily or awkwardly. — **lum′ber·ing·ly** *adv.* — **lum′ber·ing·ness** *n.*

lum·ber·jack (lum′bər·jak) *n. U.S. & Canadian* **1.** A person who fells or transports timber; a logger. **2.** A jacket of wool, leather, etc., usually hip-length and resembling those worn by loggers. Also **lum′ber·jack′et** (-jak′it) **3.** *Canadian* The Canada jay. [< LUMBER[1] + *jack* man, boy]

lum·ber·man (lum′bər·mən) *n. pl.* **·men** (mən) *U.S. & Canadian* **1.** A lumberjack (def. 1). **2.** One who is engaged in the business of lumbering.

lum·ber·yard (lum′bər·yärd′) *n. U.S. & Canadian* A yard for the storage or sale of lumber.

lum·bri·ca·lis (lum′brə·kā′lis) *n. pl.* **·les** (-lēz) *Anat.* One of the four wormlike muscles in the palm of the hand; also, one of four similar muscles in the sole of the foot. [< NL < L *lumbricus* worm] — **lum·bri·cal** (lum′brə·kəl) *adj.*

lum·bri·coid (lum′brə·koid) *adj.* **1.** Of or resembling the common earthworm. **2.** Pertaining to or designating a roundworm parasitic in the human intestine. — *n.* The roundworm. [< L *lumbricus* earthworm + -OID]

lu·men (lŏŏ′mən) *n. pl.* **·mens** or **·mi·na** (-mə·nə) **1.** *Anat.* The inner passage of a tubular organ, as a blood vessel. **2.** *Physics* A unit for measuring luminous flux, equal to the flow of light through a solid angle of one steradian from a uniform point source of one international candle. [< L, light]

Lu·mi·nal (lŏŏ′mə·nôl, -nol) *n.* Proprietary name for a brand of phenobarbital.

lu·mi·nance (lŏŏ′mə·nəns) *n. Physics* The luminous intensity of any surface, per unit of projected area of the surface as viewed in a given direction: also called *brightness.*

lu·mi·nar·y (lŏŏ′mə·ner′ē) *n. pl.* **·nar·ies** **1.** Any body that gives light, especially the sun or the moon. **2.** One who has achieved great eminence. [< OF *luminaire* < LL *luminarium* candle, torch < *lumen* light]

lu·mi·nesce (lŏŏ′mə·nes′) *v.i.* **·nesced, ·nesc·ing** To be or become luminescent. [Back formation < LUMINESCENT]

lu·mi·nes·cence (lŏŏ′mə·nes′əns) *n.* An emission of light, such as fluorescence and phosphorescence, not directly attributable to the heat that produces incandescence.

lu·mi·nes·cent (lŏŏ′mə·nes′ənt) *adj.* Characterized by, emitting, or capable of emitting luminescence. [< L *lumen* light + -ESCENT]

lumini- *combining form* Light; luminescence. Also **lumin-** (before vowels), **lumino-**. [< L *lumen, luminis* light]

lu·mi·nif·er·ous (lŏŏ′mə·nif′ər·əs) *adj.* Producing or conveying light. [< LUMINI- + -FEROUS]

lu·mi·nos·i·ty (lŏŏ′mə·nos′ə·tē) *n. pl.* **·ties** **1.** The state or quality of being luminous. **2.** That which is luminous. **3.** *Physics* The ratio of the luminous flux emitted by an object to the total radiant flux, expressed in lumens per watt.

lu·mi·nous (lŏŏ′mə·nəs) *adj.* **1.** Full of light; glowing. **2.** Giving off light; shining. **3.** Easily understood; clear: a *luminous* comment. **4.** Brilliantly intelligent or wise: *luminous* leadership. [< L *luminosus* < *lumen* light] — **lu′mi·nous·ly** *adv.* — **lu′mi·nous·ness** *n.*

luminous energy Light[1] (def. 1).

luminous flux *Physics* The time rate of the flow of visible light, expressed in lumens.

luminous intensity *Physics* The luminous flux emitted from a point source of light per steradian.

lum·mox (lum′əks) *n.* *U.S. Informal* A stupid, clumsy person. [Origin unknown]

lump¹ (lump) *n.* **1.** A shapeless mass, especially a small mass: a *lump* of dough. **2.** A protuberance or swelling. **3.** A mass of things thrown together; aggregate. **4.** A heavy, ungainly, and usually stupid person. **— a lump in one's throat** A feeling of tightness in the throat, as from emotion. **— in a** (or **the**) **lump** All together; with no distinction. **—** *adj.* Formed in a lump or lumps: *lump* sugar. **—** *v.t.* **1.** To put together in one mass, group, etc. **2.** To consider or treat as one mass, group, etc.: to *lump* all the facts together. **3.** To make lumps in or on. **—** *v.i.* **4.** To become lumpy. [< ME, prob. < Scand.]

lump² (lump) *v.t.* *Informal* To put up with; endure: You can like it or *lump* it. [Origin uncertain]

lum·pen (lum′pən) *Informal adj.* Having little genuine claim or substance; defective; shabby; phony: used in combination: *lumpen-intellectual.* **—** *n.* One who is lumpen. [< G, rag, tatter < *lump* contemptible person]

lump·fish (lump′fish′) *n.* *pl.* **·fish** or **·fish·es** A bulky fish (*Cyclopterus lumpus*) of the North Atlantic, with a sucker enabling it to cling to rocks. Also **lump′suck′er** (-suk′ər).

lump·ish (lump′ish) *adj.* **1.** Like a lump. **2.** Stupid; clumsy. **— lump′ish·ly** *adv.* **— lump′ish·ness** *n.*

lump sum A full or single sum of money paid at one time.

lump·y (lum′pē) *adj.* **lump·i·er, lump·i·est** **1.** Full of lumps. **2.** Covered with or having lumps. **3.** Lumpish. **4.** Running in rough, choppy waves: a *lumpy* sea. **— lump′·i·ly** *adv.* **— lump′i·ness** *n.*

lumpy jaw Actinomycosis.

lu·na (loo′nə) *n.* In alchemy, silver. [< L, moon]

Lu·na (loo′nə) In Roman mythology, the goddess of the moon: identified with the Greek *Selene.* [< L]

lu·na·cy (loo′nə·sē) *n.* *pl.* **·cies** **1.** Irresponsible or senseless conduct; foolishness. **2.** *Law* Insanity. **3.** Formerly, an intermittent form of mental derangement believed to depend on the changing phases of the moon. **— Syn.** See INSANITY. [< LUNATIC]

Luna moth A large North American moth (*Tropaea luna*), having light green wings with long tails and lunate spots. [So called from the crescent-shaped spots on its wings]

lu·nar (loo′nər) *adj.* **1.** Of or pertaining to the moon. **2.** Round or crescent-shaped like the moon. **3.** Measured by the revolutions of the moon: a *lunar* month. **4.** Of or pertaining to silver. [< L *lunaris* < *luna* moon]

lunar caustic *Chem.* Silver nitrate formed into pencils and used for cauterizing. [< LUNA]

lunar excursion module *Aerospace* The vehicle that transports astronauts from the orbiting command module to the moon's surface and back.

lu·nar·i·an (loo·nâr′ē·ən) *n.* **1.** A supposed inhabitant of the moon. **2.** One who studies the moon. [< L *lunaris*]

lunar month See under MONTH.

lunar year A period of twelve lunar months, one month being added at intervals to make the mean length of the astronomical year, as in the Hebrew calendar.

lu·nate (loo′nāt) *adj.* Crescent-shaped. Also **lu′nat·ed.** [< L *lunatus*]

lu·na·tic (loo′nə·tik) *adj.* **1.** Insane. **2.** Wildly foolish or irrational. **3.** Of or for the insane: a *lunatic* asylum. **—** *n.* An insane person. [< LL *lunaticus* < L *luna* moon]

lunatic fringe Those followers or devotees of a movement, idea, etc., who are extreme or fanatical in their enthusiasm.

lu·na·tion (loo·nā′shən) *n.* The interval between two returns of the new moon, averaging 29.5 days. [< Med.L *lunatio, -onis* < L *luna* moon]

lunch (lunch) *n.* **1.** A light noonday meal. **2.** Food for a lunch. **—** *v.i.* **1.** To eat lunch. **—** *v.t.* **2.** To furnish lunch for. [Short for LUNCHEON] **— lunch′er** *n.*

lunch·eon (lun′chən) *n.* A noonday meal, especially a formal one. [Origin uncertain]

lunch·eon·ette (lun′chən·et′) *n.* A restaurant, usually having a counter, booths, and small tables, where quickly prepared, light lunches and other meals may be obtained.

lunch·room (lunch′room′, -room′) *n.* A restaurant serving light lunches. Also **lunch room.**

Lun·dy's Lane (lun′dēz) A region near Niagara Falls, Ontario; scene of a battle (1814) in the War of 1812.

lune (loon) *n.* **1.** *Geom.* A figure resembling a crescent, formed on a plane or sphere by two arcs of circles. **2.** Anything shaped like a crescent. [< F < L *luna* moon]

lune² (loon) *n.* In hawking, a leash for hawks. [< OF *loigne* leash < Med.L *longea* < L *longus* long]

lu·nette (loo·net′) *n.* **1.** Something shaped like a crescent or half-moon. **2.** *Archit.* **a** A small curved or circular window or opening in a dome or in a vaulted ceiling. **b** An arched or crescent-shaped space, often ornamented with paintings or sculpture; also, the paintings or sculptures. **3.** *Mil.* A type of fieldwork. **4.** A ring in the trail plate of a towed vehicle, as a gun carriage, for receiving the towing hook. Also **lu·net** (loo′nit). [< F, dim. of *lune* moon]

Lu·né·ville (lü·nā·vēl′) A town in NE France; scene of signing of a peace treaty between Austria and France, 1801; pop. 22,961 (1968).

lung (lung) *n.* *Anat.* **1.** Either of two saclike organs of respiration in the thorax of man and other air-breathing vertebrates. ◆ Collateral adjective: *pulmonary.* **2.** An analogous organ in certain invertebrates. [OE *lungen*]

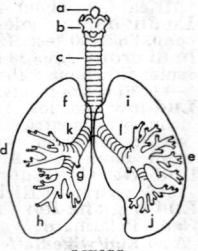

LUNGS
a Epiglottis. *b* Larynx. *c* Trachea. *d* Right lung. *e* Left lung. *f, i* Upper lobes. *g* Middle lobe. *h, j* Lower lobes. *k, l* Bronchi.

lunge¹ (lunj) *n.* **1.** A sudden pass or thrust, as with a sword, bayonet, etc. **2.** A quick movement or plunge forward. **—** *v.* **lunged, lung·ing** **—** *v.i.* **1.** To make a lunge or pass; thrust. **2.** To move with a lunge. **—** *v.t.* **3.** To cause to lunge. [Aphetic var. of obs. *allonge* < F *allonger* to prolong < L *ad* to + *longus* long]

lunge² (lunj) *n.* A rein thirty or more feet long at the end of which the horse moves for training and exercise. **—** *v.t.* **lunged, lung·ing** To cause (a horse) to circle at the end of a lunge. Also spelled *longe.* [< F < OF *lonc* long < L *longus*]

lunge³ (lunj) *n.* *U.S. & Canadian Informal* Muskellunge. Also **′lunge.**

lung·er (lung′ər) *n.* *Slang* A person having tuberculosis.

lung·fish (lung′fish′) *n.* *pl.* **·fish** or **·fish·es** A dipnoan.

lun·gi (lung′gē) *n.* In India: **a** A loincloth. **b** A long piece of fabric used as a loincloth or as a scarf or turban. Also **lun′gee.** [< Hind.]

Lung·ki (loong′kē′) A port city in southern Fukien Province, China; pop. about 100,000: formerly *Changchow.*

lung·worm (lung′wûrm′) *n.* Any of various nematode worms parasitic in the lungs of certain mammals.

lung·wort (lung′wûrt′) *n.* Any of various plants of the borage family; as: **a** A European herb (*Pulmonaria officinalis*), having white blotches on its leaves. **b** The Virginia cowslip.

luni- *combining form* Of or pertaining to the moon; lunar. [< L *luna* moon]

lu·ni·so·lar (loo′ni·sō′lər) *adj.* Of or resulting from the combined action of the sun and moon.

lu·ni·ti·dal (loo′ni·tīd′l) *adj.* Of or relating to the tides as produced by the moon's attraction.

lunitidal interval The interval between the moon's transit of a given meridian and the next lunar high tide.

lunk·er (lung′kər) *n.* *U.S. & Canadian Informal* Any very large game fish.

lunk·head (lungk′hed′) *n.* *U.S. Informal* A stupid person. [Prob. alter. of LUMP + HEAD] **— lunk′head′ed** *adj.*

lunt (lunt, loont) *n.* *Scot.* **1.** A whiff of smoke. **2.** A slow-burning match or torch.

Lunt (lunt), **Alfred,** born 1893, U.S. actor; husband of Lynn Fontanne.

lu·nu·la (loo′nyə·lə) *n.* *pl.* **·lae** (-lē) **1.** Something having the shape or appearance of a crescent. **2.** *Anat.* The whitish area at the base of the human nail: also **lu′nule** (-nyool). [< L, dim. of *luna* moon]

lu·nu·lar (loo′nyə·lər) *adj.* Crescent-shaped. [< LUNULA]

lu·nu·late (loo′nyə·lāt, -lit) *adj.* Having a crescent form or crescent-shaped markings. Also **lu′nu·lat′ed.**

lu·ny (loo′nē) See LOONY.

Lu·per·ca·li·a (loo′pər·kā′lē·ə, -kal′yə) *n.pl.* In ancient Rome, a fertility festival celebrated on February 15, in honor of a rustic deity **Lu·per·cus** (loo·pûr′kəs), often identified with Faunus. Also **Lu′per·cal** (-kal). [< L, neut. pl. of *Lupercalis* of *Lupercus* < *Lupercus* Faunus < *lupus* wolf]

lu·pine¹ (loo′pin) *adj.* **1.** Of, like, or related to a wolf or wolves. **2.** Fierce; ravenous. [< L *lupinus* < *lupus* wolf]

lu·pine² (loo′pin) *n.* Any of various plants (genus *Lupinus*) of the pea family, bearing terminal racemes of mostly blue, white, or purple flowers, as the **wild lupine** (*L. perennis*) of the United States, and the **white lupine** (*L. albus*) of Europe, whose seeds are edible. **2.** The seeds of the white lupine. Also **lu′pin** (-pin). [< F *lupin* < L *lupinus* wolflike; reason for name unknown]

lu·pu·lin (loo′pyə·lin) *n.* The glandular hairs of the hop plant, used as a sedative and stomachic. [< NL *lupulus* the hop, dim. of L *lupus* wolf; reason for name unknown]

lu·pus (loo′pəs) *n.* *Pathol.* Any of various forms of a tuberculous disease of the skin and mucous membranes, often involving the face and characterized by brownish nodules or scaly red patches. [< L, wolf]

Lu·pus (loo′pəs) *n.* A constellation, the Wolf. See CONSTELLATION. [< L]

lurch¹ (lûrch) *v.i.* **1.** To roll suddenly to one side, as a ship in a rough sea. **2.** To move unsteadily; stagger. **—** *n.* **1.** A sudden swaying or rolling to one side. **2.** A reeling or tottering. [Origin uncertain]

lurch² (lûrch) *n.* **1.** An embarrassing or difficult position; predicament: now only in the phrase **to leave (someone) in**

the lurch. 2. In cribbage, the state of a player who has made 30 points or less while his opponent has won with 61. [< F *lourche*, name of a game < *lourche* deceived < Gmc. Cf. MDu. *lurz* left-handed, unlucky.]

lurch·er (lûr′chər) *n.* **1.** One who lies in wait or lurks; a sneak thief; poacher. **2.** *Brit.* A crossbred hunting dog, especially one trained by poachers to hunt silently. [ME *lorchere* < *lorchen* to lurk]

lur·dan (lûr′dən) *Archaic adj.* Stupid or lazy. — *n.* A dull or lazy person. Also **lur′dane.** [< OF *lourdin* < *lourd* heavy]

lure (lŏŏr, lyŏŏr) *n.* **1.** Anything that attracts or entices by the prospect of advantage, pleasure, etc. **2.** In angling, an artificial bait. **3.** In falconry, a device consisting of a bunch of feathers and a bait, fastened to a long cord and used to recall a hawk. — *v.t.* **lured, lur·ing 1.** To attract or entice; allure. **2.** To recall (a hawk) with a lure. [< OF *leurre* < MHG *luoder* to bait] — **lur′er** *n.*

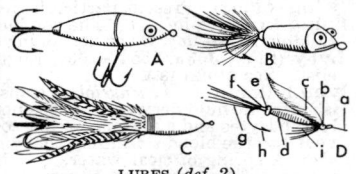

LURES (def. 2)

A Wood or plastic. B Floating cork. C Feather. D Dry fly: *a* Gut, *b* Head, *c* Wing, *d* Body, *e* Butt, *f* Tag, *g* Tail, *h* Hook, *i* Hackle.

lu·rid (lŏŏr′id, lyŏŏr-) *adj.* **1.** Shocking, vivid, or sensational: a *lurid* tale. **2.** Pale and sickly in color; sallow. **3.** Sending out or lighted up with a yellowish red glare or glow especially in smoke or darkness: a *lurid* flash. [< L *luridus* sallow] — **lu′rid·ly** *adv.* — **lu′rid·ness** *n.*

lurk (lûrk) *v.i.* **1.** To lie hidden, as in ambush. **2.** To exist unnoticed or unsuspected. **3.** To move secretly or furtively; slink. [ME *lurken.* Cf. Norw. *lurka* to sneak off.] — **lurk′ing·ly** *adv.*

Lur·lei (lŏŏr′lī) See LORELEI.

Lu·sa·ka (lŏŏ·sä′kə) The capital of Zambia, in the central part; pop. 152,000 (1963).

Lu·sa·tia (lŏŏ·sā′shə) A region of SE Germany and SW Poland between the Elbe and the Oder.

Lu·sa·tian (lŏŏ·sā′shən) *n. & adj.* Wendish.

lus·cious (lush′əs) *adj.* **1.** Very pleasurable to the sense of taste or smell. **2.** Pleasing to any sense or to the mind. **3.** Excessively sweet or rich; cloying. [? Blend of LUSH and DELICIOUS] — **lus′cious·ly** *adv.* — **lus′cious·ness** *n.*

lush[1] (lush) *adj.* **1.** Abounding in vigorous growth: a *lush* countryside. **2.** Delicious and succulent: *lush* fruit. **3.** Elaborate, luxurious, or extravagant in effects, ornamentation, etc.: *lush* prose. [? Var. of dial. E *lash* soft and watery < OF *lasche* < L *laxus* loose] — **lush′ness** *n.*

lush[2] (lush) *Slang n.* **1.** A heavy drinker; drunkard. **2.** Formerly, intoxicating liquor. — *v.t. & v.i.* To drink (alcoholic liquor), especially to excess. [Origin unknown]

Lu·si·ta·ni·a (lŏŏ′sə·tā′nē·ə) An ancient name for PORTUGAL.

lust (lust) *n.* **1.** Sexual appetite. **2.** Excessive sexual appetite, especially that seeking immediate or ruthless satisfaction. **3.** A strong, overwhelming desire or need: a *lust* for power. **4.** *Obs.* Pleasure; inclination. — **Syn.** See DESIRE. — *v.i.* To have passionate or inordinate desire, especially sexual desire: often with *after* or *for.* [OE, pleasure]

lus·ter (lus′tər) *n.* **1.** Soft, reflected light playing over a surface; sheen; gloss: the *luster* of gold. **2.** Brightness or brilliance of light; radiance. **3.** Splendor, glory, or distinction, as of achievement, renown, beauty, etc.: He brings new *luster* to the position. **4.** A source or center of light, especially a chandelier; also, one of the glass pendants of a chandelier. **5.** Any of various substances used to give a polish or gloss to a surface. **6.** In ceramics, a glossy, metallic, and often iridescent finish given to the surface of an object. **7.** A fabric of mixed wool and cotton and having a glossy finish. **8.** *Mineral.* The surface appearance of a mineral as determined by the intensity and quality of the light it reflects. — *v.* **lus·tered** or *Brit.* **tred, lus·ter·ing** or *Brit.* **tring** *v.t.* **1.** To give a luster or gloss to. — *v.i.* **2.** To be or become lustrous. Also *Brit.* **lus′tre.** [< F *lustre* < Ital. *lustro* < *lustrare* to shine, purify < L *lustrum* purification]

lus·ter·ware (lus′tər·wâr′) *n.* Pottery having a lustrous and often iridescent sheen.

lust·ful (lust′fəl) *adj.* **1.** Characterized or driven by lust; libidinous. **2.** *Archaic* Lusty; vigorous. — **lust′ful·ly** *adv.* — **lust′ful·ness** *n.*

lust·i·hood (lus′tē·hŏŏd) *n. Archaic* Lustiness.

lus·tral (lus′trəl) *adj.* **1.** Of, pertaining to, or used in purification. **2.** Occurring every five years.

lus·trate (lus′trāt) *v.t.* **trat·ed, ·trat·ing** To purify by an offering or ceremony. [< L *lustratus*, pp. of *lustrare* to purify by propitiatory offerings < *lustrum* purification] — **lus·tra′tion** *n.* — **lus·tra·tive** (lus′trə·tiv) *adj.*

lus·trous (lus′trəs) *adj.* **1.** Having a luster or sheen; glossy. **2.** Brilliant; shining: *lustrous* eyes. — **lus′trous·ly** *adv.* — **lus′trous·ness** *n.*

lus·trum (lus′trəm) *n.* **1.** A period of five years. **2.** In ancient Rome, the solemn ceremony of purification of the entire people made every five years, after the taking of the census.

lust·y (lus′tē) *adj.* **lust·i·er, lust·i·est 1.** Characterized by or full of health and vigor; robust. **2.** Strong; powerful: a *lusty* drink. — **lust′i·ly** *adv.* — **lust′i·ness** *n.*

lu·sus na·tu·rae (lŏŏ′səs nə·tŏŏr′ē, -tyŏŏr′ē) A sport or freak of nature. Also **lu′sus.** [< L, joke of nature]

Lut (lŏŏt) See DASHT-I-LUT.

Lü·ta (lü·tä′) A city in NE China, at the tip of the Liaotung Peninsula; site of a naval base operated jointly after 1945 by the Soviet Union and the People's Republic of China; formerly two cities (Port Arthur and Dairen); pop. 4,000,000 (est. 1970): formerly *Port Arthur-Dairen.*

lu·ta·nist (lŏŏt′ə·nist, lyŏŏt′-) *n.* One who plays the lute. Also **lu′te·nist.**

lute[1] (lŏŏt, lyŏŏt) *n.* An old musical instrument having strings that are plucked by the fingers, a large body shaped like half of a pear, and a long, fretted neck usually bent at a sharp angle just below the peg box. [< OF *leüt* < Pg. *laut* < Arabic al'*ūd* the piece of wood]

lute[2] (lŏŏt, lyŏŏt) *n.* A composition of finely powdered clay, used as a sealing agent for joints of pipes, etc. Also **lut′ing.** — *v.t.* **lut·ed, lut·ing** To seal with lute. [< OF *lut* < L *lutum* mud]

lu·te·al (lŏŏ′tē·əl) *adj. Anat.* Of or pertaining to the corpus luteum. [< L *luteus* yellow]

lu·te·o·lin (lŏŏ·tē·ə·lin) *n. Chem.* A yellow crystalline compound, $C_{15}H_{10}O_6$, obtained from dyer's-broom, and used as a dyestuff. [< F *lutéoline* < NL (*Reseda*) *luteola* dyer's weed < L *luteolus* yellowish < *luteus* yellow]

lu·te·ous (lŏŏ′tē·əs) *adj.* Light or moderate greenish yellow in color. [< L *luteus < lutum* weed used by dyers]

Lu·te·tia (lŏŏ·tē′shə), **Lutetia Pa·ris·i·o·rum** (pə·riz′i·ō′rəm) Ancient names for PARIS.

lu·te·ti·um (lŏŏ·tē′shē·əm, -tē′shəm) *n.* A metallic element (symbol Lu) of the lanthanide series, isolated from ytterbium. Also **lu·te′ci·um.** See ELEMENT.

lu·te·um (lŏŏ′tē·əm) *n.* Corpus luteum (which see).

Luth. Lutheran.

Lu·ther (lŏŏ′thər), **Martin**, 1483–1546, German monk, theologian, and reformer; leader of the Reformation; excommunicated by Pope Leo X, 1520.

Lu·ther·an (lŏŏ′thər·ən) *adj.* Of or pertaining to Martin Luther, his doctrines, or to the Lutheran Church. — *n.* A member of the Lutheran Church. — **Lu′ther·an·ism** *n.*

Lutheran Church A Protestant denomination founded in Germany in the 16th century by Martin Luther. Its chief doctrine is justification by faith alone.

lu·thern (lŏŏ′thərn) *n.* A dormer window. [? Alter. of LUCARNE]

lu·tist (lŏŏ′tist) *n.* One who makes or plays lutes.

Lüt·zen (lü′tsən) A town in East Germany; scene of battles in the Thirty Years' War (1632) and the Napoleonic Wars (1813); pop. about 5,000.

Lu·wi·an (lŏŏ′ē·ən, lōō′-) *n.* An extinct Anatolic language of which only a few inscriptions have been found, in Asia Minor, now considered to be closely related to Hittite. — *adj.* Of or pertaining to this language. Also spelled *Luian*: also **Lu·vi·an** (lŏŏ′vē·ən).

lux (luks) *n. pl.* **lux·es** or **lu·ces** (lŏŏ′sēz) *Physics* The unit of illumination in the metric system, equivalent to .0929 foot-candle, or 1 lumen per square meter. [< L, light]

Lux. Luxembourg.

lux·ate (luk′sāt) *v.t.* **·at·ed, ·at·ing** To put out of joint; dislocate. [< L *luxatus*, pp. of *luxare* to dislocate < *luxus* dislocated] — **lux·a′tion** *n.*

luxe (lŏŏks, luks; *Fr.* lüks) *n.* Elegance or luxury, as to quality. See DE LUXE. [< F < L *luxus* extravagance]

Lux·em·bourg (luk′səm·bûrg, *Fr.* lük·säṅ·bŏŏr′) **1.** A constitutional grand duchy between Belgium, France, and Germany; 998 sq. mi.; pop. 339,000 (est. 1970); capital, **Luxembourg**; pop. 77,458 (est. 1969). **2.** A Province in SE Belgium; 1,706 sq. mi.; pop. 219,360 (est. 1970); capital, Arlon. Also **Lux′em·burg.**

Lux·em·burg (lŏŏk′səm·bŏŏrkh), **Rosa**, 1870–1919, German socialist leader born in Poland; assassinated.

Lux·or (luk′sôr, lŏŏk′-) A city in Upper Egypt near the site of ancient Thebes, on the Nile; pop. about 30,000: Arabic *El Uksor.*

lux·u·ri·ance (lug·zhŏŏr′ē·əns, luk·shŏŏr′-) *n.* The state or quality of being luxuriant. Also **lux·u′ri·an·cy.**

LUTE

lux·u·ri·ant (lug·zhŏŏr′ē·ənt, luk·shŏŏr′-) *adj.* **1.** Growing lushly and profusely, as vegetation; prolific; rank. **2.** Abundant, exuberant, or ornate, as in design, invention, etc. **3.** *Rare* Abundantly fertile, as soil. [< L *luxurians, -antis,* ppr. of *luxuriare.* See LUXURIATE.] **— lux·u′ri·ant·ly** *adv.*

lux·u·ri·ate (lug·zhŏŏr′ē·āt, luk·shŏŏr′-) *v.i.* **·at·ed, ·at·ing** **1.** To take great pleasure; indulge oneself fully: with *in.* **2.** To live sumptuously. **3.** To grow profusely. [< L *luxuriatus,* pp. of *luxuriare* to be fruitful, abound < *luxuria.* See LUXURY.] **— lux·u′ri·a′tion** *n.*

lux·u·ri·ous (lug·zhŏŏr′ē·əs, luk·shŏŏr′-) *adj.* **1.** Characterized by or conducive to luxury or extreme comfort; opulent; sumptuous. **2.** Indulging in or given to luxury. [< L *luxuriosus.*] **— lux·u′ri·ous·ly** *adv.* **— lux·u′ri·ous·ness** *n.*

lux·u·ry (luk′shər·ē, *occasionally* lug′zhər·ē) *n. pl.* **·ries** **1.** Anything, usually expensive or rare, that ministers to comfort or pleasure but is not a necessity to life, health, etc. **2.** Free indulgence in that which is expensive, rare, or extremely gratifying. **3.** Any pleasure; also, that which produces it. [< OF *luxurie* < L *luxuria* < *luxus* extravagance]

Lu·zern (lŏŏ·tsern′) The German name for LUCERNE.

Lu·zon (lŏŏ·zon′, *Sp.* lŏŏ·sŏn′) The largest of the Philippines; 40,420 sq. mi.

lv. 1. Leave(s). **2.** Livre(s).

Lvov (lv′vôf) A city in the western Ukrainian S.S.R.; pop. 553,000 (est. 1970): German *Lemberg.* Polish **Lwów** (lvŏŏf). Also **L'vov.**

-ly[1] *suffix of adjectives* **1.** Like; characteristic of; pertaining to: *manly, godly.* **2.** Occurring every (specified interval): *weekly, daily.* Compare -LIKE. [OE -*līc*]

-ly[2] *suffix of adverbs* **1.** In a (specified) manner: used to form adverbs from adjectives, or (rarely) from nouns: *brightly, busily.* **2.** At every (specified interval): *hourly, yearly.* [OE -*līce* < -*līc* -ly[1]]

◆ In cases where an adjective already ends in *-ly,* the forms of the adjective and adverb are often identical: He spoke *kindly;* He is a *kindly* man. Occasionally, *-ly* is added to *-ly* (which is then changed to *-li*), as in *surlily,* but this is generally avoided as awkward. In the case of words derived from French adjectives in *-le,* the ending is dropped before adding *-ly,* as in *nobly, possibly.*

ly·ard (lī′ərd) *adj. Scot.* Silver-gray or streaked with gray. Also **ly′art** (-ərt). [< OF *liart*]

Lyau·tey (lyō·tā′), **Louis Hubert Gonsalve,** 1854–1934, French military commander and colonial administrator.

ly·can·thrope (lī′kən·thrōp, lī·kan′thrōp) *n.* **1.** A werewolf. **2.** One afflicted with lycanthropy. [< Gk. *lykanthrōpos* < *lykos* wolf + *anthrōpos* a man]

ly·can·thro·py (lī·kan′thrə·pē) *n.* **1.** In folklore, the power of turning oneself or another into a wolf. **2.** A form of mental illness in which the patient imagines himself to be a wolf or other wild animal. **— ly·can·throp′ic** (-throp′ik) *adj.*

Ly·ca·on (lī·kā′on) In Greek mythology, a king of Arcadia, turned by Zeus into a wolf because he tested the divinity of the disguised god by offering him human flesh as food.

Ly·ca·o·ni·a (lī′kā·ō′nē·ə, lik′ā-) An ancient district in south central Asia Minor.

ly·cée (lē·sā′) *n. French* In France, a secondary school financed by the government and preparing its students for a university. [< F < L *lyceum.* See LYCEUM.]

ly·ce·um (lī·sē′əm) *n. pl.* **·ce·ums** or **·ce·a** (-sē′ə) **1.** *U.S.* An organization providing popular instruction by lectures, concerts, etc.; also, its building. **2.** A lycée. [< LYCEUM]

Ly·ce·um (lī·sē′əm) A grove near Athens in which Aristotle taught. [< L < Gk. *Lykeion* < *lykeios,* epithet of Apollo (whose temple was near this grove)]

ly·chee (lē′chē) See LICHEE.

lych gate (lich) See LICH GATE.

lych·nis (lik′nis) *n.* Any of a large genus (*Lychnis*) of erect, ornamental herbs, as the **scarlet lychnis** (*L. chalcedonica*), or the rose campion (*L. coronaria*). [< L < Gk.]

Lyc·i·a (lish′ē·ə, lis·ē-) An ancient country on the SW coast of Asia Minor, later a Roman province.

Lyc·i·an (lish′ē·ən, lis·ē·ən) *adj.* Of or relating to ancient Lycia, its inhabitants, or their language. **—** *n.* **1.** One who lived in Lycia. **2.** The Lycian language, believed related to Hittite.

Lyc·i·das (lis′ə·dəs) The title of an elegy (1637) that Milton wrote in memory of his college friend, Edward King.

ly·co·pod (lī′kə·pod) *n.* Any of various erect or creeping evergreen plants of the club-moss family (genus *Lycopodium*), much used as Christmas decorations. [< Gk. *lykos* wolf + -POD; from the resemblance of the root to a claw]

ly·co·po·di·um (lī′kə·pō′dē·əm) *n.* **1.** A lycopod. **2.** A flammable yellow powder produced by the spores of the club moss, used in pharmacology. [< NL]

Ly·cur·gus (lī·kûr′gəs) Ninth-century B.C. Spartan lawgiver; traditional author of Spartan laws.

Lyd·da (lid′ə) A town in central Israel; site of a major airport; pop. 21,000 (est. 1963).

lyd·dite (lid′īt) *n.* A high explosive, composed chiefly of picric acid, used in shells. [after *Lydd,* a town in England, where first manufactured]

Lyd·gate (lid′gāt, -git), **John,** 1370?–1451?, English poet.

Lyd·i·a (lid′ē·ə) An ancient country in western Asia Minor, on the Aegean; famous for its wealth and luxury.

Lyd·i·an (lid′ē·ən) *adj.* **1.** Belonging or pertaining to Lydia, its inhabitants, or their language. **2.** Effeminate; gentle. **3.** Voluptuous; sensuous. **—** *n.* **1.** An inhabitant of Lydia. **2.** The language of Lydia, probably related to Hittite.

lye (lī) *n.* **1.** A solution leached from ashes, or derived from a substance containing alkali, used in making soap. **2.** Any solution obtained by leaching; a lixivium. [OE *lēah*]

Ly·ell (lī′əl), **Sir Charles,** 1797–1875, British geologist.

ly·ing[1] (lī′ing) *n.* The act of telling lies; untruthfulness. **—** *adj.* Deceitful or false; untrue: a *lying* tongue.

ly·ing[2] (lī′ing) Present participle of LIE[1].

ly·ing-in (lī′ing·in′) *n.* The confinement of women during childbirth. **—** *adj.* Of or pertaining to childbirth.

Lyl·y (lil′ē), **John,** 1554?–1606, English dramatist and novelist. See EUPHUISM.

lymph (limf) *n.* **1.** *Physiol.* A transparent, slightly yellowish alkaline fluid derived from the body tissues, consisting of lymphocytes and a plasma similar to that of blood, and conveyed to the blood stream by the lymphatic tissues. **2.** *Archaic* A spring of clear water. [< L *lympha,* var. of *limpa* water < Gk. *nymphē* nymph, goddess of moisture]

lym·phad·e·ni·tis (lim·fad′ə·nī′tis, lim′fə·də-) *n. Pathol.* Inflammation of the lymph nodes. [< NL < LYMPH(O)- + ADEN(O)- + -ITIS]

lym·phan·gi·al (lim·fan′jē·əl) *adj.* Of or pertaining to the lymphatic vessels. [< LYMPH(O)- + ANGI(O)- + -AL[1]]

lym·phat·ic (lim·fat′ik) *adj.* **1.** Containing, conveying, or pertaining to lymph. **2.** Caused by or affecting the lymph nodes. **3.** Sluggish; indifferent. **—** *n.* A vessel that conveys lymph into the veins.

lymphato- *combining form* Lymphatic. Also, before vowels, **lymphat-.**

lymph node *Anat.* Any of numerous glandlike bodies found in the course of the lymphatic vessels and producing lymphocytes and monocytes. Also **lymph gland.**

lympho- *combining form* Lymph; of or pertaining to lymph or the lymphatic system: *lymphocyte.* Also, before vowels, **lymph-.** [See LYMPH]

lym·pho·cyte (lim′fə·sīt) *n. Physiol.* A variety of nucleated, colorless leucocyte formed in the tissue of the lymph nodes and resembling white blood corpuscles. Also **lymph cell.**

lym·pho·cy·to·sis (lim′fō·sī·tō′sis) *n. Pathol.* An excess of lymphocytes in the blood. **— lym′pho·cy·tot′ic** (-tot′ik) *adj.*

lym·phoid (lim′foid) *adj.* Of, pertaining to, or resembling lymph or the tissues of a lymph node. [< LYMPH + -OID]

lyn·ce·an (lin·sē′ən) *adj.* **1.** Of or like a lynx. **2.** Sharpsighted, as a lynx. [< L *lynceus* < Gk. *lynkeios* < *lynx* lynx]

lynch (linch) *v.t.* To kill (a person accused of a crime) by mob action, as by hanging, without due process of law. [< LYNCH LAW] **— lynch′er** *n.* **— lynch′ing** *n.*

Lynch·burg (linch′bûrg) A city in south central Virginia on the James River; pop. 54,083.

lynch law The practice of administering punishment by lynching: also called *swamp law.* [? after Charles *Lynch,* 1736–96, or William *Lynch,* 1742–1820, Virginia magistrate]

Lynn (lin) **1.** A city in NE Massachusetts; pop. 90,294. **2.** See KING'S LYNN.

Lynn Re·gis (rē′jis) See KING'S LYNN.

Lyn·wood (lin′wŏŏd) A city in SW California, near Los Angeles; pop. 43,353.

lynx (lingks) *n. pl.* **lynx·es** or **lynx** A wildcat (genus *Lynx*) of Europe and North America having a short tail, tufted ears, and relatively long limbs; especially, the large, heavily furred **Canada lynx** (*L. canadensis*) or *loup-cervier,* and the North American **bay lynx** (*L. rufus*). Also called *bobcat.* [< L *lynx, lyncis* < Gk. *lynx*]

Lynx (lingks) *n.* A constellation. See CONSTELLATION. [< L -x.]

lynx-eyed (lingks′īd′) *adj.* Having sharp sight.

lyo- *combining form* A loosening; dissolution: *lyophilic.* Also, before vowels, **ly-.** [< Gk. *lyein* to loosen]

Ly·on (lī′ən), **Mary,** 1797–1849, U.S. educator.

Ly·on·nais (lē·ô·nā′) A region and former province of east central France. Also **Ly·o·nais′.**

ly·on·naise (lī′ə·nāz′, *Fr.* lē·ô·nez′) *adj.* Made with finely sliced onions; especially, designating a method of preparing potatoes with fried onions. [< F, fem. of *lyonnais* of Lyon]

Ly·on·nesse (lī′ə·nes′) In Arthurian legend, a region lying between Cornwall and the Scilly Islands, supposed to have sunk into the sea.

Ly·ons (lī′ənz) A city in east central France at the confluence of the Rhône and the Saône; pop. 527,800 (1968). Also *French* **Ly·on** (lē·ôn′). **— Ly·on·nais′** *adj.*

Lyons, Gulf of See (Gulf of) LION.

ly·o·phil·ic (lī′ə·fil′ik) *adj. Chem.* Designating a colloidal system in which the solid particles attract and hold molecules of the dispersion medium. [< LYO- + Gk. *philos* loving]

ly·o·pho·bic (lī′ə·fō′bik) *adj. Chem.* Designating a colloidal system in which the solid particles are easily precipitated out of the dispersion medium. [< LYO- + Gk. *phobos* fear]

Ly·ra (lī′rə) *n.* A constellation, the Harp or the Lyre, containing the star Vega. See CONSTELLATION. [< L < Gk.]

ly·rate (lī′rāt) *adj.* **1.** *Bot.* Designating a pinnatifid leaf, the upper lobes of which are the largest. **2.** Suggesting or resembling the shape of a lyre. Also **ly′rat·ed.** [< NL *lyratus*] — **ly′rate·ly** *adv.*

lyre (līr) *n.* An ancient harplike stringed instrument having four to ten strings and a sounding box, and usually held upright on the lap, used by the Greeks to accompany poetry and song. [< OF < L *lyra* < Gk.]

Lyre (līr) *n.* The constellation Lyra.

lyre-bird (līr′bûrd′) *n.* Either of two species of Australian passerine birds (genus *Menura*), the male of which spreads its tail feathers into the shape of a lyre.

LYRE

lyr·ic (lir′ik) *adj.* **1.** Of poetry, expressing the poet's personal or inner feelings; also, pertaining to the method, personality, etc., of a writer of such verse. **2.** Meant to be sung, or expressed in singing. **3.** *Music* Having a singing voice of a light, flexible quality: a *lyric* soprano. **4.** Pertaining to a lyre; sung or recited to the lyre. Also **lyr′i·cal.** — *n.* **1.** *Usually pl.* The words of a song. **2.** A lyric poem. [< L *lyricus* < Gk. *lyrikos* < *lyra* a lyre] — **lyr′i·cal·ly** *adv.*

lyr·i·cism (lir′ə·siz′əm) *n.* **1.** The quality of emotional self-expression in the arts, especially the expression of sweetness and rapture. **2.** *Rare* A lyrical composition.

lyr·i·cist (lir′ə·sist) *n.* **1.** One who writes the words of a song or the lyrics for a musical play. **2.** A lyric poet.

ly·ri·form (lī′rə·fôrm) *adj.* Shaped like a lyre.

lyr·ism (lir′iz·əm *for def. 1;* lī′riz·əm *for def. 2*) *n.* **1.** The playing of the lyre. **2.** Lyricism. [< F *lyrisme*]

lyr·ist (lir′ist *for def. 1;* lī′rist *for def. 2*) *n.* **1.** One who plays the lyre. **2.** A lyric poet.

Lys (lēs) A river in northern France and western Belgium, flowing 130 miles NE to the Scheldt.

Ly·san·der (lī·san′dər), died 395 B.C., Spartan general.

lyse (līs) *v.t. & v.i.* **lysed, lys·ing** To undergo or cause to undergo lysis. [< Gk. *lysis* loosening]

Ly·sen·ko·ism (li·seng′kō·iz′əm) *n.* *Biol.* A form of Neo-Lamarckism that emphasizes the inheritance of acquired characters through the action of environment on the genetic constitution of individual organisms. [after T. D. *Lysenko*, 1898–1976, Soviet biologist]

ly·ser·gic acid (lī·sûr′jik) *n.* *Biochem.* A crystalline alkaloid, $C_{16}H_{16}N_2O_2$, derived from ergot, of which it is the chief toxic principle, and forming the base of a drug; **lysergic acid di·eth·yl·am·ide-25** (dī′eth·əl·am′īd), or LSD. [< LYS- + *erg(ot)* + -IC]

lysi- *combining form* A loosening; dissolving: *lysimeter*. Also, before vowels, **lys-.** [< Gk. *lysis* a loosening]

Lys·i·as (lis′ē·əs), died 380? B.C., Athenian orator.

Ly·sim·a·chus (lī·sim′ə·kəs), 361?–281 B.C., Macedonian general under Alexander the Great; king of Thrace.

ly·sim·e·ter (lī·sim′ə·tər) *n.* An instrument for determining the solubility of a substance. [< LYSI- + METER]

ly·sin (lī′sin) *n.* *Biochem.* Any of a class of substances resembling antibodies in their action and capable of disintegrating blood cells, bacteria, etc. [< LYS(I)- + -IN]

ly·sine (lī′sēn, -sin) *n.* *Biochem.* An amino acid, $C_6H_{14}O_2N_2$, necessary to animal growth, produced by the hydrolysis of various proteins. Also **ly′sin.** [< LYS(I)- + -INE[2]]

Ly·sip·pus (lī·sip′əs) Fourth-century B.C. Greek sculptor.

ly·sis (lī′sis) *n.* **1.** *Med.* The gradual disappearing of the symptoms of a disease. **2.** *Biochem.* The process of disintegration or destruction of cells, bacteria, etc., as by lysins. [< NL < Gk., loosening < *lyein* to loosen, dissolve]

-lysis *combining form* A loosing, dissolving, etc.: *hydrolysis, paralysis.* [< Gk., loosening]

Ly·sol (lī′sôl, -sōl, -sol) *n.* Proprietary name for a saponified product of coal tar containing cresol. Also **ly′sol.**

lys·sa (lis′ə) *n.* Hydrophobia; rabies. [< Gk., frenzy]

Lys·ter bag (lis′tər) A portable waterproof bag for supplying disinfected drinking water to troops. [after W. J. L. *Lyster*, 1869–1947, U.S. Army surgeon]

-lyte *combining form* A substance decomposed by a (specified) process: *electrolyte.* [< Gk. *lytos* loosened, dissolved < *lyein* to loosen]

ly·tic (lit′ik) *adj.* **1.** Of, relating to, or effecting lysis, especially of cells. **2.** Of or relating to a lysin. [See -LYTIC.]

-lytic *combining form* Loosing; dissolving: used in adjectives corresponding to nouns in *-lysis: hydrolytic, paralytic.* [< Gk. *lytikos* loosing < *lysis* a loosening]

lyt·ta (lit′ə) *n. pl.* **lyt·tae** (lit′ē) *Anat.* A vermiform cartilage or fibrous band on the under surface of the tongue in the dog and other carnivores. [< L, a worm said to grow under a dog's tongue and cause madness < Gk., madness]

Lyt·ton (lit′n), **Earl of,** 1831–91, Edward Robert Lytton Bulwer-Lytton, son of Lord Lytton; English poet and diplomat: pseudonym **Owen Meredith.** — **Lord,** 1803–73, Edward George Earle Lytton Bulwer-Lytton, first Baron Lytton, English novelist.

Lyu·blin (lyōō′blyin) The Russian name for LUBLIN.

-lyze *suffix of verbs* To perform, cause, or undergo: formed from nouns in *-lysis: electrolyze, paralyze.* Also *esp. Brit.* **-lyse.** [< -LYSIS]

M

m, M (em) *n. pl.* **m's** or **ms, M's** or **Ms** or **ems** (emz) **1.** The thirteenth letter of the English alphabet. The shape of the Phoenician letter *mem* was adopted by the Greeks as *mu* and became Roman *M.* Also *em.* **2.** The sound represented by the letter *m,* usually a voiced, bilabial nasal. — *symbol* **1.** The Roman numeral 1,000. **2.** *Printing* An em.

m or **m.** Meter(s).

M 1. Medieval. **2.** Middle.

M. 1. Handful (L *manipulus*). **2.** Master (L *magister*). **3.** Monday. **4.** (*pl.* **MM.**) Monsieur.

M, or **m. 1.** Majesty. **2.** Male. **3.** Manual. **4.** Mark. **5.** Marquis. **6.** Married. **7.** Masculine. **8.** Mass. **9.** Medicine. **10.** Medium. **11.** Meridian. **12.** Mile. **13.** Mill. **14.** Minim. **15.** Minute. **16.** Modulus. **17.** Month. **18.** Moon. **19.** Morning. **20.** Mountain. **21.** Noon (L *meridies*).

M-1 (em′wun′) **carbine** *U.S. Mil.* The carbine (which see).

M-1 rifle *U.S. Mil.* A semiautomatic .30 caliber rifle adopted by the U.S. Army in World War II: also called *Garand rifle.* Also **M-1.**

M-14 (em′fôr′tēn′, -fōr′-) **rifle** *U.S. Mil.* An automatic or semiautomatic 7.62 mm. rifle, adopted by the U.S. Army after World War II.

ma (mä, mô) *n. Informal & Dial.* Mama.

Ma *Chem.* Masurium.

MA 1. Maritime Administration. **2.** *Psychol.* Mental age: also **M.A.**

M.A. 1. Master of Arts (L *Magister Artium*). **2.** Military Academy. **3.** *Psychol.* Mental age.

ma'am (mam, mäm, *unstressed* məm) *n.* **1.** A term of respectful address used to women; madam. **2.** *Brit.* A term of respectful address used to the queen or to a royal princess. [Contr. of MADAM]

Maas (mäs) The Dutch name for the MEUSE.

Maas·tricht (mäs′trikht, mäs·trikht′) A commune in the eastern Netherlands; pop. 90,202 (1960): also *Maestricht.*

Mab (mab), **Queen** In English folklore, the queen of the fairies.

Mab·i·no·gi·on (mab′ə·nō′gē·ən) *n.* A collection of eleven medieval Welsh bardic tales and romances translated by Lady Charlotte Guest in 1838–49. [< Welsh, pl. of *mabinogi,* bardic tales and stories of a hero's life]

Mac- *prefix* In Scottish and Irish names, son of: *MacDougal,* son of Dougal: abbr. *Mc, M*^{c}, or *M'.* See also Mc-. Compare FITZ-, O'. [< Scottish Gaelic and Irish, son]

ma·ca·bre (mə·kä′brə, -bər) *adj.* Suggesting death and decay; gruesome; ghastly. Also **ma·ca′ber.** [< F < OF (*danse*) *macabre* (dance) of death, prob. alter. of *Macabé* < LL *Maccabaeus,* ? a character in a morality play]

ma·ca·co (mə·kä′kō) *n. pl.* **-cos** Any of various lemurs or similar monkeys; especially, the **black lemur** (*Lemur macaco*) of Madagascar. [< Pg. < Tupi *macaco, macaca* monkey]

mac·ad·am (mə·kad′əm) *n.* **1.** A macadamized pavement or road. **2.** Broken stone used in macadamizing a road. [after John L. *McAdam,* 1756–1836, Scottish engineer]

mac·a·dam·i·a nut (mak′ə·dā′mē·ə) The edible nut of an Australian tree (*Macadamia ternifolio*), cultivated in Hawaii. [< L, after John *Macadam,* ?–1865, Australian chemist]

mac·ad·am·ize (mə·kad′ə·mīz) *v.t.* **-ized, -iz·ing** To pave by spreading and compacting small stones, often with a tar or asphalt binder. — **mac·ad·am·i·za′tion** *n.* — **mac·ad′·am·iz′er** *n.*

Ma·cao (mə·kou′, -kä′ō) **1.** An island in the Canton river delta, China. **2.** A Portuguese Overseas Province comprising a peninsula of Macao Island and Colôane and the Taipa

Islands; 6 sq. mi.; pop. 200,000 (est. 1971): capital, **Macao,** pop. 162,000 (1970). *Portuguese* **Ma·cáu** (mə·kou′).

ma·caque (mə·käk′) *n.* Any of several Old World monkeys (genus *Macaca*), chiefly of Asia and North Africa, with a short tail and cheek pouches. [< F < Pg. *macaco.* See MACACO.]

mac·a·ro·ni (mak′ə·rō′nē) *n.* **1.** A dried paste of wheat flour made into short tubes thicker than the strands of spaghetti and prepared as a food by boiling. **2.** A mixture or medley; farrago. **3.** An 18th-century English dandy who affected foreign dress and manners; exquisite; fop. Also **mac′ca·ro′ni.** [< Ital. *maccaroni, maccheroni,* pl. of *macherone* groats < LGk. *makaria* broth with barley groats < Gk., *blessedness < makar* blessed]

MACAQUE
(2 to 3 feet
long)

mac·a·ron·ic (mak′ə·ron′ik) *adj.* **1.** Of literary compositions, composed in a medley of languages or of words in one language humorously altered to resemble words in another; especially, made up of Latin and some vernacular. **2.** *Obs.* Resembling a medley or farrago; jumbled. Also **mac′a·ron′i·cal.** — *n.* **1.** *Usually pl.* Macaronic verse or verses. **2.** *Obs.* A jumble; medley. [< NL *macaronicus* < Ital. *maccheronico < maccheroni.* See MACARONI.]

mac·a·roon (mak′ə·rōōn′) *n.* A small cooky made of ground almonds or almond paste, white of egg, and sugar; also, an imitation of this made with coconut. [< MF *macaron* < Ital. *maccarone,* var. of *macherone.* See MACARONI.]

Mac·Ar·thur (mək·är′thər), **Douglas,** 1880–1964, U.S. general; commander in chief in the Pacific in World War II.

Ma·cas·sar (mə·kas′ər) See MAKASSAR.

Macassar oil 1. A volatile oil used as a hair dressing, originally obtained from Makassar. **2.** A substitute made from perfumed castor oil, etc.

Ma·cau·lay (mə·kô′lē), **Thomas Babington,** 1800–59, first Baron Macaulay, English historian, essayist, and statesman.

ma·caw (mə·kô′) *n.* Any of various large tropical American parrots (chiefly genus *Ara*) with a long tail, harsh voice, and brilliant plumage. [< Pg. *macao,* prob. < Tupi]

Mac·beth (mək·beth′), died 1057?, king of Scotland 1040–1057?; hero of Shakespeare's *Macbeth.*

Mac·ca·bees (mak′ə·bēz) The family of Jewish patriots who led a revolt against Syrian religious oppression; notably **Mattathias,** died 166 B.C., and his sons, **Judas Mac·ca·be·us** (mak′ə·bē·əs), died 160 B.C., whose surname was adopted by the family, **Jonathan,** died 143 B.C., and **Simon,** died 135 B.C. — *n.pl.* Four books in the Old Testament Apocrypha treating of oppression against the Jews from 222 to 135 B.C., of which the first two are regarded as canonical by Roman Catholics, but all as apocryphal by Protestants. [< LL *Machabaei,* pl. of *Machabaeus* < Gk. *Makkabaios,* prob. < Aramaic *maggābā* a hammer] — **Mac′ca·be′an** *adj.*

mac·ca·boy (mak′ə·boi) *n.* A finely ground, rose-scented, dark snuff. Also **mac′ca·baw** (-bô), **mac′co·boy.** [< F *macouba,* after *Macouba,* Martinique]

mac·chia (mak′yə) *n.* Maquis (def. 2).

Mac·Don·ald (mək·don′əld), **Sir John Alexander,** 1815–91, Canadian jurist and statesman born in Scotland.

Mac·Don·ald (mək·don′əld), **(James) Ramsay,** 1866–1937, British statesman; first Labour Party prime minister 1924, 1929–35.

Mac·Dow·ell (mək·dou′əl), **Edward Alexander,** 1861–1908, U.S. composer and pianist.

mace[1] (mās) *n.* **1.** A heavy medieval war club, usually with a spiked metal head for use against armor. **2.** A club-shaped staff of office or authority borne before officials or displayed on the table of a legislative body. **3.** A macebearer. [< OF *masse, mace.* Cf. LL *matteola* mallet.]

mace[2] (mās) *n.* An aromatic spice ground from the covering between the husk and the seed of the nutmeg. [< OF *macis* < L *macir* < Gk. *maker* a spicy bark from India]

Mace (mās) *n.* A chemical solution similar to tear gas that temporarily blinds or incapacitates one when sprayed in the face, used as a weapon. — *v.t.* **Maced, Mac·ing** To spray with Mace. [< Chemical *Mace,* a trade name]

mace·bear·er (mās′bâr′ər) *n.* An official who carries a mace, as in a procession.

Maced. Macedonia; Macedonian.

mac·é·doine (mas′i·dwän′, *Fr.* mȧ·sā·dwän′) *n.* A dish of mixed vegetables or fruits, served as a salad or dessert. **2.** Any mixture; medley; olio. [< F, a type of parsley < OF *(perresel) macedoine* Macedonian (parsley)]

Mac·e·do·ni·a (mas′ə·dō′nē·ə) **1.** A region of SE Europe, divided among Bulgaria, Greece, and Yugoslavia. **2.** The ancient kingdom of **Mac·e·don** (mas′ə·don) that became a leading world power under Alexander the Great.

Mac·e·do·ni·an (mas′ə·dō′nē·ən) *adj.* Of or pertaining to Macedonia, its people, or their language. — *n.* **1.** A native or inhabitant of Macedonia. **2.** The South Slavic language of Macedonia.

Ma·cei·ó (mä′sā·ô′) The capital of Alagoas State, Brazil, a port in the eastern part; pop. about 154,000.

mac·er (mā′sər) *n.* **1.** A macebearer. **2.** In Scotland, an

officer who keeps order in the courts and executes their orders. [< OF *maissier < masse, mace* mace]

mac·er·ate (mas′ə·rāt) *v.* **·at·ed, ·at·ing** *v.t.* **1.** To reduce (a solid substance) to a soft mass by soaking in liquid. **2.** To break down the structure of (food) in digestion. **3.** To cause to grow thin; emaciate. — *v.i.* **4.** To become macerated. [< L *maceratus,* pp. of *macerare* to make soft, knead] — **mac′er·at′er** or **mac′er·a′tor** *n.* — **mac′er·a′tion** *n.*

mach (mäk) *n. Often cap.* A mach number (which see).

mach. Machine; machinery; machinist.

Ma·cha·do y Mo·ra·les (mä·chä′thō ē mō·rä′läs), **Gerardo,** 1871–1939, Cuban statesman; president 1925–33.

ma chère (mȧ shâr′) *French fem.* My dear.

ma·chet·e (mə·shet′ē, mə·shet′; *Sp.* mä·chā′tā) *n.* A heavy knife or cutlass used as an implement and a weapon in tropical America. [< Sp., dim. of *macho* an ax, a hammer < L *marculus,* dim. of *marcus* hammer]

MACHETES

Mach·i·a·vel·li (mäk′ē·ə·vel′ē, *Ital.* mä′kyä·vel′lē), **Niccolò,** 1469–1527, Florentine statesman and writer on politics.

Mach·i·a·vel·li·an (mak′ē·ə·vel′ē·ən) *adj.* **1.** Pertaining to, resembling, or based upon the practical and amoral principles for getting and keeping political power prescribed in Niccolò Machiavelli's *The Prince.* **2.** Of or pertaining to Machiavelli. — *n.* A follower of Machiavelli's principles. Also **Mach′i·a·vel′i·an.** — **Mach′i·a·vel′li·an·ism, Mach′i·a·vel′lism** *n.* — **Mach′i·a·vel′list** *adj. & n.*

ma·chic·o·late (mə·chik′ə·lāt) *v.t.* **·lat·ed, ·lat·ing** *Archit.* To furnish with machicolations. [< Med.L *machicolatus,* pp. of *machicolare* < OF *machicoler,* prob. < *macher* to crush + *couler* to flow]

ma·chic·o·la·tion (mə·chik′ə·lā′shən) *n.* **1.** *Archit.* An opening between the corbels of a projecting parapet or in the vault of a portal or passage, through which missiles or boiling liquids may be dropped on an enemy force. For illustration see BATTLEMENT. **2.** The act of dropping missiles or pouring liquids onto an enemy party through such openings.

mach·i·nate (mak′ə·nāt) *v.t. & v.i.* **·nat·ed, ·nat·ing** To scheme or contrive. [< L *machinatus,* pp. of *machinari* to contrive < *machina* machine] — **mach′i·na′tor** *n.*

mach·i·na·tion (mak′ə·nā′shən) *n.* **1.** *Usually pl.* A concealed working and scheming for some devious purpose. **2.** The act of machinating.

ma·chine (mə·shēn′) *n.* **1.** Any combination of interrelated parts for using or applying energy to do work; especially, a mechanical unit with or without a driving motor, meant to do a particular kind of work: milling *machine;* sewing *machine.* **2.** A partisan political organization, especially the party organization of a city, county, or state: a derogatory term. **3.** In many trades and vocations, the particular mechanical device used or worked on. **4.** The organization and operating principles of a complex structure: the human *machine.* **5.** An automobile or other mechanical vehicle. **6.** A person who behaves as if he had no will of his own; a mere cog. **7.** A person whose actions are mechanically precise and undeviating. **8.** A person very well adapted for some particular activity: He is a fighting *machine.* **9.** In the ancient theater, a windlass used for the spectacular entrance and exit of gods, etc.; also, a device of supernatural intervention, etc., in a literary plot. Compare DEUS EX MACHINA. — *adj.* **1.** Of or pertaining to a machine or machines. **2.** Produced by machine: *machine* knitting. **3.** Characterized by the use of machines: *machine* age. — *v.t.* **·chined, ·chin·ing** To shape, mill, make, etc., by machine. *Abbr.* **mach.** [< F < L *machina* < Gk. *mēchanē* < *mēchos* a contrivance] — **ma·chin′a·ble, ma·chin′al** *adj.* — **ma·chin·a·bil′i·ty** *n.*

— **Syn.** (noun) **1.** *Machine, engine, motor, appliance,* and *apparatus* denote contrivances for applying energy to do work. Any device in which power is supplied at one point and does work at another may be called a *machine;* a simple lever, a cotton gin, a printing press, and a cash register are all *machines. Engine* is chiefly applied to a *machine* that transforms energy, as heat, electricity, waterpower, etc., into mechanical power: the steam *engine,* the diesel *engine.* A *motor* is a relatively small *engine,* especially one operated by electricity or a petroleum product. *Appliance* now usually refers to an electrically powered device used for housework; a vacuum cleaner and an electric mixer are *appliances. Apparatus* refers to a collection of devices organized to do some particular work; an *apparatus* may include different *machines,* or may constitute a *machine* in itself.

ma·chine-gun (mə·shēn′gun′) *v.t.* **·gunned, ·gun·ning** To fire at or shoot with a machine gun.

machine gun A rapid-firing automatic gun, usually mounted, that fires small-arms ammunition. — **machine gunner.**

ma·chin·er·y (mə·shē′nər·ē, -shēn′rē) *n.* **1.** A collection of machines or machine parts. **2.** The mechanism or operating parts and principles of a complex structure: the *machinery* of the law. **3.** In literary and dramatic works, plot devices involving gods, demons, angels, etc. *Abbr.* **mach.**

machine shop A shop where metal and other materials are cut, shaped, milled, finished, etc., with machine tools.

machine tool A power-driven tool, partly or wholly automatic in action, for cutting, shaping, boring, milling, etc.

ma·chin·ist (mə·shē′nist) *n.* **1.** One who is skilled in machine-shop practice and the operation of machine tools. **2.** One who operates, constructs, or repairs machines. **3.** In the U.S. Navy and Coast Guard, a warrant officer who is assistant to the engineer officer. *Abbr.* mach.

ma·chis·mo (mä·chiz/mō) *n.* Strong or aggressive masculinity. [< Sp. *macho* masculine + *-ismo* -ISM]

mach·me·ter (mäk/mē/tər) *n. Aeron.* A device indicating the speed of airplanes. [< MACH (NUMBER) + -METER]

mach number A number representing the ratio between the speed of an object moving through a fluid medium, as air, and the speed of sound in the same medium: *Mach number* 1 equals the speed of sound: also called *mach.* Also **Mach number.** [after Ernst *Mach,* 1838–1916, Austrian physicist]

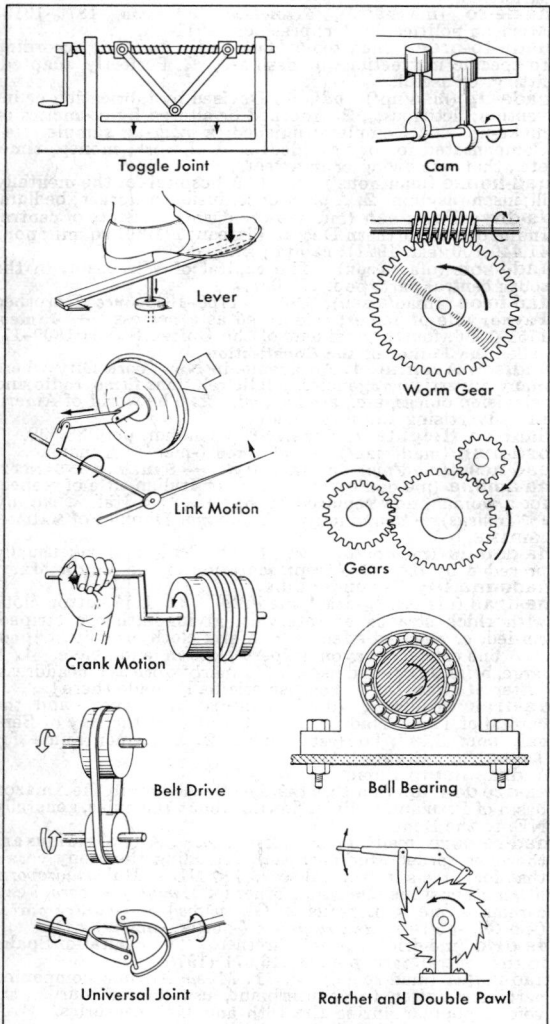

Toggle Joint   Cam

Lever

Worm Gear

Link Motion

Gears

Crank Motion

Belt Drive   Ball Bearing

Universal Joint   Ratchet and Double Pawl

MACHINE ELEMENTS

ma·chree (mə·krē/) *n.* My heart; my love: an Anglo-Irish term of endearment. [< Irish < *mo* my + *croidhe* heart < OIrish *cride*]

-machy *combining form* A fight between, or by means of: *logomachy.* [< Gk. *-machia* < *machē* a battle]

mac·in·tosh (mak/ən·tosh) See MACKINTOSH.

Mack·en·sen (mäk/ən·zən), **August von,** 1849–1945, German field marshal in World War I.

Mac·ken·zie (mə·ken/zē) A district in the Northwest Territories, Canada; 527,490 sq. mi.

Mac·Ken·zie (mə·ken/zē), **Sir Alexander,** 1755?–1820, Scottish explorer in North America.

Mackenzie River A river in NW Canada, flowing generally north 2,514 miles to the Beaufort Sea.

mack·er·el (mak/ər·əl) *n.* **1.** A food fish (*Scomber scombrus*) of the Atlantic, steel blue with blackish bars above, and silvery beneath. **2.** Any of various scombroid fishes resembling it, as the cero. [< OF *makerel*; ult. origin unknown]

mackerel sky Cirrocumulus.

Mack·i·nac (mak/ə·nô), **Straits of** A channel between Lake Michigan and Lake Huron; about 4 miles wide.

Mack·i·nac Island (mak/ə·nô) **1.** A small island in the Straits of Mackinac; a Michigan state park. **2.** A resort city on this island. Also **Mackinac.**

mack·i·naw (mak/ə·nô) **1.** A Mackinaw blanket. **2.** A Mackinaw boat. **3.** A Mackinaw coat. [< dial. F (Canadian) *Mackinac* < *Michilimackinac* Mackinac Island, ? < Algonquian (Ojibwa) *mitchimakinak* large turtle]

Mackinaw blanket A thick, heavy blanket formerly used by Indians and traders of the western United States.

Mackinaw boat A large, sharp-ended, flat-bottomed bateau, sometimes equipped with sails, and formerly used on the northern Great Lakes.

Mackinaw coat A thick, short, double-breasted woolen coat, commonly with a plaid pattern.

mack·in·tosh (mak/ən·tosh) *n. Chiefly Brit.* **1.** A waterproof overgarment or cloak; raincoat. **2.** Thin, rubber-coated cloth. Also *macintosh.* [after Charles *Macintosh,* 1766–1843, Scottish chemist, inventor of the cloth]

mack·le (mak/əl) *n.* A spot or blemish; especially, a blurred impression in printing. —*v.t. & v.i.* **mack·led, mack·ling** To print with a blurred or double image; blur; blot. Also *macule.* [< F *macule* < L *macula* spot]

Mac·lar·en (mə·klar/ən), **Ian** See (John) WATSON.

mac·le (mak/əl) *n.* A twin crystal, especially of a diamond. [< F < OF *mascle* < Med.L *mascula* a mesh of a net < L *macula* a spot]

Mac·Leish (mək·lēsh/), **Archibald,** born 1892, U.S. poet.

Mac·leod (mə·kloud/), **Fiona** See (William) SHARP. —**John James Rickard,** 1876–1935, Scottish physiologist; co-discoverer of insulin.

Mac·Ma·hon (màk·mà·ôṅ/), **Marie Edmé Patrice Maurice de,** 1808–93, Duke of Magenta, French marshal and· politician; president 1873–79.

Mac·mil·lan (mək·mil/ən), **Harold,** born 1894, British statesman; prime minister 1957–63.

Mac·Mil·lan (mək·mil/ən), **Donald Baxter,** 1874–1970, U.S. Arctic explorer.

Mac·Neice (mək·nēs/), **Louis,** 1907–1963, British poet.

Ma·con (mā/kən) A city in central Georgia, on the Ocmulgee River; pop. 122,423.

Mâ·con (mà·kôṅ/) *n.* A wine produced in the neighborhood of Mâcon, a manufacturing city in east central France.

Mac·pher·son (mək·fûr/sən), **James,** 1736–96, Scottish schoolmaster and writer. See OSSIAN.

Mac·quar·ie River (mə·kwôr/ē, -kwor/ē) A river in central New South Wales, Australia, flowing 590 miles NW to the Darling River.

mac·ra·mé (mak/rə·mā) *n.* A fringe, lace, or trimming of knotted thread or cord; knotted work. [Appar. < Turkish *maqramah* towel < Arabic *miqramah* veil]

Mac·rea·dy (mə·krē/dē), **William Charles,** 1793–1873, English actor and theatrical manager.

macro- *combining form* **1.** *Pathol.* Enlarged or overdeveloped: *macrocephaly.* **2.** Large or long in size or duration; great: *macrocosm; macroevolution.* Also, before vowels, **macr-.** [< Gk. *makros* large]

mac·ro·ceph·a·ly (mak/rō·sef/ə·lē) *n.* Abnormal largeness of the head, especially with reference to cranial capacity: opposed to *microcephaly.* [< MACRO- + Gk. *kephalē* head] —**mac/ro·ce·phal/ic** (-sə·fal/ik) *adj. & n.* —**mac/ro·ceph/a·lous** (-ləs) *adj.*

mac·ro·cli·mate (mak/rō·klī/mit) *n. Meteorol.* The general climate prevailing over a large area: distinguished from *microclimate.* —**mac/ro·cli·mat/ic** (-klī·mat/ik) *adj.*

mac·ro·cosm (mak/rə·koz/əm) *n.* **1.** The whole universe or great world, especially when regarded in contrast to man. **2.** A large system regarded as a unity. Compare MICROCOSM. [< OF *macrocosme* < Med.L *macrocosmus* < Gk. *makros* long, great + *kosmos* world] —**mac/ro·cos/mic** *adj.*

mac·ro·cyst (mak/rə·sist) *n.* **1.** An enlarged cyst. **2.** *Bot.* A large reproductive cell in certain fungi.

mac·ro·cyte (mak/rə·sīt) *n. Pathol.* An abnormally large erythrocyte, or red corpuscle. [< MACRO- + (ERYTHRO)CYTE] —**mac/ro·cyt/ic** (-sit/ik) *adj.*

mac·ro·e·co·nom·ics (mak/rō·ē/kə·nom/iks, -ek/ə-) *n.pl.* (*construed as sing.*) Economics studied in terms of large aggregates of data interpreted with reference to the behavior of the system as a whole. —**mac/ro·e/co·nom/ic** *adj.*

mac·ro·ev·o·lu·tion (mak/rō·ev/ə·lōō/shən) *n. Biol.* The processes of evolution in plants and animals above the rank of species: distinguished from *speciation.*

mac·ro·ga·mete (mak/rō·gə·mēt/, -gam/ēt) *n. Biol.* The larger, usually female, of two conjugating gametes: also called *megagamete.* [< MACRO- + GAMETE]

mac·ro·graph (mak′rə-graf, -gräf) *n.* A drawing or illustration about life size. — **mac′ro·graph′ic** *adj.*

mac·ro·mol·e·cule (mak′rə-mol′ə-kyōol) *n.* A giant molecule, as that of a protein, rubber, cellulose, starch, etc.

ma·cron (mā′krən, -kron) *n.* A straight line (—) over a vowel letter to show that it represents a long sound, as *ā* in *made.* Compare BREVE. [< Gk. *makron,* neut. of *makros* long]

mac·ro·po·di·an (mak′rə-pō′dē-ən) *Zool. adj.* Of or pertaining to any of a family (*Macropodidae*) of marsupials, especially those having enlarged hind legs for jumping and a long tail, as the kangaroos and wallabies. — *n.* A macropodian marsupial. [< NL < Gk. *makropous, -podos* long-footed < *makros* long + *pous, podos* foot]

mac·ro·scop·ic (mak′rə-skop′ik) *adj.* Visible to the naked eye: distinguished from *microscopic.* Also **mac′ro·scop′i·cal.**

mac·ro·spore (mak′rə-spôr, -spōr) *n. Bot.* The embryo sac.

ma·cru·ran (mə-krōor′ən) *adj.* Belonging to or pertaining to a suborder (*Macrura*) of decapod crustaceans with well-developed abdomens, including shrimps, prawns, lobsters, and crayfishes. Also **ma·cru′ral** (-rəl), **ma·cru′roid** (-roid), **ma·cru′rous** (-rəs). — *n.* A macruran crustacean. [< NL < Gk. *makros* long + *ourā* tail]

mac·u·la (mak′yə-lə) *n., pl.* **·lae** (-lē) A spot, as on the skin, the sun, etc. [< L, a spot]

mac·u·late (mak′yə-lāt; *for adj., also* -lit) *v.t.* **·lat·ed, ·lat·ing** To spot or blemish; stain. — *adj.* Spotted; stained.

mac·u·la·tion (mak′yə-lā′shən) *n.* **1.** The act of spotting. **2.** A spotted condition. **3.** The markings of a spotted animal or plant. **4.** A soiling; defilement.

mac·ule (mak′yōol) *n.* A mackle. — *v.t. & v.i.* **·uled, ·ul·ing** To mackle.

mad (mad) *adj.* **mad·der, mad·dest 1.** Suffering from or manifesting severe mental disorder; insane; lunatic; psychotic. **2.** *Chiefly U.S. Informal* Feeling or showing anger; angry. **3.** Going beyond the bounds of reason, decorum, or safety; wildly foolish; rash: a *mad* project. **4.** Subject to an overpowering emotion; violently moved; unhinged: *mad* with grief. **5.** Turbulent and confused; extremely disorderly: a *mad* jumble. **6.** Of animals, abnormally violent and dangerous; also, suffering from hydrophobia; rabid. **7.** *Informal* Showing a passionate infatuation with or desire for: with *about, for,* or *over.* **8.** *Informal* Flamboyant; daring. — **like mad** *Informal* As if insane; frantically. — **mad as a hatter** (or **March hare**) Totally insane; crazy. — **mad money** *Slang* Money to be used by a girl to pay her way home from a date in case she quarrels with her escort. — *n. U.S. Informal* A fit of temper: now only in the phrase **to have a mad on,** to be angry. — *v.t. & v.i.* **mad·ded, mad·ding** *Rare* To make or become mad. [Apheric var. of OE *gemǣd, gemǣded,* pp. of *gemǣden* to make mad < *gemād* insane] — **mad′ly** *adv.*

Madag. Madagascar.

Mad·a·gas·car (mad′ə-gas′kər) **1.** An island in the Indian Ocean off the SE coast of Africa. **2.** An independent Republic in this territory; 203,035 sq. mi.; pop. 7,655,134 (est. 1974); capital, Tananarive: formerly MALAGASY REPUBLIC. — **Mad′a·gas′can** *adj. & n.*

mad·am (mad′əm) *n., pl.* **mes·dames** (mā-däm′, *Fr.* mā-dăm′) *for def. 1;* **mad·ams** *for def. 2.* **1.** My lady; mistress: a title of courtesy originally addressed to a woman of rank or high position, but now used to any woman, as at the beginning of a letter. Compare SIR. See MA′AM. **2.** A woman who manages a brothel. [< OF *ma dame < ma* my (< L *meus*) + *dame* lady < L *domina.* Doublet of MADONNA, MADAME.]

mad·ame (mad′əm, *Fr.* mā-dăm′) *n., pl.* **mes·dames** (mā-däm′, *Fr.* mā-dăm′) The French title of courtesy for a married woman, equivalent to the English *Mrs.*: often used in English, especially in the plural. *Abbr.* Mme., Mme, Mdme. [< F < OF *ma dame.* Doublet of MADAM, MADONNA.]

Ma·da·ria·ga (mä′-thä-ryä′gä), **Salvador de,** born 1886, Spanish writer: full surname de Madariaga y Rojo (ē rō′hō).

mad·cap (mad′kap′) *adj.* Wild; rattlebrained. — *n.* One who acts wildly or rashly.

mad·den (mad′n) *v.t.* **1.** To rouse to anger or fury; infuriate. **2.** To make mad or insane. — *v.i.* **3.** To become mad.

mad·den·ing (mad′n·ing) *adj.* **1.** Tending to make angry or furious; exasperating. **2.** Tending to make mad or insane. — **mad·den·ing·ly** *adv.*

mad·er¹ (mad′ər) Comparative of MAD.

mad·der² (mad′ər) *n.* **1.** Any of various perennial herbs (genus *Rubia*) typical of a family (*Rubiaceae*); especially, an Old World species (*R. tinctorum*), the root of which yields a brilliant red extract. **2.** The coloring matter extracted, or its bright red hue. [OE *mædere, mæddre*]

mad·ding (mad′ing) *adj.* Being or growing mad; delirious; raging. — **mad·ding·ly** *adv.*

made (mād) Past tense and past participle of MAKE. — *adj.* **1.** Produced by fabrication, invention, or skill; not occurring naturally. **2.** Assured of success or fortune; also, successful. — **to have it made** *U.S. Slang* To be sure of success; be admirably well situated.

Ma·dei·ra (mə-dir′ə, *Pg.* mə-thä′rə) *n.* A fortified dessert wine made in the Madeira islands.

Ma·dei·ra (mə-dir′ə, *Pg.* mə-thä′rə) **1.** An archipelago west of Morocco, comprising an administrative district of Portugal. See FUNCHAL. **2.** The principal island of the archipelago; 286 sq. mi. **3.** A river in NW Brazil, the most important tributary of the Amazon, flowing NE about 2,100 miles. See map of AMAZON. — **Ma·dei′ran** *adj.*

mad·e·leine (mad′ə-len′, *Fr.* mād·len′) *n.* A small, rich pastry baked in a shell-like tin. [after *Madeleine* Paulmier, 19th c. French pastry cook]

mad·e·moi·selle (mad′ə-mə·zel′, *Fr.* mād·mwà·zel′) *n. pl.* **mad·e·moi·selles,** *Fr.* **mes·de·moi·selles** (mād·mwà·zel′) **1.** The French title of courtesy for unmarried women, equivalent to the English *Miss.* *Abbr.* Mlle, Mlle. **2.** A French nurse or governess. [< F < *ma* my + *demoiselle.* See DEMOISELLE.]

Ma·de·ro (mä·thā′rō), **Francisco Indalecio,** 1873–1913, Mexican political leader; president 1911–13.

made-to-order (mād′tōo-ôr′dər) *adj.* **1.** Made according to specific instructions or designs. **2.** Perfectly adapted, fitting, or useful.

made-up (mād′up′) *adj.* **1.** Devised by fabrication or invention; fictitious. **2.** Adorned or altered by cosmetics or make-up. **3.** Complete; finished: a *made-up* sample. **4.** Compensated for or provided: said of work, money, time, etc., that was owing or in arrears.

mad·house (mad′hous′) *n.* **1.** A hospital for the mentally ill; insane asylum. **2.** A place of confusion or uproar; bedlam.

Ma·dhya Pra·desh (mu′dyə prə-dāsh′) A State of central India, on the northern Deccan Plateau; 171,201 sq. mi.; pop. 41,449,700 (est. 1971); capital, Bhopal.

Mad·i·son (mad′ə-sən) The capital of Wisconsin, in the south central part; pop. 172,007.

Mad·i·son (mad′ə-sən), **Dolly,** 1768–1849, *née* Dorothea Payne, wife of James; celebrated as a hostess. — **James,** 1751–1836, fourth president of the United States 1809–17: called the Father of the Constitution.

Madison Avenue 1. An avenue in New York City where many advertising agencies, public relations firms, radio and television offices, etc., are located. **2.** The world of American advertising and mass media.

Madison Heights A city in SE Michigan; pop. 38,599.

mad·man (mad′man′) *n. pl.* **·men** (-men′) A maniac.

mad·ness (mad′nis) *n.* Insanity. — **Syn.** See INSANITY.

ma·don·na (mə-don′ə) *n.* A former Italian title of respect for a woman, now replaced by *signora.* [< Ital. < *ma* my (< L *meus*) + *donna* lady < L *domina.* Doublet of MADAM, MADAME.]

Ma·don·na (mə-don′ə) *n.* **1.** The Virgin Mary: usually preceded by *the.* **2.** A representation of the Virgin Mary.

Madonna lily See under LILY.

ma·dras (mə-dras′, -dräs′, mad′rəs) *n.* **1.** A cotton cloth with thick strands at intervals, giving either a striped, corded, or checked effect. **2.** A silk cloth, usually striped. **3.** A fine cotton or rayon drapery cloth in leno weave. **4.** A large, brightly colored kerchief formerly worn as a headdress. [after *Madras,* India, because originally made there]

Ma·dras (mə-dras′, -dräs′, mad′rəs) **1.** A port and the capital of Tamil Nadu State in S India, on the Bay of Bengal; pop. 2,047,700 (est. 1969). **2.** A former name for Tamil Nadu State.

Madras hemp Sunn.

Ma·dre de Dios (mä′thrä thä dyōs′) A river in the Amazon basin of Peru and Bolivia, flowing about 700 miles, generally NE, to the Beni.

mad·re·pore (mad′rə·pôr, -pōr) *n. Zool.* Any of various anthozoans (order *Madreporaria*), including the stony corals that form reefs in tropical seas. [< NL < Ital. *madrepora,* lit., mother stone < *madre* mother (< L *mater*) + *poro,* ? calcareous stone < L *porus* < Gk. *pōros*] — **mad·re·por′al** (-pôr′əl, -pō′rəl), **mad′re·po′ric** (-pôr′ik, -por′ik) *adj.*

Ma·drid (mə-drid′, *Sp.* mä-thrēth′) The capital of Spain, in the central part; pop. 3,146,071 (1970).

mad·ri·gal (mad′rə-gəl) *n.* **1.** *Music* An unaccompanied part song, often in counterpoint, usually for four to six voices, popular during the 16th and 17th centuries. **2.** A short lyric poem usually on a pastoral or amatory subject, suitable for such a musical setting. **3.** Any song, especially a part song. [< Ital. *madrigale, mandrigale* < LL *matricale* original, chief < L *matrix* womb; infl. in form by Ital. *mandra* flock < L, herd < Gk., stable, fold] — **mad′ri·gal·ist** *n.*

ma·dri·lène (mad′rə·len′, *Fr.* mä·drē·len′) *n.* Consommé madrilène (which see). [< F < Sp. *Madrileño* of Madrid]

ma·dro·ña (mə-drō′nyə) *n.* A large evergreen tree (*Arbutus menziesi*) of northern California, with shining oval or oblong leaves, white flowers, and dry, yellow berries (**madroña apples**). Also **ma·dro′ño** (-nyō). [< Sp. *madrono*]

Ma·du·ra (mad′ōo′rä) An island of Indonesia east of Java; 2,112 sq. mi. (including offshore islands): Dutch *Madoera.* — **Mad·u·rese** (maj′ōo·rēz′, -rēs′) *adj. & n.*

Ma·du·rai (maj′ōo·rī, mad·ōor′ī) A city in Tamil Nadu State, India; pop. 486,480 (est. 1971). Formerly **Ma·du·ra** (maj′ōo·rə, mə·dōor′ə). — **Mad·u·rese** (maj′ōo·rēz′, -rēs′) *adj. & n.*

ma·du·ro (mə-dōor′ō) *adj.* Strong and dark in color: said of cigars. — *n.* A maduro cigar. [< Sp. < L *maturus*]

mad·wom·an (mad′wŏŏm′ən) *n. pl.* **·wom·en** (-wim′in)
An insane woman; lunatic.

mad·wort (mad′wûrt′) *n.* **1.** Any of various shrubs or
herbs of the mustard family, as the alyssum and sweet alyssum. **2.** A low annual plant (*Asperugo procumbens*) of the
borage family. [? Trans. of NL *Alyssum*, genus name < L
< Gk. *alysson* < *a*- not + *lyssa* rabies]

mae (mā) *adj. & adv. Scot.* More.

Mae·an·der (mē·an′dər) The ancient name for the MEN-
DERES: also *Meander*.

Mae·ce·nas (mi·sē′nəs), died 8 B.C., Roman statesman;
patron of Horace and Vergil: full name **Gaius Cilnius Mae-
cenas.** — *n.* Any patron, especially of the arts.

mael·strom (māl′strəm) *n.* **1.** Any turbulent, dangerous,
and irresistible force, or a place where it prevails: the *maelstrom* of passion. **2.** A whirlpool. [< Du. *maelstrom*, *maal-
stroom* < *malen* to grind, whirl around + *stroom* a stream]

Mael·strom (māl′strəm) A famous whirlpool in the Arctic
Ocean off the NW coast of Norway.

mae·nad (mē′nad) *n.* **1.** A female votary or priestess of
Dionysus; a bacchante. **2.** Any woman beside herself with
frenzy or excitement. Also spelled *menad.* [< L *Maenas*,
-adis < Gk. *mainas* frenzied < *mainesthai* to rave] — **mae-
nad′ic** *adj.* — **mae·nad′i·cal·ly** *adv.*

ma·es·to·so (mä′es·tō′sō) *Music adj.* Majestic; stately.
— *adv.* In a stately manner: a direction to the performer.
— *n.* A stately passage or movement. [< Ital., majestic
< L *majestas* greatness < *major*, compar. of *magnus* great]

Maes·tricht (mäs′trikht) See MAASTRICHT.

ma·es·tro (mä·es′trō, mīs′trō) *n. pl.* **·tros** A master in any
art; especially, an eminent conductor, composer, or performer
of music. [< Ital., master < L *magister*]

Mae·ter·linck (mā′tər·lingk), **Count Maurice,** 1862–1949,
Belgian poet, dramatist, and essayist active in France.

Mae West (mā) An inflatable vestlike life preserver used
by aviators downed at sea in World War II. [after *Mae
West*, born 1892, U.S. actress]

Maf·e·king (maf′ə·king) A town in NE Cape of Good Hope
Province, South Africa; capital of the former Bechuanaland Protectorate (now Botswana); pop. about 7,000.

ma·fi·a (mä′fē·ä, maf′ē·ə) *n.* In Sicily, a widespread hostility toward the law and its officers; also, any of the groups,
later loosely organized into a secret society, motivated by
this attitude. Also **maf′fi·a.** [< Ital.]

Ma·fi·a (mä′fē·ä, maf′ē·ə) *n.* A secret criminal organization of Sicilians and Italians believed to exist in many countries, including the United States. Also **Maf′fi·a.** Compare
BLACK HAND, CAMORRA.

ma foi (má fwä′) *French* My faith; my goodness.

mag (mag) *n. Brit. Slang* A halfpenny. [< dial. E *make*
a halfpenny; infl. in form by *meg*, orig., a guinea]

mag. 1. Magazine. **2.** Magnet; magnetism. **3.** *Astron.*
Magnitude.

Ma·gal·la·nes (mä′gä·yä′nās) See PUNTA ARENAS.

mag·a·zine (mag′ə·zēn′, mag′ə·zēn) *n.* **1.** A periodical
publication, usually with a paper cover and illustrations,
containing articles, stories, and other features by various
writers. **2.** A warehouse or depot in which anything is
stored, especially military supplies. **3.** A building for storing explosives and ammunition; also, a storeroom in a ship
or fort serving a similar purpose. **4.** A receptacle or part of
a gun holding ammunition ready for chambering; also, a
case in which cartridges are carried. **5.** A reservoir or
supply chamber in a battery, camera, etc. [< MF *magasin*
< OF *magazin* < Arabic *makhāzin*, pl. of *makhzan* store-
house < *khazana* to store up]

mag·da·len (mag′də·lin) *n.* **1.** A reformed prostitute.
2. A house for the reformation of prostitutes. Also **mag′da-
lene** (-lēn). [after Mary *Magdalene*]

Mag·da·le·na (mäg′dä·lā′nä) A river in Colombia, flowing
about 1,000 miles north to the Caribbean Sea.

Mag·da·len College (môd′lin) A college of Oxford University, England.

Mag·da·lene (mag′də·lēn, mag′də·lē′nē) *n.* Mary Magdalene: usually preceded by *the.* Also **Mag′da·len.** See
MARY MAGDALENE.

Mag·da·lene College (môd′lin) A college of Cambridge
University, England.

Mag·da·le·ni·an (mag′də·lē′nē·ən) *adj. Anthropol.* Of or
pertaining to the most advanced culture stage of the Paleolithic period in Europe. [< F *magdalénien*, after *La Madeleine* in west central France, where artifacts were found]

Mag·de·burg (mag′də·bûrg, *Ger.* mäg′də·bŏŏrkh) A city of
west central East Germany; pop. 268,100 (est. 1967).

mage (māj) *n. Archaic* A magician. [< F < L *magus.*
See MAGI.]

Ma·gel·lan (mə·jel′ən), **Ferdinand,** 1480?–1521, Portuguese
navigator in the service of Spain. Also *Spanish* **Fernando
de Ma·gal·la·nes** (mä·gä·yä′nās). — **Mag·el·lan·ic** (maj′-
ə·lan′ik) *adj.*

Magellan, Strait of The channel between the Atlantic and
the Pacific separating the South American mainland from
Tierra del Fuego.

Magellanic cloud
Astron. Either of two
luminous aggrega-
tions of star clusters
and nebulae in the
constellations of Do-
rado and Tucana
near the south celes-
tial pole.

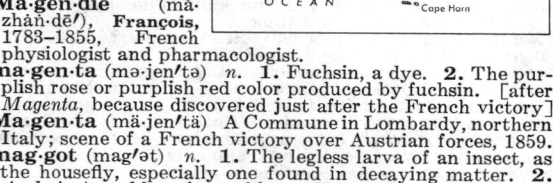

ma·gen David (mä′-
gən) See MOGEN
DAVID.

Ma·gen·die (mä·
zhän·dē′), **François,**
1783–1855, French
physiologist and pharmacologist.

ma·gen·ta (mə·jen′tə) *n.* **1.** Fuchsin, a dye. **2.** The purplish rose or purplish red color produced by fuchsin. [after
Magenta, because discovered just after the French victory]

Ma·gen·ta (mä·jen′tä) A Commune in Lombardy, northern
Italy; scene of a French victory over Austrian forces, 1859.

mag·got (mag′ət) *n.* **1.** The legless larva of an insect, as
the housefly, especially one found in decaying matter. **2.**
Archaic An odd notion; whim. [Prob. alter. of ME *mad-
dock, mathek* < ON *mathkr* worm]

mag·got·y (mag′ət·ē) *adj.* **1.** Infested with maggots.
2. *Archaic* Having odd notions. — **mag′got·i·ness** *n.*

Ma·ghreb (mug′greb) *n.* A region in NW Africa, consisting
chiefly of Morocco, Algeria, and Tunisia. Also **Ma′ghrib.**
— **Ma·ghre·bi** or **Ma·ghri·bi** (mug′rə·bē) *adj.*, *n.*

Ma·gi (mā′jī) *n. pl. of* **Ma·gus** (mā′gəs) **1.** The three "wise
men from the east" who came to Bethlehem to pay homage
to the infant Jesus. *Matt* 1 1–12. **2.** The priestly caste of
the Medes and Persians: also **ma′gi.** [< L, pl. of *magus*
< Gk. *magos* < Persian *magu* priest, magician]

mag·ic (maj′ik) *n.* **1.** Seeming control over or foresight of
natural events, forces, etc., by the ritual invocation of supernatural agencies; also, the practice of this control; thauma-
turgy. **2.** An overpowering influence; unusual effectiveness;
enchantment: the *magic* of his voice. **3.** Sleight of hand;
legerdemain. — *like* **magic** As if by magic; instantly.
— *adj.* **1.** Of, pertaining to, or used in magic. **2.** Producing the effects of magic. **3.** Mysteriously impressive; beautiful. [< OF *magique* < LL *magica* (*ars*) magic (art) < Gk.
magike (*techne*) < *magikos* of the Magi]

— **Syn.** (noun) **1.** *Magic, sorcery, witchcraft, voodoo, divination,*
and *necromancy* refer to powers that are considered supernatural.
Magic involves the belief that man can coerce nature by the use of
certain rites, formulas, actions, etc.; it can be found as an element
in all primitive religions. The study of natural phenomena, called
white or natural *magic,* developed into the modern natural sciences. Distinguished from this was black *magic* or *sorcery,* the attempt to use or invoke supernatural powers for personal or sinister
purposes. *Witchcraft* was *sorcery* as practiced by a woman possessed by a demon. *Voodoo* is one of many primitive cults combining elements of religion, *sorcery,* and *witchcraft. Divination* refers to the attempt to gain supernatural insight into the future,
while *necromancy,* or communication with the spirits of the dead,
is one of the methods of *divination.*

mag·i·cal (maj′i·kəl) *adj.* Of, pertaining to, or produced
by or as by magic. — **mag′i·cal·ly** *adv.*

ma·gi·cian (mə·jish′ən) *n.* One who performs magic; especially, an entertainer who uses illusion and legerdemain.

magic lantern *Archaic* A slide projector.

Ma·gi·not line (mazh′ə·nō, *Fr.* mà·zhē·nō′) A system of
French fortifications along the German frontier, built 1925–
35. [after André *Maginot*, 1877–1932, French statesman]

mag·is·te·ri·al (maj′is·tir′ē·əl) *adj.* **1.** Of, pertaining to,
or like a master. **2.** Dictatorial; domineering. **3.** Of or
pertaining to a magistrate, his office, or his duties. [<
Med.L *magisterialis* < LL *magisterius* < L *magister* master]
— **mag′is·te′ri·al·ly** *adv.*

mag·is·ter·y (maj′is·ter′ē) *n. pl.* **·ter·ies** In alchemy, an
agency or quality capable of transmuting other substances,
as the philosopher's stone. [< Med.L *magisterium* philosopher's stone < L *magister* master]

mag·is·tra·cy (maj′is·trə·sē) *n. pl.* **·cies** **1.** The office,
function, or term of a magistrate. **2.** Magistrates collectively. **3.** The district under a magistrate's jurisdiction.
Also **mag·is·tra·ture** (maj′is·trə·chŏŏr).

mag·is·tral (maj′is·trəl) *adj.* **1.** In pharmacy, compounded
for a specific case. **2.** *Rare* Magisterial. — *n. Mil.* Formerly, the line in a fortification plan from which the positions of fieldworks were determined: also **magistral line.**
[< F < L *magistralis* < *magister* master]

mag·is·trate (maj′is·trāt, -trit) *n.* **1.** A public official with
the power to administer and enforce the law. **2.** A minor
judicial officer having limited authority in criminal cases, as
a justice of the peace or a judge in a police court. [< L *ma-
gistratus* magisterial office < *magister* master]

Ma·gle·mo·si·an (mä′glə·mō′zē·ən) *adj. Anthropol.* Of or relating to the Mesolithic forest culture of northern Europe. [after *Maglemose*, Denmark]

mag·ma (mag′mə) *n. pl.* **-ma·ta** (-mə·tə) **1.** Any soft, doughy mixture of organic or mineral materials. **2.** *Geol.* The molten, plastic mass of rock material from which igneous rocks are formed. **3.** In pharmacy, a suspension in a relatively small volume of liquid. [< L < Gk. < root of *massein* to knead] — **mag·mat·ic** (mag·mat′ik) *adj.*

Mag·na Car·ta (mag′nə kär′tə) **1.** The Great Charter of English liberties, delivered June 19, 1215, by King John at Runnymede, on the demand of the English barons. **2.** Any document that secures liberty and rights. Also **Mag′na Char′ta.** [< Med.L, lit., Great Charter]

mag·na cum lau·de (mag′nə kum lô′dē, mäg′nä kŏŏm lou′də) See under CUM LAUDE.

Magna Grae·ci·a (grē′shē·ə) See GRAECIA MAGNA.

mag·na·nim·i·ty (mag′nə·nim′ə·tē) *n. pl.* **·ties 1.** The quality of being magnanimous. **2.** A magnanimous act.

mag·nan·i·mous (mag·nan′ə·məs) *adj.* **1.** Manifesting generosity in forgiving insults or injuries; not given to resentment or envy; great of soul; high-minded. **2.** Characterized by or arising from magnanimity. [< L *magnanimus* < *magnus* great + *animus* mind, soul] — **mag·nan′i·mous·ly** *adv.* — **mag·nan′i·mous·ness** *n.*

mag·nate (mag′nāt) *n.* **1.** One notable or powerful in a specific sphere, especially that of industry: a railroad *magnate.* **2.** A person of rank or importance. **3.** A member of the Upper House in the Diet, as formerly in Poland and Hungary. [< LL *magnas, -atis* < *magnus* great]

mag·ne·sia (mag·nē′zhə, -shə, -zē·ə) *n. Chem.* Magnesium oxide, MgO, a light, white powder used in medicine as an antacid and laxative, and in the manufacture of firebrick. [< Med.L < Gk. *Magnēsia* (*lithos*) (stone) of Magnesia] — **mag·ne′sian, mag·ne′sic** (-sik) *adj.*

Mag·ne·sia (mag·nē′zhə, -shə) The ancient name for MAGNISA.

mag·ne·site (mag′nə·sīt) *n.* A mineral composed of magnesium carbonate, $MgCo_3$, and occurring in dull white crystalline or granular masses. [< MAGNES(IA) + -ITE¹]

mag·ne·si·um (mag·nē′zē·əm, -zhē-, -shē-) *n.* A light, silver-white, malleable and ductile metallic element (symbol Mg), that burns with a very hot, bright flame and is used in lightweight alloys. See ELEMENT. [< NL < *magnesia*]

mag·net (mag′nit) *n.* **1.** A body that has a magnetic field and therefore attracts iron and other magnetic material; especially, a permanent magnet (which see). **2.** A lodestone. **3.** One who or that which exercises a strong attraction. Abbr. (for defs. 1, 2) *mag.* [< OF *magnete* < L *magnes, magnetis* < Gk. *Magnēs* (*lithos*) Magnesian (stone), i.e., a magnet < *Magnēsia* Magnesia]

mag·net·ic (mag·net′ik) *adj* **1.** Pertaining to magnetism or a magnet. **2.** Capable of exerting magnetic force. **3.** Capable of being attracted by a magnet or a lodestone. **4.** Pertaining to the magnetism of the earth. **5.** Possessing personal magnetism. **6.** *Archaic* Of or pertaining to mesmerism. Also **mag·net′i·cal.** — **mag·net′i·cal·ly** *adv.*

magnetic azimuth Azimuth from magnetic north.

magnetic chart A chart indicating the variations in the earth's magnetic field for a given area.

magnetic declination Magnetic variation (which see).

magnetic dip Dip (*n.* def. 7).

magnetic equator An imaginary irregular, unstable line on the earth's surface, encircling it nearly midway between the magnetic poles, where a free magnetic needle has no tendency to dip: also called *aclinic line.*

magnetic field That region in the neighborhood of a magnet or current-carrying body in which magnetic forces are observable.

magnetic flux The number of magnetic lines of force passing through a magnetic field, expressed in maxwells.

magnetic induction The magnetic flux per unit of area in a magnetized body, expressed in gauss.

magnetic lens *Physics* An assembly of coils and electromagnets producing a magnetic field that will focus a stream of charged particles.

magnetic meridian *Naut.* A meridian line passing through the magnetic poles.

magnetic mine An underwater mine containing a sensitive device that causes it to detonate in the proximity of any large mass of magnetic material, as a ship.

magnetic moment A measure of the magnetizing force exerted by a magnetized body or electric current.

magnetic needle A freely movable magnetized needle that tends to point to the magnetic poles of the earth.

magnetic north The direction, usually differing from true north, toward which the needle of a compass points.

magnetic permeability A number indicating the ratio of the magnetic induction of a substance or material to the magnetizing force.

magnetic pickup A phonograph pickup that employs a magnet and coils to transform vibrations into electrical impulses. Compare CRYSTAL PICKUP.

magnetic pole 1. Either of the poles of a magnet. **2.**

Either of two points (**north magnetic pole** and **south magnetic pole**) on the surface of the earth where the lines of magnetic force converge and are vertical. These poles attract the compass needle, slowly change position, and do not coincide with the geographical poles.

mag·net·ics (mag·net′iks) *n.pl.* (construed as *sing.*) Magnetism (def. 2).

magnetic storm A sudden variation in the magnetic field surrounding the earth, apparently connected with solar disturbances.

magnetic tape *Electronics* A thin ribbon of paper or plastic coated with magnetic particles that form patterns corresponding to the electromagnetic impulses generated by a tape recorder.

magnetic variation The angular difference at a given point between magnetic north and true north: also called *magnetic declination.*

MAGNETIC NEEDLE
a Magnetic north. *b* True north. *c* Magnetic needle. *d* Angle of declination.

mag·net·ism (mag′nə·tiz′əm) *n.* **1.** The specific properties of a magnet, regarded as an effect of molecular interaction. **2.** The science that treats of the laws and conditions of magnetic phenomena: also called *magnetics.* **3.** The amount of magnetic moment in a magnetized body. **4.** The personal quality that attracts, interests, or influences. **5.** *Archaic* Mesmerism. Abbr. *mag.*

mag·net·ite (mag′nə·tīt) *n.* A massive, isometric black iron oxide, Fe_3O_4, that is strongly magnetic and is called *lodestone* when it has polarity. [< MAGNET + -ITE¹] — **mag′net·it′ic** (-tit′ik) *adj.*

mag·net·ize (mag′nə·tīz) *v.t.* **ized, ·iz·ing 1.** To communicate magnetic properties to. **2.** To attract by strong personal influence; captivate. **3.** *Archaic* To hypnotize. — **mag′net·i·za′tion** *n.* — **mag′net·iz′er** *n.*

magnetizing force The ability of magnetized bodies or electric currents to produce magnetic induction, expressed in oersteds.

mag·ne·to (mag·nē′tō) *n. pl.* **·tos** Any of various alternators in which the rotation of a coil of wire between the poles of a permanent magnet induces an electric current in the coil; especially, such a device used to produce the ignition spark in some internal-combustion engines. Also **mag·ne·to·dy·na·mo** (mag·nē′tō·dī′nə·mō), and **mag·ne·to·gen·er·a·tor** (mag·nē′tō·jen′ə·rā′tər). [Short for *magnetoelectric machine*]

magneto- *combining form* Magnetic; magnetism.

mag·ne·to·chem·is·try (mag·nē′tō·kem′is·trē) *n.* The science that treats of the interrelations between magnetic and chemical phenomena. — **mag·ne·to·chem′i·cal** *adj.*

mag·ne·to·e·lec·tric·i·ty (mag·nē′tō·i·lek·tris′ə·tē) *n.* **1.** Electricity generated by the inductive action of a magnet. **2.** The science that treats of such electricity. — **mag·ne·to·e·lec′tric, mag·ne·to·e·lec′tri·cal** *adj.*

mag·ne·to·graph (mag·nē′tə·graf, -gräf) *n.* A recording magnetometer.

mag·ne·to·hy·dro·dy·nam·ics (mag·nē′tō·hī′drō·dī·nam′iks) *n.pl.* (construed as *sing.*) The branch of physics that treats of the interaction of electromagnetic, thermal, and hydrodynamic forces, as in a plasma. — **mag·ne·to·hy·dro·dy·nam′ic** *adj.*

mag·ne·tol·y·sis (mag·nə·tol′ə·sis) *n.* Chemical action in a substance placed in a magnetic field. [< MAGNETO- + -LYSIS] — **mag·net·o·lyt·ic** (mag·net′ə·lit′ik) *adj.*

mag·ne·tom·e·ter (mag·nə·tom′ə·tər) *n.* An instrument for measuring the intensity and direction of magnetic forces. — **mag′ne·tom′e·try** *n.*

mag·ne·to·mo·tive (mag·nē′tō·mō′tiv, mag′nə·tō-) *adj.* Pertaining to, having, or producing magnetic effects: distinguished from *electromotive.*

magnetomotive force The force producing a magnetic flux, equal to the intensity of flux times the reluctance.

mag·ne·to·scope (mag·nē′tə·skōp, -net′ə-) *n.* An instrument that indicates the presence of a magnetic field.

mag·ne·to·sphere (mag·nē′tə·sfir, -net′ə-) *n. Physics* A region of the atmosphere extending beyond the exosphere to a height of about 40,000 miles and forming a continuous band of ionized particles trapped by the earth's magnetic field. Compare VAN ALLEN RADIATION. — **mag·ne·to·spher′ic** (-sfir′ik, -sfer′-) *adj.*

mag·ne·to·stric·tion (mag·nē′tō·strik′shən, -net′ə-) *n. Physics* The mechanical deformation produced in certain materials when subjected to the action of a magnetic field.

mag·ne·tron (mag′nə·tron) *n. Electronics* An electron tube in which the flow of electrons is subject to the control of steady magnetic and electric fields acting at right angles to each other, used to generate alternating current output. [< MAGNET + (ELEC)TRON]

magni- *combining form* Great; large; long. [< L *magnus* great]

mag·nif·ic (mag·nif′ik) *adj. Archaic* **1.** Magnificent; sumptuous. **2.** Grandiloquent; pompous. Also **mag·nif′i·cal.** [< F *magnifique* < L *magnificus* < *magnus* great + *fic-,* stem of *facere* to make] — **mag·nif′i·cal·ly** *adv.*

Mag·nif·i·cat (mag·nif'ə·kat) *n.* **1.** The canticle of the Virgin Mary beginning *Magnificat anima mea dominum,* "My soul doth magnify the Lord." *Luke* i 46–55. **2.** A musical setting for this. [< L, it magnifies]

mag·ni·fi·ca·tion (mag'nə·fə·kā'shən) *n.* **1.** The act, process, or degree of magnifying. **2.** The state of being magnified. **3.** The magnifying power of a lens or other optical device. **4.** A magnified representation of an object, as in a drawing, photograph, etc. [< L *magnificatio, -onis* < *magnificare* < *magnificus* great. See MAGNIFIC.]

mag·nif·i·cence (mag·nif'ə·səns) *n.* The state or quality of being magnificent; splendor; impressiveness. [< OF < L *magnificentia* < *magnificus* noble. See MAGNIFIC.]

mag·nif·i·cent (mag·nif'ə·sənt) *adj.* **1.** Presenting an extraordinarily imposing appearance; splendid; beautiful. **2.** Exceptionally pleasing; superb. **3.** Exalted or sublime in expression or concept. **4.** *Usually cap.* High in rank; exalted: used as a title for a ruler. [< OF < LL *magnificens,* var. of *magnificus.* See MAGNIFIC.] — **mag·nif'i·cent·ly** *adv.*

mag·nif·i·co (mag·nif'ə·kō) *n. pl.* **·coes** **1.** A nobleman of the Venetian republic. **2.** Any lordly personage. [< Ital. < L *magnificus.* See MAGNIFIC.]

mag·ni·fy (mag'nə·fī) *v.* **·fied, ·fy·ing** — *v.t.* **1.** To increase the perceived size of, as by a lens. **2.** To increase the size of; enlarge. **3.** To cause to seem greater or more important; exaggerate. **4.** *Archaic* To extol; exalt. — *v.i.* **5.** To increase or have the power to increase the apparent size of an object, as a lens. — **Syn.** See INCREASE. [< OF *magnifier* < L *magnificare* < *magnificus* great. See MAGNIFIC.] — **mag'ni·fi'a·ble** *adj.* — **mag'ni·fi'er** *n.*

magnifying glass A lens that magnifies the image of objects or print seen through it.

mag·nil·o·quent (mag·nil'ə·kwənt) *adj.* Speaking or spoken in a grandiose style; grandiloquent. — **Syn.** See RHETORICAL. [< L *magnus* great + *loquens, -entis,* ppr. of *loqui* to speak] — **mag·nil'o·quence** *n.* — **mag·nil'o·quent·ly** *adv.*

Mag·ni·to·gorsk (məg·nyi·tō·gôrsk') A city in the southern R.S.F.S.R., on the Ural; pop. 364,000 (est. 1970).

mag·ni·tude (mag'nə·tood, -tyood) *n.* **1.** Size or extent. **2.** Greatness or importance: the *magnitude* of the achievement. **3.** *Math.* A number given to a quantity in order that it may be used as a basis for comparison with other quantities of the same class. **4.** *Astron.* The relative brightness of a star, ranging from one for the brightest to six for those just visible to the naked eye. See LIGHT RATIO. Abbr. (for def. 4) *mag.* [< L *magnitudo* < *magnus* large]

mag·no·li·a (mag·nō'lē·ə, -nōl'yə) *n.* **1.** An ornamental flowering shrub or tree (genus *Magnolia*) with large fragrant flowers. **2.** The magnolia blossom, as the white flower of the **evergreen magnolia** (*M. grandiflora*), the State flower of Louisiana and Mississippi. [< NL, genus name, after Pierre *Magnol,* 1638–1715, French botanist]

mag·no·li·a·ceous (mag·nō'lē·ā'shəs) *adj. Bot.* Of or pertaining to a family (*Magnoliaceae*) of trees and shrubs, including the magnolias and tulip trees, with large axillary or terminal flowers. [< NL *Magnoliaceae,* family name < *magnolia.* See MAGNOLIA.]

Magnolia State Nickname of MISSISSIPPI.

mag·num (mag'nəm) *n.* **1.** A wine bottle of twice the ordinary size, holding about 2/5 gallon; also, the quantity such a bottle will hold. **2.** *Anat.* The largest bone in the distal row of the carpus at the center of the wrist. [< L, neut. of *magnus* great]

magnum o·pus (ō'pəs) A great work; masterpiece; especially, the greatest single work of a writer, artist, etc. [< L]

mag·nus hitch (mag'nəs) A clove hitch with one extra turn.

Ma·gog (mā'gog) See GOG AND MAGOG.

ma·got (mà·gō') *n.* The Barbary ape. [< F, ? < *Magog* Magog]

mag·pie (mag'pī) *n.* **1.** Any of various large, noisy corvine birds (genus *Pica*) having a long tapering tail and black and white plumage; especially, the common **black-billed magpie** (*P. pica*) of Europe and America, and the **yellow-billed magpie** (*P. nuttalli*) of California: sometimes called *pie.* **2.** A chatterbox. [< *Mag,* diminutive of MARGARET + PIE²]

M.Agr. Master of Agriculture.

Mag·say·say (mäg·sī'sī), **Ramon,** 1907–57, Philippine statesman; president 1953–57.

mag·uey (mag'wā, *Sp.* mä·gā'ē) *n.* **1.** Any of the agaves of Mexico with fleshy leaves, especially the species (*Agave atrovirens*) yielding pulque, and the century plant. **2.** Any of a related group of plants (genus *Furcraea*). **3.** Any of several tough fibers taken from these plants and used in rope, etc. [< Sp., prob. < Taino]

Ma·gus (mā'gəs) Singular of MAGI.

Mag·yar (mag'yär, mäg'-; *Hungarian* mud'yär) *n.* **1.** A member of the dominant group of the population of Hungary. **2.** Hungarian, a Finno-Ugric language. — *adj.* Of or pertaining to the Magyars or their language.

Mag·yar·or·szag (mud'yär·ôr'säg) The Hungarian name for HUNGARY.

Ma·ha·bha·ra·ta (mə·hä'bä'rə·tə) One of the two great epics of ancient India, written in Sanskrit, relating mainly to the wars of the Pandava and Kaurava dynasties of northern India. Compare RAMAYANA. Also **Ma·ha'bha'ra·tam** (-təm). [< Skt., lit., the great story]

Ma·han (mə·han'), **Alfred Thayer,** 1840–1914, U. S. naval officer and historian.

ma·ha·ra·ja (mä'hə·rä'jə, *Hind.* mə·hä'rä'jə) *n.* A title of certain princes of India, particularly one ruling an Indian state. Also **ma·ha·ra'jah.** [< Hind. < Skt. *mahārāja* < *maha* great + *rājā* king]

ma·ha·ra·ni (mä'hə·rä'nē, *Hind.* mə·hä'rä'nē) *n.* **1.** The wife of a maharaja. **2.** A sovereign princess of India. Also **ma'ha·ra'nee.** [< Hind. < *maha* great + *rāni* queen]

Ma·ha·rash·tra (mə·hä'räsh'trə) A State in western India; 118,903 sq. mi.; pop. 50,295,000 (est. 1971); capital, Bombay. See BOMBAY.

ma·hat·ma (mə·hat'mə, -hät'-) *n.* In theosophy and some Asian religions, one of a group of holy men possessed of special occult knowledge: often a title of respect. [< Skt. *mahātman* < *maha* great + *ātman* soul] — **ma·hat'ma·ism** *n.*

Mahatma Gandhi See GANDHI.

Mah·di (mä'dē) *n.* **1.** In Islam, a prophet or messiah expected to appear before the end of the world. **2.** Any of various persons claiming this title, especially **Mohammed Ahmed,** 1843–85, Sudanese sheik who defeated the British under General Gordon at Khartoum, 1885. [< Arabic *mahdīy,* lit., he who is guided aright, pp. of *hadā* to lead rightly] — **Mah'dism** *n.* — **Mah'dist** *adj. & n.*

Ma·hi·can (mə·hē'kən) *n.* One of a tribe of North American Indians of Algonquian stock formerly occupying the territory from the Hudson River to Lake Champlain: also called *Mohican.* [< Algonquian, lit., wolf]

mah·jong (mä'zhong', -zhông') *n.* A game of Chinese origin, resembling dominoes, usually played by four persons with 144 pieces or tiles; also, a winning hand in this game. Also **mah'-jong', mah'jongg'.** [< dial. Chinese < Chinese *ma ch'iao* house sparrow; from the design on one of the tiles]

Mah·ler (mä'lər), **Gustav,** 1860–1911, Austro-Hungarian composer and conductor, active in Austria and Germany.

mahl·stick (mäl'stik', môl'-) See MAULSTICK.

Mah·mud II (mä·mood', mä'mood), 1785–1839, sultan of Turkey 1808–39; defeated in Greek war for independence.

ma·hog·a·ny (mə·hog'ə·nē) *n. pl.* **·nies** **1.** Any of various tropical meliaceous trees (genus *Swietenia*) yielding fine-grained reddish hardwood much used for furniture and cabinet work. **2.** The wood itself. **3.** Any of various trees yielding a similar wood, as the **African mahogany** (*Khaya ivorensis*). **4.** Any of the various shades of brownish red of the finished wood. — *adj.* Having a mahogany color. [< obs. Sp. *mahogani,* prob. < Arawakan]

Ma·hom·et (mə·hom'it) Mohammed.

Ma·hom·e·tan (mə·hom'ə·tən) *adj. & n.* Mohammedan.

Ma·hound (mə·hound', -hoond') *n.* **1.** *Archaic* The prophet Mohammed. **2.** *Scot.* The Devil. [< OF *Mahon, Mahum* < *Mahomet* Mohammed]

ma·hout (mə·hout') *n.* In India and the East Indies, the keeper and driver of an elephant. [< Hind. *mahāut, mahāvat* < Skt. *mahāmātra,* lit., great in measure]

Mah·rat·i (mə·rat'ē) See MARATHI.

Mah·rat·ta (mə·rat'ə) *n.* One of a Hindu people of SW and central India: also *Maratha.* [< Hind. *Marhaṭa* < Marathi *Marāṭhi* < Skt. *Mahārāṣṭra,* lit., great country]

Mäh·ren (mä'rən) The German name for MORAVIA.

Mäh·risch-Os·trau (mä'rish-ôs'trou) The German name for MORAVSKÁ OSTRAVA.

Mai·a (mā'yə, mī'ə) **1.** In Greek mythology, the eldest of the Pleiades, and mother by Zeus of Hermes. **2.** In Roman mythology, a goddess of spring sometimes identified with the Greek Maia. — *n.* One of the six visible stars in the Pleiades cluster.

maid (mād) *n.* **1.** A young unmarried woman or girl; maiden. **2.** A female servant. [Short for MAIDEN]

maid·en (mād'n) *n.* **1.** An unmarried woman, especially if young. **2.** A virgin. **3.** A race horse that has never won an event. **4.** A machine for beheading criminals, used in Scotland in the 16th and 17th centuries: also **the Maiden.** **5.** In cricket, an over in which no runs are scored: also **maiden over.** — *adj.* **1.** Of, pertaining to, or befitting a maiden. **2.** Unmarried: said of women: a *maiden* aunt. **3.** Of or pertaining to the first use, trial, or experience: *maiden* effort. **4.** Untried; unused. **5.** Of horses, never having won a race. [OE *mægden,* prob. dim. of *mægeth* virgin]

maid·en·hair (mād'n·hâr') *n.* A very delicate and graceful fern (genus *Adiantum*) with an erect black stem, common in damp, rocky woods. Also **maidenhair fern.**

maidenhair tree The ginkgo.

maid·en·head (mād'n·hed') *n.* **1.** The hymen. **2.** *Archaic* Maidenhood; virginity.

maid·en·hood (mād'n·hood) *n.* The state or time of being a

maid·en·ly (mād′n·lē) *adj.* Of, pertaining to, or befitting a maiden or young girl. — **maid′en·li·ness** *n.*

maiden name A woman's surname before marriage.

Maid Mar·i·on (mar′ē·ən) 1. The female companion of Robin Hood. 2. Formerly, a character in morris dances and May-day games, as a May queen, a boy acting a girl, or a buffoon.

maid of honor 1. The chief unmarried attendant of a bride at a wedding. 2. An unmarried woman, usually of noble birth, attendant upon an empress, queen, or princess.

Maid of Orléans See JOAN OF ARC.

maid·serv·ant (mād′sûr′vənt) *n.* A female servant.

Maid·stone (mād′stən, -stōn) The county seat of Kent, England, a municipal borough in the central part of the county; pop. 124,700 (1976).

ma·ieu·tic (mā·yōō′tik) *adj.* Of or pertaining to the Socratic method. Also **ma·ieu′ti·cal.** [< Gk. *maieutikos,* lit., obstetric < *maieuesthai* to act as a midwife < *maia* midwife]

mai·gre (mā′gər) *adj.* Not consisting of flesh or its juices. [< OF. See MEAGER.]

maigre day In the Roman Catholic Church, a day of abstinence on which only maigre food may be eaten.

mai·hem (mā′hem) See MAYHEM.

mail¹ (māl) *n.* 1. Letters, printed matter, parcels, etc., sent or received through a governmental postal system. 2. The postal system itself. 3. Postal matter collected or delivered at a specified time: the morning *mail.* 4. A conveyance, as a train, plane, etc., for carrying postal matter. — *adj.* Pertaining to or used for the handling or conveyance of mail: a *mail* truck. — *v.t. U.S.* To send by mail, as letters; deposit in a mailbox or at a post office; post. [< OF *male* < OHG *malha* wallet] — **mail′a·ble** *adj.*

mail² (māl) *n.* 1. Flexible armor made of interlinked rings or overlapping scales. 2. Loosely, any defensive armor. 3. A defensive covering, as the shell of a turtle. — *v.t.* To cover with or as with mail. [< OF *maille* < L *macula* spot, mesh of a net]

mail³ (māl) *n. Scot. & Brit. Dial.* That which is paid; rent; wages. Also **maill.** [OE *māl* < ON, speech, agreement; infl. in sense by ON *māle* contract, stipend]

mail·bag (māl′bag′) *n.* A bag in which mail is carried or shipped. Also **mail′pouch′** (-pouch′).

mail·box (māl′boks′) *n. U.S.* 1. A box in which letters, etc., are deposited for collection: also called *postbox.* 2. A box into which private mail is delivered. Also **mail box.**

mail car A railroad car for carrying mail.

mail·catch·er (māl′kach′ər) *n.* A device for transferring mailbags to or from a moving train. Also **mail catcher.**

mailed (māld) *adj.* Covered or armed with or as with mail.

mailed fist Aggressive force, or a threat of force, especially between nations. [Trans. of G *gepanzerte faust*]

mail·er (mā′lər) *n.* 1. A mail boat. 2. A mailing machine. 3. One who addresses and mails letters, packages, etc.

mail·ing (mā′ling) *n. Scot.* A rented piece of ground or farm; also, the rent paid for it.

mailing machine Any of various machines that address, stamp, seal, etc., envelopes and other types of mail.

Mail·lol (mà·yôl′), **Aristide,** 1861–1944, French sculptor.

mail·lot (mī·yō′) *n.* 1. A woman's tightly fitted, sometimes strapless, one-piece swim suit. 2. A garment similar to this used by gymnasts, dancers, etc. [< F]

mail·man (māl′man′, -mən) *n. pl.* **·men** (-men′, -mən) One who carries and delivers letters: also called *postman.*

mail order An order for merchandise, received and filled by mail.

mail-or·der house (māl′ôr′dər) A business enterprise that sells its merchandise wholly or in part by mail order.

maim (mām) *v.t.* 1. To deprive of the use of a bodily part; mutilate; disable. 2. To render imperfect; make defective. — *n. Rare* A maiming; crippling. [< OF *mahaignier, mayner;* ult. origin uncertain. Akin to MAYHEM.] — **maim′er** *n.*

Mai·mon·i·des (mī·mon′ə·dēz), 1135–1204, Spanish rabbi, physician, and philosopher: original name **Moses ben Maimon** (mī′mŏn). Called **RaM·BaM** (ram·bam′).

main¹ (mān) *adj.* 1. First or chief in size, rank, importance, strength, etc.; principal; leading: the *main* building; *main* event. 2. Fully exerted; sheer: by *main* force. 3. Of or pertaining to a broad expanse of land, sea, etc. 4. *Naut.* Of or connected with the mainsail or mainmast. 5. *Obs.* Very important; momentous. — *n.* 1. A principal conduit or pipe in a system conveying gas, water, etc. 2. Utmost effort; force: now chiefly in the phrase **with might and main.** 3. The chief or most important point or part. 4. *Naut.* The mainmast. 5. *Poetic* The open sea. 6. *Archaic* The mainland. — **in** (or **for**) **the main** For the most part; on the whole; chiefly. [OE *mægen*]

main² (mān) *n.* 1. In cockfighting, a match of several battles. 2. In the games of hazard and craps: **a** A hand or throw of dice. **b** A number selected by the caster before he throws the dice. [? < MAIN¹]

Main (mān, *Ger.* mīn) A river in south central West Germany, flowing 305 miles, generally west, to the Rhine.

main clause *Gram.* An independent clause. See under CLAUSE.

main deck *Naut.* The chief deck of a vessel.

main drag *U.S. Slang* The principal street of a city.

Maine (mān) *n.* A U.S. battleship blown up in Havana harbor, Feb. 15, 1898, with the loss of 260 lives.

Maine (mān) 1. A State of the extreme NE United States; 32,562 sq. mi.; pop. 993,663; capital, Augusta; entered the Union March 15, 1820; nickname, *Pine-Tree State.* 2. An ancient province of western France.

main·land (mān′land, -lənd) *n.* A principal land mass, as of a continent, as distinguished from an island or peninsula.

Main·land (mān′lənd) 1. See POMONA ISLAND. 2. The largest of the Shetland Islands, Scotland; 407 sq. mi.

main line The principal line of a railroad or highway.

Main Line An upper-class suburban strip west of Philadelphia along the railroad from Philadelphia to Pittsburgh.

main-line (mān′līn′) *v.* **·lined, ·lin·ing** *Slang v.t.* To inject (a narcotic) into a large vein. — *v.i.* To make a narcotic injection into a large vein. — **main′lin′er** *n.* — **main′-line′** *adj.*

main·ly (mān′lē) *adv.* Chiefly; principally.

main·mast (mān′məst, -mast′, -mäst′) *n. Naut.* 1. The second mast from the bow in a schooner, brig, etc. 2. The larger mast nearer the bow in a ketch or yawl.

main·sail (mān′səl -sāl′) *Naut.* 1. A sail bent to the main yard of a square-rigged vessel: also **main course.** 2. The principal sail on a mainmast.

main sequence *Astron.* The area of the Hertzsprung-Russel diagram that includes the sun and the majority of stars.

main·sheet (mān′shēt′) *n. Naut.* The sheet by which the mainsail is trimmed and set.

main·spring (mān′spring′) *n.* 1. The principal spring of a mechanism, as of a watch. 2. The principal or most compelling cause or agency.

main·stay (mān′stā′) *n.* 1. *Naut.* The rope from the mainmast head forward. 2. A chief support.

main·stream (mān′strēm′) *n.* The main or middle course or direction: in the *mainstream* of American political thought.

Main Street 1. The principal business street of a town. 2. The typical manners, customs, etc., of a small town.

main·tain (mān·tān′) *v.t.* 1. To carry on or continue; keep in existence: to *maintain* friendly relations. 2. To preserve or keep: to *maintain* an open mind. 3. To keep in proper condition: to *maintain* roads. 4. To supply with a livelihood; pay the expenses of; support. 5. To claim to be true; uphold: He *maintains* his innocence. 6. To assert or state; affirm. 7. To hold or defend (a position, place, etc.) against attack. [< OF *maintenir* < L *manu tenere* to hold in one's hand < *manu,* ablative of *manus* hand + *tenere* to hold]

main·te·nance (mān′tə·nəns) *n.* 1. The act of maintaining, or the state of being maintained. 2. Means of support or subsistence; livelihood. 3. The work of keeping roads, machines, buildings, etc., in good condition. 4. *Law* Officious meddling in a suit by one who does not concern. [< OF *maintenance* < *maintenir.* See MAINTAIN.]

maintenance of membership A stipulation in some labor-union contracts that all employees who are members of the union shall continue their membership or be dismissed by the employer.

Main·te·non (mant·nôn′), **Marquise de,** 1635–1719, Françoise d'Aubigné, mistress and second wife of Louis XIV.

main·top (mān′top′) *n. Naut.* A platform at the head of the lower section of the mainmast.

main·top·gal·lant (mān′tə·gal′ənt, -top′-) *n. Naut.* The maintopgallantmast, or its sail, yard, or shroud.

main·top·gal·lant·mast (mān′tə·gal′ənt·məst, -mast′, -mäst′, -top′-) *n. Naut.* On a square-rigged vessel, the section of the mast next above the maintopmast.

main·top·mast (mān′top′məst) *n. Naut.* 1. On a square-rigged vessel, the upper section of the mainmast.

main·top·sail (mān′top′səl) *n. Naut.* The sail set on the maintopmast.

main yard *Naut.* The lower yard on the mainmast.

Mainz (mīnts) The capital of Rhineland-Palatinate, West Germany; pop. 176,720 (est. 1970): French *Mayence.*

ma·iol·i·ca (mä·yol′ē·kä) See MAJOLICA.

mai·son de san·té (mā·zôn′ də sän·tā′) *French* A sanitarium.

maist (māst) *adj., n., & adv. Scot.* Most; almost.

Mai·sur (mī·sōōr′) See MYSORE.

Mait·land (māt′lənd), **Frederic William,** 1850–1906, English jurist and historian.

maître d'hô·tel (me′tr′ dō·tel′) 1. A headwaiter or steward. Also *U.S. Informal* **mai·tre d'** (mā′trə dē′). 2. The proprietor or manager of a hotel. 3. Having a sauce of melted butter, parsley, and lemon juice or vinegar. [< F]

maize (māz) *n.* 1. Corn (def. 1). 2. The deep shade of yellow of ripe corn. [< Sp. *maiz* < Taino *mahiz*]

ma·jes·tic (mə·jes′tik) *adj.* Having or exhibiting majesty; stately; royal. Also **ma·jes′ti·cal.** — **ma·jes′ti·cal·ly** *adv.*

maj·es·ty (maj′is·tē) *n. pl.* **·ties** 1. Exalted dignity; stateliness; grandeur. 2. Sovereign authority: the *majesty* of the law. Abbr. **m.** [< OF *majeste* < L *majestas, -tatis.* Akin to *majus,* neut. compar. of *magnus* great.]

CHAIN MAIL ARMOR

Maj·es·ty (maj′is·tē) *n. pl.* **·ties** A title or form of address for a sovereign: preceded by *His, Her, Your,* etc. Abbr. *M.*

ma·jol·i·ca (mə·jol′i·kə, -yol′-) *n.* **1.** A kind of glazed and colorfully decorated Italian pottery. **2.** Pottery made in imitation of this. Also *maiolica.* [< Ital. *maiolica,* prob. < *Majolica,* early name of *Majorca,* where formerly made]

ma·jor (mā′jər) *adj.* **1.** Greater in quantity, number, or extent. **2.** Having primary or greater importance, excellence, rank, etc.: a *major* writer. **3.** Of, relating to, or making up a majority. **4.** *Music* Denoting the larger of two similarly named intervals: *major* second; *major* third. **b** Denoting a triad in which the third above the fundamental is major. **c** Denoting a type of diatonic scale, or a key based on this scale. Compare MINOR. **5.** *Logic* Having a greater degree of generality; of less restricted scope: *major* term; *major* premise. See SYLLOGISM. **6.** *U.S.* In education, pertaining to the principal area of specialized study of a degree candidate in a college or university. **7.** Having attained the age of one's majority. **8.** In English public schools, of or pertaining to the elder of two students with the same surname. — *n.* **1.** *Mil.* An officer ranking next above a captain and next below a lieutenant colonel. Abbr. *Maj., Maj* See tables at GRADE. **2.** *Music* **a** The larger of two identically named intervals. **b** A triad in which the third above the fundamental is major. **c** A type of diatonic scale. **3.** *U.S.* In education: **a** The principal area of specialized study of a degree candidate in a college or university. **b** The student himself: a chemistry *major.* **4.** One who has reached his majority or full legal age. **5.** One of superior status within a given group. **6.** *Logic* A major term or premise. **7.** In English public schools, the elder of two students with the same surname; senior. **8.** *pl. U.S.* The major leagues. — *v.i. U.S.* In education, to study as a major: with *in.* [< L, compar. of *magnus* great. Doublet of MAYOR.]

Ma·jor·ca (mə·jôr′kə, -yôr′-) The largest of the Balearic Islands; 1,405 sq. mi.: Spanish *Mallorca.* — **Ma·jor′can** *adj. & n.*

ma·jor-do·mo (mā′jər-dō′mō) *n. pl.* **·mos** The chief steward or butler, especially of a royal or noble household. [< Sp. *mayordomo* < Med.L *major domus* chief of a house < *major* an elder (< L, greater) + *domus* house]

ma·jor·ette (mā′jər-et′) *n. U.S. Informal* A girl who marches and twirls a baton with a band, as in a parade.

major general *Mil.* An officer ranking next above a brigadier or brigadier general and next below a lieutenant general. Also *Brit. & Canadian* **ma·jor-gen·er·al** (mā′jər-jen′ər-əl). *Maj. Gen., MajGen.* See tables at GRADE.

ma·jor·i·ty (mə·jôr′ə·tē, -jor′-) *n. pl.* **·ties 1.** More than half of a given number or group; the greater part. **2.** The number of jurors, voters, etc., in accord who compose more than half of the total group. **3.** The number of votes cast for a particular candidate, bill, etc., over and above the total number of remaining votes. Distinguished from *plurality.* **4.** The party or group having the most power. **5.** The time or fact of reaching the age when full civil and personal rights may be legally exercised. **6.** The rank, commission, or office of a major. [< MF *majorité* < L *majoritas, -tatis* < *major.* See MAJOR.]

major key A key based on a major scale. See SCALE[2].

major league *U.S.* **1.** In baseball, either of the two main groups of professional teams in the United States, the **National League** or the **American League. 2.** Any league of major importance in other professional sports.

major mode An arrangement of tones found in or characteristic of a major key or scale. See SCALE[2].

major orders See under HOLY ORDERS.

major penalty In hockey, a five-minute penalty.

major premise *Logic* The more general premise in a syllogism, the predicate of which is used as the predicate of the conclusion. See SYLLOGISM.

major scale See under SCALE[2].

major suit In bridge, either spades or hearts.

major term *Logic* The predicate of both the major premise and the conclusion of a syllogism. See SYLLOGISM.

ma·jus·cule (mə·jus′kyōōl) *adj.* **1.** Large, as either capital or uncial letters. **2.** Written in such letters. — *n.* A majuscule letter. Compare MINUSCULE. [< F < L *majuscula (littera),* fem. of *majusculus* somewhat larger, dim. of *major.* See MAJOR.] — **ma·jus′cu·lar** *adj.*

Ma·kas·sar (mə·kas′ər) A port city on SW Celebes, Indonesia; pop. 473,000 (1968): also *Macassar.* Also **Ma·kas′sar.**

make[1] (māk) *v.* **made, mak·ing** *v.t.* **1.** To bring about the existence of by shaping or combining of materials; produce; build; construct; fashion. **2.** To bring about; cause: Don't *make* trouble. **3.** To bring to some state or condition; cause to be: The wind *makes* him cold. **4.** To appoint or assign; put into a specified rank or position: They *made* him

MAJUSCULES

president. **5.** To form or create in the mind, as a plan, conclusion, or judgment. **6.** To compose (a poem). **7.** To entertain mentally, as doubts, scruples, etc.: *Make* no mistake about it. **8.** To understand the meaning or significance; interpret: with *of:* What do you *make* of this story? **9.** To utter or express, as for the record: to *make* an announcement. **10.** To represent as being or appearing: That hat *makes* you look old. **11.** To put forward or proffer: to *make* friendly overtures. **12.** To carry on; engage in: to *make* war. **13.** To earn or acquire: to *make* a fortune. **14.** To act in such a way as to win or gain: to *make* new friends. **15.** To amount to; add up to: Four quarts *make* a gallon. **16.** To bring the total to: That *makes* four attempts. **17.** To draw up, enact, or frame, as laws, wills, treaties, etc. **18.** To effect or form, as an agreement or arrangement. **19.** To estimate to be; reckon: He *made* the height twenty feet. **20.** To prepare or arrange for use: to *make* a bed. **21.** To induce or force; compel: The teacher *made* him leave the room. **22.** To be the essential element or determinant of: Nourishing food *makes* strong bodies. **23.** To afford or provide: Venison *makes* good eating. **24.** To become through development; have the essential qualities of: He will *make* a good soldier. **25.** To cause the success of: His last book *made* him. **26.** To perform (a specific physical movement): to *make* a gesture. **27.** To cover (distance) by traveling: to *make* three hundred miles before dark. **28.** To travel at the rate of: to *make* sixty miles per hour. **29.** To arrive at; reach: to *make* Boston. **30.** To arrive in time for: He barely *made* the train. **31.** In games and sports, to achieve as a score. **32.** *Electr.* To complete (a circuit). **33.** *U.S. Informal* To win a place or position, as on a team; also, to achieve the rank or status of: to *make* colonel. **34.** In bridge and some other card games: **a** To declare as trump. **b** To capture a trick with (a card). **c** To win (a bid). **d** To shuffle: to *make* the deck. **35.** *Slang* To have sexual intercourse with. — *v.i.* **36.** To cause something to assume a specified condition: to *make* sure. **37.** To act or behave in a certain manner: to *make* merry. **38.** To start, or appear to start, to do something: They *made* to go. **39.** To be made: It *makes* easily. **40.** To rise, as the tide. **41.** In bridge and other card games, to win a trick: said of a card. — **to make after** To pursue; follow. — **to make as if** (or **as though**) To act as if; pretend. — **to make away with 1.** To carry off; steal. **2.** To kill. **3.** To get rid of; destroy. — **to make believe** To pretend; feign. — **to make do** To get along with what is available, especially with an inferior substitute. — **to make for 1.** To go toward, especially rapidly. **2.** To rush at in order to attack. — **to make it** *Informal* To succeed in doing something. — **to make like** *U.S. Slang* To assume the character of; impersonate. — **to make off** To leave suddenly; run away. — **to make off with** To steal. — **to make or break** To bring about the success or failure of. — **to make out 1.** To see; discern. **2.** To comprehend; understand. **3.** To establish by evidence. **4.** To fill out or draw up, as a document, bank check, etc. **5.** To succeed. **6.** To do well enough; get by. **7.** *U.S. Slang* To do well in sexual conquest. — **to make over 1.** To renovate; refashion. **2.** To transfer title or possession of. — **to make shift** To make do. — **to make up 1.** To compose; compound, as a prescription. **2.** To be the parts of; constitute. **3.** To settle differences and become friendly again. **4.** To devise; invent; fabricate: to *make up* an answer. **5.** To supply what is lacking in. **6.** To compensate; atone. **7.** To settle; decide: to *make up* one's mind. **8.** *Printing* To arrange lines of type, illustrations, etc., for (a book, etc.). **9.** To put cosmetics on (the face). **10.** In education: **a** To repeat (an examination or course one has failed). **b** To take (an examination one has missed). — **to make up to** *Informal* To make a show of friendliness and affection toward; flatter. — **to make with** *U.S. Slang* To give, do, or show (something). — *n.* **1.** Style or type; brand: a good *make* of car. **2.** The manner in which something is made. **3.** The quantity produced; output. **4.** The act or process of making. **5.** The closing of an electric circuit. **6.** In bridge, the declaration. — **on the make** *Informal* **1.** Greedy for profit or advancement. **2.** Eager for amorous conquest. [OE *macian*]

make[2] (māk) *n. Obs.* **1.** An equal. **2.** A mate. [OE *gemaca*]

make-be·lieve (māk′bi·lēv′) *n.* **1.** Pretense; feigning; sham. Also **make′-be·lief′** (-lēf′). **2.** One who pretends or feigns. — *adj.* Pretended; feigned; unreal.

make·fast (māk′fast′, -fäst′) *n. Naut.* An object, such as a buoy, post, etc., to which a boat is tied up.

make-peace (māk′pēs′) *n. Rare* A peacemaker.

mak·er (mā′kər) *n.* **1.** One who or that which makes. **2.** *Law* One who signs a promissory note. **3.** *Archaic* A poet. In the following list, *maker* is used in combination with nouns to form self-explanatory words and phrases:

ballad maker	**boilermaker**	**cakemaker**
bedmaker	**bottlemaker**	**candymaker**
beermaker	**breadmaker**	**capmaker**
beltmaker	**button maker**	**cheese maker**

cigar maker	ice maker	phrasemaker
coffinmaker	lacemaker	playmaker
diemaker	lampmaker	sailmaker
dollmaker	map maker	tentmaker
glassmaker	mythmaker	tilemaker
harness maker	patternmaker	wine maker

Mak·er (māʹkər) *n.* God, the creator.

make-read·y (mākʹredʹē) *n. Printing* The operation of fixing and adjusting forms, plates, etc., on the press to insure clear, uniform impression.

make·shift (mākʹshiftʹ) *n.* A temporary means devised for an emergency; stopgap. — *adj.* Having the nature of or used as a temporary substitute: also **makeʹshiftʹy.**

make-up (mākʹupʹ) *n.* **1.** The arrangement or combination of parts or qualities of which anything is composed. **2.** The cosmetics, etc., used by an actor in a specific role; also, the art of applying or assuming them. **3.** Cosmetics used by women. **4.** Physical or mental constitution. **5.** *Printing* The arranging of composed type and cuts into pages, columns, or forms. **6.** *U.S. Informal* A special examination given to a student who has failed or been absent from the scheduled examination. Also **makeʹupʹ.**

make·weight (mākʹwātʹ) *n.* **1.** That which is placed on a scale to make the required weight. **2.** One who or that which is made use of to fill up a deficiency.

Ma·ke·yev·ka (mä·kāʹif·kə) A city in the Donbas, eastern Ukrainian S.S.R.; pop. 393,000 (1971).

Ma·khach·ka·la (mä·khächʹkä·läʹ) The capital of the Dagestan A.S.S.R., on the Caspian Sea; pop. 186,000 (1971).

mak·ing (māʹking) *n.* **1.** The act of one who or that which makes, fashions, or constructs. **2.** That which contributes to improvement or success: Discipline is the *making* of a soldier. **3.** *Usually pl.* The materials or qualities from which something can be made; constituents. **4.** A quantity made at one time; batch. **5.** Composition; structure. **6.** *pl. U.S. & Canadian* Paper and tobacco from which a cigarette can be made. — **in the making** In the process of being made.

In the following list, *making* is used in combination with nouns to form self-explanatory words and phrases:

ballad making	capmaking	lampmaking
bedmaking	cheese making	map making
beermaking	cigar making	mythmaking
beltmaking	coffinmaking	patternmaking
boilermaking	diemaking	phrasemaking
bottlemaking	dollmaking	playmaking
breadmaking	glassmaking	sailmaking
button making	harness making	tentmaking
cakemaking	ice making	tilemaking
candymaking	lacemaking	wine making

mal- *prefix* **1.** Bad; ill; evil; wrong. **2.** Defective; imperfect. **3.** Signifying simple negation, and forming words directly from Latin and mediately through French. [< F *mal-* < L *male-* < *malus* bad]

Many words containing the prefix *mal-* are self-explaining, the prefix simply adding the meaning "defective" or "bad":

maladaptation	malconformation	malfortune
maladministration	malconstruction	malinfluence
malalignment	malcreated	malinstruction
malapplication	malcultivation	malnourished
malappropriate	maldevelopment	malobservation
malaroma	maldigestion	malodor
malarrangement	maldirection	maloperation
malassimilation	maleducation	malplaced
malassociation	maleruption	malproportioned
malbehavior	malexecution	malshaped
malconceived	malfed	malvolition

Mal. **1.** Malachi. **2.** Malay; Malayan. **3.** Malta.

Mal·a·bar (malʹə·bär) A long, narrow coastal plain in the SW part of India, extending 450 miles in the States of Mysore and Kerala. Also **Malabar Coast.**

Ma·lac·ca (mə·lakʹə) *n.* The stem of a rattan palm (*Calamus rotang*), used for walking sticks, umbrella handles, etc. Also **Malacca cane.** [after *Malacca,* Malaya]

Ma·lac·ca (mə·lakʹə) A port city in western Malaya, on the **Strait of Malacca,** a channel separating Sumatra from the Malay Peninsula; pop. about 70,000.

ma·la·ceous (mə·lāʹshəs) *adj.* Of or belonging to a former family (*Malaceae*) of trees bearing pomes, as the apple, pear, quince, etc. [< NL < L *malum* apple < Gk. *mēlon*]

Mal·a·chi (malʹə·kī) Fifth-century B.C. Hebrew prophet. — *n.* A book of the Old Testament containing his prophecies. Also, in the Douai Bible, **Ma·la·chi·as** (mal·ə·kīʹəs).

mal·a·chite (malʹə·kīt) *n.* A green basic cupric carbonate, $Cu_2CO_3(OH)_2$, a common ore of copper. [< OF *melochite,* ult. < L *malache* mallow < Gk. *malachē*; so called because resembling mallow leaves in color]

malachite green A pigment made of malachite, having an intense bluish green color.

malaco- *combining form* **1.** Soft: *malacophyllous.* **2.** Mollusk: *malacology.* Also, before vowels, **malac-.** [< Gk. *malakos* soft]

mal·a·co·phyl·lous (mal·ə·kofʹi·ləs) *adj. Bot.* Having soft or fleshy leaves. [< MALACO- + -PHYLLOUS]

mal·a·col·o·gy (mal·ə·kolʹə·jē) *n.* The branch of zoology that treats of mollusks. [< MALACO- + -LOGY] — **malʹa·colʹo·gist** *n.*

mal·a·cos·tra·can (mal·ə·kosʹtrə·kən) *Zool. adj.* Of or pertaining to a division or subclass (*Malacostraca*) of crustaceans, including crabs, lobsters, etc. Also **malʹa·cosʹtra·cous.** — *n.* A malacostracan crustacean. [< NL < Gk. *malakostrakos* soft-shelled < *malakos* soft + *ostrakon* shell]

mal·ad·just·ed (mal·ə·jusʹtid) *adj.* **1.** Poorly adjusted. **2.** *Psychol.* Poorly adapted to one's environment through conflict between personal desires and external circumstances.

mal·ad·just·ment (mal·ə·justʹmənt) *n.* Poor adjustment.

mal·a·droit (mal·ə·droitʹ) *adj.* Lacking skill; clumsy; blundering. — **Syn.** See AWKWARD. [< F < *mal-* mal- + *adroit* clever] — **mal·a·droitʹly** *adv.* — **mal·a·droitʹness** *n.*

mal·a·dy (malʹə·dē) *n. pl.* **·dies 1.** A disease, especially when chronic or deep-seated; sickness; illness. **2.** Any disordered or disturbed condition: a *malady* of the soul. — **Syn.** See DISEASE. [< OF *maladie* < LL *male habitus* < L *male* ill + *habitus,* pp. of *habere* to have]

ma·la fi·de (māʹlə fīʹdē) In bad faith; fraudulent. [< L]

Mál·a·ga (malʹə·gə, *Sp.* mäʹlä·gä) A port city in southern Spain, on the Mediterranean; pop. 340,600 (est. 1967).

Mal·a·ga (malʹə·gə) *n.* **1.** A rich, sweet white wine made in Málaga, Spain. **2.** A white, sweet grape of the muscat variety, grown in Spain and California.

Mal·a·gas·y (mal·ə·gasʹē) *n. pl.* **·gas·y** or **·gas·ies 1.** A native or citizen of Madagascar. **2.** The Indonesian language of Madagascar. — *adj.* Of or pertaining to Madagascar, its inhabitants, or their language.

Malagasy Republic Former name of the Republic of MADAGASCAR.

mal·aise (mal·āzʹ, *Fr.* mà·lezʹ) *n.* A feeling of vague discomfort or lassitude, sometimes indicating the beginning of an illness. [< F < *mal* ill + *aise.* See EASE.]

ma·la·mute (māʹlə·myoot, malʹə-) *n. U.S. & Canadian* A large Alaskan sled dog with a thick, long coat: also spelled *malemute, malemiut.* [Orig. name of an Innuit tribe, alter. of Eskimo *Mahlemut* < *Mahle,* the tribe's name + *mut* village]

mal·an·ders (malʹən·derz) *n.pl. Vet.* Sores on a horse's foreleg: also spelled *mallenders.* [< OF *malandre* < L *malandria*]

mal·a·pert (malʹə·pûrt) *Archaic adj.* Impudent; forward; bold. — *n.* An impudent, bold person. [< OF < *mal-* mal- + *apert, espert* clever, able < L *expertus.* See EXPERT.] — **malʹa·pertʹly** *adv.* — **malʹa·pertʹness** *n.*

Mal·a·prop (malʹə·prop), **Mrs.** A character in Sheridan's play *The Rivals* (1775), who uses words in an absurdly inappropriate manner. [< MALAPROPOS]

mal·a·prop·ism (malʹə·prop·izʹəm) *n.* **1.** The absurd misuse of words. **2.** An instance of this. [after Mrs. *Malaprop*] — **malʹa·propʹi·an** (-propʹē·ən, -prōʹpē-) *adj.*

mal·ap·ro·pos (mal·apʹrə·pōʹ) *adj.* Out of place; not appropriate. — *adv.* Inappropriately. [< F *mal à propos* not to the point < *mal* ill + *à* to + *propos* purpose]

ma·lar (māʹlər) *Anat. adj.* Of or pertaining to the cheekbone. — *n.* The cheekbone: also **malar bone.** [< NL *malaris* < L *mala* jaw, cheek]

Mäl·ar (melʹär) A lake in eastern Sweden; 440 sq. mi. *Swedish* **Mäl·ar·en** (melʹär-ən).

ma·lar·i·a (mə·lârʹē·ə) *n.* **1.** *Pathol.* Any of several forms of a disease caused by certain species of a parasitic protozoan (genus *Plasmodium*) introduced into the blood by the bite of the infected female anopheles mosquito and characterized by intermittent paroxysms of chills, fever, and profuse sweating: also called *paludism, swamp fever.* **2.** Foul or noxious vapors; miasma. [< Ital. *mal' aria, mala aria,* lit., bad air] — **ma·larʹi·al, ma·larʹi·an, ma·larʹi·ous** *adj.*

ma·lar·key (mə·lärʹkē) *n. U.S. Slang* Insincere or senseless talk; bunk. Also **ma·larʹky.** [Origin unknown]

Mal·a·spi·na (mal·ə·spēʹnə) A glacier in SE Alaska, on the Gulf of Alaska south of Mt. St. Elias, 1,500 square miles in extent.

mal·ate (malʹāt, māʹlāt) *n. Chem.* A salt or ester of malic acid. [< MAL(IC) + -ATE³]

Ma·la·wi (mäʹlä·wē) An independent member of the Commonwealth of Nations in SE Africa; 49,177 sq. mi.; pop. 5,040,000 (est.1975); capital, Lilongwe: formerly *Nyasaland.*

Ma·lay (māʹlā, mə·lāʹ) *n.* **1.** A member of a people dominant in Malaysia, and a Malayan. **2.** The language spoken on the Malay Peninsula and now adopted as the official language of Indonesia, belonging to the Indonesian subfamily of Austronesian languages. **3.** A variety of domestic fowl. — *adj.* Of or pertaining to the Malays; Malayan. Abbr. *Mal.*

Ma·lay·a (mə·lāʹə) A former independent Federation within the British Commonwealth, consisting of nine states on the Malay Peninsula; about 50,700 sq. mi.: now **West Malaysia.** See maps of SINGAPORE, THAILAND.

Mal·a·ya·lam (mal·ə·yäʹləm) *n.* The language of the Malabar coast, India, related to Tamil, and belonging to the Dravidian family of languages.

Ma·lay·an (mə·lāʹən) *adj.* **1.** Malay. **2.** Indonesian. — *n.* **1.** A Malay (def. 1). **2.** An Indonesian. **3.** The Indonesian subfamily of Austronesian languages. Abbr. *Mal.*

Malayan bear The honey bear (def. 1).

Malay Archipelago An island group in the Indian and Pacific oceans SE of Asia, including Java, Borneo, Sumatra, Celebes, Timor, Nusa Tenggara, and the Philippines; about 773,000 sq. mi.: also the *East Indies Malaysia.*

Ma·lay·o-Pol·y·ne·sian (mə·lā′ō·pol′ə·nē′zhən, -shən) *adj.* & *n.* Austronesian. [< MALAY + -o- + POLYNESIAN]

Malay Peninsula The southernmost peninsula of Asia, including the Federation of Malaya, Singapore, and part of Thailand.

Ma·lay·sia (mə·lā′zhə, -shə) **1.** An independent Federation within the British Commonwealth of Nations, consisting of Malaya (now **West Malaysia**) and Sarawak and Sabah in northern Borneo (together forming **East Malaysia**); 128,429 sq. mi.; pop. 11,196,000 (est. 1973); capital, Kuala Lumpur. See map of INDONESIA. See MALAY ARCHIPELAGO. — **Ma·lay′sian** *adj.* & *n.*

Mal·colm X (mal′kəm eks) Name adopted by Malcolm Little, 1925-65, U.S. political and religious leader, active in the Black Muslim movement; assassinated.

mal·con·tent (mal′kən·tent) *adj.* Discontented or dissatisfied, especially with a government or economic system. — *n.* One who is malcontent. [< OF < *mal-* + *content*. See MAL- and CONTENT.]

mal de mer (mȧl′də mâr′) *French* Seasickness.

Mal·dive Islands (mal′dīv) An archipelago in the Indian Ocean, comprising an independent Republic; 115 sq. mi.; pop. 114,000 (est. 1973); capital, Malé. Officially **Maldives.**

mal du pays (mȧl′ dü pā·ē′) *French* Homesickness.

male (māl) *adj.* **1.** Of or belonging to the sex that begets young or produces sperm. **2.** Of, characteristic of, or suitable for members of this sex; masculine. **3.** Made up of men or boys: a *male* chorus. **4.** *Bot.* **a** Designating a plant having stamens but no pistil. **b** Adapted to fertilize, but not to produce fruit, as stamens. **5.** *Mech.* Denoting a part, as in some electric plugs, etc., designed to be inserted into a correlated slot or bore known as *female*. — **Syn.** See MASCULINE. — *n.* **1.** A male person or animal. **2.** *Bot.* A plant with only staminate flowers. Abbr. *M., m.* [< OF *male, mascle* < L *masculus.* Doublet of MASCULINE.] — **male′ness** *n.*

Male·branche (mȧl′brän̈sh′), **Nicolas de,** 1638-1715, French philosopher.

mal·e·dict (mal′ə·dikt) *Archaic adj.* Accursed; detestable. — *v.t.* To curse. [< L *maledictus.* See MALEDICTION.]

mal·e·dic·tion (mal′ə·dik′shən) *n.* **1.** The pronouncing of a curse against someone: opposed to *benediction.* **2.** Slander; calumny. — **Syn.** See CURSE. [< L *maledictio, -onis* < *maledictus,* pp. of *maledicere* < *male* ill + *dicere* to speak] — **mal′e·dic′to·ry** (-tər·ē) *adj.*

mal·e·fac·tor (mal′ə·fak′tər) *n.* **1.** One who commits a crime; criminal. **2.** An evildoer. [< L < *malefactus,* pp. of *malefacere* < *male* ill + *facere* to do] — **mal′e·fac′tion** *n.* — **mal′e·fac′tress** (-tris) *n.fem.*

male fern A fern (*Dryopteris filixmas*) yielding an oleoresin used in medicine to poison tapeworms.

ma·lef·ic (mə·lef′ik) *adj.* Producing or causing evil or disaster; baleful. [< L *maleficus* < *malefacere.* See MALEFACTOR.]

ma·lef·i·cent (mə·lef′ə·sənt) *adj.* Causing or doing evil or mischief; harmful: opposed to *beneficent.* [< L *maleficus.* See MALEFIC.]

ma·le·ic acid (mə·lē′ik) *Chem.* A white, crystalline, astringent acid, $C_4H_4O_4$, used in textile dyeing and finishing. [< F *maléique* < *malique.* See MALIC.]

ma·le·mute (mä′lə·myo͞ot, mal′ə-) See MALAMUTE. Also **ma′le·miut.**

Mal·en·kov (mal′ən·kôv, *Russ.* mä′lyin·kôf), **Georgi Maximilianovich,** born 1902, Soviet statesman; premier 1953-55.

mal·en·ten·du (mȧl·än̈·tän̈·dü′) *n. French* Misunderstanding; misconception.

ma·lev·o·lent (mə·lev′ə·lənt) *adj.* **1.** Wishing evil toward others; malicious; ill-disposed. **2.** In astrology, ill-omened. — **Syn.** See MALICIOUS. [< OF < L *malevolens, -entis* < *male* ill + *volens, -entis,* ppr. of *velle* to wish, will] — **ma·lev′o·lence** *n.* — **ma·lev′o·lent·ly** *adv.*

mal·fea·sance (mal·fē′zəns) *n. Law* The performance of some act that is wrongful or that one has specifically contracted not to perform: said usually of official misconduct. Compare MISFEASANCE, NONFEASANCE. [< AF *malfaisance* < OF *malfaisant* < *mal* ill + *faisant,* ppr. of *faire* to do < L *malus* bad + *facere* to do] — **mal·fea′sant** *adj.* & *n.*

mal·for·ma·tion (mal′fôr·mā′shən) *n.* Defective structure, especially in an organism. [< MAL- + FORMATION]

mal·formed (mal·fôrmd′) *adj.* Badly formed; deformed.

mal·func·tion (mal·fungk′shən) *n.* **1.** Failure to function. **2.** Defective functioning. — *v.i.* **1.** To fail to function. **2.** To function improperly. [< MAL- + FUNCTION]

Mal·gache (mȧl·gȧsh′) *n.* & *adj. French* Madagascan.

mal·gré (mȧl·grā′) *prep. French* In spite of.

malgré lui (lwē) *French* In spite of himself.

Mal·herbe (mȧl·erb′), **François de,** 1555-1628, French poet and critic.

Ma·li (mä′lē), **Republic of** A Republic in western Africa; 464,872 sq. mi.; pop. 5,361,000 (est. 1973); capital, Bamako: formerly *French Sudan, Sudanese Republic. French République du Mali.* See map of GULF OF GUINEA.

mal·ic (mal′ik, mā′lik) *adj.* Of, pertaining to, or made from apples. [< F *malique* < L *malum* apple]

malic acid *Chem.* A deliquescent crystalline acid, $C_4H_6O_5$, with a pleasant taste, contained in the juice of many fruits.

mal·ice (mal′is) *n.* **1.** An intention or desire to injure another; specific ill will; spite. **2.** *Law* A wilfully formed design to do another an injury: also **malice aforethought, malice prepense.** [< OF < L *malitia* < *malus* evil]

ma·li·cious (mə·lish′əs) *adj.* **1.** Revealing or characterized by malice; spiteful. **2.** *Law* Resulting from or prompted by malice. [< OF *malicius* < L *malitiosus* < *malitia.* See MALICE.] — **ma·li′cious·ly** *adv.* — **ma·li′cious·ness** *n.* — **Syn.** *Malicious, malevolent, malign,* and *malignant* mean tending to produce or inflict evil. *Malicious* is chiefly applied to actions and motives, and *malevolent* to personal disposition. *Malevolent* also has a more sinister connotation; we speak of the *malicious* destruction of another's property, but of a *malevolent* enemy. The influence of a thing or of a person may be described as *malign* if it tends to destroy or corrupt; *malignant* has much the same meaning and is frequently used of pathological conditions.

ma·lign (mə·līn′) *v.t.* To speak slander of; defame; traduce. — **Syn.** See ASPERSE. — *adj.* **1.** Having an evil disposition toward others; ill-disposed; malevolent. **2.** Tending to injure; pernicious. — **Syn.** See MALICIOUS. [< OF *malignier, maliner* to plot, deceive < LL *malignare* to contrive maliciously < L *malignus* ill-disposed < *malus* evil] — **ma·lign′ly** *adv.* — **ma·lign′er** *n.*

ma·lig·nan·cy (mə·lig′nən·sē) *n. pl.* **·cies 1.** The state of being malignant. **2.** A malignant tumor. Also **ma·lig′nance.**

ma·lig·nant (mə·lig′nənt) *adj.* **1.** *Pathol.* **a** Of tumors, rapidly growing and liable to metastasize: opposed to *benign.* **b** Becoming progressively worse; virulent. **2.** Tending to do great harm; deleterious. **3.** Having an evil disposition toward others; malign; malevolent. — **Syn.** See MALICIOUS. — *n.* A malcontent. — **ma·lig′nant·ly** *adv.*

ma·lig·ni·ty (mə·lig′nə·tē) *n. pl.* **·ties 1.** The state or character of being malign; intense ill will. **2.** A harmful tendency; virulence. **3.** *Often pl.* Something evil.

ma·li·hi·ni (mä′lə·hē′nē) *n.* A newcomer to Hawaii. [< Hawaiian]

ma·lines (mə·lēn′, *Fr.* mȧ·lēn′) *n.* **1.** Mechlin lace. **2.** A gauzelike veiling for trimming hats, etc.: also **ma·line′.** [< F, after *Malines* Mechlin]

Ma·lines (mȧ·lēn′) The French name for MECHLIN.

ma·lin·ger (mə·ling′gər) *v.i.* To pretend sickness so as to avoid work or duty. [< F *malingre* sickly, ? < *mal* ill (< L *malus*) + OF *heingre* lean] — **ma·lin′ger·er** *n.*

mal·i·son (mal′ə·zən, -sən) *n. Archaic* A curse. [< OF *maleison* < L *maledictio.* See MALEDICTION.]

mall¹ (môl, mal) See MAUL.

mall² (môl, mal, mel) *n.* **1.** A promenade or walk, usually public and often shaded. **2.** *U.S. & Canadian* A street of shops closed off to vehicles and enhanced with trees, benches, etc. **3.** The game of pall-mall or an alley in which it was played. [Short for PALL-MALL]

mal·lard (mal′ərd) *n. pl.* **·lards** or **·lard 1.** A common wild duck (*Anas platyrhynchos*), the ancestor of the domestic breeds, having brownish plumage, and, in the male, a bright green head. **2.** The male or drake of this duck. [< OF *malart* < *masle.* See MALE.]

Mal·lar·mé (mȧ·lȧr·mā′), **Stéphane,** 1842-1898, French poet.

mal·le·a·ble (mal′ē·ə·bəl) *adj.* **1.** Capable of being hammered or rolled out without breaking: said especially of metals. **2.** Capable of being shaped or molded; flexible; pliable. — **Syn.** See PLASTIC. [< OF < L *malleare* to hammer < *malleus* hammer] — **mal′le·a·bil′i·ty, mal′le·a·ble·ness** *n.*

malleable iron Cast iron made tough and malleable by gradual heating and slow cooling. Also **malleable cast iron.**

mal·lee (mal′ē) *n.* **1.** Any one of several scrubby species of eucalyptus of South Australia and Victoria; especially, *Eucalyptus dumosa* and *E. oleosa.* **2.** The dense brushwood composed of such trees. [< native Australian name]

mal·le·muck (mal′ə·muk) *n.* Any of several sea birds, as the fulmar. [< Du. *mallemok* < *mal* foolish + *mok* gull]

mal·len·ders (mal′ən·dərz) See MALANDERS.

mal·le·o·lus (mə·lē′ə·ləs) *n. pl.* **·li** (-ə·lī) *Anat.* The rounded bone process of the tibia or fibula on each side of the ankle. [< L, dim. of *malleus* hammer] — **mal·le′o·lar** *adj.*

MALLARD

(To 28 inches long; wing-spread 40 inches)

MALAY PENINSULA

mal·let (mal′it) *n* **1.** A hammer having a head of wood, rubber, etc. **2.** A long-handled wooden hammer used in the game of croquet. **3.** A wooden-headed flexible stick used in the game of polo. [< OF *maillet*, dim. of *mail*. See MAUL.]

mal·le·us (mal′ē·əs) *n*. *pl.* **·le·i** (-lē·ī) *Anat.* The club-shaped largest ossicle of the middle ear, articulating with the incus: also called *hammer*. For illustration see EAR. [< L, hammer]

Mal·lor·ca (mä·lyôr′kä) The Spanish name for MAJORCA.

mal·low (mal′ō) *n.* **1.** Any of a genus (*Malva*) of herbs having roundish leaves, pale pink flowers, and disklike fruit; especially, the North American **dwarf** or **running mallow** (*M. rotundifolia*). **2.** Any other plant of the same family (*Malvaceae*), as the abutilon, the cotton plant, and the hibiscus. [OE *mealuwe* < L *malva*. Doublet of MAUVE.]

mallow rose Any of several species of hibiscus having pink or rose-colored flowers, as *Hibiscus moscheutos*.

malm (mäm) *n. Brit. Dial.* A soft, friable limestone; also, the whitish loam resulting from its disintegration. [OE *mealm(stān)* sandstone or limestone] — **mal′my** *adj.*

Mal·mé·dy (mäl·mā·dē′) A district on the Belgian-German frontier; awarded to Belgium under the Versailles Treaty.

Malmes·bur·y (mämz′bər·ē), **William of,** 1095?–1143?, English monk and historian.

Mal·mö (mal′mō, *Sw.* mäl′mœ) A port city in SW Sweden; pop. 254,300 (est. 1968).

malm·sey (mäm′zē) *n. pl.* **·seys** A rich, sweet wine made in the Canary Islands, Madeira, etc.; also, the grape used for this wine. [< Med.L *malmasia* < Gk. *Monembasia* Monemvasia, Greece, a town formerly exporting wine]

mal·nu·tri·tion (mal′nōō·trish′ən, -nyōō-) *n.* Faulty or inadequate nutrition; undernourishment.

mal·oc·clu·sion (mal′ə·klōō′zhən) *n. Dent.* Faulty meeting or closing, as of the upper and lower teeth. [< MAL- + OCCLUSION]

mal·o·dor·ous (mal·ō′dər·əs) *adj.* Having a disagreeable smell. — **mal·o′dor·ous·ly** *adv.* — **mal·o′dor·ous·ness** *n.*

Ma·lone (mə·lōn′), **Edmond,** 1741–1812, Irish Shakespearean scholar. — **Kemp,** 1889–1971, U.S. philologist.

ma·lon·ic acid (mə·lon′ik, -lō′nik) *Chem.* A white crystalline acid, CH₂(CO₂H)₂, obtained chiefly by oxidizing malic acid. [< F *malonique*, alter. of *malique*. See MALIC.]

mal·o·nyl·u·re·a (mal′ə·nil·yŏŏr′ē·ə) *n. Chem.* Barbituric acid. [< MALON(IC) + -YL + UREA]

Mal·o·ry (mal′ər·ē), **Sir Thomas,** died 1470?, English author and translator.

Mal·pi·ghi (mäl·pē′gē), **Marcello,** 1628–94, Italian anatomist. — **Mal·pigh′i·an** (-pig′ē·ən) *adj.*

mal·pigh·i·a·ceous (mal·pig′ē·ā′shəs) *adj. Bot.* Of or pertaining to a family (*Malpighiaceae*) of tropical trees or shrubs. [< NL *Malpighiaceae*, family name < *Malpighia*, genus name, after Marcello *Malpighi*]

Malpighian body *Anat.* Any of a number of small rounded bodies, consisting of a tuft of blood vessels, at the commencement of the uriniferous tubules in the kidney. Also **Malpighian capsule** or **corpuscle.** [after Marcello *Malpighi*]

Malpighian layer *Anat.* The deeper, softer layer of the epidermis.

Malpighian tube *Entomol.* One of the tubular structures composing the excretory organ of an insect. Also **Malpighian vessel.**

mal·po·si·tion (mal′pə·zish′ən) *n. Pathol.* A wrong or faulty position, as of a fetus. — **mal·posed** (-pōzd′) *adj.*

mal·prac·tice (mal·prak′tis) *n.* **1.** In medicine or surgery, the improper, injurious, or negligent treatment of a patient. **2.** Improper or immoral conduct in a professional or public position. Also **mal·prax′is** (-prak′sis). — **mal·prac·ti·tion·er** (mal′prak·tish′ən·ər) *n.*

Mal·raux (mȧl·rō′), **André,** 1901–1976, French novelist, art critic, and politician: full name **Georges André Malraux.**

malt (môlt) *n.* **1.** Grain, usually barley, germinated by soaking and then kiln-dried. **2.** Liquor made with malt, as beer, ale, whisky, etc. — *v.t.* **1.** To cause (grain) to become malt. **2.** To treat or combine with malt or malt extract. — *v.i.* **3.** To become malt. **4.** To change grain into malt. [OE *mealt*. Akin to MELT.]

Mal·ta (môl′tə) An independent member of the Commonwealth of Nations in the Mediterranean, comprising the islands of **Malta** (95 sq. mi., pop. 323,000: ancient *Melita*), Gozo, Comino, and two islets; 122 sq. mi.; pop. 324,350 (est. 1973); capital, Valletta. Also **Maltese Islands.**

Malta fever Undulant fever (which see).

mal·tase (môl′tās) *n. Biochem.* A digestive enzyme that hydrolyzes maltose into glucose. [< MALT + -ASE]

malt·ed milk (môl′tid) **1.** A beverage made of milk, a powder of malted cereals and dried milk, and usually ice cream: also **malt′ed.** **2.** The powder used in this beverage.

Mal·tese (môl·tēz′, -tēs′) *adj.* **1.** Of or pertaining to Malta, its inhabitants, or their language. **2.** Of or pertaining to the Hospitalers on Malta. — *n. pl.* **·tese 1.** A native or inhabitant of Malta. **2.** The language of Malta, a North Arabic dialect with elements of Italian. **3.** A Maltese cat or dog.

Maltese cat A cat with long, silky, bluish gray hair.

Maltese cross An eight-pointed cross formed by four arrowheads joining at their points, used as a badge by the Hospitalers on Malta. For illustration see CROSS.

Maltese dog A breed of toy dog with long, white hair, originally developed in Malta.

malt extract Wort (def. 2).

mal·tha (mal′thə) *n.* A dark and viscid bitumen. [< L < Gk., mixture of wax and pitch]

Mal·thus (mal′thəs, môl′-), **Thomas Robert,** 1766–1834, English political economist.

Mal·thu·si·an (mal·thōō′zē·ən, môl′-, -zhən) *adj.* Of or pertaining to the theory of T. R. Malthus that population tends to outrun its means of support, and will be checked by disaster unless restricted by sexual restraint. — *n.* A believer in the theories of Malthus. — **Mal·thu′si·an·ism** *n.*

malt liquor Liquor made from malt by fermentation.

malt·ose (môl′tōs) *n. Biochem.* A white, dextrorotatory, crystalline sugar, C₁₂H₂₂O₁₁·H₂O, formed by the action of diastase on starch. Also **malt sugar.** [< MALT + -OSE²]

mal·treat (mal·trēt′) *v.t.* To treat badly, roughly, or unkindly; abuse. [< F *maltraiter* < *mal-* mal- + *traiter*. See MAL- and TREAT.] — **mal·treat′ment** *n.*

malt·ster (môlt′stər) *n.* A maker of or dealer in malt.

malt·y (môl′tē) *adj.* **malt·i·er, malt·i·est** Of, resembling, or containing malt.

mal·va·ceous (mal·vā′shəs) *adj.* Of or pertaining to the mallow family (*Malvaceae*) of plants. [< LL *malvaceus* < *malva* mallow]

mal·va·si·a (mal′və·sē′ə) *n.* **1.** The grape used to make malmsey. **2.** Malmsey wine. [< Ital. *Malvasia*, alter. of Gk. *Monembasia*. See MALMSEY.] — **mal′va·si′an** *adj.*

Mal·vern Hill (mal′vərn) A plateau near Richmond, Virginia; scene of a Confederate defeat in the Civil War, 1862.

Malvern Hills A range of hills in western England, in Hereford and Worcester; highest point Worcestershire Beacon, 1,395 ft.

mal·ver·sa·tion (mal′vər·sā′shən) *n. Rare* Misconduct in a public office. [< MF *malverser* < L *male versari* < *male* wrongly + *versari* to behave, busy oneself]

mal·voi·sie (mal′voi·zē, -və-) *n.* Malmsey, the wine and the grape. [< OF *malvesia* < Ital. *malvasia*. See MALVASIA.]

ma·ma (mä′mə, mə·mä′) *n.* Mother: used familiarly. Also **mamma.** [Repetition of infantile syllable *ma*]

mam·ba (mäm′bə) *n.* Any of various long and venomous tree snakes (genus *Dendraspis*) of southern Africa; especially, *D. angusticeps*, having a black and a green phase. [< Zulu *in-amba*]

mam·bo (mäm′bō) *n. pl.* **·bos** A dance resembling the rumba; also the syncopated four-beat music for this dance — *v.i.* To dance the mambo. [< Haitian Creole]

Mam·e·luke (mam′ə·lōōk) *n.* A member of a military caste, originally composed of slaves, that dominated Egypt from 1254 to 1811. Also **Mam′a·luke.** [< F *mameluk* < Arabic *mamlūk* a slave, passive of *malaka* to possess]

ma·mey (mä·mā′, -mē′) *n. pl.* **·meys** or **·mey·es** (-mā′ās) **1.** A tropical American tree (*Mammea americana*) bearing edible yellow fruit like the pomelo in size and shape: also **mamey de Santo Domingo. 2.** A fruit of this tree: also **mamey apple, mamey colorado, mamey sapota. 3.** The marmalade tree. Also **ma·mie′, mam·mee′, mam·mey′.** [< Sp. < Taino]

mam·ma¹ (mam′ə) *n. pl.* **·mae** (-mē) In mammals, the organ that secretes milk; a breast; udder. [< L, breast]

mam·ma² (mä′mə) *n.* Mama.

mam·mal (mam′əl) *n.* Any of a class (*Mammalia*) of vertebrates whose females have mammae to nourish their young, including man, all warm-blooded quadrupeds, seals, etc. [< NL < LL *mammalis* of the breast < L *mamma* breast] — **mam·ma·li·an** (ma·mā′lē·ən, -māl′yən) *adj. & n.*

mam·mal·o·gy (ma·mal′ə·jē) *n.* The branch of zoology that treats of mammals. [< MAMMAL + -LOGY] — **mam·ma·log·i·cal** (mam′ə·loj′i·kəl) *adj.* — **mam·mal′o·gist** *n.*

mam·ma·ry (mam′ər·ē) *adj.* Of, pertaining to, or of the nature of a mamma or breast, or the mammae.

mam·ma·to·cu·mu·lus (ma·mā′tō·kyōō′myə·ləs) *n. pl.* **-li** (-lī) *Meteorol.* Cumulonimbus mammatus (which see).

mam·ma·tus (ma·mā′təs) *n. Meteorol.* A cloud form having pouchlike protuberances along the lower surface. [< L < *mamma* breast]

mam·met (mam′it) *n.* A maumet.

mam·mie (mam′ē) *n.* See MAMMY.

mam·mif·er·ous (ma·mif′ər·əs) *adj.* Having mammae or breasts; mammalian. [< MAMM(A) + -FEROUS]

mam·mil·la (ma·mil′ə) *n. pl.* **·mil·lae** (-mil′ē) *Anat.* **1.** A nipple or teat. **2.** Any nipplelike or teat-shaped protuberance. [< L *mamilla, mammilla*, dim. of *mamma* breast]

mam·mil·lar·y (mam′ə·ler′ē) *adj.* **1.** Of, pertaining to, or resembling a mammilla or a mamma. **2.** Studded with or composed of breast-shaped or rounded protuberances.

mam·mil·late (mam′ə·lāt) *adj.* **1.** Having a mammilla, mammillae, or nipplelike processes. **2.** Shaped like a nipple.

Also **mam′mil·lat′ed.** [< MAMMILL(A) + -ATE[1]] — **mam′-mil·a′tion** n.

mam·mi·tis (mə·mī′tis) n. Pathol. Mastitis. [< MAMM(A) + -ITIS]

mam·mock (mam′ək) Archaic n. A fragment. — v.t. To tear; shred. [< dial. E; ult. origin uncertain.]

mam·mon (mam′ən) n. **1.** Riches regarded as an evil influence and ignoble goal. **2.** Worldliness; avarice. Matt. vi 24; Luke xvi 9. [< LL < Gk. mammōnas < Aramaic māmōnā riches] — **mam′mon·ish** adj.

Mam·mon (mam′ən) The personification of riches or greed.

mam·mon·ism (mam′ən·iz′əm) n. Devotion to the pursuit of wealth. — **mam′mon·ist, mam′mon·ite** n. — **mam′mon·is′tic** adj.

mam·moth (mam′əth) n. Paleontol. A large, once very abundant, now extinct elephant (genus Mammuthus) related to the Indian elephant; especially, the **woolly mammoth** (M. primigenius), known from frozen cadavers, the **Columbian mammoth** (M. columbi) of the United States, and the huge **imperial mammoth** (M. imperator) that stood 14 feet high. — adj. Huge; gigantic. [< Russian mammot, mamant]

WOOLLY MAMMOTH
(9 to 12 feet high at shoulder)

Mammoth Cave National Park A national park in west central Kentucky, comprising a series of underground caverns; 79 sq. mi.

mam·my (mam′ē) n. pl. **·mies 1.** Mother: used familiarly. **2.** Southern U.S. A Negro nurse or foster mother of white children. Also spelled mammie. [Dim. of MAMA]

Ma·mo·ré (mä′mō·rā′) A river in Bolivia, flowing about 1,200 miles, generally north, to the Madeira.

man (man) n. pl. **men** (men) **1.** An adult male human being. **2.** Human beings collectively; the human race; mankind. **3.** Anthropol. Any of a genus (Homo, family Hominidae) of mammals representing the highest stage in the evolution of the primates, characterized by erect posture, exceptional development of the brain, and the power of articulate speech. H. sapiens is the only living species. **4.** A person or individual; human being: The style is the man. **5.** One having pronounced masculine traits and virtues; a genuine male. **6.** Theol. A material creature having an immortal soul, distinct from angels, etc., that are entirely spiritual and immaterial, and from other animals that are entirely material. **7.** An adult male subordinate or employee; as: **a** A worker in a factory, office, etc. **b** A servant, especially a valet. c Obs. A liegeman; vassal. **8.** An enlisted soldier, sailor, etc., in the armed forces. **9.** A husband or lover. **10.** A member of a team. **11.** You; you there: used in direct address to males to express impatience, encouragement, contempt, etc., and sometimes as a meaningless expletive. **12.** A piece or counter used in certain games, as chess, checkers, etc. **13.** Naut. A ship or vessel: used in combination: man-of-war. **14.** In Christian Science, the compound idea of infinite Spirit. — **as one man** Unanimously. — **to a man** Unanimously. — **to be one's own man** To be independent. — **the man** Slang A white man, used especially by Negroes. — interj. Slang An exclamation of surprise, pleasure, etc.: Man, what a show! — adj. Male. — v.t. **manned, man·ning 1.** To supply with men, as for work, defense, etc.: to man the fort. **2.** To take stations on, at, or in for work, defense, etc.: Man the pumps! **3.** In falconry, to accustom (a hawk) to the presence or handling of men. [OE monn, mann. ? Akin to L mens mind.]

Man may appear as a combining form in many self-explanatory compounds, where it is an object or means "by man":

man-abhorring	man-devised	manhunter
man-baiting	man-eating	manhunting
man-catching	man-enslaved	mankiller
man-chasing	man-fearing	mankilling
man-created	man-grown	manmade
man-degrading	man-hater	man-ridden
man-destroyer	man-hating	manstealing
man-destroying	manhunt	man-taught

Man (man), **Isle of** One of the British Isles in the Irish Sea; 227 sq. mi.; pop. 50,000 (1969); capital, Douglas: ancient Mona: a native of the island is a Manxman. Abbr. I.M.

Man. 1. Manila (paper). **2.** Manitoba.

ma·na (mä′nə) n. Anthropol. A pervasive supernatural power that may inhere in persons or things. [< Polynesian]

man about town A man who frequents night clubs, theaters, etc.

man·a·cle (man′ə·kəl) n. **1.** Usually pl. A device for confining or restraining the hands; shackle; handcuff. **2.** Anything that constrains or fetters. — v.t. **·cled, ·cling 1.** To put manacles on. **2.** To constrain or hamper. [< OF manicle < L manicula, dim. of manus hand]

man·age (man′ij) v. **·aged, ·ag·ing** v.t. **1.** To direct or control the affairs or interests of; be manager of; administer: to manage a hotel. **2.** To be able; arrange; contrive: usually with an infinitive as object: He managed to stay. **3.** To control or guide the operation or performance of: to manage a campaign. **4.** To cause to do one's bidding; control: to manage a crowd. **5.** To handle or wield; use, as a weapon, one's language, etc. **6.** Archaic To train and handle (a horse). — v.i. **7.** To direct or control business, affairs, etc.; be a manager. **8.** To be able to continue or thrive; make out; get by: They managed despite low pay. — n. Obs. **1.** Management. **2.** Behavior. **3.** Manège. [< Ital. maneggiare to handle, train horses, ult. < L manus hand]

man·age·a·ble (man′ij·ə·bəl) adj. Capable of being managed. — **man′age·a·bil′i·ty, man′age·a·ble·ness** n. — **man′age·a·bly** adv.

managed currency A monetary system in which the amount in circulation is regulated in an attempt to control prices, credit, etc.

man·age·ment (man′ij·mənt) n. **1.** The act, art, or practice of managing; administration. **2.** The person or persons who manage a business, institution, etc.; the administration. **3.** Managers collectively, especially in their relations with labor unions. **4.** The skillful use of means; ingenuity.

man·ag·er (man′ij·ər) n. **1.** One who manages; especially, one who directs or controls an enterprise, business, institution, etc.; director. **2.** One who is skilled in managing, especially business affairs. Abbr. Mgr. — **man′ag·er·ship** n.

man·ag·er·ess (man′ij·ər·is, -ij·ris; Brit. man′ij·ər·es′) n. Chiefly Brit. A female manager.

man·a·ge·ri·al (man′ə·jir′ē·əl) adj. Of or pertaining to a manager or management. — **man′a·ge′ri·al·ly** adv.

Ma·na·gua (mä·nä′gwä) The capital of Nicaragua, in the SW part on **Lake Managua** (390 sq. mi.); pop. 318,000 (est. 1970); city destroyed by an earthquake, 1972; being rebuilt.

man·a·kin (man′ə·kin) n. **1.** Any of numerous small tropical American birds (family Pipridae) of brilliant plumage. **2.** See MANIKIN. [Orig. var. of MANIKIN]

ma·ña·na (mä·nyä′nä) n. & adv. Spanish Tomorrow; some other time.

Ma·nas·sas (mə·nas′əs) A town in NE Virginia; scene of two battles of Bull Run in the Civil War, July 21, 1861, and Aug. 29–30, 1862.

Ma·nas·seh (mə·nas′ə) **1.** In the Old Testament, a son of Joseph. Gen. xli 51. **2.** A seventh-century B.C. king of Judah. II Kings xxi. — n. The tribe of Israel descended from Manasseh, son of Joseph. Also **Ma·nas·ses** (mə·nas′is). [< Hebrew Menasheh making forget]

man-at-arms (man′ət·ärmz′) n. pl. **men-at-arms** (men′-) A soldier; especially, an armed medieval mounted soldier.

man·a·tee (man′ə·tē′) n. A sluggish, heavily built aquatic mammal (genus Trichechus) of the coastal waters of Florida, the Gulf of Mexico, and the West Indies: also called sea cow. [< Sp. manati < Carib manattoui]

MANATEE
(8 to 10 feet long)

Ma·naus (mä·nous′) The capital of Amazonas, NW Brazil, on the Rio Negro; pop. 174,163 (est. 1958). Formerly **Ma·ná·os** (mä·nä′ōs).

Man·ches·ter (man′ches·tər, -chis-) **1.** A county borough and city in NW England; pop. 530,580 (1973). A native of Manchester is known as a Mancunian. **2.** A city in southern New Hampshire, on the Merrimack River; pop. 87,754. **3.** A town in northern Connecticut; pop. 47,994.

Manchester terrier A small, short-haired, black-and-tan terrier: formerly called Black-and-Tan terrier.

man·chet (man′chit) n. Archaic A small loaf or roll of fine white bread. [ME manchett; origin uncertain]

man·chi·neel (man′chi·nēl′) n. A tropical American tree (Hippomane mancinella) having an acrid, milky, poisonous sap. [< F mancenille < Sp. manzanilla, dim. of manzana apple < L (mala) matiana (apples) of Matius < Matius, a Roman culinary author]

Man·chu (man·chōō′, man′chōō) n. **1.** One of a Mongoloid people that conquered China in 1643 and established the dynasty overthrown in 1912. **2.** The language of the people, belonging to the Manchu-Tungusic subfamily of Altaic languages. — adj. Of or pertaining to Manchuria, its people, or its language. Also **Man·choo′.** [< Manchu, lit., pure]

Man·chu·kuo (man′chōō′kwō′, Chinese män′jō′kwō′) A former empire in NE Asia, 1932–45, established under Japanese auspices; comprising Manchuria and the Chinese province of Jehol and part of Inner Mongolia. Also **Man′chou′kuo′.**

Man·chu·ri·a (man·chŏŏr′ē·ə) A former division of NE China. See MANCHUKUO. — **Man·chu′ri·an** adj. & n.

Man·chu-Tun·gus·ic (man·chōō′tŏŏn·gŏŏz′ik) n. A subfamily of the Altaic languages, consisting of Manchu and Tungus.

man·ci·ple (man′sə·pəl) n. A steward, as of an English college. [< OF manciple, mancipe < L mancipium < manceps a buyer < manus hand + capere to take]

Man·cu·ni·an (man·kyōō′nē·ən) *n.* A native of Manchester, England. [< Med.L *Mancunium* Manchester]

-mancy *combining form* Divining or foretelling by means of: *necromancy.* [< OF *-mancie* < LL *mantia* < Gk. *manteia* power of divination]

Man·dae·an (man·dē′ən) See MANDEAN.

Man·da·lay (man′də·lā, man′də·lā′) A city in central Burma, on the Irrawaddy; pop. 182,367 (1960).

man·da·mus (man·dā′məs) *n. Law* A writ issued by courts of superior jurisdiction and directed to subordinate courts, corporations, officials, etc., commanding them to do something therein specified. —*v.t. Informal* To command by or serve with a mandamus. [< L, we command < *mandare.* See MANDATE.]

Man·dan (man′dan) *n.* **1.** One of an extinct tribe of North American Indians of Siouan stock, of the NW United States. **2.** The Siouan language of this tribe.

man·da·rin (man′də·rin) *n.* **1.** A member of any of the nine grades of exquisitely well-educated officials of the Chinese Empire. **2.** A powerful person; especially, a literary or intellectual arbiter. **3.** A tangerine: also **mandarin orange. 4.** An orange or reddish yellow dye. [< Pg. *mandarim* < Malay *mantri* minister of state; ult. < Skt. *mantra* counsel]

Man·da·rin (man′də·rin) *n.* **1.** The Chinese language of north and west China, including the Peking dialect upon which the official language of the country is based. **2.** Formerly, the court language of the Chinese Empire.

mandarin duck A crested duck (*Aix galericulata*), with variously colored plumage.

man·da·tar·y (man′də·ter′ē) *n. pl.* **·tar·ies** One having or receiving a mandate.

man·date (man′dāt; *for n.,* also -dit) *n.* **1.** In politics, an instruction from an electorate to its representative, expressed by the result of an election. **2.** Formerly, a charge to a nation from the League of Nations authorizing the administration and development of a territory, colony, etc.; also, the territory given in charge. Compare TRUSTEESHIP, TRUST TERRITORY. **3.** An authoritative command, as of a sovereign; order; charge. **4.** *Law* A judicial command issued by a higher court or official to a lower one. **b** In contract and early Roman law, a contract by which one individual acts for another gratuitously. **c** In canon law, a decree of the Pope, especially regarding preferment to a benefice. **d** In Roman law, a decree by the emperor. —*v.t.* **·dat·ed, ·dat·ing** To assign (a territory, etc.) to a specific nation under a mandate. [< L *mandatum,* pp. neut. of *mandare* to command, lit., to put in one's hand < *manus* hand + *dare* to give] — **man·da·tor** (-dā′tər) *n.*

man·da·to·ry (man′də·tôr′ē, -tō′rē) *adj.* **1.** Required by or as if by command or mandate; obligatory. **2.** Of or pertaining to a mandate. **3.** Holding a mandate. —*n. pl.* **·ries** A mandatary. — **man′da·to′ri·ly** *adv.*

Man·de·an (man·dē′ən) *n.* **1.** A member of an ancient Gnostic sect that still exists in the Tigris-Euphrates valley. **2.** The Aramaic dialect used in the writings of the Mandeans: also **Man·da′ic** (-dā′ik). —*adj.* Of or pertaining to the Mandeans, their language, or their doctrines. Also **Man·dae′an.** [< Mandean *mandayyā,* lit., having knowledge (< *mandā* knowledge), trans. of Gk. *gnōstikoi* Gnostics] — **Man·de′an·ism, Man·de′ism** *n.*

Man·de·ville (man′də·vil), **Bernard,** 1670?-1733, English author born in the Netherlands. — **Sir John,** pseudonym of a reputed English traveler whose *Narrative of Travels* appeared in Latin and French, 1357-71, and in English in the 15th century.

man·di·ble (man′də·bəl) *n. Biol.* **1.** The lower jaw bone, or its equivalent. For illustration see SKULL. **2.** Either the upper or the lower part of the beak of a bird or cephalopod. **3.** Either one of the upper or outer pair of jaws in an insect. **4.** One of the mouth part appendages of an arthropod. [< LL *mandibula* jaw < L *mandere* to chew]

man·dib·u·lar (man·dib′yə·lər) *adj.* Of, pertaining to, or formed by a mandible. Also **man·dib′u·lar·y** (-ler′ē). —*n.* The lower jaw; mandible. [< L *mandibula* jaw + -AR]

man·dib·u·late (man·dib′yə·lit, -lāt) *adj.* Having mandibles adapted for biting and chewing: said of certain insects. Also **man·dib′u·lat′ed.** —*n.* A mandibulate insect.

Man·din·go (man·ding′gō) *n. pl.* **·gos** or **·goes 1.** One of a Negroid people of western Sudan. — **Man·din′gan** *adj. & n.*

man·do·lin (man′də·lin, man′də·lin′) *n.* A musical instrument with a fretted neck, a pear-shaped body, and eight metal strings. [< F *mandoline* < Ital. *mandolino,* dim. of *mandola* < L *pandura.* See BANDORE.] — **man′do·lin′ist** *n.*

man·drake (man′drāk) *n.* **1.** A short-stemmed Old World plant (*Mandragora officinarum*) of the nightshade family with narcotic properties and fleshy forked roots sometimes resembling the human form. **2.** The May apple. Also **man·drag·o·ra** (man·drag′ō·rə). [Alter. of ME *mandrag(e),* < OE *mandragora* < LL < L *mandragoras* < Gk.; infl. in form by folk etymology < MAN + DRAKE[2]]

man·drel (man′drəl) *n. Mech.* **1.** A shaft or spindle on which material may be fixed for working on a machine. **2.** A metal bar used as a core about which wire, glass, metal, etc., may be bent, forged, or shaped. **3.** Any of various devices used to preserve the inner shape and regularity of tubing that is being welded, driven, etc. Also **man′dril.** [Prob. alter. of F *mandrin* lathe]

man·drill (man′dril) *n.* A large, ferocious West African baboon (*Mandrillus sphinx*), having large canine teeth and bony prominences on the cheeks striped with blue and scarlet. [< MAN + DRILL[4]]

MANDRILL
(About 2½ feet high at shoulder; 3 to 4 feet long)

man·du·cate (man′jōō·kāt) *v.t.* **·cat·ed, ·cat·ing** *Rare* To chew. [< L *manducatus,* pp. of *manducare* to chew] — **man′du·ca′tion** *n.* — **man′du·ca·to·ry** (-tôr·ē, -tō·rē) *adj.*

mane (mān) *n.* The long hair growing on and about the neck of some animals, as the horse, lion, etc. [OE *manu.* Akin to OE *mene* and L *monile* necklace.] — **maned** *adj.* — **mane′less** *adj.*

man-eat·er (man′ē′tər) *n.* **1.** A cannibal. **2.** An animal, as a lion, tiger, shark, etc., that devours or is said to devour human flesh. **3.** The great white shark: see under SHARK[1]. — **man′-eat′ing** *adj.*

ma·nège (ma·nezh′) *n.* **1.** The art of training and riding horses; also, a school for horsemanship. **2.** The movements of a trained horse. Also **man·ege′.** [< F < Ital. *maneggio* < *maneggiare.* See MANAGE.]

ma·nes (mā′nēz) *n.pl. Often cap.* In ancient Roman religion: **a** The spirits of the dead, especially of ancestors. **b** (*construed as sing.*) The spirit of a dead person. [< L]

Ma·nes (mā′nēz, man′ēz), 216?-276?, Persian prophet; founder of Manicheism. Also *Mani, Manichaeus.*

Ma·net (ma·nā′, *Fr.* mȧ·ne′), **Édouard,** 1833-83, French painter.

ma·neu·ver (mə·nōō′vər, -nyōō′-) *n.* **1.** *Mil.* **a** A planned movement or shift, as of troops, warships, etc. **b** *pl.* Large-scale tactical exercises simulating war; war games. **2.** Any skillful or artful move or stroke; an adroit action; instance of clever management. — **Syn.** See ARTIFICE. —*v.t.* **1.** To manage or conduct skillfully; handle; manipulate. **2.** To put (troops, vessels, etc.) through a maneuver or maneuvers. —*v.i.* **3.** To perform a maneuver or maneuvers. **4.** To use artful moves or strokes. Also, *esp. Brit.,* manoeuver, manoeuvre. [< F *manoeuvre* < OF *maneuvre* < LL *manopera* < *manopere* < L *manu operari* to work with the hand < *manus* hand + *operari.* See OPERATE. Doublet of MAINOR, MANURE.] — **ma·neu′ver·a·bil′i·ty** or **·vra·bil′i·ty** *n.* — **ma·neu′ver·a·ble** or **·vra·ble** *adj.* — **ma·neu′ver·er** *n.*

man Friday A person devoted or subservient to another, like Robinson Crusoe's servant of that name; a factotum.

man·ful (man′fəl) *adj.* Having a manly spirit; sturdy. — **Syn.** See MANLY. — **man′ful·ly** *adv.* — **man′ful·ness** *n.*

man·ga·bey (mang′gə·bā) *n.* Any of a genus (*Cercocebus*) of large monkeys having grayish brown bodies, partially webbed fingers and toes, and conspicuous white eyelids. Also **man′ga·by** (-bē). [after *Mangaby,* Madagascar]

man·ga·nate (mang′gə·nāt) *n.* *Chem.* A salt of manganic acid, as of sodium. [< MANGAN(IC) + -ATE[3]]

man·ga·nese (mang′gə·nēs, -nēz) *n. Chem.* A hard, brittle, grayish white metallic element (symbol Mn), oxidizing readily and forming an important component of certain alloys, as manganese steel. See ELEMENT. [< F *manganèse* < Ital. *manganese,* alter. of Med.L *magnesia.* See MAGNESIA.]

manganese steel A very hard, ductile steel containing from 12 to 14 per cent of manganese.

man·gan·ic (mang·gan′ik) *adj. Chem.* Of, pertaining to, or containing manganese in its highest valence.

manganic acid *Chem.* An acid, H_2MnO_4, known only by its salts.

man·ga·nite (mang′gə·nīt) *n.* **1.** A dark, steel-gray to iron-black orthorhombic manganese hydroxide, $MnO(OH)$. **2.** *Chem.* Any of a series of salts containing quadrivalent manganese as a constituent of the anion.

man·ga·nous (mang′gə·nəs) *adj.* Of, pertaining to, or containing manganese in its lowest valence.

Man·ga·re·va (mäng′ä·rā′vä) See GAMBIER ISLANDS.

mange (mānj) *n. Vet.* An itching skin disease of dogs and other domestic animals, caused by parasitic mites. [< OF *manjue* an itch, eating < *manjuer, mangier.* See MANGER.]

man·gel-wur·zel (mang′gəl·wûr′zəl) *n. Chiefly Brit.* A large-rooted European beet (*Beta vulgaris*), fed to cattle. Also **man′gel.** [< G < *mangoldwurzel* < *mangold* beet + *wurzel* root]

man·ger (mān′jər) *n.* A trough or box for feeding horses or cattle. [< OF *mangeoire, mangeure* < *mangier* to eat < L *manducare* to chew]

man·gle[1] (mang′gəl) *v.t.* **·gled, ·gling 1.** To disfigure or mutilate by cutting, bruising, crushing, etc. **2.** To mar or ruin; spoil: to *mangle* a word. [< AF *mangler, mahangler,* appar. freq. of *mahaignier.* See MAIM.] — **man′gler** *n.*

man·gle[2] (mang′gəl) *n.* A machine for smoothing and pressing fabrics by passing them between rollers. —*v.t.* **·gled, ·gling** To smooth with a mangle. [< Du. *mangel* < MDu. *mange* < Ital. *mangano* < LL *manganum* < Gk. *manganon* a pulley, a war machine. Doublet of MANGONEL.]

man·go (mang′gō) *n. pl.* **·goes** or **·gos 1.** An edible tropical fruit having a slightly acid taste. **2.** The tree (*Mangifera indica*) of the cashew family producing this fruit. **3.** A pickled melon or cucumber. [< Pg. *manga* < Malay *manga* < Tamil *mān-kāy* < *mān* a mango tree + *kāy* a fruit]

man·go·nel (mang′gə-nel) *n.* A medieval military engine for throwing stones and other missiles. [< OF, dim. of LL *manganum.* Doublet of MANGLE².]

man·go·steen (mang′gə-stēn) *n.* **1.** An edible tropical fruit having a thick rind and white, juicy pulp. **2.** The East Indian tree (*Garcinia mangostana*) producing this fruit. [< Malay *mangustan*]

man·grove (mang′grōv, man′-) *n.* **1.** Any of a genus (*Rhizophora*) of evergreen shrubs and trees growing in marshy and coastal areas in the tropics, especially the **American mangrove** (*R. mangle*), which throws out many aerial roots. **2.** A small evergreen tree of the vervain family, as the **black mangrove** (*Avicennia marina*): also called *blackwood.* [< Sp. *mangle* < Taino; infl. in form by *grove*]

man·gy (mān′jē) *adj.* **·gi·er, ·gi·est 1.** Affected with or resembling mange. **2.** Poverty-stricken; squalid; shabby. — **man′gi·ly** *adv.* — **man′gi·ness** *n.*

man·han·dle (man′han′dəl) *v.t.* **·dled, ·dling 1.** To handle with rough force. **2.** To handle by manpower alone.

Man·hat·tan (mən-hat′ən, man-) *n.* **1.** An island in SE New York at the mouth of the Hudson River; 22 sq. mi.; comprising a borough of New York City: also **Manhattan Island. 2.** One of a tribe of Algonquian Indians. **3.** A cocktail made of whisky and vermouth.

Manhattan Beach A resort city in SW California, near Los Angeles; pop. 35,352.

Manhattan District In World War II, the project that developed the atomic bomb.

man·hole (man′hōl′) *n.* A usually circular and covered opening by which a man may enter a sewer, boiler, etc.

man·hood (man′hood) *n.* **1.** The state of being an adult male human being. **2.** The masculine qualities collectively. **3.** Men collectively. **4.** The state of being human.

manhood suffrage Suffrage of all adult male citizens not disqualified by insanity, criminality, etc.

man-hour (man′our′) *n.* The amount of work a man can do in an hour.

Ma·ni (mā′nē, man′ē) See MANES.

ma·ni·a (mā′nē·ə, mān′yə) *n.* **1.** An extraordinary interest, enthusiasm, absorption, craving, etc. **2.** *Psychiatry* An exaggerated sense of well-being with excessive but disordered mental and physical activity, often alternating with melancholia, as in manic-depressive psychosis. **3.** *Rare* Violent madness. — **Syn.** See FRENZY. [< L < Gk., madness < *mainesthai* to rage. Akin to MANTIC.]

-mania *combining form* An exaggerated or irrational craving for or infatuation with. [< Gk. *mania* madness]

In the following list each entry denotes a mania for what is indicated:

acromania high places	**hippomania** horses
agoramania open places	**hodomania** travel
agyiomania streets	**hylomania** woods
ailuromania cats	**hypnomania** sleep
amaxomania being in vehicles	**ichthyomania** fish
anthomania flowers	**ideomania** ideas
apimania bees	**kainomania** novelty
arithromania counting things	**kathisomania** sitting down
automania oneself or solitude	**kinesomania** movement
ballistomania missiles	**lalomania** speech
bathomania depths	**necromania** death or the dead
cheromania gaiety or happiness	**noctimania** night
chionomania snow	**nostomania** one's home
choreomania dancing	**ochlomania** crowds
chrematomania money	**oikomania** home
cremnomania cliffs	**ophidiomania** reptiles
cynomania dogs	**ornithomania** birds
demomania crowds	**pantomania** everything
dromomania roaming	**pedomania** infants or children
entomomania insects	**pharmacomania** taking medicine
eremiomania stillness	**phonomania** noise
erythromania red	**phronemomania** thinking
gamomania marriage	**plutomania** wealth
gephyromania crossing bridges	**polymania** many things
graphomania writing	**siderodromomania** railroad traveling
gymnomania nakedness	**sitomania** food
gynemania women	**stasibasimania** walking or standing upright
hamartomania sin	**thalassomania** ocean or sea
hedonomania pleasure	**xenomania** strangers or foreigners
heliomania exposure to sun's rays	**zoomania** animals

ma·ni·ac (mā′nē·ak) *n.* A violently insane person; madman. — *adj.* Suffering from violent insanity; mad. [< LL *maniacus* < L *mania.* See MANIA.] — **ma·ni·a·cal** (mə·nī′ə·kəl) *adj.* — **ma·ni′a·cal·ly** *adv.*

-maniac *combining form* Used to form nouns and adjectives from nouns ending in *-mania*: *kleptomaniac.*

man·ic (man′ik, mā′nik) *adj. Psychiatry* Pertaining to, like, or affected by mania. [< MAN(IA) + -IC]

man·ic-de·pres·sive (man′ik-di-pres′iv) *adj. Psychiatry* Denoting or characteristic of a mental disorder in which periods of depression alternate with periods of excitement. — *n.* One who suffers from this disorder.

Ma·ni·chae·us (ma·ni·kē′əs) See MANES.

Man·i·che·an (man′ə·kē′ən) *n.* A follower of the prophet Manes: also **Man′i·chee.** — *adj.* Of or pertaining to Manicheism. Also **Man′i·chae′an.**

Man·i·che·ism (man′ə·kē′iz·əm) *n.* A dualistic and ascetic religion developed by Manes and his followers from Zoroastrian, Mandean, and other elements. Also **Man′i·chae′ism, Man′i·chae′an·ism, Man′i·che′an·ism.**

man·i·cure (man′ə·kyoor) *n.* **1.** The care of the hands and fingernails. **2.** A manicurist. — *v.t. & v.i.* **·cured, ·cur·ing** To take care of (the hands and nails). [< F < L *manus* hand + *cura* care]

man·i·cur·ist (man′ə·kyoor′ist) *n.* One whose work is to care for the hands and fingernails.

man·i·fest (man′ə·fest) *adj.* Plainly apparent to sight or understanding; evident; obvious. — *v.t.* **1.** To reveal; show; display. **2.** To prove; be evidence of. **3.** To record in a manifest. — *n.* In shipping and transportation: **a** An itemized account of a carrier's cargo, showing ports of lading, consignees, etc. **b** The list of passengers, cargo, etc., for an airplane flight. **c** A detailed list of the cars of a train. **d** A fast freight train. [< L *manifestus* evident, lit., struck by the hand] — **man′i·fes′ta·ble** *adj.* — **man′i·fest′ly** *adv.* — **Syn.** (adj.) patent, visible, palpable, plain. See EVIDENT.

man·i·fes·ta·tion (man′ə·fes·tā′shən) *n.* **1.** The act of manifesting, or the state of being manifested. **2.** That which reveals; sign; indication. **3.** A public display or avowal, as of political views. **4.** The materialization of a spirit, etc. — **man′i·fest′ant** *n.* — **man′i·fes·ta′tion·al** *adj.*

man·i·fes·to (man′ə·fes′tō) *n. pl.* **·toes** or **·tos** A public and formal declaration or explanation of principles, intentions, etc., usually by a political faction or similar group. [< Ital. < L *manifestus.* See MANIFEST.]

man·i·fold (man′ə·fōld) *adj.* MANIFOLD. **1.** Having many and varied forms, types, instances, etc.; multiple: *manifold* sorrows. **2.** Having an assortment of features, elements, etc. — **Syn.** See COMPLEX, MANY. — *n.* **1.** *Mech.* A pipe or chest having several or many openings, as for exhaust gas, air, steam, etc. **2.** A copy made by manifolding. **3.** Something that is manifold. — *v.t.* **1.** To make more than one copy of, as with carbon paper. **2.** To multiply. — *adv.* By many or by much: to increase *manifold.* [OE *manigfeald* varied, numerous] — **man′i·fold′ly** *adv.* — **man′i·fold·ness** *n.*

man·i·fold·er (man′ə·fōl′dər) *n.* A device for making manifold copies, as of a document.

man·i·hot (man′ē·hot) *n.* Any of a large genus (*Manihot*) of tropical American herbs or woody plants of the spurge family, as *M. glaziovi,* the source of Ceará rubber. [< NL < F < Tupi *mandioca* manioc root]

man·i·kin (man′ə·kin) *n.* **1.** A model of the human body used for demonstrating anatomy. **2.** A little man; dwarf. **3.** See MANNEQUIN. Also spelled *manakin, mannikin.* [< Du. *manneken,* dim. of *man* man]

ma·nil·a (mə·nil′ə) *n. Often cap.* **1.** A cheroot made in Manila. Also **Manila cigar. 2.** The fiber of the abaca. Also **Manila hemp. 3.** Manila paper (which see). Also **ma·nil′la.**

Ma·nil·a (mə·nil′ə, *Sp.* mä·nē′lä) A port city on SW Luzon, former capital of the Philippines; pop. 1,310,602 (1969).

Manila Bay An inlet of the China Sea in SW Luzon, Philippines.

Manila paper A heavy, light brown paper originally made of Manila hemp, now made of various fibers. Abbr. *Man.*

Manila rope Rope made of Manila hemp.

man in the street The common or ordinary person.

man·i·oc (man′ē·ok, mā′nē-) *n.* Cassava (def. 1). [< F < Tupi *mandioca* manioc root]

man·i·ple (man′ə·pəl) *n.* **1.** *Eccl.* A band worn on the left arm as a eucharistic vestment, usually by Roman Catholic clergymen. **2.** A subdivision of the Roman legion containing 60 or 120 men. [< OF *maniple, manipule* < L *manipulus* a handful < *manus* hand + base of *plere* to fill]

ma·nip·u·lar (mə·nip′yə·lər) *adj.* **1.** Pertaining to manipulation. Also **ma·nip′u·la·ry. 2.** Pertaining to a Roman maniple. [< L *manipularis* < *manipulus.* See MANIPLE.]

ma·nip·u·late (mə·nip′yə·lāt) *v.* **·lat·ed, ·lat·ing** *v.t.* **1.** To manage (persons, figures, stocks, etc.) shrewdly and deviously for one's own profit. **2.** To control, move, treat, etc., with the hands; handle; especially, to handle skillfully. **3.** To deal with (ideas, relations, etc.) by means of the mind; especially, to handle (ideas, etc.) skillfully. — *v.i.* **4.** To perform manipulation. [Back formation < MANIPULATION] — **ma·nip′u·la·ble** *adj.* — **ma·nip′u·la·tive, ma·nip′u·la·to′ry** *adj.* — **ma·nip′u·la′tor** *n.*

ma·nip·u·la·tion (mə·nip′yə·lā′shən) *n.* **1.** The act of manipulating, or the state of being manipulated. **2.** *Surg.* A manual procedure, especially in orthopedics or obstetrics. [< F, ult. < L *manipulus*. See MANIPLE.]

Ma·ni·pur (mun′i·poŏr) A Territory of NE India; 8,628 sq. mi.; pop. 1,035,000 (est. 1971); capital, Imphal.

Ma·ni·sa (mä′nē·sä′) A city in western Turkey; pop. about 45,000: ancient *Magnesia.* Also **Ma′nis·sa′.**

Man·i·to·ba (man′ə·tō′bə, -tō·bä′) A Province in central Canada; 246,512 sq. mi.; pop. 988,000; capital, Winnipeg. *Abbr. Man.* — **Man′i·to′ban** *adj. & n.*

Manitoba, Lake A lake in SW Manitoba; 1,817 sq. mi.

Manitoba maple *Canadian* The box elder.

Man·i·tou (man′ə·toŏ) *n.* Among the Algonquian Indians, any of various definitely conceived spiritual beings governing life and nature. Also **man′i·to** (-tō), **man′i·tu.** [< Algonquian (Massachuset) *manitto* He is god]

Man·i·tou·lin Island (man′ə·toŏ′lin) An island of Canada in Lake Huron, south central Ontario; 1,600 sq. mi.

Man·i·to·woc (man′ə·tə·wok′) A port city in eastern Wisconsin, on Lake Michigan; pop. 33,430.

Ma·ni·za·les (mä′nē·sä′lās) A city in west central Colombia; pop. 170,900 (1961).

man·kind (man′kīnd′; *for def. 1*, also man′kīnd′) **1.** The whole human species. **2.** Men collectively, as distinguished from women. [< MAN + KIND².]

man·like (man′līk′) *adj.* **1.** Having the qualities of a man; manly. **2.** Resembling a human being. **3.** Mannish. — *Syn.* See MASCULINE. — **man′like·ness** *n.*

man·ly (man′lē) *adj.* **·li·er, ·li·est 1.** Pertaining to or appropriate for a man; virile: *manly* charm. **2.** Having the qualities and virtues of a man, as courage, determination, strength, etc. — **the manly art** Boxing. — *adv. Archaic* Manfully. — **man′li·ly** *adv.* — **man′li·ness** *n.*
— *Syn.* (adj.) **1.** See MASCULINE. **2.** *Manly, manful,* and *mannish* characterize qualities proper or peculiar to men. *Manly* may be applied to almost any admired quality: *manly* fortitude, *manly* gentleness. *Manful* is used chiefly in referring to prowess or valor: a *manful* struggle. *Mannish* is a disparaging word, applied only to women, and suggesting the presence of some quality or trait usually associated with men: a *mannish* stride. Compare MASCULINE.

Mann (män), **Heinrich,** 1871–1950, and his brother **Thomas,** 1875–1955, German novelists active in the United States.

Mann (man), **Horace,** 1796–1859, U.S. educator.

man·na (man′ə) *n.* **1.** The food miraculously given to the Israelites in the wilderness as they fled from Egypt (*Ex.* xvi 14–36); also, any nourishment, help, etc., received as by divine bounty. **2.** A sweetish substance obtained from incisions in the stems of various plants, especially of the flowering ash, and used as a mild laxative. [< LL < Gk. < Aramaic *mannā* < Hebrew *mān* What is it?]

manna ash The flowering ash (which see).

Mann Act (man) *U.S.* A bill of 1910 prohibiting the interstate transportation of women for immoral purposes: also called *White-slave Act.* [after James R. *Mann,* 1856–1922, U.S. congressman]

man·ne·quin (man′ə·kin) *n.* **1.** A full-sized model of a complete or partial human figure used for cutting, fitting, or displaying garments. **2.** A woman who models clothing; model. **3.** A lay figure. Also spelled *manikin.* [< F < Du. *mannekin.* See MANIKIN.]

man·ner (man′ər) *n.* **1.** A way of doing or a way in which something happens or is done; mode; fashion. **2.** One's bearing and behavior; style of speech and action: a grave *manner.* **3.** *pl.* Social conduct; etiquette; especially, polite and civil social behavior: to learn *manners* from Emily Post. **4.** *pl.* The modes of social behavior prevailing in a group, nation, period, etc.: used especially of literary works: novel of *manners.* **5.** Typical or customary practice; especially, a characteristic style in literature, music, art, etc. **6.** *Archaic* Kind; sort. **7.** *Rare* Distinguished or fashionable behavior. **8.** *Obs.* Character; nature; disposition. — **by all manner of means** Certainly; by all means. — **in a manner of speaking** Approximately; more or less. — **to the manner born** Familiar or fitted from or as from birth. [< AF *manere,* OF *maniere,* ult. < L *manuarius* of the hand < *manus* hand]

man·nered (man′ərd) *adj.* **1.** Having (a specific kind of) manner or manners: used in combination: *mild-mannered.* **2.** Having mannerisms in writing, speaking, etc.

Man·ner·heim (män′ər·hīm) **Baron Carl Gustaf Emil von,** 1867–1951, Finnish field marshal and statesman; president 1944–46.

man·ner·ism (man′ər·iz′əm) *n.* **1.** Marked use of a distinctive style, especially in writing, music, or art. **2.** A distinctive trait of speech or behavior; idiosyncrasy; quirk. — **man′ner·ist** *n.* — **man′ner·is′tic** or **·ti·cal** *adj.*

man·ner·less (man′ər·lis) *adj.* Lacking good manners.

man·ner·ly (man′ər·lē) *adj.* Well-behaved; polite. — *adv.* With good manners; politely. — **man′ner·li·ness** *n.*

Mann·heim (män′hīm) A city in NW Baden-Württemberg, West Germany, on the Rhine; pop. 323,700 (1967).

man·ni·kin (man′ə·kin) See MANIKIN.

Man·ning (man′ing), **Henry Edward,** 1808–92, English Roman Catholic cardinal and writer.

man·nish (man′ish) *adj.* Resembling a man; masculine: said of women. — *Syn.* See MANLY. [OE *mennisc*] — **man′nish·ly** *adv.* — **man′nish·ness** *n.*

man·ni·tol (man′ə·tōl, -tol) *n. Biochem.* A slightly sweet crystalline alcohol, $C_6H_{14}O_6$, found especially in the dried sap of the flowering ash. Also **man′nite** (-īt). [< MANNA (def. 2) + -ITE³ + -OL¹] — **man·nit·ic** (mə·nit′ik) *adj.*

man·nose (man′ōs) *n. Biochem.* A hexose, $C_6H_{12}O_6$, obtained from the seed coat of the ivory nut and certain plant glycosides. [< MANN(ITOL) + -OSE]

ma·noeu·ver (mə·noŏ′vər, -nyoŏ′-), **ma·noeu·vre** See MANEUVER.

Man of Destiny Napoleon Bonaparte: so regarded by himself.

Man of Sorrows A name supposed to allude to the Messiah (*Isa.* liii 3), and applied to Jesus Christ.

man of the world A worldly-wise and sophisticated man.

man-of-war (man′əv·wôr′, -ə·wôr′) *n.* *pl.* **men-of-war** (men′-) **1.** *Chiefly Archaic* An armed ship; warship. **2.** A Portuguese man-of-war (which see). Also **man′-′o′-war′.**

man-of-war bird A frigate bird (which see). Also **man-of-war hawk.**

ma·nom·e·ter (mə·nom′ə·tər) *n.* Any of various instruments used to measure pressure, as of gases, liquids, vapors, etc. [< F *manomètre* < Gk.. *manos* thin, rare + *-mètre* -meter] — **man·o·met·ric** (man′ə·met′rik) or **·ric·al** *adj.*

man on horseback A military leader whose popularity is a threat to the civil government.

man·or (man′ər) *n.* **1.** In England: **a** Formerly, a feudal domain. **b** A landed estate. **2.** A manor house. **3.** A mansion. **4.** *U.S.* A landed estate with hereditary feudal rights, granted by royal charter in certain colonies. Compare PATROON. [< OF *manoir,* orig. a verb < L *manere* to dwell] — **ma·no·ri·al** (mə·nôr′ē·əl, -nō′rē-) *adj.*

manor house The chief residence of a manor. Also **manor seat.**

man·pow·er (man′pou′ər) *n.* **1.** The force of human physical strength. **2.** The number of men whose strength and skill are available to a nation, army, project, etc.; personnel. **3.** A unit of work equal to 1/10 horsepower.

man·qué (mäṅ·kā′) *adj. French* Lacking fulfillment; in wish but not in fact: a writer *manqué.*

man·rope (man′rōp) *n. Naut.* A rope rigged as a handrail.

man·sard (man′särd) *n. Archit.* **1.** A curb roof having the lower slope almost vertical and the upper almost horizontal, with the same profile on all four sides of the building. **2.** A room within such a roof. [< F *mansarde,* after François *Mansard,* 1598–1666, French architect who revived it]

manse (mans) *n.* **1.** A clergyman's house. **2.** *Archaic* A manor house. [< Med.L *mansa,* pp. of L *manere* to dwell]

man·ser·vant (man′sûr′vənt) *n.* An adult male servant.

Mans·field (manz′fēld, mans′-) **1.** A municipal borough in western Nottinghamshire, England; pop. 53,222 (1961). **2.** A city in north central Ohio; pop. 55,047.

Mans·field (manz′fēld, mans′-), **Katherine** Pseudonym of **Kathleen Beauchamp Mur·ry** (mûr′ē), 1888–1923, British short-story writer born in New Zealand. — **Richard,** 1854–1907, U.S. actor born in England.

Mans·field (manz′fēld, mans′-), **Mount** The highest peak of the Green Mountains, Vermont; 4,393 ft.

man·sion (man′shən) *n.* **1.** A large and impressive house, typically that of a wealthy person or family. **2.** A manor house. **3.** In astrology: **a** A house (def. 16). **b** One of the 28 places on the ecliptic occupied by the moon on successive days. **4.** *pl. Brit.* An apartment house. **5.** *Archaic* Any dwelling. [< OF < L *mansio, -onis* a dwelling < *mansus,* pp. of *manere* to dwell. Doublet of MENAGE.]

man-sized (man′sīzd′) *adj. Informal* Big enough for a man; large.

man·slaugh·ter (man′slô′tər) *n.* **1.** *Law* The unlawful killing of a human being without malice. **2.** Slaying of men.

man·slay·er (man′slā′ər) *n.* One who or that which kills a human being. — **man′slay′ing** *n. & adj.*

man·stop·ping (man′stop′ing) *adj.* Having sufficient impact to stop a man's advance: said of a bullet.

man·sue·tude (man′swə·toŏd, -tyoŏd) *n. Archaic* Mildness; gentleness. [< L *mansuetudo, -inis* < *mansuetus,* pp. of *mansuescere* to tame < *manus* hand + *suescere* to accustom]

man·ta (man′tə) *n.* **1.** Any of several very large rays (genus *Manta*) common in tropical American waters, especially *M. birostris,* that often reach a width of over 20 feet: also called *devilfish.* Also **manta ray.** **2.** A coarse and cheap cotton cloth used for garments in Spanish America; especially, a woman's shawl made of this fabric. **3.** *SW U.S.* A canvas covering for the load of a pack animal. **4.** *Obs.* A mantelet (def. 2). [< Sp., blanket < LL *mantum* cloak, back formation < L *mantellum.* See MANTLE.]

MANTA
(To 20 feet long)

man·teau (man′tō, *Fr.* mäṅ·tō′) *n. pl.* **·teaus** (-tōz) or **·teaux** (*Fr.* -tō′) **1.** A cloak or mantle. **2.** *Obs.* A woman's gown; mantua. [< F < OF *mantel.* See MANTLE.]

Man·te·gna (män·tā′nyä), **Andrea**, 1431–1506, Italian painter and engraver.

man·tel (man′təl) *n.* **1.** The shelf above a fireplace. **2.** A facing of wood, brick, stone, etc., around a fireplace: also called *chimney piece.* Also **man′tel·piece′** (-pēs′). [Var. of MANTLE; infl. in meaning by F *manteau* mantelpiece]

MANTEL

man·tel·et (man′təl·et, mant′lit) *n.* **1.** A short cloak. **2.** A screen, shield, or enclosure used by hunters, soldiers, etc. Also spelled *mantlet.* [< OF, dim. of *mantel.* See MANTLE.]

man·tel·let·ta (man′tə·let′ə) *n.* In the Roman Catholic Church, a sleeveless vestment reaching almost to the knees, worn by cardinals, bishops, and other church dignitaries. [< Ital., dim. of *mantello* < L *mantellum.* See MANTLE.]

man·tel·tree (man′təl·trē′) *n.* An arch, beam, stone, etc., serving as a lintel above a fireplace.

man·tic (man′tik) *adj.* Of, pertaining to, or having powers of divination or prophecy; prophetic: *mantic* frenzy. [< Gk. *mantikos* < *mantis* a prophet. Akin to MANIA.]

-mantic *combining form* Used to form adjectives from nouns ending in *-mancy*: *necromantic.* [< Gk. *mantikos* prophetic < *mantis* divination]

man·til·la (man·til′ə) *n.* **1.** A light scarf often of black lace worn over the head and shoulders of women in Spain and Spanish America and often supported by a high comb. **2.** Any short cloak. [< Sp., dim. of *manta.* See MANTA.]

man·tis (man′tis) *n. pl.* **·tis·es** or **·tes** (-tēz) A carnivorous, orthopterous, long-bodied insect (family *Mantidae*) with large eyes and swiveling head, that stands with its forelegs folded as if in prayer: also called *praying mantis.* For illustrations, see INSECTS (beneficial). [< NL < Gk., a prophet, also a kind of insect]

man·tis·sa (man·tis′ə) *n. Math.* The decimal part of a logarithm that, with the characteristic, completes the logarithm. [< L, makeweight, trifling addition, ? < Etruscan]

mantis shrimp A squill. Also **mantis crab.**

man·tle (man′təl) *n.* **1.** A loose and usually sleeveless garment worn over other garments; a cloak. **2.** Anything that clothes, envelops, or conceals. **3.** *Zool.* **a** The variously modified flap or folds of the membranous covering of a mollusk. **b** The soft external body wall in the tunic of ascidians. **4.** *Ornithol.* The back, scapulars, and folded wings of a bird, when distinguished by color, as in gulls. **5.** The outer covering of a wall. **6.** The outer masonry of a blast furnace. **7.** A sheath of clay laid over a wax model, forming a mold when the wax is melted out. **8.** A mantel. **9.** A gas mantle (which see). — *v.* **·tled**, **·tling** *v.t.* **1.** To cover with or as with a mantle; conceal. — *v.i.* **2.** To overspread or cover the surface of something. **3.** To be or become covered, overspread, or suffused, as a blush, etc. **4.** To spread out one wing at a time over the corresponding outstretched leg: said of hawks. [OE *mentel* < OF *mantel* < L *mantellum*]

mant·let (mant′lit) See MANTELET.

man·tu·a (man′chōō·ə, -tōō·ə) *n.* A woman's cloak, worn about 1700. [Alter. of F *manteau*; infl. in form by *Mantua*]

Man·tu·a (man′chōō·ə, -tōō·ə) A commune in Lombardy, northern Italy; birthplace of Vergil; pop. 61,580 (1961). *Italian* **Man·to·va** (män′tō·vä). — **Man′tu·an** *n. & adj.*

Mantuan the Vergil.

man·u·al (man′yōō·əl) *adj.* **1.** Involving the hand or hands; as: **a** Done or effected by hand. **b** Used by hand. **c** Operated by hand. Also *Obs.* **man′u·ar′y** (-er′ē). **2.** *Law* Actually possessed; in one's own hands. — *n.* **1.** A small guidebook, reference book, or book of instructions; handbook. **2.** An organ keyboard. **3.** A prescribed drill in manipulating a rifle, guidon, etc. Abbr. *m.*, *M.* [< OF *manuel* < L *manualis* < L *manus* hand] — **man′u·al·ly** *adv.*

manual alphabet A series of manual signs or gestures representing the letters of the written alphabet, used by the deaf and by deaf-mutes as a substitute for vocal speech: sometimes called *deaf-and-dumb alphabet.* For illustration see DEAF-AND-DUMB ALPHABET.

manual training In U.S. schools, practical training in carpentry, woodworking, etc.

ma·nu·bri·um (mə·nōō′brē·əm, -nyōō′-) *n. pl.* **·bri·a** (-brē·ə) *Anat.* A handle-shaped part; as: **a** The uppermost part of the sternum: also called *episternum.* For illustration see THORAX. **b** The lower part of the malleus. [< L, handle < *manus* hand] — **ma·nu′bri·al** *adj.*

manuf. Manufacture(d); manufacturer; manufacturing.

man·u·fac·to·ry (man′yə·fak′tər·ē) *n. pl.* **·ries** *Archaic* A factory. [< MANUFACTURE; on analogy with FACTORY]

man·u·fac·ture (man′yə·fak′chər) *v.* **·tured**, **·tur·ing** *v.t.* **1.** To make or process a product, especially on a large scale and with machinery. **2.** To fabricate or invent (a lie, false theory, alibi, etc.). **3.** To produce (poetry, art, etc.) by mere technical means. — *v.i.* **4.** To make or process something. — *n.* **1.** The act or process of manufacturing. **2.** Something that is manufactured. Abbr. *manuf.*, *mfr.* [<

MF < Med.L *manufactura* < L *manus* hand + *factura* a making < *factus*, pp. of *facere* to make] — **man′u·fac′tur·a·ble** *adj.* — **man′u·fac′tur·er** *n.*

man·u·mit (man′yə·mit′) *v.t.* **·mit·ted**, **·mit·ting** To free from bondage, as a slave; emancipate; liberate. [< L *manumittere*, lit., to send forth from one's hand < *manus* hand + *emittere* < *ex* away from + *mittere* to send] — **man′u·mis′sion** (-mish′ən) *n.*

ma·nure (mə·nōōr′, -nyōōr′) *n.* Dung, compost, etc., used to fertilize soil. — *v.t.* **·nured**, **·nur·ing** To apply manure or other fertilizer to, as soil. [< AF *maynoverer* to work with the hands < OF *manouvrer* < L *manuoperare.* Doublet of MANEUVER, MAINOR.] — **ma·nur′er** *n.*

ma·nus (mā′nəs) *n. pl.* **ma·nus** **1.** *Anat.* The hand, or the corresponding part in vertebrates, as a forefoot, claw, hoof, etc. **2.** In Roman law, authoritative control of the husband over his wife. [< L, hand]

man·u·script (man′yə·skript) *n.* **1.** A usually typewritten copy of a book, article, document, etc., prepared or submitted for publication. **2.** A book or document written by hand; especially, a document, etc., made before the use of printing. **3.** Something written by hand. Abbr. *ms* (pl. *mss*), *MS* (pl. *MSS*), *ms.* (pl. *mss.*), *MS.* (pl. *MSS.*). — *adj.* Written by hand. [< Med.L *manuscriptum* < LL *manuscriptio* < L *manus* hand + *scriptus*, pp. of *scribere* to write]

Ma·nu·ti·us (mə·nōō′shē·əs, -shəs, -nyōō′-), **Aldus**, 1450–1515, Venetian scholar and printer; invented italic letters.

man·ward (man′wərd) *adv.* To or toward man. — *adj.* Directed toward man. Also **man′wards.**

man·wise (man′wīz′) *adv.* After the manner of a man.

Manx (mangks) *adj.* Of or pertaining to the Isle of Man, its people, or their language. — *n.* **1.** The people of the Isle of Man collectively: with *the.* **2.** The Gaelic language of the Manx, nearly extinct. [< Scand. *Mansk*, alter. of *Manisk*, ult. < Celtic *Man* Isle of Man]

Manx cat A type of domestic cat having no tail.

Manx·man (mangks′mən) *n. pl.* **·men** (-mən) A native of the Isle of Man.

man·y (men′ē) *adj.* **more**, **most** Adding up to a large number; numerous. — *n.* **1.** A large number: *Many* of those present left early. **2.** The masses; crowd; multitude: with *the.* — **a great many** Many: with plural verb. — **many a** (or **an** or **another**) Many: with singular noun. — *pron.* A large number of persons or things. [OE *manig*]

— **Syn.** (adj.) *Many*, *numerous*, *manifold*, and *multifarious* mean indefinitely large in number. *Many* suggests an aggregate taken as a whole, while *numerous* suggests an aggregate taken one by one: *many* persons attended the meeting and heard *numerous* speeches. *Manifold* suggests diversity: the *manifold* aspects of a problem. *Multifarious* is somewhat stronger than *manifold*; it suggests great diversity, and sometimes even incongruity: a *multifarious* collection of china, the *multifarious* interests and investments of a great financier. Compare SEVERAL. — **Ant.** few.

man·y·plies (men′i·plīz′) *n.pl.* (construed as *sing.*) *Zool.* The omasum. [< MANY + *plies*, pl. of PLY[1], n.]

man·za·ni·ta (man′zə·nē′tə, *Sp.* män′sä·nē′tä) *n.* **1.** Any of several evergreen shrubs or trees (genus *Arctostaphylos*) of the western United States. **2.** The fruit of these shrubs. [< Sp., dim. of *manzana* apple. See MANCHINEEL.]

Mao·ism (mou′iz′əm) *n.* The militant communist doctrines or practices of Mao Tse-tung, characterized especially by a rejection of the possibility of coexistence with capitalist states. — **Mao′ist** *n.*, *adj.*

Ma·o·ri (mä′ō·rē, mou′rē) *n.* **1.** One of an aboriginal, light brown people of New Zealand, chiefly Polynesian mixed with Melanesian. **2.** The Polynesian language of these people. — *adj.* Of or pertaining to the Maoris or their language.

Mao Tse-tung (mou′ dzu′dŏong′), 1893–1976, Chinese Communist leader, chairman of the People's Republic of China 1949–59.

map (map) *n.* **1.** A representation on a plane surface of any region, as of the earth's surface; a chart. **2.** Anything resembling a map in form or purpose. **3.** *Slang* The face. — **off the map** Out of existence; out of the running. — *v.t.* **mapped**, **map·ping** **1.** To make a map of. **2.** To plan in detail: often with *out.* [< OF *mappe(monde)* < Med.L *mappa (mundi)* map (of the world) < L, cloth, napkin]

Map (map), **Walter**, 1140?–1209?, Welsh writer and satirist at the court of Henry II of England. Also **Ma·pes** (mā′pēz).

ma·ple (mā′pəl) *n.* **1.** Any of a large genus (*Acer*) typifying a family (*Aceraceae*) of deciduous trees of the north temperate zone, with opposite leaves and a fruit of two joined samaras, as the sugar maple, red maple, white maple, and Norway maple. **2.** The wood of this tree. **3.** The amber-yellow color of the finished wood. **4.** The flavor of the sap of the sugar maple. [OE *mapul* (*trēow*) maple (tree)]

maple sugar Sugar made from the sap of the sugar maple.

maple syrup The refined and concentrated sap of the sugar maple, in liquid form.

ma·quis (mä·kē′) *n.* A zone of shrubby, mostly evergreen plants in the Mediterranean region, known as cover for game, bandits, etc.: also called *macchia.* [< F < Ital. *macchia* thicket, orig., spot < L *macula* spot]

Ma·quis (má·kē′) *n.* *pl.* ·**quis 1.** The French resistance movement against the Germans during World War II. **2.** A member of this group. [< MAQUIS]

mar (mär) *v.t.* **marred, mar·ring 1.** To do harm to; impair; damage. **2.** To injure so as to deface; disfigure. — **Syn.** See INJURE. — *n.* A disfiguring mark; blemish; injury. [OE *mierran* to hinder] — **mar′rer** *n.*

mar. 1. Marine. **2.** Maritime. **3.** Married.

Mar. March.

mar·a·bou (mar′ə·boo) *n.* **1.** A stork of the genus *Leptoptilos*, especially the **African marabou** (*L. crumeniferus*), whose soft, white, lower tail and wing feathers are used in millinery. **2.** A plume from the marabou. **3.** A delicate, white silk that can be dyed without being freed from gum. **4.** The adjutant (def. 2). Also **mar′a·bout** (-boot). [< F *marabou, marabout.* See MARABOUT.]

Mar·a·bout (mar′ə·boot) *n.* A Moslem hermit or holy man of northern Africa, revered by the Berbers. [< F < Arabic *murābit* a hermit]

ma·ra·ca (mə·rä′kə, *Pg.* mä·rä·kä′) *n.* A percussion instrument made of a gourd or gourd-shaped rattle with beans or beads inside it. [< *Pg. maracá,*? < Tupi]

MARABOU
(About 3½ feet high)

Ma·ra·cai·bo (mä′rä·kī′bō) A port city in NW Venezuela, on the narrows between **Lake Maracaibo** (about 5,000 sq. mi.) and the Gulf of Venezuela; pop. 625,100 (est. 1968).

Maracaibo, Gulf of See (Gulf of) VENEZUELA.

Mar·a·can·da (mar′ə·kan′də) The ancient name for SAMARKAND.

Ma·ran·hão (mä′rə·nyoun′) A State of NE Brazil; 128,252 sq. mi.; pop. 3,314,000 (est. 1968); capital, São Luis de Maranhão.

Ma·ra·ñón (mä′rä·nyōn′) One of the main headstreams of the Amazon in Peru, flowing about 1,000 miles north.

ma·ras·ca (mə·ras′kə) *n.* A small, wild cherry (*Prunus cerasus marasca*) of the Dalmatian mountains. [< Ital., aphetic var. of *amarasca* < *amaro* bitter < L *amarus*]

mar·a·schi·no (mar′ə·skē′nō) *n.* A cordial distilled from the fermented juice of the marasca and flavored with the cracked pits. [< Ital. < *marasca.* See MARASCA.]

maraschino cherries Cherries preserved in a syrup usually flavored with imitation maraschino.

ma·ras·mus (mə·raz′məs) *n.* *Pathol.* A gradual and continuous wasting away of the body; emaciation. [< NL < Gk. *marasmos* < *marainein* to waste] — **ma·ras′mic** *adj.*

Ma·rat (má·rä′), **Jean Paul,** 1744–93, French Revolutionary leader born in Switzerland; assassinated by Charlotte Corday.

Ma·ra·tha (mə·rä′tə) See MAHRATTA.

Ma·ra·thi (mə·rä′tē) *n.* The Indic language of the Mahratta of India; the predominant language in the state of Maharashtra: also *Mahrati.*

mar·a·thon (mar′ə·thon) *n.* **1.** A footrace of 26 miles, 385 yards: a feature of the Olympic games: so called from a messenger's run from Marathon to Athens to announce the Athenian victory over the Persians, 490 B.C. **2.** Any endurance contest.

Mar·a·thon (mar′ə·thon) A plain in Attica, Greece, on the Aegean; scene of decisive victory of the Athenians over the Persians, 490 B.C.

ma·raud (mə·rôd′) *v.i.* **1.** To rove in search of plunder; make raids for booty. — *v.t.* **2.** To invade for plunder; raid. — *n.* A foray. [< F *marauder* < *maraud* rogue] — **ma·raud′er** *n.*

mar·ble (mär′bəl) *n.* **1.** A compact, granular, partly crystallized limestone occurring in many colors, used for building, sculpture, etc. **2.** A piece, block, statue, etc., of this stone. **3.** A small ball of this stone, or of glass, porcelain, etc. **4.** *pl.* A boys' game played with balls of glass, etc. **5.** Marbling (def. 1). — *v.* **·bled, ·bling** *v.t.* **1.** To color or vein in imitation of marble, as book edges. — *v.i.* **2.** To be flecked with fat: said of meat. — *adj.* **1.** Made of or consisting of marble. **2.** Resembling marble as to chilliness, lack of feeling, etc. [< OF *marble, marbre* < L *marmor* < Gk. *marmaros,* lit., sparkling stone, orig., stone; infl. in sense by *marmairein* to sparkle] — **mar′bly** *adj.*

marble cake A cake made of light and dark batter mixed to give a marblelike appearance.

mar·bled (mär′bəld) *adj.* **1.** Veined, clouded, colored, etc., like marble. **2.** Flecked with traces of fat: said of meat.

Mar·ble·head (mär′bəl·hed′) A resort town on the east coast of Massachusetts; pop. 21,295.

mar·ble·ize (mär′bəl·īz) *v.t. & v.i.* **·ized, ·iz·ing** *U.S.* To marble.

mar·bling (mär′bling) *n.* **1.** A marking, mottling, or coloring resembling that of marble. **2.** The act or method of imitating marble. **3.** In bookbinding, the imitation of marble on the edges or binding of a book.

Mar·burg (mär′bûrg, *Ger.* mär′boorkh) A city in western Hesse, West Germany; pop. 45,400 (est. 1960). Also **Mar′· burg an der Lahn** (än der län′).

marc (märk) *n.* **1.** Solid refuse remaining from grapes or other fruit after pressing. **2.** A brandy distilled from this. **3.** Any residue from a substance treated with a solvent. [< F, prob. < *marcher* to tread, press (grapes). See MARCH[1].]

Marc Antony See (Mark) ANTONY.

mar·ca·site (mär′kə·sīt) *n.* **1.** A pale, bronze-yellow, orthorhombic iron disulfide, FeS$_2$: also called *white iron pyrites.* **2.** An ornament made of crystallized marcasite or of polished steel, as the corollas of heaths, etc. [< Med.L *marcasita,* prob. < Arabic *marquashītā,* ? < Aramaic]

mar·cel (mär·sel′) *v.t.* **·celled, ·cel·ling** To dress (the hair) in even, continuous waves by means of special irons. [after M. *Marcel,* 19th c. French hairdresser] — **mar·cel′ler** *n.*

marcel wave In hairdressing, a style of dressing the hair in tiers of even, continuous waves.

Mar·cel·lus (mär·sel′əs), **Marcus Claudius,** 268?–208 B.C., Roman general in the Second Punic War.

mar·ces·cent (mär·ses′ənt) *adj.* *Bot.* Withering without falling off, as the corollas of heaths, etc. [< L *marcescens, -entis,* ppr. of *marcescere,* inceptive of *marcere* to be faint, languid] — **mar·ces′cence** *n.*

march[1] (märch) *v.i.* **1.** To walk or proceed with measured, regular steps, as a soldier or organized body of troops. **2.** To walk in a solemn or dignified manner. **3.** To proceed or advance steadily. — *v.t.* **4.** To cause to march: He *marched* his men vigorously. — *n.* **1.** The act of marching. **2.** A regular, measured step, as of a body of troops. **3.** A movement, as of soldiers, from one place to another. **4.** The distance passed over in marching: a full day's *march.* **5.** Onward progress; forward advance: the *march* of events. **6.** A musical composition in accented duple meter suitable for accompanying the movements of marching persons. [< MF *marche* < *marcher* to walk, orig., to trample, ult. < LL *marcus* hammer < L *marculus*]

march[2] (märch) *n.* **1.** A region or district lying along a boundary line; frontier. Also **march′land′** (-land′). **2.** *pl.* The border regions of England and Wales, or of England and Scotland. **3.** *Scot.* The boundary or boundary marks between lands or estates. [< OF *marche,* prob. < OHG *marka.* Akin to MARK[1], MARGIN.]

March (märch) The third month of the year, containing 31 days. Abbr. *Mar.* [< AF *marche,* OF *marz* < L *Martius* (*mensis*) (month) of Mars < *Mars* Roman god of war]

March (märkh) A river in Czechoslovakia forming part of the Austria-Czechoslovakia boundary and flowing 180 miles NW to the Danube: Czech *Morava.*

March. Marchioness.

Marche (màrsh) A region and former province of central France.

Mär·chen (mer′khən) *n.* *pl.* **Mär·chen** *German* A story; especially, a fairy tale or folk tale.

mar·cher[1] (mär′chər) *n.* One who marches. [< MARCH[1]]

mar·cher[2] (mär′chər) *n.* **1.** Formerly, an officer administering a march. **2.** A dweller in a march. [< MARCH[2]]

Mar·ches (mär′chiz), **the** A Region of central Italy; 3,742 sq. mi.; pop. 1,347,234 (1961); capital, Ancona. *Italian* **Mar·che** (mär′kā).

mar·che·se (mär·kā′zā) *n.* *pl.* **·che·si** (-kā′zē) *Italian* A marquis. — **mar·che′sa** (-zä) *n.fem.*

Mar·ches·van (mär·khesh′vən) Heshvan. See (Hebrew) CALENDAR.

mar·chion·ess (mär′shən·is) *n.* **1.** The wife or widow of a marquis. **2.** A woman having in her own right the rank corresponding to that of a marquis. Abbr. *March.* [< Med.L *marchionissa* < *marchio, -onis* captain of the marches]

march·pane (märch′pān) *n.* Marzipan. [< MF *marcepain* < Ital. *marzapane.* See MARZIPAN.]

Mar·co Po·lo (mär′kō pō′lō) See POLO.

Mar·co·ni (mär·kō′nē), **Marchese Guglielmo,** 1874–1937, Italian inventor; developed a system of wireless telegraphy.

Marconi rig *Naut.* In yachting, a fore-and-aft rig having a triangular, easily removable sail or sails with no gaff, bent on a mast or masts with stays, spreaders, etc. Also, *Brit., Bermudan rig, Bermudian rig.*

Mar·cus Antonius (mär′kəs) See ANTONY.

Marcus Aurelius See AURELIUS.

Mar·cy (mär′sē), **Mount** The highest peak in New York and in the Adirondack Mountains; 5,344 ft.

Mar·di gras (mär′dē grä′) Shrove Tuesday, the last day before Lent, celebrated as a carnival in certain cities. [< F, lit., fat Tuesday]

Mar·duk (mär′dook) In Babylonian mythology, the chief deity, originally a local sun god.

mare[1] (mâr) *n.* The female of the horse and other equine animals. [OE *miere,* fem. of *mearh* horse]

mare[2] (mâr) *n.* *Obs.* A hag or goblin supposed to produce nightmare; also, nightmare. [OE]

ma·re[3] (mä′rē) *n.* *pl.* **ma·ri·a** (mâr′ē·ə) Any of a number of dark, seemingly flat areas of the moon's surface. [< L, sea; because of their resemblance to seas]

ma·re clau·sum (mâr′ē klô′səm) *Latin* A closed sea; a sea subject to one nation: distinguished from **mare liberum** an open sea.

Mare Island (mâr) An island in San Pablo Bay, northern California; site of a U.S. Navy yard.

ma·rem·ma (mə·rem′ə) *n. pl.* **·rem·me** (-rem′ē) A marshy coastal region. [< Ital. < L *maritimus.* See MARITIME.]

Ma·ren·go (mä·reng′gō) A village in Piedmont, NW Italy; scene of Napoleon's defeat of the Austrians, 1800.

ma·re nos·trum (mâr′ē nos′trəm) *Latin* Our sea: the Roman and Fascist name for the Mediterranean.

mare's nest **1.** A seemingly important discovery that proves worthless or false. **2.** Loosely, a cluttered and confusing mess; rat's nest.

mare's-tail (mârz′tāl′) *n.* **1.** *Meteorol.* Long, fibrous, cirrus clouds, supposed to indicate rain. **2.** A perennial aquatic herb (*Hippuris vulgaris*) with leaves in whorls.

marg. Margin; marginal.

Mar·ga·ret (mär′gə·rət) In Goethe's *Faust*, Margarethe, the heroine: also *Gretchen.*

Margaret of Anjou, 1430–82, French wife of Henry VI of England.

Margaret of Navarre, 1492–1549, queen of Navarre, 1544–1549; patroness of literature.

Margaret of Valois, 1553–1615, queen of France; wife of Henry IV; divorced in 1599: called **Queen Mar·got** (mär′gō, -gət; *Fr.* mȧr′gō)

mar·gar·ic (mär·gar′ik, -gär′-) *adj.* Of, pertaining to, or resembling pearl; pearly. Also **mar·ga·rit·ic** (mär′gə·rit′ik). [< F *margarique*, ult. < Gk. *margaron* pearl]

margaric acid A white, crystalline, fatty acid, $C_{17}H_{34}O_2$, obtained from the wax of lichens or made synthetically. [< F *margarique.* See MARGARIC.]

mar·ga·rine (mär′jə·rin, -rēn, -gə-) *n.* A butter substitute, made from vegetable oils, milk, seasonings, and often containing vitamin A or D enrichments: also called *oleomargarine.* Also **mar·ga·rin** (mär′jə·rin, -gə-). [< F < the belief that it contained a derivative of margaric acid]

mar·ga·rite (mär′gə·rīt) *n.* **1.** A hydrated silicate of calcium and aluminum. **2.** Minute spherical crystals arranged as a beadlike pattern in glassy igneous rocks. **3.** *Obs.* A pearl. [< OF < L *margarita* a pearl, ult. < Gk. *margaron*]

Mar·gate (mär′git) A municipal borough, port, and resort in NE Kent, England; pop. 45,780 (1961).

mar·gay (mär′gā) *n.* Any of various South and Central American striped and spotted wild cats, especially the long-tailed *Felis tigrina*: also called *tiger cat.* [< F < *margaia* < Pg. *maracajá* < Tupi *mbaracaïa*]

marge (märj) *n. Poetic* A margin. [< MF < L *margo*]

mar·gin (mär′jin) *n.* **1.** The part of a page around the body of printed or written text. **2.** A bounding line or surface; border; verge; edge. **3.** An extra amount or allowance of something, as space, time, money, etc. **4.** A limiting or end point; limit: *margin* of endurance. **5.** In commerce: **a** The difference between the cost and selling price of a commodity. **b** The minimum return below which an enterprise is judged unprofitable. **6.** In the stock market, security deposited with a broker to protect him against loss in trading. Abbr. *marg.* — *v.t.* **1.** To furnish with a margin; form a margin to; border. **2.** To enter, place, or specify on the margin of a page, as a note. **3.** In the stock market, to deposit a margin upon, especially an additional margin. Also *Archaic* **mar′gent** (-gənt). [< L *margo*, *-inis.* Akin to MARK[1], MARCH[2].]

mar·gi·nal (mär′jə·nəl) *adj.* **1.** Pertaining to or constituting a margin. **2.** Situated at or near a margin; especially, written or printed on a margin. Also *Archaic* **mar′gent** (-jənt). **3.** Having relatively low quality or value; meager; minimal: a *marginal* talent. **4.** *Econ.* Barely profitable. **5.** *Psychol.* Relating to the fringe of consciousness. Abbr. *marg.* [< F] — **mar′gin·al′i·ty** *n.* — **mar′gin·al·ly** *adv.*

mar·gi·na·li·a (mär′jə·nā′lē·ə, -nāl′yə) *n.pl.* Marginal notes. [< NL, pl. of *marginalis* marginal < L *margo* margin]

marginal land *Econ.* Land so poor as to remain unused until the lack of more desirable land forces its development.

mar·gi·nate (mär′jə·nāt) *v.t.* **·nat·ed**, **·nat·ing** To provide with a margin or margins. — *adj. Biol.* Having a margin, especially one of a distinct character, appearance, or color: also **mar′gi·nat′ed.** [< L *marginatus*, pp. of *marginare* < *margo*, *-inis* margin] — **mar′gi·na′tion** *n.*

mar·grave (mär′grāv) *n.* **1.** Formerly, the lord or governor of a German mark, march, or border. **2.** A hereditary title of certain princes of the Holy Roman Empire. [< MDu. *marcgrave* < *marke* march[2] + *graf* count] — **mar′·gra·vine** (-grə·vēn) *n.fem.*

mar·gra·vi·ate (mär·grā′vē·it) *n.* The territory of a margrave. Also **mar·gra·vate** (mär′grə·vāt). [< Med.L *margravius* < MDu. *marcgrave* margrave]

mar·gue·rite (mär′gə·rēt′) *n.* Any of several flowers, especially the oxeye daisy and *Chrysanthemum frutescens*. [< F pearl, daisy, etc. < Gk. *margaron* pearl]

Ma·ri·a de′ Medici (mə·rī′ə, -rē′ə) See under MEDICI.

ma·ri·age de con·ve·nance (mȧ·ryȧzh′ də kôǹv·näǹs′)

French A marriage of convenience; an advantageous marriage; not a love match.

Mar·i·an (mâr′ē·ən) *n.* **1.** A worshiper or devotee of the Virgin Mary. **2.** An adherent of Mary I, queen of England, or a defender of Mary Queen of Scots. — *adj.* **1.** Of or pertaining to the Virgin Mary, or characterized by a special devotion to her. Also **Mar′i·an′ic.** **2.** Pertaining to Queen Mary of England, or to Mary Queen of Scots.

Ma·ri·a·na·o (mä′ryä·nä′ō) A city in western Cuba; pop. 348,000 (est. 1966).

Ma·ri·a·nas Islands (mär′ē·ä′näs) An archipelago in the western Pacific Ocean, including Guam, Saipan, Tinian, and Rota; comprising part of the UN Trust Territory of the Pacific Islands (excluding Guam); total, 246 sq. mi.; Japanese mandate, 1919–44: formerly *Ladrone Islands, Ladrones.* Also **Ma′ri·a′nas** or **Ma′ri·an′ne Islands** (-rē·än′ə).

Ma·ri·anne (mâr′ē·an′) **1.** A feminine personal name. **2.** The French Republic, as personified on coins, etc.

Ma·ri·a The·re·sa (mə·rē′ə te·rā′zə), 1717–80, queen of Hungary and Bohemia; wife of Francis I.

Maria Theresa dollar See under DOLLAR.

Ma·rie An·toi·nette (mȧ·rē′ äṅ·twȧ·net′), 1755–93, queen of France; daughter of Maria Theresa; wife of Louis XVI; guillotined.

Marie Lou·ise (lōō·ēz′), 1791–1847, empress of France; second wife of Napoleon Bonaparte.

Mar·i·et·ta (mar′ē·et′ə, mar′ē-) A city in NW Georgia, near Atlanta; pop. 27,216.

mar·i·gold (mar′ə·gōld) *n.* **1.** Any of several plants of the composite family (genus *Tagetes*), with golden-yellow flowers; especially, the **French marigold** (*T. patula*), and the **Aztec** or **African marigold** (*T. erecta*). **2.** Any plant resembling these, as the marsh marigold. [< MARY, prob. with ref. to the Virgin Mary + GOLD]

mar·i·jua·na (mar′ə·wä′nə, *Sp.* mä′rē·hwä′nä) *n.* **1.** Hemp (def. 1). **2.** The dried leaves and flower tops of this plant, capable of producing disorienting or hallucinogenic effects when smoked in cigarettes or ingested. Also **ma′·ri·hua′na.** [< Am. Sp. *marihuana, mariguana*]

ma·rim·ba (mə·rim′bə) *n.* A form of xylophone having a resonator beneath each tuned bar. [< Bantu *marimba, malimba,* pl. of *limba,* kind of musical instrument]

Ma·rin (mä′rin), **John**, 1872–1953, U.S. painter.

ma·ri·na (mə·rē′nə) *n. U.S.* A docking area or basin for small vessels. [< Ital., seacoast < L *marinus.* See MARINE.]

Ma·ri·na (mä·rē′nä) The former name for ESPÍRITU SANTO.

mar·i·nade (mar′ə·nād′) *n.* **1.** A brine pickle sometimes flavored with wine, oil, spices, and herbs, in which meat or fish are soaked before cooking, to improve their flavor. **2.** Pickled meat or fish. — *v.t.* **·nad·ed, ·nad·ing** To marinate. [< F < Sp. *marinada* < *marinar* to pickle in brine < *marino* marine < L *marinus.* See MARINE.]

mar·i·nate (mar′ə·nāt) *v.t.* **·nat·ed, ·nat·ing** **1.** To soak (food) in marinade. **2.** To allow, as salad, to soak in French dressing before serving. [< Ital. *marinare*]

Ma·rin·du·que (mä′rin·dōō′kā) An island of the Philippines south of Luzon; 346 sq. mi.

ma·rine (mə·rēn′) *adj.* **1.** Of, pertaining to, or characteristic of the sea. **2.** Native to, existing in, or formed by the sea: *marine* salt. **3.** Of or pertaining to the commercial, legal, etc., aspects of the sea; maritime. **4.** Pertaining to the navigation or handling of ships on the sea; nautical: *marine* currents. **5.** Relating to the navy; naval. **6.** Used or intended for use at sea or in navigation: *marine* compass. **7.** Serving aboard ship. — *n.* **1.** A soldier trained for service at sea and on land; a member of the Marine Corps: also **Ma·rine′. 2.** Shipping vessels, shipping, or the navy collectively. See MERCHANT MARINE. **3.** A seascape. **4.** The department of naval affairs in some countries. Abbr. *mar.* [< OF *marin* < L *marinus* < *mare, maris* sea]

— **Syn.** (adj.) *Marine, maritime, nautical,* and *naval* all refer to the sea, though they are not strictly synonymous. Anything that relates to the sea is *marine*: a *marine* animal, *marine* warfare. *Maritime* suggests some nearness or relation to the sea; we speak of a *maritime* province, or the *maritime* industries of fishing and navigation. *Nautical* has to do with ships and navigation: a *nautical* term, a *nautical* chart. *Naval* refers to the sea as a theater of war, and to the men and ships of a nation's armed forces upon the sea: a *naval* base, a *naval* career. Compare OCEANIC.

Marine Corps A separate service within the U.S. Department of the Navy, made up of combat troops, air forces, etc., under their own officers: officially, the *United States Marine Corps.* Abbr. *USMC, U.S.M.C.*

marine insurance Insurance covering loss or damage to ship, cargo, or freight by shipwreck or perils of the sea.

mar·i·ner (mar′ə·nər) *n.* One who navigates or assists in navigating a ship; sailor; seaman. [< OF *marinier*, ult. < Med.L *marinarius* < L *marinus.* See MARINE.]

Mar·i·ol·a·try (mâr′ē·ol′ə·trē) *n.* Worship of the Virgin Mary: usually an opprobrious term: also spelled *Maryolatry.* [< *Mario-* (< MARY) + -LATRY] — **Mar′i·ol′a·ter** *n.* — **Mar′i·ol′a·trous** *adj.*

Mar·i·ol·o·gy (mâr′ē·ol′ə·jē) *n.* The whole body of religious belief and dogma relating to the Virgin Mary: also spelled *Maryology*. [< *Mario-* (< MARY) + -LOGY]

Mar·i·on (mar′ē·ən, mâr′-) 1. A city in east central Indiana; pop. 39,607. 2. A city in central Ohio; pop. 38,646.

Mar·i·on (mar′ē·ən), **Francis,** 1732?–95, American Revolutionary general: called *the Swamp Fox.*

mar·i·o·nette (mar′ē·ə·net′) *n.* A small jointed human or animal figure of wood, cloth, etc., used in shows and animated by manipulating strings: also called *puppet.* [< F *marionnette,* dim. of *Marion,* dim. of *Marie;* prob. orig. a small image of the Virgin Mary. See MARY.]

Mar·i·po·sa lily (mar′ə·pō·sə, -zə) Any of a genus (*Calochortus*) of showy liliaceous Mexican and Californian plants. Also **Mariposa tulip.**·

mar·ish (mar′ish) *Obs. adj.* Marshy; boggy. — *n.* A marsh. [< OF *marais, mareis,* prob. < Med.L *mariscus* a marsh < Gmc.]

Mar·ist (mâr′ist) *adj.* 1. Of, pertaining to, or dedicated to the Virgin Mary. 2. Of or pertaining to the Marist Fathers. — *n.* A member of a Roman Catholic order (**Marist Fathers**) devoted to instruction and foreign missions. [< (the VIRGIN) MAR(Y) + -IST]

Ma·ri·tain (mà·rē·taṅ′), **Jacques,** 1882–1973, French philosopher.

mar·i·tal (mar′ə·təl) *adj.* 1. Of or pertaining to marriage. 2. *Rare* Of or pertaining to a husband. [< L *maritalis* < *maritus* husband, orig., married] — **mar′i·tal·ly** *adv.*

mar·i·time (mar′ə·tīm) *adj.* 1. Situated on or near the sea. 2. Of or pertaining to the sea, its navigation, commerce, etc. *Abbr. mar.* — **Syn.** See MARINE. [< MF < L *maritimus* < *mare, maris* sea]

Maritime Alps The part of the Alps between France and Italy, extending to the Mediterranean coast; highest peak Punta Argentera, 10,817 ft.

Maritime Provinces New Brunswick, Nova Scotia, and Prince Edward Island, on the Atlantic coast of Canada. Also **Mar·i·times** (mar′ə·tīmz).

Mar·i·tim·er (mar′ə·tī′mər) *n.* A resident or native of the Maritime Provinces.

Ma·ri·tsa (mä·rē′tsä) A river in SE Europe, flowing 300 miles SE to the Aegean. Also **Ma·rí·tza.**

Ma·ri·u·pol (mə·ryi·ōō′pəly′) The former name for ZHDANOV.

Mar·i·us (mâr′ē·əs), **Gaius,** 155?–86 B.C., Roman general.

Ma·ri·vaux (mà·rē·vō′), **Pierre Carlet de Chamblain de,** 1688–1763, French dramatist and novelist.

mar·jo·ram (mär′jər·əm) *n.* Any of several perennial herbs of the mint family (genera *Majorana* and *Origanum*), with dense oblong spikes of flowers, and colored bracts; especially, the **sweet marjoram** (*M. hortensis*), used for seasoning in cookery. [< OF *majorane,* ult. origin uncertain]

mark¹ (märk) *n.* 1. A visible trace, impression, or figure on something, as a line, scratch, spot, stain, or dot; any physical feature made by drawing, indenting, stamping, etc. 2. A symbol, seal, inscription, or label placed on or attached to something to identify its owner or maker; distinguish it from others, etc.; trademark. 3. A cross or other sign made by one who cannot write. 4. A letter, number, or symbol used to indicate achievement, quality, defect, etc., as of a student's work or conduct; grade; rating. 5. A symbol, point, sign, etc., serving to indicate, guide, or direct: a *mark* for lost ships. 7. That which indicates the presence of a thing, quality, process, etc.; characteristic; symptom; token: a *mark* of distinction. 8. A visible indication of some quality, trait, position, etc., assumed or imposed on a person: the *mark* of an outcast. 9. That which is aimed at, or toward which effort is directed, as in shooting, throwing, etc.; target; goal: the hunter's *mark.* 10. That which one strives to attain or achieve; a desired object or goal; end: to fall short of one's *mark.* 11. A standard or criterion of quality, performance, proficiency, etc.: His behavior was below the *mark.* 12. *Usually cap.* Model; type: with a Roman numeral: *Mark* II. 13. *Informal* A person easily duped or victimized: a *mark* for every schemer. 14. In track sports, the starting line of the contest. 15. In boxing, the pit of the stomach. 16. In the game of bowls, the jack. 17. *Naut.* A knot, twist, rag, etc., on a lead line at intervals to indicate fathoms of depth. 18. Notice; attention; heed: worthy of *mark.* 19. In medieval times among the Germanic peoples, a piece of land held in common by a village community. 20. *Archaic* A boundary; frontier. — **beside the mark** 1. Missing the point aimed at. 2. Irrelevant. — **hit the mark** 1. To be accurate. 2. To achieve one's goal; be successful. — **to leave (or make) a mark** To leave or make an impression; influence. — **to make one's mark** To succeed; achieve distinction. — **of mark** Having, or worthy of distinction, renown, etc.: a man of little *mark.* — **save (or God save) the mark!** May my words be understood as ironical! — **up to the mark** Up to standard; in good health or condition, etc. — **wide of the mark** 1. Striking far from the point aimed at. 2. Irrelevant. — *v.t.* 1. To make a mark or marks on: to *mark* the walls with chalk. 2. To trace the boundaries of; set limits to: often with *out:*

to *mark* out an area. 3. To indicate or show by a mark or sign; denote; specify: He *marked* the word in red. 4. To characterize; distinguish: a year *marked* by great events. 5. To designate, appoint, or select, as if by marking; destine: to be *marked* for death. 6. To pay attention to; notice; heed: to *mark* his warning. 7. To make known or clear; manifest; display: Angry looks *marked* his displeasure. 8. To apply or attach a price tag, identification label, etc., to an article: to *mark* a dress as washable. 9. To evaluate by giving marks to; grade; rate. 10. To keep (record or score) in various games. 11. To make form, or produce by drawing, writing, etc. — *v.i.* 12. To take notice; pay attention; consider. 13. To make a mark or marks. 14. To keep score in games. — **to mark down** 1. To note down by writing or making marks. 2. To put a lower price on, as for sale. — **to mark time** 1. To keep time by moving the feet but not advancing. 2. To pause in action or progress temporarily. — **to mark up** 1. To make marks on; scar. 2. To increase the price of. [ME *marken* < OE *mearc,* orig., boundary. Akin to MARGIN, MARCH².]

mark² (märk) *n.* 1. The former standard monetary unit and silver coin of Germany, equivalent to 100 pfennigs and worth about 24 U.S. cents: superseded in 1924 by the reichsmark and after World War II by the deutschemark in West Germany and a deutschemark of different value in East Germany. 2. A former silver coin of Scotland and England, worth 13s. 4d. 3. A former European unit of weight, equal to 256.27 grains. 4. A markka. *Abbr. m., M., mk.* [OE *marc* a unit of weight, prob. < LL *marca,* ? < Gmc. ? Akin to MARK¹.]

Mark (märk) The evangelist who wrote the second of the gospel narratives in the New Testament: called **Saint Mark.** — *n.* The second Gospel of the New Testament.

Mark Antony See (Mark) ANTONY.

marked (märkt) *adj.* 1. Clearly evident; noticeable; prominent. 2. Having a mark or marks. — **a marked man** One singled out for vengeance, punishment, etc. — **mark·ed·ly** (mär′ked·lē) *adv.* — **mark·ed·ness** *n.*

mark·er (mär′kər) *n.* 1. That which marks; especially, a bookmark, a milestone, a gravestone, etc. 2. One who marks, as a scorekeeper, grader, etc.

mar·ket (mär′kit) *n.* 1. Trade and commerce in a specific service or commodity: the boat *market*; also, trade and commerce generally: with *the.* 2. A region where one can buy or sell: the Canadian *market*; also, a category of persons, institutions, etc., considered as buyers: the college *market.* 3. A stock exchange; stock market (which see). 4. The state of trade: a brisk *market*; buyer's *market.* 5. A place where something is offered for sale; especially, an open space or large hall with stalls, counters, etc. 6. A store; shop. 7. A public gathering, often weekly or otherwise periodic, for buying and selling. 8. Market value (which see). *Abbr. mkt.* — **in the market** Seeking to buy. — **on the market** Up for sale. — *v.t.* 1. To sell. — *v.i.* 2. To deal in a market. 3. To buy household provisions. [ME < AF < L *mercatus,* orig. pp. of *mercari* to trade < *merx, mercis* merchandise. Doublet of MART.]

mar·ket·a·ble (mär′kit·ə·bəl) *adj.* Suitable for sale; in demand. — **mar′ket·a·bil′i·ty** *n.*

market order An order to a broker to buy or sell at the current market price.

mar·ket·place (mär′kit·plās′) *n.* 1. A market (def. 5). 2. The imagined place where ideas, opinions, works, etc., are tested and traded. Also **market place.**

market research The research and analysis of information concerning consumer needs, preferences, etc., especially for or by a company intending to introduce a new product.

market value The amount that can be obtained for goods, services, or securities on the open market: distinguished from *book value, face value, par value.* Also **market price.**

Mark·ham (mär′kəm), **(Charles) Edwin,** 1852–1940, U.S. poet.

Mark·ham (mär′kəm), **Mount** An Antarctic peak on the west edge of Ross Shelf Ice; 15,100 ft.

mark·ing (mär′king) *n.* 1. A mark or an arrangement of marks. 2. *Often pl.* The color pattern on a bird, animal, etc. 3. The act of making a mark.

mark·ka (märk′kä) *n.* The standard monetary unit of Finland, equivalent to 100 pennia; also, a coin of this value. Also called *mark.* *Abbr. mk.* [< Finnish < Sw. *mark.* Akin to MARK².]

marks·man (märks′mən) *n. pl.* **·men** (-mən) 1. One skilled in hitting the mark. 2. *Mil.* a In the U.S. Army, the lowest grade for skill in the use of small arms. b The soldier having this grade. Compare SHARPSHOOTER, EXPERT. — **marks′man·ship** *n.* **marks′wom·an** (-wōōm′ən) *n. fem.*

Mark Twain (märk twān) Pseudonym of Samuel Langhorne Clemens, 1835–1910, U.S. humorist and novelist.

mark·up (märk′up′) *n.* 1. A raising of price. 2. The amount of price increase. 3. In computing selling price, the sum added to cost to cover overhead and profit.

marl¹ (märl) *v.t. Naut.* To wrap with marline, tying each turn with a hitch. [< MARLINE]

marl² (märl) *n.* 1. An earthy deposit containing lime, clay, and sand, used as fertilizer. **2.** A soft, earthy, crumbling stratum of varying composition. **3.** *Poetic* Earth. — *v.t.* To fertilize or spread with marl. [< OF *marle* < LL *margila*, dim. of L *marga*, ? of Celtic origin] — **marl′y, mar·la′ceous** (-lā′shəs) *adj.*

Marl·bor·ough (märl′bûr·ō, -bər·ə), **Duke of,** 1650–1722, John Churchill, English general and statesman; defeated the French at Blenheim, 1704.

marled (märld) *adj. Scot.* Variegated; marbled; mottled.

mar·lin (mär′lin) *n.* Any of various deep-sea game fishes (genus *Makaira*); especially, the **blue marlin** (*M. nigricans*) of the Atlantic, and the **striped marlin** (*M. mitsukuri*) of the Pacific. [< MARLINE(SPIKE); because of its shape]

mar·line (mär′lin) *n. Naut.* A small rope of two strands loosely twisted together, used for winding ropes, cables, etc. [< Prob. fusion of Du. *marlijn* (< *marren* to tie + *lijn* a line) and E *marling* binding < Du. < *marlen*]

mar·line·spike (mär′lin·spīk′) *n. Naut.* A sharp-pointed iron pin used in splicing ropes. Also **mar′· lin·spike′, mar′ling·spike′** (-ling-).

marl·ite (märl′īt) *n.* A variety of marl that remains solid on exposure to air. — **mar·lit·ic** (mär·lit′ik) *adj.*

MARLINESPIKES

Mar·lowe (mär′lō), **Christopher,** 1564–93, English poet and dramatist. — **Julia,** 1866–1950, U.S. actress born in England: original name **Sarah Frances Frost.**

mar·ma·lade (mär′mə·lād) *n.* A preserve made by boiling with sugar the pulp and rind of fruits, usually citrus fruits, to the consistency of jam. [< MF *marmelade* < Pg. *marmelada* < *marmelo* quince < L *melimelum* < Gk. *melimēlon* < *meli* honey + *mēlon* apple]

marmalade tree A tall sapotaceous evergreen tree (*Calocarpum sapota*) of tropical America that bears plumlike fruits used chiefly for preserving: also called *mamey.*

Mar·ma·ra (mär′mə·rə), **Sea of** A sea between Europe and Asia, leading to the Black Sea, and by the Bosporus to the Dardanelles to the Aegean: ancient *Propontis.* Also **Mar·mo·ra** (mär′mə·rə, mär·môr′ə, -mō·rə). See maps of BLACK SEA, BOSPORUS.

Mar·mo·la·da (mär′mō·lä′dä) The highest mountain in the Dolomites, northern Italy; 10,964 ft.

mar·mo·re·al (mär·môr′ē·əl, -mō′rē-) *adj.* Pertaining to, made of, or resembling marble. Also **mar·mo′re·an** (-môr′ē-, -mō′rē-). [< L *marmoreus* < *marmor.* See MARBLE.]

mar·mo·set (mär′mə·zet) *n.* **1.** A small Central and South American monkey (family *Callithricidae*) with soft, woolly hair and a long hairy tail. **2.** A related species, **Goeldi's marmoset** (*Callimico goeldii*). **3.** The tamarin. **4.** The ouistiti. [< OF *marmouset* grotesque figure, prob. ult. < Gk. *mormō, -ous* she-monster, bogey]

mar·mot (mär′mət) *n.* Any of various rodents of the genus *Marmota,* as the woodchuck, the **yellow-bellied marmot** (*Marmota flaviventris*) of South Dakota and Wyoming, and the **hoary** or **whistling marmot** (*M. caligata*) of the western United States and Canada. [< F *marmotte,* fusion of OF *marmotte* monkey and Romansch *murmont* marmot < L *mus, muris* mouse + *mons, montis* mountain]

MARMOSET
(About 12 inches long; tail 12 inches)

Marne (märn) A river in NE France, flowing 325 miles NW to the Seine; scene of two decisive battles of World War I, 1914, 1918.

Ma·roc (mȧ·rôk′) The French name for MOROCCO.

ma·roon[1] (mə·rōōn′) *v.t.* **1.** To put ashore and abandon on a desolate island or coast. **2.** To abandon; leave helpless. — *n.* One of a class of Negroes, chiefly fugitive slaves or their descendants, living wild in the mountains of some West Indies islands and of Guiana. [< Am.Sp. *cimarron* wild]

ma·roon[2] (mə·rōōn′) *n.* A dull, dark red color. — *adj.* Having a dull, dark red color. [< F *marron* chestnut]

mar·plot (mär′plot′) *n. Archaic* One who mars or frustrates a plan or scheme, especially by meddling.

Marq. Marquis.

Mar·quand (mär′kwänd), **J(ohn) P(hillips),** 1893–1960, U.S. novelist.

marque (märk) *n. Obs.* Reprisal. See LETTER OF MARQUE. [< F < Provençal *marca* seizure < *marcar* to seize as a pledge < *marc* a pledge < Gmc. Akin to MARK[1].]

mar·quee (mär·kē′) *n.* **1.** A canopy, usually heavy and made of metal, used as a signboard and shelter over the sidewalk in front of a theater, hotel, etc. **2.** A large field tent, as one used at outdoor parties. [< *marquise* canopy, mistaken as pl. < F]

Mar·que·sas Islands (mär·kā′säs, -kē′-) A group of islands in French Polynesia; 492 sq. mi. Also **Mar·que′zas Islands.** — **Mar·que′san** (-sən) *adj. & n.*

mar·quess (mär′kwis) See MARQUIS.

mar·que·try (mär′kə·trē) *n.* Inlaid work of wood often

interspersed with stones, ivory, etc., especially as used in furniture. Also **mar′que·te·rie.** — *v.t.* [< MF *marqueterie* < *marqueter* to variegate, inlay < *marque* mark[1], ult. < Gmc.]

Mar·quette (mär·ket′), **Jacques,** 1637–75, French Jesuit missionary and explorer in North America: called **Père Marquette.**

mar·quis (mär′kwis, *Fr.* mȧr·kē′) *n.* The title of a nobleman next in rank below a duke. Also, *Brit., marquess.* Abbr. *m., M., Marq.* [< OF *marchis, marquis* < Med.L *markensis* commander of the marches < *marca* march[2]]

Mar·quis (mär′kwis) *n.* An important variety of wheat, first developed in Canada.

Mar·quis (mär′kwis), **Don,** 1878–1937, U.S. journalist and humorist: full name **Donald Robert Perry Marquis.**

mar·quis·ate (mär′kwiz·it) *n.* The rank of a marquis.

mar·quise (mär·kēz′) *n.* **1.** The wife or widow of a French marquis. **2.** An ornamental hood over a door; a marquee. **3.** In gem cutting, a pointed oval form, especially for diamonds. For illustration see DIAMOND. **4.** A ring set with an oval cluster of gemstones. [< F, fem. of *marquis* marquis]

mar·qui·sette (mär′ki·zet′, -kwi-) *n.* A lightweight, open-mesh fabric of cotton, silk, rayon, or nylon, or a combination of these, used for curtains and women's and children's garments. [< F, dim. of *marquise* a marquise]

Marquis of Queensberry Rules A widely observed boxing code devised in 1869 by John Sholto Douglas, 1844–1900, eighth **Marquis of Queensberry.**

Mar·ra·kesh (mä·rä′kesh) One of the traditional capitals of Morocco, in the SW part; pop. 295,000 (est. 1969): formerly also *Morocco.* Also **Mar·ra′kech.**

Mar·ra·no (mä·rä′nō) *n. pl.* **·nos** or **·noes** During the Spanish Inquisition, a Jew who professed Catholicism in public but observed the Jewish faith in secret. [< Sp., lit., pig; so called contemptuously by steadfast Jews because Marranos ate forbidden pork]

mar·riage (mar′ij) *n.* **1.** The state of being married; a legal contract, entered into by a man and a woman, to live together as husband and wife; wedlock. ◆ Collateral adjectives: *hymeneal, marital.* **2.** The act of marrying; also, the accompanying rites or festivities; wedding; nuptials. **3.** Any close union. **4.** In pinochle, the king and queen of any suit. [< OF *mariage* < *marier* < L *maritare* to marry]
— **Syn. 1.** *Marriage, matrimony,* and *wedlock* denote the relation of husband and wife. *Marriage* is the general and also the legal term; *matrimony* is more ecclesiastical or religious, and has to do with the estate into which married persons enter. We speak of the laws and customs of *marriage* among different peoples, but we say that two persons are joined in holy *matrimony,* rather than holy *marriage.* *Wedlock* is often used as a close synonym for *matrimony,* but it stresses the legal and moral obligations of the relationship: children born out of *wedlock.* **2.** *Marriage, wedding,* and *nuptials* denote the ceremony by which two persons are joined in wedlock. *Marriage* is the appropriate word for any ceremony, whether simple or elaborate, civil or religious. *Wedding* and *nuptials* refer to the *marriage* proper as well as to the attendant festivities; of the two, *nuptials* is the more formal or bookish term.

marriage broker One who arranges marriages, as by finding suitable partners, for a fee.

mar·riage·a·ble (mar′ij·ə·bəl) *adj.* Fitted or suitable for marriage. — **mar′riage·a·bil′i·ty, mar′riage·a·ble·ness** *n.*

marriage lines *Brit.* A certificate of marriage.

mar·ried (mar′ēd) *adj.* **1.** United in matrimony; having a spouse: a *married* man. **2.** Of or pertaining to marriage or to persons united in marriage. **3.** Closely related or joined. Abbr. *m., M., mar.*

mar·ron (mar′ən, *Fr.* mȧ·rôn′) *n. Often pl.* A large variety of chestnut, especially when candied, preserved in syrup, etc. [< F. See MAROON[2].]

marron gla·cé (glȧ·sā′) *French* A candied chestnut.

mar·row[1] (mar′ō) *n.* **1.** A soft, vascular tissue found in the central cavities of bones. **2.** The essence of anything; pith. **3.** Vitality. [OE *mearg*] — **mar′row·y** *adj.*

mar·row[2] (mar′ō) *v.t. & v.i. Scot. & Brit. Dial.* To associate or marry. [Origin uncertain]

mar·row·bone (mar′ō·bōn′) *n.* **1.** A bone containing marrow fit to be eaten. **2.** *pl.* One's knees: used humorously. **3.** *pl.* Crossbones.

mar·row·fat (mar′ō·fat′) *n.* A variety of green pea, having a large, succulent seed. Also **marrow pea.**

marrow squash *U.S.* A vegetable marrow (which see).

Mar·rue·cos (mär·rwä′kōs) The Spanish name for MOROCCO.

mar·ry[1] (mar′ē) *v.* **·ried, ·ry·ing** *v.t.* **1.** To accept as husband or wife; take in marriage. **2.** To join as husband and wife in marriage. **3.** To give in marriage. **4.** To unite closely. **5.** *Naut.* To fasten end to end, as rope, without increasing the diameter. — *v.i.* **6.** To take a husband or wife. **7.** To join or unite closely. [< OF *marier* < L *maritare* < *maritus* husband, married] — **mar′ri·er** *n.*

mar·ry[2] (mar′ē) *interj. Archaic* An exclamation of surprise, indignation, etc. [Alter. of MARY; with ref. to the Virgin Mary]

Mar·ry·at (mar′ē·it, -at), **Frederick**, 1792–1848, British naval officer and novelist: called **Captain Marryat**.

Mars (märz) In Roman mythology, the god of war: identified with the Greek *Ares*. — *n.* **1.** The seventh largest planet of the solar system and fourth in order from the sun. See PLANET. **2.** *Obs.* Iron.

Mar·sa·la (mär·sä′lä) *n.* A dark-colored, sweet, heavy wine, originally made in Marsala, Sicily.

Mar·sa·la (mär·sä′lä) A port city in western Sicily; pop. about 32,000.

Mar·seil·laise (mär′sə·lāz′, *Fr.* mȧr·sĕ·yez′) The national anthem of France, written in 1792 by Rouget de Lisle.

mar·seille (mär·sāl′) *n.* A thick cotton fabric. Also **mar·seilles** (mär·sālz′). [after *Marseille*, France]

Mar·seille (mȧr·sā′y′) A port city in SE France, on the Gulf of the Lion; pop. 889,029 (1968). Also **Mar·seilles** (mär·sā′, -sālz′).

marsh (märsh) *n.* A tract of low, wet land; swamp. [OE *mersc, merisc.* Akin to MORASS.]

Marsh (märsh), **Othniel Charles**, 1831–99, U.S. paleontologist. — **Reginald**, 1898–1954, U.S. painter.

mar·shal (mär′shəl) *n.* **1.** In various foreign countries, a military officer of high rank, usually just below the commander in chief: also *field marshal*. **2.** *U.S.* **a** An officer of the Federal courts, assigned to a judicial district and having duties similar to those of a sheriff. **b** In some cities, the chief of the police or fire department; also, an officer in either of these departments. **3.** An officer authorized to organize or regulate processions, ceremonies, etc. **4.** A title of certain royal court or household officials, often in charge of matters of protocol. **5.** *Obs.* One who tends horses. — *v.t.* **mar·shaled** or **·shalled, mar·shal·ing** or **·shal·ling 1.** To arrange or dispose in order, as facts. **2.** To array or draw up, as troops for battle. **3.** To lead; usher. [< OF *mareschal* < Med.L *mariscalcus* < OHG *marahscalh,* lit., a horse-servant < *marah* horse + *scalh* servant] — **mar′shal·cy, mar′shal·ship** *n.* — **mar′shal·er, mar′shal·ler** *n.*

Mar·shall (mär′shəl), **Alfred**, 1842–1924, English economist. — **George Catlett**, 1880–1959, U.S. general and diplomat; chief of staff in World War II; secretary of state 1947–1949. — **John**, 1755–1835, American Revolutionary statesman and jurist; secretary of state 1800–01; chief justice of the Supreme Court 1801–35. — **Thurgood**, born 1908, U.S. lawyer; associate justice of the Supreme Court 1967–.

Mar·shall Islands (mär′shəl) An island group in the NW Pacific comprising an administrative district of the UN Trust Territory of the Pacific Islands; 66 sq. mi.; pop. 14,907 (1960); capital, Jaluit; formerly a Japanese mandate.

Marshall Plan The European Recovery Plan (which see).

Marshal of the Royal Canadian Air Force In the Royal Canadian Air Force, a commissioned officer of the highest rank. See table at GRADE.

Mar·shal·sea (mär′shəl·sē) *Brit.* **1.** A debtor's prison in London, abolished 1842. **2.** Formerly, a court held by the marshal of the royal household. [Var. of MARSHALCY.]

marsh elder 1. Any of a genus (*Iva*) of American salt-marsh plants, especially the shrub (*I. frutescens*) of the SE United States: also called *sumpweed.* **2.** The guelder-rose.

marsh frog A pickerel frog (which see).

marsh gas Methane.

marsh hawk A marsh-dwelling American hawk (*Circus cyaneus*) having gray or brown plumage.

marsh hen Any of various birds (family *Rallidae*) that inhabit salt-water marshes along the American sea coasts, as the rail, coot, gallinule, etc.: also called *mud hen.*

marsh·mal·low (märsh′mel′ō, -mal′ō) *n.* **1.** A confection made of starch, sugar, corn syrup, and gelatin, and coated with powdered sugar. **2.** A sweetmeat formerly made from the root of the marsh mallow.

marsh mallow A plant of the mallow family (*Althaea officinalis*) growing in marshy places.

marsh marigold A showy swamp plant (*Caltha palustris*) of the crowfoot family, having yellow flowers and found in swamps and meadows: also called *cowslip, kingcup.*

marsh·y (mär′shē) *adj.* **marsh·i·er, marsh·i·est 1.** Of, pertaining to, or containing a marsh. **2.** Like a marsh; swampy; boggy. **3.** Growing or produced in a marsh. — **marsh′i·ness** *n.*

Mar·si·an (mär′sē·ən) *n.* The Indo-European language of the **Mar·si** (mär′sī), a people of ancient Italy.

Mar·ston (mär′stən), **John**, 1575?–1634, English divine, dramatist, and satirist: pseudonym **W. Kin·say·der** (kin′sā′dər, kin′sā·dər).

Mar·ston Moor (mär′stən) An area in central Yorkshire, England, where Cromwell defeated the Royalists in a battle of the Civil War, July 2, 1644.

mar·su·pi·al (mär·sōō′pē·əl) *n.* Any member of an order (*Marsupialia*) of viviparous mammals, as the kangaroos, opossums, wombats, etc., whose females typically lack a placenta, carrying their undeveloped young in a marsupium. — *adj.* **1.** Having a marsupium or pouch. **2.** Of, pertaining to a marsupium or the *Marsupialia.* [< NL *marsupialis* < L *marsupium.* See MARSUPIUM.] — **mar·su′pi·a′li·an** (-ā′lē·ən), **mar·su′pi·an** *adj. & n.*

mar·su·pi·um (mär·sōō′pē·əm) *n. pl.* **·pi·a** (-pē·ə) **1.** A pouchlike receptacle on the abdomen of female marsupials, containing the teats and used for carrying the young. **2.** A similar receptacle for carrying eggs, etc., as on some fishes. [< L, pouch, purse < Gk. *marsypion,* dim. of *marsipos* bag]

mart (märt) *n.* **1.** A market. **2.** *Archaic* **a** Buying and selling. **b** A fair. [< MDu. *markt, mart* < L *mercatus.* Doublet of MARKET.]

mar·ta·gon (mär′tə·gon) *n.* The Turk's-cap lily (def. 2).

Mar·ta·ban (mär′tə·bän′), **Gulf of** An inlet of the Andaman Sea in SE Burma.

mar·tel·lo tower (mär·tel′ō) A fort shaped like a circular tower, formerly erected on coasts for defense against invasion. Also **mar·tel′lo.** [after Cape *Mortella,* in Corsica, where such a tower was erected]

mar·ten (mär′tən) *n.* **1.** A weasellike carnivorous mammal (genus *Martes*) having arboreal habits, as the **pine marten** (*M. americana*) of eastern North America. **2.** The valuable, dark brown fur of a marten: also called *baum marten.* [< OF *martrine* of the marten < *martre* marten < WGmc.]

mar·tens·ite (mär′tənz·īt) *n. Metall.* The hardest constituent of quenched steel, consisting of a solid solution of iron and carbon. [after A. *Martens,* died 1914, German metallurgist + -ITE¹] — **mar′ten·sit′ic** (-tən·zit′ik) *adj.*

Mar·tha (mär′thə) A sister of Lazarus and Mary, who served Jesus at Bethany. *Luke* x 38–41.

Martha's Vineyard An island off Cape Cod in SE Massachusetts; 20 mi. long; a summer resort area.

Mar·ti (mär·tē′), **José Julian**, 1853–95, Cuban patriot.

mar·tial (mär′shəl) *adj.* **1.** Of, pertaining to, or concerned with war or the military life. **2.** Suggestive of or suitable for war or military operations. **3.** Of or characteristic of a warrior: *martial* attire. [< OF < L *martialis* pertaining to Mars < *Mars, Martis* Mars] — **mar′tial·ism** *n.* — **mar′tial·ist** *n.* — **mar′tial·ly** *adv.*

Mar·tial (mär′shəl) *adj.* **1.** Pertaining to the god Mars. **2.** In astrology, under the evil influence of the planet Mars.

Mar·tial (mär′shəl), 43–104?, Latin poet and epigrammatist: full name **Marcus Valerius Mar·ti·a·lis** (mär′shē·ā′lis).

martial law Temporary jurisdiction or rule by military forces over the citizens of an area where civil law and order no longer function or exist. Compare MILITARY LAW.

Mar·tian (mär′shən) *adj. Astron.* Of or pertaining to the planet Mars. — *n.* One of the supposed inhabitants of Mars. [< L *Martius* < *Mars, Martis* Mars]

mar·tin (mär′tən) *n.* **1.** Any of certain birds of the swallow family, having a tail that is less forked than that of the common swallow; especially, the **house martin** (*Chelidon urbica*) of Europe, and the **purple martin** (*Progne subis*) of North America. **2.** Any of various similar birds. [< F *Martin,* the bird having been thought to depart on Martinmas]

Mar·tin (mär′tən), **Saint**, 316?–397?, bishop of Tours: called **Martin of Tours.** See MARTINMAS.

Mar·tin (mär′tən), **Homer Dodge**, 1836–97, U.S. painter.

Mar·tin du Gard (mȧr·taṅ′ dü gȧr′), **Roger**, 1881–1958, French novelist and dramatist.

Mar·ti·neau (mär′ti·nō), **Harriet**, 1802–76, English author. — **James**, 1805–1900, English Unitarian clergyman and writer; brother of the preceding.

mar·ti·net (mär′tə·net′) *n.* **1.** A strict military disciplinarian. **2.** One who demands rigid adherence to rules, etc. [after General Jean *Martinet,* 17th c. French drillmaster]

mar·tin·gale (mär′tən·gāl) *n.* **1.** A forked strap that prevents a horse from rearing its head, connecting the head gear with the bellyband. For illustration see HARNESS. **2.** *Naut.* A dolphin striker (def. 1). **3.** A system of gambling in which one doubles the stakes to recover previous losses. Also **mar·tin·gal** (-gal). [< F < Provençal *martengalo,* appar. fem. of *martengo* an inhabitant of Martigues, miserly person < Sp. *almartaga* < Arabic]

mar·ti·ni (mär·tē′nē) *n. pl.* **·nis** A cocktail made of gin and dry vermouth, usually served with a green olive or a twist of lemon peel. [after *Martini* and Rossi, a company making vermouth]

Mar·ti·ni (mär·tē′nē), **Simone di**, 1283–1344, Sienese painter.

Mar·ti·nique (mär′ti·nēk′) An island in the Lesser Antilles, comprising a French Overseas Department; 421 sq. mi.; pop. 332,000 (est. 1969); capital, Fort-de-France.

Mar·tin·mas (mär′tən·məs) *n.* November 11, the feast of St. Martin. [< Saint *Martin* + -MAS]

mart·let (märt′lit) *n.* **1.** A martin. **2.** *Heraldry* A martin or swallow without feet, used as a bearing, crest, or mark of cadency. [< F *martelet,* alter. of *martinet,* dim. of *martin* martin; ? infl. in form by *roitelet* wren]

mar·tyr (mär′tər) *n.* **1.** One who submits to death rather than renounce his religion. **2.** One who dies, suffers, or sacrifices everything for a principle, cause, etc. **3.** One who suffers much, as from ill health or misfortune. — *v.t.* **1.** To make a martyr of. **2.** To torture or persecute. [OE < LL < Gk. *martyr,* Aeolic form of *martyrs, martyros* witness]

mar·tyr·dom (mär′tər·dəm) *n.* **1.** The state or condition of being a martyr. **2.** The death and afflictions of a martyr. **3.** Protracted or extreme suffering. [OE *martyrdōm*]

mar·tyr·ize (mär′tər·īz) *v.* **·ized, ·iz·ing** *v.t.* **1.** To make a martyr of. — *v.i.* **2.** To become a martyr.

mar·tyr·ol·o·gy (mär′tə·rol′ə·jē) *n.* *pl.* **·gies 1.** A list of martyrs, especially Christian religious martyrs. **2.** An account of the lives and sufferings of religious martyrs; also, such accounts collectively. **3.** That branch of ecclesiastical history dealing with the lives of martyrs. [< Med.L *martyrologium* < LGk. *martyrologion* < *martyr* martyr + Gk. *logos* word, account] — **mar·tyr·o·log·ic** (mär′tər·ə·loj′ik) or **·i·cal** *adj.* — **mar′tyr·ol′o·gist** *n.*

mar·tyr·y (mär′tər·ē) *n.* *pl.* **·tyr·ies** A construction, as a chapel or shrine, built to honor a martyr.

mar·vel (mär′vəl) *v.* **mar·veled** or **·velled, mar·vel·ing** or **·vel·ling** *v.i.* **1.** To be filled with wonder, surprise, etc. — *v.t.* **2.** To wonder at or about: with a clause as object. — *n.* **1.** That which excites wonder; a prodigy. **2.** *Archaic* Wonder. [< OF *merveillier* < *merveille* a wonder < L *mirabilia* neut. pl. of *mirabilis* wonderful < *mirari* to wonder at]

Mar·vell (mär′vəl), **Andrew,** 1621–78, English poet

mar·vel-of-Pe·ru (mär′vəl·əv·pə·rōō′) *n.* The four-o'clock.

mar·vel·ous (mär′vəl·əs) *adj.* **1.** Causing astonishment and wonder; amazing; extraordinary. **2.** Miraculous; incredible. **3.** *Informal* Very good; excellent; admirable. Also **mar′vel·lous.** — **mar′vel·ous·ly** *adv.* — **mar′vel·ous·ness** *n.*

Mar·war (mär′wär) See JODHPUR.

Marx (märks), **Karl (Heinrich),** 1818–83, German philosopher and theorist of modern socialism.

Marx·ism (märk′siz·əm) *n.* The body of socialist doctrines formulated by Karl Marx and Friedrich Engels, the basic tenets of which are dialectical materialism, the theory of class struggle, and the labor theory of value.

Marx·ist (märk′sist) *adj.* Of, pertaining to, or like Karl Marx or his theories. — *n.* An adherent of Karl Marx or of his theories. Also **Marx·i·an** (märk′sē·ən).

Mar·y (mâr′ē) The mother of Jesus: also *Virgin Mary.*

Mary The sister of Lazarus and Martha. *Luke* x 39–42.

Mary I, 1516–58, queen of England 1553–58: called **Mary Tudor, Bloody Mary.**

Mary II, 1662–94, queen of England 1689–94; ruled jointly with her husband, William III.

Mary Jane *U.S. Slang* Marijuana.

Mar·y·land (mâr′i·lənd, mer′i-) An eastern State of the United States, on Chesapeake Bay; 10,577 sq. mi.; pop. 3,922,399; capital, Annapolis; entered the Union April 28, 1788, one of the original thirteen States; nickname, *Cockade State* or *Old Line State.* Abbr. *Md.*

Mar·y·le·bone (mâr′i·lə·bon′, mär′lə·bən, *Brit.* mal′ə·bōn′) A metropolitan borough of west central London, England; pop. 68,834 (1961): also called *St. Marylebone.*

Mary Magdalene A woman from Magdala out of whom Jesus cast seven devils (*Luke* viii 2), often identified with the penitent sinner whom Jesus forgave (*Luke* vii 36–50).

Mar·y·ol·a·try (mâr′ē·ol′ə·trē), **Mar·y·ol·o·gy** (-ol′ə·jē) See MARIOLATRY, etc.

Mary, Queen of Scots, 1542–87, queen of Scotland 1542–67; beheaded. Also *Mary Stuart.*

mar·zi·pan (märt′sə·pan, mär′zə-) *n.* A confection of grated almonds, sugar, and white of eggs, usually made into a paste and molded into various shapes: also called *marchpane.* [< G < Ital. *marzapane,* orig., a small box, dry measure, weight < Med.L *matapanus* a Venetian coin stamped with an enthroned Christ < Arabic *mauthabān* seated king, coin < *wathaba* to sit]

mas. or **masc.]** Masculine.

-mas *combining form* Mass; a (specified) festival or its celebration: *Christmas.* [< MASS²]

Ma·sac·cio (mä·sät′chō), 1401–29?, Florentine painter: original name **Tommaso Gui·di** (gwē′dē).

Ma·san (mä′sän) A port city in southern South Korea; pop. 136,000 (est. 1958). Formerly **Ma·sam·po** (mä·säm·pō).

Ma·sa·ryk (mä′sä·rik), **Jan (Garrigue),** 1886–1948, Czechoslovak statesman. — **Tomas (Garrigue),** 1850–1937, Czechoslovak patriot and statesman born in Moravia; first president 1918–35; father of the preceding.

Mas·ba·te (mäz·bä′tā) One of the Visayan Islands, Philippines; 1,262 sq. mi.

masc. Masculine.

Mas·ca·gni (mäs·kä′nyē), **Pietro,** 1863–1945, Italian composer.

mas·car·a (mas·kar′ə) *n.* A cosmetic preparation used to darken or tint the eyelashes and eyebrows. [< Sp. *mascara* mask < Arabic *maskharah* buffoon]

mas·con (mas′kon) *n.* A concentration of dense mass beneath the moon's surface. [< MAS(S) CON(CENTRATION)]

mas·cot (mas′kot, -kət) *n.* A person, animal, or object thought to bring good luck by its presence. [< F *mascotte* < Provençal *mascot,* dim. of *masco* sorcerer, lit., mask]

mas·cu·line (mas′kyə·lin) *adj.* **1.** Of or pertaining to the male sex; male. **2.** Of, pertaining to, typical of, or appropriate for men or boys: *masculine* sports. **3.** Mannish: said of a female. **4.** *Gram.* Applicable to males only or to persons or

things classified, as in declension, as male. Abbr. *masc.* — *n. Gram.* **1.** The masculine gender. **2.** A word or form belonging to the masculine gender. [< OF *masculin* < L *masculinus* < *masculus* male < *mas.* Doublet of MALE.] — **mas′cu·line·ly** *adv.* — **mas′cu·lin′i·ty, mas′cu·line·ness** *n.*
— **Syn.** (adj.) **1.** *Masculine, male, manlike,* and *virile* refer to the qualities of men. *Masculine* is applied to qualities regarded as belonging particularly to men: a *masculine* voice, *masculine* strength. *Male* denotes gender, without other implication: a *male* employee. In *manlike,* comparison is made to the human race or to males: a *manlike* ape, *manlike* stubbornness. *Masculine* and *male* may refer to men of all ages, but *virile* refers especially to the qualities of the adult male, as strength, vigor, and sexual potency. Compare MANLY. — **Ant.** See synonyms for FEMININE.

masculine ending 1. The termination of a line of verse with an accented syllable. **2.** *Gram.* A termination or final syllable indicating masculine gender.

masculine gender See under GENDER.

masculine rhyme Rhyme in which the primary stress and the rhyme fall upon the final or only syllable, as in *breaks, takes* and *alert, convert.*

Mase·field (mās′fēld, māz′-), **John,** 1878–1967, English poet, novelist, and dramatist; poet laureate 1930–67.

ma·ser (mā′zər) *n.* *Physics* Any of various devices that generate electromagnetic waves of precise frequency or that amplify such waves while maintaining frequency and phase, by using the excess energy of a resonant atomic or molecular system. [< *m(icrowave) a(mplification by) s(timulated) e(mission of) r(adiation)*]

mash (mash) *n.* **1.** A soft, pulpy mixture or mass. **2.** A mixture of meal, bran etc., and water, fed warm to horses and cattle. **3.** Crushed or ground grain or malt, steeped in hot water to produce wort for making beer. — *v.t.* **1.** To crush into a mash or pulp. **2.** To steep (malt, grain meal, etc.) in hot water to produce wort. **3.** *Archaic Slang* To flirt with. [OE *max-, mǣsc(wyrt)* mash (wort) infused malt]

mash·er (mash′ər) *n.* **1.** One who or that which mashes. **2.** *Slang* A man who flirts or attempts familiarities, usually with women unknown to him.

Mash·had (mäsh·häd) See MESHED.

mash·ie (mash′ē) *n.* In golf, a five iron. For illustration see GOLF CLUB. Also **mash′y.** [? Alter. of F *massue* club < Celtic]

Mas·i·nis·sa (mas′ə·nis′ə), 238?–148 B.C., king of Numidia; ally of Scipio against the Carthaginians. Also *Massinissa.*

mas·jid (mus′jid) *n.* *Arabic* A mosque: also spelled *musjid.*

mask¹ (mask, mäsk) *n.* **1.** A covering used to conceal all or part of the face; especially: **a** A covering, often grotesque or comic, worn at a masquerade, at Halloween, etc.; a false face.

MASKS
a Greek tragedy. *b* Greek comedy. *c* Tibetan ceremonial. *d* Ancient Shinto. *e* Domino.

b A large, headlike covering for an actor's face, used to represent a specific character or trait, as in Greek and Roman drama. **c** A covering made of heavy wire or other material, worn to protect the face from a fencing foil, baseball, dust, glass, etc. **d** A gas mask (which see). **2.** A cast of a face, usually made of plaster. **3.** That which hides or conceals something from the sight or mind: a *mask* of darkness; under the *mask* of piety. **4.** One who wears a mask. **5.** A masquerade. **6.** See MASQUE (def. 1). **7.** *Mil.* A screen or cover for concealing any military installation or operation. **8.** *Archit.* A reproduction, usually exaggerated or grotesque, of a face or head, used as a decorative device. **9.** The head of an animal, as a fox or dog. **10.** *Photog.* A screen of opaque paper, used to cover or modify part of a plate during printing. — *v.t.* **1.** To cover (the face, head, etc.) with a mask. **2.** To conceal with or as with a mask; disguise. — *v.i.* **3.** To put on a mask; assume a disguise. [< F *masque* < Ital. *maschera, mascara* < Arabic *maskharah* buffoon]

mask² (mask, mäsk) *v.t. & v.i. Brit. Dial.* To infuse or be infused. [Var. of MASH]

mas·ka·longe (mas′kə·lonj) *n.* The muskellunge, a fish.

masked (maskt, mäskt) *adj.* **1.** Covered or hidden by a mask. **2.** Disguised; camouflaged. **3.** *Bot.* Personate. **4.** *Zool.* Having markings resembling a mask.

masked ball A ball at which the guests wear masks.

masked hunter The kissing bug.

mas·keg (mas′keg) *n.* Muskeg (which see).

mask·er (mas′kər, mäs′-) *n.* One who wears a mask or participates in a masque. Also spelled **masquer.**

mask·ing tape (mas′king, mäs′-) An adhesive tape used to cover those parts of a surface that are not to be painted, sprayed, etc.

mas·ki·nonge (mas′kə·nonj) *n.* The muskellunge, a fish.

mas·o·chism (mas′ə·kiz′əm) *n.* **1.** *Psychol.* A condition in which sexual gratification depends largely on undergoing physical pain or humiliation. **2.** A tendency to derive pleasure from one's own suffering. Compare SADISM. [after Leopold von Sacher-*Masoch*, 1835–95, Austrian novelist, who described this condition] — **mas′o·chist** *n.* — **mas′o·chis′tic** *adj.* — **mas′o·chis′ti·cal·ly** (-kə·lē, -klē) *adv.*

ma·son (mā′sən) *n.* **1.** One skilled in building with stone, brick, concrete, etc. **2.** A stonecutter. — *v.t.* To build of or strengthen with brick, stone, etc. [< OF *masson, macon* < Med.L *matio, macio, -onis*, prob. < Gmc.]

Ma·son (mā′sən) *n.* Freemason (which see).

Ma·son (mā′sən) **George**, 1725–92, American Revolutionary statesman. — **John**, 1586–1635, English colonial administrator in America; founded New Hampshire.

mason bee Any of various solitary bees (genus *Chalicodoma*) that build their nests of sand, clay, etc.

Mason City A city in northern Iowa; pop 30,379.

Ma·son-Dix·on line (mā′sən·dik′sən) The boundary between Pennsylvania and Maryland, surveyed by the Englishmen Charles Mason and Jeremiah Dixon in 1763 and popularly regarded as dividing the North from the South. Also **Mason and Dixon's line.**

ma·son·ic (mə son′ik) *adj.* **1.** *Usually cap.* Of, pertaining to, or like Freemasons or Freemasonry. **2.** Of or pertaining to masons or masonry.

Ma·son·ite (mā′sən·īt) *n.* A tough fiberboard made from wood fibers, used as a building and construction material: a trade name. Also **ma′son·ite.**

Ma·son jar (mā′sən) A glass jar having a tightly fitting screw top, used for canning and preserving. [after John L. Mason, 19th c. American inventor]

ma·son·ry (mā′sən·rē) *n.* *pl.* **·ries** **1.** The art or work of a mason. **2.** That which is built by masons.

Ma·son·ry (mā′sən·rē) *n.* Freemasonry (which see).

Ma·so·ra (mə·sô′rə) *n.* **1.** The body of traditional information relied on by Jews to insure correct textual reading of the Old Testament. **2.** The collection of marginal notes on which this information is based, made by Jewish scholars before the tenth century. Also **Ma·so′rah.** [< Hebrew (modern) *māsōrah* < Hebrew *māsōreth* tradition, orig., bond (of the covenant)] — **Mas·o·ret·ic** (mas′ə·ret′ik) or **·i·cal** *adj.*

Mas·o·rete (mas′ə·rēt) *n.* One of the Jewish scholars who made the notations constituting the Masora. Also **Mas′o·rite** (-rīt).

Mas·pe·ro (mäs′pə·rō, *Fr.* más·pə·rō′), **Sir Gaston Camille Charles,** 1846–1916, French Egyptologist.

masque (mask, mäsk) *n.* **1.** An elaborately staged dramatic performance, popular during the 16th and 17th centuries in England, originally in pantomime only, but later adding dialogue, poetry, and song; also, something written for such a performance. **2.** A masquerade. Also spelled **mask.** [See MASK¹.]

mas·quer (mas′kər, mäs-) See MASKER.

mas·quer·ade (mas′kə·rād′, mäs′-) *n.* **1.** A social gathering in which the guests are masked and dressed in fancy costumes. **2.** The costumes worn at such a gathering. **3.** A false show, disguise, or pretense: a *masquerade* of piety. Also called **mask, masque.** — *v.i.* **·ad·ed, ·ad·ing** **1.** To take part in a masquerade. **2.** To wear a mask or disguise. **3.** To disguise one's true character; assume a false appearance. [Alter. of F *mascarade* < Sp. *mascarada* < *máscara* mask. See MASCARA.] — **mas′quer·ad′er** *n.*

mass (mas, mäs) *n.* **1.** A coherent body of matter having no definite shape but relatively large in size: a *mass* of clay. **2.** An assemblage of individual parts or objects that collectively make up a single body: a *mass* of flowers. **3.** A great amount or number of anything: a *mass* of evidence. **4.** The principal or greater part of anything; majority: the *mass* of spectators. **5.** The volume or magnitude of a solid body; bulk; size: the overwhelming *mass* of the mountain. **6.** In painting, the solid, unified portions of color or light in a composition. **7.** In pharmacy, the thick, pastelike combination of drugs used for making pills. **8.** *Physics* The measure of the inertia of a body, as indicated by the acceleration imparted to it when acted upon by a given force and which may be expressed as the quotient of the weight of the body divided by the acceleration due to gravity. — **the masses** The great body or majority of ordinary people. — *adj.* **1.** Attended by, designed for, characteristic of, or affecting a large mass of people. **2.** Done in a large-scale manner; produced in large amounts. **3.** Total; all-over: the *mass* effect. — *v.t. & v.i.* To form into a mass; assemble. [< OF *masse* < L *massa*, prob. < Gk. *maza* barley cake]

Mass (mas, mäs) *n.* *Eccl.* **1.** In the Roman Catholic and some Anglican churches, the eucharistic liturgy, consisting of various prayers and ritual ceremonies and regarded as a commemoration or repetition of Christ's sacrifice on the Cross. See HIGH MASS, LOW MASS. **2.** A celebration of this liturgy. **3.** A musical setting for some of the fixed portions of this liturgy, usually including the Credo, Sanctus, Kyrie eleison, Gloria, Benedictus, and Agnus Dei. — **black mass** **1.** *Usually cap.* A Mass for the dead at which the celebrant

wears black vestments. **2.** A blasphemous ceremony performed as a burlesque of the Mass in so-called worship of Satan. [OE *mæsse* < LL *messa* dismissal < L *missa*, pp. fem. of *mittere* to send, dismiss < *ite, missa est* go, you are dismissed; said by the priest after the Eucharist is ended]

Mass. Massachusetts.

Mas·sa·chu·set (mas′ə·choo′sit) *n.* **1.** One of a large tribe of North American Indians of Algonquian stock, formerly inhabiting the region around Massachusetts Bay. **2.** The language of this tribe. Also **Mas′sa·chu′sett.** [< Algonquian (Massachuset) *Massa-adchu-es-et*, lit., at the big hill < *mass* big + *wadchu* hill + *es*, dim. suffix + *et* at the]

Mas·sa·chu·setts (mas′ə·choo′sits) A NE State of the United States on the Atlantic; 8,257 sq. mi.; pop. 5,689,170; capital, Boston; entered the Union Feb. 6, 1788, one of the thirteen original States; nickname, *Bay State.* Officially **Commonwealth of Massachusetts.** Abbr. *Mass.*

Massachusetts Bay A wide inlet of the Atlantic on the eastern coast of Massachusetts, extending from Cape Ann to Cape Cod.

mas·sa·cre (mas′ə·kər) *n.* **1.** A savage and indiscriminate killing of human beings, as in warfare, acts of persecution, revenge, etc. **2.** *U.S. Informal* A crushing defeat, as in sports. — *v.t.* **·cred** (-kərd), **·cring** **1.** To kill indiscriminately or in great numbers. **2.** *U.S. Informal* To defeat severely, as in sports. [< MF < OF *macacre, macecle*, ? < *mache-col* butcher < *macher* to smash + *col* neck < L *collum*] — **mas′sa·crer** *n.*
— **Syn.** (noun) *Massacre, slaughter, butchery,* and *carnage* refer to killing on a large scale. A *massacre* is the killing of those who are defenseless or unresisting, as in barbarous warfare. *Slaughter* may be used in the same sense, but frequently is applied to any great loss of life in battle, riot, etc. In a more restricted sense, *slaughter* is used of the killing of animals for food. *Butchery* stresses ruthlessness and wantonness, and compares the killing of men to the *slaughter* of cattle. *Carnage* retains much of its original sense of the heaped up bodies of the slain, and refers to the result rather than to the process of a *massacre* or *slaughter.*

mas·sage (mə·säzh′) *n.* A manual or mechanical manipulation of parts of the body, as by rubbing, kneading, slapping or the like, used to promote circulation, relax muscles, etc. — *v.t.* **·saged, ·sag·ing** To treat by massage. [< F < *masser* to massage < *masse* mass < L *massa*, ? < Gk. *massein* to knead] — **mas·sag′er, mas·sag′ist** *n.* — **mas·sa·geuse** (mas′ə·zhœz′) *n.fem.*

Mas·sa·pe·qua (mas′ə·pē′kwə) A village in SE New York, on Long Island; pop. 26,951.

mas·sa·sau·ga (mas′ə·sô′gə) *n.* **1.** *U.S. & Canadian* A small rattlesnake (*Sistrurus catenatus*) found near the Great Lakes region and south to Texas and Mexico. **2.** The pygmy rattlesnake. [< Ojibwa name of a river in Ontario, Canada]

Mas·sa·soit (mas′ə·soit), 1580?–1661, American Indian chief of Massachusetts; friendly with the Pilgrims of Plymouth Colony.

Mas·sa·wa (mäs·sä′wä) A port city in N. Ethiopia, in Eritrea, on the Red Sea; the former capital; pop. about 25,000. Also **Mas·sa′ua.** Formerly **Mas·so′wa.**

mass defect *Physics* The difference between the mass number of a nuclide and its nucleon mass.

mas·sé (mə·sā′) *n.* In billiards, a stroke with a cue held perpendicularly, causing the cue ball to return in a straight line or describe a curve. Also **massé shot.** [< F < *masser* to make a massé shot < *masse* billiard cue, lit., mace]

Mas·sé·na (má·sā·ná′), **André,** 1758?–1817, Prince d'Essling, French general under Napoleon.

Mas·se·net (mas′nā′, *Fr.* más·ne′), **Jules Émile Frédéric,** 1842–1912, French composer.

mas·se·ter (ma·sē′tər) *n.* *Anat.* A powerful muscle that is connected to and helps raise the lower jaw, as in chewing, etc. [< NL < Gk. *masētēr* chewer < *masasthai* to chew] — **mas·se·ter·ic** (mas′ə·ter′ik), **mas′se·ter′ine** (-ēn, -īn) *adj.*

mas·seur (ma·sûr′, *Fr.* má·sœr′) *n.* A man who practices or gives massage. [< F] — **mas·seuse** (ma·sōōz′, -sōōs′; *Fr.* má·sœz′) *n.fem.*

Mas·sey (mas′ē), **Raymond,** born 1896, U.S. actor born in Canada. — **Vincent,** 1887–1967, Canadian diplomat and statesman; governor general 1952–59; brother of Raymond.

mas·si·cot (mas′ə·kot) *n.* Lead monoxide, PbO, a mineral associated with galena and used in powdered form as a yellowish paint pigment similar to litharge. [< F < Sp. *mexacote* < Arabic *shabb qubti* Coptic alum]

mas·sif (mas′if, *Fr.* má·sēf′) *n.* *Geol.* **1.** The central mass of a mountainous area, having one or more longitudinal or transverse valleys. **2.** A diastrophic block of the earth's crust, isolated by boundary faults. [< F]

Mas·sil·lon (mas′ə·lən) A city in NE Ohio, near Canton; pop. 32,539.

Mas·sine (mä·sēn′), **Léonide,** born 1896, U.S. ballet dancer and choreographer, born in Russia.

Mas·sin·ger (mas′ən·jər), **Philip,** 1583–1640, English dramatist.

Mass·i·nis·sa (mas′ə·nis′ə) See MASINISSA.

mas·sive (mas′iv) *adj.* **1.** Forming or constituting a large mass; having great bulk and weight; ponderous. **2.** Relatively large or heavy: a *massive* head. **3.** Imposing or impressive in scale, scope, degree, intensity, etc. **4.** *Mineral.* Lacking definite or externally observable crystalline form. **5.** *Geol.* Homogeneous, as certain rock formations. **6.** *Pathol.* Extending over or affecting a large area. [< F *massif*] — **mas′sive·ly** *adv.* — **mas′sive·ness** *n.*

mass media The various means of disseminating information to a very wide public audience, as newspapers, magazines, radio, television, etc.

mass meeting A large public gathering for the discussion or promotion of some topic or cause, usually political.

mass noun *Gram.* A noun, such as *greed* or *water*, that refers to an abstraction or unknown quantity and that cannot be used in the plural or with an indefinite article.

mass number *Physics* The total number of nucleons of an atom; the integer nearest the observed mass of an isotope.

mas·so·ther·a·py (mas′ō-ther′ə·pē) *n.* Treatment by massage. [< Gk. *massein* to knead + THERAPY] — **mas′so·ther′a·peu′tic** (-ther′ə·pyoo′tik) *adj.*

mass production The manufacture or production, usually by machinery, of goods or articles in great numbers or quantities. — **mass-pro·duced** (mas′prə-doost′, -dyoost′) *adj.*

mass ratio *Aerospace* The ratio of the mass of a rocket at the time of liftoff to its mass after the fuel has been used up.

mass spectrograph *Physics* An instrument for determining the relative masses of electrically charged particles.

mass·y (mas′ē) *adj.* **mass·i·er, mass·i·est** Massive. — **mass′i·ness** *n.*

mast[1] (mast, mäst) *n.* **1.** *Naut.* A pole or spar, usually of round timber or tubular iron or steel, set upright in a sailing vessel to sustain the yards, sails, etc. **2.** Any large, upright pole, as of a derrick, crane, etc. — **before the mast** Serving as a common sailor: from the fact that common sailors were quartered forward of the foremast. — *v.t.* To furnish with a mast or masts. [OE *mæst*]

mast[2] (mast, mäst) *n.* The fruit of the oak, beech, etc., when used as food for swine. [OE *mæst* mast, fodder]

mast- Var. of MASTO-.

mas·ta·ba (mas′tə·bə) *n.* In ancient Egypt, an oblong building with sloping sides and a flat top, covering the mouth of a burial pit and used as a mortuary chapel and place of offering. Also **mas′ta·bah.** [< Arabic *mastabah* bench]

MASTABA

mas·tec·to·my (mas·tek′tə·mē) *n. pl.* **·mies** *Surg.* The operation of removing a breast. [< MAST- + -ECTOMY]

mast·ed (mast′id, mäst′-) *adj.* Having (a specified number of) masts: used in combination: a *two-masted* vessel.

mas·ter (mas′tər, mäs′-) *n.* **1.** One who has control, direction, or authority over someone or something, as over workers, a household, an animal, etc. **2.** One exceptionally gifted or skilled in an art, craft, science, etc.: a *master* of oratory. **3.** A craftsman or worker whose skill or experience qualifies him to practice his craft on his own and to train apprentices. **4.** One who has the ability to control or dispose of something to good advantage: a *master* of his time and money. **5.** A teacher or leader in philosophy, religion, etc., who has followers or disciples. **6.** *Chiefly Brit.* A male teacher. **7.** One who has received an academic degree more advanced than a bachelor's but less advanced than a doctor's; also, the degree itself. Abbr. *M.* **8.** One who has charge of or presides over a place, institution, ceremony, function, etc.: a *master* of ceremonies. **9.** Something considered as having the power to control or influence: Never let fear be your *master.* **10.** Something, as a matrix, mold, stencil, etc., from which copies or impressions are made. **11.** *Usually cap.* A youth or boy; also, a title prefixed to a boy's name: *Master* John Brown. **12.** *Usually cap.* A title of respect or of address, formerly used alone or prefixed to a man's name but now generally replaced by *Mister.* **13.** In the Scottish peerage, the title of the eldest son or heir apparent of a viscount or baron. **14.** A victor or conqueror. **15.** *Law* An officer of the court who assists the judge by undertaking any of various tasks. **16.** *Naut.* The captain of a ship. **17.** *Archaic* A work, as a painting or sculpture, by a master. — **Syn.** See CHIEF. — *v.t.* **1.** To bring under control; defeat. **2.** To become expert in: to *master* Greek. **3.** To control or govern as a master. — *adj.* **1.** Of, pertaining to, or characteristic of a master. **2.** Having or exercising control. **3.** Principal; main: the *master* plan. **4.** Designating a device or mechanism that controls, operates, or acts as a pattern or norm for something else: a *master* switch; a *master* copy. [Fusion of OE *mægister* and OF *maistre*, both < L *magister*, orig., a double compar. of *magnus* great] — **mas′ter·dom** *n.* — **mas′ter·hood** *n.*

mas·ter-at-arms (mas′tər·ət·ärmz′, mäs′-) *n. pl.* **mas·ters-at-arms** A petty officer assigned to police duty on a naval vessel.

master builder 1. An architect. **2.** One who supervises building construction.

mas·ter·ful (mas′tər·fəl, mäs′-) *adj.* **1.** Vigorously bold or authoritative in conduct, decision, manner, etc. **2.** Domineering; imperious. **3.** Having or displaying the skill of a master. — **mas′ter·ful·ly** *adv.* — **mas′ter·ful·ness** *n.*

master hand 1. An expert. **2.** The skill of an expert.

master key A key that will unlock two or more locks, each of which has its own key that fits no other lock.

mas·ter·ly (mas′tər·lē, mäs′-) *adj.* Characteristic of or befitting a master: a *masterly* performance. — *adv.* In a masterly manner; as befits a master. — **mas′ter·li·ness** *n.*

master mason A skilled mason.

Master Mason A Freemason of the third degree.

master mechanic An able, experienced mechanic, usually in charge of other mechanics.

mas·ter·mind (mas′tər·mīnd′, mäs′-) *n.* A person of great executive ability; especially, one who plans and directs at the highest levels of policy and strategy. — *v.t.* To plan and direct (a project, etc.) at the highest strategic level.

Master of Arts 1. A degree given by a college or university to a person who has completed a prescribed course of graduate study of at least one year in the humanities, social sciences, etc. **2.** A person who has received this degree. Abbr. *M.A., A.M.*

master of ceremonies 1. A person presiding over an entertainment or dinner and introducing the performers or speakers. **2.** A person who supervises the ceremonies at a public or formal function. Also called *emcee.* Abbr. *M.C.*

Master of Science 1. A degree given by a college or university to a person who has completed a prescribed course of graduate study of at least one year in science. **2.** A person who has received this degree. Abbr. *M.S., M.Sc., Sc. M., S.M.*

mas·ter·piece (mas′tər·pēs′, mäs′-) *n.* **1.** Something of notable excellence; an unusually brilliant achievement: a musical *masterpiece.* **2.** Something considered to be the greatest achievement of its creator: It was her *masterpiece.* **3.** Anything remarkable for some particular quality or feature: a *masterpiece* of bad taste. [Trans. of G *meisterstück*]

Mas·ters (mas′tərz, mäs′-), **Edgar Lee,** 1869–1950, U.S. poet and biographer.

mas·ter·ship (mas′tər·ship, mäs′-) *n.* **1.** The state or condition of being a master or ruler. **2.** The office, status, or function of a master. **3.** The skill, experience, or authority of a master.

mas·ter·sing·er (mas′tər·sing′ər, mäs′-) *n.* A Meistersinger (which see). [Trans. of G *meistersinger*]

mas·ter·stroke (mas′tər·strōk′, mäs′-) *n.* A masterly or decisive action or achievement.

mas·ter·work (mas′tər·wûrk′, mäs′-) *n.* A masterpiece.

master workman 1. A skilled workman, craftsman, or artist. **2.** A foreman or overseer over other workmen.

mas·ter·y (mas′tər·ē, mäs′-) *n. pl.* **·ter·ies 1.** The state of being master; dominion; control: to gain *mastery* of the entire world. **2.** Superior knowledge or skill: a *mastery* of languages. **3.** Victory or superiority, as in a contest. **4.** The act of mastering a craft, technique, etc.

mast·head (mast′hed′, mäst′-) *n.* **1.** *Naut.* **a** The head or top of a mast. **b** A sailor acting as a lookout at the masthead. **2.** The part of a newspaper or other periodical that gives the names of the editors, staff, and owners. — *v.t.* **1.** To raise to or display at the masthead, as a flag. **2.** To send to a masthead for punishment.

mas·tic (mas′tik) *n.* **1.** A small Mediterranean evergreen tree (*Pistacia lentiscus*) of the cashew family. **2.** The aromatic resin obtained from this tree, used in varnishes and sometimes as a flavoring agent in alcoholic liquors. **3.** A quick-drying, pastelike cement. [< F < LL *mastichum* < Gk. *mastichē*]

mas·ti·cate (mas′tə·kāt) *v.t.* **·cat·ed, ·cat·ing 1.** To grind (food) for swallowing; chew. **2.** To reduce, as rubber, to a pulp by crushing or kneading. [< LL *masticatus,* pp. of *masticare* to chew < Gk. *mastichaein* to gnash the teeth < *mastax* jaw] — **mas′ti·ca′tion** *n.* — **mas′ti·ca′tor** *n.*

mas·ti·ca·to·ry (mas′tə·kə·tôr′ē, -tō′rē) *adj.* **1.** Of, pertaining to, or used in mastication. **2.** Adapted for chewing. — *n. pl.* **·ries** A substance chewed to increase salivation.

mas·tiff (mas′tif, mäs′-) *n.* One of an old English breed of large hunting dogs, having a thickset, heavy body, a broad skull, drooping ears, and pendulous lips. [< OF *mastin* < L *mansuetus* gentle < pp. of *mansuescere* to tame < *manus* hand; infl. in form by OF *mestif* mongrel]

mas·ti·goph·o·ran (mas′ti·gof′ər·ən) *n. Zool.* Any of a class (*Mastigophora,* formerly *Flagellata*) of protozoa having one or more flagella. — *adj.* Of or pertaining to the *Mastigophora.* [< Gk. *mastix, mastigos* whip + *phoros* bearing < *pherein* to bear]

mas·ti·tis (mas·tī′tis) *n.* **1.** *Pathol.* Inflammation of the breast or mammary gland: also called *mammitis.* **2.** *Vet.* Garget. [< MAST- + -ITIS]

masto- *combining form* Med. The breast or the mammary glands. Also, before vowels, **mast-**, as in *mastitis*. [< Gk. *mastos* the breast]

mas·to·don (mas′tə·don) *n. Paleontol.* Any of various large, extinct mammals (genus *Mammut*), distinguished from elephants and mammoths chiefly by the structure of the molar teeth. [< NL < MAST- + Gk. *odous, odontos* tooth; from the nipple-shaped projections on its molar teeth]

mas·toid (mas′toid) *adj.* **1.** *Anat.* **a** Designating a nipple-shaped process of the temporal bone located behind the ear. **b** Of, pertaining to, or situated near this process. For illustration see SKULL. **2.** Having the shape of a breast or nipple. — *n.* The mastoid process. [< Gk. *mastoeidēs* < *mastos* breast + *eidos* form]

MASTODON
(About 9 feet high at shoulder)

mas·toid·ec·to·my (mas′toid·ek′tə·mē) *n. pl.* **·mies** *Surg.* The removal of mastoid cells or of the mastoid process. [< MASTOID + -ECTOMY]

mas·toid·i·tis (mas′toid·ī′tis) *n. Pathol.* Inflammation of the mastoid process. [< MASTOID + -ITIS]

mas·tur·bate (mas′tər·bāt) *v.i.* **·bat·ed, ·bat·ing** To perform masturbation. [< L *masturbatus,* pp. of *masturbari;* ult. origin uncertain]

mas·tur·ba·tion (mas′tər·bā′shən) *n.* Stimulation of the sexual organs, usually by oneself: also called *onanism, self-abuse.* [< L *masturbatio, -onis*] — **mas′tur·ba′tor** *n.* — **mas·tur·ba·to·ry** (mas′tər·bə·tôr′ē, -tō′rē) *adj.*

Ma·su·ri·a (mə·zŏŏr′ē·ə, -sŏŏr′-) A region of NE Poland on the Soviet border, containing the many **Masurian Lakes:** Polish *Mazury.* German **Ma·su·ren** (mä·zŏŏ′rən).

ma·su·ri·um (mə·sŏŏr′ē·əm) *n.* A supposed metallic element whose place in the periodic table is now occupied by technetium. Abbr. **Ma.** [after *Masuria,* where first found]

mat¹ (mat) *n.* **1.** A flat piece of material made of fiber, rushes, leather, rubber, etc., and used primarily to cover floors; also, a smaller piece of this, used to sit or lie on. **2.** A thickly padded piece of material placed on the floor for protection in various gymnastic sports. **3.** A small, flat piece of material, as lace, straw, or plastic, used as a table protection, ornament, etc. **4.** Any dense, twisted, or tangled mass, as of hair. **5.** *Naut.* A weblike material of rope yarn, used to protect rigging from friction. — *v.* **mat·ted, mat·ting** *v.t.* **1.** To cover with or as with a mat or mats. **2.** To knot or entangle into a mat. — *v.i.* **3.** To become knotted or entangled together. [OE *matt(e)* < LL *matta*]

mat² (mat) *n.* **1.** A border of cardboard or other material, serving as the frame or part of the frame of a picture. **2.** *Printing* A matrix. **3.** A lusterless, dull, or roughened surface, as on metal or glass; also, a tool for producing such a surface. — *v.t.* **mat·ted, mat·ting** **1.** To produce a dull surface on, as on metal or glass. **2.** To furnish (a picture) with a mat. — *adj.* Having a lusterless surface. Also spelled *matte.* [OF, defeated, overcome]

mat. **1.** Matinée. **2.** Matins. **3.** Maturity.

Mat·a·be·le (mat′ə·bē′lē) *n. pl.* **·be·le** or **·be·les** (-bē′lēz) One of a Zulu people who were forced by the Boers to leave the Transvaal in 1837.

mat·a·dor (mat′ə·dôr) *n.* **1.** In bullfighting, the man who kills the bull after completing various maneuvers with a cape in order to tire the animal. **2.** In various card games, one of the highest trumps. [< Sp., killer < *matar* to slay]

Ma·ta·mo·ros (mä′tä·mô′rōs) A city in NE Mexico, near the mouth of the Rio Grande; pop. about 46,000.

Mat·a·nus·ka Valley (mat′ə·nŏŏs′kə) A region of southern Alaska, site of an experimental colonization project by the United States government in 1935.

Ma·tan·zas (mä·tän′säs) A Province of western Cuba; 3,259 sq. mi.; pop. 483,300 (est. 1970); capital, **Matanzas,** a port; pop. 84,100 (est. 1967).

Ma·ta·pan (mä′tä·pän′), **Cape** The southernmost point of the mainland of Greece: also *Cape Tainaron.*

match¹ (mach) *n.* **1.** One who or that which is similar to another in some quality or characteristic. **2.** One who or that which is exactly equal to another; facsimile. **3.** One who or that which is able to cope with or oppose another as an equal; a peer. **4.** Either of two things that harmonize or correspond with each other: The hat is a good *match* for the coat. **5.** A suitable or fit pair: The hat and coat are a good *match.* **6.** A game or contest. **7.** A marriage or mating; also, an agreement to marry or mate. **8.** A possible partner in marriage. — *v.t.* **1.** To be similar to or in accord with in quality, degree, etc.: His looks *match* his mood. **2.** To make, provide, or select as equals or as suitable for one another: to *match* pearls. **3.** To cause to correspond; adapt: *Match* your expenses to your income. **4.** To compare so as to decide superiority; test: to *match* wits. **5.** To set (equal opponents) in opposition: to *match* boxers. **6.** To equal; oppose successfully: No one could *match* him. **7.** To flip (a coin or coins) so as to compare or bet on the faces that land upright; also, to flip coins in this manner with (another

person). **8.** To fit or place (boards, etc.) together. **9.** To place together as mates or companions; marry. — *v.i.* **10.** To be equal or similar; correspond. **11.** To be married; mate. [OE *gemæcca* companion] — **match′a·ble** *adj.* — **match′er** *n.*

match² (mach) *n.* **1.** A splinter of soft wood or a piece of waxed thread or cardboard tipped with a combustible composition that ignites by friction. **2.** A wick or cord prepared to burn quickly or slowly, formerly used for firing cannon. [< OF *mesche* wick, prob. < L *myxa* wick of a candle]

match·board (mach′bôrd′, -bōrd′) *n.* A board made with a groove along one edge and a tongue along the other so that the tongue of one board fits into the groove of another, used for floors, etc.

match·book (mach′bŏŏk′) *n.* A small paper folder containing safety matches. Also **match·fol·der** (mach′fōl′dər).

match·box (mach′boks′) *n.* A small box for matches.

match·less (mach′lis) *adj.* Having no match or equal; peerless. — **match′less·ly** *adv.* — **match′less·ness** *n.*

match·lock (mach′lok′) *n.* **1.** An old type of musket fired by igniting the powder with a slow-burning wick or match. **2.** The gunlock on such a musket.

match·mak·er (mach′mā′kər) *n.* **1.** One who tries to bring about a marriage between other persons. **2.** One who arranges an athletic match. — **match′mak′ing** *adj. & n.*

match·mak·er² (mach′mā′kər) *n.* One who makes matches for lighting. — **match′mak′ing** *adj. & n.*

match·mark (mach′märk′) *n.* A distinguishing mark placed on separable parts of machinery as a guide for assembling. — *v.t.* To put a matchmark upon.

match play In golf, a form of competitive play in which the score is computed by totaling the number of holes won or lost by each side. Compare MEDAL PLAY.

match point In tennis and similar games, the final point needed to win a match.

match·wood (mach′wŏŏd′) *n.* **1.** Wood suitable for making matches. **2.** Splinters.

mate¹ (māt) *n.* **1.** Something matched, paired, or joined in some way with another: a shoe and its *mate.* **2.** A husband or wife. **3.** The male or female of two animals paired for propagation. **4.** A companion; comrade. **5.** An officer of a merchant vessel, ranking next below the captain. **6.** *Naval* An assistant to a warrant officer; a petty officer. — **Syn.** See ASSOCIATE. — *v.* **mat·ed, mat·ing** *v.t.* **1.** To join or match closely together; pair. **2.** To join in marriage. **3.** To unite for breeding, as animals. — *v.i.* **4.** To marry. **5.** To pair. **6.** To consort; associate. [< MLG < *gemate* < *ge-* together + *mat* meat, food. Prob. akin to MEAT.]

mate² (māt) *v.t.* **mat·ed, mat·ing** In chess, to checkmate. — *n.* A checkmate. — *interj.* Checkmate. [< CHECKMATE]

ma·te (mä′tā, mat′ā) *n.* **1.** An infusion of the leaves of a Brazilian holly (*Ilex paraguariensis*), much used as a beverage in South America: also called *Paraguay tea, yerba.* **2.** The plant itself. [< Sp. < Quechua *mati* calabash (in which it was steeped)] Also **ma·té.**

mat·e·lote (mat′ə·lōt) *n.* A stew of fish in wine and oil. Also **mat′e·lotte** (-lot). [< F *matelot* sailor]

ma·ter (mā′tər, mä′-) *n. Brit. Informal* Mother. [< L]

ma·ter do·lo·ro·sa (mä′tər dō′lə·rō′sə) *Latin* **1.** Sorrowful mother. **2.** *Usually cap.* In art or music, the Virgin Mary as the sorrowing mother.

ma·ter·fa·mil·i·as (mā′tər·fə·mil′ē·əs) *n. Latin* The mother of a family; a matron.

ma·te·ri·al (mə·tir′ē·əl) *n.* **1.** That of which anything is or may be composed or constructed; the component part or constituent element: building *material.* **2.** Anything that may be used in creating, working up, or developing something: fresh *material* for a novel. **3.** *pl.* The tools, instruments, implements, etc., for doing something: drawing *materials.* **4.** Cloth or fabric. — *adj.* **1.** Of, pertaining to, or composed of matter; corporeal; physical. **2.** Of, related to, or affecting the body or sensual appetites: *material* well-being. **3.** Concerned with or devoted to things primarily physical rather than spiritual or intellectual: a *material* culture. **4.** Substantial; important: a *material* gain. **5.** Relevant; pertinent: with *to.* **6.** *Law* Having an important or pertinent influence on the decision of a case or cause. **7.** *Philos.* Pertaining to matter as opposed to form. [< LL *materialis* < L *materia* matter, stuff]

ma·te·ri·al·ism (mə·tir′ē·əl·iz′əm) *n.* **1.** *Philos.* **a** The doctrine that everything in the universe is reducible to matter and can be explained in terms of physical laws. **b** The doctrine that physical well-being and material possessions constitute the highest good. **2.** Undue regard for the material rather than the spiritual or intellectual aspects of life.

ma·te·ri·al·ist (mə·tir′ē·əl·ist) *n.* **1.** One who believes in materialism (def. 1). **2.** One excessively or exclusively interested in the material or physical aspects of life. — **ma·te′ri·al·is′tic** *adj.* — **ma·te′ri·al·is′ti·cal·ly** *adv.*

ma·te·ri·al·i·ty (mə·tir′ē·al′ə·tē) *n. pl.* **·ties** **1.** The state or quality of being material. **2.** Something composed of matter. **3.** *Obs.* Matter; substance. Also **ma·te′ri·al·ness.**

ma·te·ri·al·ize (mə·tir′ē·əl·īz′) *v.* **·ized, ·iz·ing** *v.t.* **1.** To give material or actual form to; invest with material charac-

MATHEMATICAL SYMBOLS

$+$	Plus; positive; sign of addition
$-$	Minus; negative; sign of subtraction
$\pm$	Plus or minus
$\mp$	Minus or plus
$\times,\ \cdot$	Multiplied by
$\div,\ :$	Divided by
$=,\ ::$	Equals
$\cong$	Approximately equal; congruent
$>$	Greater than
$<$	Less than
$/$	Is not; does not: drawn through another symbol, as $a \neq b$, a is not equal to b
$\geqq$	Greater than or equal to
$\leqq$	Less than or equal to
$\sim$	Similar to; equivalent
$\therefore$	Therefore
$\because$	Since; because
$\equiv$	Identical; identically equal to
$\propto$	Directly proportional to; varies directly as
∞	Infinity
i	Square root of minus one
a_1, a_2, etc.	Particular values of a (a variable)
a^n	a raised to the n power
$\frac{a}{b}$	a divided by b
$\sqrt{a}$	Square root of a. See RADICAL SIGN.
$\sqrt[n]{a}$	nth root of a
e, ϵ	Base of natural system of logarithms; 2.718...
Σ	Summation of
$\sum_1^n$	Summation of n terms, one for each positive integer from 1 to n
Π	Product of
$\prod_1^n$	Product of n terms, one for each positive integer from 1 to n
$\int$	Integral of
$\int_b^a$	Definite integral between limits a and b
$\doteq, \rightarrow$	Approaches as a limit
$f(x), F(x), \phi(x)$	Function of x
Δ	Increment of, as Δy
d	Differential, as dx
$\frac{dy}{dx}, f'(x)$	Derivative of $y = f(x)$ with respect to x
δ	Variation, as δy
π	Pi; the ratio of the circumference and a diameter of the same circle; 3.14159...
$n!, \lfloor n$	n factorial; factorial n
$(), [], \{\}$	Indicate that the enclosed symbols are to be treated as a single number
$-$	Indicates that the symbols below it are to be treated as a single number, as $\overline{PQ}^2$. See VINCULUM.
$\angle$	Angle
$\parallel$	Parallel to
$\perp$	Perpendicular to; perpendicular
$\triangle$	Triangle
$\llcorner$	Right angle
$'$	Minutes of arc; prime
$''$	Seconds of arc; double prime

teristics. **2.** In spiritualism, to cause (a spirit, etc.) to appear in visible form. **3.** To make materialistic. — *v.i.* **4.** To assume material or visible form; appear. **5.** To take form or shape; be realized: Our plans never *materialized*. — **ma·te′ri·al·i·za′tion** *n.* — **ma·te′ri·al·iz′er** *n.*

ma·te·ri·al·ly (mə·tir′ē·əl·ē) *adv.* **1.** In an important manner or to a considerable degree. **2.** With regard to that which is physical or material; physically. **3.** *Philos.* In respect to matter as distinguished from form.

ma·te·ri·a med·i·ca (mə·tir′ē·ə med′i·kə) *Med.* **1.** Substances, as drugs, etc., employed as remedial agents. **2.** The branch of medicine that treats of these substances. [< Med.L < *materia* matter + *medica*, fem. of *medicus* medical]

ma·te·ri·el (mə·tir′ē·el′) *n.* **1.** The equipment and supplies of a military force, as distinguished from its personnel. **2.** The equipment and supplies of any business or organization. Also *Fr.* **ma·té·riel** (mà·tā·ryel′). [< F, material]

ma·ter·nal (mə·tûr′nəl) *adj.* **1.** Pertaining to a mother; motherly. **2.** Inherited from one's mother. **3.** Coming through the relationship of a mother. [< F *maternel* < L *maternus* < *mater* mother] — **ma·ter′nal·ly** *adv.*

ma·ter·nal·ize (mə·tûr′nəl·īz) *v.t.* **·ized**, **·iz·ing** To make maternal.

ma·ter·ni·ty (mə·tûr′nə·tē) *n.* *pl.* **·ties 1.** The state or condition of being a mother. **2.** The qualities or characteristics of a mother. — *adj.* **1.** Fashioned for pregnant women: *maternity* clothes. **2.** Designed to accommodate women and newborn babies during and after childbirth: a *maternity* ward. [< F *maternité* < L *maternitas*]

ma·tey (mā′tē) *Brit. Informal adj.* Friendly; chummy. — *n.* Friend; chum.

math[1] (math) *n.* *Dial.* A mowing. [OE *mǣth*]

math[2] (math) *n.* *U.S. Informal* Mathematics.

math. Mathematical; mathematician; mathematics.

math·e·mat·i·cal (math/ə·mat′i·kəl) *adj.* **1.** Of, pertaining to, or like mathematics. **2.** Used in or connected with mathematics. **3.** Rigidly exact or precise. Also **math′e·mat′ic.** *Abbr. math.* [< L *mathematicus* < Gk. *mathēmatikos* disposed to learn, mathematical < *mathēma* learning < *manthanein* to learn] — **math′e·mat′i·cal·ly** *adv.*

mathematical expectation *Stat.* The sum of each possible value or outcome of a given event multiplied by the probability of a particular outcome.

mathematical logic Symbolic logic (which see).

math·e·ma·ti·cian (math/ə·mə·tish′ən) *n.* One who specializes or is expert in mathematics. *Abbr. math.*

math·e·mat·ics (math/ə·mat′iks) *n.pl. (construed as sing.)* The study of quantity, form, arrangement, and magnitude; especially, the methods and processes for disclosing, by rigorous concepts and self-consistent symbols, the properties and relations of quantities and magnitudes, whether in the abstract, **pure mathematics**, or in their practical connections, **applied mathematics**. *Abbr. math.*

Math·er (math/ər), **Cotton**, 1663?–1728?, and his father, **Increase**, 1639–1723, American Congregational clergymen and writers active in New England.

maths (maths) *n. Brit. Informal* Mathematics.

Ma·til·da (mə·til′də), 1102–67, daughter of Henry I and mother of Henry II, disputed the English throne with Stephen of Blois: called **the Lady of England.**

Matilda of Flanders, died 1083, wife of William the Conqueror.

mat·in (mat′in) *n.* **1.** *pl. Eccl.* **a** The prescribed prayers that, together with lauds, constitute the first of the seven canonical hours, usually said or sung at midnight or dawn. **b** In the Anglican Church, the order for public worship in the morning. **2.** *Poetic* Any morning song, as of birds. — *adj.* Of or pertaining to matins or to the morning: also **mat′in·al.** Also spelled **mattin.** *Abbr.* (n. def. 1) **mat.** [< OF *matin* early, < L *matutinus (tempus)* (time) of the morning, appar. < *Matuta*, goddess of morning]

mat·i·nee (mat/ə·nā′) *n.* A performance or entertainment, as a play, movie, concert, etc., held in the daytime, usually in the afternoon. Also **mat′i·née′.** *Abbr. mat.* [< F < *matin* morning. See MATIN.]

mat·ing (mā′ting) *n.* The act of pairing or matching.

Ma·tisse (mà·tēs′), **Henri**, 1869–1954, French painter.

mat-knife (mat′nīf′) *n.* *pl.* **-knives** (-nīvz′) A knife having the edge ground at an angle, used for cutting engravings, heavy paper, artist's mats, etc. For illustration see KNIFE.

Ma·to Gros·so (mat/ə grō′sō, *Pg.* mä′tŏō grō′sŏō) A State of western Brazil; 486,908 sq. mi.; pop. 650,000 (est. 1960); capital, Cuiabá: formerly *Matto Grosso.*

mat·rass (mat/rəs) *n.* A round-bodied glass vessel having a long neck, used for distilling, etc.: also called *bolthead:* also spelled *mattrass.* [< F *matras* bolt]

matri- *combining form* Mother: *matricide.* [< L *mater, matris* mother]

ma·tri·arch (mā′trē·ärk) *n.* A woman holding the position corresponding to that of a patriarch in her family or tribe. [< MATRI- + (PATRI)ARCH] — **ma′tri·ar′chal, ma′tri·ar′chic** *adj.* — **ma′tri·ar′chal·ism** *n.*

ma·tri·ar·chate (mā′trē·är′kit) *n.* A community, system of government, etc., ruled by a matriarch. [< MATRIARCH + -ATE²]

ma·tri·ar·chy (mā′trē·är′kē) *n. pl.* **·chies** **1.** A social organization having the mother as the head of the family, in which descent, kinship, and succession are reckoned through the mother, instead of the father. **2.** A matriarchate.

ma·tri·ces (mā′trə·sēz, mat′rə-) Alternative plural of MATRIX.

mat·ri·cide (mat′rə·sīd) *n.* **1.** The killing of one's mother. **2.** One who kills his mother. [< L *matricidium* < *mater, matris* mother + *caedere* to kill; def. 2 < L *matricida*] — **mat′ri·ci′dal** *adj.*

mat·ri·cli·nous (mat′rə·klī′nəs) *adj. Biol.* Showing characteristics inherited from the maternal side. Compare PATRICLINOUS. Also **mat′ro·cli′nal, mat′ro·cli′nous.**

ma·tric·u·lant (mə·trik′yə·lənt) *n.* One who has matriculated or is a candidate for matriculation.

ma·tric·u·late (mə·trik′yə·lāt) *v.t. & v.i.* **·lat·ed, ·lat·ing** To register or enroll in a college or university as a candidate for a degree. — *n.* One who is so enrolled. [< Med.L *matriculatus,* pp. of *matriculare* to enroll < *matricula,* dim. of *matrix* womb, origin, public roll < *mater* mother] — **ma·tric′u·la′tion** *n.* — **ma·tric′u·la′tor** *n.*

mat·ri·lin·e·al (mat′rə·lin′ē·əl) *adj.* Pertaining to, descended from, or characteristic of the maternal line. Compare PATRILINEAL.

mat·ri·lo·cal (mat′rə·lō′kəl) *adj. Anthropol.* Denoting or pertaining to the residence of a married couple with or near the wife's family or community. Compare PATRILOCAL.

mat·ri·mo·ni·al (mat′rə·mō′nē·əl) *adj.* Of or pertaining to matrimony. — **mat′ri·mo′ni·al·ly** *adv.*

mat·ri·mo·ny (mat′rə·mō′nē) *n. pl.* **·nies** **1.** The state or condition of being married. **2.** The act, ceremony, or sacrament of marriage. **3.** A card game played by any number of persons; also, a combination of king and queen in this game. — **Syn.** See MARRIAGE. [< L *matrimonium* < *mater, matris* mother]

matrimony vine The boxthorn.

ma·trix (mā′triks) *n. pl.* **ma·trix·es** or **ma·tri·ces** (mā′trə·sēz, mat′rə-) **1.** That in which anything originates, develops, takes shape, or is contained. **2.** *Biol.* The intercellular substance of tissue. **3.** *Anat.* The formative cells from which a structure, as a fingernail, grows. **4.** The womb. **5.** A mold in which anything is cast or shaped. **6.** *Printing* **a** A mold in which the face of a type is cast. **b** In stereotyping, a papier-mâché, plaster, or other impression of a form, from which a plate for printing may be made: also called *mat.* **7.** A mold made from a disk by electroforming and serving as a master for the production of phonograph records. **8.** *Geol.* An impression or mold left in a rock by a fossil, crystal, or other mineral; also, the rock in which a fossil, crystal, etc., is embedded. **9.** *Mining* Gangue. **10.** *Math.* A rectangular array of numbers or terms enclosed between parentheses or double vertical bars to facilitate the study of relationships. [< L, womb, breeding animal < *mater, matris* mother]

ma·tron (mā′trən) *n.* **1.** A married woman who is usually a mother and more or less mature in age and manner. **2.** A female attendant or guard, as in a woman's prison, rest room, etc. **3.** A female superintendent of an institution, etc. [< OF *matrone* < L *matrona* < *mater, matris* mother] — **ma′tron·al** *adj.* — **ma′tron·like′** *adj.*

ma·tron·age (mā′trən·ij) *n.* **1.** The state of being a matron. **2.** Matronly attention. **3.** Matrons collectively.

ma·tron·ize (mā′trən·īz) *v.t.* **·ized, ·iz·ing** **1.** To make matronlike. **2.** To chaperon.

ma·tron·ly (mā′trən·lē) *adj.* Of or like a matron. — *adv.* In a matronly manner. — **ma′tron·li·ness** *n.*

matron of honor A married woman acting as chief attendant to a bride at a wedding.

mat·ro·nym·ic (mat′rō·nim′ik) *n. & adj.* Metronymic.

MATS Military Air Transport Service.

Ma·tsu (mä′tsōō′) An island of the Republic of China, in Formosa Strait, 12 miles east of mainland China; 4 sq. mi.

Ma·tsu·ya·ma (mä·tsōō·yä·mä) A port city on NW Shikoku island, Japan; pop. 238,514 (1960).

Matt. Matthew.

matte¹ (mat) *n. Metall.* An impure metallic product obtained in smelting sulfide ores of copper, lead, etc. [< F]

matte² (mat) See MAT².

mat·ted (mat′id) *adj.* **1.** Covered with or made from mats or matting. **2.** Tangled or twisted in a mass. **3.** Covered with a dense or twisted growth. — **mat′ted·ness** *n.*

mat·ter (mat′ər) *n.* **1.** That which makes up the substance of anything, especially of material things; constituent material: the *matter* of the stars. **2.** That which is material and physical, occupies space, and is perceived by the senses,

as distinguished from that which is mental, spiritual, etc. **3.** A specific kind or form of material or substance: organic *matter.* **4.** A subject, event, or situation that is or may be an object of discussion, concern, feeling, etc.: a *matter* of faith. **5.** Cause, occasion, or reason: usually with *of* or *for*: a *matter* of great concern. **6.** Importance, consequence, or moment: It's of no *matter* what happens. **7.** Something of importance or consequence. **8.** A usually unpleasant or unfortunate condition or circumstance: with *the*: What's the *matter* with you? **9.** The ideas, content, or meaning of a book, speech, etc., as distinguished from the style or form. **10.** An indefinite amount, quantity, or extent: a *matter* of a few dollars. **11.** Pus. **12.** *Philos.* The undifferentiated or formless material of the universe of sensory experience, generally regarded as the substratum of physical phenomena. **13.** That which is written, printed, or copied in some way: *matter* for reading. **14.** Anything sent or to be sent by mail: third-class *matter.* **15.** *Printing* **a** Type that is set up or composed. **b** Material to be set up; copy. **16.** In Christian Science, the opposite of God; illusion. — *v.i.* **1.** To be of concern or importance; signify: It *matters* little. **2.** To form or discharge pus. [< OF *matere* < L *materia* stuff]

Mat·ter·horn (mat′ər·hôrn, *Ger.* mä′ter·hôrn) A mountain in the Alps on the Swiss-Italian border: 14,701 ft.: French *Mont Cervin.*

mat·ter-of-course (mat′ər·əv·kôrs′, -kōrs′) *adj.* **1.** Following or occurring as a natural or logical result. **2.** Accepting or regarding things as a matter of course.

matter of course Something expected to follow as a natural or logical result.

mat·ter-of-fact (mat′ər·əv·fakt′) *adj.* Closely adhering to facts; not fanciful; unimaginative; practical.

matter of fact Something having actual and undeniable existence or reality.

Mat·thew (math′yōō) One of the twelve apostles and author of the first Gospel: called **Saint Matthew.** — *n.* The first Gospel of the New Testament. Abbr. *Matt.*

Matthew of Paris, died 1259, English monk and chronicler. Also **Matthew Paris.**

Mat·thews (math′yōōz), **(James) Brander,** 1852–1929, U.S. scholar, author, and educator.

Mat·thi·as (mə·thī′əs) The apostle chosen by lot to succeed Judas Iscariot. *Acts* i 23–26.

mat·tin (mat′in) See MATIN.

mat·ting¹ (mat′ing) *n.* **1.** A woven fabric of fiber, straw, or other material, used as a floor covering, for packing, etc. **2.** The act of making mats. **3.** Mats collectively.

mat·ting² (mat′ing) *n.* **1.** A mat for framing a picture. **2.** A dull, lusterless, or roughened surface, as on metal or glass; also, the act or process of producing such a surface.

mat·tock (mat′ək) *n.* Either of two tools resembli·.g a pickax, as the **pick mattock,** having a blade on one end and a pick on the other, or the **cutter mattock,** having a blade on each end. [OE *mattuc*]

MATTOCK

Mat·to Gros·so (mat′ə grō′sō, *Pg.,* mä′tōō grō′sōō) See MATO GROSSO.

mat·toid (mat′oid) *n.* A mentally unbalanced person. [< Ital. *mattoide* < *matto* mad < L *mattus* intoxicated]

mat·trass (mat′rəs) See MATRASS.

mat·tress (mat′rəs) *n.* **1.** A large pad made of a strong fabric and filled with a resilient material, as cotton, rubber, hair, feathers, etc., used on or as a bed. **2.** A mat woven of brush, poles, etc., used to make dikes or jetties, protect embankments from erosion, etc. [< OF *materas* < Ital. *materasso* < Arabic *matrah* place where something is thrown]

mat·u·rate (mach′ōō·rāt, mat′yōō-) *v.i.* **·rat·ed, ·rat·ing** **1.** To form pus; suppurate. **2.** To ripen or mature. [< L *maturatus,* pp. of *maturare* to ripen < *maturus* ripe, fully developed] — **mat′u·ra′tive** *adj.*

mat·u·ra·tion (mach′ōō·rā′shən, mat′yōō-) *n.* **1.** The formation of pus. **2.** The process of ripening or coming to maturity. **3.** *Biol.* The final stages in the preparation of gametes for fertilization, during which time the number of chromosomes in the germ cells is reduced by half.

ma·ture (mə·tyōōr′, -tōōr′, -chōōr′) *adj.* **1.** Completely developed or grown; fully ripe, as plants, fruit, animals, etc. **2.** Highly developed or advanced in intellect, moral qualities, outlook, etc.: a *mature* thinker. **3.** Fully or thoroughly developed, perfected, detailed, etc.: a *mature* scheme. **4.** Having reached its time limit; due and payable: a *mature* bond. **5.** *Geog.* **a** Designating or exhibiting the maximum development of the earth's topography, as produced by the forces of erosion at full vigor. **b** Adjusted to local topography, as the course of a river. — *v.* **·tured, ·tur·ing** *v.t.* **1.** To cause to ripen or come to maturity; bring to full development. **2.** To perfect; complete. — *v.i.* **3.** To come to maturity or full development. **4.** To become due, as a note. [< L *maturus* ripe, of full age] — **ma·ture′ly** *adv.*

ma·tur·i·ty (mə·tyōōr′ə·tē, -tōōr′-, -chōōr′-) *n.* **1.** The state or quality of being mature. **2.** Full physical development of the body. **3.** The time at which a note, bill, etc., becomes due; also, the state of being due. Also **ma·ture′ness.** Abbr. *mat.* [< F *maturité* < L *maturitas*]

ma·tu·ti·nal (mə·tōō′tə·nəl, -tyōō′-, mach·ə·tī′nəl) *adj.* Of, pertaining to, or taking place in the morning; early. [< L *matutinalis* < *matutinus* early in the morning < *Matuta*, goddess of morning] **—ma·tu′ti·nal·ly** *adv.*

mat·zo (mät′sə) *n.* *pl.* **·zos** or **·zot** (-sōt) or **·zoth** (-sōth, -sōt) A large, flat piece of unleavened bread, traditionally eaten during Passover. Also **mat′za, mat′zah, mat′zoh.** [< Hebrew *matstäh* unleavened bread]

mat·zoon (mat·sōōn′) *n.* Yogurt.

Mau·beuge (mō·bœzh′) A city in northern France; pop. about 24,000.

maud·lin (môd′lin) *adj.* **1.** Excessively and tearfully emotional or sentimental. **2.** Overly sentimental or emotional from too much liquor. **— Syn.** See SENTIMENTAL. [< *Maudlin* < OF *Maudelene, Madeleine* (Mary) Magdalen, often depicted with eyes swollen from weeping]

Maugham (môm), **W**(illiam) **Somerset,** 1874–1965, English novelist and dramatist.

mau·gre (mô′gər) *prep. Obs.* In spite of. [< OF]

Mau·i (mou′ē) The second largest of the Hawaiian Islands; 728 sq. mi.

maul (môl) *n.* A heavy mallet for driving wedges, piles, etc. **—***v.t.* **1.** To beat and bruise; batter. **2.** To handle roughly; manhandle; abuse. **3.** *U.S.* To split by means of a maul and wedges, as logs or rails. Also spelled *mall.* [< OF *mail* < L *malleus* hammer. ? Akin to L *molere* to grind into pieces, crush.] **— maul′er** *n.*

Maul·main (môl·mān′) See MOULMEIN.

maul·stick (môl′stik′) *n.* A staff, often padded at one end with leather, that rests on a painting or easel and steadies the hand of a painter while doing delicate brush work: also *mahlstick.* [< Du. *maalstok* < *malen* to paint + *stok* stick]

STEEL FENCE-POST MAUL

Mau Mau (mou′ mou′) *pl.* **Mau Mau** or **Mau Maus** A member of a secret organization of Kikuyu tribesmen, active from approximately 1952 to 1956 in terrorist activities directed against European colonists in Kenya, Africa. [< native name]

mau·met (mô′mit) *n. Obs.* An idol: also spelled *mammet* [OF, contr. of MAHOMET, from the early belief that the Moslems worshiped images] **— mau′met·ry** *n.*

maun (môn) *v.i. Scot.* Must.

mau·na (mô′nə) *Scot.* Must not. Also **maun′na.**

Mau·na Ke·a (mou′nä kā′ä) An extinct volcano on Hawaii; highest mountain in the Hawaiian Islands; 13,825 ft.

Mau·na Lo·a (mou′nä lō′ä) An active volcano on Hawaii; 13,675 ft.

maund (mônd) *n.* A unit of weight used in India, varying from 24.7 to 82.28 lbs. avoirdupois. [< Hind. *mān* < Skt. *manā*]

maun·der (môn′dər) *v.i.* **1.** To talk in a wandering or incoherent manner; drivel. **2.** To move dreamily or idly. [? Freq. of obs. *maund* to beg; infl. in meaning by MEANDER] **— maun′der·er** *n.*

maun·dy (môn′dē) *n.* The religious ceremony of washing the feet of others in commemoration of the washing of the disciples' feet by Christ at the Last Supper. [< OF *mande* < L *mandatum* command; from the use of *mandatum* at the beginning of the ceremony. See MANDATE.]

Maundy Thursday The day before Good Friday, commemorating the Last Supper of Christ. [See MAUNDY]

Mau·pas·sant (mō·pá·sän′), **(Henri René Albert) Guy de,** 1850–93, French novelist and short-story writer.

Mau·re·ta·ni·a (môr′ə·tā′nē·ə) An ancient country of North Africa, including the northern part of modern Morocco and the western part of Algeria.

Mau·re·ta·ni·an (môr′ə·tā′nē·ən) *adj.* Of or pertaining to ancient Mauretania or its inhabitants. **—***n.* **1.** One of the ancient people of Mauretania. **2.** The Libyan dialect spoken by these people.

Mau·riac (mô·ryák′), **François,** 1885–1970, French novelist.

Mau·rice (mə·rēs′ môr′is, mor′is), 1521–53, elector of Saxony; helped secure religious freedom for the Protestants.

Maurice of Nassau, 1567–1625, Prince of Orange; Dutch general; son of William the Silent.

Mau·ri·ta·ni·a (môr′ə·tā′nē·ə) A Republic in western Africa; 397,850 sq. mi.; pop. 1,140,000 (est. 1969); capital, Nouakchott. Officially **Islamic Republic of Mauritania.** French *République Islamique de Mauritanie.* **French Mau·ri·ta·nie** (mō·rē·tá·nē′). **— Mau·ri′ta/ni·an** *adj. & n.*

Mau·ri·ti·us (mô·rish′ē·əs) A parliamentary state within the British Commonwealth, comprising the island of Mauritius in the Indian Ocean about 500 miles east of Madagascar; 720 sq. mi.; pop. 823,000 (est. 1969); capital, Port Louis. *French* **Mau·rice** (mō·rēs′). **— Mau·ri′ti·an** *adj. & n.*

Mau·rois (mō·rwá′), **André** Pseudonym of **Émile Salomon Wilhelm Her·zog** (er′zōg′), 1885–1967, French biographer and novelist.

Maur·ya (mour′yə) An Indian dynasty, 325?–184 B.C. founded by Chandragupta I.

Mau·ser (mou′zər) *n.* A magazine rifle having great range and velocity; also, a type of automatic pistol: a trade name. [after P. S. Mauser, 1838–1914, German inventor]

mau·so·le·um (mô′sə·lē′əm) *n.* *pl.* **·le·ums** or **·le·a** (-lē′ə) A large, stately tomb. [< L < Gk. *Mausōleion,* tomb of King Mausolus of Caria, erected by Queen Artemisia at Halicarnassus about 350 B.C., one of the Seven Wonders of the World] **— mau′so·le′an** *adj.*

maut (môt) *n. Scot.* Malt.

mau·vais goût (mō·ve′ gōō′) *French* Bad taste.

mauve (mōv) *n.* **1.** *Chem.* A coal-tar violet dyestuff obtained by oxidizing aniline and considered the first successful coal-tar dye. **2.** Any of various purplish rose shades. [< F, mallow < L *malva.* Doublet of MALLOW.]

mauve decade The 1890's as a social and cultural period. [< title of a book (1926) by Thomas Beers]

mav·er·ick (mav′ər·ik) *n.* **1.** *U.S.* An unbranded or orphaned animal, as a calf, traditionally belonging to the first person to claim or brand it. **2.** *U.S. Informal* One who is unorthodox in his ideas, attitudes, etc. [after Samuel A. *Maverick,*1803–70, Texas lawyer who did not brand his cattle]

ma·vis (mā′vis) *n.* The song thrush. [< F *mauvis*]

ma·vour·neen (mə·vŏŏr′nēn, -vôr′-) *n.* My darling. Also **ma·vour′nin.** [< Irish *mo muirnin*]

maw¹ (mô) *n.* **1.** The jaws, mouth, or gullet of a voracious mammal or fish. **2.** The craw of a bird. **3.** The stomach. [OE *maga* stomach]

maw² (mô) *v.t. Scot.* To mow, as hay.

maw³ (mô) *n. Informal & Dial.* Mama; mother.

mawk·ish (mô′kish) *adj.* **1.** Characterized by false or feeble sentimentality; lacking in strength or vigor. **2.** Sickening or insipid in taste or flavor. **— Syn.** See SENTIMENTAL. [< obs. *mawk* < ON *mathkr* maggot] **— mawk′ish·ly** *adv.* **— mawk′ish·ness** *n.*

Maw·son (mô′sən), **Sir Douglas,** 1882–1958, Australian Antarctic explorer and geologist.

max. Maximum.

max·il·la (mak·sil′ə) *n.* *pl.* **max·il·lae** (mak·sil′ē) **1.** *Anat.* In vertebrates, the upper jaw or jawbone. For illustration see SKULL. **2.** *Zool.* In arthropods, either of one or two pairs of jointed, jawlike appendages that lie behind the mandibles. [< L, dim. of *mala* jaw]

max·il·lar·y (mak′sə·ler′ē, mak·sil′ər·ē) *adj.* Of, pertaining to, or situated near the upper jaw or a maxilla: a *maxillary* artery. **—***n.* *pl.* **·lar·ies** The upper jaw or a maxilla.

max·im (mak′sim) *n.* A brief statement of a general principle, truth, or rule of conduct. **— Syn.** See PROVERB. [< F *maxime* < L *maxima* (*sententia, propositio*) greatest (authority, premise), fem. of *maximus.* See MAXIMUM.]

Max·im (mak′sim), **Sir Hiram (Stevens)**, 1840–1916, British engineer and inventor born in the United States; originated the Maxim gun. **— Hudson,** 1853–1927, U.S. engineer and inventor; developed maximite; brother of the preceding.

max·i·mal (mak′sə·məl) *adj.* Of or being a maximum; greatest or highest possible. **— max′i·mal·ly** *adv.*

Max·i·mal·ist (mak′sə·məl·ist) *n.* A member of a radical faction of the Russian Social Revolutionary Party, active in the Revolution of 1905. [< MAXIMAL + -IST]

Maxim gun A water-cooled machine gun that utilizes the recoil of each shot to fire the next. [after Sir Hiram *Maxim,* its inventor]

Max·i·mil·ian I (mak′sə·mil′yən), 1459–1519, Holy Roman Emperor 1493–1519.

Maximilian II, 1527–76, Holy Roman Emperor 1564–76.

Maximilian of Mexico, 1832–67, archduke of Austria; emperor of Mexico 1864–67; executed: full name **Ferdinand Maximilian Joseph.**

max·im·ite (mak′sim·īt) *n.* A high explosive made of picric acid, formerly used in armor-piercing projectiles. [after Hudson *Maxim* + -ITE]

max·i·mize (mak′sə·mīz) *v.t.* **·mized, ·miz·ing** To make as great as possible; increase or intensify to the maximum.

max·i·mum (mak′sə·məm) *n.* *pl.* **·mums** or **·ma** (-mə) **1.** The greatest possible quantity, amount, or degree. **2.** The greatest quantity, degree, number, etc., reached or recorded. **3.** *Math.* A value of a function that is greater than any neighboring value; also, the greatest possible value of a function. **4.** *Astron.* The moment of greatest brightness of a variable star; also, its magnitude at such a time. **—***adj.* **1.** Consisting of or showing the greatest amount or degree possible, permissible, attainable, etc. **2.** Of or pertaining to a maximum or maximums. *Abbr.* **max.** [< L *maximus,* superl. of *magnus* great]

ma·xi·xe (mə·shēsh′, màk·sēks′, mə·shē′shä) *n.* A Brazilian dance resembling the two-step. [< Brazilian Pg.]

Max Mül·ler (mäks mül′er), **Friedrich** See MÜLLER.

max·well (maks′wel) *n.* The cgs unit of magnetic flux, equal to the flux through one square centimeter normal to a magnetic induction of one gauss. [after James C. *Maxwell*]

Max·well (maks′wel), **James Clerk**, 1831–79, Scottish physicist.

Maxwell's demon *Physics* An imaginary being of molecular proportions, devised by James Clerk Maxwell to illustrate the kinetic theory of gases.

may[1] (mā) *v.* Present: *sing.* **may, may** (*Archaic* **may·est** or **mayst**) **may,** *pl.* **may;** past: **might** A defective verb now used only in the present and past tenses as an auxiliary followed by the infinitive without *to*, or elliptically with the infinitive understood, to express: **1.** Permission or allowance: *May* I go? You *may.* **2.** Desire, prayer, or wish: *May* your tribe increase! **3.** Contingency, especially in clauses of result, concession, purpose, etc.: He died that we *might* live. **4.** Possibility: You *may* be right. **5.** *Law* Obligation or duty: the equivalent of *must* or *shall.* **6.** *Obs.* Ability; power: now usually *can.* ◆ See usage notes under CAN and MIGHT[1]. [OE *mæg*]

may[2] (mā) *n. Brit.* A species of hawthorn (*Crataegus oxyacantha*), having white, rose, or crimson flowers. Also **may′bush′** (-bŏŏsh′). [< MAY, when it blooms]

May (mā) *n.* **1.** The fifth month of the year, containing 31 days. **2.** The prime of life; youth. **3.** May Day festivities. [< OF *mai* < L (*mensis*) *Maius* (month of) May, prob. < *Maia*, goddess of growth]

May (mā), **Cape** The southernmost point of New Jersey between the Atlantic and Delaware Bay.

Ma·ya (mä′yə) In Hinduism, the mother of the world, an aspect of Devi. — *n.* In Hindu philosophy, illusion, often personified as a maiden: also **ma′ya.** [< Skt. *māyā* illusion]

Ma·ya (mä′yə) *n.* **1.** One of a tribe of Central American Indians, having an early advanced civilization and still comprising a large percentage of the population of Yucatán, northern Guatemala, and British Honduras. **2.** The historical or modern language of the Mayas. — *adj.* Of or pertaining to the Mayas, their culture, or their language.

Ma·ya·güez (mä′yä-gwäs′) A port city in western Puerto Rico; pop. 69,485 (est. 1970).

Ma·yan (mä′yən) *adj.* Of or pertaining to the Mayas, their culture, or their language. — *n.* **1.** A Maya. **2.** A family of Central American Indian languages, including Maya and Quiché.

May apple 1. A North American herb (*Podophyllum peltatum*) whose roots yield podophyllin. **2.** The ovoid, yellowish, edible fruit of this herb. Also called *mandrake.*

Ma·ya·ri iron (mä-yä′rē) An iron made from Cuban ores, used in high-grade machine castings. [after *Mayari*, a Cuban town]

may·be (mā′bē) *adv.* Perhaps; possibly. [< (*it*) *may be*]

May·day (mā′dā′) *n.* The international radio telephonic call for immediate help, sent out by an aircraft or ship in distress. [< F *m'aidez* help me]

May Day The first day of May, traditionally celebrated as a spring festival by crowning a May Queen, dancing around a Maypole, etc., and, in recent times, celebrated in some countries by demonstrations commemorating labor.

Ma·yence (mȧ·yäns′) The French name for MAINZ.

May·er (mī′ər), **Julius Robert von**, 1814–78, German physicist.

may·est (mā′ist) *May:* archaic or poetic second person singular, present tense of MAY: used with *thou.* Also spelled *mayst.*

May·fair (mā′fâr) A fashionable residential district of the West End, London.

may·flow·er (mā′flou/ər) *n.* Any of various plants that blossom in the spring; especially: **a** In the United States, the **Canada mayflower** (*Maianthemum canadense*), having clusters of small, white flowers, and the trailing arbutus. **b** In Great Britain, the blossom of the hawthorn.

Mayflower The ship on which the Pilgrims came to America in 1620.

May fly 1. Any of a widespread order (*Ephemerida* or *Plectoptera*) of insects, having large, transparent forewings, a relatively long nymphal life, and a short-lived adult stage: also called *dayfly, ephemerid.* **2.** An artificial fly in imitation of this insect. **3.** *Brit.* A caddis fly (which see). Also **may·fly** (mā′flī′) *n.*

MAY FLY (def. 1)

may·hap (mā′hap) *adv. Archaic* It may happen; perhaps. Also **may′hap′pen** (-ən). [< (*it*) *may hap*(*pen*)]

may·hem (mā′hem) *n.* **1.** *Law* The offense of violently injuring or maiming a person's body so as to render him less able to defend himself or to annoy his adversary. **2.** Any situation characterized by violence, confusion, noise, etc.; also, such violence, confusion, or noise. Also spelled *maihem.* [< OF *mehaing, mahaym.* Akin to MAIM.]

May·ing (mā′ing) *n.* The celebration of May Day.

May·o (mā′ō) A county of western Connacht, Ireland; 2,084 sq. mi.; pop. 123,330 (1966); county seat, Castlebar.

May·o (mā′ō), **Charles Horace**, 1865–1939, and his brother, **William James**, 1861–1939, U.S. surgeons.

Ma·yon (mä·yôn′), **Mount** An active volcano in SE Luzon, Philippines; 7,926 ft.

may·on·naise (mā′ə·nāz′, mī′-) *n.* **1.** A dressing, as for salads, made by beating together raw egg yolk, butter or

olive oil, lemon juice or vinegar, and condiments. **2.** A dish, as of meat or fish, mixed with this dressing. [< F, ? < *Mahón*, Balearic port]

may·or (mā′ər, mâr) *n.* The chief magistrate of a city, borough, or municipal corporation. [< F *maire* < L *major* greater. Doublet of MAJOR.] — **may′or·al** *adj.*

may·or·al·ty (mā′ər·əl·tē, mâr′əl-) *n. pl.* **·ties** The office or term of service of a mayor. [< OF *mairalté*]

mayor of the palace The chief Frankish royal official, especially powerful under the late Merovingian kings. [Trans. of Med.L *mayor palatii*]

Ma·yotte (mȧ·yôt′) The easternmost of the Comoro Islands; 137 sq. mi.

May·pole (mā′pōl′) *n.* A pole decorated with flowers and ribbons, around which dancing takes place on May Day. Also **may′pole′.**

may·pop (mā′pop) *n.* **1.** The passionflower (*Passiflora incarnata*) of the southern United States. **2.** Its small, yellow, edible fruit. [Alter. of N. Am. Ind. *maracock*]

May queen A young woman or girl chosen to preside over May Day festivities.

mayst (māst) See MAYEST.

May·time (mā′tīm′) *n.* The month of May. Also **May′·tide′** (-tīd′).

may tree *Brit.* The hawthorn.

may·weed (mā′wēd′) *n.* A bitter, malodorous weed (*Anthemis cotula*) bearing daisylike flowers of white rays on a yellow disk: also called *dogfennel, stinking camomile.* [Alter. of *maid weed* < *maytheweed* < OE *magothe* + WEED]

May wine Any still, white wine flavored with woodruff, to which pineapple and orange slices are sometimes added; also, a punch made with this wine. [Named for the month of May, when the woodruff flowers]

May·wood (mā′wŏŏd) A village in NE Illinois, near Chicago; pop. 30,036.

maz·ard (maz′ərd) *n. Obs.* **1.** A mazer. **2.** The head, skull, or face. Also spelled *mazzard.* [Var. of MAZER]

Maz·a·rin (maz′ə·rin, *Fr.* má·zȧ·raṅ′), **Jules**, 1602–61, French cardinal and statesman born in Italy; prime minister under Louis XIV; patron of Descartes and Corneille: original name **Giulio Ma·za·ri·ni** (mä′dzä·rē′nē).

Maz·da·ism (maz′də·iz′əm) *n.* Zoroastrianism. Also **Maz′de·ism.** [< OPersian *Aura mazda* principle of good]

maze (māz) *n.* **1.** An intricate network of paths or passages; a labyrinth. **2.** A state of bewilderment, uncertainty, or perplexity. — *v.t.* **mazed, maz·ing** *Archaic* To daze or stupefy; bewilder. [< AMAZE]

Ma·zep·pa (mə·zep′ə, mä·zyep′ə), **Ivan Stepanovich**, 1644–1709, Russian Cossack chief; hero of a poem by Byron.

ma·zer (mā′zər) *n.* A bowl, goblet, or drinking cup, originally made of wood: also called *mazard.* [< OF *masere* maple wood < Gmc.]

ma·zu·ma (mə·zōō′mə) *n. Slang* Money. [< Yiddish *m′zumon* the ready necessary]

ma·zur·ka (mə·zûr′kə, -zŏŏr′-) *n.* **1.** A lively Polish dance in 3/4 time. **2.** The music for such a dance. Also **ma·zour′ka.** [< Polish, woman from Mazovia, a province in Poland]

Ma·zu·ry (mä·zŏŏ′ri) The Polish name for MASURIA.

ma·zy (mā′zē) *adj.* **·zi·er, ·zi·est** Of or like a maze; winding; confusing. — **maz′i·ly** *adv.* — **maz′i·ness** *n.*

mazzard cherry See under CHERRY.

Maz·zi·ni (mät·tsē′nē), **Giuseppe**, 1805?–72, Italian patriot and revolutionary; helped unify Italy.

M.B. Bachelor of Medicine (L *Medicinae Baccalaureus*).

M.B.A. Master in (or of) Business Administration.

MBS Mutual Broadcasting System.

mc or **m.c.** or **mc.** **1.** Megacycle. **2.** Millicurie.

Mc- See also MAC-.

M.C. **1.** Maritime Commission. **2.** Master of Ceremonies. **3.** Medical Corps. **4.** Member of Congress.

Mc·A·doo (mak′ə·dōō), **William Gibbs**, 1863–1941, U.S. lawyer and politician.

Mc·Al·len (mək·al′ən) A city in southern Texas; pop. 37,636.

Mc·Car·thy·ism (mə·kär′thē·iz′əm) *n.* **1.** The practice of making public and sensational accusations of disloyalty or corruption, usually with little or no proof or with doubtful evidence. **2.** The practice of conducting inquisitorial investigations, ostensibly to expose pro-Communist activity. [after Joseph *McCarthy*, 1909–57, U.S. Senator]

Mc·Clel·lan (mə·klel′ən), **George Brinton**, 1826–85, Union general in the Civil War and politician.

Mc·Cor·mack (mə·kôr′mik), **John**, 1884–1945, U.S. tenor born in Ireland.

Mc·Cor·mick (mə·kôr′mik), **Cyrus (Hall)**, 1809–1884, U.S. inventor; developed the reaping machine. — **Joseph Medill**, 1877–1925, U.S. newspaper publisher and politician.

Mc·Coy (mə·koi′), **the (real)** *U.S. Slang* The authentic person or thing. [Appar. from an episode, existing in many versions, in which a celebrated American boxer, Kid McCoy, spectacularly established his identity]

Mc·Dou·gall (mək·dōō′gəl), **William**, 1871–1938, U.S. psychologist born in England.

Mc·Dow·ell (mək·dou′əl), **Irvin**, 1818–85, Union general in the Civil War.

McGill Fence *Canadian* A trans-Canadian radar warning system.

Mc·Guf·fey (mə·guf′ē), **William Holmes**, 1800–73, U.S. educator; author of children's readers.

M.Ch. Master of Surgery (L *Magister Chirurgiae*).

Mc·In·tosh (mak′ən·tosh) *n. U.S. & Canadian* A red, early autumn, eating apple. Also **McIntosh red.** [after John *McIntosh* of Ontario, who discovered it about 1796]

Mc·Kees·port (mə·kēz′pôrt, -pōrt) A city in SW Pennsylvania, near Pittsburgh; pop. 37,977.

Mc·Kin·ley (mə·kin′lē), **Mount** A peak in central Alaska, highest in North America; 20,300 feet.

Mc·Kin·ley (mə·kin′lē), **William**, 1843–1901, 25th president of the United States 1897–1901; assassinated.

Mc·Lu·han (mə·klōō′ən), **(Herbert) Marshall**, born 1911, Canadian educator and communications theorist.

M.C.L. Master of Civil Law.

Mc·Mas·ter (mək·mas′tər, -mäs′-), **John Bach**, 1852–1932, U.S. historian.

Mc·Pher·son (mək·fûr′sən), **James Birdseye**, 1828–64, Union general in the Civil War.

Md *Chem.* Mendelevium.

Md or **M.D.** Middle Dutch.

Md. Maryland.

M/D or **m/d** 1. Memorandum of deposit. 2. Months' date.

M.D. 1. Doctor of Medicine (L *Medicinae Doctor*). 2. Medical Department. 3. Mentally deficient.

M-Day (em′dā′) *n. Mil.* Mobilization day, the day the Department of Defense orders mobilization for war.

Mddx. or **Mdx.** Middlesex.

Mdme. (*pl.* **Mdmes.**) *Brit.* Madame.

M.D.S. Master of Dental Surgery.

mdse. Merchandise.

MDu. Middle Dutch.

me (mē) *pron.* The objective case of the pronoun *I.* [OE *mē*, dat. sing.]

◆ **It's me,** etc. Anyone who answers the question "Who's there?" by saying "It's me" is using acceptable informal idiom. Here *It is I* would seem stilted, although at the formal level of writing it is expected: They have warned me that *it is I,* and not he, who will have to bear the brunt of the criticism. After a finite impersonal form of the verb *to be,* as *it is, it was,* etc., a personal pronoun should, according to prescriptive grammar, be in the nominative case as is the subject; accordingly, at the formal level, we find *It is he, It is we, It is they,* etc. In informal speech and writing we find *It's him, It's them* and so forth, but these forms are not so widely accepted as *It's me.*

m.e. Marbled edges (bookbinding).

Me *Chem.* Methyl.

Me. Maine (unofficial).

ME or **ME.** or **M.E.** Middle English.

M.E. 1. Mechanical Engineer. 2. Methodist Episcopal. 3. Mining Engineer.

Mea. Meath.

me·a cul·pa (mē′ə kul′pə) *Latin* My fault; my blame.

mead[1] (mēd) *n.* An alcoholic beverage of fermented honey and water: also called *metheglin.* [OE *medu*]

mead[2] (mēd) *n. Poetic* A meadow. [OE *mǣd*]

Mead (mēd), **Lake** A reservoir formed by Hoover Dam in the Colorado River in Arizona and Nevada; 246 sq. mi.; largest artificial lake in the world.

Mead (mēd), **Margaret**, born 1901, U.S. anthropologist.

Meade (mēd), **George Gordon**, 1815–72, Union general in the Civil War, born in Spain.

mead·ow (med′ō) *n.* 1. A tract of grassland, usually used for grazing or for growing hay. 2. A low or level piece of land, as near a river, used for growing grass or hay. [OE *mǣdwe,* oblique case of *mǣd*] — **mead′ow·y** *adj.*

mead·ow·lark (med′ō·lärk′) *n.* Any of various songbirds (genus *Sturnella*) of North America; especially, the **eastern meadowlark** (*S. magna*), and the **western meadowlark** (*S. neglecta*), both marked with black on a yellow breast.

meadow lily The Canada lily (which see).

meadow mouse The field mouse (which see).

meadow rue Any species of a genus (*Thalictrum*) of the crowfoot family, having leaves like those of rue.

mead·ow·sweet (med′ō·swēt′) *n.* 1. A shrub (genus *Spiraea*) of the rose family. Also **meadow queen.** 2. Any plant of a related genus (*Filipendula*).

mea·ger (mē′gər) *adj.* 1. Deficient in quantity or quality; scanty; inadequate. 2. Lacking in fertility, strength, or richness: *meager* soil. 3. Thin; emaciated. Also *Brit.* **mea′gre.** [< OF *maigre* < L *macer* lean] — **mea′ger·ly** *adv.*

meal[1] (mēl) *n.* 1. The edible seeds of any grain, coarsely ground and unbolted. 2. Any powdery material produced by grinding: sulfur *meal.* [OE *melu*]

meal[2] (mēl) *n.* 1. The food served or eaten regularly at certain times during the day. 2. The time or occasion of taking such food. ◆ Collateral adjective: *prandial.* [OE *mǣl* measure, time, meal]

-meal *suffix* A quantity or a unit of measurement taken at one time: now obsolete except in *piecemeal, inchmeal.* [OE *-mǣlum,* oblique case of *mǣl* measure, time]

meal·ie (mē′lē) *n.* In Africa: **a** An ear of corn (def. 1). **b** *pl.* Corn. [< Afrikaans *milje* < Pg. *milho* millet < L *milium*]

meal ticket 1. A ticket or card bought for a specified price and redeemable at a restaurant for food. 2. *U.S. Slang* One who or that which provides a livelihood for another.

meal·time (mēl′tīm′) *n.* The habitual time for a meal.

meal worm The larva of a beetle (*Tenebrio molitor*) that infests and is destructive to flour, meal, etc.

meal·y (mē′lē) *adj.* **meal·i·er, meal·i·est** 1. Resembling or having the qualities of meal; dry; powdery; soft. 2. Containing meal. 3. Sprinkled or covered with or as with meal. 4. Covered or flecked with spots. 5. Anemic or pale in color, etc. 6. Mealy-mouthed. — **meal′i·ness** *n.*

meal·y·bug (mē′lē·bug′) *n.* Any of a large family (*Pseudococcidae*) of coccids, destructive to plants and having soft, oval bodies that are usually covered with a flourlike powder.

meal·y-mouthed (mē′lē·moutht′, -mouthd′) *adj.* Unwilling to express facts or opinions plainly and frankly; insincere; euphemistic.

mean[1] (mēn) *v.* **meant** (ment), **mean·ing** *v.t.* 1. To have in mind as a purpose or intent: I *meant* to visit him. 2. To intend or design for some purpose, destination, etc.: Was that remark *meant* for me? 3. To intend to express or convey: That's not what I *meant.* 4. To have as the particular sense or significance; denote. — *v.i.* 5. To have disposition or intention; be disposed: He *means* well. 6. To be of specified importance or influence: Her work *means* everything to her. [OE *mǣnan* to tell, wish, intend]

mean[2] (mēn) *adj.* 1. Poor or inferior in grade or quality. 2. Having little worth or consequence. 3. Ignoble in mind or character; lacking magnanimity; base. 4. Miserly; stingy. 5. Poor or undistinguished in appearance; shabby. 6. Humble in birth, rank, or station; lowly. 7. *Informal* Selfishly unwilling to oblige or accommodate; disagreeable; nasty. 8. *Informal* Ashamed; humiliated. 9. *U.S. Informal* Ill; out of sorts: to feel *mean.* 10. *U.S. Informal* Vicious; ill-tempered; dangerous: a *mean* man when drunk; a *mean* animal. 11. *U.S. Informal* Difficult; troublesome: a *mean* corner to cross. 12. *U.S. Slang* Excellent; expert: He plays a *mean* game of golf. [OE (*ge*)*mǣne* ordinary]

— **Syn.** 3. *Mean, ignoble, base, sordid,* and *abject* describe persons or actions regarded as being far below common worth or dignity. *Mean* and *ignoble,* which originally meant of low birth, now seldom refer to social status. *Mean* suggests a contemptible smallness of mind, a petty, ungenerous quality; *ignoble* denotes a lack of noble or praiseworthy qualities, and frequently implies a failure to meet ordinarily accepted standards of worth or excellence: to repeat *mean* gossip, the *ignoble* betrayal of a trust. *Base* is a strong word, used to condemn that which is openly evil, selfish, or dishonorable: *base* cowardice. *Sordid* suggests drabness, dirt, or unrelieved squalor which repels and blunts the senses: a *sordid* story of official corruption. *Abject* is the least derogatory of these words; it denotes a low condition, degree, or estate, often without further implication: the *abject* spirits of the conquered.

mean[3] (mēn) *n.* 1. *pl.* The medium, method, or instrument by which some end is or may be accomplished: used often with a singular sense and construction: He is the *means* of our achieving victory. 2. *pl.* Money, property, or other resources; wealth: a man of *means.* 3. The middle point or state between two extremes. 4. Avoidance of excess or extremes; moderation. 5. *Math.* **a** A number or quantity contained within the range of a set of numbers or quantities and representative, by some method, of each of the set; an average. **b** Arithmetic mean (which see). **c** Geometric mean (which see). **d** The second or third term in a proportion containing four terms. 6. *Stat.* The average value of a large number of observed data. 7. *Logic* The middle term in a syllogism. — **by all means** Without hesitation; certainly. — **by any means** In any manner possible; at all; somehow. — **by means of** With the help of; through using. — **by no** (or **no manner of**) **means** Most certainly not; on no account whatever. — *adj.* 1. Intermediate or average in size, degree, quality, etc.; medium. 2. Intermediate or occurring halfway between extremes of time, position, value, etc.; average. [< OF *meien* < L *medianus* < *medius* middle. Doublet of MEDIAN, MESNE, MIZZEN]

me·an·der (mē·an′dər) *v.i.* 1. To wind and turn in a course. 2. To wander aimlessly. — *n.* 1. *Often pl.* A tortuous or winding course or labyrinth. 2. A rambling or zigzag movement. 3. An interlocking, geometric pattern much used in early Greek frets or fretwork. [< L *mæander* < Gk. *maiandros* < *Maiandros,* the river Meander, proverbial for its windings] — **me·an′der·er** *n.*

Me·an·der (mē·an′dər) The ancient name for the MENDERES (def. 1): also *Maeander.*

mean distance *Astron.* **a** The arithmetic mean of the maximum and minimum distance of a planet from the sun, or of any satellite from the planet around which it revolves. **b** The average distance between the two components of a binary star.

mean·ie (mē'nē) *n. Informal* A mean or cruel person. Also **mean·y.**

mean·ing (mē'ning) *n.* **1.** That which is intended or meant; aim; purpose; end: the *meaning* of his actions. **2.** That which is signified; sense; import: the *meaning* of a word. **3.** Interpretation or significance: the *meaning* of a dream. — *adj.* **1.** Having purpose or intention: usually in combination: *well-meaning.* **2.** Significant; suggestive; expressive. — **mean'ing·ly** *adv.*

mean·ing·ful (mē'ning·fəl) *adj.* Full of meaning. — **mean'ing·ful·ness** *n.* — **mean'ing·ful·ly** *adv.*

mean·ing·less (mē'ning·lis) *adj.* Having no meaning, significance, or importance. — **mean'ing·less·ly** *adv.* — **mean'ing·less·ness** *n.*

mean·ly (mēn'lē) *adv.* In a mean, poor, or ignoble manner.

mean·ness (mēn'nis) *n.* **1.** The state or quality of being mean. **2.** A mean act.

mean sun *Astron.* A fictitious sun considered to be always moving a uniform distance around the celestial equator.

meant (ment) Past tense and past participle of MEAN[1].

mean·time (mēn'tīm') *n.* Intervening time. — *adv.* **1.** In or during the intervening time. **2.** At the same time.

mean time Time based upon the rotation of the earth with reference to the mean sun, and measured by successive 12–hour periods reckoned from midnight and noon, or 24–hour periods reckoned from midnight: also called *astronomical time, civil time.* Also **mean solar time.**

mean·while (mēn'hwīl') *n. & adv.* Meantime.

Mean·y (mē'nē), **George,** born 1894, U.S. labor leader.

Mearns (mûrnz), **The** See KINCARDINE.

meas. Measure.

mea·sled (mē'zəld) *adj.* Affected with measles.

mea·sles (mē'zəlz) *n.pl.* (construed as *sing.* or *pl.*) **1.** An acute, highly contagious virus disease affecting children and sometimes adults, characterized by an extensive eruption of small red macules: also called *rubeola.* **2.** Any of various similar eruptive diseases, as German measles. **3.** *Vet.* A disease affecting swine and cattle, caused by larval tapeworms; also, the larval tapeworms. [ME *maseles,* pl. of *masel* blister < LG. Cf. MDu. *masel* spot on the skin.]

mea·sly (mēz'lē) *adj.* **·sli·er, ·sli·est** **1.** Affected with measles. **2.** Containing tapeworm larvae: said of meat. **3.** *Slang* Contemptibly stingy, scanty, or petty; worthless.

meas·ur·a·ble (mezh'ər·ə·bəl) *adj.* **1.** Capable of being measured or compared. **2.** Limited; moderate. — **meas'ur·a·bil'i·ty, meas'ur·a·ble·ness** *n.* — **meas'ur·a·bly** *adv.*

meas·ure (mezh'ər) *n.* **1.** The extent, range, dimensions, capacity, etc., of anything. **2.** A standard or unit of measurement, as a yard, pound, gallon, etc. **3.** Any standard or criterion of criticism, comparison, or judgment. **4.** A system of measurements: liquid *measure.* **5.** An instrument or vessel for taking measurements: a pint *measure.* **6.** The act of measuring; measurement. **7.** A specific quantity measured out or regarded as measured out: a full *measure* of wheat. **8.** A fixed, reasonable, or suitable limit or bound: talkative beyond all *measure.* **9.** A certain amount, extent, or degree of anything: a *measure* of freedom. **10.** Often *pl.* A specific action, step, or procedure used as a means to an end: to take *measures* for his removal. **11.** A legislative bill or decree: a senate *measure.* **12.** Rhythmic movement or beat, as in music or literature. **13.** *Music* **a** A group of beats marked off by regularly recurring primary accents. **b** The portion of music contained between two bar lines; bar. **14.** In prosody: **a** Meter (def. 1). **b** A metrical foot. **15.** *Poetic* A melody or tune. **16.** *Archaic* A dance, especially a slow, stately one. **17.** *pl. Geol.* A series of rock strata having some common feature. — **for good measure** As something additional or extra. — **in a measure** To some degree or extent. — **to take one's measure** To estimate or form an opinion of one's character, skill, etc. — *v.* **·ured, ·ur·ing** *v.t.* **1.** To take or ascertain the dimensions, quantity, capacity, etc., of, especially by means of a measure. **2.** To set apart, mark off, allot, etc., by or as by measuring: often with *off* or *out.* **3.** To estimate by comparison; judge; weigh: to *measure* a risk. **4.** To serve as the measure of. **5.** To bring into competition or comparison. **6.** To traverse as if measuring; travel over. **7.** To adjust; regulate: *Measure* your actions to your aspirations. — *v.i.* **8.** To make or take measurements. **9.** To yield a specified measurement: The table *measures* six by four feet. **10.** To admit measurement. — **to measure one's length** To fall or lie prostrate at full length. — **to measure swords** **1.** To fight with swords. **2.** To fight or contend as in a debate. — **to measure up to** To fulfill, or meet, as expectations. Abbr. *meas.* [< F *mesure* < L *mensura* < *metiri* measure] — **meas'ur·er** *n.*

meas·ured (mezh'ərd) *adj.* **1.** Determined, adjusted, or proportioned by some standard. **2.** Slow and stately; rhythmical: a *measured* step. **3.** Carefully considered or weighed; deliberate: to speak in *measured* terms. **4.** Moderate; limited.

5. Metrical. — **meas'ured·ly** *adv.* — **meas'ured·ness** *n.*

meas·ure·less (mezh'ər·lis) *adj.* Incapable of being measured; very great; immense. — **Syn.** See INFINITE.

meas·ure·ment (mezh'ər·mənt) *n.* **1.** The act or process of measuring anything. **2.** The amount, capacity, or extent determined by measuring. **3.** A system of measures.

measurement ton See TON[1] (def. 3).

measuring worm The larva of a geometrid moth, so called because it advances its body by a succession of loops as though measuring the surface along which it moves: also called *inchworm, looper, spanworm.*

meat (mēt) *n.* **1.** The flesh of animals used as food, especially the flesh of mammals as opposed to fish or fowl. **2.** The edible part of anything: the *meat* of a crab. **3.** Anything eaten for nourishment: now usually in the phrase **meat and drink. 4.** The essence, gist, or main idea of something: the *meat* of the story. **5.** *Informal* Anything one particularly enjoys or does with ease: Dancing is his *meat.* **6.** *Archaic* A meal, especially the main meal. [OE *mete*]

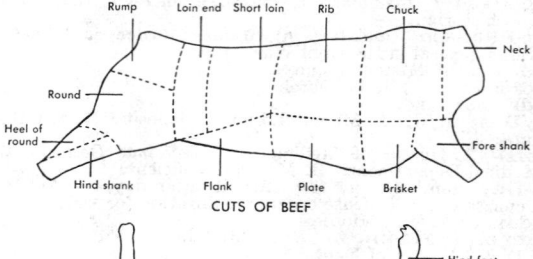

CUTS OF BEEF

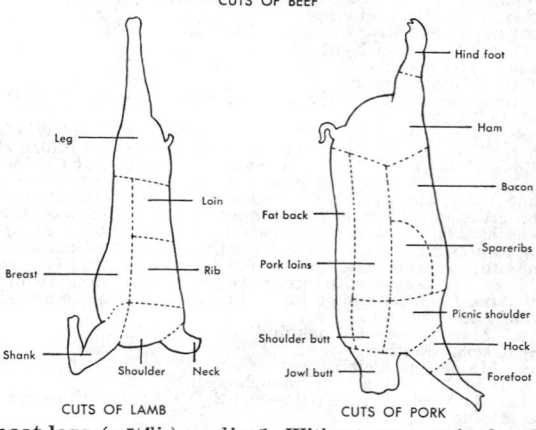

CUTS OF LAMB   CUTS OF PORK

meat·less (mēt'lis) *adj.* **1.** Without meat or food. **2.** When the eating of meat is prohibited: a *meatless* day.

meat packing *U.S.* The commercial slaughtering of meat-producing animals and the processing, packaging, and distribution of meat and meat products. — **meat packer**

me·a·tus (mē·ā'təs) *n.* *pl.* **·tus** or **·tus·es** *Anat.* A passage, duct, or canal. [< L, passage, pp. of *meare* to go]

meat·y (mē'tē) *adj.* **meat·i·er, meat·i·est** **1.** Of, pertaining to, or like meat. **2.** Full of meat. **3.** Full of substance; significant. — **meat'i·ness** *n.*

mec·ca (mek'ə) *n.* **1.** A place or attraction visited by many people. **2.** The goal of one's aspirations. [after *Mecca*]

Mec·ca (mek'ə) One of the capitals of Saudi Arabia; birthplace of Mohammed and a holy city of Islam to which Moslems make pilgrimages; pop. 185,000 (1965): also *Mek-ka.* — **Mec·can** *adj. & n.*

mech. **1.** Mechanical; mechanics. **2.** Mechanism.

me·chan·ic (mə·kan'ik) *n.* **1.** One skilled in the making, operation, or repair of tools or machinery. **2.** *Archaic* **a** An artisan. **b** A vulgar, lowly fellow. — *adj.* **1.** Involving or pertaining to manual labor or skill. **2.** Of or pertaining to mechanics; mechanical. [< L *mechanicus* < Gk. *mēchanikos* < *mēchanē* machine]

me·chan·i·cal (mə·kan'i·kəl) *adj.* **1.** Of, involving, or having to do with the construction, operation, design, etc., of machinery or tools: a *mechanical* engineer. **2.** Operated or produced by a machine. **3.** Of, pertaining to, or in accordance with the science of mechanics. **4.** Made or performed as if by a machine; done without spontaneity or by force of habit; automatic: a lifeless and *mechanical* speech. **5.** Explaining or interpreting all phenomena by means of physical forces and laws: a *mechanical* philosophy. **6.** *Archaic* Of or relating to craftsmen or to the working class. — **me·chan'i·cal·ly** *adv.* — **me·chan'i·cal·ness** *n.*

mechanical advantage In a machine, the ratio of the force used to produce work (output force) to the force applied (input force).

mechanical drawing A drawing, usually of mechanical objects or parts, done with the aid of compasses, squares, etc.; also, the craft of making such drawings.

mech·a·ni·cian (mek′ə·nish′ən) *n.* One who builds, operates, or repairs machines or tools.

me·chan·ics (mə·kan′iks) *n.pl.* (*construed as sing. in defs. 1 and 2*) **1.** The branch of physics that treats of motion and of the action of forces on material bodies, including statics, kinetics, and kinematics. **2.** The body of knowledge dealing with the design, operation, and maintenance of machinery. **3.** The mechanical or technical aspects of anything: the *mechanics* of music. Abbr. *mech.*

Me·chan·ics·ville (mə·kan′iks·vil) A hamlet near Richmond, Virginia; site of a Civil War battle (June 26, 1862).

mech·a·nism (mek′ə·niz′əm) *n.* **1.** The parts or arrangement of parts of a machine: the *mechanism* of a watch. **2.** Something similar to a machine in the arrangement and working of its parts: The human body is a magnificent *mechanism.* **3.** The process or technique by which something works or produces an action or effect: the complicated *mechanism* of democracy. **4.** The technique or the mechanical method of execution of an artist, writer, etc. **5.** A theory that all natural phenomena can be explained by the laws of chemistry and physics. **6.** *Psychol.* The mental processes, conscious or unconscious, by which certain actions or results are effected. Abbr. *mech.*

mech·a·nist (mek′ə·nist) *n.* **1.** A mechanician. **2.** A believer in mechanism (def. 5). — *adj.* Mechanistic.

mech·a·nis·tic (mek′ə·nis′tik) *adj.* **1.** Of, pertaining to, or of the nature of mechanics. **2.** Pertaining to or based on mechanism (def. 5). — **mech′a·nis′ti·cal·ly** *adv.*

mech·a·ni·za·tion (mek′ə·nə·zā′shən, -ni-) *n.* The act or process of mechanizing, or the state of being mechanized.

mech·a·nize (mek′ə·nīz) *v.t.* **·nized, ·niz·ing 1.** To make mechanical. **2.** To convert (an industry, etc.) to machine production. **3.** *Mil.* To equip with tanks, trucks, etc.

Mech·lin (mek′lin) A commune in northern Belgium; pop. 65,728 (est. 1967): French *Malines.* Flemish **Mech·e·len** (mekh′ə·lən).

Mech·lin lace (mek′lin) A lace having a fine net ground on which designs are outlined by thread or flat cord: also called *malines.* [after *Mechlin,* Belgium, where made]

Meck·len·burg (mek′lən·bûrg, *Ger.* mek′lən·bŏŏrkh) A former state of northern Germany, comprising the former grand duchies of **Meck′len·burg-Schwe·rin′** (-shvä·rēn′), **Meck′len·burg-Stre′litz** (-shtrā′lits), and western Pomerania; now included in East Germany.

me·cop·ter·ous (mə·kop′tər·əs) *adj. Entomol.* Of or belonging to an order (*Mecoptera*) of predacious insects with long, narrow wings, including the scorpion fly. [< NL < Gk. *mēkos* length + *pteron* wing]

med. **1.** Medical; medicine. **2.** Medieval. **3.** Medium.

M.Ed. Master of Education.

med·al (med′l) *n.* A small piece of metal, bearing an image, inscription, etc., usually commemorative of some event, deed, or person, and often given as an award for some outstanding act or service. — *v.t.* **med·aled** or **·alled, med·al·ing** or **·al·ling** To confer a medal upon. [< F *médaille* < Ital. *medaglia,* ult. < L *metallum.* Doublet of METAL.] — **me·dal·lic** (mə·dal′ik) *adj.*

Medal for Merit A medal awarded by the United States to civilians for exceptional services in times of peace or war.

med·al·ist (med′l·ist) *n.* **1.** A collector, engraver, or designer of medals. **2.** The recipient of a medal awarded for services or merit. **3.** In golf, the winner at medal play. Also *Brit.* **med′al·list.**

me·dal·lion (mə·dal′yən) *n.* **1.** A large medal. **2.** An ornamental subject usually set in a circular or oval frame or design, and used as a decorative element in fabrics, on walls, etc. [< F *médaillon* < Ital. *medaglione,* aug. of *medaglia.* See MEDAL.] — **me·dal′lion·ist** *n.*

Medal of Honor The highest U.S. military decoration, awarded to one who risked his life in action beyond the call of duty. It is awarded in the name of Congress and usually presented personally by the President. Also called *Congressional Medal of Honor.* See DECORATION. Abbr. *MH*

medal play In golf, a form of competitive play in which the score is computed by counting only the total number of strokes played by each competitor in playing the designated number of holes. Compare MATCH PLAY.

Me·dan (me·dän′) A city on NE Sumatra, Indonesia; pop. 568,000 (est. 1968).

med·dle (med′l) *v.i.* **·dled, ·dling 1.** To participate or interfere officiously; intrude impertinently: often with *in* or *with.* **2.** To tamper. [< OF *medler, mesdler,* var. of *mesler,* ult. < L *miscere* to mix] — **med′dler** *n.*

med·dle·some (med′l·səm) *adj.* Inclined to meddle; interfering; intrusive. — **med′dle·some·ly** *adv.* — **med′dle·some·ness** *n.*

Mede (mēd) *n.* A native or inhabitant of ancient Media.

Me·de·a (mə·dē′ə) In Greek legend, a sorceress of Colchis who helped Jason obtain the Golden Fleece.

Me·del·lín (mā′thā·yēn′) A city in NW central Colombia; pop. 651,240 (est. 1961).

Med·ford (med′fərd) A city in NE Massachusetts, near Boston; pop. 64,971.

Med.Gk. Medieval Greek.

me·di·a¹ (mē′dē·ə) Alternative plural of MEDIUM.

me·di·a² (mē′dē·ə) *n. pl.* **·di·ae** (-dē·ē) **1.** *Anat.* The medial layer of the wall of an artery or lymphatic vessel. **2.** *Phonet.* A medial (def. 2).

Me·di·a (mē′dē·ə) An ancient country of SW Asia, corresponding to NW Iran. — **Me′di·an** *adj. & n.*

me·di·a·cy (mē′dē·ə·sē) *n.* **1.** The state or quality of being mediate. **2.** Mediation.

me·di·ae·val (mē′dē·ē′vəl, med′ē-), **me·di·ae·val·ism,** etc. See MEDIEVAL.

me·di·al (mē′dē·əl) *adj.* **1.** Of, pertaining to, or situated in the middle. **2.** Of or pertaining to a mathematical average; mean. **3.** Designating a sound, syllable, or letter, neither initial nor final. — *n. Phonet.* **1.** A noninitial, nonfinal element. **2.** Any of a group of voiced stops (b, d, g), conceived as intermediate between the voiceless stops (p, t, k) and the rough or aspirate group (bh, dh, gh, ph, th, kh). [< LL *medialis* < L *medius* middle] — **me′di·al·ly** *adv.*

me·di·an (mē′dē·ən) *adj.* **1.** Pertaining to or situated in the middle; medial. **2.** *Anat. & Zool.* Of or pertaining to the plane that divides a body longitudinally into symmetrical halves. **3.** *Stat.* Designating the middle point in a series of values: 8 is the *median* number of 2, 5, 8, 10, 13. — *n.* A median point, line, or number. [< L *medianus* < *medius* middle. Doublet of MEAN³, MIZZEN.] — **me′di·an·ly** *adv.*

Me·di·an (mē′dē·ən) *adj.* Of or pertaining to ancient Media or the Medes. — *n.* A Mede.

me·di·as·ti·num (mē′dē·as·tī′nəm) *n. pl.* **·na** (-nə) *Anat.* **1.** A partition or septum separating two cavities of the body. **2.** The space separating the two pleural sacs of the chest, extending from the breastbone back to the thoracic vertebrae and downward to the diaphragm, and containing all the viscera of the thorax except the lungs. [< NL < Med.L *mediastinus* medial < *medius*] — **me′di·as·ti′nal** *adj.*

me·di·ate (*v.* mē′dē·āt; *adj.* -it) *v.* **·at·ed, ·at·ing *v.t.* 1.** To settle or reconcile (differences) by intervening as a peacemaker. **2.** To bring about or effect by one's intervention. **3.** To serve as the medium for effecting (a result) or conveying (an object, information, etc.). — *v.i.* **4.** To act between disputing parties in order to bring about a settlement, compromise, etc. **5.** To occur or be in an intermediate relation or position. — *adj.* **1.** Acting as an intervening agency; indirect. **2.** Occurring or effected as a result of indirect or median agency. **3.** *Rare* Intermediate. [< LL *mediatus,* pp. of *mediare* to stand between, mediate] — **me′di·ate·ly** *adv.*

me·di·a·tion (mē′dē·ā′shən) *n.* The act of mediating; intercession; interposition.

— **Syn. 2.** *Mediation, conciliation,* and *arbitration* come into comparison as they denote the effort of a third party to reconcile two disputants. *Mediation* seeks to find a middle ground on which two persons at odds can agree. *Conciliation* seeks to dispel anger and suspicion, and to persuade each side to make concessions to the other. *Arbitration* listens to the arguments of both sides and then renders a quasi-judicial decision, which both sides have previously agreed to accept.

me·di·a·tive (mē′dē·ā′tiv) *adj.* Mediating; mediatory.

me·di·a·tize (mē′dē·ə·tīz) *v.t.* **·tized, ·tiz·ing** To annex (one state) to another, allowing the former ruler to retain his title and certain authority. — **me′di·a·ti·za′tion** *n.*

me·di·a·tor (mē′dē·ā′tər) *n.* One who mediates.

me·di·a·tor·y (mē′dē·ə·tôr′ē, -tō′rē) *adj.* **1.** Of or pertaining to mediation. **2.** Serving to mediate. Also **me′di·a·to′ri·al** (-tôr′ē·əl, -tō′rē·əl). — **me·di·a·to′ri·al·ly** *adv.*

med·ic¹ (med′ik) *n.* Any of several cloverlike plants (genus *Medicago*) of the bean family, especially alfalfa and black medic. [< L *medicus* < Gk. *Mēdikē (poa)* Median (grass) < *Mēdos* a Mede]

med·ic² (med′ik) *n. Informal* **1.** A physician or intern. **2.** A medical student. **3.** A corpsman.

med·i·ca·ble (med′ə·kə·bəl) *adj.* Capable of being relieved by medical treatment; curable.

Med·i·caid (med′i·kād) *n. U.S.* A governmental health program financed by State and Federal funds and providing hospitalization and health insurance to persons having a low income. [< MEDIC(AL) + AID]

med·i·cal (med′i·kəl) *adj.* **1.** Of or pertaining to medicine. **2.** Having curative properties. — **med′i·cal·ly** *adv.*

medical examiner 1. An official who examines the bodies of those dead as a result of suicide, crime, or unknown causes to establish the cause and circumstances of the death. **2.** A physician authorized by a life insurance company to determine the physical fitness of insurance applicants.

medical jurisprudence The application of medical principles in law, as in the determination of the cause of death in a murder: also called *forensic medicine, legal medicine.*

med·i·ca·ment (med′ə·kə·mənt, mə·dik′ə-) *n.* Any substance for the cure of disease or the alleviation of pain; a medicine. [< L *medicamentum* < *medicare*. See MEDICATE.]

med·i·care (med′i·kâr) *n. U.S. & Canadian* Government medical care or health insurance.

med·i·cate (med′ə·kāt) *v.t.* **·cat·ed**, **·cat·ing** **1.** To treat medicinally. **2.** To tincture or impregnate with medicine. [< L *medicatus*, pp. of *medicare* to heal < *medicus* physician] — **med′i·ca′tive** *adj.*

med·i·ca·tion (med′ə·kā′shən) *n.* **1.** The act or process of medicating. **2.** A medicine or medicament.

Med·i·ci (med′ə·chē, *Ital.* mä′dē·chē) A family of Florentine bankers and statesmen prominent in Italian Renaissance history, notably **Giovanni de' Medici**, died 1429, and his sons, **Cosimo**, 1389–1464, and **Lorenzo**, 1395–1440; **Lorenzo**, 1449?–92, grandson of Cosimo, patron of the arts: called **the Magnificent**; **Giovanni**, 1475–1521, son of Lorenzo the Magnificent (see LEO X); **Giulio**, 1478?–1534 (see CLEMENT VII); **Cosimo**, 1519–74, grand duke of Tuscany: called **the Great**; **Catherine**, 1519–89, queen of Henry II of France; **Maria**, 1573–1642, second wife of Henry IV of France; exiled by Richelieu, 1631: also **Marie de Medicis**.

me·dic·i·nal (mə·dis′ə·nəl) *adj.* Pertaining to or having the properties of medicine, curative, or alleviating.

med·i·cine (med′ə·sən, *Brit.* med′sən) *n.* **1.** Any substance used in the treatment of disease, in healing, or in the relief of pain; medicament. **2.** The science of the preservation and restoration of health and of treating disease, especially measures other than those employed in surgery or obstetrics. **3.** The profession of medicine. **4.** Among American Indians, any object or rite supposed to produce supernatural effects, protection, healing, etc.; also, a magic spell or power. **5.** *Obs.* Drugs, herbs, etc., used for other than healing purposes, as love potions, elixirs, or poisons. Abbr. *m., M., med.* — **to take one's medicine** To endure hardship, discomfort, or punishment. [< OF *medecine* < L *medicina* < *medicus* physician < *mederi* to heal]

medicine ball A large, heavy, leather-covered ball, thrown and caught for physical exercise.

medicine lodge A lodge in a North American Indian village, used for ritualistic, religious ceremonies.

medicine man Among North American Indians, one professing supernatural powers of healing and of invoking the spirits; a shaman; magician; wizard.

med·i·co (med′ə·kō) *n. pl.* **·cos** *Informal* A physician or a medical student. [< Ital. or Sp., physician]

medico- *combining form* Pertaining to medical science and: *medico-legal*, medical and legal. Also, before vowels, **medic-**. [< L *medicus* physician]

me·di·e·val (mē′dē·ē′vəl, med′ē-) *adj.* Belonging to, like, or characteristic of the Middle Ages: also spelled *mediaeval.* Abbr. *M, med.* [< L *medius* middle + *aevum* age] — **me′di·e′val·ly** *adv.*

Medieval Greek See under GREEK.

me·di·e·val·ism (mē′dē·ē′vəl·iz′əm, med′ē-) *n.* **1.** The spirit, beliefs, customs, and practices of the Middle Ages. **2.** Devotion to the institutions, ideas, or characteristics of the Middle Ages. **3.** Any custom, idea, etc., surviving from the Middle Ages. Also spelled *mediaevalism.*

me·di·e·val·ist (mē′dē·ē′vəl·ist, med′ē-) *n.* **1.** A scholar or specialist in medieval history, literature, or art. **2.** One devoted to the spirit and thought of the Middle Ages. Also spelled *mediaevalist.*

Medieval Latin See under LATIN.

Me·di·na (mə·dē′nə) A Moslem holy city in western Saudi Arabia; goal of Mohammed's Hegira and the place of his tomb; pop. about 80,000.

medio- *combining form* Middle. Also, before vowels, **medi-**. [< L *medius* middle]

me·di·o·cre (mē′dē·ō′kər, mē′dē·ō′kər) *adj.* Of only average quality; ordinary; commonplace. [< F *médiocre* < L *mediocris* < *medius* middle]

me·di·oc·ri·ty (mē′dē·ok′rə·tē) *n. pl.* **·ties** **1.** The condition or quality of being mediocre. **2.** Mediocre ability or performance. **3.** A mediocre person.

Medit. Mediterranean.

med·i·tate (med′ə·tāt) *v.* **·tat·ed**, **·tat·ing** *v.i.* **1.** To engage in continuous and contemplative thought; muse; cogitate. — *v.t.* **2.** To think about doing; plan: to *meditate* mischief. — **Syn.** See DELIBERATE. [< L *meditatus*, pp. of *meditari* to muse, ponder] — **med′i·tat′er, med′i·ta′tor** *n.* — **med′i·ta′tive** *adj.* — **med′i·ta′tive·ly** *adv.*

med·i·ta·tion (med′ə·tā′shən) *n.* The act of meditating; reflection upon a subject; contemplation.

med·i·ter·ra·ne·an (med′ə·tə·rā′nē·ən) *adj.* Enclosed nearly or wholly by land, as a sea or other large body of water; landlocked. [< L *medius* middle + *terra* earth]

Med·i·ter·ra·ne·an (med′ə·tə·rā′nē·ən) *adj.* **1.** Of or pertaining to the Mediterranean Sea. **2.** Situated on or inhabiting the shores of the Mediterranean. — *n.* **1.** The Mediterranean Sea. **2.** One who lives in a Mediterranean country, or belongs to the Mediterranean race. — **Key of the Mediterranean** Gibraltar.

Mediterranean fever Undulant fever (which see).

Mediterranean race A subdivision of the Caucasoid race or stock inhabiting the shores of the Mediterranean Sea, including the ancient Iberian, Ligurian, Pelasgian, and Hamitic stocks and their modern descendants.

Mediterranean Sea An inlet of the Atlantic comprising a great inland sea between Europe, Asia, and Africa; 965,000 sq. mi.

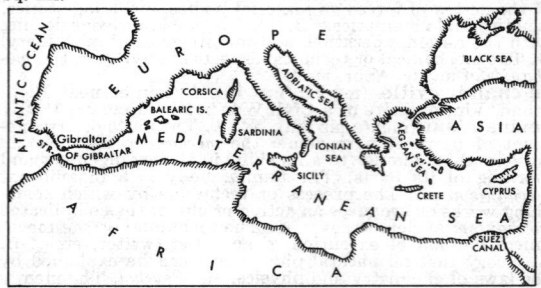

me·di·um (mē′dē·əm) *n. pl.* **·di·ums** (always for def. 5) or **·di·a** (-dē·ə) **1.** An intermediate degree or condition; mean. **2.** The surrounding or enveloping element; condition of life; environment. **3.** An intervening substance through or in which something may act or an effect be produced: Air is a *medium* of sound. **4.** A means or agency; instrument: Radio is an advertising *medium.* **5.** One through whom the spirits of the dead are believed to communicate with the material world. **6.** An area or form of artistic expression, or the materials used: This sculptor's favorite *medium* is wood. **7.** In painting, a liquid with which pigments are mixed to make them fluid enough to be applied. **8.** *Biol.* **a** A culture medium (which see). **b** Any of various substances by means of which specimens are mounted for preservation or study. — *adj.* Intermediate in quantity, quality, position, size, or degree; middle. Abbr. *m., M., med.* [< L, orig. neut. sing. of *medius* middle]

medium frequency *Telecom.* Radio waves ranging in frequency from 300 to 3000 kilocycles. Abbr. *mf.*

Med.L. or **Med.L** Medieval Latin.

med·lar (med′lər) *n.* **1.** A small, European tree (*Mespilus germanica*) of the rose family. **2.** The fruit of this tree, hard and bitter when ripe, but agreeably acid when it begins to decay. [< OF *medler*, var. of *meslier* < *mesle* fruit of the medlar < L *mespila* < Gk. *mespilē*]

med·ley (med′lē) *n.* **1.** A mingled and confused mass of elements; jumble. **2.** A musical composition made up of different airs or parts of songs arranged to run as a continuous whole. **3.** *Archaic* A melee. — *adj.* **1.** Made up of heterogeneous parts; jumbled; mixed. **2.** *Obs.* Motley. [< OF *medlee*, orig. fem. pp. of *medler.* See MEDDLE.]

Mé·doc (mā·dôk′) *n.* A red wine made in Médoc, France.

Mé·doc (mā·dôk′) A region of SW France.

me·dul·la (mə·dul′ə) *n. pl.* **·lae** (-lē) **1.** *Anat.* **a** The soft inner portion of an organ or part, such as the kidney or suprarenal. **b** The marrow of bones. **c** The pith of a hair. **d** The medulla oblongata. **2.** *Bot.* Pith (def. 1). [< L, marrow, pith < *medius* middle] — **med·ul·lar·y** (med′ə·ler·ē, mi·dul′ər·ē), **me·dul′lar** *adj.*

medulla ob·lon·ga·ta (ob′lông·gä′tə) *Anat.* The hindmost and lowest part of the brain, narrowing down into the spinal cord, and controlling breathing, circulation, etc.

medullary rays *Bot.* The vertical bands or plates of parenchymatous tissue proceeding from the pith to the surface, characteristic of exogenous plants.

medullary sheath **1.** *Bot.* The innermost ring of xylem. For illustration see EXOGEN. **2.** *Anat.* Myelin.

med·ul·lat·ed (med′ə·lā′tid, mi·dul′ā·tid) *adj.* Provided with a myelin sheath: said of nerve fibers.

me·du·sa (mə·doo′sə, -zə, -dyoo′-) *n. pl.* **·sas** or **·sae** (-sē, -zē) A jellyfish. [< L] — **me·du′san** *adj. & n.*

Me·du·sa (mə·doo′sə, -zə, -dyoo′-) In Greek mythology, one of the Gorgons, killed by Perseus.

me·du·soid (mə·doo′soid, -zoid, -dyoo′-) *adj.* Resembling a medusa or jellyfish. — *n.* **1.** A medusa-shaped gonophore of a hydrozoan. **2.** Any medusa.

meed (mēd) *n. Archaic* **1.** A well-deserved reward; recompense. **2.** A present, gift, or bribe. [OE *mēd*]

meek (mēk) *adj.* **1.** Having a patient, gentle disposition; mild. **2.** Lacking spirit or backbone; submissive; compliant. **3.** *Obs.* Compassionate; kind. [ME *meoc* < ON *miukr* gentle, soft] — **meek′ly** *adv.* — **meek′ness** *n.*

Meer (mār), **Jan van der** See VERMEER.

meer·schaum (mir′shəm, -shôm, -shoum) *n.* **1.** A soft, light, heat-resisting magnesium silicate, $H_4Mg_2Si_3O_{10}$, used for tobacco pipes, etc.: also called *sepiolite.* **2.** A tobacco pipe made from this mineral. [< G < *meer* sea + *schaum* foam]

Mee·rut (mē′rət) A city in NW Uttar Pradesh, India; pop. 283,878 (1961).

meet[1] (mēt) *v.* **met, meet·ing** *v.t.* **1.** To come upon; come face to face with; encounter: He *met* her by chance. **2.** To be at, or go to the place of arrival of: to *meet* him at the station. **3.** To make the acquaintance of; be introduced to. **4.** To come into the company of or in association with, as for a conference. **5.** To come into contact or conjunction with: where the path *meets* the road. **6.** To keep an appointment with. **7.** To come into the observation, perception, or recognition of (the eye, ear, etc.). **8.** To experience; undergo: to *meet* adversity. **9.** To oppose in battle; fight with. **10.** To answer (a blow, move, etc.) by another in return; counter. **11.** To deal or cope with; handle: He *meets* the accusation with scorn. **12.** To comply or act in accordance with; conform to: to *meet* the requirements for a diploma. **13.** To pay (a bill, debt, etc.). **14.** To fulfill (an obligation, responsibility, need, etc.). — *v.i.* **15.** To come together; come face to face. **16.** To come together in contact, conjunction, or union; join. **17.** To assemble. **18.** To make acquaintance or be introduced. **19.** To come together in conflict or opposition; contend. **20.** *Archaic* To agree; concur. — **to meet up with** *U.S. Informal* **1.** To come upon; encounter. **2.** To experience; undergo. — **to meet with 1.** To come upon; encounter. **2.** To deal or confer with. **3.** To experience. — *n.* An assembling for a sport or an athletic contest; also, the persons so assembled, or the place of assembly: a track *meet*. [OE *mētan*]

meet[2] (mēt) *adj.* Suitable; proper. — **Syn.** See APPROPRIATE. — *adv. Obs.* Suitably. [OE *gemēte*] — **meet′ly** *adv.*

meet·ing (mē′ting) *n.* **1.** A coming together. **2.** An assembly or gathering of persons; also, the persons present. **3.** A joining or conjunction of things. **4.** An assembly of Quakers for religious services; also, their meeting house.

meeting house 1. A house used for public meetings. **2.** A place of worship used by the Quakers.

meg. 1. Megacycle. **2.** Megohm.

mega- *combining form* **1.** Great; large: *megaphone*. **2.** In the metric system, a million times (a specified unit):

megabar	mega·erg	megampere
megacurie	megafarad	megavolt
megadyne	megameter	megohm

Also, before vowels, **meg-.** [< Gk. *megas* large]

meg·a·ce·phal·ic (meg′ə·sə·fal′ik) *adj.* Large-headed. Also **meg′a·ceph′a·lous** (-sef′ə·ləs).

meg·a·cy·cle (meg′ə·sī′kəl) *n.* **1.** *Telecom.* A unit of electromagnetic wave frequency of 1,000,000 cycles per second. **2.** One million cycles.

Me·gae·ra (mə·jir′ə) In Greek mythology, one of the three Furies. [< L < Gk. *Megaira* < *megairein* to bear a grudge]

meg·a·ga·mete (meg′ə·gə·mēt′, -gam′ēt) *n.* A macrogamete (which see).

meg·a·hertz (meg′ə·hûrts′) *n.* A megacycle. Abbr. *MHz.*

meg·a·lith (meg′ə·lith) *n. Archeol.* A huge stone, especially one used in various types of prehistoric monuments. — **meg′a·lith′ic** *adj.*

megalo- *combining form* Big; indicating excessive or abnormal size: *megalocephalic.* Also, before vowels, **megal-.** [< Gk. *megas, megalou* big]

meg·a·lo·ceph·a·ly (meg′ə·lō·sef′ə·lē) *n.* **1.** Unusual largeness of the head. **2.** *Pathol.* Progressive enlargement of the bones and soft tissues of the head. Also **meg′a·lo·ce·pha′li·a** (-sə·fā′lē·ə). [< MEGALO- + Gk. *kephalē* head] — **meg′a·lo·ce·phal′ic** (-sə·fal′ik), **meg′a·lo·ceph′a·lous** *adj.*

meg·a·lo·ma·ni·a (meg′ə·lō·mā′nē·ə, -mān′yə) *n.* **1.** *Psychiatry* A mental disorder in which the subject thinks himself great or exalted. **2.** A tendency to magnify and exaggerate. — **meg′a·lo·ma′ni·ac** *adj. & n.* — **meg′a·lo·ma·ni′a·cal** (-mə·nī′ə·kəl) *adj.*

meg·a·lop·o·lis (meg′ə·lop′ə·lis) *n.* An urban complex encompassing several major cities.

meg·a·lop·ter·ous (meg′ə·lop′tər·əs) *adj. Entomol.* Pertaining or belonging to an order (*Megaloptera*) of soft-bodied insects with large wings and aquatic larvae, as the hellgrammite. [< MEGALO- + -PTEROUS]

meg·a·lo·saur (meg′ə·lə·sôr) *n. Paleontol.* A gigantic, terrestrial, carnivorous dinosaur (genus *Megalosaurus*) that flourished in the Jurassic period. [MEGALO- + Gk. *sauros* lizard] — **meg′a·lo·saur′i·an** *adj. & n.*

Meg·an·thro·pus (meg·an′thrə·pəs) *n. Paleontol.* An extinct hominid primate of the Pleistocene, represented by massive fossil jawbones found in central Java. [< NL < Gk. *megas* great + *anthropos* man]

meg·a·phone (meg′ə·fōn) *n.* A funnel-shaped device for amplifying or directing sound. — *v.t. & v.i.* **·phoned, ·phon·ing** To speak through or as through a megaphone.

meg·a·pod (meg′ə·pod) *adj.* Having large feet.

meg·a·pode (meg′ə·pōd) *n.* Any of a family (*Megapodidae*) of large-footed gallinaceous birds of Australia, noted for incubating their eggs in earthen mounds.

Meg·a·ra (meg′ər·ə) An ancient city in east central Greece, capital of Megaris. — **Me·gar·i·an** (mə·gâr′ē·ən), **Me·gar·ic** (mə·gar′ik) *adj.*

Meg·a·ris (meg′ə·ris) A mountainous region of ancient Greece on the isthmus of Corinth.

meg·a·spo·ran·gi·um (meg′ə·spə·ran′jē·əm) *n. pl.* **·gi·a** (-jē·ə) *Bot.* A sporangium that bears only megaspores.

meg·a·spore (meg′ə·spôr, -spōr) *n. Bot.* The embryo sac.

meg·a·spo·ro·phyll (meg′ə·spôr′ə·fil, -spōr′rə-) *n. Bot.* A leaf or sporophyll that produces only megasporangia.

me·gass (mə·gas′, -gäs′) *n. Brit.* Bagasse. Also **me·gasse′.**

meg·a·there (meg′ə·thir) *n. Paleontol.* A gigantic, extinct, ground sloth (genus *Megatherium*), that ranged from South to North America in the Pleistocene. Also **meg·a·the·ri·um** (meg′ə·ther′ē·əm). [< MEGA- + Gk. *thērion* wild animal]

meg·a·ton (meg′ə·tun′) *n.* **1.** One million tons. **2.** A unit equal to the explosive power of one million tons of TNT.

Me·gid·do (mə·gid′ō) An ancient city in NW Palestine at the western edge of the Plain of Jezreel, probably Armageddon of the Bible.

MEGATHERES
(Probably up to
20 feet long)

me·gilp (mə·gilp′) *n.* A mixture of mastic varnish and linseed oil, used as a vehicle for oil colors in art work: also spelled *magilp.* Also **me·gilph′** (-gilf′). [Origin unknown]

me·grim (mē′grim) *n.* **1.** *pl.* Depression of spirits; dullness. **2.** *Archaic* A whim. **3.** *Obs.* Migraine. [< F *migraine* < L *hemicrania* < Gk. *hēmi* half + *krania* skull]

Me·hem·et A·li (mə·hem′et ä′lē, me·met′), 1769–1849, viceroy of Egypt 1805–49. Also *Mohammed Ali.*

Mei·ji (mā·jē) *n.* The reign, 1867–1912, of the Emperor Mutsuhito, 1852–1912, of Japan, regarded as a historic era. [< Japanese, lit., enlightened peace]

Meik·le·john (mik′əl·jon), **Alexander,** 1872–1964, U.S. educator born in England.

Meil·hac (me·yàk′), **Henri,** 1832–97, French playwright.

Mein Kampf (mīn kämpf′) A book by Adolf Hitler, written in 1924. [< G, my battle]

mei·ny (mā′nē) *n. pl.* **·nies 1.** *Obs.* A retinue; attendants; household. **2.** *Scot.* A multitude. Also **mei′nie.** [< OF *mesnee, meyné,* ult. < L *mansio* dwelling. See MANSION.]

mei·o·sis (mī·ō′sis) *n. Biol.* The cell divisions leading to the formation of gametes in which the number of chromosomes is reduced from the diploid to the haploid number. Compare MITOSIS. [< Gk. *meiosis* lessening < *meiōn* less]

Me·ir (mī·ir′), **Golda,** born 1898, Israeli government official born in Russia; prime minister, 1969–1974.

Meis·sen (mī′sən) *n.* A kind of porcelain or chinaware made in Meissen, Germany. Also **Meissen ware.**

Meis·sen (mī′sən) A city in SE East Germany, on the Elbe; pop. about 50,000.

Meis·so·nier (mā·sô·nyā′), **Jean Louis Ernest,** 1815–91, French painter.

Meis·ter·sing·er (mīs′tər·sing′ər, *Ger.* mīs′tər·zing′ər) *n. pl.* **·sing·er** *German* Any of the poets and musicians, mainly artisans and tradesmen, active in the principal cities of Germany between the 14th and 16th centuries, and claiming to be successors of the minnesingers. — **Die Meistersinger von Nürnberg** A comic opera by Richard Wagner.

Meit·ner (mīt′nər), **Lise,** 1878–1968, Austrian nuclear physicist active in Sweden.

Mé·ji·co (mā′hē·kō) The Spanish name for MEXICO.

Mek·ka (mek′ə) See MECCA.

Mek·nès (mek·nes′) One of the traditional capitals of Morocco, in the NW part; pop. 200,000 (est. 1966): formerly also *Mequinez.*

Me·kong (mā·kong′) A river in SE Asia, flowing 2,600 miles south to the China Sea: Chinese *Lantsang.*

mel (mel) *n.* Honey. [< L]

mel·a·mine (mel′ə·mēn, -min) *n. Chem.* A colorless, crystalline nitrogen compound, $C_3N_2(NH_2)_3$, that reacts with formaldehyde to produce a high-grade thermosetting resin. [< *mel(am),* a chemical compound + AMINE]

melan- Var. of MELANO-.

mel·an·cho·li·a (mel′ən·kō′lē·ə) *n. Psychiatry* Mental disorder characterized by great depression of spirits and excessive brooding without apparent or sufficient cause. [< L. See MELANCHOLY.] — **mel′an·cho′li·ac** *adj. & n.*

mel·an·chol·y (mel′ən·kol′ē) *adj.* **1.** Excessively gloomy; dejected; sad. **2.** Suggesting or promoting sadness: a *melancholy* day. **3.** Somberly thoughtful; pensive. — *n. pl.* **·chol·ies 1.** Low spirits; despondency; depression. **2.** Pensive contemplation; sober reflection. **3.** *Archaic* Black bile, the humor once believed to be secreted by the kidneys and responsible for depression of spirits. [< F *mélancolie* < L *melancholia* < Gk. < *melas, -anos* black + *cholē* bile] — **mel′an·chol′ic** *adj.* — **mel′an·chol′li·cal·ly** *adv.*

Me·lanch·thon (mə·langk′thən), **Philipp,** Hellenized name of **Philip Schwarz·erd** (shvärts′ärt), 1497–1560, German religious reformer, associate of Luther. Also **Me·lanc′thon.**

Mel·a·ne·sia (mel/ə-nē/zhə, -shə) The islands of the western Pacific south of the equator, one of the three main divisions of the Pacific Islands; about 60,000 sq. mi. See map of AUSTRALASIA.

Mel·a·ne·sian (mel/ə-nē/zhən, -shən) *adj.* Of or pertaining to Melanesia, its native inhabitants, or their languages. — *n.* **1.** A member of any of the dark-skinned, kinky-haired peoples of Melanesia. **2.** Any of the languages of the Austronesian group spoken in Melanesia.

mé·lange (mā-länzh/) *n. French* A mixture or medley.

me·lan·ic (mə-lan/ik) *adj.* Relating to or resembling melanosis or melanism; melanoid.

mel·a·nin (mel/ə-nin) *n. Biochem.* A brownish black pigment contained in animal tissues, as the skin and hair.

mel·a·nism (mel/ə-niz/əm) *n. Physiol.* Excessive pigmentation of the skin, eyes, or hair. — **mel·a·nis/tic** *adj.*

mel·a·nite (mel/ə-nīt) *n.* A deep black variety of garnet.

melano- *combining form* Black; dark-colored: *melanosis.* Also, before vowels, *melan-.* [< Gk. *melas, melanos* black]

Mel·a·noch·ro·i (mel/ə-nok/rō-ī) *n.pl.* Caucasians having fair skins and dark hair. [< MELAN- + Gk. *ōchros* pale] — **Mel/a·noch/roid** *adj.*

mel·a·noid (mel/ə-noid) *adj.* **1.** Of or characterized by melanosis. **2.** Having a dark appearance; darkly pigmented.

mel·a·no·ma (mel/ə-nō/mə) *n. Pathol.* A black-pigmented tumor. [< MELAN- + -OMA]

mel·a·no·sis (mel/ə-nō/sis) *n. Pathol.* A condition in which dark pigment is deposited in the skin and other tissues.

mel·a·nous (mel/ə-nəs) *adj.* Having dark or black skin and hair. — **mel·a·nos·i·ty** (mel/ə-nos/ə-tē) *n.*

mel·an·tha·ceous (mel/ən-thā/shəs) *adj. Bot.* Of or pertaining to a former family (*Melanthaceae*) of monocotyledonous plants resembling the lilies but distinguished from them by the absence of bulbs, including the bunchflower, hellebore, etc. [< NL < Gk. *melas, -anos* + *anthos* flower]

mel·a·phyre (mel/ə-fīr) *n.* Any igneous porphyry with a dark groundmass. [< F < Gk. *melas* black + F (*por*)*phyre* porphyry]

Mel·ba (mel/bə), **Dame Nellie,** 1861–1931, Australian operatic soprano: original name **Helen Porter Mit·chell** (mich/əl).

Mel·ba toast (mel/bə) Thinly sliced bread toasted until brown and crisp.

Mel·bourne (mel/bərn) The capital of Victoria, Australia, a port in the southern part; pop. 2,108,499 (1967, including suburbs).

Mel·bourne (mel/bərn), **Viscount,** 1779–1848, William Lamb, English statesman, prime minister 1834, 1835–41.

Mel·chi·or (mel/kē-ôr) Traditionally, one of the three Magi.

Mel·chi·or (mel/kē-ôr), **Lauritz (Lebrecht Hommel),** born 1890, Danish operatic tenor active in the United States.

Mel·chis·e·dec (mel-kiz/ə-dek) **1.** In Old Testament history, a priest; king of Salem. *Gen.* xiv 18. **2.** Of or denoting the greater priesthood of the Mormon Church. Also **Mel·chiz/e·dek.**

meld (meld) *v.t. & v.i.* In pinochle and other card games, to announce or declare (a combination of cards) for inclusion in one's total score. — *n.* A group of cards to be declared, or the act of declaring them. [< G *melden* to announce]

mel·der (mel/dər) *n. Scot.* The quantity of grain ground at one time; a grist.

Mel·e·a·ger (mel/ē-ā/jər) In Greek mythology, the son of Oeneus and Althea and slayer of the Calydonian boar.

me·lee (mā/lā, mā-lā/) A confused, general hand-to-hand fight; affray. Also *Fr.* **mê·lée** (me-lā/). — **Syn.** See ROW³. [< F < OF *meslee,* var. of *medlee.* See MEDLEY.]

me·li·a·ceous (mē/lē-ā/shəs) *adj. Bot.* Of or pertaining to the mahogany family (*Meliaceae*) of trees and shrubs. [< NL < Gk. *melia* ash tree]

mel·ic (mel/ik) *adj.* Suitable for singing, or meant to be sung: said of poetry, especially of ancient Greek lyrical poetry written in strophes. Compare ELEGIAC, IAMBIC. [< Gk. *melikos* < *melos* song]

mel·i·lot (mel/ə-lot) *n.* Any one of several cloverlike herbs (genus *Melilotus*); especially, the yellow melilot (*M. officinalis*): also called *sweet clover.* [< OF *melilot* < LL *melilotos* < Gk. *melilōtos* < *meli* honey + *lōtos* lotus]

mel·i·nite (mel/ə-nīt) *n.* A high explosive of guncotton and picric acid. [< Gk. *mēlinos* yellow + -ITE]

me·li·o·rate (mēl/yə-rāt) *v.t. & v.i.* **·rat·ed, ·rat·ing** To improve, as in quality or condition; ameliorate. [< LL *melioratus,* pp. of *meliorare* to improve < *melior* better] — **mel/io·ra·ble** *adj.* — **mel/io·ra/tive** *adj.* — **mel/io·ra/tor** *n.*

mel·io·ra·tion (mēl/yə-rā/shən) *n.* **1.** Betterment. **2.** *Ling.* An improvement or elevation in the meaning of a word, as in *nice* (formerly "foolish"): opposed to *pejoration.*

mel·io·rism (mēl/yə-riz/əm) *n.* The belief that the world tends to improve and that man can further this improvement. Compare OPTIMISM, PESSIMISM. [< L *melior* better] — **mel/io·rist** *adj. & n.* — **mel/io·ris/tic** *adj.*

mel·ior·i·ty (mēl/yôr/ə-tē, -yor/-) *n.* The state of being better; superiority.

Mel·i·ta (mel/ə-tə) The ancient name for MALTA.

Me·li·to·pol (myi-lyi-tô/pəly/) A city in southern Ukrainian S.S.R.; pop. about 95,000 (1959). Also **Me·li·to/pol'.**

mel·lif·er·ous (mə-lif/ər-əs) *adj.* Producing or bearing honey. Also **mel·lif/ic.** [< L *mellifer* honey-bearing < *mel* honey + *ferre* to bear]

mel·lif·lu·ent (mə-lif/lōō-ənt) *adj.* Mellifluous. — **mel·lif/lu·ence** *n.* — **mel·lif/lu·ent·ly** *adv.*

mel·lif·lu·ous (mə-lif/lōō-əs) *adj.* Sweetly or smoothly flowing; dulcet: *mellifluous speech.* [< L *mellifluus* < *mel* honey + *fluere* to flow] — **mel·lif/lu·ous·ly** *adv.* — **mel·lif/lu·ous·ness** *n.*

Mel·lon (mel/ən), **Andrew William,** 1855–1937, U.S. banker and public administrator.

mel·low (mel/ō) *adj.* **1.** Soft, sweet, and full-flavored by reason of ripeness, as fruit. **2.** Well-matured, as wines. **3.** Rich and soft in quality, as colors or sounds; not harsh. **4.** Made gentle and sympathetic by maturity or experience. **5.** Made jovial or genial by liquor. **6.** Soft and friable, as soil. — *v.t. & v.i.* To make or become mellow; ripen; soften. [ME *melwe,* ? < OE *melu* meal. Akin to Flemish *meluw* soft, tender.] — **mel/low·ly** *adv.* — **mel/low·ness** *n.*

me·lo·de·on (mə-lō/dē·ən) *n.* A small reed organ or harmonium. [A pseudo-Greek formation < MELODY]

me·lo·di·a (mə-lō/dē·ə) *n.* An organ stop having wood pipes and a clear, flutelike tone. [< LL]

me·lod·ic (mə-lod/ik) *adj.* **1.** Pertaining to or containing melody. **2.** Melodious. — **me·lod/i·cal·ly** *adv.*

me·lo·di·ous (mə-lō/dē·əs) *adj.* **1.** Producing or characterized by melody; tuneful. **2.** Pleasant to hear. — **me·lo/di·ous·ly** *adv.* — **me·lo/di·ous·ness** *n.*

mel·o·dize (mel/ə-dīz) *v.* **·dized, ·diz·ing** *v.t.* **1.** To make melodious. **2.** To compose melody for. — *v.i.* **3.** To make melody or melodies. — **mel/o·diz/er, mel/o·dist** *n.*

mel·o·dra·ma (mel/ə-drä/mə, -dram/ə) *n.* **1.** A play or drama in which the emotions displayed are violent or extravagantly sentimental, and the plot is made up of sensational incidents. **2.** Formerly, a romantic drama with sensational incidents, usually including music and songs. **3.** Sensational and highly emotional behavior or language. [< F *mélodrame* < Gk. *melos* song + *drama* drama] — **mel/o·dram/a·tist** *n.*

mel·o·dra·mat·ic (mel/ə-drə-mat/ik) *adj.* Of, pertaining to, or like melodrama; sensational; exaggerated. — **mel/o·dra·mat/i·cal·ly** *adv.*

mel·o·dra·mat·ics (mel/ə-drə-mat/iks) *n.pl.* Melodramatic behavior.

mel·o·dy (mel/ə-dē) *n. pl.* **·dies 1.** Pleasing sounds, or an agreeable succession of such sounds. **2.** *Music* **a** An organized succession of tones, usually in the same voice or instrument. **b** Musical structure in terms of the relations between successive tones. **c** The leading part in a homophonic composition; the air. **3.** A poem written to be set to music. [< OF *melodie* < LL *melodia* < Gk. *melōidia* choral song < *melōidos* melodious < *melos* song + *aoidos* singer]
— **Syn. 2.** *Melody, tune, air, theme, subject,* and *motif* denote various combinations of tones. *Melody* has the implication of esthetically pleasing organization, and is often used to denote the leading voice of a composition. An *air* is often the same as a *melody,* but more often refers to a song. A *tune* is usually a simple, easily sung *melody.* A *theme* is the basic melodic, harmonic, or rhythmic idea from which a composition is derived, though it is often used synonymously with *subject,* a melody that undergoes development. A *motif* is the shortest recognizable melodic or rhythmic element.

mel·on (mel/ən) *n.* **1.** The large fruit of any of various plants of the gourd family, as the muskmelon and the watermelon. **2.** Any of these plants. **3.** *Slang* Profits, dividends, or spoils for distribution among stockholders, members of a party, etc.: chiefly in the phrase **to cut the melon.** [< F < LL *melo, melonis* < L *melopepo* < Gk. *mēlopepōn* apple-shaped melon < *mēlon* apple + *pepōn* melon]

Me·los (mē/los) See MILO.

Mel·pom·e·ne (mel-pom/ə-nē) In Greek mythology, the Muse of tragedy. [< Gk. *Melpomenē,* lit., the songstress < *melpein* to sing]

Mel·rose (mel/rōz) **1.** A burgh in SE Scotland; site of a ruined Cistercian abbey, founded 1136; pop. about 2,000. **2.** A city in NE Massachusetts, near Boston; pop. 33,180.

melt (melt) *v.t. & v.i.* **melt·ed, melt·ed** (*Archaic* **mol·ten** (mōl/tən)), **melt·ing 1.** To reduce or change from a solid to a liquid state by heat; fuse. **2.** To dissolve, as in water. **3.** To disappear or cause to disappear; dissipate: often with *away.* **4.** To blend by imperceptible degrees; merge: often with *into.* **5.** To make or become softened in feeling or attitude. — *n.* **1.** Something melted. **2.** A single operation of fusing. **3.** The amount of a single fusing. [OE *meltan, mieltan.* Akin to MALT.] — **melt/a·ble** *adj.* — **melt/a·bil/i·ty** *n.* — **melt/er** *n.*
— **Syn.** (verb) 1. *Melt, fuse, thaw,* and *liquefy* mean to pass into a liquid from a solid state. *Melt* suggests a slow softening, often, though not always, from heat. *Fuse* is a close synonym of *melt,* but applied only to metals. *Thaw* is applied only to those things that are regarded as frozen, and often means only to become unfrozen; it may therefore be applied to things such as frozen foods, which do not necessarily become liquid when heated. *Liquefy* means specifically to become a liquid, but may be said of matter in either the gaseous or solid state. — **Ant.** solidify, harden, congeal, freeze.

melt·age (mel′tij) *n.* **1.** The process of melting. **2.** The amount or substance resulting from melting.

melting point The temperature at which a specified solid substance melts or fuses. Abbr. *m.p.*, *M.P.*

melting pot **1.** A vessel in which a substance is melted. **2.** A country, city, or region in which immigrants of various racial and cultural backgrounds are assimilated.

mel·ton (mel′tən) *n.* A heavy woolen cloth with a short nap, used for overcoats. [after *Melton* Mowbray, England]

Me·lun·geon (mə·lun′jən) *n.* One of a dark-skinned people of mixed white, Negro, and Indian stock, living in the mountains of Tennessee. [? < F *mélange* mixture]

Mel·ville (mel′vil), **Herman**, 1819–91, U.S. novelist and poet.

Mel·ville Island (mel′vil) An island of Canada in the Arctic Ocean; 16,503 sq. mi.

Melville Peninsula A peninsula in the northern Northwest Territories, Canada; 24,156 sq. mi.; 250 mi. long.

mem (mem) *n.* The thirteenth letter in the Hebrew alphabet. See ALPHABET.

mem. **1.** Member. **2.** Memoir. **3.** Memorandum. **4.** Memorial.

mem·ber (mem′bər) *n.* **1.** One who belongs to a society, club, party, etc. **2.** *Usually cap.* One who belongs to a legislative body, especially the U.S. House of Representatives, the Canadian Parliament, or the British House of Commons. **3.** *Biol.* A part or organ of an animal body, especially a limb. **4.** A part or element of a structural or composite whole. **5.** *Math.* Either side of an algebraic equation. Abbr. *mem.* [< OF *membre* < L *membrum* limb]

mem·ber·ship (mem′bər·ship) *n.* **1.** The state or fact of being a member. **2.** The members of an organization, etc., collectively; also, the total number of members.

mem·brane (mem′brān) *n.* A thin, pliable, sheetlike layer of animal or vegetable tissue serving to cover or line an organ or part, separate adjoining cavities, or connect adjoining structures. [< L *membrana*, lit., limb coating < *membrum* member]

membrane bone *Anat.* A bone originating in the connective tissue of which membranes are formed: distinguished from *cartilage bone*.

membrane theory *Physiol.* The theory that nerve impulses are initiated by a critical difference in electric potential between the outer and inner walls of the membrane enclosing each neuron, resulting in the passage of a current through the neuron.

mem·bra·nous (mem′brə·nəs) *adj.* **1.** Of, pertaining to, or like a membrane. **2.** Marked by the formation of a membrane. Also **mem·bra·na·ceous** (mem′brə·nā′shəs).

Mem·el (mem′əl, *Ger.* mā′məl) **1.** See KLAIPEDA. **2.** The German name for the NEMAN.

me·men·to (mə·men′tō) *n. pl.* **·tos** or **·toes** **1.** Anything that serves as a hint or reminder of the past; souvenir. **2.** In the Roman Catholic Church, either of two prayers in the canon of the Mass beginning with the word *Memento*, the first being for the living, and the second for the deceased. [< L, remember, imperative of *meminisse* to remember]

memento mo·ri (môr′ī) *Latin* An emblem or reminder of death, as a skull, etc.: literally, remember that you must die.

Mem·ling (mem′ling), **Hans**, 1430?–95?, Flemish painter. Also **Mem·linc** (mem′lingk).

Mem·non (mem′non) **1.** In Greek legend, a king of the Ethiopians killed by Achilles and made immortal by Zeus. **2.** A huge statue at Thebes, Egypt, said to emit a musical note when touched by the sun at dawn. — **Mem·no·ni·an** (mem·nō′nē·ən) *adj.*

mem·o (mem′ō) *n. pl.* **mem·os** *Informal* A memorandum.

memo. Memorandum.

mem·oir (mem′wär) *n.* **1.** *pl.* Personal reminiscences or records; especially, a narrative of events based on the writer's personal observations and experiences. **2.** A biography. **3.** *pl.* An account of the proceedings of a learned society. **4.** A report or dissertation on a learned subject; monograph. [< F *mémoire* < L *memoria* memory. Doublet of MEMORY.]

mem·o·ra·bil·i·a (mem′ə·rə·bil′ē·ə) *n.pl.* Things or events worthy of remembrance and record. [< L, neut. pl. of *memorabilis* memorable]

mem·o·ra·ble (mem′ər·ə·bəl) *adj.* Worthy to be remembered; noteworthy. [< L *memorabilis*] — **mem′o·ra·bil′i·ty, mem′o·ra·ble·ness** *n.* — **mem′o·ra·bly** *adv.*

mem·o·ran·dum (mem′ə·ran′dəm) *n. pl.* **·dums** or **·da** (-də) **1.** A brief note of a thing or things to be remembered. **2.** An account or record of observations, transactions, etc., especially for future use. **3.** An informal letter, usually sent between departments in an office. **4.** *Law* A brief written outline of the terms of a transaction or contract. **5.** In business, a statement of goods sent from a consignor to a consignee. **6.** In diplomacy, an informal statement or summary of an issue, action, or decision. Abbr. *mem.*, *memo*. [< L, a thing to be remembered]

me·mo·ri·al (mə·môr′ē·əl, -mō′rē-) *adj.* **1.** Serving to keep in memory a deceased person or an event; commemorative.

2. Of or pertaining to memory. — *n.* **1.** Something serving to keep in remembrance a person, event, etc. **2.** A written summary or presentation of facts addressed to a legislative body, official, etc., as the grounds for or in the form of a petition. Abbr. *mem.* [< OF < L *memorialis* < *memoria*]

Memorial Day *U.S.* **1.** May 30, a day set apart in most States to honor the dead of any American war. **2.** April 26, May 10, or June 3, similarly observed in various States of the South. Also called *Decoration Day*.

me·mo·ri·al·ist (mə·môr′ē·əl·ist, -mō′rē-) *n.* **1.** One who writes memoirs. **2.** One who writes, signs, or presents a memorial.

me·mo·ri·al·ize (mə·môr′ē·əl·īz′, -mō′rē-) *v.t.* **·ized, ·iz·ing** **1.** To commemorate. **2.** To present a memorial to; petition. Also *Brit.* **me·mo′ri·al·ise′**. — **me·mo′ri·al·i·za′tion** *n.*

mem·o·rize (mem′ə·rīz) *v.t.* **·rized, ·riz·ing** To commit to memory; learn by heart. — **mem′o·ri·za′tion** *n.* — **mem′·o·riz′er** *n.*

mem·o·ry (mem′ər·ē) *n. pl.* **·ries** **1.** The mental function or capacity of recalling or recognizing previously learned behavior or past experience. **2.** The total of what is remembered. **3.** One who or that which is remembered. **4.** The period of time covered by the faculty of remembrance: beyond the *memory* of man. **5.** The state of being remembered; posthumous reputation. **6.** Remembrance or commemoration: in *memory* of our mother. **7.** *Obs.* A memorial. **8.** *Electronics* Storage, a computer part. [< OF *memorie* < L *memoria* < *memor* mindful. Doublet of MEMOIR.]

— **Syn. 1.** *Memory, remembrance, retrospect, recollection*, and *reminiscence* refer to the recalling of one's past experiences. *Memory* is the mental faculty by which this recall takes place; *remembrance* is the act of bringing something to mind: a good *memory* for names, the *remembrance* of past follies. *Retrospect* is the turning of the mind to the past, and *recollection* the voluntary calling back to mind of what has been learned or experienced. Of the two, *retrospect* suggests contemplation or careful consideration of the past, while *recollection* is more specific and aims to recapture a single fact or event for some immediate practical purpose: his childhood seemed happy in *retrospect*, his *recollection* of the event has been corroborated. *Reminiscence* implies the narration and savoring of past events: to exchange *reminiscences* of college days with a friend. — **Ant.** oblivion, forgetfulness.

Mem·phi·an (mem′fē·ən) *adj.* Of or pertaining to ancient Memphis, Egypt, or to its inhabitants.

Mem·phis (mem′fis) **1.** A port city in SW Tennessee, on the Mississippi; pop. 623,530. **2.** The ancient capital of Egypt, on the Nile above the apex of its delta.

Mem·phre·ma·gog (mem′frə·mā′gog), **Lake** A lake in northern Vermont and southern Quebec; about 30 mi. long.

mem-sah·ib (mem′sä·ib) *n.* *Anglo-Indian* A European lady: a name given by native servants. [< MA′AM + Hind. *sāhib* master < Arabic]

men (men) Plural of MAN.

men·ace (men′is) *v.* **·aced, ·ac·ing** *v.t.* **1.** To threaten with evil or harm. — *v.i.* **2.** To make threats; appear threatening. — **Syn.** See THREATEN. — *n.* **1.** A threat. **2.** *Informal* A troublesome person; pest. [< OF *manace* < L *minacia* < *minax, -acis* threatening < *minari* to threaten] — **men′ac·er** *n.* — **men′ac·ing·ly** *adv.*

me·nad (mē′nad), etc. See MAENAD, etc.

mé·nage (mā·nazh′, *Fr.* mā·nàzh′) *n.* **1.** The persons of a household, collectively; a domestic establishment. **2.** Household management; housekeeping. Also **me·nage′**. [< F < L *mansio, -onis* house. Doublet of MANSION.]

me·nag·er·ie (mə·naj′ər·ē) *n.* **1.** A collection of wild animals kept for exhibition. **2.** The enclosure in which they are kept. [< F]

Men·ai Strait (men′ī) A channel between the island of Anglesey and the mainland in NW Wales.

Me·nan·der (mə·nan′dər), 343?–291? B.C., Greek comic dramatist.

me·nar·che (mə·när′kē) *n.* *Physiol.* The first menstruation in girls. [< Gk. *mēn* month + *archē* beginning]

Men·cius (men′shəs) Latinized name of *Meng-tse*, died 289? B.C., Chinese philosopher.

Menck·en (meng′kən), **H(enry) L(ouis)**, 1880–1956, U.S. author and editor.

mend (mend) *v.t.* **1.** To make sound or serviceable again by repairing; repair. **2.** To correct errors or faults in; reform; improve. *Mend* your ways. **3.** To correct (some defect). — *v.i.* **4.** To become better, as in health. **5.** To improve: said of conditions. — *n.* **1.** A repairing. **2.** A mended place, as on a garment. — **on the mend** Recovering health; recuperating. [Aphetic var. of AMEND] — **mend′a·ble** *adj.* — **mend′er** *n.*

men·da·cious (men·dā′shəs) *adj.* **1.** Lying; deceitful. **2.** Untrue; false. [< L *mendax, -acis* lying] — **men·da′cious·ly** *adv.* — **men·da′cious·ness** *n.*

men·dac·i·ty (men·das′ə·tē) *n. pl.* **·ties** **1.** The quality of being mendacious. **2.** A lie; untruth. [< L *mendacitas*]

Men·del (men′dəl), **Gregor Johann**, 1822–84, Austrian monk and botanist; formulated laws of genetics.

Men·de·ley·ev (men'də·lā'əf), **Dmitri Ivanovich**, 1834–1907, Russian chemist; developed the periodic law. Also **Men·de·le'ev**.

men·de·le·vi·um (men'də·lē'vē·əm) n. A short-lived radioactive element (symbol Md). See ELEMENT. [after Dmitri Ivanovich *Mendeleyev*]

Men·de·li·an (men·dē'lē·ən) adj. **1.** Of or pertaining to Mendel. **2.** Relating to or according with Mendel's laws.

Men·del·ism (men'dəl·iz'əm) n. Mendel's theory of heredity. Also **Men·de·li·an·ism** (men·dē'lē·ən·iz'əm).

Mendel's laws *Genetics* Principles formulated by Gregor Mendel, stating that alternative hereditary factors, or unit characters, of hybrids segregate from one another in transmission to offspring and that different pairs of such characters segregate independently of each other.

Men·dels·sohn (men'dəl·sən, *Ger.* men'dəl·zōn), **Felix**, 1809–47, German composer: full name **Jakob Ludwig Felix Men'dels·sohn-Bar·thol·dy** (-bär·tōl'dē). — **Moses**, 1729–1786, German Jewish theologian and philosopher.

Men·de·res (men'də·res') **1.** A river in western Turkey in Asia, flowing about 240 miles SW to the Aegean: ancient *Meander*. **2.** A river in NW Turkey, flowing 60 miles NW to the Dardanelles: ancient *Scamander*.

men·di·cant (men'də·kənt) adj. **1.** Begging; depending on alms for a living. **2.** Pertaining to or characteristic of a beggar. — n. **1.** A beggar. **2.** A begging friar. [< L *mendicans*, *-antis*, ppr. of *mendicare* to beg < *mendicus* needy] — **men'di·can·cy**, **men·dic·i·ty** (men·dis'ə·tē) n.

men·di·go (men'di·gō) n. *Canadian* The splake, a fish.

Men·do·ci·no (men'də·sē'nō), **Cape** A cape in NW California, the westernmost point of the state.

Men·do·za (men·dō'sä) A Province of western Argentina; 52,839 sq. mi.; pop. 825,535 (1960); capital, **Mendoza**, pop. 109,122 (1960).

Men·do·za (men·dō'thä), **Pedro de**, 1487?–1537, Spanish explorer and colonist in South America; founded Buenos Aires.

Men·e·la·us (men'ə·lā'əs) In Greek legend, a king of Sparta, who, after the abduction of his wife Helen by Paris, became one of the Greek leaders in the Trojan War.

Men·e·lik II (men'e·lik), 1844–1913, emperor of Ethiopia 1889–1910; defeated Italians at Aduwa 1896.

me·ne, me·ne, tek·el, u·phar·sin (mē'nē mē'nē tek'əl yoō·fär'sin) *Aramaic* Literally, numbered, numbered, weighed, (and) divided; in the Bible, the words that appeared on the wall at Belshazzar's feast, and that Daniel interpreted to mean that God had judged and doomed Belshazzar's kingdom. *Dan.* v 25–28.

Me·nén·dez de A·vi·lés (mā·nen'dāth thä ä·vē'lās), **Pedro**, 1519–74, Spanish explorer; founded St. Augustine, Florida.

Me·nes (mē'nēz) Fifth-millennium B.C. Egyptian king, founder of the first dynasty of Egypt. Also **Me·ni** (mē'nē).

men·folk (men'fōk') n.pl. *Informal* Men collectively. Also **men'folks'**.

Meng-tse (mung'dzu') See MENCIUS.

men·ha·den (men·hād'n) n. A marine fish (*Brevoortia tyrannus*) resembling the herring, found in North Atlantic and West Indian waters, used as a source of oil, as fertilizer, and as bait: also called *fatback*, *hardhead*, *mossbunker*, *pogy*. [Alter. of Algonquian *munnawhat* fertilizer]

men·hir (men'hir) n. *Archeol.* A prehistoric monument, consisting of a single tall, rough stone standing alone or with others. [< F < Celtic (Breton) *men* stone + *hir* long]

me·ni·al (mē'nē·əl, mēn'yəl) adj. **1.** Pertaining to or appropriate to servants. **2.** Servile; abject. — n. **1.** A domestic servant. **2.** One who has a servile nature. [< AF < OF *meisniee*, *maisnie* household < LL *mansionata* < L *mansio* house] — **me'ni·al·ly** adv.

Mé·nière's syndrome (mā·nyârz') *Pathol.* A disorder of the labyrinth of the ear characterized by recurrent attacks of deafness, tinnitus, vertigo, and sometimes nausea. [after Prosper *Ménière*, 1799–1862, French physician]

me·nin·ges (mə·nin'jēz) n. pl. of **me·ninx** (mē'ningks) *Anat.* The three membranes, dura mater, pia mater, and arachnoid, enveloping the brain and spinal cord. [< NL < Gk. *mēninx*, *mēningos* membrane] — **me·nin'ge·al** adj.

men·in·gi·tis (men'ən·jī'tis) n. *Pathol.* Inflammation of the meninges, especially of the pia mater and arachnoid. [< MENING(ES) + -ITIS] — **men'in·git'ic** (-jit'ik) adj.

me·nis·cus (mə·nis'kəs) n. pl. **·nis·cus·es** or **·nis·ci** (-nis'ī) **1.** A crescent or crescent-shaped body. **2.** *Optics* A lens concave on one side and convex on the other, either convexo-concave (**converging meniscus**) or concavo-convex (**diverging meniscus**). For illustration see LENS. **3.** *Physics* The surface or upper part of a liquid column made convex or concave by capillarity. **4.** *Anat.* A disk of cartilage found in some joints, serving to adapt the articular surfaces to each other. [< L < Gk. *mēniskos* crescent, dim of *mēnē* moon]

men·i·sper·ma·ceous (men'e·spər·mā'shəs) adj. *Bot.* Of or belonging to the moonseed family (*Menispermaceae*) of mostly tropical woody or herbaceous climbing plants. [< NL *menispermaceae* < Gk. *mēnē* moon + *sperma* seed]

Men·lo Park (men'lō) **1.** A city in western California; pop. 26,734. **2.** A village in central New Jersey; former site of Thomas Edison's laboratory.

Men·nin·ger (men'ing·ər), **Karl Augustus**, born 1893, U.S. psychiatrist. — **William Claire**, 1899–1966, U.S. psychiatrist; brother of the preceding.

Men·non·ite (men'ən·īt) n. A member of a Protestant Christian sect founded in the 16th century and still active in Europe and the United States, opposing the taking of oaths, the holding of public office, and military service. [after *Menno* Simons, 1492–1559, a leader of the sect]

me·no (mā'nō) adv. *Music* Less. [< Ital. < L *minus*]

me·nol·o·gy (mə·nol'ə·jē) n. pl. **·gies** **1.** A calendar of the months. **2.** A register or collection of the lives of the saints arranged in a calendar. [< LL *menologium* < Gk. *mēn* month + -LOGY]

me·nom·i·nee (mə·nom'ə·nē) n. *Canadian* Wild rice. [< Algonquian (Cree)]

Me·nom·i·nee (mə·nom'ə·nē) n. pl. **·nee** **1.** One of an Algonquian tribe of North American Indians, inhabiting central Wisconsin. **2.** The Algonquian language of this tribe. Also **Me·nom·i·ni** (-nē).

men·o·pause (men'ə·pôz) n. *Physiol.* The final cessation of menstruation, occurring normally between the ages of 45 and 50. [< Gk. *mēn* month + *pauein* to cause to cease]

Me·no·rah (mə·nôr'ə, -nô'rə) n. **1.** In the Jewish religion, a candelabrum; as: **a** The seven-branched ceremonial candelabrum of the Jewish temple (*Ex.* xxxvii 17–24), symbolizing the seven days of the Creation. **b** A candelabrum having nine candles lighted in increasing numbers on the eight successive days of Chanukah. **2.** An organization concerned with Jewish cultural affairs. [< Hebrew, candlestick]

Me·nor·ca (mā·nôr'kä) The Spanish name for MINORCA.

men·or·rha·gi·a (men'ə·rā'jē·ə) n. *Pathol.* Excessive menstrual flow. [< Gk. *mēn* month + -RRHAGIA]

Me·not·ti (mə·not'ē), **Gian Carlo**, born 1911, U.S. composer and librettist born in Italy.

men·sa (men'sə) n. *Dent.* The biting or chewing surface of a tooth. [< L, table]

Men·sa (men'sə) n. A constellation, the Table. See CONSTELLATION. [< L]

men·sal¹ (men'səl) adj. Belonging to or used at the table. [< L *mensalis* < *mensa* table]

men·sal² (men'səl) adj. Monthly. [< L *mensis* month]

mense (mens) n. *Scot. & Brit. Dial.* Dignified conduct; decorum. [ME *mensk*] — **mense'ful** adj. — **mense'less** adj.

men·ses (men'sēz) n.pl. *Physiol.* Menstruation. [< L, pl. of *mensis* month]

Men·she·vik (men'shə·vik) n. pl. **·vi·ki** (-vē'kē) or **·viks** A member of the conservative element in the Russian Social Democratic Party. Compare BOLSHEVIK, MAXIMALIST. Also **Men'she·vist**. [< Russian *menshe* smaller, minority] — **Men'she·vism** n.

mens sa·na in cor·po·re sa·no (menz sā'nə in kôr'pə·rē sā'nō) *Latin* A sound mind in a sound body.

men·stru·al (men'stroō·əl) adj. **1.** *Physiol.* Of or pertaining to menstruation. Also **men'stru·ous**. **2.** Monthly. [< L *menstrualis* < *menstruus* monthly < *mensis* month]

men·stru·ate (men'stroō·āt) v.i. **·at·ed**, **·at·ing** To undergo menstruation. [< L *menstruatus*, pp. of *menstruare* < *menstruus*. See MENSTRUAL.]

men·stru·a·tion (men'stroō·ā'shən) n. *Physiol.* **1.** The periodical flow of bloody fluid from the uterus, occurring normally about every 28 days: also called *catamenia*, *menses*. **2.** An occurrence of this flow: also called *period*.

men·stru·um (men'stroō·əm) n. pl. **·stru·ums** or **·stru·a** (-stroō·ə) The medium in which a substance is dissolved; a solvent. [< L, neut. of *menstruus*. See MENSTRUAL.]

men·su·ra·ble (men'shər·ə·bəl) adj. That can be measured. [< LL *mensurabilis* < *mensurare* to measure < *mensura*. See MEASURE.] — **men'su·ra·bil'i·ty** n.

men·su·ral (men'shər·əl) adj. **1.** Pertaining to measure. **2.** *Music* Having notes that, in relation to each other, are of fixed rhythmic value. See PLAINSONG.

men·su·ra·tion (men'shə·rā'shən) n. **1.** The art, act, or process of measuring. **2.** The branch of mathematics having to do with determining length, area, and volume. [< LL *mensuratio*, *-onis*]

men·su·ra·tive (men'shə·rā'tiv) adj. Adapted or suitable for measuring.

-ment *suffix of nouns* **1.** The product or result of: *achievement*. **2.** The instrument or means of: *atonement*. **3.** The process or action of: *government*. **4.** The quality, condition, or state of being: *astonishment*. [< F < L *-mentum*]

men·tal¹ (men'təl) adj. **1.** Of or pertaining to the mind or intellect. **2.** Effected by or taking place in the mind, especially without the aid of written symbols: *mental* calculations. **3.** Affected by mental illness: a *mental* patient. **4.** For the care of the mentally ill: *mental* hospital. [< F < LL *mentalis* < L *mens*, *mentis* mind]

men·tal² (men'təl) adj. Of, pertaining to, or situated near the chin. [< L *mentum* chin]

mental age See under AGE.

mental deficiency *Psychol.* A condition including all types of idiocy, imbecility, and moronism, characterized by subnormal intelligence to the extent that the individual is handicapped from participating fully in ordinary life.

mental healing The alleged curing of any disorder, ailment, or disease by mental concentration and suggestion.

mental hygiene The scientific study and application of methods to preserve and promote mental health.

men·tal·i·ty (men·tal′ə·tē) *n. pl.* **·ties 1.** The mental faculties or powers; mental activity. **2.** Intellectual capacity or power: an average *mentality*. **3.** Cast or habit of mind.

men·tal·ly (men′tə·lē) *adv.* **1.** In or with regard to the mind; intellectually. **2.** By the action of the mind alone, especially without the use of symbols or speech.

men·tha·ceous (men·thā′shəs) *adj.* Designating or belonging to a genus (*Mentha*) of odorous perennial herbs of the mint family, including the peppermint, spearmint, etc. [< L *mentha* mint + -ACEOUS]

men·thene (men′thēn) *n. Chem.* A colorless, liquid, oily hydrocarbon, $C_{10}H_{18}$, synthesized from menthol. [< L *mentha* mint + -ENE]

men·thol (men′thôl, -thōl, -thol) *n. Chem.* A white, waxy, crystalline alcohol, $C_{10}H_{19}OH$, obtained from and having the odor of oil of peppermint, used as a flavoring agent, in perfumery, and in medicine. [< G < L *mentha* mint + -OL]

men·tho·lat·ed (men′thə·lā′tid) *adj.* Treated with, containing, or impregnated with menthol.

men·tion (men′shən) *v.t.* To refer to incidentally, briefly, or in passing. — *n.* **1.** The act of one who mentions. **2.** Slight reference; casual allusion: to get only a *mention*. [< OF < L *mentio*, *-onis* < *mens*, *mentis* mind] — **men′tion·a·ble** *adj.* — **men′tion·er** *n.*

Men·ton (män·tôṅ′) A resort town on the French Riviera; pop. 23,401 (1968). Italian **Men·to·ne** (män·tō′nā).

men·tor (men′tər, -tôr) *n.* A wise and trusted teacher or guide. [< MENTOR] — **men·to′ri·al** (-tôr′ē·əl, -tō′rē-) *adj.*

Men·tor (men′tər, -tôr) In the *Odyssey*, the sage guardian of Telemachus, appointed by Odysseus before he departed for the Trojan War. [< Gk., lit., adviser]

men·u (men′yōō, mān′-; *Fr.* mə·nü′) *n.* A bill of fare; also, the dishes included in it. [< F, small, detailed < L *minutus*. See MINUTE².]

Men·u·hin (men′yōō·in), Yehudi, born 1917, U.S. violinist.

me·ow (mē·ou′, myou) *n.* The crying sound made by a cat. — *v.t.* To make the sound of a cat. Also spelled *miaou, miaow.* [Imit.]

me·per·i·dine hydrochloride (mə·per′ə·dēn, -din) A white, odorless, crystalline compound, $C_{15}H_{21}NO_2·HCl$, used in medicine as an analgesic and sedative.

Me·phis·to·phe·le·an (mə·fis′tə·fē′lē·ən) *adj.* Of, pertaining to, or like Mephistopheles; cynical; crafty; sardonic; fiendish. Also **Me·phis′to·phe·li·an.**

Meph·is·toph·e·les (mef′ə·stof′ə·lēz) **1.** In medieval legend, a devil to whom Faust sold his soul for wisdom and power. **2.** A leading character in Marlowe's *Dr. Faustus*, Goethe's *Faust*, and Gounod's *Faust*. — **n.** A diabolical or crafty person. Also **Me·phis·to** (mə·fis′tō).

me·phit·ic (mə·fit′ik) *adj.* **1.** Poisonous; foul. **2.** Offensive to the sense of smell. Also **me·phit′i·cal.**

me·phi·tis (mə·fī′tis) *n.* **1.** A noxious or foul exhalation from the earth. **2.** A foul odor; stench.

me·pro·ba·mate (mə·prō′bə·māt, me·prō·ba′māt) *n. Chem.* A white, nearly odorless, bitter powder, $C_9H_{18}N_2O_4$, that is an ester of carbamic acid, used in medicine as a tranquilizer. [< ME(THYL) + PRO(PANEDIOL) + (DI-) + (CAR)BAMATE]

Me·qui·nez (mā′kē·nāth′) The former name for MEKNÈS.

mer- Var. of MERO-.

mer. 1. Meridian. **2.** Meridional.

Me·rak (mē′rak) A star, Beta in the constellation Ursa Major.

mer·can·tile (mûr′kən·til, -tīl) *adj.* **1.** Of, pertaining to, or characteristic of merchants or commerce. **2.** Of or pertaining to the mercantile system. [< F < Ital. < L *mercans, -antis*, pp. of *mercari* to traffic. See MERCHANT.]

mercantile agency A firm that collects and furnishes to regular clients information about the financial standing, credit ratings, etc., of individuals, firms, and corporations.

mercantile law The laws having to do with merchants or with their business affairs.

mercantile paper Negotiable commercial paper originating solely in regular buying and selling transactions.

mercantile system The theory in political economy, developed after the decline of feudalism, that the wealth of a country consists in its quantity of gold and silver, and that the importation of precious metals, the increased exportation of goods, and the establishment of colonies should be encouraged by the state. Also called *mercantilism.*

mer·can·til·ism (mûr′kən·til·iz′əm) *n.* **1.** The mercantile system. **2.** The spirit or theory of mercantile life or trade; commercialism.

mer·cap·tan (mər·kap′tan) *n. Chem.* Thiol. [< G < Med.L *mer(curium) captan(s)* seizing mercury]

Mer·ca·tor (mər·kā′tər, *Flemish* mer·kà′tôr), **Gerardus**, 1512–94, Flemish geographer and cartographer: original name Gerhard Kre·mer (krā′mər).

Mercator projection A map projection in which the earth is shown as projected on a cylinder tangent to it at all points on the equator, the meridians and parallels forming a rectangular grid, with areas and distances being less truly represented the farther they are from the equator.

MERCATOR PROJECTION

mer·ce·nar·y (mûr′sə·ner′ē) *adj.* **1.** Influenced by a desire for gain or reward; greedy. **2.** Serving for pay: now said only of soldiers hired by a foreign state. — *n. pl.* **·nar·ies** A hireling; especially, a hired soldier in foreign service. [< L *mercenarius < merces* reward, hire] — **mer′ce·nar′i·ly** *adv.* — **mer′ce·nar′i·ness** *n.*

mer·cer (mûr′sər) *n. Brit.* A dealer in cloth or silks. [< F *mercier* < L *merx, mercis* wares]

mer·cer·ize (mûr′sə·rīz) *v.t.* **·ized, ·iz·ing** To treat (cotton fabrics) under tension with caustic soda so as to increase strength, impart a gloss, and render more receptive to dyes. [after John *Mercer*, 1791–1866, English inventor] — **mer·cer·i·za·tion** (mûr′sər·ə·zā′shən, -ī·zā′shən) *n.*

mer·cer·y (mûr′sər·ē) *n. pl.* **·cer·ies** *Brit.* A mercer's wares or place of business. [< OF *mercerie*]

mer·chan·dise (mûr′chən·dīz, -dīs) *n.* **1.** Anything bought and sold for profit; goods; wares. **2.** *Obs.* Commerce; trade. — *v.t. & v.i.* **·dised, ·dis·ing 1.** To buy and sell; trade. **2.** To promote the sale of (goods) through advertising, etc. Also **mer′chan·dize.** Abbr. *mdse.* [< F *merchandise.* See MERCHANT.] — **mer′chan·dis′er** *n.*

mer·chant (mûr′chənt) *n.* **1.** One who buys and sells commodities for profit; a trader. **2.** A storekeeper. — *adj.* **1.** Of or pertaining to merchants or trade. **2.** Of or pertaining to the merchant marine. [< OF *marchant* < L *mercari* to traffic, buy < *merx, mercis* wares]

mer·chant·a·ble (mûr′chən·tə·bəl) *adj.* That can be bought or sold; marketable.

mer·chant·man (mûr′chənt·mən) *n. pl.* **·men** (-mən) **1.** A trading or merchant vessel. **2.** *Archaic* A merchant.

merchant marine 1. All the merchant or trading vessels of a nation, collectively. **2.** The officers and men employed on these vessels.

mer·ci (mer·sē′) *interj. French* Thank you.

Mer·ci·a (mûr′shē·ə, -shə) An ancient Anglo-Saxon kingdom of central England.

Mer·ci·an (mûr′shē·ən, -shən) *adj.* Of or pertaining to Mercia, its people, or their dialect. — *n.* **1.** An inhabitant of Mercia. **2.** The Anglo-Saxon dialects spoken in Mercia.

Mer·cier (mer·syā′), **Désiré Joseph**, 1851–1926, Belgian cardinal and patriot.

mer·ci·ful (mûr′sə·fəl) *adj.* **1.** Full of or exercising mercy; compassionate. **2.** Characterized by or indicating mercy: a *merciful* death. — **mer′ci·ful·ly** *adv.* — **mer′ci·ful·ness** *n.*

mer·ci·less (mûr′sə·lis) *adj.* Having or showing no mercy; pitiless. — **mer′ci·less·ly** *adv.* — **mer′ci·less·ness** *n.*

mer·cu·ri·al (mər·kyŏŏr′ē·əl) *adj.* **1.** Lively; volatile; clever: a *mercurial* wit. **2.** Of, pertaining to, containing, or caused by the action of mercury, or quicksilver. **3.** *cap.* Of or pertaining to the god Mercury or the planet Mercury. — *n. Med.* A preparation containing mercury. [< L *mercurialis < Mercurius* Mercury] — **mer·cu′ri·al·ly** *adv.* — **mer·cu′ri·al·ness** *n.*

mer·cu·ri·al·ism (mər·kyŏŏr′ē·əl·iz′əm) *n. Pathol.* Poisoning produced by excessive amounts of mercury.

mer·cu·ri·al·ize (mər·kyŏŏr′ē·əl·īz′) *v.t.* **·ized, ·iz·ing 1.** To make mercurial. **2.** To treat with mercury. — **mer·cu′ri·al·i·za′tion** *n.*

mer·cu·ric (mər·kyŏŏr′ik) *adj. Chem.* Of, pertaining to, or containing mercury in its highest valence.

mercuric chloride *Chem.* A white, crystalline, very poisonous compound, $HgCl_2$, formed by sublimating a mixture of sodium chloride and sulfate of mercury, used in industry, the arts, and as a strong disinfectant: also called *bichloride of mercury, corrosive sublimate.* Also **mercury chloride.**

mercuric sulfide Cinnabar.

mer·cu·rous (mər·kyŏŏr′əs) *adj. Chem.* Of, pertaining to, or containing mercury in its lowest valence.

mer·cu·ry (mûr′kyə·rē) *n. pl.* **·ries 1.** A heavy, silver-white metallic element (symbol Hg), remarkable for being liquid at ordinary temperatures: also called *hydrargyrum,* and (when liquid) *quicksilver.* See ELEMENT. **2.** The quicksilver in a thermometer or barometer, as indicating temperature, etc. **3.** A messenger. **4.** Any of various Old World herbs (genus *Mercurialis*) of the spurge family; especially, the poisonous **dog's mercury** (*M. perennis*).

Mer·cu·ry (mûr′kyₐ·rē) In Roman mythology, the herald and messenger of the gods, god of commerce, eloquence, and skill, and patron of travelers, merchants, and thieves: identified with the Greek *Hermes*. — *n*. The smallest planet of the solar system, and that nearest the sun. See PLANET.

mer·cu·ry-va·por lamp (mûr′kyₐ·rē·vā′pₐr) A glass tube or bulb containing mercury vapor in which an electric discharge produces a light high in ultraviolet and actinic rays.

Mer·cu·ti·o (mₐr·kyōō′shē·ō) In Shakespeare's *Romeo and Juliet*, a witty and brave young nobleman, friend of Romeo.

mer·cy (mûr′sē) *n. pl.* **·cies** **1.** Kind or compassionate treatment of an offender, adversary, prisoner, etc., in one's power; compassion where severity is expected or deserved. **2.** A disposition to be kind, forgiving, or helpful. **3.** The power to show mercy or compassion: to throw myself on his *mercy.* **4.** A thing to be thankful for: It's a *mercy* he has returned. **— at the mercy of** Wholly in the power of. [< OF < L *merces, mercedis* hire, payment, reward; with reference to the heavenly reward for compassion]
— Syn. 1. *Mercy, clemency, lenity,* and *leniency* denote mildness in dealing with others, where severity might be expected or deserved. *Mercy* comes from compassion, kindness, or other ennobling sentiment. *Clemency* is a colder word, chiefly applied to moderation in the exercise of legal power to punish; it may be merely the expression of a shrewd or selfish policy, or a means of gaining favor or support from others. *Lenity,* and the more common *leniency,* denote easygoing forbearance, sometimes with a suggestion of undue laxity or indulgence. **— Ant.** harshness, severity, implacability, punishment, chastisement, vengeance.

mercy killing Euthanasia.

mercy seat **1.** In the Old Testament, the golden lid of the ark of the covenant, regarded as the resting place of God: also *propitiary. Ex.* xxv 17–22. **2.** The throne of God.

mere[1] (mir) *adj. superl.* **mer·est** **1.** Being nothing more or less than; being nothing but: a *mere* trifle. **2.** *Obs.* Absolute or unqualified. [< L *merus* unmixed, bare]

mere[2] (mir) *n. Archaic or Poetic* A lake, pond, or marsh. [OE *mere*]

-mere *combining form Zool.* A part or division: *blastomere.* [< Gk. *meros* part]

Mer·e·dith (mer′ₐ·dith), **George,** 1828–1909, English novelist and poet.

mere·ly (mir′lē) *adv.* **1.** Nothing more than; solely; only. **2.** *Obs.* Absolutely; wholly.

mer·e·tri·cious (mer′ₐ·trish′ₐs) *adj.* **1.** Artificially and vulgarly attractive. **2.** *Archaic* Of, pertaining to, or resembling a prostitute. **— Syn.** See GAUDY. [< L *meretricius < meretrix, -icis* prostitute < *merere* to earn, gain] — **mer′e·tri′cious·ly** *adv.* — **mer′e·tri′cious·ness** *n.*

Me·rezh·kov·ski (mi′rish·kôf′skē), **Dmitri,** 1865–1941, Russian man of letters active in France. Also **Me′rej·kow′ski.**

mer·gan·ser (mₐr·gan′sₐr) *n.* Any of several fish-eating, diving ducks (subfamily *Merginae*) having toothlike processes along the upper edge of the bill, and the head usually crested, as the **hooded merganser** (*Lophodytes cucullatus*) of North America. Also called *goosander.* [< NL < L *mergus* diver < *mergere* to plunge + *anser* goose]

merge (mûrj) *v.t. & v.i.* **merged, merg·ing** To combine or be combined so as to lose separate identity; blend. [< L *mergere* to dip, immerse] — **mer′gence** *n.*

Mer·gen·tha·ler (mûr′gₐn·thä′lₐr, *Ger.* mer′gₐn·tä′lₐr), **Ottmar,** 1854–99, U.S. inventor born in Germany; developed the Linotype typesetting machine.

merg·er (mûr′jₐr) *n.* **1.** *Law* The extinguishment of a lesser estate, liability, right, or offense in a greater one. **2.** The combining of two or more commercial interests or corporations into one, by which all the properties are transferred to the surviving corporation. **3.** The act of merging.

Mer·gui Archipelago (mₐr·gwē′) A Burmese island group in the eastern Andaman Sea.

Meri. or **Merions.** Merionethshire.

Me·ri·da (mā′rē·thä) The capital of Yucatan State, SE Mexico; pop. 253,856 (1970).

Mer·i·den (mer′ₐ·dₐn) A city in south central Connecticut; pop. 55,959.

me·rid·i·an (mₐ·rid′ē·ₐn) *n.* **1.** *Geog.* **a** A great circle drawn from any point on the earth's surface and passing through both poles. **b** Half of a circle so drawn between the poles. **2.** *Astron.* An imaginary great circle of the celestial sphere passing through its poles and the zenith of an observer at any point. **3.** The highest or culminating point of anything; zenith: the *meridian* of life. **4.** *Obs.* Midday. — *adj.* **1.** Of or pertaining to a meridian. **2.** Pertaining to or at the highest or culminating point of development, eminence, etc. **3.** Of or pertaining to midday: *meridian* heat. [< OF *meridien* < L *meridianus* < *meridies* noon, south < *medidies* < *medius* middle + *dies* day]

Me·rid·i·an (mₐ·rid′ē·ₐn) A city in eastern Mississippi; pop. 45,083.

me·rid·i·o·nal (mₐ·rid′ē·ₐ·nₐl) *adj.* **1.** Of or pertaining to or resembling a meridian. **2.** Of, relating to, or characteristic of the south; southern. **3.** Situated or lying in the south; southerly. — *n.* An inhabitant of a southern area; especially, a resident of southern France. Abbr. *mer.* [< OF < LL *meridionalis* southern] — **me·rid′i·o·nal·ly** *adv.*

Mé·ri·mée (mā·rē·mā′), **Prosper,** 1803–70, French novelist, archeologist, and historian.

me·ringue (mₐ·rang′) *n.* **1.** The stiffly beaten white of eggs blended with sugar and usually baked, used as a topping for pastry or pies. **2.** A small cake or tart shell made of this. [< F < G *meringe,* lit. cake of Mehringen (in Germany)]

me·ri·no (mₐ·rē′nō) *n. pl.* **·nos** **1.** A breed of sheep, originating in Spain, having fine, closely set, silky wool and heavy curled horns in the male; also, the wool of this sheep. **2.** A fine wool fabric originally made of merino wool. **3.** A type of fine yarn used for knitted underwear, hosiery, etc. — *adj.* Made of merino wool, yarn or cloth. [< Sp., roving from pasture to pasture, shepherd, inspector of sheepwalks < Med.L *majorinus* steward < L *major* greater]

Mer·i·on·eth·shire (mer′ē·on′ith·shir) A former county in NW Wales; 660 sq. mi.; pop. 35,277 (1971); county seat, Dolgelly. Also **Mer′i·on′eth.**

mer·i·stem (mer′ₐ·stem) *n. Bot.* Undifferentiated plant tissue cells in a state of active division and growth. [< Gk. *meristos* divided < *merizein* to divide < *meros* part] — **mer′i·ste·mat′ic** (-stₐ·mat′ik) *adj.*

mer·it (mer′it) *n.* **1.** Worth or excellence; high quality: a novel of *merit.* **2.** That which deserves esteem, praise, or reward; a commendable act or quality. **3.** *Sometimes pl.* The quality or fact of deserving or being entitled to reward, praise, etc. **4.** *pl.* The actual rights or wrongs of a matter, especially a legal matter, considered exclusively of extraneous details or technicalities: Consider the case on its *merits.* **5.** *Obs.* A reward or recompense. — *v.t.* To earn as a reward or punishment; deserve. [< OF *merite* < L *meritum* < *meritus,* pp. of *merere* to deserve] — **mer′it·ed** *adj.* — **mer′it·ed·ly** *adv.*

mer·i·to·ri·ous (mer′ₐ·tôr′ē·ₐs, -tō′rē-) *adj.* Deserving of reward or praise; having merit. — **mer′i·to′ri·ous·ly** *adv.* — **mer′i·to′ri·ous·ness** *n.*

merit system A system adopted in the U.S. Civil Service whereby appointments and promotions are made on the basis of merit, ascertained through qualifying examinations.

merle (mûrl) *n.* The European blackbird. Also **merl.** [< F < L *merula* blackbird]

mer·lin (mûr′lin) *n.* A small European falcon (*Falco columbarius aesalon*) related to the pigeon hawk. [< OF *merillon,* dim. of *esmeril* < OHG *smirl*]

Mer·lin (mûr′lin) In the Arthurian cycle and other medieval legends, a magician and prophet. [< Med.L *Merlinus* < Welsh *Myrddin,* lit., sea fortress]

mer·lon (mûr′lₐn) *n. Mil.* The solid part of a battlement, between any two embrasures. For illustration see BATTLEMENT. [< F < Ital. *merlone,* aug. of *merlo* battlement]

mer·maid (mûr′mād′) *n.* A legendary marine creature having the head and upper body of a woman and the tail of a fish. Also **mer′maid′en** (-mād′n). [< MERE[2] + MAID]

Mermaid Tavern A famous inn in London, England, frequented by Jonson, Shakespeare, and other celebrated Elizabethan writers.

mer·man (mûr′man′) *n. pl.* **·men** (-men′) A legendary marine creature, having the head and upper body of a man and the tail of a fish. [< MERE[2] + MAN]

mero- *combining form* Part; partial: *meroblastic.* Also, before vowels, **mer-.** [< Gk. *meros* a part, division]

mer·o·blas·tic (mer′ₐ·blas′tik) *adj. Biol.* Of or designating ova that undergo partial or incomplete segmentation: opposed to *holoblastic.*

Mer·o·ë (mer′ō·ē) An archeological site in northern Sudan, on the Nile; the ancient capital of Ethiopia.

Mer·o·pe (mer′ₐ·pē) In Greek mythology, one of the Pleiades, who supposedly hid her face in shame at having married a mortal. — *n.* The seventh, and only invisible, star of the Pleiades cluster: also called the *Lost Pleiade.*

-merous *suffix Zool.* Having (a specified number or kind of) parts: *trimerous.* [< Gk. *meros* part, division]

Mer·o·vin·gi·an (mer′ō·vin′jē·ₐn, -jₐn) *adj.* Designating or pertaining to the first Frankish dynasty founded by Clovis I about A.D. 500 and lasting until 751. — *n.* A member of the Merovingian dynasty. Also **Mer′o·win′gi·an** [< L *Merovingi,* descendants of Marovaeus, a legendary Frankish king]

mer·o·zo·ite (mer′ₐ·zō′īt) *n. Zool.* One of the mature spores liberated in the asexual stage of certain protozoa, as the malaria parasite. [< MERO- + (SPORO)ZO(A) + -ITE[1]]

Mer·ri·mack (mer′ₐ·mak) *n.* The first U.S. armored warship, a Confederate vessel, that fought the *Monitor* at Hampton Roads, 1862: Confederate name *Virginia.*

THE MERRIMACK

Mer·ri·mack River (mer′ₐ·mak) A River in New Hampshire and Massachusetts, flowing 110 miles to the Atlantic. Also **Mer′ri·mac.**

mer·ri·ment (mer′i·mənt) *n.* **1.** Laughter; fun. **2.** *Obs.* The act of making merry.

mer·ry (mer′ē) *adj.* **·ri·er, ·ri·est 1.** Full of mirth and laughter; joyous; gay. **2.** Characterized by or conducive to mirth, cheerfulness, and gay spirits; festive. [OE *myrige* pleasant] — **mer′ri·ly** *adv.* — **mer′ri·ness** *n.*
— **Syn. 1.** mirthful, hilarious, gleeful, blithe, gay, jolly, jovial.

mer·ry-an·drew (mer′ē·an′drŏō) *n.* A clown or buffoon.

mer·ry-go-round (mer′i·gō·round′, mer′ē-) *n.* **1.** A revolving platform fitted with wooden horses, seats, etc., on which people, especially children, ride for amusement; carousel. **2.** A whirl of activity. Also, *Brit.*, *roundabout.*

mer·ry·mak·ing (mer′ē·mā′king) *n.* The act of having fun and making merry; revelry; festivity. — *adj.* Festive; gay. — **mer′ry·mak′er** *n.*

mer·ry·thought (mer′ē·thôt′) *n. Brit.* The wishbone.

Mer·sey (mûr′zē) A river, in NW England, flowing 70 miles NW to the Irish Sea.

Mer·sey·side (mûr′zē·sīd′) A metropolitan county in NW England; 249 sq. mi.; pop. 1,602,700 (1976); includes Liverpool.

Mer·thyr Tyd·fil (mûr′thər tid′vil) A borough in Mid Glamorgan, Wales; pop. 61,500 (1976).

mes- Var. of MESO-.

me·sa (mā′sə, *Sp.* mä′sä) *n.* A high, broad, and flat tableland with sharp, usually rocky, slopes descending to the surrounding plain, common in the SW United States. [< Sp. < L *mensa* table]

Me·sa (mā′sə) A city in south central Arizona, near Phoenix; pop. 62,853.

Me·sa·bi Range (mə·sä′bē) A long, narrow range of hills in NE Minnesota; site of iron ore deposits.

mé·sal·li·ance (mā·zal′ē·əns, *Fr.* mā·zȧ·lyäns′) *n.* A marriage with one of inferior position; misalliance. [< F]

Me·sa Verde National Park (mā′sə vûrd′) An area in SW Colorado containing ruins of prehistoric cliff dwellings: 80 sq. mi.; established 1906.

mes·cal (mes·kal′) *n.* **1.** A spineless cactus (*Lophophora williamsii*), native to the SW United States and northern Mexico, whose dried tops, **mescal buttons**, are chewed for narcotic effect, especially during religious ceremonies: also called *peyote.* **2.** An intoxicating liquor distilled from certain species of agave. [< Sp. *mezcal* < Nahuatl *mexicalli*]

mes·ca·line (mes′kə·lēn, -lin) *n. Chem.* A crystalline narcotic alkaloid, $C_{11}H_{17}O_3N$, extracted from mescal buttons: also spelled *mezcaline.* [< MESCAL]

mes·dames (mā·däm′, *Fr.* mā·dàm′) Plural of MADAME. Abbr. *Mmes, Mmes.*

mes·de·moi·selles (mād·mwȧ·zel′) *French* Plural of MADEMOISELLE. Abbr. *Mlles, Mlles.*

mes·en·ceph·a·lon (mes′en·sef′ə·lon′) *n. Anat.* One of the three principal divisions of the central nervous system of the embryo: also called *midbrain.* [< NL < MES- + ENCEPHALON] — **mes·en·ce·phal·ic** (mes·en′sə·fal′ik) *adj.*

mes·en·chyme (mes′eng·kim) *n. Biol.* The portion of the mesoderm that produces the connective tissues of the body, the blood vessels, lymphatic system, and heart. Also **mes·en·chy·ma** (mes·eng′kə·mə). [< NL *mesenchyma* < MES- + Gk. *en-* in + *chein* to pour] — **mes·en′chy·mal, mes′en·chym′a·tous** (-kim′ə·təs) *adj.*

mes·en·ter·i·tis (mes′en·tə·rī′tis) *n. Pathol.* Inflammation of the mesentery. [< MESENTER(ON) + -ITIS]

mes·en·ter·on (mes·en′tər·on) *n. pl.* **·ter·a** (-tər·ə) *Biol.* The middle portion, lined with endoderm, of the intestinal cavity of the embryo. [< MES- + ENTERON] — **mes·en′·ter·on′ic** (-tə·ron′ik) *adj.*

mes·en·ter·y (mes′ən·ter′ē) *n. pl.* **·ter·ies** *Anat.* A fold of the peritoneum that invests an intestine and connects it with the posterior abdominal wall. Also **mes′en·te′ri·um** (-tir′ē·əm). [< Med.L *mesenterium* < Gk. *mesenterion* < *mesos* middle + *enteron* intestine] — **mes′en·ter′ic** *adj.*

Me·se·ta (mā·sā′tä) An interior plateau covering almost three fourths of Spain.

mesh (mesh) *n.* **1.** One of the open spaces between the cords of a net or the wires of a screen. **2.** *pl.* The cords or wires bounding such a space or spaces. **3.** A net or network. **4.** *Usually pl.* Anything that entangles or involves; a snare. **5.** *Mech.* The engagement of gear teeth. — *v.t. & v.i.* **1.** To make or become entangled, as in a net. **2.** To make or become engaged, as gear teeth. — **in mesh** In gear; interlocked. [< MDu. *maesche* mesh. Cf. OE *max* net.] — **mesh′y** *adj.*

Me·shach (mē′shak) Hebrew captive in Babylon. See *SHADRACH.*

Me·shed (me·shed′) A walled city in NE Iran; site of a Moslem shrine; pop. 409,616 (1966): also *Mashhad.* Also **Mesh·hed** (mesh·hed′).

mesh·work (mesh′wûrk′) *n.* Meshes; network.

me·si·al (mē′zē·əl, mes′ē·əl) *adj. Anat.* Medial. Also **me′si·an.** [< Gk. *mesos* middle] — **me′si·al·ly** *adv.*

mes·ic (mes′ik, mē′zik) *adj. Bot.* Pertaining to or characterized by a medium moisture supply, as in certain plants. [< Gk. *mesos* middle]

me·sit·y·lene (mə·sit′ə·lēn, -lin) *n. Chem.* A colorless, liquid hydrocarbon, C_9H_{12}, prepared from acetone. [< *mesityl* a hypothetical organic radical (< Gk. *mesitēs* mediator + -YL) + -ENE]

mes·mer·ism (mes′mə·riz′əm, mez′-) *n.* **1.** The theory that one person can produce in another a condition resembling sleep: also called *animal magnetism, magnetism.* **2.** Loosely, hypnotism. [after Franz Anton *Mesmer,* 1733–1815, German physician] — **mes·mer·ic** (mes·mer′ik, mez-) *adj.* — **mes·mer′i·cal·ly** *adv.* — **mes′mer·ist** *n.*

mes·mer·ize (mes′mə·rīz, mez′-) *v.t.* **·ized, ·iz·ing** To hypnotize. Also *Brit.* **mes′mer·ise.** — **mes′mer·i·za′tion** *n.* — **mes′mer·iz′er** *n.*

mesn·al·ty (mē′nəl·tē) *n. pl.* **·ties** The estate of a mesne lord. Also **mesn·al·i·ty** (mē·nal′ə·tē). [< MF *mesnalte*]

mesne (mēn) *adj. Law* Being between two periods or extremes; intermediate. [< MF, alter. of AF *meen* < L *medianus* mean. Doublet of MEAN³, MEDIAN, MIZZEN.]

mesne lord A feudal lord holding land from a superior lord.

meso- *combining form* **1.** Situated in the middle: *mesocarp.* **2.** Intermediate in size or degree: *mesognathous.* Also, before vowels, **mes-.** [< Gk. *mesos* middle]

mes·o·blast (mes′ə·blast, mē′sə-) *n. Biol.* The mesoderm in its early stages. [< MESO- + Gk. *blastos* sprout] — **mes′o·blas′tic** *adj.*

mes·o·carp (mes′ə·kärp, mē′sə-) *n. Bot.* The middle layer of a pericarp, as the fleshy part of certain fruits.

mes·o·ce·phal·ic (mes′ō·sə·fal′ik, mē′sō-) *adj.* Having a head of intermediate size; having a cephalic index of from 76 to 80.9. Also **mes′o·ceph′a·lous** (-sef′ə·ləs). — **mes′o·ceph′a·ly** *n.*

mes·o·crat·ic (mes′ə·krat′ik, mē′sə-) *adj. Geol.* Having dark and light mineral constituents in almost equal amounts: said of certain igneous rocks.

mes·o·derm (mes′ə·dûrm, mē′sə-) *n.* The middle of the three primary germ layers in the embryo of metazoan animals, developing into the skeletal and muscular systems, heart, kidneys, etc. Compare ECTODERM, ENDODERM.

mes·o·gas·tri·um (mes′ə·gas′trē·əm, mē′sə-) *Anat.* **1.** Either of the two mesenteries in the stomach of an embryo. **2.** The umbilical region. [< MESO- + Gk. *gastēr* belly] — **mes′o·gas′tric** *adj.*

me·sog·na·thous (mə·sog′nə·thəs) *adj.* **1.** Having moderately projecting jaws. **2.** Having an intermediate gnathic index of 98° to 103°. [< MESO- + -GNATHOUS] — **me·sog′na·thism, me·sog′na·thy** *n.*

Mes·o·lith·ic (mes′ə·lith′ik, mē′sə-) *adj. Anthropol.* Pertaining to or designating the period of human culture immediately following the Magdalenian stage of the Paleolithic, characterized by delicately worked tools and an economy transitional between food gathering and a settled agriculture. [< MESO- + LITH(O)- + -IC]

Mes·o·lon·ghi (mes′ō·lông′gē) See MISSOLONGHI.

mes·o·morph (mes′ə·môrf, mē′sə-) *n.* A mesomorphic person.

mes·o·mor·phic (mes′ə·môr′fik, mē′sə-) *adj.* **1.** *Physics* Of or pertaining to a state of matter intermediate between the true liquid and the crystal: also **mes′o·mor′phous.** **2.** Of human body types, characterized by a sturdy body structure as developed from the mesodermal layer of the embryo, associated with a predominance of the skeletal and muscular system. — **mes′o·mor′phy** *n.*

mes·on (mē′son, mes′on) *n. Physics* Any of a group of short-lived, unstable nucleons having a mass intermediate between that of the electron and the proton. They may be electrically neutral or carry either a positive or negative charge: formerly called *mesotron.* [< Gk. *mesos* middle]

mes·o·neph·ros (mes′ə·nef′rəs, mē′sə-) *n. Biol.* The middle of three tubular organs found in connection with the genitourinary apparatus of the vertebrate embryo: also called *Wolffian body.* [< NL < MESO- + Gk. *nephros* kidney] — **mes′o·neph′ric** *adj.*

mes·o·pause (mez′ō·pôz) *n. Meteorol.* A transition zone between the mesosphere and the ionosphere, beginning at a height of about 50 miles.

mes·o·phyll (mes′ə·fil, mē′sə-) *n. Bot.* The soft, inner, parenchymatous tissue of a leaf, lying between the upper and lower epidermis. Also **mes′o·phyl, mes′o·phyl′lum.** [< MESO- + Gk. *phyllon* leaf]

mes·o·phyte (mes′ə·fit, mē′sə-) *n. Bot.* A plant requiring medium conditions of moisture. — **mes′o·phyt′ic** (-fit′ik) *adj.*

Mes·o·po·ta·mi·a (mes′ə·pə·tā′mē·ə) An ancient country of Asia comprising the region between the lower Tigris and lower Euphrates, part of modern Iraq. [< Gk. < *mesos* middle + *potamos* river] — **Mes′o·po·ta′mi·an** *n. & adj.*

mes·or·rhine (mes′ə·rīn, -rin; mē′sə-) *adj.* Having a relatively broad, high-bridged nose. [< MESO- + Gk. *rhis, rhinos* nose]

---

mes·o·sphere (mes′ə·sfir, mē′sə-) *n. Meteorol.* A layer of the atmosphere between the stratopause and the mesopause. — **mes′o·spher′ic** (-sfir′ik, -sfer′-) *adj.*

mes·o·the·li·um (mes′ə·thē′lē·əm, mē′sə-) *n. pl.* **·li·a** *Anat.* Ephithelium that is derived from the mesoderm and lines the peritoneum, pleurae, and pericardium. [< NL < MESO- + (EPI)THELIUM] — **mes′o·the′li·al** *adj.*

mes·o·tho·rax (mes′ə·thôr′aks, -thō′raks; mē′sə-) *n. Entomol.* The middle one of the three segments of the thorax in insects, bearing the anterior wings and the middle legs. — **mes′o·tho·rac′ic** (-thô·ras′ik, -thō·ras′ik) *adj.*

mes·o·tho·ri·um (mes′ə·thôr′ē·əm, -thō′rē-; mē′sə-) *n.* Either of two isotopes resulting from the radioactive disintegration of thorium, intermediate between thorium and radiothorium. *Abbr. Ms-Th*

mes·o·tron (mes′ə·tron, mē′sə-) *n. Physics* Meson. [< MESO- + (ELEC)TRON]

Mes·o·zo·ic (mes′ə·zō′ik, mē′sə-) *Geol. adj.* Pertaining to the era between the Paleozoic and the Cenozoic, characterized by the dominance of the reptiles, the rise of flowering plants, and the beginnings of archaic mammals. — *n.* This era, including the Triassic, Jurassic, and Cretaceous periods. [< MESO- + ZOIC]

mes·quite (mes·kēt′, mes′kēt) *n.* **1.** A spiny, leguminous shrub or small tree (*Prosopis glandulosa*), found in SW United States and extending southward to Peru, that yields sweet pods used for cattle fodder: also called *algarroba, honey mesquite.* **2.** The screw bean. Also spelled *mezquit, mezquite.* Also **mes·quit** (mes·kēt′, mes′-kēt). [< Sp. *mezquite* < Nahuatl *mizquitl*]

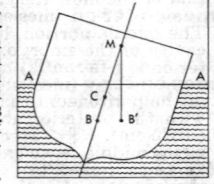

HONEY MESQUITE
a Flower.
b Fruit.

Mes·quite (mes·kēt′) A town in northern Texas, near Dallas; pop. 55,131.

mess (mes) *n.* **1.** A state of disorder; especially, a condition of dirty or untidy confusion: His clothes were in a *mess.* **2.** A confusing, difficult, or embarrassing situation or condition; muddle. **3.** An unpleasant or confused mixture or collection; jumble; hodgepodge. **4.** A quantity of food sufficient for a meal or dish. **5.** A portion of soft, partly liquid food. **6.** A disagreeable or unpleasant preparation of food; a sloppy concoction. **7.** A number of persons who regularly take their meals together, as in the military; also, a meal taken by them, or the place in which the meal is served. — *v.i.* **1.** To busy oneself; dabble: often with *around* or *about.* **2.** To make a mess; bungle: often with *up.* **3.** To interfere; meddle: often with *around.* **4.** To eat with as a member of a mess. — *v.t.* **5.** To make a mess of; muddle; botch: often with *up.* **6.** To make dirty; befoul: often with *up.* **7.** To provide meals for. **8.** To interfere with: used with *up.* **9.** To treat roughly. [< OF *mes* < L *missus* course at a meal, orig. pp. of *mittere* to send]

mes·sage (mes′ij) *n.* **1.** An oral or written communication, as of information, advice, or warning, sent by any of various means. **2.** An official or formal communication, as from a chief executive to a legislative body. **3.** A communication divinely inspired or embodying important principles or counsel: Christ's *message.* *Abbr. msg.* [< OF < Med.L *missaticum* < *missus*, pp. of *mittere* to send]

Mes·sa·li·na (mes′ə·lī′nə), **Valeria**, died 48 A.D., Roman empress; third wife of Claudius, notorious for profligacy; executed. Also **Mes·sal·li·na.**

mes·sa·line (mes′ə·lēn′, mes′ə·lēn) *n.* A lightweight, lustrous, twilled silk fabric.

Mes·se·ne (me·sē′nē) A town in the SW Peloponnesus, Greece; the capital of ancient Messenia; pop. about 7,000. Also **Mes·si′ni.**

mes·sen·ger (mes′ən·jər) *n.* **1.** One sent with a message or on an errand; especially, one whose work is running errands. **2.** A bearer of official dispatches; courier. **3.** *Archaic* A herald; harbinger. [ME *messanger, messanger* < OF *messagier* < *message.* See MESSAGE. The *n* is nonhistoric]

Mes·se·ni·a (me·sē′nē·ə) A Department of Greece, in the SW Peloponnesus, a country of ancient times; 1,119 sq. mi.; pop. about 228,000; capital, Messene. Also **Mes·si′ni·a.** See map of ATTICA.

Mes·ser·schmitt (mes′ər·shmit), **Wilhelm**, born 1898, German aircraft designer and manufacturer.

mess hall A place where a group of persons regularly take their meals, as in the army, navy, etc.

Mes·si·ah (mə·sī′ə) *n.* **1.** In Judaism, the Anointed One, a deliverer and ruler of Israel promised by God and expected by the Jews; the Christ. **2.** In Christianity, Jesus regarded as this deliverer. **3.** An expected liberator of a country, people, etc. Also **Mes·si′as.** [< LL *Messias* < Gk. < Aramaic *mĕshīhā,* Hebrew *māshīah* anointed] — **Mes·si′ah·ship** *n.* — **Mes·si·an·ic** (mes′ē·an′ik) *adj.*

Mes·si·dor (me·sē·dôr′) *n.* The tenth month of the Republican calendar. See (Republican) CALENDAR. [< F < L *messis* harvest + Gk. *dōron* gift]

mes·sieurs (mes′ərz, *Fr.* mā·syœ′) *n.pl. of Fr.* **mon·sieur** (mə·syœ′) Sirs; gentlemen: in English in the contracted form *Messrs.,* used as plural of *Mr. Abbr. MM.*

Mes·si·na (mə·sē′nə, *Ital.* mäs·sē′nä) A port city in NE Sicily, on the **Strait of Messina,** the channel between Italy and Sicily; pop. 269,300 (est. 1967).

Mes·sines (me·sēn′) A village in western Belgium, scene of two battles in World War I, 1914 and 1917.

mess jacket A man's tailored jacket, usually white and terminating at the waistline, worn on semiformal occasions.

mess kit A small, compactly arranged unit containing cooking and eating utensils, used by soldiers in the field and campers.

mess·mate (mes′māt′) *n.* An associate at a mess, especially on board ship.

Messrs. or **Messrs** Messieurs.

mess sergeant A noncommissioned officer who plans meals, issues rations, and superintends the company mess.

mes·suage (mes′wij) *n. Law* A dwelling house, with its outbuildings and adjacent lands. [< OF *mesuage,* prob. alter. of *mesnage.* See MÉNAGE.]

mes·sy (mes′ē) *adj.* Being in or causing a condition of dirt or confusion; untidy. — **mess′i·ly** *adv.* — **mess′i·ness** *n.*

mes·tee (mes·tē′) *n.* A mustee. [< Sp. *mestizo* hybrid]

mes·ti·zo (mes·tē′zō) *n. pl.* **·zos** or **·zoes** Any one of mixed blood; in Mexico and the western United States, a person of Spanish and Indian blood: also called *Ladino* (def. 2). Also **mes·te′so, mes·ti′no** (-nō). [< Sp. < LL *misticius* < L *mixtus,* pp. of *miscere* to mix] — **mes·ti′za** (-zə) *n.fem.*

Meš·tro·vić (mesh′trô·vēch), **Ivan,** 1883–1962, Yugoslav sculptor.

met (met) Past tense and past participle of MEET[1].

met- Var. of META-.

met. **1.** Metaphor. **2.** Metaphysics. **3.** Meteorological. **4.** Metronome. **5.** Metropolitan.

meta- *prefix* **1.** Changed in place or form; reversed; altered: *metamorphosis.* **2.** *Anat. & Zool.* Behind; after; on the farther side of; later: often equivalent to *post-* or *dorso-*: *metathorax, metaplasis.* **3.** With; alongside: *metabiosis.* **4.** Beyond; over; transcending: *metaphysics, metapsychology.* **5.** *Chem.* **a** A modification, usually polymeric, of. **b** A derivative of: *metaprotein.* **c** The least hydrated derivative of an acid anhydride: *metaphosphoric* acid: distinguished from *ortho-.* **d** A benzene derivative in which the substituted atoms or radicals occupy alternate positions: abbr. *m-.* Also, before vowels and *h, met-.* [< Gk. < *meta* after, beside, with]

met·a·bol·ic (met′ə·bol′ik) *adj.* **1.** *Biol. & Physiol.* Of, pertaining to, or having the nature of metabolism. **2.** *Zool.* Pertaining to or undergoing metamorphosis.

me·tab·o·lism (mə·tab′ə·liz′əm) *n. Biol. & Physiol.* The aggregate of all chemical processes constantly taking place in a living organism, including those that use energy to convert nutritive materials into protoplasm (anabolism) and those that release energy for vital processes in breaking down protoplasm into simpler substances (catabolism). [< Gk. *metabolē* < *meta-* beyond + *ballein* to throw]

me·tab·o·lite (mə·tab′ə·līt) *n.* A product of metabolism.

me·tab·o·lize (mə·tab′ə·līz) *v.t. & v.i.* **·lized, ·liz·ing** To subject to or change by metabolism.

met·a·car·pal (met′ə·kär′pəl) *adj.* Of or pertaining to the metacarpus. — *n.* One of the bones of the metacarpus.

met·a·car·pus (met′ə·kär′pəs) *n. Anat.* The part of the forelimb between the carpus or wrist and the phalanges or bones of the finger. [< NL < Gk. *metakarpion* < *meta-* beyond + *karpos* wrist]

met·a·cen·ter (met′ə·sen′tər) *n. Physics* The point at which the center of buoyancy of a floating body in equilibrium with its supporting liquid intersects the vertical line through the center when the body is displaced from equilibrium. For stability, this point must be above the center of gravity of the body. — **met′a·cen′tric** *adj.*

met·a·chro·ma·tism (met′ə·krō′mə·tiz′əm) *n.* An alteration in color; especially, such alteration due to temperature changes. — **met′a·chro·mat′ic** (-krō·mat′ik) *adj.*

met·a·gal·ax·y (met′ə·gal′ək·sē) *n. pl.* **·ax·ies** *Astron.* The entire material universe, regarded especially as a system including all the galaxies.

met·age (mē′tij) *n.* The official measurement of contents or weight of grain, coal, etc.; also, the price charged for such measurement. [< METE[1] + -AGE]

met·a·gen·e·sis (met′ə·jen′ə·sis) *n. Biol.* A type of reproduction in which one generation is produced asexually by cell division or budding and the next by union of male and female gametes from different individuals: also called *alternation of generations, digenesis, heterogenesis, exenogenesis.* — **met′a·ge·net′ic** (-jə·net′ik) *adj.*

me·tag·na·thous (mə·tag′nə·thəs) *adj. Ornithol.* Having the points of the mandibles crossing each other, as in the crossbill. [< META- + -GNATHOUS] — **me·tag′na·thism** *n.*

METACENTER
AA Water line.
B Center of buoyancy of a floating body.
B′ Center of buoyancy when body is tilted.
C Center of gravity.
M Metacenter at intersection of *MB* and *MB′.*

met·al (met′l) *n.* **1.** Any of a class of elements characterized by a distinctive luster, malleability, ductility, thermal and electrical conductivity, and capable of forming positive ions. **2.** A composition of such metallic elements; alloy. **3.** Molten glass. **4.** *Printing* **a** Type metal. **b** The state of being set in type. **5.** *Naval* The weight of the projectiles that the guns of a battleship can throw at once. **6.** *Chiefly Brit.* Broken stone for road surfaces or for railway ballast. **7.** *Heraldry* Gold (*or*) or silver (*argent*) tincture. **8.** The constituent material of anything; essential quality. **— white metal** Any one of the various white alloys, such as pewter, Babbitt metal, britannia, etc., used for making ornaments, small castings, etc. **— v.t.** **met·aled** or **·alled, met·al·ing** or **·al·ling** To furnish or cover with metal. [< OF < L *metallum* mine < Gk. *metallon*. Doublet of MEDAL.]

met·a·lin·guis·tics (met′ə·ling·gwis′tiks) *n.* An area of linguistic study concerned with the interrelationship of linguistic and other cultural factors in a society.

met·al·ist (met′l·ist) *n.* **1.** One who works with or has special knowledge of metals. **2.** An advocate of metallic money as against a paper currency. Also **met′al·list.**

met·al·ize (met′l·īz) *v.t.* **·ized, ·iz·ing** To turn into or treat with metal. Also **met′al·lize, Brit. met′al·ise.**

metall. or **metal.** Metallurgical; metallurgy.

me·tal·lic (mə·tal′ik) *adj.* **1.** Of, pertaining to, or consisting of metal. **2.** Resembling or having the nature of metal: *a metallic* sound. **3.** Yielding or containing metal.

metallic soap A soapy, waxlike material made by combining the salts of certain metals, as lead or aluminum, with various fatty acids, used in the manufacture of textiles, varnish, and paint.

met·al·lif·er·ous (met′ə·lif′ər·əs) *adj.* Yielding or containing metal.

met·al·line (met′ə·lin, -līn) *adj.* **1.** Relating to, having the properties of, or resembling metal; metallic. **2.** Impregnated with metals or metallic salts.

met·al·log·ra·phy (met′ə·log′rə·fē) *n.* **1.** The science that treats of metallic substances; especially, the microscopic study of the structure of metals and alloys. **2.** A printing process similar to lithography, using metal plates instead of stones. [< L < Gk. *metallon* mine, metal + -GRAPHY] — **me·tal·lo·graph·ic** (mə·tal′ə·graf′ik) *adj.*

met·al·loid (met′ə·loid) *n.* **1.** A nonmetal. **2.** Any nonmetallic element, as arsenic, silicon, etc., that resembles the metals in some of its properties. **— adj. 1.** Of, pertaining to, or having the properties of a metalloid. **2.** Resembling a metal. Also **met′al·loi′dal.**

me·tal·lo·ther·a·py (mə·tal′ō·ther′ə·pē) *n.* Medical treatment by the use of metals, especially metal salts. [< Gk. *metallon* mine, metal + THERAPY]

met·al·lur·gy (met′ə·lûr′jē) *n.* **1.** The art or science of extracting a metal or metals from ores. **2.** The art or science of working with metals and alloys for the purpose of their development, improvement, etc. Abbr. *metal., metall.* [< NL *metallurgia* < Gk. *metallourgos* working in mines < *metallon* mine + *-ergos* working] — **met·al·lur·gic** or **·gi·cal** *adj.* — **met′al·lur′gi·cal·ly** *adv.* — **met′al·lur′gist** *n.*

met·al·work (met′l·wûrk′) *n.* **1.** Articles made of metal. **2.** Metalworking.

met·al·work·ing (met′l·wûr′king) *n.* The making or the business of making things out of metal. **—met′al·work′er** *n.*

met·a·mere (met′ə·mir) *n. Biol.* A somite. [< META- + -MERE] **— me·tam·er·al** (mə·tam′ə·rəl), **met·a·mer·ic** (met′-ə·mer′ik) *adj.*

me·tam·er·ism (mə·tam′ə·riz′əm) *n. Biol.* **1.** Segmentation. **2.** The state of being composed of metameres.

met·a·mor·phic (met′ə·môr′fik) *adj.* **1.** Of or pertaining to metamorphosis. **2.** *Geol.* Of, pertaining to, or exhibiting metamorphism. Also **met′a·mor′phous.**

met·a·mor·phism (met′ə·môr′fiz·əm) *n.* **1.** *Geol.* The changes in the composition and texture of rocks caused by force, heat, pressure, moisture, etc. **2.** Metamorphosis.

met·a·mor·phose (met′ə·môr′fōz) *v.* **·phosed, ·phos·ing —** *v.t.* **1.** To change the form of; transmute. **2.** *Geol.* To cause to undergo metamorphism. **—** *v.i.* **3.** To undergo metamorphosis. Also **met′a·mor′phize.** [< MF *métamorphoser*]

met·a·mor·pho·sis (met′ə·môr′fə·sis) *n. pl.* **·pho·ses** (-fə·sēz) **1.** Change from one form, shape, or substance into another by any means. **2.** Complete transformation of character, purpose, circumstances, etc. **3.** One who or that which is metamorphosed. **4.** *Biol.* Any marked change in the form and structure of an animal in its development from embryo to adult, as from chrysalis to butterfly, or tadpole to frog. **5.** *Pathol.* An abnormal, often degenerative change in the tissues of an organ or part. [< L < Gk. *metamorphōsis* < *metamorphoein* to transform < *meta-* beyond + *morphē* form]

met·a·neph·ros (met′ə·nef′ros) *n. Biol.* The posterior of three tubular organs in connection with the genitourinary apparatus of the vertebrate embryo. [< NL < META- + Gk. *nephros* kidney]

metaph. **1.** Metaphor; metaphorical. **2.** Metaphysics.

met·a·phase (met′ə·fāz) *n. Biol.* The middle stage of mitotic cell division, during which the chromosomes split along the equatorial plane between the two poles of the spindle. [< META- + -PHASE]

met·a·phor (met′ə·fôr, -fər) *n.* A figure of speech in which one object is likened to another by speaking of it as if it were that other, as *He was a lion in battle*: distinguished from *simile* by not employing any word of comparison, such as "like" or "as." **— Syn.** See SIMILE. **— mixed metaphor** A figurative expression in which two or more incongruous metaphors are used, as *He kept a tight rein on his boiling passions.* [< F *métaphore* < L *metaphora* < Gk. < *metapherein* < *meta-* beyond, over + *pherein* to carry] **— met′a·phor′ic** (-fôr′ik, -for′ik) or **·i·cal** *adj.* **— met′a·phor′i·cal·ly** *adv.*

met·a·phos·phate (met′ə·fos′fāt) *n. Chem.* A salt of metaphosphoric acid.

met·a·phos·phor·ic acid (met′ə·fos·fôr′ik, -for′ik) *Chem.* A colorless, deliquescent acid, HPO_3, obtained by heating orthophosphoric acid and used as a chemical reagent.

met·a·phrase (met′ə·frāz) *v.t.* **·phrased, ·phras·ing 1.** To translate word for word. **2.** To alter the wording of. **—** *n.* A literal translation. [< L < Gk. *metaphrasis* < *metaphrazein* to paraphrase < *meta-* beyond + *phrazein* to phrase]

met·a·phrast (met′ə·frast) *n.* One who metaphrases, as by rendering prose into verse or by changing the meter of verse. [< Gk. *metaphrastēs*] **— met′a·phras′tic** or **·ti·cal** *adj.*

met·a·phys·ic (met′ə·fiz′ik) *n.* Metaphysics. **— adj.** *Rare* Metaphysical.

met·a·phys·i·cal (met′ə·fiz′i·kəl) *adj.* **1.** Of, pertaining to, or of the nature of metaphysics. **2.** Of or pertaining to ultimate reality or basic knowledge. **3.** Beyond or above the physical or the laws of nature; transcendental. **4.** Of or designating certain English poets of the 17th century, including Donne, Herbert, and Crashaw, whose poetry is characterized by complex, intellectual imagery, paradox, and subtlety of thought: term originating with Samuel Johnson. [See METAPHYSICS.] **— met′a·phys′i·cal·ly** *adv.*

met·a·phys·ics (met′ə·fiz′iks) *n.pl.* (construed as sing.) **1.** The branch of philosophy that investigates principles of reality transcending those of any particular science, traditionally including cosmology and ontology. Compare EPISTEMOLOGY. **2.** All speculative philosophy. **3.** Popularly, abstruse and bewildering discussion. Also *metaphysic.* Abbr. *met., metaph.* [< Med.L *metaphysica* < Med.Gk. < *ta meta ta physika* the (works) after the physics; in ref. to Aristotle's ontological treatises, which came after his *Physics*]

met·a·plasm (met′ə·plaz′əm) *n.* **1.** *Biol.* The lifeless material of a cell, as inclusions of fats and carbohydrates. **2.** *Gram.* The alteration of a word by the transposition, addition, or removal of letters or syllables. [< L *metaplasmus* < Gk. *metaplasmos* < *meta-* beyond + *plassein* to mold] **— met′a·plas′mic** *adj.*

met·a·pro·te·in (met′ə·prō′tē·in, -tēn) *n. Biochem.* A substance produced by the action of an acid or an alkali on a protein, and soluble in weak acid or alkaline solutions, but not in neutral ones.

met·a·psy·chic (met′ə·sī′kik) *adj.* Of or pertaining to phenomena apparently resulting from mental action and having no physical basis or explanation. Also **met′a·psych′i·cal.**

met·a·psy·chol·o·gy (met′ə·sī·kol′ə·jē) *n. Psychol.* **1.** Psychology restricted to philosophic speculation on the origin, structure, function, purpose, etc., of the mind. **2.** According to Freud, any comprehensive description of mental processes. **— met′a·psy′cho·log′i·cal** (-sī′kə·loj′i·kəl) *adj.*

met·a·so·ma·tism (met′ə·sō′mə·tiz′əm) *n. Geol.* Metamorphism in which a rock or mineral undergoes chemical change as a result of the introduction of external materials. Also **met′a·so′ma·to′sis** (-sō′mə·tō′sis). [< META- + SOMAT- + -ISM]

met·a·sta·ble (met′ə·stā′bəl) *adj. Physics* **1.** Designating an apparent state of equilibrium, as of water cooled below its freezing point without changing into ice. **2.** Designating certain excited states of an atom in which radiation seldom or never occurs. **— met′a·sta·bil′i·ty** *n.*

me·tas·ta·sis (mə·tas′tə·sis) *n. pl.* **·ses** (-sēz) **1.** *Pathol.* **a** The transfer of a disease or its manifestations from one part of the body to another, as in certain types of cancer. **b** A site to which such a transfer has been made. **2.** Change into another form, state, etc.; transformation. **3.** *Rare* Metabolism. [< L < Gk. < *methistanai* to place differently, change < *meta-* after + *histanai* to place] **— met′a·stat′ic** (-stat′ik) *adj.* **— met′a·stat′i·cal·ly** *adv.*

me·tas·ta·size (mə·tas′tə·sīz) *v.i.* **·sized, ·siz·ing** *Pathol.* To shift or spread from one part of the body to another, as a malignant growth.

met·a·tar·sal (met′ə·tär′səl) *Anat. adj.* Of or pertaining to the metatarsus. **—** *n.* One of the bones of the metatarsus. For illustration see FOOT.

met·a·tar·sus (met′ə·tär′səs) *n. pl.* **·si** (-sī) *Anat.* **1.** In man, the part of the foot situated between the tarsus and the bones of the toes. **2.** An analogous part in the hind or pelvic limb of animals or birds. [< NL < META- + TARSUS]

metath. Metathesis; metathetic(al).

met·a·the·ri·an (met′ə·thir′ē·ən) *n. Zool.* Any of a group (*Metatheria*) of mammals whose young are carried in pouches; a marsupial. — *adj.* Of or pertaining to the *Metatheria*. [< META- + Gk. *thērion* beast]

me·tath·e·sis (mə·tath′ə·sis) *n. pl.* **·ses** (-sēz) **1.** The transposition of letters, syllables, or sounds in a word: Old English *bridd* became *bird* by *metathesis*. **2.** *Chem.* Double decomposition. **3.** Any reversal of conditions. [< LL < Gk. < *metatithenai* to transpose < *meta-* over + *tithenai* to place] — **met·a·thet·ic** (met′ə·thet′ik) or *·i·cal adj.*

met·a·tho·rax (met′ə·thôr′aks, -thō′raks) *n. pl.* **·rax·es** or **·ra·ces** (-rə·sēz) *Entomol.* The hindmost of the three segments of the thorax in insects. — **met′a·tho·rac′ic** (-thō-ras′ik, -thō-) *adj.*

Me·tax·as (mə·tak′səs, *Greek* me′täk·säs′), **Joannes,** 1871–1941, Greek general, chief of state 1936–41.

met·a·xy·lem (met′ə·zī′ləm) *n. Bot.* The portion of the tissues of plants consisting of thick-walled cells developed outside the xylem. [< META- + XYLEM]

met·a·zo·an (met′ə·zō′ən) *n. Zool.* Any of a primary division (*Metazoa*) of multicellular animals, including those higher than protozoans. Also **met′a·zo′on.** — *adj.* Of or pertaining to the metazoans: also **met′a·zo′ic.** [< META- + Gk. *zōion* animal]

Metch·ni·koff (mech′ni·kôf), **Élie,** 1845–1916, Russian physiologist and bacteriologist active in France: original name **Ilya Ilich Mechnikov.**

mete¹ (mēt) *v.t.* **met·ed, met·ing 1.** To allot or distribute by or as by measure: usually followed by *out.* **2.** *Archaic* To measure. — *n. Obs.* Measure. [OE *metan* to measure]

mete² (mēt) *n.* A boundary line; limit: now chiefly in the phrase **metes and bounds.** [< OF < L *meta* goal, boundary]

met·em·pir·i·cal (met′em·pir′i·kəl) *adj.* **1.** Lying beyond the bounds of experience; not derived from experience. **2.** Of or pertaining to metempiricism. Also **met′em·pir′ic.**

met·em·pir·i·cism (met′em·pir′ə·siz·əm) *n. Philos.* Doctrine concerned with the nature of things lying beyond, though connected with, those within the scope of experience. Also **met′em·pir′ics.**

me·tem·psy·cho·sis (mə·temp′sə·kō′sis, met′əm·sī-) *n.* Transmigration of souls. [< LL < Gk. *metempsychōsis* < *metempsychoein* < *meta-* over + *empsychoein* to animate < *en-* in + *psychē* soul, life]

met·en·ceph·a·lon (met′en·sef′ə·lon) *n. pl.* **·la** (-lə) *Anat.* The fifth cerebral vesicle of the brain and the parts derived therefrom, comprising the cerebellum and the pons Varolii: also called *afterbrain.* [< NL < MET- + ENCEPHALON] — **met′en·ce·phal′ic** (-sə·fal′ik) *adj.*

me·te·or (mē′tē·ər, -ôr) *n.* **1.** *Astron.* A meteoroid that on entering the earth's atmosphere at great speed is heated to luminosity and is visible as a streak of light: also called *shooting star.* **2.** Loosely, a meteorite or meteoroid. **3.** *Obs.* Any phenomenon of the atmosphere, as snow, lightning, etc. [< Med.L *meteorum* < Gk. *meteōron* thing in the air < *meteōros* high in the air < *meta-* beyond + *eōra* suspension]

me·te·or·ic (mē′tē·ôr′ik, -or′ik) *adj.* **1.** Of, pertaining to, or consisting of meteors. **2.** Resembling a meteor; brilliant, rapid, and dazzling: a *meteoric* career. **3.** Of or pertaining to atmospheric phenomena. — **me′te·or′i·cal·ly** *adv.*

me·te·or·ite (mē′tē·ə·rīt′) *n.* The stony or metallic remaining portion of a meteor that has not been completely destroyed by combustion and has fallen to earth. — **me′te·or·it′ic** (-ə·rit′ik) *adj.*

me·te·or·o·graph (mē′tē·ər·ə·graf′, -gräf′, mē′tē·ôr′ə-, -or′ə-) *n.* An instrument that records simultaneously information concerning several meteorological elements, as temperature, humidity, air pressure, etc. [< F *météorographe*] — **me′te·or′o·graph′ic** (-ôr′ə·graf′ik, -or′-) or *·i·cal adj.*

me·te·or·oid (mē′tē·ə·roid′) *n. Astron.* One of the pieces of matter moving through outer space, that upon entering the earth's atmosphere form meteors.

meteorol. or **meteor.** Meteorologic(al); meteorology.

me·te·or·ol·o·gy (mē′tē·ə·rol′ə·jē) *n.* **1.** The science that treats of atmospheric phenomena, especially those that relate to weather. **2.** The weather conditions of any particular place. [< Gk. *meteōrologia* < *meteōros* high in the air + *logos* discourse] — **me′te·or·o·log′ic** (-ō′rə·loj′ik) or *·i·cal adj.* — **me′te·or·o·log′i·cal·ly** *adv.* — **me′te·or·ol′o·gist** *n.*

meteor shower *Astron.* Any of various displays of meteors that recur at definite intervals and appear to radiate from a single point or region, as the Leonids, Perseids, etc.

me·ter¹ (mē′tər) *n.* An instrument or device used to measure and indicate quantity or variation in amount, as of a liquid or gas, electric current, light, etc.; also, a similar device for measuring speed, time, distance, etc. — *v.t.* To measure or test by means of a meter. [< METE¹]

me·ter² (mē′tər) *n.* **1.** A measured verbal rhythm constituting one of the chief characteristics of verse, and, in prosody, forming definite groups (feet) of accented and unaccented syllables, usually of a specified number for each line. **2.** *Music* The combining of rhythmic pulses into successive

groups having like arrangement and duration. **Duple meter** has two pulses per group, **triple meter** has three pulses per group, **quadruple meter** has four pulses per group with a stronger accent on the first, **quintuple meter** and **septuple meter**, with other meters having prime numbers of pulses, usually divide into arrangements of duple and triple meter, and **compound meter** is a duple or other meter with the pulses subdivided into three, or rarely, five groups. Also, *esp. Brit., metre.* — **Syn.** See RHYTHM. [OE < L *metrum* a measure < Gk. *metron*]

me·ter³ (mē′tər) *n.* The basic unit of length in the metric system, originally defined as one ten-millionth of the distance on the earth's surface from the pole to the equator, and equivalent to 39.37 inches. Also, *esp. Brit., metre.* Abbr. *m, m.* See table inside back cover. [< F *mètre* < Gk. *metron*]

-meter *combining form* **1.** A device for measuring (a specified quality, thing, etc.): *calorimeter.* **2.** Division into (a specified number of) prosodic feet: *pentameter.* **3.** A (specified kind of) unit in the metric system: *kilometer:* also, *esp. Brit., -metre.* [< L *metrum* < Gk. *metron* a measure]

me·ter·age (mē′tər·ij) *n.* The process or result of measuring by or as by a meter.

me·ter-kil·o·gram-sec·ond (mē′tər·kil′ə·gram′sek′ənd) *adj.* See MKS.

meter maid A woman employed by a city authority to check parking meters and issue tickets for overtime parking.

meth- *combining form Chem.* Used to indicate the presence of a methyl group in a compound: *methane.* Also, before consonants, **metho-.** [< METHYL]

Meth. Methodist.

meth·ac·ry·late (meth·ak′rə·lāt) *n. Chem.* A salt or ester of methacrylic acid.

meth·a·cryl·ic acid (meth′ə·kril′ik) *Chem.* A colorless acid, $C_4H_6O_2$, the esters of which are extensively used in the making of plastics. [< METH(YL) + ACRYLIC]

meth·ane (meth′ān) *n. Chem.* A colorless, odorless, flammable gas, CH_4, the first member of the methane series, the chief constituent of firedamp and marsh gas, and commercially obtained from natural gas. [< METH(YL) + -ANE²]

methane series *Chem.* A group of saturated aliphatic hydrocarbons having the general formula C_nH_{2n+2}: also called *alkane series, paraffin series.*

meth·a·nol (meth′ə·nōl, -nol) *n. Chem.* A colorless, volatile, flammable, highly toxic alcohol, CH_3OH, obtained by the destructive distillation of wood or by catalytic treatment of hydrogen and carbon monoxide, and widely used in industry and the arts: also called *carbinol, methyl alcohol, wood alcohol, wood spirit.* [< METHANE + -OL¹]

me·theg·lin (mə·theg′lin) *n. Mead.* [< Welsh *meddyglyn* < *meddyg* doctor (< L *medicus*) + *llyn* juice, liquor]

met·he·mo·glo·bin (met·hē′mə·glō′bin, -hem′ə-) *n. Biochem.* A brownish red, crystalline compound formed by the decomposition of blood and by oxidation of hemoglobin. Also **met·hae′mo·glo′bin.** [< MET- + HEMOGLOBIN]

me·the·na·mine (mə·thē′nə·mēn, -min) *n. Chem.* An organic compound, $C_6H_{12}N_4$, crystallized from a mixture of formalin and ammonia, and used in the vulcanization of rubber, in making synthetic resins, and as an antiseptic: also called *hexamethylenetetramine, hexamine.* [< *methene* methylene (< METHYL + -ENE) + AMINE]

me·thinks (mē·thingks′) *v. impersonal,* **me·thought** *Archaic & Poetic* It seems to me. [OE *me thynch* < *thyncan* to seem]

me·thi·o·nine (mə·thī′ə·nēn, -nin) *n. Biochem.* An amino acid, $C_5H_{11}O_2NS$, closely related to cystine, and obtained from various proteins. [< ME(THYL) + THIO- + -INE²]

metho- Var. of METH-.

meth·od (meth′əd) *n.* **1.** A way, means, or manner of proceeding; especially, a regular, systematic, or orderly way of doing anything. **2.** System, order, or regularity in action or thought; plan or design: to study without *method.* **3.** The procedures or techniques used in or characteristic of a particular field of knowledge, thought, practice, etc.: the scientific *method.* **4.** Systematic and orderly arrangement, as of ideas, facts, topics, etc. — **the method** A system or style of acting, originated by Constantin Stanislavsky, in which the actor draws on his own experience to make a strong emotional identification with the role portrayed. [F *méthode* < L *methodus* < Gk. *methodos* < *meta-* after + *hodos* way]

me·thod·i·cal (mə·thod′i·kəl) *adj.* **1.** Arranged in or proceeding according to a regular, systematic order. **2.** Characterized by orderly habits, behavior, etc. Also **me·thod′ic.** — **me·thod′i·cal·ly** *adv.* — **me·thod′i·cal·ness** *n.*

Meth·od·ism (meth′əd·iz′əm) *n.* The doctrines, system, and worship of the Methodists.

meth·od·ist (meth′əd·ist) *n. Rare* One who adheres to or advocates systematic procedure. — **meth′od·ism** *n.*

Meth·od·ist (meth′əd·ist) *n.* A member of any of the Protestant denominations having their origin in a religious movement begun in England in the first half of the 18th century by John and Charles Wesley and their followers. — *adj.* Pertaining to or characteristic of Methodism or Methodists. Abbr. *Meth.* [< METHOD + -IST] — **Meth′od·ism** *n.* — **Meth′od·is′tic** or *·ti·cal adj.*

meth·od·ize (meth′ə·dīz) *v.t.* **·ized, ·iz·ing** To reduce to or arrange in accordance with a method. — **meth′od·i·za′tion** *n.*

meth·od·ol·o·gy (meth′ə·dol′ə·jē) *n. pl.* **·gies 1.** The principles, practices, etc., of orderly thought or procedure applied to a particular branch of learning and arrived at by systematic analysis and application of the techniques of logic. **2.** The branch of logic dealing with such procedures. [< Gk. *methodos* method + -LOGY] — **meth·od·o·log·i·cal** (meth′ə·də·loj′i·kəl) *adj.* — **meth′od·o·log′i·cal·ly** *adv.*

me·thought (mē·thôt′) Past tense of METHINKS.

Me·thu·en (mə·thyōō′ən) A city in NE Massachusetts, near Lowell; pop. 35,456.

Me·thu·se·lah (mə·thōō′zə·lə) In the Old Testament, a Hebrew patriarch reputed to have lived 969 years. *Gen.* v 27. — *n.* A very old man.

meth·yl (meth′əl) *n. Chem.* A univalent organic radical, CH_3, existing chiefly in combination, as in methanol, etc. *Abbr. Me.* [< METHYLENE] — **me·thyl·ic** (mə·thil′ik) *adj.*

methyl acetate *Chem.* A volatile, combustible, fragrant liquid, $CH_3CO_2CH_3$, derived from acetic acid and used as a solvent.

meth·yl·al (meth′əl·al) *n. Chem.* A colorless, volatile, flammable liquid, $C_3H_8O_2$, with a pungent taste and the odor of chloroform, used in medicine and in perfumery: also called *formal.* [< METHYL + AL(COHOL)]

methyl alcohol *Chem.* Methanol.

meth·yl·am·ine (meth′əl·am′ēn, -in) *n. Chem.* A colorless, gaseous, flammable amine, CH_3NH_2, with a strong odor, derived from ammonia by replacement of hydrogen by methyl. [< METHYL + AMINE]

meth·yl·ate (meth′əl·āt) *Chem. n.* A compound derived from methanol by replacing the hydroxyl group with a metal: potassium *methylate.* — *v.t.* **·at·ed, ·at·ing 1.** To mix with methanol. **2.** To combine with the methyl radical. [< METHYL + -ATE] — **meth′yl·a′tion** *n.*

methylated spirit Denatured alcohol prepared by the admixture of methanol. Also **methylated spirits.**

meth·yl·ene (meth′əl·ēn) *n. Chem.* A bivalent organic radical, CH_2, derived from methane. [< F *méthylène* < Gk. *methy* wine + *hylē* wood]

methylene blue *Chem.* A dark, blue-green aniline dye, $C_{16}H_{18}N_3ClS·3H_2O$, used as an antidote in cyanide poisoning, as a chemical indicator, and as a bacteriological stain.

methyl methacrylate *Chem.* A polymerized methacrylate forming transparent plastics resembling glass.

meth·yl·naph·tha·lene (meth′əl·naf′thə·lēn) *n. Chem.* A methyl compound, $C_{10}H_7CH_3$, occurring in two isomeric forms, one of which, the alpha form, is used in the determination of cetane numbers. [< METHYL + NAPHTHALENE]

me·tic·u·lous (mə·tik′yə·ləs) *adj.* Extremely or overly precise about details, especially in minor or trivial matters; minutely painstaking. [< F *méticuleux* < L *meticulosus* fearful < *metus* fear] — **me·tic′u·los′i·ty** (-los′ə·tē), **me·tic′u·lous·ness** *n.* — **me·tic′u·lous·ly** *adv.*

— **Syn.** *Meticulous, scrupulous, punctilious,* and *fastidious* all mean careful or painstaking in regard to one's own actions. *Meticulous* implies concern with details in order to avoid making errors, while *scrupulous* implies an anxious concern to do the right thing. *Punctilious* means carefully or fussily observant of the details of correct behavior, while *fastidious* implies finicky attention to one's own appearance, cleanliness, tastes, etc.

mé·tier (mā·tyā′) *n.* **1.** One's occupation, trade, or profession. **2.** Work or activity for which one is especially well suited; forte. [< OF *mestier* < L *ministerium* service, employment]

Me·tis (mā·tēs′) *n. pl.* **·tis** A person of mixed racial ancestry, especially of French-Canadian and American Indian descent. Also **mé·tis′.** [< F, < LL *misticius* mixed. See MESTIZO.] — **mé·tisse′** (-tēs′) *n. fem.*

meton. Metonymy.

Me·ton·ic cycle (mə·ton′ik) A period of 19 years, at the conclusion of which the phases of the moon recur on the same dates. [after *Meton,* fifth-century B.C. Athenian astronomer]

met·o·nym (met′ə·nim) *n.* A word used in metonymy.

met·o·nym·i·cal (met′ə·nim′i·kəl) *adj.* **1.** Pertaining to or characterized by metonymy. **2.** Used in metonymy. Also **met′o·nym′ic.** — **met′o·nym′i·cal·ly** *adv.*

me·ton·y·my (mə·ton′ə·mē) *n.* A figure of speech that consists in the naming of a thing by substituting one of its attributes or an associated term for the name itself, as in "the *crown* decrees" for "the *ruler* decrees." [< L *metonymia* < Gk. *metōnymia* < *meta-* altered + *onyma* name]

me·too·ism (mē′tōō′iz′əm) *n.* The practice of representing as one's own the popular or successful policies of another, especially a political rival. — **me′-too′er** *n.*

met·o·pe (met′ə·pē) *n. Archit.* A square slab, sculptured or plain, between triglyphs in a Doric frieze. [< Gk. *metopē* < *meta-* between + *opē* opening]

me·top·ic (mə·top′ik) *adj. Anat.* Of or pertaining to the forehead or frontal bone. [< Gk. *metōpon* forehead < *meta-* between + *ōps* eye + -IC]

metr- Var. of METRO-.

me·tral·gi·a (mə·tral′jē·ə) *n. Pathol.* Pain in the uterus. [< METR(O)-[1] + -ALGIA]

Met·ra·zol (met′rə·zōl, -zol) *n.* Proprietary name of a synthetic drug, $C_6H_{10}N_4$, used in medicine as a heart stimulant and in the shock treatment of certain mental disorders. Also **met′ra·zol.**

me·tre[1] (mē′tər) See METER[2].

me·tre[2] (mē′tər) See METER[3].

-metre See -METER (def. 3).

met·ric[1] (met′rik) *adj.* Of, pertaining to, or using the meter as a unit of measurement. [< F *métrique*]

met·ric[2] (met′rik) *adj.* Metrical. [< L *metricus* < Gk. *metrikos*]

met·ri·cal (met′ri·kəl) *adj.* **1.** Of, pertaining to, or characterized by meter; rhythmic. **2.** Composed in or constituting a unit of poetic meter. **3.** Of, pertaining to, or involving measurement. Also *metric.* — **met′ri·cal·ly** *adv.*

metrical foot A foot (def. 8).

metric centner A unit of weight equal to 100 kilograms.

metric hundredweight A unit of weight equal to 50 kilograms.

me·tri·cian (mə·trish′ən) *n.* One versed in metrics or skilled in the use of meter; a metrist.

met·rics (met′riks) *n.pl.* (construed as *sing.*) **1.** The art or branch of learning concerned with meter in prosody. **2.** The science or theory of measurement.

metric system A decimal system of weights and measures having as fundamental units the gram, from which measures of weight and mass are derived, and the meter, from which measures of length, area, and volume are derived. The liter, originally conceived of as equal to one cubic decimeter, serves as the unit of capacity. See table inside back cover.

metric ton A unit of weight equal to 1,000 kilograms, or 2,204.62 pounds avoirdupois. *Abbr. M.T.*

met·ri·fy (met′rə·fī) *v.t.* **·fied, ·fy·ing** To put into or render in meter. [< F *métrifier* < L *metrificare*]

met·rist (met′rist) *n.* One who is skillful in using poetic meter. Also **met′ri·cist** (-rə·sist). [< Med.L *metrista*]

me·tri·tis (mə·trī′tis) *n. Pathol.* Inflammation of the uterus. [< NL < METR(O)-[1] + -ITIS]

met·ro (met′rō) *n. Often cap. Informal* An underground railroad; subway; especially, the subway system of Paris. Also **mé·tro** (mā·trō′). [< F *métro* < (*chemin de fer*) *métro-* (*politain*) metro(politan railroad)]

metro-[1] *combining form* The uterus; pertaining to the uterus. Also, before vowels, **metr-.** [< Gk. *metra* uterus]

metro-[2] *combining form* Measure: *metrology.* Also, before vowels, **metr-.** [< Gk. *metron* a measure]

me·trol·o·gy (mə·trol′ə·jē) *n.* **1.** The science that treats of weights and measures. **2.** A system of weights and measures. [< METRO-[2] + -LOGY] — **met·ro·log·i·cal** (met′rə·loj′i·kəl) *adj.* — **me·trol′o·gist** *n.*

met·ro·nome (met′rə·nōm) *n.* An instrument for indicating exact tempo in music, usually producing audible clicks controlled by a reversed pendulum whose motion is regulated by a sliding weight. *Abbr. met.* [< Gk. *metron* measure + *nomos* law] — **met′ro·nom′ic** (-nom′ik) *adj.*

me·tro·nym·ic (mē′trə·nim′ik, met′rə-) *adj.* Derived from the name of one's mother or a female ancestor. — *n.* A metronymic name or designation. Also *matronymic.* Compare PATRONYMIC. [< Gk. *mētrōnymikos* < *mētēr* mother + *onyma* name]

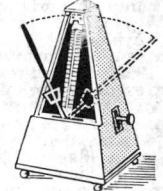

METRONOME

me·trop·o·lis (mə·trop′ə·lis) *n. pl.* **·lis·es 1.** A principal city; especially, the capital or the largest or most important city of a country, state, or area. **2.** An urban center of activity, culture, trade, etc. **3.** The see or city over which a metropolitan has authority. **4.** In ancient Greece, the mother city of a colony. [< Gk. *mētropolis* city < *mētēr* mother + *polis* city]

met·ro·pol·i·tan (met′rə·pol′ə·tən) *adj.* **1.** Of, pertaining to, or characteristic of a metropolis. **2.** Constituting a major urban center and its environs: the *metropolitan* area. **3.** Pertaining to or designating a bishop having authority over a metropolis (def. 3). **4.** Of, pertaining to, or constituting a mother country, as distinguished from its colonies. — *n.* **1.** In various churches, an archbishop or hierarch of similar rank having authority over the bishops within his jurisdiction. **2.** One who lives in or has the characteristics, viewpoint, etc., of one living in a metropolis. **3.** A citizen of a metropolis (def. 4). *Abbr. met.* [< LL *metropolitanus* < Gk. *metropolis.* See METROPOLIS.]

me·tror·rha·gi·a (mē′trə·rā′jē·ə, met′rə-) *n. Pathol.* A flow of blood from the uterus, especially when not menstrual. [< METRO-[1] + -RRHAGIA]

-metry *combining form* The process, science, or art of measuring: *geometry.* [< Gk. *metria* < *metron* a measure]

Met·su (met′sü), **Gabriel**, 1630?–67, Dutch painter. Also **Met′zu.**

Met·ter·nich (met′ər·niḵh), **Prince von**, 1773–1859, Klemens Wenzel Nepomuk Lothar von Metternich-Winneburg, Austrian statesman and diplomat.

met·tle (met′l) *n.* **1.** Inherent quality, as of character or temperament. **2.** Dauntless spirit; courage; pluck. **— on one's mettle** Aroused to one's best efforts; putting forth one's utmost. [Var. of METAL]

met·tle·some (met′l·səm) *adj.* Full of spirit; courageous; valiant. Also **met·tled** (met′əld).

me·tump (mə·tump′) *n. U.S. & Canadian* A tumpline.

Metz (mets, *Fr.* mes) A city in NE France on the Moselle river; pop. 85,701 (1954).

Meuse (myōōz, *Fr.* mœz) A river in western Europe, flowing about 580 miles north from France to the North Sea: Dutch *Maas.*

mev or **Mev** or **m.e.v.** Million electron volts.

mew[1] (myōō) *n.* **1.** A cage in which molting hawks are kept. **2.** *pl.* Stables built around a court or alley: so called from the royal stables in London. **3.** *pl.* (*construed as sing.*) *Chiefly Brit.* A narrow street or alley, often with dwellings converted from stables. **4.** *Rare* A place of concealment or confinement. **—** *v.t.* **1.** To confine in or as in a cage; often with *up.* **2.** *Archaic* To shed or change (feathers, etc.); molt. **—** *v.i.* **3.** *Obs.* To molt. [< OF *muer* to change, molt < L *mutare*]

mew[2] (myōō) *v.i.* To utter the high-pitched cry of a cat. **—** *n.* The high-pitched, plaintive cry of a cat. [Imit.]

mew[3] (myōō) *n.* A gull; especially the common gull (*Larus canus*) of Europe: also called *sea mew.* [OE *mǣw*]

mewl (myōōl) *v.i.* To whimper or cry feebly, as an infant. **—** *n.* A whimper or feeble cry. [Freq. of MEW[2]]

Mex. Mexican; Mexico.

Mex·i·can (mek′sə·kən) *n.* **1.** A native or inhabitant of Mexico. **2.** A language indigenous to Mexico, as Nahuatl. **—** *adj.* Of or pertaining to Mexico, its inhabitants, or their language or culture.

Mexican bean beetle A ladybird (*Epilachna varivestis*) that has spotted wings and feeds on the leaves and green pods of beans. For illustration see INSECTS (injurious).

Mexican hairless One of a breed of small dogs, hairless except for a tuft on the head and the end of the tail.

Mexican War See table for WAR.

Mex·i·co (mek′sə·kō) **1.** A Republic in southern North America; 760,373 sq. mi.; pop. 48,313,438 (1970); capital, Mexico (also **Mexico City**) in the Federal District of Mexico (573 sq. mi.), pop. 3,025,564 (1970). **2.** A state in central Mexico; 8,267 sq. mi.; pop. 3,833,185 (1970); capital, Toluca. Spanish *Méjico. Mexican Spanish* **Mé·xi·co** (mā′hē·kō).

Mexico, Gulf of An inlet of the Atlantic, nearly enclosed by the United States, Mexico, and Cuba; 700,000 sq. mi.

Mey·er·beer (mī′ər·bâr), **Giacomo**, 1791–1864, German composer: original name **Jakob Liebmann Beer** (bâr).

Mey·er·hof (mī′ər·hōf), **Otto Fritz**, 1884–1951, German physiologist.

Meyn·ell (men′əl), **Alice Christiana**, *née* Thompson, 1847–1922, English poet and essayist.

mez·cal (mez·kal′), **mez·ca·line** (mez′kə·lēn, -lin) See MESCAL, MESCALINE.

me·ze·re·on (mə·zir′ē·ən) *n.* A cultivated shrub (*Daphne mezereum*) native to the Old World, having clusters of fragrant, lilac-purple flowers: also called *mezereum.* [< Med.L < Arabic *māzarīyūn* camellia, ? < Persian]

me·ze·re·um (mə·zir′ē·əm) *n.* **1.** The dried bark of mezereon, used as an irritant and vesicant. **2.** Mezereon.

mez·quit (mez·kēt′, mez′kēt), **mez·quite** See MESQUITE.

me·zu·zah (mə·zōō′zə, -zōō′zä) *n. pl.* **·zahs** or **·zoth** (-zōth) In Judaism, a parchment that has been inscribed with the passages Deuteronomy vi 4–9 and xi 13–21 and marked on the outside with the word "Shaddai," a name for God, rolled up in a case or tube and affixed to a doorpost. Also **me·zu′za.** [< Hebrew *mezūzāh* doorpost]

mez·za·nine (mez′ə·nēn, -nin) *n.* **1.** An intermediate story, usually not of full width, between two main floors, especially the ground floor and the one above it. **2.** In a theater, the first balcony, or the front rows of the balcony. [< F < Ital. *mezzanino*, dim. of *mezzano* middle < L *medianus*]

mez·zo (met′sō, med′zō, mez′ō) *adj.* Half; medium; moderate: often used in combination: *mezzo-soprano.* **—** *adv. Music* Moderately: *mezzo forte.* **—** *n. pl.* **·zos** A mezzo-soprano. [< Ital., < L *medius* middle]

mez·zo·re·lie·vo (met′sō·ri·lē′vō, med′zō-, mez′ō-) *n. pl.* **·vos** A type of sculpture in which the figures project halfway from the background: also called *demirelief, half relief.* See RELIEF. [< Ital. *mezzo rilievo.* See MEZZO and RELIEF.]

mez·zo·ri·lie·vo (met′sō·rē·lyä′vō) *n. pl.* **mez·zi·ri·lie·vi** (med′zē·rē·lyä′vē) *Italian* Mezzo-relievo.

mez·zo·so·pra·no (met′sō·sə·pran′ō, -prä′nō, med′zō-, mez′ō-) *n. pl.* **·pran·os** or **·pra·ni** (-nē) **1.** A female voice intermediate between a soprano and a contralto. **2.** A person having such a voice. **—** *adj.* Of or pertaining to the voice or range of a mezzo-soprano. [< Ital. See MEZZO and SOPRANO.]

mez·zo·tint (met′sō·tint′, med′zō-, mez′ō-) *n.* **1.** A method of engraving in which the roughened surface of a copper or steel plate is scraped or burnished to produce effects of light and shade. **2.** A print produced from such a plate. **—** *v.t.* To engrave by or represent in mezzotint. [< Ital. *mezzo-tinto* < *mezzo* middle + *tinto* painted] **— mez′zo·tint′er** *n.*

mf or **mfd** Microfarad(s).

mf. or **mf 1.** *Music* Moderately loud (Ital. *mezzo forte*). **2.** Millifarad.

MF or **MF.** or **M.F.** Middle French.

mfg. Manufacturing.

mfr. Manufacture; manufacturer.

mg. or **mg** or **mgm** Milligram(s).

Mg *Chem.* Magnesium.

Mgr. 1. Manager. **2.** Monseigneur. **3.** Monsignor.

MH *Mil.* Medal of Honor.

MHG or **MHG.** or **M.H.G.** Middle High German.

mho (mō) *n.* The practical unit of electrical conductance, the reciprocal of the ohm. [< OHM reversed]

MHz Megahertz.

mi (mē) *n. Music* The third syllable used in solmization; the third tone of a major scale; also, the tone E.

mi. 1. Mile(s). **2.** Mill(s).

Mi·am·i (mī·am′ē, -am′ə) *n. pl.* **Mi·am·i** or **Mi·am·is** A member of an Algonquian tribe of North American Indians formerly inhabiting Wisconsin, Indiana, and Ohio.

Mi·am·i (mī·am′ē, -am′ə) A city in SE Florida, on Biscayne Bay; pop. 334,859.

Miami Beach A resort city on an island between the Atlantic and Biscayne Bay, SE Florida; pop. 87,072.

Miami River A river in SW Ohio, flowing 160 miles SW to the Ohio River.

mi·a·na bug (mē·ä′nə) A tick (genus *Argas*), parasitic on poultry and inflicting a bite injurious to man: also called *tampan.* Also **Mi·a′na bug.** [after *Miana*, an Iranian town]

mi·aou, mi·aow (mē·ou′) See MEOW.

mi·as·ma (mī·az′mə, mē-) *n. pl.* **·mas** or **·ma·ta** (-mə·tə) **1.** Noxious or unwholesome emanation, atmosphere, influence, etc. **2.** The poisonous effluvium once supposed to rise from putrid matter, swamps, etc. Also **mi′asm** (-az·əm). [< NL < Gk., pollution < *miainein* to stain, defile] **— mi·as′mal, mi·as·mat·ic** (mī′əz·mat′ik), **mi·as′mic, mi·as′mic** *adj.*

mi·aul (mē·ôl′, -oul′) *v.i.* To cry as a cat; meow. **—** *n.* The meowing of a cat. [Imit.]

mib (mib) *n. U.S. Dial.* **1.** A marble. **2.** *pl.* The game of marbles. [? Alter. of MARBLE]

Mic. Micah.

mi·ca (mī′kə) *n.* Any of a class of hydrous silicates of widely varying composition, cleaving into tough, thin, often transparent and flexible laminae: sometimes called *isinglass.* [< L, crumb; infl. by *micare* to glitter]

mi·ca·ceous (mī·kā′shəs) *adj.* **1.** Of, pertaining to, consisting of, or containing mica. **2.** Resembling mica.

Mi·cah (mī′kə) Eighth-century B.C. Hebrew prophet. **—** *n.* A book of the Old Testament bearing his name. Also, in the Douai Bible, **Mi·che·as** (mī·kē′əs).

Mi·caw·ber (mə·kô′bər), **Wilkins** In Dickens's *David Copperfield* (1850), an improvident family man, always waiting for "something to turn up."

mice (mīs) Plural of MOUSE.

mi·celle (mi·sel′) *n.* **1.** *Biol.* One of the theoretical molecular units said to make up organized structures. **2.** *Chem.* A particle in a colloidal dispersion, consisting of a charged nucleus surrounded by ions. Also **mi·cell′, mi·cel′la** (-sel′ə). [< NL *micella*, dim. of L *mica* crumb] **— mi·cel′lar** *adj.*

Mich. Michigan.

Mi·chael (mī′kəl) One of the archangels, represented as a militant protector and defender of the faithful: sometimes called *the Archangel. Dan.* x 10–12, *Rev.* xii 7–9.

Michael I, born 1921, King of Rumania 1927–30, 1940–47.

Mich·ael·mas (mik′əl·məs) *n.* September 29, the church festival of the archangel Michael, in Great Britain serving as the fall quarter day. Also **Michaelmas Day.** [< MICHAEL + -MAS]

Michaelmas daisy *Chiefly Brit.* Any of various wild or cultivated asters blooming in early fall.

Mi·chel·an·ge·lo (mī′kəl·an′jə·lō, *Ital.* mē′kel·än′je·lō), 1475–1564, Italian sculptor, painter, architect, and poet: full name **Michelangelo Buo·nar·ro·ti** (bwô′när·rô′tē).

Miche·let (mēsh·le′), **Jules**, 1798–1874, French historian.

Mi·chel·son (mī′kəl·sən), **Albert Abraham**, 1852–1931, U.S. physicist born in Germany.

Mich·i·gan (mish′ə·gən) A north central State of the United States; 58,216 sq. mi.; pop. 8,875,083; capital, Lansing; entered the Union Jan. 26, 1837; nickname, *Wolverine State.* Abbr. *Mich.* **— Mich′i·gan·ite** (-īt), **Mich′i·gan′der** (-gan′· dər) *n.*

Michigan City A city in northern Indiana, on Lake Michigan; pop. 39,369.

Michigan, Lake The third in size of the Great Lakes, the only one entirely within the United States, located between Michigan and Wisconsin; 22,400 sq. mi.

mick (mik) *n. Sometimes cap. Slang* An Irishman: an offensive term. [< *Michael*, a personal name]

mick·ey[1] (mik′ē) *n. pl.* **·eys** *U.S. Slang* A Mickey Finn.

mick·ey[2] (mik′ē) *adj. U.S. Slang* **1.** Having the characteristics of the music for an animated cartoon. **2.** Corny; square. Also **Mick′ey Mouse.** [< *Mickey Mouse,* an animated cartoon character]

Mick·ey Finn (mik′ē fin′) *U.S. Slang* An alcoholic drink secretly drugged so as to render the drinker unconscious. Also **mick′ey finn.** [Origin unknown]

Mic·kie·wicz (mits·kyä′vich), **Adam,** 1798–1855, Polish poet.

mick·le (mik′əl) *Scot. or Archaic adj.* **1.** Large; great. **2.** Much; many. — *adv.* Much. — *n.* A large amount. Also *muckle.* [OE *micel*]

Mic·mac (mik′mak) *n. pl.* **·mac** or **·macs** A member of an Algonquian tribe of North American Indians living in Nova Scotia, New Brunswick, and Newfoundland. [< N.Am.Ind., lit., allies]

mi·cra (mī′krə) Plural of MICRON.

mi·cri·fy (mī′krə·fī) *v.t.* **·fied, ·fy·ing** *Rare* To make small or insignificant. [< MICR(O)- + -FY]

micro- *combining form* **1.** Very small; minute: *microsome.* **2.** Enlarging or magnifying size or volume: *microscope, microphone.* **3.** *Pathol.* Abnormally small or underdeveloped: *microcephaly.* **4.** Of a science, depending on, using, or requiring a microscope, as in the following list of self-explanatory compounds:

microbotany	micrometallurgy	micropetrology
microgeology	micromineralogy	microphysiography
microhistology	micropathology	microphysiology
micromechanics	micropetrography	microzoology

5. In the metric system and in technical usage, one millionth of (a specified unit), as in the following list of self-explanatory compounds:

microampere	microfarad	microlux
microangstrom	microhenry	micromho
microbar	microhm	micromicron
microcoulomb	microjoule	microvolt
microcurie	microliter	microwatt

Sometimes, before vowels, **micr-.** [< Gk. *mikros* small]

mi·cro·anal·y·sis (mī′krō·ə·nal′ə·sis) *n.* The chemical analysis of minute quantities. — **mi′cro·an′a·lyst** (-an′ə·list) *n.* — **mi′cro·an′a·lyt′ic** (-an′ə·lit′ik) or **·i·cal** *adj.* — **mi′cro·an′a·lyt′i·cal·ly** *adv.*

mi·cro·bal·ance (mī′krō·bal′əns) *n.* A balance used to weigh minute quantities, as in microanalysis.

mi·cro·bar·o·graph (mī′krō·bar′ə·graf, -gräf) *n.* A barograph that records very small fluctuations in atmospheric pressure.

mi·crobe (mī′krōb) *n.* A microscopic organism; especially, one of the bacteria that cause disease; a germ. [< F < Gk. *mikros* small + *bios* life] — **mi·cro′bi·al, mi·cro′bi·an, mi·cro′bic** *adj.*

— Syn. *Microbe, germ, microorganism, bacterium, bacillus,* and *virus* denote organisms of microscopic size and smaller. Though not strictly synonymous, these words are frequently confused. *Microbe* was originally a general term, applied at first to protozoa, and then to *bacteria; germ* originally denoted a reproductive cell. Both words are now popularly used to refer to disease-producing *bacteria. Microorganism* developed as a general term for protozoa, *bacteria,* and *viruses. Bacteria* are unicellular organisms, distinguished from protozoa because they possess both plant and animal characteristics. *Bacillus* is sometimes used incorrectly as a synonym of *bacterium,* but properly denotes one class only of *bacteria.* A *virus* is a complex protein molecule capable of invading the cells of a living organism and there reproducing itself.

mi·cro·bi·cide (mī·krō′bə·sīd) *n.* Any substance or agent that destroys microbes. [< MICROBE + -CIDE] — **mi·cro′·bi·ci′dal** *adj.*

mi·cro·bi·ol·o·gy (mī′krō·bī·ol′ə·jē) *n.* The branch of biology concerned with the study of microorganisms. — **mi′·cro·bi′o·log′i·cal** (-bī′ə·loj′i·kəl) *adj.* — **mi′cro·bi·ol′o·gist** *n.*

mi·cro·ceph·a·ly (mī′krō·sef′ə·lē) *n.* Abnormal smallness of the head, especially in regard to cranial capacity: opposed to *macrocephaly.* [< MICRO- + Gk. *kephalē* head] — **mi′·cro·ce·phal′ic** (-sə·fal′ik) *adj. & n.* — **mi′cro·ceph′a·lous** *adj.*

mi·cro·chem·is·try (mī′krō·kem′is·trē) *n.* A branch of chemistry dealing with minute quantities. — **mi′cro·chem′·i·cal** *adj.*

mi·cro·cir·cuit (mī′krō·sûr′kit) *n. Electronics* A circuit consisting of highly miniaturized elements. — **mi′cro·cir′·cuit·ry** *n.*

mi·cro·cli·mate (mī′krō·klī′mit) *n. Meteorol.* The climate of a very small area, as a forest, field, or lake, considered with reference to the general climate of a region: distinguished from *macroclimate.* — **mi′cro·cli·mat′ic** (-klī·mat′ik) *adj.*

mi·cro·cli·ma·tol·o·gy (mī′krō·klī′mə·tol′ə·jē) *n.* The study of microclimates. — **mi′cro·cli′ma·to·log′ic** (-klī′mə·tə·loj′ik) or **·i·cal** *adj.*

mi·cro·cline (mī′krə·klīn) *n.* A variously colored, brittle, translucent mineral resembling orthoclase but of different crystal form. [< MICRO- + Gk. *klinein* to slope, bend]

mi·cro·coc·cus (mī′krə·kok′əs) *n. pl.* **·coc·ci** (-kok′sī) Any member of a genus (*Micrococcus*) of spherical bacteria that occur in irregular masses and are often pathogenic. [< NL]

mi·cro·cop·y (mī′krə·kop′ē) *n. pl.* **·cop·ies** A reduced photographic copy of a letter, manuscript, etc. — *v.t. & v.i.* **·cop·ied, ·cop·y·ing** To reproduce in the form of microcopy.

mi·cro·cosm (mī′krə·koz′əm) *n.* **1.** A little world; the universe in miniature. **2.** Man regarded as epitomizing the universe. **3.** A small group or community regarded as representing the world in miniature. Also **mi′cro·cos′mos** (-koz′məs). Compare MACROCOSM. [< LL *microcosmus* < Gk. *mikros cosmos,* lit., little world] — **mi′cro·cos′mic** *adj.*

microcosmic salt *Chem.* A white, crystalline sodium-ammonium phosphate, $NaNH_4HPO_4 \cdot 4H_2O$, originally derived from human urine.

mi·cro·crys·tal·line (mī′krō·kris′tə·lin, -lēn) *adj.* Having a crystalline structure visible only under a microscope.

mi·cro·cyte (mī′krə·sīt) *n. Pathol.* An abnormally small red blood corpuscle, usually found in cases of anemia.

mi·cro·de·tec·tor (mī′krō·di·tek′tər) *n. Elect.* An instrument used to measure small charges, as a galvanometer.

mi·cro·dont (mī′krə·dont) *adj.* Having unusually small teeth. Also **mi′cro·don′tous** (-don′təs).

mi·cro·fiche (mī′krə·fēsh′) *n.* A piece of film suitable for a card file, containing images of 24, 48, 96, or more pages of microcopy. Also *fiche.*

mi·cro·film (mī′krə·film) *n.* A photographic reproduction on film of a printed page, document, or other object, highly reduced for ease in transmission and storage, and capable of reenlargement. — *v.t. & v.i.* To reproduce on microfilm.

mi·cro·form (mī′krə·fôrm′) *n.* Any standard form, such as roll film or microfiche, in which microcopy is reproduced on film.

mi·cro·ga·mete (mī′krō·gə·mēt′, -gam′ēt) *n. Biol.* The smaller, usually male, of two conjugating gametes.

mi·cro·gram (mī′krə·gram) *n.* In the metric system, a unit of weight equal to one millionth of a gram. Also **mi′cro·gramme.**

mi·cro·graph (mī′krə·graf, -gräf) *n.* **1.** A device used to produce minute writing, drawing, etc. **2.** A picture of an object as seen through a microscope. — **mi′cro·graph′ic** *adj.*

mi·crog·ra·phy (mī·krog′rə·fē) *n.* **1.** The study, description, or representation of microscopic objects. **2.** The act or process of producing very minute writing.

mi·cro·groove (mī′krə·grōōv) *n.* An extremely fine groove cut in the surface of a phonograph record.

Mi·cro·groove (mī′krə·grōōv) *n.* A long-playing record: a trade name.

mi·cro·inch (mī′krō·inch′) *n.* A unit of linear measure equal to one millionth of an inch.

mi·crol·o·gy[1] (mī·krol′ə·jē) *n.* Undue attention to minute and unimportant matters. [< Gk. *mikrologia* < *mikros* small + *-logia.* See -LOGY.] — **mi·cro·log′ic** (mī′krə·loj′ik) or **·i·cal** *adj.* — **mi′cro·log′i·cal·ly** *adv.*

mi·crol·o·gy[2] (mī·krol′ə·jē) *n.* A branch of science dealing with or depending on the use of the microscope. [< MICRO-(SCOPE) + -LOGY.] — **mi·cro·log·ic** (mī′krə·loj′ik) or **·i·cal** *adj.* — **mi′cro·log′i·cal·ly** *adv.* — **mi·crol′o·gist** *n.*

mi·cro·me·te·or·ol·o·gy (mī′krō·mē′tē·ə·rol′ə·jē) *n.* The study of climatic conditions in very small areas.

mi·crom·e·ter (mī·krom′ə·tər) *n.* **1.** An instrument used for measuring very small distances or dimensions, as in conjunction with a microscope or telescope. **2.** A micrometer caliper. [< MICRO- + -METER]

micrometer caliper A caliper or gauge having a micrometer screw, used to make very precise measurements.

micrometer screw A screw with a very accurately cut thread and a graduated head, used in micrometers, etc.

MICROMETER

a Frame. *b* Anvil.
c Movable spindle.
d Sleeve. *e* Thimble.

mi·crom·e·try (mī·krom′ə·trē) *n.* Measurement by means of a micrometer. — **mi·cro·met·ric** (mī′krō·met′rik) or **·ri·cal** *adj.* — **mi′cro·met′ri·cal·ly** *adv.*

mi·cro·mil·li·me·ter (mī′krō·mil′ə·mē′tər) *n.* A millimicron. Also *esp. Brit.* **mi′cro·mil′li·me′tre.**

mi·cro·mod·ule (mī′krō·moj′ōol) *n. Electronics* A tiny component in microcircuitry.

mi·cron (mī′kron) *n. pl.* **·cra** (-krə) A unit of measurement equal to one thousandth of a millimeter: also spelled *mikron.* [< NL < Gk. *mikron,* neut. of *mikros* small]

Mi·cro·ne·sia (mī′krə·nē′zhə, -shə) One of the three main divisions of Pacific islands, in the western Pacific north of the equator, including the Caroline, Gilbert, Marshall, and Marianas islands. See map of AUSTRALASIA.

Mi·cro·ne·sian (mī′krə·nē′zhən, -shən) *adj.* Of or pertaining to Micronesia, its people, or their languages. — *n.* **1.** A native of Micronesia. **2.** Any of the Austronesian languages spoken in Micronesia.

---

mi·cro·nu·tri·ent (mī'krō·nōō'trē·ənt, -nyōō'-) *n.* A substance essential in nutrition, but only in very small amounts. — *adj.* Of or pertaining to such a substance.

mi·cro·or·gan·ism (mī'krō·ôr'gən·iz'əm) *n.* Any microscopic or ultramicroscopic organism, as a bacterium or protozoan. Also **mi'cro-or'gan·ism.** — **Syn.** See MICROBE.

mi·cro·pa·le·on·tol·o·gy (mī'krō·pā'lē·ən·tol'ə·jē) *n.* The study of microscopic fossils. — **mi'cro·pa'le·on'to·log'ic** (-on'tə·loj'ik) or **·i·cal** *adj.* — **mi'cro·pa'le·on·tol'o·gist** *n.*

mi·cro·par·a·site (mī'krō·par'ə·sīt) *n.* A parasitic microorganism. — **mi'cro·par'a·sit'ic** (-par'ə·sit'ik) *adj.*

mi·cro·phone (mī'krə·fōn) *n.* A device for converting sound waves into electric currents, forming the principal element of a telephone transmitter or of any sound-reproducing system, as in broadcasting. — **mi·cro·phon'ic** (-fon'ik) *adj.*

mi·cro·pho·to·graph (mī'krō·fō'tə·graf, -gräf) *n.* **1.** A very small or microscopic photographic reproduction of any object, picture, or writing, as on microfilm. **2.** Loosely, a photomicrograph. — **mi'cro·pho'to·graph'ic** *adj.* — **mi'cro·pho·tog'ra·phy** (-fə·tog'rə·fē) *n.*

mi·cro·pho·tom·e·ter (mī'krō·fō·tom'ə·tər) *n.* An instrument that measures very small luminous intensities, used in the comparative study of spectral lines. — **mi'cro·pho'to·met'ric** (-fō'tə·met'rik) *adj.* — **mi'cro·pho'to·met'ri·cal·ly** *adv.* — **mi'cro·pho·tom'e·try** *n.*

mi·cro·phys·ics (mī'krə·fiz'iks) *n.pl. (construed as sing.)* A branch of physics that is concerned with the structure, characteristics, and behavior of minute particles, as molecules, atoms, electrons, etc. — **mi'cro·phys'i·cal** *adj.*

mi·cro·print (mī'krə·print) *n.* A microphotograph reproduced in a print that may be examined or read by means of a magnifying glass. — *v.t. & v.i.* To represent or reproduce by means of a microprint.

mi·cro·pyle (mī'krə·pīl) *n.* **1.** *Bot.* The aperture in the coats of a plant ovule through which the pollen tube penetrates. **2.** *Zool.* An aperture in the enveloping membrane of the ovum, permitting entry of a spermatozoon. [< MICRO- + Gk. *pylē* gate] — **mi'cro·py'lar** *adj.*

mi·cro·py·rom·e·ter (mī'krō·pī·rom'ə·tər) *n.* An optical instrument for observing the temperature, etc., of minute bodies that radiate light or heat.

micros. Microscopy.

mi·cro·scope (mī'krə·skōp) *n.* An optical instrument consisting of a single lens or a combination of lenses, used for magnifying objects too small to be seen or clearly observed by ordinary vision. [< NL *microscopium*]

mi·cro·scop·ic (mī'krə·skop'ik) *adj.* **1.** So minute as to be visible only under a microscope: distinguished from *macroscopic*. **2.** Exceedingly small; minute. **3.** Of, pertaining to, or of the nature of a microscope or microscopy. **4.** Performed with or depending on use of a microscope. **5.** Characterized by or done with minute observation or attention to details: a *microscopic* search. Also **mi'cro·scop'i·cal.** — **Syn.** See SMALL. — **mi'cro·scop'i·cal·ly** *adv.*

Mi·cro·sco·pi·um (mī'krə·skō'pē·əm) *n.* A constellation, the Microscope. See CONSTELLATION. [< NL]

mi·cros·co·py (mī·kros'kə·pē, mī'krə·skō'pē) *n.* **1.** The process or technique of using the microscope. **2.** Investigation by means of the microscope. — **mi·cros·co·pist** (mī·kros'kə·pist, mī'krə·skō'pist) *n.*

mi·cro·sec·ond (mī'krə·sek'ənd) *n.* An interval of time equal to one millionth of a second.

mi·cro·seism (mī'krə·sīz'əm, -sīs'-) *n.* A very slight tremor or vibration of the earth's crust. [< MICRO- + SEISM] — **mi'cro·seis'mic** (-sīz'mik, -sīs'-) or **·mi·cal** *adj.*

mi·cro·some (mī'krə·sōm) *n. Biol.* A minute particle in the cytoplasm of a living cell. Also **mi'cro·so'ma** (-sō'mə).

mi·cro·spo·ran·gi·um (mī'krō·spə·ran'jē·əm) *n. pl.* **·gi·a** (-jē·ə) *Bot.* A sporangium producing microspores.

mi·cro·spore (mī'krə·spôr, -spōr) *n. Bot.* A small, asexually produced spore in seed plants, usually male in function.

mi·cro·spo·ro·phyll (mī'krə·spôr'ə·fil, -spō'rə-) *n. Bot.* A sporophyll producing microsporangia.

mi·cros·to·mous (mī·kros'tə·məs) *adj.* Having an unusually small mouth. Also **mi·cro·stom·a·tous** (mī'krō·stom'ə·təs). [< MICRO- + -STOMOUS]

mi·cro·tome (mī'krə·tōm) *n.* An instrument for cutting very thin sections of organic tissue, etc., for microscopic observations. — **mi'cro·tom'ic** (-tom'ik) or **·i·cal** *adj.*

mi·crot·o·my (mī·krot'ə·mē) *n.* The act or process of preparing material for microscopic examination with or as with a microtome. — **mi·crot'o·mist** *n.*

mi·cro·wave (mī'krə·wāv) *n.* An electromagnetic wave having a frequency between about 1,000 and 30,000 megacycles. Compare RADIO WAVE.

mi·crur·gy (mī'krûr·jē) *n.* The delicate technique of dissection, manipulation, etc., performed under high magnification. [< MICR(O)- + -URGY] — **mi·crur'gic** (mī·krûr'jik) or **·gi·cal** *adj.* — **mi'crur·gist** *n.*

mic·tu·rate (mik'chə·rāt) *v.i.* **·rat·ed, ·rat·ing** To urinate. [< MICTURITION; an erroneous formation]

mic·tu·ri·tion (mik'chə·rish'ən) *n.* The act of urinating. [< L *micturitus*, pp. of *micturire* to desire to urinate < *mingere* to urinate]

mid¹ (mid) *adj.* **1.** Being approximately in the middle; central. **2.** *Phonet.* Of a vowel sound, produced with the tongue in a position approximately half-way between high and low, as (ō) in *boat*. — *n. Archaic* The middle. [OE *midd-*]

mid² (mid) *prep. Chiefly Poetic* Amid; among. Also **'mid.**

mid- *combining form* **1.** Middle point or part of, as in:

mid-act	midforenoon	mid-Renaissance
midafternoon	mid-hour	mid-river
mid-April	mid-ice	mid-road
mid-August	mid-January	mid-sea
midautumn	mid-July	midseason
mid-block	mid-June	midsentence
mid-breast	mid-lake	mid-September
mid-career	midleg	mid-sky
mid-century	mid-length	mid-slope
mid-channel	mid-life	mid-sole
mid-chest	mid-March	midspace
mid-column	mid-May	mid-span
mid-continent	midmonth	midstory
mid-course	midmorning	midstream
mid-court	mid-mouth	midstreet
mid-crowd	mid-movement	mid-stride
mid-current	mid-November	mid-sun
mid-December	mid-ocean	mid-swing
mid-dish	mid-October	mid-thigh
mid-Empire	mid-orbit	mid-volley
midevening	mid-periphery	mid-walk
mid-February	mid-pillar	mid-wall
mid-field	midrange	mid-water
mid-flight	mid-refrain	mid-zone

2. Being in the middle or center, as in:

mid-incisor	mid-period	mid-time
mid-line	mid-position	mid-value
mid-part	mid-region	mid-world

3. With adjectives, of or pertaining to the middle part of that which is modified or implied, as in:

mid-African	mid-diastolic	midmonthly
mid-Arctic	middorsal	mid-Pacific
mid-Asian	mid-estral	mid-Pleistocene
mid-Atlantic	mid-European	mid-Siberian
midaxillary	midfacial	midtarsal
mid-Cambrian	midfrontal	mid-Tertiary
midcarpal	mid-Italian	mid-thoracic
mid-Devonian	midmandibular	midventral

mid. **1.** Middle. **2.** Midshipman.

mid·air (mid'âr') *n.* A point or region seemingly in the middle or midst of the air. Also **mid'-air'.**

Mi·das (mī'dəs) In Greek legend, a king of Phrygia who had the power of turning whatever he touched into gold.

mid·brain (mid'brān') *n. Anat.* The mesencephalon.

mid·day (mid'dā') *n.* The middle of the day; noon. — *adj.* Of, pertaining to, or occurring in the middle of the day.

mid·den (mid'n) *n.* **1.** A kitchen midden (which see). **2.** *Brit. Dial.* A dunghill or heap of refuse. [ME *midding* < Scand. Cf. Dan. *mödding* < *mög* dung + *dynge* heap]

mid·dle (mid'l) *adj.* **1.** Equally distant from the extremes, periphery, etc.; central. **2.** Intermediate in position, status, etc. **3.** Intervening between the first or earlier part and the latter part of a sequence, series, period of time, etc. **4.** Moderate, as in size or effect. **5.** *Usually cap.* Designating a language in a stage between an earlier and a recent form: *Middle* English. **6.** *Gram.* In Greek and Sanskrit, designating a voice of the verb indicating action of the subject for his own sake. — *n.* **1.** The area or point equally distant from the extremes, periphery, etc. **2.** The intermediate section or portion of anything. **3.** The middle part of the body; the waist. **4.** *Gram.* The middle voice. Abbr. *M, mid.* — **Syn.** See CENTER. — *v.t.* **·dled, ·dling** **1.** To place in the middle. **2.** *Naut.* To fold or double in the middle. [OE *middel*]

middle age The time of life between youth and old age, usually thought of as the years between 40 and 60.

mid·dle-aged (mid'l·ājd') *adj.* **1.** Being of middle age. **2.** Of, pertaining to, or characteristic of persons of middle age.

Middle Ages The period in European history between classical antiquity and the Renaissance, usually regarded as extending from the downfall of Rome, in 476, to about 1450 or 1500.

Middle America **1.** The part of North America south of the United States. **2.** The American middle class, especially that segment holding moderate political views.

Middle Atlantic States New York, New Jersey, and Pennsylvania.

mid·dle·brow (mid'l·brou') *Informal n.* One whose cultural interests or tastes are more conventional than those of a highbrow: sometimes a term of derision. — *adj.* Pertaining to, characteristic of, or suitable for a middlebrow: also **mid'dle·browed'.** — **mid'dle·brow'ism** *n.*

middle C *Music* The note written on the first ledger line above the bass staff and the first ledger line below the treble staff; also, the corresponding tone.

middle class The part of a society occupying a social or economic position between the laboring class and the very wealthy or the nobility. — **mid'dle·class'** *adj.*

Middle Congo A former French Overseas Territory in central Africa; capital, Pointe Noire. See (Republic of the) CONGO (BRAZZAVILLE).

middle distance **1.** The area between the foreground and the background in a painting, photograph, etc. **2.** In track sports, a race of 440 yards or more and less than a mile.

Middle Dutch The pre-Reformation literary language of Flanders, Brabant, and Limburg. Abbr. *MD, M.D., MDu.*

middle ear *Anat.* The portion of the ear between the tympanic membrane and the opening of the Eustachian tube; also, the membrane itself: also called *tympanum.*

Middle East **1.** The region including Egypt and the countries of SW Asia west of Pakistan and India: not used officially. **2.** *Brit.* This region with the exception of Turkey and including India, Pakistan, Burma, Tibet, Libya, Ethiopia, and Somaliland.

Middle English See under ENGLISH.

Middle French See under FRENCH.

Middle High German See under GERMAN.

Middle Irish See under IRISH.

Middle Kingdom **1.** A kingdom of ancient Egypt, 2400–1580 B.C., having first Heracleopolis, then Thebes, for its capital: also **Middle Empire. 2.** The former Chinese Empire, regarded as occupying the center of the world; later, the 18 provinces of China proper.

Middle Latin Medieval Latin. See under LATIN.

Middle Low German See under GERMAN.

mid·dle·man (mid′l·man′) *n. pl.* **·men** (-men′) **1.** One who acts as an agent; intermediary; go-between. **2.** One who buys in bulk from producers and sells to retailers or consumers. **3.** In a minstrel troupe, the interlocutor.

mid·dle·most (mid′l·mōst′) *adj.* Situated exactly or most nearly in the middle: also *midmost.*

mid·dle-of-the-road (mid′l·əv·thə·rōd′) *adj.* Tending toward neither side or extreme; taking a moderate or middle course, especially in politics. Also **mid′dle-road′ing.**

middle of the road A moderate position or course.

mid·dle-of-the-road·er (mid′l·əv·thə·rō′dər) *n.* One who endorses a moderate or middle course, especially in politics. Also **mid·dle-road·er** (mid′l·rō′dər).

Middle Paleolithic See under PALEOLITHIC.

Middle Persian See under PERSIAN.

Mid·dles·brough (mid′lz·brə) A county borough and port in Cleveland, England; pop. 153,900 (1976).

Mid·dle·sex (mid′l·seks) A former county in SE England forming part of the London metropolitan area; 232 sq. mi.; county seat, none (administrative functions are performed at **Middlesex Guildhall,** Westminster). Abbr. *Mdx., Mddx., Middlx., Midx.*

mid·dle-sized (mid′l·sīzd′) *adj.* Of moderate size.

Middle Temple A London legal society, or the set of buildings occupied by it. See INNS OF COURT.

Mid·dle·ton (mid′l·tən), **Thomas,** 1570?–1627, English dramatist.

Mid·dle·town (mid′l·toun′) **1.** A city in SW Ohio; pop. 48,767. **2.** A city in south central Connecticut, on the Connecticut River; pop. 36,924. **3.** A village in eastern New Jersey; pop. 54,623. **4.** A borough in southern Pennsylvania, on the Susquehanna River; pop. 9,080.

mid·dle·weight (mid′l·wāt′) *n.* **1.** A person or animal of average weight. **2.** A boxer or wrestler weighing between 147 and 160 pounds.

Middle West The section of the United States between the Rockies and the Alleghenies and north of the Ohio River and the southern borders of Kansas and Missouri: also *Midwest.* — **Middle Western** — **Middle Westerner**

mid·dling (mid′ling) *adj.* **1.** Of middle size, quality, or condition; ordinary; mediocre. **2.** *Informal* In fair health. — *adv. Informal* Fairly; moderately; tolerably. — *n.* **1.** *pl.* Any of various commodities regarded as intermediate in quality, size, price, etc. **2.** The coarser part of ground grain. **3.** *pl.* Pork or bacon cut from between the shoulder and ham of a hog. [< MID- + -LING²] — **mid′dling·ly** *adv.*

Middlx. Middlesex.

mid·dy (mid′ē) *n. pl.* **·dies** *Informal* **1.** A midshipman. **2.** A middy blouse (which see).

middy blouse A loosely fitting blouse with a sailor collar.

Mid·gard (mid′gärd) In Norse mythology, the earth as the abode of mankind, considered to be encircled by a great serpent: also called *Mithgarth.* Also **Mid′garth** (-gärth). [< ON *Mithgarthr* < *mithr* mid + *garthr* yard, house]

midge (mij) *n.* **1.** A gnat or small fly; especially, any of various small, dipterous insects (family *Chironomidae*). For illustration see INSECTS (injurious). **2.** An extremely small person or creature. [OE *mycge*]

midg·et (mij′it) *n.* **1.** A person of abnormally small size but of normal physical proportions. **2.** Anything very small of its kind. — *adj.* Very small. Compare DWARF, PYGMY.

Mid Glamorgan A county in SE Wales; 393 sq. mi.; pop. 542,000 (1976); administrative headquarters, Cardiff.

mid·gut (mid′gut′) *n. Anat.* The embryonic intestinal structure between the foregut and the hindgut.

Mi·di (mē·dē′) *n. French* The south of France.

Mid·i·an·ite (mid′ē·ən·īt′) *n.* One of an ancient nomadic tribe of NW Arabia. *Gen.* xxv 2. [< *Midian* a son of Abraham < Hebrew *Midhyān*] — **Mid′i·an·it′ish** *adj.*

mi·di·nette (mē·dē·net′) *n. French* A Parisian girl employed in the fashion industry as a seamstress, shopgirl, etc.

mid·i·ron (mid′ī′ərn) *n.* In golf, a five iron.

mid·land (mid′lənd) *n.* The central or interior part of a country or region. — *adj.* Of, pertaining to, or situated in an inland or interior region.

Mid·land (mid′lənd) *n.* The dialects of Middle English spoken in London and the Midlands; especially, **East Midland,** the direct predecessor of Modern English.

Mid·land (mid′lənd) **1.** A city in western Texas; pop. 59,463. **2.** A city in east central Michigan; pop. 35,176.

Mid·lands (mid′ləndz) A region comprising the middle counties of England.

Mid·lo·thi·an (mid·lō′thē·ən) A county in SE Scotland; 366 sq. mi.; pop. 595,590 (est. 1969); county seat, Edinburgh.

mid·most (mid′mōst′) *adj.* Middlemost. — *adv.* In the midst or middle. [OE *mydmest*]

mid·night (mid′nīt′) *n.* The middle of the night; twelve o'clock at night. — *adj.* **1.** Of, pertaining to, or occurring at midnight. **2.** Resembling or suggestive of midnight; very dark. — **to burn the midnight oil** To continue to work or study late into the night.

midnight sun The sun when visible at midnight during the summer months at latitudes greater than about 70° north or south of the equator.

mid·noon (mid′nōōn′) *n.* The middle of the day; noon.

mid·point (mid′point′) *n.* A point at the center or halfway between the extremes, as of a line. Also **mid′-point′.**

Mid·rash (mid′rash, -räsh) *n. pl.* **Mis·rash·im** (mid·rash′-im, -räsh′-, mid′rä·shēm′) or **Mid·rash·oth** (mid·rash′ōth, -räsh′-) In Judaism, the traditional body of commentaries on the Old Testament, dating from the fourth to the twelfth century. Compare HAGGADAH, HALAKAH.

mid·rib (mid′rib′) *n. Bot.* The central vein of a leaf.

mid·riff (mid′rif) *n.* The part of the body between the chest and the abdomen, near the diaphragm; also, the diaphragm itself. [OE *midhrif* < *midd* mid + *hrif* belly]

mid·ship (mid′ship′) *adj. Naut.* Of, pertaining to, or situated in the middle of a ship.

mid·ship·man (mid′ship′mən) *n. pl.* **·men** (-mən) **1.** In the U.S. Navy, a student training to be commissioned as an officer, especially at the U.S. Naval Academy at Annapolis. **2.** In the Royal, Royal Canadian, and other Commonwealth navies, an officer ranking between a naval cadet and the lowest commissioned officer. See table at GRADE. **3.** *Brit.* Formerly, in the Royal Navy, a youth who worked on shipboard to train for a commission. Abbr. *mid.* [< *amidshipman;* so called from being amidships when on duty]

mid·ships (mid′ships′) *Naut. adv.* Amidships. — *n.pl.* The middle part of a vessel.

midst (midst) *n.* **1.** The condition of being surrounded, as by people or things, engaged or involved, as in an activity, or beset, as by troubles or difficulties: used chiefly in the phrase **in the midst of. 2.** The central or interior part; middle. — **Syn.** See CENTER. — **in our** (**your, their**) **midst** Among us (you, them). — *prep.* Amid. [ME < OE *midd* + adverbial *-es* + intrusive or superlative *-t*]

mid·sum·mer (mid′sum′ər) *n.* The middle of summer.

Mid·sum·mer Day (mid′sum′ər) June 24, in Great Britain the summer quarter day.

mid·term (mid′tûrm′) *n.* **1.** The middle of a term. **2.** *U.S.* An examination given in the middle of a school term.

mid·town (mid′toun′) *n.* The central section of a city or town. — *adj.* Located in midtown.

mid-Vic·to·ri·an (mid′vik·tôr′ē·ən, -tō′rē-) *adj.* **1.** Of or pertaining to the middle period of Queen Victoria's reign, about 1850–80. **2.** Victorian in character; prudishly or pompously old-fashioned. — *n.* **1.** One who lived or flourished during this period. **2.** One having mid-Victorian tastes, standards, or ideas.

mid·watch (mid′woch) *n. Naut.* The watch aboard ship between midnight and 4 A.M.

mid·way (mid′wā′; *for adj. and adv., also* mid′wā′) *adv.* In, to, or at the middle of the way or distance. — *adj.* Being in the middle of the way or distance. — *n.* **1.** *U.S.* At a fair, exposition, etc., the area or mall where amusements, side shows, or exhibitions are situated. **2.** *Obs.* The middle or the middle course. [OE *midweg*]

Mid·way Islands (mid′wā′) Two islets NW of Honolulu, belonging to the United States and under jurisdiction of the U.S. Navy; 2 sq. mi.; scene of one of the decisive battles of World War II, June, 1942.

mid·week (mid′wēk′) *n.* The middle of the week.

Mid·week (mid′wēk′) *n.* In the Society of Friends, Wednesday.

Mid·west (mid′west′) *n.* The Middle West (which see). — **Mid′west′ern** *adj.* — **Mid′west′ern·er** *n.*

Midwest City A town in central Oklahoma, a suburb of Oklahoma City; pop. 48,114.

---

mid·wife (mid′wīf′) *n. pl.* **·wives** (-wīvz′) A woman whose occupation is the assisting of women in childbirth. [OE *mid* with + *wif* woman]

mid·wife·ry (mid′wī′fər-ē, -wīf′rē) *n.* The skill or practice of assisting women in childbirth; obstetrics.

mid·win·ter (mid′win′tər) *n.* The middle of winter.

Midx. Middlesex.

mid·year (mid′yir′) *n.* **1.** The middle of the year. **2.** *U.S.* An examination given in the middle of a school year.

mien (mēn) *n.* Manner, bearing, expression, or outward appearance. **— Syn.** See AIR[1]. [? Aphetic form of DEMEAN; infl. by F *mine* < Celtic (Breton) *min* beak, muzzle]

Mies van der Ro·he (mēs′ van dər rō′ə), **Ludwig,** 1886–1969, U.S. architect and industrial designer born in Germany.

miff (mif) *Informal v.t.* **1.** To cause to be offended or annoyed. **— *v.i.* 2.** To take offense. **— *n.* 1.** An ill-tempered mood; huff. **2.** A minor quarrel; tiff. [Origin uncertain. Cf. G *muffen* to sulk.]

mif·fy (mif′ē) *adj.* **·fi·er, ·fi·est** *Informal* Easily offended; very sensitive. **— mif′fi·ness** *n.*

mig (mig) *n. U.S. Dial.* **1.** A marble. **2.** *pl.* The game of marbles. Also **mig·gle** (mig′əl). [Origin uncertain]

might¹ (mīt) Past tense of MAY¹. ♦ Both *may* and *might* are now considered subjunctives with present or future sense, the difference between the two being one of degree rather than of time. *May* implies a greater probability than *might*, the latter indicating possibility but less likelihood: He *might* be on time, but don't depend on it. As a request for permission, *might* is felt to be more hesitant in approach: *Might* we expect your reply by Tuesday?

might² (mīt) *n.* **1.** Power or capacity to dominate, be pre-eminent, etc.; force; strength. **2.** Physical strength. **— with (all one's) might and main** With all one's strength or ability; with utmost endeavor. [OE *meaht, miht*]

might·i·ly (mī′tə-lē) *adv.* **1.** With might, great force, energy or earnestness. **2.** To a great degree; greatly.

might·y (mī′tē) *adj.* **might·i·er, might·i·est 1.** Possessed of or characterized by might; powerful; strong. **2.** Of great or unusual size, importance, etc.; imposing. **— *adv. Informal* Very; exceedingly: a *mighty* fine person. **— might′i·ness** *n.*

mi·gnon (min′yon, Fr. mē-nyôn′) *adj.* Delicately small; dainty. [< F, ? Celtic. Doublet of MINION.] **— mi·gnonne** (min′yon, Fr. mē-nyun′) *adj. fem.*

mi·gnon·ette (min′yən-et′) *n.* **1.** Any of various plants of the genus *Reseda*; especially, *R. odorata*, having racemes of fragrant, yellowish green flowers. **2.** A light yellowish or grayish green. Also called *reseda.* [< F]

mi·graine (mī′grān) *n.* A type of severe, recurrent headache, usually in one side of the head and often accompanied by nausea; also called *hemicrania*. [< F < LL *hemicrania* < Gk. *hēmikrania* < *hēmi* half + *kranion* skull]

mi·grant (mī′grənt) *adj.* Migratory. **— *n.*** One who or that which migrates, as a bird or animal, an itinerant worker, etc. [< L *migrans, -antis,* ppr. of *migrare* to roam, wander]

mi·grate (mī′grāt) *v.i.* **·grat·ed, ·grat·ing 1.** To move from one country, region, etc., to settle in another. **2.** To move periodically or seasonally from one region or climate to another, as birds or fish. [< L *migratus,* pp. of *migrare*] **— mi′gra·tor** *n.*

— Syn. 1. *Migrate, emigrate,* and *immigrate* agree in meaning to change one's place of abode. One may *migrate* to or from a place, whether permanently or transiently. *Emigrate* and *immigrate* imply a more or less permanent change. They are both applied to the same action performed by the same person, but *emigrate* refers to the place of departure and *immigrate* to the new home.

mi·gra·tion (mī-grā′shən) *n.* **1.** The act or procedure of migrating; also, an instance of this. **2.** Those participating in a single instance of migrating. **3.** *Chem.* **a** The shifting of one or more atoms from one position in a molecule to another. **b** The movement of ions under the influence of electromotive force toward one or the other electrode. [< L *migratio, -onis*] **— mi·gra′tion·al** *adj.*

mi·gra·to·ry (mī′grə-tôr′ē, -tō′rē) *adj.* **1.** Characterized by migration; migrating regularly. **2.** Pertaining to or characteristic of migration or those that migrate. **3.** Roving; nomadic; itinerant.

mijn·heer (mə-nir′) *n. Dutch* Mynheer (which see).

mi·ka·do (mi-kä′dō) *n. pl.* **·dos** The emperor of Japan. [< Japanese *mi* august + *kado* door]

mike (mīk) *n. Informal* A microphone.

Mi·khai·lo·vich (mē-khī′lō-vich), **Draja,** 1893–1946, Serbian Chetnik leader in World War II; executed. Also **Draža Mihailović.**

Mi·ko·yan (mi-kô′yän), **Anastas Ivanovich,** born 1895, Soviet statesman and administrator born in Armenia.

mi·kron (mī′kron) See MICRON.

mil (mil) *n.* **1.** A unit of length or diameter, equal to one thousandth of an inch, or 25.4001 microns. See table inside back cover. **2.** A milliliter, or one cubic centimeter. **3.** *Mil.* **a** A unit of angular measure equal to 1/6400 of a circle, or about 0.0560 degree. **b** A unit of angular measure equal to 0.001 radian. **4.** A former monetary unit of Palestine, equal to one thousandth of a pound; also the coin having this value. [< L *mille* thousand]

mil. 1. Mileage. **2.** Military. **3.** Militia. **4.** Million.

mi·la·dy (mi-lā′dē) *n. pl.* **·dies 1.** An English noblewoman or gentlewoman: a Continental term used in addressing or speaking of such a woman. **2.** A fashionable woman. Also **mi·la′di.** [< F < E *my lady*]

mil·age (mī′lij) See MILEAGE.

Mi·lan (mi-lan′, -län′, mil′ən) A Commune in Lombardy, northern Italy, the second largest in the country; pop. 1,683,700 (est. 1967). *Italian* **Mi·la·no** (mē-lä′nō).

Mil·an·ese (mil′ən-ēz′, -ēs′) *adj.* Of or pertaining to Milan, or its people, culture, products, etc. **— *n. pl.* ·ese** A native or inhabitant of Milan.

Mi·laz·zo (mē-lät′sō) A port town in NE Sicily; pop. about 13,000: ancient *Mylae.*

milch (milch) *adj.* Giving milk, as a cow. [OE *-milc*]

mild (mīld) *adj.* **1.** Kind or amiable in behavior, disposition, or manners; not rough or severe; gentle. **2.** Expressing or signifying kindness or gentleness, as words, behavior, etc. **3.** Gentle or moderate in action, effect, or degree; temperate; clement: *mild* weather. **4.** Not harmful, extremely painful, or dangerous: a *mild* headache. **5.** Not strong, sharp, or bitter, as in flavor or odor: a *mild* cigar. **6.** Not intense or strong; tempered; limited: *mild* interest. **7.** *Obs.* Kind or considerate. [OE *milde*] **— mild′ly** *adv.* **— mild′ness** *n.*

mil·den (mīl′dən) *v.t. & v.i.* To make or become mild.

mil·dew (mil′dōō, -dyōō) *n.* **1.** A disease of plants usually caused by a parasitic fungus that deposits a whitish or discolored coating. **2.** Any of the fungi causing such a disease. **3.** Any moldy coating or discoloration appearing on walls, fabric, etc. **— *v.t. & v.i.*** To affect or be affected with mildew. [OE *meledēaw* honeydew] **— mil′dew·y** *adj.*

mild steel *Metall.* A strong and tough but malleable steel containing not more than 0.4 percent carbon.

mile (mīl) *n.* **1.** A measure of distance used in the United States and other English-speaking countries, equal to 5,280 feet, 1,760 yards, or 1,609.35 meters: also called *statute mile.* Abbr. *M., m., mi.* See table inside back cover. **2.** Any considerable distance. **— air mile** or **geographical mile** or **nautical mile** A unit of distance equal to 6,080.2 feet, considered as 1/60 of a degree of the earth's equator. **— international nautical mile** A unit of distance by sea, official in the U.S., equal to 1,852 meters or 6,076.103 feet. **— Roman mile** An ancient Roman distance equal to about 1,620 yards. [OE *mīl* < LL *milia, millia* < *mille* (*passuum*) thousand (paces)]

mile·age (mī′lij) *n.* **1.** Total length or distance, as of a track, a road, a journey, etc., measured or expressed in miles. **2.** Number of miles traveled by an automobile, etc., as estimated for each gallon of fuel used. **3.** Period of usefulness, durability, or wear, estimated by miles used or traveled. **4.** *U.S. Informal* Present and future use or value: an idea with lots of *mileage.* **5.** *U.S.* A traveling allowance estimated at a fixed amount per mile. **6.** The rate per mile charged for the use of a car, for railroad transportation, etc. Also spelled *milage.* Abbr. *mil.*

mileage ticket *U.S.* A ticket, often one of a number forming a **mileage book,** entitling the holder to railroad transportation for a specific number of miles.

mile·post (mīl′pōst′) *n.* A post or similar marker indicating distance in miles, as along a highway.

mil·er (mī′lər) *n.* A runner, racehorse, etc., trained to compete in mile races.

mi·les glo·ri·o·sus (mī′lēz glôr′ē-ō′səs, -glō′rē-) *Latin* A swaggering, boastful soldier, appearing as a stock comic character in drama, etc.

mile·stone (mīl′stōn′) *n.* **1.** A post, pillar, or stone set up to indicate distance in miles from a given point. **2.** An important event or turning point in a lifetime, a career, etc.

Mi·le·tus (mī-lē′təs) An ancient city in western Asia Minor. **— Mi·le′sian** (-zhən, -shən) *adj. & n.*

mil·foil (mil′foil) *n.* The yarrow, a plant. [< OF < L *millefolium* < *mille* thousand + *folium* leaf]

Mil·ford (mil′fərd) A city in SW Connecticut, near Bridgeport; pop. 50,858.

Mil·ford Ha·ven (mil′fərd hā′vən) An urban district and port in southern Pembroke, Wales; pop. 12,802 (1961).

Mil·haud (mē-yō′), **Darius,** 1892–1974, French composer.

mil·i·a (mil′ē-ə) Plural of MILIUM.

mil·i·a·ri·a (mil′ē-âr′ē-ə) *n. Pathol.* An inflammation of the sweat glands, with eruption of small papules and vesicles, and often redness and itching; especially, prickly heat. [< NL, fem of L *miliarius.* See MILIARY.]

mil·i·ar·y (mil′ē-er′ē, mil′yə-rē) *adj.* **1.** Resembling millet seeds. **2.** *Pathol.* Accompanied by a rash of pimples the size of millet seeds. [< L *miliarus* < *milium* millet]

miliary tuberculosis A form of tuberculosis marked by the discharge of bacillary tubercles into one or more organs.

mi·lieu (mē-lyœ′) *n.* Environment; surroundings. [< F < OF *mi* middle (< L *medius*) + *lieu* place < L *locus*]

MILESTONE
(Brooklyn,
N.Y., 17th
century)

milit. Military.

mil·i·tant (mil′ə-tənt) *adj.* **1.** Combative or warlike in nature or tendency; aggressive. **2.** Positive and forceful in action; resolute. **3.** Engaged in conflict; fighting. — *n.* One who is militant. [< L *militans, -antis,* ppr. of *militare* to be a soldier] — **mil′i·tan·cy** *n.* — **mil′i·tant·ly** *adv.*

mil·i·ta·rism (mil′ə-tə-riz′əm) *n.* **1.** The ideals or tendencies characteristic of a military class; glorification of or emphasis on martial qualities or standards. **2.** A national policy that promotes a powerful military position, a large standing army, and constant preparation for war. **3.** Domination by a strong military class, its policies, and its ideals. — **mil′i·ta·rist** (mil′ə-tə-rist) *n.* **1.** An advocate or adherent of militarism. **2.** One devoted to or expert in military matters. — **mil′i·ta·ris′tic** *adj.* — **mil′i·ta·rist′i·cal·ly** *adv.*

mil·i·ta·rize (mil′ə-tə-rīz) *v.t.* **·rized, ·riz·ing 1.** To convert to a military system or adapt for military purposes. **2.** To train, prepare, or equip for warfare. **3.** To imbue with militarism. — **mil′i·ta·ri·za′tion** *n.*

mil·i·tar·y (mil′ə-ter′ē) *adj.* **1.** Of or pertaining to the armed forces, their activities, personnel, equipment, etc. **2.** Of, pertaining to, or characteristic of warfare. **3.** Characteristic of or befitting a soldier or soldiers; martial. **4.** Belonging to or connected with the army. — *n.* Soldiers collectively; armed forces: preceded by *the.* [< F *militaire* < L *militaris* < *miles, militis* soldier] — **mil′i·tar·i·ly** *adv.*

military academy A school for boys or young men combining military and academic training; especially, the **U.S. Military Academy** at West Point, New York. Abbr. *M.A.*

military governor A military officer serving as the civil governor of a state or territory under martial law.

military law A system or body of laws relating to the administration and discipline of the armed forces. Compare MARTIAL LAW.

military police Members of the army who perform police duty. Abbr. *MP*

mil·i·tate (mil′ə-tāt) *v.i.* **·tat·ed, ·tat·ing** To have influence or effect: with *against,* or, more rarely, *for*: The evidence *militated* against him. [< L *militatus,* pp. of *militare* to be a soldier < *miles, militis* soldier]

mi·li·tia (mə-lish′ə) *n.* **1.** A body of citizens enrolled and drilled in military organizations other than the regular military forces, and called out only in emergencies. **2.** *U.S.* Able-bodied male citizens between eighteen and forty-five years of age not members of the regular military forces, and legally subject to call for military duty. Abbr. *mil.* [< L, military service < *miles, militis* soldier]

mi·li·tia·man (mə-lish′ə-mən) *n.* *pl.* **·men** (mən) A member of the militia.

mil·i·um (mil′ē-əm) *n.* *pl.* **mil·i·a** (mil′ē-ə) *Pathol.* A small, whitish globule on the surface of the skin, containing retained sebaceous material. [< L, millet; from its resemblance to a millet seed]

milk (milk) *n.* **1.** The opaque, whitish liquid secreted by the mammary glands of female mammals for the nourishment of their young; especially, cow's milk, drunk or used by human beings. **2.** Any of various liquids resembling this, as: **a** The sap of certain plants. **b** The liquid contained in a coconut. **c** Any of various emulsions or suspensions used in medicine, etc. — *v.t.* **1.** To draw or express milk from the mammary glands of. **2.** To draw off or drain by or as by milking. **3.** To draw or extract something from: to *milk* someone of information. **4.** To exploit; take advantage of: to *milk* a client. — *v.i.* **5.** To milk (a cow, cows, etc.). **6.** To yield milk. [OE *meolc, milc*]

milk adder The milk snake (which see).

milk-and-wa·ter (milk′ən-wô′tər, -wot′ər) *adj.* Lacking force or character; weak; mawkish; namby-pamby.

milk·er (mil′kər) *n.* **1.** One who milks. **2.** A mechanical device for milking cows. **3.** A domestic animal, as a cow, that gives milk.

milk fever **1.** *Pathol.* Fever due to puerperal infection, occurring shortly after childbirth when milk is first secreted. **2.** *Vet.* A similar disease of cows, etc.

milk·fish (milk′fish) *n.* *pl.* **·fish** or **·fish·es** A large fish (*Chanos chanos*) of South Pacific waters, allied to the herring.

milk glass Whitish glass having a milky appearance.

milk leg A painful swelling of the leg in women shortly after childbirth, resulting from phlebitis of the femoral vein: also called *phlegmasia dolens.*

milk·maid (milk′mād′) *n.* A woman or girl who milks cows or works in a dairy.

milk·man (milk′man′) *n.* *pl.* **·men** (-men′) **1.** A man who sells or delivers milk. **2.** A man who milks cows.

milk of magnesia A white, aqueous suspension of magnesium hydroxide, $Mg(OH)_2$, used as a laxative and antacid.

milk punch A beverage made with milk, liquor, sugar, etc.

milk run *Slang* In the U.S. Air Force, a routine mission of little danger.

milk shake A drink made of chilled, flavored milk, sometimes ice cream, shaken, beaten, or whipped.

milk sickness *Pathol.* A disease caused by drinking milk from cows that have fed on certain poisonous plants.

milk snake A nonpoisonous snake (*Lampropeltis doliata*) of eastern North America, feeding on small rodents, frogs, etc., and often frequenting houses: also called *milk adder.*

milk·sop (milk′sop′) *n.* A weak, timorous fellow; sissy.

milk sugar Lactose.

milk·toast (milk′tōst′) *n.* **1.** A dish of buttered toast served in hot milk. **2.** See MILQUETOAST.

milk tooth One of the temporary or deciduous teeth of a mammal.

milk vetch Any of various leguminous plants (genus *Astragalus*) supposed to promote greater production of milk in goats; especially, a European species (*A. glycyphyllos*).

milk·weed (milk′wēd′) *n.* **1.** Any of a genus (*Asclepias*) of plants typical of a family (*Asclepiadaceae*) of herbs, shrubs, and vines having milky juice; especially, the **common milkweed** (*A. syriaca*), having clusters of dull purple flowers. **2.** Any of various other plants having milky juice.

milkweed butterfly A monarch (def. 4).

milk·wort (milk′wûrt′) *n.* **1.** One of a genus (*Polygala*) typifying a family (*Polygalaceae*) of plants of temperate or tropical regions, as the **purple milkwort** (*P. sanguinea*), and the **whorled milkwort** (*P. verticillata*) of eastern North America. **2.** The sea milkwort (which see).

milk·y (mil′kē) *adj.* **milk·i·er, milk·i·est 1.** Resembling or suggestive of milk in color, appearance, etc. **2.** Containing or yielding milk or a milklike substance. **3.** Very mild, bland, or spiritless. — **milk′i·ly** *adv.* — **milk′i·ness** *n.*

Milky Way A luminous band visible across the night sky, composed of distant stars and nebulae not separately distinguishable to the naked eye: also called the *Galaxy.*

milk-white (milk′hwīt′) Having the white or bluish white color of milk.

mill¹ (mil) *n.* **1.** A machine or mechanical device by means of which a solid or coarse substance is ground, crushed, or reduced to a pulp. **2.** A device, machine, building, or establishment in which grain is ground. **3.** Any of various machines that process materials, perform a continuous operation, etc., often by means of rotary parts or action: often used in combination: *sawmill; windmill.* **4.** A building or establishment equipped with machinery for manufacturing, performing an industrial process, etc.; factory. **5.** A hardened steel roller bearing a design in relief, by which a printing plate or a die is produced by pressure. **6.** A process, agency, etc., that operates mechanically or in a routine fashion. **7.** A trying or grueling experience; ordeal: used chiefly in the phrase **through the mill. 8.** *Archaic Slang* A boxing contest; fist fight. — *v.t.* **1.** To grind, roll, shape, polish, etc., in or with a mill. **2.** To raise, indent, or ridge the edge of (a coin, etc.). **3.** To cause to move in a circle, as cattle. **4.** To beat or whip to a froth, as chocolate. **5.** *Archaic Slang* To strike with the fists; thrash. — *v.i.* **6.** To move with a circular or surging motion, as a herd of cattle, a crowd, etc. **7.** *Archaic Slang* To box or fight. [OE *myln, mylen* < LL *molina* < L *mola* millstone]

mill² (mil) *n.* A monetary denomination of the United States, one tenth of a cent, or one thousandth of a dollar. Abbr. *m., M., mi.* [< L *mille* thousand]

Mill (mil), **James,** 1773–1836, British philosopher, historian, and political economist. — **John Stuart,** 1806–73, English philosopher and political economist, son of the preceding.

Mil·lais (mi-lā′), **Sir John Everett,** 1829–96, English painter.

Mil·lay (mi-lā′), **Edna St. Vincent,** 1892–1950, U.S. poet.

mill·board (mil′bôrd′, -bōrd′) *n.* Heavy pasteboard used for the covers of books.

Mill·creek (mil′krēk′) A borough in south central Pennsylvania, on the Juniata River; pop. 28,441.

mill·dam (mil′dam′) *n.* **1.** A dam constructed across a watercourse to raise its level sufficiently to turn a mill wheel. **2.** The pond formed by such a dam; millpond.

milled (mild) *adj.* **1.** Ground, mixed, worked, shaped, etc., in a mill. **2.** Ridged or grooved, as the edge of a coin.

mil·le·nar·i·an (mil′ə-nâr′ē-ən) *adj.* Of or pertaining to a thousand, especially to the years of the millennium. — *n.* One who believes in the millennium. — **mil′le·nar′i·an·ism** *n.*

mil·le·nar·y (mil′ə-ner′ē) *adj.* **1.** Of or pertaining to a thousand, especially a thousand years; millenary; millennial. **2.** Pertaining to the millennium or the millenarians. — *n.* *pl.* **·nar·ies 1.** A thousand; especially, a space of a thousand years or a millennium. **2.** A millenarian. [< LL *millenarius* < L *milleni* a thousand each < *mille* thousand]

mil·len·ni·al (mi-len′ē-əl) *adj.* Of or pertaining to the millennium or to any period of a thousand years. — *n.* A thousandth anniversary. — **mil·len′ni·al·ist** *n.* — **mil·len′ni·al·ly** *adv.*

mil·len·ni·um (mi-len′ē-əm) *n.* *pl.* **·ni·a** (-nē-ə) or **·ni·ums 1.** A period of a thousand years. **2.** The thousand years during which Christ is to rule the world, according to the New Testament. *Rev.* xx 1–5. **3.** Any period of happiness, prosperity, etc. [< NL < *mille* thousand + *annus* year]

mil·le·ped (mil'ə·ped), **mil·le·pede** (mil'ə·pēd) See MILLIPEDE.

mil·le·pore (mil'ə·pôr, -pōr) *n. Zool.* Any of a group of coralline hydrozoans (genus *Millepora*) that form large branching structures containing numerous tiny surface cavities. [< F *millepore* < *mille* thousand + *pore* pore]

mill·er (mil'ər) *n.* 1. One who operates or tends a mill, especially a gristmill. 2. A milling machine. 3. Any of various moths having pale, dusty wings.

Mil·ler (mil'ər), **Arthur,** born 1915, U.S. novelist and playwright. — **Henry,** born 1891, U.S. author. — **Joaquin,** 1839–1913, U.S. poet: original name **Cincinnatus Heine Miller.** — **Joe,** 1684–1738, English comedian: original name **Josias Miller.** — **William,** 1782–1849, U.S. religious leader; founder of the Millerites.

Mil·le·rand (mēl·rän'), **Alexandre,** 1859–1943, French statesman; president 1920–24.

mil·ler·ite (mil'ər·īt) *n.* A metallic, brass-yellow, brittle nickel sulfide, NiS, crystallizing in the hexagonal system. [after W. H. *Miller,* 1801–80, British mineralogist]

Mil·ler·ite (mil'ər·īt) *n.* A follower of William Miller, who announced in 1831 that Christ's second coming and the end of the world would take place in 1843. See ADVENTIST. — **Mil'ler·ism** *n.*

miller's-thumb (mil'ərz·thum') *n.* A small, fresh-water fish (genus *Cottus*), having a broad, flattened head and spiny fins: also called *bullhead.*

mil·les·i·mal (mi·les'ə·məl) *adj.* 1. Of, pertaining to, or consisting of a thousandth. 2. Thousandth. — *n.* A thousandth. [< L *millesimus* < *mille* thousand]

mil·let (mil'it) *n.* 1. A grass (*Panicum miliaceum*) cultivated in the United States for forage, and in many parts of the Old World for its small, edible seeds. 2. Any of various similar grasses, as the **foxtail** or **Italian millet** (*Setaria italica*); **pearl millet** (*Pennisetum glaucum*), etc. 3. The seed of these grasses. [< F, dim. of *mil* < L *milium*]

Mil·let (mē·le'), **Jean François,** 1814–75, French painter.

milli- *combining form* 1. In the metric system and in technical use, one thousandth of (a specified unit), as in the following list of self-explanatory compounds:

milliampere	millifarad	milliphot
milliangstrom	millihenry	millivolt
millicurie	millilux	milliwatt

2. *Obs.* A thousand. [< L *mille* thousand]

mil·liard (mil'yərd) *n. Brit.* A thousand millions: called a *billion* in the U.S. [< F < Provençal *milhar* thousand]

mil·li·ar·y (mil'ē·er'ē) *adj.* Pertaining to or indicating a Roman mile. See under MILE.

mil·li·bar (mil'ə·bär) *n.* A unit of atmospheric pressure equal to one thousandth of a bar.

mil·li·gram (mil'ə·gram) *n.* A unit of weight in the metric system, equal to one thousandth of a gram. Also **mil'li·gramme.** Abbr. *mg, mg., mgm.* See table inside back cover.

Mil·li·kan (mil'ə·kən), **Robert Andrews,** 1868–1955, U.S. physicist.

mil·li·li·ter (mil'ə·lē'tər) *n.* A unit of capacity in the metric system, equal to one thousandth of a liter. Also *esp. Brit.* **mil'li·litre.** Abbr. *ml, ml.* See table inside back cover.

mil·li·me·ter (mil'ə·mē'tər) *n.* A unit of length in the metric system, equal to one thousandth of a meter. Also *esp. Brit.* **mil'li·me·tre.** Abbr. *mm, mm.* See table inside back cover.

mil·li·mi·cron (mil'ə·mī'kron) *n.* A unit of length equal to one thousandth of a micron, or one millionth of a millimeter: also called *micromillimeter.*

mil·li·ner (mil'ə·nər) *n.* One who makes or sells women's hats. [< *Milaner* an inhabitant of Milan, Italy; hence, one from Milan who imported silks, etc.]

mil·li·ner·y (mil'ə·ner'ē, -nər·ē) *n.* 1. The articles made or sold by milliners. 2. The business of a milliner.

mill·ing (mil'ing) *n.* 1. The act or process of one who or that which mills; especially, the operation of grinding, cutting, shaping, or finishing something in, with, or as with a mill. 2. Ridges or grooves on the edge of a coin, etc.

milling machine A machine for cutting or shaping metal, etc., usually by means of a rotary cutter.

mil·lion (mil'yən) *n.* 1. A thousand thousands, written as 1,000,000: a cardinal number. Abbr. *mil.* 2. A million units of money, as of dollars, francs, or pounds: He is worth a *million.* 3. An indefinitely great number. — **the million** The common people. — *adj.* 1. Being a million in number. 2. Very many. [< OF < Ital. *millione* (now *milione*), aug. of *mille* thousand]

mil·lion·aire (mil'yən·âr') *n.* One whose wealth is valued at a million or more, as of dollars, pounds, etc. Also **mil'lion·naire'.** [< F *millionnaire*] — **mil'lion·air'ess** *n.fem.*

mil·lionth (mil'yənth) *adj.* 1. Having the number one million: the ordinal of *million.* 2. Being one of a million equal parts. — *n.* 1. One of a million equal parts. 2. That which is numbered one million.

mil·li·pede (mil'ə·pēd) *n.* Any of various myriapods (class *Diplopoda*) having a rounded body divided into numerous segments, nearly all of which bear two pairs of appendages: also spelled *milleped, mil-*

lepede. Also **mil'li·ped** (-ped). [< L *millepeda* < *mille* thousand + *pes, pedis* foot]

mill·pond (mil'pond') *n.* A body of water dammed up to supply power for running a mill.

mill·race (mil'rās') *n.* 1. The current of water that operates a mill wheel. 2. The channel or sluiceway through which such a current runs.

Mills bomb (milz) A type of highly explosive hand grenade. Also **Mills grenade.** [after Sir William *Mills,* 1856–1932, English inventor]

mill·stone (mil'stōn') *n.* 1. One of a pair of thick, heavy, stone disks used for grinding grain, etc. 2. That which crushes or bears down. 3. A heavy or burdensome weight.

mill·stream (mil'strēm') *n.* 1. A stream whose current is used to operate a mill. 2. The water in a millrace.

mill wheel A water wheel that drives a mill.

mill·work (mil'wûrk') *n.* Objects or material finished or processed in a mill; especially, woodwork ready for use.

mill·wright (mil'rīt') *n.* One who plans, builds, or repairs mills or mill machinery.

Milne (miln), **A**(**lan**) **A**(**lexander**), 1882–1956, English playwright, novelist, and writer of children's books.

mi·lo (mī'lō) *n.* A variety of hardy, drought-resistant grain sorghum bearing dense heads of bearded white or yellow seeds. [Var. of *milo-maize* < MILLET + MAIZE]

Mi·lo (mī'lō) Sixth-century B.C. Greek athlete.

Mi·lo (mī'lō) The southwesternmost island of the Cyclades group; 61 sq. mi.: also *Melos.* Also **Mi'los** (-lôs).

mi·lord (mi·lôrd') *n.* An English nobleman or gentleman: a Continental term used in addressing or speaking of such a man. [< F < E *my lord*]

milque·toast (milk'tōst') *n.* A timid, meek, or very apologetic person: also spelled *milktoast.* [after Caspar *Milquetoast,* a creation by H. T. Webster, U.S. cartoonist]

mil·reis (mil'rās') *n. pl.* **·reis** 1. A former Brazilian monetary unit, equivalent to 1,000 reis; also, a coin of this value. 2. A former Portuguese monetary unit and coin. [< Pg., lit., a thousand reis, pl. of REAL²]

milt (milt) *n.* 1. The seminal secretion of a fish. 2. The reproductive organs of a male fish when filled with seminal fluid. 3. *Obs.* The spleen. — *v.t.* To impregnate (fish roe) with milt. [OE *milte*]

milt·er (mil'tər) *n.* A male fish at spawning time.

Mil·ti·a·des (mil·tī'ə·dēz), died 489? B.C., Athenian general; defeated the Persians at Marathon 490 B.C.

Mil·ton (mil'tən) A town in eastern Massachusetts, near Boston; pop. 27,190.

Mil·ton (mil'tən), **John,** 1608–74, English poet and essayist.

Mil·ton·ic (mil·ton'ik) *adj.* Of, pertaining to, or characteristic of the poet Milton or his works or style; sublime; majestic. Also **Mil·to'ni·an** (-tō'nē·ən).

Mil·town (mil'toun) *n.* Proprietary name for a brand of meprobamate used in pill form as a tranquilizer.

Mil·wau·kee (mil·wô'kē) A port city in SE Wisconsin, on Lake Michigan; pop. 717,372.

mim (mim) *adj. Brit. Dial.* Primly modest. [Imit.]

mime (mīm) *n.* 1. An actor, comedian, etc., who specializes in mimicry or pantomime. 2. A type of dramatic farce popular in classical times, in which actual persons or events were mimicked or ludicrously represented. 3. An actor in such performances. — *v.* **mimed, mim·ing** — *v.i.* 1. To play a part with gestures and, usually, without words; act as a mimic. — *v.t.* 2. To portray by mimicry or pantomime. [< L *mimus* < Gk. *mimos*] — **mim'er** *n.*

mim·e·o·graph (mim'ē·ə·graf', -gräf') *n.* 1. A duplicating device that reproduces copies of written or typewritten matter, tracings, etc., by means of a stencil wrapped around a rotary drum: also **Mim'e·o·graph'.** 2. A copy made by such a device. — *v.t. & v.i.* To reproduce by mimeograph. [< *Mimeograph,* a trade name]

mi·me·sis (mi·mē'sis, mī-) *n.* 1. Imitation or representation of the speech, carriage, gestures, etc., of an individual or a people, as in art and literature. 2. *Biol.* Mimicry. [< NL < Gk. *mimēsis* imitation]

mi·met·ic (mi·met'ik, mī-) *adj.* 1. Tending to imitate or mimic; imitative. 2. Pertaining to, characterized by, or of the nature of imitation, mimicry, or mimesis. 3. Mimic (*adj.* def. 2). [< Gk. *mimētikos*] — **mi·met'i·cal·ly** *adv.*

mim·ic (mim'ik) *v.t.* **·icked, ·ick·ing** 1. To imitate the speech or actions of, as in ridicule. 2. To copy closely; ape. 3. To have or assume the color, shape, etc., of; simulate: Some insects *mimic* leaves. — *n.* 1. One who mimics or imitates; especially, one clever at mimicry, as an actor or buffoon. 2. A copy; imitation. — *adj.* 1. Of the nature of mimicry; imitative; mimetic: a *mimic* gesture. 2. Copying something real; simulated; mock. [< L *mimicus* < Gk. *mimikos* < *mimos* mime] — **mim'i·cal** *adj.* — **mim'ick·er** *n.*

mim·ic·ry (mim'ik·rē) *n. pl.* **·ries** 1. The act, practice, or art of mimicking or imitating. 2. *Biol.* An imitative superficial resemblance of an organism to another or to its immediate environment, for purposes of concealment or protection: also called *mimesis.*

Mi·mir (mē'mir) In Norse mythology, the giant who guarded the well of wisdom flowing from the root of Ygdrasil.

mi·mo·sa (mi·mō′sə, -zə) *n.* **1.** Any of a large genus (*Mimosa*) of leguminous tropical herbs, shrubs, or trees with feathery, bipinnate foliage, and clusters of small, often yellow, flowers; especially, the sensitive plant (def. 1). **2.** Any of various similar or related plants. [< NL < L *mimus* mime; from its supposed mimicry of animal life]

min. **1.** Mineralogical; mineralogy. **2.** Minim(s). **3.** Minimum. **4.** Mining. **5.** Minor. **6.** Minute(s).

mi·na[1] (mī′nə) *n.* *pl.* **·nae** (-nē) or **·nas** An ancient Greek and Asian weight or sum of money of varying amount or value, often equal to 100 drachmas. [< L < Gk. *mna*]

mi·na[2] See MYNA.

mi·na·cious (mi·nā′shəs) *adj.* Threatening; menacing. [< L *minax, minacis.* See MENACE.] — **mi·na′cious·ly** *adv.* — **mi·na′cious·ness, mi·nac·i·ty** (mi·nas′ə·tē) *n.*

min·a·ret (min′ə·ret′) *n.* **1.** A high, slender tower attached to a Muslim mosque and surrounded by one or more balconies, from which a muezzin calls the summons to prayer. **2.** Any similar structure. [< Sp. *minarete* < Turkish *manārat* < Arabic *manārah* lamp, lighthouse < *minār* candlestick]

Mi·nas Basin (mī′nəs) The southern inlet of the Bay of Fundy, Nova Scotia; connected to it by the **Minas Channel** (24 mi. long).

Mi·nas de Ri·o·tin·to (mē′näs thā rē′ō·tēn′tō) A commune in SW Spain; site of copper mines; pop. about 9,000: also *Riotinto*.

Mi·nas Ge·rais (mē′näzh zhə·rīs′) A State of eastern Brazil; 224,701 sq. mi.; pop. 8,642,000 (est. 1958); capital, Belo Horizonte. Formerly **Mi′nas Ge·raes′**.

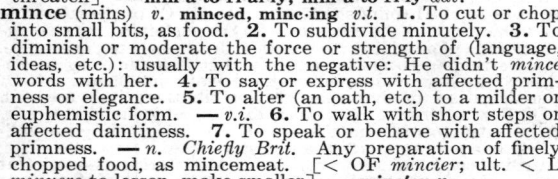

MINARETS ON A MOSQUE

min·a·to·ry (min′ə·tôr′ē, -tō′rē) *adj.* Conveying or expressing a threat; menacing. Also **min′a·to′ri·al.** [< OF *minatoire* < LL *minatorius* < *minatus,* pp. of *minari* to threaten] — **min′a·to′ri·al·ly, min′a·to′ri·ly** *adv.*

mince (mins) *v.* **minced, minc·ing** *v.t.* **1.** To cut or chop into small bits, as food. **2.** To subdivide minutely. **3.** To diminish or moderate the force or strength of (language, ideas, etc.): usually with the negative: He didn't *mince* words with her. **4.** To say or express with affected primness or elegance. **5.** To alter (an oath, etc.) to a milder or euphemistic form. — *v.i.* **6.** To walk with short steps or affected daintiness. **7.** To speak or behave with affected primness. — *n.* *Chiefly Brit.* Any preparation of finely chopped food, as mincemeat. [< OF *mincier*; ult. < L *minuere* to lessen, make smaller] — **minc′er** *n.*

mince·meat (mins′mēt′) *n.* A mixture of chopped apples, raisins, spices, etc., used as a pie filling. — **to make mince·meat of** To cut up, destroy, or annihilate utterly.

mince pie A pie filled with mincemeat.

minc·ing (min′sing) *adj.* Affectedly precise, refined, or dainty, as in manner, gait, etc. — **minc′ing·ly** *adv.*

mind (mīnd) *n.* **1.** The aggregate of processes originating in or associated with the brain, involving conscious and subconscious thought, interpretation of perceptions, insight, imagination, etc. **2.** Memory; remembrance; recollection: within the *mind* of man. **3.** Opinion; sentiment; conviction: to change one's *mind.* **4.** Desire; inclination; wish: to have a *mind* to leave. **5.** Way or state of thinking or feeling; mental disposition; temper: a liberal *mind*; a logical *mind.* **6.** Intellectual power or capacity; intelligence: He has the *mind* for such work. **7.** The faculty of cognition and intellect, as opposed to the will and emotions: a noble heart and a cultivated *mind.* **8.** A person regarded as having intellect; a highly intelligent individual: the great *minds* of our time. **9.** Sound mental condition; sanity; reason: to lose one's *mind.* **10.** Attention: to keep one's *mind* on a subject. **11.** *Philos.* Spirit or intelligence regarded as the basic substance of the universe, and sometimes distinguished from matter; psychical being. **12.** *Cap.* In Christian Science, the divine Principle; God: also *Divine* **Mind.** — *Syn.* See INTELLECT. — **a piece of one's mind** **1.** One's bluntly or candidly expressed opinion. **2.** A severe scolding. — **on one's mind** In one's thoughts, especially so as to cause concern or worry. — **out of one's mind** **1.** Insane; mad. **2.** Distracted; frantic. — **to bear** (or **keep**) **in mind** To focus one's thoughts or attention on; remember. — **to be of one mind** To be in accord; agree. — **to be of two minds** To be indecisive or uncertain. — **to have a good** (or **great**) **mind** To feel strongly disposed (to do something). — **to have in mind** To be thinking about. — **to make up one's mind** To decide; be determined. — *v.t.* **1.** To pay attention to; occupy oneself with: *Mind* your own business. **2.** To be careful or wary concerning: *Mind* your step. **3.** To give heed to, as commands; obey: *Mind* your leaders. **4.** To care for; look after; tend: to *mind* the children. **5.** To be concerned about; care about. **6.** To

object to: Do you *mind* the noise? **7.** *Dial.* To be aware of; notice; perceive. **8.** *Dial.* To remember. **9.** *Archaic* To remind. **10.** *Obs.* To intend or purpose. — *v.i.* **11.** To pay attention; take notice; heed: *Mind* you now, not a word. **12.** To be obedient. **13.** To be concerned; care; object: I don't *mind.* **14.** To be careful. [OE *gemynd*] — **mind′er** *n.*

Min·da·na·o (min′də·nä′ō) The southernmost and second largest island in the Philippines; 36,537 sq. mi.

Mindanao Trench A depression in the ocean floor just east and SE of the Philippines; 34,440 ft.: also *Philippine Trench.* Also **Mindanao Deep.**

mind·ed (mīn′did) *adj.* **1.** Having or characterized by a (specified kind of) mind: used in combination: *evil-minded.* **2.** Having an inclination; disposed: often with *to.*

mind·ful (mīnd′fəl) *adj.* Keeping in mind; heeding; aware. — **mind′ful·ly** *adv.* — **mind′ful·ness** *n.*

mind·less (mīnd′lis) *adj.* **1.** Devoid of intelligence; senseless. **2.** Not giving heed or attention; careless. — **mind′less·ly** *adv.* — **mind′less·ness** *n.*

Min·do·ro (min·dô′rō) An island in the central Philippines; 3,759 sq. mi.

mind reader One supposedly or apparently able to perceive the thoughts or intentions of others without their being overtly or consciously made known. — **mind reading**

Mind·szen·ty (mind′sen·tē), **Joseph,** born 1892, Hungarian cardinal.

mine[1] (mīn) *n.* **1.** An excavation in the earth dug to obtain coal, metallic ores, precious stones, etc. **2.** The site of such an excavation, together with its buildings, equipment, etc. **3.** Any deposit of material that may be excavated or obtained from the earth, as ore or coal. **4.** Any productive source or abundant store of something: a *mine* of talent. **5.** *Mil.* **a** An encased explosive charge placed in the earth or water to destroy enemy personnel, equipment, ships, etc., and designed to be actuated by contact, a time fuse, or remote control. **b** Formerly, an underground tunnel dug beneath an enemy's fortifications, as for the placement of explosives. **6.** A channel or groove made by an insect in a leaf, etc. — *v.* **mined, min·ing** *v.t.* **1.** To dig (coal, ores, etc.) from the earth. **2.** To dig into (the earth, etc.) for coal, ores, etc. **3.** To make by digging, as a tunnel; burrow. **4.** To obtain useful material or information from, as by purposeful effort, diligent search, etc. **5.** To dig a tunnel under, as for placing an explosive mine. **6.** To attack or destroy by slow or secret means; undermine. **7.** To place an explosive mine or mines in or under. — *v.i.* **8.** To dig in a mine for coal, ores, etc.; work in a mine. **9.** To make a tunnel, etc., by digging. **10.** To place explosive mines. [< OF < Celtic. Cf. Irish *mein* vein of metal]

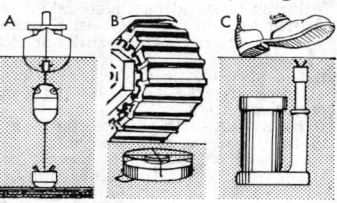

MINES (def. 5a)
A Contact moored-type submarine mine. *B* Antitank land mine. *C* Antipersonnel mine.

mine[2] (mīn) *pron.* **1.** The possessive case of the pronoun *I,* used predicatively: That book is *mine.* **2.** The one or ones belonging or relating to me: His work is better than *mine*; Fortune has been good to me and *mine.* — **of mine** Belonging or relating to me; my. — *pronominal adj.* *Archaic* My: used before a vowel or *h: mine* eyes. [OE *mīn*]

mine detector An electromagnetic device used to locate the position of explosive mines. — **mine detection**

mine·field (mīn′fēld′) *n.* An area on land or in water in which explosive mines have been systematically placed.

mine·lay·er (mīn′lā′ər) *n.* A vessel provided with special equipment for laying explosive mines.

min·er (mīn′ər) *n.* **1.** One who mines; especially, one whose occupation is working in a mine. **2.** Any of various insects whose larvae feed upon and are destructive to plants.

min·er·al (min′ər·əl) *n.* **1.** A naturally occurring, homogeneous substance formed by inorganic processes and having a characteristic set of physical properties, a definite and limited range of chemical composition, and a molecular structure usually expressed in crystalline form. **2.** Inorganic material, especially as distinguished from animal or vegetable matter. **3.** *Mining* Any ore. **4.** *pl. Brit. Informal* Carbonated drinks. — *adj.* **1.** Pertaining to, consisting of, or of the nature of a mineral or minerals. **2.** Impregnated with mineral constituents. [< OF < Med.L *minerale,* neut. sing. of *mineralis* of a mine < *minera* a mine]

mineral. Mineralogy.

min·er·al·ize (min′ər·əl·īz′) *v.* **·ized, ·iz·ing** *v.t.* **1.** To convert (a metal) to a mineral. **2.** To convert to a mineral substance; petrify. **3.** To impregnate with minerals. — *v.i.* **4.** To observe, study, and collect minerals: also **min·er·al·o·gize** (min′ə·ral′ə·jīz). — **min′er·al·i·za′tion** *n.*

min·er·al·iz·er (min′ər-əl-īz′ər) *n.* **1.** An element that combines with a metal to form an ore, as sulfur. **2.** A substance that facilitates the recrystallization of rocks.

mineral jelly A type of petrolatum used as a stabilizer for certain explosives.

mineral kingdom The division of nature comprising all inorganic and nonliving materials, as rocks, metals, minerals, etc. Compare ANIMAL KINGDOM, VEGETABLE KINGDOM.

min·er·al·o·gist (min′ə-ral′ə-jist, -rol′-) *n.* One who specializes in mineralogy.

min·er·al·o·gy (min′ə-ral′ə-jē, -rol′-) *n. pl.* **·gies 1.** The science of minerals, embracing their origin, structure, characteristics, properties, and classification. **2.** A treatise on minerals. Abbr. *min., mineral.* **— min′er·a·log′i·cal** (-ər-ə-loj′i-kəl) *adj.* **— min′er·a·log′i·cal·ly** *adv.*

mineral oil Any of various oils, especially petroleum, derived from minerals and used as a fuel, in medicine, etc.

mineral pitch Asphalt (def. 1).

mineral spring A spring containing natural mineral water.

mineral water Any water naturally containing or artificially impregnated with mineral salts or gases, especially those considered to have therapeutic value.

mineral wax Ozocerite.

mineral wool A fibrous, woollike material made from a mixture of stone and molten slag, used as packing and as insulation in buildings: also called *rock wool, slag wool.*

Mi·ner·va (mi-nûr′və) In Roman mythology, the goddess of wisdom, invention, and handicraft: identified with the Greek *Athena.*

min·e·stro·ne (min′ə-strō′nē, *Ital.* mē′nä-strō′nä) *n. Italian* A thick vegetable soup having a meat stock and containing vermicelli, barley, etc.

mine·sweep·er (mīn′swē′pər) *n.* **1.** A ship equipped to detect, destroy, and remove marine mines. **2.** A heavy roller attached to the front of a tank for exploding land mines.

Ming (ming) *n.* In Chinese history, the last ruling dynasty (1368–1644) of truly Chinese origin, noted for its scholarly and artistic achievements, especially for its porcelains. [< Chinese, lit., luminous]

min·gle (ming′gəl) *v.* **·gled, ·gling** *v.t.* **1.** To mix or unite together; blend. **2.** To join or combine in intimate association; bring into close relation: to *mingle* cultures. **3.** To make or form by combining; compound: to *mingle* drugs in a mortar. **— *v.i.* 4.** To be or become mixed, united, or closely joined. **5.** To enter into company; mix or associate, as with a crowd. **6.** To take part; become involved, as in a dispute. [Freq. of ME *mengen* < OE *mengan*] **— min′gler** *n.*

Mi·nho (mē′nyŏŏ) A river of NW Spain and northern Portugal, flowing 210 miles, generally west, to the Atlantic: Spanish *Miño.*

Min·how (min′hō′) A former name for FOOCHOW.

mini- *combining form* Small; tiny: *miniskirt.* [< L *minimus* least, smallest]

min·i·a·ture (min′ē-ə-chər, min′ə-chər) *n.* **1.** A portrayal or representation of anything on a small scale. **2.** Reduced dimensions, form, or extent: This ship model is done in *miniature.* **3.** In art: **a** A painting, usually a portrait, done on a very small scale and with much delicate detail. **b** The art of executing such paintings. **4.** In illuminated manuscripts, a small drawing, painting, or decorative letter. **— *adj.* On a very small or reduced scale; minute. **— Syn.** See SMALL. [< F < Ital. *miniatura* < L *miniatus* painted red < *minium* red lead; later infl. in meaning by L *minuere* to lessen]

miniature camera *Photog.* A small camera using film measuring 35 millimeters or less in width.

min·i·a·tur·ize (min′ē-ə-chər·īz′, min′ə-chər·īz′) *v.t.* **·ized, ·iz·ing** To reduce the size of, as the parts of an instrument or machine. **— min′i·a·tur′i·za′tion** *n.*

Mi·nié ball (min′ē-ā, min′ē; *Fr.* mē-nyā′) A conical lead bullet with a hollow base that expands, when discharged, to fill the rifling in the bore, used in the 19th century. [after Capt. Claude Etienne *Minié,* 1814–79, French inventor]

min·i·fy (min′ə-fī) *v.t.* **·fied, ·fy·ing 1.** To make small or less. **2.** To lessen the worth of. [< L *minor* less + -FY]

min·i·kin (min′ə-kin) *adj. Obs.* **1.** Dainty. **2.** Affectedly prim; mincing. **— *n. Rare* One who or that which is very small or delicate. [< Du. *minneken,* dim. of *minne* love]

min·im (min′im) *n.* **1.** A small liquid measure, ⅟₆₀ of a fluid dram, or about one drop. See table inside back cover. Abbr. *m., M., min.* **2.** *Music Chiefly Brit.* A half note. **3.** One who or that which is very small or insignificant. **4.** The smallest particle or part; jot. **5.** In handwriting, a downstroke, as in the letter *n.* **— *adj.* Extremely small. [< L *minimus* least, smallest. Doublet of MINIMUM.]

min·i·mal (min′ə-məl) *adj.* Of a minimum amount, degree, etc.; least possible; smallest. **— min′i·mal·ly** *adv.*

min·i·mal·ist (min′ə-məl·ist) *n. Sometimes cap.* A moderate or conservative socialist, especially one formerly active in Russia. Compare MAXIMALIST.

min·i·mize (min′ə-mīz) *v.t.* **·mized, ·miz·ing 1.** To reduce to the smallest possible amount or degree. **2.** To regard or represent as of the least possible importance, amount, size, etc. Also *Brit.* **min′i·mise. — min′i·mi·za′tion** *n.* **— min′·i·miz′er** *n.*

min·i·mum (min′ə-məm) *n. pl.* **·mums** or **·ma** (-mə) **1.** The least possible quantity, amount, or degree. **2.** The lowest quantity, degree, number, etc., reached or recorded. **3.** *Math.* A value of a function that is smaller than any neighboring value; also, the smallest possible value of a function. **— *adj.* 1.** Consisting of or showing the least amount or degree possible, permissible, attainable, etc. **2.** Of or pertaining to a minimum or minimums. Abbr. *min.* [< L, neut. of *minimus.* Doublet of MINIM.]

minimum wage The smallest hourly wage, set by law or by labor contract, that an employer may legally pay an employee of a certain category.

min·ing (mī′ning) *n.* **1.** The act, process, or business of extracting coal, ores, etc., from mines. **2.** The act of laying explosive mines. Abbr. *min.*

min·ion (min′yən) *n.* **1.** A servile favorite or follower: a term of contempt. **2.** *Printing* A size of type, 7-point. **3.** *Obs.* A mistress or paramour. **4.** *Obs.* Any favorite object. **— minion of the law** A policeman. **— *adj. Rare* Dainty; delicate; fine. [< F *mignon.* Doublet of MIGNON.]

min·ish (min′ish) *v.t. & v.i. Archaic* To diminish. [< F *menuisier* to make small < L *minutus,* pp. of *minuere* to lessen]

min·i·skirt (min′i·skûrt′) *n.* A short skirt worn by women, with the hemline well above the knee. Also **min′i-skirt′.** [< MINI- + SKIRT]

min·is·ter (min′is·tər) *n.* **1.** One who is authorized to administer the sacraments, preach, conduct services of worship, etc., in a church; clergyman; pastor. **2.** One appointed to head an executive or administrative department of a government. **3.** One authorized to represent his government to another government in diplomatic matters and having a rank next below an ambassador. **4.** One who or that which acts as the servant or agent of another person or thing. **— Syn.** See AMBASSADOR. **— *v.i.* 1.** To give attendance or aid; provide for the wants or needs of someone: to *minister* to the sick. **2.** To be helpful or useful; contribute. **— *v.t.* 3.** To administer or apply (a sacrament, medicine, etc.). **4.** *Archaic* To supply; furnish. [< OF *ministre* < L *minister* attendant < *minor* less] **—min′is·ter·ship′** *n.*

min·is·te·ri·al (min′is·tir′ē·əl) *adj.* **1.** Of or pertaining to a minister or to the ministry. **2.** Of, pertaining to, or characteristic of administrative duties, functions, etc.; executive. **3.** Pertaining to an act or duty that is mandatory or imposed by law and involves no private judgment. **4.** Of ministration or service. **5.** Contributive; instrumental. [< F *ministériel* < L *ministerialis*] **— min′is·te′ri·al·ly** *adv.*

min·is·te·ri·al·ist (min′is·tir′ē·əl·ist) *n.* In English politics, one who supports the ministry.

min·is·trant (min′is·trənt) *adj.* Ministering. **— *n.* One who ministers. [< L *ministrans, -antis,* ppr. of *ministrare* to serve]

min·is·tra·tion (min′is·trā′shən) *n.* **1.** The act of ministering or serving, especially in religion. **2.** *Often pl.* Help or aid. [< L *ministratio, -onis*] **— min′is·tra′tive** *adj.*

min·is·try (min′is·trē) *n. pl.* **·tries 1.** The profession, duties, length of service, etc., of a minister of religion. **2.** Ministers of religion collectively; the clergy. **3.** *Govt.* **a** An executive or administrative department presided over by a minister; also, its building. **b** A body of ministers collectively. **c** The duties or functions of a minister or body of ministers; also, their term of office. **4.** The act of ministering; ministration; service. [< L *ministerium*]

min·i·track (min′i·trak′) *n. Aerospace* A sensitive electronic system for tracking the paths of earth satellites by the timing of radio signals received from the satellite at properly spaced ground stations. Also **Min′i·track′.**

min·i·um (min′ē·əm) *n.* **1.** A vivid, opaque, red lead oxide, Pb₃O₄, used chiefly as a pigment: also called *red lead.* **2.** The color vermilion. **3.** *Obs.* Cinnabar. [< L]

min·i·ver (min′ə·vər) *n.* **1.** A white or gray and white fur, used in the Middle Ages as trimming, etc. **2.** Any white fur, as ermine. [< OF *menu vair,* lit., little spotted (fur) < L *minutus* small + *varius* variegated]

mink (mingk) *n.* **1.** A semiaquatic, slender-bodied, carnivorous mammal (genus *Mustela*), resembling but slightly larger than a weasel; especially, a species (*M. vison*) common in North America. **2.** The valuable, soft, thick, glossy brown fur of this mammal. [< Scand. Cf. Sw. *menk.*]

Minn. Minnesota.

Min·ne·ap·o·lis (min′ē·ap′ə·lis) A city in eastern Minnesota, on the Mississippi; pop. 434,400.

min·ne·sing·er (min′ə·sing′ər) *n.* A lyric poet and singer of medieval Germany. **— Syn.** See TROUBADOUR. [< G *minne* love + *singer* singer]

Min·ne·so·ta (min′ə·sō′tə) A State in the north central United States bordering on Canada and Lake Superior; 84,068 sq. mi.; pop. 3,805,069; capital, St. Paul; entered the Union May 11, 1858; nickname, *Gopher State.* **— Min′ne·so′tan** *n. & adj.*

Min·ne·ton·ka (min′ə·tong′kə) A village in eastern Minnesota; pop. 35,737.

min·now (min′ō) *n. pl.* **min·nows** (*Rare* **min·now**) **1.** A small European cyprinoid fish (*Phoxinus phoxinus*). **2.** Any of various other small cyprinoid fishes. **3.** Any small fish.

Also *U.S. Dial.* **min·ny** (min′ē). [ME *menawe.* Akin to OE *myne* small fish; prob. infl. in meaning by F *menu* small.]

Mi·ño (mē′nyō) The Spanish name for the MINHO.

Mi·no·an (mi·nō′ən) *adj.* **1.** Of or pertaining to an advanced Bronze Age civilization that flourished in Crete from about 3000 to 1100 B.C. **2.** Designating two varieties of linear script, one (**Linear A**) deciphered in 1957 and thought to be Akkadian, the other (**Linear B**) deciphered in 1952 and found to be an Achaean dialect of Greek.

mi·nor (mī′nər) *adj.* **1.** Less in quantity, number, or extent. **2.** Of secondary or lesser importance: a *minor* poet. **3.** Under legal age. **4.** *Music* **a** Denoting an interval smaller by a half step than the corresponding major interval, as a minor second, minor third, etc. **b** Denoting a triad in which the third above the fundamental is minor. **c** Denoting a type of diatonic scale, or a key based on this scale. Compare MAJOR. **5.** Sad or plaintive; mournful: said of a sound or voice. **6.** *Logic* More restricted or narrow in scope; having a greater degree of particularity. See SYLLOGISM. **7.** *U.S.* In education, of or pertaining to an area of specialized study undertaken by a degree candidate in a college or university, usually requiring fewer class hours than a major field of study. **8.** Of, relating to, or constituting a minority. **9.** In English public schools, denoting the younger of two students having the same surname. — *n.* **1.** One who is below the age when full civil and personal rights can be legally exercised. **2.** *U.S.* In education, a minor subject or area of study. **3.** *Music* A minor chord, interval, scale, key, etc. **4.** *Logic* A minor term or premise. **5.** In U.S. sports: **a** A minor league (which see). **b** *pl.* The minor leagues collectively. — *v.i. U.S.* In education, to study as a minor subject: with *in:* to *minor* in philosophy. Abbr. *min.* [< L]

Mi·nor·ca (mi·nôr′kə) *n.* One of a breed of large domestic fowls having black or white feathers and producing abundant white eggs. [after *Minorca*]

Mi·nor·ca (mi·nôr′kə) Second largest of the Balearic islands; 271 sq. mi.: Spanish *Menorca.* — **Mi·nor′can** *adj. & n.*

Mi·nor·ite (mī′nə·rīt) *n.* A Franciscan friar. Also **Mi′nor·ist.** [< Med.L (*Fratres*) *Minores* Lesser (Brethren)]

mi·nor·i·ty (mə·nôr′ə·tē, -nor′-, mī-) *n. pl.* **·ties** **1.** The smaller in number of two parts or parties: opposed to *majority.* **2.** A racial, religious, political, or national group smaller than and usually different in some ways from the larger group of which it is a part. **3.** The state or period of being under legal age. [< F *minorité* or L *minoritas*]

minor key *Music* A key or mode based on the minor scale in any of its various forms.

minor league *U.S.* Any professional sports league not having the standing of a major league. — **mi·nor-league** (mī′nər·lēg′) *adj.*

minor mode An arrangement of tones as found in and characteristic of a minor key or scale. Compare SCALE².

minor orders See under HOLY ORDERS.

minor penalty In hockey, a two-minute penalty.

minor premise *Logic* The more particular premise in a syllogism, whose subject is used as the subject of the conclusion. See SYLLOGISM.

minor scale See under SCALE².

minor suit In bridge, diamonds or clubs.

minor term *Logic* The subject of both the minor premise and the conclusion of a syllogism. See SYLLOGISM.

Mi·nos (mī′nəs, -nos) In Greek mythology: **a** A king of Crete, son of Zeus and Europa, who became a judge of the lower world after his death. **b** His grandson, the husband of Pasiphae. [< Gk. *Mīnōs*]

Mi·not (mī′nət) A city in north North Dakota; pop. 32,290.

Min·o·taur (min′ə·tôr) In Greek mythology, a monster with the body of a man and the head of a bull, conceived through the union of Pasiphae and a bull sent by Poseidon. Minos confined the Minotaur in the Labyrinth, where it was annually fed seven youths and seven maidens from Athens, until it was killed by Theseus. [< L *Minotaurus* < Gk. *Mīnōtauros* < *Mīnōs* Minos + *tauros* bull]

Minsk (minsk, *Russ.* myēnsk) The capital of the Byelorussian S.S.R., in the central part; pop. 916,000 (est. 1970).

min·ster (min′stər) *n. Chiefly Brit.* **1.** A monastery church. **2.** A cathedral or large, important church: often used in combination: *Axminster.* [OE *mynster* < LL *monasterium.* Doublet of MONASTERY.]

min·strel (min′strəl) *n.* **1.** In the Middle Ages, a wandering musician who made his living by singing and reciting poetry, usually to the accompaniment of a harp. **2.** A performer in a minstrel show. **3.** *Poetic* A poet, singer, or musician. [< OF *menestrel* < LL *ministerialis* servant, jester < L *minister* attendant]
— **Syn.** **2.** *Minstrel, gleeman,* and *jongleur* denote types of wandering musicians and poets who wrote their own songs, often of a highly romantic character. The *minstrels* arose in England in the 14th century; the *gleemen* were of an earlier period; and the *jongleurs* were French contemporaries of the *gleemen.* Compare BARD, TROUBADOUR.

minstrel show A comic variety show of songs, dances, jokes, etc., given by a company of performers in blackface.

min·strel·sy (min′strəl·sē) *n. pl.* **·sies** **1.** The art or occupation of a minstrel. **2.** Ballads or lyrics collectively, especially those sung by minstrels. **3.** A troupe of minstrels. [< AF *menestralcie,* OF *menestralsie*]

mint¹ (mint) *n.* **1.** A place where the coin of a country is lawfully manufactured. **2.** An abundant supply, especially of money. **3.** A source of manufacture, invention, or inspiration. — *v.t.* **1.** To make (money) by stamping; to coin. **2.** To invent or fabricate (a word, etc.). — *adj.* In original condition; unused: a *mint* stamp. [OE *mynet* coin < L *moneta* mint < *Moneta* epithet of Juno, whose temple at Rome was used as a mint. Doublet of MONEY.] — **mint′er** *n.*

mint² (mint) *n.* **1.** Any of several aromatic herbs (genus *Mentha*) of the mint family; especially, spearmint and peppermint, used as a flavoring, garnish, etc. **2.** A mint-flavored candy. [OE *minte* < L *menta, mentha* < Gk. *mintha*]

mint³ (mint) *v.t. Scot.* To hint; intend.

mint·age (min′tij) *n.* **1.** The act or process of minting. **2.** The money manufactured by a mint. **3.** The fee paid for coining. **4.** The authorized impression stamped upon a coin.

mint julep A drink made of bourbon mixed with crushed ice and sugar and flavored with sprigs of fresh mint.

mint par of exchange *Econ.* The reduction of the monetary unit of one country to expression in terms of that of another. Also called *par of exchange.*

min·u·end (min′yōo·end) *n. Math.* The number from which another (the subtrahend) is to be subtracted. [< L *minuendus* to be lessened, gerundive of *minuere* to lessen]

min·u·et (min′yōo·et) *n.* **1.** A stately dance for couples, introduced in France in the 17th century. **2.** Music for or in the manner of this dance, in moderate triple meter, often used as a movement of a symphony, sonata, or suite. [< F *menuet,* dim. of *menu* small < L *minutus*]

Min·u·it (min′yōo·it), Peter, 1580–1638, Dutch administrator in America; purchased Manhattan Island from the Indians 1626: original name Peter Min·new·it (min′ō·it).

mi·nus (mī′nəs) *prep.* **1.** Lessened or reduced by; less: ten *minus* five. **2.** *Informal* Lacking; deprived of: *minus* a tooth. — *adj.* **1.** Of or denoting subtraction: the *minus* sign. **2.** Negative or in a negative direction: a *minus* value. **3.** Less in quality or value than: I got a C *minus* in the course. **4.** *Informal* Non-existent; lacking: His chances were *minus.* **5.** *Bot.* Designating or pertaining to certain strains of mycelia that, in fungi, are assumed to be female in the reproductive function. — *n.* **1.** The minus sign (−). **2.** A minus quantity. **3.** A deficit or loss. [< L, neut. of *minor*]

mi·nus·cule (mi·nus′kyōol, min′ə·skyōol) *n.* **1.** A cursive script, developed from the uncial in the 7th–9th centuries and forming the basis of the modern small Roman and Greek letters. **2.** A letter in this script. **3.** Any small or lowercase letter. Compare MAJUSCULE. — *adj.* **1.** Of, pertaining to, like, or composed of minuscules. **2.** Very small; miniature. [< L *minusculus,* dim. of *minor* less]

minus sign A sign (−) denoting subtraction or a negative quantity.

min·ute¹ (min′it) *n.* **1.** The 60th part of an hour; 60 seconds. **2.** Any very brief period of time; moment. **3.** A specific instant of time: Do it this *minute!* **4.** A unit of angular measure equal to the 60th part of a degree, indicated by the sign (′) and called a *minute* of arc. **5.** A brief note of something to be remembered; memorandum. **6.** *pl.* An official record of the business discussed and transacted at a meeting, conference, etc. **7.** The distance normally covered in a minute: five *minutes* away. — **up to the minute** In accord with the latest fashion, equipment, etc. — *v.t.* **·ut·ed, ·ut·ing** **1.** To make a minute or brief note of; record. **2.** To time to the minute. Abbr. (for n. defs. 1, 4) *m., M., min.* [< F < Med.L *minuta (pars)* small (part), minute < L *minutus* small]

mi·nute² (mi·nōot′, -nyōot′, mī-) *adj.* **1.** Exceedingly small; tiny. **2.** Having little importance or value; insignificant; trifling. **3.** Demonstrating or characterized by careful scrutiny and treatment of small details or components: a *minute* examination. — **Syn.** See SMALL. [< L *minutus* small, little, orig. pp. of *minuere* to lessen] — **mi·nute′ness** *n.*

min·ute gun (min′it) A gun fired at intervals of a minute, as a sign of mourning at a funeral or as a signal of distress.

min·ute hand (min′it) The hand that indicates the minute on a clock or similar timepiece.

min·ute·ly¹ (min′it·lē) *adj. & adv.* At intervals of a minute.

mi·nute·ly² (mī·nōot′lē, -nyōot′-, mi-) *adv.* In a minute manner or degree; with great detail, precision, or exactness.

min·ute·man (min′it·man′) *n. pl.* **·men** (-men′) At the time of the American Revolution, one of the colonial militiamen or armed citizens who pledged themselves to be ready for combat at a minute's notice.

min·ute steak (min′it) A small, thin cut of steak that can be cooked quickly.

mi·nu·ti·ae (mi·nōo′shi·ē, -nyōo′-) *n. pl.* of **mi·nu·ti·a** (-shē·ə, -shə) Small or unimportant details; trifles. [< L]

minx (mingks) *n.* A saucy, bold, or flirtatious girl. [Prob. < LG *minsk* impudent woman. Akin to G *mensch* person.]

Mi·o·cene (mī′ə·sēn) *adj.* Pertaining to or designating the fourth geological epoch of the Tertiary period, associated with a great development of modern mammals. See chart for GEOLOGY. — *n.* The Miocene epoch or series. [< Gk. *meiōn* less + *kainos* recent]

mi·o·sis (mī·ō′sis) *n. Pathol.* **1.** Excessive contraction of the pupil of the eye: also spelled *myosis.* **2.** The period in the course of a disease when the symptoms begin to diminish. [< Gk. *myein* to close + -OSIS] — **mi·ot′ic** (-ot′ik) or **my·ot′ic** *adj.*

Mi·que·lon (mik′ə·lon, *Fr.* mē·kə·lôn′) See ST. PIERRE AND MIQUELON.

mir (mir) *n.* In Russia before the Revolution, a peasant commune. [< Russian]

Mi·ra·beau (mē·rȧ·bō′), **Comte de,** 1749–91, Honoré Gabriel Riqueti, French Revolutionary statesman and orator.

mi·ra·bi·le dic·tu (mi·rab′ə·lē dik′tōō, -tyōō) *Latin* Wonderful to relate.

mi·ra·bil·i·a (mir′ə·bil′ē·ə) *n.pl. Latin* Miracles; wonders.

mir·a·cle (mir′ə·kəl) *n.* **1.** An event that appears to be neither a part nor result of any known natural law or agency and is therefore often attributed to a supernatural or divine source. **2.** Any wonderful or amazing thing, fact, or event; marvel. **3.** One who or that which is of surpassing merit or excellence: often with *of.* **4.** A miracle play. [< F < L *miraculum* < *mirari* to wonder < *mirus* wonderful]

miracle play A medieval play dealing with the lives of saints and with their miracles. Compare MYSTERY PLAY.

mi·rac·u·lous (mi·rak′yə·ləs) *adj.* **1.** Wonderful and amazing; extraordinary. **2.** Apparently caused by the direct intervention of a supernatural or divine power. **3.** Having the power to work miracles. — **Syn.** See SUPERNATURAL. [< F *miraculeux* < Med.L *miraculosus* < L *miraculum*] — **mi·rac′u·lous·ly** *adv.* — **mi·rac′u·lous·ness** *n.*

mir·a·dor (mir′ə·dôr′, -dōr′) *n.* In Spanish architecture, a window, balcony, porch, etc., that commands a view. [< Sp. < *mirar* to behold < L *mirari* to wonder at]

Mir·a·flo·res Lake (mir′ə·flôr′əs, -flō′rəs) An artificial lake in the southern Canal Zone.

mi·rage (mi·räzh′) *n.* **1.** An optical illusion, as of a body or sheet of water, upside-down ship, etc., that sometimes appears in a desert, on a highway, or in the air, and is caused by such distant objects being reflected from layers of atmosphere having different densities. **2.** Anything that appears to be real but is not. — **Syn.** See DELUSION. [< F < *se mirer* to be reflected < L *mirari* to wonder at]

mire (mīr) *n.* **1.** An area of wet, yielding earth; swampy ground. **2.** Deep mud or slush. — *v.* **mired, mir·ing** *v.t.* **1.** To cause to sink or become stuck in mire. **2.** To smear or soil with mud; defile. **3.** To entangle or entrap. — *v.i.* **4.** To sink in mire; bog down. [< ON *myrr* swampy ground]

Mir·i·am (mir′ē·əm) Sister of Moses and Aaron. *Ex.* xv 20.

mirk[1] (mûrk), **mirk·i·ly** (mûrk′i·lē), etc. See MURK, etc.

mirk[2] (mûrk) *Scot. adj.* Dark, gloomy. — *n.* Darkness.

Mi·ró (mē·rō′), **Joan** (hwän), born 1893, Spanish painter.

mir·ror (mir′ər) *n.* **1.** Any smooth reflecting surface, as of polished metal or more usually of glass backed with a coating of silver, aluminum, etc. **2.** Whatever reflects or depicts truly. **3.** *Rare* Something deserving imitation. — *v.t.* To reflect or show an image of, as in a mirror. [< OF *mirour* < LL *mirare* to look at < L *mirari* to wonder at, admire]

mirth (mûrth) *n.* **1.** Spirited gaiety, especially when accompanied by jesting or laughter; social merriment. **2.** *Obs.* Joy. [OE *myrgth* < *myrig* pleasant, merry]

mirth·ful (mûrth′fəl) *adj.* Full of or characterized by mirth; merry. — **mirth′ful·ly** *adv.* — **mirth′ful·ness** *n.*

mirth·less (mûrth′lis) *adj.* Lacking mirth; joyless; sad; dismal. — **mirth′less·ly** *adv.* — **mirth′less·ness** *n.*

MIRV (mûrv) Multiple Independently-targeted Reentry Vehicle.

mir·za (mir′zä) *n.* A Persian title of honor, placed after a name to denote a prince or before a name to denote a hero, scholar, etc. [< Persian, contr. of *mīrzādah* < *mīr* prince (< Arabic *amir* ruler) + *zādah* son of]

mis-[1] *prefix* Bad; amiss; badly; wrongly; unfavorably. [OE *mis-* prefix, infl. in meaning by ME *mes-* mis-[2]] *Mis-* may appear as a combining form, as in the self-explanatory words in the list below:

misaccent	miscensure	misdesire	mis-hallowed	misoccupy	misrehearsal
misaccentuation	miscenter	misdetermine	mishear	misopinion	misrehearse
misachievement	mischallenge	misdevise	mis-heed	misordination	misrelate
misacknowledge	mischaracterize	misdevoted	mis-hit	misorganization	misrelation
misact	mischarge	misdevotion	mis-hold	misorganize	misreliance
misadapt	mischoose	misdispose	misidentification	mispage	misrely
misadaptation	mischristen	misdisposition	misidentify	mispagination	misrender
misadd	miscipher	misdistinguish	misimagination	mispaint	misrepeat
misaddress	miscite	misdistribute	misimagine	misparse	misreprint
misadjust	misclaim	misdistribution	misimpression	mispart	misrepute
misadmeasurement	misclass	misdivide	misimputation	mispassion	misresemblance
misadministration	misclassification	misdraw	misimpute	mispatch	misresolved
misaffection	misclassify	misdrive	misincite	mispen	misresult
misaffirm	miscoin	miseat	misinclination	misperceive	misseason
misagent	miscoinage	misedit	misincline	misperception	misseat
misaim	miscollate	miseducate	misinfer	misperform	mis-see
misalienate	miscollation	miseducation	misinference	misperformance	mis-seed
misalinement	miscollocation	miseffect	misinflame	mispersuade	missemblance
misallegation	miscommand	misencourage	misingenuity	misperuse	mis-send
misallege	miscommit	misendeavor	misinspired	misphrase	mis-sense
misallotment	miscommunicate	misenforce	misinstruct	misplant	missentence
misallowance	miscompare	misengrave	misinstruction	mispoint	mis-sheathed
misalphabetize	miscomplain	misenrol	misinstructive	mispoise	mis-ship
misalter	miscomplaint	misenter	misintend	mispolicy	misshod
misanalyze	miscompose	misentitle	misintention	misposition	mis-sing
misanswer	miscomputation	misentry	misinter	mispossessed	missolution
misapparel	miscompute	misenunciation	misinterment	mispractice	missort
misappear	misconclude	misevent	misintimation	misprejudiced	missound
misappearance	misconclusion	misexample	misjoin	mispresent	misspace
misappellation	misconfer	misexecute	miskeep	misprincipled	misstart
misappoint	misconfident	misexecution	miskindle	misproceeding	missteer
misappointment	misconfiguration	misexpectation	mislabel	misproduce	misstop
misappraisal	misconjecture	misexpend	mislabor	misproportion	misstrike
misappraise	misconjugate	misexpenditure	mislanguage	misproposal	misstroke
misappraisement	misconjugation	misexplain	mislearn	mispropose	misstyle
misascribe	misconjunction	misexplanation	mislie	misprovide	missuggestion
misascription	misconsecrate	misexplication	mislight	misprovidence	missuit
misassay	misconsequence	misexposition	mislikeness	misprovoke	missummation
misassent	miscook	misexpound	mislive	mispunctuate	missuppose
misassert	miscopy	misexpress	mislocate	mispunctuation	mis-sway
misassign	miscounsel	misexpression	mislocation	mispurchase	missyllabication
misassociate	miscultivated	misexpressive	mislodge	mispursuit	missyllabify
misassociation	misculture	misfaith	mismark	misqualify	mistaught
misatone	miscurvature	misfashion	mismeasure	misraise	misteach
misattribute	miscut	misfeature	mismeasurement	misrate	mistend
misattribution	misdecide	misfield	mismeet	misrealize	misterm
misauthorization	misdecision	misfile	mismenstruation	misreason	misthread
misauthorize	misdeclaration	misform	misminded	misreceive	misthrive
misaver	misdeclare	misformation	mismingle	misrecital	misthrow
misaward	misdeem	misframe	mismotion	misrecite	mistitle
misbegin	misdefine	misgauge	mismove	misrecognition	mistouch
misbestow	misdeliver	misgesture	misnavigation	misrecognize	mistranscribe
misbetide	misdelivery	misgraft	misnumber	misrecollect	mistranscription
misbias	misdention	misground	misnurture	misrefer	mistune
misbill	misderive	misgrow	misnutrition	misreference	mistutor
misbind	misdescribe	misgrown	misobservance	misreform	misunion
misbuild	misdescription	misguess	misobserve	misregulate	misyoke

mis-² *prefix* Bad; amiss; not: found with negative or depreciatory force in words borrowed from Old French: *misadventure, miscreant.* [< OF *mes-* < L *minus* less]

mis-³ Var. of MISO-.

mis·ad·ven·ture (mis′əd·ven′chər) *n.* **1.** A disastrous or unfortunate event; misfortune; mischance. **2.** Bad luck. — **Syn.** See MISFORTUNE. [< OF *mesaventure*]

mis·ad·vise (mis′ad·vīz′) *v.t.* ·**vised,** ·**vis·ing** To give bad advice or erroneous information to.

mis·al·li·ance (mis′ə·lī′əns) *n.* An undesirable alliance or marriage. [< F *mésalliance*]

mis·al·ly (mis′ə·lī′) *v.t.* ·**lied,** ·**ly·ing** To ally badly or improperly.

mis·an·thrope (mis′ən·thrōp, miz′-) *n.* One who hates or does not trust his fellow men. Also **mis·an·thro·pist** (mis·an′thrə·pist). [< Gk. *misanthrōpos* hating mankind < *misein* to hate + *anthrōpos* man]

mis·an·throp·ic (mis′ən·throp′ik) *adj.* Of, pertaining to, or like a misanthrope. Also **mis·an·throp′i·cal.** — **mis′· an·throp′i·cal·ly** *adv.*

mis·an·thro·py (mis·an′thrə·pē) *n.* Hatred or distrust of mankind.

mis·ap·ply (mis′ə·plī′) *v.t.* ·**plied,** ·**ply·ing** **1.** To use or apply incorrectly or inefficiently. **2.** To use or apply wrongfully. — **mis·ap·pli·ca·tion** (mis′ap·li·kā′shən) *n.*

mis·ap·pre·hend (mis′ap·ri·hend′) *v.t.* To apprehend or interpret wrongly; misunderstand.

mis·ap·pre·hen·sion (mis′ap·ri·hen′shən) *n.* A failure in apprehending; misunderstanding.

mis·ap·pro·pri·ate (mis′ə·prō′prē·āt) *v.t.* ·**at·ed,** ·**at·ing** To use or take improperly or dishonestly; misapply. — **mis′ap·pro′pri·a′tion** *n.*

mis·ar·range (mis′ə·rānj′) *v.t.* ·**ranged,** ·**rang·ing** To arrange wrongly. — **mis′ar·range′ment** *n.*

mis·be·come (mis′bi·kum′) *v.t.* ·**came,** ·**come,** ·**com·ing** To be unbecoming or not appropriate to.

mis·be·got·ten (mis′bi·got′n) *adj.* Unlawfully begotten; especially, born out of wedlock. Also **mis′be·got′.**

mis·be·have (mis′bi·hāv′) *v.i. & v.t.* ·**haved,** ·**hav·ing** To behave badly.

mis·be·hav·ior (mis′bi·hāv′yər) *n.* Bad or improper conduct. Also *Brit.* **mis′be·hav′iour.**

mis·be·lief (mis′bi·lēf′) *n.* False belief or opinion.

mis·be·lieve (mis′bi·lēv′) *v.* ·**lieved,** ·**liev·ing** *v.i.* **1.** To hold a false, unorthodox, or heretical belief or opinion. — *v.t.* **2.** *Archaic* To disbelieve or distrust. — **mis′be·liev′er** *n.*

mis·brand (mis·brand′) *v.t.* To label or brand incorrectly.

misc. **1.** Miscellaneous. **2.** Miscellany.

mis·cal·cu·late (mis·kal′kyə·lāt) *v.t. & v.i.* ·**lat·ed,** ·**lat·ing** To calculate wrongly. — **mis′cal·cu·la′tion** *n.*

mis·call (mis·kôl′) *v.t.* **1.** To call by a wrong name. **2.** *Brit. Dial.* To revile; abuse.

mis·car·riage (mis·kar′ij) *n.* **1.** A premature delivery of a nonviable fetus. **2.** Failure to bring about a proper or expected conclusion. **3.** Failure to reach an intended destination. **4.** Improper handling or shipment of goods.

mis·car·ry (mis·kar′ē) *v.i.* ·**ried,** ·**ry·ing** **1.** To fail to arrive at an expected or proper conclusion; go wrong: The plan *miscarried.* **2.** To bring forth a fetus prematurely; have a miscarriage. **3.** To fail to reach an intended destination, as freight, mail, etc.

mis·cast (mis·kast′, -käst′) *v.t.* ·**cast, cast·ing** In the theater, movies, etc., to cast (a play or a role) inappropriately; also, to cast (an actor) in a role not suited to him.

mis·ce·ge·na·tion (mis′i·jə·nā′shən) *n.* Interbreeding of ethnic stocks or races. [< L *miscere* to mix + *genus* race] — **mis′ce·ge·net′ic** (-jə·net′ik) *adj.*

mis·cel·la·ne·a (mis′ə·lā′nē·ə) *n.pl.* A miscellaneous collection of things, especially of literary works. [< L]

mis·cel·la·ne·ous (mis′ə·lā′nē·əs) *adj.* **1.** Composed of various and diverse things or elements; mixed. **2.** Possessing diverse qualities or capabilities; many-sided. Abbr. *misc.* — **Syn.** See HETEROGENEOUS. [< L *miscellaneus* < *miscellus* mixed < *miscere* to mix] — **mis′cel′la·ne·ous·ly** *adv.* — **mis′cel·la′ne·ous·ness** *n.*

mis·cel·la·nist (mis′ə·lā′nist, -lə·nist) *n.* A writer of miscellanies.

mis·cel·la·ny (mis′ə·lā′nē) *n. pl.* ·**nies** A miscellaneous collection. Abbr. *misc.*

mis·chance (mis·chans′, -chäns′) *n.* Bad luck; also, an instance of bad luck; mishap. — **Syn.** See MISFORTUNE. [< OF *mescheance*]

mis·chief (mis′chif) *n.* **1.** Action or conduct, often of a playful nature, that causes some usually slight irritation, harm, or trouble; also, a specific instance of such action or conduct. **2.** The mood or disposition to annoy, tease, or disturb, as from high spirits. **3.** One who causes harm, trouble, or petty vexation. **4.** Harm, trouble, or injury attributed to a particular cause or agent: High winds can cause great *mischief.* **5.** A cause or source of damage, evil, or petty annoyance. **6.** *Informal* Satan. [< OF *meschef*

bad result < *meschever* to come to grief < *mes-* mis-² (< L *minus* less) + *chief* head, end < L *caput* head]

mis·chief-mak·er (mis′chif-mā′kər) *n.* One who causes mischief, especially by exciting quarrels, bearing gossip, etc. — **mis′chief-mak′ing** *adj. & n.*

mis·chie·vous (mis′chi·vəs) *adj.* **1.** Inclined to or full of mischief: a *mischievous* child. **2.** Troubling or annoying, usually in a petty way. **3.** Having a playful, teasing nature or quality: a *mischievous* look. **4.** Causing or tending to cause harm or injury: a *mischievous* rumor. — **mis′chie·vous·ly** *adv.* — **mis′chie·vous·ness** *n.* [< AF *meschevous*]

mis·ci·ble (mis′i·bəl) *adj.* Capable of being mixed. [< L *miscere* to mix]

mis·col·or (mis·kul′ər) *v.t.* **1.** To give a wrong color to. **2.** To misrepresent. Also *Brit.* **mis·col′our.**

mis·con·ceive (mis′kən·sēv′) *v.t. & v.i.* ·**ceived,** ·**ceiv·ing** To conceive wrongly; misunderstand. — **mis′con·ceiv′er** *n.*

mis·con·cep·tion (mis′kən·sep′shən) *n.* A false or mistaken notion, idea, concept, etc.

mis·con·duct (*n.* mis·kon′dukt; *v.* mis′kən·dukt′) *n.* **1.** Improper or immoral behavior; often, in legal proceedings, adultery. **2.** Unlawful conduct by one holding some official or administrative position. **3.** Mismanagement, as of duties, responsibilities, etc. — *v.t.* **1.** To behave (oneself) improperly. **2.** To mismanage.

mis·con·struc·tion (mis′kən·struk′shən) *n.* **1.** A wrong interpretation or understanding of something: a *misconstruction* of his actions. **2.** The act of misconstruing.

mis·con·strue (mis′kən·strōō′) *v.t.* ·**strued,** ·**stru·ing** **1.** To interpret wrongly; give a false or unwarranted meaning to; misunderstand. **2.** *Gram.* To construe incorrectly.

mis·count (mis·kount′) *v.t. & v.i.* To count incorrectly; miscalculate. — *n.* An incorrect count or reckoning.

mis·cre·ance (mis′krē·əns) *n.* *Archaic* False belief or faith. [< OF *miscreant* disbelieving, ppr. of *mescroire* < *mes-* mis-² (< L *minus* less) + *croire* to believe < L *credere*]

mis·cre·an·cy (mis′krē·ən·sē) *n.* *Archaic* **1.** The act or the condition of a miscreant. **2.** Miscreance.

mis·cre·ant (mis′krē·ənt) *n.* **1.** An unscrupulous wretch; evildoer. **2.** *Archaic* An unbeliever; infidel. — *adj.* **1.** Villainous; vile. **2.** *Archaic* Unbelieving; faithless.

mis·cre·ate (mis′krē·āt′) *v.t. & v.i.* ·**at·ed,** ·**at·ing** To create or shape amiss. — *adj. Archaic* Miscreated.

mis·cre·at·ed (mis′krē·ā′tid) *adj.* Badly formed or made.

mis·cue (mis·kyōō′) *n.* **1.** In billiards, a stroke spoiled by a slipping of the cue. **2.** *Informal* An error; slip-up. — *v.i.* ·**cued,** ·**cu·ing** **1.** To make a miscue. **2.** In the theater, etc., to miss one's cue or to answer another's cue.

mis·date (mis·dāt′) *v.t.* ·**dat·ed,** ·**dat·ing** To date incorrectly; assign a wrong date to. — *n.* An incorrect date.

mis·deal (mis·dēl′) *v.t. & v.i.* ·**dealt** (-delt′), ·**deal·ing** In card games, to deal incorrectly or improperly. — *n.* An incorrect deal. — **mis·deal′er** *n.*

mis·deed (mis·dēd′) *n.* An evil or immoral act.

mis·de·mean (mis′di·mēn′) *v.t. & v.i.* To misbehave.

mis·de·mean·ant (mis′di·mē′nənt) *n.* **1.** One who is guilty of misconduct. **2.** *Law* One who is guilty or convicted of a misdemeanor.

mis·de·mean·or (mis′di·mē′nər) *n.* **1.** *Law* Any offense less serious than a felony, or for which the punishment is less severe. **2.** *Archaic* Misbehavior, or a specific instance of it. Also *Brit.* **mis′de·mean′our.**

mis·di·rect (mis′di·rekt′, -dī·rekt′) *v.t.* To direct or guide wrongly, as a letter, person, etc.

mis·di·rec·tion (mis′di·rek′shən, -dī-) *n.* **1.** The act of misdirecting or the state of being misdirected. **2.** A wrong direction or guidance. **3.** *Law* A legal error in the judge's charge to a jury.

mis·do (mis·dōō′) *v.t. & v.i.* ·**did,** ·**done,** ·**do·ing** To do wrongly. [OE *misdōn*] — **mis·do′er** *n.* — **mis·do′ing** *n.*

mis·doubt (mis·dout′) *v.t.* *Archaic* **1.** To doubt; call in question. **2.** To fear; suspect. — *v.i.* **3.** To be in doubt; suspect. — *n.* Doubt or suspicion.

mise (mīz) *n.* **1.** *Law* The issue in a writ of right. **2.** An agreement or settlement. [< AF < OF *mis* put, laid out, pp. of *mettre* < L *mittere* to send]

mis·ease (mis·ēz′) *n.* **1.** *Archaic* Lack of ease; discomfort; misery. **2.** *Obs.* Poverty.

mise en scène (mēz än sen′) *French* **1.** In a play, movie, etc.: **a** The set and the properties for any particular scene. **b** The arrangement of the actors, set, properties, etc. **2.** Physical surroundings generally; environment.

mis·em·ploy (mis′im·ploi′) *v.t.* To put to a wrong or improper use. — **mis′em·ploy′ment** *n.*

Mi·se·no (mē·zā′nō), **Cape** A promontory in southern Italy on the northern shore of the Bay of Naples; site of ruins of **Mi·se·num** (mī·sē′nəm), an ancient city.

mi·ser (mī′zər) *n.* **1.** One who saves or hoards avariciously. **2.** One who lives miserably for the sake of adding to his wealth. **3.** *Obs.* An unhappy wretch. [< L, wretched]

mis·er·a·ble (miz′ər·ə·bəl, miz′rə-) *adj.* **1.** Being in a state of misery, poverty, or wretched unhappiness. **2.** *Informal* In poor health; not well: *He has been* miserable *all year.* **3.** Causing misery or extreme discomfort: *a miserable headache.* **4.** Proceeding from or exhibiting misery: *a miserable life.* **5.** Of inferior quality; worthless: *a miserable play.* **6.** Paltry or meager; skimpy. **7.** Deserving of pity: *a miserable creature.* **8.** Disreputable; shameful: *a miserable scoundrel.* —*n. Obs.* A miserable person. [< OF < L *miserabilis* pitiable < *miserari* to pity < *miser* wretched] —**mis′er·a·ble·ness** *n.* —**mis′er·a·bly** *adv.*

mis·e·re·re (miz′ə·râr′ē, -rir′ē) *n.* **1.** A misericord (def. 2). **2.** A request or prayer for mercy.

Mis·e·re·re (miz′ə·râr′ē, -rir′ē) *n.* **1.** The 51st Psalm (in the Vulgate and Douai versions, the 50th): from the opening word of the Latin version. **2.** A musical setting of this psalm. [< L, imperative of *misereri* to have mercy]

mis·er·i·cord (miz′ər·i·kôrd′, mi·zer′i·kôrd) *n.* **1.** A small dagger, used in the Middle Ages to give the death stroke to a wounded knight. **2.** In a church stall, a small wooden ledge so fixed to the underside of a hinged seat that when the seat is turned up, the ledge offers support for one standing. **3.** Formerly, a dispensation, especially from fasting, given to a member of a monastic order. **4.** A room in a monastery where meals are served to monks dispensed from fasting. Also **mis·er·i·corde** (miz′ər·i·kôrd′, mi·zer′i·kôrd). [< OF < L *misericordia* < *misereri* to have pity + *cor, cordis* heart]

mis·e·ri·cor·di·a (miz′ə·ri·kôr′dē·ə) *n. Latin* Pity; compassion; mercy.

mi·ser·ly (mī′zər·lē) *adj.* Of, like, or characteristic of a miser; grasping; avaricious. —**mi′ser·li·ness** *n.*

mis·er·y (miz′ər·ē) *n. pl.* **·er·ies 1.** A condition of great wretchedness or suffering, as caused by poverty, pain, etc. **2.** Intense mental or emotional anguish; extreme unhappiness. **3.** A cause or source of suffering or unhappiness. **4.** *Dial.* A physical pain: *a misery in the back.* —**Syn.** See SUFFERING. [< OF *miserie* < L *miseria* < *miser* wretched]

mis·es·ti·mate (*v.* mis·es′tə·māt; *n.* mis·es′tə·mit) *v.t.* **·mat·ed, ·mat·ing** To estimate wrongly. Also **mis·es·teem** (mis′es·tēm′). —*n.* A wrong estimate.

mis·fea·sance (mis·fē′zəns) *n. Law* The performance of a lawful act in an unlawful or culpable manner. Compare MALFEASANCE, NONFEASANCE. [< OF *mesfaisance* < *mesfaire* to do wrong < *mes-* mis- + *faire* to do < L *facere*] —**mis·fea·sor** (mis·fē′zər) *n.* One guilty of misfeasance.

mis·fire (*v.* mis·fīr′; *n.* mis′fīr) *v.i.* **·fired, ·fir·ing 1.** To fail to fire, ignite, or explode at the desired time, as a firearm, internal-combustion engine, etc. **2.** To fail in achieving the proper or desired effect: *The final scene* misfires *badly.* —*n.* The act of misfiring; also, a specific instance of this.

mis·fit (mis·fit′; *for n. def. 2,* mis′fit) *v.t. & v.i.* **·fit·ted, ·fit·ting** To fail to fit or make fit. —*n.* **1.** Something that fits badly. **2.** One who is not well adjusted to his environment. **3.** The act or condition of fitting badly.

mis·for·tune (mis·fôr′chən) *n.* **1.** Adverse or ill fortune; bad luck; adversity. **2.** A calamity; mishap. — **Syn. 2.** *Misfortune, mishap, mischance,* and *misadventure* characterize unwelcome events regarded as coming from bad luck or adverse fate. *Misfortune* suggests a long-lasting condition: *the misfortune of being born blind. Mishap* and *mischance* suggest a single unforeseen occurrence: *a mishap on the road interrupted our trip. Misadventure* is much the same, but is sometimes applied to the adverse consequences of erroneous planning or calculation. Compare DISASTER.

mis·give (mis·giv′) *v.* **·gave** (-gāv′), **·giv·ing** *Archaic v.t.* **1.** To make fearful, suspicious, or doubtful: *My heart* misgives *me.* —*v.i.* **2.** To be apprehensive.

mis·giv·ing (mis·giv′ing) *n.* A feeling of doubt, distrust, or apprehension. —**Syn.** See DOUBT, ANXIETY.

mis·gov·ern (mis·guv′ərn) *v.t.* To govern badly; administer improperly. —**mis·gov′ern·ment** *n.*

mis·guide (mis·gīd′) *v.t.* **·guid·ed, ·guid·ing** To guide wrongly in action or thought; mislead. —**mis·guid′ance** *n.* —**mis·guid′er** *n.*

mis·guid·ed (mis·gī′did) *adj.* Guided or led wrongly in thought or action. —**mis·guid′ed·ly** *adv.*

mis·han·dle (mis·han′dəl) *v.t.* **·dled, ·dling** To handle, treat, or manage badly; abuse.

mis·han·ter (mis·han′tər) *n. Scot.* Misfortune; ill luck. [< MISADVENTURE]

mis·hap (mis′hap, mis·hap′) *n.* An unfortunate accident. — **Syn.** See MISFORTUNE. [< MIS-¹ + HAP]

Mish·a·wa·ka (mish′ə·wô′kə) A city in northern Indiana, near South Bend; pop. 35,517.

mis·hear (mis·hir′) *v.t.* **·heard** (-hûrd′), **·hear·ing** To hear wrongly or poorly.

mish·mash (mish′mash′, -mosh′) *n.* A confused mixture or collection of things; hodgepodge. Also **mish′-mash**. [Reduplication of MASH]

Mish·nah (mish′nə) *n. pl.* **Mish·na·yoth** (mish′nä·yōth′) **1.** The first part of the Talmud, consisting of a collection of early rabbinical traditions and decisions compiled chiefly by Rabbi Judah ha-Nasi (born about A.D. 150). **2.** A paragraph of this collection. **3.** The teachings of any notable expounder of the Jewish law. Also **Mish′na**. [< Hebrew

mishnāh repetition, oral law < *shānāh* to repeat, teach] — **Mish·na·ic** (mish·nā′ik), **Mish′nic** or **-ni·cal** *adj.*

mis·in·form (mis′in·fôrm′) *v.t.* To give false or erroneous information to. —**mis′in·form′ant, mis′in·form′er** *n.* —**mis·in·for·ma′tion** *n.*

mis·in·ter·pret (mis′in·tûr′prit) *v.t.* To interpret or understand incorrectly. —**mis′in·ter′pre·ta′tion** *n.* —**mis′in·ter′pret·er** *n.*

mis·join·der (mis·join′dər) *n. Law* In an action or suit, the improper joining of parties or causes of action.

mis·judge (mis·juj′) *v.t. & v.i.* **·judged, ·judg·ing** To judge wrongly or unfairly. —**mis·judg′ment** or *Brit.* **mis·judge′ment** *n.*

mis·kal (mis·käl′) *n.* An Oriental weight equivalent to 4.7 grams in Persia, and to 4.8 grams in Turkey. [< Arabic *mithqāl* weight]

Mis·kolc (mish′kôlts) A county borough in NE Hungary; pop. 170,000 (est. 1967). Formerly **Mis′kolcz**.

mis·lay (mis·lā′) *v.t.* **·laid, ·lay·ing 1.** To put or lay in a place not remembered; misplace. **2.** To place or put down incorrectly: *He* mislaid *the carpet.* —**mis·lay′er** *n.*

mis·lead (mis·lēd′) *v.t.* **·led** (-led′), **·lead·ing 1.** To guide or lead in the wrong direction. **2.** To lead into error, as of judgment or conduct. —**mis·lead′er** *n.* —**mis·lead′ing** *adj.* —**mis·lead′ing·ly** *adv.*

mis·leared (mis·lird′) *adj. Scot.* Ill-bred or ill-mannered.

mis·like (mis·līk′) *v.t.* **·liked, ·lik·ing 1.** To dislike. **2.** To displease. —*n.* Dislike, disapproval: also **mis·lik′ing**. — **mis·lik′er** *n.* —**mis·lik′ing·ly** *adv.*

mis·man·age (mis·man′ij) *v.t. & v.i.* **·aged, ·ag·ing** To manage badly or improperly. —**mis·man′age·ment** *n.* — **mis·man′ag·er** *n.*

mis·mar·riage (mis·mar′ij) *n.* An unhappy or incongruous marriage.

mis·match (mis·mach′) *v.t.* To match badly or inappropriately, as in marriage. —*n.* A bad or incongruous match.

mis·mate (mis·māt′) *v.t. & v.i.* **·mat·ed, ·mat·ing** To mate unsuitably.

mis·name (mis·nām′) *v.t.* **·named, ·nam·ing** To call by a wrong name.

mis·no·mer (mis·nō′mər) *n.* **1.** A name wrongly applied to someone or something. **2.** The act of misnaming, especially in a legal document. [< AF < OF *mesnomer* to misname < *mes-* wrongly + *nomer* < L *nominare* to name]

miso- combining form Hating; hatred: *misogynist.* Also, before vowels, **mis-**. [< Gk.*misein* to hate]

mis·og·a·my (mis·og′ə·mē) *n.* Hatred of marriage. [< MISO- + -GAMY] —**mis·og′a·mist** *n.*

mis·og·y·ny (mis·oj′ə·nē) *n.* Hatred of women. [< Gk. *misogynia* < *misein* to hate + *gynē* woman] —**mis·og′y·nist** *n.* —**mis·og′y·nous** *adj.*

mis·ol·o·gy (mis·ol′ə·jē) *n.* Hatred of debate, enlightenment, or reasoning. [< Gk. *misologia* < *misein* to hate + *logos* discourse] —**mis·ol′o·gist** *n.*

mis·o·ne·ism (mis′ō·nē′iz·əm, mī′sō-) *n.* Hatred of change or novelty. [< MISO- + Gk. *neos* new] —**mis′o·ne′ist** *n.*

mis·pick·el (mis′pik·əl) *n.* Arsenopyrite, a mineral. [< G; ult. origin unknown]

mis·place (mis·plās′) *v.t.* **·placed, ·plac·ing 1.** To put in a wrong place. **2.** To put (confidence, faith, trust, etc.) in an unworthy or unsuitable person, thing, or idea. **3.** To mislay (def. 1). —**mis·place′ment** *n.*

mis·play (mis·plā′; *for n., also* mis′plā) *v.t. & v.i.* In games or sports, to play badly or incorrectly. —*n.* A bad play or move.

mis·plead (mis·plēd′) *v.t. & v.i.* **·plead·ed** or **·pled** (-pled′), **·plead·ing** To plead incorrectly.

mis·plead·ing (mis·plē′ding) *n. Law* An error in pleading, or the omission of anything required for the support or defense of an action.

mis·print (mis·print′; *for n., also* mis′print′) *v.t.* To print incorrectly. —*n.* An error in printing.

mis·pri·sion (mis·prizh′ən) *n.* **1.** *Law* **a** Concealment of a crime, especially of treason or felony. **b** Misconduct of a public official; often, a clerical error. **2.** *Archaic* Misconception; misunderstanding. [< OF *mesprision* mistake < *mesprendre* to do wrong, take amiss < *mes-* + *prendre* to take < L *prehendere*]

mis·prize (mis·prīz′) *v.t.* **·prized, ·priz·ing** To fail to appreciate the worth of; undervalue; despise.

mis·pro·nounce (mis′prə·nouns′) *v.t. & v.i.* **·nounced, ·nounc·ing** To pronounce incorrectly or in an unorthodox manner. —**mis·pro·nun·ci·a·tion** (mis′prə·nun′sē·ā′shən) *n.*

mis·quote (mis·kwōt′) *v.t. & v.i.* **·quot·ed, ·quot·ing** To quote incorrectly. —**mis·quo·ta·tion** (mis′kwō·tā′shən) *n.*

mis·read (mis·rēd′) *v.t.* **·read** (-red′), **·read·ing** (-rē′ding) To read incorrectly or with the wrong sense; misinterpret.

mis·reck·on (mis·rek′ən) *v.t. & v.i.* To reckon incorrectly; miscalculate.

mis·re·mem·ber (mis′ri·mem′bər) *v.t. & v.i.* To remember incorrectly or imperfectly.

mis·re·port (mis′ri·pôrt′, -pōrt′) *v.t.* To report erroneously or falsely. —*n.* An erroneous or false report.

mis·rep·re·sent (mis′rep·ri·zent′) *v.t.* **1.** To give an incorrect or false representation of. **2.** To represent inadequately or poorly: to *misrepresent* one's country or one's client. **— mis/rep·re·sen·ta/tion** *n.* **— mis/rep·re·sen/ta·tive** *adj.* & *n.* **— mis/rep·re·sent/er** *n.*

mis·rule (mis·rool/) *v.t.* **·ruled, ·rul·ing** To rule unwisely or unjustly; misgovern. **—** *n.* **1.** Bad or unjust rule or government. **2.** Disorder or confusion, as from lawlessness.

miss[1] (mis) *v.t.* **1.** To fail to hit, strike, reach, or land upon (a specified object). **2.** To fail to meet or catch: to *miss* a train. **3.** To fail to obtain, accomplish, or achieve: to *miss* the presidency by a few votes. **4.** To fail to see, hear, perceive, etc.: to *miss* the point. **5.** To fail to attend, keep, perform, etc.: to *miss* church. **6.** To overlook or fail to take advantage of: to *miss* an opportunity. **7.** To discover the absence of, usually belatedly: to *miss* one's wallet. **8.** To feel the loss or absence of: to *miss* one's friend. **9.** To escape; avoid: He narrowly *missed* being killed. **—** *v.i.* **10.** To fail to hit; strike wide of the mark. **11.** To be unsuccessful; fail. **12.** *Archaic* To fail to possess, acquire, find, reach, etc.: used with *of.* **—** *n.* **1.** A failure to hit, find, attain, succeed, etc. **2.** *Obs.* Loss; lack. [OE *missan*]

miss[2] (mis) *n.* **1.** *Often cap.* A title used in speaking to an unmarried woman or girl: used without name. **2.** A young girl: chiefly informal or trade usage: clothing for *misses.* [Contraction of MISTRESS]

Miss (mis) *n.* A title of address used before the name of a girl or unmarried woman. ◆ In referring to two or more unmarried women bearing the same name, either *the Misses Brown* or *the Miss Browns* is acceptable. The latter is less formal and probably more widely used.

Miss. Mississippi.

mis·sal (mis/əl) *n.* **1.** A book containing all the prayers, responses, etc., for celebrating Mass throughout the year. **2.** Loosely, any prayer book. [< Med.L *missale*, neut. of *missalis* (*liber*) mass (book) < LL *missa* mass]

mis·say (mis·sā/) *v.t.* & *v.i.* **·said, ·say·ing** *Archaic* **1.** To say wrongly or incorrectly. **2.** To malign; slander.

mis·sel thrush (mis/əl) A large European thrush (*Turdus viscivorus*) that feeds largely on mistletoe berries: also called *wood thrush.* Also **mis/sel.** [OE *mistel* mistletoe]

mis·shape (mis·shāp/) *v.t.* **·shaped, ·shaped** or **·shap·en, ·shap·ing** To shape badly; deform.

mis·shap·en (mis·shā/pən) *adj.* Shaped badly; deformed.

mis·sile (mis/əl, *Brit.* mis/īl) *n.* **1.** An object, especially a weapon, intended to be thrown or discharged, as a bullet, arrow, stone, etc. **2.** A guided missile (which see). **—** *adj.* **1.** Such as may be thrown or discharged: a *missile* weapon. **2.** Used or adapted for throwing or discharging missiles. [< L *missilis* < *missus*, pp. of *mittere* to send]

mis·sile·man (mis/əl·mən) *n.* *pl.* **·men** (-mən) One trained or skilled in the design, construction, use, etc., of missiles.

mis·sil·ry (mis/əl·rē) *n.* The science and art of designing, building, and operating missiles, especially rockets and guided missiles. Also **mis/sile·ry.**

miss·ing (mis/ing) *adj.* **1.** Not present; absent; lacking. **2.** *Mil.* Absent: said of one whose whereabouts or fate in battle has not been determined: also **missing in action.**

missing link **1.** A hypothetical animal assumed to be intermediate in development between man and the anthropoid apes. **2.** Something lacking that if found would complete a chain or series.

mis·sion (mish/ən) *n.* **1.** Any body of persons sent some place in order to perform or accomplish a specific work or service; especially, such a body sent to a foreign country to conduct business, negotiations, etc., on behalf of its own country. **2.** The specific task, business, or responsibility that a person or body of persons is assigned to do or fulfill: Our *mission* was to aid the victims of the flood. **3.** A body of missionaries sent by a religious organization to a foreign country or region to convert, aid, or instruct the inhabitants. **4.** *pl.* The organized work of such missionaries: to assist the *missions.* **5.** The place or establishment where missionaries carry on their work and often live; also, the entire district or locality that they serve. **6.** An organized church or congregation without a resident minister or priest of its own. **7.** A special program or series of religious services or exercises for stimulating piety or converting unbelievers. **8.** *U.S.* The permanent foreign office of an ambassador or envoy; embassy. **9.** A center or place, chiefly in cities, where the destitute and underprivileged may go for aid, counsel, etc. **10.** The particular work or goal that one is or feels destined to do or accomplish; a calling. **11.** *Mil.* A definite task or field of operation assigned to an individual or unit of the armed forces. **12.** *Aeron.* A flight operation of a single aircraft or formation, especially in wartime. **13.** The act of sending, or the state of being sent. **—** *adj.* **1.** Pertaining or belonging to a mission. **2.** Of or similar to the early Spanish missions of the SW United States: *mission* architecture. **—** *v.t.* **1.** To send on a mission. **2.** To establish a mission in or among. [< L *missio, -onis* < *missus*, pp. of *mittere* to send] **— mis/sion·er** *n.*

mis·sion·ar·y (mish/ən·er/ē) *n.* *pl.* **·ar·ies** **1.** A person sent to propagate religion or to do educational or charitable work in some foreign country or region. **2.** One who advocates or spreads any new system or doctrine. **3.** One who is sent on a mission. **—** *adj.* Of, pertaining to, or characteristic of religious missions or missionaries.

Mis·sion·ar·y Ridge (mish/ən·er/ē) A ridge in Tennessee and Georgia; a Civil War battleground, 1863.

mis·sis (mis/əz) *n.* *Informal* & *Dial.* **1.** A wife: often with *the.* **2.** The female head of a household: with *the.* Also spelled *missus.* [Alter. of MISTRESS]

Mis·sis·sip·pi (mis/ə·sip/ē) A State in the south central United States, on the Gulf of Mexico; 47,716 sq. mi.; pop. 2,216,912; capital, Jackson; entered the Union Dec. 10, 1817: nickname *Bayou State.* Abbr. *Miss.*

Mis·sis·sip·pi·an (mis/ə·sip/ē·ən) *adj.* **1.** Of or pertaining to the Mississippi River or to the State. **2.** *Geol.* Relating to the earliest of the two geological periods or systems in the American Carboniferous division of the Paleozoic era. See chart for GEOLOGY. **—** *n.* **1.** One born or residing in Mississippi. **2.** The Lower Carboniferous or Mississippian geological formation.

Mississippi River A river in the central United States, flowing about 2,330 miles to the Gulf of Mexico; from the headwaters of the Missouri River, flowing about 3,872 miles.

THE MISSISSIPPI and Its Tributaries

mis·sive (mis/iv) *n.* A letter, especially one of an official nature. **—** *adj.* Sent or designed to be sent. [< Med.L *missivus* < L *missus*, pp. of *mittere* to send]

Mis·so·lon·ghi (mis/ə·lông/gē) A port city in west central Greece; here Byron died, April 29, 1824; pop. about 14,000. Greek *Mesolonghi.*

Mis·sou·la (mi·zoo/lə) A city in western Montana, on Clark Fork; pop. 29,497.

Mis·sou·ri (mi·zoor/ē, -zoor/ə) *n.* *pl.* **·ri** One of a tribe of North American Indians of the Siouan family, formerly inhabiting northern Missouri.

Mis·sou·ri (mi·zoor/ē, -zoor/ə) A State in the west central United States west of the Mississippi; 69,674 sq. mi.; pop. 4,677,399; capital, Jefferson City; entered the Union Aug. 10, 1821: nickname, *Ozark State* or *Show Me State.* Abbr. *Mo.* **— from Missouri** *U.S. Informal* Skeptical or unbelieving until furnished with definite proof. **— Mis·sou/ri·an** *adj.* & *n.*

Missouri River The longest river of the United States, flowing 2,714 miles from the Rocky Mountains to the Mississippi River near St. Louis. See map of MISSISSIPPI RIVER.

mis·speak (mis·spēk/) *v.t.* & *v.i.* **·spoke, ·speak·ing** To speak or pronounce incorrectly.

mis·spell (mis·spel/) *v.t.* & *v.i.* **·spelled** or **·spelt, ·spell·ing** To spell incorrectly.

mis·spell·ing (mis·spel/ing) *n.* An incorrect spelling.

mis·spend (mis·spend/) *v.t.* **·spent, ·spend·ing** To spend wrongfully or wastefully.

mis·spent (mis·spent/) *adj.* Spent or used foolishly or wastefully.

mis·state (mis·stāt/) *v.t.* **·stat·ed, ·stat·ing** To state wrongly or falsely. **— mis·state/ment** *n.*

mis·step (mis·step/) *n.* **1.** A false step; a stumble. **2.** An error or blunder, as in conduct.

mis·sus (mis/əs) *n.* Same as MISSIS.

miss·y (mis/ē) *n.* *pl.* **miss·ies** Miss: an informal or diminutive form.

mist (mist) *n.* **1.** An aggregation of fine drops of water suspended in the atmosphere at or near the earth's surface. **2.** *Meteorol.* A very thin fog with a horizontal visibility arbitrarily set by international agreement at not more than two kilometers. **3.** Watery vapor condensed on and blurring a surface. **4.** Any colloidal suspension of a liquid in a gas. **5.** Any cloud of particles forming a haze, as of dust, smoke, etc. **6.** A film or haze before the eyes that blurs one's vision: a *mist* of tears. **7.** Anything that clouds or obscures one's memory, perceptions, etc. **—** *v.i.* **1.** To be or become dim or misty; blur. **2.** To rain in very fine drops. **—** *v.t.* **3.** To make dim or misty; blur. [OE]

mis·tak·a·ble (mis·tāk/ə·bəl) *adj.* Capable of being mistaken or misunderstood. **— mis·tak/a·bly** *adv.*

mis·take (mis·tāk/) *n.* An error or fault in action, judgment, perception, understanding, etc. **—** *v.* **·took, ·tak·en, ·tak·ing** *v.t.* **1.** To understand wrongly; acquire a wrong conception of; misinterpret. **2.** To take (a person or thing) to be another: to *mistake* friends for enemies. — *v.i.* **3.** To make a mistake. [< ON *mistaka*]

mis·tak·en (mis-tā'kən) *adj.* **1.** Based on or arising from error, as of judgment, understanding, perception, etc.: *mistaken* views. **2.** Wrong in opinion, action, etc.: He is *mistaken* in his views. — **mis·tak'en·ly** *adv.*

Mis·tas·si·ni Lake (mis'tä-sē'nē) A lake in central Quebec, Canada; 840 sq. mi.

mis·ter (mis'tər) *n. Informal* Sir: used without the name. [Var. of MASTER]

Mis·ter (mis'tər) *n.* **1.** Master: a title of address prefixed to the name and to some official titles of a man: commonly written *Mr.: Mr.* Darwin; The Reverend *Mr.* Younge. **2.** The official term of address for certain military and naval persons; as: **a** Warrant officers. **b** Flight officers. **c** Cadets and midshipmen. **d** All officers beneath the rank of commander in the U.S. Navy. **e** All officers beneath the rank of captain in the Merchant Marine.

mist·flow·er (mist'flou'ər) *n.* A tall perennial herb (*Eupatorium coelestinum*) of the composite family, having clusters of light blue or violet flowers.

mis·think (mis-thingk') *v.* **·thought** (-thôt'), **·think·ing** *Archaic v.i.* **1.** To think wrongly. — *v.t.* **2.** To think ill of.

Mis·ti (mēs'tē), **El** See EL MISTI.

mis·time (mis-tīm') *v.t.* **·timed**, **·tim·ing** **1.** To time wrongly or inappropriately: We *mistimed* our visit. **2.** To misjudge the time of: I *mistimed* your arrival by two hours.

mis·tle·toe (mis'əl·tō) *n.* **1.** A European parasitic shrub (*Viscum album*), found growing on various deciduous trees and having yellowish green leaves, inconspicuous flowers, and glutinous white berries, used as a Christmas decoration. **2.** An American plant (*Phoradendron flavescens*) related to this shrub, used as a Christmas decoration and the State flower of Oklahoma. [OE *misteltān* mistletoe twig]

MISTLETOE

mis·took (mis-tŏŏk') Past tense of MIS-TAKE. Also *Scot.* **mis·teuk** (-tyŏŏk').

mis·tral (mis'trəl, *Fr.* mēs·tral') *n.* A cold, dry, violent northerly wind blowing down the Rhône Valley through Southern France and adjacent areas. [< F < Provençal, lit., master wind < L *magistralis* < *magister* master]

Mis·tral (mēs·tral'), **Frédéric**, 1830–1914, French Provençal poet and lexicographer. — **Gabriela**, 1889–1957, Chilean poet: original name **Lucila Go·doy' Al'ca·ya'ga** (gō-thoi' äl'kä-yä'gä).

mis·trans·late (mis'trans·lāt', -tranz-, mis·trans'lāt, -tranz'-) *v.t.* **·lat·ed**, **·lat·ing** To translate incorrectly. — **mis'trans·la'tion** *n.*

mis·treat (mis-trēt') *v.t.* To treat badly or improperly. — **mis·treat'ment** *n.*

mis·tress (mis'tris) *n.* **1.** A woman in a position of authority or control; as: **a** The head of a household, institution, or estate. **b** The head of a staff of servants. **c** The owner of an animal or slave: the dog's *mistress.* **2.** A woman who unlawfully cohabits with a man, usually over an extended period of time. **3.** A woman having supreme control over anything: She was *mistress* of his heart. **4.** *Often cap.* Anything considered feminine that has actual or potential power over something else: Louisiana, *mistress* of the Mississippi. **5.** A woman who has mastered a skill, craft, or branch of learning: a *mistress* of embroidery. **6.** *Chiefly Brit.* A female schoolteacher. **7.** *Archaic* A sweetheart. **8.** *Scot.* A married woman. [< OF *maistresse*, fem. of *maistre.* See MASTER.]

Mis·tress (mis'tris) *n.* Formerly, a title of address applied to women, now generally supplanted by *Mrs.* for married and *Miss* for unmarried women.

Mistress of the Adriatic Venice.
Mistress of the Seas Great Britain.
Mistress of the World Rome, when it embraced the known world.

mis·tri·al (mis-trī'əl) *n. Law* **1.** A trial made void because of some legal errors or defects. **2.** A trial terminated by the jury's inability to agree on a verdict.

mis·trust (mis-trust') *v.t.* **1.** To regard (someone or something) with suspicion or doubt; be skeptical of. **2.** *Obs.* To have foreboding of. — *v.i.* **3.** To be wary or suspicious. — *n.* Lack of trust or confidence. — **mis·trust'er** *n.*

mis·trust·ful (mis-trust'fəl) *adj.* Full of mistrust; suspicious. — **mis·trust'ful·ly** *adv.* — **mis·trust'ful·ness** *n.*

mis·trust·ing·ly (mis-trus'ting·lē) *adv.* With mistrust.

mis·tryst (mis-trist') *v.t. Scot.* **1.** To fail to keep an engagement with. **2.** To perplex.

mist·y (mis'tē) *adj.* **mist·i·er**, **mist·i·est** **1.** Consisting of, characterized by, or having the nature of mist. **2.** Dimmed or obscured by or as by mist. **3.** Lacking clarity; indistinct; vague. — **mist'i·ly** *adv.* — **mist'i·ness** *n.*

mis·un·der·stand (mis'un·dər·stand', mis·un'-) *v.t. & v.i.* **·stood**, **·stand·ing** To understand wrongly; misinterpret.

mis·un·der·stand·ing (mis'un·dər·stan'ding, mis·un'-) *n.* **1.** A failure to understand the meaning, motive, etc., of someone or something. **2.** A disagreement or quarrel.

mis·un·der·stood (mis'un·dər·stŏŏd', mis·un'-) *adj.* **1.** Wrongly understood. **2.** Not valued or appreciated.

mis·us·age (mis-yŏŏ'sij, -zij) *n.* **1.** Incorrect or improper use: His *misusage* of words is hilarious. **2.** Ill-treatment.

mis·use (*n.* mis·yŏŏs'; *v.* mis·yŏŏz') *n.* **1.** Erroneous or improper use; misapplication. **2.** *Obs.* Ill-treatment; abuse. — *v.t.* **·used**, **·us·ing** **1.** To use or apply wrongly or improperly. **2.** To treat badly; abuse; maltreat.

mis·us·er (mis-yŏŏ'zər) *n.* **1.** One who misuses. **2.** *Law* A misuse or abuse of a privilege, franchise, office, etc.

mis·val·ue (mis-val'yŏŏ) *v.t.* **·ued**, **·u·ing** To value wrongly.

mis·ven·ture (mis-ven'chər) *n.* A misadventure.

mis·word (mis-wûrd') *v.t.* To word wrongly.

mis·write (mis-rīt') *v.t.* **·wrote** (*Archaic* or *Dial.* **·writ**), **·writ·ten** (*Archaic* or *Dial.* **·writ**), **·writ·ing** To write incorrectly.

Mitch·ell (mich'əl), **John**, 1870–1919, U.S. labor leader. — **William**, 1879–1936, U.S. general born in France; early advocate of air power: called **Billy Mitchell**.

Mitch·ell (mich'əl), **Mount** A peak in the Black Mountains, western North Carolina; the highest point in the United States east of the Mississippi; 6,684 ft.

mite¹ (mīt) *n.* Any of various small arachnids (order *Acarina*), many of which are parasitic on men, animals, plants, and stored grain. [OE *mīte*] — **mit'y** *adj.*

mite² (mīt) *n.* **1.** A very small particle, object, or creature. **2.** Any very small coin or sum of money. **3.** A widow's mite (which see). [< Du. *mijt*]

mi·ter (mī'tər) *n.* **1.** A tall ornamental headdress, rising in peaks at the front and back, worn by popes, bishops, and abbots. **2.** The office or dignity of a bishop. **3.** The official headdress of the ancient Jewish high priest. **4.** In ancient Greece, a headband commonly worn by women. **5.** A device used on the top of a chimney to keep out the wind and rain and still permit the smoke to leave. **6.** In carpentry: **a** A miter joint. **b** The beveled edges that come together to form a miter joint. **c** A miter square. — *v.t.* **1.** To confer a miter upon; raise to the rank of bishop. **2.** To make or join with a miter joint. Also, *Brit.*, **mitre**. [< OF *mitre* < L *mitra* < Gk., belt, turban] — **mi'ter·er** *n.*

miter box A troughlike device whose sides are slotted to guide a handsaw in the making of accurate miter joints.

mi·tered (mī'tərd) *adj.* **1.** Shaped like an ecclesiastical miter. **2.** Wearing or permitted to wear a miter. Also, *Brit.*, **mitred**.

miter joint A joint made of two pieces of material whose joined ends have been beveled at equal angles, as at the corner of a picture frame.

miter square A square having either a blade adjustable to any angle or an immovable blade set at a 45° angle, used in marking the angles of miter joints.

mi·ter·wort (mī'tər·wûrt') *n.* **1.** Any of a genus (*Mitella*) of low, slender, saxifragaceous herbs, growing mainly in North America and having small flowers with capsules resembling a bishop's miter: also called *bishop's-cap.* **2.** A loganiaceous plant (*Cynoctonum mitreola*) of the SE United States. Also, *Brit.*, **mitrewort**.

Mit·ford (mit'fərd), **Mary Russell**, 1787–1855, English author.

mith·er (mith'ər) *n. Scot.* Mother.

Mith·gar·thr (mith'gär·thər) See MIDGARD.

Mith·ra·ism (mith'rā·iz'əm) *n.* The worship of Mithras. Also **Mith·ra·i·cism** (mith·rā'ə·siz'əm). — **Mith·ra·ic** (mith-rā'ik), **Mith·ra·is·tic** (mith'rā·is'tik) *adj.*

Mith·ras (mith'rəs) The ancient Persian god of light and truth, often identified with the sun. Also **Mith'ra** (-rə). [< L < Gk. *Mithras* < OPersian *Mithra*]

mith·ri·date (mith'rə·dāt) *n.* Formerly, a substance considered to be an antidote for all poisons. [< Med.L *mithridatum*, ult. < L *Mithridatius* of Mithridates]

Mith·ri·da·tes VI (mith'rə·dā'tēz), 132?–63 B.C., king of Pontus; defeated by Pompey: called **the Great**.

mith·ri·dat·ism (mith'rə·dā'tiz·əm) *n.* Immunity against poisons by the administration of gradually increasing doses: so called from King Mithridates VI of Pontus who is said to have immunized himself by this method. — **mith'ri·dat'ic** (-dat'ik) *adj.*

mit·i·gate (mit'ə·gāt) *v.t. & v.i.* **·gat·ed**, **·gat·ing** To make or become milder or less severe. — **Syn.** See ALLEVIATE. [< L *mitigatus*, pp. of *mitigare* < *mitis* mild + *agere* to do, drive] — **mit'i·ga·ble** *adj.* — **mit'i·ga'tor** *n.*

mit·i·ga·tion (mit'ə·gā'shən) *n.* **1.** The act of mitigating, or the state of being mitigated. **2.** Something that mitigates.

mit·i·ga·tive (mit'ə·gā'tiv) *adj.* Tending to mitigate. — *n.* Something that mitigates pain, discomfort, etc. Also **mit'i·gant** (-gənt), **mit'i·ga·to·ry** (-gə·tôr'ē, -tō'rē).

mi·tis iron (mī'tis, mē'-) *Metall.* Wrought iron improved in malleability by the addition of a small amount of aluminum. [< L *mitis* mild]

mi·to·chon·dri·a (mī'tə·kon'drē·ə) *n.pl. Biol.* Small granular bodies found in the cytoplasm of a cell, believed to function in certain phases of oxidative metabolism: also called *chondriosomes.* For illustration see CELL. [< NL < Gk. *mitos* thread + *chondros* cartilage, granule]

mi·to·sis (mī-tō′sis) *n. Biol.* The series of changes in cell division by which the chromatin is modified into two sets of chromosomes that split longitudinally, one set going to each pole before the cell divides into two mature daughter cells: also called *karyokinesis*. Compare MEIOSIS. [< NL < Gk. *mitos* thread + -OSIS] — **mi·tot·ic** (mī-tot′ik) *adj.* — **mi·tot′i·cal·ly** *adv.*

mi·trail·leur (mē-trà-yœr′) *n.* **1.** A soldier who operates a mitrailleuse. **2.** A mitrailleuse. [< F < *mitrailler* to fire grapeshot < *mitraille* grapeshot, small coins < OF *mitre, mite* small coin]

mi·trail·leuse (mē-trà-yœz′) *n.* **1.** A breechloading machine gun with a group of barrels that may be fired simultaneously or in quick succession, introduced in the 19th century. **2.** Any machine gun. [< F]

mi·tral (mī′trəl) *adj.* **1.** Pertaining to or resembling a miter. **2.** Of or pertaining to a mitral valve.

mitral valve *Anat.* A membranous valve between the left atrium and the left ventrical of the heart, that prevents the blood from flowing back into the atrium.

mi·tre (mī′tər), **mi·tred** (mī′tərd), etc. See MITER, etc.

Mi·trop·ou·los (mi-trop′ə-ləs), Dimitri, 1896–1960, U.S. orchestra conductor born in Greece.

mitt (mit) *n.* **1.** In baseball, a covering constructed somewhat like a mitten, to protect the hand catching the ball, as a **catcher's mitt** or **first baseman's mitt**. **2.** A woman's glove, often of lace or knitwork, sometimes extending to or above the elbow but without fully covering the fingers. **3.** A mitten (def. 1). **4.** *Slang* Usually *pl.* A hand. **5.** *Slang* A boxing glove. [< MITTEN]

mit·ten (mit′n) *n.* **1.** A covering for the hand, encasing the four fingers together and the thumb separately. **2.** A mitt (def. 2). **3.** *Usually pl. Slang* A mitt (def. 4). — **to get the mitten** *Archaic Informal* To be rejected as a lover. — **to give the mitten** *Archaic Informal* To reject or jilt as a lover. [< F *mitaine*]

mit·ti·mus (mit′ə-məs) *n.* **1.** *Law* A warrant committing a person to jail: also *commitment*. **2.** *Brit. Informal* A dismissal, as from a job. [< L, we send < *mittere* to send]

mitz·vah (mits′vä) *n. pl.* **·vahs** or **·voth** (-vōth) In Judaism: **a** A commandment or rule of conduct, as found in the Bible or issued by a rabbi. **b** The fulfillment of such a commandment. **c** Any meritorious act. Also **mits′vah**. [< Hebrew *miswah* commandment < *şiwa* to command]

Mi·vart (mī′vərt, miv′ərt), St. George Jackson, 1827–1900, English biologist.

mix (miks) *v.* **mixed** or **mixt**, **mix·ing** *v.t.* **1.** To combine or put together in one mass or compound so as to render the constituent parts wholly or partially indistinguishable from one another. **2.** To make by combining ingredients: to *mix* cake batter. **3.** To put or add, as an ingredient: to *mix* two eggs into the batter. **4.** To combine or join: to *mix* age with wisdom. **5.** To bring into contact with; cause to mingle: to *mix* the old and the young. **6.** To crossbreed. — *v.i.* **7.** To become mixed or have the capacity to become mixed; mingle: This paste *mixes* well with water. **8.** To associate; get along: He does not *mix* well with others. **9.** To take part; become involved. **10.** To crossbreed. — **to mix it up** *Slang* To fight or exchange blows. — **to mix up 1.** To mix or blend together. **2.** To confuse. **3.** To mistake for another or others: He *mixed up* the meanings of those two words. **4.** To implicate or involve: He is *mixed up* in politics. — *n.* **1.** The act or product of mixing. **2.** A combination or mixture of ingredients, often prepared and sold commercially: a cake *mix*. **3.** A beverage, as water, soda, ginger ale, etc., used in the making of cocktails and other mixed drinks. **4.** Confusion or bewilderment; a muddle; mess. **5.** *Telecom.* The correct blending of the outputs of two or more microphones. [Back formation < MIXED] — **mix′a·ble** or **mix′i·ble** *adj.*

mixed (mikst) *adj.* **1.** Mingled or blended together in a single mass or compound. **2.** Composed of different, dissimilar, or incongruous elements, qualities, classes, races, etc.: *mixed* motives. **3.** Made up of or involving persons of both sexes: *mixed* school; *mixed* foursome. **4.** Mentally confused; bewildered: followed by *up*. **5.** *Law* Composed of or applying to more than one class or type of statute, property, or action. **6.** *Phonet.* Designating a vowel produced with neither front nor back articulation predominating; central. **7.** *Bot.* Denoting a combination of cymose and racemose inflorescence. Also **mixt**. — **Syn.** See HETEROGENEOUS. [< F *mixte* < L *mixtus*, pp. of *miscere* to mix]

mixed marriage Marriage between persons of different religions or races.

mixed metaphor See under METAPHOR.

mixed number A number, as 3½, 5¾, that is the sum of an integer and a fraction.

mix·er (mik′sər) *n.* **1.** One who or that which mixes. **2.** *Informal* A person with ability to mix socially or get along well in various groups. **3.** *Informal* A dance or gathering for the purpose of getting acquainted. **4.** A mix (def. 3).

mix·ture (miks′chər) *n.* **1.** Something formed by or resulting from mixing. **2.** Anything composed of unlike or various elements; as: **a** A cloth made of several types or colors of yarn. **b** A blend of different kinds or qualities of tea, tobacco, etc. **3.** *Chem.* A commingling of two or more substances in varying proportions, in which the components retain their individual chemical properties: distinguished from *compound*. **4.** In pharmacy, an aqueous solution in which an insoluble compound is suspended. **5.** The act of mixing, or the state of being mixed. [< F < L *mixtura* < *miscere* to mix]

mix·up (miks′up′) *n.* **1.** A state of confusion; also, an instance of this. **2.** *Informal* A fight.

Mi·ya·za·ki (mē-yä-zä-kē) A city on SE Kyushu island, Japan; pop. 212,000 (est. 1968).

miz·zen (miz′ən) *Naut. n.* **1.** A triangular sail set on the mizzenmast. **2.** A mizzenmast. — *adj.* Of or pertaining to the mizzen or mizzenmast. Also **miz′en**. [< F *misaine* < Ital. *mezzana*, fem. of *mezzano* middle, ? < L *medianus*. Doublet of MEDIAN, MEAN³, MESNE.]

miz·zen·mast (miz′ən-məst′, -mast′, -mäst′) *n. Naut.* **1.** In a ship with three masts, the mast nearest the stern. **2.** In a ship having more than three masts, the third mast from the forward end of the ship. **3.** In a ketch or yawl, the shorter of the two masts. Also **miz′en·mast′**.

mizzen sail *Naut.* The lowest sail on the mizzenmast of a full-rigged ship: also called *crossjack*. Also **mizen sail**.

Mjol·nir (myol′nir) *n.* In Norse mythology, Thor's hammer. Also **Mjoll′nir**, **Mjöll·nir** (myœl′nir), **Mjol·ner**.

mk. 1. Mark(s). **2.** Markka(s).

Mk. Mark.

mks The meter-kilogram-second system of measurement in which the unit of length is the meter, the unit of mass is the kilogram, and the unit of time is one second. Also **m.k.s.**, MKS, M.K.S.

mkt. Market.

ml. 1. Mail. **2.** Milliliter(s).

ML or ML. or M.L. Medieval (or Middle) Latin.

M.L.A. 1. Member of the Legislative Assembly. **2.** Modern Language Association.

MLG or MLG. or M.L.G. Middle Low German.

Mlle. or Mlle Mademoiselle.

Mlles. or Mlles Mesdemoiselles.

M.L.S. Master of Library Science.

mm. or mm 1. Millimeter(s). **2.** Thousands (L *millia*).

m.m. With the necessary changes (L *mutatis mutandis*).

MM. Messieurs.

Mme. or Mme Madame.

Mmes. or Mmes Mesdames.

Mn *Chem.* Manganese.

mne·mon·ic (nē-mon′ik, ni-) *adj.* **1.** Aiding or designed to aid the memory. **2.** Of or relating to mnemonics or memory. Also **mne·mon′i·cal**. — *n.* **1.** A device to assist memory. **2.** Mnemonics. [< Gk. *mnēmonikos* < *mnēmōn* mindful < *mnasthai* to remember]

mne·mon·ics (nē-mon′iks, ni-) *n.pl.* (construed as sing.) A system of principles and formulas designed to assist or improve the memory. Also **mne·mo·tech·nics** (nē′mō-tek′niks).

Mne·mos·y·ne (nē-mos′ə-nē, -moz′-) In Greek mythology, the goddess of memory and, by Zeus, mother of the Muses. [< L < Gk. *mnēmosynē* memory < *mnasthai* to remember]

mo. Month(s).

Mo *Chem.* Molybdenum.

Mo. 1. Missouri. **2.** Monday.

M.O. 1. Medical Officer. **2.** Money order: also **m.o.**

mo·a (mō′ə) *n.* Any of a family (*Dinornithidae*) of extinct, flightless birds of New Zealand, resembling the ostrich and having very powerful legs. [< Maori]

Mo·ab (mō′ab) An ancient country east of the Dead Sea.

Mo·ab·ite (mō′əb-īt) *n.* **1.** One of the descendants of Moab, son of Lot (*Gen.* xix 37). **2.** An inhabitant of Moab. **3.** The language of Moab. — *adj.* Of or relating to Moab, the Moabites, or to their language: also **Mo·ab·it·ic** (mō′əb-it′ik), **Mo·ab·it·ish** (mō′əb-īt′ish). — **Mo·ab·it·ess** (mō′əb-īt′is) *n.fem.*

moan (mōn) *n.* **1.** A low, sustained, mournful sound, as from grief or pain. **2.** Any similar sound: the *moan* of the wind. **3.** *Obs.* Lamentation; complaint. — *v.i.* **1.** To utter moans. **2.** To make a low, mournful sound, as wind. **3.** To complain or lament. — *v.t.* **4.** To lament; bewail. **5.** To utter with moans. [Cf. OE *mǣnan* to lament, moan]

moat (mōt) *n.* A deep, wide, and usually water-filled trench around a castle, fortress, or town, designed to discourage attempts at invasion. — *v.t.* To surround with or as with a moat. [< OF *mote* embankment]

mob¹ (mob) *n.* **1.** A disorderly or lawless crowd or throng; a rabble. **2.** Any large assemblage, group, or class of indi-

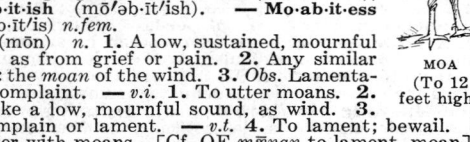

MOA
(To 12 feet high)

viduals or things: the ruling *mob*. **3.** The lower class or classes of people; the masses. **4.** *Informal* A gang of thieves, hoodlums, etc. — *v.t.* **mobbed, mob·bing 1.** To attack in a mob. **2.** To crowd around and jostle or molest, as from adulation or curiosity. **3.** To attend or crowd into (a hall, theater, etc.). [< L *mob*(*ile vulgus*) movable crowd] — **mob′ber** *n.* — **mob′bish** *adj.* — **mob′bish·ly** *adv.*

mob² (mob) *n.* A large, high-crowned, frilly cap or headdress formerly worn by women and usually tied under the chin. Also **mob′cap′** (-kap′). [Cf. Du. *mop* coif, cap]

mo·bile (*adj.* mō′bəl, -bēl; *n.* mō′bēl; *Brit.* mō′bīl) *adj.* **1.** Characterized by freedom of movement; movable. **2.** Flowing freely: a *mobile* liquid. **3.** Capable of changing or responding easily or quickly, as to emotions, etc.: a very *mobile* face; a *mobile* personality. **4.** Moving easily from one thing to another; versatile: a *mobile* mind. **5.** Capable of being easily and quickly moved: a *mobile* hospital. **6.** Capable of moving with relative ease from one social group, class, or status to another. **7.** Of, pertaining to, or like a mobile. — *n.* A form of sculpture consisting of movable parts that are suspended from or balanced on rods, wires, etc., and are capable of being set or sustained in motion by slight air currents or by mechanical means. Compare STABILE. [< F < L *mobilis* movable < *movere* to move]
— **Syn.** (adj.). **1.** motile. **3.** variable, volatile, fickle. — **Ant.** immobile, immovable, fixed, stolid.

Mo·bile (mō-bēl′) A port city in SW Alabama; pop. 190,026; on **Mobile Bay**, an inlet of the Gulf of Mexico.

mobile home A trailer (def. 3).

mo·bil·i·ty (mō-bil′ə-tē) *n.* The quality, character, or state of being mobile.

mo·bi·lize (mō′bə-līz) *v.* **·lized, ·liz·ing** *v.t.* **1.** To make ready for war, as an army, industry, men, etc. **2.** To assemble for use; organize: to *mobilize* the nation's resources. **3.** To put into activity, circulation, or use: to *mobilize* one's talents. — *v.i.* **4.** To undergo mobilization. Also *Brit.* **mo′bi·lise.** [< F *mobiliser*] — **mo′bi·li·za′tion** (-lə-zā′shən, -lī-zā′-) *n.*

Mö·bi·us strip (mœ′bē-ŏŏs) *Geom.* A band having only one side, made by turning one end of a rectangular ribbon 180° and then fastening it to the other end. Also **Möbius band.** [after August Ferdinand *Möbius*, 1790–1868, German mathematician and astronomer]

mob·oc·ra·cy (mob-ok′rə-sē) *n. pl.* **·cies 1.** Rule by a mob. **2.** The dominant or ruling mob. Also called *ochlocracy*. [< MOB¹ + -(O)CRACY] — **mob·o·crat·ic** (mob′ə-krat′ik) or **·i·cal** *adj.*

mob·ster (mob′stər) *n. Slang* A gangster.

Mo·çam·bi·que (mōō′səm-bē′kə) The Portuguese name for MOZAMBIQUE.

moc·ca·sin (mok′ə-sin) *n.* **1.** A heelless foot covering, made of buckskin or of any soft leather and formerly worn by North American Indians. **2.** A shoe or slipper resembling a moccasin. **3.** The water moccasin (which see). [< Algonquian *mohkisson*]

moccasin flower Any of certain lady's-slippers, common in the United States; especially, a hardy species (*Cyprideum acaule*), having a pink, fragrant flower.

mo·cha (mō′kə) *n.* **1.** A choice, pungent coffee, originally brought from Mocha, Arabia. **2.** A flavoring made of an infusion of coffee or of coffee and chocolate. **3.** A fine sheepskin leather used for making gloves. [after *Mocha*]

Mo·cha (mō′khə) A port city in SW Yemen Arab Republic; pop. about 5,000: also *Mokha, Mukha.*

mo·chi·la (mō-chē′lə) *n. U.S.* A leather covering that fits over a saddle. [< Sp.]

mock (mok) *v.t.* **1.** To treat or address scornfully or derisively; hold up to ridicule. **2.** To mimic, as in sport, derision, or contempt. **3.** To deceive or disappoint; delude. **4.** To defy; make futile or meaningless. **5.** *Poetic* To imitate; counterfeit. — *v.i.* **6.** To express or show ridicule, scorn, or contempt; scoff. — *adj.* Merely imitating or resembling the reality; sham: a *mock* wedding. — *n.* **1.** An act of mocking or derision; a jeer. **2.** One who or that which is mocked. **3.** An imitation or counterfeit. [< OF *mocquer*] — **mock′er** *n.* — **mock′ing·ly** *adv.*
— **Syn.** (verb). **1.** taunt¹, twit, banter, rally². **4.** flout.

mock·er·y (mok′ər-ē) *n. pl.* **·er·ies 1.** Derision; ridicule. **2.** A contemptuous or derisive speech or action. **3.** An object of derision or ridicule. **4.** A deceitful, impudent, or contemptible imitation: His trial was a *mockery*. **5.** Something ludicrously futile, inadequate, or unsuitable.

mock-he·ro·ic (mok′hi-rō′ik) *adj.* Imitating or satirizing the heroic manner, style, attitude, or character. — *n.* Something mock-heroic in nature or manner, as a literary work, utterance, etc. Also **mock′-he·ro′i·cal.** — **mock′-he·ro′i·cal·ly** *adv.*

mock·ing·bird (mok′ing-bûrd′) *n.* **1.** A bird (*Mimus polyglottos*) common in the southern United States, noted for its ability to imitate the calls of other birds. **2.** Any of various other birds of the same family (*Mimidae*).

mock moon *Meteorol.* A paraselene.

mock orange The syringa.

mock sun *Meteorol.* A parhelion.

mock turtle soup A soup prepared from calf's head or other meat and seasoned to taste like green turtle soup.

mock-up (mok′up′) *n.* A model, usually full-scale, of a proposed structure, machine, apparatus, etc., constructed for purposes of study, testing, or training of personnel.

mod. 1. Moderate. **2.** *Music* Moderato. **3.** Modern.

mo·dal (mōd′l) *adj.* **1.** Of or pertaining to mode or a mode. **2.** *Gram.* **a** Of or pertaining to mood. **b** Conveying a meaning similar to those meanings conveyed by a mood. **3.** *Music* **a** Of or pertaining to the modes. **b** Written or performed in a mode, as plain song and other early music. **4.** *Philos.* Pertaining to form without reference to substance. **5.** *Logic* Expressing or involving modality. **6.** *Stat.* Most frequent; typical. — **mo′dal·ly** *adv.*

mo·dal·i·ty (mō-dal′ə-tē) *n. pl.* **·ties 1.** The fact, quality, or state of being modal. **2.** *Logic* The character of a proposition in respect to its asserting relations of necessity (including impossibility) or of contingency (including probability and possibility). **3.** *Med.* **a** Any of certain forms of physical therapy, as diathermy. **b** The apparatus used in such therapy. **4.** A tendency to belong or conform to a particular group or category.

mode (mōd) *n.* **1.** Manner or form of being, doing, etc.; way; method: a *mode* of political thought. **2.** Prevailing or current style or fashion, as in dress. **3.** *Gram.* Mood. **4.** *Music* **a** Any of the arrangements of tones achieved by starting at various points in a given scale and proceeding through one octave; especially, the modes of the diatonic scale, as major mode, minor mode, etc. Compare SCALE. **b** One of the twelve conventional scales of ancient and medieval Western music. **5.** *Philos.* The manner, appearance, or form in which a basic substance is manifested. **6.** *Logic* **a** Modality. **b** The arrangement of the propositions in a syllogism according to their quantity and quality. **7.** *Stat.* The value, magnitude, or score that occurs the greatest number of times in a given series of observations: also called *norm.* **8.** *Geol.* The actual mineral composition of an igneous rock, expressed in percentages by weight: distinguished from *norm.* [< L *modus* measure, manner]

mod·el (mod′l) *n.* **1.** An object, usually in miniature and often built according to scale, that represents something to be made or something already existing. **2.** A pattern, example, or standard that is or may be used for imitation or comparison: He is a *model* of industry. **3.** Information, data, principles, etc., arranged or grouped, usually mathematically, so as to represent or describe a certain thing, idea, or condition: weather *models*. **4.** A representation in clay, plaster, etc., of something later to be reproduced in more permanent material. **5.** One who or that which serves as a figure or pattern for an artist, sculptor, etc. **6.** One who is employed to display or advertise merchandise; especially, one who displays articles of clothing by wearing them. **7.** A representative style, plan, or design: houses built on the colonial *model*. **8.** In merchandise, a particular style or design: last year's *model*. — *v.* **mod·eled** or **·elled, mod·el·ing** or **·el·ling** *v.t.* **1.** To plan or fashion after a model or pattern. **2.** To make a model of. **3.** To shape or fashion; make. **4.** To display by wearing, as a coat or hat. **5.** In painting, drawing, etc., to show or accentuate, as by use of light and shadow, the three-dimensional appearance or quality of. — *v.i.* **6.** To make a model or models. **7.** To pose or serve as a model (defs. 5 & 6). — *adj.* **1.** Serving or used as a model. **2.** Worthy or suitable to be used as a model. [< F *modèle* < Ital. *modello*, dim. of *modo* < L *modus* measure, manner] — **mod′el·er** or **mod′el·ler** *n.*
— **Syn.** (noun) **2.** archetype, prototype. See EXAMPLE. **4.** sitter. **5.** manikin. Compare DUPLICATE.

mod·el·ing (mod′ling, -əl·ing) *n.* **1.** The act or art of making a model, especially a sculptor's clay or wax model. **2.** In painting, drawing, etc., the representation of depth or three-dimensional solidity. **3.** The surfaces or planes of a solid form or shape: the *modeling* of a person's features. **4.** The act or occupation of being a model (defs. 5 & 6). Also **mod′el·ling.**

Model T *U.S.* The Ford car of 1908–1928; a tin lizzie.

Mo·de·na (mō′dā-nä) A commune in north central Italy.

mod·er·ate (*adj. & n.* mod′ər·it; *v.* mod′ə-rāt) *adj.* **1.** Keeping or kept within reasonable limits; not extreme or excessive; temperate. **2.** Holding or characterized by ideas or convictions that are not extreme or radical: a *moderate* religious group; *moderate* political views. **3.** Of medium or average quality, quantity, scope, extent, etc.: a *moderate* intelligence; *moderate* incomes. **4.** *Meteorol.* Designating a breeze (No. 4) or a gale (No. 7) on the Beaufort scale. See BEAUFORT SCALE. — *n.* One who is characterized by moderate views, opinions, or practices, especially in politics or religion. — *v.* **·at·ed, ·at·ing** *v.t.* **1.** To reduce the violence, severity, etc., of; make less extreme; restrain. **2.** To preside over. — *v.i.* **3.** To become less intense or violent; abate. **4.** To act as a moderator. Abbr. **mod.** [< L *moderatus,* pp. of *moderare* to regulate < *modus* measure] — **mod′er·ate·ly** *adv.* — **mod′er·ate·ness** *n.*

mod·er·a·tion (mod′ə-rā′shən) *n.* **1.** The state or quality of being moderate. **2.** The act of moderating. **3.** *pl. Brit.*

moderato

The first public examinations for degrees at Oxford University: also *mods.* **—in moderation** Within reasonable limits; temperately. **Moder**e. **—adv.**
mod·e·ra·to (mod′ə·rä′tō) *Music adj.* Moderate In moderate time; moderately. **—n.** *pl.* **·tos** [< Ital.] that which passage or movement. Abbr *mod.* **1.** One who, forum, debate, or a Presbyterian assembly. **3.** Tas graphite or
mod·er·a·tor (mod′ə·rā′tər) *n.* **2.** One who presides over a mediator of a moderates. **4.** *Physics* A substatomic-energy bate, or a Presbyterian assembly.
dispute; mediator. **4.** *Physics* A sing to the present beryllium, used to slow down neutrons stic of or serving reactor. **—mod′er·a′tor·ship** *n.* Of or Poned; up-to-date.
mod·ern (mod′ərn) *adj.* **1.** Of or Poned; up-to-date. or recent times; not ancient; not at of a language: to express the current times; ts in modern times. **3.** *Usually cap.* Of, pertaining dices, etc., character-most recent period in the yle of type face char-Modern French. **—n. 1.** Ontely thin serifs. Abbr. **2.** One who has opinions, hanodo, ablative of *modus* istic of modern times. **3.** **·od′ern·ness** *n.* acterized by heavy stems *late* refer to time not long *mod.* [< LL *modernus* rent fields. *Modern* history, measure] **—mod′ern** re considered to have begun **—Syn.** (adj.) **1.** M′er contexts *modern* art, *modern* past or to time includer to schools arising in the late these terms varies .es. *Recent* usually includes the literature, and art′iod within the life of those now after the Middle close to *recent* in meaning, but usu-music, or moderge before the present time. Compare nineteenth or for ANCIENT.
present and of theatrical or concert dance that alive; in gestional ballet technique but has its of the lastvement.
ally impl′ under ENGLISH.
NEW. **—under** GREEK.
moderander IRISH.
is n′′ərn·iz′əm) *n.* **1.** The character or ov′, action, etc., that is peculiar to modern ming characteristic of modern times, as an rom, attitude, etc. **3.** *Theol.* **a** Often *cap.* Catholic Church, a humanistic movement, e late 19th century, that reinterpreted the and other church teachings in order to make nt with modern developments in science and Pope Pius X declared it a heresy in 1907. **b** A movement in Protestantism. Compare LIBERALISM.
.ern·ist (mod′ərn·ist) *n.* **1.** One who is sympathetic with or has a preference for modern things, practices, ideas, etc. **2.** *Often cap.* An advocate of religious modernism. **—mod′ern·is′tic** *adj.*
mo·der·ni·ty (mo·dûr′nə·tē) *n. pl.* **·ties 1.** The condition or quality of being modern. **2.** Something modern.
mod·ern·ize (mod′ərn·īz) *v.* **·ized, ·iz·ing** *v.t.* **1.** To make modern in method, style, character, etc.; bring up to date. **—v.i. 2.** To accept or adopt modern ways, ideas, idioms, etc. **—mod′ern·i·za′tion** *n.* **—mod′ern·iz′er** *n.*
modern pentathlon In the modern Olympic games, a contest consisting of five events, riding, shooting, fencing, swimming, and jumping.
mod·est (mod′ist) *adj.* **1.** Having or displaying a moderate or unexaggerated regard for oneself or one's abilities, accomplishments, etc.; unassuming; humble. **2.** Not showy, gaudy, or ostentatious: a *modest* meal. **3.** Not excessive or extreme; moderate: a *modest* price. **4.** Reserved, chaste, or pure in speech, manner, dress, etc. [< L *modestus* moderate < *modus* measure] **—mod′est·ly** *adv.*
—Syn. 1. unassuming, diffident, meek. **2.** unpretentious, unostentatious. **4.** proper, seemly, decent. **—Ant.** immodest, conceited, arrogant, showy.
Mo·des·to (mō·des′tō) A city in central California; pop. 61,712.
mod·es·ty (mod′is·tē) *n. pl.* **·ties 1.** The state or quality of being modest. **2.** Freedom from vanity or excessive pride. **3.** Freedom from showiness or ostentation: the *modesty* of his rooms. **4.** Propriety or decorum in speech, manner, dress, etc. **5.** Moderation.
Mod. Gr. Modern Greek.
mod·i·cum (mod′i·kəm) *n. pl.* **·cums** or **·ca** (-kə) A moderate or small amount. [< L < *modus* measure]
mod·i·fi·ca·tion (mod′ə·fə·kā′shən) *n.* **1.** The act of modifying, or the state of being modified. **2.** That which results from modifying: It is a *modification* of his old theory. **3.** A small adjustment, alteration, or qualification: His words need some *modification* before being taken literally. **4.** *Biol.* A noninheritable change in the structure or function of an organism, resulting from its own activity or environment. **5.** *Ling.* Alteration of a vowel by umlaut.

mod·i·fi·ca·to·ry (mod′ə·fə·kā′tər·ē) *adj.* Modifying or tending to modify. Also **mod′i·fi·ca′tive.**
mod·i·fi·er (mod′ə·fī′ər) *n.* **1.** One who or that which modifies. **2.** *Gram.* A word, phrase, or clause that restricts or qualifies the meaning of another word or group of words: Adjectives and adverbs are *modifiers*. Compare UNIT MODIFIER.
mod·i·fy (mod′ə·fī) *v.* **·fied, ·fy·ing** *v.t.* **1.** To make somewhat different in form, character, etc.; vary. **2.** To revise by making less extreme, severe, or uncompromising; moderate: to *modify* one's views. **3.** *Gram.* To qualify the meaning of; restrict; limit. **4.** *Ling.* To alter (a vowel) by umlaut. **—v.i. 5.** To be or become modified; change. **—Syn.** See CHANGE. [< F *modifier* < L *modificare* < *modus* measure + *facere* to make] **—mod′i·fi′a·ble** *adj.*
Mo·di·glia·ni (mō′dē·lyä′nē), **Amedeo**, 1884–1920, Italian painter and sculptor.
mo·dil·lion (mō·dil′yən) *n. Archit.* An ornamental block or horizontal bracket used in series under a cornice of the Corinthian or other orders. [< F *modillon* < Ital. *modiglione* < L *mutulus*]
mo·di·o·lus (mō·dī′ə·ləs) *n. pl.* **·li** (-lī) *Anat.* In the internal ear, the central bony stem around which winds the cochlea. [< NL < L, dim. of *modus* measure]
mod·ish (mō′dish) *adj.* Conforming to the current mode or fashion; stylish. **—mod′ish·ly** *adv.* **—mod′ish·ness** *n.*
mo·diste (mō·dēst′) *n.* A woman who deals in fashionable women's clothing, especially hats or dresses. [< F]
Mo·djes·ka (mō·jes′kə), **Helena**, 1840–1909, *née* Opid, Polish actress active in the United States.
Mo·djo·ker·to Man (mō′jō·kâr′tō) A primitive hominid identified from the fossil skull of an infant found in 1931 near Modjokerto, Java, and bearing anatomical resemblances both to Pithecanthropus and to Neanderthal man.
Mo·dred (mō′drid) In Arthurian legend, King Arthur's treacherous nephew, slain in battle by Arthur, who was himself mortally wounded: also spelled *Mordred*.
mods (modz) *n.pl. Brit.* Moderation (def. 3).
mod·u·lar (moj′oo·lər) *adj.* Of, like, or pertaining to a module or modulus.
mod·u·late (moj′oo·lāt) *v.* **·lat·ed, ·lat·ing** *v.t.* **1.** To vary the tone, inflection, pitch, or volume of. **2.** To regulate or adjust; modify; soften. **3.** To sing or intone, as a prayer. **4.** *Telecom.* To alter some characteristic of (a radio carrier wave). **—v.i. 5.** *Music* To change from one key to another. **6.** *Telecom.* To alter some characteristic of a carrier wave. [< L *modulatus*, pp. of *modulari* to regulate < *modulus* small measure] **—mod′u·la·to·ry** (-lə·tôr′ē, -tō′rē) *adj.*
mod·u·la·tion (moj′oo·lā′shən) *n.* **1.** The act of modulating, or the state of being modulated. **2.** *Music* A change from one key to another. **3.** A melodious or rhythmical inflection of the voice. **4.** A melodious use of language, as in prose or poetry. **5.** *Ling.* The use of suprasegmental phonemes. **6.** *Telecom.* **a** The process whereby some characteristic of one carrier wave is varied in accordance with another wave. **b** The result of this process.
mod·u·la·tor (moj′oo·lā′tər) *n.* **1.** One who or that which modulates. **2.** *Telecom.* A device for effecting modulation.
mod·ule (moj′ool) *n.* **1.** A standard or unit of measurement. **2.** *Archit.* A unit of measure used to determine the proportion among parts of a classical order, and usually equal to the diameter or semidiameter of the base of column shaft. **3.** A standard structural component repeatedly used, as in a building, computer, etc. [< L *modulus*, dim. of *modus* measure. Doublet of MOLD[1].]
mod·u·lus (moj′oo·ləs) *n. pl.* **·li** (-lī) **1.** *Physics* A number, coefficient, or quantity that measures a force, function, or effect: the *modulus* of elasticity. **2.** *Math* **a** The absolute value of a complex number $(a + bi)$, where a and b are numbers and $i = \sqrt{-1}$. **b** An integer that leaves the same remainder when it is the divisor of different numbers. **c** factor by which a Napierian logarithm is multiplied to vert it to a logarithm of the base 10. Abbr. m., M. [< dim. of *modus* measure]
mo·dus (mō′dəs) *n. pl.* **·di** (-dī) *Latin* Mode; ma
modus op·er·an·di (op′ə·ran′dī) *Latin* A manne operating or proceeding.
modus vi·ven·di (vi·ven′dī) *Latin* **1.** A manner of **2.** A temporary agreement between parties in dispute ing a final settlement of the issues involved.
Moe·ro (mwe·rō′) The French name for MWERU.
Moe·si·a (mē′shē·ə) An ancient country and former province in SE Europe south of the Danube.
Moe·so·goth (mē′sə·goth) *n.* A member of the tribe that settled in Moesia in the latter part of th century. Also **Moe′so-Goth.**
Moe·so·goth·ic (mē′sə·goth′ik) *n.* The langua Moesogoths, into which Bishop Ulfilas translated in the fourth century. **—adj.** Of or like the Moe their language. Also **Moe′so-Goth′ic** *n. & adj.*

mo·fette (mō·fet′) *n.* **1.** An emanation of carbon dioxide and other gases from a fissure in the earth and usually marking the final stages of volcanic activity. **2.** An opening through which such gases escape. Also **mof·fette′**. [< F < Ital. *mofetta* < *muffare* to decay < G *muff* mold]

Mo·ga·di·scio (mō′gä·dē′shō) The capital and chief port of Somalia, in the eastern part on the Indian Ocean; pop. 200,000 (1966). Also **Mog·a·di·shu** (mog′ə·dish′ōō).

Mog·a·dor (mog′ə·dôr′, -dōr′; *Fr.* mô·gà·dôr′) A port city in SW Morocco; pop. 26,392 (1960).

mo·gen Da·vid (mō′gən dä′vid, duv′id) A six-pointed star in the form of a hexagram, used as a symbol of Judaism: also called *shield of David, star of David:* also spelled *magen David.* For illustration see HEXAGRAM. Compare SOLOMON'S SEAL. [< Hebrew, shield of David]

Mo·gi·lev (mo·gyi·lyôf′) A city in the eastern Byelorussian S.S.R., on the Dnieper; pop. 202,000 (1970). Also **Mo·gi·lëv′, Mogilev on the Dnieper.**

mo·gul[1] (mō′gul, -gəl, mō·gul′) *n.* **1.** A very important person. **2.** A type of freight locomotive. [< MOGUL]

mo·gul[2] (mō′gəl) *n.* In skiing, a bump and dip on the slope, made by the skis of turning skiers. Compare BUNNY HOP. [< dial. G., bump]

Mo·gul (mō′gul, mō·gul′) *n.* **1.** One of the conquerors of India, followers of Baber, who in 1526 founded a Moslem empire that formally endured until 1857. **2.** Any of their descendants. **3.** A member of the Mongoloid race; a Mongol. — *adj.* Of or pertaining to the Moguls or their empire. Also spelled *Mughal, Mughul:* also **Mo·ghal′, Mo·ghul′.** — **the Great** or **Grand Mogul** Any of the former Mogul emperors of Delhi. [< Persian *mugal* Mongol]

mo·hair (mō′hâr) *n.* **1.** The hair of the Angora goat. **2.** A glossy, wiry fabric made of mohair and cotton in a plain or twill weave. **3.** A fabric having a mohair pile, used for upholstery. **4.** A garment made of mohair. [Earlier *mocayare* < Arabic *mukhayyar;* infl. in form by *hair*]

Moham. Mohammedan.

Mo·ham·med (mō·ham′id), 570?-632, Arabian founder and prophet of Islam whose revelations are collected in the Koran: also *Mahomet, Mahound, Muhammad.*

Mohammed II, 1430?-81, sultan of Turkey 1451-81; captured Constantinople, 1453; patron of the arts; founded Ottoman power in Europe: called **the Conqueror, the Great.**

Mohammed Ah·med (ä′med) See under MAHDI.

Mohammed Ali See MEHEMET ALI.

Mo·ham·me·dan (mō·ham′ə·dən) *adj.* Of or pertaining to Mohammed or to his religion and institutions. — *n.* A follower of Mohammed or a believer in Islam; a Muslim. Also *Mohometan, Muhammadan, Muhammedan.*

Mohammedan calendar See under CALENDAR.

Mo·ham·me·dan·ism (mō·ham′ə·dən·iz′əm) *n.* Islam.

Mo·har·ran (mə·här′ən) *n.* Muharram.

Mo·ha·ve (mō·hä′vē) *n.* One of a tribe of North American Indians of Yuman stock, formerly living along the Colorado River: also spelled *Mojave.*

Mohave Desert See MOJAVE DESERT.

Mo·hawk (mō′hôk) *n.* **1.** One of a tribe of North American Indians of Iroquoian stock, one of the original Five Nations, formerly ranging from the Mohawk River to the St. Lawrence. **2.** The language of this tribe. [< N.Am.Ind. Cf. Narragansett *mohowaicuck*, lit., they eat animate things, eaters of human flesh.]

Mohawk River A river in central New York, flowing about west to the Hudson River.

Mo·he·gan (mō·hē′gən) *n.* **1.** One of a tribe of North American Indians of Algonquian stock, formerly living along the Thames River in Connecticut. **2.** Loosely, Mahican. [< Algonquian, wolf]

Mo·hen·jo-Da·ro (mō·hen′jō·dä′rō) An ancient site of Indus civilization in West Pakistan.

Mo·hi·can (mō·hē′kən) *n.* A Mahican.

Mo·hock (mō′hok) *n.* One of a band of ruffians, often aristocratic, who attacked people on the streets of London in the early 18th century. [Var. of MOHAWK]

mo·hole (mō′hōl) *n.* A hole drilled or to be drilled through the earth's crust to the level of the Mohorovicic discontinuity.

Mo·ho·ro·vi·cic discontinuity (mō·hôr′ə·vis′ik, -vich′ik) The surface or boundary zone between the earth's crust and mantle, of undetermined composition and of varying depths of from about 6 to 25 miles. It is marked by certain changes in the character and velocity of seismic waves. Also **Mo·ho** (mō′hō). [after Andrija Mohorovicic, Yugoslavian geologist]

Mohs' scale (mōz) *Mineral.* A qualitative scale in which the hardness of a mineral is determined by its ability to scratch another, any one of 15 minerals arranged in order of increasing hardness:

11. fused zirconia
12. fused alumina
13. silicon carbide
14. boron carbide
15. diamond

pure silica

[after F. Mohs, 1773-1839, German mineralogist who devised the scale]

mo·hur (mō′hər) *n.* A gold coin used in British India in the 19th and early 20th centuries, equal in value to 15 rupees. [< Hind. < Persian *muhr*]

M.O.I. Ministry of Information.

moi·dore (moi′dôr, -dōr) *n.* A former Portuguese or Brazilian gold coin. [< Pg. *moeda d'ouro* coin of gold < L *moneta* money + *aurum* gold]

moi·e·ty (moi′ə·tē) *n. pl.* **·ties** **1.** A half. **2.** Any portion, part, or share. **3.** *Anthropol.* Either of two basic groups that together constitute a tribe. [< F *moitié* < L *medietas* < *medius* half]

moil (moil) *v.i.* **1.** To work hard; toil; slave. **2.** To move about ceaselessly; churn. — *n.* **1.** Hard work; toil. **2.** Confusion; dampness. [< OF *moillier, muiller* < L *molliare* to make wet; soil with dampness]

moi·ra (moi′rə) *n.* **1.** Confusion; uproar. **2.** Fate or destiny; the power of fate. [< L *mollis* soft; infl. in meaning by *toil*]

Moi·rai (moi′rī) In Greek religion, the three Fates. [< Gk., lit. parts, shares]

moi·ré (mwä·rā′) *adj.* Having a watered or wavy appearance, as certain fabrics; watered. — *n.* A watered fabric, usually silk or rayon, having a wavy pattern. **2.** A wavy pattern, as on watered silk, etc. Also spelled *moire.* [< F *moire* mohair]

moist (moist) *adj.* **1.** Slightly wet; damp; humid. **2.** Tearful; also, tearfully sentimental. [< OF *moiste* < L *mucidus* moldy < *mucus* mucus]

mois·ten (mois′ən) *v.t. & v.i.* To make or become moist. — **mois′ten·er** *n.*

mois·ture (mois′chər) *n.* **1.** Water or other liquid diffused as a vapor in the air or as a liquid through the interstices of objects. **2.** Dampness. [< OF *moisteur*]

Mo·ja·ve (mō·hä′vē) See MOHAVE.

Mojave Desert An arid region comprising part of the Great Basin in southern California; about 15,000 sq. mi. Also *Mohave Desert.*

Mo·ji (mō·jē) A port city on northern Kyushu island, Japan; pop. 165,000 (est. 1959).

moke (mōk) *n. Slang* **1.** *U.S.* A Negro: an offensive term. **2.** A dull or easy-going person. **3.** *Brit.* A donkey. **4.** *Austral.* A second-rate horse; nag. [Origin unknown]

Mo·kha (mō′khə) See MOCHA.

Mo·ki (mō′kē) See MOQUI.

mol (mōl) See MOLE[5].

mo·lal (mō′ləl) *adj. Chem.* **1.** Of or pertaining to the mole or gram molecule. **2.** Designating a solution that has a concentration equivalent to one mole of the solute in 1,000 grams of the solvent. [< MOL(E) + -AL] — **mo·lal·i·ty** (mō·lal′ə·tē) *n.*

mo·lar[1] (mō′lər) *adj.* **1.** *Physics* Of or pertaining to a mass of matter considered as a whole. **2.** *Chem.* **a** Having or containing a gram-molecular weight or mole. **b** Denoting a solution containing one mole of solute per liter of solution. [< MOL(E) + -AR] — **mo·lar·i·ty** (mō·lar′ə·tē) *n.*

mo·lar[2] (mō′lər) *n.* A grinding tooth, of which there are 12 in man, situated behind the canine and incisor teeth and having a broad, flattened crown. For illustration see TOOTH. — *adj.* **1.** Grinding or adapted for grinding. **2.** Pertaining to a molar. [< L *molaris* < *mola* mill]

mo·las·ses (mə·las′iz) *n. pl.* **mo·las·ses** Any of various thick, dark-colored syrups obtained from sugar, sorghum, etc., during the refining process: also, *Brit.*, treacle. [< Pg. *melaço* < L *mellaceus* honeylike < *mel* honey]

mold[1] (mōld) *n.* **1.** A form or matrix that gives a particular shape to anything in a fluid or plastic condition. **2.** A frame or model on or around which something is shaped or made: a basket *mold.* **3.** That which is shaped or made in or on a mold. **4.** The shape or pattern rendered by a mold. **5.** General shape, form, or pattern. **6.** Distinctive nature, character, or type: He is of the New England *mold.* **7.** *Archit.* A molding or set of moldings. — *v.t.* **1.** To work into a particular shape or form; shape. **2.** To shape or form in or as in a mold; make on a mold. **3.** To influence, determine, or direct: to *mold* public sentiment. **4.** To follow the contours of; cling to: a dress that *molds* the figure. **5.** In founding, to form a mold of or from, preparatory to casting. **6.** To ornament with moldings. — **Syn.** See INFLUENCE. — *v.i.* **7.** To assume or come to fit a particular shape or pattern. Also, *Brit.,* mould. [< OF *modle* < L *modulus* < *modus* measure, limit. Doublet of MODULE.] — **mold′a·ble** *adj.*

mold[2] (mōld) *n.* **1.** Any of a variety of fungous growths commonly found on the surfaces of decaying food or in warm, moist places, and usually having a woolly or furry texture. **2.** A fungus producing one of these growths. — *v.i.* To become moldy. Also *Brit.,* mould. [< obs. *mouled*, pp. of *moulen* to grow moldy. Cf. Dan. *mugle* to grow moldy.]

mold[3] (mōld) *n.* **1.** Soft, loose earth that is especially suitable for plants because it is rich in decaying organic matter. **2.** *Poetic* **a** The earth; ground. **b** A grave. — *v.t.* To cover with mold. Also, *Brit.,* mould. [OE *molde* earth]

Mol·dau (môl′dou) The German name for the VLTAVA.

Mol·da·vi·a (mol·dā′vē·ə) **1.** A historical province of eastern Rumania. **2.** The Moldavian S.S.R. Also **Mol·do·va** (môl·dô′vä).

Mol·da·vi·an (mol·dā′vē·ən) *adj.* Of or relating to Moldavia. — *n.* **1.** A native or naturalized inhabitant of Moldavia. **2.** The Rumanian language of the Moldavians.

Moldavian S.S.R. A constituent Republic of the Soviet Union, in the extreme SW part; 13,000 sq. mi.; pop. 3,572,-000 (1970); capital, Kishinev: also *Moldavia. Russian* **Mol·dav·ska·ya S.S.R.** (mol·däf′ska·yə).

mol·da·vite (mol′də·vīt) *n.* A dull green, natural glass thought to be of meteoritic origin. [after the *Moldau*, near which it is found]

mold·board (mōld′bôrd′, -bōrd′) *n.* The curved metal plate of a plow that digs into and turns over the soil. Also, *Brit.*, *mouldboard*. [< MOLD³ + BOARD]

mold·er¹ (mōl′dər) *v.i.* **1.** To decay gradually and turn to dust; crumble. **2.** To atrophy from lack of use. — *v.t.* **3.** To cause to crumble. **4.** To waste or squander. Also, *Brit.*, *moulder.* — **Syn.** See DECAY. [Freq. of obs. *mold* to crumble]

mold·er² (mōl′dər) *n.* **1.** One who molds or makes molds. **2.** One who or that which influences: a *molder* of public taste. **3.** *Printing* An electrotype plate from which duplicate plates are made. Also, *Brit.*, *moulder.*

mold·ing (mōl′ding) *n.* **1.** The act or process of one who or that which molds. **2.** That which is molded. **3.** *Archit.* **a** A cornice or other depressed or projecting member, used to decorate the surface or angle of a building, room, etc. **b** The decoratively molded surface of a cornice, jamb, etc. **4.** A strip of decoratively shaped wood or other material, used to decorate or finish walls, doors, etc. Also, *Brit.*, *moulding.*

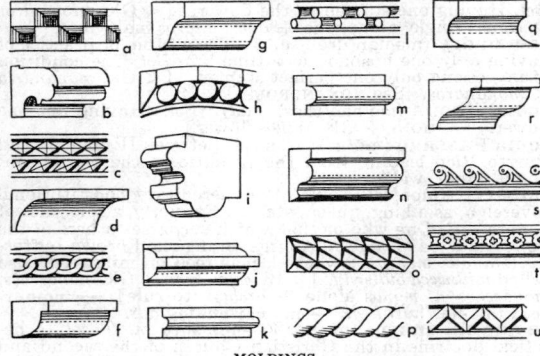

MOLDINGS

a Square billet. *b* Roll and fillet. *c* Nailhead. *d* Cavetto. *e* Chain. *f* Roman ovolo. *g* Cyma Recta. *h* Pellet. *i* Roll and scroll. *j* Fillet. *k* Astragal. *l* Round billet. *m* Torus. *n* Ogee. *o* Hatched. *p* Cable. *q* Scotia. *r* Cyma reversa. *s* Vitruvian scroll. *t* Rose. *u* Chevron.

molding board A board for the kneading, rolling, or cutting of dough in the preparation of bread, etc.

mold·warp (mōld′wôrp) *n. Brit. Dial.* The common mole of Europe (*Talpa europaea*): also spelled *mouldwarp.* [ME < OE *molde* soil + *weorpan* to throw]

mold·y (mōl′dē) *adj.* **mold·i·er, mold·i·est** **1.** Covered with or containing mold. **2.** Musty, as from age, lack of use, etc. Also, *Brit., mouldy.* — **mold′i·ness** *n.*

mole¹ (mōl) *n.* A small, permanent spot on the human skin, slightly protuberant and often dark and hairy; especially, a pigmented nevus. [OE *māl*]

mole² (mōl) *n.* Any of a number of small insectivorous mammals, chiefly of the family *Talpidae*, that live mainly underground and have soft fur, small eyes, and broad forefeet adapted for digging and burrowing: also called *taupe.* [ME *molle.* Akin to MLG and MDu. *mol.* Prob. related to MOLD³.]

COMMON MOLE
(6 to 8 inches long; tail 1 inch)

mole³ (mōl) *n.* **1.** A massive, usually stone barricade in the sea, built to partially enclose an anchorage or harbor for which it acts as a breakwater or pier. **2.** An anchorage or harbor so enclosed. [< F *môle* < L *mola* great mass < Gk. *mylē* millstone]

mole⁴ (mōl) *n. Pathol.* A fleshy mass formed in the uterus by the degeneration of a partly developed ovum. [See MOLE³.]

mole⁵ (mōl) *Chem.* The gram molecule: also spelled *mol.*

Mo·lech (mō′lek) See MOLOCH.

mole cricket 1. A burrowing cricket (family *Gryllotalpidae*) whose front legs are large and molelike. For illustration see INSECTS (injurious). **2.** Any of several related species.

mo·lec·u·lar (mə·lek′yə·lər) *adj.* Pertaining to, consisting of, or caused by molecules. [< NL *molecularis*]

molecular beam *Physics* A stream of electrically neutral molecules passed through one or more slits in a vacuum chamber and moving almost parallel to each other, used to determine various properties of atoms, etc.

molecular film A layer having the thickness of one molecule: also called *monolayer.*

molecular volume *Chem.* The volume occupied by the gram-molecular weight of a substance, equal to its molecular weight divided by its density.

molecular weight *Chem.* The sum of the atomic weights of all the atoms in a molecule.

mol·e·cule (mol′ə·kyōol) *n.* **1.** *Chem.* **a** The smallest particle of an element or compound that can exist separately without losing the physical or chemical properties of the original element or compound. **b** A gram molecule (which see). **2.** Any very small particle. [< F *molécule* < NL *molecula*, dim. of L *moles* mass]

mole·hill (mōl′hil′) *n.* **1.** A small heap or mound of earth raised by a burrowing mole. **2.** Something trivial or inconsequential: to make a mountain out of a *molehill.*

mole·skin (mōl′skin′) *n.* **1.** The dark gray pelt of a mole, very soft and fragile and used as a fur. **2.** A heavy, twilled cotton fabric with a thick, soft nap on one side that resembles moleskin. **3.** *Usually pl.* Items of clothing, especially trousers, made of this fabric.

mo·lest (mə·lest′) *v.t.* **1.** To disturb or annoy by unwarranted, excessive, or malicious interference. **2.** To interfere with improperly or illicitly, especially with a sexual motive. [< OF *molester* < L *molestare* < *molestus* troublesome < *moles* mass, burden] — **mo·les·ta·tion** (mō′les·tā′shən, mol′es-) *n.* — **mo·lest′er** *n.*

Mo·lière (mō·lyâr′) Pseudonym of **Jean Baptiste Po·que·lin** (pō·klaṅ′), 1622–73, French dramatist and actor.

Mo·line (mō·lēn′) A city in NW Illinois, on the Mississippi near Rock Island; pop. 46,237.

moll (mol) *n. Slang* **1.** The girl friend or female accomplice of a gangster. **2.** A prostitute. [< *Moll*, dim. of *Mary*, fem. personal name]

mol·lah (mol′ə) See MULLAH.

mol·les·cent (mə·les′ənt) *adj.* Having a tendency to soften; softening. [< L *mollescens, -entis*, ppr. of *mollescere* to soften] — **mol·les′cence** *n.*

mol·lie (mol′ē) *n.* Any of a variety of tropical fishes (genus *Mollienisia*), often raised in aquariums. Also **mol′ly.**

mol·li·fy (mol′ə·fī) *v.t.* **·fied, ·fy·ing** **1.** To make less angry, violent, or agitated; soothe: to *mollify* someone. **2.** To reduce the harshness, severity, or intensity of; mitigate: to *mollify* pain, demands, etc. [< F *mollifier* < LL *mollificare* < L *mollis* soft + *facere* to make] — **mol′li·fi′a·ble** *adj.* — **mol′li·fi·ca′tion** *n.* — **mol′li·fi′er** *n.* — **mol′li·fy·ing·ly** *adv.*

mol·lus·coid (mə·lus′koid) *adj.* **1.** Of or like a mollusk. **2.** Pertaining or belonging to a phylum (*Molluscoidea*) of marine bivalve animals that include the brachiopods. Also **mol·lus·coi·dal** (mol′əs·koid′l).

mol·lusk (mol′əsk) *n. Zool.* A large phylum of unsegmented, soft-bodied invertebrates, usually protected by a calcareous shell of one or more pieces, and including snails, mussels, oysters, clams, cuttlefish, squids, octopi, whelks, etc. Also **mol′lusc.** [< F *mollusque* < L *molluscus (nux)* soft, thin-shelled (nut) < *mollis* soft] — **mol·lus·can** (mə·lus′kən) *adj. & n.* — **mol·lus′cous** *adj.*

mol·ly·cod·dle (mol′ē·kod′l) *n.* Any overprotected or pampered person; also, an effeminate man or boy. — *v.t.* **·dled, ·dling** To pamper; coddle. [< *Molly*, dim. of *Mary*, a personal name + CODDLE] — **mol′ly·cod′dler** *n.*

Mol·ly Pitch·er (mol′ē pich′ər), 1754–1832, the American Revolutionary heroine, **Mary Ludwig Hays Mc·Cau·ley** (mə·kô′lē), who carried water for the American soldiers at the Battle of Monmouth, 1778.

Mol·nár (mōl′när), **Ferenc**, 1878–1952, Hungarian novelist and playwright.

mo·loch (mō′lok) *n.* A spiny Australian lizard (genus *Moloch*), resembling the horned toad. [< NL *Moloch*, genus name < MOLOCH]

Mo·loch (mō′lok) **1.** In the Bible, a god of the Ammonites and Phoenicians to whom parents offered their children to be burnt in sacrifice. **2.** Anything having the power to exact merciless sacrifices. Also *Molech.* [< LL < Gk. < Hebrew *Mōlekh* a king]

Mo·lo·kai (mō′lə·kī′) An island in the central Hawaiian Islands; 259 sq. mi.; site of a leper colony.

Mo·lo·tov (mō′lə·tôf) See PERM.

Mo·lo·tov (mō′lə·tôf), **Vyacheslav Mikhailovich**, born 1890, Soviet statesman and diplomat: original name **Vyacheslav Mikhailovich Skria·bin** (skryä′bēn).

Molotov cocktail A small, crude bomb, consisting of a bottle filled with a flammable liquid and a rag wick.

molt (mōlt) *v.t. & v.i.* To cast off or shed (feathers, horns, skin, etc.) in preparation for periodic replacement by new growth. — *n.* **1.** The act or process of molting. **2.** That which is molted. Also *Brit.*, **moult.** [ME *mouten,* OE *bemūtian* to exchange for < L *mutare* to change] — **molt′er** *n.*

mol·ten (mōl′tən) Archaic past participle of MELT. — *adj.* **1.** Made liquid by heat; melted: *molten* metal. **2.** Made by melting and casting in a mold: *molten* images.

Molt·ke (mōlt′kə), **Count Helmuth Johannes Ludwig von,** 1848–1916, German general; chief of staff in World War I. — **Count Helmuth Karl Bernhard von,** 1800–91, Prussian general; chief of staff 1858–88; uncle of the preceding.

mol·to (mōl′tō) *adv. Music* Much; very: *molto* adagio. [< Ital. < L *multum* much]

Mo·luc·ca Islands (mə-luk′ə) A widely scattered island group of Indonesia, between Celebes and New Guinea; 33,315 sq. mi.: formerly *Spice Islands. Malay* **Ma·lu·ku** (mä-lōō′kōō). Also **Mo·luc′cas.** See map of INDONESIA.

mo·ly (mō′lē) *n. pl.* **·lies** **1.** A legendary herb possessing magical power and, according to Homer in the *Odyssey,* given by Hermes to Odysseus for protection against the enchantments of Circe. **2.** A wild garlic found in Europe. **3.** *Informal* Molybdenum. [< L < Gk. *mōly*]

mo·lyb·date (mə-lib′dāt) *n. Chem.* A salt of molybdic acid.

mo·lyb·de·nite (mə-lib′də-nīt) *n.* A soft, lead-gray molybdenum disulfide, MoS₂, occurring in scales or foliated masses that resemble graphite. It is the chief ore of molybdenum.

mo·lyb·de·num (mə-lib′də-nəm, mol′ib-dē′nəm) *n.* A hard, heavy, silver-white, metallic element (symbol Mo) of the chromium group, occurring only in combination, used to harden steel. See ELEMENT. [< NL, alter. of L *molybdaena* lead, galena < Gk. *molybdaina* < *molybdos* lead]

mo·lyb·dic (mə-lib′dik) *adj. Chem.* Of, pertaining to, or containing molybdenum, especially in its higher valence.

mo·lyb·dous (mə-lib′dəs) *adj. Chem.* Of or pertaining to molybdenum, especially in its lower valence.

mom (mom) *n.* Mother: used familiarly. [< MAMA]

Mom·ba·sa (mom-bä′sə, -bas′ə) A port city in SE Kenya, on **Mombasa Island** (7 sq. mi.); pop. 152,150 (est. 1959).

mome (mōm) *n. Archaic* A lout; fool. [Origin uncertain]

mo·ment (mō′mənt) *n.* **1.** A very short or relatively short period of time: a *moment* later. **2.** A particular point in time, usually the present time: He is busy at the *moment.* **3.** A particular period or stage in a series of events: a great *moment* in history. **4.** Importance; consequence; substance: matters of great *moment.* **5.** A brief period of excellence, distinction, enjoyment, etc.: Everyone has his *moments.* **6.** *Physics* **a** The product of a quantity, as a force, mass, etc., and its perpendicular distance from some significant, related point: *moment* of area; *moment* of inertia. **b** The tendency to produce rotatory motion. **c** A measure of such a tendency. **7.** *Stat.* The arithmetic mean of the powers of the deviations in a frequency distribution. **8.** *Philos.* An essential element or constituent. [< F < L *momentum* movement. Doublet of MOMENTUM.]

mo·men·tar·i·ly (mō′mən-ter′ə-lē, mō′mən-ter′ə-lē) *adv.* **1.** For a moment: *momentarily* at a loss. **2.** In a moment; at any moment. **3.** From moment to moment; progressively.

mo·men·tar·y (mō′mən-ter′ē) *adj.* **1.** Lasting no more than a moment; fleeting. **2.** Occurring or operating at every moment. — **Syn.** See TRANSIENT. — **mo′men·tar′i·ness** *n.*

mo·ment·ly (mō′mənt-lē) *adv.* **1.** From moment to moment; at any instant. **2.** For a moment.

mo·men·tous (mō-men′təs) *adj.* Of great importance or consequence: a *momentous* year. — **mo·men′tous·ly** *adv.* — **mo·men′tous·ness** *n.*

mo·men·tum (mō-men′təm) *n. pl.* **·ta** (-tə) or **·tums** **1.** *Physics* The quantity of motion in a body as measured by the product of its mass and velocity. **2.** Impetus, as of a body in motion. **3.** *Philos.* Moment. [< L. Doublet of MOMENT.]

mom·ism (mom′iz·əm) *n.* An excessive and sentimental worship of mothers and motherhood, resulting in a psychologically harmful prolongation of maternal influences. [< MOM + -ISM; coined by Philip Wylie, born 1902, U.S. author]

Momm·sen (mom′sən, -zən; *Ger.* mom′zən), **Theodor,** 1817–1903, German historian.

mo·mus (mō′məs) *n. pl.* **·mus·es** or **·mi** (-mī) *Often cap.* One who is quick to criticize; faultfinder. [< MOMUS]

Mo·mus (mō′məs) In Greek mythology, the god of blame and mockery. [< L < Gk. *momos* blame, ridicule]

mon (mon) *n. Scot.* Man.

mon- *combining form* Var. of MONO-.

mon. **1.** Monastery. **2.** Monetary.

Mon (mōn) *n.* **1.** One of the dominant native peoples of the Pegu region in Burma. **2.** The Austro-Asiatic language of the Mons, related to Khmer. Also called *Peguan.*

Mon. **1.** Monday. **2.** Monmouthshire. **3.** Monsignor.

Mo·na (mō′nə) The ancient name for the (Isle of) MAN.

mon·a·chism (mon′ə-kiz′əm) *n.* Monasticism. [< L *monachus* monk + -ISM] — **mon′a·chal** (-kəl) *adj.*

mon·ac·id (mon-as′id) *adj. Chem.* Designating a base or alcohol that is able to react with only one molecule of a monobasic acid. — *n.* A base or alcohol characterized by a single hydroxyl group. Also called *monoacid.*

Mon·a·co (mon′ə-kō, mə-nä′kō; *Fr.* mô·nà·kō′) An indepen-

dent principality in SE France, on the Mediterranean; 368 acres; pop. 23,035 (1968).

mon·ad (mon′ad, mō′nad) *n.* **1.** An indestructible unit; a simple and indivisible substance. **2.** *Biol.* A minute, simple, single-celled organism, especially a flagellate protozoan. **3.** *Chem.* An atom, radical, or element with a valence of one. **4.** In metaphysics, a fundamental unit or individual; an indivisible and ultimate substance. — *adj.* Of, pertaining to, or consisting of a monad: also **mo·nad′ic** or **·i·cal.** [< LL *monas, monadis* < Gk. *monas* unit < *monos* alone]

mon·a·del·phous (mon′ə-del′fəs) *adj. Bot.* **1.** Having the stamens united by their filaments into a single set or tube. **2.** United in this manner: said of stamens. [< MON- + Gk. *adelphos* brother]

mon·ad·ism (mon′ad·iz·əm, mō′nad-) *n.* In metaphysics, the theory that the universe is composed of monads, especially as formulated by Leibnitz. Also **mon′a·dol′o·gy** (mon′-ə·dol′ə·jē, mō′nad·ol′-). — **mon′ad·is′tic** *adj.*

mo·nad·nock (mə-nad′nok) *n. Geog.* A hill or mass of rock rising above a peneplain. [after Mt. *Monadnock*]

Mo·nad·nock (mə-nad′nok), **Mount** An isolated peak in SW New Hampshire; 3,165 ft.

Mo·na·gas (mō-nä′gäs), **José Tadeo,** 1784–1868, Venezuelan general and statesman; president 1847–51, 1855–58.

Mon·a·ghan (mon′ə·gən, -hən) A county in southern Ulster Province, Ireland; 498 sq. mi.; pop. 47,088 (1966); county seat, **Monaghan,** pop. 4,013 (1966).

Mo·na Li·sa (mō′nə lē′zə) A portrait by Leonardo da Vinci of a Neapolitan woman, renowned for her inscrutable expression, often regarded as a smile: also called *La Gioconda.*

mo·nan·drous (mə-nan′drəs) *adj.* **1.** Having one male or husband at a time. **2.** Of or characterized by monandry. **3.** *Bot.* Having one stamen to the flower. [< Gk. *monandros* < *monos* single, alone, one + *anēr, andros* male, man]

mo·nan·dry (mə-nan′drē) *n.* **1.** The custom or practice of having only one husband at a time. **2.** *Bot.* The condition of possessing only one perfect stamen. [< Gk. *monandria* < *monandros.* See MONANDROUS.]

mo·nan·thous (mə-nan′thəs) *adj. Bot.* Having but one flower. [< MON- + Gk. *anthos* flower]

Mo·na Passage (mō′nə) A strait between Hispaniola and Puerto Rico leading from the Atlantic to the Caribbean; about 80 mi. wide.

mon·arch (mon′ark) *n.* **1.** A hereditary constitutional sovereign, as a king, queen, etc. **2.** Formerly, a sole ruler of a state. **3.** One who or that which surpasses others of the same kind. **4.** *Entomol.* A large, orange and brown butterfly (*Danaus menippe*) whose larvae feed on milkweed: also called *milkweed butterfly.* [< LL *monarcha* < Gk. *monarchēs, monarchos* < *monos* alone + *archein* to rule] — **mo·nar·chal** (mə-när′kəl) *adj.* — **mo·nar′chal·ly** *adv.*

mo·nar·chi·an·ism (mə-när′kē-ən-iz′əm) *n. Theol.* A heretical doctrine in the Christian Church of the second and third centuries that denied the concept of the Trinity. [< LL *monarchianus* < *monarchia* sovereignty of a single person < *monarcha.* See MONARCH.] — **mo·nar′chi·an·is′tic** *adj.*

mo·nar·chi·cal (mə-när′ki·kəl) *adj.* **1.** Of, pertaining to, or characteristic of a monarchy or monarch. **2.** Governed by or favoring a monarch or monarchy. Also **mo·nar′chi·al, mo·nar′chic.** — **mo·nar′chi·cal·ly** *adv.* [< F *monarchique* < Gk. *monarchikos* < *monarchos.* See MONARCH.]

mon·arch·ism (mon′ark·iz′əm) *n.* **1.** The principles or system of a monarchy. **2.** The advocacy of a monarchy. — **mon′arch·ist** *n.* — **mon′arch·is′tic** *adj.*

mon·ar·chy (mon′ər·kē) *n. pl.* **·chies** **1.** Government by a monarch; sovereign control. **2.** A government or territory ruled by a monarch. — **absolute monarchy** A government in which the will of the monarch is positive law; a despotism. — **constitutional** or **limited monarchy** A monarchy in which the power and prerogative of the sovereign are limited by constitutional provisions. [< F < LL *monarchia* < Gk. *monarchos.* See MONARCH.]

mo·nar·da (mə-när′də) *n.* Any of a genus (*Monarda*) of aromatic American herbs of the mint family, including the horsemint and Oswego tea. [< NL, after N. *Monardes,* 1493–1588, Spanish botanist]

mon·as (mon′əs, mō′nəs) *n. pl.* **monades** (mon′ə-dēz) A monad. [< LL. See MONAD.]

mon·as·ter·y (mon′əs-ter′ē) *n. pl.* **·ter·ies** **1.** A dwelling place occupied in common by persons, especially monks, living under religious vows and in seclusion. **2.** The community of persons living in such a place. Abbr. *mon.* [< LL *monasterium* < LGk. *monastērion* < Gk. *monastēs* monk < *monazein* to live alone < *monos* alone. Doublet of MINSTER.]

mo·nas·tic (mə-nas′tik) *adj.* **1.** Of, pertaining to, or characteristic of monasteries or their inhabitants; monkish; ascetic. **2.** Characteristic of a life of religious seclusion. Also **mo·nas′ti·cal.** — *n.* A monk or other religious recluse. [< F *monastique* < LL *monasticus* < Gk. *monastikos.* See MONASTERY.] — **mo·nas′ti·cal·ly** *adv.*

mo·nas·ti·cism (mə-nas′tə-siz′əm) *n.* The monastic life or system.

Mon·as·tir (mon′əs-tēr′) The Turkish name for BITOLJ.

mon·a·tom·ic (mon′ə-tom′ik) *adj. Chem.* **1.** Consisting of

a single atom, as the molecules of certain elements. **2.** Containing one replaceable or reactive atom. **3.** Monovalent.
mon·au·ral (män'ôr·əl, mōn'-) *adj.* **1.** Pertaining to or characterized by the perception of sound by one ear only. **2.** *Electronics* Designating a system of sound reproduction in which the sound is perceived as coming from one direction only: also *monophonic:* distinguished from *stereophonic.*
mon·ax·i·al (mon-ak'sē·əl) *adj.* **1.** Having but one axis. **2.** *Bot.* Uniaxial.
mon·a·zite (mon'ə·zīt) *n.* A resinous, brownish red or brown phosphate of the lanthanide metals, chiefly cerium, lanthanum, and didymium, an important source of thorium. [< G *monazit* < Gk. *monazein* to live alone < *monos* alone]
Mon·chen·glad·bach (mœn'khən·glät'bäkh) A city in west central North Rhine–Westphalia, West Germany; pop. 152,400 (est. 1960): also *München-Gladbach.*
mon cher (môn shâr') *French masc.* My dear.
Monck (mungk), **George** See MONK.
Mon·dale (mon'dāl'), **Walter Frederick**, born 1928, U.S. senator; vice president, 1977–.
Mon·day (mun'dē, -dā) *n.* The second day of the week. Abbr. *M., Mo., Mon.* [OE *mōn(an)dæg* day of the moon; trans. of L *lunae dies*]
monde (môńd) *n. French* The world; society.
Mon·dri·an (môn'drē·än), **Piet**, 1872–1944, Dutch painter. Also **Mon'dri·aan.**
mo·ne·cious (mə·nē'shəs, mō-) See MONOECIOUS.
Mo·né·gasque (mō'nə·gask, *Fr.* mô·nā·gàsk') *n. French* A citizen of Monaco.
Mo·nel metal (mō·nel') A corrosion-resistant nickel alloy containing copper, iron, and manganese, used for industrial equipment machine parts, etc.: a trade name. [after Ambrose *Monel,* d. 1921, U.S. manufacturer]
Mo·net (mō·ne'), **Claude**, 1840–1926, French painter.
mon·e·tar·y (mon'ə·ter'ē, mun'-) *adj.* **1.** Of or pertaining to currency or coinage. **2.** Pertaining to or concerned with money; pecuniary. Abbr. *mon.* [< L *monetarius* of a mint < *moneta* mint. See MINT.] — **mon'e·tar'i·ly** *adv.*
mon·ey (mun'ē) *n. pl.* **mon·eys** or **mon·ies** **1.** Officially issued coins and paper currency that serve as a medium of exchange and a measure of value and may be used as payment for goods and services and for settlement of debts. ◆ Collateral adjective: *pecuniary.* **2.** Any substance or object used similarly, as checks, money orders, wampum, etc. **3.** Property of any type having value in terms of money. **4.** Money of account. **5.** A system of coinage. **6.** *pl.* Sums of money. **7.** Pecuniary profits: to make *money* on a transaction. — **to be in the money** *Slang* To have lots of money; be prosperous or wealthy. — **to put money into** To invest money in. — **to put money on** To place a bet on. [< OF *moneie* < L *moneta.* Doublet of MINT.]
— **Syn.** *Money, coin, coinage, specie, cash,* and *currency* refer to pieces of metal, paper, etc., used as a medium of exchange. *Money* is the general term; it includes the wampum of the primitive American Indians, as well as the pieces of stamped metal and the paper notes issued by a modern government for use within its domain. Pieces of metal used as *money* are called collectively *coin, coinage,* or *specie. Cash* refers to *money* in hand and ready for use, as opposed to *money* obtainable by sale of property, collection of debts, etc. *Currency* is *money* in actual circulation, as distinguished from that held in reserve, as in government vaults.
mon·ey·bag (mun'ē·bag) *n.* **1.** A bag for holding money. **2.** *pl. Slang* A wealthy person; also, wealth.
money belt A belt with pouches for carrying money.
mon·ey·chang·er (mun'ē·chān'jər) *n.* **1.** One whose business it is to change money at a prescribed rate. **2.** A device for holding and dispensing coins.
money cowry See under COWRY.
mon·ey·ed (mun'ēd) *adj.* **1.** Possessed of money; wealthy. **2.** Consisting of, arising from, or representing money or wealth: *moneyed* interests. Also spelled *monied.*
mon·ey·er (mun'ē·ər) *n.* **1.** A coiner of money; minter. **2.** *Obs.* A broker; banker. [< OF *monoier* maker of coins < L *monetarius* < *moneta* mint. See MINT.]
mon·ey·lend·er (mun'ē·len'dər) *n.* One whose business is the lending of money at interest.
mon·ey·mak·ing (mun'ē·mā'king) *adj.* **1.** Bent upon or successful in accumulating wealth. **2.** Likely to bring in money; profitable: a *moneymaking* proposition. — *n.* The acquisition of money or wealth. — **mon'ey·mak'er** *n.*
money of account A monetary denomination used in keeping accounts, usually not represented by a coin, as the mill of the United States.
money order An order for the payment of a specified sum of money; especially, such an order issued at one post office or telegraph office and payable at another. Abbr. *m.o., M.O.*
mon·ey·wort (mun'ē·wûrt') *n.* A trailing primulaceous herb (*Lysimachia nummularia*) with solitary yellow flowers and rounded leaves. [< MONEY + WORT; trans. of NL *Nummularia* < *nummus* coin]
mon·ger (mung'gər, mong'-) *n.* **1.** *Brit.* A dealer or trader: chiefly in combination: *fishmonger.* **2.** One who engages in

discreditable matters: chiefly in compounds: a *scandalmonger.* [OE *mangere* < *mangian* to traffic < L *mango* dealer]
mon·ger·ing (mung'gər·ing, mong'-) *n. & adj.* Dealing; trading: chiefly in combination: *warmongering.*
Mon·gol (mong'gəl, -gol, -gōl) *n.* **1.** A member of any of the native tribes of Mongolia; especially, one inhabiting eastern Mongolia or a Kalmuck. **2.** Any of the Mongolian languages. **3.** A member of the Mongoloid division of mankind. — *adj.* Mongolian (def. 1). [< Mongolian *mong* brave]
Mon·go·li·a (mong·gō'lē·ə, mon-) A region of east central Asia; about 1 million sq. mi.; divided into the **Mongolian People's Republic** (formerly *Outer Mongolia*) in the northern and western part; 604,247 sq. mi.; pop. 1,240,000 (est. 1969); capital, Ulan Bator; and **Inner Mongolia,** a region of northern China, most of which comprises the **Inner Mongolian Autonomous Region**; about 400,000 sq. mi.; pop. 6,100,104 (1953); capital, Huhehot. See map of UNION OF SOVIET SOCIALIST REPUBLICS.
Mon·go·li·an (mong·gō'lē·ən, -gōl'yən, mon-) *adj.* **1.** Of or pertaining to Mongolia, its people, or their languages. **2.** Exhibiting Mongolism. — *n.* **1.** A native of Mongolia. **2.** A subfamily of the Altaic languages, including the languages of the Mongols. **3.** A person afflicted with Mongolism.
Mon·gol·ic (mong·gol'ik, mon-) *adj.* Of or peculiar to the Mongols. — *n.* Any of the Mongolian languages.
Mon·gol·ism (mong'gəl·iz'əm) *n.* A form of congenital mental deficiency in a child characterized by a broad flat face and skull, obliquely set, narrow eyes, etc.: also called *Down's syndrome.*
Mon·go·loid (mong'gə·loid) *adj.* **1.** *Anthropol.* Of, pertaining to, or belonging to a major ethnic division of the human species, characterized by yellowish skin, slanting eyes, straight head hair, a broad nose, high cheek bones, etc. **2.** Resembling, related to, or characteristic of Mongols or Mongolians. **3.** Characterized by Mongolism. — *n.* A Mongoloid person.
mon·goose (mong'gōos, mung'-) *n. pl.* **·goos·es** A small, ferretlike, carnivorous mammal (family *Viverridae*); especially, the **Indian mongoose** (*Herpestes nyula*) that destroys rats and is noted for its ability to kill venomous snakes without injury to itself. [< Marathi *mangus*]

MONGOOSE
(To 18 inches long; tail 18 inches)

mon·grel (mung'grəl, mong'-) *n.* **1.** An animal or plant of mixed breed; especially, a crossbred dog. **2.** Any incongruous mixture. — *adj.* Of mixed breed, origin, nature, etc.: often a contemptuous term: a *mongrel* language. [ME < obs. *mong* mixture < OE *gemang* + *-rel,* dim. suffix]
'mongst (mungst) *prep. Poetic* Amongst.
Mon·gu (mong'gōo) The capital of Barotseland, Northern Rhodesia; pop. about 1,750.
mon·ied (mun'ēd) See MONEYED.
Mon·i·er-Wil·liams (mun'ē·ər·wil'yəmz, mon'-), **Sir Monier,** 1819–99, British Sanskrit scholar born in India.
mon·i·ker (mon'ə·kər) *n. Informal* A name, signature, or nickname. Also **mon'ick·er.** — **Syn.** See NAME. [Prob. blend of MONOGRAM and MARKER]
mo·nil·i·form (mō·nil'ə·fôrm) *adj. Biol.* Contracted or jointed at regular intervals so as to resemble a string of beads, as the branches of certain roots, the nuclei of some infusoria, etc. [< L *monile* necklace + -FORM]
mon·ish (mon'ish) *v.t. Archaic* To admonish. [See ADMONISH.]
mon·ism (mon'iz·əm, mō'niz·əm) *n. Philos.* **1.** The doctrine that there is but one principle of being or ultimate substance, as mind or matter. **2.** The theory that reality is a unified whole: opposed to *pluralism.* [< NL *monismus* < Gk. *monos* single] — **mon'ist** *n.* — **mo·nis'tic** or **·ti·cal** *adj.* — **mo·nis'ti·cal·ly** *adv.*
mo·ni·tion (mō·nish'ən) *n.* **1.** A warning or admonition, as of impending danger. **2.** An official, legal, or formal notice. **3.** *Law* A summons or citation in civil law and admiralty practice. [< OF < L *monitio, -onis* < *monitus,* pp. of *monere* to warn] — **mon·i·tive** (mon'ə·tiv) *adj.*
mon·i·tor (mon'ə·tər) *n.* **1.** In some schools, a student selected to perform certain duties in class, as helping to keep records, maintain order, etc. **2.** One who advises or cautions, especially in matters of conduct. **3.** Something that warns or reminds. **4.** Formerly, an ironclad warship having a low, flat deck and low freeboard, and fitted with one or more revolving turrets carrying heavy guns; especially, the first vessel of this type, **the Monitor,** a Union ship used in the Civil War against the Merrimack (1862). **5.** A servo. **6.** *Zool.* Any of several large, carnivorous lizards (family *Varanidae*) of Africa, Asia, and Australia; especially, the kabarogoya of the East Indies. **7.** A contrivance consisting of a nozzle and holder whereby the direction of a stream of water can be readily changed, used in mining and fighting fires. **8.** *Telecom.* A receiver, loudspeaker, or other apparatus used to check radio or television broadcasts for quality of transmis-

sion, frequency, compliance with laws, material transmitted, etc. — *v.t. & v.i.* **1.** *Telecom.* To listen to or watch (a broadcast) with or as with a monitor. **2.** To act or supervise as a monitor (def. 1). [< L < *monitus.* See MONITION.] — **mon′i·tor·ship′** *n.* — **mon′i·tress** *n.fem.*

mon·i·to·ri·al (mon′ə·tôr′ē·əl, -tō′rē-) *adj.* **1.** Pertaining to or performed by a school monitor or monitors. **2.** Monitory.

mon·i·to·ry (mon′ə·tôr′ē, -tō′rē) *adj.* Conveying a warning or monition; admonitory: a *monitory* look. — *n.* A monitory letter. [< L *monitorius < monitor.* See MONITOR.]

monitory letter *Eccl.* A letter of monition from an ecclesiastical superior.

monk (mungk) *n.* **1.** One who has taken the religious vows of poverty, chastity, and obedience, usually a member of a monastic order. **2.** Formerly, a religious hermit. [OE *munuc* < LL *monachus* < LGk. *monachos* solitary < *monos* alone] — **monk′ish** *adj.* — **monk′ish·ly** *adv.*

Monk (mungk), **George,** 1608–70, first Duke of Albemarle, English general and admiral. Also **Monck.**

monk·er·y (mungk′ər·ē) *n. pl.* **·er·ies 1.** Monastic life, ways, or beliefs: generally a contemptuous term. **2.** A monastery or its inmates.

mon·key (mung′kē) *n.* **1.** Any member of an extensive suborder (*Anthropoidea*) of primates, excluding the anthropoid apes, having elongate limbs, hands and feet adapted for grasping, and a highly developed nervous system; especially, the marmosets, baboons, macaques, etc. **2.** One who acts in a way suggestive of a monkey, as a mischievous child. **3.** Any of various mechanical devices, especially an iron block or ram with a catch, used in pile-driving. — *v.i.* **1.** *Informal* To play or trifle; meddle; fool: often with *with* or *around.* — *v.t.* **2.** *Rare* To imitate or ape; mimic. [? < MLG *Moneke,* name of the son of Martin the Ape in *Reynard the Fox.* Cf. MF *monne,* Sp. *mona* female ape. Perhaps < Du. *monnik* monk, on account of the brown-capped head]

monkey bread The baobab, or its fruit.

monkey business *Slang* Foolish tricks; deceitful or mischievous behavior.

monkey flower Any of various plants (genus *Mimulus*) of the figwort family, with gaping corollas; especially, *M. ringens,* with violet flowers, **scarlet monkey flower** (*M. cardinalis*).

monkey jacket *Informal* A short, snug jacket formerly worn by sailors.

monkey nut *Brit.* A peanut.

mon·key·pot (mung′kē·pot′) *n.* **1.** The hard, woody, potshaped seed vessel of several tropical American trees (genus *Lecythis*). **2.** Any of these trees.

monkey puzzle A large Chilean tree (*Araucaria araucana*) yielding a hard, durable yellowish wood and edible seeds.

mon·key·shine (mung′kē·shīn′) *n. Usually pl. Slang* A mischievous or playful trick, prank, or joke. [< MONKEY + SHINE, n. (def. 4)]

monkey suit *U.S. Slang* A formal suit of men's clothing; especially, a full dress Army or Navy uniform.

monkey wrench A wrench having an adjustable jaw for grasping nuts, bolts, etc., of various sizes. For illustration see WRENCH. — **to throw a monkey wrench into** *U.S. Informal* To disrupt (normal or proper procedure).

Mon-Khmer (mon′kmer′) *n.* A subfamily of the Austro-Asiatic family of languages, spoken chiefly in Indochina.

monk·hood (mungk′hŏŏd) *n.* **1.** The character or condition of a monk. **2.** Monks collectively. [< MONK + -HOOD]

Monk Lewis See (Matthew Gregory) LEWIS.

monk's cloth (mungks) A sturdy cotton fabric with a basket weave, used for drapes, curtains, etc.

monks·hood (mungks′hŏŏd′) *n.* Any of various plants (genus *Aconitum*) having the upper sepal arched like a hood; especially, *A. napellus,* a poisonous variety: also called *aconite.*

Mon·mouth (mon′məth) **1.** A county in east central New Jersey; scene of the Revolutionary War Battle of **Monmouth Courthouse,** June 28, 1778; pop. 459,379. **2.** Monmouthshire or its county seat.

Mon·mouth (mon′məth), **Duke of,** 1649–85, James Scott, English general and rebel; illegitimate son of Charles II of England; claimed the throne and led an insurrection against James II; beheaded: called the **Protestant Duke.**

Mon·mouth·shire (mon′məth·shir) A former county in SE Wales; 546 sq. mi.; pop. 461,459 (1971); county seat, **Monmouth,** pop. 66,090 (1976); also **Monmouth.**

MONKSHOOD
(To 4 feet high)

mono- *combining form* **1.** Single; one: *monocotyledon.* **2.** *Chem.* **a** Denoting the presence in a compound of a single atom, or an equivalent of the element or radical to the name of which it is prefixed: *monobasic.* **b** Having the thickness of one molecule: *monolayer.* Also, before vowels, **mon-.** [< Gk. < *monos* single, one, alone]

Mono Monotype.

mon·o·ac·id (mon′ō·as′id) *n. & adj.* Monacid (which see).

mon·o·ba·sic (mon′ə·bā′sik) *adj. Chem.* Possessing but a single hydrogen atom replaceable by a metal or positive radical: applied to acids.

mon·o·carp (mon′ə·kärp) *n. Bot.* A plant that yields fruit only once before dying. [< MONO- + -CARP] — **mon′o·car′pic** *adj.*

mon·o·car·pel·lar·y (mon′ə·kär′pə·ler′ē) *adj. Bot.* Consisting of a single carpel.

mon·o·car·pous (mon′ə·kär′pəs) *adj. Bot.* **a** Having a gynoecium composed of a single carpel. **b** Yielding fruit only once before dying; monocarpic.

Mo·noc·er·os (mə·nos′ər·əs) A constellation, the Unicorn. See CONSTELLATION. [< OF < L < Gk. *monokēros < monos* single + *keras* horn]

mon·o·cha·si·um (mon′ə·kā′zē·əm, -zhē-) *n. Bot.* A cymose inflorescence having only one lateral axis. [< NL < Gk. *monos* single + *chasis* division] — **mon′o·cha′si·al** *adj.*

mon·o·chlo·ride (mon′ə·klôr′īd, -klō′rīd) *n. Chem.* A chloride that contains one chlorine atom in each molecule.

mon·o·chord (mon′ə·kôrd) *n. Music* An acoustical instrument with one string and a movable bridge, used for measuring intervals. [< F < Med.L *monochordus* < Gk. *monos* single + *chorde* string]

mon·o·chro·mat·ic (mon′ə·krō·mat′ik) *adj.* **1.** Of or having only one color. **2.** Consisting of one wave length. Also **mon′o·chro′ic** (-krō′ik). [< Gk. *monochrōmatos*] — **mon′o·chro·mat′i·cal·ly** *adv.*

mon·o·chrome (mon′ə·krōm) *n.* **1.** A painting or drawing in a single color or in various shades of the same color. **2.** The art or technique of producing such pictures. [< L < Gk. *monochrōmos < monos* single + *chrōma* color] — **mon′o·chro′mic, mon′o·chro′mi·cal** *adj.* — **mon′o·chro′mist** *n.*

mon·o·cle (mon′ə·kəl) *n.* An eyeglass for one eye. [< F < LL *monoculus* one-eyed < Gk. *monos* single + L *oculus* eye] — **mon′o·cled** *adj.*

mon·o·cli·nal (mon′ə·klī′nəl) *Geol. adj.* Having an inclination in only one direction, or composed of rock strata so inclined. — *n.* A monocline. — **mon′o·cli′nal·ly** *adv.*

mon·o·cline (mon′ə·klīn) *n. Geol.* A monoclinal rock structure. [< MONO- + Gk. *klinein* to incline]

mon·o·clin·ic (mon′ə·klin′ik) *adj. Crystall.* Pertaining to or designating a crystal system having two oblique axes and a third perpendicular to both, as in gypsum and augite. [< MONO- + Gk. *klinein* to incline]

mon·o·cli·nous (mon′ə·klī′nəs) *adj. Bot.* Containing both stamens and pistils in the same flower; hermaphroditic. [< NL *monoclinus* < MONO- + Gk. *klinē* bed, couch]

mon·o·cot·y·le·don (mon′ə·kot′ə·lēd′n) *n. Bot.* Any of a great subclass (*Monocotyledones*) of seed plants bearing one cotyledon in the embryo, including palms, orchids, lilies, etc. Also **mon′o·cot′.** [< NL] — **mon′o·cot′y·le′do·nous** *adj.*

mon·o·crat (mon′ə·krat) *n. Rare* **1.** An autocrat. **2.** A monarchist. — **mon′o·crat′ic** *adj.* [< Gk. *monokratēs < monos* single + *krateein* to rule]

mon·oc·u·lar (mon·ok′yə·lər) *adj.* **1.** One-eyed. **2.** Of or pertaining to one eye. Also **mo·noc′u·lous.** [< LL *monoculus.* See MONOCLE.]

mon·o·cul·ture (mon′ə·kul′chər) *n. Agric.* The use of a given tract of land for the cultivation of only one crop.

mon·o·cy·cle (mon′ə·sī′kəl) *n.* A cycle or velocipede having a single wheel propelled by pedals: also called *unicycle.*

mon·o·cyte (mon′ə·sīt) *n. Anat.* A large leucocyte, having a horseshoe-shaped nucleus surrounded by clear cytoplasm.

mon·o·dra·ma (mon′ə·drä′mə, -dram′ə) *n.* A drama written for and acted by a single performer.

mon·o·dy (mon′ə·dē) *n. pl.* **·dies 1.** A poem in which the poet laments the death of another. Compare THRENODY. **2.** In Greek literature, an ode performed by one voice; especially, a lyric ode in a tragedy; dirge. **3.** *Music* **a** A composition in which there is only one vocal part; also, the style of such a composition; homophony: opposed to *polyphony.* **b** A composition for a single voice or part, with or without instrumental accompaniment. **4.** A monotonous sound. [< LL *monodia* < Gk. *monōida < monōidos* singing alone < *monos* alone + *aeidein* to sing] — **mo·nod′ic** (mə·nod′ik) or **·i·cal** *adj.* — **mo·nod′i·cal·ly** *adv.* — **mon′o·dist** *n.*

mo·noe·cious (mə·nē′shəs) *adj.* **1.** *Biol.* Hermaphroditic. **2.** *Bot.* Monoclinous. Also **monoicous, monoicous.** Also **mo·ne′cian.** [< MON- + Gk. *oikos* house]

mo·nog·a·mist (mə·nog′ə·mist) *n.* One who believes in or practices monogamy. — **mo·nog′a·mis′tic** *adj.*

mo·nog·a·mous (mə·nog′ə·məs) *adj.* **1.** Pertaining to or characteristic of monogamy. **2.** Holding to monogamy; having only one spouse. **3.** *Zool.* Having or paired with but one mate. Also **mon·o·gam·ic** (mon′ə·gam′ik). [< LL *monogamus* < Gk. *monogamos*] — **mo·nog′a·mous·ly** *adv.*

mo·nog·a·my (mə·nog′ə·mē) *n.* **1.** The condition or practice of having only one wife or husband at a time. Compare POLYGAMY. **2.** *Rare* The practice of marrying only once during a lifetime: opposed to *digamy.* **3.** *Zool.* The habit of pairing with or having but one mate. [< F *monogamie* < LL *monogamia* < Gk. < *monos* single + *gamos* marriage]

mon·o·gen·e·sis (mon′ə·jen′ə·sis) *n. Biol.* **1.** The doctrine that all living beings are descended from a single cell. **2.**

Asexual reproduction, as by budding, etc. **3.** Direct development, without metamorphosis, of an ovum into an organism that resembles the parent. **4.** The doctrine that the whole human race is of one blood or species. Also **mo·nog·e·ny** (mə·noj′ə·nē). [< NL]

mon·o·ge·net·ic (mon′ə·jə·net′ik) *adj.* **1.** Pertaining to or exhibiting monogenesis. **2.** Asexual. Also **mo·nog·e·nous** (mə·noj′ə·nəs). **3.** *Geol.* Resulting from one developmental process, as a group of mountains.

mon·o·gram (mon′ə·gram) *n.* A character consisting of two or more letters intertwined into one; especially, the initials of one's name, used on clothing, stationery, etc. — *v.t.* **mon·o·gramed** or **·grammed**, **mon·o·gram·ing** or **·gram·ming** To mark or decorate with a monogram. [< LL *monogramma* < Gk. *monos* single + *grammē* letter] — **mon′o·gram·mat·ic** (-grə·mat′ik) *adj.*

mon·o·graph (mon′ə·graf, -gräf) *n.* A book, pamphlet, or treatise on one subject or on a single aspect of a subject. — **mo·nog·ra·pher** (mə·nog′rə·fər) *n.* — **mon′o·graph·ic** *adj.* — **mo·nog·ra·phy** (mə·nog′rə·fē) *n.* [< MONO- + -GRAPH]

mo·nog·y·ny (mə·noj′ə·nē) *n.* The condition or practice of having only one wife at a time: opposed to *polygyny.* [< MONO- + Gk. *gynē* woman] — **mo·nog′y·nist** *n.* — **mo·nog′y·nous** *adj.*

mon·o·hy·drate (mon′ō·hī′drāt) *n. Chem.* The union of a single molecule of water with an element or a compound.

mon·o·hy·dric (mon′ō·hī′drik) *adj. Chem.* Possessing a single hydroxyl radical.

mo·noi·cous (mə·noi′kəs) *adj.* Monoecious.

mo·nol·a·try (mə·nol′ə·trē) *n.* Worship of one of several gods. Compare MONOTHEISM. [< MONO- + -LATRY] — **mo·nol′a·ter**, **mo·nol′a·trist** *n.* — **mo·nol′a·trous** *adj.*

mon·o·lay·er (mon′ō·lā′ər) *n.* A monomolecular film.

mon·o·lith (mon′ə·lith) *n.* A single block of stone, usually very large, used in architecture and sculpture. [< LL *monolithus* < Gk. *monolithos* < *mono-* + *lithos* stone]

mon·o·lith·ic (mon′ə·lith′ik) *adj.* **1.** Of, pertaining to, or resembling a monolith. **2.** Consisting of one kind of rock. **3.** Having a massive, uniform structure that does not permit individual variations: a *monolithic* state.

mon·o·logue (mon′ə·lôg, -log) *n.* **1.** A lengthy speech by one person, especially one that interferes with conversation. **2.** A play or dramatic composition for one actor only. **3.** A soliloquy. **4.** A poem, etc., written as a soliloquy. Also **mon′o·log.** [< F < Gk. *monologos* speaking alone < *monos* alone + *-logos* speech] — **mon′o·log′ic** (-loj′ik) or **·i·cal** *adj.* — **mo·nol·o·gist** (mə·nol′ə·jist) *n.* — **mo·nol′o·gy** *n.*

mon·o·ma·ni·a (mon′ə·mā′nē·ə, -mān′yə) *n.* **1.** A mental disorder in which a person, otherwise rational, is obsessed with one idea or subject. **2.** An exaggerated fondness for or irrational enthusiasm for something; craze. [< NL] — **mon′o·ma′ni·ac** *n.* — **mon′o·ma·ni′a·cal** (-mə·nī′ə·kəl) *adj.*

mon·o·mer (mon′ə·mər) *n. Chem.* The structural unit of a polymer. [< MONO- + Gk. *mēros* part]

mo·nom·er·ous (mə·nom′ər·əs) *adj. Bot.* Having a single member in each whorl: said of a flower. Sometimes written **1-merous.** [< MONO- + -MEROUS]

mon·o·met·al·ism (mon′ō·met′əl·iz′əm) *n.* The theory or system of a single metallic standard in coinage. Also **mon′o·met′al·lism.** — **mon′o·met′al·ist** *n.*

mon·o·me·tal·lic (mon′ō·mə·tal′ik) *adj.* **1.** Consisting of one metal. **2.** Using or advocating monometalism.

mo·no·mi·al (mō·nō′mē·əl) *adj. Math.* Consisting of a single algebraic term. **2.** *Biol.* Consisting of a single word or term, as the names of some plants and animals. — *n.* A monomial term or expression. [< MO(NO)- + -NOMIAL, as in *binomial*; an irregular formation]

mon·o·mo·lec·u·lar (mon′ō·mə·lek′yə·lər) *adj. Chem.* Having a thickness of only one molecule.

mon·o·mor·phic (mon′ə·môr′fik) *adj. Biol.* **1.** Having the same or an essentially similar type of structure. **2.** Having the same form throughout successive stages of development. Also **mon′o·mor′phous.** [< MONO- + -MORPHIC]

Mo·non·ga·he·la River (mə·nong′gə·hē′lə) A river in West Virginia and western Pennsylvania, flowing 128 miles NE to the Allegheny River at Pittsburgh.

mon·o·nu·cle·ar (mon′ō·nōō′klē·ər, -nyōō′-) *adj.* Having only one nucleus, as certain cells of the blood.

mon·o·nu·cle·o·sis (mon′ō·nōō·klē·ō′sis, -nyōō′-) *n. Pathol.* **1.** The presence in the blood of an abnormal number of mononuclear leucocytes. **2.** Infectious mononucleosis (which see). [< NL < MONO- + NUCLE(US) + -OSIS]

mon·o·pet·al·ous (mon′ə·pet′əl·əs) *adj. Bot.* **1.** Gamopetalous (which see). **2.** Having a single petal, as certain flowers. [< NL *monopetalus*]

mon·o·phon·ic (mon′ə·fon′ik) *adj.* **1.** Of or pertaining to a monody; monodic. **2.** *Electronics* Monaural. [< MONO- + Gk. *phōnē* sound]

mon·oph·thong (mon′əf·thông, -thong) *n. Phonet.* **1.** A vowel, or single vowel sound; pure vowel: distinguished from *diphthong, triphthong.* **2.** Loosely, a digraph representing a

single vowel sound. [< MONO- + Gk. *phthongos* sound] — **mon′oph·thon′gal** *adj.*

mon·o·phy·let·ic (mon′ō·fī·let′ik) *adj. Biol.* **1.** Of or pertaining to a single phylum of animals or plants. **2.** Derived from one parent form. [< MONO- + *phylē* tribe]

mon·o·phyl·lous (mon′ə·fil′əs) *adj. Bot.* Having or composed of one leaf. [< MONO- + Gk. *phyllon* leaf]

Mo·noph·y·site (mə·nof′ə·sīt) *n. Theol.* One who believes in the doctrine that Christ had one nature, the divine, or a composite nature made up of both the human and the divine, as a member of the Coptic Church of Egypt. [< LGk. *monophysitēs* < *monos* single + *physis* nature] — **Mon·o·phy·sit·ic** (mon′ō·fi·sit′ik) *adj.* — **mo·noph′y·sit·ism** *n.*

mon·o·plane (mon′ə·plān) *n. Aeron.* An airplane with only one wing or pair of wings: distinguished from *biplane.*

mon·o·ple·gi·a (mon′ə·plē′jē·ə) *n. Pathol.* Paralysis of one extremity or part of the body. [< NL < MONO- + Gk. *plēgē* stroke] — **mon′o·ple′gic** *adj.*

mon·o·pode (mon′ə·pōd) *n.* **1.** A creature with only one foot. **2.** *Bot.* A monopodium. — *adj.* One-footed: also **mo·nop·o·dous** (mə·nop′ə·dəs). [< L *monopodius* < Gk. *monos* single + *pous, podos* foot]

mon·o·po·di·um (mon′ə·pō′dē·əm) *n. pl.* **·di·a** (-dē·ə) *Bot.* A stem or axis of growth, as in the pine and other conifers, giving off lateral branches formed by the continued development of a terminal bud. [< NL] — **mon′o·po′di·al** *adj.*

mo·nop·o·lize (mə·nop′ə·līz) *v.t.* **·lized, ·liz·ing** **1.** To obtain or exercise a monopoly of. **2.** To assume exclusive possession or control of. Also *Brit.* **mo·nop′o·lise.** — **mo·nop′o·li·za′tion** *n.* — **mo·nop′o·liz′er** *n.*

mo·nop·o·ly (mə·nop′ə·lē) *n. pl.* **·lies** **1.** The exclusive control of a commodity, service, or means of production in a particular market, with the resulting power to fix prices and eliminate competition. **2.** *Law* An exclusive right or privilege, granted by a government, of buying, selling, making, or using anything. **3.** A company or group of persons having a monopoly. **4.** The commodity, service, etc., controlled under a monopoly. **5.** Exclusive possession or control of anything. [< L *monopolium* < Gk. *monopōlion* < *monos* alone + *pōlein* to sell] — **mo·nop′o·lism** *n.* — **mo·nop′o·list** *n. & adj.* — **mo·nop′o·lis′tic** *adj.*

mon·o·pro·pel·lant (mon′ō·prə·pel′ənt) *n. Aerospace* A liquid rocket propellant consisting of fuel and oxidizer mixed and ready for simultaneous ignition.

mon·o·rail (mon′ō·rāl′) *n.* **1.** A single rail serving as a track for cars either suspended from it or balanced upon it. **2.** A railway using such a track.

mon·o·sac·cha·ride (mon′ə·sak′ə·rīd, -rid) *n. Biochem.* Any of a class of simple sugars that cannot be decomposed by hydrolysis, as glucose and fructose.

mon·o·sep·a·lous (mon′ə·sep′ə·ləs) *adj. Bot.* **1.** Gamosepalous (which see). **2.** Having a single sepal, as a calyx.

mon·o·sil·ane (mon′ə·sil′ān) *n. Chem.* Silane (which see).

mon·o·so·di·um glu·ta·mate (mon′ə·sō′dē·əm glōō′tə·māt) A crystalline salt, $C_5H_8NNaO_4$, of glutamic acid, used to enhance the flavor of foods or to impart a meat taste.

mon·o·sper·mous (mon′ə·spûr′məs) *adj. Bot.* One-seeded. Also **mon′o·sper′mal.**

mon·o·stome (mon′ə·stōm) *adj. Zool.* Of or belonging to a suborder (*Monostomata*) of flatworms, having only one mouth or sucker. Also **mo·nos·to·mous** (mə·nos′tə·məs). — *n.* A flatworm with a single mouth or sucker. [< F < Gk. *monōstomos* < *monos* single + *stōma* mouth]

mo·nos·tro·phe (mə·nos′trə·fē, mon′ə·strōf′) *n.* A poem in which the strophes all have the same metrical form. [< MONO- + STROPHE] — **mon·o·stroph·ic** (mon′ə·strof′ik) *adj.*

mon·o·sty·lous (mon′ə·stī′ləs) *adj. Bot.* Having only one style. [< MONO- + Gk. *stylos* pillar]

mon·o·syl·la·bic (mon′ə·si·lab′ik) *adj.* **1.** Having only one syllable: said of words. **2.** Using or speaking in monosyllables. **3.** Composed of monosyllables. — **mon′o·syl·lab′i·cal·ly** *adv.* — **mon′o·syl·la·bism** (mon′ə·sil′ə·biz′əm) *n.*

mon·o·syl·la·ble (mon′ə·sil′ə·bəl) *n.* A word of one syllable, as *no.*

mon·o·the·ism (mon′ə·thē·iz′əm) *n.* The doctrine or belief that there is but one God. [< MONO- + Gk. *theos* god] — **mon′o·the′ist** *n.* — **mon′o·the·is′tic** or **·ti·cal** *adj.* — **mon′o·the·is′ti·cal·ly** *adv.*

mon·o·tone (mon′ə·tōn) *n.* **1.** The utterance of a succession of sounds, syllables, words, etc., in a single tone. **2.** Sameness or lack of variety in expression, style, color, etc. **3.** A single musical tone unvaried in pitch; also, a chant. [< LGk. *monotonos* < Gk. *monos* single + *tonos* tone] — **mon·o·ton·ic** (mon′ə·ton′ik) *adj.*

mo·not·o·nous (mə·not′ə·nəs) *adj.* **1.** Unvaried in inflection, cadence, or pitch, as in tone, etc. **2.** Tiresome by reason of monotony and lack of variety. [< LGk. *monotonos*] — **mo·not′o·nous·ly** *adv.* — **mo·not′o·nous·ness** *n.*

mo·not·o·ny (mə·not′ə·nē) *n.* **1.** Tiresome uniformity or lack of variety; irksome sameness. **2.** Lack of variety in cadence, pitch, or inflection.

---

mon·o·treme (mon′ə·trēm) *n.* A member of the lowest order of mammals (*Monotremata*), comprising the oviparous duckbills and echidnas, without true teeth in the adult stage, and having a cloaca. [< MONO- + Gk. *trēma* hole] **— mon′·o·trem′a·tous** (-trem′ə·təs) *adj.*

mo·not·ri·chous (mə·not′rə·kəs) *adj.* Having a flagellum at only one pole, as certain bacteria: also **mon·o·trich·ic** (mon′ə·trik′ik). [< MONO- + Gk. *thrix, trichos* hair]

mon·o·type (mon′ə·tīp) *n.* **1.** *Biol.* The only representative of its kind, as a single species making up a genus. **2.** *Printing* **a** A print from a metal plate on which a design, painting, etc., has been made; also, the method of producing such prints. **b** A Monotype. Abbr. *Mono.*

Mon·o·type (mon′ə·tīp) *n.* *Printing* A machine that automatically casts and sets type in single characters or units: a trade name.

mon·o·typ·ic (mon′ə·tip′ik) *adj. Biol.* **1.** Containing but one representative; having only one type: a *monotypic* genus. **2.** Being a monotype.

mon·o·va·lent (mon′ə·vā′lənt) *adj.* **1.** *Chem.* Univalent. **2.** *Bacteriol.* Denoting a type of antibody capable of dissolving a specific bacterium or cell in the presence of a suitable complement. **— mon′o·va′lence, mon′o·va′len·cy** *n.* [< MONO- + L *valens, -entis,* ppr. of *valere* to be strong]

mon·ox·ide (mon·ok′sīd, mə·nok′-) *n. Chem.* An oxide containing a single atom of oxygen in each molecule.

Mon·roe (mən·rō′) A city in northern Louisiana; pop. 56,374.

Mon·roe (mən·rō′), **James,** 1758–1831, fifth president of the United States 1817–25.

Monroe Doctrine The doctrine, essentially formulated by President Monroe in his message to Congress (December 2, 1823), that any attempt by European powers to interfere in the affairs of the American countries or to acquire territory on the American continents would be regarded by the United States as an unfriendly act.

Mon·ro·vi·a (mən·rō′vē·ə) **1.** The capital of Liberia, a port in the eastern part on the Atlantic; pop. 85,000 (est. 1966). **2.** A city in SW California, near Los Angeles; pop. 30,015.

mons (monz) *n. pl.* **mon·tes** (mon′tēz) *Anat.* The rounded fatty eminence over the pubic symphysis, covered with hair in the adult; the **mons pu·bis** (pyōō′bis) of the male, or the **mons ven·er·is** (ven′ər·is) of the female. [< L, hill]

Mons (mons) The capital of Hainaut Province, SW Belgium; pop. 26,049 (est. 1959).

Mons. **1.** Monmouthshire. **2.** Monsieur.

Mon·sei·gneur (mon·sēn′yər; *Fr.* môṅ·se·nyœr′) *n. pl.* **Mes·sei·gneurs** (me·se·nyœr′) **1.** My lord: a French title given to the higher nobility, bishops, cardinals, etc. **2.** One having this title. Abbr. *Mgr.* [< F < *mon* my + *seigneur* lord < L *senior* older. See SENIOR.]

mon·sieur (mə·syûr′, *Fr.* mə·syœ′) *n. pl.* **mes·sieurs** (mes′ərz, *Fr.* me·syœ′) The French title of courtesy for men, equivalent to *Mr.* and *sir.* Abbr. *M., Mons.* [< F < *mon* + *sieur,* short for *seigneur.* See MONSEIGNEUR.]

Monsig. Monsignor.

Mon·si·gnor (mon·sēn′yər, *Ital.* môṅ′sēn·nyōr′) *n. pl.* **-gnors** or *Ital.* **-gno·ri** (-nyō′rē) **1.** In the Roman Catholic Church, a title of honor of certain prelates. **2.** One having this title. Abbr. *Mgr., Mon., Monsig., Msgr.* Also **Mon·si·gno·re** (môṅ′sē·nyō′rā). [< Ital. *monsignore* < F *monseigneur.* See MONSEIGNEUR.]

mon·soon (mon·sōōn′) *n. Meteorol.* **1.** A seasonal wind that blows along the Asian coast of the Pacific and from the Indian Ocean, in winter from the northeast, in summer from the southwest. **2.** The summer monsoon, characterized by heavy rains. **3.** Any wind reversing in direction with the season, especially one between land and water. [< MDu. *monssoen* < Pg. *monção* < Arabic *mausim* season]

mon·ster (mon′stər) *n.* **1.** One who or that which is abnormal, unnatural, or hideous in form or appearance. **2.** An animal or plant that is malformed or has an excess or lack of certain parts; monstrosity. **3.** One who or that which inspires hate or horror because of cruelty, wickedness, depravity, etc. **4.** A huge or unwieldy person or thing. **5.** *Pathol.* A fetus so malformed at birth as to be either incapable of performing vital functions or of developing normally; a teratism. **6.** A fabulous creature, compounded of parts from various animals, as a centaur, dragon, etc. — *adj.* Enormous in size or number; huge: a *monster* rally. [< OF *monstre* < L *monstrum* divine warning or omen, hence supernatural, monster < *monere* to warn]

mon·strance (mon′strəns) *n.* In Roman Catholic ritual, a vessel in which the consecrated Host is exposed for adoration. [< OF < Med.L *monstrantia* < L *monstrare* to show]

mon·stros·i·ty (mon·stros′ə·tē) *n. pl.* **·ties** **1.** One who or that which is monstrous; also, a monster. **2.** The condition or character of being monstrous. [< L *monstrositas*]

mon·strous (mon′strəs) *adj.* **1.** Deviating greatly from the natural or normal in form, structure, or character. **2.** Of extraordinary size or number; enormous; huge: a *monstrous* gathering. **3.** Hideous; horrible; atrocious: a *monstrous* cruelty. **4.** Strikingly wrong; ridiculous; absurd: a *monstrous* error. **5.** Having the appearance or nature of a

fabulous monster. — *adv. Archaic* Extremely. [< OF *monstreux* < LL *monstrosus* < L *monstrum.* See MONSTER.] **— mon′strous·ly** *adv.* **— mon′strous·ness** *n.*

Mont. **1.** Montana. **2.** Montgomeryshire.

mon·tage (mon·täzh′) *n.* **1.** A picture made by superimposing or arranging a number of different pictorial elements; also, the art or process of making such a picture. **2.** In motion pictures or television: **a** A rapid sequence of images used to illustrate a group of associated ideas. **b** The revolving of several images around a central, focused picture. **3.** Similar techniques in radio and writing. [< F < *monter* to mount]

Mon·ta·gu (mon′tə·gyōō), **Lady Mary Wortley,** 1689–1762, *née* Pierrepont, English writer.

Mon·ta·gue (mon′tə·gyōō) The family of Romeo, in Shakespeare's *Romeo and Juliet.*

Mon·taigne (mon·tān′, *Fr.* môṅ·ten′y′), **Michel Eyquem de,** 1533–92, French essayist.

Mon·tan·a (mon·tan′ə) A State in the NW United States bordering on Canada; 147,138 sq. mi.; pop. 694,409; capital, Helena; entered the Union Nov. 8, 1889; nickname, *Treasure State.* Abbr. *Mont.* **— Mon·tan′an** *adj. & n.*

mon·tane (mon′tān) *adj.* Pertaining to or living in the mountains: said especially of plants and animals. [< L *montanus* of the mountain < *mons, montis* mountain]

mon·tan wax (mon′tən) A dark brown or whitish hydrocarbon wax of high melting point, extracted from lignite and peat and used in making polishes, candles, etc. [< L *montanus* of the mountain]

Mon·tauk Point (mon′tôk) The easternmost point of New York, at the tip of Long Island.

Mont-aux-Sources (môṅ·tō·sōōrs′) The highest peak, 11,425 feet, of the Drakensberg mountain range.

Mont Blanc (mont blangk′, *Fr.* môṅ bläṅ′) The highest mountain of the Alps, on the French-Italian border; 15,781 ft.; site of **Mont Blanc Tunnel,** a vehicular tunnel between France and Italy; length 7.5 mi. *Italian* **Mon·te Bian·co** (môn′tä byäng′kō).

Mont·calm (mont·käm′, *Fr.* môṅ·kälm′), **Louis Joseph,** 1712–59, Marquis de Montcalm de Saint Veran, French general; fell in defense of Quebec against the British under Wolfe.

Mont Cer·vin (môṅ ser·vaṅ′) The French name for the MATTERHORN.

Mont Ce·nis (môṅ sə·nē′) An Alpine pass in SE France on the Italian frontier; site of the **Mont Cenis tunnel** between France and Italy; 8.5 mi., *Italian* **Mon·te Ce·ni·sio** (môn′tä chā·nē′zyō).

Mont·clair (mont·klâr′, mont′klâr) A town in NE New Jersey, near Newark; pop. 44,043.

mont-de-pié·té (môṅ·də·pyä·tā′) *n. French* A government pawnshop; literally, mount of piety. Also *Italian* **mon·te di pie·tá** (môn′tä dē pyä·tä′).

mon·te (mon′tē) *n.* A Spanish or Spanish-American gambling game of cards. Also **monte bank.** [< Sp., lit., mountain < L; in ref. to the pile of unplayed cards]

Mon·te·bel·lo (mon′ti·bel′ō) A city in SW California, near Los Angeles; pop. 42,807.

Mon·te Car·lo (mon′tē kär′lō, *Ital.* môn′tä kär′lō) A resort commune in Monaco, on the Mediterranean; pop. 9,948 (1968).

Monte Cassino See under CASSINO.

Mon·te Cor·no (môn′tä kôr′nō) The highest peak of the Apennines, south central Italy; 9,560 ft.: also *Corno Grande.*

Mon·te·ne·gro (mon′tə·nē′grō) A constituent Republic of southern Yugoslavia; 5,343 sq. mi.; pop. 471,800 (est. 1965); capital, Titograd. **— Mon·te·ne′grin** *adj. & n.*

Mon·te·rey (mon′tə·rā′) A city in western California, at the southern end of **Monterey Bay,** an inlet of the Pacific; pop. 26,302.

Monterey Park A city in SW California, a suburb of Los Angeles; pop. 49,166.

mon·te·ro (mon·târ′ō) *n. pl.* **·ros** A huntsman's cap with a round crown and a flap. [< Sp. *montero* hunter, mountaineer < *monte* hill + *-ero* (< L *-arius*)]

Mon·te Ro·sa (môn′tä rō′zä) The highest mountain mass of the Pennine Alps, on the Swiss-Italian border; highest peak, Dufourspitze, 15,216 ft.

Mon·ter·rey (mon′tə·rā′, *Sp.* mōn′ter·rā′) The capital of Nuevo León State, NE Mexico; captured by United States troops (1846) in the Mexican War; pop. 830,336 (1970).

Mon·tes·pan (mon′tə·span′, *Fr.* môṅ·tes·päṅ′), **Marquise de,** 1641–1707, Françoise Athénaïs de Rochechouart, mistress of Louis XIV of France.

Mon·tes·quieu (mon′tas·kyōō′, *Fr.* môṅ·tes·kyœ′), **Baron de la Brède et de,** 1689–1755, Charles de Secondat, French jurist, political philosopher, and man of letters.

Mon·tes·so·ri (mon′tes·sôr′ē, -sō′rē; *Ital.* mon′tes·sō′rē), **Maria,** 1870–1952, Italian educator.

Montessori method A system of teaching preschool children, devised in 1907 by Maria Montessori, in which their sense perceptions are trained and their activities guided rather than controlled. Also **Montessori system.**

Mon·teux (moǹ·tü′), **Pierre**, 1875–1964, French conductor.

Mon·te·ver·di (mon′tɑ·vûr′dē, *Ital.* môn′tä·ver′dē), **Claudio** (**Giovanni Antonio**), 1567–1643, Italian composer.

Mon·te·vi·de·o (mon′tɑ·vi·dā′ō, -vid′e·ō; *Sp.* môn′tä-vē·thä′ō) The capital of Uruguay, a port in the southern part at the mouth of the Río de la Plata; pop. 1,348,000 (est. 1968).

Mon·tez (mon·tez′), **Lola**, 1818–61, Irish dancer; mistress of King Ludwig of Bavaria; active in the United States: original name **Marie Dolores Eliza Rosanna Gil·bert** (gil′bərt).

Mon·te·zu·ma II (mon′tɑ·zōō′mɑ), 1479?–1520, last Aztec emperor of Mexico, dethroned by Cortés.

Mont·fort (mont′fərt, *Fr.* môǹ·fôr′), **Simon de**, 1160?–1218, Earl of Leicester, French general and crusader. — **Simon de**, 1208?–65, Earl of Leicester, English general and statesman born in France; son of the preceding.

mont·gol·fi·er (mont·gol′fi·ər) *n.* A hot-air balloon. [after the *Montgolfier* brothers Jacques and Joseph, 18th c. French inventors, who made the first ascent (1783)]

Mont·gom·er·y (mont·gum′ər·ē, mənt-, man-) 1. The capital of Alabama, in the central part, on the Alabama River; pop. 133,386. 2. Montgomeryshire or its county seat.

Mont·gom·er·y (mont·gum′ər·ē, mən-). **Sir Bernard Law**, 1887–1976, first Viscount Montgomery of Alamein, British field marshal in World War II: called **Mont·y** (mon′tē). — **Richard**, 1736?–75, American Revolutionary general born in Ireland; killed at Quebec.

Mont·gom·er·y·shire (mont·gum′ər·ē·shir, mənt-, mən-) A former county in central Wales; 797 sq. mi.; pop. 42,761 (1971); county seat, Montgomery, pop. 970.

month (munth) *n.* 1. One of the parts (**calendar month**) usually 12 in number, into which the calendar year is divided. 2. A period of thirty days or four weeks. 3. The twelfth part (**solar month**) of the solar year. 4. The period (**lunar month**), equivalent to 29.53 days, during which the moon makes a complete revolution with reference to a fixed point; also, the interval between two new moons (**synodic month**). Abbr. *m.*, *M.*, *mo.* ◆ Collateral adjective *mensal.* [OE *mōnath.* Akin to MOON.]

month·ly (munth′lē) *adj.* 1. Happening, done, appearing, etc., once a month or every month: a *monthly* payment. 2. Of or pertaining to a month. 3. Pertaining to the menses. 4. Continuing or lasting for a month. — *adv.* Once a month. — *n. pl.* **·lies** 1. A periodical published once a month. 2. *pl.* The menses.

Mon·ti·cel·lo (mon′tɑ·sel′ō, -chel′ō) The estate and residence of Thomas Jefferson, near Charlottesville, Virginia.

Mont·mar·tre (môǹ·mȧr′tr′) A northern district of Paris, on a hill, a former artists′ quarter.

Mont·pel·ier (mont·pēl′yər) The capital of Vermont, in the north central part, on the Winooski River; pop. 8,609.

Mont·pel·lier (môǹ·pe·lvä′) A city in southern France, on the Lez; pop. 152,105 (1968).

Mont·re·al (mon′trē·ôl′) A city in southern Quebec, Canada, on Montreal Island at the confluence of the St. Lawrence and Ottawa rivers; pop. 1,197,753. French **Mont·ré·al** (môǹ·rā·ȧl′).

Mont Saint Mi·chel (môǹ saǹ mē·shel′) A rocky islet in the Gulf of Saint Malo, NW France, site of an ancient fortress and abbey.

Mont·ser·rat (mont′sɑ·rat′) 1. An island in the Leeward Islands, a British Colony; about 32 sq. mi.; pop. 15,000 (est. 1969); capital, Plymouth. 2. A mountain in NE Spain, 4,054 ft.; site of an 11th-century Benedictine monastery.

mon·u·ment (mon′yɑ·mənt) *n.* 1. A statue, pillar, plaque, etc., erected to perpetuate the memory of a person, event, or historical period. 2. A tombstone. 3. Any conspicuous or fine structure surviving from the past. 4. A work of art, literature, scholarship, etc., regarded as having enduring value. 5. A stone or other permanent mark to indicate a boundary. 6. An area or plot of land having some special or historical interest and set aside by a government as public property. 7. *Obs.* A statue. 8. *Obs.* A tomb. [< L *monumentum* monument, memorial < *monere* to remind]

mon·u·men·tal (mon′yɑ·men′tɑl) *adj.* 1. Of, pertaining to, or serving as a monument. 2. Like a monument; enduring; imposing; massive. 3. Having great significance; prominent; notable: a *monumental* study. 4. In fine arts, larger than life-size. 5. *Informal* Very large; huge: a *monumental* fraud. [< L *monumentalis*] — **mon′u·men′tal·ly** *adv.*

mon·u·men·tal·ize (mon′yɑ·men′tɑl·īz) *v.t.* **·ized**, **·iz·ing** To establish a lasting record or memorial of.

mon·y (mon′ē) *adj. & n. Scot.* Many. Also **mon′ie**.

-mony *suffix of nouns* The condition, state, or thing resulting from: parsimony. [< L *-monia*, *-monium*]

Mon·za (môn′tsä) A commune in Lombardy, northern Italy; pop. about 14,000.

mon·zo·nite (mon′zɑ·nīt) *n.* A coarse-grained, igneous rock containing approximately equal amounts of orthoclase and plagioclase, with inclusions of colored silicates. [after Mount *Monzoni*, in the Tirol] — **mon′zo·nit′ic** (-nit′ik) *adj.*

moo (mōō) *v.i.* To make the deep, moaning sound of a cow; to low. — *n. pl.* **moos** The sound made by a cow. [Imit.]

mooch (mōōch) *Slang v.t.* 1. To obtain without paying; beg; cadge. 2. To steal. — *v.i.* 3. To loiter or rove about. 4. To skulk; sneak. Also spelled *mouch.* [Akin to dial. *miche* to pilfer < OF *muchier* to hide, skulk] — **mooch′er** *n.*

mood[1] (mōōd) *n.* 1. A specific state of mind or feeling, especially a temporary one. 2. *pl.* Fits of sullen or morose behavior: to have *moods.* 3. *Obs.* Anger. — **in the mood** Disposed; inclined. [OE *mōd* mind, heart, courage. Cf. G *mut.*]

mood[2] (mōōd) *n.* 1. *Gram.* The set of distinctive forms of a verb showing the attitude and understanding of the speaker regarding the action or condition expressed: also *mode.* See IMPERATIVE, INDICATIVE, SUBJUNCTIVE. Compare ASPECT. 2. *Logic* Mode. 3. *Obs. Music* Mode. [Var. of MODE]

mood·y (mōō′dē) *adj.* **mood·i·er**, **mood·i·est** 1. Given to sudden moods of moroseness. 2. Expressive or characteristic of such moods: a *moody* glance. [OE *mōdig* courageous < *mōd* courage] — **mood′i·ly** *adv.* — **mood′i·ness** *n.*

Mood·y (mōō′dē), **Dwight Lyman** (**Ryther**), 1837–99, U.S. evangelist. — **William Vaughn**, 1869–1910, U.S. poet.

Moog synthesizer (mōg) A keyboard musical instrument comprising audio oscillators and other electronic sound generators. [After Robert A. *Moog*, U.S. engineer, the inventor]

moo·lah (mōō′lɑ) *n. Slang* Money. [Origin unknown]

moo·ley (mōō′lē) *n.* See MULEY.

moon (mōōn) *n.* 1. A celestial body revolving around the earth from west to east in a lunar month of 29.53 days, and accompanying the earth in its yearly revolution about the sun; mean diameter, 2,160 miles; mean distance from earth, 238,900 miles. Sign for new moon, ●; for first quarter, ☽; for full, ○; for last quarter, ☾. 2. This celestial body at a specific time of the month, or during a particular lunar month or point of time: new *moon*; full *moon*. 3. Any satellite revolving about a planet: the *moons* of Jupiter. 4. A month; especially, a lunar month. 5. Something resembling a full moon or crescent. 6. Moonlight. Abbr. *m.*, *M.* — **man in the moon** The fancied appearance of a face in the disk of a full moon. — **to reach for the moon** To attempt the impossible. — *v.i.* 1. *Informal* To stare or wander about in an abstracted or listless manner. — *v.t.* 2. To pass (time) in such a way. [OE *mōna.* Akin to MONTH.]

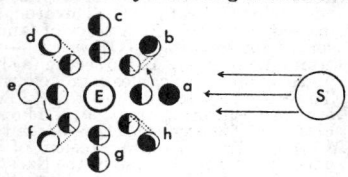

PHASES OF THE MOON
E Earth.   *S* Sun.
a New. *b* Crescent (waxing). *c* First quarter. *d* Gibbous. *e* Full. *f* Gibbous. *g* Third quarter. *h* Crescent (waning).
The inner circle represents the moon in its orbit; the outer circle shows the moon's phases as seen from the earth.

Moon, Mountains of the See RUWENZORI.

moon·beam (mōōn′bēm′) *n.* A ray of moonlight.

moon·blind (mōōn′blīnd′) *adj.* Affected with moon blindness.

moon blindness 1. Nyctalopia. 2. *Vet.* A periodic inflammation of the eyes of a horse, usually ending in blindness.

moon·calf (mōōn′kaf′, -käf′) *n.* 1. A congenital idiot; born imbecile. 2. *Obs.* A monster; deformity. [With ref. to the supposed bad influence of the moon]

mooned (mōōnd) *adj.* 1. Moonlike; crescent-shaped. 2. Ornamented with moonlike marks.

Moo·ney (mōō′nē), **Thomas J. Zechariah**, 1882–1942, U.S. labor leader, convicted of murder in 1917; pardoned in 1939.

moon·eye (mōōn′ī′) *n.* 1. An eye affected with moon blindness. 2. Moon blindness.

moon·eyed (mōōn′īd′) *adj.* 1. Moonblind. 2. Having eyes wide open, as with amazement, awe, etc.

moon·fish (mōōn′fish′) *n. pl.* **·fish** or **·fish·es** 1. Any of various carangoid fishes found on either coast of the Western Hemisphere, having a silvery or yellowish, much compressed body, especially a species (*Vomer setipinnis*) of the Atlantic: also called *dollarfish*, *horsefish.* 2. The opah. 3. A top minnow (*Platypoecilus maculatus*) of Mexican waters.

moon·flow·er (mōōn′flou′ər) *n.* Any of a genus (*Calonyction*) of perennial climbing herbs of the morning glory family, especially *C. aculeatum*, bearing fragrant white flowers that open at night.

moon·ish (mōō′nish) *adj.* Variable like the moon; fickle.

moon·light (mōōn′līt′) *n.* The light of the moon. — *adj.* Pertaining to, illuminated by, or performed by moonlight: a *moonlight* excursion. — **moon′lit′** (-lit′) *adj.*

moon·light·ing (mōōn′līt′ing) *n. Slang* The act of one who holds a job in addition to the regular day's work. — **moon′light′er** *n.*

moon·rise (mōōn′rīz′) *n.* The rising of the moon above the horizon; also, the time when this occurs.
moon·seed (mōōn′sēd′) *n.* A North American climbing plant (genus *Menispermum*), with crescent-shaped seeds.
moon·set (mōōn′set′) *n.* The setting of the moon below the horizon; also, the time when this occurs.
moon·shine (mōōn′shīn′) *n.* **1.** Moonlight. **2.** Something visionary or unreal; pretense; nonsense. **3.** *Informal* Smuggled or illicitly distilled spirits, especially whisky.
moon·shin·er (mōōn′shī′nər) *n. U.S. Informal* One who conducts an illegal trade by night, especially distilling.
moon·shin·y (mōōn′shī′nē) *adj.* **1.** Moonlit. **2.** White as moonlight. **3.** Nonsensical; visionary; silly.
moon·shot (mōōn′shot′) *n.* The act of launching a rocket to the moon.
moon·stone (mōōn′stōn′) *n.* A pearly, opalescent variety of orthoclase and albite, valued as a gemstone: also called *adularia*.
moon·struck (mōōn′struk′) *adj.* Affected in the mind, supposedly by the influence of the moon; lunatic; deranged. Also **moon′strick′en** (-strik′ən).
moon·wort (mōōn′wûrt′) *n.* **1.** Any fern of the genus *Botrychium*, especially *B. lunaria*, having crescent-shaped fronds. **2.** Honesty (def. 4).
moon·y (mōō′nē) *adj.* **moon·i·er, moon·i·est** **1.** Moonlit. **2.** Like moonlight, or giving out light resembling moonlight. **3.** Shaped like the moon. **4.** *Informal* Dreamy.
moor[1] (mōōr) *n. Brit.* **1.** A tract of wasteland sometimes covered with heath, often elevated, marshy, and abounding in peat; a heath. **2.** A tract of land on which game is preserved for shooting. [OE *mōr*] — **moor′ish** *adj.*
moor[2] (mōōr) *v.t.* **1.** To secure (a ship, aircraft, etc.) in one place by means of cables attached to shore, anchors, etc. **2.** To secure in place; fix. — *v.i.* **3.** To secure a ship, aircraft, etc., in position; anchor. **4.** To be secured by chains or cables. [ME *moren* < MDu. *māren* to fasten]
Moor (mōōr) *n.* **1.** A Moslem of mixed Berber and Arab ancestry, especially one of the Saracen invaders of Spain in the 8th century or a descendant of the Saracens. **2.** A native of Morocco. [< OF *More, Maure* < L *Maurus* Moor, Mauritanian < Gk. *Mauros*, lit., dark]
moor·age (mōōr′ij) *n.* **1.** The act of mooring or the condition of being moored. **2.** A mooring place. **3.** A charge for mooring.
moor cock The male of the red grouse: also called *gorcock.*
Moore (mōōr, môr, mōr), **George**, 1852–1933, Irish novelist, poet, and dramatist. — **Henry**, born 1898, English sculptor. — **Sir John**, 1761–1809, British general. — **John Bassett**, 1860–1947, U.S. educator, jurist, and statesman. — **Marianne (Craig)**, 1887–1972, U.S. poet. — **Thomas**, 1779–1852, Irish poet: pseudonym **Thomas Little.**
moor·fowl (mōōr′foul′) *n.* The red grouse. See under GROUSE.
moor hen *n.* **1.** The female of the red grouse: also called *gorhen.* **2.** The European gallinule (*Gallinula chloropus*): also called *water hen.*
moor·ing (mōōr′ing) *n.* **1.** The act of one who or that which moors a vessel, aircraft, etc. **2.** *Chiefly pl.* A mooring place. **3.** *Chiefly pl.* That which secures or fastens an object.
mooring mast The tower to which a dirigible or blimp may be secured when not in flight. Also **mooring tower.**
Moor·ish (mōōr′ish) *adj.* **1.** Of or pertaining to the Moors. **2.** In the architectural or artistic style of the Moors.
moor·land (mōōr′land′) *n. Brit.* A moor (def. 1).
moor·wort (mōōr′wûrt′) *n.* A low, smooth shrub (*Andromeda polifolia*) of the heath family, with narrow, thick, evergreen leaves, growing in wet bogs: also called *marsh rosemary.*
moose (mōōs) *n. pl.* **moose** **1.** A large, heavily built mammal (*Alces americana*) of the deer family, found in northern U.S. and Canada, the male of which bears huge palmate antlers. **2.** The elk (def. 1). [< Algonquian (Massachusetts) *moosu* he strips off; because it eats the bark of trees]
moose·bird (mōōs′bûrd′) *n. Canadian* The Canada jay.
moose·milk (mōōs′milk′) *n. Canadian* A cocktail containing rum and milk.
moose pasture *Canadian slang.* A mining claim of little or no value.
moot (mōōt) *adj.* Open to or intended for discussion: debatable: a *moot* point. — *v.t.* **1.** To bring up for discussion; raise for debate. **2.** To argue (a case) in a moot court. — *n.* **1.** Discussion or argument; especially, a discussion of a hypothetical case by law students. **2.** In early English history, a meeting of freemen to discuss local affairs. [OE *mōt* assembly, court. Akin to *mētan* to meet.] — **moot′er** *n.*
moot court A court for the trial of hypothetical legal cases by law students.
mop[1] (mop) *n.* **1.** A device for washing or dusting floors, usually consisting of a bunch of heavy cotton yarn, rags, or the like, attached to a handle. **2.** Any loosely tangled bunch or mass, especially of hair. — *v.t.* **mopped, mop′ping** To rub

MOOSE
(To 7 feet high at shoulder)

or wipe with or as with a mop. — **to mop up** **1.** *Informal* To finish. **2.** *Mil.* To wipe out remnants of enemy resistance in (captured areas). — **to mop (up) the floor with** *Slang* To defeat easily and decisively. [ME *mappe,* ? var. of earlier *mapple.* Cf. L *mappula,* dim. of *mappa* napkin, cloth.]
mop[2] (mop) *n.* A wry mouth; grimace. — *v.i.* To make a wry face; grimace. [Cf. Du. *moppen* to pout, ? imit.]
mop·board (mop′bôrd′, -bōrd′) *n.* A baseboard (def. 1).
mope (mōp) *v.* **moped, mop·ing** *v.i.* **1.** To be gloomy, listless, or dispirited. — *v.t.* **2.** To make gloomy or dispirited. — *n.* **1.** One who mopes. **2.** *pl.* Dejection; depression. [Origin unknown. Cf. Sw. *mopa* to sulk, Dan. *maabe* to be stupid, unaware.] — **mop′er** *n.* — **mop′ish** *adj.* — **mop′ish·ly** *adv.* — **mop′ish·ness** *n.*
mo·poke (mō′pōk′) *n. Austral.* The frogmouth. [Imit.]
mop·pet (mop′it) *n.* **1.** *Informal* A child; youngster. **2.** *Obs.* A rag doll. [Dim. of MOP[1]]
mo·quette (mō·ket′) *n.* A woolen fabric with a velvety pile, used for carpets and upholstery. [< F]
Mo·qui (mō′kē) *n.* A Hopi Indian: also spelled *Moki.*
mor. Morocco (bookbinding).
Mor. Morocco.
mo·ra (môr′ə, mō′rə) *n. pl.* **mo·rae** (môr′ē, mō′rē) or **mo·ras** In prosody, a unit of meter, the common short foot, usually indicated by the breve. [< L, delay]
mo·ra·ceous (mō·rā′shəs, mō-) *adj. Bot.* Denoting or belonging to the mulberry family (*Moraceae*) of herbs, shrubs, and trees, including the common fig, hop, hemp, etc. [< NL *moraceae* < L *morus* mulberry]
Mo·rad·a·bad (mō·rad′ə·bad, mo·rad′ä·bäd′) A city in north central Uttar Pradesh, India; pop. 205,509 (est. 1969).
mo·raine (mə·rān′, mō-) *n. Geol.* Debris in various topographic forms that has been carried by a glacier, either along its course, at its edges, or at its lower terminus. [< F < dial. *morēna*] — **mo·rain′al, mo·rain′ic** *adj.*
mor·al (môr′əl, mor′-) *adj.* **1.** Of or related to conduct or character from the point of view of right and wrong; concerned with the goodness and badness of an action, character, disposition, etc.: *moral* goodness. **2.** Of good character or disposition; right or proper in behavior; righteous. **3.** Sexually virtuous; chaste. **4.** Teaching or attempting to teach standards of right and wrong; moralizing: a *moral* lecture. **5.** Capable of distinguishing between right and wrong: Man is a *moral* agent. **6.** Concerned with the establishment of principles of right and wrong, and their application; dealing with the study of ethics: *moral* theology. **7.** Arising from a sense of duty and right conduct; based on principles of right and wrong: a *moral* obligation. **8.** Acting not by physical force or practical means but by appeal to character, conduct, or disposition: *moral* support. **9.** Based on probability or on a general knowledge of human nature rather than on objective evidence or clear demonstration: *moral* certainty. — *n.* **1.** The lesson or teaching contained in or to be derived from a fable, poem, etc. **2.** *pl.* Conduct or behavior with regard to right and wrong, especially in sexual matters: a person of doubtful *morals.* **3.** A maxim; aphorism. [< OF < L *moralis* < *mos, moris* custom; in the pl., manners, morals] — **mor′al·ly** *adv.*
— **Syn.** (adj.) **2.** ethical, conscientious, scrupulous, upright, just, honest. — **Ant.** See synonyms for IMMORAL.
mo·rale (mə·ral′, -räl′, mô-) *n.* **1.** State of mind, especially of persons associated in some enterprise, with reference to confidence, courage, hope, zeal, etc.: the high *morale* of the workers. **2.** Formerly, morality. [< F. See MORAL.]
moral hazard In insurance, a risk resulting from doubt as to the honesty of the person insured.
mor·al·ism (môr′əl·iz′əm, mor′-) *n.* **1.** The practice of a nonreligious morality. **2.** The practice of moralizing. **3.** A moral maxim.
mor·al·ist (môr′əl·ist, mor′-) *n.* **1.** A teacher of morals. **2.** One who practices moralism. — **mor′al·is′tic** *adj.*
mo·ral·i·ty (mə·ral′ə·tē, mô-) *n. pl.* **·ties** **1.** The quality of being morally right; rightness; virtue. **2.** Conformity to standards of right conduct. **3.** Virtuous conduct, often sexual virtue. **4.** The doctrine or a system of the principles and duties of right and wrong conduct; ethics. **5.** An instruction or lesson in morals; a moral. **6.** A morality play. [< OF *moralite* < L *moralitas, -tatis* < *moralis.* See MORAL.]
morality play A form of allegorical drama of the 15th and 16th centuries in which the characters were personified virtues, vices, mental attributes, etc.
mor·al·ize (môr′əl·īz, mor′-) *v.* **·ized, ·iz·ing** *v.i.* **1.** To make moral reflections; talk about morality. — *v.t.* **2.** To explain in a moral sense; derive a moral from. **3.** To improve the morals of. Also *Brit.* **mor′al·ise.** [< MF *moraliser*] — **mor′al·i·za′tion** *n.* — **mor′al·iz′er** *n.*
moral philosophy Ethics.
Moral Rearmament Buchmanism.
mo·rass (mə·ras′, mô-, mō-) *n.* **1.** A tract of low-lying, soft, wet ground; marsh; bog. **2.** Anything that impedes, perplexes, or traps, as a difficult situation. [< Du. *moeras,* earlier *marasch* < OF *maresc* < Gmc. Akin to MARSH.]
mor·a·to·ri·um (môr′ə·tôr′ē·əm, -tō′rē-, mor′-) *n. pl.* **·ri·a** (-rē·ə) or **·ri·ums** **1.** A legal authorization to a debtor to sus-

pend payments for a given period; especially, such authorization to a bank in an emergency. **2.** The period during which such suspension of payments is in effect. **3.** Any authorized suspension or deferment of action. [< NL < LL *moratorius*. See MORATORY.]

mor·a·to·ry (môr′ə·tôr′ē, -tō′rē, mor′-) *adj.* Pertaining to or intended to delay; especially, designating legislation authorizing a moratorium. [< LL *moratorius* < L *morari* to delay < *mora* delay]

Mo·ra·va (mô′rä·vä) **1.** The Czech name for the river MARCH. **2.** The Czech name for MORAVIA.

Mo·ra·vi·a (mô·rā′vē·ə, mō-) A region of central Czechoslovakia; a former Austrian crownland: German *Mähren*, Czech *Morava*.

Mo·ra·vi·an (mô·rā′vē·ən, mō-) *adj.* Pertaining to Moravia, the Moravians, or the Moravian Church. — *n.* **1.** A native of Moravia. **2.** A member of the Moravian Church.

Moravian Church A denomination organized in Germany in 1722 by survivors of the Bohemian Brethren and by Count Nicholas von Zinzendorf: also called *Unitas Fratrum*.

Moravian Gate A mountain pass between the Carpathian and the Sudeten mountains in central Europe.

Mo·rav·ská O·stra·va (mô′räf·skä ôs′trä·vä) A city in central Czechoslovakia; pop. 271,905 (est. 1967): German *Mährisch-Ostrau*: also *Ostrava*.

mo·ray (môr′ā, mō·rā′) *n.* A brightly colored, voracious eel (family *Muranidae*), inhabiting tropical and subtropical waters; especially, *Muraena helena*, of Mediterranean waters esteemed as a food fish, and the **banded moray** (*Gymnothrax waialuoe*) of Hawaiian waters: also called *murry.* Also **mo′ray eel.** [Origin uncertain]

Mor·ay (mûr′ē, *Scot.* mûr′ā) A county of NE Scotland; 476 sq. mi.; pop. 49,156 (1961); county seat, Elgin. Formerly *Elgin.* Also **Mor′ay·shire** (-shir).

mor·bid (môr′bid) *adj.* **1.** Taking or showing an excessive interest in matters of a gruesome or unwholesome nature; being in an abnormally impressionable state of mind. **2.** Grisly; gruesome: a *morbid* fantasy. **3.** Pertaining to, arising from, or affected by disease. [< L *morbidus* < *morbus* disease] — **mor′bid·ly** *adv.* — **mor′bid·ness** *n.*

mor·bid·i·ty (môr·bid′ə·tē) *n.* *pl.* **·ties 1.** The state or quality of being morbid; also, a specific instance of this. **2.** The rate of disease or proportion of diseased persons in a community.

mor·bif·ic (môr·bif′ik) *adj.* *Rare* Producing disease. Also **mor·bif′i·cal.** [< F *morbifique* or LL *morbificus*] — **mor·bif′i·cal·ly** *adv.*

mor·bil·li (môr·bil′ī) *n.pl. Pathol.* The measles. [< Med.L, pl. of *morbillus*, dim. of *morbus* disease]

mor·ceau (môr·sō′) *n.* *pl.* **·ceaux** (-sō) *French* **1.** A small bit or fragment. **2.** A short composition, as of music.

mor·da·cious (môr·dā′shəs) *adj.* **1.** Biting, or given to biting. **2.** Sarcastic. [< L *mordax, -acis* < *mordere* to bite] — **mor·da′cious·ly** *adv.* — **mor·dac′i·ty** (-das′ə·tē) *n.*

mor·dan·cy (môr′dən·sē) *n.* The quality of being biting or sarcastic; pungency.

mor·dant (môr′dənt) *adj.* **1.** Biting; cutting; sarcastic: a *mordant* wit. **2.** Acting to fix colors in dyeing. — *n.* **1.** A substance, such as tannic acid or aluminum hydroxide, that, by combining with a dyestuff to form an insoluble compound or lake, serves to produce a fixed color in a textile, leather, etc. **2.** In etching, a corrosive used to bite into the lines traced on a metal plate. — *v.t.* To treat or imbue with a mordant. [< F, ppr. of OF *mordre* to bite < L *mordere*]

Mor·de·cai (mor′də·kī, -kā·ī) In the Old Testament, Esther's cousin, instrumental in saving the Jews from the extermination planned by Haman. *Esth.* ii 5.

mor·dent (mor′dənt) *n.* *Music* A melodic ornamentation consisting of a rapid single or double alternation of a tone with the tone immediately below it, ending on the principal tone; also, the symbol that indicates this. — **inverted mordent** A mordent in which the subsidiary tone is the tone immediately above; also called *pralltriller.* [< G < Ital. *mordente*, ppr. of *mordere* to bite]

Mor·dred (môr′drid) See MODRED.

more (môr, mōr) *adj.* *superlative* **most 1.** Greater in amount, extent, degree, or number: comparative of *much* and *many.* **2.** Additional; further; extra: *More* coffee, please. — *n.* **1.** A greater or additional quantity, amount, etc. **2.** That which exceeds or excels something else: This is *more* than enough. — *adv.* **1.** In or to a greater extent or degree: used to form the comparative of many adjectives and adverbs of two or more syllables: *more* beautiful, *more* tactfully. **2.** In addition; further; again. — **more or less 1.** In some undetermined degree. **2.** Approximately. [OE *māra*]

More (môr, mōr) **Paul Elmer,** 1864–1937, U.S. critic and essayist. — **Sir Thomas,** 1478?–1535, English statesman and author; lord chancellor of England; friend of Erasmus; beheaded by Henry VIII; canonized in 1935.

Mo·re·a (mô·rē′ə, mō-) A former name for the PELOPONNESUS.

Mo·reau (mô·rō′), **Jean Victor,** 1761–1813, French general; opposed Napoleon Bonaparte; exiled.

mo·reen (mə·rēn′) *n.* A sturdy, ribbed, cotton, wool, or wool and cotton fabric, often with a watered or embossed finish, used for clothing, upholstery, etc. [Prob. < MOIRE + *-een*, a suffix indicating similarity as in *velveteen*]

mo·rel (mə·rel′) *n.* Any of a group of edible mushrooms (genus *Morchella*) resembling a sponge on a stalk. [< MF *morille*, ult. < Gmc. Cf. OHG *morhila* little carrot.]

mo·rel·lo (mə·rel′ō) *n.* A variety of cultivated cherry (*Prunus cerasus austera*), with a dark red skin, flesh, and juice, used in cooking, etc. [< Flemish *marelle*, aphetic var. of *amarelle* < Ital. *amarello*, dim. of *amaro* bitter < L *amarus*]

more·o·ver (môr·ō′vər, mōr-) *adv.* Beyond what has been said; further; besides; likewise; in addition.

mo·res (môr′āz, mō′rāz, môr′ēz, mō′rēz) *n.pl. Sociol.* **1.** The established, traditional customs or folkways regarded by a social group as essential to its preservation and welfare. **2.** The accepted conventions of a group or community. [< L, pl. of *mos, moris* custom]

Mo·resque (mô·resk′, mə-) *adj.* Moorish. [< F < Ital. *moresco* < L *Maurus.* See MOOR.]

Mor·gan (môr′gən) *n.* One of an American breed of light horses of Arabian strain. Also **Morgan horse.** [after Justin *Morgan,* 1747–98, U.S. owner of the stallion that became the direct progenitor of the breed]

Mor·gan (môr′gən), **Daniel,** 1736–1802, American Revolutionary general. — **Sir Henry,** 1635?–88, English buccaneer born in Wales; raided the Spanish Main. — **John Hunt,** 1825–64, Confederate general in the Civil War. — **John Pierpont,** 1837–1913, U.S. banker, art collector, and philanthropist. — **Thomas Hunt,** 1866–1945, U.S. zoologist.

MORESQUE
DECORATION

mor·ga·nat·ic (môr′gə·nat′ik) *adj.* Of or designating a form of legitimate marriage between a member of certain royal families of Europe and a person of inferior rank, in which the titles and estates are not shared by the inferior partner or their children. Also **mor·gan′ic·al.** [< NL *morganaticus* < LL (*matrimonium ad*) *morganaticam* (wedding with) morning gift < OHG *morgangeba* morning gift (in lieu of a share in the estate)] — **mor′ga·nat′i·cal·ly** *adv.*

mor·gan·ite (môr′gən·īt) *n.* A rose-colored variety of beryl, used as a gemstone. [after John Pierpont *Morgan*]

Morgan le Fay (lə fā′) In Arthurian legend, the fairy half-sister of King Arthur, often depicted as an evil enchantress: also called *Fata Morgana.* Also **Morgain** (mor′gān, -gən) **le Fay.** [< OF *Morgain la fée* Morgan the fairy < Celtic]

mor·gen (môr′gən) *n.* *pl.* **·gen** or **·gens 1.** A land measure equal to about two acres, formerly used by the Dutch and still employed in South Africa. **2.** A land measure equal to about two thirds of an acre, formerly used in Prussia, Norway, and Denmark. [< Du. & G, morning; hence, area plowed in one morning]

Mor·gen·thau (môr′gən·thô), **Henry,** 1891–1967, U.S. public official.

morgue (môrg) *n.* **1.** A place where the bodies of unknown dead persons and of those killed in accidents or by other violent means are kept for identification before burial. **2.** In a newspaper editorial office, the department in charge of filed items and biographical material used for obituary notices, etc.; also, the room used for this purpose. [< F, orig. the building in Paris for keeping the bodies of unidentified dead]

mor·i·bund (môr′ə·bund, -bənd, mor′-) *adj.* **1.** At the point of death; dying. **2.** Approaching extinction; coming to an end: a *moribund* enterprise. [< L *moribundus* < *mori* to die] — **mor′i·bun′di·ty** *n.* — **mor′i·bund·ly** *adv.*

mo·ri·on¹ (môr′ē·on, mō′rē-) *n.* An open, crested, visorless helmet with a curved brim that is peaked in front and in back, worn in the 16th and 17th centuries: also spelled *morrion.* [< MF < Sp. *morrion* < *morra* crown of the head]

mo·ri·on² (môr′ē·on, mō′rē-) *n.* A dark variety of smoky quartz. [< F < LL, a misreading of L *mormorion*]

Mo·ris·co (mə·ris′kō) *adj.* Moorish. — *n.* *pl.* **·cos** or **·coes 1.** A Moor, especially one of Spain. **2.** The Moorish style of architecture or decoration. [< Sp. < *moro* Moor.]

Mo·ri·son (môr′ə·sən, mor′-), **Samuel Eliot,** 1887–1976, U.S. historian and biographer.

mo·ri·tu·ri te sa·lu·ta·mus (môr′i·tyŏŏr′ī tē sal′yŏŏ·tā′məs) *Latin* We (who are) about to die salute thee: salutation of the gladiators to the Roman emperor.

Mor·ley (môr′lē), **Christopher** (**Darlington**), 1890–1957, U.S. writer. — **John,** 1838–1923, first Viscount Morley of Blackburn, English statesman and man of letters.

Mor·mon (môr′mən) *n.* **1.** A member of the Mormon Church; a Latter-day Saint. **2.** In Mormon belief, a prophet of the fourth century who wrote, on golden tablets, a history of the early American people. The tablets, called the **Book of Mormon,** a holy book of the Mormon faith, were found by Joseph Smith near Palmyra, New York, and translated and published by him in 1830. — *adj.* Of or pertaining to the Mormons or their religion. — **Mor'mon·ism** *n.*

Mormon Church The Church of Jesus Christ of Latter-day Saints, founded by Joseph Smith in 1830. See MORMON.

Mormon State Nickname of UTAH.

Mormon Trail The trail taken by the Mormons, 1847, from Iowa to Utah.

morn (môrn) *n. Poetic* The morning. [OE *morne*]

Mor·nay (môr·nā'), **Philippe de**, 1549–1623, Seigneur du Plessis-Marly, French statesman and Huguenot leader: also *Duplessis-Mornay.*

morn·ing (môr'ning) *n.* **1.** The early part of the day; the time from midnight to noon, or from sunrise to noon. **2.** The early part or stage of anything: the *morning* of the world. — *adj.* Pertaining to or occurring in the morning: *morning* exercises. Abbr. **m., M.** ◆ Collateral adjective: *matutinal*. [ME *morwening* < *morwen* + *-ing* by analogy with evening]

Morn·ing (môr'ning) The goddess Eos or Aurora.

morn·ing-glo·ry (môr'ning-glôr'ē, -glō'rē) *n.* Any of various twining plants (genus *Ipomoea*) with funnel-shaped flowers of various colors, typical of a family (*Convolvulaceae*) of shrubs and twining herbs, including the moonflower.

morning report *Mil.* A daily report made by a unit of company size or above, giving information as to troop strength, changes in status, etc.

morning sickness Vomiting and nausea in the morning, common in early pregnancy.

morning star **1.** A planet, especially Venus, when rising in the east shortly before the sun. **2.** An annual herb (*Mentzelia aurea*) native to California, having yellow flowers.

Mo·ro (môr'ō, mō'rō) *n. pl.* **·ros** **1.** A member of any of the various Moslem Malay tribes of the southern Philippines. **2.** The language of the Moros. — *adj.* Of or pertaining to the Moros or their language. [< Sp., Moor]

mo·roc·co (mə·rok'ō) *n.* **1.** A fine flexible leather, made originally in Morocco from goatskin tanned with sumac. **2.** Any soft, grained leather of calfskin or sheepskin made in imitation of morocco. Also **morocco leather**. Abbr. *mor.*

Mo·roc·co (mə·rok'ō) **1.** A kingdom in NW Africa; about 160,000 sq. mi.; pop. 15,577,000 (est. 1970); capital, Rabat; French *Maroc*, Spanish *Marruecos*. **2.** A former name for MARRAKESH. — **Mo·roc'can** *adj.* & *n.*

mo·ron (môr'on, mō'ron) *n.* **1.** A person exhibiting the mildest degree of mental deficiency, permitting adequacy in simple life activities. **2.** Loosely, a very foolish or stupid person. — **Syn.** See IDIOT. [< Gk. *mōron*, neut. of *mōros* stupid] — **mo·ron·ic** (mô·ron'ik, mō-) *adj.* — **mo·ron'i·cal·ly** *adv.* — **mo·ron·ism** *n.*

mo·rose (mə·rōs') *adj.* Ill-humored; sullen; gloomy, as a person, mood, etc. [< L *morosus* < *mos, moris* manner, mood] — **mo·rose'ly** *adv.* — **mo·rose'ness** *n.* — **Syn.** glum, dour, crabbed. — **Ant.** cheerful, genial.

morph. or **morphol.** Morphological; morphology.

-morph *combining form* Having the form or shape of: *allomorph*. [< Gk. *morphē* form]

mor·pheme (môr'fēm) *n. Ling.* The smallest meaningful unit of a language or dialect, whether a word, base, or affix. *Man, scamper, pro-, -ess, -ing, ouch,* etc., are morphemes. See ALLOMORPH. [< F *morphème* < Gk. *morphē* form]

morpheme alternant *n.* An allomorph. Also **morpheme variant.**

Mor·pheus (môr'fē·əs, -fyōōs) In Greek mythology, the god of dreams, son of Hypnos, the god of sleep. [< L < Gk. *morphē* form; from the shapes he calls up in dreams] — **Mor'phe·an** *adj.*

-morphic *combining form* Having the form or shape of: *anthropomorphic.* [< Gk. *morphē* form]

mor·phine (môr'fēn) *n. Chem.* A bitter, white crystalline compound, $C_{17}H_{19}NO_3$, the principal alkaloid of opium, used as an analgesic and narcotic. Also **mor'phi·a** (-fē-ə), **mor'phin** (-fin). [< F < L *Morpheus* god of dreams]

mor·phin·ism (môr'fin·iz'əm) *n. Pathol.* **1.** An abnormal condition of the system produced by the habitual use of morphine. **2.** Addiction to morphine.

morpho- *combining form* Form; shape: *morphogenesis.* Also, before vowels, **morph-.** [< Gk. *morphē* form]

mor·pho·gen·e·sis (môr'fō·jen'ə·sis) *n. Biol.* The structural changes in the evolution and development of an organism or part. — **mor'pho·ge·net'ic** (-jə·net'ik) *adj.*

mor·phol·o·gy (môr·fol'ə·jē) *n. pl.* **·gies** **1.** *Biol.* The study of the form and structure of plants and animals considered apart from function; also, a particular theory or work dealing with this subject. **2.** The form and structure of an organism regarded as a whole. **3.** *Ling.* **a** The arrangement and interrelationship of morphemes in words. **b** The branch of linguistics dealing with this. Compare SYNTAX. **4.** Geomorphology (which see). [< MORPHO- + -LOGY] — **mor·pho·log·ic** (môr'fə·loj'ik) or **·i·cal** *adj.* — **mor·phol'o·gist** *n.*

mor·pho·pho·neme (môr'fō·fō'nēm) *n. Ling.* A set of phonemes alternating in a morpheme according to context; also, a symbol for this, as the /D/ that may represent /t/ after unvoiced consonants and /d/ elsewhere. — **mor'pho·pho·nem'ic** *adj.*

-morphous *combining form* Having a (specified) form: often equivalent to *-morphic*: *anthropomorphous.* [< Gk. *morphē* form]

mor·ri·on (môr'ē·on, mō'rē-) See MORION[1].

mor·ris (môr'is, mor'-) *n.* An old English dance, performed especially on May Day, in which the performers impersonate various characters in English folklore. Also **morris dance.** [Earlier *morys, morish* Moorish]

Mor·ris (môr'is, mor'-), **Gouverneur**, 1752–1816, American Revolutionary statesman and diplomat. — **Lewis**, 1726–98, American patriot, signer of the Declaration of Independence; half brother of Gouverneur. — **Robert**, 1734–1806, American patriot, signer of the Declaration of Independence; chief financier of the American Revolution. — **William**, 1834–96, English poet, painter, and socialist writer.

Morris chair A large wooden armchair with removable cushions and an adjustable back. [after William *Morris*, who invented it]

Mor·ris Jes·up (môr'is jes'əp, mor'is), **Cape** The world's northernmost point of land, at the northern extremity of Greenland. Also **Cape Morris K. Jesup.**

Mor·ri·son (môr'ə·sən, mor'-), **Herbert Stanley**, 1888–1965, English statesman and Labour Party leader.

Mor·ri·son (môr'ə·sən, mor'-), **Mount** The highest mountain of Taiwan; 13,599 ft. *Chinese* **Sin·kao** (shin'kou'), *Japanese* **Ni·i·ta·ka** (nē-ē-tä·kä).

Morris Plan bank *U.S.* A bank organized to extend small loans to industrial wage earners.

mor·ro (môr'ō, mor'ō; *Sp.* môr'rō) *n. pl.* **mor·ros** (môr'ōz, mor'-; *Sp.* môr'rōs) A round hill or promontory. [< Sp.]

Morro Castle A fort at the entrance to Havana harbor.

mor·row (môr'ō, mor'ō) *n. Archaic & Poetic* **1.** The next succeeding day. **2.** A time immediately following a specified event. **3.** Formerly, morning: good *morrow*. [ME *morwen*. See MORNING.]

Mors (môrs) In Roman mythology, death personified as a god: identified with the Greek *Thanatos*. [< L, death]

Morse (môrs), **Samuel Finley Breese**, 1791–1872, U.S. artist and inventor; constructed the first practical telegraph.

Morse code **1.** A system of telegraphic signals invented by S.F.B. Morse, composed of dots and dashes or short and long flashes representing the letters of the alphabet, numerals, etc., and used in transmitting messages. **2.** International Morse Code (which see). Also **Morse, Morse alphabet.**

mor·sel (môr'səl) *n.* **1.** A small fragment or bite of food. **2.** A tempting dish; tidbit. **3.** A small piece or bit of something: a choice *morsel* of gossip. — *v.t.* **mor·seled** or **·selled, mor·sel·ing** or **·sel·ling** To divide into small pieces. [< OF, dim. of *mors* bite < L *morsus* < *mordere* to bite]

mort[1] (môrt) *n.* **1.** In hunting, a flourish on the horn to announce the killing of game. **2.** *Obs.* Death. [< OF *mort* < L *mors, mortis* death]

mort[2] (môrt) *n.* A salmon in its third year. [Orig. unknown]

mort[3] (môrt) *n. Brit. Dial.* A great quantity or number. [? < MORTAL (def. 10)]

mor·tal (môr'tal) *adj.* **1.** Subject to death: opposed to *immortal*: *mortal* man. **2.** Of or pertaining to humanity as subject or liable to death; human. **3.** Of or relating to this life or world: *mortal* existence. **4.** Causing or liable to cause death; fatal: He has received a *mortal* blow. **5.** Relating to or accompanying death. **6.** Arising from or as from fear of death; dire: *mortal* terror. **7.** Likely to remain so until death; implacable: a *mortal* enemy. **8.** Ending in death: a *mortal* contest. **9.** *Theol.* Incurring spiritual death unless repented of and forgiven: distinguished from *venial*: *mortal* sin. **10.** *Informal* Very great. **11.** *Informal* Long and tedious: He talked for two *mortal* hours. **12.** *Informal* Possible; conceivable: There's no *mortal* reason for his action. — *n.* One who is mortal; a human being. — *adv. Informal* Very; exceedingly: *mortal* tired. [< OF < L *mortalis* < *mors, mortis* death]

mor·tal·i·ty (môr·tal'ə·tē) *n. pl.* **·ties** **1.** The condition of being mortal or subject to death; mortal nature. **2.** Loss of life on a large scale, as caused by war, disease, etc. **3.** Frequency of death; the proportion of deaths in a specified portion of the population; death rate. **4.** Humanity; mankind. **5.** *Obs.* Death. [< OF *mortalite* < L *mortalitas*]

mortality table A statistical table showing the average length of life, probable death rate, etc., for various population groups or categories of individuals: also called *life table*.

mor·tal·ize (môr'təl·īz) *v.t.* **·ized, ·iz·ing** To make mortal; consider as mortal.

mor·tal·ly (môr'təl·ē) *adv.* **1.** Fatally. **2.** After the manner of a mortal. **3.** Extremely: *mortally* offended.

mor·tar[1] (môr'tər) *n.* **1.** A strong bowl-shaped vessel in which substances are crushed or pounded with a pestle. For illustration see PESTLE. **2.** *Mining* A tublike receptacle with grated sides, in which ore is stamped. [OE *mortere* < L *mortarium* mixing trough]

mor·tar[2] (môr'tər) *n.* A building material consisting of a mixture of lime, cement, etc., with sand and water, used in bricklaying, plastering walls, etc. [< OF *mortier* < L *mortarium* trough, mixture of sand and lime]

mor·tar[3] (môr′tər) *n.* **1.** *Mil.* A smooth-bored or rifled muzzleloading weapon, firing a relatively heavy shell, having a shorter range and higher trajectory than a howitzer: also called *trench mortar.* **2.** Any of several devices for hurling pyrotechnic shells, life lines, etc. [< F *mortier*]

mor·tar·board (môr′tər·bôrd′, -bōrd′) *n.* **1.** A square board with a handle, on which a mason holds mortar. **2.** A type of academic cap topped by a stiff, flat, four-cornered piece covered with cloth, worn at high-school and college graduations.

mortar hoe A hoe with openings in the blade, used for mixing mortar, cement, etc. For illustration see HOE.

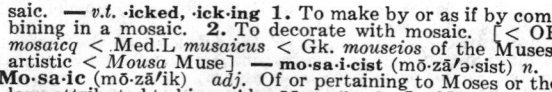

MORTAR[3] (*def.* 1)
A Shell. *B* Mortar: *a* Base plate. *b* Tube. *c* Sight. *d* Bipod.

Morte d'Arthur (môrt′där′thər) A collection of stories about King Arthur compiled by Sir Thomas Malory.

mort·gage (môr′gij) *n. Law* **1.** A conditional transfer of property pledged as security for the repayment of a loan. **2.** The contract specifying such a pledge. **3** The claim that the mortgagee has on the property. Abbr. *mtg., mtge.* — *v.t.* **·gaged, ·gag·ing 1.** To make over or pledge (property) by mortgage. **2.** To pledge; stake: to *mortgage* one's future. [< OF, dead pledge]

mort·ga·gee (môr′gi·jē′) *n.* One to whom a mortgage is given; the holder of a mortgage.

mort·ga·gor (môr′gi·jər) *n.* One who mortgages his property to another as security for a loan. Also **mort′gag·er.**

mor·tice (môr′tis) *n.* A mortise. — *v.t.* **·ticed, ·tic·ing** To mortise.

mor·ti·cian (môr·tish′ən) *n. U.S.* A funeral director; undertaker. [< L *mors, mortis* death + -ICIAN]

mor·ti·fi·ca·tion (môr′tə·fə·kā′shən) *n.* **1.** A feeling of loss of self-esteem through failure, disappointment, or embarrassment; humiliation; shame. **2.** That which causes such humiliation. **3.** The ascetic practice of subduing the appetites and strengthening the will against sin by fasting or other disciplines. **4.** *Pathol.* The death of one part of a living animal body by gangrene or necrosis. — **Syn.** See CHAGRIN. [< OF < LL *mortificatio, -onis*]

mor·ti·fy (môr′tə·fī) *v.* **·fied, ·fy·ing** *v.t.* **1.** To affect with humiliation, shame, or chagrin; humiliate. **2.** To discipline or punish (the body, appetites, etc.) by fasting or other ascetic practices. **3.** *Pathol.* To cause mortification in (part of an animal body). — *v.i.* **4.** To practice ascetic self-discipline. **5.** *Pathol.* To undergo mortification. [< OF *mortifier* < LL *mortificare* < L *mors, mortis* death + *facere* to make] — **mor′ti·fi′er** *n.* — **mor′ti·fy′ing·ly** *adv.*

Mor·ti·mer (môr′tə·mər), **Roger de,** 1287–1330, first Earl of March, English nobleman; opponent of Edward II of England; lover of Isabella, Edward's queen; hanged.

mor·tise (môr′tis) *n.* A space hollowed out in a piece of timber, stone, etc., and shaped to fit a tenon to which it is to be joined. — *v.t.* **·tised, ·tis·ing 1.** To cut or make a mortise in. **2.** To join by a tenon and mortise. Also spelled *mortice.* [< F *mortaise,* ? < Arabic *murtazz* joined, fixed in]

MORTISE (*a*) AND TENON (*b*)

mort·main (môrt′mān) *n. Law* The holding of lands and buildings in perpetual ownership, as by a religious or charitable corporation; inalienable possession: also called *dead hand.* [< OF *mortemain* < Med.L *mortua manus* dead hand]

Mor·ton (môr′tən), **William Thomas Green,** 1819–68, U.S. dentist; pioneer in use of ether as an anesthetic.

mor·tu·ar·y (môr′chōō·er′ē) *n. pl.* **·ar·ies 1.** A place for the temporary reception of the dead before burial. **2.** Formerly, a gift claimed by or given to a parish priest upon the death of a parishioner. — *adj.* **1.** Of or pertaining to the burial of the dead. **2.** Relating to death. [< MF *mortuaire* < L *mortuarius* of the dead < *mortuus* dead]

mor·u·la (môr′yōō·lə, -ōō-) *n. pl.* **·lae** (-lē) *Zool.* The compact, spherical mass of cells formed by the cleavage of the ovum of many animals in the early stages of embryonic development: also called *mulberry body.* [< NL, dim. of L *morum* mulberry] — **mor′u·lar** *adj.*

mos. Months.

MOS Military occupational specialty.

mo·sa·ic (mō·zā′ik) *n.* **1.** Inlaid work composed of bits of stone, glass, etc., forming a pattern or picture; also, the process of making this. **2.** A design, arrangement, etc., resembling such work. **3.** *Photog.* An assemblage of aerial photographs joined so as to form a single, continuous picture of a terrain. **4.** *Telecom.* An array of minute, photosensitive granules or elements mounted in the image-scanning section of a television camera. **5.** *Bot.* Any of several destructive virus diseases of plants, characterized by a pale, mottled appearance of the foliage: tobacco *mosaic*: also **mosaic disease.** — *adj.* Of, pertaining to, or resembling mo-

saic. — *v.t.* **·icked, ·ick·ing 1.** To make by or as if by combining in a mosaic. **2.** To decorate with mosaic. [< OF *mosaicq* < Med.L *musaicus* < Gk. *mouseios* of the Muses, artistic < *Mousa* Muse] — **mo·sa·i·cist** (mō·zā′ə·sist) *n.*

Mo·sa·ic (mō·zā′ik) *adj.* Of or pertaining to Moses or the laws attributed to him. Also **Mo·sa′i·cal.** [< NL *Mosaicus* < L *Moses* Moses < Hebrew *Mōsheh*]

mosaic gold 1. Stannic sulfide. **2.** Ormolu (def. 1).

Mosaic Law The code of civil and religious laws contained in the Pentateuch and traditionally attributed to Moses: also called *Law of Moses, the Law.*

Mo·san (mō′sən) *n.* A phylum of North American Indian languages spoken from the Columbia River valley to southern Alaska.

Mos·by (môz′bē), **John Singleton,** 1833–1916, American Confederate cavalry officer and author.

mos·chate (mos′kāt, -kit) *adj.* Having the odor of musk; musky. [< NL *moschatus* < Med.L *moschus* musk]

mos·cha·tel (mos′kə·tel′, mos′kə·tel) *n.* A low, perennial herb (*Adoxa moschatellina*), with greenish flowers and a musky odor. [< F *moscatelle* < Ital. *moscatella*]

Moś·cic·ki (mōsh·tsits′kē), **Ignacy,** 1867–1946, Polish chemist and statesman; president 1926–39.

Mos·cow (mos′kou, -kō) The capital of the Soviet Union and the R.S.F.S.R., in the western R.S.F.S.R.; pop. 6,942,-000 (est. 1970). *Russian* **Mos·kva** (mos·kvä′).

Mose·ley (mōz′lē), **Henry Gwyn-Jeffreys,** 1887–1915, English physicist.

Mo·selle (mō·zel′) *n.* A light, dry wine made in the valley of the Moselle, chiefly in Germany.

Mo·selle (mō·zel′) A river in NE France, Luxembourg, and western Germany, flowing 320 miles, generally NE, to the Rhine. *German* **Mo·sel** (mō′zəl).

Mo·ses (mō′zis, -ziz) In the Old Testament, the younger son of Amram and Jochebed, who led the Israelites out of Egypt to the Promised Land, received the Ten Commandments from God, and gave laws to the people. **2.** A leader; legislator. [< Hebrew *Mōsheh,* ? < Egyptian *mesu* son]

Mo·ses (mō′zis, -ziz), **Anna Mary Robertson,** 1860–1961, U.S. painter: called **Grandma Moses.**

mo·sey (mō′zē) *v.i.* **·seyed, ·sey·ing** *U.S. Slang* **1.** To saunter, or stroll; shuffle along. **2.** To go away; move off. [Origin unknown]

Mos·lem (moz′ləm, mos′-) *n. pl.* **·lems** or **·lem** A Muslim. — *adj.* Muslim.

Mos·lem·ism (moz′ləm·iz′əm) *n.* Islam.

Mos·ley (mōz′lē), **Sir Oswald Ernald,** born 1896, English Fascist politician.

mosque (mosk) *n.* A Muslim temple of worship. For illustration see MINARET. Also **mosk.** [< F *mosquée* < Ital. *moschea* < Arabic *masjid* < *sajada* to worship, pray]

mos·qui·to (məs·kē′tō) *n. pl.* **·toes** or **·tos** Any of various dipterous insects (family *Culicidae*), having in the female a long proboscis capable of puncturing the skin of man and animals for extracting blood, certain species of which transmit malaria, yellow fever, etc., by their bite. For illustration see INSECTS (injurious). [< Sp., dim. of *mosca* fly < L *musca*] — **mos·qui′tal** *adj.*

mosquito boat A patrol torpedo boat (which see).

mosquito fleet *Naut. Slang* An assemblage of small craft.

mosquito hawk A nighthawk (which see).

mosquito net A fine net or gauze (**mosquito netting**) placed around beds or over windows and the like to keep out mosquitoes.

moss (môs, mos) *n.* **1.** A delicate bryophytic plant (class *Musci*), having a stem and distinct leaves, and growing in tufts or clusters on the ground, decaying wood, rocks, etc. **2.** A clump or tuft of such plants. **3.** Any of several other cryptogamous plants, as certain lichens, clubmosses, etc. **4.** *Chiefly Scot.* A peat bog. [OE *mos* marsh. Akin to OE *mēos* moss.] — **moss′y** *adj.* — **moss′i·ness** *n.*

moss agate A variety of agate containing mineral oxides and showing patterns arranged in mosslike forms.

moss·back (môs′bak′, mos′-) *n.* **1.** An old fish or turtle on whose back is a growth of algae or the like. **2.** *U.S. Slang* A very conservative or old-fashioned person; fogy. — **moss·backed** (môs′bakt′, mos′-) *adj.*

Möss·bau·er effect (mœs′bou′ər) The absorption of gamma rays emitted from a radioactive isotope by nuclei of the same isotope, with resonance between the emitting and absorbing nuclei, both of which are anchored in crystals. It is used in the exact determination of wavelengths, time intervals, the red shift, and in testing various concepts of relativity and quantum theory. [after Rudolf L. *Mössbauer,* born 1929, German physicist.]

moss·bunk·er (môs′bungk·ər, mos′-) *n.* A fish, the menhaden. Also **moss′bank·er.** [Alter. of Du. *marsbanker*]

moss green Any of various shades of dull yellowish green.

moss-grown (môs′grōn′, mos′-) *adj.* **1.** Overgrown with moss. **2.** Old-fashioned; antiquated.

moss hag *Scot.* A pit or slough in a peat bog.

mos·so (môs′so) *adj. Music* Rapid; literally, moved. [< Ital., pp. of *movere* to move < L]

moss pink A low plant (*Phlox subulata*) of the eastern United States, that has white, pink, or purplish flowers: also called *ground pink*. Also **moss phlox.**

moss rose A cultivated variety (*Rosa centifolia muscosa*) of the rose with a mossy calyx and stem.

moss·troop·er (môs′trōō′pər, mos′-) *n.* In the 17th century, one of a group of marauders who infested the mosses or marshes between Scotland and England.

most (mōst) *adj.* **1.** Consisting of the greatest number: superlative of *many.* **2.** Consisting of the greatest amount or degree: superlative of *much*: to have the *most* power. **3.** In the greatest number of instances: *Most* people are honest. **— for the most part** Generally; mostly. **—** *n.* **1.** (construed as *pl.*) The greatest number; the largest part: *most* of my belongings. **2.** (construed as *pl.*) The greatest number of persons: too difficult for *most.* **3.** The greatest amount, quantity or degree; utmost: the *most* in quality. **— at (the) most** Not more than; at the extreme point or limit. **— to make the most of 1.** To use to the fullest advantage; get the greatest use from. **2.** To exaggerate the importance of. **—** *adv.* **1.** In or to the greatest or highest degree, quantity, extent, etc.: used with adjectives and adverbs to form the superlative degree: *most* honorable. **2.** Very: a *most* delicious meal. **3.** *Informal* Almost: *Most* everyone says so. [OE *mǣst, māst*]

-most *suffix* Most: added to adjectives and adverbs to form superlatives: *innermost; outmost.* [OE *-mest < -ma + -est,* earlier superlative suffixes]

most·ly (mōst′lē) *adv.* For the most part; principally.

Mo·sul (mō·sōōl′) A city in northern Iraq, on the Tigris; near the site of ancient Nineveh; pop. 243,311 (1965). Also **Mos·sul′.**

mot (mō) *n.* **1.** A witty or pithy saying: bon *mot.* **2.** *Archaic* A bugle note. [< F, word < LL *muttum* uttered sound cognate with *muttire* to murmur]

mote[1] (mōt) *n.* A minute particle or speck, especially of dust. [OE *mot* dust]

mote[2] (mōt) *v.i. Archaic* May; might. [OE *mōt* it is permitted]

mo·tel (mō·tel′) *n. U.S.* A roadside hotel for motorists, often comprising private cabins that open on parking facilities: also called *motor court.* [< MO(TOR) + (HO)TEL]

mo·tet (mō·tet′) *n. Music* A polyphonic vocal composition of a sacred nature, usually unaccompanied. [< OF, dim. of *mot* word. See MOT[1].]

moth (môth, moth) *n. pl.* **moths** (môthz, môths, mothz, moths) **1.** Any of a large group of lepidopterous insects, usually with nocturnal habits, distinguished from the butterflies by having smaller wings, stouter bodies, and duller coloring. **2.** The clothes moth (which see). [OE *moththe*]

moth-ball (môth′bôl′, moth′-) *Mil. & Nav. adj.* Designating ships or military equipment laid up in reserve and covered or coated with protective materials. **—** *v.t.* To put in reserve and protective storage.

moth ball A small ball of camphor or naphthalene used to repel moths from clothing, etc., during storage.

moth-eat·en (môth′ēt′n, moth′-) *adj.* **1.** Eaten or damaged by moths. **2.** Used up or worn out; decrepit. **3.** Old-fashioned. Also *mothy.*

moth·er[1] (muth′ər) *n.* **1.** A female who has borne offspring; female parent. **2.** A female who adopts a child, or who otherwise holds a maternal relationship toward another. **3.** The characteristics regarded as belonging to a mother: It appealed to the *mother* in her. **4.** Anything that creates, nurtures, or protects something else. **5.** *Usually cap.* A title given to nuns of certain rank, especially to the head of a female religious community. **6.** In Christian Science, the divine and eternal Principle; God. **—** *adj.* **1.** Native: mother tongue. **2.** Relating to or characteristic of a mother: *mother* love. **3.** Holding a maternal relation: the *mother* church. **4.** That is a mother: a *mother* goat. **—** *v.t.* **1.** To bring forth as a mother; produce; create. **2.** To care for or protect as a mother. **3.** To admit or claim parentage, authorship, etc., of. [OE *mōdor* from a common base in many languages akin to G *mutter*, Du. *moeder*, L *mater*, Gk. *mētēr*, Skt. *mātr*]

moth·er[2] (muth′ər) *n.* A slimy film composed of bacteria and yeast cells that forms on the surface of fermenting liquids and is active in the production of vinegar: also called *mother of vinegar.* [Special use of MOTHER[1]. Akin to MDu. *moeder, modder* mud.] **— moth′er·y** *adj.*

Mother Car·ey's chicken (kâr′ēz) Any of various small petrels, especially the storm petrel. [Alter. of L *mater cara* dear mother, an epithet for the Virgin Mary]

Mother Goose 1. The imaginary narrator of a volume of folk tales, compiled in French by Charles Perrault in 1697. **2.** The imaginary writer or compiler of a collection of nursery rhymes (**Mother Goose's Nursery Rhymes**) of English folk origin, originally known as **Mother Goose's Melodies** and first published in London about 1790.

moth·er·hood (muth′ər·hŏŏd) *n.* **1.** The state of being a mother. **2.** The spirit or qualities of a mother. **3.** Mothers collectively.

Mother Hub·bard (hub′ərd) **1.** The main character in an old nursery rhyme. **2.** A woman's loose, flowing gown, unconfined at the waist: also **mother hubbard.**

moth·er-in-law (muth′ər·in·lô′) *n. pl.* **moth·ers-in-law** The mother of one's spouse.

moth·er·land (muth′ər·land′) *n.* **1.** The land of one's birth; native land. **2.** The land of one's ancestors.

mother lode In mining, any principal or very rich vein.

moth·er·ly (muth′ər·lē) *adj.* **1.** Resembling or having the nature of a mother: a *motherly* woman. **2.** Characteristic of or befitting a mother: *motherly* care. **—** *adv.* In the manner of a mother. **— moth′er·li·ness** *n.*

Mother of God The Virgin Mary: an official title given at the Council of Ephesus in 431.

moth·er-of-pearl (muth′ər·əv·pûrl′) *n.* The pearly, iridescent internal layer of certain shells, especially those of the pearl oyster and abalone, used in ornamental work, for buttons, etc.: also called *nacre.* **—** *adj.* Of mother-of-pearl.

mother of vinegar Mother[2].

Mother's Day *U.S.* A memorial day in honor of mothers, observed annually on the second Sunday in May.

mother superior The head of a female religious community.

mother tongue 1. One's native language. **2.** A parent language.

Moth·er·well and Wish·aw (muth′ər·wel ənd wish′ô) A burgh in northern Lanarkshire, Scotland, on the Clyde; formerly two towns; pop. 72,799 (1961).

mother wit Inherent or native intelligence; common sense.

moth·er·wort (muth′ər·wûrt′) *n.* An Old World herb (*Leonurus cardiaca*) of the mint family, having small purple or pink flowers, common in the U.S. [ME *moderwort*]

moth-proof (môth′prōōf′, moth′-) *adj.* Resistant to the attack of moths, as certain textiles. **—** *v.t.* **·proofed, ·proof·ing** To render (textiles) resistant to moths.

moth·y (môth′ē, moth′ē) *adj.* **moth·i·er, moth·i·est 1.** Moth-eaten. **2.** Full of moths.

mo·tif (mō·tēf′) *n.* **1.** The underlying theme or main element in a literary or artistic work. **2.** In decoration, a distinct element of design. **3.** *Music* The shortest intelligible and significant melodic or rhythmic fragment of a theme or subject. Also *motive.* **— Syn.** See MELODY. [< F]

mo·tile (mō′til, -təl) *adj. Zool.* Having the power of or demonstrating motion, as certain minute organisms. **—** *n. Psychol.* One in whose mind motor images are especially distinct. [< L *motus,* pp. of *movere* to move] **— mo·til′i·ty** *n.*

mo·tion (mō′shən) *n.* **1.** The act or process of changing position; movement; also, an instance of this. **2.** Change of place or position in the body or any of its parts, as in walking, etc. **3.** A significant movement of the limbs, eyes, etc.; gesture. **4.** A formal proposal or suggestion in an assembly or meeting: to second the *motion.* **5.** *Mech.* An arrangement of parts in a mechanism to produce a particular result: link *motion.* **6.** *Music* Melodic progression, as a change of pitch in a voice part. **7.** *Law* An application to a court to obtain an order, ruling, etc. **8.** An impulse; inclination. **9.** The power of moving. **— in motion** Moving; in operation. **—** *v.i.* **1.** To make a gesture of direction or intent, as with the hand. **—** *v.t.* **2.** To direct or guide by a gesture. [< OF < L *motio, -onis < motus,* pp. of *movere* to move]

— Syn. (noun) **1.** *Motion, movement, move, locomotion,* and *translation* are compared as they denote change of position in space. *Motion* is most commonly used abstractly, while *movement* is always used concretely. We refer to the laws of planetary *motion* (not *movement*), but speak of a sudden *movement* (or *motion*) of a person's head. A *move* is an instance of changing position, especially when such a change is one of a series comprising a greater change: the army's next *move* was to positions across the river. *Locomotion* is moving from place to place: animals have the power of *locomotion,* an airplane is a means of *locomotion. Translation* is used in a technical sense to refer to *motion* in which all axes of the moving body remain parallel to their original position; this contrasts with curvilinear and rotational *motion.*

motion picture 1. A sequence of pictures of moving objects, each slightly different from the last, photographed by a special camera on a strip of film, that, when projected on a screen, gives the optical illusion of continuous movement. **2.** A specific drama, story, etc., made by means of such photographs: also called *cinema, film, movie, moving picture, photoplay, picture, screen play.*

motion sickness Nausea, dizziness, etc., caused by the effects of motion, as in travel on land, water, and in the air.

motion study See TIME AND MOTION STUDY.

mo·ti·vate (mō′tə·vāt) *v.t.* **·vat·ed, ·vat·ing** To provide with a motive; instigate; induce. [< F *motiver*]

mo·ti·va·tion (mō′tə·vā′shən) *n.* **1.** The act of motivating or providing an incentive. **2.** That which motivates; incentive; drive. **— mo′ti·va′tion·al** *adj.*

motivational research In advertising and marketing, the use of sampling and psychoanalytic techniques to find out why people choose or reject a product. Also **motivation research.** Abbr. *MR, M.R.*

mo·tive (mō′tiv) *n.* **1.** A conscious or unconscious need, drive, etc., that incites a person to some action or behavior; incentive; goal. **2.** A motif. **— Syn.** See CAUSE, REASON. **—** *adj.* **1.** Causing or having the power to cause motion:

motive force. **2.** Relating to or acting as a motive. — *v.t.* **1.** To provide with a motive; motivate. **2.** To relate to the leading idea or motif in a work of art, etc. [< OF *motif* < Med.L *motivus* < *motus*, pp. of *movere* to move]

motive power 1. Any power that imparts motion; any source of mechanical energy. **2.** The locomotives of a railroad collectively. **3.** An impelling force.

mo·tiv·i·ty (mō-tiv′ə-tē) *n.* The power of moving or of producing motion.

mot juste (mō zhüst′) *French* The precise or most suitable word; exactly the right expression.

mot·ley (mot′lē) *adj.* **1.** Made up of diverse elements; heterogeneous: a *motley* crew. **2.** Variegated in color; parti-colored. **3.** Clothed in varicolored garments. — *n.* **1.** A heterogeneous mixture or collection. **2.** A woolen cloth of mixed colors worn between the 14th and 17th centuries. **3.** A garment of various colors such as formerly worn by court jesters. **4.** *Obs.* A jester or fool in motley garments. [ME *motteley*; ult. origin uncertain]

Mot·ley (mot′lē), **John Lothrop**, 1814–77, U.S. historian and diplomat.

mot·mot (mot′mot) *n.* One of a family (*Momotidae*) of tropical American birds related to the kingfishers, and having a long, racket-shaped tail and a serrate bill: also called *sawbill*. [Imit. of its note]

MOTLEY (*n. def.* 3)

mo·to·neu·ron (mō′tō-nōōr′on, -nyōōr′-) *n. Anat.* A neuron specialized for the innervation of muscle tissue; a motor nerve cell.

mo·tor (mō′tər) *n.* **1.** An engine; especially, an internal-combustion engine propelling an automobile, motor boat, etc. **2.** An electric motor (which see). **3.** Something that imparts or produces motion; especially, a steam engine, etc., that receives and converts power from some natural source. **4.** *Chiefly Brit.* An automotive vehicle. **5.** *pl.* Stocks and bonds issued by automobile companies. — **Syn.** See MACHINE. — *adj.* **1.** Causing, producing, or imparting motion: *motor* power. **2.** Equipped with or driven by a motor: a *motor* scooter. **3.** Of, pertaining to, or for automotive vehicles: *motor* oil. **4.** *Physiol.* Transmitting impulses from nerve centers to the muscles. **5.** *Psychol.* Relating to or involving the movements of muscles. — *v.i.* To travel or ride in an automobile. [< L < *motus*, pp. of *movere* to move]

mo·tor·bike (mō′tər-bīk′) *n. Informal* **1.** A bicycle driven by a small motor. **2.** A motorcycle.

mo·tor·boat (mō′tər-bōt′) *n.* A boat propelled by an internal-combustion engine or by an electric motor: also called *power boat*.

mo·tor·bus (mō′tər-bus′) *n.* A passenger bus powered by a motor, especially by an internal-combustion engine. Also **motor bus, motor coach.**

mo·tor·cade (mō′tər-kād) *n.* A procession of automobiles. [< MOTOR + (CAVAL)CADE]

mo·tor·car (mō′tər-kär′) *n.* An automobile. Also **motor car.**

motor court A motel.

mo·tor·cy·cle (mō′tər-sī′kəl) *n.* A two-wheeled vehicle, larger and heavier than a bicycle, propelled by an internal-combustion engine and having one or two saddles and sometimes an attached sidecar with a third wheel. — *v.i.* **·cled, ·cling** To travel or ride on a motorcycle. — **mo′tor·cy′clist** *n.*

motor drive A power unit consisting of an electric motor and auxiliaries, used to operate a machine or machines.

mo·tor·drome (mō′tər-drōm′) *n.* An enclosure, course, or track where motor-driven vehicles are tested or raced.

mo·tored (mō′tərd) *adj.* Equipped with a specified type of motor or number of motors: used in combination.

mo·tor·ist (mō′tər-ist) *n.* One who drives or travels by automobile.

mo·tor·ize (mō′tər-īz) *v.t.* **·ized, ·iz·ing 1.** To equip with a motor. **2.** To equip with motor-propelled vehicles in place of horses or horse-drawn vehicles. — **mo′tor·i·za′tion** *n.*

mo·tor·man (mō′tər-mən) *n. pl.* **·men** (-mən) **1.** One who operates an electric street car or electric railway locomotive. **2.** One who operates a motor.

motor scooter A two-wheeled vehicle similar to a child's scooter, having a driver's seat and powered by an internal-combustion engine.

mo·tor·ship (mō′tər·ship′) *n.* A vessel propelled by an internal-combustion diesel or gas engine.

Mott (mot), **Lucretia**, 1793–1880, *née* Coffin, U.S. social reformer, preacher, and abolitionist.

motte (mot) *n. SW U.S.* A small growth of trees on a prairie. Also **mott.** [< Am. Sp. *mata* bush, shrub]

Mot·teux (mô·tœ′), **Peter Anthony**, 1663–1718, English dramatist and translator born in France.

mot·tle (mot′l) *v.t.* **·tled, ·tling** To mark with spots or streaks of different colors or shades; blotch. — *n.* **1.** A spotted, blotched, or variegated appearance, as of skin or marble. **2.** A spot, blotch, etc. [back formation < MOTLEY]

mot·tled (mot′ld) *adj.* Marked with spots of different color or shade; blotched; spotted.

mot·to (mot′ō) *n. pl.* **·toes** or **·tos 1.** A word or phrase expressing a rule of conduct, principle, etc.; a maxim. **2.** An appropriate or indicative phrase inscribed on something, prefixed to a literary work, etc. [< Ital. < F *mot.* See MOT.]

mouch (mōōch) See MOOCH.

mou·choir (mōō-shwär′) *n. French* A pocket handkerchief.

moue (mōō) *n.* A pouting grimace, as of disdain. [< F]

mouf·lon (mōōf′lon) *n.* A hairy wild sheep (*Ovis musimon*) of the mountains of Corsica and Sardinia, having very large, curved horns in the male. Also **mouf′flon.** [< F < dial. Ital. *muffolo, muffione* < LL *mufro, -onis*]

mouil·lé (mōō-yā′) *adj. Phonet.* **1.** Having a palatalized quality: said especially of laterals and nasals. **2.** Characterizing the letters *ll* when they represent (y). [< F, pp. of *mouiller* to moisten < L *mollis* soft]

mou·jik (mōō-zhēk′) See MUZHIK.

mou·lage (mōō-läzh′) *n.* The making of a cast or mold of footprints, tire marks, etc., for use in criminal identification; also, such a cast or mold. [< F]

mould (mōld), **mould·board** (mōld′bôrd′), etc. See MOLD, etc.

mould goose The musk duck (def. 2).

mou·lin (mōō-lan′) *n. Geol.* A nearly vertical well in a glacier, formed by surface waters trickling down through a crevice. [< F, mill < LL *molina.* See MILL.]

Moul·mein (mōōl-mān′) A port city in Lower Burma, on the Andaman Sea; pop. 101,720 (1960): also *Maulmain.*

moult (mōlt) See MOLT, etc.

Moul·ton (mōl′tən), **Forest Ray**, 1872–1952, U.S. astronomer.

Moul·trie (mōōl′trē, mōō′-, mōl′-), **William**, 1730–1805, American Revolutionary general; builder and defender of **Fort Moultrie**, Charleston Harbor, South Carolina, in 1776.

mound[1] (mound) *n.* **1.** A heap or pile of earth, debris, etc., either natural or artificial. **2.** A small natural elevation; a hillock. **3.** Any pile or mass: a *mound* of flesh. **4.** In baseball, the slightly raised ground from which the pitcher pitches. **5.** One of the earthworks built by the Mound Builders for burial or fortification. — **Syn.** See BANK[1]. — *v.t.* **1.** To fortify or enclose with a mound. **2.** To heap up in a mound. [Origin unknown. Cf. MDu. *mond*, var. of *mont, munt* protection.]

mound[2] (mound) *n.* A jeweled ball or globe, often surmounted by a cross, forming part of the regalia of a king or emperor and symbolizing his sovereignty; orb. [< F *monde* < L *mundus* world]

Mound Builder One of the prehistoric Indians who built the burial mounds and fortifications found in the Mississippi basin and adjoining regions.

mount[1] (mount) *v.t.* **1.** To ascend or climb (a slope, stairs, etc.). **2.** To get up on; climb upon. **3.** To put or set on horseback. **4.** To furnish with a horse. **5.** To set or place in an elevated position: to *mount* a picture on a wall. **6.** To prepare or place in position for use or operation: to *mount* a motor. **7.** To set, fix, or secure in or on a support, frame, etc., as for exhibition: to *mount* a drawing. **8.** To furnish with scenery, costumes, etc.: to *mount* a play. **9.** In microscopy: **a** To place or fix (a specimen) on a slide. **b** To prepare (a slide) for examination. **10.** *Mil.* **a** To set or raise into position, as a gun. **b** To carry or be equipped with: a turret *mounting* two machine guns. **c** To stand or post (guard). **d** To prepare and begin: to *mount* an offensive. **11.** To copulate with (a female). — *v.i.* **12.** To rise or ascend; go or come up. **13.** To increase in amount, number, or degree: His anger *mounted.* **14.** To get up on something; especially, to get on horseback. — *n.* **1.** Anything on or in which an object is placed for use, preparation, display, etc., as a gun support, microscopic slide, or setting for a jewel. **2.** A horse or other animal used for riding; sometimes, a bicycle. **3.** The act or style of mounting. **4.** The opportunity of riding a horse, especially in a race. [< OF *monter* < L *mons, montis* mountain] — **mount′a·ble** *adj.* — **mount′er** *n.*

mount[2] (mount) *n.* A mountain or hill: used poetically or as part of a proper name. Abbr. *mt., Mt.* [OE *munt*; infl. by OF *mont*; both < L *mons, montis* mountain]

Mount, Mount of, etc. See specific name, as (Mount) EVEREST, (Mount of) OLIVES, etc.

moun·tain (moun′tən) *n.* **1.** A natural elevation of the earth's surface, typically having steep sides and a narrow summit, and rising higher than a hill. Abbr. *m., M., mt., mtn.* **2.** Any large heap or pile: a *mountain* of paper. **3.** Anything of great size: a *mountain* of a man. — **the Mountain** The ultrarevolutionary party of the French National Assembly in 1793, whose members sat highest in the chamber. — *adj.* **1.** Of or pertaining to mountains. **2.** Living, growing, or situated in or on mountains. **3.** Suggesting a mountain, as in size. [< OF *montaigne* < L *montanus* mountainous < *mons, montis* mountain]

mountain ape *Paleontol.* Oreopithecus.

mountain ash   1. A small tree (*Sorbus americana*), of the rose family, having white flowers and orange-red berries. 2. Any of various related trees, as the rowan. 3. A large eucalyptus tree (*Eucalyptus regnans*) of Australia.

mountain avens   A small evergreen plant (*Dryas octopetala*) of the rose family, growing in arctic and alpine regions.

mountain bluebird   A songbird (*Sialia curricoides*), of western North America, the male of which is azure blue.

mountain cat   1. The puma. 2. The lynx.

mountain chain   A connected series of mountains having some common characteristics.

mountain cork   A variety of asbestos occurring in light sheets that will float on water. Also **mountain leather.**

mountain cranberry   A variety of cowberry having edible red berries, evergreen leaves, and pink or red flowers.

mountain dew   *Slang* Illicitly distilled whiskey.

moun·tain·eer (moun′tən·ir′)   *n.* 1. An inhabitant of a mountainous district. 2. One who climbs mountains. — *v.i.* To climb mountains.

mountain goat   The Rocky Mountain goat (which see).

mountain laurel   A low-growing evergreen shrub (*Kalmia latifolia*) of the eastern United States, having white or pink flowers: the State flower of Connecticut and Pennsylvania: also called *calico bush, calico tree.*

mountain lion   The puma.

moun·tain·ous (moun′tən·əs)   *adj.* 1. Full of mountains. 2. Huge; gigantic. — **moun′tain·ous·ly** *adv.*

mountain range   1. One of the components of a mountain chain, usually a group of more or less parallel ridges of similar origin and structure. 2. A land area dominated by such a group of mountains.

mountain rat   The pack rat (which see).

mountain sheep   The bighorn.

mountain sickness   *Pathol.* A form of anoxia with nausea and lassitude, caused by rarefied air at high altitudes.

Mountain Standard Time   See under STANDARD TIME. Abbr. *MST*, *m.s.t.*, *M.S.T.*

Mountain View   A city in western California, near San José; pop. 51,092.

Mount Athos (ath′os, ā′thos)   An autonomous monastic district in Macedonia, comprising a department of Greece; 131 sq. mi.; pop. 3,086 (1951); capital, Karyai.

Mount·bat·ten (mount·bat′n), **Lord Louis,** born 1900, first Earl Mountbatten of Burma, British admiral in World War II, last viceroy of India 1947: original name **Louis Albert Victor Nicholas of Bat·ten·berg** (bat′ən·bûrg).

Mount Desert   An island in Acadia National Park off the SE coast of Maine; about 100 sq. mi.

moun·te·bank (moun′tə·bangk)   *n.* 1. One who sells quack medicines at fairs after drawing a crowd with jokes, tricks, etc. 2. Any charlatan. [< Ital. *montimbanco* < *montare* to mount + *in* upon + *banco* bench]

mount·ed (moun′tid)   *adj.* 1. Riding or seated on a horse. 2. Serving on or equipped with some means of transportation, especially horses: *mounted* police. 3. Set in position, adjusted, or fitted for use or operation: *mounted* machine guns. 4. Placed on or in a support, setting, backing, etc.

mount·ing (moun′ting)   *n.* 1. Something used as a mount, support, basis, etc. 2. The act of one who or that which mounts.

Mount Leb·a·non (leb′ə·nən)   An urban township in SW Pennsylvania, near Pittsburgh; pop. 39,596.

Mount McKinley National Park   A region in south central Alaska; 3,030 sq. mi.; established 1917.

Mount Rainier National Park   A region in the Cascade Mountains of Washington; 378 sq. mi.; established 1899.

Mount Rob·son Provincial Park (rob′sən)   A park in eastern British Columbia, Canada.

Mount Ver·non (vûr′nən)   1. The home and burial place of George Washington, near Washington, D.C., on the Potomac River. 2. A city in SE New York, a suburb of New York City; pop. 72,778.

Moun·ty (moun′tē)   *n.* *pl.* **·ties** *Informal* A member of the Royal Canadian Mounted Police. Also **Mount′ie.**

mourn (môrn, mōrn)   *v.i.* 1. To feel or express grief or sorrow, especially for the dead; grieve. 2. To display the conventional signs of grief after someone's death; wear mourning. — *v.t.* 3. To lament or sorrow for (someone dead). 4. To grieve over or bemoan (misfortune, failure, etc.); bewail; deplore. 5. To utter in a sorrowful manner. [OE *murnan*]
— **Syn.** *Mourn, regret, rue, deplore,* and *bewail* mean to regard with sorrow or remorse. One *mourns* in sorrow, as at the death of a friend or close relative; the word implies deep emotion felt over a period of time. *Regret* is much milder, and may involve self-reproach, pity, or disappointment. We may *regret* an angry word said to another, or our inability to attend a party. *Rue* refers to one's own actions, and suggests remorse or chagrin at some personal failure or fault. *Deplore* means to express regret strongly; it usually refers to the actions of others, and suggests a feeling of righteous indignation: to *deplore* a statesman's vacillating policies. *Bewail,* like *deplore,* points to the open expression of sorrow, and suggests tears and loud complaints. — **Ant.** rejoice, exult.

mourn·er (môr′nər, mōr′-)   *n.* 1. One who mourns; especially, one who attends a funeral. 2. A penitent at a revival meeting.

mourners' bench   *U.S.* At revival meetings, a bench near the preacher, reserved for penitents: also called *anxious seat.*

mourn·ful (môrn′fəl, mōrn′-)   *adj.* 1. Indicating, expressing, or exciting grief. 2. Doleful; melancholy; sad. — **mourn′ful·ly** *adv.* — **mourn′ful·ness** *n.*

mourn·ing (môr′ning, mōr′-)   *n.* 1. The act of one who expresses grief or sorrow, especially for the dead; lamentation; sorrow. 2. The symbols or outward manifestations of grief, as the wearing of black dress, etc. 3. The period during which one mourns. — **in mourning** 1. Wearing mourning. 2. Observing a period of mourning. — **mourn′ing·ly** *adv.*

mourning cloak   A brownish black butterfly (*Nymphalis antiopa*) of Europe and North America, having wings with a wide yellow border: also called *Camberwell beauty.*

mourning dove   A dove (*Zenaidura macroura*) common in North America, having a mournful cry: also called *turtledove.*

mourning warbler   A warbler (*Oporornis philadelphia*) of the eastern United States, having a plaintive note.

mouse (*n.* mous; *v.* mouz)   *n.* *pl.* **mice** (mīs) 1. One of various small rodents (family *Muridae*) frequenting human habitations throughout the world; especially, the common **house mouse** (*Mus musculus*). ◆ Collateral adjective: *murine.* 2. Any of various similar animals, as the American **harvest mouse** (genus *Reithrodontomys*), or the **lemming mouse** (genus *Synaptomys*). 3. *U.S. Informal* A timid person. 4. *Slang* A black eye (def. 2). 5. *Naut.* **a** A knot or knob on a rope to prevent its slipping. **b** Mousing. — *v.* **moused, mous·ing** *v.i.* 1. To hunt or catch mice. 2. To hunt for something cautiously and softly; prowl. — *v.t.* 3. *Naut.* To secure (a hook) with mousing. [OE *mūs,* pl. *mȳs*]

mouse·bird (mous′bûrd′)   *n.* 1. An African bird (genus *Colius*) with a conical bill, long medial tail feathers, and soft plumage: also called *coly.* 2. A shrike.

mouse deer   The chevrotain.

mouse-ear (mous′ir′)   *n.* Any of various plants having soft, hairy leaves; especially, a species of hawkweed (*Hieracium pilosella*).

mous·er (mou′zər)   *n.* An animal, especially a cat, that catches mice.

mouse·tail (mous′tāl′)   *n.* One of a genus (*Myosurus*) of plants of the crowfoot family, having a slender spike.

mouse·trap (mous′trap′)   *n.* 1. A trap for catching mice. 2. A snare or entrapment. — *v.t.* **·trapped, ·trap·ping** To trap or ensnare.

mous·ing (mou′zing)   *n.* 1. The act of hunting mice. 2. *Naut.* A lashing or shackle passed around the shank and point of a hook, to prevent its spreading or unhooking.

mousse (mōōs)   *n.* Any of various light, frozen desserts made with whipped cream, egg white, etc., and sugar and flavoring. [< F < L *mulsus* sweetened with honey]

mousse·line (mōōs·lēn′)   *n.* 1. Fine French muslin. 2. A thin glass blown to resemble lace. [< F. See MUSLIN.]

mousseline de laine (də len′)   *French* Fine woolen muslin, often figured.

mousseline de soie (də swä′)   *French* A gauzelike silk fabric, often figured.

Mous·sorg·sky (mōō·sôrg′skē), **Modest Petrovich,** 1835–1881, Russian composer. Also *Mussorgsky.*

mous·tache (məs·tash′, mus′tash)   See MUSTACHE.

Mous·te·ri·an (mōō·stir′ē·ən)   *adj.* *Anthropol.* Pertaining to or describing the culture stage of the Middle Paleolithic, represented in western Europe by artifacts of stone and other materials and generally found associated with Neanderthal men. [< F *moustérien* < *Le Moustier,* a village in France where such remains were found]

mous·y (mou′sē, -zē)   *adj.* **mous·i·er, mous·i·est** 1. Of, pertaining to, or resembling a mouse, as in color, smell, etc. 2. Characterized by timidity, shyness, drabness, etc.: a *mousy* voice. 3. Infested with mice. Also **mous′ey.**

mouth (*n.* mouth; *v.* mouth)   *n.* *pl.* **mouths** (mouthz) 1. The orifice or opening at which food is taken into the body; also, the cavity between the lips and throat containing the lingual and masticating structures. ◆ Collateral adjective: *oral.* 2. The organ of eating, tasting, etc.; also, one who needs food: so many *mouths* to feed. 3. The organ or instrument of speech: to shut one's *mouth.* 4. Something resembling a mouth in shape or function; as: **a** The part of a stream where its waters are discharged into another body of water. **b** The entrance or opening of a cave, mine, etc. **c** The opening of a vessel or container: the *mouth* of a jar. **d** The slit in an organ pipe; also, the aperture in a flute across which the player blows. **e** The opening in the muzzle of a firearm. **f** The space between the jaws of a vise. — **down in (or at) the mouth** *Informal* Disconsolate; dejected. — **to have a big mouth** *Informal* 1. To speak loudly or rudely

HUMAN MOUTH
a Hard palate. *b* Pharynx. *c* Soft palate. *d* Uvula. *e* Tonsil. *f* Epiglottis. *g* Esophagus. *h* Trachea. *i* Tongue. *j* Hyoid bone. *k* Larynx.

2. To be loud or rude. **3.** To talk too much. — *v.t.* **1.** To speak in a forced or affected manner; declaim: to *mouth* platitudes. **2.** To seize or take in the mouth. **3.** To caress or rub with the mouth. **4.** To form (words, etc.) silently with the lips and tongue. **5.** To accustom (a horse) to the bit. — *v.i.* **6.** To speak in a forced or affected manner. **7.** *Rare* To distort the face; grimace. [OE *mūth*] — **mouth′er** (mou′-thər) *n.*

mouth·breed·er (mouth′brē′dər) *n.* Any of various cichlid fishes (genera *Tilapia* and *Haplochromis*) that carry the eggs of their young in their mouths.

mouthed (mou*th*d, moutht) *adj.* **1.** Having a mouth or mouths. **2.** Having or characterized by a (specified kind of) mouth or speech or (a specified number of) mouths: used in combination: *evil-mouthed.*

mouth·ful (mouth′fŏŏl′) *n.* *pl.* **·fuls** (-fŏŏlz′) **1.** As much as can be held in the mouth. **2.** As much as is usually taken or put in the mouth at one time. **3.** A small quantity. **4.** *Slang* An important or perceptive remark or observation: chiefly in the phrase **to say a mouthful. 5.** *Informal* A word, phrase, etc., that is difficult to articulate.

mouth organ 1. A harmonica. **2.** A set of panpipes.

mouth·piece (mouth′pēs′) *n.* **1.** That part of a musical instrument, telephone, etc., that is applied to or used in or near the mouth. **2.** One who acts as spokesman for an individual, group, belief, etc. **3.** *Slang* A criminal lawyer. **4.** A rubber guard placed in the mouth of a boxer.

mouth·wash (mouth′wosh′, -wôsh′) *n.* An antiseptic and scented solution used for cleaning the mouth.

mouth·y (mou′thē, -thē) *adj.* **mouth·i·er, mouth·i·est** Garrulous; bombastic. — **mouth′i·ly** *adv.* — **mouth′i·ness** *n.*

mou·ton (moo′ton) *n.* Sheepskin processed to simulate beaver or seal, used for women's coats, etc. [< F, sheep]

mou·ton·née (moo′tô·nā′) *adj.* *Geol.* Having the form of a sheep's back: said of rock. Also **mou′ton·need′** (-nād′). [< F]

mov·a·ble (moo′və·bəl) *adj.* **1.** Capable of being moved; not fixed or fast; transportable. **2.** *Eccl.* Varying in date from year to year: *movable* feast. **3.** *Law* Pertaining to personal property as distinguished from real property: opposed to *immovable.* — *n.* **1.** *Usually pl.* Anything that can be moved; especially, an article of furniture. **2.** *pl.* *Law* Personal property. Also **move′a·ble.** — **mov′a·bil′i·ty, mov′a·ble·ness** *n.* — **mov′a·bly** *adv.*

movable feast *Eccl.* A church feast that does not fall on the same date each year.

move (moov) *v.* **moved, mov·ing** *v.i.* **1.** To change place or position; go to or from a place; transfer; shift. **2.** To change one's residence. **3.** To make progress; proceed; advance. **4.** To live or carry on one's life; be active; associate: to *move* in cultivated circles. **5.** To operate, work, revolve, etc., as a machine: to *move* on a pivot. **6.** *Informal* To depart or go away; start off: often with *on:* We ought to *move* on. **7.** To take or begin to take action; act: to *move* on an important matter. **8.** In commerce, to be disposed of by sale: Some products *move* quickly. **9.** To make an application, appeal, or proposal, especially formally: usually with *for:* to *move* for adjournment. **10.** To evacuate: said of the bowels. **11.** In checkers, chess, etc., to transfer a piece from one position to another. **12.** *Informal* To be active or busy; hum. **13.** *Informal* To go fast. — *v.t.* **14.** To change the place or position of, as by carrying, pushing, pulling, etc. **15.** To set or keep in motion; actuate or stir. **16.** To dislodge, budge, or force from a set position, conviction, etc.: to *move* him from his purpose. **17.** To rouse, influence, or impel to some action; prompt; urge: to *move* her to agree. **18.** To affect or arouse the emotions, sympathies, etc., of; stir; touch: The sight *moved* him to tears. **19.** To propose for action, deliberation, etc., especially formally: I *move* that we accept the offer. **20.** To cause (the bowels) to evacuate. **21.** In checkers, chess, etc., to transfer (a piece). — **Syn.** See IN-FLUENCE. — *n.* **1.** An act of moving; movement. **2.** An action for some purpose or design; step; maneuver: a clever *move.* **3.** A change in residence. **4.** In checkers, chess, etc., the transfer of a piece. — **Syn.** See MOTION. — **to be on the move** *Informal* **1.** To move about continually. **2.** To make progress; advance. — **to get a move on** *Informal* To hurry; get going. — **to make one's move 1.** To go into action; get started. **2.** To commit oneself; become involved. [< AF *mover*, OF *movoir* < L *movere* to set in motion]

move·ment (moov′mənt) *n.* **1.** The act of moving; any change of place or position. **2.** A specific instance or manner of moving: a population *movement;* a dance *movement.* **3.** A series of actions, plans, etc., tending toward some end: the temperance *movement;* also, organizations, persons, etc., of a particular tendency: the right-wing *movement.* **4.** An inclination or tendency; trend: a *movement* toward greater freedom. **5.** *Mech.* A particular arrangement of related moving parts; especially, the mechanism of a clock or watch. **6.** In literature and the other fine arts, the quality or effect of motion, action, progression, etc. **7.** *Music* **a** One of the

sections of a work, as of a symphony, string quartet, etc. **b** Tempo. **c** Rhythm. **8.** In prosody, rhythm or meter; cadence. **9.** An emptying of the bowels; also, the matter so emptied. **10.** *Mil.* A tactical change of position; maneuver. — **Syn.** See MOTION. [< OF < *movoir.* See MOVE.]

mov·er (moo′vər) *n.* One who or that which moves; especially, one whose business is moving household goods.

mov·ie (moo′vē) *Informal n.* **1.** A motion picture. **2.** A motion-picture theater. **3.** *pl.* The motion-picture industry. **4.** *pl.* A showing of motion pictures. — *adj.* Pertaining to, appearing in, or used for motion pictures. [Contraction of MOVING PICTURE]

mov·ie·go·er (moo′vē·gō′ər) *n.* *Informal* One who watches motion pictures regularly or often. — **mov′ie·go′ing** *n.*

mov·ing (moo′ving) *adj.* **1.** Going or capable of going from place to place, position to position, etc. **2.** Causing or producing motion or change. **3.** That actuates, impels, or influences: a *moving* principle. **4.** Arousing or touching the feelings or passions. **5.** Exciting or stirring up controversy, debate, etc. — **mov′ing·ly** *adv.* — **mov′ing·ness** *n.*

moving picture A motion picture (which see).

moving staircase An escalator.

mow¹ (mō) *v.* **mowed, mowed** or **mown, mow·ing** *v.t.* **1.** To cut down (grain, grass, etc.) with a scythe or machine. **2.** To cut the grain or grass of (a field, lawn, etc.). **3.** *Informal* To cut down or kill rapidly or indiscriminately: with *down:* to *mow* down the enemy. — *v.i.* **4.** To cut down grass or grain. [OE *māwan*] — **mow′er** *n.*

mow² (mō, mou) *Archaic v.i.* To make faces; grimace. — *n.* A grimace. [< OF *moue* mouth, lip, pout]

mow³ (mou) *n.* Hay or grain stored in a barn; also, the place of storage. — *v.t.* To store in a mow. [OE *mūga*]

mowing machine A farm machine for mowing hay, etc.

mox·a (mok′sə) *n.* **1.** Cottony material burned on the skin as a counterirritant or cautery. **2.** Any of various plants yielding such material, especially *Artemisia moxa* of China. [< Japanese *mogusa* a caustic < *moe kusa* burning herb]

mox·ie (mok′sē) *n.* *U.S. Slang* Spirit or courage; pluck [< *Moxie* trade name for a soft drink]

moy·en âge (mwä·yen äzh′) *French* The Middle Ages.

Mo·zam·bique (mō′zam·bēk′) **1.** An independent Republic in SE Africa; 297,731 sq. mi.; pop. 9,240,000 (est. 1975); capital, Maputo: formerly *Portuguese East Africa.* See map of SOUTH AFRICA. **2.** A port city in Northern Mozambique, on **Mozambique Island,** in **Mozambique Channel,** a strait separating Africa from Madagascar; pop. 12,166 (1960). Portuguese *Moçambique.*

Moz·ar·ab (mōz·ar′əb) *n.* A Spanish Christian permitted to practice a modified form of his religion after the Moslem conquest. [< Sp. *Mozárabe* < Arabic *musta'rib* would-be Arab] — **Moz·ar′ab·ic** *adj.*

Mo·zart (mō′tsärt, -zärt), **Wolfgang Amadeus,** 1756–91, Austrian composer.

mo·zet·ta (mō·zet′ə) *n.* A short, hooded cape worn by prelates of the Roman Catholic Church. Also **moz·zet′ta.** [< Ital. *almozetta* < L *almutia* amice]

moz·za·rel·la (môd′dzä·rel′lä) *n.* A soft Italian curd cheese that is very stringy when cooked. [< Ital.]

mp *Music* Mezzo piano.

MP *Mil.* Military Police.

M.P. 1. Melting point: also **m.p. 2.** Member of Parliament.

M.Pd. Master of Pedagogy.

M.P.E. Master of Physical Education.

m.p.h. or **mph** Miles per hour.

Mr. (mis′tər) *n.* The contracted form of MISTER.

MR or **M.R.** Motivation Research.

Mrs. (mis′iz) *n.* A title prefixed to the name of a married woman: a contracted form of *Mistress.*

Ms. or **Ms** (miz) *n.* A title prefixed to the name of a woman, especially when her marital status is unknown.

MS. or **MS, ms.** or **ms** Manuscript.

M.S. 1. Master of Science: also **M.Sc. 2.** Master in Surgery.

msg. Message.

Msgr. Monsignor.

M.Sgt. or **M/Sgt** *Mil.* Master Sergeant.

m.s.l. or **M.S.L.** Mean sea level.

MSS. or **MSS, mss.** or **mss** Manuscripts.

MST or **M.S.T.** or **m.s.t.** Mountain standard time.

Ms-Th Mesothorium.

MSTS Military Sea Transportation Service.

Mt. or **mt.** (pl. **mts.**) Mount; mountain.

M.T. 1. Metric ton. **2.** Mountain time: also **m.t.**

mtg. 1. Meeting. **2.** Mortgage: also **mtge.**

mtn. Mountain.

Mt.Rev. Most Reverend.

mu (myoo, moo) *n.* **1.** The twelfth letter in the Greek alphabet (M, μ), corresponding to the English *m.* See ALPHABET. **2.** The micron (symbol μ).

muc- Var. of MUCO-.

much (much) *adj.* **more, most 1.** Great in quantity, amount, extent, etc.: *much* noise. **2.** *Obs.* Many in number. — *n.* **1.** A considerable quantity or amount; a great deal: It leaves *much* out. **2.** A remarkable or important thing: It isn't *much.* — **to make much of 1.** To treat as very important. **2.** To treat (someone) with great courtesy, regard, etc. — *adv.* **1.** To a great degree; greatly: *much* obliged. **2.** For the most part; nearly; almost: to come to *much* the same conclusion. [ME *muchel* < OE *mycel*] — **much′ness** *n.*

muci- Var. of MUCO-.

mu·cic acid (myoo′sik) *Chem.* A crystalline acid, $C_6H_{10}O_8$, formed by the oxidation of milk sugar, various gums, etc. [< F *mucique* < L *mucus* mucus]

mu·cid (myoo′sid) *adj.* Moldy; also, slimy. [< L *mucidus* < *mucere* to be moldy] — **mu·cid′i·ty, mu′cid·ness** *n.*

mu·ci·lage (myoo′sə·lij) *n.* **1.** An aqueous solution of vegetable gum or the like, used as an adhesive. **2.** Any of various gummy or gelatinous substances found in some plants. [< F < LL *mucilago* musty juice < L *mucus* mucus]

mu·ci·lag·i·nous (myoo′si·laj′ə·nəs) *adj.* **1.** Of, pertaining to, or producing mucilage. **2.** Resembling or characteristic of mucilage; soft, slimy, and viscid. [< F *mucilagineux*] — **mu′ci·lag′i·nous·ness** *n.*

mu·cin (myoo′sin) *n. Biochem.* A glycoprotein secreted by the mucous membranes. [< F *mucine* < L *mucus* mucus] — **mu′cin·ous** *adj.*

muck (muk) *n.* **1.** Any wet and clinging material that soils; especially, viscid mud; filth. **2.** Moist dung mixed with decomposed vegetable matter, used as a soil fertilizer; manure. **3.** A dark brown to black soil consisting largely of decomposing peat and other vegetable materials. **4.** A confusing or uncertain state or condition; jumble; mess: to be all in a *muck.* — *v.t.* **1.** To fertilize with manure. **2.** *Informal* To make dirty; pollute. **3.** To remove manure, dirt, rocks, etc., from. [ME *muk*; of Scand. origin. Cf. ON *myki* dung.]

muck·er (muk′ər) *n. Brit. Slang* A coarse, rude person.

muck·le (muk′əl) *adj. & n. Scot.* Mickle.

muck·rake (muk′rāk′) *v.i.* **·raked, ·rak·ing** To search for or expose real or alleged corruption on the part of political officials, businessmen, etc. — *n. Obs.* A rake used for collecting muck or dung. [Back formation < *muckrakes*, slang term in late 19th c. U.S. politics, prob. in allusion to "man with a muckrake" in Bunyan's *Pilgrim's Progress*] — **muck′rak′er** *n.* — **muck′rak′ing** *n.*

muck·worm (muk′wûrm′) *n.* The larva of a beetle (*Ligyrus gibbosus*) found in manure.

muck·y (muk′ē) *adj.* **muck·i·er, muck·i·est 1.** Foul; nasty. **2.** Containing or resembling muck. — **muck′i·ly** *adv.* — **muck′i·ness** *n.*

muco- *combining form* Mucus; mucus and: *mucopurulent*: also, *muc-* (before vowels), *muci-*. [< L *mucus* mucus]

mu·coid (myoo′koid) *adj.* Like mucus. — *n. Biochem.* A compound glycoprotein similar to mucin, found in connective tissue, cysts, etc. [< MUC(O)- + -OID]

mu·co·pro·te·in (myoo′kō·prō′tē·in, -tēn) *n. Biochem.* Any of a group of proteins containing a carbohydrate group.

mu·co·pu·ru·lent (myoo′kō·pyoor′ə·lənt, -yə·lənt) *adj.* Containing both mucus and purulent matter.

mu·co·sa (myoo·kō′sə) *n. pl.* **·sae** (-sē) *Anat.* A mucous membrane. [< NL fem. of L *mucosus* mucous] — **mu·co′sal** *adj.*

mu·cous (myoo′kəs) *adj.* **1.** Secreting mucus: *mucous* membrane. **2.** Pertaining to, consisting of, or resembling mucus. Also **mu′cose** (-kōs). [< L *mucosus* slimy < *mucus* mucus] — **mu·cos′i·ty** (-kos′ə·tē) *n.*

mucous membrane *Anat.* A membrane secreting or producing mucus, that lines passages communicating with the exterior, as the alimentary and respiratory passages, etc.

mu·cro (myoo′krō) *n. pl.* **·cro·nes** (-krō′nēz) *Biol.* A small, sharp point, as at the end of a leaf. [< NL < L, point]

mu·cro·nate (myoo′krō·nāt) *adj. Biol.* Having a short, straight point, as a leaf, feather, etc. Also **mu′cro·nat′ed.** [< L *mucronatus* < *mucro* point]

mu·cus (myoo′kəs) *n. Biol.* A viscid substance secreted by the mucous membranes. [< L]

mud (mud) *n.* **1.** Soft and sticky wet earth; mire; muck. **2.** *Informal* Slanderous or abusive charges; defamation: to sling *mud.* **3.** *Informal* The most degrading place or situation: to drag one into the *mud.* **4.** In well-drilling, a fluid forced into the hole to cool and lubricate the bit, flush up chips, etc. — **clear as mud** Absolutely incomprehensible. — **(one's) name is mud** (One) is defeated or in disgrace. — *v.t.* **mud·ded, mud·ding** To soil or cover with or as with mud. [ME *mudde* < MLG *mudde* or MDu. *modde*]

mud·cap (mud′kap′) *v.t.* **·capped, ·cap·ping** To cover (a charge of high explosive) with mud before detonating. — *n.* A mud covering thus used.

mud cat A large catfish of the Mississippi valley.

mud dauber 1. Any of various wasps (family *Sphecidae*) that build mud cells in which their larvae develop. For illustration see INSECTS (beneficial). **2.** The cliff swallow.

mud·der (mud′ər) *n.* A race horse that runs well on a muddy track.

mud·dle (mud′l) *v.* **·dled, ·dling** *v.t.* **1.** To mix in a confused or disordered way; jumble. **2.** To confuse, bewilder, or confound (the mind, speech, etc.); befuddle. **3.** To mess up or mismanage; bungle. **4.** To make muddy or turbid. **5.** To stir or mix, as a drink. — *v.i.* **6.** To act or think in a confused or ineffective manner. — **to muddle through** *Chiefly Brit.* To achieve one's object despite confusion or mistakes. — *n.* **1.** A state or condition of confusion, disorder, or uncertainty; jumble; mess. **2.** A state of mental or intellectual disorder; confused thinking. [< MUD + freq. suffix -*le*. Cf. MDu. *moddelen* to make muddy.]

mud·dle·head·ed (mud′l·hed′id) *adj.* Mentally confused; addlebrained; stupid. — **mud′dle·head′ed·ness** *n.*

mud·dler (mud′lər) *n.* **1.** A stick for stirring liquids, especially drinks. **2.** One who muddles.

mud·dy (mud′ē) *adj.* **·di·er, ·di·est 1.** Covered, spattered, or filled with mud. **2.** Not clear, bright, or distinct, as color, liquid, texture, etc. **3.** Confused or obscure in thought, expression, meaning, etc.; muddled; vague: a *muddy* style. — *v.t. & v.i.* **·died, ·dy·ing** To become or cause to become muddy. — **mud′di·ly** *adv.* — **mud′di·ness** *n.*

mud eel An eel-shaped amphibian (*Siren lacertina*), with very small forelegs and no hind legs, that inhabits swamps of the southern United States: also called *siren.*

mud·fish (mud′fish′) *n. pl.* **·fish** or **·fish·es** Any of various fishes that inhabit mud or muddy waters, as the bowfin.

mud flat A low-lying strip of muddy ground, especially one between high and low tide.

mud·guard (mud′gärd′) *n.* A fender (def. 2).

mud hen The marsh hen (which see).

mud·lark (mud′lärk′) *n. Brit. Informal* A street urchin.

mud puppy A tailed amphibian (*Necturus maculosus*) having bushy external gills and short legs, found in streams and lakes of North America.

mud·rock (mud′rok′) *n.* Argillite.

mud·sill (mud′sil′) *n.* The foundation timber of a structure placed directly on the ground.

mud·sling·er (mud′sling′ər) *n.* One who casts malicious slurs, especially at a political opponent. — **mud′sling′ing** *n.*

MUD PUPPY
(12 to 18
inches long)

mud snake A North American snake (*Farancia abacura*) having black and red markings: sometimes called *hoop snake*: also *wampum snake.*

mud·stone (mud′stōn′) *n.* A gray, sandy shale that readily decomposes into mud.

mud·suck·er (mud′suk′ər) *n.* A fish (*Gillicthys mirabilis*), of California, commonly used as bait.

mud turtle Any of various turtles (family *Kinosternidae*), inhabiting muddy waters in North and Central America.

mu·ez·zin (myoo·ez′in) *n.* In Islam, a crier who calls the faithful to prayer, as from a minaret of a mosque. Also **mu·ed′din** (-ed′in). [< Arabic *mu'adhdhin* < *adhana* to call]

muff [1] (muf) *v.t. & v.i.* To perform (some act) clumsily; especially, to fail to catch (a ball). — *n.* An awkward action. [< MUFF [2]; prob. to handle as if with muffs]

muff [2] (muf) *n.* **1.** A pillowlike or tubular case of fur or cloth, open at the ends, into which the hands are put for warmth. **2.** A tuft of feathers on the head or legs of certain birds. [< Du. *mof* < F *moufle* mitten]

muf·fin (muf′in) *n.* **1.** A small, cup-shaped portion of light bread, usually eaten hot with butter. **2.** An English muffin (which see). [Origin uncertain]

muffin stand A small tiered stand used in tea service for holding and passing cakes, sandwiches, etc.

muf·fle [1] (muf′əl) *v.t.* **·fled, ·fling 1.** To wrap up in a blanket, scarf, etc., as for warmth or concealment: often with *up.* **2.** To deaden the sound of by or as by wrapping: to *muffle* a cry. **3.** To deaden (a sound). **4.** To prevent (someone) from seeing, hearing, etc., by wrapping the head. — *n.* **1.** Something used for muffling. **2.** A chamber in a kiln or furnace that protects its contents from flame, gases, etc. [< F *enmoufler* < *moufle* mitten]

muf·fle [2] (muf′əl) *n.* The hairless upper lip and nose of ruminants and certain other animals. [< F *mufle*; origin uncertain. Prob. infl. by MF *museau* muzzle]

muf·fler (muf′lər) *n.* **1.** A device to reduce noise, as from the exhaust of an engine. **2.** A heavy scarf worn about the neck for warmth. **3.** Anything that muffles. [< MUFFLE [1]]

muf·ti [1] (muf′tē) *n.* In Islam, an expounder of religious law. [< Arabic, active participle of *aftā* to expound the law]

muf·ti [2] (muf′tē) *n.* Civilian dress; plain clothes, especially when worn by one who normally wears a uniform. [< MUFTI [1]; prob. from the fact that a mufti is a civil official]

mug [1] (mug) *n.* **1.** A large drinking cup. **2.** As much as will fill a mug. [Origin unknown]

mug [2] (mug) *Slang n.* **1.** The face, especially the mouth and chin. **2.** *U.S.* A photograph of the face. Also **mug shot. 3.** *U.S.* A man; guy. **4.** *Brit.* A dupe; victim. **5.** *U.S.* A criminal. — *v.* **mugged, mug·ging 1.** *U.S.* To photograph (someone's face), especially for police files. **2.** To assault viciously and rob. — *v.i.* **3.** To make funny faces; overact to win an audience. Also **mugg.** [< MUG [1], prob. because drinking mugs often were made to resemble faces]

mug·ger[1] (mug′ər) *n.* A large crocodile (*Crocodilus palustris*) of India and the East Indies. Also **mug′gar, mug′gur.** [< Hind. *magar* < Skt. *makara* sea monster]

mug·ger[2] (mug′ər) *n. Slang* **1.** One who assaults another with an intent to rob. **2.** In the theater, etc., one who overacts in order to gain attention. [< MUG[2]]

mug·gins (mug′inz) *n.* **1.** One of several card games in which exposed cards are matched or suits are built. **2.** A variant of dominoes. **3.** *Brit. Slang* A dupe; simpleton. [Prob. < *Muggins*, a surname used in arbitrary allusion to *mug* a cardsharper's dupe]

mug·gy (mug′ē) *adj.* **·gi·er, ·gi·est** Warm, humid, and close; sultry. [< dial. E *mug* drizzle; of Scand. origin. Cf. ON *mugga* drizzle.] — **mug′gi·ness** *n.*

Mu·ghal (mōō′gəl) *n. & adj.* Mogul. Also **Mu′ghul.**

mug·wump (mug′wump′) *n. U.S.* **1.** *Usually cap.* A Republican who bolted the party when James G. Blaine was its candidate in the presidential election of 1884. **2.** One who is independent, especially in politics. [< Algonquian *mugquomp* great man, chief] — **mug′wump′er·y, mug′·wump′ism** *n.*

Mu·ham·mad (mōō·ham′əd) Mohammed. — **Elijah,** born 1897, U.S. leader of the Black Muslims: original name *Elijah Poole.*

Mu·ham·ma·dan (mōō·ham′ə·dən) *adj. & n.* Mohammedan. Also **Mu·ham′me·dan.**

Mu·har·ram (mōō·har′əm) *n.* The first month of the Moslem year, or its first ten days, a period of lamentation: also *Moharran.* See (Moslem) CALENDAR.

muh·ly (myōō′lē) *n. pl.* **·lies** Any of a genus (*Muhlenbergia*) of wiry grasses growing in the SW United States and Mexico, as the **ring muhly** (*M. torreyi*), and **spike muhly** (*M. wrighti*), valued as forage. Also **muhly grass.** [after G. H. E. *Muhlenberg*, 1753–1815, American botanist]

Muir (myōōr), **John,** 1838–1914, U.S. naturalist born in Scotland.

Muir Glacier (myōōr) A glacier in the St. Elias Mountains, SE Alaska; about 350 sq. mi.

mu·jik (mōō·zhēk′, mōō′zhik) See MUZHIK.

Muk·den (mook′den′, mook′dən, mōōk′-) A former name for SHENYANG.

Mu·kha (mō′khə) See MOCHA.

muk·luk (muk′luk) *n. U.S. & Canadian* **1.** An Eskimo boot of sealskin or reindeer skin. **2.** *pl.* Casual shoes of the soft moccasin type. [< Alaskan Eskimo *makliak, muklok* large seal]

mu·lat·to (mə·lat′ō, myōō-, -lä′tō) *n. pl.* **·toes 1.** A person having one white and one Negro parent. **2.** Anyone having mixed white and Negro ancestry. — *adj.* Of or pertaining to a mulatto; especially, having the light brown color of a mulatto. [< Sp. *mulato* of mixed breed < *mulo* mule < L *mulus*]

mul·ber·ry (mul′ber′ē, mul′bər·ē) *n. pl.* **·ries 1.** Any of various trees (genus *Morus*) typical of a widely distributed family (*Moraceae*) of plants whose leaves are valued for silkworm culture; especially, the **white mulberry** (*M. alba*), and the **red mulberry** (*M. rubra*), having edible, purplish red fruit. **2.** The berrylike fruit of any of these trees. **3.** A purplish red color. [ME *mulberie*, dissimilated var. of *murberie*, < OF *mure* < L *morum* mulberry + OE *berie* berry]

mulberry body *Zool.* A morula.

mulch (mulch) *n.* Any loose material, as straw, leaves, peat moss, etc., placed about the stalks of plants to protect their roots from drying, freezing, etc. — *v.t.* To cover with mulch. [ME *molsh* soft, OE *milisc.* Akin to L *mollis.*]

mulct (mulkt) *v.t.* **1.** To defraud or cheat (someone). **2.** To punish with a fine. — *n.* A fine or similar penalty. [< L *mulctare* to inflict a fine upon < *mulcta, multa* fine]

mule[1] (myōōl) *n.* **1.** A hybrid between the ass and horse: especially, a hybrid between a jackass and mare. Compare HINNY[1]. **2.** *Biol.* Any hybrid or cross, especially one that is sterile: said usually of the hybrid between the canary and a related bird. **3.** *U.S. Informal* A stubborn or stupid person. **4.** A textile machine that draws and spins fibers into yarn and winds it on spindles: also called *spinning mule:* also **mule′·jen′ny** (-jen′ē). **5.** A small electric engine or tractor for towing canal boats. [< OF *mul* < L *mulus*]

mule[2] (myōōl) *n.* A backless lounging slipper. [< F < L *mulleus* reddish (shoe)]

mule deer A black-tailed deer (*Odocoileus hemionus*) of the western United States, having long ears: also called *blacktail.*

mule skinner *U.S. Informal* One who drives mules.

mu·le·teer (myōō′lə·tir′) *n.* A mule driver. [< F *muletier* < MF *mulet,* dim. of OF *mul.* See MULE.] — **mu′le·tress** (-tris) *n.fem.*

mule train A train of mules carrying packs; also, a train of freight wagons drawn by mules.

mu·ley (myōō′lē, mōōl′ē, mōō′lē) *adj.* Hornless: said of cattle. — *n.* A hornless cow. Also spelled *mooley, mulley.* [< Irish *maol, moile* hornless, dismantled]

muley saw *U.S.* A long ripsaw not mounted in a gate.

Mül·heim-an-der-Ruhr (mül′hīm-än-der-rōōr′) A city in western North Rhine–Westphalia, West Germany, on the Ruhr; pop. 182,300 (est. 1960). Also **Mül′heim.**

Mul·house (mül·ōōz′) A city in eastern France, near the German border; pop. 115,632 (1968). *German* **Mül·hau·sen** (mül′hou·zən).

mu·li·eb·ri·ty (myōō′lē·eb′rə·tē) *n.* **1.** The state of being a woman; womanhood. **2.** The qualities of a woman; femininity. [< LL *muliebritas, -tatis* < L *muliebris* womanly < *mulier* woman]

mul·ish (myōō′lish) *adj.* Resembling a mule; stubborn. — Syn. See OBSTINATE. — **mul′ish·ly** *adv.* — **mul′ish·ness** *n.*

mull[1] (mul) *v.t.* To heat and spice, as wine or cider. [Origin uncertain]

mull[2] (mul) *v.t.* To ponder; cogitate: usually with *over.* [ME *mullen* to pulverize < OE *myl* dust]

mull[3] (mul) *n.* A thin, soft, cotton, rayon, or silk fabric. [Short for *mulmull* < Hind. *malmal* < Persian]

Mull (mul) An island o' the Inner Hebrides in NW Argyllshire, Scotland; 351 sq. mi.

mul·lah (mul′ə, mōōl′ə) *n.* A Moslem religious leader or teacher, or any man of learned reputation: used as a title of respect: also *mollah.* Also **mul′la.** [< Turkish, Persian, and Hind. *mullā* < Arabic *mawlā* master, sir]

mul·lein (mul′ən) *n.* Any of various herbs (genus *Verbascum*) of the figwort family; especially, the **great mullein** (*V. thapsus*) and the **moth mullein** (*V. blattaria*). Also **mul′len.** [< AF *moleine,* prob. < OF *mol* soft < L *mollis*]

mull·er (mul′ər) *n.* **1.** A pestlelike implement used to grind paints, etc. **2.** A mechanical pulverizer or grinder. [ME *mullen* to pulverize < OE *myl* dust]

Mul·ler (mul′ər), **Hermann Joseph,** 1890–1967, U.S. geneticist.

Mül·ler (mül′ər), **(Friedrich) Max,** 1823–1900, English philologist and Orientalist born in Germany.

mul·let (mul′it) *n. pl.* **·lets** or **·let** Any of various marine and fresh-water fish (family *Mugilidae*), as the **striped mullet** (*Mugil cephalus*) of the Atlantic and Pacific. [< OF *mulet* < L *mullus* red mullet. Cf. Gk. *myllos.*]

mul·ley (mōōl′ē, mōō′lē) See MULEY.

mul·li·gan stew (mul′i·gən) *U.S. Slang* A stew, originally made by tramps, composed of odds and ends of meat, vegetables, etc. Also **mul′li·gan.** [? from personal name]

mul·li·ga·taw·ny (mul′i·gə·tô′nē) *n.* A strongly flavored soup of the East Indies, made of meat and curry. [< Tamil *milagutannir* pepper water]

mul·lion (mul′yən) *n. Archit.* A vertical dividing piece in an opening, especially in a window. Also, *Archaic, munnion.* — *v.t.* To furnish with or divide by means of mullions. [? Var. of *monial* < OF *moienel* medial < L *medianus*]

mul·lock (mul′ək) *n.* Waste rock or earth left from mining. [ME *mull* dust + -OCK] — **mul′lock·y** *adj.*

Mu·lock (myōō′lok), **Miss** See CRAIK.

Mul·tan (mōōl·tän′) A city in east central West Pakistan; pop. 358,000 (1961).

multi- *combining form* **1.** Much; many; consisting of many; as in:

MULLION

multiangular	multidimensional	multilocular
multiareolate	multidirectional	multiloculate
multiarticulate	multifaced	multimedial
multiarticulated	multifaceted	multimetallic
multiaxial	multifactorial	multimillion
multiblade	multifistular	multimolecular
multibladed	multiflagellate	multinational
multibranchiate	multiflow	multinervate
multicapital	multiflue	multinodal
multicapitate	multifocal	multinodous
multicapsular	multifurcate	multinodular
multicarinate	multigranulate	multiovular
multicellular	multigyrate	multiovulate
multicentral	multihead	multipartisan
multicentric	multihearth	multiperforate
multicharge	multihued	multiperforated
multichord	multi-infection	multipersonal
multichrome	multijet	multipinnate
multiciliate	multijugate	multipointed
multiciliated	multilaciniate	multipolar
multicircuit	multilamellar	multipurpose
multicoil	multilaminar	multiradial
multicolor	multilaminate	multiradiate
multiconductor	multilaminated	multiramified
multicore	multilighted	multiramose
multicorneal	multilineal	multiramous
multicourse	multilinear	multirange
multicrystalline	multilobar	multirate
multidentate	multilobate	multireflex
multidenticulate	multilobed	multirooted
multidenticulated	multilobular	multisaccate
multidigitate	multilobulate	multisacculate

multisection	multispiculate	multisulcated
multisegmental	multispindle	multisyllable
multisensitivity	multispinous	multiterminal
multiseptate	multispiral	multititular
multiserial	multispired	multituberculate
multiserially	multistaminate	multituberculated
multiseriate	multistoried	multitubular
multishot	multistratified	multivaned
multispermous	multistriate	multivoiced
multispicular	multisulcate	multivolumed

2. Having more than two (or more than one); as in:

multicostate	multiengine	multinuclear
multicuspid	multiexhaust	multinucleate
multicuspidate	multimammae	multinucleolar
multicylinder	multimammate	multinucleolate
multielectrode	multimotor	multispeed

3. Many times over: *multimillionaire.* **4.** *Med.* Affecting many; as in:

multiarticular	multiganglionic
multifamilial	multiglandular

Also, before vowels, sometimes **mult-**. [< L *multus* much]
mul·ti·col·ored (mul′ti·kul′ərd) *adj.* Having many colors.
mul·ti·far·i·ous (mul′tə·fâr′ē·əs) *adj.* Having great diversity or variety. — **Syn.** See MANY. [< LL *multifarius*] — **mul′ti·far′i·ous·ly** *adv.* — **mul′ti·far′i·ous·ness** *n.*
mul·ti·fid (mul′tə·fid) *adj. Bot.* Cut into many lobes or segments, as a leaf. Also **mul·tif·i·dous** (mul·tif′ə·dəs). [< MULTI- + -FID]
mul·ti·fold (mul′tə·fōld) *adj.* Many times doubled.
mul·ti·form (mul′tə·fôrm) *adj.* Having many forms or appearances. [< L *multiformis*] — **mul′ti·for′mi·ty** *n.*
Mul·ti·graph (mul′tə·graf, -gräf) *n.* An office duplicator that is used chiefly to reproduce copies of typewritten matter by means of a rotary drum into which metal type is inserted: a trade name. Also **mul′ti·graph.**
mul·ti·lat·er·al (mul′ti·lat′ər·əl) *adj.* **1.** Having many sides. **2.** *Govt.* Involving more than two nations: also *multipartite.* — **mul′ti·lat′er·al·ly** *adv.*
mul·ti·lin·gual (mul′ti·ling′gwəl) *n. & adj.* Polyglot.
Mul·ti·lith (mul′tə·lith) *n.* An office offset duplicator that reproduces copies of written or typewritten matter, tracings, etc., by means of a master wrapped around a rotary drum: a trade name. Also **mul′ti·lith.**
mul·ti·me·di·a (mul′ti·mē′dē·ə) *n. pl.* (*construed as sing.*) The simultaneous use of various communications media, such as slides, film, television, etc., especially for instructional presentations.
mul·ti·mil·lion·aire (mul′ti·mil′yən·âr′) *n.* One having a fortune of many millions; a very rich person.
mul·ti·nom·i·al (mul′ti·nō′mē·əl) *adj.* Polynomial (which see). [< MULTI- + -*nomial* as in BINOMIAL]
mul·tip·a·ra (mul·tip′ə·rə) *n. pl.* **·rae** (-rē) A woman who has borne more than one child, or who is bearing her second. Compare NULLIPARA, PRIMIPARA. [< NL, fem. of *multiparus* < MULTI- + L *parere* to give birth. Cf. PARENT.]
mul·tip·a·rous (mul·tip′ə·rəs) *adj.* **1.** Giving birth to many at one time: *multiparous opossums.* **2.** Of or relating to a multipara. [< NL *multiparus*]
mul·ti·par·tite (mul′ti·pär′tīt) *adj.* **1.** Divided into many parts. **2.** *Govt.* Multilateral (def. 2).
mul·ti·ped (mul′ti·ped) *adj.* Having many feet. — *n.* *Rare* A many-footed animal. Also **mul′ti·pede** (-pēd). [< L *multipes, -edis* < *multus* many + *pes* foot]
mul·ti·phase (mul′ti·fāz) *adj.* Polyphase (which see).
mul·ti·ple (mul′tə·pəl) *adj.* **1.** Having, consisting of, or relating to more than one part, aspect, individual, etc.; manifold. **2.** Happening more than once; repeated: *multiple* echoes. **3.** *Electr.* Denoting a circuit having two or more conductors arranged in parallel. — *n.* **1.** *Math.* Any of the products of a given number and some other number: 8 and 12 are *multiples* of 4. **2.** *Electr.* Parallel (def. 8). [< F < L *multiplex.* See MULTIPLEX.]
multiple allele *Genetics* One of three or more alleles, only one of which may pass from each parent to a normal diploid offspring.
mul·ti·ple-choice (mul′tə·pəl·chois′) *adj.* Giving several answers from which the correct one is to be selected: a *multiple-choice* test.
multiple factors *Genetics* Two or more distinct genes that may act as a unit or with cumulative effect in the production of certain characteristics, as size, pigmentation, etc.
multiple fruit *Bot.* Collective fruit (which see).
multiple neuritis *Pathol.* Neuritis involving several nerves simultaneously.
multiple sclerosis *Pathol.* Sclerosis occurring in various areas of the brain or spinal cord or both, and characterized by tremors, failure of coordination, etc.
multiple star *Astron.* A system of three or more stars, usually revolving around a common gravitational center.
mul·ti·plex (mul′tə·pleks) *adj.* **1.** Multiple; manifold. **2.** *Telecom.* Designating a system for the simultaneous transmission of two or more signals over the same wire or radio frequency channel. **3.** *Photog.* Designating a method in which three cameras are used to facilitate the construction of accurate maps on the stereoscopic principle. — *v.t. & v.i.*

Telecom. To send (two or more signals) at the same time over the same wire or radiofrequency channel. [< L < *multus* much + -*plex* < *plicare* to fold]
mul·ti·pli·cand (mul′tə·plə·kand′) *n. Math.* A number to be multiplied, by another: also called *faciend.* [< L *multiplicandus* to be multiplied, gerundive of *multiplicare.* See MULTIPLY[1].]
mul·ti·pli·ca·tion (mul′tə·plə·kā′shən) *n.* **1.** The act of multiplying, or the state of being multiplied. **2.** *Math.* The process of finding the sum (the *product*) of a number (the *multiplicand*) repeated a given number of times (the *multiplier*). [< OF < L *multiplicatio, -onis*]
multiplication sign The symbol (×) placed between two numbers or quantities to denote a multiplication of the first by the second, as $4 \times 2 = 8$.
mul·ti·pli·ca·tive (mul′tə·plə·kā′tiv) *adj.* **1.** Tending to multiply. **2.** Involving multiplication. — **mul′ti·pli·ca′tive·ly** *adv.*
mul·ti·plic·i·ty (mul′tə·plis′ə·tē) *n. pl.* **·ties 1.** The condition or quality of being manifold or various; multiple character. **2.** A large number: a *multiplicity* of tasks. [< OF *multiplicite* < LL *multiplicitas* < L *multiplicare* to multiply]
mul·ti·pli·er (mul′tə·plī′ər) *n.* **1.** One who or that which multiplies or causes multiplication. **2.** *Math.* The number by which a quantity is multiplied. **3.** *Physics* An instrument or device for increasing or intensifying an effect.
mul·ti·ply[1] (mul′tə·plī) *v.* **·plied, ·ply·ing** *v.t.* **1.** To increase the quantity, amount, or degree of. **2.** *Math.* To determine the product of by multiplication. — *v.i.* **3.** To become more in number, amount, or degree; increase. **4.** *Math.* To determine the product by multiplication. **5.** To grow in number by procreation; propagate. — **Syn.** See INCREASE. [< OF *multiplier* < L *multiplicare* < *multiplex.* See MULTIPLEX.] — **mul′ti·pli′a·ble** *adj.*
mul·ti·ply[2] (mul′tə·plē) *adv.* So as to be multiple; in many ways.
mul·ti·pro·pel·lant (mul′ti·prə·pel′ənt) *Aerospace n.* A rocket propellant consisting of two or more chemicals separately fed into the combustion chamber.
mul·ti·stage (mul′ti·stāj) *adj.* **1.** Having or characterized by a number of definite stages in the completion of a process or action. **2.** *Aerospace* Having several sections, as in a rocket, each of which fulfills a given task before burnout.
mul·ti·tude (mul′tə·tōod, -tyōod) *n.* **1.** A great number; host: a *multitude* of ideas. **2.** A large gathering of people; crowd; throng. **3.** The state or quality of being many or numerous. — **Syn.** See ARMY, COMPANY. — **the multitude** The common people. [< OF < L *multitudo* < *multus* many]
mul·ti·tu·di·nous (mul′tə·tōo′də·nəs, -tyōo′-) *adj.* **1.** Existing in great numbers; numerous; myriad. **2.** Consisting of or exhibiting many parts, features, etc. **3.** *Poetic* Crowded. [< L *multitudo, -inis* crowd] — **mul′ti·tu′di·nous·ly** *adv.* — **mul′ti·tu′di·nous·ness** *n.*
mul·ti·va·lent (mul′ti·vā′lənt) *adj. Chem.* Having three or more valences: also *polyvalent.* — **mul′ti·va′lence** *n.*
mul·ti·valve (mul′ti·valv) *n. Zool.* A shell with many valves. — *adj.* Having many valves. — **mul′ti·val′vu·lar** (-val′vyə·lər) *adj.*
Mult·no·mah Falls (mult·nō′mə) A waterfall in NW Oregon in a tributary of the Columbia River; 850 ft. high.
mul·tum in par·vo (mul′təm in pär′vō) *Latin* Much in little.
mul·ture (mul′chər) *n.* Formerly, a fee paid to a miller for grinding grain, usually a portion of the grain or flour. [< OF *moulture* < Med.L *molitura* < L *molere* to grind]
mum[1] (mum) *adj.* Silent; saying nothing. — *interj.* Hush! Be quiet! — **mum's the word** Keep silent; be secretive. [Imit.]
mum[2] (mum) *v.i.* **mummed, mum·ming** To play or act in a mask or disguise; be a mummer. Also **mumm.** [Prob. < MUM[1]. Cf. OF *momer* to act in dumb show.]
mum[3] (mum) *n.* A strong, sweet beer. [? after Christian *Mumme,* 15th c. German brewer]
mum[4] (mum) *n. Informal or Dial.* Ma'am; madam.
mum[5] (mum) *n. Informal* A chrysanthemum.
mum[6] (mum) *n. Chiefly Brit. Informal* Mother.
mum·ble (mum′bəl) *v.t. & v.i.* **·bled, ·bling 1.** To speak low and indistinctly; mutter. **2.** *Rare* To chew slowly and ineffectively, as with toothless gums. — *n.* A low, indistinct speech or sound; mutter. [ME *momelen.* Cf. MUM[1]] — **mum′bler** *n.* — **mum′bling·ly** *adv.*
mum·ble·ty-peg (mum′bəl·tē·peg′) *n.* A game played by manipulating a jackknife in various ways so as to stick it into the ground: so called because the loser was originally required to draw a peg out of the ground with his teeth. Also **mum′ble-peg′, mum·ble-the-peg** (mum′bəl·thə·peg′). [< MUMBLE, v. (def. 2) + PEG]
mum·bo jum·bo (mum′bō jum′bō) **1.** Meaningless, complicated, or obscure ritual, observance, incantation, etc. **2.** *Informal* Needlessly involved or unintelligible language; gibberish. **3.** Any object of superstitious devotion or fear; a fetish. **4.** *Usually cap.* In certain African tribes, a village god or idol who opposes evil and terrifies the women into subjection. [< Mandingo *mama dyambo* a tutelary god]

mu·mes·on (myōō′mes′on, -mē′son) *n. Physics* An unstable, short-lived subatomic particle formed from the decay of a pi-meson and having a mass about 210 times that of the electron: also called *muon.* [< MU + MESON]

mum·mer (mum′ər) *n.* **1.** One who acts or makes sport in a mask or disguise. **2.** An actor. [< OF *momeur*]

mum·mer·y (mum′ər·ē) *n. pl.* **·mer·ies 1.** A performance by mummers. **2.** A pretentious or hypocritical ritual. [< MF *mommerie* dumb show]

mum·mi·fy (mum′ə·fī) *v.* **·fied, ·fy·ing** *v.t.* **1.** To make a mummy of; preserve by embalming, drying, etc. **2.** To make dry and lifeless, as an idea, institution, etc. — *v.i.* **3.** To dry up; shrivel. [< F *momifier*] — **mum′mi·fi·ca′tion** *n.*

mum·my (mum′ē) *n. pl.* **·mies 1.** A human or animal body embalmed in the ancient Egyptian manner. **2.** Any dead body that has been well preserved, as by heat, cold, special preparation, etc. **3.** One who is lifeless, withered, or torpid. — *v.t. & v.i.* **·mied, ·my·ing** To mummify. [< F *momie* < Med.L *mumia* < Arabic *mumiya* < Persian *mum* wax] — **mum′mi·form** *adj.*

mumps (mumps) *n.pl.* (*construed as sing.*) *Pathol.* An acute contagious virus disease usually occurring in childhood, characterized by fever, inflammation, and swelling of the parotid and other facial glands, and occasionally of the ovaries and testicles: also called *parotitis.* [Pl. of obs. *mump* grimace]

mun¹ (mun) *n. Brit. Dial.* Man.

mun² (mun, mōōn) *n. Scot. & Brit. Dial.* Must.

mun. Municipal; municipality.

munch (munch) *v.t. & v.i.* To chew steadily with a crunching noise. [ME *monchen, manchen,* ? < MF *manger;* prob. ult. imit.] — **munch′er** *n.*

Mun·chau·sen (mun-chô′zən, mun′chou′zən), **Baron,** 1720–1797, German nobleman and cavalry officer whose extravagant stories of his exploits formed the basis of the *Tales of Munchausen,* collected by Rudolf Erich Raspe in 1785. Also **Münch·hau·sen** (münkh′hou′zən). — **Mun′chau′sen·ism** *n.*

Mün·chen-Glad·bach (mün′khən glät′bäkh) See MÖNCHEN-GLADBACH.

Mun·cie (mun′sē) A city in eastern Indiana; pop. 69,082.

Mun·da (mōōn′də) *n.* A subfamily of the Austro-Asiatic family of languages, spoken in central India.

mun·dane (mun′dān, mun·dān′) *adj.* **1.** Pertaining to or characterized by that which is practical, routine, or ordinary: *mundane* concerns. **2.** Of or relating to the world or earth; earthly. [< F *mondain* < L *mundanus* < *mundus* world] — **mun·dane′ly** *adv.* — **mun·dane′ness** *n.*

Mun·de·lein (mun′də-līn), **George William,** 1872–1939, U.S. cardinal.

mun·dun·go (mun·dung′gō) *n. Archaic* A black, malodorous tobacco. Also **mun·dun′gus.** [Jocular use of Sp. *mondongo* tripe]

mun·go (mung′gō) *n.* Short fibers recovered from wool waste; also, cloth made from these. Compare SHODDY. [Origin uncertain]

mun·goose (mung′gōōs) *n. pl.* **·goos·es** A mongoose.

Mu·nich (myōō′nik) The capital of Bavaria, SE West Germany, on the Isar; pop. 1,326,300 (est. 1970). *German* **München** (mün′khən).

Mu·nich (myōō′nik) *n.* An instance or act of ignoble political appeasement or concession. [< MUNICH PACT]

Munich Pact The pact of September 29, 1938, signed by Nazi Germany, Great Britain, France, and Italy, in which the Sudetenland was ceded to Germany. Also **Munich Agreement.**

mu·nic·i·pal (myōō·nis′ə·pəl) *adj.* **1.** Of or pertaining to a town or city or its local government. **2.** Having local self-government. Abbr. **mun.** [< L *municipalis < municeps, -cipis* free citizen < *munia* duties + *capere* to take] — **mu·nic′i·pal·ly** *adv.*

municipal borough See under BOROUGH.

mu·nic·i·pal·ism (myōō·nis′ə·pəl·iz′əm) *n.* **1.** Municipal government. **2.** The theory that advocates greater powers for municipal governments. — **mu·nic′i·pal·ist** *n.*

mu·nic·i·pal·i·ty (myōō·nis′ə·pal′ə·tē) *n. pl.* **·ties 1.** An incorporated borough, town, or city. **2.** In Cuba and some other Latin-American countries, an administrative area somewhat like a county. Abbr. *mun.* [< F *municipalité* < L *municipalis.* See MUNICIPAL.]

mu·nic·i·pal·ize (myōō·nis′ə·pəl·īz′) *v.t.* **·ized, ·iz·ing 1.** To place within municipal authority or transfer to municipal ownership. **2.** To make a municipality of. — **mu·nic′i·pal·i·za′tion** *n.*

mu·nif·i·cent (myōō·nif′ə·sənt) *adj.* Extraordinarily generous or bountiful; liberal. — **Syn.** See GENEROUS. [< L *munificens, -entis < munificus < munus* gift + *facere* to make] — **mu·nif′i·cence** *n.* — **mu·nif′i·cent·ly** *adv.*

mu·ni·ment (myōō′nə·mənt) *n.* **1.** *Usually pl. Law* A deed, charter, or other document that serves to defend title to property, maintain rights and privileges, etc. **2.** *Archaic* Something that defends or protects. [< OF < L *munimentum* fortification, support < *munire* to fortify]

mu·ni·tion (myōō·nish′ən) *n. Usually pl.* Ammunition and all other necessary war materiel. — *v.t.* To furnish with munitions. [< F < L *munitio, -onis < munire* to fortify]

mun·nion (mun′yən) *n. Archaic* A mullion.

Mun·ro (mən·rō′), **H(ector) H(ugh)** See SAKI.

Mun·sey (mun′sē), **Frank Andrews,** 1854–1925, U.S. publisher.

Mun·ster (mun′stər) A Province in southern Ireland; 9,317 sq. mi.; pop. 916,750 (est. 1960).

Mün·ster (mün′stər) A city in northern North Rhine–Westphalia, West Germany; pop. 204,571 (est. 1970). Also **Mün′ster-in-West·fa′len** (-in·vest·fä′lən).

Mün·ster·berg (mün′stər·berkh), **Hugo,** 1863–1916, U.S. philosopher and psychologist born in Germany.

Mun·the (mun′te), **Axel (Martin Fredrik),** 1857–1949, Swedish physician and writer.

munt·jac (munt′jak) *n.* Any of various small. horned deer (genus *Muntiacus*) of southeastern Asia and the East Indies. Also **munt′jak.** [< Javanese *mĕnjañan*]

mu·on (myōō′on) *n. Physics* A mu-meson.

mu·ral (myŏŏr′əl) *n.* A painting or decoration applied to a wall or ceiling. — *adj.* **1.** Placed or executed on a wall: a *mural* painting. **2.** Of, pertaining to, or resembling a wall: *mural* precipices. [< F < L *muralis < murus* wall]

mu·ral·ist (myŏŏr′əl·ist) *n.* A painter of murals.

Mu·ra·sa·ki Shi·ki·bu (mōō·rä·sä·kē shē·kē·bōō), **Lady** Eleventh-century Japanese novelist and poet.

Mu·rat (mōō·rät′) A river in east central Turkey, flowing 380 miles west to the Euphrates. Also **Mu·rad** (-räd′).

Mu·rat (mü·rå′), **Joachim,** 1771–1815, French marshal; brother-in-law of Napoleon Bonaparte; king of Naples as Joachim I in 1808.

Mur·cia (mûr′shə, mōōr′-; *Sp.* mōōr′thyä) **1.** A region and former kingdom of southern Spain. **2.** A city in SE Spain, capital of the former kingdom; pop. 170,000 (est. 1967).

mur·der (mûr′dər) *n.* **1.** The unlawful, malicious, and intentional killing of one human being by another. **2.** *U.S. Informal* Something exceedingly difficult, painful, or hazardous: That road is *murder* in winter. — **to get away with murder** *U.S. Slang* To avoid or elude punishment or responsibility. — *v.t.* **1.** To kill (a human being) unlawfully and with deliberate malice. **2.** To kill or slaughter in a brutal manner, as in war. **3.** To spoil, ruin, or mar by a bad performance, improper pronunciation, etc.; mangle; butcher: to *murder* the English tongue. **4.** *U.S. Slang* To defeat decisively; trounce. — *v.i.* **5.** To commit murder. — **Syn.** See KILL. [< OE *morthor.* Akin to L *mors, mortis* death.] — **mur′der·er** *n.* — **mur′der·ess** *n.fem.*

mur·der·ous (mûr′dər·əs) *adj.* **1.** Of, pertaining to, or involving murder. **2.** Capable of or given to murder: a *murderous* fiend. **3.** Having the characteristics of or resembling murder; brutal; bloody; deadly: *murderous* gunfire. **4.** Extremely difficult or dangerous: a *murderous* curve in the road. — **mur′der·ous·ly** *adv.* — **mur′der·ous·ness** *n.*

mu·rex (myŏŏr′eks) *n. pl.* **mu·ri·ces** (myŏŏr′ə·sēz) or **·rex·es** Any of various marine gastropods (genus *Murex*) of warm seas, used as a source of a purple dye in ancient times. [< L, purple fish. Akin to Gk. *myax* sea mussel.]

Mur·frees·bor·o (mûr′frēz·bûr′ō) A city in central Tennessee; site of the Civil War battle of Stones River, December 31, 1862, and January 2, 1863; pop. 26,360.

mu·ri·ate (myŏŏr′ē·āt) *n. Obs.* Chloride. [< F]

mu·ri·at·ed (myŏŏr′ē·ā′tid) *adj. Archaic* Salted; pickled.

mu·ri·at·ic acid (myŏŏr′ē·at′ik) *n.* Hydrochloric acid, especially an impure grade used commercially. [< L *muriaticus* pickled < *muria* brine]

Mu·ril·lo (myŏŏ·ril′ō, *Sp.* mōō·rē′lyō), **Bartolomé Esteban,** 1617–82, Spanish painter.

mu·rine (myŏŏr′īn, -in) *adj.* Of or pertaining to a family (*Muridae*) or a subfamily (*Murinae*) of rodents that includes the true mice and rats. — *n.* A murine rodent. [< L *murinus < mus, muris* mouse]

murk (mûrk) *n.* Darkness; gloom. — *adj. Archaic & Poetic* Murky; dark. Also spelled *mirk.* [OE *mirce*] — **murk′ly** *adv.*

murk·y (mûr′kē) *adj.* **murk·i·er, murk·i·est 1.** Dark, gloomy, or obscure: the *murky* depths. **2.** Hazy, thick, or misty, as atmosphere, color, etc. **3.** Not clear or distinct to the mind; confused; abstruse. Also *mirky.* — **Syn.** See DARK. — **murk′i·ly** *adv.* — **murk′i·ness** *n.*

Mur·man Coast (mōōr′mən) A generally ice-free part of the Arctic coast of the NW R.S.F.S.R.; site of the city **Murmansk** (mōōr·mänsk′; *Russ.* mōōr′mənsk), a port, pop. 309,000 (1970). Also **Murmansk Coast.** *Russian* **Murman·skiy Be·reg** (mōōr′mən·skye bye′ryik).

mur·mur (mûr′mər) *n.* **1.** A low, indistinct, continuously repeated sound, as of many voices, a quiet brook, etc.: the *murmur* of bees. **2.** An indistinct or mumbled complaint; grumbling. **3.** *Med.* A soft, low sound heard on auscultation of certain organs and blood vessels: especially, an abnormal, rasping sound produced within the heart. — *v.i.* **1.**

To make a low, indistinct sound. **2.** To complain in low, muttered tones; grumble. — *v.t.* **3.** To utter in a low, indistinct voice; mutter. [< OF *murmure* < L *murmur,* ? ult. imit. Cf. Gk. *mormȳrein* to boil, crackle.] — **mur′mur·er** *n.* — **mur′mur·ing·ly** *adv.*

mur·mur·ous (mûr′mər-əs) *adj.* Characterized by, filled with, or making murmurs. — **mur′mur·ous·ly** *adv.* — **mur′mur·ous·ness** *n.*

mur·phy (mûr′fē) *n.* *pl.* **·phies** *Slang* A potato. [after *Murphy,* an Irish surname]

Mur·phy (mûr′fē), **Frank,** 1890–1949, U.S. jurist; associate justice of the Supreme Court 1940–49. — **William Parry,** born 1892, U.S. physician.

Murphy bed A bed that folds or slides into a closet for concealment. [after W. *Murphy,* 20th c. U.S. inventor]

Murphy's Law *U.S. Informal* The principle that whatever can possibly go wrong will. [Origin unknown]

mur·ra (mûr′ə) *n.* A material of ancient Rome that has been variously supposed to be Chinese jade, porcelain, iridescent glass, or artificially colored chalcedony, used for cups, vases, etc. Also **mur′rha.** [< L]

mur·rain (mûr′in) *n.* **1.** Any of various contagious diseases affecting cattle, as anthrax, Texas fever, etc. **2.** *Archaic* Any plague or pestilence. [< OF *morine* < L *mori* to die]

Mur·ray (mûr′ē), **Gilbert,** 1866–1957, British classical scholar: full name George Gilbert Aimé Murray. — **Sir James Augustus Henry** 1837–1915, Scottish philologist and lexicographer. — **Lindley,** 1745–1826, U.S. grammarian. — **Philip,** 1866–1952, U.S. labor leader born in Scotland.

Murray River The principal river of Australia, forming part of the Victoria–New South Wales boundary and flowing 1,600 miles, generally west, to the Indian Ocean.

murre (mûr) *n.* *pl.* **murres** or **murre** Either of two North American diving birds (genus *Uria*), the **common murre** (*U. aalge*) of coastal regions, and the **thick-billed murre** (*U. lomvia*) of arctic regions. Also **murr.** [Origin uncertain]

murre·let (mûr′lit) *n.* Any of certain small sea birds (family *Alcidae*) of the North Pacific, especially the **marbled murrelet** (*Brachyramphus marmoratus*). [Dim. of MURRE]

mur·rey (mûr′ē) *adj.* Of a purplish red color. — *n.* A dark purplish red. [< OF *moree* < L *morum* mulberry]

mur·rhine glass (mûr′in, -īn) **1.** Glassware with embedded flowers, ribbons, etc., of colored glass. **2.** Glassware thought to resemble the murra ware of ancient Rome. Also **mur′rine glass.**

Mur·rum·bidg·ee (mûr′əm-bij′ē) A river in New South Wales, Australia, rising in the Great Dividing Range and flowing 1,050 miles west to the Murray River.

mur·ry (mûr′ē) *n.* The moray, an eel.

mur·ther (mûr′thər) *Obs.* *n.* Murder. — *v.t.* & *v.i.* To murder. — **mur′ther·er** *n.*

Mur·vie·dro (mōōr-vyä′thrō) A former name for SAGUNTO.

mus. **1.** Museum. **2.** Music; musician.

mu·sa·ceous (myōō-zā′shəs) *adj.* *Bot.* Of or pertaining to a family (*Musaceae*) of plants that include the banana. [< NL *Musaceae* < *Musa* < Arabic *mawzah* banana]

Mus.B. or **Mus.Bac.** Bachelor of Music (L *Musicae Baccalaureus*).

mus·ca (mus′kə) *n.* *pl.* **mus·cae** (mus′sē) Any of a genus (*Musca*) of dipterous insects (family *Muscidae*) including the housefly. [< L, fly] — **mus·cid** (mus′id) *adj.* & *n.*

Mus·ca (mus′kə) *n.* A constellation, the Fly. See CONSTELLATION. [< NL]

mus·ca·dine (mus′kə-din, -dīn) *n.* **1.** A North American grape (*Vitis rotundifolia*) having a thick skin and a strong flavor, especially scuppernong. **2.** *Obs.* Muscatel wine. [Prob. < Provençal *muscade,* fem. of *muscat.* See MUSCAT.]

mus·cae vol·i·tan·tes (mus′sē vol′ə·tan′tēz) Specks or motes apparently moving before the eyes, caused by defects or impurities in the vitreous humor. [< L, flying flies]

mus·ca·rine (mus′kə-rēn, -rin) *n.* *Chem.* A deliquescent, poisonous, white crystalline alkaloid, $C_9H_{20}NO_2$, found in certain fungi. [< L *muscarius* of flies < *musca* fly]

mus·cat (mus′kat, -kət) *n.* **1.** Any of several varieties of musk-flavored Old World grapes. **2.** A sweet wine made from such cultivated grapes. Also called *muscatel.* [< F < Provençal, smelling like musk < LL *muscus* musk]

Mus·cat (mus·kät′) The capital of the sultanate of Oman, on the Arabian peninsula; port on the Gulf of Oman; pop. 6,000 (est. 1968).

Muscat and Oman (mus·kät′ ənd ō·män′) See OMAN.

mus·ca·tel (mus′kə·tel′) *n.* **1.** A rich, sweet wine made from the muscat grape. **2.** The muscat grape. Also **mus′·ca·del′** (-del′). [< OF, dim. of *muscat.* See MUSCAT.]

mus·cle (mus′əl) *n.* **1.** *Anat.* A contractile tissue composed of bundles of elongated cells (**muscle fibers**) that functions to produce bodily movements. **2.** An organ or structure consisting of such tissue: leg *muscles.* **3.** Muscular strength; brawn. — *v.i.* **·cled, ·cling** *U.S. Slang* To force one's way by or as by sheer brawn: often with *in.* [< F < L *musculus,* lit., little mouse, dim. of *mus.* Doublet of MUSSEL.]

mus·cle-bound (mus′əl·bound′) *adj.* Having enlarged and inelastic muscles, as from excessive exercise.

mus·cled (mus′əld) *adj.* Having or supplied with muscles.

muscle plasma *Physiol.* A liquid from muscle tissue, sometimes injected as a stimulant.

muscle sense Kinesthesia.

Muscle Shoals Rapids in the Tennessee River, NW Alabama; site of the Wilson Dam.

muscle spindle *Anat.* One of various terminal sense organs in muscle.

mus·co·va·do (mus′kə·vā′dō) *n.* Raw cane sugar. Also **mus′ca·va′da** (-də), **mus′co·vade** (-vād). [< Sp. *mascabado* unrefined (sugar)]

mus·co·vite (mus′kə·vīt) *n.* A common light or colorless mica, $KAl_3Si_3O_{10}(OH)_2$, used as an insulator. [< earlier *Muscovy glass*]

Mus·co·vite (mus′kə·vīt) *n.* **1.** An inhabitant of Muscovy or of Moscow. **2.** *Archaic* A Russian. — *adj.* **1.** Of or pertaining to Muscovy. **2.** *Archaic* Russian. — **Mus′co·vit′ic** (-vit′ik) *adj.*

Mus·co·vy (mus′kə·vē) *n.* Ancient Russia.

Muscovy duck A large, greenish black duck (*Cairina moschata*) of Central and South America, now widely domesticated: also called *musk duck.* [Alter. of MUSK DUCK]

mus·cu·lar (mus′kyə·lər) *adj.* **1.** Pertaining to or involving muscle. **2.** Composed of muscle. **3.** Having strong muscles; brawny; powerful. [< L *muscularis*] — **mus′cu·lar′i·ty** (-lar′ə·tē) *n.* — **mus′cu·lar·ly** *adv.*

muscular dystrophy *Pathol.* One of various diseases of undetermined cause, characterized by a progressive wasting degeneration of muscle tissue, lordosis of the spine, and usually terminating in severe physical helplessness.

mus·cu·la·ture (mus′kyə·lə·chŏŏr) *n.* **1.** The disposition or arrangement of muscles in a part or organ. **2.** The muscle system as a whole. Also **mus′cu·la′tion.** [< F]

Mus.D. or **Mus.Doc.** or **Mus.Dr.** Doctor of Music (L *Musicae Doctor*)

muse[1] (myōōz) *n.* A spirit or power regarded as inspiring artists, poets, etc. [< MUSE]

muse[2] (myōōz) *v.t.* & *v.i.* **mused, mus·ing** To consider thoughtfully or at length; ponder; meditate. — *Syn.* See DELIBERATE. [< OF *muser* to reflect, loiter; prob. orig. to stay with muzzle in the air < OF *mus* animal's mouth < LL *musus*] — **muse′ful** *adj.* — **muse′ful·ly** *adv.*

Muse (myōōz) *n.* In Greek mythology, any of the nine daughters of Mnemosyne (Memory) and Zeus who preside over the arts and sciences, including Calliope, Clio, Erato, Euterpe, Melpomene, Polyhymnia, Terpsichore, Thalia, and Urania. [< F < L *Musa* < Gk. *Mousa* a Muse, eloquence, music]

mu·sette (myōō·zet′) *n.* **1.** A gentle pastoral air written in imitation of bagpipe tunes. **2.** A small bagpipe formerly popular in France. **3.** A small canvas or leather bag for carrying provisions, etc., worn suspended from a shoulder strap, especially by soldiers: also **musette bag.** [< F, dim. of OF *muse* bagpipe]

mu·se·um (myōō·zē′əm) *n.* A place or building for preserving and exhibiting works of art, scientific objects, curiosities, etc. Abbr. Mus. [< L < Gk. *mouseion* shrine of the Muses < *Mousa* Muse]

mush[1] (mush) *n.* **1.** *U.S.* A thick porridge made with meal, especially corn meal, boiled in water or milk. **2.** Anything soft, thick, and pulpy. **3.** *Informal* Maudlin or mawkish sentimentality. [Var. of MASH]

mush[2] (mush) *Chiefly Canadian* *v.i.* In arctic regions, to travel on foot, especially over snow with a dog sled. — *interj.* Get along!: a command to a dog team. [Prob. < *mush on,* alter. of F (Canadian) *marche,* the cry of voyageurs and trappers to their dogs] — **mush′er** *n.*

mush·mel·on (mush′mel′ən) *n.* *U.S. Dial.* A muskmelon (which see).

mush·room (mush′rōōm, -rŏŏm) *n.* **1.** A fleshy, rapidly growing, umbrella-shaped fungus (order *Agaricales*); especially, the common, edible **field mushroom** (*Agaricus campestris*) and certain poisonous varieties loosely called toadstools. **2.** Anything resembling a mushroom in shape or rapid growth. — *v.i.* **1.** To grow or spread rapidly, like a mushroom: The town *mushroomed* overnight. **2.** To expand or sprout out into a mushroomlike shape, as a bullet, smoke, etc. [ME *muscheron,* prob. < OF *mousse* moss]

MUSHROOMS

a Pileus (whole and in section). *b* Stipe in velum. *ca* Ruptured velum. *cb* Velum forming ring. *d* Gill. *da* Cross-section of gill. *e* Mycelia. *f, f* Young mushrooms.

mushroom cloud A rapidly rising, mushroom-shaped column of smoke and debris, especially from a nuclear explosion.

mush·y (mush′ē) *adj.* **mush·i·er, mush·i·est** **1.** Soft; pulpy. **2.** *Informal* Mawkishly sentimental. — **mush′i·ly** *adv.* — **mush′i·ness** *n.*

mu·sic (myōō′zik) *n.* **1.** The art of producing significant arrangements of sounds, usually with reference to rhythm, pitch, and tone color. **2.** A musical composition or body of compositions; also, a musical score. **3.** A succession or combination of musical sounds, especially if pleasing to the ear. **4.** *Obs.* A band of musicians. Abbr. *mus.* — **absolute music** Music wholly without representation of or dependence on title, program, etc. — **electronic music** Music in which all or part of the sound is either generated as an audio-frequency electronic signal or altered beyond ready recognition by electronic means. — **program music** Music intended to be heard with reference to an extramusical idea, situation, event, etc. — **to face the music** To accept the consequences of one's acts. For symbols used in music see Special Signs and Symbols section. [< OF *musique* < L *musica* < Gk. *mousikē* (*technē*), lit., the art of the Muse < Mousa. See MUSE.]

mu·si·cal (myoo′zi·kəl) *adj.* **1.** Of, pertaining to, or capable of creating music: *musical* instrument. **2.** Having the nature or characteristics of music; melodious; harmonious: a *musical* voice. **3.** Fond of or versed in music. **4.** Set to or accompanied by music: *musical* comedy. — *n.* **1.** A musical comedy. **2.** *Archaic* A musicale. [< OF < Med.L *musicalis* < L *musica*. See MUSIC.] — **mu′si·cal·ly** *adv.* — **mu′si·cal·i·ty, mu′si·cal·ness** *n.*

musical chairs A game in which the players circle a row of chairs to music and rush to sit down when the music stops, the one not finding an empty chair being eliminated.

musical comedy A show with music, songs, dances, jokes, colorful staging, etc., often based on a tenuous plot.

mu·si·cale (myoo′zi·kal′) *n.* A private concert or recital, as in a home. [< F (*soirée*) *musicale*]

music box A mechanism that plays tunes, usually by means of pins that strike the tuned teeth of a comblike metal plate as they revolve on a cylinder or disk.

music drama An opera, especially one by Richard Wagner.

music hall **1.** A public building for musical performances. **2.** *Brit.* A vaudeville theatre.

mu·si·cian (myoo·zish′ən) *n.* **1.** A professional performer or composer of music. **2.** One skilled in the performance or composition of music. Abbr. *mus.* [< OF *musicien*] — **mu·si′cian·ly** *adj.* — **mu·si′cian·ship** *n.*

music of the spheres According to Pythagorean philosophy, the harmony or music produced by the movements of the celestial spheres.

mu·si·col·o·gy (myoo′zə·kol′ə·jē) *n. pl.* **·gies** The scientific and historical study of the forms, theory, methods, etc., of music. — **mu′si·col′o·gist** *n.*

music stand A rack to hold music for a performer.

mus·ing (myoo′zing) *adj.* Thoughtful; meditative; reflective. — *n.* The act of one who muses. — **mus′ing·ly** *adv.*

mus·jid (mus′jid) See MASJID.

musk (musk) *n.* **1.** A soft, powdery, reddish brown secretion with a penetrating odor, obtained from the sac (**musk bag**) of the male musk deer, and used in making perfumes and in medicine. **2.** Any similar substance from some other animals, as the muskrat or civet. **3.** Any of several synthetic compounds used to imitate natural musk. **4.** The musk deer. **5.** Any of various plants having a musky odor, as the grape hyacinth. **6.** The odor of musk. [< OF *musc* < LL *muscus* < LGk. *moskos*, ? < Persian *mushk*, ? < Skt. *mushka* testicle, dim. of *mus* mouse]

musk deer A small, hornless deer (*Moschus moschiferus*) of central and eastern Asia, of which the male has a musk-secreting gland.

musk duck **1.** A Muscovy duck (which see). **2.** A duck (*Biziura lobata*) of Australia with a musky odor in the breeding season: also called *mould goose.*

mus·keg (mus′keg) *n. U.S. & Canadian* A bog or marsh formed by successive deposits of leaves, mosses, muck, etc., filling a depression in the land; especially, such a bog having much sphagnum: also *maskeg.* [of Algonquian origin]

Mus·ke·gon (mə·skē′gən) A port city in western Michigan, on Lake Michigan; pop. 44,631.

mus·kel·lunge (mus′kə·lunj) *n. pl.* **·lunge** or **·lung·es** A large North American pike (*Esox masquinongy*), valued as a game fish: also called *maskalonge, maskinonge.* Also **mus′kal·lunge, mus′kie** (-kē). [< Algonquian *maskinonge* < *mas* great + *kinong* pike]

mus·ket (mus′kit) *n.* An archaic smoothbore, usually muzzleloading, firearm designed to be fired from the shoulder, as the flintlock and matchlock, now superseded by the rifle. Compare RIFLE[1] (def. 1). [< MF *mosquet* < Ital. *moschetto* crossbow, dart, orig., sparrow hawk < L *musca* fly]

mus·ket·eer (mus′kə·tir′) *n.* Formerly, a soldier armed with a musket; especially, a member of the French royal bodyguard between 1622 and 1786. [< F *mousquetaire*]

mus·ket·ry (mus′kit·rē) *n.* **1.** Muskets collectively. **2.** The technique of firing small arms. **3.** Musketeers collectively.

Mus·ko·ge·an (mus·kō′gē·ən, mus′kō·gē′ən) *n.* One of the principal North American Indian linguistic stocks, including the Chickasaw, Choctaw, Creek, and Seminole tribes, formerly inhabiting the Gulf region of the SE United States. Also **Mus·ko·gi·an** (mus·kō′gē·ən, mus′kō·gē′ən).

mus·kit (mus·kēt′) *n.* Mesquite.

musk·mel·on (musk′mel′ən) *n.* **1.** Any of several varieties of juicy, edible fruits of a trailing herb (*Cucumis melo*) of the gourd family, as the cantaloupe. **2.** The plant bearing this fruit.

Mus·ko·gee (mus·kō′gē) A city in eastern Oklahoma, on the Arkansas River; pop. 37,331.

musk ox A shaggy, hollow-horned ruminant (*Ovibos moschatus*) of arctic America and Greenland, combining the characteristics of the sheep and ox and emitting a strong odor of musk: also called *ovibos.*

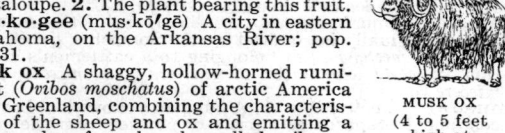

MUSK OX
(4 to 5 feet
high at
shoulder)

musk·rat (musk′rat) *n. pl.* **·rats** or **·rat** **1.** An aquatic rodent (*Ondatra zibethica*) of North America, having dark, glossy brown fur and a musky odor: also called *musquash, water rat.* **2.** The valuable fur of this rodent. [By folk etymology < Algonquian *musquash*]

musk rose A cultivated climbing rose (*Rosa moschata*) from Europe, with clusters of large, white, fragrant flowers.

musk turtle A small turtle (*Sternotherus odoratus*) of the eastern United States and Canada, having a musky odor. Also **musk terrapin, musk tortoise.**

musk·y (mus′kē) *adj.* **musk·i·er, musk·i·est** Resembling musk in odor or taste. — **musk′i·ly** *adv.* — **musk′i·ness** *n.*

Mus·lim (muz′lim, mooz′-, moos′-) *n. pl.* **·lims** or **·lim** A believer in Islam; Mohammedan. — *adj.* Of or pertaining to Islam or the Muslims. Also called *Moslem:* also **Mus′lem.** [< Arabic, one who submits < *aslama* to surrender (to God)]

Mus·lim·ism (muz′lem·iz′əm, mooz′-, moos′-) *n.* Islam.

mus·lin (muz′lin) *n.* Any of several plain-weave cotton fabrics of varying fineness, especially a sturdier variety used for sheets, etc. [< F *mousseline* < Ital. *mussolino* < *Mussolo* Mosul, city in Iraq, where it was made]

Mus.M. Master of Music (L *Musicae Magister*).

mus·pike (mus′pīk′) *n. Canadian* A hybrid cross of the pike and the muskellunge.

mus·quash (mus′kwosh) *n.* **1.** The muskrat. **2.** *Brit.* Muskrat fur. [< Algonquian]

muss (mus) *U.S. Informal n.* **1.** A state of disorder or untidiness; mess. **2.** A commotion or tumult; row; squabble. — *v.t.* To make messy or untidy; rumple: often with *up:* to *muss* up her hair. [Alter. of MESS]

mus·sel (mus′əl) *n.* **1.** A bivalve marine mollusk (family Mytilidae), especially the common edible **blue mussel** (*Mytilus edulis*). **2.** Any of several fresh-water mollusks (family Unionidae). [OE *musle, muscelle* < L *musculus,* dim. of *mus* mouse. Doublet of MUSCLE.]

Mus·set (mü·se′), (**Louis Charles**) **Alfred de,** 1810–57, French poet, dramatist, and novelist.

Mus·so·li·ni (mōōs′ə·lē′nē, *Ital.* mōōs′sō·lē′nē), **Benito,** 1883–1945, Italian Fascist leader; premier 1922–43; executed: called *Il Duce* (the Leader).

Mus·sorg·sky (mōō·sôrg′skē), **Modest Petrovich** See MOUSSORGSKY.

Mus·sul·man (mus′əl·mən) *n. pl.* **·mans** (-mənz) or **·men** (-mən) A Muslim; Mohammedan. — *adj.* Belonging or relating to the Muslims. [< Persian and Turkish *musulmān* < Arabic *muslimān.* pl. of *muslim.* See MUSLIM.]

muss·y (mus′ē) *adj. U.S. Informal* **muss·i·er, muss·i·est** Rumpled; messy. — **muss′i·ly** *adv.* — **muss′i·ness** *n.*

must[1] (must) *v. Present 3rd person sing.* **must** A defective verb now used only as an auxiliary followed by the infinitive without *to,* or elliptically with the infinitive understood, to express: **a** Compulsion: *Must* you go? I *must;* also, a weaker obligation: I *must* try harder. **b** Requirement: You *must* be healthy to be accepted. **c** Probability or supposition: You *must* be tired. **d** Conviction or certainty: War *must* follow. ◆ A past conditional is formed by placing the following verb in the perfect infinitive: *He must have gone.* — *n. Informal* Anything that is required or vital: Safety is a *must.* — *adj. Informal* Important and essential: a *must* book. [OE *mōste,* pl. of *mōtan* to be able, to be obliged to]

must[2] (must) *n.* Mustiness; mold. — *v.t. & v.i. Obs.* To make or become musty. [Back formation < MUSTY]

must[3] (must) *n.* The pressed unfermented juice of the grape or other fruit. [OE < L *mustum* (*vinum*) new (wine)]

must[4] (must) *n.* **1.** A state of dangerous sexual frenzy, especially in male elephants. **2.** An elephant in this condition. — *adj.* Being in a state of must. Also spelled *musth.* [< Hind. *mast* drunk, lustful < Persian]

mus·tache (məs·tash′, mus′tash) *n.* **1.** The growth of hair on the upper lip or on either half of the upper lip; especially, such a growth when cultivated or groomed. **2.** The hair or bristles growing near the mouth of an animal. **3.** A marking, etc., resembling a mustache. Also **mus·ta·chio** (məs·tä′shō). Also, *Chiefly Brit., moustache.* [< F *moustache* <

Ital. *mostaccio* face, prob. < Med.L *mustacia* < Gk. *mystax* jaws, mustache] — **mus·tached** (məs·tasht′) *adj.*

Mus·ta·fa Ke·mal (mōō′stä·fä ki·mäl′) See KEMAL ATA-TÜRK.

Mus·tagh (mōōs·tä′) See KARAKORAM.

mus·tang (mus′tang) *n.* A wild horse of the American plains, originally introduced by the Spanish. [< Sp. *mes-teño*, obs. *mestengo*, lit., belonging to a cattlemen's associa-tion < *mesta* association of graziers < L *mixtus*, pp. of *miscere* to mix]

mus·tard (mus′tərd) *n.* **1.** A pungent yellowish or brownish condiment prepared as a paste or powder from the ground seed of the mustard plant. **2.** Any of several plants (genus *Brassica*), typical of a large family (*Cruciferae*) that includes broccoli, cabbage, cress, etc.; especially, **white mustard** (*B. hirta*) and **black mustard** (*B. nigra*). **3.** The yellowish or brownish color of ground mustard. [< MF *moustarde* < L *mustum* (see MUST³); orig. prepared with must]

mustard gas *Chem.* An oily amber liquid, dichlorethyl sulfide, $C_4H_8Cl_2S$, having an odor of mustard or garlic, and used in warfare because of its powerful blistering effect.

mustard oil A fixed oil extracted from mustard seeds and used in making soap, as a lubricant, etc.

mustard plaster A mixture of powdered black mustard and a suitable adhesive, to be spread on a cloth for use as a counterirritant and rubefacient.

mus·tee (mus·tē′, mus′tē) *n.* **1.** The offspring of a white person and a quadroon. **2.** Any half-breed. Also spelled *mestee*. [Alter. of Sp. *mestizo* mongrel, hybrid]

mus·te·line (mus′tə·lin, -līn) *adj.* Of or pertaining to a family (*Mustelidae*) of fur-bearing, predacious mammals, including weasels, skunks, badgers, otters, wolverines, etc. [< L *mustelinus* < *mustela* weasel. Akin to L *mus* mouse.]

mus·ter (mus′tər) *v.t.* **1.** To summon or assemble (troops, etc.), for service, review, roll call, etc. **2.** To collect, gather, or summon: often with *up*: to *muster* facts; to *muster up* courage. — *v.i.* **3.** To gather or assemble, as troops for ser-vice, review, etc. — **Syn.** See CONVOKE. — **to muster in** (or **out**) To enlist in (or release from) military service. — *n.* **1.** An assembling or gathering, as of troops for inspection, parade, etc. **2.** An assemblage or collection; especially, an assemblage of troops for inspection, etc. **3.** An official list of officers and men in a military unit or ship's crew: also **muster roll.** [< OF *mostrer* < L *monstrare* to show]

musth (must) See MUST⁴.

must·y (mus′tē) *adj.* **must·i·er, must·i·est 1.** Having a moldy odor or flavor, as a close room, spoiled food, etc. **2.** Dull or stale with age; old-fashioned; antiquated. **3.** Without vigor; lifeless; apathetic. [? Alter. of obs. *moisty* < MOIST] — **must′i·ly** *adv.* — **must′i·ness** *n.*

mu·ta·ble (myōō′tə·bəl) *adj.* **1.** Capable of or subject to change; alterable. **2.** Liable or prone to frequent change; fickle: *mutable* desires. [< L *mutabilis* < *mutare* to change] — **mu′ta·ble·ness, mu·ta·bil′i·ty** *n.* — **mu′ta·bly** *adv.*

mu·ta·gen·ic (myōō′tə·jen′ik) *adj. Genetics* Having the power to produce mutations in plant or animal organisms, as X-rays, ionization from radioactive elements, and certain chemicals. [< L *mutare* to change + -GENIC]

mu·tant (myōō′tənt) *n.* **1.** That which admits of or under-goes mutation or change. **2.** *Biol.* **a** A plant or animal or-ganism differing from its parents in one or more character-istics that are inheritable; mutation; sport. **b** A modified gene resulting in a mutant organism. — *adj.* Pertaining to, resulting from, or undergoing mutation. [< L *mutans, -antis*, ppr. of *mutare* to change]

mu·tate (myōō′tāt) *v.t. & v.i.* **·tat·ed, ·tat·ing** To undergo or subject to change or mutation. [< L *mutatus*, pp. of *mutare* to change] — **mu′ta·tive** (-tə·tiv) *adj.*

mu·ta·tion (myōō·tā′shən) *n.* **1.** The act or process of changing; alteration. **2.** A change or modification in form, structure, function, etc. **3.** *Biol.* **a** A sudden, transmissible variation in a plant or animal, especially as the result of new modifications or combinations of genes and chromosomes. **b** An individual, species, etc., resulting from such a variation. **4.** *Ling.* The modification of one vowel or consonant by another or by its position; especially, umlaut. [< OF < L *mutatio, -onis* < *mutare* to change] — **mu·ta′tion·al** *adj.*

mu·ta·tis mu·tan·dis (myōō·tā′tis myōō·tan′dis) *Latin* The necessary changes having been made. Abbr. *m.m.*

mutch (much) *n. Scot.* A close-fitting linen cap worn by women and children. [< MDu. *mutse*]

mutch·kin (much′kin) *n. Scot.* A liquid measure equal to ¾ of a Scottish pint. [< Du. *mudsekin*]

mute (myōōt) *adj.* **1.** Not producing speech or sound; silent. **2.** Lacking the power of speech; dumb. **3.** Ex-pressed or conveyed without speech; unspoken: a *mute* appeal. **4.** *Law* Deliberately refusing to plead on arraignment: chief-ly in the phrase **to stand mute. 5.** *Phonet.* **a** Not pronounced; silent, as the *e* in *gone*. **b** Plosive. — *n.* **1.** One who is un-able to speak; especially, one who is a deaf-mute. **2.** A pro-fessional or hired mourner at a funeral. **3.** *Law* One who re-fuses to plead on arraignment. **4.** *Phonet.* **a** A silent or un-pronounced letter. **b** A plosive. **5.** *Music* A device used to muffle or attenuate the tone of an instrument, as the cone-

shaped contrivance inserted into the bell of a trumpet. — *v.t.* **mut·ed, mut·ing 1.** To muffle or deaden the sound of (a musical instrument, etc.). **2.** In art, to soften (a color, a shade, etc.). [< L *mutus* dumb] — **mute′ly** *adv.* — **mute′ness** *n.*

mu·ti·late (myōō′tə·lāt) *v.t.* **·lat·ed, ·lat·ing 1.** To deprive (a person, animal, etc.) of a limb or essential part; maim. **2.** To damage or injure, especially by the removal of an im-portant part or parts: to *mutilate* a speech. [< L *mutilatus*, pp. of *mutilare* to maim < *mutilus* dehorned, hence maimed] — **mu′ti·la′tion** *n.* — **mu′ti·la′tive** *adj.* — **mu′ti·la′tor** *n.*

mu·ti·neer (myōō′tə·nir′) *n.* One guilty of mutiny: also *Obs.* **mu·tine** (myōō′tin). — *v.i.* To mutiny. [< MF *mutinier* < (*se*) *mutiner* to rebel. See MUTINY.]

mu·ti·nous (myōō′tə·nəs) *adj.* **1.** Disposed to mutiny; seditious. **2.** Characterized by, expressing, or constituting mutiny. — **mu′ti·nous·ly** *adv.* — **mu′ti·nous·ness** *n.*

mu·ti·ny (myōō′tə·nē) *n. pl.* **·nies** Rebellion against con-stituted authority; insubordination; especially, a revolt of soldiers or sailors against their commanders. — **Syn.** See REBELLION. — *v.i.* **·nied, ·ny·ing** To revolt against con-stituted authority, as in the army or navy; take part in a mutiny. [< MF (*se*) *mutiner* to rebel < *mutin* rebellious < OF *muete* a riot < Med.L *movita* hostile movement < L *movere* to move]

mut·ism (myōō′tiz·əm) *n.* **1.** The state of not speaking; muteness; dumbness. **2.** *Psychol.* A refusal to talk, a symp-tom of negativism. [< F *mutisme*]

Mu·tsu·hi·to (mōō·tsōō·hē·tō), 1852–1912, emperor of Ja-pan 1867–1912.

mutt (mut) *n. Slang* **1.** A cur; mongrel dog. **2.** A stupid person; blockhead. Also **mut.** [< MUTT(ONHEAD)]

mut·ter (mut′ər) *v.i.* **1.** To speak in a low, indistinct tone and with compressed lips, as in complaining or talking to oneself. **2.** To complain; grumble. **3.** To make a low, rum-bling sound. — *v.t.* **4.** To say in a low, indistinct tone. — *n.* A low, indistinct utterance or tone; murmur. [ME *muteren*. Akin to L *muttire*, G *muttern*; ult. init.] — **mut′-ter·er** *n.* — **mut′ter·ing·ly** *adv.*

mut·ton (mut′n) *n.* The flesh of sheep used as food; espe-cially, the flesh of mature sheep as distinguished from lambs. [< OF *molton* sheep < Celtic. Cf. OIrish *molt*, Breton *maout*.] — **mut·ton·y** *adj.*

mutton chop A piece of mutton from the rib for broiling.

mut·ton-chops (mut′n·chops′) *n.pl.* Side whiskers nar-row at the temples and broad at the lower cheeks.

mut·ton-fish (mut′n·fish′) *n. pl.* **·fish** or **·fish·es 1.** The ocean pout. **2.** An abalone (*Haliotis iris*) said to taste like mutton. **3.** A snapper (*Lutianus analis*) of tropical Atlantic waters: also **mutton snapper.**

mut·ton-head (mut′n·hed′) *n. Slang* A stupid, dense per-son. [< MUTTON + HEAD; from the traditional stupidity of sheep] — **mut′ton·head′ed** (-hed′id) *adj.*

mu·tu·al (myōō′chōō·al) *adj.* **1.** Felt, expressed, or per-formed for or toward each other by the persons, sides, or parties concerned; reciprocal: *mutual* dislike. **2.** Having the same attitude toward or relationship with each other or others: *mutual* friends. **3.** Possessed or held in common: *mutual* interests. [< OF *mutuel* < L *mutuus* borrowed, exchanged, reciprocal < *mutare* to change] — **mu′tu·al·ly** *adv.* — **mu′tu·al′i·ty** *n.*

— **Syn. 1, 2.** *Mutual, reciprocal,* and *common* mean pertaining to both or all the persons or things mentioned. *Mutual* may prop-erly be applied to the relation between two persons, or to feelings, views, etc., they both entertain: *mutual* esteem, *mutual* distrust o' strangers. *Reciprocal* is properly limited to relations between two persons or things, where whatever is directed by one to the other is returned in kind: *reciprocal* vows of friendship. If more than two are concerned, *common* is properly used: the *common* attitude of the guests was polite boredom, the *common* concern of the citi-zens for good government. In strict usage, *mutual* and *reciprocal* are avoided in application to three or more unless the intention is to denote a relationship true of *every* possible combination of two.

mutual fund An open-end investment company. See un-der INVESTMENT COMPANY.

mutual insurance A method of insurance in which all policyholders become members of the company, contracting to indemnify one another against designated losses. Also **mutual plan.**

mu·tu·al·ism (myōō′chōō·al·iz′əm) *n. Biol.* Symbiosis ad-vantageous to both or all participants.

mu·tu·al·ize (myōō′chōō·al·īz) *v.t. & v.i.* **·ized, ·iz·ing 1.** To make or become mutual. **2.** *Econ.* To put (a firm or corpor-ation) on the basis of majority employee or consumer owner-ship of common stock. — **mu′tu·al·i·za′tion** *n.*

mutual savings bank A savings bank having no capital and sharing its profits with the depositors.

mu·tule (myōō′chool) *n. Archit.* One of a series of rectan-gular blocks projecting under the corona of a Doric cornice. [< F < L *mutulus* modillion]

muu-muu (mōō′mōō′) *n.* A loose, flowing gown for women, gathered from the neckline. [< Hawaiian]

mu·zhik (mōō·zhēk′, mōō′zhēk) *n.* A Russian peasant in Czarist times: also spelled *moujik, mujik.* Also **mu·zjik′.** [< Russian]

muz·zle (muz′əl) *n.* **1.** The projecting part of an animal's head, including the jaws, mouth, and nose; snout. For illustration see HORSE. **2.** A guard or covering for the snout of an animal to prevent biting or eating. **3.** The front end of the barrel of a firearm. — *v.t.* **zled, ·zling 1.** To put a muzzle on (an animal, etc.). **2.** To restrain from speaking, expressing opinions, etc.; gag. [< OF *musel* < Med.L *musellum*, dim. of *musus* snout] — **muz′zler** *n.*

muz·zle·load·er (muz′əl·lō′dər) *n.* A gun loaded through the muzzle. — **muz′zle·load′ing** *adj.*

muzzle velocity The velocity of a bullet or projectile at the instant of leaving the barrel of a gun.

muz·zy (muz′ē) *adj.* **·zi·er, ·zi·est** *Informal* **1.** Muddled; confused. **2.** Blurred.

m.v. *Music* Softly (Ital. *mezzo voce*).

MVD The Ministry of Internal Affairs of the Soviet Union; the secret police: formerly called *Cheka, OGPU, NKVD.* Also **M.V.D.**

M.W. 1. Most Worshipful. **2.** Most Worthy.

M.W.A. Modern Woodmen of America.

Mwer·u (mwä′rōo) A lake between the SE Republic of Zaire and the Republic of Zambia; 173 sq. mi.: French *Moéro.* See map of CONGO.

Mx. Middlesex.

my (mī) *pronominal adj.* The possessive case of the pronoun *I,* used attributively: also used in certain forms of address: *my* lord; *my* good man. — *interj.* An exclamation of surprise, dismay, etc.: Oh, *my!* [OE *mīn*]

my- Var. of MYO-.

my·al·gi·a (mī·al′jē·ə) *n. Pathol.* Pain in a muscle; cramp. [< MY- + -ALGIA] — **my·al′gic** *adj.*

my·as·the·ni·a (mī′əs·thē′nē·ə) *n. Pathol.* Muscular debility. — **myasthenia gra·vis** (gra′vis) Muscular debility accompanied by general and usually progressive exhaustion but without marked sensory disturbance or atrophy. [< MY(O) + ASTHENIA]

my·ce·li·um (mī·sē′lē·əm) *n. pl.* **·li·a** (-lē·ə) *Bot.* The thallus or vegetative portion of a fungus, consisting of hyphae. For illustration see MUSHROOM. Also **my′cele** (-sēl). [< NL < Gk. *mykēs* fungus] — **my·ce′li·al, my·ce′li·an** *adj.* — **my·ce′li·oid, my·ce·loid** (mī′sə·loid) *adj.*

My·ce·nae (mī·sē′nē) An ancient city in the NE Peloponnesus, Greece; first excavated 1876–77.

My·ce·nae·an (mī′sə·nē′ən) *adj.* **1.** Of or relating to the ancient city of Mycenae. **2.** Of, pertaining to, or characteristic of an ancient civilization that flourished in various parts of the Mediterranean area, including Greece, Asia Minor, and Sicily, from about 1400 B.C. to 1100 B.C.

-mycete *combining form Bot.* A member of a class of fungi, corresponding in use to class names in *-mycetes: Basidiomycete.* [See -MYCETES]

-mycetes *combining form Bot.* Used to form class names of fungi: *Basidiomycetes.* [< Gk. *mykētes,* pl. of *mykēs* fungus]

my·ce·to·zo·an (mī·sē′tō·zō′ən) *n.* A myxomycete. — *adj.* Myxomycetous. [< Gk. *mykēs, mykētos* fungus + -ZOA]

myco- *combining form* Fungus: *mycology.* Also, before vowels, **myc-.** [< Gk. *mykēs* fungus]

my·co·bac·te·ri·um (mī′kō·bak·tir′ē·əm) *n. pl.* **·ri·a** (-rē·ə) One of a genus (*Mycobacterium*) of slender, typically aerobic bacteria difficult to stain, including the bacterium of tuberculosis and that of leprosy. [< MYCO- + BACTERIUM]

my·col. Mycological; mycology.

my·col·o·gy (mī·kol′ə·jē) *n. pl.* **·gies 1.** The branch of botany dealing with fungi. **2.** The fungus life of a region. **3.** The properties and attributes of a type of fungus. [< MYCO- + -LOGY] — **my·co·log·ic** (mī′kə·loj′ik) or **·i·cal** *adj.* — **my·col′o·gist** *n.*

my·cor·rhi·za (mī′kə·rī′zə) *n. Bot.* **1.** A mass of fungus hyphae often found in symbiotic association with the roots of certain trees. **2.** The symbiosis itself. Also **my′co·rhi′za.** [< MYCO- + Gk. *rhiza* root] — **my′cor·rhi′zic** *adj.*

my·co·sis (mī·kō′sis) *n. Pathol.* **1.** A fungous growth within the body. **2.** A disease caused by such a growth, as ringworm. [< MYC(O)- + -OSIS] — **my·cot′ic** (-kot′ik) *adj.*

my·dri·a·sis (mī·drī′ə·sis, mī-) *n. Pathol.* An abnormal or prolonged dilatation of the pupil of the eye. [< LL < Gk.]

myd·ri·at·ic (mid′rē·at′ik) *adj. Med.* Relating to or causing mydriasis. — *n.* A drug that causes mydriasis.

my·e·len·ceph·a·lon (mī′ə·len·sef′ə·lon) *n. Anat.* The posterior part of the rhombencephalon or that portion of the medulla oblongata lying behind the pons Varolii and cerebellum. [< MYEL(O)- + ENCEPHALON]

my·e·lin (mī′ə·lin) *n. Anat.* A semisolid fatlike substance surrounding the axillary portion of medullated nerve fibers: also called *medullary sheath.* Also **my′e·line** (-lēn, -lin), **myelin sheath.** [< Gk. *myelos* marrow] — **my·e·lin′ic** *adj.*

my·e·li·tis (mī′ə·lī′tis) *n. Pathol.* **1.** Inflammation of the spinal cord. **2.** Inflammation of the bone marrow. [< MYEL(O)- + -ITIS]

myelo- *combining form Anat.* The spinal cord or bone marrow. Also, before vowels, **myel-.** [< Gk. *myelos* marrow]

my·e·loid (mī′ə·loid) *adj. Anat.* **1.** Of, pertaining to, or resembling marrow. **2.** Of or pertaining to the spinal cord [< MYEL(O)- + -OID]

my·i·a·sis (mī′yə·sis) *n. Pathol.* Infestation by flies or maggots. [< NL < Gk. *myia* fly + -(O)SIS]

My·lae (mī′lē) The ancient name for MILAZZO; scene of a Roman naval victory over Carthage, 260 B.C.

my·lo·nite (mī′lə·nīt) *n. Geol.* A hard, fine-grained, laminated rock produced by the crushing and re-forming of earth material under pressure. [< Gk. *mylōn* mill + -ITE¹]

my·na (mī′nə) *n.* One of various starlinglike Oriental birds (genera *Acridotheres* and *Eulabes*); especially, the hill **myna** (*E. religiosa*) of India, often taught to speak words: sometimes spelled *mina.* Also **my′nah.** [< Hind. *mainā*]

myn·heer (mīn·hâr′, -hir′) *n.* **1.** *Cap.* The Dutch equivalent of *Mr.* **2.** A title of courtesy, equivalent to *sir.* Also, Dutch, *mijnheer.* [< Du. *mijnheer* < *mijn* my + *heer* lord, master]

myo- *combining form* Muscle: *myology.* Also, before vowels, **my-.** [< Gk. *mys, myos* muscle]

my·o·car·di·al (mī′ō·kär′dē·əl) *adj. Anat.* Of or pertaining to the heart muscle. [< MYO- + Gk. *kardia* heart]

my·o·car·di·o·graph (mī′ō·kär′dē·ə·graf′, -gräf′) *n.* An instrument for registering the muscular action of the heart.

my·o·car·di·tis (mī′ō·kär·dī′tis) *n. Pathol.* Inflammation of the myocardium. [< NL] — **my′o·car·dit′ic** (-dit′ik) *adj.*

my·o·car·di·um (mī′ō·kär′dē·əm) *n. Anat.* The muscular tissue of the heart. [< MYO- + Gk. *kardia* heart]

my·o·gen·et·ic (mī′ō·jə·net′ik) *adj. Physiol.* Originating in muscle or in muscle tissue. Also **my′o·gen′ic** (-jen′ik), **my·og·e·nous** (mī·oj′ə·nəs).

my·o·graph (mī′ə·graf, -gräf) *n.* An instrument for recording the contractions and dilatations of the muscles.

my·oid (mī′oid) *adj.* Resembling muscle.

my·ol·o·gy (mī·ol′ə·jē) *n.* The study of the structure, functions, and diseases of the muscles. [< MYO- + -LOGY] — **my·o·log·ic** (mī′ə·loj′ik) or **·i·cal** *adj.* — **my·ol′o·gist** *n.*

my·o·ma (mī·ō′mə) *n. pl.* **·ma·ta** (-mə·tə) *Pathol.* A tumor affecting muscle tissue. [< MY- + -OMA] — **my·om′a·tous** (-om′ə·təs) *adj.*

my·o·mec·to·my (mī′ō·mek′tə·mē) *n. pl.* **·mies** *Surg.* The removal of a myoma. [< MYOMA + -ECTOMY]

my·ope (mī′ōp) *n.* One who is nearsighted. [< F < LL *myops* < Gk. *myōps* < *myein* to close + *ōps* eye]

my·o·pi·a (mī·ō′pē·ə) *n.* **1.** *Pathol.* A visual defect in which images are focused in front of instead of on the retina, so that objects are seen clearly only when close to the eye; nearsightedness. **2.** Lack of insight or discernment; obtuseness. Also **my·o·py** (mī′ə·pē). [< NL] — **my·op′ic** (-op′ik) *adj.*

my·o·scope (mī′ə·skōp) *n. Med.* An instrument for observing the contraction of muscles.

my·o·sin (mī′ə·sin) *n. Biochem.* A globulin found in contractile muscular tissue. [< Gk. *mys, myos* muscle + -IN]

my·o·sis (mī·ō′sis) See MIOSIS.

my·o·so·tis (mī′ə·sō′tis) *n.* Any of several plants (genus *Myosotis*) of the borage family, especially the forget-me-not. Also **my′o·sote** (-sōt). [< L < Gk. *myosōtis,* lit., mouse ear < *mys, myos* mouse + *ous, ōtos* ear]

My·ra (mī′rə) An ancient city of Lycia, Asia Minor.

myria- *combining form* **1.** Very many; of great number: *myriapod.* **2.** In the metric system, ten thousand. Also, before vowels, **myri-.** [< Gk. *myrios* numberless, *myrioi* ten thousand]

myr·i·ad (mir′ē·əd) *adj.* Composed of a very large indefinite number; innumerable. — *n.* **1.** A vast indefinite number. **2.** A vast number of persons or things. **3.** Ten thousand. [< Gk. *myrias, myriados* < *myrios* numberless]

myr·i·a·pod (mir′ē·ə·pod) *n. Zool.* One of a class or group of arthropods (*Myriapoda*) whose bodies are made up of a certain number of segments, each of which bears one or two pairs of jointed appendages, including the centipedes and millipedes. — **myr·i·ap·o·dan** (mir′ē·ap′ə·dən) *adj. & n.* — **myr′i·ap′o·dous** *adj.*

myr·i·ca (mi·rī′kə) *n.* The dried bark or root of wax myrtle, sometimes used in medicine. [< L < Gk. *myrikē* tamarisk]

myrmeco- *combining form* Ant: *myrmecophagous.* Also, before vowels, **myrmec-.** [< Gk. *myrmēx, myrmēkos* ant]

myr·me·col·o·gy (mûr′mə·kol′ə·jē) *n.* The branch of entomology treating of ants. [< MYRMECO- + -LOGY] — **myr′me·co·log′i·cal** (-kə·loj′i·kəl) *adj.* — **myr′me·col′o·gist** *n.*

myr·me·coph·a·gous (mûr′mə·kof′ə·gəs) *adj.* Feeding on ants. [< MYRMECO- + -PHAGOUS]

myr·mi·don (mûr′mə·don, -dən) *n.* A faithful adherent; especially, a follower who carries out his chief's orders without scruple or question. [< MYRMIDON]

Myr·mi·don (mûr′mə·don, -dən) *n.* In Greek legend, one of a warlike people of Thessaly, followers of Achilles in the Trojan War. [< L < Gk., pl. *Myrmidones*] — **Myr′mi·do′ni·an** (-dō′nē·ən) *adj.*

my·rob·a·lan (mī·rob′ə·lən, mi-) *n.* Any of the prunelike fruits of certain tropical plants (genus *Terminalia*), including the broadleaf, used in tanning and dyeing. [< F < L *myrobalanum* < Gk. *myrobalanos* < *myron* juice, ointment + *balanos* acorn]

My·ron (mī′rən) Fifth-century B.C. Greek sculptor. — **My·ron′ic** (-ron′ik) *adj.*

myrrh (mûr) *n.* **1.** An aromatic gum resin that exudes from certain small trees (genus *Commiphora*) of Arabia and eastern Africa, used as incense, perfume, and in medicine. **2.** Any shrub or tree that yields this gum, especially *C. myrrha* and *C. abyssinica.* [OE *myrra* < L *murrha* < Gk. *mýrra* < Semitic. Cf. Arabic *murr,* Hebrew *mōr, mar* bitter.]

myr·ta·ceous (mûr-tā′shəs) *adj. Bot.* Of, belonging to, or designating the myrtle family (*Myrtaceae*) of trees and shrubs, widely distributed in tropical and semitropical countries and including the pimento, eucalyptus, and clove. [< NL *Myrtaceae* < L *myrtus* myrtle tree]

myr·tle (mûr′təl) *n.* Any of a group of shrubs (genus *Myrtus*) typical of a large family (*Myrtaceae*); especially, the true myrtle, (*M. communis*) of southern Europe, with evergreen leaves, white or rose-colored flowers, and black berries. **2.** One of various other plants, as the periwinkle and the California laurel. [< F *myrtille* whortleberry < Med.L *myrtillus* myrtle, dim. of L *myrtus* < Gk. *myrtos* < Semitic]

my·self (mī-self′) *pron.* A form of the first person singular pronoun, used: **1.** As a reflexive or as the object of a preposition in a reflexive sense: I saw *myself* in the mirror; I was alone with *myself.* **2.** As an emphatic or intensive form of *I:* I *myself* invented the yo-yo. **3.** Informally as part of a direct compound object of a verb, or as an emphatic form of *me:* He asked John and *myself* to come along; They saw *myself* on television. **4.** As a designation of a normal, proper, or usual state: Once out of uniform, I was *myself* again in no time. [OE *mē* + *sylf*]

My·si·a (mish′ē-ə) An ancient region of NW Asia Minor on the Aegean Sea and the Sea of Marmara.

My·sore (mī-sôr′, -sōr′) **1.** A State in southern India; 74,122 sq. mi.; pop. 27,985,000 (1971); capital, Bangalore. **2.** A city in southern India; former dynastic capital of Mysore State; pop. 262,136 (1969). Also *Maisur.*

mys·ta·gogue (mis′tə-gôg, -gog) *n.* One who teaches, interprets, or initiates into religious mysteries. Also **mys′ta·gog.** [< F < L *mystagogus* < Gk. *mystagōgos* < *mystēs* an initiate + *agein* to lead. See MYSTERY.] — **mys′ta·gog′ic** (-goj′ik) or **i·cal** *adj.* — **mys′ta·go′gy** (-gō′jē) *n.*

mys·te·ri·ous (mis-tir′ē-əs) *adj.* **1.** Implying or characterized by mystery. **2.** Unexplained; puzzling. [< L *mysterium*] — **mys·te′ri·ous·ly** *adv.* — **mys·te′ri·ous·ness** *n.*
— **Syn.** *Mysterious, obscure, inscrutable, abstruse, esoteric, occult,* and *arcane* mean difficult to understand or explain. A *mysterious* occurrence contains something unknown, but not necessarily unknowable, while something *obscure* is hidden but may be brought to light. *Inscrutable* refers to that which is quite beyond the power of perception; *abstruse,* to that which is difficult to understand because of its complexity or profundity. *Esoteric* suggests something that is understood only by a small and select group possessing special knowledge or sensitivity. *Occult* and *arcane* mark those things which are considered to belong to a realm beyond human experience, and are therefore hidden from normal perception. — **Ant.** clear, evident, understandable, comprehensible.

mys·ter·y¹ (mis′tər-ē) *n. pl.* **·ter·ies 1.** Something that is not or cannot be known, understood, or explained: the *mystery* of the human spirit. **2.** Any action, affair, or thing that arouses curiosity or suspense because it is not fully revealed or explained. **3.** A story, play, movie, etc., narrating or dramatizing such an affair: a murder *mystery.* **4.** Obscurity or darkness, especially that which conceals a secret: an incident shrouded in *mystery.* **5.** Baffling character or property, as of a glance, gesture, etc. **6.** *Theol.* A truth that can be known only through divine revelation, and that cannot be fully understood by men. **7.** *Eccl.* **a** A sacrament, especially the Eucharist. **b** *pl.* The Eucharistic elements. **c** Any of fifteen events in the life of Christ, forming the substance of devotion during the recital of the rosary. **8.** *Usually pl.* In ancient times, one of certain religious cults whose rites were kept secret from all but initiates: the Orphic *mysteries.* **9.** A secret rite of such a cult. **10.** *Often pl.* A secret rite, doctrine, or practice of certain secular or quasi-religious societies. — **Syn.** See PUZZLE. [< L *mysterium* < Gk. *mysterion* secret rite. Akin to Gk. *myein* to shut the eyes or lips.]

mys·ter·y² (mis′tər-ē) *n. pl.* **·ter·ies 1.** A mystery play. **2.** *Archaic* A trade or occupation; also, a guild. [< Med.L *misterium* < L *ministerium* service, occupation; infl. by L *mysterium.* See MYSTERY¹.]

mystery play A medieval dramatic representation dealing with Scriptural events or characters and typically presented by a craft guild on a holiday. Compare MIRACLE PLAY.

mys·tic (mis′tik) *adj.* **1.** Of the nature of or pertaining to mysteries. **2.** Of or designating an occult or esoteric rite, practice, belief, religion, etc. **3.** Of or pertaining to mystics or mysticism. **4.** Baffling or enigmatic in character or meaning; mysterious; inscrutable. **5.** Mystical (def. 1). — *n.* **1.** One who believes in or expounds mysticism, or professes to have had mystical experiences. **2.** One who participates in occult or mystic rites; an initiate. [< L *mysticus* pertaining to secret rites < *mystēs* initiate]

mys·ti·cal (mis′ti-kəl) *adj.* **1.** Of the nature of a direct, intuitive, or subjective perception beyond the ordinary range of human experience, especially one of a religious character. **2.** Having a spiritual character or reality beyond the comprehension of human reason. **3.** Mystic (defs. 1, 2 & 3) **4.** *Rare* Obscure in meaning or origin; mysterious. — **mys′ti·cal·i·ty** (-kal′ə-tē), **mys′ti·cal·ness** *n.* — **mys′ti·cal·ly** *adv.*

mys·ti·cism (mis′tə-siz′əm) *n.* **1.** The doctrine or belief that through contemplation and love man can achieve a direct and immediate consciousness of God or of divine truth, etc., without the use of reason or of any of the ordinary senses. **2.** Any theory affirming that spiritual truths may be directly apprehended by intuition or meditation. **3.** Vague or confused thinking; fanciful speculation.

mys·ti·fi·ca·tion (mis′tə-fi-kā′shən) *n.* **1.** The act of mystifying, or the state of being mystified. **2.** Something that mystifies. — **mys·tif′i·ca·to·ry** (mis-tif′ik-ə-tôr′ē, -tō′rē) *adj.*

mys·ti·fy (mis′tə-fī) *v.t.* **·fied, ·fy·ing 1.** To confuse or perplex, especially deliberately. **2.** To make obscure or mysterious; complicate. [< F *mystifier* < *mystique* mystic] — **mys′ti·fi′er** *n.* — **mys′ti·fy′ing·ly** *adv.*

mys·tique (mis-tēk′) *n.* **1.** A body of attitudes, opinions, or ideas that become associated with a person, thing, institution, etc., and give it a superhuman or mythical status: the *mystique* of bullfighting. **2.** A peculiar or mystical way of viewing reality, especially when adopted as a doctrine or guide to behavior by an organization, religion, etc. **3.** A highly specialized or difficult skill or accomplishment in a given occupation: the *mystique* of good cookery. [< F]

myth (mith) *n.* **1.** A traditional story, usually focusing on the deeds of gods or heroes, often in explanation of some natural phenomenon, as the origin of the sun, etc. It purports to be historical, but is useful to historians principally for what it reveals of the culture of the peoples it describes or among whom it was current. **2.** A theme, motif, character type, etc., in modern literature that expresses or is felt to express significant truths about human life or human nature: the *myth* of the alienated man. **3.** Myths collectively. **4.** An imaginary or fictitious person, thing, event, or story. **5.** A collective opinion, belief, or ideal that is based on false premises or is the product of fallacious reasoning. **6.** An allegory or parable used to explain or illustrate a philosophic concept, as in Plato's dialogues. — **Syn.** See FICTION. [< LL *mythos* < Gk., word, speech, story]

myth. or **mythol.** Mythology.

myth·i·cal (mith′i-kəl) *adj.* **1.** Of the nature of or pertaining to myth. **2.** Derived from or contained in a myth or myths, as distinguished from historical records. **3.** Existing only in the imagination; fictitious. Also **myth′ic.** [< LL *mythicus*] — **myth′i·cal·ly** *adv.*

myth·i·cize (mith′ə-sīz) *v.t.* **·cized, ·ciz·ing** To convert into or explain as myth.

mytho- *combining form* Myth: *mythography.* Also, before vowels, **myth-.** [< Gk. *mythos* story]

myth·o·log·i·cal (mith′ə-loj′i-kəl) *adj.* **1.** Of, pertaining to, or described in mythology. **2.** Imaginary. Also **myth′o·log′ic.** [< LL *mythologicus* < Gk. *mythologikos* < *mythologia.* See MYTHOLOGY.] — **myth′o·log′i·cal·ly** *adv.*

my·thol·o·gize (mi-thol′ə-jīz) *v.* **·gized, ·giz·ing** *v.i.* **1.** To narrate, classify, or explain myths. **2.** To make or disseminate myths. — *v.t.* **3.** To mythicize. Also *Brit.* **my·thol′o·gise.** [< F *mythologiser*] — **my·thol′o·giz′er** *n.*

my·thol·o·gy (mi-thol′ə-jē) *n. pl.* **·gies 1.** The collective myths and legends of a particular people, usually describing the exploits of gods and heroes and often including an account of how the world or life originated: Greek *mythology.* **2.** The scientific collection and study of myths. **3.** A volume of myths. **4.** A body of myths associated with a person, institution, etc.: the *mythology* of democracy. [< F *mythologie* < LL *mythologia* < Gk., storytelling < *mythos* story + *logos* to speak, tell] — **my·thol′o·gist** *n.*

myth·o·ma·ni·a (mith′ə-mā′nē-ə, -mān′yə) *n.* An abnormal tendency to tell lies. — **myth′o·ma′ni·ac** *n. & adj.*

myth·o·poe·ic (mith′ə-pē′ik) *adj.* Of, pertaining to, or contributing to the making of myths. Also **myth′o·pe′ic.** [< Gk. *mythopoios* < *mythos* story + *poieein* to make] — **myth′o·poe′ia** (-pē′ə) *n.*

my·thos (mith′os, mī′thos) *n. pl.* **·thoi** (-thoi) **1.** The traits, values, ideals, etc., of a group as embodied in myth. **2.** Myth. **3.** Mythology.

Myt·i·le·ne (mit′ə-lē′nē) **1.** Lesbos. **2.** The capital of the Aegean Islands Division of Greece, a port on SE Lesbos; pop. about 27,000; formerly *Kastro.* Also **Myt′i·li′ni** (-lē′nē).

myx·e·de·ma (mik′sə-dē′mə) *n. Pathol.* A form of hypothyroidism characterized by dryness and wrinkling of the skin, swelling and thickening of the features of the face, and progressive mental deterioration. Also **myx′oe·de′ma.** [< MYX(O)- + EDEMA] — **myx·e·dem′ic** (-dem′ik), **myx′e·dem′a·tous** (-dem′ə-təs, -dē′mə-təs) *adj.*

myxo- *combining form* Slimy; like mucus. Also, before vowels, **myx-.** [< Gk. *myxa* mucus]

myx·o·ma (mik-sō′mə) *n. pl.* **·ma·ta** (-mə-tə) *Pathol.* A soft, elastic tumor composed of mucous tissue. [< MYX(O)- + -OMA] — **myx·om·a·tous** (mik-som′ə-təs) *adj.*

myx·o·ma·to·sis (mik/sō·mə·tō/sis) *n.* **1.** *Pathol.* The condition of having myxomas. **2.** A usually fatal disease of rabbits, caused by a virus.

myx·o·my·cete (mik/sō·mī·sēt/) *n.* One of the slime molds

(*Myxomycetes*), a class of chiefly saprophytic fungi having both plant and animal traits and classified by some authorities as *Mycetozoa*: also called *mycetozoan*. [< MYXO- + -MYCETE] — **myx/o·my·ce/tous** *adj.*

N

n, N (en) *n.* *pl.* **n's** or **ns, N's** or **Ns, ens** (enz) **1.** The fourteenth letter of the English alphabet. The shape of the Phoenician letter *nun* was adopted by the Greeks as *nu* and became Roman *N.* Also *en.* **2.** The sound represented by the letter *n*, a voiced, alveolar nasal. — *symbol* **1.** *Printing* An *en.* **2.** *Chem.* Nitrogen (symbol N). **3.** *Math.* An indefinite number.

n. **1.** Born (L *natus*). **2.** Name. **3.** Nephew. **4.** Net. **5.** Neuter. **6.** New. **7.** Nominative. **8.** Noon. **9.** *Chem.* Normal. **10.** Note. **11.** Number. **12.** Noun.

N **1.** Knight (chess). **2.** North; northern.

N. **1.** Nationalist. **2.** Navy. **3.** Noon. **4.** *Chem.* Normal (strength solution). **5.** Norse. **6.** North; northern. **7.** November.

na (nä) *Scot. & Brit. Dial. adv.* No; not. — *conj.* Nor. [OE *ne* + *ā* ever]

Na *Chem.* Sodium (L *natrium*).

N.A. **1.** National Academician. **2.** North America.

N.A.A. **1.** National Aeronautic Association. **2.** National Automobile Association.

NAACP or **N.A.A.C.P.** National Association for the Advancement of Colored People.

nab (nab) *v.t.* **nabbed, nab·bing** *Informal* **1.** To catch or arrest, as a fugitive or criminal. **2.** To take or seize suddenly; snatch. — **Syn.** See CATCH. [Prob. of Scand. origin. Cf. Norw., Sw. *nappa* to snatch.]

NAB National Association of Broadcasters.

Nab·a·te·an (nab/ə·tē/ən) *n.* **1.** One of an ancient Arabic people of Palestine. **2.** Their Aramaic language.

Na·blus (nä·blōōs/) The chief town of Samaria, in Israeli-occupied Jordan; pop. about 42,000; ancient *Shechem.*

na·bob (nā/bob) *n.* **1.** A European who has become rich in India. **2.** Any very rich or powerful man. **3.** A nawab, viceroy, or governor in India under the old Mogul empire. [< Hind. *nawwāb* < Arabic *nuwwab*, pl. of *nā'ib* viceroy] — **na·bob·er·y** (nā/bob/ər·ē, nä·bob/ər·ē), **na/bob·ism** *n.*

Na·bo·kov (nä/bə·kof/, nä·bô/kôf) Vladimir Vladimirovich, born 1899, U.S. novelist and poet, born in Russia.

Na·both (nā/both) In the Bible, the owner of a vineyard that Ahab coveted. I *Kings* xxi.

NACA National Advisory Committee for Aeronautics.

na·celle (nə·sel/) *n.* *Aeron.* A separate enclosure on an aircraft, especially one for an engine. [< F, small boat < LL *navicella*, dim. of L *navis* ship]

na·cre (nā/kər) *n.* Mother-of-pearl. [< F < Ital. *naccara* < Arabic *naqqāra* drum] — **na·cre·ous** (nā/krē·əs), *adj.*

N.A.D. National Academy of Design.

Na·Dene (nä·dēn/) *n.* A group of related North American Indian languages comprising Athapascan, Haida, and Tlingit. Also **Na·Dé·né/** (-dā·nā/).

Na·der (nā/dər), Ralph, born 1934, U.S. advocate of consumers' rights.

na·dir (nā/dər, -dir) *n.* **1.** The point of the celestial sphere directly beneath the position of an observer, and opposite to the zenith. **2.** The lowest possible point: opposed to *zenith.* [< MF < Arabic *nazīr* (*as-samt*) opposite (the zenith)]

nae (nā) *adj. & adv. Scot.* No; not.

nae·void (nē/void), **nae·vus** (nē/vəs) See NEVOID, NEVUS.

nag¹ (nag) *v.* **nagged, nag·ging** *v.t.* **1.** To bother or annoy by repeatedly urging, scolding, carping, etc.; harass. **2.** To keep in a state of agitation or discomfort by continually impinging on one's consciousness, as an idea, ache, image, etc.: The memory *nags* him. — *v.i.* **3.** To urge, scold, or carp continually. **4.** To provoke discomfort or pain by continually impinging on one's consciousness: often with *at.* — *n.* One who nags, especially a woman. [< Scand. Cf. Sw. and Norw. *nagga* to gnaw.] — **nag/ger** *n.* — **nag/ging·ly** *adv.*

nag² (nag) *n.* **1.** A pony or small horse used for riding. **2.** Any horse. **3.** An old, broken-down, or worthless horse. [ME *nagge*; origin uncertain. Cf. OE *hnægan* to neigh]

na·ga·na (nə·gä/nə) *n. Vet.* An infectious disease of horses and other domestic animals in Africa. [< Zulu]

Na·ga·ri (nä/gə·rē) *n.* **1.** Any one of a group of vernacular alphabets in India. **2.** Devanagari (which see).

Na·ga·sa·ki (nä·gä·sä·kē) A port city on NW Kyushu island, Japan; largely destroyed by a U.S. atomic bomb, Aug. 9, 1945; pop. 422,000 (est. 1968).

Na·go·ya (nä·gō·yä) A city on south central Honshu island, Japan, on Ise Bay; pop. 2,036,000 (est. 1970).

Nag·pur (näg/pŏŏr) A city in NE Maharashtra, India, former capital of Madhya Pradesh; pop. 876,020 (est. 1969).

Nagy·vá·rad (nôd/y'·vä/rôd) The Hungarian name for ORADEA.

Nah. Nahum.

Na·ha (nä·hä) The capital of the Japanese prefecture of Ryukyu Islands, on the SW coast of Okinawa; pop. 257,177 (1965).

Na·hua (nä/wä) *n.* *pl.* **·hua** One of a group of Indian peoples of Mexico and Central America of the Uto-Aztecan stock, including the Aztecs, Toltecs, etc. — *adj.* Designating or pertaining to the Nahua: also **Na/huan.**

Na·hua·tl (nä/wät/l) *n.* **1.** The Uto-Aztecan language of the Aztecs and certain other Indian peoples. **2.** The peoples whose native language is Nahuatl. — *adj.* Of or pertaining to Nahuatl or the people who speak it.

Na·hua·tlan (nä/wät·lən) *n.* **1.** A branch of the Uto-Aztecan linguistic family of North and Central American Indians, including the Aztec dialects. **2.** Nahuatl. — *adj.* Of or pertaining to Nahuatl or Nahuatlan.

Na·hum (nā/əm, -hum) Seventh-century B.C. Hebrew prophet. — *n.* A book of the Old Testament containing his prophecies. [< Hebrew, comfort]

nai·ad (nā/ad, nī/-) *n.* *pl.* **·ads** or **·a·des** (-ə·dēz) **1.** In classical mythology, one of the water nymphs who were believed to dwell in and preside over fountains, brooks, springs, rivers, lakes, and wells. **2.** *Entomol.* The aquatic nymphal stage in the life cycle of certain insects. **3.** *Bot.* Any of a genus (*Naias*) of aquatic plants common in the United States. [< L < Gk. *Naias, -ados.* Akin to Gk. *naein* to flow.]

na·if (nä·ēf/) *adj. French* Masculine form of NAIVE. Also **na·if/.**

nail (nāl) *n.* **1.** A slender piece of metal, usually pointed at one end and broadened at the other, used for driving into or through wood, etc., so as to hold or fasten one piece to another or to project as a peg. **2.** Something resembling a nail in shape or function. **3.** A thin, horny plate growing on one side of the ends of the fingers and toes of men and other primates. **4.** An animal part corresponding to the nail of a primate in structure or composition, as a claw, talon, or hoof. **5.** A unit of length for measuring cloth, equal to 2¼ inches. — **hard as nails** **1.** In good physical condition; tough; rugged. **2.** Not to be moved by sentiment, pity, etc.; unfeeling; merciless. — **to hit the nail on the head** To do or say something exactly to the point. — *v.t.* **1.** To fasten or fix in place with a nail or nails. **2.** To close up or shut in by means of nails: often with *up.* **3.** To secure or make certain through quick or decisive action: often with *down:* to *nail* down a contract. **4.** To fix firmly or immovably: Terror *nailed* him to the spot. **5.** *Slang* To catch or arrest; intercept: He *nailed* me on my way to lunch. **6.** *Slang* To detect and expose, as a lie or liar. **7.** *Slang* To succeed in hitting or striking. **8.** *Slang* To seize or steal. **9.** To focus or bring to bear on an object or subject, as the eyes, intellect, etc. [OE *nægl*, orig., fingernail.]

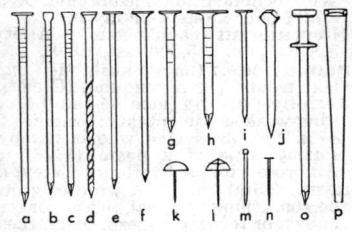

NAILS

a Common. *b* Finishing. *c* Casing. *d* Screw (flooring). *e* Box. *f* Countersunk. *g* Shingle. *h* Roofing. *i* Lath. *j* Horseshoe. *k* Upholstery. *l* Hobnail. *m* Brad. *n* Flathead. *o* Duplex head (for temporary construction). *p* Cut.

nail brush A small brush for cleaning the fingernails.
nail file A small, fine file for shaping the fingernails.
nail·fold (nāl′fōld′) *n. Anat.* The circular fold of skin around the base of a fingernail or toenail; cuticle. For illustration see FINGERNAIL.
nail polish A clear or colored lacquer or other substance applied to the nails to give a glossy finish. Also **nail enamel.**
nail·set (nāl′set′) *n.* A punch for driving the head of a nail below or even with a surface. Also **nail set.**
nain·sook (nān′sŏŏk, nan′-) *n.* A soft, lightweight cotton fabric similar to but heavier than batiste. [< Hind. *nain-sukh,* lit., pleasure of the eye]
nai·ra (nī′rə) *n.* The monetary unit of Nigeria, equivalent to 100 kobo.
Nairn (nârn) A county in NE Scotland; 163 sq. mi.; pop. 7,991 (est. 1969); county seat, Nairn, pop. 5,000 (est. 1969). Also **Nairn′shire** (-shir).
Nai·ro·bi (nī-rō′bē) The capital of Kenya, in the SW part; pop. 535,200 (est. 1970).
na·ive (nä-ēv′) *adj.* **1.** Having an unaffected or simple nature that lacks worldly experience; candid; artless. **2.** Lacking or revealing the lack of deliberate or careful analysis; uncritical: a *naive* idea. **3.** Uninstructed: a *naive* observer. Also **na·ïve′.** — *Syn.* See INGENUOUS. [< F, fem. of *naïf* < L *nativus* natural, inborn < *nasci* to be born. Doublet of NATIVE.] — **na·ive′ly** *adv.* — **na·ive′ness** *n.*
na·ive·té (nä-ēv′tā′, nä-ēv′tā) *n.* **1.** The state or quality of being naive. **2.** An incident, remark, etc., of a naive character. Also **na·ive·té′, na·ive·ty** (nä-ēv′tē). [< F]
na·ked (nā′kid) *adj.* **1.** Having no clothes or garments on; nude. **2.** Having no covering, or lacking the usual covering; exposed. **3.** Bare or stripped, as of vegetation, furnishings, ornaments, etc.: *naked* ground. **4.** Without addition, adornment, or qualification; plain; stark: the *naked* truth. **5.** Unaided by an optical instrument: the *naked* eye. **6.** Open or exposed to view; undisguised: a *naked* sword; *naked* jealousy. **7.** Without defense or protection; vulnerable. **8.** Being without means of sustenance; destitute. **9.** *Law* Lacking conditions necessary for validation, as of a contract, promise, etc. **10.** *Bot.* **a** Not enclosed in an ovary or case: said of seeds. **b** Without protective scales: said of buds. **c** Without a perianth: said of flowers. **d** Without leaves: said of stalks. **e** Having no hairs; smooth: said of leaves. **11.** *Zool.* Lacking fur, hair, feathers, etc. [OE *nacod*] — **na′ked·ly** *adv.* — **na′ked·ness** *n.*
naked eye The eye unaided by optical instruments.
N.Am. North American.
NAM or **N.A.M.** National Association of Manufacturers.
Na·ma (nä′mä) *n.* **1.** A dialect of the Hottentot language. **2.** One of a tribe of Hottentots of southern Africa: also **Na·ma·qua** (nə-mä′kwə).
nam·a·ble (nā′mə-bəl) *adj.* **1.** Capable of being named. **2.** Worthy of mention; memorable. Also **name′a·ble.** — **nam′a·bil′i·ty** or **name′a·bil′i·ty** *n.*
Na·man·gan (nə-män-gän′) A city in the eastern Uzbek S.S.R.; pop. 175,000 (est. 1970).
nam·ay·cush (nam′ə-kush, -ā-) *n. Canadian Rare* The lake trout. [< Algonquian (Cree) *namekus*]
nam·by-pam·by (nam′bē-pam′bē) *adj.* **1.** Full of or exhibiting weak sentimentality; insipid. **2.** Timid and irresolute. — *n., pl.* **·bies** One who is namby-pamby. [< *Namby-Pamby,* title of a poem (1726), referring satirically to Ambrose Philips, by Henry Carey, died 1743.]
name (nām) *n.* **1.** A word or group of words by which a person, thing, animal, class, or concept is distinctively known or referred to; especially, the proper appellation of a person or family. **2.** A usually derogatory word or phrase evaluating character or quality: to call someone *names.* **3.** Popular or general reputation: to have a bad *name.* **4.** A famous or important person, organization, or thing: a big *name* in industry. **5.** Mere semblance or outward form, as distinguished from essence or actuality: a wife in *name* only **6.** The sacred and powerful appellation of God or a god or goddess. **7.** Fame or distinction; eminence: to seek *name* and position. *Abbr. n.* — **by the name of** Named. — **in the name of 1.** For the sake of: *in the name of* peace. **2.** By the authority of: *in the name of* the Queen. — **to make a name for oneself** To achieve distinction or fame. — **to one's name** Of one's own: He hasn't a friend *to his name.* — *v.* **named, nam·ing** *v.t.* **1.** To give a name to; call; entitle; style; term. **2.** To mention or refer to by name; cite. **3.** To give the name of; identify. **4.** To fix or determine; specify: to *name* the day. **5.** To designate for a particular job, duty, or office; nominate; appoint. — *adj.* **1.** Having or known by a name. **2.** *U.S. Informal* Having high prestige or popularity; famous: a *name* performer. **3.** Lending its title to a collection or miscellany: the *name* story. [OE *nama.* Cf. OHG *namo,* ON *namn,* L *nomen,* Gk. *onoma.*] — **nam′er** *n.*
— *Syn.* (noun) *Name, appellation, designation, title, style, cognomen, eponym,* and *moniker* denote a word, words, or phrase by which a person or thing is called. *Name* is fairly general, being used of both persons and things, but it is also specific, in that we think of a *name* as being peculiarly appropriate to its object in some sense, whether familial, legal, traditional, taxonomic, etc. *Appella-*

tion is more general than *name;* it refers to that by which any entity is called, and so includes nicknames, epithets, pseudonyms, and the like, that are usually separate and distinct from proper *names.* A *designation* is an arbitrarily given *name* that serves to distinguish one thing or kind from others in the same class. *Title* has many shades of meaning; it may be the *designation* given to a book, painting, drama, or other creative work, or a *designation* that indicates office or rank, and is added to a personal *name.* A *style* is also a *designation,* usually of some corporate entity, and is largely limited to legal usage. *Cognomen,* originally a personal surname, is now used in the general sense of a personal *appellation;* personal *names* (frequently modified), when used to designate a whole people, race, era, culture, etc., are *eponyms. Moniker* is a slang term close in meaning to *appellation;* it refers to that by which a person is identified, as a *name,* nickname, signature, or the like. Compare NICKNAME, PSEUDONYM.
name day The feast day of the saint for whom one is named.
name-drop·ping (nām′drop′ing) *n. Informal* The practice of trying to impress others by referring to prominent people as friends or acquaintances. — **name′-drop′per** *n.*
name·less (nām′lis) *adj.* **1.** Undistinguished or obscure; anonymous: a *nameless* multitude. **2.** That cannot be named; inexpressible; indescribable: *nameless* terror. **3.** Not fit to be spoken of; unmentionable: *nameless* atrocities. **4.** Unmentioned by name: The guilty party shall be *nameless.* **5.** Having no name; especially, having no legal name; illegitimate. — **name′less·ly** *adv.* — **name′less·ness** *n.*
name·ly (nām′lē) *adv.* That is to say; to wit.
name·sake (nām′sāk′) *n.* One who is named after or has the same name as another.
Nam·hoi (näm′hoi′) See FATSHAN.
Na·mib·i·a (nà-mĭb′ē-ə) The official UN name for SOUTH-WEST AFRICA.
N.Am.Ind. North American Indian.
Na·mur (nä-mōōr′, *Fr.* nà-mür′) A commune in south central Belgium; pop. 33,331 (est. 1959). *Flemish* **Na·men** (nä′mən).
nan·a (nan′ə) *n. U.S.* Grandmother: used familiarly, chiefly by children.
Nan·chang (nän′chäng′) The capital of Kiangsi Province, SE China; pop. 900,000 (est. 1970).
Nan·cy (nan′sē, *Fr.* näN-sē′) A city in NE France; pop. 121,910 (1968).
Nan·da De·vi (nun′dä dā′ve) A mountain in northern Uttar Pradesh, India; 25,645 ft.
Nan·ga Par·bat (nung′gä pûr′bət) A mountain in western Kashmir; 26,660 ft.
nan·ism (nan′iz-əm) *n.* Abnormal smallness; dwarfishness. [< F *nanisme* < L *nanus* dwarf < Gk. *nānos*]
nan·keen (nan-kēn′) *n.* **1.** A buff-colored Chinese cotton fabric. **2.** *pl.* Clothes made of nankeen. **3.** A buff or yellowish color: also **nankeen yellow.** Also **nan·kin′** (-kēn′). [after *Nanking,* where originally made]
Nan·king (nan′king′, nän′-) A port city in eastern China, on the Yangtze; former capital of Kiangsu Province; capital of China, 1928–37; pop. 1,450,000 (est. 1968).
Nanking porcelain A Chinese porcelain painted in blue on white. Also **Nankeen porcelain.**
Nan Ling (nän′ ling′) A mountain chain in SE China, on the northern border of Kwangtung Province: also *Nan Shan.*
Nan·ning (nän′ning′) A city in southern China; former capital of Kwangsi Province; pop. 375,000 (est. 1970).
nan·ny (nan′ē) *n., pl.* **·nies 1.** *Informal* A female goat: also **nanny goat.** **2.** *Brit.* A child's nurse. [after *Nanny,* a personal name, dim. of *Ann*]
nano- *combining form* **1.** Exceedingly or abnormally small: *nanoplankton.* **2.** In the metric system and in technical usage, one billionth of (a specified unit). Also, before vowels, **nan-.** [< Gk. *nānos* dwarf]
na·no·plank·ton (nā′nə-plangk′tən, nan′ə-) *n.* Floating plant and animal organisms of microscopic size. Also **nan′no·plank′ton** (nan′ə-). [< NANO- + PLANKTON]
Nan·sen (nän′sən), **Fridtjof,** 1861–1930, Norwegian Arctic explorer, naturalist, and humanitarian.
Nansen passport A passport issued by the League of Nations after World War I to persons having no official status of nationality. [after F. *Nansen*]
Nan Shan (nän′ shän′) **1.** A mountain range in Tsinghai and Kansu provinces, China. **2.** See NAN LING.
Nantes (nants, *Fr.* näNt) A city in western France, on the Loire; pop. 253,105 (1968). — **Edict of Nantes** An order granting religious freedom and political equality to the Huguenots, issued by Henry IV of France in 1598 and revoked by Louis XIV in 1685.
Nan·tuck·et (nan-tuk′it) An island and summer resort off the SE coast of Massachusetts; 57 sq. mi.
Na·o·mi (nā-ō′mē, nā′ə-mē, -mī) In the Bible, the mother-in-law of Ruth. *Ruth* i 2. [< Hebrew, my delight]
nap¹ (nap) *n.* A short sleep; doze. — *v.i.* **napped, nap·ping 1.** To take a nap; doze. **2.** To be unprepared or off one's guard. [OE *hnappian* to doze. Akin to OHG *hnaffezen.*]
nap² (nap) *n.* **1.** The short fibers forming a downy or fuzzy surface on flannel and certain other fabrics. **2.** A covering resembling this, as upon some plants. — *v.t.* **napped, nap·ping** To raise a nap on. [< MDu. *noppe*]

nap

nap³ (nap) *n.* Napoleon (def. 3).

na·palm (nā′päm) *n.* A jellylike mixture that is combined with gasoline to form an incendiary fuel, as in bombs, flame throwers, etc. [< *na(phthenic)* and *palm(itic) acids*, chemical compounds used in its manufacture]

nape (nāp) *n.* The back of the neck [Origin uncertain]

na·per·y (nā′pər·ē) *n.* *pl.* **·per·ies** household linen, especially napkins, tablecloths, etc. [< F *naperie* < *nape.*]

See NAPKIN.

Naph·ta·li (naf′tə·li, -lē) In the Old Testament, a son of Jacob and Bilhah, Rachel's maid. Geby the tribe of Naphtali. [< Hebrew, my wrestling]

naph·tha (naf′thə, nap′-) *n.* The land occupied by the tribe of Israel. **2.** Any similar volatile, colorless petroleum distillate intermediate source, as from coal tar. **3.** used as a solvent, cleaning in gasoline and benzene, substance obtained from any < Persian *naft petroleum*]

Petroleum. [< L < Gk, *n.* *Chem.* A colorless.

naph·tha·lene (naf′thə·lēn) *n.* $C_{10}H_8$, obtained from coal-tar distillates and us making of dyes, moth balls, etc.: also called *tar* odorous crystalline hy. Also **naph·tha·line** (-lin, -lēn)

naph·thene (naf′thēn) *n.* *Chem.* Any of a group of saturated hydrocarbons, general formula C_nH_{2n}.

naph·thol (naf′thol, nap′-) *n.* *Chem.* **1.** Either of two isomeric hydro's, $C_{10}H_7OH$, derived from naphthalene and us pentane and hig dyes. **2.** Any of a class of naphthalene derivatives containing the hydroxyl group. Also **naph·thol** (-pir′). [< NAPTH(ALENE) + -OL²]

tol (nafgarithms (nə·pir′ē·ən) *Math.* The logarithms Sir Charles James, 1782–1853, colonial administrator. — **John**, 1550– mathematician; invented logarithms.

Na·pi·er (nā·pir′ē·ən) *Math.* The logarithms Brit' employing the base *e* (2.71828...): also **Na·pe′ri·an logarithms.** Also **Na·pe′ri·an logarithms.**

Nif (nā′pə·fôrm) *adj.* Turnip-shaped: a *napiform* napus turnip + -FORM]

nap(ăp′kin) *n.* **1.** A small, usually square cloth or d at meals for wiping the hands and mouth or pro- the clothes. **2.** A small piece of toweling or cloth, as: *y Brit.* A diaper. **b** *Scot.* A neckerchief. **c** *Brit. Dial.* A handkerchief. **3.** A sanitary napkin (which see). *napekun*, dim. of OF *nape* < L *mappa* a cloth]

Na·ples (nā′pəlz) A port commune in SW Italy on the **Bay of Naples,** an inlet of the Tyrrhenian Sea; pop. 1,263,400 (est. 1967). *Italian* **Na·po·li** (nä′pō·lē).

na·po·le·on (nə·pō′lē·ən, *Fr.* nȧ·pô·lā·ôN′) *n.* **1.** A rich pastry composed of layers of puff paste filled with cream, custard, etc. **2.** A former French gold coin, equivalent to 20 francs. **3.** A card game in which the highest bidder named trumps; also, a bid to take all five tricks in this game: also called *nap.* [after *Napoleon* Bonaparte]

Na·po·le·on I (nə·pō′lē·ən; *Fr.* nȧ·pô·lā·ôN′) See under BONAPARTE.

Napoleon II See under BONAPARTE.

Napoleon III See under BONAPARTE.

Na·po·le·on·ic (nə·pō′lē·on′ik) *adj.* Characteristic of, pertaining to, or suggesting Napoleon Bonaparte. — **Na·po′le·on′i·cal·ly** *adv.*

Napoleonic Wars See table for WAR.

nappe (nap) *n.* **1.** *Geol.* A recumbent anticline, a portion of which has been moved by overthrusting for a distance of at least a mile. **2.** The sheet of water overlying the top of a weir. **3.** *Geom.* In a cone, one of the two conical surfaces divided by the vertex. [< F, *sheet*]

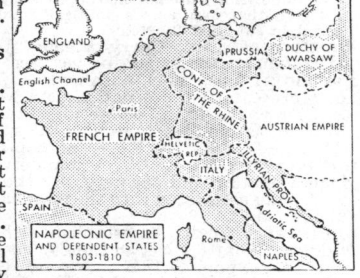

nap·per¹ (nap′ər) *n.* One who takes naps.

nap·per² (nap′ər) *n.* One who or that which raises a nap.

nap·py¹ (nap′ē) *adj.* **·pi·er, ·pi·est 1.** Strong; heady, as ale. **2.** Intoxicated; tipsy. — *n. Scot.* Strong ale or beer.

nap·py² (nap′ē) *adj.* **·pi·er, ·pi·est 1.** Having or coated with nap. **2.** Having a coarse or kinky quality, as hair.

nap·py³ (nap′ē) *n.* *pl.* **·pies** A shallow dish used for cooking or serving food. [OE *hnæp* bowl]

nap·py⁴ (nap′ē) *n.* *pl.* **·pies** *Brit. Informal* A baby's diaper. Also **nap/pie.** [< NAPKIN]

na·prap·a·thy (nə·prap′ə·thē) *n.* *Med.* A system of therapy based on the theory that all disease is caused by disordered ligaments and connective tissue. [< Czechoslovakian *napra-(va)* correction + -PATHY] — **nap·ra·path** (nap′rə·path′) *n.*

Nar·bonne (nȧr·bôn′) A town in S France; pop. 35,236 (1968). Ancient **Nar·bo Mar·ti·us** (nar′bō mär′shē·əs).

nar·ce·ine (när′si·ēn, -in) *n.* *Chem.* A bitter, crystalline opium derivative, $C_{23}H_{27}NO_8$, used as a hypnotic. Also **nar′ce·in** (-in). [< F (< Gk. *narkē* numbness) + -INE²]

nar·cis·sism (när′sis·əm, när·sis/iz·əm) *n.* **1.** Excessive admiration for or fascination with oneself; self-love. **2.** *Psychoanal.* The infantile stage of development in which the self is the object of one's erotic interest; also, the persistence of this stage into later years. Also **nar·cism** (när′siz·əm). [< NARCISSUS] — **nar′cis·sist** *n.* — **nar′cis·sis/tic** *adj.*

nar·cis·sus (när·sis′əs) *n.* *pl.* **·cis·sus·es** or **·cis·si** (-sis/ī) Any of a genus (*Narcissus*) of bulbous flowering plants of the amaryllis family, including the daffodil and jonquil.

Nar·cis·sus (när·sis′əs) In Greek mythology, a youth who caused the death of Echo by spurning her love. Nemesis caused him to fall in love with his own image in water and pine away for it until he died and changed into the narcissus.

narco- *combining form* Torpor; insensibility: *narcomania.* Also, before vowels, **narc-.** [< Gk. *narkē* numbness]

nar·co·lep·sy (när′kə·lep′sē) *n.* *Pathol.* A condition marked by sudden, uncontrollable attacks of sleep of brief duration.

nar·co·ma·ni·a (när′kō·mā/nē·ə, -mān/yə) *n.* A morbid craving for narcotics. — **nar′co·ma/ni·ac** *adj. & n.*

nar·co·sis (när·kō′sis) *n.* Deep stupor produced by a drug.

nar·co·syn·the·sis (när′kō·sin′thə·sis) *n.* *Psychiatry* Therapy using narcotics to enable the patient to recall and relive painful experiences and minimize their hidden effects.

nar·cot·ic (när·kot′ik) *n.* **1.** A drug, as opium or morphine, that in medicinal doses relieves pain and induces sleep, and in toxic doses causes convulsions, coma, or death. **2.** One who is addicted to the use of narcotics. **3.** Anything that deadens or soothes; an anodyne. — *adj.* **1.** Capable of producing narcosis or stupor. **2.** Pertaining to, like, or induced by a narcotic or narcotics. **3.** Of, relating to, or for narcotic addicts or their treatment. [< L *narcoticus* < Gk. *narkōtikos* < *narkē* torpor] — **nar·cot/i·cal·ly** *adv.*

nar·co·tism (när′kə·tiz/əm) *n.* **1.** The state of being under the influence of narcotics. **2.** Addiction to narcotics. **3.** Narcosis. **4.** Any method or influence inducing narcosis.

nar·co·tize (när′kə·tiz) *v.t.* **·tized, ·tiz·ing** To bring under the influence of a narcotic; stupefy. — **nar′co·ti·za/tion** *n.*

nard (närd) *n.* **1.** Spikenard (def. 1). **2.** Any of several aromatic plants or roots formerly used in medicine. [< OF *narde* < L *nardus* < Gk. *nardos*, prob. < Semitic] — **nar·dine** (när′din, -din) *adj.*

nar·es (nâr′ēz) *n.* *pl.* of **nar·is** (nâr′is) *Anat.* Openings into the nasal cavities; especially, the nostrils. [< L, nostrils] — **nar·i·al** (nâr′ē·əl), **nar·ine** (nâr′in, -īn) *adj.*

Na·rew (nä′ref) A river in the western Belorussian S.S.R. and NE Poland, flowing about 275 miles NW to the Vistula. *Russian* **Na·rev** (nä′ryif).

nar·ghi·le (när′ ə·lā) *n.* A hookah. Also **nar′gi·le, nar′gi·leh.** [< F < Persian *nārgileh* < *nārgil* coconut; because originally made of coconut shell]

nark (närk) *Brit. Slang n.* A stool pigeon. — *v.i.* To spy or inform. [< Romany *nāk* nose]

Nar·ra·gan·set (nar′ə·gan′sit) *n.* *pl.* **·set** or **·sets 1.** One of a tribe of North American Indians of Algonquian stock, formerly inhabiting Rhode Island. **2.** The Algonquian language of this tribe. **3.** One of a breed of small riding horses originally bred in Rhode Island. Also **Nar′ra·gan′sett.**

Nar·ra·gan·sett Bay (nar′ə·gan′sit) An inlet of the Atlantic Ocean in SE Rhode Island.

nar·rate (na·rāt′, nar′āt) *v.* **·rat·ed, ·rat·ing** *v.t.* **1.** To tell or relate, as a story. **2.** To speak in accompaniment and explanation of (a motion picture, television program, etc.). — *v.i.* **3.** To tell a story, etc. [< L *narratus*, pp. of *narrare* to relate] — **nar·ra·tor** or **nar·rat·er** (na·rāt′ər, nar′ā·tər) *n.* — *Syn.* **1.** recount, state, recite.

nar·ra·tion (na·rā′shən) *n.* **1.** The act or technique of narrating. **2.** That which is narrated; narrative. **3.** An account that narrates, as in fiction, history, etc.

nar·ra·tive (nar′ə·tiv) *n.* **1.** Something narrated, as an account, story, or tale. **2.** The act, art, or process of narrating. — *adj.* Of the nature of, pertaining to, or dealing with narration: a *narrative* poem. — **nar′ra·tive·ly** *adv.*

nar·row (nar′ō) *adj.* **1.** Having little width, especially in comparison with length; not wide or broad. **2.** Limited or small, as in extent or scope: *narrow* space; *narrow* ambition. **3.** Lacking breadth of vision or tolerance; illiberal. **4.** Nearly unsuccessful or disastrous; precarious: a *narrow* escape. **5.** Exhibiting or characterized by small means or resources; straitened: *narrow* circumstances. **6.** Minute or detailed: careful; painstaking: *narrow* search. **7.** *Brit. Dial.* Stingy; tight-fisted; niggardly. **8.** *Phonet.* Tense. — *v.t. & v.i.* To make or become narrow or narrower, as in width or scope. — *n.* **1.** *Usually pl.* A narrow passage; especially, the narrowest part of a strait, isthmus, etc. **2.** A narrow or contracted part, as of a street or valley. — **The Narrows 1.** A

---

strait connecting Upper New York Bay with Lower New York Bay, between the western end of Long Island and Staten Island. **2.** The narrowest part of the Dardanelles. [OE *nearu*] — **nar'row·ness** *n.*

nar·row-gauge (nar'ō-gāj') *adj.* **1.** Designed for or having a width of railroad track less than the standard gauge of 56½ inches. **2.** *U.S. Informal* Petty; narrow-minded. Also **nar'- row-gage', nar'row-gaged', nar'row-gauged'.**

narrow gauge A narrow-gauge railway, locomotive, or car. Also **narrow gage.**

nar·row·ly (nar'ō-lē) *adv.* **1.** Barely; hardly. **2.** So as to be narrow. **3.** In a narrow manner.

nar·row-mind·ed (nar'ō-mīn'did) *adj.* Having or characterized by narrow views or sentiments; illiberal; bigoted. — **nar'row-mind'ed·ly** *adv.* — **nar'row-mind'ed·ness** *n.*

nar·thex (när'theks) *n. Archit.* **1.** In early Christian and Byzantine churches, a porch or vestibule just inside the main entrance, and at the opposite end from the altar. **2.** Any vestibule leading to the nave of a church. [< Gk. *narthēx*, orig., a plant with a hollow stalk]

Nar·va (när'vä, *Russ.* när'və) A city in the NE Estonian S.S.R.; pop. 43,600 (1959).

Nar·vá·ez (när-vä'eth), **Pánfilo de,** 1478?–1528, Spanish conquistador defeated by Cortés in Mexico; explored Florida.

nar·whal (när'wəl, -hwəl) *n.* A large, arctic cetacean (*Monodon monoceros*), having in the male a long, straight, spiral tusk, and valued for its oil and ivory. Also **nar'wal, nar·whale** (när'wāl', -hwāl'). [< Dan. or Sw. *narhval*]

nar·y (nâr'ē) *adj. Dial.* Not one; never a: opposed to *ary*.

NASA National Aeronautics and Space Administration.

na·sal[1] (nā'zəl) *adj.* **1.** Of or pertaining to the nose. **2.** *Phonet.* Produced with the voice passing partially or wholly through the nose, as (m), (n), and (ng), and the French nasal vowels. **3.** Characterized by or suggestive of a sound so produced. — *n.* **1.** *Phonet.* A nasal sound. **2.** *Anat.* A part of the nose, as a bone. [< NL *nasalis* < L *nasus* nose] — **na·sal·i·ty** (nā-zal'ə-tē) *n.* — **na'sal·ly** *adv.*

na·sal[2] (nā'zəl) *n.* A nosepiece of a helmet. [< OF *nasal*, *nasel* < L *nasus* nose]

nasal index A number expressing the ratio of the greatest breadth of the nose (multiplied by 100) to the length.

na·sal·ize (nā'zəl-īz) *v.* **·ized, ·iz·ing** *v.t.* **1.** To give a nasal sound to. — *v.i.* **2.** To produce nasal or orinasal sounds instead of oral ones. — **na'sal·i·za'tion** *n.*

nas·cent (nā'sənt, nas'ənt) *adj.* **1.** Beginning to exist or develop; newly conceived. **2.** *Chem.* Of, pertaining to, or being in the nascent state. [< L *nascens, -centis,* ppr. of *nasci* to be born] — **nas'cence, nas'cen·cy** *n.*

nascent state *Chem.* The uncombined condition of an atom in its most active state at the moment of its liberation from a compound. Also **nascent condition.**

nase·ber·ry (nāz'ber'ē, -bər·ē) *n. pl.* **·ries** The sapodilla. [< Sp. *níspero* medlar < L *mespilus*]

Nase·by (nāz'bē) A village in Northamptonshire, central England; site of defeat of royalists by Cromwell, 1645.

Nash (nash), **Ogden,** 1902–71, U.S. poet and humorist. — **Thomas,** 1567–1601, English pamphleteer, poet, and dramatist: pseudonym **Pas·quil** (pas'kwil): also **Nashe.**

Nash·u·a (nash'ōō-ə) A city in southern New Hampshire, on the Merrimack River; pop. 55,820.

Nash·ville (nash'vil) The capital of Tennessee, in the north central part, on the Cumberland River; pop. 447,877.

na·si·on (nā'zē-on) *n. Anat.* The point in the skull where the two nasal bones meet the frontal bone. [< NL < L *nasus* nose] — **na'si·al** *adj.*

naso- *combining form* **1.** Nose. **2.** Nasal and: *nasofrontal.* [< L *nasus* nose]

na·so·fron·tal (nā'zō-frun'təl) *adj. Anat.* Of or pertaining to the nasal and frontal bones.

na·so·phar·ynx (nā'zō-far'ingks) *n. pl.* **·pha·ryn·ges** (-fə-rin'jēz) or **·phar·ynx·es** *Anat.* The part of the pharynx above the soft palate and behind the nose. — **na'so·pha·ryn'ge·al** (-fə-rin'jē-əl) *adj.*

Nas·sau (nä'sou *for def.* 1; nas'ô *for def.* 2) **1.** A former duchy in western Germany, now part of Hesse. **2.** The capital of the Bahama Islands, a port on New Providence; pop. 100,000 (est. 1967, with suburbs).

Nas·ser (näs'ər, nas'-), **Gamal Abdel,** 1918–1970, Egyptian army officer and political leader; prime minister 1954–58; president of the United Arab Republic 1958–70.

Nast (nast), **Thomas,** 1840–1902, U.S. political cartoonist born in Germany.

nas·tic (nas'tik) *adj. Bot.* Of, pertaining to, or exhibiting an automatic response of plants, the direction and character of which is determined by internal cellular pressure. [< Gk. *nastos* close-pressed]

-nastic *combining form* Nastic toward or by: *epinastic.*

na·stur·tium (nə-stûr'shəm) *n.* **1.** Any of various garden plants (genus *Tropaeolum*) with funnel-shaped flowers, commonly yellow, orange, or red. **2.** A rich yellow or reddish orange color. [< L, cress < *nasus* nose + *tortus,* pp. of *torquere* to twist; from the pungent odor of the plant]

nas·ty (nas'tē) *adj.* **·ti·er, ·ti·est** **1.** Offensive to the sense of taste or smell; disgusting. **2.** Indecent; obscene: *nasty* lan-

guage. **3.** Disagreeable; disturbing; unpleasant: *nasty* weather; a *nasty* situation. **4.** Mean, spiteful, or ill-natured: a *nasty* remark. **5.** Serious or painful; bad: a *nasty* cut. **6.** Filthy or offensive; dirty. [< Du. *nestig* or Sw. *naskug* filthy] — **nas'ti·ly** *adv.* — **nas'ti·ness** *n.* — **Syn. 1.** foul, nauseating. **2.** gross, vulgar.

-nasty *combining form Biol.* An automatic response to a (specified) stimulus in a (specified) direction or character: *epinasty.* [< Gk. *-elos* close-pressed]

nat. **1.** National. **2.** Native. **3.** Natural. **4.** Naturalist.

na·tal (nāt'l) *adj.* **1.** Of or pertaining to one's birth; dating from birth. **2.** *Poetic* Native: said of a place. [< L *natalis* < *nasci* to be born]

Na·tal (nə-tal'; *for def.* 1 nā-tal') **1.** A Province of eastern South Africa; 33,578 sq. mi.; cap. Pietermaritzburg; pop. 2,933,447 (1960); capital, Pietermaritzburg. **2.** A seaport of Rio Grande do Norte, NE Brazil (including Zululand); pop. 172,667 (est. 1958). **2.** The capital and a port on the Atlantic.

na·tal·i·ty (nā-tal'ə-tē, nā-) *n.* Birth rate. Also **na'tal·ness.**

na·tant (nā'tənt) *adj.* Floating; swimming.

na·ta·tion (nā-tā'shən) *n.* The art or act of swimming in water. [< L *natatio, -onis < natare* to swim]

na·ta·to·ri·um (nā'tə-tôr'ē-əm, -tō'rē-ə) *n. pl.* **·to·ri·ums** or **·to·ri·a** (-tôr'ē·ə, -tō'rē·ə) A place for swimming, especially indoors; a swimming pool. — **na·ta'tion·al** *adj.*

na·ta·to·ry (nā'tə-tôr'ē, -tō'rē) *adj.* **1.** Adapted for swimming, or characteristic of swimming. **2.** Adapted, especially as an organ. Also **na'ta·to'ri·al.**

Natch·ez (nach'iz) *n. pl.* **Natch·ez** One belonging to, or a member of, a tribe of American Indians of Muskhogean stock, formerly living in the lower Mississippi valley.

Natch·ez (nach'iz) A port city in SW Mississippi, on the Mississippi River; pop. 19,704.

na·tes (nā'tēz) *n.pl.* The buttocks. [< L, pl. of *natis*]

Na·than (nā'thən) In the Bible, a prophet who chid David for the death of Uriah. II *Sam.* xii 1. [< Hebrew *nāthān* he gave]

Na·than (nā'thən), **George Jean,** 1882–1958, U.S. editor and dramatic critic.

Na·than·a·el (nə-than'ē-əl, -than'yəl) A disciple of Jesus. *John* xxi 2. [< Hebrew, gift of God]

nathe·less (nāth'lis, nath'-) *Archaic adv.* Nevertheless. — *prep.* Notwithstanding. Also **nath'less** (nath'lis).

Na·tick (nā'tik) A town in NE Massachusetts; pop. 31,057.

na·tion (nā'shən) *n.* **1.** A body of persons associated with a particular territory, usually organized under a government, and possessing a distinctive cultural and social way of life. **2.** A body of persons having a common origin and language. **3.** A tribe or federation, especially of American Indians; also, the territory it occupies. [< F < L *natio, -onis* birth, race < *nasci* to be born]

— **Syn. 1.** *Nation, state, country,* and *land* denote a people and the portion of the earth they inhabit. A *nation* is primarily the people under one government; a *state* is an independent *nation.* The words are often interchanged, but *nation* stresses ethnic unity, while *state* stresses political autonomy. We may speak of the many *nations* that made up the ancient Roman *state. Country* is primarily geographical, a region of the earth distinct from others by its topographical features or political character; Montenegro is a *country,* but no longer a *state.* Since *country* is used loosely for *nation* or *state, land* is often preferable to indicate a region that cuts across political boundaries: the *land* of the midnight sun. See PEOPLE.

Na·tion (nā'shən), **Carry Amelia,** 1846–1911, *née* Moore, U.S. temperance leader and lecturer: also *Carrie Nation.*

na·tion·al (nash'ən-əl, nash'nəl) *adj.* **1.** Of, belonging to, or representative of a nation as a whole: *national* anthem. **2.** Characteristic of or peculiar to a particular nation. **3.** *Rare* Nationalistic. — *n.* A subject or citizen of a nation. Abbr. *nat., natl.* [< F] — **na'tion·al·ly** *adv.*

national bank **1.** *U.S.* A commercial bank organized by federal statute and chartered by the national government. **2.** A bank associated with the national finances, as the Bank of France.

national church An established church (which see).

National City A city in the SW corner of California, near San Diego; pop. 43,184.

national committee *U.S.* The executive committee of a political party, responsible for directing campaigns, etc.

national debt The debt owed by any state: also called *public debt.*

National Guard An organized militia force of a State, a Territory, or the District of Columbia, maintained in part by the U.S. government and subject to federal service in national emergencies. Abbr. *NG, N.G.*

National Guard of the United States That part of the U.S. Army or Air Force reserve consisting of federally recognized units and members of the National Guard.

national income The aggregate income of a nation over a specified period of time, usually a year, consisting of salaries, wages, profits, dividends, rent, interest, etc.

na·tion·al·ism (nash'ən-əl-iz'əm, nash'nəl-) *n.* **1.** Devotion, often chauvinistic, to one's own nation and its political and economic interests or aspirations, social and cultural traditions, etc. **2.** The belief or doctrine that among nations the common welfare is best served by independent rather than collective or cooperative action: distinguished from *internationalism*. **3.** A desire or movement for national independence.

na·tion·al·ist (nash/ən-əl-ist, nash/nəl-) *n.* One who advocates or practices nationalism. — *adj.* Of or pertaining to nationalists or nationalism: also **na/tion·al·is/tic.** — **na/tion·al·is/ti·cal·ly** *adv.*

Nationalist China See the Republic of China under CHINA.

na·tion·al·i·ty (nash/ən-al/ə-tē) *n. pl.* **·ties 1.** A body of people having the same traditions, language, or ethnic origin, and potentially or actually constituting a nation. **2.** The state, quality, or fact of being related to a particular nation, as by birth or citizenship. **3.** National character or quality. **4.** The fact or quality of existing as a nation; national independence.

na·tion·al·ize (nash/ən·əl·īz/, nash/nəl-) *v.t.* **·ized, ·iz·ing 1.** To place (the industries, resources, etc., of a nation) under the control or ownership of the state. **2.** To make national, as in character or scope. **3.** To accept as a national; naturalize. Also *Brit.* **na/tion·al·ise/.** — **na/tion·al·i·za/tion** *n.* — **na/tion·al·iz/er** *n.*

National Labor Relations Board A U.S. government board empowered to investigate and compel correction of unfair labor practices. *Abbr. NLRB, N.L.R.B.*

National League See under MAJOR LEAGUE.

Nation of Islam See under BLACK MUSLIM.

national park A tract of land preserved and maintained by a national government because of its historical or scientific interest, great natural beauty, etc.

National Road The Cumberland Road (which see).

National Socialism See under NAZI.

na·tion-wide (nā/shən·wīd/) *adj.* Extending throughout the nation.

na·tive (nā/tiv) *adj.* **1.** Born in a particular place or region: a *native* New Yorker. **2.** Linked to one by birth or by conditions existing at the time and place of one's birth: *native* land; *native* language. **3.** Produced, originated, or grown in a particular region or country; not foreign; indigenous. **4.** Of, pertaining to, or characteristic of any particular area or its inhabitants: *native* New England architecture. **5.** Natural rather than acquired; inborn: *native* shrewdness. **6.** Of, pertaining to, or characteristic of the original inhabitants, chiefly nonwhites, of areas recently discovered or settled by foreigners: *native* ritual. **7.** Characterized by naturalness or simplicity: the peasants' *native* charm. **8.** Occurring in nature in a pure state; also, not obtained artificially: *native* copper. **9.** *Archaic* Closely related, as by birth. — *n.* **1.** A permanent or lifelong resident of a country or region. **2.** One who was born or that which was produced in a specified country or place. **3.** An original inhabitant of a country or region; aborigine. **4.** An animal, plant, or mineral found only in a specified country or place. *Abbr. nat.* [< F *natif* < L *nativus* < *nascito* be born. Doublet of NAIVE.] — **na/tive·ly** *adv.* — **na/tive·ness** *n.*

— **Syn.** (adj.) **1, 3.** *Native, indigenous, endemic, aboriginal,* and *autochthonous* describe persons or things that belong to the place where they are found. That which is born or produced in a place is *native* to it; yet the word may also be used of things which have been naturalized in a place, so that we may speak of the coffee plant as *native* to Brazil although it was introduced into that country from Africa several hundred years ago. *Indigenous* is more restricted than *native*, in that it excludes the possibility of introduction from elsewhere; the kangaroo is *indigenous* to Australia. *Endemic* is used of plants or diseases that are *native* to a place and seem peculiarly adapted to flourish there. *Aboriginal* is chiefly used of human beings, and designates the peoples inhabiting a region at the earliest known historical time. *Autochthonous* is applied to rock and minerals, and indicates that they were produced where they are found, rather than brought in by some external agency, as a glacier.

native bear *Austral.* The koala.

na·tive-born (nā/tiv-bôrn/) *adj.* Born in the region or country specified.

Native States See INDIAN STATES.

na·tiv·ism (nā/tiv-iz/əm) *n.* **1.** The favoring of native-born persons over the foreign-born. **2.** *Philos.* The doctrine of innate ideas. — **na/tiv·ist** *n.* — **na/tiv·is/tic** *adj.*

na·tiv·i·ty (nā-tiv/ə-tē, nə-) *n. pl.* **·ties 1.** Birth, especially with regard to the time, place, or circumstances surrounding it; origin. **2.** In astrology, a horoscope taken at the time of one's birth. [< OF *nativite* < L *nativitas*]

Na·tiv·i·ty (nā-tiv/ə-tē, nə-) *n. pl.* **·ties 1.** The birth of Christ: preceded by *the*. **2.** A representation of the birth of Christ. **3.** Christmas Day.

natl. National.

NATO (nā/tō) North Atlantic Treaty Organization.

na·tri·um (nā/trē-əm) *n.* Sodium. [< NL < F *natron*. See NATRON.]

nat·ro·lite (nat/rə-līt, nā/trə-) *n. Mineral.* A white or colorless, orthorhombic zeolite occurring in needlelike crystals: also called *needlestone*. [< NATRON + -LITE]

na·tron (nā/tron) *n. Mineral.* A hydrous sodium carbonate, $Na_2CO_3 \cdot 10H_2O$, found in solution in salt lakes and crystallizing in the monoclinic system. [< F < Sp. *natrón* < Arabic *natrūn, nitrūn* < Gk. *nitron* niter]

nat·ter (nat/ər) *v.i. Brit.* To chatter idly or fretfully.

nat·ty (nat/ē) *adj.* **·ti·er, ·ti·est** Neat and smart, as in dress or appearance: a *natty* vest. — **Syn.** See NEAT[1]. [? Akin to NEAT[1]] — **nat/ti·ly** *adv.* — **nat/ti·ness** *n.*

nat·u·ral (nach/ər·əl, nach/rəl) *adj.* **1.** Produced by or existing in nature; not artificial: a *natural* bridge. **2.** Of, pertaining to, or involving nature or the study of nature. **3.** Derived from or defined by nature: *natural* day. **4.** Belonging to or existing in one's nature; not acquired; innate: *natural* talent. **5.** Being so because of one's inherent ability, disposition, etc.: a *natural* athlete. **6.** Conforming to nature or to its usual or expected course; not exceptional; normal: death from *natural* causes. **7.** Closely resembling nature; free from distortion; lifelike: a *natural* pose. **8.** Untouched by man or by the influences of civilization; wild; untutored: *natural* passions. **9.** Free from affectation or awkwardness; not forced; easy: *natural* manner. **10.** Derived from or consistent with the nature or essence of a thing; reasonable or expected: *natural* conclusion; *natural* tendency. **11.** *Music* **a** Not sharped or flatted. **b** Denoting a scale or mode that is unaltered by accidentals. **c** Denoting instruments without valves or keys, especially brass instruments. **12.** Physical or actual, as distinguished from spiritual, etc.: *natural* man. **13.** Determined by innate moral conviction: *natural* rights. **14.** Related by blood rather than through adoption: *natural* mother. **15.** Founded upon reason rather than faith: *natural* religion. **16.** Born out of wedlock: *natural* child. — **Syn.** See NORMAL. — *n.* **1.** *Music* **a** A note that is affected by neither a sharp nor a flat. **b** A character (♮) that cancels a sharp or flat at a specific line or space on the staff. **2.** In keyboard musical instruments, a white key. **3.** *U.S. Informal* One who or that which is naturally gifted, especially well suited to some purpose, or obviously destined for success. **4.** *Archaic* One who is subnormal in intellect; an idiot. *Abbr. nat.* [< F *naturel* < L *naturalis* < *natura* nature, character. See NATURE.] — **nat/u·ral·ness** *n.*

Natural Bridge A rock-and-earth natural bridge over Cedar Creek in western Virginia; span, 90 ft.; width, 50–100 ft.; height, 215 ft.

Natural Bridges National Monument A region in SE Utah with three natural bridges; 4 sq. mi.; established 1908.

natural childbirth Childbirth conducted as a relaxed, relatively painless natural function; also, the prenatal program that prepares the mother physically and psychologically for such childbirth.

natural gas A gas consisting chiefly of methane, generated naturally in underground oil deposits and used as a fuel.

natural gender See under GENDER.

natural history 1. The observation and study of the phenomena of the material universe, especially the biological and earth sciences. **2.** The sum of knowledge regarding such phenomena.

nat·u·ral·ism (nach/ər·əl·iz/əm, nach/rəl-) *n.* **1.** Close adherence to nature in literature, painting, etc.; especially, the doctrine or belief that life should be represented in works of art with an objectivity comparable to that employed in scientific description. **2.** The quality or effect of a work of art created in accordance with such a doctrine. **3.** *Philos.* The doctrine that all phenomena are derived from natural causes and can be explained by scientific laws without reference to a plan or purpose. **4.** *Theol.* The doctrine that all religious truth stems from the natural world and can be attained without the aid of revelation. **5.** Action or thought derived exclusively from natural desires and instincts.

nat·u·ral·ist (nach/ər·əl·ist, nach/rəl-) *n.* **1.** One who is versed in natural history, as a zoologist or botanist. **2.** An adherent of the doctrine of naturalism. *Abbr. nat.*

nat·u·ral·is·tic (nach/ər·əl·is/tik, nach/rəl-) *adj.* **1.** Of, according to, or characteristic of naturalism. **2.** In accordance with or closely resembling nature. **3.** Of or pertaining to naturalists or natural history.

nat·u·ral·ize (nach/ər·əl·īz/, nach/rəl-) *v.* **·ized, ·iz·ing** *v.t.* **1.** To confer the rights and privileges of citizenship upon, as an alien. **2.** To adopt (a foreign word, custom, etc.) into the common use of a country or area. **3.** To adapt (a foreign plant, animal, etc.) to the environment of a country or area. **4.** To attribute to natural rather than supernatural causes; explain by natural laws: to *naturalize* a miracle. **5.** To make natural or lifelike. — *v.i.* **6.** To become as if native; adapt. **7.** To observe or study nature. Also *Brit.* **nat/u·ral·ise/.** [< MF *naturaliser*] — **nat/u·ral·i·za/tion** *n.*

natural law A rule of conduct supposed to be inherent in man's nature and discoverable by reason alone.

natural logarithms Napierian logarithms (which see).

nat·u·ral·ly (nach/ər·əl·ē, nach/rəl-ē) *adv.* **1.** In a natural, normal, or expected manner. **2.** By inherent nature. **3.** Of course; certainly.

---

natural number *Math.* A positive integer, as 1,2,3, etc.
natural philosophy **1.** The study of nature in general. **2.** The physical sciences collectively.
natural religion Deism (def. 1).
natural resource *Usually pl.* **1.** A source of wealth provided by nature, as forests, minerals, and water supply. **2.** Any natural ability or talent.
natural science **1.** The sciences collectively that deal with the physical universe. **2.** Any one of these sciences, as biology, chemistry, or physics.
natural selection *Biol.* The process whereby individual variations advantageous to an organism in a certain environment tend to become perpetuated in later generations; survival of the fittest forms.
natural theology Theology that depends for its knowledge of God on a study of nature rather than on revelation.
natural year An astronomical year (which see).
na·ture (nā′chər) *n.* **1.** The fundamental qualities or characteristics that together define the identity of something; essential character: the *nature* of democracy. **2.** *Sometimes cap.* The overall pattern or system of natural objects, existences, forces, events, etc.; also, the principle or power that appears to guide it: laws of *nature*. **3.** The entire material universe and its phenomena. **4.** The basic character or disposition of a person or animal; heart: His is a generous *nature*. **5.** *Sometimes cap.* A force, drive, or tendency that influences or determines the behavior or condition of a person or thing; instinct. **6.** Sort; kind; variety: nothing of that *nature*. **7.** A wild, naked, or uncivilized condition: a state of *nature*. **8.** A particular character or temperament; also, the person possessing it. **9.** Bodily functions, activities, or powers essential to life: a call of *nature*. **10.** That which is within the accepted or legal limits of morality; normality: an act against *nature*. **11.** Natural aspect or appearance, as of a person or scene. **12.** *Theol.* The unregenerate state of man, as distinguished from a state of grace. **— by nature** By birth or disposition; innately. [< OF < L *natura* < *natus*, pp. of *nasci* to be born]
-natured *combining form* Possessing a (specified) nature, disposition, or temperament: *good-natured.*
nature study An elementary study of objects and conditions in nature, especially through field trips.
na·tur·op·a·thy (nā′chə·rop′ə·thē) *n.* A system of treatment that avoids drugs in favor of sunshine, air, massage, etc. [< NATURE + -PATHY] **— na·tur·o·path** (nə·choor′ə·path) *n.* **— na·tur·o·path′ic** *adj.*
Nau·cra·tis (nô′krə·tis) An ancient Greek city in the Nile delta, Egypt. Also **Nau′kra·tis.**
naught (nôt) *n.* **1.** Nothing. **2.** A cipher; zero; the character 0. *— adj.* **1.** *Archaic* Of no value or account; worthless. **2.** *Obs.* Bad; wicked. *— adv.* *Archaic* Not in the least. Also spelled *nought*. [OE *nāwiht* < *nā* not + *wiht* thing]
naugh·ty (nô′tē) *adj.* **·ti·er, ·ti·est** **1.** Mischievous; disobedient; bad: a *naughty* child. **2.** Indecent or improper: a *naughty* word. [< NAUGHT, adj.] **—naugh′ti·ly** *adv.* **— naugh′ti·ness** *n.*
nau·ma·chi·a (nô·mā′kē·ə) *n.* *pl.* **·chi·ae** (-kē·ē) or **·chi·as** **1.** In ancient Rome, a mock sea battle fought before spectators. **2.** A place suitable for such a display, as a flooded arena. Also **nau·ma·chy** (nô′mə·kē). [< L < Gk. *naumachia* sea battle < *naus* ship + *machē* battle]
Nau·pak·tos (nô·pak′təs, näf′päk·tôs) A town in west central Greece, on the Gulf of Corinth; pop. about 7,000: Italian *Lepanto.* Also *Navpaktos.*
nau·pli·us (nô′plē·əs) *n.* *pl.* **·pli·i** (-plē·ī) *Zool.* A larval form of certain crustaceans, usually the first stage after leaving the egg, characterized by an unsegmented body, a median eye, and three pairs of legs. [< L, a kind of shellfish < Gk. *nauplios*]
Na·u·ru (nä·ōō′rōō) An island west of the Gilbert Islands, comprising an independent Republic; 8 sq. mi.; pop. 7,000 (est. 1969); capital, *Nauru*: formerly *Pleasant Island.*
nau·se·a (nô′zē·ə, -zhē·ə, -sē·ə, -shə) *n.* **1.** A sick feeling in the stomach accompanied by an impulse to vomit; queasiness. **2.** Strong disgust or loathing. [< L < Gk. *nausia, nautia* seasickness < *naus* ship]
nau·se·ate (nô′zē·āt, -sē-, -zhē-, -shē-) *v.t. & v.i.* **·at·ed, ·at·ing** To affect with or feel nausea or disgust. [< L *nauseatus*, pp. of *nauseare* < *nausea*] **— nau·se·a′tion** *n.*
nau·seous (nô′shəs, -zhē·əs, -zē·əs, -sē·əs) *adj.* **1.** Affected with nausea; queasy; sick. **2.** Nauseating; disgusting. **— nau′seous·ly** *adv.* **— nau′seous·ness** *n.*
Nau·sic·a·a (nô·sik′ā·ə, -ē·ə) In Homer's *Odyssey,* the Phaeacian princess who finds the shipwrecked Odysseus and guides him to her father, King Alcinoüs, from whom he receives aid to return to Ithaca.
nautch (nôch) *n.* In India, an entertainment consisting chiefly of a dancing exhibition, performed by professional dancing girls called **nautch girls.** [< Hind. *nāch* dance]
naut. Nautical.
nau·ti·cal (nô′ti·kəl) *adj.* Pertaining to or involving ships, seamen, or navigation. **— Syn.** See MARINE. [< L < Gk. *nautikos* < *naus* ship] **— nau′ti·cal·ly** *adv.*

nautical mile See under MILE.
nau·ti·lus (nô′tə·ləs) *n.* *pl.* **·lus·es** or **·li** (-lī) **1.** Any of a group of cephalopod mollusks (genus *Nautilus*) with a spiral shell whose chambers are lined with mother-of-pearl; especially, the **chambered** or **pearly nautilus. 2.** The paper nautilus (which see). [< L < Gk. *nautilos* sailor]

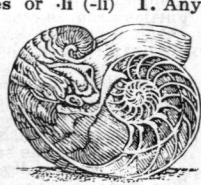

CHAMBERED NAUTILUS
(Cross-section; diameter to 10 inches)

Nau·ti·lus (nô′tə·ləs) *n.* The first atomic-powered submarine, built for the U.S. Navy; made the first undersea crossing of the North Pole, August 3, 1958.
nav. **1.** Naval. **2.** Navigation.
Nav·a·ho (nav′ə·hō) *n.* *pl.* **·hos** or **·hoes** or **·ho** One of a tribe of North American Indians of Athapascan stock, now living on reservations in Arizona, New Mexico, and Utah. Also **Nav′a·jo.**
na·val (nā′vəl) *adj.* **1.** Of, involving, or having a navy: a *naval* power. **2.** Of or pertaining to ships: a *naval* convoy. Abbr. *nav.* **— Syn.** See MARINE. [< L *navalis* < *navis* ship]
naval academy A school where young men are trained for service in the navy; especially, the **U.S. Naval Academy** at Annapolis, Maryland.
Na·var (nā′vär) *n.* *Aeron.* A system of air navigation and control in which ground radar stations transmit their radarscope images to radarscopes in aircraft. [< NAV(IGATION) + (RAD)AR]
Na·varre (nə·vär′, *Fr.* nà·vàr′) **1.** A region and former kingdom in northern Spain and SW France. **2.** A Province of northern Spain; 4,024 sq. mi.; pop. 402,042 (1960); capital, Pamplona. *Spanish* **Na·var·ra** (nä·vär′rä). **— Na·var·rese** (nä′və·rēz′, -rēs′, nav′ə-) *adj. & n.*
nave¹ (nāv) *n.* *Archit.* The main body of a church, situated between the side aisles and usually having a clerestory. [< L *navis* ship]
nave² (nāv) *n.* The hub of a wheel. [OE *nafu.* Cf. NAVEL.]
na·vel (nā′vəl) *n.* **1.** The depression on the abdomen where the umbilical cord was attached; umbilicus. **2.** A central part or point. **3.** *Heraldry* The nombril. [OE *nafela* < *nafu* nave². Akin to G *nabel* and L *umbilicus.*]
navel orange An orange, usually seedless, having a navellike depression that contains a small, secondary fruit.
na·vel·wort (nā′vəl·wûrt′) *n.* **1.** A succulent herb (*Umbilicus pendulinus*) with yellowish or greenish tubular flowers. **2.** Any of various other plants, as the pennywort.
nav·i·cert (nav′ə·sûrt) *n.* *Brit.* A safe-conduct authorizing a vessel of a friendly or neutral nation to pass through a naval blockade. [< NAVI(GATION) + CERT(IFICATE)]
na·vic·u·lar (nə·vik′yə·lər) *Anat.* *n.* **1.** A carpal bone on the proximal row of the radial side of the wrist. **2.** A tarsal bone in front of the talus on the instep of the foot: for illustration see FOOT. Also called *scaphoid*: also **na·vic·u·lar·e** (nə·vik′yə·lā′rē). *— adj.* Shaped like a boat. [< LL *navicularis* < L *navicula,* dim. of *navis* ship]
navig. Navigation.
nav·i·ga·ble (nav′ə·gə·bəl) *adj.* Capable of being navigated; as: **a** Broad or deep enough to admit of passage: said of a body of water. **b** Capable of being steered. [< F < L *navigabilis*] **— nav′i·ga·bil′i·ty, nav′i·ga·ble·ness** *n.* **— nav′i·ga·bly** *adv.*
nav·i·gate (nav′ə·gāt) *v.* **·gat·ed, ·gat·ing** *v.t.* **1.** To travel or move across, over, on, or through, as by ship or aircraft. **2.** To plot the course of (a ship, aircraft, etc.). **3.** To manage or direct the course of; guide: to *navigate* a missile. *— v.i.* **4.** To guide or steer a ship, aircraft, etc. **5.** To compute and plot the course, position, etc., as of a ship or aircraft. **6.** To travel by ship; sail. [< L *navigatus,* pp. of *navigare* < *navis* boat + *agere* to direct]
nav·i·ga·tion (nav′ə·gā′shən) *n.* **1.** The act or practice of navigating. **2.** The art or science of charting the course of ships, aircraft, etc. **3.** Commerce by ship; shipping. Abbr. *nav., navig.* [< L *navigatio, -onis*] **— nav′i·ga′tion·al** *adj.*
navigation light *Aeron.* One of the colored lights on an aircraft, indicating its size, position, and course at night: also called *position light, running light.*
nav·i·ga·tor (nav′ə·gā′tər) *n.* **1.** One who navigates. **2.** One who is trained in or practices navigation. **3.** *Brit.* A navvy. **— Syn.** See PILOT. [< L]
Nav·pak·tos (nav′päk·tôs). See NAUPAKTOS.
nav·vy (nav′ē) *n.* *pl.* **·vies** *Brit.* A laborer, especially in construction work on railways, roads, etc. [< NAVIGATOR]
na·vy (nā′vē) *n.* *pl.* **·vies** **1.** *Often cap.* The entire military sea force of a country, including vessels, servicemen, yards, etc.; also, the agency of government charged with its supervision. **2.** The warships of a nation, taken collectively. **3.** Navy blue. **4.** *Archaic* A fleet of ships. Abbr. *N.* **— United States Navy** The U.S. naval force administered by the Department of the Navy under the Department of Defense, including the Regular Navy, the Naval Reserve, the United States Marine Corps, and the United States Coast Guard when operating as a component of the Navy. Abbr. *USN, U.S.N.* [< OF *navie* < L *navis* ship]

navy bean   A small, dried, white bean related to the common kidney bean. [from its use in the U.S. Navy]
navy blue   A very dark blue: also *navy*.
Navy Cross   A decoration in the form of a bronze cross, awarded by the U.S. Navy for extraordinary heroism in action against the enemy. See DECORATION.
navy yard   A government-owned dockyard for the building, repairing, docking, and equipping of warships.
na·wab (nə-wôb′)   *n.*   **1.** A Moslem ruler or viceroy in India under the Moguls. **2.** Any person of wealth or distinction; a nabob. [< Hind. *nawwāb.* See NABOB.]
Nax·os (nak′sos)   The largest island of the Cyclades group; 169 sq. mi. Formerly **Nax·i·a** (nak′sē-ə).
nay (nā)   *adv.*   **1.** *Archaic* No. **2.** Not exactly that, but rather; not only that, but also; indeed: She is a pretty, *nay,* a beautiful woman. — *n.*   **1.** A negative vote or voter: opposed to *yea.* **2.** A denial or refusal. [ME < ON *nei* < *ne* not + *ei* ever]
na·ya pai·sa (nä-yä′ pī′sä)   *n. pl.* **na·ye pai·se** (nä-yä′ pī-sā′)   A monetary unit and coin of India and Pakistan, equal to one hundredth of a rupee. [< Hind.]
Naz·a·rene (naz′ə-rēn)   *n.*   **1.** A native or inhabitant of Nazareth. **2.** A Christian. **3.** One of a sect of early Christians of Jewish origin who continued to observe much of the Jewish ritual. — **the Nazarene** Jesus Christ. — *adj.* Of or pertaining to Nazareth or the Nazarenes. Also **Naz′a·re′an** (-rē′ən).
Naz·a·reth (naz′ə-rith)   A town in Lower Galilee, northern Israel; scene of Christ's childhood; pop. 26,400 (est. 1963).
Naz·a·rite (naz′ə-rīt)   *n.*   **1.** An ancient Hebrew who took vows of abstinence. *Num.* vi. **2.** Erroneously, a Nazarene. Also **Naz′i·rite.** [< Hebrew *nazīr* < *nāzar* to abstain]
na·zi (nä′tsē, nat′sē, na′zē)   *Often cap.* *n. pl.* **·zis** One who advocates or practices Nazism. — *adj.* Of the nature of, pertaining to, or involving Nazism. [< NAZI]
Na·zi (nä′tsē, nat′sē, na′zē)   *n. pl.* **·zis**   A member of the National Socialist German Workers' Party, founded in 1919, whose fascistic program (called **National Socialism**) was dominant in Germany from 1933 to 1945 under the dictatorship of Hitler, and was characterized by extreme nationalism, militarism, racism, totalitarian direction of all political, economic, and cultural activity, and a belief in German world leadership. — *adj.*   **1.** Of or pertaining to the Nazis or their party. **2.** Caused or committed by Nazis: *Nazi* atrocities. [< G, short for *nationalsozialist* National Socialist] — **Na′zism** or **Na′zi·ism** *n.*
na·zi·fy (nä′tsə-fī, nat′sə-)   *v.t.* **·fied, ·fy·ing** *Often cap.* To subject to Nazi influence or control; cause to be like the Nazis — **na′zi·fi·ca′tion** *n.*
Na·zim·o·va (nə-zim′ə-və), **Alla,** 1879–1945, Russian actress active in the United States.
Nb   *Chem.* Niobium.
N.B.   **1.** New Brunswick. **2.** Note well (L *nota bene*).
NBC   National Broadcasting Company.
NbE   North by east.
NBS or **N.B.S.**   National Bureau of Standards.
NbW   North by west.
N.C.   North Carolina: also **N.Car.** (unofficial).
NCAA or **N.C.A.A.**   National Collegiate Athletic Association.
NCO   Noncommissioned Officer.
Nd   *Chem.* Neodymium.
N.D. or **n.d.**   No date.
N.Dak.   North Dakota: also **N.D.** (unofficial).
N.D.P.   New Democratic Party (Canada).
Ne   *Chem.* Neon.
NE   Northeast.
NEA   National Education Association.
Ne·an·der·thal (nē-an′dər-täl, -thôl; *Ger.* nā-än′dər-täl)   *adj.* Of or characteristic of Neanderthal man.
Ne·an·der·thal·er (nē-an′dər-täl′ər, -thôl′-, -thol′-/)   *n.*   **1.** A Neanderthal man. **2.** Any rude or rugged person.
Neanderthal man   *Anthropol.* An extinct species of man (*Homo neanderthalensis*) that typifies the paleolithic cavedwellers preceding modern man. [< G *Neanderthal,* Neander valley, Germany, where the first bones of this species were found]
neap¹ (nēp)   *adj.* Designating or pertaining to a neap tide. — *n.* A neap tide. [OE *nēp-* in *nēpflōd* low tide]
neap² (nēp)   *n. U.S. Dial.* The harnessing pole of a wagon. [? < Scand. Cf. dial. Norw. *neip* forked pole.]
Ne·a·pol·i·tan (nē′ə-pol′ə-tən)   *adj.* Of, relating to, or characteristic of Naples. — *n.* A native or resident of Naples.
neap tide   The tide occurring shortly after the first and third quarters of the moon, when the rise and fall are minimal: also called *neap.* Compare SPRING TIDE.
near (nir)   *adv.*   **1.** At, to, or within a little distance; not remote in place, time, or degree. **2.** Nearly; almost; approx-

NEANDERTHAL SKULL

imately: a team of *near* championship caliber. **3.** In a close relation; intimately. **4.** Stingily or frugally. — *adj.* **1.** Not distant in place, time, or degree. **2.** Closely approximating; almost achieved: a *near* success. **3.** Narrow; close; precarious: a *near* escape. **4.** Closely related, as by blood: someone *near* and dear. **5.** Closely touching one's interests or affections; intimate: a *near* friend. **6.** That saves distance or time; short; direct. **7.** Stingy; miserly; parsimonious. **8.** On the left: used in riding or driving: the *near* ox: opposed to *off.* — *prep.* Close by or to. — *v.t. & v.i.* To come or draw near (to); approach. — **Syn.** See APPROXIMATE. Abbr. *nr.* [OE *nēar,* compar. of *nēah* nigh] — **near′ness** *n.*
near·by (*adj.* nir′bī′, *adv.* nir′bī′)   *adj. & adv.* Close by; near; adjacent.
Ne·arc·tic (nē-ärk′tik)   *adj.* Of or pertaining to a zoogeographic realm including North America, Greenland, Iceland, and the arctic region. [< NE(O)- + ARCTIC]
Near East   **1.** The countries lying east of the Mediterranean, mostly in SW Asia, including Turkey, Syria, Lebanon, Israel, Jordan, Saudi Arabia, etc., and sometimes the Balkans and Egypt. **2.** *Brit.* The Balkans.
near-hand (nir′hand′)   *Scot. & Brit. Dial. adj.* Close at hand; adjacent. — *adv.* **1.** Nearby. **2.** Nearly; almost.
near·ly (nir′lē)   *adv.* **1.** Almost; practically. **2.** Closely, as in distance, time, degree, similarity, etc.
near rhyme   A rhyme based upon an imperfect or incomplete correspondence of sounds, as on consonance or assonance: also called *half rhyme, oblique rhyme, slant rhyme.*
near·sight·ed (nir′sī′tid)   *adj.* Able to see distinctly at short distances only; myopic. — **near′sight′ed·ly** *adv.* — **near′sight′ed·ness** *n.*
neat¹ (nēt)   *adj.*   **1.** Characterized by or in a state of orderliness, tidiness, and cleanliness. **2.** Free from sloppiness, vagueness, or embellishment; precise. **3.** Ingeniously done or said; clever; smart: a *neat* trick. **4.** Free from admixture; undiluted, as liquor. **5.** Remaining after all deductions; net. **6.** *Slang* Wonderful; splendid. [< OF *net* < L *nitidus* shining] — **neat′ly** *adv.* — **neat′ness** *n.*
— **Syn.** **1.** *Neat, tidy, trim, trig, spruce, dapper,* and *natty* mean pleasing in appearance because clean, orderly, or smart. That which is *neat* is clean, simple, and well cared for, while *tidy* stresses good order or condition. *Trim* combines the meanings of both *neat* and *tidy,* and in addition suggests pictorial attractiveness. *Trig, spruce, dapper,* and *natty* are chiefly applied to persons, and suggest varying degrees of neatness or smartness in dress; *dapper,* however, sometimes has a slightly pejorative overtone, and may imply merely superficial attractiveness. — **Ant.** untidy, disorderly, slovenly, unkempt.
neat² (nēt)   *Obs.* *n.* Bovines collectively; also, a bovine. — *adj.* Pertaining to bovines. [OE *nēat*]
'neath (nēth)   *prep. Dial.* or *Poetic* Beneath. Also **neath.**
neat·herd (nēt′hûrd′)   *n.* *Archaic* A cowherd (which see).
neat's-foot oil (nēts′fŏŏt′)   A pale yellow oil obtained by boiling the shinbones and feet of cattle, used as a lubricant and softening agent for leather.
neb (neb)   *n. Dial.*   **1.** The beak or bill, as of a bird; nose; snout: also *nib.* **2.** The tip end of a thing; nib, as of a pen. **3.** A person's mouth. [OE *nebb*]
NEB or **N.E.B.**   New English Bible.
Nebr.   Nebraska: also **Neb.** (unofficial).
Neb·i·im (neb′i-ēm′, *Hebrew* nə-vē′ēm′)   *n.pl. Hebrew* The Prophets. See under PROPHET.
Ne·bo (nē′bō), **Mount**   A mountain in Moab from which Moses saw the Promised Land just before his death. *Deut.* xxxii 49. See PISGAH.
Ne·bras·ka (nə-bras′kə)   A State in the central United States; 77,237 sq. mi.; pop. 1,483,791; capital, Lincoln; entered the Union Feb. 9, 1867; nicknames, *Tree Planter State* and *Cornhusker State.* Abbr. *Nebr.* — **Ne·bras′kan** *adj. & n.*
Neb·u·chad·nez·zar (neb′yŏŏ-kəd-nez′ər), died 562 B.C., king of Babylonia 605–562 B.C.; conquered Judea and destroyed Jerusalem. II *Kings* xxiv and xxv. Also **Neb′u·chad·rez′zar** (-rez′ər).
neb·u·la (neb′yə-lə)   *n. pl.* **·lae** (-lē) or **·las**   **1.** *Astron.* **a** Any interstellar mass of cloudlike appearance and vast extent, often luminous, and composed of gaseous matter in various degrees of density. **b** A galaxy (def. 1). **2.** *Pathol.* **a** A cloudy spot on the cornea; visual opacity. **b** Cloudiness of the urine. **3.** *Med* A liquid preparation used as a spray. [< L, vapor, mist. Akin to Gk. *nephelē* cloud.] — **neb′u·lar** *adj.*
nebular hypothesis   *Astron.* The hypothesis, as formulated by Laplace, that the solar system was formed from the cooling and consolidation of great masses of matter thrown off in successive rings by a rotating nebula.
neb·u·lize (neb′yə-līz)   *v.t.* **·lized, ·liz·ing**   **1.** To spray (a wound, etc.) with medicated liquid. **2.** To reduce to a spray; atomize. — **neb′u·li·za′tion** *n.* — **neb′u·liz′er** *n.*
neb·u·los·i·ty (neb′yə-los′ə-tē)   *n. pl.* **·ties**   **1.** The state or quality of being nebulous. **2.** A nebula. [< LL *nebulositas*]
neb·u·lous (neb′yə-ləs)   *adj.*   **1.** Vague or confused; unclear; hazy: a *nebulous* idea. **2.** Cloudlike; misty. **3.** Of,

pertaining to, or like a nebula; nebular. [< L *nebulosus*] — **neb′u·lous·ly** *adv.* — **neb′u·lous·ness** *n.*

nec·es·sar·i·ly (nes′ə·ser′ə·lē) *adv.* **1.** As a necessary consequence: Great actors are not *necessarily* handsome. **2.** Of necessity; unavoidably: Taxes must *necessarily* be levied.

nec·es·sar·y (nes′ə·ser′ē) *adj.* **1.** Absolutely essential to accomplish a certain result; essential; indispensable. **2.** Being of such a nature that it must exist or occur; of necessity so; inevitable: a *necessary* belief. **3.** Caused by or acting under obligation or compulsion; required. **4.** That cannot be logically denied. — *n. pl.* **·sar·ies 1.** *Often pl.* That which is indispensable; an essential requisite: the *necessaries* of life. **2.** *pl. Law* Such things necessary for a person's maintenance in a condition suitable to his station in life. **3.** *Dial.* A water closet; privy. [< L *necessarius* < *necesse* needful] — **Syn.** (adj.) *Necessary, essential, indispensable, requisite,* and *needful* refer to a person or thing whose presence is urgently desired or required in a system, series, group, arrangement, etc. A *necessary* thing may supply a wide range of wants, from mere convenience to logical completeness. *Essential* refers to that which is required for the continued existence of a thing; *indispensable* may denote that which is only an adjunct, but which cannot be spared. Air is *essential* to human life; warmth and shelter from the elements are *indispensable*. *Requisite* is a more subjective word pointing to the judgment of a thing's value made by a person who desires it. *Needful* points to a concrete need or want, as for food or money, but is the weakest of these words in degree of urgency; it may take careful planning and a long period of time to provide everything *needful* for a journey. — **Ant.** unnecessary, needless, dispensable, optional.

ne·ces·si·tar·i·an (nə·ses′ə·târ′ē·ən) *adj.* Of or pertaining to necessitarianism. — *n.* One who professes or believes in necessitarianism. Also **nec·es·sar·i·an** (nes′ə·sâr′ē·ən).

ne·ces·si·tar·i·an·ism (nə·ses′ə·târ′ē·ən·iz′əm) *n. Philos.* The doctrine that all acts, including those of the will, are necessarily determined by a fixed progression of causes. Also **nec·es·sar·i·an·ism** (nes′ə·sâr′ē·ən·iz′əm).

ne·ces·si·tate (nə·ses′ə·tāt) *v.t.* **·tat·ed, ·tat·ing 1.** To make necessary: The rain *necessitated* a postponement. **2.** To compel or oblige: No man is *necessitated* to lie. [< Med.L *necessitatus*, pp. of *necessitare* to compel < L *necessitas* necessity] — **ne·ces′si·ta′tion** *n.* — **ne·ces′si·ta′tive** *adj.*

ne·ces·si·tous (nə·ses′ə·təs) *adj.* **1.** Extremely needy; destitute; poverty-stricken. **2.** Urgent; compelling. — **ne·ces′si·tous·ly** *adv.* — **ne·ces′si·tous·ness** *n.*

ne·ces·si·ty (nə·ses′ə·tē) *n. pl.* **·ties 1.** *Often pl.* That which is indispensable or requisite, especially toward the attainment of some end: the *necessities* of life. **2.** The quality, condition, or fact of being necessary: the *necessity* for truth. **3.** The conditions that make compulsory a particular course of action; inescapable obligation: to resign out of *necessity*. **4.** Urgent or desperate need, as because of poverty or accident; also, a time of such need. **5.** That which is unavoidable because it is part of an invariable process, as in nature, logic, etc.; also, the process itself. **6.** *Philos.* The doctrine that all events, including acts of volition, are necessarily determined. — **of necessity** By necessity; inevitably: It is of *necessity* so. [< OF *necessite* < L *necessitas*] — **Syn. 1.** need, exigency, requirement. Compare NECESSARY.

neck (nek) *n.* **1.** *Anat.* **a** The part of an animal that connects the head with the trunk. **b** Any similarly constricted part of an organ, bone, etc.: the *neck* of the uterus. ◆ Collateral adjective: *cervical.* **2.** The narrowed part of an object, especially if near one end: the *neck* of a bottle. **3.** Something likened to a neck, as from its position or shape; as: **a** A narrow passage of water between two larger bodies of water. **b** A narrow strip of land, as a peninsula, isthmus, or cape. **4.** The part of a garment close to or covering the neck. **5.** The part of a violin, guitar, etc., that carries the fingerboard and tuning pegs. **6.** *Archit.* The upper part of the shaft of a column, just below the capital. **7.** *Dent.* The constricted part of a tooth between the crown and the root. **8.** *Printing* The beard. — **neck and crop** Entirely. — **neck and neck** Abreast of one another, as horses in a race; closely contested. — **neck of the woods** *U.S. Informal* A neighborhood or region. — **neck or nothing** Willing to risk all. — **to get it in the neck** To receive the full force of some one's anger, contempt, etc. — **to save one's (own) neck** To extricate oneself from difficult or dangerous circumstances, often without concern for others. — **to win by a neck 1.** In horse racing, to win by the length of a horse's head and neck. **2.** To win by a close margin. — *v.i.* **1.** *U.S. Slang* To kiss and caress in lovemaking. — *v.t.* **2.** *U.S. Slang* To make love to (someone) in such a manner. **3.** To behead or strangle, as a fowl. [OE *hnecca.* Akin to OHG *hnac*, ON *hnakki*.]

neck·band (nek′band′) *n.* **1.** The part of a garment that fits around the neck. **2.** A band around the neck.

neck·cloth (nek′klôth′) *n. Archaic* A necktie.

necked (nekt) *adj.* **1.** Having a neck or necks. **2.** Having or characterized by (a specified kind of) neck or (a specified number of) necks: used in combination: *long-necked.*

Neck·er (nek′ər, Fr. ne·kâr′), **Jacques,** 1732–1804, French statesman and financier born in Switzerland; father of Madame de Staël.

neck·er·chief (nek′ər·chif) *n.* A kerchief for the neck.

neck·ing (nek′ing) *n.* **1.** *U.S. Slang* Kissing and caressing in lovemaking. **2.** *Archit.* A gorgerin.

neck·lace (nek′lis) *n.* An ornament worn around the neck and usually consisting of a string of beads, shells, gems, etc.

neck·line (nek′līn′) *n.* The line or contour formed by the fit of a garment around the neck.

neck·piece (nek′pēs′) *n.* An article of clothing, usually of fur, worn around the neck like a scarf.

neck·tie (nek′tī′) *n.* **1.** A strip of material worn knotted around the neck or collar and hanging down the front of a shirt. **2.** Any bow or tie worn under the chin.

necktie party *U.S. Slang* An execution by hanging, especially by lynching.

neck·wear (nek′wâr′) *n.* Articles worn around the neck, as ties, collars, mufflers, etc.

necro- *combining form* Corpse; the dead; death: *necropolis.* Also, before vowels, **necr-.** [< Gk. *nekros* corpse]

nec·ro·bac·il·lo·sis (nek′rō·bas′ə·lō′sis) *n. Vet.* A disease of cattle, sheep, horses, elk, and swine due to invasion of the body by a bacillus (*Actinomyces* or *Spherophorus necrophorus*) that produces large areas of gangrenous and necrotic tissue.

ne·crol·a·try (ne·krol′ə·trē) *n.* Worship of the dead.

ne·crol·o·gy (ne·krol′ə·jē) *n. pl.* **·gies 1.** A list of persons who have died in a certain place or time. **2.** An obituary notice. **3.** A treatise on or an account of the dead. [< NE-CRO- + -LOGY²] — **nec·ro·log·ic** (nek′rə·loj′ik) or **·i·cal** *adj.* — **nec′ro·log′i·cal·ly** *adv.* — **ne·crol′o·gist** *n.*

nec·ro·man·cy (nek′rə·man′sē) *n.* **1.** The art of divining the future through alleged communication with the dead. **2.** Black magic; sorcery. — **Syn.** See MAGIC. [ME < OF *nygromancie*; infl. by L *necromantia* < Gk. *nekromanteia* < *nekros* corpse + *manteia* divination] — **nec′ro·man′cer** *n.* — **nec′ro·man′tic** *adj.*

ne·croph·a·gous (ne·krof′ə·gəs) *adj.* Subsisting on carrion. [< NECRO- + -PHAGOUS]

nec·ro·phile (nek′rə·fil, -fil) *n.* One who is afflicted with necrophilia. Also **ne·croph·il** (-fil).

nec·ro·phil·i·a (nek′rō·fil′ē·ə) *n.* An abnormal attraction, especially of an erotic nature, to corpses. Also **ne·croph·i·lism** (ne·krof′ə·liz′əm). — **nec′ro·phil′ic** *adj.*

ne·crop·o·lis (ne·krop′ə·lis) *n.* A large burial area for the dead, especially of an ancient city; cemetery. [< Gk. *nekropolis* < *nekros* corpse + *polis* city]

nec·rop·sy (nek′rop·sē) *n. pl.* **·sies** An examination of a dead body; an autopsy. Also **ne·cros·co·py** (ne·kros′kə·pē). [< NECRO- + -OPSY]

ne·crose (ne·krōs′, nek′rōs) *v.t. & v.i.* **·crosed, ·cros·ing.** To affect with or undergo necrosis. Also **nec′ro·tize** (-tīz).

ne·cro·sis (ne·krō′sis) *n.* **1.** *Pathol.* The death of tissue in a living animal, resulting from infection or burns; gangrene. **2.** *Bot.* A disease of plants and trees manifested by the decay and death of tissue. [< Gk. *nekrōsis* death < *nekroein* to make dead] — **ne·crot·ic** (-krot′ik) *adj.*

ne·crot·o·my (ne·krot′ə·mē) *n. pl.* **·mies 1.** The dissection of a dead body. **2.** *Surg.* The excision of dead bone. [< NECRO- + -TOMY]

nec·tar (nek′tər) *n.* **1.** In Greek mythology, the drink of the gods. **2.** Any delicious drink. **3.** *Bot.* The saccharine secretion of plants, collected by bees to make honey. [< L < Gk. *nektar*] — **nec·tar·e·an** (nek·târ′ē·ən), **nec·tar·e·ous** (nek·târ′ē·əs), **nec·tar·ous** (nek′tər·əs) *adj.*

nec·tar·ine (nek′tə·rēn′, nek′tə·rēn) *n.* A variety of peach having a smooth, waxy skin and a firm pulp.

nec·ta·ry (nek′tər·ē) *n. pl.* **·ries 1.** *Bot.* **a** A gland that secretes nectar. **b** The part in which such a gland is situated. **2.** *Entomol.* One of the abdominal tubes by which an aphid secretes honeydew. — **nec·tar·i·al** (nek·târ′ē·əl) *adj.*

NED or **N.E.D.** New English Dictionary (Oxford English Dictionary).

Ne·der·land (nā′dər·länt) The Dutch name for the NETH-ERLANDS.

née (nā) *adj.* Born with the name of: used chiefly to note the maiden name of a married woman: Mrs. Mary Lincoln, *née* Todd. Also **nee.** [< F, pp. fem. of *naître* to be born]

need (nēd) *v.t.* **1.** To have an urgent or essential use for (something lacking); want; require. — *v.i.* **2.** To be in want. **3.** To be obliged or compelled; have to. ◆ In this sense *need* is used as an uninflected auxiliary verb only in questions and in sentences with negative import, followed by the infinitive without *to*: He *need* not go; You *need* hardly ask; *Need* he come? **4.** *Archaic* To be necessary: It *needs* not. — *n.* **1.** The fact, quality, or condition of lacking or feeling the lack of something necessary or desirable. **2.** An intense or compulsive desire or longing: the *need* for revenge. **3.** Obligation; necessity: no *need* to be afraid. **4.** A condition of want, danger, or helplessness: a friend in *need*. **5.** Something wanted or required: modest *needs*. **6.** Poverty; hardship; indigence: in time of *need*. — **Syn.** See NECESSITY, POVERTY. [OE *nīed, nēd.* Akin to OHG *nōt*, ON *nauthr* distress, compulsion.] — **need′er** *n.*

need·ful (nēd′fəl) *adj.* **1.** Needed; requisite; necessary. **2.** *Archaic* Needy. — **Syn.** See NECESSARY. — **need′ful·ly** *adv.* — **need′ful·ness** *n.*

Need·ham (nēd′əm) A town in NE Massachusetts; pop. 29,748.
Need·ham (nēd·əm), **Joseph,** born 1900, English biochemist and philosopher.
need·i·ness (nē′dē·nis, -di·nis) n. The state of being needy; poverty; want.
nee·dle (nēd′l) n. 1. A small, slender, pointed instrument, usually of steel, with an eye at one end to carry thread through fabric in sewing. 2. A hypodermic needle (which see). 3. A pointer or index, as in a gauge or compass. Compare MAGNETIC NEEDLE. 4. A small, pointed instrument of steel, diamond, etc., that traverses the grooves of a phonograph record and transmits sound vibrations: sometimes called *stylus.* 5. A slender rod of steel, bone, etc., pointed at one or both ends and used in knitting; also, a similar rod with a hook at one end used in crocheting. 6. A needle-shaped leaf, as that of a pine tree. 7. Any object suggesting a needle in shape, as a pinnacle of rock, an obelisk, etc. 8. An electric needle (which see). 9. A fine-pointed instrument used in etching. See DRY POINT (def. 1). 10. *Mech.* A needle valve (which see). — **on the needle** *U.S. Slang* Addicted to narcotics. — v. **·dled, ·dling** v.t. 1. To sew or pierce with a needle. 2. *Informal* To tease or heckle repeatedly, especially so as to annoy, embarrass, or goad into action. 3. *U.S. Informal* To increase the alcoholic content of: to *needle* the beer. — v.i. 4. To sew or work with a needle. 5. To crystallize in the form of needles. [OE *nǣdle.* Akin to OHG *nāian* to sew, MDu. *nayen,* ? L *nere* to spin.]
nee·dle·fish (nēd′l·fish′) n. pl. **·fish** or **·fish·es** 1. Any of a family (*Belonidae*) of sea fishes having slender bodies, elongated jaws, and needlelike teeth. 2. The pipefish.
needle grass Feather grass (def. 2).
nee·dle·point (nēd′l·point′) n. 1. A stitch used in the embroidery of canvas, as in a tapestry; also, the embroidery itself. 2. Lace made entirely with a sewing needle rather than bobbins and worked with buttonhole stitches on a paper pattern: also called *point lace.* 3. Anything resembling the point of a needle.
need·less (nēd′lis) adj. Not needed or necessary; useless. — **need′less·ly** adv. — **need′less·ness** n.
nee·dle·stone (nēd′l·stōn′) n. Natrolite.
needle valve *Mech.* A valve having a cone-shaped or needlelike plug that fits into a cone-shaped opening, capable of closely regulating the flow of a liquid or gas.
nee·dle·wom·an (nēd′l·wŏŏm′ən) n. pl. **·wom·en** (-wim′in) A seamstress.
nee·dle·work (nēd′l·wûrk′) n. 1. Work done with a needle, as embroidery. 2. The business or occupation of sewing, crocheting, etc., with a needle. — **nee′dle·work′er** n.
need·n't (nēd′nt) Need not.
needs (nēdz) adv. *Archaic* Of necessity; necessarily: often with *must.* [OE *nīedes,* genitive of *nīed*]
need·y (nē′dē) adj. **need·i·er, need·i·est** Being in need, want, or poverty; necessitous.
neep (nēp) n. *Scot.* & *Brit. Dial.* A turnip. [OE *nǣp* < L *napus*]
ne′er (nâr) adv. *Poetic* Never.
ne′er-do-well (nâr′dōō·wel′) n. A worthless, unreliable person. — adj. Shiftless; good-for-nothing.
ne·far·i·ous (ni·fâr′ē·əs) adj. Extremely wicked; vile; villainous. [< L *nefarius* < *nefas* sin, crime < *ne-* not + *fas* divine law] — **ne·far′i·ous·ly** adv. — **ne·far′i·ous·ness** n.
Ne·fer·ti·ti (ne′fer·tē′tē) Fourteenth-century B.C. Egyptian queen; wife of Ikhnaton: also *Nofretete.*
neg. Negative(ly).
ne·gate (ni·gāt′, nē′gāt) v.t. **·gat·ed, ·gat·ing** 1. To render ineffective or void; nullify. 2. To deny; contradict; rule out. [< L *negatus,* pp. of *negare* to deny]
ne·ga·tion (ni·gā′shən) n. 1. The absence or opposite of something considered affirmative or existent: Sleep is the *negation* of consciousness. 2. The act of denying or contradicting; also, an instance of this. 3. That which is negative; a nullity. [< L *negatio, -onis* < *negatus.* See NEGATE.] — **ne·ga′tion·al, neg′a·to·ry** (-tôr′ē, -tō′rē) adj.
neg·a·tive (neg′ə·tiv) adj. 1. Expressing, containing, or characterized by negation, denial, or refusal: a *negative* reply. 2. Marked by the absence of or opposition to positive or affirmative qualities: a *negative* attitude. 3. Denoting a direction or position opposite to that taken as positive: *negative* rotation. 4. *Math.* Less than zero; to be subtracted; minus: said of quantities and usually denoted by the sign (−). 5. *Electr.* Having the kind of electricity exhibited by a resinous object when rubbed with wool, characterized by an excess of electrons on a charged body. 6. *Med.* Not indicating the presence of a particular disease, organism, etc.: a *negative* blood test. 7. *Biol.* Designating a response directed away from or in opposition to a stimulus. 8. *Photog.* Having the lights and darks reversed. 9. *Chem.* Tending to attract electrons: a *negative* element. 10. *Logic* Affirming that all or part of one class of things is excluded from another class: a *negative* proposition. — n. 1. *Photog.* An image showing

the lights and darks reversed; also, the film or plate on which it appears and from which positive prints are made. 2. An expression of denial or refusal, as by word or gesture. 3. The side of a question that denies or contradicts what the other side affirms, as in a debate. 4. *Math.* A negative symbol or quantity. 5. *Electr.* A negative pole, plate, terminal, etc. 6. Any object or impression that is the inverse of another, as a mold made from a sculpture. 7. *Gram.* A negative particle, as *not.* 8. *Archaic* The right to veto. — adv. No; not so: a military usage. — **double negative** *Gram.* The use of two negatives in the same statement, as in "I didn't see nobody." ◆ This usage is a descendant of a formation native to the Germanic languages and was regularly used in Old and Middle English to intensify negation. It survives in Modern English, but is now considered nonstandard on analogy with Latin, where a double negative becomes an affirmative. Such statements as "I am not unhappy," however, are standard English and have the effect of weak affirmatives. — **in the negative** 1. By or with an expression of refusal; no: to answer *in the negative.* 2. On the negative or opposing side. — v.t. **·tived, ·tiv·ing** 1. To refuse to sanction or support, as a bill or a candidate for office; reject; veto. 2. To deny; contradict. 3. To prove to be false; disprove. 4. To make ineffective; counteract. [< F < L *negativus* < *negare* to deny] — **neg′a·tive·ly** adv. — **neg′a·tive·ness, neg′a·tiv′i·ty** n.
negative angle *Geom.* An angle measured clockwise from the reference line.
negative correlation *Stat.* A correlation in which the large values of one variable tend to be accompanied by small values of another variable: also called *inverse correlation.*
negative number A number preceded by the minus sign, as −3, −7, etc.
neg·a·tiv·ism (neg′ə·tiv·iz′əm) n. 1. An attitude or body of opinions characterized by the denial or questioning of traditional beliefs; skepticism. 2. A tendency to deny, contradict, oppose, etc. 3. *Psychol.* An attitude or type of behavior characterized by resistance to suggestion. — **neg′a·tiv·ist** n. & adj. — **neg′a·tiv·is′tic** adj.
Neg·ev (neg′ev, ne·gev′) A triangular desert region in southern Israel; 4,700 sq. mi. Also **Neg·eb** (neg′eb, nə·geb′). [< Hebrew *South*]
neg·lect (ni·glekt′) v.t. 1. To fail to heed or take note of; disregard: They *neglected* their father's advice. 2. To fail to give proper attention to or take proper care of: to *neglect* one's business. 3. To fail to do or perform, as through carelessness or oversight; leave undone. — n. 1. Habitual want of attention or care; negligence. 2. The act of neglecting, or the state of being neglected. 3. An instance of neglect. [< L *neglectus,* pp. of *negligere* < *nec-* not + *legere* to gather] — **neg·lect′er** or **neg·lec′tor** n.
— **Syn.** (verb) *Neglect, disregard, ignore,* and *overlook* mean to give little or no attention to a specified person or object. *Neglect* always indicates a culpable omission: to *neglect* one's studies, to *neglect* household duties. *Disregard* may refer to a culpable or a justifiable omission, by deliberation or by oversight: he *disregarded* the warning, this theory *disregards* some of the known data. *Ignore* always implies a deliberate disregard of a fact or action: to *ignore* an insult, to *ignore* a greeting. *Overlook* usually indicates oversight and lack of conscious intent; it may also be used, however, as a close synonym of *ignore,* with a connotation of leniency or concession: to *overlook* one item in paying a bill, to *overlook* an injury. — **Ant.** heed, attend (to), care (for), cherish. — (noun) 1, 2. *Neglect, negligence, dereliction,* and *remissness* denote a failure to give due attention or care, and they all imply culpability. *Neglect* refers to the act, and *negligence* to the disposition, of one who does not give due attention; of the two, *neglect* is the stronger word. *Neglect* of one's appearance suggests slovenliness, while *negligence* as to one's appearance indicates only a lack of smartness. *Dereliction* is reprehensible *neglect* of duty or responsibility. *Remissness* is a milder word for *dereliction,* indicating either omission or poor performance of duty.
neg·lect·ful (ni·glekt′fəl) adj. Exhibiting or indicating neglect: often with *of.* — **neg·lect′ful·ly** adv. — **neg·lect′ful·ness** n.
neg·li·gee (neg′li·zhā′, neg′li·zhā) n. 1. A loose, flowing, usually decorative dressing gown worn by women. 2. Any informal or negligent attire. Also **neg′li·gé,** *French* **né·gli·gé** (nā·glē·zhā′). — adj. Carelessly or negligently dressed. [< F *négligé,* pp. of *négliger* to neglect]
neg·li·gence (neg′lə·jəns) n. 1. The state, quality, or fact of being negligent. 2. A negligent act or omission. 3. *Law* Unreasonable or imprudent action or failure to act; especially, the failure to take reasonable precautions to avoid injury to persons or property. — **Syn.** See NEGLECT. [< OF]
neg·li·gent (neg′lə·jənt) adj. 1. Habitually neglecting to do what ought to be done; neglectful. 2. Free-and-easy; informal; nonchalant. [< L *negligens, -entis,* ppr. of *negligere.* See NEGLECT.] — **neg′li·gent·ly** adv.
neg·li·gi·ble (neg′lə·jə·bəl) adj. Not worth considering, as because of trifling size, amount, or extent. — **neg′li·gi·bil′-i·ty, neg′li·gi·ble·ness** n. — **neg′li·gi·bly** adv.

ne·go·ti·a·ble (ni·gō′shē·ə·bəl, -shə·bəl) *adj.* **1.** Capable of being negotiated. **2.** Open to negotiation. **3.** That can be legally transferred to another party by endorsement or delivery: *negotiable* instruments. — **ne·go′ti·a·bil′i·ty** *n.*

ne·go·ti·ate (ni·gō′shē·āt) *v.* **·at·ed, ·at·ing** *v.i.* **1.** To bargain or confer with another party or parties with the aim of reaching an agreement. — *v.t.* **2.** To arrange or conclude by negotiation: to *negotiate* a treaty; to *negotiate* the sale of a property. **3.** To transfer (a note, bond, etc.) to another for a value received; sell; assign. **4.** To manage to execute, traverse, or cope with (something difficult): to *negotiate* a steep hill. [< L *negotiatus*, pp. of *negotiari* to do business < *negotium* business < *nec* not + *otium* leisure] — **ne·go′ti·a·tor** *n.* — **ne·go′ti·a·to/ry** *adj.*
— **Syn. 1.** deal, parley, dicker, consult.

ne·go·ti·a·tion (ni·gō′shē·ā′shən) *n.* **1.** The act or process of negotiating. **2.** A conference or discussion designed to produce an agreement.

Ne·gress (nē′grəs) *n.* A female Negro: usually considered an offensive term. [< F *négresse* < L *niger* black]

Ne·gri Sem·bi·lan (nā′grē sem·bē·län′) A state in Malaysia, in the SW part of the Malay peninsula; 2,565 sq. mi.; pop. 488,318 (1968); capital, Seremban.

Ne·grit·ic (ni·grit′ik) *adj.* Of, pertaining to, or having the characteristics of Negroes or Negritos.

Ne·gri·to (ni·grē′tō) *n.* *pl.* **·tos** or **·toes** *Anthropol.* **1.** A Pygmy of central Africa. Also **Ne·gril′lo** (-gril′ō). **2.** One of the Pygmy peoples of the Malay Peninsula, the Philippine Islands, and other parts of southeast Asia. [< Sp., dim. of *negro* black < L *niger*] — **Ne·gri·toid** (nē′gri·toid) *adj.*

ne·gri·tude (nē′grə·tōōd′, -tyōōd′) *n.* *Often cap.* **1.** Awareness of and pride in one's black African heritage. **2.** Black African or Negro values and culture. **3.** The fact of being a Negro; Negroness. Also *French* **né·gri·tude** (nā′grə·tüd′). [< F *négritude* < *nègre* Negro < L *niger*]

Ne·gro (nē′grō) *n.* *pl.* **·groes 1.** A member of the Negroid ethnic division of mankind, especially one inhabiting the Congo and Sudan regions of Africa. **2.** One who is of Negroid stock or has Negro ancestors. — *adj.* **1.** Of, pertaining to, or having the characteristics of a Negro or Negroes. **2.** Of Negroid ethnic stock. Also **ne′gro.** [< Sp. < L *niger*, neuter *nigrum* black]

Ne·gro (nā′grō), **Río** See RÍO NEGRO.

Ne·groid (nē′groid) *adj.* **1.** *Anthropol.* Of, pertaining to, or belonging to a major ethnic division of the human species characterized by skin color ranging from dark brown to almost black, hair black and usually woolly or frizzly, slight body hair, a broad or flat nose, full, often everted lips, and a generally prognathous face. **2.** Resembling, related to, or characteristic of Negroes. — *n.* A Negroid person.

Ne·gro·ness (nē′grō·nis) *n.* The fact or condition of being a Negro.

Ne·gros (nā′grōs) One of the Visayan Islands, Philippines; 4,905 sq. mi.

ne·gus (nē′gəs) *n.* A drink made of wine, hot water, and lemon juice, sweetened and flavored with spices. [after Col. Francis *Negus*, died 1732, the inventor]

Ne·gus (nē′gəs) *n.* A title of the ruler of Ethiopia.

Neh. Nehemiah.

Ne·he·mi·ah (nē′hə·mī′ə) Fifth-century B.C. Hebrew statesman and historian. — *n.* A book of the Old Testament describing the rebuilding of Jerusalem: also, in the Douai Bible, II *Esdras*. [< Hebrew *Nehemyāh* Jehovah comforts]

Neh·ru (nā′rōō), **Ja·wa·har·lal** (jə·wä′hər·läl), 1889–1964, Indian nationalist leader and statesman; first prime minister 1947–1964. — **Motilal,** 1861–1931, Indian nationalist and statesman; father of the preceding: called **Pandit Nehru.**

neif (nēf) See NIEVE.

neigh (nā) *v.i.* To utter the cry of a horse; whinny. — *n.* The cry of a horse. [OE *hnǣgan*; imit.]

neigh·bor (nā′bər) *n.* **1.** One who lives near another. **2.** One who or that which is near another. **3.** *Chiefly Dial.* Friend; mister: a term of address. **4.** A fellow human being. — *adj.* Living nearby. — *v.t.* **1.** To live or be near to or next to; adjoin: Ohio *neighbors* Indiana. **2.** To bring or locate near to. — *v.i.* **3.** To live or be nearby. **4.** To associate with a neighbor in a friendly way; be sociable. Also *Brit.* **neigh′bour.** [OE *nēahgebur* < *nēah* near + *gebur* dweller < *ge* together + *būr* dwelling]

neigh·bor·hood (nā′bər·hŏŏd) *n.* **1.** A comparatively small populated region or district possessing some quality or character that distinguishes it from other areas. **2.** The community of people who live in such a region. **3.** Any region or area considered as distinct from other areas; vicinity. **4.** The quality or condition of being near; proximity. **5.** *Archaic* Friendly relations. Also *Brit.* **neigh′bour·hood.** — **in the neighborhood of 1.** In the vicinity of; near. **2.** *Informal* Approximately: *in the neighborhood of* $30,000.
— **Syn. 1.** locality, section. **4.** Nearness.

neigh·bor·ing (nā′bər·ing) *adj.* Situated or living nearby; adjacent. — **Syn.** See ADJACENT.

neigh·bor·ly (nā′bər·lē) *adj.* Acting in a way appropriate to good neighbors; kind, considerate, sociable, etc. — **neigh′bor·li·ness** *n.* — **Syn.** See AMICABLE.

Neil·son (nēl′sən), **William Allan,** 1869–1946, U.S. educator and scholar born in Scotland.

Neis·se (nī′sə) A river in Czechoslovakia, East Germany, and Poland, flowing 140 miles to the Oder: Polish *Nysa*.

neist (nēst) *adj., adv., & prep. Brit. Dial. & Scot.* Next; nearest. [OE *nēhst*]

nei·ther (nē′thər, nī′-) *adj.* Not the one nor the other; not either: *Neither* eye has perfect vision. — *pron.* Not the one nor the other: *Neither* of the hats is becoming. — *conj.* **1.** Not either; not: used with the correlative *nor* to list alternatives and to signify their negation: He *neither* reads nor writes. **2.** Nor yet: He cannot write; *neither* can he read. — *adv. Illit. & Dial.* Any more so: used in place of *either* after the denial of an alternative, or to emphasize a preceding negative: No one else can do it *neither*. ♦ See usage note under EITHER. [ME *naither, neyther* < OE *nāhwæther*]

Nejd (nejd) A Province of Saudi Arabia comprising a viceroyalty; about 450,000 sq. mi.; pop. about 4 million; capital, Riyadh.

nek·ton (nek′tən) *n. Biol.* The aggregate of marine animal organisms capable of swimming freely, relatively independent of currents, waves, etc., ranging in size from microorganisms to whales. Compare PLANKTON. [< NL < Gk. *nēktos,* neuter *nēkton* swimming] — **nek·ton′ic** *adj.*

nel·son (nel′sən) *n.* One of several wrestling holds, as the full nelson or half nelson. [? < *Nelson*, personal name]

Nel·son (nel′sən), **Viscount Horatio,** 1758–1805, English admiral; killed at the battle of Trafalgar.

Nelson River A river in NE Manitoba, Canada, flowing 400 miles NE from Lake Winnipeg to Hudson Bay.

ne·lum·bo (ni·lum′bō) *n. pl.* **·bos** A member of a genus (*Nelumbo*) of aquatic herbs of the water-lily family, as the water chinkapin and the sacred lotus of India. Also **ne·lum·bi·um** (ni·lum′bē·əm). [< NL < Singhalese *nelumbu*]

Ne·man (nye′mən) A river in the Byelorussian and Lithuanian S.S.R., flowing 597 miles, generally west, to the Baltic: Polish *Nieman*, Lithuanian *Nemunas*, German *Memel*.

nem·a·thel·minth (nem′ə·thel′minth) *n. Zool.* One of a phylum or major division (*Nemathelminthes*) of worms having a round, slender, unsegmented body, and including the nematodes. Also **nem′a·tel′minth** (-tel′-). [< NL < Gk. *nēma, -matos* thread + *helmins, -inthos* worm]

nemato- *combining form* Thread; filament: *nematocyst*: also, before vowels, **nemat-**. Also **nema-**. [< Gk. *nēma, -matos* thread]

nem·a·to·cyst (nem′ə·tō·sist′) *n. Zool.* One of the cells in jellyfishes, polyps, and other hydrozoans that contain a long filament whose instantaneous release gives a sharp sting: also called *nettle cell*. — **nem′a·to·cys′tic** *adj.*

nem·a·tode (nem′ə·tōd) *Zool. adj.* Of or belonging to a phylum or class (*Nematoda*) of roundworms having a mouth and intestinal canal, and including some specimens parasitic in man and other animals, as the hookworm. — *n.* A nematode worm. [< NL *Nematoda*]

Ne·me·a (nē′mē·ə, nə·mē′ə) A valley in ancient Argolis, Greece; celebrated for the **Nemean** games, one of the four great pan-Hellenic festivals. — **Ne·me′an** *adj.*

Nemean lion In Greek legend, a fierce lion that Hercules strangled as one of his twelve labors.

ne·mer·te·an (ni·mûr′tē·ən) *Zool. adj.* Of or belonging to a phylum or class (*Nemertinea*) of unsegmented nonparasitic flatworms, having ciliated skin and a rectractile proboscis, and living chiefly in mud or sand near the sea. — *n.* A nemertian flatworm: also called *ribbon worm*. Also **ne·mer′ti·an, ne·mer·tine** (nem′ər·tən, -tēn), **ne·mer·tin·e·an** (nem′-ər·tin′ē·ən). [< NL < Gk. *Nēmertēs*, a sea nymph]

nem·e·sis (nem′ə·sis) *n. pl.* **·ses** (-sēz) **1.** An unusually tenacious or fearsome opponent or antagonist. **2.** An instrument of just retribution or vengeance. [< Gk., retributive justice < *nemein* to distribute]

Nem·e·sis (nem′ə·sis) In Greek mythology, the goddess of retributive justice or vengeance. [< NEMESIS]

ne·mi·ne con·tra·di·cen·te (nem′ə·nē kon′trə·di·sen′tē) *Latin* No one opposing; unanimously.

ne·mi·ne dis·sen·ti·en·te (nem′ə·nē di·sen′shē·en′tē) *Latin* No one dissenting; unanimously.

Ne·mu·nas (nye′mŏŏ·näs) The Lithuanian name for the NEMAN.

neo- *combining form* **1.** New; recent; a modern or modified form of: *Neo-Platonism*. **2.** *Geol.* Denoting the most recent subdivision of a period: *Neocene*. Also, before vowels, usually **ne-**. [< Gk. < *neos* new]

ne·o·ars·phen·am·ine (nē′ō·ärs′fen·ə·mīn, -fen·ə·mēn) *n. Chem.* A modified compound of arsphenamine, $C_{13}H_{13}O_4N_2$·SAs_2Na, similarly used, but less toxic and more soluble.

Ne·o·cene (nē′ə·sēn) *adj. Geol.* Of or pertaining to the later of the two epochs into which the Tertiary was formerly divided, or to the corresponding strata. — *n.* The Neocene epoch, equivalent to the Miocene and Pliocene taken together. Also **Ne′o·gene** (-jēn). [< NEO- + Gk. *kainos* new]

ne·o·clas·sic (nē′ō·klas′ik) *adj.* Of, pertaining to, or denoting a revival of classical style in literature, art, music, etc. Also **ne′o·clas′si·cal.**

ne·o·clas·si·cism (nē′ō·klas′ə·siz′əm) *n.* **1.** A revival of classical style in literature, art, etc. **2.** *Often cap.* A neo-classical movement of the late 17th and 18th centuries in European literature, art, etc. — **ne′o·clas′si·cist** *n.*

Ne·o-Dar·win·ism (nē′ō-där′win·iz′əm) *n. Biol.* Darwinism as modified by more recent students, who hold that evolution is a consequence of natural selection and that acquired characteristics are not inheritable. — **Ne′o-Dar′win′i·an** (-där·win′ē·ən) *adj. & n.* — **Ne′o-Dar′win·ist** *n.*

ne·o·dym·i·um (nē′ō-dim′ē·əm) *n.* A metallic element (symbol Nd) forming rose-colored salts, found in combination with cerium and other elements of the lanthanide series. See ELEMENT. [< NEO- + (DI)DYMIUM]

Ne·o·gae·a (nē′ō-jē′ə) *n.* A zoogeographical realm coextensive with the Neotropical region. [< NEO- + Gk. *gaia* earth] — **Ne′o·gae′an** *adj.*

Ne·o-He·bra·ic (nē′ō-hē-brā′ik) *n.* The form of the Hebrew language used in Hebraic literature after the Bible. — *adj.* Pertaining to post-Biblical Hebrew.

ne·o·im·pres·sion·ism (nē′ō·im-presh′ən·iz′əm) *n.* The doctrines and methods of a group of artists of the late 19th century, derived from impressionism but based on a more strictly scientific practice. Compare POINTILLISM, POSTIMPRESSIONISM. — **ne·o·im·pres′sion·ist** *n. & adj.*

Ne·o-La·marck·ism (nē′ō·lə-mark′iz·əm) *n. Biol.* Lamarckism as modified by students who hold that acquired characteristics can be inherited and thus influence the course of evolution. Also **Ne′o-La·marck′i·an·ism** (-ē·ən·iz·əm). — **Ne′o-La·marck′i·an** *adj. & n.* — **Ne′o-La·marck′ist** *n.*

Ne·o-Lat·in (nē′ō-lat′n) See under LATIN.

ne·o·lith (nē′ə·lith) *n.* A Neolithic stone implement.

Ne·o·lith·ic (nē′ə·lith′ik) *adj. Anthropol.* Of or pertaining to the period of human culture following the Mesolithic, characterized by a great variety of polished stone implements and the development of new social forms based upon a settled agriculture. [< Gk.*neos* new + *lithos* stone]

ne·ol·o·gism (nē·ol′ə·jiz′əm) *n.* **1.** A new word or phrase. **2.** The use of new words or of new meanings for old words. **3.** A new doctrine, especially in theology. Also called *neology.* [< F *néologisme*] — **ne·ol′o·gis′tic** or **-ti·cal** *adj.*

ne·ol·o·gist (nē·ol′ə·jist) *n.* **1.** One who invents or uses new words, or new meanings for old words. **2.** One who adopts a new doctrine, especially in theology. [< F *néologiste*]

ne·ol·o·gize (nē·ol′ə·jīz) *v.i.* **·gized, ·giz·ing** To use, introduce, or adopt a neologism. [< F *néologiser*]

ne·ol·o·gy (nē·ol′ə·jē) *n. pl.* **·gies** A neologism. [< F *néologie,* ult. < Gk. *neos* new + *logos* word] — **ne·o·log·i·cal** (nē′ə·loj′i·kəl) *adj.* — **ne′o·log′i·cal·ly** *adv.*

Ne·o-Mal·thu·sian (nē′ō·mal·thōō′zhən, -zē·ən) *n.* An advocate of population control through birth control. — *adj.* Of or pertaining to Neo-Malthusians, their doctrines, etc. — **Ne′o-Mal′thu·sian·ism** *n.*

ne·o·my·cin (nē′ə·mī′sin) *n.* An antibiotic related to streptomycin, used in the treatment of certain infections.

ne·on (nē′on) *n.* A gaseous element (symbol Ne) occurring in the atmosphere in very small amounts. See ELEMENT. — *adj.* **1.** Of or pertaining to neon. **2.** Composed of or employing neon, especially in display lights. [< NL < Gk., neut. of *neos* new]

ne·o·or·tho·dox·y (nē′ō·ôr′thə·dok′sē) *n.* A 20th-century Protestant theological movement devoted to reviving traditional doctrines. — **ne′o·or′tho·dox** *adj.*

ne·o·phyte (nē′ə·fīt) *n.* **1.** A recent convert, especially in the early Christian Church. **2.** One who is newly ordained or admitted into a religious or mystic order. **3.** Any novice or beginner. — *Syn.* See CONVERT, NOVICE. [< LL *neophytus* < Gk. *neophytos* newly planted] — **ne′o·phyt′ic** (-fit′ik) *adj.*

ne·o·plasm (nē′ə·plaz′əm) *n. Pathol.* Any abnormal growth of tissue in the body; a tumor. — **ne′o·plas′tic** *adj.*

ne·o·plas·ty (nē′ə·plas′tē) *n. pl.* **·ties** The formation of new parts or the restoration of old parts through plastic surgery. [< NEO- + -PLASTY]

Ne·o-Pla·to·nism (nē′ō·plā′tə·niz′əm) *n.* A system of philosophy elaborated by Plotinus and others in the third century, based chiefly on Platonic concepts modified by the influence of later Greek philosophers and by Oriental thought. Also **Ne′o·pla′to·nism.** — **Ne·o-Pla·ton·ic** (nē′ō·plə·ton′ik) *adj.* — **Ne′o-Pla′to·nist** *n.*

ne·o·prene (nē′ə·prēn) *n. Chem.* Any of various types of synthetic rubber obtained by polymerizing chloroprene. [< NEO- + (CHLORO)PRENE]

Ne·op·tol·e·mus (nē′op·tol′ə·məs) In Greek legend, a son of Achilles: also called *Pyrrhus.*

Ne·o·sal·var·san (nē′ō·sal′vər·san) *n.* Proprietary name for a brand of neoarsphenamine. Also **ne′o·sal′var·san.**

Ne·o-Scho·las·ti·cism (nē′ō·skə·las′tə·siz′əm) *n.* A modern movement to revive and extend Scholasticism, especially that of Thomas Aquinas, and so as to make it more applicable to contemporary problems. — **Ne′o-Scho·las′tic** *adj.*

ne·o·ter·ic (nē′ə·ter′ik) *Rare adj.* Recent in origin. Also **ne′o·ter′i·cal.** — *n.* One of modern times; a modern. [< LL < Gk. *neōterikos* youthful] — **ne′o·ter′i·cal·ly** *adv.*

Ne·o·trop·i·cal (nē′ō·trop′i·kəl) *adj.* Of, pertaining to, or designating a zoogeographical realm that includes Central and South America and the adjacent islands.

Ne·o·zo·ic (nē′ə·zō′ik) *adj. Geol. Rare* The Cenozoic era.

Nep (nep) *n.* The New Economic Policy.

NEP or **N.E.P.** New Economic Policy.

Ne·pal (ne·päl′) A kingdom between Tibet and India; 54,362 sq. mi.; pop. 11,000,000 (1968); capital, Katmandu. See map of TIBET. — **Nep·a·lese** (nep′ə·lēz′, -lēs′) *adj. & n.*

ne·pen·the (ni·pen′thē) *n.* **1.** A drug or potion supposed by the ancient Greeks to banish pain and sorrow. **2.** Anything causing oblivion. [< L *nepenthes* < Gk. *nēpenthes* free from sorrow < *nē-* not + *penthos* sorrow] — **ne·pen′the·an, ne·pen′thic** *adj.*

Neph·e·le (nef′ə·lē) In Greek legend, the wife of Athamas and mother of Phrixus and Helle.

neph·e·line (nef′ə·lin) *n.* A hexagonal sodium aluminum silicate, NaAlSiO₄, found in various igneous rocks. Also **neph′e·lite′** (-līt′). [< F *néphéline* < Gk. *nephelē* cloud]

neph·e·lin·ite (nef′ə·lin·īt′) *n.* A dark gray volcanic rock composed of the minerals nepheline, augite, and magnetite. Also **neph′e·lin·yte′.**

neph·e·lom·e·ter (nef′ə·lom′ə·tər) *n. Physics* An instrument for measuring the quantity or size of particles in suspension, by means of light transmitted or reflected from such particles. [< Gk. *nephelē* cloud + METER] — **neph·e·lo·met·ric** (nef′ə·lə·met′rik) *adj.* — **neph′e·lom′e·try** *n.*

neph·ew (nef′yoo, *esp. Brit.* nev′yoo) *n.* **1.** The son of a brother or brother-in-law or of a sister or sister-in-law Abbr. *n.* **2.** An illegitimate son, as of a churchman: a euphemistic term. **3.** *Obs.* A cousin. [< OF *neveu* < L *nepos* grandson, nephew. Akin to OE *nefa.*]

nepho- *combining form* Cloud: *nephology.* Also, before vowels, **neph-.** [< Gk. *nephos* cloud]

neph·o·gram (nef′ə·gram) *n. Meteorol.* A photograph of a cloud.

neph·o·graph (nef′ə·graf, -gräf) *n. Meteorol.* An electrically operated camera for photographing clouds.

ne·phol·o·gy (ne·fol′ə·jē) *n.* The branch of meteorology that treats of clouds. — **neph·o·log·i·cal** (nef′ə·loj′i·kəl) *adj.*

neph·o·scope (nef′ə·skōp) *n. Meteorol.* An instrument for indicating the direction of cloud movements, especially with a view to determining their velocity.

ne·phral·gi·a (ni·fral′jē·ə, -jə) *n. Pathol.* Pain in the kidney or kidneys. [< NEPHR(O)- + -ALGIA]

ne·phrec·to·my (ni·frek′tə·mē) *n. pl.* **·mies** *Surg.* The removal of a kidney. [< NEPHR(O)- + -ECTOMY]

ne·phrid·i·um (ni·frid′ē·əm) *n. pl.* **·phrid·i·a** (-frid′ē·ə) *Biol.* **1.** A primitive excretory organ in annelid worms, mollusks, and other invertebrates. **2.** The embryonic tube that develops into the kidney in vertebrates. [< NL < Gk. *nephros* kidney] — **ne·phrid′i·al** *adj.*

neph·rism (nef′riz·əm) *n. Pathol.* General ill health caused by chronic kidney disease.

neph·rite (nef′rīt) *n.* A very hard, compact, white to dark green mineral formerly worn as a remedy for diseases of the kidney: also called *kidney stone.* Compare JADE¹. [< G *nephrit* < Gk. *nephros* kidney]

ne·phrit·ic (ni·frit′ik) *adj.* **1.** Of or pertaining to the kidney or kidneys; renal: also **neph′ric. 2.** Of, pertaining to, or suffering from nephritis. Also **ne·phrit′i·cal.** — *n.* Any medicine applicable to disease of the kidney.

ne·phri·tis (ni·frī′tis) *n. Pathol.* Inflammation of the kidneys. [< LL < Gk. *nephros* kidney]

nephro- *combining form* A kidney: *nephrotomy.* Also, before vowels, **nephr-.** [< Gk. *nephros* kidney]

ne·phro·sis (ni·frō′sis) *n. Pathol.* Disease of the kidney, especially one characterized by degenerative lesions of the renal tubules. — **ne·phrot′ic** (-frot′ik) *adj.*

ne·phrot·o·my (ni·frot′ə·mē) *n. pl.* **·mies** *Surg.* Incision into the kidney. [< NL *nephrotomia* < Gk.]

ne plus ul·tra (nē plus ul′trə) *Latin* The extreme or utmost point; perfection; literally, nothing more beyond.

Ne·pos (nē′pos, nep′os), **Cornelius** First-century B.C. Roman historian.

nep·o·tism (nep′ə·tiz′əm) *n.* Favoritism; especially, governmental patronage extended toward relatives: The senator denied the charge of *nepotism.* [< F *népotisme* or Ital. *nepotismo* < L *nepos, -potis* grandson, nephew] — **ne·pot·ic** (ni·pot′ik) *adj.* — **nep′o·tist** *n.*

Nep·tune (nep′toon, -tyoon) In Roman mythology, the god of the sea: identified with the Greek *Poseidon.* — *n.* The fourth largest planet of the solar system and eighth in order from the sun. See PLANET. [< L *Neptunus*]

Nep·tu·ni·an (nep·too′nē·ən, -tyoo′-) *adj.* **1.** Of or pertaining to Neptune or his domain, the sea. **2.** Of or pertaining to the planet Neptune. **3.** *Geol.* Of or pertaining to a theory that the principal rock features of the earth were determined by water: distinguished from *Plutonic.* — **Nep′tun·ist** *adj. & n.*

nep·tu·ni·um (nep·too′nē·əm, -tyoo′-) *n.* A radioactive element (symbol Np), artificially produced from a uranium isotope by neutron bombardment and decaying to plutonium by emission of a beta particle. See ELEMENT.

neptunium series *Physics* A sequence of radioactive elements beginning with plutonium 241 and continuing to the stable isotope bismuth 209: named from its longest-lived member, neptunium 237, with a half life of 2.2 million years.

Ne·re·id (nir′ē·id) *pl.* **Ne·re·i·des** (ni·rē′ə·dēz) or **Ne·re·ids** In Greek mythology, one of the fifty daughters of Nereus, sea nymphs who attend Poseidon. [< L *Nereis, -idis* < Gk. *Nēreis* < *Nēreus*]

ne·re·is (nir′ē·is) *n.* Any of a genus (*Nereis*) of burrowing annelid worms having a long, flattened body and a distinct head: also called *clamworm*. [< L < Gk., *Nēreis*]

Ne·reus (nir′ŏŏs, -ē·əs) In Greek mythology, a sea god, father of the Nereides.

Ne·ri (nā′rē), **Saint Philip**, 1515–95, Italian priest; founded the Oratorians 1564; canonized, 1622: original name **Filippo Romolo de' Neri**. Also **San Filippo de' Neri**.

ne·rit·ic (ni·rit′ik) *adj.* Of or pertaining to the coastline or to shallow water. — **Syn.** See OCEANIC. [? < L *nerita* mussel < Gk. *nērítēs* < *Nēreus*]

Nernst (nernst), **Walther Hermann**, 1864–1941, German physicist and chemist.

Ne·ro (nir′ō), 37–68, Nero Claudius Caesar Drusus Germanicus, Roman emperor 54–68; committed suicide: original name **Lucius Domitius A·he·no·bar·bus** (ə·hē·nō·bär′bus). — **Ne·ro′ni·an**, **Ne·ron·ic** (ni·ron′ik) *adj.*

ner·o·li (ner′ə·lē) *n.* The essential oil distilled from orange blossoms, used in perfumery. Also **neroli oil.** [after Princess *Neroli*, Italian noblewoman said to have discovered it]

ner·va·tion (nûr·vā′shən) *n.* **1.** The arrangement of nerves. **2.** Venation. Also called *neuration*: also **ner·va·ture** (nûr′və·chŏŏr).

nerve (nûrv) *n.* **1.** *Physiol.* Any of the cordlike bundles of nerve fibers that convey impulses of sensation, etc., between the brain or spinal cord and other parts or organs. **2.** Courage or boldness; daring. **3.** *Informal* Arrogant assurance; brashness; effrontery: He has some *nerve*. **4.** *Usually pl.* The source of sensitivity, patience, emotional steadiness, etc.: frayed *nerves*. **5.** *Usually pl.* Unsteadiness of mind and muscle; nervousness: a case of *nerves*. **6.** Muscle; sinew: now only in the phrase **to strain every nerve**. **7.** *Biol.* A nervure. — **to get on one's nerves** *Informal* To irritate; exasperate; upset. — *v.t.* **nerved, nerv·ing** To provide with nerve or nerves. — **to nerve oneself** To summon up one's courage or energy to do something difficult or unpleasant. [< L *nervus* nerve. Akin to Gk. *neuron* sinew.]

nerve cell *Physiol.* A neuron.

nerve center **1.** *Physiol.* An aggregation of neurons having a specific function, as hearing, sight, etc. **2.** The focus of command and communication; headquarters.

nerved (nûrvd) *adj.* Provided with nerve or nerves. Also **ner·vate** (nûr′vāt).

nerve fiber *Physiol.* Any of the threadlike processes called axons and dendrites arising from a neuron and of which a nerve is composed.

nerve gas In chemical warfare: **a** A gas that paralyzes or affects the central nervous system. **b** A gas that causes frivolous and irresponsible behavior among its victims.

nerve impulse *Physiol.* A wave of electrical disturbance propagated along a nerve fiber by a potential difference between the outer and inner layers, and continuing until the resulting current has been discharged into the appropriate sensory or motor channels.

nerve·less (nûrv′lis) *adj.* **1.** Lacking force; feeble. **2.** Completely controlled and calm in crises; cool. **3.** *Anat.* Having no nerves. — **nerve′less·ly** *adv.* — **nerve′less·ness** *n.*

nerve-rack·ing (nûrv′rak′ing) *adj.* Extremely irritating; harrowing. Also **nerve′-wrack′ing.**

ner·vine (nûr′vēn, -vīn) *adj.* **1.** Pertaining to the nerves. **2.** Calming or quieting to the nerves. — *n.* Any medicine that calms or soothes the nerves. [< Med.L *nervinus*]

nerv·ing (nûr′ving) *n. Vet.* Removal of part of a nerve trunk.

ner·vous (nûr′vəs) *adj.* **1.** Characterized by or exhibiting restlessness, anxiety, tension, etc.; high-strung; excitable. **2.** Neural. **3.** Caused by or acting on the nerves or nervous system: a *nervous* disorder. **4.** *Archaic* Having vigor, force, and vitality. [< L *nervosus* sinewy] — **ner′vous·ly** *adv.* — **ner·vos·i·ty** (-vos′ə·tē), **ner′vous·ness** *n.* — **Syn. 1.** uneasy, fidgety, jittery, skittish.

nervous breakdown Popularly, any severe mental or emotional disturbance, short of psychosis, usually requiring hospitalization. Also **nervous prostration.**

nervous system *Physiol.* A system in animals that coordinates, controls, and regulates various organic activities by means of the reception and transmission of stimuli; especially, the aggregate of neurons and neuroglia in vertebrates, divided into the central and autonomic nervous systems, and having the additional function in man of directing and conditioning consciousness.

ner·vure (nûr′vyŏŏr) *n. Biol.* A vein, as on a leaf or an insect's wing: also called *nerve*. Also **ner′vule** (-vyŏŏl). [< F < L *nervus* sinew] — **ner·vu·ra·tion** (nûr′vyə·rā′shən) *n.*

nerv·y (nûr′vē) *adj.* **nerv·i·er, nerv·i·est** **1.** *U.S. Informal* Brazen; impudent; brash. **2.** *Brit. Informal* Nervous; jumpy. **3.** Having or requiring courage. **4.** *Archaic* Sinewy.

nes·cience (nesh′əns, -ē·əns) *n.* **1.** Lack or absence of knowledge; ignorance. **2.** Agnosticism. [< L *nesciens*, ppr. of *nescire* to be ignorant of < *ne-* not + *scire* to know] — **nes′cient** *adj. & n.* — **nes′cient·ist** *n.*

ness (nes) *n.* A promontory or cape: frequently used as a suffix in the proper name of a headland: *Inverness*. [OE *naes*. Akin to OE *nosu* nose.]

-ness *suffix of nouns* **1.** State or quality of being: *darkness*. **2.** An example of this state or quality: to do someone a *kindness*. [OE *-ness(s)*, *-nis(s)*]

Nes·sel·rode pudding (nes′əl·rōd) A custard made with preserved fruits and nuts, and flavored with rum, used in pies, ice cream, etc. [after Count K. R. *Nesselrode*, 1780–1862, Russian diplomat]

Nes·sus (nes′əs) In Greek legend, a centaur who tried to abduct Deianira and was killed by her husband Hercules. A shirt that Deianira dipped in Nessus's blood and used as a charm to preserve her husband's love killed Hercules when he wore it. [< L < Gk. *Nessos*]

nest (nest) *n.* **1.** The habitation prepared or the place selected by a bird for the hatching of its eggs and the rearing of its young. **2.** A place used by fishes, insects, turtles, mice, etc., for laying eggs and rearing young. **3.** The group of animals, birds, etc., occupying such a place or habitation; swarm; brood; colony: a *nest* of wasps. **4.** A cozy or snug place; retreat. **5.** A place containing or fostering something bad, vulgar, or dangerous; haunt; den; also, those occupying such a place: a *nest* of thieves. **6.** A series or set of similar things designed to fit into one another, as bowls, trays, boxes, etc. **7.** A concentration of troops in battle. — *v.t.* **1.** To place in or as in a nest. **2.** To pack or place one inside another. — *v.i.* **3.** To build or occupy a nest. **4.** To hunt for nests. [OE. Akin to G *nest* and to L *nidus*.]

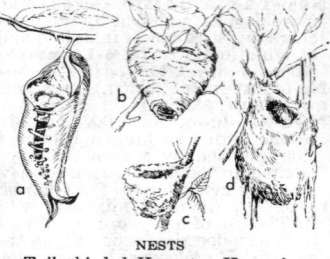

NESTS
a Tailorbird. *b* Hornet. *c* Hummingbird. *d* Oriole.

n'est-ce pas (nes pä′) *French* Isn't that so?

nest egg **1.** A sum of money set aside or saved for reserve, emergencies, or as a basis for future accumulation. **2.** An artificial or natural egg kept in a nest to induce a hen to lay more eggs in the same place.

nes·tle (nes′əl) *v.* **tled, ·tling** *v.i.* **1.** To lie or press closely and snugly; cuddle; snuggle. **2.** To settle down in comfort and pleasure: to *nestle* among the pillows. **3.** To lie or be embedded, sheltered, or half-hidden: The cottage *nestled* in a quiet valley. — *v.t.* **4.** To place or press snugly or lovingly. **5.** To place, settle, or shelter in or as in a nest. [OE *nestlian* to nest] — **nes′tler** *n.*

nest·ling (nest′ling, nes′-) *n.* **1.** A bird too young to leave the nest. **2.** A young child. — *adj.* Recently hatched.

Nes·tor (nes′tər) In Greek legend, a king of Pylos and one of the Argonauts, the oldest and wisest Greek chief in the Trojan War. — *n.* Any wise old man.

Nes·to·ri·an·ism (nes·tôr′ē·ən·iz′əm, -tō′rē-) *n. Theol.* The doctrines of Nestorius or of the sect he founded; especially, the doctrine that the divine and human exist in Christ as distinct, independent natures and are not joined in the unity of a single personality. — **Nes·to′ri·an** *n. & adj.*

Nes·tor·i·us (nes·tôr′ē·əs, -tō′rē-), died 451?, Syrian theologian; patriarch of Constantinople 428–31; banished as a heretic, 431.

net[1] (net) *n.* **1.** A fabric of thread, cord, rope, etc., woven or knotted to form an open pattern or meshwork; network. ◆ Collateral adjective: *reticular*. **2.** A contrivance of meshed fabric used to catch fish, birds, etc. **3.** Anything that traps or entangles; a snare: a *net* of political intrigue. **4.** A piece of fine openwork fabric, as lace. **5.** Any of various devices constructed with meshes: cargo *net*; tennis *net*. **6.** Something resembling a net, as a mass of intersecting lines. **7.** In tennis, etc., a ball hit into the net. — *v.t.* **net·ted, net·ting** **1.** To catch in or as in a net; ensnare. **2.** To make into a net. **3.** To cover, enclose, or shelter with a net. **4.** In tennis, etc., to hit (the ball) into the net. [OE. Akin to G *netz*, ON *net*. Cf. L *nodus* knot and *nectere* to bind.]

net[2] (net) *adj.* **1.** Obtained after deducting all expenses, losses, taxes, etc.: distinguished from *gross*: *net* proceeds. **2.** Free from anything extraneous; fundamental; basic: *net* results. — *n.* A net profit, amount, weight, etc. — *v.t.* **net·ted, net·ting** To earn or yield as clear profit: to *net* $5,000 a year. Abbr. *n.* [< F. See NEAT[1].]

Net (net) *n.* The constellation Reticulum.

Neth. Netherlands.

neth·er (neth′ər) *adj.* Situated beneath or below. [OE *nither, nithor* < Gmc.]

Neth·er·lands (neth′ər·ləndz) A country in NW Europe; 15,780 sq. mi.; pop. 13,077,000 (est. 1970); capital, Amsterdam; seat of government, The Hague: also, popularly, *Holland.* Dutch *Nederland.* — **Neth′er·land′er** *n.* — **Neth′er·land′ish** *adj.*

Netherlands, Kingdom of the A Kingdom comprising the Netherlands, the Netherlands Antilles, and Surinam as autonomous parts; capital, Amsterdam.

Netherlands Antilles Three islands north of Venezuela and three in the Leeward Islands group; 336 sq. mi.; pop. 220,000 (1970); capital, Willemstad: formerly *Dutch West Indies.* Also *Netherlands West Indies.*

Netherlands East Indies The former Netherlands colonial possessions in the Malay Archipelago: also *Dutch East Indies.* Also **Netherlands Indies.** See INDONESIA.

Netherlands Guiana See SURINAM.

Netherlands New Guinea A former name for WEST IRIAN.

Netherlands West Indies See NETHERLANDS ANTILLES.

neth·er·most (neth′ər·mōst′) *adj.* Lowest.

neth·er·ward (neth′ər·wərd) *adv.* In a downward course.

nether world 1. The world of the dead. 2. The world of punishment after death; hell.

ne·tsu·ke (nē·tsōō·kē, ne-) *n.* A small toggle or button, used to attach a purse or small case to the girdle or sash of a kimono. [< Japanese]

net·ting (net′ing) *n.* 1. A fabric of openwork; a net; network. 2. The act or operation of making net. 3. The act, practice, or right of using nets, as in fishing.

net·tle (net′l) *n.* 1. An herb (genus *Urtica*), with opposite leaves and minute stinging hairs. 2. Any of various plants having some real or fancied resemblance to those of the nettle family (*Urticaceae*). 3. A condition of irritation. — *v.t.* **·tled, ·tling** 1. To annoy or irritate; provoke. 2. To sting like nettle. [OE *netle* < Gmc.] — **net′tler** *n.*

nettle cell A nematocyst.

nettle rash Urticaria. Also **nettle fever.**

net ton A short ton. See under TON[1].

net·work (net′wûrk′) *n.* 1. A system of interlacing lines, tracks, or channels: a *network* of arteries. 2. An openwork fabric; netting. 3. *Telecom.* A chain of broadcasting stations. 4. Any interconnected system: an espionage *network.*

Neu·châ·tel (nōō′shə·tel′, *Fr.* nœ·shà·tel′) A Canton in western Switzerland; 309 sq. mi.; pop. 161,000 (est. 1965); capital, **Neuchâtel** on the **Lake of Neuchâtel** (24 mi. long, 4–5 mi. wide); pop. 36,300 (est. 1966). German **Neu·en·burg** (noi′ən·bŏŏrkh).

Neuf·châ·tel (nōō′shə·tel′, *Fr.* nœ·shà·tel′) *n.* A soft, white cheese produced in Neufchâtel, a town in northern France.

Neuil·ly-sur-Seine (nœ·yē′sür·sen′) A city in north central France, a suburb of Paris; pop. 70,787 (1968).

neume (nōōm, nyōōm) *n. Music* 1. One of the symbols in a system of notation to aid singers of Gregorian chants, indicating direction of melody and later including pitch and manner of performance. 2. *pl.* This system. Also **neum.** [< OF < Med.L *neuma* < Gk. *pneuma* breath]

Neu-Meck·len·burg (noi′mek′lən·bŏŏrkh) A former name for New IRELAND.

Neu·pest (noi′pest) The German name for ÚJPEST.

Neu-Pom·mern (noi′pom′ərn) The former name for NEW BRITAIN.

neu·ral (nŏŏr′əl, nyŏŏr′-) *adj.* Of or pertaining to the nerves or nervous system. [< Gk. *neuron* cord, sinew]

neu·ral·gi·a (nŏŏ·ral′jē·ə, -jə, nyŏŏ-) *n. Pathol.* Acute, paroxysmal pain along the course of a nerve. [< NEUR(O)- + -ALGIA] — **neu·ral′gic** *adj.*

neu·ras·the·ni·a (nŏŏr′əs·thē′nē·ə, -then′yə, nyŏŏr′-) *n. Obs. Psychiatry* A condition marked by general debility, depression, and bodily disturbances, formerly believed to be due to weakness or exhaustion of the nervous system. Compare NEUROSIS. [< NL < Gk. *neuron* cord, sinew + *astheneia* weakness] — **neu′ras·then′ic** (-then′ik) *adj. & n.*

neu·ra·tion (nŏŏ·rā′shən, nyŏŏ-) *n.* Nervation.

neu·rec·to·my (nŏŏ·rek′tə·mē, nyŏŏ-) *n. pl.* **·mies** *Surg.* The removal of a nerve or part of a nerve. [< NEURO- + -ECTOMY]

neu·ri·lem·ma (nŏŏr′ə·lem′ə, nyŏŏr′-) *n. Anat.* The delicate sheath of a nerve fiber. Also **neu′ri·lem′a, neu′ro·lem′ma.** [< NL < Gk. *neuron* sinew + *eilēma* sheath] — **neu′ri·lem′mic** *adj.*

neu·ri·tis (nŏŏ·rī′tis, nyŏŏ-) *n. Pathol.* Inflammation of a nerve. — **neu·rit′ic** (-rit′ik) *adj.*

neuro- *combining form* Nerve: *neurology.* Also **neur-** (before vowels), **neuri-.** [< Gk. *neuron* sinew]

neu·ro·blast (nŏŏr′ə·blast, nyŏŏr′-) *n. Biol.* An embryonic cell that develops into a neuron.

neu·rog·li·a (nŏŏ·rog′lē·ə, nyŏŏ-) *n. Anat.* The supporting tissue of the central nervous system, composed of finely branched ectodermic cells with thin interlacing processes. [< NEURO- + LGk. *glia* glue]

neu·roid (nŏŏr′oid, nyŏŏr′-) *adj.* Nervelike.

neu·rol·o·gy (nŏŏ·rol′ə·jē, nyŏŏ-) *n.* The branch of medicine that deals with the nervous system and its disorders. [< NL *neurologia*] — **neu·ro·log·i·cal** (nŏŏr′ə·loj′i·kəl, nyŏŏr′-) *adj.* — **neu·rol′o·gist** *n.*

neu·ro·ma (nŏŏ·rō′mə, nyŏŏ-) *n. pl.* **·ma·ta** (-mə·tə) *Pathol.* A tumor composed of nerve tissue. [< NL]

neu·ron (nŏŏr′on, nyŏŏr′-) *n. Physiol.* The fundamental cellular unit of the nervous system, consisting of a nucleus with all its processes and extensions: also called *nerve cell.* Also **neu′rone** (-ōn). [< NL < Gk. *neuron* sinew] — **neu·ron·ic** (nŏŏ·ron′ik, nyŏŏ-) *adj.*

neu·ro·path (nŏŏr′ə·path, nyŏŏr′-) *n.* One suffering from or predisposed to disease of the nervous system. — **neu′ro·path′ic, neu′ro·path′i·cal** *adj.* — **neu′ro·path′i·cal·ly** *adv.*

neu·ro·pa·thol·o·gy (nŏŏr′ō·pə·thol′ə·jē, nyŏŏr′-) *n.* The pathology of the nervous system. — **neu′ro·pa·thol′o·gist** *n.*

neu·ro·phys·i·ol·o·gy (nŏŏr′ō·fiz′ē·ol′ə·jē, nyŏŏr′-) *n.* The physiology of the nervous system. — **neu′ro·phys′i·o·log′i·cal** (-fiz′ē·ə·loj′i·kəl) *adj.* — **neu′ro·phys′i·ol′o·gist** *n.*

neu·ro·psy·chi·a·try (nŏŏr′ō·sī·kī′ə·trē, nyŏŏ′-) *n.* A combination of the specialties of neurology and psychiatry. — **neu′ro·psy′chi·at′ric** (-sī′kē·at′rik) *adj.*

neu·ro·psy·cho·sis (nŏŏr′ō·sī·kō′sis, nyŏŏr′-) *n. Obs.* A psychosis (which see).

neu·rop·ter·an (nŏŏ·rop′tər·ən, nyŏŏ-) *n.* A neuropterous insect. Also **neu·rop′ter, neu·rop′ter·on** (-on). — *adj.* Neuropterous. Also **neu·rop′ter·oid.**

neu·rop·ter·ous (nŏŏ·rop′tər·əs, nyŏŏ-) *adj.* Of or pertaining to an order (*Neuroptera*) of insects having two pairs of membranous net-veined wings and chewing mouth parts, as ant lions, lacewings, etc.: also *neuropteran.* Also **neu·rop′ter·al.** [< NL *Neuroptera*]

neu·ro·sis (nŏŏ·rō′sis, nyŏŏ-) *n. pl.* **·ses** (-sēz) *Psychiatry* Any of various emotional disturbances, less severe than the psychoses, due to unresolved unconscious conflicts and typically involving anxiety, depression, somatic disturbances, etc.: also called *psychoneurosis.* [< NL] — **neu·ro′sal** *adj.*

neu·rot·ic (nŏŏ·rot′ik, nyŏŏ-) *adj.* 1. Pertaining to or suffering from neurosis. 2. *Informal* Exhibiting erratic, eccentric, or obsessive tendencies. 3. Of or pertaining to the nerves; neural. — *n.* A neurotic person.

neu·rot·o·my (nŏŏ·rot′ə·mē, nyŏŏ-) *n. pl.* **·mies** *Surg.* The severing of a nerve, as to relieve pain. [< NL *neurotomia*] — **neu·ro·tom·ic** (nŏŏr′ə·tom′ik, nyŏŏr′-) *adj.*

Neu·satz (noi′zäts) The German name for Novi SAD.

Neus·tri·a (nōōs′trē·ə, nyōōs′-) The western part of the Frankish Empire, comprising north and NW France.

neut. Neuter.

neu·ter (nōō′tər, nyōō′-) *adj.* 1. *Gram.* a Neither masculine nor feminine in gender. See GENDER. b Neither active nor passive; intransitive: said of verbs. 2. *Biol.* a Having no sexual organs; asexual. b Having nonfunctioning or imperfectly developed sex organs, as a worker bee. 3. *Obs.* Neutral. — *n.* 1. *Biol.* A neuter plant or animal. 2. A castrated animal. 3. *Gram.* a The neuter gender. b A word in this gender. 4. *Obs.* A neutral person. Abbr. *n., neut.* [ult. < L *neuter* < *ne-* not + *uter* either]

neu·tral (nōō′trəl, nyōō′-) *adj.* 1. Not interfering with or taking the part of either side in a dispute, contest, controversy, etc.; especially, refraining from aiding or siding with any belligerent in a war. 2. Of or belonging to neither side in a dispute, quarrel, war, etc.: *neutral* territory. 3. Having no marked characteristics; neither one nor the other; indefinite; middling. 4. Having no decided hue or color; without chroma; grayish. 5. *Biol.* Neuter; especially, without stamens or pistils. 6. *Chem.* Having or exhibiting neither acid nor alkaline properties: a *neutral* solution. 7. *Electr.* Neither positive nor negative. 8. *Mech.* Having a disengaged gear transmission. 9. *Phonet.* Produced with the tongue in a relaxed, midcentral position, as the *a* in *about.* — *n.* 1. One who or that which is neutral. 2. *Mech.* The state in which transmission gears are disengaged: a car in *neutral.* [< L *neutralis* < *neuter* neither] — **neu′tral·ly** *adv.*

neu·tral·ism (nōō′trəl·iz′əm, nyōō′-) *n.* In foreign affairs, the policy of not associating or aligning a nation with any side of a power conflict. — **neu′tral·ist** *adj. & n.*

neu·tral·i·ty (nōō·tral′ə·tē, nyōō-) *n. pl.* **·ties** Neutral condition, status, attitude, policy, etc., as of a nation during a war. [< F *neutralité* < Med.L *neutralitas. -tatis*]

neu·tral·i·za·tion (nōō′trəl·ə·zā′shən, -ī·zā′-, nyōō′-) *n.* 1. The act of neutralizing, or the state of being neutralized. 2. *Ling.* The suspension under given conditions of an otherwise functioning opposition or phonemic contrast between two phonemes, as /t/ and /d/ in *latter* and *ladder* in the speech of many Americans.

neu·tral·ize (nōō′trəl·īz, nyōō′-) *v.t.* **·ized, ·iz·ing** **1.** To counteract, nullify, or destroy the force, influence, effect, etc., of; render ineffective. **2.** To declare or render (a nation, area, etc.) neutral during a war. **3.** *Chem.* To make neutral or inert. **4.** *Electr.* To render electrically neutral or inert by combining equal negative and positive units. Also *Brit.* **neu·tral·ise.** [< F *neutraliser*] **— neu·tral·iz′er** *n.*

neutral spirits Ethyl alcohol of at least 190 proof.

neu·tri·no (nōō·trē′nō, nyōō′-) *n.* *pl.* **·nos** *Physics* An atomic particle associated with the radioactive emission of beta rays, carrying no electric charge and having a mass approaching zero. [< Ital., little neutron]

neu·tron (nōō′tron, nyōō′-) *n.* *Physics* An electrically neutral particle of the atomic nucleus having a mass approximately equal to that of the proton. [< NEUT(RAL) + (ELEC)TRON]

neutron number *Physics* The number of neutrons in the nucleus of an atom.

neutron star *Astron.* A hypothetical star of density approximating a billion tons per cubic inch, collapsed from a larger star, and a strong source of X-rays.

Nev. Nevada.

Ne·va (nē′və, *Russ.* nye-vä′) A river in the NW R.S.F.S.R., flowing west 46 miles from Lake Ladoga to its delta at Leningrad.

Ne·vad·a (nə-vad′ə, -vä′də) A State in the western United States; 110,540 sq. mi.; pop. 488,738; capital, Carson City; entered the Union Oct. 31, 1864; nickname, *Sagebrush State.* **— Ne·vad′an** *adj. & n.*

Ne·va·do de Co·li·ma (nā-vä′thō thä kō-lē′mä) An inactive volcano in western Mexico; 14,240 ft.: also *Colima.*

né·vé (nā-vā′) *n.* The granular snow found on the upper part of a mountain, eventually forming glacial ice; also, a field composed of this type of snow: also called *firn.* [< F < dial. F (Swiss), ult. < L *nix, nivis* snow]

nev·er (nev′ər) *adv.* **1.** Not at any time; not ever: also used in combination to form adjectives: *never-ending.* **2.** Not at all; positively not: *Never* fear. [OE *næfre*]

nev·er·more (nev′ər·môr′, -mōr′) *adv.* Never again.

nev·er·the·less (nev′ər·thə·les′) *adv.* Nonetheless; however; yet. **— Syn.** See BUT¹.

Ne·vis (nē′vis, nev′is) See ST. CHRISTOPHER, NEVIS, AND ANGUILLA.

ne·void (nē′void) *adj.* Of, pertaining to, or resembling a nevus: also spelled *naevoid.*

Nev·ski (nev′skē, nef′-), **Alexander** See ALEXANDER NEVSKI.

ne·vus (nē′vəs) *n.* *pl.* **·vi** (-vī) A birthmark or congenital mole: also spelled *naevus.* [< L *naevus* blemish]

new (nōō, nyōō) *adj.* **new·er, new·est** **1.** Having recently or lately been made, used, developed, etc.; recent. **2.** Having never existed, occurred, appeared, etc., before: a *new* day. **3.** Recently discovered, known, observed, experienced, etc.: a *new* river. **4.** Different or distinguished from that which is older, former, or previous: a *new* dispensation. **5.** Unfamiliar; strange; novel: a *new* approach. **6.** Not accustomed or experienced: *new* at the job. **7.** Having recently come into a certain place, position, condition, relationship, etc.: a *new* member. **8.** Built, made, etc., in place of something older: a *new* post office. **9.** Fresh; unspoiled. **10.** Repeated; resumed; renewed: a *new* plea. **11.** Additional; further; increased: a *new* supply. **12.** Rejuvenated or invigorated; refreshed: a *new* man. **13.** Modern; current; fashionable: the *new* taste in music. **14.** *Usually cap.* Of or designating the most recent form, development, or period: said of languages: *New* Latin. Abbr. *n.* **— *adv.* Newly; freshly; recently. — *n.* That which is new. [OE *nīwe, nēowe* < Gmc. Akin to L *novus*, Gk. *neos.*] **— new′ness** *n.*

— Syn. (adj.) *New, novel, original, fresh,* and *modernistic* characterize what has only recently come into existence, use, or notice. *New* is very broad, and may vary greatly in meaning in different contexts: a *new* house, a *new* rug, a *new* star, a *new* wife, a *new* baby. *Novel* refers to something *new* that is also unfamiliar, odd, or striking: a *novel* scheme to harness the tides, a *novel* approach to a problem. *Original* describes that which is the first of its kind: the *original* edition of a book. *Fresh* suggests the newness of youth, that may lose its vigor as it ages: a *fresh* view of a situation, a *fresh* coat of paint. *Modernistic* refers to the immediate present, and the latest fashions, and suggests the utmost novelty: *modernistic* music. Compare MODERN. **— Ant.** old.

New Albany A city in southern Indiana, on the Ohio River; pop. 38,402.

New Amsterdam The Dutch capital of New Netherland; taken by the English in 1664 and renamed *New York.*

New·ark (nōō′ərk, nyōō′-) **1.** A port city in NE New Jersey, on Newark Bay; pop. 381,930. **2.** A city in central Ohio; pop. 41,836.

New Bedford A city in SE Massachusetts, on Buzzards Bay; pop. 101,777.

new blue Ultramarine.

new·born (nōō′bôrn′, nyōō′-) *adj.* **1.** Newly born; in the first few days or weeks of life. **2.** Born again; reborn. **—** *n.* A newborn infant or animal.

New Britain **1.** The largest island in the Bismarck Archipelago; 14,600 sq. mi.; chief city, Rabaul: formerly *Neu-Pommern.* **2.** A city in central Connecticut; pop. 83,441.

New Brunswick **1.** A Province of SE Canada on the Bay of Fundy; 27,836 sq. mi.; pop. 632,000; capital, Fredericton. Abbr. *N.B.* **2.** A city in east central New Jersey, on the Raritan River; pop. 41,885.

New·burg (nōō′bûrg, nyōō′-) See À LA NEWBURG.

New·burgh (nōō′bûrg, nyōō′-) A city in SE New York, on the Hudson River; pop. 26,219.

New Caledonia **1.** An island east of Australia, comprising with its dependencies a French Overseas Territory; 9,401 sq. mi.; pop. 98,000 (est. 1969); capital, Nouméa: French *Nouvelle Calédonie.* **2.** Formerly, a part of British Columbia.

New Castile A region of central Spain.

New Castle A city in western Pennsylvania, on the Shenango River; pop. 38,559.

New·cas·tle-up·on-Tyne (nōō′kas·əl·ə·pon′tīn′, nyōō′-) The county seat of Northumberland and of Tyne and Wear, England; pop. 297,000 (1976). Also **Newcastle, Newcastle-on-Tyne. — to carry coals to Newcastle** To provide something already in abundant supply.

New Church The Swedenborgian Church. See under SWEDENBORGIANISM.

new·com·er (nōō′kum′ər, nyōō′-) *n.* One who has recently arrived.

New Criticism A type of literary analysis based upon an intensive textual examination and evaluation of the intrinsic elements of a work, as structure, symbols, imagery, etc.

New Deal **1.** The political, economic, and social policies and principles of the administration under Franklin D. Roosevelt. **2.** The Roosevelt administration. **— New Dealer**

New Delhi The capital of India in Delhi Territory, an administrative center SW of (old) Delhi; pop. 324,283 (1967).

New Democratic Party The socialist party of Canada: before 1961 called *Cooperative Commonwealth Federation.*

New Economic Policy The policy adopted by the Soviet government in 1921–1928 permitting limited capitalism: also called *Nep.* Abbr. *NEP, N.E.P.*

new·el (nōō′əl, nyōō′-) *n.* *Archit.* **1.** The post that terminates the handrail of a staircase. **2.** The central pillar or upright of a spiral staircase. Also **newel post.** [< OF *nouel* newel, kernel < LL *nucalis* nutlike < L *nux, nucis* nut]

New England The NE section of the United States, including Maine, New Hampshire, Vermont, Massachusetts, Rhode Island, and Connecticut. **— New Englander**

New England aster A perennial aster (*Aster novae-angliae*) of eastern North America, having purple flowers.

New English Bible A modern translation of the Bible done by a group of interdenominational scholars in Great Britain. The New Testament was published in 1961.

Newf. Newfoundland (unofficial).

new·fan·gled (nōō′fang′gəld, nyōō′-) *adj.* **1.** Lately come into fashion; new-fashioned; novel: a derogatory term: *newfangled* notions. **2.** *Rare* Disposed to or fond of novelty: a derogatory term: *newfangled* salesmen. **— new′fan′gled·ness** *n.* [ME *newefangel* novelty < *newe* new + *fangel* contrivance, prob. dim. < *fangen,* pp. of *fōn* to seize, grasp]

new-fash·ioned (nōō′fash′ənd, nyōō′-) *adj.* Made in a new style; recently become fashionable.

New Forest A partly wooded region in SW Hampshire, England; about 145 sq. mi.

New·found·land (nōō′fənd·lənd, nyōō′-) *n.* A large dog of a breed originating in Newfoundland, having a broad head, square muzzle, and thick, abundant, usually black coat.

New·found·land (nōō′fənd·land′, nyōō′-) The easternmost Province of Canada, comprising the island of New-foundland (42,734 sq. mi.) and its dependency, Labrador, on the mainland; total, 152,734 sq. mi.; pop. 524,000; capital, St. John's. Abbr. *Nfld., N.f., Newf.* **— New·found′land·er** (-found′-) *n.*

New France The region discovered and settled by the French in North America, including Canada, the Great Lakes region, and Louisiana, from 1534 to 1763.

New·gate (nōō′git, -gāt, nyōō′-) Formerly, a London prison.

New Georgia An island group in the British Solomon Islands; about 2,000 sq. mi.; chief island, **New Georgia.**

New Granada A former Spanish viceroyalty, now divided into Ecuador, Colombia, Panama, and Venezuela.

New Guinea The world's second largest island, north of Australia; 304,200 sq. mi.: also *Papua.* See WEST IRIAN, PAPUA NEW GUINEA, maps of AUSTRALASIA, INDONESIA.

New Guinea, Territory of A former United Nations Trust Territory, comprising NE New Guinea, the Bismarck Archipelago, and Bougainville and Buka in the Solomon Islands; an integral part of the independent nation of Papua New Guinea since 1974; formerly governed administratively with the Territory of Papua: see PAPUA NEW GUINEA.

New Hampshire A State of the NE United States; 9,304 sq. mi.; pop. 737,681; capital, Concord; entered the Union June 21, 1788, one of the thirteen original States; nickname, *Granite State.* Abbr. *N.H.*

New Hanover A town in NE New Jersey; pop. 27,410.
New Haven A port city in southern Connecticut on Long Island Sound; pop. 137,707.
New Hebrides An island group in the SW Pacific, comprising an Anglo-French condominium; about 5,700 sq. mi.; pop. 80,000 (est. 1969); capital, Vila.
New High German See under GERMAN.
New Iberia A city in southern Louisiana; pop. 30,147.
New Ireland An island of the Bismarck Archipelago; 3,340 sq. mi.: formerly *Neu-Mecklenburg.*
new·ish (nōō'ish, nyōō'-) *adj.* Rather new.
New Jersey A State of the eastern United States on the Atlantic; 7,836 sq. mi.; pop. 7,168,164; capital, Trenton; entered the Union Dec. 18, 1787, one of the thirteen original States; nickname, *Garden State.* Abbr. *N.J.* **— New Jer·sey·ite** (jûr'zē-ĭt)
New Jerusalem The city of God; heaven. *Rev.* xxi 2.
New Jerusalem Church The Swedenborgian Church. See under SWEDENBORGIANISM.
New Latin See under LATIN.
New London A port city in SE Connecticut, at the mouth of the Thames River; site of a U.S. naval base; pop. 31,630.
new·ly (nōō'lē, nyōō'-) *adv.* **1.** Very recently; lately. **2.** Once more; anew; afresh. **3.** In a new or different way.
new·ly·wed (nōō'lē·wĕd', nyōō'-) *n.* A person recently married.
New·man (nōō'mən, nyōō'-), **John Henry,** 1801–90, English cardinal, theologian, and author.
new·mar·ket (nōō'mär·kĭt, nyōō'-) *n.* **1.** Formerly, a long, close-fitting coat. Also **Newmarket coat. 2.** A card game resembling Pope Joan. [after *Newmarket*]
New·mar·ket (nōō'mär·kĭt, nyōō'-) An urban district in West Suffolk, England; pop. 20,887 (1961).
new math *U.S.* A system of teaching arithmetic and mathematics by related sequences that was introduced into many schools in the 1950's.
New Mexico A State of the SW United States on the Mexican border; 121,666 sq. mi.; pop. 1,016,000; capital, Santa Fé; entered the Union Jan. 6, 1912; nickname, *Land of Enchantment.* Abbr. *N.Mex.* **— New Mexican**
new moon 1. The phase of the moon when it is between the earth and the sun, its disk being invisible; also, its first visible crescent. **2.** The period when the moon is new.
new·mown (nōō'mōn', nyōō'-) *adj.* Recently mown, as hay.
New Neth·er·land (nĕth'ər·lənd) The Dutch colony in North America, 1613–1664, near the mouth of the Hudson River; capital, New Amsterdam.
New Norwegian Landsmål, a language.
New Order The political, economic, and social system of the Axis Powers, especially Nazi Germany.
New Or·le·ans (ôr'lē·ənz, ôr·lēnz', ôr'lənz) A port city in SE Louisiana, on the Mississippi; pop. 593,471; a native of the city is sometimes known as an *Orleanian.* **— New Or·lean·i·an** (ôr·lē'nē·ən)
new penny A penny (def. 3).
New Philharmonic pitch See under PITCH.
New·port (nōō'pôrt, -pōrt, nyōō'-) **1.** A port city of SE Rhode Island, on Narragansett Bay; site of a United States naval base; pop. 94,228. **2.** A city in northern Kentucky, on the Ohio River; pop. 25,998. **3.** The county seat of Isle of Wight, England; pop. 21,440. **4.** A county borough and port in southern Gwent, Wales; pop. 134,700 (1976).
Newport Beach A resort city in SW California, on San Pedro Channel; pop. 49,422.
Newport News A city in SE Virginia, on the James River; pop. 138,177.
New Providence Island The chief island of the Bahamas; 58 sq. mi.
New Quebec See UNGAVA.
New Ro·chelle (rə·shĕl') A city in SE New York, on Long Island Sound; pop. 75,385.
news (nooz, nyooz) *n.pl.* (construed as *sing.*) **1.** Information of a recent event, development, etc., especially as reported in a newspaper, on the radio, etc. **2.** Any new or unfamiliar information. [< NEW, ? trans. of OF *nouvelles.*]
New Sar·um (sâr'əm) See SALISBURY.
news·boy (nōōz'boi', nyōōz'-) *n.* A boy who sells or delivers newspapers.
news·cast (nōōz'kăst', -käst', nyōōz'-) *n.* A radio or television broadcast of news. **— news'cast'er** *n.*
news·deal·er (nōōz'dē'lər, nyōōz'-) *n. U.S.* One who sells newspapers, etc. Also *Brit.* **news'ag'ent** (-â'jənt)
New Siberian Islands An archipelago off the Arctic coast of the Yakut S.S.R.; 11,000 sq. mi.
news·let·ter (nōōz'lĕt'ər, nyōōz'-) *n.* A brief, specialized, periodical news report or set of reports sent by mail.
news·mag·a·zine (nōōz'măg'ə·zēn, -măg'ə·zēn', nyōōz'-) *n.* A periodical, especially a weekly, that summarizes the news.
news·man (nōōz'măn', -mən, nyōōz'-) *n. pl.* **·men** (-mĕn', -mən) **1.** A news reporter. **2.** A newsdealer.

New South Wales A State of SE Australia; 309,433 sq. mi.; pop. 4,595,400 (est. 1970); capital, Sydney.
New Spain The former Spanish possessions in the SW United States, Central America north of Panama, the West Indies, and the Philippines.
news·pa·per (nōōz'pā'pər, nyōōz'-) *n.* **1.** A printed publication usually issued daily or weekly, containing news, editorials, advertisements, etc. **2.** Newsprint.
news·pa·per·man (nōōz'pā'pər·măn, -mən, nyōōz'-) *n. pl.* **·men** (-mĕn', -mən) **1.** One who is a writer or editor on a newspaper. **2.** One who owns or operates a newspaper.
news·print (nōōz'prĭnt', nyōōz'-) *n.* The thin, unsized paper on which the ordinary newspaper is printed.
news·reel (nōōz'rēl', nyōōz'-) *n.* A short motion picture showing current events.
news·stand (nōōz'stănd', nyōōz'-) *n. U.S.* A stand or stall at which newspapers and periodicals are offered for sale.
New Style See (Gregorian) CALENDAR.
news·worth·y (nōōz'wûr'thē, nyōōz'-) *adj.* Having sufficient importance to be reported in a newspaper or newscast.
news·y (nōō'zē, nyōō'-) *Informal adj.* **news·i·er, news·i·est** Full of news. **—** *n. pl.* **news·ies** *U.S.* A newsboy.
newt (nōōt, nyōōt) *n.* Any of various semiaquatic salamanders, especially of the genus *Triturus:* also called *eft.* [Earlier *ewt, evet,* OE *efete;* in ME *an ewt* was taken as *a newt*]
New Test. New Testament.
New Testament That portion of the Bible containing the life and teachings of Christ, consisting of the following books: Matthew, Mark, Luke, John, The Acts, Romans, I Corinthians, II Corinthians, Galatians, Ephesians, Philippians, Colossians, I Thessalonians, II Thessalonians, I Timothy, II Timothy, Titus, Philemon, Hebrews, James, I Peter, II Peter, I John, II John, III John, Jude, Revelation (Apocalypse). Abbr. *New Test., NT, N.T.*
new·ton (nōō'tən, nyōō'-) *n. Physics* The unit of force in the mks system, equal to the force needed to accelerate a mass of 1 kilogram 1 meter per second per second. A newton equals 10⁵ or 100,000 dynes. [after Isaac *Newton*]
New·ton (nōō'tən, nyōō'-), **Sir Isaac,** 1642–1727, English philosopher and mathematician; formulated the basic laws of dynamics and the law of gravitation, and discovered the dispersion of white light by a prism. **— New·to·ni·an** (nōō·tō'nē·ən, nyōō-) *adj. & n.*
New World The Western Hemisphere.
New Year The first day of the year; in the Gregorian calendar, January 1. Also **New Year's Day** (yirz). Compare CALENDAR.
New Year's Eve The night of December 31.
New York 1. A State of the NE United States on the Atlantic; 49,576 sq. mi.; pop. 18,190,740; capital, Albany; entered the Union July 26, 1788; one of the thirteen original States; nickname, *Empire State.* Abbr. *N.Y.* **2.** A port city at the mouth of the Hudson River in SE New York, divided into the five boroughs of the Bronx, Brooklyn, Manhattan, Queens, and Richmond (Staten Island), constituting the largest city of the United States; 365 sq. mi.; pop. 7,895,563: also *Greater New York.*

NEW YORK HARBOR

New York Bay An inlet of the Atlantic Ocean at the mouth of the Hudson River, forming **New York Harbor** and divided by the Narrows into **Upper New York Bay** and **Lower New York Bay.**
New York City New York (def. 2).
New York·er (yôr'kər) An inhabitant of New York; especially, a native or resident of New York City.
New York State Barge Canal A waterway system of central New York, connecting the Hudson River with Lakes Erie, Champlain, and Ontario; total length, 525 mi.
New Zea·land (zē'lənd) A self-governing member of the Commonwealth of Nations, comprising a group of islands, principally North Island and South Island, SE of Australia; 103,416 sq. mi., excluding island territories; pop. 2,949,000 (est. 1973); capital, Wellington.
New Zea·land·er (zē'lən·dər) **1.** A resident of New Zealand. **2.** Formerly, a Maori.
Nex·ö (nĕk'sœ), **Martin Andersen,** 1869–1954, Danish novelist born in Germany.
next (nĕkst) *adj.* **1.** Coming directly after in time, order, position, etc.; immediately following or succeeding. **2.** Nearest or closest in space. **3.** Adjacent or adjoining: the *next* room. **—** *adv.* **1.** Immediately afterward or subsequently. **2.** On the first succeeding occasion: when *next* we meet. **—** *prep.* Nearest to: *next* his heart. **— next door 1.** The adjacent house, building, apartment, etc. **2.** In, at, or to the adjacent house, etc. **— next to** Almost; nearly: *next to* impossible. [OE *niehst,* superl. of *neah* near]

next friend *Law* One who though not a guardian appears to prosecute an action in behalf of someone under legal disability, as a minor child, etc.

next of kin 1. *Law* The kindred of a person who would share in his estate according to the statutes of distribution. 2. The person most closely related to one.

nex·us (nek'səs) *n. pl.* **·us·es** or **·us** 1. A bond or tie between the several members of a group or series; link. 2. A connected series. [< L, pp. of *nectere* to tie]

Ney (nā), **Michel**, 1769–1815, Duc d'Elchingen, Prince de la Moskova, French marshal under Napoleon Bonaparte; executed.

Nez Per·cé (nez' pûrs', *Fr.* nā per·sā') One of a tribe of North American Indians of Shahaptian stock, formerly living in Idaho, Oregon, and Washington. [< F, pierced nose]

N.F. 1. National Formulary. 2. Newfoundland (unofficial). 3. No funds: also **n.f.** 4. Norman French: also **NF.**

Nfld. Newfoundland.

NG or **N.G.** National Guard.

N.G. or **n.g.** No good.

NGk. or **N.Gk.** New Greek.

N.H. New Hampshire.

N.Heb. New Hebrides.

NHI *Brit.* National Health Insurance.

Ni *Chem.* Nickel.

N.I. Northern Ireland.

ni·a·cin (nī'ə·sin) *n.* Nicotinic acid.

Ni·ag·a·ra Falls (nī·ag'rə. ·ər·ə) 1. A resort city in western New York, on the Niagara River; pop. 85,615. 2. See under NIAGARA RIVER.

Niagara River A river between Ontario province Canada, and New York State, flowing 34 miles from Lake Erie to Lake Ontario; in its course occurs **Niagara Falls**, a cataract divided by Goat Island into the American Falls, about 167 ft. high and 1,000 ft. wide, and Horseshoe Falls on the Canadian side, about 160 ft. high and 2,500 ft. wide.

Nia·mey (nyä·mā') The capital of the Republic of Niger, in the western part on the Niger river; pop. 42,000 (1968).

nib (nib) *n.* 1. The point of a pen. 2. The projecting, pointed part of anything; tip. 3. A neb (def. 1). — *v.t.* **nibbed, nib·bing** 1. To furnish with a nib. 2. To sharpen or mend the nib of. [Var. of NEB < OE *nebb* beak]

nib·ble (nib'əl) *v.* **·bled, ·bling** *v.t.* 1. To eat with small, quick, gentle bites: to *nibble* grass. 2. To take little, soft bites of: to *nibble* an ear. — *v.i.* 3. To eat or bite, especially with small, gentle bites: often with *at.* — *n.* 1. A little bit or morsel. 2. The act of one who or that which nibbles. [< Gmc. Cf. LG *nibbelen*] — **nib'bler** *n.*

Ni·be·lung (nē'bə·lŏong) *n. pl.* **·lungs** or **·lung·en** (-lŏong'- en) 1. In Teutonic mythology, one of a dwarf people who held a magic ring and a hoard of gold, taken from them by Siegfried. 2. Any of the followers of Siegfried. 3. In the *Nibelungenlied*, one of the Burgundian kings.

Ni·be·lung·en·lied (nē'bə·lŏong'ən·lēt') The lay of the Nibelungs, a Middle High German epic poem written by an unknown author during the early 13th century, embodying legends of Siegfried, Kriemhild, and the Burgundian kings.

nib·lick (nib'lik) *n.* In golf, a nine iron. [? < Du. *kneppe-lig* < *kneppel* club]

Nic. or **Nicar.** Nicaragua.

Ni·cae·a (nī·sē'ə) 1. An ancient town of Bithynia in Asia Minor on the site of modern Iznik. 2. An ancient name for NICE. — **Council of Nicaea** A council held at Nicaea, Asia Minor, in A.D. 325, that condemned Arianism and promulgated the Nicene Creed.

Nic·a·ra·gua (nik'ə·rä'gwə) A Republic in Central America; about 57,100 sq. mi.; pop. 1,915,000 (est. 1969); capital, Managua.

Nicaragua, Lake A lake in SW Nicaragua; 3,100 sq. mi.

Nic·a·ra·guan (nik'ə·rä'gwən) *adj.* Of or pertaining to Nicaragua. — *n.* A native of Nicaragua.

nic·co·lite (nik'ə·līt) *n.* A metallic nickel arsenide, NiAs: also called *copper nickel.* [< NL *niccolum* nickel]

nice (nīs) *adj.* **nic·er, nic·est** 1. Agreeable; commendable; pleasing; respectable; suitable. 2. Friendly; kind. 3. Characterized by, revealing, or demanding discrimination, delicacy, or subtlety: a *nice* distinction. 4. Precise, accurate, or minute, as an instrument or measurement. — **nice and Gratifyingly:** properly: *nice and dry.* [< OF, innocent, foolish < L *nescius* ignorant < *ne* not + *scire* to know] — **nice'ly** *adv.* — **nice'ness** *n.*

Nice (nēs) A port city in SE France; pop. 322,422 (1968): ancient *Nicaea.*

Ni·cene (nī'sēn, nī·sēn') *adj.* Of or pertaining to Nicaea, a town in Asia Minor. Also **Ni·cae·an** (nī·sē'ən).

Nicene Creed *Eccl.* 1. A Christian confession of faith, adopted against the Arian heresy by the first Council of Nicaea, A.D. 325. 2. A similar creed, later attributed to the Council of Constantinople, A.D. 381, and accepted by the Greek Church: also called *Constantinopolitan Creed.* Also **Ni·ce·no-Con·stan·ti·no·pol·i·tan Creed** (nī·sēn'ō·kon·stan'-tə·nō·pol'ə·tən) 3. A modification of this, adopted by the Council of Toledo, A.D. 589, and accepted by the Anglican, Roman Catholic, and various Protestant churches.

ni·ce·ty (nī'sə·tē) *n. pl.* **·ties** 1. *Usually pl.* A minute or subtle point, detail, or distinction; a fine point: the *niceties* of pedagogy. 2. *Usually pl.* A delicacy or refinement: *niceties* of living. 3. Excessive delicacy or refinement; fastidiousness: a *nicety* of taste. 4. The quality of requiring careful and delicate treatment: a question of utmost *nicety.* 5. Precision or accuracy; exactness: rendered with great *nicety.* 6. The quality of being nice. — **to a nicety** Exactly; precisely. [< OF *nicete* folly < *nice.* See NICE.]

niche (nich) *n.* 1. A recessed space or hollow, usually in a wall, for a statue or the like. 2. Any position specially adapted to its occupant: to find one's *niche.* — *v.t.* **niched, nich·ing** To put in a niche. [Prob. < F < *nicher* to nest, ult. < L *nidus* nest]

NICHE

Nich·o·las (nik'ə·ləs), **Saint** Fourth-century prelate; bishop of Myra; patron of Russia, seamen, and children. In Dutch nursery lore, the Santa Claus who brings presents to children on Christmas Eve. See SANTA CLAUS.

Nicholas I, 1796–1855, czar of Russia 1825–55.

Nicholas I, Saint, died 867, pope 858–867: called **the Great**.

Nicholas II, 1868–1918, czar of Russia 1894–1917; executed by the Bolsheviks.

Nicholas V, 1397–1455, pope 1447–55; patron of learning and the arts: original name **Tommaso Pa·ren·tu·cel·li** (pä'ren·tōo·chel'lī).

Nicholas of Cusa, 1401?–64, German bishop and scholar: original name **Nikolas Chrypffs** (kripfs) or **Krebs** (kreps).

Ni·chrome (nī'krōm) *n.* An alloy of nickel, chromium, and iron, highly resistant to electricity, heat, and corrosion: a trade name. Also **ni'chrome.**

nicht wahr (nikht vär') *German* Isn't that so?

Ni·ci·as (nish'ē·əs), died 413 B.C., Athenian general and statesman in the Peloponnesian War.

nick (nik) *n.* 1. A slight cut, chip, or indentation on a surface or edge. 2. *Printing* A groove or notch on the shank of a type character. 3. *Archaic* A score or tally. — **in the nick of time** At the exact or crucial moment. — *v.t.* 1. To make a nick in or on. 2. *Brit. Slang* To arrest; catch. 3. *Slang* To rob or steal. — **to nick (someone) for** *U.S. Slang* To take or exact from (someone), as a fee, price, tax, etc. [Prob. var. of NOCK] — **nick'er** *n.*

nick·el (nik'əl) *n.* 1. A hard, ductile, malleable, silver-white metallic element (symbol Ni) of the iron-cobalt group, having a wide variety of uses. See ELEMENT. 2. A five-cent coin of the United States, made of an alloy of nickel and copper. — *v.t.* **·eled** or **·elled, ·el·ing** or **·el·ling** To plate with nickel. [< Sw. < G < (*kupfer*)*nickel*, lit., copper demon; because its ore looks like copper]

nick·el·bloom (nik'əl·blōom') *n.* Annabergite.

nick·el·ic (nik'əl·ik, ni·kel'-) *adj.* Containing nickel, especially in its trivalent state.

nick·el·if·er·ous (nik'ə·lif'ər·əs) *adj.* Containing or yielding nickel, as ore.

nick·el·o·de·on (nik'əl·ō'dē·ən) *n. U.S.* 1. Formerly, a motion-picture theater charging an admission fee of five cents. 2. Formerly, a jukebox or other automatic music machine. [< NICKEL (def. 2) + odeon < F *odéon* theater < LL *odeum.* See ODEUM.]

nick·el·ous (nik'əl·əs) *adj.* Containing nickel, especially in its bivalent state.

nick·el·plate (nik'əl·plāt') *v.t.* **-plat·ed, -plat·ing** To cover with nickel by electroplating.

nickel plate A thin layer of nickel deposited on the surface of objects by electroplating.

nickel silver German silver (which see).

nick·er (nik'ər) *n.* 1. A neigh. 2. A neighing laugh. — *v.i.* 1. To neigh. 2. To snicker. [Imit.]

nick·nack (nik'nak') See KNICKKNACK.

nick·name (nik'nām') *n.* 1. A familiar form of a proper name, as *Tom* for *Thomas.* 2. A descriptive name given instead of or in addition to the actual name of a person, place, or thing, in acclaim, derision, etc., as *Honest Abe* or *Empire State.* — *v.t.* **·named, ·nam·ing** 1. To give a nickname to or call by a nickname. 2. To misname. [ME *ekename* surname, *an ekename* becoming a *nickname*]

— **Syn.** (noun) *Nickname, agnomen, epithet,* and *sobriquet* denote a shortened or descriptive name of a person or thing. A *nickname* is usually a shortened or traditional hypocoristic form, as Beth for Elizabeth or Dick for Richard, but it may also be a general term including the meanings of the other synonyms. *Agnomen* is merely the Latin form of *nickname,* and is generally to be found in more formal or learned usage. An *epithet* is a descriptive adjective or phrase that serves as a nickname; "the Red" is an *epithet* in Eric the Red. A humorous or elaborate *nickname* is called a *sobriquet;* "the Manassa Mauler" was the *sobriquet* of Jack Dempsey. Compare PSEUDONYM, ACRONYM.

Nic·o·bar Islands (nik'ə·bär') See under ANDAMAN AND NICOBAR ISLANDS.

Nic·o·de·mus (nik'ə·dē'məs) A ruler of the Jews and disciple of Christ. *John* iii 1.

Nic·o·lay (nik'ə·lā), **John George**, 1832–1901, U.S. biographer born in Germany.

Nic·ol prism (nik'əl) *Optics* A set of two prisms of Iceland spar cemented together, used for producing plane-polarized light. Also **nic′ol.** [after Wm. *Nicol*, 1768?–1851, Scottish physicist]

Nic·ol·son (nik′əl·sən), **Harold,** born 1886, English diplomat, biographer, and critic born in Persia.

Nic·o·si·a (nik′ə·sē′ə) The capital of Cyprus, in the north central part; pop. 86,300 (est. 1959).

nic·o·tine (nik′ə·tēn, -tin) *n.* An acrid, poisonous, oily alkaloid, $C_{10}H_{14}N_2$, contained in the leaves of tobacco. Also **nic′o·tin.** [< F, after Jean *Nicot*, 1530–1600, French courtier, who introduced tobacco into France from Portugal] — **nic·o·tin·ic** (nik′ə·tin′ik) *adj.*

nicotinic acid *Biochem.* A colorless, water-soluble compound, $C_6H_5NO_2$, prepared by the oxidation of nicotine and forming part of the vitamin B complex, used to prevent pellagra: also called *niacin*.

nic·o·tin·ism (nik′ə·tin·iz′əm) *n.* Nicotine poisoning, as from excessive use of tobacco.

Nic·the·roy (nē′tə·roi′) See NITERÓI.

nic·ti·tate (nik′tə·tāt) *v.i.* **·tat·ed, ·tat·ing** To wink. Also **nic′tate.** [< Med.L *nictitatus*, pp. of *nictitare*, freq. of L *nictare* to wink] — **nic′ti·ta′tion** *n.*

nictitating membrane A transparent third eyelid at the inner corner of the eye in various birds, reptiles, etc.: also called *haw*. Also **nictating membrane.**

Ni·da·ros (nē′dä·rōs) A former name for TRONDHEIM.

nid·der·ing (nid′ər·ing) *Archaic n.* A coward. — *adj.* Cowardly; base. Also **nid′er·ing.** [Alter. of ME *nithing* < OE *nīthing*]

nide (nīd) *n.* A nest or brood of young pheasants. — *v.i.* **nid·ed, nid·ing** *Rare* To nest. [< L *nidus* nest]

nid·i·fy (nid′ə·fī) *v.i.* **·fied, ·fy·ing** To build a nest. Also **nid′i·fi·cate′.** [< L *nidificare* < *nidus* a nest + *facere* to make] — **nid′i·fi·cant** (-fi·kənt) *adj.* — **nid′i·fi·ca′tion** *n.*

ni·dus (nī′dəs) *n. pl.* **·dus·es** or **·di** (-dī) **1.** A nest where an insect, spider, etc., deposits eggs. **2.** *Pathol.* A focus of infection or infestation. [< L, nest]

Nie·buhr (nē′bōōr), **Barthold Georg,** 1776–1831, German historian, philologist, and critic born in Denmark. — **Reinhold,** 1892–1972, U.S. Protestant theologian.

niece (nēs) *n.* **1.** The daughter of a brother or brother-in-law or of a sister or sister-in-law. **2.** An illegitimate daughter, as of a churchman: a euphemistic term. [< OF, ult. < L *neptis* niece, granddaughter]

Nie·der·ös·ter·reich (nē′dər·œs′tə·rīkh) The German name for LOWER AUSTRIA.

Nie·der·sach·sen (nē′dər·zäk′sən) The German name for LOWER SAXONY.

ni·el·lo (nē·el′ō) *n. pl.* **·li** (-lī) or **·los 1.** The art of decorating metal plates with incised linear designs filled in with a black alloy. **2.** A work produced by this method. **3.** A black alloy used in this work. — *v.t.* **·loed, ·lo·ing** To decorate with or by means of niello. [< Ital. < L *nigellus* dark, dim. of *niger* black] — **ni·el′list** *n.*

Niel·sen (nēl′sən), **Carl August,** 1865–1931, Danish composer.

Nie·men (nē′mən, *Polish* nye′men) The Polish name for the NEMAN.

Nie·möl·ler (nē′mœl·ər), **Martin,** born 1892, German Protestant leader; opposed the Nazis.

Nier·stein·er (nir′stī·nər, -shtī-) *n.* A white Rhine wine. [after *Nierstein*, village in Germany]

Nie·tzsche (nē′chə), **Friedrich Wilhelm,** 1844–1900, German philosopher.

Nie·tzsche·ism (nē′chi·iz′əm) *n.* The principles propounded in the philosophy of Nietzsche; especially, the doctrine of the superman. Also **Nie′tzsche·an·ism.** — **Nie′tzsche·an** *adj. & n.*

nieve (nēv) *n. Scot. & Brit. Dial.* The fist or hand: also *neif*. [ME < ON *hnefi*]

nif·fer (nif′ər) *Scot. v.t.* To barter; exchange. — *n.* An exchange or barter. [? < NIEVE, NEIF]

Nif·l·heim (niv′əl·hām) In Norse mythology, the world of eternal chill, fog, and darkness; the realm of Hel. Also **Nif′el·heim.** [< ON < *nifl* fog + *heimr* world]

nif·ty (nif′tē) *adj.* **·ti·er, ·ti·est** *Slang* Stylish; pleasing. [Origin unknown]

Nig. Nigeria, Nigerian.

Ni·ger (nī′jər, -gər) A river of western Africa flowing generally east, south, and west in a great arc about 2,600 miles to the Gulf of Guinea.

Niger, Republic of An independent Republic in west central Africa; 489,069 sq. mi.: pop. 4,016,000 (est. 1970); capital, Niamey: French *République du Niger*.

Ni·ge·ri·a (nī·jir′ē·ə), **Federation of** An independent member of the British Commonwealth, in western Africa north of the Gulf of Guinea; 356,574 sq. mi.: pop. 63,870,000 (est. 1969); capital, Lagos. See map of (Gulf of) GUINEA. — **Ni·ge′ri·an** *adj. & n.*

Niger seed The seed of an African herb (*Guizotia abyssinica*) cultivated as birdseed and for its oil: also called *ramtil seed*.

nig·gard (nig′ərd) *n.* A stingy person. — *adj.* Niggardly. [? < AF, ? ult. < ON *hnøggr*]

nig·gard·ly (nig′ərd·lē) *adj.* **1.** Meanly covetous or avaricious; parsimonious; stingy. **2.** Meanly insufficient; scanty: a *niggardly* portion. — *adv.* In the manner of a niggard. — **nig′gard·li·ness** *n.*

nig·ger (nig′ər) *n.* A Negro or member of any dark-skinned people: a vulgar and offensive term. [Earlier *neger* < F *nègre* < Sp. *negro*. See NEGRO.]

nig·gle (nig′əl) *v.i.* **·gled, ·gling** To occupy oneself with trifles; behave trivially. [Cf. dial. Norw. *nigla*]

nig·gling (nig′ling) *adj.* **1.** Fussy; overprecise. **2.** Mean; petty. **3.** Annoying; nagging. — *n.* Overelaborate or overprecise work or behavior. — **nig′gling·ly** *adv.*

nigh (nī) *Chiefly Archaic & Dial. adj.* **nigh·er, nigh·est** or next **1.** Close; near. **2.** Convenient; direct. — *adv.* **1.** Near in time or place. **2.** Almost: often with *on* or *onto*: *nigh* on a year. — *prep.* Near. — *v.t. & v.i.* To draw near; approach. [OE *nēah, nēh*] — **nigh′ness** *n.*

night (nīt) *n.* **1.** The period from sunset to sunrise, especially the part that is dark. ♦ Collateral adjective: *nocturnal*. **2.** The period of evening and darkness before midnight of a given day. **3.** Darkness; the dark. **4.** A condition of ignorance, gloom, painful confusion, etc.: the dark *night* of the soul. [OE *niht, neaht*. Akin to OHG *naht*, ON *nätt*, Gk. *nux, nuktos*.]

night blindness Nyctalopia.

night-bloom·ing cereus (nīt′blōō′ming) See under CEREUS.

night·cap (nīt′kap′) *n.* **1.** A cap to be worn in bed. **2.** *Informal* A drink of liquor taken just before going to bed.

night·clothes (nīt′klōz′, -klōth z′) *n.pl.* Clothes to be worn in bed.

night·club (nīt′klub′) *n.* A restaurant open until late at night, providing entertainment, food, and drink. Also **night club.**

night crawler *U.S. Informal* Any large earthworm that emerges at night: also called *nightwalker*.

night·fall (nīt′fôl′) *n.* The close of day.

night·glass (nīt′glas′, -gläs′) *n.* A spyglass or telescope having concentrating lenses, for use at night.

night·gown (nīt′goun′) *n.* A loose gown worn in bed by women and children. Also **night′dress′** (-dres′).

night·hawk (nīt′hôk′) *n.* **1.** Any of various goatsuckers (genus *Chordeiles*) of North and South America, related to the whippoorwill; especially, the **common nighthawk** (*C. minor*): also called *bullbat, mosquito hawk*. **2.** The nightjar. **3.** A night owl (def. 2).

night heron Any of various short, stocky herons (genus *Nycticorax*), of nocturnal habits; especially, the **black-crowned night heron** (*N. nycticorax*) of the Old and New Worlds: also *night raven*.

night·in·gale (nī′tən·gāl, nī′ting-) *n.* A small, Old World migratory bird (genus *Luscinia*), allied to the thrushes; especially, *L. megarhynchos* of Europe, noted for the sweet melodious song of the male. [OE *nihtegale* < *niht* night + *galan* to sing]

Night·in·gale (nī′tən·gāl, nī′ting-), **Florence,** 1820–1910, English nurse born in Italy; served in the military hospitals during the Crimean War; pioneer of modern nursing.

night·jar (nīt′jär′) *n.* Any of various goatsuckers (genus *Caprimulgus*) of Europe: also called *nighthawk*.

night latch A spring latch operated from the outside by a key and from the inside by a knob. Also **night lock.**

night letter A telegram transmitted at night, at reduced rates.

night-light (nīt′līt′) *n.* A light, usually a dim one, kept burning all night.

night-long (nīt′lông′, -long′) *adj.* Lasting through the night. — *adv.* Through the whole night.

night·ly (nīt′lē) *adj.* **1.** Of, pertaining to, or occurring each night. **2.** Pertaining to or occurring at night. — *adv.* **1.** By night. **2.** Each night: to take place *nightly*.

night·mare (nīt′mâr) *n.* **1.** A horrible and frightening dream. **2.** Any experience, condition, or tendency resembling a nightmare: the *nightmare* of total war. **3.** Formerly, an evil spirit supposed to suffocate people during sleep; an incubus. [< NIGHT + MARE^2] — **night′mar·ish** *adj.*

night owl 1. An owl having nocturnal habits. **2.** One who stays up late: also called *nighthawk*.

night raven Any of various nocturnal birds, especially the night heron.

night-ri·der (nīt′rī′dər) *n.* In the southern or western United States, one of a band of masked, mounted men performing lawless acts of violence at night for purposes of intimidation, vengeance, etc. — **night′rid′ing** *n.*

nights (nīts) *adv. Informal* At night. [OE *nihtes*, adverbial genitive]

night school A school that holds classes during the evening, especially for those who cannot attend day school.

night·shade (nīt/shād/) *n.* **1.** Any of various flowering plants (genus *Solanum*); especially, the **black** or **common nightshade** (*S. nigrum*), having white flowers and black berries, and the **woody** or **bittersweet nightshade** (*S. dulcamara*), with purple flowers and red berries. The nightshade typifies a large family (*Solanaceae*) of plants, including tobacco, pepper, jimsonweed, the potato, and the tomato. **2.** Belladonna (def. 1).

COMMON NIGHT-SHADE (*a*) Spray showing blossom (*b*) and fruit (*c*).

night·shirt (nīt/shûrt/) *n.* A long, loose garment worn in bed, usually by men or boys.
night soil The contents of privies, cesspools, etc., usually removed at night.
night·spot (nīt/spot/) *U.S. Informal* A night club.
night·stick (nīt/stik/) *n. U.S.* A long, heavy club carried by policemen.
night table A bedside table or stand. Also **night/stand/**.
night·time (nīt/tīm/) *n.* The time from sunset to sunrise, or from dark to dawn. Also *Archaic & Poetic* **night/tide/**.
night·walk·er (nīt/wô/kər) *n.* **1.** *U.S. Informal* A night crawler. **2.** *Rare* One who walks about at night.
night watch 1. A watch or guard kept at night. **2.** A night watchman. **3.** A period of watch or guard.
night·wear (nīt/wâr/) *n.* Nightclothes.
night·y (nī/tē) *n. pl.* **night·ies** *U.S. Informal* A nightgown.
ni·gres·cence (nī-gres/əns) *n.* The process of becoming black; also blackness or darkness. [< L *nigrescere* to become black < *niger* black] — **ni·gres/cent** *adj.*
nigri- *combining form* Black. Also, before vowels, **nigr-.** [< L *niger, nigris* black]
nig·ri·fy (nig/rə-fī) *v.t.* **·fied, ·fy·ing** To make black. [< LL *nigrificare* < L *niger* black + *facere* to make] — **nig/ri·fi·ca/tion** *n.*
Ni·gri·ti·a (ni-grish/ē-ə) A former name for the region of the SUDAN.
nig·ri·tude (nig/rə-tōōd, -tyōōd) *n.* Blackness; darkness.
ni·hil (nī/hil, nĭ/-) *n.* Nothing; nil. [< L]
ni·hil ad rem (nī/hil ad rem) *Latin* Nothing to the point.
ni·hil·ism (nī/əl·iz/əm, nĭ/hil-) *n.* **1.** *Philos.* **a** A doctrine that denies existence. **b** A doctrine that denies any basis for knowledge or truth. **c** Total denial of all traditional and existing principles, values, and institutions. **2.** In politics: **a** A doctrine holding that reform is possible only through the destruction of all political, economic, and social institutions. **b** *Usually cap.* A revolutionary movement in Russia in the 19th century advocating violence and terror. **3.** Any revolutionary movement or propaganda advocating terror and violence. — **ni/hil·ist** *n.* — **ni/hil·is/tic** *adj.*
ni·hil·i·ty (nī-hil/ə-tē, ni-) *n.* Nothingness.
Ni·hon (nē/hon/) In JAPAN.
Ni·i·ga·ta (nē/i·gä/tä) A port city on NW Honshu island, Japan; pop. 379,000 (est. 1968).
Ni·jin·sky (nə·jin/skē, *Russian* ni·zhēn/skē), **Vaslav,** 1890–1950, Russian ballet dancer and choreographer.
Nij·me·gen (nī/mā·gən, *Du.* nī/mä·khən) A city in the eastern Netherlands, on the Waal; pop. 148,790 (1970): German *Nimwegen*.
Ni·ke (nī/kē) In Greek mythology, the winged goddess of victory: identified with the Roman *Victoria*. — *n.* An antiaircraft guided missile. [< Gk. *Nikē* victory]
Nik·ko (nēk/kō) A town and religious center on central Honshu island, Japan; pop. about 33,000.
Ni·ko·la·ev (nyi·kō·lä/yəf) A port city in the southern Ukrainian S.S.R., on the Bug estuary; pop. 331,000 (1970): formerly *Vernoleninsk*. Also *Nikolayev*.
nil (nil) *n.* Nothing. [< L, contr. of *nihil* nothing]
nil des·pe·ran·dum (nil des/pə·ran/dəm) *Latin* Nothing to be despaired of; never despair.

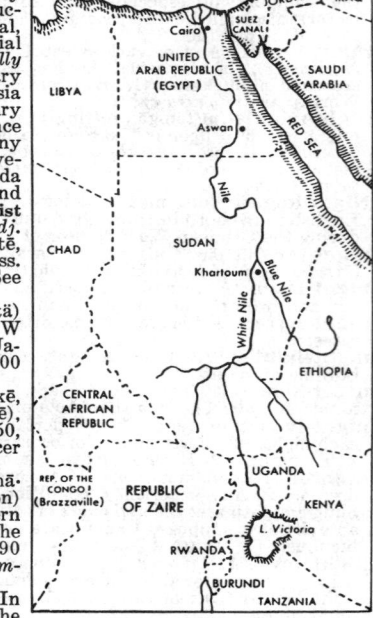

THE NILE

Nile (nīl) The longest river in Africa, rising in Lake Victoria and flowing 3,485 miles north to the Mediterranean; between Lake Victoria and Lake Albert it is known as the **Victoria Nile;** between Lake Albert and the Sudan as the **Albert Nile,** between Lake No and Khartoum as the **White Nile;** at Khartoum it receives the **Blue Nile,** a tributary flowing 850 miles from Ethiopia, and is known as the Nile for the rest of its course. — **Battle of the Nile** A British naval victory over the French, near the mouth of the Nile on August 1, 1798.
Nile green Any of several light green tints.
nil·gai (nil/gī) *n.* A large, short-maned antelope (*Boselaphus tragocamelus*) of India: also spelled *nylghai, nylghau.* Also **nil/gau** (-gô), **nil/ghai, nil/ghau** (-gô). [< Hind. *nīlgāi* < *nīl* blue + *gāi* cow]
Nil·gi·ri Hills (nil/gi·rē) A mountainous plateau district in SW Madras, India; highest peak, Dodabetta, 8,460 ft. Also **the Nil/gi·ris.**
nill (nil) *v.t. & v.i. Archaic* To be unwilling. See WILLY-NILLY. [OE *nyllan* < *ne-* not + *willan* to will]
nil ni·si bo·num (nil nī/sī bō/nəm) *Latin* Short for DE MORTUIS NIL NISI BONUM.
Ni·lom·e·ter (nī·lom/ə·tər) *n.* A gauge for measuring the height of the Nile floods. [< Gk. *Neilometrion* < *Neilos* Nile + *metron* measure] — **Ni·lo·met/ric** (nī/lō·met/rik) *adj.*
Ni·lot·ic (nī·lot/ik) *adj.* **1.** Of, pertaining to, or characteristic of the Nile or the peoples native to the Nile basin. **2.** Of or pertaining to a subfamily of Sudanic languages.
nim·ble (nim/bəl) *adj.* **·bler, ·blest 1.** Light and quick in movement; lively. **2.** Characterized by a quick and ready intellect: a *nimble* mind. [OE *numel* quick at grasping, and *næmel* receptive; both < *niman* to take] — **nim/ble·ness** *n.* — **nim/bly** *adv.*
— **Syn. 1.** Nimble, agile, brisk, and spry mean moving easily and quickly. *Nimble* stresses lightness and rapidity: the *nimble* fingers of a concert pianist; *agile*, dexterity in the use of the limbs: Are you *agile* enough to climb that tree? *Brisk* describes that which is lively, animated, and rapid: a *brisk* walk before dinner. *Spry* refers to suppleness or agility which is unusual or unexpected: a *spry* old man. — **Ant** slow, heavy, ponderous, awkward.
nim·bo·stra·tus (nim/bō·strā/təs, -strat/əs) *n. Meteorol.* A low, formless, dark gray cloud layer, precipitating continuous rain or snow. See table for CLOUD.
nim·bus (nim/bəs) *n. pl.* **·bus·es** or **·bi** (-bī) **1.** A luminous emanation or atmosphere believed to envelop a deity or holy person; glory; also, the representation of this in art. **2.** Any atmosphere or aura, as of fame, glamor, etc., about a person or thing. **3.** Formerly, a nimbostratus. [< L, cloud]
Nîmes (nēmz, *Fr.* nēm) A city in south France; pop. 115,561 (1968): formerly *Nismes.*
ni·mi·e·ty (ni·mī/ə·tē) *n. pl.* **·ties** *Rare* Excess. [< L *nimis* too much] — **nim·i·ous** (ni/mē·əs) *adj.*
nim·i·ny-pim·i·ny (nim/ə·nē·pim/ə·nē) *adj.* Affectedly nice or delicate; effeminate; mincing. [Imit.]
Nim·itz (nim/its), **Chester William,** 1885–1966, U.S. admiral; chief of naval operations, 1945.
n'im·porte (naṅ·pôrt/) *French* It is of no importance.
Nim·rod (nim/rod) Grandson of Ham, described as a mighty hunter. *Gen.* x 8. — *n.* A hunter. Also **nim/rod.**
Nim·u·e (nim/ōō·ā) See VIVIAN.
Nim·we·gen (nim/vā·gən) The German name for NIJMEGEN.
Ni·ña (nē/nə, *Sp.* nē/nyä) *n.* One of the three ships of Columbus on his first voyage to America.
nin·com·poop (nin/kəm·pōōp/) *n.* An idiot; dolt; fool. [Origin unknown] — **nin/com·poop/er·y, nin/com·poop/ish·ness** *n.* — **nin/com·poop/ish** *adj.*
nine (nīn) *n.* **1.** The sum of eight and one: a cardinal number. **2.** Any symbol of this number, as 9, ix, IX. **3.** Anything consisting of or representing nine units, as a baseball team, etc. — **the Nine** The Muses. — *adj.* Being one more than eight. [OE *nigon.* Cf. OHG *niun,* ON *niu,* L *novem.*]
nine iron In golf, an iron with an extremely slanted face, used for lofting the ball: also called *niblick.* For illustration see GOLF CLUB.
nine·pence (nīn/pəns) *n. Brit.* **1.** The sum of nine pennies. **2.** A coin of this value, no longer minted.
nine·pin (nīn/pin/) *n.* One of the pins used in ninepins.
nine·pins (nīn/pinz/) *n.pl.* (construed *as sing.*) A bowling game similar to tenpins, using nine large wooden pins.
nine·teen (nīn/tēn/) *n.* **1.** The sum of eighteen and one: a cardinal number. **2.** Any symbol of this number, as 19, xix, XIX. **3.** Anything consisting of or representing nineteen units, as an organization, game token, etc. — *adj.* Being one more than eighteen. [OE *nigontīene,* lit., nine plus ten]
nine·teenth (nīn/tēnth/) *adj.* **1.** Next after the eighteenth: the ordinal of *nineteen.* **2.** Being one of nineteen equal parts. — *n.* **1.** One of nineteen equal parts. **2.** That which follows the *eighteenth.*
nine·ti·eth (nīn/tē·ith) *adj.* **1.** Tenth in order after the eightieth: the ordinal of *ninety.* **2.** Being one of ninety equal parts. — *n.* **1.** One of ninety equal parts. **2.** That which is tenth in order after the eightieth.
nine·ty (nīn/tē) *n. pl.* **·ties 1.** The sum of eighty and ten: a cardinal number. **2.** Any symbol of this number, as 90,

xc, XC. **3.** Anything consisting of or representing ninety units, as an organization, game token, etc. — *adj.* Being ten more than eighty. [OE *nigontig,* lit., nine by ten]

Nin·e·veh (nin′ə·və) An ancient city on the Tigris, capital of Assyria: Latin *Ninus.* — **Nin′e·vite** (-vīt) *n.*

Ning·po (ning′pō′) A port city in NE Chekiang province, China; pop. 280,000 (est. 1958).

Ning·sia (ning′shyä′) See YINCHWAN. Also **Ning′hsia′.**

nin·ny (nin′ē) *n. pl.* **·nies** A dunce. [? < (*a*)*n inn*(*ocent*)]

ninth (nīnth) *adj.* **1.** Next after the eighth: the ordinal of *nine.* **2.** Being one of nine equal parts. — *n.* **1.** One of nine equal parts. **2.** That which follows the eighth.

Ni·nus (nī′nəs) **1.** In Assyrian legend, the founder of Nineveh and husband of Semiramis. **2.** The Latin name for NINEVEH.

Ni·o·be (nī′ə·bē) In Greek mythology, the mother whose children were killed by Apollo and Artemis after she had vaunted their superiority to Leto. She was turned by Zeus into a stone from which tears continued to flow.

ni·o·bi·um (nī·ō′bē·əm) *n.* A rare, steel gray, metallic element (symbol Nb), valuable as an alloy metal: formerly called *columbium.* See ELEMENT. [< NIOBE]

ni·o·bous (nī·ō′bəs) *adj. Chem.* Denoting a compound containing trivalent niobium.

Ni·o·brar·a River (nī′ə·brâr′ə) A river in east Wyoming and north Nebraska, flowing 431 miles east to the Missouri.

nip[1] (nip) *v.* **nipped, nip·ping** *v.t.* **1.** To catch or compress tightly between two surfaces or points; bite; pinch. **2.** To sever or remove by pinching, biting, or clipping: usually with *off:* to *nip* off a shoot. **3.** To check, arrest, or destroy the growth or development of: to *nip* the rumor. **4.** To affect painfully or injuriously, as by cold: A sharp wind *nipped* his ears. **5.** *Slang* To steal; pilfer. **6.** *Slang* To catch; take. — *v.i.* **7.** *Brit. Informal* To move nimbly or rapidly: with *off, away,* etc. — **to nip in the bud** To stop or suppress at the outset. — *n.* **1.** The act of one who or that which nips; a bite. **2.** That which is nipped off; a little piece or bit. **3.** Any small portion or fragment: a *nip* of tea. **4.** A sharp, stinging quality, as in cold air. **5.** Severe cold or frost: winter's *nip.* **6.** A cutting remark or saying; gibe. **7.** A sharp, pungent flavor; tang. — **nip and tuck** *U.S.* Very close or even; precariously uncertain. [Cf. Du. *nijpen* to pinch]

nip[2] (nip) *n.* A small quantity of liquor. — *v.t. & v.i.* To sip (liquor). [? < earlier *nipperkin* a small liquid measure]

Nip (nip) *n. & adj. Slang* Japanese: an offensive term.

ni·pa (nī′pə, nē′-) *n.* A palm (*Nipa fruticans*) of tropical SE Asia, having feathery leaves and bunches of edible fruit, and used for weaving, thatching, etc. An alcoholic beverage made from this palm. [ult. < Malay *nipah*]

Nip·i·gon (nip′ə·gon), **Lake** A lake in Ontario, Canada, north of Lake Superior; 1,870 sq. mi.

Nip·is·sing (nip′ə·sing), **Lake** A lake in Ontario, Canada, between Georgian Bay and the Ottawa River; 330 sq. mi.

nip·per (nip′ər) *n.* **1.** One who or that which nips. **2.** *pl.* Any of various implements used for nipping, as pliers, pincers, etc. **3.** The large claw of a crab or lobster. **4.** One of the incisors of a horse. **5.** *pl. Slang* Handcuffs. **6.** *Brit. Informal* A small boy; lad.

nip·ping (nip′ing) *adj.* **1.** That pinches or nips. **2.** Biting or sharp, as cold wind; nippy. **3.** Sarcastic or stinging.

nip·ple (nip′əl) *n.* **1.** The protuberance on the breasts of higher mammals, especially that of the female; mammilla; teat. **2.** The rubber teatlike mouthpiece of a nursing bottle. **3.** Something resembling a nipple, as a short pipe coupling with threaded ends. [Earlier *nible,* ? dim. of NIB]

Nip·pon (nip′on, ni·pon′; *Japanese* nēp·pōn′) See JAPAN. — **Nip′pon·ese′** (-ēz′, -ēs′) *adj. & n.*

Nip·pur (ni·pōōr′) An ancient Sumerian city of southern Babylonia, the earliest religious capital of the area.

nip·py (nip′ē) *adj.* **·pi·er, ·pi·est** **1.** Biting or sharp, as cold weather. **2.** *Brit. Informal* Active; alert. — **nip′pi·ly** *adv.* — **nip′pi·ness** *n.*

N. Ire. Northern Ireland.

nir·va·na (nir·vä′nə, nər·van′ə) *n.* **1.** In Buddhism, the state of absolute felicity, characterized by freedom from passion, desire, suffering, etc., and attained through the annihilation of the self or through the liberation of the individual from all passions and desires. **2.** Loosely, a similar state in Hinduism, achieved through the merging of the self into Brahma. **3.** Freedom from care and pain; bliss. [< Skt. *nirvāna* extinction < *nirvā* to blow]

Ni·san (nē·sän′, nis′ən) *n.* The seventh month of the Hebrew year: also called *Abib.* Also **Nis′san.** See (Hebrew) CALENDAR.

Ni·sei (nē·sā) *n. pl.* **·sei** or **·seis** A native American of immigrant Japanese parentage. Compare ISSEI, KIBEI.

Nish (nēsh) A city in SE central Serbia, Yugoslavia; pop. 74,500 (est. 1959). *Serbo-Croatian* **Niš.** Formerly also **Nis·sa** (nis′ə).

Ni·sha·pur (nē′shä·pōōr′) A town in NE Iran; pop. about 24,000.

ni·si (nī′sī) *conj. Law* Unless: used after the word *order, rule, decree,* etc., signifying that it shall become effective at a certain time, unless modified or avoided. [< L]

ni·si pri·us (nī′sī prī′əs) *Law* A term meaning, literally, unless sooner, but used now to describe the trying of an issue of fact before a single judge and jury. [< L]

Nismes (nēm) See NÎMES.

Nis·sen hut (nis′ən, nēs′-) A prefabricated sheet steel building resembling a long half-cylinder lying flat on the ground. Compare QUONSET HUT. [after P. N. *Nissen,* 1871–1930, Canadian Army engineer, who invented it]

ni·sus (nī′səs) *n. pl.* **·sus** *Latin* The exercise of power in acting or attempting to act; an effort, endeavor, or exertion.

nit (nit) *n.* **1.** The egg of a louse or other parasitic insect, especially when attached to body hairs, etc. **2.** An immature louse. [OE *hnitu*] — **nit′ty** *adj.*

nit·chie (nich′ē) *n. Canadian* An Indian: an offensive term.

ni·ter (nī′tər) *n.* **1.** Potassium or sodium nitrate; saltpeter. **2.** *Obs.* Natron. Also **ni′tre.** [< OF *nitre* < L *nitrum* < Gk. *nitron.* Cf. Hebrew *nether.*]

Ni·te·rói (nē′te·roi′) The capital of Rio de Janeiro State, SE Brazil, on Guanabara Bay; pop. 228,826 (1960): formerly *Nictheroy.*

ni·ton (nī′ton) *n.* Radon (which see). Abbr. *Nt* [< *nit-* (< L *nitere* to shine) + -ON]

nit-pick (nit′pik′) *Informal v.t.* **1.** To fuss over, especially with the aim of picking out petty faults. — *v.i.* **2.** To engage in nitpicking. Also **nit′pick.** [Back formation < NIT-PICKING] — **nit′-pick′er** *n.*

nit-pick·ing (nit′pik′ing) *n. Informal* A fussing over trivial details, often with the aim of finding fault.

ni·trate (nī′trāt) *Chem. n.* **1.** A salt or ester of nitric acid. **2.** Niter. — *v.t.* **·trat·ed, ·trat·ing** To treat or combine with nitric acid or a compound. [< F < OF *nitre.* See NITER.]

ni·tric (nī′trik) *adj. Chem.* **1.** Of, pertaining to, or obtained from nitrogen. **2.** Containing nitrogen in the higher valence.

nitric acid *Chem.* A colorless, highly corrosive liquid, HNO_3, having strong oxidizing properties.

nitric oxide *Chem.* A colorless, gaseous compound, NO, liberated when certain metals are dissolved in nitric acid.

ni·tride (nī′trīd, -trid) *n. Chem.* A compound of nitrogen with some more electropositive element. Also **ni′trid** (-trid).

ni·tri·fi·ca·tion (nī′trə·fə·kā′shən) *n. Chem.* The oxidation of ammonium salts into nitrites and nitrates, especially by soil bacteria. [< F]

ni·tri·fy (nī′trə·fī) *v.t.* **·fied, ·fy·ing** *Chem.* **1.** To treat or combine with nitrogen. **2.** To convert, as ammonium salts in the soil, into nitrates or nitrites by oxidation. **3.** To treat or impregnate (soil, etc.) with nitrates. [< F *nitrifier*] — **ni′tri·fi′a·ble** *adj.*

ni·trile (nī′tril, -trēl, -tril) *n. Chem.* Any of a group of cyanogen compounds, corresponding to the formula RCN, in which R is a univalent organic radical. Also **ni′tril** (-tril).

ni·trite (nī′trīt) *n. Chem.* A salt of nitrous acid.

nitro- *combining form Chem.* Containing the univalent radical NO_2: *nitrobenzene.* Also before vowels, **nitr-.** Also **nitri-.** [< L *nitrum* < Gk. *nitron*]

ni·tro·bac·te·ri·um (nī′trō·bak·tir′ē·əm) *n. pl.* **·ri·a** (-rē·ə) Any of various soil bacteria involved in the process of nitrification, especially any bacteria of the genera *Nitrosomonas* and *Nitrobacter.* Also **nitric bacterium.**

ni·tro·ben·zene (nī′trō·ben′zēn, -ben·zēn′) *n. Chem.* A yellow, oily compound, $C_6H_5NO_2$, formed by the nitration of benzene and used in the making of aniline.

ni·tro·cel·lu·lose (nī′trō·sel′yə·lōs) *n.* Cellulose nitrate.

ni·tro·gen (nī′trə·jən) *n.* An odorless, colorless, gaseous element (symbol N) forming about four-fifths of the atmosphere by volume and playing a decisive role in the formation of compounds essential to life. See ELEMENT. [< F *nitrogène* < *nitro-* NITRO- + *-gène* -GEN]

nitrogen fixation **1.** The conversion of atmospheric nitrogen into nitrates by soil bacteria, either free-living or in root nodules of certain leguminous plants. **2.** The production of nitrogen compounds, as for fertilizers and explosives, by processes utilizing free nitrogen. — **ni′tro·gen-fix′ing** *adj.*

ni·trog·en·ize (nī·troj′ən·īz, nī′trə·jən·īz′) *v.t.* **·ized, ·iz·ing** To treat or combine with nitrogen.

ni·trog·e·nous (nī·troj′ə·nəs) *adj.* Pertaining to or containing nitrogen. Also **ni·tro·ge·ne·ous** (nī′trō·jē′nē·əs).

ni·tro·glyc·er·in (nī′trō·glis′ər·in) *n. Chem.* A colorless to pale yellow, oily liquid, $C_3H_5(ONO_2)_3$, made by nitrating glycerol, used as an explosive and propellant, combined with kieselguhr to form dynamite, and used in medicine. Also **ni′tro, ni′tro·glyc′er·ine.** [< NITRO- + GLYCERIN]

nitro group *Chem.* The univalent NO_2 radical.

ni·tro·hy·dro·chlo·ric acid (nī′trō·hī′drə·klôr′ik, -klō′rik) Aqua regia.

ni·trol·ic (nī·trol′ik) *adj. Chem.* Noting a class of acids containing a nitro group combined with an oxime group and having the general formula $RC(:NOH)NO_2.$

---

ni·tro·par·af·fin (nī'trō·par'ə·fin) *n. Chem.* Any derivative of the methane series in which hydrogen has been replaced by a nitro group.

ni·tro·phe·nol (nī'trō·fē'nōl, -nol) *n. Chem.* Any of a group of phenol compounds derived by the replacement of one or more hydrogen atoms by the nitro group, used in the making of dyestuffs.

ni·tros·a·mine (nī·tros'ə·mēn, -min) *n. Chem.* Any of a group of organic compounds containing the bivalent radical N:NO. Also **ni·tros'a·min** (-min).

nitroso- *combining form Chem.* Of or containing nitrosyl. Also, before vowels, **nitros-.** [< NL *nitrosus* nitrous]

ni·tro·syl (nī·trō'sil, nī'trə·sēl', nī'trə·sil) *n. Chem.* The univalent radical NO, known only in its combinations. [< NITROS(O)- + -YL]

ni·trous (nī'trəs) *adj. Chem.* Of, pertaining to, or derived from nitrogen: especially applied to those compounds containing less oxygen than the nitric compounds.

nitrous acid *Chem.* An unstable compound, HNO_2, occurring only in solution.

nitrous oxide A gas, N_2O, used as an anesthetic in dental surgery, etc., and sometimes having an exhilarating effect when inhaled: also called *laughing gas*.

nit·wit (nit'wit') *n.* A silly or stupid person. [< NIT + WIT¹]

Ni·u·e (nē·ōō'ā) An island dependency of New Zealand SE of Samoa; about 100 sq. mi.: also *Savage Island*.

ni·val (nī'vəl) *adj.* Pertaining to the snow; also, growing under the snow. [< L *nivalis* < *nix, nivis* snow]

niv·e·ous (niv'ē·əs) *adj.* Snowy; like snow.

Ni·ver·nais (nē·ver·nā') A region and former province of central France.

Ni·vôse (nē·vôz') *n.* The fourth month of the Republican calendar. See (Republican) CALENDAR. [< F < L *nivosus* snowy]

nix¹ (niks) *n.* In Germanic mythology, a water sprite appearing in male or female form, and sometimes appearing as part fish. [< G] — **nix'ie** *n.fem.*

nix² (niks) *Slang n.* **1.** Nothing. **2.** No. — *adv.* No. — *interj.* Stop! Watch out!: an exclamation urging someone to stop saying or doing something. — *v.t.* To forbid or disagree with: He *nixed* our suggestions. [< G *nichts* nothing]

Nix·on (nik'sən), **Richard Milhous,** born 1913, vice president of the United States 1953–1960; 37th president of the United States 1969–.

ni·zam (ni·zäm', -zam', nī-) *n. pl.* **·zam** A Turkish regular soldier. [< Urdu and Turkish *nizäm* < Arabic]

Ni·zam (ni·zäm', -zam', nī-) *n.* The title of the former hereditary rulers of Hyderabad, India.

Nizam's Dominions A former name for HYDERABAD. Also **Ni·zam'ate.**

Nizh·niy Nov·go·rod (nyēzh'nyē nôv'gə·rət) A former name for GORKIY.

Nizh·niy Ta·gil (nyēzh'nyē tä·gyēl) A city in the west central R.S.F.S.R.; pop. 338,000 (1959). Also **Nizh'ni Ta·gil'.**

N.J. New Jersey.

Njord (nyôrd) In Norse mythology, one of the Vanir, god of the winds and sea, father of Frey and Freya. Also **Njorth.**

NKVD Formerly, the MVD. Also **N.K.V.D.** [< Russian *N(arodni) K(ommissariat) V(nutrennikh) D(el)* People's Commissariat for Internal Affairs]

n.l. **1.** *Printing* New line. **2.** North latitude. **3.** Not clear (L *non liquet*). **4.** Not lawful (L *non licet*).

NL or **NL.** or **N.L.** New Latin.

N. lat. North latitude.

NLRB or **N.L.R.B.** National Labor Relations Board.

N.Mex. New Mexico: also **N.M.** (unofficial).

NMU or **N.M.U.** National Maritime Union.

NNE or **nne, N.N.E.,** or **n.n.e.** North-northeast.

NNW or **nnw, N.N.W.,** or **n.n.w.** North-northwest.

no¹ (nō) *adv.* **1.** Nay; not so: opposed to *yes.* **2.** Not at all; not in any wise: used with comparatives: *no* better than the other. **3.** Not: used to express an alternative after *or*: whether or *no.* — *n. pl.* **noes 1.** A negative reply; a denial: He will not take *no* for an answer. **2.** A negative vote or voter: The *noes* have it. [OE *nā* < *ne* not + *ā* ever]

no² (nō) *adj.* Not any; not one: *No* seats are left. [OE *nān* < *ne* not + *ān* one]

no³ (nō) *n. pl.* **no** *Sometimes cap.* The classical drama of Japan, traditionally tragic or noble in theme, having music and dancing: also spelled *noh.* Also **nō.** Compare KABUKI.

No *Chem.* Nobelium.

No. **1.** North; northern. **2.** Number: also **no.**

No·a·chi·an (nō·ā'kē·ən) *adj.* Of or pertaining to Noah or to his time. Also **No·ach'ic** (-ak'ik), **No·ach'i·cal** (-ak'-).

No·ah (nō'ə) In the Old Testament, a patriarch who at God's command built an ark that saved him, his family, and every kind of animal from the Flood. *Gen.* v–ix. [< Hebrew *Nōăh* rest or comfort]

nob¹ (nob) *n.* **1.** *Slang* The head. **2.** In cribbage, a jack of the same suit as the card turned face up, worth one point. [Var. of KNOB]

nob² (nob) *n. Slang* One who is rich, influential, etc. [Origin unknown]

no-ball (nō'bôl') *n.* In cricket, a ball unfairly bowled.

nob·ble (nob'əl) *v.t.* **·bled, ·bling** *Brit. Slang* **1.** To disable (a horse) to prevent its winning a race, as by drugging, etc. **2.** To gain or influence by underhand means. **3.** To swindle. **4.** To catch. [Origin uncertain] — **nob'bler** *n.*

nob·by (nob'ē) *adj.* **·bi·er, ·bi·est** *Slang* Elegant or flashy; showy; stylish. [< NOB²]

No·bel (nō·bel'), **Alfred Bernhard,** 1833–96, Swedish industrialist, inventor of dynamite; founded by his will the **Nobel Prizes,** awarded annually in the fields of physics, chemistry, medicine, literature, and the furtherance of world peace.

no·be·li·um (nō·bē'lē·əm) *n.* An unstable radioactive element (symbol No) of the actinide series, originally produced by the bombardment of curium by an isotope of carbon. See ELEMENT. [after A. B. *Nobel*]

No·bi·le (nō'bē·lā), **Umberto,** born 1885, Italian aeronautical engineer and Arctic explorer.

no·bil·i·ar·y (nō·bil'ē·er'ē, -bil'yə·rē) *adj.* Of or pertaining to the nobility. [< F *nobiliaire*]

no·bil·i·ty (nō·bil'ə·tē) *n. pl.* **·ties 1.** A class in society composed of persons having hereditary title, rank, and privileges; the aristocracy. **2.** In Great Britain, the peerage. **3.** The state or quality of being noble. **4.** The state or quality of being elevated in birth, rank, or title. [< OF *nobilite* < L *nobilitas* < *nobilis* noble]

no·ble (nō'bəl) *adj.* **·bler, ·blest 1.** Having or indicative of excellence or dignity; eminent; illustrious; worthy: a *noble* effort. **2.** Characterized by or displaying superior moral qualities; magnanimous; lofty. **3.** Magnificent and imposing in appearance; grand; stately. **4.** Of or pertaining to the nobility; aristocratic. **5.** Chemically inert. **6.** Comparatively high in value: said of metals. — *n.* **1.** One who belongs to the nobility; a nobleman. **2.** In Great Britain, a peer. **3.** A former English gold coin, equivalent to 6 shillings, 8 pence. [< MF < L *nobilis* noble, well-known. Akin to L *noscere* to know.] — **no'ble·ness** *n.* — **no'bly** *adv.*

no·ble·man (nō'bəl·mən) *n. pl.* **·men** (-mən) A man of noble rank; in England, a peer.

no·blesse (nō·bles') *n.* **1.** *Obs.* Noble birth or condition. **2.** The nobility. [< F]

no·blesse o·blige (nō·bles' ō·blēzh') *French* Those of high birth, wealth, or social position must behave generously or nobly toward others; literally, nobility obligates.

no·ble·wom·an (nō'bəl·wŏom'ən) *n. pl.* **·wom·en** (-wim'in) **1.** A woman of noble rank. **2.** In England, a peeress.

no·bod·y (nō'bod'ē, -bəd·ē) *pron.* Not anybody. — *n. pl.* **·bod·ies** A person of no importance or influence.

no·cent (nō'sənt) *adj. Rare* **1.** Injurious; hurtful. **2.** Guilty. [< L *nocens, -entis,* ppr. of *nocere* to harm]

nock (nok) *n.* **1.** The notch for the bowstring on the butt end of an arrow. **2.** The notch on the horn of a bow for securing the bowstring. — *v.t.* **1.** To notch (an arrow or bow). **2.** To fit (an arrow) to the bowstring, as for shooting. [ME *nocke,* prob. < Sw. *nock.* Akin to MDu. *nocke.*]

noc·tam·bu·la·tion (nok·tam'byə·lā'shən) *n.* Somnambulism. Also **noc·tam'bu·lism.** [< L *nox, noctis* night + *ambulare* to walk] — **noc·tam'bu·list** *n.*

nocti- *combining form* By or at night: *noctilucent.* Also, before vowels, **noct-.** [< L *nox, noctis* night]

noc·ti·lu·ca (nok'tə·lōō'kə) *n.* Any of a genus (*Noctiluca*) of bioluminescent marine flagellates producing a phosphorescent luminosity. [< L *noctiluca* something that shines at night < *nox, noctis* night + *lucere* to shine]

noc·ti·lu·cent (nok'tə·lōō'sənt) *adj. Meteorol.* Luminous by night: said especially of certain high-altitude clouds.

noc·tu·id (nok'chōō·id) *n.* Any of a large family (*Noctuidae*) of medium-sized moths, especially those whose larvae, as the army worm and the cutworm, are very destructive pests. — *adj.* Of or pertaining to this family of moths. [< NL *noctuidae* < L *noctua* night owl] — **noc·tu·id'e·ous** (-id'ē·əs), **noc·tu'id·ous, noc·tu·oid** (nok'chōō·oid) *adj.*

noc·tule (nok'chōōl) *n.* A large insectivorous bat (*Nyctalus noctula*) of Europe and Asia. [< F < Ital. *nottola* bat]

noc·turn (nok'tûrn) *n. Often cap. Eccl.* One of the three divisions of the office of matins. [< L *nocturnus* nightly]

noc·tur·nal (nok·tûr'nəl) *adj.* **1.** Of, pertaining to, or occurring at night: *nocturnal* activities. **2.** *Biol.* Active, blooming, etc., by night, as certain animals and plants. [< LL *nocturnalis* < L *nocturnus* nightly] — **noc·tur'nal·ly** *adv.*

noc·turne (nok'tûrn) *n.* **1.** In painting, a night scene. **2.** *Music* A composition of a pensive or romantic nature.

noc·u·ous (nok'yōō·əs) *adj.* Causing harm; noxious. [< L *nocuus* injurious < *nocere* to harm] — **noc'u·ous·ly** *adv.* — **noc'u·ous·ness** *n.*

nod (nod) *v.* **nod·ded, nod·ding** *v.i.* **1.** To lower the head forward briefly, as in agreement, assent, invitation, etc. **2.** To let the head fall forward slightly and involuntarily, as when drowsy or sleepy. **3.** To be inattentive or careless; make an error or slip. **4.** To sway or bend the top or upper part, as trees in the wind. — *v.t.* **5.** To lower (the head) by nodding. **6.** To express or signify (assent, agreement, etc.) by nodding the head. **7.** To invite, guide, etc., by nodding: to *nod* him into the room. — *n.* The act of one who or that which nods. — **to give** (or **get**) **the nod** *U.S. Slang* **1.** To give (or receive) the sign to go ahead, assent, approval, etc. **2.** In boxing, to award (or gain) the decision. [ME *nodden.* Prob. akin to OHG *hnŏtŏn* to shake.] — **nod′der** *n.*

nod·dle (nod′l) *Informal n.* The head; noodle. — *v.t. & v.i.* **·dled, ·dling** To nod frequently. [Freq. of NOD]

nod·dy (nod′ē) *n. pl.* **·dies 1.** A dunce; a fool. **2.** One of several terns (subfamily *Sterninae*), especially *Anous stolidus* of the Atlantic coast. [? < NOD]

node (nōd) *n.* **1.** A knot, knob, or swelling; protuberance. **2.** *Bot.* A joint or knob of a stem; especially, a joint from which leaves grow. **3.** *Math.* A point at which a curve crosses itself; crunode. **4.** *Astron.* Either of two points at which the orbit of a heavenly body intersects the ecliptic, known as the **ascending node** when crossed by a body moving northward and as the **descending node** when crossed by a body moving southward. **5.** *Physics* A point, line, or surface in a standing wave system at which some component wave has virtually zero amplitude. **6.** *Anat.* A swelling. [< L *nodus* knot] — **nod·al** (nōd′l) *adj.* — **nod′al·ly** *adv.*

nod·i·cal (nod′i·kəl, nō′di-) *adj. Astron.* Nodal.

nod·ose (nō′dōs, nō-dōs′) *adj.* Having nodes or knots; knobby. Also **no′dous** (-dəs). [< L *nodosus* full of knots < *nodus* knot] — **no·dos·i·ty** (nō-dos′ə·tē) *n.*

nod·ule (noj′ōōl, nod′yōōl) *n.* **1.** A little knot or node. **2.** *Bot.* A tubercle. [L *nodulus,* dim. of *nodus* knot] — **nod·u·lar** (noj′ōō·lər), **nod·u·lose** (-lōs), **nod·u·lous** (-ləs) *adj.*

no·dus (nō′dəs) *n.* **1.** A node. **2.** A difficulty. [< L]

no·ël (nō-el′) *n.* A Christmas carol. Also **no·el′.**

No·ël (nō-el′) *n.* Christmas. Also **No·el′.** [< F < LL (*dies*) *natalis* birthday]

no·et·ic (nō-et′ik) *Philos. adj.* Of, pertaining to, or originating in intellectual or rational activity. [< Gk. *noētikos* intellectual, ult. < *nous* mind] — **no·e·sis** (nō-ē′sis) *n.*

Nof·re·te·te (nof′rə·tē′tē) See NEFERTITI.

nog¹ (nog) *n.* A peg or block of wood, especially when placed into a wall to hold nails, etc. [Origin unknown]

nog² (nog) *n.* **1.** Eggnog (which see). **2.** *Brit. Dial.* A strong ale. Also **nogg.** [Origin unknown]

nog·gin (nog′in) *n.* **1.** *Informal* A person's head. **2.** A small mug or cup. **3.** A measure of liquor equal to about one fourth of a pint or a gill. [Origin unknown]

nog·ging (nog′ing) *n.* **1.** Pieces of wood inserted in a masonry wall to receive nails. **2.** Brick filling in the spaces of a frame wall. [< NOG¹]

No·gu·chi (nō·gōō·chē), Hideyo, 1876–1928, Japanese bacteriologist active in the United States.

noh (nō) See NO³.

no·how (nō′hou′) *adv. Dial.* In no way; not by any means.

noil (noil) *n.* Short fibers combed out during the preparation of wool, silk, or cotton yarns. [Origin unknown]

noise (noiz) *n.* **1.** Loud, confused, or disturbing sound of any kind. **2.** In communication theory, any random disturbance that causes a received signal to differ from what was transmitted. **3.** *Obs.* Slander; scandal; gossip. — *v.* **noised, nois·ing** *v.t.* **1.** To spread, report, or rumor: often with *about* or *abroad.* — *v.i.* **2.** To be noisy; make a noise. **3.** To talk loudly or volubly. [< OF, ? < L *nausea*] — **Syn.** (noun) **1.** din, clamor, uproar, hubbub, racket, clatter, blare. See SOUND.

noise·less (noiz′lis) *adj.* Causing or making little or no noise; quiet; silent. — **noise′less·ly** *adv.* — **noise′less·ness** *n.*

noise·mak·er (noiz′mā′kər) *n.* **1.** A horn, bell, etc., for making noise at celebrations. **2.** One who or that which makes noise. — **noise′mak′ing** *n. & adj.*

noise pollution A persistent, often excessive, level of noise considered as a harmful factor in a given environment.

noi·some (noi′səm) *adj.* **1.** Offensive or disgusting, especially in smell; stinking. **2.** Injurious; noxious. [ME *noy* annoyance + OE *-sum* like, resembling] — **noi′some·ly** *adv.* — **noi′some·ness** *n.*

— **Syn.** **1.** malodorous, fetid, rank.

nois·y (noi′zē) *adj.* **nois·i·er, nois·i·est 1.** Making a loud noise. **2.** Characterized by or full of noise. — **nois′i·ly** *adv.* — **nois′i·ness** *n.*

— **Syn.** **1.** vociferous, obstreperous, clamorous. **2.** uproarious, tumultuous, riotous.

no·lens vo·lens (nō′lenz vō′lenz) *Latin* Willy-nilly.

no·li-me-tan·ge·re (nō′lī·mē·tan′jə·rē) *n.* **1.** A warning or caution against touching or meddling. **2.** Any of various pictures showing Christ appearing to Mary Magdalene after the Resurrection. **3.** The touch-me-not, a plant. [< L *noli me tangere* touch me not]

nol·le pros·e·qui (nol′ē pros′ə·kwī) *Law* An entry of record in a civil or criminal case, to signify that the plaintiff or prosecutor will not press it. Abbr. *nol. pros.* Compare NON PROSEQUITUR. [< L, to be unwilling to prosecute]

no·lo con·ten·de·re (nō′lō kən·ten′də·rē) *Law* A plea by a defendant in a criminal action that has the same legal effect as an admission of guilt but does not debar him from deny-

ing the truth of the charges in any other proceedings. [< L, I am unwilling to contend]

nol-pros (nol′pros′) *v.t.* **-prossed, -pros·sing** *Law* To subject to a nolle prosequi. [Short for NOLLE PROSEQUI]

nol. pros. Nolle prosequi.

nom (nôn) *n. French* Name.

nom- Var. of NOMO-.

nom. Nominative.

no·ma (nō′mə) *n. Pathol.* Gangrenous inflammation of the mouth, a form of stomatitis found especially in young children. [< NL < Gk. *nomē* < *nemein* to feed]

no·mad (nō′mad, nom′ad) *n.* **1.** One of a group of people that habitually shifts its abode to find food, avoid drought, etc., usually moving with the seasons and in a well-defined area. **2.** One who constantly moves about, usually without purpose; a wanderer. — *adj.* Nomadic. [< Gk. *nomas, -adis* < Gk. *nomas* < *nemein* to graze] — **no′mad·ism** *n.*

no·mad·ic (nō-mad′ik) *adj.* Of, pertaining to, or like nomads; roaming; unsettled. Also **no·mad′i·cal.** [< Gk. *nomadikos* pastoral] — **no·mad′i·cal·ly** *adv.*

no man's land 1. A tract of waste or unowned land. **2.** In war, the land between opposing armies. **3.** An area of human activity characterized by ambiguity, uncertainty, or peril: the *no man's land* of political controversy.

nom·arch (nom′ärk) *n.* The head of a nomarchy or nome. [< Gk. *nomarchēs* < *nomos* province + *archein* to rule]

nom·ar·chy (nom′är·kē) *n. pl.* **·chies** A province of modern Greece; nome. [< Gk. *nomarchia.* See NOMARCH.]

nom·bles (nom′bəlz, num′-) *n.pl.* Numbles.

nom·bril (nom′bril) *n. Heraldry* The point between the fess point and the base point on an escutcheon: also called navel. For illustration see ESCUTCHEON. [< F, navel < L *umbilicus*]

nom de guerre (nôn də gâr′) *French* A pseudonym; literally, a war name. — **Syn.** See PSEUDONYM.

nom de plume (nom′ də plōōm′, *Fr.* nôn də plüm′) A pen name; a writer's assumed name. — **Syn.** See PSEUDONYM. [< F *nom* name + *de* of + *plume* pen]

nome (nōm) *n.* A province or department of ancient Egypt or modern Greece. Also, *Greek, nomos.* [< Gk. *nomos* province < *nemein* to divide, graze]

Nome (nōm) A city in western Alaska; pop. 2,488; near Cape Nome, a promontory of the southern Seward Peninsula.

no·men·cla·tor (nō′mən·klā′tər) *n.* **1.** One who gives or assigns names to things, as a taxonomist. **2.** *Rare* One who announces guests at a social gathering. [< L < *nomen* name + *calator* < *calare* to summon]

no·men·cla·ture (nō′mən·klā′chər, nō-men′klə-) *n.* **1.** The system of names used to describe the various elements of a science, art, etc.; terminology. **2.** The specific names for the parts or stages of a device, process, etc.

nom·i·nal (nom′ə·nəl) *adj.* **1.** Existing in name only; not actual: a *nominal* peace. **2.** Slight or inconsiderable; trifling: a *nominal* sum. **3.** Of, pertaining to, or containing a name or names. **4.** *Gram.* Of, pertaining to, or like a noun. [< L *nominalis* of a name < *nomen* name]

nom·i·nal·ism (nom′ə·nəl·iz′əm) *n. Philos.* The doctrine that universals (abstract concepts) exist only as names and without a basis in reality: opposed to *realism.* Compare CONCEPTUALISM. [< F *nominalisme*] — **nom′i·nal·ist** *adj. & n.* — **nom′i·nal·is′tic** *adj.*

nom·i·nal·ly (nom′ə·nəl·ē) *adv.* In name only; not actually.

nominal wages Wages evaluated in terms of money paid: distinguished from *real wages.*

nom·i·nate (nom′ə·nāt) *v.t.* **·nat·ed, ·nat·ing 1.** To name or propose as a candidate for elective office. **2.** To appoint to some office or duty. **3.** *Obs.* To name; call. — *adj.* Having a particular or special name. [< L *nominatus,* pp. of *nominare* to name < *nomen* *-inis* name] — **nom′i·na′tor** *n.*

nom·i·na·tion (nom′ə·nā′shən) *n.* The act of nominating or the condition of being nominated.

nom·i·na·tive (nom′ə·nə·tiv, nom′ə·nā′-) *adj.* **1.** *Gram.* Designating the case of the subject of a finite verb, or of a word agreeing with or in apposition to the subject; subjective. **2.** Appointed by nomination; nominated. **3.** Bearing the name of a person, as an invitation, etc. — *n. Gram.* **1.** The nominative case. **2.** A word in this case. Abbr. *n., nom.* [< OF < L *nominativus*]

nom·i·nee (nom′ə·nē′) *n.* One who receives a nomination.

no·mism (nō′miz·əm) *n.* Strict adherence to religious or moral law in human conduct. [< Gk. *nomos* law, custom] — **no·mis·tic** (nō-mis′tik) *adj.*

nomo- *combining form* Law; custom; usage: *nomography.* Also, before vowels, *nom-.* [< Gk. *nomos* law, custom]

no·mo·graph (nō′mə·graf, -gräf) *n.* A graphic representation of numerical relations; especially, a graph having graduated scales for three interrelated variables, so arranged that a straight line joining values of two of the variables will cut the scale of the third variable at its related value. Also **no·mo·gram** (nō′mə·gram). [< NOMO- + -GRAPH]

no·mog·ra·phy (nō·mog'rə·fē) *n. pl.* **·phies** **1.** The art of drafting laws; also, a treatise on that art. **2.** The science of constructing nomographs for the solution of related problems. — **no·mo·graph·ic** (nō'mə·graf'ik) or **·i·cal** *adj.*

no·mol·o·gy (nō·mol'ə·jē) *n.* **1.** The science of law and lawmaking. **2.** The branch of any science that formulates its own laws. — **nom·o·log·i·cal** (nom'ə·loj'i·kəl) *adj.*

no·mos (nō'mos) See NOME[1].

nom·o·thet·ic (nom'ə·thet'ik) *adj.* **1.** Of, involving, or leading to the formulation or enactment of laws; legislative. **2.** Pertaining to a science or study of general or universal laws. Also **nom'o·thet'i·cal.** [< Gk. *nomothetikos* < *nomo-thetēs* lawgiver < *nomos* law + *tithēnai* to establish]

No·mu·ra (nō·mōō·rä), **Kichisaburo,** 1877–1964, Japanese admiral and diplomat.

-nomy *combining form* The science or systematic study of: *astronomy, economy.* [< Gk. *nomos* law]

non- *prefix* Not. [< F < L *non* not]
◆ *Non-* is the Latin negative adverb adopted as an English prefix. It denotes in general simple negation or absence of, as in *nonheroic,* not heroic, *nonattendance,* lack of attendance. Compare UN-, IN-, and A-[4], which are commonly more emphatic and often imply a contrary condition or quality, as in *unheroic, uninspired,* etc. Numerous words beginning with *non-* are self-explaining, as in the list beginning below.

non·age (non'ij, nō'nij) *n.* **1.** The period of legal minority. **2.** A period of immaturity. [< OF < *non* not + *age* age]

non·a·ge·nar·i·an (non'ə·jə·nâr'ē·ən, nō'nə-) *n.* A person between 90 and 100 years of age. — *adj.* **1.** Being ninety years old, or between 90 and 100. **2.** Of or pertaining to a nonagenarian. [< L *nonagenarius* of ninety]

non·a·ge·nar·y (non·aj'ə·ner'ē, nō·naj'-) *adj.* **1.** Of or pertaining to the number ninety; progressing by nineties. **2.** Nonagenarian. — *n. pl.* **·nar·ies** A nonagenarian.

non·a·gon (non'ə·gon) *n. Geom.* A polygon having nine sides and nine angles: also called *ennagon.* [< L *nonus* ninth + Gk. *gōnia* angle]

no·na·no·ic acid (nō'nə·nō'ik) Pelargonic acid.

non·ap·pear·ance (non'ə·pir'əns) *n.* Failure to appear.

non-book (non'book') *n.* A book that bears little resemblance to a standard book, such as a cookbook published as a series of cards, etc.

nonce (nons) *n.* Present time or occasion: now chiefly in the phrase **for the nonce.** [ME *for then ones* for the one (occasion), misread as *for the nones*]

nonce word A word coined for a single occasion.

non·cha·lance (non'shə·ləns, non'shə·läns') *n.* The state of being nonchalant; unconcern. [< F < *nonchalant*]

non·cha·lant (non'shə·lənt, non'shə·länt') *adj.* Marked by or exhibiting a lack of interest or excitement; casually indifferent. [< F, ppr. of *nonchaloir* < L *non* not + *calere* to be warm, to be desirous] — **non'cha·lant·ly** *adv.*
— **Syn.** imperturbable, cool, composed, detached.

non·com (non'kom') *U.S. Informal n.* A noncommissioned officer. — *adj.* Noncommissioned.

noncom. Noncommissioned (officer).

non·com·bat·ant (non'kəm·bat'ənt, non'kom'bə·tənt, -kum'-) *n.* **1.** One whose military duties do not entail fighting, as a chaplain. **2.** A civilian in wartime.

non·com·mis·sioned (non'kə·n·ish'ənd) *adj.* Not holding a commission: said of certain grades and men of the armed forces.

noncommissioned officer *Mil.* An enlisted man appointed to a noncommissioned grade, as from corporal to sergeant major in the U.S. Army. Abbr. *NCO* See table for GRADE.

non·com·mit·tal (non'kə·mit'l) *adj.* Not involving or revealing a commitment to any particular attitude, opinion, etc. — **non'com·mit'tal·ly** *adv.*

non·com·pli·ance (non'kəm·pli'əns) *n.* Failure or neglect to comply. — **non'·com·pli'ant** *adj. & n.*

non com·pos men·tis (non kom'pəs men'tis) *Law* Not of sound mind; mentally unbalanced: often **non compos.** [< L]

non·con·duc·tor (non'kən·duk'tər) *n.* A substance that offers resistance to the passage of some form of energy, as of heat or electricity. — **non'con·duct'ing** *adj.*

non·con·form·ist (non'kən·fôr'mist) *n.* **1.** One who does not conform to a manner of behaving or thinking that is expected or approved by a majority of the society. **2.** *Often cap.* An English Protestant who refuses to conform to the Church of England; dissenter. **3.** Anyone who refuses to conform to the principles or practices of an established church. — **Syn.** See HERETIC. — **non'con·form'ing** *adj.*

non·con·for·mi·ty (non'kən·fôr'mə·tē) *n.* **1.** Neglect or refusal to conform. **2.** *Often cap.* Failure to conform to the Church of England.

non·co·op·er·a·tion (non'kō·op'ə·rā'shən) *n.* Failure to cooperate; especially, resistance to a government through civil disobedience, including the refusal to pay taxes. — **non'co·op'er·a'tion·ist** *n.* — **non'co·op'er·a·tive** (-kō·op'rə·tiv, -kō·op'ə·rā'tiv) *adj.* — **non'co·op'er·a'tor** *n.*

non·de·script (non'di·skript) *adj.* Not distinctive enough to be described; lacking individual character. — *n.* A nondescript person or thing: often used disparagingly. [< NON- + L *descriptus,* pp. of *describere.* See DESCRIBE.]

non·dis·junc·tion (non'dis·jungk'shən) *n. Biol.* The failure of paired chromosomes to separate during cell mitosis.

non·dis·tinc·tive (non'dis·tingk'tiv) *adj.* Not distinctive.

none (nun) *pron. (construed as sing. or pl.)* **1.** Not one; no one: *None* will arrive today. **2.** No or not one (specified person or thing); not any (of a class of things): *None* of them have finished their drawings; *None* of the apples is rotten. **3.** No part or portion; not any: I want *none* of it; It is *none* of my business. — **none** of *Archaic* Not at all; nothing like. — *adv.* By no means; not at all: He is *none* too bright. — *adj. Archaic* Not one; not any; no: used before vowels: *none* other choice but to flee. [OE *nān* < *ne* not + *an* one]

non·ef·fec·tive (non'i·fek'tiv) *adj.* **1.** Not effective. **2.** Unfit or unavailable for active service or duty, as in the army or navy. — *n.* A noneffective soldier, sailor, etc.

non·e·go (non·ē'gō, -eg'ō) *n. pl.* **·gos** **1.** Everything that is not part of the conscious self or ego; the object of the ego. **2.** The objective or external world.

non·en·ti·ty (non·en'tə·tē) *n. pl.* **·ties** **1.** One who or that which is of little or no account; a nothing. **2.** That which does not exist, or exists solely in the imagination. **3.** The negation of being; nonexistence.

nones (nōnz) *n.pl.* **1.** In the ancient Roman calendar, the ninth day before the ides. **2.** *Often cap. Eccl.* Prescribed prayers constituting the fifth of the seven canonical hours, originally recited at 3 P.M., or the ninth hour by ancient Roman reckoning. [< OF < L *nonae,* fem. pl. of *nonus* ninth < *novem* nine]

non est (non est) *Latin* It is not; it is wanting.

nonabsolute	nonallegorical	nonattention	non-Calvinist	noncoercive	noncomplying
nonabsorbable	nonallergic	non-Attic	noncannibalistic	noncognition	noncompressible
nonabsorbent	nonalliterative	nonattributive	noncanonical	noncognitive	noncompression
nonabstainer	nonalphabetic	nonaugmentative	noncapitalistic	noncoherent	noncompulsion
nonaccent	nonamateur	nonauricular	noncarnivorous	noncohesive	nonconcealment
nonacceptance	nonamendable	nonauriferous	noncategorical	noncoincident	nonconcentration
nonaccomplishment	non-American	non-Australian	non-Catholic	noncollaborative	nonconception
nonacid	non-Anglican	nonauthoritative	non-Caucasian	noncollapsible	nonconciliating
nonacquaintance	nonannexation	nonautomatic	noncelestial	noncollectable	nonconcordant
nonacquiescence	nonantagonistic	nonautomotive	noncellular	noncollegiate	nonconcurrence
nonactinic	nonapologetic	nonbacterial	non-Celtic	noncolloid	nonconcurrency
nonaction	nonapostolic	non-Baptist	noncensored	noncollusive	nonconcurrent
nonactive	nonappearing	nonbasic	noncentral	noncolonial	noncondensable
nonadherence	nonapprehension	nonbeliever	noncereal	noncombat	noncondensation
nonadherent	nonapprehensive	nonbelieving	noncerebral	noncombining	noncondensible
nonadhesive	nonaquatic	nonbelligerent	nonceremonial	noncombustible	noncondensing
nonadjacent	non-Arab	nonbenevolent	noncertified	noncombustion	nonconditioned
nonadjectival	non-Arabic	non-Biblical	nonchargeable	noncommendable	nonconducive
nonadministrative	nonaristocratic	nonblending	nonchemical	noncommercial	nonconductibility
nonadmission	nonarithmetical	nonblooming	non-Chinese	noncommunicable	nonconductible
nonadult	nonarrival	non-Bolshevik	non-Christian	noncommunicant	nonconducting
nonadvantageous	non-Aryan	non-Bolshevist	nonchurch	noncommunicating	nonconductive
nonadverbial	non-Asiatic	non-Brahmanical	nonciliate	noncommunist	nonconferrable
nonaffiliated	nonassertive	nonbreakable	noncitizen	non-Communist	nonconfidential
non-African	nonassessable	non-British	noncivilized	noncompensating	nonconfiscable
nonaggression	nonassignable	non-Buddhist	nonclassifiable	noncompensation	nonconflicting
nonaggressive	nonassimilable	nonbudding	noncleistogamic	noncompetency	nonconforming
nonagreement	nonassimilation	nonbureaucratic	nonclerical	noncompetent	noncongealing
nonagricultural	nonassociable	nonburnable	nonclinical	noncompeting	noncongenital
nonalcoholic	nonathletic	nonbusiness	nonclotting	noncompetitive	noncongestion
nonalgebraic	nonatmospheric	noncaffeine	noncoagulable	noncomplaisance	non-Congressional
nonaligned	nonattached	noncaking	noncoagulating	noncomplaisant	nonconjugate
nonalienation	nonattendance	noncalcareous	noncoalescing	noncompletion	nonconnective

none·such (nun'such') *n.* **1.** One who or that which has no equal and cannot be compared to anything else; nonpareil. **2.** Black medic. **3.** A variety of apple. Also *nonsuch.*

none·the·less (nun'tho·les') *adv.* In spite of everything; nevertheless. Also **none the less.**

non·ex·is·tence (non'ig·zis'təns) *n.* **1.** The condition of not existing. **2.** That which does not exist. **— non·ex'is·tent** *adj.*

non·fea·sance (non·fē'zəns) *n. Law* The nonperformance of some act that one is legally bound to perform. Compare MALFEASANCE, MISFEASANCE. **— non·fea'sor** *n.*

non·fer·rous (non·fer'əs) *adj.* Not consisting of or containing iron; especially, pertaining to metals other than iron, as copper, tin, platinum, etc.

non·fic·tion (non'fik'shən) *n.* Prose literature other than fiction, as historical works, biographies, etc. **— non'fic'tion·al** *adj.* **— non'fic'tion·al·ly** *adv.*

non·flam·ma·ble (non'flam'ə·bəl) *adj.* Not flammable.

no·nil·lion (nō·nil'yən) *n.* **1.** *U.S.* A thousand octillions, written as 1 followed by thirty zeros: a cardinal number. **2.** *Brit.* A million octillions (def. 2), written as 1 followed by fifty-four zeros: a cardinal number. **— adj.** Being a nonillion in number. [< MF < L *nonus* ninth + F (*m*)*illion* million] **— no·nil'lionth** (-yənth) *adj. & n.*

non·in·duc·tive (non'in·duk'tiv) *adj. Electr.* Not inductive.

non·in·ter·ven·tion (non'in·tər·ven'shən) *n.* **1.** The refusal or failure to intervene; especially, the policy or practice of a nation of not intervening in the affairs of other nations. **2.** An instance of this. **— non'in·ter·ven'tion·ist** *adj. & n.*

non·join·der (non·join'dər) *n. Law* An omission to join an action or suit, as by a person who should be a party to it.

non·ju·ror (non·jŏor'ər) *n.* **1.** One who refuses to take an oath, as of allegiance, supremacy, or abjuration. **2.** *Sometimes cap.* One of the body of persons, consisting mainly of Anglican clergymen, who refused to take the oath of allegiance to William and Mary after the revolution of 1688. [< NON- + JUROR, in obs. sense "one who takes an oath"]

non li·cet (non lī'sit) *Latin* It is not lawful. Abbr. *n.l.*

non li·quet (non lī'kwit, lik'wit) *Latin* The case is not clear. Abbr. *n.l.*

non·met·al (non·met'l) *n. Chem.* Any element, as nitrogen, carbon, or sulfur, that has acid rather than basic properties and is incapable of forming monatomic cations.

non·me·tal·lic (non'mə·tal'ik) *adj.* **1.** Not metallic. **2.** *Chem.* Pertaining to a nonmetal.

non·mor·al (non·môr'əl, -mor'-) *adj.* Having no relation to morals; neither moral nor immoral. **— non·mo·ral·i·ty** (non'mə·ral'ə·tē) *n.*

non·ni·trog·e·nous (non'nī·troj'ə·nəs) *adj.* Containing no nitrogen.

non·ob·jec·tive (non'əb·jek'tiv) *adj.* Not objective; especially, denoting a style of art that does not seek to represent objects as they appear in nature. **— non·ob·jec·tiv·i·ty** (non'ob'jek·tiv'ə·tē) *n.*

non ob·stan·te (non ob·stan'tē) *Latin* Notwithstanding.

non·pa·reil (non'pə·rel') *adj.* Having no equal; matchless; unrivaled. **— n. 1.** One who or that which has no equal; a paragon. **2.** Any of various brilliantly colored finches of the southern United States; especially, the painted bunting. **3.** *Printing* **a** A size of type, 6 points, between agate and minion. **b** A 6-point slug. [< MF < *non* not + OF *pareil* equal < LL *pariculus*, dim. of L *par* equal]

non·par·ous (non·par'əs) *adj.* Not having borne children.

non·par·tic·i·pat·ing (non'pär·tis'ə·pā'ting) *adj.* Not participating; especially, not conveying the right to participate in the surplus or profits of an insurance company.

non·par·ti·san (non·pär'tə·zən) *adj.* Not partisan; especially, not controlled by, associated with, or in support of the interests of any one political party. Also **non·par'ti·zan.**

non·plus (non·plus', non'plus) *v.t.* **·plused** or **·plussed, ·plus·ing** or **·plus·sing** To cause to be at a loss; baffle; perplex. **— n.** A mental standstill; bewilderment, especially as causing speechlessness or indecision. [< L *non plus* no further] **— Syn.** (verb) dumfound, mystify, puzzle, confound.

non pos·su·mus (non pos'ə·məs) *Latin* We cannot.

non·pro·duc·tive (non'prə·duk'tiv) *adj.* **1.** Not productive; especially, pertaining to that part of the labor force that does not directly contribute to the production of goods, as office workers, salesmen, etc. **2.** Unproductive. **— non'·pro·duc'tive·ly** *adv.* **— non'pro·duc'tive·ness** *n.*

non·prof·it (non·prof'it) *adj.* Not organized or maintained for the making of a profit: *nonprofit* charities.

non·pros (non·pros') *v.t.* **·prossed, ·pros·sing** *Law* To enter judgment against (a plaintiff who fails to prosecute). [Short for NON PROSEQUITUR]

non pros. Non prosequitur.

non pro·se·qui·tur (non prō·sek'wi·tər) *Law* A judgment entered against a plaintiff who fails to prosecute an action. Compare NOLLE PROSEQUI. [< L, lit., he does not prosecute]

non·rep·re·sen·ta·tion·al (non'rep'ri·zen·tā'shən·əl) *adj.* Not representational; especially, denoting a style of art that does not seek to represent objects as they appear in nature. **— non'rep're·sen·ta'tion·al·ism** *n.*

non·res·i·dent (non·rez'ə·dənt) *adj.* Not resident; especially, not residing permanently in the locality where one works, owns property, attends school, etc. **— n.** One who is nonresident. **— non·res'i·dence, non·res'i·den·cy** *n.*

non·re·sis·tant (non'ri·zis'tənt) *adj.* **1.** Not resistant; especially, incapable of resistance, as to infection or disease. **2.** Of, pertaining to, or characteristic of a nonresistant. **— n. 1.** One who believes in or practices total obedience to authority. **2.** One who is passive in the face of violence. **— non're·sis'tance** *n.*

non·re·stric·tive (non'ri·strik'tiv) *adj.* **1.** Not restrictive. **2.** *Gram.* Denoting a word or word group, especially an adjective clause, that describes but does not limit the identity of its antecedent and may be omitted without loss of essential meaning, as *which is for sale* in *Our house, which is for sale, needs repairs:* also *descriptive.* Compare RESTRICTIVE.

non·rig·id (non·rij'id) *adj.* **1.** Not rigid. **2.** *Aeron.* Designating an airship whose form is not supported by a frame but is maintained by internal gas pressure alone.

non·sec·tar·i·an (non'sek·târ'ē·ən) *adj.* Not restricted to or associated with any one religion, sect, or faction.

non·sense (non'sens, -səns) *n.* **1.** That which is without sense, or without good sense; especially, words or actions that are meaningless or absurd. **2.** Things of no importance or use; trifles. **3.** Foolish or frivolous conduct: He'll stand for no *nonsense.* **— non·sen'si·cal** *adj.* **— non·sen'si·cal·ly** *adv.* **— non·sen'si·cal·ness** *n.*

non·sep·a·ra·tist (non·sep'rə·tist) *n.* In Quebec, one who does not support the separation of the Province from Confederation.

non seq. Non sequitur.

nonconnivance	noncontrolled	noncultivation	nondepreciating	nondiscovery	noneclectic
nonconnotative	noncontroversial	noncumulative	nonderivable	nondiscrimination	noneconomic
nonconnubial	nonconventional	noncurrency	nonderivative	nondiscriminatory	nonedible
nonconscious	nonconvergent	non-Czech	nonderogatory	nondisfranchised	noneditorial
nonconsecutive	nonconversant	nondamageable	nondespotic	nondisinterested	noneducable
nonconsent	nonconversion	non-Darwinian	nondestructive	nondisparaging	noneducational
nonconsenting	nonconvertible	nondecaying	nondetachable	nondisparate	noneffervescent
nonconsequence	nonconviction	nondeceptive	nondetonating	nondispersion	nonefficacious
nonconservative	nonconvivial	nondeciduous	nondevelopable	nondisposal	nonefficacy
nonconsideration	noncoordinating	nondefamatory	nondevelopment	nondisqualifying	nonefficiency
nonconsistorial	noncoordination	nondefensive	nondevotional	nondissenting	nonefficient
nonconspiring	noncorrective	nondeferential	nondialectical	nondistribution	non-Egyptian
nonconstitutional	noncorresponding	nondeferrable	nondiatomaceous	nondistributive	nonelastic
nonconstructive	noncorroborative	nondefilement	nondichotomous	nondivergence	nonelect
nonconsular	noncorrodible	nondefining	nondictatorial	nondivergent	nonelection
nonconsultative	noncorroding	nondefinitive	nondidactic	nondiversification	nonelective
nonconsumption	noncorrosive	nondegeneration	nondifferentiable	nondivisibility	nonelectric
noncontagious	noncosmic	nondehiscent	nondifferentiation	nondivisible	nonelectrical
noncontemplative	noncotyledonous	nondelineation	nondiffractive	nondivision	nonelectrified
noncontemporary	noncreative	nondeliquescent	nondiffusing	nondivisional	nonelementary
noncontentious	noncredible	nondelirious	nondilatable	nondoctrinal	nonelimination
noncontiguous	noncreditor	nondelivery	nondiphtheritic	nondocumentary	nonembryonic
noncontinental	noncriminal	nondemand	nondiplomatic	nondogmatic	nonemotional
noncontinuance	noncrinoid	nondemocratic	nondirectional	nondomesticated	nonemphatic
noncontinuous	noncritical	nondepartmental	nondirigible	nondramatic	nonempirical
noncontraband	noncrucial	nondeparture	nondisappearing	nondrying	nonemulative
noncontradiction	noncrystalline	nondependence	nondischarging	nondutiable	nonencyclopedic
noncontradictory	noncrystallized	nondepletion	nondisciplinary	nondynastic	nonendemic
noncontributing	nonculpable	nondeportation	nondiscontinuance	nonearning	nonenforceable
noncontributory	noncultivated	nondepositor	nondiscountable	nonecclesiastical	nonenforcement

non·seq·ui·tur (non sek′wə-tər) **1.** *Logic* An inference that does not follow from the premises; an irrelevant conclusion. **2.** Any spoken or written comment marked by a lack of relevance to what has preceded it. [< L, it does not follow]

non·sked (non′sked′) *n. Informal* An airline without scheduled flying times. [Short for *nonscheduled*]

non·skid (non′skid′) *adj.* Having a surface that resists skidding.

non·stan·dard (non′stan′dərd) *adj.* **1.** Varying or deviating from the standard. **2.** *Ling.* Designating or belonging to those usages or varieties of a language that differ from the standard: *nonstandard* English.

nonstandard English *Ling.* Those usages in English that differ from standard English: also called *substandard English.*

non·stop (non′stop′) *adj.* Making, having made, or scheduled to make no stops: a *nonstop* flight; *nonstop* train.

non·stri·at·ed (non-strī′ā-tid) *adj.* Lacking striations, as certain muscle fibers.

non·such (nun′such′) See NONESUCH.

non·suit (non′sōōt′) *Law v.t.* To order the dismissal of the suit of. — *n.* **1.** The abandonment of a suit. **2.** A judgment dismissing a suit, when the plaintiff either abandons it or fails to establish a cause of action. [< AF *nonsute*, OF *nonsuite* < *non* not + *suite.* See SUIT.]

non·sup·port (non′sə-pôrt′, -pōrt′) *n.* Failure to provide for the support of a legal dependent.

non trop·po (non trop′ō, *Ital.* nōn trôp′pō) *Music* Not too much: allegro ma *non troppo.* [< Ital.]

non·un·ion (non-yōōn′yən) *adj.* **1.** Not belonging to or associated with a trade union. **2.** Not recognizing or contracting with any trade union; also, not employing the members of any union: *nonunion* shop. **3.** Not produced or maintained by union labor. — *n. Surg.* Failure to join or unite: said of fractured bones.

non·un·ion·ism (non-yōōn′yən-iz′əm) *n.* Nonsupport of or opposition to the establishment or practices of trade unions. — **non·un′ion·ist** *n.*

non·u·ple (non′yə-pəl) *adj.* Consisting of nine; having nine parts or members; ninefold; also, taken by nines. — *n.* A number or sum nine times as great as another. [< F < L *nonus* ninth; on analogy with *quadruple, quintuple,* etc.]

non·u·pli·cate (non-yōō′plə-kit) *adj.* **1.** Ninefold. **2.** Raised to the ninth power. [< L *nonus* ninth; on analogy with *duplicate*]

non·white (non′hwīt′) *n.* One who is not a member of the Caucasoid ethnic division of mankind. — *adj.* **1.** Of or pertaining to nonwhites. **2.** Not white.

noo (nōō) *adv. Scot.* Now.

noo·dle¹ (nōōd′l) *n.* **1.** A simpleton. Also **noo′dle·head′** (-hed′). **2.** *Informal* The head. [? < NODDY; infl. in form by NODDLE and in pronun. by FOOL]

noo·dle² (nōōd′l) *n.* A thin strip of dried dough, usually containing egg, used in soup, etc. [< G *nudel*]

nook (nŏŏk) *n.* **1.** An interior corner or angle, as in a room. **2.** Any narrow or retired place, as a recess. [ME *nok* corner]

noon (nōōn) *n.* **1.** The middle of the day; twelve o'clock in the daytime. *Abbr. n., N.* **2.** The highest or culminating point; zenith: the *noon* of life. **3.** *Poetic* The peak or middle, as of the night. **4.** Formerly, the ninth hour after sunrise, or midway between 12 A.M. and sunset. — *adj.* Of, pertaining to, or occurring at or about noon. [OE *nōn* < L *nona (hora)* ninth (hour)]

noon·day (nōōn′dā′) *n.* Noon. — *adj.* Of or at noon.

no one Not anyone; no person.

noon·ing (nōō′ning) *n. Archaic* **1.** A time of rest taken at noon. **2.** A midday meal. **3.** The time of noon.

noon·time (nōōn′tīm′) *n.* **1.** The time of noon; midday. **2.** The culminating point or period. **3.** *Poetic* Midnight. Also *Archaic* **noon′tide′** (-tīd′). [OE *nōntīd*]

Noord·bra·bant (nōrt′brä-bänt′) The Dutch name for NORTH BRABANT.

noose (nōōs) *n.* **1.** A loop furnished with a running knot, as in a hangman's halter or a snare. **2.** Anything that entraps, restrains, or binds. — *v.t.* **noosed, noos·ing 1.** To capture or secure with a noose. **2.** To make a noose in or with. [< Provençal *nous* < L *nodus* knot]

Noot·ka fir (nōōt′kə) The Douglas fir (which see).

no·pal (nō′pəl) *n.* Any of various cacti (especially of genus *Nopalea*), as *N. cochenillifer*, eaten by the cochineal insect. **2.** A prickly pear. [< Sp. < Nahuatl *nopalli*]

no·par (nō′pär′) *adj.* Having no par or face value.

no-par stock Stock issued without a face value on the certificate and sold at whatever price it will command.

nope (nōp) *adv. Chiefly U.S. Slang* No.

nor¹ (nôr) *conj.* And not; likewise not. ◆ *Nor* is used chiefly as a correlative of a preceding negative, as *neither, not,* or *never:* He is neither tall *nor* short; He has not come, *nor* will he. For poetical effect the correlative is sometimes omitted: Friend *nor* foe could stop him. *Nor* is also used to introduce a clause following an affirmative clause: He hates me, *nor* does he hide it. In older writing and in poetry, it often appears as an introductory negative instead of neither: He heeded *nor* praise nor blame. [Contr. of ME *nother* neither]

nor² (nôr) *conj. Brit. Dial.* Than: He does better *nor* you

nor- *combining form Chem.* A normal or a parent compound.

Nor. 1. Norman. **2.** North. **3.** Norway; Norwegian.

Nor·dau (nôr′dou) **Max Simon,** 1849–1923, German physician, author, and Zionist leader born in Hungary: original name **Max Simon Süd·feld** (süt′felt).

Nor·den·skjöld (nŏŏr′dən-shœld), **Baron Nils Adolf Erik,** 1832–1901, Swedish Arctic explorer born in Finland.

Nor·den·skjöld Sea (nŏŏr′dən-shœld) A former name for the LAPTEV SEA.

Nord·hau·sen (nôrt′hou-zən) A city in western East Germany; pop. 39,200 (est. 1959).

Nor·dic (nôr′dik) *adj. Anthropol.* Pertaining or belonging to the tall, long-headed, blond-haired subdivision of the Caucasian ethnic stock, distributed mainly in NW Europe. — *n.* A Nordic person. [< NL *nordicus.* Cf. F *nordique* < *nord* north.]

Nord·kyn (nôr′kün), **Cape** A cape in northern Norway, the northernmost point of the European mainland. See NORTH CAPE.

Nord·rhein-West·fa·len (nôrt′rīn-vest-fä′lən) The German name for NORTH RHINE–WESTPHALIA.

nor′·east·er (nôr-ēs′tər), etc. See NORTHEASTER, etc.

Norf. Norfolk, England.

Nor·folk (nôr′fək) **1.** A county in eastern England; 2,054 sq. mi.; pop. 650,300 (1976); county seat, Norwich. **2.** A port city in SE Virginia, near Hampton Roads; site of a United States naval base; pop. 307,951.

Norfolk Island An island dependency of Australia north of New Zealand; 13 sq. mi.; pop. 1,000 (est. 1969).

Norfolk jacket A loose-fitting men's jacket with a belt and two box pleats at the back and front. Also **Norfolk coat.**

non-English	noneviction	nonextradition	nonfluctuating	nonhabitual	nonimpairment
nonentailed	nonevolutionary	nonextraneous	nonflying	nonharmonious	nonimperative
nonenteric	nonexcessive	nonfacetious	nonfocal	nonhazardous	nonimperial
nonentry	nonexchangeable	nonfactual	nonforfeitable	nonheading	nonimportant
nonephemeral	nonexciting	nonfading	nonforfeiting	nonheathen	nonimportation
nonepicurean	nonexclusive	nonfanatical	nonforfeiture	nonhedonistic	nonimporting
nonepiscopal	nonexcusable	nonfanciful	nonformal	non-Hellenic	nonimpregnated
nonequal	nonexecution	non-Fascist	nonfortuitous	nonhereditary	nonimprovement
nonequation	nonexecutive	nonfastidious	nonfossiliferous	nonheretic	nonincandescent
nonequatorial	nonexemplary	nonfatal	nonfraudulent	nonheretical	noninclusive
nonequilateral	nonexempt	nonfatalistic	nonfreedom	nonheritable	nonincrease
nonequilibrium	nonexercise	nonfederal	nonfreezing	nonheritor	nonindependent
nonequivalent	nonexisting	nonfederated	non-French	nonheroic	non-Indian
nonequivocating	nonexotic	nonfermentable	nonfricative	non-Hibernian	nonindictable
nonerasure	nonexpansive	nonfermentative	nonfulfillment	nonhistoric	nonindictment
nonerotic	nonexpendable	nonfermented	nonfunctional	nonhistorical	nonindividual
nonerudite	nonexperienced	nonfertile	nonfundamental	nonhomogeneous	nonindividualistic
nonessential	nonexperimental	nonfertility	nongaseous	nonhostile	non-Indo-European
nonesthetic	nonexpert	nonfestive	nongelatinous	nonhouseholder	nonindustrial
noneternal	nonexploitation	nonfeudal	nongenealogical	nonhuman	noninfallible
noneternity	nonexplosive	nonfiduciary	nongenerative	nonhumorous	noninfected
nonethereal	nonexportable	nonfigurative	nongenetic	nonhygroscopic	noninfection
nonethical	nonexportation	nonfilamentous	nongentile	nonidentical	noninfectious
nonethnological	nonextant	nonfimbriate	non-Gentile	nonidentity	noninfinite
non-Euclidean	nonextended	nonfinancial	non-German	nonidiomatic	noninflammable
noneugenic	nonextensile	nonfinite	non-Germanic	nonidolatrous	noninflammatory
non-European	nonextension	nonfireproof	nongovernmental	nonignitible	noninflected
nonevacuation	nonexternal	nonfiscal	nongranular	nonimaginary	noninflectional
nonevanescent	nonextinct	nonfissile	non-Greek	nonimitative	noninformative
nonevangelical	nonextinction	nonfissionable	nongreen	nonimmune	noninheritable
nonevasion	nonextortion	nonflowering	nongregarious	nonimmunity	noninjurious
nonevasive	nonextraditable	nonflowing	nonhabitable	nonimmunized	noninjury

Nor·ge (nôr′gə) The Norwegian name for NORWAY.

no·ri·a (nō′rē·ə) *n.* An undershot water wheel having buckets on its rim to raise water, used in Spain and the Orient: also called *Persian wheel.* [< Sp. < Arabic *nā′ūrah*]

Nor·i·cum (nôr′i·kəm, nor′-) An ancient Roman province south of the Danube, corresponding to southern Austria.

Nor·land (nôr′lənd) *n.* *Chiefly Poetic* Northland; also, northlander. — **Nor′land·er** *n.*

norm (nôrm) *n.* **1.** A pattern, model, or standard regarded as typical of a specified group. **2.** *Psychol.* The standard of performance in a given function or test, usually taken from the average or median achievement for the group concerned. **3.** *Stat.* The mode. **4.** *Geol.* The theoretical standard of chemical composition of igneous rocks, expressed in terms of oxides: distinguished from *mode.* [< L *norma* rule, carpenter's square]

Nor·ma (nôr′mə) *n.* A constellation, the Square. See CONSTELLATION. [< L]

nor·mal (nôr′məl) *adj.* **1.** Conforming to or consisting of a pattern, process, or standard regarded as usual or typical; regular; natural. **2.** *Psychol.* a Well adjusted to the outside world; without marked or persistent mental aberrations. **b** Of average skill, ability, intelligence, etc. **3.** *Biol.* a Not exposed to infection or modified by experimental treatment: a *normal* animal. **b** Occurring naturally. **4.** *Chem.* a Denoting a solution containing one gram equivalent weight of solute per liter: used as a unit, as *two normal, three normal,* etc. **b** Denoting an aliphatic hydrocarbon having a straight, unbranched chain of carbon atoms: *normal* butane. **5.** *Math.* Perpendicular. — *n.* **1.** *Math.* A perpendicular; especially, a perpendicular to a tangent line or plane at the point of tangency. **2.** The common or natural condition, amount, form, degree, etc. **3.** The usual or accepted rule or process; standard. [< L *normalis* < *norma* rule] — **nor·mal·i·ty** (nôr·mal′ə·tē), **nor′mal·ness** *n.*
— **Syn.** (adj.) **1.** *Normal, natural, regular,* and *typical* denote conformity to what is expected or usual. *Normal* suggests conformity to the process or pattern typical for the class of things to which one belongs: the *normal* development of a child. *Natural* stresses the agreement between an action and the innate character of the agent involved: the *natural* tendency to gloat over one's triumphs. *Regular* points to accordance with some rule, plan, or method, and emphasizes symmetry, constancy, etc.: a *regular* army; a *regular* pulse. *Typical* indicates possession of those properties or characteristics that represent a particular class of things and differentiate it from all other classes of things: the *typical* clubbed antennae of the butterflies. — **Ant.** abnormal, exceptional, irregular, unnatural, unusual.

normal curve *Stat.* A bell-shaped curve representing the distribution of a series of values of a variable: also called *Gaussian curve.*

nor·mal·cy (nôr′məl·sē) *n.* The condition or fact of being normal; normality.

normal distribution *Stat.* A frequency distribution represented by a normal curve.

nor·mal·ize (nôr′məl·īz) *v.t.* **·ized, ·iz·ing** To bring into accord with a norm or standard form; make normal. — **nor′·mal·i·za′tion** *n.* — **nor′mal·iz′er** *n.*

nor·mal·ly (nôr′mə·lē) *adv.* **1.** As a rule; usually: The mail *normally* comes before noon. **2.** In a normal manner.

normal salt *Chem.* A salt containing no hydrogen replaceable by a metal, as sodium carbonate.

normal school A school that prepares secondary-school graduates to become teachers.

normal solution *Chem.* A solution containing one gram equivalent of the solute per liter of solution.

Nor·man (nôr′mən) *n.* **1.** One of the Scandinavian people who conquered Normandy in the tenth century. **2.** One of the people of mixed Scandinavian and French descent who conquered England in 1066. **3.** A resident of Normandy. **4.** Norman French (which see). Abbr. *Nor.* — *adj.* **1.** Of or pertaining to Normandy or the Normans. **2.** *Archit.* Designating the form of Romanesque architecture that developed in Normandy and in England during the 11th and 12th centuries. [< OF *Normans,* pl. of *Normant* Northman]

Nor·man (nôr′mən) A city in central Oklahoma; pop. 52,117.

Nor·man (nôr′mən), **Montagu Collet,** 1871–1950, first Baron Norman of St. Clare, English financier.

Norman Conquest The subjugation of England by William the Conqueror after the Battle of Hastings in 1066. See table for WAR.

Nor·man·dy (nôr′mən·dē) A region and former province of NW France, comprising the Cotentin peninsula and the region to the southeast and east.

Norman French **1.** The dialect of French spoken by the Normans in the Middle Ages. **2.** The legal parlance of England from the Norman Conquest to the 17th century, still existing in certain phrases. **3.** The dialect of French spoken in Normandy. Also called *Norman.* Abbr. *NF, N.F.*

Nor·man·ize (nôr′mən·īz) *v.t. & v.i.* **·ized, ·iz·ing** To make or become Norman or like the Normans.

nor·ma·tive (nôr′mə·tiv) *adj.* **1.** Of, pertaining to, or based upon a norm, especially one regarded as a standard or rule of usage: *normative* grammar. **2.** Implying, supporting, or establishing a norm: a *normative* science. [< NORM + -ATIVE]

Norn (nôrn) *n.* *pl.* **Norns** (nôr′nir) or **Norns** In Norse mythology, any of the three goddesses of fate.

Nor·ris (nôr′is, nor′-), **Frank,** 1870–1902, U.S. novelist and journalist: full name **Benjamin Franklin Norris.** — **George William,** 1861–1944, U.S. statesman and legislator. — **Kathleen,** 1880–1966, U.S. novelist.

Nor·ris·town (nôr′is·toun′, nor′-) A borough in SE Pennsylvania, on the Schuylkill River; pop. 68,169.

Norr·kö·ping (nôr′chœ·ping) A port city in SE Sweden; pop. 94,300 (est. 1968).

Norse (nôrs) *adj.* **1.** Scandinavian. **2.** Of or pertaining to Norway, Iceland, and the Faroe Islands; West Scandinavian. — *n.* **1.** The Scandinavians or West Scandinavians collectively: used with *the.* **2.** The Scandinavian or North Germanic group of the Germanic languages; especially, Norwegian. **3.** The West Scandinavian languages. Abbr. *N.* — **Old Norse 1.** The ancestor of the North Germanic languages, best represented by runic inscriptions of the third to eighth centuries, and by Old Icelandic: also called *Old Scandinavian.* **2.** Old Icelandic: see under ICELANDIC. Abbr. *ON, ON., O.N.* [< Du. *Noorsch* a Norwegian < *noordsch* northern < MDu. *nordsch, nortsch*]

Norse·man (nôrs′mən) *n.* *pl.* **·men** (-mən) A Scandinavian of Viking times.

noninquiring	nonirritating	nonluminosity	nonmembership	nonmythical	nonoffensive
noninstruction	non-Islamic	nonluminous	nonmercantile	nonnational	nonofficial
noninstructional	nonisolation	nonlustrous	nonmetalliferous	nonnative	nonoperating
noninstrumental	nonisolationist	non-Lutheran	nonmetaphysical	nonnatural	nonoperative
noninsurance	non-Israelite	nonmagnetic	nonmeteoric	nonnautical	nonoptional
nonintellectual	non-Italian	nonmagnetizable	non-Methodist	nonnaval	nonorganic
nonintelligent	non-Japanese	nonmaintenance	nonmetrical	nonnavigable	nonoriental
noninterchangeable	non-Jew	nonmalignant	nonmetropolitan	nonnecessity	non-Oriental
nonintercourse	non-Jewish	non-Malay	nonmigratory	nonnegotiable	nonorthodox
noninterference	nonjudicial	non-Malayan	nonmilitant	nonnegotiation	nonowner
nonintermittent	nonjuristic	nonmalicious	nonmilitary	non-Negro	nonownership
noninternational	nonlaminated	nonmalleable	nonmimetic	nonneutral	nonoxidizable
noninterrupted	non-Latin	nonmarital	nonmineral	non-Norman	nonoxidizing
nonintersecting	nonlegal	nonmaritime	nonministerial	non-Norse	nonoxygenated
nonintestinal	nonlethal	nonmarriageable	nonmiraculous	nonnotional	nonpacific
nonintoxicant	nonliberation	nonmarrying	nonmischievous	nonnuclear	nonpagan
nonintoxicating	nonlicensed	nonmartial	nonmissionary	nonnucleated	nonpalatal
nonintrospective	nonlicentiate	nonmaterial	nonmobile	nonnutrient	nonpalatalization
nonintuitive	nonlife	nonmaterialistic	nonmodal	nonnutritious	nonpapal
noninverted	nonlimiting	nonmateriality	nonmodulated	nonnutritive	nonpapist
noninvidious	nonliquefying	nonmaternal	non-Mohammedan	nonobedience	nonpar
noniodized	nonliquidating	nonmathematical	non-Mongolian	nonobedient	nonparallel
nonionized	nonliquidation	nonmatrimonial	non-Mormon	nonobligatory	nonparalytic
non-Irish	nonliterary	nonmechanical	nonmortal	nonobservable	nonparasitic
nonirradiated	nonlitigious	nonmechanistic	non-Moslem	nonobservance	nonparental
nonirrigable	nonliturgical	nonmedical	nonmotile	nonobservant	nonparishioner
nonirrigated	nonliving	nonmelodious	nonmunicipal	nonobstructive	nonparliamentary
nonirrigation	nonlocal	nonmember	nonmuscular	nonoccupational	nonparochial
nonirritant	nonloving		nonmyelinic	nonoccurrence	nonparticipant
	nonluminescent		nonmystical	nonodorous	nonparticipation

north (nôrth) *n.* **1.** The direction along a meridian that falls to the left of an observer on earth facing the sun at sunrise. **2.** One of the four cardinal points of the compass, directly opposite *south* and 90° counterclockwise from *east*. See COMPASS CARD. **3.** Any direction near this point. **4.** *Sometimes cap.* Any region north of a specified point. — **the North** In the United States: **a** The population or territory of the northern or northeastern States; especially, the region north of Maryland, the Ohio River, and Missouri. **b** The Free States opposed to the Confederacy (*the South*) in the Civil War. — *adj.* **1.** To, toward, facing, or in the north; northern. **2.** Coming from the north: the *north* wind. — *adv.* In or toward the north; northward. Abbr. *N, N., No., Nor.* [OE]

North (nôrth), **Christopher** See (John) WILSON. — **Lord Frederick**, 1732–92, earl of Guilford, English statesman; prime minister during the American Revolution: called **Lord North.** — **Sir Thomas**, 1535?–1601?, English translator.

North America The northern continent of the western hemisphere; 9.3 million sq. mi. (including adjacent islands); pop. 314,000,000 (est. 1969). — **North American**

North American Indian An Indian of any of the tribes formerly inhabiting North America north of Mexico, now the United States and Canada. Abbr. *N.Am.Ind.*

North·amp·ton (nôr·thamp′tən) **1.** A city in western Massachusetts, on the Connecticut River; pop. 29,664. **2.** Northamptonshire or its county seat.

North·amp·ton·shire (nôr·thamp′tən·shir) A county in south central England; 914 sq. mi.; pop. 496,400 (1976); county seat, **Northampton**, a county borough, pop. 137,600 (1976); also *Northampton*.

Northants. Northamptonshire.

North Atlantic Drift The terminal current of the Gulf Stream system, flowing from near Newfoundland northeast to western Europe. Also **North Atlantic Current.** See map at OCEAN CURRENT.

North Atlantic Treaty Organization A military and naval alliance of Belgium, Canada, Denmark, France, Greece, Iceland, Italy, Luxemburg, the Netherlands, Norway, Portugal, Turkey, the United Kingdom, the United States, and West Germany, organized under the **North Atlantic Treaty** of Washington, Apr. 4, 1949. Abbr. *NATO*

North Ber·gen (bûr′gən) A township in NE New Jersey, near Newark; pop. 47,751.

North Borneo See under BORNEO.

north·bound (nôrth′bound′) *adj.* Going northward. Also **north′-bound′.**

North Brabant A Province of the southern Netherlands; 1,894 sq. mi.; pop. 1,787,800 (est. 1970); capital, 's Hertogenbosch: Dutch *Noordbrabant.*

north by east A point on the mariner's compass, one point or 11° 15′ clockwise from due north. See COMPASS CARD. Abbr. *NbE*

north by west A point on the mariner's compass, one point or 11° 15′ counterclockwise from due north. See COMPASS CARD. Abbr. *NbW*

North Cape A cape on a Norwegian island in the Barents Sea, popularly considered the northernmost point of Europe. See (Cape) NORDKYN.

North Car·o·li·na (kar′ə·lī′nə) A SE State of the United States on the Atlantic; 52,712 sq. mi.; pop. 5,082,059; capital, Raleigh; entered the Union Nov. 21, 1789, one of the thirteen original States; nickname, *Tarheel State.* Abbr. *N.C.* — **North Car′o·lin′i·an** (-lin′ē·ən)

North·cliffe (nôrth′klif), **Viscount**, 1865–1922, Alfred Charles William Harmsworth, British newspaper magnate.

North Da·ko·ta (də·kō′tə) A north central State of the United States, bordering on Canada; 70,665 sq. mi.; pop. 617,761; capital, Bismarck; entered the Union Nov. 2, 1889; nickname, *Flickertail State.* Abbr. *N. Dak.* — **North Da·ko′tan**

north·east (nôrth′ēst′, *Naut.* nôr·ēst′) *n.* **1.** The direction midway between north and east. **2.** A point on the mariner's compass, four points or 45° clockwise from due north. See COMPASS CARD. **3.** Any region lying in or toward this point. — *adj.* **1.** To, toward, facing, or in the northeast. **2.** Coming from the northeast: a *northeast* wind. — *adv.* In or toward the northeast. Abbr. *ne, n.e., NE, N.E.* — **north′east′ern** *adj.*

northeast by east A point on the mariner's compass, five points or 56° 15′ clockwise from due north. See COMPASS CARD.

northeast by north A point on the mariner's compass, three points or 33° 45′ clockwise from due north. See COMPASS CARD.

north·east·er (nôrth′ēs′tər, *Naut.* nôr·ēs′tər) *n.* **1.** A gale or storm from the northeast. **2.** A waterproof hat with a sloping brim worn by sailors in stormy weather. Also spelled *nor′easter.*

north·east·er·ly (nôrth′ēs′tər·lē, *Naut.* nôr·ēs′tər·lē) *adj.* **1.** In, of, or toward the northeast. **2.** From the northeast, as a wind. — *adv.* Toward or from the northeast. — *n.* A wind or storm from the northeast. Also spelled *nor′easterly.*

Northeast Passage A water route from the Atlantic to the Pacific along the northern coast of Europe and Asia.

north·east·ward (nôrth′ēst′wərd, nôr·ēst′wərd) *adv.* Toward the northeast. Also **north′east′wards** (-wərdz). — *adj.* To, toward, facing, or in the northeast. — *n.* Northeast.

north·east·ward·ly (nôrth′ēst′wərd·lē, *Naut.* nôr·ēst′wərd·lē) *adj. & adv.* Toward or from the northeast.

north·er (nôr′thər) *n.* **1.** A gale or storm from the north. **2.** *U.S.* A violent, cold north wind blowing over the plains of the SW States.

north·er·ly (nôr′thər·lē) *adj.* **1.** In, of, toward, or pertaining to the north. **2.** From the north, as a wind. — *adv.* Toward or from the north. — *n.* A wind or storm from the north. — **north′er·li·ness** *n.*

north·ern (nôr′thərn) *adj.* **1.** To, toward, or in the north. **2.** Native to or inhabiting the north: a *northern* species. **3.** *Sometimes cap.* Of, pertaining to, or characteristic of the north or the North. **4.** From the north, as a wind. **5.** *Astron.* North of the celestial equator. Abbr. *N, N., No.* [OE *northerne*]

northern canoe *Canadian* A large freight canoe.

Northern Caucasus The part of the R.S.F.S.R. north of the Caucasus: also *Ciscaucasia.*

Northern Cross The constellation Cygnus, so called from the cross formed by its principal stars.

Northern Crown Corona Borealis.

Northern Dvina See DVINA.

north·ern·er (nôr′thər·nər) *n.* **1.** One who is native to or lives in the north. **2.** *Usually cap.* One who lives in or comes from the North.

Northern Hemisphere See under HEMISPHERE.

nonpartisanship	nonpigmented	nonproficiency	nonreceiving	nonreprehensible	nonrhyming
nonpasseriform	nonpinaceous	nonproficient	nonreceptive	nonrepresentative	nonrhythmic
nonpasserine	nonplanetary	nonprofiteering	nonreciprocal	nonreproductive	nonritual
nonpaternal	nonplastic	nonprogressive	nonreciprocating	nonrequital	nonritualistic
nonpathogenic	nonplausible	nonprohibitive	nonrecital	nonresemblance	nonrival
nonpaying	nonplutocratic	nonprolific	nonrecognition	nonresidential	non-Roman
nonpayment	nonpoetic	nonpromiscuous	nonrecourse	nonresidual	nonromantic
nonpelagic	nonpoisonous	nonprophetic	nonrecoverable	nonresinous	nonrotatable
nonpenalized	nonpolarizable	nonpropitiation	nonrectangular	nonresisting	nonrotating
nonpensionable	non-Polish	nonpropitiatory	nonrecurrent	nonresistive	nonroyal
nonperceptual	nonpolitical	nonproportional	nonrecurring	nonresolvable	nonruminant
nonperforated	nonporous	nonproprietary	nonredeemable	nonresonant	nonrural
nonperforating	non-Portuguese	nonproscriptive	nonrefillable	nonrespirable	non-Russian
nonperformance	nonpractical	nonprotection	nonrefueling	nonrestraint	nonrusting
nonperformer	nonpredatory	nonprotective	nonregenerating	nonrestricted	nonsacerdotal
nonperforming	nonpredicative	non-Protestant	nonregenerative	nonretention	nonsacramental
nonperiodical	nonpredictable	non-Prussian	nonregent	nonretentive	nonsacred
nonperishable	nonpreferential	nonpsychic	nonregimented	nonretinal	nonsacrificial
nonperishing	nonprehensile	nonpublication	nonregistered	nonretiring	nonsalable
nonpermanent	nonprejudicial	nonpulmonary	nonregistrable	nonretraceable	nonsalaried
nonpermeability	nonprepositional	nonpuncturable	nonreigning	nonretractile	nonsalutary
nonpermeable	non-Presbyterian	nonpunishable	nonrelative	nonretrenchment	nonsaturated
nonpermissible	nonprescriptive	nonpunishment	nonrelevant	nonretroactive	non-Scandinavian
nonperpendicular	nonpreservative	nonpurulent	nonreligious	nonreturnable	nonscheduled
nonperpetual	nonpresidential	nonracial	nonremission	nonrevealing	nonschismatic
nonpersecution	nonpressure	nonradical	nonremunerative	nonreversible	nonscholastic
nonperseverance	nonprevalent	nonratable	nonrenewable	nonrevertible	nonscientific
nonpersistence	nonpriestly	nonrated	nonrepatriable	nonreviewable	nonscoring
nonpersistent	nonproducer	nonrational	nonrepayable	nonrevival	nonseasonal
nonphilanthropic	nonproducing	nonrationalized	nonrepentance	nonrevolting	nonsecret
nonphilosophical	nonprofane	nonreactive	nonrepentant	nonrevolving	nonsecretarial
nonphysical	nonprofessional	nonreality	nonrepetition	nonrhetorical	nonsecretive
nonphysiological	nonprofessorial	nonreasonable	nonrepetitive	nonrhymed	nonsecretory

Northern Ireland A part of the United Kingdom of Great Britain and Northern Ireland occupying the NE section of Ireland; 5,238 sq. mi.; pop. 1,512,500 (est. 1969); capital, Belfast.

northern lights The aurora borealis.

north·ern·most (nôr′thərn·mōst′) *adj.* Farthest north.

Northern Rhodesia The former name of ZAMBIA.

Northern Spy A large, yellowish red variety of apple.

Northern Territories A former British protectorate in western Africa, included since 1957 in Ghana.

Northern Territory A Territory of Australia in the north central part; 523,620 sq. mi.; pop. 73,000 (est. 1970); capital, Darwin.

North Germanic See under GERMANIC.

North Holland A Province of the NW Netherlands; 1,016 sq. mi.; pop. 2,244,405 (est. 1970); capital, Haarlem.

north·ing (nôr′thing, -thing) *n.* **1.** *Chiefly Naut.* **a** Difference in latitude between two positions resulting from a northward movement. **b** Deviation or progression toward the south. **2.** *Astron.* North declination: see DECLINATION.

North Island The northernmost of the principal islands of New Zealand; 44,281 sq. mi.

North Korea See under KOREA.

north·land (nôrth′lənd) *n.* A land or region in the north. [OE] — **north′land·er** *n.*

North·land (nôrth′land) *n. Canadian* The Far North.

North Little Rock A city in central Arkansas, on the Arkansas River; pop. 60,040.

North·man (nôrth′mən) *n. pl.* **·men** (-mən) A Scandinavian; especially, a Scandinavian of the Viking period. Compare NORSEMAN. [OE]

North Miami A town in SE Florida, a suburb of Miami; pop. 34,767.

north-north·east (nôrth′nôrth′ēst′, *Naut.* nôr′nôr′ēst′) *n.* **1.** The direction midway between north and northeast. **2.** A point on the mariner's compass, two points or 22°30′ clockwise from due north. See COMPASS CARD. — *adj. & adv.* In, toward, or from the north-northeast. Abbr. *nne, n.n.e., NNE, N.N.E.*

north-north·west (nôrth′nôrth′west′, *Naut.* nôr′nôr′west′) *n.* **1.** The direction midway between north and northwest. **2.** A point on the mariner's compass, two points or 22°30′ counterclockwise from due north. See COMPASS CARD. — *adj. & adv.* In, toward, or from the north-northwest. Abbr. *nnw, n.n.w., NNW, N.N.W.*

North Platte A river in northern Colorado, SE Wyoming, and western Nebraska, flowing 680 miles SE to join the South Platte, forming the Platte River.

North Pole The northern extremity of the earth's axis, whose zenith is a little more than 1° from Polaris.

North Rhine-West·pha·lia (rīn′west·fāl′yə) A State of West Germany, in the western part; 13,157 sq. mi; pop. 17,129,800 (est. 1970); capital, Düsseldorf: German *Nord-rhein-Westfalen.*

North Rid·ing (rīd′ing) A former administrative division of Yorkshire, England; 2,127 sq. mi.; pop. 724,463 (1971).

North River The estuary of the Hudson River.

North Sea The part of the Atlantic Ocean between Great Britain and Europe: formerly *German Ocean.*

North Star Polaris (def. 1).

North Ton·a·wan·da (tŏn′ə·won′də) A port city in western New York, on the Niagara River; pop. 36,012.

Northum. or **Northumb.** Northumberland.

North·um·ber·land (nôr·thum′bər·lənd) A county of northern England; 2,019 sq. mi.; pop. 285,700 (1976); county seat, Newcastle-upon-Tyne.

North·um·bri·a (nôr·thum′brē·ə) An ancient Anglo-Saxon kingdom, extending from the Humber to the Firth of Forth.

North·um·bri·an (nôr·thum′brē·ən) *adj.* **1.** Of or pertaining to Northumbria or Northumberland, or to its inhabitants. **2.** Of or pertaining to the Old English dialect used in Northumbria. **3.** Of or pertaining to the modern dialect in use in Northumberland. — *n.* **1.** A native or inhabitant of Northumbria or Northumberland. **2.** The Old English or modern Northumbrian dialect.

North Vietnam See under VIETNAM.

north·ward (nôrth′wərd, *Naut.* nôr′thərd) *adv.* Toward the north. Also **north′wards** (-wərdz). — *adj.* To, toward, facing, or in the north. — *n.* A northward direction or point; also, a northern part or region.

north·ward·ly (nôrth′wərd·lē, *Naut.* nôr′thərd·lē) *adj. & adv.* **1.** Toward the north. **2.** Coming from the north.

north·west (nôrth′west′, *Naut.* nôr′·west′) *n.* **1.** The direction midway between north and west. **2.** A point on the mariner's compass, four points or 45° counterclockwise from due north. See COMPASS CARD. **3.** Any region lying in or toward this point. — *adj.* **1.** To, toward, facing, or in the northwest. **2.** Coming from the northwest: a *northwest* wind. — *adv.* In or toward the northwest. Abbr. *nw, n.w., NW, N.W.* — **north′west′ern** *adj.*

northwest by north A point on the mariner's compass, three points or 33°45′ counterclockwise from due north. See COMPASS CARD.

northwest by west A point on the mariner's compass, five points or 56°15′ counterclockwise from due north. See COMPASS CARD.

north·west·er (nôrth′wes′tər, *Naut.* nôr′·wes′tər) *n.* A gale or storm from the northwest: also spelled *nor′wester.*

north·west·er·ly (nôrth′wes′tər·lē, *Naut.* nôr′·wes′tər·lē) *adj.* **1.** In, of, or toward the northwest. **2.** From the northwest, as a wind. — *adv.* Toward or from the northwest. Also spelled *nor′westerly.*

North-West Frontier Province A former province of West Pakistan on the Afghanistan border, included in West Pakistan Province, 1955.

North West Mounted Police Original name of the ROYAL CANADIAN MOUNTED POLICE.

Northwest Passage A water route from the Atlantic to the Pacific along the northern coast of North America.

Northwest Semitic See under SEMITIC.

Northwest Territories An administrative division of northern Canada east of the Yukon Territory; 1,304,903 sq. mi.; pop. 36,000. Abbr. *N.W.T.*

Northwest Territory A region awarded to the United States by Britain in 1783, extending from the Great Lakes south to the Ohio River and from Pennsylvania west to the Mississippi: also *Old Northwest.*

north·west·ward (nôrth′west′wərd, *Naut.* nôr·west′wərd) *adv.* Toward the northwest. Also **north′west′wards** (-wərdz). — *adj.* To, toward, facing, or in the northwest. — *n.* Northwest.

north·west·ward·ly (nôrth′west′wərd·lē, *Naut.* nôr·west′wərd·lē) *adj. & adv.* Toward or from the northwest.

NORTHWEST TERRITORY

North Yorkshire A county in northern England; 3,210 sq. mi.; pop. 648,600 (1976); county seat, Northallerton.

Nor·ton (nôr′tən), **Charles Eliot,** 1827–1908, U.S. educator, editor, and author. — **Thomas,** 1532–84, English author and translator.

Norw. Norway; Norwegian.

Nor·walk (nôr′wôk) **1.** A town in SW Connecticut, on Long Island Sound; pop. 79,113. **2.** A city in SW California, near Los Angeles; pop. 91,827.

Nor·way (nôr′wā) A kingdom of northern Europe; 119,240 sq. mi.; pop. 3,893,000 (est. 1971); capital, Oslo: Norwegian *Norge.*

Norway maple A tall European maple (*Acer platanoides*), an excellent shade tree.

Norway spruce See under SPRUCE.

Nor·we·gian (nôr·wē′jən) *adj.* Of or pertaining to Norway, its people, or their language. — *n.* **1.** A native or inhabitant of Norway. **2.** The North Germanic language of Norway. See LANDSMÅL, RIKSMÅL. Abbr. *Nor., Norw.* [< Med.L *Norwegia* (earlier *Norvegia*) Norway < ON *Norvegr* < *nor(thr)* north + *vegr* way]

nor′·west·er (nôr·wes′tər), etc. See NORTHWESTER, etc.

Nor·wich (nor'ij, -ich *for def. 1*; nôr'wich *for def. 2*) **1.** The county seat of Norfolk, England, a county borough in the east central part; pop. 121,688 (1976). **2.** A town in SE Connecticut, on the Shetucket River; pop. 41,739.

Nor·wood (nôr'wŏŏd) A city in SW Ohio, near Cincinnati; pop. 30,420.

nos- Var. of NOSO-.

Nos. or **nos.** Numbers.

nose (nōz) *n.* **1.** The part of the face or forward end of an animal that contains the nostrils and the organ of smell, and that in man encloses cavities used in the respiratory process. ◆ Collateral adjectives: *nasal, rhinal.* **2.** The sense of smell or the power of smelling; scent. **3.** The ability to perceive or discover by or as if by the sense of smell: a *nose* for scandal. **4.** That which resembles a nose because of its prominence, position, or shape, as a spout or nozzle. **5.** *Aeron.* The forward part of an aircraft. **6.** The prow of a ship. **7.** *Informal* The nose (def. 1), considered as its owner's agent for prying or interfering: Keep your *nose* out of this. — **by a nose** *Slang* By a narrow margin. — **on the nose** *Slang* **1.** Designating a racing bet on a horse, etc., to win. **2.** Exactly; precisely. — **to pay through the nose** *Slang* To pay an excessively high price. — *v.* **nosed, nos·ing** *v.t.* **1.** To sniff, touch, or rub with the nose; nuzzle. **2.** To make (one's way) carefully with the front end foremost. **3.** To perceive or discover by or as if by smell; scent. — *v.i.* **4.** To pry or interfere; snoop: with *around* or *about.* **5.** To move forward, especially carefully. **6.** To smell; sniff. — **to nose out** To defeat by a narrow margin. — **to nose over** To turn over on its nose, as an airplane. [OE *nosu*]

nose·bag (nōz'bag') *n.* Feedbag (which see).

nose·band (nōz'band') *n.* The part of a bridle that passes over the nose of a horse: also called *nosepiece.* For illustration see HARNESS.

nose·bleed (nōz'blēd') *n.* Bleeding from the nose: also called *epistaxis.*

nose cone *Aerospace* The cone-shaped forward section of a rocket or missile, separable from the main body and carrying the payload, and equipped to withstand very high temperatures.

nose-dive (nōz'dīv') *v.i.* **-dived, -div·ing** To take a nose dive; plunge downward.

nose dive **1.** A steep, downward plunge of an aircraft, nose end foremost. **2.** Any steep, sudden drop.

nose·gay (nōz'gā') *n.* A small bunch of flowers; bouquet. [< NOSE + GAY, in obs. sense "a pretty thing"]

nose-heavy (nōz'hev'ē) *adj.* Tending to fly or move with the nose down, because of weight, poor trim, etc.

nose·piece (nōz'pēs') *n.* **1.** Any piece or part, as of a helmet, that covers or protects the nose. **2.** The part of a microscope, often rotatable, to which the object lens or lenses are fastened. **3.** The part of a pair of eyeglasses that fits over the bridge of the nose. **4.** A noseband.

nos·ey (nō'zē) See NOSY.

no-show (nō'shō') *n.* *U.S. Informal* One who reserves a seat, especially for an airplane flight, but neither claims it nor cancels the reservation by the time of departure.

nos·ing (nō'zing) *n.* **1.** The part of a stair tread projecting beyond the riser. **2.** Any similarly projecting part, as the rounded edge of a molding. **3.** A band of metal, rubber, etc., covering the edge of a stair tread. [< NOS(E) + -ING¹]

noso- *combining form* Disease: nosology. Also, before vowels, *nos-.* [< NL < Gk. *nosos* disease]

no·sog·ra·phy (nō·sog'rə·fē) *n.* *pl.* **·phies** A classification and description of diseases. [< NL] — **no·sog'ra·pher** *n.* — **no·so·graph·ic** (nō'sə·graf'ik) or **·i·cal** *adj.*

no·sol·o·gy (nō·sol'ə·jē) *n.* *pl.* **·gies** **1.** The branch of medical science dealing with the systematic classification of diseases. **2.** A scientific classification of diseases. **3.** The characteristics of a particular disease. [< NL *nosologia* < Gk. *nosos* disease + -*logia* -logy] — **nos·o·log·i·cal** (nos'ə·loj'i·kəl) *adj.* — **no·sol'o·gist** *n.*

nos·tal·gi·a (nos·tal'jə, -jē·ə) *n.* **1.** A longing for familiar or beloved circumstances that are now remote or irrecoverable. **2.** Any longing for something far away or long ago. **3.** Severe homesickness. [< NL < Gk. *nostos* return home + *algos* pain] — **nos·tal'gic** *adj.*

nos·toc (nos'tok) *n.* Any of a genus (*Nostoc*) of blue-green

fresh-water algae that form jellylike masses in or near water, as on moist rocks. [< NL; coined by Paracelsus]

nos·tol·o·gy (nos·tol'ə·jē) *n.* Gerontology (def. 1). — **nos·to·log·ic** (nos'tə·loj'ik) *adj.*

Nos·tra·da·mus (nos'trə·dā'məs), 1503–66, French astrologer: original name **Michel de No·tre·dame** (də nô'trə·däm').

nos·tril (nos'trəl) *n.* One of the external openings of the nose. [OE *nosthyrl* < *nos(u)* nose + *thyrel* hole < *thurh* through]

nos·trum (nos'trəm) *n.* **1.** A medicine of one's own invention or preparation; also, a quack medicine. **2.** A favorite remedy or plan. **3.** A cure-all. [< L *nostrum,* neut. of *noster* our own < *nos* we, us]

nos·y (nō'zē) *adj.* **nos·i·er, nos·i·est** *Informal* Prying; snooping; inquisitive: also spelled *nosey.* — **nos'i·ly** *adv.* — **nos'i·ness** *n.*

not (not) *adv.* In no way, or to no extent or degree: used to note the absence, reverse, or opposite of something or to express negation, prohibition, or refusal. [OE *nāwiht* < *ne* not + *ā* ever + *wiht* thing however small]

not- Var. of NOTO-.

no·ta be·ne (nō'tə bē'nē) *Latin* Note well. Abbr. **n.b.,** *N.B.*

no·ta·bil·i·ty (nō'tə·bil'ə·tē) *n.* *pl.* **·ties** **1.** The quality of being notable. **2.** A distinguished or notable person.

no·ta·ble (nō'tə·bəl) *adj.* **1.** Worthy of note; remarkable; distinguished. **2.** Capable of being noted or perceived. **3.** *Archaic* Industrious or efficient. — *n.* **1.** One who is distinguished, famous, or socially prominent. **2.** *Rare* That which is notable. [< OF < L *notabilis* < *notare* to note < *nota* mark] — **no·ta·ble·ness** *n.* — **no'ta·bly** *adv.*

no·tar·i·al (nō·târ'ē·əl) *adj.* Of, pertaining to, or done by a notary. — **no·tar'i·al·ly** *adv.*

no·ta·rize (nō'tə·rīz) *v.t.* **·rized, ·riz·ing** To attest to or authenticate as a notary. — **no'ta·ri·za'tion** *n.*

no·ta·ry (nō'tə·rē) *n.* *pl.* **·ries** **1.** Notary public (which see). **2.** In Quebec, a lawyer whose functions do not include pleading. **3.** Formerly, one who drew up legal papers. [< OF *notarie* < L *notarius* secretary < *notare* to note]

notary public *pl.* **notaries public** One who is legally authorized to administer oaths, take depositions, certify contracts, etc. Abbr. *N.P.*

no·ta·tion (nō·tā'shən) *n.* **1.** A system of signs, figures, or abbreviations used for convenience in recording a quantity, relation, process, etc.: musical *notation*; algebraic *notation.* **2.** The act or process of using notation. **3.** A note or comment. [< L *notatio, -onis* < *notatus,* pp. of *notare.* See NOTABLE.] — **no·ta'tion·al** *adj.*

notch (noch) *n.* **1.** A hollow or V-shaped cut in a surface; indentation. **2.** A nick cut into a stick, etc., as for keeping count. **3.** A narrow passage between mountains; a defile. **4.** *Informal* A degree; level: He is a *notch* above the others. — *v.t.* **1.** To make a notch or notches in. **2.** To record by or as if by notches; score. [Prob. ME *an oche* a notch < OF *osche* < *oschier* to notch] — **notch'er** *n.*

note (nōt) *n.* **1.** *Often pl.* A brief record or summary of facts set down for future study or reference: to take *notes.* **2.** A brief account or jotting to aid the memory. **3.** *Music* **a** A symbol representing a tone or sound of a given duration, usually in terms of an established time unit, the pitch of the tone being indicated by the position of the symbol on a staff, with possible modification by a key signature or accidental. **b** A tone or sound of a definite pitch. **c** A key of the keyboard. **4.** Any more or less musical sound, as the call of a bird. **5.** Any distinctive vocal sound, as the cry of an animal. **6.** A sign, suggestion, or element by which a quality, condition, fact, etc., may be recognized or known; a distinctive mark: a *note* of sadness; a *note* of spring in the air. **7.** A piece of paper currency issued by a government or authorized bank and negotiable as money: a bank *note.* **8.** A promissory note (which see). **9.** A formal, written communication of an official or diplomatic nature. **10.** A brief letter, especially of an informal character. **11.** *pl.* A record of impressions, observations, reflections, etc. **12.** A written comment amending, criticizing, or explaining a passage in a book, manuscript, etc., as in the margin of a page. **13.** Distinction; importance; reputation: a gentleman of *note.* **14.** Notice; observation; attention: worthy of *note.*

nonsymptomatic	nonterrestrial	nontransparent	non-Unitarian	nonvenous	nonvocal
nonsynchronous	nonterritorial	nontransposing	nonunited	nonverbal	nonvocalic
nonsyntactic	nontestamentary	nontransposition	nonuniversal	nonverminous	nonvocational
nonsyntactical	nontextual	nontreasonable	non-Universalist	nonvernacular	nonvolatile
nonsynthesized	nontheatrical	nontributary	nonuniversity	nonvertical	nonvolcanic
nonsystematic	nontheological	nontropical	nonuser	nonvesicular	nonvolition
nonarnishable	nontheosophical	nontruth	nonviable	nonvibratory	nonvoluntary
nontax	nontherapeutic	nontuberculous	nonusing	nonviolation	nonvortical
nontaxability	nonthinking	non-Turkish	nonuterine	nonviolence	nonvoter
nontaxable	nontitular	non-Tuscan	nonutilitarian	nonvirulent	nonvoting
nonteachable	nontitular	nontypical	nonutilization	nonviscous	nonvulcanizable
nontechnical	nontraditional	nontypographical	nonutilized	nonvisiting	nonwaterproof
nonteleological	nontragic	nontyrannical	nonvalidity	nonvisual	nonworker
nontemporal	nontransferability	nonulcerous	nonvascular	nonvisualized	nonworking
nontemporizing	nontransferable	nonunderstandable	nonvegetative	nonvenereal	nonvisualized	nonwoven
nonterminating	nontransitional	nonunderstanding	nonvenomous	nonvitreous	nonyielding

15. A mark or character used in writing or printing to call attention to something. **16.** An artist's sketch. **17.** *Archaic* An itemized bill or list. **18.** *Archaic* Manner of speaking; attitude. **19.** *Archaic* or *Poetic* A melody or song. Abbr. *n.* — **Syn.** See RE-MARK. — *v.t.* **not·ed**, **not·ing 1.** To become aware of; observe. **2.** To pay attention to; heed carefully: to *note* well. **3.** To state; remark; make special mention of. **4.** To set down for remembering; make a note of. **5.** To annotate. **6.** To point out or indicate. **7.** To set down in musical notation. [< OF *noter* < L *notare* < *nota* mark] — **no'ter** *n.*

	NOTE	DENOMINATION	REST
	O	Whole	
or	♩	Half	
or	♩	Quarter	
or	♫	Eighth	
or	♫	Sixteenth	
or	♫	Thirty-second	
or	♫	Sixty-fourth	

note·book (nōt'- boŏk') *n.* **1.** A book with blank pages on which notes may be entered. **2.** A book in which notes of hand are registered; bill book.

not·ed (nō'tid) *adj.* **1.** Well known by reputation; famous. **2.** Taken note of. — **not'ed·ly** *adv.* — **not'ed·ness** *n.*

note·less (nōt'lis) *adj.* **1.** Not noted or distinguished; obscure. **2.** Unmusical.

note of hand A promissory note.

note paper Paper for writing notes or letters.

note·wor·thy (nōt'wûr'thē) *adj.* Remarkable; significant. — **note'wor'thi·ly** *adv.* — **note'wor'thi·ness** *n.*

noth·ing (nuth'ing) *n.* **1.** Not anything; not something; naught. **2.** No part, piece, or element: He knew *nothing* of it. **3.** One who or that which is of little or no importance; a trifle. **4.** Insignificance or unimportance: to rise from *nothing.* **5.** A cipher; zero. **6.** A state of nonexistence; also, that which is nonexistent. — **for nothing 1.** Without charge; free. **2.** To no avail; fruitlessly. **3.** Without cause; inexplicably. — **in nothing flat** *U.S. Slang* In a very short time. — **nothing doing** *Informal* **1.** No: an emphatic refusal to acquiesce in something. **2.** Nothing happening or of interest, excitement, etc. — **to know from nothing** (or **not to know from nothing**) *U.S. Slang* To know nothing. — *adv.* In no degree; not at all: now only in the expression **nothing like.** [ME < OE *nān thing*]

noth·ing·ness (nuth'ing·nis) *n.* **1.** The condition, quality, or fact of being nothing; nonexistence. **2.** Utter worthlessness or insignificance; meaninglessness. **3.** That which is petty, trivial, or nonexistent. **4.** The absence of consciousness, as unconsciousness or death.

no·tice (nō'tis) *v.t.* **·ticed**, **·tic·ing 1.** To pay attention to or become aware of. **2.** To refer to or comment on; mention. **3.** To treat courteously or with favor. **4.** *Archaic* To serve with a notice; notify. — *n.* **1.** The act of noticing or observing; attention; cognizance: to take *notice* of. **2.** Announcement; information; warning: *notice* of an approaching storm. **3.** A formal announcement, as of the termination or intended termination of an agreement, contract, etc.: to give *notice.* **4.** A written or printed communication publicly displayed: *notice* of sale. **5.** A short, literary advertisement or review. **6.** Respectful treatment; civility. [< OF < L *notitia* fame, renown < *notus* known]

no·tice·a·ble (nō'tis·ə·bəl) *adj.* **1.** That can be noticed; perceptible. **2.** Worthy of notice. — **no'tice·a·bly** *adv.*

no·ti·fi·ca·tion (nō'tə·fə·kā'shən) *n.* **1.** The act of notifying. **2.** Notice given. **3.** A sign, advertisement, etc., by which notice is conveyed. [< OF < Med.L *notificatio*, *-onis* < L *notificare.* See NOTIFY.]

no·ti·fy (nō'tə·fī) *v.t.* **·fied**, **·fy·ing 1.** To give notice to; inform. **2.** *Chiefly Brit.* To give information of; make known. [< OF *notifier* < L *notificare* < *notus* known + *fa·cere* to make] — **no'ti·fi'er** *n.*

no·tion (nō'shən) *n.* **1.** A general idea or impression; a vague conception. **2.** An opinion, belief, or idea. **3.** Intention; inclination. **4.** *pl. U.S.* Small miscellaneous articles for sale, as ribbons, thread, pins, etc. — **Syn.** See IDEA. [< LL *notio*, *-onis* < *notus*, pp. of *noscere.* See NOTIFY.]

no·tion·al (nō'shən·əl) *adj.* **1.** Pertaining to, expressing, or consisting of notions or concepts. **2.** Existing in imagination only. **3.** *Archaic U.S.* Given to entertaining pet ideas. **4.** *Gram.* **a** Based upon meaning rather than form or

syntax. **b** Of a verb, etc., having meaning of its own, independent of contextual words. — **no'tion·al·ly** *adv.*

noto- *combining form* Back: *notochord.* Also, before vowels, *not-.* [< Gk. *nōton* back]

no·to·chord (nō'tə·kôrd) *n. Biol.* In vertebrate embryos, a flexible rod of cells along the median line on the dorsal side, a precursor of the spinal column, that persists in adult protochordates.

No·to·gae·a (nō'tə·jē'ə) *n.* A zoogeographical realm including the Australian and Neotropical regions. [< Gk. *notos* south + *gaia* earth] — **No'to·gae'al**, **No'to·gae'an**, **No'to·gae'ic** *adj.*

no·to·ri·e·ty (nō'tə·rī'ə·tē) *n. pl.* **·ties 1.** The state or character of being notorious. **2.** One who or that which is notorious. — **Syn.** See FAME. [< F *notoriété* < Med.L *notorietas*, *-tatis* < LL *notorius.* See NOTORIOUS.]

no·to·ri·ous (nō·tôr'ē·əs, -tō'rē-) *adj.* **1.** Widely known and generally disapproved of or deplored. **2.** Generally known; acknowledged. [< Med. L *notorius* < *notus*, pp. of *noscere* to know] — **no·to'ri·ous·ly** *adv.*

no·tor·nis (nō·tôr'nis) *n.* A flightless bird (genus *Notornis*) of New Zealand and neighboring islands, with rudimentary wings. [< NL < Gk. *notos* south + *ornis* bird]

no·to·un·gu·late (nō'tō·ung'gyə·lāt) *n. Paleontol.* Any member of an extinct order (*Notoungulata*) of herbivorous mammals of the Tertiary. — *adj.* Of or pertaining to the Notoungulata. Also **no·tun·gu·late** (nō·tung'gyə·lāt). [< NOTO- + UNGULATE]

No·tre Dame (nō'trə däm', nō'tər däm'; *Fr.* nô'tr' däm') **1.** French Our Lady (Mary, mother of Jesus). **2.** A famous early Gothic cathedral in Paris, built 1163–1257.

no-trump (nō'trump') *n.* **1.** In bridge, a bid calling for play without a trump suit. **2.** Play without a trump suit. — *adj.* **1.** Of, suitable for, or denoting a bid or play of no-trump. **2.** Being without a trump suit.

no-trump·er (nō'trump'ər) *n.* A no-trump bid or hand.

Not·ting·ham·shire (not'ing·əm·shir') A county of north central England; 844 sq. mi.; pop. 981,000 (1976); county seat, **Nottingham,** a county borough, pop. 287,000 (1976): also **Nottingham.** Abbr. *Notts.*

Notts. Nottinghamshire.

not·with·stand·ing (not'with·stan'ding, -with-) *prep.* In spite of: He left *notwithstanding* your orders. — *adv.* All the same; nevertheless: Though closely guarded, he escaped *notwithstanding.* — *conj.* In spite of the fact that; although. — **notwithstanding that** Although.

— **Syn.** (prep.) *Notwithstanding, in spite of,* and *despite* introduce a person, agency, or circumstance that acts in unsuccessful opposition. These words are largely interchangeable, differing chiefly in force. *Notwithstanding* is the weakest, suggesting merely some obstacle, while *in spite of* indicates active, often violent opposition, and is the strongest synonym. *Despite* is intermediate in force. — (conj.) nevertheless, still, though. Compare BUT¹.

Nouak·chott (nwäk·shôt') The capital of Mauritania, in the western part; pop. 70,000 (est. 1976).

nou·gat (nōō'gət, *Fr.* nōō·gä') *n.* A confection made with chopped almonds, pistachios, etc., mixed in a honey or sugar paste. [< F < Provençal, ult. < L *nux, nucis* nut]

nought (nôt) See NAUGHT.

Nou·mé·a (nōō·mē'ə, -mä'ə) The capital of New Caledonia, a port on the southwestern coast; pop. 22,272 (est. 1959).

nou·me·nal (nōō'mə·nəl, nou'-) *adj.* Of or pertaining to noumena or the noumenon. — **nou'me·nal·ly** *adv.* — **nou'me·nal·ism** *n.* — **nou'me·nal·ist** *n.*

nou·me·non (nōō'mə·non, nou'-) *n. pl.* **·me·na** (-mə·nə) *Philos.* **1.** An object of intuition that can be apprehended by the intellect only and not by the senses. **2.** The necessarily postulated ground or cause of phenomena, transcending sense perception and theoretically unknowable. **3.** An object in itself, independent of our perception of it. Compare PHENOMENON. [< NL < Gk. *nooumenon,* neut. ppr. passive of *noein* to conceive]

noun (noun) *n.* **1.** *Gram.* **a** A word used as the name of a thing, quality, or action. **b** Anything that can be used either as subject, object, or appositive, as a noun clause. **2.** *Ling.* One of a form class the members of which can take inflectional endings for number, case, and gender, or can occupy certain syntactic positions in sentences and phrases, or can be identified by a combination of morphological and syntactic criteria. In English, *boy, boys, boy's* are nominal forms by virtue of inflection; *The boy went home* and *I saw the boy* illustrate typical syntactic positions for a noun such as *boy.* See SUBSTANTIVE. — *adj.* Of or pertaining to a noun or nouns: also **noun'al.** [< AF, OF *nun* < L *nomen* name] — **noun'al·ly** *adv.*

noun clause *Gram.* A dependent clause that functions as a noun in a sentence, as *That he is wrong* in *That he is wrong is obvious* and *Whoever finds my wallet* in *Whoever finds my wallet will be rewarded.*

nour·ish (nûr'ish) *v.t.* **1.** To furnish food or other material to sustain the life and promote the growth of (a living plant

or animal). **2.** To support; maintain; foster. [< OF *noriss-*, stem of *norir* < L *nutrire* to nourish] — **nour'ish·a·ble** *adj.* — **nour'ish·er** *n.* — **nour'ish·ing·ly** *adv.*
— **Syn. 1.** feed, nurture. **2.** nurse, cherish.
nour·ish·ment (nûr'ish-mənt) *n.* **1.** That which nourishes; nutriment. **2.** The act of nourishing, or the state of being nourished. [< OF *norrissement*]
nous (nōōs, nous) *n. Philos.* Mind; intellect; reason. [< Gk. *nous, noos* mind]
nou·veau riche (nōō'vō' rēsh') *French pl.* **nou·veaux riches** (nōō'vō' rēsh') One who has recently become rich.
nou·veau·té (nōō·vō·tā') *n. pl.* **·tés** (-tā') *French* A new thing; a novelty.
Nou·velle Ca·lé·do·nie (nōō·vel' kà·lā·dô·nē') The French name for NEW CALEDONIA.
nov. Novelist.
Nov. or **Nov** November.
no·va (nō'və) *n. pl.* **·vae** (-vē) or **·vas** *Astron.* A star that suddenly flares up and fades away after a period of a few weeks or months. [< L, fem. of *novus* new]
no·vac·u·lite (nō·vak'yə·līt) *n.* An extremely fine-grained siliceous rock used for honing. [< L *novacula* razor]
No·va·lis (nō·vä'lis) Pseudonym of **Georg Friedrich Philipp von Har·den·berg** (här'den·berk), 1772–1801, German poet.
No·va Lis·bo·a (nō'və lēzh·bō'ə) A city in Angola, in the west central part, on the Cuvo River; pop. 109,000 (est. 1964): formerly *Huambo.*
No·va·ra (nō·vä'rä) A commune in Piedmont, northern Italy; pop. 86,190 (1961). Ancient **No·va'ri·a** (-rē·ä).
No·va Sco·tia (nō'və skō'shə) A province of eastern Canada; 21,068 sq. mi.; pop. 770,000; capital, Halifax. Abbr. *N.S.* — **No'va Sco'tian**
no·va·tion (nō·vā'shən) *n.* **1.** *Law* A substitution of a new obligation for an old one, as by transferring a debt from one creditor to another. **2.** *Rare* A making anew. [< L *novatio, -onis* making new < *novare* to make new < *novus* new]
No·va·ya Zem·lya (nō'və·yə zyim·lyä') An Arctic archipelago in the R.S.F.S.R., separating the Kara and Barents seas; 35,000 sq. mi.
nov·el[1] (nov'əl) *n.* **1.** A fictional prose narrative of considerable length, relating a series of events or circumstances in a self-consistent sequence incorporating some overall pattern or plot, and usually displaying the thoughts and sensations as well as the acts of the characters. **2.** The particular type of literature represented by fiction of this kind: with *the.* **3.** *Usually pl. Archaic* A novella. [< F *nouvelle* < Ital. *novella* < Med.L < L *novus* new]
nov·el[2] (nov'əl) *adj.* New, strange, or unusual. [< OF < L *novellum* < *novum* new] — **nov'el·ly** *adv.*
nov·el[3] (nov'əl) *n.* In Roman law, a new constitution or a decree supplemental to a code. [< Med.L *novellus* < L *novus* new]
nov·el·ette (nov'əl·et') *n.* A short novel: also *novella.*
nov·el·ist (nov'əl·ist) *n.* A writer of novels. Abbr. *nov.*
nov·el·is·tic (nov'əl·is'tik) *adj.* Of, pertaining to, characteristic of, or found in novels. — **nov'el·is'ti·cal·ly** *adv.*
nov·el·ize (nov'əl·īz) *v.t.* **·ized, ·iz·ing** To put into the form of a novel. — **nov'el·i·za'tion** *n.*
no·vel·la (nō·vel'ə, *Ital.* nō·vel'lä) *n. pl.* **·vel·las**, *Ital.* **·vel·le** (-vel'lā) **1.** A short tale or narrative, usually with a moral and often satiric, as the stories in Boccaccio's *Decameron.* **2.** A novelette. [< Ital. See NOVEL[1].]
Nov·els (nov'əlz) *n.pl.* **1.** The amendments and supplementary laws to the Justinian Code decreed by Justinian and his immediate successors. Also *Latin* **No·vel·lae Con·sti·tu·ti·o·nes** (nō·vel'ē kon'sti·tōō'shē·ō'nēz). See CORPUS JURIS CIVILIS. **2.** Similar decrees proclaimed by other Roman emperors.
nov·el·ty (nov'əl·tē) *n. pl.* **·ties 1.** Something novel or unusual; innovation. **2.** The quality of being novel or new; freshness. **3.** *Usually pl.* A small manufactured article, as for adornment. [< F *novelté* < LL *novellitas, -tatis*]
No·vem·ber (nō·vem'bər) *n.* The eleventh month of the year, containing 30 days. Abbr. *N., Nov, Nov.* [< L, ninth month (of the old Roman calendar) < *novem* nine]
no·ve·na (nō·vē'nə) *n.* In the Roman Catholic Church, devotions made on nine successive days, for some special religious purpose. [< Med.L < L *novem* nine]
Nov·go·rod (nov'gə·rod) A city in the NW R.S.F.S.R., on the Volkhov; pop. about 61,000 (1959).
nov·ice (nov'is) *n.* **1.** A beginner in any occupation; an inexperienced person. **2.** *Eccl.* **a** One who enters a religious order or community on probation. **b** One recently converted or recently accepted as a member of a church. [< F < L *novicius* new < *novus*] — **nov'ice·hood** (-hŏŏd) *n.*
— **Syn. 1.** *Novice, beginner, tyro, novitiate,* and *neophyte* denote a person of little experience, or one who is newly embarked on learning a trade, craft, skill, etc *Novice* is a general term, often used as the official designation for those who have yet to demonstrate proficiency in a game or sport. *Beginner* is a homelier synonym for *novice*, sometimes implying depreciation; even more depreciatory is *tyro.* In special senses, *novice*, and *novitiate* denote one newly entered into a religious order, and *neophyte* refers to a new member of a mystic or fraternal society. Compare AMATEUR.

No·vi Sad (nô'vē säd') The capital of Vojvodina, NE Yugoslavia, on the Danube; pop. 119,000 (est. 1968): German *Neusatz.*
no·vi·ti·ate (nō·vish'ē·it, -āt) *n.* **1.** The state or period of being a novice. **2.** *Eccl.* **a** The period of probation of a novice in a religious order or community. **b** The quarters occupied by such novices. **3.** A novice (defs. 1 and 2a). — **Syn.** See NOVICE. Also **no·vi'ci·ate.** [< F *novicat* or Med.L *novitiatus* < *novitius*]
No·vo·cain (nō'və·kān) *n.* Proprietary name for a brand of procaine used as a local anesthetic, less toxic than cocaine. Also **no'vo·cain, no'vo·caine, No'vo·caine.**
No·vo·Kuz·netsk (nə·və·kōōz·nyetsk') A city in the southern R.S.F.S.R., on the Tom; pop. 499,000 (1970): from 1932–61 called *Stalinsk.*
No·vo·ros·siysk (nə·və·ro·syēsk') A port city in the SW R.S.F.S.R., on the Black Sea; pop. 133,000 (1970). Also **No·vo·ros·siisk, No·vo·ros·sisk.**
No·vo·si·birsk (nə·və·syi·byērsk') A city in the southern R.S.F.S.R., on the Ob; pop. 1,161,000 (1970).
no·vus or·do se·clo·rum (nō'vəs ôr'dō sə·klôr'əm, -klō'rəm) *Latin* A new order of the ages: motto on the Great Seal of the United States.
now (nou) *adv.* **1.** At once. **2.** At or during the present time. **3.** Nowadays. **4.** In the immediate past: He said so just *now.* **5.** In the immediate future: He is going just *now.* **6.** In such circumstances; things being as they are: *Now* we can be sure of getting home. **7.** At this point in the proceedings, narrative, etc.: The war was *now* virtually over. — *conj.* Seeing that; since: *Now* that you've come, stay a while. — *n.* The present time, moment, or occasion. — **now and then** From time to time; occasionally: also **now and again.**
◆ *Now* is often used as an expletive, as in a command: Come *now,* don't make me angry! [OE *nū*]
now·a·days (nou'ə·dāz') *adv.* In the present time or age.
no·way (nō'wā') *adv.* **1.** In no way, manner, or degree. **2.** *U.S. Dial.* By any means. Also **no'ways'** (-wāz').
no·where (nō'hwâr') *adv.* In no place; not anywhere. — *n.* No place. Also *U.S. Dial.* **no'wheres'** (-hwârz').
no·whith·er (nō'hwith'ər) *adv.* Toward no definite place.
no·wise (nō'wīz') *adv.* In no manner or degree.
nowt (nout) *n. Scot.* An ox. [ME < ON *naut*]
Nox (noks) In Roman mythology, the goddess of night: identified with the Greek *Nyx.*
nox·ious (nok'shəs) *adj.* Causing or tending to cause injury to health or morals; hurtful. — **Syn.** See PERNICIOUS. [< L *noxius* < *noxa* harm < *nocere* to hurt] — **nox'ious·ly** *adv.* — **nox'ious·ness** *n.*
noy·ade (nwà·yàd') *n. French* Execution by drowning, especially as practiced during the Reign of Terror (1793–94) in Nantes, France.
Noyes (noiz), **Alfred**, 1880–1958, English poet.
Noy·on (nwà·yôn') A town in northern France; scene of Charlemagne's coronation; birthplace of Calvin; pop. 11,567 (1968).
noz·zle (noz'əl) *n.* **1.** A projecting spout or pipe serving as an outlet or opening, as of a teapot, hose, or rifle. **2.** *Slang* The nose. [Dim. of NOSE.]
n.p. No place (of publication).
n.p. or d. No place or date (of publication.)
Np *Chem.* Neptunium.
NP Neuropsychiatric.
N.P. Notary Public.
n.p.t. Normal pressure and temperature.
nr. Near.
NRA or **N.R.A.** National Recovery Administration.
Ns *Meteorol.* Nimbostratus.
N.S. 1. New Style. **2.** Not specified: also **n.s. 3.** Nova Scotia.
NSA National Shipping Authority.
NSC National Security Council.
NSF National Science Foundation.
N.S.F. or **N/S/F/** Not sufficient funds.
NSLI National Service Life Insurance.
N.S.P.C.A. National Society for the Prevention of Cruelty to Animals.
N.S.P.C.C. National Society for the Prevention of Cruelty to Children.
N.S.W. New South Wales.
Nt *Chem.* Niton.
N.T. 1. New Testament: also **NT. 2.** Northern Territory.
nth (enth) *adj.* **1.** *Math.* Representing an ordinal equivalent to *n.* **2.** Infinitely or indefinitely large (or small); most extreme: to the *nth* degree.
nt.wt. Net weight.
nu (nōō, nyōō) *n.* The thirteenth letter in the Greek alphabet (N, ν), corresponding to English *n.* See ALPHABET.
nu·ance (nōō·äns', nōō'äns, nyōō'-; *Fr.* nü·äns') *n.* A fine or subtle variation, as in color, tone, or meaning; a gradation. [< F < OF *nuer* to shade < *nue* cloud < L *nubes*]
nub (nub) *n.* **1.** A knob or protuberance. **2.** A small piece, as of coal. **3.** *U.S. Informal* Core; gist; point: the *nub* of the story. [Var. of *knub*, var. of KNOB.] — **nub'by** *adj.*
Nu·ba (nōō'bä) *n.* **1.** A Nubian. **2.** One of a Negro tribe of

the central Sudan, related to the Nubians. **3.** The language of the Nuba peoples: also called *Berberi*.

nub·bin (nub′in) *n. U.S.* **1.** An imperfectly developed fruit or ear of corn. **2.** Anything small, stunted, or depleted from use. **3.** *Informal* Nub (def. 3). [< NUB]

nub·ble (nub′əl) *n.* **1.** A small protuberance or lump; nub. **2.** *Dial.* A small island. [Dim. of NUB]

nub·bly (nub′lē) *adj.* Having small knobs or knots, as the surface of a fabric.

nu·bi·a (nōō′bē·ə, nyōō′-) *n.* A soft, light scarf for covering the head, worn by women. [< L *nubes* cloud]

Nu·bi·a (nōō′bē·ə, nyōō′-) A region and ancient country of NE Africa in the northern Sudan and southern Egypt.

Nu·bi·an (nōō′bē·ən, nyōō′-) *adj.* Of or pertaining to Nubia, its people, or their language. — *n.* **1.** A native of Nubia; especially, a member of any of the Negroid tribes formerly ruling the territory between Egypt and Abyssinia. **2.** The Sudanic language of the Nubians. **3.** A Nubian horse or goat.

Nubian Desert A sandstone plateau in the NE Sudan between the Nile valley and the Red Sea.

nu·bile (nōō′bil, nyōō′-) *adj.* Ready or suitable for marriage, as because of age or physical maturity: said of young women. [< L *nubilis* < *nubere* to wed] — **nu·bil′i·ty** *n.*

nu·bi·lous (nōō′bə·ləs, nyōō′-) *adj.* **1.** Cloudy; foggy. **2.** Obscure; indefinite. Also **nu′bi·lose** (-lōs). [< LL *nubilosus* < *nubes* cloud]

nu·cel·lus (nōō·sel′əs, nyōō-) *n.* pl. **·cel·li** (-sel′ī) *Bot.* The essential part of a plant ovule, containing the embryo sac. [< NL < L *nucella*, dim. of *nux, nucis* nut] — **nu·cel′lar** *adj.*

nu·cha (nōō′kə, nyōō′-) *n.* pl. **·chae** (-kē) The nape or back of the neck. [< Med.L < Arabic *nukhā′* spinal marrow] — **nu′chal** *adj.*

nu·cle·ar (nōō′klē·ər, nyōō′-) *adj.* **1.** Of, pertaining to, or resembling a nucleus or nuclei. Also **nu′cle·al** (-klē·əl). **2.** Of or using atomic energy: *nuclear* reactor. [< F *nucléaire*]

nuclear fission *Physics* Fission (which see).

nuclear fusion *Physics* Fusion (which see).

nuclear physics The branch of physics that investigates the structure and properties of the atomic nucleus.

nuclear reaction *Physics* A change in the properties of one or more atomic nuclei, especially as a result of a collision between two nuclei.

nu·cle·ase (nōō′klē·ās, nyōō′-) *n. Biochem.* An enzyme that hydrolyzes nucleic acids.

nu·cle·ate (nōō′klē·āt, nyōō′-) *adj.* Having a nucleus. — *v.t.* & *v.i.* **·at·ed, ·at·ing** To form or gather into a nucleus. [< L *nucleatus*, pp. of *nucleare* to form a kernel] — **nu′cle·a′tion** *n.* — **nu′cle·a′tor** *n.*

nu·cle·ic acid (nōō·klē′ik, nyōō-) *Biochem.* Any of a group of complex noncrystalline acids derived from nucleoproteins and containing carbohydrates combined with phosphoric acids and bases derived from purine or pyrimidine.

nu·cle·in (nōō′klē·in, nyōō′-) *n. Biochem.* A colorless, amorphous protein containing nucleic acid, found as a normal constituent of cell nuclei.

nucleo- *combining form* Nucleus: *nucleoprotein*. [< L *nucleus* kernel]

nu·cle·o·late (nōō′klē·ə·lāt, nyōō′-) *adj.* Having a nucleolus or nucleoli. Also **nu′cle·o·lat′ed.**

nu·cle·o·lus (nōō·klē′ə·ləs, nyōō-) *n.* pl. **·li** (-lī) *Biol.* A rounded body sometimes found within the nucleus of a cell. Also **nu′cle·ole** (-ōl). For illustration see CELL. [< L, dim. of *nucleus.* See NUCLEUS.] — **nu·cle·o′lar** *adj.*

nu·cle·on (nōō′klē·on, nyōō′-) *n. Physics* Any of the particles composing the nucleus of an atom, as the proton, neutron, neutrino, etc.

nu·cle·on·ics (nōō′klē·on′iks, nyōō′-) *n.pl.* (*usually construed as sing.*) The practical applications of nuclear physics in any field of science, engineering, or technology. — **nu′cle·on′ic** *adj.*

nu·cle·o·plasm (nōō′klē·ə·plaz′əm, nyōō′-) *n. Biol.* The protoplasm of a cell nucleus: also called *karyoplasm.* — **nu′cle·o·plas′mic** *adj.*

nu·cle·o·pro·te·in (nōō′klē·ə·prō′tē·in, -tēn, nyōō′-) *n. Biochem.* Any of a class of substances found in the nuclei of plant and animal cells, containing one or more protein molecules combined with nucleic acid.

nu·cle·us (nōō′klē·əs, nyōō′-) *n.* pl. **·cle·i** (-klē·ī) **1.** A central point or part around which other things are gathered; inner or essential element; core. **2.** A center of growth or development; basis; kernel. **3.** *Biol.* A complex spherical body surrounded by a thin membrane and embedded in the protoplasm of most plant and animal cells, containing chromatin and essential to the processes of heredity and to other vital activities of the cell, as assimilation, metabolism, growth, and reproduction. For illustration see CELL. **4.** *Anat.* Any of certain masses of gray matter composed of nerve cells and found in the brain and spinal cord. **5.** *Astron.* The brightest portion in the head of a comet or in the center of a nebula. **6.** *Physics* The central core of an atom, containing nucleons

that provide its effective mass and carrying a positive electric charge balanced by the negative charge of the surrounding electrons. **7.** *Chem.* A group or ring of atoms so related structurally that their fundamental arrangement remains intact through a series of chemical changes. **8.** *Bot.* The central point of a starch granule around which circular markings appear. [Contr. of L *nuculeus*, dim. of *nux, nucis* nut]

nu·clide (nōō′klīd, nyōō′-) *n. Physics* A nuclear species as marked by the atomic number and mass number.

nude (nōōd, nyōōd) *adj.* **1.** Without clothing or covering; naked; bare. **2.** *Law* Lacking an essential legal requisite; naked. — *n.* **1.** A nude figure, especially as represented in painting, sculpture, etc. **2.** The state of being nude. [< L *nudus* naked, bare] — **nude′ly** *adv.* — **nude′ness** *n.*

nudge (nuj) *v.t.* **nudged, nudg·ing** To touch or push gently, as with the elbow, in order to attract attention, convey a meaning, etc. — *n.* A gentle push, as with the elbow. [? < Scand. Cf. dial. Norw. *nugga* to push gently.]

nudi- *combining form* Without covering; naked; bare: *nudicaulous.* [< L *nudus* naked]

nu·di·branch (nōō′di·brangk, nyōō′-) *n.* One of a suborder (*Nudibranchiata*) of marine gastropods lacking shells and true gills in the adult stage. [< NL *Nudibranchiata*, suborder name] — **nu′di·bran′chi·ate** (-brang′kē·it) *adj. & n.*

nu·di·cau·lous (nōō′di·kô′ləs, nyōō′-) *adj. Bot.* Having naked or leafless stems. Also **nu′di·caul.** [< NUDI- + L *caulis* stem]

nud·ism (nōō′diz·əm, nyōō′-) *n.* The doctrine or practice of living in the state of nudity.

nud·ist (nōō′dist, nyōō′-) *n.* One who believes in or practices nudism. — *adj.* Of or pertaining to nudism.

nu·di·ty (nōō′də·tē, nyōō′-) *n.* pl. **·ties** **1.** The state or fact of being nude. **2.** A naked part; anything uncovered. **3.** A nude (def. 1). [< MF *nudité* < L *nuditas, -tatis* < L *nudus*]

nud·nik (nōōd′nik) *n. U.S. Slang* A pestiferous or annoying person. Also **nud′nick.** [< Yiddish]

nu·dum pac·tum (nōō′dəm pak′təm, nyōō′-) *Latin* A contract made without a consideration; literally, nude pact.

Nu·e·ces River (nōō·ā′səs) A river in southern Texas, flowing 315 miles SE to **Nueces Bay**, an inlet of Corpus Christi Bay.

Nue·vo Le·ón (nwā′vō lā·ōn′) A State in NE Mexico; 25,-136 sq. mi.; pop. 1,653,808 (1970); capital, Monterrey.

nue·vo pe·so (nwā′vō pā′sō) The monetary unit of Uruguay, equivalent to 100 centesimos.

nu·ga·to·ry (nōō′gə·tôr′ē, -tō′rē, nyōō′-) *adj.* **1.** Having no power; inoperative. **2.** Having no worth or meaning. [< L *nugatorius* < *nugari* to trifle < *nugae* trifles, nonsense] — **nu′ga·to′ri·ly** *adv.* — **nu′ga·to′ri·ness** *n.*

nug·get (nug′it) *n.* A lump; especially, a lump of gold found in its native state. [? < dial. E *nug* lump]

nug·get·y (nug′it·ē) *adj.* **1.** Found in the form of nuggets. **2.** Nugget-shaped. [< NUGGET + -Y]

nui·sance (nōō′səns, nyōō′-) *n.* **1.** Anything that annoys, bothers, or irritates; a cause of trouble or vexation. **2.** *Law* That which by its use or existence works annoyance or damage to another. [< F < *nuire* to harm < L *nocere*]

nuisance ground *Canadian* In the West, a garbage or trash dump.

nuisance tax A tax on various consumer goods and services, etc., regarded as more of a bother than a burden.

null (nul) *adj.* **1.** Of no legal force or effect; void; invalid. **2.** Nonexistent; absent; negative. **3.** Of no avail; without effect; useless. **4.** Having no distinction or individuality; featureless. — **null and void** Without legal force or effect. [< L *nullus* < *ne* not + *ullus* any]

nul·lah (nul′ə) *n. Anglo-Indian* **1.** The dry bed of a small stream, or the stream itself. **2.** A ravine. [< Hind. *nālā*]

nul·li·fi·ca·tion (nul′ə·fə·kā′shən) *n.* **1.** The act of nullifying, or the state of being nullified. **2.** In U.S. history, the refusal of a State to obey an act of Congress, or the doctrine that such refusal is legal. [< LL *nullificatio, -onis* < *nullificare.* See NULLIFY.] — **nul′li·fi·ca′tion·ist, nul′li·fi·ca′tor** *n.*

nul·li·fid·i·an (nul′ə·fid′ē·ən) *adj.* Having no religious faith. — *n.* A nullifidian person. [< L *nullus* no + *fides* faith]

nul·li·fy (nul′ə·fī) *v.t.* **·fied, ·fy·ing** **1.** To make useless or ineffective; bring to naught; undo. **2.** To deprive of legal force or effect; annul. — **Syn.** See ANNUL. [< LL *nullificare* < *nullus* none + *facere* to make] — **nul′li·fi′er** *n.*

nul·lip·a·ra (nu·lip′ər·ə) *n.* pl. **·rae** (-rē) A woman who has never given birth. Compare PRIMIPARA, MULTIPARA. [< NL < L *nullus* none + *parere* to bring forth] — **nul·li·par′i·ty** (nul′ə·par′ə·tē) *n.* — **nul·lip′a·rous** *adj.*

nul·li·pore (nul′ə·pôr, -pōr) *n. Bot.* A red-spored, coralline seaweed (family *Rhodophyceae*) that secretes lime. [< L *nullus* none + *porus* pore] — **nul′li·po′rous** *adj.*

nul·li·ty (nul′ə·tē) *n.* pl. **·ties** **1.** The state of being null. **2.** That which is null. **3.** *Law* A void act or instrument. [< F *nullité* < Med.L *nullitas, -tatis* < *nullus* none]

num. Numeral(s).

Num. Numbers.

Nu·man·ti·a (nōō·man′shē·ə, nyōō-) An ancient ruined city in north central Spain.

Nu·ma Pom·pil·i·us (nōō′mə pom·pil′ē·əs, nyōō′-) Legendary second king of Rome 715–675 B.C.

numb (num) *adj.* 1. Having no sensation; without feeling. 2. Unable to move; paralyzed. — *v.t.* To make numb. [ME *nume*, pp. of *numen* < OE *numen*, pp. of *niman* to take] — **numb′ly** *adv.* — **numbed′ness, numb′ness** *n.*

num·ber (num′bər) *n.* 1. A specific quantity or place in a sequence, usually designated by one of a series of symbols or words called *numerals*. 2. A symbol or word used to designate number; a numeral. 3. *Often pl.* A sizable collection or grouping of persons or things: *numbers* of people. 4. An indefinite quantity or collection: a *number* of facts. 5. A specific sum or total count of units or individuals. 6. *pl.* A large group or aggregation; multitude: They came in *numbers.* 7. One of a series of things to which numbers are assigned or that are considered to be in numerical sequence: the March *number* of a magazine. 8. A numeral used to identify or distinguish a person or thing: a serial *number.* 9. Any of the separate, successive parts of which a program of music or entertainment is composed. 10. Quantity, as composed of units: a difference in *number* between two and ten. 11. A particular group, especially one of a select or privileged character. 12. *Sometimes pl.* Numerical force or strength: to rely on *numbers.* 13. *Gram.* The representation in a language, by inflection or otherwise, of singleness or plurality. English has the singular and the plural number. Some other languages, as Sanskrit and Greek, also have a dual number. 14. *pl.* In poetry, metrical feet or rhythm; also, verse or verses. 15. *pl.* The science of numerals; arithmetic. 16. *pl.* (*sometimes construed as sing.*) A lottery in which bets are made on the appearance of some particular, unpredictable number, as the last digits in the parimutuel racing totals of a given day: also called *policy.* Also **numbers game, numbers pool.** 17. *Informal* Any item or article, as of merchandise, that is specially selected or pointed out. 18. *Chiefly U.S. Slang* A person; especially, a girl: a cute little *number.* 19. *pl. Archaic* Musical rhythms, measures, or groups of notes. Symbol #. Abbr. n., no., No. — **any number of** A good many; rather a lot: *Any number of* insects circled beneath the light. — **beyond** (or **without**) **number** Too numerous to be counted; innumerable. — **by the numbers** 1. *Mil.* Step by step upon the calling out of consecutive numbers. 2. *Slang* In a mechanical or overprecise manner. — **number one** *Sometimes cap. Informal* 1. Oneself. 2. Anything of the best quality. 3. *Brit.* The second in command of a ship; executive officer. — **to get** (or **have**) **one's number** *Informal* To have insight into a person's motives, character, etc. — *v.t.* 1. To determine the total number of; count; reckon. 2. To assign a number to; designate by number. 3. To include as one of a collection or group; comprise. 4. To amount to; total: We *number* fifty men. 5. To set or limit the number of: Your days are *numbered.* 6. To be (a number of years, etc.) old or older: He *numbered* 80 years. — *v.i.* 7. To make a count; total. 8. To be included, as in a particular group. 9. To count off or call out numbers. [< OF *nombre* < L *numerus*] — **num′ber·er** *n.*

num·ber·less (num′bər·lis) *adj.* 1. Very numerous; countless. 2. Having no number. — **Syn.** See INFINITE.

Num·bers (num′bərz) *n.pl.* (*construed as sing.*) The fourth book of the Old Testament, giving the two censuses of Israel.

numb·fish (num′fish′) *n.* *pl.* **·fish** or **·fish·es** The electric ray.

num·bles (num′bəlz) *n.pl. Archaic* The entrails of an animal, as a deer; especially, the heart, liver, etc.: also *nombles.* [< OF *nombles,* ult. < LL *lumbellus,* dim. of L *lumbus* loin]

numb·skull (num′skul′) See NUMSKULL.

nu·men (nōō′mən, nyōō′-) *n.* *pl.* **·mi·na** (-mə·nə) 1. In ancient Roman religion, a local divinity or presiding spirit. 2. An indwelling force or quality that animates or guides: the *numen* of his career. [< L, divine nod < *nuere* to nod]

nu·mer·a·ble (nōō′mər·ə·bəl, nyōō′-) *adj.* That can be numbered. [< L *numerabilis* < *numerare* to count]

nu·mer·al (nōō′mər·əl, nyōō′-) *n.* 1. A symbol, letter, or word that is used alone or in combination with others to express a number. 2. *pl.* The numerals, usually only the last two, of the year in which a class of a college or school is graduated. — *adj.* 1. Used in expressing or representing a number. 2. Of or pertaining to number. Abbr. *num.* [< LL *numeralis* < *numerus* number] — **nu′mer·al·ly** *adv.*

nu·mer·ar·y (nōō′mə·rer′ē, nyōō′-) *adj.* Pertaining to a number or numbers. [< Med.L *numerarius* < *numerus*]

nu·mer·ate (nōō′mə·rāt, nyōō′-) *v.t.* **·at·ed, ·at·ing** 1. To enumerate; count. 2. To read, as a numerical expression, according to some system of numeration. [< L *numeratus,* pp. of *numerare* to number < *numerus* number]

nu·mer·a·tion (nōō′mə·rā′shən, nyōō′-) *n.* 1. The act, process, or system of reading or naming numbers. 2. An instance or example of this. [< L *numeratio, -onis* < *numerare.* See NUMERATE.]

nu·mer·a·tor (nōō′mə·rā′tər, nyōō′-) *n.* 1. *Math.* The term

of a fraction indicating how many of the parts of a unit are to be taken. In a common fraction it appears above or to the left of the line. Compare DENOMINATOR. 2. One who or that which numbers. [< LL]

nu·mer·i·cal (nōō·mer′i·kəl, nyōō-) *adj.* 1. Pertaining to or denoting number. 2. Numerable. 3. Represented by or consisting of numbers or figures rather than letters. 4. *Math.* Designating a value irrespective of sign: −8 has a numerical value greater than +4. [< NL *numericus* < L *numerus* number] — **nu·mer′i·cal·ly** *adv.*

nu·mer·ol·o·gy (nōō′mər·ol′ə·jē, nyōō′-) *n.* A system that purports to explain the occult influence of numbers. — **nu·mer·o·log·i·cal** (nōō′mər·ə·loj′i·kəl, nyōō′-) *adj.*

nu·mer·ous (nōō′mər·əs, nyōō′-) *adj.* Consisting of a great number of units; being many or multiple. — **Syn.** See MANY. [< L *numerosus*] — **nu′mer·ous·ly** *adv.* — **nu′mer·os·i·ty** (nōō′mə·ros′ə·tē, nyōō′-), **nu′mer·ous·ness** *n.*

Nu·mid·i·a (nōō·mid′ē·ə, nyōō-) An ancient kingdom and Roman province in northern Africa, roughly corresponding to modern Algeria.

Nu·mid·i·an (nōō·mid′ē·ən, nyōō-) *adj.* Of or pertaining to Numidia, its inhabitants, or their language. — *n.* 1. An inhabitant of Numidia. 2. The Libyan dialect of Numidia.

Numidian crane The demoiselle (def. 2).

nu·mi·nous (nōō′mə·nəs, nyōō′-) *adj.* 1. Of, pertaining to, or of the nature of a numen. 2. Evoking awe or reverence, as the presence of something holy or divine. 3. Irrational; mysterious; inscrutable. — **the numinous** The part of religious experience that is characterized by feelings of fascination and awe. [< L *numen, -inis.* See NUMEN.]

numis. Numismatic(s).

nu·mis·mat·ics (nōō′miz·mat′iks, -mis-, nyōō′-) *n.pl.* (*construed as sing.*) The study of coins, medals, and related objects, as paper money. Abbr. *numis.* [< F *numismatique* < L *numisma* coin < Gk. *nomisma* < *nomos* law] — **nu′mis·mat′ic** *adj.* — **nu·mis′ma·tist** *n.*

nu·mis·ma·tol·o·gy (nōō·miz′mə·tol′ə·jē, -mis′-, nyōō′-) *n.* Numismatics. — **nu·mis′ma·tol′o·gist** *n.*

num·ma·ry (num′ər·ē) *adj.* Of or pertaining to coins.

num·mu·lar (nu′ə·lər) *adj.* Suggesting a coin in shape; circular: *nummular* sputa. Also **num′mu·lar′y.** [< L *nummulus,* dim. of *nummus* coin]

num·mu·lite (num′yə·līt) *n. Paleontol.* A large foraminifer of a family (*Nummulitidae*) of the older Tertiary, having a thin, coinlike shell. [< L *nummulus.* See NUMMULAR.] — **num′mu·lit′ic** (-lit′ik) *adj.*

num·skull (num′skul′) *n.* A blockhead; a dunce: also spelled *numbskull.*

nun[1] (nŏon, noon) *n.* The fourteenth letter in the Hebrew alphabet. See ALPHABET.

nun[2] (nun) *n.* 1. A woman belonging to a religious order and living under vows of poverty, chastity, and obedience. 2. Any of various types of pigeons or other birds. [OE *nunne* < LL *nonna,* child's nurse, fem. of *nonnus,* orig., old man] — **nun′nish** *adj.*

NUMMULITES

nu·na·tak (nōō′nə tak′) *Canadian* A mountain peak showing above surrounding glacial ice. [< Eskimo]

nun buoy (nun) See under BUOY.

nunc di·mit·tis (nungk′ di·mit′is) *Latin* A dismissal or departure.

Nunc Dimittis The song or canticle of Simeon (*Luke* ii 29–32), so called from the first two words of the Latin version. [< L, now let depart]

nun·ci·a·ture (nun′shē·ə·chŏor) *n.* The office or term of a nuncio. [< Ital. *nunziatura* < *nunzio.* See NUNCIO.]

nun·ci·o (nun′shē·ō, -sē·ō, nŏon′-) *n.* *pl.* **·ci·os** 1. A permanent diplomatic envoy of the Pope to a foreign court or government. 2. *Obs.* Any messenger. — **Syn.** See AMBASSADOR. [< Ital. *nunzio* < L *nuntius* messenger]

nun·cle (nung′kəl) *n. Dial.* An uncle. [< *an uncle,* taken as *a nuncle*]

nun·cu·pa·tive (nung′kyə·pā′tiv, nung·kyōō′pə·tiv) *adj. Law* Oral as distinguished from written. [< LL *nuncupativus* < *nuncupare* to call by name] — **nun′cu·pa′tive·ly** *adv.*

nun·na·tion (nu·nā′shən) *n.* The addition of the letter *n* to a word, as in the declension of Arabic nouns. [< NL *nunnatio, -onis* < Arabic *nūn,* the letter *n*]

nun·ner·y (nun′ər·ē) *n.* *pl.* **·ner·ies** A convent for nuns. [ME *nunnerie* < AF *nonnerie*]

nup·tial (nup′shəl) *adj.* Of or pertaining to marriage or the marriage ceremony. — *n.* *Usually pl.* A marriage or wedding. — **Syn.** See MARRIAGE. [< L *nuptialis* < *nuptus,* pp. of *nubere* to marry] — **nup′tial·ly** *adv.*

Nu·rem·berg (nŏor′əm·bûrg, nyŏor′-) A city in north central Bavaria, West Germany; pop. 477,100 (est. 1970). German **Nürn·berg** (nürn′berkh).

Nu·ris·tan (nŏor′is·tan) A mountainous district of NE Afghanistan; 5,000 sq. mi.; formerly *Kafiristan.*

nurse (nûrs) *n.* 1. A person who cares for the sick, injured, or infirm; especially, one who is trained to do such work. 2. One who is a graduate of a school of nursing: also called *graduate nurse.* **3.** A nursemaid. **4.** A wet nurse (which see). **5.** One who or that which fosters, nourishes, protects, or promotes. **6.** *Entomol.* A sexually incomplete bee, ant, etc., whose function in the colony is to care for the young. — *v.* **nursed, nurs·ing** *v.t.* **1.** To take care of (the sick, injured or infirm.) **2.** To feed (an infant) at the breast; suckle. **3.** To promote the growth and development of; foster; cherish. **4.** To feed and care for, as an infant or child; bring up; raise. **5.** To look after the wants of; minister to. **6.** To take steps to cure. **7.** To use or operate carefully so as to preserve from injury, damage, or strain: to *nurse* a weak wrist. **8.** To preserve or prolong deliberately: to *nurse* a grudge. **9.** To hold or clasp carefully or caressingly; fondle. **10.** To suckle at the breast of. **11.** In billiards, to keep (the balls) in a close group for a series of caroms. — *v.i.* **12.** To act or serve as a nurse. **13.** To take nourishment from the breast. **14.** To suckle an infant. [Earlier *nurice* < OF < LL *nutricia*, fem. of L *nutricius*. See NUTRITIOUS.] — **nurs′er** *n.*

nurse·maid (nûrs′mād′) *n.* A girl or woman employed to care for children. Also **nurs·er·y·maid** (nûr′sər·ē·mād′, nûrs′rē·).

nurs·er·y (nûr′sər·ē, nûrs′rē) *n. pl.* **·er·ies** **1.** A place where trees, shrubs, etc., are raised, as for sale or transplanting. **2.** A room or area set apart for the use or occupancy of children. **3.** A nursery school. **4.** A place, as in a store, where children may be temporarily left under adult supervision while their parents shop, etc. **5.** Anything that fosters, breeds, or develops; also, the place where this occurs.

nurs·er·y·man (nûr′sər·ē·mən, nûrs′rē-) *n. pl.* **·men** (-mən) One who raises or cultivates plants in a nursery.

nursery rhyme A simple story, riddle, proverb, etc., presented in rhymed verse or jingle for children.

nursery school A place where children of preschool age regularly meet for training and supervised play.

nurs·ing (nûrs′ing) *n.* The profession, occupation, or duties of a nurse, especially one who cares for the sick, injured, or infirm, assists physicians, etc.

nursing bottle A bottle fitted with a rubber nipple for feeding infants milk, or other liquids.

nursing home **1.** A residence for persons who are unable to care for themselves without some personal or medical assistance, as the aged or the infirm. **2.** *Chiefly Brit.* A small private hospital.

nurs·ling (nûrs′ling) *n.* **1.** An infant or animal in the stage of being nursed. **2.** Anything that is carefully tended or supervised. Also **nurse′ling.**

nur·ture (nûr′chər) *n.* **1.** That which nourishes; food; sustenance. **2.** The act or process of promoting growth or development; breeding; education. **3.** *Biol.* The aggregate of environmental conditions and influences acting on an organism subsequent to its conception. — *v.t.* **·tured, ·tur·ing** **1.** To feed or support; nourish; rear. **2.** To bring up or train; educate. [< OF *norriture, norreture* < LL *nutritura* < L *nutrire* to nourish] — **nur′tur·er** *n.*

Nu·sa Teng·ga·ra (nōō′sä teng·gä′rə) A division of Indonesia comprising all of the smaller islands east of Bali, and including the western part of Timor; 61,995 sq. mi.: formerly *Lesser Sunda Islands.*

nut (nut) *n.* **1.** A dry fruit consisting of a kernel or seed enclosed in a woody shell. **2.** The kernel of such fruit, especially when edible, as of the peanut, walnut, or chestnut. **3.** A small block of metal having an internal screw thread so that it may be fitted upon a bolt, screw, or the like. **4.** *Bot.* A hard, indehiscent, one-seeded pericarp generally resulting from

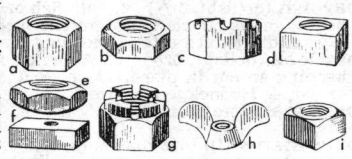

NUTS

a Soft hexagonal. *b* Lock. *c* Slotted hexagonal. *d* Plain square. *e* Double-cupped. *f* Untapped joint. *g* Castle. *h* Thumb. *i* Chamfered square.

a compound ovary, as the chestnut or acorn. **5.** A person or matter difficult to deal with; a problem. **6.** In stringed instruments, the ridge at the upper end of the neck, serving to elevate the strings; also, the end of a fiddle bow that contains a screw for adjusting the tautness of the hairs. **7.** *U.S. Slang* A crazy, irresponsible, or eccentric person. **8.** *Slang* The head. **9.** *Usually pl. Slang* A testicle. — *v.t.* **nut·ted, nut·ting** To seek or gather nuts. [OE *hnutu*] — **nut′ter** *n.*

nu·ta·tion (nōō·tā′shən, nyōō-) *n.* **1.** The act of nodding. **2.** *Astron.* The periodic oscillation of the earth's axis in its precessional motion around the pole of the ecliptic. **3.** *Bot.* A spontaneous rotatory movement, as of growing plants. [< L *nutatio, -onis* < *nutare* to nod] — **nu·ta′tion·al** *adj.*

nut·brown (nut′broun′) *adj.* Of a dark shade of brown suggesting the color of certain nuts, as the walnut.

nut·crack·er (nut′krak′ər) *n.* **1.** *Sometimes pl.* A device for cracking the hard shells of nuts. **2.** Any of certain crow-

like birds (genus *Nucifraga*), as the common nutcracker (*N. caryocatactes*) of Europe, or Clark's nutcracker (*N. columbiana*) of western North America. **3.** A nuthatch.

Nutcracker Man *Anthropol.* Zinjanthropus: so called from his massive jaws and teeth.

nut·gall (nut′gôl′) *n.* A nut-shaped gall, as on an oak tree: also called *Aleppo gall*

nut·grass (nut′gras′, -gräs′) *n.* A perennial herb (*Cyperus rotundus*) of the sedge family, bearing nutlike tubers: also called *cocograss.*

nut·hatch (nut′hach′) *n.* A small, short-tailed bird (family *Sittidae*) related to the titmouse, having a slender bill and feeding on nuts and insects: also called *nutcracker.*

nut·let (nut′lit) *n.* **1.** A small nut. **2.** The stone in a peach, plum, etc.

Nut·ley (nut′lē) A town in NE New Jersey, a suburb of Newark; pop. 32,099.

nut·meg (nut′meg) *n.* **1.** The aromatic kernel of the fruit of various tropical trees (genus *Myristica*), especially the nutmeg tree (*M. fragrans*) of the Molucca Islands. **2.** The tree itself. [ME *notemuge*, partial trans. of OF *nois mugue* < *nois* nut + *mugue* musk < L *muscus*]

Nutmeg State Nickname of CONNECTICUT.

nut·pick (nut′pik′) *n.* A small, sharp-pointed instrument for picking out the kernels of nuts.

nut pine The piñon (def. 1).

nu·tri·a (nōō′trē·ə, nyōō′-) *n.* **1.** The soft brown fur of the coypu, often dyed to resemble beaver. **2.** The coypu. [< Sp., otter < L *lutra*]

nu·tri·ent (nōō′trē·ənt, nyōō′-) *adj.* **1.** Giving nourishment; nutritious. **2.** Conveying nutriment. — *n.* Something that nourishes; food. [< L *nutriens, -entis*, ppr. of *nutrire* to nourish]

nu·tri·ment (nōō′trə·mənt, nyōō′-) *n.* **1.** That which nourishes or sustains; food. **2.** Anything that promotes development. [< L *nutrimentum* < *nutrire* to nourish] — **nu′-tri·men′tal** *adj.*

nu·tri·tion (nōō·trish′ən, nyōō-) *n.* **1.** The act or process of nourishing or of taking nourishment; especially, the processes by which food is assimilated and converted into tissue in living organisms. **2.** That which nourishes; nutriment. — **Syn.** Compare FOOD. [< L *nutritio, -onis* < *nutrire* to nourish] — **nu·tri′tion·al** *adj.* — **nu·tri′tion·al·ly** *adv.*

nu·tri·tion·ist (nōō·trish′ən·ist, nyōō-) *n.* One who specializes in the processes and problems of nutrition.

nu·tri·tious (nōō·trish′əs, nyōō-) *adj.* Promoting growth and repairing the waste of living organisms; nourishing. [< L *nutricius, nutritius* < *nutrix* nursing mother] — **nu·tri′tious·ly** *adv.* — **nu·tri′tious·ness** *n.*

nu·tri·tive (nōō′trə·tiv, nyōō′-) *adj.* **1.** Having nutritious properties. **2.** Of or relating to nutrition. — **nu′tri·tive·ly** *adv.* — **nu′tri·tive·ness** *n.*

nuts (nuts) *Chiefly U.S. Slang adj.* **1.** Crazy; demented; eccentric. **2.** Madly in love: with *about.* **3.** Extremely enthusiastic: with *about*: He's absolutely *nuts* about baseball. — *interj.* An exclamation of contempt, disappointment, etc. [< pl. of NUT]

nut·shell (nut′shel′) *n.* The shell of a nut. — **in a nutshell** In brief and concise statement or form.

nut·ter (nut′ər) *n.* One who gathers nuts.

nut·ty (nut′ē) *adj.* **·ti·er, ·ti·est** **1.** Abounding in or producing nuts. **2.** Having the flavor of nuts. **3.** *Chiefly U.S. Slang* Crazy; eccentric. — **nut′ti·ly** *adv.* — **nut′ti·ness** *n.*

nut·wood (nut′wŏŏd′) *n.* **1.** Any tree bearing nuts, as walnut, hazel, hickory, etc. **2.** The wood of such a tree.

nux vom·i·ca (nuks′ vom′i·kə) **1.** The silky disklike seed of an Indian tree (*Strychnos nux-vomica*), containing strychnine, brucine, and other alkaloidal poisons. **2.** The tree itself. [< Med.L < L *nux* nut + *vomere* to vomit]

nuz·zle (nuz′əl) *v.* **·zled, ·zling** *v.i.* **1.** To rub, press, or dig with or as with the nose. **2.** To nestle or snuggle; lie close. — *v.t.* **3.** To push or rub the nose, etc., into or against. **4** To root up with the nose or snout. **5.** *Archaic* To cherish; foster. [Freq. of NOSE, v.]

NW or **nw, N.W.** or **n.w.** Northwest; northwestern.

N.W.T. Northwest Territories, Canada.

N.Y. New York.

Nya·sa (nyä′sä, nī·as′ə), **Lake** A lake in eastern Africa between Tanzania, Malawi, and Mozambique; about 11,000 sq. mi. Also, **Lake Malawi.** Formerly **Nyas′sa.**

Nya·sa·land (nyä′sä·land, nī·as′ə-) A former British Protectorate in SE Africa. See MALAWI.

N.Y.C. New York City.

nyc·ta·gi·na·ceous (nik′tə·ji·nā′shəs) *adj. Bot* Pertaining or belonging to the four-o'clock family (*Nyctaginaceae*) of plants. [< NL < Gk. *nyx, nyktos* night]

nyc·ta·lo·pi·a (nik′tə·lō′pē·ə) *n. Pathol.* Vision that is abnormally poor in dim light but normal in daylight: distinguished from *hemeralopia.* Also called *moon blindness. night blindness.* [< LL < Gk. *nyctalōps* < *nyx, nyktos* night + *alaos* blind + *ōps* eye] — **nyc′ta·lop′ic** (-lop′ik) *adj.*

nyc·tit·ro·pism (nik-tit′rə-piz′əm) *n. Bot.* The tendency of the leaves of certain plants to change position at dusk or at night. Also **nyc′ti·nas′ty** (-ti-nas′tē). — **nyc′ti·trop′ic** (-trop′ik) *adj.*

nycto- *combining form* Night; nocturnal. Also, before vowels, **nyct-**. Also **nycti-**. [< Gk. *nyx, nyktos* night]

Nye (nī), **Edgar Wilson**, 1850–96, U.S. humorist: called Bill Nye.

nyet (nyet) *adv. Russian* No.

nyl·ghai (nil′gī), **nyl·ghau** (nil′gô) See NILGAI.

ny·lon (nī′lon) *n.* **1.** A synthetic thermoplastic polyamide yielding fibers and bristles of great toughness, strength, and elasticity; especially, cloth made from these fibers. **2.** *pl. Informal* Stockings made of nylon. [< *Nylon*, a trade name]

nymph (nimf) *n.* **1.** In Greek and Roman mythology, any of a class of minor female divinities dwelling in groves, forests, fountains, etc., usually depicted as beautiful maidens. **2.** *Chiefly Poetic* **a** A young woman or girl, especially one who is beautiful or comely. **b** A maiden. **3.** *Entomol.* The young of an insect undergoing incomplete metamorphosis, at which stage the wing pads are first evident: also called *nympha*. [< OF < L *nympha* < Gk. *nymphē* nymph, bride] — **nymph′al, nym·phe·an** (nim-fē′ən) *adj.*

nym·pha (nim′fə) *n. pl.* **·phae** (-fē) **1.** *pl. Anat.* The inner folds of the mucous membrane of the female pudenda; the labia minora. **2.** *Entomol.* A nymph.

nym·phae·a·ceous (nim′fē-ā′shəs) *adj. Bot.* Pertaining or belonging to the water-lily family (*Nymphaeaceae*) of plants. [< NL < L *nymphaea* waterlily < Gk. *nymphaia*]

nym·pha·lid (nim′fə-lid) *n.* Any of a large family (*Nymphalidae*) of butterflies, having small, functionless front legs, and including the monarch and admiral butterflies.

nympho- *combining form* Nymph; bride: *nympholepsy.* Also, before vowels, **nymph-**. [< Gk. *nymphē* bride, nymph]

nym·pho·lep·sy (nim′fə-lep′sē) *n. pl.* **·sies** **1.** A state of ecstasy or frenzy believed to be inspired by nymphs. **2.** An emotional frenzy, as that caused by desiring something unattainable. [< Gk. *nympholeptos* frenzied < *nymphē* nymph + *lambanein* to take] — **nym′pho·lep′tic** *adj.*

nym·pho·lept (nim′fə-lept) *n.* One afflicted with nympholepsy.

nym·pho·ma·ni·a (nim′fə-mā′nē-ə, -mǎn′yə) *n. Psychiatry* An extreme and ungovernable sexual desire in women. — **nym′pho·ma′ni·ac** *adj. & n.*

Ny·sa (nē′sä) The Polish name for the NEISSE.

nys·tag·mus (nis-tag′məs) *n. Pathol.* A spasmodic movement of the eyes, rotatory or from side to side. [< NL < Gk. *nystagmos* drowsiness < *nystazein* to nod, grow drowsy] — **nys·tag′mic** *adj.*

Nyx (niks) In Greek mythology, the goddess of night: identified with the Roman *Nox.*

N.Z. or **N.Zeal.** New Zealand.

O

o, O (ō) *n. pl.* **o's** or **os, O's** or **Os, oes** (ōz) **1.** The fifteenth letter of the English alphabet. The shape of the Phoenician consonant *ayin* was adopted by the Greeks as *omicron* and became Roman O. **2.** Any sound represented by the letter *o.* **3.** Anything shaped like an *O*; an oval, circle, or spot. — *symbol* **1.** *Math.* Zero or nought. **2.** *Chem.* Oxygen.

o Ohm.

o' (ō, ə) *prep.* Of: one o'clock, man-o'-war, jack-o'-lantern.

o- Var. of OB-.

o. **1.** Octavo. **2.** Off. **3.** Old. **4.** Only. **5.** Order. **6.** Out(s) (baseball). **7.** Pint (L *octarius*).

-o *suffix* **1.** A suffix found in the first word or element of compounds, as in *pedometer, clinometer,* or *Afro-Asian.* **2.** One who or that which is similar to, connected with, or sometimes smaller than (what is indicated by the stem), as in *combo, bucko.* **3.** An ending of many interjections, often British in origin, as in *cheerio, righto.*

O (ō) *interj.* **1.** An exclamation used in direct address, especially in earnest or solemn appeal, as in prayer or invocation: *O Lord!; O my countrymen!* **2.** An exclamation of surprise, disappointment, fear, longing, etc.: *O dear!; O to be twenty-one!* — *n. pl.* **O's** An exclamation or lamentation.

◆ *O* and *oh* are sometimes used indiscriminately, but *O* is the generally accepted form for direct address. *O* is always capitalized but never followed directly by a punctuation mark. *Oh* is capitalized only at the beginning of a sentence and is followed by a comma or an exclamation mark, as *Oh! How could you?*

O' A descendant of: *O'Conor:* a patronymic prefix commonly used in Irish surnames, equivalent to the English and Scandinavian suffixes *-son, -sen.* Compare FITZ-, MAC-. [< Irish *ó* grandson, descendant]

O. **1.** Ocean. **2.** Octavo. **3.** October. **4.** Ohio (unofficial).

oaf (ōf) *n. pl.* **oafs** or *Rare* **oaves** (ōvz) **1.** A stupid, bungling person; a dunce or lummox. **2.** *Obs.* A changeling. [Earlier *auf* < ON *álfr* elf. Akin to ELF.] — **oaf′ish** *adj.* — **oaf′ish·ly** *adv.* — **oaf′ish·ness** *n.*

O·a·hu (ō-ä′hōō) An island in the north central Hawaiian Islands on which Honolulu is located; 589 sq. mi.

oak (ōk) *n.* **1.** An acorn-bearing tree or shrub (genus *Quercus*) of the beech family, valued for the hardness, strength, and durability of its timber. ◆ Collateral adjective: *quercine.* **2.** The wood of the oak. **3.** Any of various plants resembling or suggesting the oak. **4.** Oaken furniture or woodwork. **5.** Any of various shades of finished oak wood. **6.** The leaves of the oak, as in a garland. [OE *āc*]

oak apple A rounded gall produced on an oak by an insect. Also **oak gall.**

oak·en (ō′kən) *adj.* Made or consisting of oak.

Oak·ham (ō′kəm) Formerly, the county seat of Rutland, England; pop. 4,571.

Oak·land (ōk′lənd) A port city in western California, on San Francisco Bay; pop. 361,561.

Oak Lawn A village in NE Illinois, near Chicago; pop. 60,305.

oak leaf cluster A bronze decoration given to holders of certain U.S. military medals in recognition of acts meriting a further award of the same medal.

Oak·ley (ōk′lē), **Annie**, 1860–1926, U.S. markswoman: original name Phoebe Anne Oakley Mo·zee (mō′zē).

Oak Park **1.** A village in NE Illinois, near Chicago; pop. 62,511. **2.** A city in SE Michigan, near Detroit; pop. 36,762.

Oak Ridge A town in eastern Tennessee; site of an atomic research center; pop. 28,319.

oak·um (ō′kəm) *n.* Hemp fiber obtained by untwisting and picking out the fibers of old rope, used for caulking seams, etc. [OE *ācumba* < *ā-* out + *cemban* to comb < *camb* comb]

oar (ôr, ōr) *n.* **1.** A wooden implement for propelling or occasionally for steering a boat, consisting of a long shaft with a blade at one end. **2.** A person using an oar; oarsman. **3.** An oarlike part or appendage, as in certain worms. — *v.t.* **1.** To propel with or as with oars; row. **2.** To make (one's way) or traverse (water) with or as with oars. — *v.i.* **3.** To proceed by or as by rowing; row. [OE *ār*]

oared (ôrd, ōrd) *adj.* Having or equipped with oars.

oar·fish (ôr′fish′, ōr′-) *n. pl.* **·fish** or **·fish·es** Any of several fishes (genus *Regalecus*) of northern seas, with oarlike dorsal rays and a length often exceeding twenty feet.

oar·lock (ôr′lok′, ōr′-) *n.* A device on the side of a boat for keeping an oar in place. Also, *Brit.,* **rowlock.** [OE *ārloc* < *ār* oar + *loc* lock, enclosure]

oars·man (ôrz′mən, ōrz′-) *n. pl.* **·men** (-mən) One who rows.

oars·man·ship (ôrz′mən-ship, ōrz′-) *n.* The art of rowing.

OAS Organization of American States.

o·a·sis (ō-ā′sis, ō′ə-sis) *n. pl.* **·ses** (-sēz) **1.** An area in a desert made fertile by groundwater or by irrigation. **2.** Any place of shelter or relief; refuge. [< L < Gk.]

oat (ōt) *n.* **1.** *Usually pl.* A cereal grass (*Avena sativa*) widely cultivated for its edible grain. **2.** *Usually pl.* The grain itself. **3.** Any other grass of the genus *Avena,* as the wild oat. **4.** A musical pipe made from the stem of an oat. — **to feel one's oats** *Informal* **1.** To be exuberant or high-spirited, especially in an unruly way. **2.** To feel bold or self-assured, or to behave in a way that suggests such a feeling. — **to sow one's wild oats** *Informal* To experience the adventures and follies characteristic of youth. [OE *āte*] — **oat·en** *adj.*

oat·cake (ōt′kāk′) *n.* A thin, hard cake of oatmeal.

Oates (ōts), **Titus,** 1649–1705, English impostor: fabricated the Popish Plot, a supposed Catholic conspiracy to massacre Protestants, burn London, and kill the king; convicted by James II; pardoned by William III.

oat grass Any uncultivated kind of oats or oatlike grass.

oath (ōth) *n. pl.* **oaths** (ōths, ōthz) **1.** A formal declaration or attestation in support of a pledge or promise, usually based on an appeal to God or some other higher institution or figure; also, the form of the declaration. **2.** The careless or profane use of the name of God or other sacred person or thing. **3.** A profane or vulgar utterance; imprecation; curse. [OE *āth* < Gmc. Cf. OHG *eid,* ON *eithr,* OS *eth.*]

oat·meal (ōt'mēl') *n.* A cereal food made from the cooked meal of oats; also, the meal itself. Also **oat meal.**

Oa·xa·ca (wä·hä'kä) A state in SW Mexico on the Pacific; 36,355 sq. mi.; pop. 2,011,946 (1970); capital, **Oaxaca.** Also **Oa·xa'ca de Juá·rez** (thä hwä'räs).

ob- *prefix* **1.** Toward; to; facing: *obvert.* **2.** Against; in opposition to: *object, obstruct.* **3.** Over; upon: *obliterate.* **4.** Completely: *obdurate.* **5.** Inversely: *obovate:* prefixed to adjectives in scientific terms. Also: *o-* before *m,* as in *omit; oc-* before *c,* as in *occur; of-* before *f,* as in *offend; op-* before *p,* as in *oppress.* [< L *ob* toward, for, against]

ob. **1.** He (or she) died (L *obiit).* **2.** Incidentally (L *obiter).* **3.** *Music* Oboe.

Ob (ōb') A river in the west central R.S.F.S.R., flowing about 2,500 miles NW to the **Ob Gulf,** *Russian* **Ob·ska·ya Gu·ba** (ôp'skə·yə gŏō·bä'), an inlet of the Kara Sea.

Obad. Obadiah.

O·ba·di·ah (ō'bə·dī'ə) Sixth-century B.C. minor Hebrew prophet. — *n.* A book of the Old Testament containing his prophecies. Also, in the Douai Bible, *Abdias.*

obb. *Music* Obbligato.

ob·bli·ga·to (ob'lə·gä'tō, *Ital.* ôb'blē·gä'tō) *Music adj.* **1.** Denoting a part or accompaniment essential to the performance of a composition. **2.** Loosely, ad libitum. — *n.* An obbligato part or accompaniment. Also spelled *obligato.* [< *Ital. obbligato* < L *obligatus,* pp. of *obligare.* See OBLIGE.]

ob·cor·date (ob·kôr'dāt) *adj. Bot.* Heart-shaped, as a leaf attached by the pointed end. [< OB- + CORDATE]

obdt. Obedient.

ob·du·ra·cy (ob'dyə·rə·sē) *n.* The condition or quality of being obdurate; unyielding stubbornness; hardheartedness.

ob·du·rate (ob'dyə·rit, -rāt) *adj.* **1.** Unmoved by or hardened against human feelings or moral influence; hardhearted. **2.** Difficult to handle or manage; intractable: *obdurate* materials. — **Syn.** See OBSTINATE. [< L *obduratus,* pp. of *obdurare* to harden < *ob-* against + *durare* to harden < *durus* hard] — **ob'du·rate·ly** *adv.* — **ob'du·rate·ness** *n.*

o·be (ō'bē) *n.* **ob·be·ah** (ō'bē·ə) See OBI[1].

O.B.E. Officer (of the Order) of the British Empire.

o·be·di·ence (ō·bē'dē·əns, ə·bē'-) *n.* **1.** The act of obeying, or the condition of being obedient; submission; compliance. **2.** *Eccl.* Spiritual jurisdiction or control; also, an area or group of persons under such jurisdiction.

o·be·di·ent (ō·bē'dē·ənt, ə·bē'-) *adj.* **1.** Complying with or conforming to a command, restraint, etc.; dutiful. **2.** Deferring habitually to laws, superiors, etc.; docile; compliant. Abbr. *obdt., obt.* [< OF *obedient* < L *obediens, -entis,* ppr. of *obedire.* See OBEY.] — **o·be'di·ent·ly** *adv.*

o·bei·sance (ō·bā'səns, ō·bē'-) *n.* Courtesy, reverence, or homage; also, an act or gesture expressing this: chiefly in phrases **to do (make,** or **pay) obeisance.** [< OF *obeissance* < *obeissant,* ppr. of *obeir.* See OBEY.] — **o·bei'sant** *adj.*

ob·e·lisk (ob'ə·lisk) *n.* **1.** A square shaft of stone with a pyramidal top, usually monolithic and tapering, and often used as a monument in ancient Egypt. **2.** *Printing* The dagger sign (†), used as a mark of reference; obelus. [< L *obeliscus* < Gk. *obeliskos,* dim. of *obelos* a spit, hence pointed pillar] — **ob'e·lis'cal, ob'e·lis'koid** (-koid) *adj.*

ob·e·lize (ob'ə·līz) *v.t.* **·lized, ·liz·ing** To mark or indicate with an obelus. [< Gk. *obelizein* to mark with an obelus < *obelos* obelus]

ob·e·lus (ob'ə·ləs) *n. pl.* **·li** (lī) **1.** A critical mark, as — or ÷ used in ancient manuscripts to designate a spurious or doubtful passage or reading. **2.** *Printing* An obelisk. [< LL < Gk. *obelos,* lit., a spit]

O·ber·am·mer·gau (ō'bər·äm'ər·gou) A village in Bavaria, West Germany; noted for its Passion play, performed by the villagers every ten years.

O·ber·hau·sen (ō'bər·hou'zən) A city in North Rhine–Westphalia, West Germany; pop. 256,-700 (est. 1960).

O·ber·land (ō'bər·länt) A mountainous region of central Switzerland.

O·ber·on (ō'bə·ron) In medieval legend and folklore, the king of the fairies, husband of Titania.

O·ber·ös·ter·reich (ō'bər·œs'tə·rīkh) The German name for UPPER AUSTRIA.

o·bese (ō·bēs') *adj.* Very fat or corpulent; exceedingly stout. — **Syn.** See FAT. [< L *obesus* fat, orig. pp. of *obedere* to devour < *ob-* completely + *edere* to eat] — **o·bese'ly** *adv.*

o·bes·i·ty (ō·bē'sə·tē, ō·bes'ə-) *n.* The condition of being obese; corpulence. Also **o·bese'ness.**

o·bey (ō·bā', ə-) *v.t.* **1.** To comply with or carry out the command, request, etc., of; be obedient to: to *obey* one's superiors. **2.** To comply with or execute (a command, request, etc.). **3.** To be guided, controlled, or actuated by; act in ac-cordance with: to *obey* one's instincts. — *v.i.* **4.** To be obedient; comply. [< OF *obeir* < L *obedire,* var. of *oboedire* to give ear, obey < *ob-* towards + *audire* to hear] — **o·bey'er** *n.*

ob·fus·cate (ob·fus'kāt, ob'fəs-) *v.t.* **·cat·ed, ·cat·ing** **1.** To confuse or perplex; bewilder. **2.** To darken or obscure. [< L *obfuscatus,* pp. of *obfuscare* to darken, obscure < *ob-* + *fuscare* to darken < *fuscus* dark] — **ob'fus·ca'tion** *n.*

o·bi¹ (ō'bē) *n.* **1.** A kind of sorcery practiced by Negroes of the West Indies and SE United States. **2.** A charm or fetish used in these practices. Also called *obe, obeah.* Also **o'bi·a** (-bē·ə). [Var. of *obeah,* of West African origin] — **o'bi·ism** *n.*

o·bi² (ō'bē) *n.* A broad sash tied with a stylized bow or loop in the back, worn by Japanese women. [< Japanese *ōbi*]

ob·i·it (ō'bē·it) *Latin* He (or she) died. Abbr. *ob.*

o·bit (ō'bit, ob'it) *n. Informal* An obituary.

obit. Obituary.

ob·i·ter dic·tum (ob'ə·tər dik'təm) *Latin pl.* **ob·i·ter dic·ta** (dik'tə) **1.** *Law* A judicial opinion not bearing on the elements of a case and therefore not binding. **2.** Any remark made by the way or in passing; comment; observation.

o·bit·u·ar·y (ō·bich'ōō·er'ē) *n. pl.* **·ar·ies** A published notice of a death, especially in a newspaper, usually including a biographical sketch of the deceased. — *adj.* Of, pertaining to, or recording a death. [< Med.L *obituarius* < L *obitus* a going down, death < *obire* < *ob-* down + *ire* to go]

obj. **1.** Object. **2.** Objection. **3.** Objective.

ob·ject¹ (əb·jekt') *v.t.* **1.** To offer an argument in opposition or disagreement; raise an objection: usually with *to:* to *object* to his remarks. **2.** To feel or state disapproval; disapprove; be averse. — *v.t.* **3.** To offer in opposition or criticism; charge. [< L *objectus,* pp. of *objicere, obicere* < *ob-* towards, against + *jacere* to throw] — **ob·jec'tor** *n.*

ob·ject² (ob'jikt, -jekt) *n.* **1.** Anything that is or may be apprehended by the senses; especially, a tangible or visible thing. **2.** The purpose or end of an action; goal; aim. **3.** One who or that which is the focus or center of thought, action, etc. **4.** *Gram.* **a** A substantive that receives or is affected by the action of the verb, called the **direct object** when it receives the direct action, as *pie* in *She gave him the pie,* and the **indirect object** when it receives the secondary action, as *him* in the same sentence. **b** A substantive following a preposition, as *mountain* in the phrase *on the mountain.* In passive constructions, the substantive corresponding to the direct or indirect object is called the **retained object,** as *pie* in *He was given the pie.* Abbr. *obj.* **5.** One who or that which evokes pity, ridicule, etc.; a sight; spectacle. **6.** *Philos.* Anything that is apprehended or perceived by the mind. — **Syn.** See PURPOSE. [< Med.L *objectum* something thrown in the way < L *objectus.* See OBJECT¹.]

object ball In billiards or pool, the ball that the player aims to hit with his cue ball.

object glass *Optics* An objective (*n.* def. 3).

ob·jec·ti·fy (əb·jek'tə·fī) *v.t.* **·fied, ·fy·ing** To render or express in an external or concrete form; make objective; externalize. [< OBJECT² + FY] — **ob·jec'ti·fi·ca'tion** *n.*

ob·jec·tion (əb·jek'shən) *n.* **1.** A statement or feeling of disagreement, opposition, etc. **2.** The cause or reason for disagreement. **3.** The act of objecting. Abbr. *obj.* [< OF < LL *objectio, -onis* < L *objectus.* See OBJECT¹.]

ob·jec·tion·a·ble (əb·jek'shən·ə·bəl) *adj.* Deserving of disapproval; offensive. — **ob·jec'tion·a·bil'i·ty** *n.* — **ob·jec'tion·a·bly** *adv.*

ob·jec·tive (əb·jek'tiv) *adj.* **1.** Free from or independent of personal feelings, opinions, prejudice, etc.; detached; unbiased. **2.** Pertaining to what is external to or independent of the mind; real: opposed to *subjective.* **3.** Treating, stressing, or dealing with external or actual phenomena, as distinct from inner or imaginary feelings and thoughts. **4.** *Gram.* Denoting the case of the object of a transitive verb or preposition; accusative. **5.** Pertaining to a goal or end: *objective* position. — *n.* **1.** That which is striven for or aimed at; a goal; end. **2.** *Gram.* **a** The objective or accusative case. **b** A word in this case; object. **3.** *Optics* A lens or combination of lenses, as in a telescope, that is nearest to the object being viewed: also called *object glass.* **4.** In a camera or projector, the lens that makes the image of the object. — **Syn.** See PURPOSE. [< Med.L *objectivus* < *objectum.* See OBJECT².] — **ob·jec'tive·ly** *adv.*

ob·jec·tiv·ism (əb·jek'tə·viz'əm) *n.* **1.** *Philos.* **a** The doctrine that reality is objective or external to the mind. **b** The theory that knowledge, morals, etc., are based on external reality, as distinct from subjective existence. **c** The view that human knowledge is universally valid. Opposed to *solipsism.* **2.** The tendency to deal with or stress objective or external elements, as in art, literature, etc. — **ob·jec'tiv·ist** *n.* — **ob·jec'tiv·is'tic** *adj.*

ob·jec·tiv·i·ty (ob'jek·tiv'ə·tē) *n.* **1.** The state or quality of being objective. **2.** Material reality. Also **ob·jec'tive·ness.**

ob·ject·less (ob'jikt·lis, -jekt-) *adj.* **1.** Having or containing no object. **2.** Purposeless.

OBELISK (Washington monument, Washington, D.C.; 555 feet, 5½ inches high)

object lesson An example of a principle or moral in a concrete form or striking instance.

ob·jet d'art (ôb-zhe′ där′) *French* *pl.* **ob·jets d'art** (ôb-zhe′) Any object or article of artistic value.

ob·jur·gate (ob′jər·gāt, əb·jûr′-) *v.t.* **·gat·ed, ·gat·ing** To rebuke severely; scold sharply; berate; chide. [< L *objurgatus*, pp. of *objurgare* to rebuke < *ob-* against + *jurgare* to scold] — **ob·jur·ga′tion** *n.* — **ob·jur·ga′tor** *n.* — **ob·jur·ga·to·ri·ly** (əb·jûr′gə·tôr′ə·lē, -tō′rə·lē) *adv.* — **ob·jur′ga·to′ry** (-tôr′e, -tō′re) *adj.*

obl. 1. Oblique. 2. Oblong.

ob·lan·ce·o·late (ob·lan′sē·ə·lit, -lāt′) *adj. Bot.* Inversely lance-shaped, as the leaves of certain plants. [< OB- inversely + LANCEOLATE]

ob·last (ob′lăst; *Russian* ô′bləsty′) *n.* An administrative division of the Soviet Union corresponding to a region or province. Also **o′blast′**. [< Russian, region]

ob·late[1] (ob′lāt, ob·lāt′) *adj.* Flattened at the poles: opposed to *prolate*. [< NL *oblatus* < L *ob-* towards + (*pro*)*latus* lengthened out] — **ob·late·ly** (ob′lāt·lē, ob·lāt′-) *adv.*

ob·late[2] (ob′lāt, ob·lāt′) *adj.* Consecrated or devoted to a religious life. — *n.* A person so devoted, as in a monastery. [< Med.L *oblatus* < L, pp. of *offerre* to OFFER.]

ob·la·tion (ob·lā′shən) *n.* 1. The act of offering religious worship, sacrifice, etc., especially in the Eucharist. 2. That which is offered, especially the elements of the Eucharist. 3. Any grateful or solemn offering. [< OF < Med.L *oblatio*, *-onis* < *oblatus*. See OBLATE[2].] — **ob·la′tion·al** *adj.* — **ob·la·to·ry** (ob′lə·tôr′ē, -tō′rē) *adj.*

ob·li·gate (ob′lə·gāt; for *adj.*, *also* -git) *v.t.* **·gat·ed, ·gat·ing** To bind or compel, as by contract, conscience, promise, etc. — *adj.* 1. Bound or restricted. 2. *Biol.* Restricted to one mode of life, as certain parasites: opposed to *facultative*. [< L *obligatus*, pp. of *obligare*. See OBLIGE.] — **ob′li·ga′tor** *n.*

ob·li·ga·tion (ob′lə·gā′shən) *n.* 1. The act of obligating, or the state of being obligated. 2. The duty, promise, contract, etc., by which one is bound. 3. Any duty or requirement imposed by society, law, etc. 4. The constraining or binding power of a law, promise, conscience, etc. 5. *Law* a An agreement or tie binding one to pay a certain amount or perform some duty. b The document, as a bond, contract, deed, etc., containing the terms of such an agreement. 6. What one owes in return for a service, favor, etc.; also, the service or favor itself. 7. The condition of being indebted for a kindness, benefit, etc. — **Syn.** See DUTY. [< OF < LL *obligatio*, *-onis* < L *obligare*. See OBLIGE.]

ob·li·ga·tive (ob′lə·gā′tiv) *adj.* Implying or expressing obligation: opposed to *facultative*.

ob·li·ga·to (ob′lə·gä′tō, *Ital.* ôb′blē·gä′tō) See OBBLIGATO.

ob·li·ga·to·ry (ə·blig′ə·tôr′ē, -tō′rē, ob′lə·gə-) *adj.* Of the nature of or constituting a duty or obligation; imperative: opposed to *facultative*. [< LL *obligatorius* < L *obligatus*, pp. of *obligare*. See OBLIGE.]

o·blige (ə·blīj′) *v.t.* **o·bliged, o·blig·ing** 1. To place (one) under obligation, as for a service, favor, etc.; give (one) cause for gratitude: with *to*: I am *obliged* to you. 2. To compel, bind, or constrain, as by command, promise, etc.; obligate. 3. To do a favor or service for. [< OF *obliger* < L *obligare*, orig. to tie around < *ob-* towards + *ligare* to bind] — **o·blig′er** *n.*

ob·li·gee (ob′lə·jē′) *n.* 1. One who is obliged. 2. *Law* The person to whom one is obligated: compare *obligor*.

o·blig·ing (ə·blī′jing) *adj.* Disposed to do favors; accommodating; kind. — **o·blig′ing·ly** *adv.* — **o·blig′ing·ness** *n.*

ob·li·gor (ob′lə·gôr′, ob′lə·gôr′) *n. Law* The person who is bound to perform an obligation: distinguished from *obligee*.

ob·lique (ə·blēk′, *in military usage* ə·blīk′) *adj.* 1. Deviating from the perpendicular or horizontal; slanting; sloping. 2. Not direct or straightforward in meaning, expression, etc.: *oblique* praise. 3. Indirectly aimed at or attained: *oblique* results. 4. *Geom.* Having an acute or obtuse angle. 5. Not in the direct line of descent; collateral. 6. *Bot.* Having unequal sides, as a leaf. 7. *Anat.* Designating several muscles whose fibers run at an angle to the lateral or longitudinal plane of the body. 8. *Gram.* Designating the oblique cases. — *n.* 1. An oblique thing, as a line, muscle, etc. 2. *Naut.* The act of veering less than ninety degrees. — *v.i.* **·liqued, ·li·quing** 1. To deviate from the perpendicular or horizontal; slant. 2. *Mil.* To march or advance in an oblique direction. Abbr. *obl.* [< L *obleiquus*] — **ob·lique′ly** *adv.* — **ob·lique′ness** *n.*

oblique angle *Geom.* An angle not a right angle; an acute or obtuse angle.

oblique case *Gram.* Any case other than the nominative or vocative.

oblique rhyme Near rhyme (which see).

oblique sailing *Naut.* Navigation at an oblique angle to the meridian.

oblique triangle Any triangle not a right triangle.

ob·liq·ui·ty (ə·blik′wə·tē) *n. pl.* **·ties** 1. The state or quality of being oblique. 2. Inclination from a vertical or horizontal line or plane; also, the amount or angle of such inclination. 3. Mental or moral deviation. — **ob·liq′ui·tous** *adj.*

ob·lit·er·ate (ə·blit′ə·rāt) *v.t.* **·at·ed, ·at·ing** 1. To destroy

utterly; leave no trace of. 2. To blot or wipe out; erase, as writing. — **Syn.** See ABOLISH, CANCEL. [< L *obliteratus*, pp. of *obliterare* to efface < *ob-* against + *littera* letter] — **ob·lit′er·a′tion** *n.* — **ob·lit′er·a′tive** *adj.* — **ob·lit′er·a′tor** *n.*

ob·liv·i·on (ə·bliv′ē·ən) *n.* 1. The state or fact of being completely forgotten. 2. The state or fact of forgetting completely; forgetfulness. 3. Heedlessness; disregard. [< OF < L *oblivio*, *-onis* < *oblivisci* to forget]

ob·liv·i·ous (ə·bliv′ē·əs) *adj.* 1. Not conscious or aware; unmindful: with *of* or *to*: *oblivious* to his surroundings. 2. Forgetful or given to forgetfulness. 3. Of or pertaining to oblivion. — **Syn.** See ABSTRACTED. [< L *obliviosus*] — **ob·liv′i·ous·ly** *adv.* — **ob·liv′i·ous·ness** *n.*

ob·long (ob′lông, -long) *adj.* 1. Longer in one dimension than in another: said usually of rectangles. 2. Having one principal axis longer than the other or others. 3. *Bot.* Bluntly elliptical, as a leaf. See illustration of LEAF. — *n.* An oblong figure, object, etc. Abbr. *obl.* [< L *oblongus* somewhat long < *ob-* towards + *longus* long]

ob·lo·quy (ob′lə·kwē) *n. pl.* **·quies** 1. Abusive and defamatory language, especially when directed against one by a large group of people; vilification. 2. The state or condition resulting from such abuse; disgrace. [< LL *obloquium* contradiction < *obloqui* < *ob-* against + *loqui* to speak] — **Syn.** opprobrium, odium, infamy, disgrace.

ob·nox·ious (əb·nok′shəs) *adj.* 1. Highly disagreeable; objectionable; offensive. 2. *Obs.* Liable or exposed to punishment, harm, etc. [< L *obnoxiosus* < *ob-* towards + *noxius* harmful < *noxa* injury] — **ob·nox′ious·ly** *adv.* — **ob·nox′ious·ness** *n.* — **Syn.** detestable, abhorrent, repugnant, abominable.

o·boe (ō′bō, ō′boi) *n.* A double-reed woodwind instrument with a conical bore, having a high, penetrating tone. Abbr. *ob.* [< Ital. < F *hautbois*. See HAUTBOY.] — **o′bo·ist** *n.*

ob·o·lus (ob′ə·ləs) *n. pl.* **·li** (-lī) A silver coin and unit of weight of ancient Greece, equivalent to one sixth of a drachma. Also **ob·ol** (ob′əl). [< L < Gk. *obolos*]

ob·o·vate (ob·ō′vāt) *adj. Bot.* Inversely ovate, with the broad end upward, as a leaf. [< OB- inversely + OVATE]

ob·o·void (ob·ō′void) *adj. Bot.* Inversely ovoid, with the broader end upward or outward, as certain fruits. [< OB- inversely + OVOID]

O·bre·gón (ō′brā·gōn′), **Alvaro,** 1880–1928, Mexican politician; president 1920–24, 1928; assassinated.

obs. 1. Observation. 2. Observatory. 3. Obsolete.

ob·scene (əb·sēn′, ob-) *adj.* 1. Offensive or abhorrent to prevailing concepts of morality or decency; indecent; lewd. 2. Stressing or suggesting indecency, lust, or depravity. 3. Inciting or aiming to incite indecency, lust, etc. 4. Offensive to the senses; disgusting; loathsome; foul. [< MF *obscène* < L *obscenus* ill-omened, filthy, ? < *obs-*, var. of *ob-* towards + *caenum* filth] — **ob·scene′ly** *adv.* — **ob·scene′ness** *n.*

ob·scen·i·ty (əb·sen′ə·tē, -sē′nə-, ob-) *n. pl.* **·ties** 1. The quality or state of being obscene; indecency; lewdness. 2. An obscene act, expression, word, etc. [< MF *obscénité* < L *obscenitas* < *obscenus*. See OBSCENE.]

ob·scur·ant (əb·skyŏor′ənt) *n.* One who or that which obscures, especially by opposing or hindering educational progress, free thought, etc. — *adj.* 1. Causing obscurity. 2. Of or pertaining to an obscurant. [< L *obscurans*, *-antis*, ppr. of *obscurare* to darken]

ob·scur·ant·ism (əb·skyŏor′ən·tiz′əm) *n.* 1. The act or principles of an obscurant. 2. Opposition to learning and inquiry. — **ob·scur′ant·ist** *n. & adj.*

ob·scu·ra·tion (ob′skyə·rā′shən) *n.* The act of obscuring, or the state of being obscured.

ob·scure (əb·skyŏor′) *adj.* **·scur·er, ·scur·est** 1. Not clear or plain to the mind; hard to understand; abstruse: an *obscure* statement. 2. Not clear or distinct to the senses, difficult to discern; indistinct; faint: *obscure* sounds; *obscure* outline. 3. Not readily discovered; hidden; remote: an *obscure* nook. 4. Without distinction or fame; inconspicuous; humble: an *obscure* artist. 5. Having little or no light; dark; dim; dusky. — *v.t.* **·scured, ·scur·ing** 1. To render obscure, vague, indefinite, etc. 2. To cover or darken so as to make dim, indistinct, etc. 3. *Phonet.* To articulate (a vowel) as (ə). — *n. Rare* Obscurity. [< OF *obscur, oscur* < L *obscurus*. Akin to Skt. *skutás* covered.] — **ob·scure′ly** *adv.* — **ob·scure′ness** *n.* — **Syn.** (adj.) 1. equivocal. See MYSTERIOUS. 5. See DARK. — **Ant.** clear, distinct, lucid, obvious.

ob·scu·ri·ty (əb·skyŏor′ə·tē) *n. pl.* **·ties** 1. The state or quality of being obscure. 2. One who or that which is obscure.

ob·se·crate (ob′sə·krāt) *v.t.* **·crat·ed, ·crat·ing** *Rare* To supplicate. [< L *obsecratus*, pp. of *obsecrare* to beseech < *ob-* on account of + *sacrare* to make sacred < *sacer* sacred] — **ob′se·cra′tion** *n.* — **ob′se·cra·to·ry** (-krā′tər·ē) *adj.*

ob·se·quies (ob′sə·kwēz) *n.pl.* Funeral rites. [< OF *obseques* < Med.L *obsequiae*, pl., funeral rites, confusion of LL *exsequiae* funeral rites and L *obsequium* dutiful service. See OBSEQUIOUS.]

ob·se·qui·ous (əb·sē′kwē·əs) *adj.* 1. Excessively obedient or submissive; sycophantic; servile. 2. *Rare* Dutiful; obedi-

ent. [< L *obsequiosus* compliant < *obsequium* compliance < *obsequi* to comply with < *ob-* towards + *sequi* to follow]
— **ob·se′qui·ous·ly** *adv.* — **ob·se′qui·ous·ness** *n.*
— **Syn.** fawning, toadyish, slavish.

ob·serv·a·ble (əb·zûr′və·bəl) *adj.* **1.** Capable of being observed; noticeable; discernible: an *observable* change. **2.** Worthy of notice or mention; noteworthy; notable. **3.** That may or must be observed or celebrated, as a holiday. — **ob·serv′a·bly** *adv.* — **ob·serv′a·ble·ness** *n.*

ob·ser·vance (əb·zûr′vəns) *n.* **1.** The act of following, heeding, or complying with a command, law, etc. **2.** The act of celebrating or keeping a holiday, ceremony, etc. **3.** A customary rite, ceremony, etc. **4.** Observation; notice; attention. **5.** *Eccl.* **a** The rule or constitution of a religious order. **b** The order or the house of such an order. **6.** *Archaic* Respectful attention. [< OF < L *observantia* attention, reverence < *observans, -antis,* ppr. of *observare.* See OBSERVE.]

ob·ser·vant (əb·zûr′vənt) *adj.* **1.** Attentive, careful, or quick in observing or noting; heedful; alert. **2.** Strict or careful in obeying or keeping a custom, law, ceremony, etc.: often with *of: observant* of ritual. [< MF < L *observans, -antis,* ppr. of *observare.* See OBSERVE.] — **ob·serv′ant·ly** *adv.*

Ob·ser·van·tine (ob·zûr′vən·tin, -tēn) *n.* A member of a branch of the Franciscan order that observes the original rule strictly, especially with regard to the vow of poverty. Also **Ob·ser′vant.** [< F *Observantin* < *observant,* ppr. of *observer.* See OBSERVE.]

ob·ser·va·tion (ob′zər·vā′shən) *n.* **1.** The act or faculty of observing, or the fact of being observed. **2.** Close examination, especially of natural phenomena, for the purpose of scientific analysis and interpretation; also, the record or data of such an examination. **3.** An opinion or judgment in the form of a comment; a remark. **4.** *Rare* That which is acquired or learned from observing. **5.** *Obs.* Observance. Abbr. *obs.* — **Syn.** See REMARK. — **to take** (or **work out**) **an observation** *Naut.* To calculate the latitude and longitude from angular measurements of the altitude and position of the sun or other celestial body.

ob·ser·va·tion·al (ob′zər·vā′shən·əl) *adj.* **1.** Of or pertaining to observation. **2.** Based on or involving observation.

observation balloon See under BALLOON.

observation car A railroad car with an open or glass-enclosed top or rear section, used for sight-seeing, etc.

observation post *Mil.* An open or concealed position for observing enemy movements, directing fire, etc. Abbr. *OP*

ob·ser·va·to·ry (əb·zûr′və·tôr′ē, -tō′rē) *n. pl.* **·ries 1.** A building or station for the systematic observation of natural phenomena; especially, one for astronomical observation. **2.** A place affording a panoramic view. Abbr. *obs.* [< NL *observatorium* < L *observatus,* pp. of *observare.* See OBSERVE.]

ob·serve (əb·zûrv′) *v.* **·served, ·serv·ing** *v.t.* **1.** To see or notice; perceive. **2.** To watch attentively; keep under surveillance: to *observe* the enemy. **3.** To make careful observation of, especially for scientific purposes. **4.** To say or comment; remark. **5.** To follow or comply with (a law, custom, etc.); abide by: to *observe* silence. **6.** To celebrate or solemnize in the proper or customary manner, as a holiday or ceremony. — *v.i.* **7.** To make a remark; comment: often with *on* or *upon.* **8.** To take notice. **9.** To look on or attend without taking part, as at a meeting, conference, etc. — **Syn.** See CELEBRATE, SEE¹. [< OF *observer* < L *observare* to watch < *ob-* towards, against + *servare* to keep, protect] — **ob·serv′er** *n.* — **ob·serv′ing·ly** *adv.*

ob·sess (əb·ses′) *v.t.* To occupy or trouble the mind of to an excessive degree; preoccupy; harass; haunt. [< L *obsessus,* pp. of *obsidere* to occupy, besiege < *ob-* before + *sedere* to sit] — **ob·ses′sive** *adj.* — **ob·ses′sor** *n.*

ob·ses·sion (əb·sesh′ən) *n.* **1.** That which obsesses, preoccupies, or vexes, as a persistent idea or feeling. **2.** *Psychiatry* **a** An unwanted or compulsive idea or emotion persistently coming to awareness. **b** The compulsive state itself. **3.** The act of obsessing, or the state of being obsessed.

ob·sid·i·an (əb·sid′ē·ən, ob-) *n.* A glassy volcanic rock, usually black and having a conchoidal fracture without individualized crystals. [< L *obsidianus,* after *Obsidius,* alter. of *Obsius,* said by Pliny to be its discoverer]

ob·so·les·cent (ob′sə·les′ənt) *adj.* Growing or tending to grow obsolete. — **Syn.** See OBSOLETE. [< L *obsolescens, -entis,* ppr. of *obsolescere* to wear out < *ob-* against + *solere* to use] — **ob·so·les′cence** *n.* — **ob·so·les′cent·ly** *adv.*

ob·so·lete (ob′sə·lēt, ob′sə·lēt′) *adj.* **1.** Gone out of fashion; out-of-date; outmoded: an *obsolete* weapon. **2.** No longer used or practiced; not current: an *obsolete* word. **3.** *Biol.* Imperfectly developed; atrophied or vestigial: said of certain organs, parts, etc., no longer functional in living forms of the same species or sex. Abbr. *obs.* [< L *obsoletus* grown old, worn-out, pp. of *obsolescere.* See OBSOLESCENT.] — **ob′so·lete′ly** *adv.* — **ob′so·lete′ness** *n.* — **ob′so·let′ism** *n.*
— **Syn. 1.** *Obsolete, obsolescent, archaic,* and *rare* are applied to words that are now seldom or never used. An *obsolete* word is no longer used either in speech or writing, usually because it has been

supplanted by a different word; *oscitate,* meaning to yawn, is now *obsolete.* An *obsolescent* word, though still in use, is becoming obsolete; *mercaptan,* a former chemical term, is such a word. *Archaic* words were current at some time in the past, and appear in the works of Shakespeare, the Bible, etc., but unlike obsolete words they are still used for effect because they have an unmistakable flavor of their period or milieu, or are used by persons whose vocabularies were formed in a distinctively earlier era. *Rare* words may be *archaic* or current, but are little used; *trow* is an archaic word, and *obsecrate* is an example of a *rare* word.

ob·sta·cle (ob′stə·kəl) *n.* That which stands in the way; a hindrance or obstruction. — **Syn.** See IMPEDIMENT. [< OF < L *obstaculum* < *obstare* to stand before, withstand < *ob-* before, against + *stare* to stand]

obstet. Obstetrical; obstetrics.

ob·stet·ric (əb·stet′rik) *adj.* Of or pertaining to obstetrics or childbirth. Also **ob·stet′ri·cal.** [< L *obstetricius* < *obstetrix, -icis* midwife, lit., one who stands by < *obstare.* See OBSTACLE.] — **ob·stet′ri·cal·ly** *adv.*

ob·ste·tri·cian (ob′stə·trish′ən) *n.* A medical and surgical specialist in obstetrics.

ob·stet·rics (əb·stet′riks) *n.pl.* (construed as sing.) The branch of medicine dealing with pregnancy and childbirth.

ob·sti·na·cy (ob′stə·nə·sē) *n. pl.* **·cies 1.** The state or quality of being obstinate. **2.** An obstinate act, feeling, etc.

ob·sti·nate (ob′stə·nit) *adj.* **1.** Unreasonably fixed in one's purpose or opinion; unyielding; inflexible; stubborn. **2.** Difficult to overcome, control, or cure: an *obstinate* habit. [< L *obstinatus* stubborn < *obstinare* to persist < *obstare.* See OBSTACLE.] — **ob′sti·nate·ly** *adv.* — **ob′sti·nate·ness** *n.*
— **Syn. 1.** *Obstinate, stubborn, dogged, pertinacious, headstrong, obdurate, pig-headed,* and *mulish* mean unyielding in opinion or action. One may be *obstinate* in a particular instance, but is *stubborn* by disposition. *Dogged* also refers to character or disposition, but it alone of all these words is not necessarily deprecatory, and frequently refers to a commendable perseverance: a *dogged* determination to overcome a handicap. *Pertinacious* refers to perseverance in action that annoys others, while *headstrong* implies persistence in behavior that is foolish, reckless, or arrogant. *Obdurate* describes a person who is hard and unfeeling, and unmoved by compassion, pity, etc. *Pig-headed* usually suggests a stupid obstinacy, *mulish,* an irrational stubbornness. See INFLEXIBLE. — **Ant.** compliant, amenable, tractable, docile.

ob·sti·pant (ob′stə·pənt) *n. Med.* Anything inducing obstipation.

ob·sti·pa·tion (ob′stə·pā′shən) *n. Med.* Persistent or acute constipation. [< L *obstipatio, -onis* a stopping up, ult. < *ob-* against + *stipare* to press together]

ob·strep·er·ous (əb·strep′ər·əs) *adj.* Unruly, noisy, or boisterous, especially in resistance to control, advice, etc. [< L *obstreperus* < *obstrepere* to make noise at < *ob-* towards + *strepere* to make noise] — **ob·strep′er·ous·ly** *adv.* — **ob·strep′er·ous·ness** *n.*

ob·struct (əb·strukt′) *v.t.* **1.** To stop or impede movement through (a way or passage) by obstacles or impediments; barricade; choke; clog. **2.** To block or retard the progress or way of; impede; check. **3.** To come or be in front of so as to prevent a clear view or hide from sight. [< L *obstructus,* pp. of *obstruere* to block up < *ob-* before + *struere* to pile, build] — **ob·struct′er** or **ob·struc′tor** *n.* — **ob·struc′tive** *adj.* — **ob·struc′tive·ly** *adv.* — **ob·struc′tive·ness** *n.*

ob·struc·tion (əb·struk′shən) *n.* **1.** That which obstructs; an impediment; hindrance; obstacle. **2.** The act of obstructing, or the state of being obstructed; blockage.

ob·struc·tion·ist (əb·struk′shən·ist) *n.* One who makes a practice of obstructing; especially, in politics, one who obstructs debate, legislation, etc. — **ob·struc′tion·ism** *n.*

ob·stru·ent (ob′strōō·ənt) *Med. adj.* Causing obstruction or impediment, as of the stomach. — *n.* Any substance or agent that obstructs. [< L *obstruens, -entis,* ppr. of *obstruere.* See OBSTRUCT.]

obt. Obedient.

ob·tain (əb·tān′) *v.t.* **1.** To gain possession of, especially by effort; acquire; get. **2.** *Archaic* To arrive at; reach. — *v.i.* **3.** To be prevalent or in effect: Old customs still *obtain* there. **4.** *Archaic* To succeed; prevail. — **Syn.** See GET. [< OF *obtenir* < L *obtinere* < *ob-* towards + *tenere* to hold] — **ob·tain′a·ble** *adj.* — **ob·tain′er** *n.* — **ob·tain′ment** *n.*

ob·tect (ob·tekt′) *adj. Entomol.* Covered with a hard, glutinous secretion, as the pupa of most flies. Also **ob·tect′ed.** [< L *obtectus,* pp. of *obtegere* < *ob-* over + *tegere* to cover]

ob·test (ob·test′) *Rare v.t.* **1.** To invoke as a witness. **2.** To beseech; implore. — *v.i.* **3.** To protest. [< L *obtestari* to call to witness < *ob-* towards + *testari* to testify] — **ob′tes·ta′tion** *n.*

ob·trude (əb·trōōd′) *v.* **·trud·ed, ·trud·ing** *v.t.* **1.** To thrust or force (oneself, an opinion, etc.) upon another without request or warrant. **2.** To push forward or out; eject. — *v.i.* **3.** To intrude oneself. [< L *obtrudere* < *ob-* towards + *trudere* to thrust] — **ob·trud′er** *n.* — **ob·tru′sion** *n.*

ob·tru·sive (əb·trōō′siv) *adj.* Tending to obtrude. — **ob·tru′sive·ly** *adv.* — **ob·tru′sive·ness** *n.*

ob·tund (ob·tund′) *v.t. Rare* To dull; deaden. [< L *obtundere* < *ob-* towards + *tundere* to beat] —**ob·tund′ent** *adj. & n.*

ob·tu·rate (ob′tyə·rāt, -tə-) *v.t.* ·**rat·ed**, ·**rat·ing** *Rare* To close or stop up. [< L *obturatus*, pp. of *obturare*] —**ob′tu·ra′tion** *n.* —**ob′tu·ra′tor** *n.*

ob·tuse (ab·tōōs′, -tyōōs′) *adj.* 1. Lacking acuteness of intellect or feeling; not sharp or perceptive; insensible. 2. Not clear or distinct to the senses; dull, as a sound or pain. 3. Blunt in form; not sharp. 4. *Bot.* Blunt or rounded at the extremity, as a leaf or petal: opposed to *acute.* See illustration of LEAF. [< L *obtusus* blunt, dulled, pp. of *obtundere.* See OBTUND.] —**ob·tuse′ly** *adv.* —**ob·tuse′ness** *n.*

obtuse angle *Geom.* An angle greater than a right angle and less than a straight angle.

ob·verse (ob′vûrs; *for adj., also* ob·vûrs′) *adj.* 1. Turned toward or facing one. 2. Narrower at the base than at the apex; inverse: an *obverse* leaf. 3. Constituting a counterpart: an *obverse* impression. — *n.* 1. The front or principal side of anything; especially, the side of a coin bearing the main design or device: distinguished from *reverse.* 2. A counterpart. 3. *Logic* A proposition derived by reversing the positive or negative terms of another proposition: "All men are mortal" is the *obverse* of "No men are immortal." [< L *obversus*, pp. of *obvertere.* See OBVERT.] —**ob·verse′ly** *adv.*

ob·ver·sion (ob·vûr′zhən, -shən) *n.* The act of obverting, or the state of being obverted.

ob·vert (ob·vûrt′) *v.t.* 1. *Logic* To derive the obverse of (a proposition). 2. *Obs.* To present the principal or other side of. [< L *obvertere* < *ob-* towards + *vertere* to turn]

ob·vi·ate (ob′vē·āt) *v.t.* ·**at·ed**, ·**at·ing** To prevent or counter (an objection, difficulty, etc.) by effective measures; dispose of; provide for: to *obviate* the risk of war. [< L *obviatus*, pp. of *obviare* to meet, withstand < *obvius.* See OBVIOUS.] —**ob′vi·a′tion** *n.* —**ob′vi·a′tor** *n.*
— **Syn.** preclude, forestall, avert. See PREVENT.

ob·vi·ous (ob′vē·əs) *adj.* 1. Immediately evident; palpably true; manifest. 2. Behaving without equivocation or subtlety. 3. *Obs.* Standing in the way. — **Syn.** See EVIDENT. [< L *obvius* in the way, obvious < *ob-* before + *via* way] —**ob′vi·ous·ly** *adv.* —**ob′vi·ous·ness** *n.*

ob·vo·lute (ob′və·lōōt) *adj. Bot.* Overlapping, as the margins of certain leaves or petals. [< L *obvolutus*, pp. of *obvolvere* to wrap around < *ob-* towards + *volvere* to roll] —**ob′vo·lu′tion** *n.* —**ob′vo·lu′tive** *adj.*

oc- Assimilated var. of OB-.

o/c Overcharge.

o.c. In the work cited (L *opere citato*).

Oc. or **oc.** Ocean.

o·ca·ri·na (ok′ə·rē′nə) *n.* A small musical instrument in the shape of a sweet potato, usually of terra cotta, with a mouthpiece and finger holes, and yielding soft, sonorous notes: also, *U.S. Informal, sweet potato.* [< Ital., dim. of *oca* goose < L *auca*; so called with ref. to its shape]

OCARINA

O'Ca·sey (ō·kā′sē), **Sean** (shôn), 1880–1964, Irish playwright.

Oc·cam (ok′əm), **William of** See OCKHAM.

oc·ca·sion (ə·kā′zhən) *n.* 1. The particular time of an event or occurrence; also, the event or occurrence itself: on the *occasion* of her marriage. 2. An important or extraordinary event: The inaugural ball was quite an *occasion.* 3. A favorable time or condition; opportunity: to seize the first *occasion.* 4. The immediate cause or grounds for some action or state; reason: to give one *occasion* to complain. 5. A need or requirement; exigency. 6. *pl. Obs.* Personal needs or wants. 7. *pl. Obs.* Business; affairs. — **Syn.** See OPPORTUNITY. —**by occasion of** In consequence of; by reason of. —**on occasion** On suitable opportunity; now and then. —**to take the (this, etc.) occasion** To avail oneself of the (this, etc.) opportunity. — *v.t.* To cause or bring about, especially in an accidental or incidental manner. [< L *occasio, -onis* a falling towards, opportunity < *occidere* to fall, go down < *ob-* towards + *cadere* to fall]

oc·ca·sion·al (ə·kā′zhən·əl) *adj.* 1. Occurring, appearing, etc., irregularly or now and then: an *occasional* visit. 2. Made, intended, or suitable for a special or particular occasion: *occasional* verse. 3. Pertaining to or designating a small chair, table, etc., that is not part of a set. Abbr. *occas.*

oc·ca·sion·al·ism (ə·kā′zhən·əl·iz′əm) *n. Philos.* The doctrine that the mind and body do not act upon each other but that their apparent interaction is produced by God. —**oc·ca′sion·al·ist** *n.*

oc·ca·sion·al·ly (ə·kā′zhən·əl·ē) *adv.* Now and then; sometimes. Abbr. *occas.*

oc·ci·dent (ok′sə·dənt) *n.* The west: opposed to *orient.* [< OF < L *occidens, -entis* region where the sun sets, ppr. of *occidere* to fall. See OCCASION.]

Oc·ci·dent (ok′sə·dənt) 1. The countries west of Asia; especially, Europe. 2. The western hemisphere. Distinguished from *Orient.*

oc·ci·den·tal (ok′sə·den′təl) *adj.* Of or belonging to the west, or to the countries constituting the Occident: distinguished from *oriental.* — *n.* One born or living in a western country. Also **Oc′ci·den′tal.**

Oc·ci·den·tal·ism (ok′sə·den′təl·iz′əm) *n.* The culture, institutions, etc., of the Occident. — **Oc′ci·den′tal·ist** *n.*

oc·ci·den·tal·ize (ok′sə·den′təl·īz) *v.t.* ·**ized**, ·**iz·ing** To render occidental in spirit, culture, character, etc. —**oc′ci·den′tal·i·za′tion** *n.*

oc·cip·i·tal (ok·sip′ə·təl) *adj.* Pertaining to the occiput. — *n.* The occipital bone. [< Med.L *occipitalis* < L *occiput.* See OCCIPUT.]

occipital bone *Anat.* The hindmost bone of the skull, between the parietal and temporal bones. For illustration see SKULL.

occipito- *combining form Anat.* Occipital; occipital and. [< L *occiput* back of the head]

oc·ci·put (ok′sə·put, -pət) *n. pl.* **oc·cip·i·ta** (ok·sip′ə·tə) *Anat.* The lower back part of the skull. [< L, back of the head < *ob-* against + *caput* head]

oc·clude (ə·klōōd′) *v.t.* ·**clud·ed**, ·**clud·ing** *v.t.* 1. To shut up or close, as pores or openings. 2. To shut in, out, or off. 3. *Chem.* To take up, either on the surface or internally, but without change of properties: Palladium *occludes* hydrogen. 4. *Meteorol.* To displace, as a mass of warm air by an advancing front of cold air. — *v.i.* 5. *Dent.* To meet so that the corresponding cusps fit closely together: said of the teeth of the upper and lower jaws. [< L *occludere* to shut < *ob-* against + *claudere* to close] —**oc·clu′dent** *adj.* —**oc·clu·sion** (ə·klōō′zhən) *n.*

oc·clu·sive (ə·klōō′siv) *adj.* 1. Characterized by or bringing about occlusion or closure. 2. *Phonet.* Pertaining to a stop or plosive consonant. — *n. Phonet.* A stop.

oc·cult (ə·kult′, ok′ult) *adj.* 1. Of or pertaining to various magical arts and practices, as astrology, alchemy, necromancy, etc. 2. Beyond human understanding; mysterious: *occult* powers. 3. Not divulged or disclosed; secret. — **Syn.** See MYSTERIOUS. — *n.* Occult arts or practices: usually with *the.* — *v.t.* 1. To hide or conceal from view. 2. *Astron.* To hide or conceal by occultation. — *v.i.* 3. To become hidden or concealed from view. [< L *occultus*, pp. of *occulere* to cover over, hide] —**oc·cult′ly** *adv.* —**oc·cult′ness** *n.*

oc·cul·ta·tion (ok′ul·tā′shən) *n.* 1. The act of occulting, or the state of being occulted. 2. *Astron.* Concealment of one celestial body by another interposed in the line of vision. 3. A disappearance from view or notice.

oc·cult·ism (ə·kul′tiz·əm) *n.* 1. The theory or practice of cult arts. 2. Belief in occult powers. —**oc·cult′ist** *n.*

oc·cu·pan·cy (ok′yə·pən·sē) *n. pl.* ·**cies** 1. The act of occupying, or the state of being occupied. 2. *Law* The act of taking possession of something unowned so as to become its owner. 3. The condition of being an occupant or tenant. 4. The time during which something is occupied.

oc·cu·pant (ok′yə·pənt) *n.* 1. One who occupies a place, position, etc. 2. A tenant. [< L *occupans, -antis*, ppr. of *occupare.* See OCCUPY.]

oc·cu·pa·tion (ok′yə·pā′shən) *n.* 1. One's regular, principal, or immediate business or job. 2. The act of occupying, or the state of being occupied. 3. The taking and holding of land by a military force: the *occupation* of Germany. [< OF < L *occupatio, -onis* a seizing < *occupare.* See OCCUPY.]
— **Syn.** 1. *Occupation, vocation, profession, business, trade, craft, pursuit,* and *avocation* concern the daily work one does, especially to gain a livelihood. *Occupation* and *vocation* are general terms, meaning little more than line of work. A *profession* requires special knowledge and training: Law and medicine are *professions.* A *business* is usually industrial, commercial, or mercantile, but may also be general: the clothing *business,* the *business* of government. A *trade* requires manual skill, as does a *craft,* but the latter suggests a greater degree of skill and even artistic creation: the bricklayer's *trade,* the jeweler's *craft.* A *pursuit* is an *occupation* for pleasure rather than for profit; an *avocation* is a *pursuit* additional to one's *vocation.*

oc·cu·pa·tion·al (ok′yə·pā′shən·əl) *adj.* Of, pertaining to, or caused by an occupation. —**oc′cu·pa′tion·al·ly** *adv.*

occupational therapy *Med.* The treatment of nervous, mental, or physical disabilities by means of work designed to promote recovery or readjustment.

oc·cu·py (ok′yə·pī) *v.t.* ·**pied**, ·**py·ing** 1. To take and hold possession of, as by conquest. 2. To fill or take up (space or time): The estate *occupies* ten acres. 3. To inhabit; dwell in. 4. To hold; fill, as an office or position. 5. To busy or engage; employ: He *occupies* himself with trifles. [< OF *occuper* < L *occupare* to seize, take possession of < *ob-* against + *capere* to take] —**oc′cu·pi′er** *n.*

oc·cur (ə·kûr′) *v.i.* ·**curred**, ·**cur·ring** 1. To happen or take place; come about. 2. To be found or met with; appear: Trout *occur* in this lake. 3. To suggest itself; come to mind: It just *occurred* to me. — **Syn.** See HAPPEN. [< L *occurrere* to run to, meet < *ob-* towards, against + *currere* to run]

oc·cur·rence (ə·kûr′əns) *n.* 1. The act or fact of occurring. 2. That which occurs; an event; incident. — **Syn.** See EVENT. —**oc·cur′rent** *adj.*

OCDM Office of Civil and Defense Mobilization.

o·cean (ō′shən) *n.* 1. The great body of salt water that covers about 70 percent of the earth's surface. 2. *Often cap.* Any one of the divisions of this body of water, usually reckoned as five, the Atlantic, Pacific, Indian, Arctic, and Antarctic. **3.** A very large expanse or quantity. Abbr. *O., oc., Oc.* [< OF < L *oceanus* < Gk. *ōkeanos,* orig. *Ōkeanos rhoos* stream of Oceanus encompassing the earth]

ocean current Any of a large number of riverlike masses of water flowing in all oceans, each having a characteristic direction, length, depth, speed, and temperature.

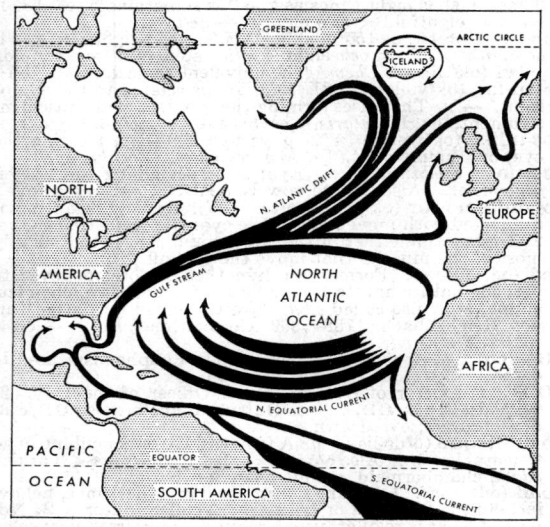

ATLANTIC OCEAN CURRENTS

O·ce·an·i·a (ō′shē·an′ē·ə) The islands of the central and South Pacific, including Melanesia, Micronesia, and Polynesia, and sometimes the Malay Archipelago and Australasia. Also **O′ce·an′i·ca** (-an′ə·kə) — **O′ce·an′i·an** *adj. & n.*
o·ce·an·ic (ō′shē·an′ik) *adj.* **1.** Of, relating to, or living in the ocean; pelagic. **2.** Resembling an ocean; vast.
  — **Syn.** *Oceanic, thalassic, neritic, pelagic,* and *abyssal* refer to the regions and life of the oceans. *Oceanic* is the general term, while the others are more restricted. *Thalassic* refers to seas and gulfs as opposed to the open ocean. *Neritic* is used of the shallow *oceanic* waters around the continents and islands; beyond these waters lie the deeper *pelagic* regions, while *abyssal* is applied to the deepest parts of the ocean beyond the continental shelves. Compare MARINE.
O·ce·an·ic (ō′shē·an′ik) *n.* A subfamily of the Austronesian family of languages, including the Melanesian languages of the Solomon Islands, Fiji, New Caledonia, the New Hebrides, etc., and the Micronesian group of languages.
O·ce·a·nid (ō·sē′ə·nid) *n.* In Greek mythology, one of the 3,000 sea nymphs, daughters of Oceanus and Tethys. [< Gk. *Ōkeanis, -idos*]
oceanog. Oceanography.
o·ce·an·og·ra·phy (ō′shē·ən·og′rə·fē, ō′shən·og′-) *n.* The branch of physical geography that treats of oceanic life and phenomena. — **o′ce·an·og′ra·pher** *n.* — **o′ce·an·o·graph′ic** (-ə·graf′ik) or **·i·cal** *adj.* — **o′ce·an·o·graph′i·cal·ly** *adv.*
ocean pout An eelpout (*Macrozoarces americanus*) of the New World, inhabiting Atlantic waters: also called *muttonfish.*
O·cean·side (ō′shən·sīd′) A resort village in SE New York, on Long Island; pop. 35,028.
O·ce·a·nus (ō·sē′ə·nəs) In Greek mythology: **a** A Titan, early god of the sea and father of the Oceanids. **b** The vast sea supposed to encircle the earth. [< L. dim. of *oculus* eye]
o·cel·lat·ed (os′ə·lā′tid, ō·sel′ā·tid) *adj.* **1.** Having an ocellus or ocelli. **2.** Resembling an ocellus. **3.** Spotted. Also **o·cel·late** (os′ə·lāt, ō·sel′āt). [< L *ocellatus* small-eyed < *ocellus.* See OCELLUS.]
o·cel·la·tion (os′ə·lā′shən) *n.* An eyelike marking.
o·cel·lus (ō·sel′əs) *n. pl.* **·li** (-lī) **1.** *Biol.* A minute simple eye, as of many invertebrates. **2.** An eyelike spot, as in the tail of a peacock. [< L. dim. of *oculus* eye] — **o·cel′lar** *adj.*
o·ce·lot (ō′sə·lot, -lot, os′ə-) *n.* A large cat (*Felis pardalis*) of Central and South America, having a spotted yellowish or reddish gray coat: also called *tiger cat.* [< F, short for Nahuatl *tlaocelotl* < *tlalli* field + *ocelotl* jaguar]
o·cher (ō′kər) *n.* **1.** A naturally occurring hydrated iron oxide mixed with various earthy materials and varying from light yellow to deep orange or red, largely used as a pigment. **2.** A dark yellow color derived from or resembling ocher. Also *Brit.* **o′chre.** [< OF *ocre* < L *ochra* < Gk. *ōchra* yellow

ocher < *ōchros* pale yellow] — **o′cher·ous, o·chre·ous** (ō′krē·əs), **o′cher·y, o·chry** (ō′krē) *adj.*
och·loc·ra·cy (ok·lok′rə·sē) *n. pl.* **·cies** Mobocracy. [< MF *ochlocratie* < Gk. *ochlokratia* mob rule < *ochlos* a crowd + *krateein* to rule] — **och′lo·crat·ic** (ok′-lə·krat′ik) or **·i·cal** *adj.* — **och′lo·crat′i·cal·ly** *adv.*
och·lo·pho·bi·a (ok′lə·fō′bē·ə) *n.* Abnormal fear of crowds. [< Gk. *ochlos* crowd + -PHOBIA]
och·one (ə·khōn′) *interj. Irish & Scot.* Alas: a cry of grief. [< Scottish Gaelic and Irish *ochōin* alas]
o·chroid (ō′kroid) *adj.* Of the color of ocher.
Ochs (oks), **Adolph Simon,** 1858–1935, U.S. newspaper publisher and philanthropist
-ock *suffix of nouns* Small; little: now often without perceptible force: *hillock.* [OE *-oc, -uc*]
Ock·ham (ok′əm), **William of,** 1300?–49?, English Franciscan and scholastic philosopher; opponent of Duns Scotus: called **the Invincible Doctor.** Also spelled *Occam.*
Ockham's razor *Philos.* A principle formulated by William of Ockham, stating that terms, concepts, assumptions, etc., must not be multiplied beyond necessity.
o′clock (ə·klok′) Of or according to the clock: six *o′clock.*
O'Con·nell (ō·kon′əl), **Daniel,** 1775–1847, Irish nationalist statesman and orator: called **the Liberator.**
O'Con·nor (ō·kon′ər), **Thomas Power,** 1848–1929, Irish journalist and patriot: called **Tay Pay** (tā′pā′).
o·co·til·lo (ō′kə·tēl′yō, ō′kō·tē′yō) *n. pl.* **·los** The candlewood tree (*Fouquiera splendens*) of California and Mexico. [< Sp., dim. of *ocote* Mexican pine < Nahuatl *ocotl*]
oc·re·a (ok′rē·ə, ō′krē·ə) *n. pl.* **oc·re·ae** (ok′rē·ē, ō′krī·ē) *Biol.* A tube-shaped sheath, as a stipule about the stem of a plant, or the boot of a bird. [< L, legging, greave]
oc·re·ate (ok′rē·it, -āt, ō′krē-) *adj.* **1.** Having ocreae. **2.** *Ornithol.* Booted: said of the tarsi of certain birds.
OCS *Mil.* Officer Candidate School.
oct-, octa- See OCTO-.
oct. Octavo.
Oct. October.
oc·tad (ok′tad) *n.* **1.** A series of eight. **2.** *Chem.* An atom, radical, or element that has a valence of eight. [< L *octas, -adis* < Gk. *oktas, -ados* a group of eight < *oktō* eight] — **oc·tad′ic** *adj.*
oc·ta·gon (ok′tə·gon) *n. Geom.* A polygon having eight sides and eight angles. [< L *octagonos* eight-cornered < Gk. *oktagōnos* < *oktō* eight + *gōnia* angle]
oc·tag·o·nal (ok·tag′ə·nəl) *adj.* **1.** Having the form of an octagon. **2.** Of solid figures, having the form of an octagon as a base; eight-sided. Also *octangular.* [< NL *octogonalis* < L *octogon* OCTAGON.] — **oc·tag′o·nal·ly** *adv.*

OCTAGON

oc·ta·he·dral (ok′tə·hē′drəl) *adj.* Having the form of an octahedron: also spelled *octohedral.*
oc·ta·he·drite (ok′tə·hē′drīt) *n.* Anatase.
oc·ta·he·dron (ok′tə·hē′drən) *n. pl.* **·dra** (-drə) *Geom.* A polyhedron bounded by eight plane faces. [< Gk. *oktaedron,* neut. of *oktaedros* eight-sided < *oktō* eight + *hedra* seat]
oc·tam·er·ous (ok·tam′ər·əs) *adj. Bot.* Having the parts in eights, as a flower with eight members in each set of organs: frequently written **8-merous.** [< Gk. *oktameres* < *oktō* eight + *meros* part]
oc·tam·e·ter (ok·tam′ə·tər) *adj.* In prosody, having eight measures or metrical feet. — *n.* A verse of eight feet. [< L < Gk. *oktametros* < *oktō* eight + *metron* measure]

OCTAHEDRON

oc·tane (ok′tān) *n. Chem.* One of a group of isomeric saturated hydrocarbons that have the formula C_8H_{18}. [< OCT- + -ANE²]
octane number A measure of the antiknock properties of gasoline, expressed as the percentage, by volume, of isooctane (2,2,4-trimethylpentane) that must be blended with normal heptane until the mixture has the same knock rating as the gasoline under test. Compare CETANE NUMBER.
oc·tan·gle (ok′tang·gəl) *n.* An octagon. [< LL *octangulus* < *octo* eight + *angulus* angle]
oc·tan·gu·lar (ok·tang′gyə·lər) *adj.* Octagonal.
Oc·tans (ok′tanz) A constellation. See CONSTELLATION. Also **Oc·tant** (ok′tənt). [< NL. See OCTANT.]
oc·tant (ok′tənt) *n.* **1.** An eighth part of a circle; an arc subtending an angle of 45 degrees. **2.** *Astron.* The position of a celestial body when it is 45° distant from another. **3.** An instrument resembling a sextant but having an arc of only 45 degrees, used for measuring the angular height of the sun, moon, etc., as an aid in navigation. **4.** *Geom.* Any of the eight areas bounded by three mutually perpendicular planes having a common origin. [< LL *octans, -antis* an eighth part < L *octo* eight] — **oc·tan′tal** (-tan′təl) *adj.*
oc·tar·chy (ok′tär·kē) *n. pl.* **·chies** **1.** A government

headed by eight persons; also, a country having such rule. **2.** A group of eight allied governments. [< OCT- + -ARCHY]

oc·tave (ok′tiv, -tāv) *n.* **1.** *Music* **a** The interval between a tone and another having twice as many or half as many vibrations per second. **b** A tone at this interval above or below any other, considered in relation to that other. **c** Two tones at this interval, sounded together; also, the resulting consonance. **d** An organ stop giving tones an octave above those normally corresponding to the keys played. **2.** *Eccl.* The eighth day from a feast day, beginning with the feast day as one; also, the lengthening of a festival so as to include a period of eight days. **3.** Any group or series of eight. **4.** In prosody, an octet. — *adj.* **1.** Composed of eight. **2.** *Music* Producing tones an octave higher. [< OF < L *octava* (*pars* or *dies*) < *octavus* eighth < *octo* eight] — **oc·ta·val** (ok-tā′vəl, ok′tə-) *adj.*

Oc·ta·vi·a (ok-tā′vē-ə), died 11 B.C., wife of Mark Antony.

Oc·ta·vi·an (ok-tā′vē-ən) See AUGUSTUS CAESAR.

oc·ta·vo (ok-tā′vō, -ä′-) *n. pl.* **-vos 1.** The page size (6 x 9½ inches except where otherwise specified) of a book made up of printer's sheets folded into eight leaves. **2.** A book consisting of pages of this size. — *adj.* In octavo. Also *eightvo*. Also written **8vo** or **8°**. Abbr. *o., O., oct.* [< L (*in*) *octavo*, ablative of *octavus* eighth < *octo* eight]

oc·ten·ni·al (ok-ten′ē-əl) *adj.* **1.** Recurring every eight years. **2.** Lasting eight years. [< L *octennium* a period of eight years < *octo* eight + *annus* year] — **oc·ten′ni·al·ly** *adv.*

oc·tet (ok-tet′) *n.* **1.** A musical composition for eight singers or instrumentalists. **2.** A group of eight singers or instrumentalists. **3.** Any group of eight. **4.** In prosody, the first eight lines of an Italian sonnet; octave. Also **oc·tette′**. [< Ital. *otetto* < L *octo* eight]

oc·til·lion (ok-til′yən) *n.* **1.** *U.S.* A thousand septillions, written as 1 followed by 27 zeros: a cardinal number. **2.** *Brit.* A million septillions (def. 2), written as 1 followed by 48 zeros: a cardinal number. — *adj.* Being an octillion in number. [< MF < L *octo* eight + (*mi*)*llion* a million]

oc·til·lionth (ok-til′yənth) *adj.* **1.** Having the number one octillion: the ordinal of *octillion*. **2.** Being one of an octillion equal parts. — *n.* **1.** One of an octillion equal parts. **2.** That which is numbered one *octillion*.

octo- *combining form* Eight: *octopus*: also, before vowels, *oct-*. Also *octa-*. [< L *octo* and Gk. *oktō* eight]

Oc·to·ber (ok-tō′bər) **1.** The tenth month of the year, containing 31 days. Abbr. *O., Oct.* **2.** *Brit.* Ale or cider made in October. [< L, eighth month of Roman calendar < *octo* eight]

October Revolution See RUSSIAN REVOLUTION under REVOLUTION.

oc·to·dec·i·mo (ok′tə-des′ə-mō) *n. pl.* **·mos 1.** The page size (approximately 4 x 6½ inches) of a book made up of printer's sheets folded into 18 leaves. **2.** A book consisting of pages of this size. — *adj.* In octodecimo; consisting of pages of this size. Also *eighteenmo*. Also written **18mo** or **18°**. [< L (*in*) *octodecimo*, ablative of *octodecimus* eighteenth < *octodecim* eighteen]

oc·to·ge·nar·i·an (ok′tə-jə-nâr′ē-ən) *adj.* Being eighty or from eighty to ninety years of age. — *n.* One between eighty and ninety years of age. [< L *octogenarius* < *octogeni* eighty each < *octoginta* eighty]

oc·tog·e·nar·y (ok-toj′ə-ner′ē) *adj.* **1.** Of or pertaining to the number eighty; progressing by eighties. **2.** Octogenarian. — *n. pl.* **·nar·ies** An octogenarian.

oc·to·he·dral (ok′tə-hē′drəl) See OCTAHEDRAL.

oc·to·lat·er·al (ok′tə-lat′ər-əl) *adj.* Eight-sided. [< OCTO- + LATERAL]

oc·to·nar·y (ok′tə-ner′ē) *adj.* **1.** Of or pertaining to the number eight. **2.** Having eight parts or members. — *n. pl.* **·nar·ies 1.** In prosody, an octet. **2.** A set or group of eight; an ogdoad. [< L *octonarius* containing eight < *octoni* eight at a time < *octo* eight]

oc·to·pod (ok′tə-pod) *n. Zool.* Any of an order or suborder (*Octopoda*) of eight-armed cephalopods, as the octopus.

oc·to·pus (ok′tə-pəs) *n. pl.* **·pus·es** or **·pi** (-pī) or **oc·top·o·des** (ok-top′ə-dēz) **1.** An eight-armed marine cephalopod (genus *Octopus*) having a large oval head and rows of suckers along the arms; a devilfish. **2.** Any organized power regarded as far-reaching and potentially destructive; especially, a powerful business organization. [< NL < Gk. *oktōpous* eight-footed < *oktō* eight + *pous* foot]

OCTOPUS
(Span from 6 inches to 32 feet, according to species)

oc·to·roon (ok′tə-rōōn′) *n.* A person who is one-eighth Negro, the offspring of a white person and a quadroon. [< L *octo* eight + (QUAD)ROON]

oc·to·syl·lab·ic (ok′tə-si·lab′ik) *adj.* **1.** Composed of eight syllables, as a line of verse. **2.** Containing lines of eight syllables. — *n.* An octosyllabic line or verse.

oc·to·syl·la·ble (ok′tə-sil′ə-bəl) *n.* **1.** A verse or line composed of eight syllables. **2.** An eight-syllabled word. [< LL *octosyllabus* < L < Gk. *oktasyllabos* < *oktō* eight + *syllabē* a syllable]

oc·troi (ok′troi, *Fr.* ôk·trwä′) *n.* **1.** A tax on certain articles

brought into a city, especially in European cities. **2.** The place or service of collection; also, the collectors of this tax. [< F < *octroyer* to grant < LL *auctorizare* < L *auctor* authority < *augere* to increase]

oc·tu·ple (ok′tōō·pəl, -tyōō-, ok·tōō′pəl, -tyōō′-) *adj.* **1.** Consisting of eight parts or copies. **2.** Multiplied by eight; eightfold. — *v.t.* **·pled, ·pling** To multiply by eight. — *n.* That which is eight times as great as something else. [< L *octuplus* eightfold < *octo* eight] — **oc′tu·ply** *adv.*

oc·tu·pli·cate (ok·tōō′plə·kit, -tyōō′-) *adj.* Eightfold. [< L *octuplicatus*, ult. < *octo* eight + *plic-* stem of *plicare* to fold]

oc·tyl (ok′til) *n. Chem.* The univalent radical $CH_3(CH_2)_7$.

oc·u·lar (ok′yə·lər) *adj.* Of, like, or related to the eye or sight. — *n.* The lens forming the eyepiece of an optical instrument. [< L *ocularis* < *oculus* eye] — **oc′u·lar·ly** *adv.*

oc·u·list (ok′yə·list) *n.* A physician skilled in treating the eye; ophthalmologist. [< MF *oculiste* < L *oculus* eye]

oculo- *combining form* Eye; or pertaining to the eye: *oculomotor*. Also, before vowels, **ocul-**. [< L *oculus* eye]

oc·u·lo·mo·tor (ok′yə·lə·mō′tər) *adj. Anat.* **1.** Causing or connected with movement of the eye: the oculomotor nerve. **2.** Designating either of the two cranial nerves that supply most of the muscles that move the eyeball.

od (od, ōd) *n.* Formerly, a hypothetical force believed to pervade nature and to be the basis of magnetism, chemical action, etc.: also called *odyl*. [< G; coined by Baron Karl von Reichenbach, 1788–1869, German chemist] — **od·ic** (od′ik, ō′dik) *adj.*

Od (od) *n. & interj. Archaic* God: a euphemism used in oaths. Also **Odd.** [Alter. of GOD]

O.D. 1. Doctor of Optometry. **2.** Officer of the Day. **3.** Olive drab: also **OD, o.d. 4.** Outside diameter: also **OD, o.d. 5.** Overdraft; overdrawn.

o·da·lisque (ō′də·lisk) *n.* A female slave or concubine in an Oriental harem. Also **o′da·lisk.** [< F *odalisque* < Turkish *ōdaliq* chambermaid < *ōdah* chamber]

odd (od) *adj.* **1.** Strange or unusual in appearance, behavior, etc.; not normal or ordinary; peculiar; queer. **2.** Not part of what is regular, usual, required, etc.; irregular; occasional; extra: an *odd* job; *odd* moments. **3.** Constituting a member of an incomplete pair, set, etc.: an *odd* slipper; *odd* volumes. **4.** Leaving a remainder when divided by two; not even: Five is an *odd* number; also, characterized by such a number. **5.** Designating an indefinite or inconsiderable amount additional to a specified round number: seventy *odd* dollars. — *n.* **1.** That which is odd. **2.** In golf: **a** One stroke more than that played by one's opponent. **b** *Brit.* An advantage of one stroke given as odds to a player. [< ON *oddi* point, hence, third point of a triangle, hence, odd number. Cf. OE *ordi*, OHG and MHG *ort*.] — **odd′ly** *adv.* — **odd′ness** *n.*

odd·ball (od′bôl′) *U.S. Slang* *n.* An eccentric or nonconforming person. — *adj.* Unusual or unconventional.

Odd Fellow A member of the Independent Order of Odd Fellows, a secret society for the mutual aid and benefit of the members, originated in England in the 18th century.

odd·i·ty (od′ə·tē) *n. pl.* **·ties 1.** One who or that which is odd. **2.** An eccentricity. **3.** The state of being odd.

odd·ment (od′mənt) *n.* **1.** *Usually pl.* A fragment, scrap, or leftover. **2.** *Printing* A part of a book other than the text, as the title page, index, etc. **3.** Something odd.

odd-pin·nate (od′pin′āt) *adj. Bot.* Pinnate with a single leaflet at the end.

odd-toed (od′tōd′) *adj.* Having an odd number of toes on each foot.

odds (odz) *n.pl.* (*sometimes construed as sing.*) **1.** An equalizing allowance or advantage given to a weaker opponent. **2.** The proportion by which one bet differs from that of another: *Odds* are three to two. **3.** The ratio between the probability for and the probability against something being true or happening. **4.** In a contest of any sort, a difference to the advantage of one side: the *odds* in his favor. — **at odds** At variance; disagreeing. — **to give** (or **lay**) **odds** To offer to bet with someone on terms apparently favorable to him. — **to take odds** To agree to a wager on terms apparently favorable to the other person. [< plural of ODD]

odds and ends Miscellaneous things; fragments; scraps.

ode (ōd) *n.* **1.** A rhymed or unrhymed lyric poem, often in the form of an elaborate address and usually characterized by loftiness of tone, feeling, and style. **2.** Formerly, a lyric poem intended to be sung or chanted. See HORATIAN ODE, PINDARIC ODE, PSEUDO-PINDARIC ODE. [< MF < LL *ode* < Gk. *ōidē, aoidē* song < *aeidein* to sing]

-ode[1] *combining form* Way; path: *anode, cathode.* [< Gk. *hodos* way]

-ode[2] *suffix* Like; resembling; having the nature of: *phyllode.* [< Gk. *-ōdēs* < *eidos* form]

O·den·se (ō′thən·sə) A port city in southern Denmark, on Fyn Island; birthplace of Hans Christian Andersen; pop. 103,900 (est. 1969).

O·der (ō′dər) A river in central Europe flowing 563 miles, generally NE, from Czechoslovakia through Germany and Poland to the Baltic; Czech and Polish *Odra.*

O·des·sa (ō·des′ə, *Russ.* o·dyes′sə) **1.** A port city in the southern Ukrainian S.S.R., on the Black Sea; pop. 892,000 (est. 1970). **2.** A city in western Texas; pop. 78,380.

O·dets (ō·dets′), Clifford, 1906–63, U.S. playwright.

o·de·um (ō′dē·əm) *n. pl.* **o·de·a** (ō′dē·ə) **1.** A theater or music hall. **2.** In ancient Greece and Rome, a roofed building for musical performances. Also **o·de·on** (ō′dē·on). [< LL < Gk. *ōideion* < *ōidē*. See ODE.]

O·din (ō′din) In Norse mythology, the supreme deity, god of war, art, culture, and the dead: also spelled *Othin*.

o·di·ous (ō′dē·əs) *adj.* Exciting hate, repugnance, or disgust; offensive; abhorrent. [< OF *odieus* < L *odiosus* < *odium*. See ODIUM.] — **o′di·ous·ly** *adv.* — **o′di·ous·ness** *n.*

o·di·um (ō′dē·əm) *n.* **1.** The state of being odious. **2.** Extreme dislike or aversion; hatred. **3.** The reproach, disgrace, or stigma associated with something hateful; opprobrium: the *odium* of being a convict. [< L, hatred < *odisse* to hate]

O·do·a·cer (ō′dō·ā′sər), 434?–493, Germanic chieftain; deposed the Roman emperor Romulus Augustulus 476. This event is considered the fall of the Western Roman Empire. Also *Odovacar.*

o·do·graph (ō′də·graf, -gräf) *n.* **1.** A device for measuring distance traveled by vehicle or foot; an odometer or pedometer. **2.** An automatic mapmaking device designed to work from a moving vehicle. [< Gk. *hodos* way + -GRAPH]

o·dom·e·ter (ō·dom′ə·tər) *n.* A device for measuring distance traveled by a vehicle. [< Gk. *hodometros* < *hodos* way, road + *metron* a measure] — **o·dom′e·try** *n.*

-odont *combining form* Toothed. [< Gk. *odous, odontos* tooth]

o·don·tal·gi·a (ō′don·tal′jē·ə, -jə) *n. Pathol.* Toothache. [ODONT(O) + Gk. *algos* pain] — **o′don·tal′gic** *adj.*

odonto- *combining form* Tooth; of the teeth: *odontology.* Also, before vowels, **odont-.** [< Gk. *odous, odontos* tooth]

o·don·to·blast (ō·don′tə·blast) *n. Anat.* A tooth cell that produces dentine. — **o·don′to·blas′tic** *adj.*

o·don·to·glos·sum (ō·don′tə·glos′əm) *n.* Any of a large genus (*Odontoglossum*) of tropical American epiphytic orchids with thick, fleshy leaves and large flowers. [< NL < Gk. *odous, odontos* tooth + *glossa* tongue]

o·don·to·graph (ō·don′tə·graf, -gräf) *n.* **1.** *Mech.* An instrument for correctly laying out gear teeth. **2.** *Dent.* A device for showing irregularities on tooth enamel.

o·don·toid (ō·don′toid) *adj.* **1.** Toothlike. **2.** *Anat.* Of or pertaining to a toothlike process extending from the second cervical vertebra and upon which the atlas rotates, found in mammals and birds.

o·don·tol·o·gy (ō′don·tol′ə·jē) *n.* The body of scientific knowledge that relates to the structure, health, and growth of the teeth. — **o·don·to·log′i·cal** (ō·don′tə·loj′i·kəl) *adj.* — **o·don′to·log′i·cal·ly** *adv.* — **o′don·tol′o·gist** *n.*

o·don·to·phore (ō·don′tə·fôr, -fōr) *n. Zool.* A tooth-bearing structure in the mouth of various mollusks, associated with the radula and serving to grind up food materials. [< Gk. *odontophoros* bearing teeth < *odous, odontos* tooth + -*phoros* bearing < *pherein* to bear] — **o·don·toph·o·ral** (ō′don·tof′ər·əl), **o′don·toph′o·rine** (-rīn, -rēn), **o′don·toph′o·rous** *adj.*

o·dor (ō′dər) *n.* **1.** That quality of a substance that renders it perceptible to the sense of smell; smell; scent. **2.** Regard or estimation. **3.** A perfume; incense. — *Syn.* See SMELL. Also *Brit.* **o′dour.** [< OF < L] — **o′dored** *adj*

o·dor·if·er·ous (ō′də·rif′ər·əs) *adj.* Having or giving off an odor, especially a pleasant odor. [< L *odorifer* < *odor* odor + *ferre* to bear] — **o′dor·if′er·ous·ly** *adv.* — **o′dor·if′er·ous·ness** *n.*

o·dor·less (ō′dər·lis) *adj.* Having no odor. — **o′dor·less·ly** *adv.* — **o′dor·less·ness** *n.*

o·dor·ous (ō′dər·əs) *adj.* Having an odor, especially a fragrant odor. [< L *odorus* < *odor* odor] — **o′dor·ous·ly** *adv.* — **o′dor·ous·ness** *n.*

O·do·va·car (ō′dō·vā′kər) See ODOACER.

Od·ra (ôd′rä) The Czech and Polish name for the ODER.

od·yl (od′il, ō′dil) *n.* The od (which see). Also **od′yle.**

-odynia *combining form Med.* Pain; chronic pain in a (specified) part of the body: *osteodynia*. [< Gk. *odynē* pain]

O·dys·seus (ō·dis′yōōs, -ē·əs) In Greek legend, king of Ithaca, one of the Greek leaders in the Trojan War and hero of the *Odyssey*: Latin *Ulysses.*

Od·ys·sey (od′ə·sē) An ancient Greek epic poem attributed to Homer, describing the wanderings of Odysseus during the ten years after the fall of Troy. — *n.* A long, wandering journey: often **od′ys·sey.** — **Od′ys·sey′an** *adj.*

oe- See also words beginning E-.

OE or **Œ** or **O.E.** Old English.

O.E.C.D. Organization for Economic Cooperation and Development.

oec·u·men·i·cal (ek′yōō·men′i·kəl, *Brit.* ē′kyōō·men′i·kəl) See ECUMENICAL.

O.E.D. Oxford English Dictionary.

oe·de·ma (i·dē′mə) See EDEMA.

Oed·i·pus (ed′ə·pəs, ē′də-) In Greek legend, the son of Laius and Jocasta, rulers of Thebes, who was abandoned at birth and reared in the court of Corinth. Returning to Thebes, he unwittingly killed his father, married his mother, and upon learning of his true relationship to her, blinded himself, later dying in exile. [< L < Gk. *Oidipous*, lit., swollen-footed < *oideein* to swell + *pous* foot]

Oedipus complex *Psychoanal.* A strong, typically unconscious attachment of a child to the parent of the opposite sex, especially of a son to his mother, with antagonism toward the other parent. Compare ELECTRA COMPLEX. — **Oed·i·pal** (ed′ə·pəl, ē′də-) *adj.*

OEEC or **O.E.E.C.** Organization for European Economic Cooperation.

Oeh·len·schlä·ger (œ′lən·shlā′gər), Adam Gottlob, 1779–1850, Danish poet and dramatist. Also *Öhlenschläger.*

oeil-de-boeuf (œ′y′də·bœf′) *n. pl.* **oeils-de-boeuf** (œ′y′-) A circular or oval window. [< F, lit., eye of an ox]

oeil·lade (œ·yàd′) *n. French* An amorous look; ogle.

Oe·ne·us (ō′nē·əs) In Greek mythology, the father of Meleager and husband of Althea.

oeno- *combining form* Wine: also spelled *oino-.* [< Gk. *oinos* wine]

oe·nol·o·gy (ē·nol′ə·jē) *n. pl.* **-gies** The science or study of wines and winemaking: also spelled *oinology.* [< Gk. *oinos* wine + LOGY] — **oe′no·log′i·cal** (ē′nə·loj′i·kəl) — **oe·nol′o·gist** *n.*

oe·no·mel (ē′nə·mel, en′ə-) *n.* **1.** In ancient Greece, a beverage of wine and honey. **2.** Anything combining sweetness and strength. Also spelled *oinomel.* [< LL *oenomeli* < Gk. *oinomeli* < *oinos* wine + *meli* honey]

Oe·no·ne (ē·nō′nē) In Greek mythology, a nymph who married Paris, later deserted by him for Helen of Troy.

o′er (ôr, ōr) *prep. & adv. Poetic* Over.

oer·sted (ûr′sted) *n.* The cgs unit of magnetizing force, equal to a force of 1 dyne exerted on a unit magnetic pole. [after Hans C. *Oersted*, 1777–1851, Danish physicist]

oe·soph·a·gus (i·sof′ə·gəs), etc. See ESOPHAGUS, etc.

oes·trin (es′trin, ēs′-) *n.* Estrone. Also **oes′trone** (-trōn).

oes·tri·ol (es′trē·ōl, ēs′-, -ol) See ESTRIOL.

oes·tro·gen (es′trə·jən, ēs′-) See ESTROGEN.

oes·trous (es′trəs, ēs′-), etc. See ESTROUS, etc.

oeu·vre (œ′vr′) *n. pl.* **oeu·vres** (œ′vr′) *French* **1.** A work, as of art or literature. **2.** The totality of works, as of an author.

of (uv, ov; *unstressed* əv) *prep.* **1.** Coming from; originating at or from: Anne *of* Cleves; an actor *of* noble birth. **2.** Associated or connected with; included among: Is he *of* your party? **3.** Located at: the Leaning Tower *of* Pisa. **4.** Away or at a distance from: within six miles *of* home. **5.** Named; specified as: the city *of* Newark; a fall *of* ten feet. **6.** Characterized by: a man *of* strength. **7.** With reference to; as to: quick *of* wit. **8.** About; concerning: Good is said *of* him. **9.** Because of: dying *of* pneumonia. **10.** Possessing: a man *of* means. **11.** Belonging to: the lid *of* a box. **12.** Pertaining to: the majesty *of* the law. **13.** Composed of: a ship *of* steel. **14.** Containing: a glass *of* water. **15.** Taken from; from the number or class of: six *of* the seven conspirators. **16.** So as to be without: relieved *of* anxiety; despoiled *of* ornaments. **17.** Proceeding from; produced by: the plays *of* Shakespeare; the work *of* a vanished hand. **18.** Directed toward: exerted upon: the massacre *of* the innocents; a love *of* opera. **19.** During, on, or at a specified time or occasion: *of* recent years. **20.** Set aside for or devoted to: a program *of* Lieder. **21.** *U.S.* Before; until: used in telling time: ten minutes *of* ten. **22.** *Archaic* By: loved *of* all men. [OE, away from, off. Akin to ON *af*, OHG *aba*. Cf. L *ab* from.]

of- Assimilated var. of OB-.

OF or **OF.** or **O.F.** Old French.

o·fay (ō′fā) *n. U.S. Slang* A white person: a contemptuous term. [?Pig latin for FOE]

of course **1.** In the usual order or procedure; naturally; as expected. **2.** Doubtless; certainly.

off (ôf, of) *adj.* **1.** Farther or more distant; remote: an *off* chance. **2.** In a (specified) circumstance or situation: to be well *off.* **3.** Not in accordance with the facts; wrong: Your reckoning is *off.* **4.** Not usual or normal; not up to standard: an *off* season for roses. **5.** Not in existence; no longer considered active or effective: The deal is *off.* **6.** Away from work; not on duty: He spent his *off* hours at the rink. **7.** In riding or driving, on the right: opposed to *near*: Pass on the *off* side. **8.** *Naut.* Seaward; farther from the coast. **9.** In cricket, toward the side of the field facing the batsman. — *adv.* **1.** To a distance; so as to be away: My horse ran *off.* **2.** To or at a (specified) future time: to put it *off* for a week. **3.** To or at a (specified) distance: to stand five feet *off.* **4.** So as to be no longer in place, connection, etc.: Take *off* your hat. **5.** So as to be no longer functioning, continuing, or in operation: to turn *off* the lights; to break *off* talks. **6.** So as to be away from one's work, duties, etc.: to take the day *off.* **7.** So as to be completed, exhausted, etc.: to kill *off* one's

enemies.   **8.** So as to deviate from or be below what is regarded as standard: His game dropped *off*.   **9.** *Naut.* Away from land, a ship, the wind, etc.: Keep her four points *off*. — **off and on** Now and then; intermittently. — **off with . . .!** Take off! Remove!: *Off with his head!* — **off with you!** Go away! Leave! — **right** (or **straight**) **off** Forthwith; immediately. — **to be off 1.** To leave; depart.   **2.** *Informal* To be insane. — *prep.* **1.** So as to be separated, detached, distant, or removed from (a position, source, etc.): twenty miles *off* course.   **2.** Not engaged in or occupied with; relieved from: *off* duty.   **3.** Extending away or out from; no longer on: *off* Broadway.   **4.** So as to deviate from or be below (what is regarded as standard): to be *off* one's game.   **5.** On or from (the material or substance of): living *off* nuts and berries.   **6.** *Informal* No longer using, engaging in, or advocating: to be *off* drinking.   **7.** *Naut.* Opposite to and seaward of: the battle *off* the eastern cape. — **off of** *Informal* Off; from: He fell *off of* the horse. — *n.* **1.** The state or condition of being off.   **2.** In cricket, the *off* side. Abbr. *o.* [ME, orig. stressed var. of OF. See OF.]
off. **1.** Offered.   **2.** Office.   **3.** Officer.   **4.** Official.
of·fal (ô′fəl) *n.* **1.** The waste parts of a butchered animal.   **2.** Rubbish or refuse of any kind. [ME *ofall* < OFF + FALL] — **Syn. 1.** leavings. **2.** trash, garbage, dross.
off·beat (ôf′bēt′, of′-) *n.* *Music* Any secondary or weak beat in a measure. — *adj.* *U.S. Slang* Out of the ordinary; strange; unconventional; unusual.
off-Broad·way (ôf′brôd′wā) *adj.* **1.** Not situated in the Broadway entertainment district: an *off-Broadway* theater.   **2.** Designating a play that is regarded as experimental, noncommercial, etc. — *n.* Any area in New York City in which off-Broadway plays are produced.
off·cast (ôf′kast′, -käst′, of′-) *adj.* Rejected; castoff. — *n.* Anything thrown away or rejected.
off chance A bare possibility.
off-col·or (ôf′kul′ər, of′-) *adj.* **1.** Unsatisfactory in color.   **2.** Indelicate or indecent; risqué. Also *Brit.* **off′-col′our.**
Of·fen·bach (ôf′ən-bäkh) A city in southern Hesse, West Germany, on the Main; pop. 113,000 (1960). Also **Of′fen·bach-am-Main′** (-äm-mīn′).
Of·fen·bach (ôf′ən-bäk, of′-; *Fr.* ô·fen·bàk′), **Jacques,** 1819–80, French composer born in Germany.
of·fence (ə·fens′) *n.* See OFFENSE.
of·fend (ə·fend′) *v.t.* **1.** To give displeasure or offense to; displease; affront; anger.   **2.** To be disagreeable to (the sense of smell, sight, etc.).   **3.** *Obs.* To transgress or violate. — *v.i.* **4.** To give displeasure or offense; be offensive.   **5.** To commit an offense, crime, or sin; err. [< OF *offendre* strike against, pp. of L *offendere* < *ob-* against + *fendere* to hit] — **of·fend′er** *n.*
— **Syn. 1.** *Offend, insult, affront, exasperate,* and *outrage* mean to deal with so as to arouse hostility, anger, resentment, etc. To *offend* is to cause displeasure, whether intentionally or not; to *insult* is to treat with deliberate contempt, in order to humiliate or mortify. One *affronts* another by belittling him to his face, by discourtesy, or by insolence. To *exasperate* is to annoy or irritate exceedingly. The strongest of these words is *outrage,* which implies the arousal of extreme resentment and indignation in the offended person. Compare IRRITATE, PIQUE[1].
of·fense (ə·fens′; *for defs. 4 & 5, also* ô′fens, of′ens) *n.* **1.** Any violation of a rule, duty, propriety, etc.; a wrong or transgression; especially, a breach of law; a crime.   **2.** The act of offending or causing displeasure.   **3.** That which offends or causes displeasure, resentment, anger, etc.: an *offense* to his ear.   **4.** The act of attacking or assaulting; attack.   **5.** In football, hockey, etc., the team possessing the ball or puck. — **to give offense** To offend or cause anger, resentment, etc. — **to take offense** To be offended; feel angry, hurt, etc. Also, *esp. Brit.,* **offence.** [< OF < L *offensa* a striking against, injury < *offendere.* See OFFEND.]
— **Syn. 1.** *Offense, crime, sin, error, fault,* and *wrong* denote a violation of what is regarded as right or proper. *Offense* is the broadest of these words, embracing any transgression of law, morals, or good manners. More specifically, a *crime* is a violation of common or statute law, such as forgery and arson, while a *sin* is a violation of moral law, such as envy or anger. An *error* is primarily a mistake as to fact or truth; the word stresses a person's ignorance, rather than his deliberation. A *fault* is a trifling or petty *offense;* a *wrong* is an *offense* with regard to the harm or injustice it does. Compare OFFEND.
of·fense·less (ə·fens′lis) *adj.* **1.** Not giving offense; harmless.   **2.** Incapable of offense or attack.
of·fen·sive (ə·fen′siv) *adj.* **1.** Unpleasant or disagreeable to the senses; obnoxious; disgusting: an *offensive* sight.   **2.** Causing anger, resentment, etc.; giving offense; insulting.   **3.** Of, pertaining to, or characterized by attack: distinguished from *defensive.* — *n.* The movement, attitude, or position of offense or attack: to launch an *offensive.* [< MF *offensif,* fem. *offensive* < L *offensus,* pp. of *offendere.* See OFFEND.] — **of·fen′sive·ly** *adv.* — **of·fen′sive·ness** *n.*
of·fer (ô′fər, of′ər) *v.t.* **1.** To present for acceptance or rejection; tender; proffer.   **2.** To suggest for consideration or action; propose.   **3.** To present with solemnity or in worship; make an offering of: often with *up.*   **4.** To show readi-

ness to do or attempt; propose or threaten: to *offer* battle.   **5.** To attempt to do or inflict; also, to do or inflict.   **6.** To suggest as payment; bid.   **7.** To present for sale. — *v.i.* **8.** To present itself; appear.   **9.** To make an offering in worship or sacrifice. — *n.* **1.** The act of offering.   **2.** That which is offered, as a bid, suggestion, etc. [OE *offrian* to offer, esp. a sacrifice, ult. < L *offerre* to present < *ob-* before + *ferre* to bring] — **of′fer·er** or **of′fer·or** *n.*
of·fer·ing (ô′fər·ing, of′ər-) *n.* **1.** The act of making an offer.   **2.** That which is offered, as a sacrifice or gift.   **3.** A contribution, as at a religious service.
of·fer·to·ry (ô′fər·tôr′ē, -tō′rē, of′ər-) *n. pl. ·ries Eccl.* **1.** *Usually cap.* A section of the eucharistic liturgy, usually following the saying of the creed, during which the bread and wine to be consecrated are offered, and the alms of the congregation are collected.   **2.** Any collection taken during a religious service; also, the part of a service when it is taken.   **3.** An antiphon, hymn, or anthem sung during this service.   **4.** A prayer of oblation said by the celebrant over the bread and wine to be consecrated. [< Med.L *offertorium* < LL, place of offerings < L *offertus,* pp. of *offerre.* See OFFER.]
off·hand (ôf′hand′, of′-) *adv.* Without preparation; unceremoniously; extempore. Also **off′hand′ed·ly.** — *adj.* **1.** Done, said, or made offhand   **2.** Casual; informal; curt. Also **off′hand′ed.** — **Syn.** See EXTEMPORANEOUS.
of·fice (ô′fis, of′is) *n.* **1.** A place in which the business of an individual, corporation, government bureau, etc., is carried out: a doctor's *office;* the post *office;* also, the staff and administrative officials working in such a place.   **2.** *Usually cap.* **a** *U.S.* An executive branch of the federal government ranking below the departments: the Patent *Office.* **b** *Brit.* A similar branch of the national government, often headed by a cabinet member.   **3.** Any post or position held by a person; especially, a position of authority or trust in the government, a corporation, etc.   **4.** The duty, charge, or trust of a person.   **5.** Any act done or intended to be done for another; a service; favor: through his kind *offices.*   **6.** *Eccl.* A prescribed religious or devotional service, as: **a** The canonical hours. **b** The Morning or Evening Prayer.   **7.** Any ceremony or rite, especially, a rite for the dead.   **8.** *pl. Brit.* The buildings or rooms of a house or estate in which domestic or farm duties are carried out. Abbr. *off.* [< OF < L *officium* service, prob. < *opus* work + *facere* to do, make]
office boy A boy hired by an office for errands, odd jobs, etc.
of·fice·hold·er (ô′fis·hōl′dər, of′-) *n.* One who holds an office under a government.
office hours 1. The number of hours one works in an office.   **2.** The hours an office is open for business.
of·fi·cer (ô′fə·sər, of′ə-) *n.* **1.** In the armed forces, one appointed to a certain rank and authority; especially, one holding a commission.   **2.** One who holds an office or post; especially, one elected or appointed to a position of authority or trust in a corporation, government, institution, etc.   **3.** On a merchant or passenger ship, the captain or any of the mates.   **4.** One who enforces the law, as a policeman, constable, etc.   **5.** In some honorary societies, a rank above the lowest. Abbr. *off.* — **Syn.** See OFFICIAL. — *v.t.* **1.** To furnish with officers.   **2.** To command; direct; manage. [< OF *officier* < Med.L *officarius* < L *officium.* See OFFICE.]
officer of the day At a military installation, the officer who on a given day is responsible for the performance of the guard, maintenance of order or security, etc. Abbr. *O.D.*
officer of the guard The officer responsible to the officer of the day for the performance of guard duty. Abbr. *O.G.*
of·fi·cial (ə·fish′əl, ō-) *adj.* **1.** Of or relating to an office or position of authority: his last *official* act.   **2.** Supported by or derived from authority; duly sanctioned; authorized; authoritative.   **3.** Authorized to carry out some special duty: the *official* timekeeper.   **4.** Having regard for or exhibiting social form, propriety, etc.; formal: *official* banquets. — *n.* One who holds an office or position; especially, one who is authorized to act for a corporation, government agency, etc., in a subordinate capacity. Abbr. *off.* [< OF < LL *officialis* < L *officium.* See OFFICE.] — **of·fi′cial·ly** *adv.*
— **Syn.** (noun) *Official* and *officer* denote one holding an office. *Official* usually refers to one or another branch of service, and *officer,* to a particular post; we speak of the *officials* of the postal service generally, or of the local chief *officer* of that service, the local postmaster. In usage, *official* is chiefly applied to members of the governmental civil service and of special groups (as security guards) in private corporations. *Officer* is chiefly applied to members of the armed forces, of the police and other paramilitary groups, and to the directing managers of private corporations.
of·fi·cial·dom (ə·fish′əl·dəm, ō-) *n.* **1.** Officials collectively or as a class.   **2.** Behavior characteristic of officials, as rigid adherence to form, routine, etc.   **3.** Officialism.
of·fi·cial·ism (ə·fish′əl·iz′əm, ō-) *n.* The condition, system, or attitude of officials; especially, rigid adherence to official forms, routines, etc.
of·fi·ci·ant (ə·fish′ē·ənt) *n.* One who conducts or officiates at a religious service, office, or ceremony; celebrant. [< Med.L *officians, -antis,* ppr. of *officiare.* See OFFICIATE.]
of·fi·ci·ar·y (ə·fish′ē·er′ē, ō-) *n. pl. ·ar·ies* A body of officials. — *adj.* Pertaining to or holding an office.

of·fi·ci·ate (ə·fish′ē·āt, ō-) *v.i.* **·at·ed, ·at·ing** **1.** To act or serve as a priest or minister; conduct a service. **2.** To perform the duties or functions of an office or position. **3.** In sports, to act as a referee, umpire, etc. [< Med.L *officiatus*, pp. of *officiare* to perform one's duty < L *officium*. See OFFICE.] — **of·fi′ci·a′tion** *n.* — **of·fi′ci·a′tor** *n.*

of·fic·i·nal (ə·fis′ə·nəl) *adj.* **1.** Prepared and kept in stock, as drug preparations. **2.** Available without prescription, as a medicine. — *n.* Any drug or medicine kept ready for sale. [< Med.L *officinalis* < L *officina* workshop, contr. of *opificina* < *opifex* workman < *opus* work + *facere* to do]

of·fi·cious (ə·fish′əs, ō-) *adj.* **1.** Unduly forward in offering one's services or advice; obtrusive. **2.** *Obs.* Disposed to serve or oblige. [< L *officiosus* obliging < *officium*. See OFFICE.] — **of·fi′cious·ly** *adv.* — **of·fi′cious·ness** *n.*

— **Syn. 1.** meddling, nosy, intrusive.

off·ing (ôf′ing, of′ing) *n.* **1.** That part of the visible sea offshore but beyond anchorage. **2.** A position some distance offshore. — **in the offing 1.** In sight and not very distant. **2.** Ready or soon to happen, arrive, etc.

off·ish (ô′fish, of′ish) *adj.* Inclined to be distant in manner; aloof. — **off′ish·ly** *adv.* — **off′ish·ness** *n.*

off·print (ôf′print′, of′-) *v.t.* To reprint (an excerpt). — *n.* A reproduction of an article or the like formerly printed in some larger publication.

off·scour·ing (ôf′skour′ing, of′-) *n.* **1.** *Usually pl.* That which is scoured off; also, rubbish; trash; garbage. **2.** A social outcast; wretch.

off·set (*n.* ôf′set′, of′-; *v.* ôf′set′, of′-) *n.* **1.** That which balances or compensates for something else; counterbalance; setoff. **2.** That which derives, develops, or springs from something else; as: **a** *Bot.* A short lateral offshoot, serving to propagate a plant. **b** *Geol.* A spur from a range of mountains or hills. **c** *Archit.* A ledge along a wall formed by a reduction in thickness above; a setoff. **d** A descendant of a family or race; offshoot; scion. **3.** *Printing* **a** Offset printing (which see). **b** An impression made by offset printing. **c** An ink smear on a surface that is in contact with a freshly printed sheet. **4.** In surveying, a short distance measured from the main line, used to help determine the area of an irregular plot. **5.** A bend or curve made in a pipe, rod, etc., to allow it to pass an obstacle. — *adj.* Pertaining to or produced by offset printing. — *v.* **·set, ·set·ting** *v.t.* **1.** To balance or compensate for; counterbalance: to *offset* a defeat. **2.** *Printing* **a** To reproduce by offset printing. **b** To transfer (an impression) by offset printing. **c** To smudge or mark with an offset. **3.** *Archit.* To make an offset in. — *v.i.* **4.** *Printing* To make an offset. **5.** To branch off or project as an offset.

offset printing A method of printing in which the inked impression from a lithographic plate is transferred to a rubber-coated cylinder, and then onto the paper.

off·shoot (ôf′shōōt′, of′-) *n.* **1.** *Bot.* A lateral shoot or branch from the main stem of a plant. **2.** Anything that derives or branches off from a principal source, stock, etc.

off·shore (ôf′shōr′, -shôr′, of′-) *adj.* **1.** Moving or directed away from the shore: an *offshore* breeze. **2.** Situated or occurring at some distance from the shore. — *adv.* **1.** At a distance from the shore. **2.** From or away from the shore.

off·side (ôf′sīd′, of′-) *adj.* **1.** In football, in front of the ball before it is put into play: said of a player, team, or play. **2.** In ice hockey, in the attacking zone ahead of the puck: said of a player, team, or play. Also **off side.**

off·spring (ôf′spring′, of′-) *n.* *pl.* **·spring** or **·springs 1.** The progeny or issue of a person, animal, or plant; descendant. **2.** Any result or product: the *offspring* of his mind.

off·stage (ôf′stāj′, of′-) *n.* The area behind or to the side of a stage, out of the view of the audience. — *adj.* In or from this area: *off-stage* dialogue. — *adv.* To this area: He went *off-stage.*

off-white (ôf′hwīt′, of′-) *n.* Oyster white (which see).

O'Fla·her·ty (ō-fla′hər·tē), **Liam,** born 1896, Irish novelist and short-story writer.

O.F.S. Orange Free State.

oft (ôft, oft) *adv.* Often: archaic or poetic except in certain combinations, as **oft-repeated, oft-recurring,** etc. [OE]

of·ten (ôf′ən, of′-) *adv.* Frequently or repeatedly; many times. — *adj. Obs.* Repeated; frequently occurring. [Var. of ME *ofte,* OE *oft.* Cf. OHG *ofto,* ON *opt.*]

of·ten·times (ôf′ən·tīmz′, of′-) *adv. Archaic* Frequently; often. Also **oft·times** (ôft′tīmz′, of′-).

Og (og) The king of Bashan; conquered by the Israelites. *Josh.* xii 4.

O.G. 1. Officer of the Guard. **2.** Original gum (philately): also **o.g.**

O·ga·sa·wa·ra Ji·ma (ō-gä·sä·wä·rä jē·mä) The Japanese name for the BONIN ISLANDS.

Og·den (og′dən) A city in northern Utah; pop. 69,478.

Og·den (og′dən), **C(harles) K(ay).** 1889–1957, English psychologist, educator, and semanticist.

og·do·ad (og′dō·ad) *n.* **1.** The number eight. **2.** Any group or set of eight. [< Gk. *ogdoas, -ados* < *oktō* eight]

o·gee (ō′jē, ō·jē′) *n. Archit.* **1.** A molding having in profile a long S-curve. For illustration see MOLDING. **2.** Any S-shaped curve used in a construction. **3.** An arch having two S-shaped curves meeting at the apex: also **ogee arch.** [Appar. alter. of OF *ogive.* See OGIVE.]

O·gil·vie (ō′gəl·vē), **John,** 1797–1867, Scottish lexicographer.

o·give (ō′jīv, ō·jīv′) *n.* **1.** *Archit.* **a** A diagonal rib of a vaulted arch or bay. **b** A pointed arch. **2.** *Stat.* A frequency curve any of whose ordinates expresses a percentage or number of observations less than or more than the corresponding abscissa. **3.** The head of a projectile. [< OF *ogive, augive,* origin uncertain; perh. < OF *auge* trough or ? < Sp. *algibe* vaulted cistern < Arabic *al* the + *g'ubb* well]

OGIVES
a Equilateral. *b* Dropped. *c* Lancet. *d* Moorish.

o·gle (ō′gəl, og′əl) *v.* **o·gled, o·gling** *v.t.* **1.** To look at with admiring or impertinent glances. **2.** To stare at; eye. — *v.i.* **3.** To look or stare in an admiring or impertinent manner. — *n.* An amorous or coquettish look. [< LG *oegeln,* freq. of *oegen* to look at < *oege* eye] — **o′gler** *n.*

O·gle·thorpe (ō′gəl·thôrp), **James Edward,** 1696–1785, English general and colonial administrator in America; founded the colony of Georgia.

OGPU (og′pōō) *n.* A former name of the MVD: also called *Gay-Pay-Oo.* [< Russian *O(b′yedinennoye) G(osudarstven-noye) P(oliticheskoye) U(pravleniye)* Unified Government Political Administration]

o·gre (ō′gər) *n.* **1.** In fairy tales, a man-eating giant or monster. **2.** One who is brutal, hideous, or feared. [< F; prob. coined by Perrault] — **o·gre·ish** (ō′gər·ish), **o·grish** (ō′grish) *adj.* — **o′gress** (-grəs) *n.fem.*

O·gyg·i·a (ō·jij′ē·ə) In the *Odyssey,* Calypso's island.

oh (ō) *interj.* An exclamation expressing surprise, sudden emotion, etc. — *n.* The interjection *oh.* ♦ See O (interj.).

O'Ha·ra (ō·hâr′ə), **John,** 1905–1970, U.S. novelist.

O. Hen·ry (ō hen′rē) Pseudonym of *William Sydney Porter,* 1862–1910, U.S. short-story writer.

OHG or **OHG.** or **O.H.G.** Old High German.

O'Hig·gins (ō·hig′ənz, *Sp.* ō·ē′gēns), **Bernardo,** 1778–1842, Chilean general and statesman; first ruler of an independent Chile 1817–23: called the **Liberator of Chile.**

O·hi·o (ō·hī′ō) A north central State of the United States, on Lake Erie; 41,222 sq. mi.; pop. 10,652,017; capital, Columbus; entered the Union March 1, 1803; nickname, *Buckeye State.* — **O·hi′o·an** *adj. & n.*

Ohio River A river in the east central United States, flowing 981 miles, generally SW, from the junction of the Allegheny and Monongahela rivers to the Mississippi.

Oh·len·schlä·ger (œ′lən·shlā′gər), **Adam Gottlob.** See OEHLENSCHLÄGER.

ohm (ōm) *n.* The unit of electrical resistance, equal to the resistance of a conductor carrying a current of one ampere at a potential difference of one volt between the terminals. Abbr. *o* — **International ohm** The resistance at 0° C. of a uniform column of mercury having a mass of 14.4521 grams and a length of 106.3 centimeters. [after G. S. *Ohm*] — **ohm′ic** *adj.*

Ohm (ōm), **Georg Simon,** 1787–1854, German physicist.

ohm·age (ō′mij) *n.* Electrical resistance of a conductor, expressed in ohms.

ohm·me·ter (ōm′mē′tər) *n.* A galvanometer for measuring the resistance in ohms.

O.H.M.S. On His (or Her) Majesty's Service.

o·ho (ō·hō′) *interj.* An exclamation expressing astonishment, exultation, etc.

O·hře (ō′hr′zhe) The Czech name for the EGER.

O.C. Officer in Charge.

-oid *suffix* Like; resembling; having the form of: *ovoid, hydroid.* [< NL *-oides* < Gk. *-oeidēs* < *eidos* form]

-oidea *combining form Zool.* Used to form the names of classes or superfamilies: *Asteroidea.* [< NL < -OID]

oil (oil) *n.* **1.** A greasy or unctuous, sometimes combustible liquid of vegetable, animal, or mineral origin, used in alcohol and ether, but not in water, variously used as food for lubricating, illuminating, and fuel, and in the manufacture of soap, candles, cosmetics, perfumery, etc. **2.** Petroleum. **3.** An oil color (which see); also, an oil painting

4. Anything of an oily consistency. — *v.t.* **1.** To smear, lubricate, or supply with oil. **2.** To bribe; flatter. — *adj.* **1.** Of, pertaining to, or resembling oil. **2.** Using, obtained from, or yielding oil: an *oil* burner. [< OF *oile* < L *oleum*, prob. < Gk. *elaion* olive oil]

Oil may appear as a combining form or as the first element in two-word phrases, as in:

oil-bearing	oil-fueled	oil refiner
oil box	oil gauge	oil-refining
oil-bright	oil gas	oil-regulating
oil-burning	oil groove	oil-rich
oilcamp	oil-harden	oil-saving
oil-carrying	oil-hardened	oil seal
oil-containing	oil-hardening	oilsk nned
oil crane	oil heater	oil-secreting
oil cup	oilhole	oil-smelling
oil derrick	oil industry	oil-soaked
oil-dispensing	oil-insulated	oil-stained
oil distiller	oil-laden	oil stove
oil-distributing	oil-ladened	oil tanker
oil drill	oil land	oil tar
oil driven	oil-lit	oil-tempered
oil engine	oilmonger	oil-testing
oil-fed	oil press	oil-thickening
oil-filled	oil-producer	oiltight
oil-finding	oil-producing	oiltightness
oil-finished	oilproof	oil tube
oil-fired	oilproofing	oilway
oil-forming	oil-pumping	oil-yielding

oil·bird (oil′bûrd′) *n.* The guacharo.

oil burner **1.** A furnace or heating unit that operates on oil fuel. **2.** An atomizer for spraying oil into such a furnace.

oil cake The mass of compressed seeds of cotton, flax, etc., or coconut pulp from which oil has been expressed, used as food (**oil meal**) for livestock, etc.

oil·can (oil′kan′) *n.* A can with a spout for lubricating machinery.

oil·cloth (oil′klôth′, -kloth′) *n.* A cotton fabric waterproofed with oils and pigments, used as a covering for tables, shelves, etc.

oil color A color or paint made of pigment ground in linseed or other oil, used chiefly by artists.

oil·er (oi′lər) *n.* **1.** One who or that which oils; especially, one who oils engines or machinery. **2.** Any automatic device for oiling machinery. **3.** An oilcan. **4.** A coat of oilskin. **5.** An oil tanker.

oil field An oil-producing area.

oil gland **1.** *Bot.* An oil-secreting gland, as in some plants. **2.** *Ornithol.* The uropygial gland (which see).

oil of vitriol Sulfuric acid.

oil painting **1.** A painting done in pigments mixed in oil. **2.** The art of painting in oils.

oil·paper (oil′pā′pər) *n.* Paper treated with oil for transparency and resistance against moisture and dryness.

Oil Rivers The Niger delta, Nigeria; governed by Britain as the **Oil Rivers Protectorate**, 1890–93.

oil shale A compact brown or black sedimentary shale impregnated with petroleum in varying proportions.

oil·skin (oil′skin′) *n.* Cloth made waterproof with oil, or a garment of such material.

oil slick A smooth area on water caused by a film of oil.

oil·stone (oil′stōn′) *n.* A smooth whetstone moistened with oil.

oil well A well that is dug or drilled to obtain petroleum.

oil·y (oi′lē) *adj.* **oil·i·er, oil·i·est** **1.** Of, pertaining to, or containing oil. **2.** Coated, smeared, or soaked with oil; greasy. **3.** Smooth or suave in behavior, speech, etc.; unctuous. — **oil′i·ly** *adv.* — **oil′i·ness** *n.*

oi·nol·o·gy (oi·nol′ə·jē) See OENOLOGY.

oi·no·mel (oi′nə·mel) See OENOMEL.

oint·ment (oint′mənt) *n.* A fatty or unctuous preparation applied to the skin as a medicine or cosmetic; unguent; salve. [< OF *oignement*, ult. < L *unguentum* < *ungere* to anoint; infl. by obs. *oint* to anoint]

Oir·each·tas (er′əkh·thəs) *n.pl.* The legislature of Ireland, consisting of the Dail Eireann (the representative assembly) and the Seanaid Eireann (the senate). [< Irish]

OIrish Old Irish.

Oise (wäz) A river of Belgium and NE France, flowing 186 miles, generally SW, to the Seine.

OIT Office of International Trade.

O·jib·wa (ō·jib′wä, -wə) *n.* *pl.* **·wa** or **·was** **1.** One of a tribe of North American Indians of Algonquian stock, formerly inhabiting the regions around Lake Superior. **2.** The Algonquian language of this tribe. Also called **Chippewa**: also **O·jib′way.** [< Algonquian (Ojibwa) *Ojibway* roast till puckered < *ojib* to pucker + *ub-way* to roast; with ref. to their puckered moccasin seams]

OK (*interj., adj., adv. & n.* ō′kā′; *v.* ō·kā′) *interj., adj., & adv.* All correct; all right: used to express approval, agreement, etc. — *v.t.* To approve, endorse, or agree to; especially, to sign with an *OK.* — *n.* Approval; agreement; endorsement: to give one's *OK*: also spelled *O.K.*, **o′kay′.** [Origin unknown. Perhaps < *o*(ll) *k*(*orrect*), humorous misspelling of "all correct," reinforced by *O*(ld) *K*(*inderhook*) in the

name of a political club (1840) supporting Martin Van Buren of Kinderhook, N.Y.]

o·ka (ō′kə) *n.* In Turkey, Egypt, Bulgaria, etc., a weight equal to about 2¾ pounds or a unit of capacity equal to about 1½ quarts. Also **oke** (ōk). [< Ital. *oca, occa* < Turkish *ogah* < Arabic *uqivah*, appar. < Gk. *oungia, ounkia* ounce]

O·ka (ō·kä′) A river in the western R.S.F.S.R., flowing 918 miles east to the Volga.

o·ka·pi (ō·kä′pē) *n.* An African ruminant (*Okapia johnstoni*) related to the giraffe, but with a smaller body and a shorter neck. [< native African name]

OKAPI

(About 5 feet high at shoulder)

O·ka·ya·ma (ō·kä·yä·mä) A port city on SW Honshu island, Japan; pop. 322,000 (est. 1968).

O·kee·cho·bee (ō′kē·chō′bē), **Lake** A lake in south central Florida; about 730 sq. mi.

Okeechobee Waterway See CROSS-FLORIDA WATERWAY.

O'Keeffe (ō·kēf′), **Georgia,** born 1887, U.S. painter.

O·ke·fi·no·kee Swamp (ō′kə·fə·nō′kē) A swamp in NE Florida and SE Georgia; about 700 sq. mi. Also **O·kee·fe·no·kee** (ō′kē·fə·nō′kē).

o·keh (ō′kā′) See OK.

O'Kel·ly (ō·kel′ē), **Seán Thomas,** 1882–1966, Irish political leader; president 1945–59.

O·ken (ō′kən), **Lorenz,** 1779–1851, German naturalist and philosopher: original name **Lorenz Ock·en·fuss** (ōk′ən·fōōs).

O·khotsk (ō·kotsk′), **Sea of** An inlet of the Pacific west of Kamchatka and the Kurile Islands. *Russian* **O·khot·sko·ye Mo·re** (o·khôt′ska·ya mô′rya).

O·kie (ō′kē) *n.* *U.S. Slang* **1.** An inhabitant of Oklahoma **2.** A migrant farmworker; originally, one from Oklahoma forced during the Depression to leave his land or to seek work elsewhere. [Dim. of *Oklahoman*]

O·ki·na·wa (ō′ki·nä′wä) The largest of the Ryukyu Islands, Japan; captured by U.S. forces, 1945; returned to Japan, 1972; 467 sq. mi.; pop. 758,777 (1965). — **O′ki·na′·wan** *adj. & n.*

Okla. Oklahoma.

O·kla·ho·ma (ō′klə·hō′mə) A State in the south central United States; 69,919 sq. mi.; pop. 2,559,253; capital, Oklahoma City; entered the Union Nov. 16, 1907; nickname, *Sooner State.* — **O′kla·ho′man** *adj. & n.*

Oklahoma City The capital of Oklahoma, in the central part, on the North Canadian River; pop. 368,856.

o·kra (ō′krə) *n.* **1.** A tall annual herb (*Hibiscus* or *Abelmoschus esculentus*) of the mallow family. **2.** Its green mucilaginous pods, used in soups and stews, or as a vegetable. **3.** Gumbo. [< West African]

-ol¹ *suffix Chem.* Denoting an alcohol or phenol: *methanol, glycerol.* [< (ALCOH)OL]

-ol² *suffix Chem.* Var. of -OLE¹, as in *benzol.*

O·laf I (ō′ləf), 969?–1000, king of Norway 995–1000; hero of Norse legend: called **Olaf Tryg·ves·son** (trüg′və·sun).

Olaf II, Saint, 995?–1030, king of Norway 1015–28, patron of Norway: called **Olaf the Fat.**

Olaf V, born 1903, king of Norway 1957–; born in England: full name **Alexander Edward Christian Frederik of Glücksburg.** Also **O·lav** (ō′läv, ō′läf).

Ö·land (œ′länd) An island of SE Sweden, in the Baltic Sea; 519 sq. mi.

old (ōld) *adj.* **old·er** or **eld·er, old·est** or **eld·est** **1.** Living, existing, made, known, etc., for a relatively long time. **2.** Exhibiting the characteristics of advanced life or an aged person. **3.** Having a specified age or duration: a child two months *old.* **4.** Worn with age or repeated use; dilapidated: worn out; shabby: an *old* suit of clothes. **5.** Familiar through long acquaintance or use: an *old* friend. **6.** Skilled, able, or cunning through long experience or practice: an *old* hand at politics. **7.** Belonging to or associated with a former or previous period, especially a relatively remote or distant period in history; ancient: *old* writings; *old* superstitions. **8.** *Usually cap.* Denoting the earlier or earliest of two or more things, periods, developments, etc.; *Old* English; the *Old* Testament. **9.** *Informal* Good; cherished; dear: a general term of affection or endearment: *old* buddy of mine. **10.** *Informal* Plentiful; great; wonderful: used to express intense pleasure, excess, etc.: a grand *old* time. **11.** *Geog.* In a late stage of a cycle of development: said of topographic features, streams, etc. — *n.* Past time: days of *old.* *Abbr.* o., O, O. [OE *ald*] — **old′ness** *n.*

— **Syn.** (adj.) **1.** *Old, aged,* and *elderly* are compared as applied to persons. *Old* and *aged* mean having lived a long time, but *old* more often suggests feebleness or senility than *aged.* An *elderly* man has passed middle age, but is generally regarded as younger than an *old* man, both in years and in vigor. — **Ant.** young, youthful, new.

Old Bailey The central criminal court of London.

Old·bridge (ōld′brij) A village in NE County Meath, Ireland; scene of the Battle of the Boyne, 1690.

Old Castile A region of central Spain.

Old·cas·tle (ōld′kas·əl, -käs·əl), **Sir John** See COBHAM.
Old Church Slavic or **Slavonic** See under SLAVIC.
old country The native country of an immigrant, especially a European country.
Old Delhi See DELHI.
Old Dominion Nickname of VIRGINIA.
old·en (ōl′dən) adj. Archaic & Poetic Old; ancient.
Old·en·burg (ōl′dən·bûrg, Ger. ōl′dən-bo͝orkh) 1. A former state of NW Germany, included after 1945 in Lower Saxony. 2. Its former capital; pop. 121,800 (est. 1960).
Old English 1. See under ENGLISH. 2. Printing Black letter.
old-fan·gled (ōld′fang′gəld) adj. Having a fondness for what is old-fashioned. [On analogy with NEWFANGLED]
old-fash·ioned (ōld′fash′ənd) adj. 1. Antiquated or obsolete in method, style, function, etc.; out-of-date. 2. Of, pertaining to, or characteristic of former times: old-fashioned notions. 3. Attached to or favoring old customs, ways, etc.: an old-fashioned wife. — Syn. See ANTIQUE.
old fashioned A cocktail made with whisky, sugar, bitters, and fruit.
old fo·gy (fō′gē) One who is extremely conservative or old-fashioned in his ideas, tastes, etc. Also **old fo′gey.**
old-fo·gy·ish (ōld′fō′gē·ish) adj. Of, pertaining to, or like an old fogy. Also **old′-fo′gey·ish.**
Old French See under FRENCH.
Old Glory The flag of the United States.
old guard The conservative element in a community, political party, etc.
Old Guard The imperial guard formed by Napoleon I in 1804, composed of veterans of three campaigns. [Trans. of F Vieille Garde; so called in contrast with Jeune Garde Young Guard, formed 1810]
Old·ham (ōl′dəm) A county borough in Greater Manchester, England; pop. 224,700 (1976).
old hat U.S. Slang Out of style; old-fashioned; obsolete.
Old Hickory Nickname of Andrew Jackson.
Old High German See under GERMAN.
Old Icelandic See under ICELANDIC.
Old Irish See under IRISH.
Old Ironsides The U.S. frigate Constitution.
old·ish (ōl′dish) adj. Somewhat old.
old lady Slang 1. One's mother. 2. One's wife.
Old Latin See under LATIN.
old-line (ōld′līn′) adj. 1. Traditional or conservative in action or thought. 2. Long-established; traditional.
Old Line State Nickname of MARYLAND.
old maid 1. A spinster. 2. Informal One who is prim, prudish, fastidious, etc. 3. A simple game involving the matching of pairs of cards.
old man Slang 1. One's father. 2. One's husband. 3. Any man in a position of authority, as an employer. 4. An affectionate term of address: Old Man River.
old master Any of the famous painters who lived between the 13th and 16th centuries, especially in Italy and the Low Countries; also, any of their paintings.
Old Nick The devil.
Old Norse See under NORSE.
Old Northwest See NORTHWEST TERRITORY.
Old Orchard Beach A summer resort town on the coast of SE Maine; pop. 4,310.
Old Pretender See (James Edward) STUART.
Old Prussian See under PRUSSIAN.
old rose Any of various shades of grayish or purplish red.
Old Sar·um (sâr′əm) An ancient ruined city in SE Wiltshire, England.
Old Saxon See under SAXON.
Old Scandinavian Old Norse. See under NORSE.
Old Slavic See under SLAVIC.
old sledge Seven-up, a card game.
Old South The South before the Civil War.
old squaw A sea duck (Clangula hyemalis) of the northern hemisphere: also called oldwife.
old·ster (ōld′stər) n. Informal An old or elderly person.
Old Stone Age The Paleolithic period of human culture.
old-style (ōld′stīl′) adj. Of a former or old-fashioned style.
old style Printing A style of type first used in the 18th century, the stems and the serifs being of nearly the same thickness. Compare MODERN.
Old Style See (Gregorian) CALENDAR.
Old Style figures Printing Hanging figures (which see).
Old Test. Old Testament.
Old Testament The first of the two main divisions of the Bible, divided into the Pentateuch, the Prophets, and the Hagiographa.
old-time (ōld′tīm′) adj. 1. Of or characteristic of a former time. 2. Of long standing; long-established.
old-tim·er (ōld′tī′mər) n. Informal 1. One who has been a member, resident, etc., for a long time. 2. An old-fashioned person.

Ol·du·vai Gorge (ōl′do͞o·vī′, ōl′do͝o·vī′) A gorge about 100 mi. southeast of Lake Victoria in Tanzania, noted as the site of many fossils of extinct mammals, including Zinjanthropus, believed to be a forerunner of early man.
old-wife (ōld′wīf′) n. 1. Any of several fishes found in West Indian waters, as the parrot fish, spot, alewife, menhaden, etc. 2. The old squaw (which see).
old wives' tale A story, anecdote, superstitious belief, etc., handed down from one generation to another.
old-wom·an·ish (ōld′wo͝om′ən·ish) adj. Characteristic of or suitable for an old woman; fussy.
old-world (ōld′wûrld′) adj. 1. Of or pertaining to the Old World or Eastern Hemisphere. 2. Ancient; antique.
Old World The Eastern Hemisphere, including Europe, Asia and Africa; especially, Europe.
-ole[1] suffix Chem. 1. Denoting a heterocyclic compound having a five-membered ring and one or more hetero atoms: pyrrole. 2. Denoting certain aldehydes and ethers: anisole. Also spelled **-ol.** [< L oleum oil]
-ole[2] suffix Small; little: nucleole. [< L -olus, dim. suffix]
o·le·a·ceous (ō′lē·ā′shəs) adj. Bot. Pertaining or belonging to the olive family (Oleaceae) of plants and including the lilac, jasmine, and ash. [< NL oleaceae < L olea olive tree]
o·le·ag·i·nous (ō′lē·aj′ə·nəs) adj. Of or pertaining to oil; oily. [< F oléagineux < L oleaginus pertaining to the olive tree < olea olive tree] — **o′le·ag′i·nous·ly** adv. — **o′le·ag′i·nous·ness** n.
o·le·an·der (ō′lē·an′dər) n. An Old World, evergreen, shrub (Nerium oleander) of the dogbane family, having leaves that yield a poisonous glycoside and clusters of fragrant rose or white flowers. [< Med.L oleander < LL lorandrum, ? alter. of L rhododendron. See RHODODENDRON.]
o·le·as·ter (ō′lē·as′tər) n. A shrub or small tree (Elaeagnus angustifolia) of western Asia and southern Europe, having fragrant, yellow flowers: also called wild olive. [< L < olea olive tree]
o·le·ate (ō′lē·āt) n. Chem. A salt or ester of oleic acid.
o·lec·ra·non (ō·lek′rə·non, ō′lə·krā′non) n. Anat. The curved process of the ulnar bone, marking its juncture with the elbow. [< Gk. ōlekranon, contr. of ōlenokranon < ōlenē elbow + kranion head] — **o·lec′ra·nal** adj.
o·le·fin (ō′lə·fin) n. Chem. An alkene. [< OLEF(IANT) + -IN] — **o′le·fin′ic** adj.
o·le·ic (ō·lē′ik, ō′lē-) adj. Of, pertaining to, or derived from oil. [< L oleum oil + -IC]
oleic acid Chem. An oily compound, $C_{17}H_{33}COOH$, contained as an ester in most mixed oils and fats.
o·le·in (ō′lē·in) n. Chem. A colorless liquid glyceride of oleic acid, the chief constituent of fatty oils: also called elain. Also **o·le·ine** (ō′lē·in, ō′li·ēn). [< F oleine < L oleum oil]
o·le·o (ō′lē·ō) Short for OLEOMARGARINE.
oleo- combining form 1. Oil; of oil: oleoresin. 2. Olein; oleic: oleomargarine. [< L oleum oil]
o·le·o·graph (ō′lē·ə·graf′, -gräf′) n. 1. A chromolithograph imitating an oil painting. 2. The pattern assumed by a drop of oil placed on water. [< OLEO- + -GRAPH] — **o·le·og·ra·pher** (ō′lē·og′rə·fər) n. — **o′le·o·graph′ic** adj. — **o′le·og′ra·phy** n.
o·le·o·mar·ga·rine (ō′lē·ō·mär′jə·rin, -rēn) n. Margarine. Also **o′le·o·mar′ga·rin.** [< OLEO- + MARGARINE]
oleo oil An oil obtained from animal fats, consisting of olein with palmitin, and used in oleomargarine, soap, etc.
o·le·o·res·in (ō′lē·ō·rez′in) n. 1. A naturally occurring compound of an essential oil and a resin. 2. A pharmaceutical preparation consisting of a resin and sometimes other active matter in solution with a fixed or volatile oil.
ol·fac·tion (ol·fak′shən) n. The act, sense, or process of smelling odors. [< L olfactus. See OLFACTORY.]
ol·fac·to·ry (ol·fak′tər·ē, -trē) adj. Of or pertaining to the sense of smell. — n. pl. ·ries Usually pl. An olfactory nerve or organ. [< L olfactus, pp. of olfacere to smell < olere to have a smell + facere to make]
o·lib·a·num (ō·lib′ə·nəm) n. Frankincense. [< Med.L < Arabic al-lubān. Cf. Gk. libanos.]
ol·i·garch (ol′ə·gärk) n. A ruler in an oligarchy. [< Gk. oligarchēs < oligos few + archein to rule]
ol·i·gar·chy (ol′ə·gär′kē) n. pl. ·chies 1. A form of government in which power is restricted to a few; also, a state so governed. 2. The ruling oligarchs. [< Gk. oligarchēs. See OLIGARCH.] — **ol′i·gar′chic,** **ol′i·gar′chal,** **ol′i·gar′chi·cal** adj.
oligo- combining form Small; few; scanty: oligocythemia. Also, before vowels, **olig-.** [< Gk. oligos few]
Ol·i·go·cene (ol′ə·gō·sēn′) Geol. adj. Pertaining to the third oldest of the epochs or series comprised in the Tertiary system. — n. This epoch, with its included rock series. [< OLIGO- + Gk. kainos new, recent]
ol·i·go·chaete (ol′ə·gō·kēt′) Zool. n. Any of a class (Oligochaeta) of fresh-water and terrestrial hermaphroditic annelid worms, including the earthworms, having bristle-

like locomotive organs. — *adj.* Of or pertaining to this group. Also **ol′i·go·chete′**. [< NL *Oligochaeta* < Gk. *oligos* few + *chaitē* bristle, mane] — **ol′i·go·chae′tous** (-kē′təs) *adj.*

ol·i·go·clase (ol′ə·gō·klās′) *n.* A massive, vitreous feldspar of the plagioclase group, occurring in whitish crystals often tinged with blue, green, or red. [< OLIGO- + Gk. *klasis* fracture < *klaein* to break]

ol·i·gop·o·ly (ol′ə·gop′ə·lē) *n. pl.* **·lies** A form of monopoly in which the effective control of a market is exercised by a limited number of competitive sellers. [< OLIGO- + (MONO)POLY] — **ol′i·gop′o·list** *n.* — **ol′i·gop′o·lis′tic** *adj.*

o·li·o (ō′lē·ō) *n. pl.* **o·li·os** A miscellaneous collection, as of musical pieces or numbers; a medley. [< Sp. *olla* pot, stew. See OLLA.]

Ol·i·phant (ol′ə·fənt), **Margaret, 1828–97,** *née* Wilson, British novelist and biographer.

ol·i·va·ceous (ol′ə·vā′shəs) *adj.* Olive green. [< NL *olivaceus* < L *oliva* an olive]

ol·i·var·y (ol′ə·ver′ē) *adj.* **1.** Olive-shaped. **2.** *Anat.* Relating to an olive-shaped body containing a nucleus of gray matter, found at either side of the medulla oblongata. [< L *olivarius* of olives < *oliva* an olive]

ol·ive (ol′iv) *n.* **1.** A small, oily fruit native to Southern Europe and the Middle East. **2.** The evergreen tree (*Olea europea*) yielding this fruit, having leathery leaves and hard yellow wood. It is typical of a family (*Oleaceae*) of trees and includes the ash and the lilac. **3.** The dull, yellowish green color of the unripe olive. Also **olive green**. **4.** A branch of this tree. — *adj.* **1.** Pertaining to or characteristic of the olive. **2.** Having a dull, yellowish green color. **3.** Tinged with this color: an *olive* complexion. [< L *oliva* an olive]

OLIVE
*a Flowering branch.
b Floret.
c Olive.*

olive branch 1. A branch of the olive tree as an emblem of peace. **2.** Anything offered as a symbol of peace. **3.** Offspring; children: alluding to *Psalms* cxxviii 3.

olive drab 1. Any of several shades of greenish brown. **2.** A woolen material of this color, formerly used by the armed services of the United States for uniforms. **3.** *Often pl.* A uniform or a pair of trousers made of this cloth. *Abbr.* o.d., OD, O.D.

olive oil Oil pressed from olives, used in cooking, soapmaking, etc.

Ol·i·ver (ol′ə·vər) A paladin of Charlemagne's court.

Olives, Mount of A hill just east of Jerusalem: *Matt.* xvi 1. Also **Ol·i·vet** (ol′ə·vet, -vit).

O·li·vi·er (ō·liv′ē·ā), **Sir Laurence (Kerr),** born 1907, English actor.

ol·i·vine (ol′ə·vēn, -vin) *n.* A vitreous, orthorhombic, often transparent, olive-green magnesium-iron silicate, (Mg,Fe)$_2$SiO$_4$, of which many varieties are used as gemstones. [< OLIVE + -INE²]

ol·la (ol′ə, *Sp.* ô′lyä, ô′yä) *n.* **1.** A wide-mouthed pot or jar, usually of earthenware. **2.** An olla podrida. [< Sp. L *olla* pot]

ol·la po·dri·da (ol′ə pə·drē′də, *Sp.* ô′lyä pô·thrē′thä, ô′yä) **1.** A dish of meat and vegetables, usually highly seasoned, cooked together. **2.** Any heterogeneous mixture or miscellany [< Sp., lit., a putrid pot]

ol·o·gy (ol′ə·jē) *n. pl.* **·gies** *Informal* A science or branch of learning: a humorous term. [< -LOGY] — **ol′o·gist** *n.*

O·lo·mouc (ō′lô·mōts) A city in north central Moravia, Czechoslovakia; pop. 73,899 (est. 1957). German **Ol·mütz** (ôl′müts).

O·lym·pi·a (ō·lim′pē·ə) **1.** A plain in the western Peloponnesus, Greece; scene of the Olympic games. **2.** The capital of Washington, in the western part, a port on Puget Sound; pop. 23,111.

O·lym·pi·ad (ō·lim′pē·ad) *n.* **1.** The interval of four years between two successive celebrations of the Olympic games, used as a means for reckoning time. **2.** Loosely, the ancient Olympic games. **3.** The modern Olympic games. [< MF *Olympiade*, ult. < Gk. *Olympias, -ados* < *Olympos* Mt. Olympus]

O·lym·pi·an (ō·lim′pē·ən) *adj.* **1.** Of or pertaining to the great gods of Olympus, or to Mount Olympus. **2.** Godlike in manner, power, etc. **3.** Of or pertaining to Olympia or the Olympic games. Also **O·lym·pic** (ō·lim′pik, ə-). **4.** Grandly disinterested, and likely to be impractical: an *Olympian* proposal to eliminate crime. — *n.* **1.** One of the twelve higher gods who dwelt on Mount Olympus. **2.** A contestant in the Olympic games. **3.** A resident or native of Olympia. [< LL *Olympianus* < L *Olympius* < Gk. *Olympios* < *Olympos* Mt. Olympus]

Olympic games 1. In ancient Greece, athletic games, races, and contests in poetry held every four years at the plain of Olympia in Elis as a pan-Hellenic festival in honor of Zeus. **2.** A modern international revival of the ancient athletic games, held every four years at some city chosen for the event. Also **Olympian games, O·lym′pics.**

Olympic National Park A heavily forested park, 1,314 sq. mi.; established 1938 in the Olympic Mountains, part of the Coast Range in NW Washington; highest peak, **Mount Olympus,** 7,954 ft.

Olympic Peninsula A peninsula bounded by Puget Sound, the Pacific, and Juan de Fuca Strait.

O·lym·pus (ō·lim′pəs) **1.** The highest mountain of Greece, between Thessaly and Macedonia on the Aegean, regarded in Greek mythology as the home of the Olympian gods; 9,570 ft. Also **Mount O·lym′pus. 2.** The sky; heaven. [< Gk. *Olympos*]

O·lyn·thus (ō·lin′thəs) An ancient city in SE Macedonia; destroyed 348 B.C. by Philip II of Macedon. — **O·lyn′thi·ac** (-thē·ak) *adj.*

Om. Ostmark(s).

O.M. *Brit.* Order of Merit.

-oma *suffix Med.* Tumor: *carcinoma*. [< Gk. *-ōma*]

O·ma·ha (ō′mə·hä, -hô) *n.* One of a Siouan tribe of North American Indians now living in Nebraska. [< Siouan (*Omaha*), lit., those going upstream]

O·ma·ha (ō′mə·hä, -hô) A city in eastern Nebraska, on the Missouri River; pop. 346,929.

O·man (ō′man, ō·man′, ō·män′) **1.** The coastal region of the eastern promontory (**Oman Promontory**) of the Arabian peninsula. See map of SAUDI ARABIA. **2.** A sultanate in SE Arabia, 82,000 sq. mi.; pop. 750,000; capital, Muscat; formerly, *Muscat and Oman*. **3.** See TRUCIAL OMAN.

Oman, Gulf of An inlet of the Arabian Sea between Oman and Iran.

O·man (ō′mən), **Sir Charles (William Chadwick),** 1860–1946, British historian.

O·mar Khay·yám (ō·mä′səm kī·äm′, ō′mər), died 1123?, Persian poet, mathematician, and astronomer; author of the *Rubáiyát*.

o·ma·sum (ō·mä′səm) *n. pl.* **·sa** (-sə) The third stomach of a ruminant: also called *manyplies, psalterium*. [< L, bullock's tripe, paunch]

O·may·yad (ō·mī′yad) See OMMIAD.

om·bre (om′bər) *n.* **1.** A gambling game played by three persons with 40 cards, popular in the 18th century. **2.** The player undertaking to win the pool in this game. Also spelled *hombre*: also **om′ber**. [< F < Sp. *hombre* man < L *homo*]

ombro- *combining form* Rain. Also, before vowels, **ombr-**. [< Gk. *ombros* rain]

om·buds·man (om·budz′mən) *n. pl.* **·men** (-mən) A government official appointed to receive and report grievances against the government. [< Sw.]

Om·dur·man (om′dŏor·män′) A city in the central Sudan, at the confluence of the White and Blue Nile; pop. 206,000 (est. 1968).

-ome *combining form Bot.* Group; mass; body. [< Gk. *-ōma*]

o·me·ga (ō·mē′gə, ō·meg′ə, ō′meg·ə) *n.* **1.** The twenty-fourth and last letter in the Greek alphabet (Ω, ω), corresponding to English long *o*. See ALPHABET. ◆ In the etymologies in this dictionary, omega is transliterated as ō. **2.** The end; the last. [< Gk. *ō mega* great o]

om·e·let (om′lit, om′ə·lit) *n.* A dish of eggs beaten together with milk and cooked in a frying pan, often with other ingredients. Also *Brit.* **om′e·lette**. [< F *omelette* < OF *amelette, alemette* < L *lamella* small metal plate]

o·men (ō′mən) *n.* A phenomenon or incident regarded as a prophetic sign. — *v.t.* To foretell as or by an omen. [< L] — **Syn.** (noun) portent, foretoken, augury, presage.

o·men·tum (ō·men′təm) *n. pl.* **·ta** (-tə) *Anat.* A fold of the peritoneum passing between certain of the viscera. The **small** or **lesser omentum** passes from the stomach to the liver, the **great omentum** from the lower border of the stomach to the transverse colon, hanging down in front of the intestines. [< L] — **o·men′tal** *adj.*

o·mer (ō′mər) *n.* A Hebrew unit of dry measure; equal to one tenth of an ephah. [< Hebrew *eōmer*]

om·i·cron (om′ə·kron, ō′mə-) *n.* The fifteenth letter of the Greek alphabet (O, o), corresponding to English short *o*. Also **om′i·kron**. See ALPHABET. [< Gk. *o mikron* little o]

om·i·nous (om′ə·nəs) *adj.* **1.** Of the nature of or foreshadowed by an omen or by a presentiment of evil; threatening. **2.** Serving as an omen; prognostic. [< L *ominosus* < *omen, ominis* omen] — **om′i·nous·ly** *adv.* — **om′i·nous·ness** *n.* — **Syn. 1.** menacing, sinister. **2.** premonitory, foreboding.

o·mis·si·ble (ō·mis′ə·bəl) *adj.* Capable of being omitted.

o·mis·sion (ō·mish′ən) *n.* **1.** The act of omitting, or the state of being omitted. **2.** Anything omitted or neglected. [< L *omissio, -onis* < *omissus*, pp. of *omittere*. See OMIT.]

o·mis·sive (ō·mis′iv) *adj.* Failing to do or include. — **o·mis′sive·ly** *adv.*

o·mit (ō·mit′) *v.t.* **o·mit·ted, o·mit·ting 1.** To leave out; fail to include. **2.** To fail to do, make, etc.; neglect. [< L *omittere* to let go < *ob-* to, toward + *mittere* to send]

om·ma·tid·i·um (om′ə·tid′ē·əm) *n. pl.* **·tid·i·a** (-tid′ē·ə) *Zool.* One of the simple elements of a compound eye, as in arthropods. [< NL, dim. of Gk. *omma, -atos* eye] — **om′·ma·tid′i·al** *adj.*

om·mat·o·phore (ə-mat′ə-fôr, -fōr) *Zool.* A stalk terminating in an eye. [< NL *ommatophorus* < Gk. *omma, -atos* eye + -*phoros* bearing < *pherein* to bear] —**om·ma·toph·o·rous** (-ə-tof′ər-əs) *adj.*

Om·mi·ad (ō-mĭ′ad) *n. pl.* **Om·mi·ads** or **Om·mi·a·des** (ō-mĭ′ə-dēz) A member of a dynasty of early Moslem caliphs who ruled at Damascus 661–750, and in southern Spain 756–1031: also spelled *Omayyad.* [after *Omayyah,* great-grandfather of the first caliph of the dynasty]

omni- *combining form* All; totally: *omnipotent.* [< L *omnis* all]

Following is a list of self-explanatory words containing the prefix *omni-*:

omniactive	omnilingual	omniproductive
omniactuality	omnilucent	omniprudence
omniarch	omnimental	omniprudent
omnibenevolence	omninescience	omniregent
omnibenevolent	omninescient	omnirevealing
omnicausality	omnimode	omnisentient
omnicompetence	omniparent	omnisignificance
omnicompetent	omniparous	omnisignificant
omnicredulous	omnipatient	omnisufficiency
omnidirectional	omnipercipience	omnisufficient
omnierudite	omnipercipiency	omnitemporal
omniessence	omnipercipient	omnitemporality
omnifacial	omniperfect	omnitenant
omniform	omnipotential	omnitonality
omniformal	omnipregnancy	omnitonic
omniformity	omnipregnant	omnivalence
omnihuman	omniprevalence	omnivalent
omnihumanity	omniprevalent	omnivision
omni-ignorant	omniproduction	omnivorousness

om·ni·a vin·cit a·mor (om′nē-ə vin′sit ä′môr) *Latin* Love conquers all things.

om·ni·bus (om′nə-bəs, -bus) *n.* **1.** A bus (which see). **2.** A printed anthology: a Conrad *omnibus.* — *adj.* Covering a full collection of objects or cases: an *omnibus* bill. [< F < L, for all, dat. pl. of *omnis* all]

omnibus bar *Electr.* A bus bar (which see).

omnibus bill Any legislative bill or part of a bill containing miscellaneous unrelated provisions.

om·ni·far·i·ous (om′nə-fâr′ē-əs) *adj.* Of all varieties, forms, or kinds. [< L *omnifarius* of all sorts]

om·nif·er·ous (om-nif′ər-əs) *adj.* Producing all kinds. [< L *omnifer* < *omnis* all + *ferre* to bear]

om·nif·ic (om-nif′ik) *adj.* All-creating. [< Med.L *omnificus* < L *omnis* all + *facere* to make]

om·nip·o·tence (om-nip′ə-təns) *n.* **1.** Unlimited and universal power, especially as a divine attribute. **2.** *Usually cap.* God. **3.** Unlimited power or authority. Also **om·nip′o·ten·cy.** [< LL *omnipotentia*]

om·nip·o·tent (om-nip′ə-tənt) *adj.* Almighty; not limited in authority or power. —**the Omnipotent** God. [< OF < L *omnipotens, -entis* < *omnis* all + *potens, -entis* able, powerful < *posse* to be able] —**om·nip′o·tent·ly** *adv.*

om·ni·pres·ence (om′nə-prez′əns) *n.* The quality of being everywhere present at the same time. [< Med.L *omnipraesentia* < L *omnis* all + *praesens, -entis* present] —**om′ni·pres′ent** *adj.*

om·ni·range (om′nə-rānj′) *n. Aeron.* A network of very-high-frequency radio signals emitted simultaneously in all directions from a transmitting station, enabling aircraft pilots to plot their bearings from the station: in full **omni-directional radio range.**

om·nis·cience (om-nish′əns) *n.* **1.** Infinite knowledge. **2.** *Usually cap.* God. **3.** Extensive knowledge. Also **om·nis′·cien·cy.** [< Med.L *omniscientia.* See OMNISCIENT.]

om·nis·cient (om-nish′ənt) *adj.* Knowing all things; all-knowing. —**the Omniscient** God. [< NL *omnisciens, -entis,* infl. by Med.L *omniscientia* < L *omnis* all + *sciens, -entis,* ppr. of *scire* to know] —**om·nis′cient·ly** *adv.*

om·ni·um–gath·er·um (om′nē-əm-gath′ər-əm) *n.* A miscellaneous collection: a humorous pseudo-Latin term.

om·niv·o·rous (om-niv′ər-əs) *adj.* **1.** Eating both animal and vegetable food. **2.** Eating food of all kinds indiscriminately. **3.** That assimilates everything: an *omnivorous* taste for literature. [< L *omnivorus* < *omnis* all + *vorare* to devour] —**om·niv′o·rous·ly** *adv.* —**om·niv′o·rous·ness** *n.*

o·mo·pha·gi·a (ō′mə-fā′jē-ə) *n.* The eating of raw flesh. Also **o·moph·a·gy** (ō-mof′ə-jē). [< NL < Gk. *ōmophagia* < *ōmos* raw + *phagein* to eat] —**o·mo·phag·ic** (ō′mə-faj′ik), **o·moph·a·gous** (ō-mof′ə-gəs) *adj.* —**o·moph·a·gist** (ō-mof′ə-jist) *n.*

Om·pha·le (om′fə-lē) In Greek mythology, a Lydian queen in whose service Hercules, dressed as a woman, did womanly tasks for three years to expiate a murder.

om·pha·los (om′fə-ləs) *n.* **1.** A round stone in the temple of Apollo at Delphi, supposed to mark the middle point of the earth. **2.** The central boss of a shield. **3.** A central point; hub. **4.** The navel. [< Gk., navel]

Omsk (ômsk) A city in the southern R.S.F.S.R., on the Irtish; pop. 821,000 (est. 1970).

O·mu·ta (ō-mōō′tä) A port city on western Kyushu island, Japan; pop. 205,766 (1960). Also **O·mu·da** (ō-mōō·dä).

on (on, ôn) *prep.* **1.** In contact with the upper surface of; above and supported by: lying *on* the ground. **2.** In contact with any surface or outer part of: a blow *on* the head. **3.** Attached to or suspended from: a puppet *on* a string. **4.** Directed or moving along the course of: Be *on* your way. **5.** Near; adjacent to: the town *on* the river bank. **6.** Within the duration of: He arrived *on* my birthday. **7.** At the occasion of; because of: *On* seeing her, I left. **8.** At the moment or point of: *on* the hour. **9.** In a state or condition of: *on* fire; *on* record. **10.** By means of: *on* wheels. **11.** Using as a means of sustenance, activity, etc.: living *on* fruit. **12.** In addition to: thousands *on* thousands of them. **13.** Sustained or confirmed by: *on* good authority; *on* my honor. **14.** With reference to; so as to affect or be affected by: to bet *on* a horse; to depend *on* someone. **15.** Concerning; about: a work *on* economics. **16.** Engaged in; occupied with: *on* a journey; *on* duty all night. **17.** As a consequence or result of: making a profit *on* tips. **18.** In accordance with or relation to; in terms of. **19.** Directed, tending, or moving toward or against: making war *on* the enemy. **20.** Following after: disease *on* the heels of famine. **21.** *Informal* With, as about one's person: Do you have five dollars *on* you? **22.** *Informal* At the expense of: The joke is *on* them; drinks *on* the house. **23.** *Informal* So as to annoy or make difficulty for: The car stalled *on* me. — **Syn.** See AT. ◆ See notes under ONTO, UPON. — **to have something on** *U.S. Informal* To have knowledge, possess evidence, etc., against. — *adv.* **1.** In or into a position or condition of contact, adherence, covering, etc.: He put his hat *on.* **2.** In the direction of an activity, performance, etc.: He looked *on* while they played. **3.** In advance; ahead, in space or time: later *on.* **4.** In continuous course or succession: The music went *on.* **5.** In or into operation, performance, or existence. — **and so on** And like what has gone before; et cetera. — **on and off** Now and then; intermittently; off and on. — **on and on** Without interruption; continuously. — **to be on to** *Informal* To be aware of, informed about, or alert to. — *adj.* **1.** Being in operation, progress, or application. **2.** Near; located nearer. **3.** In cricket, indicating or pertaining to the side of the wicket and field where the batsman stands. — *n.* **1.** The state or fact of being on. **2.** In cricket, the on side of the field or wicket. [OE *on, an.* Cf. OHG *ana,* ON *á,* Gk. *ana.*]

-on *suffix* **1.** *Physics* Atomic or charged particle: *meson.* **2.** *Chem.* Inert gas: *neon.* [< Gk., neuter -*on*]

On (on) The Egyptian name for HELIOPOLIS.

ON or **O.N.** or **O.N.** Old Norse.

on·a·ger (on′ə-jər) *n. pl.* ·**gers** or ·**gri** (-grī) **1.** A wild ass (*Equus onager*) of central Asia. **2.** An ancient military device by which stones were hurled. [< L, wild ass]

on·a·gra·ceous (on′ə-grā′shəs) *adj. Bot.* Pertaining or belonging to a family (*Onagraceae*) of plants of which the evening primrose is typical. [< NL < L *onagra,* fem. of *onager.* See ONAGER.]

o·nan·ism (ō′nən-iz′əm) *n.* **1.** Withdrawal before orgasm; incomplete coitus. **2.** Masturbation. [after *Onan.* Cf. *Gen.* xxxviii 9.] —**o′nan·ist** *n.* —**o′nan·is′tic** *adj.*

once (wuns) *adv.* **1.** One time; without repetition. **2.** At or during some past time. **3.** At any time; ever. — **once (and) for all** Finally. — **once in a while** Occasionally. — **once upon a time** At a time long past. — *adj.* Former; formerly existing; quondam. — *conj.* As soon as; whenever. — *n.* One time. — **all at once 1.** All at the same time. **2.** All of a sudden. — **at once 1.** Simultaneously. **2.** Immediately. [ME *ones* < OE *ānes,* genitive of *ān* one]

once-o·ver (wuns′ō′vər) *n. Slang* **1.** A quick glance or survey. **2.** A quick putting of things in order.

on·col·o·gy (on-kol′ə-jē) *n.* The science of tumors. [< Gk. *onkos* bulk + -LOGY]

on·com·ing (on′kum′ing, ôn′-) *adj.* Approaching. — *n.* An approach.

on·do·gram (on′də-gram) *n.* The record made by an ondograph. [< F *onde* wave (< L *unda*) + -GRAM]

on·do·graph (on′də-graf, -gräf) *n.* A device for recording electric wave forms, especially those of alternating currents. [< F *onde* wave (< L *unda*) + -GRAPH]

on·dom·e·ter (on-dom′ə-tər) *n.* A meter for registering the frequency of electromagnetic waves. [< F *onde* wave (< L *unda*) + -METER]

one (wun) *adj.* **1.** Being a single individual, object, or unit. **2.** Being or designating an unspecified or not precisely identified individual, thing, or time. **3.** Designating a person, thing, or group as contrasted with another or others. **4.** Single in kind; the same; closely united or alike. — *n.* **1.** A single unit, the first and lowest integer in the numerical series, preceding two: a cardinal number. **2.** Any symbol of this number, as 1, i, I. **3.** A single person or thing. — *pron.* **1.** Someone or something; anyone or anything. **2.** An individual or thing among persons or things already mentioned. **— all one 1.** Of equal consequence. **2.** Unimportant; of no significance. **— at one** In harmony or accord. **— one another** Each other: said of a reciprocal action or relation: They love *one another*. **— one by one** Singly and in succession. [OE *ān*]

◆ Expressions like *one of those who* may be followed by a plural or a singular verb, either *one* or *those* being regarded as the antecedent of *who* according to the sense or emphasis of the idea expressed. One may say *He is one of those who never break rules* or *He is one of those who is always sure of what he is doing.* Similarly, sentences in which *one* is contrasted with a higher number may also take a singular or plural verb, as *One out of every ten persons is* (or *are*) *mentally disturbed.*

One must work at one's own pace and *One must work at his own pace* are both correct, but the latter form is more common in the United States.

-one *suffix Chem.* Denoting an organic compound of the ketone group: *acetone*. [< Gk. *-ōnē*, fem. patronymic]

one-armed bandit (wun'ärmd') *Slang* A slot machine.

one-base hit (wun'bās') In baseball, a base hit that enables the batter to reach first base; a single. Also *Slang* **one'-bag'ger** (-bag'ər).

O·ne·ga (ô-neg'ə) A lake in the southern Karelian A.S.S.R.; about 3,800 sq. mi.

one-horse (wun'hôrs') *adj.* **1.** Drawn or adapted to be worked by one horse. **2.** *Informal* Of inferior resources or capacity; small; unimportant: a *one-horse* town.

O·nei·da (ō-nī'də) *n.* A member of a tribe of North American Indians of Iroquoian stock.

Oneida Lake A lake in central New York; 20 mi. long; about 80 sq. mi.

O'Neill (ō-nēl'), **Eugene (Gladstone),** 1888–1953, U.S. playwright.

oneiro- *combining form* Dream; of dreams: *oneiromancy*: also *oniro-*. Also, before vowels, **oneir-.** [< Gk. *oneiros* dream]

o·nei·ro·crit·ic (ō-nī'rə-krit'ik) *n.* One who interprets dreams. [< Gk. *oneirokritikos* pertaining to the interpretation of dreams < *oneiros* dream + *kritikos* able to discern < *krinein* to judge] **— o·nei'ro·crit'i·cal** *adj.*

o·nei·ro·man·cy (ō-nī'rə-man'sē) *n.* Divination by means of dreams. [< ONEIRO + -*mancy* < Gk. *manteia* divination] **— o·nei'ro·man'cer, o·nei'ro·man'tist** *n.*

one·ness (wun'nis) *n.* **1.** Singleness; unity; sameness. **2.** Agreement; concord. **3.** Quality of being unique.

one-night stand (wun'nīt') *U.S.* **1.** A performance given by a traveling show on one night only. **2.** The town or place in which such a performance is given.

on·er·ous (on'ər-əs) *adj.* **1.** Burdensome or oppressive. **2.** *Law* Legally liable for or subject to an obligation. [< OF *onereus* < L *onerosus* < *onus, oneris* burden] **— on'er·ous·ly** *adv.* **— on'er·ous·ness** *n.*

on·er·y (on'ər-ē) *adj.* Ornery.

one·self (wun'self', wunz'-) *pron.* A form of the indefinite pronoun *one*, used as a reflexive or as object of a preposition. Also **one's self.**

one-sid·ed (wun'sī'did) *adj.* **1.** Having, involving, or on one side. **2.** Biased; unfair. **3.** Having unequal or unbalanced sides. **— one'-sid'ed·ly** *adv.* **— one'-sid'ed·ness** *n.*

one-step (wun'step') *n.* **1.** A ballroom dance consisting of long, rapid steps. **2.** The ragtime music for such a dance.

one-time (wun'tīm') *adj.* Former; quondam.

one-track (wun'trak') *adj.* **1.** Having a single track. **2.** *Informal* Limited to a single idea: a *one-track* mind.

one-up·man·ship (wun'up·man·ship') *n.* The facetious idea that one should stay a hypothetical point ahead of another or others in a skill, discussion, etc.

one-way (wun'wā') *adj.* **1.** Moving in one direction only. **2.** Permitting traffic in one direction only. **3.** Providing for travel in one direction only: a *one-way* ticket.

ONI Office of Naval Intelligence.

on·ion (un'yən) *n.* **1.** The edible, succulent bulb of an herb (*Allium cepa*) of the lily family, having a pungent odor and taste. **2.** Any of various allied plants. [< OF *oignon* < L *unio, -onis* unity, pearl, onion. Doublet of UNION.]

On·ions (un'yənz), **Charles Talbut,** 1873–1965, English philologist and lexicographer.

on·ion·skin (un'yən·skin') *n.* A thin, translucent paper.

oniro- Var. of ONEIRO.

on·look·er (on'lŏŏk'ər, ôn'-) *n.* A spectator. **— on'look'ing** *adj.*

on·ly (ōn'lē) *adv.* **1.** In one manner or for one purpose alone. **2.** Solely; exclusively. **3.** Merely; just. **— adj. 1.** Alone in its class; having no fellow or mate; sole; single; solitary: an *only* child. **2.** Standing alone by reason of superior excellence. **— conj.** Except that; but. Abbr. *o.* [OE *ānlīc* < *ān* one + -LY²]

on·o·ma·si·ol·o·gy (on'ō-mā'zē·ol'ə·jē) *n.* The study of the meanings of names.

on·o·mas·tic (on'ə·mas'tik) *adj.* **1.** Of or pertaining to a name or names. **2.** *Law* Designating a signature in a handwriting other than that of the instrument to which it is appended. [< Gk. *onomastikos* of naming < *onomastos* named < *onomazein* to name < *onoma* name]

on·o·mas·tics (on'ə·mas'tiks) *n.pl.* (*construed as sing.*) The study of the origin and evolution of proper names.

on·o·mat·o·poe·ia (on'ə·mat'ə·pē'ə, ō·nom'ə·tə-) *n.* **1.** The formation of words in imitation of natural sounds, as *crack, splash,* or *bow-wow*. **2.** An imitative word. **3.** The use of such words. Also **on'o·mat'o·po·e'sis** (-pō·ē'sis), **on'o·mat'o·py** (-mat'ə·pē). [< L < Gk. *onomatopoiia* < *onoma, -atos* name + *poieein* to make] **— on'o·mat·o·poe'ic** or **on'o·mat'o·po·et'ic** (-pō·et'ik) *adj.* **— on'o·mat'o·po·et'i·cal·ly** *adv.*

On·on·da·ga (on'ən-dô'gə, -dä'-) *n. pl.* **·ga** or **·gas 1.** A tribe of North American Indians of Iroquoian stock formerly living in New York and Ontario. **2.** A member of this tribe. [< Iroquoian *ononta'gé*, lit., on top of the hill] **— On'on·da'gan** *adj.*

Onondaga Lake A salt lake in central New York; 5 mi. long.

on·rush (on'rush', ôn'-) *n.* An onward rush or flow.

on·set (on'set', ôn'-) *n.* **1.** An attack; assault. **2.** An initial stage, as of illness. **3.** A setting about; outset; start.

on·shore (on'shōr', -shôr', ôn'-) *adv. & adj.* To, toward, or on the shore.

on·slaught (on'slôt', ôn'-) *n.* A violent, often hostile assault. [< Du. *annslag,* or ON + ME *slaught* slaughter < OE *sleaht* < *slean* to slay]

Ont. Ontario.

On·tar·i·o (on-târ'ē-ō) **1.** A Province in SE Canada; 412,582 sq. mi.; pop. 7,815,000; capital, Toronto. **2.** A city in SW California; pop. 64,118 **— On·tar'i·an** *adj. & adj.*

Ontario, Lake The smallest and easternmost of the five Great Lakes; 7,540 sq. mi.

on-the-job (on·thə·job', ôn-) *adj.* Pertaining to skills acquired, especially under guidance, while actually doing the job, as distinguished from formal preparation before employment: *on-the-job* training.

on·to (on'tōō, ôn'-) *prep.* **1.** Upon the top of; to and upon: The cat jumped *onto* the table. **2.** *Informal* Aware of; informed about: I'm *onto* your tricks.

◆ **onto, on** *Onto* and *on* are now often used interchangeably when motion into position is indicated, as in *He stepped onto* (or *on*) *the platform,* although in some instances *onto* is preferable in order to avoid ambiguity, as in *They moved onto the dance floor.*

onto- *combining form* Being; existence: *ontogeny*. Also, before vowels, **ont-.** [< Gk. *ōn, ontos,* ppr. of *einai* to be]

on·tog·e·ny (on-toj'ə·nē) *n. pl.* **·nies** *Biol.* The history of the development of the individual organism: distinguished from *phylogeny*. Also **on·to·gen·e·sis** (on'tō·jen'ə·sis). [< ONTO- + -GENY] **— on·to·ge·net·ic** (on'tō·jə·net'ik), **on'to·gen'ic** (-jen'ik) *adj.* **— on·tog'e·nist** *n.*

on·to·log·i·cal (on'tə·loj'i·kəl) *adj.* Pertaining to ontology. Also **on'to·log'ic.** **— on'to·log'i·cal·ly** *adv.*

ontological argument The metaphysical argument that the real, objective existence of God is necessarily involved in the existence of the very idea of God.

on·tol·o·gy (on-tol'ə·jē) *n. pl.* **·gies** The branch of metaphysics dealing with the philosophical theory of reality, including consideration of the universal and necessary characteristics of all existence; also, a particular theory of reality. [< NL *ontologia* < Gk. *ōn, ontos* being + -*logia* < *logos* word, study] **— on·tol'o·gist** *n.*

o·nus (ō'nəs) *n.* A burden or responsibility. [< L]

o·nus pro·ban·di (ō'nəs prō·ban'dī) *Latin* Burden of proof.

on·ward (on'wərd, ôn'-) *adv.* In the direction of progress; forward in space or time; ahead. Also **on'wards.** **— adj.** Moving or tending to be forward or ahead. [ME]

on·yx (on'iks) *n.* A variety of chalcedony having layers of different colors, used as a semiprecious gemstone. [< L < Gk., nail, onyx]

oo- *combining form* **1.** Egg; pertaining to eggs: *oology.* **2.** *Biol.* An ovum: *oogenesis.* [< Gk. *ōon* egg]

o·o·cyte (ō'ə·sīt) *n. Biol.* A female gamete that has not reached full development. [< OO- + -CYTE]

oo·dles (ōōd'lz) *n.pl. Informal* A great deal; many. [< dial. E *oodle,* var. of HUDDLE, n.]

o·o·gen·e·sis (ō'ə·jen'ə·sis) *n. Biol.* The development of ova. Also **o·og·e·ny** (ō·oj'ə·nē). **— o'o·ge·net'ic** (-jə·net'ik) *adj.*

o·o·go·ni·um (ō'ə·gō'nē·əm) *n. pl.* **·ni·a** (-nē·ə) **1.** *Bot.* The female reproductive organ in thallophytic plants, within which the oospheres are developed. **2.** *Biol.* A cell whose divisions give rise to oocytes. [< NL < Gk. *ōon* egg + *gonos* offspring]

oo·la·chan (ōō'lə·kən) *n.* The eulachon, a fish.

o·o·lite (ō'ə·līt) *n.* A granular variety of limestone made up of nearly spherical concretions resembling the roe of a fish. [< F *oölithe* < Gk. *ōon* egg + *lithos* stone] **— o'o·lit'ic** (-lit'ik) *adj.*

o·ol·o·gy (ō·ol'ə·jē) *n.* The branch of ornithology that deals with the study of eggs. [< OO- + -LOGY] **— o·o·log·ic** (ō'ə·loj'ik) or **·i·cal** *adj.* **— o·ol'o·gist** *n.*

oo·long (ōō'lông') *n.* A variety of dark tea that is partly fermented before being dried. [< Chinese *wu-lung* < *wu* black + *lung* dragon]

oo·mi·ak (ōō'mē·ak) See UMIAK.

oomph (oŏmf) *n. Slang* **1.** Obvious physical attractiveness; sex appeal: said especially of women. **2.** Spirit; pep. [Prob. imit. of a grunt of pleasure]

o·o·pho·rec·to·my (ō′ə·fə·rek′tə·mē) *n. pl.* **·mies** *Surg.* Ovariotomy. [< OOPHOR(O)- + -ECTOMY]

o·o·pho·ri·tis (ō′ə·fə·rī′tis) *n. Pathol.* Inflammation of an ovary or the ovaries: also called *ovaritis.* [< OOPHOR(O)- + -ITIS]

oophoro- *combining form* Ovary; ovarian. Also, before vowels, **oophor-.** [< Gk. *ōophoros* egg-bearing]

o·o·phyte (ō′ə·fīt) *n. Bot.* The stage in the life of mosses, ferns, and liverworts during which sexual organs are developed. [< OO- + -PHYTE] — **o′o·phyt′ic** (-fit′ik) *adj.*

oo·ra·li (oō·rä′lē) *n.* Curare, a drug. [Var. of CURARE]

oo·rie (oō′rē) See OURIE.

o·o·sperm (ō′ə·spûrm) *n. Biol.* A fertilized ovum.

o·o·sphere (ō′ə·sfir) *n. Bot.* In algae and fungi, the egg cell prior to fertilization: also called *germinal vesicle.* [< OO- + SPHERE]

o·o·spore (ō′ə·spôr, -spōr) *n. Bot.* The fertilized, fully developed oosphere, produced within an oogonium. [< OO- + SPORE] — **o′o·spor′ic, o·os·po·rous** (ō·os′pər·əs) *adj.*

Oos-Lon·den (ōs′lôn′də) The Afrikaans name for EAST LONDON.

Oost–Vlaan·de·ren (ōst′vlän′də·rən) The Flemish name for EAST FLANDERS.

oot (oōt) *adv., adj., interj., n., & prep. Scot.* Out.

o·o·the·ca (ō′ə·thē′kə) *n. pl.* **·cae** (-sē) *Entomol.* The egg case of certain insects, as the cockroach. [< NL < Gk. *ōon* egg + *thēkē* case] — **o′o·the′cal** *adj.*

ooze¹ (oōz) *v.* **oozed, ooz·ing** *v.i.* **1.** To flow or leak out slowly or gradually, as through pores or small holes; seep; trickle. **2.** To exude moisture. **3.** To escape or disappear little by little. — *v.t.* **4.** To give off or exude in or as in droplets or a trickle. — *n.* **1.** A slow, gradual leak; gentle flow. **2.** That which oozes. **3.** An infusion of a substance such as oak bark, used in tanning. **4.** Ooze leather (which see). [ME *wosen* < OE *wāse* slimy mud]

ooze² (oōz) *n.* **1.** Slimy mud or moist, spongy soil. **2.** A deposit of calcareous matter found on the ocean bottom and largely made up of the remains of foraminifers. **3.** A piece of muddy or marshy ground; bog; fen. [OE *wāse* slimy mud. Akin to ON *neisa* slime, ? L *virus* sap, slime.]

ooze leather Calfskin or other leather having a soft, velvety finish on the flesh side: also called *ooze.*

oo·zy¹ (oō′zē) *adj.* **·zi·er, ·zi·est** Slowly leaking.

oo·zy² (oō′zē) *adj.* **·zi·er, ·zi·est** Of or resembling mud or ooze; slimy. — **oo′zi·ly** *adv.* — **oo′zi·ness** *n.*

op- Assimilated var. of OB-.

op. **1.** Opera. **2.** Operation. **3.** Opposite. **4.** Work(s) (L *opus, opera*).

OP *Mil.* Observation post.

O.P. (Dominican) Order of Preachers (L *Ordo Praedicatorum*).

OPA or **O.P.A.** Office of Price Administration.

o·pac·i·ty (ō·pas′ə·tē) *n. pl.* **·ties** **1.** The state or quality of being opaque. **2.** Obscurity. **3.** That which is opaque. **4.** *Photog.* The light-stopping power of the silver deposit on a negative. [< MF *opacité* < L *opacitas* < *opacus* dark]

o·pah (ō′pə) *n.* A large marine fish (*Lampris regius*), having a compressed, oviform body, and noted for the brilliance of its colors: also called *moonfish.* [< Ibo *ubà*]

o·pal (ō′pəl) *n.* An amorphous, variously colored hydrous silica, softer and less dense than quartz, and including some iridescent varieties esteemed as gemstones. [< L *opalus* < Gk. *opallios* < Skt. *upala* precious stone]

o·pal·esce (ō′pəl·es′) *v.i.* **·esced, ·esc·ing** To exhibit opalescence.

o·pal·es·cence (ō′pəl·es′əns) *n.* An iridescent play of brilliant or milky colors, as in an opal. — **o′pal·es′cent** *adj.*

o·pal·ine (ō′pəl·ēn, -in) *adj.* Resembling or characteristic of an opal; opalescent. — *n.* A milky variety of glass.

o·paque (ō·pāk′) *adj.* **1.** Impervious to light; not translucent or transparent. **2.** Impervious to reason; unintelligent. **3.** Impervious to radiant heat, electric radiation, etc. **4.** Having no luster; dull. **5.** Unintelligible; obscure. — *n.* **1.** That which is opaque. **2.** A pigment used to darken or eliminate portions of a print, photographic negative, etc. [ME *opake* < L *opacus* dark, later refashioned after F *opaque*] — **o·paque′ly** *adv.* — **o·paque′ness** *n.*

opaque projector An optical device that magnifies and projects a nontransparency, as a printed page or photograph.

op art (op) A style of art of the 1960's characterized by complex geometric patterns designed to create optical distortions, illusions, and the like: also called *optical art.* [< *op(tical) art*; infl. in form by *pop art*]

op. cit. In the work cited [L *opere citato*]

ope (ōp) *v.t. & v.i.* **oped, op·ing** *Poetic & Archaic* To open. [ME, short for OPEN]

o·pen (ō′pən) *adj.* **1.** Affording approach, view, passage, or access because of the absence or removal of barriers, restrictions, etc.; unobstructed: *open* for traffic. **2.** Public; accessible to all: the *open* market. **3.** Unconcealed; overt; not secret or hidden: *open* hostility. **4.** Expanded; unfolded: an *open* flower. **5.** Exposed; not enclosed or covered: an *open* car. **6.** Ready for business, appointment, etc. **7.** Not settled or decided; pending: an *open* question. **8.** Available: The job is still *open.* **9.** Ready to consider proof or argument; unbiased; receptive: often with *to*: an *open* mind; *open* to conviction. **10.** Generous; liberal: to give with an *open* hand. **11.** *Phonet.* **a** Produced with a wide opening above the tongue; low: said of vowels, as the *a* in *father* and *calm*: opposed to *close.* **b** Ending in a vowel or diphthong: said of a syllable. **12.** Frank; ingenuous; not deceptive: an *open* face. **13.** Eager or willing to receive: with *open* arms. **14.** In hunting or fishing, without prohibition: *open* season. **15.** Liable to attack, robbery, temptation, etc. **16.** Having openings, holes, or perforations, as woven goods or needlework; porous. **17.** Mild; free from fog, mist, or ice: an *open* winter. **18.** *Printing* **a** Widely spaced, as a line on a page. **b** Widely leaded or containing many breaks; fat: said of composed or printed matter. **19.** *Music* **a** Not stopped by the finger, as a string, a hole of a woodwind instrument, etc. **b** Not produced by the stopping of a string or hole, or the use of a valve or slide; not fingered, as the tone of an instrument. **c** Not stopped by the hand or by a mute, as a brass instrument or its tone. **d** Having the top uncovered, as an organ pipe. **20.** Unrestricted by union regulations in employment: an *open* shop. **21.** *U.S. Informal* Permitting or ineffective in controlling normally illicit activities, as gambling and prostitution: an *open* town. **22.** Out of doors. **23.** Not to be defended in war: *open* city. **24.** Not restricted by rigid classes, control, etc.: an *open* society. — **Syn.** See CANDID. — *v.t.* **1.** To set open or ajar, as a door; unclose; unfasten. **2.** To make passable; free from obstacles. **3.** To make or force (a hole, passage, etc.). **4.** To remove the covering, lid, etc., of: to *open* a package. **5.** To expand, as for viewing; unroll; unfold, as a map. **6.** To make an opening or openings into: to *open* an abscess. **7.** To make or declare ready for commerce, use, etc.: to *open* a store. **8.** To make or declare public or free of access, as a park; make available for settlement. **9.** To make less compact; expand: to *open* ranks. **10.** To make more receptive to ideas or sentiments; enlighten: to *open* the mind. **11.** To bare the secrets of; divulge; reveal: to *open* one's heart. **12.** To begin; commence, as negotiations. **13.** *Law* To undo or recall (a judgment or order) so as to permit its validity to be questioned. — *v.i.* **14.** To become open. **15.** To come apart or break open; rupture: The wound *opened* again. **16.** To come into view; spread out; unroll. **17.** To afford access or view: The door *opened* on a courtyard. **18.** To become receptive or enlightened. **19.** To begin; be started: The season *opened* with a ball. **20.** In the theater, to begin a season or tour. — *n.* Any wide space not enclosed, obstructed, or covered, as by woods, rocks, etc.; open land or water: usually with the definite article: in the *open.* [OE. Akin to OHG *offan,* ON *opinn,* ult. from root of UP.] — **o′pen·ly** *adv.* — **o′pen·ness** *n.*

o·pen-air (ō′pən·âr′) *adj.* Occurring, done, etc., out of doors: an *open-air* concert.

o·pen-and-shut (ō′pən·ən·shut′) *adj. Informal* Obvious; easily determined.

open chain *Chem.* An organic compound in which the carbon atoms are disposed in a chain open at both ends: distinguished from *closed chain.*

open city A city belonging to a nation at war, officially declared as being completely demilitarized, so as to avoid bombardment or attack.

open door **1.** The policy or practice of giving to all nations the same commercial privileges in a region or area open for trade or exploitation. **2.** Admission to all without charge.

o·pen-door (ō′pən·dôr′, -dōr′) *adj.* Of or characterized by the commercial policies or practices of the open door.

o·pen-end investment company (ō′pən·end′) See under INVESTMENT COMPANY.

o·pen·er (ō′pən·ər) *n.* **1.** An instrument for opening firmly closed containers, as bottles, jars, or cans. **2.** One who opens. **3.** In poker, etc.: **a** The player who opens the jackpot. **b** *pl.* Cards of sufficient value to enable the player to open the pot. **3.** In the theater, the first act, dance, song, etc., in a revue, vaudeville performance, etc.

o·pen-eyed (ō′pən·īd′) *adj.* **1.** Having the eyes open; aware; watchful. **2.** Amazed: in *open-eyed* wonder.

o·pen-faced (ō′pən·fāst′) *adj.* **1.** Possessing a countenance suggestive of frankness, simplicity, and honesty. **2.** Having a face or side uncovered.

o·pen-hand·ed (ō′pən·han′did) *adj.* Giving freely; liberal. — **o′pen·hand′ed·ly** *adv.* — **o′pen·hand′ed·ness** *n.*

o·pen-heart·ed (ō′pən·här′tid) *adj.* Disclosing the thoughts and intentions plainly; frank; candid. — **o′pen·heart′ed·ly** *adv.* — **o′pen·heart′ed·ness** *n.*

o·pen-hearth (ō'pən·härth') *adj. Metall.* **1.** Designating a steel-making process in which the material is melted in a shallow reverberatory furnace open at each end to admit fuel and air, and permitting close control of the finished product. **2.** Describing steel made by this process.

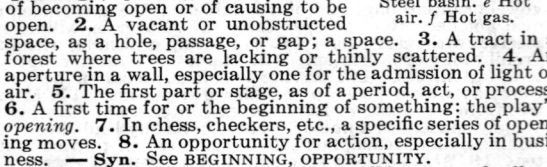

OPEN-HEARTH FURNACE

a Molten pig iron. *b* Scrap steel. *c* Limestone lining. *d* Steel basin. *e* Hot air. *f* Hot gas.

open house 1. A house or a social event in which hospitality is extended to all who wish to come. **2.** An occasion when a school, factory, institution, etc., is open to visitors.

o·pen·ing (ō'pən·ing) *n.* **1.** The act of becoming open or of causing to be open. **2.** A vacant or unobstructed space, as a hole, passage, or gap; a space. **3.** A tract in a forest where trees are lacking or thinly scattered. **4.** An aperture in a wall, especially one for the admission of light or air. **5.** The first part or stage, as of a period, act, or process. **6.** A first time for or the beginning of something: the play's *opening*. **7.** In chess, checkers, etc., a specific series of opening moves. **8.** An opportunity for action, especially in business. — **Syn.** See BEGINNING, OPPORTUNITY.

open market A market accessible to all buyers and sellers, as opposed to a market restricted to a specific group.

o·pen-mind·ed (ō'pən·mīn'did) *adj.* Free from prejudiced conclusions; amenable to reason; receptive. — **o'pen·mind'ed·ly** *adv.* — **o'pen·mind'ed·ness** *n.*

o·pen-mouthed (ō'pən·mouth̶d', -moutht') *adj.* **1.** Having the mouth open; gaping, as in wonder or surprise. **2.** Noisy; clamorous. **3.** Greedy; voracious.

open sesame An unfailing means or formula for opening secret doors and gaining entrance: an allusion to the tale of *Ali Baba and the Forty Thieves* in the *Arabian Nights*.

open shop 1. An establishment employing both union and nonunion labor: opposed to *closed shop*. **2.** An establishment whose policy is to hire only nonunion labor.

open syllable A syllable ending in a vowel or diphthong.

open stock In merchandising, extra or additional parts of a set, as of dishes, that are always kept in stock.

open timber A forest having no undergrowth.

o·pen·work (ō'pən·wûrk') *n.* Any product of art or handicraft containing numerous small openings.

op·er·a (op'ər·ə, op'rə) Plural of OPUS. — *n.* **1.** A form of drama in which music is a dominant factor, made up of arias, recitatives, choruses, etc., with orchestral accompaniment, scenery, acting, and sometimes dance. See GRAND OPERA, OPÉRA COMIQUE. **2.** A particular musical drama or its music or libretto. **3.** An opera house. Abbr. *op.* [< Ital. < L, service, work < *opus, operis* work] — **op·er·at·ic** (op·ə-rat'ik) *adj.* — **op'er·at'i·cal·ly** *adv.*

op·er·a·ble (op'ər·ə·bəl) *adj.* **1.** Capable of treatment by surgical operation. **2.** Practicable. — **op'er·a·bil'i·ty** *n.*

o·pé·ra bouffe (ō·pä·rä bōof') *French* A farcical comic opera. Also *Ital.* **o·pe·ra buf·fa** (ō'pä·rä bōof'fä).

o·pé·ra co·mique (ō·pä·rä kô·mēk') *French* **1.** Originally, an opera having spoken dialogue and usually a less serious subject than grand opera. **2.** In the nineteenth century, an opera having spoken dialogue.

opera glass Small binoculars suitable for use at the theater. Also **opera glasses.**

opera hat A man's top hat, having a collapsible crown.

opera house A theater adapted for performance of operas.

op·er·and (op'ər·and) *n. Math.* Any quantity or symbol upon which an operation is performed. [< L *operandus*, gerundive of *operari* to work]

op·er·ate (op'ə·rāt) *v.* **·at·ed, ·at·ing** *v.i.* **1.** To act or function, especially with force or influence; work. **2.** To bring about or produce the proper or intended effect. **3.** *Surg.* To perform an operation. **4.** To deal in securities, stocks, etc., especially speculatively. **5.** To carry on a military or naval operation: usually with *against*. — *v.t.* **6.** To control the working of, as a machine. **7.** To manage or conduct the affairs of: to *operate* a business. **8.** To bring about or cause; effect. [< L *operatus*, pp. of *operari* to work, have effect < *opus, operis* work] — **op'er·a·ble** *adj.*

op·er·a·ted (op'ə·rā'tid) *adj.* Made to operate by a (specified) means or agency: used in combination: *coin-operated.*

op·er·a·tion (op·ə·rā'shən) *n.* **1.** The act or process of operating. **2.** A method of exercising or applying force; a mode of action. **3.** An act or transaction, especially in the stock market. **4.** A course or series of acts to effect a certain purpose; process. **5.** The state of being in action: to be in *operation*. **6.** *Surg.* Any systematic manipulation upon or within the body, performed either with or without instruments, to restore disunited or deficient parts, to remove diseased or injured parts, or to extract foreign matter. **7.** *Math.* **a** The act of making a change in the value or form of a quantity. **b** The change itself as indicated by symbols or rules. **8.** A military or naval campaign. Abbr. *op.* [< OF, deed < L *operatio, -onis* work < *operari* to work]

op·er·a·tion·al (op·ə·rā'shən·əl) *adj.* **1.** Of or pertaining to an operation or operations. **2.** Checked and serviced for ready operation, as an aircraft.

operations research The application of scientific method, mathematical analysis, and technical skills to insure maximum efficiency in industry and government. Also called **operational research.**

op·er·a·tive (op'ər·ə·tiv, -ə·rā'tiv) *adj.* **1.** Exerting force or influence. **2.** Moving or working efficiently; effective. **3.** Being in operation or in force. **4.** Connected with operations: *operative* surgery. **5.** Concerned with practical work, mechanical or manual. — *n.* **1.** A person employed as a skilled worker, as in a mill or factory. **2.** *Informal* A detective; secret agent. [< F or < Med.L *operativus* < L *operari* to work] — **op'er·a·tive·ly** *adv.*

op·er·a·tor (op'ə·rā'tər) *n.* **1.** One who works or operates a machine or mechanism: a telegraph *operator*. **2.** One who owns or directs some commercial or industrial establishment: the *operator* of a coal mine. **3.** A broker. **4.** *Surg.* One who performs operations. **5.** *Math.* A symbol that briefly indicates a mathematical process. **6.** *Slang* One who craftily obtains things with little or no cost to himself: He's quite an *operator*. — **Syn.** See DOER. [< LL, worker < L *operari* to work]

o·per·cu·late (ō-pûr'kyōō-lit, -lāt) *adj.* Having an operculum. Also **o·per'cu·lat·ed.**

o·per·cu·lum (ō-pûr'kyōō-ləm) *n. pl.* **·la** (-lə) **1.** *Bot.* A lidlike part or organ, as of the capsule in mosses and in flowering plants. **2.** *Zool.* **a** A horny or shelly plate in many gastropods, serving to close the aperture when the animal is retracted. **b** In fishes, the gill cover. **c** In the horseshoe crab, the plate that covers the abdominal limbs. For illustration see HORSESHOE CRAB. **3.** *Anat.* A part of the cerebral cortex. Also **o·per·cele** (ō-pûr'sēl), **o·per'cule** (-kyōōl). [< L, a covering, lid < *operire* to cover] — **o·per'cu·lar** *adj.*

o·pe·re ci·ta·to (op'ə·rē sī·tä'tō) *Latin* In the work cited, or quoted. Abbr. *o.c., op. cit.*

op·e·ret·ta (op'ə·ret'ə) *n.* A type of short, humorous opera with dialogue: also called *light opera*. [< Ital., dim. of *opera*. See OPERA.]

op·er·ose (op'ə·rōs) *adj.* **1.** Involving labor; laborious. **2.** Industrious; diligent. [< L *operosus* < *opus, operis* labor] — **op'er·ose'ly** *adv.* — **op'er·ose'ness** *n.*

oph·i·cleide (of'ə·klīd) *n.* An obsolete brass musical instrument of bass range with pitches regulated by holes in the side of its tube. [< F *ophicléide* < Gk. *ophis* serpent + *kleis, kleidos* key]

o·phid·i·an (ō-fid'ē-ən) *n.* One of a group (suborder *Serpentes* or *Ophidia*) of limbless reptiles with jaws connected by elastic ligaments; a serpent or snake. — *adj.* Of or pertaining to snakes; snakelike. [< NL < Gk. *ophis* serpent]

ophio- *combining form* Serpent; of or pertaining to serpents: *ophiolatry*. Also, before vowels, **ophi-.** [< Gk. *ophis* serpent]

oph·i·ol·a·try (of'ē·ol'ə·trē) *n.* Serpent worship. [< OPHIO- + -LATRY] — **oph'i·ol'a·trous** *adj.*

O·phir (ō'fər) *n.* In the Bible, a land rich in gold from which Solomon obtained his wealth. I *Kings* x 11.

oph·ite (of'īt, ō'fīt) *n.* A variety of greenish altered diabase occurring in the Pyrenees. [< L *ophites* < Gk. *ophitēs* (*lithos*) serpentine (stone) < *ophis* serpent]

o·phit·ic (ō-fit'ik) *adj.* Describing a rock texture characterized by feldspar crystals in a matrix of pyroxene crystals. [< Gk. *ophitēs* like a serpent]

Oph·i·u·chus (of'ē·yōō'kəs, ō'fē-) *n.* A constellation, the Serpent-holder or Doctor. See CONSTELLATION. [< L < Gk. *ophiouchos* < *ophis* serpent + *echein* to hold]

ophthal. or **ophthalm.** Ophthalmology.

oph·thal·mi·a (of·thal'mē·ə) *n. Pathol.* Inflammation of the eye, its membranes, or its lids. Also **oph·thal'my** (-mē). [< LL < Gk. < *opthalmos* eye]

oph·thal·mic (of·thal'mik) *adj.* Of, for, or pertaining to the eye: an *ophthalmic* ointment.

oph·thal·mi·tis (of'thal·mī'tis) *n. Pathol.* Inflammation of the eye, including the outer and internal structures.

ophthalmo- *combining form* Eye; pertaining to the eyes: *ophthalmology*. Also, before vowels, **ophthalm-.** [< Gk. *ophthalmos* eye]

oph·thal·mol·o·gist (of'thal·mol'ə·jist) *n.* A physician specializing in ophthalmology.

oph·thal·mol·o·gy (of'thal·mol'ə·jē) *n.* The science dealing with the structure, functions, and diseases of the eye. — **oph·thal'mo·log'ic** (-mə·loj'ik) or **·i·cal** *adj.*

oph·thal·mo·scope (of·thal'mə·skōp) *n.* An optical instrument for illuminating and viewing the center of the eye. — **oph·thal'mo·scop'ic** (-skop'ik) or **·i·cal** *adj.* — **oph·thal·mos·co·py** (of'thal·mos'kə·pē) *n.*

-opia *combining form Med.* A (specified) defect of the eye, or condition of sight: *myopia*. Also spelled *-opy*. [< Gk. *-ōpia* < *ōps, ōpos* the eye]

o·pi·ate (*n. & adj.* ō'pē·it, -āt; *v.* ō'pē·āt) *n.* **1.** Medicine containing opium or one of its derivatives. **2.** Something inducing relaxation or sleep. — *adj.* **1.** Consisting of opium. **2.** Tending to induce sleep. — *v.t.* **·at·ed, ·at·ing 1.** To treat with opium or an opiate. **2.** To deaden; dull. [< Med.L *opiatus*, pp. of *opiare* to treat with opium < L *opium.* See OPIUM.]

o·pine (ō·pīn') *v.t. & v.i.* **o·pined, o·pin·ing** To hold or express as an opinion; think; conjecture: now usually humorous. [< MF *opiner* < L *opinari* to think, suppose]

o·pin·ion (ə·pin′yən, ō-) *n.* **1.** A conclusion or judgment held with confidence, but falling short of positive knowledge. **2.** An estimation or judgment given more or less formally by an expert or experts. **3.** A judgment or estimate of the excellence or value of a person or thing. **4.** A common or prevailing sentiment: public *opinion*. **5.** *Law* The formal announcement of the conclusions of a court. [< OF < L *opinio, -onis < opinari* to think]
  — **Syn. 1, 3.** *Opinion, sentiment, impression, view,* and *persuasion* relate to one's thoughts about a subject. An *opinion* may be either a judgment in a matter of objective fact or truth, or it may express one's feeling in what is a matter of evaluation rather than fact. In the latter sense, it is a close synonym of *sentiment*. *Impression* refers to the first reaction of the mind, before the due consideration that warrants an *opinion* or *sentiment*. *View* is a general term embracing both *opinions* and *sentiments*, while *persuasion* emphasizes the warmth of feeling, somewhat short of conviction or belief, with which one holds a *view*. Compare DOCTRINE, BELIEF, HYPOTHESIS.

o·pin·ion·at·ed (ə·pin′yən·ā′tid, ō-) *adj.* Obstinately attached to one's own opinion. — **o·pin′ion·at′ed·ness** *n.*

o·pin·ion·a·tive (ə·pin′yən·ā′tiv, ō-) *adj.* **1.** Opinionated. **2.** Of the nature of opinion. — **o·pin′ion·a′tive·ly** *adv.* — **o·pin′ion·a′tive·ness** *n.*

op·is·thog·na·thous (op′is·thog′nə·thəs) *adj.* Having receding jaws: opposed to *prognathous*. [< Gk. *opisthen* behind + *gnathos* jaw] — **op′is·thog′na·thism** (nə·thiz′əm) *n.*

o·pi·um (ō′pē·əm) *n.* A milky exudation from the unripe capsules of the **opium poppy** (*Papaver somniferum*), containing a mixture of alkaloids, including morphine. It is a powerful narcotic, having a bitter taste and a heavy odor. [< L < Gk. *opion* opium, dim. of *opos* vegetable juice]

opium den A room or place for opium smoking or eating.

o·pi·um·ism (ō′pē·əm·iz′əm) *n. Pathol.* **1.** Addiction to the use of opium. **2.** A morbid condition due to such addiction.

op·o·del·doc (op′ə·del′dok) *n.* A camphorated soap liniment. [? < Gk. *opos* vegetable juice]

O·por·to (ō·pôr′tō) A port city in western Portugal, on the Douro; pop. 325,400 (est. 1969): Portuguese *Porto*.

o·pos·sum (ə·pos′əm, pos′əm) *n.* An American marsupial (genus *Didelphis*) of largely arboreal and nocturnal habits, having prehensile paws and tail; especially, the **common** or **Virginia opossum** (*D. virginiana*), noted for feigning death when threatened: also called *possum*. [< Algonquian. Cf. Virginian *apasum* white animal.]

opossum shrimp A crustacean (family *Mysidae*) that carries its eggs in a pouch beneath the thorax.

opp. 1. Opposed. **2.** Opposite.

Op·pen·heim (op′ən·hīm), E(**dward**) **Phillips,** 1866–1946, English novelist.

Op·pen·heim·er (op′ən·hī′mər), **J. Robert,** 1904–1967, U.S. physicist.

op·pi·dan (op′ə·dən) *adj.* Relating to a town; civic. — *n.* At Eton College in England, a student who boards in town. [< L *oppidanus* of a town < *oppidum* town]

op·pi·late (op′ə·lāt) *v.t.* **·lat·ed, ·lat·ing** *Med.* To block or obstruct; constipate. [< L *oppilatus,* pp. of *oppilare* to stop up < *ob-* against + *pilare* to ram down] — **op′pi·lant** *adj.* — **op′pi·la′tion** *n.*

op·po·nent (ə·pō′nənt) *n.* One who opposes another, as in battle or debate; antagonist. — **Syn.** See ENEMY. — *adj.* **1.** Acting against something or someone; opposing. **2.** *Anat.* Bringing one part, as of a muscle, into opposition to another. **3.** Standing in front; opposite. [< L *opponens, -entis,* ppr. of *opponere* to set against < *ob-* against + *ponere* to place] — **op·po′nen·cy** *n.*

op·por·tune (op′ər·tōōn′, -tyōōn′) *adj.* **1.** Meeting some need; especially right or fit: an *opportune* place. **2.** Occurring at the right moment; timely. [< MF, fem. of *opportun* < L *opportunus* favorable, lit., (a wind) blowing towards port] — **op′por·tune′ly** *adv.* — **op′por·tune′ness** *n.*

op·por·tu·nist (op′ər·tōō′nist, -tyōō′-) *n.* One who uses every opportunity to contribute to the achievement of some end, and who is relatively uninfluenced by moral principles or sentiment. — **op′por·tu·nis′tic** (-tōō·nis′tik, -tyōō-) *adj.* — **op′por·tu′nism** *n.*

op·por·tu·ni·ty (op′ər·tōō′nə·tē, -tyōō′/-) *n. pl.* **·ties** A fit or convenient time; favorable occasion or circumstance. [< OF *opportunite* < L *opportunitas* fitness, advantage < *opportunus*. See OPPORTUNE.]
  — **Syn.** *Opportunity, chance, opening, break,* and *occasion* are compared as they denote a time or circumstance which is favorable to some purpose. When such a propitious moment comes in the normal course of events, we call it an *opportunity*; when it seems to come by accident or unexpectedly, we call it a *chance*. An *opening* is an *opportunity* that permits one to enter a field, launch an enterprise, embark on a career, etc. The informal *break* is quite similar, and stresses in addition the emergence of an *opportunity* in previously opposing circumstances. *Occasion* is a general term, denoting a time suitable to some action, or requiring some action. It

differs from the other synonyms in that it does not have the suggestion of good fortune which is implicit in them.

op·pos·a·ble (ə·pō′zə·bəl) *adj.* **1.** Capable of being placed opposite something else: said especially of the thumb. **2.** That can be opposed. — **op·pos′a·bil′i·ty** *n.*

op·pose (ə·pōz′) *v.* **·posed, ·pos·ing** *v.t.* **1.** To act or be in opposition to; resist; combat. **2.** To set in opposition or contrast: to *oppose* love to hatred. **3.** To place before or in front. — *v.i.* **4.** To act or be in opposition. [< OF *opposer,* ult. < L *oppositus,* pp. of *opponere* < *ob-* against + *ponere* to place] — **op·pos′er** *n.*
  — **Syn.** *Oppose, combat, fight, withstand, dispute, contradict,* and *contravene* mean to act against someone or something. *Oppose* is a general word, implying nothing as to the manner of opposition nor its object; we may *oppose* a person, an action, a cause, or an idea either by physical conflict or by intellectual argument. We *combat* or *fight* an enemy or a purpose opposed to our own, *resist* an attack on our own position, and *withstand* a siege; all these words, even in figurative use, suggest physical battle. *Dispute* sometimes has the generality of *oppose*; we may speak of boxers *disputing* in the ring, or of debaters *disputing* in the forum. But *dispute* is used chiefly, *contradict* and *contravene* always, of the conflict of ideas. One *contradicts* a statement by asserting the opposite; facts or circumstances *contravene* a principle or belief by showing it to be false or invalid. Compare CONTEND, OBSTRUCT.
  — **Ant.** support, sustain, uphold, abet, aid, foster.

op·po·site (op′ə·zit) *adj.* **1.** Situated or placed on the other side, or on each side, of an intervening space or thing; contrary in position: *opposite* ends of the room. **2.** Facing or moving the other way; contrary: *opposite* directions. **3.** Contrary in tendency or character; diametrically different: *opposite* opinions; the *opposite* sex. **4.** *Bot.* **a** Arranged in pairs, as leaves on a stem. **b** Having one part or organ immediately before or vertically over another, as a stamen before a petal. — *n.* **1.** Something or someone that is opposite, opposed, or contrary. **2.** *Obs.* An antagonist. — *adv.* In an opposite or complementary direction or position. — *prep.* **1.** Across from; facing. **2.** Complementary to, as in theatrical roles: He played *opposite* her. Abbr. *op., opp.* [< OF < L *oppositus,* pp. of *opponere*. See OPPONENT.] — **op′po·site·ly** *adv.* — **op′po·site·ness** *n.*

op·po·si·tion (op′ə·zish′ən) *n.* **1.** The act of opposing or resisting. **2.** The state of being opposite or opposed; antithesis. **3.** A position confronting another or a placing in contrast. **4.** That which is or furnishes an obstacle to some result: The stream flows without *opposition*. **5.** *Often cap.* The political party opposed to the party or administration in power. **6.** *Astron.* **a** The position of two heavenly bodies 180° apart in right ascension. **b** The position of the moon or a planet when the earth is directly between it and the sun. **7.** *Ling.* A state of contrast between any one phoneme and all the other phonemes in a language, as, /p/ is said to be in **bilateral opposition** to /b/ on the basis of the distinctive feature of voice, and in **multilateral opposition** to /d/ on the basis of the distinctive features of voice and place of articulation. **8.** *Logic* The relation between two propositions having the same subject and predicate but differing in quantity or quality or both. [< OF < L *oppositio, -onis < oppositus.* See OPPOSITE.] — **op′po·si′tion·al** *adj.* — **op′po·si′tion·ist** *n.* — **op′po·si′tion·less** *adj.*
  — **Syn. 1.** competition, hostility, antagonism. **2.** antipathy, conflict, rivalry. **4.** impediment, obstruction, hindrance, difficulty.

op·pos·i·tive (ə·poz′ə·tiv) *adj.* Placed or capable of being placed in contrast. — **op·pos′i·tive·ly** *adv.* — **op·pos′i·tive·ness** *n.*

op·press (ə·pres′) *v.t.* **1.** To burden or keep in subjugation by harsh and unjust use of force or authority; tyrannize. **2.** To lie heavy upon physically or mentally; weigh down; depress; dispirit. **3.** *Obs.* To crush or trample; overwhelm. — **Syn.** See ABUSE. [< OF *oppresser, apresser* < Med.L *oppressare,* freq. < L *oppressus,* pp. of *opprimere* to crush < *ob-* against + *premere* to press] — **op·pres′sor** (-sər) *n.*

op·pres·sion (ə·presh′ən) *n.* **1.** The act of oppressing, or the state of being oppressed. **2.** A sense of weight or constriction; mental depression. **3.** That which oppresses; privation; hardship; cruelty.

op·pres·sive (ə·pres′iv) *adj.* **1.** Burdensome; tyrannical; harsh; cruel. **2.** Producing a state of oppression. — **op·pres′sive·ly** *adv.* — **op·pres′sive·ness** *n.*

op·pro·bri·ous (ə·prō′brē·əs) *adj.* Contemptuously abusive; imputing disgrace. **2.** Shameful; disgraceful. [< OF *opprobrieux* < LL *opprobriosus* < L *opprobrium*. See OPPROBRIUM.] — **op·pro′bri·ous·ly** *adv.* — **op·pro′bri·ous·ness** *n.*

op·pro·bri·um (ə·prō′brē·əm) *n.* **1.** The state of being scornfully reproached; ignominy. **2.** Reproach mingled with disdain. **3.** A cause of disgrace or reproach. [< L < *opprobrare* to reproach < *ob-* against + *probum* disgrace]
  — **Syn. 1.** odium, obloquy, infamy, disgrace.

op·pugn (ə·pyōōn′) *v.t.* To assail or oppose with argument; call in question; controvert. [< L *oppugnare* < *ob-* against + *pugnare* to fight] — **op·pugn′er** *n.*
  — **Syn.** dispute, oppose, challenge, contest.

---

op·pug·nant (ə·pug′nənt) *adj.* Opposing in a hostile manner; combative. [< L *oppugnans, -antis,* ppr. of *oppugnare.* See OPPUGN.] — **op·pug′nance, op·pug′nan·cy** *n.*

Ops (ops) In Roman mythology, the wife of Saturn, goddess of the harvest: identified with the Greek *Rhea.*

-opsia *combining form Med.* A (specified) type or condition of sight. Also **-opsy.** [< NL < Gk. *opsis* aspect, sight]

-opsis *combining form Biol.* A thing having a (specified) appearance: often used in describing fruits: *caryopsis, coreopsis.* [< Gk. *opsis* sight, appearance]

opsonic index *Bacteriol.* The ratio of the quantity of bacteria destroyed by phagocytes in the blood serum of the tested individual to that destroyed in a normal serum.

op·son·i·fy (op·son′ə·fi) *v.t.* **·fied, ·fy·ing** *Bacteriol.* To render (bacteria) subject to phagocytosis by the action of opsonins. Also **op·son·ize** (op′sən·iz). — **op·son′i·fi·ca′tion** *n.*

op·so·nin (op′sə·nin) *n. Bacteriol.* A component of blood serum that acts upon invading cells or bacteria so as to assist in their absorption by the phagocytes. [< Gk. *opson* cooked food + -IN] — **op·son′ic** *adj.*

opt (opt) *v.i.* To choose; decide; elect. [< F *opter* < L *optare,* to choose, wish]

opt. 1. Optative. **2.** Optical; optics.

op·ta·tive (op′tə·tiv) *adj.* **1.** Expressing or indicative of desire or choice. **2.** *Gram.* Denoting the mood that expresses wish or desire, as in Greek and certain other languages. — *n. Gram.* **1.** The optative mood. **2.** A word or construction in this mood. Abbr. *opt.* [< F *optatif* < LL *optativus* < L *optare* to wish] — **op′ta·tive·ly** *adv.*

op·tic (op′tik) *adj.* Pertaining to the eye or vision. — *n. Informal* An eye. [< MF *optique* < Med.L *opticus* < Gk. *optikos* < *optos* seen < stem *op-* as in *opsomai* I shall see]

op·ti·cal (op′ti·kəl) *adj.* **1.** Pertaining to optics. **2.** Of or pertaining to eyesight. **3.** Designed to assist or improve vision. Abbr. *opt.* — **op′ti·cal·ly** *adv.*

optical activity *Chem.* The property possessed by certain compounds of rotating the plane of polarization of light.

optical art Op art (which see).

optical glass High-quality glass specialized in refractive and dispersive powers for lenses.

optical maser *Physics* A laser.

optic axis 1. *Crystall.* One of the directions along which a ray of light undergoes no double refraction within a crystal. **2.** The axis of the eye corresponding with the line of vision passing through the center of the lens and cornea.

op·ti·cian (op·tish′ən) *n.* One who makes or deals in optical goods, as one who grinds eyeglass lenses to prescription and sells frames for them. [< F *opticien* < Med.L *optica.* See OPTICS.]

optic nerve *Anat.* The special nerve of vision, connecting the retina with the cerebral centers. For illustration see EYE.

op·tics (op′tiks) *n.pl.* (construed as *sing.*) The science that treats of the phenomena of light, vision, and sight. Abbr. *opt.* [< OPTIC; trans. of Med.L *optica* < Gk. *ta optika* optics < *optikos.* See OPTIC.]

optic thalamus *Anat.* The thalamus.

op·ti·mal (op′tə·məl) *adj.* Optimum.

op·ti·me (op′tə·mē) *n.* In Cambridge University, England, one who has attained the second (**Senior optime**) or third (**Junior optime**) grade in mathematical honors. Compare WRANGLER (def. 2). [< L *optime* best]

op·ti·mism (op′tə·miz′m) *n.* **1.** A disposition to look on the bright side of things: opposed to *pessimism.* **2.** The doctrine that everything is ordered for the best. **3.** The doctrine that the universe is constantly tending toward a better state. [< F *optimisme* < L *optimus* best] — **op′ti·mist** *n.* — **op·ti·mis′tic** or **·ti·cal** *adj.* — **op′ti·mis′ti·cal·ly** *adv.*

op·ti·mize (op′tə·miz) *v.* **·mized, ·miz·ing** *v.t.* **1.** To make the most of. **2.** To plan or prepare plans for (industrial production) in order to secure maximum efficiency. — *v.i.* **3.** To be optimistic. **4.** To work toward obtaining an optimum.

op·ti·mum (op′tə·məm) *n. pl.* **·ma** (-mə) or **·mums 1.** The condition or degree producing the best result. **2.** *Biol.* The condition, amount, degree, etc., as of temperature, light, moisture, nutrition, and habitat, most favorable to the growth and development of organisms. — *adj.* Producing or conducive to the best results. [< L, neut. of *optimus* best]

op·tion (op′shən) *n.* **1.** The right, power, or liberty of choosing; discretion. **2.** The act of opting or choosing. **3.** The purchased privilege of either buying or selling something at a specified price within a specified time. **4.** A thing that is or can be chosen. — **Syn.** See ALTERNATIVE. [< MF < L *optio, -onis* < *optare* to choose]

op·tion·al (op′shən·əl) *adj.* Left to one's preference; not required; elective. — *n.* A study or course to be chosen from two or more offered; an elective. — **op′tion·al·ly** *adv.*

op·tom·e·ter (op·tom′ə·tər) *n.* An optical instrument for measuring the range of vision of the eye, and its peculiarities as a refracting medium. [< OPT(IC) + -METER]

op·tom·e·trist (op·tom′ə·trist) *n.* One who is skilled in optometry.

op·tom·e·try (op·tom′ə·trē) *n.* The profession or occupation of measuring vision and prescribing corrective lenses to compensate for visual defects.

op·u·lence (op′yə·ləns) *n.* **1.** Wealth; affluence. **2.** Luxuriance; abundance. Also **op′u·len·cy** (-lən·sē). — **Syn. 1.** riches, fortune, means, prosperity.

op·u·lent (op′yə·lənt) *adj.* **1.** Possessing great wealth; rich; affluent. **2.** Plentiful; abundant; profuse. [< L *opulentus* < *ops, opis* power, wealth] — **op′u·lent·ly** *adv.*

o·pun·ti·a (ō·pun′shē·ə) *n.* **1.** One of a large genus (*Opuntia*) of mainly tropical American cacti, having a usually flattened, much-branched stem, tubular yellow, red, or purple flowers, and an ovoid, sometimes edible fruit. **2.** A prickly pear. [< NL < L *Opuntia* (herba) (a plant) native to Opus < *Opus, Opuntis* a city in ancient Locris < Gk. *Opous*]

OPUNTIA

o·pus (ō′pəs) *n. pl.* **op·er·a** (op′ər·ə, op′rə) A literary or musical work or composition. Abbr. *op.* [< L, work]

o·pus·cule (ō·pus′kyōōl) *n.* A small or unimportant work. [< OF < L *opusculum,* dim. of *opus* work]

-opy See -OPIA.

o·quas·sa (ō·kwas′ə) *n.* A small lake trout (*Salvelinus oquassa*) of Maine, with a bluish black body. [after *Oquassa* Lake in Maine; ult. < Algonquian]

or[1] (ôr, *unstressed* ər) *conj.* **1.** Introducing an alternative: stop *or* go; red *or* white. **2.** Offering a choice of a series: Will you take milk *or* coffee *or* chocolate? **3.** Introducing an equivalent: the culinary art *or* art of cookery. **4.** Indicating uncertainty: He lives in Chicago *or* thereabouts. **5.** Introducing the second alternative of a choice limited to two: with *either* or *whether:* It must be either black *or* white; I don't care whether he goes *or* not. **6.** *Poetic* Either; whether: *or* in the heart *or* in the head. [ME, contraction of *other, auther* either, OE *āther;* infl. in meaning by OE *oththe* or]

or[2] (ôr) *adv., prep., & conj. Obs.* or *Scot.* Before; ere: chiefly in the phrase **or ever.** [OE *ār,* var. of *ær* earlier, before]

or[3] (ôr) *n. Heraldry* Gold, represented in engraving by a white surface powdered with dots. [< MF < L *aurum* gold]

o.r. Owner's risk.

-or[1] *suffix of nouns* The person or thing performing the action expressed in the root verb: *competitor.* ◆ See note under -ER[1]. [< AF *-our,* OF *-or* < L *-or, -ator*]

-or[2] *suffix of nouns* Quality, state, or condition: *favor.* [< OF < L]

OR or **O.R.** Operating room.

or·ach (ôr′əch, or′-) *n.* Any of various plants of the genus *Atriplex;* especially, the **garden orach** (*A. hortensis*), a tall, hardy annual cultivated for its spinachlike flavor. Also **or′·ache.** [< AF *arasche* < L *atriplex* < Gk. *atraphaxys*]

or·a·cle (ôr′ə·kəl, or′-) *n.* **1.** The seat of the worship of some ancient divinity, as of Apollo at Delphi, where prophecies were given out by the priests in answer to inquiries. **2.** A prophecy thus given. **3.** The deity whose prophecies were given. **4.** A person of unquestioned wisdom or knowledge, or something regarded as of infallible authority. **5.** An infallible authority: often used ironically. **6.** A wise saying. **7.** In the Bible, a divine command or communication; also, the holy of holies in the temple. [< OF < L *oraculum* < *orare* to speak, pray, ? < *os, oris* mouth]

o·rac·u·lar (ô·rak′yə·lər, ō-) *adj.* **1.** Of or pertaining to an oracle. **2.** Obscure; enigmatical. **3.** Prophetic; farseeing. — **o·rac·u·lar′i·ty** *n.* — **o·rac′u·lar·ly** *adv.*

O·ra·dea (ō·rä′dyä) A city in NW Rumania; pop. 132,250 (est. 1968): Hungarian *Nagyvarad.* Also **Oradea Ma·re** (mä′rā).

o·ral (ôr′əl, ō′rəl) *adj.* **1.** Uttered through the mouth; consisting of spoken words. **2.** Of or pertaining to the mouth; also, situated at or near the mouth. **3.** *Zool.* Designating the part of the body that contains the mouth, as in polyps. **4.** Of, pertaining to, or using speech. **5.** Taken or administered by mouth. **6.** *Phonet.* Produced through the mouth with the nasal passage closed; nonnasal. — **Syn.** See VERBAL. — *n. Usually pl.* An academic examination in which the student speaks his answers aloud. [< L *os, oris* mouth] — **o′ral·ly** *adv.*

O·ran (ō·ran′, *Fr.* ô·räṅ′) A port city in NW Algeria, on the Mediterranean; pop. 958,460 (est. 1966).

o·rang (ō·rang′) *n.* An orang-utan.

or·ange (ôr′inj, or′-) *n.* **1.** A round, juicy fruit of a low, much-branched, evergreen tree (genus *Citrus*) of the rue family, with a reddish yellow rind enclosing membranous divisions and a refreshing, sweetish or subacid pulp. **2.** Any of the trees yielding this fruit, as the **sour, bitter,** or **Seville orange** (*C. aurantium*) and the **sweet orange** (*C. sinensis*). **3.** Any of many related species, as the **trifoliate orange** (*Poncirus trifoliata*). **4.** The kumquat. **5.** The Osage orange (which see). **6.** A reddish yellow color; also, a pigment of this color. — **mandarin orange** A mandarin (def. 2). — *adj.* **1.** Reddish yellow. **2.** Of or pertaining to an orange. [< OF *orenge* < Provençal *auranja* (infl. by *aur* gold) < Sp. *naranja* < Arabic *nāranj* < Persian *nārang*]

Or·ange (ôr′inj, or′-; *Fr.* ô·räṅzh′) **1.** A former principality of western Europe, now part of SE France. **2.** A city in SE France; capital of the former principality; pop. 17,582

(1968). **3.** A city in NE New Jersey, near Newark; pop. 32,566. **4.** A city in SW California, near Santa Ana; pop. 77,374. **5.** A port city in eastern Texas, on the Sabine River; pop. 24,457.

Or·ange (ôr′inj, or′-) A European ruling family that has been sovereign in the Netherlands since 1815. Also *Dutch* **O·ran·je** (ô·rän′yə).

or·ange·ade (ôr′inj·ād′, or′-) *n.* A beverage made of orange juice, sugar, and water. [< F]

orange blossom The white, fragrant blossom of the orange tree, often worn by brides: State flower of Florida.

Orange Free State A Province of east central South Africa; 49,866 sq. mi.; pop. 1,373,790 (1960); capital, Bloemfontein; a Boer republic until 1900; known as **Orange River Colony** from 1900 to 1910. *Afrikaans* **O·ran·je Vry·staat** (ô·rän′yə frā′stät).

Or·ange·ism (ôr′inj·iz′əm, or′-) *n.* The principles of the Orangemen; Irish Protestantism. Also **Or′ang·ism.** — **Or′ange·ist, Or′ang·ist** *n.*

Or·ange·man (ôr′inj·mən, or′-) *n. pl.* **·men** (-mən) A member of a secret society founded in northern Ireland in 1795 for upholding Protestant ascendancy and succession in England. [named in honor of William III, king of England and Prince of Orange]

orange pekoe A finely sifted grade of black tea of India, Ceylon, and Java.

Orange River A river in southern Africa, flowing 1,300 miles, generally west, from NE Lesotho to the Atlantic and forming the southern boundaries of the Orange Free State and South–West Africa.

or·ange·ry (ôr′inj·rē, or′-) *n. pl.* **·ries** A place for cultivating orange trees, as a greenhouse.

or·ange·wood (ôr′inj·wŏŏd′, or′-) *n.* The fine-grained, yellowish wood of the orange tree, used in lathe work.

o·rang-u·tan (ō·rang′ə·tan, -ŏŏ·tan) *n. pl.* **·tans** or **·tan** A large, anthropoid ape (genus *Pongo* or *Simia*) of Borneo and Sumatra, having brownish red hair and extremely long arms: also called *orang, ourang.* Also **o·rang′-ou·tang** (-ə·tang, -ŏŏ·tang). [< Malay *oran utan* < *oran* man + *utan* forest]

o·ra pro no·bis (ō′rə prō nō′bis) *Latin* Pray for us.

o·rate (ôr′āt, ō·rāt′, ō′rāt; ō·rāt′) *v.i.* **o·rat·ed, o·rat·ing** To talk oratorically or pompously; speechify: chiefly humorous. [< L *oratus*, pp. of *orare*. See ORATION.]

o·ra·tion (ō·rā′shən, ō·rā′-) *n.* An elaborate public speech, especially one given at a formal occasion. — **Syn.** See SPEECH. [< L *oratio, -onis* < *oratus*, pp. of *orare* to pray, speak, ? < *os, oris* mouth. Doublet of ORISON.]

or·a·tor (ôr′ə·tər, or′-) *n.* **1.** One who delivers an oration; an eloquent public speaker. **2.** *Law* The complainant in a chancery proceeding. [< AF *oratour* < L *orator* < *orare*. See ORATION.]

or·a·tor·i·cal (ôr′ə·tôr′i·kəl, or′-, -tor′-) *adj.* Of, pertaining to, or characteristic of orators or oratory; rhetorical or eloquent. — **or′a·tor′i·cal·ly** *adv.*

or·a·to·ri·o (ôr′ə·tôr′ē·ō, -tō′rē·ō, or′-) *n. pl.* **·os** A large musical composition for solo voices, chorus, and orchestra, usually dramatizing a sacred story, but without scenery or acting. [< Ital., lit., place for prayer < LL *oratorium.* See ORATORY².]

or·a·to·ry¹ (ôr′ə·tôr′ē, -tō′rē, or′-) *n.* **1.** The art of public speaking; eloquence. **2.** Eloquent language. [< L *oratoria* (*ars*) the oratorical (art) < *orator.* See ORATOR.]

or·a·to·ry² (ôr′ə·tôr′ē, -tō′rē, or′-) *n. pl.* **·ries** A place for prayer; private chapel. [< LL *oratorium* (*templum*) (temple) for prayer < *orator* entreater < *oratus.* See ORATION.]

Or·a·to·ry (ôr′ə·tôr′ē, -tō′rē, or′-) *n. pl.* **·ries** **1.** In the Roman Catholic Church, a society of secular priests living together without vows and devoted to popular preaching and education: full name **Congregation of the Oratory.** **2.** Any of various similarly constituted religious orders.

orb (ôrb) *n.* **1.** A rounded mass; a sphere or globe. **2.** A circle or orbit; anything circular. **3.** A sphere topped by a cross, used as a symbol of royal power. **4.** *Poetic* The eye. **5.** *Obs.* The plane of the orbit or the orbit of a planet. — *v.t.* **1.** To shape into a sphere or circle. **2.** *Poetic* To enclose; encircle. [< L *orbis* circle]

or·bic·u·lar (ôr·bik′yə·lər) *adj.* **1.** Having the form of an orb or orbit. **2.** Well-rounded. **3.** *Bot.* Circular, as a leaf. [< F, or < L *orbicularis* < *orbiculus*, dim. of *orbis* circle] — **or·bic·u·lar·i·ty** (-lar′ə·tē) *n.* — **or·bic′u·lar·ly** *adv.*

or·bic·u·late (ôr·bik′yə·lit, -lāt) *adj.* Having a rounded form; orbicular. Also **or·bic′u·lat′ed.** [< L *orbiculatus* < *orbiculus.* See ORBICULAR.] — **or·bic′u·late·ly** *adv.* — **Syn.** circular, globular, spherical, spheroidal.

or·bit (ôr′bit) *n.* **1.** The path in space along which a heavenly body or artificial satellite moves about its center of attraction. **2.** *Anat.* One of the two cavities of the skull containing the eyes. **3.** *Ornithol.* The eyelid and skin surrounding the eye of a bird. **4.** *Physics* The assumed path of an electron around the atomic nucleus. **5.** A range of influence or action: the *orbit* of imperialism. — *v.t.* **1.** To cause to move in an orbit, as an artificial satellite. **2.** To revolve around (the earth, etc.), as a satellite. — *v.i.* **3.** To move in or as in an orbit. **4.** To track a wheel, orbit < *orbis* wheel, circle] — **or′bi·tal** *adj.*

orbital index *Anat.* The maximum height of the orbital cavity multiplied by 100 and divided by the width of the cavity.

orc (ôrk) *n.* A grampus or other cetacean. [ME *orgue* < L *orca* a kind of whale. Akin to OE *orc, orcneas.*]

Or·ca·gna (ôr·kä′nyä), **Andrea**, 1308?–68?, Florentine painter, sculptor, and architect: original name **Andrea di Cio·ne** (dē chō′nä).

or·ce·in (ôr′sē·in) *n. Chem.* A reddish brown coloring matter obtained from orcinol by the action of ammonium hydroxide and air. [< ORC(INOL) + -EIN]

orch. Orchestra(l).

or·chard (ôr′chərd) *n.* A plantation of trees grown for their products, as fruit, nuts, oils, etc.; also, the enclosure or ground containing them. [OE *orceard* < *ort-geard* garden < *ort* (akin to L *hortus*) + *geard* yard, enclosure]

or·chard·ist (ôr′chərd·ist) *n.* One who cultivates trees in orchards for their products. Also **or′chard·man** (-mən).

orchard oriole A common oriole (*Icterus spurius*) of eastern North America, smaller and having less brilliant plumage than the Baltimore oriole.

or·ches·tra (ôr′kis·trə) *n.* **1.** A comparatively large group of musicians playing together; especially, such a group including violins, cellos, etc., as a symphony orchestra; also, the instruments they play. **2.** *U.S.* In theaters, the place immediately before the stage, occupied by the musicians: also **orchestra pit.** **3.** The main floor of a theater. **4.** In ancient Greek and Roman theaters, the semicircular space from which the tiers of seats rose. Abbr. *orch.* [< L < Gk. *orchēstra* dancing space < *orcheesthai* to dance] — **or·ches·tral** (ôr·kes′trəl) *adj.* — **or·ches′tral·ly** *adv.*

or·ches·trate (ôr′kis·trāt) *v.t. & v.i.* **·trat·ed, ·trat·ing** **1.** To compose or arrange (music) for an orchestra. **2.** To plan, arrange, build, etc., for a specific purpose or for maximum effect: to *orchestrate* colors, buildings, etc.

or·ches·tra·tion (ôr′kis·trā′shən) *n.* The technique of writing or arranging music for an orchestra; also, an orchestral arrangement.

or·ches·tri·on (ôr·kes′trē·ən) *n.* A mechanical musical instrument, similar in action to a barrel organ, designed to imitate an orchestra. Also **or·ches·tri·na** (ôr′kis·trē′nə). [< ORCHESTRA]

or·chid (ôr′kid) *n.* **1.** Any of a widely distributed family (*Orchidaceae*) of terrestrial or epiphytic herbs of warm and temperate regions, having thickened, bulbous roots and often very showy and distinctive flowers. **2.** Any of various delicate, rosy purple colors. [< NL *orchidis*, faulty genitive of L *orchis* orchid < Gk., orig., a testicle; so called because of the shape of its rootstocks]

ORCHID

or·chi·da·ceous (ôr′ki·dā′shəs) *adj.* Of, pertaining to, or belonging to the orchid family.

orchido- *combining form* **1.** *Bot.* Orchid; pertaining to orchids: *orchidology.* **2.** *Med.* Orchio-. Also, before vowels, **orchid-.** [< ORCHID]

or·chid·ol·o·gy (ôr′ki·dol′ə·jē) *n.* The study and cultivation of orchids. — **or′chid·ol′o·gist** *n.*

or·chil (ôr′kil) *n.* **1.** A purple or blue dye obtained from archil. **2.** Archil. [< OF *orcheil, orchel.* See ARCHIL.]

orchio- *combining form* Testicle; pertaining to the testicles. Also before vowels, **orchi-.** [< Gk. *orchis* testicle]

or·chis (ôr′kis) *n.* Any plant of the genus *Orchis* having dense spikes of small flowers, frequently of striking shape and structure. [< L. See ORCHID.]

or·chi·tis (ôr·kī′tis) *n. Pathol.* Inflammation of the testicle. Also **or·chei′tis, or·chi·di·tis** (ôr′ki·dī′tis). — **or·chit′ic** (-kit′ik) *adj.*

or·ci·nol (ôr′sə·nōl, -nol) *n. Chem.* A colorless, crystalline compound, $C_7H_8O_2$, derived from certain lichens and also made synthetically. Also **or′cin** (-sən). [< Ital. *orc(ello)* archil + -IN + -OL¹]

Or·cus (ôr′kəs) In Roman mythology: **a** The abode of the dead. **b** Pluto or Dis, the god of the underworld.

Or·czy (ôr′tsē), **Baroness Emmuska**, 1865–1947, English novelist born in Hungary.

ord. **1.** Ordained. **2.** Order. **3.** Ordinal. **4.** Ordinance. **5.** Ordinary. **6.** Ordnance.

or·dain (ôr·dān′) *v.t.* **1.** To order or decree; enact; establish. **2.** To predestine; destine: said of God, fate, etc. **3.** To invest with ministerial or priestly functions. [< OF *ordener* < L *ordinare* to set in order < *ordo, -inis* order, arrangement] — **or·dain′er** *n.*

or·deal (ôr·dēl′, -dē′əl, ôr′dēl) *n.* **1.** A severe test of character or endurance; a trying course of experience. **2.** A former method of judicial trial in which the accused was subjected to painful physical tests that were supposed to do him no harm if he were innocent. [OE *ordāl, ordēl* judgment < *or-* out + *dæl* a deal].

ordeal bean Calabar bean (which see).

or·der (ôr′dər) *n.* **1.** A condition in which there is a methodical, proper, and harmonious arrangement or disposition of things. **2.** The disposition or arrangement of successive things: In what *order* shall they enter? **3.** Established method or customary procedure: the *order* of worship. **4.** Established or existing state or condition of things. **5.** A proper or working state or condition. **6.** A social condition of peace and harmony: to restore *order.* **7.** Social rank, grade, or class: every *order* of society. **8.** A kind, degree, or class: a high *order* of talent. **9.** A command, direction, or regulation. **10.** *Law* Any direction of a court, entered in the record but not included in the final judgment. **11.** A commission or instruction to supply, purchase, or sell something; also, that which is supplied or purchased. **12.** A class or body of persons united by some common bond or purpose: the *Order* of Odd Fellows. **13.** A monastic or religious body. **14.** A group of persons upon whom a government or sovereign has conferred an honor or dignity entitling them to wear specific insignia; also, the insignia so worn. **15.** *Eccl.* a *Usually pl.* Any of the various grades or degrees of the Christian ministry. **b** The rank or position of an ordained clergyman. **c** The rite or sacrament of ordination. **d** A liturgical form for a service or the performance of a rite: the *order* of confirmation. **16.** *Archit.* a A style of classical architecture, usually represented by the general character of its columns. Doric, Ionic, Corinthian, Tuscan, and Composite are the main classical orders. **b** A column with its entablature. **17.** *Biol.* A taxonomic category ranking next below the class, and above the family. **18.** *Math.* A number expressing the degree of complexity of an algebraic expression. **19.** *Gram.* The sequence of words in a sentence or construction. **20.** *Mil.* The position in which a rifle is placed at the command *order arms.* **21.** *Theol.* Any one of the nine grades or choirs of angels. See ANGEL. **22.** *Obs.* Suitable care; preparation: usually in the phrase **to take order.** Abbr. *o., ord.* — **in order** **1.** In accordance with rule or proper procedure. **2.** Neat; tidy. — **in order that** So that; to the end that. — **in order to** For the purpose of; to the end that. — **in short order** Quickly; without delay. — **on order** Ordered but not yet delivered. — **on the order of** Similar to. — **out of order** **1.** Not in working condition. **2.** Not in proper or harmonious arrangement or sequence. **3.** Not according to rule or customary procedure. **4.** Not suitable or appropriate. — **to cut orders** *U.S. Mil. Informal* To issue formal written orders, usually by mimeograph. — **to order** According to the buyer's specifications. — *v.t.* **1.** To give a command or direction to. **2.** To command to go, come, etc.: They *ordered* him out of the city. **3.** To give an order that (something) be done; prescribe. **4.** To give an order for: to *order* a new suit. **5.** To put in orderly or systematic arrangement; regulate. **6.** To decide or will: Fate *ordered* it so. **7.** To ordain: He was *ordered* deacon. — *v.i.* **8.** To give an order or orders. — **to order arms** *Mil.* To bring a rifle against the right side, with the butt on the ground. [< OF *ordre* < L *ordo, -inis* row, series, order] — **or′der·er** *n.*

or·der·ly (ôr′dər·lē) *adj.* **1.** Having regard for arrangement, method, or system. **2.** Peaceful. **3.** Characterized by neatness and order. **4.** Pertaining to orders. — *n.* *pl.* **·lies** **1.** A hospital attendant. **2.** A soldier detailed to carry orders. — *adv.* Methodically; regularly. — **or′der·li·ness** *n.*

Order of the Garter See under KNIGHTS OF THE GARTER.

or·di·nal[1] (ôr′də·nəl) *adj.* **1.** Denoting position in an order or succession. **2.** Pertaining to an order, as of plants, animals, etc. Abbr. *ord.* [< LL *ordinalis* < L *ordo, -inis* order]

or·di·nal[2] (ôr′də·nəl) *n.* *Eccl.* **1.** A book of rites for clerical ordinations, episcopal consecrations, etc. **2.** An ordo. [< Med.L *ordinale* < LL *ordinalis.* See ORDINAL[1].]

ordinal number *Math.* A number that shows the order of a unit in a given series, as first, second, third, etc.: distinguished from *cardinal number.*

or·di·nance (ôr′də·nəns) *n.* **1.** An authoritative rule; an order, decree, or law of a municipal body. **2.** A religious rite or ceremony. **3.** *Archit.* A system of arrangement. **4.** A law or command of God, or a decree of fate. Abbr. *ord.* — **Syn.** See LAW[1]. [< OF *ordenance* < Med.L *ordinantia* < L *ordinans, -antis,* ppr. of *ordinare.* See ORDAIN.]

or·di·nar·i·ly (ôr′də·ner′ə·lē, ôr′də·nâr′ə·lē) *adv.* **1.** In ordinary cases; commonly; usually. **2.** In the usual manner. **3.** To the usual extent: normally.

or·di·nar·y (ôr′də·ner′ē) *adj.* **1.** Of common or everyday occurrence; customary; usual. **2.** According to an established order; regular; normal. **3.** Common in rank or degree; of average merit or consequence; commonplace. **4.** Having immediate or ex-officio jurisdiction, as a judge. — *n.* *pl.* **·nar·ies** **1.** That which is usual or common. **2.** *Brit.* a A meal provided regularly at a fixed price. **b** An eating house where such meals are served. **3.** *Law* One who exercises jurisdiction in his own right, and not by delegation. **4.** *U.S.* In some States, a judge exercising probate jurisdiction. **5.** *Eccl.* a A rule or book prescribing the form for say-

ing Mass. **b** The practically unchangeable part of the Mass: with *the:* distinguished from the *proper.* **6.** An early type of bicycle with a large front wheel and a small rear wheel. **7.** *Heraldry* A charge of the simplest kind, usually bounded between simple lines, as a chief, pale, fess, chevron, bend, cross, or quarter. Abbr. *ord.* — **in ordinary** **1.** In actual and constant service. **2.** *Naut.* Out of commission; laid up: said of a ship. — **out of the ordinary** Not common or usual; extraordinary. [< OF *ordinarie* < L *ordinarius* regular, usual < *ordo, -inis* order, arrangement] — **or′di·nar′i·ness** *n.*

ordinary seaman A sailor having a lower rank and usually less experience than an able-bodied seaman.

or·di·nate (ôr′də·nit) *adj.* **1.** Characterized by order; regular. **2.** *Biol.* Arranged in a regular row or rows, as spots on an insect's body or wings. — *n.* *Math.* **1.** The distance of any point from the X-axis, measured on a line parallel to the Y-axis in a coordinate system. **2.** The line or number indicating such distance. Symbol *y.* [< L *ordinatus,* pp. of *ordinare.* See ORDAIN.]

or·di·na·tion (ôr′də·nā′shən) *n.* **1.** *Eccl.* The rite of consecration to the ministry. **2.** The state of being ordained, regulated, or settled. **3.** Arrangement of things in order; array. **4.** Natural or proper order. [< L *ordinatio, -onis* arrangement < *ordinare.* See ORDAIN.]

ord·nance (ôrd′nəns) *n.* **1.** Military weapons, ammunition, and associated equipment and materiel. **2.** Cannon or artillery. Abbr. *ord., ordn.* [Contr. of ORDINANCE]

or·do (ôr′dō) *n.* *pl.* **·di·nes** (-də·nēz) *Eccl.* A book containing directions for the portions of the Mass and the daily office that vary according to the calendar. [< L, order]

or·don·nance (ôr′də·nəns, *Fr.* ôr·dô·näns′) *n.* **1.** A right arranging of parts, as in a picture, so as to produce the best effect. **2.** A law or ordinance; especially, in French law, any code of laws. [< F < OF *ordenance.* See ORDINANCE.]

Or·do·vi·ces (ôr′də·vī′sēz, ôr·dov′ə·sēz) *n.pl.* An ancient Celtic tribe in Wales. [< L]

Or·do·vi·cian (ôr′də·vish′ən) *adj.* **1.** *Geol.* Of, pertaining to, or designating a period of the Paleozoic era, following the Cambrian and preceding the Silurian. **2.** Of or pertaining to the Ordovices. — *n.* An epoch of the Paleozoic era: sometimes called *Lower Silurian.* See chart for GEOLOGY. [< L *Ordovices* the Ordovices]

or·dure (ôr′jər, -dyŏŏr) *n.* Excrement; feces. [< OF < *ord* foul, nasty < L *horridus.* See HORRID.]

Or·dzho·ni·ki·dze (ôr′jə·nyi·kye′dzyi) A city in the SW R.S.F.S.R.; pop. 164,000 (1959).

ore (ôr, ōr) *n.* **1.** A natural substance, as a mineral or rock, containing a valuable metal. **2.** A natural substance containing a nonmetallic mineral: sulfur *ore.* [OE *ār, ǣr* brass, copper; infl. in meaning by OE *ōra* unwrought metal]

ö·re (œ′rə) *n.* *pl.* **öre** A coin or monetary unit equivalent to one hundredth of a krone in Denmark and Norway, and of a krona in Sweden. [< Norw., Dan., and Sw.]

o·re·ad (ôr′ē·ad, ō′rē-) *n.* In classical mythology, a mountain nymph. [< L *oreas, -adis* < Gk. *oreias, -ados* < *oros* mountain]

Ö·re·bro (œ′rə·brōō′) A city in south central Sweden; site of many medieval buildings; pop. 74,926 (1960).

o·rec·tic (ō·rek′tik) *adj. Philos.* Of or pertaining to the appetites or desires. Also **o·rec′tive.** [< Gk. *orektikos* appetitive < *orektos* reached for < *oregein* to reach for]

ore dressing *Metall.* The mechanical separation of valuable metals and materials from the ores in which they occur.

Oreg. Oregon: also **Ore.** (unofficial).

o·reg·a·no (ō·reg′ə·nō) *n.* A perennial herb (genus *Origanum*) of the mint family, resembling marjoram and having aromatic leaves used as a seasoning. [< Sp. *orégano* < L *origanum* wild marjoram]

Or·e·gon (ôr′ə·gon, -gən, or′-, ôr′ē·gən) A State of the United States on the Pacific; 96,981 sq. mi.; pop. 2,091,385; capital, Salem; entered the Union Feb. 14, 1859; nickname, *Beaver State.* — **Or′e·go′ni·an** (-gō′ne·ən) *adj. & n.*

Oregon fir The Douglas fir (which see). Also **Oregon pine.**

Oregon grape A thornless evergreen shrub (*Mahonia aquifolium*) of the barberry family, having dark blue berry clusters resembling grapes: the State flower of Oregon.

Oregon Trail A former route extending from the Missouri River about 2,000 miles NW to the Columbia River in Oregon: used by pioneers, 1804–1846.

o·re·ide (ō′rē·īd) *n.* Oroide, a metallic alloy.

O·rel (o·ryôl′) A city in the western R.S.F.S.R., on the Oka; pop. 232,000 (est. 1970): also *Oryol.*

O·ren·burg (ə·ryen·bŏŏrk′) A city in the SW R.S.F.S.R., on the Ural; pop. 345,000 (est. 1970): formerly *Chkalov.*

o·re·o·pith·e·cus (ôr′ē·ō·pith′ə·kəs, ō′rē-) *n. Paleontol* An anthropoid primate (genus *Oreopithecus*) of the Miocene or Pliocene epochs, whose fossilized bones were found in Tuscany: also called *mountain ape.* [< NL < Gk. *oros, oreos* mountain + *pithēkos* ape]

O·res·tes (ō·res′tēz, ō-) In Greek legend, the son of Agamemnon and Clytemnestra who, together with his sister Electra, avenged his father's murder by killing his mother and her lover Aegisthus. [< L < Gk.]

Ö·re·sund (œ'rə·sund′) The strait between Zealand (Denmark) and Sweden, connecting the Kattegat with the Baltic; 87 mi. long; average width 17 mi.: also *The Sound*. Danish **Ø·re·sund** (œ'rə·sōōn).

Or·fi·la (ôr·fē·là′), **Mathieu Joseph Bonaventure**, 1787–1853, French chemist; founder of toxicology.

or·gan (ôr′gən) *n.* **1.** A musical instrument consisting of a collection of pipes and reeds made to sound by means of compressed air controlled by one or more keyboards and by various knobs used to vary registration: often called *pipe organ*. **2.** Any musical instrument resembling this, either in sound or in some aspect of its mechanism. **3.** Any part of a plant or animal, as a stamen, the heart, etc., performing some definite function. **4.** An instrument or agency of communication; especially, a newspaper or periodical published in the interest of a political party, religious denomination, etc. **5.** An agency for or a means of getting something done or performing a certain function: Congress is an *organ* of government. [< OE *organa*, or < OF *organe* < L *organum* instrument, engine < Gk. *ergon* work.]

or·gan·dy (ôr′gən·dē) *n. pl.* **·dies** A thin, crisp, transparent, cotton muslin, used for dresses, collars, cuffs, etc. Also **or′gan·die.** [< F *organdi*; ult. origin uncertain]

organ grinder A street musician playing a hand organ.

or·gan·ic (ôr·gan′ik) *adj.* **1.** Of, pertaining to, or of the nature of animals and plants. **2.** Affecting or altering the structure of an organ or part: *organic* disease: distinguished from *functional*. **3.** Serving the purpose of an organ. **4.** *Chem.* Of or pertaining to compounds containing carbon. **5.** Inherent in or pertaining to the fundamental structure of something; constitutional. **6.** Of or characterized by systematic coordination of parts; organized; systematized. **7.** *Law* Designating the system of laws or principles forming the foundation of a government. **8.** *Agric.* Pertaining to the use of compost, manure, and other natural fertilizers in the cultivation of farms and gardens. Also **or·gan′i·cal.** Abbr. *org.* [< L *organicus* mechanical, musical < Gk. *organikos* < *organon*. See ORGAN.] **— or·gan′i·cal·ly** *adv.*

organic chemistry The branch of chemistry that relates to the structure, formation, and properties of compounds containing carbon.

organic disease *Pathol.* A disease that affects or alters the structure of some particular organ or part.

or·gan·i·cism (ôr·gan′ə·siz′əm) *n.* **1.** *Med.* The doctrine that all diseases are caused by specific lesions of one or more organs. **2.** *Biol.* The theory that living processes are the result of the activity of all the organs considered as an autonomous, integrated system. **3.** *Sociol.* The concept of society as an organism. **— or·gan′i·cist** *n.*

or·gan·ism (ôr′gən·iz′əm) *n.* **1.** An animal or plant considered as a totality of interdependent parts functioning to maintain vital activities. **2.** Anything that is analogous in structure and function to a living thing: the social *organism*. Abbr. *org.* **— or′gan·is′mal** *adj.*

or·gan·ist (ôr′gən·ist) *n.* One who plays the organ.

or·gan·i·za·tion (ôr′gən·ə·zā′shən, -i·zā′-) *n.* **1.** The act of organizing, or the state of being organized; also, that which is organized. **2.** A number of individuals systematically united for some end or work: a military *organization*. **3.** The officials, committeemen, etc., who control a political party: also called *machine*. **4.** An animal or vegetable organism. **5.** Any combination of parts. Also *Brit.* **or′gan·i·sa′tion.** [< Med.L *organizatio, -onis* < *organizare*. See ORGANIZE.]

or·gan·ize (ôr′gən·īz) *v.* **ized, ·iz·ing** *v.t.* **1.** To bring together or form as a whole or combination, as for a common objective. **2.** To arrange systematically; order. **3.** To furnish with organic structure. **4.** To enlist (workers) in a trade union. **5.** To unionize the workers of (a factory, etc.). **— *v.i.* 6.** To form or join an organization. Also *Brit.* **or′gan·ise.** [< MF *organiser* < Med.L *organizare* < L *organum*. See ORGAN.] **— or′gan·iz′a·ble** *adj.* **— or′gan·iz′er** *n.*

organo- *combining form* **1.** *Biol.* Related to an organ or to the organs of the body: *organogenesis*. **2.** *Chem.* Organic: *organometallic*. [< Gk. *organon* instrument, organ]

or·ga·no·gen·e·sis (ôr′gə·nō·jen′ə·sis) *n. Biol.* The development of organs in animals and plants. **— or′ga·no·ge·net′ic** (-jə·net′ik) *adj.*

or·ga·nog·ra·phy (ôr′gə·nog′rə·fē) *n.* The scientific description of organs; descriptive organology. **— or′ga·no·graph′ic** (-nō·graf′ik) or **·i·cal** *adj.*

or·ga·nol·o·gy (ôr′gə·nol′ə·jē) *n.* The branch of biology that deals with the study of the structure and function of plant and animal organs. **— or′ga·no·log′ic** (-nō·loj′ik) or **·i·cal** *adj.* **— or′ga·nol′o·gist** *n.*

or·ga·no·me·tal·lic (ôr′gə·nō·mə·tal′ik) *adj. Chem.* Designating or pertaining to a compound of metal and carbon.

or·ga·non (ôr′gə·non) *n. pl.* **·na** (-nə) or **·nons** A system of rules and principles considered as an instrument of knowledge or thought: also called *organum*. [< Gk.]

or·ga·no·sil·i·con (ôr′gə·nō·sil′ə·kon) *n. Chem.* Any of a class of compounds containing silicon and carbon.

or·ga·no·ther·a·py (ôr′gə·nō·ther′ə·pē) *n. Med.* The treatment of disease by extracts from animal organs, as the thyroid gland, pancreas, etc. Also **or′ga·no·ther′a·peu′tics** (-ther′ə·pyōō′tiks).

organ pipe One of the tubes of a pipe organ in which a column of air is made to vibrate so as to produce a tone.

or·ga·num (ôr′gə·nəm) *n. pl.* **·na** (-nə) or **·nums** **1.** An organon. **2.** In medieval music, a part sung as an accompaniment to the melody or plain song at a consistent interval, such as a fourth or fifth, above or below it; also, this method of part singing. [< L. See ORGAN.]

or·gan·za (ôr·gan′zə) *n.* A sheer, crisp fabric used for evening dresses, etc. [Prob. var. of *Lorganza*, a trade mark]

or·gan·zine (ôr′gən·zēn) *n.* **1.** A raw silk thread made of single threads twisted together. **2.** A fabric of organzine. [< F *organsin* < Ital. *organzino*; ult. origin uncertain]

or·gasm (ôr′gaz·əm) *n.* **1.** *Physiol.* The acme of excitement at the culmination of a sexual act, followed by detumescence. **2.** Immoderate or extreme excitement or behavior. [< NL *orgasmus* < Gk. *orgasmos* < *orgaein* to swell] **— or·gas′tic** (ôr·gas′tik) *adj.*

or·geat (ôr′zhat, *Fr.* ôr·zhà′) *n.* A syrup made from barley water and sugar flavored with almonds, orange flowers, etc. [< MF < Provençal *orjat* < *ordi* barley < L *hordeum*]

Or·get·o·rix (ôr·jet′ə·riks) First-century B.C. Helvetian chief, who opposed Julius Caesar.

or·gi·as·tic (ôr′jē·as′tik) *adj.* **1.** Pertaining to or resembling an orgy. **2.** Marked by orgies. Also **or′gi·ac** (-ak), **or′·gic** (-jik). [< Gk. *orgiastikos* < *orgiastes* practitioner of secret rites < *orgiazein* to celebrate < *orgia* secret rites]

or·gy (ôr′jē) *n. pl.* **·gies** **1.** Wild or wanton revelry; a drunken carousal; debauch. **2.** Any immoderate or excessive indulgence. **3.** *pl.* The secret rites in honor of certain ancient Greek and Roman deities, as Dionysus, marked by frenzied songs and dances. [Earlier *orgies*, pl. < MF < L *orgia* < Gk., secret rites. Akin to Gk. *ergon* work.]

or·i·bi (ôr′ə·bē, or′-) *n. pl.* **·bis** or **·bi** A small, dun-colored African antelope (genus *Ourebia*) having slender horns: also spelled *ourebi*. [< Afrikaans < Hottentot *arab*]

o·ri·el (ôr′ē·əl, ō′rē-) *n. Archit.* A bay window, especially one built out from a wall and resting on a bracket or similar support. [< OF *oriol* porch, gallery, ? < Med.L *oriolum*; ult. origin unknown]

o·ri·ent (*n. & adj.* ôr′ē·ənt, ō′rē-, -ent; *v.* ôr′ē·ent, ō′rē-) *n.* **1.** The east: opposed to *occident*. **2.** The eastern sky; also, dawn; sunrise. **3.** The iridescent luster of a pearl. **— *v.t.* 1.** To cause to face or turn to the east. **2.** To place or adjust, as a map, in exact relation to the points of the compass. **3.** To adjust according to recognized facts or truths. **4.** To adjust in relation to something else: His experience *oriented* his ideas toward science. Also *orientate*. **— *adj.* 1.** Resembling sunrise; bright. **2.** Ascending; rising. [< OF < L (*sol*) *oriens, -entis* rising (sun), east, ppr. of *oriri* to rise]

O·ri·ent (ôr′ē·ənt, ō′rē-, -ent) **1.** The countries east of Europe; Asia; especially, eastern Asia. **2.** The eastern hemisphere. Distinguished from *Occident*.

o·ri·en·tal (ôr′ē·en′təl, ō′rē-) *adj.* **1.** Of or pertaining to the East, or to the countries constituting the Orient: distinguished from *occidental*. **2.** Appearing or being in the eastern sky: said of stars and planets. **3.** Very bright, clear, and pure: said of gems. **4.** Denoting a variety of precious corundum, especially sapphire: an *oriental* topaz. [< OF < L *orientalis*. See ORIENT.] **— o′rien·tal′ly** *adv.*

O·ri·en·tal (ôr′ē·en′təl, ō′rē-) *adj.* **1.** Of or pertaining to the Orient; Eastern. **2.** Designating a zoogeographic realm that includes India, southern Asia, the East Indies, and the Philippine Islands. **— *n.* An inhabitant of Asia; an Asian.

Oriental alabaster Alabaster (def. 2).

Oriental amethyst Amethyst (def. 2).

O·ri·en·tal·ism (ôr′ē·en′təl·iz′əm, ō′rē-) *n.* **1.** An Oriental quality, mannerism, characteristic, etc. **2.** Knowledge of or proficiency in Oriental languages, literature, etc. Also **o′ri·en′tal·ism.** **— O′ri·en′tal·ist** *n.*

O·ri·en·tal·ize (ôr′ē·en′təl·īz, ō′rē-) *v.t. & v.i.* **ized, ·iz·ing** To make or become Oriental. Also *Brit.* **O′ri·en′tal·ise.**

Oriental ruby A ruby (def. 1).

Oriental rug 1. A rug or carpet hand-woven in one piece in the Orient. **2.** Any rug having a design or texture resembling those made in the Orient.

o·ri·en·tate (ôr′ē·en·tāt′, ō′rē-) *v.* **·tat·ed, ·tat·ing** *v.t.* **1.** To orient. **— *v.i.* 2.** To face or turn eastward or in some specified direction. **3.** To become adjusted or oriented. [< F *orienter* < OF *orient*. See ORIENT.]

o·ri·en·ta·tion (ôr′ē·en·tā′shən, ō′rē-) *n.* **1.** The act of orienting, or the state of being oriented. **2.** Position, or the determining of position, with relation to the points of the compass. **3.** The determination or adjustment of one's position with reference to circumstances, ideals, etc. **4.** A program or class introducing one to a new environment, job, school, etc. **5.** *Psychol.* Awareness of one's own temporal, spatial, and personal relationships. **6.** *Archit.* The alignment of a church upon an east-west axis, so as to have the altar in the eastern end. **7.** The homing instinct, as in pigeons. **8.** *Chem.* The particular disposition of the constituent atoms in a compound, especially as determined by electrical forces.

O·ri·en·te (ôr/ē·en/tä, ō/rē-) **1.** A Province of eastern Cuba; 14,128 sq. mi.; pop. 2,857,200 (1970); capital, Santiago de Cuba: formerly *Santiago de Cuba*. **2.** A region and former province of Ecuador, comprising all its territory east of the Andes.

or·i·fice (ôr/ə·fis, or/-) *n.* An opening into a cavity; mouth; aperture. [< MF < LL *orificium* < L *os, oris* mouth + *facere* to make]

or·i·flamme (ôr/ə·flam, or/-) *n.* **1.** The red banner of the abbey of St. Denis, used as a battle standard by the kings of France until the 15th century. **2.** *Heraldry* A blue banner charged with three fleurs-de-lis of gold. **3.** Any flag or standard. Also spelled *auriflamme*. [< F < OF *orie flambe* < *orie* golden (< L *aureus*) + *flambe* banner; infl. by Med.L *aurea flamma* the red banner of the French kings < L *aureus* golden (< *aurum* gold) + *flamma* flame]

orig. Original(ly).

or·i·ga·mi (ôr/i·gä/mē) *n.* The ancient Japanese art of folding single sheets of paper into realistic animal forms, usually without the aid of scissors or paste. [< Japanese]

or·i·gan (ôr/ə·gən, or/-) *n.* The wild marjoram. [< OF < L *origanum* < Gk. *origanon*, an herb like marjoram, ? < *oros* mountain + *ganos* brightness]

Or·i·gen (ôr/ə·jen, -jən, or/-), 185?–254?, Alexandrian theologian.

or·i·gin (ôr/ə·jin, or/-) *n.* **1.** The beginning of the existence of anything. **2.** A primary source; cause. **3.** Parentage; ancestry. **4.** *Anat.* The relatively fixed point of attachment of a muscle: distinguished from *insertion*. **5.** *Math.* **a** The point at which the axes of a Cartesian coordinate system intersect; the point where the ordinate and abscissa equal zero. **b** The point in a polar coordinate system where the radius vector equals zero. — **Syn.** See BEGINNING. [< OF *origine* < L *origo, -inis* source, beginning < *oriri* to rise. Cf. ORIENT.]

o·rig·i·nal (ə·rij/ə·nəl) *adj.* **1.** Of or belonging to the beginning, origin, or first stage of existence of a thing. **2.** Produced by one's own mind and thought; not copied or imitative. **3.** Able to produce works requiring thought without copying or imitating others; creative; inventive. — *n.* **1.** The first form of anything. **2.** An original work, as a painting, sculpture, etc., as distinct from a reproduction or copy. **3.** A person or thing represented in a painting, biography, etc. **4.** A person of unique character or genius. **5.** An eccentric. **6.** *Archaic* An originator. Abbr. *orig.* — **Syn.** See NEW. [< OF < L *originalis* < *origo*. See ORIGIN.]

o·rig·i·nal·i·ty (ə·rij/ə·nal/ə·tē) *n.* *pl.* **·ties** **1.** The power of originating; inventiveness. **2.** The quality of being original or novel. **3.** Something original. [< F *originalité*]

o·rig·i·nal·ly (ə·rij/ə·nal·ē) *adv.* **1.** At the beginning. **2.** In a new and striking manner. Abbr. *orig.*

original sin *Theol.* The corruption and depravity held to be inherent in all mankind as a consequence of Adam's first sinful disobedience.

o·rig·i·nate (ə·rij/ə·nāt) *v.* **·nat·ed, ·nat·ing** *v.t.* **1.** To bring into existence; create; initiate. — *v.i.* **2.** To come into existence; have origin; arise. — **o·rig·i·na/tion** *n.* — **o·rig/i·na/tive** *adj.* — **o·rig/i·na/tive·ly** *adv.* — **o·rig/i·na/tor** *n.* — **Syn. 1.** institute, propagate, produce.

o·ri·na·sal (ôr/ə·nā/zəl, or/-) *adj.* *Anat.* Of or pertaining to the mouth and nose: the *orinasal* duct. **2.** *Phonet.* Produced with the nasal and oral passages both open, as the French nasal vowels. — *n.* *Phonet.* An orinasal vowel. [< L *os, oris* mouth + NASAL]

O·ri·no·co (ôr/ə·nō/kō, or/-) A river in Venezuela, flowing about 1,700 miles in a great arc to the Atlantic Ocean.

o·ri·ole (ôr/ē·ōl, ō/rē-) *n.* **1.** Any of a family (Oriolidae) of black and yellow passerine birds of the Old World, related to the crows, as the common **European** (or **golden**) **oriole** (*Oriolus oriolus*). **2.** Any of various black and yellow American songbirds (family *Icteridae*) that build hanging nests: especially, the Baltimore oriole and the orchard oriole: for illustration see NEST. [< OF *oriol* < Med.L *oriolus* < L *aureolus*, dim. of *aureus* golden < *aurum* gold]

O·ri·on (ō·rī/ən) In Greek and Roman mythology, a giant hunter who pursued the Pleiades and was killed by Diana. — *n.* A constellation, containing the bright star Rigel. See CONSTELLATION. [< L < Gk.]

O·ris·ka·ny (ō·ris/kə·nē) A village on the Mohawk River in central New York; scene of a battle in the Revolutionary War, 1777; pop. 1,627.

or·i·son (ôr/i·zən, or/-) *n. Usually pl.* A devotional prayer. [< OF *oreison, orison* < LL *oratio, -onis* prayer. Doublet of ORATION.]

O·ris·sa (ō·ris/ə) A State of eastern India, on the Bay of Bengal; 60,162 sq. mi.; pop. 20,674,000 (1971); capital, Bhubaneswar.

O·ri·ya (ō·rē/yä) *n.* One of the major Indic languages of India, closely related to Bengali.

O·ri·za·ba (ō/rē·sä/vä) A city in Veracruz State, SE Mexico,

near **Pico de Orizaba** (also *Citlaltépetl*), an inactive volcano (18,700 ft.); pop. 92,728 (1970).

Ork. Orkney Islands.

Ork·ney Islands (ôrk/nē) An island group north of Scotland comprising **Orkney**, a county of Scotland; 376 sq. mi.; pop. 17,300 (1969); county seat, Kirkwall. Also **Ork·neys** (ôrk/nēz).

Or·lan·do (ôr·lan/dō) A city in east central Florida; pop. 99,006.

Or·lan·do (ôr·län/dō), **Vittorio Emanuele**, 1860–1952, Italian statesman; premier 1917–19.

orle (ôrl) *n. Heraldry* A border around a shield, half the width of a bordure. See SUBORDINARY. [< F < OF *urle, ourle* < L *ora* border]

Or·lé·a·nais (ôr·lā·á·ne/) A region and former province of north central France.

Or·le·an·ist (ôr/lē·ən·ist) *n.* A supporter of the Orléans branch of the French royal family descended from the younger brother of Louis XIV. — *adj.* Of or pertaining to Orleanists or to their point of view. — **Or/le·an·ism** *n.*

Or·lé·ans (ôr·lā·än/) A branch of the reigning Valois and Bourbon houses of France, many members of which have been prominent in French history; notably, **Louis Philippe Joseph**, 1747–93, Duc d'Orléans, Revolutionary politician; guillotined: called **Philippe É·ga·li·té** (ā·gá·lē·tā/).

Or·lé·ans (ôr·lā·än/) A commune in north central France, on the Loire; pop. 94,382 (1968).

Or·lon (ôr/lon) *n.* A synthetic fiber woven from an acrylic resin, having high resistance to heat, light, and chemicals, widely used as a textile material: a trade name. Also **or/lon.**

or·lop (ôr/lop) *n. Naut.* The lowest deck of a ship, especially of a warship. Also **orlop deck.** [< Du. *overloop*, orig., covering < *over* over + *loopen* to run; so called because it covers the hold]

Or·man·dy (ôr/mən·dē), **Eugene**, born 1899, U.S. conductor born in Hungary.

or·mer (ôr/mər) *n.* Any ear-shaped shell; especially, that of an edible abalone (*Haliotis tuberculata*) of the Channel Islands. [< dial. F (Channel Islands) and F *ormier*, contr. of *oreille de mer*, lit., ear of the sea]

or·mo·lu (ôr/mə·lōō) *n.* **1.** Any of various alloys of copper, tin, and zinc that resemble gold in appearance, used in furniture decorations, jewelry, etc.: also called *mosaic gold*. **2.** Anything appearing genuine but actually derivative or of inferior quality. [< F *or moulu*, lit., ground gold < *or* gold (< L *aurum*) + *moulu*, pp. of *moudre* to grind < L *molere*]

Or·muz (ôr/muz, ôr·mōōz/) See HORMUZ.

Or·muzd (ôr/muzd) The supreme deity of the Zoroastrian religion, the creator of the world, source of light, and embodiment of the principle of good, essentially opposed to Ahriman, the spirit of darkness and evil: also called *Ahura Mazda*. Also Or/muzd (-mäzd). [< Persian *Ormazd*, ult. < Avestan *Ahuro-Mazdao*, lit., wise lord]

or·na·ment (*n.* ôr/nə·mənt; *v.* ôr/nə·ment) *n.* **1.** Something that adorns or beautifies; a decoration. **2.** Ornaments, collectively. **3.** A person regarded as a source of honor or credit. **4.** The act of adorning, or the state of being adorned; ornamentation. **5.** *Music* A tone or group of tones used to embellish a melody without materially affecting its harmonic content, as an appoggiatura. **6.** *Eccl.* An accessory or trapping; adjunct. — *v.t.* **1.** To furnish with ornaments; decorate. **2.** To be an ornament to. — **Syn.** See ADORN. [< OF *ornement* < L *ornamentum* equipment, ornament < *ornare* to adorn] — **or/na·ment/er** (-ment/ər) *n.*

or·na·men·tal (ôr/nə·men/təl) *adj.* Of the nature of or serving as an ornament. — *n.* An ornamental object; especially, a plant used as decoration. — **or/na·men/tal·ly** *adv.*

or·na·men·ta·tion (ôr/nə·men·tā/shən) *n.* **1.** The act or result of ornamenting. **2.** The state of being ornamented. **3.** That which ornaments; also, ornaments, collectively.

or·nate (ôr·nāt/) *adj.* **1.** Elaborately or excessively ornamented; overdecorative. **2.** Florid or showy, as a style of writing. [< L *ornatus*, pp. of *ornare* to adorn] — **or·nate/ly** *adv.* — **or·nate/ness** *n.*

or·ner·y (ôr/nər·ē, ôrn/rē) *adj. Dial.* **1.** *U.S.* Disposed to be contrary or stubborn; hard to manage. **2.** *U.S.* Mean; ugly; low; snide: an *ornery* trick. **3.** Ordinary; common. Also *onery.* [Alter. of ORDINARY] — **or/ner·i·ness** *n.*

or·nis (ôr/nis) *n.* Avifauna. [< G < Gk., bird]

ornith. or **ornithol.** Ornithological; ornithology.

or·nith·ic (ôr·nith/ik) *adj.* Of or pertaining to birds. [< Gk. *ornithikos* birdlike < *ornis, ornithos* bird]

or·ni·thine (ôr/nə·thēn, -thin) *n. Biochem.* An amino acid, $C_5H_{12}O_2N_2$, obtained from arginine. [< Gk. *ornis, ornithos* bird + -INE²]

or·ni·this·chi·an (ôr/nə·this/kē·ən) *Paleontol. adj.* Of or belonging to an order (Ornithischia) of Mesozoic dinosaurs, including stegosauri, armored and horned dinosaurs, and iguanodons. — *n.* A member of this order. [< NL *ornithischia* < Gk. *ornis, ornithos* bird + *ischion* hip]

ornitho- *combining form* Bird; of or relating to birds: *ornithology.* Also, before vowels, **ornith-**. [< Gk. *ornis, onithos* bird]

or·ni·thoid (ôr′nə·thoid) *adj.* Resembling or of the nature of a bird.

ornithol. Ornithology.

or·ni·thol·o·gy (ôr′nə·thol′ə·jē) *n.* The branch of zoology that treats of birds. [< NL *ornithologia* < Gk. *ornithologos* treating of birds] **— or′ni·tho·log′ic** (-thə·loj′ik) or **·i·cal** *adj.* **— or′ni·tho·log′i·cal·ly** *adv.* **— or·ni·thol′o·gist** *n.*

or·ni·tho·pod (ôr′nə·thō·pod, ôr·ni′-) *Paleontol. adj.* Of or belonging to a group (*Ornithopoda*) of bipedal dinosaurs of herbivorous habits. **—** *n.* A member of this group. [< NL *Ornithopoda* < Gk. *ornis, ornithos* bird + *pous, podos* foot]

or·ni·thop·ter (ôr′nə·thop′tər) *n.* A theoretical type of aircraft sustained and propelled by the movement of the wings: also called *orthopter.* [< ORNITHO- + Gk. *pteron* wing]

or·ni·tho·rhyn·chus (ôr′nə·thō·ring′kəs) *n. pl.* **·chi** (-kī) Any of a genus (*Ornithorhynchus*) of monotremes of which only the duckbill survives. [< NL < Gk. *ornis, ornithos* bird + *rhynchos* beak] **— or′ni·tho·rhyn′chous** *adj.*

or·ni·tho·sis (ôr′nə·thō′sis) *n.* An infectious virus disease of turkeys and other birds that resembles psittacosis.

oro-[1] *combining form* Mouth; oral: *oropharynx.* [< L *os, oris* mouth]

oro-[2] *combining form Geol.* Mountain; of mountains: *orography.* [< Gk. *oros* mountain]

or·o·ban·cha·ceous (ôr′ō·bang·kā′shəs, or′-) *adj. Bot.* Of or belonging to the broomrape family of plants (*Orobanchaceae*). [< NL *orobanchaceae* < L *orobanche* broomrape < Gk. *orobanchē* < *orobos* kind of vetch + *anchein* to throttle]

o·rog·e·ny (ô·roj′ə·nē, ō-) *n. Geol.* The process of mountain formation. Also **o·ro·gen·e·sis** (ôr′ə·jen′ə·sis). [< ORO-[2] + -GENY] **— or·o·gen·ic** (ôr′ə·jen′ik, or′-) *adj.* **— or′o·gen′i·cal·ly** *adv.*

o·rog·ra·phy (ô·rog′rə·fē, ō-) *n.* The branch of physical geography that deals with highlands and mountain ranges. [< ORO-[2] + -GRAPHY] **— or·o·graph·ic** (ôr′ə·graf′ik, or′-) or **·i·cal** *adj.* **— or′o·graph′i·cal·ly** *adv.*

o·ro·ide (ôr′ō·īd, ō′rō-) *n.* An alloy of copper, zinc, tin, and other metals, having a golden luster: also called *oreide.* [< F *or* gold (< L *aurum*) + Gk. *eidos* form]

o·rol·o·gy (ô·rol′ə·jē, ō-) *n.* The study of mountains. [< ORO-[2] + -LOGY] **— or·o·log·i·cal** (ôr′ə·loj′i·kəl, or′-) *adj.* **— or′o·log′i·cal·ly** *adv.* **— o·rol′o·gist** *n.*

o·rom·e·ter (ô·rom′ə·tər, ō-) *n.* An aneroid barometer having a scale that gives elevations above sea level. [< ORO-[2] + -METER] **— or·o·met·ric** (ôr′ə·met′rik, or′-) *adj.*

O·ron·tes (ô·ron′tēz, ō-) A river of NW Syria and southern Turkey, flowing about 240 miles, generally north, to the Mediterranean.

o·ro·phar·ynx (ôr′ō·far′ingks, ō′rō-) *n. pl.* **·pha·ryn·ges** (-fə·rin′jēz) or **·phar·ynx·es** *Anat.* The part of the pharynx behind the mouth. [< ORO-[1] + PHARYNX]

O·ro·si·us (ə·rō′shē·əs), **Paulus,** 385?–420, Spanish theologian and historian.

o·ro·tund (ôr′ə·tund, ō′rə-) *adj.* **1.** Full, clear, rounded, and resonant: said of the voice. **2.** Pompous; inflated, as a manner of speech. [< L *ore rotundo* with well-turned speech, lit., with round mouth < *os, oris* mouth + *rotundus* round] **— o·ro·tun·di·ty** (ôr′ə·tun′də·tē) *n.*

O·roz·co (ō·rōs′kō), **José Clemente,** 1883–1949, Mexican painter.

Or·pen (ôr′pən), **Sir William (Newenham Montague),** 1878–1931, British painter born in Ireland.

or·phan (ôr′fən) *n.* **1.** A child whose parents are dead; also, less commonly, a child with one surviving parent. **2.** A cast-off or waif. **—** *adj.* **1.** That is an orphan. **2.** Of or for orphans. **—** *v.t.* To make an orphan of. [< L *orphanus* < Gk. *orphanos* orphaned] **— or′phan·hood** (-hŏŏd) *n.*

or·phan·age (ôr′fən·ij) *n.* **1.** An institution for the care of orphans or other abandoned children. **2.** The condition of being an orphan; also, orphans collectively.

Orphans' Court In some States of the United States, a court having jurisdiction over the estates of deceased persons, guardianship of orphans, etc.

Or·phe·us (ôr′fē·əs) In Greek mythology, the son of a Muse (usually Calliope), whose singing to the lyre could charm beasts and even rocks and trees. When his wife Eurydice died he was permitted to lead her back from Hades provided he did not turn to look at her until they had arrived in the upper world, but he did look back and she was lost. **— Or′phe·an** *adj.*

or·phic (ôr′fik) *adj. Sometimes cap.* Of a mystical nature; oracular. Also **or′phi·cal.** **— or′phi·cal·ly** *adv.*

Or·phic (ôr′fik) *adj.* **1.** Of, pertaining to, or associated with Orpheus. **2.** Having the quality of the music of Orpheus; enchanting. Also **Or′phi·cal.** [< L *Orphicus* < Gk. *Orphikos* < Orpheus Orpheus] **— Or′phi·cal·ly** *adv.*

Orphic mysteries The doctrines and rites observed by the worshipers of Dionysus, who identified him with Zagreus and claimed Orpheus as their founder.

Or·phism (ôr′fiz·əm) *n.* The religious system of the Orphic mysteries. **— Or′phist** *n.*

or·phrey (ôr′frē) *n.* **1.** A band of rich embroidery on certain ecclesiastical vestments. **2.** Any rich embroidery, especially of gold. [< OF *orfreis* < Med.L *aurifrisium* < L *auriphrygium* < *aurum* gold + *Phrygius* Phrygian]

or·pi·ment (ôr′pə·mənt) *n.* A lemon-yellow native arsenic trisulfide, As_2S_3, used as a pigment and as a dyestuff. [< OF < L *auripigmentum* gold pigment]

or·pine (ôr′pin) *n.* Any of a large, widely distributed family (*Crassulaceae*) of plants including the sedums and houseleeks, as the **common** or **garden orpine** (*Sedum telephium*), having succulent stems and leaves and clusters of whitish flowers. Also **or′pin.** [< OF *orpin* < *orpiment.* See ORPIMENT.]

Or·ping·ton (ôr′ping·tən) *n.* Any of a variety of large domestic fowls having single combs and unfeathered legs. [after *Orpington,* a village in Kent, England]

or·ra (ôr′ə, or′ə) *adj. Scot.* Extra and occasional; odd.

or·re·ry (ôr′ə·rē, or′-) *n. pl.* **·ries** A mechanical apparatus showing the relative positions and motions of the members of the solar system: also called *cosmoscope.* [after the fourth Earl of *Orrery,* Charles Boyle, 1676–1731, for whom an early model was made]

or·ris (ôr′is, or′-) *n.* Any of the several species of iris having a scented root; especially, *Iris florentina,* whose dried rootstock is used in medicine, as a perfume, etc. Also **or′rice.** [Prob. alter. of Ital. *ireos* < L *iris.* See IRIS.]

ort (ôrt) *n. Usually pl. Archaic* or *Dial.* A worthless scrap or leaving, as of food. [ME; ult. origin uncertain]

Or·te·gal (ôr′tā·gäl′), **Cape** A headland of NW Spain.

Or·te·ga y Gas·set (ôr·tā′gä ē gä·set′), **José,** 1883–1955, Spanish philosopher, writer, and statesman.

Orth. Orthodox.

or·thi·con (ôr′thə·kon) *n.* A sensitive television camera tube using low-velocity electrons in scanning: also called *image orthicon.* Also **or·thi·con·o·scope** (ôr′thi·kon′ə·skōp). [< ORTH(O)- + ICON(OSCOPE)]

ortho- *combining form* **1.** Straight; upright; in line: *orthotropic.* **2.** At right angles; perpendicular: *orthorhombic.* **3.** Correct; proper; right: *orthography.* **4.** *Med.* The correction of irregularities or deformities of: *orthopedics.* **5.** *Chem.* **a** Designating that one of a series of acids that is most fully hydrated: *orthophosphoric* acid: distinguished from *meta-.* **b** Noting a benzene derivative in which the substituted atoms or radicals occupy adjoining positions. Also, before vowels, **orth-.** [< Gk. *orthos* straight]

or·tho·cen·ter (ôr′thō·sen′tər) *n. Geom.* The point at which the three altitudes of a triangle intersect.

or·tho·chro·mat·ic (ôr′thō·krō·mat′ik) *adj. Photog.* **1.** Rendering natural color tones accurately in shades of lightness and darkness. **2.** Denoting an emulsion that sensitizes a film or plate to the values of green and yellow but not red. Also *isochromatic.* [< ORTHO- + Gk. *chrōmatikos*] **— or′tho·chro′ma·tism** (ôr′thō·krō′mə·tiz′əm) *n.*

or·tho·clase (ôr′thō·klās, -klāz) *n.* A brittle, vitreous, potassium-aluminum silicate of the feldspar group, a constituent of many igneous rocks: also called *potash feldspar.* [< ORTHO- + Gk. *klasis* fracture < *klaein* to break]

or·tho·don·tics (ôr′thə·don′tiks) *n.pl.* (construed as sing. or pl.) *n.* The branch of dentistry concerned with the prevention and correction of irregularities of the teeth. Also **or·tho·don·tia** (ôr′thə·don′shə, -shē-ə). [< NL < Gk. *orthos* right, straight + *odous, odontos* tooth] **— or′tho·don′tic** *adj.* **— or·tho·don′tist** *n.*

or·tho·dox (ôr′thə·doks) *adj.* **1.** Holding the commonly accepted or established faith, especially in religion; correct or sound in doctrine. **2.** Conforming to the Christian faith as represented in the early ecumenical creeds. **3.** Adhering to traditional practice or belief; conventional; proper. [< LL *orthodoxus* < Gk. *orthodoxos* < *orthos* right + *doxa* opinion < *dokeein* to think] **— or′tho·dox′ly** *adv.*

Or·tho·dox (ôr′thə·doks) *adj.* **1.** Of, belonging to, or characteristic of the Eastern Orthodox Church. **2.** Designating any of the bodies in this Church. Abbr. *Orth.*

Orthodox Church The Eastern Orthodox Church (which see).

Orthodox Judaism The branch of Judaism that accepts the Mosaic Laws and their authoritative rabbinical interpretations in the Talmud and elsewhere as binding for today.

or·tho·dox·y (ôr′thə·dok′sē) *n. pl.* **·dox·ies 1.** Orthodox belief or practice; also, an instance of it. **2.** The quality or condition of being orthodox. [< Gk. *orthodoxia* < *orthodoxos.* See ORTHODOX.] **— or′tho·dox′i·cal** *adj.*

or·tho·e·pist (ôr·thō′ə·pist, ôr′thō·ə·pist) *n.* An authority on pronunciation. **— or·tho·e·pis·tic** (ôr′thō·ə·pis′tik) *adj.*

or·tho·e·py (ôr·thō′ə·pē, ôr′thō·ep′ē) *n.* **1.** The branch of grammar dealing with pronunciation. **2.** Correct or standard pronunciation. [< Gk. *orthoepeia* correctness of diction < *orthos* right + *epos* word] **— or·tho·ep·ic** (ôr′thō·ep′ik) or **·i·cal** *adj.*

or·tho·gen·e·sis (ôr′thō·jen′ə·sis) *n.* **1.** *Biol.* The theory that the evolution of a species occurs as a series of developments in a single direction rather than as a succession of random changes subject to natural selection. **2.** *Sociol.* The doctrine that all cultures pass through the same stages of development in the same succession, regardless of their external differences. — **or/tho·ge·net/ic** (-jə-net/ik) *adj.*

or·thog·na·thous (ôr·thog/na-thəs) *adj.* Having the lower jaw in line with or not protruding beyond the upper jaw. Also **or·thog·nath·ic** (ôr/thog-nath/ik). [< ORTHO- + -GNA- THOUS] — **or·thog/na·thism, or·thog/na·thy** *n.*

or·thog·o·nal (ôr·thog/ə-nəl) *adj.* Pertaining to or consist- ing of angles or perpendicular lines: also *orthographic.* [< F < MF *orthogone* right triangle < LL *orthogonium,* neut. of *orthogonius* < Gk. *orthogōnios* < *orthos* right + *gōnia* angle] — **or·thog/o·nal·ly** *adv.*

or·tho·graph·ic (ôr/thə-graf/ik) *adj.* **1.** Of or relating to orthography. **2.** Correctly spelled. **3.** Orthogonal. Also **or/tho·graph/i·cal.** — **or/tho·graph/i·cal·ly** *adv.*

or·thog·ra·phy (ôr·thog/ra-fē) *n. pl.* **·phies 1.** A mode or system of spelling, especially of spelling correctly or accord- ing to usage. **2.** The study dealing with letters and spelling. **3.** A projection in which the lines lie at right angles to the plane of projection. [< OF *ortographie* < L *orthographia* < Gk. < *orthographos*] — **or·thog/ra·pher, or·thog/ra·phist** *n.*

or·tho·pe·dics (ôr/thə-pē/diks) *n.pl. (construed as sing.)* The branch of surgery concerned with the correction of deformities of the skeletal system, especially the spine and its associated structures. Also **or/tho·pae/dics, or·tho·pe·dy** (ôr/thə-pē/dē). [< F *orthopédique* < *orthopédic* < Gk. *orthos* + *paidion* child < *paideia* rearing of children] — **or/tho· pe/dic** *adj.* — **or/tho·pe/dist** *n.*

or·tho·phos·phor·ic acid (ôr/thō-fos-fôr/ik, -for/-) *Chem.* The common form of phosphoric acid, H_3PO_4, a colorless, syrupy liquid used in the manufacture of fertilizers.

or·tho·psy·chi·a·try (ôr/thō-sī-kī/ə-trē) *n.* The study of be- havioral disorders, with emphasis on early treatment and satisfactory social adjustment. — **or/tho·psy/chi·at/ric** (-sī/- kē-at/rik) or **·ri·cal** *adj.* — **or/tho·psy·chi/a·trist** *n.*

or·thop·ter (ôr·thop/tər) *n.* Ornithopter.

or·thop·ter·on (ôr·thop/tə-ron) *n.* An orthopterous insect.

or·thop·ter·ous (ôr·thop/tər-əs) *adj.* Designating any of an order (*Orthoptera*) of insects with membranous hind wings and leathery, usually straight, fore wings, including locusts, crickets, grasshoppers, etc. [< NL *orthoptera* < Gk. *orthos* straight + *pteron* wing] — **or·thop/ter·an** *adj. & n.*

or·thop·tic (ôr·thop/tik) *adj.* Of, pertaining to, or charac- terized by normal binocular vision. [< ORTH(O)- + OPTIC]

or·thop·tics (ôr·thop/tiks) *n.pl. (construed as sing.)* The treatment of defects in binocular vision and of poor visual habits, especially by therapeutic exercises.

or·tho·rhom·bic (ôr/thə-rom/bik) *adj. Crystall.* Pertaining to a crystal system containing three unequal axes at right an- gles, as that of sulfur or topaz: also *prismatic, rhombic.*

or·tho·scope (ôr/thə-skōp) *n.* An instrument by which a layer of water is held against the cornea to correct its refrac- tion and permit accurate examination of the eye.

or·tho·scop·ic (ôr/thə-skop/ik) *adj.* Producing a flat image free from distortion; characterized by correct vision.

or·thos·ti·chy (ôr·thos/tə-kē) *n. pl.* **·chies** *Bot.* A vertical row or rank of organs on an axis, as leaves or flowers. [< ORTHO- + Gk. *stichos* row] — **or/thos/ti·chous** *adj.*

or·tho·trop·ic (ôr/thə-trop/ik) *adj. Bot.* Tending to grow vertically, as certain roots. — **or/tho·trop/i·cal·ly** *adv.* — **or·thot·ro·pism** (ôr·thot/rə-piz/əm) *n.*

or·thot·ro·pous (ôr·thot/rə-pəs) *adj. Bot.* Having a straight axis: said of an ovule. [< ORTHO- + -TROPOUS]

Ort·ler Range (ôrt/lər) A division of the Alps in northern Italy; highest peak, **Ortler,** also **Ort/ler·spit/ze** (-shpit/sə), 12,792 ft. *Italian* **Ort·les** (ôrt/lās).

or·to·lan (ôr/tə-lən) *n.* **1.** A bunting (*Emberiza hortulana*) of Europe, having an olive-green head and breast and a yel- low throat. **2.** Loosely, any of several other birds, as the sora or bobolink. [< F < Provençal < Ital. *ortolano* gar- dener < L *hortolanus* < *hortulus,* dim. of *hortus* garden]

O·ru·ro (ō-rōō/rō) A city in western Bolivia; pop. 81,553 (1960).

Or·well (ôr/wel), **George,** pseudonym of **Eric Blair** (blâr), 1903–50, British novelist and essayist.

-ory¹ *suffix of nouns* A place or instrument for (performing the action of the main element): *dormitory, lavatory.* [< OF *-oir, -oire.* See -ORY².]

-ory² *suffix of adjectives* Related to; like; resembling: *ama- tory, laudatory.* [< F *-oir, -oire,* or < L *-orius, -oria, -orium*]

Or·yol (or·yol/) See OREL.

o·ryx (ôr/iks, or/-, ō/riks) *n. pl.* **o·ryx·es** or **o·ryx** Any of a small genus (*Oryx*) of long-horned antelopes, as the **Arabian oryx** (*O. leucoryx*) and the gemsbok. [< NL < L < Gk., a pickax, a kind of antelope; so called from its pointed horns]

os¹ (os) *n. pl.* **o·ra** (ôr/ə, ō/rə) *Anat.* A mouth or opening. [< L]

os² (os) *n. pl.* **os·sa** (os/ə) *Anat.* A bone. [< L]

os³ (ōs) *n. pl.* **o·sar** (ō/sär) *Geol.* An esker: also spelled *ose.* [< Sw. *ås* ridge, chain of hills]

OS *Chem.* Osmium.

OS or **OS.** or **O.S.** Old Saxon.

O.S. or **O/S** or **o/s** Old Style.

O.S.A. Order of St. Augustine.

O·sage (ō/sāj) *n.* **1.** One of a tribe of North American In- dians of Siouan stock, formerly inhabiting the region be- tween the Missouri and Arkansas rivers and now living in Oklahoma. **2.** The language of this tribe. [< Siouan (Osage) *Wazhazhe* war people]

Osage orange 1. A showy tree (*Maclura pomifera*) of the mulberry family, native to Arkansas and adjacent regions, widely used as a hedge. **2.** Its fruit, somewhat resembling an orange in size and color. Also called *hedge apple.*

Osage River A river in eastern Kansas and west central Missouri, flowing 500 miles east to the Missouri.

O·sa·ka (ō-sä-kä) A port city on southern Honshu island, Japan, on **Osaka Bay,** an inlet of the Inland Sea; pop. 2,980,400 (est. 1970).

O.S.B. Order of St. Benedict.

Os·born (oz/bərn), **Henry Fairfield,** 1857–1935, U.S. pale- ontologist.

Os·borne (oz/bôrn), **Thomas Mott,** 1859–1926, U.S. prison reformer.

Os·can (os/kən) *n.* **1.** One of an ancient people who in- habited SW Italy. **2.** The language of these people and of the early Samnites, belonging to the Osco-Umbrian branch of the Italic languages. — *adj.* Of or pertaining to the Oscans or their language. [< L *Oscus,* pl. *Osci* people of Campania]

Os·car (os/kər) *n.* One of the small gold statuettes awarded annually in the United States by the Academy of Motion Picture Arts and Sciences for outstanding achievements in motion pictures. [Origin uncertain]

Os·car II (os/kər), 1829–1907, king of Sweden 1872–1907, and of Norway 1872–1905.

Os·ce·o·la (os/ē-ō/lə), 1804?–38, Seminole war chief.

os·cil·late (os/ə-lāt) *v.i.* **·lat·ed, ·lat·ing 1.** To swing back and forth, as a pendulum; vibrate. **2.** To fluctuate between various courses of action or thought; waver. **3.** *Physics* To produce oscillations. — **Syn.** See FLUCTUATE. [< L *oscilla- tus,* pp. of *oscillare* to swing < *oscillum,* dim. of *os* mouth]

os·cil·la·tion (os/ə-lā/shən) *n.* **1.** The act or state of oscil- lating. **2.** A single swing of an oscillating body from one extreme position to another. **3.** *Physics* A periodic fluctua- tion between extreme values of a quantity or force, as in an electric current. [< L *oscillatio, -onis* < *oscillatus.* See OSCILLATE.] — **os/cil·la·to/ry** (-lə-tôr/ē, -tō/rē) *adj.*

os·cil·la·tor (os/ə-lā/tər) *n.* **1.** One who or that which os- cillates. **2.** Any machine producing oscillations. **3.** *Elec- tronics* A device for producing oscillations.

os·cil·lo·gram (ə-sil/ə-gram) *n.* A record made by an oscil- lograph. [< *oscillo-* < *oscillate* to oscillate + -GRAM]

os·cil·lo·graph (ə-sil/ə-graf, -gräf) *n.* A device for record- ing and measuring the instantaneous values of a rapidly varying electrical quantity as shown by the corresponding wave forms, or of any oscillating system convertible into wave forms, as sound, light, heartbeats, etc.

os·cil·lo·scope (ə-sil/ə-skōp) *n.* Any of various electronic instruments for projecting the forms of electromagnetic waves on the fluorescent screen of a cathode-ray tube.

os·cine (os/in, -īn) *adj.* Of or belonging to a suborder (*Os- cines*) of passerine birds, including those having the most highly developed vocal ability, as thrushes, sparrows, etc. Also **os/ci·nine.** — *n.* An oscine bird. [< NL < L *oscen, oscinis* singing bird < *ob-* towards + *canere* to sing]

os·ci·tan·cy (os/ə-tən-sē) *n. pl.* **·cies 1.** The act of yawn- ing or gaping. **2.** Drowsiness; dullness. Also **os/ci·tance.** [< L *oscitans, -antis,* ppr. of *oscitare* to gape, yawn < *os* mouth + *citare* to move] — **os/ci·tant** *adj.*

Os·co-Um·bri·an (os/kō-um/brē-ən) *n.* A branch of the Italic subfamily of Indo-European languages, comprising the ancient Oscan and Umbrian.

os·cu·lant (os/kyə-lənt) *adj. Biol.* **1.** Intermediate in char- acter between two groups of organisms: an *osculant* genus. **2.** Adhering closely; embracing. [< L *osculans, -antis,* ppr. of *osculari.* See OSCULATE.]

os·cu·lar (os/kyə-lər) *adj.* **1.** Of or pertaining to the mouth or kissing. **2.** *Zool.* Of or pertaining to an osculum. [< L *osculum,* dim. of *os* mouth]

os·cu·late (os/kyə-lāt) *v.t. & v.i.* **·lat·ed, ·lat·ing 1.** To kiss: used humorously. **2.** To bring or come into close contact or union. **3.** *Math.* To touch so as to have three or more points in common, as two curves. **4.** *Biol.* To have (characteris- tics) in common, as two genera or families. [< L *osculatus,* pp. of *osculari* to kiss < *osculum* little mouth, kiss]

os·cu·la·tion (os/kyə-lā/shən) *n.* **1.** The act of kissing; also, a kiss. **2.** *Math.* The point of contact between osculating curves, etc.: also called *tacnode.* — **os/cu·la·to/ry** (-lə-tôr/ē, -tō/rē) *adj.*

os·cu·lum (os/kyə-ləm) *n. pl.* **·la** (-lə) *Zool.* One of the apertures in a sponge by which water with waste products is expelled. Also **os/cule** (-kyōōl). [< L, dim. of *os* mouth]

OSD Office of the Secretary of Defense.

O.S.D. Order of St. Dominic.

ose (ōs) See OS³.

-ose¹ *suffix of adjectives* **1.** Full of or abounding in (the main element): *verbose.* **2.** Like; resembling (the main element): *grandiose.* Compare -OUS. [< L *-osus*]

-ose[2] *suffix* *Chem.* Indicating a sugar or other carbohydrate: *lactose, fructose.* [< (GLUC)OSE]

O·see (ō′zē, ō′sē) The Douai Bible name for HOSEA.

O.S.F. Order of St. Francis.

Osh·kosh (osh′kosh) A city in eastern Wisconsin, on Lake Winnebago; pop. 53,221.

o·sier (ō′zhər) *n.* **1.** Any of various willows (genus *Salix*) producing long, flexible shoots used in wickerwork; especially, the **velvet osier** (*S. viminalis*) of Europe and the **purple** or **red osier** (*S. purpurea*). **2.** A shoot of an osier. **3.** Any of various plants resembling the osier, as the squawbush; also, a shoot from such a plant. — *adj.* Consisting of or containing osier. [< OF, prob. < Med.L *ausaria, osaria* bed of willows]

O·si·jek (ō′sē·yek) A city in NE Croatia; pop. 78,000 (1963).

O·si·ris (ō·sī′ris) In Egyptian mythology, the god of the underworld and lord of the dead, husband of his sister Isis.

-osis *suffix of nouns* **1.** The condition, process, or state of: *metamorphosis.* **2.** *Med.* **a** A diseased or abnormal condition of: *melanosis.* **b** A formation of: *sclerosis.* [< L < Gk. *-ōsis*; or directly < Gk.]

-osity *suffix of nouns* Forming nouns corresponding to adjectives in *-ose: verbosity, grandiosity.* [< F *-osité* < L *-ositas*; or directly < L]

Os·ler (ōs′lər, ōz′-), **Sir William**, 1849–1919, Canadian physician active in the United States and England.

Os·lo (os′lō, oz′-; *Norw.* ōōs′lōō) The capital of Norway, in the SE part, on **Oslo Fiord**, an inlet of the Skagerrak extending 80 miles inland; pop. 487,000 (1970): formerly *Christiania, Kristiania.*

Os·man I (oz′mən, os′-; *Turkish* ōs·män′), 1259–1326, founder of the Ottoman Empire. Also *Othman.*

Os·man·li (oz·man′lē, os-) *n. pl.* **·lis 1.** An Ottoman Turk. **2.** The language of the Ottoman Turks; Turkish. — *adj.* Ottoman. [< Turkish *Osmānli* of Osman < *Osman* Osman < Arabic *'Othmān*]

os·mic (oz′mik, os′-) *adj. Chem.* Of, pertaining to, or containing osmium in its higher valence.

os·mi·ous (oz′mē·əs, os′-) *adj. Chem.* Of, pertaining to, or containing osmium in its lower valence.

os·mi·rid·i·um (os′mə·rid′ē·əm, oz′-) *n.* A mixture of iridium and osmium that occurs naturally, used in pen points: also called *iridosmine, iridosmium.* [< OSM(IUM) + IRIDIUM]

os·mi·um (oz′mē·əm, os′-) *n.* A hard, brittle, extremely heavy, white, metallic element (symbol Os) of the platinum group. See ELEMENT. [< Gk. *osmē* odor; with ref. to the pungent odor of one of its oxides]

os·mose (oz′mōs, os′-) *v.* **·mosed, ·mos·ing** *v.t.* **1.** To subject to the process of osmosis. — *v.i.* **2.** To undergo osmosis. [< *osmose, n.* See OSMOSIS.]

os·mo·sis (oz·mō′sis, os-) *n.* **1.** *Chem.* **a** The diffusion of a fluid through a semipermeable membrane, resulting in equalization of the pressures on each side. **b** The tendency of a fluid to act in such a manner. Also *os′mose.* Compare ENDOSMOSIS, EXOSMOSIS. **2.** Any gradual process of assimilation, as of facts, ideas, or habits, that seems to occur without conscious or deliberate effort. [Earlier *osmose < -osmose* (as in *endosmose, exosmose*) < Gk. *ōsmos < ōthein* to impel] — **os·mot·ic** (oz·mot′ik, os-) *adj.* — **os·mot′i·cal·ly** *adv.*

os·mund (oz′mənd, oz′-) *n.* Any of a genus (*Osmunda*) of ferns having pinnate fronds growing upright from a large crown; especially, the royal fern. [< AF *osmunde* < OF *osmonde* < Med.L *osmunda*; ult. origin unknown]

Os·na·brück (ōz′nä·brük′) A city in Lower Saxony, West Germany; pop. 135,100 (est. 1960).

os·na·burg (oz′nə·bûrg) *n.* A tough, unbleached cotton cloth, used for upholstery, grain and cement sacks, etc. [after *Osnaburg*, var. of OSNABRÜCK]

os·prey (os′prē) *n.* An American hawk (*Pandion haliaëtus*), brown above and white below, that preys upon fish: also called *fish hawk, ossifraga.* [ME < L *ossifraga < os, ossis* bone + *frangere* to break]

OSS or **O.S.S.** Office of Strategic Services.

Os·sa (ōs′ə) A mountain in eastern Thessaly, Greece; 6,490 ft.; in Greek mythology, the giant sons of Poseidon attempted to scale Olympus by piling Pelion on Ossa.

os·se·in (os′ē·in) *n. Biochem.* The protein substance forming the organic basis of bone and remaining after the removal of mineral matter. [< L *osse(us)* bony + -IN]

os·se·ous (os′ē·əs) *adj.* Containing, resembling, or composed of bone. [< L *osseus* bony < *os, ossis* bone] — **os′se·ous·ly** *adv.*

ossi- *combining form* Bone: *ossify.* [< L *os, ossis* bone]

Os·sian (osh′ən, os′ē·ən) A legendary Irish hero and bard of the third century, subject of a cycle of poems by James Macpherson, published 1760–63, purporting to be translations from the original Gaelic manuscripts of Ossian. — **Os·si·an·ic** (os′ē·an′ik) *adj.*

os·si·cle (os′i·kəl) *n. Anat.* A small bone; especially, the malleus, incus, or stapes in the tympanic cavity of the ear. [< L *ossiculum*, dim. of *os, ossis* bone] — **os·sic·u·lar** (o·sik′yə·lər) *adj.*

Os·sietz·ky (ô·syet′skē), **Carl von,** 1887–1938, German journalist and pacifist.

os·sif·er·ous (o·sif′ər·əs) *adj.* Yielding or containing bones. [< L *os, ossi(s)* + -FEROUS]

os·si·frage (os′ə·frij) *n.* **1.** The osprey. **2.** The lammergeier. [< L *ossifraga.* See OSPREY.]

os·si·fy (os′ə·fī) *v.t. & v.i.* **·fied, ·fy·ing 1.** To convert or be converted into bone. **2.** To make or become rigid or inflexible in habits, beliefs, etc.; harden. [< L *os, ossis* + *facere* to make] — **os·sif′ic** (o·sif′ik) *adj.* — **os′si·fi·ca′tion** *n.*

Os·si·ning (os′ə·ning) A village in SE New York, on the Hudson River; pop. 21,659: formerly *Sing Sing.*

Os·so·li (ōs′sō·lē), **Marchioness** See (Margaret) FULLER.

os·su·ar·y (os′ōō·er′ē, osh′-) *n. pl.* **·ar·ies** A place or receptacle for holding the bones of the dead. [< LL *ossuarium* < L *ossuarius* of or for bones < *os, ossis* bone]

os·te·al (os′tē·əl) *adj.* Of, pertaining to, or like bone; osseous; bony. [< Gk. *osteon* bone]

os·te·i·tis (os′tē·ī′tis) *n. Pathol.* Inflammation of bone. [< OSTE(O)- + -ITIS]

Os·tend (os′tend, os·tend′) A port commune in NW Belgium, on the North Sea; pop. 55,446 (est. 1959). French **Os·tende** (ô·stäṅd′).

os·ten·si·ble (os·ten′sə·bəl) *adj.* Offered as real or genuine; apparent. [< L *ostensus*, pp. of *ostendere* to show < *obstendere* to stretch] — **os·ten′si·bly** *adv.*

— **Syn.** avowed, seeming, proffered, feigned, exhibited. Compare APPARENT. — **Ant.** actual, real, veritable.

os·ten·sive (os·ten′siv) *adj.* **1.** Manifest; ostensible. **2.** *Logic* Set forth as a principle that manifestly includes the proposition to be proved. [< Med.L *ostensivus* < L *ostensus.* See OSTENSIBLE.] — **os·ten′sive·ly** *adv.*

os·ten·ta·tion (os′tən·tā′shən) *n.* **1.** The act of displaying vainly or pretentiously, as in order to excite admiration, awe, etc. **2.** Excessive or uncalled-for elaboration; showiness. [< OF *ostentacion* < L *ostentatio, -onis < ostentatus,* pp. of *ostentare,* freq. of *ostendere* to show]

— **Syn. 1.** pomp, pageantry, display, show.

os·ten·ta·tious (os′tən·tā′shəs) *adj.* **1.** Intended to attract notice; showy. **2.** Marked by ostentation. — **os′ten·ta′tious·ly** *adv.* — **os′ten·ta′tious·ness** *n.*

osteo- *combining form* Bone; pertaining to bone or bones: *osteoblast.* Also, before vowels, **oste-.** [< Gk. *osteon* bone]

os·te·o·blast (os′tē·ə·blast′) *n. Anat.* A bone-forming cell. — **os′te·o·blas′tic** *adj.*

os·te·o·cla·sis (os′tē·ok′lə·sis) *n.* **1.** *Surg.* The breaking of a bone to correct a deformity or a bad setting. **2.** *Anat.* The gradual absorption of bony tissue by osteoclasts. [< NL < Gk. *osteon* bone + *klasis* fracture < *klaein* to break]

os·te·o·clast (os′tē·ə·klast′) *n.* **1.** *Surg.* An instrument for effecting osteoclasis. **2.** *Anat.* A large multinucleate cell found in the marrow of bones and concerned in the absorption of bony tissue during the formation of canals, cavities, etc. [< G *osteoklast* < Gk. *osteon* bone + *klastos* broken < *klaein* to break] — **os′te·o·clas′tic** *adj.*

os·te·oid (os′tē·oid) *adj.* Resembling bone; bony.

os·te·ol·o·gy (os′tē·ol′ə·jē) *n.* The study of the skeleton and of the structure of bones. — **os′te·o·log′i·cal** (-ə·loj′i·kəl) *adj.* — **os′te·ol′o·gist** *n.*

os·te·o·ma (os′tē·ō′mə) *n. pl.* **·o·mas** or **·o·ma·ta** (-ō′mə·tə) *Pathol.* A tumor of bony tissue. [< OSTE(O)- + -OMA]

os·te·o·my·e·li·tis (os′tē·ō·mī′ə·lī′tis) *n. Pathol.* Suppurative inflammation of the bone, sometimes involving the marrow. [< OSTEO- + MYEL(O)- + -ITIS]

os·te·o·path (os′tē·ə·path′) *n.* One who practices osteopathy. Also **os·te·op·a·thist** (os′tē·op′ə·thist).

os·te·op·a·thy (os′tē·op′ə·thē) *n.* A system of healing based on the theory that most diseases are the result of structural abnormalities of the body that may be corrected by manipulation of the affected parts. [< OSTEO- + -PATHY] — **os·te·o·path·ic** (os′tē·ə·path′ik) *adj.*

os·te·o·phyte (os′tē·ə·fīt′) *n. Pathol.* A bony excrescence. — **os·te·o·phyt′ic** (-fit′ik) *adj.*

os·te·o·plas·tic (os′tē·ə·plas′tik) *adj.* **1.** *Surg.* Of or pertaining to osteoplasty. **2.** *Anat.* Pertaining to or consisting of bone-forming material; osteoblastic.

os·te·o·plas·ty (os′tē·ə·plas′tē) *n. pl.* **·ties** *Surg.* An operation to remedy the loss of bone, or to restore a bone temporarily removed. [< OSTEO- + Gk. *plastos* moulded]

os·te·o·tome (os′tē·ə·tōm′) *n. Surg.* An instrument for dividing or cutting bone.

os·te·ot·o·my (os′tē·ot′ə·mē) *n. pl.* **·mies** *Surg.* The operation of dividing a bone or excising part of it, as to remedy deformity. — **os′te·ot′o·mist** *n.*

Ös·ter·reich (œs′tər·rīkh) The German name for AUSTRIA.

Os·ti·a (os′tē·ə, *Ital.* ô′styä) An ancient port city of Rome, at the mouth of the Tiber.

OSPREY
(About 2 feet long; wingspread to 4½ feet)

os·ti·ar·y (ŏs′tē·er′ē) *n. pl.* **·ar·ies** **1.** In the Roman Catholic Church, one who belongs to the lowest of the minor orders. **2.** A doorkeeper, as of a church. [< L *ostiarius* doorkeeper < *ostium* door]

os·ti·na·to (ŏs′tē·nä′tō) *n. Music* A phrase continually reiterated in the same voice and pitch. [< Ital. (*basso*) *ostinato*, lit., obstinate (bass) < L *obstinatus*]

os·ti·ole (ŏs′tē·ōl) *n.* **1.** A small opening. **2.** *Zool.* Any one of the small inhalant orifices of a sponge. [< L *ostiolum*, dim. of *ostium* door] — **os′ti·o·lar** *adj.*

ost·ler (ŏs′lər) *See* HOSTLER.

ost·mark (ŏst′märk′) The deutschemark of East Germany. See MARK² (def. 1).

os·to·sis (ŏs·tō′sis) *n.* Bone formation; ossification. [< OST(EO)- + -OSIS]

Ost·preus·sen (ŏst′proi′sən) The German name for EAST PRUSSIA.

os·tra·cism (ŏs′trə·siz′əm) *n.* **1.** In ancient Greece, temporary banishment by popular vote. **2.** The act of ostracizing or the state of being ostracized. [< LL *ostracismus*, transliteration of Gk. *ostrakismos* < *ostrakizein*. See OSTRACIZE.]

os·tra·cize (ŏs′trə·sīz) *v.t.* **·cized**, **·ciz·ing** **1.** To shut out or exclude, as fron n society or fro.n a particular group; banish. **2.** To exile by ostracism. Also *Brit.* **os′tra·cise.** [< Gk. *ostrakizein* < *ostrakon* potsherd, shell, voting tablet]

Os·tra·va (ôs′trä·vä) *See* MORAVSKÁ OSTRAVA.

os·trich (ôs′trich, ŏs′-) *n. pl.* **·trich·es** or **·trich** **1.** A large, two-toed, ratite bird (genus *Struthio*) of Africa and Arabia, the largest of existing birds, having long, powerful legs and a plumage highly valued for ornamental purposes. **2.** A rhea. [< OF *ostrusce* < LL *avis struthio* < L *avis* bird + LL *struthio* ostrich < Gk. *strouthiōn* < *strouthos* sparrow, ostrich]

OSTRICH
(To about 8 feet high)

Os·tro·goth (ŏs′trə·goth) *n.* A member of the eastern branch of the Goths, who established a kingdom in Italy from 493 to 555. Compare VISIGOTH. [< LL *Ostrogothi*, earlier *Austrogoti*; ult. < Gmc.] — **Os′tro·goth′ic** *adj.*

Ost·wald (ôst′vält), **Wilhelm**, 1853–1932, German chemist born in Latvia.

Os·ty·ak (ŏs′tē·ak) *n.* **1.** One of a Finno-Ugric people inhabiting western Siberia and the Ural Mountains. **2.** The Ugric language of these people. Also **Os′ti·ak.**

Os·we·go tea (ŏs·wē′gō) A species of mint (*Monarda didyma*) with a showy head of bright red flowers, found in the eastern United States: also called *bee balm*. [after *Oswego*, city in New York State]

Oś·wię·cim (ôsy′vyăn′tzyĕm) The Polish name for AUSCHWITZ.

ot- *Var. of* OTO-.

OT or **OT.** or **O.T.** Old Testament.

O·ta·hei·te (ō′tə·hē′tē, -hā′-) A former name for TAHITI.

o·tal·gi·a (ō·tal′jē·ə) *n. Pathol.* Neuralgia of the ear; earache. Also **o·tal′gy.** [< NL < Gk. *ōtalgia* < *ous, ōtos* ear + *algos* pain] — **o·tal′gic** *adj.*

O·ta·ru (ō·tä·rōō) A port city on western Hokkaido island, Japan; pop. 204,000 (est. 1959).

OTC Organization for Trade Cooperation.

O tem·po·ra! O mo·res! (ō tem′pə·rə ō môr′ēz, mō′rēz) *Latin* O the times! O the manners!

O·thel·lo (ō·thel′ō, ə-) In Shakespeare's play of this name, the hero, a Moor of Venice, whose jealousy, inspired by Iago, provokes him to kill his innocent wife Desdemona.

oth·er (uth′ər) *adj.* **1.** Different from the one or ones specified or implied; not the same. **2.** Noting the remaining one of two persons or things: the *other* eye. **3.** Apart from that or those; additional; more: Have you no *other* children? **4.** Alternate; second: every *other* day. **5.** Different in character or quality: The truth is *other* than what you suppose. **6.** Forme.r: in *other* times. — **the other day** (night, etc.) A day (night, etc.) not long ago; recently. — *pron.* **1.** Another or different person or thing. **2.** The other person or thing: this hand, not the *other*. — *adv.* Differently; otherwise: with than. [OE *ōther*] — **oth′er·ness** *n.*

oth·er·guess (uth′ər·ges′) *Obs. adj.* Of another sort; other. — *adv.* In a different manner.

oth·er·where (uth′ər·hwâr′) *adv. Archaic* or *Dial.* Elsewhere.

oth·er·while (uth′ər·hwīl′) *adv. Archaic* or *Dial.* At another time. Also **oth′er·whiles′.**

oth·er·wise (uth′ər·wīz′) *adv.* **1.** In a different manner; by other means. **2.** In other circumstances or conditions. **3.** In all other respects: an *otherwise* sensible person. — *adj.* **1.** Other than supposed; different: The facts are *otherwise*. **2.** Other: He could not be *otherwise* than proud.

other world An unknown world; especially, a world peopled by the dead, as in a supposed afterlife.

oth·er·world·ly (uth′ər·wûrld′lē) *adj.* **1.** Of or characteristic of an ideal or spiritual world, as of heaven. **2.** Concerned with matters of the spirit or intellect, especially to the neglect of material things. — **oth′er·world′li·ness** *n.*

O·thin (ō′thin) *See* ODIN.

Oth·man (oth′man, *Arabic* ôôth·män′) **1.** *See* OSMAN I. **2.** Ottoman.

o·tic (ō′tik, ŏt′ik) *adj.* Pertaining to or situated near the ear. [< Gk. *ōtikos* < *ous, ōtos* ear]

-otic *suffix of adjectives* **1.** *Med.* Of, related to, or affected by: corresponding to nouns in *-osis*: *sclerotic*. **2.** Causing or producing: *narcotic*. [< Gk. *-ōtikos*, suffix of adjectives]

o·ti·ose (ō′shē·ōs, -tē-) *adj.* **1.** Being at rest; indolent; lazy. **2.** Having no use or effect; futile. [< L *otiosus* idle < *otium* leisure] — **o′ti·ose′ly** *adv.* — **o′ti·os′i·ty** (-ŏs′ə·tē) *n.*
— **Syn.** 1. idle, slothful. 2. vain, empty, nugatory.

O·tis (ō′tis), **James**, 1725–83, American Revolutionary patriot, orator, and pamphleteer.

o·ti·tis (ō·tī′tis) *n. Pathol.* Inflammation of the ear. [< OT(O)- + -ITIS]

oto- *combining form* Ear; pertaining to the ear: *otoscope*. Also, before vowels, *ot-*. [< Gk. *ous, ōtos* ear]

o·to·cyst (ō′tə·sist) *n. Anat.* **1.** An auditory vesicle, as in many invertebrates. **2.** A similar vesicle contained in the embryo of a vertebrate. — **o′to·cyst′ic** *adj.*

o·to·lar·yn·gol·o·gy (ō′tō·lar′ing·gol′ə·jē) *n.* The branch of medicine that treats of the ear and throat. — **o′to·lar′yn·gol′o·gist** *n.*

o·to·lith (ō′tə·lith) *n. Anat.* One of the calcareous concretions found in the internal ear of vertebrates and in the auditory organ of many invertebrates: also called *earstone*.

o·tol·o·gy (ō·tol′ə·jē) *n.* The science of the ear and its diseases. — **o·to·log·i·cal** (ō′tə·loj′i·kəl) *adj.* — **o·tol′o·gist** *n.*

o·to·scope (ō′tə·skōp) *n. Med.* An instrument for viewing or examining the interior of the ear; also, an instrument for auscultation of the ear.

O·tran·to (ō·trän′tō, *Ital.* ô′trän·tō), **Strait of** A strait between Italy and Albania, connecting the Adriatic and Ionian seas; about 43 mi. wide.

ot·tar (ot′ər) *See* ATTAR.

ot·ta·va (ō·tä′və) *n. Ital.* An octave.

ottava ri·ma (rē′mä) In prosody, a stanza form of Italian origin consisting of eight lines in iambic pentameter and rhyming in the pattern *abababcc*, used by Byron in *Don Juan* and by Keats in *Isabella.* [< Ital., octave rhyme]

Ot·ta·wa (ot′ə·wə) *n.* One of a tribe of North American Indians of Algonquian stock, originally inhabiting the region around Georgian Bay, Lake Huron, Ontario, and later the region around Lake Superior and Lake Michigan. [< dial. F *otauan*; ult. < Algonquian. Akin to Cree *atâweu* a trader.]

Ot·ta·wa (ot′ə·wə) The capital of Canada, in SE Ontario on the **Ottawa River**, that flows 696 miles SE to the St. Lawrence; pop. 298,087.

ot·ter (ot′ər) *n.* **1.** Any of various webfooted, carnivorous mammals (genus *Lutra*) of aquatic habits, related to the weasel and having a long, flattened tail. **2.** Its valuable, dark brown fur. **3.** The sea otter (which see). [OE *otor*. Akin to WATER.]

OTTER
(About 2 feet long; tail 1 foot)

Ot·ter·burn (ot′ər·bûrn) A village in Northumberland, England; scene of a defeat of the English by the Scots, 1388. *See* CHEVY CHASE.

Ot·to I (ot′ō), 912–973, king of Germany 936–973; Holy Roman Emperor 962–973: called **the Great.**

ot·to·man (ot′ə·mən) *n.* **1.** An upholstered, armless seat or sofa, usually without a back. **2.** A cushioned footrest. **3.** A heavy corded silk or rayon fabric, used for coats and trimmings. [< F *ottoman*, orig. fem. of *ottoman* Ottoman]

Ot·to·man (ot′ə·mən) *n. pl.* **·mans** A Turk: also *Othman*. — *adj.* Of or pertaining to the Turks. [< F < Ital. *Ottomano* < Med.L *Ottomanus* < Arabic *'Uthmāni, 'Othmāni* < *'Othmān* Osman]

Ottoman Empire A former empire (1300–1919) of the Turks in Asia Minor, NE Africa, and SE Europe; capital, Constantinople: also *Turkish Empire.*

Ot·tum·wa (o·tum′wə) A city in SE Iowa, on the Des Moines River; pop. 29,610.

Ot·way (ot′wā), **Thomas**, 1652–85, English dramatist.

oua·ba·in (wä·bä′in) *n. Chem.* A white, crystalline glycoside, $C_{29}H_{44}O_{12}$, derived chiefly from the seeds of a South African tree (*Strophanthus glaber*), used as a cardiac stimulant. [< F *ouabaio*, a South African tree < Somali *waba yo*]

Ouach·i·ta River (wosh′ə·tô, wŏsh′-) A river in SW Arkansas and NE Louisiana, flowing 605 miles generally SE to the Red River: also *Washita*.

Oua·ga·dou·gou (wä′gə·dōō′gōō) The capital of the Republic of Upper Volta, in the central part; pop. 124,779 (1970).

oua·na·niche (wä′nə·nēsh′, *Fr.* wȧ·nȧ·nēsh′) *n. pl.* **-niche** A small, Canadian, fresh-water salmon (*Salmo salar ouananiche*), identified with the Atlantic salmon of Maine. [< dial. F (Canadian) < Algonquian (Cree) *wananish*]

ou·bli·ette (ōō′blē·et′) *n.* A secret dungeon with an entrance only through the top. [< OF < *oublier* to forget]

ouch¹ (ouch) *interj.* An exclamation of sudden pain. [Cf. G *autsch*]

ouch² (ouch) *n. Archaic* 1. A setting of a precious stone. 2. A personal ornament, often set with jewels. [< AF *nouche* < LL *nusca* < OHG *nuscka, nuscha* buckle, clasp, appar. ult. of Celtic origin; in ME *a nouche* became *an ouche*]

Oudh (oud) A historic region of east central Uttar Pradesh, India; 24,071 sq. mi.

Oues·sant (w·sän′) The French name for USHANT.

ought¹ (ôt) *v. Present 3rd person sing.* **ought** An auxiliary followed by the infinitive with *to* expressed or understood, meaning: 1. To have a moral duty; be obliged: A person *ought* to keep his promises. 2. To be advisable, expedient, or proper: You *ought* to be careful. 3. To be expected or anticipated, as something probable, natural, or logical: The engine *ought* to run. ◆ A past is formed by placing the following verb in the perfect infinitive, as in *He ought to have been there*. [OE *āhte*, past tense of *āgan* to owe, possess]
— **Syn.** 1, 2, 3. *Ought* and *should* are often interchangeable, especially in the sense of probability or expectation: he *ought* to be (or *should* be) home by sunset. In the sense of obligation, *ought* is stronger. "You *ought* to write your mother" is more forceful than "You *should* write your mother." *Should* is more often used to express expediency: a liar *should* have a good memory.

ought² (ôt) See AUGHT¹.

ought³ (ôt) See AUGHT².

ou·gui·ya (ōō·gē′yə) *n.* The monetary unit of Mauretania, equivalent to five khoums.

oui (wē) *adv. French* Yes.

Oui·da (wē′də) Pseudonym of **Marie Louise de la Ra·mée** (rȧ·mā′), 1840–1908, English novelist.

Oui·ja (wē′jə) *n.* A device consisting of a board inscribed with the alphabet and other characters, and a planchette, the pointer of which is thought to spell out mediumistic communications: a trade name. Also **oui′ja.**

oui·sti·ti (wis′ti·tē) *n.* A monkey (genus *Callithrix*) of South America, with tufted ears and a long, banded tail: also called *marmoset.* [< F; name coined by Buffon, imit. of the animal's cry]

ounce¹ (ouns) *n.* 1. A unit of weight; one sixteenth of a pound avoirdupois, or 28.349 grams; one twelfth of a pound troy, or 31.1 grams. Abbr. *oz.* See table inside back cover. 2. A fluid ounce (which see). 3. A small quantity. [< OF *unce* < L *uncia* twelfth part (of a pound or foot), orig., unit < *unus* one. Doublet of INCH.]

ounce² (ouns) *n.* The snow leopard. [< OF *l'once*, by false division < *lonce* lynx < L *lyncea* < *lynx, lyncis* lynx]

ouphe (ōōf) *n. Archaic* A goblin or elf. [Var. of OAF]

our (our) *pronominal adj.* The possessive case of the pronoun *we*, used attributively: *our* child. [OE *ūre*, gen. of *wē*. Akin to *ūs* us]

ou·ra·ri (ōō·rä′rē) *n.* Curare. [Var. of *woorali* < Tupi]

ou·re·bi (ōō′rə·bē) See ORIBI.

ou·rie (ōō′rē) *adj. Scot.* 1. Shivering; cold. 2. Bleak; desolate. Also spelled *oorie.*

Our Lady The Virgin Mary.

ours (ourz) *pron.* 1. The possessive case of the pronoun *we*, used predicatively: That dog is *ours.* 2. The one or ones belonging or relating to us: their country and *ours.* — **of ours** Belonging or relating to us: a double possessive. [ME *ures*, orig. genitive of *ure* < OE *ūre* our]

our·self (our·self′) *pron.* Myself or ourselves, considered collectively: used in formal or regal contexts.

our·selves (our·selvz′) *pron.pl.* A form of the first person plural pronoun, used: 1. As a reflexive or as object of a preposition in a reflexive sense: We helped *ourselves.* 2. As an emphatic or intensive form of *we*: We *ourselves* want to know. 3. As a designation of a normal, proper, or usual state: We weren't *ourselves* then.

-ous *suffix of adjectives* 1. Full of, having, given to, like: *joyous, glorious.* 2. *Chem.* Having a lower valence than that indicated by *-ic*: said of elements in compounds: *nitrous* oxide. [< OF < L *-osus*; or directly < L]

Ouse (ōōz) 1. A river in North Riding, Yorkshire, England, flowing 61 miles SE to the Humber. 2. A river in eastern England, flowing 156 miles NE to the Wash.

ou·sel (ōō′zəl) See OUZEL.

oust (oust) *v.t.* To force out or remove, as from a place or position; eject. — **Syn.** See EXPEL. [< AF *ouster* to take away < LL *obstare* to obstruct < *ob-* against + *stare* to stand]

oust·er (ous′tər) *n.* 1. The act or condition of ousting. 2. One who ousts. 3. *Law* The act of putting one out of possession of real property to which he is legally entitled.

out (out) *adv.* 1. Away from the inside or center: to branch *out.* 2. In or into the open air; outside: to go *out.* 3. Away from a specified or usual place, as from one's home or place of business: *out* to lunch. 4. From a receptacle or source: to pour *out* wine. 5. From among others: to pick *out.* 6. So as to remove, deplete, or exhaust: to sweep *out*; to dry *out.* 7. To an extreme degree; thoroughly: tired *out.* 8. Into extinction or inactivity: The flame went *out*; The excitement died *out.* 9. To a result or conclusion; to the end: Hear me *out.* 10. Into being or activity, or into a state manifest to the senses: An epidemic broke *out*; The sun came *out.* 11. Into or within the realm of public knowledge: The secret leaked *out.* 12. In or into circulation: to bring *out* a new edition. 13. Aloud and boldly; without constraint: to speak *out.* 14. So as to be extended or projecting: to lean *out.* 15. Into the care or control of another or others: to deal *out* cards. 16. From a state of ease or composure to a state of tension, irritation, or dispute: to be put *out* over trifles. 17. In or into a condition of being out-of-date or retired from activity or use: Latin went *out* as a spoken language. 18. In baseball, etc., so as to be or count as an out. 19. In golf, to the end of the first half of an 18-hole circuit: *out* in par. 20. *Informal* Into unconsciousness: to pass *out.* — **out and away** By far; incomparably. — **out from under** *Informal* Past or beyond the point of danger or trouble. — **out of** 1. From or beyond the inside of; from among. 2. Beyond the limits, scope, or usual position of: *out of* sight; *out of* joint. 3. From (a material, etc.): made *out of* tin. 4. Influenced, inspired, or caused by: *out of* pity. 5. Without (any): *out of* breath. 6. From among others of: Take a shirt *out of* that pile. 7. Born of (a dam): said especially of horses. — **out to** With the intention of. — *adj.* 1. External; exterior; outer. 2. Abnormal; irregular: an *out* size. 3. Not in effective working order; unusable: The bridge is *out.* 4. At a financial loss: *out* five dollars. 5. Not to be considered; impossible: That method is altogether *out.* 6. Exposed or bare, as by tears in the clothing: *out* at the seams. 7. In error; mistaken: *out* in one's reckoning. 8. Not in office or in a position of power. 9. Used to direct outward; also, headed outwardly. 10. No longer skillful, as at a game; not in practice. 11. Distant; outlying. ◆ *Out* may also be used in many of its adverbial senses as a predicate adjective with a form of the verb *to be*, as in the following examples: *He is out to lunch* (adv., def. 3); *The fire is out* (adv., def. 8); *The stars are out* (adv., def. 10). — *prep.* 1. From within; forth from: *out* the door. 2. Along or on: Walk *out* the dirt road to the house. 3. *Archaic* On the outside of; outside. — *n.* 1. One who or that which is out. 2. A way of dodging responsibility or involvement; a means of escape. 3. In baseball, a play so made that a player is prevented from batting or running the bases until he gets another turn at bat; also, a player so prevented. 4. In tennis, etc., a return that falls outside the court. 5. *Printing* a A word, phrase, etc., of copy omitted from composed type. b Such an omission. 6. *Archaic* or *Dial.* An outing; holiday. — **on the outs** (or **at outs**) Involved in a disagreement; at odds. — *v.i.* 1. To come out; be revealed: Murder will *out.* 2. To go out or outside. 3. To make an out, as in tennis. — *v.t.* To put (someone or something) out. — *interj.* Get out! Away! [OE *ūt*]

out- *combining form* 1. Living or situated outside; external; away from the center; detached: *outlying, outpatient.* 2. Going forth; issuing; outward: *outbound, outstretch.* 3. Denoting the time, place, or result of the action expressed by the root verb: *outcome, outcry.* 4. To a greater extent; surpassing; more; better; beyond. ◆ Two-syllable nouns with this prefix are pronounced with almost even stress on each syllable, the first slightly more emphatic. In two-syllable verbs the stress is usually strongly upon the second element except when their participles are used as adjectives or nouns, when the stress becomes more or less even.
Out- is widely used to form compounds, as in the list beginning below.

outact	outbalance	outbellow	outblush	outbully	outchide	outdare
outadd	outbanter	outblaze	outbluster	outburn	outclimb	outdazzle
outambush	outbargain	outbleat	outboast	outcaper	outcompete	outdodge
outanswer	outbark	outbless	outbox	outcatch	outcook	outdream
outargue	outbawl	outbloom	outbrag	outcavil	outcrawl	outdress
outask	outbeam	outblossom	outbrazen	outcharm	outcrow	outdrink
outbabble	outbeg	outbluff	outbribe	outchatter	outcurse	outdrive
outbake	outbeggar	outblunder	outbuild	outcheat	outdance	outdrop

out-and-out (out'ənd-out') *adj.* Thoroughgoing; unqualified; outright.

out-back (out'bak') *n. Austral.* Unsettled inland country; the bush.

out-bid (out-bid') *v.t.* **·bid, ·bid·den** or **·bid, ·bid·ding** To bid more than; offer a higher bid than: also **overbid**.

out-board (out'bôrd', -bōrd') *adj. & adv.* **1.** *Naut.* **a** Outside the hull. **b** Away from the center line of a vessel. **2.** *Aeron.* Away from the fuselage. **3.** *Mech.* On the outside of a principal machine bearing.

outboard motor A portable gasoline or electric motor, equipped with a propeller and tiller, for temporary attachment to the stern of a small boat.

out-bound (out'bound') *adj.* Outward bound.

out-brave (out-brāv') *v.t.* **·braved, ·brav·ing 1.** To surpass in bravery. **2.** To stand in defiance of.

out-break (out'brāk') *n.* A sudden bursting forth, as of an emotion or a disease; an eruption.

out-breed (out'brēd, out·brēd') *v.t.* **·bred, ·breed·ing** To breed by the mating of stocks not closely related. — **out'-breed'ing** *n.*

out-build-ing (out'bil'ding) *n.* A building separate from and subordinate to a main building, as a woodshed or barn: also called **outhouse**.

out-burst (out'bûrst') *n.* A bursting out; especially, a sudden and violent display, as of anger.

out-by (out'bī') *adv. Scot.* At a distance; outlying; also, outdoors. Also **out'bye'.**

out-cast (out'kast', -käst') *n.* **1.** One who is cast out or excluded, as from society. **2.** A homeless person or vagabond. **3.** Anything cast out, as refuse. **4.** *Scot.* A quarrel; disagreement. — *adj.* Rejected; discarded; forlorn.

out-caste (out'kast', -käst') *n.* In India, one who has forfeited his caste.

out-class (out-klas', -kläs') *v.t.* To surpass decisively in skill, quality, or powers.

out-come (out'kum') *n.* That which naturally follows; consequence or result. — **Syn.** See EFFECT.

out-crop (*n.* out'krop'; *v.* out·krop') *Geol. n.* **1.** The exposure at or above the surface of the ground of any rock stratum, vein, etc. **2.** The rock so exposed. — *v.i.* **·cropped, ·crop·ping** To crop out above the ground, as rocks.

out-cross (*v.* out·krôs', -kros'; *n.* out'krôs', -kros') *Biol. v.t.* To mate (individuals) within the same breed but of different strains. — *n.* The act or result of so mating.

out-cry (*n.* out'krī'; *v.* out·krī') *n. pl.* **·cries 1.** A loud cry or clamor. **2.** A vehement outburst of alarm, indignation, etc. — *v.t.* **·cried, ·cry·ing** To surpass in noise or crying.

out-curve (out'kûrv') *n.* In baseball, a pitched ball that curves away from the batter.

out-date (out-dāt') *v.t.* **·dat·ed, ·dat·ing** To make obsolete.

out-dat-ed (out-dā'tid) *adj.* Out-of-date; old-fashioned.

out-dis-tance (out-dis'təns) *v.t.* **·tanced, ·tanc·ing 1.** To run or move far ahead of. **2.** To surpass completely.

out-do (out-dōō') *v.t.* **·did, ·done, ·do·ing** To exceed in performance; surpass. — **Syn.** See EXCEED. — **out·do'er** *n.*

out-done (out-dun') *adj. U.S. Dial.* Provoked; exasperated.

out-door (out'dôr', -dōr') *adj.* **1.** Being or done in the open air. **2.** Intended for the outdoors. Also **out-of-door.**

out-doors (out-dôrz', -dōrz') *adv.* Outside of the house; in the open air. — *n.* The world beyond the house; the open air. Also **out-of-doors.**

out-er (ou'tər) *adj.* **1.** Being on the exterior side; external. **2.** Farther from a center or from something regarded as the inside. — *n.* **1.** The part of a target outside the rings. **2.** A shot that strikes this part.

Outer Hebrides See under HEBRIDES.

Outer Mongolia The former name for the Mongolian People's Republic. See under MONGOLIA.

out-er-most (ou'tər-mōst) *adj.* Most remote from the inside or inner part; farthest out.

outer space The space beyond the extreme limits of the earth's atmosphere; interplanetary and interstellar space.

out-face (out-fās') *v.t.* **·faced, ·fac·ing 1.** To face or stare down. **2.** To defy or confront fearlessly or impudently.

out-fall (out'fôl') *n. Brit. Dial.* The place where a river, drain, etc., discharges; mouth.

out-field (out'fēld') *n.* In baseball: **a** The space beyond the infield, divided into right field, center field, and left field. **b** The outfielders collectively. Distinguished from *infield.*

out-field-er (out'fēl'dər) *n.* In baseball, any of three players whose positions are in the outfield.

out-fit (out'fit') *n.* **1.** The tools or equipment needed for any particular purpose, as a journey, trade, etc. **2.** The act of fitting out or equipping. **3.** *U.S. Informal* Any group of persons regarded as a unit; especially, a military unit. **4.** *U.S. Informal* A set of clothing. — *v.t. & v.i.* **·fit·ted, ·fit·ting** To provide with or acquire an outfit. — **out'fit'ter** *n.* — **Syn. 1.** apparatus, paraphernalia, gear.

out-flank (out-flangk') *v.t.* To get around and in back of the flank of (an opposing force or army); flank.

out-flow (out'flō') *n.* **1.** That which flows out. **2.** The act or process of flowing out.

out-foot (out·fŏŏt') *v.t.* **1.** To exceed or surpass in running, dancing, etc. **2.** *Naut.* To sail faster than; outsail.

out-fox (out-foks') *v.t. U.S. Informal* To outwit.

out-gen-er-al (out-jen'ər-əl) *v.t.* **·aled** or **·alled, ·al·ing** or **·al·ling** To surpass in generalship; outmaneuver.

out-go (*v.* out-gō'; *n.* out'gō') *v.t.* **·went, ·gone, ·go·ing** To go farther than; exceed or outstrip. — *n. pl.* **·goes 1.** That which goes out; cost or outlay. **2.** The act of going out.

out-go-ing (out'gō'ing) *adj.* **1.** Going out; leaving. **2.** Friendly; expansive; sympathetic. — *n.* **1.** The act of going out; departure. **2.** That which goes out.

out-group (out'grōōp') *n. Sociol.* Those not in an in-group.

out-grow (out-grō') *v.t.* **·grew, ·grown, ·grow·ing 1.** To grow too large for. **2.** To lose or get rid of in the course of time or growth: to *outgrow* a habit. **3.** To surpass in growth.

out-growth (out'grōth') *n.* **1.** That which grows out of something else; an excrescence. **2.** A natural result or development. **3.** The process of growing out.

out-guess (out-ges') *v.t.* **1.** To foresee or anticipate. **2.** To prove more clever than; outwit.

out-gush (out'gush') *n.* A gushing out.

out-haul (out'hôl') *n. Naut.* A rope for extending a sail along a spar.

out-house (out'hous') *n.* **1.** An outdoor privy or toilet. **2.** An outbuilding.

out-ing (ou'ting) *n.* **1.** A short pleasure trip; an excursion. **2.** The act of going out; an airing. **3.** Distance out at sea. — *adj.* Of, pertaining to, or suitable for an outing.

outing flannel A soft, lightweight cotton fabric, usually napped on both sides.

out-land (out'land'; *for adj. also* out'lənd) *n.* **1.** *pl.* Outlying areas of a country or region. **2.** *Archaic* A foreign land. — *adj.* **1.** Outlying; distant. **2.** *Archaic* Foreign. [OE *ūtland*] — **out'land'er** *n.*

out-land-ish (out-lan'dish) *adj.* **1.** Strange or unfamiliar, as in appearance or manners. **2.** *Informal* Freakish; crazy; ridiculous: an *outlandish* notion. **3.** Far-off; remote. **4.** *Archaic* Not native; foreign. [OE *ūtlendisc < ūtland*] — **out-land'ish-ly** *adv.* — **out-land'ish-ness** *n.*

out-last (out-last', -läst') *v.t.* To last longer than.

out-law (out'lô') *n.* **1.** One who habitually breaks or defies the law; a criminal. **2.** A person deprived of the protection or benefit of the law, as for having committed a crime. **3.** A vicious animal. — *v.t.* **1.** To prohibit; ban. **2.** To deprive of legal force or protection, as a contract. **3.** To declare an outlaw; proscribe. [OE *ūtlaga < ON ūtlagi*]

out-law-ry (out'lô'rē) *n. pl.* **·ries 1.** The act or process of outlawing, or the condition of being outlawed. **2.** Habitual breaking or defiance of the law.

outeat	outgnaw	outlove	outpush	outsee	outstride	outvalue
outecho	outgrin	outmanage	outquestion	outserve	outstrive	outvaunt
outfable	outguess	outmaneuver	outquibble	outshame	outstudy	outvoice
outfast	outguide	outmarch	outquote	outshout	outstunt	outvote
outfawn	outhasten	outmatch	outrace	outshriek	outsuffer	outwait
outfeast	outhear	outmove	outraise	outsin	outsulk	outwalk
outfeel	outhit	outpaint	outrave	outsing	outswagger	outwallop
outfight	outhowl	outpass	outread	outsit	outswear	outwar
outfigure	outhumor	outperform	outrange	outskirmish	outswim	outwarble
outfind	outinvent	outpity	outreason	outslander	outswindle	outwaste
outfire	outjinx	outplan	outredden	outsleep	outtalk	outwatch
outflatter	outjockey	outplod	outring	outsmile	outtask	outweary
outfool	outjourney	outpoison	outrival	outsmoke	outthank	outweep
outfrown	outjump	outpopulate	outrear	outsnore	outthieve	outwhirl
outgabble	outkeep	outpractice	outrock	outsparkle	outthink	outwile
outgain	outkiss	outpraise	outroll	outspell	outthreaten	outwill
outgallop	outlaugh	outpray	outrun	outsprint	outthrob	outwish
outgamble	outleap	outpreach	outsail	outstare	outtower	outwrangle
outgather	outlearn	outpreen	outsatisfy	outstart	outtrade	outwrestle
outgive	outlie	outpress	outsavor	outstate	outtravel	outwriggle
outglare	outlighten	outprice	outscold	outstay	outtrick	outyell
outglitter	outlinger	outproduce	outscorn	outsteer	outtrot	outyelp
outglow	outlisten	outpromise	outscream	outstrain	outtrump	outyield

out·lay (*n.* out′lā′; *v.* out·lā′) *n.* **1.** The act of disbursing or spending. **2.** The amount spent; expenditure. — *v.t.* **·laid, ·lay·ing** To expend (money, etc.).

out·let (out′let) *n.* **1.** A passage or vent for escape or discharge. **2.** A channel of expression or escape: an *outlet* for creative energy. **3.** In commerce, a market for any commodity; also, a store handling the goods of a particular manufacturer. **4.** *Electr.* The point in a wiring system at which the current is taken to supply electrical apparatuses.

out·li·er (out′lī′ər) *n.* **1.** One who or that which is beyond or excluded from the main body. **2.** *Geol.* An exposed mass of rock surrounded by older or underlying rock strata that have been worn down by erosion or denudation.

out·line (out′līn) *n.* **1.** *Sometimes pl.* A preliminary sketch showing the principal features of a thing; general plan. **2.** A systematic statement of the structure or content of an essay, story, speech, etc. **3.** The bordering line that serves to define a figure. **4.** A sketch made of such lines without shading. — *v.t.* **·lined, ·lin·ing 1.** To make or give an outline of. **2.** To draw the outline of; sketch.

out·live (out·liv′) *v.t.* **·lived, ·liv·ing 1.** To live longer than (another). **2.** To live through; survive.

out·look (out′look′) *n.* **1.** A point of view; mental attitude; an *outlook* on life. **2.** The condition or prospect of a thing; probable outcome. **3.** A place where something is viewed. **4.** The expanse in view; vista. **5.** The act of looking out.

out·ly·ing (out′lī′ing) *adj.* Far or remote from the center or main part of something: the *outlying* districts.

out·man (out·man′) *v.t.* **·manned, ·man·ning 1.** To surpass in number of men. **2.** To excel in manliness.

out·mod·ed (out·mōd′id) *adj.* Out of fashion.

out·most (out′mōst′) *adj.* Farthest out; outermost.

out·num·ber (out′num′bər) *v.t.* To be greater in quantity than: the pink ones *outnumber* the green.

out of commission Completely out of order; not working.

out-of-date (out′əv-dāt′) *adj.* Old-fashioned; archaic.

out-of-door (out′əv-dôr′, -dōr′) *adj.* Outdoor.

out-of-doors (out′əv-dôrz′, dōrz′) *adv. & n.* Outdoors.

out-of-the-way (out′əv-thə-wā′) *adj.* **1.** Remote; difficult to reach; secluded. **2.** Out of the common range; odd.

out·pa·tient (out′pā′shənt) *n.* A patient treated at but not formally admitted to a hospital, dispensary, etc.

out·play (out·plā′) *v.t.* To play better than; defeat.

out·point (out·point′) *v.t.* **1.** To score more points than. **2.** *Naut.* To sail closer to the wind than.

out·port (out′pôrt′, -pōrt′) *n. Canadian* An isolated Newfoundland fishing village.

out·post (out′pōst′) *n.* **1.** A detachment of troops stationed at a distance from the main body as a guard against surprise attack. **2.** The station occupied by such troops. **3.** Any outlying settlement, as at a frontier.

out·pour (v. out·pôr′, -pōr′; *n.* out′pôr′, -pōr′) *v.t. & v.i.* To pour out. — *n.* A free outflow. — **out′pour′er** *n.*

out·pull (out·pool′) *v.t.* To pull more strongly than.

out·put (out′pool′) *n.* **1.** The amount of anything produced in a given time, as by a mine, factory, mill, etc. **2.** The effective work done by a machine. **3.** *Electr.* The electrical energy delivered by a generator, circuit, amplifier, etc.

out·rage (*n.* out′rāj′; *v.* out·rāj′) *n.* **1.** An act of shocking violence or cruelty. **2.** A gross violation of morality or decency. **3.** A profound insult or injury. — *v.t.* **·raged, ·rag·ing 1.** To commit an outrage upon; wrong or abuse grossly. **2.** To subject to an outrage. **3.** To violate (a woman); rape. [ME < OF *ultrage,* ult. < L *ultra* beyond] — **Syn.** (noun) **1.** crime, atrocity. **2.** Indecency, indignity, abuse. — (verb) See OFFEND.

out·ra·geous (out·rā′jəs) *adj.* **1.** Of the nature of an outrage; awful; atrocious. **2.** Heedless of authority or decency. **3.** Exceeding the bounds of moderation. [< F *outrageux*] — **out·ra′geous·ly** *adv.* — **out·ra′geous·ness** *n.*

ou·trance (ōō-träns′) *n. French* The utmost extremity.

out·rank (out′rangk′) *v.t.* To be of higher rank or station than: A colonel *outranks* a major. **2.** To take precedence over: Urban poverty *outranks* all other problems.

ou·tré (ōō-trā′) *adj. French* Deviating from conventional usage; strikingly odd; exaggerated.

out·reach (v. out·rēch′, *n.* out′rēch′) *v.t.* **1.** To reach or go beyond; surpass. **2.** To extend (something). — *v.i.* **3.** To reach out. — *n.* The act or extent of reaching out.

out·ride (out·rīd′) *v.t.* **·rode, ·rid·den, ·rid·ing** To ride faster, farther, or better than.

out·rid·er (out′rī′dər) *n.* **1.** A mounted attendant who rides in advance or to one side of a carriage. **2.** One who guides or escorts. **3.** *U.S.A.* A cowboy who rides along the edge of a herd to prevent stampeding or straying.

out·rig·ger (out′rig′ər) *n.* **1.** A part built or arranged to project beyond a natural outline, as of a vessel or machine. **2.** A projecting contrivance terminating in a boatlike float, braced to the side of a canoe to prevent capsizing. **3.** *Naut.* **a** A spar for extending a sail or rope farther than the beam of the vessel would otherwise permit. **b** A boom swung out

from a vessel, to which boats are secured. **4.** A bracket projecting from the side of a narrow rowboat or shell, and provided with a rowlock for an oar or scull; also, a boat or shell so equipped. **5.** *Aeron.* A projecting frame, as a tail boom, to support various components of an airplane.

out·right (*adj.* out′rīt′; *adv.* out′rīt′) *adj.* **1.** Free from reserve or restraint; downright. **2.** Complete; entire. **3.** Going straight on. — *adv.* **1.** Without reservation or limitation; openly. **2.** Entirely; utterly. **3.** Without delay.

out·root (out·rōōt′, -rōōt′) *v.t.* To root out; eradicate.

out·run (out·run′) *v.t.* **·ran, ·run, ·run·ning 1.** To run faster than; outstrip. **2.** To exceed or surpass.

out·run·ner (out′run′ər) *n.* **1.** An attendant who runs before or beside a carriage. **2.** The leading dog in a dog team.

out·sell (out·sel′) *v.t.* **·sold, ·sell·ing 1.** To sell more readily or for a higher price than. **2.** To sell more goods than.

out·sert (out′sûrt) *n.* A folded sheet placed around a folded section of printed matter.

out·set (out′set′) *n.* A setting out; beginning; start; opening. Also **out′set·ting.**

out·shine (out·shīn′) *v.* **·shone, ·shin·ing** *v.t.* **1.** To shine brighter than. **2.** To surpass, as in wit or elegance. — *v.i.* **3.** To shine forth.

out·shoot (v. out·shōōt′; *n.* out′shōōt′) *v.* **·shot, ·shoot·ing** *v.t.* **1.** To excel in shooting. **2.** To shoot or project beyond. — *v.i.* **3.** To shoot out; project. — *n.* **1.** Something that protrudes or projects, as a branch or bud. **2.** A rushing forth, as of water. **3.** In baseball, a pitch that curves outward away from the batter.

out·side (out′sīd′, out′sīd′, out′sīd′) *n.* **1.** The outer or external part of a thing, as an exterior surface or side. **2.** The space beyond a bounding line or surface; outer region. **3.** The part or side that is seen; outward appearance. **4.** Something empty of significance or substance; mere outward display. **5.** *Canadian* The settled parts of Canada as distinguished from the Far North. — **at the outside** *Informal* At the farthest, longest, or most: no more than three days *at the outside.* — *adj.* **1.** Pertaining to, located on, or restricted to the outside; exterior. **2.** Originating, caused by, or situated beyond designated limits or boundaries; foreign. **3.** Reaching the limit; extreme: an *outside* estimate. **4.** Slight; slim: an *outside* possibility. — *adv.* **1.** On or to the outside; externally. **2.** Beyond the outside limits of. **3.** In the open air; outdoors. — *prep.* **1.** On or to the exterior of: *outside* the park. **2.** Beyond the limits of: Don't tell it *outside* the club. **3.** *Informal* Except. — **outside of 1.** *U.S. Informal* Except; besides: No one came *outside* of me. **2.** Outside.

out·sid·er (out′sī′dər) *n.* **1.** One who is outside or excluded. **2.** A race horse whose chance of winning is slight. **3.** *Canadian* A dweller in the outside (n. def. 5). — **Syn. 1.** stranger, alien, foreigner.

out sister A nun of a cloistered order who works outside the convent and looks after its external affairs.

out·sit (out·sit′) *v.t.* **·sat, ·sit·ting 1.** To sit longer than. **2.** To sit beyond the time or period of.

out·size (out′sīz′) *n.* An irregular size, as of clothing; especially, an uncommonly large size. — *adj.* Being of an outsize: also **out′sized′.**

out·skirts (out′skûrts′) *n.pl.* A place remote from the main or central area; an outlying district.

out·smart (out·smärt′) *v.t. U.S. Informal* To outwit; fool.

out·sole (out′sōl′) *n.* The outside sole of a boot or shoe. For illustration see SHOE.

out·span (out·span′) *v.t. & v.i.* **·spanned, ·span·ning** In South Africa, to unharness or unyoke (animals). — *n.* The act or the place of outspanning. [< Afrikaans *uitspannen* < Du. *uit-* out + *spannen* to stretch]

out·speak (out·spēk′) *v.* **·spoke, ·spo·ken, ·speak·ing** *v.t.* **1.** To outdo in speaking. **2.** To say openly or boldly. — *v.i.* **3.** To speak out.

out·spo·ken (out′spō′kən) *adj.* **1.** Bold or free in speech; frank. **2.** Spoken boldly or frankly. — **out′spo′ken·ly** *adv.* — **out′spo′ken·ness** *n.*

out·spread (v. out·spred′; *n.* out′spred′) *v.t. & v.i.* **·spread, ·spread·ing** To spread out. — *n.* The act of spreading out.

out·stand (out·stand′) *v.* **·stood, ·stand·ing** *v.i.* **1.** To stand out; project. **2.** *Naut.* To put to sea; sail. — *v.t.* **3.** *Archaic* To stay or last beyond. **4.** *Dial.* To withstand.

out·stand·ing (out·stan′ding) *adj.* **1.** Standing out from others of its kind; prominent; excellent. **2.** Still standing or unsettled, as a debt or claim. **3.** Projecting; abutting.

out·stretch (out·strech′) *v.t.* **1.** To stretch out; expand; extend. **2.** To extend beyond.

out·strip (out·strip′) *v.t.* **·stripped, ·strip·ping 1.** To leave behind; outrun. **2.** To excel; surpass. — **Syn.** See EXCEED.

out·tell (out·tel′) *v.t.* **·told, ·tell·ing** To say openly; declare.

out·turn (out′tûrn′) *n.* **1.** Output; product. **2.** In commerce, the quantity, condition, or quality of goods actually turned out and delivered.

out·ward (out′wərd) *adj.* **1.** Of or pertaining to the exterior or outside; outer; external.   **2.** Relating to the physical or bodily as distinguished from the mental or spiritual aspect: *outward* manner.   **3.** Readily apparent, especially to sight; clear: no *outward* sign of trouble.   **4.** Superficially evident; seeming; ostensible: *outward* display of wealth.   **5.** Derived from or depending upon something external to oneself; not inherent; extrinsic.   **6.** Moving or directed toward the outside or away from the center: an *outward* look. — *adv.* **1.** In an outward direction; toward the outside.   **2.** In an outward manner; apparently.   **3.** Away from a place regarded as central, as port or home. — *n.* External form; outward appearance. [OE *ūtweard*] — **out′ward·ness** *n.*

out·ward·ly (out′wərd·lē) *adv.* **1.** On or toward the outside.   **2.** In outward form or aspect; seemingly.

out·wards (out′wərdz) *adv.* Outward.

out·wear (out·wâr′) *v.t.* **·wore**, **·worn**, **·wear·ing 1.** To wear or stand use longer than; outlast.   **2.** To wear out, as by constant use.   **3.** To use up.   **4.** To outlive; outgrow.

out·weigh (out·wā′) *v.t.* **1.** To weigh more than.   **2.** To exceed in importance, value, etc.

out·wit (out·wit′) *v.t.* **·wit·ted**, **·wit·ting 1.** To trick or baffle by superior ingenuity or cunning.   **2.** *Archaic* To surpass in intelligence.

out·work[1] (out·wûrk′) *v.t.* **·worked** or **·wrought**, **·work·ing 1.** To work faster or better than.   **2.** To work out.

out·work[2] (out′wûrk′) *n. Mil.* Any outer defense, as beyond the ditch of a fort.

out·worn (out·wôrn′) Past participle of OUTWEAR.

ou·zel (o͞o′zəl) *n.* **1.** One of various European thrushes, as the blackbird or the **ring ouzel** (*Turdus torquatus*).   **2.** The water ouzel (which see).   Also spelled **ousel.**   [OE *ōsle*]

o·va (ō′və) Plural of OVUM.

o·val (ō′vəl) *adj.* **1.** Having the figure or shape of an egg viewed lengthwise.   **2.** Resembling an ellipse; ellipsoidal. — *n.* An oval shape or figure.   [< MF < L *ovum* egg] — **o′val·ly** *adv.* — **o′val·ness** *n.*

o·var·i·ot·o·my (ō·vâr′ē·ot′ə·mē) *n. pl.* **·mies** *Surg.* The excision of either or both ovaries, or of an ovarian tumor: also called **oophorectomy.**   Also **o·var′i·ec·to·my** (-ek′tə·mē).

o·va·ri·tis (ō′və·rī′tis) *n. Pathol.* Inflammation of the ovary.   [< OVAR(Y) + -ITIS]

o·va·ry (ō′və·rē) *n. pl.* **·ries 1.** *Zool.* The genital gland of female animals in which the essential reproductive elements or ova are produced.   **2.** *Bot.* In angiospermous plants, that portion of the pistil or gynoecium in which the ovules are contained.   For illustration see FLOWER.   [< NL *ovarium* < L *ovum* egg] — **o·var′i·an, o·var′i·al** *adj.*

o·vate (ō′vāt) *adj. Bot.* Egg-shaped: said of leaves.   See illustration of LEAF.   [< L *ovatus* < *ovum*] — **o′vate·ly** *adv.*

o·va·tion (ō·vā′shən) *n.* **1.** A spontaneous acclamation of popularity; enthusiastic applause.   **2.** In ancient Rome, a secondary triumphal honor.   [< L *ovatio, -onis* rejoicing < *ovare* to rejoice, exult] — **o·va′tion·al** *adj.*

ov·en (uv′ən) *n.* An enclosed chamber in which substances are heated, as in order to cook or dry them.   [OE *ofen*]

Ov·en (uv′ən) *n.* The constellation Fornax.

ov·en·bird (uv′ən·bûrd′) *n.* **1.** A North American warbler (*Seiurus aurocapillus*) with an olive-colored back and a golden crown, having a grassy nest suggesting an oven: sometimes called *teacher bird.*   **2.** A South American passerine bird (genus *Furnarius*) having an oven-shaped nest of clay.

o·ver (ō′vər) *prep.* **1.** In or to a place or position above; higher than: the sky *over* our heads.   **2.** From one side or end of to the other; across or along: to climb *over* a fence; walking *over* the bridge.   **3.** On the other side of: lying *over* the ocean.   **4.** Upon the surface or exterior of: a layer of varnish *over* the wood.   **5.** Here and there upon or within; through all or many parts of: traveling *over* land and sea.   **6.** At or up to a level higher than: The water is *over* my boots.   **7.** So as to close or cover: Put the lid *over* the jar.   **8.** Throughout the time of; during: a diary kept *over* the years.   **9.** Up to the end of and beyond: Stay *over* Christmas.   **10.** More than; in excess of: *over* a million dollars.   **11.** Downward beyond: to fall *over* the side of a boat.   **12.** In preference to: chosen *over* other candidates.   **13.** In a position to guide or control; above in power or authority: too many bosses *over* them.   **14.** Upon, as an effect: his influence *over* her.   **15.** Concerning or on account of: time wasted *over* trifles.   **16.** While engaged in or partaking of: a bargain made *over* a bottle of wine.   **17.** By means of: to talk *over* the phone. — **over a barrel** *U.S. Informal* In a defenseless or abject state. — **over all** From one end or aspect to the other. — **over and above** In addition to; besides. — *adv.* **1.** Above; overhead.   **2.** To another or opposite side, or to a specified place; across: Try to leap *over*; to bring *over* a friend.   **3.** At or on the other side; at a distance in a specified direction or place: *over* in France.   **4.** From one side, opinion, or attitude to another: to be won *over* by her charm.   **5.** From one person, condition, or custody to another: to make property *over* to someone.   **6.** So as to close, cover, or be covered: The pond froze *over*.   **7.** Through from beginning to end: I'll think the matter *over*.   **8.** So as to bring the underside upward: to turn *over* the boat.   **9.** Beyond and down from the edge or brim: The water is running *over*.   **10.** From an upright position: to topple *over*.   **11.** Once more; again: He added the figures *over*.   **12.** So as to constitute a surplus; in excess: to have some left *over*.   **13.** Beyond some amount or limit; more: 21 years of age and *over*.   **14.** Beyond or until a stated time: Stay *over* until tomorrow. — **over again** Once more; anew. — **over against** Opposite to; as contrasted with. — **over and over** Time and again; repeatedly. — *adj.* **1.** Finished; done; past.   **2.** On the other side; having got across.   **3.** Outer; superior; upper.   **4.** In excess or addition; extra. — **to be over with** To be finished or at an end. — *n.* **1.** Some thing remaining or in addition.   **2.** In cricket, the succession of four to six balls bowled during a turn at one end of the wicket; also, the part of the game in which this occurs.   **3.** *Mil.* A shot hitting or exploding beyond the target. — *v.t. & v.i. Rare* To go or pass over.   [OE *ofer*]

over- *combining form* **1.** Above; on top of; superior: *over-lord.*   **2.** Passing above; going beyond the top or limit of: *overarch, overflow.*   **3.** Moving or causing to move downward, as from above: *overthrow, overturn.*   **4.** Excessively; excessive; too much: *overweight, overcharge.*

Over- is widely used to form compounds, as in the following list:

overability	overbanked	overcareless	overconservatism	overdazzle	overeagerness
overable	overbarren	overcaring	overconservative	overdear	overearnest
overabound	overbarrier	overcarry	overconsiderate	overdeck	overearnestly
overabstemious	overbashful	overcasual	overconsideration	overdecorate	overeasily
overabundance	overbashfully	overcaution	overconsume	overdecorative	overeasy
overabundant	overbelief	overcautious	overconsumption	overdeepen	overeducate
overabundantly	overbet	overcautiously	overcontented	overdeeply	overelaborate
overaccentuate	overbig	overcautiousness	overcontribute	overdeliberate	overelaboration
overaccumulation	overbitter	overcentralization	overcook	overdeliberation	overelate
overactive	overblame	overcharitable	overcool	overdelicate	overelegant
overactivity	overblithe	overcheap	overcoolly	overdelicately	overembellish
overadvance	overboastful	overcherish	overcopious	overdelighted	overemotional
overagitate	overbold	overchildish	overcorrect	overdemand	overemphasis
overagitation	overboldly	overchill	overcorrupt	overdemocratic	overemphasize
overambition	overbookish	overcivil	overcostly	overdepress	overemphatic
overambitious	overboorish	overcivility	overcount	overdepressive	overempty
overambitiously	overborrow	overcivilized	overcourteous	overdesirous	overenjoy
overanalyze	overbounteous	overclean	overcovetous	overdestructive	overenrich
overanxiety	overbravely	overclever	overcoy	overdestructiveness	overenter
overanxious	overbreed	overclose	overcram	overdevoted	overenthusiastic
overanxiously	overbreed	overcloseness	overcredit	overdevotion	overesteem
overapprehension	overbright	overcold	overcredulity	overdiffuse	overexcitable
overapprehensive	overbrilliant	overcolor	overcredulous	overdignified	overexcite
overapprehensively	overbroaden	overcommend	overcritical	overdiligence	overexcitement
overapt	overbroil	overcompetitive	overcriticize	overdiligent	overexercise
overargue	overbrown	overcomplacency	overcrowd	overdilute	overexert
overassert	overbrush	overcomplacent	overcultivate	overdiscipline	overexertion
overassertive	overbulky	overcomplex	overcultivation	overdistant	overexpand
overassess	overburdensome	overcompliant	overcunning	overdiversification	overexpansion
overassessment	overbusily	overconcentration	overcunningly	overdiversify	overexpect
overassumption	overbusy	overconcern	overcured	overdogmatic	overexpectant
overattached	overbuy	overcondense	overcurious	overdominate	overexpenditure
overattention	overcapability	overconfidence	overcuriousness	overdoubt	overexpress
overattentive	overcapable	overconfident	overdaintiness	overdramatic	overexuberant
overattentively	overcapacity	overconfidently	overdainty	overdredge	overfacile
overattentiveness	overcaptious	overconscientious	overdance	overdrink	overfaithful
overbake	overcaptiousness	overconscious	overdare	overdry	overfamiliar
overballast	overcareful	overconsciousness	overdaring	overeager	overfamiliarly

o·ver·act (ō′vər·akt′) *v.t. & v.i.* To act with exaggeration.

o·ver·age¹ (ō′vər·ij) *n.* In commerce, an amount of money or goods in excess of that which is listed as being on hand.

o·ver·age² (ō′vər·āj′) *adj.* **1.** Over the usual or specified age. **2.** Too old to be of use: *overage* guns.

o·ver·all (ō′vər·ôl′) *adj.* **1.** From one end to the other. **2.** Including or covering everything. — *n. Chiefly Brit.* A loose protective outer garment.

o·ver·alls (ō′vər·ôlz′) *n.pl.* **1.** Loose, coarse trousers, often with suspenders and a piece extending over the breast, worn over the clothing as protection against soiling and wear. **2.** *Brit.* Waterproof leggings.

o·ver·arch (ō′vər·ärch′) *v.t. & v.i.* To form an arch over (something).

o·ver·arm (ō′vər·ärm′) *adj.* Done with the arm above the level of the shoulder, as a swimming stroke.

o·ver·awe (ō′vər·ô′) *v.t.* ·awed, ·aw·ing To subdue or restrain by awe.

o·ver·bal·ance (ō′vər·bal′əns) *v.* ·anced, ·anc·ing *v.t.* **1.** To exceed in weight, importance, etc. **2.** To cause to lose balance. — *v.i.* **3.** To lose one's balance. — *n.* Excess of weight or value.

o·ver·bear (ō′vər·bâr′) *v.* ·bore, ·borne, ·bear·ing *v.t.* **1.** To crush or bear down by physical weight or force. **2.** To prevail over; domineer. — *v.i.* **3.** To be too fruitful.

o·ver·bear·ing (ō′vər·bâr′ing) *adj.* **1.** Arrogant; domineering; dictatorial. **2.** Overwhelming; crushing. — **o′ver·bear′ing·ly** *adv.*

o·ver·bid (ō′vər·bid′) *v.t. & v.i.* ·bid, ·bid·den or ·bid, ·bid·ding **1.** To bid more than the value of (something). **2.** To outbid (someone).

o·ver·bite (ō′vər·bīt′) *n. Dent.* Excessive projection of the upper incisor teeth in front of the lower in occlusion.

o·ver·blow (ō′vər·blō′) *v.* ·blew, ·blown, ·blow·ing *v.t.* **1.** To blow down, over, or away. **2.** To cover by blowing, as with snow or sand. **3.** *Music* To blow (a wind instrument) so as to produce an overtone rather than a fundamental tone. — *v.i.* **4.** *Music* To produce an overtone rather than a fundamental tone with a wind instrument.

o·ver·blown (ō′vər·blōn′) *adj.* **1.** Blown up or swollen, as with conceit or pretentiousness; inflated; bombastic. **2.** Past full bloom, as a flower.

o·ver·board (ō′vər·bôrd′, -bōrd′) *adv.* Over the side of or out of a boat or ship. — **to go overboard** *U.S. Informal* To be extremely enthusiastic about someone or something.

o·ver·build (ō′vər·bild′) *v.t.* ·built, ·build·ing **1.** To build over. **2.** To erect more buildings in (an area) than are needed. **3.** To build, as a house, on too elaborate a scale.

o·ver·bur·den (ō′vər·bûr′dən) *v.t.* To load with too much weight, care, responsibility, etc. — *n.* That which overburdens.

o·ver·call (ō′vər·kôl′) *n.* In bridge, etc., a bid higher than an opponent's previous bid. — *v.t.* **1.** To bid higher than (an opponent or his previous bid). — *v.i.* **2.** To make an overcall.

o·ver·cap·i·tal·ize (ō′vər·kap′i·təl·īz′) *v.t.* ·ized, ·iz·ing **1.** To invest capital in to an extent not warranted by actual prospects. **2.** To affix an unjustifiable or unlawful value to the nominal capital of (a corporation). **3.** To estimate the value of (a property, company, etc.) too highly.

o·ver·cast (ō′vər·kast′, -käst′; *for v. defs.* **1, 2, & 4,** *also* ō′vər·kast′, -käst′) *adj.* **1.** Covered or obscured, as with clouds. **2.** Gloomy; melancholy. **3.** Sewn with long wrapping stitches to prevent raveling. — *n.* **1.** A covering or mantle, as of clouds. **2.** In mining, a support for a passage extending above another passage. **3.** *Meteorol.* A cloud or clouds covering more than nine-tenths of the sky. — *v.* ·cast, ·cast·ing *v.t.* **1.** To make overcast. **2.** To cast beyond. **3.** To sew, as the edge of a fabric, with an overcast stitch. — *v.i.* **4.** To become overcast.

o·ver·charge (*v.* ō′vər·chärj′; *n.* ō′vər·chärj′) *v.t.* ·charged, ·charg·ing **1.** To charge (someone) too high a price. **2.** To load or fill to excess; overburden. **3.** To exaggerate; overdo. — *n.* An excessive charge. *Abbr. o/c*

o·ver·check (ō′vər·chek′) *n.* A checkrein passing over a horse's head between the ears to draw the bit upward.

o·ver·clothes (ō′vər·klōz′, -klōthz′) *n.pl.* Outer garments.

o·ver·cloud (ō′vər·kloud′) *v.t.* **1.** To cover with clouds; darken. **2.** To make gloomy. — *v.i.* **3.** To become cloudy.

o·ver·coat (ō′vər·kōt′) *n.* An outdoor coat worn over a suit, etc., especially in cold weather.

o·ver·come (ō′vər·kum′) *v.t.* ·came, ·come, ·com·ing **1.** To get the better of in any conflict or struggle; defeat; conquer. **2.** To prevail over or surmount, as difficulties, obstacles, etc. **3.** To render (someone) helpless, as by emotion, sickness, etc. — *v.i.* **4.** To gain mastery; win. [OE *ofercuman*]

o·ver·com·pen·sate (ō′vər·kom′pən·sāt) *v.* ·sat·ed, ·sat·ing *v.i.* **1.** To make too great a compensation, as in balancing the arms of a scales. **2.** To engage in overcompensation. — *v.t.* **3.** To make too great a compensation to.

o·ver·com·pen·sa·tion (ō′vər·kom′pən·sā′shən) *n. Psychol.* Excessive or abnormal reaction, especially to compensate for the fact or feeling of inferiority.

o·ver·crop (ō′vər·krop′) *v.t.* ·cropped, ·crop·ping *Agric.* To exhaust (land) by continuous cropping.

o·ver·de·vel·op (ō′vər·di·vel′əp) *v.t.* **1.** To develop excessively. **2.** *Photog.* To develop (a plate or film) to too great a degree. — **o′ver·de·vel′op·ment** *n.*

o·ver·do (ō′vər·dōō′) *v.* ·did, ·done, ·do·ing *v.t.* **1.** To do excessively; carry too far; exaggerate. **2.** To overtax the strength of; exhaust. **3.** To cook too much, as meat. — *v.i.* **4.** To do too much. [OE *oferdōn*]

o·ver·dose (*v.* ō′vər·dōs′; *n.* ō′vər·dōs′) *v.t.* ·dosed, ·dos·ing To dose to excess. — *n.* An excessive dose.

o·ver·draft (ō′vər·draft′, -dräft′) *n.* **1.** The act of overdrawing an account, as at a bank. **2.** The amount by which a check or draft exceeds the sum against which it is drawn. *Abbr. O.D.* **3.** A current of air passing over and not through the ignited fuel in a furnace. Also **o′ver·draught′.**

o·ver·draw (ō′vər·drô′) *v.t.* ·drew, ·drawn, ·draw·ing **1.** To draw against (an account) beyond one's credit. **2.** To draw or strain excessively, as a bow. **3.** To exaggerate a representation of.

o·ver·dress (ō′vər·dres′) *v.t. & v.i.* To dress in clothes that are too fancy or too elaborate for the occasion.

o·ver·drive (*v.* ō′vər·drīv′; *n.* ō′vər·drīv′) *v.t.* ·drove, ·driv-

overfanciful	overfreedom	overgreediness	overhysterical	overjocular	overloud
overfast	overfreely	overgreedy	overidealism	overjoyful	overlove
overfastidious	overfreight	overgrieve	overidealistic	overjoyous	overloyal
overfastidiousness	overfrequency	overgross	overidle	overjudicious	overluscious
overfasting	overfrequent	overhandle	overillustrate	overjust	overlustiness
overfat	overfrighten	overhappy	overimaginative	overkeen	overlusty
overfatigue	overfruitful	overharass	overimitate	overkind	overluxuriant
overfatten	overfull	overhard	overimitative	overknowing	overluxurious
overfavor	overfullness	overharden	overimpress	overlabor	overmagnify
overfear	overfunctioning	overhardy	overimpressible	overlactation	overmany
overfearful	overfurnish	overharsh	overinclination	overlade	overmarch
overfeatured	overgamble	overhaste	overinclined	overlarge	overmasterful
overfed	overgarrison	overhastily	overindividualistic	overlate	overmasterfulness
overfeed	overgeneralize	overhastiness	overindulge	overladudatory	overmature
overfeminine	overgenerous	overhasty	overindulgence	overlaunch	overmeanness
overfierce	overgenial	overhate	overindulgent	overlavish	overmeasure
overfill	overgentle	overhaughty	overindustrialize	overlawful	overmeddle
overflatten	overgifted	overheap	overinflate	overlax	overmeek
overflourish	overgird	overheartily	overinflation	overlaxness	overmellow
overfluent	overglad	overhearty	overinfluence	overlearnedness	overmelt
overfond	overgloomy	overheavy	overinfluential	overlet	overmerciful
overfondle	overglorious	overhelpful	overinsistence	overlewd	overmerrily
overfondly	overgoad	overhigh	overinsistent	overliberal	overmerry
overfondness	overgodly	overhold	overinsolent	overliberality	overmighty
overfoolish	overgorge	overholy	overinstruct	overliberally	overmild
overforce	overgracious	overhomely	overinsure	overlighted	overminutely
overforged	overgraciously	overhonest	overintellectual	overlinger	overminuteness
overforward	overgrasping	overhonor	overintense	overliterary	overmix
overforwardness	overgrateful	overhope	overinterest	overliveliness	overmodest
overfoul	overgratify	overhot	overinventoried	overlively	overmodestly
overfrail	overgraze	overhotly	overinvest	overload	overmodesty
overfrank	overgreasy	overhuman	overirrigate	overlofty	overmoist
overfraught	overgreat	overhumanize	overirrigation	overlogical	overmoisten
overfree	overgreatness	overhurriedly	overjealous	overlong	overmoisture

en, ·driv·ing To drive too hard or too far. — *n. Mech.* A gearing device that turns a drive shaft at a speed greater than that of the engine, thus decreasing power output: opposed to *underdrive.*

o·ver·due (ō/vər·dōō/, -dyōō/) *adj.* **1.** Remaining unpaid after becoming due. **2.** Past due: an *overdue* plane or train.

o·ver·dye (ō/vər·dī/) *v.t.* ·**dyed, ·dye·ing 1.** To dye with too much color. **2.** To dye with a second color.

o·ver·eat (ō/vər·ēt/) *v.i.* ·**ate** (-āt/, *Brit.* -et/) or *Archaic* ·eat (-et/, -ēt/), ·eat·en, eat·ing To eat to excess.

o·ver·es·ti·mate (*v.* ō/vər·es/tə·māt; *n.* ō/vər·es/tə·mit) *v.t.* ·mat·ed, ·mat·ing To value or estimate too highly. — *n.* An estimate that is too high. — **o/ver·es/ti·ma/tion** *n.*

o·ver·ex·pose (ō/vər·ik·spōz/) *v.t.* ·**posed, ·pos·ing 1.** To expose excessively. **2.** *Photog.* To expose (a film or plate) too long. — **o/ver·ex·po/sure** (-spō/zhər) *n.*

o·ver·flight (ō/vər·flīt/) *n. Aeron.* The flight of an aircraft over a place or region, often at high altitudes and for reconnaissance or espionage purposes.

o·ver·flow (*v.* ō/vər·flō/; *n.* ō/vər·flō/) *v.* ·**flowed, ·flown, ·flow·ing** *v.i.* **1.** To flow or run over the brim or bank, as water, rivers, etc. **2.** To be filled beyond capacity; superabound. — *v.t.* **3.** To flow over the brim or bank of. **4.** To flow or spread over; cover; flood. **5.** To cause to overflow. — *n.* **1.** The act or process of overflowing. **2.** That which flows over. **3.** The amount by which a capacity is exceeded; surplus. **4.** An outlet for liquid. [OE *oferflōwan*]

o·ver·gar·ment (ō/vər·gär/mənt) *n.* An outer garment.

o·ver·glaze (ō/vər·glāz/; *for v., also* ō/vər·glāz/) *n.* A decoration or glaze applied over a first glaze, as to pottery. — *v.t.* ·**glazed, ·glaz·ing** To apply an overglaze.

o·ver·grow (ō/vər·grō/) *v.* ·**grew, ·grown, ·grow·ing** *v.t.* **1.** To grow over; cover with growth. **2.** To grow too big for; outgrow. — *v.i.* **3.** To increase excessively; grow too large.

o·ver·growth (ō/vər·grōth/) *n.* **1.** Luxuriant or excessive growth. **2.** A growth upon or over something.

o·ver·hand (ō/vər·hand/) *adj.* **1.** In baseball, etc., executed with the hand above the level of the elbow or the shoulder. Also **o/ver·hand/ed** (-han/did). **2.** Striking downward. **3.** In sewing, made by carrying the thread over both edges, as a seam. — *adv.* In an overhand manner. — *n.* **1.** An overhand stroke or delivery, as in tennis or baseball. **2.** A kind of knot. For illustration see KNOT[1].

o·ver·hang (ō/vər·hang/) *v.* ·**hung** (-hung/), ·hang·ing *v.t.* **1.** To hang or project over (something); jut over. **2.** To threaten; menace. **3.** To adorn with hangings. — *v.i.* **4.** To hang or jut over something. — *n.* **1.** An overhanging portion of a structure, as of a roof, cliff, the bow of a ship, etc.; also, the amount of such projection. **2.** *Aeron.* **a** On a biplane, etc., the span of one wing beyond another: called **positive overhang** when the upper surface is greater. **b** The distance from the outer strut attachment to the tip of a wing.

o·ver·haul (*v.* ō/vər·hôl/; *n.* ō/vər·hôl/) *v.t.* **1.** To examine carefully for needed repairs; also, to take apart for this purpose. **2.** To make all needed repairs in; renovate. **3.** To catch up with; gain on. **4.** *Naut.* **a** To slacken (a rope) by hauling in the opposite direction. **b** To prepare (a tackle) for use by separating the blocks. — *n.* **1.** A thorough inspection. **2.** Examination and complete repair. Also **o/ver·haul/ing.**

o·ver·head (*adj. & n.* ō/vər·hed/; *adv.* ō/vər·hed/) *adj.* **1.** Situated or working above the level of one's head: an *overhead* light. **2.** Of or relating to the overhead of a business. — *n.* **1.** The operating expenses of a business that cannot be attributed to any one department or product and that exclude the costs of labor and materials, as rent, light, heat, taxes, etc. **2.** *Naut.* The ceiling of a cabin or hold. — *adv.* Over or above the head.

overhead valve *Mech.* A valve located in the upper part of the combustion chamber of an engine, above the piston face.

o·ver·hear (ō/vər·hir/) *v.t.* ·**heard** (-hûrd/), ·hear·ing To hear (something said or someone speaking) without the knowledge or intention of the speaker. — **o/ver·hear/er** *n.*

o·ver·heat (ō/vər·hēt/) *v.t. & v.i.* To make or become excessively hot or excited.

o·ver·is·sue (*n.* ō/vər·ish/ōō, -yōō; *v.* ō/vər·ish/ōō, -yōō) *n.* An excessive or unauthorized issue of stocks, bonds, etc. — *v.t.* ·**sued, ·su·ing** To issue in excess.

o·ver·joy (ō/vər·joi/) *v.t.* To delight or please greatly.

o·ver·kill (ō/vər·kil/) *n.* The military capacity for destruction far beyond the resources and population of an enemy.

o·ver·lade (ō/vər·lād/) *v.t.* ·**lad·ed, ·lad·en, ·lad·ing** To overload: now used chiefly in the past participle.

o·ver·lain (ō/vər·lān/) Past participle of OVERLIE.

o·ver·land (ō/vər·land/) *adj.* Proceeding over or accomplished by land. — *adv.* Across, over, or via land. — *n.* An overland stage or train.

o·ver·lap (*v.* ō/vər·lap/; *n.* ō/vər·lap/) *v.t. & v.i.* ·**lapped, ·lap·ping 1.** To lie or extend partly over or upon (another or each other); lap over. **2.** To cover and project beyond (something). — *n.* **1.** The state or extent of overlapping. **2.** The part that overlaps. **3.** *Geol.* The extension of a rock stratum beyond the limits of an older underlying stratum.

o·ver·lay (*v.* ō/vər·lā/; *n.* ō/vər·lā/) *v.t.* ·**laid, ·lay·ing 1.** To spread something over, as with a decorative pattern or layer. **2.** To lay or place over or upon something else. **3.** To weigh down; overburden. **4.** *Printing* To put an overlay upon. — *n.* **1.** *Printing* A piece of paper placed on the tympan of a press to make the impression heavier at the corresponding part of the form, or to compensate for a depression in the form. **2.** Anything that covers or partly covers something. **3.** An ornamental layer, as veneer, applied to wood, etc. **4.** A sheet laid over a map to add or emphasize certain features, as in military operations. **5.** *Scot.* A cravat.

o·ver·leap (ō/vər·lēp/) *v.t.* ·**leaped** or ·**leapt, ·leap·ing 1.** To leap over or across. **2.** To omit; overlook. **3.** To leap farther than; outleap. — **to overleap oneself** To miss one's purpose by going too far. [OE *oferhlēapan*]

o·ver·lie (ō/vər·lī/) *v.t.* ·**lay** (-lā/), ·**lain** (-lān/), ·ly·ing **1.** To lie over or upon. **2.** To suffocate by lying upon.

o·ver·live (ō/vər·liv/) *v.* ·**lived, ·liv·ing** *v.t.* To live longer than; survive. — *v.i.* To live on; survive. [OE *oferlibban*]

o·ver·load (*v.* ō/vər·lōd/; *n.* ō/vər·lōd/) *v.t.* To load excessively; overburden. — *n.* **1.** An excessive burden. **2.** *Electr.* **a** An amperage in excess of that which a given current, device, or apparatus can safely carry. **b** A circuit breaker.

o·ver·look (*v.* ō/vər·lŏŏk/; *n.* ō/vər·lŏŏk/) *v.t.* **1.** To fail to see or notice; miss. **2.** To disregard purposely or indulgently; ignore. **3.** To look over or see from a higher place. **4.** To afford a view of: The castle *overlooks* the harbor. **5.** To supervise; oversee. **6.** To examine or inspect. **7.** To look upon or bewitch with the evil eye. — **Syn.** See NEGLECT. — *n.* **1.** The act of looking over, as from a height; an inspection; survey. **2.** An elevated place affording a view; also, the view from such a place. **3.** Oversight; neglect. **4.** The jack bean.

o·ver·lord (ō/vər·lôrd/) *n.* **1.** A superior lord or chief. **2.** One who holds supremacy over others. — **o/ver·lord/ship** *n.*

o·ver·ly (ō/vər·lē) *adv. Chiefly U.S.* To an excessive degree; too much; too.

o·ver·man[1] (ō/vər·mən *for defs. 1 & 2;* ō/vər·man/ *for def. 3*) *n. pl.* ·**men** (-mən *for defs. 1 & 2;* -men/ *for def. 3*) **1.** An overseer (def. 1). **2.** A referee. **3.** A superman (def. 1).

o·ver·man[2] (ō/vər·man/) *v.t.* ·**manned, ·man·ning** To provide with more men than necessary.

o·ver·mas·ter (ō/vər·mas/tər, -mäs/-) *v.t.* To overcome; overpower. — **o/ver·mas/ter·ing** *n. & adj.*

o·ver·match (*v.* ō/vər·mach/; *n.* ō/vər·mach/) *v.t.* To be more than a match for; surpass. — *n.* **1.** One who or that which is superior in strength, skill, etc. **2.** A contest in which one party overmatches the other.

overmortgage	overoften	overpointed	overprovide	overrefinement	oversale
overmournful	overoptimistic	overpolemical	overprovident	overreflection	oversalt
overmultiply	overornamented	overpolish	overprovision	overreflective	oversalty
overnarrow	overpainful	overponderous	overprovocation	overregulation	oversanguine
overnear	overpamper	overpopular	overprovoke	overrelax	oversaturate
overneat	overpartial	overpopulous	overpublic	overreliant	oversaturation
overneglect	overpartiality	overpositive	overpublicity	overreligious	oversaucy
overnegligence	overparticular	overpotent	overpunish	overrepresent	oversave
overnegligent	overpassionate	overpowerful	overpunishment	overreserved	overscare
overnervous	overpassionately	overpraise	overquantity	overresolute	overscented
overnervousness	overpatient	overprecise	overquick	overrestrain	overscrub
overnew	overpatriotic	overpreciseness	overquiet	overretention	overscrupulosity
overnice	overpensive	overpreoccupation	overquietness	overreward	overscrupulous
overnimble	overpeople	overpress	overrank	overrich	overscrupulousness
overnotable	overpert	overpresumptuous	overrapturous	overrife	overseason
overnourish	overpessimistic	overprocrastination	overrash	overrighteous	overseasoned
overnumerous	overpicture	overproductive	overrational	overrighteousness	oversecure
overobedient	overpiteous	overproficient	overrationalize	overrigid	overseed
overobese	overplain	overprolific	overreadily	overrigorous	oversensible
overoblige	overplausible	overprominent	overreadiness	overripe	oversensitive
overobsequious	overplease	overprompt	overready	overripen	oversensual
overobsequiousness	overplentiful	overpromptness	overrealism	overroast	oversensuality
overoffensive	overplenty	overprosperous	overrealistic	over·rough	oversententious
overofficious	overplump	overprotract	overrefine	overrude	oversentimental
overofficiousness	overply	overproud	overrefined	oversad	overserious

o·ver·much (ō′vər·much′) *adj.* Excessive; too much. — *adv.* In too great a degree. — *n.* An excess; too much.

o·ver·night (*adj. & adv.* ō′vər·nīt′; *n.* ō′vər·nīt′) *adj.* 1. Of, done during, or lasting the night: an *overnight* visit. 2. Away from home for one night: an *overnight* trip. 3. Used for short visits: an *overnight* bag. 4. Sudden: *overnight* fame. — *adv.* 1. During or through the night. 2. On the previous evening. 3. In no time; suddenly or quickly: He became famous *overnight*. — *n.* The previous evening.

o·ver·pass (*n.* ō′vər·pas′, -päs′; *v.* ō′vər·pas′, -päs′) *n.* An elevated section of highway crossing other lines of travel. — *v.t.* 1. To pass over, across, or through; cross. 2. To surpass or exceed. 3. To overlook; disregard. 4. To pass beyond a limit; transgress.

o·ver·pay (ō′vər·pā′) *v.t.* **·paid, ·pay·ing** 1. To pay more than (a sum due). 2. To pay (someone) too much. 3. To reward too highly. — **o′ver·pay′ment** *n.*

o·ver·per·suade (ō′vər·pər·swād′) *v.t.* **·suad·ed, ·suad·ing** To persuade (someone) to an action or view, especially against his judgment or inclination. — **o′ver·per·sua′sion** (-swā′zhən) *n.*

o·ver·play (ō′vər·plā′) *v.t.* 1. To play or act (a part or role) to excess; overdo; exaggerate. 2. To outplay; surpass. 3. In golf, to send (the ball) beyond the putting green.

o·ver·plus (ō′vər·plus′) *n.* That which remains after a certain part has been used or set aside; surplus; excess. [Partial trans. of OF *surplus* < *sur-* over + *plus* more]

o·ver·pop·u·late (ō′vər·pop′yə·lāt) *v.t.* **·lat·ed, ·lat·ing** To cause to have too high a population; populate to excess. — **o′ver·pop′u·la′tion** *n.*

o·ver·pow·er (ō′vər·pou′ər) *v.t.* 1. To gain supremacy over; subdue. 2. To render helpless or ineffective; overcome. 3. To supply with more power than necessary.

o·ver·pow·er·ing (ō′vər·pou′ər·ing) *adj.* 1. That overpowers. 2. Intense; overwhelming. — **o′ver·pow′er·ing·ly** *adv.*

o·ver·price (ō′ver·prīs′) *v.t.* **·priced, ·pric·ing** To set too high a price upon, as merchandise.

o·ver·print (*v.* ō′vər·print′; *n.* ō′vər·print′) *v.t.* To print additional material of another color on (sheets already printed). — *n.* 1. Anything printed over another impression. 2. Any word, symbol, etc., printed over a postage stamp, changing its value or use.

o·ver·prize (ō′vər·prīz′) *v.t.* **·prized, ·priz·ing** To value too highly.

o·ver·pro·duce (ō′vər·prə·dōōs′, -dyōōs′) *v.t.* **·duced, ·duc·ing** To produce too much of or so as to exceed demand.

o·ver·pro·duc·tion (ō′vər·prə·duk′shən) *n.* Production in excess of demand, or of the possibility of profitable sale.

o·ver·proof (ō′vər·prōōf′) *adj.* Containing a larger proportion of alcohol than proof spirit: said of liquors.

o·ver·pro·por·tion (ō′vər·prə·pôr′shən, -pōr′-) *v.t.* To make or depict in excess of true proportions. — **o′ver·pro·por′tion·ate** *adj.* — **o′ver·pro·por′tion·ate·ly** *adv.*

o·ver·pro·tect (ō′vər·prə·tekt′) *v.t.* To shelter or protect more than is necessary or proper. — **o′ver·pro·tec′tion** *n.* — **o′ver·pro·tec′tive·ness** *n.* — **o′ver·pro·tec′tive** *adj.* — **o′ver·pro·tec′tive·ly** *adv.*

o·ver·rate (ō′vər·rāt′) *v.t.* **·rat·ed, ·rat·ing** To rate or value too highly; credit with undue merit; overestimate.

o·ver·reach (ō′vər·rēch′) *v.t.* 1. To reach over or beyond. 2. To spread over; cover. 3. To defeat (oneself), as by attempting something beyond one's capability. 4. To miss by stretching or reaching too far. 5. To get the advantage of; outwit; cheat. — *v.i.* 6. To reach too far. 7. To be dishonest; cheat. 8. To hit a toe of the hind foot against the heel of the forefoot: said of horses, etc. — **o′ver·reach′er** *n.*

o·ver·ride (ō′vər·rīd′) *v.t.* **·rode** (-rōd′), **·rid·den** (-rid′ən), **·rid·ing** 1. To disregard summarily, as if trampling down; supersede; prevail over. 2. To ride (a horse, etc.) to exhaustion. 3. To ride over or across. 4. To trample down; suppress. 5. *Surg.* To slide over (the corresponding fragment), as one end of a fractured bone. [OE *oferrīdan*]

o·ver·rule (ō′vər·rōōl′) *v.t.* **·ruled, ·rul·ing** 1. To decide against or nullify by superior authority; set aside; invalidate. 2. To disallow the arguments of (someone). 3. To have control over; rule. 4. To influence or prevail over.

o·ver·run (*v.* ō′vər·run′; *n.* ō′vər·run′) *v.* **·ran** (-ran′), **·run, ·run·ning** *v.t.* 1. To spread or swarm over, especially harmfully, as vermin or invaders; ravage; invade; infest. 2. To run or flow over; overflow. 3. To spread rapidly across or throughout, as a fashion or fad. 4. To run beyond; pass the limit of. 5. *Printing* To shift or rearrange (words, lines of type, etc.) from one line, page, or column to another. 6. *Archaic* To run faster than; outrun. — *v.i.* 7. To run over; overflow. 8. To pass the usual or desired limit. — *n.* 1. An instance of overrunning; also, the amount or extent of overrunning. 2. *Aeron.* A cleared zone at the end of a runway.

o·ver·sand·ed (ō′vər·san′did) *adj.* Containing more than the normal or necessary amount of sand: said of cement.

o·ver·score (ō′vər·skôr′, -skōr′) *v.t.* **·scored, ·scor·ing** To draw a line or lines over a word, letter, etc.

o·ver·seas (ō′vər·sēz′) *adv.* Beyond the sea; abroad. — *adj.* Situated, coming from, or for use beyond the sea; foreign: also **o′ver·sea′**.

overseas cap A narrow, boat-shaped, visorless cap worn as part of the military uniform: also called *field cap*.

o·ver·see (ō′vər·sē′) *v.t.* **·saw, ·seen, ·see·ing** 1. To direct as supervisor; superintend. 2. To survey; watch. 3. *Archaic* To examine; peruse. [OE *ofersēon*]

o·ver·se·er (ō′vər·sē′ər, -sir′) *n.* 1. A person who oversees; especially, one who superintends laborers at their work: also called *overman*. 2. *Brit.* A parish officer who administrates relief funds: also **overseer of the poor**.

o·ver·sell (ō′vər·sel′) *v.t.* **·sold** (-sōld′), **·sell·ing** 1. To sell to excess. 2. To sell more of (a stock, etc.) than one can provide. 3. To praise (a product, etc.) too highly.

o·ver·set (*v.* ō′vər·set′; *n.* ō′vər·set′) *v.* **·set, ·set·ting** *v.t.* 1. To overcome or disorder mentally or physically; disconcert. 2. *Printing* **a** To set too much (type or copy) for a given space. **b** To set too much type in. 3. *Rare* To cause to overturn; capsize. — *v.i.* 4. To overturn; fall over. — *n.* 1. A turning over; upset. 2. *Printing* Excess of composed type.

o·ver·sew (ō′vər·sō′, ō′vər·sō′) *v.t.* **·sewed, ·sewed** or **·sewn, ·sew·ing** To sew overhand, especially with close stitches.

o·ver·sexed (ō′vər·sekst′) *adj.* Having, displaying, or characterized by excessive sexual desire or interest.

o·ver·shade (ō′vər·shād′) *v.t.* **·shad·ed, ·shad·ing** To overshadow; overcast.

o·ver·shad·ow (ō′vər·shad′ō) *v.t.* 1. To render unimportant or insignificant by comparison; loom above; dominate. 2. To throw a shadow over; obscure. [OE *ofersceadwian*]

o·ver·shine (ō′vər·shīn′) *v.t.* **·shone** (-shōn′), **·shin·ing** 1. To shine over or upon; illumine. 2. To excel in some respect; outshine.

o·ver·shoe (ō′vər·shōō′) *n.* A shoe worn over another for protection against water, mud, cold, etc., usually made of a pliable substance, as rubber; a galosh.

o·ver·shoot (ō′vər·shōōt′) *v.* **·shot, ·shoot·ing** *v.t.* 1. To shoot or go over or beyond (the mark, target, etc.). 2. To go beyond; exceed, as a limit. 3. To drive or force (something) beyond the proper limit. 4. *Aeron.* To fly beyond (an intended limit); land beyond (the runway). — *v.i.* 5. To shoot or go over or beyond the mark. 6. To go too far.

overservile	oversolemn	oversteadfastness	oversup	overthin	overvehement
oversettled	oversolicitous	oversteady	oversuperstitious	overthoughtful	overventilate
oversevere	oversoon	overstiff	oversupination	overthrifty	overventuresome
overseverely	oversoothing	overstimulate	oversure	overthrong	overventurous
overseverity	oversophisticated	overstimulation	oversusceptible	overthrust	overvigorous
oversexual	oversophistication	overstir	oversuspicious	overtight	overviolent
oversharp	oversorrow	overstock	oversuspiciously	overtimid	overvote
overshort	overspacious	overstore	oversweet	overtimorous	overwarm
overshorten	oversparing	overstout	oversystematic	overtinseled	overwarmed
overshrink	oversparingly	overstrain	oversystematize	overtire	overwary
oversick	overspecialization	overstress	overtalkative	overtoil	overweak
oversilent	overspecialize	overstretch	overtalkativeness	overtop	overwealthy
oversimple	overspeculate	overstrict	overtame	overtorture	overwet
oversimplicity	overspeculation	overstrident	overtart	overtrain	overwide
oversimplification	overspeculative	overstriving	overtask	overtrim	overwilling
oversimplify	overspeed	overstrong	overtaxation	overtrust	overwily
overskeptical	overspeedily	overstudious	overteach	overtrustful	overwise
overslander	overspent	overstudiousness	overtechnical	overtruthful	overwoody
overslight	overspin	overstudy	overtedious	overunionized	overworry
overslow	oversqueamish	oversublime	overtenacious	overurbanization	overworship
oversmall	oversqueamishness	oversubscribe	overtender	overurge	overyoung
oversmooth	overstaring	oversubscription	overtenderness	overuse	overyouthful
oversoak	overstately	oversubtle	overtense	overvaluable	overzeal
oversoft	oversteadfast	obersubtlety	overtension	overvaluation	overzealous
oversoftness		oversufficient	overthick	overvariety	overzealously

o·ver·shot (ō'vər·shot') *adj.* **1.** Surpassed in any way. **2.** Projecting, as the upper jaw beyond the lower jaw. **3.** Driven by water flowing over from above: an *overshot* wheel.

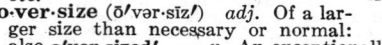

OVERSHOT WHEEL

o·ver·sight (ō'vər·sīt') *n.* **1.** An error due to inattention; an inadvertent mistake or omission. **2.** Watchful supervision; superintendence.

o·ver·signed (ō'vər·sīnd') *n.* The person whose name appears at the head of an article, document, report, etc.

o·ver·size (ō'vər·sīz') *adj.* Of a larger size than necessary or normal: also **o'ver·sized'.** — *n.* An exceptionally large size.

o·ver·skirt (ō'vər·skûrt') *n.* A skirt or drapery worn over the skirt of a dress.

o·ver·sleep (ō'vər·slēp') *v.* **·slept, ·sleep·ing** *v.i.* **1.** To sleep too long. — *v.t.* **2.** To sleep through.

o·ver·soul (ō'vər·sōl') *n. Often cap.* In Emerson's transcendentalist philosophy, the spiritual being or element of the universe that unites and influences all human souls.

o·ver·spend (ō'vər·spend') *v.* **·spent, ·spend·ing** *v.t.* **1.** To spend more than; exceed. **2.** *Archaic* To use up; exhaust. — *v.i.* **3.** To spend more than one can afford.

o·ver·spread (ō'vər·spred') *v.t.* **·spread, ·spread·ing** To spread or extend over; cover completely. [OE *ofersprǣdan*]

o·ver·state (ō'vər·stāt') *v.t.* **·stat·ed, ·stat·ing** To state in too strong terms; exaggerate. — **o'ver·state'ment** *n.*

o·ver·stay (ō'vər·stā') *v.t.* To stay beyond the limits or duration of.

o·ver·step (ō'vər·step') *v.t.* **·stepped, ·step·ping** To step over or go beyond; exceed, as a limit. [OE *ofersteppan*]

o·ver·strung (ō'vər·strung') *adj.* **1.** Strung too tightly or tensely; too sensitive. **2.** *Music* Having two sets of strings crossing obliquely at different levels, as piano bass strings.

o·ver·stuff (ō'vər·stuf') *v.t.* **1.** To stuff to excess. **2.** To cover completely with deep upholstery: said of furniture.

o·ver·sup·ply (*n.* ō'vər·sə·plī'; *v.* ō'vər·sə·plī') *n. pl.* **·plies** An excessive supply. — *v.t.* **·plied, ·ply·ing** To supply in excess.

o·vert (ō·vûrt', ō'vûrt) *adj.* Open to view; observable. **2.** *Law* Done with criminal intent. [< OF, pp. of *ovrir* to open < L *aperire*] — **o·vert·ly** (ō·vûrt'·lē, ō'vûrt'lē) *adv.* — **Syn. 1.** evident, plain, open. See MANIFEST. — **Ant.** covert, hidden, secret.

o·ver·take (ō'vər·tāk') *v.t.* **·took** (-tŏŏk'), **·tak·en, ·tak·ing 1.** To catch up with. **2.** To come upon suddenly.

o·ver·tax (ō'vər·taks') *v.t.* **1.** To tax too heavily. **2.** To put too great a strain on: to *overtax* one's strength.

o·ver-the-count·er (ō'vər·thə·koun'tər) *adj.* Not sold on the floor of a stock exchange: said of stocks, bonds, etc.

o·ver·throw (*v.* ō'vər·thrō'; *n.* ō'vər·thrō') *v.t.* **·threw** (-thrōō'), **·thrown, ·throw·ing 1.** To bring down or remove from power by force; defeat; ruin. **2.** To throw over or down; upset. — *n.* **1.** The act of overthrowing; destruction; demolition. **2.** In baseball, etc., a throwing of the ball over and beyond the player or base aimed at.

o·ver·thrust (ō'vər·thrust') *adj. Geol.* Characterized by or belonging to older and originally lower rock strata, which are pushed over younger and originally higher strata.

o·ver·time (*n., adj., & adv.* ō'vər·tīm'; *v.* ō'vər·tīm') *n.* **1.** Time used in working beyond the specified hours; also, the extra pay received for such work. **2.** In sports contests, an extra period of play to break a tie. — *adj.* Of or pertaining to overtime: *overtime* pay. — *adv.* Beyond the stipulated or regular time. — *v.t.* **·timed, ·tim·ing** *Photog.* To expose too long, as a plate or film.

o·ver·tone (ō'vər·tōn') *n.* **1.** *Music* An upper partial tone: so called because it is heard with and above the fundamental tone produced by a musical instrument. **2.** The color of the light reflected by a painted surface. **3.** The associations, connotations, implications, etc., of language, thoughts, etc. — **Syn.** See PROPOSAL. — *v.t.* **·tured, ·tur·ing 1.** To offer as an overture or proposal. **2.** To introduce with or as an overture. [< OF < *overt*. See OVERT.]

o·ver·trade (ō'vər·trād') *v.i.* **·trad·ed, ·trad·ing** To trade beyond one's capital or the requirements of the market.

o·ver·trick (ō'vər·trik') *n.* In card games, a trick more than game or than the number bid.

o·ver·trump (ō'vər·trump') *v.t. & v.i.* In card games, to trump (a player or a trump played) with a higher trump.

o·ver·ture (ō'vər·chər) *n.* **1.** *Music* a An instrumental prelude to an opera or other large work. b Any of various orchestral pieces, often having programmatic content. **2.** An act or proposal intended to initiate a relationship, negotiations, etc.

o·ver·turn (*v.* ō'vər·tûrn'; *n.* ō'vər·tûrn') *v.t.* **1.** To turn or throw over; capsize; upset. **2.** To destroy the power of; overthrow; defeat; ruin. — *v.i.* **3.** To turn over; capsize; upset. — *n.* **1.** The act of overturning, or the state of being overturned; an upset; overthrow. **2.** A subversion or destruction. **3.** Turnover (def. 6).

o·ver·view (ō'vər·vyōō') *n.* A view of the whole; survey.

o·ver·watch (ō'vər·woch', -wôch') *v.t.* **1.** To watch over. **2.** To weary with watching.

o·ver·wear (ō'vər·wâr') *v.t.* **·wore, ·worn, ·wear·ing 1.** To wear out. **2.** To grow too large for; outgrow.

o·ver·wea·ry (ō'vər·wir'ē) *adj.* Overtired; exhausted. — *v.t.* **·ried, ·ry·ing** To tire to excess.

o·ver·weath·er (ō'vər·weth'ər) *adj. Aeron.* Denoting flight conditions or activities that are above, and not affected by, storm, overcast, or other meteorological phenomena.

o·ver·ween·ing (ō'vər·wē'ning) *adj.* Characterized by presumptuous pride or conceit; arrogant; excessive; exaggerated. — *n.* Overconfidence; presumption. [OE *oferwēnan* to become insolent < *ofer-* over + *wēnan* to think, believe] — **o'ver·ween'ing·ly** *adv.*

o·ver·weigh (ō'vər·wā') *v.t.* **1.** To outweigh; overbalance. **2.** To overburden; oppress.

o·ver·weight (*n.* ō'vər·wāt'; *adj. & v.* ō'vər·wāt') *n.* **1.** Excess of weight, as beyond the legal or customary amount. **2.** Greater weight; preponderance; also, more than normal weight. — *adj.* Being more than the usual or permitted weight. — *v.t.* To weigh down; overburden.

o·ver·whelm (ō'vər·hwelm') *v.t.* **1.** To bury or submerge completely, as with a wave or flood. **2.** To overcome or defeat by or as by irresistible force or numbers; render helpless; crush. **3.** *Obs.* To overthrow. [ME *oferwhelmen* to turn upside down < OE *ofer* over. See WHELM.] — **Syn. 1.** inundate, bury. **2.** rout, vanquish.

o·ver·whelm·ing (ō'vər·hwel'ming) *adj.* Crushing by reason of force, weight, or numbers; irresistible. — **o'ver·whelm'ing·ly** *adv.*

o·ver·wind (ō'vər·wīnd') *v.t.* **·wound, ·wind·ing 1.** To wind too far or too tightly, as a watch. **2.** *Electr.* To wind (the coil of an electromagnet) to produce a maximum magnetism with a smaller current than is normally required.

o·ver·word (ō'vər·wûrd') *n.* A word or words repeated, as the burden of a song; refrain.

o·ver·work (*v.* ō'vər·wûrk'; *n.* ō'vər·wûrk') *v.* **·worked** (*Archaic* **·wrought**), **·work·ing** *v.t.* **1.** To cause to work too hard; exhaust with work or use. **2.** To work on or elaborate excessively: to *overwork* an argument. **3.** To work up or excite excessively. — *v.i.* **4.** To work too hard; do too much work. — *n.* **1.** Work done in overtime, or in excess of the stipulated amount. **2.** Excessive work. [OE *oferwiercan*]

o·ver·write (ō'vər·rīt') *v.t. & v.i.* **·wrote** (-rōt'), **·writ·ten** (-rit'ən), **·writ·ing 1.** To write in too elaborate or labored a style. **2.** To write too much about (a subject) or at too great length. **3.** To write over other writing.

o·ver·wrought (ō'vər·rôt') *adj.* **1.** Worked up or excited excessively; overstrained. **2.** Worked all over, as with embroidery. **3.** Worked too hard. **4.** Too elaborate; overdone. [Archaic pp. of OVERWORK]

ovi- combining form Egg; of or pertaining to eggs: *oviparous*. Also **ovo-**. [< L *ovum* egg]

o·vi·bos (ō'və·bos) *n.* The musk ox. [< NL < L *ovis* sheep + *bos* ox, cow]

Ov·id (ov'id), 43 B.C.–A.D. 18, Roman poet: full name **Publius Ov·id·i·us Na·so** (ō·vid'ē·əs nā'sō). — **O·vid·i·an** (ō·vid'ē·ən) *adj.*

o·vi·duct (ō'vi·dukt) *n. Anat.* A Fallopian tube.

O·vie·do (ō·vyā'thō) A city in NW Spain; pop. 127,058 (1960).

o·vif·er·ous (ō·vif'ər·əs) *adj.* Bearing or holding eggs. [< OVI- + -FEROUS]

o·vi·form (ō'vi·fôrm') *adj.* Shaped like an egg or ovum.

o·vine (ō'vīn, ō'vin) *adj.* Of or pertaining to sheep; sheeplike. — *n.* An ovine animal. [< L *ovinus* < *ovis* sheep]

o·vip·a·ra (ō·vip'ər·ə) *n.pl.* Animals that lay eggs. [< NL < L *oviparus* laying eggs < *ovum* egg + *-parus* < *parere* to bring forth]

o·vip·a·rous (ō·vip'ər·əs) *adj. Zool.* Producing eggs or ova that mature and are hatched outside the body, as birds, most fishes, and reptiles: distinguished from *ovoviviparous*, *viviparous*. — **o·vip'a·rous·ly** *adv.* — **o·vip'a·rous·ness** *n.*

o·vi·pos·it (ō'vi·poz'it) *v.i. Biol.* To lay eggs, especially by means of an ovipositor. [< OVI- + L *positus*, pp. of *ponere* to place] — **o·vi·po·si·tion** (ō'vi·pə·zish'ən) *n.*

o·vi·pos·i·tor (ō'vi·poz'ə·tər) *n. Entomol.* The tubular organ at the extremity of the abdomen in many insects by which the eggs are deposited.

o·vi·sac (ō'vi·sak) *n. Anat.* A Graafian follicle. [< OVI- + SAC]

o·void (ō'void) *adj.* Egg-shaped: also **o·voi'dal.** — *n.* An egg-shaped body.

o·vo·lo (ō'və·lō) *n. pl.* **·li** (-lē) *Archit.* A convex molding, usually a quarter of a circle or ellipse. For illustration see MOLDING. [< Ital., dim. of *ovo* egg < L *ovum*]

o·vo·vi·vip·a·rous (ō'vō·vī·vip'ər·əs) *adj. Zool.* Producing eggs that are incubated and hatched within the parent's body, but without formation of a placenta, as some reptiles and fishes: distinguished from *oviparous*, *viviparous*. [< OVO- + VIVIPAROUS] — **o'vo·vi·vip'a·rous·ly** *adv.* — **o'vo·vi·vip'a·rous·ness** *n.*

o·vu·late (ō'vyə·lāt) *v.i.* **·lat·ed, ·lat·ing** To produce ova; discharge ova from an ovary. [< NL *ovulum*. See OVULE.]

o·vu·la·tion (ō′vyə·lā′shən) *n. Biol.* **1.** The formation and discharge of ova. **2.** The period when this occurs.

o·vule (ō′vyōōl) *n.* **1.** *Bot.* **a** The rudimentary seed of a plant. **b** The body within the ovary that upon fertilization becomes the seed. For illustration see FLOWER. **2.** *Biol.* A small ovum. [< F < NL *ovulum*, dim. of L *ovum* egg] — **o′vu·lar, o·vu·lar·y** (ō′vyə·ler′ē) *adj.*

o·vum (ō′vəm) *n. pl.* **o·va** (ō′və) **1.** *Biol.* The female reproductive cell of animals, produced in the ovary; an egg. **2.** *Archit.* An egg-shaped ornament. [< L]

owe (ō) *v.* **owed** (*Obs.* **ought**), **ow·ing** *v.t.* **1.** To be indebted to the amount of; be obligated to pay or repay. **2.** To be obligated to render or offer: to *owe* an apology. **3.** To have or possess by virtue of some condition or cause: with *to*: He *owes* his success to his own efforts. **4.** To cherish (a certain feeling) toward another. **5.** *Obs.* To own; have. — *v.i.* **6.** To be in debt. [OE *āgan* to own, have < Gmc.]

Ow·en (ō′ən), **Robert,** 1771–1858, British manufacturer and social reformer. — **Wilfred,** 1893–1918, English poet.

Ow·en Falls (ō′in) A waterfall (65 ft. high) in the Victoria Nile, SE Uganda; site of a dam 2,725 ft. long, 85 ft. high, built 1949.

Ow·ens·bor·o (ō′ənz·bûr′ō) A city in NW Kentucky, on the Ohio River; pop. 50,329.

Owen Stanley Range A mountain range in SE New Guinea; highest peak, Mt. Victoria, 13,240 ft.

OWI or **O.W.I.** Office of War Information.

ow·ing (ō′ing) *adj.* Due; yet to be paid. — **owing to** Attributable to; on account of; in consequence of.

owl (oul) *n.* **1.** A predatory nocturnal bird (order *Strigiformes*), having large eyes and head, short, sharply hooked bill, long powerful claws, and a circular facial disk of radiating feathers. **2.** One of a breed of domestic pigeons having an owllike head and a prominent frill. **3.** A person with nocturnal habits. **4.** A person of solemn appearance, etc. [OE *ūle* < Gmc.; prob. imit. of bird's cry]

owl·et (ou′lit) *n.* **1.** A small owl; especially, the European owlet (*Athene noctua*), or a similar species (*A. brama*) of India. **2.** A young owl.

owl·ish (ou′lish) *adj.* **1.** Like an owl. **2.** *Brit. Dial.* Stupid. — **owl′ish·ly** *adv.* — **owl′ish·ness** *n.*

owl's-clo·ver (oulz′klō′vər) *n.* Any of a genus (*Orthocarpus*) of herbs of the figwort family of western North and South America; especially, a California species (*O. purpurascens*) with crimson or purple flowers.

own (ōn) *adj.* **1.** Belonging to oneself; peculiar; particular; individual: following the possessive (usually a possessive pronoun) as an intensive or to indicate the exclusion of others, sometimes with ellipsis of the noun: my *own* horse; his *own* idea; It is my *own.* **2.** Being of the nearest degree: *own* cousin. — **to come into one's own 1.** To obtain possession of one's property. **2.** To receive one's reward; come into one's rightful position. — **to hold one's own 1.** To maintain one's place or position. **2.** To keep up with one's work, or remain undefeated. — **on one's own** Entirely dependent on oneself for support or success. — *v.t.* **1.** To have or hold as one's own; have as a belonging; possess. **2.** To admit or acknowledge. — *v.i.* **3.** To confess: with *to.* — **to own up** *Informal* To confess forthrightly and fully. — **Syn.** See CONFESS, HAVE. [OE *āgen,* orig. pp. of *āgan* to possess, have; later, to owe. Cf. OWE.] — **own′a·ble** *adj.*

own·er (ō′nər) *n.* One who has the legal title or right to or has possession of a thing. — **own′er·less** *adj.*

own·er·ship (ō′nər·ship) *n.* **1.** The state of being an owner. **2.** Legal title; proprietorship.

owse (ouz) *n. pl.* **ow·sen** (ou′sən, -zən) *Scot.* Ox.

ox (oks) *n. pl.* **ox·en** (ok′sən) **1.** An adult castrated male of the genus *Bos,* used for draft and food. **2.** Any bovine quadruped, as a buffalo, bison, or yak. [OE *oxa*]

Ox. 1. Oxford. **2.** Oxfordshire.

oxa- *combining form Chem.* Denoting the presence of linked oxygen atoms, especially as replacing carbon in a ring compound. Also, before vowels, **ox-.** [< OXYGEN]

ox·a·late (ok′sə·lāt) *n. Chem.* A salt or ester of oxalic acid.

ox·al·ic (ok·sal′ik) *adj.* Pertaining to or derived from the oxalis or sorrel. [< F *oxalique* < L *oxalis.* See OXALIS.]

oxalic acid *Chem.* A white, crystalline, poisonous compound, $C_2H_2O_4 \cdot 2H_2O$, found in plant tissues and made artificially, used in bleaching, dyeing, etc.

ox·a·lis (ok·sal′əs, ok′sə·lis) *n.* Any of a large genus (*Oxalis*) of herbs, having purple, rose, or white flowers: also called *wood sorrel.* [< L < Gk. < *oxys* sour, acid]

ox·blood (oks′blud′) *n.* A deep red color.

ox·bow (oks′bō′) *n.* **1.** A U-shaped piece of wood in an ox yoke, that forms a collar for the ox. **2.** A bend in a river shaped like this. Also called *bow.*

Ox·en·stiern (ok′sən·stirn), **Count Axel Gustafsson,** 1583–1654, Swedish statesman. Also **Ox·en·stier·na** (-nä).

ox·eye (oks′ī′) *n.* **1.** Any of several plants of the composite family; especially, any plant of the genus *Buphthalmum,* having large yellow heads. **2.** The oxeye daisy. See under

---

DAISY. **3.** Any of various shore birds, as the least sandpiper. **4.** An oval dormer window.

ox-eyed (oks′īd) *adj.* Having large, calm eyes, as an ox.

oxeye daisy See under DAISY.

Oxf. 1. Oxford. **2.** Oxfordshire.

ox·ford (oks′fərd) *n. U.S.* **1.** A low shoe laced at the instep. Also **oxford shoe. 2.** A cotton cloth of basket weave, used for men's shirts. Also **Oxford.** [after *Oxford*]

Ox·ford (oks′fərd) County town of Oxfordshire, England, on the Thames; site of **Oxford University,** established in the 12th century; pop. 104,500.

oxford gray 1. A very dark gray. **2.** A woolen fabric of this color.

Oxford Group movement Buchmanism.

Oxford movement In the Church of England, a movement based on Tractarianism. It sought to link the Anglican Church more closely to the Roman Catholic Church and opposed liberalism in theology.

Ox·ford·shire (oks′fərd·shir) A county of south central England; 749 sq. mi.; pop. 535,300 (1976); county seat, **Oxford,** a county borough, pop. 115,100 (1976). Also **Ox′ford.**

ox·heart (oks′härt′) *n.* A variety of sweet cherry.

ox·i·dant (ok′sə·dənt) *n. Chem.* That which oxidizes or produces oxidation. Also **oxidizing agent.**

ox·i·dase (ok′si·dās) *n. Biochem.* One of many oxidizing ferments found widely distributed in plant and animal tissues. [< OXID(E) + -ASE] — **ox′i·da′sic** *adj.*

ox·i·da·tion (ok′sə·dā′shən) *n. Chem.* **1.** The process or state of undergoing combination with oxygen. **2.** The process by which atoms lose or are deprived of valence electrons, or begin sharing them with a more electronegative element.

oxidation number *Chem.* The number of electrons an atom has lost or is sharing with a more electronegative element, if electrons shared by atoms of the same element are divided equally between them.

ox·i·da·tion-re·duc·tion (ok′sə·dā′shən·ri·duk′shən) *n. Chem.* Oxidation or reduction considered in regard to their reciprocal relationship.

ox·ide (ok′sīd, -sid) *n. Chem.* Any binary compound of oxygen with another element or radical: iron *oxide.* Also **ox′id** (-sid). [< F < *ox*(*ygène*) oxygen + (*ac*)*ide* acid]

ox·i·dim·e·try (ok′sə·dim′ə·trē) *n. Chem.* A titration method that uses oxidizing agents in solution.

ox·i·dize (ok′sə·dīz) *v.* **·dized, ·diz·ing** *Chem. v.t.* **1.** To convert (an element) into its oxide; combine with oxygen. **2.** To increase the valence of an atom or group of atoms by the loss of electrons: to *oxidize* ferrous iron to ferric iron. — *v.i.* **3.** To become oxidized. — *n. Chem.* Also **ox·i·date** (ok′sə·dāt). Also *Brit.* **ox′i·dise.** — **ox′i·diz′a·ble** *adj.*

ox·ime (ok′sēm, -sim) *n. Chem.* One of a series of compounds containing the group C–NOH, formed by the action of hydroxylamine on aldehydes and ketones. Also **ox′im** (-sim). [< OX(YGEN) + IM(IDE)]

ox·lip (oks′lip′) *n.* A species of primrose (*Primula elatior*), closely resembling the cowslip: also called *five-fingers.* [OE *oxanslyppe* < *oxa, oxan* ox + *slyppe* slime]

Ox·nard (oks′närd) A city in SW California; pop. 71,225.

Oxon. 1. Oxford. **2.** Oxfordshire. **3.** Oxonian.

Ox·o·ni·an (ok·sō′nē·ən) *adj.* Of or pertaining to Oxford, England, or to its university. — *n.* A student or graduate of Oxford University. [< LL *Oxonia* Oxford]

ox·o·ni·um compound (ok·sō′nē·əm) *Chem.* Any of a class of organic compounds containing a basic oxygen atom combined with a mineral acid.

ox·peck·er (oks′pek′ər) *n.* An African bird of the starling family (genus *Buphagus*) that devours the parasites on oxen.

ox·tail (oks′tāl′) *n.* The tail of an ox, especially when skinned for use in soup.

ox·ter (ok′stər) *n. Brit. Dial. & Scot.* The armpit. [OE *ōxta, ōcusta.* Cf. OHG *ahsala,* L *axilla.*]

ox·tongue (oks′tung′) *n.* **1.** Any of various plants having rough, tongue-shaped leaves, as the European alkanet or bugloss. **2.** A short broadsword.

Ox·us River (ok′səs) The ancient name for the AMU DARYA.

oxy-¹ *combining form* **1.** Sharp; pointed; keen: *oxytone.* **2.** Acid: *oxygen.* [< Gk. *oxys* sharp, acid]

oxy-² *combining form Chem.* **1.** Oxygen; of or containing oxygen, or one of its compounds: *oxyhemoglobin.* **2.** An oxidation product of: *oxysulfide.* **3.** Containing the hydroxyl group: *oxyacid.* [< OXYGEN]

ox·y·ac·et·y·lene (ok′sē·ə·set′ə·lēn) *adj.* Designating or pertaining to a mixture of acetylene and oxygen, used to obtain high temperatures, as in welding.

ox·y·ac·id (ok′sē·as′id) *n. Chem.* An inorganic acid containing oxygen.

ox·y·cal·ci·um (ok′si·kal′sē·əm) *adj.* Pertaining to or produced by oxygen and calcium, as in the calcium light.

ox·y·gen (ok′sə·jin) *n.* A colorless, tasteless, odorless gaseous element (symbol O), occurring free in the atmosphere, and forming 21 percent of the atmosphere by volume. It is an abundant and active element, combining with hydrogen

---

to form water, supporting combustion, and essential in the respiration of plants and animals. See ELEMENT. [< F *oxygène* < *oxy-* oxy-[1] + *-gène* -gen; so called because formerly considered essential to all acids]

oxygen acid An oxyacid (which see).

ox·y·gen·ate (ok′sə·jən·āt′) *v.t.* **·at·ed, ·at·ing** To treat, combine, or impregnate with oxygen. — **ox′y·gen·a′tion** *n.*

ox·y·gen·ic (ok′sə·jen′ik) *adj.* Of, pertaining to, resembling, or containing oxygen. Also **ox·yg·e·nous** (ok·sij′ə·nəs).

ox·y·gen·ize (ok′sə·jən·īz′) *v.t.* **·ized, ·iz·ing** To oxidize.

oxygen mask A device worn over the nose and mouth to aid breathing, as at high altitudes, by conveying oxygen from a container to the user.

oxygen point *Physics* The boiling point of liquid oxygen at standard atmospheric pressure, −182.97° C.: one of the fixed points of the international temperature scale.

oxygen tent A tentlike canopy placed over a patient's head and shoulders, within which pure oxygen may be circulated for the purpose of facilitating respiration.

ox·y·he·mo·glo·bin (ok′si·hē′mə·glō·bin) *n. Biochem.* A combination of oxygen and hemoglobin, formed in the red blood corpuscles of the pulmonary capillaries and carried to body tissues by the arteries.

ox·y·hy·dro·gen (ok′si·hī′drə·jən) *n.* A mixture of oxygen and hydrogen, used in the **oxyhydrogen torch** for welding and cutting metals, and formerly in a type of limelight.

ox·y·mo·ron (ok′si·môr′on, -mō′ron) *n. pl.* **·mo·ra** (-môr′ə, -mō′rə) A figure of speech in which contradictory terms are brought together for emphasis or in an epigram, as in the phrase, "*O heavy lightness, serious vanity!*" [< Gk. *oxymoron*, neut. of *oxymoros* < *oxys* sharp + *moros* foolish]

ox·y·salt (ok′si·sôlt) *n. Chem.* A salt of an oxyacid.

ox·y·sul·fide (ok′si·sul′fīd) *n. Chem.* A compound of a sulfide with an oxide in which part of the sulfur has been replaced by oxygen. Also **ox′y·sul′phide.**

ox·y·toc·ic (ok′si·tos′ik, -tō′sik) *adj. Med.* **1.** Stimulating contraction of the uterine muscle. **2.** Bringing on or hastening parturition. — *n.* A medicine efficacious in hastening parturition. [< OXY-[1] + Gk. *tokos* birth]

ox·y·to·cin (ok′si·tō′sin) *n. Physiol.* A hormone of the posterior lobe of the pituitary gland, believed to facilitate uterine contractions during childbirth.

ox·y·tone (ok′si·tōn) *adj.* In Greek, having the acute accent on the last syllable. Compare BARYTONE[1]. — *n.* An oxytone word. [< Gk. *oxytonos* < *oxys* sharp + *tonos* pitch]

o·yer (ō′yər, oi′ər) *n. Law* **1.** A copy of a document, bond, etc., sued upon, given by the party holding the document to the party being sued. **2.** Oyer and terminer. [< AF *oyer* < OF *oir, oyr,* ult. < L *audire* to hear]

oyer and ter·min·er (tûr′mə·nər) **1.** *Brit.* A court composed of two or more judges of assize held at least twice a year in each county. **2.** *U.S.* A court of higher criminal jurisdiction. [< AF *oyer et terminer* to hear and determine]

o·yez (ō′yes, ō′yez) *interj.* Hear! hear ye! an introductory word to call attention to a proclamation, as by a court crier: usually repeated three times. Also **o′yes.** [< OF *oyez,* imperative of *oir.* See OYER.]

oys·ter (ois′tər) *n.* **1.** A bivalve mollusk (family *Ostreidae*), found in salt and brackish water and moored by the shell to stones, other shells, etc.; especially, the common edible species (genus *Ostrea*) of Europe and America. **2.** An analogous bivalve, as the **pearl oyster** (*Pinctada margaritifera*). **3.** A morsel of dark meat found in the hollows of the bone on the back of a fowl. **4.** Some delicacy; tidbit; prize. **5.** *Slang* A very uncommunicative person. — *v.i.* To gather or farm oysters. [< OF *oistre* < L *ostrea* < Gk. *ostreon.* Akin to Gk. *osteon* bone, *ostrakon* shell.]

oyster bed A place where oysters breed or are grown.

oyster catcher Any of several large, long-billed shore birds (genus *Haematopus*); especially, *H. palliatus* of America, having black-and-white plumage and feeding mainly upon small mollusks.

oyster crab A smooth-bodied crab (*Pinnotheres ostreum*) living symbiotically in the mantle of the oyster.

oyster cracker A small biscuit or hard, salted cracker served with oysters, soups, etc.

oys·ter·man (ois′tər·mən) *n. pl.* **·men** (-mən) **1.** One who dredges for, raises, or sells oysters. **2.** A vessel engaged in the oyster trade.

oyster plant Salsify.

oyster planting The placing of small oysters on submerged artificial beds for propagation.

oyster seed Seed oyster (which see).

oyster white Any of several very light gray tints: also called *off-white.*

oz. Ounce(s).

O·zark Mountains (ō′zärk) The hilly uplands in SW Missouri, NW Arkansas, and NE Oklahoma; highest point, 2,500 ft. Also **Ozark Plateau.**

Ozark State Nickname of MISSOURI.

o·zo·ce·rite (ō·zō′kə·rīt, -sə-, ō′zō·sir′ĭt) *n.* A waxy, translucent mixture of natural hydrocarbons, used in making candles, etc.: also called *mineral wax, earth wax.* Also **o·zo′ke·rite.** [< G *ozokerite* < Gk. *ozein* to smell + *keros* wax]

o·zone (ō′zōn) *n.* **1.** An unstable allotropic form of oxygen, O_3, with a pungent odor like that of chlorine, formed variously, as by the passage of electricity through the air. It is a powerful oxidizing agent, much more active than ordinary oxygen, and is used for bleaching oils, waxes, ivory, flour, and starch, and for sterilizing drinking water. **2.** *Informal* Pure or fresh air. [< F < Gk. *ozein* to smell] — **o·zon·ic** (ō·zon′ik, ō·zō′nik), **o·zo·nous** (ō′zə·nəs) *adj.*

o·zo·nide (ō′zō·nīd) *n. Chem.* Any of a group of unstable, sometimes violently explosive, organic compounds containing ozone.

o·zo·nize (ō′zō·nīz) *v.t.* **·nized, ·niz·ing 1.** To treat or charge with ozone. **2.** To convert (oxygen) into ozone. — **o′zo·ni·za′tion** *n.* — **o′zo·niz′er** *n.*

o·zon·o·sphere (ō·zon′ə·sfir) *n. Meteorol.* A narrow layer in the stratosphere at a height of about 20 miles, containing an unusually high concentration of ozone formed by the action of ultraviolet radiation on oxygen. Also called **ozone layer.** [< OZONE + (STRATO)SPHERE] — **o·zon′o·spher′ic** (-sfir′ik, -sfer′-) or **·i·cal** *adj.*

ozs. Ounces.

OYSTER
a Shell. *b* Hinge.
c Mantle. *d* Palpi.
e Anus. *f* Liver.
g Heart. *h* Adductor.
i Stomach. *j* Gills.

P

p, P (pē) *n. pl.* **p's** or **ps, P's** or **Ps, pees** (pēz) **1.** The sixteenth letter of the English alphabet. The shape of the Phoenician letter *pe* was adopted by the Greeks as *pi* and became Roman P. Also **pee.** **2.** The sound represented by the letter *p,* the voiceless bilabial stop. — *symbol* **1.** *Chem.* Phosphorus (symbol P). **2.** *Genetics* The parental generation: followed by a subscript numeral, as P_1, P_2, to indicate the first, second, etc., parental generation. — **to mind one's P's and Q's** To be careful of one's behavior.

p or **p. 1.** *Music* Piano. **2.** Pitcher (baseball).

p- *Chem.* Para-.

p. 1. After (L *post*). **2.** By (L *per*). **3.** By weight (L *pondere*). **4.** First (L *primus*). **5.** For (L *pro*). **6.** Page. **7.** Part. **8.** Participle. **9.** Past. **10.** Penny. **11.** Perch (measure). **12.** Peseta. **13.** Peso. **14.** Pint. **15.** Pole (measure). **16.** Population.

P 1. Pawn (chess). **2.** *Physics* Pressure. **3.** *Mil.* Prisoner.

P- *Mil.* Pursuit.

P. 1. Father (F *père;* L *pater*). **2.** Pastor. **3.** President. **4.** Priest. **5.** Prince. **6.** Prompter (theater).

pa (pä) *n. Informal* Papa.

p.a. 1. Participial adjective. **2.** Per annum (L, yearly).

Pa *Chem.* Protactinium.

Pa. Pennsylvania.

PA 1. Press agent. **2.** Public-address (system).

P.A. 1. Passenger Agent. **2.** Power of attorney: also **P/A. 3.** Private account: also **P/A. 4.** Purchasing Agent.

pa′·an·ga (pä·äng′gä) *n.* The monetary unit of Tonga, equivalent to 100 seniti.

Paa·si·ki·vi (pä′si·kē′vē), **Juhoo Kusti,** 1870–1956, Finnish statesman; president 1946–56.

paba or **PABA** *Biochem.* Para-aminobenzoic acid.

pab·u·lum (pab′yə·ləm) *n.* Any substance giving nourishment; aliment. [< L *pabulum* fodder; akin to *pascere* to feed] — **pab′u·lar** *adj.*

Pac. Pacific.

pa·ca (pä′kə, pak′ə) *n.* A large seminocturnal rodent (genus *Cuniculus* or *Agouti*) of Central and South America, brownish with white spots. [< Pg. or Sp. < Tupi]

Pa·ca (pä′kə), **William,** 1740–99, American patriot and jurist; signer of the Declaration of Independence.

pace[1] (pās) *n.* **1.** A step in walking; also, the distance covered in one such movement. **2.** A conventional measure of length approximating the average length of stride in walking: usually 3 feet, but sometimes 3.3 feet, making 5 paces to the rod. The **Roman pace**, measured from the point where the heel of one foot left the ground to the point where it descended in the next stride, was 5 Roman feet, equal to about 58.1 inches. Such a double step is now called a **geometrical pace**, reckoned at 5 feet. The U.S. Army **regulation pace** is 30 inches, quick time; 36 inches, double time. **3.** The manner or speed of movement in going on the legs; gait; carriage and action, especially of a horse. **4.** Rate of speed, as in movement, work, etc. **5.** The speed with which a baseball pitcher delivers the ball. **6.** A gait of a horse, etc., in which both feet on the same side are lifted and moved forward at once. — **to put (one) through his paces** To test the abilities, speed, etc., of. — v. **paced, pac·ing** v.t. **1.** To walk back and forth across: to *pace* the floor. **2.** To measure by paces: to *pace* off 20 feet. **3.** To set or make the pace for. **4.** To train to a certain gait or pace. — v.i. **5.** To walk with slow or regular steps. **6.** To move at a pace (def. 6). [< F *pas* < L *passus*, pp. of *pandere* to stretch. Doublet of PASS, n.]

pa·ce[2] (pā′sē) adv. & prep. With the permission (of): used to express courteous disagreement. [< L, ablative of *pax*, *pacis* peace, pardon]

paced (pāst) adj. **1.** Having a particular pace: used in compounds: slow-*paced*. **2.** Measured in paces or by pacing. **3.** Done alone or with the help of a pacemaker.

pace·mak·er (pās′mā′kər) n. **1.** One who makes or sets the pace for another in a race. **2.** One who or that which sets an example for others: She is a *pacemaker* in fashion. **3.** *Biochem.* A substance that determines the rate of a series of reactions. **4.** *Anat.* A mass of tissue in the right atrium of the heart that normally regulates the heartbeat. **5.** *Med.* A small, electrical device that stimulates the heart muscle so that it contracts at a certain or regular rate. — **pace′mak′ing** n. & adj.

pac·er (pā′sər) n. **1.** A pacing horse, usually five-gaited. **2.** One who paces or measures by paces. **3.** A pacemaker.

pa·cha (pə·shä′, pash′ə), **pa·cha·lic** (pə·shä′lik) See PASHA, PASHALIK.

pa·chi·si (pə·chē′zē, pä-) n. **1.** In India, a board game resembling backgammon. **2.** Parcheesi. [< Hind. *pacīsī* < *pacīs* twenty-five < Skt. *pañca* five + *viṁśati* twenty]

pach·ou·li (pach′ōō·lē, pə·chōō′lē) See PATCHOULI.

Pa·chu·ca (pä·chōō′kä) The capital of Hidalgo State, Mexico; pop. 84,543 (1970). Officially **Pa·chu′ca de So′to**.

pachy- *combining form* Thick; massive: *pachyderm*. [< Gk. *pachys* thick]

pach·y·derm (pak′ə·dûrm) n. **1.** Any of certain thick-skinned, nonruminant ungulates: especially, an elephant, hippopotamus, or rhinoceros. **2.** A stolid, thick-skinned, insensitive person. [< F *pachyderme* < Gk. *pachydermos* < *pachys* thick + *derma* skin] — **pach′y·der′ma·tous** (-dûr′mə·təs), **pach′y·der′mous** adj.

pach·y·san·dra (pak′ə·san′drə) n. A hardy, evergreen, spurgelike plant (*Pachysandra terminalis*) much cultivated for ground cover: also called *shade grass*. [< NL, with thick stamens < Gk. *pachys* thick + *anēr*, *andros* male]

pa·cif·ic (pə·sif′ik) adj. **1.** Tending or leading to peace or conciliation. **2.** Peaceful; calm. Also **pa·cif′i·cal.** [< MF *pacifique* < L *pacificus* peacemaking < *pax*, *pacis* peace + *facere* to make] — **pa·cif′i·cal·ly** adv.
— **Syn.** *Pacific, peaceable,* and *peaceful* relate to peace but differ in application. *Pacific* characterizes a tendency: *pacific* measures, a *pacific* purpose. *Peaceable* refers to disposition or temperament: *peaceable* neighbors, a *peaceable* soul. A state or condition is described by *peaceful*: *peaceful* relations between nations, a *peaceful* scene. — **Ant.** belligerent, quarrelsome.

Pa·cif·ic (pə·sif′ik) adj. Pertaining to the Pacific Ocean.

pa·cif·i·cate (pə·sif′ə·kāt) v.t. **·cat·ed, ·cat·ing** To pacify; calm. [< L *pacificatus*, pp. of *pacificare* to make peace, pacify < *pax*, *pacis* peace + *facere* to make] — **pac·i·fi·ca·tion** (pas′ə·fə·kā′shən) n. — **pa·cif′i·ca·tor** n. — **pa·cif′i·ca·to′ry** (-kə·tôr′ē, -tō′rē) adj.

Pacific Islands, Trust Territory of the A UN Trust Territory administered by the United States, comprising the Marshall Islands, the Marianas (excluding Guam), and the Caroline Islands; about 700 sq. mi.; pop. 101,600 (1971); administrative center, Saipan.

Pacific Ocean An ocean separating the American continents from Asia and Australia, and extending between the Arctic and Antarctic oceans; about 70 million sq. mi.; divided by the equator into the **North Pacific Ocean** and the **South Pacific Ocean**.

Pacific Standard Time See under STANDARD TIME. Abbr. *PST, P.S.T., p.s.t.*

pac·i·fi·er (pas′ə·fī′ər) n. **1.** One who or that which pacifies. **2.** A rubber nipple or ring, for babies to suck or bite on.

pac·i·fist (pas′ə·fist) n. One who opposes military ideals, war, or military preparedness, and proposes that all inter-national disputes be settled by arbitration. — **pac′i·fism** n. — **pac′i·fis′tic** adj.

pac·i·fy (pas′ə·fī) v.t. **·fied, ·fy·ing** **1.** To bring peace to; end war or strife in (an area). **2.** To allay the anger or agitation of; appease; calm; quiet; soothe. [< F *pacifier* < L *pacificare* < *pax*, *pacis* peace + *facere* to make.]

pack[1] (pak) n. **1.** A bundle or large package, especially one to be carried on the back of a man or animal. **2.** A collection of anything; heap. **3.** A full set of like or associated things usually handled collectively, as cards. **4.** A group of dogs or wolves that hunt together. **5.** Any gang or band, especially a criminal gang. **6.** An ice pack (which see). **7.** A cosmetic paste for the face. **8.** A wrapping of sheets or blankets about a patient, used in certain water-cure treatments; also, the sheets or blankets used. **9.** A parachute, fully assembled and folded for use. **10.** The quantity of something, as vegetables or other foods, put in containers for preservation at one time or in one season. Abbr. *pk.* — **Syn.** See FLOCK. — v.t. **1.** To make a pack or bundle of. **2.** To place compactly in a trunk, box, etc., for storing or carrying. **3.** To fill compactly, as for storing or carrying: to *pack* a suitcase. **4.** To put up for preservation or sale: to *pack* fruit. **5.** To compress tightly; crowd together. **6.** To fill completely or to overflowing; cram. **7.** To cover, fill, or surround so as to prevent leakage, damage, etc.: to *pack* a piston rod. **8.** To load with a pack; burden. **9.** To carry or transport on the back or on pack animals. **10.** To carry or wear habitually: to *pack* a gun. **11.** To send or dispatch summarily: with *off* or *away*. **12.** To treat with a pack (def. 7). **13.** *Slang* To be able to inflict: He *packs* a wallop. — v.i. **14.** To place one's clothes and belongings in trunks, boxes, etc., for storing or carrying. **15.** To be capable of being stowed or packed. **16.** To crowd together; form a pack or packs. **17.** To settle in a hard, firm mass. **18.** To leave in haste: often with *off* or *away*. — **to send packing** To send away or dismiss summarily. [ME *pakke*, appar. < LG *pak*]

pack[2] (pak) v.t. To arrange, select, or manipulate to one's own advantage: to *pack* a jury. [? < PACK[1]]

pack[3] (pak) adj. *Scot.* Intimate. — **pack′ly** adv. — **pack′ness** n.

pack·age (pak′ij) n. **1.** Something packed, wrapped up, or bound together, as for transportation. **2.** A box, case, crate, or other receptacle used for packing. **3.** The act or process of packing. **4.** A combination of items considered as a unit: a salary increase and fringe benefits all in one *package*. Abbr. *pkg.* — v.t. **·aged, ·ag·ing** To arrange or tie into a package; wrap [< PACK[1] + -AGE]

package store A store selling sealed bottles and cans of alcoholic beverages to be consumed off the premises.

pack animal An animal, as a horse or mule, used to carry packs or burdens.

pack·er (pak′ər) n. **1.** One who packs; especially one who makes a business of packing goods for transportation or preservation. **2.** One who cures and packs wholesale provisions. **3.** One who transports goods on pack animals.

pack·et (pak′it) n. **1.** A small package; parcel. **2.** A steamship for conveying mails, passengers, and freight at stated times, especially one plying up and down a coast or on a canal: also **packet boat.** Abbr. *pkt.* — v.t. To make into a packet or parcel. [< AF *pacquet*, dim. of ME *pakke*. See PACK[1].]

pack·ing (pak′ing) n. **1.** The act or operation of one who or that which packs. **2.** The canning or putting up of meat, fish, fruit, etc. **3.** Any material used in packing.

packing box 1. A stout box in which goods are packed. Also **packing case. 2.** *Mech.* A stuffing box (which see).

packing fraction *Physics* A measure of the binding force within the atomic nucleus, equivalent to the mass defect of an atom divided by the mass number, the quotient usually being multiplied by 10,000.

packing plant *U.S.* A factory where meats and meat products are processed and packed. Also *U.S.* **packing house.**

pack·man (pak′mən) n. pl. **·men** (-mən) A peddler.

pack rat A common North American rat (genus *Neotoma*) that carries off and hides small articles in its nest: also called *mountain rat, trade rat, wood rat.*

pack·sack (pak′sak′) n. A canvas or leather traveling sack for blankets, etc., usually carried across the shoulders.

pack·sad·dle (pak′sad′l) n. A saddle for a pack animal, to which the packs are fastened so as to balance evenly.

pack·thread (pak′thred′) n. Strong thread or twine used for wrapping packages.

pack·wax (pak′waks′) n. The paxwax (which see).

pact (pakt) n. An agreement; compact. — **Syn.** See CONTRACT. [< OF < L *pactum* agreement < *pactus*, pp. of *paciscere* to agree]

Pac·to·lus (pak·tō′ləs) In ancient Lydia, a river whose gold was a traditional source of Croesus' gold.

pad[1] (pad) n. **1.** A cushion; also, any stuffed, cushionlike thing serving to protect from jarring, friction, etc. **2.** A number of sheets of paper packed and gummed together at one edge; a tablet. **3.** A large floating leaf of an aquatic plant: a lily *pad*. **4.** A soft cushionlike enlargement of skin on the undersurface of the toes of many animals. **5.** The foot of a fox, otter, etc. **6.** The footprint of an animal. **7.** A pulvillus. **8.** A launching pad (which see). **9.** A stamp pad (which see). **10.** A soft saddle. **11.** *Slang* A room or apartment; lodgings. — *v.t.* **pad·ded, pad·ding 1.** To stuff, line, or protect with pads or padding. **2.** To lengthen (speech or writing) by inserting unnecessary matter. **3.** To add to (an expense account, subscription list, voting register, etc.) for fraudulent purposes. [Origin unknown]

pad² (pad) *v.i.* **pad·ded, pad·ding 1.** To travel by walking; tramp. **2.** To move with soft, almost noiseless footsteps. — *n.* A dull, padded sound, as of a footstep. [Akin to PAD³ (path); ? partly imit. Cf. LG *padden* to tread.]

pad³ (pad) *n.* **1.** An easy-paced road horse. **2.** A highwayman. **3.** *Brit. Dial.* A path; road. [< LG *pad* path]

Pa·dang (pä·däng′) A port city on the western coast of Sumatra, Indonesia; pop. 143,615 (1961).

Pa·dauk wood (pə·dôk′) Amboina wood (which see).

pad·ding (pad′ing) *n.* **1.** The act of one who or that which pads. **2.** Material with which to pad. **3.** Extraneous matter used in writing, etc., merely to fill space.

Pad·ding·ton (pad′ing·tən) A metropolitan borough of NW London; pop. 115,322 (1961).

pad·dle (pad′l) *n.* **1.** A broad-bladed implement resembling a short oar, used without a rowlock in propelling a canoe or small boat. **2.** The distance covered during one trip in a canoe over a given time. **3.** A paddle board (which see). **4.** A straight iron tool for stirring ore in a furnace. **5.** A bat or pallet, as used in tempering clay. **6.** A scoop for stirring and mixing, as used in glassmaking. **7.** A flat board for inflicting bodily punishment. **8.** A flat instrument with which clothes are beaten while being washed in a stream. **9.** A limb or appendage of a turtle, penguin, etc.; a flipper. **10.** The snout of a paddle fish. **11.** A small, rounded, flat piece of wood with a handle, used in table tennis. **12.** The act of paddling. — *v.* **·dled, ·dling** *v.i.* **1.** To move a canoe, etc., on or through water by means of a paddle. **2.** To row gently or lightly. **3.** To swim with short, downward strokes, as ducks do. **4.** To play in water with the hands or feet; dabble; wade. — *v.t.* **5.** To propel by means of a paddle or paddles. **6.** To convey by paddling. **7.** To beat with a paddle; spank. **8.** To stir. — **to paddle one's own canoe** To be independent; get along without help. [ME *padell* a small spade, ? var. of *patel* shallow pan < L *patella*] — **pad′dler** *n.*

paddle board One of the broad, paddlelike boards set on the circumference of a paddle wheel or water wheel.

paddle boat A boat propelled by paddle wheels.

paddle box The housing or box enclosing the upper part of a paddle wheel.

pad·dle·fish (pad′l·fish′) *n. pl.* **·fish** or **·fish·es** A large fish (*Polyodon spathula*) allied to the sturgeon, having a scaleless body and spatuliform snout, found in the Mississippi Valley streams: also called *spoonbill*.

paddle wheel A wheel having projecting floats or boards for propelling a vessel.

pad·dling (pad′ling) *n.* **1.** The act of propelling with a paddle. **2.** A beating or spanking.

pad·dock¹ (pad′ək) *n.* **1.** A pasture, lot, or enclosure for exercising horses, adjoining a stable. **2.** A grassed enclosure at a racecourse where horses are walked and saddled. **3.** In Australia, any enclosed piece of land, whether tilled or untilled. — *v.t.* To confine in a paddock, as horses. [Alter. of dial. E *parrock*, OE *pearruc* enclosure. Akin to PARK.]

pad·dock² (pad′ək) *n. Scot.* A toad or frog.

pad·dy¹ (pad′ē) *n. pl.* **·dies** The ruddy duck: also *paddywhack*. [after *Paddy*, a proper name]

pad·dy² (pad′ē) *n. pl.* **·dies** Rice in the husk, whether gathered or growing. [< Malay *pādī*]

Pad·dy (pad′ē) *n. Slang* An Irishman. [Nickname for *Patrick*, a proper name]

paddy wagon *U.S. Slang* A patrol wagon (which see). [Prob. < PADDY]

pad·dy·whack (pad′ē·hwak′) *n.* **1.** *Brit. Dial.* A fit of temper. **2.** *Informal* A beating or thrashing. **3.** *U.S.* The ruddy duck. [< PADDY + WHACK]

Pa·de·rew·ski (pä′də·ref′skē), **Ignace Jan,** 1860–1941, Polish pianist, composer, and statesman; premier 1919.

pa·di·shah (pä′di·shä) *n.* **1.** Lord protector; chief ruler: a title of the shah of Iran. **2.** Formerly, the title of the sultan of Turkey. **3.** Formerly, the title of the British sovereign as emperor of India. Also **pad·shah** (päd′shä). [< Persian *Pādshāh < pati* master + *shāh* king]

pad·le (päd′l) *n. Scot.* A garden hoe.

pad·lock (pad′lok′) *n.* A detachable lock, having a pivoted shackle designed to be passed through a staple or ring and then locked. — *v.t.* To fasten with or as with a padlock. [ME *padlocke*; ult. origin uncertain]

pad·nag (pad′nag′) *n. Scot.* **1.** A horse ridden with a pad instead of a saddle. **2.** An ambling nag.

Pa·douk wood (pə·dook′) Amboina wood (which see).

pa·dre (pä′drā) *n.* **1.** Father: a title used in Italy, Spain, and Spanish America in addressing or speaking of priests, and in India for all clergymen. **2.** An army or navy chaplain. [< Ital., Sp., and Pg. < L *pater, patris* father]

pa·dro·ne (pä·drō′nā) *n. pl.* **·nes** (-näs) or **·ni** (-nē) **1.** Master: an appellation of an Italian innkeeper or employer of labor. **2.** The master of a small vessel. [< Ital. < L *patronus.* See PATRON.] — **pa·dro′nism** *n.*

Pad·u·a (paj′ōō·ə, pad′yōō·ə) A commune in NE Italy; pop. 198,403 (1961). *Italian* **Pa·do·va** (pä′dō·vä).

pad·u·a·soy (paj′ōō·ə·soi′) A strong, rich silk fabric, originally made at Padua; also, an article made of it. [Prob. alter. of F *pou-de-soie* silk fabric; infl. by *Padua*]

Pa·du·cah (pə·dōō′kə) A city in western Kentucky, on the Ohio River; pop. 31,627.

Pa·dus (pā′dəs) The ancient name for the Po.

pae·an (pē′ən) *n.* **1.** A song of joy or exultation. **2.** Formerly, a song of praise honoring Apollo. Also spelled *pean*. [< L < Gk. *paian* hymn, one properly addressed to Apollo]

paed-, paedo- See PEDO-.

paed·e·rast (paj′ər·ast), etc. See PEDERAST, etc.

pae·do·gen·e·sis (pē′dō·jen′ə·sis) *n. Biol.* The reproduction of young in the larval stage, as in certain dipterous insects. [< NL < Gk. *pais, paidos* child + GENESIS]

pae·on (pē′on) *n.* In Greek and Latin prosody, a foot of four syllables, one long and three short in any order. [< L < Gk. *paiōn*, orig. *paian.* See PAEAN.]

Paes·tum (pes′təm) An ancient Greek city in southern Italy.

pa·gan (pā′gən) *n.* **1.** One who is neither a Christian, a Jew, nor a Moslem; a heathen. **2.** In early Christian use, an idol worshiper. **3.** An irreligious person. — **Syn.** HEATHEN. — *adj.* Of, pertaining to, or like pagans; heathenish; idolatrous. [< LL *paganus* heathen < L, orig., villager < *pagus* the country] — **pa′gan·dom** *n.* — **pa′gan·ish** *adj.* — **pa′gan·ism** *n.*

Pa·ga·ni·ni (pä′gä·nē′nē), **Nicolò,** 1782–1840, Italian violinist and composer.

pa·gan·ize (pā′gən·īz) *v.t. & v.i.* **·ized, ·iz·ing** To make or become pagan.

page¹ (pāj) *n.* **1.** A male servant or attendant; especially, in chivalry, a lad or young man in training for knighthood, or a youth attending a royal or princely personage. **2.** In Congress or other legislatures, a boy whose duty it is to attend upon legislators while in session. **3.** A boy employed in a hotel, club, theater, library, or private house to perform light duties. — *v.t.* **paged, pag·ing 1.** To seek or summon (a person) by calling his name, as a hotel page does. **2.** To wait on as a page. [< OF < Ital. *paggio*, ? < Gk. *paidion*, dim. of *pais, paidos* boy, child]

page² (pāj) *n.* **1.** One side of a leaf of a book, letter, etc. Abbr. *p.* (pl. *pp.*), *pg.* **2.** The printing or the type used on one side. **3.** Any event or events worthy of being noted or recorded: a sad *page* in history. **4.** *Usually pl.* Any source or record of knowledge. — *v.* **paged, pag·ing** *v.t.* **1.** To mark the pages of with numbers. — *v.i.* **2.** To turn pages: usually with *through*. [< F < L *pagina* written page < *pag-*, stem of *pangere* to fasten]

Page (pāj), **Thomas Nelson,** 1853–1922, U.S. novelist and diplomat. — **Walter Hines,** 1855–1918, U.S. journalist, publisher, and diplomat: pseudonym **Nicholas Worth** (wûrth).

pag·eant (paj′ənt) *n.* **1.** A community outdoor celebration presenting scenes from local history and tradition. **2.** An exhibition or spectacular parade devised for a public celebration. **3.** Something showy, as a float, designed for a parade. **4.** A theatrical spectacle. **5.** Unsubstantial display or cheap finery. [< Med.L *pagina* scaffold of a stage]

pag·eant·ry (paj′ən·trē) *n. pl.* **·ries 1.** Pageants collectively. **2.** Ceremonial splendor or display. **3.** Empty or showy display.

Pag·et (paj′it), **Sir James,** 1814–99, English surgeon and pathologist.

pag·i·nal (paj′ə·nəl) *adj.* **1.** Consisting of, or pertaining to, the pages of a book. **2.** Page for page. [< LL *paginalis* < L *pagina* leaf of a book, page]

pag·i·nate (paj′ə·nāt) *v.t.* **·nat·ed, ·nat·ing** To number the pages of (a book) consecutively. [< L *pagina* page + -ATE¹]

pag·i·na·tion (paj′ə·nā′shən) *n.* **1.** The numbering of the pages, as of a book. **2.** The system of figures and marks used in paging.

pa·go·da (pə·gō′də) *n.* In the Far East, a sacred tower or temple, usually pyramidal and profusely adorned. Also **pag·od** (pag′əd, pə·god′). [< Pg. *pagode < Tamil *pagavadi* < Skt. *bhagavati* belonging to a deity < *bhagavat* diety]

Pa·go Pa·go (päng′ō päng′ō) A port town on SE Tutuila island, American Samoa; pop. 2,481 (est. 1970): also *Pango Pango.* Also **Pa′go·pa′go.**

pa·gu·ri·an (pə·gyoor′ē·ən) *n.* Any of a family (*Paguridae*) of crustaceans that includes the hermit crabs. [< L *pagurus* < Gk. *pagouros* a kind of crab] — **pa·gu·rid** (pə·gyoor′id, pag′yə·rid) *n. & adj.*

pah (pä, pa) *interj.* Bah! faugh! an exclamation of contemptuous disgust or disbelief.

Pa·hang (pä·häng′) A State of Malaysia, on the SE coast

of the Malay Peninsula; 13,873 sq. mi.; pop. 405,156 (est. 1966).

pah·la·vi (pä′lə·vē) *n.* *pl.* **·vis** A former gold coin of Iran, equivalent to 100 rials. [< Persian, after Rhiza Khan *Pahlavi*, shah of Persia]

Pah·la·vi (pä′lə·vē) *n.* A literary form of Middle Persian, in use from the third to the seventh century and preserved in the Zoroastrian sacred writings, where it was transliterated into Semitic characters: also spelled *Pehlevi*. [< Persian *Pahlavī* Parthian < OPersian *Parthava* Parthia]

paid (pād) Past tense and past participle of PAY.

pai·dol·o·gy (pī·dol′ə·jē) *n.* Pedology.

paik (pāk) *n.* *Scot.* A blow. — *v.t.* To beat or strike.

pail (pāl) *n.* **1.** A cylindrical vessel for carrying liquids, etc., properly having a handle; bucket. **2.** The amount carried in this vessel. [OE *paegel* wine measure; infl. by OF *paielle* pan < L *patella* small pan] — **pail′ful** *n.*

pail·lasse (pal·yas′, pal′yas) *n.* A mattress of straw, excelsior, or the like: also spelled *palliasse*. [< MF < *paille* straw < L *palea* chaff]

pail·lette (pal·yet′) *n.* **1.** A bit of metal or colored foil, used in enamel painting. **2.** A spangle. [< F, dim. of *paille* straw] — **pail·let′ted** *adj.*

pain (pān) *n.* **1.** The unpleasant sensation or feeling resulting from or accompanying some injury, derangement, overstrain, or obstruction of the physical powers. **2.** Any distressing or afflicting emotion. **3.** *pl.* Care, trouble, effort, or exertion expended on anything: with much *pains*. **4.** *pl.* The pangs of childbirth. — **on** (or **upon** or **under**) **pain of** With the penalty of (some specified punishment). — **to take pains** To be careful; to make an effort. — *v.t.* **1.** To cause pain to; hurt or grieve; disquiet. — *v.i.* **2.** To cause pain. [< OF *peine* pain, penalty < L *poena* < Gk. *poinē* fine, penalty]
— **Syn. 1.** *Pain, ache, throe, pang, twinge,* and *stitch* denote sensations of discomfort or suffering. *Pain* is the most general term; it may refer to a bodily hurt, to mental anxiety, or to both a physical cause of discomfort, and the consequent mental anguish. The other words here given refer primarily to bodily discomfort. An *ache* is a long-lasting *pain,* usually dull rather than sharp, and often associated with a particular organ, member, etc.: a stomach *ache. Throes* are violent, usually convulsive, *pains,* such as those associated with a mortal wound, or the effects of many poisons. A *pang* is a sudden but transient *pain;* so is a *twinge,* but the latter is far milder. A sudden sharp *pain,* often followed by a cramp, is called a *stitch.*

painch (pänch) *n. Scot.* Paunch.

Paine (pān), **Robert Treat,** 1731–1814, American patriot and jurist; signer of the Declaration of Independence. — **Thomas,** 1737–1809, American patriot, author, and political philosopher born in England.

pained (pānd) *adj.* **1.** Hurt physically or mentally; distressed. **2.** Showing pain: a *pained* expression.

pain·ful (pān′fəl) *adj.* **1.** Giving or attended with pain; distressing. **2.** Requiring labor, effort, or care; arduous. **3.** Affected with pain: said of the body or of some part of it. **4.** *Archaic* Painstaking; laborious. — **pain′ful·ly** *adv.* — **pain′ful·ness** *n.*

pain·kill·er (pān′kil′ər) *n.* *U.S. Informal* A medicine that relieves pain.

pain·less (pān′lis) *adj.* Free from pain; causing no pain. — **pain′less·ly** *adv.* — **pain′less·ness** *n.*

pains·tak·ing (pānz′tā′king, pān′stā′-) *adj.* Taking pains; careful; assiduous. — *n.* Diligent and careful effort. — **pains′tak′ing·ly** *adv.*

paint (pānt) *n.* **1.** A color or pigment, either dry or mixed with oil, water, etc. **2.** A cosmetic, as rouge. **3.** Grease paint (which see). **4.** A film, layer, or coat of pigment applied to the surface of an object; also, the dry coating of such a pigment: cracked *paint.* — *v.t.* **1.** In art: **a** To make a representation of in paints or colors. **b** To make, as a picture, by applying paints or colors. **2.** To describe or depict vividly, as in words. **3.** To cover, coat, or decorate with or as with paint. **4.** To apply cosmetics to. **5.** To apply (medicine, etc.) with or as with a swab. — *v.i.* **6.** To cover or coat something with paint. **7.** To practice the art of painting; paint pictures. **8.** To apply cosmetics to the face, etc. [< OF *peint,* pp. of *peindre* < L *pingere* to paint]

paint·brush (pānt′brush′) *n.* **1.** A brush for applying paint. **2.** The painted cup, a flower.

paint·ed (pān′tid) *adj.* **1.** Covered or coated with paint. **2.** Depicted in colors. **3.** Having no reality, truth, or value; artificial: our *painted* hopes.

painted bunting A brilliantly colored finch (*Passerina ciris*) widely distributed in the southern United States. Also **painted finch.**

painted cup Any of several showy North American flowers (genus *Castilleja*) of the figwort family, usually having vivid scarlet bracts and calyxes: also called *Indian paintbrush.*

Painted Desert A large arid area in northern Arizona, extending SE along the Little Colorado River, and containing brightly colored rock formations.

painted lady The thistle butterfly.

paint·er[1] (pān′tər) *n.* **1.** One who covers surfaces with a preservative or decorative coat of paint. **2.** An artist who paints in oils, etc.

paint·er[2] (pān′tər) *n. Naut.* A rope with which to fasten a boat by its bow. [Prob. < OF *pentoir* a rope for hanging things < L *pendere* to suspend]

paint·er[3] (pān′tər) *n. U.S. Dial.* The puma, or cougar. [Var. of PANTHER]

painters' colic *Pathol.* A form of lead poisoning characterized by sharp abdominal pains and slow pulse.

paint horse In the western United States, a pied or spotted horse; a pinto.

paint·ing (pān′ting) *n.* **1.** The act of laying on paints with a brush. **2.** The art of creating meaningful effects on a surface by the use of pigments. **3.** A picture made with paints; also, such pictures collectively: eighteenth-century *painting.*

paint·y (pān′tē) *adj.* **paint·i·er, paint·i·est** Of, belonging to, or covered with paint.

pair (pâr) *v.t.* **1.** To bring together or arrange in a pair or pairs; match; couple; mate. — *v.i.* **2.** To come together as a couple or pair. **3.** To marry or mate. — **to pair off 1.** To separate into couples. **2.** To arrange by pairs. — *n.* **1.** Two persons or things of a kind, that are joined, related, correspondent, or associated; a couple; brace. **2.** A single thing having two like or correspondent parts dependent on each other: a *pair* of scissors. **3.** A married couple; also, two animals mated. **4.** In legislative bodies, two opposed members who agree to abstain from voting, and so offset each other. **5.** A set of like or similar things making a whole: a *pair* of pajamas. **6.** In some games of cards, two cards of the same denomination: a *pair* of queens. **7.** *Mech.* A combination of two elements forming a unit, as a piston and cylinder, a screw and nut, etc. Abbr. (for n.) *pr.* ◆ Current usage calls for *pair* in the plural after a numeral of two or more, as, four *pairs* of shoes, though informally the singular is often used, as, four *pair* of shoes. [< F *paire* < L *paria,* neut. plural of *par* equal]

pair-oar (pâr′ôr′, -ōr′) *n.* A boat in which two rowers sitting one behind the other pull one oar each. — **pair′-oared′** *adj.*

pair production *Physics* The instantaneous conversion of a photon into an electron and a positron by its passage through a strong electric field.

pai·sa (pī′sä) *n.* *pl.* **pai·se** (pī·sā′) A naya paisa (which see).

Pais·ley (pāz′lē) A burgh in NE Renfrew, Scotland; pop. 95,753 (1961).

Pais·ley (pāz′lē) *adj.* Made of or resembling a patterned woolen fabric originally made in Paisley, Scotland. — *n.* **1.** Paisley fabric. **2.** A Paisley shawl.

Pai·ute (pī·yōōt′) *n.* One of a tribe of North American Indians of Shoshonean stock, living in SW Utah. Also spelled *Piute.*

pa·ja·mas (pə·jä′məz, -jam′əz) *n.* *pl.* of **pa·ja·ma** (-mə) **1.** A garment consisting of loose trousers of silk, cotton, etc., and an accompanying jacket or blouse, used for sleeping and informal daytime wear. **2.** In the Orient, similar trousers worn by both men and women. Also, *Brit., pyjamas.* [< Hind. *pājāmā* a Mohammedan's loose trousers < Persian *pāi* leg + *jāmāh* garment]

Pa·ki·stan (pä′ki·stän′, pak′i·stan) A Republic of the Commonwealth of Nations, on the northwestern part of the Indian subcontinent; formerly consisting principally of two provinces: East Pakistan and West Pakistan. In January, 1972, East Pakistan became the independent Republic of Bangladesh. Area West Pakistan, 310,403 sq. mi.; pop. about 58,000,000 (1972); capital, Islamabad. — **Pa′ki·sta′ni** (-nē) *adj. & n.* See **Bangladesh.**

pal (pal) *Informal n.* A friend or chum. — **Syn.** See FRIEND. — *v.i.* **palled, pal·ling** To associate as pals. [< Romany *pal* brother, mate, ult. < Skt. *bharatr.* Akin to BROTHER.]

Pal. Palestine.

pa·la·bra (pä·lä′brä) *n. Spanish* A word; speech.

pal·ace (pal′is) *n.* **1.** A royal residence, or the official residence of some high dignitary, as of a bishop. **2.** Any splendid residence or stately building. **3.** A large building or room used as a place of refreshment and amusement. [< OF *palais* < L *palatium* < *Palatium* Palatine Hill at Rome, on which stood the palace of Caesar Augustus]

Pa·la·cio Val·dés (pä·lä′thyō väl·dās′), **Armando,** 1853–1938, Spanish novelist.

pal·a·din (pal′ə·din) *n.* **1.** Any of the twelve peers of Charlemagne. **2.** A paragon of knighthood. [< F < Ital. *paladino* < L *palatinus* of the palace < *palatium.* See PALACE.]

pa·laes·tra (pə·les′trə) See PALESTRA.

palae- Var. of PALEO-.

palaeo- See PALEO-.

Pal·a·me·des (pal/ə·mē/dēz) In Greek legend, one of the Greek warriors in the Trojan War.

pal·an·quin (pal/ən·kēn/) *n.* A type of covered litter used as a means of conveyance in the Orient, borne by poles on the shoulders of two or more men. Also **pal/an·keen/**. [< Pg. *palanquim* < Javanese *pĕlangki* < Skt. *palyanka* bed, var. of *paryanka* bed]

pal·at·a·ble (pal/it·ə·bəl) *adj.* 1. Agreeable to the taste or palate; savory. 2. Acceptable. — **pal/at·a·bil/i·ty, pal/at·a·ble·ness** *n.* — **pal/at·a·bly** *adv.*

pal·a·tal (pal/ə·təl) *adj.* 1. Pertaining to the palate. 2. *Phonet.* **a** Produced by placing the front (not the tip) of the tongue near or against the hard palate, as *y* in English *yoke*, *ch* in German *ich*. **b** Produced with the blade of the tongue near the hard palate, as *ch* in *child*, *j* in *joy*. — *n.* *Anat.* 1. A bone of the palate. 2. *Phonet.* **a** A palatal consonant. **b** A front vowel. [< F < L *palatum* palate]

pal·a·tal·ize (pal/ə·təl·īz) *v.t.* & *v.i.* **·ized**, **·iz·ing** *Phonet.* 1. To add a palatal quality to a labial, apical, or dorsal consonant, as the so-called soft consonants of Slavic languages. 2. To change a nonpalatal sound to a palatal by assimilation, as (-yŏŏr) to (-shər) in *censure*. — **pal/a·tal·i·za/tion** *n.*

pal·ate (pal/it) *n.* 1. *Anat.* The roof of the mouth, consisting of the **hard palate**, or anterior part, having a bony skeleton, and the **soft palate**, or posterior division, that is composed of muscular tissue. For illustrations see MOUTH, THROAT. 2. The sense of taste; relish: so called because the palate was originally thought to be the organ of taste. 3. Intellectual taste; mental relish. [< L *palatum*.]

pa·la·tial (pə·lā/shəl) *adj.* Of, like, or befitting a palace; magnificent. [< L *palatium* (see PALACE) + -AL] — **pa·la/tial·ly** *adv.*

pa·lat·i·nate (pə·lat/ə·nāt, -nit) *n.* 1. A political division ruled over by a prince possessing certain prerogatives of royalty within his own domain. 2. The office of a count palatine or of an elector palatine.

Pa·lat·i·nate (pə·lat/ə·nāt, -nit) *n.* A native or resident of the Palatinate.

Palatinate, the A region west of the Rhine, administered (1837–1945) by Bavaria; incorporated (1945) into the Rhineland-Palatinate: also *Rhine Palatinate*.

pal·a·tine[1] (pal/ə·tīn, -tin) *adj.* Of or pertaining to the palate. — *n.* *Anat.* Either of the two bones forming the hard palate. [< F *palatin* < L *palatum* palate]

pal·a·tine[2] (pal/ə·tīn, -tin) *adj.* 1. Of or pertaining to a royal palace or its officials. 2. Possessing royal prerogatives: a count *palatine*. — *n.* 1. A lord exercising sovereign power over a province. 2. A vassal exercising royal privileges over his territory. 3. In medieval France and Germany, a high official. See COUNT PALATINE. 4. The ruler of a palatinate or county palatine. 5. A fur tippet formerly worn by women. — **the Palatine** or **the Palatine Hill** The central hill of the seven on which ancient Rome was built. [< F *palatin* < L *palatinus* < *palatium*. See PALACE.]

Pal·a·tine (pal/ə·tīn) *adj.* Of or pertaining to the Palatinate. — *n.* An inhabitant of the Palatinate.

Pa·lau Islands (pä·lou/) An island group in the western Caroline Islands; 188 sq. mi.; also *Pelew Islands*.

pa·lav·er (pə·lav/ər) *n.* 1. Empty talk, especially that intended to flatter or deceive. 2. A public discussion or conference. 3. Originally, a parley with native or aboriginal inhabitants, as by explorers. — *v.t.* 1. To flatter; cajole. — *v.i.* 2. To talk idly and at length. [< Pg. *palavra* word, speech < LL *parabola* story, word < L, comparison. Doublet of PARABLE, PARABOLA, PAROLE.] — **pa·lav/er·er** *n.*

Pa·la·wan (pä·lä/wän) An island in the western Philippines; 4,550 sq. mi.

pale[1] (pāl) *n.* 1. A pointed stick or stake. 2. A fence enclosing a piece of ground. 3. Any boundary or limit. 4. That which is enclosed within bounds: the social *pale*. 5. *Heraldry* An ordinary consisting of a vertical band through the middle of the shield, occupying one third of its width. — **English pale** 1. The varying portion of Irish territory which the Anglo-Normans conquered and governed for several centuries after their invasion of Ireland in the 12th century: also **the Pale.** 2. Formerly, the territory of Calais in France. — *v.t.* **paled**, **pal·ing** To enclose with pales; fence in. [< OF *pal* < L *palus* stake]

pale[2] (pāl) *adj.* 1. Of a whitish or ashen appearance; pallid; wan. 2. Of a very light shade of any color; lacking in brightness or intensity of color. 3. Feeble or weak. — *v.t.* & *v.i.* **paled**, **pal·ing** To make or turn pale; blanch. [< OF *pâle* < L *pallidus* < *pallere* to be pale. Doublet of PALLID.] — **pale/ly** *adv.* — **pale/ness** *n.*
— **Syn.** 1. *Pale*, *pallid*, *wan*, and *livid* refer to lack or deprivation of natural color. *Pale* may be applied to anything more whitish than is natural or expected; a human face may be *pale* by natural complexion, or transiently *pale* through access of emotion. *Pallid* means excessively *pale*, as a result of fatigue, illness, or death. *Wan* implies not only paleness, but also a loss of vigor, and is often associated with severe or prolonged illness. *Livid* means lead-colored, dull or bluish gray, and describes a morbid change from a normal rosy hue. Compare GHASTLY.

pa·le·a (pā/lē·ə) *n.* *pl.* **·le·ae** (-li·ē) *Bot.* A tiny chafflike bract subtending the flower in a spikelet of grass. [< NL < L, chaff] — **pa·le·a/ceous** (-ā/shəs) *adj.*

Pa·le·arc·tic (pā/lē·ärk/tik) *adj.* Of or pertaining to a zoogeographical realm that includes the northern regions of Europe, Africa, and Asia.

pa·le·eth·nol·o·gy (pā/lē·eth·nol/ə·jē) *n.* Ethnology dealing with prehistoric man. — **pa/le·eth/no·log/ic** (-eth/nə·loj/ik) or **·i·cal** *adj.* — **pa/le·eth·nol/o·gist** *n.*

pale·face (pāl/fās/) *n.* A white person: a term allegedly originated by North American Indians.

Pa·lem·bang (pä/lem·bäng/) A city on SE Sumatra, Indonesia; pop. 563,000 (est. 1968).

Pa·len·que (pä·leng/kā) A village in NE Chiapas State, Mexico, on the site of extensive Mayan ruins.

paleo- *combining form* 1. Ancient; old: *paleography*. 2. Primitive: *paleolithic*. Also, before vowels, **pale-**. Also *palae-*, *palaeo-*. [< Gk. *palaios* old, ancient]

pa·le·o·bot·a·ny (pā/lē·ō·bot/ə·nē) *n.* The study of fossil plants. — **pa/le·o·bo·tan/ic** (-bə·tan/ik) or **·i·cal** *adj.* — **pa/le·o·bot/a·nist** *n.*

Pa·le·o·cene (pā/lē·ə·sēn/) *Geol.* *adj.* Of or pertaining to the oldest epoch of the Tertiary period, preceding the Eocene. — *n.* This epoch. See chart for GEOLOGY.

Pa·le·o·gene (pā/lē·ə·jēn/) *adj.* *Geol.* Eogene.

pa·le·og·ra·phy (pā/lē·og/rə·fē) *n.* 1. An ancient mode of writing; ancient writings collectively. 2. The science of describing or deciphering ancient writings. — **pa·le·og/ra·pher** *n.* — **pa/le·o·graph/ic** (-ə·graf/ik) or **·i·cal** *adj.*

pa·le·o·lith (pā/lē·ō·lith/) *n.* A chipped stone object or implement of the Paleolithic period of human culture.

Pa·le·o·lith·ic (pā/lē·ō·lith/ik) *adj.* *Anthropol.* Designating, pertaining to, or associated with a period of human culture preceding the Mesolithic and consisting of the **Lower Paleolithic, Middle Paleolithic,** and **Upper Paleolithic** periods. The culture of this period is characterized by chipped or flaked stone implements, cave paintings, etc.

paleolithic man *Anthropol.* Any of the hominine types of the Paleolithic period, as Neanderthal or Cro-Magnon men.

pa·le·ol·o·gy (pā/lē·ol/ə·jē) *n.* The study of antiquity or antiquities; archeology. [< PALEO- + -LOGY] — **pa/le·o·log/i·cal** (-ə·loj/i·kəl) *adj.* — **pa/le·ol/o·gist** *n.*

pa·le·on·tog·ra·phy (pā/lē·on·tog/rə·fē) *n.* The description of fossils; descriptive paleontology. [< PALEO- + Gk. *ŏn, ontos* being, ppr. of *einai* to be + -GRAPHY] — **pa/le·on/to·graph/ic** (-ə·graf/ik) *adj.*

paleontol- Paleontology.

pa·le·on·tol·o·gy (pā/lē·on·tol/ə·jē) *n.* *pl.* **·gies** 1. The science that treats of ancient forms of life or of fossil organisms. 2. A work dealing with this subject. [< PALEO- + Gk. *ŏn, ontos* being, ppr. of *einai* to be + -LOGY] — **pa/le·on/to·log/ic** (-on/tə·loi/ik) or **·i·cal** *adj.* — **pa/le·on·tol/o·gist** *n.*

Pa·le·o·zo·ic (pā/lē·ō·zō/ik) *adj.* *Geol.* Of or pertaining to the era following the Pre-Cambrian and preceding the Mesozoic. — *n.* The Paleozoic era, with its life forms and rock systems extending from the Cambrian to the Permian. See chart for GEOLOGY. [< PALEO- + Gk. *zōē* life]

pa·le·o·zo·ol·o·gy (pā/lē·ō·zō·ol/ə·jē) *n.* The study of fossil animals. — **pa/le·o·zo/o·log/i·cal** (-zō/ə·loj/i·kəl) *adj.*

Pa·ler·mo (pä·ler/mō) The capital of Sicily, a port on the NW coast; pop. 653,533 (est. 1968): ancient *Panormus*.

Pal·es·tine (pal/is·tīn) 1. In Biblical times, a territory on the eastern coast of the Mediterranean, the country of the Jews: Old Testament *Canaan*: also *Holy Land*. 2. Parts of this territory, placed (1920) under British mandate by the League of Nations; 10,434 sq. mi.; capital, Jerusalem; divided (1947) by the United Nations into Israel and an Arab territory that became part of Jordan in 1949. — **Pal/es·tin/i·an** (-tin/ē·ən) *adj.* & *n.*

PALESTINE
Biblical Palestine

pa·les·tra (pə·les/trə) *n.* *pl.* **·trae** (-trē) In ancient Greece, a school or practice place for athletics; a gymnasium: also spelled *palaestra*. [< L *palaestra* < Gk. *palaistra* < *palaiein* to wrestle] — **pa·les/tral, pa·les/tri·an** *adj.*

Pa·les·tri·na (pä/les·trē/nä), Giovanni Pierluigi da, 1524?–1594, Italian composer: called **Prin·ceps Mu·si·cae** (prin/seps myŏŏ/zi·sē) (Prince of Music).

pal·e·tot (pal/ə·tō, pal/tō) *n.* A loose overcoat or outer garment. [< F < OF *palletoc*]

pal·ette (pal/it) *n.* 1. A thin board or tablet with a hole for the thumb, upon which artists lay and mix their colors for painting. 2. The range of colors characteristic of a particular artist, painting, etc. Also spelled *pallet*. [< F, dim. of *pale* shovel < L *pala* spade]

palette knife   A thin, flat knife with a flexible blade, used for mixing and applying oil colors.

Pa·ley (pā′lē), **William**, 1743–1805, English theologian and philosopher.

pal·frey (pôl′frē)   *n.*   *pl.* **·freys** *Archaic* A saddle horse, especially a woman's saddle horse.   [< OF *palefrei* < LL *palafredus*, alter. of *paraveredus* < Gk. *para* beside + LL *veredus* post horse. Cf. G *pferd* horse.]

Pal·grave (pôl′grāv), **Francis Turner**, 1824–97, English poet and anthologist.

Pa·li (pä′lē)   *n.*   The sacred language of the early Buddhist writings, still surviving in the religious literature of Burma and Thailand.   [< Skt. *pāli* line, canon ; *pāli* (*bhasa*) canonical (language)]

pal·i·kar (pal′i-kär)   *n.*   A Greek soldier in the struggle against Turkey for Grecian independence.   [< Modern Gk. *palikari* lad < Gk. *pallax, pallakos* youth]

pal·imp·sest (pal′imp·sest)   *n.*   A parchment, manuscript, etc., written upon two or three times, the earlier writing having been wholly or partially erased to make room for the next.   [< L *palimpsestus* < Gk. *palimpsēstos*, lit., scraped again < *palin* again + *psaein* to rub]

pal·in·drome (pal′in·drōm)   *n.*   A word, sentence, verse, etc., that is the same read forward or backward, as "Madam, I'm Adam," or "radar."   [< Gk. *palindromos* a running back again < *palin* again + *dromos* course, run]

pal·ing (pā′ling)   *n.*   **1.** One of a series of upright pales forming a fence.   **2.** Pales or pickets collectively.   **3.** A fence or enclosure made of pales or pickets.   **4.** The act of erecting a fence with pales.

pal·in·gen·e·sis (pal′in·jen′ə·sis)   *n.*   **1.** A new or second birth, as into a higher life or form of being.   **2.** The theory or belief that souls are continually reborn.   **3.** *Biol.* The development of an individual in which ancestral forms and characteristics are repeated: distinguished from *cenogenesis*.   [< NL < Gk. *palin* again + GENESIS]   — **pal·in·ge·net′ic** (-jə·net′ik) *adj.*

pal·i·node (pal′ə·nōd)   *n.*   **1.** A poem in which the poet retracts something stated in a former poem.   **2.** A retraction or recantation.   [< LL *palinodia* < Gk. *palinōidia* < *palin* again + *ōidē* ode]

pal·i·sade (pal′ə·sād′)   *n.*   **1.** A barrier or fortification made of strong timbers set in the ground.   **2.** One of the stakes or posts forming such a barrier.   **3.** *pl.* An extended cliff or rocky precipice.   —*v.t.* **·sad·ed, ·sad·ing** To enclose or fortify with a palisade.   [< MF *palissade* < Provençal *palissa* < L *palus* stake]

Pal·i·sades (pal′ə·sādz′), **the**   The cliffs extending about 25 miles along the western bank of the Hudson River in New York and New Jersey.

pal·ish (pāl′ish)   *adj.*   Somewhat pale.

pall[1] (pôl)   *n.*   **1.** A covering, usually of black cloth, thrown over a coffin or over a tomb.   **2.** A dark, heavy covering, cloud, etc.   **3.** A gloomy or oppressive atmosphere, effect, etc.   **4.** *Eccl.* **a** A chalice cover, consisting of a square piece of cardboard faced on both sides with lawn or linen. **b** An altar cloth. **c** A pallium.   — *heraldic* **pall** A Y-shaped bearing resembling a pallium.   —*v.t.* To cover with or as with a pall; cloak < L *pallium* pallium, cloak]

HERALDIC
PALL

[OE *paell*

pall[2] (pôl)   *v.i.*   **1.** To become insipid or uninteresting.   **2.** To have a dulling or displeasing effect: followed by *on*.   —*v.t.* **3.** To satiate; cloy; disgust.   [Appar. aphetic var. of APPALL]

Pal·la·di·an (pə·lā′dē·ən)   *adj.*   **1.** Pertaining to or characteristic of the goddess Pallas.   **2.** Characterized by wisdom or learning.   [< L *Palladius* < Gk. *Palladios* of Pallas]

Pal·la·di·an (pə·lā′dē·ən)   *adj.*   *Archit.* Pertaining to or characteristic of the style of Andrea Palladio, who introduced a modification of the classic Roman style.

pal·lad·ic (pə·lad′ik)   *adj.*   *Chem.* Pertaining to or designating compounds containing tetravalent palladium.

Pal·la·dio (päl·lä′dyō), **Andrea**, 1518–80, Italian architect.

pal·la·di·um[1] (pə·lā′dē·əm)   *n.*   *pl.* **·di·a** (-dē·ə)   Any object considered essential to the safety of a community or organization; a safeguard.   [< PALLADIUM[2]]

pal·la·di·um[2] (pə·lā′dē·əm)   *n.*   A rare, silver-white, malleable and ductile metallic element (symbol Pd) occurring in combination with platinum, iridium, and rhodium. See ELEMENT.   [< NL, after the asteroid *Pallas*, discovered contemporaneously with the element]

Pal·la·di·um (pə·lā′dē·əm)   In Greek and Roman legend, a statue of Pallas Athena, especially one in Troy, on the preservation of which the safety of the city was believed to depend.   [< L < Gk. *palladion*, neut. of *palladios* of Pallas]

pal·la·dous (pal′ə·dəs)   *adj.*   *Chem.* Designating compounds containing palladium, especially in its lower valence.

Pal·las (pal′əs)   In Greek mythology, a name of Athena, the goddess of wisdom: often **Pallas Athena.**   —*n.* The second largest asteroid.   [< Gk., prob. orig. maiden]

pall·bear·er (pôl′bâr′ər)   *n.*   One who forms part of an escort for a coffin at a funeral.   [< PALL[1] + BEARER]

pal·let[1] (pal′it)   *n.*   **1.** *Mech.* **a** A click or pawl used to regulate the motion of a ratchet wheel, etc., as by converting reciprocating into rotary motion, or the reverse. For illustration see ESCAPEMENT. **b** The lip or point of a pawl.   **2.** A paddle for mixing and shaping clay for crucibles, etc.   **3.** A tool used in gilding the backs of books or for taking up gold leaf.   **4.** A movable platform for the storage or transportation of goods.   **5.** A painter's palette.   [< F *palette*. See PALETTE.]

pal·let[2] (pal′it)   *n.*   **1.** A small, mean bed or mattress, usually of straw.   **2.** A blanket laid on the floor for a bed.   [< OF *paillet* < *paille* straw < L *palea* chaff, straw]

pal·let·ize (pal′it·īz)   *v.t.*   **·ized, ·iz·ing** To load or store (goods) on pallets.   [< PALLET[1] (def. 4) + -IZE]

pal·lette (pal′it)   *n.*   In a suit of armor, one of the plates protecting the armpits.   [< F *palette*. See PALETTE.]

pal·liasse (pal·yas′, pal′yas)   See PAILLASSE.

pal·li·ate (pal′ē·āt)   *v.t.*   **·at·ed, ·at·ing**   **1.** To cause (a crime, fault, etc.) to appear less serious or offensive; extenuate.   **2.** To relieve the symptoms or effects of (a disease, etc.) without curing; alleviate; mitigate.   [< L *palliatus* cloaked, pp. of *palliare* to cloak < *pallium* cloak]   — **pal′li·a′tion** *n.*   — **pal′li·a′tor** *n.*

— **Syn. 1.** *Palliate, extenuate, gloss over,* and *whitewash* mean to make seem less wrong, evil, blameworthy, etc. *Palliate* implies concealment, as of the incriminating facts or the gravity of their consequences, while *extenuate* suggests the effort to lessen the blame incurred by an offense: to *palliate* the errors in a book, to *extenuate* past neglect by present concern. To *gloss over* stresses the disguising or misrepresentation of incriminating facts: to *gloss over* a mediocre academic record. To *whitewash* is to represent by completely false information or a dishonest judgment: the accused man went free, *whitewashed* by a packed board of investigation.

pal·li·a·tive (pal′ē·ā′tiv, -ē-ə-)   *adj.*   Tending to palliate.   —*n.* That which serves to palliate.   — **pal′li·a′tive·ly** *adv.*

pal·lid (pal′id)   *adj.*   Of a pale or wan appearance; weak or lacking in color.   — **Syn.** See PALE[2].   [< L *pallidus* < *pallere* to be pale. Doublet of PALE[2].]   — **pal′lid·ly** *adv.*   — **pal′lid·ness** *n.*

pal·li·um (pal′ē·əm)   *n.*   *pl.* **·li·a** (lē·ə) or **·li·ums**   **1.** A mantle resembling the ancient Greek himation, worn by the Romans.   **2.** *Eccl.* A vestment of the pope, archbishops, and metropolitans in the Roman Catholic Church, and of patriarchs in the Eastern Church: also called *pall.*   **3.** *Zool.* A mantle.   **4.** *Anat.* The cerebral cortex.   [< L]

pall-mall (pel′mel′)   *n.*   **1.** A game formerly played in England and France, in which a wooden ball was driven along an alley and through a raised iron ring by means of a mallet.   **2.** The alley used in this game. Also called *mall.*   [< MF *pallemail* < Ital. *pallamaglio* < *palla* ball + *maglio* mallet < L *malleus* hammer]

Pall Mall (pel′ mel′, pôl′ môl′)   A street in London, noted for its numerous clubs.   [< PALL-MALL, because the street was formerly an alley where this game was played]

pal·lor (pal′ər)   *n.*   The state of being pale or pallid; paleness.   [< L < *pallere* to be pale]

palm[1] (päm)   *n.*   **1.** The inner surface of the hand between the wrist and the base of the fingers.   **2.** A linear measure equal to the approximate breadth (3 or 4 inches) or length (about 8½ inches) of the hand.   **3.** That which covers the palm, as part of a glove or mitten.   **4.** The flattened terminal portion of the antler of a moose, etc.   **5.** The flat, expanding end of any armlike projection, as the blade of an oar.   **6.** A shield attached to the palm of the hand, used by sailmakers in pushing a needle through heavy canvas.   —*v.t.* **1.** To hide (cards, dice, etc.) in or about the hand, as in sleight of hand.   **2.** To handle or touch with the palm.   — **to palm off** To pass off or impose fraudulently.   [< F *paume* < OF *paulme* < L *palma*; refashioned after L]

palm[2] (päm)   *n.*   **1.** Any of a large and varied group (*Palmae* or *Palmaceae*) of tropical evergreen trees or shrubs usually having an unbranched trunk topped by a crown of large palmate or pinnate leaves.   **2.** A leaf or branch of the palm, used as a symbol of victory or joy.   **3.** The reward or symbol of victory or preeminence.   **4.** Triumph; victory.   [OE *palm* < L *palma* palm tree, orig., palm of the hand; so called because of the spreading fronds]

Pal·ma (päl′mä)   **1.** The capital of the Balearic Islands, a port on western Majorca; pop. 159,084 (1960). Also **Palma de Mal·lor·ca** (thä mä·lyôr′kä, mä·yôr′kä).   **2.** An island in the NW Canary group; 280 sq. mi.: also *La Palma.*

pal·ma·ceous (pal·mā′shəs, pä·mā′-)   *adj.*   Belonging to or characteristic of the group of plants comprising the palms.

pal·mar (pal′mər, pä′mər)   *adj.*   Of, pertaining to, or similar to the palm of the hand.   [< L *palmaris* < *palma* palm]

pal·mate (pal′māt, pä′māt)   *adj.*   **1.** Resembling an open hand.   **2.** Broad and flat, with fingerlike projections, as the antlers of the moose, or some corals.   **3.** *Bot.* Having lobes that diverge from the apex of the petiole: a *palmate* leaf.   **4.**

Zool. Webbed, as a bird's foot. Also **pal′mat·ed.** [< L *palmatus*, pp. of *palmare* to mark with the palm of the hand < *palma* palm] **— pal′mate·ly** *adv.*

pal·ma·tion (pal-mā′shən, pä-mā′-) *n.* **1.** The state or quality of being palmate. **2.** A division of a palmate structure.

Palm Beach (päm) A resort town in SE Florida; pop. 9,086.

Palm Beach cloth A lightweight summer fabric of cotton warp and mohair filling: a trade name.

palm civet Any of various long-tailed, arboreal civets (family *Viverridae*) of Asia and Africa, as *Paradoxurus hermaphroditus*, common in India. Also **palm cat.**

palm·er (pä′mər) *n.* In the Middle Ages, one who had visited Palestine and brought back a palm branch as a token of the pilgrimage. [< AF < L *palmarius* pertaining to palms < L *palma* palm]

Palm·er (pä′mər), **George Herbert,** 1842–1933, U.S. scholar, philosopher, and educator.

Palmer Archipelago An island group off the NW coast of Palmer Peninsula: also *Antarctic Archipelago.*

Palmer Peninsula A region of Antarctica extending about 800 miles toward South America. Also *Graham Land.*

Palm·er·ston (pä′mər·stən), **Viscount,** 1784–1865, Henry John Temple, British statesman.

Palm·er·ston (pä′mər·stən) The former name for DARWIN, Australia.

palmer worm The caterpillar of a tineid moth (*Dichomeris ligulella*) that feeds upon and damages apple leaves.

pal·mette (pal-met′) *n.* A conventional carved or painted ornament in ancient art, resembling the palm leaf. [< F, dim. of *palme* palm tree]

pal·met·to (pal-met′ō) *n. pl.* **·tos** or **·toes** Any of various palms having fanlike foliage, as the cabbage palm of the southern United States. [< Sp. *palmito*, dim. of *palma* palm tree < L; ending infl. by Ital. *-etto*, dim. suffix]

Palmetto State Nickname of SOUTH CAROLINA.

palmi- *combining form* Palm. [< L *palma* palm]

palm·ist (pä′mist) *n.* One who practices palmistry.

palm·is·try (pä′mis·trē) *n.* The art or practice of supposedly discovering a person's past or future from the lines and marks in the palm of the hand. [ME *palmestrie* < *palme* palm + *-estrie*, prob. < OF *maistrie* mastery < L *magister* master]

pal·mi·tate (pal′mə·tāt, pä′mə-) *n. Chem.* A salt or ester of palmitic acid.

pal·mit·ic acid (pal-mit′ik, pä-mit′-) *Biochem.* A crystalline fatty acid, $C_{15}H_{31}CO_2H$, contained in numerous animal and vegetable fats, and used in making candles and soaps. [< F *palmitique* < L *palma* palm]

pal·mi·tin (pal′mə·tin, pä′mə-) *n. Chem.* A colorless crystalline compound, $(C_{15}H_{31}COO)_3C_3H_5$, contained in palm oil and in natural fats that yield palmitic acid on saponification. [< F *palmitine*]

palm oil A yellowish, butterlike oil obtained from the fruit of several varieties of palm, especially *Elaeis guineensis*, and used in the manufacture of soap, candles, etc.

palm sugar Sugar made from palm sap.

Palm Sunday The Sunday before Easter, being the last Sunday in Lent and the first day in Holy Week. [Named for Christ's triumphal entry into Jerusalem, when palm branches were strewn before him]

palm·y (pä′mē) *adj.* **palm·i·er, palm·i·est 1.** Marked by prosperity; flourishing. **2.** Abounding in or characteristic of palms.

pal·my·ra (pal-mī′rə) *n.* An East Indian palm (*Borassus flabellifer*) having a crown of large fan-shaped leaves. [< Pg. *palmeira* palm tree < L *palma*; spelling infl. by PALMYRA]

Pal·my·ra (pal-mī′rə) An ancient, ruined city in central Syria, NE of Damascus.

Pa·lo Al·to (pä′lō äl′tō *for def. 1*; pal′ō al′tō *for def. 2*) **1.** A battlefield of the Mexican War (1846) in southern Texas near Brownsville. **2.** A city in western California; pop. 55,966.

Pal·o·mar (pal′ə·mär), **Mount** A mountain in southern California, 6,126 ft.; site of **Mount Palomar Observatory.**

pal·o·mi·no (pal′ə·mē′nō) *n. pl.* **·nos** A light tan or golden brown horse with a cream-colored mane and tail. [< Am. Sp., orig., dove-colored horse < Sp. *palomillo*, dim. of *paloma* dove < L *palumbus* ringdove]

pa·loo·ka (pə·loo′kə) *n. U.S. Slang* **1.** An inferior or bungling pugilist. **2.** A lout; lummox. [Coined by Jack Conway, U.S. journalist, d. 1928; ult. origin uncertain]

Pa·los (pä′lōs) A village, formerly a port, in SW Spain, where Columbus embarked in 1492. Also **Palos de la Fron·te·ra** (thä lä frōn·tā′rä).

palp (palp) *n.* A palpus. [< F *palpe* < L *palpus*. See PALPUS.]

pal·pa·ble (pal′pə·bəl) *adj.* **1.** Capable of being touched or felt. **2.** Readily perceived; obvious. **3.** Perceptible by touching. **— Syn.** See EVIDENT. [< LL *palpabilis* < L *palpare* to touch] **— pal′pa·bil′i·ty, pal′pa·ble·ness** *n.* **— pal′pa·bly** *adv.*

pal·pate (pal′pāt) *v.t.* **·pat·ed, ·pat·ing** To feel or examine

by touch, especially for medical diagnosis. **— adj.** Having a palpus or palpi. [< L *palpatus*, pp. of *palpare* to touch]

pal·pa·tion (pal-pā′shən) *n. Med.* The process of examining or exploring the body by means of touch. [< L *palpatio*, *-onis* stroking, flattery < *palpare* to touch]

pal·pe·bra (pal′pə·brə) *n. pl.* **·brae** (-brē) An eyelid. [< L] **— pal′pe·bral** *adj.*

pal·pi·tate (pal′pə·tāt) *v.i.* **·tat·ed, ·tat·ing 1.** To quiver; tremble. **2.** To beat more rapidly than normal; flutter: said especially of the heart. [< L *palpitatus*, pp. of *palpitare* to tremble, freq. of *palpare* to touch]

pal·pi·ta·tion (pal′pə·tā′shən) *n.* **1.** Rapid and irregular pulsation. **2.** A quivering or trembling.

pal·pus (pal′pəs) *n. pl.* **·pi** (-pī) *Zool.* A feeler; especially, one of the jointed sense organs attached to the mouth parts of arthropods: also called *palp.* [< NL < L *palpus* feeler. Akin to *palpare* to touch.]

pals·grave (pôlz′grāv, palz′-) *n.* A count palatine (def. 1). [< MDu. *paltsgrave* < *palts* palace (ult. < L *palatium*) + *grave* count] **— pals′gra·vine** (-grə·vēn) *n. fem.*

pal·sied (pôl′zēd) *adj.* Affected with palsy; trembling.

pal·sy (pôl′zē) *n. pl.* **·sies 1.** Paralysis. **2.** Any impairment or loss of ability to control movement. **— v.t. ·sied, ·sy·ing 1.** To paralyze. **2.** To cause to tremble or become helpless, as from fear or rage. [< OF *paralisie* < L *paralysis.* Doublet of PARALYSIS.]

pal·ter (pôl′tər) *v.i.* **1.** To speak or act insincerely; equivocate; lie. **2.** To be fickle or capricious; trifle. **3.** To haggle or quibble. [Origin unknown] **— pal′ter·er** *n.*

pal·try (pôl′trē) *adj.* **·tri·er, ·tri·est 1.** Having little or no worth or value; trifling; trivial. **2.** Contemptible; petty. [< LG *paltrig* ragged < *palte* rag.] **— pal′tri·ly** *adv.* **— pal′tri·ness** *n.*

pa·lu·dal (pə·lōōd′l) *adj.* Pertaining to a marsh; swampy. [< L *palus, paludis* marsh]

pal·u·dism (pal′yə·diz′əm) *n. Pathol.* Malaria. [< L *palus, paludis* marsh]

pal·y[1] (pā′lē) *adj. Chiefly Poetic* Pale; pallid.

pal·y[2] (pā′lē) *adj. Heraldry* Divided into an even number of vertical bands of alternating colors. [< OF *pale* < *pal* stake < L *palus*]

pal·y·nol·o·gy (pal′ə·nol′ə·jē) *n.* A branch of science dealing with pollen and spores. [< Gk. *polynein* to sprinkle]

pam (pam) *n.* **1.** In the game of loo, the jack of clubs. **2.** A game resembling napoleon, wherein the highest trump is the jack of clubs. [Short for F *pamphile* jack of clubs < Gk. *Pamphilos*, a personal name; lit., beloved of all]

pam. or **pamph.** Pamphlet.

Pa·mir (pä·mir′) An elevated region of central Asia, with high plains lying at 11,000 to 13,000 ft. and rising to Garmo Peak, 24,590 ft. Also **the Pamirs.**

Pam·li·co Sound (pam′li·kō) A body of water between eastern North Carolina and its offshore islands; 80 mi. long; greatest width, 25 mi.

pam·pas (pam′pəz, *Sp.* päm′päs) *n.pl.* The great treeless plains south of the Amazon river, extending from the Atlantic to the Andes. **— Syn.** See PLAIN[1]. [< Sp. *pampa* < Quechua, plain]

pam·pas grass (pam′pəs) A tall, ornamental, reedlike grass (*Cortaderia selloana*) native to South America, having very large, thick, silvery panicles.

pam·pe·an (pam′pē·ən, pam·pē′ən) *adj.* Of or pertaining to the pampas or to their native inhabitants. **— n.** An Indian of the pampas.

pam·per (pam′pər) *v.t.* **1.** To treat very indulgently; gratify the whims or wishes of; coddle. **2.** *Obs.* To feed with rich food; glut. [Appar. < LG *pamperen* < *pampen* to live luxuriously] **— pam′per·er** *n.*

— Syn. 1. indulge, humor, baby.

pam·pe·ro (päm·pā′rō) *n. pl.* **·ros** *Meteorol.* A strong, cold, dry, southwest wind of the Argentine pampas. [< Sp. < Quechua *pampa* plain]

pam·phlet (pam′flit) *n.* **1.** A printed work stitched or pasted, but not permanently bound. **2.** A brief treatise or essay, often on a subject of current interest, printed and published without a binding. *Abbr.* **pam., pamph., pph.** [< OF *pamphlet*, dim. of *Pamphilus*, title of a 12th c. Latin love poem]

pam·phlet·eer (pam′flə·tir′) *n.* One who writes pamphlets: sometimes a term of contempt. **— v.i.** To write and issue pamphlets.

Pam·phyl·i·a (pam·fil′ē·ə) An ancient country and Roman province in southern Asia Minor.

Pam·plo·na (päm·plō′nä) The capital of Navarre, northern Spain; pop. 97,880 (1960). Also **Pam·pe·lu·na** (päm′pā·lōō′nä).

pan[1] (pan) *n.* **1.** A wide, shallow vessel, usually of metal, used for holding liquids or in cooking. **2.** Any similar receptacle or vessel, as one used for boiling and evaporating. **3.** A natural or artificial depression in the earth, containing mud or water, or used for evaporating brine. **4.** A circular iron dish with sloping sides, in which gold is separated. **5.** The powder cavity of a flintlock. **6.** The skull; brainpan. **7.** Hardpan. **8.** Either of the two receptacles on a pair of scales or a balance. **9.** Ice broken from a large floe and floating in open water. **— v. panned, pan·ning** *v.t.* **1.** To separate (gold) by washing gold-bearing earth in a pan. **2.** To wash (earth, gravel, etc.) for this purpose. **3.** To cook and serve in a pan. **4.** *Informal* To criticize severely. — *v.i.* **5.** To search for gold by washing earth, gravel, etc., in a pan. **6.** To yield gold, as earth. — **to pan out** *U.S. Informal* To turn out well; succeed. [OE *panne* < Gmc. < LL *panna* < L *patina* pan, dish < Gk. *patanē*]

pan² (pan) *n.* **1.** Betel leaf. **2.** A preparation made from this leaf and other ingredients, chewed in India and the East Indies. [< Hind. *pān* betel leaf < Skt. *parṇa* feather, leaf]

pan³ (pan) *v.t.* **panned, pan·ning** To move (a motion-picture or television camera) so as to photograph an entire scene, follow a particular character, etc. [< PANORAMA]

pan- *combining form* **1.** All; every; the whole: *panchromatic*. **2.** Comprising, including, or applying to all: usually capitalized when preceding proper nouns or adjectives, as in:

Pan-African	Pan-Asian	Pan-Slav
Pan-Arab	Pan-Islam	Pan-Slavic
Pan-Arabian	Pan-Islamic	Pan-Slavonic
Pan-Asia	Pan-Russian	Pan-Syrian

[< Gk., neut. of *pas* all]

Pan (pan) In Greek mythology, a god of forests, flocks, and shepherds, having the horns and hoofs of a goat: identified with the Roman *Faunus*.

Pan. Panama.

pan·a·ce·a (pan′ə·sē′ə) *n.* A remedy for all diseases or ills; a cure-all. [< L < Gk. *panakeia* < *panakēs* all-healing < *pan*, neut. of *pas* all + *akos* cure < *akeomai* to heal] — **pan′·a·ce′an** *adj.*

pa·nache (pə·nash′, -näsh′) *n.* **1.** A plume or bunch of feathers, especially as an ornament on a helmet. **2.** Dash; verve. [< F < Ital. *pennacchio* < *penna* feather < L]

pa·na·da (pə·nä′də, -nā′-) *n.* A dish made of soaked, sweetened or flavored crackers or bread. [< Sp. < L *panis* bread]

Pan·a·ma (pan′ə·mä, *Sp.* pä′nä·mä′) A Republic of Central America; 28,575 sq. mi. (excluding Canal Zone); pop. 1,500,-000 (est. 1970); capital, **Panama** (also *Panama City*), near the Pacific end of the Canal, pop. 372,200 (est. 1968).

Panama, Isthmus of An isthmus connecting North and South America; 30 mi. wide at its narrowest point: formerly *Isthmus of Darien*.

Panama Canal A ship canal connecting the Atlantic and the Pacific, extending 40 miles across the Isthmus of Panama; completed (1914) by the United States on the leased territory of the Canal Zone.

Panama Canal Zone See CANAL ZONE.

Panama City **1.** See PANAMA. **2.** A city in NW Florida, on the Gulf of Mexico; pop. 32,096.

Panama hat A hat woven from the young leaves of the jipijapa tree of Central and South America.

Pan·a·ma·ni·an (pan′ə·mā′nē·ən, -mä′-) *adj.* Of or pertaining to the Isthmus of Panama or its inhabitants. — *n.* A native or naturalized inhabitant of Panama. Also **Pan·a·man** (pan′ə·män′).

Pan-A·mer·i·can (pan′ə·mer′ə·kən) *adj.* Including or pertaining to the whole of America, both North and South, or to all Americans. Also **Pan American**.

Pan-A·mer·i·can·ism (pan′ə·mer′ə·kən·iz′əm) *n.* The advocacy of a political union or alliance, or of closer political and economic cooperation, among the republics of the western hemisphere.

Pan American Union A bureau (formerly the *International Bureau of the American Republics*) established in Washington, D.C., in 1890, by the 21 American republics to promote mutual peace. *Abbr.* PAU, P.A.U.

Pan·a·mint Mountains (pan′ə·mint) A range in SE California; highest point, Telescope Peak, 11,045 ft.

pan·a·tel·a (pan′ə·tel′ə) See PANETELA.

Pa·nay (pä·nī′) An island of the central Philippines; 4,446 sq. mi.

pan-broil (pan′broil′) *v.t.* & *v.i.* To cook in a heavy frying pan placed over direct heat, using little or no fat.

pan·cake (pan′kāk′) *n.* **1.** A thin, flat cake made from batter fried in a pan or baked on a griddle. **2.** A cosmetic resembling face powder, pressed in a thin disk: also **pancake make-up**. **3.** *Aeron.* An abrupt landing in which an airplane is leveled off and stalled well above the surface so that it drops flat. — *v.i.* **caked, ·cak·ing** *Aeron.* To make a pancake landing.

pan·chro·mat·ic (pan′krō·mat′ik) *adj. Photog.* Sensitive to light of all colors of the spectrum, as film or a plate. — **pan·chro′ma·tism** (-krō′mə·tiz′əm) *n.*

pan·crat·i·um (pan·krā′shē·əm) *n. pl.* **·ti·a** (-shē·ə) In ancient Greece, an athletic contest that combined boxing and wrestling. [< L < Gk. *pankration* < *pan-* all + *kratos* bodily strength] — **pan·crat′ic** (-krat′ik) *adj.*

pan·cre·as (pan′krē·əs, pang′-) *n. Anat.* A large gland situated behind the lower part of the stomach, secreting pancreatic juice into the duodenum and producing insulin in the islands of Langerhans. [< NL < Gk. *pankreas* sweetbread < *pan-* all + *kreas* flesh] — **pan′cre·at′ic** (-at′ik) *adj.*

pancreatic juice *Biochem.* A colorless fluid secreted by the pancreas and containing enzymes important in digestion.

pan·cre·a·tin (pan′krē·ə·tin, pang′-) *n.* **1.** A mixture of the enzymes contained in pancreatic juice. **2.** A preparation made from the fresh pancreas of hogs, cattle, etc., and used as a digestant. [< Gk. *pankreas, -atos* pancreas + -IN]

pan·da (pan′də) *n. pl.* **·das** or **·da 1.** A small, raccoonlike carnivore (*Ailurus fulgens*), of the southeastern Himalayas, with long reddish brown fur and ringed tail: also called *bearcat, lesser panda.* **2.** A large, bearlike mammal (*Ailuropoda melanoleuca*) of Tibet and China, with black-and-white coat and rings around the eyes: also called *giant panda, great panda*. [Prob. < Nepalese]

GIANT PANDA (5 feet long; 2 feet high at shoulder)

pan·da·nus (pan·dā′nəs) *n.* Any of a genus (*Pandanus*) of trees and shrubs of southeastern Asia, characterized by stilt-like aerial roots and the spiral arrangement of their leaves. Also called *screwpine*. [< NL < Malay *pandan*] — **pan·da·na·ceous** (pan′də·nā′shəs) *adj.*

Pan·da·rus (pan′də·rəs) **1.** In the *Iliad*, a leader of the Lycians in the Trojan War. **2.** In medieval legend, Chaucer, and Shakespeare, a go-between who procures Cressida for Troilus. Also **Pan·dar** (pan′dər).

Pan·de·an (pan·dē′ən) *adj.* Of or pertaining to the god Pan.

Pandean pipes A panpipe (which see).

Pan·dects (pan′dekts) *n.pl.* A digest of the Roman civil law in fifty books, made by direction of the Emperor Justinian about A.D. 533: also called *the Digest*. See CORPUS JURIS CIVILIS.

pan·dem·ic (pan·dem′ik) *adj.* **1.** *Med.* Widely epidemic. **2.** Universal; general. — *n.* A pandemic disease. [< Gk. *pandēmos* pertaining to all the people < *pan-* all + *dēmos* people]

pan·de·mo·ni·um (pan′də·mō′nē·əm) *n.* **1.** The abode of all demons. **2.** Loosely, hell. **3.** A place or gathering marked by disorder and uproar. **4.** Riotous uproar. — **Pandemonium** In Milton, the palace of Satan in Hell. Also **pan′dae·mo′ni·um**. [< NL < Gk. *pan-* all + *daimōn* demon]

pan·der (pan′dər) *n.* **1.** A go-between in sexual intrigues; a procurer; pimp. **2.** One who ministers to the passions or base desires of others. Also **pan′der·er**. — *v.i.* **1.** To act as a pander. — *v.t.* **2.** To act as a pander for. [< L *Pandarus* < Gk. *Pandaros*; or < *Pandare*, character in Chaucer's Troilus and Criseyde] — **pan′der·age** (-ij), **pan′der·ism** *n.* — **pan′der·ess** *n.fem.*

Pan·dit (pun′dit), **Vijaya Lakshmi**, born 1900, Indian diplomat and administrator; sister of Jawaharlal Nehru.

Pan·do·ra (pan·dôr′ə, -dō′rə) In Greek mythology, the first mortal woman, sent to earth as a punishment to man for Prometheus' theft of the fire. She brought with her a box (**Pandora's box**) containing all human ills which, when she opened the lid, escaped into the world, leaving only hope at the bottom of the box. [< Gk., all-gifted]

pan·dore (pan′dôr, -dōr) *n.* A bandore (which see). Also **pan·do′ra, pan·du·ra** (pan·dôr′ə, -dyoor′ə). [< F *pandore* < L *pandura*. See BANDORE.]

pan·dour (pan′door) *n.* **1.** A member of a force of Croatian foot soldiers, noted for their brutality, organized locally in 1741 and later incorporated in the Austrian army. **2.** Any inhuman or marauding soldier. Also **pan′door**. [< F < Serbo-Croatian *pandūr* constable, prob. < Med.L *banderius* follower of a banner]

pan·dow·dy (pan·dou′dē) *n. pl.* **·dies** *U.S.* A deep-dish pie or pudding made of baked sliced apples and having only a top crust. Also **apple pandowdy**. [Origin unknown]

pan·du·rate (pan′dyə·rāt) *adj. Bot.* Shaped like a fiddle, as certain leaves. Also **pan·du·ri·form** (pan·door′ə·fôrm, -dyoor′-). [< L *pandura* lute + -ATE¹]

pan·dy (pan′dē) *Scot. & Dial. n. pl.* **·dies** A stroke on the palm of the hand with a cane or strap, as a punishment in schools. — *v.t.* **·died, ·dy·ing** To punish thus. [Prob. < L *pande* imperative of *pandere* to stretch]

pane (pān) *n.* **1.** One of the sections of a window, door, etc., filled with a sheet of glass. **2.** A sheet of glass for such a section. **3.** One of the flat surfaces on an object having several sides, as a nut, bolthead, or cut diamond. **4.** A panel in a door, ceiling, etc. [< OF *pan* < L *pannus* piece of cloth]

pan·e·gyr·ic (pan′ə·jir′ik) *n.* **1.** A formal public eulogy, either written or spoken. **2.** Elaborate praise; laudation. — *Syn.* See EULOGY. [< MF *panégyrique* < L *panegyricus* < Gk. *panēgyrikos* of an assembly < *panēgyris* assembly < *pan-* all + *agyris* assembly, var. of *agora* < *agein* to lead] — **pan′e·gyr′i·cal** *adj.* **pan′e·gyr′i·cal·ly** *adv.*

pan·e·gyr·ist (pan'ə·jir'ist) *n.* One who panegyrizes.

pan·e·gy·rize (pan'ə·jə·rīz') *v.* **·rized, ·riz·ing** *v.t.* **1.** To deliver or write a panegyric upon; eulogize. — *v.i.* **2.** To make panegyrics.

pan·el (pan'əl) *n.* **1.** A rectangular or square piece forming part of a wainscot, ceiling, door, etc., but distinguished from the rest of the surface by being raised above or sunk below the general level, by being surrounded by a frame or molding, or by being of a different material. **2.** A window pane. **3.** One or more pieces of the same or of a different fabric inserted lengthwise in the skirt of a woman's dress. **4.** A tablet of wood used as the surface for an oil painting; also, the picture painted on such a tablet. **5.** A picture very long for its width, often without a frame. **6.** A size of photograph longer than it is wide, usually about 8½ x 4 inches. **7.** A section of a book cover with a framed effect from having been stamped, tooled, etc. **8.** *Law* **a** The official list of persons summoned for jury duty. **b** The body of persons composing a jury. **c** In Scottish law, the person or persons indicted and tried. **9.** A small group of persons selected to hold a discussion, judge a contest, etc. **10.** *Chiefly Brit.* In systems of medical insurance, a group of doctors whom patients may consult. **11.** *Aeron.* **a** A section of an airplane wing. **b** A section of the covering of a balloon or the canopy of a parachute. **12.** *Electr.* An upright board of insulating material sustaining the controlling devices of an electric circuit. **13.** An instrument panel (which see). **14.** *Mining* A section of a coal seam separated from other sections by walls of unusual thickness. — *v.t.* **pan·eled** or **·elled, pan·el·ing** or **·el·ling 1.** To fit, furnish, or adorn with panels. **2.** To divide into panels. **3.** In Scottish law, to indict. [< OF, piece of cloth < Med.L *panellus*, dim. of L *pannus* piece of cloth]

panel discussion A discussion before an audience of a specific topic by a group of selected speakers.

panel heating Radiant heating (which see).

pan·el·ing (pan'əl·ing) *n.* **1.** Wood or other materials used in making panels. **2.** Panels collectively. Also **pan'el·ling.**

pan·el·ist (pan'əl·ist) *n.* A person serving on a panel.

pan·e·tel·a (pan'ə·tel'ə) *n.* A long, slender cigar: also spelled *panatela.* Also **pan'e·tel'la.** [< Sp.]

pan fish Any little fish that can be fried whole.

pang (pang) *n.* **1.** A sudden sharp pain. **2.** A spasm of mental anguish. — **Syn.** See PAIN. [Origin unknown]

pan·gen·e·sis (pan·jen'ə·sis) *n. Biol.* The now abandoned theory, advanced by Charles Darwin, that all the cells of an organism throw off very minute gemmules, or *pangens,* that circulate through the body and contain the units of heredity which they transmit from parent to offspring. Compare BLASTOGENESIS. — **pan'ge·net'ic** (-jə·net'ik) *adj.*

Pan-Ger·man·ism (pan·jûr'mən·iz'əm) *n.* The German idea of or movement toward political union of all neighboring territories inhabited by German-speaking peoples: also called *Pan-Teutonism.* — **Pan'-Ger'man** *adj. & n.* — **Pan'·Ger·man'ic** (-jer·man'ik) *adj.* — **Pan'Ger'man·ist** *n.*

pan·go·lin (pang·gō'lin) *n.* A heavily armored, typically long-tailed edentate mammal (genus *Manis*) of Asia and Africa: also called *scaly anteater.* [< Malay *peng-gōling* roller < *gōling* to roll, in ref. to its power of rolling itself up]

Pang·o Pang·o (päng'ō päng'ō) See PAGO PAGO.

pan·han·dle[1] (pan'han'dəl) *v.i.* **·dled, ·dling** *U.S. Informal* To beg, especially on the street. [Back formation < PANHANDLER]

pan·han·dle[2] (pan'han'dəl) *n.* **1.** The handle of a pan. **2.** *U.S.* A narrow strip of land shaped like the handle of a pan and attached to a larger region. **3.** *Usually cap.* A region of this shape in either Texas or West Virginia.

pan·han·dler (pan'han'dlər) *n. U.S. Informal* A beggar. [< PAN[1] (used to receive alms) + HANDLE, v.]

Panhandle State Nickname of West Virginia.

Pan-Hel·len·ic (pan'he·len'ik) *adj.* **1.** Of or pertaining to Pan-Hellenism or to all Greeks. **2.** Of or pertaining to college fraternities or sororities collectively.

pan-Hel·len·ic festival (pan'he·len'ik) In ancient Greece, any one of the four religious and athletic observances, the Isthmian, Nemean, Olympic, and Pythian.

Pan-Hel·le·nism (pan'hel'ə·niz'əm) *n.* The aspiration for the political union of all Greeks. — **Pan'-Hel'le·nist** *n.*

pan·ic (pan'ik) *n.* **1.** A sudden, unreasonable, overpowering fear, especially when affecting a large number simultaneously. **2.** An instance of such fear. **3.** In finance, a sudden and overpowering distrust or alarm precipitating mercantile and banking failures. — **Syn.** see FEAR. — *adj.* **1.** Of the nature of or resulting from sudden and infectious terror. **2.** *Usually cap.* Of or pertaining to the Greek god Pan. — *v.* **·icked, ·ick·ing** *v.t.* **1.** To affect with panic. **2.** *U.S. Slang* To move to great applause or laughter: He *panicked* his audience. — *v.i.* **3.** To become affected with panic. [< MF *panique* < Gk. *panikos* of or for the god Pan, who was believed to cause sudden or groundless fear] — **pan'ick·y** *adj.*

pan ice Loose fragments of ice detached from ice floes and drifting along the seacoast.

panic grass A North American grass (*Panicum capillare*) used for forage: also called *witchgrass.* [< L *panicum* kind of millet < *panus* swelling + GRASS]

pan·i·cle (pan'i·kəl) *n. Bot.* A loose compound flower cluster, produced by irregular branching. For illustration see INFLORESCENCE. [< L *panicula,* dim. of *panus* swelling, ear of millet]

pan·ic-strick·en (pan'ik·strik'ən) *adj.* Overcome by panic. Also **pan'ic-struck'** (-struk').

pa·nic·u·late (pə·nik'yə·lāt, -lit) *adj. Bot.* Arranged or borne in panicles. Also **pa·nic'u·lat'ed.** [< NL *paniculatus* < L *panicula.* See PANICLE.] — **pa·nic'u·late·ly** *adv.*

Pan·ja·bi (pun·jä'bē) See PUNJABI.

pan·jan·drum (pan·jan'drəm) *n.* A mock title for an official of exaggerated importance or great pretensions. [Coined by Samuel Foote, 1720–1777, English dramatist and actor]

Pank·hurst (pangk'hûrst), **Emmeline,** 1858–1928, *née* Goulden, English suffragist.

panne satin (pan) Silk or rayon satin with an unusually high luster because of a special finish. [< F *panne,* type of soft cloth]

panne velvet A lustrous, lightweight velvet with a flattened pile, used chiefly in millinery and as a trim.

pan·nier (pan'yər) *n.* **1.** One of a pair of baskets adapted to be slung on both sides of a beast of burden. **2.** A basket for carrying a load on the back. **3.** A light framework for extending a woman's dress at the hips; also, a skirt or overskirt extended at the hips. [< MF < L *panarium* bread basket < *panis* bread]

pan·ni·kin (pan'ə·kin) *n. Chiefly Brit.* A small saucepan or tin cup. [Dim. of PAN[1]]

Pan·no·ni·a (pə·nō'nē·ə) An ancient Roman province south and west of the Danube.

pa·no·cha (pə·nō'chə) *n.* **1.** A coarse Mexican sugar. **2.** Penuche. Also **pa·no'che.** [< Am. Sp., dim. of Sp. *pan* < L *panis* bread]

pan·o·ply (pan'ə·plē) *n. pl.* **·plies 1.** The complete equipment of a warrior. **2.** Any complete covering that protects or magnificently arrays. [< Gk. *panoplia* full armor < *pan-* all + *hopla* arms] — **pan'o·plied** *adj.*

pan·op·tic (pan·op'tik) *adj.* Including all visible objects in one view. Also **pan·op'ti·cal.** [< Gk. *panoptēs*]

pan·o·ram·a (pan'ə·ram'ə, -rä'mə) *n.* **1.** A series of pictures representing a continuous scene, arranged to unroll and pass before the spectator. **2.** A complete view in every direction; also, a complete or comprehensive view of a subject or of passing events. [< PAN- + Gk. *horama* sight < *horaein* to see] — **pan'o·ram'ic** *adj.* — **pan'o·ram'i·cal·ly** *adv.*

panoramic sight *Optics* A sight constructed on the periscope principle, intended for use in aiming guns at targets within a complete circle.

Pan·or·mus (pə·nôr'məs) The ancient name for PALERMO.

pan·pipe (pan'pīp') *n. Sometimes cap. Often pl.* An instrument consisting of a graduated series of short flutes, originally reeds, bound together in proper order to produce a scale: also called *Pandean pipes, syrinx.*

Pan-Slav·ism (pan·slä'viz·əm) *n.* The idea of uniting all Slavic peoples, especially under the hegemony of Russia. — **Pan'-Slav'ic** *adj.* — **Pan'-slav'ist** *n.*

pan·so·phism (pan'sə·fiz'əm) *n.* A pretension to pansophy. — **pan'so·phist** *n.* [< Gk. *pansophos* all-wise + -ISM]

pan·so·phy (pan'sə·fē) *n.* Comprehensive or universal knowledge. [< PAN- + Gk. *sophia* wisdom] — **pan·soph·ic** (pan·sof'ik), **pan·soph'i·cal** *adj.*

pan·sy (pan'zē) *n. pl.* **·sies 1.** A species of garden violet (*Viola tricolor hortensis*) having blossoms of a variety of colors of great beauty: also called *heartsease.* **2.** *U.S. Slang* An effeminate or homosexual man. [< MF *pensée* thought < OF *penser* < L *pensare* to weigh]

pant (pant) *v.i.* **1.** To breathe rapidly or spasmodically; gasp for breath. **2.** To emit smoke, steam, etc., in loud puffs. **3.** To gasp with desire; yearn: with *for* or *after.* **4.** To beat or pulsate rapidly; throb. — *v.t.* **5.** To breathe out or utter gaspingly. — *n.* **1.** The act of panting. **2.** A short or labored breath; gasp. **3.** A throb or palpitation, as of the heart. **4.** A puff, as from an engine. [Appar. < OF *pantoisier* to gasp, ult. < L *phantasiare* to have a nightmare]

pant- Var. of PANTO-.

Pan·tag·ru·el (pan·tag'rōō·el, pan'tə·grōō'əl; *Fr.* päṅ·tȧ·grü·el') In Rabelais' satirical romance *Gargantua and Pantagruel,* the giant son of Gargantua, characterized by his broad, somewhat cynical good humor. — **Pan·ta·gru·el·i·an** (pan'tə·grōō·el'ē·ən) *adj.* — **Pan·ta·gru·el·ism** (pan'tə·grōō'əl·iz'əm, pan·tag'rōō·el·iz'əm), **Pan'ta·gru'el·ist** *n.*

pan·ta·lets (pan'tə·lets') *n.pl.* **1.** Formerly, long ruffled or embroidered drawers extending below the hem of the skirt. **2.** Separate frilled leg coverings to be attached to drawers. Also **pan'ta·lettes'.** [Dim. of PANTALOON]

pan·ta·loon (pan'tə·lōōn') *n.* **1.** *pl.* Formerly, a tight-fitting garment for the hips and legs; trousers. **2.** In pantomimes, an absurd old man on whom the clown plays tricks. [< MF *pantalon* ⊲ Ital. *pantalone* clown < *Pantalone,* nickname for a Venetian < *Pantaleone,* popular Venetian saint]

Pan·ta·loon (pan'tə·lōōn') In early Italian comedy, a skinny, foolish old man wearing pantaloons.

pan·tech·ni·con (pan·tek'ni·kon) *n. Brit.* **1.** A van for moving furniture. **2.** A warehouse for storing furniture.

[< PAN- + Gk. *technikon*, neut. of *technikos* belonging to the arts < *technē* art, craft]

Pan·tel·le·ri·a (pän/tel·le·rē/ä) An island of Italy, off the SW coast of Sicily; 32 sq. mi.: ancient *Cossyra*.

Pan-Teu·ton·ism (pan/tōōt/n·iz/əm, -tyōōt/n-) *n.* Pan-Germanism (which see). **— Pan/-Teu·ton/ic** (-tōō·ton/ik, -tyōō-) *adj.*

pan·the·ism (pan/thē·iz/əm) *n.* **1.** The doctrine that the whole universe is God, or that every part of the universe is a manifestation of God. **2.** Worship of all the gods of various cults, etc., as in the Roman Empire. Compare DEISM, THEISM. [< PAN- + Gk. *theos* god] **— pan/the·ist** *n.* **— pan/the·is/tic, pan/the·is/ti·cal** *adj.* **— pan/the·is/ti·cal·ly** *adv.*

pan·the·on (pan/thē·on) *n.* **1.** All the gods of a people collectively. **2.** A mausoleum or temple commemorating the great of a nation. [< L *pantheon* < Gk. *pantheion*, a temple consecrated to all the gods < *pan-* all + *theios* of or sacred to a god < *theos* god]

Pan·the·on (pan/thē·on) A circular domed temple at Rome, dedicated to all the gods, built by Agrippa in 27 B.C. and since A.D. 609 used as a church, Santa Maria della Rotunda.

pan·ther (pan/thər) *n.* **1.** A leopard, especially the black variety of southern Asia. **2.** The puma or cougar. **3.** The jaguar. [< OF *pantère* < L *panthera* < Gk. *panthēr*] **— pan/ther·ess** *n.fem.*

pant·ies (pan/tēz) *n.pl.* A woman's or child's underpants. Also **pantie**.

pan·tile (pan/tīl) *n.* A roof tile displaying an S-shaped cross-section, making laps on each side with adjacent tiles.

panto- combining form All; every: *pantoscope*. Also, before vowels, **pant-**. [< Gk. *pantos*, genitive of *pas* all]

pan·tof·fle (pan/tə·fəl, pan·tof/əl, -tōō/fəl) *n.* A slipper. Also **pan/to·fle**. [< MF *pantoufle*; ult. origin uncertain]

pan·to·graph (pan/tə·graf, -gräf) *n.* **1.** An instrument consisting of a framework of four jointed rods forming a parallelogram, used for copying drawings, maps, etc., to any desired scale. **2.** A trolley, or other device for collecting current, that is mounted on a jointed, quadrilateral frame. **— pant/o·graph/ic** or **·i·cal** *adj.* **— pan·tog/ra·phy** (pan·tog/rə·fē) *n.*

pan·tol·o·gy (pan·tol/ə·jē) *n.* A system comprehending all departments of human knowledge. **— pan·tol/o·gist** *n.*

pan·to·mime (pan/tə·mīm) *n.* **1.** Any play in which the actors express their meaning by action without dialogue. **2.** *Brit.* A type of Christmas play relating a popular story against a background of satiric or exaggerated scenery and music. **3.** Gestures without speech. **4.** In ancient Roman drama, a part of a play in which the actor used only gestures to the accompaniment of the chorus. **— v.t. & v.i. ·mimed, ·mim·ing** To act or express in pantomime. [< F < L *pantomimus* pantomimist < Gk. *pantomimos* an imitator of all < *panto(s)* of all + *mimos* imitator] **— pan/to·mim/ic** (-mim/ik) or **·i·cal** *adj.* **— pan/to·mi/mist** (-mī/mist) *n.*

pan·to·scope (pan/tə·skōp) *n.* *Photog.* A lens with a very wide angle.

pan·to·scop·ic (pan/tə·skop/ik) *adj.* Giving a broad scope or sweep of vision.

pan·to·then·ic acid (pan/tə·then/ik) *Biochem.* An unstable, oily compound, $C_9H_{17}NO_5$, widely distributed in plant and animal tissues: formerly called vitamin B₃. [< Gk. *pantothen* from every side + -IC]

pan·toum (pan·tōōm/) *n.* A verse form consisting of an indefinite number of quatrains rhyming *abab, bcbc, cdcd*, etc., with the second and fourth lines of the final stanza repeating the first and third of the first stanza. [< F < Malay *pantun*]

pan·try (pan/trē) *n.* *pl.* **·tries** A room or closet for provisions, dishes, table linen, etc. [ME *pantrie* < *panetrie* < OF *paneterie* < *pain* < L *panis* bread]

pants (pants) *n.pl. Chiefly U.S.* **1.** Trousers. **2.** Drawers; underpants. [Short for PANTALOONS]

pant·suit (pant/sōōt/) *n.* A suit worn by women for casual or sports wear, consisting of a jacket and matching slacks. Also **pants suit**.

panty hose A woman's undergarment designed as a pair of tights and made of lightweight, usually sheer, material such as nylon.

pan·ty·waist (pan/tē·wāst/) *n.* **1.** A child's waist with buttons on which to fasten short pants. **2.** *Slang* An effeminate young man.

Pan·urge (pan·ûrj/) In Rabelais' *Gargantua and Pantagruel*, the boon companion of Pantagruel.

Pa·nyush·kin (pä·nyōōsh/kyin), **Aleksandr Semenovich**, born 1905, Soviet diplomat.

Pan·za (pan/zə, *Sp.* pän/thä), **Sancho** See SANCHO PANZA.

pan·zer (pan/zər, *Ger.* pän/tsər) *adj.* Armored; also, using armored tanks or mechanized troops: a *panzer* division. [< G, armor plating < MHG *panzier* < OF *pancier* < Ital. *panzia* belly < L *pantex*. Cf. PAUNCH.]

Pão de A·çú·car (poun thi ə·sōō/kar) The Portuguese name for SUGAR LOAF MOUNTAIN.

Pa·o·lo (pä/ō·lō), died 1285?, lover of Francesca da Rimini.

Pao·ting (bou/ting/) A city in Hopeh Province, NE China;

pop. 350,000 (1970). Also **Pao/-ting/**.

pap¹ (pap) *n.* **1.** *Archaic* A teat; nipple. **2.** A hill or other object having a conical shape. [ME *pappe*, appar. of Scand. origin. Cf. Lithuanian *papas*.]

pap² (pap) *n.* **1.** Any soft food for babies. **2.** *Slang* The fees, favors, and privileges of public office. [Prob. akin to L *pappa*. Cf. MDu. *pappe*.]

pa·pa¹ (pä/pə, pə·pä/) *n.* Father: used familiarly. [< F < L < Gk. *papas*, child's word for father]

pa·pa² (pä/pä) *n.* **1.** The bishop of Rome; the pope. **2.** In the Greek Church, the patriarch of Alexandria; also, a parish priest. [< Med.L < Gk. *papas* father. Doublet of POPE.]

pa·pa·cy (pā/pə·sē) *n. pl.* **·cies** **1.** The dignity, office, or jurisdiction of the pope. **2.** The succession of popes and the administration of affairs in the Roman Catholic Church. **3.** The period during which a pope is in office. [< Med.L *papatia* < *papa*. See PAPA².]

Pa·pa·cy (pā/pə·sē) *n.* The Roman Catholic system of church government.

pa·pa·in (pə·pā/in, pā/pə·in) *n.* *Biochem.* A vegetable enzyme derived from the fruit of the papaya, used in medicine as a digestant. [< PAPA(YA) + -IN]

pa·pal (pā/pəl) *adj.* **1.** Of, pertaining to, or ordered by the pope. **2.** Of or pertaining to the papacy. **3.** Of or pertaining to the Roman Catholic Church. [< OF < Med.L *papalis* belonging to the pope < *papa*. See PAPA².]

Papal cross A cross having three crossbars or transoms, the top one the shortest and the bottom one the longest. For illustration see CROSS.

papal delegate Internuncio (def. 1).

Papal States See STATES OF THE CHURCH.

pa·pav·er·a·ceous (pə·pav/ə·rā/shəs) *adj.* *Bot.* Pertaining or belonging to a widely distributed family (*Papaveraceae*) of herbs that includes the poppy. [< NL *papaveraceae* (< L *papaver* poppy) + -OUS]

pa·pav·er·ine (pə·pav/ə·rēn, -ər·in, pə·pā/və·rin) *n.* *Chem.* A white, odorless, tasteless, crystalline alkaloid, $C_{20}H_{21}O_4N$, obtained from opium and used in medicine to relieve spasms of the smooth muscles. Also **pa·pav/er·in** (pə·pav/ər·in, pə·pā/və·rin). [< L *papaver* poppy + -INE²]

pa·paw (pə·pô/, pô/pô) *n.* **1.** The fleshy, edible fruit of a North American shrub or small tree (*Asimina triloba*). **2.** The tree bearing this fruit. Also called *custard apple*: also spelled *pawpaw*. [< PAPAYA]

pa·pa·ya (pə·pä/yä, pə·pī/ə) *n.* **1.** The yellow, melonlike fruit of a tropical American evergreen tree (*Carica papaya*), valued for its flavor and nutritious qualities. **2.** The tree bearing this fruit. [< Sp. and Pg.; ult. of Carib origin]

Pa·pe·e·te (pä/pā·ā/tā, pə·pē/tē) The capital of French Polynesia, a port on Tahiti; pop. 22,278 (est. 1967).

Pa·pen (pä/pən), **Franz von**, 1879–1969, German diplomat.

pa·per (pā/pər) *n.* **1.** A substance made from pulp obtained from rags, wood, bark, or other cellulose materials, usually formed into thin sheets for writing, printing, wrapping, covering walls, etc. **2.** A sheet of this material, especially when written or printed. **3.** Something similar in appearance to paper, as papyrus or papier-mâché. **4.** Wallpaper. **5.** A small paper wrapper or card holding a limited number or amount: a *paper* of pins. **6.** A printed or written document. **7.** A newspaper; journal. **8.** A written discourse or treatise: to present a *paper* before a learned society. **9.** In schools and colleges, a piece of written work, as an assignment, a report, an examination, etc. **10.** *pl.* A collection of letters, diaries, and other writings, especially by one person: the Jefferson *papers*. **11.** *pl.* Personal documents or identification; credentials. **12.** *pl.* A ship's papers (which see). **13.** In business, written or printed pledges to pay, that are negotiable. **14.** *Slang* Collectively, free orders of admission to a place of amusement; also, an audience so admitted. **15.** *pl. U.S.* Documents leading to naturalization: see FIRST PAPERS, SECOND PAPERS. **— on paper 1.** In written or printed form. **2.** In theory, as distinguished from fact. **— v.t. 1.** To cover with wallpaper. **2.** To fold or enclose in paper. **3.** To supply with paper. **4.** *Slang* To issue free tickets of admission to (a place of amusement). **— adj. 1.** Made of paper. **2.** Existing only in writing; not actual; unsubstantial: *paper* profits. **Abbr.** *pa., pr.* [< OF *papier* < L *papyrus*. Doublet of PAPYRUS.] **— pa/per·y** *adj.*

pa·per·back (pā/pər·bak/) *adj.* Of books, having a flexible paper cover or binding. **— n.** A book so bound.

paper birch See under BIRCH.

paper clip A metal clasp for holding sheets of paper together.

pa·per·er (pā/pər·ər) *n.* One who applies wallpaper.

paper gold See under SPECIAL DRAWING RIGHTS.

PAPAYA
(Tree 15 to 25
feet high)

pa·per·hang·er (pā′pər·hang′ər) *n.* One whose business is to cover walls, etc., with paper. — **pa′per·hang′ing** *n.*

pa·per·knife (pā′pər·nīf′) *n. pl.* **·knives** (-nīvz′) A blade of bone or other hard substance for cutting open the leaves of books, creasing paper, etc.

paper money Currency consisting of paper imprinted with certain fixed values issued by a government or by authorized banks for circulation as a substitute for metallic money.

paper nautilus One of a genus (*Argonauta*) of cephalopods having delicate shells: also called *argonaut.*

paper profit In finance, a profit that would be realized if a stock were sold.

paper wasp Any of various social wasps, as the hornets, that build nests of a material resembling paper.

pa·per·weight (pā′pər·wāt′) *n.* A small, heavy object, often ornamental, placed on loose papers to secure them.

pa·per·work (pā′pər·wûrk′) *n.* Work involving the preparation or handling of reports, letters, forms, etc.

pap·e·terie (pap′ə·trē, *Fr.* pàp·trē′) *n.* A box or case containing writing materials. [< F < *papetier* papermaker < OF *papier* paper]

Paph·la·go·ni·a (paf′lə·gō′nē·ə) An ancient country and Roman province in northern Asia Minor, on the Black Sea.

Pa·phos (pā′fos) An ancient city in SW Cyprus, considered sacred to Aphrodite. — **Pa′phi·an** (-fē·ən) *adj. & n.*

pa·pier-mâ·ché (pā′pər·mə·shā′, *Fr.* pà·pyā·mà·shā′) *n.* A material consisting of paper pulp mixed with size, paste, oil, resin, etc., or from sheets of paper glued and pressed together, that can be molded into various shapes when wet and that becomes hard and tough when dry. [< F *papier* paper + *mâché,* pp. of *mâcher* to chew < L *masticare*]

pa·pil·i·o·na·ceous (pə·pil′ē·ō·nā′shəs) *adj. Bot.* **1.** Shaped like a butterfly, as the flowers of the pea and other leguminous plants. **2.** Of or belonging to a subgroup (*Papilionaceae*) of leguminous plants having such flowers. [< NL *papilionaceus* < L *papilio, -onis* butterfly]

pa·pil·la (pə·pil′ə) *n. pl.* **·pil·lae** (-pil′ē) **1.** *Anat.* **a** The nipple. **b** Any small nipplelike process of connective tissue, as on the tongue or at the root of a hair. For illustration see HAIR. **2.** *Bot.* A small nipple-shaped projection on a flower or leaf. [< L, dim. of *papula* swelling, pimple]

pap·il·la·ry (pap′ə·ler′ē) *adj.* **1.** Of, pertaining to, or having the nature of a papilla or papillae. **2.** Provided with many papillae.

pap·il·lo·ma (pap′ə·lō′mə) *n. pl.* **·ma·ta** (-mə·tə) *Pathol.* An abnormality of the skin or of various mucous membranes consisting of tumorous outgrowths from hypertrophied papillae, as corns, warts, etc. [< PAPILLA]

pap·il·lon (pap′ə·lon) *n.* A breed of toy spaniel having large fringed ears resembling the wings of a butterfly. [< F, butterfly < L *papilio, -onis*]

pap·il·lose (pap′ə·lōs) *adj.* Having many papillae. [< NL *papillosus* < L *papilla*] — **pap′il·los′i·ty** (-los′ə·tē) *n.*

pap·il·lote (pap′ə·lōt) *n. French* A small paper encircling the end of the bone of a chop or cutlet when served. [< F < *papillon* butterfly]

pa·pist (pā′pist) *n.* An adherent of the papacy; a Roman Catholic: usually a disparaging term. [< MF *papiste* or L *papista* < *papa.* See PAPA².]

pa·pis·ti·cal (pə·pis′ti·kəl) *adj.* Of or pertaining to the doctrines of the Roman Catholic Church or to the papal system: a disparaging term. Also **pa·pis′tic.** — **pa·pis′try** (pā′pis·trē) *n.*

pa·poose (pa·pōōs′) *n.* A North American Indian infant or small child. Also **pap·poose′.** [< Algonquian (Narragansett) *papoos* child]

Pap·pen·heim (päp′ən·hīm), **Count Gottfried Heinrich zu,** 1594–1632, German general in the Thirty Years' War.

pap·pus (pap′əs) *n. pl.* **pap·pi** (pap′ī) *Bot.* The peculiar limb on the calyx of a floret of a flower of the composite family, consisting either of a downy tuft of hairs, as in thistles, or of teeth, scales, bristles, or awns. [< NL < Gk. *pappos* grandfather] — **pap′pose** (-ōs), **pap′pous** (-əs) *adj.*

pap·py¹ (pap′ē) *adj.* **·pi·er, ·pi·est** Resembling pap; pulpy.

pap·py² (pap′ē) *n. pl.* **·pies** Papa; father. [Dim. of PAPA¹]

pa·pri·ka (pa·prē′kə, pap′rə·kə) *n.* A condiment made from the ripe fruit of a mild variety of red pepper (*Capsicum frutescens*). Also **pa·pri′ca.** [< Magyar, red pepper < Gk. *peperi* pepper]

Pap test *Pathol.* A method of detecting uterine cancer and precancerous conditions by use of a vaginal smear. Also **Pap smear test.** [after George N. *Papinicolaou,* ? 1884–1962, U.S. physician born in Greece]

Pap·u·a (pä′pōō·ə, pap′ōō·ə) See NEW GUINEA.

Papua, Gulf of An inlet of the Coral Sea in SE New Guinea.

Papua, Territory of An Australian Territory comprising SE New Guinea and adjacent islands, and governed in an administrative union with the Trust Territory of New Guinea; 90,540 sq. mi.; pop. 648,000 (1969); capital, Port Moresby.

Papua and New Guinea, Territory of An administrative union of the Trust Territory of New Guinea and the Territory of Papua, established 1949; capital, Port Moresby.

Pap·u·an (pä′pōō·ən, pap′ōō·ən) *adj.* Of or pertaining to the Island of Papua or New Guinea, or to the Papuan peoples. — *n.* A member of any of the dark peoples inhabiting the Melanesian Archipelago from Fiji westward to the Aru Islands, including New Guinea or Papua.

pap·u·la (pap′yə·lə) *n. pl.* **·lae** (-lē) *Pathol.* An isolated pimple. Also **pap′ule** (-yōōl). [< L, pimple] — **pap′u·lan** *adj.*

pap·y·ra·ceous (pap′ə·rā′shəs) *adj.* Like paper; papery.

pa·py·rus (pə·pī′rəs) *n. pl.* **·ri** (-rī) **1.** A tall rushlike aquatic plant (*Cyperus papyrus*) of the sedge family, found in Palestine, Ethiopia, etc., and formerly common in Egypt. **2.** A type of writing paper made by the ancient Egyptians from the pith and the long tough stems of this plant. **3.** A manuscript written on this material. [< L < Gk. *papyros.* Doublet of PAPER.]

par (pär) *n.* **1.** An accepted standard or level used for comparison: usually preceded by *on* or *upon:* His work is on a *par* with that of the other students. **2.** The normal average in amount, quality, or degree: His health is up to *par.* **3.** In commerce, the state of equality between the nominal, or face, value and the market value of shares of stock, bonds, bills of exchange, etc. They are said to be at (or up to) *par* when exchangeable at face value in money, above *par* when the market price is greater, and below *par* when less than the face value: also *parity.* **4.** In golf, the number of strokes required to hole out when the hole is quite skillfully played. Par for a course is the sum of pars for the individual holes. — *adj.* **1.** Normal; average. **2.** In commerce, equal to the standard; having the face value normal. [< L, equal]

par. 1. Paragraph. **2.** Parallel. **3.** Parenthesis. **4.** Parish.

pa·ra (pä·rä′, pä′rä) *n.* **1.** A Turkish coin and monetary unit equivalent to ¹⁄₄₀ piaster. **2.** A Yugoslavian coin and monetary unit, the hundredth part of a dinar. [< Turkish and Persian *pārah* piece]

para-¹ *prefix* **1.** Beside; nearby; along with: *paradigm.* **2.** Beyond; aside from; amiss: *paradox.* **3.** *Chem.* **a** An isomeric or polymeric modification of: *paraformaldehyde.* **b** A modification of a compound similar to (not necessarily isomeric or polymeric): *paramorphine.* **c** A benzene derivative in which the substituted atoms or radicals occupy positions directly opposite each other in the ring: *paradichlorobenzene.* **Abbr.** p-. **4.** *Med.* **a** A functionally disordered or diseased condition: *paraplegia.* **b** In an accessory or secondary capacity: *parasympathetic.* **c** Similar to but not identical with a true condition or form: *paratyphoid.* Also, before vowels and *h,* usually **par-.** [< Gk. *para* beside]

para-² *combining form* Shelter or protection against: *parasol.* [< Ital. *para,* imperative of *parare* to defend < L, to prepare]

Pa·rá (pä·rä′) **1.** The eastern estuary of the Amazon; about 200 mi. long, 40 mi. wide at its mouth. **2.** A State in northern Brazil; 469,778 sq. mi.; pop. 1,872,000 (est. 1967); capital, Belém. **3.** A former name for BELÉM.

Para. Paraguay.

par·a·a·mi·no·ben·zo·ic acid (par′ə·ə·mē′nō·ben·zō′ik, -am′ə·nō-) *Biochem.* A colorless crystalline compound, C₇H₇NO₂, forming part of the vitamin B complex, present in yeast and also made synthetically. **Abbr.** *paba,* PABA.

par·a·bi·o·sis (par′ə·bī·ō′sis) *n. Biol.* A fusion of two individuals, either naturally, as in Siamese twins, or by experimental surgery, with a sharing of circulatory and other physiological functions. — **par′a·bi·ot′ic** (-ot′ik) *adj.*

par·a·blast (par′ə·blast) *n. Biol.* The nutritive yolk of a meroblastic egg. — **par′a·blas′tic** *adj.*

par·a·ble (par′ə·bəl) *n.* A short narrative making a moral or religious point by comparison with natural or homely things. — **Syn.** See ALLEGORY. [< OF *parabole* < LL *parabola* allegory, speech < Gk. *parabolē* a placing side by side, a comparison < *para* beside + *ballein* to throw. Doublet of PALAVER, PARABOLA, PAROLE.]

pa·rab·o·la (pə·rab′ə·lə) *n. Math.* The locus of a point moving in a plane so that its distances from a fixed point (focus) and a fixed straight line (directrix) are equal; the curve formed by the edges of a plane when cutting through a right circular cone at an angle parallel to one of its sides. [< L *parabola* a placing beside < Gk. *parabolē.* Doublet of PALAVER, PARABLE, PAROLE.]

par·a·bol·ic (par′ə·bol′ik) *adj.* **1.** Pertaining to or having the nature of a parable. **2.** Pertaining to or having the form of a parabola. Also **par′a·bol′i·cal.** [< LL *parabolicus* < LGk. *parabolikos* figurative < *parabolē.* See PARABLE.] — **par′a·bol′i·cal·ly** *adv.*

pa·rab·o·lize (pə·rab′ə·līz) *v.t.* **·lized, ·liz·ing 1.** To relate in parable form. **2.** *Math.* To give the form of a parabola to.

pa·rab·o·loid (pə·rab′ə·loid) *n. Math.* A quadratic surface or solid generated by the rotation of a parabola about its axis. — **pa·rab′o·loi′dal** *adj.*

Par·a·cel·sus (par′ə·sel′səs) Pseudonym of **Theophrastus von Ho·hen·heim** (hō′ən·hīm), 1493–1541, Swiss physician and alchemist. — **Par′a·cel′si·an** *adj.*

par·a·cen·tric (par′ə·sen′trik) *adj.* Directed to or from the center: said of motion. Also **par′a·cen′tri·cal.**

par·a·chor (par′ə·kôr) *n. Chem.* A function expressing the relationship between the surface tension, density, and molecular weight of a given compound, proportional to the molecular volume. [< PARA-¹ + Gk. *chōros* space]

par·a·chute (par'ə-shoot) *n.* **1.** A large, expanding, umbrella-shaped apparatus for retarding the speed of a body descending through the air, especially from an airplane. **2.** *Zool.* A patagium. — *v.* **·chut·ed, ·chut·ing** *v.t.* **1.** To land (troops, materiel, etc.) by means of parachutes. **2.** *Canadian* In politics, to enter a candidate into an election in a constituency of which he is not a resident. — *v.i.* **3.** To descend by parachute. [< F PARA-² + *chute* fall] — **par'a·chut·ist** *n.*

parachute troops Troops organized and trained to parachute into battle, often behind enemy lines, from transport aircraft: also called *paratroops.*

par·a·clete (par'ə-klēt) *n.* One called to the aid of another; an advocate. — **the Paraclete** The Holy Spirit as a helper or comforter. [< OF *paraclet* < LL *paracletus* < LGk. *paraklētos* comforter, advocate < *parakalein* to call to one's aid < *para-* to + *kalein* to call]

pa·rade (pə-rād') *n.* **1.** A procession or march for ceremony or display. **2.** A marshaling and maneuvering of troops for display or official inspection. **3.** A ground where military reviews are held. **4.** A promenade or public walk; also, the persons promenading. **5.** Pompous show, ostenation. — **on parade** On display. — *v.* **·rad·ed, ·rad·ing** *v.t.* **1.** To walk or march through or about: to *parade* the streets. **2.** To display or show off ostentatiously; flaunt. **3.** To cause to assemble for military parade or review. — *v.i.* **4.** To march formally or with display. **5.** To walk in public for the purpose of showing oneself. **6.** To assemble in military order for inspection or review. [< MF < Sp. *parada* stopping place, exercise ground < *parar* to prepare < L *parare*]

parade rest A formal position of rest, with or without rifle, in which soldiers stand without moving or speaking.

par·a·di·chlo·ro·ben·zene (par'ə-dī-klôr'ō-ben'zēn, -klō'rō-) *n. Chem.* A white, volatile, crystalline compound, $C_6H_4Cl_2$, widely used as an insecticide.

par·a·digm (par'ə-dim, -dīm) *n. Gram.* **1.** An ordered list or table of all the inflected forms of a word or class of words, as of a particular declension, conjugation, etc. **2.** Any pattern or example. [< LL *paradigma* < Gk. *paradeigma* pattern < *para-* beside + *deiknynai* to show] — **par'a·dig·mat'ic** (-dig·mat'ik) *adj.*

par·a·dise (par'ə-dīs) *n.* **1.** Heaven, the ultimate abode of righteous souls; also, in Islam, the abode of the deceased faithful. **2.** The intermediate place or state where the souls of the saved await the Resurrection. **3.** A place of surpassing beauty. **4.** A state of rapture or great delight. [< F *paradis* < LL *paradisus* < Gk. *paradeisos* park < OPersian *pairidaēza* an enclosure, park < *pairi* around + *diz* to mould] — **par'a·di·sa'ic** (-di·sā'ik) or **·i·cal, par'a·dis'i·ac** (-dis'ē·ak) or **par'a·di·si·a·cal** (par'ə-di·sī'ə-kəl) *adj.*

Par·a·dise (par'ə-dīs) Eden.

Paradise Lost and **Paradise Regained** Epic poems by John Milton depicting the fall and redemption of man.

par·a·dos (par'ə-dos) *n.* An embankment, as behind a trench, for protection against gunfire from the rear. [< F < PARA-² + *dos* back < L *dorsam*]

par·a·dox (par'ə-doks) *n.* **1.** A statement seemingly absurd or contradictory, yet in fact true. **2.** A statement essentially self-contradictory, false, or absurd. **3.** One whose character or behavior is inconsistent or contradictory. **4.** *Rare* An opinion or statement conflicting with received opinion. [< F *paradoxe* < L *paradoxum* < Gk. *paradoxos* incredible < *para-* contrary to + *doxa* opinion < *dokein* to think] — **par'a·dox'i·cal** *adj.* — **par·a·dox'i·cal'i·ty** (-kal'ə-tē), **par'·a·dox'i·cal·ness** *n.* — **par'a·dox'i·cal·ly** *adv.*

par·a·drop (par'ə-drop) *n. Mil.* The dropping of supplies, equipment, etc., by parachute.

par·aes·the·sia (par'is-thē'zhə, -zhē-ə), etc. See PARESTHE-SIA, etc.

par·af·fin (par'ə-fin) *n. Chem.* **1.** A translucent, waxy mixture of hydrocarbons, inert to most chemical reagents, derived principally from the distillation of petroleum and widely used for candles, as a preservative, for waterproofing, etc. **2.** Any hydrocarbon of the methane series. — *v.t.* To treat or impregnate with paraffin. Also **par'af·fine** (-fin, -fēn). [< G < L *var(um)* too little + *affin(is)* related to; so named because it has little affinity for other substances]

paraffin series *Chem.* The methane series (which see).

paraffin wax Paraffin in its solid state.

par·a·for·mal·de·hyde (par'ə-fôr·mal'də-hīd) *n. Chem.* A white crystalline powder, $(CH_2O)_3$, obtained by concentrating formaldehyde, used as a disinfectant: also called *polyoxymethylene.*

par·a·gen·e·sis (par'ə-jen'ə·sis) *n. Mineral.* The development of minerals in contact in such manner as to show the order of formation of the individual crystals. Also **par'a·ge·ne'si·a** (-jə·nē'sē·ə). — **par'a·ge·net'ic** (-jə·net'ik) *adj.*

par·a·go·ge (par'ə·gō'jē) *n. Ling.* The addition of an un-

etymological sound or syllable at the end of a word without a change in meaning, as in *amongst, whilst,* etc. [< L < Gk. *paragōgē* < *para-* beyond + *agōgē* a leading < *agein* to lead] — **par'a·gog'ic** (-goj'ik) *adj.*

par·a·gon (par'ə-gon) *n.* **1.** A model or pattern of excellence, especially of a specific excellence: a *paragon* of manhood. **2.** *Printing* A size of type, 20-point. **3.** A round pearl of exceptional size. — *v.t. Archaic & Poetic* **1.** To match; equal. **2.** To surpass. **3.** To compare with. **4.** To hold up as a paragon. [< OF < Ital. *paragone* touchstone, prob. < Gk. *parakonan* to sharpen one thing against another < *para-* beside + *akonē* whetstone]

par·a·graph (par'ə-graf, -gräf) *n.* **1.** A distinct part or section of a written discourse, begun on a new and usually indented line and generally containing a unified statement on a particular point. Abbr. *par.* **2.** A short article, item, or comment, as in a newspaper. **3.** A mark (¶) used to indicate where a paragraph is to be begun, or as a reference mark. — *v.t.* **1.** To arrange in or into paragraphs. **2.** To comment on or express in a paragraph. [< OF *paragraphe* < LL *paragraphus* < Gk. *paragraphos*, orig., a short line in a text marking a break in sense < *para* beside + *graphein* to write] — **par'a·graph'er, par'a·graph'ist** *n.* — **par'a·graph'ic, par'a·graph'i·cal** *adj.*

par·a·graph·i·a (par'ə-graf'ē-ə) *n. Psychiatry* A mental disorder, generally due to cerebral injury, in which words or phrases other than those meant are written. [< NL < Gk. *para* beside + *graphein* to write]

Par·a·guay (par'ə-gwā, -gwī; *Sp.* pä-rä-gwī') **1.** A Republic in south central South America; 157,047 sq. mi.; pop. 2,400,-000 (est. 1970); capital, Asunción. **2.** A river in south central South America, flowing about 1,300 miles south to the Paraná.

Paraguay tea Maté.

par·a·hyp·no·sis (par'ə-hip·nō'sis) *n.* Abnormal sleep, as in so mnambulism. — **par'a·hyp·not'ic** (-not'ik) *adj.*

Pa·ra·í·ba (pä-rä-ē'vä) **1.** A State of NE Brazil; 21,831 sq. mi.; pop. 2,219,000 (est. 1967); capital, Jão Pessoa. **2.** A river in São Paulo and Rio de Janeiro states, flowing about 600 miles NE to the Atlantic: also **Paraíba do Sul** (thoo sool'). **3.** A river in Paraíba State, flowing about 180 miles NE to the Atlantic: also **Paraíba do Nor·te** (nôr'ti). Formerly **Pa·ra·hi'ba, Pa·ra·hy'ba.**

par·a·keet (par'ə-kēt) *n.* Any of certain small parrots, with long, wedge-shaped tails: also spelled *paraquet, paroquet, parrakeet, parroket, parroquet.* [< OF *paroquet* < Ital. *parrochetto* or Sp. *periquito*]

par·a·ki·ne·sia (par'ə-ki·nē'zhə, -zhē-ə) *n. Pathol.* Clumsy and unnatural body movements, caused by impairment of motor functions. Also **par'a·ki·ne'sis** (-nē'sis). [< NL < Gk. *para* beside + *kinēsis* movement] — **par'a·ki·net'ic** (-net'ik) *adj.*

par·al·de·hyde (pə-ral'də-hīd) *n. Chem.* A colorless, aromatic liquid, $C_6H_{12}O_3$, a polymer of acetaldehyde, used as a hypnotic and sedative.

par·a·leip·sis (par'ə-līp'sis) *n.* In rhetoric, a pretended suppression for effect of what is really said; a feigned omission, as in "not to mention his insufferable conceit." Also **par'a·lep'sis** (-lep'sis), **par'a·lip'sis** (-lip'sis). [< Gk., an omission < *paraleipein* < *para* beside + *leipein* to leave]

Par·a·li·pom·e·non (par'ə-li·pom'ə-non) *n.* The Douai Bible name for CHRONICLES.

par·al·lax (par'ə-laks) *n.* The apparent displacement of an object, especially of a star or other heavenly body, when it is viewed successively from two points not in the same line of sight. It is **diurnal** or **geocentric parallax** when the observer's change of position is caused by the earth's rotation on its axis, **annual** or **heliocentric parallax** when the change of position is caused by the earth's revolution around the sun. [< F *parallaxe* < Gk. *parallaxis* < *parallassein* to deviate < *para* beside + *allassein* to change]

par·al·lel (par'ə-lel) *adj.* **1.** Being a uniform distance away or apart throughout a certain area or extent: said of linear objects and flat surfaces: The floor is *parallel* to the ceiling. **2.** *Geom.* a Not meeting, however far extended: said of straight lines lying in the same plane, and of planes. **b** In projective geometry, meeting at infinity. **3.** Having a close resemblance or similar course; corresponding. **4.** *Music* **a** Denoting consecutive identical or similar intervals in the same two voices. **b** Denoting consecutive identical chords. **5.** *Electr.* Connected between like terminals, as a group of cells, condensers, etc. — *n.* **1.** An object or surface equidistant from another. **2.** *Geom.* A parallel line or plane. **3.** Essential likeness; correspondence. **4.** A counterpart; match. **5.** Comparison: to draw a *parallel* between two things. **6.** *Geog.* **a** Any of the circles imagined as drawn upon the earth's surface at right angles to its axis, every point on which marks a given latitude north or south of the equator. **b** A line on a map or chart representing such a circle. **7.** *Electr.* Connection between like terminals: usually in the phrase **in parallel:** also called *multiple.* **8.** *Mil.* A trench dug parallel to the line of a fortification. —*v.t.* ·**leled** or ·**lelled,** ·**lel·ing** or ·**lel·ling 1.** To place in parallel; make parallel. **2.** To be, go, or extend parallel to. **3.** To furnish with a parallel or equal; find a parallel to. **4.** To be a parallel to; correspond to. **5.** To compare; liken. —*adv.* In a parallel way or manner: often used with *with* or *to.* Abbr. *par.* [< MF *parallele* < L *parallelus* < Gk. *parallēlos* < *para* beside + *allēlos* one another]

parallel bars Two horizontal crossbars, parallel to each other and supported by upright posts, used for gymnastics.

par·al·lel·e·pi·ped (par′ə·lel′ə·pī′pid, -pĭp′id) *n.* A prism with six faces, each of which is a parallelogram. Also **par′al·lel′o·pi′ped, par′al·lel′e·pip′e·don, par′al·lel′o·pip′e·don** (-pĭp′ə·don, -pī′pə-). [< Gk. *parallēlepipedon* < *parallēlos* parallel + *epipedon* a plane surface < *epi-* upon + *pedon* ground]

par·al·lel·ism (par′ə·lel·iz′əm) *n.* **1.** The state or quality of being parallel; parallel relation or position. **2.** Essential likeness; similarity. **3.** A comparison. **4.** *Philos.* The doctrine that the relation between mind and matter is one of concomitant or parallel variation, and not of cause and effect. **5.** *Music* Frequent or characteristic use of parallel chords or intervals.

par·al·lel·o·gram (par′ə·lel′ə·gram) *n.*
1. *Geom.* A four-sided plane figure whose opposite sides are parallel and equal. **2.** Any area or object having such form. [< MF *parallélogramme* < L *parallelogrammum* < Gk. *parallēlogrammon,* orig. adj., bounded by parallel lines < *parallēlos* parallel + *grammē* line]

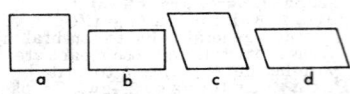

PARALLELOGRAMS
a Square. *b* Rectangle. *c* Rhombus.
d Rhomboid.

pa·ral·o·gism (pə·ral′ə·jiz′əm) *n.* False or illogical reasoning. —**Syn.** See FALLACY. [< MF *paralogisme* < LL *paralogismus* < Gk. *paralogismos < paralogizesthai* to reason falsely, ult. < *para* beside + *logos* word, reason] —**par·a·log·ic** (par′ə·loj′ik) or ·**i·cal** *adj.* —**pa·ral′o·gist** *n.*

pa·ral·y·sis (pə·ral′ə·sis) *n. pl.* ·**ses** (-sēz) **1.** *Pathol.* Partial or complete loss of motor function, especially voluntary motion, resulting from injury to the nervous system or to a muscular mechanism. **2.** Cessation or crippling of normal activities. [< L < Gk. < *paralyein* to disable < *para* beside + *lyein* to loose. Doublet of PALSY.]

paralysis a·gi·tans (aj′ə·tanz) *Pathol.* Parkinson's disease. [< L]

par·a·lyt·ic (par′ə·lit′ik) *adj.* **1.** Of or pertaining to paralysis. **2.** Affected with paralysis. —*n.* One affected with paralysis. [< OF *paralytique* < L *paralyticus* < Gk. *paralytikos* < *paralyein.* See PARALYSIS.]

par·a·lyze (par′ə·līz) *v.t.* ·**lyzed,** ·**lyz·ing 1.** To bring about paralysis in; make paralytic. **2.** To render powerless, ineffective, or inactive. [< F *paralyser,* back formation < *paralysie* palsy] —**par′a·lyz′er** *n.* —**par′a·ly·za′tion** *n.*

par·a·mag·net (par′ə·mag′net) *n.* A paramagnetic substance. [Back formation < PARAMAGNETIC]

par·a·mag·net·ic (par′ə·mag·net′ik) *Physics* Having a magnetic permeability greater than that of a vacuum yet less than that of a ferromagnetic substance or body.

Par·a·mar·i·bo (par′ə·mar′i·bō) The capital of Surinam, a port on the northern coast; pop. 110,867 (est. 1964).

par·a·mat·ta (par′ə·mat′ə) *n.* See PARRAMATTA.

par·a·me·ci·um (par′ə·mē′shē·əm, -sē·əm) *n. pl.* ·**ci·a** (-shē·ə, -sē·ə) Any of various species of ciliate protozoa (genus *Paramecium*), widely used in laboratory study, having a flattened, elongate body, and feeding by a primitive oral groove. [< NL < Gk. *paramēkēs* oblong, oval < *para* beside + *mēkos* length]

par·a·med·ic (par′ə·med′ik) *n.* A technician or other doctor's assistant trained in a variety of procedures, esp. in advanced first aid. [< PARA-¹ + MEDIC] —**par′a·med′i·cal** *adj.*

pa·ram·e·ter (pə·ram′ə·tər) *n. Math.* **1.** A constant whose values determine the operation or characteristics of a system. In $y = ax^2 + bx + c$, *a,* *b,* and *c* are the parameters of a family of parabolas. **2.** A variable *t,* such that each of a related system of variable may be expressed as a function of *t.* **3.** A fixed limit or guideline. [< NL < Gk. *para* beside + *metron* measure] —**par·a·met·ric** (par′ə·met′rik) *adj.*

par·a·mil·i·tar·y (par′ə·mil′ə·ter′ē) *adj.* Having a military structure although not officially military; capable of becoming, replacing, or supplementing a military force: said of certain political movements, etc. [< PARA-¹ + MILITARY]

par·am·ne·sia (par′am·nē′zhə, -zhē·ə) *n. Psychiatry* Distortion and falsification of memory, as the apparent memory of things not previously seen or experienced.

par·a·morph (par′ə·môrf) *n.* A crystal exhibiting paramorphism. —**par′a·mor′phic, par′a·mor′phous** *adj.*

par·a·mor·phine (par′ə·môr′fēn) *n. Chem.* Thebaine.

par·a·mor·phism (par′ə·môr′fiz·əm) *n. Mineral.* The alteration of one mineral to another having the same chemical composition but differing in molecular structure and physi-

cal properties. [< PARA-¹ + Gk. *morphē* form + -ISM]

par·a·mount (par′ə·mount) *adj.* **1.** Superior to all others; chief in importance. **2.** Having the highest authority or rank. —**Syn.** See DOMINANT. —*n.* A supreme lord; highest ruler. [< AF *paramont* above < OF *par* by (< L *per*) + *à mont* up, above < L *ad montem* to the hill] —**par′a·mount·ly** *adv.* —**par′a·mount·cy** *n.*

Par·a·mount (par′ə·mount) A city in SW California, near Los Angeles; pop. 34,734.

par·a·mour (par′ə·mŏŏr) *n.* A lover, especially one who unlawfully takes the place of a husband or wife. [< OF *par amour* with love < *par* by, with (< L *per* through) + *amour* love < L *amor*]

Pa·ra·ná (pä′rä·nä′) **1.** A State of southern Brazil; 77,717 sq. mi.; pop. 6,743,000 (est. 1967); capital, Curitiba. **2.** A river of SW Brazil and NE Argentina, flowing about 2,050 miles south to the Rio de la Plata. **3.** A city in eastern Argentina, on the Paraná; pop. 183,897 (est. 1956).

pa·rang (pä′räng) *n.* A short, heavy knife with a straight edge, used especially in Borneo. [< Malay *parang*]

par·a·noi·a (par′ə·noi′ə) *n. Psychiatry* A form of mental disorder characterized by well-systematized delusions of persecution or of grandeur, often without markedly affecting the rest of the personality. Also **par′a·noe′a** (-nē′ə). [< NL < Gk. *para* beside + *noos, nous* mind]

par·a·noi·ac (par′ə·noi′ak) *adj.* Relating to or affected by paranoia. —*n.* One affected by paranoia. Also **par′a·no′ic** (-nō′ik), **par′a·noe′ac** (-nē′ak).

par·a·noid (par′ə·noid) *adj.* Resembling or suggestive of paranoia. —*n.* One affected by paranoia.

par·a·nymph (par′ə·nimf) *n.* A best man or bridesmaid at a wedding. [< L *paranymphus* < Gk. *paranymphos* best man or, fem., bridesmaid < *para* beside + *nymphē* bride]

par·a·pet (par′ə·pit, -pet) *n.* **1.** A low wall about the edge of a roof, terrace, bridge, etc. **2.** A breastwork. —**Syn.** See BULWARK. [< MF, or < Ital. *parapetto* < *para-*² + *petto* breast < L *pectus* breast] —**par′a·pet·ed** *adj.*

par·aph (par′əf) *n.* A flourish made with the pen at the end of a signature, originally as a protection against forgery. [< F *paraphe* < Med.L *paraphus,* contr. of L *paragraphus.* See PARAGRAPH.]

par·a·pher·na·li·a (par′ə·fər·nā′lē·ə, -nāl′yə, -fə-) *n.pl.* **1.** Personal effects. **2.** A group of articles, especially as used in some activity; equipment; gear. **3.** *Law* Formerly, the personal belongings reserved to a wife over and above her dowry. [< Med.L *paraphernalia* (bona) a wife's own (goods) < Gk. *parapherna* < *para* beside + *phernē* bride's dowry]

par·a·phrase (par′ə·frāz) *n.* A restatement of the meaning of a passage, work, etc., as for clarity. —*v.t. & v.i.* ·**phrased,** ·**phras·ing** To express in or make a paraphrase. [< MF < L *paraphrasis* < Gk. < *paraphrazein* to tell the same thing in other words < *para* beside + *phrazein* to tell] —**par′a·phras′er, par′a·phrast** (-frast) *n.* —**par·a·phras′tic** or ·**ti·cal** *adj.* —**par·a·phras′ti·cal·ly** *adv.*

pa·raph·y·sis (pə·raf′ə·sis) *n. pl.* ·**ses** (-sēz) *Bot.* A sterile filamentous growth found among the reproductive organs in certain cryptogams. [< NL < Gk. *para* beside + *physis* growth]

par·a·ple·gi·a (par′ə·plē′jē·ə) *n. Pathol.* Paralysis of the lower half of the body, due to disease or injury of the spinal cord. Also **par′a·ple′gy** (-plē′jē). [< NL < Gk. *paraplēgia, paraplēxia* stroke on one side < *paraplēssein* to strike at the side < *para* beside + *plēssein* to strike] —**par·a·ple·gic** (par′ə·plē′jik, -plej′ik) *adj. & n.*

par·a·prax·is (par′ə·prak′sis) *n. Psychoanal.* A faulty action, blunder, or lapse, as a slip of the tongue, memory blocking, etc. Also **par′a·prax′i·a** (-prak′sē·ə). [< NL]

par·a·pro·fes·sion·al (par′ə·prə·fesh′ən·əl) *n.* One who assists professionals, as teachers, by performing tasks not requiring professional skills.

par·a·psy·chol·o·gy (par′ə·sī·kol′ə·jē) *n.* The study of extrasensory perception and related psychic phenomena.

pa·ra·quet (par′ə·ket) *n.* See PARAKEET.

Pa·rá rubber (pä·rä′) Rubber from the American rubber tree (*Hevea brasiliensis*). [after *Pará,* state in Brazil]

par·a·sang (par′ə·sang) *n.* An ancient Persian measure of length, varying from 2 to 4 miles. [< L *parasanga* < Gk. *parasangēs;* of Persian origin]

par·a·se·le·ne (par′ə·si·lē′nē) *n. pl.* ·**nae** (-nē) *Meteorol.* A luminous spot appearing on a lunar halo: also called *mock moon.* [< NL < Gk. *para* beside + *selēnē* moon]

par·a·shah (par′ə·shä) *n. pl.* ·**shoth** (-shōth) One of the fifty-four sections or lessons into which the Pentateuch is divided for weekly readings throughout the annual cycle, or one of the smaller sections read on festivals. [< Hebrew *pārāshāh* division < *pārash* to divide]

par·a·site (par′ə·sīt) *n.* **1.** *Biol.* An animal or plant that lives in or on another organism, the host, at whose expense it obtains nourishment and shelter. **2.** One who lives at another's expense without making proper return. **3.** In ancient Greece and Rome, one who secured a welcome at the tables of the rich in return for amusing his host. [< L *parasitus* < Gk. *parasitos,* lit., one who eats at another's table < *para* beside + *sitos* food] —**par′a·sit′i·cal·ly** *adv.*

parasite drag *Aeron.* The portion of the drag of an aircraft caused by the configuration of the nonlifting surfaces.
par·a·sit·ic (par′ə·sit′ik) *adj.* **1.** Pertaining to or designating a parasite. **2.** Designating an influence, effect, or phenomenon that subtracts from the efficiency of a system, design, etc. Also **par′a·sit′i·cal.** — *n.* A parasitic influence, effect, etc.
par·a·sit·i·cide (par′ə·sit′ə·sīd) *n.* An agent or preparation that destroys parasites. — *adj.* Efficacious for destroying parasites: also **par·a·sit′i·ci′dal.**
par·a·sit·ism (par′ə·sī′tiz·əm) *n.* **1.** The condition of being a parasite; parasitic mode of existence. **2.** The relationship, usually injurious, of a parasite to its host. **3.** *Pathol.* A diseased condition caused by parasites; infestation by parasites.
par·a·si·tol·o·gy (par′ə·sī·tol′ə·jē) *n.* The scientific study of parasites and parasitism. —**par′a·si′to·log′i·cal** (-sī′tə·loj′i·kəl) *adj.* —**par′a·si·tol′o·gist** *n.*
par·a·sol (par′ə·sôl, -sol) *n.* A small, light umbrella carried by women, used as protection against the sun. [< MF < Ital. *parasole* < *para-* para-² + *sole* sun]
pa·ras·ti·chy (pə·ras′tə·kē) *n. pl.* **·chies** *Bot.* A form of phyllotaxis in certain plants in which closely crowded leaves or scales are disposed in secondary spirals around the stem or principal axis. [< PARA¹ + Gk. *-stichia* < *stichos* row]
par·a·sym·pa·thet·ic (par′ə·sim′pə·thet′ik) *adj. Anat.* Denoting the part of the autonomic nervous system that consists of nerves originating in the cranial and sacral regions, and that has among its functions the constriction of the pupil, the slowing of the heart, the dilation of the blood vessels, and the stimulation of the digestive and genitourinary systems: also *craniosacral.* See SYMPATHETIC.
par·a·syn·ap·sis (par′ə·si·nap′sis) *n. Biol.* In meiosis, the side-by-side conjugation of chromosomes. Also **par′a·syn′· de·sis** (-sin′də·sis).
par·a·syn·the·sis (par′ə·sin′thə·sis) *n. Gram.* The formation of words by both combination and derivation; especially, the creation of a derivative word by compounding with a particle, as in *downfallen.* —**par′a·syn·thet′ic** (-sin·thet′ik) *adj.*
par·a·syph·i·lis (par′ə·sif′ə·lis) *n. Pathol.* A diseased condition following syphilis, but not in itself syphilitic. —**par′· a·syph′i·lit′ic** (-sif′ə·lit′ik) *adj.*
par·a·tax·is (par′ə·tak′sis) *n. Gram.* Independent arrangement of clauses, phrases, etc., without connectives, as in "I die, I faint, I fail." Opposed to *hypotaxis.* [< Gk., lit., a placing side by side < *paratassein* to place side by side < *para* beside + *tassein* to arrange] —**par′a·tac′tic** (-tak′tik) or **·ti·cal** *adj.* —**par′a·tac′ti·cal·ly** *adv.*
par·a·thy·roid (par′ə·thī′roid) *adj. Anat.* **1.** Lying near the thyroid gland. **2.** Of or pertaining to the parathyroid glands. — *n.* One of the parathyroid glands.
parathyroid glands Any of the several, usually four, small, bean-shaped glands found typically in pairs near the lateral lobes of the thyroid gland and serving to control the amount of calcium in the blood.
par·a·troop·er (par′ə·trōō′pər) *n.* A member of the parachute troops.
par·a·troops (par′ə·trōōps) *n.pl.* Parachute troops (which see).
par·a·ty·phoid (par′ə·tī′foid) *Pathol. adj.* Of or pertaining to paratyphoid fever. — *n.* Paratyphoid fever.
paratyphoid fever *Pathol.* An infectious disease having symptoms resembling those of typhoid fever, but caused by a different bacterium.
par·a·vane (par′ə·vān) *n.* **1.** A torpedo-shaped underwater device equipped with sharp projecting teeth for cutting the moorings of sunken mines. **2.** A similar device loaded with high explosives for use against submarines.
par a·vi·on (pár′ á·vyön′) *French* By plane: a label affixed to air mail.
par·boil (pär′boil′) *v.t.* **1.** To boil partially. **2.** To make uncomfortable with heat. [< OF *parboillir* < LL *perbullire* to boil thoroughly < *per-* through + *bullire* to bubble]
par·buck·le (pär′buk′əl) *n.* **1.** A device for raising or lowering a heavy cylindrical object, as a cask or log, along an inclined plane, consisting of a doubled rope securely looped at the top of the incline and passed around the object, the free ends being hauled in or played out as desired. **2.** A sling for vertically raising a heavy object by passing a doubled rope around it, the free ends being pulled through the loop. — *v.t.* **·led, ·ling** To hoist or lower by means of a parbuckle. [Earlier *parbunkle*; origin uncertain]
Par·cae (pär′sē) *n.pl.* In Roman mythology, the three Fates.
par·cel (pär′səl) *n.* **1.** Something that is wrapped up; package. **2.** A quantity of some commodity put up for sale; lot. **3.** An indefinite number of persons or things assembled together. **4.** A distinct portion of land. **5.** A small, distinct part of anything, especially an essential part: now only in phrase **part and parcel.** — Syn. See PORTION. — *v.t.* **par· celed** or **·celled, par·cel·ing** or **·cel·ling** **1.** To divide or dis-

tribute in parts or shares: usually with *out.* **2.** To make up a parcel or parcels. **3.** *Naut.* To wrap or cover (a rope) with canvas strips. — *adj. & adv.* Part; partly. [< F *parcelle* < L *particula,* dim. of *pars, partis* part]
parcel post A postal service for the conveying and delivering of parcels not exceeding a specified weight and size. Also **parcels post.** Abbr. *p.p., P.P.*
par·ce·nar·y (pär′sə·ner′ē) *n. Law* Coparcenary (which see).
par·ce·ner (pär′sə·nər) *n. Law* Coparcener (which see).
parch (pärch) *v.t.* **1.** To make extremely dry; shrivel with heat. **2.** To make very thirsty. **3.** To dry (corn, peas, etc.) by exposing to great heat; roast slightly. **4.** To dry up or shrivel by exposing to cold. — *v.t.* **5.** To become dry; shrivel with heat. **6.** To become dry with thirst. [ME *parchen*; ult. origin uncertain]
Par·chee·si (pär·chē′zē) *n.* A board game derived from pachisi: a trade name. Also **par·chee′si, par·che′si, par·chi′si.**
parch·ment (pärch′mənt) *n.* **1.** The skin of sheep, goats, and other animals prepared and polished with pumice stone, used as a material for writing or painting upon. **2.** A formal writing or manuscript on this material. **3.** Any of several types of paper made in imitation of parchment, especially that used in stationery or lamp shades. [< OF *parchemin* < fusion of *parthica (pellis),* lit., parthian (skin) + LL *pergamenum* parchment < L *pergamenus* of Pergamum, the city where it was first used instead of papyrus for writing on]
pard¹ (pärd) *n. Archaic* A leopard or panther. [< OF *parde* < L *pardus* < Gk. *pardos* < *pardalis.* Cf. Persian *pars* panther.]
pard² (pärd) *n. Slang* A partner. [Short for PARDNER]
par·di (pär·dē′) *adv. & interj. Archaic* By God; verily: formerly a form of profanity: also spelled *perdie, perdy.* Also **par·dee′, par·die′, par·dy′.** [< OF *par de* by God!]
pard·ner (pärd′nər) *n. U.S. Dial.* Chum; friend. [Alter. of PARTNER]
par·don (pär′dən) *v.t.* **1.** To remit the penalty of (an offense, insult, etc.). **2.** To forgive (a person) for an offense. **3.** To grant courteous allowance for or to. — *n.* **1.** The act of pardoning; forgiveness. **2.** Courteous forbearance. **3.** *Law* **a** The remission of guilt for a crime. **b** An official warrant declaring such a remission. **4.** In the Roman Catholic Church, an indulgence. [< OF *pardon* < *pardoner* < LL *perdonare* to grant < *per-* through + *donare* to give] —**par′don·a·ble** *adj.* —**par′don·a·bly** *adv.*
— Syn. (verb) **1, 2.** *Pardon, excuse, overlook, forgive,* and *remit* mean to forgo punishment of an offense or an offender. *Pardon* implies the authority to punish: the governor *pardoned* the confessed embezzler. We *excuse* slight offenses, such as breaches of courtesy, or grosser offenses that are not criminal: the company *excused* the watchman for falling asleep. To *overlook* is to ignore a just cause for censure or resentment: to *overlook* a pupil's occasional disobedience. *Forgive* implies the abandoning not only of claim to redress or retribution, but also of ill will against the offender: let us *forgive* our enemies. *Remit* is a close synonym of *pardon,* but used mostly in legal or ecclesiastical context: the judge *remitted* half the sentence; the priest *remitted* his sins. See ABSOLVE. — Ant. punish. — (noun) **1.** amnesty, absolution.
par·don·er (pär′dən·ər) *n.* **1.** One who pardons. **2.** In the Middle Ages, a layman commissioned to sell ecclesiastical indulgences.
par·don·nez-moi (pår·dôn′á·mwå′) *French* Pardon me.
pare (pâr) *v.t.* **pared, par·ing** **1.** To cut off the covering layer or part of. **2.** To cut off or trim away (a covering layer or part): often with *off* or *away.* **3.** To diminish, especially gradually or little by little. [< OF *parer* to prepare, trim < L *parare*] —**par′er** *n.*
Pa·ré (pá·rā′), **Ambroise,** 1517?–90, French surgeon, one of the founders of modern surgery.
pa·re·cious (pə·rē′shəs), etc. See PAROECIOUS, etc.
par·e·gor·ic (par′ə·gôr′ik, -gor′ik) *n. Med.* A camphorated tincture of opium, used primarily to treat diarrhea. [< LL *paregoricus* < Gk. *parēgorikos* < *parēgoros* soothing < *para* beside + *agoros* speaking < *agora* assembly, market place]
paren. *(pl.* parens.) Parenthesis.
pa·ren·chy·ma (pə·reng′ki·mə) *n.* **1.** *Biol.* The essential functioning cellular substance of an animal organ, as distinguished from connective tissue. **2.** *Bot.* The soft cell tissue of higher plants, as found in stem pith and in the pulp of fruits. Also **pa·ren′chyme** (-kīm). [< NL < Gk., lit., something poured in beside < *para* beside + *enchyma* infusion] —**par·en·chym·a·tous** (par′eng·kim′ə·təs) *adj.*
par·ent (pâr′ənt) *n.* **1.** A father or mother. **2.** One exercising the functions of a father or mother. **3.** A progenitor; forefather. **4.** Any organism that generates another. **5.** Source; cause. [< OF < L *parens, -entis* parent, ancestor, orig. ppr. of *parere* to beget]
par·ent·age (pâr′ən·tij) *n.* **1.** Descent or derivation from parents; lineage; origin. **2.** Derivation from a source or origin. **3.** Parenthood. [< OF]
pa·ren·tal (pə·ren′təl) *adj.* **1.** Of, pertaining to, or characteristic of a parent. **2.** *Genetics* Pertaining to or denoting

the generation from whose crossbreeding hybrids are produced. [< L *parentalis* < *parere*] — **pa·ren'tal·ly** *adv.*

par·en·ter·al (par·en'tər·əl) *adj. Med.* Pertaining to or denoting a mode of assimilation other than through the alimentary canal, as intravenous or intramuscular. [< Gk. *para* beside + *enteron* intestine]

pa·ren·the·sis (pə·ren'thə·sis) *n. pl.* **·ses** (-sēz) **1.** Either or both of the upright curved lines () used to enclose an interjected, explanatory, or qualifying remark or mathematical quantities to be considered as a single quantity. **2.** *Gram.* A word, phrase, or clause inserted in a sentence that is grammatically complete without it, set off usually by commas, dashes, or upright curved lines. **3.** An intervening episode or incident; interval. *Abbr. par., paren.* [< Med.L < Gk. < *parentithenai* to put in beside < *para* beside + *en* in + *tithenai* to place]

pa·ren·the·size (pə·ren'thə·sīz) *v.t.* **·sized, ·siz·ing 1.** To insert as a parenthetical statement. **2.** To insert parentheses in. **3.** To place within parentheses (def. 1).

par·en·thet·i·cal (par'ən·thet'i·kəl) *adj.* **1.** Thrown in; episodic: *parenthetical* remarks. **2.** Abounding in parentheses; also, given to using parentheses. [< Med.L *parenthet-icus* + -AL] — **par'en·thet'i·cal·ly** *adv.*

par·ent·hood (par'ənt·hŏŏd) *n.* The condition or relation of being a parent.

parent language A language from which another language has sprung.

pa·re·sis (pə·rē'sis, par'ə·sis) *n. pl.* **·ses** (-sēz) *Pathol.* **1.** Partial paralysis affecting muscular motion but not sensation. **2.** General paresis (which see). [< NL < Gk., a letting go < *parienai* to let go < *para* beside + *hienai* to let go]

par·es·the·sia (par'is·thē'zhə, -zhē·ə) *n. Pathol.* Abnormal or perverted sensation, as itching, tingling, or prickling of the skin: also spelled *paraesthesia.* Also **par'es·the'sis.** [< NL] — **par'es·thet'ic** (-thet'ik) *adj.*

pa·ret·ic (pə·ret'ik, -rē'tik) *adj.* Resulting from or afflicted with paresis or general paresis. — *n.* One who suffers from paresis or general paresis. [< NL *pareticus* < Gk. *paretos* relaxed] — **pa·ret'i·cal·ly** *adv.*

Pa·re·to (pä·rā'tō), **Vilfredo,** 1848–1923, Italian economist and sociologist.

pa·re·u (pä'rā·ōō) *n.* A rectangular, figured cotton cloth worn as a skirt or loincloth by the natives of southern Pacific islands. [< Tahitian]

par ex·cel·lence (pär ek'sə·läns, *Fr.* pär ek·se·läns') Beyond comparison; preeminently. [< F, lit., by excellence]

par ex·em·ple (pär eg·zän'pl') *French* For example.

par·fait (pär·fā') *n.* A frozen dessert or confection made with eggs, sugar, whipped cream, and fruit or other flavoring. [< F, lit. < L *perfectus.* See PERFECT.]

par·fleche (pär·flesh') *n.* **1.** Rawhide, usually of buffalo skin, which has been freed of hair by being soaked in lye, and dried on a stretcher. **2.** An article, as a shield, made from such a hide. Also **par·flesh'.** [< dial. F (Canadian) < *parer* to ward off + *flèche* arrow]

par·get (pär'jit) *n.* **1.** Gypsum. **2.** Plaster suitable for lining chimneys. **3.** Pargeting. — *v.t.* **par·get·ed** or **·get·ted, par·get·ing** or **·get·ting** To cover or adorn with pargeting. [Appar. < OF *pargeter, parjeter* to throw over a surface < *par-* all over + *jeter* to throw < L *per-* thoroughly + *jactare,* freq. of *jacere* to throw]

par·get·ing (pär'jit·ing) *n.* **1.** The act of one who pargets. **2.** Plastering, especially ornamental plasterwork or stuccowork in relief for outside walls.

par·go (pär'gō) *n. pl.* **·gos** or **·go** A fish (*Lutianus analis*), with brick-red fins and small scales, found in Atlantic waters, and esteemed as a food fish: also called *red snapper.* [< Sp. < L *pagarus* < Gk. *phagros* sea bream]

par·he·lic circle (pär·hē'lik, -hel'ik) *Meteorol.* A band of light passing through the sun and parallel to the horizon, an effect of solar reflection from the vertical faces of ice crystals in the atmosphere. Also **parhelic ring.**

par·he·li·on (pär·hē'lē·ən) *n. pl.* **·li·a** (-lē·ə) *Meteorol.* One of two bright solar images appearing on the parhelic circle: also called *mock sun, sundog.* Also **par·he'li·um** (-əm). [< L *parelion* < Gk. *parelion* < *para* beside + *hēlios* sun] — **par·he'lic, par·he·li·a·cal** (pär'hi·lī'ə·kəl) *adj.*

pari- *combining form* Equal: *parisyllabic.* [< L *par, paris* equal]

pa·ri·ah (pə·rī'ə, par'ē·ə) *n.* **1.** A member of an extensive low caste of southern India and Burma, often employed as servants or farm workers. **2.** A social outcast. [< Tamil *paraiyar,* pl. of *paraiyon,* lit., (hereditary) drummer < *parai* large festival drum]

Par·i·an (pâr'ē·ən) *adj.* **1.** Of or pertaining to Paros or the white marble mined there. **2.** Denoting a fine, unglazed porcelain (**Parian ware**) resembling this marble. — *n.* **1.** A native or inhabitant of Paros. **2.** Parian ware.

Pa·ri·cu·tin (pä'rē·kōō·tēn') A volcano in Michoacán state, Mexico; 8,200 ft.; first erupted February, 1943.

pa·ri·es (pâr'i·ēz) *n. pl.* **pa·ri·e·tes** (pə·rī'ə·tēz) *Usually pl. Biol.* A wall, as of a hollow organ. [< L, wall]

pa·ri·e·tal (pə·rī'ə·təl) *adj.* **1.** *Anat.* **a** Of, pertaining to, or forming the walls of a cavity or hollow organ. **b** Of or per-

taining to the parietal bones or the side of the skull. **2.** *Bot.* Attached to the wall of the ovary, as the ovules of certain plants. **3.** *U.S.* Pertaining to residence or authority within the walls or precincts of a college. — *n.* A parietal bone. [< MF *parietal* < L *parietalis* < *paries* wall]

parietal bone *Anat.* Either of two bones between the occipital and frontal bones that form a part of the top and sides of the cranium. For illustration see SKULL.

parietal lobe *Anat.* The portion of each hemisphere of the brain, lying just beneath the parietal bones.

pa·ri·e·tes (pə·rī'ə·tēz) Plural of PARIES.

par·i·mu·tu·el (par'i·myōō'chōō·əl) *n.* **1.** A system of betting at races in which those who have bet on the winners share in the total amount wagered. Also **par'i·mu·tu·el. 2.** A pari-mutuel machine. [< F, stake or mutual wager]

pari-mutuel machine A machine for recording bets under the pari-mutuel system: also called *pari-mutuel, totalizator, totalizer, tote.*

par·ing (pâr'ing) *n.* **1.** The act of one who pares. **2.** *Often pl.* The part pared off.

pa·ri pas·su (pâr'i pas'ōō, par'ē) *Latin* With equal pace; of the same speed.

par·i·pin·nate (par'i·pin'āt) *adj. Bot.* Equally or abruptly pinnate: said of leaves.

par·is (par'is) *n.* The herb Paris (which see). [< NL]

Par·is (par'is) In Greek mythology, a son of Priam and Hecuba who carried off Helen, wife of Menelaus, thus causing the Trojan War. See APPLE OF DISCORD.

Par·is (par'is, *Fr.* pà·rē') The capital of France, in the northern part, on the Seine; pop. 2,590,771 (1968): ancient *Lutetia, Lutetia Parisiorum.*

Pa·ris (pä·rēs'), **Bruno Paulin Gaston,** 1839–1903, French philologist.

Par·is (par'is), **Matthew** See MATTHEW OF PARIS.

Paris Basin The depression of north and north central France, surrounding Paris.

Paris blue Prussian blue (which see).

Paris green A poisonous compound prepared from copper acetate and arsenic trioxide, used chiefly as an insecticide.

par·ish (par'ish) *n.* **1.** *Eccl.* In the Anglican, Roman Catholic, and some other churches, a district, usually part of a diocese, with its own church. **2.** *U.S.* **a** A religious congregation, comprising all those who worship at the same church. **b** The district in which they live. **3.** *Brit.* A political subdivision of a county, often corresponding to an ecclesiastical parish. **4.** In Louisiana, a civil district corresponding to a county. **5.** The people of a parish. *Abbr. par.* ◆ Collateral adjective: *parochial.* [< OF *paroche, paroisse* < LL *parochia* < Gk. *paroikia,* orig., neighborhood, later diocese < *para* beside + *oikein* to dwell] — **pa·rish'ion·al** *adj.*

parish clerk A clerk (def. 5).

pa·rish·ion·er (pə·rish'ən·ər) *n.* A member of a parish.

Pa·ri·sian (pə·rizh'ən, -riz'ē·ən) *adj.* Of or pertaining to the city of Paris. — *n.* A native or resident of Paris.

par·i·ty (par'ə·tē) *n. pl.* **·ties 1.** Equality, as of condition, rank, value, etc.; also, a like state or degree. **2.** The equivalence in legal weight and quality of the legal tender of one class of money to another. **3.** Par (def. 3). **4.** Equality between the currency or prices of commodities of two countries or cities. **5.** Perfect analogy; close resemblance. **6.** *U.S.* A level for farm prices that gives to the farmer the same purchasing power that he averaged during each year of a chosen base period, originally the five years of farm prosperity prior to World War I. **7.** *Math.* The symmetrical relationship between two integers both of which are either odd or even. **8.** *Physics* The property of a wave whereby its function is symmetrically unchanged by inversion in a coordinate system (**even parity**), or changed only in sign (**odd parity**). [< MF *parité* < L *paritas* equality < *par* equal]

par·i·ty[2] (par'ə·tē) *n. pl.* **·ties** *Med.* Fitness or ability to bear offspring. [< L *parere* to bear + -ITY]

park (pärk) *n.* **1.** A tract of land for public use in or near a city, usually laid out with walks, drives, playgrounds, athletic fields, etc. **2.** An open square in a city, usually containing shade trees, benches, etc. **3.** A national park (which see). **4.** An amusement park (which see). **5.** A large tract of land containing woods and fields, surrounding a country estate. **6.** *Mil.* An open area where guns, trucks, etc., are assembled for servicing and storage. **7.** In English law, a tract of enclosed land stocked with game animals and birds, and held through royal grant or by prescription. *Abbr. pk.* — *v.t.* **1.** To place or leave (an automobile, etc.) standing for a time, as on a street. **2.** *U.S. Slang* To place; set: *Park* your hat on the table. **3.** To assemble or mass together: to *park* artillery. **4.** To enclose in or as in a park. — *v.i.* **5.** To park an automobile, etc. [< OF *parc* game preserve, ult. of Gmc. origin. Akin to PADDOCK.]

par·ka (pär'kə) *n. U.S. & Canadian* **1.** A hooded outer garment of undressed skins worn by Eskimos. **2.** A similar garment worn for skiing and other winter sports. [< Aleut]

Park Avenue A thoroughfare running north and south in New York City, regarded as a symbol of wealth and fashion.

Par·ker (pär'kər), **Dorothy,** 1893–1968, *née* Rothschild, U.S. writer. — **Sir Gilbert,** 1862–1932, Canadian poet, novelist.

and dramatist: full name **Horatio Gilbert George Parker.**
— **Matthew,** 1504–75, English prelate; archbishop of Canterbury 1559–75.
Par·kers·burg (pär′kərz·bûrg) A city in western West Virginia; pop. 44,208.
Parkes (pärks), **Sir Henry,** 1815–96, Australian statesman born in England; premier 1872–75, 1877, 1878–83, 1887–89, 1889–91.
Park Forest A village in NE Illinois, near Chicago; pop. 30,638.
parking lot A plot of land used to park automobiles.
parking meter A device that meters time for the rental of a parking space, usually having a slot for coins.
Par·kin·son's disease (pär′kən·sənz) *Pathol.* A form of paralysis characterized by muscular rigidity, tremor, and weakness: also called *paralysis agitans, shaking palsy.* Also **Park′in·son·ism.** [after James *Parkinson,* 1755–1824, English physician]
park·land (pärk′land′) *n. Often pl.* **1.** Land used or designated for use as a park: federal *parklands;* urban *parkland.* **2.** Grassland with trees, suitable for use as a park.
Park·man (pärk′mən), **Francis,** 1823–93, U.S. historian.
Park Range A part of the Rocky Mountains in western Colorado; highest peak, Mt. Lincoln, 14,284 ft.
Park Ridge A city in NE Illinois; pop. 42,614.
Park·ville-Car·ney (pärk′vil·kär′nē) A village in northern Maryland, a suburb of Baltimore; pop. 33,589.
park·way (pärk′wā′) *n.* A wide thoroughfare adorned with spaces planted with turf and trees.
Parl. 1. Parliament. **2.** Parliamentary: also **parl.**
par·lance (pär′ləns) *n.* **1.** Manner of speech; language: legal *parlance.* **2.** *Archaic* Conversation. — **Syn.** See DICTION. [< OF < *parler* to speak < ML *parabolare* < *parabola.* See PARABLE.]
par·lay (pär·lā′, pär′lā) *v.t. & v.i.* To place (an original bet and its winnings) on a later race, contest, etc. — *n.* Such a bet. [Alter. of earlier *paroli* < F < Ital., grand cast at dice < *paro* equal < L *par*]
par·ley (pär′lē) *n.* A conference, as with an enemy; a discussion of terms. — **Syn.** See CONVERSATION. — *v.i.* To hold a conference, especially with an enemy. Also *Obs.* **parle** (pärl). [< F *parlée,* fem. pp. of *parler* to speak < LL *parabolare* < *parabola.* See PARABLE.]
par·lia·ment (pär′lə·mənt) *n.* **1.** An assembly for consultation and deliberation. **2.** A national legislature, especially when composed of various estates. **3.** In pre-Revolutionary France, one of several principal courts of justice. Also *Obs.* **par′le·ment.** [< OF *parlement* speaking < *parler* to speak < Med.L *parabolare* < LL *parabola.* See PARABLE.]
Par·lia·ment (pär′lə·mənt) *n.* **1.** The supreme legislature of Great Britain and Northern Ireland, composed of the House of Lords and the House of Commons. **2.** The legislature in any of Great Britain's self-governing colonies or dominions. **3.** In France, before the French Revolution, one of several tribunals of justice. **4.** The legislative assembly of Scotland until 1707, or that of Ireland until 1800. Abbr. *Parl.* — **Long Parliament** The British Parliament that first assembled in 1640 and dissolved by its own consent in 1660. After the expulsion (Pride's Purge) of some of its members in 1648, it was known as the **Rump Parliament.**
par·lia·men·tar·i·an (pär′lə·men·târ′ē·ən) *n.* **1.** One versed in parliamentary procedure or debate. **2.** *Usually cap.* During the reign of Charles I, an adherent of the parliamentary party as opposed to the king's party.
par·lia·men·tar·i·an·ism (pär′lə·men·târ′ē·ən·iz′əm) *n.* The system of government, developed in England, in which the position of the head of the government, as the prime minister or premier, and of the other members of the cabinet depend upon the confidence of the majority in the lower house.
par·lia·men·ta·ry (pär′lə·men′tər·ē) *adj.* **1.** Of, pertaining to, or enacted by a parliament. **2.** According to the rules of a parliament: *parliamentary* procedure. **3.** Of a government, having a parliament. Abbr. *parl.*
parliamentary procedure The rules by which meetings and business of deliberative assemblies, societies, boards, clubs, etc. are formally conducted. Also **parliamentary law.**
par·lor (pär′lər) *n.* **1.** A room for reception of callers or entertainment of guests. **2.** A room in an inn, hotel, etc., for private conversation, appointments, etc. **3.** *U.S.* Formerly, a smartly furnished room for the performance of personal or professional services: a tonsorial *parlor.* Also *Brit.* **par′lour.** [< AF *parlur,* OF *parleor* < Med.L *parlatorium* < *parlare* < ML *parabolare* to speak < LL *parabola.* See PARABLE.]
parlor car A railway car fitted with luxurious chairs, and run as a day coach: also called *chair car.*
par·lous (pär′ləs) *Archaic adj.* **1.** Dangerous or exciting; perilous. **2.** Shrewd; venturesome; waggish. — *adv.* Exceedingly; very. [Var. of PERILOUS] — **par′lous·ly** *adv.*
Par·ma (pär′mä *for def. 1;* pär′mə *for def. 2*) **1.** A Province of Emilia-Romagna, north central Italy, formerly a duchy;

1,333 sq. mi.; pop. 389,110 (1961); capital, **Parma,** a commune, pop. 140,844. **2.** A city in NE Ohio, a suburb of Cleveland; pop. 100,216.
Par·men·i·des (pär·men′ə·dēz) Fifth-century B.C. Greek philosopher.
Par·me·san (pär′mə·zan′) *adj.* Of or pertaining to Parma. Also **Par·mese** (pär·mēs′). [< F < Ital. *parmegiano* < *Parma*]
Parmesan cheese A hard, dry Italian cheese made from skim milk, grated and used to flavor spaghetti, soups, etc.
Par·nas·si·an (pär·nas′ē·ən) *adj.* **1.** Of or pertaining to Mount Parnassus or to poetry. **2.** Of or pertaining to the Parnassians. — *n.* A member of a school of poetry, founded in France during the last half of the 19th century, that emphasized technique and form: so called from the title of its first collection, *Le Parnasse contemporain,* 1866. [< L *Parnas(s)ius*] — **Par·nas′si·an·ism** *n.*
Par·nas·sus (pär·nas′əs), **Mount 1.** A mountain north of the Gulf of Corinth in central Greece, anciently regarded as sacred to Apollo and the Muses; 8,062 ft. *Greek* **Par·nas·sos** (pär·nə·sôs′) **2.** The domain of poetry or of literature. **3.** A collection of poems or other literary works.
pa·ro·chi·al (pə·rō′kē·əl) *adj.* **1.** Pertaining to, supported by, or confined to a parish. **2.** Narrow; provincial; restricted in scope: *parochial* ideas. [< OF < LL *parochialis* < *parochia.* See PARISH.]
pa·ro·chi·al·ism (pə·rō′kē·əl·iz′əm) *n.* The quality of being parochial; narrowness of view; provincialism.
parochial school A school, usually elementary, supported and directed by the parish of a church.
par·o·dy (par′ə·dē) *n. pl.* **·dies 1.** A humorous or burlesque imitation of a piece of serious literary work or of a musical composition, or of the style of a particular writer or composer. **2.** An incompetent attempt to imitate another's work or style. — *v.t.* **·died, ·dy·ing** To make a parody of. — **Syn.** See CARICATURE. [Ult. < Gk. *parōidia* burlesque poem or song < *para-* beside + *ōidē* song, poem] — **pa·rod·ic** (pə·rod′ik) or **·i·cal** *adj.* — **par′o·dist** *n.*
pa·roe·cious (pə·rē′shəs) *adj. Bot.* Having the male and female sexual organs developed side by side or in the same inflorescence: also spelled *parecious.* Also **pa·roi′cous.** [< Gk. *paroikos* dwelling side by side < *paroikein* < *para-* beside + *oikein* to dwell] — **pa·roe′cious·ly** *adv.* — **pa·roe′cious·ness** *n.* — **pa·roe′cism** (-siz′əm) *n.*
par of exchange Mint par of exchange (which see).
pa·rol (pə·rōl′) *Law n.* **1.** The pleadings filed in an action. **2.** A word: now only in phrase **by parol,** by word of mouth. — *adj.* Given or expressed by word of mouth; oral. Also **pa·role′.** [< OF *parole* < ML *parabola* word. See PARABLE.]
pa·role (pə·rōl′) *n.* **1.** The conditional release of a prisoner with an unexpired or indeterminate sentence from a penal or correctional institution. **2.** The duration of such conditional freedom. **3.** *Mil.* **a** A pledge of honor by a prisoner of war that he will return at a specified date or will not serve against his captors. **b** A watchword used only by officers of the guard or of the day. **4.** Word of honor. **5.** *Law* Parol. — **on parole** Freed from prison under conditions of parole. — *v.t.* **·roled, ·rol·ing** To release (a prisoner) on parole. [< F *parole* (*d'honneur*) word (of honor) < OF < L *parabola.* Doublet of PALAVER, PARABLE, PARABOLA.]
pa·role d'hon·neur (pȧ·rôl′ dô·nœr′) *French* Word of honor.
pa·rol·ee (pə·rō′lē) *n.* One released from prison on parole.
par·o·no·ma·si·a (par′ə·nō·mā′zhē·ə, -zē·ə) *n.* **1.** Play on words; punning. **2.** A pun. [< L < Gk. < *para-* beside + *onomasia* naming < *paronomazein* to alter slightly in naming] — **par′o·no·ma′si·al, par′o·no·mas′tic** (-mas′tik) or **·ti·cal** *adj.* — **par′o·no·mas′ti·cal·ly** *adv.*
par·o·nym (par′ə·nim) *n.* A word having the same root as another; a cognate word. [< Gk. *parōnymon,* orig. neut. of *parōnymos* derivative < *para-* beside + *onoma* name] — **par′o·nym′ic** (-nim′ik), **pa·ron·y·mous** (pə·ron′ə·məs) *adj.*
par·o·quet (par′ə·ket) *n.* See PARAKEET.
Pa·ros (pā′ros) An island of the central Cyclades, Greece; 77 sq. mi.
pa·rot·ic (pə·rot′ik, -rō′tik) *adj.* Situated about or near the ear: the *parotic* region. [< NL *paroticus* < Gk. *para-* beside + *otikos* of the ear < *ous, ōtos* ear]
pa·rot·id (pə·rot′id) *Anat. adj.* **1.** Situated near the ear. **2.** Designating one of the paired salivary glands in front of and below the external ear in mammals. — *n.* A parotid gland. [< F *parotide* or < L *parotis, -idis* < Gk. *parōtis, -idos* tumor near the ear < *para-* beside + *ous, ōtos* ear]
par·o·ti·tis (par′ə·tī′tis) *n. Pathol.* Mumps. Also **par′o·ti·di′tis** (-ti·dī′tis). — **par′o·tit′ic** (-tit′ik) *adj.*
pa·ro·toid (pə·rō′toid) *Biol. adj.* Designating a cutaneous gland situated behind the eye and above the tympanum in some toads and frogs. — *n.* A parotoid gland.
par·ox·ysm (par′ək·siz′əm) *n.* **1.** A sudden and violent outburst, as of emotion or action: a *paroxysm* of tears. **2.** *Pathol.* A sudden intensification of the symptoms of a dis-

ease, usually occurring at intervals. [< MF *paroxysme* < Med.L *paroxysmus* irritation < Gk. *paroxysmos* < *paroxynein* to goad < *para-* beside + *oxynein* to goad < *oxys* sharp] **— par′ox·ys′mal** (-siz′məl) *adj.* **— par′ox·ys′mal·ly** *adv.*

par·ox·y·tone (par-ok′sə-tōn) *adj.* In Greek grammar, having the acute accent on the penultimate syllable. **—** *n.* A word thus accented. [< NL *paroxytonus* < Gk. *paroxytonos* < *para-* beside, past + *oxytonos*. See OXYTONE.]

par·quet (pär-kā′, -ket′) *n.* **1.** Flooring of parquetry. **2.** The main floor of a theater, especially the section from the orchestra pit to the parquet circle: also called *orchestra.* **—** *v.t.* **·quet·ed** (-kād′, -ket′id), **·quet·ing** (-kā′ing, -ket′ing) To make (a floor, etc.) of parquetry. [< F < OF *parchet* small compartment, dim. of *parc*. See PARK.]

parquet circle The section of theater seats at the rear of the parquet and under the balcony.

par·quet·ry (pär′kit·rē) *n. pl.* **·ries** Inlaid mosaic of wood, used especially for floors. [< F *parqueterie* < *parquet*. See PARQUET.]

PARQUETRY

parr (pär) *n.* **1.** A young salmon before its first migration seaward. **2.** The young of some other fishes, as the cod or pollack. [? < dial. E (Scottish)]

Parr (pär), **Catherine,** 1512?–48, sixth and last wife of Henry VIII of England.

par·ra·keet (par′ə-kēt) See PARA-KEET.

par·ra·mat·ta (par′ə-mat/ə) *n.* A kind of light, twilled dress fabric of cotton and wool or formerly of silk and wool: also spelled *paramatta.* [after *Parramatta*, a town in New South Wales, Australia]

par·rel (par′əl) *n. Naut.* A sliding hoop, rope, or chain by which a yard or spar is attached to a mast. Also **par′ral.** [ME *parail*, aphetic var. of *aparail* equipment]

par·ri·cide (par′ə-sīd) *n.* **1.** The killing of a parent. **2.** One who has killed a parent. [< F < L *pariicidium* killing of a relative, and *paricida* killer of a relative] **— par′ri·ci′·dal** *adj.* **— par′ri·ci′dal·ly** *adv.*

Par·ring·ton (par′ing·tən), **Vernon Louis,** 1871–1929, U.S. literary historian.

Par·rish (par′ish), **Maxfield,** 1870–1966, U.S. painter and illustrator.

Par·ris Island (par′is) One of the Sea Islands in southern South Carolina; site of a U.S. Marine Corps training camp.

par·ritch (par′ich) *n. Scot.* Porridge. Also **par′ridge** (-ij).

par·ro·quet (par′ə·ket) See PARAKEET.

par·rot (par′ət) *n.* **1.** Any of certain birds (order *Psittaciformes*), native in warm regions, having a fleshy tongue, hooked bill, paired toes, and often brilliant plumage, including the macaws, parakeets, cockatoos, etc., some of which are noted for their ability to imitate human speech and laughter. ◆ Collateral adjective: *psittacine.* **2.** One who repeats or imitates without understanding. **—** *v.t.* To repeat or imitate by rote. [ME, var. of *Perrot* < F *Pierrot* < *Pierre* < LL *Petrus*) *—par′rot·er n.*

parrot fish **1.** Any of many small fishes (family *Scaridae*) inhabiting warm seas and so called from their vivid coloring and beaklike jaws. **2.** A labroid fish (genus *Labrichthys*), especially the **parrot perch** (*L. psittacula*) of Australasia.

par·ry (par′ē) *v.* **·ried, ·ry·ing** *v.t.* **1.** To ward off (a thrust, blow, etc.) in fencing. **2.** To avoid or evade. **—** *v.i.* **3.** To ward off a thrust or blow. **—** *n. pl.* **·ries 1.** A defensive movement, as in fencing. **2.** An evasion or diversion in a contest of wits. [< Ital. *parare* to ward off, prevent < OF *parer* to prepare [< L *parare*]

Par·ry (par′ē), **Sir William Edward,** 1790–1855, English Arctic explorer.

parse (pärs) *v.t.* **parsed, pars·ing 1.** To analyze (a sentence) grammatically by giving the form, function, and syntactical relation of each of its words. **2.** To describe and analyze (a word) grammatically. [< L *pars, partis* part]

par·sec (pär′sek) *n. Astron.* A unit of length used in expressing stellar distances, corresponding to an annual parallax of one second of arc, almost exactly 206,265 times the mean distance of the earth from the sun, or 3.26 light-years: also called *secpar.* Compare LIGHT-YEAR. [< PAR(ALLAX) + SEC(OND)[1] (def. 2)]

Par·see (pär′sē, pär·sē′) *n.* A member of a religious sect practicing a form of Zoroastrianism, descendants of Persians who fled to India in the eighth century to escape Moslem persecution. Also **Par′si.** [< Persian *Pārsī* a Persian < *Pārs* Persia] **— Par′see·ism, Par′si·ism, Par′sism** *n.*

Par·si·fal (pär′si·fäl, -fəl) In Wagner's opera (1882) of this name, based on the *Parzifal* of Wolfram von Eschenbach, a knight who heals Amfortas' wound with the sacred spear he has recovered from the magician Klingsor.

par·si·mo·ni·ous (pär′sə·mō′nē·əs) *adj.* Characterized by or showing parsimony; penurious; niggardly. **— par′si·mo′·ni·ous·ly** *adv.* **— par′si·mo′ni·ous·ness** *n.*

par·si·mo·ny (pär′sə·mō′nē) *n. pl.* **·nies** Undue sparingness in the expenditure of money; niggardliness; stinginess. [< L *parsimonia* < *parsus*, pp. of *parcere* to spare]

Par·sip·pa·ny (pär·sip′ə·nē) A town in northern New Jersey; pop. 55,112.

pars·ley (pärs′lē) *n.* A cultivated herb (*Petroselinum latifolium* or *crispum*), having aromatic leaves, widely used to garnish and flavor foods. It is typical of a family that includes the carrot, parsnip, etc. [Fusion of OE *petersilie* and OF *peresil* < LL *petrosilum*, alter. of L *petroselinum* < Gk. *petroselinon* < *petros* stone + *selinon* parsley]

pars·nip (pärs′nip) *n.* A European herb (*Pastinaca sativa*) of the parsley family, with a large, sweetish, edible root. [ME *parsnepe* < OF *pasnaie* (< L *pastinaca* carrot) + OE *næp* turnip (< L *napus*)]

par·son (pär′sən) *n.* **1.** A clergyman; minister. **2.** In the Anglican Church, a clergyman having full charge of a parish; a rector. [< OF *persone* < Med.L *persona* rector. Doublet of PERSON.] **— par·son·i·cal** (pär·son′i·kəl), **par·son′ic** *adj.*

par·son·age (pär′sən·ij) *n.* **1.** A clergyman's dwelling; especially, a free official residence provided by the church. **2.** In English ecclesiastical law, the benefice of a parson.

Par·sons (pär′sənz), **Sir Charles (Algernon),** 1854–1931, English engineer; invented the steam turbine. **— William Barclay,** 1859–1932, U.S. engineer; chief designer of the New York subway system.

parson's nose *Informal* The rump of a fowl, especially when cooked: also called *pope's nose.*

part (pärt) *n.* **1.** A portion of a whole; piece; segment. **2.** *Math.* One of a specified number of equal divisions; an aliquot division. **3.** A distinct piece or portion of a machine that fulfills a specific function in the working of the whole. **4.** Something less than the whole: She has regained *part* of the weight she lost. **5.** An organ, member, or other portion of an animal or plant body. **6.** *Usually pl.* A region; territory: in foreign *parts*. **7.** One's proper share, as of obligation, business, or performance: If he'll do his *part*, we will win. **8.** Individual concern or participation in something. **9.** The role or lines assigned to an actor in a play; also, a role played in actual life. **10.** *Usually pl.* An endowment of mind or character: a man of *parts*. **11.** *Music* **a** The melody intended for a single voice or instrument in a concerted piece: sometimes called *voice.* **b** The written or printed copy for the performer's use. **c** One of the voices of a polyphonic composition. **12.** Division or section of a literary work; also, an instalment of a literary work issued at intervals. **13.** The dividing line on the scalp made by combing sections of the hair in opposite directions. **— for one's part** As far as one is concerned; in general. **— for the most part** To the greatest extent; in general. **— in good part** With good grace; good-naturedly: He took our teasing *in good part*. **— in part** Partly. **— part and parcel** An essential part: an emphatic phrase. **— to take part** To participate; share or cooperate: usually with *in*. **— to take someone's part** To support someone in a contest or disagreement; side with someone. **—** *v.t.* **1.** To divide or break (something) into parts. **2.** To sever or discontinue (a relationship or connection): to *part* company. **3.** To separate by being or coming between; keep or move apart: The referee *parted* the two men. **4.** To comb (the hair) so as to leave a dividing line on the sides or elsewhere on the scalp. **5.** To separate (mingled substances) chemically or mechanically: to *part* gold and silver. **6.** *Archaic* To divide into shares or portions. **7.** *Obs.* To depart from; leave. **—** *v.i.* **8.** To become divided or broken into parts; come apart; divide. **9.** To go away from each other; cease associating; separate. **10.** To depart; leave. **— to part from** To separate from; leave. **— to part with 1.** To give up; relinquish. **2.** To part from. **—** *adv.* To some extent; partly. Abbr. *p., pt.* [< OF and OE < L *pars, partis* part]

part. **1.** Participle. **2.** Particular.

par·take (pär·tāk′) *v.* **took, ·tak·en, ·tak·ing** *v.i.* **1.** To take part or have a share: with *in*. **2.** To receive or take a portion or share: with *of*. **3.** To have something of the quality or character: with *of*: replies *partaking* of insolence. **—** *v.t.* **4.** To take or have a part in; share. [Back formation < *partaker*, var. of *part taker* < L *particeps* < *pars, partis* part + *capere* to take] **— par·tak′er** *n.*

par·tan (pär′tən) *n. Scot.* A crab. [< Celtic]

part·ed (pär′tid) *adj.* **1.** Situated or placed apart; separated. **2.** *Bot.* Cut almost but not quite to the base, as certain leaves. **3.** Divided into parts. **4.** *Archaic* Deceased.

par·terre (pär·târ′) *n.* **1.** A flower garden having beds arranged in a pattern. **2.** The part of a theater on the main floor under the balcony and behind the parquet. [< MF < *par terre* on (the) ground < L *per* through, all over + *terra* land]

par·the·no·gen·e·sis (pär′thə·nō·jen′ə·sis) *n. Biol.* Reproduction by means of unfertilized eggs, seeds, or spores, as in many rotifers, insects, and algae: also called *virgin birth.* Also **par′the·nog′e·ny** (-noj′ə·nē). [< Gk. *parthenos* virgin + GENESIS] **— par′the·no·ge·net′ic** (-jə·net′ik), **par′the·no·gen′ic** *adj.* **— par′the·no·ge·net′i·cal·ly** *adv.*

Par·the·non (pär′thə·non) The temple of Athena on the Acropolis at Athens, dedicated in 438 B.C., regarded as one of the finest examples of Doric architecture

Par·the·no·pae·us (pär′thə·nō·pē′əs) An ancient Greek hero. See SEVEN AGAINST THEBES. Also **Par′·the·no·pæ′us.**

Par·then·o·pe (pär·then′ə·pē) In Greek legend, one of the sirens, who, unable to charm Odysseus by her singing, cast herself into the sea. [< Gk. *Parthenopē*]

THE PARTHENON

Par·the·nos (pär′thə·nos) *n.* A virgin: epithet of several Greek goddesses, especially of Athena. [< Gk.]

Par·thi·a (pär′thē·ə) An ancient kingdom occupying what is now NE Iran.

Par·thi·an (pär′thē·ən) *n.* An inhabitant of Parthia. — *adj.* Of or pertaining to Parthia or the Parthians. — **Parthian shot** Any aggressive remark or action made in leaving or fleeing, after the manner of Parthian cavalry who shot at their enemies while retreating.

par·tial (pär′shəl) *adj.* **1.** Pertaining to, constituting, or involving a part only. **2.** Favoring one side; prejudiced; biased. **3.** Having a special liking: usually with *to.* — *n.* In acoustics, a partial tone (which see). [< OF *parcial* < LL *partialis* < L *pars, partis* part] — **par′tial·ly** *adv.*

partial eclipse *Astron.* An eclipse in which only part of the disk of a celestial body is obscured from view. Compare TOTAL ECLIPSE.

partial fraction *Math.* One of a set of fractions whose algebraic sum is a given fraction.

par·ti·al·i·ty (pär′shē·al′ə·tē) *n. pl.* **·ties 1.** The state of being partial. **2.** Unfairness; bias. **3.** A particular fondness; predilection. Also **par′tial·ness** (-shəl·nis). [< OF *partialite* < Med.L *partialitas* < LL *partialis.* See PARTIAL.]

partial tone In acoustics, a simple sinusoidal component of a complex tone. — **upper partial tone** Any partial tone other than the fundamental.

part·i·ble (pär′tə·bəl) *adj.* That can be parted or separated; divisible. [< L *partibilis* < L *partiri* to divide < *pars* part] — **part′i·bil′i·ty** *n.*

par·ti·ceps cri·mi·nis (pär′ti·seps krim′i·nis) *Latin* A sharer in crime; accomplice.

par·tic·i·pant (pär·tis′ə·pənt) *adj.* Sharing; taking part in. — *n.* One who participates; a sharer. [< L *participans, -antis,* ppr. of *participare.* See PARTICIPATE.]

par·tic·i·pate (pär·tis′ə·pāt) *v.* **·pat·ed, ·pat·ing** *v.i.* **1.** To take part or have a part or share in common with others: with *in.* — *v.t.* **2.** *Rare* To take or have a part or share of; partake of. [< L *participatus,* pp. of *participare* < *particeps, -cipis* partaker < *pars, partis* part + *capere* to take] — **par·tic′i·pa′tion, par·tic′i·pance** *n.* — **par·tic′i·pa′tor** *n.* — **par·tic′i·pa·to·ry** *adj.*

par·ti·cip·i·al (pär′tə·sip′ē·əl) *Gram. adj.* **1.** Having the nature, form, or use of a participle. **2.** Characterized by, consisting of, or based on a participle. — *n.* A participle. Abbr. **ppl.** [< L *participialis* < *participium.* See PARTICIPLE.] — **par′ti·cip′i·al·ly** *adv.*

par·ti·ci·ple (pär′tə·sip′əl) *n. Gram.* A verbal adjective, often retaining some of the attributes of a verb, such as tense and the power of taking an object, but often also having the adjectival function of qualifying nouns. The **present participle** ends in *-ing* and the **past participle** commonly in *-d, -ed, -en, -n,* or *-t.* Abbr. **p., part.** — **dangling participle** A participle that modifies the wrong substantive, as in "*Opening* the door, the *room* looked large" instead of "*Opening* the door, *I* saw that the room looked large." [< OF, var. of *participe* < L *participium* a sharing, partaking < *participare.* See PARTICIPATE.]

par·ti·cle (pär′ti·kəl) *n.* **1.** A minute part, piece, or portion, as of matter; a speck. **2.** A very small amount or slight degree: a *particle* of truth. **3.** *Physics* Any of a number of extremely small entities of which all matter is composed, as an electron, proton, neutron, meson, etc. **4.** *Gram.* **a** A short, uninflected part of speech, as an article, preposition, interjection, or conjunction. **b** A prefix or suffix. **5.** A small section or clause, as of a document. **6.** In the Roman Catholic Church: **a** A fragment of the Host. **b** The small Host given to each lay communicant. [< L *particula,* dim. of *pars, partis* part]
— **Syn. 1.** atom, mite, iota, jot, tittle, whit, smidgen, scintilla.

par·ti-col·ored (pär′tē·kul′ərd) *adj.* **1.** Differently colored in different parts. **2.** Diversified; varied. Also spelled **party-colored.** [< F *parti,* pp. of *partir* to divide + COLORED]

par·tic·u·lar (pər·tik′yə·lər) *adj.* **1.** Peculiar or pertaining to a specified person, thing, time, or place; not common or general; specific: my *particular* hobby. **2.** Referring to one as distinguished from others: Why did you choose this *particular* subject? **3.** Especially noteworthy; exceptional: of *particular* importance. **4.** Comprising all details or circumstances; circumstantial: a *particular* description. **5.** Requiring or giving minute attention to details; precise; fastidious: *particular* in dress. **6.** *Law* Separate or separable; being apart from others; limited; specific. **7.** *Logic* Including some, not all, of a class: opposed to *universal.* "Some trees are oaks" is a *particular* proposition. — *n.* **1.** Usually *pl.* An item; detail: to go into *particulars.* **2.** An individual instance; a single or separate case; a given fact that may be brought under or be the ground of a generalization. **3.** *Logic* A particular proposition. — **in particular** Particularly; especially. Abbr. **part.** [< OF *particuler* < LL *particularis* concerning a part < *particula.* See PARTICLE.]
— **Syn. 1.** special, distinctive, especial. **3.** distinct, peculiar. **4.** accurate, exact. **5.** discriminating, careful.

par·tic·u·lar·ism (pər·tik′yə·lə·riz′əm) *n.* **1.** Exclusive devotion to the interests of one's particular state, party, people, or religion. **2.** *Govt.* The policy of allowing individual states in a federation to act independently. **3.** *Theol.* The doctrine that only certain individuals attain divine grace. — **par·tic′u·lar·ist** *n.* — **par·tic′u·lar·is′tic** *adj.*

par·tic·u·lar·i·ty (pər·tik′yə·lar′ə·tē) *n. pl.* **·ties 1.** The state, character, or quality of being particular, as: **a** Exactitude in description; circumstantiality. **b** Strict or careful attention to details; fastidiousness. **2.** That which is particular, as: **a** A circumstance or detail; a particular. **b** A special characteristic; peculiarity.

par·tic·u·lar·ize (pər·tik′yə·lə·rīz′) *v.* **·ized, ·iz·ing** *v.t.* **1.** To speak of or treat individually or in detail. — *v.i.* **2.** To give particulars or details; be specific. — **par·tic′u·lar·i·za′tion** *n.* — **par·tic′u·lar·iz′er** *n.*

par·tic·u·lar·ly (pər·tik′yə·lər·lē) *adv.* **1.** With specific reference; distinctly: a fact *particularly* mentioned. **2.** In an unusually great degree: *particularly* difficult. **3.** Part by part; in detail. **4.** Severally; personally.

par·tic·u·late (pər·tik′yə·lāt) *adj.* **1.** Consisting of minute, separate particles. **2.** *Genetics* Acting as a unit in inheritance, as certain genes. [< L *particulatus,* pp. of *particulare* to divide into particles < *particula.* See PARTICLE.]

part·ing (pär′ting) *adj.* **1.** Given or done at parting: a *parting* glance. **2.** Of or pertaining to a parting or a going away. **3.** Departing; declining. **4.** Separating; dividing. — *n.* **1.** The act of separating, or the state of being separated. **2.** A leave-taking; a departure; especially, a final separation. **3.** A place, line, or surface of separation or division. **4.** That which serves to part or separate objects. **5.** *Archaic* Death.

parting shot Any retort or aggressive action made as one is leaving or fleeing. [< PARTHIAN SHOT by folk etymology]

parting strip A strip or piece of thin wood or metal separating contiguous parts.

par·ti pris (pär·tē′ prē′) *French* An opinion formed beforehand; a foregone conclusion.

par·ti·san (pär′tə·zən) *n.* **1.** One who supports or upholds a party, cause, etc.; especially, an overly zealous adherent or devotee. **2.** *Mil.* A member of a body of detached or irregular troops, especially in certain occupied areas of southern and eastern Europe during World War II; a guerrilla. — *adj.* **1.** Of, relating to, or characterstic of a partisan or adherent. **2.** Advocated by or composed of members of one party. **3.** *Mil.* Of, pertaining to, or carried on by partisans. Also **par′ti·zan.** — **Syn.** See ADHERENT. [< F < Ital. *partisano,* var. of *partigiano* < *parte* part < L *pars, partis*] — **par′ti·san·ship** *n.*

par·tite (pär′tīt) *adj.* **1.** Divided into or composed of parts: used in combination: *bipartite, tripartite.* **2.** *Bot.* Parted [< L *partitus,* pp. of *partire* to divide]

par·ti·tion (pär·tish′ən) *n.* **1.** The act of dividing, separating, distributing; also, the state of being divided, etc. **2.** Something that divides or separates, as a light interior wall dividing a room, an enclosure, a septum in a plant or animal structure, etc. **3.** One of the parts, sections, compartments, etc., into which a thing is divided. **4.** *Law* A division into severalty of property, especially of real estate, held in joint ownership. **5.** *Math.* Any of the ways of expressing a positive integer as the sum of positive integers: a *partition* of 5 is 3+2. **6.** *Logic* The systematic analysis of a whole into its constituent parts. — *v.t.* **1.** To divide into parts, sections, segments, etc. **2.** To separate by a partition: often with *off.* **3.** *Law* To divide (property) into severalty. [< OF *particion* < L *partitio, -onis* < *partire* to divide] — **par·ti′tion·er** *n.* — **par·ti′tion·ment** *n.*

par·ti·tive (pär′tə·tiv) *adj.* **1.** Separating into integral parts or distinct divisions. **2.** *Gram.* Denoting a part as distinct from the whole. Example: *Of them* is the *partitive* genitive in the sentence "Many of them were there." — *n.*

Gram. A partitive word or case. [< F *partitif* or L *partitivus* < *partitus,* pp. of *partire* to divide] — **par'ti·tive·ly** *adv.*

part·let (pärt'lit) *n.* A garment worn by women in the 16th century, covering the throat and breast. [Var. of obs. *patlet* < OF *patelette* band of stuff, dim. of *patte* paw, flap]

part·ly (pärt'lē) *adv.* In some part; partially.

part·ner (pärt'nər) *n.* **1.** One who is united or associated with another or others in some action, enterprise, etc.; as: **a** *Law* A member of a partnership. **b** A husband or wife; spouse. **c** One of a couple who dance together. **d** One of two or more players on the same side in a game, as tennis, bridge, etc. **e** A colleague or associate in some undertaking; a sharer. **2.** *Usually pl. Naut.* A framework of timber used to strengthen a deck for the support of a mast, capstan, etc. — **Syn.** See ASSOCIATE. — *v.t. Rare* **1.** To make a partner. **2.** To be the partner of. [ME *partener* < fusion of *parcener* and *part*]

part·ner·ship (pärt'nər·ship) *n.* **1.** The state or relationship of being a partner; joint interest; association. **2.** *Law* **a** A contractual relationship in which two or more persons combine capital, labor, etc., to carry on a business, usually sharing the profits and losses in certain proportions. **b** The contract that creates such a relationship. **c** The persons associated in such a relationship.

part of speech **1.** *Gram.* One of the eight traditional classes of words in English, noun, pronoun, verb, adverb, adjective, conjunction, preposition, and interjection. Some grammarians consider the article a ninth part of speech rather than an adjective. **2.** *Ling.* Any of the form classes of a language marked by certain morphological and syntactic features and serving to perform semantic functions in sentences and phrases.

par·took (pär·took') Past tense of PARTAKE.

par·tridge (pär'trij) *n.* **1.** Any of certain small, plump game birds (family *Perdicidae*) of the Old World, especially the **Hungarian** or **gray partridge** (*Perdix perdix*). **2.** Any of various similar birds, as the ruffed grouse or the bobwhite. **3.** A tinamou of the South American pampas. [< OF *perdriz,* var. of *perdis* < L *perdix, -icis* < Gk. *perdix, -ikos* partridge]

PARTRIDGE

(16 to 18 inches long)

par·tridge·ber·ry (pär'trij·ber'ē) *n. pl.* **·ries** **1.** One of the scarlet double berries of a small, trailing evergreen herb (*Mitchella repens*) of the madder family. **2.** The herb bearing this berry. Also called *checkerberry, twinberry.*

part song A song of three or more parts; especially, a secular choral piece without accompaniment.

part-time (pärt'tīm') *adj.* For, during, or by part of the time: a *part-time* student.

par·tu·ri·ent (pär·tyoor'ē·ənt, -toor'-) *adj.* **1.** Bringing forth or about to bring forth young. **2.** Of or pertaining to parturition. **3.** Producing or about to produce an idea, discovery, etc. [< L *parturiens, -entis,* ppr. of *parturire* to be in labor, desiderative of *parere* to bring forth] — **par·tu'ri·en·cy** *n.*

par·tu·ri·fa·cient (pär·tyoor'ə·fā'shənt, -toor'-) *Med. adj.* Promoting or facilitating childbirth. — *n.* A medicine promoting or facilitating childbirth. [< L *parturire* to be in labor + -FACIENT]

par·tu·ri·tion (pär'tyoo·rish'ən, -choo-) *n.* The act of bringing forth young; delivery; childbirth. [< L *parturitio, -onis* < *parturire* to be in labor]

par·ty (pär'tē) *n. pl.* **·ties** **1.** A social gathering for pleasure or entertainment: a lawn *party.* **2.** A group of persons associated or gathered together for some common purpose; as: **a** A group united in promoting or maintaining a cause, policy, system, etc.; especially, a political group organized to gain control of a government through the election of its candidates to public office. **b** A small body of persons selected for some special mission or assignment: a landing *party;* a demolition *party.* **c** A group formed for a sport or other diversion: a hunting *party.* **3.** *Law* Either of the persons or groups involved in legal proceedings. **4.** One who takes part or participates in an action, plan, etc.: a *party* to his crime. **5.** *Informal* A person. — *adj.* **1.** Of or pertaining to a party or parties. **2.** *Heraldry* Divided; parted: said of a shield. [< OF *partie,* orig., fem. pp. of *partir* to divide < L *partire* < *pars, partis* part]

par·ty-col·ored (pär'tē·kul'ərd) See PARTI-COLORED.

party line **1.** A telephone line or circuit serving two or more subscribers. Also **party wire.** **2.** A boundary line between the properties of two or more owners. **3.** The essential beliefs or policies of a political party, usually regarded as limiting the actions of its members.

party politics Policies and acts aimed at furthering the interests of one political party.

party wall A wall erected on a line between adjoining properties and used in common.

party whip A whip (def. 4a).

pa·rure (pə·roor', *Fr.* pà·rür') *n.* A set of ornaments or of jewels. Also **pa·ru'ra** (-roor'ə). [< OF *pareure* peeling < L *paratura* preparation < *parare* to make ready]

par value The nominal or stated value of stock; face value: distinguished from *book value, market value.*

par·ve·nu (pär'və·noo, -nyoo) *n.* One who has risen above his class through the sudden attainment of wealth or position; an upstart. — *adj.* **1.** Being a parvenu. **2.** Characteristic of or resembling a parvenu. [< F, orig., pp. of *parvenir* to arrive < L *pervenire*]

par·vis (pär'vis) *n.* **1.** An enclosed or raised area in front of a church. **2.** A portico or colonnade before a church. [< F < L *paradisum* paradise; later, the court in front of St. Peter's, Rome]

par·vo·line (pär'və·lēn, -lin) *n. Chem.* An oily liquid, $C_9H_{13}N$, obtained either from decaying fish or as a product of the destructive distillation of certain shales and coals. Also **par'vo·lin** (-lin). [< L *parvus* small + (QUIN)OLINE; so named because of its low volatility]

Par·zi·val (pär'tsi·fäl) An epic poem written by Wolfram von Eschenbach.

pas (pä) *n.* **1.** A dance step. **2.** A dance. **3.** Right of going before; precedence. [< F, step < L *passus*]

Pas·a·de·na (pas'ə·dē'nə) **1.** A city in SW California; a suburb of Los Angeles; pop. 113,327. **2.** A city in SE Texas; near Houston; pop. 89,277.

Pa·sar·ga·dae (pə·sär'gə·dē) A ruined city of ancient Persia in south central Iran; site of the tomb of Cyrus the Great. Also **Pa·sar'ga·dæ.**

Pas·cal (pas·kal', pas'kəl; *Fr.* pàs·kàl'), **Blaise,** 1623–62, French mathematician, philosopher, and author.

Pasch (pask) *n.* The feast of the Passover; also, Easter. Also **Pas·cha** (pas'kə). [< OF *pasche* < L *pascha* < Gk. < Hebrew *pesakh* a passing over, the Passover < *pāsakh* to pass over]

pas·chal (pas'kəl) *adj.* Pertaining to the Jewish Passover or to Easter: *paschal* sacrifice. [< OF *pascal* < LL *paschalis* < L *pascha.* See PASCH.]

paschal flower The pasqueflower (which see).

paschal lamb The lamb eaten at the feast of the Passover.

Paschal Lamb **1.** Jesus Christ. **2.** Any symbolic representation of Christ.

Pas-de-Ca·lais (pä·də·kà·le') The French name for the Strait of Dover. See under DOVER.

pas de deux (pä də dœ') *French* A dance or ballet figure for two persons.

pas du tout (pä dü too') *French* Not at all.

pash[1] (pash) *Obs.* or *Dial.* *v.t.* To strike violently; dash to pieces. — *n.* A crushing blow. [Imit.]

pash[2] (pash) *n. Scot.* The head. [ME; origin unknown]

pash[3] (pash) *n. Slang* An infatuation or crush [< PASSION]

pa·sha (pə·shä', pash'ə, pä'shə) *n.* Formerly, a Turkish honorary title placed after the name of generals, governors of provinces, etc.: also called *bashaw:* also spelled *pacha.* [< Turkish *pāshā* < *bāsh* head]

pa·sha·lik (pə·shä'lik) *n.* The province or jurisdiction of a pasha: also spelled *pachalic.* Also **pa·sha'lic.** [< Turkish *pāshālik*]

Pash·to (push'tō) *n.* The Iranian language dominant in Afghanistan: also called *Afghan:* also *Pushtu.*

Pa·siph·a·e (pə·sif'ē·ē) In Greek mythology, the wife of Minos and mother of the Minotaur.

pasque·flow·er (pask'flou'ər) *n.* Any of several plants (genus *Anemone*) of the crowfoot family, having showy white, red, or purple flowers blooming about Easter; especially *A. pulsatilla* of Europe or *A. ludoviciana,* the State flower of South Dakota: also called *paschal flower.* Also **pasch'flow'er.** [Earlier *passeflower* < F *passefleur* < OF *pasque,* var. of *pasche.* See PASCH.]

pas·quil (pas'kwil) *n.* A pasquinade. [< Med.L *Pasquillus* < Ital. *Pasquillo,* dim. of *Pasquino.* See PASQUINADE.]

pas·quin·ade (pas'kwin·ād') *n.* An abusive or coarse personal satire posted in a public place. — **Syn.** See LAMPOON. — *v.t.* **·ad·ed, ·ad·ing** To attack or ridicule in pasquinades; lampoon. [< Ital. *pasquinata* < *Pasquino,* orig., a disinterred statue at Rome on which satirical verses were pasted] — **pas'quin·ad'er** *n.*

pass (pas, päs) *v.t.* **1.** To go by or move past: We *passed* him. **2.** To succeed in meeting the requirements of (a test, trial, etc.). **3.** To go beyond or surpass; exceed; transcend: It *passes* all comprehension. **4.** To cause or allow (a specified period of time) to elapse; spend: to *pass* the summer in Europe. **5.** To cause or allow to move, go past, proceed, advance, etc.: to *pass* a mop over the floor; to *pass* him through the ranks. **6.** To approve or sanction; ratify; enact: to *pass* a bill. **7.** To be approved or sanctioned by: The bill *passed* the senate. **8.** To cause or allow to get through (a test, trial, etc.). **9.** To convey or transfer from one to another; circulate; transmit: to *pass* the word; to *pass* a bad check. **10.** In football, hockey, etc., to transfer (the ball, etc.) to another player on the same team. **11.** In baseball, to walk (a batter). **12.** To utter or pronounce, especially judicially: to *pass* sentence. **13.** To discharge or excrete (waste); void. **14.** To omit paying (a dividend). **15.** *Law* To transfer ownership or title of to another; make over. **16.** *Rare* To permit to go unnoticed or unmentioned.

17. *Rare* To pledge or promise. — *v.i.* **18.** To go or move; proceed; advance. **19.** To go by or move past: to *pass* in procession. **20.** To obtain or force a way; secure passage: to *pass* through a crowd. **21.** To lead or extend; run: The river *passes* under a bridge. **22.** To go by or elapse; glide by: The years *passed* slowly. **23.** To come to an end; draw to a close; terminate: His fear *passed* abruptly. **24.** To die. **25.** To go about or circulate; be current. **26.** To change or move from one condition, place, form, etc., to another; be altered or transferred: to *pass* from hot to cold. **27.** To be mutually exchanged or transacted: Whispers *passed* between them. **28.** To take place; happen; occur: It came to *pass*. **29.** To be allowed or permitted without challenge, censure, etc. **30.** To undergo a test, etc., successfully; fulfill the requirements. **31.** To be approved, sanctioned, ratified, etc. **32.** To be excreted or voided. **33.** *Law* **a** To give or pronounce sentence, judgment, etc.: with *on* or *upon*. **b** To sit in inquest: with *on* or *upon*. **c** To adjudicate: with *between*. **d** To be transferred to another by will, deed, etc. **34.** In football, hockey, etc., to transfer the ball, etc., to another player on the same team. **35.** In fencing, to make a pass or thrust; lunge. **36.** In card games, to decline to make a play, bid, etc. — **to pass away 1.** To come to an end; terminate. **2.** To die. **3.** To allow (time) to elapse. — **to pass for** To be accepted or regarded as, usually erroneously. — **to pass off 1.** To come to an end; disappear. **2.** To give out or circulate as genuine; palm off. **3.** To be emitted, as vapor. — **to pass out 1.** To distribute or circulate. **2.** *Informal* To faint. — **to pass over** To fail to notice or consider, as an applicant. — **to pass up** *U.S. Informal* **1.** To reject or fail to take advantage of, as an offer or opportunity. **2.** To pass over. — *n.* **1.** A way or opening through which one can pass; especially, a narrow passage between the peaks of a mountain range. **2.** A permit, order, or license giving the bearer authority to enter, move about, depart, etc., without the usual restrictions; as: **a** *Mil.* A written form granting permission to the holder to be absent from duty; also, the permission itself or the period of absence covered by it. **b** A ticket allowing one to enter a theater, movie, train, etc., free of charge; a complimentary ticket. **3.** The passing of an examination or course. **4.** In British universities, a degree without honors: also **pass degree. 5.** In magic, hypnotism, etc.: **a** A movement of the hand, a wand, etc., over a person or thing. **b** The manipulation or transference of objects by sleight of hand or other trickery. **6.** A state of affairs; condition; situation: to bring events to a critical *pass*. **7.** In fencing, a thrust or lunge. **8.** In cards, a refusal to bid or raise a bid. **9.** In football, hockey, etc., the passing of the ball, etc., from one player to his teammate. **10.** In baseball, a walk. **11.** *Aeron.* A dive, sweep, or run by an aircraft. **12.** *Archaic* A witty sally or stroke. — **to bring to pass** To cause to be fulfilled, accomplished, or realized. — **to come to pass** To happen; come about. — **to make a pass 1.** To attempt to hit. **2.** *Slang* To invite intimacies; proposition. [< OF *passer* < L *passus* step; n., doublet of PACE] **pass. 1.** Passage. **2.** Passenger. **3.** Passive.

pass·a·ble (pas′ə-bəl, päs′-) *adj.* **1.** Capable of being passed, penetrated, crossed, etc.: *passable* rivers. **2.** Fairly good or acceptable; tolerable. **3.** Fit for general circulation, as money. — **pass′a·ble·ness** *n.* — **pass′a·bly** *adv.*

pas·sa·ca·glia (pas′ə-cal′yə, päs′sä-cäl′lyä) *n.* A musical form identical with or similar to the chaconne, probably derived from a Spanish street dance. [< Ital. < Sp. *pasacalle* < *pasar* to pass + *calle* street]

pas·sade (pə-sād′) *n.* **1.** In horsemanship, the moving of a horse back and forth over the same ground. **2.** *Obs.* In fencing, a forward thrust made by advancing the body: also **pas·sa·do** (pə-sä′dō). [< F < Ital. *passata* or Provençal *passada* < *passare* to pass]

pas·sage¹ (pas′ij) *n.* **1.** A portion of a writing, speech, or musical composition, usually of small or moderate length. **2.** *Music* A short section of a composition designed primarily to display the performer's skill, as a run or flourish. **3.** A way, route, channel, duct, etc., by which a person or thing may pass. **4.** A hall, corridor, etc., between apartments in a building; passageway. **5.** The act of passing, moving, changing, etc.; especially, the transition from one state, or period to another: the *passage* from winter to summer. **6.** A journey, especially by sea; voyage: a stormy *passage*; also, the right or privilege of making a journey: to secure *passage*. **7.** The right, power, or freedom to pass: to refuse him safe *passage*. **8.** The passing or enactment of a legislative measure. **9.** An evacuation of the bowels. **10.** *Archaic* An incident or occurrence. **11.** *Rare* An encounter or interchange. Abbr. *pass.* — *v.i.* **·saged**, **·sag·ing** *Rare* **1.** To make a journey. **2.** To engage in a physical or verbal interchange. [< OF < *passer*. See PASS.]

pas·sage² (pas′ij) *v.* **·saged**, **·sag·ing** *v.t.* **1.** In horsemanship, to cause (a horse) to sidle or walk sideways. — *v.i.* **2.** In horsemanship: **a** To move sideways; sidle. **b** To cause

a horse to move sidewise. — *n.* A sideways movement made by a horse in which diagonal pairs of feet are raised alternately. [< F *passager*, alter. of *passéger* < Ital. *passeggiare* to walk < L *passus* step]

pas·sage·way (pas′ij·wā′) *n.* A way affording passage, especially a hall or corridor.

Pas·sa·ic (pə-sā′ik) A city in NE New Jersey; pop. 55,124; on the **Passaic River**, that flows about 80 miles generally south and east to Newark Bay.

Pas·sa·ma·quod·dy Bay (pas′ə-mə·kwod′ē) An inlet of the Bay of Fundy between NE Maine and SW New Brunswick.

pas·sant (pas′ənt) *adj.* *Heraldry* Walking and looking toward the dexter, with the fore paw raised: said of a beast. [< F, ppr. of *passer*. See PASS.]

pass·book (pas′bŏŏk′, päs′-) *n.* **1.** A bankbook (which see). **2.** A book given by a merchant to a customer, showing all items bought on credit.

pas·sé (pa·sā′, pas′ā; *Fr.* pà·sā′) *adj.* **1.** Past the prime; faded. **2.** Out-of-date; old-fashioned. [< F, orig., pp. of *passer*. See PASS.] — **pas·sée′** *adj. fem.*

passed ball (past, päst) In baseball, a misplay charged to the catcher for allowing a runner to advance by failing to catch a pitch that passes reasonably close to him. Compare WILD PITCH.

passe·men·terie (pas·men′trē, *Fr.* päs·män·trē′) *n.* Trimming for dresses, as beaded lace, tinsel, etc. [< MF < *passement* lace]

pas·sen·ger (pas′ən·jər) *n.* **1.** One who travels in a conveyance. **2.** *Rare* A traveler; passer-by. Abbr. *pass.* [< MF *passager* (with intrusive -*n*), orig., passing < *passage*. See PASSAGE.]

passenger pigeon The extinct wild pigeon (*Ectopistes migratorius*) of North America.

passe par·tout (pas pär·tōō′, *Fr.* päs pär·tōō′) **1.** In picture framing: **a** A light frame consisting of a glass, the picture, and a pasteboard back put together with strips of tape pasted around the edges. **b** The tape. **c** A pasteboard mat. **2.** That which enables one to pass everywhere, especially, a master key. [< MF < *passe*, imperative of *passer* to pass + *partout* everywhere]

passe·pied (päs′pyā′) *n.* *Music* **1.** A quick, lively French dance of the 17th century. **2.** The music for or in the manner of this dance. [< MF < *passe*, imperative of *passer* to pass + *pied* foot]

pas·ser·by (pas′ər·bī′, päs′-) *n. pl.* **pas·sers·by** One who passes by, usually casually.

pas·ser·ine (pas′ər·ēn, -in) *adj.* **1.** Of or pertaining to an order of birds (*Passeriformes*) including all singing birds, and more than half of the living birds of various sizes ranging from crows and jays to sparrows and titmice. **2.** Resembling or characteristic of a sparrow. — *n.* A passerine bird. [< L *passer* sparrow + -INE¹]

pas seul (pä sœl′) *French* A dance or ballet figure by a single person.

Pass·field (pas′fēld), **Baron** See (Sidney James) WEBB.

pas·si·ble (pas′ə·bəl) *adj.* Capable of feeling or of suffering. [< OF < LL *passibilis* < L *passus*, pp. of *pati* to suffer] — **pas′si·bil′i·ty, pas′si·ble·ness** *n.*

pas·si·flo·ra·ceous (pas′i·flô·rā′shəs) *adj.* *Bot.* Pertaining or belonging to the passionflower family of climbing vines and erect herbs. [< NL *Passifloraceae* < *Passiflora* < L *passio, -onis* suffering + *flos, floris* flower]

pas·sim (pas′im) *adv.* *Latin* Here and there; in various passages: a reference note in books.

pass·ing (pas′ing, päs′-) *adj.* **1.** Going by or away. **2.** Transitory; fleeting. **3.** Happening or occurring; current. **4.** Done, said, etc., in a cursory or casual manner: a *passing* glance. **5.** Fulfilling all requirements; satisfactory: a *passing* grade. **6.** *Obs.* Surpassing. — **Syn.** See TRANSIENT. — *n.* **1.** The act of one who or that which passes. **2.** A means or place of passing, as a ford. — **in passing** Incidentally. — *adv.* *Archaic* In a surpassing degree or manner.

passing bell A death bell (which see).

passing tone *Music* An unaccented tone, foreign to the harmony, that occurs in a stepwise progression between two harmonic tones.

pas·sion (pash′ən) *n.* **1.** Any intense, extreme, or overpowering emotion or feeling. **2.** Ardent affection or love. **3.** Intense sexual desire or lust. **4.** Overwhelming anger or rage. **5.** An outburst of strong feeling, especially of violence or anger: to fly into a *passion*. **6.** A strong desire or affection for some object, cause, etc.: a *passion* for art. **7.** The object of such a desire or affection. **8.** Formerly, in philosophy and psychology, the state or condition of being acted upon. [< OF *passiun* < L *passio, -onis* suffering < *passus* pp. of *pati* to suffer] — **Syn. 3.** Compare LOVE. **4.** fury. Compare ANGER. **6.** propensity, fanaticism. Compare APPETITE, ENTHUSIASM.

Pas·sion (pash′ən) *n.* **1.** The sufferings of Christ, especially after the Last Supper and on the Cross. **2.** The part

of the Gospels that relates the sufferings and death of Christ.
3. A representation of Christ's sufferings in art, music, etc.
pas·sion·al (pash'ən·əl) *adj.* Of, pertaining to, or characterized by passion. — *n.* A book descriptive of the sufferings of saints.
pas·sion·ate (pash'ən·it) *adj.* **1.** Capable of or inclined to strong passion; susceptible of vehement emotion; excitable. **2.** Easily moved to anger; quick-tempered. **3.** Expressing, displaying, or characterized by passion or strong emotion; intense; ardent. **4.** Strong or vehement, as a feeling or emotion. — **Syn.** See ARDENT. [< Med.L *passionatus*, ult. < L *passio*, *-onis*. See PASSION.] — **pas'sion·ate·ly** *adv.* — **pas'sion·ate·ness** *n.*
pas·sion·flow·er (pash'ən·flou'ər) *n.* Any of various vines or shrubs (genus *Passiflora*) typical of a tropical American family (*Passifloraceae*), having showy flowers and sometimes edible berries: so called from the fancied resemblance of certain parts of the flower to the wounds, crown of thorns, etc., of Christ. [Trans. of Med.L *flos passionis*]
passion fruit The berries of the passion flower.
pas·sion·less (pash'ən·lis) *adj.* **1.** Without feeling or emotion; cold. **2.** Objective or detached; unbiased.
Passion play A religious drama representing the Passion of Christ.
Passion Sunday *Eccl.* The second Sunday before Easter.
Passion Week *Eccl.* **1.** The week that begins with Passion Sunday. **2.** Formerly, Holy Week.
pas·sive (pas'iv) *adj.* **1.** Not acting, working, or operating; inactive; inert. **2.** Acted upon, affected, or influenced by something external. **3.** Receiving or receptive to an external force, etc. **4.** Submitting or yielding without resistance or opposition; submissive: *passive* surrender. **5.** *Chem.* Characterized by passivity; inactive; inert. **6.** *Med.* Designating certain abnormal conditions characterized by impaired vitality and reaction. **7.** *Gram.* Designating a voice of the verb that indicates that the subject is receiving the action, as *was killed* is in the passive voice in *Caesar was killed by Brutus*: distinguished from *active*. **8.** Denoting various bonds, shares, etc., that do not bear interest. — *n.* *Gram.* **1.** The passive voice. **2.** A verb or construction in this voice. *Abbr.* pass. [< L *passivus* < *passus* pp. of *pati* to suffer] — **pas'sive·ly** *adv.* — **pas'sive·ness** *n.*
passive resistance A method of demonstrating opposition to some authority or law by nonviolent acts as voluntary fasting, etc.
pas·siv·i·ty (pa·siv'ə·tē) *n.* *pl.* **·ties** **1.** The state or condition of being passive. **2.** *Chem.* The decrease in reactivity of certain metals after immersion in strong nitric acid or other oxidizing agents.
pass·key (pas'kē', päs'-) *n.* **1.** A latchkey (which see). **2.** A master key (which see).
Pas·so Bren·ner·o (päs'sō brān·nā'rō) The Italian name for the BRENNER PASS.
pass·o·ver (pas'ō'vər, päs'-) *n.* The sacrifice offered at the paschal feast; the paschal lamb.
Pass·o·ver (pas'ō'vər, päs'-) *n.* **1.** A Jewish feast commemorating the night when God, smiting the first-born of the Egyptians, "passed over" the houses of the children of Israel. *Ex.* xii. **2.** The entire festival of seven days following the paschal supper, during which only unleavened bread is eaten. Also *Pesach, Pesah.*
pass·port (pas'pôrt', -pōrt', päs'-) *n.* **1.** An official warrant certifying the citizenship of the bearer and affording protection to him when traveling abroad. **2.** A permit to travel or convey goods through a foreign country. **3.** A documentary permission for a ship to proceed on a voyage. **4.** Anything that enables one to gain entrance, acceptance, etc. [< MF *passeport* < *passer* to pass + *port* harbor]
pas·sus (pas'əs) *n.* *pl.* **·sus** or **·sus·es** A part or canto, as of a poem. [< Med.L, passage of a book < L, step]
pass·word (pas'wûrd', päs'-) *n.* **1.** A secret word or phrase enabling the speaker to pass a guard or sentry. **2.** Anything that gains entrance or access for one.
Pas·sy (pà·sē'), **Paul Edouard**, 1859–1940, French philologist; chief originator of the International Phonetic Alphabet.
past (past, päst) *adj.* **1.** Ended or finished; gone by; done with; over: His hopes are *past*. **2.** Having existed in or belonging to a former time; bygone: *past* civilizations; *past* sorrows. **3.** Just passed or gone by; immediately preceding: the *past* few days. **4.** Having formerly served in a public office, committee, etc.: a *past* governor. — *n.* **1.** Past or antecedent time, conditions, or events: usually with *the*: in the remote *past*. **2.** Something, as a former life or career, that is kept secret: a woman with a *past*. **3.** *Gram.* **a** A verb tense denoting any action or condition that occurred at a former time. **b** A verb or construction in this tense. — *adv.* In such a manner as to go by; so as to pass: to run *past*. — *prep.* **1.** Beyond in time; at a later period than; after: It is now *past* noon. **2.** Beyond in place or position; farther than: walking *past* the house. **3.** Beyond the reach, scope, power, or influence of: The matter is *past* hope. **4.** Beyond in amount or degree: He couldn't count *past* ten. *Abbr.* p. [Orig. pp. of PASS]

pas·ta (päs'tə) *n.* Any of several noodlelike pastes or doughs containing semolina, as spaghetti, macaroni, etc. [< Ital. < LL, dough, paste]
paste¹ (pāst) *n.* **1.** A mixture, usually of flour and water, used as an adhesive for paper, etc. **2.** Any of various soft, moist, smooth preparations used as foods, in cooking, etc.; as: **a** Dough, especially when used in making pastry. **b** A soft, creamy mass made from fish, fruit, etc., used as a relish, seasoning, or spread: almond *paste*. **c** A soft, jellylike confection or candy. **3.** A vitreous composition used in making imitation gems; strass; also, a gem made of this composition. **4.** A variety of clay used in making stoneware or porcelain. — *v.t.* **past·ed, past·ing** **1.** To stick or fasten with or as with paste. **2.** To cover by applying pasted material. [< OF < LL *pasta* pap. < Gk. *pastē* barley porridge < *pastos* sprinkled < *passein*]
paste² (pāst) *Slang* *v.t.* **past·ed, past·ing** To strike, as with the fist; beat. — *n.* A hard blow. [< BASTE³]
paste·board (pāst'bôrd', -bōrd') *n.* **1.** Paper pulp compressed, or paper pasted together and rolled into a stiff sheet. **2.** A board on which dough for pastry is rolled. **3.** *Informal* A visiting card; also, a playing card. — *adj.* **1.** Made of or resembling pasteboard. **2.** Thin and flimsy.
pas·tel¹ (pas·tel', pas'tel) *n.* **1.** A picture drawn with colored crayons. **2.** The art of drawing such pictures. **3.** A dried paste made of pipe clay, pigment, and gum water, used for crayons; also, a hard crayon made of this paste: also called *pastille*. **4.** A sketchy poetic study in prose. **5.** A delicate, soft, or slighly grayish tint. — *adj.* **1.** Of or pertaining to a pastel. **2.** Having a delicate, soft, or slightly grayish tint. [< MF < Ital. *pastello*. See PASTEL².] — **pas'tel·ist** or **pas'tel·list** *n.*
pas·tel² (pas·tel') *n.* Woad, a plant and a dye. [< MF < Ital. *pastello*, dim. of *pasta* < LL. See PASTE¹.]
past·er (pās'tər) *n.* **1.** One who pastes. **2.** A strip of gummed paper, to cover a portion of a circular, an election ballot, or the like; a sticker.
pas·tern (pas'tərn) *n.* **1.** The part of a horse's foot that is between the fetlock and the hoof. For illustration see HORSE. **2.** A hobble for a horse's foot. [< OF *pasturon* < *pasture* tether for a grazing animal]
Pas·ter·nak (päs·tir·näk'), **Boris Leonidovich**, 1890–1960, Soviet poet and novelist.
pastern bone Either the proximal or first phalanx (**great pastern bone**) or the median or second phalanx (**small pastern bone**) of a horse's foot.
pastern joint The joint between the pastern bones.
Pas·teur (päs·tœr'), **Louis**, 1822–95, French chemist; founder of modern bacteriology.
pas·teu·rel·la (pas'tə·rel'ə) *n.* Any of a genus (*Pasteurella*) of Gram-negative, rod-shaped, aerobic bacteria parasitic in animals and man; especially *P. pestis*, the bubonic plague bacillus, and *P. tularensis*, the cause of tularemia. [< NL, after Louis *Pasteur*]
pas·teur·ism (pas'tə·riz'əm) *n.* *Med.* A method of progressive inoculation for the prevention or cure of certain diseases, as hydrophobia. [after Louis *Pasteur*]
pas·teur·i·za·tion (pas'tər·ə·zā'shən, -chər-) *n.* A process of arresting or preventing fermentation in liquids, as beer, milk, wine, etc., by heating from 140° to about 155° F., so as to destroy the vitality of the ferment.
pas·teur·ize (pas'tə·rīz, -chə·rīz) *v.t.* **·ized, ·iz·ing** **1.** To treat by pasteurization. **2.** *Med.* To prevent or treat (certain diseases) by pasteurism. Also *Brit.* **pas'teur·ise.**
pas·teur·iz·er (pas'tə·rī'zər, -chə-) *n.* **1.** One who pasteurizes. **2.** An apparatus for pasteurizing milk, beer, etc.
pas·tic·cio (päs·tē'chō) *n.* *pl.* **·ci** (-chē) A work of art, music, or literature made up of fragments from various sources. [< Ital., paste < Med.L *pasticium* < LL *pasta*. See PASTE¹.]
pas·tiche (pas·tēsh', päs-) *n.* A pasticcio, especially one imitating or satirizing the style of other artists. [< F < Ital. *pasticcio*. See PASTICCIO.]
pas·tille (pas·tēl', -til') *n.* **1.** A compound of aromatic substances with niter for fumigating. **2.** A troche; lozenge. **3.** A flavored confection. **4.** A small paper disk coated with a chemical that changes color on exposure to X-rays, used to determine X-ray dosages. **5.** Pastel¹ (def. 3). Also **pas·til** (pas'til). [< MF < L *pastillus* little loaf, lozenge, ? dim. of *pasta*. See PASTE¹.]
pas·time (pas'tīm', päs'-) *n.* Something that serves to make time pass agreeably; a recreation or sport. [< PASS, v. + TIME; trans. of F *passe-temps*]
past·i·ness (pās'tē·nis) *n.* The aspect or quality of paste.
past master **1.** One who has held the office of master in certain social or benevolent organizations. **2.** One who has thorough experience in something; an expert; adept. *Abbr.* P.M.
Pas·to (päs'tō) A city in SW Colombia; pop. 119,600 (est. 1961); at the foot of the active **Pasto Volcano** (also *Galeras Volcano*); 13,996 ft.
pas·tor (pas'tər, päs'-) *n.* **1.** A Christian clergyman who has a church or congregation under his official charge. *Abbr.* P. **2.** *Obs.* A shepherd. [< AF *pastour*, OF *pastur* < L *pastor*, *-oris* shepherd, lit., feeder < *pascere* to feed]

pas·tor·al (pas'tər·əl, päs'-) *adj.* **1.** Of or pertaining to shepherds, rustics, or rural life. **2.** Having the characteristics usually associated with rural life, as innocence, simplicity, charm, etc. **3.** Dealing with or portraying rural life, scenes, or manners: a *pastoral* poem. **4.** Pertaining to a clergyman or to his duties. — *n.* **1.** A literary work, especially a poem, dealing with rural life, scenes, etc., usually in an artificial or conventional manner; an idyl. **2.** A picture illustrating rural scenes. **3.** *Eccl.* **a** A letter from a pastor to his flock or from a bishop to the clergy or people of his diocese. **b** A book or treatise on the function of a pastor. **c** A crosier. **d** *pl.* The pastoral epistles (which see). [< L *pastoralis* < *pastor*. See PASTOR.] — **pas'tor·al·ism** *n.* — **pas'tor·al·ist** *n.* — **pas'tor·al·ly** *adv.*

pas·to·ra·le (pas'tə·rä'lē, -lā; pas'tə·ral') *n.* *pl.* **·li** (-lē) or **·les** A cantata or operetta on a rustic theme; also, a piece of instrumental music, simple and idyllic in character. [< Ital., lit., pastoral < L *pastoralis*. See PASTORAL.]

pastoral epistles In the New Testament, the three epistles addressed to Timothy and Titus, and ascribed to St. Paul: so called because they deal almost entirely with the office of a Christian pastor.

pas·tor·ate (pas'tər·it) *n.* **1.** The office or jurisdiction of a pastor. **2.** The duration of a pastoral charge. **3.** Pastors collectively. [< Med.L *pastoratus*]

pas·to·ri·um (pas·tôr'ē·əm, -tō'rē·əm, päs-) *n.* *pl.* **·ums** *Southern U.S.* A parsonage (def. 1).

pas·tor·ship (pas'tər·ship, päs'-) *n.* The place, dignity, or work of a pastor.

past participle See under PARTICIPLE.

past perfect *Gram.* The verb tense indicating an action completed prior to the occurrence of some other past action or before some specified past time, as *had finished* is the past perfect in *He had finished before the bell rang*, or, *He had finished by last Friday*. Also called *pluperfect*.

pas·tra·mi (pə·strä'mē) *n.* Heavily seasoned, smoked beef, usually cut from the shoulder. [< Yiddish < Rumanian]

pas·try (pās'trē) *n.* *pl.* **·tries** Articles of food that are sweet, baked, and are usually made with a crust of shortened dough, as pies, tarts, etc.; also, any sweet baked foods, as cakes, cookies, rolls, etc. [Appar. < PAST(E)¹ + -(E)RY. Cf. OF *pastaierie*.]

pas·tur·age (pas'chər·ij, päs'-) *n.* **1.** Grass and herbage for cattle. **2.** Ground used or suitable for grazing. **3.** The business or right of grazing cattle. [< OF < *pasturer* to feed < *pasture*. See PASTURE.]

pas·ture (pas'chər, päs'-) *n.* **1.** Ground for the grazing of domestic animals. **2.** Grass or herbage that cattle or other grazing domestic animals eat. — *v.t.* **·tured, ·tur·ing 1.** To lead to or put in a pasture to graze. **2.** To graze on (grass, land, etc.). **3.** To provide pasturage for (cattle, etc.): said of land. [< OF < LL *pastura*, lit., feeding < *pastus*, pp. of *pascere* to feed] — **pas'tur·a·ble** *adj.* — **pas'tur·er** *n.*

past·y¹ (pās'tē) *adj.* **past·i·er, past·i·est 1.** Like paste. **2.** Pale and unhealthy, as in appearance.

past·y² (pās'tē, *Brit.* pas'tē, päs'tē) *n.* *pl.* **past·ies** A meat pie. [< OF *pastée* < LL *pasta*. See PASTE¹.]

pat¹ (pat) *v.* **pat·ted, pat·ting** *v.t.* **1.** To touch or tap lightly with something flat, especially with the hand in caressing, soothing, etc. **2.** To shape or mold by a pat or pats. **3.** To strike or tap with lightly sounding steps, as in running. — *v.i.* **4.** To tap or strike gently. **5.** To run or walk with light steps. — *n.* **1.** A light, caressing stroke; a gentle tap. **2.** The sound of patting or pattering. **3.** A small, molded mass, as of butter. — *adj.* **1.** Exactly suitable; fitting; apt. **2.** Formulated in a customary way without much thought; too neat; facile: a *pat* response to a complex question. **3.** Satisfactory; needing no change: a *pat* hand in poker. — *adv.* **1.** Firm; steadfast: to stand *pat*. **2.** Aptly; also, perfectly: to know one's lesson *pat*. [ME *patte*; prob. imit.] — **pat'ly** *adv.* — **pat'ter** *n.*

pat² (pat) *n.* *Scot.* A pot.

pat. **1.** Patent(ed). **2.** Patrol. **3.** Pattern.

pa·ta·ca (pä·tä'kä) *n.* The monetary unit of Macao, equivalent to 100 avas.

pa·ta·gi·um (pə·tā'jē·əm) *n.* *pl.* **·gi·a** (-jē·ə) *Zool.* **1.** The wing membrane of a bat. **2.** A lateral extension of skin, as in flying squirrels, enabling them to glide. **3.** The membranous expansion of a bird's wing. Also called *parachute*. [< NL < L, gold edging of a tunic < Gk. *patageion*]

Pat·a·go·ni·a (pat'ə·gō'nē·ə) The region at the southern extremity of South America; especially, the part in Argentina (300,000 sq. mi.). — **Pat'a·go'ni·an** *adj.* & *n.*

pat·a·mar (pat'ə·mär) *n.* A coasting vessel with great stem and stern rake, used from Bombay to Ceylon: also spelled *pattamar*. [< Pg. < Malayalam *pattamāri*]

patch (pach) *n.* **1.** A small piece of material, especially of cloth, used to repair a garment, etc. **2.** A piece of court-plaster or the like, applied to the skin to hide a blemish or to set off the complexion; a beauty spot. **3.** A small piece of ground; also, the plants growing on it: a *patch* of corn. **4.** A piece of material worn over an injured eye. **5.** Any small part of a surface not sharing the general character or appearance of the whole. **6.** A shred or scrap. — *v.t.* **1.** To put a patch or patches on. **2.** To repair or put together, especially hurriedly or crudely: often with *up* or *together*: to *patch* up their differences. **3.** To make of patches, as a quilt. [ME *pacche*; origin uncertain] — **patch'a·ble** *adj.* — **patch'er** *n.*

patch·head (pach'hed') *n.* The surf scoter, a bird. Also **patchhead coot**.

patch·ou·li (pach'ŏo·lē, pə·choo'lē) *n.* **1.** An East Indian herb (*Pogostemon heyneanus* or *patchouly*) of the mint family. **2.** A perfume obtained from it. Also spelled *pachouli*. Also **patch'ou·ly.** [< F < Tamil *paccilai* < *paccu* green + *ilai* leaf]

patch pocket A pocket sewn to the outside of a garment.

patch test *Med.* A test for allergy made by applying to an area of unbroken skin a small patch of linen or blotting paper impregnated with the suspected substance, and upon removal of the patch observing the skin reaction.

patch·work (pach'wûrk') *n.* **1.** A fabric made of patches of cloth, as for quilts, etc. **2.** Work made up of heterogeneous materials; work done hastily or carelessly; a jumble.

patch·y (pach'ē) *adj.* **patch·i·er, patch·i·est 1.** Made up of or abounding in patches. **2.** Careless; jumbled. **3.** Peevish; irritable. — **patch'i·ly** *adv.* — **patch'i·ness** *n.*

patd. Patented.

pate (pāt) *n.* The head or top of the head; also, the brains or intellect: usually humorous or derogatory. [ME; origin uncertain]

pâte (pät) *French* Paste; especially, porcelain paste.

pâ·té (pä·tā') *n.* A little pie or pasty; a patty. [< F < OF *paste* < LL *pasta*. See PASTE¹.]

pâté de foie gras (də fwä grä') *French* A paste of fat goose liver.

pa·tel·la (pə·tel'ə) *n.* *pl.* **·tel·lae** (-tel'ē) **1.** *Anat.* The flat, movable, oval bone in front of the knee joint; kneecap. **2.** *Biol.* Any of various panlike formations. **3.** In ancient Rome, a small pan or dish. [< L, dim. of *patina* pan, bowl < Gk. *patanē*] — **pa·tel'lar** *adj.* — **pa·tel·late** (pə·tel'āt, -it) *adj.*

pa·tel·li·form (pə·tel'i·fôrm) *adj.* **1.** Having the form of a patella; saucer-shaped. **2.** Having the shape of a limpet shell. [< NL *patelliformis* < L *patella* patella + *forma* form]

pat·en (pat'n) *n.* **1.** A plate; especially, a plate for the eucharistic bread, or one held beneath the chin of the person receiving it: also called *patina*: also spelled *patin, patine*. **2.** A thin, metallic plate or disk. [< OF *patène* < L *patena, patina* pan < Gk. *patanē*]

pa·ten·cy (pāt'n·sē) *n.* **1.** The condition of being patent or evident. **2.** *Chiefly Med.* The state of being open, spread, enlarged, or without obstruction.

pat·ent (pat'nt, *Brit.* pāt'nt; for *adj.* defs. 1, 4, & 5, usually pāt'nt) *n.* **1.** A government protection to an inventor, securing to him for a specific time the exclusive right of manufacturing, exploiting, using, and selling an invention; also, the right granted. **2.** Any official document securing a right. **3.** A government grant or franchise of land; also, land so granted or the official certificate of such a grant. **4.** That which is protected by a patent or its distinctive marks or features. — *v.t.* **1.** To obtain a patent on (an invention). **2.** *Rare* To grant a patent for or to. — *adj.* **1.** Manifest or apparent to everybody. **2.** Protected or conferred by letters patent. **3.** Open for general inspection or use: letters *patent*. **4.** Expanded; spreading widely, as leaves from the stem of a plant. **5.** *Chiefly Med.* Open; unobstructed, as an intestine. **6.** Designating grades of flour, usually those of superior quality. — Syn. See EVIDENT. ♦ In British English, pāt'nt is the usual pronunciation, except in *patent office* and *letters patent*. Abbr. *pat.* [< F < L *patens, -entis*, ppr. of *patere* to lie open] — **pat'ent·a·bil'i·ty** *n.* — **pat'ent·a·ble** *adj.*

pat·en·tee (pat'n·tē') *n.* One who holds a patent.

patent leather Leather finished with a glossy, varnishlike coat.

patent log *Naut.* A torpedo-shaped device with projecting rotary fins that when trailed from the stern of a vessel records the distance traveled: also called *screw log, taffrail log*.

pa·tent·ly (pāt'nt·lē, pat'nt-) *adv.* Manifestly; clearly; obviously.

patent medicine A medicine manufactured and sold under patent and available without a prescription.

Patent Office A bureau of the U.S. Department of Commerce where applications for patents are examined and patents are issued. Abbr. *Pat. Off.*

pat·en·tor (pat'n·tər) *n.* One who grants a patent.

patent right **1.** An exclusive right conferred by a government grant. **2.** The exclusive privilege, for a limited time, to the use, control and manufacture of an invention.

PATELLA
a Femur.
b Patella.
c Tibia.
d Fibula.

pa·ter (pā′tər) *n. Brit. Informal* Father. Abbr. **P.** [< L]

Pa·ter (pā′tər), **Walter Horatio,** 1839–94, English essayist and critic.

pa·ter·fa·mil·i·as (pā′tər·fə·mil′ē·əs) *n.* **1.** The father of a family or master of a house. **2.** In Roman law, an independent person. [< L < *pater* father + *familias*, archaic genitive of *familia* family, household]

pa·ter·nal (pə·tûr′nəl) *adj.* **1.** Of, pertaining to, or characteristic of a father; fatherly. **2.** Derived from, related through, or connected with one's father. **3.** [< L *paternalis* < L *paternus* fatherly < *pater* father] **— pa·ter′nal·ly** *adv.*

pa·ter·nal·ism (pə·tûr′nəl·iz′əm) *n.* The care or control of a country, community, group of employees, etc., in a manner suggestive of a father looking after his children. **— pa·ter′nal·is′tic** *adj.* **— pa·ter′nal·is′ti·cal·ly** *adv.*

pa·ter·ni·ty (pə·tûr′nə·tē) *n.* **1.** The condition of being a father. **2.** Parentage on the male side; descent from a father. **3.** Origin in general; authorship. [< OF *paternite* < L *paternitas, -tatis* < *paternus*. See PATERNAL.]

pa·ter·nos·ter (pā′tər·nos′tər) *n.* **1.** The Lord's Prayer: the prayer taught to his disciples by Jesus. *Matt.* vi 9–13. Also **Pa′ter Nos′ter. 2.** A recitation of this prayer. **3.** A large bead of the rosary, indicating that a paternoster is to be recited. **4.** Any formula or prayer repeated in a low voice. [< L *pater noster* our father, the opening words of the prayer in Latin]

pa·ter pa·tri·ae (pā′tər pā′tri·ē) *Latin* Father of his country.

Pat·er·son (pat′ər·sən) A city in NE New Jersey, on the Passaic River; pop. 144,824.

path (path, päth) *n.* *pl.* **paths** (pathz, päthz, paths, päths) **1.** A walk or way used by man or animals on foot. **2.** Any road, track, or course. **3.** A course of life or action. [OE *pæth*]

Pa·than (pə·tän′, pət·hän′) *n.* An Afghan; especially, one of a people of Afghanistan of Indo-Iranian stock and Moslem religion. [< Hind. *Pathān* < Afghan *Pĕstāna,* pl. of *Pĕstūn* an Afghan]

pa·thet·ic (pə·thet′ik) *adj.* Of the nature of, expressing, or arousing sadness, pity, tenderness, etc. Also **pa·thet′i·cal.** **— Syn.** See PITIFUL. [< LL *patheticus* < Gk. *pathētikos* sensitive < *pathētos* < *pathos* suffering] **— pa·thet′i·cal·ly** *adv.* **— pa·thet′i·cal·ness** *n.*

pathetic fallacy The ascribing of human emotions and characteristics to nature or things of nature, as *a sad day.*

path·find·er (path′fīn′dər, päth′-) *n.* **1.** One skilled in leading or finding a way, especially in unknown regions. **2.** One who opens new fields, as in science, philosophy, or art.

-pathia See -PATHY.

path·less (path′lis, päth′-) *adj.* Trackless; untrodden: the *pathless* forest. **— path′less·ness** *n.*

patho- *combining form* Suffering; disease: *pathogenesis.* Also, before vowels, **path-.** [< Gk. *pathos* suffering]

Pat. Off. Patent Office.

path·o·gen (path′ə·jən) *n.* Any disease-producing bacterium or microorganism. Also **path′o·gene** (-jēn).

path·o·gen·e·sis (path′ə·jen′ə·sis) *n. Med.* The production or development of any diseased condition. Also **pa·thog·e·ny** (pə·thoj′ə·nē).

path·o·gen·ic (path′ə·jen′ik) *adj. Med.* Productive of or pertaining to the production of disease. Also **path′o·ge·net′· ic** (-jə·net′ik).

pathol. or path. Pathology.

path·o·log·i·cal (path′ə·loj′i·kəl) *adj.* **1.** Pertaining to pathology. **2.** Related to, involving, concerned with, or caused by disease. Also **path′o·log′ic.** Abbr. *path., pathol.* **— path′o·log′i·cal·ly** *adv.*

pa·thol·o·gist (pə·thol′ə·jist) *n.* One skilled in pathology.

pa·thol·o·gy (pə·thol′ə·jē) *n. pl.* **·gies 1.** The branch of medical science that treats of the origin, nature, causes, and development of disease. **2.** The sum of the conditions, processes, and effects in the course of a disease. Abbr. *path., pathol.* [< PATHO- + -LOGY]

pa·thos (pā′thos) *n.* **1.** The quality, especially in literature or art, that arouses feelings of pity, sorrow, compassion, etc. **2.** *Obs.* Suffering. [< Gk. suffering < *path-,* stem of *pathein* to suffer]

path·way (path′wā′, päth′-) *n.* A path; footway.

-pathy *combining form* **1.** Suffering; affection: *sympathy.* **2.** *Med.* Disease, or the treatment of disease: *psychopathy.* Also spelled *-pathia.* [< Gk. *-patheia* < *pathos* suffering]

Pat·i·a·la (put′ē·ä′lə) **1.** A former princely state now included in Punjab, India. **2.** A city in Punjab; former capital of Patiala; pop. 124,948 (1961).

pa·tience (pā′shəns) *n.* **1.** The state, quality, or fact of being patient; also, the ability to be patient. **2.** *Chiefly Brit.* Solitaire (def. 2). [< OF *pacience* < L *patientia* < *patiens.* See PATIENT.]

pa·tient (pā′shənt) *adj.* **1.** Possessing or demonstrating quiet, uncomplaining endurance under distress or annoyance; long-suffering. **2.** Tolerant, tender, and forbearing. **3.** Capable of tranquilly awaiting results or outcomes. **4.** Capable of bearing: with *of.* **5.** Persevering; diligent. **— *n.* 1.** A person undergoing treatment for disease or in-

jury. **2.** Anything passively affected by external actions or impressions. [< OF *pacient* < L *patiens, -entis,* ppr. of *pati* to suffer] **— pa′tient·ly** *adv.*

pat·in (pat′n) See PATEN (def. 1).

pat·i·na¹ (pat′ə·nə) *n. pl.* **·nae** (-nē) **1.** An earthenware or metal bowl or basin used as a domestic utensil by the Romans; a patella. **2.** A paten (def. 1). [< L < Gk. *pat-anē*]

pat·i·na² (pat′ə·nə, pə·tē′nə) *n.* **1.** A green rust or aerugo that covers ancient bronzes, copper coins, medals, etc. **2.** Any surface of antique appearance. Also called *patine.* [< F *patine,* prob. < L *patina* plate]

pat·ine (pə·tēn′ *for def. 1,* pat′n *for def. 2*) *n.* **1.** Patina². **2.** See PATEN (def. 1).

Pa·ti·ño (pä·tē′nyō), **Simón Ituri,** 1868?–1947, Bolivian industrialist, banker, and diplomat: called **the Tin King.**

pa·ti·o (pä′tē·ō, pat′ē·ō; *Sp.* pä′tyō) *n. pl.* **·ti·os 1.** The open inner court of a Spanish or Spanish-American dwelling. **2.** *U.S.* The paved area adjoining a house, used for parties, barbecues, etc. [< Sp., ? < L *patere* to lie open]

pa·tis·se·rie (pə·tis′ər·ē, *Fr.* pä·tēs·rē′) *n.* A pastry shop; also, one in which light luncheons are served. [< F *pâtisserie* < *pâtissier* pastry cook < Med.L *pasticium* pastry < LL *pasta.* See PASTE¹.]

Pat·more (pat′môr, -mōr), **Coventry,** 1823–96, English poet: full name **Coventry Kersey Dighton Patmore.**

Pat·mos (pat′mos, -môs, pät′-) An island in the northern Dodecanese off the western coast of Turkey; place of St. John's exile. *Rev.* i 9. *Italian* **Pat·mo** (pät′ mō).

Pat·na (put′nə) The capital of Bihar, India, on the Ganges in the northern part of the State; pop. 449,470 (est. 1971).

pat·ois (pat′wä, *Fr.* pä·twä′) *n. pl.* **pat·ois** (pat′wäz, *Fr.* pä·twä′) A type of local dialect, especially one that is rustic or illiterate. **— Syn.** See DIALECT. [< F; origin uncertain]

Pa·tras (pə·träs′, pat′rəs) A port city in the northern Peloponnesus, Greece, on the Gulf of Patras; pop. about 79,000. *Greek* **Pa·trai** (pä′tre).

Patras, Gulf of An inlet of the Ionian Sea in the northern Peloponnesus, Greece: also *Gulf of Calydon.* Ancient *Sinus Calydonius.*

patri- *combining form* Father: *patricide.* [< L *pater, -tris* father]

pa·tri·arch (pā′trē·ärk) *n.* **1.** The leader of a family or tribe who rules by paternal right. **2.** One of the earliest fathers of the human race, from Adam to Noah: also **ante-diluvian patriarch. 3.** One of the fathers of the Hebrew race, Abraham, Isaac, or Jacob. **4.** One of the twelve sons of Jacob considered as the progenitors of the tribes of Israel. **5.** A venerable man; especially, the founder of a religion, order, etc. **6.** In later Jewish history, the title of the president of the Sanhedrin in Syria and Babylon. **7.** *Eccl.* **a** In the primitive Christian church, any of the bishops of Antioch, Alexandria, Rome, Constantinople, or Jerusalem. **b** In the Roman Catholic Church, a prelate inferior only to the pope and the cardinals, appointed as head of one of the ancient eastern patriarchates or of some modern Uniat churches. **c** In the Greek Orthodox Church, any of the bishops of Constantinople, Alexandria, Antioch, or Jerusalem, sometimes also a prelate of other cities. The bishop of Constantinople, the highest ranking dignitary in the Greek Church, is titled the **ecumenical patriarch. d** The title of the heads of other Eastern churches, as the Coptic, Armenian, Jacobite, or Nestorian churches. **8.** In the Mormon Church, one of the superior order of priests, with special authority and jurisdiction in bestowing blessings. [< OF *patriarche* < L *patriarcha* < Gk. *patriarchēs* head of a family < *patria* family, clan + *archein* to rule]

pa·tri·ar·chal (pā′trē·är′kəl) *adj.* **1.** Of, pertaining to, or governed by a patriarch: a *patriarchal* see. **2.** Of the nature of a patriarchy. **3.** Having the nature or character of a patriarch; venerable. [< LL *patriarchalis* < L *patriarcha.* See PATRIARCH.] **— pa′tri·ar′chal·ly** *adv.*

pa·tri·ar·chate (pā′trē·är′kit) *n.* **1.** The office, dominion, or residence of a patriarch. **2.** A patriarchal system of government. [< Med.L *patriarchatus*]

pa·tri·ar·chy (pā′trē·är′kē) *n. pl.* **·chies 1.** A system of government in which the father or the male heir of his choice rules. **2.** Government by men. [< Gk. *patriarchia* office of a patriarch]

pa·tri·cian (pə·trish′ən) *adj.* **1.** Of or pertaining to the aristocracy. **2.** Noble or aristocratic. **— *n.* 1.** An aristocrat; especially, in ancient Rome, a member of the hereditary aristocracy. **2.** Any one of the upper classes. **3.** An honorary title bestowed by the later Roman emperors. **4.** In medieval history, one of the upper class in the Italian republics, German free cities, etc. [< OF *patricien* < L *patricius* belonging to the senatorial class < *pater, -tris* senator, lit., father] **— pa·tri′cian·ly** *adv.*

pa·tri·ci·ate (pə·trish′ē·it, -āt) *n.* **1.** The patricians as a class; the nobility. **2.** The rank, dignity, or term of office of a patrician.

pat·ri·cide (pat′rə·sīd) *n.* **1.** The killing of one's father. **2.** One who has killed his father. [< LL *patricidium*] **— pat′ri·ci′dal** *adj.*

Pat·rick (pat′rik), **Saint**, 389?–461?, Christian missionary; patron of Ireland: called **the Apostle of Ireland.**

pat·ri·cli·nous (pat′rə·klī′nəs) *adj.* Showing characteristics inherited from the paternal side. Compare MATRICLINOUS. Also **pat·ro·cli′nous.** [< PATRI- + Gk. *klinein* to lean]

pat·ri·lin·e·al (pat′rə·lin′ē·əl) *adj.* Derived from or descending through the male line. Compare MATRILINEAL.

pat·ri·lo·cal (pat′rə·lō′kəl) *adj. Anthropol.* Denoting or pertaining to the residence of a married couple with or near the husband's family or community. Compare MATRILOCAL.

pat·ri·mo·ny (pat′rə·mō′nē) *n. pl.* **·nies** **1.** An inheritance from a father or an ancestor; also, anything inherited. **2.** An endowment, as of a church. [< OF *patrimoine* < L *patrimonium* < *pater*, -*tris* father] — **pat·ri·mo′ni·al** *adj.*

pa·tri·ot (pā′trē·ət, -ot) *n.* One who loves his country and zealously guards its welfare; especially, a defender of popular liberty. [< F *patriote* < LL *patriota* fellow countryman < Gk. *patriōtēs* < *patrios* < *patris* fatherland]

pa·tri·ot·ic (pā′trē·ot′ik) *adj.* Pertaining to or characterized by patriotism. [< LL *patrioticus* < Gk. *patriōtikos* < *patriōtēs*. See PATRIOT.] — **pa·tri·ot′i·cal·ly** *adv.*

pa·tri·ot·ism (pā′trē·ə·tiz′əm) *n.* Devotion to one's country.

Patriots' Day The day of the battle of Lexington, April 19, 1775: a legal holiday in Maine and Massachusetts.

pa·tris·tic (pə·tris′tik) *adj.* Of or pertaining to the fathers of the Christian church or to their writings. Also **pa·tris′ti·cal.** [< L *pater*, -*tris* father + -IST + -IC. Cf. F *patristique.*] — **pa·tris′ti·cal·ly** *adv.*

pa·tris·tics (pə·tris′tiks) *n.pl.* (*construed as sing.*) The study of the doctrines, writings, and lives of the early Fathers of the Church.

Pa·tro·clus (pə·trō′kləs) In the *Iliad*, a Greek soldier and friend of Achilles in the Trojan War who, wearing Achilles' armor, was mistaken for him and killed by Hector.

pa·trol (pə·trōl′) *v.t. & v.i.* **·trolled, ·trol·ling** To walk or go through or around (an area, town, etc.) for the purpose of guarding or inspecting. — *n.* **1.** One or more soldiers, policemen, etc., patrolling a district. **2.** A reconnaissance or combat group sent out from the main body in air, ground, or naval warfare. **3.** The act of patrolling. **4.** A division of a troop of Boy or Girl Scouts. Abbr. *pat.* [< MF *patrouille* night watch < *patrouiller*, var. of *patouiller*, orig., to paddle in mud < *patte* paw, foot] — **pa·trol′er** *n.*

patrol car A squad car (which see).

pa·trol·man (pə·trōl′mən) *n. pl.* **·men** (-mən) **1.** One who patrols. **2.** *U.S.* A policeman assigned to a beat.

patrol torpedo boat A small, highly maneuverable vessel, armed with torpedoes for action against enemy shipping: also called *PT boat.*

patrol wagon A motor vehicle for conveying prisoners.

pa·tron (pā′trən) *n.* **1.** One who protects, fosters, countenances, or supports some person, thing, or enterprise; a protector or benefactor. **2.** A regular customer. **3.** A patron saint (which see). **4.** In ancient Rome, a master who freed his slave and sustained toward him a relation analogous to that of father. [< OF *patrun* < L *patronus* protector < *pater*, -*tris* father] — **pa′tron·al** *adj.*

pa·tron·age (pā′trən·ij, pat′rən-) *n.* **1.** The protection, support, or position of a patron. **2.** In the public service, the power or right to distribute offices, especially political offices; also, the offices so distributed. **3.** The financial support given by customers to a commercial establishment: the *patronage* of a hotel. **4.** An overly condescending manner.

pa·tron·ess (pā′trən·is, pat′rən-) *n.* A female patron.

pa·tron·ize (pā′trən·īz, pat′rən-) *v.t.* **·ized, ·iz·ing 1.** To act as a patron toward; give support to. **2.** To treat in an offensively superior way. **3.** To trade with as a regular customer; frequent. — **pa′tron·iz′er** *n.* — **pa′tron·iz′ing·ly** *adv.*

patron saint A saint regarded as the special protector of a country, city, person, cause, etc.

pat·ro·nym·ic (pat′rə·nim′ik) *adj.* Pertaining to or derived from the name of one's father or paternal ancestor. — *n.* **1.** A name derived from that of an ancestor; a family name. **2.** A name formed by adding a prefix or suffix to a proper name, as *Fitzhugh*, son of Hugh, or *Johnson*, son of John. [< L *patronymicus* < Gk. *patrōnymikos* < *patrōnymos* < *patēr*, -*tros* father + *onoma* name] — **pat′ro·nym′i·cal·ly** *adv.*

pa·troon (pə·troon′) *n.* Formerly, under the old Dutch law, a holder of entailed estates, having some manorial rights. [< Du. < F *patron* < L *patronus*. See PATRON.]

pat·sy (pat′sē) *n. Slang* **1.** A person who has been taken advantage of in some way; sucker; fool. **2.** A weak or effeminate man. [? < Ital. *pazzo* madman, fool]

pat·ten (pat′n) *n.* A shoe having a thick, wooden sole. [< OF *patin*, prob. dim. of *patte* paw, foot]

pat·ter¹ (pat′ər) *v.i.* **1.** To make a succession of light, sharp sounds. **2.** To move with light, quick steps. — *v.t.* **3.** To cause to patter. — *n.* The act or sound of pattering. [Freq. of PAT¹]

pat·ter² (pat′ər) *v.t. & v.i.* To speak or say glibly or rapidly; mumble or recite (prayers, etc.) mechanically or indistinctly. — *n.* **1.** Glib and rapid talk, as used by comedians, etc. **2.** Patois or dialect. **3.** Any professional jargon. **4.** Rapid speech set to music. [Short for PATERNOSTER; from the rapid repetition of the prayer] — **pat′ter·er** *n.*

pat·tern (pat′ərn) *n.* **1.** An original or model proposed for or worthy of imitation. **2.** Anything shaped or designed to serve as a model or guide in making something else: a *pattern* for a coat. **3.** Any decorative design or figure; also, such design worked on something: a vase with a geometrical *pattern.* **4.** Arrangement of natural or accidental markings: the *pattern* of a butterfly's wings. **5.** The stylistic composition or design of a work of art: the *pattern* of Hardy's novels. **6.** A complex of integrated parts functioning as a whole: the behavior *pattern* of a five-year-old. **7.** In gunnery, the distribution of shot or shots about a target. **8.** A representative example, sample, or instance. **9.** *U.S.* Material in sufficient quantity to make a garment, especially a dress. Abbr. *pat.* — **Syn.** See EXAMPLE. — *v.t.* **1.** To make after a model or pattern: with *on, upon*, or *after.* **2.** To decorate or furnish with a pattern. [< F *patron.* See PATRON.]

Pat·ter·son (pat′ər·sən), **Joseph Medill**, 1879–1946, U.S. newspaper publisher. — **Robert Porter**, 1891–1952, U.S. lawyer, jurist, and statesman.

Pat·ti (pät′tē), **Adelina**, 1843–1919, Baroness Cederstrom, Italian soprano born in Spain.

Pat·ton (pat′n), **George Smith**, 1885–1945, U.S. general in World War II: called **Old Blood and Guts.**

pat·ty (pat′ē) *n. pl.* **·ties 1.** A small, flat piece of chopped meat, fish, etc. **2.** A small pie. [Alter. of F *pâté.* See PÂTÉ.]

pat·ty·pan (pat′ē·pan) *n.* A pan in which patties, small cakes, etc., are baked. Also **patty pan.**

pat′typan squash The cymlin.

patty shell A small puff-paste shell in which creamed meat, fish, vegetables, or fruit are served.

pat·u·lous (pach′ŏŏ·ləs, -ə-) *adj.* **1.** Spreading; gaping. **2.** *Bot.* Spreading slightly, as a calyx. **3.** Having a wide aperture. [< L *patulus* standing open < *patere* to lie open] — **pat′u·lous·ly** *adv.* — **pat′u·lous·ness** *n.*

Pau (pō) A resort city in SW France; pop. about 48,000.

pau·cis ver·bis (pô′sis vûr′bis) *Latin* In few words.

pau·ci·ty (pô′sə·tē) *n.* **1.** Smallness of number or quantity; fewness. **2.** Scarcity; insufficiency. [< OF *paucite* or < L *paucitas*, -*tatis* < *paucus* few]

paugh·ty (pôkh′tē) *adj. Scot.* Haughty; insolent.

PAU or **P.A.U.** Pan American Union.

Pau·ker (pou′kər), **Ana**, 1894?–1960, Rumanian Communist leader.

Paul (pôl), died 67? A.D., one of the apostles; the chief early Christian missionary to the Gentiles; author of several New Testament epistles: original name *Saul.* Also **Saint Paul, Paul the Apostle, Saul of Tarsus.**

Paul I, 1754–1801, czar of Russia 1796–1801; assassinated.

Paul I, born 1901, king of Greece 1947– .

Paul III, 1468–1549, pope 1534–49; excommunicated Henry VIII of England: original name *Alessandro Farnese.*

Paul VI, born 1897, pope 1963–: original name **Giovanni Battista Mon·ti·ni** (mōn·tē′nē).

Paul Bunyan The famous hero lumberjack of American folklore, of superhuman size and strength.

Paul·ding (pôl′ding), **James Kirke**, 1778–1860, U.S. author and politician.

paul·dron (pôl′drən) *n.* A detachable piece of plate armor to protect the shoulder. [Aphetic var. of OF *espauleron* < *espaule* shoulder]

Pau·li (pou′lē), **Wolfgang**, 1900–1958, U.S. physicist born in Austria.

pau·lin (pô′lin) *n.* A sheet of tarpaulin.

Paul·ine (pô′lēn, -līn) *adj.* Of or relating to the apostle Paul, his teachings, or writings. — **Paul′in·ism** *n.* — **Paul′in·ist** *n.*

Pau·ling (pô′ling), **Linus Carl**, born 1901, U.S. chemist.

Pau·li·nus (pô·lī′nəs), **Saint**, died 644, Roman prelate; missionary to England; bishop of York: called **Saint Paulinus of York.**

Paul·ist (pô′list) *n.* A member of the Congregation of the Missionary Priests of St. Paul the Apostle, founded in New York in 1858.

pau·low·ni·a (pô·lō′nē·ə) *n.* Any of a genus (*Paulownia*) of Chinese trees of the figwort family, with heart-shaped leaves and panicles of handsome, fragrant, purple flowers. [< NL, after Anna *Paulovna*, daughter of Czar Paul I]

Pau·lus (pou′loos), **Friedrich von**, 1890–1957, German field marshal in World War II.

Pa·u·mo·tu Archipelago (pä′ŏŏ·mō′tōō) A former name for the TUAMOTU ARCHIPELAGO.

paunch (pônch) *n.* **1.** The abdomen or the belly, especially if protruding. **2.** The first stomach of a ruminant; rumen. [< OF *panche* < L *pantex*, -*ticis* belly, bowels] — **paunch′y** *adj.* — **paunch′i·ness** *n.*

pau·per (pô′pər) *n.* **1.** One who receives, or is entitled to receive, public charity. **2.** Any very poor person. [< Med.L (*in forma*) *pauperis* (in the character) of a poor man < *pauper* poor; orig. a legal phrase. Doublet of POOR.]

pau·pered (pô′pərd) *adj.* Made a pauper.

pau·per·ism (pô′pə·riz′əm) *n.* **1.** Poverty. **2.** Paupers collectively.

pau·per·ize (pô′pər·īz) *v.t.* **·ized, ·iz·ing** To make a pauper of.

Pau·sa·ni·as (pô·sā′nē·əs) Second-century Greek geographer and travel writer.

pause (pôz) *v.i.* **paused, paus·ing** **1.** To cease action or utterance temporarily; stop; hesitate; delay. **2.** To dwell or linger: with *on* or *upon*: to *pause* on a word. — *n.* **1.** A temporary ceasing of action; an intermission; rest; stop. **2.** A holding back because of doubt or irresolution; suspense; hesitation. **3.** A momentary cessation in speaking or music for the sake of meaning or expression; also, a character or sign indicating such cessation. **4.** *Music* A hold. **5.** In prosody, a calculated interval of silence in a meter, or the place at which the voice naturally pauses in reading a verse: see CAESURA. [< OF < L *pausa* stop < Gk. *pausis* < *pauein* to stop] — **paus′er** *n.*

pav·an (pə·van′, -vän′) *n.* **1.** A slow, stately dance of the 16th and 17th centuries. **2.** Music for or in the manner of this dance, written in duple meter. Also **pav·ane** (pə·van′, -vän′; *Fr.* pȧ·vȧn′). [< MF *pavane* < Sp. *pavana*, ? < *pavo* peacock < L *pavo, -onis*]

pave (pāv) *v.t.* **paved, pav·ing** To cover or surface with asphalt, gravel, concrete, etc., as a road. — **to pave the way (for)** To make preparation (for); lead up to. [< OF *paver* < L *pavire* to ram down] — **pav′er** *n.*

pa·vé (pä·vā′) *n.* **1.** A street pavement. **2.** A close setting of jewels in which no metal shows. [< F, orig. pp. of *paver*. See PAVE.]

pave·ment (pāv′mənt) *n.* **1.** A hard, solid, surface covering for a road or footway. **2.** A paved road or footway. **3.** The material with which a surface is paved. [< OF < L *pavimentum* rammed floor < *pavire* to ram down]

Pa·vi·a (pä·vē′ä) A commune in Lombardy, northern Italy; pop. 73,305 (1961).

pa·vil·ion (pə·vil′yən) *n.* **1.** A movable or open structure, as a large tent or summerhouse. **2.** A related or connected part of a principal building, as for patients at a hospital. **3.** A canopy. **4.** The external ear. **5.** The sloping surface of a brilliant-cut gem between the girdle and the culet. — *v.t.* **1.** To provide with a pavilion. **2.** To shelter by a pavilion. [< OF *paveillon* < L *papilio, -onis* butterfly, tent]

pav·ing (pā′ving) *n.* **1.** The laying of a pavement. **2.** A pavement; also, the material used for pavement.

pav·ior (pāv′yər) *n.* A pavement layer. Also *esp. Brit.* **pav′iour.** [Alter. of PAVER]

pav·is (pav′is) *n.* A large, medieval shield protecting the whole body. Also **pav′ise.** [< OF *pavais* < Ital. *pavese*, appar. < *Pavia* Pavia, where these shields were made]

pav·is·er (pav′is·ər) *n.* A soldier bearing a pavis.

Pav·lov (päv′lôf), Ivan Petrovich, 1849–1936, Russian physiologist.

Pav·lo·va (päv·lō′və), Anna, 1885?–1931, Russian ballet dancer.

Pa·vo (pā′vō) A constellation, the Peacock, containing the bright star Peacock. See CONSTELLATION. [< L]

pav·o·nine (pav′ə·nīn, -nin) *adj.* **1.** Resembling or characteristic of the peacock. **2.** Iridescent like the tail of a peacock. [< L *pavoninus* < *pavo, -onis* peacock]

paw (pô) *n.* **1.** The foot of an animal having nails or claws. **2.** *Informal* A human hand. — *v.t. & v.i.* **1.** To strike or scrape with the feet or paws: to *paw* the air. **2.** *Informal* To handle or caress rudely or clumsily; maul. [< OF *powe*, prob. of Gmc. origin] — **paw′er** *n.*

pawk·y (pô′kē) *adj. Scot.* **pawk·i·er, pawk·i·est** Cunning; sly; humorous. — **pawk′i·ly** *adv.* — **pawk′i·ness** *n.*

pawl (pôl) *n. Mech.* A hinged or pivoted member shaped to engage with ratchet teeth, either to drive a ratchet wheel or to stop its reverse motion; a click or detent. [Origin uncertain]

pawn¹ (pôn) *n.* **1.** A chessman of the least value, that moves on file but captures diagonally. Abbr. *P* **2.** Any insignificant person used at another's will. [< AF *poun*, OF *paon*, var. of *peon* foot soldier < LL *pedo, -onis* < L *pes, pedis* foot. Doublet of PEON.]

pawn² (pôn) *n.* **1.** Something pledged as security for a loan. **2.** The condition of being held as a pledge for money loaned. **3.** The act of pawning. **4.** One who or that which serves as security. — *v.t.* **1.** To give as security for a loan. **2.** To

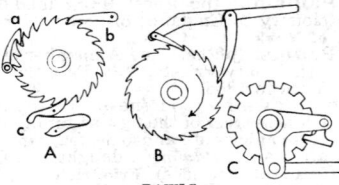

PAWLS
A Types: *a* Hook, *b* Straight gravity, *c* Spring. *B* Double pawl. *C* Reversible double pawl.

risk or stake; pledge. [< OF *pan*, var. of early Frisian *pand* pledge] — **pawn′a·ble** *adj.* — **pawn′age** *n.*

pawn·brok·er (pôn′brō′kər) *n.* One engaged in the business of lending money at interest on pledged personal property.

pawn·ee (pô·nē′) *n. Law* A pawnbroker.

Paw·nee (pô·nē′) *n. pl.* **·nees** or **·nee** A member of one of four tribes of North American Indians of Caddoan stock, formerly inhabiting the region between the Arkansas River and the Platte River, Nebraska, now living in Oklahoma.

pawn·er (pô′nər) *n.* One who pawns personal property.

pawn·shop (pôn′shop′) *n.* The place of business of a pawnbroker.

pawn ticket A receipt for goods pawned.

paw-paw (pô′pô) See PAPAW.

Paw·tuck·et (pô·tuk′it) A city in NE Rhode Island, near Providence, on the Blackstone River; pop. 76,984.

pax (paks) *n.* **1.** In the Mass, a symbolic embrace in which the participants place their hands on each other's shoulders. **2.** A plaque or tablet containing a representation of a sacred subject and sometimes used in the Mass during the pax. **3.** Peace. [< L, peace]

Pax (paks) In Roman mythology, the goddess of peace: identified with the Greek *Irene*.

pax vo·bis·cum (paks vō·bis′kəm) *Latin* Peace be with you.

pax·wax (paks′waks) *n.* A strong, fibrous ligament supporting the head in many mammals: also called *pack-wax*. [ME, alter. of *fax-wax* < OE *feax* hair + *weaxan* to grow]

pay¹ (pā) *v.* **paid** or (*Obs.* except for def. 2 of *to pay out*) **payed, pay·ing** *v.t.* **1.** To give (someone) what is due for a debt, purchase, etc.; recompense; remunerate. **2.** To give (money, etc.) for a purchase, service rendered, etc. **3.** To provide or hand over the amount of; discharge, as a debt, bill, etc. **4.** To yield as return or recompense. **5.** To afford profit or benefit to: It wouldn't *pay* me to do it. **6.** To defray, as expenses. **7.** To requite, as for an insult. **8.** To render or give, as a compliment, attention, etc. **9.** To make, as a call or visit. — *v.i.* **10.** To make recompense or payment. **11.** To afford compensation or profit; be worthwhile: It *pays* to be honest. — **to pay back** To repay. — **to pay off** **1.** To pay the entire amount of (a debt, mortgage, etc.). **2.** To pay the wages of and discharge. **3.** To gain revenge upon or for. **4.** *U.S. Informal* To afford full return; be fully effective. **5.** *Naut.* To turn or cause to turn to leeward. **6.** *U.S. Slang* To bribe. — **to pay out** **1.** To disburse or expend. **2.** *Naut.* To let out by slackening, as a rope or cable. — **to pay up** To make full payment (of). — *n.* **1.** That which is given as a recompense; compensation; wages. **2.** The act of paying, or the state of being paid. **3.** Paid employment. **4.** Requital; reward; also, retribution. **5.** A person considered with respect to his ability to pay or his promptness in paying. — *adj.* **1.** Of or pertaining to payments, persons who pay, or services paid for: *pay* day; *pay* students; a *pay* library. **2.** Constructed so as to require payment on use: a *pay* phone. **3.** Yielding enough metal to be worth mining: *pay* dirt. [< OF *payer* to pay, appease < L *pacare* to appease < *pax, pacis* peace] — **pay′er** *n.*
— **Syn.** (verb) **1.** compensate, indemnify. **2.** spend, expend, disburse. **3.** settle, liquidate. — (noun) **1.** See SALARY.

pay² (pā) *v.t.* **paid** or **payed, pay·ing** To coat with pitch or other waterproof composition, as the seams of a vessel, etc. [< AF *peier* < L *picare* < *pix, picis* pitch]

pay·a·ble (pā′ə·bəl) *adj.* **1.** Due and unpaid. **2.** That can or will be paid. **3.** Likely to be profitable. — **pay′a·bly** *adv.*

pay·day (pā′dā′) *n.* The day on which wages are distributed.

pay dirt **1.** Soil containing enough metal, especially gold, to be profitable to mine. **2.** Anything profitable.

pay·ee (pā·ē′) *n.* A person to whom money has been or is to be paid.

pay·load (pā′lōd′) *n.* **1.** That part of a cargo producing revenue. **2.** The warhead of a guided missile.

pay·mas·ter (pā′mas′tər, -mäs′-) *n.* One who has charge of paying employees. Abbr. *P.M*

pay·ment (pā′mənt) *n.* **1.** The act of paying, or that which is paid. **2.** Recompense. **3.** Punishment. Abbr. *payt., pt.*

Payne (pān), John Howard, 1791–1852, U.S. actor and writer, author of the song *Home, Sweet Home*.

pay·nim (pā′nim) *n. Archaic* A non-Christian, pagan, or heathen; especially, a Moslem. [< OF *paienime* < LL *paganismus* heathenism < *paganus*. See PAGAN.]

pay·off (pā′ôf′, -of′) *n.* **1.** The time or act of paying wages to employees; also, the time or act of paying an employee in full and discharging him. **2.** *Informal* Any settlement, reward, or punishment. **3.** *Informal* The climax or outcome of an incident or narrative. **4.** *U.S. Slang* A bribe.

pay·o·la (pā·ō′lə) *n. U.S. Slang* A secret or undercover payment for favors.

pay·roll (pā′rōl′) *n.* A list of those entitled to receive pay with the amounts due them; also, the total sum of money needed to make the payments. Also **pay roll.**

Pb *Chem.* [L *plumbum*].

PBX or **P.B.X.** Private branch (telephone) exchange.

pc. **1.** (*pl.* **pcs.**) Piece. **2.** Price(s).

p.c. **1.** Percent. **2.** Petty cash. **3.** Postal card. **4.** Price(s) current.

P/C or **p/c** 1. Petty cash. 2. Prices current.
P.C. 1. *Brit.* Police Constable. 2. Post Commander. 3. Privy Council.
pct. Percent.
pd. Paid.
p.d. 1. Per diem. 2. Potential difference.
Pd *Chem.* Palladium.
P.D. 1. Per diem. 2. Police Department.
Pd.B. Bachelor of Pedagogy (L *Pedagogiae Baccalaureus*).
Pd.D. Doctor of Pedagogy (L *Pedagogiae Doctor*).
Pd.M. Master of Pedagogy (L *Pedagogiae Magister*).
pe (pā) *n.* The seventeenth letter in the Hebrew alphabet. See ALPHABET.
P.E. 1. Petroleum Engineer. 2. Presiding Elder. 3. *Printing* Printer's error. 4. *Stat.* Probable error. 5. Protestant Episcopal.
pea (pē) *n. pl.* **peas** or **pease** 1. A climbing annual leguminous herb (*Pisum sativum*) having pinnate leaves. 2. Its round, green, edible seed. 3. The seed of any one of various other plants of the same family (*Leguminosae*), as the chick-pea or cowpea. [< PEASE, incorrectly taken as a plural]
Pea·bod·y (pē'bod'ē, -bəd-ē), **George**, 1795–1869, U.S. financier and philanthropist.
Pea·bod·y (pē'bod'ē, -bəd-ē) A city in NE Massachusetts; pop. 48,080.
pea·bod·y bird (pē'bod-ē) The white-throated sparrow.
peace (pēs) *n.* 1. A state of mental or physical quiet or tranquillity; calm; repose. 2. The absence or cessation of war. 3. Public order and tranquillity; freedom from riot or violence. 4. A state of reconciliation after strife or enmity. 5. Freedom from mental agitation or anxiety. — **at peace** 1. In a quiet state; tranquil. 2. In a state or condition of order and harmony. — **to hold** (or **keep**) **one's peace** To be silent. — *v.i. Obs. except as an imperative* To be or become quiet or silent. [< OF *pais* < L *pax, pacis*]
 Peace may appear as a combining form or as the first element in two-word phrases; as in:

peace-abiding	peace-giving	peace movement
peace-bearer	peace-inspiring	peace offer
peacebreaker	peace-keeper	peace party
peacebreaking	peace-keeping	peace plan
peace-bringer	peace-lover	peace-preserver
peace conference	peace-loving	peace-restoring
peace congress	peace-minded	peace-seeker
peace-destroying	peacemonger	peacetime

Peace Corps A U.S. government organization, established in 1961, that trains and sends volunteers to live in and aid underdeveloped countries by teaching, farming, building, etc.
peace·a·ble (pē'sə·bəl) *adj.* 1. Inclined to peace. 2. Peaceful; tranquil. — **Syn.** See AMICABLE, PACIFIC. — **peace'a·ble·ness** *n.* — **peace'a·bly** *adv.*
peace·ful (pēs'fəl) *adj.* 1. Not in a state of war, riot, or commotion; undisturbed. 2. Averse to strife. 3. Inclined to or characteristic of peace. — **Syn.** See PACIFIC. — **peace'ful·ly** *adv.* — **peace'ful·ness** *n.*
peace·mak·er (pēs'mā'kər) *n.* One who effects, or seeks to effect, a reconciliation between unfriendly parties. — **peace'mak'ing** *n. & adj.*
peace offering 1. An offering made for the sake of peace or reconciliation. 2. Formerly, a Levitical sacrificial offering.
peace officer One entrusted to preserve civil peace, as a justice of the peace, sheriff, etc.
peace pipe The calumet.
Peace River (pēs) A river in western Canada, flowing 1,054 miles NE to the Slave River.
peace·time (pēs'tīm') *n.* A time of peace. — *adj.* Of, characterized by, or used in such a time.
peach¹ (pēch) *n.* 1. The drupaceous, edible fruit of a tree (*Prunus persica*) of the rose family, widely cultivated in many varieties. 2. The tree itself. 3. The yellowish pink color characteristic of the fruit. 4. *Slang* Any particularly beautiful, pleasing, or excellent person or thing. [< OF *peche, pesche* < LL *persica* < L *persicum* < Gk. *Persikon* (*mēlon*) Persian (fruit)]
peach² (pēch) *v.i.* 1. *Slang* To inform against an accomplice; turn informer. — *v.t.* 2. *Obs.* To impeach; inform against. [Aphetic var. of obs. *appeach* to accuse]
peach·bloom (pēch'blōōm') *n.* 1. A monochrome glaze used on Chinese porcelain etc., having various tones of pinkish red. 2. A delicate pink color. — **peach'bloom'** (*adj.*)
peach·y (pē'chē) *adj.* **peach·i·er**, **peach·i·est** 1. Resembling a peach, especially in color or downiness. 2. *Slang* Delightfully pleasant, beautiful, etc. — **peach'i·ness** *n.*
pea·coat (pē'kōt') *n.* A pea jacket. Also **pea coat.** [< PEA (JACKET) + COAT]
pea·cock (pē'kok') *n.* The male of a gallinaceous crested bird (genus *Pavo*), having erectile, brilliantly iridescent tail coverts enormously elongated and marked with ocelli or eye-like spots, and the neck and breast of a greenish blue. ◆ Collateral adjective: *pavonine.* — *v.i.* To strut vainly; make a display. [OE *pēa, pāwa* peacock (< L *pavo*) + COCK¹]

Pea·cock (pē'kok') A star of 2.12 magnitude in the constellation Pavo. See STAR.
Pea·cock (pē'kok'), **Thomas Love**, 1785–1866, English novelist.
peacock blue A vivid greenish blue.
pea·cock·ish (pē'kok·ish) *adj.* Vain; pretentious. Also **pea'cock·y** (-kok'ē).
peacock ore Bornite.
pea·fowl (pē'foul') *n.* A peacock or pea-hen.
peag (pēg) *n.* Wampum. [< Algonquian (Massachuset) *piak,* pl of *pi* strung bead of shell money]
pea green A light yellowish green.
pea·hen (pē'hen') *n.* A female peafowl.
pea jacket A short coat of thick woolen cloth, worn by seamen. Also called *peacoat.* [< Du *pij* coat of coarse wool < MDu. *pie* + JACKET]
peak¹ (pēk) *n.* 1. A projecting point or edge; an end terminating in a point. 2. A conspicuous or precipitous mountain; also, the summit of such a mountain. 3. A point formed by the growth or cut of hair. 4. The maximum development, strength, value, etc., of something: at the *peak* of his powers. 5. *Electr.* The maximum value of a specified quantity: a *peak* of voltage. 6. *Naut.* **a** The after upper corner of a fore-and-aft sail. **b** The upper end of a gaff. **c** The sharply narrowed part of a vessel at the bow or stern. — *v.t.* 1. *Naut.* To raise to or almost to a vertical position, as a gaff or yard. 2. To make into a peak or point — *v.i.* 3. To assume the form of a peak or peaks. [Var. of PIKE⁴]
peak² (pēk) *v.i.* To become sickly, weak, or dispirited. [Origin uncertain]
peak·ed (pē'kid pēkt) *adj.* Having a thin or sickly appearance. [< PEAK²]
peak load *Electr.* The maximum power load consumed or produced by a generating unit, etc., during a specified time.
peal (pēl) *n.* 1. A prolonged, sonorous sound, as of a bell, trumpet, or thunder. 2. A set of large bells attuned to the major scale. 3. A change rung on a set of bells. — *v.t. & v.i.* To sound with a peal or peals; ring out; resound. [ME *pele,* aphetic var. of *apele* < OF *apeler.* See APPEAL.]
Peale (pēl) A family of American artists; notably **Charles Willson,** 1741–1827, and his brother, **James,** 1749–1831; **Rembrandt,** 1778–1860, son of Charles Willson.
pe·an (pē'ən) See PAEAN.
pea·nut (pē'nut') *n.* 1. The nutlike seed or seed pod of an annual herbaceous vine (*Arachis hypogaea*) of the pea family, ripening underground from the pistillate flowers that bury themselves after fertilization. 2. The plant bearing this nut. 3. *Informal* A small or insignificant person. 4. *pl. U.S. Slang* An insignificant sum of money.
peanut brittle A hard candy containing roasted peanuts.
peanut butter A spread resembling butter in consistency, made from ground, roasted peanuts.
peanut gallery *U.S. Slang* The highest balcony or row of seats in a theater.
peanut oil Oil from the seeds of the peanut.
pear (pâr) *n.* 1. The juicy, edible, fleshy fruit of a tree (*Pyrus communis*) of the rose family, widely cultivated in many varieties. 2. The tree bearing this fruit. [OE *pere* < W Gmc. *pera* < LL *pera, pira* < L *pira,* pl. of *pirum* pear]
pearl¹ (pûrl) *n.* 1. A smooth, rounded, variously tinted nacreous concretion formed as a deposit around a foreign body in the shells of various mollusks, and largely used as a gem. 2. Something like or likened to such a jewel in form, luster, value, etc. 3. Nacre or mother-of-pearl. 4. A very pale bluish gray: also **pearl blue, pearl gray.** 5. *Printing* A size of type smaller than agate, 5 points. — *adj.* 1. Pertaining to, consisting of, set with, or made of pearl or mother-of-pearl: a *pearl* button; a *pearl* ring. 2. Shaped like a pearl: *pearl* barley. — *v.i.* 1. To seek or fish for pearls. 2. To form beads like pearls. — *v.t.* 3. To adorn or set with or as with pearls. 4. To color or shape like pearls. 5. To make into small round grains, as barley. [< OF *perle* < Med.L *perna* pearl < L, mussel]
pearl² (pûrl) See PURL².
Pearl See CANTON (def. 3).
pearl·ash (purl'ash') *n.* Commercial potassium carbonate.
pearl barley Barley reduced to a round shotlike form by pearling. Also **pearled barley.**
pearl·er (pûr'lər) *n.* 1. A diver for or trader in pearls. 2. A boat engaged in pearling.
Pearl Harbor An inlet on the southern coast of Oahu, near Honolulu, Hawaii; site of a U.S. naval base, bombed by Japanese, December 7, 1941.
pearl·ite (pûr'līt) *n.* 1. A cast-iron alloy of low carbon content and high tensile strength, formed of ferrite and cementite in alternate layers. 2. See PERLITE.

MALE PEACOCK
(Body to 36 inches long; tail coverts to 6 feet)

pearl millet A tall East Indian and African cereal grass (*Pennisetum glaucum*) having edible seeds, used in the United States as a forage grass.

pearl oyster See under OYSTER.

Pearl River A river in central Mississippi, flowing 480 miles SW to the Gulf of Mexico.

pear·ly (pûr′lē) *adj.* **·li·er**, **·li·est** **1.** Resembling a pearl or pearls. **2.** Adorned with pearls.

pearly nautilus See under NAUTILUS.

pear·main (pâr′mān) *n.* A variety of apple. [< OF *permain*, *parmain*, lit., of Parma, Italy]

pear oil Isoamyl acetate.

Pearse (pirs), **Patrick Henry**, 1879–1916, Irish educator and patriot; executed: called **Padraic Pearse**.

Pear·son (pir′sən), **Karl**, 1857–1936, English scientist.

peart (pirt, pûrt) *adj.* *Dial.* In good health and spirits; active; lively. [Var. of PERT] **— peart′ly** *adv.*

Pea·ry (pir′ē), **Robert Edwin**, 1856–1920, U.S. Arctic explorer; first to reach the North Pole, April 6,1909.

peas·ant (pez′ənt) *n.* **1.** In Europe, a farmer, farm laborer, or rustic workman. **2.** *Informal* A boorish, uncouth, or simple-minded person. **3.** *Obs.* A rascal; base character. [< AF *paisant* < *pais* country < LL *pagensis* (*ager*) (territory) of a canton < *pagus* district]

peas·ant·ry (pez′ən·trē) *n.* **1.** The peasant class; a body of peasants. **2.** Rusticity.

pease (pēz) Alternate plural of PEA. ◆ *Pease* is now used only in the collective sense. **—** *n. pl.* **peas·es** or **peas·en** (pēz′ən) *Obs.* A pea. [OE *pise* < LL *pisa* < L, pl. of *pisum* < Gk. *pison* < *pisos* pulse, pease]

Pease (pēz), **Francis Gladheim**, 1881–1938, U.S. astronomer.

pease·cod (pēz′kod) *n.* A pea pod. Also **peas′cod**. [< PEASE + COD²]

pea·shoot·er (pē′shōō′tər) *n.* A toy blowgun through which small pellets, as dried peas, are blown.

pea·soup·er (pē′sōōp′ər) *n.* **1.** *Canadian* A French Canadian. **2.** *Brit.* A thick fog.

peat¹ (pēt) *n.* **1.** A substance consisting of partially carbonized vegetable material, chiefly mosses, found usually in bogs. **2.** A block of this substance, pressed and dried for fuel: also called *turf*. [ME *pete* < Med.L *peta* piece of peat. Prob. akin to *petia* fragment.]

peat² (pēt) *n. Obs.* A pet; favorite. [Origin uncertain]

peat bog A marsh with an accumulation of peat.

peat moss 1. A moss of which peat is largely composed. **2.** *Brit.* A peat bog.

peat·y (pē′tē) *adj.* **peat·i·er**, **peat·i·est** Resembling or containing peat.

pea·vey (pē′vē) *n. pl.* **·vies** An iron-pointed lever fitted with a movable hook and used for handling logs. Also **pea′vy.** [after Joseph *Peavey*, its inventor]

peb·ble (peb′əl) *n.* **1.** A small, rounded fragment of rock, shaped by the action of water, ice, etc. **2.** Quartz crystal; also, a lens made of it. **3.** Leather that has been pebbled. **4.** Pebbleware. **—** *v.t.* **·bled**, **·bling 1.** To impart a rough grain to (leather). **2.** To cover or pelt with pebbles. [Back formation of OE *papol*(*stān*) pebble(stone)]

peb·ble·ware (peb′əl·wâr′) *n.* A ware having various colored clays in the paste.

peb·bly (peb′lē, peb′əl·ē) *adj.* **·bli·er**, **·bli·est 1.** Covered with or full of pebbles. **2.** Having a texture resembling pebbles.

pe·can (pi·kan′, -kän′, pē′kan) *n.* **1.** A large hickory (*Carya illinoensis*) of the central and southern United States, with edible, oval, thin-shelled nuts. **2.** The nut of this tree. [Earlier *paccan* < Algonquian (Cree) *pacan*]

pec·ca·ble (pek′ə·bəl) *adj.* Capable of sinning. [< OF or < Med.L *peccabilis* < L *peccare* to sin] **— pec′ca·bil′i·ty** *n.*

pec·ca·dil·lo (pek′ə·dil′ō) *n. pl.* **·los** or **·loes** A slight or trifling sin; a fault. [< Sp. *pecadillo*, dim. of *pecado* sin < L *peccatum* < *peccare* to sin]

pec·cant (pek′ənt) *adj.* **1.** Guilty of sin; sinful. **2.** Corrupt and offensive. **3.** Diseased; morbid. **4.** Violating some rule or principle. [< L *peccans*, *-antis*, ppr. of *peccare* to sin] **— pec′can·cy** *n.* **— pec′cant·ly** *adv.*

pec·ca·ry (pek′ə·rē) *n. pl.* **·ries** Either of two pugnacious, hoglike ungulates of Central and South America, the **collared peccary** (*Pecari angulatus*), or the **white-lipped peccary** (*Tayassus pecari*). [< Sp. *pecari* < Carib *pakira*]

pec·ca·vi (pe·kä′vī, -kä′vē) *n. pl.* **·vis** *Latin* A confession of guilt; literally, I have sinned.

pech (pekh) *v.i. Scot. & Brit. Dial.* To pant; puff.

pech·an (pekh′an) *n. Scot.* The gullet; stomach.

Pe·cho·ra (pyi·chôr′ə) A river in the NW R.S.F.S.R., flowing 1,110 miles north to the Barents Sea.

peck¹ (pek) *v.t.* **1.** To strike with the beak, as a bird does, or with something pointed. **2.** To make by striking thus: to *peck* a hole in a wall. **3.** To pick up, as food, with the beak. **—** *v.i.* **4.** To make strokes with the beak or with something

COLLARED PECCARY
(16 inches high at shoulder; to 38 inches long)

pointed. **5.** To eat in small amounts or without appetite: with *at*. **—** *n.* **1.** A quick, sharp blow, as with a beak. **2.** A mark or hole made by such a blow. **3.** *Informal* A quick kiss. [ME. Var. of PICK.]

peck² (pek) *n.* **1.** A measure of capacity: the fourth of a bushel, 8 quarts, or 8.8 liters. Abbr. *pk.* See table inside back cover. **2.** A vessel for measuring a peck. **3.** *Slang* A great quantity. [< OF *pek*; ult. origin uncertain]

peck·er (pek′ər) *n.* **1.** One who or that which pecks. **2.** *Brit. Slang* Courage; spirits.

peck·er·wood (pek′ər·wŏŏd′) *n. U.S. Dial.* **1.** A woodpecker. **2.** A poor white.

peck·ing order (pek′ing) **1.** A hierarchy among a flock of chickens, characterized by the right of the more aggressive to peck at and dominate those lower in the scale. **2.** Any similar hierarchy among human social groups.

Peck·sniff·i·an (pek·snif′ē·ən) *adj.* Unctuously hypocritical; insincere. [after Seth *Pecksniff*, a character in Dickens's *Martin Chuzzlewit*]

Pe·cos Bill (pā′kōs bil) A legendary cowboy of the American West, who performed many fantastic feats.

Pe·cos River (pā′kəs, -kōs) The principal tributary of the Rio Grande, flowing 926 miles from New Mexico to western Texas.

Pécs (pāch) A county borough in southern Hungary; pop. 114,713 (1960): German *Fünfkirchen*.

pec·tase (pek′tās) *n. Biochem.* An enzyme obtained from fruits, and combining with pectin to yield pectic acid. [< PECT(IN) + (DIAST)ASE]

pec·tate (pek′tāt) *n. Chem.* A salt or ester of pectic acid. [< PECT(IC) + -ATE³]

pec·ten (pek′tən) *n. pl.* **·ti·nes** (-tə·nēz) *Zool.* **1.** A comb, or comblike part or process. **2.** In birds and reptiles, a vascular pigmented membrane of the eyeball. **3.** A scallop (def. 1). [< L, comb, scallop < *pectere* to comb, dress the hair]

pec·tic (pek′tik) *adj.* Of, pertaining to, or derived from pectin. [< F *petique* < Gk.*pēktikos* < *pēktos* congealed < *pēguyein* to make firm]

pectic acid *Chem.* Any of a group of compounds derived from pectin by the hydrolysis of methyl ester.

pec·tin (pek′tin) *n. Biochem.* Any of a class of carbohydrates of high molecular weight contained in the cell walls of various fruits and vegetables, as apples, lemons, or carrots, used as the basis of fruit jellies. [< PECT(IC) + -IN]

pec·ti·nate (pek′tə·nāt) *adj.* Toothed, as a comb; comblike. Also **pec′ti·nat′ed.** [< L *pectinatus*, pp. of *pectere* to comb]

pec·tize (pek′tīz) *v.t. & v.i.* **·tized**, **·tiz·ing** To coagulate. [< Gk. *pēktos* congealed + -IZE]

pec·to·ral (pek′tər·əl) *adj.* **1.** Of or pertaining to the breast or chest. **2.** Adapted to, efficacious in, or designed for relieving or curing diseases of the lungs or chest. **3.** Emotional and subjective in manner, content, etc.: *pectoral* theology. **—** *n.* **1.** An ornament worn on the breast; especially, the **pectoral cross** worn on the breast by bishops, abbots, etc. **2.** A pectoral organ, fin, or muscle. **3.** Any medicine for ailments of the chest. [< L *pectoralis* < *pectus*, *-oris* breast]

pectoral arch *Anat.* **1.** The arch formed by the collar bone and shoulder blade in man. **2.** That part of the skeleton with which the forelimbs of a vertebrate animal are articulated. Also **pectoral girdle.**

pectoral fin *Zool.* One of the anterior paired fins of fishes, homologous with the anterior limb of higher vertebrates.

pectoral sandpiper An American sandpiper (*Erolia melanotos*), occasional in Europe, having a gray breast with dusky streaks: also called *fatbird*, *grass snipe*, *jacksnipe*.

pec·u·late (pek′yə·lāt) *v.t. & v.i.* **·lat·ed**, **·lat·ing** To steal or appropriate wrongfully (funds, especially public funds entrusted to one's care); embezzle. [< L *peculatus*, pp. of *peculari* to embezzle < *peculium*. See PECULIUM.] **— pec′u·la′tion** *n.* **— pec′u·la′tor** *n.*

pe·cu·liar (pi·kyōōl′yər) *adj.* **1.** Having a character exclusively its own; unlike anything else or anything of the same class or kind; specific. **2.** Singular; odd; strange. **3.** Select or special; separate. **4.** Belonging particularly or exclusively to one. **—** *n.* **1.** A person or thing that is peculiar; formerly, any private possession. **2.** A member of the sect known as the Peculiar People. [< MF *peculier* or < L *peculiaris* < *peculium*. See PECULIUM.] **— pe·cul′iar·ly** *adv.*

pe·cu·li·ar·i·ty (pi·kyōō′lē·ar′ə·tē) *n. pl.* **·ties 1.** A characteristic. **2.** The quality of being peculiar. **— Syn.** See CHARACTERISTIC.

Peculiar People 1. A denomination of Christians who hold that sinless perfection is immediately obtainable by those willing to seek and accept it. **2.** In the Scripture, the Jews, as being God's chosen people and separated from the rest of mankind. *Deut.* xxvi 18.

pe·cu·li·um (pi·kyōō′lē·əm) *n.* In Roman law, property that a slave, a wife, or a child was permitted to hold as his own. [< L, private property, orig., one's cattle < *pecus* cattle, money]

pe·cu·ni·ar·y (pi·kyōō′nē·er′ē) *adj.* **1.** Consisting of or relating to money. **2.** Having a monetary penalty; entailing a fine. [< L *pecuniarius* < *pecunia* money < *pecus* cattle]

ped-¹ Var. of PEDI-¹.
ped-² Var. of PEDO-.
ped. 1. Pedal. 2. Pedestal.
-ped Var. of -PEDE.
ped·a·gog·ic (ped′ə·goj′ik, -gō′jik) *adj.* 1. Of or pertaining to the science or art of teaching. 2. Of or belonging to a pedagogue; affected with a conceit of learning. Also **ped′a·gog′i·cal.** — **ped′a·gog′i·cal·ly** *adv.*
ped·a·gog·ics (ped′ə·goj′iks) *n.pl.* (construed as sing.) The science and art of teaching; pedagogy.
ped·a·gog·ism (ped′ə·gog′iz·əm, -gōg′-) *n.* The nature, character, or business of teachers or a teacher.
ped·a·gogue (ped′ə·gog, -gôg) *n.* 1. A schoolmaster; educator. 2. A pedantic, narrow-minded teacher. 3. In ancient Greece and Rome, a slave who attended children to school. Also **ped′a·gog.** [< OF *pedagoge* < L *paedagogus* < Gk. *paidagogos* trainer of boys < *pais, paidos* child + *agōgos* leader < *agein* to lead]
ped·a·go·gy (ped′ə·gō′jē, -goj′ē) *n.* 1. The science or profession of teaching. 2. The theory of how to teach.
ped·al (ped′l) *adj.* 1. Of or pertaining to a foot, feet, or a footlike part. 2. Of or pertaining to a pedal. — *n.* 1. *Mech.* A lever operated by the foot and having various functions: a bicycle *pedal*; a piano *pedal*. Abbr. **ped.** 2. A pedal point. — *v.t.* **·aled** or **·alled, ped·al·ing** or **·al·ing** To move or operate by working pedals. [< L *pedalis* < *pes, pedis* foot]
ped·al·fer (pi·dal′fər) *n.* A type of soil characterized by a downward shifting of alumina and iron oxide, with an absence of carbonate of lime accumulations. [< Gk. *ped(on)* ground + AL(UMINA) + L *fer(rum)* iron]
ped·a·lier (ped′ə·lir′) *n.* A pedal keyboard for a pianoforte. [< F *pédalier* < *pédale* pedal < L *pedalis*. See PEDAL.]
pedal point *Music* A tone sustained, usually in the bass, while other parts proceed with varying harmonies. Also **pedal.**
ped·al-push·ers (ped′l·pŏŏsh′erz) *n.pl.* Slacks that come to just below the knees, worn by women and girls.
ped·ant (ped′ənt) *n.* 1. One who makes needless display of his learning, or who insists upon the importance of trifling points of scholarship. 2. *Obs.* A schoolmaster. [< MF *pédant* < Ital. *pedante*, prob. < Med.L *paedagogans, -antis,* ppr. of *paedagogare* to teach < L *paedagogus.* See PEDAGOGUE.] — **pe·dan·tic** (pi·dan′tik) *adj.* — **pe·dan′ti·cal·ly** *adv.*
ped·ant·ry (ped′ən·trē) *n. pl.* **·ries** 1. Ostentatious display of knowledge. 2. Undue or slavish adherence to forms or rules. [< Ital. *pedanteria* < *pedante.* See PEDANT.]
ped·ate (ped′āt) *adj.* 1. Resembling or having the functions of a foot; also, having feet. 2. *Bot.* Divided or parted as a fan, the lateral divisions being subdivided: said especially of leaves. [< L *pedatus* having feet < *pes, pedis* foot] — **ped′ate·ly** *adv.*
pedati- *combining form Bot.* Pedately: *pedatifid.* [< L *pedatus* having feet < *pes, pedis* foot]
pe·dat·i·fid (pi·dat′ə·fid, -dā′tə-) *adj. Bot.* Having the subdivisions of a simple leaf, which is pedately nerved, extending halfway to the base.
ped·dle (ped′l) *v.* **·dled, ·dling** *v.i.* 1. To travel about selling small wares. 2. To occupy oneself with trifles; piddle. — *v.t.* 3. To carry about and sell in small quantities. — **peddle your papers** *U.S. Slang* Get out of here! [Appar. back formation < ME *pedlere* peddler]
ped·dler (ped′lər) *n.* One who peddles; a hawker: also spelled *pedlar, pedler.* [ME *pedlere* < *pedder* < *ped* basket]
ped·dling (ped′ling) *adj.* Small; trifling; piddling.
-pede *combining form* Footed: *centipede.* Also spelled *-ped,* as in *quadruped.* [< L *pes, pedis* foot]
ped·er·ast (ped′ə·rast, pē′də-) *n.* One addicted to pederasty: also spelled *paederast.*
ped·er·as·ty (ped′ə·ras′tē, pē′də-) *n.* Sex relations between men, especially between men and boys. [< NL *paederastia* < Gk. *paiderastia* < *paiderastēs* lover of boys < *pais, paidos* boy + *erastēs* lover < *eraein* to love] — **ped′er·as′tic** *adj.* — **ped′er·as′ti·cal·ly** *adv.*
pe·des (pē′dēz) Plural of PES.
ped·es·tal (ped′is·təl) *n.* 1. A base or support for a column, statue, or vase. 2. Any foundation, base, or support, either material or immaterial. Abbr. **ped.** — **to put on a pedestal** To hold in high estimation; to put in the position of an idol or hero. — *v.t.* **·taled** or **·talled, ·tal·ing** or **·tal·ling** To place on a pedestal. [< MF *piédestal* < Ital. *piedestallo* < *pie di stallo* < *piè, piede* foot + *di* of + *stallo* stall, standing place]
pe·des·tri·an (pə·des′trē·ən) *adj.* 1. Moving on foot; walking. 2. Pertaining to common people; plebeian. 3. Commonplace, prosaic, or dull, as prose. — *n.* One who journeys or moves from place to place on foot; a walker. [< L *pedester, -tris* on foot < *pes, pedis* foot] — **pe·des′tri·an·ism** *n.*
pedi-¹ *combining form* Foot; related to the foot or feet: *pedicure.* Also, before vowels, **ped-.** [< L *pes, pedis* foot]
pedi-² Var. of PEDO-.

pe·di·a·tri·cian (pē′dē·ə·trish′ən, ped′ē-) *n.* A physician specializing in pediatrics. Also **pe·di·at·rist** (pē′dē·at′rist).
pe·di·at·rics (pē′dē·at′riks, ped′ē-) *n.pl.* (construed as sing.) That branch of medicine dealing with the diseases and hygienic care of children: also spelled *paediatrics.* [< Gk. *pais, paidos* child + -IATRICS] — **pe′di·at′ric** *adj.*
ped·i·cab (ped′i·kab) *n.* A three-wheeled vehicle operated by pedaling and having an attached seat for one or two passengers, available for public hire in some Asian countries. [< PEDI-¹ + CAB¹]
ped·i·cel (ped′ə·səl) *n.* 1. A stalk or supporting part. 2. *Bot.* **a** The stalk supporting a single flower in an inflorescence composed of flowers arranged upon a common peduncle. **b** A small or delicate support of various special organs, as of a sporangium in ferns or a capsule in mosses. Also called *footstalk.* 3. *Zool.* A footlike sucker or part. [< NL *pedicellus,* dim. of L *pediculus,* dim. of *pes, pedis* foot] — **ped′i·cel′lar** (-sel′ər) *adj.*
ped·i·cel·late (ped′ə·sə·lit, -lāt′) *adj.* On or having a pedicel.
ped·i·cle (ped′i·kəl) *n.* 1. *Anat.* One of two short bony processes connecting either side of the body of a vertebra with the posterior spinal process. For illustration see VERTEBRA. 2. A pedicel. [< L *pediculus.* See PEDICEL.]
pe·dic·u·lar (pə·dik′yə·lər) *adj.* Pertaining to or caused by lice. [< L *pedicularis* < *pediculus,* dim. of *pedis* louse]
pe·dic·u·late (pə·dik′yə·lit, -lāt) *adj.* Of, pertaining, or belonging to an order (*Pediculati*) of teleost fishes having a spinous dorsal fin with the front ray adapted as a lure. [< L *pediculus* footstalk + -ATE¹]
pe·dic·u·lo·sis (pə·dik′yə·lō′sis) *n. Pathol.* The condition of being infested with lice; lousiness: also called *phthiriasis.* [< L *pediculus* little louse + -OSIS] — **pe·dic′u·lous** *adj.*
ped·i·cure (ped′i·kyoŏr) *n.* 1. Chiropody. 2. A chiropodist; podiatrist. 3. The cosmetic treatment of the feet and toenails. — *v.t.* **·cured, ·cur·ing** To treat (the feet) for corns, bunions, etc. [< F *pédicure* < L *pes, pedis* foot + *curare* to care for] — **ped′i·cur′ist** *n.*
ped·i·form (ped′i·fôrm) *adj.* Resembling a foot in shape.
ped·i·gree (ped′ə·grē) *n.* 1. A line of ancestors; lineage. 2. A list or table of descent and relationship; a genealogical register, especially of an animal of pure breed. [< MF *pié de grue* a crane's foot; from a three line mark denoting succession in pedigrees]
ped·i·greed (ped′ə·grēd) *adj.* Having a pedigree; of notable ancestry.
ped·i·ment (ped′ə·mənt) *n. Archit.* 1. A broad triangular part above a portico or door. 2. Any similar piece with a long base surmounting a door, screen, bookcase, etc. [Earlier *periment,* prob. alter. of PYRAMID; infl. in form by L *pes, pedis* foot] — **ped′i·men′tal** (-men′təl) *adj.*

PEDIMENT
(Supreme Court Building, Washington, D.C.)

ped·lar (ped′lər), **ped·ler** See PEDDLER.
pedo- *combining form* Child; children; offspring: also, before vowels, **ped-,** as in *pedagogy.* Also spelled *paedo-.* [< Gk. *pais, paidos* child]
pe·dol·o·gy¹ (pi·dol′ə·jē) *n.* The scientific study of the development and behavior of children: also called *paidology.* [< PEDO-² + -LOGY] — **ped·o·log·i·cal** (ped′ə·loj′i·kəl) *adj.* — **ped′o·log′i·cal·ly** *adv.* — **pe·dol′o·gist** *n.*
pe·dol·o·gy² (pi·dol′ə·jē) *n.* The science that treats of the origin, nature, properties, and classification of soils. [< Gk. *pedon* ground + -LOGY] — **ped·o·log·i·cal** (ped′ə·loj′i·kəl) *adj.* — **ped′o·log′i·cal·ly** *adv.* — **pe·dol′o·gist** *n.*
pe·dom·e·ter (pi·dom′ə·tər) *n.* An instrument that measures distance traveled by recording the number of steps taken by the person who carries it. [< F *pédomètre* < L *pes, pedis* foot + Gk. *metron* measure]
ped·o·sphere (ped′ə·sfir) *n.* The soil-bearing layer of the earth's surface. [< Gk. *pedon* ground + -SPHERE] — **ped′o·spher′ic** (-sfir′ik, -sfer′-) or **·i·cal** *adj.*
pe·dro (pē′drō) *n. pl.* **·dros** 1. The five of trumps in the card game of cinch. 2. A game of seven-up in which the five of trumps counts five. [< Sp. *Pedro* Peter, a personal name]
pe·dun·cle (pi·dung′kəl) *n.* 1. *Bot.* The general stalk or support of an inflorescence: also called *footstalk.* 2. *Anat.* A stalk or stem, as for the attachment of an organ or organism: the *peduncles* of the brain. 3. *Zool.* A stalk or stalklike part. [< NL *pedunculus* footstalk, dim. of *pes, pedis* foot] — **pe·dun′cled, pe·dun′cu·lar** (-kyə·lər) *adj.*
pe·dun·cu·late (pi·dung′kyə·lit, -lāt) *adj.* Borne on or having a peduncle. Also **pe·dun′cu·lat′ed.**

pee¹ (pē) *n.* The letter P.

pee² (pē) *Informal n.* Urine. — *v.i.* **peed, pee·ing** To urinate. [Euphemism for PISS]

pee·been (pē′bēn) *n.* A large hardwood evergreen tree (*Syncarpia hilli*) of the myrtle family, native to Australia: also called *turpentine tree.*

Pee·bles (pē′bəlz) A county in SE Scotland; 347 sq. mi.; pop. 13,339 (1969); county seat, **Peebles,** pop. 5,598 (1969): also *Tweeddale.* Also **Pee′bles·shire** (-shir).

Pee Dee River (pē dē) A river in southern North Carolina and NE South Carolina, flowing 435 miles, generally SE, to Winyah Bay.

peek (pēk) *v.i.* To look furtively, slyly, or quickly; peep. — *n.* A peep, glance. [ME *piken*; origin uncertain]

peek·a·boo (pē′kə·boō′) *n.* A children's game in which one hides one's face and calls out "peekaboo!"

peel¹ (pēl) *n.* The natural coating of certain kinds of fruit, as oranges and lemons; skin; rind. — *v.t.* **1.** To strip off the bark, skin, etc., of. **2.** To strip off; remove. — *v.i.* **3.** To lose bark, skin, etc. **4.** To come off: said of bark, skin, etc. **5.** *Slang* To undress. — **to keep one's eye peeled** *Informal* To keep watch; be alert. — **to peel off** *Aeron.* To veer off from a flight formation so as to dive or prepare for a landing. [ME *pelen,* prob. < OE *pilian* and OF *peler* (< *pel,* var. of *peau* skin < L *pellis*) and < L *pilare* to deprive of hair < *pilus* hair]

peel² (pēl) *n.* **1.** A long-handled, shovellike implement used by bakers in moving bread, etc., about an oven. **2.** The blade or broad part of an oar. [< OF *pele* < L *pala* shovel]

peel³ (pēl) *n.* A square stronghold or tower of the 16th century, especially on the borders of Scotland and England: also **peel/house/** (-hous/). [< AF *pel* < L *palus* stake]

Peel (pēl) A port and resort town on the west coast of the Isle of Man; site of an ancient castle; pop. about 3,000.

Peel (pēl), **Sir Robert,** 1788–1850, English statesman, introduced police reforms.

Peele (pēl), **George,** 1558?–97?, English playwright and poet.

peel·ing (pē′ling) *n.* Something peeled off; a strip of rind, bark, skin, or outer layer.

peel·er (pē′lər) *n. Brit. Slang* A policeman. [after Sir Robert *Peel*]

peen (pēn) *n.* The end of a hammer head opposite the flat, striking face, usually shaped for indenting, riveting, chipping, etc. For illustration see HAMMER. — *v.t.* To beat, bend, or shape with the peen. [< ON. Cf. Norw. *pen* end of a hammer, Sw. *pæna* to beat out.]

peep¹ (pēp) *v.i.* **1.** To utter the small, sharp cry of a young bird or chick; chirp; cheep. **2.** To speak in a weak, small voice. — *n.* **1.** The cry of a chick or small bird, or of a young frog; chirp. **2.** A small sandpiper. [ME *pepen*; imit.]

peep² (pēp) *v.i.* **1.** To look through a small hole, from concealment, etc.; peek. **2.** To look furtively or quickly; peek. **3.** To begin to appear; be just visible. — *v.t.* **4.** *Rare* To cause to stick out slightly. — *n.* **1.** A furtive look; a glimpse or glance. **2.** An aperture or crevice through which one may look; peephole. **3.** The earliest appearance: the *peep* of day. [Prob. alter. of PEEK]

peep³ (pēp) *n. Slang* A jeep.

peep·er¹ (pē′pər) *n.* An animal that peeps or makes a chirping sound; especially, a chick or any of several tree frogs.

peep·er² (pē′pər) *n.* **1.** One who peeps or peeks; a spying person. **2.** *Slang* An eye.

peep·hole (pēp′hōl′) *n.* An aperture, as a hole or crack, through which one may peep; also, a small window in a door.

peep·ing Tom (pē′ping tom′) An overly inquisitive or prying person; especially, one who peeps in at windows.

Peeping Tom of Coventry In British legend, a curious tailor who peeped at Lady Godiva during her ride through Coventry and was struck blind.

peep·show (pēp′shō′) *n.* An exhibition of pictures, etc., viewed through a small orifice fitted with a magnifying lens.

peep sight An adjustable rear gunsight with a small aperture through which the front sight is aligned when aiming.

peer¹ (pir) *v.i.* **1.** To look narrowly or searchingly, as in an effort to see clearly. **2.** To come partially into view: The sun *peers* over the horizon. **3.** *Poetic* To appear. — **Syn.** See LOOK. [Origin uncertain]

peer² (pir) *n.* **1.** An equal, as in natural gifts or in social rank. **2.** An equal before the law. **3.** A noble; especially, a member of a hereditary legislative body. **4.** In the United Kingdom, a duke, marquis, earl, viscount, or baron; also, a prelate having a seat in the House of Lords. **5.** *Obs.* A companion; mate; also, rival. — *adj. Sociol.* Made up of people having approximately the same age, education, social standing, etc.: a *peer* group. [< OF *per* < L *par* equal]

peer³ (pir) *n. Scot.* **1.** A pear. **2.** A peg top.

peer·age (pir′ij) *n.* **1.** In the United Kingdom, the office or rank of a peer of the realm, or nobleman. **2.** Peers collectively; the nobility. **3.** A book containing a genealogical list of the nobility.

peer·ess (pir′is) *n.* A woman who holds a title of nobility, either in her own right or by marriage with a peer.

peer·less (pir′lis) *adj.* Of unequaled excellence. — **peer′less·ly** *adv.* — **peer′less·ness** *n.*

peer of the realm One of the lords of Parliament.

peer·y (pir′ē) *n. pl.* **peer·ies** *Scot.* A child's top spun with a string. Also **peer′ie.**

pees·weep (pēz′wēp′) *n. Scot.* The pewit or lapwing.

peet·weet (pēt′wēt′) *n.* The spotted sandpiper. See under SANDPIPER. [Imit.]

peeve (pēv) *v.t.* **peeved, peev·ing** *Informal* To make peevish. — *n. Informal* A complaint, annoyance, or grievance. [Back formation < PEEVISH]

peeved (pēvd) *adj.* Vexed; discontented; disagreeable: to be *peeved* at someone.

pee·vish (pē′vish) *adj.* **1.** Irritable or querulous; fretful; cross. **2.** Showing or marked by petulant discontent and vexation. [ME *pevische*; origin uncertain] — **pee′vish·ly** *adv.* — **pee′vish·ness** *n.*

pee·wee (pē′wē) *n.* **1.** See PEWEE. **2.** *Informal* Anything or anyone especially small or diminutive. — *adj.* Tiny; insignificant. [Imit.]

peg (peg) *n.* **1.** A pin, usually of wood or metal, used to fasten articles together, to stop a hole, etc. **2.** A projecting pin upon which something may be fastened or hung, or which may serve to mark a boundary or keep a score, etc. **3.** In a stringed musical instrument, a pin for holding fast the end of a string and adjusting its tension. **4.** A reason or excuse for an action: a *peg* to hang an argument upon. **5.** A degree or step, as in rank or estimation. **6.** *Brit.* A drink of brandy and soda or of whisky and soda. **7.** *Informal* A leg, often one of wood. **8.** *Informal* A throw, as in baseball. — **to take (one) down a peg** To lower the self-esteem of (a person), as by humiliating. — *v.* **pegged, peg·ging** *v.t.* **1.** To drive or force a peg into; fasten with pegs. **2.** To mark or designate with pegs. **3.** To strike or pierce with a peg or sharp instrument. **4.** *Informal* To throw: to *peg* stones. — *v.i.* **5.** To work or strive hard and perseveringly: usually with *away.* **6.** In croquet, to hit a peg. **7.** In cribbage, etc., to mark the score with pegs. — *adj.* Peg-topped. [ME *pegge* < MDu. *pegge*]

Peg·a·sus (peg′ə·səs) In Greek mythology, a winged horse sprung from the blood of Medusa, a blow of whose hoof caused Hippocrene, the fountain of poetic inspiration, to spring from Mount Helicon; also, poetic inspiration. See BELLEROPHON. — *n.* A constellation, the Winged Horse. See CONSTELLATION. [< L < Gk. *Pēgasos*]

peg·board (peg′bôrd) *n.* **1.** Any perforated board into which pegs may be inserted for holding things, keeping score, etc. **2.** *Brit.* A game in which a player arranges pegs in certain patterns on a perforated board: also called *solitaire.*

peg leg *Informal* **1.** An artificial leg of rodlike or tapering shape. **2.** A person with such a leg.

peg·ma·tite (peg′mə·tīt) *n.* A very coarse-grained granitic rock composed chiefly or orthoclase, quartz, and mica, commonly occurring in veins or dikes. [< Gk. *pegma, -atos* solid mass + -ITE¹] — **peg′ma·tit′ic** (-tit′ik) *adj.*

peg-top (peg′top′) *adj.* Having the shape of a peg top: applied especially to trousers that are narrow at the ankle.

peg top A child's wooden spinning top, pear-shaped and having a sharp metal peg.

Pe·gu·an (pe·goō′ən) *n.* Mon.

Peh·le·vi (pä′lə·vē) See PAHLAVI.

P.E.I. Prince Edward Island.

pei·gnoir (pān·wär′, pān′wär) *n.* A loose dressing gown or negligée worn by women. [< F < *peigner* to comb < L *pectinare* < *pecten, pectinis* comb]

Pei·ping (bā′ping′) See PEKING.

Pei·pus (pī′pəs), Lake A lake on the border between the Estonian S.S.R. and the R.S.F.S.R.; 1,357 sq. mi.: Russian *Chudskoye Ozero.* Estonian *Peip·si Järv* (pāp′sē yarv).

Pei·rai·evs (pē′rē·efs′) The Greek name for PIRAEUS.

Peirce (pûrs), **Charles Sanders,** 1839–1914, U.S. mathematician and logician; founder of pragmatism.

Pei·sis·tra·tus (pī·sis′tra·təs, pi-) See PISISTRATUS.

pe·jo·ra·tion (pē′jə·rā′shən, pej′ə-) *n.* **1.** The condition of becoming worse; deterioration. **2.** *Ling.* A degeneration or lowering in the meaning of a word, as in *silly* (formerly "blessed"): opposed to *melioration.* [< Med.L *pejoratio, -onis* < LL *pejoro.* See PEJORATIVE.]

pe·jo·ra·tive (pē′jə·rā′tiv, pej′ə-, pi·jôr′ə·tiv, -jor′-) *adj.* Having any derogatory or disparaging meaning or sense: a *pejorative* statement. — *n.* A pejorative word. [< LL *pejoratus,* pp. of *pejorare* to make worse < L *pejor* worse] — **pe′jo·ra′tive·ly** *adv.*

pek·an (pek′ən) *n.* The fisher (def. 2). [< dial. F (Canadian) < Algonquian *pékané*]

pe·kin (pē′kin′) *n.* A silk fabric, usually striped. [< F *pékin* < *Pékin* Peking, China]

Pe·kin (pē′kin) A city in central Illinois, on the Illinois River, near Peoria; pop. 31,375.

Pe·king (pē′king′, Chinese bā′jing′) The capital of the People's Republic of China, in northern Hopeh Province; pop. 7,000,000 (est. 1968): from 1928–49 *Peiping.*

Pe·king·ese (pē′kə·nēz′ for def. 1; pē′king·ēz′ for defs. 2, 3) *n. pl.* **·ese** **1.** A Pekingese dog. **2.** A native or inhabitant of Peking. **3.** The dialect spoken in Peking. — *adj.* Of or pertaining to Peking or to a Pekingese dog. Also **Pe·kin·ese** (pē′kə·nēz′).

Pekingese dog A variety of the Chinese (or Pekingese) pug, having long silky hair, especially upon the ears, diminutive snub nose, and short legs.

Peking man *Paleontol.* Sinanthropus.

pe·koe (pē′kō, *Brit.* pek′ō) *n.* A superior black tea of India, Ceylon, and Java, made from the downy tips of the young buds of the tea plant. [< dial. Chinese (Amoy) *pek-ho* < *pek* white + *ho* hair]

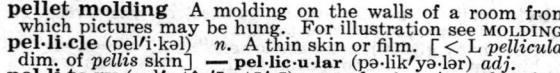

PEKINGESE DOG
(About 8 inches high
at shoulder)

pel·age (pel′ij) *n.* The coat or covering of a mammal, as fur, wool, etc. [< MF < OF *pel*, var. of *peau* skin < L *pellis*]

Pe·la·gi·an·ism (pə·lā′jē·ən·iz′əm) *n. Theol.* The body of doctrines held by the followers of **Pe·la·gi·us** (pə·lā′jē·əs), died 420?, a British monk who denied original sin, confined grace to forgiveness, and affirmed that man's unaided will is capable of spiritual good. **— Pe·la′gi·an** *n & adj.*

pe·lag·ic (pə·laj′ik) *adj.* Of, pertaining to, or inhabiting the sea or ocean far from land; oceanic. **— Syn.** See OCEANIC. [< L *pelagicus* < Gk. *pelagos* the sea]

Pe·la·gie Islands (pə·lā′jē) An island group of Sicily between Tunis and Malta; 10 sq. mi.

pel·ar·gon·ic acid (pel′är·gon′ik) *Chem.* A colorless oily, organic compound, $CH_3(CH_2)_7 \cdot COOH$, obtained as an ester from the leaves of pelargonium: also called *nonanoic acid.*

pel·ar·go·ni·um (pel′är·gō′nē·əm) *n.* Any of a number of strong-scented, ornamental evergreen herbs or shrubs (genus *Pelargonium*), generally known in cultivation as *geraniums*, having entire lobed or dissected leaves, and handsome, variously colored flowers: also called *stork's-bill.* [< NL < Gk. *pelargos* stork] **— pel′ar·gon′ic** (-gon′ik) *adj.*

Pe·las·gi (pə·laz′jī) *n. pl.* A prehistoric, seafaring people who inhabited the coasts of Greece, Asia Minor, and islands of the eastern Mediterranean. Also **Pe·las′gi·ans. — Pe·las′gi·an** *& n.* **— Pe·las′gic** *adj.*

Pe·le (pā′lā) In Polynesian mythology, the goddess of volcanoes.

Pe·lée (pə·lā′), **Mount** A volcano in northern Martinique; 4,429 ft.

pel·er·ine (pel′ə·rēn′) *n.* A woman's cape of waist length, usually having long, pointed ends in front. [< F *pèlerine*, fem. of *pèlerin* < OF *pelerin*. See PILGRIM.]

Pe·le's hair (pā′lāz) Molten lava drawn out into long, fine, glasslike threads by the action of wind. [after PELE]

Pe·leus (pē′yŏŏs, pē′lē·əs) In Greek legend, a king of the Myrmidons and father of Achilles.

Pe·lew Islands (pē·lōō′) See PALAU ISLANDS.

pelf (pelf) *n.* Money; wealth, especially if dishonestly acquired. [< OF *pelfre* booty; ult. origin uncertain]

Pe·li·as (pē′lē·əs, pel′ē·əs) In Greek mythology, a son of Poseidon and king of Iolcus, who sent his nephew Jason to get the Golden Fleece.

pel·i·can (pel′i·kən) *n.* A large, gregarious, web-footed bird (genus *Pelecanus*) of warm regions, having a distensible membranous pouch on the lower jaw for the temporary storage of fish. [OE *pellican* < LL *pelicanus, pelecanus* < Gk. *pelekan.* ? Akin to Gk. *pelekys* ax; in ref. to its bill]

Pelican State Nickname of LOUISIANA.

Pel·i·des (pel′ə·dēz) In Greek mythology, any male descended from Peleus, especially his son Achilles.

Pe·li·on (pē′lē·on) A mountain range on the coast of SE Thessaly; highest peak, 5,252 ft. See OSSA.

PELICAN
(4 to 5
feet high)

pe·lisse (pə·lēs′) *n.* A long outer garment or cloak, originally made of fur or lined with fur. [< F < Med.L *pellicia* < L (*vestis*) *pellicia* (a garment) of skins or fur < *pellis* skin]

pe·lite (pē′līt) *n.* Argillite (which see). [< Gk. *pēlos* clay + -ITE¹] **— pe·lit·ic** (pi·lit′ik) *adj.*

Pel·la (pel′ə) A city of ancient Greece; capital of Macedonia, birthplace of Alexander the Great.

pel·la·gra (pə·lā′grə, -lag′rə) *n. Pathol.* A disease characterized by gastric disturbance, skin eruptions, etc., caused by a deficiency of nicotinic acid. [< NL, prob. < Ital. *pelle agra* rough skin; ? infl. by Gk. *-agra* < *agra* a seizure, as in *podagra* gout, lit., a seizure in the feet] **— pel·la′grous** *adj.*

pel·la·grin (pə·lā′grin, -lag′rin) *n.* One who suffers from pellagra.

Pel·le·as (pel′ē·əs), **Sir** In Arthurian legend, one of the Knights of the Round Table.

pel·let (pel′it) *n.* **1.** A small round ball, as of wax, paper, bread, etc. **2.** A small bullet or shot. **3.** A very small pill. **4.** A stone for a slingshot. **5.** A cannonball. **— v.t. 1.** To make into pellets. **2.** To strike or hit with pellets. [< OF *pelote* ball < Med.L *pelota, pilota* < L *pila*]

pellet molding A molding on the walls of a room from which pictures may be hung. For illustration see MOLDING.

pel·li·cle (pel′i·kəl) *n.* A thin skin or film. [< L *pellicula*, dim. of *pellis* skin] **— pel·lic·u·lar** (pə·lik′yə·lər) *adj.*

pel·li·to·ry (pel′ə·tôr′ē, -tō′rē) *n. pl.* **·ries** Any of various weedlike herbs (genus *Parietaria*) of the nettle family; especially, the **wall pellitory** (*P. officinalis*) of Europe, that grows on old walls. [< OF *paritoire, paritaire* < L *parietaria* < *parietarius* of a wall < *paries, -etis* wall]

pellitory of Spain A perennial herb (*Anacyclus pyrethrum*) of the composite family, with procumbent stems, dissected leaves, and white flowers, cultivated for its pungent roots used as a local irritant and as a sialogogue.

pell-mell (pel′mel′) *adv.* **1.** In a confused or disordered way or manner; indiscriminantly; higgledy-piggledy. **2.** With a headlong rush; in wild haste. **— adj.** Devoid of order or method; confused: a *pell-mell* assortment of things. **— n.** A confused crowd or mixture; a jumble; disorder. Also **pell′mell′.** [< F *pêlemêle* < OF *pesle-mesle*, varied reduplication of *mester* to mix]

pel·lu·cid (pə·lōō′sid) *adj.* **1.** Permitting to a certain extent the passage of light; translucent; limpid. **2.** Transparently clear and simple; understandable: a *pellucid* style. **— Syn.** See CLEAR. [< L *pellucidus* transparent < *perlucere* < *per-* through + *lucere* to shine] **— pel·lu′cid·ly** *adv.* **— pel·lu′cid·ness, pel·lu·cid·i·ty** (pel′ōō·sid′ə·tē) *n.*

Pel·ly River (pel′ē) A river in south central Yukon, Canada, flowing 330 miles NW to a confluence with the Lewes River, and forming the Yukon River.

pe·lon (pə·lōn′) *adj.* Hairless: said of animals. [< Am. Sp. < Sp. *pelón* bald]

Pe·lop·i·das (pə·lop′i·dəs), died 364 B.C., Theban general.

Pel·o·pon·ne·sian (pel′ə·pə·nē′zhən, -shən) *adj.* Of or pertaining to the Peloponnesus. **— n.** A native or inhabitant of the Peloponnesus.

Peloponnesian War See table for WAR.

Pel·o·pon·ne·sus (pel′ə·pə·nē′səs) The peninsula between the Aegean and Ionian seas comprising one of the main divisions of southern Greece; 8,603 sq. mi.; pop. 1,096,390 (1961): formerly *Morea*. Also **Pel′o·pon·nese′** (-nēs′, -nēz′). *Greek* **Pe·lo·pon·ne·sos** (pā′lô·pôn′nyĕ·sôs).

Pe·lops (pē′lops) In Greek mythology, the son of Tantalus, killed by his father and served as food to the gods but later restored to life by Demeter.

pe·lo·ri·a (pə·lôr′ē·ə, -lō′rē·ə) *n. Bot.* Abnormal regularity of a flower form, by development of complementary irregularities or by the loss of the irregular parts. [< NL < Gk. *pelōros* monstrous < *pelōr* monster] **— pe·lor·ic** (pə·lôr′ik, -lor′-) *adj.*

pe·lo·rus (pə·lôr′əs) *n.* A navigational instrument by which bearings are taken, on a horizontal graduated circle.

pe·lo·ta (pe·lō′tə) *n.* The game of jai alai. [< Sp., lit., a ball, aug. of *pella* < L *pila*]

pelt[1] (pelt) *n.* **1.** The skin of an animal, usually with the fur or hair left on. **2.** A garment made of skins. **3.** The human skin: a humorous term. [Prob. back formation < PELTRY]

pelt[2] (pelt) *v.t.* **1.** To strike repeatedly with or as with missiles or blows. **2.** To throw or hurl (missiles). **3.** To assail with words. **— v.i. 4.** To beat or descend with violence. **5.** To move rapidly; hurry. **— n. 1.** A blow, as one given by something thrown. **2.** A steady or swift pace: especially in the phrase **full pelt.** [ME *pelten*, ? var. of *pulten* to thrust < L *pultare*, freq. of *pellere* to beat, drive] **— pelt′er** *n.*

pel·tast (pel′tast) *n.* In ancient Greece, a lightly armed soldier. [< L *peltasta* < Gk. *peltastēs* < *peltē* shield]

pel·tate (pel′tāt) *adj. Bot.* Attached to the stalk at or near the center of the lower surface, as a leaf. Also **pel′tat·ed.** [< L *peltatus* armed with a shield < Gk. *peltē* shield] **— pel′tate·ly** *adv.*

Pel·ti·er effect (pel′tē·ər, -tē·ā) *Physics* The liberation or absorption of heat resulting from the passage of an electric current across the junction of two dissimilar metals. Also called **Peltier heat.** Compare SEEBECK EFFECT. [after Jean Charles Athanase *Peltier*, 1785–1845, French physicist]

Pel·ton wheel (pel′tən) *Mech.* A type of water wheel that is made to rotate by the impingement of high-pressure jets of water on a succession of buckets shaped to obtain maximum efficiency in operation.

pelt·ry (pel′trē) *n. pl.* **·ries 1.** Pelts collectively. **2.** A pelt. **3.** A place for keeping or storing pelts. [< OF *pelterie* < *peletier* furrier < *pel* skin < L *pellis*]

pelvi- *combining form* Pelvis: *pelvimetry*. [< L *pelvis* basin]

pel·vic (pel′vik) *adj.* Of, pertaining to, or near the pelvis.

pelvic arch *Anat.* In vertebrates, that part of the skeleton to which the hind limbs (in man, the lower limbs) are attached. Also **pelvic girdle.**

pel·vim·e·ter (pel·vim′ə·tər) *n. Med.* An instrument used in pelvimetry. [< PELVI- + -METER]

pel·vim·e·try (pel·vim′ə·trē) *n. Med.* The measurement of the size and capacity of the pelvis, especially prior to childbirth. **— pel·vi·met·ric** (pel′vi·met′rik) *adj.*

pel·vis (pel′vis) *n.* *pl.* **·vis·es** (-və·səz) or **·ves** (-vēz) **1.** *Anat.* **a** The part of the skeleton that forms a bony girdle joining the lower or hind limbs to the body, composed, in man, of the two innominate bones and the sacrum. **b** The hollow interior portion of the kidney, into which the urine is discharged before going into the ureter: for illustration see KIDNEY. **2.** A basin or basinlike structure. [< L, basin]

Pemb. Pembrokeshire.

Pem·ba (pem′bə) An island off the NE coast of Tanganyika, in the Zanzibar protectorate; 380 sq. mi.

Pem·ber·ton (pem′bər·tən), **John Clifford**, 1814–81, Confederate general in the Civil War.

pem·bi·na (pem·bē′nə) *n. Canadian* A variety of cranberry.

Pem·broke (pem′brŏŏk) County town of Pembrokeshire, Wales; pop. 13,800.

Pem·broke·shire (pem′brŏŏk-shir) A former county of SW Wales; 614 sq. mi.; pop. 97,295 (1971); county seat, Pembroke, pop. 14,200 (1969). Also **Pem′broke.**

pem·mi·can (pem′ə·kən) *n. U.S. & Canadian* **1.** Lean meat, usually venison, cut into strips, dried, pounded into paste with fat and a few berries, and pressed into cakes. **2.** A similar concentrated and nutritious food made from beef and dried fruits, used by Arctic explorers, etc. Also **pem′i·can.** [< Algonquian (Cree) *pimekan* < *pime* fat]

pem·phi·gus (pem′fə·gəs, pem·fī′-) *n. Pathol.* A skin disease characterized by watery blisters successively formed on various parts of the body. Also **pem′phix** (-fiks). [< NL < Gk. *pemphix, -igos* pustule]

pen¹ (pen) *n.* **1.** An instrument for writing with fluid ink; formerly, one made of a quill that had been pointed and split, but now usually a metal point split in the middle and fitted to a holder; also, a pen and its holder together. **2.** A ball-point pen (which see). **3.** The quality of one's penmanship. **4.** The pen regarded as the means of literary work: verse from the *pen* of a novice. **5.** The profession of writing. **6.** The style of writing. **7.** A writer. **8.** *Bot.* The midrib of a leaf. **9.** *Zool.* The internal shell of a cuttlefish. **10.** *Ornithol.* **a** A feather; quill. **b** *pl.* Wings. —*v.t.* **penned, pen·ning** To write with a pen. [< OF *penne* pen, feather < LL *penna* < L, wing, feather] —**pen′ner** *n.*

pen² (pen) *n.* **1.** A small enclosure, as for pigs; also, the animals contained in a pen. **2.** Any small place of confinement. **3.** *Slang* A penitentiary. —*v.t.* **penned** or **pent, pen·ning** To enclose in or as in a pen; confine. [OE *penn.* Akin to OE *pinn* pin, peg.]

pen³ (pen) *n.* A female swan. [Origin unknown]

Pen. or **pen.** Peninsula.

P.E.N. International Association of Poets, Playwrights, Editors, Essayists, and Novelists.

pe·nal (pē′nəl) *adj.* **1.** Of or pertaining to punishment. **2.** Liable, or rendering liable, to punishment: a *penal* act. **3.** Enacting or prescribing punishment: a *penal* code. **4.** Relating to the means, method, or place of punishment: a *penal* colony. [< OF < L *poenalis* < *poena* penalty < Gk. *poinē* fine]

penal code See under CODE.

pe·nal·ize (pē′nəl-īz, pen′əl-) *v.t.* **·ized, ·iz·ing** **1.** To subject to a penalty, as for a violation. **2.** To declare, as an action, subject to a penalty. **3.** To put at a disadvantage. Also *Brit.* **pe′nal·ise.** —**pe′nal·i·za′tion** *n.*

pen·al·ty (pen′əl·tē) *n. pl.* **·ties** **1.** The legal punishment for having committed a crime or having violated a law. **2.** A sum of money fixed by statute to be forfeited as punishment for illegal acts; fine; mulct. **3.** The disadvantage, loss, or suffering incurred by some act, error, state of being, etc.: the *penalty* of sin; the *penalty* of fame. **4.** In sports: **a** Any handicap imposed for a violation of rules. **b** In hockey, the removal of an offending player fom the ice for a certain period, leaving his team shorthanded. **5.** In games, a number of points, etc., lost for failure to fulfill some condition. [< Med.L *poenalitas* < *poenalis.* See PENAL.]

penalty box In hockey, the bench for players serving penalties.

penalty killer In hockey, a player particularly skilled at preventing the opponents from scoring while his own team is shorthanded, and often used for this purpose.

pen·ance (pen′əns) *n.* **1.** *Eccl.* **a** A sacramental rite involving contrition, confession of sins to a priest, the acceptance of penalties, and absolution. **b** The penalty or penalties imposed. **2.** A feeling of sorrow for sin or fault, evinced by some outward act. **3.** Any penalty, mortification, or act of piety, imposed or voluntarily undertaken as an atonement or outward sign of repentance for sin. —**to do penance** To perform an act or acts of penance. —*v.t.* **·anced, ·anc·ing** To impose a penance upon. [< OF < L *paenitentia.* Doublet of PENITENCE.]

Pe·nang (pē·nang′) A State in the NW Federation of Malaya; 398 sq. mi., including **Penang Island** (formerly *Prince of Wales Island*), 110 sq. mi.; pop. 616,294 (est. 1959); capital, George Town.

pe·na·tes (pə·nā′tēz) *n.pl.* In the ancient Roman religion, the household gods: associated with the *lares.* [< L *penus* innermost part of a temple of Vesta]

pence (pens) *Brit.* The plural of PENNY: used mostly in combination: *twopence.*

pen·cel (pen′səl) *n.* A small flag or streamer: also spelled *pensil.* [< AF, alter. of *penoncel.* See PENNONCEL.]

pen·chant (pen′chənt, *Fr.* päṅ·shäṅ′) *n.* A strong liking or inclination for or in favor of something. [< F, orig. ppr. of *pencher* to incline, ult. < L *pendere* to hang]

pen·cil (pen′səl) *n.* **1.** A writing, drawing, or marking implement consisting of a stick or thin strip of graphite, colored chalk, slate, etc., encased in wood or inserted in a mechanically operated holder. **2.** A pencillike instrument for applying cosmetics: an eyebrow *pencil.* **3.** A small stick of some substance having medicinal properties: a styptic *pencil.* **4.** A set of rays, as of light, diverging from or converging upon a given point. **5.** In drawing or painting, the artist's skill, technique, or characteristic style. **6.** *Archaic* A small, finely pointed brush for painting. —*v.t.* **pen·ciled** or **·cilled, pen·cil·ing** or **·cil·ling** **1.** To mark, write, draw, or color with or as with a pencil. **2.** To use a pencil on. [< OF *pincel* < L *penicillum* paintbrush, dim. of *peniculus* brush, dim. of *penis* tail] —**pen′cil·er** or **pen′cil·ler** *n.*

pen·ciled (pen′səld) *adj.* **1.** Marked with fine lines, with or as if with a finely pointed pencil. **2.** Having pencils or rays. Also **pen′cilled.**

pend (pend) *v.i.* **1.** To await or be in process of adjustment or settlement. **2.** *Dial.* To hang; depend. [< MF *pendre* to hang < L *pendere*]

pen·dant (pen′dənt) *n.* **1.** Anything that hangs from something else, either for ornament or for use. **2.** One of a pair; a parallel; match. **3.** Something hanging from a chandelier, ceiling, lamp, etc., by which a light is turned on and off. **4.** The stem of a watchcase and the ring by which it is attached to a chain. **5.** *Archit.* An ornament hanging from a ceiling, roof, etc., used especially in late Perpendicular architecture. Also spelled *pendent.* —*adj.* See PENDENT. [< OF, orig. ppr. of *pendre.* See PEND.]

pen·dent (pen′dənt) *adj.* **1.** Hanging downward; suspended. **2.** Projecting; overhanging. **3.** Undetermined; pending. **4.** *Rare* Impending. Also spelled *pendant.* —*n.* See PENDANT. [Var. of PENDANT; refashioned after L *pendens, -entis,* ppr. of *pendere* to suspend] —**pen′dent·ly** *adv.*

pen·den·te li·te (pen·den′tē lī′tē) *Law* Pending or during suit. [< L]

pen·den·tive (pen·den′tiv) *n. Archit.* **1.** One of the four triangularly concave sections of vaulting arising from the corners of a square or oblong area and permitting the area to be completely covered by a dome. **2.** The principle or system of such vaulting. [< MF *pendentif* < L *pendens, -entis,* ppr. of *pendere* to hang]

pend·ing (pen′ding) *adj.* **1.** Remaining unfinished or undecided. **2.** Imminent; impending. —*prep.* **1.** During the process or continuance of. **2.** While awaiting; until: *pending* the verdict.

pen·drag·on (pen·drag′ən) *n.* In ancient Britain, a supreme head, ruler, or chief. [< Welsh, a chief leader in war < *pen* head + *dragon* a war chief < L *draco, -onis,* orig. a dragon (used as a military standard)] —**pen·drag′on·ish** *adj.* —**pen·drag′on·ship** *n.*

pen·du·lous (pen′jŏŏ·ləs) *adj.* **1.** Hanging, especially so as to swing. **2.** Undecided; wavering. [< L *pendulus* hanging < *pendere* to hang] —**pen′du·lous·ly** *adv.* —**pen′du·lous·ness** *n.*

pen·du·lum (pen′jŏŏ·ləm, -də-) *n.* **1.** An inert body suspended from a fixed point and free to oscillate, under the action of gravity, in equal times between two extremes. **2.** Such a device serving to regulate the movement of a clock. **3.** Something that changes often from one view, extreme, etc., to another: the fickle *pendulum* of public taste. [< NL < L, neut. of *pendulus.* See PENDULOUS.]

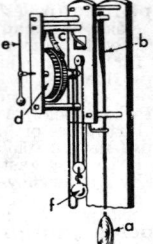

PENDULUM
a Bob (adjustable on rod).
b Rod. *c* Pallet.
d Escape wheel.
e Second hand.
f Weight.

Pe·nel·o·pe (pə·nel′ə·pē) In the *Odyssey,* the faithful wife of Odysseus, who, during her husband's absence kept her many suitors in check under pretext of having to complete a shroud she was weaving.

pe·ne·plain (pē′nə·plān′, pē′nə·plān′) *n. Geol.* An area worn down by erosion until it is almost a plain. Also **pe′ne·plane′.** [< L *paene* almost + PLAIN]

pen·e·tra·ble (pen′ə·trə·bəl) *adj.* That can be penetrated. —**pen′e·tra·bil′i·ty** *n.* —**pen′e·tra·bly** *adv.*

pen·e·tra·li·a (pen′ə·trā′lē·ə) *n.pl.* **1.** The inmost parts of anything, especially of a house or temple. **2.** Secret things. [< L, orig. neut. pl. of *penetralis* innermost < *penetrare.* See PENETRATE.]

HUMAN PELVIS
a Crest of ilium. *b* Ilium. *c* Coccyx. *d* Acetabulum. *e* Ischium. *f* Pubic symphysis. *g* Head of femur. *h* Sacrum. *i* Lumbar vertebrae.

pen·e·trance (pen'ə·trəns) *n. Genetics* A measure of the frequency with which a given gene will show its effects, expressed as a percentage of the total number of cases in which it is present. [< L *penetrans, -antis,* ppr. of *penetrare.* See PENETRATE.]

pen·e·trate (pen'ə·trāt) *v.* **·trat·ed, ·trat·ing** *v.t.* **1.** To force a way into or through: pierce; enter. **2.** To spread or diffuse itself throughout. **3.** To perceive the meaning of; understand. **4.** To affect or move profoundly. **5.** To see through: Our eyes could not *penetrate* the darkness. — *v.i.* **6.** To enter or pass through something. **7.** To have an effect on the mind or emotions. — **Syn.** See PERMEATE. [< L *penetratus,* pp. of *penetrare* to put within. Akin to L *penes* inside.] — **pen'e·tra·ble** (-trə·bəl) *adj.* — **pen'e·tra·bil'i·ty** *n.*

pen·e·trat·ing (pen'ə·trā'ting) *adj.* **1.** Tending or having power to penetrate. **2.** Acute; discerning: a *penetrating* mind. — **pen'e·trat'ing·ly** *adv.* — **pen'e·trat'ing·ness** *n.*

pen·e·tra·tion (pen'ə·trā'shən) *n.* **1.** The act or power of penetrating physically. **2.** Ability to penetrate mentally; acuteness: discernment. **3.** The depth to which a bullet or other projectile sinks in a target. **4.** The repeated commercial or diplomatic assault of a strong country upon a weaker one until definite influence is established. [< LL *penetratio, -onis* < L *penetrare.* See PENETRATE.] — **Syn. 2.** perspicacity, perception, acumen, keenness.

pen·e·tra·tive (pen'ə·trā'tiv) *adj.* Tending or having power to penetrate, physically or mentally: a *penetrative* odor; *penetrative* wisdom. [< Med.L *penetrativus* < L *penetratus,* pp. of *penetrare.* See PENETRATE.] — **pen'e·tra'tive·ly** *adv.* — **pen'e·tra'tive·ness** *n.*

pen·e·trom·e·ter (pen'ə·trom'ə·tər) *n.* **1.** *Med.* An instrument for indicating the quality and measuring the strength of X-rays. **2.** A device for testing the hardness of relatively semisolid substances. Also **pen·e·tram·e·ter** (pen'ə·tram'ə·tər). [< L *penetrare* (see PENETRATE) + -METER]

Pe·ne·us (pē·nē'əs) A river in Thessaly, Greece, flowing 135 miles SE to the Aegean: formerly *Salambria.*

pen·gö (pen'gœ') *n. pl.* **·gö** or **·gös** A former monetary unit of Hungary; a coin equivalent to 100 fillér: now replaced by the forint.

pen·guin (pen'gwin, peng'-) *n.* **1.** A web-footed, flightless, aquatic bird (family *Spheniscidae*) of the southern hemisphere, with flipperlike wings, short legs, and plantigrade feet: especially, the **Adélie penguin** (*Pygoscelis adeliae*) and the **emperor penguin** (*Aptenodytes patagonica*). **2.** Originally, the great auk. [Appar. < Welsh *pen* head + *gwyn* white]

EMPEROR
PENGUIN
(3 to 4
feet high)

pen·hold·er (pen'hōl'dər) *n.* **1.** A handle with a device for inserting a metallic pen. **2.** A rack for pens.

pen·i·cil·late (pen'ə·sil'it, -āt) *adj.* **1.** Pencilshaped. **2.** *Biol.* Bordered or tufted with fine hairs, as on a caterpillar. Also **pen'i·cil'li·form** (-sil'ə·fôrm). [< L *penicillus* paintbrush + -ATE¹] — **pen'i·cil'late·ly** *adv.* — **pen'i·cil·la'tion** (-sil'ā'shən) *n.*

pen·i·cil·lin (pen'ə·sil'in) *n.* A powerful antibiotic found in the mold fungus *Penicillium* and produced in several forms for the treatment of a wide variety of bacterial infections. [< PENICILL(IUM) + -IN]

pen·i·cil·li·um (pen'ə·sil'ē·əm) *n. pl.* **·cil·li·a** (-sil'ē·ə) Any of a genus (*Penicillium*) of ascomycetous fungi characterized by feltlike masses growing on decaying fruits, ripening cheese, etc.; especially, *P. notatum,* the principal source of penicillin. [< NL < L *penicillus* paintbrush, so called because of resemblance of its tufts to small paint brushes. See PENCIL.]

pe·nin·su·la (pə·nin'sə·lə, -syə-) *n.* A piece of land almost surrounded by water, and connected with the mainland by an isthmus. Abbr. *pen., Pen.* [< L *paeninsula < paene* almost + *insula* island] — **pen·in'su·lar** *adj.*

Peninsula, the **1.** The Iberian Peninsula. See IBERIA. **2.** The region between the James and York rivers, SE Virginia: scene of several Civil War battles, 1862.

Peninsula State A nickname for FLORIDA.

pe·nis (pē'nis) *n. pl.* **·nis·es** or **·nes** (-nēz) The copulatory organ of male animals. [< L, origin, tail] — **pe'ni·al** (-nē·əl), **pe'nile** (-nil, -nīl) *adj.*

pen·i·tence (pen'ə·təns) *n.* The state of being penitent; contrition. — **Syn.** See REPENTANCE. [< OF *penitence* < L *paenitentia < paenitens,* ppr. of *paenitere* to repent. Doublet of PENANCE.]

pen·i·tent (pen'ə·tənt) *adj.* Affected by a sense of one's own guilt, and resolved on amendment. — *n.* **1.** One who is penitent. **2.** One who confesses his sins to a priest and submits to the penance prescribed. [< MF < L *paenitens, -entis.* See PENITENCE.] — **pen'i·tent·ly** *adv.* — **Syn.** (adjective) rueful, regretful, remorseful, repentant.

pen·i·ten·tial (pen'ə·ten'shəl) *adj.* Of, pertaining to, or expressing penitence or penance. — *n.* **1.** *Eccl.* A book of

rules relating to penance and the reconciliation of penitents to the church. **2.** A penitent. [< LL *paeniten'tialis* (*presbyter*) confessor < L *paenitentia.* See PENITENCE.] — **pen'i·ten'tial·ly** *adv.*

pen·i·ten·tia·ry (pen'ə·ten'shər·ē) *n. pl.* **·ries** **1.** A prison, especially one operated by a state or federal government for those convicted of serious crimes. **2.** *Eccl.* In the Roman Catholic Church: **a** An office, having as its head a cardinal called the **Grand Penitentiary,** whose purpose is to decide questions of conscience, absolution, special dispensation, etc. **b** One who has authority to prescribe or superintend penances in cases normally handled by a bishop or the Holy See. — *adj.* **1.** Of or pertaining to penance. **2.** Relating to or used for the punishment and discipline of criminals or penitents. **3.** Rendering the offender liable to imprisonment in a penitentiary. [< Med.L *paenitentiaria* < L *paenitentia.* See PENITENCE.]

pen·knife (pen'nīf) *n. pl.* **·knives** (-nīvz') A small pocketknife, formerly used for making or sharpening quill pens. For illustration see KNIFE.

pen·man (pen'mən) *n. pl.* **·men** (-mən) **1.** A person considered with regard to his handwriting. **2.** One skilled in penmanship. **3.** An author.

pen·man·ship (pen'mən·ship) *n.* **1.** The art of writing. **2.** The style or quality of handwriting.

Penn (pen), **William,** 1644–1718, English Quaker, founder of Pennsylvania.

Penn. or **Penna.** Pennsylvania (unofficial).

pen·na (pen'ə) *n. pl.* **pen·nae** (pen'ē) *Ornithol.* Any of the feathers that determine the shape of a bird. [< NL < L, feather] — **pen·na·ceous** (pə·nā'shəs) *adj.*

pen name An author's assumed name; pseudonym; nom de plume. — **Syn.** See PSEUDONYM.

pen·nant (pen'ənt) *n.* **1.** A long, narrow flag, usually triangular, used as a signal on naval vessels, as a school emblem, etc. **2.** A similar flag awarded to the winners in some sports contests; also, the championship thus symbolized. **3.** *Music* Any hook on the stem of a note briefer in duration than a quarter note. [< PENNON; infl. by PENDANT]

pen·nate (pen'āt) *adj.* Having wings or feathers. Also **pen'nat·ed.** [< L *pennatus* winged < *penna* feather]

-pennate *combining form* Having wings or feathers: *longipennate.* [< L *pennatus* winged < *penna* feather]

Pen·nell (pen'əl), **Joseph,** 1860–1926, U.S. etcher and illustrator.

Penn Hills An urban township in SW Pennsylvania, near Pittsburgh; pop. 62,886.

pen·ni (pen'ē) *n. pl.* **pen·nis** or **pen·ni·a** (pen'ē·ə) A Finnish coin and monetary unit, the hundredth part of a markka. [< Finnish < G *pfennig* penny]

pen·ni·less (pen'i·lis) *adj.* Proverty-stricken.

Pen·nine Alps (pen'in, -īn) A SW division of the Alps on the Swiss-Italian border; highest peak, Dufourspitze, 15,203 ft.

Pennine Chain (pen'in, -īn) A long hill range, called "the backbone of England," extending south from the Cheviot Hills on the Scottish border to Derbyshire and Staffordshire; highest point, Cross Fell, 2,930 ft.

pen·non (pen'ən) *n.* **1.** A small, pointed or swallow-tailed flag, borne by medieval knights on their lances and displaying a personal device. **2.** Any banner or flag. **3.** A wing. [< OF *penon* streamer, feather of an arrow < L *penna* feather]

pen·non·cel (pen'ən·sel) *n.* A small, narrow pennon: also spelled *penoncel.* Also **pen'non·celle.** [< OF *penoncel,* dim. of *penon.* See PENNON.]

Penn·sau·ken (pen·sô'kən) A town in SW New Jersey, near Camden; pop. 36,394.

Penn·syl·va·ni·a (pen'səl·vā'nē·ə, -vān'yə) An eastern State of the United States; 45,333 sq. mi.; pop. 11,793,909; capital, Harrisburg; entered the Union Dec. 12, 1787; one of the thirteen original States; nickname, *Keystone State* or *Quaker State.* Officially **Commonwealth of Pennsylvania.** Abbr. *Pa.*

Penn·syl·va·ni·a-Dutch (pen'səl·vā'nē·ə·duch', -vān'yə-) *adj.* **1.** Of or pertaining to the Pennsylvania Dutch. **2.** Denoting a style of furniture, pottery, etc., made by these people, characterized by carved or gaily colored decorations of flowers, fruits, etc.

Pennsylvania Dutch **1.** Descendants of immigrants from the Palatinate, SW Germany, and from Switzerland, who settled in Pennsylvania in the 17th and 18th centuries. **2.** The language spoken by these people, a High German dialect with an admixture of English. Also **Pennsylvania German.** [< early and dial. *Dutch* < *Deutsch*) German]

Penn·syl·va·ni·an (pen'səl·vā'nē·ən, -vān'yən) *adj.* **1.** Of or relating to the State of Pennsylvania. **2.** *Geol.* Belonging to or denoting a Paleozoic period following the Mississippian and preceding the Permian periods. See table for GEOLOGY. — *n.* **1.** A native or inhabitant of Pennsylvania. **2.** *Geol.* The Pennsylvanian period or rock system.

pen·ny (pen′ē) *n. pl.* **pen·nies** or *Brit.* **pence** (pens) **1.** In the United States and Canada, a cent. **2.** A coin of Great Britain, Ireland, and various members of the Commonwealth of Nations, equivalent to ¹⁄₁₂ shilling. Abbr. *d.* **3.** In the United Kingdom, a coin equal in value to ¹⁄₁₀₀ pound: also *new penny.* **4.** Money in general. Abbr. *p.* — **a pretty penny** *Informal* A large or relatively large amount of money. — **to turn an honest penny** To gain money honestly. [OE *penning, penig, pending.* Cf. ON *penningr,* OHG *pfenning.*]

-penny *combining form* Costing (a specified number of) pennies: formerly designating the cost of nails per hundred, but now denoting their length, beginning at 1 inch for two-penny nails, increasing by quarter-inches up to tenpenny, and thereafter irregularly. [< PENNY]

pen·ny-a-lin·er (pen′ē-ə-lī′nər) *n.* A hack writer.

penny ante 1. A poker game in which the ante is limited to one cent. **2.** *Informal* Any piddling transaction.

penny dreadful *Brit. Informal* A cheap book or magazine containing popular, usually sensational fiction.

penny pincher A parsimonious person. — **pen·ny-pinch·ing** (pen′ē-pinch′ing) *adj. & n.*

pen·ny·roy·al (pen′ē-roi′əl) *n.* **1.** A low, erect, strong-scented herb (*Hedeoma pulegioides*), growing in North America and yielding oil of pennyroyal, used in medicine. **2.** A European species of mint (*Mentha pulegium*), resembling the American pennyroyal in odor and uses. [Alter. of earlier *pulyole ryale* < AF *puliol real* royal fleabane < L *pulegium* fleabane < *pulex* flea]

pen·ny·weight (pen′ē-wāt′) *n.* In troy weight, the twentieth part of an ounce, 24 grains, or 1.56 grams. Abbr. *dwt., pwt.* See table inside back cover.

pen·ny-wise (pen′ē-wīz′) *adj.* Unduly economical in small matters. — **penny-wise and pound-foolish** Economical in small matters, but wasteful in large ones.

pen·ny·wort (pen′ē-wûrt′) *n.* Any one of various plants with round or peltate leaves, as the several species of *Hydrocotyle,* of the parsley family, the navelwort, and a small plant (*Obolaria virginica*) of the gentian family.

pen·ny·worth (pen′ē-wûrth′) *n.* **1.** As much as can be bought for a penny. **2.** A bargain. **3.** A small amount.

Pe·nob·scot (pə-nob′skot) *n.* One of a tribe of North American Indians of the Algonquian confederacy of 1749.

Penobscot River A river in central Maine, flowing about 350 miles generally south to **Penobscot Bay,** an inlet of the Atlantic Ocean.

pe·nol·o·gy (pē-nol′ə-jē) *n. pl.* **·gies** The science that treats of the punishment and prevention of crime and of the management of prisons and reformatories: also spelled *poenology.* [< L *poena* penalty + -LOGY] — **pe·no·log·i·cal** (pē′nə-loj′i-kəl) *adj.* — **pe·nol′o·gist** *n.*

pen·on·cel (pen′ən-sel) See PENNONCEL.

pen-pal (pen′pal′) *n.* A friend to whom one writes letters, usually without ever having met. Also **pen pal.**

Pen·sa·co·la (pen′sə-kō′lə) A port city in NW Florida, on **Pensacola Bay,** an inlet of the Gulf of Mexico; site of a U.S. naval and air base; pop. 59,507.

pen·sil (pen′səl) See PENCEL.

pen·sile (pen′sil) *adj.* **1.** Hanging loosely; pendulous; suspended: a *pensile* nest. **2.** Constructing pensile nests: said of birds. [< L *pensilis* hanging down < *pensus,* pp. of *pendere* to hang] — **pen′sile·ness, pen·sil′i·ty** *n.*

pen·sion[1] (pen′shən) *n.* **1.** A periodic allowance to an individual or to his family, given because of some meritorious work or when certain conditions, as age, length of service, etc., have been fulfilled. **2.** A grant or allowance paid to someone of recognized ability in the arts or sciences. — *v.t.* **1.** To grant a pension to. **2.** To dismiss with a pension: with *off.* [< OF < L *pensio, -onis* payment < *pensus,* pp. of *pendere* to weigh, pay] — **pen′sion·a·ble** *adj.*

pen·sion[2] (pen′shən, *Fr.* pän-syôn′) *n. French* A boarding house; also, a boarding school. [< OF, payment, rent. See PENSION[1].]

pen·sion·ar·y (pen′shən·er′ē) *adj.* **1.** Living by means of a pension; pensioned. **2.** Consisting of or like a pension. — *n. pl.* **·ar·ies 1.** A pensioner. **2.** A hireling. [< Med.L *pensionarius* < L *pensio, -onis.* See PENSION[1].]

pen·sion·er (pen′shən·ər) *n.* **1.** One who receives a pension or is dependent on the bounty of another. **2.** At Cambridge University, a student who pays his own expenses. Compare COMMONER (def. 2). **3.** A boarder, as in a convent or school. **4.** *Obs.* A gentleman-at-arms. [< AF *pensionner* < OF *pension.* See PENSION[1].]

pen·sive (pen′siv) *adj.* **1.** Engaged in or addicted to serious, quiet reflection, often with a touch of sadness. **2.** Expressive of, suggesting, or causing a sad or melancholy thoughtfulness. [< OF *pensif, pensive* < *penser* to think < L *pensare*] — **pen′sive·ly** *adv.* — **pen′sive·ness** *n.*

pen·ste·mon (pen-stē′mən, pen′stem·ən) *n.* Any member of a North American genus (*Penstemon*) of perennial or shrubby plants of the figwort family, with opposite leaves and variously colored flowers: also called *beardtongue:* also spelled *pentstemon.* [Var. of NL *pentstemon* < Gk. *pente* five + *stēmōn* thread; so called from the rudimentary fifth stamen of this genus]

pen·stock (pen′stok′) *n.* **1.** A trough or conduit for carrying water to a water wheel. **2.** A sluice or floodgate controlling the discharge of water, as from a pond.

pent (pent) Past tense and past participle of PEN[2]. — *adj.* Penned up or in; closely confined.

penta- *combining form* Five: *pentahedron.* Also, before vowels, **pent-.** [< Gk. *pente* five]

pen·ta·cle (pen′tə-kəl) *n.* **1.** A figure composed of five straight lines, making a star that includes a pentagon. **2.** In magic, any similar figure of symbol. Also called *pentagram.* [< Med.L *pentaculum,* prob. infl. by LL *pentagonus* five-cornered, ult. < Gk. *pente* five]

pen·tad (pen′tad) *n.* **1.** The number five; also, a group of five things. **2.** A period of five years. **3.** *Chem.* An atom, radical, or element having a valence of five. — *adj.* Having a combining power of five. [< Gk. *pentas, -ados* a group of five < *pente* five]

PENTACLE

pen·ta·dac·tyl (pen′tə-dak′til) *adj.* Having five fingers or toes on each hand or foot. Also **pen′ta·dac′ty·late** (-lit, -lāt). [< L *pentadactylus* < Gk. *pentadactylos* < *pente* five + *dactylos* finger]

pen·ta·gon (pen′tə-gon) *n. Geom.* A polygon having five sides and five angles. [< L *pentagonum* < Gk. *pentagōnon* < *pente* five + *gōnia* angle] — **pen·tag·o·nal** (pen·tag′ə-nəl) *adj.* — **pen·tag′o·nal·ly** *adv.*

Pentagon, the 1. A five-sided building in Arlington, Virginia, housing the U.S. Department of Defense and other military, naval, and air force offices. Also **Pentagon Building. 2.** The military leadership of the United States.

pen·ta·gram (pen′tə-gram) *n.* A pentacle. [< *penta-* + -gram[1]]

pen·ta·he·dron (pen′tə-hē′drən) *n. pl.* **·dra** (-drə) *Geom.* A polyhedron bounded by five plane faces. — **pen′ta·he′dral** *adj.* [< PENTA- + -HEDRON]

pen·tam·er·ous (pen·tam′ər·əs) *adj.* **1.** Composed of or having five similar parts. **2.** *Bot.* Having whorls divided into five parts or into multiples of five: also written 5-merous. [< PENTA- + -MEROUS]

pen·tam·e·ter (pen·tam′ə·tər) *n.* **1.** In prosody, a line of verse consisting of five metrical feet: Ā bŏŏk | ŏf vēr | sĕs ŭn | dĕrnēath | thĕ bŏugh. **2.** Verse comprised of pentameters; heroic verse. — *adj.* Having five metrical feet. [< L < Gk. *pentametros* (a verse) of five measures < *pente* five + *metron* a measure]

pen·tane (pen′tān) *n. Chem.* Any one of three isomeric, volatile, liquid hydrocarbons of the methane series, C_5H_{12}, two of which are contained in petroleum.

pen·tar·chy (pen′tär·kē) *n. pl.* **·chies 1.** A government having five joint rulers; also, the five rulers. **2.** An association of five kingdoms, each ruled separately. [< Gk. *pentarchia* < *pente* five + *archein* to rule] — **pen·tar′chi·cal** *adj.*

pen·ta·stich (pen′tə-stik) *n.* A stanza or a poem consisting of five lines. [< NL *pentastichus* < Gk. *pentastichos* of five lines < *pente* five + *stichos* row, line]

pen·ta·style (pen′tə-stīl) *Archit. adj.* Having five columns in front — *n.* A pentastyle portico or other edifice. [< PENTA- + Gk. *stylos* pillar]

Pen·ta·teuch (pen′tə-tōōk, -tyōōk) *n.* The first five books of the Old Testament collectively, consisting of Genesis, Exodus, Leviticus, Numbers, and Deuteronomy. [< LL *pentateuchus* < Gk. *pentateuchos* (*biblos*) (the book) of five books < *pente* five + *teuchos* book, orig., implement, vessel] — **Pen′ta·teuch′al** *adj.*

pen·tath·lon (pen·tath′lən) *n.* **1.** An athletic contest consisting of five separate events, in all of which each contestant must participate. **2.** The modern pentathlon (which see). **3.** Formerly, in the modern Olympic games, a contest of five events, the 200-meter run, the 1,500-meter run, the discus throw, the javelin throw, and the running broad jump. [< Gk. < *pente* five + *athlos* contest]

pen·ta·ton·ic (pen′tə·ton′ik) *adj. Music* Consisting of five tones: a *pentatonic* scale.

pentatonic scale *Music* A scale consisting of the first, second, third, fifth, and sixth tones of the diatonic scale.

pen·ta·va·lent (pen′tə-vā′lənt, pen-tav′ə-) *adj. Chem.* Having a valence of five: also *quinquevalent.* [< PENTA- + L *valens, -entis,* ppr. of *valere* to have power or value]

Pen·te·cost (pen′tə-kôst, -kost) *n.* **1.** A Christian festival occurring the seventh Sunday after Easter and commemorating the descent of the Holy Ghost upon the apostles (*Acts* ii): also called *Whitsunday.* **2.** A Jewish festival occurring fifty days after the first day of Passover: also called *Shabuoth.* [< LL *pentecoste* < Gk. *pentēkostē* (*hēmera*) the fiftieth (day) < *pentēkonta* fifty]

Pen·te·cos·tal (pen′tə·kôs′təl, -kos′-) *adj.* **1.** Of, pertaining to, or occurring at Pentecost. **2.** Of or pertaining to any of several Christian sects whose revivallike form of worship is highly emotional and whose doctrines are basically fundamentalist in character.

Pen·tel·i·kon (pen·tel′i·kon) A mountain NW of Athens, Greece; famous for its marble; 3,637 ft. *Latin* **Pen·tel′i·cus** (-tel′i·kəs).

Pen·the·si·le·a (pen′thə·si·lē′ə) In Greek legend, a queen of the Amazons who aided the Trojans against the Greeks and was killed by Achilles.

pent·house (pent′hous′) *n.* **1.** An apartment or dwelling on the roof of a building. **2.** A structure built on a roof to conceal or cover a water tank, elevator machinery, etc. **3.** A small building, or a sloping rooflike structure, attached to the wall of another building. **4.** A canopy or awning above a doorway or window. [Alter. of ME *pentis*, aphetic form of OF *apentis, apendis*, ? < LL *appendicium* appendage < L *appendere*. See APPEND.]

pen·tom·ic (pen·tom′ik) *adj. Mil.* Of or designating a U.S. Army division designed primarily for use in nuclear warfare and consisting of five self-contained battle groups of high mobility, supported by atomic weapons. [< PENT(A) + (AT)OMIC]

pen·to·san (pen′tə·san) *n. Biochem.* One of a group of polysaccharides, found in foods and plant juices, that yield pentoses on hydrolysis. [< PENTOS(E) + -AN]

pen·tose (pen′tōs) *n. Biochem.* Any of a class of monosaccharides having four carbon atoms in the molecule. [< Gk. *pent(e)* five + -OSE²]

Pen·to·thal Sodium (pen′tə·thôl) A proprietary name for a brand of thiopental sodium. Also **pen′to·thal sodium.**

pent·ste·mon (pent·stē′mən, pent′stem·ən) See PENSTEMON.

pent-up (pent′up′) *adj.* Confined; repressed: *pent-up* emotions.

pe·nu·che (pə·nōō′chē) *n.* A candy made from brown sugar and milk, often with chopped nuts: also called *panocha.* Also **pe·nu′chi.** [< Am. Sp. *panocha* brown or raw sugar]

pe·nuch·le (pē′nuk·əl), **pe·nuck·le** See PINOCHLE.

pe·nult (pē′nult, pi·nult′) *n.* The syllable next to the last in a word. Also **pe·nul·ti·ma** (pi·nul′tə·mə). [Short for *penultima* < L *paenultima (syllaba)* next to the last (syllable) < *paene* almost + *ultimus* last]

pe·nul·ti·mate (pi·nul′tə·mit) *adj.* **1.** Next to the last. **2.** Of or belonging to the next to the last syllable. — *n.* A penultimate syllable or part. [< L *paene* almost + ULTIMATE, on analogy with L *paenultimus* next to the last]

pe·num·bra (pi·num′brə) *n. pl.* **·brae** (-brē) or **·bras** **1.** A partial shadow within which the rays of light from an illuminating body are partly but not wholly intercepted. **2.** *Astron.* **a** In an eclipse, the partial shadow between the region of total eclipse and the region of unobstructed light. **b** The dark fringe around the central part of a sunspot. **3.** In painting, the point or line at which light and shade are blended together. [< NL < L *paene* almost + *umbra* shadow] — **pe·num′bral, pe·num′brous** (-brəs) *adj.*

pe·nu·ri·ous (pə·nŏŏr′ē·əs, -nyŏŏr′-) *adj.* **1.** Excessively sparing in the use of money; stingy. **2.** Extremely poor; needy. **3.** Affording or yielding little; scanty. [< MF *penurieux* < Med.L *penuriosus* < L *penuria* want, poverty] — **pe·nu′ri·ous·ly** *adv.* — **pe·nu′ri·ous·ness** *n.*

pen·u·ry (pen′yə·rē) *n.* Extreme poverty or want. [< OF *penurie* < L *penuria* want] — **Syn.** indigence, destitution, need.

Pe·nu·ti·an (pə·nōō′tē·ən, -shən) *n.* A phylum of northwestern North American Indian languages, including the Chinookan and Shahaptian linguistic stocks.

Pen·za (pyen′zə) A city in the western R.S.F.S.R., on the Sura; pop. 254,000 (1959).

Pen·zance (pen·zans′) A municipal borough and port in western Cornwall, England; pop. 19,433 (1961).

pe·on (pē′ən) *n.* **1.** In Latin America: **a** A laborer; servant. **b** Formerly, a debtor kept in servitude until he had worked out of his debt. **2.** In India: **a** A foot soldier. **b** A messenger, attendant, or orderly. **c** A native police officer or constable. — **Syn.** See SLAVE. [< Sp. *peón* < LL *pedo, -onis* foot soldier < L *pes, pedis* foot. Doublet of PAWN¹.]

pe·on·age (pē′ən·ij) *n.* **1.** The condition of being a peon. **2.** The system by which debtors are held in servitude until they have worked out their debt. Also **pe′on·ism** (-iz′əm).

pe·o·ny (pē′ə·nē) *n. pl.* **·nies** **1.** Any of a genus (*Paeonia*) of plants of the crowfoot family, having large crimson, rose, or white flowers. **2.** The flower. [OE *peonie* < L *paeonia* < Gk. *paiōnia* < *Paion* Paeon, the Healer]

peo·ple (pē′pəl) *n. pl.* **peo·ple;** *for defs. 1 & 2, also* **peo·ples** **1.** The entire body of human beings living in the same country, under the same government, and speaking the same language: the *people* of England. **2.** A body of human beings having the same history, culture, and traditions, and usually speaking the same language: the Polish *people.* **3.** In a state or nation, the whole body of persons invested with political rights; the enfranchised. **4.** A group or body of persons having the same interests, profession, condition of life, place of residence, etc.: poor *people.* **5.** Persons considered collectively and not as individuals: *people* say. **6.** Ordinary persons as distinguished from those who are wealthy, privileged, titled, etc.; the populace: usually with *the.* **7.** Those persons connected with someone as subjects, attendants, etc.: the Queen's *people.* **8.** One's family or

relatives. **9.** Human beings as distinguished from animals· **10.** Animals collectively: the ant *people.* — **good people** In Ireland, the fairies: also **little people.** — *v.t.* **·pled, ·pling** To fill with inhabitants; populate. [< OF *pueple, poeple* < L *populus* populace] — **peo′pler** *n.*

— **Syn.** *People, folk, nation, population,* and *race* are compared as they denote a large number of persons collectively. A group having a common descent, language, culture, habitat, or government may be called a *people;* this word evades stress on any one aspect, but may also be used in a more restricted sense to indicate specifically an ethnic, cultural, linguistic, or other community. *Folk* is a homelier word for *people,* nearly as broad, and usually stressing common traditions, customs, or behavior. A *nation* is a political entity, comprising the *people* (or *peoples*) under one government. *Population* refers to habitat, and comprises all the members of a group found in one region; it is the only one of the synonyms commonly used of human and nonhuman groups alike. *Race* refers to descent, and includes all those of roughly similar physical features who are considered to have a common ancestry. Compare TRIBE.

people's front A popular front (which see).

People's Party A political organization formed in the United States in 1891, and advocating an increase in currency, free coinage of silver, public control of railways, an income tax, and limitation of ownership of land: also called *Populist Party.*

Pe·o·ri·a (pē·ôr′ē·ə, -ō′rē·ə) A city in north central Illinois, on the Illinois River; pop. 126,963.

pep (pep) *n. Informal* Energy and high spirits; vigorous activity. — *v.t.* **pepped, pep·ping** To fill or inspire with energy or pep: usually with *up.* [Short for PEPPER]

Pep·in the Short (pep′in), died 768, king of the Franks 751–768; father of Charlemagne.

pep·los (pep′ləs) *n.* In ancient Greece, a woman's shawl or large scarf worn draped about the upper part of the body: also *peplum.* Also **pep′lus.** [< Gk.]

pep·lum (pep′ləm) *n. pl.* **·lums** or **·la** (-lə) **1.** A short overskirt, ruffle, or flounce attached to a blouse or coat at the waist, and extending down over the hips. **2.** A peplos. [< L < Gk. *peplos* peplos]

pe·po (pē′pō) *n. pl.* **·pos** The fleshy fruit of plants of the gourd family, with hardened rind and numerous enclosed seeds, as the squash, cucumber, pumpkin, melon, etc. Also **pe·pon′i·da** (pi·pon′ə·də), **pe·po·ni·um** (pi·pō′nē·əm). [< L, pumpkin < Gk. *pepon (sikyos)* ripe (gourd)]

pep·per (pep′ər) *n.* **1.** A pungent, aromatic condiment consisting of the dried immature berries of a plant (*Piper nigrum*). When ground entire it is **black pepper,** but when the outer coating of the seeds is removed, the product is **white pepper. 2.** Any plant of the pepper family (*Piperaceae*), native to India, now widely distributed. **3.** Red pepper (which see). **4.** Green pepper (which see). — *v.t.* **1.** To sprinkle or season with pepper. **2.** To sprinkle freely. **3.** To shower, as with missiles; spatter; pelt. **4.** To make (speech or writing) vivid or pungent, as with humor, sarcasm, etc. — *v.i.* **5.** To discharge missiles at something [OE *pipor,* ult. < L *piper* < Gk. *peperi.* Cf. Skt. *pippali* peppercorn.]

pep·per-and-salt (pep′ər·ən·sôlt′) *adj.* Having or consisting of a mixture of white and black, so intermingled as to present a grayish appearance: said of cloth, hair, etc. — *n.* A pepper-and-salt cloth.

pep·per·box (pep′ər·boks′) *n.* **1.** A cylindrical container with a perforated lid for sprinkling pepper. **2.** A quick-tempered person.

pep·per·corn (pep′ər·kôrn′) *n.* **1.** A berry of the pepper plant. **2.** Anything trifling or insignificant.

pep·per·grass (pep′ər·gras′, -gräs′) *n.* Any of a genus (*Lepidium*) of plants of the mustard family, having a pungent flavor, and used as a salad vegetable. Also **pep′per·wort** (-wûrt).

pep·per·idge (pep′ər·ij) *n.* The black gum, a tree. [Origin unknown]

pepper mill A hand mill, often designed for table use, in which peppercorns are ground.

pep·per·mint (pep′ər·mint′) *n.* **1.** A pungent, aromatic herb (*Mentha piperita*), used in medicine and confectionery. **2.** An oil or other preparation made from this herb. **3.** A confection flavored with peppermint.

pepper pot 1. A pepperbox. **2.** A West Indian stew of meat or fish with okra, chilis, and other vegetables, flavored with Cayenne pepper, etc. **3.** In the United States, a soup of tripe and vegetables, highly seasoned with pepper.

pep·per·root (pep′ər·rōōt′, -rŏŏt′) *n.* Crinkleroot (which see).

pepper tree 1. A Tasmanian and Australian shrub (*Drimys aromatica*) of the magnolia family, having small, greenish yellow flowers and globular berries sometimes used as a substitute for pepper. **2.** A tree (*Schinus molle*), of Central and South America, whose seeds are used as a spice and whose fruit yields an intoxicating beverage: also called *Peruvian mastic.*

pep·per·y (pep′ər-ē) *adj.* **1.** Pertaining to or like pepper; pungent. **2.** Quick-tempered; hasty. **3.** Spicy and vivid, as speech or writing. **— pep′per·i·ness** *n.*

pep·py (pep′ē) *adj.* **·pi·er, ·pi·est** *Informal* Full of energy.

pep·sin (pep′sin) *n.* **1.** *Biochem.* An enzyme secreted by the gastric juices of the stomach, that changes proteins into proteoses and peptones. **2.** A medicinal preparation obtained from the stomachs of various animals, as the pig and the calf, used to aid digestion. **3.** A similar enzyme found in the cells of certain plants. Also **pep′sine** (-sin). [< Gk. *pepsis* digestion]

pep·sin·ate (pep′sin-āt) *v.t.* **·at·ed, ·at·ing** To treat, make up, or prepare with pepsin.

pep·sin·o·gen (pep·sin′ə·jən) *n.* *Biochem.* The inactive form of pepsin, found in the stomach mucosa and converted into pepsin in a slightly acid solution.

pep talk *Informal* A brief talk meant to inspire confidence, spark interest or enthusiasm, etc.

pep·tic (pep′tik) *adj.* **1.** Of, pertaining to, or promotive of digestion. **2.** Of, pertaining to, or caused by pepsin. **3.** Able to digest. **— n.** An agent that promotes digestion. [< Gk. *peptikos* able to digest < *pepsis* digestion]

pep·tide (pep′tīd, -tid) *n.* *Biochem.* Any combination of amino acids in which the carboxyl group of one is joined with the amino group of another. [< PEPT(ONE) + -IDE]

pep·tize (pep′tīz) *v.t.* **·tized, ·tiz·ing** *Chem.* To bring about or increase the colloidal dispersion of (a substance); especially, to convert (a sol) into a gel.

pep·tone (pep′tōn) *n.* *Biochem.* Any of the soluble compounds into which proteins are converted when acted upon by pepsin, by acids and alkalis, by putrefaction, etc. [< Gk. *pepton* < Gk., neut. of *peptos* digested, cooked] **— pep·ton·ic** (pep·ton′ik) *adj.*

pep·to·nize (pep′tə·nīz) *v.t.* **·nized, ·niz·ing 1.** To change into peptones. **2.** To subject, as food, to the action of a peptone or other proteolytic enzyme. **3.** To subject to partial predigestion. **— pep′to·ni·za′tion** *n.*

Pepys (pēps, peps, pep′is), Samuel, 1633–1703, English diarist. **— Pepys′i·an** *adj.*

Pe·quot (pē′kwot) *n.* One of a tribe of North American Indians of Algonquian stock, formerly inhabiting southern New England. Also **Pe′quod** (-kwod).

per (pûr) *prep.* **1.** By; by means of; through: used in commercial and business English: *per* bearer. **2.** To or for each: ten cents *per* yard. **3.** By the; every: especially in Latin phrases: *per diem.* Abbr. *p.* [< L, through, by]

per- *prefix* **1.** Through; throughout: *pervade, perennial.* **2.** Thoroughly; completely: *perturb.* **3.** Away: *pervert, peremptory.* **4.** Very: *perfervid.* **5.** *Chem.* **a** Indicating the higher valence of a designated element in a compound: potassium *permanganate.* **b** Indicating an excess amount of a specified element in a compound: hydrogen *peroxide.* [< L *per* through, by means of]

per. **1.** Period. **2.** Person.

Pe·ra (pā′rä) A residential section of Istanbul, formerly the foreign quarter.

per·a·cid·i·ty (pûr′a·sid′ə·tē) *n.* Excessive acidity, as of the stomach.

per·ad·ven·ture (pûr′əd·ven′chər) *adv.* *Archaic* Perchance; it may be; perhaps. **— n.** Possibility of failure, miscarriage, or error; doubt; question. [< OF *par aventure* by chance; infl. in form by L *adventura* chance]

Pe·rak (pā′rak, *Malay* pe′rä) A State in the NW Federation of Malaya; 7,980 sq. mi.; pop. 1,327,120 (est. 1959); capital, Ipoh.

per·am·bu·late (pə·ram′byə·lāt) *v.* **·lat·ed, ·lat·ing** *v.t.* **1.** To walk through or over. **2.** To walk through or around so as to inspect, etc. **— v.i. 3.** To walk about; stroll. [< L *perambulatus,* pp. of *perambulare* < *per* through + *ambulare* to walk] **— per·am′bu·la·to′ry** (-tôr′ē, -tō′rē) *adj.*

per·am·bu·la·tion (pə·ram′byə·lā′shən) *n.* **1.** The act of perambulating. **2.** That which is perambulated.

per·am·bu·la·tor (pə·ram′byə·lā′tər) *n.* **1.** One who perambulates. **2.** *Chiefly Brit.* A baby carriage. **3.** A chair equipped with wheels for rolling. **4.** A surveyor's wheellike instrument that measures the distance over which it travels.

per an·num (pûr an′əm) *Latin* By the year. Abbr. *p.a., per an., per ann.*

per·bo·rate (pər·bôr′āt, -bō′rāt) *n.* *Chem.* A salt containing the boron radical BO₃, as **sodium perborate,** NaBO₃·4H₂O, used as a bleaching agent and disinfectant.

per·cale (pər·kāl′, -kal′) *n.* A closely woven cotton fabric without gloss. [< F, prob. < Persian *pergālah*]

per·ca·line (pûr′kə·lēn′) *n.* A glossy cotton cloth, used chiefly as lining. [< F, dim. of *percale* PERCALE]

per cap·i·ta (pûr kap′ə·tə) *Latin* For each person; literally, by heads.

per·ceive (pər·sēv′) *v.t. & v.i.* **·ceived, ·ceiv·ing 1.** To become aware of (something) through the senses; see, hear, feel, taste, or smell. **2.** To come to understand; apprehend with the mind. [< OF *perceivre* < L *percipere* to seize, perceive < *per-* thoroughly + *capere* to take] **— per·ceiv′a·ble** *adj.* **— per·ceiv′a·bly** *adv.* **— per·ceiv′er** *n.*

— Syn. 1. sense. Compare SEE, DISCERN. **2.** comprehend.

per·cent (pər·sent′) *n.* **1.** Number of parts in or to every hundred, often specified: fifty *percent* of the people. **2.** Amount or quantity commensurate with the number of units in proportion to one hundred: ten *percent* of fifty is five: symbol, %. **3.** *pl.* Securities bearing a certain percentage of interest. Also **per cent.** Abbr. *p.c., pct.* [Short for L *per centum* by the hundred]

per·cent·age (pər·sen′tij) *n.* **1.** Rate per hundred, or proportion in a hundred parts. **2.** A proportion or part considered in its quantitative relation to the whole. **3.** In commerce, the allowance, commission, duty, or interest on a hundred. **4.** *Informal* Advantage; profit.

per·cen·tile (pər·sen′tīl, -til) *n.* *Stat.* Any of 100 points spaced at equal intervals within the range of a plotted variable, each point denoting that percentage of the total cases lying below it in the series. Thus, 1, 2, 3, etc., percent of the cases are in the first, second, third, etc., percentile. Also called *centile.* **— adj.** Of or pertaining to a percentile.

per·cept (pûr′sept) *n.* *Psychol.* **1.** Something perceived. **2.** Immediate knowledge derived from perceiving. **— Syn.** See SENSATION. [< L *perceptum,* neut. pp. of *percipere.* See PERCEIVE.]

per·cep·ti·ble (pər·sep′tə·bəl) *adj.* That can be perceived; perceivable; cognizable; appreciable. [< LL *perceptibilis* < L *percipere.* See PERCEIVE.] **— per·cep′ti·bil′i·ty, per·cep′ti·ble·ness** *n.* **— per·cep′ti·bly** *adv.*

— Syn. apparent, manifest, palpable, noticeable.

per·cep·tion (pər·sep′shən) *n.* **1.** The act or process of perceiving. **2.** The result or effect of perceiving. **3.** Any insight, knowledge, or intuitive judgment arrived at by or as by perceiving. **4.** The capacity for perceiving. **5.** *Law* The taking of something, as crops or profits, into possession. [< L *perceptio, -onis* a receiving < *percipere.* See PERCEIVE.] **— per·cep′tion·al** *adj.*

— Syn. 1. See SENSATION. **2.** See KNOWLEDGE. **3.** penetration, discernment, discrimination. See ACUMEN.

per·cep·tive (pər·sep′tiv) *adj.* **1.** Having the power of perception. **2.** Having a quick, ready capacity for perceiving. **3.** Of or pertaining to perception; perceptional. **— per·cep′tive·ly** *adv.* **— per·cep·tiv·i·ty** (pûr′sep·tiv′ə·tē), **per·cep′tive·ness** *n.*

per·cep·tu·al (pər·sep′chōō·əl) *adj.* Of, pertaining to, or involving perception. **— per·cep′tu·al·ly** *adv.*

Per·ce·val (pûr′sə·vəl) In Arthurian legend, a knight of the Round Table and an archetype of chivalry and purity who, together with Galahad, accomplished the quest for the Grail. Also spelled *Percival, Percivale.*

perch¹ (pûrch) *n.* **1.** A horizontal staff or pole used as a roost for poultry. **2.** Any place on which birds alight or rest. **3.** Any place for sitting or standing, especially if elevated. **4.** A pole connecting the fore gear and hind gear of a spring carriage. **5.** A frame on which cloth is examined for imperfections. **6.** Any long pole or rod: an acrobat's balancing *perch.* **7.** A linear measure equal to one rod or 16.5 feet. **8.** A square rod. **9.** In stonework, a variable measure, usually about 25 cubic feet. **— v.i. 1.** To alight or sit on or as on a perch; roost. **— v.t. 2.** To set on or as on a perch. **3.** To examine (cloth) on a perch. Abbr. (for n. def. 7, 8) *p.* [< OF *perche* < L *pertica* pole]

perch² (pûrch) *n. pl.* **perch** or **perches 1.** Any of various small, spiny-finned fresh-water food fishes (genus *Perca*); especially, the **yellow perch** (*P. flavescens*) of central and eastern United States, and *P. fluviatilis* of Europe. **2.** Any of various other related fishes. [< OF *perche* < L *perca* < Gk. *perkē.* Akin to Gk. *perknos* dark, speckled]

per·chance (pər·chans′, -chäns′) *adv.* **1.** Possibly; perhaps. **2.** *Obs.* By chance. [< OF *par chance* by chance < *par* (< L *per* through) + *chance.* See CHANCE.]

Perche (persh) A region of northern France, mostly in Maine and Normandy.

perch·er (pûr′chər) *n.* **1.** One who or that which perches. **2.** A bird whose feet are adapted for perching.

Per·che·ron (pûr′chə·ron, -shə-) *n.* Any of a breed of large, usually dapple-gray or black draft horses. [< F (*cheval*) *percheron* (horse) from Perche]

per·chlo·rate (pər·klôr′āt, -klō′rāt) *n.* *Chem.* A salt of perchloric acid.

per·chlo·ric acid (pər·klôr′ik, -klō′rik) *Chem.* A colorless, liquid, unstable acid, HClO₄, formed by the addition of one oxygen atom to chloric acid.

per·chlo·ride (pər·klôr′īd, -klō′rīd) *n.* *Chem.* A chloride having a larger proportion of chlorine than any other chloride of the same series. Also **per·chlo′rid** (-klôr′id, -klō′rid).

per·cip·i·ent (pər·sip′ē·ənt) *adj.* **1.** Having the power of perception. **2.** Perceiving rapidly or keenly. **— n.** One who or that which perceives. [< L *percipiens, -entis,* ppr. of *percipere.* See PERCEIVE.] **— per·cip′i·ence** or **·en·cy** *n.*

Per·ci·val, Per·ci·vale (pûr′sə·vəl) See PERCEVAL.

per·coid (pûr′koid) *adj.* Of or pertaining to an order (*Percomorphi* or *Perciformes*) of spiny-finned teleost fishes, including the fresh-water perches; perchlike. **— n.** A percoid fish. Also **per·coi′de·an** (-dē′ən). [< L *perca* perch² + -OID]

per·co·late (pûr′kə·lāt; *for n., also* pûr′kə·lət) *v.t. & v.i.*

·**lat·ed**, ·**lat·ing** Of a liquid, to pass or cause to pass through fine interstices; filter. — *n.* That which has percolated. [< L *percolatus*, pp. of *percolare* < *per-* through + *colare* to strain < *colum* strainer] — **per'co·la'tion** *n.*

per·co·la·tor (pûr'kə·lā'tər) *n.* **1.** A type of coffeepot in which boiling water rises constantly to the top in a tube and then filters down through finely ground coffee to a container below. **2.** That which percolates.

per con·tra (pûr kon'trə) *Latin* On the contrary.

per·cur·rent (pər·kûr'ənt) *adj. Bot.* Extending from one end to another or from base to apex, as the veins of certain leaves. [< L *percurrens, -entis*, ppr. of *percurrere* < *per-* through + *currere* to run]

per·cuss (pər·kus') *v.t.* **1.** To strike or tap quickly or forcibly. **2.** *Med.* To test or treat by percussion. [< L *percussus*, pp. of *percutere* to strike < *per-* through + *quatere* to shake] — **per·cus'sor** *n.*

per·cus·sion (pər·kush'ən) *n.* **1.** The sharp striking of one body against another, especially so as to cause a shock or sound. **2.** The shock, vibration, or sound produced by a striking of one body against another. **3.** *Med.* A light, quick tapping of the finger tips upon the back, chest, or abdomen, for determining by resonance the condition of the organ beneath. **4.** The act of striking the percussion cap in a firearm. **5.** *Music* Percussion instruments (which see). — *adj.* Of, pertaining to, or operating by percussion. [< L *percussio, -onis* < *percutere*. See PERCUSS.] — **per·cus'sive** *adj.*

percussion cap A small cap of thin metal, containing mercury fulminate or some other detonator, formerly used in ammunition to explode the propelling charge.

percussion figure *Mineral.* The figure assumed in a crystal or mineral by the various cracks made by the impact of a dull point: also called *strike figure.*

percussion fuse A fuse within a projectile or bomb, causing it to explode on impact.

percussion instruments Musical instruments whose tone is produced by striking or hitting, as the timpani, cymbals, piano, etc.

Per·cy (pûr'sē), **Sir Henry,** 1364–1403, English military commander; appears as a character in Shakespeare's *Henry IV*: called **Hot·spur** (hot'spûr). — **Thomas,** 1729–1811, English poet, bishop, and antiquary.

per·die, per·dy (pər·dē') See PARDI.

per di·em (pər dē'əm, dī'əm) **1.** By the day. **2.** An allowance for expenses each day. Abbr. *p.d., P.D.* [< L]

per·di·tion (pər·dish'ən) *n.* **1.** Eternal damnation; the utter loss of a soul. **2.** The place of eternal damnation; hell. **3.** *Archaic* Utter destruction or ruin. **4.** *Obs.* Lessening; diminution. [< OF *perdiciun* < L *perditio, -onis* < *perditus*, ppr. of *perdere* to destroy, lose < *per-* through, away + *dare* to give]

per·du (pər·dōō') *adj.* Hidden; concealed. — *n. Obs.* A soldier on a dangerous assignment. Also **per·due.** [< F *perdu*, pp. of *perdre* to lose < L *perdere.* See PERDITION.]

per·du·ra·ble (pər·dōōr'ə·bəl, -dyōōr'-) *adj.* Very durable; lasting. [< OF < LL *perdurabilis* < L *perdurare* < *per-* through + *durare* to endure < *durus* hard] — **per'du·ra·bil'i·ty** *n.* — **per·du'ra·bly** *adv.*

père (pâr) *n. French* Father: often used after a surname to distinguish father from son: Dumas *père.* Abbr. *P.*

per·e·gri·nate (per'ə·gri·nāt') *v.* ·**nat·ed**, ·**nat·ing** *v.i.* **1.** To travel from place to place. — *v.t.* **2.** To travel through or along. — *adj. Obs.* Foreign. [< L *peregrinatus*, pp. of *peregrinari* to travel abroad < *peregrinus.* See PEREGRINE.] — **per'e·gri·na'tion** *n.* — **per'e·gri·na'tor** *n.*

per·e·grine (per'ə·grin) *adj.* **1.** Coming from foreign regions: a *peregrine* bird. **2.** Traveling; wandering. — *n.* The peregrine falcon. Also **per'e·grin.** [< L *peregrinus* foreign < *peregre* abroad < *per-* through + *ager, agri* land]

peregrine falcon **1.** A falcon (*Falco peregrinus*) generally blackish blue above and white or gray below, formerly much used in falconry. **2.** An American subspecies (*F. p. anatum*) of this falcon: also called *duck hawk.*

pe·rei·ra bark (pə·rā'rə) The bark of a tropical American tree (*Geissospermum vellosii*), valued for its medicinal properties. [< NL *pereira*, former genus name, after J. Pereira, 1804–53, English medical professor]

per·emp·to·ry (pə·remp'tər·ē, per'əmp·tôr'ē, -tō'rē) *adj.* **1.** Not admitting of debate or appeal; decisive; absolute. **2.** Positive and assured in opinion, manner, judgment, etc.; imperious. **3.** Intolerant of opposition; dictatorial. **4.** *Law* Precluding or putting an end to debate or discussion; final. [< L *peremptorius* destructive < *peremptus*, pp. of *perimere* to destroy < *per-* entirely + *emere* to take] — **per·emp'to·ri·ly** *adv.* — **per·emp'to·ri·ness** *n.*

per·en·ni·al (pə·ren'ē·əl) *adj.* **1.** Continuing or enduring through the year or through many years. **2.** Perpetual; everlasting; unceasing. **3.** *Bot.* Lasting more than two years. — *n.* A plant that grows for three or more years, usually blossoming and fructifying annually. [< L *perennis* < *per-* through + *annus* year] — **per·en'ni·al·ly** *adv.*

Pé·rez Gal·dós (pā'rāth gäl·thōs'), **Benito,** 1843–1920, Spanish novelist and dramatist.

perf. **1.** Perfect. **2.** Perforated. **3.** Performer.

per·fect (*adj. & n.* pûr'fikt; *v.* pər·fekt') *adj.* **1.** Having all the elements or qualities requisite or necessary to its nature or kind; complete. **2.** Without defect, blemish, or any imperfection: *perfect* weather. **3.** Thoroughly and completely skilled or informed: a *perfect* violinist. **4.** Accurately or closely reproducing or corresponding to a type or original; exact: a *perfect* replica. **5.** Thorough; total; utter: He made a *perfect* nuisance of himself. **6.** Thoroughly meeting the requirements of the occasion; completely effective: a *perfect* answer. **7.** *Informal* Very great; excessive: a *perfect* horror of spiders. **8.** *Gram.* Denoting the tense of a verb expressing action completed in the past. Grammarians note in English a present perfect, past perfect (or pluperfect), and a future perfect tense. **9.** *Music* **a** Denoting the three intervals whose accuracy of intonation the human ear can recognize within precise limits, the **perfect octave,** containing 13 semitones, the **perfect fifth,** containing seven, and the **perfect fourth,** containing five. See illustration of INTERVAL. **b** Complete: a *perfect* cadence. **10.** *Bot.* **a** Having all essential organs or parts: said of flowers. **b** Monoclinous. **11.** *Obs.* Assured; positive. — *n. Gram.* The perfect tense; also, a verb in this tense. — *v.t.* **1.** To bring to perfection; complete; finish. **2.** To make thoroughly skilled or accomplished: to *perfect* oneself in an art. Abbr. *perf.* [< OF < L *perfectus*, pp. of *perficere* to complete < *per-* thoroughly + *facere* to do, make] — **per·fect'er** *n.* — **per·fect·ness** *n.*
— **Syn.** (adj.) **1.** whole, entire, intact, finished. **2.** faultless, unblemished, ideal.

per·fect·i·ble (pər·fek'tə·bəl) *adj.* Capable of being made perfect or of arriving at perfection. — **per·fect'i·bil'i·ty** *n.*

per·fec·tion (pər·fek'shən) *n.* **1.** The state or quality of being perfect. **2.** The embodiment of something that is perfect: As a hostess, she is *perfection.* **3.** Any quality, characteristic, or trait considered to be perfect. **4.** The highest degree of something: the *perfection* of rudeness. **5.** The act or process of perfecting, or the fact of having been perfected. [< OF < L *perfectio, -onis* < *perficere.* See PERFECT.]

per·fec·tion·ism (pər·fek'shən·iz'əm) *n.* **1.** A theory that moral perfection may be or has been attained by men in this life. **2.** The practice of setting exceedingly high goals or standards for oneself or for others.

per·fec·tion·ist (pər·fek'shən·ist) *n.* **1.** One who demands of himself or of others an exceedingly high degree of excellence. **2.** One who believes in perfectionism.

per·fec·tive (pər·fek'tiv) *adj.* **1.** Tending to make perfect. **2.** *Gram.* Denoting an aspect of the verb expressing the completion of an action. — *n. Gram.* **1.** The perfective aspect. **2.** A verb in this aspect. — **per·fec'tive·ly** *adv.* — **per·fec'tive·ness** *n.*

per·fect·ly (pûr'fikt·lē) *adv.* **1.** In a perfect manner. **2.** Wholly; completely; altogether: *perfectly* new. ◆ The use of *perfectly* as an intensive, as in "a *perfectly* beautiful day," should be avoided in formal writing, although it is standard in informal speech or writing.

per·fec·to (pər·fek'tō) *n. pl.* ·**tos** A cigar of medium size, shaped to taper at either end. [< Sp., perfect < L *perfectus.* See PERFECT.]

perfect participle Past participle. See under PARTICIPLE.

perfect pitch Absolute pitch (def. 2).

per·fer·vid (pər·fûr'vid) *adj.* Very or excessively fervid; ardent; zealous. [< NL *perfervidus* < L *per-* thoroughly + *fervidus.* See FERVID.]

per·fid·i·ous (pər·fid'ē·əs) *adj.* Marked by or guilty of perfidy; treacherous. [< L *perfidiosus* < *perfidia.* See PERFIDY.] — **per·fid'i·ous·ly** *adv.* — **per·fid'i·ous·ness** *n.*
— **Syn.** *Perfidious, faithless, unfaithful, disloyal, false, traitorous,* and *treacherous* refer to the breaking of a promise, pledge, vow, etc. *Perfidious,* the strongest of these words, suggests that the person who breaks his word has acted deliberately, and is of a mean and despicable character: a *perfidious* attack on an ally. *Faithless* and *unfaithful* may be as strong as *perfidious,* but more often they stress a person's failure to abide by his word or his duty: a *faithless* friend, an *unfaithful* wife. *Disloyal* means *faithless* in allegiance, as to an institution, nation, sovereign, superior, or the like. *False* is close to *faithless,* but implies even more strongly a failure to meet an expected standard of devotion or loyalty. *False* also frequently suggests deceit or betrayal, ideas which are always present in *traitorous* and *treacherous. Traitorous* is the more neutral word, describing an actual betrayal or breach of confidence; *treacherous* denotes a tendency or disposition to imperil or betray another, and its use involves the passing of an ad-erse moral judgment.

per·fi·dy (pûr'fə·dē) *n. pl.* ·**dies** The act of violating faith, trust, or allegiance; treachery. [< MF *perfidie* < L *perfidia* < *per* through, under pretext of + *fides* faith]

per·fo·li·ate (pər·fō'lē·it, -āt) *adj.* **1.** *Bot.* Growing so that the stem seems to pass through it, as a leaf. [< NL *perfoliatus* < L *per-* through + *folium* leaf] — **per·fo'li·a'tion** *n.*

per·fo·rate (*v.* pûr'fə·rāt; *adj.* pûr'fə·rit) *v.t.* ·**rat·ed**, ·**rat**-

ing 1. To make a hole or holes through, by or as by stamping or drilling. **2.** To pierce with holes in rows or patterns, as sheets of stamps, etc. — *adj.* Perforated. [< L *perforatus*, pp. of *perforare* < *per-* through + *forare* to bore] — **per′fo·ra·ble** *adj.* — **per′fo·ra·tive, per′fo·ra·to·ry** (-rə-tôr′ē, -tō′rē) *adj.* — **per′fo·ra′tor** *n.*

per·fo·rat·ed (pûr′fə·rā′tid) *adj.* Pierced with a hole or holes; especially, pierced with lines of holes, as sheets of stamps, to facilitate tearing. Abbr. *perf.*

per·fo·ra·tion (pûr′fə·rā′shən) *n.* **1.** The act of perforating, or the state of being perforated. **2.** A hole or series of holes drilled in or stamped through something.

per·force (pər·fôrs′, -fōrs′) *adv.* By or of necessity; necessarily. [< OF *par force* < *par* by (< L *per-*) + *force* force]

per·form (pər·fôrm′) *v.t.* **1.** To carry out in action; execute; do: to *perform* an operation. **2.** To act in accord with the requirements or obligations of; fulfill; discharge, as a duty or command. **3.** To act (a part) or give a performance of (a play, piece of music, acrobatic feats, etc.). — *v.i.* **4.** To carry through to completion an action, undertaking, etc. **5.** To give an exhibition or performance. — **Syn.** See ACCOMPLISH. [< OF *parfournir* to accomplish entirely < *par-* thoroughly (< L *per-*) + *fournir* to accomplish; infl. in form by L *performare* to form thoroughly] — **per·form′a·ble** *adj.*

per·form·ance (pər·fôr′məns) *n.* **1.** An entertainment of some kind before an audience or spectators. **2.** A public presentation: The music had its first *performance* here. **3.** The act or manner of performing a play, part, piece of music, etc. **4.** Manner of operating or functioning: The car's *performance* improved. **5.** Any act, deed, or accomplishment.

per·form·er (pər·fôr′mər) *n.* One who performs; especially, an actor, musician, etc. Abbr. *perf.* — **Syn.** See DOER.

per·fume (pər·fyoom′; *for n., usually* pûr′fyoom) *n.* **1.** A fragrant substance, usually a volatile liquid, prepared to emit a pleasant odor; scent. **2.** A pleasant odor, as from flowers; fragrance. — **Syn.** See SMELL. — *v.t.* **fumed, fuming** To fill or scent with a fragrant odor. [< MF *parfum* < Ital. *perfumare*, lit., to impregnate with smoke < *per-* through (< L) + *fumare* to smoke < LL *fumus* smoke]

per·fum·er (pər·fyoo′mər) *n.* **1.** One who makes or deals in perfumes. **2.** One who or that which perfumes.

per·fum·er·y (pər·fyoo′mər·ē) *n. pl.* **·er·ies 1.** The art or business of preparing perfumes. **2.** Perfumes in general, or a specific perfume. **3.** A place where perfumes are made.

per·func·to·ry (pər·fungk′tər·ē) *adj.* **1.** Done or performed mechanically and merely for the sake of getting through; careless; superficial; cursory. **2.** Having no zest or enthusiasm; dull. [< LL *perfunctorius* < *perfungi* to get through with < *per-* through + *fungi* to perform] — **per·func′to·ri·ly** *adv.* — **per·func′to·ri·ness** *n.*

per·fuse (pər·fyooz′) *v.t.* **fused, fus·ing 1.** To permeate, suffuse, or sprinkle with a liquid, color, etc. **2.** To spread (a liquid, etc.) over or through something; diffuse. [< L *perfusus*, pp. of *perfundere* < *per-* throughout + *fundere* to pour] — **per·fu′sion** (-fyoo′zhən) *n.* — **per·fu′sive** (-fyoo′siv) *adj.*

Per·ga·mum (pûr′gə·məm) **1.** An ancient kingdom of western Asia Minor, later a Roman province. **2.** Its capital, a Greek city on the site of modern Bergama. Also **Per′ga·mon** (-mon), **Per′ga·mos** (-mos), **Per′ga·mus** (-məs).

per·go·la (pûr′gə·lə) *n.* An arbor or covered walk made of trelliswork covered with vegetation or flowers. [< Ital., arbor < L *pergula* projecting roof, arbor, ? < *pergere* to proceed < L *per-* through + *regere* to keep straight]

PERGOLA

Per·go·le·si (per′gō·lā′zē), **Giovanni Battista**, 1710–36, Italian composer. Also **Per′go·le′se** (-zā).

perh. Perhaps.

per·haps (pər·haps′) *adv.* Maybe; possibly. [< PER + *happes, haps,* pl. of HAP]

pe·ri (pir′ē) *n.* **1.** In Persian mythology, a beautiful fairy or elf descended from the disobedient angels and doing penance until readmitted into paradise. **2.** Any beautiful elflike creature. [< Persian *pari, peri*]

peri- *prefix* **1.** Around; encircling: *periphery.* **2.** Situated near; adjoining: *perihelion.* [< Gk. < *peri* around]

Per·i·an·der (per′ē·an′dər), died 585 B.C., tyrant of Corinth 625–585 B.C.

per·i·anth (per′ē·anth) *n. Bot.* The envelope of a flower, especially one in which the calyx and corolla are so alike as to be indistinguishable. [< F *périanthe* < NL *perianthium* < Gk. *peri-* around + *anthos* flower]

per·i·apt (per′ē·apt) *n.* A charm; amulet. [< F *périapte* < Gk. *periapton* < *peri-* around + *haptos* fastened < *haptein* to fasten]

per·i·blem (per′ə·blem) *n. Bot.* A sheath of meristematic tissue surrounding the plerome of a plant and giving rise to the cortex. [< G < Gk. *periblēma* a covering < *periballein* to put on or around < *peri-* around + *ballein* to throw]

per·i·car·di·al (per′ə·kär′dē·əl) *adj.* Of or pertaining to the pericardium. Also **per′i·car′di·ac** (-ak), **per′i·car′di·an.**

per·i·car·di·tis (per′ə·kär·dī′tis) *n. Pathol.* Inflammation of the pericardium.

per·i·car·di·um (per′ə·kär′dē·əm) *n. pl.* **·di·a** (-dē·ə) *Anat.* A membranous bag that surrounds and protects the heart. [< NL < Gk. *perikardion,* neut. of *perikardios* around the heart < *peri-* around + *kardia* heart]

per·i·carp (per′ə·kärp) *n. Bot.* The wall of a ripened ovary or fruit, usually consisting of three layers, the epicarp, mesocarp, and endocarp: also called *seedcase, seed vessel.* [< NL *pericarpium* < Gk. *perikarpion* husk < *peri-* around + *karpos* fruit] — **per′i·car′pi·al** *adj.*

per·i·chon·dri·um (per′ə·kon′drē·əm) *n. pl.* **·dri·a** (-drē·ə) *Anat.* The vascular membrane that envelops the surface of a cartilage between neighboring joints. [< NL < Gk. *peri-* around + *chondros* cartilage] — **per′i·chon′dri·al** *adj.*

Per·i·cle·an (per′ə·klē′ən) *adj.* Pertaining to or characteristic of Pericles or his period, when Greek art, drama, etc. are considered to have been at their height.

Per·i·cles (per′ə·klēz), died 429 B.C., Athenian statesman.

Pericles, Prince of Tyre Hero of Shakespeare's play of that name.

per·i·cline (per′ə·klīn) *n.* A variety of albite found in the Swiss Alps in the form of white twinned crystals. [< NL *periklinēs* sloping all around < *peri-* around + *klinein* to lean]

pe·ric·o·pe (pə·rik′ə·pē) *n.* A selection from a book, especially a passage of Scripture read as part of a religious service. [< LL, < Gk. *perikopē* < *peri* around + *koptō* cut]

per·i·cra·ni·um (per′ə·krā′nē·əm) *n. pl.* **·ni·a** (-nē·ə) *Anat.* The periosteum of the external surface of the cranium. [< NL < Gk. *perikranion* < *perikranios* around the skull < *peri-* around + *kranion* skull] — **per′i·cra′ni·al** *adj.*

per·i·cy·cle (per′ə·sī′kəl) *n. Bot.* The outer portion of the central cylinder in plants, capable of active growth. [< Gk. *perikyklos* all around, spherical < *peri-* around + *kyklos* circle] — **per′i·cy′clic** *adj.*

per·i·derm (per′ə·dûrm) *n. Bot.* The tissue produced by the phellogen in plants and giving rise to the outer bark. — **per′i·der′mal** or **·der′mic** *adj.* [< Gk. *peri-* around + *derma* skin]

pe·rid·i·um (pə·rid′ē·əm) *n. pl.* **·i·a** (-ē·ə) *Bot.* The two-layered outer coat enveloping the fruit body in certain fungi, as in puffballs. [< NL < Gk. *péridion,* dim. of *pēra* leather bag] — **pe·rid′i·al** *adj.*

per·i·dot (per′ə·dot, -dō) *n.* A yellowish green variety of chrysolite, used as a gemstone. [< F *péridot* < OF *peritot;* ult. origin uncertain] — **per′i·dot′ic** (-dot′ik) *adj.*

per·i·do·tite (per′ə·dō′tīt) *n.* A granular igneous rock composed essentially of olivine. [< PERIDOT + -ITE¹]

per·i·gee (per′ə·jē) *n. Astron.* That point in the orbit of a celestial body, such as the moon or an artificial satellite, which is nearest to the earth: opposed to *apogee.* [< MF *périgee* < Med.L *perigaeum* < Gk. *perigeion,* neut. of *perigeios* near the earth < *peri-* near + *gē* earth] — **per′i·ge′al, per′i·ge′an** *adj.*

per·i·gon (per′ə·gon) *n. Geom.* An angle equal to two straight angles or 360 degrees. [PERI- + -GON]

Per·i·gor·di·an (per′ə·gôr′dē·ən) *adj. Anthropol.* Of or pertaining to either of two extensions of the Upper Paleolithic stage. [after *Périgord,* a region of France]

pe·rig·y·nous (pə·rij′ə·nəs) *adj. Bot.* **1.** Situated in a cuplike organ that surrounds the pistil, as stamens. **2.** Having stamens or petals arranged in this way. [< NL *perigynus* < Gk. *peri-* around + *gynē* female] — **pe·rig′y·ny** *n.*

per·i·he·li·on (per′ə·hē′lē·ən) *n. pl.* **·li·a** (-lē·ə) *Astron.* The point in the orbit of a planet or comet where it is nearest the sun: opposed to *aphelion.* [< NL *perihelium* < Gk. *peri-* around, near + *hēlios* sun; refashioned after Greek]

per·il (per′əl) *n.* Exposure to the chance of injury, loss, or destruction; danger; jeopardy; risk. — **Syn.** See DANGER. — *v.t.* **·iled** or **·illed, ·il·ing** or **·il·ling** To expose to danger; imperil. [< OF *peril* < L *periculum* trial, danger]

per·il·ous (per′əl·əs) *adj.* Full of, involving, or attended with peril; hazardous. [< OF *perillous* < L *periculosus.* See PERIL.] — **per′il·ous·ly** *adv.* — **per′il·ous·ness** *n.*

per·i·lune (per′ə·loon′) *n.* That point in the lunar orbit of an artificial satellite or other celestial body which is nearest to the moon. [< PERI- + Fr. *lune* moon]

pe·rim·e·ter (pə·rim′ə·tər) *n.* **1.** The boundary line of any figure of two dimensions. **2.** The sum of the sides of a plane figure. **3.** An instrument for testing the scope of the field of vision. [< L *perimetros* < Gk. < *peri-* around + *metron* measure] — **per′i·met′ric** (per′ə·met′rik) or **·ri·cal** *adj.* — **per′i·met′ri·cal·ly** *adv.*

— **Syn. 1.** *Perimeter, circumference,* and *periphery* denote a bounding line, as of a plane figure. *Perimeter* is the most general term, used both for the boundary and for its total length. *Circumference* is the *perimeter* of a circle or an ellipse; in extension, it may be the *perimeter* of any curvilinear figure. *Periphery* may be substituted for *perimeter* in most cases, but is more often used in the sense of the bounding surface of a solid.

pe·rim·e·try (pə·rim′ə·trē) *n.* Measurement by a perimeter.

per·i·morph (per′ə·môrf) *n. Mineral.* A mineral that encloses another. [< PERI- + -MORPH] — **per′i·mor′phic** or **·phous** *adj.* — **per′i·mor′phism** *n.*

per·i·neph·ri·um (per′ə·nef′rē·əm) *n. Anat.* The capsule of adipose tissue that surrounds the kidney. [< NL < Gk.

peri- around + *nephros* kidney] **—per′i·neph′ral** or **·ri·al** or **·ric** *adj.*

per·i·ne·um (per′ə·nē′əm) *n. pl.* **·ne·a** (-nē′ə) *Anat.* **1.** The region of the body at the lower end of the trunk, between the genital organs and the rectum. **2.** The entire region at the outlet of the pelvis, comprising the anus and the internal genitals. Also **per′i·nae′um.** [< LL < Gk. *perineos* < *peri* around + *inein* to empty out] **—per′i·ne′al** *adj.*

per·i·neu·ri·tis (per′ə·nŏŏ·rī′tis, -nyŏŏ-) *n. Pathol.* Inflammation of the perineurium.

per·i·neu·ri·um (per′ə·nŏŏr′ē·əm, -nyŏŏr′-) *n. pl.* **·ri·a** (-ē·ə) *Anat.* The connective tissue investing any of the bundles of fibers composing a nerve. [< NL < Gk. *peri-* around + *neuron* nerve] **—per′i·neu′ri·al** *adj.*

per in·ter·im (pər in′tər·im) *Latin* In the meantime.

pe·ri·od (pir′ē·əd) *n.* **1.** A portion of time marked or defined by certain conditions, events, etc.: a *period* of rest. **2.** A portion or lapse of time, as in a process or development; a stage. **3.** A portion of time marked by some recurring action or phenomenon. **4.** A portion of time into which something is divided: Our new school day has seven *periods.* **5.** *Astron.* The time it takes a planet or satellite to revolve once about its primary. **6.** *Geol.* One of the divisions of geologic time, intermediate between the shorter *epoch* and the longer *era.* **7.** *Physics* The time that elapses between any two successive similar phases of an oscillation or other regularly repeated cyclical motion. **8.** A dot (.) placed on the line, used as a mark of punctuation after every complete declarative sentence, after most abbreviations, etc. **9.** A portion of speech or writing, especially if composed of a full sentence or sentences having several clauses. **10.** The pause at the end of a sentence. **11.** In Greek verse, a unit of two or more cola. **12.** *Music* A group of two or more related phrases. **13.** *Pathol.* A stage distinguishable in the course of a disease. **14.** Menstruation (def. 2). **15.** The completion or end of something. *Abbr. per.* [< OF *periode* < L *periodus* < Gk. *periodos* a going around, < *peri-* around + *hodos* way]

per·i·o·date (pə·rī′ə·dāt) *n. Chem.* A salt of periodic acid. [< PERIOD(IC ACID) + -ATE³]

period furniture Furniture in the style of a given period.

pe·ri·od·ic (pir′ē·od′ik) *adj.* **1.** Of, pertaining to, or like a period. **2.** Recurring at regular intervals. **3.** Intermittent. **4.** Of, pertaining to, or expressed in periodic sentences. **5.** *Physics* Recurring after a definite interval, as a phase in a cyclical system. [< OF *periodique* < L *periodicus* < Gk. *periodikos.* See PERIOD.] **—pe′ri·od′i·cal·ly** *adv.*

per·i·od·ic acid (pûr′ī·od′ik) *Chem.* Any of various acids containing heptavalent iodine, the principal forms being H_5IO_6 and HIO_4. [< PER- (def. 5) + IODIC]

pe·ri·od·i·cal (pir′ē·od′i·kəl) *adj.* **1.** Of or pertaining to publications, as magazines, etc., that appear at fixed intervals of more than one day; also, published at regular intervals. **2.** Periodic. **—** *n.* A periodical publication.

pe·ri·o·dic·i·ty (pir′ē·ə·dis′ə·tē) *n.* The quality of being periodic or of recurring at definite intervals of time.

periodic law *Chem.* The statement that the physical and chemical properties of the elements are related to their atomic numbers, and that they recur periodically when the elements are arranged in the order of these numbers.

periodic sentence A sentence so constructed as to suspend completion of both sense and structure until the close: distinguished from *loose sentence.*

periodic system *Chem.* A classification of the elements in accordance with the periodic law.

periodic table *Chem.* A table in which the elements are arranged in physicochemical groups as determined by the periodic law. See page 1004.

per·i·o·dide (pə·rī′ə·dīd) *n. Chem.* An iodide having a larger proportion of iodine than any other compound of the same series. Also **per′i′o·did** (-did).

per·i·o·don·tics (per′ē·ə·don′tiks) *n.* The branch of dentistry concerned with diseases of the gums and of the bones that support the teeth. Also **per′i·o·don′ti·a** (-don′shə, -shē·ə). [< NL < Gk. *peri-* around + *odous, odontos* tooth] **—per′i·o·don′tic** *adj.* **—per′i·o·don′tist** *n.*

per·i·os·te·um (per′ē·os′tē·əm) *n. Anat.* A tough, fibrous, two-layered vascular membrane that surrounds and nourishes the bones. [< NL < LL *periosteon* < Gk., neut. of *periosteos* around the bones < *peri-* around + *osteon* bone] **—per′i·os′te·al, per′i·os′te·ous** *adj.*

per·i·os·ti·tis (per′ē·os·tī′tis) *n. Pathol.* Inflammation of the periosteum. [< PERIOST(EUM) + -ITIS] **—per′i·os·tit′ic** (-tit′ik) *adj.*

per·i·o·tic (per′ē·ō′tik, -ot′ik) *adj. Anat.* **1.** Surrounding the ear, especially the inner ear. **2.** Denoting the bony structure protecting the inner ear, part of the mastoid bone. [< Gk. *peri-* around and *ōtikos* of the ear < *ous, ōtos* ear]

per·i·pa·tet·ic (per′i·pə·tet′ik) *adj.* **1.** Walking about from place to place. **2.** *Rare* Rambling, as of speech. **—** *n.* One given to walking about. [< MF *péripatétique* < L *peripateticus* < Gk. *peripatētikos.* < *peri-* around + *pateein* to walk]

Per·i·pa·tet·ic (per′i·pə·tet′ik) *adj.* Of or pertaining to the philosophy of Aristotle, who lectured to his disciples while walking in the Lyceum at Athens. **—** *n.* A disciple of Aristotle or of his teachings.

pe·riph·er·al (pə·rif′ər·əl) *adj.* **1.** Of, pertaining to, or consisting of a periphery. **2.** Describing the ability to perceive images laterally that are not directly in one's line of sight: *peripheral* vision. **3.** Not central; marginal: of *peripheral* importance. **4.** *Anat.* Located on or at the surface; outer; external. Also **per·i·pher·ic** (per′ə·fer′ik) or **·i·cal** (-i·kəl). **—pe·riph′er·al·ly** *adv.*

pe·riph·er·y (pə·rif′ər·ē) *n. pl.* **·er·ies** **1.** The outer part, surface, or boundary of something. **2.** The perimeter of a curvilinear figure. **3.** A surrounding region, area, or country. **— Syn.** See PERIMETER. [< OF *periferie* < LL *peripheria* < Gk. *periphereia* circumference < *peri-* around + *pherein* to carry]

pe·riph·ra·sis (pə·rif′rə·sis) *n. pl.* **·ses** (-sēz) **1.** A roundabout method of expressing something; circumlocution. **2.** An instance of this. Also **per·i·phrase** (per′i·frāz′). **— Syn.** See CIRCUMLOCUTION. [< L < Gk. < *periphrazein* < *peri-* around + *phrazein* to declare]

per·i·phras·tic (per′i·fras′tik) *adj.* **1.** Of the nature of or involving periphrasis; employing indirect words; circumlocutory. **2.** *Gram.* Denoting a construction in which a phrase is substituted for an inflected form of similar function, as, *the hat of John* for *John's hat.* Also **per′i·phras′ti·cal. — per′i·phras′ti·cal·ly** *adv.* [< Med.L *periphrasticus* < Gk. *periphrastikos < periphrazein.* See PERIPHRASIS.]

periphrastic conjugation *Gram.* A conjugation formed by simple verbs with the aid of auxiliaries, instead of by inflection of the verb itself, as, *he did run* for *he ran.*

pe·rip·ter·al (pə·rip′tər·əl) *Archit. adj.* Having a row of columns around all sides. **—** *n.* A peripteral temple; peristyle: also **pe·rip′ter, pe·rip′ter·os** (-tər·os). [< L *peripteros* < Gk., lit., flying around < *peri-* around + *pteron* a wing]

pe·rique (pə·rēk′) *n.* A dark, strongly flavored tobacco grown in Louisiana. [after nickname of Pierre Chenet, American tobacco grower who introduced this variety]

per·i·sarc (per′ə·särk) *n. Zool.* The hard, chitinous excretion of a hydroid colony. [< Gk. *peri-* around + *sarx, sarkos* flesh] **—per′i·sar′cal, per′i·sar′cous** *adj.*

per·i·scope (per′ə·skōp) *n.* An instrument consisting of totally reflecting prisms or mirrors so arranged as to reflect light rays down a vertical tube, used to guide submarines, observe objects from a trench, etc. [< Gk. *peri-* around + *skopos* looker < *skopeein* to look]

PERISCOPE

per·i·scop·ic (per′ə·skop′ik) *adj.* **1.** *Optics* Denoting a special type of lens permitting oblique or peripheral vision of an object in its field. **2.** Of or pertaining to a periscope. Also **per′i·scop′i·cal.**

per·ish (per′ish) *v.i.* **1.** To suffer a violent or untimely death. **2.** To pass from existence. [< OF *periss-*, stem of *perir* < L *perire* < *per-* away + *ire* to go]

per·ish·a·ble (per′ish·ə·bəl) *adj.* **1.** Liable to perish. **2.** Liable to speedy decay, as fruit in transportation. **—** *n.* Usually *pl.* Something liable to decay, as food. **—per′ish·a·ble·ness, per′ish·a·bil′i·ty** *n.* **—per′ish·a·bly** *adv.*

per·i·sperm (per′ə·spûrm) *n. Bot.* Tissue surrounding the embryo sac in an ovule, in which nutrient material is stored. [< F *périsperme* < NL *perispermum* < Gk. *peri-* around + *sperma* seed] **—per′i·sper′mic** *adj.*

pe·ris·so·dac·tyl (pə·ris′ō·dak′til) *adj.* **1.** Odd-toed. **2.** *Zool.* Of or pertaining to an order of ungulates (*Perissodactyla*) having an odd number of toes or digits on each foot and an enlarged cecum, including horses, tapirs, and rhinoceroses. **—** *n.* An ungulate mammal belonging to this order. Also **pe·ris′so·dac′tyle.** [< NL *perissodactylus* < Gk. *perissos* unusual, odd + *dactylos* finger, toe] **—pe·ris′so·dac·tyl′ic** or **·dac′ty·lous** *adj.* **—pe·ris′so·dac′ty·lism** *n.*

per·i·stal·sis (per′ə·stôl′sis, -stal′-) *n. pl.* **·ses** (-sēz) *Physiol.* A contractile muscular movement of any hollow organ of the body, as of the alimentary canal, whereby the contents are gradually propelled toward the point of expulsion. [< NL < Gk. *peristaltikos < peristellein* to surround < *peri-* around + *stellein* to place] **—per′i·stal′tic** *adj.*

per·i·stome (per′ə·stōm) *n.* **1.** *Bot.* The fringe of delicate teeth around the mouth of the capsule of mosses. **2.** *Zool.* The parts that surround the mouth or form the margins of a mouthlike opening, as in a univalve or sea anemone. Also **pe·ris·to·ma** (pə·ris′tə·mə), **per′i·sto′mi·um.** [< NL *peristoma* < Gk. *peri-* around + *stoma* mouth]

per·i·style (per′ə·stīl) *n. Archit.* **1.** A system of columns about a building or an internal court. **2.** An area or space so enclosed. [< MF *péristyle* < L *peristylum* < Gk. *peristylon,* neut. of *peristylos* surrounded by a colonnade < *peri-* around + *stylos* pillar]

per·i·the·ci·um (per′ə·thē′shē·əm, -sē′əm) *n. pl.* **·ci·a** (-shē·ə, -sē·ə) *Bot.* A closed or narrow-mouthed, flask-shaped

PERIODIC TABLE OF ELEMENTS

The atomic number will be found in the upper left corner of each box; the atomic weight (1961), based on carbon 12.01115, in the lower right (numbers in the table in parentheses are mass numbers of the most stable isotopes); and the symbol in the lower left.

Period	Group 1	Group 2	Group 3	Group 4	Group 5	Group 6	Group 7	Group 8			Group 0
1	1 Hydrogen, H 1.00797										2 Helium, He 4.0026
2	3 Lithium, Li 6.939	4 Beryllium, Be 9.0122	5 Boron, B 10.811	6 Carbon, C 12.01115	7 Nitrogen, N 14.0067	8 Oxygen, O 15.9994	9 Fluorine, F 18.9994				10 Neon, Ne 20.183
3	11 Sodium, Na 22.9898	12 Magnesium, Mg 24.312	13 Aluminum, Al 26.9815	14 Silicon, Si 28.086	15 Phosphorus, P 30.9738	16 Sulfur, S 32.064	17 Chlorine, Cl 35.453				18 Argon, Ar 39.948
4A	19 Potassium, K 39.102	20 Calcium, Ca 40.08	21 Scandium, Sc 44.956	22 Titanium, Ti 47.90	23 Vanadium, V 50.942	24 Chromium, Cr 51.996	25 Manganese, Mn 54.938	26 Iron, Fe 55.847	27 Cobalt, Co 58.9332	28 Nickel, Ni 58.71	
4B	29 Copper, Cu 63.54	30 Zinc, Zn 65.37	31 Gallium, Ga 69.72	32 Germanium, Ge 72.59	33 Arsenic, As 74.9216	34 Selenium, Se 78.96	35 Bromine, Br 79.909				36 Krypton, Kr 83.80
5A	37 Rubidium, Rb 85.47	38 Strontium, Sr 87.62	39 Yttrium, Y 88.905	40 Zirconium, Zr 91.22	41 Niobium, Nb 92.906	42 Molybdenum, Mo 95.94	43 Technetium, Tc (99)	44 Ruthenium, Ru 101.07	45 Rhodium, Rh 102.905	46 Palladium, Pd 106.40	
5B	47 Silver, Ag 107.87	48 Cadmium, Cd 112.40	49 Indium, In 114.82	50 Tin, Sn 118.69	51 Antimony, Sb 121.75	52 Tellurium, Te 127.60	53 Iodine, I 126.9044				54 Xenon, Xe 131.30
6A	55 Cesium, Cs 132.905	56 Barium, Ba 137.34	57–71 Lanthanide Series	72 Hafnium, Hf 178.49	73 Tantalum, Ta 180.948	74 Tungsten, W 183.85	75 Rhenium, Re 186.20	76 Osmium, Os 190.20	77 Iridium, Ir 192.2	78 Platinum, Pt 195.09	
6B	79 Gold, Au 196.967	80 Mercury, Hg 200.59	81 Thallium, Tl 204.37	82 Lead, Pb 207.19	83 Bismuth, Bi 208.98	84 Polonium, Po 210.00	85 Astatine, At (210)				86 Radon, Rn 222.00
7	87 Francium, Fr (223)	88 Radium, Ra 226.05	89–103 Actinide Series								

Lanthanide Series						
57 Lanthanum, La 138.91	58 Cerium, Ce 140.12	59 Praseodymium, Pr 140.907	60 Neodymium, Nd 144.24	61 Promethium, Pm (147)	62 Samarium, Sm 150.35	63 Europium, Eu 151.96
64 Gadolinium, Gd 157.25	65 Terbium, Tb 158.924	66 Dysprosium, Dy 162.50	67 Holmium, Ho 164.93	68 Erbium, Er 167.26	69 Thulium, Tm 168.934	70 Ytterbium, Yb 173.04
71 Lutetium, Lu 174.97						

Actinide Series						
89 Actinium, Ac 227.0	90 Thorium, Th 232.038	91 Protactinium, Pa 231	92 Uranium, U 238.03	93 Neptunium, Np (237)	94 Plutonium, Pu (242)	95 Americium, Am (243)
96 Curium, Cm (247)	97 Berkelium, Bk (249)	98 Californium, Cf (251)	99 Einsteinium, Es (254)	100 Fermium, Fm (253)	101 Mendelevium, Md (256)	102 Nobelium, No (253)
103 Lawrencium, Lw (257?)						

receptacle containing the asci of certain fungi, as the powdery mildews. [< NL < Gk. *peri-* around + *thēkē* case < *tithenai* to put] — **per′i·the′ci·al** *adj.*

per·i·to·ne·um (per′ə·tə·nē′əm) *n. pl.* **·ne·a** (-nē′ə) *Anat.* A serous membrane that lines the abdominal cavity in mammals and is a more or less complete covering or investment for the viscera. Also **per′i·to·nae′um.** [< LL *peritonaeum* < Gk. *peritonaion* < *peritonos* stretched round < *peri-* around + *teinein* to stretch] — **per′i·to·ne′al** or **·nae′al** *adj.*

per·i·to·ni·tis (per′ə·tə·nī′tis) *n. Pathol.* Inflammation of the peritoneum. [< *periton-* (< PERITONEUM) + -ITIS]

pe·rit·ri·cha (pə·rit′rə·kə) *n.pl.* Bacteria having flagella all around the body. [< NL < Gk. *peri-* around + *thrix, trichos* hair] — **pe·rit′ri·chous** *adj.*

per·i·wig (per′ə·wig) *n.* A peruke or wig. [Earlier *perwyke,* alter. of *perruck* < MF *perruque*. See PERUKE.]

per·i·win·kle[1] (per′ə·wing′kəl) *n.* **1.** A small marine snail (genus *Littorina*), especially the edible **European periwinkle** (L. *littorea*), now common on the east coast of the United States, or the **American periwinkle** (L. *palliata*). **2.** Any of various other small univalves. Also called *winkle.* [OE *pinewincle,* ? < L *pina* mussel (< Gk.) + OE *wincle* a shellfish; ? infl. in form by PERIWINKLE[2]]

per·i·win·kle[2] (per′ə·wing′kəl) *n.* **1.** A plant (genus *Vinca*) of the dogbane family, especially *V. minor,* having shining, evergreen leaves and blue or sometimes white flowers: also called *myrtle.* **2.** A similar plant (*V. major*), having trailing foliage. [OE *perwince* < L *pervinca* < *vinca pervinca,* prob. < *pervincire* < *per-* thoroughly + *vincire* to bind]

per·jure (pûr′jər) *v.t.* **·jured, ·jur·ing 1.** To make (oneself) guilty of perjury. **2.** To find guilty of or involved in perjury: usually in the passive: if they are *perjured.* [< OF *parjurer* < L *perjurare* < *per-* thoroughly + *jurare* to swear; reshaped after L] — **per′jur·er** *n.*

per·jured (pûr′jərd) *adj.* **1.** Guilty of perjury; having sworn falsely; forsworn: a *perjured* witness. **2.** Involving perjury; fake: *perjured* testimony. — **per′jured·ly** *adv.*

per·ju·ry (pûr′jə·rē) *n. pl.* **·ries** *Law* The wilful and voluntary giving of false testimony or the withholding of material facts or evidence in regard to a matter or thing material to the issue or point of inquiry in a legal document or while under oath in a judicial proceeding. [< OF *parjurie* < *parjurer.* See PERJURE.]

perk[1] (pûrk) *v.i.* **1.** To recover one's spirits or vigor: with *up.* **2.** To carry oneself or lift one's head jauntily. — *v.t.* **3.** To raise quickly or smartly, as the ears: often with *up.* **4.** To make (oneself) trim and smart in appearance: often with *up* or *out.* — *adj.* Perky. [ME *perken;* ? var. of PERCH[1]]

perk[2] (pûrk) *v.i. Informal* To percolate. [Short for PERCOLATE]

Per·kin (pûr′kin), **Sir William Henry,** 1838–1907, English chemist; founded the aniline dye industry.

Per·kins (pûr′kinz), **Frances,** 1882–1965, U.S. social worker; secretary of labor 1933–45; first woman in the U.S. cabinet. — **Maxwell Evarts,** 1884–1947, U.S. editor.

perk·y (pûr′kē) *adj.* **perk·i·er, perk·i·est 1.** Jaunty; sprightly; pert. **2.** Spirited and self-assured. Also *perk.* — **perk′i·ly** *adv.* — **perk′i·ness** *n.*

Per·lis (pûr′lis) The northernmost State of Malaysia, on the Malay peninsula; 310 sq. mi.; pop. 113,350 (est. 1966); capital, Kangar.

per·lite (pûr′līt) *n.* An acid, igneous, glassy rock of the composition of obsidian, usually occurring in masses of small globules: also spelled *pearlite.* [< F < *perle* pearl] — **per·lit′ic** (-lit′ik) *adj.*

Perm (pyermy′) A city in the western R.S.F.S.R., on the Kama; pop. 628,000 (1959): from 1940–57 *Molotov.* Also **Perm′.**

perm. Permanent.

per·ma·frost (pûr′mə·frôst, -frost) *n.* The part of the earth's surface in arctic regions that is permanently frozen. [< PERMA(NENT) + FROST]

Perm·al·loy (pûr′mə·loi) *n.* Any of a group of iron and nickel alloys having small quantities of other metals and characterized by high magnetic permeability: a trade name. Also **perm′al·loy.** [< PERM(EABLE) + ALLOY]

per·ma·nence (pûr′mə·nəns) *n.* The state or quality of being permanent. [< OF < Med.L *permanentia* < L *permanens.* See PERMANENT.]

per·ma·nen·cy (pûr′mə·nən·sē) *n. pl.* **·cies 1.** Permanence. **2.** Something permanent.

per·ma·nent (pûr′mə·nənt) *adj.* Continuing in the same state or without essential change; enduring; durable; fixed. — *n.* A permanent wave (which see). [< OF, or < L *permanens, -entis* < *permanere* to stay to the end < *per-* through + *manere* to remain] — **per′ma·nent·ly** *adv.*

— **Syn.** (adj.) *Permanent, lasting, enduring, durable, stable,* and *fixed* characterize that which does not change or pass away. *Permanent* and *lasting* suggest long continuance of something that might be expected to end soon, rather than perpetual existence:

a *permanent* dye, a *lasting* friendship. That which is *enduring* resists both time and change: *enduring* social institutions. *Durable* stresses resistance to destructive agencies: a *durable* fabric. *Stable* and *fixed* denote firmness of character or position, or of both, such as resists change or displacement: a *stable* government, a *fixed* attitude toward a question. — **Ant.** temporary, transient, transitory. Compare CONTINUAL, EVERLASTING.

Permanent Court of Arbitration A court established at The Hague in 1899 for the arbitration of disputes between nations, whose jurists now select the nominees from which members of the International Court of Justice are elected: also called *Hague Tribunal.*

Permanent Court of International Justice An international tribunal established under the Covenant of the League of Nations (1921) and superseded in 1945 by the International Court of Justice: also called *World Court.*

permanent magnet A magnet that retains its magnetism indefinitely; especially, a magnetized piece of a special alloy steel: distinguished from *electromagnet.*

permanent wave An artificial wave mechanically or chemically set in the hair and lasting several months.

per·man·ga·nate (pər·mang′gə·nāt) *n. Chem.* A dark purple salt of permanganic acid.

per·man·gan·ic acid (pûr′man·gan′ik) *Chem.* An acid, HMnO₄, that is a powerful oxidizer in aqueous solutions.

per·me·a·bil·i·ty (pûr′mē·ə·bil′ə·tē) *n.* **1.** The quality or condition of being permeable. **2.** *Physics* **a** The property of being easily traversed by magnetic lines of force; susceptibility to magnetization. **b** The measure of the rate of diffusion of a gas through a fabric under standard conditions, generally given in liters per square meter per 24 hours.

per·me·a·ble (pûr′mē·ə·bəl) *adj.* **1.** Allowing passage, especially of fluids. **2.** Designating a type of protective clothing treated to resist penetration by vapors and gases, but not by liquids. [< L *permeabilis* < *permeare.* See PERMEATE.] — **per′me·a·bly** *adv.*

per·me·ance (pûr′mē·əns) *n.* **1.** The act of permeating. **2.** *Electr.* The ability to be traversed by magnetic lines of force: the reciprocal of *reluctance.*

per·me·ate (pûr′mē·āt) *v.* **·at·ed, ·at·ing** *v.t.* **1.** To spread thoroughly through; pervade. **2.** To pass through the pores or interstices of. — *v.i.* **3.** To spread itself. [< L *permeatus,* pp. of *permeare* < *per-* through + *meare* to pass] — **per′me·ant** *adj.* — **per′me·a′tion** *n.* — **per′me·a′tive** *adj.*

— **Syn. 1.** *Permeate, pervade, penetrate, saturate,* and *impregnate* are compared in their physical sense. *Permeate* refers to an action like that of a gas which diffuses through all the pores or intermolecular spaces of a solid or another gas; *pervade* describes the action of a gas which fills all the open space of a chamber. Therefore a gas *pervades* a room by *permeating* the air in the room. *Penetrate* means to pass through or into, and usually implies the overcoming of resistance. A solution is said to be *saturated* when it can hold no more of the solute; *impregnate* is midway between *permeate* and *saturate,* and stresses the new qualities or characteristics gained by a substance through which some other substance has been diffused.

per men·sem (pûr men′səm) *Latin* By the month.

Per·mi·an (pûr′mē·ən) *Geol. adj.* Of or pertaining to the latest period of the Paleozoic era, following the Pennsylvanian and succeeded by the Triassic. — *n.* The Permian rock system or period. See table for GEOLOGY. [after *Perm,* former E. Russian province]

per mill (pûr mil′) By the thousand; in a thousand. Also **per mil.** [< L *per* by + *mille* thousand]

per·mil·lage (pər·mil′ij) *n.* Proportion or rate per thousand.

per·mis·si·ble (pər·mis′ə·bəl) *adj.* That can be permitted; allowable. — **per·mis′si·bil′i·ty** *n.* — **per·mis′si·bly** *adv.*

per·mis·sion (pər·mish′ən) *n.* **1.** The act of permitting or allowing. **2.** Formal authorization or consent. [< L *permissio, -onis* < *permissus,* pp. of *permittere.* See PERMIT[1].] — **Syn.** leave, license, sanction, allowance, authorization.

per·mis·sive (pər·mis′iv) *adj.* **1.** Permitting; granting permission. **2.** Permitted; optional. **3.** Not strict in discipline; lenient: *permissive* parents. — **per·mis′sive·ly** *adv.* — **per·mis′sive·ness** *n.*

per·mis·so·ry (pər·mis′ər·ē) *adj.* **1.** Pertaining to or of the nature of permission. **2.** *Law* Arising from or founded on permission; authorized; licensed.

per·mit[1] (*v.* pər·mit′; *n.* pûr′mit) *v.* **·mit·ted, ·mit·ting** *v.t.* **1.** To allow the doing of; consent to. **2.** To give (someone) leave or consent; authorize. **3.** To afford opportunity for: His answer *permits* no misinterpretation. — *v.i.* **4.** To afford possibility or opportunity. **5.** To allow. — *n.* **1.** Permission or warrant; especially, a written authorization to do something. **2.** An official document or certificate authorizing performance of a specified activity; license. [< L *permittere* < *per-* through < *mittere* to send, let go] — **per·mit′ter** *n.*

— **Syn.** (verb) See ALLOW. — **Ant.** prohibit, forbid.

per·mit[2] (pûr′mit) *n.* A pompano (genus *Trachinotus*) of Caribbean and Atlantic waters. [< Sp. *palometa,* dim. of *paloma* dove]

---

per·mut·a·ble (pər·myōō′tə·bəl) *adj.* Capable of being changed or of undergoing change or interchange.

per·mu·ta·tion (pûr′myōō·tā′shən) *n.* **1.** The act of rearranging; transformation. **2.** *Math.* **a** Change in the order of sequence of elements or objects in a series; especially, the making of all possible changes of sequence, as *abc, acb, bac,* etc. **b** Any one of the arrangements thus made. See COMBINATION. [< OF *permutacion* < L *permutatio, -onis* < *permutatus,* pp. of *permutare.* See PERMUTE.]

per·mute (pər·myōōt′) *v.t.* **·mut·ed, ·mut·ing** To subject to permutation; especially, to change the order of. [< OF, or < L *permutare* < *per-* thoroughly + *mutare* to change]

Per·nam·bu·co (pûr′nam·bōō′kō, *Pg.* per′nəm·bōō′kŏō) **1.** A State of NE Brazil; 37,458 sq. mi.; pop. 4,107,000 (est. 1958); capital, Recife. **2.** See RECIFE.

per·ni·cious (pər·nish′əs) *adj.* **1.** Having the power of destroying or injuring; tending to kill or hurt; very injurious; deadly. **2.** Malicious; wicked. [< MF *pernicieux* < L *perniciosus* < *pernicies* destruction < *per-* thoroughly + *nex, necis* death] **— per·ni′cious·ly** *adv.* **— per·ni′cious·ness** *n.*
— Syn. 1. *Pernicious, noxious, baneful, deleterious,* and *detrimental* mean causing harm. *Pernicious* is the strongest word, implying the power to kill or destroy utterly: *pernicious* anemia, *pernicious* gossip. *Noxious* refers to something unpleasant as well as injurious: the *noxious* vapors given off by gas engines. *Baneful* literally means poisonous, but most often suggests a weakening rather than a lethal effect: a *baneful* climate. *Deleterious* is chiefly applied to what we ingest: a *deleterious* ingredient in a prepared food. *Detrimental* suggests less extreme harm, and often denotes mere adversity; it is more widely applicable than the other words: this tax will be *detrimental* to business. **— Ant.** innocuous, beneficial, wholesome.

pernicious anemia *Pathol.* Macrocytic anemia characterized by inadequate development of red blood corpuscles, degenerative lesions in the posterior and lateral columns of the spinal cord, and progressive disturbances in the muscular, nervous, and gastrointestinal systems.

per·nick·e·ty (pər·nik′ə·tē) *adj.* Persnickety.

Pe·rón (pā·rōn′), **Juan Domingo,** born 1895, Argentine army officer and politician; president 1946–55.

per·o·ne·al (per′ə·nē′əl) *adj. Anat.* Of, pertaining to, or near the fibula. [< NL *peronaeus* < *perone* fibula < Gk. *peronē,* orig., a pin]

per·o·rate (per′ə·rāt) *v.i.* **·rat·ed, ·rat·ing** **1.** To speak at length; harangue. **2.** To sum up or conclude a speech. [< L *peroratus.* See PERORATION.]

per·o·ra·tion (per′ə·rā′shən) *n.* The concluding portion of an oration; the recapitulation and summing up of an argument. [< L *peroratio, -onis* < *peroratus,* pp. of *perorare* to speak to the end < *per-* through + *orare* to speak]

per·ox·ide (pə·rok′sīd) *n. Chem.* **1.** An oxide having the highest proportion of oxygen for a given series. Compare PROTOXIDE. **2.** Hydrogen peroxide (which see). Also **per·ox′id** (-sid). **— v.t. ·id·ed, ·id·ing** To bleach, as hair, with peroxide.

per·pend¹ (pər·pend′) *v.t. & v.i. Archaic* To ponder. [< L *perpendere* < *per-* thoroughly + *pendere* to weigh]

per·pend² (pûr′pənd) *n.* In masonry, a stone extending through a wall so that one end appears on each side of it. Also **perpend stone, per′pent** (-pənt). [< OF *parpaing;* origin uncertain]

per·pen·dic·u·lar (pûr′pən·dik′yə·lər) *adj.* **1.** Being at right angles to the plane of the horizon; upright or vertical. **2.** *Math.* Meeting a given line or plane at right angles. **3.** *Often cap.* Pertaining to or designating a style of English late Gothic architecture characterized by accentuation of vertical lines. **— n. 1.** A perpendicular line or plane. **2.** An appliance or instrument used to indicate the vertical line from any point; a plumb rule. **3.** A line at right angles to another line or to a plane. **4.** A vertical or nearly vertical plane or surface, as a steep incline. **5.** Perpendicular position. **6.** *Rare* Moral uprightness. [< OF *perpendiculer* < L *perpendicularis* < *perpendiculum* plumb line < *pendiculus* cord, dim. of *pendulus* hanging < *pendere* to suspend] **— per′pen·dic′u·lar′i·ty** (-lar′ə·tē) *n.* **— per·pen·dic′u·lar·ly** *adv.*

per·pe·trate (pûr′pə·trāt) *v.t.* **·trat·ed, ·trat·ing** To do, perform or commit (a crime, etc.). [< L *perpetratus,* pp. of *perpetrare* to carry through < *per-* thoroughly + *patrare* to accomplish] **— per′pe·tra′tion** *n.* **— per′pe·tra′tor** *n.*

per·pet·u·al (pər·pech′ōō·əl) *adj.* **1.** Continuing or lasting forever or for an unlimited time. **2.** Incessant; ceaseless. **3.** In horticulture, flowering during all or nearly all the year, as certain hybrid flowers. **— n.** Any of certain perpetual hybrid roses. [< OF *perpetuel* < L *perpetualis* < *perpetuus* < *per-* through + *petere* to seek] **— per·pet′u·al·ly** *adv.*
— Syn. (adj.) **1.** eternal, endless, interminable. Compare EVERLASTING. **2.** See CONTINUAL. **— Ant.** transitory, evanescent.

perpetual calendar A calendar or similar table arranged so that the day of the week can be ascertained for any given date over an extended period.

perpetual motion Continuous motion, especially of a mechanism, conceived of as a condition in which energy would be inexhaustible or constantly replenished.

per·pet·u·ate (pər·pech′ōō·āt) *v.t.* **·at·ed, ·at·ing** **1.** To make perpetual or enduring. **2.** To cause to remain known,

current, etc.: to *perpetuate* a myth. [< L *perpetuatus,* pp. of *perpetuare* to perpetuate < *perpetuus.* See PERPETUAL.] **— per·pet′u·a′tion** *n.* **— per·pet′u·a′tor** *n.*

per·pe·tu·i·ty (pûr′pə·tōō′ə·tē, -tyōō′-) *n. pl.* **·ties** **1.** The quality or state of being perpetual. **2.** Something that has perpetual existence or worth. **3.** Unending or unlimited time. **4.** *Law* **a** A limitation rendering property inalienable. **b** The property so limited. **5.** In finance: **a** A perpetual annuity. **b** The number of years in which the simple interest of a sum becomes equal to the principal. [< OF *perpetuite* < L *perpetuitas* < *perpetuus.* See PERPETUAL.]

Per·pi·gnan (per·pē·nyän′) A city in southern France; pop. 100,086 (1968).

per·plex (pər·pleks′) *v.t.* **1.** To cause to hesitate or become confused, as from doubt, difficulties encountered, etc.; puzzle. **2.** To make complicated, intricate, or confusing. [Back formation < PERPLEXED]
— Syn. 1. bewilder, mystify, confound. Compare BAFFLE.

per·plexed (pər·plekst′) *adj.* **1.** Confused; puzzled; bewildered. **2.** Of a complicated character; involved. [Appar. alter. of obs. *perplex,* adj., intricate < L *perplexus* involved < *per-* thoroughly + *plexus,* pp. of *plectere* to braid] **— per·plex′ed·ly** (-plek′sid·lē) *adv.*

per·plex·ing (pər·plek′sing) *adj.* Confusing; puzzling. **— Syn.** See DIFFICULT. **— per·plex′ing·ly** *adv.*

per·plex·i·ty (pər·plek′sə·tē) *n. pl.* **·ties** **1.** The state, quality, or condition of being perplexed; doubt; confusion; bewilderment. **2.** That which perplexes. **3.** The quality or condition of being intricate or complicated.

per·qui·site (pûr′kwə·zit) *n.* **1.** Any incidental profit, payment, etc., beyond what is earned as salary or wages. **2.** Any privilege or benefit owed or claimed as one's due. [< L *perquisitum* a thing diligently sought, orig. pp. neut. of *perquirere* < *per-* thoroughly + *quaerere* to seek]

Per·rault (pe·rō′), **Charles,** 1628–1703, French writer and compiler of fairy tales.

Per·rin (pe·raň′), **Jean Baptiste,** 1870–1942, French physicist.

per·ron (per′ən, *Fr.* pe·rôṅ′) *n. Archit.* A flight of external steps and a platform before the entrance door of a building. [< OF, large stone < *pierre* stone < L *petra*]

per·ry (per′ē) *n.* A fermented drink made from the juice of pears. [< OF *pere* < LL *pera.* See PEAR.]

Perry (per′ē), **Bliss,** 1860–1954, U.S. author and critic. **— Matthew Calbraith,** 1794–1858, U.S. naval commodore; opened Japan to American commerce. **— Oliver Hazard,** 1785–1819, U.S. naval commander; defeated British on Lake Erie, Sept. 10, 1813; brother of the preceding. **— Ralph Barton,** 1876–1957, U.S. philosopher and educator.

pers. 1. Person. **2.** Personal.

Pers. Persia; Persian.

per·salt (pûr′sôlt′) *n. Chem.* One of a series of salts in which the metal or negative radical is at a high, or its highest, state of oxidation.

perse (pûrs) *adj.* Dark grayish blue. **— n.** A dark grayish blue. [< OF *pers* < LL *persus* < *Persicus* Persian]

per se (pûr sē′, sā′) *Latin* By itself; intrinsically.

per·se·cute (pûr′sə·kyōōt) *v.t.* **·cut·ed, ·cut·ing** **1.** To harass with cruel or oppressive treatment. **2.** To maltreat or oppress because of race, religion, or beliefs. **3.** To annoy or harass persistently. [< F *persecuter* < L *persecutus,* pp. of *persequi* to pursue < *per-* thoroughly + *sequi* to follow] **— per′se·cu′tive** *adj.* **— per′se·cu′tor** *n.*
— Syn. 1. oppress. See ABUSE. **3.** harry, torment.

per·se·cu·tion (pûr′sə·kyōō′shən) *n.* The act or process of persecuting, or the condition of being persecuted. [< OF < L *persecutio, -onis* < *persecutus.* See PERSECUTE.] **— per′se·cu′tion·al, per·se·cu·to·ry** (pûr′sə·kyōō′tər·ē) *adj.*

Per·se·id (pûr′sē·id) *n. pl.* **Per·se·ids** or **Per·se·i·des** (pər·sē′ə·dēz) *Astron.* One of the meteors of a meteor shower having its radiant point in the constellation Perseus, and appearing annually about August 12. [< NL *Perseis,* pl. *Perseides* < Gk. *Persēis,* pl. *Persēides* daughter of Perseus]

Per·seph·o·ne (pər·sef′ə·nē) In Greek mythology, the daughter of Zeus and Demeter, abducted to the underworld by Pluto, but allowed to return to the earth for part of each year: identified with the Roman *Proserpine.*

Per·sep·o·lis (pər·sep′ə·lis) An ancient, ruined capital of Persia in central Iran.

Per·seus (pûr′syōōs, -sē·əs) In Greek mythology, the son of Zeus and Danae, slayer of Medusa and rescuer of Andromeda. **— n.** A northern constellation. See CONSTELLATION.

per·se·ver·ance (pûr′sə·vir′əns) *n.* **1.** The act or habit of persevering; persistence. **2.** *Theol.* In Calvinism, the continuance in grace and certain salvation of those chosen by God. [< OF *perseverance* < L *perseverantia* < *perseverans, -antis,* pp. of *perseverare.* See PERSEVERE.]
— Syn. 1. constancy, tenacity, resolution.

per·sev·er·a·tion (pər·sev′ə·rā′shən) *n. Psychol.* **1.** Continuation or repetition of an activity or mental state to an unusual degree. **2.** The spontaneous recurrence in the mind of the same idea, phrase, tune, mental image, etc. [< OF < LL *perservatio, -onis* < *perservare.* See PERSEVERE.]

per·se·vere (pûr/sə·vir/) *v.i.* **·vered, ·ver·ing** To persist in any purpose or enterprise; continue striving in spite of difficulties, etc. [< OF *perseverer* < L *perseverare* < *perseverus* very strict < *per-* thoroughly + *severus* strict]
— **Syn.** *Persevere* and *persist* mean to exert continual effort toward a purpose. To *persevere* is always commendable; to *persist* points to a trait which is at best tolerable, but which more often includes obstinacy or harassment, and is considered blameworthy. — **Ant.** falter, hesitate.

per·se·ver·ing (pûr/sə·vir/ing) *adj.* Persistent in effort or purpose; steadfast. — **per'se·ver'ing·ly** *adv.*

Per·shing (pûr/shing) John Joseph, 1860–1948, U.S. General of the Armies: called **Black Jack.**

Per·sia (pûr/zhə, -shə) A former and now unofficial name for IRAN. See PERSIAN EMPIRE.

Per·sian (pûr/zhən, -shən) *adj.* Of or pertaining to Persia (now Iran), or its people, language, or culture. — *n.* **1.** A native or inhabitant of Persia or Iran. **2.** The Iranian language of the Persians, historically divided into **Old Persian,** recorded in the cuneiform inscriptions of Darius I, **Middle Persian,** chiefly represented by Pahlavi, and **Modern Persian,** or Iranian, containing many Arabic loan words and written in Arabic script. **3.** *Usually pl.* A Persian blind. Abbr. **Pers.** [< OF *persien,* ult. < L *Persia* Persia < Gk. *Persis* < OPersian *Pārsa*]

Persian blind *Usually pl.* **1.** A window shutter of thin, movable slats fastened in a frame. **2.** A slatted window shade similar to a Venetian blind. Also, *pl., persiennes.*

Persian carpet An Oriental carpet having an all-over design, with the warp and filling of silk, wool, or cotton, and the pile of wool. Also **Persian rug.**

Persian Empire An empire of SW Asia, extending from the Indus to the Mediterranean: founded by Cyrus the Great (sixth century B.C.) and destroyed by Alexander the Great (331 B.C.).

Persian Gulf An inlet of the Arabian Sea between Iran and Arabia.

Persian lamb **1.** The lamb of the karakul sheep. **2.** The black, gray, or brown curled fur obtained from this lamb, usually when three to four days old. Compare BROADTAIL.

Persian wheel A noria.

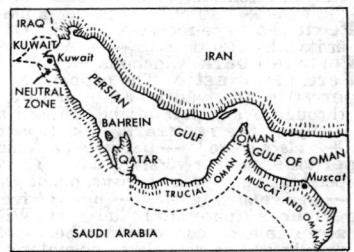

per·si·car·i·a (pûr/sə·kâr/ē·ə) *n.* Any of several plants (genus *Polygonum*) of the buckwheat family, as the lady's-thumb: also called *heartsease.* Also **per·si·car·y** (pûr/sə·ker/ē). [< NL *persicaria* < L *persicum (malum)* peach]

per·si·enne (pûr/zē·en/, *Fr.* per·syen/) *n.* **1.** A printed cotton fabric formerly made in the Orient. **2.** *pl.* Persian blinds. [< F, fem. of *persien* Persian]

per·si·flage (pûr/sə·fläzh) *n.* A light, flippant style of conversation or writing. [< F < *persifler* to banter < L *per-* through + *siffler* to whistle < L *sifilare;* ult. imit.]

per·sim·mon (pər·sim/ən) *n.* **1.** Any of several trees (genus *Diospyros*) having reddish orange fruit with an astringent taste when not completely ripe; especially, *D. virginiana,* of SE North America, and the Japanese persimmon (which see). **2.** The fruit of these trees. [< Algonquian. Cf. Cree *pasiminan* dried fruit.]

per·sist (pər·sist/, -zist/) *v.i.* **1.** To continue firmly in some course, state, etc., especially despite opposition or difficulties. **2.** To be insistent, as in repeating or continuing an action. **3.** To continue to exist; endure. [< L *persistere* < *per-* thoroughly + *sistere* causative of *stare* to stand]
— **Syn. 1, 2.** See PERSEVERE. **3.** remain, last. — **Ant.** cease, stop.

per·sis·tence (pər·sis/təns, -zis/-) *n.* **1.** The act, condition, or quality of persisting; lasting or enduring state. **2.** Fixed adherence to a resolve, course of conduct, etc; perseverance. **3.** The continuance of an effect longer than the cause that first produced it. Also **per·sis/ten·cy.**

per·sis·tent (pər·sis/tənt, -zis/-) *adj.* **1.** Persevering or stubborn in a course or resolve. **2.** Enduring; permanent; continuous. **3.** *Bot.* Not falling away; remaining past the time of maturity, as the leaves or petals in certain plants. **4.** *Zool.* Retained throughout life, as the gills of fishes and some amphibians. [< L *persistens, -entis,* ppr. of *persistere.* See PERSIST.] — **per·sis/tent·ly** *adv.*

Per·si·us (pûr/shē·əs, -shəs), A.D. 34–62, Roman satirist: full name Aulus Persius Flaccus (flak/us).

per·snick·e·ty (pər·snik/ə·tē) *adj. Informal* **1.** Unduly fastidious; fussy; overprecise. **2.** Demanding minute care or pains. Also *pernickety.* [< dial. E, ? alter. of PARTICULAR] — **per·snick/e·ti·ness** *n.*

per·son (pûr/sən) *n.* **1.** Any human being considered as a distinct entity or personality; an individual. **2.** The body of a human being: to clothe one's *person* in rags. **3.** One's characteristic appearance or physical condition. **4.** One considered as somewhat inferior in status; a mere nobody. **5.** *Law* Any human being, corporation, or body politic having legal rights and duties. **6.** *Theol.* One of the three individualities in the Trinity; hypostasis. **7.** *Gram.* **a** A modification of the pronoun and verb that distinguishes the speaker (**first person**), the person or thing spoken to (**second person**), and the person or thing spoken of (**third person**). **b** Any of the forms or inflections indicating this, as *I* or *we, you, he, she, it.* Abbr. *per., pers.* — **in person 1.** Physically present. **2.** Acting for oneself. [< F *personne* < L *persona* actor's mask, character. Doublet of PARSON.]

per·so·na (pər·sō/nə) *n.* *pl.* **·nae** (-nē) **1.** *Usually pl.* A character in a drama, novel, etc. **2.** *Psychol.* The personality assumed by an individual for purposes of concealment, defense, deception, or adaptation to his environment. [L, person, orig., mask. See PERSON.]

per·son·a·ble (pûr/sən·ə·bəl) *adj.* Attractive or pleasing in personal appearance. — **per'son·a·bly** *adv.*

per·son·age (pûr/sən·ij) *n.* **1.** A man or woman of importance or rank. **2.** A person; individual. **3.** A character in fiction, drama, history, etc. [< F *personnage.* See PERSON.]

per·so·na gra·ta (pər·sō/nə grä/tə, grā/tə) *Latin* An acceptable or welcome person.

per·son·al (pûr/sən·əl) *adj.* **1.** Pertaining to or concerning a particular person; not general or public: a purely *personal* matter. **2.** Relating to, having the qualities of, or constituting a person or persons. **3.** Done to, for, or by the person directly concerned; done in person: a *personal* service. **4.** Characteristic of or relating to a single individual. **5.** Of or pertaining to the body or appearance: *personal* beauty. **6.** Directly characterizing or referring to an individual, especially in a critical or disparaging manner: *personal* remarks. **7.** *Law* Pertaining to property regarded as movable or temporary: distinguished from *real.* **8.** *Gram.* Denoting or indicating person: *personal* pronouns. — *n.* **1.** *Law* A movable or temporary article or property; chattel. **2.** A paragraph or advertisement of personal reference or application. Abbr. *pers.* [< OF < LL *personalis* < L *persona* a person]

personal effects Possessions of an individual of a private nature, as clothing, etc.

personal equation The tendency to error in observations, reasoning, etc., resulting from individual characteristics.

per·son·al·i·ty (pûr/sən·al/ə·tē) *n.* *pl.* **·ties 1.** Distinctive qualities or characteristics of a person. **2.** A person, especially one of outstanding or distinctive qualities. **3.** That which constitutes a person; personal existence. **4.** *Often pl.* A remark or reference, often disparaging, of a personal nature. — **double** or **multiple personality** *Psychiatry* A condition in which two or more relatively distinct sets of experiences and behavior patterns reveal themselves alternately in the same individual. [< OF *personalite* < Med.L *personalitas, -tatis* < LL *personalis* < L *persona* a person]

per·son·al·ize (pûr/sən·əl·īz/) *v.t.* **·ized, ·iz·ing 1.** To make personal. **2.** To personify. **3.** To mark with one's name, initials, etc., as stationery or handkerchiefs.

per·son·al·ly (pûr/sən·əl·ē) *adv.* **1.** In person; not through an agent. **2.** As regards one's own opinions, tastes, etc. **3.** With regard to a person as an individual. **4.** As though intended for or directed toward oneself.

personal pronoun *Gram.* A pronoun that varies in form according to person, gender, case, and number, as *we, their, him.*

per·son·al·ty (pûr/sən·əl·tē) *n.* *pl.* **·ties** *Law* Personal property. [< AF *personaltie* < OF *personalite* < Med.L *personalitas.* See PERSONALITY.]

per·so·na non gra·ta (pər·sō/nə non grä/tə, grā/tə) *Latin* A person who is not welcome or acceptable.

per·son·ate (pûr/sən·āt) *v.t.* **·at·ed, ·at·ing 1.** To act the part of, as a character in a play. **2.** To personify, as in poetry, art, etc. **3.** *Law* To impersonate with intent to deceive. — *adj. Bot.* Masklike, as the bilabiate corolla of certain plants, in which the mouth of the tube is closed by an inflated projection of the throat: also *masked.* [< L *personatus* masked < *persona.* See PERSON.] — **per'son·a'tion** *n.* — **per'son·a'tive** *adj.* — **per'son·a'tor** *n.*

per·son·i·fi·ca·tion (pər·son/ə·fə·kā/shən) *n.* **1.** The figurative endowment of inanimate objects or qualities with personality or human attributes, especially as a literary device: sometimes called *prosopopeia.* **2.** Exemplification of a quality or attribute in one's person; embodiment: She was the *personification* of joy. **3.** The representation of an abstract quality or idea by a human figure. **4.** Impersonation.

per·son·i·fy (pər·son/ə·fī) *v.t.* **·fied, ·fy·ing 1.** To think of or represent as having life or human qualities. **2.** To represent (an abstraction or inanimate object) as a person. **3.** To be the embodiment of; typify. [< F *personnifier* < L *persona* mask, person + *facere* to make] — **per·son'i·fi'er** *n.*

per·son·nel (pûr′sə·nel′) n. The persons employed in a business, engaged in military service, etc. [< F < OF personal. See PERSONAL.]

per·spec·tive (pər·spek′tiv) n. **1.** The art or theory of representing solid objects on a flat surface in such a way as to convey the impression of depth and distance. **2.** The effect of distance upon the appearance of objects, by means of which the eye judges spatial relations. **3.** The relationship or relative importance of facts or matters from any special point of view. **4.** Judgment of facts, circumstances, etc., with regard to their proportional importance. **5.** A distant view, vista, or prospect. **6.** A picture giving the illusion of space or depth. — **aerial perspective** The representation of relative distances of objects by gradations of tone and color. — **linear perspective** The representation of an appearance of distance by means of converging lines. — adj. Pertaining to, characterized by, or represented in perspective. [< Med.L perspectiva (ars) optical (art) < LL perspectivus optical < L perspectus, pp. of perspicere to look through < per- through + specere to look] — **per·spec′tive·ly** adv.

PERSPECTIVE
ab Horizon.
c Vanishing point. dc Line of sight. ef Ground line.

per·spi·ca·cious (pûr′spə·kā′shəs) adj. **1.** Keenly discerning or understanding. **2.** Archaic Sharp-sighted. — **Syn.** See ASTUTE. [< L perspicax, -acis sharp-sighted < perspicere. See PERSPECTIVE.] — **per′spi·ca′cious·ly** adv. — **per′spi·ca′cious·ness** n.

per·spi·cac·i·ty (pûr′spə·kas′ə·tē) n. Keenness in mental penetration or discernment. — **Syn.** See ACUMEN.

per·spi·cu·i·ty (pûr′spə·kyōō′ə·tē) n. **1.** Clearness of expression or style; lucidity. **2.** Perspicacity.

per·spic·u·ous (pər·spik′yōō·əs) adj. Having the quality of perspicuity; clear; lucid. [< L perspicuus clear, transparent < perspicere. See PERSPECTIVE.] — **per·spic′u·ous·ly** adv. — **per·spic′u·ous·ness** n.

per·spi·ra·tion (pûr′spə·rā′shən) n. **1.** The act or process of exuding the saline fluid secreted by the sweat glands. **2.** The fluid excreted; sweat. **3.** Arduous physical effort. [< MF < perspirer < L perspirare. See PERSPIRE.] — **per·spir′a·to·ry** (pər·spī′rə·tôr′ē, -tō′rē) adj.

per·spire (pər·spīr′) v. **·spired**, **·spir·ing** v.i. **1.** To give off perspiration through the pores of the skin; sweat. — v.t. **2.** To give off through pores; exude. [< MF perspirer < L perspirare to breathe constantly < per- through + spirare to breathe]

per·suade (pər·swād′) v.t. **·suad·ed**, **·suad·ing** **1.** To induce (someone) to do something. **2.** To induce to a belief; convince. — **Syn.** See CONVINCE, INFLUENCE. [< MF suader < L persuadere < per- thoroughly + suadere to advise] — **per·suad′a·ble** adj. — **per·suad′er** n.

per·sua·si·ble (pər·swā′sə·bəl) adj. Open to persuasion; persuadable. — **per·sua·si·bil′i·ty, per·sua′si·ble·ness** n.

per·sua·sion (pər·swā′zhən) n. **1.** The act of persuading or of using persuasive methods. **2.** Ability to persuade; power of convincing. **3.** The state of being persuaded; settled opinion; conviction. **4.** An accepted creed or belief. **5.** A religious sect or denomination. **6.** Party; group; faction. — **Syn.** See OPINION. [< L persuasio, -onis < persuasus, pp. of persuadere. See PERSUADE.]

per·sua·sive (pər·swā′siv) adj. Having power or tendency to persuade. — n. That which persuades or tends to persuade. — **per·sua′sive·ly** adv. — **per·sua′sive·ness** n.

per·sul·fate (pər·sul′fāt) n. Chem. A salt of persulfuric acid. Also **per·sul′phate**.

per·sul·fu·ric acid (pûr′sul·fyŏŏr′ik) Chem. An acid, $H_2S_2O_8$, formed by the electrolysis of concentrated sulfuric acid. Also **per′sul·phu′ric acid**.

pert (pûrt) adj. **1.** Disrespectfully forward; impertinent; saucy. **2.** Dial. Of fine appearance; handsome and lively. [Aphetic var. of ME apert < OF, open, impudent < L apertus, pp. of aperire to open] — **pert′ly** adv. — **pert′ness** n.

pert. Pertaining.

per·tain (pər·tān′) v.i. **1.** To have reference; relate. **2.** To belong as an adjunct, function, quality, etc. **3.** To be fitting or appropriate. — **pertaining to** Having to do with; characteristic of; belonging or relating to. [< OF partenir < L pertinere to extend < per- through + tenere to hold]

Perth (pûrth) **1.** A county of central Scotland; 2,493 sq. mi.; pop. 124,199 (1969); county seat, Perth, a burgh, pop. 41,654 (1969). Also **Perth′shire** (-shir). **2.** The capital of Western Australia, near the SW coast; pop. 499,969 (1966, including suburbs).

Perth Am·boy (pûrth am′boi) A port city in eastern New Jersey, on Raritan Bay; pop. 38,798.

per·ti·na·cious (pûr′tə·nā′shəs) adj. **1.** Tenacious of purpose; adhering fixedly to a pursuit or opinion. **2.** Stubbornly or doggedly persistent. — **Syn.** See OBSTINATE. [< L pertinax, -acis per- thoroughly, very + tenax, -acis tenacious] — **per′ti·na′cious·ly** adv.

per·ti·nac·i·ty (pûr′tə·nas′ə·tē) n. pl. **·ties 1.** Tenacity of purpose; unyielding adherence. **2.** Obstinacy.

per·ti·nent (pûr′tə·nənt) adj. Related to or properly bearing upon the matter in hand; relevant. — **Syn.** See APPROPRIATE. [< OF < L pertinens, -entis, ppr. of pertinere. See PERTAIN.] — **per′ti·nence, per′ti·nen·cy** n. — **per′ti·nent·ly** adv.

per·turb (pər·tûrb′) v.t. **1.** To disquiet or disturb greatly; alarm; agitate. **2.** To throw into disorder; cause confusion in. [< OF perturber < L perturbare < per- thoroughly + turbare to disturb < turba turmoil] — **per·turb′a·ble** adj.

per·tur·ba·tion (pûr′tər·bā′shən) n. **1.** The act of perturbing or the state of being perturbed; agitation. **2.** A cause of disquiet or agitation. **3.** Astron. Deviation in the motion of a heavenly body, caused by the attraction of some body other than that about which it revolves. [< OF perturbacion < L perturbatio, -onis < perturbare. See PERTURB.]

per·tus·sis (pər·tus′is) n. Pathol. Whooping cough. [< NL < L per- thoroughly, very great + tussis a cough] — **per·tus′sal** adj.

Pe·ru (pə·rōō′, Sp. pā·rōō′) A Republic in western South America; 496,093 sq. mi.; pop. 13,600,000 (1970); capital, Lima.

Peru Current See HUMBOLDT CURRENT.

Pe·ru·gia (pā·rōō′jä) The capital of Umbria, central Italy; pop. 109,596 (1961).

Perugia, Lake of See TRASIMENO.

Pe·ru·gi·no (pā·rōō·jē′nō), 1446–1523, Italian painter: original name Pietro Ban·nuc·ci (bän·nōōt′chē).

pe·ruke (pə·rōōk′) n. A wig; especially, one worn by men in the 17th and 18th centuries: also periwig. [< MF perruque < Ital. perrucca]

pe·rus·al (pə·rōō′zəl) n. The act or procedure of reading or examining carefully; a thorough reading or scrutiny.

pe·ruse (pə·rōōz′) v.t. **·rused**, **·rus·ing 1.** To read carefully or attentively. **2.** To read. **3.** To examine; scrutinize. [< PER- + USE, v.] — **pe·rus′a·ble** adj. — **pe·rus′er** n.

Pe·ru·vi·an (pə·rōō′vē·ən) adj. Of or pertaining to Peru or its inhabitants, etc. — n. A native or inhabitant of Peru.

Peruvian bark Cinchona (def. 2).

Peruvian mastic The pepper tree (def. 2).

per·vade (pər·vād′) v.t. **·vad·ed**, **·vad·ing** To spread through every part of; be diffused throughout; permeate. — **Syn.** See PERMEATE. [< L pervadere < per- through + vadere to go] — **per·va′sion** (-zhən) n.

per·va·sive (pər·vā′siv) adj. Thoroughly penetrating or permeating. [< L pervasus, pp. of pervadere. See PERVADE.] — **per·va′sive·ly** adv. — **per·va′sive·ness** n.

per·verse (pər·vûrs′) adj. **1.** Willfully deviating from acceptable or conventional behavior, opinion, etc.; waywardly or unreasonably nonconforming; contrary. **2.** Refractory; capricious. **3.** Petulant; cranky. **4.** Morally wrong or erring; wicked; perverted. [< OF pervers < L perversus turned the wrong way, orig. pp. of pervertere. See PERVERT.] — **per·verse′ly** adv. — **per·verse′ness** n.

per·ver·sion (pər·vûr′zhən, -shən) n. **1.** The act of perverting, or the state of being perverted. **2.** A perverted form, act, use, etc. **3.** Deviation from the normal in sexual desires or activities. **4.** Pathol. A deviation from the normal in structure or function.

per·ver·si·ty (pər·vûr′sə·tē) n. pl. **·ties 1.** The state or quality of being perverse. **2.** Perverse nature or behavior. **3.** An instance of perverseness.

per·vert (v. pər·vûrt′; n. pûr′vərt) v.t. **1.** To turn to an improper use or purpose; misapply. **2.** To distort the meaning or intent of; misconstrue. **3.** To turn from approved opinions or conduct; lead astray. **4.** To deprave; debase; corrupt. — n. One characterized by or practicing sexual perversion. [< F pervertir < L pervertere to turn around < per- away + vertere to turn] — **per·vert′er** n. — **per·vert′i·ble** adj.

per·vert·ed (pər·vûr′tid) adj. **1.** Deviating widely from what is right or acceptable; especially, willfully distorted. **2.** Characterized by viciousness, sexual perversion, etc. — **per·vert′ed·ly** adv.

per·vi·ous (pûr′vē·əs) adj. **1.** Capable of being penetrated; permeable. **2.** Open to reason, suggestions, etc. [< L pervius having a way through < per- through + via way] — **per′vi·ous·ly** adv. — **per′vi·ous·ness** n.

pes (pēz) n. pl. **pe·des** (pē′dēz) Zool. **1.** A footlike organ, appearance, or part. **2.** In prosody, the name for each of the first two quatrains of a sonnet. [< L, foot]

Pe·sach (pä′säkh) n. Passover, a Jewish festival. Also **Pe′sah**. [< Hebrew pesakh, lit., a passing over < pāsakh to pass over]

pe·sade (pə·säd′, -zäd′, -zäd′) n. The act or position of a saddle horse in rearing. [< F, alter. of posade < Ital. posata a pause < posare to pause < L pausare to halt < pausa a stop]

Pes·ca·do·res (pes′kä·dō′rās, pes′kə·dôrz) An island group in Taiwan Strait, a dependency of Taiwan; 49 sq. mi.

pe·se·ta (pə·sā′tə, Sp. pā·sā′tä) n. The standard monetary unit of Spain, equivalent to 100 centimos; also, a silver coin of this value. Abbr. p. [< Sp., dim. of pesa weight]

Pe·sha·war (pə·shä′wər, pā′shä·vər) A city in northern Pakistan, in ancient times a Greco-Buddhist cultural center; pop. 296,000 (est. 1969).

Pe·shi·to (pə·shē'tō) *n.* The oldest Syriac version of the Bible. Also **Pe·schi'to, Pe·shit'ta** (-shē'tä), **Pe·shit·to.** [< Syriac *p'shī(t̬)to,* lit., plain, simple]

pes·ky (pes'kē) *adj.* **·ki·er, ·ki·est** *U.S. Informal* Annoying; troublesome; plaguy. [Prob. < PEST + -Y²] — **pes'ki·ly** *adv.*

pe·so (pā'sō) *n. pl.* **·sos 1.** The standard monetary unit of Argentina, Bolivia, Chile, Colombia, Cuba, Dominican Republic, Guinea-Bissau, Mexico, and the Philippines, equivalent to 100 centavos. **2.** A coin or note of this denomination. **3.** The obsolete silver dollar used in the Spanish and British colonies in America during the Revolutionary War, equal to 8 reals: also called **piece of eight.** [< Sp., orig., a weight < L *pensum,* orig. pp. neut. of *pendere* to weigh]

pes·sa·ry (pes'ə·rē) *n. pl.* **·ries** *Med.* **1.** A device worn internally to remedy a uterine displacement. **2.** A medicated suppository for use in the vagina. **3.** A contraceptive device worn over or in the uterine cervix. [< Med.L *pessarium* < L *pessum* < Gk. *pessos* oval stone]

pes·si·mism (pes'ə·miz'əm) *n.* **1.** A disposition to take a gloomy or cynical view of affairs: opposed to *optimism.* **2.** The doctrine that the world and life are essentially evil. **3.** The theory that the existing universe is the worst possible world. [< L *pessimus* worst + -ISM] — **pes'si·mist** *n.* — **pes'si·mis'tic** or **·ti·cal** *adj.* — **pes'si·mis'ti·cal·ly** *adv.*

pest (pest) *n.* **1.** An annoying or vexatious person or thing; nuisance. **2.** A destructive or injurious insect, plant, etc. **3.** A virulent epidemic, especially of plague. [< MF *peste* < L *pestis* plague]

Pes·ta·loz·zi (pes'tä·lôt'tsē), **Johann Heinrich,** 1746–1827, Swiss educational reformer.

pes·ter (pes'tər) *v.t.* To harass with petty and persistent annoyances; bother; plague. [Var. of obs. *impester* to entangle < OF *empestrer,* orig., to hobble a grazing horse < *em-* (< L *in-* in) + LL *pastorium* foot shackles < L *pastus,* pp. of *pascere* to feed; infl. in meaning by PEST.] — **pes'ter·er** *n.*

pest·hole (pest'hōl') *n.* A squalid or insanitary place in which disease is likely to occur and spread.

pest·house (pest'hous') *n.* Formerly, a public hospital for patients suffering from plague or infectious disease.

pes·ti·cide (pes'tə·sīd) *n.* A chemical or other substance used to destroy plant and animal pests. — **pes'ti·ci'dal** *adj.*

pes·tif·er·ous (pes·tif'ər·əs) *adj.* **1.** *Informal* Annoying; bothersome. **2.** Carrying or spreading infectious disease. **3.** Having an evil or harmful influence. [< L *pestiferus* bringing plague < *pestis* plague + *ferre* to bear] — **pes·tif'er·ous·ly** *adv.* — **pes·tif'er·ous·ness** *n.*

pes·ti·lence (pes'tə·ləns) *n.* **1.** Any widespread, often fatal infectious or contagious disease, as cholera or the bubonic plague. **2.** A noxious or malign doctrine, influence, etc.

pes·ti·lent (pes'tə·lənt) *adj.* **1.** Tending to produce infectious or epidemic disease; pestilential. **2.** Having a malign influence or effect. **3.** Making trouble; causing irritation; vexatious. [< OF < L *pestilens, -entis* < *pestis* plague] — **pes'ti·lent·ly** *adv.*

pes·ti·len·tial (pes'tə·len'shəl) *adj.* **1.** Pertaining to, causing, or resembling pestilence. **2.** Harmful or pernicious; baneful. **3.** Exasperating; annoying.

pes·tle (pes'əl) *n.* **1.** An implement used for crushing, pulverizing, or mixing substances in or as in a mortar. **2.** A vertical moving bar employed in pounding, as in a stamp mill, etc. — *v.t. & v.i.* **·tled, ·tling** To pound, grind, or mix with or as with a pestle. [< OF *pestel* < L *pistillum* < *pistus,* pp. of *pinsere* to pound] **PESTLE** (a) **MORTAR** (b)

pet¹ (pet) *n.* **1.** A tame animal treated lovingly or kept as a companion or playmate. **2.** Any loved and cherished creature or thing. **3.** A favorite: *teacher's pet.* — *adj.* **1.** Tamed or kept as a pet. **2.** Regarded as a favorite; cherished: my *pet* hobby. — *v.* **pet·ted, pet·ting** — *v.t.* **1.** To stroke or caress. **2.** To treat indulgently; coddle. — *v.i.* **3.** *U.S. Slang* To make love by kissing and caressing. [< dial. E (Scottish), ? < F *petit* little one]

pet² (pet) *n.* A fit of pique or ill temper. [Origin unknown]

pet³ (pet) *n. Southern U.S.* An inflamed sore; boil.

Pet. Peter.

Pé·tain (pā·tan'), **Henri Philippe,** 1856–1951, French marshal; chief of the Vichy government 1940–44; convicted of treason 1945.

pet·al (pet'l) *n. Bot.* One of the divisions or leaflike parts of a corolla. For illustration see FLOWER. [< NL *petalum* < Gk. *petalon* leaf. Akin to *petannynai* Gk. to expand.] — **pet'aled** or **pet'alled** *adj.*

-petal *combining form* Seeking: *centripetal.* [< L *petere* to seek]

pet·a·lif·er·ous (pet'ə·lif'ər·əs) *adj.* Bearing petals. [< PETAL + -FEROUS]

pet·a·line (pet'ə·lin, -līn) *adj.* Of, pertaining to, or like a petal.

pet·a·lo·dy (pet'ə·lō'dē) *n. pl.* **·dies** *Bot.* A metamorphosis of sepals, stamens, etc., into petals, as in cultivated roses. [< Gk. *petalōdēs* leaflike < *petalon* leaf + *eidos* a form] —

pet·a·lod·ic (-lod'ik) *adj.*

pet·al·oid (pet'l·oid) *adj.* **1.** Resembling a petal. **2.** Consisting of petals.

pet·al·ous (pet'l·əs) *adj.* Having petals.

pe·tard (pi·tärd') *n.* **1.** An explosive device formerly used to break through walls, gates, etc. **2.** A small firecracker exploding with a loud report. — **hoist with** (or **by**) **one's own petard** Victimized or harmed by one's own plans or actions. [< MF *pétard* < *péter* to break wind < OF *pet* fart < L *peditum,* orig. pp. neut. of *pedere* to break wind]

PETARD

pet·a·sus (pet'ə·səs) *n.* **1.** A hat with a broad brim and low crown, worn in ancient Greece. **2.** The winged hat of the god Mercury. Also **pet'a·sos.** [< L < Gk. *petasos.* Akin to Gk. *petannynai* to expand.]

pet·cock (pet'kok') *n. Mech.* A small valve or faucet, used for draining, releasing pressure, etc. Also **pet cock.** [? < obs. *pet* a fart + COCK¹]

pe·ter (pē'tər) *v.i. Informal* To diminish gradually and then cease or disappear: followed by *out.* [Orig. U.S. mining slang, ? < F *péter* (dans la main) to come to nothing]

Pe·ter (pē'tər) One of the twelve apostles, reputed author of two epistles of the New Testament: called **Saint Peter.** Also **Simon Peter.** — *n.* Either of the two books of the New Testament that bear his name. Abbr. **Pet.** [< LL *Petrus* < Gk. *Petros* < *petros* stone]

Peter I. 1672–1725, czar of Russia 1682–1725: called **Peter the Great.**

Peter II, 1923–1970, king of Yugoslavia 1934–45; deposed.

Peter III, 1728–62, czar of Russia 1762; husband of Catherine II; assassinated.

Pe·ter·bor·ough (pē'tər·bûr'ō, -bər·ə) A city in NE Northamptonshire, England; pop. 62,031 (1961).

Peterborough, Soke of See SOKE OF PETERBOROUGH.

pe·ter·head boat (pē'tər·hed') *Canadian* A small single-masted sailboat of the eastern Arctic region.

Peter Pan The hero of J. M. Barrie's play (1904) of the same name, a little boy who remained perpetually a child.

Peter Pan collar A flat collar with rounded ends, used on girls' and women's blouses, dresses, etc.

Peter Principle The rule that persons in a hierarchy are generally promoted just beyond the limit of their competence. [after Laurence J. *Peter,* U.S. author]

Pe·ters·burg (pē'tərz·bûrg) A port city in SE Virginia, on the Appomattox River; scene of Civil War battles, 1864, 1865; pop. 36,103.

pe·ter·sham (pē'tər·shəm) *n.* **1.** A heavy, rough, tufted woolen cloth. **2.** Formerly, a heavy greatcoat of such cloth. [after Lord *Petersham,* who introduced it about 1812]

Peter's pence **1.** Voluntary contributions collected annually by Roman Catholics for the Pope. **2.** Formerly, a tribute or tax of a penny for every house, paid by the English to the papal see: also called *hearth money.* Also **Peter pence.**

Peter the Hermit, 1050?–1115, French monk; preacher of the first Crusade. Also **Peter of Amiens.**

pet·i·o·lar (pet'ē·ə·lər) *adj.* Pertaining to or borne on a petiole.

pet·i·o·late (pet'ē·ə·lāt) *adj.* Having a petiole. Also **pet'i·o·lat'ed.**

pet·i·ole (pet'ē·ōl) *n.* **1.** *Bot.* The stem or slender stalk of a leaf; a leafstalk. **2.** *Anat.* A peduncle. [< L *petiolus,* orig. dim. of *pes, pedis* foot]

pe·tite (pə·tēt') *adj. fem.* Diminutive; little. — **Syn.** See SMALL. [< F, fem. of *petit.* See PETIT.]

pet·it four (pet'ē fôr', fŏr'; *Fr.* pə·tē'fŏŏr') *pl.* **pet·its fours** or **pet·it fours** (pet'ē fôrz', fŏrz'; *Fr.* pə·tē'fŏŏr') A little, decoratively iced cake. [< F, lit., little oven]

pe·ti·tion (pə·tish'ən) *n.* **1.** A formal request, supplication, or prayer. **2.** A formal request addressed to a person or group in authority and asking for some grant or benefit, the redress of a grievance, etc. **3.** *Law* A formal application in writing made to a court, requesting judicial action concerning some matter therein set forth. **4.** Something formally requested or entreated. — *v.t.* **1.** To make a petition to; entreat. **2.** To ask for. — *v.i.* **3.** To make a petition. [< OF *peticiun* < L *petitio, -onis* < *petere* to seek] — **pe·ti'tion·ar'y** *adj.* — **pe·ti'tion·er** *n.*

pe·ti·ti·o prin·cip·i·i (pə·tish'ē·ō prin·sip'ē·ī) *Logic* Begging the question; assuming in the premise that which is yet to be proved. [< L]

petit juror A member of a petit jury: also spelled *petty juror.*

petit jury The jury that sits at a trial in civil and criminal cases: also called *trial jury;* also spelled *petty jury.*

petit larceny See under LARCENY.

pe·tit mal (pə·tē′ màl′)   *Pathol.* A mild form of epilepsy characterized by a momentary loss of consciousness: distinguished from *grand mal.*   [< F, lit., little sickness]

pet·it point (pet′ē)   1. A fine tapestry stitch used in decorative needlework: also called *tent stitch.*   2. Needlework done in this stitch.

pe·tits pois (pə·tē′ pwä′)   *French* Selected small peas.

Pe·tö·fi (pe′tœ·fi), **Sándor,** 1823–49, Hungarian poet and national hero: original name **Sandor Pet·ro·vics** (pet′rovich).

Pe·tra (pē′trə)   A ruined ancient city of SW Jordan.

Pe·trarch (pē′trärk), **Francesco,** 1304–74, Italian poet and scholar. Also **Pe·trar·ca** (pā·trär′kä).

Pe·trar·chan sonnet (pə·trär′kən)   A sonnet having the rhyme scheme *abbaabba* in the octave, and having in the sestet a set of two or three different, variously combined rhymes, as *cdcdcd*, or *cdecde*, etc.: also called *Italian sonnet.*

pet·rel (pet′rəl)   *n.* Any of various small sea birds (order *Procellariiformes*), as the storm petrel (which see).   [? < LL *Petrellus*, dim. of *Peter*, after St. Peter, in an allusion to his walking on the water.   *Matt.* xiv 29]

Pe·tri dish (pē′trē, pä′-, pet′rē)   A round, flat, glass container used to hold bacteria cultures for laboratory study. [after Julius *Petri*, 1852–1922, German bacteriologist]

Pe·trie (pē′trē), **Sir (William Matthew) Flinders,** 1853–1942, English Egyptologist.

pet·ri·fac·tion (pet′rə·fak′shən)   *n.*   1. The act or process of petrifying, or the state of being petrified.   2. Anything petrified. Also **pet′ri·fi·ca′tion** (-fə·kā′shən). [< PETRIFY.]   — **pet′ri·fac′tive** *adj.*

Petrified Forest National Monument   A region of eastern Arizona containing petrified flora; 133 sq. mi.

pet·ri·fy (pet′rə·fī)   *v.*   **·fied, ·fy·ing**   *v.t.*   1. To convert (organic material) into a substance of stony character.   2. To make fixed and unyielding; deaden; harden.   3. To daze or paralyze with fear, surprise, etc.   — *v.i.*   4. To become stone or like stone.   [< MF *pétrifier* < L *petra* a rock (< Gk.) + *facere* to make]

petro-   *combining form*   Rock; stone: *petroglyph.* Also, before vowels, **petr-.**   [< F < L < Gk. *petra* rock and *petros* stone]

pet·ro·chem·is·try (pet′rō·kem′is·trē)   *n.* The chemistry of petroleum and its derivatives, especially the natural and synthetic hydrocarbons.   — **pet′ro·chem′i·cal** *adj. & n.*

petrog.   Petrography.

pet·ro·glyph (pet′rə·glif)   *n.* A prehistoric carving, usually pictorial, gouged into a rock surface.   [< F *pétroglyphe* < Gk. *petra* rock + *glyphē* carving]   — **pet′ro·glyph′ic** *adj.*

Pet·ro·grad (pet′rə·grad, *Russ.* pyi·tro·grät′)   A former name for LENINGRAD.

pet·ro·graph (pet′rə·graf, -gräf)   *n.*   1. A carving or inscription on a rock.   2. Loosely, a petroglyph.

pe·trog·ra·phy (pə·trog′rə·fē)   *n.* The systematic description and classification of rocks.   — **pe·trog′ra·pher** *n.*   — **pet·ro·graph·ic** (pet′rə·graf′ik) or **·i·cal** *adj.*   — **pet′ro·graph′i·cal·ly** *adv.*

pet·rol (pet′rəl)   *n.*   1. *Brit.* Gasoline.   2. *Obs.* Petroleum. [< OF *petrole* < Med.L *petroleum.* See PETROLEUM]

petrol.   Petrology.

pet·ro·la·tum (pet′rə·lā′təm)   *n.* A greasy, semisolid substance obtained from petroleum, used as a stabilizer for certain explosives and in ointments and protective dressings: sometimes called *mineral jelly.* Also **petroleum jelly.**

pe·tro·le·um (pə·trō′lē·əm)   *n.* An oily, liquid mixture of numerous hydrocarbons, found in subterranean deposits, used in its natural state for heat and light, and as the source of many economically important substances, as gasoline, benzine, kerosene, paraffin, etc.: also called *naphtha, rock oil.* [< Med.L < L *petra* rock (< Gk.) + *oleum* oil]

petroleum ether   *Chem.* A distillate of petroleum used as a solvent of fats, waxes, etc.: also called *ligroin.*

petroleum spirit   Benzine.

Pe·tro·le·um V. Nas·by (pə·trō′lē·əm vē naz′bē)   Pseudonym of David Ross Locke, 1833–88, U.S. political satirist.

pe·trol·ic (pə·trol′ik)   *adj.* Of or pertaining to petroleum.

pe·trol·o·gy (pə·trol′ə·jē)   *n.* The science of the origin, structure, constitution, and characteristics of rocks.   — **pet·ro·log·ic** (pet′rə·loj′ik) or **·i·cal** *adj.*   — **pet′ro·log′i·cal·ly** *adv.*   — **pe·trol′o·gist** *n.*

pet·ro·nel (pet′rə·nəl)   *n.* Formerly, a firearm about the size of a large pistol, fired with the stock against the breast. [< MF *petrinal* pectoral < *poitrine* chest, ult. < L *pectus*]

Pe·tro·ni·us (pə·trō′nē·əs), **Gaius,** died A.D. 66?, Roman author: called **Ar·bi·ter E·le·gan·ti·ae** (är′bə·tər el′ə·gan′shi·ē) (Arbiter of Elegance).

Pet·ro·pav·lovsk (pet′rō·päv·lôfsk′, *Russ.* pyi·tro·päv′ləfsk)   A city in the northern Kazakh S.S.R., on the Ishim; pop. 154,000 (est. 1970).

pet·rous (pet′rəs, pē′trəs)   *adj.*   1. Resembling stone; hard.   2. *Anat.* Pertaining to or situated near the hard portion of the temporal bone that encloses the organs of hearing and equilibrium. Also **pe·tro·sal** (pə·trō′səl).   [< L *petrosus* rocky < L *petra* rock < Gk.]

Pet·ro·za·vodsk (pyi·tra·zə·vôtsk′)   The capital of the Karelian A.S.S.R., in the southern part on Lake Onega; pop. 185,000 (1970). *Finnish* **Pet·ro·skoi** (pet′rô·skoi).

pet·ti·coat (pet′ē·kōt)   *n.*   1. A skirt or skirtlike garment hanging from the waist; especially, a woman's underskirt.   2. Something resembling a petticoat.   3. A woman: a humorous or disparaging term.   4. An electric insulator shaped like an inverted cup, for use on high-tension wires.   — *adj.* Of or influenced by women: *petticoat* politics.   [< PETTY + COAT]

pet·ti·fog (pet′i·fog, -fôg)   *v.i.*   **fogged, fog·ging**   1. To be unduly concerned over trivial matters; fuss.   2. To be a pettifogger. [Appar. back formation < PETTIFOGGER]

pet·ti·fog·ger (pet′i·fog′ər, -fôg′ər)   *n.*   1. An inferior lawyer, especially one dealing with insignificant cases, or resorting to tricks.   2. One who quibbles or fusses over trivialities. [Earlier *petty fogger* < PETTY + *fogger* a trickster for gain. Cf. LG *fokker* usurer.]   — **pet′ti·fog′ger·y** *n.*

pet·tish (pet′ish)   *adj.* Capriciously ill-tempered; petulant; peevish. [Prob. < *PET* + -ISH]   — **pet′tish·ly** *adv.*

pet·ti·toes (pet′ē·tōz′)   *n.pl.*   1. Pig's feet, prepared as food.   2. Toes, especially a child's.   [? < F *petit oie* giblets, lit., little goose; later mistakenly understood as *petty toes*]

pet·tle (pet′l)   *v.t. & v.i.*   **pet·tled, pet·tling**   *Scot.* To cuddle.

pet·to (pet′ō)   *n.* *pl.* **·ti** (tē) The breast.   — **in petto** Within one's own breast; to oneself.   [< Ital., breast < L *pectus*]

pet·ty (pet′ē)   *adj.*   **·ti·er, ·ti·est**   1. Having little worth or importance; trifling; insignificant.   2. Having little scope or generosity; narrow-minded.   3. Mean; spiteful.   4. Having a comparatively low rank or position; minor.   5. *Law* Petit.   [< F *petit* small]   — **pet′ti·ly** *adv.*   — **pet′ti·ness** *n.*

petty cash   A supply of money kept for minor expenses, as in a business office.   Abbr. *p.c., p/c, P/C.*

petty juror, petty jury   See PETIT JUROR, PETIT JURY.

petty larceny   See under LARCENY.

petty officer   *Naval* Any of a class of noncommissioned officers. See table at GRADE.   Abbr. *p.o., P.O.*

pet·u·lance (pech′ŏŏ·lens)   *n.*   1. The condition or quality of being petulant; fretfulness; peevishness.   2. *Obs.* Insolence; pertness. Also **pet′u·lan·cy.**

pet·u·lant (pech′ŏŏ·lant)   *adj.*   1. Displaying or characterized by capricious fretfulness; peevish.   2. *Obs.* Saucily rude; insolent; pert.   [< OF < L *petulans, -antis* forward, ult. < *petere* to rush at]   — **pet′u·lant·ly** *adv.*

pe·tu·ni·a (pə·tōō′nē·ə, -tyōō′-)   *n.* Any of various tropical American plants (genus *Petunia*) of the nightshade family, cultivated widely for their funnel-shaped, variously colored flowers.   [< NL < F *petun* tobacco < Guarani *petŭñ*; so called because of its close relation to tobacco]

pe·tun·tze (pə·tōŏn′tse, *Chinese* bĭ′dun′dzu′)   *n.* A variety of feldspar that, when ground and mixed with kaolin, is used in the manufacture of Chinese porcelain. Also **pe·tun′tse.**   [< Chinese *pai-tun-tze*, lit., white stone]

peu à peu (pœ à pœ′)   *French* Little by little.

peu de chose (pœ də shōz′)   *French* A small matter; a trifle.

pew¹ (pyōō)   *n.*   1. A bench for seating people in church, frequently with a kneeling rack attached.   2. Formerly, a boxlike enclosure with seats on three sides, occupied by a family attending church. [ME *pewe* < OF *puye* parapet < LL *podia*, pl. of *podium* height, balcony < Gk. *podion* base, dim. of *pous, podos* foot]

pew² (pyōō)   *interj.* An expression of disgust or displeasure, as at a bad odor. [Origin unknown]

pe·wee (pē′wē)   *n.* Any of various small, greenish gray flycatchers; especially, the **wood pewee** (*Contopus virens*) of eastern North America: also spelled *peewee.* [Imit.]

pe·wit (pē′wit, pyōō′it)   *n.* Any of various birds having a high or shrill cry, as the lapwing. [Imit.]

pew·ter (pyōō′tər)   *n.*   1. An alloy, usually of tin and lead, formerly much used for tableware.   2. Pewter articles collectively.   3. The characteristic dull gray of pewter.   — *adj.*   1. Made of pewter.   2. Dull gray.   [< OF *peutre, pialtre*; ult. origin unknown]

pew·ter·er (pyōō′tər·ər)   *n.* One who makes articles of pewter.

pe·yo·te (pā·ō′tē, *Sp.* pā·yō′tä)   *n.* Mescal. Also **pe·yo′tl** (-yot′l).   [< Am. Sp., mescal < Nahuatl *peyotl*, lit., caterpillar; so called from the downy center of the mescal button]

pf.   Pfennig.

p.f.   1. *Music* Louder (Ital. *più forte*).   2. Power factor.

Pfc or **Pfc.**   *Mil.* Private, first class.

pfen·nig (pfen′ikh)   *n.* *pl.* **·nigs** or **pfen·ni·ge** (pfen′i·gə) A small bronze coin of Germany, equivalent to one hundredth of a deutschemark. Compare REICHSPFENNIG.   Abbr. *pf., pfg.*   [< G, penny]

pfg.   Pfennig.

Pforz·heim (pfôrts′hīm)   A city in Baden-Württemberg, West Germany; pop. 80,200 (est. 1960).

pg.   Page.

Pg.   Portugal; Portuguese.

PGA or **P.G.A.**   Professional Golfers Association.

pH   *Chem.* A symbol denoting the negative logarithm of the hydrogen ion concentration, in grams per liter, of a solution: used in expressing relative acidity and alkalinity.

A *p*H of 7 is regarded as neutral.   [< P(OTENTIAL OF) H(YDROGEN)]

Ph *Chem.* Phenyl.

PH *Mil.* Purple Heart.

PHA Public Housing Administration.

Phae·a·cia (fē·ā′shə)   In the Odyssey, an island visited by Odysseus after the fall of Troy.   Also **Phæ·a′cia.** — **Phae· a′cian** *adj. & n.*

Phae·dra (fē′drə)   In Greek mythology, a daughter of Minos and Pasiphaë and wife of Theseus, who fell in love with her stepson Hippolytus and killed herself because he spurned her.   Also **Phæ′dra.**

Phae·drus (fē′drəs)   First-century A.D. Roman fabulist; chief transmitter of Aesop's fables.

Pha·e·thon (fā′ə·thon)   In Greek mythology, the son of Helios, who borrowed his father's chariot of the sun, and would have set heaven and earth on fire by his careless driving if Zeus had not slain him with a thunderbolt.

pha·e·ton (fā′ə·tən), *esp. Brit.* fā′tən)   *n.*   **1.** A light, four-wheeled carriage, open at the sides, and sometimes having a top.   **2.** An open auto-mobile having front and back seats.   [< F *phaéton,* ult. < Gk. *Phaethōn* Phaethon]

-phage   *combining form*   One who or that which eats or consumes: *bacteriophage.*   [< Gk. *phagein* to eat]

phag·e·de·na (faj′ə·dē′nə)   *n.* *Pathol.* A widely spreading ulcer.   Also **phag′e·dae′na.**   [< L *phagedaena* an eating ulcer < Gk. *phagedaina* < *phagein* to eat]   — **phag′e·den′ic** (-den′ik) *adj.*

AMERICAN TWO–SPRING PHAETON

phago-   *combining form*   Eating: *phagocyte.*   Also, before vowels, **phag-.**   [< Gk. *phagein* to eat]

phag·o·cyte (fag′ə·sīt)   *n.* *Physiol.* A leucocyte that in-gests and destroys harmful bacteria, etc., in the blood and tissues of the body.   — **phag′o·cyt′ic** (-sit′ik) or **-i·cal** *adj.*

phagocytic index   The average number of bacteria in-gested by a single leucocyte under specified conditions.

phag·o·cy·to·sis (fag′ə·sī·tō′sis)   *n.*   The destruction and absorption of bacteria or microorganisms by phagocytes.

-phagous   *combining form*   Consuming; tending to eat: *rhizophagous.*   [< Gk. *phagein* to eat]

-phagy   *combining form*   The consumption or eating of: *geophagy.*   Also **-phagia.**   [< Gk. *-phagia* < *phagein* to eat]

phal·ange (fal′ənj, fə·lanj′)   *n. Anat.* A phalanx.   [< F < L *phalanx, phalangis.* See PHALANX.]

pha·lan·ge·al (fə·lan′jē·əl)   *adj.* Of, pertaining to, or re-sembling the phalanges of the fingers and toes.   Also **pha·lan′gal** (-gəl), **pha·lan′ge·an.**

pha·lan·ger (fə·lan′jər)   *n.* Any one of a family (*Phalan-geridae*) of small marsupials of Australia and New Guinea, having long, often prehensile tails: also, *Austral.,* possum.   [< NL < *phalanges,* pl. of *phalanx* phalanx (def. 4); in ref. to the phalangeal structure of its hind feet]

phal·an·ges (fə·lan′jēz)   Plural of PHALANX.

phal·an·ster·y (fal′ən·ster′ē)   *n. pl.* **·ster·ies**   **1.** A com-munity of Fourierites, or the building inhabited by them.   **2.** Any similar group or community.   [< F *phalanstère* < *phalan(x)* phalanx (< L) + (*mona*)*stère* < LL *monaste-rium* monastery]   — **phal′an·ste′ri·an** (-stir′ē·ən) *adj. & n.*   — **phal′an·ste′ri·an·ism** *n.*

pha·lanx (fā′langks, *esp. Brit.* fal′angks)   *n. pl.* **pha·lan·ges** (fə·lan′jēz) or **pha·lanx·es**   **1.** In ancient Greece, a marching order of heavy infantry, with close ranks and files, joined shields, and spears overlapping.   **2.** Any massed or compact body or corps.   **3.** A community of Fourierites.   **4.** *Anat.* One of the bones articulating with the joints of the fingers or toes: also called *phalange.* For illustrations see FINGERNAIL, FOOT.   [< L *phalanx, phalangis* < Gk. *phalanx, phalangos* line of battle]

phal·a·rope (fal′ə·rōp)   *n.* Any of several swimming birds (family *Phalaropodidae*) resembling the sandpiper, but hav-ing lobate toes.   [< F < NL *Phalaropus* < Gk. *phalaris* coot + *pous* foot]

phal·lic (fal′ik)   *adj.* Of, pertaining to, or resembling a phallus.   Also **phal′li·cal.**

phal·lism (fal′iz·əm)   *n.* Worship of the generative power in nature as symbolized by the phallus, as in the Dionysian festivals of ancient Greece.   Also **phal′li·cism.**   [< PHAL-L(US) + -ISM]   — **phal′li·cist, phal′list** *n.*

phal·lus (fal′əs)   *n. pl.* **·li** (-ī)   **1.** A representation of the male generative organ, used in many systems of religion as a symbol of the generative power of nature.   **2.** *Anat.* **a** The penis or the clitoris.   **b** The sexually undifferentiated genital structure of the embryo.   [< L < Gk. *phallos* penis]

-phane   *combining form*   Something resembling or similar to (a specified substance or material): *cellophane.*   [< Gk. *-phanēs* < *phainein* to show]

phanero-   *combining form*   Visible: *phanerogam.* Also, before vowels, **phaner-.**   [< Gk. *phaneros* visible < *phainein* to show]

phan·er·o·crys·tal·line (fan′ər·ō·kris′tə·lin, -līn)   *adj. Mineral.* Obviously crystalline: opposed to *cryptocrystalline.*

phan·er·o·gam (fan′ər·ə·gam′)   *n. Bot.* Any member of a former division of plants (*Phanerogamia*), embracing all those with flowers having stamens and pistils: distinguished from *cryptogam.*   [< F *phanérogame* < NL *phanerogamus* < Gk. *phaneros* visible (< *phainein* to show) + *gamos* mar-riage]   — **phan′er·o·gam′ic, phan·er·og·a·mous** (fan′ə-rog′ə·məs) *adj.*

phan·tasm (fan′taz·əm)   *n.*   **1.** An imaginary appearance; phantom.   **2.** A mental image; fancy.   Also spelled *fantasm.*   [< Gk. *phantasma.* Doublet of PHANTOM.]

phan·tas·ma·go·ri·a (fan·taz′mə·gôr′ē·ə, -gō′rē·ə)   *n.*   **1.** A changing, incoherent series of apparitions or phantasms, as in a dream.   **2.** An exhibition of pictures projected on a screen and made to increase or diminish in size rapidly while continously in focus; also, any exhibition of optical effects.   **3.** An apparition. Also spelled *fantasmagoria.* Also **phan·tas′ ma·go′ry.**   [< NL < Gk. *phantasma* apparition (See PHAN-TOM) + (probably) *agora* assembly, crowd]   — **phan·tas′ma-go′ri·al, phan·tas′ma·gor′ic** (-gôr′ik, -gor′ik) or **-i·cal** *adj.*

phan·tas·mal (fan·taz′məl)   *adj.* Of or like a phantasm; unreal or illusive; spectral.   Also spelled *fantasmal:* also **phan·tas′mic.**

phan·ta·sy (fan′tə·sē, -zē)   See FANTASY.

phan·tom (fan′təm)   *n.*   **1.** Something that exists only in appearance.   **2.** An apparition; specter.   **3.** The visible rep-resentative of an abstract state or incorporeal person.   — **Syn.** See GHOST.   — *adj.* Illusive; ghostlike: a *phantom* ship.   Also spelled *fantom.*   [< OF *fantosme* < L *phantasma* < Gk. apparition < *phantazein* to make visible < *phantos* visible < *phainein* to show. Doublet of PHANTASM.]

-phany   *combining form*   Appearance; manifestation: *theo-phany.*   [< Gk. *-phaneia* < *phainein* to appear]

Phar. or **phar., Pharm.,** or **pharm.**   **1.** Pharmaceutical.   **2.** Pharmacopoeia.   **3.** Pharmacy.

Phar·a·mond (far′ə·mənd)   A legendary king of the Franks during the fifth century.

Phar·aoh (fâr′ō, fā′rō, fär′ē·ō)   *n.* Any one of the monarchs of ancient Egypt.   [< LL *Pharao* < Gk. *Pharaō* < Hebrew *Par'ōh* < Egyptian *pr-'ōh* the great house]   — **Phar′a·on′ic** (-ē·on′ik) or **-i·cal** *adj.*

Phar. B. Bachelor of Pharmacy (L *Pharmaciae Bacca-laureus*).

Phar. D. Doctor of Pharmacy (L *Pharmaciae Doctor*).

phar·i·sa·ic (far′ə·sā′ik)   *adj.*   **1.** Of or pertaining to the Pharisees.   **2.** Observing the form, but neglecting the spirit, of religion; self-righteous.   Also **phar′i·sa′i·cal**   [< LL *pharisaïcus* < LGk. *pharisaïkos* < *pharisaios.* See PHARI-SEE.]   — **phar′i·sa′i·cal·ly** *adv.*   — **phar′i·sa′i·cal·ness** *n.*

phar·i·sa·ism (far′ə·sā·iz′əm)   *n.*   **1.** *Often cap.* The prin-ciples and practices of the Pharisees.   **2.** Formality, self-righteousness, censoriousness, or hypocrisy.   Also **phar′i· see·ism** (-sē·iz′əm).   — **Syn.** See HYPOCRISY.

Phar·i·see (far′ə·sē)   *n.*   **1.** A member of an ancient Jewish sect that accepted the Mosaic law and the oral traditions as-sociated with it, and emphasized strict observance of ritual.   Compare SADDUCEE.   **2.** A formal, sanctimonious, hypo-critical person: also **phar′i·see.**   [OE *fariseus,* infl. by OF *pharise,* both < L *pharisaeus* < Gk. *pharisaios* < Aramaic *perīshayā,* pl. of *perish.* Akin to Hebrew *pārūsh* separated < *parash* to cleave.]

phar·ma·ceu·ti·cal (fär′mə·sōō′ti·kəl)   *adj.* Pertaining to, using, or relating to pharmacy or the pharmacopoeia: also **phar·ma·cal** (fär′mə·kəl).   Also **phar′ma·ceu′tic.**   — *n.* A pharmaceutical product.   Abbr. *phar., pharm., Phar., Pharm.*   [< L *pharmaceuticus* < Gk. *pharmakeutikos* of drugs < *pharmakeuein* to give drugs < *pharmakon* drug]   — **phar′ma·ceu′ti·cal·ly** *adv.*   — **phar′ma·ceu′tist** *n.*

phar·ma·ceu·tics (fär′mə·sōō′tiks)   *n.pl.* (construed as *sing.*)   Pharmacy (def. 1).

phar·ma·cist (fär′mə·sist)   *n.* A qualified druggist; phar-maceutist.

pharmaco-   *combining form*   A drug; of or pertaining to drugs: *pharmacology.*   Also, before vowels, **pharmac-.**   [< Gk. *pharmakon* drug]

phar·ma·co·dy·nam·ics (fär′mə·kō·dī·nam′iks)   *n.pl.* (con-strued as *sing.*)   The experimental science of the action and effects of drugs.

phar·ma·cog·no·sy (fär′mə·kog′nə·sē)   *n.* The knowledge of drugs, especially their origin, structure, and chemical consitution.   [< NL *pharmacognosia* < Gk. *pharmakon* drug + *gnōsis* knowledge]   — **phar′ma·cog′no·sist** *n.*

phar·ma·col·o·gy (fär′mə·kol′ə·jē)   *n.* The science of the nature, preparation, administration, and effects of drugs.   — **phar′ma·co·log′ic** (-kə·loj′ik) or **-i·cal** *adj.*   — **phar′ma· co·log′i·cal·ly** *adv.*   — **phar′ma·col′o·gist** *n.*

phar·ma·co·poe·ia (fär′mə·kə·pē′ə)   *n.*   **1.** A book, usually published by an authority, containing standard formulas and methods for the preparation of medicines, drugs, and other remedial substances.   **2.** A collection of drugs.   Abbr.

phar., pharm., Phar., Pharm. [< NL < Gk. *pharmakopoiia* making of drugs < *pharmakon* drug + *poieein* to make] — **phar'ma·co·poe'ial** *adj.* — **phar'ma·co·poe'ist** *n.*

phar·ma·cy (fär'mə-sē) *n. pl.* **·cies** **1.** The art or business of compounding, preserving, and identifying drugs, and of compounding and dispensing medicines: also called *pharmaceutics.* **2.** A drugstore. *Abbr.* phar., pharm., Phar., Pharm. [< OF *farmacie* < LL *pharmacia* < Gk. *pharmakeia* < *pharmakon* drug]

Phar·na·ces II (fär'nə-sēz), died 47 B.C., king of Pontus; defeated by Julius Caesar.

pha·ros (fâr'os, fā'rŏs, fā'-) *n.* A lighthouse; beacon. [< L < Gk. < *Pharos* Pharos]

Pha·ros (fâr'os, fā'rŏs, fā'-) A peninsula of Alexandria, Egypt; formerly an island, the site of an ancient lighthouse that was considered one of the Seven Wonders of the World.

Phar·sa·la (fär'sä·lä) A city of southern Thessaly, Greece; chief town of the ancient district of **Phar·sa·li·a** (fär-sā'lē-ə) and scene of Caesar's victory over Pompey, 48 B.C., also *Farsala.* Ancient **Phar·sa·lus** (fär-sā'ləs).

pha·ryn·ge·al (fə-rin'jē-əl, far'in·jē'əl) *adj.* **1.** Of or pertaining to the pharynx. **2.** *Phonet.* Denoting a sound produced in the pharynx. — *n.* A sound produced in the pharynx. Also **pha·ryn'gal** (-gəl). [< NL *pharyngeus* < *pharynx, -yngis.* See PHARYNX.]

phar·yn·gi·tis (far'in·jī'tis) *n. Pathol.* Inflammation of the pharynx, as in diphtheria and malignant sore throat. [< NL < *pharynx, -yngis* pharynx]

pharyngo- *combining form* The throat; related to the throat: *pharyngoscope.* Also, before vowels, **pharyng-**. [< Gk. *pharynx* throat]

pha·ryn·gol·o·gy (far'ing·gol'ə·jē) *n.* The study of the pharynx and its diseases.

pha·ryn·go·scope (fə-ring'gə·skōp) *n.* An apparatus for examining the pharynx. — **phar·yn·gos·co·py** (far'ing·gos'kə·pē) *n.*

phar·yn·got·o·my (far'ing·got'ə·mē) *n. pl.* **·mies** *Surg.* The operation of making an incision into the pharynx.

phar·ynx (far'ingks) *n. pl.* **pha·ryn·ges** (fə-rin'jēz) or **phar·ynx·es** *Anat.* The part of the alimentary canal between the palate and the esophagus, serving as a passage for air and food. For illustrations see MOUTH, THROAT. [< NL *pharynx, -yngis* < Gk. *pharynx, -yngos* throat. Akin to Gk. *pharanx* ravine.]

phase (fāz) *n.* **1.** The view that anything presents to the eye; any one of varying distinctive manifestations of an object. **2.** *Astron.* One of the appearances or forms presented periodically by the moon and planets. **3.** *Physics* **a** Any particular stage in the complete cycle of a periodic system. **b** The fraction of a cycle through which a wave has passed at any instant: often measured as an angle, 360° or 2π radians representing one complete cycle. **4.** *Chem.* Any homogeneous part of a material system separated from other parts by physical boundaries, as water in ice, with water vapor above. **5.** *Biol.* **a** One of the distinct stages in the reduction or division process of a cell. **b** Any characteristic or decisive stage in the growth, development, or life pattern of an organism. Also **pha·sis** (fā'sis). ◆ In formal writing *phase* should not be loosely used as a synonym for *part,* as *a phase of his book.* — *v.t.* **phased, phas·ing** *U.S.* To plan, organize, or execute (a process, project, program, etc.) by phases. — **in phase** *Physics* Reaching corresponding phases simultaneously, as two waves. — **out of phase** *Physics* Not in phase. — **to phase out** (or **in**) *U.S.* To plan and execute the orderly and gradual completion or initiation of an enterprise. [< NL *phasis* < Gk., appearance < *phainein* to show] — **pha·sic** (fā'zik) *adj.*

— **Syn.** (noun) 1, 4. Phase, aspect, side, facet, and stage denote one of a number of different appearances presented by an object. *Phases* differ through change in the object; *aspects* differ through change in the position of the observer. *Side* is used particularly of one or two contrasted or opposed *aspects,* while a *facet* is one of many aspects. A *stage* is a step or period in development or progress. *Stage* does not derive from the metaphor of vision, but it is close to *phase* in implying change in that which is seen.

phase meter An instrument for measuring the difference in phase between two alternating oscillations of the same frequency.

phase modulation *Electronics* Modulation of a carrier wave by varying its phase.

phase rule In physical chemistry, a generalization of the equilibrium relations between phases of a material system, by which the number of phases plus the variance equals the number of components plus 2, or $P + V = C + 2$.

-phasia *combining form Med.* Defect or malfunction of speech: *dysphasia.* Also **-phasy.** [< Gk. *-phasia* < *phanai* to speak]

Ph.B. Bachelor of Philosophy (L *Philosophiae Baccalaureus*).

Ph.C. Pharmaceutical Chemist.

Ph.D. Doctor of Philosophy (L *Philosophiae Doctor*).

pheas·ant (fez'ənt) *n.* **1.** A long-tailed, gallinaceous bird (family *Phasianidae*), originally of Asia, noted for the gorgeous plumage of the male; especially, the **ring-necked**

pheasant (*Phasianus colchicus torquatus*), widely bred in the United States. **2.** One of various other birds, as the ruffed grouse. [< AF *fesant* < L *Phasianus* < Gk. *Phasianos* (*ornis*) the Phasian (bird) < *Phasis* the Phasis, a river in the Georgian S.S.R., now called Rion, where it was first found]

Phe·be (fē'bē) See PHOEBE.

Phei·dip·pi·des (fī·dip'ə·dēz) Fifth-century B.C. Athenian athlete; ran from Athens to Sparta to secure help against the Persians 490 B.C.: sometimes confused with the runner, whose name is not preserved, who carried news of victory at Marathon to Athens. Also spelled *Phidippides.*

phel·lo·derm (fel'ə·dûrm) *n. Bot.* A layer of green parenchymatous tissue sometimes developed on the inner side of a layer of cork. [< Gk. *phellos* cork + *derma* skin] — **phel'lo·der'mal** *adj.*

phel·lo·gen (fel'ə·jən) *n. Bot.* The active meristematic tissue out of which cork is developed: also called *cork cambium.* [< Gk. *phellos* cork + -GEN] — **phel'lo·ge·net'ic** (-jə·net'ik), **phel'lo·gen'ic** *adj.*

Phelps (felps), **William Lyon,** 1865–1943, U.S. educator.

phen- Var. of PHENO-.

phe·na·caine (fē'nə·kān) *n.* A white, odorless, crystalline substance, $C_{18}H_{22}N_2O_2$, used in the form of a hydrochloride as a local anesthetic. [< PHEN- + A(CETO)- + (CO)CAINE]

phe·nac·e·tin (fə·nas'ə·tin) *n. Chem.* Acetophenetidin. Also **phe·nac'e·tine.**

phen·a·cite (fen'ə·sīt) *n.* A brittle, vitreous, crystalline beryllium silicate, Be_2SiO_4, sometimes used as a gemstone. [< Gk. *phenax, -akos* cheat + -ITE¹; so called because mistaken for quartz]

phe·nan·threne (fə·nan'thrēn) *n. Chem* A crystalline isomer, $C_{14}H_{10}$, of anthracene, a coal-tar product used in the synthesis of drugs and dyes. [< PHEN(YL) + ANTHR(AC)-ENE]

phen·a·zine (fen'ə·zēn, -zin) *n. Chem.* A yellowish basic compound, $C_{12}H_8N_2$, on which many dyestuffs are based. Also **phen'a·zin** (-zin). [< PHEN(YL) + AZ(O)- + -INE²]

phe·net·i·dine (fə·net'ə·dēn, -din) *n. Chem.* Any one of three isomeric liquid derivatives, $C_8H_{11}ON$, of phenetole; especially the *para* form, which is the base of acetophenetidin. Also **phe·net'i·din** (-din). [< PHEN(OL) + ET(HYL) + (AM)ID(O)- + -INE²]

phen·e·tole (fen'ə·tōl, -tol) *n. Chem.* An aromatic liquid compound, $C_6H_5OC_2H_5$, the ethyl ether of phenol. Also **phen'e·tol.** [< PHEN(YL) + ET(HYL) + -OLE]

Phe·ni·cia (fə·nē'shə, -nish'ə), **Phe·ni·cian,** etc. See PHOENICIA, etc.

phe·nix (fē'niks) See PHOENIX.

Phe·nix City (fē'niks) A city in eastern Alabama, on the Chattahoochee River; pop. 25,281.

pheno- *combining form Chem.* Related to benzene; a derivative of benzene: *phenobarbital.* Also, before vowels, **phen-**. [< Gk. *phaino-* shining < *phainein* to show]

phe·no·bar·bi·tal (fē'nō·bär'bə·tal, -tôl) *n. Chem.* A white, odorless, slightly bitter, crystalline powder, $C_{12}H_{12}O_3N_2$, a derivative of barbituric acid, used as a sedative. Also **phe'no·bar'bi·tone** (-tōn). [< PHENO- + BARBITAL]

phe·no·cop·y (fē'nə·kop'ē) *n. Genetics* An environmentally induced, non-inherited modification similar to one that is genetically produced. [< PHENO(TYPE) + COPY]

phe·no·cryst (fē'nō·krist) *n. Geol.* A constituent of an igneous rock, usually occurring as large crystals embedded in a fine-grained groundmass. [< F *phénocryste* < Gk. *phainein* to show + *krystallos* crystal] — **phe'no·crys'tic** *adj.*

phe·nol (fē'nōl, -nol) *n. Chem.* **1.** A white, crystalline, caustic compound, C_6H_5OH, with a characteristic odor, derived from coal tar and used as a disinfectant: also called *carbolic acid.* **2.** Any of a series of aromatic hydroxyl derivatives of benzene or its homologs. [< Gk. *phaino-* shining < *phainein* to show + -OL¹; so called because derived from coal tar, a by-product of illuminating gas]

phe·no·late (fē'nə·lāt) *n. Chem.* A salt of phenol: also called *phenoxide.*

phe·nol·ic (fi·nol'ik, -nō'lik) *adj. Chem.* Of, pertaining to, derived from, or containing phenol.

phenolic resin Any of a large and important class of resins and synthetic plastics made from an aldehyde-phenol base.

phe·nol·o·gy (fi·nol'ə·jē) *n.* The study of the periodic phenomena of plant and animal life, as migrations, breeding, etc., in relation to seasonal changes, climatic and other ecological factors. [Contr. of PHENOMENOLOGY, with a restricted application] — **phe·no·log·ic** (fē'nə·loj'ik) or **·i·cal** *adj.* — **phe'no·log'i·cal·ly** *adv.* — **phe·nol'o·gist** *n.*

phe·nol·phthal·ein (fē'nōl·thal'ēn, fē'nolf·thal'ē·in) *n. Chem.* A yellowish white derivative of phenol, $C_{20}H_{14}O_4$, used as a laxative, an indicator in acid-base titrations, etc. [< PHENOL + PHTALEIN]

phe·nom·e·na (fi·nom'ə·nə) Plural of PHENOMENON: erroneously used as a singular.

phe·nom·e·nal (fi·nom'ə·nəl) *adj.* **1.** Pertaining to phenomena. **2.** Extraordinary or marvelous. **3.** *Philos.* Perceptible through the senses. — **phe·nom'e·nal·ly** *adv.*

phe·nom·e·nal·ism (fi·nom'ə·nəl·iz'əm) *n. Philos.* The doctrine that denies either our knowledge or the existence of a reality beyond phenomena. Compare POSITIVISM. — **phe·nom′e·nal·ist** *n.* — **phe·nom′e·nal·is′tic** *adj.* — **phe·nom′e·nal·is′ti·cal·ly** *adv.*

phe·nom·e·nol·o·gy (fi·nom′ə·nol′ə·jē) *n.* **1.** The scientific investigation or description of phenomena. **2.** *Philos.* The general doctrine of phenomena, as distinguished from ontology. [< PHENOMENO(N) + -LOGY] — **phe·nom′e·no·log′i·cal** (-nə·loj′i·kəl) *adj.* — **phe·nom′e·no·log′i·cal·ly** *adv.*

phe·nom·e·non (fi·nom′ə·non) *n. pl.* **phe·nom·e·na** (-nə); *for defs. 2 & 3, often* **phe·nom·e·nons** **1.** Something visible or directly observable, as an appearance, action, change, etc. **2.** Any unusual occurrence; an inexplicable fact; marvel. **3.** *Informal* A person having some remarkable talent, power, or ability; prodigy. **4.** *Philos.* **a** Anything that can be apprehended by the senses; an appearance. **b** An object as it seems to us on the basis of our perception of it. Compare NOUMENON. **5.** *Med.* Any notable characteristic or disease. [< LL *phaenomenon* < Gk. *phainomenon,* ppr. neut. of *phainesthal* to appear, passive of *phainein* to show]

phe·no·type (fē′nə·tīp) *n. Biol.* The aggregate of genetic characteristics visibly manifested by an organism through environmental influences. Compare GENOTYPE. [< F *phéno-* (< Gk. *phaino-* < *phainein* to show) + -TYPE] — **phe′no·typ′ic** (-tip′ik) *or* **·i·cal** *adj.* — **phe′no·typ′i·cal·ly** *adv.*

phe·nox·ide (fi·nok′sīd) *n. Chem.* Phenolate.

phen·yl (fen′əl, fē′nəl) *n. Chem.* The univalent radical C_6H_5, regarded as the basis of numerous aromatic derivatives. Abbr. *Ph* [< PHEN(O) + -YL]

phen·yl·a·mine (fen′əl·ə·mēn′, -am′in, fē′nəl-) *n. Chem.* Aniline.

phen·yl·ke·to·nu·ri·a (fen′əl·kēt′n·yŏŏr′ē·ə, fē′nəl-) *n. Pathol.* A rare, inherited metabolic disorder that can cause permanent mental impairment if untreated within a few weeks after birth: also called *PKU*. [< PHENYL + KETON(E) + -URIA]

phen·yl·ene (fen′əl·ēn, fē′nəl-) *n. Chem.* A bivalent radical, C_6H_4, contained in certain benzene derivatives.

phew (fyŏŏ, fŏŏ) *interj.* An exclamation of disgust or surprise.

phi (fī, fē) *n.* The twenty-first letter in the Greek alphabet (Φ, φ): corresponding to English *ph* and *f.* See ALPHABET.

phi·al (fī′əl) See VIAL.

Phi Be·ta Kap·pa (fī bā′tə kap′ə, bē′tə) An American honorary society founded in 1776, having its membership based on conditions of high academic standing.

Phid·i·as (fid′ē·əs) Fifth-century B.C. Greek sculptor and architect; designed the *Athena Parthenos,* a chryselephantine statue of Athena in the Parthenon. — **Phid′i·an** *adj.*

Phi·dip·pi·des (fi·dip′ə·dēz) See PHEIDIPPIDES.

phil- Var. of PHILO-.

phil. Philosopher; philosophical; philosophy.

-phil Var. of -PHILE.

Phil. **1.** Philippians. **2.** Philippine.

Phila. Philadelphia.

phil·a·beg, (fil′ə·beg), **phil·i·beg** See FILIBEG.

Phil·a·del·phi·a (fil′ə·del′fē·ə) A city in SE Pennsylvania, on the Delaware River, the fourth largest city in the United States; pop. 1,950,098. — **Phil′a·del′phi·an** *adj. & n.*

Philadelphia lawyer *U.S. Slang* An unusually sharp lawyer, especially one adept in phrasing legal technicalities.

Phi·lae (fī′lē) An island in the Nile river, near Aswan; submerged half the year by the backwater from the Aswan Dam; site of the temples of Isis and Hathor. Also **Phi′læ.**

phi·lan·der (fi·lan′dər) *v.i.* To make love without serious intentions: said of a man. — *n.* A male flirt or suitor: also **phi·lan′der·er.** [< Gk. *philandros,* orig., loving men < *phileein* to love + *anēr, andros* man; from its use as a proper name for a lover in drama and romance]

phi·lan·thro·py (fi·lan′thrə·pē) *n. pl.* **·pies** **1.** Disposition or effort to promote the happiness or social elevation of mankind, as by making donations, etc. **2.** Love or benevolence toward mankind in general. — **Syn.** See ALTRUISM, BENEVOLENCE. [< LL *philanthropia* < Gk. *philanthrōpia* < *phileein* to love + *anthropos* man] — **phil·an·throp·ic** (fil′ən·throp′ik) *or* **·i·cal** *adj.* — **phil′an·throp′i·cal·ly** *adv.* — **phi·lan′thro·pist** *n.*

phi·lat·e·ly (fi·lat′ə·lē) *n.* The study and collection of postage stamps, stamped envelopes, wrappers, etc.; stamp collecting. [< F *philatélie* < Gk. *philos* loving + *ateleia* exemption from tax; with ref. to prepaid postage, indicated by a stamp] — **phil·a·tel·ic** (fil′ə·tel′ik) *or* **·i·cal** *adj.* — **phil′a·tel′i·cal·ly** *adv.* — **phi·lat′e·list** *n.*

-phile *combining form* One who supports or is fond of; one devoted to: *bibliophile.* Also *-phil.* [< Gk. *-philos* loving < *phileein* to love]

Philem. Philemon (bible).

Phi·le·mon (fi·lē′mən) In Greek mythology, the husband of Baucis.

Philemon A Greek of Colossae, converted to Christianity by Saint Paul. — *n.* A book of the New Testament consisting of an epistle addressed by Saint Paul to him.

phil·har·mon·ic (fil′här·mon′ik, -ər·mon′-) *adj. Sometimes cap.* Fond of music: often used in the names of musical societies. [< F *philharmonique* < Ital. *filarmonico* < Gk. *philos* loving + *harmonikos* musical < *harmonia* music]

Phil·hel·lene (fil·hel′ēn) *n.* One who loves and supports Greece or the Greeks. Also **Phil·hel′le·nist.** [< Gk. *philellēn* loving Greeks < *phileein* to love + *Hellēn* a Greek] — **Phil·hel·len·ic** (fil′he·len′ik) *adj.* — **Phil·hel·le·nism** *n.*

Phil. I. Philippine Islands.

-philia *combining form* **1.** A tendency toward: *hemophilia.* **2.** An excessive affection or fondness for: *necrophilia.* Also spelled *-phily.* [< Gk. *-philia* < *phileein* to love]

Phil·ip (fil′ip) One of the twelve apostles: called **Saint Philip.**

Philip, King, died 1676, American Indian chief; leader in King Philip's War, 1675–76, against the New England colonists: original name **Met·a·com·et** (met′ə·kom′it).

Philip, Prince, born 1921, Duke of Edinburgh; consort of Queen Elizabeth II of England.

Philip, Saint First-century A.D. Christian martyr; one of the seven deacons of the early Christian Church: called **Philip the Evangelist.** *Acts* viii 5.

Philip II, 382–336 B.C., king of Macedon 359–336 B.C.; conquered Thessaly and Greece; father of Alexander the Great: called **Philip of Macedon.**

Philip II, 1165–1223, king of France 1180–1223; subdued the barons; defeated King John of England: called **Philip Augustus.**

Philip II, 1527–98, king of Spain 1556–98, king of Portugal 1580–98; sent the Armada against England.

Philip IV, 1268–1314, king of France 1285–1314; supported Pope Clement V at Avignon: called **the Fair.**

Philip V, 1683–1746, king of Spain 1700–46; first of the Bourbon line in Spain.

Phi·lip·pi (fi·lip′ī) An ancient town in northern Macedonia, Greece; scene of the defeat of Brutus and Cassius by Octavian and Antony, 42 B.C., and of Saint Paul's first preaching in Europe. *Acts* xvi 12. — **Phi·lip′pi·an** *adj. & n.*

Phi·lip·pi·ans (fi·lip′ē·ənz) *n.pl.* (*construed as sing.*) A book of the New Testament consisting of an epistle of Saint Paul addressed to Christians at Philippi. Abbr. *Phil.*

phi·lip·pic (fi·lip′ik) *n.* An impassioned speech characterized by invective. — **·he Philippics** A series of twelve speeches in which Demosthenes denounced Philip of Macedon. [< L *Philippicus* < Gk. *Philippikos* pertaining to Philip]

Phil·ip·pine (fil′ə·pēn) *adj.* Of or pertaining to the Philippine Islands or their inhabitants: also spelled *Filipine.* Abbr. *Phil.*

Philippine Sea A part of the western Pacific between the Philippines and the Marianas.

Philippines, Republic of the A Republic occupying the **Philippine Islands,** a Pacific archipelago of some 7,000 islands, SE of China; 115,707 sq. mi.; pop. 38,153,000 (est. 1970); capital, Quezon City; seat of administration, Manila.

Philippine Trench, Philippine Deep See MINDANAO TRENCH.

Phil·ip·pop·o·lis (fil′i·pop′ə·ləs) An ancient name for PLOVDIV.

Philip the Bold, 1342–1404, duke of Burgundy; acquired Flanders through marriage.

Philip the Good, 1396–1467, duke of Burgundy; supported Louis XI of France; suppressed revolts in the Netherlands.

Phi·lis·ti·a (fi·lis′tē·ə) An ancient region on the Mediterranean, SW Palestine. *Ps.* lx 8.

Phi·lis·tine (fi·lis′tin, -tēn, -tīn, fil′əs-) *n.* One of a warlike race of ancient Philistia. I *Sam.* xvii 23. [< F *Philistin* < LL *Philistinus,* pl. *Philistini* < Gk. *Philistinoi, Palaistinoi* < Hebrew *p'lishtim*]

Phi·lis·tine (fi·lis′tin, -tēn, -tīn, fil′əs-) *n.* An ignorant, narrow-minded person, devoid of culture and indifferent to art. [< G student slang *Philister* one of the ancient Philistines]

Phi·lis·tin·ism (fi·lis′tin·iz′əm) *n.* Blind conventionalism; lack of culture, taste, etc.

Phil·lips (fil′ips), **Stephen,** 1868–1915, English poet and dramatist. — **Wendell,** 1811–84, U.S. orator and reformer.

Phillips screw (fil′ips) A screw having a head (called a **Phillips head**) with crossing grooves for use with a special screwdriver. [after *Phillips* Screws, a trademark]

philo- *combining form* Loving; fond of: *philomath.* Also, before vowels, *phil-.* [< Gk. *philos* loving < *phileein* to love]

Phil·oc·te·tes (fil′ok·tē′tēz) In Greek legend, a Greek hero who killed Paris with a poisoned arrow in the Trojan War.

phil·o·den·dron (fil′ə·den′drən) *n.* Any of a genus (*Philodendron*) of tropical American climbing plants of the arum family, having thick, glossy, evergreen leaves and cultivated as an ornamental house plant. [< NL < Gk., neut. of *phil-odendros* fond of trees < *philos* fond + *dendron* tree]

phi·log·y·ny (fi·loj′ə·nē) *n.* Fondness for or devotion to women. [< Gk. *philogynia* < *philos* loving + *gynē* woman] — **phi·log′y·nist** *n.* — **phi·log′y·nous** *adj.*

Phi·lo Ju·dae·us (fī′lō jōō·dē′əs), 20? B.C.–A.D. 50?, Jewish Platonist philosopher. Also **Philo of Alexandria.**

philol. Philology.

phi·lol·o·gy (fi·lol′ə·jē) *n.* **1.** The scientific study of written records, chiefly of literary works, in order to set up accurate texts and determine their meaning. **2.** Literary scholarship, especially classical scholarship. **3.** Linguistics, especially comparative and historical. **4.** Loosely, etymology. [< F *philologie* < L *philologia* < Gk. *philologos* fond of argument or words < *philos* fond + *logos* word] — **phil·o·log·ic** (fil′ə·loj′ik) or **·i·cal** *adj.* — **phil′o·log′i·cal·ly** *adv.* — **phi·lol′o·gist, phi·lol′o·ger** *n.*

phil·o·mel (fil′ə·mel) *n. Poetic* The nightingale. Also **phil′·o·me′la** (-mē′lə). [< F *philomèle* < L *philomela* < Gk. *philomēla*, ? < *philos* loving + *melos* song]

Phil·o·me·la (fil′ə·mē′lə) In Greek mythology, a princess of Athens who was raped by her sister Procne's husband, Tereus, who then tore out her tongue. When, in revenge, she and Procne killed his son Itys, the gods changed Tereus into a hoopoe, Procne into a swallow, and Philomela into a nightingale.

phil·o·pe·na (fil′ə·pē′nə) *n.* **1.** A game in which twin kernels of a nut are shared by two people, one of whom must pay a forfeit to the other if certain conditions are not met. **2.** The twin kernels shared. **3.** The gift made as a forfeit. Often spelled *fillipeen.* Also **phil′lip·pine, phil/li·peen′er.** [Appar. < Du. *phillipine*, alter. of G *vielliebchen* very dear < *viel* much + *liebchen*, dim. of *liebe* love; infl. by Gk. *philos* loving and L *poena* penalty]

Phil·o·poe·men (fil′ə·pē′mən), 252?–183 B.C., Greek general and patriot; advocated unity among the Greeks: called **the Last of the Greeks.**

phil·o·pro·gen·i·tive (fil′ə·prō·jen′ə·tiv) *adj.* **1.** Fond of offspring or of children in general. **2.** Prolific. [< PHILO- + L *progenitus*, pp. of *progignere* to beget] — **phil′o·pro·gen′i·tive·ly** *adv.* — **phil′o·pro·gen′i·tive·ness** *n.*

philos. Philosopher; philosophical; philosophy.

phi·los·o·pher (fi·los′ə·fər) *n.* **1.** A student of or specialist in philosophy. **2.** The creator of a system of philosophy. **3.** One who lives, thinks, makes judgments, etc., according to a system of philosophy. **4.** One who is calm and patient under all circumstances. Abbr. *phil., philos.* [< OF *philosophe* < L *philosophus* < Gk. *philosophos* lover of wisdom < *philos* loving + *sophos* wise]

philosopher's stone An imaginary stone or substance capable of transmuting the baser metals into gold, sought by the alchemists.

phil·o·soph·i·cal (fil′ə·sof′i·kəl) *adj.* **1.** Pertaining to or founded on the principles of philosophy. **2.** Proper to or characteristic of a philosopher. **3.** Self-restrained and serene; rational; thoughtful. **4.** *Archaic* Of or used in natural philosophy or physics. Also **phil′o·soph′ic.** Abbr. *phil., philos.* — **phil′o·soph′i·cal·ly** *adv.* — **phil′o·soph′i·cal·ness** *n.*

phi·los·o·phism (fi·los′ə·fiz′əm) *n.* Unsound or pretended philosophy; sophistry.

phi·los·o·phize (fi·los′ə·fīz) *v.i.* **·phized, ·phiz·ing** To speculate like a philosopher; seek ultimate causes and principles; moralize. — **phi·los′o·phiz′er** *n.*

phi·los·o·phy (fi·los′ə·fē) *n. pl.* **·phies** **1.** The inquiry into the most comprehensive principles of reality in general, or of some limited sector of it such as human knowledge or human values. **2.** The love of wisdom, and the search for it. **3.** A philosophical system; also, a treatise on such a system. **4.** The general laws that furnish the rational explanation of anything: the *philosophy* of banking. **5.** Practical wisdom; fortitude, as in enduring reverses and suffering. **6.** *Archaic* Reasoned science; a scientific system: natural *philosophy.* **7.** *Archaic* The sciences as formerly studied in the universities. Abbr. *phil., philos.* [< OF *filosofie, philosophie* < L *philosophia* < Gk. < *philosophos.* See PHILOSOPHER.]

-philous *combining form* Loving; fond of: *anemophilous.* [< Gk. *-philos.* See -PHILE.]

phil·ter (fil′tər) *n.* **1.** A charmed draft supposed to have power to excite sexual love; a love potion. **2.** Any magic potion. — *v.t.* To charm with a philter. Also **phil′tre.** [< MF *philtre* < L *philtrum* < Gk. *philtron* < *phileein* to love]

-phily Var. of -PHILIA.

phi·mo·sis (fi·mō′sis) *n. Pathol.* The abnormal constriction of the opening of the prepuce, preventing the uncovering of the glans penis. [< NL < Gk. *phimōsis* a muzzling < *phimos* muzzle] — **phi·mot′ic** (-mot′ik) *adj.*

Phin·ti·as (fin′tē·əs) Pythias. See DAMON AND PYTHIAS.

Phips (fips), Sir William, 1651–95, English colonial administrator in America. Also **Phipps.**

phiz (fiz) *n. Archaic Slang* Visage; face. [Short for *phiznomy*, obs. var. of PHYSIOGNOMY]

phle·bi·tis (fli·bī′tis) *n. Pathol.* Inflammation of the inner membrane of a vein. [< NL < Gk. *phleps, phlebos* blood vessel + -ITIS] — **phle·bit′ic** (-bit′ik) *adj.*

phlebo- *combining form* Venous: *phlebotomy.* Also, before vowels, **phleb-.** [< Gk. *phleps, phlebos* blood vessel]

phleb·o·scle·ro·sis (fleb′ō·skli·rō′sis) *n. Pathol.* Thickening and hardening of the walls of the veins. [< PHLEBO- + Gk. *sklērōsis* a hardening < *sklēros* hard] — **phleb′o·scle·rot′ic** (-rot′ik) *adj.*

phle·bot·o·mize (fli·bot′ə·mīz) *v.t.* **·mized, ·miz·ing** To treat by phlebotomy.

phle·bot·o·my (fli·bot′ə·mē) *n. Surg.* The practice of opening a vein for letting blood as a remedial measure; bloodletting: also called *venesection.* [< OF *flebothomie* < L *phlebotomia* < Gk. < *phleps, phlebos* blood vessel + *temnein* to cut] — **phleb·o·tom·ic** (fleb′ə·tom′ik) or **·i·cal** *adj.* — **phle·bot′o·mist** *n.*

Phleg·e·thon (fleg′ə·thon, flej′-) In Greek mythology, the river of fire, one of the five rivers surrounding Hades. [< Gk. *Phlegethōn*, lit., blazing]

phlegm (flem) *n.* **1.** *Physiol.* A viscid, stringy mucus secreted in the air passages, especially when produced as a discharge through the mouth. **2.** Apathy; indifference. **3.** Cold, undemonstrative temper; self-possession. **4.** One of the four natural humors (the cold and moist) in ancient physiology. [< MF *fleugme* < LL *phlegma* < Gk., flame, phlegm < *phlegein* to burn; reshaped after Gk.]

phleg·ma·si·a do·lens (fleg·mā′zhē·ə dō′lənz) *Pathol.* Milk leg. Also **phlegmasia alba dolens.** [< L < *phlegmasia* inflammation + *dolens, -entis* painful, ppr. of *dolere* to feel pain]

phleg·mat·ic (fleg·mat′ik) *adj.* Not easily moved or excited; sluggish; indifferent. Also **phleg·mat′i·cal.** [< OF *fleumatique* < L *phlegmaticus* < Gk. *phlegmatikos* < *phlegma, -matos.* See PHLEGM.] — **phleg·mat′i·cal·ly** *adv.*

phlegm·y (flem′ē) *adj.* **1.** Relating to, resembling, or containing phlegm. **2.** Phlegmatic in temperament.

phlo·em (flō′em) *n. Bot.* The complex plant tissue composed of sieve tubes with associated cells, serving for the conduction of the sap: also called *bast, liber.* Compare XYLEM. [< G < Gk. *phloos* bark]

phlo·gis·tic (flō·jis′tik) *adj.* **1.** Pertaining to phlogiston or to the theory of its existence. **2.** *Med.* Inflammatory; inflamed. [< Gk. *phlogistos* inflammable. See PHLOGISTON.]

phlo·gis·ton (flō·jis′tən) *n.* The hypothetical substance formerly assumed to be a necessary constituent of all combustible bodies, and to be given up by them in burning. [< NL < Gk., neut. of *phlogistos* flammable < *phlogizein* to set on fire < *phlox, phlogos* flame < *phlegein* to burn]

phlog·o·pite (flog′ə·pīt) *n.* A light brown or reddish brown hydrous silicate of potassium, magnesium, and aluminum resembling muscovite. [< G *phlogopit* < Gk. *phlogōpos* fiery < *phlox, phlogos* flame + *ōps* eye, face]

phlor·i·zin (flôr′ə·zin, flor′-, flə·rī′-) *n. Chem.* A bitter crystalline glycoside, $C_{21}H_{24}O_{10}$, contained in the root bark of the apple, pear, plum, and cherry tree, formerly used in medicine as a tonic. Also **phlo·rid·zin** (flə·rid′zin), **phlo·rhi·zin** (flə·rē′zin). [< Gk. *phloos* bark + *rhiza* root + -IN]

phlox (floks) *n.* Any of a North American genus (*Phlox*) of herbs, with opposite leaves and clusters of variously colored flowers. [< NL < L, kind of flower < Gk., wallflower, lit., flame < *phlegein* to burn]

phlyc·te·na (flik·tē′nə) *n. pl.* **·nae** (-nē) *Pathol.* A small blister containing watery or serous fluid. Also **phlyc·tae′na.** [< NL < Gk. *phlyktaina* blister < *phlyein* to swell]

Phnôm·penh (pə·nôm′pen′) See PNOM-PENH.

-phobe *combining form* One who fears or has an aversion to: *Anglophobe.* [< LL < Gk. *-phobos* fearing < *phobeesthai* to fear]

pho·bi·a (fō′bē·ə) *n.* **1.** A compulsive and persistent fear of any specified type of object, stimulus, or situation. **2.** Any strong aversion or dislike. [< L < Gk. < *phobos* fear] — **pho′bic** (-bik) *adj.*

-phobia *combining form* An exaggerated and persistent dread of or aversion to. [< Gk. *phobos* fear]

In the following list each entry denotes a phobia for what is indicated:

PHLOX
(Plant 2 to 6 feet tall)

acrophobia high places		**hypnophobia** sleep	
agoraphobia open spaces		**kinesophobia** movement	
aichinophobia sharp objects		**lalophobia** speaking	
ailurophobia cats		**musophobia** mice	
androphobia men		**mysophobia** contamination	
apeirophobia infinity		**necrophobia** dead bodies	
astraphobia thunderstorms		**neophobia** new things	
astrophobia stars		**nyctophobia** night, darkness	
autophobia self, being alone		**ophidiophobia** reptiles	
ballistophobia missiles		**pedophobia** infants or children	
bathophobia depths		**phagophobia** eating	
chionophobia snow		**phonophobia** noise	
cynophobia dogs		**psychrophobia** cold	
demophobia crowds		**pyrophobia** fire	
erythrophobia red		**taphephobia** being buried alive	
gamophobia marriage		**thalassophobia** ocean or sea	
gynophobia women		**thanatophobia** death	
haptephobia being touched		**toxicophobia** poison	
hemophobia blood		**zoophobia** animals	

Pho·cae·a (fō-sē′ə) An ancient Ionian port and important maritime state on the Aegean in western Asia Minor.

pho·cine (fō′sīn, -sin) adj. Zool. Of or pertaining to seals.

Pho·ci·on (fō′shē-on), 402?–317 B.C., Athenian statesman and general; executed.

Pho·cis (fō′sis) A region of central Greece north of the Gulf of Corinth.

pho·co·me·li·a (fō′kō-mē′lē-ə, -lyə) n. Pathol. A congenital deformity in which the hands or feet are attached to the trunk by single, very short bones. [< Gk. phōkē seal + NL -melia condition of the limbs < Gk. melos limb]

phoe·be (fē′bē) n. An American flycatcher (Sayornis phoebe) having grayish brown plumage and a slightly crested head, common throughout the eastern United States. Also **phoebe bird.** [Imit. of its cry; infl. in form by PHOEBE]

Phoe·be (fē′bē) In Greek mythology: **a** A Titaness, mother of Leto. **b** A name for Artemis as goddess of the moon. — n. **1.** Poetic The moon. **2.** Saturn's ninth satellite. Also spelled Phebe. [< L < Gk., bright]

Phoe·bus (fē′bəs) In Greek mythology, Apollo as god of the sun. Also **Phoebus Apollo.** — n. Poetic The sun.

Phoe·ni·cia (fə-nē′shə, -nish′ə) An ancient country at the eastern end of the Mediterranean in modern Syria and Lebanon, comprising a group of city-states that flourished around 1200 B.C.: also Phenicia.

Phoe·ni·cian (fə-nē′shən, -nish′ən) adj. Of or pertaining to ancient Phoenicia, its people, or its language. — n. **1.** One of the people of ancient Phoenicia or any of its colonies, as Carthage, ethnically belonging to the Canaanite branch of the Semitic peoples. **2.** The Northwest Semitic language of these people. Also spelled Phenician.

phoe·nix (fē′niks) n. **1.** In Egyptian mythology, a bird of great beauty, said to live for 500 or 600 years in the Arabian Desert and then consume itself by fire, rising from its ashes young and beautiful to live through another cycle, often used as a symbol of immortality. **2.** A person of matchless beauty or excellence; a paragon. Also spelled phenix. [OE fenix < Med.L phenix < L phoenix < Gk. phoinix phoenix, Phoenician, purple red, crimson]

Phoe·nix (fē′niks) A constellation. See CONSTELLATION.

Phoe·nix (fē′niks) The capital of Arizona, in the south central part; pop. 581,562.

Phoenix Islands An island group of the central Pacific administered by Great Britain; Canton and Enderbury are controlled jointly with the United States; 11 sq. mi.

phon- Var. of PHONO-.

phon. **1.** Phonetic(s). **2.** Phonology.

pho·nate (fō′nāt) v.i. ·nat·ed, ·nat·ing **1.** To make speech sounds; articulate. **2.** To set the vocal cords into vibration. [< Gk. phōnē voice + -ATE¹] — **pho·na′tion** n.

phone¹ (fōn) Informal n. A telephone. — v.t. & v.i. **phoned, phon·ing** To telephone. [Short for TELEPHONE]

phone² (fōn) n. Phonet. A sound used in human speech, whether defined in terms of articulatory processes or acoustic attributes. [< Gk. phōnē a sound, voice]

-phone combining form Voice; sound: used in names of musical instruments and other sound-transmitting devices: saxophone, microphone. [< Gk. phōnē voice]

pho·neme (fō′nēm) n. Ling. A class of phonetically similar phones that alternate with each other according to phonetic environment; the smallest contrastive unit in the sound system of language, functioning to distinguish utterances from one another. The English phonemes /t/ and /p/ distinguish the words tin and pin, whereas the varying phonetic qualities of (t) in tip, stop, and pit do not so function and are members of the one phoneme /t/. See ALLOPHONE. [< F phonème < Gk. phōnēma utterance < phōnē voice]

pho·ne·mic (fə-nē′mik, fō-) adj. **1.** Of or referring to phonemes: the phonemic pattern of a language. **2.** Involving distinctive speech sounds: a phonemic difference. — **pho·ne′mi·cal·ly** adv.

pho·ne·mics (fə-nē′miks, fō-) n.pl. (construed as sing.) **1.** A phonemic system. **2.** The study of phonemic systems. Also called phonology.

phonet. Phonetic(s).

pho·net·ic (fə-net′ik, fō-) adj. **1.** Of or pertaining to phonetics, or to speech sounds and their production. **2.** Representing the sounds of speech; especially, designating the representation of each speech sound by a distinct character, or by a distinctive spelling or mark: a phonetic alphabet. Also spelled phonet·ic·al. Abbr. phon., phonet. [< NL < Gk. phōnētikos < phōnē sound] — **pho·net′i·cal·ly** adv.

pho·ne·ti·cian (fō′nə-tish′ən) n. A specialist in phonetics. Also **pho·net·i·cist** (fə-net′ə-sist), **pho′ne·tist.**

phonetic law A description of a pattern of sound changes occurring under given conditions in a language or group of languages, as Grimm's law.

pho·net·ics (fə-net′iks, fō-) n.pl. (construed as sing.) **1.** The branch of linguistics dealing with the analysis, description, and classification of the sounds of speech, including **articulatory phonetics,** the study of the physiological processes in-

volved in speech production, and **acoustic phonetics,** the study of the physical attributes of speech sounds by the use of laboratory instruments. **2.** The system of sounds of a language, roughly equivalent to phonemics: the phonetics of American English. **3.** Loosely, phonetic transcription. Abbr. phon., phonet.

pho·ney (fō′nē) See PHONY.

-phonia See -PHONY.

phon·ic (fon′ik, fō′nik) adj. Pertaining to or of the nature of sound, especially speech sounds.

phon·ics (fon′iks, fō′niks) n.pl. (construed as sing.) **1.** The phonetic rudiments used in teaching reading and pronunciation. **2.** The science of sound; acoustics.

phono- combining form Sound; speech; voice: phonograph. Also, before vowels, phon-. [< Gk. phōnē voice]

pho·no·gram (fō′nə-gram) n. A character symbolizing a speech sound, word, etc. — **pho′no·gram′ic** or **·gram′mic** adj. — **pho′no·gram′i·cal·ly** or **·gram′mi·cal·ly** adv.

pho·no·graph (fō′nə-graf, -gräf) n. A record player.

pho·no·graph·ic (fō′nə-graf′ik) adj. **1.** Pertaining to or produced by a phonograph. **2.** Pertaining to or written in phonography. — **pho′no·graph′i·cal·ly** adv.

phonograph record A grooved disk that reproduces sounds on a record player.

pho·nog·ra·phy (fō-nog′rə-fē, fə-) n. **1.** The art or science of representing words according to a system of sound elements that reduces their graphic reproduction to the simplest form; especially a style of shorthand developed by Isaac Pitman. **2.** The art of representing speech sounds by marks or letters. **3.** The art of making or using phonographs. — **pho·nog′ra·pher, pho·nog′ra·phist** n.

phonol. Phonology.

pho·no·lite (fō′nə-līt) n. A grayish green compact igneous rock composed essentially of orthoclase, nepphelite, and augite. — **pho′no·lit′ic** (-lit′ik) adj.

pho·nol·o·gy (fō-nol′ə-jē) n. **1.** Phonemics. **2.** Phonemics and phonetics taken together. **3.** The history of the sound changes that have taken place in a language, or the study thereof. Abbr. phon., phonol. — **pho·no·log·ic** (fō′nə-loj′ik) or **·i·cal** adj. — **pho′no·log′i·cal·ly** adv. — **pho·nol′o·gist** n.

pho·nom·e·ter (fō-nom′ə-tər, fə-) n. An instrument for measuring the intensity of sounds or the frequency of sound vibrations. — **pho·nom′e·try** n.

pho·no·scope (fō′nə-skōp) n. An instrument for observing, testing, or exhibiting the properties of sounds.

pho·no·type (fō′nə-tīp) n. **1.** A writing or printing alphabet having a distinct character for each speech sound. **2.** Something written or printed in such characters. — **pho′no·typ′ic** (-tip′ik) or **·i·cal** adj. — **pho′no·typ′i·cal·ly** adv.

pho·no·typ·y (fō′nə-tī′pē) n. Phonetic transcription. — **pho′no·typ′ist** n.

pho·ny (fō′ne) U.S. Slang adj. ·ni·er, ·ni·est Fake; false; spurious; counterfeit. — n. pl. ·nies **1.** Something fake or not genuine. **2.** One who tries to be something he is not. Also spelled phoney. [? < British slang fawney man peddler of imitation jewelry, ult. < Irish fainne ring]

-phony combining form A (specified) type of sound or sounds: cacophony. Also -phonia, as in aphonia. [< Gk. phōnē sound, voice]

phoo·ey (foo′ē) interj. An exclamation of disgust, contempt, disappointment, etc.

-phore combining form A bearer or producer of: semaphore. [< NL < Gk. -phoros < pherein to bear]

-phorous combining form Bearing or producing: found in adjectives corresponding to nouns in -phore. [See -PHORE]

phos·gene (fos′jēn) n. Chem. A colorless, highly toxic gas, $COCl_2$, having a suffocating odor, used in organic chemistry and as a chemical warfare agent: also called carbonyl chloride. [< Gk. phōs light + -gene -GEN]

phos·ge·nite (fos′jə-nīt) n. A white, adamantine carbonate and chloride of lead, $Pb_2Cl_2CO_3$, crystallizing in the tetragonal system. [< PHOSGENE + -ITE¹]

phosph- Var. of PHOSPHO-.

phos·pha·tase (fos′fə-tās) n. Biochem. An enzyme found in various animal tissues, as in the kidneys and intestines, that hydrolyzes phospholipids. [< PHOSPHAT(E) + -ASE]

phos·phate (fos′fāt) n. **1.** Chem. A salt or ester of phosphoric acid. **2.** Agric. Any fertilizer valued for its phosphoric acid. **3.** A beverage of carbonated water, containing small amounts of phosphoric acid. [< F] — **phos·phat′ic** adj.

phos·pha·tide (fos′fə-tīd, -tid) n. A phospholipid. [< PHOSPHAT(E) + -IDE]

phos·pha·tize (fos′fə-tīz) v.t. ·tized, ·tiz·ing **1.** To treat with phosphates. **2.** To reduce to a phosphate. — **phos′·pha·ti·za′tion** n.

phos·pha·tu·ri·a (fos′fə-töor′ē-ə, -työor′-) n. Pathol. Excess of phosphates in the urine. [< NL < phosphatum phosphate + Gk. ouron urine] — **phos′pha·tu′ric** adj.

phos·phene (fos′fēn) n. Physiol. The luminous image made by pressing the eyeball through the closed lid, due to

phos·phide (fos'fīd, -fid) *n. Chem.* A compound of phosphorus with a metal, as **calcium phosphide**, Ca_3P_2. Also **phos'phid** (-fid).

phos·phine (fos'fēn, -fin) *n. Chem.* **1.** A colorless, gaseous, flammable, highly toxic hydride of phosphorus, PH_3, with an odor resembling that of putrid fish. **2.** One of a class of compounds derived from phosphine. Also **phos'phin** (-fin).

phos·phite (fos'fīt) *n.* A salt of phosphorous acid.

phospho- *combining form* Phosphorus; of or containing phosphorus, or any of its compounds: *phospholipid.* Also, before vowels, **phosph-**. [< PHOSPHORUS]

phos·pho·cre·a·tine (fos'fō-krē'ə-tēn, -tin) *n. Biochem.* An organic compound, $C_4H_{10}O_5N_3P$, present in muscle tissue, to which it supplies the energy for contraction. [< PHOSPHO(RIC ACID) + CREATINE]

phos·pho·lip·id (fos'fō-lip'id) *n. Biochem.* Any of a group of fatty substances widely distributed in plant and animal tissue: also called *phosphatide.* [< PHOSPHO- + LIPID]

phos·pho·ni·um (fos·fō'nē·əm) *n. Chem.* The univalent radical PH_4, resembling ammonium and forming crystalline halides. [< PHOSPH(ORUS) (AMM)ONIUM]

phos·pho·pro·te·in (fos'fō-prō'tē-in, -tēn) *n. Biochem.* Any of a class of conjugated proteins containing phosphoric acid combined with the hydroxyl group of certain amino acids, as the casein of milk.

phos·phor (fos'fər) *n.* **1.** Phosphorus. **2.** Any of a class of substances that will emit light under the action of certain chemicals or radiations. — *adj.* Phosphorescent. [< L *phosphorus.* See PHOSPHORUS.]

Phos·phor (fos'fər) *n. Poetic* The morning star, especially Venus, as the harbinger of day. Also **Phos'phore**. [< L *Phosphorus* < Gk. *phōsphoros.* See PHOSPHORUS.]

phos·pho·rate (fos'fə-rāt') *v.t.* **·rat·ed, ·rat·ing** To combine with phosphorus.

phosphor bronze An alloy of copper and tin containing small amounts of phosphorus, noted for its toughness, durability, and high tensile strength.

phos·phor·esce (fos'fə-res') *v.i.* **·esced, ·esc·ing** To glow with a faint light unaccompanied by sensible heat. [? Back formation < PHOSPHORESCENT]

phos·phor·es·cence (fos'fə-res'əns) *n.* **1.** The emission of light without sensible heat; also, the light so emitted. **2.** The property of continuing to shine in the dark after exposure to light, shown by many mineral substances: distinguished from *fluorescence.*

phos·phor·es·cent (fos'fə-res'ənt) *adj.* Exhibiting phosphorescence: also *phosphor.* [< PHOSPHORUS + -ESCENT]

phos·phor·et·ed (fos'fə-ret'id) *adj. Chem.* Combined with phosphorus: *phosphoreted* hydrogen. Also **phos'phor·et·ted, phos'phu·ret·ed** (-fyə·ret'id) or **·ret'ted.**

phos·phor·ic (fos·fôr'ik, -for'-) *adj. Chem.* Pertaining to or derived from phosphorus, especially in its highest valence.

phosphoric acid *Chem.* One of three acids of phosphorus known respectively as *metaphosphoric acid* (HPO_3), *orthophosphoric acid* (H_3PO_4), and *pyrophosphoric acid* ($H_4P_2O_7$).

phos·phor·ism (fos'fə-riz'əm) *n. Pathol.* Chronic phosphorus poisoning.

phos·phor·ite (fos'fə-rīt) *n.* **1.** A massive fibrous variety of apatite. **2.** Phosphate rock in general.

phos·phor·o·scope (fos'fər·ə·skōp') *n.* An apparatus for measuring the duration of phosphorescent light after the source is withdrawn. [< PHOSPHOR(ESCENT) + -SCOPE]

phos·pho·rous (fos'fər·əs, fos·fôr'əs, -fō'rəs) *adj. Chem.* Of, pertaining to, resembling, containing, or derived from phosphorus, especially in its lower valence.

phosphorous acid *Chem.* A crystalline acid, H_3PO_3, with a garlic taste, obtained by the oxidation of phosphorus.

phos·pho·rus (fos'fər·əs) *n.* **1.** A soft, nonmetallic element (symbol P), occurring in several allotropic forms. White or yellow phosphorus is luminous in the dark, highly flammable, and poisonous. Red phosphorus does not glow, is less flammable, and nonpoisonous. See ELEMENT. **2.** Any phosphorescent substance. Also called *phosphor.* [< NL < L *Phosphorus* morning star < Gk. *phōsphoros* light-bringing < *phōs* light + *-phoros* bearing < *pherein* to bear]

phot (fot, fōt) *n.* The cgs unit of illumination, equal to one lumen per square centimeter. [< Gk. *phōs, phōtos* light]

phot. Photograph; photographic; photography.

pho·tic (fō'tik) *adj.* **1.** Of or relating to light or to the production of light. **2.** Designating those underwater regions penetrated by sunlight: the *photic* zone.

Pho·ti·us (fō'shē·əs, -shəs) died 891? patriarch of Constantinople; his dispute with the Pope marked the beginning of the schism between the Greek and Latin churches.

pho·to (fō'tō) *n. pl.* **·tos** *Informal* A photograph. [Short for PHOTOGRAPH]

photo- *combining form* **1.** Light; of, pertaining to, or produced by light: *photometer.* **2.** Photograph; photographic: *photoengrave.* [< Gk. *phōs, phōtos* light]

pho·to·ac·tin·ic (fō'tō·ak·tin'ik) *adj.* Capable of emitting actinic radiation.

pho·to·bath·ic (fō'tō·bath'ik) *adj.* Of or pertaining to ocean depths to which sunlight reaches. [< PHOTO- + Gk. *bathos* depth < *bathys* deep]

pho·to·bi·ot·ic (fō'tō·bī·ot'ik) *adj.* **1.** Living in the light. **2.** Requiring light for life or development.

pho·to·cath·ode (fō'tō·kath'ōd) *n. Electronics* The electrode in a photoelectric cell that emits electrons.

pho·to·cell (fō'tō·sel') *n.* A photoelectric cell (which see).

pho·to·chem·is·try (fō'tō·kem'is·trē) *n.* The branch of chemistry dealing with chemical reactions produced or influenced by light. — **pho'to·chem'i·cal** *adj.*

pho·to·chro·mat·ic (fō'tō·krō·mat'ik) *adj. Physics* Exhibiting photochromatism.

pho·to·chro·ma·tism (fō'tō·krō'mə·tiz'əm) *n. Physics* The property of changing color under irradiation by the light of a suitable wavelength or in some cases simply by removal of the stimulating radiation.

pho·to·chron·o·graph (fō'tō·kron'ə·graf, -gräf) *n.* **1.** An instrument for taking a sequence of instantaneous, regularly timed photographs of a body in motion, as of a star. **2.** A photograph so taken. **3.** A device for measuring very brief intervals of time. — **pho'to·chro·nog'ra·phy** (-krə·nog'rə·fē) *n.*

pho·to·com·pos·er (fō'tō·kəm·pō'zər) *n.* Any machine or apparatus used in the process of photocomposition.

pho·to·com·po·si·tion (fō'tō·kom'pə·zish'ən) *n.* The composing of printed matter by photographic means rather than directly from movable type.

pho·to·con·duc·tion (fō'tō·kən·duk'shən) *n. Physics* The property whereby a substance exhibits increased electrical conductivity when subjected to light waves. — **pho'to·con·duc'tive** (-duk'tiv) *adj.* — **pho'to·con·duc·tiv'i·ty** *n.*

pho·to·cop·y (fō'tō·kop'ē) *n. pl.* **·cop·ies** A photographic reproduction of printed or illustrative matter. — *v.t. & v.i.* **·cop·ied, ·cop·y·ing** To copy (printed matter, etc.) by a photographic process.

pho·to·cur·rent (fō'tō·kûr'ənt) *n.* An electric current produced by the action of light or by a photoelectric cell.

pho·to·dra·ma (fō'tə·drä'mə, -dram'ə) *n.* A motion picture or photoplay. — **pho'to·dra·mat'ic** (-drə·mat'ik) *adj.*

pho·to·dy·nam·ic (fō'tō·dī·nam'ik, -di·nam'-) *adj.* Of, pertaining to, or operating by the energy of light.

pho·to·dy·nam·ics (fō'tō·dī·nam'iks, -di·nam'-) *n.pl.* (*construed as sing.*) The study of the action and influence of light on plants and animals.

pho·to·e·lec·tric (fō'tō·i·lek'trik) *adj.* Of or pertaining to the electrical or electronic effects due to the action of light. Also **pho'to·e·lec'tri·cal.**

photoelectric cell An electron tube, one of whose electrodes is sensitive to variations in the intensity of light falling upon it, incorporated in electrical circuits as a controlling, testing, and counting device: also called *electric eye, photocell, phototube.*

pho·to·e·lec·tron (fō'tō·i·lek'tron) *n.* An electron emitted from a metal surface when exposed to suitable radiation.

pho·to·e·lec·tro·type (fō'tō·i·lek'trə·tīp) *n.* **1.** An electrotype produced by a photomechanical process. **2.** A picture printed from such a block.

pho·to·en·grave (fō'tō·in·grāv') *v.t.* **·graved, ·grav·ing** To reproduce by photoengraving. — **pho'to·en·grav'er** *n.*

pho·to·en·grav·ing (fō'tō·in·grā'ving) *n.* **1.** The act or process of producing by the aid of photography a relief block or plate for printing. **2.** A plate or picture so produced.

photo finish **1.** A race so closely contested that only a photograph of the finish can determine the winner. **2.** *Informal* Any race or competition decided by a slim margin.

pho·to·flash bulb (fō'tō·flash') *Photog.* A flash bulb (which see).

pho·to·flood lamp (fō'tō·flud') *Photog.* An electric lamp operating at excess voltage to give high illumination.

photog. Photograph; photographic; photography.

pho·to·gel·a·tin process (fō'tō·jel'ə·tin) *Printing* Collotype (def. 1).

pho·to·gene (fō'tō·jēn) *n. Physiol.* An afterimage (def. 1).

pho·to·gen·ic (fō'tō·jen'ik) *adj.* **1.** Being a good subject for a photograph, especially for esthetic reasons. **2.** *Biol.* Producing phosphorescence, as fireflies. [< PHOTO- + -GENIC] — **pho'to·gen'i·cal·ly** *adv.*

pho·to·ge·ol·o·gy (fō'tō·jē·ol'ə·jē) *n. Geol.* The study of aerial photographs for the purpose of obtaining geological data. — **pho'to·ge'o·log'i·cal** (-jē'ə·loj'i·kəl) *adj.*

pho·to·gram·me·try (fō'tō·gram'ə·trē) *n.* The art and technique of making surveys or maps by means of photographs. [< *photogram,* var. of PHOTOGRAPH + -METRY]

pho·to·graph (fō'tə·graf, -gräf) *n.* A picture taken by photography. Abbr. *phot., photog.* — *v.t.* **1.** To take a photograph of. — *v.i.* **2.** To practice photography. **3.** To be depicted in photographs: He *photographs* beautifully. [< PHOTO- + -GRAPH]

pho·tog·ra·pher (fə·tog'rə·fər) *n.* One who takes photographs or makes a business of photography.

pho·to·graph·ic (fō'tə·graf'ik) *adj.* **1.** Of, pertaining to, used in, or produced by photography. **2.** Of or like a photograph. Also **pho'to·graph'i·cal.** Abbr. *phot., photog.* — **pho'to·graph'i·cal·ly** *adv.*

pho·tog·ra·phy (fə·tog′rə·fē) *n.* **1.** The process of forming and fixing an image of an object or objects by the chemical action of light and other forms of radiant energy on photo-sensitive surfaces. **2.** The art or business of producing and printing photographs. Abbr. *phot., photog.*

pho·to·gra·vure (fō′tō·grə·vyŏŏr′, -grāv′yər) *n.* **1.** The process of making an intaglio plate from a photograph for use in printing. **2.** A picture produced from such a plate. [< F]

pho·to·he·li·o·graph (fō′tō·hē′lē·ə·graf′, -gräf′) *n.* A telescopic camera for taking pictures of the sun.

pho·to·jour·nal·ism (fō′tō·jûr′nəl·iz′əm) *n.* A form of journalism in which a story or news item is recounted largely by means of photographs. — **pho′to·jour′nal·ist** *n.*

pho·to·ki·ne·sis (fō′tō·ki·nē′sis) *n. Biol.* Movement under the influence of light. — **pho′to·ki·net′ic** (-ki·net′ik) *adj.*

pho·to·lith·o·graph (fō′tō·lith′ə·graf, -gräf) *v.t.* To reproduce by photolithography. — *n.* A picture produced by photolithography.

pho·to·li·thog·ra·phy (fō′tō·li·thog′rə·fē) *n.* The art or operation of producing on stone, largely by photographic means, a printing surface from which impressions may be taken by a lithographic process. — **pho′to·lith′o·graph′ic** (-lith′ə·graf′ik) *adj.*

pho·tol·y·sis (fō·tol′ə·sis) *n.* Chemical or biological decomposition due to the action of light. [< NL < Gk. *phōs, phōtos* light + *lysis* a loosening < *lyein* to loosen] — **pho·to·lyt·ic** (fō′tō·lit′ik) *adj.*

photom. Photometrical; photometry.

pho·to·map (fō′tō·map′) *n.* A map composed of one or more aerial photographs.

pho·to·me·chan·i·cal (fō′tō·mi·kan′i·kəl) *adj.* Designating or pertaining to any of various processes by which plates may be prepared for printing with the aid of photography. — **pho′to·me·chan′i·cal·ly** *adv.*

pho·tom·e·ter (fō·tom′ə·tər) *n.* Any instrument for measuring the intensity of light or comparing the relative intensity of several lights.

pho·tom·e·try (fō·tom′ə·trē) *n.* **1.** The measurement of the intensity of light, especially with a photometer. **2.** The branch of optics that treats of such measurement. — **pho·to·met·ric** (fō′tə·met′rik) or **-ri·cal** *adj.* — **pho·tom′e·trist** *n.*

pho·to·mi·cro·graph (fō′tō·mī′krə·graf, -gräf) *n.* A photograph taken through a microscope; a microphotograph. — **pho·to·mi·crog·ra·phy** (fō′tō·mī·krog′rə·fē) *n.*

pho·to·mon·tage (fō′tō·mon·täzh′, -môn-) *n.* **1.** The process of montage with photographs. **2.** A picture produced by this process.

pho·to·mu·ral (fō′tō·myŏŏr′əl) *n.* A photograph enlarged to a considerable size, used for wall decoration.

pho·ton (fō′ton) *n. Physics* A quantum of radiant energy moving with the velocity of light and an energy proportional to its frequency: also called *light quantum.* [< PHOTO- + (ELECTR)ON] — **pho·ton′ic** *adj.*

Pho·ton (fō′ton) *n.* A keyboard-operated machine assembly for the composition of printed matter by means of high-speed photography and photoelectric action: a trade name.

pho·to·nu·cle·ar (fō′tō·nōō′klē·ər, -nyōō′-) *adj. Physics* Of, pertaining to, or designating a reaction initiated in an atomic nucleus by a photon.

pho·to·off·set (fō′tō·ôf′set, -of′-) *n.* Offset printing from a metal surface on which the text or design has been imprinted by photography.

pho·to·pe·ri·od (fō′tō·pir′ē·əd) *n.* The length of day most favorable to the growth of a specified plant. — **pho′to·pe′ri·od′ic** (-pir′ē·od′ik) *adj.*

pho·toph·i·lous (fō·tof′ə·ləs) *adj. Biol.* Flourishing in light. — **pho·toph′i·ly** (-fō·fil′ik) — **pho·toph′i·ly** *n.*

pho·to·pho·bi·a (fō′tə·fō′bē·ə) *n.* **1.** Aversion to or intolerance of light. **2.** *Pathol.* Abnormal sensitivity of the eye to light. — **pho′to·pho′bic** *adj.*

pho·to·pi·a (fō·tō′pē·ə) *n.* Vision under lighting conditions that permit color discrimination. [< NL < Gk. *phōs, phōtos* light + *ōps, ōpos* eye] — **pho·top′ic** (-top′ik) *adj.*

pho·to·play (fō′tō·plā′) *n.* A play arranged for or presented in a motion-picture performance.

pho·to·re·cep·tor (fō′tō·ri·sep′tər) *n. Physiol.* A nerve receptor sensitive to light stimuli.

pho·to·sen·si·tive (fō′tō·sen′sə·tiv) *adj.* Sensitive to light. — **pho′to·sen′si·tiv′i·ty** *n.*

pho·to·spec·tro·scope (fō′tō·spek′trə·skōp) *n.* A spectrograph (def. 1).

pho·to·sphere (fō′tə·sfir′) *n. Astron.* The visible shining surface of the sun. — **pho′to·spher′ic** (-sfir′ik, -sfer′-) *adj.*

pho·to·sta·ble (fō′tə·stā′bəl) *adj.* Unaffected by or resistant to the influence of light.

pho·to·stat (fō′tə·stat) *v.t. & v.i.* **·stat·ed** or **·stat·ted, ·stat·ing** or **·stat·ting** To make a reproduction (of) with a Photostat. — *n.* The reproduction so produced. [< PHOTO- + -STAT] — **pho′to·stat′ic** *adj.*

Pho·to·stat (fō′tə·stat) *n.* A camera designed to reproduce facsimiles of documents, drawings, etc., directly as positives: a trade name. Also **pho′to·stat.**

pho·to·syn·the·sis (fō′tō·sin′thə·sis) *n. Biochem.* The process by which plants form carbohydrates from carbon dioxide, inorganic salts, and water through the agency of sunlight acting upon chlorophyll. — **pho′to·syn·thet′ic** (-sin·thet′ik) *adj.*

pho·to·tax·is (fō′tō·tak′sis) *n. Biol.* The reaction of an organism with reference to a source of light, called **negative phototaxis** when the movement is away from the light and **positive phototaxis** when the movement is toward the light. Also **pho′to·tax′y.** [< NL < Gk. *phōs, phōtos* light + *taxis* arrangement] — **pho′to·tac′tic** (-tak′tik) *adj.*

pho·to·tel·e·graph (fō′tō·tel′ə·graf, -gräf) *v.t. & v.i.* To transmit by phototelegraphy. — *n.* Something so transmitted.

pho·to·te·leg·ra·phy (fō′tō·tə·leg′rə·fē) *n.* The electrical or telegraphic transmission of messages, photographs, etc., by facsimile; telephotography. — **pho′to·tel′e·graph′ic** (-tel′ə·graf′ik) *adj.*

pho·to·tel·e·scope (fō′tō·tel′ə·skōp) *n.* A telescope equipped with a device for photographing the heavenly bodies. — **pho′to·tel′e·scop′ic** (-tel′ə·skop′ik) *adj.*

pho·to·ther·a·peu·tic (fō′tō·ther′ə·pyōō′tik) *adj. Med.* Of or pertaining to phototherapy.

pho·to·ther·a·py (fō′tō·ther′ə·pē) *n. Med.* Treatment of diseases, especially skin diseases, by the application of light. Also **pho′to·ther′a·peu′tics** (-ther′ə·pyōō′tiks) *n.*

pho·to·ther·mic (fō′tō·thûr′mik) *adj.* **1.** Denoting the thermic activity of light rays. **2.** Of or involving the combined action of heat and light.

pho·to·tim·er (fō′tō·tī′mər) *n.* **1.** An electrical device that photographs the finish of a race and records the exact time of the winner. **2.** A device that automatically adjusts the amount of exposure in X-ray machines, etc.

pho·tot·o·nus (fō·tot′ə·nəs) *n. Biol.* **1.** The influence of light upon the movement and growth of plants. **2.** Increased irritability or motility induced by exposure to light. [< NL < Gk. *phōs, phōtos* light + *tonos* tension. See TONE.] — **pho·to·ton·ic** (fō′tə·ton′ik) *adj.*

pho·to·pog·ra·phy (fō′tō·tə·pog′rə·fē) *n.* The art and technique of preparing topographic maps with the aid of photographs. — **pho′to·top′o·graph′ic** (-top′ə·graf′ik) *adj.*

pho·to·tran·sis·tor (fō′tō·tran·zis′tər) *n.* A transistorlike device in which one pair of electrodes is replaced by a beam of light that controls the current between another pair.

pho·to·trop·ic (fō′tə·trop′ik) *adj. Biol.* Turning in a particular direction under the influence of light. — **pho′to·trop′i·cal·ly** *adv.*

pho·tot·ro·pism (fō·tot′rə·piz′əm) *n. Biol.* Phototropic growth or response.

pho·to·tube (fō′tō·tōōb′, -tyōōb′) *n.* A photoelectric cell.

pho·to·type (fō′tə·tīp′) *n.* **1.** A relief plate made for printing by photography. **2.** The process by which it is produced. **3.** A picture printed from such a plate. — **pho′to·typ′ic** (-tip′ik) *adj.*

pho·to·ty·pog·ra·phy (fō′tō·tī·pog′rə·fē) *n.* Any photomechanical process of engraving in relief that may be reproduced along with type on a printing press. — **pho′to·ty′po·graph′ic** (-tī′pə·graf′ik) *adj.*

pho·to·typ·y (fō′tō·tī′pē) *n.* The production or use of phototypes.

pho·to·vol·ta·ic (fō′tō·vol·tā′ik) *adj.* Capable of producing an electromotive force under the action of light.

pho·to·zin·cog·ra·phy (fō′tō·zing·kog′rə·fē) *n.* Photoengraving in which a sensitized zinc plate is used.

phr. Phrase.

phras·al (frā′zəl) *adj.* Of the nature of, pertaining to, or composed of a phrase or phrases.

phrase (frāz) *n.* **1.** *Gram.* A group of two or more associated words, not containing a subject and predicate: distinguished from *clause.* **2.** In speaking and reading aloud, a word or group of words spoken in one breath, preceded and followed by pauses. **3.** A concise, catchy, often original expression: a happy *phrase.* **4.** A series of dance movements considered as a unit in a dance pattern. **5.** *Music* A short division of time comprising several statements of one or more motifs. — *v.t. & v.i.* **phrased, phras·ing** **1.** To express or be expressed in words or phrases. **2.** To divide (a sentence, etc.) into phrases when speaking or reading aloud. **3.** *Music* To execute or divide (a melody) into phrases. [< LL *phrasis* diction < Gk., speech < *phrazein* to point out, tell]

phra·se·o·gram (frā′zē·ə·gram′) *n.* A symbol or combination of signs standing for a phrase, as in shorthand. [< PHRASE + -GRAM; on analogy with PHRASEOLOGY]

phra·se·o·graph (frā′zē·ə·graf′, -gräf′) *n.* A phrase having a symbol or phraseogram. — **phra′se·o·graph′ic** *adj.*

phra·se·ol·o·gist (frā′zē·ol′ə·jist) *n.* **1.** One who makes or collects phrases.

phra·se·ol·o·gy (frā′zē·ol′ə·jē) *n. pl.* **·gies** **1.** The choice and arrangement of words and phrases in expressing ideas.

2. A compilation or handbook of phrases. — **Syn.** See DICTION. [< NL *phraseologia* < Gk., irregularly formed < Gk. *phrasis, -eos* speech + *logos* word] — **phra′se·o·log′i·cal** (-ə-loj′i·kəl) *adj*

phrase structure *Ling.* The basic structure of a sentence as determined by a series of progressive breakdowns into immediate constituents.

phras·ing (frā′zing) *n.* **1.** The act of making phrases; wording. **2.** Manner or form of verbal expression. **3.** *Music* The rendition of musical phrases in performance.

phra·try (frā′trē) *n.* *pl.* **·tries 1.** A tribal unit among primitive peoples, as a group of clans. **2.** In ancient Athens, a clan or subdivision of a phyle. [< Gk. *phratria* < *phratēr* clansman, brother] — **phra′tric** *adj*.

phre·at·ic (frē·at′ik) *adj.* Of or pertaining to underground waters, especially those accessible through wells: distinguished from *vadose*. [< Gk. *phrear, phreatos* well]

phren. Phrenological; phrenology.

phre·net·ic (frə·net′ik) See FRENETIC.

phren·ic (fren′ik) *adj.* **1.** Of or pertaining to the mind. **2.** *Anat.* Of or pertaining to the diaphragm. [< NL *phrenicus* or F *phrénique* < Gk. *phrēn, phrenos* diaphragm, mind]

phre·ni·tis (fri·nī′tis) *n.* *Pathol.* **1.** Wild delirium; frenzy. **2.** Inflammation of the diaphragm. [< LL < Gk., delirium < *phrēn, phrenos* diaphragm, mind]

phreno- *combining form* **1.** Mind; brain: *phrenotropic.* **2.** Diaphragm; of or related to the diaphragm. Also, before vowels, **phren-.** [< Gk. *phrēn, phrenos* the diaphragm (thought to be the seat of intellect)]

phre·nol·o·gy (fri·nol′ə·jē) *n.* The doctrine that the conformation of the human skull indicates the position and degree of development of various mental faculties and characteristics. [< Gk. *phrēn, phrenos* mind + -LOGY] — **phren·o·log·ic** (fren′ə·loj′ik) or **·i·cal** *adj.* — **phre·nol′o·gist** *n.*

phren·sy (fren′zē) See FRENZY.

phren·o·tro·pic (fren′ə·trop′ik) *adj. Med.* Acting upon, influencing, or affecting the mind, as certain drugs.

Phrix·us (frik′səs) In Greek legend, son of Athamas and Nephele, who escaped his stepmother on a ram with a golden fleece and sacrificed the ram upon his safe arrival in Colchis.

Phryg·i·a (frij′ē·ə) An ancient country in West Central Asia Minor divided into **Greater Phrygia**, the central part, and **Lesser Phrygia**, the NW section.

Phryg·i·an (frij′ē·ən) *adj.* Of or pertaining to Phrygia or its people. — *n.* **1.** A native or inhabitant of Phrygia. **2.** The Indo-European language of this people, known from a few inscriptions.

Phrygian cap A liberty cap (which see).

PHS Public Health Service.

phthal·e·in (thal′ē·in, -ēn, fthal′-) *n. Chem.* Any of a series of compounds formed by combining a phenol with phthalic acid or its anhydride, and yielding dyes in some derivatives. Also **phthal′e·ine.** [< PHTHAL(IC) + -ein, var. of -IN]

phthal·ic (thal′ik, fthal′-) *adj. Chem.* Of, pertaining to, or derived from naphthalene. [Short for NAPHTHALIC]

phthalic acid *Chem.* One of three aromatic crystalline compounds, $C_8H_6O_4$, derived variously, as by the oxidation of naphthalene.

phthal·in (thal′in, fthal′-) *n. Chem.* Any of several colorless crystalline compounds obtained by reducing phthalein. Also **phthal′ine.** [< PHTHAL(EIN) + -IN]

phthi·ri·a·sis (thi·rī′ə·sis, fthi-) *n. Pathol.* Pediculosis. [< L < Gk. *phtheiriasis* < *phtheirian* to be lousy < *phtheir* louse]

phthis·ic (tiz′ik) *n.* **1.** *Pathol.* Phthisis (def. 1). **2.** Difficulty in breathing; asthma. — *adj.* Phthisical. [< OF *tisike* < L *phthisicus* < Gk. *phthisikos* consumptive < *phthisis.* See PHTHISIS.]

phthis·i·cal (tiz′i·kəl) *adj.* **1.** *Pathol.* Of, relating to, or affected by phthisis. **2.** Asthmatic; wheezy. Also *phthisic.* Also **phthis·ick·y** (tiz′ik·ē).

phthi·sis (thī′sis, fthī′-) *n. Pathol.* **1.** Tuberculosis of the lungs: also called *phthisic.* **2.** Any continuous destruction of tissue; progressive emaciation. [< L < Gk., a wasting away < *phthinein* to decay]

-phyceae *combining form Bot.* Seaweed: used in the names of various classes of algae: *Rhodophyceae.* [< Gk. *phykos* seaweed]

phyco- *combining form* Seaweed; of or related to seaweed: *phycology.* [< Gk. *phykos* seaweed]

phy·col·o·gy (fī·kol′ə·jē) *n.* The branch of botany dealing with seaweeds or algae. — **phy·col′o·gist** *n.* — **phy′co·log′i·cal** *adj.*

phy·co·my·ce·tous (fī′kō·mī·sē′təs) *adj. Bot.* Pertaining or belonging to a class of fungi (*Phycomycetes*) resembling algae but destitute of chlorophyll, and including the water molds and downy mildews. [< NL < Gk. *phykos* seaweed + *mykēs, -ētos* mushroom]

Phyfe (fīf), **Duncan**, 1768?–1854, U.S. cabinetmaker born in Scotland.

phy·la (fī′lə) Plural of PHYLUM.

phy·lac·ter·y (fi·lak′tər·ē) *n.* *pl.* **·ter·ies 1.** In traditional Judaism, one of two small leather cases containing a strip or strips of parchment inscribed with Scriptural passages, and having thongs for binding on the forehead or around the left arm during morning prayer, except on Sabbath and holy days. *Deut.* vi 8 and xi 18; *Ex.* xiii 9, 16. **2.** An inscribed scroll represented in medieval art as held in the hands or issuing from the mouths of angels. **3.** A charm or amulet. **4.** Among the early Christians, a case containing a relic. [< LL *phylacterium* < Gk. *phylaktērion* safeguard < *phylaktēr* guard < *phylassein* to guard]

phy·le (fī′lē) *n.* *pl.* **·lae** (-lē) A political subdivision in ancient Athens. [< Gk. *phylē* tribe]

phy·let·ic (fi·let′ik) *adj.* **1.** *Biol.* Of or pertaining to a phylum or to a genetic type or strain; racial. **2.** Pertaining to a phyle or clan. Also **phy·lic** (fī′lik). [< Gk. *phyletikos* < *phyletēs* tribesman < *phylē* tribe] — **phy·let′i·cal·ly** *adv.*

Phyl·lis (fil′is) A country girl in Vergil's *Eclogues.*

phyl·lite (fil′īt) *n.* A lustrous schistose rock containing small particles of mica. [< Gk. *phyllon* leaf + -ITE[1]]

phyllo- *combining form* Leaf; pertaining to a leaf: *phyllotaxis.* Also, before vowels, **phyll-.** [< Gk. *phyllon* leaf]

phyl·lo·clade (fil′ə·klād) *n. Bot.* A flat branch that functions as a leaf, as in the cacti. Also **phyl′lo·clad** (-klad). [< NL *phyllocladium* < Gk. *phyllon* leaf + *klados* branch]

phyl·lode (fil′ōd) *n.* *pl.* **phyl·lo·di·a** (fi·lō′dē·ə) *Bot.* A petiole that flattens out and assumes the shape and function of a leaf. [< F < NL *phyllodium* < Gk. *phyllōdēs* leaflike < *phyllon* leaf + *eidos* form] — **phyl·lo′di·al** *adj.*

phyl·loid (fil′oid) *adj.* Resembling a leaf; foliaceous. [< NL *phylloma* < Gk. *phyllōma* foliage < *phyllon* leaf]

phyl·lome (fil′ōm) *n. Bot.* A leaf or its equivalent. [< NL *phylloma* < Gk. *phyllōma* foliage < *phyllon* to clothe with leaves < *phyllon* leaf] — **phyl·lom·ic** (fi·lom′ik) *adj.*

phyl·lo·pod (fil′ə·pod) *n.* Any of a suborder of crustaceans (*Phyllopoda*), characterized by elongated bodies and leaflike swimming and respiratory organs. — *adj.* **1.** Having leaflike feet. **2.** Of or pertaining to the phyllopods. [< NL *Phyllopoda* < Gk. *phyllon* leaf + *pous, podos* foot] — **phyl·lop·o·dan** (fi·lop′ə·dən) *n. & adj.*

phyl·lo·tax·is (fil′ə·tak′sis) *n. Bot.* **1.** The arrangement of leaves upon a stem. **2.** The laws of this arrangement. **phyl′lo·tax′y.** [< NL < Gk. *phyllon* leaf + *taxis* arrangement < *tassein* to arrange] — **phyl′lo·tac′tic** (-tak′tik) *adj.*

-phyllous *combining form* Having (a specified kind or number of) leaves: *monophyllous.* [< Gk. *phyllon* leaf]

phyl·lox·e·ra (fil′ək·sir′ə, fi·lok′sər·ə) *n.* *pl.* **·rae** (-rē) A minute plant louse (family *Phylloxeridae*); especially, the **grape phylloxera** (*Dactylosphaera vitifoliae*), that is very destructive to grapevines. For illustration see INSECTS (injurious). [< NL < Gk. *phyllon* leaf + *xēros* dry]

phylo- *combining form* Tribe; race; species: *phylogeny.* Also, before vowels, **phyl-.** [< Gk. *phylē, phylon* tribe]

phy·log·e·ny (fī·loj′ə·nē) *n.* *pl.* **·nies 1.** *Biol.* The history of the evolution of a species or group: distinguished from *ontogeny.* **2.** Tribal or racial history. Also **phy·lo·gen·e·sis** (fī′lə·jen′ə·sis). [< G *phylogenie* < Gk. *phylon* race + *-geneia* birth, origin] — **phy′lo·ge·net′ic** (-jə·net′ik) *adj.* — **phy′lo·ge·net′i·cal·ly** *adv.* — **phy′lo·gen′ic** *adj.*

phy·lum (fī′ləm) *n.* *pl.* **·la** (-lə) **1.** *Biol.* A great division of animals or plants ranking next below a subkingdom and above a class, of which the members are believed to have a common evolutionary ancestor. **2.** *Ling.* A broad division of languages in which apparently related linguistic stocks or families are grouped. [< NL < Gk. *phylon* race]

-phyre *combining form Geol.* A porphyritic rock: *granophyre.* [< F < *porphyre* < OF *porfire.* See PORPHYRY.]

phys. **1.** Physical. **2.** Physician. **3.** Physicist; physics.

physi- Var. of PHYSIO-.

phys·ic (fiz′ik) *n.* **1.** Medicine in general. **2.** A cathartic; a purge. **3.** *Archaic* The art or practice of medicine. **4.** *Obs.* Physics. — *v.t.* **·icked, ·ick·ing 1.** To treat with medicine, especially with a cathartic. **2.** To cure or relieve. [< OF *fisique* < L *physica* < Gk. *physikē* (*epistēmē*) (the knowledge) of nature < *physis* nature < *phyein* to produce]

phys·i·cal (fiz′i·kəl) *adj.* **1.** Of or relating to the human body, as distinguished from the mind or spirit; carnal: a *physical* defect; *physical* love. **2.** Of the nature of or pertaining to matter or material things. **3.** Of or relating to the material universe or to the sciences that treat of it. **4.** Of or pertaining to physics: a *physical* law. **5.** Apparent to the senses; external; *physical* changes. — *n.* A physical examination of the body. Abbr. *phys.* [< Med.L *physicalis* < L *physica.* See PHYSIC.] — **phys′i·cal·ly** *adv.*

— **Syn. 1.** *Physical, bodily, corporeal,* and *corporal* refer to the body as opposed to the mind or spirit. *Physical* and *bodily* are largely interchangeable, but *bodily* makes clearer reference to the human body: *physical* distress, *bodily* discomfort. *Corporeal* more clearly contrasts with spiritual or immaterial; it also means having a body, or organized into a whole: the *corporeal* law. *Corporal* was originally interchangeable with *bodily,* but is now restricted to that which is applied to or inflicted on the body: *corporal* punishment. **2.** *Physical* and *material* refer to the matter of which the universe is composed. *Physical* suggests form, structure, relation, as *material* does not; we speak of *physical* properties, or *physical* forces, but of *material* substances such as chemical elements. The *physical* world is always perceptible to the senses, but the *material* world may not be: the *physical* geography of a region, the *material* side of life.

physical anthropology The branch of anthropology that deals with the evolution of man, his zoological position, physical and anatomical characteristics, racial differentiation, and the genetic relationships among ethnic groups.

physical chemistry The branch of chemistry that deals with the physical properties of substances, especially with reference to the laws governing their quantitative energy transformations and chemical interactions.

physical education Athletic training and development of the human body; also, education in hygiene.

physical geography Geography dealing with the natural features of the earth, as vegetation, land forms, drainage, ocean currents, climate, etc.: also called *physiography*.

physical science Any of the sciences that treat of the structure, properties, and energy relations of matter apart from the phenomena of life, as physics, astronomy, chemistry, geology, etc.

physical therapy The treatment of disability, injury, and disease by external physical means, as by electricity, heat, light, massage, exercise, etc.: also called *physiotherapy*.

phy·si·cian (fi·zish′ən)   *n.* **1.** One who is legally authorized to practice medicine; a doctor. **2.** A doctor engaged in general practice, as distinguished from a surgeon. **3.** Any healer. Abbr. *phys.* [< OF *fisicien* < L *physica.* See PHYSIC.]

phys·i·cist (fiz′ə·sist)   *n.* A student of or specialist in physics. Abbr. *phys.*

physico- *combining form* Physics: *physicochemical.* [< Gk. *physikos* < *physis* nature. See PHYSIC.]

phys·i·co·chem·i·cal (fiz′i·kō·kem′i·kəl) *adj.* **1.** Of or pertaining to the physical and chemical properties of matter. **2.** Pertaining to physical chemistry.

phys·ics (fiz′iks) *n.pl.* (*construed as sing.*) The science that treats of the laws governing motion, matter, and energy under conditions susceptible to precise observation, generally considered in distinction from chemistry and the sciences dealing with living matter. Abbr. *phys.*

physio- *combining form* Nature; related to natural functions or phenomena: *physiology.* Also, before vowels, *physi-.* [< Gk. *physis* nature. See PHYSIC.]

phys·i·oc·ra·cy (fiz′ē·ok′rə·sē)   *n.* The doctrine of François Quesnay that land and its natural products are the only true wealth and that the best society maintains freedom of trade, person, opinion, and property. [< F *physiocratie*]

phys·i·o·crat (fiz′ē·ə·krat′)   *n.* A believer in physiocracy. — **phys′i·o·crat′ic** *adj.*

phys·i·og·no·my (fiz′ē·og′nə·mē, *esp.* Brit. fiz′ē·on′ə·mē) *n. pl.* **·mies 1.** The face or features considered as revealing character or disposition. **2.** The outward look of a thing. **3.** The practice of discerning character in the features of the face or form of the body. [< OF *fiznomie* < Med.L *phisnomia* < Gk. *physiognōmonia* the judging of a man's nature (by his features) < *physis* nature + *gnōmōn, -onos* judge] — **phys′i·og·nom′ic** (-og·nom′ik, *esp.* Brit. -ō·nom′ik) or **·i·cal** *adj.* — **phys′i·og·nom′i·cal·ly** *adv.* — **phys′i·og′no·mist** *n.*

phys·i·og·ra·phy (fiz′ē·og′rə·fē)   *n.* **1.** A description of nature. **2.** Physical geography (which see). **3.** Geomorphology. [< PHYSIO- + -GRAPHY] — **phys′i·og′ra·pher** *n.* — **phys′i·o·graph′ic** (-ə·graf′ik) or **·i·cal** *adj.* — **phys′i·o·graph′i·cal·ly** *adv.*

physiol. Physiological; physiology.

phys·i·o·log·i·cal (fiz′ē·ə·loj′i·kəl)   *adj.* **1.** Of or pertaining to physiology. **2.** Promoting or in accord with the proper functioning of an organism. Also **phys′i·o·log′ic.** Abbr. *physiol.* — **phys′i·o·log′i·cal·ly** *adv.*

phys·i·ol·o·gy (fiz′ē·ol′ə·jē) *n. pl.* **·gies 1.** The science that treats of the processes and mechanisms by which living animals and plants function under varied conditions; also, a work dealing with this subject. **2.** The aggregate of vital processes: the *physiology* of the frog. Abbr. *physiol.* [< F *physiologie* < L *physiologia* < Gk., natural philosophy < *physiologos* speaker on nature < *physis* nature + *logos* word] — **phys′i·ol′o·gist** *n.*

phys·i·o·ther·a·py (fiz′ē·ō·ther′ə·pē)   *n.* Physical therapy (which see).

phy·sique (fi·zēk′)   *n.* The structure, strength, or appearance of the body. [< F, orig. adj., physical < L *physicus* < Gk. *physikos* natural < *physis.* See PHYSIC.]

phy·so·clis·tous (fī′sō·klis′təs) *adj. Zool.* Having no connection between the air bladder and the digestive tract, as in most teleost fishes. [< NL *Physoclisti,* a genus of fishes < Gk. *physa* bladder + *kleistos* closed < *kleiein* to close]

phy·so·stig·mine (fī′sō·stig′mēn, -min) *n. Chem.* A white, tasteless, toxic alkaloid, $C_{15}H_{21}N_3O_2$, derived from the Calabar bean, used as a miotic: also called *eserine.* [< NL *Physostigma,* genus of the Calabar bean (< Gk. *physa* bladder + *stigma* mark) + -INE²]

phy·sos·to·mous (fī·sos′tə·məs) *adj. Zool.* Having the air bladder united by a duct with the intestinal canal, as in certain teleost fishes. Also **phy·so·stom·a·tous** (fī′sō·stom′ə·təs). [< NL *physostomus* < Gk. *physa* bladder + *stoma* mouth]

-phyte *combining form* A (specified) kind of plant; a plant having a (specified) habitat: *thallophyte, hydrophyte.* [< Gk. *phyton* plant]

Phy·tin (fī′tin)   *n.* Proprietary name of a calcium-magnesium salt containing phosphorus, isolated from the seeds of various plants, and used in medicine. Also **phy′tin.**

phyto- *combining form* Plant; of or related to vegetation: *phytogenesis.* Also, before vowels, **phyt-.** [< Gk. *phyton* plant]

phy·to·gen·e·sis (fī′tō·jen′ə·sis)   *n.* The science of the origin and development of plants. Also **phy·tog·e·ny** (fī·toj′-ə·nē). — **phy′to·ge·net′ic** (-jə·net′ik) or **·i·cal** *adj.* — **phy′to·ge·net′i·cal·ly** *adv.*

phy·to·gen·ic (fī′tō·jen′ik)   *adj.* Of plant origin, as coal and peat. Also **phy·tog·e·nous** (fī·toj′ə·nəs).

phy·to·ge·og·ra·phy (fī′tō·jē·og′rə·fē)   *n.* The study of the geographical distribution and relationships of plants: also called *geobotany.*

phy·tog·ra·phy (fī·tog′rə·fē)   *n.* The systematic description of plants; descriptive botany. [< NL *phytographia* < Gk. *phyton* plant + *graphein* to write]

phy·toid (fī′toid)   *adj.* Plantlike.

phy·to·kin·in (fī′tō·kī′nin)   *n. Biochem.* Any of a group of organic compounds, chiefly purine derivatives, that act to promote cell division in the process of plant growth: sometimes called *kinin.*

phy·tol·o·gy (fī·tol′ə·jē)   *n. Obs.* Botany. [< NL *phytologia* < Gk. *phyton* plant + *logos* word, study] — **phy·to·log′ic** (fī′tə·loj′ik) or **·i·cal** *adj.*

phy·to·pa·thol·o·gy (fī′tō·pə·thol′ə·jē)   *n.* **1.** The study of the diseases of plants and their control. **2.** The pathology of diseases caused by plant organisms.

phy·toph·a·gous (fī·tof′ə·gəs)   *adj. Biol.* Feeding on plants; herbivorous. [< PHYTO- + -PHAGOUS]

phy·to·plank·ton (fī′tō·plangk′tən) *n.* Free-floating aquatic plants. — **phy′to·plank·ton′ic** (-plangk·ton′ik) *adj.*

phy·to·tron (fī′tə·tron)   *n.* A field laboratory for the study of plant growth under a wide range of artificially produced conditions. [< PHYTO- + -tron, instrumental suffix]

pi¹ (pī)   *n.* **1.** The sixteenth letter in the Greek alphabet (Π, π): corresponding to English *p.* See ALPHABET. **2.** *Math.* **a** This letter used to designate the ratio of the circumference of a circle to its diameter. **b** The ratio itself (3.14159 . . .). [def. 2 < Gk. *p(eriphereia)* periphery]

pi² (pī)   *n.* **1.** *Printing* Type that has been thrown into disorder. **2.** Any jumble or disorder. — *v.t.* **pied, pie·ing** To jumble or disorder, as type. Also spelled *pie.* [Var. of PIE¹]

P.I. Philippine Islands.

Pia·cen·za (pyä·chen′tsä) A commune in northern Italy, on the Po; pop. 87,930 (1961): ancient *Placentia.*

pi·ac·u·lar (pī·ak′yə·lər)   *adj.* **1.** Having power to atone; expiatory. **2.** Requiring expiation; criminal. [< L *piacularis* < *piaculum* expiation < *piare* to appease]

piaffe (pyaf)   *v.i.* **piaffed, piaf·fing** To perform or move by performing the piaffer. [< MF *piaffer* to paw the ground, lit., to strut; ult. origin uncertain]

piaf·fer (pyaf′ər)   *n.* In horsemanship, a movement in which the horse lifts one forefoot and the opposite hind foot in unison and slowly places them forward, backward, or to the side. [< F *piaffer.* See PIAFFE.]

pi·a ma·ter (pī′ə mā′tər) *Anat.* The delicate inner vascular membrane that envelops the brain and spinal cord and is overlaid by the arachnoid and dura mater. [< Med.L, inexact trans. of Arabic *umm raqīqah* tender mother]

pi·an·ism (pē·an′iz·əm, pē′ə·niz′əm)   *n.* **1.** Arrangement of music for the pianoforte. **2.** Performance on the piano; the technique of piano playing.

pi·a·nis·si·mo (pē′ə·nis′i·mō, *Ital.* pyä·nē′sē·mō) *Music adj. & adv.* Very soft or very softly: a direction to the performer. Abbr. *pp, pp.* — *n. pl.* **·mos** A passage so played. [< Ital. < L *planissimus,* superl. of *planus* soft]

pi·an·ist (pē·an′ist, pē′ə·nist)   *n.* One who plays the piano; especially, an expert or professional performer on the piano. [< F *pianiste* and < Ital. *pianista*]

pi·an·o¹ (pē·an′ō)   *n. pl.* **·os** A musical instrument having felt-covered hammers operated from a manual keyboard that strike upon steel wires to produce musical tones; a pianoforte. See GRAND PIANO, SQUARE PIANO, UPRIGHT PIANO. [< Ital., short for *pianoforte.* See PIANOFORTE.]

pi·an·o² (pē·ä′nō, *Ital.* pyä′nō) *Music adj. & adv.* Soft or softly: a direction to the performer. Abbr. *p.* — *n. pl.* **·os** A passage so played. [< Ital. < L *planus* flat, soft]

pi·an·o·for·te (pē·an′ə·fôr′tā, -fôr′-, -fôrt′, -fôrt′)   *n.* A piano. [< Ital. < *piano e forte* soft and loud]

Pi·a·no·la (pē′ə·nō′lə)   *n.* A small, portable, cabinetlike, piano-playing mechanism: a trade name. Also **pi′a·no′la.** [Appar. dim. of PIANO¹]

Pi·a·rist (pī′ə·rist)   *n.* One of a Roman Catholic monastic order, the members of which are known as Regular Clerks of the Scuole Pie, an institute of instruction founded in Rome about 1600. [< NL (*patres scholarum*) *piarum* (fathers of the) religious (schools)]

PRONUNCIATION KEY: add, āce, câre, pälm; end, ēven; it, īce; odd, ōpen, ôrder; tŏŏk, pōōl; up, bûrn; ə = a in *above,* e in *sicken,* i in *flexible,* o in *melon,* u in *focus;* yōō = u in *fuse;* oil; pout; check; go; ring; thin; this; zh, vision. For å, œ, ü, kh, ṅ, see inside front cover.

pi·as·sa·va (pē/ə·sä/və) *n.* **1.** A coarse, stiff fiber obtained from two Brazilian palms (*Attalea funifera* and *Leopoldinia piassaba*) used for making ropes, brooms, etc. **2.** Either of these palms. Also **pi/a·sa/ba** (-bə), **pi/as·sa/ba, pi/a·sa/va.** [< Pg. *piassava, piassaba* < Tupi *piaçába*]

pi·as·ter (pē·as/tər) *n.* **1.** A monetary unit of various countries, as Egypt, Libya, Sudan, and Syria: the hundredth part of a pound. **2.** A Turkish coin and monetary unit: also called *kurus.* **3.** The Spanish peso or dollar. Also **pi·as/tre.** [< F *piastre* < Ital. *piastra,* lit., plate of metal, short for *piastra d'argento* plate of silver, ult. < L *emplastrum* plaster]

Pia·ve (pyä/vā) A river in NE Italy, flowing 137 miles, generally SE, to the Adriatic; scene of World War I battles, 1917–18.

pi·az·za (pē·az/ə, *Ital.* pyät/tsä) *n.* **1.** An open area or public square in a city or town, especially in Italy. **2.** A covered outer walk or gallery. **3.** *Chiefly U.S.* A veranda or porch. [< Ital., square, market place, ult. < L *platea* broad street < Gk. *plateia* (*hodos*). Doublet of PLACE, PLAZA.]

pi·broch (pē/brokh) *n.* A martial air played on the bagpipe. [< Gaelic *piobaireachd* art of playing the bagpipe < *piobair* piper + -*achd,* suffix of function]

pi·ca[1] (pī/kə) *n.* **1.** A size of type; 12-point; about ⅙ inch; also, a standard unit of measurement for thickness and length of leads, borders, etc. **2.** A size of typewriter type equivalent to 12-point, with 10 characters to the inch. — **small pica** A size of type; 11-point. — **two line** or **double pica** Type having a depth equal to two lines of pica; 24-point. [< Med.L, *pie*[4]; ? because used in printing pies]

pi·ca[2] (pī/kə) *n. Pathol.* A morbid appetite for unusual or unfit food, as clay, chalk, ashes, etc., occurring in some cases of hysteria and pregnancy. [< L *pica* magpie, ? trans. of Gk. *kissa, kitta* magpie, craving for strange food; with ref. to the bird's omnivorousness] — **pi/cal** *adj.*

pi·ca·cho (pē·kä/chō) *n. pl.* **·chos** *SW U.S.* An isolated peak of a hill or butte. [< Am. Sp. < Sp. *pico* peak]

pi·ca·dor (pik/ə·dôr, *Sp.* pē/kä·thôr/) *n.* **1.** In bullfighting, a horseman who seeks to weaken the bull by pricking him with a lance. **2.** A clever debater; a wit. [< Sp., lit., pricker < *picar* to prick, pierce < *pica.* Akin to PIKE[1].]

Pi·card (pē·kàr/), **Jean,** 1620–82, French astronomer.

Pic·ar·dy (pik/ər·dē) A region and former province of northern France. — **Pic/ard** *adj. & n.*

pic·a·resque (pik/ə·resk/) *adj.* **1.** Characteristic of or involving rogues or picaroons. **2.** Denoting a form of fictional narrative of Spanish origin in which the hero is a rogue whose adventures are described in a series of episodes. [< Sp. *picaresco* roguish < *picaro*; ult. origin uncertain]

pic·a·roon[1] (pik/ə·rōōn/) *n.* **1.** One who lives by cheating or robbery; a pirate, rogue, or adventurer. **2.** A pirate vessel. [< Sp. *picarón,* aug. of *picaro* rogue]

pic·a·roon[2] (pik/ə·rōōn/) *n.* A piked pole used by log drivers: also spelled *pickaroon.* [? < MF *piqueron* spur < *pique* pike[1]]

Pi·cas·so (pē·kä/sō), **Pablo,** born 1881, Spanish painter and sculptor active in France: full name **Pablo Ru·iz y Picasso** (rōō·ēth/ ē).

pic·a·yune (pik/i·yōōn/) *adj. U.S.* **1.** Of small value; paltry; contemptible. **2.** Petty; niggling; mean. Also **pic/a·yun/ish.** — *n.* **1.** A former small Spanish-American coin; a half real. **2.** *U.S.* A coin of little value, as a 5-cent piece. **3.** *U.S.* Anything of trifling value. [< F *picaillon* old Piedmontese coin, farthing < Provençal *picaioun, picalhoun,* dim. of *picalo* money]

Pic·ca·dil·ly (pik/ə·dil/ē) A famous thoroughfare of London, running from Piccadilly Circus to Hyde Park Corner.

pic·ca·lil·li (pik/ə·lil/ē) *n.* A highly seasoned relish of chopped vegetables. [? < PICKLE[1]]

Pic·card (pē·kàr/), **Auguste,** 1884–1962, and his twin brother, **Jean Félix,** 1884–1963, Swiss physicists and aeronauts.

pic·co·lo (pik/ə·lō) *n. pl.* **·los 1.** A small flute pitched an octave higher than the ordinary flute. **2.** An organ stop of similar tone. [< Ital., small] — **pic/co·lo·ist** *n.*

Pic de Néthou (pēk də nā·tōō/) The French name for PICO DE ANETO.

pice (pīs) *n. pl.* **pice** (pīs) A former coin of India and Pakistan, equal to one-fourth of an anna. [< Hind. *paisā,* ? < *pāi, pai* quarter < Skt. *pad, padī*]

pic·e·ous (pis/ē·əs, pī/sē-) *adj.* **1.** Relating to or resembling pitch. **2.** Pitch-black. [< L *piceus* < *pix, picis* pitch]

pich·i·ci·a·go (pich/ə·sē·ä/gō, -ā/gō) *n. pl.* **·gos** Either of two small burrowing armadillos of southern South America (genera *Chlamyphorus* and *Burmeisteria*). Also **pich/i·ci·e/go** (-ā/gō). [< Sp. *pichiciego* < Guarani *pichey* the little armadillo + Sp. *ciego* blind < L *caecus*]

pick[1] (pik) *v.t.* **1.** To choose; select; cull, as from a group or number. **2.** To detach or pluck, as with the fingers: to *pick* a flower. **3.** To clear (a field, tree, etc.) in such a manner. **4.** To clear of or harvest; gather: to *pick* cotton. **5.** To prepare by removing the feathers, hulls, leaves, etc.: to *pick* a chicken. **6.** To remove extraneous matter from (the teeth, etc.), as with the fingers or with a pointed instrument. **7.** To touch, irritate, or remove (something) with a pointed instru-

ment, a fingernail, etc. **8.** To nibble at or peck, as a bird. **9.** To eat in a dainty or overfastidious manner. **10.** To break up, penetrate, or indent with or as with a pointed instrument. **11.** To form or make in this manner: to *pick* a hole. **12.** To pull apart, as rags. **13.** To point out critically: to *pick* flaws. **14.** To remove the contents of by stealth: to *pick* a pocket. **15.** To open (a lock) by means other than the key. **16.** To pluck the strings of: to *pick* a ukulele. **17.** *Informal* To provoke: to *pick* a fight. — *v.i.* **18.** To work with a pick. **19.** To pluck or remove fruit, flowers, etc. **20.** To eat daintily or without appetite. **21.** To select carefully: to *pick* and choose. **22.** To pilfer. — **Syn.** See CHOOSE. — **to pick apart** (or **to pieces**) **1.** To pull apart. **2.** To destroy the arguments of by shrewd or critical analysis. — **to pick at 1.** To touch or toy with. **2.** To eat without appetite. **3.** *U.S. Informal* To nag at. — **to pick off 1.** To remove by picking. **2.** To hit, as with a bullet, after taking careful aim. **3.** In baseball, to catch (a base runner) off base. — **to pick on 1.** To determine on; choose. **2.** *Informal* To tease or annoy, as with carping criticism; also, to single out for harassment. — **to pick one's way** (or **steps**) To advance by careful selection of one's course or actions. — **to pick out 1.** To choose or select. **2.** To distinguish (something) from its surroundings. **3.** To produce the notes of (a tune, etc.) singly or slowly, as by ear. — **to pick over** To examine carefully or one by one. — **to pick up 1.** To take up, as with the hand. **2.** To take up or receive into a group, vehicle, etc. **3.** To acquire casually or by chance. **4.** To gain speed; accelerate. **5.** To be able to perceive or receive, as a distant radio station. **6.** To break (ground, etc.) with a pick. **7.** *U.S.* To make (a room, etc.) tidy. **8.** *Informal* To recover spirits, health, etc.; improve. **9.** *Informal* To make the acquaintance of (a stranger, especially of the opposite sex) under casual or informal circumstances. — *n.* **1.** Right of selection; choice. **2.** That which is selected; especially, the choicest or best part. **3.** The quantity of certain crops that are picked by hand. **4.** The act of picking. [ME *piken, pikken* < OE *pīcan, pīcian* (assumed); infl. by OF *piquer* to pierce. Akin to PIKE[1].]

pick[2] (pik) *n.* **1.** A double-headed, pointed metal tool mounted on a wooden handle, used for breaking ground, etc. **2.** Any of various implements for picking, as an ice pick or toothpick. **3.** A plectrum. [Appar. var. of PIKE[1]]

pick[3] (pik) *n.* **1.** In weaving, the blow that drives a loom shuttle. **2.** A single weft thread. [< dial. E *pick,* v., var. of PITCH[2]]

PICKS

a Pickax. *b* Mandolin pick. *c* Guitar thumb pick. *d* Ice pick. *e* Quill tooth pick.

pick·a·back (pik/ə·bak/) *adv.* Piggyback. [Earlier *pickback, pickpack.* Cf. dial. E *pick* to throw, toss.]

pick·a·dil (pik/ə·dil) *n.* A standing collar, usually with a scalloped edge, as worn in the 17th century. Also **pick/a·dill.** [Var. of *piccadil* < MF *piccadilles* pieces fastened on edge of a doublet's collar < dim. of Sp. *picado* pierced]

pick·a·nin·ny (pik/ə·nin/ē) *n. pl.* **·nies** A Negro child: a condescending or offensive term. Also **pic/ca·nin/ny.** [Alter. of Sp. *pequeñito* or Pg. *pequenino,* dims. of *pequeño* or *pequeno* little, small]

pick·a·roon (pik/ə·rōōn/) See PICAROON.

pick·ax (pik/aks/) *n.* A pick or mattock with one end of the head edged like a chisel and the other pointed; also, a pick with both ends pointed. Also **pick/axe/.** [ME *pikoys* < OF *picois,* ? < *pic* pike[1]; infl. in form by *ax*]

pick·ed[1] (pik/id, pikt) *adj.* Archaic or *Dial.* Sharp-pointed, as a stick. [< PICK[2], n.]

pick·ed[2] (pikt) *adj.* **1.** Carefully selected; chosen for a purpose. **2.** Cleaned by picking out refuse, stalks, etc., as cotton. [Orig. pp. of PICK[1], v.]

pick·ed-o·ver (pikt/ō/vər) *adj.* **1.** Handled; left after the best have been removed. **2.** Left after the undesirable ones have been removed, as berries.

Pick·ens (pik/inz), **Andrew,** 1739–1817, American Revolutionary general.

pick·er[1] (pik/ər) *n.* **1.** One who or that which picks. **2.** A machine for loosening up fibrous material. [< PICK[1]]

pick·er[2] (pik/ər) *n.* In a loom, the part that strikes the shuttle. [< dial. E *pick,* v. See PICK[3].]

pick·er·el (pik/ər·əl, -rəl) *n. pl.* **·el** or **·els 1.** Any of various North American fresh-water fishes of the pike family, especially the smaller species having a narrow snout and sharp teeth, as the **mud pickerel** (*Esox vermiculatus*) and the **chain pickerel** (*E. niger*). **2.** *U.S. Dial.* A pike perch. **3.** *Brit.* A young pike. [Dim. of PIKE[1] < AF or formed in ME]

pickerel frog A frog (*Rana palustris*) of the eastern United States: also called *marsh frog.*

pick·er·el·weed (pik/ər·əl·wēd/) *n.* Any of various perennial plants (genus *Pontederia*) found in the shallows of North

American lakes; especially, the common pickerelweed (*P. cordata*), having a spike of blue flowers.

Pick·er·ing (pik′ər·ing), **Timothy,** 1745–1829, American Revolutionary general and politician. — **Edward Charles,** 1846–1919, U.S. astronomer and physicist. — **William Henry,** 1858–1938, U.S. astronomer; brother of Edward Charles.

pick·et (pik′it) *n.* **1.** A pointed stick or post, used as a fence paling, tent peg, etc.; a stake. **2.** A person stationed by a labor organization at the outside of a place affected by a strike, for the purpose of publicizing alleged grievances, persuading the public not to do business with the affected establishment, etc. **3.** A person engaged in publicly protesting a proposed law, policy, etc., by posting himself outside a place associated with the controversy. **4.** *Mil.* A soldier or detachment of soldiers posted to guard a camp, army, etc. — *v.t.* **1.** To post oneself or be posted outside of as a picket. **2.** To station a picket or pickets outside of. **3.** To fence or fortify with pickets or pointed stakes. **4.** To tie to a picket, as a horse. **5.** *Mil.* **a** To guard by means of a picket. **b** To post as a picket. — *v.i.* **6.** To act as a picket (defs. 2 & 3). [< F *piquet* pointed stake < *piquer* to pierce]

pick·et·er (pik′it·ər) *n.* A picket (defs. 2 & 3).

picket fence A fence made of upright pickets.

picket line A line or procession of people picketing a place of business, etc.

picket pin A long iron pin or wooden stake driven into the ground and having a swivel loop at the upper end, used for tethering horses.

Pick·ett (pik′it), **George Edward,** 1825–75, Confederate general in the Civil War.

Pick·ford (pik′fərd), **Mary,** born 1893, U.S. motion-picture actress born in Canada: original name **Gladys Smith.**

pick glass A magnifying glass for determining the thread count of fabrics.

pick·ing (pik′ing) *n.* **1.** The act of picking; also, that which is or may be picked. **2.** *pl.* That which is left to be picked up or gleaned: scanty *pickings*. **3.** The act of pilfering, or that which is pilfered. **4.** *Usually pl.* That which is taken by questionable means; spoils.

pick·le¹ (pik′əl) *n.* **1.** A cucumber that has been preserved and flavored in a liquid solution, usually of brine or vinegar. **2.** Any article of food so preserved or flavored. **3.** A liquid preservative, as brine or vinegar, sometimes spiced, for meat, fish, vegetables, etc. **4.** *Metall.* Diluted acid or other chemicals used in cleaning metal castings, etc. **5.** *Informal* An embarrassing condition or position. **6.** *Chiefly Brit. Informal* A troublesome child. — *v.t.* **·led, ·ling 1.** To preserve or flavor in pickle. **2.** *Metall.* To treat with a pickle. — **Syn.** See PREDICAMENT. [Appar. < MDu. *pekel, peeckel*]

pick·le² (pik′əl) *n. Scot.* A grain of corn; a small quantity.

pick·led (pik′əld) *adj.* **1.** Preserved in pickle. **2.** Of wood work, etc., having a bleached finish. **3.** *Slang* Drunk.

pick·lock (pik′lok′) *n.* **1.** A special implement for opening a lock. **2.** One who picks locks, especially illegally.

pick-me-up (pik′mē·up′) *n. Informal* A drink, especially an alcoholic drink, taken to renew one's energy or spirits.

pick-off (pik′ôf′, -of′) *n.* In baseball, a play in which a runner is caught off base, as by a quick throw from the pitcher or catcher.

pick·pock·et (pik′pok′it) *n.* One who steals from pockets.

pick·up (pik′up′) *n.* **1.** Acceleration, as in the speed of an automobile, engine, etc. **2.** *Electronics* A crystal, ceramic, or magnetic device that converts the oscillations of a needle in a record groove into electrical impulses. **3.** The tone arm of a record player. **4.** A small, usually open truck for light loads. **5.** *Telecom.* **a** In radio, the location of microphones in relation to program elements. **b** The system for broadcasting material gathered outside the studio. **c** In television, the scanning of an image by the electron beam. **d** The scanning apparatus. **6.** In baseball, the act of fielding a ball that has touched the ground. **7.** *Informal* A period of renewed or increased activity: a *pickup* in business. **8.** *Informal* Something that stimulates or renews in spirit. **9.** *Slang* A stranger with whom a casual acquaintance is made, usually in a public place and for the purposes of lovemaking.

Pick·wick (pik′wik), **Mr.** (**Samuel**) In Dickens' *Pickwick Papers*, the stout, goodhearted president of the Pickwick Club, distinguished for his blundering simplicity.

Pick·wick·i·an (pik·wik′ē·ən) *adj.* Relating to or characteristic of Mr. Pickwick.

Pickwickian sense A technical or esoteric sense; not the common sense: usually said of a word or a phrase.

pic·nic (pik′nik) *n.* **1.** An outdoor social outing for which food is usually provided by the people participating. **2.** *Slang* An easy or pleasant time or experience. — *v.i.* **·nicked, ·nick·ing** To have or attend a picnic. [< F *pique-nique*, prob. reduplication of *piquer* to nick, peck] — **pic′nick·er** *n.*

pico- *combining form* One trillionth (10⁻¹²) of a specified quantity or dimension. [< NL < Sp., small quantity, peak]

Pi·co de A·ne·to (pē′kō thä ä·nā′tō) The highest peak of the Pyrenees, NE Spain; 11,169 ft.: French *Pic de Néthou*.

Pi·co del·la Mi·ran·do·la (pē′kō del′lä mē·rän′dō·lä), **Count Giovanni,** 1463–94, Italian humanist and scholar.

pic·o·line (pik′ə·lēn, -lin) *n. Chem.* Any of three isomeric liquid compounds, C_6H_7N, contained in coal tar, naphtha, bone oil, etc., and homologous with pyridine. Also **pic′o·lin** (-lin). [< L *pix, picis,* PITCH¹ + -OL² + -INE²]

Pi·co Ri·ve·ra (pē′kō ri·vä′rə) A city in SW California, near Los Angeles; pop. 54,170.

pi·cot (pē′kō) *n.* A small thread loop on ornamental edging, ribbon, etc. — *v.t. & v.i.* **·coted** (-kōd), **·cot·ing** (-kō·ing) To sew with this edging. [< F, dim. of OF *pic* point]

pic·o·tee (pik′ə·tē′) *n.* A variety of carnation, having white or light-colored petals edged with a darker color, as scarlet. [< F *picotée,* pp. fem. of *picoter* to mark with pricks or dots < *picot.* See PICOT.]

picot stitch A loop stitch (which see).

pic·quet (pi·kā′, -ket′) See PIQUET.

pic·rate (pik′rāt) *n. Chem.* One of the salts or esters of picric acid, exploding when heated or struck.

pic·ric (pik′rik) *adj.* Of, pertaining to, or having an exceedingly bitter taste. [< Gk. *pikros* bitter]

picric acid *Chem.* A yellow, crystalline, bitter compound, $C_6H_2(NO_2)_3OH$, used in dyeing and in certain explosives.

pic·rite (pik′rīt) *n.* A variety of peridotite containing some magnetite or ilmenite, biotite, and brown hornblende. [< Gk. *pikros* bitter + -ITE¹]

picro- *combining form* Bitter: *picrotoxin.* Also, before vowels, **picr-.** [< Gk. *pikros* bitter]

pic·ro·tox·in (pik′rə·tok′sin) *n. Chem.* A bitter, very poisonous crystalline compound, $C_{30}H_{34}O_{13}$, used in medicine as a respiratory stimulant, etc. — **pic′ro·tox′ic** *adj.*

Pict (pikt) *n.* One of an ancient people of uncertain origin who inhabited Britain and the Scottish Highlands, waged war on the Romans, and were conquered in 846 by the Scots. [< LL *Picti,* ? < L *pictus,* pp. of *pingere* to paint; with ref. to their being painted or tattooed]

Pict·ish (pik′tish) *n.* The language of the Picts, of undetermined relationship. — *adj.* Of or pertaining to the Picts.

pic·to·graph (pik′tə·graf, -gräf) *n.* **1.** A picture representing an idea, as a hieroglyph. **2.** A record consisting of such pictures. [< L *pictus,* pp. of *pingere* to paint + -GRAPH] — **pic′to·graph′ic** *adj.* — **pic′to·graph′i·cal·ly** *adv.* — **pic·tog′·ra·phy′** *n.*

Pic·tor (pik′tər) A constellation, the Painter. See CONSTELLATION. [< L]

pic·to·ri·al (pik·tôr′ē·əl, -tō′rē-) *adj.* **1.** Pertaining to, composed of, or concerned with pictures. **2.** Representing in or as if in pictures; graphic. **3.** Containing or illustrated by pictures. — *n.* A periodical that devotes considerable space to pictures. — **Syn.** See GRAPHIC. [< LL *pictorius* < L *pictor* painter < *pictus,* pp. of *pingere* to paint] — **pic·to′ri·al·ly** *adv.*

pic·ture (pik′chər) *n.* **1.** A visual representation of an object or scene upon a flat surface, as a painting, drawing, engraving, or photograph. **2.** A vivid or graphic verbal description. **3.** A mental image or impression of the nature of a situation, event, etc. **4.** An overall situation, especially as perceived or understood from a particular vantage point: In the 1930's Hitler came into the *picture*. **5.** One who or that which bears a striking resemblance to another person or thing, or that seems to embody a quality or idea: She is the *picture* of despair. **6.** A motion picture (which see). **7.** The image on a television screen. **8.** Something attractive or pleasant: pretty as a *picture*. **9.** A tableau vivant. — *v.t.* **·tured, ·tur·ing 1.** To form a mental image of. **2.** To describe graphically; depict verbally. **3.** To make a picture of. [< L *pictura* < *pictus,* pp. of *pingere* to paint]

picture gallery A room or hall for exhibiting pictures.

picture hat A woman's hat having a very wide brim and often trimmed with plumes, seen in certain paintings.

Pic·ture·phone (pik′chər·fōn′) *n.* A device or system for transmitting two-way televised pictures of persons having a telephone conversation allowing visual as well as sound contact: a trade name.

pic·tur·esque (pik′chə·resk′) *adj.* **1.** Having a striking, irregular beauty, quaintness, or charm. **2.** Abounding in striking or original expression or imagery; richly graphic. **3.** Like or suitable for a picture; having pictorial quality. — **Syn.** See GRAPHIC. [< F *pittoresque* < Ital. *pittoresco* < *pittore* painter < L *pictor.* See PICTORIAL.] — **pic′tur·esque′ly** *adv.* — **pic′tur·esque′ness** *n.*

picture tube Kinescope (def. 1).

picture window A large window of a single pane of glass.

picture writing 1. The use of pictures or pictorial symbols in writing. **2.** A writing so made.

pic·ul (pik′ul) *n.* A varying commercial weight, usually about 100 catties, or 133⅓ pounds, used in China, Japan, and other Asian countries. [< Malay *nikul* man's load]

pid·dle (pid′l) *v.* **·dled, ·dling** *v.t.* **1.** To trifle; dawdle: usually with *away*. — *v.i.* **2.** To trifle; dawdle. **3.** To urinate. [Origin uncertain]

pid·dling (pid′ling) *adj.* Unimportant; trivial; trifling.

pid·dock (pid′ək) *n.* A bivalve, typically marine mollusk (genus *Pholas*), having an elongated shell and burrowing in clay and sand. [Origin uncertain]

pidg·in (pij′ən) *n.* A mixed language, such as bêche-de-mer, combining the vocabulary and grammar of dissimilar languages and providing a simplified, mutually intelligible form of communication for use as a lingua franca. Compare CRE- OLIZED LANGUAGE. [Elliptical for Pidgin English; with ref. to Chinese pronun. of *business*]

Pidgin English A jargon composed of English and ele- ments of local non-English dialects, used as the language of commerce or lingua franca between indigenous peoples and foreigners in areas of China, Melanesia, Northern Australia, and West Africa. Also called **Pidgin.**

pie¹ (pī) *n.* **1.** A baked food consisting of one or two layers or crusts of pastry with a filling of fruit, custard, meat, etc. **2.** A layer cake filled with cream, jam, etc. **3.** See PI². **4.** *Slang* Anything very good or very easy. **5.** *Slang* Political graft. [ME *pie, pye,* ? < PIE²; with ref. to the variety of ob- jects collected by magpies and of foods baked in pies]

pie² (pī) *n.* A magpie. [< OF < L *pica* magpie]

pie³ (pī) *n.* A former coin of India and Pakistan of the small- est value, equal to one-third of a pice. [< Hind. *pā′ī* < Skt. *pad, padī* a fourth]

pie⁴ (pī) *n.* In the pre-Reformation English church, a book of rules for determining the correct service for the day: also spelled *pye.* [< L *pica* magpie; ? because its pages resem- bled the bird's black-and-white plumage]

pie·bald (pī′bôld′) *adj.* Having spots, especially of white and black. — *n.* A spotted or mottled animal, especially a horse. [< PIE² + BALD; because like a magpie's plumage]

piece (pēs) *n.* **1.** A portion or quantity existing as an indi- vidual entity or mass: a *piece* of paper. **2.** A small portion considered as forming or having formed a distinct part of a whole. **3.** A coin: a fifty-cent *piece.* **4.** An instance; speci- men; example: a *piece* of luck. **5.** One of a class or group: a *piece* of furniture, luggage, etc. **6.** A work of esthetic inter- est, as a literary or musical composition, a play, a painting, etc. **7.** Point of view; attitude; opinion: to speak one's *piece.* **8.** A firearm, as a cannon or rifle. **9.** One of the disks or counters used in checkers, backgammon, etc. **10.** In chess, any figure other than a pawn. **11.** A quantity or length, as of wallpaper, in which an article is manufactured or sold. **12.** *Dial.* A short time, space, or distance: to walk a *piece.* **13.** *Dial.* A snack between regular meals. **14.** *Ar- chaic* or *Dial.* A person; individual. **15.** *Canadian* Former- ly, an eighty-pound package, as of furs. — **a piece of one's mind** *Informal* Criticism or censure frankly expressed. — **in one piece** Whole; intact: lucky to get out *in one piece.* — **of a (or one) piece 1.** Of the same kind, sort, or class. **2.** Of the same piece; undivided. — **to go to pieces 1.** To fall apart. **2.** *Informal* To lose moral or emotional self-control. — **to have a piece of** *U.S. Slang* To have a financial inter- est in. — *v.t.* **pieced, piec·ing 1.** To add or attach a piece or pieces to, as for enlargement. **2.** To unite or reunite the pieces of, as in mending. **3.** To unite (parts or fragments) into a whole. — *v.i.* **4.** *Dial.* To eat between meals. *Abbr.* *pc.* [< OF *pece* < Med.L *pecia*; ult. origin uncertain]

pièce de résistance (pyes də rā·zē·stäns′) *French* **1.** The principal or most important work in a collection, as of art, poems, etc. **2.** The most substantial dish of a dinner.

piece goods Fabrics of various widths, cut and sold from bolts in lengths specified by the customer.

piece·meal (pēs′mēl′) *adv.* **1.** Piece by piece; gradually. **2.** In pieces. — *adj.* Made up of pieces. [ME *pece-mele* < *pece* piece + -*mele* < OE *mælum* < *mæl* measure]

piece of eight Peso (def. 3).

piec·er (pē′sər) *n.* One who or that which pieces; especially, one who ties broken threads in a spinning mill.

piece·work (pēs′wûrk′) *n.* Work done or paid for by the piece or quantity. — **piece′work′er** *n.*

pie chart *Stat.* A graph in the form of a circle divided into sectors, each of which is proportional in area and subtended angle to a component part of an entire series.

piec·ing (pē′sing) *n.* Pieces of cloth, especially those col- lected and saved to be sewed together, as for a quilt.

Pieck (pēk), **Wilhelm,** 1876–1960, German Communist lead- er; president of the German Democratic Republic 1949–1960.

pie·crust table (pī′krust′) A small table having a top, usu- ally round, with a raised scalloped edge.

pied (pīd) *adj.* Spotted; piebald; mottled. [< PIE²]

pied à-terre (pyā·dà·târ′) *n. French* A temporary or sec- ondary lodging; literally, foot on the ground.

pied·mont (pēd′mont) *adj. Geog.* At the foot of a mountain or mountain range. [< *Piedmont,* Italy < L *Pedimontium* < *pes, pedis* foot + *mons, montis* mountain]

Pied·mont (pēd′mont) **1.** A Region of northern Italy; 9,817 sq. mi.; pop. 3,889,962 (1961); capital, Turin. *Italian* **Pie·** **mon·te** (pyä·môn′tā). **2.** A region of the eastern United States extending from New Jersey to Alabama east of the Appalachian Mountains; about 80,000 sq. mi.

Pied·mont·ese (pēd′mont·ēz′, -ēs′) *adj.* Of or pertaining to Piedmont, Italy, or to its people. — *n.* A native or in- habitant of Piedmont, Italy.

Pied Piper of Hamelin In medieval legend, a piper who rid the town of Hamelin of its rats by leading them with his music into the river. When not rewarded as promised, he led the town's children to a hill into which they disappeared.

pie plant *U.S. Dial.* The common variety of rhubarb.

pier (pir) *n.* **1.** A structure extending over the water, secured by piles and serving as a landing place for vessels; wharf. **2.** A plain, detached mass of masonry, usually serving as a sup- port: the *pier* of a bridge. **3.** An upright projecting portion of a wall; a buttress. **4.** A solid portion of a wall between window openings, etc. [< OF *per* < Med.L *pera*]

pierce (pirs) *v.* **pierced, pierc·ing** *v.t.* **1.** To pass into or through; penetrate with or as if with a knife or other pointed instrument; puncture; stab. **2.** To force a way into or through: to *pierce* the wilderness. **3.** To make an opening or hole in, into, or through. **4.** To make or cut (an opening or hole) in or through something. **5.** To cut through as if stabbing; cleave: Lightning *pierced* the sky. **6.** To affect sharply or deeply, as with emotion, pain, etc. **7.** To pene- trate to the source or meaning; solve; understand: to *pierce* a mystery. — *v.i.* **8.** To enter; penetrate. [< OF *percer,* var. of *percier* < L *pertusus,* pp. of *pertundere* to perforate < *per-* through + *tundere* to beat] — **pierc′er** *n.* — **pierc′- ing·ly** *adv.* — **pierc′ing·ness** *n.*

Pierce (pirs), **Franklin,** 1804–69, 14th president of the Unit- ed States 1853–57.

pier glass A large, high mirror intended to fill the space, or pier, between two windows.

Pi·e·ri·a (pī·ir′ē·ə) A coastal region of ancient Macedon, at the base of Mount Olympus, legendary birthplace of the nine Muses. — **Pi·e′ri·an** *adj.*

Pierian Spring A spring in Pieria, supposed to give poetic inspiration to those who drank from it.

Pi·er·i·des (pī·er′ə·dēz) *n.pl.* **1.** In Greek mythology, the nine Muses. **2.** The nine daughters of Pierus, vanquished by the Muses in a musical contest and changed into magpies.

pi·er·i·dine (pī·er′ə·dīn, -din) *adj.* Of or pertaining to a fam- ily (*Pieridae*) of butterflies, including species of predom- inantly white or yellow color. [< NL *Pieridinae,* subfamily name < *Pieris,* genus name < Gk., one of the Pierian Muses]

Pie·ro del·la Fran·ces·ca (pyä′rō del′lä frän·ches′kä), 1420?–92, Umbrian painter. Also **Piero de·i Fran·ces·chi** (dā′ē frän·ches′kē).

Pierre (pir) The capital of South Dakota, in the central part, on the Missouri River; pop. 10,088.

pier·rot (pye·rō′) *n.* A white-faced clown or buffoon dressed in the costume of Pierrot. [< PIERROT]

Pier·rot (pye·rō′) Formerly, a stock character in French pantomimes, wearing white pantaloons and a loose white jacket with big buttons. [< F, dim. of *Pierre* Peter < L *Petrus*]

pier table A low table occupying the space between two wall openings, usually under a pier glass.

Pi·er·us (pī′ər·əs) In Greek mythology, a king of Thrace, father of the nine Pierides.

Pie·tà (pyä·tä′) *n.* In painting, sculpture, etc., a representa- tion of Mary mourning over the body of Christ in her arms. [< Ital., lit., pity < L *pietas, -tatis.* See PIETY.]

Pie·ter·mar·itz·burg (pē′tər·mär′its·bootkh) The capital of Natal, South Africa, in the south central part of the Prov- ince; pop. 111,000 (est. 1967).

pi·e·tism (pī′ə·tiz′əm) *n.* **1.** Piety or godliness; devotion, as distinguished from insistence on religious creeds or forms. **2.** Affected or exaggerated piety. [< G *pietismus*] — **pí·e· tist** *n.* — **pi′e·tis′tic** or ·**ti·cal** *adj.* — **pi·e·tis′ti·cal·ly** *adv.*

Pi·e·tism (pī′ə·tiz′əm) *n.* A movement in the Lutheran Church in Germany during the later 17th century, advocat- ing a revival of the devotional ideal. — **Pi′e·tist** *n.* — **Pi′e· tis′tic** or ·**ti·cal** *adj.* — **Pi·e·tis′ti·cal·ly** *adv.*

pi·e·ty (pī′ə·tē) *n. pl.* **·ties 1.** Reverence toward God or the gods; religious devoutness. **2.** Honor and obedience due to parents, superiors, etc. **3.** A pious act, wish, etc. **4.** The state or quality of being pious. [< OF *piete* < L *pietas, -tatis* dutifulness < *pius* dutiful. Doublet of PITY.]

piezo- *combining form* Pressure; related to or produced by pressure: *piezometer.* [< Gk. *piezein* to press]

pi·e·zo·chem·is·try (pī·ē′zō·kem′is·trē) *n.* The study of chemical reactions under the influence of high pressures.

pi·e·zo·e·lec·tric·i·ty (pī·ē′zō·i·lek′tris′ə·tē, -ē′lek-) *n.* Elec- tricity or electric phenomena resulting from pressure upon certain bodies, especially crystals. — **pi·e′zo·e·lec′tric** or **·tri·cal** *adj.* — **pi·e′zo·e·lec′tri·cal·ly** *adv.*

pi·e·zom·e·ter (pī′ə·zom′ə·tər) *n.* Any instrument for the determination and measurement of pressure. — **pi′e·zo· met′ric** (-zō·met′rik) or **·ri·cal** *adj.* — **pi′e·zom′e·try** *n.*

pif·fle (pif′əl) *Informal v.i.* **fled, fling** To talk nonsensi- cally; babble. — *n.* Nonsense; babble. [? Blend of PID- DLE and TRIFLE]

pig (pig) *n.* **1.** A cloven-hoofed mammal (genus *Sus*), hav- ing a long, mobile snout; especially, a small, young one weighing less than 120 pounds: also called *hog, swine.* ◆

Collateral adjective: *porcine.* **2.** The flesh of a pig, used as food; pork. **3.** An oblong mass of metal, especially iron or lead, just run from the smelter and cast in a rough mold, usually in sand; also, the mold. **4.** Pig iron or iron pigs in general. **5.** *Informal* A person regarded as like a pig, especially one who is filthy, gluttonous, or coarse. **6.** An animal likened to a pig, as the guinea pig. **7.** *Informal* A railroad locomotive: also called *hog.* **8.** *U.S. Slang* A woman of loose morals; also, a slovenly or unattractive woman. — *v.i.* **pigged, pig·ging 1.** To bring forth pigs. **2.** To act or live like pigs: with *it.* [ME *pigge*; ult. origin uncertain]
pig bed The bed of sand in which iron pigs are cast.
pig·boat (pig′bōt′) *n. Slang* A submarine.
pig·eon (pij′ən) *n.* **1.** Any of a widely distributed family (*Columbidae*) of birds, having short legs, a small head and a sturdy body; especially, the domestic pigeon or rock dove. **2.** *Slang* One who is easily swindled. [< OF *pijon* < LL *pipio, -onis* young chirping bird < L *pipire* to chirp]
pigeon breast *Pathol.* A deformity in which the chest is narrow and pointed: also called *chicken breast.* — **pig′eon-breast′ed** *adj.*
pigeon hawk A small American falcon (*Falco columbarius*) related to the merlin.
pig·eon-heart·ed (pij′ən-här′tid) *adj.* Timid; fearful.
pig·eon-hole (pij′ən-hōl′) *n.* **1.** A hole for pigeons to nest in, especially in a compartmented pigeon house. **2.** A small compartment, as in a desk, for filing papers. — *v.t.* **-holed, -hol·ing 1.** To place in a pigeonhole; file. **2.** To file away and ignore. **3.** To place in categories; classify mentally.
pig·eon-liv·ered (pij′ən-liv′ərd) *adj.* Weak-spirited.
pig·eon-toed (pij′ən-tōd′) *adj.* Having the toes or feet turned inward.
pig·eon·wing (pij′ən-wing′) *n. U.S.* **1.** A fancy dance step in which one jumps and strikes the feet together. **2.** A figure in skating resembling the outline of a pigeon's wing.
pig·fish (pig′fish′) *n. pl.* **·fish** or **·fish·es** A species of grunt (*Orthopristis chrysopterus*) common off the southern Atlantic coasts of the United States: also called *hogfish.*
pig·ger·y (pig′ər-ē) *n. pl.* **·ger·ies** A place for keeping or raising pigs.
pig·gin (pig′in) *n.* A small wooden vessel having one stave projecting above the rim for a handle: also called *pipkin.* [? Dim. of dial. E *pig* crock]
pig·gish (pig′ish) *adj.* Like a pig; greedy; dirty; selfish. — **pig′gish·ly** *adv.* — **pig′gish·ness** *n.*
pig·gy (pig′ē) *n. pl.* **·gies** A little pig. Also **pig′gie.**
pig·gy·back (pig′ē-bak′) *adv.* On the back or shoulders: to ride *piggyback:* also *pickaback.*
pig·gy·back·ing (pig′ē-bak′ing) *n. U.S.* Transshipment of loaded truck bodies on railway flat cars.
piggy bank A coin bank in the shape of a pig with a slot in its back for inserting coins.
pig·head·ed (pig′hed′id) *adj.* Stupidly obstinate. — **Syn.** See OBSTINATE. — **pig′head′ed·ly** *adv.* — **pig′head′ed·ness** *n.*
pig iron Crude iron poured from a blast furnace into variously shaped molds or pigs of sand or the like.
pig latin A jargon in which the initial sound of a word is usually transposed to the end and to which *-ay* (ā) is added, as in *Illkay the umbay* for *Kill the bum.* Also **pig Latin.**
pig·ment (pig′mənt) *n.* **1.** Any of a class of finely powdered, insoluble coloring matters suitable for making paints, enamels, oil colors, etc. **2.** Any substance that imparts color to animal or vegetable tissues, as melanin and chlorophyll. **3.** Any substance used for coloring. [< L *pigmentum* < *pingere* to paint. Doublet of PIMENTO.]
pig·men·tar·y (pig′mən-ter′ē) *adj.* Of, producing, or containing pigment, as a cell. [< L *pigmentarius*]
pig·men·ta·tion (pig′mən-tā′shən) *n.* **1.** Coloration resulting from pigment. **2.** *Biol.* Deposition of pigment by cells. [< L *pigmentatus* < *pigmentum.* See PIGMENT.]
pigment cell *Biol.* A chromatophore.
pig·my (pig′mē) See PYGMY.
Pig·my (pig′mē) See PYGMY.
pig·nus (pig′nəs) *n. pl.* **·no·ra** (-nər-ə) *Law* A contract of pawn or personal property; also, personal property pawned. [< L, pledge, pawn]
pig·nut (pig′nut′) *n.* **1.** The fruit of a species of hickory (*Carya glabra*) common in the United States. **2.** The tree. **3.** St. Anthony's nut (which see).
pig·pen (pig′pen′) *n.* A pen or sty where pigs are kept.
pig·skin (pig′skin′) *n.* **1.** The skin of a pig. **2.** Something made of this skin, as a saddle. **3.** *U.S. Informal* A football.
pig·stick·ing (pig′stik′ing) *n.* The spearing of wild boars.
pig·sty (pig′stī′) *n. pl.* **·sties** A sty or pen for pigs.
pig·tail (pig′tāl′) *n.* **1.** A braid or plait of hair extending down from the back of the head. **2.** A twist of tobacco. **3.** The tail of a pig.
pig·tailed (pig′tāld′) *adj.* Having hair braided in a pigtail or pigtails.
pig·weed (pig′wēd′) *n.* **1.** Any of several American goose-

foots; especially, the **white pigweed** (*Chenopodium album*). **2.** Redroot (def. 3).
pi·ka (pī′kə) *n.* Any of various small, harelike mammals (family *Ochotonidae*) without tails, mostly of North America and Asia; especially, the little chief hare. [< Tungus (East Siberian) *piikd*]
pike[1] (pīk) *n.* A long pole having a metal spearhead, used by foot soldiers in medieval warfare. — *v.t.* **piked, pik·ing** To run through or kill with a pike. [< MF *pique.* Akin to OF *pic* pike[5], and *piquer* to pierce.]
pike[2] (pīk) *n.* **1.** Any of various widely-distributed, voracious freshwater food fishes (family *Esocidae*) having a slender body, a long snout, and spiny fins, as the **northern pike** (*Esox lucius*) and the muskellunge: also, *Canadian, jackfish.* **2.** Any of several other fishes resembling the pike, as the garpike. [Appar. short for *pikefish* < PIKE[5] + FISH with ref. to its pointed snout]

PIKE HEADS

pike[3] (pīk) *n.* **1.** A turnpike (which see). **2.** The fee for using a turnpike road. — *v.i.* **piked, pik·ing** *Slang* To go in haste: usually with *along.* [Short for TURNPIKE]
pike[4] (pīk) *n. Brit. Dial.* A mountain peak or pointed hill. [Appar. < PIKE[1]]
pike[5] (pīk) *n.* A spike or sharp point, as the end of a spear. [OE *pīc*]
Pike (pīk), **Zebulon Montgomery,** 1779–1813, U.S. general; explored the American West.
piked (pīkt, pī′kid) *adj.* Having a pike; pointed. [< PIKE[5]]
pike·man (pīk′mən) *n. pl.* **·men** (-mən) A soldier armed with a pike. [< PIKE[1] + MAN]
pike perch A pikelike percoid fish, as the walleyed pike or the sauger.
pik·er (pī′kər) *n. U.S. Slang* **1.** One who bets or speculates in a small, niggardly way. **2.** One who acts in a petty or niggling way. [Appar. after *Pike* County, Missouri, whose inhabitants were considered lazy, poor, suspicious, etc.]
Pike's Peak A mountain in central Colorado; 14,110 ft.
pike·staff (pīk′staf′, -stäf′) *n. pl.* **·staves** (-stāvz′) **1.** A piked staff, formerly carried by pilgrims, travelers, etc. **2.** The wooden handle of a pike. [< PIKE[5] + STAFF[1]]
pi·laf (pi·läf′) *n.* An Oriental dish of rice, raisins, spice, and a meat or fowl sauce. Also **pi·laff′, pi·lau** (pi·lou′, -lô′), **pi·law′** (-lô′). [< Persian and Turkish *pilāw*]
pi·lar (pī′lər) *adj.* Of, pertaining to, or covered with hair. [< NL *pilaris* < L *pilus* hair]
pi·las·ter (pi·las′tər) *n. Archit.* A rectangular column, with capital and base, engaged in a wall. [< MF *pilastre* < Ital. *pilastro* < L *pila* column]

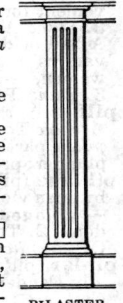

PILASTER

Pi·late (pī′lət), **Pontius** See PONTIUS PILATE.
Pi·la·tus (pē·lä′toos), **Mount** A peak near the Lake of Lucerne, Switzerland; 6,994 ft.
pil·chard (pil′chərd) *n.* **1.** A small, herringlike food fish (*Sardina* or *Arengus pilchardus*), the sardine of Mediterranean and European Atlantic waters. **2.** Any of various related fishes, as the **false pilchard** (*Harengula clupeola*) of American Atlantic waters, and the Pacific or California sardine. [Earlier *pilcher*; origin uncertain]
Pil·co·ma·yo (pēl′kō·mä′yō) A river in south central South America, flowing about 700 miles, generally SE, to the Paraguay, and forming part of the boundary between Argentina and Paraguay.
pile[1] (pīl) *n.* **1.** A quantity of anything gathered or thrown together in one place; a heap. **2.** A funeral pyre. **3.** A massive building or group of buildings. **4.** *Informal* A large accumulation, quantity, or number of something. **5.** *Physics* A reactor. **6.** *Slang* A large amount of money; a fortune. — *v.* **piled, pil·ing** *v.t.* **1.** To make a heap or pile of: often with *up.* **2.** To cover or burden with a pile or piles: to *pile* a plate with food. — *v.i.* **3.** To form a heap or pile. **4.** To proceed or go in a confused mass: with *in, on, off, out,* etc. — **to pile up 1.** To accumulate. **2.** *Informal* To reduce or become reduced to a pile or wreck: He *piled* the ship *up* on a reef. [< OF < L *pila* pillar, pier]
pile[2] (pīl) *n.* **1.** A heavy timber forced into the earth to form a foundation for a building, pier, etc.: also called *spile.* **2.** Any similar supporting structure, as of steel or concrete. **3.** *Heraldry* A charge in the shape of a wedge, usually pointed downward. — *v.t.* **piled, pil·ing 1.** To drive piles into. **2.** To furnish or strengthen with piles. [OE *pīl* dart, pointed stake < L *pilum* javelin used by the Roman foot soldier]
pile[3] (pīl) *n.* **1.** The cut or uncut loops that form the surface of certain fabrics, as velvets, plushes, and corduroys. **2.** The surface so formed. **3.** Hair collectively; fur; wool. **4.** Soft, fine hair; down. [< L *pilus* hair] — **piled** *adj.*
pi·le·at·ed (pī′lē·ā′tid, pil′ē-) *adj.* **1.** *Bot.* Provided with a pileus or cap. **2.** *Ornithol.* Having the feathers of the pileum

elongated or conspicuous; crested: the *pileated* woodpecker. Also **pi·le·ate.** [< L *pileatus* capped < *pileus* felt cap]

pile driver A machine for driving piles, usually with a heavy weight raised by a hoist between upright guides and released, so as to fall and strike the head of the pile.

pi·le·ous (pī′lē·əs) *adj.* Pilose.

piles (pīlz) *n.pl.* Hemorrhoids. [< LL *pila* ball]

pi·le·um (pī′lē·əm, pil′ē-) *n.* *pl.* **·le·a** (-lē·ə) *Ornithol.* The top of the head of a bird, from the base of the bill to the nape and above the eyes. [< L, var. of *pileus* felt cap]

pi·le·us (pī′lē·əs, pil′ē-) *n.* *pl.* **·le·i** (-lē·ī) **1.** *Bot.* The cap or expanded umbrella-shaped portion of a mushroom. For illustration see MUSHROOM. **2.** In ancient Rome, a brimless round felt cap. [< L, felt cap]

pile·wort (pīl′wûrt′) *n.* **1.** Celandine (def. 2). **2.** An American species of fireweed (*Erechtites hieracifolia*). [From its reputed ability to cure hemorrhoids]

pil·fer (pil′fər) *v.t. & v.i.* To steal in small quantities. — **Syn.** See STEAL. [Appar. < OF *pelfrer* to rob < *pelfre* plunder] — **pil′fer·er** *n.*

pil·fer·age (pil′fər·ij) *n.* **1.** The act of pilfering, or such acts collectively. **2.** Goods lost through pilfering.

pil·gar·lic (pil·gär′lik) *n.* *Dial.* One regarded with mock pity or contempt. **2.** *Obs.* A bald man. [< PILL² + GARLIC; with ref. to a peeled head of garlic]

pil·grim (pil′grim) *n.* **1.** One who journeys to some sacred place from religious motives. **2.** Any wanderer. [ME *pele-grim* < OF *pelerin* < L *peregrinus.* See PEREGRINE.]

Pil·grim (pil′grim) *n.* One of the English Puritans who founded Plymouth Colony in 1620.

pil·grim·age (pil′grə·mij) *n.* **1.** A journey made to a shrine or sacred place. **2.** Any long or arduous journey. — **Syn.** See JOURNEY. [ME < OF *pelrimage, pelerinage < peleriner* to go as a pilgrim < *pelerin.* See PILGRIM.]

Pilgrim Fathers The founders of Plymouth Colony, Massachusetts, in 1620.

Pilgrim's Progress A religious allegory in two parts (1678 and 1684) by John Bunyan.

pi·li (pē·lē′) *n.* **1.** An edible nut of a Philippine tree (*Canarium ovatum*), considered a delicacy after roasting. **2.** The tree. [< Tagalog]

pili- *combining form* Hair; related to hair. [< L *pilus* hair]

pi·lif·er·ous (pī·lif′ər·əs) *adj.* Having hairs.

pil·i·form (pil′ə·fôrm) *adj.* Resembling a hair in form.

pil·ing (pī′ling) *n.* **1.** Piles collectively. **2.** A structure formed of piles. **3.** The process of driving piles. [< PILE²]

pill¹ (pil) *n.* **1.** A pellet or globule containing medicine, convenient for swallowing whole. **2.** A disagreeable necessity. **3.** *Slang* A person difficult to bear with; a bore. **4.** *Slang* A ball or disk, as a baseball. — **the pill** or **the Pill** Any of various oral contraceptive drugs in tablet form, taken by women. — *v.t.* **1.** To form into pills. **2.** To dose with pills. **3.** *Slang* To blackball. [< L *pilula,* dim. of *pila* ball]

pill² (pil) *v.t. & v.i.* **1.** *Archaic* or *Dial.* To peel off; scale. **2.** *Archaic* To pillage. **3.** *Obs.* To make or become bald. [ME *pillen,* partly < OE *pylian* to strip, and partly < MF *piller* to plunder; prob. ult. < L *pilleum* rag or < *pilum* javelin]

pil·lage (pil′ij) *n.* **1.** The act of taking money or property by open violence, especially in war; looting. **2.** Spoil; booty. — *v.* **·laged, ·lag·ing** *v.t.* **1.** To rob openly, as in war; plunder. **2.** To take as loot. — *v.i.* **3.** To take plunder. [< OF < *piller* to plunder < L *pilare*] — **pil′lag·er** *n.*

pil·lar (pil′ər) *n.* **1.** A vertical, freestanding support, usually slender in relation to its height, made of wood, stone, clay, etc.; column; shaft. **2.** A structure of similar form used as a decoration or monument. **3.** Anything resembling a pillar in form or function. **4.** One who strongly supports a work or cause: a *pillar* of society. — **from pillar to post** From one predicament to another; hither and thither. — *v.t.* To support or adorn with or as with pillars. [< OF *piler* < LL *pilare* < L *pila* pillar]

pillar box *Brit.* A public mailbox in the shape of a pillar.

Pillars of Hercules Two promontories on opposite sides of the eastern entrance to the Strait of Gibraltar, identified with Gibraltar and Jebel Musa.

pill·box (pil′boks′) *n.* **1.** A small box for pills. **2.** A small, round, concrete emplacement for a machine gun, antitank gun, etc. **3.** A small, round hat with a flat top.

pill bug A small isopod crustacean (family *Armadillidiidae*), found under logs, etc., capable of rolling up into a tiny ball when disturbed.

pil·lion (pil′yən) *n.* A pad or seat behind the saddle of a horse or motorcycle for a second rider. [Appar. < Scottish Gaelic *pillean,* dim. of *pell* cushion < L *pellis* skin]

pil·li·winks (pil′ē·wingks) *n.* An old instrument of torture for the thumbs and fingers: also called *pinnywinkle.* [ME *pyrwykes;* origin unknown]

pil·lo·ry (pil′ə·rē) *n.* *pl.* **·ries** A framework in which an offender was fastened by the neck and wrists and exposed to public scorn. — *v.t.* **·ried, ·ry·ing** **1.** To set in the pillory. **2.** To hold up to public scorn or ridicule. [< OF *pellori, pilori;* origin uncertain]

pil·low (pil′ō) *n.* **1.** A case, usually of cloth, filled with a soft or yielding material, as feathers or foam rubber, used to prop up or cushion the head or other part of the body, as during sleep. **2.** A small, usually decorative cushion used chiefly as an ornament, as for a made-up bed. **3.** Any body rest. **4.** Anything resembling a pillow, as a cushion used in making bobbin lace. — *v.t.* **1.** To rest on or as on a pillow. **2.** To act as a pillow for. — *v.i.* **3.** To recline on or as on a pillow. [ME *pilwe* < OE *pyle, pylu,* ult. < L *pulvinus* cushion] — **pil′low·y** *adj.*

pillow block *Mech.* A block or other device designed to support a journal or shaft; a bearing.

pil·low·case (pil′ō·kās′) *n.* A covering drawn over a pillow. Also **pillow slip.**

pillow lace Bobbin lace (which see).

pi·lo·car·pine (pī′lō·kär′pēn, -pin, pil′ō-) *n.* *Chem.* A colorless to yellow liquid or crystalline alkaloid, $C_{11}H_{16}N_2O_2$, contained in jaborandi. Also **pi′lo·car′pin** [< NL *Pilocarpus,* genus of the jaborandi (< Gk. *pilos* felt + *karpos* fruit) + -INE²]

pi·lose (pī′lōs) *adj.* Covered with hair, especially with fine, soft hair; hairy; also *pileous, pilous.* [< L *pilosus < pilus* hair] — **pi·los·i·ty** (pī·los′ə·tē) *n.*

pi·lot (pī′lət) *n.* **1.** One who operates or guides an aircraft or spacecraft during flight. **2.** One who is trained and licensed to conduct ships in and out of port or through certain waters difficult to navigate. **3.** The helmsman of a ship. **4.** Any guide. **5.** *Mech.* A part that steadies or guides the action of a tool or other part. **6.** A pilot light (which see). **7.** A cowcatcher. — *v.t.* **1.** To act as the pilot of; steer. **2.** To guide or conduct, as through difficult circumstances. **3.** To serve as a pilot on, over, or in. — *adj.* **1.** Serving as a guide or control. **2.** Serving as a trial situation: a *pilot* project. [< MF *pillotte, pilot* < Ital. *pilota,* ? < *pedota,* ult. < Gk. *pēda* rudder, orig. pl. of *pēdon* oar]" — **Syn.** (noun) **2.** *Pilot, navigator, helmsman,* and *steersman* denote one who steers a ship. In specific usage, a *pilot* is one licensed to guide a ship in specified coastal or inland waters; a *navigator* is one qualified to operate on the high seas. A *helmsman* or *steersman* is a subordinate who handles a steering wheel at the direction of a superior.

pi·lot·age (pī′lət·ij) *n.* **1.** The act of piloting a vessel or aircraft. **2.** The fee for such service. **3.** Aerial navigation by reference to ground features.

pilot balloon A small balloon sent aloft to show the direction and velocity of the wind.

pilot bread Hardtack. Also **pilot biscuit.**

pilot engine A locomotive that precedes a train.

pilot fish **1.** An oceanic fish (*Naucrates ductor*), often seen in warm latitudes in company with sharks. **2.** A whitefish (*Prosopium cylindraceum*) of North American waters.

pi·lot·house (pī′lət·hous′) *n.* An enclosed structure, usually in the forward part of a ship, containing the steering wheel and compass: also called *wheelhouse.*

pi·lot·ing (pī′lət·ing) *n.* **1.** The occupation of a pilot. **2.** The branch of navigation that has to do with steering vessels in and out of ports or along coasts, or finding a ship's position by knowledge of landmarks, buoys, etc.

pilot lamp A small electric light that shows whether a given circuit, motor, etc., is functioning: also called *pilot light.*

pilot light **1.** A minute jet of gas kept burning for igniting an ordinary burner as soon as the gas is turned on: also **pilot burner.** **2.** A pilot lamp (which see).

pilot officer In the Royal, Royal Canadian, and other Commonwealth air forces, a commissioned officer ranking next below a flight officer. See table at GRADE.

pilot whale The blackfish (def. 1).

pi·lous (pī′ləs) *adj.* Pilose.

Pil·sen (pil′zən) A city in western Bohemia, Czechoslovakia; pop. 135,282 (est. 1958); Czech *Plzeň.*

pil·sner (pil′znər) *n.* *Often cap.* Beer of a kind originally brewed in Pilsen, Czechoslovakia. Also **pil′sen·er** (-zə·nər).

Pil·sud·ski (pēl·sŏŏt′skē), **Jozef,** 1867–1935, Polish general and statesman; first president of Poland.

Pilt·down (pilt′doun) A locality of eastern Sussex, England. Also **Pilt Down.**

Piltdown man Eoanthropus.

pil·ule (pil′yōŏl) *n.* A little pill; pellet. [< F < L *pilula.* See PILL¹.] — **pil′u·lar** *adj.*

pi·ma (pē′mə) *n.* *Often cap.* A strong, fine U.S. cotton grown from Egyptian strains; also, the fabric woven from it. Also **pima cotton.** [< *Pima* county, Arizona]

Pi·ma (pē′mə) *n.* *pl.* **Pi·mas** or **Pi·ma 1.** One of a tribe of North American Indians of southern Arizona and Northern Mexico. **2.** The Uto-Aztecan language of this tribe.

Pi·man (pē′mən) *n.* A branch of the Uto-Aztecan stock of North American Indians of southern Arizona and northern Mexico. — *adj.* Of or pertaining to Pima or Piman.

pi·men·to (pi·men′tō) *n.* *pl.* **·tos 1.** The dried, unripe, aromatic berries of a West Indian tree (*Pimenta officinalis*) of the myrtle family. **2.** Allspice. **3.** A sweet pepper or its ripe fruit, used as a relish and as a stuffing in olives: also called *pimiento.* [< Sp. *pimienta* pepper < Med.L *pigmentum* spiced drink, spice < L, paint, juice of plants. Doublet of PIGMENT.]

pimento cheese Cheese made from processed Neufchâtel curds, cream cheese, or cheddar with pimentos added.

pi·mes·on (pī′mes′on, -mē′son) *n. Physics* A short-lived, highly unstable, radioactive nucleon having a mass about 275 times that of the electron and an electric charge that may be either positive or negative. It decays spontaneously into mu-mesons and neutrinos: also called *pion.*

pi·mien·to (pi-myen′tō) *n. pl.* **·tos** Pimento. [< Sp. < *pimienta.* See PIMENTO.]

pimp (pimp) *n.* A pander; especially, one who solicits for a prostitute in exchange for part of her earnings. — *v.i.* To act as a pimp. [? < F *pimpant* seductive, ppr. of *pimper* to dress smartly, alter. of MF *piper* < L *pipare*, var. of *pipire* to murmur seductively]

pim·per·nel (pim′pər·nel) *n.* A plant (genus *Anagallis*) of the primrose family, usually with red flowers, as the common **scarlet pimpernel** or eyebright (*A. arvensis*). [< OF *pimprenele, piprenelle* < Med.L *pimpernella* < LL *pimpinella,* ? < L *piper* pepper]

pimp·ing (pim′ping) *adj. Informal* 1. Puny; sickly. 2. Mean; paltry. [Origin uncertain]

pim·ple (pim′pəl) *n.* A small swelling or elevation of the skin, with an inflamed base. [ME *pinple* < OE *piplian* to break out in pimples]

pim·ply (pim′plē) *adj.* Marked by many pimples: a *pimply* face. Also **pim·pled** (pim′pəld).

pin (pin) *n.* 1. A short, stiff piece of wire with a sharp point and a round, usually flattened head, used for fastening together parts of clothing, sheets of paper, etc. 2. An ornament mounted on a pin or having a pin with a clasp. 3. Anything resembling a pin in form or use, as a hairpin or clothespin. 4. A peg or bar, as of metal or wood, used in fastening or supporting, as the bolt of a door, a linchpin, etc. 5. A rolling pin (which see). 6. Something of no importance; a trifle. 7. In bowling and other ball-throwing games, one of the rounded wooden clubs, usually tapering toward the top, that are set up as the target. 8. In golf, a pole with a small flag attached to mark the position of a hole. 9. *pl. Informal* The legs. 10. *Music* A peg. 11. *Naut.* a A belaying pin. b A thole. — **on pins and needles** Uneasy or anxious; on edge; nervous. — *v.t.* **pinned, pin·ning** 1. To fasten with or as with a pin or pins. 2. To seize and hold firmly; make unable to move. 3. To transfix with a pin, spear, etc. 4. To force (someone) to make up his mind; follow a definite course of action, etc.: usually with *down.* 5. *U.S. Slang* In colleges and universities, to give one's fraternity pin to (a girl) as an expression of the intention to become engaged. 6. *U.S. Slang* To hold responsible for (a wrongdoing, etc.); accuse of: with *on.* [OE *pinn* peg]

pi·ña (pē′nyä) *n. Spanish* 1. The pineapple. 2. A sweet drink prepared from the pineapple.

pi·na·ceous (pī-nā′shəs) *adj. Bot.* Pertaining or belonging to the pine family (*Pinaceae*) of widely distributed coniferous trees and shrubs having needlelike leaves and bearing hard, woody cones. [< NL *Pinaceae* < L *pinus* pine]

piña cloth A soft, delicate fabric for scarfs, handkerchiefs, etc., made from the fibers of the pineapple leaf. [< PIÑA]

pin·a·fore (pin′ə·fôr, -fōr) *n.* A sleeveless apronlike garment, worn to protect a child's dress. [< PIN + AFORE]

pi·nang (pi·nang′) *n.* The betel palm, or its fruit. [< Malay *areca* betel nut]

Pi·nar del Rí·o (pē·när thel rē′ō) A Province in western Cuba; 5,211 sq. mi.; pop. 448,422 (1953); capital, **Pinar del Río.**

pi·nas·ter (pī·nas′tər, pi-) *n.* A pine (*Pinus pinaster*) of Europe common in the Mediterranean region. [< L, wild pine < *pinus* pine]

pin·ball (pin′bôl′) *n.* A game in which a ball is propelled by a spring to the top of an inclined board, and in its descent touches any of various numbered pins, holes, etc., the contacts so made determining the player's score.

pince-nez (pans′nā′, pins′-, *Fr.* pańs-nā′) *n. pl.* **pince-nez** Eyeglasses held upon the nose by a spring. [< F, lit., pinch-nose < *pincer* to pinch + *nez* nose]

pin·cer·like (pin′sər-līk′) *adj.* Resembling the action or form of one or both jaws of pincers: a *pincerlike* movement.

pin·cers (pin′sərz) *n.pl.* (*sometimes construed as sing.*) 1. An instrument having two handles and a pair of jaws working on a pivot, used for holding objects. 2. *Zool.* A nipper-

like organ, as the claw of a lobster. Also **pinch·ers** (pin′- chərz). [ME *pinsours,* appar. < AF *pincer* to pinch]

pinch (pinch) *v.t.* 1. To squeeze between two hard edges or surfaces, as a finger and thumb, etc. 2. To bend or compress painfully: This collar *pinches* my neck. 3. To affect with pain or distress: The cold *pinched* his fingers. 4. To contract or make thin, as from cold or hunger. 5. To reduce in means; distress, as for lack of money; straiten. 6. To move by means of a pinch bar. 7. *Slang* To capture or arrest. 8. *Slang* To steal. 9. *Naut.* To sail (a vessel) closehauled. — *v.i.* 10. To squeeze; hurt. 11. To be careful with money; be stingy. 12. *Mining* Of veins, to become narrow; also, to disappear: with *out.* — **Syn.** See STEAL. — **to pinch pennies** To be economical or stingy. — *n.* 1. The act of pinching, or the state of being pinched. 2. So much of a substance as can be taken between the finger and thumb; a small amount. 3. A time or instance of need or distress; an emergency. 4. *Slang* A theft. 5. *Slang* An arrest or raid. [< AF *pincher,* OF *pincier*] — **pinch′er** *n.*

pinch bar A crowbar with a short projection and a heel or fulcrum at the end for prying forward heavy objects.

pinch·beck (pinch′bek) *n.* 1. An alloy of copper, zinc, and tin, forming a cheap imitation of gold. 2. Anything spurious or pretentious. — *adj.* 1. Made of pinchbeck. 2. Cheap; spurious. [after Christopher *Pinchbeck,* 1670?–1732, English inventor]

pinch·bug (pinch′bug′) *n.* A stag beetle.

pinch·cock (pinch′kok′) *n.* A clamp used to compress a flexible tube and control the flow of liquid through it.

pinch effect *Physics* The self-constriction of a group of charged particles moving in such a way as to produce a unidirectional current, used in magnetohydrodynamics.

pinch-hit (pinch′hit′) *v.i.* **-hit, -hit·ting** 1. In baseball, to go to bat in place of a regular player, as when a hit is needed. 2. *U.S. Informal* To substitute for another in an emergency. [< PINCH (n. def. 3) + HIT]

pinch hitter One who pinch-hits.

Pin·chot (pin′shō), **Gifford,** 1865–1946, U.S. conservationist and politician.

Pinck·ney (pingk′nē), **Charles Cotesworth,** 1746–1825, and his brother, **Thomas,** 1750–1828, American Revolutionary soldiers and statesmen.

pin·cush·ion (pin′koosh′ən) *n.* A small cushion into which pins are stuck when they are not in use.

Pin·dar (pin′dər), 522?–443 B.C., Greek lyric poet.

Pin·dar·ic (pin·dar′ik) *adj.* 1. Of, pertaining to, or characteristic of Pindar. 2. Having a complex metrical structure. — *n.* A Pindaric ode (which see).

Pindaric ode An ode consisting of a strophe and antistrophe of similar structure and an epode of contrasting structure: also called *Pindaric, regular ode.*

pin·der (pin′dər) *n.* Pinner[2].

pind·ling (pind′ling) *adj. Dial.* 1. *U.S.* Delicate; sickly; pinched. 2. *Brit.* Peevish; fretful. [? Var. of PIDDLING or SPINDLING]

Pin·dus (pin′dəs) A mountain range in northern Greece, between Epirus and Thessaly; highest point, Smolikas, 8,650 ft.

pine[1] (pīn) *n.* 1. Any of a genus (*Pinus*) of cone-bearing trees having needle-shaped evergreen leaves growing in clusters, and including many important timber trees. 2. Loosely, any tree of the pine family (*Pinaceae*), including the cedar, fir, etc. 3. The wood of any pine tree. 4. *Informal* The pineapple. [Fusion of OE *pīn* and OF *pin,* both < L *pinus* pine tree]

pine[2] (pīn) *v.* **pined, pin·ing** *v.i.* 1. To grow thin or weak with longing, grief, etc. 2. To have great desire or longing: usually with *for.* — *v.t.* 3. *Archaic* To grieve for. [OE *pīn* torment, ult. < L *poena* punishment]

pin·e·al (pin′ē·əl) *adj.* 1. Shaped like a pine cone. 2. Pertaining to the pineal body. [< F *pinéal* < L *pinea* pine cone < *pinus* pine tree]

pineal body *Anat.* A small, reddish gray, vascular, conical body of rudimentary glandular structure found behind the third ventricle of the brain and having no known function: sometimes called *epiphysis.* Also **pineal gland.**

pineal eye *Biol.* The pineal body that in certain reptiles emerges as an eyelike structure.

pine·ap·ple (pīn′ap′əl) *n.* 1. A tropical American plant (*Ananas comosus*) having spiny, recurved leaves and a cone-shaped fruit consisting of the inflorescence clustering densely around a fleshy axis tipped with a rosette of spiked leaves. 2. Its edible fruit. 3. *Slang* A hand grenade resembling a pineapple in appearance. [< PINE[1] + APPLE]

PINEAPPLE

Pine Bluff A city in central Arkansas; pop. 57,389.

pine cone The cone-shaped fruit of the pine tree.

pine·drops (pīn′drops′) *n. pl.* **·drops** 1. A purplish brown

PINS

a Greek. *b* Roman. *c* Early French. *d* Russian. *e* Scandinavian. *f* Safety. *g* Hairpins. *h* Roundhead. *i* Hatpin.

saprophytic plant (*Pterospora andromedea*) with terminal clusters of nodding white flowers. **2.** Beechdrops (def. 1).

pine grosbeak A North American finch (*Pinicola enucleator*) having a slate-gray plumage that in the male is tinged with red.

pine knot 1. A knot in pine wood. **2.** Any person or thing as tough as a pine knot.

Pi·nel (pē·nel′), **Philippe,** 1745–1826, French physician, noted for reforms in treatment of the insane.

pine mouse The reddish brown vole (*Microtus pinetorum*) of the eastern United States.

pi·nene (pī′nēn) *n. Chem.* Either of two isomeric terpenes, $C_{10}H_{16}$, the principal constituent of turpentine and an ingredient of many essential oils. [< PIN(E)¹ + -ENE]

pine needle The needle-shaped leaf of a pine tree.

Pi·ner·o (pi·nâr′ō, -nir′ō), **Sir Arthur Wing,** 1855–1934, English dramatist.

pin·er·y (pī′nər·ē) *n. pl.* **·er·ies 1.** A hothouse for growing pineapples. **2.** A pine forest, especially one where lumbering is carried on.

Pines, Isle of An island of Cuba SE of Pinar del Río; 1,182 sq. mi.: Spanish *Isla de Pinos.*

pine·sap (pīn′sap′) *n.* A low, fragrant plant (*Hypopitys latisquama*), whitish or reddish, parasitic on roots or living on dead vegetable material. [< PINE¹ + SAP²]

pine siskin A finch (*Spinus pinus*) of North America having streaked plumage, showing yellow on the wings and tail. Also **pine finch.**

pine squirrel See under SQUIRREL.

pine tar A dark, viscous tar obtained by the destructive distillation of the wood of pine trees, used in the treatment of skin ailments.

Pine-Tree State Nickname of MAINE.

pi·ne·tum (pī·nē′təm) *n. pl.* **·ta** (-tə) A plantation of pine trees. [< L, pine grove < *pinus* pine tree]

pine warbler A small warbler (*Dendroica pinus*) common in the pine forests of the eastern United States.

pine·y (pī′nē) See PINY.

Pine·y (pī′nē) *n. U.S.* A poor white living in a pine woods area of New Jersey or the South. Also **Pin·er** (pī′nər).

pin·feath·er (pin′feth′ər) *n. Ornithol.* **1.** A rudimentary feather. **2.** A feather just beginning to grow through the skin.

pin·fish (pin′fish′) *n. pl.* **·fish** or **·fish·es** A sparoid fish (*Lagodon rhomboides*) allied to the porgy, common on the Atlantic coast of the southern United States.

pin·fold (pin′fōld′) *n.* A pound for stray animals, especially for cattle. — *v.t.* To shut in a pinfold. [OE *pundfald.* See POUND², FOLD²; infl. in form by *pyndan* to enclose.]

ping (ping) *n.* A brief, sharp, high-pitched sound. — *v.i.* To make this sound. [Imit.]

pin·go (ping′gō) *n. Canadian* A conical hill formed by frost action.

ping-pong (ping′pong′, -pông′) *n.* The game of table tennis. [< *Ping Pong,* a trade name]

pin·grass (pin′gras′, -gräs′) *n.* Alfilleria.

pin·guid (ping′gwid) *adj.* Containing or resembling oil or fat; unctuous. [< L *pinguis* fat] — **pin·guid′i·ty** *n.*

pin·head (pin′hed′) *n.* **1.** The head of a pin. **2.** Any small or insignificant object. **3.** A small minnow. **4.** A person afflicted with microcephaly; a microcephalic. **5.** *Slang* A brainless or stupid person; a fool.

pin·hole (pin′hōl′) *n.* A minute puncture made by or as by a pin.

pinhole camera A camera consisting of a box having a small aperture functioning as a lens at one end, the image being projected on the film at the other end.

pin·ion¹ (pin′yən) *n.* **1.** The wing of a bird. **2.** A feather; quill. **3.** The outer segment of a bird's wing, bearing the flight feathers. **4.** The anterior border of the wing of an insect. — *v.t.* **1.** To cut off one pinion or bind the wings of (a bird) so as to prevent flight. **2.** To cut or bind (the wings) of a bird. **3.** To bind or hold the arms of (someone) so as to render helpless. **4.** To shackle; confine. [< OF *pignon* streamer, feather < L *penna, pinna* feather]

pin·ion² (pin′yən) *n. Mech.* A toothed wheel driving or driven by a larger cogwheel. For illustration see DIFFERENTIAL GEAR. [< F *pignon,* orig., battlement < OF *pinun* < L *pinna,* orig., pinnacle]

pin·ite (pin′īt, pī′nīt) *n.* A hydrous potassium-aluminum silicate. [< G *pinit* < *Pin(i),* a mine in Saxony + -ITE¹]

pink¹ (pingk) *n.* **1.** A pale hue of crimson. **2.** Any of several garden plants (genus *Dianthus*) with narrow, grasslike leaves and fragrant flowers, as the **garden pink** (*D. plumarius*) and the **China** or **rainbow pink** (*D. chinensis*). **3.** The flower of any of these plants, as the carnation. **4.** The highest or best condition, degree, or example: the *pink* of fashion. **5.** *Informal* A person who holds somewhat radical economic or political views: a contemptuous term. Also *U.S. Slang* **pink·o** (pingk′ō). **6.** *Brit.* The scarlet displayed by fox hunters; also, a scarlet hunting coat. **7.** *Brit.* A fox hunter. — **in the pink (of condition)** *Informal* In excellent health. — *adj.* **1.** Being pink in color. **2.** *Informal* Moderately radical. [Origin uncertain]

pink² (pingk) *v.t.* **1.** To prick or stab with a pointed weapon. **2.** To decorate, as cloth or leather, with a pattern of holes. **3.** To cut or finish the edges of (cloth) with a notched pattern, as to prevent raveling or for decoration. **4.** *Brit.* To adorn; deck. [ME *pynken.* Cf. OE *pyngan* to prick.]

pink³ (pingk) *n. Naut.* A sailing vessel with a narrow stern, originally flat-bottomed with bulging sides: also called *pink-stern.* Also **pink′ie, pink′y.** [Appar. < MDu. *pincke* a small seagoing ship; ult. origin unknown]

pink⁴ (pingk) *v.i. Brit. Dial.* **1.** To blink; peer. **2.** To draw in; fade, as daylight: with *in.* [Cf. Du. *pinken* to blink, glimmer]

pink bollworm *n.* A bollworm (def. 1).

Pink·er·ton (pingk′ər·tən), **Allan,** 1819–84, U.S. private detective born in Scotland.

pink·eye (pingk′ī′) *n.* **1.** *Pathol.* An acute, contagious conjunctivitis marked by redness of the eyeball. **2.** *Vet.* A febrile, contagious keratitis of sheep.

pink·ie (pingk′ē) *n. U.S. Informal* The little or fifth finger. Also **pink′y.** [Prob. < obs. *pink* small]

pink·ing (pingk′ing) *n.* **1.** The act or process of pinking fabrics. **2.** The act of stabbing. [Orig. ppr. of PINK²]

pinking shears Shears with serrated blades for scalloping the edges of fabrics.

pink·ish (pingk′ish) *adj.* Somewhat pink.

pink rhododendron A tall rhododendron (*Rhododendron macrophyllum*) having rosy purple flowers, common on the Pacific coast: State flower of Washington.

pink·root (pingk′rōōt′, -rōōt′) *n.* **1.** The root of any of several perennial herbs (genus *Spigelia*), especially the **Carolina pinkroot** (*S. marilandica*), used as an anthelmintic: also called *wormroot.* **2.** A plant yielding such a root.

Pink·ster (pingk′stər) *n. U.S. Dial.* Whitsunday or Whitsuntide: also spelled *Pinxter.* [< Du. *pinkster,* ult. < Gothic *paintekuste* < Gk. *pentēkostē.* See PENTECOST.]

pink·ster flower (pingk′stər) See PINXTER FLOWER.

pink-stern (pingk′stûrn′) *n.* Pink³.

pink tea *U.S. Informal* An elegant social gathering or tea, especially one for women.

pin money 1. An allowance of money for minor incidental expenses. **2.** An allowance made by a husband to his wife for her personal expenses.

pin·na (pin′ə) *n. pl.* **pin·nae** (pin′ē) **1.** *Bot.* A single leaflet of a pinnate leaf. **2.** *Anat.* The auricle of the ear. **3.** *Zool.* A feather, wing, fin, or the like. [< NL < L *pinna, penna* feather] — **pin′nal** *adj.*

pin·nace (pin′is) *n. Naut.* **1.** Any ship's boat. **2.** Formerly, a small schooner-rigged vessel used as a tender, scout, etc. [< OF *pinasse* < Ital. *pinaccia,* prob. < L *pinus* pine]

pin·na·cle (pin′ə·kəl) *n.* **1.** A small turret or tall ornament, as on a parapet. **2.** Anything resembling a pinnacle, as a mountain peak. **3.** The highest point or place; apex; summit. — *v.t.* **·cled, ·cling 1.** To place on or as on a pinnacle. **2.** To furnish with a pinnacle; crown. [< OF *pinacle* < LL *pinnaculum,* dim. of L *pinna* wing, pinnacle]

pin·nate (pin′āt, -it) *adj.* **1.** Like a feather. **2.** *Bot.* Having the shape or arrangement of a feather: said of compound leaves or leaflets arranged on each side of a common axis. See illustration of LEAF. Also **pin′nat·ed.** [< L *pinnatus* feathered < *pinna* feather, wing] — **pin′nate·ly** *adv.* — **pin·na′tion** *n.*

pinnati- *combining form* **1.** *Bot.* Feathered; resembling a feather: *pinnatifid.* **2.** *Zool.* Pinni-. [< L *pinnatus* feathered < *pinna* feather]

pin·nat·i·fid (pi·nat′ə·fid) *adj. Bot.* Pinnately cleft, with the incisions halfway down or more to the midrib.

pin·nat·i·lo·bate (pi·nat′ə·lō′bāt) *adj. Bot.* Pinnately lobed, the lobes extending less than halfway to the midrib.

pin·nat·i·par·tite (pi·nat′ə·pär′tīt) *adj. Bot.* Pinnately parted.

pin·nat·i·ped (pi·nat′ə·ped) *adj. Ornithol.* Having lobed membranes to the toes.

pin·nat·i·sect (pi·nat′ə·sekt) *adj. Bot.* Pinnately divided as far as the rachis.

pin·ner¹ (pin′ər) *n.* **1.** One who or that which pins. **2.** A headdress with long flaps at each side, worn by women in the 18th century. **3.** *Dial.* A pinafore.

pin·ner² (pin′ər) *n. Obs.* An officer who impounded stray animals; a poundkeeper: also called *pinder.* [Var. of obs. *pinder* < OE *pyndan* to enclose]

pinni- *combining form Zool.* Web; fin: *pinniped.* Also *pinnati.* [< L *pinna* feather]

pin·ni·grade (pin′ə·grād) *adj. Biol.* Moving by means of flippers, as a seal. [< PINNI- + L *gradi* to walk]

pin·ni·ped (pin′ə·ped) *adj.* **1.** Having finlike locomotive organs. **2.** Of or pertaining to a suborder (*Pinnipedia*) of aquatic, carnivorous mammals, including the seals and walruses. — *n.* A pinniped animal. [< NL *Pinnipes, -pedis* < L *pinnipes* wing-footed, fin-footed < *pinna* wing, fin + *pes, pedis* foot] — **pin′ni·pe′di·an** (-pē′dē·ən) *adj. & n.*

pin·nu·la (pin′yə·lə) *n. pl.* **·lae** (-lē) **1.** A pinnule. **2.** *Ornithol.* A barb of a feather.

pin·nu·late (pin′yə-lāt) *adj.* Having pinnules. Also **pin′nu·lat′ed**.

pin·nule (pin′yōōl) *n.* **1.** *Zool.* **a** A small, detached fin, as in a mackerel. **b** A finlike appendage. **2.** *Bot.* One of the smaller or ultimate divisions of a pinnate leaf or frond; a secondary pinna. Also called *pinnula.* [< NL *pinnula,* dim. of *L pinna* wing] **— pin′nu·lar** *adj.*

pin·ny·win·kle (pin′ē-wing′kəl) *n.* Pilliwinks.

pin oak An oak (*Quercus palustris*) common in the eastern United States, having long pendulous branches.

pi·noch·le (pē′nuk-əl, -nok-) *n.* A card game for two, three, or four persons, played with a double deck of 48 cards with no card below a nine: also spelled *penuchle, penuckle.* Also **pi′noc·le.** [Origin uncertain]

pi·no·le (pi·nō′lā) *n.* *SW U.S.* A meal ground from corn, mesquite beans, or other plant seeds, and roasted. [< Am. Sp. < Nahuatl *pinolli*]

pi·ñon (pin′yən, pēn′yōn; *Sp.* pē·nyōn′) *n.* **1.** Any of various pine trees of the southwestern United States, having edible seeds: also called *nut pine:* also spelled *pinyon.* **2.** A seed from such a tree. [< Sp., pine nut < L *pinea* pine cone < *pinus* pine tree]

pin·point (pin′point′) *n.* **1.** The point of a pin. **2.** Something extremely small. **—** *v.t.* To locate or define precisely.

pins and needles A tingling or prickling sensation in some part of the body, as the fingers or toes; paresthesia. **— on pins and needles** Uneasy; nervous; anxious.

pin·scher (pin′shər) *n.* A Doberman pinscher (which see). [< G, terrier]

pin·set·ter (pin′set′ər) *n.* An automatic device used in a bowling alley to reset the bowling pins. Also **pin′spot′ter.**

pint (pīnt) *n.* **1.** A dry and liquid measure of capacity equal to half a quart. See table inside back cover. Abbr. *p., pt.* **2.** A container having such a capacity. **3.** *Scot.* A measure equivalent to three English pints. [< OF *pinte;* ult. origin uncertain. Cf. Sp. *pinta,* MDu. *pinte.*]

pin·ta (pin′tə, *Sp.* pēn′tä) *n.* *Pathol.* A tropical skin disease caused by a treponema and characterized by patches of discoloration: also called *carate.* [< Sp., spot < LL *pincta* < L *picta,* fem. pp. of *pingere* to paint]

Pin·ta (pin′tə, *Sp.* pēn′tä) *n.* One of the three ships of Columbus on his initial voyage to America.

pin·ta·do (pin·tä′dō) *n.* *pl.* **·dos** or **·does** The cero. [< Pg., lit., painted, pp. of *pintar* to paint, ult. < L *pingere* to paint]

pin·tail (pin′tāl′) *n.* **1.** A duck (*Anas acuta*) of the northern hemisphere, the male of which has a long, sharp tail. **2.** A sharp-tailed grouse (*Pedioecetes phasianellus*) of northern North America. **3.** The ruddy duck.

pin·ta·no (pin·tä′nō) *n.* *pl.* **·nos** or **·no** A green tropical fish (genus *Abudefduf*) marked with dark bands, found among coral reefs: also called *cow pilot.* [< Am. Sp.]

Pin·ter (pin′tər), **Harold,** born 1930, English playwright.

pin·tle (pin′təl) *n.* **1.** A pin upon which anything pivots. **2.** One of the metal braces or hooks upon which a rudder swings. **3.** The pin of a hinge of a gunlock. [OE *pintel* penis. Akin to PIN.]

pin·to (pin′tō) *adj.* *SW U.S.* Piebald; pied, as an animal. **—** *n.* *pl.* **·tos** **1.** *SW U.S.* A pied animal: said especially of a horse or pony. **2.** A kind of spotted bean (*Phaseolus vulgaris*) of the southwestern United States: also **pinto bean.** [< Am. Sp. < Sp., lit., painted, ult. < L *pingere* to paint]

Pintsch gas (pinch) A fuel and illuminating gas made by the destructive distillation of petroleum or shale oil. [after Richard *Pintsch,* 1840–1919, German inventor]

Pin·tu·ric·chio (pēn′tōō-rēk′kyō) 1454–1513, Perugian painter: original name *Bernadino di Bet·ti* (dē bāt′tē).

pin-up (pin′up′) *n.* *Slang* **1.** A picture of a sexually attractive young woman hung on the wall, as of a barracks. **2.** A young woman who is the subject of a picture used as a pinup. **—** *adj.* **1.** Capable of being affixed to a wall, etc. **2.** *U.S. Slang* Having the qualities for a pinup: a *pinup* girl.

pin·weed (pin′wēd′) *n.* Any of various perennial herbs (genus *Lechea*), having small greenish or purplish flowers.

pin·wheel (pin′hwēl′) *n.* **1.** A firework that revolves when ignited. **2.** A child's toy resembling a windmill.

pin·worm (pin′wûrm′) *n.* A nematode worm (*Enterobius vermicularis*) parasitic in the lower intestines and rectum of man, especially of children.

pinx. Pinxit.

pinx·it (pingk′sit) *Latin* He (or she) painted (it). Abbr. *pinx., pnxt., pxt.*

Pinx·ter (pingk′stər) See PINKSTER.

pinx·ter flower (pingk′stər) A North American shrub (*Rhododendron nudiflorum*) of the heath family, having showy pink or purplish flowers: also spelled *pinkster flower.*

pin·y (pī′nē) *adj.* **pin·i·er, pin·i·est** Pertaining to, suggestive of, or covered with pines: also spelled *piney.*

pin·yon (pin′yən) See PIÑON (def. 1).

pinvon jav A small, dark-colored jay (*Gymnorhinus cyanocephala*) of the Rocky Mountain region, having a long bill.

Pin·zón (pēn·thōn′), **Martín Alonzo,** 1441?–93, Spanish navigator; commanded the *Pinta* of Columbus' fleet. — **Vicente Yáñez,** 1460?–1524?, Spanish navigator; commanded the *Nina;* brother of the preceding.

pi·on (pī′on) *n.* *Physics* A pi-meson. [< PI + (MES)ON]

pi·o·neer (pī′ə-nir′) *n.* **1.** One of the first explorers, settlers, or colonists of a new country or region. **2.** One of the first investigators or developers in a new field of research, enterprise, etc. **3.** *Mil.* An engineer who goes before the main body, building roads, bridges, etc. **—** *v.t.* **1.** To prepare (a way, etc.). **2.** To prepare the way for. **3.** To be a pioneer of. **—** *v.i.* **4.** To act as a pioneer. [< OF *peonier* foot soldier < *peon* < ML *pedo, -onis* < L *pes, pedis* foot]

pi·ous (pī′əs) *adj.* **1.** Actuated by reverence for a Supreme Being; religious; godly. **2.** Marked by a reverential spirit. **3.** Practiced in the name of religion. **4.** *Obs.* Exhibiting filial respect and affection; filial. [< L *pius* dutiful, respectful] **— pi′ous·ly** *adv.* **— pi′ous·ness** *n.*

Pi·oz·zi (pē·ôz′ē, *Ital.* pyôt′tsē), **Hester Lynch Thrale,** 1741–1821, English writer, friend of Samuel Johnson: called *Mrs. Thrale.*

pip[1] (pip) *n.* **1.** The seed of an apple, orange, etc. **2.** *Slang* An admirable person or thing. [Short for PIPPIN]

pip[2] (pip) *n.* **1.** A spot, as on a playing card, domino, or die. **2.** Any of the small buds of the lily-of-the-valley. **3.** Any dormant rootstock of several flowering plants, as anemones and peonies. **4.** One of the diamond-shaped sections on the rind of a pineapple. **5.** A sharp audible or visible signal produced mechanically or electronically, as in radar. [< earlier *peep;* origin unknown]

pip[3] (pip) *v.* **pipped, pip·ping** *v.t.* **1.** To break through (the shell), as a chick in the egg. **—** *v.i.* **2.** To peep; chirp. [Prob. var. of PEEP[1]]

pip[4] (pip) *n.* **1** *Vet.* A contagious disease of fowls marked by mucus in the throat or by a scale on the tongue. **2** *Slang* A mild human ailment: used humorously. [< MDu. *pippe* < LL *pipita* < L *pituita* mucus, the pip]

pip·age (pī′pij) *n.* **1.** Pipes collectively; a system of pipes. **2.** The carriage of oil, gas, water, etc., through pipes.

pi·pal (pē′pəl) *n.* The sacred fig tree (*Ficus religiosa*) of India: also spelled *peepul.* [< Hind. *pipal* < Skt. *pippala*]

pipe (pīp) *n.* **1.** An apparatus, usually a small bowl with a hollow stem, for smoking tobacco, opium, etc. **2.** Enough tobacco to fill the bowl of a pipe. **3.** A long conducting passage of wood, metal, tiling, etc., for conveying a fluid. **4.** A single tube or long, hollow case. **5.** Any hollow or tubular part in an animal or plant body. **6.** *Music* **a** A tubular flute or woodwind instrument. **b** An organ pipe (which see). **c** *pl.* The bagpipe. **7.** The voice; also, a bird's note or call. **8.** A large cask for wine; also, a liquid measure of half a tun. **9.** *Metall.* A conical cavity in the head of a steel ingot, made by an escape of gas while the metal was cooling. **10.** *Slang* An easy college course. **11.** A boatswain's whistle. **12.** *Mining* An elongated, usually vertical or highly inclined body of mineral or rich ore. **—** *v.* **piped, pip·ing** *v.i.* **1.** To play on a pipe. **2.** To make a shrill sound. **3.** *Naut.* To signal the crew by means of a boatswain's pipe. **4.** *Metall.* To form conical cavities in hardening, as ingots. **—** *v.t.* **5.** To convey by or as by means of pipes. **6.** To provide with pipes. **7.** To play, as a tune, on a pipe. **8.** To utter shrilly or in a high key. **9.** *Naut.* To call to order by means of a boatswain's pipe. **10.** To lead, entice, or bring by piping. **11.** To trim, as a dress, with piping. **— to pipe down** *Slang* To become silent; stop talking or making noise. **— to pipe up** **1.** To start playing or singing: *Pipe up* the band! **2.** To speak out, especially in a shrill voice. [OE *pipe* (verb *pipian*), ult. < L *pipare* to cheep, ult. imit. of bird's cry. Doublet of FIFE.]

pipe-clay (pīp′klā′) *v.t.* To whiten with pipe clay.

pipe clay A white clay used for pottery, for making tobacco pipes, and for whitening military accouterments: also called *terra alba.*

pipe dream A groundless hope or wish; a daydream.

pipe·fish (pīp′fish′) *n.* *pl.* **·fish** or **·fish·es** Any of a family (*Syngnathidae*) of slender marine and fresh-water fishes having a straight, tubelike snout and bodies enclosed in a series of bony rings: also called *needlefish.*

pipe·fit·ting (pīp′fit′ing) *n.* **1.** A piece of pipe used to connect two or more pipes together. **2.** The work of joining pipes together. **— pipe′fit′ter** *n.*

pipe·line (pīp′līn′) *n.* **1** A line of pipe, as for the transmission of water, oil, etc. **2.** A channel for the transmission of information, usually private or secret. **—** *v.t.* **·lined, ·lining** **1.** To convey by pipeline. **2.** To furnish with a pipeline.

pipe of peace The calumet.

pipe organ An organ having pipes, as distinguished from an electric organ, etc.

pip·er (pī′pər) *n.* **1.** One who plays upon a pipe, especially a bagpipe. **2.** One who installs pipes. [OE *pipere* < *pipe.* See PIPE.]

pi·per·a·ceous (pī′pə-rā′shəs, pip′ə-) *adj.* *Bot.* Of or belonging to a family (*Piperaceae*) of tropical aromatic herbs and shrubs, including the common pepper plant of Asia and South America. [< NL *Piperaceae* < L *piper* pepper]

pi·per·i·dine (pi·per′ə·dēn) *n. Chem.* A colorless liquid alkaloid, $C_5H_{11}N$, with a strong odor and caustic taste, contained in piperine and also made synthetically. [< L *piper* pepper + -ID(E) + -INE²]

pip·er·ine (pip′ər·ēn, -in) *n. Chem.* A colorless crystalline alkaloid, $C_{17}H_{19}NO_3$, contained in pepper and made synthetically. [< L *piper* pepper + -INE²]

pip·er·o·nal (pip′ər·ə·nal′) *n. Chem.* A white crystalline aldehyde, $C_8H_6O_3$, derived from benzene, used in making perfumes. [< G < *piper(in)* piperine]

pipe stem 1. The stem of a tobacco pipe. **2.** Anything resembling the stem of a pipe, as a skinny leg. Also **pipe-stem** (pīp′stem′).

pipe·stone (pīp′stōn′) *n.* An indurated red clay much valued by the American Indians for making tobacco pipes.

pi·pette (pī·pet′, pi-) *n.* **1.** A small tube, often graduated, for removing or transferring measured quantities of a liquid. **2.** A funnellike can used in applying liquid decoration. Also **pi·pet′.** [< F, dim. of *pipe* pipe]

pip·ing (pī′ping) *adj.* **1.** Playing on the pipe. **2.** Having a shrill sound. **3.** Characterized by peaceful rather than martial music. — **piping hot** Extremely hot; red hot. — *n.* **1.** The act of one who pipes. **2.** Music of or suggesting that of pipes; a wailing or whistling sound. **3.** A system of pipes, as for drainage. **4.** A narrow strip of cloth folded on the bias, used for trimming dresses, etc. **5.** A cordlike decoration of icing on a cake.

piping plover See under RING PLOVER.

pip·it (pip′it) *n.* One of various larklike singing birds (genus *Anthus*) widely distributed in North America; especially, the common American pipit (*A. spindetta*): also called *titlark.* [Prob. imit. of its call]

pip·kin (pip′kin) *n.* **1.** A small earthenware jar. **2.** A piggin. [? Dim. of PIPE]

pip·pin (pip′in) *n.* **1.** An apple of many varieties. **2.** A seed; pip. **3.** *Slang* An admirable person or thing. [< OF *pepin* seed of a fruit; origin uncertain]

pip·sis·se·wa (pip·sis′ə·wə) *n.* An evergreen (genus *Chimaphila*) of the heath family, with white or pink flowers and thick leaves, used in medicine as an astringent and diuretic. [< Algonquian. Cf. Cree *pipisisikweu*, lit., it breaks it (gallstone) into pieces.]

pip-squeak (pip′skwēk′) *n.* **1.** A petty and contemptible person or thing. **2.** A small, insignificant person. [Orig. imit. name for a small German high-velocity shell employed in World War I]

pip·y (pī′pē) *adj.* **pip·i·er, pip·i·est 1.** Pipelike; tubular; containing pipes. **2.** Piping; thin and shrill.

pi·quant (pē′kənt, -känt, -kwənt, pē·känt′) *adj.* **1.** Having an agreeably pungent or tart taste. **2.** Tart; racy. **3.** Lively and charming; interesting. **4.** *Obs.* Stinging; sharp. — **Syn.** See RACY. [< F, orig. ppr. of *piquer* to sting. See PIQUE.¹] — **pi′quan·cy** *n.* — **pi′quant·ly** *adv.*

pique¹ (pēk) *n.* A feeling of irritation or resentment. — *v.t.* **piqued, pi·quing 1.** To excite resentment in. **2.** To stimulate or arouse; provoke. **3.** To pride (oneself): with *on* or *upon.* [< MF < *piquer* to sting, prick. ? ult. < L *picus* woodpecker]
  — **Syn.** (noun) displeasure, offense, umbrage, huff. — (verb) **1.** gall, nettle, peeve, roil, vex. Compare BOTHER, IRRITATE.

pique² (pēk) *n.* In piquet, the scoring of 30 points in one hand before the other side scores at all. — *v.t.* **piqued, pi·quing** To win a pique from. [< F *pic* < MF *piquer*. See PIQUE.¹]

pi·qué (pē·kā′) *n.* A fabric of cotton, rayon, or silk, with raised cord or welts running lengthwise in the fabric. [< F, lit., quilted, orig. pp. of *piquer* to prick, backstitch]

pi·quet (pē·ket′, Fr. pē·kā′) *n.* A two-handed game of cards in which the cards below the seven are excluded: also spelled *picquet.* [< F, ? dim. of *pique* spade in cards, pike < MF *piquer*. See PIQUE.¹]

pi·ra·cy (pī′rə·sē) *n. pl.* **·cies 1.** Robbery on the high seas. **2.** The unauthorized publication, reproduction, or use of another's invention, idea, or literary creation. [< Med.L *piratia* < Gk. *peirateia* < *peiratēs.* See PIRATE.]

Pi·rae·us (pī·rē′əs) A port city in southern Greece, near Athens; pop. about 186,000: Greek *Peiraievs.*

pi·ra·gua (pi·rä′gwə) *n.* **1.** A dugout canoe. **2.** A flat-bottomed boat with two masts, used in the Caribbean Sea. [< Sp. < Carib, dugout]

Pi·ran·del·lo (pē′rän·del′lō), **Luigi,** 1867–1936, Italian dramatist and novelist.

pi·ra·nha (pi·rä′nyə) *n.* A small, voracious, fresh-water fish of tropical South America (genus *Serrasalmo*), with massive jaws and sharp, trenchant teeth, that in schools will attack man or the larger animals: also called *caribe.* Also **pi·ra′ña, pi·ra′ya** (-rä′yä). [< Pg. (Brazilian) < Tupi, toothed fish < *piro* fish + *sainha* tooth]

pi·rate (pī′rit) *n.* **1.** A rover and robber on the high seas. **2.** A vessel engaged in piracy. **3.** A person who appro-

priates without right the work of another. — *v.t. & v.i.* **·rat·ed, ·rat·ing 1.** To practice or commit piracy (upon). **2.** To publish or appropriate (the work, ideas, etc., of another) wrongfully or illegally; plagiarize. [< L *pirata* < Gk. *peiratēs* < *peiran* to attempt] — **pi·rat·ic** (pī·rat′ik) or **·i·cal** *adj.* — **pi·rat′i·cal·ly** *adv.*

Pi·rith·o·us (pī·rith′ō·əs) In Greek mythology, a king of the Lapithae who with his friend Theseus attempted to carry off Persephone from Hades, and was punished by Pluto by being bound to a rock. See LAPITHAE.

pirn (pûrn) *n. Scot.* **1.** A small spindle. **2.** Yarn on a shuttle. **3.** A spinning-wheel bobbin. **4.** A fishing-rod reel. [ME]

pi·rogue (pē′rōg) *n.* A dugout or a canoelike boat. [< Sp. *piragua.* See PIRAGUA.]

pir·ou·ette (pir′ōō·et′) *n.* A rapid whirling upon the toes in dancing. — *v.i.* **·et·ted, ·et·ting** To make a pirouette. [< F spinning top, origin uncertain; ? blend of *pivot* pivot + *girouette* weathervane]

Pi·sa (pē′sä) A commune in Tuscany, NE Italy, on the Arno; noted for its leaning tower; pop. 91,108 (1961).

pis al·ler (pē zà·lā′) *French* Last resort.

Pi·sa·nel·lo (pē·sä·nel′lō), died 1456, Italian painter and medalist: original name **Antonio Pi·sa·no** (pē·sä′nō).

Pi·sa·no (pē·sä′nō), **Andrea,** 1270–1349?, Italian sculptor: original name **Andrea da Pon·te·de·ra** (pôn·tā·dā′rä). — **Nicola,** 1220?–78?, and his son **Giovanni,** 1240–1320, Italian sculptors and architects.

pis·ca·ry (pis′kər·ē) *n. pl.* **·ries 1.** *Law* The right of fishing in waters that belong to another: now usually in the phrase **common of piscary. 2.** A fishing place; fishery. [< Med.L *piscaria* < L *piscarius* of fishing < *piscis* fish]

pis·ca·tol·o·gy (pis′kə·tol′ə·jē) *n.* The science of fishing. [< L *piscatus*, pp. of *piscari* to fish + -LOGY]

pis·ca·to·ri·al (pis′kə·tôr′ē·əl, -tō′rē-) *adj.* **1.** Pertaining to fishes or fishing. **2.** Engaged in fishing. Also **pis′ca·to′ry.** [< L *piscatorius* < *piscator* fisherman < *piscari* to fish < *piscis* fish] — **pis′ca·to′ri·al·ly** *adv.*

Pis·ces (pis′ēz, pī′sēz) *n.pl.* **1.** A constellation, the Fish or Fishes; also, the twelfth sign of the zodiac. See CONSTELLATION, ZODIAC. **2.** A class of vertebrates that includes the teleosts or true fishes. [< L, pl. of *piscis* fish]

pisci- *combining form* Fish; of or related to fish: *piscivorous.* Also, before vowels, **pisc-.** [< L *piscis* fish]

pis·ci·cul·ture (pis′i·kul′chər) *n.* The hatching and rearing of fish. — **pis′ci·cul′tur·al** *adj.* — **pis′ci·cul′tur·ist** *n.*

pis·ci·na (pi·sī′nə, -sē′-) *n. pl.* **·nae** (-nē) *Eccl.* A stone basin in which the priest drains and washes the chalice after communion: also called *sacrarium.* [< Med.L < L, fish pond, tank < *piscis* fish] — **pis·ci·nal** (pis′ə·nəl) *adj.*

pis·cine (pis′īn, -ēn, -in) *adj.* Of, pertaining to, or resembling a fish < *piscis* a fish + -INE¹]

Pis·cis Aus·tri·nus (pis′is ô·stri′nəs) A constellation, the Southern Fish, containing the bright star Fomalhaut. See CONSTELLATION. [< L]

pis·civ·o·rous (pi·siv′ər·əs) *adj.* Feeding on fish.

Pis·gah (piz′gə), **Mount** A mountain ridge in Jordan, NE of the Dead Sea; highest peak, Mount Nebo, from which Moses saw the Promised Land.

pish (pish) *interj.* An exclamation of contempt. — *v.t. & v.i.* To use this exclamation.

Pi·sid·i·a (pi·sid′ē·ə) An ancient country, later a Roman province, of south central Asia Minor. — **Pi·sid′i·an** *adj.*

pi·si·form (pī′sə·fôrm) *adj.* Shaped like a pea. — *n. Anat.* A pea-shaped bone on the inner or ulnar side of the carpus. [< NL *pisiformis* < L *pisum* pea + *forma* form]

Pi·sis·tra·tus (pī·sis′trə·təs, pi-), 605?–527 B.C., Athenian statesman and tyrant. Also *Peisistratus.*

pis·mire (pis′mīr) *n. Archaic & Dial.* An ant. Also **piss·ant** (pis′ant). [ME *pissemire* < *pisse* urine + *mire* an ant; with ref. to its ejection of formic acid]

pis·mo clam (piz′mō) A clam (*Tivela stultorum*) of the southwestern coast of North America. [after *Pismo* beach, California]

pi·so·lite (pī′sə·līt) *n.* A concretionary limestone, composed of globules with a pealike structure. [< NL *pisolithus* < Gk. *pison* pea + *lithos* stone] — **pi′so·lit′ic** (-lit′ik) *adj.*

piss (pis) *n.* Urine. — *v.i.* **1.** To urinate. — *v.t.* **2.** To discharge as or with the urine. A vulgar term. [< OF *pissier*; prob. ult. imit.]

Pis·sar·ro (pē·sà·rō′), **Camille,** 1830–1903, French painter born in the West Indies.

pis·ta·chi·o (pis·tä′shē·ō, -tash′ē·ō) *n. pl.* **·chi·os 1.** A small tree (genus *Pistacia*) of western Asia and the Levant. **2.** Its edible nut. **3.** The flavor produced by or a delicacy flavored with the pistachio nut. **4.** A delicate shade of green, the color of the pistachio nut. Also **pis·tache** (-täsh′). [< Ital. *pistacchio* < L *pistacium* < Gk. *pistakion* < *pistakē* a pistachio tree, prob. < OPersian *pistah* a pistachio nut]

pis·ta·reen (pis′tə·rēn′) *n.* An old Spanish coin worth about 20 cents, used in the West Indies and United States in the 18th century. [Appar. alter. of Sp. *peseta* peseta]

pis·til (pis′til) *n. Bot.* The seed-bearing organ of flowering plants, composed of the ovary, with its contained ovules, and the stigma, usually with a style. For illustration see FLOWER. [< F < L *pistillum* pestle]

pis·til·late (pis′tə·lit, -lāt) *adj. Bot.* **1.** Having a pistil. **2.** Having pistils and no stamens. [< NL *pistillatus* < L *pistillum* pestle] Also **pis·til·lar·y** (-ler′ē).

Pis·to·ia (pēs·tô′yä) A commune in Tuscany, north central Italy; pop. 82,401 (1961).

pis·tol (pis′təl) *n.* A small firearm having a stock to fit the hand, and a short barrel, now either the revolver or automatic type fired from one hand. — *v.t.* **pis·toled** or **·tolled**, **pis·tol·ing** or **·tol·ling** To shoot with a pistol. [< MF *pistole* < MHG *pischol* < Czechoslovakian *pišt′al*; prob. ult. imit.]

pis·tole (pis·tōl′) *n.* A former European gold coin of varying value. [< F, short for MF *pistolet* pistol]

pis·to·leer (pis′tə·lir′) *n.* One who fires a pistol; formerly, a soldier carrying a pistol. Also **pis′to·lier′**.

pis·tol-whip (pis′təl·hwip′) *v.t.* **-whipped** or **-whipt**, **-whip·ping** To strike or beat with the barrel of a pistol.

pis·ton (pis′tən) *n.* **1.** *Mech.* A thick disk fitted to slide in a cylinder, and connected with a rod for receiving the pressure of or exerting pressure upon a fluid in the cylinder. **2.** A valve in a wind instrument for altering the pitch of tones. [< F, orig., pounder < Ital. *pistone* < *pistare* to pound < LL *pistare*, freq. of L *pinsere* to pound]

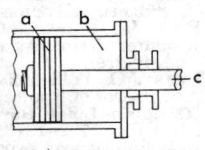

STEAM-ENGINE PISTON
a Piston. *b* Cylinder.
c Piston rod.

piston ring *Mech.* An adjustable metal ring fitted into a groove around the piston and designed to prevent leakage between the piston and the cylinder wall.

piston rod *Mech.* A connecting rod (which see).

pit[1] (pit) *n.* **1.** A natural or artificial cavity in the ground, especially when relatively wide and deep. **2.** A pitfall for snaring animals: snare. **3.** An abyss so deep that one cannot return from it, as the grave or hell. **4.** Great distress or trouble. **5.** In theaters: **a** Orchestra (def. 2). **b** *Brit.* The main floor of the auditorium, especially the rear part; also, the audience occupying this area. **6.** An enclosed space in which fighting cocks, etc., are pitted against each other. **7.** Any natural cavity or depression in the body: the *pit* of the stomach. **8.** An indention like a pockmark; any slight depression or excavation. **9.** A thin spot in the cell walls of some plants. **10.** That part of the floor of an exchange where a special line of trading is done: the wheat *pit*. **11.** A mining excavation, or the shaft of a mine. — *Syn.* See HOLE. — *v.* **pit·ted**, **pit·ting** *v.t.* **1.** To mark with dents, pits, or hollows. **2.** To put, bury, or store in a pit. **3.** To match as antagonists; set in opposition. — *v.i.* **4.** To become marked with pits. [OE *pytt* < L *puteus* a well]

pit[2] (pit) *n.* The kernel of certain fruits, as the plum. — *v.t.* **pit·ted**, **pit·ting** To remove pits from, as fruits. [< Du. < MDu. *pitte* kernel, pith. Akin to PITH.]

pi·ta (pē′tə) *n.* **1.** Istle (def. 1). **2.** The plant yielding istle. **3.** The fiber obtained from several kinds of yucca. [< Sp. < Quechua, a fine thread made from vegetable fiber]

pit-a-pat (pit′ə·pat′) *v.i.* **·pat·ted**, **·pat·ting** To move or sound with light, quick steps or pulsations. — *n.* A tapping or succession of taps, steps, or similar sounds. — *adv.* With a pitapat; flutteringly. Also *pitty-pat*. [Imit.]

Pit·cairn Island (pit′kârn) A British Colony in the South Pacific, settled in 1790 by mutineers of the British ship *Bounty*; 2 sq. mi.; pop. 76 (1969).

pitch[1] (pich) *n.* **1.** A thick, viscous, dark substance obtained by boiling down tar from the residues of distilled turpentine, etc., used in coating seams. **2.** Any of a class of residues obtained from the refining of fats, oils, and greases. **3.** The resinous sap of pines. **4.** Bitumen or asphalt, especially when unrefined. — *v.t.* To smear, cover, or treat with or as with pitch. [OE *pic* < L *pix, picis* pitch]

pitch[2] (pich) *v.t.* **1.** To throw or hurl; toss; fling. **2.** To erect or set up (a tent, camp, etc.). **3.** To set the level, angle, degree, etc., of. **4.** To put in a definite place or position. **5.** To set in order; arrange: now chiefly in the phrase **pitched battle**. **6.** In baseball, to deliver (the ball) to the batter. **7.** To set or be set in a pitch or key. **8.** In card games, to determine or announce (the trump suit) by leading a card of that suit. — *v.i.* **9.** To fall or plunge forward or headlong. **10.** To lurch; stagger. **11.** To rise and fall alternately at the bow and stern, as a ship: to *pitch* and roll. **12.** To incline downward; slope. **13.** To encamp; settle. **14.** To decide, especially at random: with *on* or *upon*. **15.** In baseball, to deliver the ball to the batter; act as pitcher. — **to pitch in** *Informal* **1.** To work together; cooperate. **2.** To start vigorously. — **to pitch into** To attack; assail. — *n.* **1.** Point or degree of elevation or depression. **2.** The extreme top or bottom point; the ultimate reach. **3.** The degree of descent of a declivity; also, a descent, slope, or inclination to the horizon. **4.** In building, the inclination of a roof. **5.** *Aeron.* **a** The movement of an aircraft about its

lateral axis. **b** The angle of attack of the blade of a propeller or rotor. **6.** *Mech.* **a** The amount of advance of a screw thread in a single turn. **b** The distance between two corresponding points on the teeth of a gearwheel. **7.** *Physics* The dominant frequency of a sound wave perceived by the ear, ranging from a low tone of about 20 cycles per second to a maximum high approaching 30,000 cycles. **8.** *Music* **a** The sensory impression of the acuteness or gravity of a tone or sound. **b** The exact vibration frequency of a tone expressed in cycles per second. **c** Any of various standards used for establishing the frequency of each tone in the gamut, as **International** (or **Concert** or **New Philharmonic**) **pitch**, with the A above middle C at 435 cycles per second, widely used in Europe, and **standard pitch**, with A at 440 cycles per second, used in the United States. **9.** The act of pitching; a throw. **10.** In baseball: **a** The delivery of the ball by the pitcher. **b** The place of pitching. **c** The distance pitched. **11.** *Geol.* The inclination or dip of a rock stratum or vein of ore. **12.** The act of dipping or plunging downward, as a ship: opposed to *scend*. **13.** Seven-up, a card game. **14.** A location or station for a vender, as on a sidewalk. **15.** A short, steep stretch of a mountain climb. **16.** *U.S. Slang* A practiced talk or appeal intended to influence or persuade: a sales *pitch*. — **auction pitch** A variety of the game of pitch in which the privilege of pitching is sold at auction by the player entitled to it. — **full pitch** In cricket, bowled to hit the wicket before touching the ground. [ME *picchen*; origin uncertain. Cf. ME *piken* to pierce. ? Akin to PICK[1].]

pitch accent *Phonet.* The stress given a speech sound, syllable, etc., by variations of pitch: also called *tonic accent*.

pitch-black (pich′blak′) *adj.* Intensely black, as pitch.

pitch·blende (pich′blend′) *n.* A black or brown variety of uraninite occurring in the massive form and resembling pitch in luster, the chief source of uranium and radium. [< G *pechblende* < *pech* pitch[1] + *blende* blende]

pitch-dark (pich′därk′) *adj.* Very dark; as black as pitch.

pitch·er[1] (pich′ər) *n.* One who pitches; especially, in baseball, the player who delivers the ball to the batter. Abbr. *p, p.* [< PITCH[2]]

pitch·er[2] (pich′ər) *n.* **1.** *Chiefly U.S.* A container with a spout and a handle, used for holding liquids to be poured out. **2.** A form of leaf suggestive of a pitcher. For illustration see PITCHER PLANT. [< OF *pichier* < LL *bicarium* jug < Gk. *bikos* wine jar. Akin to PECK[2], BEAKER.]

pitcher plant **1.** Any of several carnivorous plants having tubular leaves arranged in the form of pitchers that function as insect traps. **2.** The common American pitcher plant (genus *Sarracenia*): also called *huntsman's-cup.*

pitch·fork (pich′fôrk′) *n.* A large fork with which to handle hay, straw, etc. — *v.t.* To lift and throw with or as with a pitchfork. [< PITCH[2] + FORK]

Pitch Lake A deposit of natural asphalt in SW Trinidad; 114 acres; greatest depth, 285 ft.

pitch·man (pich′mən) *n. pl.* **·men** (-mən) *Slang* One who sells small articles from a temporary stand, as at a fair, etc.; a sidewalk vender.

PITCHER PLANT
(About 2 feet tall)

pitch pine Any of several American pines that yield pitch or turpentine; especially, the longleaf pine.

pitch pipe *Music* A small pipe that sounds a particular tone when blown, used to adjust the pitch of a voice or instrument; also, a group of such pipes combined in a unit.

pitch·stone (pich′stōn′) *n.* A volcanic glass having a resinous luster and the appearance of hardened pitch. [Trans. of G *pechstein* < *pech* pitch[1] + *stein* stone]

pitch·y (pich′ē) *adj.* **pitch·i·er**, **pitch·i·est** **1.** Resembling pitch; intensely dark; pitchlike. **2.** Full of or daubed with pitch. — **pitch′i·ly** *adv.* — **pitch′i·ness** *n.*

pit·e·ous (pit′ē·əs) *adj.* **1.** Exciting pity, sorrow, or sympathy. **2.** *Archaic* Affected with or feeling pity. — *Syn.* See PITIFUL. [< OF *pitos, piteus* < Med.L *pietosus* < L *pietas, -tatis.* See PITY.] — **pit′e·ous·ly** *adv.* — **pit′e·ous·ness** *n.*

pit·fall (pit′fôl′) *n.* **1.** A hidden danger or unexpected difficulty. **2.** A pit for entrapping wild beasts or men. [ME *pitfalle, putfal* < PIT[1] + *falle, fal* < OE *fealle* a trap]

pith (pith) *n.* **1.** *Bot.* The cylinder of soft, spongy tissue in the center of the stems and branches of certain plants. **2.** *Ornithol.* The spongy substance of the interior of the shaft of a feather. **3.** The marrow of bones or of the spinal cord. **4.** Concentrated force; vigor; substance. **5.** The essential part; quintessence; gist. — *v.t.* **1.** To destroy the central nervous system or spinal cord of (a frog, etc.) by passing a wire through the vertebral column. **2.** To remove the pith from, as a plant stem. **3.** To kill (cattle) by severing the spinal cord. [OE *pitha.* Akin to PIT[2].]

pith·e·can·thrope (pith′ə·kan·thrōp′) *n. Paleontol.* A member of the genus *Pithecanthropus.*

Pith·e·can·thro·pus (pith/ə·kan/thrə·pəs, -kan·thrō/pəs)
n. pl. ·pi (-pī) *n. Paleontol.* The genus of a small-brained
Pleistocene hominid represented by a fossil cranium, femur,
and other skeletal remains discovered near Trinil, central
Java, especially, *P. erectus*: also called *Java man, Trinil
man.* [< NL < Gk. *pithēkos* ape + *anthropos* man] —
pith/e·can/thro·pine (-pēn, -pin) *adj.*

pith helmet A topi.

pith·less (pith/lis) *adj.* Having no pith; lacking force.

pith·y (pith/ē) *adj.* **pith·i·er, pith·i·est** 1. Consisting of pith;
like pith. 2. Forceful; effective: a *pithy* remark. — **Syn.**
See TERSE. — **pith/i·ly** *adv.* — **pith/i·ness** *n.*

pit·i·a·ble (pit/ē·ə·bəl) *adj.* 1. Arousing or meriting pity or
compassion; pathetic. 2. Insignificant; contemptible. —
Syn. See PITIFUL. [< OF *piteable* < *piteer, pitier* to pity <
pitie. See PITY.] — **pit/i·a·ble·ness** *n.* — **pit/i·a·bly** *adv.*

pit·i·ful (pit/i·fəl) *adj.* 1. Calling forth pity or compassion;
miserable; wretched. 2. Evoking a feeling of contempt;
contemptible. 3. *Archaic* Full of pity; compassionate. —
pit/i·ful·ly *adv.* — **pit/i·ful·ness** *n.*
— **Syn.** 1, 2. *Pitiful, piteous, pitiable,* and *pathetic* are compared as they mean arousing or deserving pity. Something *pitiful*
actually arouses pity; that which is *piteous* or *pitiable* will probably
do so. *Pathetic* describes that which excites a more complicated
feeling of compassion, tenderness, etc., that surpasses mere pity.
All these words may be used contemptuously in deprecation of
weakness or sham, but *pitiable* and *pathetic* are more often used in
this way than the other two.

pit·i·less (pit/i·lis) *adj.* Having no pity or mercy; ruthless.
— **pit/i·less·ly** *adv.* — **pit/i·less·ness** *n.*
— **Syn.** inexorable, unrelenting, merciless.

pit·man (pit/mən) *n. pl. ·men* (-mən) *for def. 1,* **·mans**
(-mənz) *for def. 2* 1. One who works in a pit, as in a mine.
2. *Mech.* A rod that connects a rotary with a reciprocating
part; a connecting rod.

Pit·man (pit/mən), **Sir Isaac,** 1813–97, English educator, inventor of a system of shorthand.

pi·ton (pē·ton/, *Fr.* pē·tôn/)   *n.* An
iron spike, with an eye or ring in one
end, that can be driven into a crack in
rock or ice, used in mountaineering as
a hold or support for hand or foot, or
for karabiner and rope. See KARA-
BINER. [< F, staple, peak; origin
uncertain]

PITON HAMMER (*a*)
AND PITON WITH
KARABINER (*b*)

Pi·tot tube (pē·tō/) A device for measuring the velocity of a
fluid flow, consisting of a narrow bent tube with its opening
against the current and its upper portion above the surface
of the fluid. [after Henri *Pitot,* 1695–1771, French hydraulic engineer]

pit saw A two-handled saw for cutting logs over a pit, one
man standing on the log, the other in the pit.

Pitt (pit) *n.* Regent (def. 5).

Pitt (pit) See under CHATHAM ISLANDS.

Pitt (pit) **William,** 1708–78, first Earl of Chatham, English
statesman, prime minister 1766–68: called **the Elder, the
Great Commoner.** — **William,** 1759–1806, English statesman, prime minister 1783–1801, 1804–1806, son of the preceding: called **the Younger.**

pit·tance (pit/əns) *n.* 1. A small allowance of money. 2.
Any meager income or remuneration. [< OF *pitance,*
monk's food allotment, pity < *pite.* See PITY.]

pit·ter-pat·ter (pit/ər·pat/ər) *n.* A rapid series of light
sounds or taps. [Varied reduplication of PATTER[1]]

Pitts·burgh (pits/bûrg) A city in SW Pennsylvania, at the
confluence of the Allegheny, Monongahela, and Ohio rivers;
a major iron and steel center; pop. 520,117.

Pittsburg Landing A village in SW Tennessee; scene of
the Civil War battle of Shiloh, 1862.

Pitts·field (pits/fēld) A city in western Massachusetts, on
the Housatonic River; pop. 57,020.

pit-ty-pat (pit/ē·pat/) See PITAPAT.

pi·tu·i·tar·y (pi·too/ə·ter/ē, -tyoo/-) *adj. Physiol.* 1. Secreting mucus; mucous. 2. *Anat.* Of or pertaining to the pituitary gland. — *n. pl. ·tar·ies* 1. *Anat.* The pituitary
gland. 2. *Med.* Any of various preparations made from extracts of the anterior or posterior lobe of the pituitary gland.
[< L *pituitarius* pertaining to mucus < *pituita* mucus]

pituitary gland *Anat.* A small, rounded body at the base
of the brain in vertebrates, consisting of an anterior and a
posterior lobe that secrete hormones having a wide range of
effects upon the growth, metabolism, and other functions of
the body: also called *pituitary.* Also **pituitary body.**

pi·tu·i·tous (pi·too/ə·təs, -tyoo/-) *adj.* Containing, like, or
discharging mucus. [< L *pituitosus* < *pituita* mucus]

pit viper One of a family (*Crotalidae*) of venomous snakes,
as the rattlesnake, bushmaster, copperhead, etc., characterized by a small depression between the nostril and the eye.

pit·y (pit/ē) *n. pl. pit·ies* 1. Grief or pain awakened by the
misfortunes or sorrows of others; compassion. 2. That
which arouses compassion; misfortune. — *v.t. & v.i.* **pit·ied,**
pit·y·ing To feel compassion or pity (for). [< OF *pitet,
pitie* pity; piety < L *pietas, -tatis* dutiful conduct < *pius* dutiful. Doublet of PIETY.] — **pit/i·er** *n.* — **pit/y·ing·ly** *adv.*

— **Syn.** (noun) 1. *Pity, compassion, commiseration, condolence,*
and *sympathy* are compared as they denote mental distress caused
by the plight of another. Both *pity* and *compassion* are keen regret or sorrow, but *compassion* more strongly suggests the inclination to give aid or support, or to show mercy. *Commiseration* is
now largely confined to the expression of *pity* in sympathetic words,
etc., and *condolence* to a formal expression of regret, as to a bereaved family. *Sympathy* is a sharing of the feelings of another; it
becomes akin to *pity* when those feelings are sorrow, chagrin,
disappointment, etc. Compare MERCY.

pit·y·ri·a·sis (pit/i·rī/ə·sis) *n.* 1. *Pathol.* A skin disease in
which the epidermis sheds thin, branlike scales. 2. *Vet.* A
disease of domestic animals, characterized by dry scales. [<
NL < Gk. < *pityron* bran]

più (pyoo) *adv. Music* More: a direction to performers, as
in *più allegro* (faster), etc. [< Ital. < L *plus*]

Pi·us II (pī/əs), 1405–64, pope 1458–64; poet, diplomat, and
historian: original name **Enea Silvio Pic·co·lo·mi·ni** (pēk/-
kō·lô·mē/·nē). Also, *Lat., Aeneas Sylvius.*

Pius IV, 1499–1565, pope 1559–65; issued the Tridentine
Creed: original name **Giovanni Angelo Med·i·ci** (mä/dē·chē).

Pius V, Saint, 1504–72, pope 1566–72; promoted the
Counter Reformation: original name **Michele Ghis·lie·ri**
(gēz·lyä/rē).

Pius VII, 1742–1823, pope 1800–23; consecrated Napoleon
as emperor of France, later imprisoned by him: original name
Gregorio Luigi Barnaba Chia·ra·mon·ti (kyä/rä·mōn/tē).

Pius IX, 1792–1878, pope 1846–78; the doctrine of papal
infallibility was proclaimed by his Vatican Council 1870:
original name **Giovanni Maria Ma·stai-Fer·ret·ti** (mäs·tä/-
ē·fer·ret/tē).

Pius X, 1835–1914, pope 1903–14; canonized in 1954: original name **Giuseppe Sar·to** (sär/tō).

Pius XI, 1857–1939, pope 1922–39; signed treaty with Mussolini establishing Vatican City as a sovereign state: original
name **Achille Rat·ti** (rät/tē).

Pius XII, 1876–1958, pope 1939–58: original name **Eugenio
Pa·cel·li** (pä·chel/lē).

Pi·ute (pī·oot/) See PAIUTE.

piv·ot (piv/ət)   *n.* 1. *Mech.* Something
upon which a related part turns, oscillates,
or rotates, as a pin or short cylindrical
bearing fixed on only one end, for carrying
or rotating a swinging part. 2. A person
or thing upon which an important matter
hinges or turns. 3. *Mil.* In wheeling
troops, the soldier, officer, or point upon which the line turns.
4. The act of pivoting. — *v.t.* 1. To place on, attach by, or
provide with a pivot or pivots. — *v.i.* 2. To turn on a pivot;
swing. [< F, origin unknown]

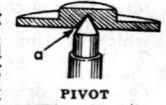

PIVOT
a Pivot point.

piv·ot·al (piv/ə·təl) *adj.* 1. Of, pertaining to, or being a
pivot. 2. Crucially important. — **piv/ot·al·ly** *adv.*

pix (piks) *n.pl. U.S. Slang* 1. Motion pictures. 2. Photographs. [Short for PICTURES]

pix·i·la·ted (pik/sə·lā/tid) *adj.* 1. Affected by the pixies;
mentally unbalanced; fey. 2. *Slang* Drunk. [Prob. alter.
of dial. E (Cornish) *pixy-led* bewitched]

pix·y (pik/sē) *n. pl. pix·ies* A fairy or elf. Also **pix/ie.** [<
dial. E *pixey, pisky;* origin uncertain.]

Pi·zar·ro (pi·zär/ō, *Sp.* pē·thär/rō), **Francisco,** 1471?–1541,
Spanish conquistador, conqueror of Peru.

piz·azz (pə·zaz/) *n. Slang* Exuberant energy; vitality; pep.

pizz. *Music* Pizzicato.

piz·za (pēt/sə, *Ital.* pēt/sä) *n.* An Italian food comprising a
doughy crust overlaid with a mixture of cheese, tomatoes,
spices, etc., and baked. [< Ital.]

piz·ze·ri·a (pēt/sə·rē/ə) *n.* A place where pizzas are prepared, sold, and eaten. [< Ital. < *pizza* pizza]

piz·zi·ca·to (pit/sə·kä/tō, *Ital.* pēt/tsē·kä/tō)   *Music adj.*
Plucked with the fingers rather than played with a bow. —
adv. In a pizzicato manner: a direction to the performer. —
n. pl. ·ti (-tē) A tone or passage played in a pizzicato manner. [< Ital., pp. of *pizzicare* to pluck, pinch]

pk. (*pl.* **pks.**) 1. Pack. 2. Park. 3. Peak. 4. Peck.

PK Psychokinesis.

pkg. Package(s).

PKU Phenylketonuria.

pl. 1. Place. 2. Plate. 3. Plural.

pla·ca·ble (plā/kə·bəl, plak/ə-) *adj.* Appeasable; yielding;
forgiving. [< OF < L *placabilis* < *placare* to appease] —
pla/ca·bil/i·ty, pla/ca·ble·ness *n.* — **pla/ca·bly** *adv.*

plac·ard (plak/ärd; *for v.,* also plə·kärd/) *n.* 1. A printed or
written paper publicly displayed, as a proclamation or
poster. 2. A tag or plate bearing the owner's name. — *v.t.*
1. To announce by means of placards. 2. To post placards
on or in. [< F *plaquer* to plate < MDu *placken*]

pla·cate (plā/kāt, plak/āt, plak/ət) *v.t.* **·cat·ed, ·cat·ing** To
appease the anger of; pacify. [< L *placatus,* pp. of *placare*
to appease] — **pla/cat·er** *n.* — **pla·ca/tion** *n.*

pla·ca·to·ry (plā/kə·tôr/ē, -tō/rē, plak/ə-) *adj.* Tending or
intended to placate. Also **pla/ca·tive.** [< LL *placatorius* <
L *placare* to appease]

place (plās) *n.* 1. A particular point or portion of space, especially that part of space occupied by or belonging to a

thing under consideration. **2.** A city, town, or other locality: *What places* did you visit? **3.** A house or dwelling: our *place* at the shore. **4.** Any building or area used for a special purpose: an eating *place*. **5.** A particular point, part, passage, etc.: The play was bad in several *places*. **6.** Position, rank, or status: his *place* in history. **7.** Social class, rank, or station. **8.** The right or proper position, location, or time: no *place* for laughter. **9.** Right or duty: It is not your *place* to ask. **10.** A job or appointment: Find him a good *place* in your company. **11.** An open square, court, or small street. **12.** A position or space left open or unfilled; stead: He is going in my *place*. **13.** *Math.* The relative position of a numeral by which it is assigned a certain value. *Abbr. pl.* — **in place 1.** In its natural or original position. **2.** Right or suitable; proper. — **in place of** In substitution or exchange for; instead of. — **out of place** Removed from or not situated in the natural or appropriate place, order, or relation; unsuitable; inappropriate; ill-timed. — **to go places** *Slang* To rise to success. — **to take place** To happen; occur. — *v.* **placed, plac·ing** *v.t.* **1.** To put in a particular place or position. **2.** To put or arrange in a particular relation or sequence. **3.** To find a place, situation, home, etc., for. **4.** To appoint to a post or office. **5.** To identify; classify: Historians *place* him in the time of Nero. **6.** To arrange for the satisfaction, handling, or disposition of: to *place* an order for a garbage truck. **7.** To bestow or entrust: I *place* my life in your hands. **8.** To invest, as funds. **9.** To emphasize or resonate tones of (the voice) consciously, as in singing or speaking. — *v.i.* **10.** In racing: **a** To finish second: distinguished from *show, win.* **b** To finish among the first three finishers. [< OF, ult. < L *platea* wide street < Gk. *plateia* < *platys* wide. Doublet of PIAZZA, PLAZA.] — **Syn.** (noun) **1.** locale, position, post, site, spot, station.
pla·ce·bo (plə-sē′bō) *n. pl.* **·bos** or **·boes 1.** In the Roman Catholic Church, the opening antiphon of the vespers for the dead. **2.** *Med.* Any harmless substance given to humor a patient or as a test in controlled experiments on the effects of drugs. **3.** Anything said in order to flatter or please. [< L *placebo* I shall please < *placere* to please]
place kick In football, a kick for a goal in which the ball is placed on the ground for kicking.
place·man (plās′mən) *n. pl.* **·men** (-mən) *Chiefly Brit.* An officeholder: often derogatory.
place mat A mat on which a table setting is placed.
place·ment (plās′mənt) *n.* **1.** The act of placing, or the state of being placed. **2.** Relative position; arrangement. **3.** The business or function of placing persons in jobs. **4.** In football, a place kick, or the play in which it is attempted.
place name The name of a geographic place.
pla·cen·ta (plə-sen′tə) *n. pl.* **·tas** or **·tae** (-tē) **1.** *Anat.* In higher mammals, the vascular, spongy organ of interlocking fetal and uterine membranes by which the fetus is nourished in the uterus. **2.** *Bot.* **a** The part of the ovary that supports the ovules. **b** The tissue from which sporangia develop in cryptogams. [L, cake < Gk. *plakous, -ountos* flat cake < *plax, plakos* flat object] — **pla·cen′tal, plac·en·tar·y** (plas′ən·ter′ē, plə·sen′tər·ē) *adj.*
pla·cen·tate (plə-sen′tāt) *adj.* Having a placenta. [< NL *placentatus.* See PLACENTA.]
plac·en·ta·tion (plas′ən·tā′shən) *n.* **1.** *Anat.* **a** The process of fetal attachment to the uterus. **b** The type of placenta or manner of its structure. **2.** *Bot.* The way in which the seeds are arranged in the pericarp of a plant, or the manner in which the placentas are attached. [< F. See PLACENTA.]
Pla·cen·tia (plə·sen′shə) The ancient name for PIACENZA.
Pla·cen·tia Bay (plə·sen′shə) An inlet of the Atlantic extending NE 100 miles into SE Newfoundland.
plac·er¹ (plā′sər) *n.* One who or that which places.
plac·er² (plas′ər) *n. Mining* **1.** An alluvial or glacial deposit of sand, gravel, etc., containing gold in particles large enough to be obtained by washing. **2.** Any place where deposits are washed for valuable minerals. [Var. of Sp. *placel* sandbank < *plaza* place, ult. < L *platea.* See PLACE.]
placer digging The act of obtaining minerals from deposits by washing. Also **placer mining.**
pla·cet (plā′sit) *n. Latin* **1.** Literally, it pleases; permission given by authority; sanction. **2.** A vote of assent, as by a council: expressed by saying the word *placet.*
plac·id (plas′id) *adj.* Having a smooth, unruffled surface or nature; unruffled; calm. — **Syn.** See CALM. [< L *placidus* pleasing < *placere* to please] — **pla·cid·i·ty** (plə·sid′ə·tē), **plac′id·ness** *n.* — **plac′id·ly** *adv.*
plack (plak) *n.* A small copper coin, formerly current in Scotland. [Prob. < MDu. *plak* coin, flat disk. Doublet of PLAQUE.]
plack·et (plak′it) *n.* **1.** The opening in the upper part of a dress, blouse, or skirt to make it easy to put on and take off. Also **placket hole. 2.** A pocket in a woman's skirt. [Origin unknown]
plac·oid (plak′oid) *adj. Zool.* Platelike, as the hard, spiny scales resembling teeth found on sharks and rays. — *n.* A

fish having platelike scales; an elasmobranch. [< Gk. *plax, plakos* flat object + -OID]
pla·fond (plà·fôn′) *n. Archit.* **1.** A flat or arched ceiling considered as the underside of the floor above, and usually elaborately decorated with painting or carving; also, a painting or carving on such a ceiling. [< F < *plat* flat + *fond* bottom]
pla·gal (plā′gəl) *adj. Music* Designating a type of medieval mode having its final a fourth above its lowest tone. [< Med.L *plagalis* < *plaga* plagal mode < Med.Gk. *plagios* < Gk., oblique < *plagos* side]
plagal cadence *Music* A cadence in which the subdominant chord immediately precedes the tonic chord.
pla·gia·rism (plā′jə·riz′əm, -jē-ə-) *n.* **1.** The act of plagiarizing. **2.** Something plagiarized. — **pla′gia·rist** *n.* — **pla′gia·ris′tic** *adj.*
pla·gia·rize (plā′jə·rīz, -jē-ə-) *v.* **·rized, ·riz·ing** *v.t.* **1.** To appropriate and pass off as one's own (the writings, ideas, etc., of another). **2.** To appropriate and use passages, ideas, etc., from. — *v.i.* **3.** To commit plagiarism. Also *Brit.* **pla′·gia·rise.** — **pla′gia·riz′er** *n.*
pla·gia·ry (plā′jər·ē, -jē-ər-ē) *n. pl.* **·ries 1.** The act or result of plagiarism. **2.** One who plagiarizes; a plagiarist. [< L *plagiarius* kidnapper, plagiarist < L *plagium* kidnapping < Gk. *plagios* oblique, crooked, treacherous]
plagio- *combining form* Oblique; slanting: *plagiotropism.* Also, before vowels, **plagi-.** [< Gk. *plagios* oblique]
pla·gi·o·clase (plā′jē·ə·klās′) *n.* Feldspar consisting chiefly of the silicates of sodium, calcium, and aluminum, and crystallizing in the triclinic system. [< PLAGIO- + Gk. *klasis* cleavage] — **pla′gi·o·clas′tic** (-klas′tik) *adj.*
pla·gi·ot·ro·pism (plā′jē·ot′rə·piz′əm) *n. Bot.* Geotropism in which growth occurs at an angle from the vertical. — **pla·gi·o·trop·ic** (plā′jē·ə·trop′ik), **pla·gi·ot′ro·pous** *adj.*
plague (plāg) *n.* **1.** Anything troublesome or harassing, producing mental distress; affliction. **2.** *Pathol.* Any of various forms of a virulent, febrile, highly contagious, and often pandemic disease caused by a bacillus (*Pasteurella pestis*), especially the bubonic plague. **3.** The Black Death. **4.** Any great evil or calamity. **5.** *Informal* Nuisance; bother. — *v.t.* **plagued, pla·guing 1.** To harass or torment; vex; annoy. **2.** To afflict with plague or disaster. [< OF *plage, plague* < LL *plaga* pestilence < L, stroke, blow, prob. < Gk. *plēgē* stroke < *plēssein* to strike]
— **Syn. 1.** irritation, vexation, worry.
pla·guy (plā′gē) *Informal adj.* Characterized by vexation or annoyance; troublesome. — *adv.* Vexatiously; intolerably: also **pla′gui·ly.** Also **pla′guey.**
plaice (plās) *n.* **1.** A flounder (*Pleuronectes platessa*) of European waters. **2.** Any of various American flatfishes, as the summer flounder (*Paralichthys dentatus*). [< OF *plais* < LL *platessa* flatfish, ult. < Gk. *platys* broad]
plaid (plad) *adj.* Having a tartan pattern; checkered. — *n.* An oblong woolen scarf of tartan or checkered pattern, worn in the Scottish Highlands as a cloak over one shoulder; also, any fabric of this pattern. [< Scottish Gaelic *plaide* blanket. ? < *peallaid* sheepskin < *peall* skin] — **plaid′ed** *adj.*
plain¹ (plān) *adj.* **1.** Having no noticeable elevation or depression; flat; smooth. **2.** Presenting few difficulties; easy. **3.** Clear; understandable: *plain* English. **4.** Straightforward; guileless. **5.** Lowly in condition or station; unlearned. **6.** Having no conspicuous ornamentation; unadorned; unvariegated. **7.** Not figured or twilled: *plain* cloth. **8.** Homely; unbecoming; unattractive. **9.** Not rich; simple: *plain* food. — *n.* An expanse of level, treeless land; a prairie. [< OF < L *planus* flat] — **plain′ly** *adv.* — **plain′ness** *n.*
— **Syn.** (adj.) See CLEAR, LEVEL. — (noun) *Plain, steppe, prairie, pampas,* and *tundra* denote a large tract of treeless land. Though derived from particular regions, the terms are now applied generally in physical geography. *Plain* is the general English term for a fairly level, unforested region; *steppe* is the Russian term for the same thing. Neither word implies anything about the soil, which may vary from barren to extremely fertile. The other words describe *plains* with differing soil. The *prairies* of the central United States are very fertile; the *pampas* of South America are not, affording some forage but little in cereal crops. The Siberian *tundra* that borders the Arctic region and has permanently frozen subsoil is poor in vegetation.
plain² (plān) *v.i.* **1.** *Dial.* To complain. **2.** *Obs.* To mourn. [< OF *plaindre* < L (*se*) *plangere* to strike (oneself, one's breast), to lament]
plain·clothes man (plān′klōz′, -klōthz′) A member of a police force not in uniform; especially, a detective.
plain-deal·ing (plān′dē′ling) *adj.* Dealing frankly and sincerely. — **plain dealing**
Plain·field (plān′fēld) A city in NE New Jersey; pop. 46,862.
plain-laid (plān′lād′) *adj.* Consisting of strands twisted together in the ordinary way: a *plain-laid* rope.
plain people *U.S.* The Amish, Mennonites, and Dunkers: so called from their plain dress.
plain sailing *Informal* Any kind of progress or advance-

ment in which no difficulties or setbacks are encountered.

Plains Indian A member of any of the tribes of American Indians formerly inhabiting the Great Plains of North America, belonging variously to the Algonquian, Athapascan, Caddoan, Kiowan, Siouan, and Uto-Aztecan stocks, but having in common the nomadic culture of the plains and dependence on the buffalo: also called *Buffalo Indian.*

plains·man (plānz′mən) *n. pl.* **-men** (-mən) A dweller on the plains.

plain·song (plān′sông, -song) *n.* The old ecclesiastical chant, having simple melody, not governed by strict rules of meter but by accentuation of the words. Also **plain·chant** (plān′chant, -chänt). [Trans. of Med.L *cantus planus*]

plain-spo·ken (plān′spō′kən) *adj.* Candid; frank.

plain-stanes (plān′stānz′) *n.pl. Scot.* A pavement; flagstones, as opposed to cobbles. Also **plain′stones′** (-stōnz′).

plaint (plānt) *n.* **1.** Audible utterance of sorrow or grief; lamentation; a complaint. **2.** *Brit. Law* A writ setting forth a grievance and asking redress. [< OF *plainte* < L *planctus* striking, lamentation < *plangere*. See PLAIN².]

plain text In cryptography, the original text of a message before conversion into or after reconversion from a code.

plain·tiff (plān′tif) *n. Law* The party that begins an action at law; the complaining party in an action: opposed to *defendant.* Abbr. *plf., plff.* [< OF *plaintif, plaintive* plaintive < L *planctus.* See PLAINT.]

plain·tive (plān′tiv) *adj.* Expressing a subdued sadness; mournful. [< OF, fem. of *plaintif*] — **plain′tive·ly** *adv.* — **plain′tive·ness** *n.*

Plain·view (plān′vyōō) A village in SE New York, on Long Island; pop. 32,195.

plait (plat, plāt) *v.t.* **1.** To **braid** (hair, etc.). **2.** To pleat. **3.** To make by pleating or braiding. — *n.* **1.** A braid, especially of hair. **2.** A pleat. [< OF *pleit* < L *plicitus,* pp. of *plicare* to fold]

plan (plan) *n.* **1.** A scheme, method, or design for the attainment of some object. **2.** A drawing showing the proportion and relation of parts, as of a building. **3.** Any sketch; draft. **4.** A mode of action. **5.** *pl.* Intentions or arrangements worked out in advance: holiday *plans;* I have *plans* for that evening. **6.** One of a number of hypothetical planes perpendicular to the line of vision between an object and the viewer. — *v.* **planned, plan·ning** *v.t.* **1.** To form a scheme or method for doing, achieving, etc. **2.** To make a plan of, as a building; design. **3.** To have as an intention or purpose. — *v.i.* **4.** To make plans. [< MF < OF, plane < L *planum* level ground < *planus* flat] — **plan′ner** *n.*

pla·nar (plā′nər) *adj.* Of or pertaining to a plane; lying in one plane; flat. [< LL *planaris* < L *planus* flat]

pla·nar·i·an (plə-nâr′ē-ən) *n. Zool.* Any of an order (*Tricladida*) of chiefly aquatic flatworms having trifid intestines, elongate flattened bodies, and the power of regenerating themselves when cut apart. [< NL *Planaria,* genus name of the flatworm < L, fem. of *planarius* level < *planus* flat]

planch (planch, plänch) *n.* A plank; board. Also **planche.** [< OF *planche* < L *planca*]

planch·et (plan′chit) *n.* A piece of metal ready to receive an impression. [Dim. of PLANCH]

plan·chette (plan·chet′, -shet′) *n.* A small board, usually resting on a vertical pencil and two casters, believed by some to spell out messages involuntarily when the fingers are rested lightly upon it. [< F, dim. of *planche* plank]

Planck (plängk), **Max** (**Karl Ernst Ludwig**), 1858–1947, German physicist; formulated the quantum theory.

Planck's constant *Physics* A universal constant (symbol *h*) having the value of approximately 6.624×10^{-27} erg per second. For any specified radiation, the magnitude of the energy emitted is given by the product *hv*, where *v* is the frequency of the radiation in cycles per second.

Plan·çon (plän·sôn′), **Pol** (**Henri**), 1854–1914, French basso.

plane¹ (plān) *n.* **1.** *Geom.* A surface such that a straight line joining any two of its points lies wholly within the surface. **2.** Any flat surface. **3.** A grade of development; stage; level: a *plane* of thought. **4.** *Aeron.* A supporting surface of an airplane: often used in combination: *monoplane.* **5.** An airplane. — *adj.* **1.** Lying in a plane; level; flat. **2.** Having a flat surface. **3.** Dealing only with flat surfaces: *plane* geometry. — **Syn.** See LEVEL. [< L *planus* flat]

plane² (plān) *n.* **1.** A tool used for smoothing boards or other surfaces of wood. **2.** A trowellike tool for striking off clay that projects above the mold. — *v.* **planed, plan·ing** *v.t.* **1.** To make smooth or even with or as with a plane. **2.** To remove with or as with a plane. — *v.i.* **3.** To use a plane. **4.** To do the work of a plane. [< F < LL *plana,* < OF *planer,* both ult. < L *planare* to level < *planus* flat]

plane³ (plān) *n.* A plane tree (which see). [< OF *plasne* < L *platanus* < Gk. *platanos* < *platys* broad]

plane⁴ (plān) *v.i.* **planed, plan·ing** **1.** To rise partly out of the water, as a power boat when driven at high speed. **2.** To glide; soar. **3.** To travel by airplane. [< F *planer* < OF *plan* plane < L *planum* level ground < *planus* flat]

plane angle Angle² (def. 1a).

plan·er (plā′nər) *n.* **1.** A machine for planing wood or metal. **2.** A smooth wooden block used for leveling a form of type, etc. **3.** One who or that which planes. [< PLANE²]

planer tree A small tree (*Planera aquatica*) allied to the elm, growing in wet places in the southern United States, having nutlike fruit and small ovate leaves: also called *water elm.* [after J. J. *Planer,* 1743–89, German botanist]

plane sailing *Naut.* A system for ascertaining a vessel's position on the supposition that the earth's surface is plane, not spherical.

plane-sheer (plān′shir′) *n. Naut.* Plank-sheer (which see).

plan·et (plan′it) *n.* **1.** *Astron.* One of the celestial bodies revolving around the sun and shining only by reflected light. Those within the Earth's orbit, Mercury and Venus, are called **inferior planets.** Those beyond it, the **superior planets,** are Mars, Jupiter, Saturn, Uranus, Neptune, and Pluto. Between Mars and Jupiter are the asteroids or **minor planets.** **2.** In ancient astronomy, one of the seven heavenly bodies (the Sun, Moon, Mercury, Venus, Mars, Jupiter, and Saturn) having a motion relative to the fixed stars. **3.** In astrology, a planet considered as an influence on human beings and their affairs. [< OF *planete* < LL *planeta* < Gk. *planētēs* wanderer < *planaesthai* to wander]

TABLE OF PLANETS

Name	MERCURY	VENUS	EARTH	MARS	JUPITER	SATURN	URANUS	NEPTUNE	PLUTO
Symbol	☿	♀	⊕	♂	♃	♄	♅	♆	♇
Distance from sun, millions of miles	36	67	93	142	483	886	1780	2790	3670
Mean diameter, miles	3000	7600	7918	4200	87,000	72,000	33,200	31,000	4000
Period of sidereal revolution	88 days	225 days	365.25 days	687 days	12 years	29.5 years	84 years	165 years	248 years
Period of rotation	88 days	20–30 days?	23 hr., 56 min.	24 hr., 37 min.	9 hr., 50 min.	10 hr., 14 min.	10 hr., 45 min.	15 hr., 48 min.	?
No. of satellites	0	0	1	2	12	9	5	2	0
Mass, Earth considered as 1.	0.0543	0.8148	1.0000	0.1069	318.35	95.3	14.58	17.26	0.1?
Escape velocity, miles per second	2	6.3	6.95	3.1	37	22	13	15	?
Mean density, water = 1	5.3	4.95	5.52	3.95	1.33	0.69	1.56	2.27	5?
Surface gravity, Earth = 1	0.38	0.87	1.00	0.39	2.65	1.17	1.05	1.23	0.5?
Mean orbital velocity, miles per second	29.76	21.78	18.52	15.00	8.12	6.00	4.23	3.37	2.95

plane table A surveying instrument used in mapping in the field.

plan·e·tar·i·um (plan/ə·târ/ē·əm) *n. pl.* **·i·ums** or **·i·a** (-ē-ə) **1.** An apparatus for exhibiting the features of the heavens as they exist at any time and for any place on earth, consisting of an array of suitably mounted stereopticons installed in a room having a circular dome. **2.** A room or building having such an apparatus. **3.** An apparatus or model representing the planetary system. [< PLANET + -ARIUM]

plan·e·tar·y (plan/ə·ter/ē) *adj.* **1.** Of or pertaining to a planet or the planets. **2.** Mundane; terrestrial. **3.** Wandering; erratic: a *planetary* career. **4.** *Mech.* Pertaining to or denoting a type of gearing in which one or more small wheels mesh with the toothed circumference of a larger wheel, around which they revolve, at the same time rotating axially. **5.** In astrology, under the influence of some of the planets. [< MF *planétaire* < OF *planete*. See PLANET.]

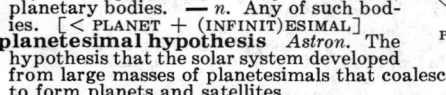

plan·e·tes·i·mal (plan/ə·tes/ə·məl) *Astron. adj.* Of or pertaining to very small, solid, planetary bodies. — *n.* Any of such bodies. [< PLANET + (INFINIT)ESIMAL]

PLANETARY GEARING

planetesimal hypothesis *Astron.* The hypothesis that the solar system developed from large masses of planetesimals that coalesced gradually to form planets and satellites.

plan·et·fall (plan/it·fôl/) *n.* The descent of a rocket or artificial satellite to the surface of a planet.

plan·e·toid (plan/ə·toid) *n. Astron.* An asteroid. — **plan/·e·toi/dal** *adj.*

plane tree Any of various large deciduous trees (genus *Platanus*) characterized by broad, lobed leaves and spreading growth, as the buttonwood: also called *plane, platan.* [See PLANE³]

plan·et·struck (plan/it·struk/) *adj.* Affected by the influence of planets. Also **plan/et·strick/en** (-strik/ən).

planet wheel One of the smaller wheels in an epicyclic train.

plan·gent (plan/jənt) *adj.* Dashing noisily; resounding, as the sound of bells. [< L *plangens, -entis,* ppr. of *plangere* to lament, strike] — **plan/gen·cy** *n.* — **plan/gent·ly** *adv.*

plan·gor·ous (plang/gər·əs) *adj.* Wailing; lamenting. [< L *plangor* lamentation < *plangere*. See PLANGENT.]

pla·ni·form (plā/nə·fôrm, plan/ə-) *adj.* Having the surfaces nearly flat.

pla·nim·e·ter (plə·nim/ə·tər) *n.* An instrument for measuring the area of any plane surface, however irregular, by moving a pointer around its boundary and reading the indications of a scale. [< F *planimètre*] — **pla·ni·met·ric** (plā/·nə·met/rik, plan/ə-) or **·ri·cal** *adj.* — **pla·nim/e·try** *n.*

plan·ish (plan/ish) *v.t.* To condense, smooth, toughen, or polish, as metal, by hammering, rolling, etc. [< MF *planiss-,* stem of *planir* to flatten < L *planare*. See PLANE².]

plan·i·sphere (plan/ə·sfir/) *n.* A plane projection of the sphere; especially, a polar projection of the heavens on a chart, showing the stars visible at a given time. [< OF < Med.L *planisphaerium* < L *planus* flat + *sphaera* sphere] — **plan/i·spher/ic** (-sfir/ik, -sfer/-) *adj.*

plank (plangk) *n.* **1.** A broad piece of sawed timber, thicker than a board. **2.** Anything that sustains or upholds; a support. **3.** One of the principles of a political platform. — **to walk the plank** To walk off a plank projecting from the side of a ship, a method once used by pirates for executing prisoners. — *v.t.* **1.** To cover, furnish, or lay with planks. **2.** To broil or bake and serve on a plank, as fish. **3.** *Informal* To put down emphatically or forcibly. **4.** *Informal* To pay: with *out, down,* etc. [< OF *planke* < LL *planca*]

plank·ing (plangk/ing) *n.* **1.** The act of laying planks. **2.** Anything made of planks. **3.** Planks collectively.

plank·sheer (plangk/shir/) *n. Naut.* A timber extending around a vessel's deck, covering and fastening the timberheads: also called *plane-sheer.*

plank·ton (plangk/tən) *n. Biol.* The marine animal and plant organisms that drift or float with currents, waves, etc., unable to influence their own course, ranging in size from microorganisms to jellyfish: distinguished from *benthos.* Compare NEKTON. [< G < Gk., neut. of *planktos* drifting, wandering < *plazesthai* to wander] — **plank·ton/ic** *adj.*

plano-¹ *combining form* Roaming; wandering. Also, before vowels, **plan-.** [< Gk. *planos* wandering]

plano-² *combining form* Flat; level; plane: *plano-convex*: also, before vowels, **plan-.** Also **plani-.** [< L *planus* flat]

pla·no·con·cave (plā/nō·kon/kāv) *adj.* Plane on one side and concave on the other. For illustration see LENS. [< PLANO-² + CONCAVE]

pla·no·con·vex (plā/nō·kon/veks) *adj.* Plane on one side and convex on the other. For illustration see LENS. [< PLANO-² + CONVEX]

pla·nom·e·ter (plə·nom/ə·tər) *n.* A device for gauging a plane surface, especially as used in metalworking. [< PLANO-² + -METER] — **pla·nom/e·try** *n.*

plant (plant, plänt) *n.* **1.** A living organism belonging to the vegetable kingdom, as distinguished from the animal kingdom, having typically rigid cell walls and characterized by growth chiefly from the synthesis of simple, usually inorganic food materials from soil, water, and air. **2.** One of the smaller forms of vegetable life, as distinct from shrubs and trees. **3.** A set of machines, tools, apparatus, etc., necessary to conduct a manufacturing enterprise or other business: a chemical *plant.* **4.** The buildings, grounds, and permanent appliances needed for any institution, as a post office, college, etc. **5.** A slip or cutting from a tree or bush; sapling. **6.** A person placed in a theater audience to encourage applause, speak lines, or contribute to the action of a play. **7.** An apparently trivial passage early in a story or play that later becomes important in shaping the outcome of the action. **8.** *Slang* A trick; dodge; swindle. — *v.t.* **1.** To set in the ground for growing. **2.** To furnish with plants or seed: to *plant* a field. **3.** To set or place firmly; put in position. **4.** To found; establish. **5.** To introduce into the mind; implant, as an idea or principle. **6.** To introduce into a country, as a breed of animal. **7.** To deposit (fish or spawn) in a body of water. **8.** To stock, as a river. **9.** To bed (oysters). **10.** *Slang* To deliver, as a blow. **11.** *Slang* To place or station for purposes of deception, observation, etc.: to *plant* evidence. **12.** *Slang* To hide; bury. [OE *plante* < L *planta* a sprout, cutting; ult. origin uncertain]

Plan·tag·e·net (plan·taj/i·net) A patronymic of the Angevin dynasty of English sovereigns from Henry II (1154) to the accession of the House of Tudor (1485). See table for ENGLAND. [< Med.L *planta genista* sprig of broom; with ref. to the habit of Geoffrey of Anjou, founder of the line, of wearing one]

plan·tain¹ (plan/tin) *n.* An annual or perennial herb (genus *Plantago*) widely distributed in temperate regions; especially, the **common** or **greater plantain** (*P. major*) with large, ovate, ribbed leaves. [< OF < L *plantago, -ginis* < *planta* sole of the foot; with ref. to the shape of the leaves]

plan·tain² (plan/tin) *n.* **1.** A tropical, perennial herb (*Musa paradisiaca*), sometimes growing to 30 feet. **2.** The long, bananalike fruit of this plant, edible when cooked. [< Sp. *plátano*; infl. in form by PLANTAIN¹]

plantain lily A cultivated plant (genus *Hosta*) of the lily family, having broad, ovate leaves and lavender or white flowers: also called *day lily.*

plan·tar (plan/tər) *adj.* Pertaining to the sole of the foot. [< L *plantaris* < *planta* sole of the foot]

plan·ta·tion (plan·tā/shən) *n.* **1.** Any place that is planted. **2.** A farm or estate of many acres, planted in cotton, tobacco, rice, etc., worked by resident laborers. **3.** A group of early settlers; a colony. **4.** An oyster bed or oyster farm. **5.** A grove cultivated for its wood. **6.** The act of planting. [< L *plantatio, -onis* a planting < *plantare* to plant]

plant·er (plan/tər) *n.* **1.** One who plants. **2.** An early settler or colonizer. **3.** An owner of a plantation. **4.** An agricultural implement for dropping seed in soil. **5.** A decorative container in which shrubs and flowers are planted, especially outdoors. **6.** *Canadian* In Newfoundland, a trader who hires and provisions fishermen in return for a share of the catch.

plan·ti·grade (plan/tə·grād) *Zool. adj.* Walking on the whole sole of the foot, as men, bears, etc. — *n.* A plantigrade animal. Distinguished from *digitigrade.* [< F < L *planta* sole of the foot + *gradi* to walk]

plant louse **1.** An aphid. **2.** Any of a family (*Chermidae*) of leaping insects that infest plants and suck their juices.

plan·u·la (plan/yə·lə) *n. pl.* **·lae** (-lē) *Zool.* The freely moving, ciliated embryo of certain coelenterates, as the hydroids. [< NL < L, dim. of *planus* flat] — **plan/u·lar, plan/u·late** (-lit, -lāt) *adj.*

plaque (plak) *n.* **1.** A plate, disk, or slab of metal, porcelain, ivory, etc., artistically ornamented, as for wall decoration. **2.** A small plate or brooch worn as a badge of membership, etc. [< F < MDu. *placke* flat disk, tablet < *placken* to piece together. Doublet of PLACK.]

plash¹ (plash) *n.* A slight splash. — *v.t. & v.i.* To splash lightly, as water. [Prob. imit.] — **plash/y** *adj.*

plash² (plash) *n.* A small pool. [OE *plæsc* pool. Prob. akin to PLASH¹.]

plash³ (plash) *v.t.* **1.** To bend down and interweave, as twigs or branches, so as to form a hedge or arbor. **2.** To form or trim (a hedge) in this manner. [< OF *plaissier,* ult. < L *plectere* to weave] — **plash/er** *n.*

-plasia *combining form* Growth; development; formative action: *hypoplasia*: also spelled *-plasy.* Also **-plasis.** [< Gk. *plasis* molding < *plassein* to mold, form]

-plasm *combining form Biol.* The viscous material of an animal or vegetable cell: *protoplasm.* [< LL *plasma* < Gk., form, figure < *plassein* to mold, form]

plas·ma (plaz′mə) *n.* **1.** The liquid portion of nutritive animal fluids, as blood, lymph, or intercellular fluid. **2.** The clear, fluid portion of blood, freed from blood cells and used for transfusions. **3.** The viscous material of a cell; protoplasm. **4.** A green, translucent variety of chalcedony, used among the Romans as a gem. **5.** *Physics* **a** The region in a gas-discharge tube in which there are approximately equal numbers of positive ions and electrons. **b** Any gas composed of such particles. Also **plasm** (plaz′əm). [< LL, a molded thing < Gk. *plasma* < *plassein* to mold, form] —**plas·mat·ic** (plaz·mat′ik), **plas′mic** *adj.*

plasma engine A reaction engine producing a small but sustained thrust by emission of a plasma jet. Compare ION ENGINE.

plasma jet *Physics* A beam of plasma ejected from a specially constructed generator that utilizes the pinch effect in forming a brilliantly luminous jet of extremely high energy and temperature.

plasmo- *combining form* Plasma; of or pertaining to plasma: *plasmolysis.* Also, before vowels, **plasm-.** [See PLASMA]

plas·mo·di·um (plaz·mō′dē·əm) *n.* *pl.* **·di·a** (-dē·ə) **1.** A mass of protoplasm resulting from the fusion of ameboid organisms, typical of the slime molds. **2.** Any of a genus (*Plasmodium*) of parasitic protozoans that include the causative agents of malaria. [< NL < PLASM(O)- + Gk. *eidos* form]

plas·moid (plaz′moid) *n.* *Physics* A small particle of plasma ejected from a plasma jet and capable of reacting as a unit under magnetohydrodynamic forces.

plas·mol·y·sis (plaz·mol′ə·sis) *n.* *Bot.* The withdrawal of water from a living plant cell, resulting in shrinkage of the protoplasm and cell wall. [< PLASMO- + -LYSIS]

plas·mo·lyze (plaz′mə·līz) *v.t.* & *v.i.* **·lyzed, ·lyz·ing** To subject to or undergo plasmolysis.

plas·mon (plaz′mon) *n.* *Biol.* The cytoplasm of a plant or animal cell, considered as a determinant of inheritance.

plas·mo·some (plaz′mə·sōm) *n.* *Biol.* The true, acid-staining nucleolus of a cell. [< PLASMO- + -SOME²]

-plast *combining form* An organized living particle or cell: *protoplast.* [< Gk. *plastos* formed < *plassein* to form]

plas·ter (plas′tər, pläs′-) *n.* **1.** A composition of lime, sand, and water, sometimes mixed with hair, for coating walls and partitions. **2.** Plaster of Paris. **3.** A viscid substance spread on linen, silk, etc., and applied to some part of the body, used for healing purposes. — *v.t.* **1.** To cover or overlay with or as with plaster. **2.** To apply a plaster to, as a boil or part of the body. **3.** To apply like plaster or a plaster: to *plaster* posters on a fence. **4.** To cause to adhere or lay flat like plaster. **5.** *Slang* To strike with great force or effect. [OE reinforced by OF *plastre* < LL *plastrum* < L *emplastrum* < Gk. *emplastron* < *emplessain* < *en* upon, into + *plassein* to mold] —**plas′ter·er** *n.* —**plas′ter·ing** *n.*

plas·ter·board (plas′tər·bôrd′, pläs′-, -bōrd′) *n.* A board made of a slab of gypsum mixed with fibers or of plaster between sheets of fibrous paper, used as wallboard or as backing for a plaster finish on walls.

plaster cast **1.** A cast or model of a person or object made by molding plaster of Paris. **2.** *Surg.* A cast (def. 7).

plas·tered (plas′tərd, pläs′-) *adj.* *Slang* Drunk.

plaster of Paris Calcined gypsum, setting readily when mixed with water, useful in making molds, casts, bandages, etc.: also called *plaster.* [With ref. to use of gypsum from Montmartre, Paris, in its preparation]

plas·ter·y (plas′tər·ē, pläs′-) *adj.* Like plaster; viscid.

plas·tic (plas′tik) *adj.* **1.** Giving form or fashion to matter. **2.** Capable of being molded; pliable. **3.** Pertaining to modeling or molding; sculptural. **4.** *Surg.* Efficacious in recreating or remodeling injured or destroyed parts: *plastic* surgery. — *n.* **1.** Any substance or material that may be molded. **2.** *Chem.* One of a large class of organic compounds synthesized from hydrocarbons, proteins, cellulose, or resins, capable of being molded, extruded, cast, or otherwise fabricated into various shapes, or of being drawn into filaments for textiles and fabrics. [< L *plasticus* < Gk. *plastikos* moldable < *plassein* to form, mold] —**plas′ti·cal·ly** *adv.*

—**Syn.** (adj.) **2.** *Plastic, pliable, malleable,* and *ductile* mean capable of being shaped. *Plastic* suggests the consistency of clay or wax, substances which are soft enough to be molded, yet capable of being hardened. *Pliable* suggests the flexibility of wood, while *malleable* and *ductile* are applied chiefly to metals. A metal which can be hammered or pressed into shape without fracturing is *malleable;* one that can be drawn into a wire without breaking is *ductile.* In extension, *plastic* and *malleable* persons can be trained, disciplined, or bent to another's will; *pliable* is used chiefly of the last of these extended senses. Compare ELASTIC. — **Ant.** rigid.

-plastic *combining form* Growing; developing; forming: *cytoplastic.* [< Gk. *plastikos* plastic, moldable]

plas·tic·i·ty (plas·tis′ə·tē) *n.* **1.** The quality or state of being plastic. **2.** Capacity for being shaped or molded.

plas·ti·cize (plas′tə·sīz) *v.t.* & *v.i.* **·cized, ·ciz·ing** To make or become plastic.

plas·ti·ciz·er (plas′tə·sī′zər) *n.* **1.** That which functions to make a substance plastic. **2.** *Chem.* Any of a class of substances adapted to preserve the softness and flexibility of materials to which they are added.

plastic surgery Surgery that deals with the restoration or healing of lost, wounded, or deformed parts of the body.

plas·tid (plas′tid) *n.* *Biol.* **1.** Any of various small, specialized masses in the cytoplasm of a cell: formerly called *protoplast.* For illustration see CELL. **2.** An elementary organism, as a cell. [< G *plastiden* < Gk. *plastēs, plastidos* molder < *plassein* to mold]

plas·tom·e·ter (plas·tom′ə·tər) *n.* An instrument for measuring the plasticity of a substance or material.

plas·tron (plas′trən) *n.* **1.** An ornamental addition to the front of a woman's dress, reaching from the throat to the waist. **2.** A leather shield worn on the breast by fencers. **3.** *Zool.* The ventral part of the shell of a turtle or tortoise: also **plas′trum.** **4.** The starched front of a man's shirt. **5.** An iron breastplate worn under a coat of mail. [< F, orig., breastplate < Ital. *piastrone* < *piastra* sheet of metal, ult. < L *emplastrum.* See PLASTER.] —**plas′tral** (-trəl) *adj.*

-plasty *combining form* *Surg.* An operation involving: **a** A (specified) part of the body: *osteoplasty.* **b** Tissue from a (specified) source: *zooplasty.* **c** A (specified) process or formation: *neoplasty.* [< Gk. *-plastia* formation < *plastos.* See -PLAST.]

-plasy See -PLASIA.

plat¹ (plat) *v.t.* **plat·ted, plat·ting** To plait or braid. — *n.* A plait; braid. [Var. of PLAIT]

plat² (plat) *Archaic* *n.* **1.** Plot (def. 1). **2.** A plotted map, chart, or plan. — *v.t.* **plat·ted, plat·ting** To make a plot or plan of. [Var. of PLOT; infl. in form by obs. *plat* flat thing or area < OF. See PLATE.]

plat. **1.** Plateau. **2.** Platoon.

plat- Var. of PLATY-.

Pla·tae·a (plə·tē′ə) An ancient city NW of Athens, Greece; scene of a Spartan and Athenian victory over the Persians, 479 B.C. Also **Pla·tae′ae** (-tē′ē). — **Pla·tae′an** *adj.*

plat·an (plat′ən) *n.* The plane tree. Also **plat′ane** (-ən). [< L *platanus* < Gk. *platanus.* See PLANE³.]

plate (plāt) *n.* **1.** A flat, extended, rigid body of metal or any material of slight but even thickness. **2.** A shallow vessel made of crockery, wood, glass, etc., in which food is served or from which it is eaten at table. **3.** Household articles, as trays, carving sets, etc., that are plated with a precious metal. **4.** A portion of food served at table; a dish; a plateful; also, a whole course served on one plate. **5.** A cup or other article of silver or gold offered as a prize in a race or other contest. **6.** A piece of flat metal bearing a design or inscription or intended for reproduction, as in a bookplate. **7.** Metal in sheets. **8.** An impression from an engraving, woodcut, etc., as reproduced in a book. **9.** An electrotype or stereotype. **10.** A full-page illustration printed on special paper in a book. **11.** A horizontal timber laid on a wall to receive a framework. **12.** *Dent.* A piece of metal, vulcanite, or plastic fitted to the mouth and holding one or more artificial teeth. **13.** A thin part of the brisket of beef. **14.** *Photog.* A sensitized sheet of glass, metal, or the like, for taking photographs. **15.** In baseball, the home base, usually flat and pentagonal in shape. **16.** *Biol.* A platelike part or structure; a lamina. **17.** A dish like a table plate used in taking up collections, as in churches; also, a collection. **18.** *Electronics* The principal anode in an electron tube. **19.** *Geol.* One of the huge blocks thought to make up the crust and upper mantle of the earth and, by their drift, determine the shape and position of the continents. **20.** *Obs.* A piece of silver money. Abbr. *pl.* — *v.t.* **plat·ed, plat·ing** **1.** To coat with a thin layer of gold, silver, etc. **2.** To cover or sheathe with metal plates for protection. **3.** In papermaking, to give a high gloss to (paper) by pressure between metal plates. **4.** *Printing* To make an electrotype or stereotype from. [< OF, sheet of metal < *plat* flat < LL *plattus*]

Plate (plāt), **River** The British name for the RÍO DE LA PLATA.

pla·teau (pla·tō′, *esp. Brit.* plat′ō) *n.* *pl.* **·teaus** or **·teaux** (-tōz′) **1.** An extensive stretch of elevated and comparatively level land; mesa. **2.** A stage or period of leveling off in the development of something. **3.** A broad, low stand for table decorations; also, a decorative plaque. **4.** *Psychol.* A relatively stable interval in the progress of a subject's learning ability, indicated by a flat portion on the graph of performance. Abbr. *plat.* [< F < OF *plat.* See PLATE.]

plat·ed (plā′tid) *adj.* **1.** Coated with a layer of gold, silver, etc.: often used in combination: *gold-plated.* **2.** Provided with plates, as of metal. **3.** Having one kind of yarn on the face and another on the back: said of certain fabrics.

plate·ful (plāt′fōōl′) *n.* *pl.* **·fuls** The quantity that fills a plate.

plate glass Glass in clear, thick sheets, suitable for mirrors, display windows, etc.

plate hinge A hinge with one long, narrow plate as the movable unit. For illustration see HINGE.

plate·let (plāt′lit) *n.* **1.** A small, platelike object. **2.** *Physiol.* A blood platelet (which see). [Dim. of PLATE]

plat·en (plat′n) *n.* *Mech.* **1.** The part of a printing press, typewriter, or the like, on which the paper is supported to receive the impression. **2.** In a machine tool, the adjustable table that carries the work. [< OF *platine* flat piece, metal plate < *plat.* See PLATE.]

plat·er (plā/tər) *n.* **1.** One who or that which plates articles with a layer of gold, silver, etc. **2.** One who makes or works upon metallic plates. **3.** An inferior race horse.

plate rail A shelflike molding around a room, for holding ornamental plates or bric-à-brac.

plate tectonics *Geol.* The theory that the earth's crust consists of a few huge plates that are slowly moving relative to one another.

plat·form (plat/fôrm) *n.* **1.** Any floor or flat surface raised above the adjacent level, as a stage for public speaking or a raised walk upon which railroad passengers alight. **2.** A projecting stage at the end of a car or similar vehicle. **3.** A formal scheme of principles put forth by a religious, political, or other body; also, the document stating the principles of a political party. **4.** The business of public speaking. [< MF *plateforme* < *plate* flat + *forme* form]

platform car A flatcar (which see).

pla·ti·na (plat/ə-nə, plə-tē/nə) *n.* **1.** A white, brittle alloy of zinc and copper. **2.** *Archaic* Platinum. [< NL < Sp. *plata* silver]

plat·ing (plā/ting) *n.* **1.** A layer or coating of metal: silver *plating.* **2.** A sheathing of metal plates, as armor. **3.** The act or process of sheathing or coating with plates or metal.

pla·tin·ic (plə-tin/ik) *adj. Chem.* Of, pertaining to, or containing platinum, especially in its higher valence.

plat·i·nif·er·ous (plat/ə-nif/ər-əs) *adj.* Containing or yielding platinum. [< PLATIN(UM) + -FEROUS]

plat·in·i·rid·i·um (plat/in-i-rid/ē-əm) *n.* A whitish to gray native alloy of iridium, platinum, and other allied metals.

plat·i·nize (plat/ə-nīz) *v.t.* **·nized, ·niz·ing** To coat or combine with platinum, especially by electroplating.

platino- *combining form* Platinum; of, related to, or containing platinum: *platinocyanide.* Also, before vowels, **platin-.** [< PLATINUM]

plat·i·no·cy·an·ic acid (plat/ə-nō-sī-an/ik) *Chem.* An acid containing platinum and cyanogen.

plat·i·no·cy·a·nide (plat/ə-nō-sī/ə-nīd, -nid) *n. Chem.* A salt of platinocyanic acid. Also **plat/i·no·cy/a·nid** (-nid). [< PLATINO- + CYANIDE]

plat·i·noid (plat/ə-noid) *adj.* Like platinum. — *n.* **1.** An alloy of German silver and a small amount of tungsten, used in the manufacture of resistance coils and other electrical appliances. **2.** Any of the heavy metallic elements resembling platinum in certain chemical properties, especially osmium, iridium and palladium.

plat·i·no·type (plat/ə-nō-tīp/) *n. Photog.* **1.** A process in which the positive print is obtained by a deposit of finely precipitated platinum. **2.** A print made by this process.

plat·i·nous (plat/ə-nəs) *adj. Chem.* Of, pertaining to, or containing platinum, especially in its lower valence.

plat·i·num (plat/ə-nəm) *n.* **1.** A heavy, steel-gray, malleable and ductile metallic element (symbol Pt) that is very infusible, resistant to most acids, and that has a high electrical resistance. It is widely used as a catalyst, in industry and the arts, and in jewelry. See ELEMENT. **2.** A color resembling that of platinum, but having a slightly bluish tone. [< NL < Sp. *platina* < *plata* silver]

platinum black Finely divided metallic platinum in the form of black powder, used as a catalyst.

platinum blond **1.** A very light, almost white blond. **2.** One having platinum blond hair.

plat·i·tude (plat/ə-tood, -tyood) *n.* **1.** A flat, dull, or commonplace statement; an obvious truism. **2.** Dullness; triteness. [< F, flatness < *plat* flat]

plat·i·tu·di·nize (plat/ə-too/də-nīz, -tyoo/-) *v.i.* **·nized, ·niz·ing** To utter platitudes.

plat·i·tu·di·nous (plat/ə-too/də-nəs, -tyoo/-) *adj.* **1.** Of the nature of platitude. **2.** Abounding in or given to platitudes.

Pla·to (plā/tō, 427?-347? B.C., Greek philosopher; founder of the Academy; friend of Socrates. See PLATONISM.

pla·ton·ic (plə-ton/ik) *adj. Often cap.* Purely spiritual, or devoid of sensual feeling: a *platonic* relationship. — **pla·ton/i·cal·ly** *adv.*

Pla·ton·ic (plə-ton/ik) *adj.* Of, pertaining to, or characteristic of Plato or of Platonism; academic; theoretical. Also **Pla·ton/i·cal.** — **Pla·ton/i·cal·ly** *adv.*

Platonic year See under PRECESSION OF THE EQUINOXES.

Pla·to·nism (plā/tə-niz/əm) *n.* **1.** The philosophy of Plato; especially, the doctrine that objects are merely copies or images of eternal ideas and that these ideas are the ultimate metaphysical realities and therefore the object of true knowledge. **2.** A tenet or maxim of the Platonic philosophy. **3.** The doctrine or practice of platonic love. — **Pla·to·nist** *n.*

Pla·to·nize (plā/tə-nīz) *v.* **·nized, ·niz·ing** *v.t.* **1.** To make Platonic; idealize. — *v.i.* **2.** To conform to Platonism.

pla·toon (plə-toon/) *n.* **1.** A subdivision of a company, troop, or other military unit, commanded by a lieutenant. **2.** A group or set of people; especially, in football, a group of players assigned to play either defense or offense and put into or taken from the game as a unit. *Abbr.* **plat.** [< F *peloton* ball, group of men < *pelote* ball]

platoon sergeant In the U.S. Army, the senior noncommissioned officer in a platoon or unit of equivalent size. See table for GRADE.

Platt·deutsch (plät/doich/) *n.* The low German vernacular of the north of Germany. [< G]

Plat·ten·see (plät/ən-zā) The German name for (Lake) BALATON.

plat·ter (plat/ər) *n.* **1.** *Chiefly U.S.* An oblong shallow dish on which meat or fish is served. **2.** *Informal* A phonograph record. [< AF *plater* < *plat* dish]

Platte River (plat) A river in Nebraska formed by the confluence of the North Platte and the South Platte and flowing 310 miles generally east to the Missouri River.

Platts·burgh (plats/bûrg) A city in NE New York, on Lake Champlain; scene of a U.S. naval victory over the British (1814) in the War of 1812; pop. 18,715. Also **Platts/burg.**

platy- *combining form* Flat: *platyrrhine.* Also, before vowels, *plat-.* [< Gk. *platys* flat]

plat·y·hel·minth (plat/ē-hel/minth) *n. Zool.* Any of a phylum (*Platyhelminthes*) of soft-bodied, usually flattened worms. [< PLATY- + Gk. *helmins, -inthos* worm]

plat·y·pus (plat/ə-pəs) *n. pl.* **·pus·es** A burrowing, egg-laying, aquatic monotreme (*Ornithorhynchus anatinus*) of Australia, having a duck-like bill: also called *duckbill, duck-billed platypus.* [< NL < Gk. *platypous* < *platus* flat + *pous* foot]

plat·yr·rhine (plat/ə-rīn, -rin) *adj.* **1.** Having a broad nose, with widely separated nostrils. **2.** *Zool.* Designating a former suborder (*Platyrrhini*) of primates, the ceboid monkeys of the New World, having broad, flat noses: distinguished from *catarrhine.* — *n.* A broad-nosed person or monkey. Also **plat/yr·rhin/i·an** (-rin/ē-ən). [< NL *platyrrhinus* < Gk. *platus* wide, flat + *rhis, rhinos* nose]

PLATYPUS
(To 2 feet long; tail about 5½ inches)

plau·dit (plô/dit) *n.* An expression of applause; praise bestowed. — **Syn.** See APPLAUSE. [< L *plaudite*, pl. imperative of *plaudere* to applaud]

Plau·en (plou/ən) A city in south central East Germany; pop. about 82,000. Also **Plauen im Vogt·land** (im fōkht/länt).

plau·si·ble (plô/zə-bəl) *adj.* **1.** Seeming to be likely or probable, but open to doubt. **2.** Apparently trustworthy or believable: a *plausible* speaker. [< L *plausibilis* deserving applause < *plaudere* to applaud] — **plau/si·bil/i·ty, plau/si·ble·ness** *n.* — **plau/si·bly** *adv.*

plau·sive (plô/siv) *adj.* **1.** Manifesting praise; applauding. **2.** *Obs.* Plausible.

Plau·tus (plô/təs), 254?-184 B.C., Roman comic dramatist: full name **Titus Maccius Plautus.**

play (plā) *v.i.* **1.** To engage in sport or diversion; amuse oneself; frolic; gambol. **2.** To take part in a game of skill or chance; gamble. **3.** To act in a way that is not to be taken seriously. **4.** To act or behave in a specified manner: to *play* false. **5.** To deal carelessly; behave lightly or insincerely: with *with.* **6.** To make love sportively. **7.** To move quickly or irregularly as if frolicking: lights *playing* along a wall. **8.** To discharge or be discharged freely or continuously: a fountain *playing* in the square. **9.** To perform on a musical instrument. **10.** To give forth music or sound: The radio is *playing.* **11.** To be performed or exhibited: *Hamlet* is *playing* tonight. **12.** To act on or as on a stage; perform. **13.** To move freely or loosely, especially within limits, as part of a mechanism. — *v.t.* **14.** To engage in (a game etc.). **15.** To pretend to be; imitate in play: to *play* cowboys and Indians. **16.** To perform sportively or wantonly: to *play* a trick. **17.** To oppose in a game or contest. **18.** To move or employ (a piece, card, etc.) in a game. **19.** To employ (someone) in a game as a player. **20.** To cause; bring about: to *play* havoc. **21.** To perform upon (a musical instrument). **22.** To perform or produce, as a piece of music, a play, etc. **23.** To act the part of or on as on the stage; assume the character of: to *play* the fool. **24.** To perform or act in: to *play* Chicago. **25.** To cause to move quickly or irregularly: to *play* lights over a surface. **26.** To put into or maintain in action; wield; ply. **27.** In angling, to let (a hooked fish) tire itself by maintaining pressure on the line. **28.** To bet or bet on. — **to play at 1.** To take part in. **2.** To pretend to be doing; do half-heartedly. — **to play down** To treat as being of little importance; minimize. — **to play into the hands of** To act to the advantage of (a rival or opponent). — **to play off 1.** To oppose against one another. **2.** To decide (a tie) by playing one more game. — **to play on 1.** To take unscrupulous advantage of (another's hopes, emotions, etc.) for one's own advantage. **2.** To continue: The band *played* on. — **to play out 1.** To come to an end; be exhausted. **2.** To continue to the end; finish. — **to play the game** To behave in a fair manner. — **to play up** *Informal* To emphasize. — **to play up to** *Informal* To try to win the favor of by flattery, etc. — *n.* **1.** A dramatic composition; drama. **2.** The performance of such a composition. **3.** Exercise or action for recreation or diversion; sport. **4.** A move, maneuver, or turn in a game: his *play*. **5.** Manner of playing: rough *play*. **6.** In sports, a state of being actively and legitimately in use or motion: in *play*; out of *play*. **7.** The act of playing a game, especially gambling. **8.** Fun; jest; joking: to say something in *play*. **9.** The active operation of something: the *play* of one's mind. **10.** Action or operation that is light, free, and unencumbered: the *play* of muscles. **11.** Light, quick, fitful movement: the *play* of shadows. **12.** Manner of acting toward or dealing with others: fair *play*. **— to make a play for** *Informal* **1.** To attempt to gain something, as a favor, votes, etc. **2.** To attempt to seduce. [OE *plegan*; prob. akin to MDu. *playen* to frolic; ult. origin uncertain] **— play′a·ble** *adj.*

pla·ya (plä′yä) *n.* A plain with a hard clayey surface intermittently covered by a shallow lake. [< Sp., beach < Med.L *plagia* hillside, shore line]

play·back (plä′bak′) *n.* **1.** The act of reproducing a sound recording, as from a record or tape. **2.** A method or machine for reproducing sound recordings.

play·bill (plä′bil′) *n.* **1.** A bill or poster advertising a play. **2.** A program of a play.

play·boy (plä′boi′) *n. Informal* One who constantly seeks pleasure at nightclubs, social gatherings, etc.

play-by-play (plä′bī-plä′) *adj.* Dealing with each play or event as it happens: a *play-by-play* report.

play·day (plä′dā′) *n.* A holiday.

play·down (plä′doun′) *n. Canadian* A playoff (def. b).

play·er (plä′ər) *n.* **1.** One who takes part or specializes in a game: a tennis *player*. **2.** One who performs on the dramatic stage; an actor. **3.** A performer on a musical instrument. **4.** One who works without a purpose or makes idle pretensions; also, an idler; a trifler. **5.** A gambler. **6.** An automatic device for playing a musical instrument.

player piano A piano having a mechanical device by which it may be played automatically.

play·fel·low (plä′fel′ō) *n.* An associate in play; playmate.

play·ful (plä′fəl) *adj.* **1.** Lightly humorous; joking: a *playful* remark. **2.** Full of high spirits and play; frolicsome: a *playful* puppy. **— play′ful·ly** *adv.* **— play′ful·ness** *n.*

play·go·er (plä′gō′ər) *n.* One who goes often to the theater.

play·ground (plä′ground′) *n.* An area, usually adjoining a school, used for playing games and for recreation.

play·house (plä′hous′) *n.* **1.** A theater. **2.** A small house for children to play in. **3.** A toy house.

playing card One of a pack of cards used in playing various games, the pack usually consisting of 52 cards divided into four suits (spades, hearts, diamonds, clubs) of 13 cards each.

play·let (plä′lit′) *n.* A short play.

play·mate (plä′māt′) *n.* A companion in sports or in play.

play·off (plä′ôf′, -of′) *n.* In sports: **a** A decisive game or contest to break a tie. **b** A series of games to decide a championship, award, etc.

play·pen (plä′pen′) *n.* A small, usually collapsible enclosure in which a baby or small child is left to amuse himself.

play·thing (plä′thing′) *n.* A thing to play with; a toy.

play·time (plä′tīm′) *n.* Time for play or amusement.

play upon words Words used with double meaning; a pun.

play·wright (plä′rīt′) *n.* A writer of plays.

pla·za (plä′zə, plaz′ə; *Sp.* plä′thä) *n.* An open square or market place in a town or city. [< Sp. < L *platea* wide street < Gk. *plateia*. Doublet of PIAZZA, PLACE.]

plea (plē) *n.* **1.** An appeal or entreaty: a *plea* for aid. **2.** An excuse, pretext, or justification: the tyrant's *plea*. **3.** *Law* **a** An allegation made by either party in a cause; a pleading. **b** A statement made by or for the defendant concerning the charge or indictment against him. **c** In common-law practice, a defendant's answer of fact to the plaintiff's declaration. **d** In equity, a special answer, showing a reason why the writ should be dismissed, delayed, or barred. **e** *Usually pl.* A suit or action. [< OF *plaid* < L *placitum* opinion, orig. pp. of *placere* to please]

pleach (plēch) *v.t.* To plait (vines or twigs) together, as in forming a hedge or arbor; interweave. [< AF *plechier*, OF *plaissier* < L *plectere* to weave]

pleached (plēcht) *adj.* Interwoven; covered with interwoven branches.

plead (plēd) *v.* **plead·ed** or **pled** (pled), **plead·ing** *v.i.* **1.** To make earnest entreaty; implore; beg. **2.** *Law* **a** To advocate a case in court. **b** To file a pleading. **— v.t.** **3.** To allege as as an excuse or defense: to *plead* insanity. **4.** *Law* To discuss or maintain (a case) by argument. [< OF *plaider* < *plaid*. See PLEA.] **— plead′a·ble** *adj.* **— plead′er** *n.*
— Syn. 1. sue, petition. Compare ENTREAT.

plead·ing (plē′ding) *n.* **1.** The act of making a plea. **2.** *Law* **a** The art, science, or system of preparing the formal written statements of the parties to an action. **b** *Usually pl.* Any one of such statements. **— plead′ing·ly** *adv.*

pleas·ance (plez′əns) *n.* **1.** A secluded garden. **2.** *Archaic* Pleasure, or that which pleases. Also **pleas′aunce.** [< OF *plaisance* < *plaisant*. See PLEASANT.]

pleas·ant (plez′ənt) *adj.* **1.** Giving or promoting pleasure; pleasing. **2.** Agreeable in manner, act, appearance, etc. **3.**

Merry; gay. [< OF *plaisant*, ppr. *plaisir* to please < L *placere*] **— pleas′ant·ly** *adv.* **— pleas′ant·ness** *n.*
— Syn. 1. pleasurable, enjoyable, delightful, satisfying. **2.** congenial, welcome. **— Ant.** unpleasant, disagreeable, repulsive.

Pleasant Island A former name for NAURU.

pleas·an·try (plez′ən·trē) *n. pl.* **·tries 1.** A playful, amusing, or good-natured remark, jest, or trick. **2.** The quality or spirit of pleasant conversation or companionship.

please (plēz) *v.* **pleased, pleas·ing** *v.t.* **1.** To give pleasure to; be agreeable to; gratify. **2.** To be the wish or will of: May it *please* you. **3.** To be so kind as to; be willing to: usually in the imperative and followed by a request: *Please* pass the bread. **— v.i.** **4.** To give satisfaction or pleasure. **5.** To have the will or preference; wish: Go when you *please*. [< OF *plaisir* < L *placere* to please]
— Syn. 1. cheer, gladden, delight, rejoice, exhilarate. Compare PLEASURE. **— Ant.** displease, offend, anger.

pleas·ing (plē′zing) *adj.* Affording pleasure or satisfaction; gratifying. **— pleas′ing·ly** *adv.* **— pleas′ing·ness** *n.*

pleas·ur·a·ble (plezh′ər·ə·bəl) *adj.* Gratifying; pleasant; satisfying. **— pleas′ur·a·ble·ness** *n.* **— pleas′ur·a·bly** *adv.*

pleas·ure (plezh′ər) *n.* **1.** An agreeable sensation or emotion; gratification; enjoyment. **2.** Something that gives a feeling of enjoyment, delight, or satisfaction. **3.** Amusement or diversion: a search for *pleasure*. **4.** Sensual gratification. **5.** One's preference; choice. **— v.** **·ured, ·ur·ing** *Archaic v.t.* **1.** To give or afford pleasure to; please; gratify. **— v.i.** **2.** To take pleasure; delight. [< OF *plaisir*. See PLEASE.]
— Syn. (noun) **1.** *Pleasure, delight, joy, rapture, ecstasy, enjoyment,* and *delectation* denote feelings of satisfaction or happiness. *Pleasure* is the general term; it is also the weakest, often indicating little more than the absence of pain or dissatisfaction. *Delight* is a poignant feeling of *pleasure*, often sudden and transient; we feel *delight* at a friend's visit. *Joy* is deeper and more lasting delight; we may find *joy* in following a certain vocation, as law or writing, or in the successful completion of a difficult task. The extreme of pleasurable feeling is *rapture* or *ecstasy,* both of which suggest an otherworldly exaltation. *Enjoyment* and *delectation* more often denote action than feeling; *enjoyment* is the savoring of that which pleases, and *delectation,* the yielding to that which amuses or diverts: the *enjoyment* of good food, the *delectation* of the theater. Compare SATISFACTION, HAPPINESS. **— Ant.** displeasure, pain, sorrow.

pleasure principle *Psychoanal.* The concentration of the ego on securing a maximum of pleasure with a minimum of pain and effort. Compare REALITY PRINCIPLE.

pleat (plēt) *n.* A fold of cloth doubled on itself and pressed or sewn in place. **— v.t.** To make a pleat or pleats in. Also *plait*. [Var. of PLAIT]

pleat·er (plē′tər) *n.* **1.** One who pleats. **2.** A sewing-machine attachment for pleating.

pleb (pleb) *n.* **1.** A plebeian. **2.** A plebe.

plebe (plēb) *n.* **1.** *U.S.* A member of the lowest class in the academies at West Point and Annapolis. **2.** *Obs.* Plebs. [Short for PLEBEIAN]

ple·be·ian (pli-bē′ən) *adj.* **1.** Of or pertaining to the common people, especially those of ancient Rome. **2.** Common or vulgar. **— n.** **1.** One of the common people, especially of ancient Rome. **2.** Anyone who is coarse or vulgar. [< L *plebeius* < *plebs* the common people] **— ple·be′ian·ism** *n.*

pleb·i·scite (pleb′ə·sīt, -sit) *n.* An expression of the popular will by means of a vote by the whole people, usually resorted to in changes of the constitution, sovereignty, etc. [< F *plébiscite* < L *plebiscitum* < *plebs* plebs + *scitum* decree < *scire* to know] **— pleb·is·ci·tar·y** (plə·bis′ə·ter′ē) *adj.*

plebs (plebz) *n. pl.* **ple·bes** (plē′bēz) **1.** The lower order of the ancient Roman people. **2.** The populace or common people. [< L]

ple·cop·ter·an (plə·kop′tər·ən) *n.* Any of an order (*Plecoptera*) of insects of which the nymphs are aquatic, as the stone fly. [< Gk. *plekein* to twine + *pteron* wing]

plec·tog·nath (plek′tog·nath) *n.* Any of an order or suborder (*Plectognathi*) of teleost fishes having spiny bodies, short, powerful jaws, and including the triggerfishes and globefishes. **— adj.** Of or pertaining to the plectognaths. [< NL *Plectognathi* < Gk. *plektos* twisted + *gnathos* jaw]

plec·trum (plek′trəm) *n. pl.* **·trums** or **·tra** (-trə) A small implement with which the player on a lyre, guitar, etc., picks or strikes the strings to set them in vibration: also called *pick.* Also **plec′tron** (-tron). [< L < Gk. *plēktron* < *plessein* to strike]

pled (pled) Alternate past tense and past participle of PLEAD.

pledge (plej) *v.t.* **pledged, pledg·ing 1.** To give or deposit as security for a loan, etc.; pawn. **2.** To bind by or as by a pledge. **3.** To promise solemnly, as assistance. **4.** To offer (one's word, life, etc.) as a guaranty or forfeit. **5.** To drink a toast to. **6.** To promise to join (a fraternity). **7.** To accept (someone) as a pledge (def. 6). **— n.** **1.** A promise or agreement to perform or fulfill some act, contract, or duty. **2.** A formal promise to do or not to do something. **3.** The drinking of a toast to one's health, etc. **4.** Something given as security for a debt or obligation. **5.** The state of being given or held as security: to put property in *pledge*. **6.** One who has promised to join a fraternity but who has not yet been formally inducted. —**Syn.** See SECURITY. [< OF *plege* guarantee < Med.L *plebium*, prob. < Gmc.]

pledg·ee (plej·ē′) *n.* **1.** One to whom something is pledged. **2.** One with whom a pledge is deposited. **3.** *U.S. Informal* A pledge (def. 6).

pledg·er (plej′ər) *n.* One who gives a pledge.

pledg·or (plej′ər) *n. Law* A pledger. Also **pledge′or.**

pledg·et (plej′it) *n.* A compressed wad of lint, cotton, etc., as for a wound. [Origin unknown]

-plegia *combining form Pathol.* A (specified) kind of paralysis, or paralytic condition: *hemiplegia.* Also **-plegy.** [< Gk. < *plēgē* stroke]

Plei·ad (plē′ad, plī′ad) *n. pl.* **Plei·a·des** (plē′ə·dēz, plī′-). **1.** One of the Pleiades. **2.** One of any cluster of brilliant persons, usually seven.

Plei·a·des (plē′ə·dēz, plī′-) *n.pl.* **1.** In Greek mythology, the seven daughters of Atlas (Maia, Electra, Taygeta, Alcyone, Celaeno, Sterope, and Merope), who were set by Zeus among the stars. **2.** *Astron.* A loose cluster of many hundred stars in the constellation Taurus, six of which are visible to ordinary sight.

plein-air (plān′âr′) *adj.* Characterizing the work of a school of French impressionist painters concerned with the representation of objects seen under brilliant sunlight, and other outdoor effects. [< F, open-air] —**plein-air·ism** (plān′âr′iz·əm) *n.* —**plein′-air′ist** *n.*

Plei·o·cene (plī′ə·sēn) See PLIOCENE.

Pleis·to·cene (plīs′tə·sēn) *Geol. adj.* Of or pertaining to the earlier of the two epochs of the Quaternary, characterized by the glacial epoch of northern Asia, Europe, and North America. —*n.* The rock series of this epoch. See chart for GEOLOGY. [< Gk. *pleistos* most + *kainos* recent]

ple·na·ry (plē′nə·rē, plen′ə-) *adj.* **1.** Full in all respects or requisites; entire; absolute; complete. **2.** Fully or completely attended, as an assembly. [< LL *plenarius* < L *plenus* full] —**ple′na·ri·ly** *adv.* —**ple′na·ri·ness** *n.*

plenary indulgence In the Roman Catholic Church, the remission of all temporal penalties incurred by sin.

ple·nip·o·tent (plə·nip′ə·tənt) *adj.* Possessing full power or authority.

plen·i·po·ten·ti·a·ry (plen′i·pə·ten′shē·er′ē, -shə·rē) *adj.* Possessing or conferring full powers. —*n. pl.* **·ar·ies** A person fully empowered to represent a government, as an ambassador, minister, or envoy. [< Med.L *plenipotentiarius* < LL *plenipotens, -entis* < L *plenus* full + *potens* powerful < *potere* to be able]

plen·ish (plen′ish) *v.t. Scot. & Brit. Dial.* To fill or stock; replenish.

ple·nism (plē′niz·əm) *n.* The doctrine that space is fully occupied by matter. —**ple′nist** *n.*

plen·i·tude (plen′ə·tood, -tyood) *n.* The state of being full, complete, or abounding. [< OF < L *plenitudo* < *plenus* full]

plen·te·ous (plen′tē·əs) *adj.* **1.** Characterized by plenty; amply sufficient. **2.** Yielding an abundance. —**Syn.** See PLENTIFUL. [< OF *plentieus, plentivous* < *plente.* See PLENTY.] —**plen′te·ous·ly** *adv.* —**plen′te·ous·ness** *n.*

plen·ti·ful (plen′ti·fəl) *adj.* **1.** Existing in great quantity; abundant. **2.** Yielding or containing plenty; affording ample supply. —**plen′ti·ful·ly** *adv.* —**plen′ti·ful·ness** *n.*
—**Syn. 1.** *Plentiful, plenteous, abundant, copious,* and *ample* mean more than enough in amount. These words are largely interchangeable, but some shades of difference can be felt. *Plentiful* suggests comparison with a need or demand, and can be applied to almost anything concrete: wheat is *plentiful* this year, aspirants for movie jobs are always *plentiful. Plenteous* is a bookish or poetic word for *plentiful. Abundant* suggests, in the concrete, the works of nature rather than of man: *abundant* foliage. It is preferred to *plentiful* in the abstract: *abundant* errors in a book, *abundant* argument. *Copious* often requires, for clarity, the interpolation of "supply of," "number of," etc., before the operative noun: the squirrel gathered a *copious* store of nuts (not *copious* nuts). However, the interpolation is unnecessary when reference is made to a volume or flow: *copious* rain, *copious* tears. *Ample* means both just enough and more than enough, and so tends to imply an amount between enough and *plentiful.* Compare PROFUSE. —**Ant.** scanty, scarce.

plen·ty (plen′tē) *n.* **1.** The state of being sufficient and in abundance. **2.** As much as can be required; an abundance or sufficiency: now generally without the article: I have *plenty.* —*adj. Informal* Existing in abundance; plentiful. —*adv. Informal* In a sufficient degree: The house is *plenty* large. [< OF *plente* < L *plenitas, -tatis* < *plenus* full]

ple·num (plē′nəm) *n. pl.* **·nums** or **·na** (-nə) **1.** Space considered as fully occupied by matter: opposed to *vacuum.* **2.** An enclosed body of gas under greater pressure than the pressure outside. **3.** A completely attended meeting, as of a legislative body. **4.** Fullness. —*adj.* Pertaining to or utilizing fullness (of air, etc.). [< L < *plenus* full]

ple·och·ro·ism (plē·ok′rō·iz′əm) *n. Mineral.* The property exhibited by crystals of showing different colors when the transmitted light is viewed along different axes. [< Gk.

pleōn more + *chrōs* color + *-ISM*] —**ple·o·chro·ic** (plē′ə·krō′ik) *adj.*

ple·o·nasm (plē′ə·naz′əm) *n.* **1.** The use of needless words; redundancy; also, an instance of it. **2.** A redundant word or phrase. **3.** Superabundance; excess. —**Syn.** See CIRCUMLOCUTION. [< L < Gk. *pleonasmos* < *pleōn* more] —**ple·o·nas′tic** (-nas′tik) *adj.* —**ple′o·nas′ti·cal·ly** *adv.*

ple·o·pod (plē′ə·pod) *n. Zool.* A swimmeret. [< Gk. *pleōn,* ppr. of *pleein* to swim + *pous, podos* foot]

ple·si·o·sau·rus (plē′sē·ə·sôr′əs) *n. pl.* **·rus·es** *Paleontol.* Any of an extinct suborder (*Plesiosauria*) of fish-eating marine reptiles of the Mesozoic era, typically having a small head and long neck, and limbs modified into swimming paddles. Also **ple′si·o·saur.** [< Gk. *plēsios* near + *sauros* lizard]

ples·sor (ples′ər) *n. Med.* Plexor.

pleth·o·ra (pleth′ər·ə) *n.* **1.** A state of excessive fullness; superabundance; excess; superfluity. **2.** *Med.* Superabundance of blood in the whole system or in an organ or part. [< LL < Gk. *plēthōre* fullness < *plēthein* to be full]

ple·thor·ic (ple·thôr′ik, -thor′-, pleth′ə·rik) *adj.* **1.** Affected or characterized by plethora. **2.** Excessively full; overloaded; turgid; inflated. —**ple·thor′i·cal·ly** *adv.*

ple·thys·mo·graph (ple·thiz′mə·graf, -gräf, -this′-) *n.* An instrument for recording variations in the size of various parts of the body, especially such variation as is caused by the circulation of the blood. [< Gk. *plēthysmos* enlargement (< *plēthyein* to increase) + *-GRAPH*]

pleu·ra (ploor′ə) *n. pl.* **pleu·rae** (ploor′ē) *Anat.* The serous membrane that infolds the lungs and is folded back upon the walls of the thorax and upon the diaphragm. [< Gk. *pleura* side] —**pleu′ral** *adj.*

pleu·ri·sy (ploor′ə·sē) *n. Pathol.* Inflammation of the pleura, commonly attended with fever, pain in the chest, difficult breathing, exudation, etc. [< OF *pleurisie* < LL *pleurisis* < L *pleuritis* < Gk. < *pleura* side] —**pleu·rit·ic** (ploo·rit′ik) *adj.*

pleurisy root **1.** Butterfly weed (def. 1). **2.** Its root, formerly used in treating pleurisy.

pleuro- *combining form* **1.** Of or pertaining to the side: *pleurodont.* **2.** *Med.* Of, related to, or affecting the pleura: *pleurotomy.* Also, before vowels, **pleur-.** [< Gk. *pleura* side]

pleu·ro·dont (ploor′ə·dont) *Zool. adj.* Having teeth attached to the inner side of the jaw, as certain lizards. —*n.* A pleurodont lizard. [< PLEUR(O)- + -ODONT]

pleu·ron (ploor′on) *n. pl.* **pleu·ra** (ploor′ə) *Entomol.* The lateral plate or plates of a thoracic segment in insects. [< NL < Gk., rib]

pleu·ro·pneu·mo·ni·a (ploor′ō·nŏŏ·mō′nē·ə, -mōn′yə), -nyŏŏ-) *n. Pathol.* Pleurisy combined with pneumonia.

pleu·rot·o·my (ploo·rot′ə·mē) *n. pl.* **·mies** *Surg.* The operation of making an incision into the pleura, for drawing off effused liquids.

pleus·ton (ploos′tən) *n. Bot.* Vegetation that consists of large aquatic plants floating on bodies of fresh water. [< NL < Gk. *pleus-,* stem of *pleein* to swim]

Plev·en (plev′ən, *Bulgarian* ple′veny′) A city in northern Bulgaria; surrendered by the Turks after a siege, 1877; pop. 57,758 (1956). Also **Plev·na** (plev′nä).

plex·i·form (plek′sə·fôrm) *adj.* Having the form of a plexus or network; complicated.

Plex·i·glas (plek′si·glas′, -gläs′) *n.* A lightweight thermoplastic acrylic resin, very weather-resistant and highly transparent: a trade name. Also **plex′i·glas, plex′i·glass.**

plex·im·e·ter (plek·sim′ə·tər) *n. Med.* A plate to be placed against the body to receive the blows in percussion. [< Gk. *plēxis* stroke + -METER] —**plex·i·met·ric** (plek′si·met′rik) *adj.* —**plex·im′e·try** *n.*

plex·or (plek′sər) *n. Med.* A small, hammerlike instrument, used on the body in diagnostic percussion: also called *plessor.* [< NL < Gk. *plēxis* stroke]

plex·us (plek′səs) *n. pl.* **plex·us·es** or **plex·us** **1.** A network or complicated interlacing of parts. **2.** *Anat.* A network of cordlike structures, as blood vessels or nerves. [< L, pp. of *plectere* to intertwine]

pli·a·ble (plī′ə·bəl) *adj.* **1.** Easily bent or twisted; flexible. **2.** Easily persuaded or controlled; tractable. —**Syn.** See PLASTIC. —**pli′a·bil′i·ty, pli′a·ble·ness** *n.* —**pli′a·bly** *adv.*

pli·an·cy (plī′ən·sē) *n.* The state or quality of being pliant.

pli·ant (plī′ənt) *adj.* **1.** Capable of being bent or twisted with ease; supple; lithe. **2.** Easily yielding to influence; compliant. —**Syn.** See DOCILE. [< OF, ppr. of *plier.* See PLY.] —**pli′ant·ly** *adv.*

pli·ca (plī′kə) *n. pl.* **·cae** (-sē) **1.** *Anat.* A fold of skin, membrane, etc., as between the fingers. **2.** *Pathol.* A condition in which the hair becomes crusted and matted due to disease and vermin. [< Med.L < *plicare* to fold]

pli·cate (plī′kāt) *adj.* Folded or pleated, as a fan. Also **pli′cat·ed.** [< L *plicatus,* pp. of *plicare* to fold] —**pli′cate·ness** *n.* —**pli′cate·ly** *adv.*

pli·ca·tion (plī·kā′shən) *n.* **1.** A folding or fold. **2.** The condition of being folded. Also **plic·a·ture** (plik′ə·chŏŏr).

pli·er (plī′ər) *n.* **1.** *pl.* Small pincers for bending, holding, or cutting: also **pair of pliers**. **2.** One who or that which plies.

plight[1] (plīt) *n.* A condition, state, or circumstance, usually of a dangerous or complicated nature. — **Syn.** See PREDICAMENT. [< AF *plit* fold, condition < OF *pleit*. See PLAIT.]

plight[2] (plīt) *n. Rare* A pledge. — *v.t.* **1.** To pledge (one's word, faith, etc.). **2.** To promise, as in marriage; betroth. — **to plight one's troth** To pledge one's solemn word. **2.** To promise oneself in marriage. [OE *plihtan* to expose to danger, *pliht* danger] — **plight′er** *n.*

Plim·soll (plim′sol, -sal), **Samuel**, 1824–1898, English merchant and statesman.

Plimsoll mark A mark painted on the outside of the hull of a British vessel to show how deeply she may be loaded; load line. Also **Plimsoll line**. [after Samuel *Plimsoll*]

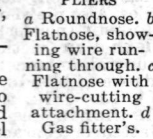

PLIERS

a Roundnose. *b* Flatnose, showing wire running through. *c* Flatnose with wire-cutting attachment. *d* Gas fitter's.

plinth (plinth) *n. Archit.* **1.** The slab, block, or stone, usually square, on which a column, pedestal, or statue rests. For illustration see TUSCAN ORDER. **2.** A thin course, as of slabs, usually projecting beneath a wall: also **plinth course**. [< L *plinthus* < Gk. *plinthos* brick]

Plin·y (plin′ē) Anglicized name of two Roman authors, **Pliny the Elder**, A.D. 23–79, naturalist: full name **Gaius Plin·i·us Se·cun·dus** (sē·kun′dəs); and his nephew **Pliny the Younger**, 62–113, statesman and author: full name **Gaius Plinius Cae·cil·i·us** (sē·sil′ē·əs) **Secundus.**

Pli·o·cene (plī′ə·sēn) *Geol. adj.* Of or pertaining to the latest epoch of the Tertiary, following the Miocene and succeeded by the Pleistocene. — *n.* The Pliocene epoch or rock series. Also spelled *Pleiocene*. See chart for GEOLOGY. [< Gk. *pleiōn* more + *kainos* new] — **Pli·o·cen′ic** (-sen′ik) *adj.*

plod (plod) *v.* **plod·ded, plod·ding** *v.i.* **1.** To walk heavily or laboriously; trudge. **2.** To work in a steady, laborious manner; drudge. — *v.t.* **3.** To walk along heavily or laboriously. — *n.* **1.** The act or duration of plodding. **2.** The sound of a heavy step, as of a horse. [Imit.] — **plod′ding·ly** *adv.*

plod·der (plod′ər) *n.* **1.** One who plods; a drudge. **2.** A slow but persevering person.

Plo·eș·ti (plô·yesht′) A city in south central Rumania; pop. 156,382 (est. 1968). Also **Plo·esh′ti.**

-ploid *combining form Biol.* In cytology and genetics, having a (specified) number of chromosomes: *polyploid* Corresponding nouns end in **-ploidy**. [< Gk. *-ploos* fold + -OID]

plop (plop) *v.t. & v.i.* **plopped, plop·ping** To drop with a sound like that of something striking the water without making a splash. — *n.* The act or sound of plopping. — *adv.* Suddenly with the sound of plop: They fell *plop* into the river. [Imit.]

plo·sion (plō′zhən) *n. Phonet.* The sudden release of breath after closure of the oral passage in the articulation of a stop consonant, as after the *p* in *pat*: also called *explosion*: distinguished from *implosion*. [< EXPLOSION]

plo·sive (plō′siv) *Phonet. adj.* Designating a sound produced by plosion. — *n.* A consonant so produced; a stop. Also *explosive, mute.*

plot (plot) *n.* **1.** A piece or patch of ground, usually used for some special purpose: also called *plat*. **2.** A chart or diagram, as of a building, for showing certain data; also, a surveyor's map. **3.** A secret plan to accomplish some questionable purpose; conspiracy. **4.** The scheme or pattern of the events, incidents, or situations of a story, play, poem, etc. — *v.* **plot·ted, plot·ting** *v.t.* **1.** To make a map, chart, or plan of, as of a ship's course, a building, etc. **2.** To plan for secretly: to *plot* an enemy's ruin. **3.** To arrange the plot of (a novel, etc.). **4.** *Math.* **a** To represent graphically the position of (a measured value) by a point located with reference to its coordinates on graph paper. **b** To draw (a curve) through a series of such points. — *v.i.* **5.** To form a plot. [OE] — **Syn.** (noun) **1.** field. **3.** scheme, intrigue, conspiracy.

Plo·ti·nus (plō·tī′nəs), 204?–270?, Greek philosopher born in Egypt, active in Rome; formulated Neo-Platonism.

plot·ter (plot′ər) *n.* **1.** One who plots or contrives; a conspirator. **2.** A maker of a plot or map. **3.** A contrivance, as for plotting coordinates.

plotting paper Graph paper (which see).

plot·ty (plot′ē) *n. Scot.* A hot, spiced beverage.

plough (plou) See PLOW.

Plough (plou) The constellation Ursa Major. Also **Plow.**

Plov·div (plôv′dif) A city in south central Bulgaria; pop. 236,627 (est. 1968): ancient *Philippopolis.*

plov·er (pluv′ər, plō′vər) *n.* **1.** Any of various shore birds (family *Charadriidae*), having long, pointed wings and a short tail, especially the **American golden plover** (*Pluvialis dominica*) whose upper plumage is speckled in summer with yellow and white, and the **Eurasian golden plover** (*P. apricaria*), having similar markings. **2.** Any of certain related shore birds, as the **upland plover** (*Bartramia longicauda*). [< OF *plovier*, ult. < L *pluvia* rain]

plow (plou) *n.* **1.** An implement for cutting, turning over, stirring, or breaking up the soil, usually drawn by horses or oxen, or by mechanical power. **2.** Any implement that operates like a plow: often in combination: a *snowplow*. **3.** Any of various furrowing or grooving tools. — *v.t.* **1.** To turn up the surface of (land) with a plow. **2.** To make or form (a furrow, ridge, one's way, etc.) by or as by means of a plow. **3.** To furrow or score the surface of: Shot *plowed* the field. **4.** To dig out or remove with a plow: with *up* or *out*. **5.** To move or cut through (water): to *plow* the waves. — *v.i.* **6.** To turn up soil with a plow. **7.** To undergo plowing in a specified way, as land. **8.** To move or proceed as a plow does: usually with *through* or *into*. **9.** To advance laboriously; plod. — **to plow back** To reinvest (profits, etc.) in a business, equipment, etc. — **to plow into** *Informal* **1.** To hit hard: The car *plowed into* us. **2.** To undertake vigorously to accomplish, finish, or solve (a piece of work, a meal, problem, etc.). — **to plow under** *U.S.* To put from sight by or as by plowing: obliterate. Also, *esp. Brit.*, **plough.** [OE *plōh*, prob. < ON *plógr*. Cf. OHG *pfluog*, MDu. *ploech*.] — **plow′a·ble** *adj.* — **plow′er** *n.*

plow beam The horizontal projecting part of a plow frame, whose front end is attached to the whiffletree. For illustration see WHIFFLETREE.

plow·boy (plou′boi′) *n.* **1.** A boy who drives or guides a team in plowing. **2.** A country boy. Also **plough′boy′.**

plow·man (plou′mən) *n. pl.* **·men** (-mən) **1.** One who plows. **2.** A farmer; rustic. Also **plough′man.**

plow·share (plou′shâr′) *n.* The blade of a plow. Also **plough′share′.**

plow·staff (plou′staf′, -stäf′) *n.* The handle of a plow. Also **plough′staff′.**

ploy[1] (ploi) *n.* A maneuver or stratagem, as in a game or conversation. [< EMPLOY]

ploy[2] (ploi) *n. Chiefly Scot.* Sport; merrymaking.

plu. Plural.

pluck (pluk) *v.t.* **1.** To pull out or off; pick: to *pluck* a flower. **2.** To pull with force; snatch or drag: with *off, away*, etc. **3.** To pull out the feathers, hair, etc., of: to *pluck* a chicken. **4.** To give a twitch or pull to, as a sleeve. **5.** To cause the strings of (a musical instrument) to sound by quickly pulling or picking them. **6.** *Slang* To rob; swindle. **7.** *Brit. Slang* To reject (a candidate) for failure to pass an examination. — *v.i.* **8.** To give a sudden pull; tug: with *at*: a beggar *plucking* at his sleeve. — **to pluck up** To rouse or summon (one's courage). — *n.* **1.** Confidence and spirit in the face of difficulty or danger; courage. **3.** The heart, liver, windpipe, and lungs of an animal. **3.** A sudden pull; twitch. [OE *pluccian* to pick out, ? ult. < LL *piluccare* < *pilus* hair. Cf. Ital. *piluccare*, MHG *pflücken*.] — **pluck′er** *n.*

Plück·er (plük′ər), **Julius**, 1801–68, German scientist.

pluck·y (pluk′ē) *adj.* **pluck·i·er, pluck·i·est** Brave and spirited; courageous. — **pluck′i·ly** *adv.* — **pluck′i·ness** *n.*

plug (plug) *n.* **1.** Anything, as a piece of wood or a cork, used to stop a hole. **2.** *Electr.* A usually two-pronged device attached to the end of a wire or cable and inserted in a socket or jack to make a connection. **3.** A spark plug (which see). **4.** A fireplug (which see). **5.** A flat cake of pressed or twisted tobacco. **6.** A piece of tobacco for chewing. **7.** *Informal* Anything useless or defective. **8.** *Informal* An old, worn-out horse. **9.** *Slang* A favorable word, recommendation, or piece of publicity for someone or something. **10.** *Slang* A shot: to take a *plug* at a rabbit. **11.** *Slang* A punch or blow. **12.** *Archaic Slang* A man's high silk hat: also **plug hat. 13.** *Geol.* A core of hard, igneous rock that has filled the neck of a volcano. **14.** In angling, a type of lure, usually cylindrical and with several hooks attached. — *v.* **plugged, plug·ging** *v.t.* **1.** To stop or close, as a hole, by inserting a plug: often with *up*. **2.** To insert as a plug. **3.** *Slang* To shoot a bullet into. **4.** *Slang* To hit or punch. **5.** *Slang* To advertise frequently or insistently; publicize. — *v.i.* **6.** *Informal* To work doggedly; persevere. **7.** *Slang* To hit or shoot. **8.** *Slang* To favor or work for a cause, person, etc.: root: usually with *for*: to *plug* for peace. — **to plug in** To insert the plug of (a lamp, etc.) in an electrical outlet. [< MDu. *plugge*] — **plug′ger** *n.*

plug-ug·ly (plug′ug′lē) *n. pl.* **·lies** *U.S. Slang* A gangster, ruffian, or rowdy.

plum[1] (plum) *n.* **1.** The edible drupaceous fruit of any of various trees (genus *Prunus*) of the rose family, especially *P. domestica*. **2.** The tree itself. **3.** The plumlike fruit of any of various other trees; also, a tree bearing such fruit. **4.** A raisin, especially as used in cooking. **5.** Any of various shades of dark, reddish purple. **6.** The best or most choice part of anything. **7.** Something desirable, as a post or appointment. **8.** A sugarplum (which see). [OE *plūme* < LL *pruna* < L *prunum* < Gk. *pronon*. Doublet of PRUNE[1].]

plum[2] (plum) See PLUMB (*adj.* def. 2 and *adv.* def. 2).

plum·age (plōō′mij) *n.* **1.** The feathers of a bird; especially, a bird's entire covering of feathers. **2.** Gaudy costume or adornment. [< F < *plume* plume]

plu·mate (plōō′māt) *adj.* Resembling plumage or feathers. [< L *plumatus* feathered]

plumb (plum) *n.* A lead weight on the end of a line used to find the exact perpendicular, to sound the depth of water, etc.: a plumb bob; a plummet. — **off** (or **out of**) **plumb** Not exactly vertical; not in alignment. — *adj.* **1.** Conforming to a true vertical or perpendicular. **2.** *Informal* Sheer; absolute; complete: also spelled *plum.* — *adv.* **1.** In a line perpendicular to the plane of the horizon; vertically. **2.** *Informal* Utterly; completely; entirely: also spelled *plum.* — *v.t.* **1.** To test the perpendicularity of with a plumb. **2.** To make vertical; straighten: usually with *up.* **3.** To test the depth of; sound. **4.** To reach the lowest level or extent of; fathom: to *plumb* the depths of despair. **5.** To seal with lead. [< F *plomb* < L *plumbum* lead]

plumb- Var. of PLUMBO-.

plum·ba·go (plum·bā′gō) *n. pl.* **·gos 1.** Graphite. **2.** A drawing made with a lead-pointed instrument. **3.** Any of a genus (*Plumbago*) of hardy, shrubby plants, typical of a family (*Plumbaginaceae*), and cultivated for their showy blue, white, or purplish flowers: also called *leadwort.* [< L *plumbum* lead] — **plum·bag′i·nous** (-baj′ə-nəs) *adj.*

plumb bob The weight used at the end of a plumb line.

plum·be·ous (plum′bē-əs) *adj.* **1.** Resembling or containing lead; heavy. **2.** Lead-colored. [< L *plumbeus* < *plumbum* lead]

plumb·er (plum′ər) *n.* One whose occupation is the installing or repairing of plumbing.

plumb·er's friend (plum′ərz) A plunger (def. 3).

plumb·er·y (plum′ər-ē) *n. pl.* **·er·ies 1.** The work of a plumber. **2.** A plumber's place of business. **3.** Leadwork.

plum·bic (plum′bik) *adj. Chem.* Of, pertaining to, or containing lead, especially in its higher valence.

plum·bif·er·ous (plum·bif′ər-əs) *adj.* Containing or yielding lead.

plumb·ing (plum′ing) *n.* **1.** The art or trade of putting into buildings the tanks, pipes, etc., for water, gas, sewage, etc. **2.** The pipe system of a building. **3.** The act of sounding for depth, etc., with a plumb line.

plumb·ism (plum′biz·əm) *n. Pathol.* Lead poisoning.

plumb line 1. A cord by which a weight is suspended to test the perpendicularity or depth of something. **2.** Such a cord, indicating the direction of the earth's center from any point on its surface.

plumbo- *combining form* Lead; of or containing lead. Also, before vowels, **plumb-.** [< L *plumbum* lead]

plum·bous (plum′bəs) *adj. Chem.* Of, pertaining to, or containing lead, especially in its lower valence. [< L *plumbosus* full of lead < *plumbum* lead]

plumb rule A narrow rule having a plumb line, with which masons and carpenters test the verticality of their work.

plum·bum (plum′bəm) *n.* Lead. [< L]

plum duff A suet and flour pudding with raisins, currants, etc., boiled in a cloth bag.

plume (ploōm) *n.* **1.** A feather, especially when long and ornamental. **2.** A large feather or tuft of feathers used as an ornament, especially on a helmet or shield. **3.** *Biol.* A featherlike form or part. **4.** Plumage. **5.** Anything resembling a plume or feather. **6.** A decoration of honor or achievement; a prize. — *v.t.* **plumed, plum·ing 1.** To adorn, dress, or furnish with or as with plumes. **2.** To smooth or dress (itself or its feathers); preen. **3.** To congratulate or pride (oneself): with *on* or *upon.* [< F < L *pluma*]

plume·let (ploōm′lit) *n.* A little plume.

plu·mi·ped (ploō′mə-ped) *adj.* Having feathered feet. — *n.* A plumiped bird, as an owl. Also **plu′mi·pede** (-pēd). [< L *pluma* feather + -PED]

plum·met (plum′it) *n.* **1.** A piece of lead or heavy substance attached to a line for making soundings, adjusting walls to the vertical, etc.; a plumb bob. **2.** A plumb rule. **3.** Something that oppresses or weighs down. — *v.i.* To drop straight down; plunge. [< OF *plommet,* dim. of *plom* lead < L *plumbum*]

plum·my (plum′ē) *adj.* **·mi·er, ·mi·est 1.** Full of plums. **2.** *Informal* Full of desirable things; profitable.

plu·mose (ploō′mōs) *adj.* **1.** Bearing feathers or plumes. **2.** Plumelike; feathery. [< L *plumosus* < *pluma* feather] — **plu′mose·ly** *adv.* — **plu·mos·i·ty** (ploō·mos′ə·tē) *n.*

plump¹ (plump) *adj.* **1.** Somewhat fat; chubby: a *plump* girl. **2.** Well filled or rounded out: a *plump* purse. — **Syn.** See FAT. — *v.t. & v.i.* To make or become plump: often with *up* or *out.* [< MDu., var. of *plomp* blunt] — **plump′ly** *adv.* — **plump′ness** *n.*

plump² (plump) *v.i.* **1.** To fall suddenly or heavily; drop with full impact. **2.** To give one's complete support: with *for.* **3.** To come or go abruptly or in a hurry: with *in* or *out.* — *v.t.* **4.** To drop or throw down heavily or all at once. **5.**

To utter bluntly or abruptly: often with *out.* — *n.* **1.** The act of plumping or falling. **2.** The sound made by this. — *adj.* Containing no reservation or qualification; blunt; downright. — *adv.* **1.** With a sudden impact or fall. **2.** Straightforwardly; bluntly. **3.** Straight down. [< MDu. *plompen;* ult. imit.] — **plump′ly** *adv.*

plump³ (plump) *n. Archaic* or *Brit. Dial.* A small group; cluster. [Origin uncertain]

plump·er¹ (plum′pər) *n.* **1.** A heavy fall or drop. **2.** Votes cast all for one candidate, when more than one candidate may be voted for; also, a person so voting. **3.** *Brit. Slang* An unqualified lie.

plump·er² (plum′pər) *n.* A pad placed in the mouth to distend the cheek and give it an appearance of plumpness.

plum pudding A boiled pudding made with flour, suet, raisins, currants, spices, etc.

plu·mule (ploō′myoōl) *n.* **1.** *Ornithol.* A down feather. **2.** *Bot.* The rudimentary or first bud of a plant embryo, appearing on the ascending axis. [< L *plumula,* dim. of *pluma* feather]

plum·y (ploō′mē) *adj.* **plum·i·er, plum·i·est 1.** Made of, covered, or adorned with feathers. **2.** Like a plume or feather.

plun·der (plun′dər) *v.t.* **1.** To rob of goods or property by open violence, as in war; pillage; loot. **2.** To despoil by robbery or fraud. **3.** To take as plunder. — *v.i.* **4.** To take plunder; steal. — *n.* **1.** That which is taken by plundering; booty. **2.** The act of plundering or robbing. **3.** *U.S. Informal* Personal belongings or goods, etc. [< G *plündern* < MHG *plundern,* orig., to remove household goods < *plunder* household goods] — **plun′der·age** *n.* — **plun′der·er** *n.*

plunge (plunj) *v.* **plunged, plung·ing** *v.t.* **1.** To thrust or force suddenly into a fluid, penetrable substance, hole, etc. **2.** To force into some condition or state: to *plunge* a nation into debt. — *v.i.* **3.** To dive, jump, or fall into a fluid, chasm, etc. **4.** To move suddenly or with a rush. **5.** To move violently forward and downward, as a horse or ship. **6.** To descend abruptly or steeply, as a road or cliff. **7.** *Informal* To gamble or speculate heavily and recklessly. — *n.* **1.** The act of plunging; a leap; dive. **2.** A sudden and violent motion, as of a breaking wave. **3.** A place, tank, or pool for diving or swimming. **4.** A swim. **5.** An exceptionally heavy or extravagant bet, expenditure, or speculation. [< OF *plongier,* ult. < L *plumbum* lead]

plung·er (plun′jər) *n.* **1.** One who or that which plunges. **2.** *Informal* One who gambles or speculates recklessly. **3.** A cuplike device made of rubber and attached to a stick, used to clean out clogged drains, etc.: also called *plumber's friend.* **4.** *Mech.* Any appliance having or adapted for a plunging motion, as a piston.

plunk (plungk) *Informal v.t.* **1.** To pluck, as a banjo or its strings; strum. **2.** To place or throw heavily and suddenly: with *down.* — *v.i.* **3.** To emit a twanging sound. **4.** To fall heavily or suddenly; plump. — *n.* **1.** A heavy blow, or its sound. **2.** *Slang* A dollar. — *adv.* Directly; exactly: *plunk* in the middle. [Imit.]

plu·per·fect (ploō·pûr′fikt) *n. Gram.* The past perfect (which see). [< L *plus quam perfectus,* lit., more than completed]

plur. 1. Plural. **2.** Plurality.

plu·ral (ploōr′əl) *adj.* **1.** Containing, consisting of, or designating more than one. **2.** Involving or being more than one. **3.** *Gram.* Of or designating a linguistic form that denotes more than one (in languages that have dual number, as Sanskrit and Greek, more than two): distinguished from *dual, singular.* — *n. Gram.* The plural number or a word in this number. *Abbr. pl., plu., plur.* [< OF < L *pluralis* < *plus, pluris* more] — **plu′ral·ly** *adv.*

◆ English nouns regularly form their plurals by adding *s* to the singular. However, nouns that end in *y* preceded either by a consonant or by *qu* form their plurals by changing the *y* to *i* and adding *es,* as, body, *bodies,* city, *cities,* colloquy, *colloquies;* if the *y* is preceded by a vowel (other than *u*), the plural is formed by adding *s,* as, day, *days,* monkey, *monkeys.* Nouns ending in *ss, sh, ch, s, x,* and *zz* usually form their plurals by adding *es,* as, brass, *brasses,* crash, *crashes,* crutch, *crutches,* gas, *gases,* box, *boxes,* buzz, *buzzes.* Many nouns ending in *f* change the *f* to *v* and add *es,* as, wolf, *wolves,* half, *halves.* Nouns ending in *o* form their plurals by adding either *s* or *es,* and the preferable form will be found at the word entry. Some nouns of Old English origin have an irregular plural in *en,* as, child, *children,* and some form the plural by a vowel change, as mouse, *mice;* goose, *geese;* man, *men.* A few nouns retain the singular form unchanged in the plural, as, deer, hose, moose, series. Some such nouns, especially the names of animals, have also an alternative plural regularly formed, as fish, *fish* or *fishes. Fish* is the usual collective plural; *fishes* is used to indicate more than one genus, variety, species, etc. Many words of foreign derivation retain the plural forms peculiar to the languages from which they are derived, as, addendum, *addenda;* crisis, *crises;* datum, *data.* Many nouns of this class have also a plural of the regular English form, as, appendix, *appendixes* or *appendices*; beau, *beaus* or *beaux*; cherub, *cherubs* or *cherubim*; focus, *focuses* or *foci*. Compounds commonly form the plural regularly by adding *s* or *es* to the complete word, as, armful, *armfuls*; football, *footballs*. If the last element of the compound forms its plural irregularly, the same form usually appears in the plural of the compound, as, footman, *footmen*. Some nouns that end in -*man*, but are not compounds, form the plural regularly by adding *s*, as, Mussulman, *Mussulmans*. Hyphenated compounds in which the principal word forms the first element change that element to form the plural, as, father-in-law, *fathers-in-law*.

plu·ral·ism (plŏor'əl·iz'əm) *n.* **1.** The quality or condition of being plural. **2.** A social condition in which disparate religious, ethnic, and racial groups are geographically intermingled and united in a single nation, as in the United States. Also **pluralistic society, pluralistic culture.** **3.** *Eccl.* The holding at the same time of more than one office, or, in the Anglican Church, of more than one living. **4.** *Philos.* The doctrine that there are several ultimate substances. Compare DUALISM, MONISM.

plu·ral·ist (plŏor'əl·ist) *n.* **1.** *Eccl.* One who holds more than one office or ecclesiastical benefice at the same time. **2.** A believer in philosophical pluralism. — **plu'ral·is'tic** *adj.*

plu·ral·i·ty (plŏo·ral'ə·tē) *n. pl.* **·ties 1.** In U.S. politics: **a** The number of votes cast for a candidate over and above the number cast for his nearest opponent. **b** In a contest having more than two candidates, the greatest number of votes cast for any one candidate but not more than half the total number of votes cast. Distinguished from *majority.* **2.** The larger or greater portion or number of anything. **3.** The state or condition of being plural or numerous. **4.** *Eccl.* Pluralism; also, a living held by a pluralist. Abbr. *plur.*

plu·ral·ize (plŏor'əl·īz) *v.t.* **·ized, ·iz·ing 1.** To make plural. **2.** To express in the plural. — **plu'ral·i·za'tion** *n.*

pluri- *combining form* More; many; several: *pluriaxial.* [< L *plus, pluris* more]

plu·ri·ax·i·al (plŏor'ē·ak'sē·əl) *adj.* **1.** Having more than one axis. **2.** *Bot.* Having flowers on secondary shoots.

plus (plus) *prep.* **1.** Added to or to be added to: Three *plus* two equals five. **2.** Increased by: salary *plus* commission. — *adj.* **1.** Of, pertaining to, or involving addition. **2.** Extra; supplemental: The *plus* values were many. **3.** Denoting a value higher than ordinary in a specified grade: B *plus.* **4.** Positive: a *plus* quantity. **5.** *Informal* More of something than can be stated or described: He has personality *plus.* **6.** *Informal* Possessing something in addition: He was *plus* a new hat. **7.** *Electr.* Positive. **8.** *Bot.* Designating a form of sexual differentiation in certain plants: the *plus* strain of heterothallic fungi. — *n. pl.* **plus·es** The plus sign (which see). **2.** An addition or an extra quantity. **3.** A positive quantity. — *adv. Electr.* Positively. [< L, more]

plus fours Knickerbockers cut very full and bagging below the knees. [Orig. tailor's cant; because they were four inches longer than ordinary knickerbockers]

plush (plush) *n.* A pile fabric of silk, rayon, mohair, etc., having a deeper pile than velvet. — *adj.* **1.** Of or made of plush. **2.** *Slang* Luxurious. [< MF *pluche* < OF *peluche* < Ital. *peluzzo,* dim. of *pelo* hair < L *pilus*]

plush·y (plush'ē) *adj.* **plush·i·er, plush·i·est** Of or resembling plush. — **plush'i·ly** *adv.*

plus sign A sign (+) denoting addition or a positive quantity.

Plu·tarch (plŏo'tärk) A.D., 46?–120?, Greek biographer.

Plu·to (plŏo'tō) In Greek and Roman mythology, the god of the dead: identified with the Greek *Hades* and the Roman *Dis.* — *n.* A planet of the solar system, having an undetermined size and ninth in order from the sun. See PLANET.

plu·toc·ra·cy (plŏo·tok'rə·sē) *n. pl.* **·cies 1.** Government by the wealthy. **2.** A class that, by means of its wealth, controls the government. [< Gk. *ploutokratia* < *ploutos* wealth + *kratein* to rule]

plu·to·crat (plŏo'tə·krat) *n.* **1.** A member of a plutocracy. **2.** *Informal* Any wealthy person.

plu·to·crat·ic (plŏo'tə·krat'ik) *adj.* Of, pertaining to, or like a plutocrat or plutocracy. Also **plu'to·crat'i·cal.** — **plu'to·crat'i·cal·ly** *adv.*

Plu·to·ni·an (plŏo·tō'nē·ən) *adj.* **1.** Of or pertaining to Pluto and the lower world. **2.** Plutonic (def. 2). [< L *Plutonius* < Gk. *Ploutonios* < *Ploutōn* Pluto]

plu·ton·ic (plŏo·ton'ik) *adj. Geol.* **1.** Deeply subterranean in original position and crystallized, probably from a fused condition: said of igneous rocks. **2.** *Sometimes cap.* Of or pertaining to a theory that the principal rock features of the earth were formed by the agency of heat: distinguished from *Neptunian.* [< L *Pluto, -onis*]

plu·to·ni·um (plŏo·tō'nē·əm) *n.* A radioactive element (symbol Pu), occurring in several isotopes, especially Pu-239, formed in the bombardment of neptunium by deuterons and produced by fission of uranium 238. See ELEMENT. [< NL < *Pluto* (the planet)]

Plu·tus (plŏo'təs) In Greek mythology, the god of riches, blinded by Zeus so that his gifts should be distributed without discrimination. [< L < Gk. *Ploutos* < *ploutos* wealth]

plu·vi·al (plŏo'vē·əl) *adj.* **1.** Of or pertaining to rain. **2.** Caused by the action of rain. [< L *pluvialis* < *pluvia* rain]

pluvio- *combining form* Rain; pertaining to rain: *pluviometer.* Also, before vowels, **pluvi-.** [< L *pluvia* rain]

plu·vi·om·e·ter (plŏo'vē·om'ə·tər) *n.* A rain gauge. [< PLUVIO- + -METER] — **plu'vi·o·met'ric** (-ə·met'rik) or **·ri·cal** *adj.* — **plu'vi·o·met'ri·cal·ly** *adv.* — **plu'vi·om'e·try** *n.*

Plu·vi·ôse (plŏo'vē·ōs, *Fr.* plü·vyōz') *n.* The fifth month of the Republican calendar. See (Republican) CALENDAR. [< F < L *pluviosus* rainy]

plu·vi·ous (plŏo'vē·əs) *adj.* Pertaining to rain; rainy. Also **plu'vi·ose** (-ōs). [< L *pluviosus* < *pluvia* rain]

ply¹ (plī) *v.* **plied, ply·ing** *v.t.* To bend; mold; shape. — *v.i. Obs.* To bend or yield. — *n. pl.* **plies 1.** A layer, fold, or thickness, as of cloth, etc. **2.** A strand of rope, yarn, thread, etc.; used in combination to mean (a certain) number of folds, twists, or strands: three-*ply* yarn. **3.** A bent or bias; inclination. [< F *plier* < L *plicare* to fold]

ply² (plī) *v.* **plied, ply·ing** *v.t.* **1.** To use in working, fighting, etc.; wield; employ. **2.** To work at; be engaged in: He *plies* the trade of shoemaker. **3.** To supply with or offer repeatedly: to *ply* a person with drink. **4.** To address (a person) repeatedly with questions, requests, etc. **5.** To strike or assail persistently: He *plied* the donkey with a whip. **6.** To traverse regularly: ferryboats that *ply* the river. — *v.i.* **7.** To make regular trips; sail: usually with *between.* **8.** To work steadily; do one's work. **9.** To proceed; steer. **10.** *Naut.* To beat; tack. [< APPLY]

Plym·outh (plim'əth) **1.** A town of eastern Massachusetts, on **Plymouth Bay,** an inlet of Massachusetts Bay; first settlement (*Plymouth Colony*) in New England; pop. 18,606. **2.** A county borough and port in SW Devonshire, England, on **Plymouth Sound,** an inlet of the English Channel; pop. 248,470 (est. 1969).

Plymouth Colony The colony on the shore of Massachusetts Bay founded by the Pilgrim Fathers who sailed from Plymouth, England, in 1620.

Plymouth Rock 1. The rock at Plymouth, Massachusetts, on which the Pilgrim Fathers are said to have stepped when landing from the *Mayflower* in 1620. **2.** One of a breed of domestic fowls having variously colored, often barred plumage.

ply·wood (plī'wŏod') *n.* A structural material consisting of sheets or layers of wood glued together, the grains of adjoining layers usually being at right angles to each other.

Pl·zeň (pul'zeny') The Czech name for PILSEN.

Pm *Chem.* Promethium.

P.M. 1. Afternoon (L *post meridiem*): also **p.m.** **2.** Past Master. **3.** Paymaster. **4.** Police Magistrate. **5.** Postmaster: also **PM.** **6.** Post-mortem: also **p.m.** **7.** Prime Minister. **8.** *Mil.* Provost Marshal: also **PM.**

P.M.G. 1. Postmaster General. **2.** Provost Marshal General.

P/n or **p.n.** Promissory note.

pneu·ma (nŏo'mə, nyŏo'-) *n.* The breath of life; the soul or spirit. [< Gk., wind, breath < *pneein* to blow]

pneu·mat·ic (nŏo·mat'ik, nyŏo-) *adj.* **1.** Pertaining to pneumatics. **2.** Operated by or making use of compressed air: a *pneumatic* engine. **3.** Pertaining to or containing air or gas, especially compressed air. **4.** Having or equipped with pneumatic tires. **5.** Of or pertaining to the pneuma; spiritual. **6.** Containing air, as cavities in the bones of certain birds. Also **pneu·mat'i·cal.** — *n.* A tire inflated with compressed air: also **pneumatic tire.** [< L *pneumaticus* < Gk. *pneumatikos* < *pneuma* breath, wind < *pneein* to blow] — **pneu·mat'i·cal·ly** *adv.*

pneu·ma·tics (nŏo·mat'iks, nyŏo-) *n.pl.* (*construed as sing.*) The branch of physics that treats of the mechanical properties of air and other gases, and also of pneumatic mechanisms: also called *aeromechanics, pneumodynamics.*

pneumato- *combining form* **1.** Air: *pneumatophore.* **2.** Breath; breathing: *pneumatometer.* **3.** Spirit; spirits: *pneumatology.* Also, before vowels, **pneumat-.** [< Gk. *pneuma, pneumatos* air, spirit, breath < *pneein* to blow]

pneu·ma·tol·o·gy (nŏo'mə·tol'ə·jē, nyŏo'-) *n. pl.* **·gies 1.** *Theol.* The doctrine or doctrines treating of the Holy Ghost. **2.** The doctrine or study of the nature and operation of spirit and spiritual beings. **3.** *Archaic Psychology.* **4.** *Obs.* Pneumatics. — **pneu'ma·to·log'ic** (-tə·loj'ik) or **·i·cal** *adj.* — **pneu'ma·tol'o·gist** *n.*

pneu·ma·tol·y·sis (nŏo'mə·tol'ə·sis, nyŏo'-) *n. Geol.* The process of forming minerals under the action of the gases present in the magma of igneous rocks.

pneu·ma·to·lyt·ic (nŏo'mə·tō·lit'ik, nyŏo'-) *adj.* Of, pertaining to, formed by, or characteristic of pneumatolysis.

pneu·ma·tom·e·ter (nŏo'mə·tom'ə·tər, nyŏo'-) *n.* An instrument for measuring the volume of air exhaled or inhaled at one breath. — **pneu'ma·tom'e·try** *n.*

pneu·ma·to·phore (nŏo'mə·tə·fôr, -fōr, nyŏo'-; nŏo·mat'ə-, nyŏo-) *n.* **1.** *Zool.* In a siphonophore, a sac containing air and serving to keep the organism afloat. **2.** *Bot.* A structure on the roots of certain swamp plants, acting as a respiratory organ. — **pneu'ma·toph'o·rous** (-tof'ər·əs) *adj.*

pneu·ma·to·ther·a·py (nŏo'mə·tō·ther'ə·pē, nyŏo'-) *n. Med.* The treatment of disease by rarefied or condensed air.

pneu·mec·to·my (nōō-mek′tə-mē, nyōō-) *n. pl.* **·mies** *Surg.* The operation of removing lung tissue or a part of the lung. [< PNEUM(O)- + -ECTOMY]

pneumo- *combining form* Lung; related to the lungs; respiratory: *pneumobacillus.* Also **pneum-** (before vowels), **pneumono-.** [< Gk. *pneumōn, pneumonos* a lung]

pneu·mo·ba·cil·lus (nōō′mō-bə-sil′əs, nyōō′-) *n. pl.* **·cil·li** (-sil′ī) A bacillus (*Klebsiella pneumoniae*) found in infections of the respiratory tract.

pneu·mo·coc·cus (nōō′mə-kok′əs, nyōō′-) *n. pl.* **·coc·ci** (-kok′sī) Any of a group of bacteria (genus *Diplococcus*) that inhabit the respiratory tract of man and animals; especially, *D. pneumoniae*, the cause of lobar pneumonia. — **pneu·mo·coc′cal, pneu′mo·coc′cous, pneu′mo·coc′cic** (-kok′sik) *adj.*

pneu·mo·co·ni·o·sis (nōō′mō-kon′ē-ō′sis, nyōō′-) *n. Pathol.* A lung disorder resulting from the inhalation of dust or other minute particles. Also **pneu′mo·no·con′i·o′sis** (nōō′mə-nō-, nyōō′-). [< PNEUMO- + Gk. *konia* dust + -OSIS]

pneu·mo·dy·nam·ics (nōō′mō-dī-nam′iks, nyōō′-) *n.pl.* (*construed as sing.*) Pneumatics.

pneu·mo·gas·tric (nōō′mō-gas′trik, nyōō′-) *Anat. adj.* **1.** Of or pertaining to the lungs and the stomach. **2.** Of or pertaining to the vagus nerve. — *n.* The vagus: also **pneu·mogastric nerve.**

pneu·mo·nec·to·my (nōō′mə-nek′tə-mē, nyōō′-) *n. pl.* **·mies** *Surg.* The total removal of a lung.

pneu·mo·nia (nōō-mōn′yə, nyōō-) *n. Pathol.* Inflammation of the lungs, a disease of bacterial or viral origin occurring in many forms, as **bronchial pneumonia** or **lobar pneumonia.** [< NL < Gk. < *pneumōn* lung]

pneu·mon·ic (nōō-mon′ik, nyōō-) *adj.* **1.** Of, pertaining to, or affected with pneumonia. **2.** Pulmonary (def. 1). [< NL *pneumonicus* < Gk. *pneumonikos* < *pneumōn* lung]

pneu·mo·tho·rax (nōō′mō-thôr′aks, -thō′raks, nyōō′-) *n. Pathol.* An accumulation of air or gas within the pleural cavity, sometimes artificially induced to collapse the lung.

Pnom-Penh (nom′pen′, pnōōm-pen′y′) The capital of Cambodia, in the south central part on the Mekong; pop. 500,-000 (est. 1966): also *Phnômpenh.*

pnxt. He (or she) painted (L *pinxit*).

Pnyx (niks) The place in ancient Athens where the people met to deliberate and vote upon public affairs.

p.o. or **po** Put-out(s).

Po (pō) A river in northern Italy, flowing 405 miles, generally SE, to the Adriatic: ancient *Padus.*

Po *Chem.* Polonium.

P.O. or **p.o.** **1.** Personnel officer. **2.** Petty officer. **3.** Postal order. **4.** Post office.

po·a·ceous (pō-ā′shəs) *adj. Bot.* Of, pertaining to, or characteristic of plants of the grass family (*Gramineae*, formerly *Poaceae*). [< Gk. *poa* grass + -ACEOUS]

poach[1] (pōch) *v.t.* To cook (eggs without their shells, fish, etc.) in boiling water, milk, or other liquid. [< OF *pochier* to pocket < *poche* pocket, pouch; because the egg white forms a pouch around the yolk]

poach[2] (pōch) *v.i.* **1.** To trespass on another's property, etc., especially for the purpose of taking game or fish. **2.** To take game or fish unlawfully. **3.** To become soft and muddy by being trampled: said of land. **4.** To sink into mud or soft earth while walking. — *v.t.* **5.** To trespass on, as for taking game or fish. **6.** To take (game or fish) unlawfully. **7.** To make muddy or tear up by trampling, as land. **8.** To reduce to a uniform consistency by mixing with water, as clay. [< OF *pocher* to thrust, encroach upon < MLG *poken* to poke] — **poach′er** *n.*

poach·y (pō′chē) *adj.* **poach·i·er, poach·i·est** Soft and miry; swampy. [< POACH[2] (def. 3)] — **poach′i·ness** *n.*

Po·ca·hon·tas (pō′kə-hon′təs), 1595?–1617, American Indian princess in Virginia, daughter of Powhatan; reputedly saved the life of Captain John Smith.

Po·ca·tel·lo (pō′kə-tel′ō, -tel′ə) A city in SE Idaho; pop. 40,036.

po·chard (pō′chərd, -kərd) *n.* Any of various sea ducks (genus *Aythya*), having a reddish head and neck; especially, the **common pochard** (*A. ferina*) of the Old World. [Origin uncertain]

pock[1] (pok) *n.* **1.** A pustule in an eruptive disease, as in smallpox. **2.** A pockmark. [OE *pocc*]

pock[2] (pok) *n. Scot.* A bag; pouch.

pock·et (pok′it) *n.* **1.** A small pouch inserted in and forming part of a garment, for carrying money, etc. **2.** A small bag or pouch. **3.** Any opening, receptacle, or container. **4.** Money, means, or financial interests. **5.** *Mining* **a** A cavity containing gold or other ore. **b** An accumulation in one spot of alluvial gold or other ore. **6.** One of the pouches in a billiard or pool table, into which the balls are driven. **7.** In racing, a position in which a horse, runner, car, etc., is behind the leading contender or contenders and is unable to go past because of others at the side. **8.** An air pocket (which see). **9.** A region or area, usually small and differentiated in some way from the surrounding area. **10.** A bin for holding

grain, coal, etc., for storage. — **in one's pocket 1.** On terms of close intimacy. **2.** Under one's influence or control. — *adj.* **1.** Diminutive, as if pocketable. **2.** Pertaining to, for, or carried in a pocket: *pocket* lining, *pocketknife.* — *v.t.* **1.** To put into or confine in a pocket. **2.** To appropriate as one's own, especially dishonestly, as profits or funds. **3.** To enclose as if in a pocket. **4.** To accept or endure without open resentment or reply, as an insult. **5.** To conceal or suppress: *Pocket* your pride. **6.** To retain without signing. See POCKET VETO. **7.** In billiards, to drive (a ball) into a pocket. [< AF *pokete*, dim. of OF *poque, poche* pouch < Gmc.] — **pock′et·a·ble** *adj.* — **pock′et·er** *n.*

pocket billiards Pool[2] (def. 5).

pock·et·book (pok′it-book′) *n.* **1.** A small case for carrying money and papers in the pocket; wallet. **2.** A woman's purse or handbag. **3.** A book, usually paperbound and smaller than standard size. **4.** Money or financial resources.

pocket borough In England before the Reform Bill of 1832, a Parliamentary borough owned or controlled by a single individual or family; also, any constituency so controlled.

pocket edition An edition or copy of a book small enough to be carried in the pocket.

pock·et·ful (pok′it-fool′) *n. pl.* **-fuls** As much as a pocket will hold.

pocket gopher See under GOPHER.

pock·et·knife (pok′it-nīf′) *n. pl.* **-knives** (-nīvz′) A knife having one or more blades that fold into the handle. For illustration see KNIFE.

pocket money Money for small expenses.

pocket veto 1. *U.S.* An act whereby the President, on being presented a bill by Congress for his signature of approval, retains ("pockets") it unsigned until the session has adjourned, thus causing it to fail without a direct veto. **2.** Any similar act by a chief executive.

pock·mark (pok′märk′) *n.* A pit or scar left on the skin by smallpox or a similar disease. — **pock′-marked** *adj.*

pock·y (pok′ē) *adj.* **pock·i·er, pock·i·est 1.** Pertaining to, resembling, or affected with smallpox. **2.** Marked by pocks.

po·co (pō′kō) *adv. Music* Slightly; a little. [< Ital. < L *paucus*]

po·co a po·co (pō′kō ä pō′kō) *Music* Little by little; gradually. [< Ital.]

po·co·cu·ran·te (pō′kō-koo-ran′tē, *Ital.* pō′kō-koo-rän′tā) *adj.* Indifferent; not caring. — *n.* An indifferent person. [< Ital. *poco curante*, lit., caring little] — **po′co·cu·ran′te·ism** or **·ran′tism** *n.*

pod[1] (pod) *n.* **1.** A seed vessel or capsule, especially of a leguminous plant. **2.** Any dry and many-seeded dehiscent fruit. **3.** *Aeron.* A separate enclosure on an aircraft, for housing a gun, engine, fuel, etc.; especially, one beneath the wing for a jet engine. — *v.i.* **pod·ded, pod·ding 1.** To fill out like a pod. **2.** To produce pods. [Origin unknown; replaced earlier *cod*]

pod[2] (pod) *n.* A flock or collection of animals, especially of seals, whales, or walruses. [Origin unknown]

pod[3] (pod) *n. Mech.* **1.** The lengthwise groove in certain augers, bits, etc. **2.** An auger so grooved. [Origin unknown]

-pod *combining form* **1.** One who or that which has (a specified number or kind of) feet: *arthropod.* **2.** A (specified kind of) foot: *pleopod.* Also **-pode.** [< Gk. *pous, podos* foot]

P.O.D. Pay on delivery: also **p.o.d.**

-poda *combining form Zool.* Plural of -POD: used in names of phyla, orders, classes, etc.: *Arthropoda.*

po·dag·ra (pō-dag′rə, pod′ə-grə) *n. Pathol.* Gout in the foot. [< L < Gk. < *pous, podos* foot + *agra* seizure] — **po·dag′ral, po·dag′ric** *adj.*

po·des·ta (pō-des′tə, *Ital.* pō′des-tä′) *n.* **1.** A chief magistrate in the medieval Italian republics or towns. **2.** One of the governors of the Lombard cities appointed by Frederick I. **3.** In Fascist Italy, a mayor or chief executive of a town. [< Ital. *podestà* < L *potestas* power]

Pod·go·ri·ca (pôd′gô′rē-tsä) The former name for TITO-GRAD. Also **Pod′go·re·tsa.**

podg·y (poj′ē) *adj.* **podg·i·er, podg·i·est** Pudgy. [< dial. *podge* to walk slowly and heavily] — **podg′i·ness** *n.*

po·di·a·try (pə-dī′ə-trē, pō-) *n.* Chiropody. [< Gk. *pous, podos* foot + -IATRY] — **po·di′a·trist** *n.*

po·di·um (pō′dē-əm) *n. pl.* **·di·a** (-dē-ə) **1.** A small platform or dais for the conductor of an orchestra, a speaker, etc. **2.** *Archit.* **a** A solid foundation supporting a structure. **b** A wall surrounding the arena of an ancient amphitheater or circus. **3.** *Zool.* A foot, or any footlike structure. [< L < Gk. *podion*, dim. of *pous, podos* foot. Akin to PEW.]

-podium *combining form* A footlike part: *pseudopodium.* [< NL < Gk. *podion*, dim. of *pous, podos* a foot]

Po·dolsk (pō-dôlsk′, *Russ.* pō-dôlv′sk′) A city in the western R.S.F.S.R.; pop. 124,000 (1959). Also **Po·dol′sk′.**

pod·o·phyl·lin (pod′ə-fil′in) *n.* A bitter, resinous substance obtained from the dried root of the May apple, used in medicine as a purgative. [< NL *Podophyllum*, genus name < Gk. *pous, podos* foot + *phyllon* leaf]

-podous *combining form* -footed: used in adjectives corresponding to nouns in *-pod* and *-poda*: *arthropodous*. [< -POD + -OUS]

Po·dunk (pō'dungk) *n.* One of a tribe of North American Indians of Algonquian stock, formerly inhabiting parts of Connecticut and Massachusetts.

Po·dunk (pō'dungk) *n.* Any small town regarded as dull and nonprogressive. [? after *Podunk*, Massachusetts]

pod·zol (pod'zol) *adj.* Of, pertaining to, or designating a major soil type of northern regions, characterized by a strongly acid, infertile humus underlying a thin mat of leaves and decayed vegetation. Also **pod·zol'ic.** — *n.* Podzol soil. Also **pod'sol** (-sol). [< Russian, ashlike < *zola* ashes]

pod·zol·i·za·tion (pod'zol-ə-zā'shən, -ī-zā'-) *n.* The processes by which a soil develops podzol characteristics.

Poe (pō), **Edgar Allan,** 1809–49, U.S. poet, critic, and short-story writer.

P.O.E. **1.** *Mil.* Port of Embarkation. **2.** Port of Entry.

po·e·chore (pō'ə-kôr, -kōr) *n.* *Ecol.* The semiarid regions of the steppes. [< Gk. *poa* grass + *chōra* region] — **po'e·chor'ic** (-kôr'ik, -kōr'ik) *adj.*

po·em (pō'əm) *n.* **1.** A composition in verse, characterized by the imaginative treatment of experience and a condensed use of language that is more vivid and intense than ordinary prose. **2.** Any composition in verse. **3.** Any composition characterized by intensity and beauty of language or thought: a prose *poem.* **4.** Any experience that produces an effect upon the mind similar or likened to that of a poem: a *poem* in stone. [< F *poème* < L *poema* < Gk. *poiēma* work, product < *poiein* to make]

poe·nol·o·gy (pē·nol'ə·jē) See PENOLOGY.

po·e·sy (pō'ə·sē, -zē) *n.* *pl.* **·sies** **1.** *Poetic* Poetry taken collectively. **2.** *Poetic* The art of writing poetry. **3.** *Obs.* A poem. **4.** *Obs.* A motto or conceit, as one engraved on jewelry. [< OF *poesie* < L *poesia* < Gk. *poiēsis* creation, production < *poiein* to make, do]

po·et (pō'it) *n.* **1.** One who writes poems. **2.** One especially endowed with imagination and the creative faculty or power of artistic expression. [< OF *poete* < L *poeta* < Gk. *poiētēs* maker < *poiein* to make] — **po'et·ess** *n.fem.*

poet. Poetic; poetical; poetry.

po·et·as·ter (pō'it·as'tər) *n.* An inferior poet. [< NL]

po·et·ic (pō·et'ik) *adj.* **1.** Of or pertaining to poetry. **2.** Having the nature or quality of or expressed in poetry: a *poetic* theme. **3.** Pertaining to, befitting, or characteristic of a poet: *poetic* fire. **4.** Fit to be described in poetry; of a nature to evoke poetic expression: a *poetic* incident or scene. **5.** Having or showing the sensibility, feelings, faculty, etc., of a poet. **6.** Celebrated or recounted in poetry or verse. Also **po·et'i·cal.** — *n.* Poetics. *Abbr.* poet. [< F *poétique* < L *poeticus* < Gk. *poiētikos* < *poiein* to make]

poetic justice The ideal distribution of rewards to the good and punishment to the evil as often represented in literature.

poetic license The departure from the rules of diction, pronunciation, or from what is regarded as fact, for the sake of rhyme, meter, or an overall enhancement of effect.

po·et·ics (pō·et'iks) *n.pl.* (*usually construed as sing.*) **1.** The nature, principles, and forms of poetry or, by extension, of any art. **2.** A treatise on poetry. Also *poetic.*

po·et·ize (pō'it·īz) *v.* **·ized, ·iz·ing** *v.i.* **1.** To write poetry. — *v.t.* **2.** To turn into or express by means of poetry; express in poetic form. **3.** To make poetic. — **po'et·iz'er** *n.* [< MF *poétiser*]

poet laureate *pl.* **poets laureate** **1.** In Great Britain, the official poet of the realm, a member of the royal household charged with writing verses for particular occasions. **2.** A poet acclaimed as the most eminent in a locality.

po·et·ry (pō'it·rē) *n.* **1.** The art or craft of writing poems. **2.** Poems collectively. **3.** The quality, effect, or spirit of a poem or of anything poetic. **4.** Something that resembles a poem in nature, form, or spirit. *Abbr.* poet. [< OF *poetrie* < LL *poetria* < L *poeta* poet. See POET.]

Po·ga·ny (pō·gä'nē, *Hungarian* pō'gän·y'), **Willy,** 1882–1955, U.S. illustrator, mural painter, and theatrical designer born in Hungary: full name **William Andrew Pogany.**

po·gey (pō'gē) *n.* *Canadian Slang* **1.** The public welfare rolls; dole. **2.** Unemployment insurance.

po·go·ni·a (pə·gō'nē·ə, -gōn'yə) *n.* One of a genus (*Pogonia*) of terrestrial orchids, especially the North American species, *P. ophioglossoides,* having fragrant, rose-pink flowers. [< NL < Gk. *pōgōn* beard]

pog·o·nip (pog'ə·nip) *n.* *Meteorol.* A cold fog containing particles of ice, characteristic of the Sierra Nevada mountains and valleys of California: also called *frost fog.* [< Shoshonean (Paiute)]

po·go stick (pō'gō) A stiltlike toy, with a spring at the base and fitted with two projections for the feet, on which a person may stand and propel himself in a series of hops.

po·grom (pō'grəm, pō·grom') *n.* An organized and often officially instigated local massacre, especially one directed against the Jews. [< Russian, destruction]

po·gy (pō'gē, pog'ē) *n.* *pl.* **·gies** or **·gy** The menhaden, a fish. [< Algonquian *pauhagen*]

poh (pō) *interj.* Pshaw! bah!: an expletive signifying disgust.

Po Hai (bō' hī'), **Gulf of** An inlet of the Yellow Sea in NE China: also *Gulf of Chihli.*

poi (poi, pō'ē) *n.* A native Hawaiian food made from the root of the taro that is first cooked, ground to a paste, then fermented. [< Hawaiian]

-poietic *combining form* Making; producing; creating: *hematopoietic.* [< Gk. *poiētikos* forming < *poieein* to make]

poign·ant (poin'yənt, poi'nənt) *adj.* **1.** Painful and afflicting to the feelings: *poignant* grief. **2.** Piercing, sharp, and cutting: *poignant* sarcasm. **3.** Penetrating and apt: *poignant* observations. **4.** *Archaic* Sharp or stimulating to the taste; pungent; piquant. [< OF, ppr. of *poindre* to prick < L *pungere*] — **poign'an·cy** *n.* — **poign'ant·ly** *adv.*

poi·ki·lo·ther·mal (poi'kə·lō·thûr'məl) *adj.* *Zool.* Having blood that varies in temperature in accordance with that of the surrounding medium: distinguished from *homoiothermal:* also *cold-blooded.* [< Gk. *poikilos* variegated + THERMAL]

poi·lu (pwà·lü') *French adj.* Hairy; bearded. — *n.* A French soldier; originally, an experienced French soldier of World War I.

Poin·ca·ré (pwaṅ·kà·rā'), **Jules Henri,** 1854–1912, French mathematician. — **Raymond,** 1860–1934, French statesman, president in World War I.

poin·ci·a·na (poin'sē·a'nə, -än'ə) *n.* **1.** One of a small genus (*Poinciana*) of tropical trees or shrubs of the bean family, especially the flowerfence. **2.** A similar tree of the bean family, the **royal poinciana** (*Delonix regia*), now widely distributed and having bright orange and scarlet flowers and large flat pods. [< NL, after M. de *Poinci,* a 17th c. governor of the West Indies]

poind (poind) *v.t.* *Scot.* **1.** To seize and sell (the property of a debtor) to satisfy a debt. **2.** To distrain the property of. **3.** To impound. — *n.* Distraint. [OE *pyndan*]

poin·set·ti·a (poin·set'ē·ə) *n.* Any of a genus (*Euphorbia*) of American plants of the spurge family, having large, showy bracts and inconspicuous flowers, especially *E. pulcherrima,* an ornamental evergreen shrub from Mexico and South America, having richly colored red, leaflike bracts. [after J. R. *Poinsett,* 1779–1851, U.S. statesman]

point (point) *n.* **1.** The sharp, tapering end of a thing: the *point* of a needle. **2.** Something having a sharp or tapering end, as a needle or dagger. **3.** In printing or writing, a dot, mark, etc.: a decimal *point.* **4.** Any mark of punctuation, especially a period. **5.** A vowel point (which see). **6.** That which is conceived to have position, but not parts, dimension, or extent, as the extremity of a line. **7.** A spot, place, or locality: a *point* of interest. **8.** A tapering tract of land extending into water; a promontory; cape. **9.** A fixed place from which position and distance are reckoned. **10.** A particular degree, state, or limit reached or determined: tired to the *point* of exhaustion; the boiling *point.* **11.** One of the 32 equal divisions that indicate direction on a mariner's compass card, each division equal to an angular distance of 11° 15', reckoning from north at 0°. For illustration see COMPASS CARD. **12.** A particular moment of time, as when something is about or likely to be done or take place: on the *point* of starting; at the *point* of death. **13.** The important or main purpose or aim: the whole *point* of the inquiry. **14.** Purpose or advantage: What's the *point* of telling her? **15.** The main idea; gist: the *point* of the joke. **16.** An important, striking, or effective fact, idea, etc.: She has some good *points* in her argument. **17.** A tip, idea, or suggestion: *points* on how to win. **18.** Any single item or particular; detail. **19.** A prominent or distinguishing feature, attribute, or peculiarity. **20.** An important or essential physical characteristic: the *points* of a thoroughbred animal. **21.** *pl.* The extremities of an animal, as a horse. **22.** A spike or prong on the antler of a deer. **23.** A unit, as in measuring, evaluating, rating, etc.: the number of *points* in a hand of bridge. **24.** In games and sports, a unit of counting or scoring: A touchdown equals six *points.* **25.** In schools and colleges, a unit of credit equal to a certain number of hours of academic work. **26.** *Printing* A unit of type size, about ½₇ of an inch. **27.** In commerce, a unit used in quoting prices of stocks, etc.: Wheat went down four *points.* **28.** In cricket: **a** A fielder stationed nearest to the right and slightly in advance of the wicket. **b** The position thus occupied. **29.** A cross-country run; also, the place where it terminates. **30.** The attitude of a pointer or setter when it finds game: The dog came to a *point.* **31.** In craps, the number a player must throw to win. **32.** *Electr.* **a** A contact or conducting part for making or breaking a circuit, as in a distributor, relay, etc. **b** *Brit.* An outlet or socket. **33.** *Brit.* In railroads, a movable rail that tapers to a point, as in a switch. **34.** In the 16th- and 17th-century costume, a ribbon or string having an aglet on one end, used to fasten pieces of clothing together. **35.** Point lace (which see). **36.** *Mil.* The individual or group that goes ahead of an advance guard. **37.** The act of pointing. **38.** *Electr.* Any of a set of contacts determining the direction of current flow in a circuit. **39.** In hockey, the position at the opponent's blueline taken by an offensive player when the puck is within the opposing team's defensive zone. — **at** (or **on, upon**) **the point of** On the verge of. — **beside the point**

Irrelevant. — **in point** Pertinent. — **in point of** In the matter of; as regards. — **to make a point of** To treat as vital or essential. — **to see the point** To understand the purpose of a course of action; get the important meaning of a story, joke, etc. — **to stretch a point** To make an exception. — **to the point** Relevant; apt. — *v.t.* **1.** To direct or aim, as a finger or weapon. **2.** To indicate; direct attention to: often with *out*: to *point* the way; to *point* out errors. **3.** *Chiefly U.S.* To give force or point to, as a meaning or remark: often with *up*. **4.** To shape or sharpen to a point. **5.** To punctuate, as writing. **6.** To mark or separate with points, as decimal fractons: with *off*. **7.** In hunting, to indicate the presence or location of (game) by standing rigid and directing the muzzle toward it: said of dogs. **8.** In masonry, to fill and finish the joints of (brickwork) with mortar. **9.** *Ling.* To mark with a vowel point. — *v.i.* **10.** To call attention or indicate direction by or as by extending the finger: usually with *at* or *to*. **11.** To direct the mind: Everything *points* to your being wrong. **12.** To be directed; have a specified direction; tend; face: with *to* or *toward*. **13.** To point game: said of hunting dogs. **14.** *Med.* To come to a head, as an abscess. **15.** *Naut.* To sail close to the wind. *Abbr. pt.* [< OF *point* dot (< L *punctum*) and *pointe* sharp tip (< L *puncta*), both ult. < L *pungere* to prick]

Point Bar·row (bar'ō) See (Point) BARROW.

point·blank (point'blangk') *adj.* **1.** Aimed directly at the mark; in gunnery, fired horizontally without allowing for dropping. **2.** Close enough to aim directly at the mark: *pointblank* range. **3.** Direct; plain: a *pointblank* question. — *n.* A shot with direct aim. — *adv.* **1.** In a straight line; from close range. **2.** Directly; without circumlocution. [? < F *de pointe en blanc* from a point into the white (of a target)]

point blanket *Canadian* A Hudson's Bay blanket (which see).

point d'ap·pui (pwaǹ dȧ·pwē') *French* Point of support; base.

Point de Galle (pwaǹ də gäl) A former name for GALLE.

point d'es·prit (pwaǹ des·prē') *French* Net, tulle, or lace with small scattered dots.

point-de·vice (point'di·vīs') *adj.* Scrupulously neat or precise; finical. — *adv.* Precisely; exactly. Also **point'-de·vise'.** [ME (*at point*) *devis*, i.e., (at an) exact (point)]

Pointe-à-Pi·tre (pwaǹ·tȧ·pē'tr') A port city on SE Grande-Terre, Guadeloupe; pop. 50,000 (est 1969).

point·ed (poin'tid) *adj.* **1.** Having a point. **2.** Sharply precise and cutting, as an epigram. **3.** Made clearly evident; emphasized. **4.** Directed or aimed, as at a particular person. **5.** Of or pertaining to a type of medieval architecture, characterized by use of a pointed arch. — **point'ed·ly** *adv.* — **point'ed·ness** *n.*

Pointe-Noire (pwaǹt·nwàr') A port city in the SW Republic of the Congo (Brazzaville); capital of the former Middle Congo, French Equatorial Africa; pop. 100,000 (1967).

point·er (poin'tər) *n.* **1.** One who or that which points. **2.** A hand, index finger, or other indicator, as on a clock or scale. **3.** A long tapering rod used in classrooms to point out things on wall maps, charts, diagrams, etc. **4.** One of a breed of smooth-haired dogs trained to scent and point out game, usually having a white coat with brown spots. **5.** *Informal* A useful bit of information; hint; tip. **6.** In the U.S. Navy, the member of a gun crew who controls the elevation of the gun: compare TRAINER.

Point·ers (poin'tərz) *n.pl. Astron.* Two stars (Dubhe and Merak), Alpha and Beta in the constellation Ursa Major, whose connecting line points to the polestar.

pointes (points) *n.pl.* In ballet, dancing on tiptoe. [< F]

poin·til·lism (pwan'tə·liz'əm) *n.* In painting, a method of producing effects of light by placing small spots of varying hues close together on a surface, the eye blending them together. [< F *pointillisme* < *pointiller* to mark with dots] — **poin'til·list** *n.*

point lace Needlepoint (def. 2). — **point-laced** (point'lāst') *adj.*

point·less (point'lis) *adj.* **1.** Having no point; blunt. **2.** Having no relevance or meaning: a *pointless* remark. **3.** Having no force; ineffective: *pointless* attempts at wit. **4.** Having no points scored: a *pointless* game. — **point'less·ly** *adv.* — **point'less·ness** *n.*

point·man (point'man') *n. pl.* **·men** (-men') In hockey, the player at the point.

point of honor Something that vitally affects one's honor.

point of no return That stage or position in any enterprise, course, action, etc., beyond which there can be no return to the starting point; a state of total commitment.

point of order In a deliberative assembly, a question as to whether or not the correct parliamentary procedure is being observed.

point of view **1.** The place or position from which one views an object, situation, etc. **2.** An attitude or set of principles or ideas by which one looks at, judges, or evaluates a person, circumstance, situation, etc.

point system **1.** *Printing* A standard system of sizes for type bodies, 996 points of which are equal to 35 centimeters, one point being .0138 inch (or approximately ½ inch), as adopted by the Typefounders' Association of the United States. **2.** Any system of raised letters for the blind, as Braille, in which the alphabet is formed of groups of raised dots or points. **3.** An academic system of allowing students to progress according to points or credits earned.

point·y (poin'tē) *adj.* **point·i·er, point·i·est** Coming to a point: *pointy* shoes.

poise[1] (poiz) *v.* **poised, pois·ing** *v.t.* **1.** To bring into or hold in balance; maintain in equilibrium. **2.** To hold; support, as in readiness. **3.** *Rare* To weigh. — *v.i.* **4.** To be balanced or suspended; hover. — *n.* **1.** The state or quality of being balanced; equilibrium; equipoise. **2.** Repose and dignity of manner; self-possession. **3.** Physical ease or balance in bearing or movement. **4.** Any condition or position of hovering or suspended motion. **5.** A state of indecision; suspense. [< OF, (it) weighs < *peser* to weigh, ult. < L *pensare*, freq. of *pendere* to weigh, suspend]

poise[2] (poiz) *n. pl.* **poise** The unit of viscosity in the cgs system, equal to 1 dyne-second per square centimeter. [after Jean Marie *Poiseuille*, 1797?–1869, French physiologist]

poi·son (poi'zən) *n.* **1.** Any substance that, either taken internally by or coming into contact with an organism, acts chemically upon the tissues in such a way as to harm or destroy; toxin. **2.** Anything that tends to harm, destroy, or corrupt. — *v.t.* **1.** To administer poison to; kill or injure with poison. **2.** To put poison into or on. **3.** To affect wrongfully; corrupt; pervert: to *poison* one's mind. — *adj.* Poisonous. [< OF < L *potio, -onis* drink, esp. a poisonous one < *potus* having drunk. Akin to *potare* to drink. Doublet of POTION.] — **poi'son·er** *n.*

poison dogwood Poison sumac. Also **poison elder.**

poison hemlock See under HEMLOCK.

poison ivy A climbing shrub (*Toxicodendron radicans* or *Rhus toxicodendron*) related to sumac, having glossy, variously notched, trifoliate leaves, greenish flowers, whitish berries, and a powerful blistering poison.

poison oak **1.** Any of various shrubs related to poison ivy or poison sumac, especially *Toxicodendron quercifolium*. **2.** A species of poison ivy (*T. rydlerii*) common in the western United States.

poi·son·ous (poi'zən·əs) *adj.* **1.** Containing or being a poison. **2.** Having the effect of a poison; toxic. — **poi'son·ous·ly** *adv.* — **poi'son·ous·ness** *n.*

poison sumac A shrub or small tree (*Toxicodendron vernix* or *Rhus vernix*), growing in swamps in the United States and Canada, having smooth, entire leaflets, loose panicles of smooth greenish yellow berries, and a strong poison.

POISON IVY (*a*) AND POISON SUMAC (*b*)

Poi·tiers (pwä·tyä') A city in west central France; former capital of Poitou; pop. 68,082 (1968).

Poi·tou (pwä·tōō') A region and former province of west central France.

poke[1] (pōk) *v.* **poked, pok·ing** *v.t.* **1.** To push or prod, as with the elbow; jab: to *poke* a person in the ribs. **2.** To make by or as by thrusting: to *poke* a hole. **3.** To thrust or push in, out, through, from, etc.: to *poke* one's head from a window. **4.** To stir (a fire, etc.) by prodding: often with *up*. — *v.i.* **5.** To make thrusts, as with a stick or weapon: often with *at*. **6.** To intrude or meddle. **7.** To go or look curiously; pry: often with *about* or *around*. **8.** To appear or show: logs *poking* above the surface. **9.** To proceed slowly; dawdle; putter: often with *along*. — **to poke one's nose into** To meddle in. — **to poke fun at** To ridicule, especially slyly. — *n.* **1.** A push; prod. **2.** One who moves sluggishly; a dawdler. **3.** *Informal* A punch. [< MLG *poken*. Prob. akin to MDu. *pochen* to boast.]

poke[2] (pōk) *n.* A pocket or small bag. [< OF < Gmc. Cf. On *poki* and MDu. *poke*. ? Akin to OE *pohha* bag.]

poke[3] (pōk) *n.* The pokeweed. [< Algonquian (Virginian) *pakon* weed used for staining < *pak* blood]

poke[4] (pōk) *n.* A large bonnet with projecting front or brim. Also **poke bonnet.** [Prob. < POKE[1]]

poke·ber·ry (pōk'ber'ē) *n. pl.* **·ries** **1.** A berry of the pokeweed. **2.** The pokeweed plant.

pok·er[1] (pō'kər) *n.* **1.** One who or that which pokes. **2.** A metal rod for poking a fire.

po·ker[2] (pō'kər) *n.* Any of several games of cards in which the players bet on the value of the cards dealt them, the winner being he whose hand contains the cards of highest value. [Cf. G *pochspiel*, lit., boast game < *pochen* to boast. Cf. also *brag*, a form of this game; also F *poque*, a card game.]

---

poker face *Informal* A face that reveals nothing: so called from the inscrutable faces of skillful poker players.

poke·weed (pōk′wēd′) *n.* A stout perennial North American herb (*Phytolacca americana*), having purple berries, edible shoots, and a medicinal root: also called *inkberry, pokeberry.* Also **poke′root′** (-rōōt′, -rŏŏt′). [See POKE³]

pok·y¹ (pō′kē) *adj.* **pok·i·er, pok·i·est** *Informal* **1.** Lacking briskness; dull; slow. **2.** Shabby or dowdy, as dress. **3.** Cramped; stuffy. Also **poke′y.**

pok·y² (pō′kē) *n. pl.* **pok·ies** *Slang* Jail: usually with *the.* Also **pok′ey.** [Origin uncertain]

pol. Political; politics.

Pol. Poland; Polish.

Po·la (pō′lä) The Italian name for PULA.

Po·lack (pō′lŏk, -lak) *n. Slang* A Pole; especially, an immigrant from Poland: an offensive term. — *adj.* Polish. [< Polish *polak*]

Po·land (pō′lənd) A Republic of north central Europe; 120,359 sq. mi.; pop. 33,000,000 (est. 1970); capital, Warsaw: Polish *Polska.* Officially **Polish People's Republic.**

Poland China An American mixed breed of large pigs, similar to Berkshires.

Po·land·er (pō′lən·dər) *n.* A Pole.

po·lar (pō′lər) *adj.* **1.** Of or pertaining to the poles of a sphere, magnet, etc. **2.** Pertaining to, coming from, or found near the North or South Pole. **3.** Directly opposite in action, tendency, character, etc. **4.** Guiding or directing, as a polestar. **5.** Central. **6.** *Chem.* Exhibiting ionization; ionized. [< Med.L *polaris* < L *polus* pole. See POLE¹.]

polar angle *Math.* In a polar coordinate system, the angle subtended between the polar axis and the radius vector of a point.

polar axis *Math.* A fixed line directed from the pole in the polar coordinate system from which angles are measured in a counterclockwise direction.

polar bear A large, amphibious, white bear (*Thalarctus maritimus*) of arctic regions.

polar body *Biol.* One of the two spherical bodies that separate from the ovum at the time of its maturation.

polar circles *Geog.* The Arctic and Antarctic circles.

polar compound *Chem.* Any of a class of compounds that will conduct an electric current when either fused or in solution, as most inorganic acids, bases, and salts.

polar coordinate system. **1.** A system of coordinates whereby a point is located by its linear distance from the pole and by the angle made by the radius vector of the point with the polar axis. **2.** A curve or an equation traced or traceable by means of such coordinates.

polar distance. *Astron.* Codeclination.

polar front *Meteorol.* The boundary line or surface separating an air mass originating in polar regions from one of temperate or tropical origin.

po·lar·im·e·ter (pō′lə·rim′ə·tər) *n.* **1.** An instrument for measuring the proportion of polarized light in a beam. **2.** A form of polariscope for measuring the amount of rotation of the plane of polarization. [< L *polaris* polar + -METER]

Po·lar·is (pō·lar′is, -lâr′-) *n.* **1.** One of the 20 brightest stars, 2.12 magnitude; Alpha in the constellation Ursa Minor: also called *Cynosure, polar star, polestar, North Star.* **2.** An intermediate range ballistic missile of the U.S. Navy. [< L]

po·lar·i·scope (pō·lar′ə·skōp) *n.* An optical instrument for exhibiting or measuring the polarization of light, or for examining substances in polarized light.

po·lar·i·ty (pō·lar′ə·tē, -lâr′-) *n. pl.* **·ties** **1.** The quality or condition of having poles. **2.** *Physics* The possession by a body of two poles at either extremity of a line of direction passing through its mass, the properties at one pole being of opposite or contrasting nature to the properties at the other pole, as in a magnet. **3.** The quality or condition of being attracted to one pole and repelled from the other. **4.** The possession or demonstration of two directly opposite or contrary qualities, tendencies, etc.

po·lar·i·za·tion (pō′lər·ə·zā′shən, -ī·zā′-) *n.* **1.** The state

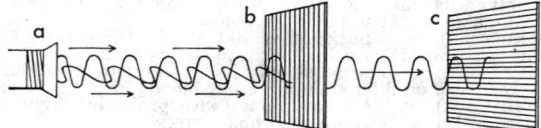

POLARIZATION
Of the light emitted at *a*, only the part whose electric oscillations are parallel to the axis of polarizing medium *b* can pass through it. This is blocked at polarizing medium *c*, whose axis is at right angles to that of *b*.

or condition of possessing polarity; also, the bestowal of polarity on or in something. **2.** *Physics* A condition of electromagnetic waves, most noticeable in light, in which the electric component of its oscillation is limited to a certain plane, as by transmission through variously oriented crystals or other suitable media. **3.** *Electr.* A change in the potential of a cell due to the accumulation of liberated gases. — **angle of polarization** or **polarizing angle** The angle of reflection from a plane surface at which light is polarized. — **plane of polarization** The plane in which the light vibrations occur when polarized.

po·lar·ize (pō′lə·rīz) *v.* **·ized, ·iz·ing** *v.t.* **1.** To develop polarization in; give polarity to. **2.** To give a special meaning or direction to. — *v.i.* **3.** To acquire polarity. Also *Brit.* **po′lar·ise.** — **po′lar·iz′a·ble** *adj.* — **po′lar·iz′er** *n.*

polar lights The aurora borealis or the aurora australis.

Po·lar·oid (pō′lə·roid) *n.* A plastic capable of polarizing the light passing through: a trade name. Also **po′lar·oid.**

Polar Regions The areas within the Arctic and Antarctic circles.

polar star Polaris (def. 1).

pol·der (pōl′dər) *n.* A tract of marshy land, lower than the sea, that has been reclaimed for cultivation by the erection of dikes. Also **pol′der·land** (-land′). [< Du.]

pole¹ (pōl) *n.* **1.** Either of the two extremities of the axis of a sphere or any spheroidal body. **2.** One of the two points where the earth's axis of rotation meets the surface, called the North *Pole* and the South *Pole.* Compare CELESTIAL POLE. **3.** *Physics* One of the two points at which opposite qualities or forces are concentrated, especially a point of maximum intensity of electric or magnetic force. **4.** *Biol.* Either extremity of an imaginary axis within an ovum or cell, at or near which certain structures are symmetrically located. **5.** *Physiol.* The point of a nerve cell where a process has its origin.

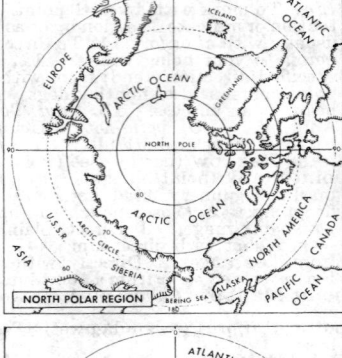

NORTH POLAR REGION

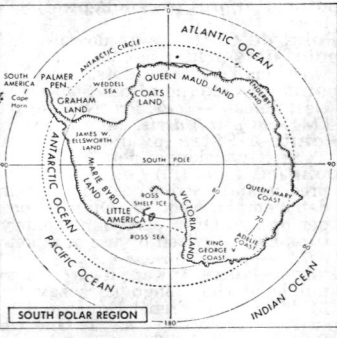

SOUTH POLAR REGION

6. Either one of two diametrically opposite forces, tendencies, opinions, etc. **7.** A central or fixed point of reference. **8.** *Math.* In a polar coordinate system, that point where all radius vectors equal zero. — **to be poles apart** (or **asunder**) To have widely different opinions, views, tastes, etc.; differ greatly. [< OF *pole* < L *polus* < Gk. *polos* pivot, pole. Akin to *pelein* to turn.]

pole² (pōl) *n.* **1.** A long, comparatively slender piece of wood or metal, often tapering and more or less rounded. **2.** A tongue (def. 18). **3.** A unit of linear measure, usually equal to 16.5 feet. **4.** A unit of square measure equal to a square rod or 30.25 square yards. — *v.* **poled, pol·ing** *v.t.* **1.** To propel, push, or strike with a pole. **2.** To support on poles, as growing beans. — *v.i.* **3.** To push a boat, raft, etc., with a pole. [OE *pāl* < L *palus* stake]

Pole (pōl) *n.* A native or inhabitant of Poland.

Pole (pōl), **Reginald,** 1500–58, English Roman Catholic prelate, archbishop of Canterbury 1556–58.

pole·ax (pōl′aks′) *n.* A medieval weapon consisting of an ax, or a combined ax and pick, set on a long pole; a battle-ax. — *v.t.* To strike or fell with a poleax. Also **pole′·axe′.** [ME *pollax* < *pol* poll¹ + AX]

pole bean Any variety of climbing bean supported by poles.

pole·cat (pōl′kat′) *n.* **1.** One of certain European carnivores (genus *Mustela*) allied to the weasel, noted for its offensive odor when irritated or alarmed. **2.** *U.S.* A skunk. [< F *poule* pullet + CAT; from its predacity]

pol. econ. Political economy.

pole fence A fence made of horizontal unsplit poles.

pole horse A horse hitched beside the tongue of a vehicle.

pole jump A pole vault.

pole line A line of telephone or telegraph poles.

po·lem·ic (pō·lem′ik) *adj.* Of or pertaining to controversy; disputatious. Also **po·lem′i·cal.** — *n.* **1.** An argument or controversy, especially one about theology. **2.** One who engages in argument or controversy. [< Gk. *polemikos* warlike < *polemos* war]

po·lem·i·cist (pō·lem′ə·sist) *n.* One skilled or engaged in polemics. Also **pol·e·mist** (pol′ə·mist).

po·lem·ics (pō·lem′iks) *n.pl.* (*construed as sing.*) The art or practice of disputation; especially, the use of aggressive argument to refute errors of doctrine.

pol·e·mo·ni·a·ceous (pol′ə·mō′nē·ā′shəs) *adj. Bot.* Designating or belonging to a family (*Polemoniaceae*) of herbs, as the phlox. [< Gk. *polemōnion* a kind of plant]

pole plate *Archit.* A wall plate resting on the tie beams of a roof and serving as a support for the rafters.

pole·star (pōl′stär′) *n.* 1. Polaris (def. 1). 2. That which governs, guides, or directs; a controlling principle.

pole-vault (pōl′vôlt′) *v.i.* To perform a pole vault. — **pole′-vault′er** *n.*

pole vault An athletic field event in which a vault or jump over a high, horizontal bar is made with the help of a long pole: also called *pole jump.*

po·lice (pə·lēs′) *n.* 1. An official civil force or department organized to maintain order, prevent and detect crime, and enforce law. 2. (*construed as pl.*) The members of such a force. 3. In a community, the maintenance of order, law, health, safety, etc.; also, those whose duty it is to see such order maintained. 4. In the U.S. Army: **a** The condition of a camp or garrison as to cleanliness. **b** The cleaning or keeping clean of a camp or garrison. **c** A group of soldiers assigned to some specific duty or duties: kitchen *police.* — *v.t.* ·**liced,** ·**lic·ing** 1. To protect, regulate, or maintain order in (a city, country, etc.) with or as with police. 2. *U.S.* To make clean or orderly, as a military camp. [< MF, orig. political organization < LL *politia* administration < Gk. *politeia* polity < *politēs* citizen < *polis* city]

police court A municipal court having the power to try minor criminal cases and to hold in custody for trial those charged with more grave offenses.

police dog A German shepherd dog (which see).

po·lice·man (pə·lēs′mən) *n. pl.* ·**men** (-mən) A member of a police force.

police state A country whose citizens are rigidly supervised by a national police, often working secretly.

police station The headquarters of a community police force, to which arrested persons are taken and from which policemen operate: also called *station house.*

police village *Canadian* In Ontario, a municipal district administered by an appointive rather than an elective council.

po·lice·wom·an (pə·lēs′wŏŏm′ən) *n. pl.* ·**wom·en** (-wim′in) A woman member of a police force.

pol·i·clin·ic (pol′i·klin′ik) *n.* The department of a hospital in which outpatients are treated. Compare POLYCLINIC. [< G *poliklinik* < Gk. *polis* city + G *klinik* clinic]

pol·i·cy¹ (pol′ə·sē) *n. pl.* ·**cies** 1. Any course or plan of action, especially, in governmental or business administration, such a course or plan designed to influence future decisions, actions, etc.: a nation's foreign *policy.* 2. Prudence, wisdom, or shrewdness, as in conduct or the management of one's affairs; also, any act or plan based on such principles: It was his *policy* always to be silent. [< OF *policie* political organization < LL *politia.* See POLICE.]

pol·i·cy² (pol′ə·sē) *n. pl.* ·**cies** 1. A written contract of insurance. 2. In gambling: **a** Number (def. 16). **b** A game in which numbers are taken from a wheel to decide bets: also **policy racket.** [< MF *police* < Ital. *polizza* < Med.L *apodixa* receipt < Gk. *apodeixis* proof < *apodeiknynai* to show forth]

pol·i·cy·hol·der (pol′ə·sē·hōl′dər) *n.* One who holds a policy of insurance.

po·li·o (pō′lē·ō) *n. Informal* Poliomyelitis.

polio- *combining form Med.* Of or pertaining to the gray matter of the brain or the spinal cord: *polioencephalitis.* [< Gk. *polios* gray]

pol·i·o·en·ceph·a·li·tis (pol′ē·ō·en·sef′ə·lī′tis, pō′lē-) *n. Pathol.* Inflammation of the gray matter of the brain. Also **pol′i·en·ceph′a·li′tis.** [< POLIO- + ENCEPHALITIS]

pol·i·o·my·e·li·tis (pol′ē·ō·mī′ə·lī′tis, pō′lē-) *n. Pathol.* An acute, infectious virus disease, occurring especially in children, and characterized by inflammation of the gray matter of the spinal cord, followed by paralysis and atrophy of various muscle groups: also called *infantile paralysis.* [< NL < POLIO- + Gk. *myelos* marrow + -ITIS]

pol·ish (pol′ish) *n.* 1. Smoothness or glossiness of surface; finish. 2. A substance used to produce a bright, smooth, or glossy surface. 3. Refinement or elegance of manner, style, etc. 4. The process of polishing. — *v.t.* 1. To make smooth or lustrous, as by rubbing. 2. To make complete; finish; perfect. 3. To free from crudity, imperfection, etc.: to *polish* a poem. — *v.i.* 4. To take a gloss; shine. 5. To become elegant or refined. — **to polish off** 1. To do or finish completely or quickly. 2. To dispose of; overwhelm. — **to polish up** To make better; improve. [< OF *poliss-,* stem of *polir* < L *polire* to smooth] — **pol′ish·er** *n.*

Po·lish (pō′lish) *adj.* Of or pertaining to Poland, its inhabitants, or their language. — *n.* The West Slavic language of the Poles. *Abbr. Pol.*

Polish Corridor A strip of land in NW Poland, extending to the Baltic between Germany and East Prussia 1919–1939; part of Germany prior to 1919, and from 1939 to 1945; now a part of Poland.

pol·ished (pol′isht) *adj.* 1. Made smooth by polishing. 2. Naturally smooth and glossy. 3. Refined and polite. 4. Having no flaws, crudities, or errors: a *polished* style.

polit. Political; politics.

Po·lit·bu·ro (pol′it·byŏŏr′ō) *n.* The leading policy-forming committee of the Communist party in the Soviet Union until 1952, when it was replaced by the Presidium. [< Russian *polit(icheskoe) buro*]

po·lite (pə·līt′) *adj.* ·**lit·er,** ·**lit·est** 1. Exhibiting in manner or speech a considerate regard for others; courteous; mannerly. 2. Refined; cultured; cultivated: *polite* society. 3. Polished; elegant; refined: *polite* letters. [< L *politus,* pp. of *polire* to polish] — **po·lite′ly** *adv.* — **po·lite′ness** *n.*

— **Syn.** 1. *Polite, civil, courteous* and *courtly* characterize a manner of social intercourse that is designed to please, or at least not to give offense. *Polite* implies punctilious observance of the forms of speech and action customary among well-bred persons. *Civil* is weaker, implying little more than the avoidance of rudeness. To be *courteous* is to be *polite* while having also a warmer regard for the feelings and dignity of others, while *courtly* means *polite* or *courteous* in a ceremonial way, as befits a royal court. — **Ant.** impolite, rude, boorish.

polit. econ. Political economy.

po·li·tesse (pô·lē·tes′) *n. French* Politeness; civility.

Po·li·tian (pō·lish′ən), 1454–94, Florentine humanist and poet: original name **Angelo Am·bro·gi·ni** (äm·brō·jē′nē).

pol·i·tic (pol′ə·tik) *adj.* 1. Skillful, ingenious, or shrewd; artful: a *politic* statesman. 2. Crafty; sly; cunning. 3. Wise, prudent, or expedient, as in conception or execution; judicious: a *politic* move. 4. Political: see BODY POLITIC. [< OF *politique* < L *politicus* < Gk. *politikos* civic < *politēs* citizen < *polis* city] — **pol′i·tic·ly** *adv.*

— **Syn.** 1. diplomatic, discreet. 2. wily. 3. See EXPEDIENT.

po·lit·i·cal (pə·lit′i·kəl) *adj.* 1. Of, pertaining to, or concerned with the science, organization, or activities of government. 2. Of, relating to, or involved in politics. 3. Characteristic of or similar to politics or politicians. 4. Pertaining to or having an organized system of government. *Abbr. pol., polit.* [< L *politicus.* See POLITIC.] — **po·lit′i·cal·ly** *adv.*

political economist A person skilled in political economy.

political economy Economics.

political science The science of the form and principles of civil government, and the extent and manner of its intervention in public and private affairs; politics.

pol·i·ti·cian (pol′ə·tish′ən) *n.* 1. One who is engaged in politics, especially professionally. 2. One who engages in politics for personal or partisan aims rather than for reasons of principle; a political opportunist. 3. One who is skilled in the science of government or politics; a statesman.

po·lit·i·cize (pə·lit′ə·sīz) *v.* ·**cized,** ·**ciz·ing** *v.i.* 1. To take part in or discuss politics. — *v.t.* 2. To make political.

po·lit·ick (pol′ə·tik) *v.i. U.S. Informal* To engage in political activity; be a politician.

po·lit·i·co (pə·lit′i·kō) *n. pl.* ·**cos** A politician. [< Sp. *politico* < L *politicus*]

politico- *combining form* Political and: *politico-economical.*

pol·i·tics (pol′ə·tiks) *n.pl.* (*Usually construed as sing.*) 1. The science or art of government or of the administration and management of public or state affairs. 2. The affairs or activities of those who are engaged in controlling or seeking to control a government or its offices or departments; also, the life, profession, or area of activity of such persons. 3. The principles, aims, or policies of a government or of the parties or groups within a government. 4. The acts or practices of those who seek any position of power, authority, or advantage: campus *politics.* 5. Political sentiments or opinions. *Abbr. pol., polit.* [< POLITIC]

pol·i·ty (pol′ə·tē) *n. pl.* ·**ties** 1. The form or method of government of a nation, state, church, etc. 2. Any community living under some definite form of government. [< MF *politie, policie* < L *politia.* See POLICY¹.]

Polk (pōk), **James Knox,** 1795–1849, eleventh president of the United States 1845–49.

pol·ka (pōl′kə, pō′-) *n.* 1. A lively round dance of Bohemian origin, consisting of three quick steps and a hop. 2. Music for or in the manner of this dance, in duple meter. — *v.i.* ·**kaed,** ·**ka·ing** To dance the polka. [< F < Czech *pulka* half step or *Polka,* fem. of *Polak* a Pole.]

polka dot 1. One of a series of round dots of various sizes and spacing on a textile fabric. 2. A pattern or fabric made up of such dots.

poll¹ (pōl) *n.* 1. The voting at an election. 2. The total number of votes cast or registered. 3. *pl.* The place where votes are cast and counted. 4. A survey of public opinion on a given subject, usually obtained from a sample group. 5. A person, especially one of a group. 6. A list of persons.

7. The head, especially the top or back of the head where hair grows. **8.** The blunt or flat end of a hammer or ax. **9.** A poll tax. — *v.t.* **1.** To receive (a specified number of votes). **2.** To enroll, as for taxation or voting; register. **3.** To cast (a vote) at the polls. **4.** To canvass in a poll (def. 4). **5.** To cut off or trim, as hair, horns, etc.; clip; shear. **6.** To cut off or trim the hair, horns, top, etc., of: to poll cattle. — *v.i.* **7.** To vote at the polls; cast one's vote. [< MDu. *polle* top of the head] — **poll′er** *n.*

poll² (pol) *n.* In Cambridge University, England, a student who contents himself with a pass degree. Such students are called collectively **the poll.** [< Gk. *(hoi) polloi* (the) many]

pol·lack (pol′ək) *n.* A gadoid food fish (*Pollachius virens*) of the North Atlantic: also spelled **pollock.** [< Scot. *podlok*, prob. infl. by Scottish Gaelic *pollag* fresh water fish]

pol·lard (pol′ərd) *n.* **1.** A tree shorn of its top so that it puts out a dense head of slender shoots. **2.** An animal that has lost its horns. — *v.t.* To convert into a pollard. [< POLL¹]

polled (pōld) *adj.* **1.** Shorn of the head or top. **2.** Shorn of the hair; bald. **3.** Shorn of horns.

poll·ee (pōl′ē′) *n.* A person whose opinion is polled.

pol·len (pol′ən) *n.* The male or fertilizing element in a seed plant, consisting of fine yellowish powder formed within the anther of the stamen. [< L, fine flour]

pollen count A measure of the relative concentration of pollen grains in the atmosphere at a given locality and date, usually expressed as the number of grains per cubic yard.

pol·lex (pol′eks) *n.*, *pl.* **pol·li·ces** (pol′ə·sēz) The first or radial digit of the hand or forelimb of a vertebrate; the thumb. [< L, thumb or big toe] — **pol′li·cal** *adj.*

pol·li·nate (pol′ə·nāt) *v.t.* **·nat·ed, ·nat·ing** *Bot.* To supply or convey pollen to. Also **pol′len·ate.**

pol·li·na·tion (pol′ə·nā′shən) *n.* *Bot.* The fertilization of plants by the transfer of pollen from anthers to stigmas. Also **pol′len·a′tion.**

pol·li·nif·er·ous (pol′ə·nif′ər·əs) *adj.* **1.** Producing pollen. **2.** Bearing or carrying pollen. Also **pol′len·if′er·ous.**

pol·lin·i·um (pə·lin′ē·əm) *n.*, *pl.* **·i·a** (-ē·ə) *Bot.* A mass of pollen grains. [< NL < L *pollen, -inis* fine flour]

pol·li·no·sis (pol′ə·nō′sis) *n.* *Pathol.* Hay fever. [< NL < L *pollen, -inis* pollen + -OSIS]

Pol·li·o (pol′ē·ō), **Gaius Asinius,** 76? B.C.–A.D. 5, Roman politician, general, and author.

pol·li·wog (pol′ē·wog) *n.* A tadpole. Also **pol′ly·wog.** [ME *polwygle.* Cf. POLL¹ (head), WIGGLE.]

pol·lock (pol′ək) See POLLACK.

Pol·lock (pol′ək), **Channing,** 1880–1946, U.S. dramatist, novelist, and critic. — **Sir Frederick,** 1845–1937, English jurist and philosopher. — **Jackson,** 1912–56, U.S. painter.

poll·ster (pōl′stər) *n.* One who takes polls. Also **poll′ist.**

poll tax A tax on a person, as distinguished from that on property, especially as a prerequisite for voting.

pol·lut·ant (pə·lōō′tənt) *n.* **1.** That which pollutes. **2.** Any of various noxious chemicals and refuse materials that impair the purity of water, soil, or the atmosphere.

pol·lute (pə·lōōt′) *v.t.* **·lut·ed, ·lut·ing** To make unclean or impure; dirty; corrupt; profane. [< L *pollutus,* pp. of *polluere* to defile] — **pol·lut′er** *n.* — **pol·lu′tion** *n.*

— **Syn.** *Pollute, contaminate, taint, infect, defile,* and *debase* refer to the process of making a thing dirty, impure, or worthless. *Pollute* suggests the end of this process, and *contaminate,* its beginning. A *polluted* stream is completely unfit for swimming, drinking, fishing, etc. because of impure foreign substances in it, while a *contaminated* stream is only partially or temporarily unsafe for the same reason. A similar distinction exists between *taint* and *infect,* both of which suggest the presence of decay- or disease-causing organisms. That which is *tainted* is already decayed or corrupt, but that which is *infected* in in the early stages of decay or disease and may be cured or restored. *Defile* often suggests the malicious or thoughtless dirtying or profanation of that which should be pure, clean, or held in reverence: to *defile* a temple. *Debase* suggests a loss of dignity, value, honor, etc. by a person or thing formerly held in high esteem.

Pol·lux (pol′əks) In Greek mythology, one of the Dioscuri. See CASTOR AND POLLUX. — *n.* One of the 20 brightest stars, 1.16 magnitude; Beta in the constellation Gemini: see STAR.

Pol·ly·an·na (pol′ē·an′ə) *n.* One who finds good in everything. [after the heroine of stories by Eleanor H. Porter, 1868–1920]

po·lo (pō′lō) *n.* **1.** A hockeylike game played on horseback, usually with a light wooden ball and long-handled mallets. **2.** A similar game played on ice, roller skates, in the water, etc. [Prob. < Tibetan *pulu* ball] — **po′lo·ist** *n.*

Po·lo (pō′lō), **Marco,** 1254?–1323?, Venetian traveler.

polo coat A tailored overcoat of camel's hair or of a fabric imitating camel's hair.

pol·o·naise (pol′ə·nāz′, pō′lə-) *n.* **1.** A stately, marchlike Polish dance. **2.** Music for or in the manner of this dance, in triple meter. **3.** An 18th-century, coatlike garment for women, consisting of a fitted bodice and a cutaway skirt, worn over another dress or skirt. [< F (*danse*) *polonaise* Polish (dance)]

po·lo·ni·um (pə·lō′nē·əm) *n.* A radioactive element (symbol Po) produced by the disintegration of various uranium minerals, discovered in 1898 by Pierre and Marie Sklodowska Curie. See ELEMENT. [< NL < Med.L *Polonia* Poland]

Po·lo·ni·us (pə·lō′nē·əs) In Shakespeare's *Hamlet,* the chamberlain to the king and father of Ophelia and Laertes.

polo shirt A sport shirt that pulls on over the head, usually has short sleeves, a soft, turnover collar or sometimes a collarless, round neck.

Pol·ska (pôl′skä) The Polish name for POLAND.

Pol·ta·va (pol·tä′və) A city in the central Ukrainian S.S.R.; scene of Peter the Great's victory over the Swedes, 1709; pop. 220,000 (est. 1970).

pol·ter·geist (pōl′tər·gīst) *n.* A ghost or spirit reputed to make its presence known by any kind of clatter, as knockings and the noise of moving objects. [< G, lit., noisy ghost < *poltern* to make a noise + *geist* spirit]

pol·troon (pol·trōōn′) *n.* A mean-spirited coward; craven; dastard. — *adj.* Cowardly; contemptible. [< F *poltron* < Ital. *poltrone* coward < *poltro* colt < L *pullus* young of an animal] — **pol·troon′er·y** *n.*

poly- *combining form* **1.** Many; several; much: *polygamy, polygon.* **2.** Excessive; abnormal: *polydactylism.* [< Gk. *polys* much, many]

pol·y·al·co·hol (pol′ē·al′kə·hôl, -hol) *n.* *Chem.* Any of a class of alcohols containing more than one hydroxyl radical.

pol·y·am·ide (pol′ē·am′īd) *n.* *Chem.* A polymer derived from compounds containing amine and carboxyl groups, used in the making of various synthetic fibers.

pol·y·an·dry (pol′ē·an′drē) *n.* **1.** The condition or practice of having more than one husband at the same time. **2.** *Bot.* The condition of having 20 or more stamens. [< Gk. *polyandria* < *polys* many + *anēr, andros* man, husband] — **pol′y·an′drous** *adj.*

pol·y·an·thus (pol′ē·an′thəs) *n.* **1.** A variety of primrose (*Primula polyantha*), having many-flowered umbels. **2.** A widely distributed narcissus (*Narcissus tazetta*). [< NL < Gk. *polys* many + *anthos* blossom]

pol·y·a·tom·ic (pol′ē·ə·tom′ik) *adj.* *Chem.* Having more than one atom in the molecule.

po·ly·ba·sic (pol′ē·bā′sik) *adj.* *Chem.* Containing two or more atoms of hydrogen replaceable by a base or basic radicals: said of certain acids.

pol·y·ba·site (pol′ē·bā′sīt) *n.* A metallic, iron-black ore of silver crystallizing in the monoclinic system. [< G *polybasit*]

Po·lyb·i·us (pə·lib′ē·əs), 204?–122? B.C., Greek historian.

pol·y·brid (pol′i·brid) *n.* *Bot.* A hybrid plant derived from the crossing of two particular genera, species, or varieties.

Pol·y·carp (pol′i·kärp), **Saint,** 69?–155?, Christian martyr, bishop of Smyrna.

pol·y·car·pel·lar·y (pol′i·kär′pə·ler′ē) *adj.* *Bot.* Made up of many carpels.

pol·y·car·pous (pol′i·kär′pəs) *adj.* *Bot.* **1.** Having the fruit composed of two or more distinct carpels. **2.** Fruiting many times. Also **pol′y·car′pic.**

pol·y·cen·trism (pol′i·sen′triz·əm) *n.* The existence of several centers of power in the Communist world, as Peking and Belgrade, where Moscow had formerly been the single undisputed center. — **pol′y·cen′trist** *n. & adj.*

pol·y·chae·tous (pol′i·kē′təs) *adj.* *Zool.* **1.** Having several setae. **2.** Of or pertaining to a class (*Polychaeta*) of annelids having swimming appendages covered with bristles, including most marine worms. Also **pol′y·chae′tal, pol′y·chae′tan.** [< NL *Polychaeta* < Gk. *polychaitēs* having much hair < *polys* much + *chaitēs* mane] — **pol′y·chaete** *adj. & n.*

pol·y·cha·si·um (pol′i·kā′zē·əm, -zhē·əm) *n.*, *pl.* **·si·a** (-zē·ə, -zhē·ə) *Bot.* A form of cymose inflorescence in which, below each flower, more than two branches are given off from the main axis. [< NL < POLY- + Gk. *chasis* division]

pol·y·chrome (pol′i·krōm) *adj.* Having or made in several or many colors. — *n.* A polychrome object.

pol·y·chro·mic (pol′i·krō′mik) *adj.* Having or exhibiting many colors or changes of color. Also **pol′y·chro·mat′ic** (-krō·mat′ik), **pol′y·chro′mous.**

pol·y·chro·my (pol′i·krō′rē) *n.* The art of decorating in several or many colors, as in statuary and architecture.

pol·y·clin·ic (pol′i·klin′ik) *n.* A general hospital or clinic in which all forms of diseases are treated and in which clinical instruction is furnished. Compare POLICLINIC.

Pol·y·cli·tus (pol′i·klī′təs) Fifth-century B.C. Greek sculptor. Also **Pol′y·cle′tus** (-klē′təs). — **Pol′y·cli′tan** *adj.*

pol·y·con·ic projection (pol′i·kon′ik) A type of map projection in which the parallels of latitude are arcs of circles that are not concentric and the meridians, except the central one, are curved lines.

Po·lyc·ra·tes (pə·lik′rə·tēz), died 522? B.C., tyrant of Samos 536?–522? B.C., crucified.

pol·y·dac·tyl (pol′i·dak′til) *adj.* Having more than the usual or normal number of fingers or toes: also **pol′y·dac′ty·lous.** — *n.* A polydactyl animal. — **pol′y·dac′tyl·ism** *n.*

pol·y·dem·ic (pol′i·dem′ik) *adj.* *Ecol.* Occurring or dwelling in two or more regions. [< POLY- + Gk. *dēmos* region]

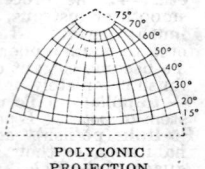

POLYCONIC
PROJECTION

Pol·y·do·rus (pol/i·dôr/əs, -dō/rəs) First-century B.C. Greek sculptor.

pol·y·em·bry·o·ny (pol/ē·em/brē·ō/nē, -brē·ə·nē) *n. Biol.* The production of two or more viable embryos in a seed, or of two or more offspring from a single fertilized ovum.

pol·y·es·ter fiber (pol/ē·es/tər) *Chem.* A synthetic fiber of high tensile strength made by the esterification of ethylene glycol and other organic compounds.

pol·y·eth·y·lene (pol/ē·eth/ə·lēn) *n. Chem.* A tough, flexible thermoplastic resin, made by the polymerization of ethylene, used in the making of moistureproof plastics for electrical insulation, packaging, etc.

po·lyg·a·la (pə·lig/ə·lə) *n.* Any of a large genus (*Polygala*) of herbs and shrubs of the milkwort family; especially, the **fringed polygala** (*P. paucifolia*) of North America, having purplish rose flowers. [< NL *Polygala* < Gk. *polys* much + *gala* milk]

po·lyg·a·mous (pə·lig/ə·məs) *adj.* 1. Of, pertaining to, practicing, or characterized by polygamy. 2. *Bot.* Bearing unisexual and bisexual or hermaphrodite flowers on the same plant. — **po·lyg/a·mous·ly** *adv.* [< Gk. *polygamos* much-married. See POLYGAMY.]

po·lyg·a·my (pə·lig/ə·mē) *n.* 1. The condition or practice of having more than one wife or husband at the same time. 2. *Zool.* The state of having more than one mate at the same time. Compare MONOGAMY. [< F *polygamie* < LL *polygamia* < Gk. *polygamia* < *polygamos* < *polys* many + *gamos* marriage] — **po·lyg/a·mist** *n.*

pol·y·gen·e·sis (pol/i·jen/ə·sis) *n. Biol.* The doctrine that new types or species of organisms originate from more than one ancestral species. — **pol/y·ge·net/ic** (-jə·net/ik), **pol/y·gen/ic, po·lyg·e·nous** (pə·lij/ə·nəs) *adj.*

pol·y·glot (pol/i·glot) *adj.* Expressed in several tongues or speaking several languages; multilingual. — *n.* 1. A book giving versions of the same text, as of the Scriptures, in several languages. 2. One who speaks or writes several languages. 3. A mixture of several languages. [< Gk. *polyglōttos* < *polys* many + *glōtta* tongue] — **pol/y·glot/ism** *n.*

Pol·y·gno·tus (pol/ig·nō/təs) Fifth-century B.C. Greek painter. — **Pol/yg·no/tan** *adj.*

pol·y·gon (pol/i·gon) *n. Geom.* A closed, usually plane, figure bounded by straight lines or arcs, especially by more than four. [< L *polygonum* < Gk. *polygōnon* < *polys* many + *gōnia* angle] — **po·lyg·o·nal** (pə·lig/ə·nəl), **po·lyg/o·nous** *adj.* — **po·lyg/o·nal·ly** *adv.*

pol·y·go·na·ceous (pol/i·gə·nā/shəs) *adj. Bot.* Pertaining or belonging to the buckwheat family (*Polygonaceae*) of plants. [< POLYGONUM]

po·lyg·o·num (pə·lig/ə·nəm) *n.* Any of a large and widely distributed genus (*Polygonum*) of annual or perennial herbs, including the common smartweed, the prince's-feather, and the bistort. Also **po·lyg/o·ny** (-nē). [< NL < L *polygonos* < Gk. *polygonon* knotgrass < *poly-* many + *gony* knee; from its many joints]

pol·y·graph (pol/i·graf, -gräf) *n.* 1. A device for multiplying or reproducing a drawing or writing. 2. A versatile or prolific author. 3. An electrical device for simultaneously recording variations in the heartbeat, blood pressure, muscle reflexes, and respiratory movements, sometimes used as a lie detector. [< Gk. *polygraphos* writing much] — **pol/y·graph/ic** or **-i·cal** *adj.*

po·lyg·ra·phy (pə·lig/rə·fē) *n.* 1. The use of a polygraph. 2. The art of writing in or of interpreting various ciphers.

po·lyg·y·nous (pə·lij/ə·nəs) *adj.* 1. Of, pertaining to, or practicing polygyny. 2. *Bot.* Having many pistils or styles.

po·lyg·y·ny (pə·lij/ə·nē) *n.* 1. The condition or practice of having more than one wife at the same time: opposed to monogyny. 2. *Bot.* The condition of having many pistils or styles. [< POLY- + *gynē* woman]

pol·y·he·dral (pol/i·hē/drəl) *adj.* Of or pertaining to a polyhedron; many-faced.

polyhedral angle *Geom.* The angle formed by three or more planes passing through a point; an angle at a vertex of a polyhedron. Compare SOLID ANGLE.

pol·y·he·dron (pol/i·hē/drən) *n. pl.* **-dra** (-drə) or **-drons** *Geom.* A solid bounded by plane faces, especially by more than four. [< NL < Gk. *polyedros* < *polys* many + *hedra* base, side]

Pol·y·hym·ni·a (pol/i·him/nē·ə) The Muse of sacred song. Also **Po·lym·ni·a** (pə·lim/nē·ə).

pol·y·mer (pol/i·mər) *n. Chem.* Any of two or more compounds formed by polymerization, especially one of higher molecular weight than the parent substance. [< Gk. *polymerēs* manifold < *polys* many + *meros* part]

pol·y·mer·ic (pol/i·mer/ik) *adj. Chem.* Having the same chemical composition but different molecular weights and different properties, as acetylene and benzene.

po·lym·er·ism (pə·lim/ə·riz/əm, pol/i·mə-) *n. Chem.* The condition of being polymeric.

po·lym·er·i·za·tion (pə·lim/ər·ə·zā/shən, pol/i·mər·ə-) *n. Chem.* The process of changing the molecular arrangement of a compound so as to form new compounds having the same percentage composition as the original, but of greater molecular weight and different properties.

po·lym·er·ize (pə·lim/ə·rīz, pol/i·mə·rīz/) *v.t. & v.i.* **-ized, -iz·ing** To subject to or undergo polymerization. Also *Brit.* **po·lym/er·ise.**

po·lym·er·ous (pə·lim/ər·əs) *adj.* 1. *Biol.* Consisting of many parts. 2. *Bot.* Having many parts or members in each whorl or series.

pol·y·morph (pol/i·môrf) *n.* A substance or organism that exhibits polymorphism. [< Gk. *polymorphos* < *poly-* many + *morphē* form]

pol·y·morph·ism (pol/i·môr/fiz·əm) *n.* 1. *Biol.* The property of assuming or passing through several forms, as an animal or plant exhibiting seasonal changes in coloration. 2. *Chem.* The occurrence in a substance of two or more distinct crystal forms of identical chemical composition. — **pol·y·mor/phic, pol/y·mor/phous** *adj.*

Pol·y·ne·sia (pol/i·nē/zhə, -shə) The islands of Oceania in the central and SE Pacific, extending east of Melanesia and Micronesia from the Hawaiian Islands to New Zealand.

Pol·y·ne·sian (pol/i·nē/zhən, -shən) *n.* 1. One of the native brown-skinned people of Polynesia, believed to be either of Malay stock originally stemming from a Caucasian strain of Asia, or of mixed Melanesian, Malay, and Caucasian stock. 2. A subfamily of the Austronesian family of languages spoken by these people. — *adj.* Of or pertaining to Polynesia, its people, or their languages.

pol·y·neu·ri·tis (pol/i·nŏŏ·rī/tis, -nyŏŏ-) *n. Pathol.* Simultaneous inflammation of many peripheral nerves.

Pol·y·ni·ces (pol/i·nī/sēz) An ancient Greek hero. See SEVEN AGAINST THEBES.

pol·y·no·mi·al (pol/i·nō/mē·əl) *adj.* Of, pertaining to, or consisting of many names or terms. — *n.* 1. *Math.* An expression, as in algebra, containing two or more terms. 2. *Biol.* A scientific name consisting of more than two terms. [< POLY- + *-nomial*, as in BINOMIAL]

pol·y·nu·cle·ar (pol/i·nŏŏ/klē·ər, -nyŏŏ/-) *adj.* Having many nuclei. Also **pol·y·nu/cle·ate** (-klē·it).

pol·y·ox·y·meth·yl·ene (pol/i·ok/sē·meth/əl·ēn) *n. Chem.* Paraformaldehyde.

pol·yp (pol/ip) *n.* 1. *Pathol.* **a** A smooth growth of hypertrophied mucus found in mucous membrane, as in the nasal passages. **b** A tumor. Also called *polypus.* 2. *Zool.* **a** A single individual forming part of a colonial coelenterate, especially a hydrozoan. **b** A hydra. [< MF *polype* < L *polypus* < Gk. *polypous* < *polys* many + *pous* foot]

pol·y·par·y (pol/i·per/ē) *n. pl.* **·par·ies** *Zool.* The solid calcareous or chitinous framework of a colony of polyps, especially of coral: also called *polypidom.* [< NL *polyparium* < L *polypus* polyp]

pol·y·pep·tide (pol/i·pep/tīd) *n. Chem.* A peptide formed by the union of two or more amino acids.

pol·y·pet·al·ous (pol/i·pet/əl·əs) *adj. Bot.* Having the petals free and distinct. [< NL *polypetalus* < Gk. *polys* many + *petalon* leaf]

pol·y·pha·gi·a (pol/i·fā/jē·ə) *n.* 1. *Pathol.* Excessive craving for food; voracity. 2. *Zool.* The practice of eating many kinds of food. [< NL < Gk. < *polyphagos* eating to excess < *polys* much + *phagein* to eat] — **pol/y·pha/gi·an** *n. & adj.* — **pol/y·phag/ic, po·lyph·a·gous** (pə·lif/ə·gəs) *adj.*

pol·y·phase (pol/i·fāz) *adj. Electr.* Having or producing several phases, as an alternating current.

pol·y·phe·mus (pol/i·fē/məs) *n.* 1. An animal, or sometimes a person, having but one eye. 2. A large American silkworm moth (*Telea polyphemus*) having a conspicuous eyelike spot on each hind wing. For illustration see COCOON. [< NL < L, POLYPHEMUS]

Pol·y·phe·mus (pol/i·fē/məs) In Homer's *Odyssey*, the Cyclops who imprisoned Odysseus and his companions in a cave, from which they escaped after blinding him in his sleep. [< L < Gk. *Polyphēmos*]

pol·y·phon·ic (pol/i·fon/ik) *adj.* 1. Representing more than one sound or combination of sounds, as some written characters. 2. Consisting of many sounds or voices. 3. *Music* **a** Designating or involving the simultaneous combination of two or more independent melodic parts: opposed to homophonic. **b** Denoting an instrument, as a piano, by which two or more sounds may be produced simultaneously. Also **po·lyph·o·nous** (pə·lif/ə·nəs). [< Gk. *polyphōnos* many-toned < *polys* many + *phōnē* voice]

po·lyph·o·ny (pə·lif/ə·nē, pol/i·fō/nē) *n. pl.* **·nies** 1. Multiplicity of sounds, as in an echo. 2. The representation by one written character or sign of more than one sound. 3. Polyphonic music. [< Gk. *polyphōnia* < *polyphōnos.* See POLYPHONIC.]

pol·y·phy·let·ic (pol/i·fī·let/ik) *adj. Biol.* Coming from or showing characteristics of more than one ancestral type. [< POLY- + Gk. *phyletikos* of a tribe < *phylē* tribe]

po·lyp·i·dom (pə·lip/ə·dəm) *n.* A polypary. [< L *polypus* polyp + *domus* house < Gk.]

pol·y·ploid (pol′i·ploid′) *adj. Genetics* Having more than twice the normal (haploid) number of chromosomes. — *n.* An organism with more than two chromosome sets.

pol·y·pod (pol′i·pod) *adj.* **1.** Having many feet. **2.** *Zool.* Pertaining to many-footed organisms. — *n.* A myriapod. [< POLY- + -POD]

pol·y·po·dy (pol′i·pō′dē) *n. pl.* **·dies** Any of a genus (*Polypodium*) of widely distributed ferns, typically epiphytic, and having unenclosed sori. [< L *polypodium* < Gk. *polypodion* < *polus* many + dim. of *pous, podos* foot]

pol·y·pous (pol′i·pəs) *adj.* **1.** Pertaining to or resembling a polyp. **2.** *Pathol.* Pertaining to, afflicted with, or resembling polyps. [< L *polypus.* See POLYP.]

pol·yp·tych (pol′ip·tik) *n.* An altarpiece or panel having more than three folds or leaves. [< Gk. *polyptychos* having many folds < *poly-* many + *ptyx, ptychos* a fold]

pol·y·pus (pol′i·pəs) *n. pl.* **·pi** (-pī) *Pathol.* A polyp (def. 1). [< NL < L, polyp. See POLYP.]

pol·y·sac·cha·ride (pol′i·sak′ə·rīd, -rid) *n. Biochem.* Any of a class of carbohydrates formed by the union of three or more monosaccharide molecules and including starch. Also **pol′y·sac′cha·rid** (-rid), **pol′y·sac′cha·rose** (-rōs).

pol·y·se·my (pol′i·sē′mē) *n. pl.* **·mies** Acquisition or possession of several different meanings by one word. — **pol′y·se·man′tic, pol′y·se′mous** *adj.* [Ult. < Gk. *polysēmos* with many meanings < *polys* many + *sēma* sign]

pol·y·sty·rene (pol′i·stī′rēn) *n. Chem.* A thermoplastic polymer of styrene, C_8H_8, used in the making of plastics, etc.

pol·y·sul·fide (pol′i·sul′fīd, -fid) *n. Chem.* A binary compound having more than one sulfur atom in the molecule.

pol·y·syl·lab·ic (pol′i·si·lab′ik) *adj.* **1.** Having or pertaining to several syllables, especially to more than three. **2.** Characterized by words of more than three syllables. Also **pol′y·syl·lab′i·cal.** [< MF *polysyllabe* < Med.L *polysyllabus* < Gk. *polysyllabos* < *polys* many + *syllabē* syllable]

pol·y·syl·la·ble (pol′i·sil′ə·bəl) *n.* A polysyllabic word. — **pol′y·syl′la·bism** or **·syl·lab′i·cism** (pol′i·sil′lab′ə·siz′əm) *n.*

pol·y·syn·de·ton (pol′i·sin′də·ton) *n.* Repetition of connectives or conjunctions for rhetorical effect, as, "east and west and south and north." Compare ASYNDETON. [< NL < Gk. *polys* much + *syndetos* bound together < *syndeein* < *syn-* together + *deein* to bind]

pol·y·syn·thet·ic (pol′i·sin·thet′ik) *adj. Ling.* Describing a language, such as Eskimo, in which the subject, object, verb, etc., of a sentence are combined into a single utterance and have no existence as separate elements: also *holophrastic, incorporating.* Compare SYNTHETIC. [< Gk. *polysynthetos* much compounded < *polys* much + *syntithenai* < *syn-* together + *tithenai* to put]

pol·y·tech·nic (pol′i·tek′nik) *adj.* Embracing many arts: also **pol′y·tech′ni·cal.** — *n.* A school of applied science and the industrial arts. [< F *polytechnique* < Gk. *polytechnos* < *polys* many + *technē* craft, art]

pol·y·the·ism (pol′i·thē·iz′əm) *n.* The belief in and worship of more gods than one. [< F *polythéisme* < Gk. *polytheos* of many gods < *polys* many + *theos* god] — **pol′y·the′ist** *n.* — **pol′y·the·is′tic** or **·is′ti·cal** *adj.*

pol·y·troph·ic (pol′i·trof′ik, -trō′fik) *adj.* Obtaining nourishment from several sources. [< Gk. *polytrophos* highly nourished < *polus* much + *trephein* to feed]

pol·y·typ·ic (pol′i·tip′ik) *adj.* Having many forms. Also **pol′y·typ′i·cal.** [< POLY- + Gk. *typos* a type]

pol·y·un·sat·u·rat·ed (pol′i·un·sach′ə·rā′tid) *adj.* Designating any of a class of fats having more than two double bonds in its molecule.

pol·y·u·re·thane (pol′ē·yŏŏr′ə·thān′) *n.* Any of various thermoplastic or thermosetting resins, made by polymerization, used as insulation, cushion padding, etc. [< POLY- + URETHANE]

pol·y·u·ri·a (pol′i·yŏŏr′ē·ə) *n. Pathol.* Excessive urination. [< NL < Gk. *polys* much + *ouron* urine] — **pol′y·u′ric** *adj.*

pol·y·va·lent (pol′i·vā′lənt) *adj.* **1.** *Bacteriol.* Designating a type of vaccine containing antibodies derived from two or more different strains of microorganisms. **2.** *Chem.* Multivalent. — **pol′y·va′lence** *n.*

pol·y·vi·nyl (pol′i·vī′nil) *adj. Chem.* Designating any of a group of polymerized vinyl derivatives extensively used in the production of high-quality resins: *polyvinyl* acetate.

Po·lyx·e·na (pə·lik′sə·nə) In Greek legend, a daughter of Priam, betrothed to Achilles.

pol·y·zo·an (pol′i·zō′ən) *n. Zool.* A bryozoan.

pol·y·zo·ar·i·um (pol′i·zō·âr′ē·əm) *n. pl.* **·ar·i·a** (-âr′ē·ə) *Zool.* The entire colony of a compound bryozoan, or its supporting skeleton. Also **pol′y·zo′a·ry** (-zō′ə·rē). [< NL < *polyzoa* bryozoan < Gk. *poly-* many + *zōion* animal]

pol·y·zo·ic (pol′i·zō′ik) *adj. Zool.* **1.** Of or pertaining to the *Bryozoa.* **2.** Denoting a spore that produces many sporozoites. [< NL *polyzoa.* See POLYZOARIUM.]

pom·ace (pum′is) *n.* **1.** The pulpy substance of apples or similar fruit after grinding. **2.** The pulpy substance of anything ground. [< Med.L *pomacium* cider < L *pomum* apple]

po·ma·ceous (pō·mā′shəs) *adj.* **1.** Relating to or made of apples. **2.** Of or pertaining to a pome, or to trees that produce pomes. [< NL *pomaceus* < L *pomum* apple]

po·made (pō·mād′, -mäd′) *n.* A perfumed dressing for the hair or an ointment for the scalp. — *v.t.* **·mad·ed, ·mad·ing** To anoint with pomade. [< MF *pommade* < Ital. *pomata* < *pomo* apple < L *pomum*]

po·man·der (pō′man·dər, pō·man′dər) *n.* **1.** A ball or powder of aromatic substances, formerly worn as a guard against infection. **2.** A small box or case for carrying such perfume. [Earlier *pomamber* < OF *pomme d'ambre* apple of amber]

pome (pōm) *n. Bot.* A fleshy fruit with a core, as an apple, quince, pear, or the like. [< OF, apple < L *pomum*]

pome·gran·ate (pom′gran·it, pum′-, pəm·gran′it) *n.* **1.** The fruit of a tropical Asian and African tree (*Punica granatum*), about the size of an orange and having a hard rind enclosing a pleasantly subacid red pulp with many seeds. **2.** The tree itself. [< OF *pome grenate* < *pome* apple (< L *pomum*) + *grenate* < L *granatum* seeded < *granum* a grain, seed]

pom·e·lo (pom′ə·lō) *n. pl.* **·los** **1.** The grapefruit. **2.** The shaddock. [Prob. < POME]

Pom·e·ra·ni·a (pom′ə·rā′nē·ə) A region of north central Europe extending along the Baltic from Stralsund to the Vistula: German *Pommern.*

Pom·e·ra·ni·an (pom′ə·rā′nē·ən) *adj.* Relating to Pomerania or its inhabitants. — *n.* **1.** A native or inhabitant of Pomerania. **2.** One of a breed of small dog with pointed ears, a bushy tail, and long, straight, silky coat.

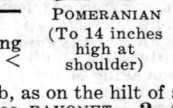
POMERANIAN
(To 14 inches high at shoulder)

po·mi·cul·ture (pō′mi·kul′chər) *n.* The cultivation and growing of fruit. [< *pomi-* (< L *pomum* apple, fruit) + CULTURE] — **po′mi·cul′tur·ist** *n.*

po·mif·er·ous (pō·mif′ər·əs) *adj.* Bearing pomes or pomelike fruit. [< L *pomifer* < *pomum* apple, fruit + *ferre* to bear]

pom·mel (pum′əl, pom′-) *n.* **1.** A knob, as on the hilt of a sword, bayonet, etc. For illustration see BAYONET. **2.** A knob at the front and on the top of a saddle. For illustration see SADDLE. — *v.t.* **pom·meled** or **·melled, pom·mel·ing** or **·mel·ling** To beat with or as with the fists or the pommel of a sword. Also spelled *pummel.* [< OF *pomel* rounded knob, dim. of *pome.* See POME.]

Pom·mern (pôm′ərn) The German name for POMERANIA.

po·mol·o·gy (pō·mol′ə·jē) *n.* The science that deals with fruits and fruit culture. [< NL *pomologia* < L *pomum* an apple, fruit + *-logia* -LOGY] — **po·mo·log′i·cal** (pō′mə·loj′i·kəl) *adj.* — **po·mo·log′i·cal·ly** *adv.* — **po·mol′o·gist** *n.*

Po·mo·na (pə·mō′nə) In Roman mythology, the goddess of fruit and fruit trees.

Po·mo·na (pə·mō′nə) A city in SW California; pop. 87,384.

Po·mo·na Island (pə·mō′nə) Largest of the Orkney Islands, Scotland; about 189 sq. mi.: also *Mainland.*

pomp (pomp) *n.* **1.** Magnificent or stately display; splendor. **2.** Ostentatious display; vain show. **3.** *Obs.* A grand procession or pageant. [< OF *pompe* < L *pompa* < Gk. *pompē* a sending, procession < *pempein* to send]

pom·pa·dour (pom′pə·dôr, -dŏŏr, -dōr) *n.* **1.** A style of arranging a man's hair by brushing it straight up from the forehead. **2.** A style of arranging a woman's hair by puffing it out at the forehead over a pad or roller. **3.** A shade of rosy pink. [after the Marquise de *Pompadour*]

Pom·pa·dour (pôṅ·pȧ·dōōr′), **Marquise de,** 1721–64, mistress of Louis XV of France: original name **Jeanne Antoinette Pois·son** (pwä·sôṅ′).

pom·pa·no (pom′pə·nō) *n. pl.* **·nos** **1.** Any of various carangoid food fishes (genus *Trachinotus*) of warm seas, especially one species (*T. carolinus*) found along the coasts of the South Atlantic States. **2.** A highly prized food fish (*Palometa simillima*) of the California coast. [< Sp. *pámpano* < L *pampinus* tendril]

Pom·pe·ii (pom·pā′, -pā′ē) An ancient city of southern Italy SE of Naples; destroyed by an eruption of Vesuvius, A.D. 79. — **Pom·pe·ian** (pom·pā′ən, -pē′ən) *adj. & n.*

pom·pel·mous (pom′pəl·mŏŏs) *n.* A large variety of shaddock, a fruit grown in the East Indies. [< Du. *pompelmoes,* ? < Du. *pompoen* pumpkin + *limoes* lemon]

Pom·pey (pom′pē) Anglicized name of **Gnaeus Pompeius Mag·nus** (mag′nəs), 106–48 B.C., Roman general, statesman, and triumvir; defeated by Julius Caesar: called **the Great.**

pom-pom (pom′pom′) *n. Brit.* A rapid-fire, automatic, antiaircraft cannon. [Imit. of its sound]

pom·pon (pom′pon, *Fr.* pôṅ·pôṅ′) *n.* **1.** In millinery, a tuft or ball, as of feathers or ribbon. **2.** The colored ball of wool on the front of a shako, or on top of a sailor's cap. **3.** A variety of chrysanthemum or dahlia having a small, compact, globe-shaped flower head. [< F, prob. reduplication of *pompe* pomp; infl. by MF *pomper* to dress magnificently]

pom·pos·i·ty (pom·pos′ə·tē) *n. pl.* **·ties** The state or quality of being pompous in manner or speech. [< Med.L *pompositas* < LL *pomposus.* See POMPOUS.]

pom·pous (pom′pəs) *adj.* **1.** Marked by exaggerated dignity or self-importance; pretentious. **2.** Bombastic and florid, as speech. **3.** Full of pomp; marked by ceremonious or impressive display. [< LL *pomposus* < L *pompa.* See POMP.] — **pom′pous·ness** *n.* — **pom′pous·ly** *adv.*

Pon·ce (pôn′sä) A port city in southern Puerto Rico; pop. 125,900 (1970).

Ponce de Le·ón (pons′ də lē′ən, *Sp.* pôn′thä thä lā·ôn′), **Juan,** 1460?–1521, Spanish explorer; discovered Florida, 1513.

pon·cho (pon′chō) *n. pl.* **·chos** **1.** A South American cloak like a blanket with a hole in the middle for the head. **2.** A similar garment, waterproofed or rubberized, and used as a raincoat by soldiers, sportsmen, etc. [< Sp. < Araucan]

pond (pond) *n.* A body of still water, smaller than a lake. [ME *ponde,* var. of POUND[2]]

pon·der (pon′dər) *v.t.* **1.** To weigh in the mind; consider carefully. —*v.i.* **2.** To meditate; reflect. —**Syn.** See DE-LIBERATE. [< OF *ponderer* < L *ponderare* to weigh < *pondus, ponderis* weight] —**pon′der·er** *n.*

pon·der·a·ble (pon′dər·ə·bəl) *adj.* Capable of being weighed; having appreciable weight. —**pon′der·a·bil′i·ty** *n.*

pon·der·ous (pon′dər·əs) *adj.* **1.** Having great weight; also, huge; bulky. **2.** Heavy to the extent of dullness; lumbering. [< F *pondereux* < L *ponderosus* < *pondus, ponderis* weight] —**pon′der·os′i·ty** (-də·ros′ə·tē), **pon′der·ous·ness** *n.* —**pon′der·ous·ly** *adv.* —**Syn. 1.** gigantic, massive, behemothian. **2.** awkward, clumsy, unwieldy, lumpish.

pond hockey *Canadian* **1.** Unorganized hockey played on what ice is available. **2.** *Slang* Hockey badly played.

Pon·di·cher·ry (pon′di·cher′ē, -sher′ē) A former French settlement in SE India; a free city 1947–54; incorporated into India, July 29, 1962; 196 sq. mi.; pop. about 380,000. *French* **Pon·di·che·ry** (pôn·dē·shä·rē′)

pond lily Any of various aquatic plants of the water-lily family; especially, the **yellow pond lily** (genus *Nuphar* or *Nymphaea*) having cup-shaped yellow flowers: also called *frog lily, spatterdock.*

pond scum Any of a group of free-floating, fresh-water green algae (*Spirogyra* and related genera) that form a scum on ponds.

pond·weed (pond′wēd′) *n.* Any of various submersed or partially floating perennial aquatic plants (genus *Potamogeton*) that grow in ponds and streams.

pone (pōn) *n. Southern U.S.* Corn pone (which see).

po·nent (pō′nənt) *adj. Logic* Affirmative; constructive. [< L *ponens, -entis,* ppr. of *ponere* to place]

pon·gee (pon·jē′) *n.* A thin, natural, unbleached silk with a knotty, rough weave, originally made in China from the product of wild silkworms. [? Alter. of dial. Chinese *pen chi* home loom < Chinese *pen-chi*]

pon·iard (pon′yərd) *n.* A dagger. —*v.t.* To stab with a poniard. [< MF *poignard* < OF *poing* fist < L *pugnus*]

pons (ponz) *n. pl.* **pon·tes** (pon′tēz) *Latin* **1.** A bridge: used in Latin phrases. **2.** *Anat.* The pons Varolii.

pons Va·ro·li·i (ponz və·rō′lē·ī) *Anat.* A broad band of nerve fibers that connect the cerebrum, cerebellum, and medulla oblongata. Also called *pons.* [< NL, bridge of Varoli; after Costanzo *Varoli,* 1543?–75, Italian anatomist]

Pon·selle (pon·sel′), **Rosa Melba,** born 1895?, U.S. operatic soprano: original name **Rosa Pon·zil·lo** (pon·zil′lō).

Pon·ta Del·ga·da (pon′tə del·gä′də) A port city on São Miguel in the Azores; pop. about 22,000.

Pont·char·train (pon′chər·trān), **Lake** A shallow lake in SE Louisiana, joined with the Mississippi at New Orleans by a canal; about 40 by 25 mi.

Pon·ti·ac (pon′tē·ak), died 1769, Ottawa Indian chief; made war on the British.

Pon·ti·ac (pon′tē·ak) A city in SE Michigan; pop. 85,279.

Pon·tic (pon′tik) *adj.* Of or pertaining to the Black Sea or adjacent regions. [< L *Ponticus* < Gk. *Pontikos* < *Pontos* the Black Sea, Pontus < *pontos* open sea]

pon·ti·fex (pon′tə·feks) *n. pl.* **pon·tif·i·ces** (pon·tif′ə·sēz) In ancient Rome, a priest of the Pontifical College that was headed by a high priest, the **Pontifex Max·i·mus** (mak′sə·məs) [< L *pontifex, -ficis,* ? < Osco-Umbrian *puntis* sacrificial offering, or ? < L *pons, pontis* bridge + *facere* to make]

pon·tiff (pon′tif) *n.* **1.** In the Roman Catholic Church: **a** The Pope. **b** Any bishop. **2.** In ancient Rome, a pontifex. [< MF *pontife* < L *pontifex* pontifex] —**pon·tif′ic** *adj.*

pon·tif·i·cal (pon·tif′i·kəl) *adj.* **1.** Of, pertaining to, or suitable for a pope or bishop. **2.** Haughty; pompous; dogmatic. [< L *pontificalis* < *pontifex* pontifex] —**pon·tif′i·cal·ly** *adv.*

Pontifical College In ancient Rome, the highest priestly group that had supreme jurisdiction in religious matters.

pon·tif·i·cate (*n.* pon·tif′ə·kit, -kāt′; *v.* -kāt′) *v.i.* **·cat·ed, ·cat·ing** **1.** To act or speak pompously or dogmatically. **2.** To perform the office of a pontiff. —*n.* The office or term of a pontiff. [< L *pontificatus,* pp. of *pontificare* to be a pontiff < *pontifex* pontifex]

pon·til (pon′til) *n.* A punty. [< F < Ital. *pontello* < L *punto* point]

pon·tine (pon′tīn) *adj.* Of or pertaining to a bridge or bridges. [< L *pons, pontis* bridge + -INE[1]]

Pon·tine Marshes (pon′tin, -tīn) A plain in west central Italy; about 300 sq. mi.; formerly a swamp, but now drained.

Pon·tius Pilate (pon′shəs, -tē·əs) Roman procurator of Judea 26–36 A.D., condemned Jesus to be crucified. Also *Pilate.*

pon·ton (pon′tən) *n. U.S. Mil.* A pontoon. [< OF. See PONTOON.]

pon·to·nier (pon′tə·nir′) *n. Mil.* An engineer or other member of the armed services in charge of pontoons or of building pontoon bridges. [< F *pontonnier* < *ponton*]

pon·toon (pon·tōōn′) *n.* **1.** *Mil.* A flat-bottomed boat, air-tight metal cylinder, or the like, used in the construction of temporary floating bridges over rivers. **2.** A pontoon bridge (which see). **3.** Either of the floats on the landing gear of a seaplane. [< MF *ponton* < L *ponto, pontonis* < *pons, pontis* bridge]

pontoon bridge A bridge supported on pontoons: also called *bateau bridge.* Also **ponton bridge.**

Pon·top·pi·dan (pôn·tôp′i·dän), **Henrik,** 1857–1943, Danish novelist.

Pon·tus (pon′təs) An ancient country, later a Roman province, on the Black Sea in NE Asia Minor.

Pon·tus Eux·in·us (pon′təs yōōk·sī′nəs) The ancient name for the BLACK SEA.

PONTOON BRIDGE
a Pontoons. *b* Locking bridge sections. *c* Shore.

po·ny (pō′nē) *n. pl.* **·nies 1.** A breed of very small horse, especially one not over 14 hands high. **2.** Any small type of horse. **3.** *U.S. Slang* A translation used in the preparation of foreign language lessons: also called *trot.* **4.** Anything that is small for its kind. **5.** *Informal* A very small glass for liquor; also, the amount of liquor such a glass will hold. **6.** *Brit. Slang* In racing, the sum of 25 pounds. —*v.t. & v.i.* **·nied, ·ny·ing** *U.S. Slang* **1.** To translate lessons with the aid of a pony or trot. **2.** To pay (money) that is due: with *up.* [< dial. E (Scottish) *powney,* prob. OF *poulenet,* dim. of *poulain* colt < LL *pullanus* < L *pullus* young animal]

pony engine *U.S.* A small switching locomotive.

pony express In 1860–61, a postal system by which mail was relayed from Missouri to California by riders mounted on swift ponies; also, the rider.

po·ny·tail (pō′nē·tāl′) *n.* A girl's or woman's hairstyle in which the hair is drawn back and tied close behind the head, hanging free like a pony's tail.

pooch (pōōch) *n. Slang* A dog; especially a small mongrel. [? < dial. E and obs. *pooch,* var. of POUCH; ? with ref. to appetite]

pood (pōōd) *n.* A Russian weight equivalent to 36.1 pounds. [< Russian *pud* < LG *pund* ult. < L *pondo* a pound]

poo·dle (pōōd′l) *n.* One of a breed of dogs of high intelligence, with long, curly, usually white or black hair. [< G *pudel* < LG, short for *pudelhund* < *pudeln* to splash in water; with ref. to its being a water dog]

pooh (pōō) *interj.* An exclamation of disdain, scorn, etc.

Pooh-Bah (pōō′bä′) *n. Informal* A pompous official. [after a character in Gilbert and Sullivan's *The Mikado*]

pooh-pooh (pōō′pōō′) *v.t.* To reject or speak of disdainfully. [Reduplication of POOH]

pool[1] (pōōl) *n.* **1.** A small body, usually of fresh water, as a spring. **2.** A deep place in a stream. **3.** Any small, isolated body of liquid; a puddle: a *pool* of blood. **4.** A swimming pool (which see). [OE *pōl* < Gmc.]

pool[2] (pōōl) *n.* **1.** In certain gambling games, a collective stake. **2.** In business, a combination whereby companies or corporations agree to fix rates or prices in order to overcome the effects of excessive competition. **3.** In finance, any combination formed for a speculative operation, as in stocks or the like. **4.** Any combining of efforts or resources: a typists' *pool.* **5.** Any of various games played on a six-pocket billiard table, in which the object is to drive balls numbered from 1 to 15 into the pockets: also *pocket billiards.* See BILLIARDS. —*v.t.* **1.** To combine in a mutual fund or pool, so as to satisfy a mutual need: to *pool* one's resources for a common cause. —*v.i.* **2.** To form a pool. [< F *poule* stake, orig., hen < L *pulla*]

Poole (pōōl) A municipal borough of SE Dorsetshire, England, on the English Channel; pop. 88,088 (1961).

pool·room (pōōl′rōōm′, -rōōm′) *n.* A commercial establishment or room equipped for the playing of pool, billiards, etc.

pool table A six-pocket billiard table for playing pool.

pool train *Canadian* A train operated by more than one railroad. Also **pooled train** (pōōld′).

poon (pōōn) *n.* **1.** Any of various East Indian trees (genus *Calophyllum*) from which is obtained a hard, light wood used for masts and spars. **2.** The wood itself. Also called *puna.* [< Singhalese *pūna*]

Poo·na (pōō′nä) A city in W India; pop. 1,123,399 (1971).

poop[1] (pōōp) *Naut. n.* **1.** The after part or stern of a ship. **2.** A short deck built over the main deck at the stern of a ship: also **poop deck**. — *v.t.* **1.** To break over the stern or poop of: said of a wave. **2.** To take (a wave) over the stern. [< OF *pope* < OProvençal *poppa* < L *puppis*]

poop² (poop) *U.S. Slang v.t.* To bring to exhaustion; weary: usually in the passive. *He was pooped by the long climb.* [Origin unknown]

Po·o·pó (pō'ō·pō') **Lake**   A lake in west central Bolivia; 12,106 ft. above sea level; 60 mi. long, 20 to 30 mi. wide.

poor (poor) *adj.* **1.** Lacking means of comfortable subsistence; indigent; needy. **2.** Characterized by or indicative of poverty: *a poor neighborhood.* **3.** *Law* Depending upon charity or public relief. **4.** Lacking in abundance or good qualities; scanty; meager: *a poor crop.* **5.** Lacking in fertility; sterile: *poor soil.* **6.** Inferior in workmanship or quality: *a poor watch.* **7.** Deficient in vigor; feeble; frail: *poor health.* **8.** Thin from bad feeding; lean, as cattle. **9.** Lacking in nobility of character; contemptible; mean. **10.** Lacking proper ability; unsatisfactory. **11.** Deserving of pity; wretched; unhappy. — *n.* Indigent or needy people collectively: preceded by *the.* [< OF *povre, poure* < L *pauper.* Akin to *paucus* few. Doublet of PAUPER.] — **poor'ness** *n.*
— **Syn. 1.** destitute, wanting, impoverished. **4.** deficient, scrimpy, spare. **9.** base, lily-livered, dastardly. **11.** miserable.

Poor Clare A nun belonging to an order founded in 1212 by St. Clare of Assisi following a rule prescribed by St. Francis.

poor farm A farm where paupers are cared for at public expense.

poor·house (poor'hous') *n.* A public establishment maintained as a dwelling for paupers.

poor·ly (poor'lē) *adv.* **1.** With poor or unsatisfactory results. **2.** Disparagingly. — *adj. Informal* Poor in health.

Poor Richard's Al·ma·nack (ôl'mə·nak) An almanac issued by Benjamin Franklin from 1732 to 1757 in which he wrote many wise precepts and proverbs.

poor-spir·it·ed (poor'spir'it·ed) *adj.* Having little spirit or courage. — **Syn.** See COWARDLY. — **poor'spir'it·ed·ness** *n.*

poor·tith (poor'tith) *n. Scot.* Poverty.

poor white In the southern United States, a member of a class of poverty-stricken white farmers or laborers: an offensive term. Also **poor white trash.**

pop¹ (pop) *v.* **popped, pop·ping** *v.i.* **1.** To make a sharp, explosive sound. **2.** To burst open or explode with such a sound. **3.** To move or go suddenly or quickly: with *in, out,* etc. **4.** To protrude; bulge: *His eyes popped.* **5.** In baseball, to bat the ball high into the air so that an opposing player can easily catch it, thus retiring the batter: with *up* or *out.* — *v.t.* **6.** To cause to burst or explode, as kernels of corn by roasting. **7.** To thrust or put suddenly: with *in, out,* etc. *He popped his head in the door.* **8.** To fire (a gun, etc.). **9.** To shoot. **10.** In baseball, to bat (the ball) short but high so that it is easily caught. — **to pop the question** *Informal* To make a proposal of marriage. — *n.* **1.** A sharp, explosive noise. **2.** A shot with a firearm. **3.** A soft drink containing carbonated water and flavoring. — *adv.* **1.** Like or with the sound of a pop. **2.** Suddenly or unexpectedly. [Imit.]

pop² (pop) *n. Slang* **1.** Papa. **2.** A familiar term of address for an old man. [Short for *poppa,* var. of PAPA]

pop³ (pop) *n.* A concert of popular or light classical music. — *adj.* Featuring popular or light classical music: *a pop concert; a pop orchestra.* Also **pops.** [Short for POPULAR]

pop. **1.** Popular(ly). **2.** Population.

POP Point of purchase.

pop art *Sometimes cap.* A dadaistic style of art of the 1960's characterized by the representation, often in life-size or larger, of popular commercial products, images, and people, as cans of soup, comic-strip characters, movie stars, etc.

pop·corn (pop'kôrn') *n.* A variety of maize, the kernels of which explode when heated, forming large white balls; also, the corn after popping, eaten as a confection.

pope (pōp) *n.* **1.** *Often cap.* In the Roman Catholic Church, the bishop of Rome and the head of the Church. **2.** One who assumes, or is considered to have, similar great authority. **3.** In the Eastern Orthodox Church, a parish priest. [OE *pāpa* < LL < LGk. *papas* bishop < Gk. *pappas* child's word for father]

Pope (pōp), **Alexander,** 1688–1744, English poet and satirist: called **the Wasp of Twickenham.** — **John,** 1822–92, Union general in the Civil War.

pope·dom (pōp'dəm) *n.* The office, dominion, or tenure of a pope.

pop·er·y (pō'pər·ē) *n.* The practices, doctrines, etc., of the Roman Catholic Church: an offensive term.

pope's nose Parson's nose (which see).

pop·eyed (pop'īd') *adj.* **1.** Having bulging or protruding eyes. **2.** Filled with astonishment; amazed.

pop group A group of musicians specializing in pop music.

pop·gun (pop'gun') *n.* A child's toy gun that expels a pellet with a popping sound by compressed air.

pop music Popular music, especially commercially produced songs, ballads, etc.

pop·in·jay (pop'in·jā) *n.* **1.** A fop; coxcomb. **2.** The figure of a bird, formerly used as a mark in archery. **3.** *Archaic* A parrot. [< OF *papegai* < OProvençal *papagai* < Sp. *papagayo* < Arabic *babaghā;* infl. by JAY¹]

pop·ish (pō'pish) *adj.* Pertaining to popes or popery: an offensive term. — **pop'ish·ly** *adv.* — **pop'ish·ness** *n.*

Popish Plot See (Titus) OATES.

pop·lar (pop'lər) *n.* **1.** Any of a genus (*Populus*) of dioecious trees and bushes of the willow family, widely distributed in the northern hemisphere, especially the Lombardy poplar and the white poplar. **2.** The wood of any of these trees. **3.** Any of several trees resembling the poplar in some ways, as the tuliptree. [< OF *poplier* < L *populus*]

poplar bluff *Canadian* A poplar grove.

pop·lin (pop'lin) *n.* A durable silk, cotton, or rayon fabric with a ribbed surface, used for dresses, upholstery, etc. [< F *papeline,* ? < Ital. *papalina* papal; because made in Avignon, a papal residence]

pop·lit·e·al (pop·lit'ē·əl, pop'li·tē'əl) *adj.* Of or pertaining to the back part of the leg behind the knee. Also **pop·li·te·al** (pop'li·tē'əl), **pop·lit·ic.** [< NL *popliteus* < L *poples, poplitis* the back of the knee]

Po·po·cat·e·pet·l (pō'pə·kat'ə·pet'l, pō·pō'kä·tā'pet'l) A dormant volcano in central Mexico; crater 250 ft. deep, 2,000 ft. across; 17,887 ft. high.

pop·o·ver (pop'ō'vər) *n.* A very light egg muffin, so named because it rises over the edge of the baking tin.

pop·per (pop'ər) *n.* **1.** One who or that which pops. **2.** A container or device for popping corn.

pop·pet (pop'it) *n.* **1.** *Mech.* A poppet valve. **2.** *Chiefly Brit.* A dainty little person; pretty child: a pet name. **3.** Any of the small bits of wood on the gunwale of a boat for supporting an oarlock. **4.** *Obs.* A doll. [Var. of PUPPET.]

poppet valve *Mech.* A valve mounted on a stem and having a reciprocating motion in the direction of the longitudinal axis, used in various types of steam and gasoline engines.

pop·pied (pop'ēd) *adj.* **1.** Abounding in or adorned with poppies. **2.** Drowsy with or as with opium.

popping crease In cricket, a line 4 feet in front of and parallel to the wicket, marking the limit of the batsman's position. For illustration see CRICKET².

pop·ple (pop'əl) *v.i.* **·pled, ·pling** To have a heaving motion; ripple; bubble, as agitated water. — *n.* Rippling or bubbling water; bubbling, or its sound. [ME *poplen.* Cf. Du. *popeln* to murmur, Med.L *populare.*]

pop·py (pop'ē) *n. pl.* **·pies 1.** Any of various plants (genus *Papaver*), typical of a widely distributed family (*Papaveraceae*), having lobed or toothed leaves and showy red, violet, orange, or white flowers, as the **opium poppy** (*P. somniferum*), the **oriental poppy** (*P. orientale*) and the **Iceland poppy** (*P. nudicaule*). ◆ Collateral adjective: *papaverous.* **2.** A medicinal extract, as opium, from such a plant. **3.** The bright scarlet color of certain poppy blossoms: also **poppy red.** [OE *popig* < L *papaver*]

pop·py·cock (pop'ē·kok) *n. Informal* Pretentious talk; humbug; nonsense. [< Dial. Du. *pappekak,* lit., soft dung]

pop·py·head (pop'ē·hed') *n.* A small, carved wooden finial, especially at the end of a church pew.

poppy seed The small, black seed of the poppy plant used to flavor and top rolls, bread, etc.

Pop·si·cle (pop'si·kəl) *n.* Ice cream or flavored ice on a stick: a trade name. Also **pop·si·cle.**

pop·u·lace (pop'yə·lis) *n.* The common people of a community, etc.; the masses. [< MF < Ital. *popolaccio,* pejorative of *popolo* people < L *populus*]

pop·u·lar (pop'yə·lər) *adj.* **1.** Approved of, admired, or liked by most people: *popular music.* **2.** Having many friends and acquaintances; well-liked. **3.** Of, pertaining to, or engaged in by the people at large: *popular government.* **4.** Suited to the intelligence and taste of ordinary people: *popular lectures.* **5.** Prevalent among the people in general: *popular superstitions.* **6.** Suited to the means of the people: *popular prices.* **7.** Of folk origin. **8.** Of language, used by ordinary people; nonstandard or substandard: said also of many borderline usages. Abbr. *pop.* [< L *popularis* of the people < *populus* the people] — **pop'u·lar·ly** *adv.*

popular etymology Folk etymology (which see).

popular front A coalition of leftist, labor, and liberal parties formed to combat fascism or conservatism in a government by promoting social reform: also called *people's front.*

pop·u·lar·i·ty (pop'yə·lar'ə·tē) *n.* The condition of being popular, especially of possessing the confidence and favor of the people or of a set of people. [MF *popularité* < L *popularitas* fellow-citizenship < *popularis.* See POPULAR.]

pop·u·lar·ize (pop'yə·lə·rīz') *v.t.* **·ized, ·iz·ing** To make popular. Also *Brit.* **pop'u·lar·ise'.** — **pop'u·lar·i·za'tion** *n.* — **pop'u·lar·iz'er** *n.*

pop·u·late (pop'yə·lāt) *v.t.* **·lat·ed, ·lat·ing 1.** To furnish with inhabitants, as by colonization; people. **2.** To inhabit. [< Med.L *populatus,* pp. of *populare* < L *populus* the people]

pop·u·la·tion (pop'yə·lā'shən) *n.* **1.** The total number of persons living in a country, city, or other specified area. **2.** The total number of persons of a particular group, class, race, etc., residing in a place. Abbr. *p., pop.* **3.** The act or process of populating or furnishing with inhabitants. **4.** *Biol.* The total number of organisms living in a given region; also, the total aggregate of those studied by statistical or biometric methods. **5.** *Stat.* A group of items or individuals to be studied. — **Syn.** See PEOPLE. [< LL *populatio, -onis* < L *populus* the people]

Pop·u·list (pop′yə·list) *adj.* Of or pertaining to the Populist or People's Party. — *n.* A member of the People's Party. [< L *populus* the people] — **Pop′u·lism** *n.* — **Pop′u·lis′tic** *adj.*

Populist Party People's Party (which see).

pop·u·lous (pop′yə·ləs) *adj.* Containing many inhabitants; thickly settled. [< L *populosus* < *populus* the people] — **pop′u·lous·ly** *adv.* — **pop′u·lous·ness** *n.*

por·bea·gle (pôr′bē·gəl) *n.* A large voracious shark (*Lamna nasus*) of northern waters, sometimes 10 feet long. [< dial. E (Cornish); ult. origin unknown]

porce·lain (pôrs′lin, pôrs′-, pôr′sə-, pôr′-) *n.* 1. A white, hard, translucent ceramic ware, usually glazed, existing in many varieties; china; chinaware. 2. An object made of this material. [< MF *porcelaine* < Ital. *porcellana* shell < L *porcella*, dim. fem. of *porcus* pig; semantic connection unclear] — **por·ce·la·ne·ous** (pôr′sə·lā′nē·əs, pôr′-) or **por′cel·la′ne·ous** *adj.*

porch (pôrch, pōrch) *n.* 1. A covered structure or recessed space at the entrance to a building; a stoop. 2. *U.S.* A veranda. 3. A covered walk or portico. — **the Porch** The Stoic school of philosophy in ancient Athens, named from the Stoa Poecile, or Painted Porch. See STOIC. [< OF *porche* < L *porticus* colonnade < *porta* gate. Doublet of PORTICO.]

por·cine (pôr′sīn, -sin) *adj.* 1. Of, pertaining to, or characteristic of swine. 2. Swinish; hoggish; piggish. [< F, fem. of *porcin* < L *porcinus* < *porcus* pig]

por·cu·pine (pôr′kyə·pīn) *n.* Any of various large, clumsy rodents covered with erectile spines or quills used for defense, as the **African porcupine** (*Hystrix cristata*), and the **Canada porcupine** (*Erethizon dorsatum*) common to the U.S. and Canada: also, *U.S.*, **hedgehog.** [< OF < OProvençal *porc-espin* < It. *porcospino*, lit., spiny pig < *porco* pig (< L *porcus*) + *spino* thorn < L *spina*]

CANADA
PORCUPINE
(To 3 feet long;
tail 6 inches)

porcupine anteater An echidna.

porcupine fish A globefish (which see).

porcupine grass A tall grass (*Stipa spartea*) of the western United States, yielding good forage and hay.

pore[1] (pôr, pōr) *v.i.* **pored, por·ing** 1. To gaze steadily or intently. 2. To study or read with care and application: with *over*: to *pore* over one's accounts. 3. To meditate; ponder: with *on, over,* or *upon.* [ME *pouren*; origin unknown]

pore[2] (pôr, pōr) *n.* 1. A minute orifice or opening, as in the skin or a leaf, serving as an outlet for perspiration or as a means of absorption. 2. Any similar opening, as in rock. [< OF *pore, porre* < L *porus* < Gk. *poros* pore, passage]

por·gy (pôr′gē) *n.* *pl.* **·gies** or **·gy** 1. Any of various sparoid, salt-water food fishes, especially the **red porgy** (*Pagrus pagrus*) of Mediterranean and European waters. 2. Any of various related fishes, as the scup. [< PARGO]

po·rif·er·ous (pô·rif′ər·əs, pō-) *adj.* 1. Bearing or having pores. 2. Belonging or relating to a phylum (*Porifera*) of primitive aquatic, and chiefly marine, animals comprising the sponges. [< NL *porifer* < L *porus* pore + *ferre* to bear]

po·rism (pôr′iz·əm, pō′riz-) *n.* *Math.* One of an ancient class of propositions that asserted a relation between variables or affirmed the possibility of finding conditions under which a problem would become indeterminate. [< Med.L < Gk *porisma* corollary < *porizein* to carry, deduce < *poros* way]

pork (pôrk, pōrk) *n.* 1. The flesh of swine used as food. 2. *U.S. Slang* Government money, distinctions, favors, etc., obtained by a representative for his constituents: a form of political patronage. [< OF *porc* < L *porcus* pig]

pork barrel *U.S. Slang* A Federal appropriation for some local enterprise that will favorably impress a representative's constituents.

pork·eat·er (pôrk′ē·tər) *n. Canadian Slang* A voyageur.

pork·er (pôr′kər, pōr′-) *n.* A pig or hog, especially one fattened for slaughter.

pork·pie (pôrk′pī′, pōrk′-) *n.* 1. A pie filled with chopped pork and having a thick crust. 2. A man's hat with a low, flat crown. Also **pork pie.**

pork·wood (pôrk′wōōd′, pōrk′-) *n.* 1. The brown, coarsegrained wood of a small tropical American tree (*Torrubia longifolia*) with small cymose flowers. 2. The tree.

pork·y (pôr′kē, pōr′-) *adj.* **pork·i·er, pork·i·est** 1. Of or like pork. 2. Obese; fat, as from overeating. [< PORK]

por·no (pôr′nō) *n. Slang* Pornography. Also **porn.**

por·nog·ra·phy (pôr·nog′rə·fē) *n.* *pl.* **·phies** Obscene literature or art. [< Gk. *pornographos* writing of prostitutes < *pornē* prostitute + *graphein* to write] — **por·no·graph·ic** (pôr′nō·graf′ik) *adj.*

po·ros·co·py (pô·ros′kə·pē, pō-) *n.* The study of the character and arrangement of the sweat glands, especially in finger-

print identification. [< *poro-* (Gk. *poros* pore) + -SCOPY]

po·ro·scop·ic (pôr′ə·skop′ik, pō′rə-) or **·i·cal** *adj.*

po·ros·i·ty (pô·ros′ə·tē, pō-) *n.* *pl.* **·ties** 1. The property of being porous; porousness. 2. A porous part or structure. [< L *porositas* < *porus* pore]

po·rous (pôr′əs, pō′rəs) *adj.* 1. Having pores. 2. Permeable by fluids or light. — **po′rous·ly** *adv.* — **po′rous·ness** *n.*

por·phy·rin (pôr′fə·rin) *n. Biochem.* Any of a class of widely distributed pyrrole compounds derived from the breakdown of hemoglobin and chlorophyll. [< (*hemato*) *porphyrin* < HEMATO- + Gk. *porphyra* purple + -IN]

por·phy·rit·ic (pôr′fə·rit′ik) *adj.* 1. Of, relating to, or resembling porphyry. 2. *Mineral.* Containing well-defined, relatively large crystals in a fine-grained, glassy base or groundmass. Also **por′phy·rit′i·cal.** [< Med.L *porphyriticus* < L *porphyrites* porphyry < Gk. *porphyrītēs* (*lithos*), purple stone < *porphyros* purple]

por·phy·roid (pôr′fə·roid) *n.* A variously colored sedimentary rock exhibiting a well-defined porphyritic structure.

por·phy·ry (pôr′fə·rē) *n.* *pl.* **·ries** An igneous rock that has a groundmass enclosing crystals of feldspar or quartz. [< OF *porfire* < Med.L *porphyreus* < Gk. *porphyros* purple < *porphyra* the purple-fish and its dye]

Por·phy·ry (pôr′fə·rē) Anglicized name of **Malchus Porphy·ri·us** (pôr·fir′ē·əs), 233?–305?, Neo-Platonic philosopher; disciple of Plotinus; opposed Christianity.

por·poise (pôr′pəs) *n.* *pl.* **·pois·es** or **·poise** 1. A dolphinlike cetacean (genus *Phocaena*) with a blunt, rounded snout; especially, the **common** or **harbor porpoise** (*P. phocaena*) of the North Atlantic and Pacific, from five to six feet long, blackish above and white below: also called *sea hog, snuffer.* 2. Loosely, any small cetacean, as the common dolphin. [< OF *porpeis, porpois* < L *porcus pisces,* lit., hog fish]

PORPOISE (def. 1)
(To 6 feet long)

por·ridge (pôr′ij, por-) *n.* 1. *Chiefly Brit.* A soft food made by boiling oatmeal or other meal in water or milk until thickened. 2. Originally, pottage. [Alter. of POTTAGE; infl. in form by ME *porray* leek soup]

por·rin·ger (pôr′in·jər, por′-) *n.* A small, relatively shallow bowl for porridge or soup; especially, such a bowl of silver or other material used by small children. [Earlier *pottanger* < MF *potager* soup bowl; infl. in form by PORRIDGE]

Por·se·na (pôr′sə·nə), **Lars** A semilegendary Etruscan king of the sixth century B.C. who marched against Rome to restore the Tarquins. Also **Por·sen·na** (pôr·sen′ə).

Por·son (pôr′sən), **Richard,** 1759–1808, English classical scholar.

port[1] (pôrt, pōrt) *n.* 1. A city or place of customary entry and exit of ships, especially for commerce. 2. A harbor or haven. 3. *Law* A port of entry (which see). Abbr. *pt.* [OE reinforced by F *port,* both < L *portus* harbor]

port[2] (pôrt, pōrt) *n. Naut.* The left side of a vessel as one faces the front or bow: formerly called *larboard:* opposed to *starboard.* — *v.t. & v.i.* To put or turn to the port or larboard side. — *adj.* Left: *port* side. [Prob. < PORT[1]]

port[3] (pôrt, pōrt) *n.* 1. *Naut.* **a** A porthole (which see). **b** A covering for a porthole. 2. *Mech.* An orifice for the passage of air, gas, etc.: a steam *port.* 3. *Scot.* A gate; portal. [Prob. < OF *porte* < L *porta* gate, door]

port[4] (pôrt, pōrt) *n.* A variety of sweet wine, usually dark red. [Short for *Oporto* wine, after *Oporto,* Portugal]

port[5] (pôrt, pōrt) *v.t. Mil.* To carry (a rifle, saber, etc.) diagonally across the body and sloning to the left shoulder. — *n.* 1. *Mil.* The position of a rifle or other weapon when ported. 2. The way in which one bears or carries himself. [< MF *porter* to carry < L *portare*]

Port. Portugal; Portuguese.

Por·ta (pôr′tä), **Giambattista della,** 1540?–1615, Italian scientist and alchemist.

port·a·ble (pôr′tə·bəl, pōr′-) *adj.* 1. That can be readily carried or moved. 2. *Obs.* Endurable; supportable. — *n.* Something portable, as a typewriter or radio. [< MF < LL *portabilis* < L *portare* to carry] — **port′a·bil′i·ty, port′a·ble·ness** *n.* — **port′a·bly** *adv.*

port·age (pôr′tij, pōr′-) *n.* *U.S. & Canadian* 1. The act of transporting (canoes, boats, and goods) from one navigable water to another: also, that which is transported. 2. The route over which and the place where such transportation is made: also, *Canadian, carrying place.* 3. The charge for transportation. [< MF < *porter* to carry < L *portare*]

por·tal (pôr′təl, pōr′-) *n.* 1. *Often pl.* An entrance, door, or gate, especially one that is grand and imposing. 2. The portal vein. — *adj.* Pertaining to the portal vein. [< MF < Med.L *portale* city gate, ult. < L *porta* gate]

por·tal-to-por·tal pay (pôr′təl·tə·pôr′təl, pōr′-) A wage computed on the full time spent on mine or factory property from arrival to departure.

portal vein *Anat.* The large vein that conveys blood from the intestines, stomach, and pancreas to the liver.

por·ta·men·to (pôr′tə·men′tō, pōr′-; *Ital.* pôr′tä·men′tō) *n. pl.* **·ti** (-tē) *Music* **1.** A legato connection of two successive tones, produced by a subtle sliding between them. **2.** Loosely, a legato passage or effect. [< Ital., lit., a carrying]

port·ance (pôr′təns, pōr′-) *n. Archaic* Personal carriage; deportment; mien. [< MF, a carrying, support < *porter* to carry < L *portare*]

Port Ar·thur (är′thər) A port city on Sabine Lake in SE Texas, pop. 57,371.

por·ta·tive (pôr′tə·tiv, pōr′-) *adj.* **1.** Of or pertaining to carrying; capable of carrying. **2.** Portable. [< OF, fem. of *portatif* portable < L *portatus*, pp. of *portare* to carry]

Port-au-Prince (pôrt′ō·prins′, pōrt′-; *Fr.* pôr·tō·praṅs′) The capital of Haiti, a port in the southern part; pop. 250,-000 (est. 1970).

port authority Any official body having charge of the co-ordination of all rail and water traffic of a port.

Port Blair (blâr) The capital of the Andaman and Nicobar Islands, a port on SE South Andaman Island; pop. about 3,500.

port·cul·lis (pôrt·kul′is, pōrt-) *n.* A grating made of strong bars of wood or iron that can be let down suddenly to close the gateway of a fortified place. [< OF *porte coleïce* < *porte* gate (< L *porta*) + fem. of *coleïs*, pp. of *couler* to slide < L *colare* to filter]

MEDIEVAL PORTCULLIS

Port du Sa·lut (pôrt də sə·lōōt′, sə·lōō′) A creamy, compact cheese with a flavor similar to that of Gouda.

Porte (pôrt, pōrt) *n.* The former Ottoman Turkish government: with *the*: officially called **the Sublime Porte**. [< F (*la Sublime*) *Porte* (the High) Gate, trans. of Turkish *Babi Ali*, the chief office of the Ottoman Empire]

porte-co·chère (pôrt′kō·shâr′, pōrt′-; *Fr.* pôrt·kô·shâr′) *n.* **1.** A large covered gateway for vehicles, leading into a courtyard. **2.** A porch over a driveway at the entrance of a building for sheltering persons entering or leaving vehicles. [< F < *porte* gate + *cochère*, fem. adj. < *coche* coach]

Port Elizabeth A port city in SE Cape of Good Hope Province, South Africa; pop. 374,100 (1967).

porte-mon·naie (pôrt′mŭn′ē, pōrt′-; *Fr.* pôrt·mô·ne′) *n. French* A pocketbook for money; especially, a small purse with clasps.

por·tend (pôr·tend′, pōr-) *v.t.* **1.** To warn of as an omen; presage; forebode. **2.** *Obs.* To mean; signify. — **Syn.** See AUGUR. [< L *portendere* to foretell, var. of *protendere* < *pro-* forth + *tendere* to stretch]

Por·te·ño (pôr·tā′nyō) *n.* A native or inhabitant of Buenos Aires.

por·tent (pôr′tent, pōr′-) *n.* **1.** An indication or sign of what is to happen, especially of something momentous or calamitous. **2.** Ominous significance. **3.** A prodigy; marvel. [< L *portentum* < *portendere*. See PORTEND.]

por·ten·tous (pôr·ten′təs, pōr-) *adj.* **1.** Having the nature of a portent; ominous; foreboding. **2.** Causing astonishment or awe; prodigious; extraordinary. [< L *portentosus*] — **por·ten′tous·ly** *adv.* — **por·ten′tous·ness** *n.*

por·ter[1] (pôr′tər, pōr′-) *n.* **1.** One who carries travelers' luggage, etc., for hire, as in a hotel or at a railroad station. **2.** *U.S.* An attendant in a Pullman car. [< OF *porteour* < LL *portator* to carry]

por·ter[2] (pôr′tər, pōr′-) *n.* A keeper of a door or gate; janitor. [< OF *portier* < LL *portarius* < L *porta* gate, door]

por·ter[3] (pôr′tər, pōr′-) *n.* A dark brown, heavy, English malt liquor resembling ale. [< PORTER[1]; so called because formerly drunk chiefly by porters]

Por·ter (pôr′tər, pōr′-), **Cole**, 1893–1964, U.S. song writer. — **David**, 1780–1843, U.S. naval officer. — **David Dixon**, 1813–91, U.S. admiral, son of David Porter. — **Fitz-John**, 1822–1901, U.S. general in the Civil War. — **Jane**, 1776–1850, English novelist. — **Katherine Anne**, born 1890, U.S. short-story writer and novelist. — **Noah**, 1811–92, U.S. educator and lexicographer. — **William Sydney** See O. HENRY.

por·ter·age (pôr′tər·ij, pōr′-) *n.* **1.** The work of a porter. **2.** The charge for such work.

por·ter·house (pôr′tər·hous′, pōr′-) *n.* **1.** A place where porter, ale, etc., are retailed. **2.** A restaurant; chophouse. **3.** A choice cut of beefsteak including a part of the tenderloin, usually next to the sirloin: also **porterhouse steak**. [< PORTER[3] + HOUSE]

port·fo·li·o (pôrt·fō′lē·ō, pōrt-) *n. pl.* **·li·os** **1.** A portable case for holding drawings, papers, etc. **2.** Such a case for carrying documents of a department of state. **3.** The position or office of a minister of state or a cabinet member. **4.** An itemized list of investments, securities, etc., of a bank or investor. [Earlier *porto folio* < Ital. *portafoglio* < *portare* to carry (< L) + *foglio* leaf, sheet of paper < L *folium*]

port·hole (pôrt′hōl′, pōrt′-) *n.* **1.** A small opening in a ship's side for admitting light and air, for shooting a weapon through, or for loading cargo. **2.** A loophole in the wall of a fort for shooting through; embrasure. **3.** An opening into a furnace, engine, or the like, shaped like a porthole.

Port Huron A city in SE Michigan, on the St. Clair River, pop. 35,794.

Por·tia (pôr′shə, -shē·ə, pōr′-) In Shakespeare's *Merchant of Venice*, the heroine who acts the part of a lawyer and defeats Shylock's claim for a pound of Antonio's flesh.

por·ti·co (pôr′ti·kō, pōr′-) *n. pl.* **·coes** or **·cos** An open space or ambulatory with roof upheld by columns; a porch. [< Ital. < L *porticus* < *porta* door. Doublet of PORCH.] — **por′ti·coed** *adj.*

por·tière (pôr·tyâr′, pōr-; *Fr.* pôr·tyâr′) *n.* A curtain for a doorway, used instead of a door or as an ornament. Also **por·tiere′.** [< F]

Por·ti·le de Fier (pôr·tsē′le de fyer′) The Rumanian name for the IRON GATE.

por·tion (pôr′shən, pōr′-) *n.* **1.** A part of a whole, whether separated from it or not. **2.** An allotment or share. **3.** The quantity of food usually served to one person. **4.** The part of an estate coming to an heir or next of kin. **5.** A dowry (def. 1). — *v.t.* **1.** To divide into shares for distribution; parcel: usually with *out*. **2.** To give a dowry or inheritance to. **3.** To assign; allot. [< OF *portion* < L *portio, -onis.* Akin to PART.] — **por′tion·a·ble** *adj.* — **por′tion·less** *adj.* — **Syn.** (noun) **1.** *Portion, fraction, segment, sector, section, division, subdivision,* and *parcel* denote a part of a whole. A *portion* was originally an alloted share, and so suggests a measured quantity: to devote a *portion* of one's time to study. A *fraction,* originally a very small part, now denotes a part taken away: the first *fraction* in the distillation of petroleum. Unlike the other synonyms, *fraction* has little or no suggestion of measurement. *Segment* and *sector* are influenced by their geometric meanings. Thus *segment* is a piece marked out on something regarded as having one principal dimension; a *segment* of a rod, a *segment* of the population. A *sector* is two-dimensional; it describes an area, region, etc. A *section* is the part lying between two cuts; hence, any clearly demarcated part: a *section* of a book. *Division* and *subdivision* stress even more strongly than *section* the dividing of a whole into parts, and are preferred when the dividing is abstract or conceptual: the *subdivisions* of the phylum *Mollusea. Parcel* was originally an integral part of a whole, not separable from it; this sense has been preserved in legal usage: a *parcel* of land. Compare PIECE. See DESTINY.

por·tion·er (pôr′shən·ər, pōr′-) *n.* One who divides in shares or holds a share or shares.

Port Jackson (jak′sən) An inlet on the southern shore of New South Wales, Australia, forming the harbor of Sydney.

Port·land (pôrt′lənd, pōrt′-) **1.** A port city in NW Oregon, on the Willamette River; pop. 382,619. **2.** A port city in SW Maine, on Casco Bay; pop. 65,116.

Portland cement See under CEMENT.

Port Lou·is (lōō′is, lōō′ē) The capital of Mauritius, a port on the SW coast; pop. 137,650 (est. 1968).

port·ly (pôrt′lē, pōrt′-) *adj.* **·li·er, ·li·est** **1.** Somewhat corpulent; stout. **2.** Having a stately appearance and carriage; impressive. [< PORT[5] + -LY] — **port′li·ness** *n.*

port·man·teau (pôrt·man′tō, pōrt-) *n. pl.* **·teaus** or **·teaux** (-tōz) *Chiefly Brit.* **1.** A large, leather suitcase hinged at the back to form two distinct compartments. **2.** Formerly, a case for carrying clothes, etc., on horseback. [< MF < *porter* to carry + *manteau* coat < L *mantellum*]

portmanteau word *Ling.* A blend.

Port Mores·by (môrz′bē, mōrz′-) A port town on the SE coast of New Guinea; administrative center of the Territory of Papua and New Guinea; pop. 56,206 (1966).

Pôr·to (pôr′tōō) The Portuguese name for OPORTO.

Pôr·to A·le·gre (pôr′tōō ä·le′grə) The capital of Río Grande do Sul, southern Brazil, a port in the eastern part of the State; pop. 932,800 (est. 1968, with suburbs).

Por·to Bel·lo (pôr′tō bel′ō) A port town on the Caribbean coast of Panama; pop. 626 (1970). Also **Por·to·be·lo** (pôr′-tō·bā′lō).

port of call A port where vessels put in for supplies, repairs, discharge or taking on of cargo, etc.

port of entry *Law* A place, whether on the coast or inland, designated as a point at which persons or merchandise may enter or pass out of a country under the supervision of customs and other authorities: also called *port.* Abbr. *P.O.E.*

Port-of-Spain (pôrt′əv·spān′, pōrt′-) The capital of Trinidad and Tobago, a port on NW Trinidad; pop. 100,000 (est. 1968). Also **Port of Spain.**

Por·to-No·vo (pôr′tō·nō′vō) The capital of Dahomey, a port in the SE part; pop. 74,000 (est. 1967).

Por·to Ri·co (pôr′tō rē′kō) The former official name for PUERTO RICO.

por·trait (pôr′trit, pōr′-, -trāt) *n.* **1.** A likeness of a person, especially of the face, produced, usually from life, by an artist or photographer. **2.** A vivid word description, especially of a person. [< MF, orig. pp. of *portraire* < OF *pourtraire.* See PORTRAY.]

por·trait·ist (pôr′trā·tist, pōr′-) *n.* One who makes portraits; a portrait painter or photographer.

por·trai·ture (pôr′tri·chər, pōr′-) *n.* **1.** The art or practice of making portraits. **2.** A portrait. **3.** Portraits collectively. [< OF < *pourtrait,* pp. of *pourtraire.* See PORTRAY.]

por·tray (pôr·trā′, pōr-) *v.t.* **1.** To represent by drawing, painting, etc. **2.** To describe or depict in words. **3.** To represent, as in a play; act. [< OF *pourtraire* to design <

Med.L *protrahere* < L, to draw forth < *pro-* forward + *trahere* to draw] **— por·tray'a·ble** *adj.* **— por·tray'er** *n.*
por·tray·al (pôr·trā'əl, pōr-) *n.* **1.** The act or process of portraying. **2.** A picture or description.
por·tress (pôr'tris, pōr'-) *n.* A woman porter or door-keeper. Also **por·ter·ess** (pôr'tris, -tər·is, pōr'-).
Port-Roy·al (pôr'roi'əl, pōrt'-; *Fr.* pôr·rwá·yál') A Cistercian abbey SW of Paris, France; noted as a Jansenist center in the 17th century; suppressed, 1709. Also **Port-Royal-des-Champs** (-dä·shän').
Port Royal **1.** A town and naval station in Jamaica, The West Indies; destroyed by earthquake, 1692. **2.** The former name for ANNAPOLIS ROYAL.
Port Sa·id (sä·ēd') A port city in NE Egypt, at the Mediterranean end of the Suez Canal; pop. 283,400 (1966).
Ports·mouth (pôrts'məth, pōrts'-) **1.** A county borough and port in SE Hampshire, England; site of the chief British naval station; pop. 214,800 (1969). **2.** A port city and naval station in SE New Hampshire; site of the signing of the **Treaty of Portsmouth**, ending the Russo-Japanese war, Sept. 5, 1905; pop. 25,717. **3.** A port city in SE Virginia, site of a U.S. naval base; pop. 110,963. **4.** A city in southern Ohio, on the Ohio River; pop. 27,633.
Por·tu·gal (pôr'chə·gəl, pōr'-; *Pg.* pôr'tŏŏ·gäl') A Republic on the western Iberian Peninsula, and including the Azores and Madeira islands; 35,419 sq. mi.; pop. 9,600,000 (est. 1970). Capital Lisbon: ancient *Lusitania*.
Por·tu·guese (pôr'chə·gēz', -gēs', pōr'-) *adj.* Pertaining to Portugal, its inhabitants, or their language. **— n. 1.** A native or inhabitant of Portugal. **2.** The people of Portugal collectively: with *the*. **3.** The Romance language of Portugal and Brazil. Abbr. *Pg., Port.*
Portuguese East Africa A former name for MOZAMBIQUE.
Portuguese Guin·ea (gin'ē) A Portuguese Overseas Province on the coast of western Africa; 13,948 sq. mi.; pop. 530,000 (est. 1969); capital, Bissau.
Portuguese India A former Portuguese Overseas Province on the west coast of India, comprising Gôa, Damâo, Diu, and their dependencies.
Portuguese man-of-war Any of several large marine organisms (genus *Physalia*), having long, stinging tentacles hanging down from a bladderlike float.
Portuguese Timor See under TIMOR.
Portuguese West Africa See ANGOLA.
por·tu·lac·a (pôr'chə·lak'ə, pōr'-) *n.* Any plant of a genus (*Portulaca*) of low, fleshy herbs of the purslane family, with flowers of many colors and a globular pod. [< L, purslane]
pos. **1.** Positive. **2.** Possessive.
po·sa·da (pō·sä'thä) *n. Spanish* An inn.
pose¹ (pōz) *n.* **1.** The position of the whole or part of the body, especially such a position assumed for or represented by an artist or photographer. **2.** A mental attitude adopted for effect. **— Syn.** See ATTITUDE. **— v.** posed, pos·ing *v.i.* **1.** To assume or hold an attitude or position, as for a portrait. **2.** To affect mental attitudes. **3.** To represent oneself: to *pose* as an expert. **— v.t. 4.** To cause to assume an attitude or position, as an artist's model. **5.** To state or propound; put forward as a question, etc. [< OF < *poser* to put down, rest, place; fusion of LL *pausare* to place < L, to pause < *pausa* pause and *pos-*, stem of L *ponere* to put]
pose² (pōz) *v.t.* posed, pos·ing **1.** To puzzle or confuse by asking a difficult question. **2.** *Obs.* To question closely. [< obs. *appose*, var. of OPPOSE]
Po·sei·don (pō·sī'dən) In Greek mythology, brother of Zeus and husband of Amphitrite, god of the sea and of horses: identified with the Roman *Neptune*. **— Po'sei·do'ni·an** (-dō'nē·ən) *adj.*
Po·sen (pō'zən) The German name for POZNAŃ.
pos·er¹ (pō'zər) *n.* One who poses. [< POSE¹, v.]
pos·er² (pō'zər) *n.* A question that baffles. [< POSE²]
po·seur (pō·zœr') *n.* One who affects a particular attitude to make an impression on others. [< F < *poser* to pose]
posh (posh) *adj. Chiefly Brit. Informal* Smart, stylish, and exclusive; first-class. [? Acronym of *p(ort) o(ut), s(tarboard) h(ome)*; with ref. to preferred accommodations on ships from England to India and back]
pos·it (poz'it) *v.t.* **1.** To put in position; place. **2.** To lay down or assume as a fact or basis of argument; postulate. [< L *positus*, pp. of *ponere* to place]
po·si·tion (pə·zish'ən) *n.* **1.** The manner in which a thing is placed. **2.** Disposition of the body or of parts of the body: a sitting *position*. **3.** The locality or place occupied by a person or thing. **4.** *Med.* The placement or arrangement of the body of a patient in order to facilitate therapeutic, surgical, or obstetrical procedures. **5.** The proper or appropriate place: in *position*. **6.** State or situation in relation to other conditions: to be in a false *position*. **7.** The act of positing a principle or proposition; also, the proposition or principle posited. **8.** An attitude or point of view; stand. **9.** Relative social standing; rank; status; also, high social standing. **10.** Employment; job. **11.** *Music* **a** The arrangement and

spacing of tones of a chord, as in voice parts. **b** The location of the left hand on the fingerboard of a stringed instrument. **c** Any of the various locations of the slide on a trombone. **12.** In sports, the assignment of an area covered by a particular player. **13.** In Greek and Latin prosody, the situation causing a prolonged utterance: In "texunt" the vowels are long by *position*. **— to be in a position to** To have the means or opportunity to. **— v.t. 1.** To place in a particular or appropriate position. **2.** *Rare* To locate. [< OF < L *positio, -onis* < *ponere* to place] **— po·si'tion·al** *adj.* **— Syn.** (noun) **1.** See PLACE. **2.** See ATTITUDE. **10.** office, post, situation, place, berth, billet.
positional variant *Ling.* Allophone.
position light A navigation light (which see).
pos·i·tive (poz'ə·tiv) *adj.* **1.** That is or may be directly affirmed; real; actual. **2.** Expressing, containing, or characterized by affirmation: a *positive* attitude. **3.** Inherent in a thing by and of itself, regardless of its relations to other things. **4.** Openly and plainly expressed; explicit: a *positive* denial. **5.** Imperative. **6.** Not admitting of doubt or denial: incontestable: *positive* proof. **7.** Noting one of two opposite directions, qualities, properties, etc., which is taken as primary, or as indicating increase or progression. **8.** *Law* Dependent on authority, agreement, or convention: *positive* law. **9.** *Math.* Greater than zero; plus: said of quantities and usually denoted by the sign (+). **10.** *Med.* Denoting the presence of a specific condition or organism: a *positive* Wasserman reaction. **11.** *Photog.* Having the lights and darks in their original relation, as in a print made from a negative. **12.** *Biol.* Noting the response of an organism toward a stimulus: a *positive* tropism. **13.** *Philos.* Pertaining to positivism (def. 2). **14.** *Electr.* Having the kind of electricity exhibited by a glass object when rubbed with silk; characterized by a deficiency of electrons on a charged body. **15.** *Chem.* Basic. **16.** *Mech.* Operated by or communicating power through intermediate parts that are fixed and under exact control. **17.** *Gram.* Denoting the simple, uncompared degree of the adjective or adverb. **18.** *Stat.* Designating a correlation in which the values of two variables tend to increase or decrease together: also called *direct*. **— n. 1.** That which is positive or capable of being directly or certainly affirmed. **2.** *Philos.* In positivism, that which is cognizable by the senses. **3.** *Math.* A positive symbol or quantity. **4.** *Electr.* A positive pole, plate, terminal, etc. **5.** *Photog.* A positive picture or print. **6.** *Gram.* The positive degree of an adjective or adverb; also, a word in this degree. [< OF, fem. of *positif* < L *positivus* < *ponere* to place] **— pos'i·tive·ly** *adv.* **— pos'i·tive·ness** *n.*
positive angle *Geom.* An angle measured counterclockwise from the reference line.
positive rays *Physics* Canal rays (which see).
pos·i·tiv·ism (poz'ə·tiv·iz'əm) *n.* **1.** A way of thinking that regards nothing as ascertained or ascertainable beyond the facts of physical science or of sense. **2.** *Philos.* A system of philosophy elaborated by Auguste Comte, holding that man can have no knowledge of anything but actual phenomena and facts and their interrelations, rejecting all speculation concerning ultimate origins or causes. **3.** Certitude, or the claim of certitude, in knowledge. [< F *positivisme*] **— pos'i·tiv·ist** *n.* **— pos'i·tiv·is'tic** *adj.*
pos·i·tron (poz'ə·tron) *n. Physics* An antiparticle corresponding to an electron. [< POSI(TIVE) + (ELEC)TRON]
pos·i·tron·i·um (poz'ə·trō'nē·əm) *n. Physics* An unstable, shortlived subatomic system consisting of a positron and an electron closely bound together. [< POSITRON + -IUM]
po·sol·o·gy (pō·sol'ə·jē) *n.* The branch of medicine that treats of the dosages of drugs. [< F *posologie* < Gk. *posos* how much + *-logie* -logy] **— pos·o·log·ic** (pos'ə·loj'ik) or **·i·cal** *adj.*
poss. **1.** Possession; possessive. **2.** Possible; possibly.
pos·se (pos'ē) *n.* **1.** A posse comitatus (which see). **2.** A force of men; squad. **3.** *Law* Possibility: chiefly in the phrase in posse. [< Med.L, armed force < L, to be able]
pos·se com·i·ta·tus (pos'ē kom'ə·tā'təs) The body of men that a sheriff or other peace officer calls or may call to his assistance in the discharge of his official duty, as to quell a riot or make an arrest. [< Med.L, power of the county < *posse* power + *comitatus* county]
pos·sess (pə·zes') *v.t.* **1.** To have as property; own. **2.** To have as a quality, attribute. etc.: to *possess* a conscience. **3.** To enter and exert control over; dominate: often used passively: The idea *possessed* him. **4.** To maintain control over (oneself, one's mind, etc.): *Possess* yourself in patience. **5.** To put in possession, as of property, news, etc.: with *of*. **6.** To have knowledge of; gain mastery of, as a language. **7.** To imbue or impress, as with wonder or an idea: with *with*. **8.** To have sexual intercourse with. **9.** *Obs.* To seize: gain. **— Syn.** See HAVE. [< F < L *possessus*, pp. of *possidere* to possess < *potis* master + *sedere* to sit (as)] **— pos·ses'sor** *n.*
pos·sessed (pə·zest') *adj.* **1.** Having; owning: *possessed* of a ready tongue. **2.** Calm; cool: to be *possessed* in time of

danger. 3. Controlled by or as if by evil spirits; beyond self-control; frenzied. — **like all possessed** *U.S. Informal* As if driven by the devil; frenziedly.

pos·ses·sion (pə·zesh′ən) *n.* 1. The act or fact of possessing. 2. The state of being possessed. 3. That which is possessed or owned. 4. *pl.* Property; wealth. 5. The state of being possessed by, or as by, evil spirits. 6. Self-possession.

pos·ses·sive (pə·zes′iv) *adj.* 1. Of or pertaining to possession or ownership. 2. Having a strong desire for complete emotional domination of another person. 3. *Gram.* Designating a case of the noun or pronoun that denotes possession, origin, or the like. In English, this is formed in nouns by adding 's to the singular and plural or irregular plurals: *John's* book; *men's* souls; the *boss's* office; and a simple apostrophe to the regular plural and sometimes to singulars and proper names ending in a sibilant: *boys'* shoes; *Dickens'* (or *Dickens's*) writings; *James'* (or *James's*) brother. See also -'s¹. Pronouns in the possessive case have special forms, as *my, mine, his, her, hers, its, our, ours, your, yours, their, theirs, whose*. By some grammarians possessive nouns and pronouns are called **possessive adjectives.** — *n. Gram.* 1. The possessive case. 2. A possessive form or construction. Abbr. *pos., poss.*

pos·ses·sive·ness (pə·zes′iv·nis) *n.* 1. Strong or excessive concern with one's own possessions. 2. A strong desire for emotional domination of another person.

pos·ses·so·ry (pə·zes′ər·ē) *adj.* 1. Pertaining to or having possession. 2. *Law* Proceeding from or depending upon possession. [< LL *possessorius*]

pos·set (pos′it) *n.* A drink of hot milk curdled with wine or ale, sweetened and spiced. [ME *poshote, possot*]

pos·si·bil·i·ty (pos′ə·bil′ə·tē) *n. pl.* **·ties** 1. The fact or state of being possible. 2. That which is possible. [< OF *possibilite* < L *possibilitas* < *possibilis*. See POSSIBLE.]

pos·si·ble (pos′ə·bəl) *adj.* 1. Capable of happening or proving true: not contrary to fact, natural laws, or experience: It is *possible* to die young. 2. Capable of being done or of coming about; feasible: Improvement is always *possible.* 3. That may or may not happen; uncertain but not unlikely: A storm is *possible* tonight. Abbr. *poss.* — **Syn.** See PROBABLE. [< OF < L *possibilis* < *posse* to be able < *potis* able + *esse* to be] — **pos′si·bly** *adv.*

pos·sum (pos′əm) *n.* 1. *Informal* An opossum. 2. *Austral.* A phalanger. — **to play possum** To feign death, illness, etc.; dissemble. [< OPOSSUM]

pos·sum·haw (pos′əm·hô′) *n.* The bearberry (def. 2). [< POSSUM + HAW²]

post¹ (pōst) *n.* An upright piece of timber or other material; as: **a** A support for a sign. **b** A bearing or framing member in a building. **c** An indicator of the starting or finishing point of a racecourse, etc. — *v.t.* 1. To put up (a poster, etc.) in some public place. 2. To fasten posters upon; placard. 3. To announce by or as by a poster: to *post* a reward. 4. To denounce publicly: to *post* one as a coward. 5. To publish the name of on a list. 6. To publish the name of (a ship) as lost or overdue. [OE < L *postis* door post]

post² (pōst) *n.* 1. A position or employment, especially a public office. 2. *Mil.* **a** A place occupied by a detachment of troops. **b** The buildings and grounds of such a place. 3. An assigned beat, position, or station, as of a sentry, policeman, etc. 4. A trading post or settlement. 5. *U.S.* A local unit of a veterans' organization. 6. *Brit.* One of the two bugle calls known respectively as **first post** and **last post,** the latter of which corresponds to *taps* in the army. — *v.t.* 1. To assign to a particular post or position; station, as a sentry. 2. Formerly, to appoint to a military or naval command. [< MF *poste* post, station < Ital. *posto* < LL *postum,* contraction of L *positum.* pp. neut. of *ponere* to place]

post³ (pōst) *n.* 1. *Chiefly Brit.* A single delivery of mail to a home, office, etc.; also, the mail itself. 2. *Chiefly Brit.* An established, usually government, system, for transporting the mails; also, a local post office. 3. *Brit.* A mailbox. 4. A rider or courier who carries mail over a fixed route. 5. Any of the stations furnishing relays of men and horses on such a route. — *v.t.* 1. *Chiefly Brit.* To place in a mailbox or post office, mail. 2. To inform: He *posted* us on the latest news. 3. In bookkeeping: **a** To transfer (items or accounts) to the ledger. **b** To make the proper entries in (a ledger). — *v.i.* 4. To travel with post horses. 5. To travel with speed; hasten. 6. In horseback riding, to rise from the saddle in rhythm with a horse's gait when trotting. — *adv.* 1. By post horses. 2. Speedily; rapidly. [< MF *poste* relay of horses < Ital. *posta,* orig., a station < LL, contraction of L *posita,* pp. fem. of *ponere* to place]

post- *prefix* 1. After in time or order; following: *postdate, postwar.* 2. Chiefly in scientific terms, after in position; behind: *postorbital.* [< L *post* behind, after]

Post (pōst), **Emily,** 1873–1960, *née* Price, U.S. columnist and writer on social etiquette.

post·age (pōs′tij) *n.* 1. The charge levied on mail matter. 2. The act of going by post.

postage meter A machine that facilitates the preparation of large amounts of outgoing mail by printing the amount of postage on each piece. Also **postal meter.**

postage stamp A small, printed label issued and sold by a

government to be affixed to letters, parcels, etc., in payment of postage.

pos·tal (pōs′təl) *adj.* Pertaining to the mails or to mail service. — *n.* A postal card.

postal card A card, issued officially, for carrying a written or printed message through the mails under government stamp. Compare POST CARD. Abbr. *p.c.*

post·ax·i·al (pōst·ak′sē·əl) *adj. Anat. & Zool.* Pertaining to or situated behind an axis, as the fibula of the leg.

post·bel·lum (pōst′bel′əm) *adj.* Coming or occurring after a war, especially after the Civil War. [< L *post* after + *bellum* war]

post·box (pōst′boks′) *n.* A mailbox (def. 1).

post card 1. A postal card (which see). 2. An unofficial card of any regulation size, usually having a picture on the front side, transmissible through the mails on prepayment of the same postage as for a postal card.

post chaise A closed carriage used for traveling and drawn by post horses.

post·com·mun·ion (pōst′kə·myōōn′yən) *n. Often cap.* In the Roman Catholic or Anglican Mass, a prayer that comes after the distribution of the Eucharist.

post·date (pōst′dāt′) *v.t.* **·dat·ed, ·dat·ing** 1. To assign or fix a date later than the actual date to (a check, document, etc.). 2. To follow in time.

post·di·lu·vi·an (pōst′di·lōō′vē·ən) *adj.* Existing or happening after the Flood. — *n.* A person, plant, or animal living after the Flood. [< POST- + L *diluvium* deluge]

pos·teen (pos·tēn′) *n.* An Afghan outer garment made of sheepskin with the fleece left on the outside: also spelled *postin.* [< Persian *pōstīn* of leather < *pōst* skin]

post·er¹ (pōs′tər) *n.* 1. A placard or bill used for advertising, public information, etc., to be posted on a wall or other surface. 2. A billposter (which see). [< POST¹]

post·er² (pōs′tər) *n.* 1. One who travels post. 2. A post horse. [< POST³, v.]

poste res·tante (pōst res·tänt′, *Fr.* pôst res·tänt′) 1. A direction written on mail that is to be held until called for. 2. *Chiefly Brit.* A department in a post office having charge of mail matter to be called for. [< F, remaining post]

pos·te·ri·or (pos·tir′ē·ər) *adj.* 1. Situated behind or toward the hinder part. 2. Coming after another in a series. 3. Subsequent in time; later. 4. *Anat.* **a** In animals, pertaining to the caudal end of the body. **b** In man, pertaining to the dorsal side of the body. 5. *Bot.* Situated or growing on the side next to the parent axis: said of an axillary flower. — *n. Sometimes pl.* The buttocks. [< L, compar. of *posterus* coming after < *post* after, behind]

pos·te·ri·or·i·ty (pos·tir′ē·ôr′ə·tē, -or′ə-) *n.* The state of being posterior in position or point of time.

pos·te·ri·or·ly (pos·tir′ē·ər·lē) *adv.* 1. Subsequently. 2. Behind.

pos·ter·i·ty (pos·ter′ə·tē) *n.* 1. Future generations taken collectively. 2. All of one's descendants. [< OF *posterite* < L *posteritas* < *posterus.* See POSTERIOR.]

pos·tern (pōs′tərn, pos′-) *n.* A small back gate or door, especially in a fortification or castle. — *adj.* Situated at the back or side. [< OF *posterne, posterle* < LL *posterula,* dim. of *postera* back door, gate < L *posterus.* See POSTERIOR.]

post exchange *Mil.* An establishment for the sale of merchandise and services to military personnel. Abbr. *PX*

post·ex·il·i·an (pōst′eg·zil′ē·ən) *adj.* Pertaining to the period of Jewish history following the Babylonian captivity (after 597 B.C.). Also **post′ex·il′ic.**

post·fix (*v.* pōst·fiks′; *n.* pōst′fiks′) *v.t.* To add at the end of a word, as a letter, syllable, etc. — *n. Rare* A suffix.

post·gla·cial (pōst′glā′shəl) *adj. Geol.* Existing or happening since the glacial or Pleistocene epoch.

post·grad·u·ate (pōst′graj′ōō·it, -āt) *adj.* Of or pertaining to studies pursued after the taking of an advanced degree, especially in the fields of medicine, dentistry, etc. — *n.* One who pursues such studies.

post·haste (pōst′hāst′) *Archaic adj.* Done with speed; instant. — *n.* Great haste or speed, like that of the post. — *adv.* With utmost speed; hurriedly.

post horse A horse kept at a post house for postriders or for hire to travelers: also called *poster.*

post house A house where post horses were kept for relay; also, formerly, a post office.

post·hu·mous (pos′chōō·məs) *adj.* 1. Denoting a child born after the father's death. 2. Published after the author's death, as a book. 3. Arising or continuing after one's death: a *posthumous* reputation. [< LL *posthumus* < *posthumus* latest, last, superl. of *posterus*; infl. by L *humus* earth. See POSTERIOR.] — **post′hu·mous·ly** *adv.*

pos·tiche (pos·tēsh′) *adj.* 1. Added after the completion of the work, as an inappropriate architectural ornament. 2. Spurious; artificial. — *n.* 1. Pretense; sham. 2. An imitation; artificial substitute. Also **pos·tique′** (-tēk′). [< F < Ital. *posticcio* < L *posticus*]

pos·ti·cous (pos·tī′kəs) *adj. Bot.* Hinder; posterior. [< L *posticus* < *post* after]

pos·til·ion (pōs·til′yən, pos-) *n.* One who guides a team drawing a carriage or other heavy vehicle by riding the near horse when one pair is used or the near horse of the leaders when two or more pairs are used. Also **pos·til′lion.** [< MF *postillon* < Ital. *postiglione* < *posta* post, station]

post·im·pres·sion·ism (pōst′im-presh′ən-iz′əm) *n.* The theories and practice of a group of expressionist painters of the late 19th century, originating in France and including Cézanne, Van Gogh, Gauguin, and others, who rejected the objective naturalism of the Impressionists and emphasized the subjective point of view of the artist. **— post′im·pres′·sion·ist** *n. & adj.* **— post′im·pres′sion·is′tic** *adj.*

pos·tin (pos-tēn′, -tin′) See POSTEEN.

post·li·min·i·um (pōst′li·min′ē·əm) *n.* In international law, a right whereby persons or things seized in war by the enemy are restored to their former status when returned to their own country. Also **post·lim·i·ny** (pōst·lim′ə·nē). [< L < *post* behind + *limen, liminis* threshold]

post·lude (pōst′lōōd) *n. Music* 1. An organ voluntary concluding a church service. 2. Loosely, a coda. [< POST- + (PRE)LUDE]

post·man (pōst′mən) *n. pl.* **·men** (-mən) A mailman.

post·mark (pōst′märk′) *n.* Any official mark stamped on mail to cancel stamps and to give the date and place of sending or receiving. **— v.t.** To stamp with a postmark.

post·mas·ter (pōst′mas′tər, -mäs′-) *n.* 1. An official having charge of a post office. Abbr. *PM, P.M.* 2. One who provides horses for posting. **— post′mis′tress** (-mis′tris) *n.fem.*

postmaster general *pl.* **postmasters general** The executive head of the postal service of a government. Abbr. *P.M.G.*

post·me·rid·i·an (pōst′mə·rid′ē·ən) *adj.* Pertaining to or occurring in the afternoon. Also **post′me·rid′i·o·nal.** [< L *postmeridianus* < *post* after + *meridies* noon]

post me·rid·i·em (pōst mə·rid′ē·əm) After midday. Abbr. *p.m., P.M.* [< L]

post·mil·len·ni·al (pōst′mi·len′ē·əl) *adj.* Happening or existing in the period following the millennium. Also **post′·mil·len′ni·an.**

post·mil·len·ni·al·ism (pōst′mi·len′ē·əl·iz′əm) *n. Theol.* The tenet that Christ's second coming will follow the millennium: opposed to *premillennialism.* Also **post·mil·le·nar·i·an·ism** (pōst·mil′ə·nâr′ē·ən·iz′əm). **— post′mil·len′ni·al·ist** *n.*

post·mor·tem (pōst·môr′təm) *adj.* 1. Happening or performed after death. 2. Of or pertaining to a post-mortem examination. **— n.** 1. A post-mortem examination. 2. *Informal* An analysis or discussion of an accomplished fact. [< L *post mortem* after death]

post-mortem examination *Med.* A thorough examination of a human body after death: also called *autopsy, necropsy.* Abbr. *p.m., P.M.*

post·na·tal (pōst·nāt′l) *adj.* Occurring after birth.

post·nup·tial (pōst·nup′chəl) *adj.* Happening or occurring after marriage; made after marriage.

post-o·bit (pōst-ō′bit) *adj.* 1. Made or done after death. 2. Taking effect only after death: also **post′-o·bit′u·ar′y** (ō·bich′ōō·er′ē). **— n.** A bond given by a borrower to repay money after the death of a designated person from whose estate he expects to inherit: also **post-obit bond.** [< L *post obitum* after decease]

post office 1. The branch of the civil service of a government charged with carrying and delivering the mails. 2. Any local office that receives, transmits, sorts, and delivers mail, sells stamps, etc. 3. Any town or place having a post office. Abbr. (for defs. 1, 2) *p.o., P.O.*

post·op·er·a·tive (pōst·op′ər·ā·tiv, -ə·rā′-) *adj. Surg.* Occurring or done after a surgical operation: *postoperative* care.

post·or·bi·tal (pōst·ôr′bi·təl) *adj. Anat.* Situated behind the orbit or socket of the eye. **— n.** In some reptiles, a postorbital bone or scale.

post·paid (pōst′pād′) *adj.* Having postage prepaid. Abbr. *p.p., P.P., ppd.*

post·par·tum (pōst′pär′təm) *adj. Med.* After childbirth. [< POST- + L *partus* childbirth < *parere* to bear]

post·pone (pōst·pōn′) *v.t.* **·poned, ·pon·ing** 1. To put off to a future time; defer; delay. 2. To subordinate. [< L *postponere* < *post-* after + *ponere* to put] **— post·pon′a·ble** *adj.* **— post·pone′ment** *n.* **— post·pon′er** *n.*

— Syn. 1. *Postpone, adjourn,* and *defer* agree in meaning to put off or delay. To *postpone* is strictly to put aside until something else occurs, or is done, known, obtained, etc. However, it is often used without this limitation, and suggests the intention to perform the *postponed* act at some future time: to *postpone* a club meeting. To *adjourn* is literally to put off to another day, but often suggests suspension of present activity without the necessary implication of later resumption: to *adjourn* a court session. The implication of later performance is weakest of all in *defer,* which means to refrain from dealing with, and frequently suggests reluctance to take any action. Compare PROCRASTINATE.

post·po·si·tion (pōst′pə·zish′ən) *n.* 1. The act of placing after, or the state of being so placed. 2. *Gram.* A word placed after another word, as an enclitic; especially, a suffixed element that functions as a preposition, as *-de* in Greek

oikade homeward. [< LL *postpositio, -onis* < *postponere.* See POSTPONE.]

post·pos·i·tive (pōst·poz′ə·tiv) *Gram. adj.* Appended to something; suffixed; enclitic. **— n.** An appended word; a postposition. [< L *postpositus.* See POSTPOSITION.]

post·pran·di·al (pōst·pran′dē·əl) *adj.* After-dinner. [< POST- + L *prandium* lunch + -AL[1]]

post·rid·er (pōst′rī′dər) *n.* One who journeys by relays of horses, especially to carry mail.

post road A road built for the transportation of mail, formerly having post houses at specified distances.

post·script (pōst′skript′) *n.* 1. A sentence or paragraph added to a letter after the writer's signature. 2. A supplemental addition to a written or printed document. Abbr. *p.s., P.S.* [< L *postscriptum,* pp. of *postscribere* to write after]

post time The starting time of a horse or dog race.

pos·tu·lant (pos′chə·lant) *n.* 1. One who presents a request. 2. *Eccl.* An applicant for admission into a religious order. Compare NOVICE. [< L *postulans, -antis,* ppr. of *postulare,* freq. of *poscere* to ask] **— pos′tu·lant·ship** *n.*

pos·tu·late (*v.* pos′chə·lāt; *n.* pos′chə·lit) *v.t.* **·lat·ed, ·lat·ing** 1. To claim, demand, or require. 2. To set forth as self-evident or already known. 3. To assume the truth or reality of; take for granted. **— n.** 1. A position claimed or basis of argument laid down as well known or too plain to require proof; a self-evident truth. 2. A prerequisite: Peace is a *postulate* of prosperity. 3. A fundamental principle. [< L *postulatus,* pp. of *postulare.* See POSTULANT.] **— pos′·tu·la′tion** *n.* **— pos′tu·la′tor** *n.*

pos·ture (pos′chər) *n.* 1. The position or carriage of the body or of parts of the body: a sitting *posture.* 2. Such a position assumed during posing for an artist, etc. 3. The visible disposition of the various parts of a material thing. 4. A mental attitude; frame of mind: a *posture* of Olympian indifference. 5. Situation or condition, especially when considered as indicative of attitude or policy: to criticize the national defense *posture.* **— Syn.** See ATTITUDE. *v.* **·tured, ·tur·ing. — v.t.** 1. To place (a person) in a specific position or pose. **— v.i.** 2. To assume or adopt a bodily pose or a character not natural to one; attitudinize. [< F < L *positura* position < *ponere* to place] **— pos′tur·al** *adj.* **— pos′tur·er, pos′tur·ist** *n.*

pos·tur·ize (pos′chə·rīz) *v.t. & v.i.* **·ized, ·iz·ing** To posture; pose.

post·war (pōst′wôr′) *adj.* After a war.

po·sy (pō′zē) *n. pl.* **·sies** 1. A single flower or a bouquet. 2. *Archaic* A brief inscription or motto, especially one inscribed on a ring or other trinket. [Contraction of POESY]

pot (pot) *n.* 1. A round, fairly deep vessel of metal, earthenware, or glass, generally having a handle, used for cooking and other domestic purposes. 2. Such a vessel and its contents: a *pot* of stew. 3. The amount a pot will hold; potful. 4. A large drinking cup, as a tankard; also, drink or liquor. 5. In cardplaying, the amount of stakes wagered or played for, especially in poker; kitty; pool. 6. *Informal* A large sum of money. 7. In fishing, a basketlike trap for catching lobsters, eels, etc. 8. *Brit.* A chimney pot (which see). 9. *Informal* A pot shot. 10. *Slang* Marijuana. 11. *Informal* A potentiometer. 12. A chamber pot (which see). 13. *Slang* A potbelly. **— to go to pot** To deteriorate. **— v. pot·ted, pot·ting** *v.t.* 1. To put into a pot or pots: to *pot* plants. 2. To preserve (meat, etc.) in pots or jars. 3. To cook in a pot. 4. To shoot (game) for food rather than for sport. 5. To shoot or kill with a pot shot. 6. *Informal* To secure, capture, or win; bag. **— v.i.** 7. To take a pot shot; shoot. [OE *pott*]

pot. Potential.

po·ta·ble (pō′tə·bəl) *adj.* Suitable for drinking: said of water. **— n.** *Often pl.* Something drinkable; a drink. [< MF < LL *potabilis* < *potare* to drink]

po·tage (pō·täzh′) *n. French* Any thick soup.

pot·ash (pot′ash′) *n.* 1. Potassium hydroxide. 2. Crude potassium carbonate: called *pearl ash* when purified. 3. Oxide of potassium, K_2O. [< Du. *potasch,* lit., potash]

potash feldspar Orthoclase.

po·tas·si·um (pə·tas′ē·əm) *n.* A bluish white, highly reactive, metallic element (symbol K), never found free in nature, but yielding many compounds of great practical value in industry, medicine, etc.: also called *kalium.* See ELEMENT. [< NL < *potass* potash] **— po·tas′sic** *adj.*

potassium bitartrate *Chem.* A white crystalline compound, $HKC_4H_4O_6$, having an acid taste; an ingredient in baking powder: also called *cream of tartar.*

potassium bromide *Chem.* A crystalline compound, KBr, used in photography, and in medicine as a sedative.

potassium carbonate *Chem.* A white, strongly alkaline compound, K_2CO_3, prepared from wood ashes and from potassium sulfate, used in the manufacture of soap and glass.

potassium cyanide *Chem.* An intensely poisonous, white, crystalline compound, KCN, used in photography, in electrometallurgy, and as a reagent.

---

potassium dichromate *Chem.* A reddish crystalline salt, $K_2Cr_2O_7$, used in the arts as an oxidizing agent and in making sensitive coatings for photographs.

potassium hydroxide *Chem.* A whitish deliquescent solid, KOH, yielding a strong caustic solution: used in salt-making, electroplating, as a chemical reagent, etc. Also called *caustic potash, potash.*

potassium nitrate *Chem.* A crystalline white salt, KNO_3, produced by nitrification in soil, used in gunpowder, fertilizers, and in medicine. Also called *niter, saltpeter.*

potassium permanganate *Chem.* A purple red crystalline salt, $KMnO_4$, used as an oxidizing agent in antiseptics and deodorizing substances.

potassium sulfate *Chem.* A salt, K_2SO_4, used in the manufacture of glass and alum, and in the crude state as a component of fertilizer.

po·ta·tion (pō·tā′shən) *n.* **1.** The act of drinking; also, a drink, especially of an alcoholic beverage. **2.** A drinking bout. [< OF < L *potatio, -onis* < *potare* to drink]

po·ta·to (pə·tā′tō) *n. pl.* **·toes 1.** One of the edible tubers of a plant (*Solanum tuberosum*) of the nightshade family: also called *Irish potato, white potato.* **2.** The plant. **3.** The sweet potato (which see). [< Sp. *patata*, orig. sweet potato < Arawakan (Taino) *batata*]

potato beetle 1. A beetle (*Leptinotarsa decemlineata*), that has long black stripes on the wing covers, feeds on the leaves of the potato, tomato, and similar plants, and is among the world's greatest agricultural pests: also called *Colorado beetle.* Also **potato bug.** For illustration see INSECTS (injurious). **2.** Any of several beetles feeding on the foliage of the potato, especially *Lema trilineata*, with three long black stripes on the wing covers.

potato chip *U.S.* A very thin slice of potato fried crisp and salted.

potato rot A disease of the potato caused by a mildew (genus *Phytophthora*).

po·ta·to·ry (pō′tə·tôr′ē, -tō′rē) *adj.* **1.** Pertaining to or given to drinking. **2.** *Rare* Potable. [< L *potatorius* < *potator* drinker < *potare* to drink]

pot-au-feu (pô·tō·fœ′) *n. French* A variety of beef stew; literally, pot on the fire.

Pot·a·wot·o·mi (pot′ə·wot′ə·mē) *n.* One of a tribe of North American Indians of Algonquian stock, formerly inhabiting the western shores of Lake Michigan.

pot·bel·ly (pot′bel′ē) *n. pl.* **·lies 1.** A protuberant belly. **2.** A person having a potbelly. **3.** An upright wood- or coal-burning stove with bulging sides: also **potbelly stove, potbellied stove.** — **pot′bel′lied** *adj.*

pot·boil·er (pot′boi′lər) *n. Informal* A literary or artistic work produced simply to obtain the means of subsistence.

pot bottle A bell-shaped bottle holding 17 ounces, intermediate between the half bottle and the full bottle.

pot·boy (pot′boi′) *n. Chiefly Brit.* In a public house, a boy or young man who cleans the pots, serves customers, etc.

pot cheese Cottage cheese (which see).

po·teen (pō·tēn′) *n.* In Ireland, illicitly manufactured whiskey: also spelled *potheen:* also called *potheen.* [< Irish *poitín*, dim. of *poite* pot]

Po·tem·kin (pō·tem′kin, *Russ.* pô·tyôm′kin), **Prince Grigori Alexandrovich,** 1739–91, Russian general; favorite of Catherine II.

po·ten·cy (pōt′n·sē) *n. pl.* **·cies 1.** Mental, moral, or physical power. **2.** Authority. **3.** Strength and effectiveness, as of a drug, liquor, etc. **4.** One who or that which is powerful. **5.** Latent power; potentiality. **6.** In the male, sexual competency. Also **po′tence.** [< L *potentia* < *potens, -entis.* See POTENT.]

po·tent (pōt′nt) *adj.* **1.** Physically powerful. **2.** Having great authority. **3.** Capable of influencing greatly; very convincing: a *potent* argument. **4.** Of a drug, liquor, etc., strong in its physical and chemical effects. **5.** Sexually competent: said of the male. [< L *potens, -entis*, ppr. of *posse* to be able < *potis* able + *esse* to be] — **po′tent·ly** *adv.* — **po′tent·ness** *n.*

po·ten·tate (pōt′n·tāt) *n.* One having great power or sway; a sovereign. [< LL *potentatus*]

po·ten·tial (pə·ten′chəl) *adj.* **1.** Possible but not actual. **2.** Having capacity for existence, but not yet existing; latent. **3.** *Gram.* Indicating possibility or power. See POTENTIAL MOOD. **4.** Having force or power. — *n.* **1.** A possible development; potentiality. **2.** *Gram.* The potential mood. **3.** *Electr.* The charge on a body as referred to another charged body or to a given standard, as the earth, considered as having zero potential. Abbr. *pot.* [< LL *potentialis*] — **po·ten′tial·ly** *adv.*

po·ten·ti·al·i·ty (pə·ten′chē·al′ə·tē) *n. pl.* **·ties 1.** Inherent capacity for development or accomplishment. **2.** That which is potential or capable of being realized.

potential mood *Gram.* The verb phrase made up by means of the auxiliaries *may, can, could, must, should,* or *would*, with an infinitive, and expressing power, liberty, or possibility: I could say it; it may be.

po·ten·til·la (pō′tən·til′ə) *n.* Any of a large genus (*Potentilla*) of herbs or, rarely, shrubs of the rose family, including the cinquefoils. [< Med.L < L *potens, -entis,* ppr. of *posse* to be able + *-illa,* dim. suffix]

po·ten·ti·om·e·ter (pə·ten′chē·om′ə·tər) *n. Electr.* **1.** A device similar to a rheostat but having three terminals, used to vary the ratio of two resistances, and sometimes having an incorporated on-off switch. **2.** A device for measuring voltage. Also, *Informal,* pot.

poth·e·car·y (poth′ə·ker′ē) *n. pl.* **·car·ies** *Scot. & Brit. Dial.* Apothecary.

po·theen (pō·thēn′) *n.* Poteen.

poth·er (poth′ər) *n.* Excitement mingled with confusion; bustle; fuss. — *v.t. & v.i.* To worry; bother. [Origin uncertain]

pot·herb (pot′ûrb′, -hûrb′) *n.* Any plant or herb, especially greens, when cooked or used to flavor boiled foods.

pot·hole (pot′hōl′) *n.* **1.** A pot-shaped cavity in a rock, as that worn by loose stones whirling in an eddy. **2.** A deep hole, as in a road. **3.** *Canadian* A slough; also, a large prairie dugout.

pothole trout *Canadian* A trout stocked in a pothole.

pot·hook (pot′hook′) *n.* **1.** A curved or hooked piece of iron for lifting or hanging pots. **2.** A curved mark or elementary stroke used in teaching penmanship; also, a scrawl, or popularly, any curved stroke in stenography.

pot·house (pot′hous′) *Brit. n.* An alehouse; saloon. — *adj.* Of or pertaining to a pothouse; vulgar: *pothouse* politics.

pot·hunt·er (pot′hun′tər) *n.* **1.** One who kills game for food rather than for sport: usually a contemptuous term. **2.** One who engages in a competition simply to win the prizes offered. — **pot′hunt′ing** *adj. & n.*

po·tiche (pō·tēsh′) *n.* A vase having an elongated round body, a cylindrical neck, and a detached cover. [< F]

po·tion (pō′shən) *n.* A draft, as a large dose of liquid medicine: often used of a magic or poisonous draft. [< OF < L *potio, -onis* < *potare* to drink. Doublet of POISON.]

Pot·i·phar (pot′i·fär, -fər) An officer of Pharaoh, who bought Joseph as a slave. *Gen.* xxxix 1.

pot·latch (pot′lach) *n. U.S. & Canadian* **1.** Among American Indians of the northern Pacific coast: **a** A gift. **b** *Often cap.* A winter festival. **2.** A ceremonial feast in which gifts are exchanged and property destroyed in a competitive show of wealth. **3.** *Informal* A party. Also **pot′lach, pot′lache.** [< Chinook *patshatl* gift]

pot liquor The liquid left in a pot after cooking greens and meat (usually pork or bacon) together.

pot·luck (pot′luk′) *n.* Whatever food may have been prepared for the family and not especially for guests; also, any events, consequences, etc., that may be in store: usually in the phrase **to take potluck.**

pot marigold A calendula (*Calendula officinalis*), whose dried florets are sometimes used as a seasoning in cooking.

Po·to·mac River (pə·tō′mək) A river forming the boundaries between Maryland, West Virginia, and Virginia, and flowing 287 miles to Chesapeake Bay. — **Army of the Potomac** The chief Union army in the Civil War, commanded at first by General George McClellan.

Po·to·sí (pō′tō·sē′) A city in south central Bolivia; elevation 13,255 ft.; pop. 70,000 (est. 1966).

pot·pie (pot′pī′) *n.* **1.** A pie, baked in a deep dish, containing meat and vegetables and having only a top crust. **2.** Meat stewed with dumplings.

pot·pour·ri (pot·poor′ē, *Fr.* pô·pōo·rē′) *n.* **1.** A mixture of dried flower petals kept in a jar and used to perfume a room. **2.** A medley of musical airs. **3.** A literary production composed of miscellaneous parts. **4.** Any mixture of incongruous or disparate elements. **5.** A stew of meat and potatoes. [< F, lit., rotten pot. See OLLA PODRIDA.]

pot roast Meat braised and cooked in a covered pot until tender, often with vegetables.

Pots·dam (pots′dam, *Ger.* pôts′däm) A city in East Germany; scene of a United Nations conference, July–August, 1945; pop. 110,670 (est. 1968).

pot·sherd (pot′shûrd) *n.* A bit of broken earthenware. Also **pot′shard** (-shärd). [ME < POT + SHARD]

pot shot 1. A shot fired to kill, without regard to the rules of sports. **2.** A shot fired, as from ambush, at a person or animal within easy range. **3.** A random shot. [Orig. a pothunter's shot]

pot·stone (pot′stōn′) *n.* A variety of steatite or soapstone.

pot·sy (pot′sē) *n.* A variation of hopscotch as played in the eastern U.S. Also **pot′sie.** [Origin unknown]

pot·tage (pot′ij) *n.* **1.** A thick broth or stew of vegetables with or without meat. **2.** *Archaic* Porridge. [< OF *potage* < *pot* pot]

pot·ted (pot′id) *adj.* **1.** Placed or kept in a pot. **2.** Cooked or preserved in a pot. **3.** *Slang* Drunk.

pot·teen (pot·tēn′) *n.* See POTEEN.

pot·ter¹ (pot′ər) *v.t. & v.i. Chiefly Brit.* To putter. [Freq. of dial. *pote*, var. of POKE¹] — **pot′ter·er** *n.*

pot·ter² (pot′ər) *n.* One who makes earthenware or porcelain vessels.

Pot·ter (pot′ər), **Paul,** 1625–54, Dutch painter.

potter's field A piece of ground appropriated as a burial ground for the destitute and the unknown. *Matt.* xxvii 7.

potter's wheel A horizontal rotating disk used by potters for holding and manipulating prepared clay.

potter wasp A digger wasp (genus *Eumenes*) that constructs vaselike cells of mud as a nest, especially the **North American potter wasp** (*E. fraterna*). For illustration see INSECTS (beneficial).

pot·ter·y (pot′ər·ē) *n. pl.* **·ter·ies** **1.** Ware molded from clay and hardened by intense heat. **2.** The art or technique of making earthenware or porcelain. **3.** A place where pottery is made. [< OF *poterie* < *potier* *potter* < Med.L *potaria* < *pot* pot]

POTTER'S WHEEL
a Molding clay. *b* Rotating wheel. *c* Shaft. *d* Treadle.

pot·tle (pot′l) *n.* **1.** A drinking vessel, pot, or tankard holding about half a gallon. **2.** An old liquid measure of half a gallon. **3.** *Chiefly Brit.* A small vessel or basket for holding fruit. **4.** Liquor. [< OF *potel*, dim. of *pot* pot]

pot·to (pot′ō) *n. pl.* **·tos** A small, slow-moving lemur (genus *Perodicticus*) of tropical Africa, having a rudimentary tail and large hands and feet. [< West African]

Potts·town (pots′toun) A borough in SE Pennsylvania, on the Schuylkill River; pop. 25,355.

Pott's disease (pots) *Pathol.* Caries or osteitis of the vertebrae, usually of tubercular origin and characterized by curvature of the spine. [after Percival *Pott*, 1714–88, English surgeon, who first described it]

pot·ty¹ (pot′ē) *adj. Brit. Informal* **1.** Insignificant. **2.** Slightly drunk; also, a little silly. [Prob. < POT, in connection with drunkenness]

pot·ty² (pot′ē) *n. pl.* **·ties** **1.** A receptacle, as of plastic, that fits under a child's toilet seat. **2.** A child's toilet seat, sometimes part of a small chair called a **pot·ty-chair** (pot′ē-châr′).

pot·val·iant (pot′val′yənt) *adj.* Courageous from drink. — **pot′-val′ian·cy**, **pot′-val′ian·try**, **pot′-val′or** (-val′ər) *n.*

pot-wal·lo·per (pot′wol′ə-pər, pot′wol′-) *n. Brit.* Formerly, by the requirements of some boroughs before 1832, a parliamentary voter who was a householder (not a tenant), having his own fireplace as a qualification for suffrage. [< POT + WALLOP (def. 5)]

pouch (pouch) *n.* **1.** A small bag, sack, or container. **2.** A small purse. **3.** A receptacle of leather, plastic, etc., for carrying loose pipe tobacco. **4.** *Zool.* **a** A saclike part for temporarily containing food, as in gophers and pelicans. **b** A marsupium. **5.** *Bot.* Any baglike cavity, as the silique of the mustard plant. **6.** A leather receptacle for carrying small-arms ammunition. **7.** A mailbag. **8.** *Scot.* A pocket. — *v.t.* **1.** To put in or as in a pouch. **2.** To fashion or arrange in pouchlike form. **3.** To swallow. — *v.i.* **4.** To take on a pouchlike shape; form a pouchlike cavity. [< OF *poche* < Gmc.] — **pouch′y** *adj.*

pouched (poucht) *adj.* **1.** Having pouches or sacs. **2.** Having pouched cheeks, as gophers and kangaroo rats.

pouf (poof) *n.* **1.** A hair arrangement in high rolled puffs, popular in the 18th century. **2.** Any puffed part of a dress. **3.** An upholstered ottoman. [< F, a puff]

Pough·keep·sie (pə-kip′sē) A city in SE New York, on the Hudson River; pop. 32,029.

pou·lard (poo-lärd′) *n.* **1.** A pullet that has been spayed in order to improve the quality of the flesh for eating. Compare CAPON. **2.** A fattened pullet. [< F *poularde* < *poule* hen]

Pou·lenc (poo-länk′) **Francis**, 1899–1963, French composer.

poult (pōlt) *n.* A young turkey, chicken, etc. [ME *pulte* < MF *polet*, var. of *poulet*, dim. of *poule* hen]

poul·ter·er (pōl′tər·ər) *n.* A dealer in poultry.

poul·tice (pōl′tis) *n.* A moist, mealy mass of flour, mustard, etc., applied hot to a sore or inflamed part of the body. — *v.t.* **·ticed**, **·tic·ing** To cover or treat with a poultice. [< L *pultes*, pl. of *puls* porridge]

poul·try (pōl′trē) *n.* Domestic fowls, as hens, ducks, etc. [< OF *pouleterie* < *poulet*, dim. of *poule* hen]

pounce¹ (pouns) *v.i.* **pounced**, **pounc·ing** To swoop or spring in or as in seizing prey: with *on*, *upon*, or *at*. — *n.* **1.** A talon or claw of a bird of prey. **2.** The act of pouncing; a sudden leap, swoop, or spring. — **pounc′er** *n.*

pounce² (pouns) *v.t.* To emboss (metalwork) with a design hammered on the reverse side. [< OF *poinçonner* < *poinçon* puncheon < ME *punchon* < MF *poinçon*. See PUNCHEON.]

pounce³ (pouns) *n.* **1.** A powder, as of cuttlebone, formerly used to absorb excess of ink, as on a manuscript. **2.** A finely pulverized substance used in transferring designs. — *v.t.* To sprinkle, smooth, or rub with pounce. [< F *ponce* < L *pumex*, *pumicis* pumice]

pounce box A box with a perforated lid formerly used for dusting powder or sand on freshly written paper.

poun·cet box (poun′sit) A scent box with perforated lid.

pound¹ (pound) *n.* **1.** A unit of weight varying in different countries and at different periods. **2.** In Great Britain and the United States, either of two legally fixed units, the avoirdupois pound and the troy pound. *Abbr. lb.* See table inside back cover. **3.** The standard monetary unit of the United Kingdom, equivalent to 100 new pence: also **pound sterling**. *Symbol £. Abbr. l., L.* Compare SOVEREIGN. **4.** A similar monetary unit of the Republic of Ireland, equivalent to 100 new pence. *Symbol £.* **5.** A standard monetary unit of various other governments, including Cyprus, Falkland Islands, Gibraltar, Lebanon, Malta, Sudan, and Syria; especially: **a** The Egyptian pound, equivalent to 100 piasters. *Symbol £E.* **b** The Israeli pound, equivalent to 100 agorot. *Symbol £I.* **c** The Turkish pound, equivalent to 100 piasters: also called *lira. Symbol £T.* **6.** A former monetary unit of Scotland, equivalent originally to the English pound, and later to 20 English pence: more fully **pound Scots**. [OE *pund* < L *pondo* in weight, ablative of *pondus* weight]

pound² (pound) *n.* **1.** A place, enclosed by authority, in which stray or trespassing cattle and distrained cattle or goods are left until redeemed; also, a similar enclosure for stray dogs. **2.** A place of confinement for lawbreakers. **3.** A trap for wild animals. **4.** An area or place in which to catch or stow fish; a pound net. — *v.t.* To confine in or as in a pound; impound; restrain. [OE *pund-*. Akin to *pyndan* to enclose.]

pound³ (pound) *v.t.* **1.** To strike heavily and repeatedly, as with a hammer; beat. **2.** To reduce to a pulp or powder by beating; pulverize. **3.** To force or impress by drill; make sink in, as a fact or idea. **4.** To walk tediously or lumberingly: to *pound* the pavements. — *v.i.* **5.** To strike heavy, repeated blows: with *on*, *at*, etc. **6.** To move or proceed heavily or vigorously. **7.** To rise and fall heavily, as a ship in rough water. **8.** To throb heavily or resoundingly. — *Syn.* See BEAT. — *n.* **1.** A heavy blow; thump; thud. **2.** The act of pounding. [OE *punian* to bruise]

Pound (pound) **Sir Dudley**, 1877–1943, English admiral in World War II. — **Ezra (Loomis)**, 1885–1972, U.S. poet. — **Louise**, 1872–1958, U.S. linguist.

pound·age¹ (poun′dij) *n.* **1.** A rate on the pound sterling. **2.** Formerly, in England, a subsidy to the crown on each pound of merchandise exported or imported.

pound·age² (poun′dij) *n.* **1.** The charges for the redemption of impounded cattle. **2.** The act of impounding cattle.

pound·al (poun′dəl) *n. Physics* A unit of force that, acting on a mass of one pound, changes its velocity by one foot per second per second.

pound·cake (pound′kāk′) *n.* A rich cake having ingredients equal in weight, as a pound each of flour, butter, and sugar, with eggs added.

pound·er¹ (poun′dər) *n.* One who or that which pounds.

pound·er² (poun′dər) *n.* **1.** Anything weighing a pound. **2.** One who or that which weighs, has, etc., a given number of pounds: used in combination: an eight-*pounder*.

pound-fool·ish (pound′foo′lish) *adj.* Extravagant with large sums, but watching small sums closely.

pound-keep·er (pound′kē′pər) *n.* One who has charge of a pound². Also **pound′mas′ter** (-mas′tər, -mäs′-).

pound net A weir or arrangement of nets supported upon stakes to form a trap for fish.

pour (pôr, pōr) *v.t.* **1.** To cause to flow in a continuous stream, as water, sand, etc. **2.** To send forth, emit, or utter profusely or continuously. — *v.i.* **3.** To flow in a continuous stream; gush. **4.** To rain heavily. **5.** To move in great numbers; swarm. **6.** To serve as host or hostess at a social tea. — *n.* A pouring, flow, or downfall. [ME *pouren* ? < MF *purer* to filter, ult. < L *purus* pure] — **pour′er** *n.*

pour·boire (pōōr-bwàr′) *n. French* A gratuitous gift of money, as a tip. [< F, lit., in order to drink]

pour·par·ler (pōōr-pàr-lā′) *n. French* A preliminary or informal conference or consultation.

pour·point (pōōr′point′, *Fr.* pōōr-pwàn′) *n.* A quilted cloth doublet worn by men in the 14th and 15th centuries. [< F, prob. < *pourpoindre* to perforate < L *pungere* to puncture]

pousse-ca·fé (pōōs-kà-fā′) *n. French* A drink, commonly a mixture of cordials and brandy in successive layers, served after the coffee at dinner.

pous·sette (pōō-set′) *n.* A dance figure in which a couple or couples swing round and round while holding hands. — *v.i.* **·set·ted**, **·set·ting** To perform a poussette. [< F, dim. of *pousse* a push]

Pous·sin (pōō-saň′) **Nicolas**, 1594–1665, French painter.

pou sto (pōō′ stō′, pou′) A place to stand on; a foundation for operations. [< Gk. *pou stō* where I may stand; from the alleged saying of Archimedes: "Give me a place where I may stand and I will move the earth."]

pout¹ (pout) *v.i.* **1.** To thrust out the lips, especially in ill humor. **2.** To look sullen. **3.** To swell out; protrude. — *v.t.* **4.** To thrust out (the lips, etc.). **5.** To utter with a

pout. — *n.* **1.** A pushing out of the lips as in pouting. **2.** A fit of ill humor. [ME *pouten*, prob. < ON]

pout² (pout) *n.* **1.** Any of various fresh-water catfishes having a pouting appearance. **2.** The eelpout (which see). [OE (*æle*)*pūte* eelpout]

pout·er (pou'tər) *n.* **1.** One who or that which pouts. **2.** A breed of pigeon: also spelled *powter*.

pov·er·ty (pov'ər·tē) *n.* **1.** The condition or quality of being poor or without sufficient subsistence. **2.** Scantiness of supply: a *poverty* of imagination. **3.** Absence or scarcity of necessary qualities, elements, etc.: *poverty* of soil. [< OF *poverte* < L *paupertas* < *pauper* poor]
— **Syn. 1.** *Poverty, privation, indigence, penury, want, destitution, pauperism, beggary,* and *mendicancy* denote the state of being very poor. *Poverty* is a condition below that of comfortable living. *Privation* describes a painful lack of what is useful or desirable, while *indigence* is the lack of ordinary means of subsistence, and *penury* refers to a *poverty* that cramps or hampers. Extreme *poverty,* the lack of the very necessities of life, is *want* or *destitution,* and *pauperism* is *destitution* that throws a person on public charity for support. *Beggary* and *mendicancy* are *poverty* that appeals indiscriminately for public charity. — **Ant.** comfort, affluence, riches.

pov·er·ty-strick·en (pov'ər·tē-strik'ən) *adj.* Suffering from poverty; destitute.

pow (pou) *n. Scot.* The poll; head.

POW or **P.O.W.** Prisoner of War.

pow·der (pou'dər) *n.* **1.** A finely ground or pulverized mass of loose particles formed from a solid substance in the dry state. **2.** Any of various substances prepared in this form, as a cosmetic, medicine, or gunpowder. — **to take a powder** *U.S. Slang* To run away; depart. — *v.t.* **1.** To reduce to powder; pulverize. **2.** To sprinkle or cover with or as with powder. **3.** To sprinkle with small objects or ornaments. — *v.i.* **4.** To be reduced to powder. **5.** To use powder as a cosmetic. [< OF *poudre* < L *pulvis, pulveris* dust. Akin to POLLEN.] — **pow'der·er** *n.*

powder blue A soft medium blue.

pow·dered sugar (pou'dərd) Granulated sugar that has been ground into a powder less fine than confectioner's sugar.

powder flask A metallic or other flask for gunpowder.

powder horn The hollow horn of an ox or cow, formerly fitted with a cover and used for holding gunpowder.

powder metallurgy The science and technique of manufacturing objects from finely powdered metals and alloys.

powder puff A soft pad used to apply powder to the skin.

pow·der room A woman's toilet and washroom in a public building.

pow·der·y (pou'dər·ē) *adj.* **1.** Consisting of or like fine powder or dust. **2.** Mealy or dusty. **3.** Friable.

Pow·ell (pou'əl), **Lewis Franklin, Jr.,** born 1907, U.S. jurist; associate justice of the Supreme Court 1971–.

pow·er (pou'ər) *n.* **1.** Ability to act; capability. **2.** Potential capacity. **3.** Strength or force actually put forth. **4.** The right, ability, or capacity to exercise control; legal authority, capacity, or competency. See POWER OF APPOINTMENT. **5.** Any agent that exercises power, as in control or dominion; a military or naval force; an important and influential sovereign nation. **6.** Great or telling force or effect. **7.** *Dial.* A great number or quantity. **8.** *Often pl.* A mental or physical faculty. **9.** Any form of energy available for doing work; especially, electrical energy. **10.** *Physics* The time rate at which energy is transferred, or converted into work. **11.** *Math.* **a** The product of a number multiplied by itself a given number of times: The third *power* of 2 is 8. **b** An exponent. **12.** *Optics* Magnifying capacity, as of a lens. **13.** *pl. Theol.* The sixth of the nine orders of angels. See ANGEL. — *v.t.* To provide with means of propulsion. Abbr. *pr.* [< OF *poeir* < LL *potere* < L *posse* to be able]
— **Syn.** (noun) **1.** efficacy. Compare ABILITY. **2.** faculty, function. **3.** energy, might, puissance. **4.** jurisdiction, dominion, sway. **6.** impact.

power boat A motorboat (which see).

power brakes An automobile braking system in which a power source, such as compressed air, facilitates the braking of the vehicle.

power dive *Aeron.* A dive accelerated by the engine.

power drill A motor-operated drill.

pow·er·ful (pou'ər·fəl) *adj.* **1.** Possessing great force; strong. **2.** Having great intensity or energy. **3.** Exercising great authority, or manifesting high qualities. **4.** Convincing. — *adv. Dial. & Informal* Very. — **pow'er·ful·ly** *adv.*
— **Syn.** (adj.) **1.** forceful, forcible. **2.** potent, effective. Compare EFFICIENT. **3.** commanding, influential, puissant. **4.** impressive, cogent. — **Ant.** powerless, weak.

pow·er·house (pou'ər·hous') *n.* **1.** *Electr.* A station where electricity is generated. **2.** *Slang* A powerful person or thing.

pow·er·less (pou'ər·lis) *adj.* **1.** Destitute of power; unable to accomplish an effect; impotent. **2.** Without authority. — **pow'er·less·ly** *adv.* — **pow'er·less·ness** *n.*

power loading *Aeron.* The gross weight of an aircraft divided by its rated engine horsepower.

power loom A loom operated by power-driven machinery.

power of appointment *Law* Authority conferred, as by

power of attorney, deed, or will, to appoint or designate a person or persons to make disposition of an estate or interest in the property of another.

power of attorney *Law* **1.** The authority or power to act conferred upon an agent. **2.** The instrument or document by which that power or authority is conferred or guaranteed. Abbr. *P/A, P.A.*

power pack A compact assemblage of electrical units to provide requisite steady power.

power plant Any source of power, together with its housing, installations and accessory equipment.

power play In hockey, an offensive combination and tactic designed to score while the opposing team is shorthanded.

power politics The use or threatened use of superior force to exact international concessions.

power steering An automobile steering system in which a power source facilitates the turning of the steering wheel.

power tool A machine or tool, as a drill, saw, planer, etc., driven by a motor, usually electric.

Pow·ha·tan (pou/hə·tan') 1550?–1618, Algonquian Indian chief in Virginia; father of Pocahontas.

pow·ter (pou'tər) See POUTER (def. 2).

pow·wow (pou'wou') *U.S. n.* **1.** *Informal* Any meeting or conference. **2.** A North American Indian medicine man or priest. **3.** The ceremony of a medicine man to cure the sick or effect success in hunting, war, etc. **4.** A conference with or of American Indians. — *v.i.* To hold a powwow. [< Algonquian (Massachusetts) *pauwau,* lit., he dreams]

Pow·ys (pō'is) A county in east central Wales; 1,960 sq. mi.; pop. 100,200 (1976); county seat, Llandrindod Wells.

Pow·ys (pō'is), **John Cowper,** 1872–1963, and his brothers **Llewelyn,** 1884–1939, and **Theodore Francis,** 1875–1953, English authors.

pox (poks) *n.* **1.** Any disease characterized by eruptions of a purulent nature: *chickenpox.* **2.** Syphilis. [Var. of *pocks,* pl. of POCK]

Po·yang (pō'yäng') A lake in northern Kiangsi province, China; 1,070–3,600 sq. mi., varying with seasons.

poy·ou (poi'ōō) *n.* The six-banded armadillo (*Dasypus sexcinctus*) of Argentina and Brazil. [< Guarani]

Poz·nań (pōz'näny') A city in western Poland; pop. 457,000 (est. 1969); German Posen.

Po·zsony (pō'zhôny') The Hungarian name for BRATISLAVA.

poz·zuo·la·na (pot'swə·lä'nə, *Ital.* pōt'tswô·lä'nä) *n.* A volcanic ash used in hydraulic cement, also made artificially. Also **poz'zo·la·na** (pot'sə-). [< Ital., after *Pozzuoli,* Italy, where first collected] — **poz'zuo·lan'ic** *adj.*

pp. **1.** Pages. **2.** Past participle. **3.** *Music* Pianissimo: also **pp** **4.** Privately printed.

p.p. **1.** Parcel post. **2.** Past participle. **3.** Postpaid.

P.P. **1.** Parcel post. **2.** Parish Priest. **3.** Postpaid.

P.P.C. or **p.p.c.** To take leave (F *pour prendre congé*).

ppd. **1.** Postpaid. **2.** Prepaid.

pph. Pamphlet.

ppl. Participial.

p.p.m. or **ppm.** or **ppm** Parts per million.

ppr. or **p.pr.** Present participle.

P.P.S. or **p.p.s.** Additional postscript (L *post postscriptum*).

p.q. Previous question.

P.Q. Province of Quebec.

pr. **1.** Pair(s). **2.** Paper. **3.** Power. **4.** Present. **5.** Price. **6.** Priest. **7.** Prince. **8.** Printing. **9.** Pronoun.

Pr *Chem.* Praseodymium.

Pr. **1.** Prince. **2.** Provençal.

PR Public relations.

P.R. **1.** Proportional Representation. **2.** Puerto Rico.

praam (präm) See PRAM².

prac·ti·ca·ble (prak'ti·kə·bəl) *adj.* **1.** That can be put into practice; feasible. **2.** That can be used for an intended purpose; usable. [< F *praticable* < *pratiquer.* See PRACTICE.] — **prac'ti·ca·bil'i·ty, prac'ti·ca·ble·ness** *n.* — **prac'ti·ca·bly** *adv.*
— **Syn. 1, 2.** *Practicable* and *practical* overlap because the latter includes the former as one of its senses. Ideas, plans, contrivances, etc., are said to be *practicable* if they can be put into effect, or if they will serve their purposes. Persons are *practical* but never *practicable.* A man is *practical* by reason of his ability to execute a plan of action, or to deal easily and effectively with ordinary matters. An idea may also be *practical* because derived from experience rather than from theory. *Practicable* contrasts only with *unworkable; practical* contrasts as well with *theoretical, visionary, unreal, inexpert, clumsy,* etc.

prac·ti·cal (prak'ti·kəl) *adj.* **1.** Pertaining to or governed by actual use and experience or action, as contrasted with ideals and speculations. **2.** Trained by or derived from practice or experience. **3.** Having reference to useful ends to be attained; applicable to use. **4.** Manifested in practice. **5.** Being such to all intents and purposes; virtual. — **Syn.** See PRACTICABLE. [< obs. *practic* < MF *practique* < LL *practicus* < Gk. *praktikos* < *prassein* to do] — **prac'ti·cal'i·ty** (-kal'ə·tē), **prac'ti·cal·ness** *n.*

practical joke A joke involving action instead of wit or words; a prank or trick having a victim or victims.

prac·ti·cal·ly (prak′tik·lē) *adv.* **1.** In a practical manner. **2.** To all intents and purposes; in fact or effect; virtually.

practical nurse One who has some training and practical experience in caring for the sick, but who is not a graduate of a nursing school. Compare REGISTERED NURSE.

prac·tice (prak′tis) *v.* ·ticed, ·tic·ing *v.t.* **1.** To make use of habitually or often: to *practice* economy. **2.** To apply in action; make a practice of: *Practice* what you preach. **3.** To work at or pursue as a profession: to *practice* law. **4.** To do or perform repeatedly in order to acquire skill or training; rehearse. **5.** To instruct, as pupils, by repeated exercise or lessons. — *v.i.* **6.** To repeat or rehearse something in order to acquire skill or proficiency: to *practice* for a concert. **7.** To work at or pursue a profession: He *practiced* for twenty years. **8.** *Rare* To conspire; scheme. Also **prac′tise.** — *n.* **1.** Any customary action or proceeding regarded as individual; habit. **2.** An established custom or usage. **3.** The act or process of executing or accomplishing; doing or performance: distinguished from *theory.* **4.** The regular prosecution of a business pursuit requiring education; professional business. **5.** Frequent and repeated exercise in any matter. **6.** *pl.* Stratagems or schemes for bad purposes; tricks. **7.** A rule or method in arithmetic to facilitate multiplying quantities in different denominations. **8.** The rules by which legal proceedings are governed. Also *Brit.* **prac′tise.** [< MF *practiser* < *practiquer* < Med.L *practicare* < LL *practicus.* See PRACTICAL.] — **prac′tic·er** *n.*
— **Syn.** (noun) **1.** See HABIT. **5.** *Practice, exercise,* and *drill* are compared as they denote repeated action. *Practice* is the putting into action of what one has learned in theory, to gain skill and facility: gunnery *practice,* daily *practice* at the piano. *Exercise* is primarily physical action to gain strength and vigor; in extension, it becomes *practice* to maintain a facility already acquired. *Drill* is systematic and rigorous *practice* under a teacher or commander.

prac·ticed (prak′tist) *adj.* **1.** Expert by practice; experienced. **2.** Acquired by practice. Also **prac′tised.**

prac·ti·tion·er (prak·tish′ən·ər) *n.* **1.** One who practices an art or profession. **2.** A Christian Science healer. [< earlier *practician* < MF < *practiquer.* See PRACTICE.]

prae- See PRE-.

prae·di·al (prē′dē·əl) *adj.* Of, pertaining to, or attached to land. [< Med.L *praedialis* < L *praedium*]

prae·fect (prē′fekt) See PREFECT.

prae·mu·ni·re (prē·myoō·nī′rē) *n.* In English law: **a** A writ charging the offense of appealing to the jurisdiction of a foreign court, especially the papal court. **b** The offense so charged. **c** The statute of Richard II punishing this offense. [< Med.L *praemunire* (*facias*) (see that you) warn, alter. of L *praemonere* < *prae* before + *monere* to advise]

prae·no·men (prē·nō′mən) *n.* *pl.* ·nom·i·na (-nom′ə·nə) The first name of an ancient Roman, as *Publius* Vergilius Maro; also, any given name: also spelled *prenomen.* [< L]

prae·pos·i·tor (prē·poz′ə·tər) See PREPOSITOR.

prae·pos·tor (prē·pos′tər) *n. Brit.* A prepositor.

praeter- See PRETER-.

prae·tor (prē′tər) *n.* A city magistrate of ancient Rome, having charge of the administration of justice: also spelled *pretor.* [< L *praetor* < *praeire* to go before] — **prae·to·ri·al** (pri·tôr′ē·əl, -tō′rē-) *adj.* — **prae′tor·ship** *n.*

prae·to·ri·an (pri·tôr′ē·ən, -tō′rē-) *adj.* Of or pertaining to a praetor; praetorial. — *n.* A praetor or ex-praetor. Also spelled *pretorian.*

Prae·to·ri·an (pri·tôr′ē·ən, -tō′rē-) *adj.* Denoting the Praetorian Guard. — *n.* A soldier of the Praetorian Guard. Also spelled *Pretorian.*

Praetorian Guard **1.** The bodyguard of the Roman emperors, organized by Augustus and disbanded by Constantine I. **2.** A member of this bodyguard.

prag·mat·ic (prag·mat′ik) *adj.* **1.** Pertaining to the study of events with emphasis on cause and effect: the *pragmatic* method. **2.** *Philos.* Of or pertaining to pragmatism. **3.** Pragmatical. **4.** *Rare* Of or pertaining to the affairs of a community or state. [< L *pragmaticus* active or skilled in business < Gk. *pragmatikos* < *pragma, pragmatos* thing done < *prassein* to do]

prag·mat·i·cal (prag·mat′i·kəl) *adj. Rare* **1.** Officious or meddlesome; self-important; busy. **2.** Relating to everyday business; practical; commonplace.

prag·mat·i·cal·ly (prag·mat′i·kəl·ē) *adv.* In a pragmatic or pragmatical manner. — **prag·mat′i·cal·ness** *n.*

pragmatic sanction An imperial or royal edict or decree having the force of a fundamental law.

prag·ma·tism (prag′mə·tiz′əm) *n.* **1.** *Philos.* The doctrine that ideas have value only in terms of their practical consequences, and that results are the sole test of the validity or truth of one's beliefs. **2.** The quality or condition of being pragmatic. — **prag′ma·tist** *n.*

Prague (präg) The capital of Czechoslovakia, in central Bohemia, on the Vltava; pop. 1,031,870 (1967): *Czech* **Pra·ha** (prä′hä). *German* **Prag** (präkh).

pra·hu (prä·hoō′) *n.* A proa. [< Malay *prau*]

Prai·ri·al (pre·rē·äl′) *n.* The ninth month of the Republican calendar. See (Republican) CALENDAR. [< F < *prairie* meadow]

prai·rie (prâr′ē) *n.* *U.S. & Canadian* A tract of grassland; especially, the broad, grassy plain of central North America. — **Syn.** See PLAIN. [< F, large meadow < *pré* meadow < L *pratum*]

prairie chicken Either of two gallinaceous game birds (genus *Tympanuchus*) inhabiting the plains of western North America, the **greater prairie chicken** (*T. cupido*), and the **lesser prairie chicken** (*T. pallidicinctus*). Also **prairie hen.**

prairie dog A burrowing rodent (genus *Cynomys*) of the plains of North America; especially, *C. ludovicianus,* that lives in large communities and is very destructive to vegetation. Also **prairie squirrel.**

prairie oysters *U.S. & Canadian* The testicles of bull calves used as food.

Prairie Provinces Manitoba, Saskatchewan, and Alberta, western Canada.

prairie schooner *U.S.* A covered wagon used for travel by pioneers.

prairie state One of the States of the prairie regions of the Western and Middle Western United States.

Prairie State Nickname of ILLINOIS.

prairie wolf A coyote.

praise (prāz) *n.* **1.** An expression of approval or commendation. **2.** The glorifying and honoring of a god, ruler, hero, etc.; especially, worship of God expressed in song. **3.** *Archaic* The ground or reason for praise. — *v.t.* **praised,** **prais·ing** **1.** To express approval and commendation of; applaud; eulogize. **2.** To express adoration of; glorify, especially in song. [< OF *preisier* < LL *pretiare* to prize < L *pretium* price] — **prais′er** *n.*
— **Syn.** (verb) **1.** *Praise, laud, extol, eulogize, applaud, acclaim,* and *celebrate* mean to commend highly. *Praise* is the weakest word, and may refer to the mere speaking of compliments. To *laud* is to *praise* highly, possibly to excess. *Extol* stresses the intention to elevate or magnify a person or thing by praise; *eulogize* is to *extol* in a formal way, especially by a public speech. *Applaud* and *acclaim* point to a public show of approval, as by clapping the hands or shouting. *Celebrate* almost always implies the use of poetry, and refers to the singing of hymns or the writing of a poem in another's honor. — **Ant.** blame, decry. — (noun) **1.** approbation, encomium. Compare APPLAUSE, EULOGY.

praise·wor·thy (prāz′wûr′thē) *adj.* Worthy of praise. — **praise′wor·thi·ly** *adv.* — **praise′wor·thi·ness** *n.*

Pra·ja·dhi·pok (prä·jä′di·pôk), 1893–1941, king of Siam 1925–35; abdicated: reigned as **Ra·ma VII** (rä′mä).

Pra·krit (prä′krit) *n.* Any of several vernacular languages of ancient India, forming a link between Sanskrit and the modern Indic languages. [< Skt. *prakrtā* natural, lit., created before < *pra-* before + *kr* to make. Cf. SANSKRIT.]

pra·line (prä′lēn, prä′-) *n.* A confection made of pecans or other nuts browned in boiling sugar. [< F, after Marshal Duplessis-*Praslin*, 1598–1675, whose cook invented it]

prall·tril·ler (präl′tril·ər) *n. Music* An inverted mordent. See under MORDENT. [< G, lit., elastic trill]

pram¹ (pram) *n. Chiefly Brit. Informal* A baby carriage. [Short for PERAMBULATOR]

pram² (präm) *n. Naut.* A small rowboat having a blunt bow and a flat bottom: also spelled *praam.* [< Du. *praam*]

prance (prans, präns) *v.* **pranced, pranc·ing** *v.i.* **1.** To move proudly with high steps, as a spirited horse; spring from the hind legs; also, to ride a horse moving thus. **2.** To move in an arrogant or elated manner; swagger. **3.** To gambol; caper. — *v.t.* **4.** To cause to prance. — *n.* The act of prancing; a high step; caper. [ME *prauncen*; origin uncertain. ? Akin to dial. Dan. *pranse.*] — **pranc′er** *n.*

pran·di·al (pran′dē·əl) *adj.* Of or pertaining to a meal, especially dinner. [< L *prandium* breakfast or lunch]

prank¹ (prangk) *v.t.* **1.** To decorate gaudily; deck with showy ornaments. — *v.i.* **2.** To make an ostentatious show. [Prob. < MLG *prank* pomp]

prank² (prangk) *n.* A mischievous or frolicsome act; a trick. — *v.i.* To play pranks or tricks. [Origin uncertain; ? < PRANK¹] — **prank′ish** *adj.*

pra·se·o·dym·i·um (prā′zē·ō·dim′ē·əm, prā′sē-) *n.* A yellowish white metallic element (symbol Pr) of the lanthanide series, having olive-green salts. See ELEMENT. [< NL < Gk. *prasios* light green (< *prason* leek) + (DI)DYMIUM]

prate (prāt) *v.* **prat·ed, prat·ing** *v.i.* **1.** To talk idly and at length; chatter. — *v.t.* **2.** To utter idly or emptily. — *n.* Idle talk; prattle. [< MDu.-MLG *praten*] — **prat′er** *n.* — **prat′ing·ly** *adv.*

prat·fall (prat′fôl′) *n. U.S. Slang* A fall on the buttocks.

prat·in·cole (prat′ing·kōl, prā′tin-) *n.* Any of a genus (*Glareola*) of ternlike, Old World shore birds having long pointed wings and a deeply forked tail. [< L *pratum* meadow + *incola* inhabitant]

pra·tique (pra·tēk′, prat′ik; *Fr.* prȧ·tēk′) *n. Naut.* Permission granted to a ship to enter a port, load and unload, etc., after passing quarantine. [< F]

prat·tle (prat′l) *v.* **·tled, ·tling** *v.i.* **1.** To talk foolishly or like a child; prate. — *v.t.* **2.** To utter in a foolish or childish way. — **Syn.** See BABBLE. — *n.* **1.** Childish speech; babble. **2.** Idle or foolish talk. [Freq. of PRATE. Akin to MLG *pratelen.*] — **prat′tler** *n.*

prawn (prôn) *n.* Any of various shrimplike decapod crustaceans (genera *Pandalus, Palaemon, Peneus,* etc.) abundant in tropical and temperate waters, and used as food. — *v.i.* To fish for prawns. [ME *prane, prayne;* origin unknown]

PRAWN
(To 6 inches long)

prax·is (prak′sis) *n.* **1.** Practical, as distinguished from theoretical, application of rules. **2.** Accepted or habitual practice; custom. [< NL < Gk. < *prassein* to do]

Prax·it·e·les (prak·sit′ə·lēz) Fourth-century B.C. Greek sculptor.

pray (prā) *v.i.* **1.** To address prayers to a deity, idol, etc.; say prayers. **2.** To make earnest request or entreaty; beg. — *v.t.* **3.** To address by means of prayers; say prayers to. **4.** To ask (someone) earnestly; entreat. **5.** To ask for by prayers or entreaty. **6.** To cause to move by prayer: to *pray* a soul out of purgatory. [< OF *preier* < LL *precare* < L *precari* < *prex, precis* request, prayer] — **pray′er** *n.* — **Syn. 4.** beseech, implore. Compare ENTREAT.

prayer (prâr) *n.* **1.** A devout request or petition to a deity. **2.** The act of offering devout petitions, expressions of adoration, etc., especially to God. **3.** A set form of words used for a devout request, petition, etc. **4.** Spiritual communion with God, and awareness of his presence, as in praise, thanksgiving, confession, etc. **5.** *Often pl.* A religious service in which praying plays the most prominent part: evening *prayers.* **6.** Something prayed for. **7.** Any earnest request. **8.** *Law* In a bill of equity, the request that the court will grant the aid sought by the complainant; also the part of the bill containing this request. [< OF *preiere,* ult. < L *precarius* obtained by prayer < *precari.* See PRAY.]

prayer book **1.** A book of prayers for divine service. **2.** *Usually cap.* The Book of Common Prayer. *Abbr.* P.B.

prayer·ful (prâr′fəl) *adj.* Inclined or given to prayer; devotional. — **prayer′ful·ly** *adv.* — **prayer′ful·ness** *n.*

prayer wheel A wheel, cylinder, or vertical drum containing written prayers, used by the Buddhists of Tibet. Each revolution of the wheel represents one repetition of a prayer.

praying mantis The mantis (which see).

pre- *prefix* **1.** Before in time or order; prior to; preceding; as in:

preaccept	preattune	precondition
preaccomplish	preaver	preconditioned
preaccusation	preavowal	preconfiguration
preachieved	prebaptismal	preconfirm
preacknowledge	prebaptize	preconnection
preacquaint	prebasal	preconnubial
preacquaintance	prebasilar	preconsent
preacquire	preblooming	preconsideration
preact	preboding	preconsign
preaction	preboil	preconstitute
preadapt	prebranchial	preconstruct
preadaptation	pre-British	preconstruction
preaddress	prebronchial	preconsult
preadjust	prebuccal	preconsultation
preadjustment	precalculable	preconsume
preadmit	precalculate	precontract
preadmonish	precalculation	precontrive
preadmonition	precampaign	preconviction
preadopt	precancerous	precool
preadult	precast	precorrupt
preadulthood	pre-Celtic	precounsel
preadvertise	precensure	precreate
preadvertiser	precensus	precreation
preadvise	pre-Centennial	precultivation
preadviser	precerebellar	precultural
preaestival	precheck	pre-Darwinian
preaffirm	prechill	predawn
preaffirmation	pre-Christian	predecision
preallege	precirculate	prededication
preannounce	precited	prededuction
preannouncer	preclassical	predeliberation
preantiquity	precogitate	predemand
preappearance	precogitation	predescribe
preappoint	precognizable	predesign
preappointment	precognizant	predetect
preapproval	precollect	predeterminable
preaptitude	precollection	predevised
prearm	precompose	predinner
prearrange	precomputation	predirect
prearrangement	precompute	prediscipline
pre-Aryan	preconceal	prediscovery
preassigned	preconcealment	predusk
preassume	preconcert	preelect
preassumption	preconception	preelection
preassurance	preconclusion	preembodiment
preassure	precondemn	preembody
preattachment	precondemnation	preemploy

preenact	preinhabitation	preseason
preengage	preinstruct	preselect
preengagement	preinstruction	preset
preenlist	preintimation	preshadow
preenlistment	prekindergarten	preshape
pre-epic	premeasurement	preshow
preexamination	premorning	pre-shrink
preexamine	prenumber	prestamp
preexpose	pre-Paleozoic	presuccess
prefashion	preparticipation	presurmise
prefertile	preplan	pretaste
preform	prepublish	pre-Tertiary
prefrank	prepurchase	pretribal
prefranked	pre-Reformation	pretypify
prefurnish	pre-Renaissance	preunion
preglacial	prerequire	preunite
pregrowth	prerevolutionary	pre-Victorian
preheat	pre-Roman	prewarm
preheater	preromantic	prewarn
preinaugural	prescholastic	prewrap

2. Before in position; anterior: chiefly in scientific terms; as in:

preabdomen	precardiac	prerectal
preanal	precerebral	prerenal
preaortic	precostal	preretinal
preauricular	prepatellar	prevertebral

3. Preliminary to; preparing for; as in:

precollege	preengineering	prelexical
predoctorate	prelegal	premilitary

Also *prae-.* [< L *prae* before]

preach (prēch) *v.t.* **1.** To advocate or recommend urgently: to *preach* temperance. **2.** To proclaim or expound upon: to *preach* the gospel. **3.** To deliver (a sermon, etc.). — *v.i.* **4.** To deliver a sermon. **5.** To give advice, especially in an officious or moralizing manner. [< OF *prechier* < L *praedicare* to proclaim < *prae-* before + *dicare* to make known]

preach·er (prē′chər) *n.* **1.** *Informal* A clergyman, especially a Protestant minister or revivalist. **2.** One who preaches. [< OF *prechor*]

preach·i·fy (prē′chə·fī) *v.i.* **·fied, ·fy·ing** *Informal* To preach or discourse tediously. — **preach′i·fi·ca′tion** *n.*

preach·ment (prēch′mənt) *n.* A sermon or moral lecture, especially a tedious one.

preach·y (prē′chē) *adj.* **preach·i·er, preach·i·est** Given to preaching; sanctimonious.

pre·ad·am·ite (prē·ad′əm·īt) *adj.* **1.** Existing before Adam. **2.** Relating to the preadamites. Also **pre·a·dam·ic** (prē′ə·dam′ik), **pre·ad·am·it·ic** (-it′ik). — *n.* **1.** A preadamite person or thing. **2.** One who believes that there were men on earth before Adam.

pre·ag·o·nal (prē·ag′ə·nəl) *adj.* Immediately preceding the death agony. [< PRE- + AGON(Y) + -AL¹]

pre·am·ble (prē′am·bəl) *n.* **1.** An introductory statement or preface; especially, the introduction to a formal document, statute, etc., explaining its purpose. **2.** An introductory act, event, fact, etc.; a preliminary. [< OF *preamble* < Med. L *praeambulum,* orig. neut. of LL *praeambulus* walking before < *praeambulare* < L *prae-* before + *ambulare* to walk] — **pre·am′bu·lar·y** (-byə·ler′ē) *adj.*

pre·am·pli·fi·er (prē·am′plə·fī′ər) *n.* In a sound reproduction system, an auxiliary amplifier used to reinforce very weak signals before sending them into the main amplifier. Also **pre·amp** (prē′amp).

pre·ax·i·al (prē·ak′sē·əl) *adj. Anat.* Situated in front of the axis of a limb or body.

preb·end (preb′ənd) *n.* **1.** A stipend allotted from the revenues of a cathedral or conventual church to a clergyman. **2.** The land or tithe yielding the stipend; the tenure of which is a benefice. **3.** A prebendary. [< MF *prébende* < Med.L *praebenda,* lit., things to be furnished, neut. pl. of L *praebendus,* gerundive of *praebere* to supply < *prae-* before + *habere* to have] — **preb′en·dal** *adj.*

preb·en·dar·y (preb′ən·der′ē) *n. pl.* **·dar·ies 1.** A canon or clergyman who holds a prebend. **2.** In the Church of England, a canon who holds the honorary title of prebend without a stipend. Also called *prebend.*

Pre-Cam·bri·an (prē·kam′brē·ən) *adj. Geol.* Of or pertaining to all geological time and rock formations preceding the Cambrian: also *primary.* See table for GEOLOGY. — *n.* Pre-Cambrian rocks.

precanc. Precanceled.

pre·can·cel (prē·kan′səl) *v.t.* **·celed** or **·celled, ·cel·ing** or **·cel·ling** To cancel (stamps) before use on mail. — *n.* A precanceled stamp.

pre·car·i·ous (pri·kâr′ē·əs) *adj.* **1.** Subject to continued risk; uncertain. **2.** Subject or exposed to danger; hazardous. — **Syn.** See RISKY. **3.** Without foundation or basis; untrustworthy. **4.** *Archaic* Dependent upon the will of another. [< L *precarius.* See PRAYER.] — **pre·car′i·ous·ly** *adv.* — **pre·car′i·ous·ness** *n.*

prec·a·to·ry (prek′ə·tôr′ē, -tō′rē) *adj.* Expressing entreaty; supplicatory. Also **prec′a·tive.** [< LL *precatorius*]

pre·cau·tion (pri·kô′shən) *n.* **1.** A step or preparation taken to avoid a possible danger, evil, etc. **2.** Caution observed in preparation for a possible emergency. [<

précaution < LL *praecautio, -onis* < L *praecavere* < *prae-* before + *cavere* to take care]
— **Syn.** 2. vigilance, circumspection, care, concern.
pre·cau·tion·ar·y (pri·kô′shən·er′ē) *adj.* 1. Of or pertaining to precaution. 2. Expressing, advising, or using precaution. Also **pre·cau′tion·al.**
pre·cau·tious (pri·kô′shəs) *adj.* Exercising precaution. — **pre·cau′tious·ly** *adv.* — **pre·cau′tious·ness** *n.*
pre·cede (pri·sēd′) *v.* ·**ced·ed,** ·**ced·ing** *v.t.* 1. To go or be before in order, place, rank, time, etc. 2. To preface; introduce. — *v.i.* 3. To go or be before; take precedence. [< F < L *praecedere* < *prae-* before + *cedere* to go]
pre·ce·dence (pri·sēd′əns, pres′ə·dəns) *n.* 1. The act or right of preceding, or the state of being precedent; priority in place, time, or rank. 2. The ceremonial order observed by persons of different ranks on formal occasions. Also **pre·ce·den·cy** (pri·sēd′ən·sē, pres′ə·dən·sē).
— **Syn.** *Precedence, priority,* and *antecedence* mean the fact or right of going ahead of another. *Precedence* is chiefly used of matters of etiquette and protocol: the *precedence* in seating ambassadors at a table. *Priority* usually refers to relation in time: this telegram has *priority,* i.e., it must be transmitted before others. *Antecedence* is a preceding in time or logical sequence; *priority* may be fixed by human decision, but *antecedence* is a fact of the external world: the *antecedence* of life to the Cambrian period is inferred but not proved.
prec·e·dent (*n.* pres′ə·dənt; *adj.* pri·sēd′nt) *n.* 1. An act or instance capable of being used as a guide or standard in evaluating future actions. 2. *Law* A judicial decision taken as a guiding principle or example for subsequent decisions. — *adj.* Former. [< F *précédent* < L *praecedens, -entis,* ppr. of *praecedere.* See PRECEDE.]
prec·e·den·tial (pres′ə·den′shəl) *adj.* 1. Of the nature of a precedent; serving as a guide. 2. Having precedence.
pre·ced·ing (pri·sē′ding) *adj.* Going before, as in time, place, or rank; earlier; foregoing. — **the preceding** That which precedes or has been mentioned before. Abbr. *prec.*
pre·cent (pri·sent′) *v.i.* To act as precentor.
pre·cen·tor (pri·sen′tər) *n.* One who leads the singing of a church choir or congregation. [< LL *praecentor* < L *praecinere* < *prae-* before + *canere* to sing] — **pre·cen·to·ri·al** (prē′sen·tôr′ē·əl, -tō′rē-) — **pre·cen′tor·ship** *n.*
pre·cept (prē′sept) *n.* 1. A rule prescribing a particular kind of conduct or action. 2. A proverbial standard or guide to morals; a maxim. — **Syn.** See PROVERB. 3. A direction, as for a technical procedure. 4. *Law* A judicial command in writing; writ. [< L *praeceptus,* pp. of *praecipere* to prescribe < *prae-* before + *capere* to take]
pre·cep·tive (pri·sep′tiv) *adj.* 1. Consisting of or expressing a precept or precepts. 2. Pertaining to or of the nature of a precept.
pre·cep·tor (pri·sep′tər) *n.* 1. A teacher; instructor. 2. The principal of a school. 3. The head of a preceptory. [< L *praeceptor*] — **pre·cep·to·ri·al** (prē′sep·tôr′ē·əl, -tō′rē-) *adj.* — **pre·cep′tress** (-tris) *n.fem.*
pre·cep·to·ry (pri·sep′tər·ē) *n.* *pl.* ·**ries** A subordinate religious house of the Knights Templars. [< Med.L *praeceptoria*]
pre·ces·sion (pri·sesh′ən) *n.* 1. The act of preceding. 2. *Astron.* The precession of the equinoxes (which see). [< LL *praecessio, -onis* < L *praecedere.* See PRECEDE.]
pre·ces·sion·al (pri·sesh′ən·əl) *adj.* Relating to or resulting from the precession of the equinoxes.
precession of the equinoxes *Astron.* A slow retrograde motion of the equinoctial points from east to west, causing the time between successive equinoxes to be appreciably shorter than it would otherwise be. It is due to the combined attractive forces of the moon, sun, and planets upon the equatorial protuberance of the earth and completes a full cycle in about 26,000 years, a period known as the **Platonic** (or **great**) **year.**
pre·cinct (prē′singkt) *n.* 1. *U.S.* An election district of a town, township, county, etc. 2. *U.S.* **a** A subdivision of a city or town under the jurisdiction of a police unit. **b** The police station for such an area. 3. A minor administrative or jurisdictional district. 4. A place or enclosure marked off by fixed limits; also, the boundary of such a place. 5. *pl.* Neighborhood; environs. 6. *Chiefly Brit.* The immediate neighborhood of a church or temple. 7. A limited area of thought, action, etc. 8. An enclosure bounded by walls. [< Med.L *praecinctum* enclosure < L *praecingere* < *prae-* before + *cingere* to encircle]
pre·ci·os·i·ty (presh′ē·os′ə·tē) *n.* *pl.* ·**ties** Extreme fastidiousness or affected refinement, as in speech, style, or taste.
pre·cious (presh′əs) *adj.* 1. Highly priced or prized; valuable: a *precious* gem. 2. Greatly esteemed, as for moral or spiritual qualities: the *precious* ideal of truth. 3. Beloved; cherished. 4. Affectedly delicate or sensitive, as a style of writing. 5. *Informal* Flagrant; surpassing: a *precious* scoundrel. — *n.* Precious one; sweetheart. — *adv.*

Extremely; very. [< OF *precios* < L *pretiosus* < *pretium* price] — **pre′cious·ly** *adv.* — **pre′cious·ness** *n.*
precious stone A valuable, rare gem, as the diamond, ruby, sapphire, or emerald.
prec·i·pice (pres′i·pis) *n.* 1. A high vertical or overhanging face of rock; the brink of a cliff. 2. A perilous situation. [< F *précipice* < L *praecipitium* < *praeceps* headlong < *prae-* before + *caput* head]
pre·cip·i·ta·ble (pri·sip′ə·tə·bəl) *adj.* *Chem.* Capable of being precipitated: a *precipitable* salt.
pre·cip·i·tance (pri·sip′ə·təns) *n.* 1. The quality of being precipitant; rashness. 2. A rash act. Also **pre·cip′i·tan·cy.**
pre·cip·i·tant (pri·sip′ə·tənt) *adj.* 1. Rushing or falling quickly or heedlessly: *precipitant* speed. 2. Rash in thought or action; overhasty; impulsive. 3. Very sudden; abrupt. — *n.* *Chem.* Any substance, as a reagent, that when added or applied to a solution results in the formation of a precipitate. [< L *praecipitans, -antis,* ppr. of *praecipitare.* See PRECIPITATE.] — **pre·cip′i·tant·ly** *adv.*
pre·cip·i·tate (pri·sip′ə·tāt; *for adj. & n., also* pri·sip′ə·tit) *v.* ·**tat·ed,** ·**tat·ing** *v.t.* 1. To bring about before expected or needed; hasten the occurrence of: to *precipitate* a quarrel. 2. To hurl from or as from a height; throw headlong. 3. *Meteorol.* To cause (vapor, etc.) to condense and fall as dew, rain, etc. 4. *Chem.* To separate (a substance) in solid form, as from a solution. — *v.i.* 5. *Meteorol.* To fall as condensed vapor, etc. 6. *Chem.* To separate and settle, as a substance held in solution. 7. To fall headlong. — *adj.* 1. Moving speedily or hurriedly; rushing headlong. 2. Lacking due deliberation; done prematurely; hasty; rash. 3. Sudden and brief, as a disease. — *n.* *Chem.* A deposit of solid matter formed by precipitation: also called *precipitation.* [< L *praecipitatus,* pp. of *praecipitare* < *praeceps.* See PRECIPICE.] — **pre·cip′i·tate·ly** *adv.* — **pre·cip′i·tate·ness** *n.* — **pre·cip′i·ta·tive** *adj.* — **pre·cip′i·ta·tor** *n.* — **Syn.** (adj.) 2. impetuous, rushed.
pre·cip·i·ta·tion (pri·sip′ə·tā′shən) *n.* 1. *Meteorol.* **a** The depositing of moisture from the atmosphere upon the surface of the earth. **b** The amount of rain, snow, etc., deposited. 2. *Chem.* **a** The process of separating any of the constituents of a solution, as by reagents or mechanical means. **b** A precipitate. 3. The act of precipitating, or the state of being precipitated. 4. Rash haste or hurry; precipitancy. 5. In spiritualism, the act of materializing; materialization.
pre·cip·i·tin (pri·sip′ə·tin) *n.* *Biochem.* An antibody produced in the blood serum by injection with a soluble antigen, capable of precipitating certain proteins, etc.
pre·cip·i·tous (pri·sip′ə·təs) *adj.* 1. Consisting of or like a precipice; very steep. 2. Having many precipices. 3. Precipitate; hasty. — **Syn.** See STEEP¹. — **pre·cip′i·tous·ly** *adv.* — **pre·cip′i·tous·ness** *n.*
pré·cis (prā′sē, prā·sē′) *n.* *pl.* **pré·cis** (prā′sēz, prā·sēz′) A concise summary of a book, article, or document; abstract. — **Syn.** See ABRIDGMENT. [< F]
pre·cise (pri·sīs′) *adj.* 1. Sharply and clearly determined or defined; strictly accurate. 2. No more and no less than; exact in amount. 3. Noting or confined to a certain thing; particular; identical. 4. Exact or distinct in sound, statement, etc.: a *precise* voice. 5. Scrupulously observant of rule; also, overexact; finicky. — **Syn.** See CORRECT. [< F *précis* < L *praecisus,* pp. of *praecidere* to cut off < *prae-* before + *caedere* to cut] — **pre·cise′ness** *n.*
pre·cise·ly (pri·sīs′lē) *adv.* 1. In a precise manner. 2. Yes, indeed; quite so.
pre·ci·sian (pri·sizh′ən) *n.* A strict adherent to rules and forms of religion, etc.; especially, an English Puritan.
pre·ci·sion (pri·sizh′ən) *n.* The state or quality of being precise; accuracy; definition. — *adj.* 1. Designed for extremely accurate measurement: *precision* instruments. 2. *Mech.* Of low tolerance. 3. Characterized by precision.
precision bombing *Mil.* Aerial bombing of comparatively small targets by the use of precision instruments.
pre·ci·sion·ist (pri·sizh′ən·ist) *n.* One who is or believes in being precise.
pre·clin·i·cal (prē·klin′i·kəl) *adj.* 1. *Med.* In the period of disease before the appearance of symptoms sufficient for diagnosis. 2. Pertaining to medical studies that precede the practical study of patients.
pre·clude (pri·klood′) *v.t.* ·**clud·ed,** ·**clud·ing** 1. To make impossible or ineffectual by prior action. 2. To shut out; exclude. — **Syn.** See PREVENT. [< L *praecludere* < *prae-* before + *cludere* to shut] — **pre·clu′sion** (-kloo′zhən) *n.* — **pre·clu′sive** (-kloo′siv) *adj.* — **pre·clu′sive·ly** *adv.*
pre·co·cial (pri·kō′shəl) *adj.* *Ornithol.* Of or pertaining to newly hatched birds that are down-covered and able to run about: distinguished from *altricial.*
pre·co·cious (pri·kō′shəs) *adj.* 1. Unusually developed or advanced, especially for one's age: a *precocious* child. 2. Pertaining to or showing premature development. 3. *Bot.* Flowering or ripening early, as certain plants. [< L *praecox, praecocis* < *praecoquere* < *prae-* beforehand, early + *coquere*

to cook] — **pre·co′cious·ly** adv. — **pre·co′cious·ness**, **pre·coc′i·ty** (-kos′ə·tē) n.

pre·cog·ni·tion (prē′kog·nish′ən) n. Prior cognition, especially as a form of extrasensory perception.

pre·con·ceive (prē′kən·sēv′) v.t. **·ceived**, **·ceiv·ing** To conceive in advance; form an idea or opinion of beforehand.

pre·con·cep·tion (prē′kən·sep′shən) n. 1. An idea or opinion formed or conceived in advance. 2. A prejudice or misconception; bias. — **pre′con·cep′tion·al** adj.

pre·con·di·tion (prē′kən·dish′ən) n. A condition or requirement that must be met before a certain end or result is attained; prerequisite. — v.t. To prepare or condition (a person or thing) in advance for some special purpose, use, etc.

pre·con·scious (prē·kon′shəs) n. Psychoanal. Those areas of the mind not in immediate awareness but capable of being recalled readily into consciousness.

pre·cook (prē·kook′) v.t. To cook beforehand; especially, to cook and package before selling to the consumer.

pre·crit·i·cal (prē·krit′i·kəl) adj. Med. Preceding the crisis of a disease.

pre·cur·sor (pri·kûr′sər) n. One who or that which precedes and suggests the course of future events. [< L praecursor < praecurrere < prae- before + currere to run]

pre·cur·so·ry (pri·kûr′sər·ē) adj. Going before as a precursor or harbinger; preliminary. Also **pre·cur′sive** (-kûr′siv).

pre·da·cious (pri·dā′shəs) adj. Living by preying upon others, as a beast or bird; raptorial: also **predatory**. Also **pre·da′ceous**. [< L praeda prey] — **pre·da′cious·ness**, **pre·dac′i·ty** (-das′ə·tē) n.

pre·date (prē′dāt′) v.t. **·dat·ed**, **·dat·ing** 1. To date before the actual time. 2. To precede in time.

pre·da·tion (pri·dā′shən) n. The act or result of preying or plundering; especially, the natural act of animals that kill other animals for food; also, the result of such killing. [< L praedation-, < praedatus, pp. of praedari to prey upon]

pred·a·tor (pred′i·tər) n. A predatory person, animal, or thing.

pred·a·to·ry (pred′ə·tôr′ē, -tō′rē) adj. 1. Of, relating to, or characterized by plundering. 2. Accustomed to or living by pillaging. 3. Predacious. [< L predatorius < praeda prey] — **pred′a·to′ri·ly** adv. — **pred′a·to′ri·ness** n.

pre·de·cease (prē′di·sēs′) v.t. **·ceased**, **·ceas·ing** To die before: She predeceased her husband by five years.

pred·e·ces·sor (pred′ə·ses′ər) n. 1. One who goes or has gone before another in point of time, as a previous holder of an office. 2. A thing succeeded by something else. 3. An ancestor; forefather. [< OF predecesseur < LL praedecessor < prae- before + decessor withdrawer < decedere to go away]

pre·des·ig·nate (prē·dez′ig·nāt) v.t. **·nat·ed**, **·nat·ing** To designate beforehand. — **pre·des′ig·na′tion** n.

pre·des·ti·nar·i·an (prē·des′tə·nâr′ē·ən) adj. 1. Pertaining to predestination. 2. Believing in the doctrine of predestination. — n. A believer in the doctrine of predestination; also, a fatalist. — **pre·des′ti·nar′i·an·ism** n.

pre·des·ti·nate (prē·des′tə·nit; for adj., also prē·des′tə·nit) v.t. **·nat·ed**, **·nat·ing** 1. Theol. To foreordain by divine decree or purpose. 2. To destine or decree beforehand; predestine. — adj. Predestined. [< L praedestinatus, pp. of praedestinare < prae- before + destinare to determine]

pre·des·ti·na·tion (prē·des′tə·nā′shən) n. 1. The act of predestining, or the state of being predestined; destiny; fate. 2. Theol. The foreordination of all things by God, including the salvation or damnation of men.

pre·des·tine (prē·des′tin) v.t. **·tined**, **·tin·ing** To destine or decree beforehand; foreordain; predestinate.

pre·de·ter·mi·nate (prē′di·tûr′mə·nit, -nāt) adj. Decided or decreed beforehand.

pre·de·ter·mine (prē′di·tûr′min) v.t. **·mined**, **·min·ing** 1. To determine beforehand; decide in advance; foreordain. 2. To urge to accept (a point of view, etc.) beforehand; influence; bias. — **pre′de·ter′mi·na′tion** n.

pre·di·al (prē′dē·əl) adj. See PRAEDIAL.

pred·i·ca·ble (pred′i·kə·bəl) adj. Capable of being predicated or affirmed. — n. 1. Anything predicable. 2. Logic Any of the various kinds of predicates that may be affirmed or denied of a subject, as genus, species, difference, property, and accident. — **pred′i·ca·bil′i·ty**, **pred′i·ca·ble·ness** n.

pre·dic·a·ment (pri·dik′ə·mənt) n. 1. A trying or embarrassing situation; plight. 2. A specific state, position, or situation. 3. Logic A category. [< LL praedicamentum that which is predicated < praedicare to proclaim. See PREACH.]
— Syn. 1. Predicament, plight, scrape, fix, jam, dilemma, quandary, and pickle denote an unpleasant or perplexing situation. Predicament is a general term that includes all the others. A plight is unpleasant or unfortunate and complicated, defying easy solution; the word is often used humorously. A scrape is an unfortunate situation due, at least in part, to one's own fault; the word often suggests difficulties arising from the violation of some rule, or the defiance of authority. Fix and jam (both informal) are close to scrape, but stress instead the difficulty of extricating oneself. Dilemma refers to an unavoidable choice between two unwelcome alternatives. Quandary refers to the subjective aspect of a dilemma, and emphasizes perplexity or vacillation, while the informal pickle, also often subjective, suggests the embarrassment of a person in a predicament.

pred·i·cant (pred′i·kənt) adj. Preaching. — n. A preacher. [< L praedicans, -antis, ppr. of praedicare to proclaim. See PREACH.]

pred·i·cate (v. pred′i·kāt; n. & adj. pred′i·kit) v. **·cat·ed**, **·cat·ing** v.t. 1. U.S. To found or base (an argument, proposition, etc.): with on or upon. 2. To affirm as a quality or attribute of something. 3. To imply or connote. 4. To declare; affirm; proclaim. 5. Logic To state or affirm concerning the subject of a proposition. — v.i. 6. To make a statement or affirmation. — n. 1. Gram. The verb in a sentence or clause together with its objects, complements, and modifiers; the word or words in a sentence that express what is stated about a subject, as is short in the sentence Life is short. 2. Logic In a proposition, that which is stated about a subject. — adj. 1. That predicates. 2. Gram. Of, relating to, or of the nature of a predicate: a predicate adjective. Abbr. pred. [< L praedicatus, pp. of praedicare to proclaim. See PREACH.] — **pred′i·ca·tive** adj. — **pred′i·ca′tive·ly** adv.

predicate adjective Gram. An adjective that describes the subject of a linking verb, as sad in He is sad.

predicate noun Gram. A noun that designates or identifies the subject of a linking verb, as king in He was king.

pred·i·ca·tion (pred′i·kā′shən) n. 1. The act of predicating. 2. Something predicated. — **pred′i·ca′tion·al** adj.

pred·i·ca·to·ry (pred′i·kə·tôr′ē, -tō′rē) adj. 1. Of or pertaining to a preacher or preaching. 2. Proclaimed; preached.

pre·dict (pri·dikt′) v.t. 1. To make known beforehand; prophesy; foretell. 2. To assert on the basis of theory, data, or experience but in advance of proof: to predict the winning candidate on the basis of public opinion polls. — v.i. 3. To make a prediction; prophesy. — Syn. See AUGUR. [< L praedictus, pp. of praedicere < prae- before + dicere to say] — **pre·dict′a·ble** adj. — **pre·dict′a·bly** adv.

pre·dic·tion (pri·dik′shən) n. 1. The act of predicting. 2. Something predicted; a prophecy; forecast. [< L praedictio, -onis] — **pre·dic′tive** adj. — **pre·dic′tive·ly** adv.

pre·dic·tor (pri·dik′tər) n. 1. One who or that which predicts. 2. Mil. A mechanism used with antiaircraft guns for automatically determining the position, speed, and course of approaching aircraft.

pre·di·gest (prē′di·jest′, -dī-) v.t. To treat (food) by a process of partial digestion before introduction into the stomach. — **pre′di·ges′tion** n.

pre·di·lec·tion (prē′də·lek′shən, pred′ə-) n. A preference or bias in favor of something; a partiality: with for. [< F < Med.L praedilectus, pp. of praediligere to prefer < L prae- before + diligere to love, choose]
— Syn. liking, penchant, inclination, bent.

pre·dis·pose (prē′dis·pōz′) v.t. **·posed**, **·pos·ing** 1. To give a tendency or inclination to; make susceptible or liable: Exhaustion predisposes one to sickness. 2. To dispose beforehand. 3. To dispose of beforehand; bequeath.

pre·dis·po·si·tion (prē′dis·pə·zish′ən) n. The state or fact of being predisposed; tendency.

pre·dom·i·nance (pri·dom′ə·nəns) n. The state or quality of being predominant; ascendancy. Also **pre·dom′i·nan·cy**.

pre·dom·i·nant (pri·dom′ə·nənt) adj. Superior in power, influence, effectiveness, number, or degree; prevailing over others. — Syn. See DOMINANT. — **pre·dom′i·nant·ly** adv.

pre·dom·i·nate (pri·dom′ə·nāt) v.i. **·nat·ed**, **·nat·ing** 1. To have governing influence or control; be in control: often with over. 2. To be superior to all others, as in power, height, number, etc. 3. To prevail; preponderate. — **pre·dom′i·nat′ing·ly** adv. — **pre·dom′i·na′tion** n.

pree (prē) v.t. preed pree·ing Scot. To test, especially by tasting; also, to kiss.

pre·em·i·nent (prē·em′ə·nənt) adj. Supremely eminent; distinguished above all others; outstanding; conspicuous. [< L praeëminens, -entis, ppr. of praeëminere < prae- before + eminere to stand out] — **pre·em′i·nent·ly** adv. — **pre·em′i·nence** n.

pre·empt (prē·empt′) v.t. 1. To acquire or appropriate beforehand. 2. To secure by preemption; occupy (public land) so as to acquire by preemption. — v.i. 3. In bridge, to make a preemptive bid. [Back formation < PREEMPTION] — **pre·emp′tor** n. — **pre·emp′to·ry** (-tər·ē) adj.

pre·emp·tion (prē·emp′shən) n. 1. The right to purchase something before others; also, the act of so purchasing. 2. Public land obtained by exercising the right of preemption. [< Med.L preëmptio, -onis < L prae- before + emptus, pp. of emere to buy]

pre·emp·tive (prē·emp′tiv) adj. 1. Pertaining to or capable of preemption. 2. In bridge, designating a bid that is unnecessarily high, intended to discourage subsequent bidding.

preen[1] (prēn) v.t. 1. To trim and dress (feathers, etc.) with the beak, as a bird. 2. To dress or adorn (oneself) carefully; primp; prink. 3. To pride or congratulate (oneself): with on. — v.i. 4. To primp; prink. [ME proyne, preyn, prene. Prob. var. of PRUNE[3].]

preen[2] (prēn) Scot. n. A pin; brooch. — v.t. To pin. [OE prēon]

pre·ex·il·i·an (prē′eg·zil′ē·ən) adj. Pertaining to the period of Jewish history before the Babylonian captivity at the end of the sixth century B.C. Also **pre′ex·il′ic**.

pre·ex·ist (prē'ig·zist') *v.t. & v.i.* To exist before. — **pre'·ex·is'tence** *n.* — **pre·ex·is'tent** *adj.*

pref. 1. Preface. 2. Prefatory. 3. Preference. 4. Prefix.

pre·fab (prē'fab') *n.* A prefabricated structure or part.

pre·fab·ri·cate (prē·fab'rə·kāt) *v.t.* **·cat·ed, ·cat·ing** 1. To fabricate or build beforehand. 2. To manufacture in standard sections that can be rapidly assembled. — **pre·fab'ri·ca'tion** *n.*

pref·ace (pref'is) *n.* 1. A statement or brief essay, usually by the author, included in the front matter of a book, etc., and dealing primarily with the purpose and scope of the work. Abbr. *pref.* 2. Any introductory speech, writing, etc. — *v.t.* **·aced, ·ac·ing** 1. To introduce or furnish with a preface. 2. To serve as a preface for. [< OF < L *praefatio* < *prae-* + *fari* to speak]

Pref·ace (pref'is) *n. Eccl.* 1. The prayer of thanksgiving, ending with the Sanctus, that introduces the canon of the Mass. 2. The corresponding section in other Eucharistic liturgies.

pref·a·to·ry (pref'ə·tôr'ē, -tō'rē) *adj.* Of the nature of a preface; introductory. Also **pref'a·to'ri·al.** Abbr. *pref.* — **pref'a·to'ri·ly** *adv.*

pre·fect (prē'fekt) *n.* 1. In ancient Rome, any of various civil and military officials, as certain magistrates, governors, and commanders. 2. Any magistrate, chief official, etc.; especially, in France: **a** The chief administrator of a department. **b** The head of the Paris police. 3. The dean of certain private or religious schools. 4. In British schools, a senior monitor. Also spelled *praefect.* [< OF < L *praefectus*, orig. pp. of *praeficere* to set over < L *prae-* before + *facere* to do]

pre·fec·ture (prē'fek·chər) *n.* 1. The office, jurisdiction, or province of a prefect. 2. The residence of a prefect. [< L *praefectura*] — **pre·fec'tur·al** *adj.*

pre·fer (pri·fûr') *v.t.* **·ferred, ·fer·ring** 1. To hold in higher regard or esteem; value more. 2. To choose (something) over another or others; like better. 3. To give priority to, as one creditor or form of securities over others. 4. To advance or promote, as in status or rank. 5. To offer or put forward for consideration or decision, as a suit or charge. — **Syn.** See CHOOSE. [< F *préférer* < L *praeferre* < *prae-* before + *ferre* to carry] — **pre·fer'rer** *n.*

pref·er·a·ble (pref'ər·ə·bəl) *adj.* That is preferred; more desirable; worthy of choice. — **pref'er·a·ble·ness, pref'er·a·bil'i·ty** *n.* — **pref'er·a·bly** *adv.*

pref·er·ence (pref'ər·əns) *n.* 1. The choosing of one person or thing over another or others; also, the privilege or opportunity of so choosing. 2. One who or that which is preferred. 3. *Law* **a** A priority of payment given to one or to a certain class of creditors by an insolvent debtor. **b** The right of a creditor to priority of payment. 4. The granting of special advantage to one over others, as to one country or group of countries in international trade. 5. The act of preferring, or the state of being preferred. Abbr. *pref.* — **Syn.** See ALTERNATIVE. [< F *préférence* < L *praeferentia*, orig. neut. pl. of *praeferens, -entis*, ppr. of *praeferre.* See PREFER.]

pref·er·en·tial (pref'ə·ren'shəl) *adj.* 1. Showing or arising from preference or partiality. 2. Giving preference, as in tariffs. — **pref'er·en'tial·ism** *n.* — **pref'er·en'tial·ly** *adv.*

preferential shop A shop that gives preferential treatment to union members when hiring, laying off, promoting, etc.

preferential voting A form of voting in which an order of choice of candidates may be indicated by a voter.

pre·fer·ment (pri·fûr'mənt) *n.* 1. The act of promoting or appointing to higher office; advancement; promotion. 2. A position, rank, or office of social prestige or profit. 3. The act of preferring.

preferred stock Stock on which dividends must be paid before dividends can be paid on common stocks, usually also receiving preference in the distribution of assets on liquidation. Also *Brit.* **preference shares.**

pre·fig·u·ra·tion (prē·fig'yə·rā'shən) *n.* 1. The act of prefiguring. 2. That which prefigures; a prototype. — **pre·fig·u·ra·tive** (prē·fig'yər·ə·tiv) *adj.* — **pre·fig'ur·a·tive·ly** *adv.* — **pre·fig'ur·a·tive·ness** *n.*

pre·fig·ure (prē·fig'yər) *v.t.* **·ured, ·ur·ing** 1. To represent in advance; serve as an indication or suggestion of; foreshadow. 2. To imagine or picture to oneself beforehand. [< LL *praefigurare* < L *prae-* before + *figurare* to form < *figura.* See FIGURE.]

pre·fix (*n.* prē'fiks; *v.* prē·fiks') *n.* 1. *Gram.* A bound form affixed to the beginning of a base, stem, or root, altering or modifying its meaning, as *re-* in *renew.* Compare COMBINING FORM, SUFFIX. 2. Something placed before, as a title before a name. Abbr. *pref.* — *v.t.* 1. To put or attach before or at the beginning; add as a prefix. 2. *Obs.* To arrange or settle beforehand. [< OF *prefixer* < L *praefixus*, pp. of *praefigere* < *prae-* before + *figere* (pp. *fixus*) to fasten, fix] — **pre'fix·al** *adj.* — **pre'fix·al·ly** *adv.* — **pre·fix·ion** (prē·fik'shən) *n.*

pre·flight (prē'flīt') *adj.* Preparing for or occurring before flight, as of an airplane: *preflight training.*

pre·for·ma·tion (prē'fôr·mā'shən) *n.* 1. The act of forming in advance, or the state of being formed in advance. 2. *Biol.* An early theory that an organism exists fully formed in the germ cell, developing only by increase in size.

Pre·gl (prā'gəl), Fritz, 1869–1930, Austrian chemist.

preg·na·ble (preg'nə·bəl) *adj.* 1. Capable of being captured, as a fort. 2. Open to attack; vulnerable; assailable. [< OF *prenable* < *prendre* to take < L *prehendere* to seize] — **preg'na·bil'i·ty** *n.*

preg·nan·cy (preg'nən·sē) *n. pl.* **·cies** 1. The state or quality of being pregnant.

preg·nant (preg'nənt) *adj.* 1. Carrying a growing fetus in the uterus; being with child or with young. 2. Having considerable weight or significance; full of meaning. 3. Teeming with ideas; imaginative; inventive. 4. Bearing issue or results; fruitful; prolific. 5. Full or filled; replete: *pregnant with meaning.* [< L *praegnans, -antis*, ult. < *prae-* before + *gnasci* to be born] — **preg'nant·ly** *adv.*

pre·hen·si·ble (pri·hen'sə·bəl) *adj.* Capable of being grasped.

pre·hen·sile (pri·hen'sil) *adj.* Adapted for grasping or holding, especially by coiling around, as the tail of a monkey. [< F *préhensile* < *préhension* < L *prehensio.* See PREHENSION.] — **pre·hen·sil·i·ty** (prē'hen·sil'ə·tē) *n.*

pre·hen·sion (pri·hen'shən) *n.* The act of grasping, physically or mentally. [< L *prehensio, -onis* < *prehendere* to seize]

pre·his·tor·ic (prē'his·tôr'ik, -tor'-) *adj.* Of or belonging to the period before written history. Also **pre'his·tor'i·cal.** — **pre'his·tor'i·cal·ly** *adv.*

pre·his·to·ry (prē·his'tə·rē) *n. pl.* **·ries** The history of mankind in the period preceding written records, based mainly on archeological and ethnological findings.

pre·ig·ni·tion (prē'ig·nish'ən) *n.* Ignition of the charge in the cylinder of an internal-combustion engine before the completion of the compression stroke.

pre·judge (prē·juj') *v.t.* **·judged, ·judg·ing** To judge beforehand or without proper inquiry. [< F *préjuger* < Med.L *praejudicare* < *prae-* before + *judicare* to judge] — **pre·judg'er** *n.* — **pre·judg'ment** or **pre·judge'ment** *n.*

prej·u·dice (prej'oo·dis) *n.* 1. A judgment or opinion formed beforehand or without thoughtful examination of the pertinent facts, issues, or arguments; especially, an unfavorable, irrational opinion. 2. The act or state of holding preconceived, irrational opinions. 3. Hatred of or dislike for a particular group, race, religion, etc. 4. Injury or damage to a person arising from a hasty and unfair judgment by others. — **in** (or **to**) **the prejudice of** To the injury or detriment of. — **without prejudice** *Law* Without damaging a person's legal rights or claims. — *v.t.* **·diced, ·dic·ing** 1. To cause to have a prejudice; bias; influence. 2. To damage or impair by some act, judgment, etc. [< OF < L *praejudicium* prior judgment, precedent < *prae-* before + *judicium* judgment] — **Syn.** (noun) *Prejudice, bias, partiality,* and *prepossession* are compared as they denote an attitude of mind that interferes with fair judgment. Only *prejudice* is necessarily a term of opprobrium; literally, it signifies prejudgment without adequate hearing or consideration, but it is chiefly used to refer to a strong emotional *bias.* A *bias* is an imbalance of mind, an inclination in some direction that prevents a fair weighing of issues. *Partiality* is an inclination to favor one person or view unfairly. A *bias* may be for or against someone or something, but *partiality* always implies favor. *Prepossession* is domination of the mind by some familiar or favorite idea which excludes new ideas.

prej·u·di·cial (prej'oo·dish'əl) *adj.* Tending to prejudice or injure; detrimental. — **prej'u·di'cial·ly** *adv.*

prel·a·cy (prel'ə·sē) *n. pl.* **·cies** 1. The system of church government by prelates: sometimes used disparagingly. 2. The dignity or function of a prelate; also, prelates collectively: also **prel·a·ture** (prel'ə·chər). [< AF *prelacie* < Med.L *praelatia* < *praelatus.* See PRELATE.]

prel·ate (prel'it) *n.* An ecclesiastic of high rank, as a bishop, archbishop, etc. [< OF *prelat* < L *praelatus*, pp. of *praeferre* to set over. See PREFER.] — **prel'ate·ship** *n.* — **pre·lat·ic** (pri·lat'ik) or **·i·cal** *adj.*

prel·a·tism (prel'ə·tiz'əm) *n.* Prelacy; episcopacy.

prel·a·tist (prel'ə·tist) *n.* An advocate of or believer in prelacy (def. 1): sometimes used disparagingly.

pre·lect (pri·lekt') *v.i.* To lecture; discourse. [< L *praelectus*, pp. of *praelegere* < *prae-* before + *legere* to read] — **pre·lec'tion** *n.* — **pre·lec'tor** *n.*

pre·li·ba·tion (prē'li·bā'shən) *n.* 1. A preliminary offering. 2. A tasting beforehand; foretaste. [< LL *praelibatio, -onis* < *prae-* before + *libare* to taste]

prelim. Preliminary.

pre·lim·i·nar·y (pri·lim'ə·ner'ē) *adj.* Before or introductory to the main event, proceeding, or business; prefatory; preparatory. — *n. pl.* **·nar·ies** 1. A preparatory step or act. 2. A preliminary examination. 3. *pl. Printing* Front matter. 4. In sports, a minor, introductory event, as a boxing match. [< F *préliminaire* < *pré-* pre- + *liminaire* < L *liminaris* pertaining to a threshold < *limen, liminis* threshold] — **pre·lim'i·nar'i·ly** *adv.*

pre·lit·er·ate (prē·lit′ər·it) *adj.* Of a culture, lacking or predating the existence of written language or records.

prel·ude (prel′yōod, prē′lōod) *n.* **1.** *Music* **a** An instrumental composition of moderate length, in a free style. **b** An opening piece at the start of a church service; a voluntary. **c** An opening section or movement of a musical composition. **2.** Any introductory or opening performance or event; also, that which foreshadows a coming event: also **pre·lu·sion** (pri·lōo′zhən). — *v.* **·ud·ed, ·ud·ing** *v.t.* **1.** To introduce with a prelude. **2.** To serve as a prelude to. — *v.i.* **3.** To serve as a prelude. **4.** To provide or play a prelude. [< Med.L *praeludium* < L *praeludere* < *prae-* before + *ludere* to play] — **pre·lud·er** (pri·lōo′dər, prel′yə·dər) *n.* — **pre·lu·di·al** (pri·lōo′dē·əl) *adj.*

pre·lu·sive (pri·lōo′siv) *adj.* Serving as a prelude; introductory. Also **pre·lu′so·ry** (-sər·ē). — **pre·lu′sive·ly, pre·lu′so·ri·ly** *adv.*

pre·ma·ture (prē′mə·chŏŏr′, -tŏŏr′, -tyŏŏr′; *Brit.* prem′ə·tyŏŏr′) *adj.* Existing, happening, or developed before the natural or proper period; unusually early; untimely. [< L *praematurus* < *prae-* before + *maturus* ripe, seasonable] — **pre′ma·ture′ly** *adv.* — **pre′ma·ture′ness, pre′ma·tu′ri·ty** *n.*

pre·max·il·la (prē′mak·sil′ə) *n. pl.* **·max·il·lae** (-mak·sil′ē) *Anat.* One of the two bones set between the maxillae in front of the upper jaw of vertebrates. [< NL] — **pre·max·il·lar·y** (prē·mak′sə·ler′ē) *adj.*

pre·med·i·cal (prē·med′i·kəl) *adj.* Preparatory to or preparing for the study of medicine: a *premedical* student. Also *Informal* **pre·med′.**

pre·med·i·tate (prē·med′ə·tāt) *v.t. & v.i.* **·tat·ed, ·tat·ing** To plan or consider beforehand. [< L *praemeditatus*, pp. of *praemeditari* < *prae-* before + *meditari*. See MEDITATE.] — **pre·med′i·tat′ed·ly** *adv.* — **pre·med′i·ta′tive** *adj.* — **pre·med′i·ta′tor** *n.*

pre·med·i·ta·tion (prē·med′ə·tā′shən) *n.* **1.** The act of premeditating. **2.** *Law* The deliberation and planning of a crime before its commission, showing intent to commit the crime.

pre·mier (pri·mir′, -myir′, prē′mē·ər, prim′ē-, *esp. Brit.* prem′yər) *adj.* **1.** First in rank or position; principal: *premier* officer. **2.** First in order of occurrence; earliest; senior: the *premier* duke of England. — *n.* **1.** Prime minister (def. 2). **2.** In Canada, the head of a Provincial cabinet. **3.** In Australia, the head of a State government. [< F < L *primarius* < L *primus* first] — **pre′mier·ship′** *n.*

pre·miere (pri·mir′, -myâr′) *n.* **1.** The first public performance of a play, movie, etc. **2.** The leading lady in a theatrical company. — *v.t. & v.i.* **·miered, ·mier·ing** To show or perform (a play, movie, etc.) publicly for the first time. Also **pre·mière** (prə·myâr′). [< F, fem. of *premier* first]

pre·mil·le·nar·i·an (prē′mil·ə·nâr′ē·ən) *adj.* **1.** Existing or occurring before the millennium. **2.** Pertaining to premillennialism. — *n.* One who believes in premillennialism: also **pre′mil·len′ni·al·ist.**

pre·mil·len·ni·al (prē′mi·len′ē·əl) *adj.* Pertaining to or occurring before the millennium.

pre·mil·len·ni·al·ism (prē′mi·len′ē·əl·iz′əm) *n.* The doctrine that the second coming of Christ will precede and introduce the millennium: opposed to *postmillennialism.*

prem·ise (prem′is; *for v.*, also pri·mīz′) *n.* **1.** A proposition that serves as a ground for argument or for a conclusion. **2.** *pl.* A definite portion of real estate; land with its appurtenances; also, a building or part of a building. **3.** *Logic* **a** In a syllogism, either of the two propositions that combine to form a conclusion. **b** A hypothesis in a deductive argument. **4.** *pl. Law* **a** Foregoing statements or facts. **b** That part in a deed that sets forth the date, names of parties, the land or thing conveyed or granted, and the consideration. **c** The property mentioned in a deed. Also **prem′iss.** — *v.* **·mised, ·mis·ing** *v.t.* **1.** To state beforehand, as by way of introduction or explanation. **2.** To state or assume as a premise or basis of argument. — *v.i.* To make a premise. [< MF *premisse* < Med.L *praemissa*, orig. fem. of L *praemissus*, pp. of *praemittere* < *prae-* before + *mittere* to send]

pre·mi·um (prē′mē·əm) *n.* **1.** An object or service offered free as an inducement to buy, rent, or contract for another object or service. **2.** The amount paid or payable for insurance, usually in periodical installments. **3.** An extra amount or bonus paid in addition to a fixed price, wage, etc. **4.** A price paid for a loan, usually in addition to interest. **5.** The rate or price at which stocks, shares, or money are valued in excess of their nominal or par value: bank shares at a *premium* of five percent. **6.** High regard or value: to put a *premium* on truth. **7.** A reward or prize awarded in a competition. **8.** A fee for instruction in a trade or profession. *Abbr.* **prem.** — **at a premium 1.** Valuable and in demand. **2.** Above par. [< L *praemium*, profit, reward, ult. < *prae-* before + *emere* to take, buy]

pre·mo·lar (prē·mō′lər) *Anat. n.* One of the teeth situated in front of the molars and behind the canines: also called *bicuspid.* — *adj.* Situated in front of the molar teeth.

pre·mon·ish (pri·mon′ish) *v.t. Rare* To admonish in advance; forewarn.

pre·mo·ni·tion (prē′mə·nish′ən, prem′ə-) *n.* **1.** A presenti-

ment of the future not based on information received; an instinctive foreboding. **2.** An actual warning of something yet to occur. [< LL *praemonitio, -onis* < *praemonere* < *prae-* before + *monere* to advise] — **pre·mon·i·to·ry** (pri·mon′ə·tôr′ē, -tō′rē) *adj.* — **pre·mon′i·to′ri·ly** *adv.*

pre·morse (pri·môrs′) *adj. Biol.* Terminating abruptly, as if bitten off: a *premorse* root. [< L *praemorsus*, pp. of *praemordere* to bite off < *prae-* before + *mordere* to bite]

pre·mun·dane (prē·mun′dān) *adj.* Antemundane.

pre·na·tal (prē·nāt′l) *adj.* Prior to birth: *prenatal* care. — **pre·na′tal·ly** *adv.*

pre·no·men (prē·nō′mən) See PRAENOMEN.

pre·nom·i·nate (prē·nom′ə·nāt) *Obs. v.t.* **·nat·ed, ·nat·ing** To mention beforehand. — *adj.* Named beforehand.

pre·no·tion (prē·nō′shən) *n.* A preconception.

pren·tice (pren′tis) *n. Archaic* or *Dial.* An apprentice. Also **'pren′tice.** [Aphetic var. of APPRENTICE.]

pre·oc·cu·pa·tion (prē·ok′yə·pā′shən) *n.* **1.** The state of being preoccupied, as in mind, attention, or attitude. **2.** The act of occupying before others, or the state of having a prior occupant: also **pre·oc′cu·pan·cy** (-pən·sē). **3.** Something that preoccupies. [< L *praeoccupatio, -onis*]

pre·oc·cu·pied (prē·ok′yə·pīd) *adj.* **1.** Engrossed in thought or in some action; absorbed. **2.** Previously occupied. **3.** *Biol.* Already in use, as a scientific name. — **Syn.** See ABSTRACTED.

pre·oc·cu·py (prē·ok′yə·pī) *v.t.* **·pied, ·py·ing 1.** To engage fully; engross. **2.** To occupy or take possession of first. [< L *praeoccupare* to seize beforehand]

pre·or·dain (prē′ôr·dān′) *v.t.* To ordain beforehand; foreordain. — **pre·or·di·na·tion** (prē′ôr·də·nā′shən) *n.*

prep (prep) *adj. Informal* Preparatory: a *prep* school.

prep. 1. Preparation; preparatory; prepare. **2.** Preposition.

pre·pack·age (prē·pak′ij) *v.t.* **·aged, ·ag·ing** To package (meats, vegetables, etc.) before offering them for sale, as in large food stores or supermarkets.

prep·a·ra·tion (prep′ə·rā′shən) *n.* **1.** The act or process of preparing. **2.** An act or proceeding undertaken in advance of some event; a precaution; provision. **3.** The fact or state of being prepared; readiness. **4.** Something made or prepared, as a medicine. **5.** Preliminary study or training, as for college or business. **6.** *Music* **a** The practice of arranging a dissonant tone so that it is either held over or repeated from a consonance immediately preceding. **b** The tone so treated before it becomes a dissonance. **7.** *Eccl.* Devotional exercises introducing an office, as that of the Eucharist. **8.** In the New Testament, the day preceding the Sabbath or a feast day. *Abbr.* **prep.** [< MF *préparation* < L *praeperatio, -onis* < *praeparare.* See PREPARE.]

pre·par·a·tive (pri·par′ə·tiv) *adj.* Serving or tending to prepare. — *n.* **1.** That which is preparatory. **2.** An act of preparation. — **pre·par′a·tive·ly** *adv.*

pre·par·a·tor (pri·par′ə·tər) *n.* One who prepares specimens or objects for scientific purposes.

pre·par·a·to·ry (pri·par′ə·tôr′ē, -tō′rē) *adj.* **1.** Serving as preparation. **2.** Occupied in preparation: a *preparatory* scholar. *Abbr.* **prep.** — *adv.* As a preparation: *Preparatory* to writing, I will consider this: also **pre·par′a·to′ri·ly** *adv.*

preparatory school A private school that prepares students for college admission.

pre·pare (pri·pâr′) *v.* **·pared, ·par·ing** *v.t.* **1.** To make ready, fit, or qualified; put in readiness. **2.** To provide with what is needed; outfit; equip: to *prepare* an expedition. **3.** To bring to a state of completeness: to *prepare* a meal. **4.** *Music* To introduce (a dissonance) by using preparation. — *v.i.* **5.** To make preparations; get ready. *Abbr.* **prep.** [< F *préparer* < L *praeparare* < *prae-* before + *parare* to produce] — **pre·par·ed·ly** (pri·pâr′id·lē) *adv.* — **pre·par′er** *n.*

pre·par·ed·ness (pri·pâr′id·nis, -pârd′-) *n.* Readiness; especially, a condition of military readiness for war.

pre·pay (prē·pā′) *v.t.* **·paid, ·pay·ing** To pay or pay for in advance. — **pre·pay′ment** *n.*

pre·pense (pri·pens′) *adj.* Considered beforehand; premeditated: chiefly in the phrase **malice prepense.** [< OF *purpense*, pp. of *purpenser* < *pur-* (< L *pro-*) ahead + *penser* to think < L *pensare*] — **pre·pense′ly** *adv.*

pre·pon·der·ance (pri·pon′dər·əns) *n.* Superiority in weight, influence, quantity, etc. Also **pre·pon′der·an·cy.**

pre·pon·der·ant (pri·pon′dər·ənt) *adj.* Having superior force, weight, importance, quantity, etc.; predominant. — **Syn.** See DOMINANT. — **pre·pon′der·ant·ly** *adv.*

pre·pon·der·ate (pri·pon′də·rāt) *v.i.* **·at·ed, ·at·ing 1.** To be of greater weight. **2.** To incline downward or descend, as the scale of a balance. **3.** To be of greater power, importance, quantity, etc.; predominate; prevail. [< L *praeponderatus*, pp. of *praeponderare* < *prae-* before + *ponderare* to weigh < *pondus, ponderis* weight] — **pre·pon′der·a′tion** *n.*

prep·o·si·tion (prep′ə·zish′ən) *n. Gram.* **1.** In some languages, a word functioning to indicate the relation of a substantive (the object of the preposition) to another substantive, verb, or adjective. Some English prepositions are *by, for, from, in, to, with.* A preposition is usually placed before its object, and together they constitute a prepositional phrase that serves as an adjectival or an adverbial modifier as in the following phrases: sitting *beside the fire*; sick *at heart*; a man *of honor*. **2.** Any word or construction that functions in a similar manner, as *in reference to* in *He telephoned in reference to your letter.* Abbr. *prep.*

◆ It was once maintained that a sentence should never end with a preposition, but natural English sentences often do. The terminal position need not be avoided if it does not put undue emphasis on the preposition or if other possible positions are awkward. *What did you laugh at?* is good English. *At what did you laugh?* is awkward and unnatural. [< F *préposition* < L *praepositio, -onis* < *praeponere* < *prae-* before + *ponere* to place]

prep·o·si·tion·al (prep′ə·zish′ən·əl) *adj.* Pertaining to, formed with, or functioning as a preposition. — **prep′o·si′tion·al·ly** *adv.*

pre·pos·i·tive (prē·poz′ə·tiv) *Gram. adj.* Placed before the word qualified. — *n.* A prepositive word or particle.

pre·pos·i·tor (prē·poz′ə·tər) *n.* In some British schools, a student having authority over others; a prefect: also *praepositor.* Also **pre·pos·tor** (prē·pos′tər). [Alter. of L *praepositus,* pp. of *praeponere.* See PREPOSITION.]

pre·pos·i·to·ri·al (prē·poz′ə·tôr′ē·əl, -tō′rē-) *adj.*

pre·pos·sess (prē′pə·zes′) *v.t.* **1.** To preoccupy to the exclusion of other ideas, beliefs, etc.; prejudice; bias. **2.** To impress or influence beforehand or at once, especially favorably. **3.** *Rare* To take possession of in advance of others.

pre·pos·sess·ing (prē′pə·zes′ing) *adj.* Inspiring a favorable opinion; pleasing. — **pre′pos·sess′ing·ly** *adv.*

pre·pos·ses·sion (prē′pə·zesh′ən) *n.* **1.** A preconceived opinion; bias. **2.** A preoccupation with an idea, opinion, etc. **3.** *Rare* Prior possession.

pre·pos·ter·ous (pri·pos′tər·əs) *adj.* Contrary to nature, reason, or common sense; utterly absurd or impracticable. — **Syn.** See ABSURD. [< L *praeposterus* inverted < *prae-* before + *posterus* last] — **pre·pos′ter·ous·ly** *adv.* — **pre·pos′ter·ous·ness** *n.*

pre·po·ten·cy (pri·pō′tən·sē) *n.* **1.** The state or quality of being prepotent. **2.** *Biol.* The pronounced capacity of one parent, strain, or breed to transmit its own characteristics to the offspring. Also **pre·po′tence.**

pre·po·tent (pri·pō′tənt) *adj.* **1.** Having superior power, force, influence, etc.; predominant. **2.** *Biol.* Pertaining to or exhibiting prepotency. Also **pre·po·ten·tial** (prē′pə·ten′shəl). [< L *praepotens, -entis* < *prae-* before + *potens.* See POTENT.] — **pre·po′tent·ly** *adv.*

pre·puce (prē′pyoōs) *n. Anat.* The fold of skin covering the glans of the penis or clitoris: also called *foreskin.* [< F *prépuce* < L *praeputium.*] — **pre·pu·tial** (pri·pyoō′shəl) *adj.*

Pre-Raph·a·el·ite (prē·raf′ē·ə·līt, -rā′fē-) *n.* **1.** A follower or adherent of the **Pre-Raphaelite Brotherhood,** a society of artists formed in England, 1847–49, by D. G. Rossetti, W. Holman Hunt, John Millais, and others, stressing characteristics supposedly typical of Italian art before the time of Raphael. **2.** Any modern artist with similar aims. — *adj.* **1.** Of or pertaining to the Pre-Raphaelites. **2.** Before the time of Raphael. — **Pre-Raph′a·el·it′ism** *n.*

pre·req·ui·site (prē·rek′wə·zit) *adj.* Required as an antecedent condition; necessary to something that follows. — *n.* Something prerequisite, as a course that a student must pass before enrolling in a more advanced course.

pre·rog·a·tive (pri·rog′ə·tiv) *n.* **1.** An exclusive and unquestionable right belonging to a person or body of persons; especially, a hereditary or official right: the royal *prerogative.* **2.** Any characteristic privilege peculiar to a person or class: It is a woman's *prerogative* to change her mind. **3.** Precedence; preeminence. — *adj.* Of, pertaining to, or possessing a prerogative. [< OF < L *praerogativa* right of voting first < *praerogare* < *prae-* before + *rogare* to ask]

prerogative court 1. *Brit.* Formerly, a court having jurisdiction over testamentary matters. **2.** *U.S.* The New Jersey probate court.

pres. 1. Present. **2.** Presidency; presidential.

Pres. President.

pre·sa (prā′sä) *n. Music* A sign, ♯, +, or ⁑, used in fugues or canons to indicate where the voices are successively to take up the theme. [< Ital., lit., seizure, taking < *prendere* to take]

pres·age (*n.* pres′ij; *v.* pri·sāj′) *n.* **1.** An indication of something to come; portent; omen. **2.** A presentiment; foreboding. **3.** Prophetic meaning or import. **4.** *Rare* A prediction. — *v.* **·saged, ·sag·ing** *v.t.* **1.** To give a presage or portent of; betoken; foreshadow. **2.** To have a presentiment of. **3.** To predict; foretell. — *v.i.* **4.** To make a prediction. — **Syn.** See AUGUR. [< MF *présage* < L *praesagium* omen < *praesagire* to perceive beforehand < *prae-* before + *sagire* to perceive keenly. Akin to SAGACIOUS.] — **pre·sag′er** *n.*

Presb. Presbyterian.

pres·by·o·pi·a (prez′bē·ō′pē·ə, pres′-) *n. Pathol.* Farsightedness associated with aging and due to rigidity of the crystalline lens. [< NL < Gk. *presbys* old + -OPIA] — **pres′·by·op′ic** (-op′ik) *adj.*

pres·by·ter (prez′bə·tər, pres′-) *n. Eccl.* **1.** In the early Christian church, one of the elders of a church. **2.** In various hierarchical churches, a priest. **3.** In the Presbyterian Church: **a** An ordained clergyman: also called *teaching elder.* **b** A layman who is a member of the governing body of a congregation: also called *ruling elder.* [< LL < Gk. *presbyteros* elder, compar. of *presbys* old, important. Doublet of PRIEST.]

pres·byt·er·ate (prez·bit′ər·it, -ə·rāt, pres-) *n.* **1.** The office or dignity of a presbyter. **2.** A body of presbyters.

pres·by·te·ri·al (prez′bə·tir′ē·əl, pres′-) *adj.* Pertaining to a presbytery or a presbyter. Also **pres·byt′er·al.** — **pres′by·te′ri·al·ly** *adv.*

pres·by·te·ri·an (prez′bə·tir′ē·ən, pres′-) *adj.* Pertaining to or characterized by church government by presbyters. — **pres′by·te′ri·an·ism** *n.*

Pres·by·te·ri·an (prez′bə·tir′ē·ən, pres′-) *adj.* Pertaining to or designating any of various Protestant churches, mostly Calvinist in doctrine, that have church government by presbyters. — *n.* A member of a Presbyterian church. — **Pres′by·te′ri·an·ism** *n.*

pres·by·ter·y (prez′bə·ter′ē, pres′-) *n. pl.* **·ter·ies 1.** In the Presbyterian Church: **a** A court composed of the ministers and one or two presbyters of each church in a district. **b** The district so represented. **2.** Presbyters collectively. **3.** Government of a church by presbyters: distinguished from *episcopacy.* **4.** That part of a church set apart for the clergy. **5.** *Brit.* In the Roman Catholic Church, the residence of a priest. [< OF *presbiterie* < LL *presbyterium* assembly of elders < Gk. *presbyterion* < *presbyteros* elder]

pre·school (prē′skoōl′) *adj.* Of, intended for, or designating a child past infancy but under school age, usually between the ages of two and five.

pre·sci·ence (prē′shē·əns, presh′ē-) *n.* Knowledge of events before they take place; foreknowledge. [< OF < L *praescientia* < *prae-* before + *scire* to know]

pre·sci·ent (prē′shē·ənt, presh′ē-) *adj.* Having prescience; farseeing. [< F < L *presciens, -entis* < *praescire.* See PRESCIENCE.] — **pre′sci·ent·ly** *adv.*

pre·scind (pri·sind′) *v.t.* **1.** To set apart in thought; consider separately. **2.** To cut off; remove. — *v.i.* **3.** To withdraw the attention: with *from.* [< L *praescindere* < *prae-* before + *scindere* to cut]

Pres·cott (pres′kət), **William,** 1726–95, American Revolutionary soldier; commanded at the battle of Bunker Hill. — **William Hickling,** 1796–1859, U.S. historian.

pre·scribe (pri·skrīb′) *v.* **·scribed, ·scrib·ing** *v.t.* **1.** To set down as a direction or rule to be followed; ordain; enjoin. **2.** *Med.* To order the use of (a medicine, treatment, etc.). **3.** *Law* To render invalid by lapse of time. — *v.i.* **4.** To lay down laws or rules; give directions. **5.** *Med.* To order a remedy; give prescriptions. **6.** *Law* **a** To assert a title to something on the basis of prescription: with *for* or *to.* **b** To become invalid or unenforceable by lapse of time. [< L *praescribere* < *prae-* before + *scribere* to write] — **pre·scrib′er** *n.*

pre·script (prē′skript; *for adj., also* pri·skript′) *n.* Something prescribed; a rule or regulation, especially a rule of conduct. — *adj.* Laid down; prescribed. [< L *praescriptus,* pp. of *praescribere.* See PRESCRIBE.]

pre·scrip·ti·ble (pri·skrip′tə·bəl) *adj.* **1.** Derived from or acquirable by prescription. **2.** Depending on or subject to prescription. — **pre·scrip′ti·bil′i·ty** *n.*

pre·scrip·tion (pri·skrip′shən) *n.* **1.** *Med.* **a** A physician's formula for compounding a medicine or his designation of a medicine by name, including directions regarding its administration. **b** The remedy so prescribed. **c** A formula issued by a licensed oculist or optometrist giving directions for the grinding of eyeglass lenses. **2.** The act of prescribing. **3.** That which is prescribed; a prescript. **4.** Old or continued custom. **5.** A claim based on long usage. **6.** *Law* **a** A title to property, or a mode of acquiring title to property, founded on immemorial or uninterrupted possession. **b** A mode of losing a right or title by failure to assert it within a given time. **c** The period after which a neglected right or title cannot be asserted. [< L *praescriptio, -onis*]

SYMBOLS USED IN MEDICAL PRESCRIPTIONS

℞ take (L *recipe*)
S, Sig. write: indicates directions to be given on the label of a prescription (L *signa*)
ĀĀ, Ā, āā of each (Gk. *ana*)
a.c. before meals (L *ante cibum*)
ad up to; so as to make (L)
ad. add; let there be added (L *adde*)
aq. water (L *aqua*)
b.i.d. twice daily (L *bis in die*)
t.i.d. three times daily (L *ter in die*)
q.i.d. four times daily (L *quater in die*)
p.r.n. when required; according to circumstances (L *pro re nata*)
gtt. drops (L *guttae*)

pre·scrip·tive (pri·skrip′tiv) *adj.* **1.** Making strict requirements or rules: *prescriptive* grammar. **2.** Sanctioned by custom or long use: a *prescriptive* right. **3.** *Law* Acquired by immemorial use; based on prescription: a *prescriptive* title. **— pre·scrip′tive·ly** *adv.*

pres·ence (prez′əns) *n.* **1.** The state or fact of being present. **2.** The area immediately surrounding a person or thing; close proximity. **3.** The immediate vicinity of a person of superior rank, especially a sovereign; also, the person or personality of a sovereign, ruler, etc. **4.** Personal appearance; bearing; especially, a pleasing or dignified bearing. **5.** An invisible spirit or influence felt to be near. **6.** *Obs.* An assembly of persons; audience. **7.** *Obs.* A presence chamber. [< OF < L *praesentia,* < *praeesse.* See PRESENT.]

presence chamber The room or apartment in which a high dignitary or ruler receives assemblies.

presence of mind Full command of one's faculties, especially in an emergency; coolness, alertness, and readiness.

pres·ent[1] (prez′ənt) *adj.* **1.** Now going on; not past or future. **2.** Of or pertaining to time now occurring; current; contemporary. **3.** Being in the place or company referred to or considered; being at hand. **4.** Being actually considered, written, discussed, etc.; now in mind: the *present* issue. **5.** *Gram.* Denoting a tense or verb form that expresses a current or habitual action or state. **6.** *Archaic* Ready at hand; prompt in emergency: a *present* wit. **7.** *Archaic* Not delayed; immediate; instant. **—** *n.* **1.** Present time; the time being; now. **2.** *Gram.* The present tense; also, a verb form denoting it. **3.** *pl. Law* Present writings: a term for the document in which the word occurs: Know all men by these *presents*. **4.** *Obs.* A present matter or affair. Abbr. (for adj. def. 4, n. def. 2) *pr., pres.* **— at present** Now. **— for the present** For the time being. [< OF < L *praesens, -entis,* ppr. of *praeesse* < *prae-* before + *esse* to be]

pre·sent[2] (v. pri·zent′; n. prez′ənt) *v.t.* **1.** To bring into the presence or acquaintance of another; introduce, especially to one of higher rank: The ambassador was *presented* to the king. **2.** To exhibit to view or notice; display. **3.** To suggest to the mind: This *presents* a problem. **4.** To put forward for consideration or action; submit, as a petition. **5.** To make a gift or presentation of or to, usually formally. **6.** To aim or level (a weapon, etc.). **7.** *Law* **a** To offer, as a charge, for judicial action or inquiry. **b** To bring a charge or indictment against. **8.** *Eccl.* To nominate to a benefice. **9.** *Archaic* To represent on the stage; act. **— Syn.** See GIVE. **— to present arms** *Mil.* To salute by holding a gun vertically in front of one's body with the muzzle up and the trigger facing forward. **—** *n.* Something presented or given; a gift; donation. [< OF *presenter* < L *praesentare* to exhibit < *praesens.* See PRESENT[1].] **— pre·sent′er** *n.*

pre·sent·a·ble (pri·zen′tə·bəl) *adj.* **1.** Fit to be presented; in suitable condition or attire for company. **2.** Capable of being offered, exhibited, or bestowed. **— pre·sent′a·bil′i·ty, pre·sent′a·ble·ness** *n.* **— pre·sent′a·bly** *adv.*

pres·en·ta·tion (prez′ən·tā′shən, prē′zən-) *n.* **1.** The act of presenting or proffering for acceptance, approval, etc., or the state of being presented. **2.** The formal offering of a complimentary gift. **3.** The act of introducing or bringing to notice, especially to one of higher rank: *presentation* at court. **4.** *Eccl.* The nomination of a clergyman to a benefice; also, the right of such nomination. **5.** An exhibition or representation, as of a play. **6.** The fact or process of being present in consciousness; also, something present in consciousness, as a perception. **7.** *Med.* The position of the fetus at birth, designated by the part that is first presented at the mouth of the womb: breech *presentation.* **8.** Presentment (def. 4). **9.** *Often cap. Eccl.* A representation or commemoration of a ceremony of being presented to God: the *Presentation* of the Virgin. **10.** *Rare.* A gift; present.

pres·en·ta·tion·al (prez′ən·tā′shən·əl, prē′zən-) *adj.* Relating to or composed of presentations.

pres·en·ta·tion·ism (prez′ən·tā′shən·iz′əm, prē′zən-) *n. Philos.* The doctrine that the mind has an immediate and direct awareness of objects perceived. Also **pres′en·ta′tion·al·ism** (-əl·iz′əm). **— pres′en·ta′tion·ist** *adj. & n.*

pre·sen·ta·tive (pri·zen′tə·tiv) *adv.* **1.** Having to do with the mental awareness or knowledge of an activity, power, or object. **2.** *Eccl.* Having the right to present a benefice; also, admitting the presentation of a clergyman. **— pre·sen′ta·tive·ness** *n.*

pres·ent-day (prez′ənt·dā′) *adj.* Of the present time; current.

pres·en·tee (prez′ən·tē′) *n.* **1.** One who is presented, as to a benefice or at court. **2.** The recipient of a gift.

pre·sen·ti·ment (pri·zen′tə·mənt) *n.* A prophetic sense of something to come; a foreboding. [< F *pressentiment* < *pressentir* to perceive beforehand < L *praesentire* < *prae-* before + *sentire* to perceive]

pre·sen·tive (pri·zen′tiv) *adj.* Conveying a distinct and complete conception: said of words: distinguished from *symbolic.* **— pre·sen′tive word. — pre·sen′tive·ly** *adv.* **— pre·sen′tive·ness** *n.*

pres·ent·ly (prez′ənt·lē) *adv.* **1.** After a little time; shortly. **2.** At the present time; now. **3.** *Archaic* or *Dial.* At once.

pre·sent·ment (pri·zent′mənt) *n.* **1.** The act of presenting; also, the state or manner of being presented; presentation. **2.** Something represented or exhibited; a representation or picture. **3.** *Law* A report made by a grand jury concerning some wrongdoing, based on the jury's own knowledge and presented to the court without an indictment. **4.** In commerce, the presenting of a note, bill, etc., for payment: also called *presentation.*

present participle See under PARTICIPLE.

present perfect *Gram.* The verb tense expressing an action completed by the present time, usually constructed with a form of the verb *to have,* as *has finished* in *By now he has finished the task.*

present tense *Gram.* The verb tense marking present time, as *am* in *I am here,* or *are going* in *You are going home.*

pre·ser·va·tive (pri·zûr′və·tiv) *adj.* Serving or tending to preserve. **—** *n.* A preservative agent; especially, a chemical substance added to food to retard spoilage.

pre·serve (pri·zûrv′) *v.* **·served, ·serv·ing** *v.t.* **1.** To keep in safety; protect from danger or harm; guard: May the gods *preserve* you. **2.** To keep intact or unimpaired; maintain: to *preserve* appearances. **3.** To prepare (food) for future consumption, as by boiling with sugar or by salting. **4.** To keep from decomposition or change, as by chemical treatment: to *preserve* a specimen in alcohol. **5.** To keep for one's private hunting or fishing: to *preserve* foxes. **—** *v.i.* **6.** To make preserves, as of fruit. **7.** To maintain a game preserve. **—** *n.* **1.** *Usually pl.* Fruit that has been cooked, usually with sugar, to prevent its fermenting. **2.** Something that preserves or is preserved. **3.** An area set apart for the protection of wildlife, natural resources, forests, etc.; also, such an area reserved for restricted or private hunting or fishing. [< OF *preserver* < LL *praeservare* < L *prae-* before + *servare* to keep] **— pre·serv′a·bil′i·ty** *n.* **— pre·serv′a·ble** *adj.* **— pres·er·va·tion** (prez′ər·vā′shən) *n.* **— pre·serv′er** *n.* **— Syn.** (verb) **1.** save, secure, defend.

pre-shrunk (prē′shrungk′) *adj.* Shrunk during manufacture to minimize later shrinkage during washing or cleaning.

pre·side (pri·zīd′) *v.i.* **·sid·ed, ·sid·ing** **1.** To sit in authority, as over a meeting; act as chairman or president. **2.** To exercise direction or control. **3.** To occupy a featured place, as an instrumentalist on a program. [< F *présider* < L *praesidere* < *prae-* before + *sedere* to sit] **— pre·sid′er** *n.*

pres·i·den·cy (prez′ə·dən·sē) *n. pl.* **·cies 1.** The office, function, or term of office of a president. **2.** *Often cap.* The office of president of the United States. **3.** *Often cap.* Formerly, any of the three original provinces of British India, consisting of Bengal, Madras, and Bombay. **4.** In the Mormon Church: **a** A local council of three men. **b** The highest governing body of the church (**First Presidency**), consisting of the president and two counselors. Abbr. *pres.*

pres·i·dent (prez′ə·dənt) *n.* **1.** One who is chosen to preside over an organized body. **2.** *Often cap.* The chief executive of a republic. **3.** The chief executive officer of a government department, corporation, society, board of trade or trustees, or similar body. **4.** The chief officer of a college or university. **5.** The chairman of a meeting conducted under parliamentary rules. Abbr. *P. Pres.* [< OF < L *praesidens, -entis,* ppr. of *praesidere.* See PRESIDE.] **— pres·i·den·tial** (prez′ə·den′shəl) *adj.* **— pres′i·dent·ship′** *n.*

THE PRESIDENTS OF THE UNITED STATES

Number—Name	Birthplace—Inaugurated: year		Age
1 George Washington	Westmoreland Co., Va.	1789	57
2 John Adams	Quincy, Mass.	1797	61
3 Thomas Jefferson	Shadwell, Va.	1801	57
4 James Madison	Port Conway, Va.	1809	57
5 James Monroe	Westmoreland Co., Va.	1817	58
6 John Quincy Adams	Quincy, Mass.	1825	57
7 Andrew Jackson	Union Co., N.C.	1829	61
8 Martin Van Buren	Kinderhook, N.Y.	1837	54
9 William H. Harrison	Berkeley, Va.	1841	68
10 John Tyler	Greenway, Va.	1841	51
11 James K. Polk	Little Sugar Creek, N.C.	1845	49
12 Zachary Taylor	Orange Co., Va.	1849	64
13 Millard Fillmore	Summerhill, N.Y.	1850	50
14 Franklin Pierce	Hillsboro, N.H.	1853	48
15 James Buchanan	Cove Gap, Pa.	1857	65

16	Abraham Lincoln		
	Hardin Co., Ky.	1861	52
17	Andrew Johnson		
	Raleigh, N.C.	1865	56
18	Ulysses S. Grant		
	Point Pleasant, O.	1869	46
19	Rutherford B. Hayes		
	Delaware, O.	1877	54
20	James A. Garfield		
	Cuyahoga Co., O.	1881	49
21	Chester A. Arthur		
	Fairfield, Vt.	1881	50
22	Grover Cleveland		
	Caldwell, N.J.	1885	47
23	Benjamin Harrison		
	North Bend, O.	1889	55
24	Grover Cleveland		
	Caldwell, N.J.	1893	55
25	William McKinley		
	Niles, O.	1897	54
26	Theodore Roosevelt		
	New York, N.Y.	1901	42
27	William H. Taft		
	Cincinnati, O.	1909	51
28	Woodrow Wilson		
	Staunton, Va.	1913	56
29	Warren G. Harding		
	Corsica, O.	1921	55
30	Calvin Coolidge		
	Plymouth, Vt.	1923	51
31	Herbert C. Hoover		
	West Branch, Ia.	1929	55
32	Franklin D. Roosevelt		
	Hyde Park, N.Y.	1933	51
33	Harry S Truman		
	Lamar, Mo.	1945	60
34	Dwight D. Eisenhower		
	Denison, Tex.	1953	62
35	John F. Kennedy		
	Brookline, Mass.	1961	43
36	Lyndon B. Johnson		
	Stonewall, Texas	1963	55
37	Richard M. Nixon		
	Yorba Linda, Calif.	1969	56
38	Gerald R. Ford		
	Omaha, Nebr.	1974	61
39	Jimmy (James Earl, Jr.) Carter		
	Plains, Ga.	1977	52

pre·sid·i·al (pri·sid′ē·əl) *adj.* **1.** Of, pertaining to, or having a garrison. Also **pre·sid′i·ar′y** (-er′ē). **2.** Presidential. **3.** Provincial. [< F *présidial* < LL *praesidialis* < *praesidium* a presiding over < *praesidere*. See PRESIDE.]

pre·sid·i·o (pri·sid′ē·ō) *n. pl.* **·sid·i·os** A fort or garrisoned post in countries formerly or currently under Spanish control. [< Am.Sp. < L *praesidium*]

pre·sid·i·um (pri·sid′ē·əm) *n.* An executive committee in the Soviet Union serving as the permanent organ of a larger governmental body. [< L *praesidium*. See PRESIDIAL.]

Pre·sid·i·um (pri·sid′ē·əm) *n.* **1.** The administrative cabinet of the Soviet Union, headed by the premier, that exercises executive powers between sessions of the Supreme Soviet. **2.** The supreme policy-making committee of the Communist party of the Soviet Union, headed by the party secretary. See POLITBURO.

pre·sig·ni·fy (prē·sig′nə·fī) *v.t.* **·fied, ·fy·ing** To signify or give token of in advance; presage; foreshadow.

press¹ (pres) *v.t.* **1.** To act upon by weight or pressure: to *press* a button. **2.** To compress so as to extract the juice: to *press* grapes. **3.** To extract by pressure, as juice. **4.** To exert pressure upon so as to smooth, shape, make compact, etc. **5.** To smooth or shape by heat and pressure, as clothes; iron. **6.** To embrace closely; hug. **7.** To force or impel; drive. **8.** To distress or harass; place in difficulty: He was *pressed* by circumstances. **9.** To urge persistently; importune; entreat: They *pressed* me for an answer. **10.** To advocate persistently; insist on; emphasize. **11.** To put forward insistently: to *press* a claim. **12.** To urge onward; hasten. **13.** To proceed further in, as a lawsuit. **14.** To produce (a phonograph record) from a matrix. **15.** *Obs.* To crowd. **16.** *Obs.* To oppress. — *v.i.* **17.** To exert pressure; lie heavily. **18.** To advance forcibly or quickly. **19.** To press clothes. **20.** To take a press. **21.** To crowd; cram. **22.** To seek eagerly or urgently. **23.** To be urgent or importunate. — *n.* **1.** Any medium or agency, as newspapers, periodicals, broadcasting, etc., whose function

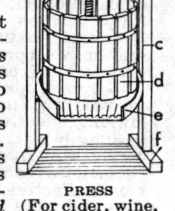

PRESS
(For cider, wine, and fruit)
a Press screw. *b* Crosshead. *c* Frame. *d* Tub. *e* Grooved drain tray. *f* Base.

is to collect and disseminate news. **2.** The people, as reporters, editors, broadcasters, etc., who gather or disseminate such news. **3.** Criticism, comments, news, etc., in newspapers or periodicals. **4.** A place where printing is carried on. **5.** The art, process, or business of printing. **6.** A printing press (which see). **7.** An apparatus or machine by which pressure is applied to form, shape, or cut objects, to compress bulky substances, to extract liquids, etc. **8.** The act of pressing, pushing, or crowding together; also, the condition that results: the *press* of the crowd. **9.** Hurry or pressure of affairs; urgency. **10.** The proper creases or folds in a pressed garment. **11.** A movable, upright closet or case. **12.** A frame or framelike device that by the use of pressure prevents warping: a ski *press*. **13.** In weightlifting, a lift in two movements of the weight off the floor, first to shoulder height, then vertically over the head with the arms fully extended: also called *military press*. **14.** *Archaic* A dense throng. [< OF *presser* < L *pressare*, freq. of *premere* (pp. *pressus*) to press]

press² (pres) *v.t.* **1.** To force into military or naval service; impress. **2.** To put to use in a manner not intended or desired. — *n.* A commission to impress men into the public service; also, the impressment of men. [< obs. *prest* enlistment for advance pay < OF *prest* loan < L *praestare* to be at hand < *prae-* before + *stare* to stand]

press agent A person employed to advance the interests of an actor, singer, etc., by means of publicity; also, a publicity agent for any person or business. Abbr. *PA*

press·board (pres′bôrd′, -bōrd′) *n.* **1.** A strong cardboard or paper, used for covers on printing presses, for packing, etc. **2.** An ironing board, especially a small one.

press box A section reserved for reporters, especially at a sports event.

Press·burg (pres′bŏŏrkh) German name for BRATISLAVA.

press conference An interview granted by a celebrity, official, etc., to a number of journalists at the same time.

press·er (pres′ər) *n.* One who or that which presses.

press gang A detachment of men detailed to press men into naval or military service. Also **press·gang** (pres′gang′).

press·ing (pres′ing) *adj.* **1.** Demanding immediate attention; urgent. **2.** Importunate. — **press′ing·ly** *adv.*

press·man (pres′mən) *n. pl.* **·men** (-mən) **1.** A man who has charge of a press, as a printing press. **2.** *Brit.* Journalist.

press·mark (pres′märk′) *n.* A mark in a book to locate its particular place in a library.

press money The king's shilling. See under SHILLING.

press of canvas *Naut.* The maximum spread of sail that can be carried with safety under wind pressure.

press·or (pres′ər) *adj. Physiol.* Increasing the functional activities of an organ. [< PRESS¹]

pressor nerve *Physiol.* A nerve that when stimulated raises the arterial blood pressure.

press proof **1.** The last proof taken before printing. **2.** A proof taken on a press.

press release A bulletin prepared by a press agent, public relations department, etc., announcing an event, development, decision, etc.

press·room (pres′rŏŏm′, -rŏŏm′) *n.* A room containing the presses of a printing concern.

pres·sure (presh′ər) *n.* **1.** The act of pressing, or the state of being pressed. **2.** Any force that acts against an opposing force. **3.** An impelling or constraining moral force: bringing *pressure* to bear. **4.** Urgent demands on one's time or strength: the *pressure* of business. **5.** The oppressive influence or depressing effect of something hard to bear; weight: the *pressure* of grief. **6.** *Physics* The force acting upon a surface per unit of area. Abbr. *P* **7.** Electromotive force (which see). **8.** *Obs.* A printed character; an impression; stamp. — *Syn.* See STRESS. — *v.t.* **·sur·ed, ·sur·ing** *Informal* To compel, as by forceful persuasion or influence. [< OF < L *pressura* < *premere* to press]

pressure cabin *Aeron.* An enclosed compartment in an aircraft in which air pressure is artificially maintained to compensate for the low pressure at high altitudes.

pressure cooker A strong, airtight pot for cooking food at high temperature under pressure: also called *autoclave.*

pressure gauge **1.** An instrument for measuring the pressure of a gas or liquid; a manometer. **2.** A device for measuring explosive pressure, as in the bore of a gun.

pressure gradient *Meteorol.* The rate of change in barometric pressure per unit of distance along a given atmospheric plane, usually horizontal.

pressure group A group that seeks through propaganda and lobbying to influence legislators and public opinion in behalf of its own special interests.

pres·sur·ize (presh′ər·īz) *v.t.* **·ized, ·iz·ing** **1.** To subject to high pressure. **2.** To establish (in an aircraft compartment, special suit, etc.) an air pressure higher than the low atmospheric pressure at high altitudes. — **pres′sur·i·za′tion** *n.*

press·work (pres′wûrk′) *n.* **1.** The operating or management of a printing press. **2.** The work done by it.

prest[1] (prest) *adj. Obs.* Ready; prepared; at hand. [< OF < L *praesto* ready]

prest[2] (prest) *n.* **1.** An advance or loan; also, ready money. **2.** The king's shilling. See under SHILLING: also **prest money.** [< OF. See PRESS[2].]

pres·ter (pres′tər) *n. Obs.* A priest or presbyter. [< OF *prestre* < LL *presbyter.* See PRIEST.]

Pres·ter John (pres′tər jon′) A legendary medieval Christian king and priest, traditionally of central Asia or Abyssinia.

pres·ti·dig·i·ta·tion (pres′tə·dij′ə·tā′shən) *n.* The practice of sleight of hand; jugglery; legerdemain. [< F < *preste* (< Ital. *presto* < LL *praestus*) nimble + L *digitus* finger] — **pres′ti·dig′i·ta′tor** *n.*

pres·tige (pres·tēzh′, pres′tij, pres·tēj′) *n.* **1.** Authority or importance based on past achievements, reputation, power, etc.; renown. **2.** Importance, respect, etc., due to the appearance of wealth or power: a car that gives *prestige.* [< F < L *praestigium* illusion, juggler's trick < *praestringere* < *prae*- before + *stringere* to bind] — **Syn. 1.** distinction, name, repute.

pres·tig·ious (pres·tij′əs, -tē′jəs) *adj.* Having a famous reputation or name; honored or well-known; illustrious. — **pres·tig′ious·ly** *adv.* — **pres·tig′ious·ness** *n.*

pres·tis·si·mo (pres·tis′i·mō, *Ital.* pres·tēs′sē·mō) *Music adj.* Very fast; as fast as possible. — *adv.* In a prestissimo manner: a direction to the performer. — *n.* A movement or passage so played. [< Ital.]

pres·to (pres′tō) *adj. Music* Quick; faster than allegro. — *adv.* **1.** *Music* In a presto manner: a direction to the performer. **2.** At once; speedily. — *n. Music* A presto movement or passage. [< Ital. < L *praesto* at hand]

Pres·ton (pres′tən) A county borough and river port in central Lancashire, England; pop. 132,000 (1976).

Pres·ton·pans (pres′tən·panz′) A burgh in East Lothian, Scotland, on the Firth of Forth; scene of a Scottish victory over the English, 1745; pop. 6,816 (est. 1969).

pre·sum·a·ble (pri·zōō′mə·bəl) *adj.* That may be assumed or presumed; reasonable. — **pre·sum′a·bly** *adv.*

pre·sume (pri·zōōm′) *v.* **·sumed, ·sum·ing** *v.t.* **1.** To take for granted; assume to be true until disproved: I *presume* you are right. **2.** To take upon oneself without warrant or permission; dare; venture: usually with the infinitive: Do you *presume* to address me? **3.** To indicate the probability of; seem to prove: A concealed weapon *presumes* the intent to commit a crime. — *v.i.* **4.** To act or proceed presumptuously or overconfidently. **5.** To make excessive demands; rely too heavily: with *on* or *upon:* He *presumes* on my good nature. [< OF *presumer* < L *praesumere* < *prae*- before + *sumere* to take] — **pre·sum·ed·ly** (pri·zōō′mid·lē) *adv.* — **pre·sum′er** *n.*

pre·sump·tion (pri·zump′shən) *n.* **1.** Offensively forward or arrogant conduct or speech; effrontery; insolence. **2.** The act of presuming; also, something presumed. **3.** A ground or reason for presuming. **4.** That which may be logically assumed to be true until disproved. **5.** *Law* The inference of a fact from circumstances that usually or necessarily attend such a fact. [< OF *presomption* < L *praesumtio, -onis* < *praesumere.* See PRESUME.] — **Syn. 1.** arrogance, boldness, impudence, impertinence.

pre·sump·tive (pri·zump′tiv) *adj.* **1.** Creating or affording reasonable grounds for belief. **2.** Based upon presumption: an heir *presumptive.* Abbr. **pres.** [< F *présomptif*] — **pre·sump′tive·ly** *adv.*

pre·sump·tu·ous (pri·zump′chōō·əs) *adj.* Unduly confident or bold; audacious; arrogant. — **Syn.** See ARROGANT. — **pre·sump′tu·ous·ly** *adv.* — **pre·sump′tu·ous·ness** *n.*

pre·sup·pose (prē′sə·pōz′) *v.t.* **·posed, ·pos·ing** **1.** To take for granted; assume to start with. **2.** To imply or involve as a necessary antecedent or condition: Death *presupposes* life. [< F *présupposer*] — **pre·sup·po·si·tion** (prē′sup·ə·zish′ən) *n.*

pret. Preterite.

pre·tend (pri·tend′) *v.t.* **1.** To assume or display a false appearance of; feign: to *pretend* friendship for an enemy. **2.** To claim or assert falsely: He *pretended* that there was gold on his property. **3.** To feign in play; make believe. — *v.i.* **4.** To make believe, as in play or deception. **5.** To put forward a claim: with *to.* [< L *praetendere* < *prae*- before + *tendere* to spread out] — **Syn. 1.** affect, counterfeit, profess, sham, simulate.

pre·tend·ed (pri·ten′did) *adj.* **1.** Alleged or asserted; professed. **2.** Deceptive; false. — **pre·tend′ed·ly** *adv.*

pre·tend·er (pri·ten′dər) *n.* **1.** One who advances a claim or title; a claimant; especially, a claimant to a throne. **2.** One who pretends.

pre·tense (pri·tens′, prē′tens) *n.* **1.** A pretended claim; a ruse or wile; pretext. **2.** A false assumption of a character or condition; affectation. **3.** The act or state of pretending. **4.** A right or title asserted; a claim. **5.** The condition of being a claimant. Also *Brit.* **pre·tence′.** [< AF *pretensse* < Med.L *praetensus* < L *praetendere.* See PRETEND.]

pre·ten·sion (pri·ten′shən) *n.* **1.** A claim put forward, as to an office, privilege, rank, etc. **2.** Affectation; display. **3.** A bold or presumptuous assertion.

pre·ten·tious (pri·ten′shəs) *adj.* **1.** Making an ambitious outward show; ostentatious. **2.** Making claims, especially when exaggerated or false. [< F *prétentieux*] — **pre·ten′tious·ly** *adv.* — **pre·ten′tious·ness** *n.*

preter- *prefix* Beyond; past; more than: *preternatural:* also spelled *praeter-.* [< L *praeter* beyond < *prae* before]

pret·er·hu·man (prē′tər·hyōō′mən) *adj.* Beyond what is human.

pret·er·it (pret′ər·it) *adj.* **1.** *Gram.* Signifying past time or completed past action. **2.** *Rare* Belonging to the past; bygone. — *n. Gram.* The tense that expresses absolute past time; the past tense; also, a verb in this tense. Also **pret′er·ite.** Abbr. **pret., pt.** [< OF *preterit* < L *praeteritus* past, pp. of *praeterire* < *praeter*- beyond + *ire* to go]

pret·er·i·tion (pret′ə·rish′ən) *n.* **1.** The act of passing over or omitting. **2.** *Law* The omission or passing by of a natural heir in a will. **3.** *Theol.* In the doctrine of predestination, the passing over of the nonelect. [< LL *praeteritio, -onis* < L *praeteritus.* See PRETERIT.]

pret·er·i·tive (pri·ter′ə·tiv) *adj. Gram.* Used only in a past tense or past tenses: said of certain verbs.

pret·er·mit (prē′tər·mit′) *v.t.* **·mit·ted, ·mit·ting** **1.** To fail or cease to do; neglect; omit. **2.** To let pass without noticing; overlook; disregard. [< L *praetermittere* < *praeter*- beyond + *mittere* to send] — **pre′ter·mis′sion** (-mish′ən) *n.*

pre·ter·nat·u·ral (prē′tər·nach′ər·əl) *adj.* **1.** Diverging from or exceeding the common order of nature, but not outside the natural order: distinguished from *supernatural.* **2.** Outside the natural order; supernatural. — **Syn.** See SUPERNATURAL. — **pre′ter·nat′u·ral·ism** *n.* — **pre′ter·nat′u·ral·ly** *adv.*

pre·text (prē′tekst) *n.* **1.** A fictitious reason or motive advanced to conceal a real one. **2.** A specious excuse or explanation. [< F *prétexte* < L *praetextus,* pp. of *praetexere* to allege < *prae* before + *texere* to weave]

pre·tor (prē′tər), **pre·to·ri·an** (pri·tôr′ē·ən, -tō′rē-), etc. See PRAETOR, etc.

Pre·to·ri·a (pri·tôr′ē·ə, -tō′rē·ə) The administrative capital of the Republic of South Africa and the capital of Transvaal, in the south central part of the Province; pop. 571,541 (1970).

Pre·to·ri·us (prə·tōō′rē·ŏŏs), **Andries Wilhelmus Jacobus,** 1799–1853, Boer pioneer and leader. — **Martinius Wessels,** 1819–1901, Boer statesman; first president of the South African Republic; son of the preceding.

pret·ti·fy (prit′i·fī) *v.t.* **·fied, ·fy·ing** To make pretty; embellish overmuch. [< PRETTY + -FY]

pret·ty (prit′ē) *adj.* **·ti·er, ·ti·est** **1.** Characterized by delicacy, gracefulness, or proportion rather than by striking beauty: a *pretty* face. **2.** Pleasant; attractive: a *pretty* melody. **3.** Decent; good; sufficient: often used ironically: A *pretty* mess you've made of it! **4.** *Informal* Rather large in size or degree; considerable. **5.** Characterized by effeminacy; affected; foppish. **6.** *Archaic* Fine; elegant. **7.** *Archaic* or *Scot.* Bold; vigorous; strong. — **Syn.** See BEAUTIFUL. — *adv.* **1.** To a fair extent; moderately; somewhat; rather: He looked *pretty* well. **2.** *Dial.* Prettily; finely. — **sitting pretty** *Informal* In good circumstances. — *n. pl.* **·ties** (-tēz) A pretty person or thing. [OE *prættig* sly, cunning < *praet* deceit] — **pret′ti·ly** *adv.* — **pret′ti·ness** *n.*

pret·zel (pret′səl) *n.* A glazed, salted biscuit, usually baked in the form of a loose knot. [< G *brezel*]

Preus·sen (proi′sən) The German name for PRUSSIA.

pre·vail (pri·vāl′) *v.i.* **1.** To gain mastery; be victorious; triumph: with *over* or *against.* **2.** To be effective or efficacious; succeed. **3.** To use persuasion or influence successfully: with *on, upon,* or *with.* **4.** To be or become a predominant feature or quality; be prevalent. **5.** To have general or widespread use or acceptance; be in force. [< OF *prevaloir* or L *praevalere* < *prae*- before + *valere* to be strong] — **Syn. 1.** defeat, conquer, vanquish, overthrow.

pre·vail·ing (pri·vā′ling) *adj.* **1.** Current; prevalent. **2.** Having effective power or influence; efficacious. — **pre·vail′ing·ly** *adv.* — **pre·vail′ing·ness** *n.*

prev·a·lent (prev′ə·lənt) *adj.* **1.** Of wide extent or frequent occurrence; common. **2.** Predominant; superior. **3.** Efficacious; effective. — **prev′a·lence** *n.* — **prev′a·lent·ly** *adv.*

pre·var·i·cate (pri·var′ə·kāt) *v.i.* **·cat·ed, ·cat·ing** To speak or act in a deceptive, ambiguous, or evasive manner; quibble; lie. [< L *praevaricatus,* pp. of *praevaricari* to walk crookedly < *prae*- before + *varicare* to straddle < *varicus* straddling < *varus* crooked] — **pre·var′i·ca′tor** *n.*

pre·var·i·ca·tion (pri·var′ə·kā′shən) *n.* **1.** The act of prevaricating. **2.** A misleading or equivocal statement. — **Syn. 2.** deception, sophistry, deceit, lie.

pré·ve·nance (prā′və·näns′) *n. French* Attention to or anticipation of the needs of others: also called *prevenience.*

pre·ven·ience (pri·vēn′yəns) *n.* **1.** The act or state of going before; anticipation. **2.** Prévenance.

pre·ven·ient (pri·vēn′yənt) *adj.* **1.** Going before; preceding. **2.** Anticipatory; expectant. **3.** Preventive. [< L *praeveniens, -entis,* ppr. of *praevenire.* See PREVENT.]

pre·vent (pri·vent′) *v.t.* **1.** To keep from happening, as by

previous measures or preparations; preclude; thwart. **2.** To keep from doing something; forestall; hinder. **3.** *Obs.* To anticipate; precede. [< L *praeventus*, pp. of *praevenire* < *prae-* before + *venire* to come] — **pre·vent′a·ble** or **pre·vent′i·ble** *adj.* — **pre·vent′a·bil′i·ty** or **pre·vent′i·bil′i·ty** *n.* — **pre·vent′er** *n.*
— **Syn. 1.** *Prevent, preclude, forestall, avert,* and *obviate* mean to hinder or stop from happening or doing. *Prevent* suggests forcible restraint and complete stoppage: armed guards *prevented* us from entering the palace. The sense of anticipation, originally understood in *prevent,* is now to be found in *preclude* and *forestall.* An event is *precluded* by circumstances which make its occurrence impossible; to *forestall* is to make advance preparation to deal with, especially to restrain. *Avert* suggests a thrusting aside or warding off of something, while *obviate* refers to a risk, difficulty, objection, or the like, which is met squarely and cleared out of the way. Compare HINDER, BAFFLE. — **Ant.** permit, facilitate.
pre·ven·tion (pri·ven′shən) *n.* **1.** The act of preventing. **2.** A hindrance; obstruction.
pre·ven·tive (pri·ven′tiv) *adj.* Intended or serving to ward off harm, disease, etc.: *preventive* medicine. — *n.* That which prevents or hinders, as a medicine to ward off disease; a precautionary measure. Also **pre·vent·a·tive** (pri·ven′tə·tiv). — **pre·ven′tive·ly** *adv.* — **pre·ven′tive·ness** *n.*
pre·view (prē′vyōō′) *n.* **1.** An advance showing of a motion picture, a fashion show, etc., to invited guests before it is presented publicly. **2.** Any advance display or viewing; especially, the showing of scenes or parts of scenes to advertise a forthcoming motion picture. — *v.t.* To view in advance. Also spelled *prevue.*
pre·vi·ous (prē′vē·əs) *adj.* **1.** Existing or taking place before something else in time or order; antecedent; prior to. **2.** *Informal* Acting, occurring, or speaking too soon; premature. — **previous** to Antecedent to; before. [< L *praevius* going before < *prae-* before + *via* way] — **pre′vi·ous·ly** *adv.* — **pre′vi·ous·ness** *n.*
— **Syn. 1.** preceding, earlier, former, anterior. — **Ant.** subsequent, later.
previous question The parliamentary motion to proceed to an immediate vote on the main question under consideration, often used to force the immediate question to a vote by cutting off debate. Abbr. *p.q.* Compare CLOTURE.
pre·vise (prē·vīz′) *v.t.* **·vised, ·vis·ing 1.** To see beforehand; foresee. **2.** To notify beforehand; forewarn. [< L *praevisus,* pp. of *praevidere* < *prae-* before + *videre* to see]
pre·vi·sion (prē·vizh′ən) *n.* **1.** The act or power of foreseeing; prescience; foresight. **2.** A prophetic or anticipatory vision. [< L *praevisus*]
pre·vo·ca·tion·al (prē′vō·kā′shən·əl) *adj.* Of or pertaining to the training given or required before admission to vocational schools.
Pré·vost (prā·vō′), **Marcel (Eugène),** 1862–1941, French novelist.
Pré·vost d′Ex·iles (prā·vō′ deg·zēl′), **Antoine François,** 1697–1763, French novelist: called **Abbé Prévost.**
pre·vue (prē′vyōō) See PREVIEW.
pre·war (prē′wôr′) *adj.* Of or pertaining to a condition, arrangement, time, etc., before a war.
prex·y (prek′sē) *pl.* **·ies** *n. Slang* A president; especially, a college president. Also **prex.**
prey (prā) *n.* **1.** Any animal seized by another for food. **2.** A person or thing made the victim of a harmful or hostile person or influence. **3.** *Obs.* The act of preying; depredation; robbery. **4.** *Obs.* Booty; plunder; pillage. — *v.i.* **1.** To seek or take prey for food: Cats *prey* on birds. **2.** To make someone a victim, as by cheating. **3.** To exert a wearing or harmful influence: His losses *preyed* on his mind. **4.** *Obs.* To plunder. [< OF *preie* < L *praeda* booty] — **prey′er** *n.*
Pri·am (prī′əm) In Greek legend, the son of Laomedon, husband of Hecuba, and father of fifty sons including Hector and Paris. He was the last king of Troy and was killed during its capture at the end of the Trojan War.
Pri·a·pe·an (prī′ə·pē′ən) *adj.* Of or pertaining to Priapus; phallic.
pri·a·pism (prī′ə·piz′əm) *n. Pathol.* A persistent erection of the penis, usually without sexual desire, usually resulting from certain injuries and diseases of the spinal cord.
pri·a·pus (prī·ā′pəs) *n.* A representation of the male generative organ; phallus. [< PRIAPUS]
Pri·a·pus (prī·ā′pəs) In Greek and Roman mythology, the god of male procreative power, son of Dionysus and Aphrodite. [< L < Gk. *Priapos*]
Prib·i·lof Islands (prib′i·lof) A group of four islands of Alaska in the SE Bering Sea; major breeding ground of the Alaska fur seal.
price (prīs) *n.* **1.** The amount of money, goods, etc., for which something is bought or sold. **2.** The cost at which something is obtained: Death is the *price* of glory. **3.** Value; worth; especially, high value. **4.** A bribe, or anything used for a bribe. **5.** A reward for the capture or death of someone. Abbr. *pc., pr.* — **beyond price 1.** Invaluable; priceless. **2.** Not bribable. — **to price out of the market** To lose one's

share of a market by overpricing (oneself, a product, etc.). — **to set a price on one's head** To offer a reward for the capture of a person, dead or alive. — *v.t.* **priced, pric·ing 1.** To set a price on; establish a price for. **2.** *Informal* To ask the price of. [< OF *pris* < L *pretium.* Akin to PRAISE.]
— **Syn.** (noun) **1.** *Price, charge, cost,* and *expense* denote the money or other valuable consideration exchanged for goods or services. The *price* is the amount asked by the seller of an article; the amount asked for a service is a *charge.* That which a buyer must pay is the *cost; expense* is a *cost,* or *costs* collectively, with emphasis on the deduction from the buyer's funds. All these words are extended freely to a person's resources in energy, labor, time, and the like.
Price may appear as a combining form or as the first element in two-word phrases, as in the following examples:

price adjustment	price-making
price administration	price manipulation
price boom	price notice
price control	price reduction
price cut	price-ruling
price fixer	price stabilizer
price freeze	price-stabilizing
price history	price support
price level	price-supporting
price maintenance	price tag

price cutting The act of reducing the price of an article below the price at which it is usually advertised or sold.
price fixing 1. The establishment and maintenance of a scale of prices agreed upon by specified groups of producers or distributors. **2.** The establishing by government action of maximum or minimum or fixed prices for certain goods and services. **3.** The fixing by a manufacturer or producer of the price at which retailers must sell his product. — *adj.* Of or pertaining to price fixing.
price·less (prīs′lis) *adj.* **1.** Beyond price or valuation; invaluable. **2.** *Informal* Wonderfully amusing or absurd.
price list A catalogue of goods listing their prices.
price rigging The concealed illegal fixing of prices.
Prich·ard (prich′ərd) A city in SW Alabama, near Mobile; pop. 41,578.
prick (prik) *v.t.* **1.** To pierce slightly, as with a sharp point; puncture. **2.** To affect with sharp mental pain; sting; spur. **3.** To mark, outline, or indicate by or as by punctures. **4.** In farriery: **a** To drive a nail into the quick of (a horse's hoof), causing lameness. **b** To nick (a horse's tail). **5.** To transplant (young plants) preparatory to later planting. **6.** To trace (a ship's course, etc.) on a chart: with *off.* **7.** *Obs.* To urge on with or as with a spur; goad. — *v.i.* **8.** To have or cause a stinging or piercing sensation. **9.** *Archaic* To ride at full speed; go at a gallop. — **to prick up one's (or its) ears 1.** To raise the ears erect. **2.** To listen attentively. — *n.* **1.** The act of pricking; also, the sensation of being pricked. **2.** A mental sting or spur: the *prick* of conscience. **3.** A slender, sharp-pointed thing, as a thorn or pointed weapon. **4.** A mark made by a sharp, pointed instrument; puncture; dot. **5.** The footprint of an animal, as a rabbit or deer. **6.** *Archaic* A goad or spur. [OE *prica* point, dot] — **prick′er** *n.*
prick·et (prik′it) *n.* **1.** A buck in its second year. **2.** A sharp point upon which to stick a candle; also, a candlestick having such a point. [Dim. of PRICK]
prick·le (prik′əl) *n.* **1.** A small, sharp point, as on the bark of a plant. **2.** A tingling or stinging sensation. — *v.* **·led, ·ling** *v.t.* **1.** To prick; pierce. **2.** To cause a tingling or stinging sensation in. — *v.i.* **3.** To have a stinging sensation; tingle. [OE *pricel*]
prick·ly (prik′lē) *adj.* **1.** Furnished with prickles. **2.** Stinging, as if from a prick or sting: a *prickly* sensation.
prickly ash 1. A prickly shrub or tree (*Xanthoxylum americanum*) of the rue family, with pungent and aromatic bark. **2.** Hercules'-club.
prickly heat A form of miliaria characterized by redness, itching, and small eruptions: also called *heat rash.*
prickly lettuce A species of lettuce (*Lactuca serriola*) growing wild in the United States: also called *compass plant.*
prickly pear 1. A flat-stemmed cactus (genus *Opuntia*) bearing a pear-shaped and often prickly fruit: also called *nopal.* **2.** The fruit itself.
prickly poppy A weedlike annual (*Argemone mexicana*) of the poppy family, with prickly stem and leaves, showy flowers, and yellow juice.
prick song *Archaic* **1.** Written music. **2.** Counterpoint.
pride (prīd) *n.* **1.** An undue sense of one's own superiority; inordinate self-esteem; arrogance; conceit. **2.** A proper sense of personal dignity and worth; honorable self-respect. **3.** That of which one is justly proud; a cause of exultation. **4.** The best or most excellent part of anything: the nation's *pride.* **5.** The best time or the flowering of something: the *pride* of summer. **6.** *Obs.* Sexual desire. **7.** *Archaic* Ostentatious splendor; display. **8.** A group or company: said of lions. — *v.t.* **prid·ed, prid·ing** To take pride in (oneself) for something: with *on* or *upon.* [OE *prȳte < prūt* proud]

— **Syn.** (noun) **1.** *Pride, self-esteem, conceit, vanity,* and *vainglory* denote an unwarranted sense of one's superiority. *Pride* manifests itself in disdain or haughtiness toward others; *self-esteem,* in more deference to one's opinions than others grant. *Conceit* is an exaggerated opinion of one's ability or worth. *Vanity* is seen in an excessive desire for admiration and praise, while *vainglory* points to undue boasting about one's accomplishments. **8.** See FLOCK. — **Ant.** humility, modesty.

Pride (prīd), **Thomas,** died 1658, English Roundhead general; led **Pride's Purge** in 1648, expelling Royalist members from the House of Commons; signed the death warrant of Charles I.

pride·ful (prīd′fəl) *adj.* Full of pride; haughty; disdainful.

pride of China The azedarach tree.

Prid·win (prid′win) King Arthur's shield.

prie-dieu (prē-dyœ′) *n.* A small desk with a shelf for a book, at which to kneel at prayers. [< F, pray God]

pri·er (prī′ər) *n.* One who pries: also spelled *pryer.*

PRIE-DIEU

priest (prēst) *n.* **1.** One especially consecrated to the service of a divinity, and serving as mediator between the divinity and his worshipers in sacrifice, worship, prayer, teaching, etc. **2.** In the Anglican, Greek, and Roman Catholic churches, a clergyman in the second order of the ministry, ranking next below a bishop, and having authority to administer the sacraments. **3.** Any ordained clergyman or pastor, as distinguished from a layman. **4.** In the early Christian church, an elder or presbyter. **5.** One who performs functions or duties similar to those of a priest. Abbr. *P., pr.* [OE *prēost,* ult. < L *presbyter.* Doublet of PRESBYTER.]

priest·craft (prēst′kraft′, -kräft′) *n.* **1.** Priestly arts and wiles: a disparaging term. **2.** The knowledge and skill of priests.

priest·ess (prēs′tis) *n.* A woman or girl who exercises priestly functions.

priest·hood (prēst′hŏŏd) *n.* **1.** The priestly office or character. **2.** Priests collectively. [OE *prēosthad*]

Priest·ley (prēst′lē), **J(ohn) B(oynton),** born 1894, English author. — **Joseph,** 1733–1804, English clergyman, philosopher, and chemist; discovered oxygen.

priest·ly (prēst′lē) *adj.* **1.** Of or pertaining to a priest or the priesthood; sacerdotal. **2.** Suitable to or befitting a priest. — **priest′li·ness** *n.*

priest-rid·den (prēst′rid′n) *adj.* Completely under the influence or domination of priests.

prig[1] (prig) *n.* A formal and narrow-minded person who assumes superior virtue and wisdom. [Origin uncertain]

prig[2] (prig) *v.* **prigged, prig·ging** *v.t.* **1.** *Brit. Slang* To steal. — *v.i.* **2.** *Scot. & Brit. Dial.* To bargain; haggle. — *n. Brit. Slang* A thief.

prig·gish (prig′ish) *adj.* Like a prig; smug. — **prig′gish·ly** *adv.* — **prig′gish·ness** *n.*

prig·gism (prig′iz·əm) *n.* The characteristics or manners of a prig.

prim (prim) *adj.* Minutely or affectedly precise and formal; stiffly proper and neat. — *v.* **primmed, prim·ming** *v.i.* **1.** To fix the face or mouth in a precise or prim expression; be prim. — *v.t.* **2.** To fix in a precise or prim manner. [Origin uncertain] — **prim′ly** *adv.* — **prim′ness** *n.*

prim. **1.** Primary. **2.** Primitive.

pri·ma·cy (prī′mə·sē) *n. pl.* **·cies 1.** The state of being first, as in rank or excellence. **2.** The office or province of a primate; archbishopric: also **pri′mate·ship** (-mit·ship). **3.** In the Roman Catholic Church, the office and jurisdiction of the Pope. [< OF *primacie* < Med.L *primatia* < LL *primas, primatis* one of the first. See PRIMATE.]

pri·ma don·na (prē′mə don′ə) **1.** A leading female singer, as in an opera company. **2.** *Informal* A temperamental or vain person. [< Ital., lit., first lady]

pri·ma fa·ci·e (prī′mə fā′shi·ē, fā′shē) *Latin* At first view; so far as at first appears. — **pri′ma-fa′ci·e** *adj.*

prima-facie evidence Evidence that, if unexplained or uncontradicted, would establish the fact alleged.

pri·mage (prī′mij) *n.* An allowance in addition to wages, formerly paid by a shipper to the master and crew of a vessel for taking care of the goods, now paid to the owner of the vessel as an addition to freight charges. [< Med.L *primagium*]

pri·mal (prī′məl) *adj.* **1.** Being at the beginning or foundation; first; original. **2.** Most important; chief. — **Syn.** See PRIMEVAL. [< Med.L *primalis* < L *primus*]

pri·ma·ri·ly (prī′mer·ə·lē, -mər·ə·lē, *emphatic* prī·mâr′ə·lē) *adv.* **1.** In the first place; originally; essentially.

pri·ma·ry (prī′mer·ē, -mər·ē) *adj.* **1.** First in time or origin; primitive; original. **2.** First in a series or sequence. **3.** First in degree, rank, or importance; chief. **4.** Constituting the fundamental or original elements of which a whole is composed; basic; elemental: the *primary* forces of life. **5.** Of the first stage of development; elementary; lowest: *primary* school. **6.** *Ornithol.* Of or pertaining to the principal flight feather of a bird's wing. **7.** *Geol.* Pre-Cambrian. **8.**

Electr. Of or pertaining to an inducing current or its circuit: a *primary* coil. **9.** *Chem.* **a** Having some characteristic in the first degree, as an initial replacement of one atom or radical. **b** Having a carbon atom directly joined to only one other carbon atom in a molecule. — **Syn.** See PRIMEVAL. — *n. pl.* **·ries 1.** That which is first in rank, dignity, or importance. **2.** *U.S.* An election in which the voters of a political party choose its candidates for public office or select delegates to a nominating convention. Compare DIRECT PRIMARY. **3.** One of the primary colors. **4.** A primary cell. **5.** *Ornithol.* One of the large flight feathers of the pinion of a bird's wings. For illustration see BIRD. **6.** *Astron.* A body, as a planet, as distinguished from a body that revolves around it. [< L *primarius* < *primus* first]

primary accent See under ACCENT.

primary cell *Electr.* Any of several devices consisting of two electrodes of dissimilar materials immersed in an electrolyte and capable of generating a current by chemical action when the electrodes are in contact through a conducting wire. Also called *galvanic cell, voltaic cell.*

primary colors Any of several sets of colors considered basic to all other colors, as red, green, and blue (**physiological, fundamental,** or **additive primaries**); red, yellow, green, blue, black, and white (**psychological** or **subtractive primaries**); and red, yellow, and blue (**painting primaries**).

primary school A school for very young pupils, usually the first four grades of elementary school.

pri·mate (prī′mit, -māt) *n.* **1.** The prelate highest in rank in a nation or province. **2.** Any of an order (*Primates*) of mammals, including the tarsiers, lemurs, marmosets, monkeys, apes, and man. [< OF *primat* < LL *primas, primatis* of the first < L *primus*] — **pri·ma·tial** (prī·mā′shəl) *adj.*

pri·ma·tol·o·gy (prī′mə·tol′ə·jē) *n.* The study of the origin, structure, evolution, and classification of primates. — **pri′ma·tol′o·gist** *n.*

prime[1] (prīm) *adj.* **1.** First in rank, dignity, or importance; chief. **2.** First in value or excellence; of excellent quality; first-rate. **3.** First in time or order; original; primitive; primeval. **4.** *Math.* Divisible by no whole number except itself and unity. Two or more numbers are said to be *prime* to each other when they have no common factor but unity. **5.** Having or pertaining to the strength and vigor of fresh maturity; blooming. **6.** Original; not derived; first. **7.** Marked with the sign (′). — **Syn.** See PRIMEVAL. — *n.* **1.** The period of full vigor, beauty, and power succeeding youth and preceding age; formerly, youth. **2.** The period of full perfection in anything. **3.** The beginning of anything, as of the day; dawn; spring. **4.** The best or pick of anything. **5.** A prime number. **6.** A mark or accent (′) written above and to the right of a letter or figure; also, an inch, a minute, etc., as indicated by that sign. **7.** *Music* The tonic; the interval of unison; also, a note in unison with another. — *v.* **primed, prim·ing** *v.t.* **1.** To prepare; make ready for some new purpose. **2.** To put a primer into (a gun, mine, etc.) preparatory to firing. **3.** To pour water into (a pump) so as to displace air and promote suction. **4.** To cover (a surface) with sizing, a first coat of paint, etc. **5.** To supply beforehand with facts, information, etc.; brief: to *prime* a witness. — *v.i.* **6.** To carry water along with the steam into the cylinder: said of a steam boiler or engine. **7.** To make something ready, as for firing, pumping, etc. **8.** To become prime. [< OF < L *primus*] — **prime′ly** *adv.* — **prime′ness** *n.*

prime[2] (prīm) *n.* *Often cap. Eccl.* Prescribed prayers constituting the second of the seven canonical hours. [OE *prīm* < LL *prima* (*hora*) first (hour)]

prime cost The direct cost of labor and material in producing something, exclusive of capital and overhead expenses.

prime meridian A meridian from which longitude is reckoned, now, generally, the one that passes through Greenwich, England.

prime minister 1. In the British Commonwealth, the head of the national or federal cabinet and principal minister of the sovereign, as in Great Britain, Australia, Canada, etc. **2.** The chief minister and head of a cabinet, and often the chief executive of a government: also called *premier.* Abbr. *P.M.*

prime ministry The office of a prime minister.

prime mover 1. An original or chief force in an undertaking. **2.** That which is regarded as an original source of the energy required to perform work or develop power, as muscular force, wind, water, etc. **3.** *Mech.* Any apparatus or machine by which the energy obtained from a natural source may be converted into work, as a steam engine, turbine, etc. **4.** In Aristotelian philosophy, the cause of all movement, which does not itself move. Also called *primum mobile.*

prime number *Math.* A number divisible without remainder by no whole number except itself and unity: opposed to *composite number.*

prim·er[1] (prim′ər) *n.* **1.** An elementary textbook; especially, a beginning reading book. **2.** *Printing* Either of two sizes of type, **great primer** (18-point) and **long primer** (10-point): see POINT SYSTEM. [< Med.L *primarius* < L *primus*]

prim·er[2] (prī′mər) *n.* **1.** Any device, as a cap, tube, etc., used to detonate the main charge of a gun, mine, etc. For illustration see SHRAPNEL. **2.** One who or that which primes.

pri·me·ro (prï-mâr′ō) *n.* An old card game. [< Sp. < L *primarius*]

prime time The evening hours of television or radio broadcasting, when the largest audience is available.

pri·me·val (prï-mē′vəl) *adj.* Belonging to the first ages; primitive. [< L *primaevus* youthful < *primus* first + *aevum* age] — **pri·me′val·ly** *adv.*

— **Syn.** *Primeval, prime, primary, primal, primitive, primordial,* and *pristine* refer to the beginning or earliest period. *Primeval* is used chiefly of time before the appearance of man on earth: the *primeval* hills of Appalachia. *Prime* is a very general word, applicable to the first in time, magnitude, degree, rank, choice, importance, etc. That which is *primary* is first in development, progress, or sequence: *primary* schools, *primary* principles. *Primal* is a rare word signifying initial or fundamental: the *primal* observations of Galileo in dynamics. *Primitive* characterizes early times or early man, and contains a note of simplicity or crudeness: *primitive* pottery, *primitive* tribes. *Primordial* points to the first stage of development, especially when reference is made to organic growth: a *primordial* leaf, *primordial* swamps. *Pristine* speaks of the freshness of that which has newly come into existence: tears like the *pristine* dew. Compare ANCIENT.

primi- *combining form* First. [< L *primus* first]

pri·mi·ge·ni·al (prï′mə-jē′nē-əl) *adj.* Being the first or first-born; primal; original. [< L *primigenius* first, original < *primus* + *genus* kind]

pri·mine (prï′mĭn) *n. Bot.* The outermost integument of an ovule. [< L *primus* first]

prim·ing (prï′mĭng) *n.* **1.** That with which anything is primed. **2.** A combustible composition used to ignite an explosive charge. **3.** The ground or first layer of paint laid on a surface that is to be painted.

pri·mip·a·ra (prï-mĭp′ər-ə) *n. pl.* **·a·rae** (-ə-rē) A woman pregnant for the first time or one who has borne just one child. [< L *primus* first + *parere* to give birth to] — **pri·mi·par·i·ty** (prï′mĭ-păr′ə-tē) *n.* — **pri·mip′a·rous** *adj.*

prim·i·tive (prĭm′ə-tĭv) *adj.* **1.** Pertaining to the beginning or origin; first; earliest; primary. **2.** Resembling the manners or style of long ago; old-fashioned; simple; plain. **3.** *Anthropol.* Of or pertaining to the earliest anthropological forms or civilizations: *primitive* man; *primitive* culture. **4.** *Biol.* **a** Being or occurring at an early stage of development or growth; first-formed; rudimentary. **b** Not much changed by evolution: a *primitive* species. **5.** *Ling.* **a** Standing in original relation, as a word from which a derivative is made; radical. **b** Designating the unrecorded or reconstructed parent language, or Ursprache, of a language family: *Primitive* Germanic. **6.** *Theol.* Adhering to strictly traditional interpretation of doctrine and Scripture: the *primitive* church. — **Syn.** See PRIMEVAL. — *n.* **1.** *Ling.* A primary or radical word; also, a word from which another is derived. **2.** *Math.* A form in algebra or geometry from which another is derived. **3.** An artist, or a work of art, belonging to a very early period; also, a work resembling or imitating such art, or an artist producing it, often characterized by simplicity or a childlike quality. **4.** One who or that which is primitive. Abbr. *prim.* [< F *primitif* < L *primitivus* < *primus* first] — **prim′i·tive·ly** *adv.* — **prim′i·tive·ness, prim′i·tiv′i·ty** *n.*

Primitive Germanic See under GERMANIC.

prim·i·tiv·ism (prĭm′ə-tĭv-ĭz′əm) *n.* Belief in or adherence to primitive forms and customs.

pri·mo (prē′mō) *n. & adj. pl.* **·mi** (-mē) *Italian* First. — **pri′ma** (-mä) *n. & adj. fem.*

pri·mo·gen·i·tor (prï′mə-jen′ə-tər) *n.* An earliest ancestor; a forefather. [< Med.L < L *primo* first + *genitor* father]

pri·mo·gen·i·ture (prï′mə-jen′ə-chər) *n.* **1.** The state of being the first-born child. **2.** The right of the eldest son to inherit the property, title, etc., of a parent, to the exclusion of all other children. Compare ULTIMOGENITURE. [< Med.L *primogenitura* < L *primo* first + *genitura* birth < *genitus,* pp. of *gignere* to beget]

pri·mor·di·al (prï-môr′dē-əl) *adj.* **1.** First in order or time; original; elemental. **2.** *Biol.* First in order of appearance in the growth or development of an organism. — **Syn.** See PRIMEVAL. — *n.* An elementary principle. [< LL *primordialis* < *primordius* original < *primordium* beginning < *primus* first + *ordiri* to begin a web] — **pri·mor′di·al·ly** *adv.*

primp (prĭmp) *v.t. & v.i.* To prink; dress up, especially with superfluous attention to detail. [Akin to PRIM]

prim·rose (prĭm′rōz) *n.* **1.** An early-blossoming perennial herb (genus *Primula*) with tufted basal leaves and variously colored flowers. **2.** The evening primrose (which see). **3.** A pale yellow color, named for the common primrose of England. — *adj.* **1.** Pertaining to a primrose. **2.** Of primrose color. **3.** Flowery; gay. [Alter. of ME *primerole* < OF < Med.L *primula,* fem. dim. of L *primus* first; infl. by ROSE]

primrose path The life of worldly or sensual pleasures.

prim·sie (prĭm′zē) *adj. Scot.* Demure; prim.

prim·u·la·ceous (prĭm′yə-lā′shəs) *adj. Bot.* Designating or belonging to the primrose family (*Primulaceae*) of herbs, including the pimpernel, cyclamen, and loosestrife. [< NL *Primulaceae* < Med.L *primula* primrose]

pri·mum mo·bi·le (prï′məm mō′bĭ-lē) **1.** A prime mover. **2.** *Astron.* In the Ptolemaic cosmology, the tenth and outermost of the concentric spheres of the universe, regarded as causing all the other spheres to repeat its own revolution around the earth once in 24 hours. [< L, first moving thing]

pri·mus in·ter pa·res (prï′məs ĭn′tər pâr′ēz) *Latin* First among equals.

prin. **1.** Principal(ly). **2.** Principle.

prince (prĭns) *n.* **1.** A nonreigning male member of a royal family. **2.** A male monarch or sovereign. **3.** *Brit.* The son of a sovereign or of a son of the sovereign. **4.** One of a high order of nobility. **5.** The ruler of a small state. **6.** A chief or leader, or one of the highest rank of any class: a merchant *prince.* Abbr. *P., pr., Pr.* [< OF < L *princeps* first, principal < *primus* first + stem of *capere* to take]

Prince Albert A long, double-breasted frock coat.

Prince Albert National Park A park in central Saskatchewan, Canada; 1,496 sq. mi.; established 1927.

prince consort The husband of a reigning female sovereign.

Prince Edward Island An island in the Gulf of St. Lawrence, comprising a Province of Canada; 2,184 sq. mi.; pop. 111,000; capital, Charlottetown. Abbr. *P.E.I.*

prince·kin (prĭns′kĭn) *n.* A little or inferior prince.

prince·ling (prĭns′lĭng) *n.* **1.** A young prince. **2.** A subordinate prince. Also **prince′let** (-lĭt).

prince·ly (prĭns′lē) *adj.* **·li·er, ·li·est** **1.** Liberal; generous. **2.** Like or suitable for a prince. **3.** Having the rank of a prince. — **Syn.** See KINGLY. — *adv.* In a princely manner. — **prince′li·ness** *n.*

Prince of Darkness Satan.

Prince of Peace Jesus Christ.

Prince of Wales The eldest son of the British sovereign, who is born Duke of Cornwall, and becomes Prince of Wales, or male heir apparent, only by creation.

Prince of Wales, Cape A promontory at the tip of Seward Peninsula, Alaska, the westernmost point of North America.

Prince of Wales Island **1.** A former name for Penang Island. See under PENANG. **2.** An island in the Arctic Ocean, Northwest Territories, Canada; 13,736 sq. mi.; the north magnetic pole was located on it in 1948. **3.** The largest island of the Alexander Archipelago, SE Alaska; 2,231 sq. mi.

Prince Rupert A port city in western British Columbia, Canada; pop. 14,677.

prin·ce's-feath·er (prĭn′sĭz-feth′ər) *n.* A tall, hardy plant (*Polygonum orientale*) having plumelike inflorescences and crimson flowers, growing wild in eastern North America.

prin·cess (prĭn′sĭs) *n.* **1.** A nonreigning female member of a royal family. **2.** The consort of a prince. **3.** A female sovereign. **4.** *Brit.* A daughter of the sovereign or of a son of the sovereign. [< F *princesse*]

prin·cesse (prĭn-ses′, prĭn′sĭs) *adj.* Designating a woman's close-fitting garment hanging in an unbroken line from shoulder to flared hem. Also **prin′cess.** [< F, princess]

princess royal The eldest daughter of a sovereign.

Prince·ton (prĭns′tən) A borough in west central New Jersey; scene of an American victory in the Revolutionary War (1777) and seat of Princeton University; pop. 12,311.

prin·ci·pal (prĭn′sə-pəl) *adj.* First in rank, character, or importance; chief. — *n.* **1.** One who takes a leading part or who is a leader or chief in some action. **2.** *Law* **a** The actor in a crime, or one present aiding and abetting. **b** The employer of one who acts as an agent. **c** One primarily liable for whom another has become surety. **d** The most important thing, or part of a given property, to which other things or parts are incidental. **e** The capital or body of an estate. **3.** One who is at the head of some body or society; one in authority. **4.** The head teacher or master in a public or private school. **5.** The chief executive of some colleges and universities in Great Britain. **6.** Property or capital, as opposed to interest or income. **7.** The chief or most important truss or rafter of a roof. **8.** *Music* The chief metal organ stop, an octave higher in pitch than the other diapasons. Abbr. *prin.* [< F < L *principalis* < *princeps.* See PRINCE.] — **prin′ci·pal·ly** *adv.* — **prin′ci·pal·ship** *n.*

principal axis *Optics* The imaginary line passing through the center of a lens or mirror at right angles to each surface.

principal clause *Gram.* An independent clause. See under CLAUSE.

prin·ci·pal·i·ty (prĭn′sə-pal′ə-tē) *n. pl.* **·ties** **1.** The territory of a reigning prince, or one that gives to a prince a title of courtesy. **2.** *pl. Theol.* The seventh of the nine orders of angels. See ANGEL. **3.** The state, office, or jurisdiction of a prince; sovereignty.

principal parts The inflected forms of a verb from which all other inflected forms may be derived. In English, the principal parts of a verb are the infinitive (*go, walk*), the past tense (*went, walked*), and the past participle (*gone, walked*). In this dictionary, when appropriate, the past, past participle, and present participle are shown (*gave, given, giving*). When, however, the principal parts are entirely regular in formation, adding *-ed* and *-ing* directly to the infinitive without spelling modification, they are not shown. In cases where the past tense and past participle are identical, only the one is shown (*behaved, behaving*).

principal verb *Gram.* The part of a verb phrase that has the basic meaning: I will *go*; They are *going*; He has *gone*.

Prin·ci·pe (prin′si·pē, *Pg.* prēn′sē·pə) See under SÃO TOMÉ E PRINCIPE.

prin·cip·i·um (prin·sip′ē·əm) *n.* *pl.* **·cip·i·a** (-sip′ē·ə) 1. First principle; beginning. 2. *pl.* Fundamentals. [< L]

prin·ci·ple (prin′sə·pəl) *n.* 1. A general truth or law, basic to other truths: the *principle* of self-government. 2. A law or rule of personal conduct. 3. Moral standards collectively: a man of *principle*. 4. That which is inherent in anything, determining its nature; essence. 5. A source or cause from which a thing proceeds; fundamental cause. 6. An established mode of action or operation in natural phenomena: the *principle* of relativity. 7. *Chem.* An essential constituent of a compound or substance that gives its character to it. 8. In Christian Science, God. *Abbr.* **prin.** — **Syn.** See AXIOM. [< L *principium* a beginning]

prin·ci·pled (prin′sə·pəld) *adj.* Having or characterized by ethical principles: often in combination: *high-principled*.

prin·cock (prin′kok) *n.* *Obs.* A coxcomb; fop. Also **prin′·cox** (-koks). [Origin uncertain]

prink (pringk) *v.t.* 1. To dress or adorn (oneself) for show. — *v.i.* 2. To dress oneself showily or fussily. [Prob. alter. of PRANK¹] — **prink′er** *n.*

print (print) *n.* 1. An impression with ink from type, plates, etc.; printed characters collectively; also, any printed matter. 2. Anything printed from an engraved plate or lithographic stone; a proof; also, a printed picture or design. 3. A newspaper, pamphlet, or the like. 4. An impression or mark made upon or sunk into a substance by pressure; imprint: the *print* of a shoe in the snow. 5. A reproduction made by printing or by pressure: a *print* of butter. 6. Any fabric stamped with a design by means of dyes used on engraved rollers, wood blocks, or screens. 7. Any tool or device bearing a pattern or design, or that upon which it is impressed. 8. *Photog.* A positive picture made from a negative. 9. Newsprint. — **in print** 1. Printed; also, for sale in printed form. 2. *Obs.* In an exact or formal manner. — **out of print** No longer on sale, the edition being exhausted: said of books, etc. — *v.t.* 1. To mark, as with inked type, a stamp, die, etc. 2. To stamp or impress (a mark, seal, etc.) on or into a surface. 3. To fix as if by impressing: The scene is *printed* on my memory. 4. To produce (a book, newspaper, etc.) by the application of inked type, plates, etc., to paper or similar material. 5. To cause to be put in print; publish: The newspaper *printed* the story. 6. To write in letters similar to those used in print: Please *print* your name and address. 7. *Photog.* To produce (a positive picture) by transmitting light through a negative onto a sensitized surface. — *v.i.* 8. To be a printer. 9. To take or give an impression in printing. 10. To form letters similar to printed ones. [< OF *preinte, priente,* pp. of *preindre* < L *premere* to press] — **print′a·ble** *adj.*

print. Printing.

printed circuit An electronic circuit in which fixed components and the connecting wiring are printed on an insulating board.

print·er (prin′tər) *n.* 1. One who or that which prints; especially, one who sets type or runs a printing press. 2. *Electronics* The element of a computer that delivers information in the form of printed characters, words, etc.

printer's devil Devil (def. 8).

print·er·y (prin′tər·ē) *n.* *pl.* **·er·ies** 1. A place where cotton goods, as calico, are printed. 2. A printing office.

print·ing (prin′ting) *n.* 1. The making and issuing of matter for reading by means of type and the printing press. 2. The act of reproducing a design upon a surface by any process. 3. That which is printed. 4. The number of copies of anything printed at one time. 5. Writing that resembles printed matter. 6. The act of one who or that which prints. *Abbr.* **pr., print., ptg.**

printing press A mechanism for printing from an inked surface and operating by pressure, either against a flat bed, as in the platen press, or against a series of revolving cylinders, as in the rotary press.

print·less (print′lis) *adj.* Making, bearing, or retaining no print or impression.

print·out (print′out′) *n.* Information delivered in printed form by a computer or any similar apparatus.

pri·or¹ (prī′ər) *adj.* Preceding in time, order, or importance. — **prior to** Before: The theater closed *prior* to our arrival. [< L, earlier, superior]

pri·or² (prī′ər) *n.* 1. A monastic officer next in rank below an abbot. 2. Formerly, an Italian magistrate. [OE < L]

Pri·or (prī′ər), **Matthew,** 1664–1721, English poet and diplomat.

pri·or·ate (prī′ər·it) *n.* 1. The rank, office, or term of office of a prior. 2. A priory.

pri·or·ess (prī′ər·is) *n.* A woman holding a position corresponding to that of a prior; a nun next below an abbess.

pri·or·i·ty (prī·ôr′ə·tē, -or′-) *n.* *pl.* **·ties** 1. Antecedence; precedence. 2. A first right established on emergency or need: Defense plants have *priorities*. 3. A certificate giving a first right to a manufacturer or contractor. 4. A restriction on the use of a commodity or service. — **Syn.** See PRECEDENCE. [< F *priorité* < Med.L *prioritas* < L *prior*]

pri·o·ry (prī′ər·ē) *n.* *pl.* **·ries** A monastic house presided over by a prior or prioress. — **Syn.** See CLOISTER. [< OF *priorie* < Med.L *prioria*]

Prip·et (prip′ət) A river in NE Ukrainian S.S.R. and southern Byelorussian S.S.R., flowing about 500 miles east through the **Pripet Marshes** to the Dnieper.

Pris·cian (prish′ən) Sixth-century Latin grammarian: full name **Priscianus Cae·sar·i·en·sis** (sē-zâr′i·en′sis).

Pris·cil·la (pri·sil′ə) In Longfellow's poem *The Courtship of Miles Standish,* the Puritan maiden, Priscilla Mullens, courted by John Alden as proxy for Standish.

Pris·cil·li·an (pri·sil′ē·ən, -sil′yən) died 385?, Spanish prelate; bishop of Avila.

prise (prīz) See PRIZE².

prism (priz′əm) *n.* 1. *Geom.* A solid whose bases or ends are any similar equal and parallel plane figures, and whose lateral faces are parallelograms. 2. *Optics* An instrument consisting of such a solid, usually having triangular ends and made of glass or other transparent substance, used to produce a spectrum or to refract light beams. 3. Any medium that resolves a substance or material into its elements. 4. *Mineral.* A crystal form consisting of three or more intersecting planes whose intersections are parallel and vertical. [< LL *prisma* < Gk., something sawed < *prixein* to saw]

pris·mat·ic (priz·mat′ik) *adj.* 1. Refracted or formed by a prism. 2. Resembling the spectrum; exhibiting rainbow tints. 3. Pertaining to or shaped like a prism. 4. *Crystall.* Orthorhombic. Also **pris·mat′i·cal.** [< Gk. *prisma, prismatos*] — **pris·mat′i·cal·ly** *adv.*

pris·moid (priz′moid) *n.* A body resembling a prism in form. — **pris·moi·dal** (priz·moid′l) *adj.*

pris·on (priz′ən) *n.* 1. A public building for the safekeeping of persons in legal custody; a penitentiary. 2. A State prison (which see). 3. Any place of confinement. 4. Imprisonment. — *v.t.* To imprison. [< OF *prisun* < F *prehensio, -onis* seizure < *prehendere* to seize]

pris·on·er (priz′ən·ər, priz′nər) *n.* 1. One who is confined in a prison or whose liberty is forcibly restrained. 2. A prisoner of war (which see). 3. A person confined for any reason to a place or position. [< OF *prisonier*]

prisoner of war A person who is captured by, or surrenders to, the enemy in time of war. *Abbr.* **POW, P.O.W.**

prisoner's base A game played in various forms and popular in England as early as the 14th century: also called *chevy*.

pris·sy (pris′ē) *Informal* *adj.* **·si·er, ·si·est** Effeminate; overprecise; prim. — *n.* *pl.* **·sies** A person who acts, dresses, or speaks very meticulously: also **priss.** [Blend of PRIM or PRECISE + SISSY]

pris·tine (pris′tēn, -tin, pris·tēn′; *Brit.* pris′tīn) *adj.* 1. Of or pertaining to the earliest state or time; primitive. 2. Extremely pure; untouched; unspoiled. — **Syn.** See PRIMEVAL. [< L *pristinus* primitive]

prith·ee (prith′ē) *interj.* *Archaic* I pray thee.

priv. Privative.

pri·va·cy (prī′və·sē) *n.* *pl.* **·cies** 1. The condition of being private; seclusion. 2. The state of being secret; secrecy.

Pri·vat·do·zent (prē-vät′dō·tsent′) *n.* *German* A lecturer or tutor recognized by a university but unsalaried and dependent on his student fees. Also **Pri·vat′do·cent′.**

pri·vate (prī′vit) *adj.* 1. Removed from public view; secluded: a *private* parlor. 2. Not for public or common use: *private* property. 3. Having no official rank, character, office, etc.: a *private* citizen. 4. Not generally known; secret. 5. Not common or usual; special: a *private* interpretation. 6. Individual; personal: one's *private* opinion. — *n.* 1. *Mil.* An enlisted man ranking below a corporal. *Abbr.* **Pvt.** See table at GRADE. 2. *pl.* The private parts; genitals. — **in private** In secret; privately. [< L *privatus* apart from the state, orig. pp. of *privare* to set apart < *privus* single, one's own. Doublet of PRIVY.] — **pri′vate·ly** *adv.* — **pri′vate·ness** *n.*

private detective A detective employed by a private citizen, business enterprise, etc., rather than by a city or state.

private enterprise Free enterprise (which see).

pri·va·teer (prī′və·tir′) *n.* 1. A vessel owned and commanded by private persons, but carrying on maritime war under letters of marque. 2. The commander or one of the crew of a privateer: also **pri′va·teers′man** (-tirz′mən). — *v.i.* To cruise in or as a privateer. — **pri′va·teer′ing** *n.*

private eye *Informal* A private detective (which see).

private first class A soldier ranking next above a private and below a corporal. *Abbr.* **Pfc, Pfc.** See table at GRADE.

private member *Brit. & Canadian* A member of parliament who is not a cabinet member.

private school *U.S.* A school maintained under private or corporate management.

private secretary A secretary who works for one individual only and is usually entrusted with confidential matters.

pri·va·tion (prī·vā′shən) *n.* **1.** The state of lacking something necessary or desirable; especially, want of the common comforts of life. **2.** *Rare* Deprivation. **3.** *Logic* The absence from an object of what ordinarily belongs to objects of that kind. [< L *privatio, -onis* < *privare*. See PRIVATE.]

priv·a·tive (priv′ə·tiv) *adj.* **1.** Causing privation, want, or destitution; depriving. **2.** *Gram.* Altering a word so as to express a negative instead of a positive meaning; also, denoting negation: *privative* particles (such prefixes and suffixes as *a-, an-, in-, -less*). **3.** *Logic* Noting or denoting negation or privation. — *n.* *Gram.* A private prefix or suffix. [< L *privativus*] — **priv′a·tive·ly** *adv.* — **priv′a·tive·ness** *n.*

priv·et (priv′it) *n.* **1.** An ornamental, bushy European shrub (*Ligustrum vulgare*) of the olive family, with white flowers and black berries, used for hedges, naturalized in the U.S. **2.** Any other plants of the same genus. **3.** The swamp privet (which see). [Earlier *primet*; origin unknown]

priv·i·lege (priv′ə·lij) *n.* **1.** A special or peculiar benefit, favor, or advantage enjoyed only under special conditions: the *privileges* of the rich. **2.** A special right or power conferred on or possessed by one or more individuals, in derogation of the general right; also, the law or grant conferring it. **3.** An exemption or immunity by virtue of one's office or station. **4.** A fundamental or basic civil, legal, or political right; the *privilege* of voting. **5.** A form of contract for buying or selling a stock, as a call, put, spread, or straddle. Compare OPTION. **6.** An advantage. — *v.t.* **·leged, ·leg·ing 1.** To grant a privilege to. **2.** To exempt or free: with *from*. [< OF *privilege* < L *privilegium* a piece of special legislation < *privus* one's own + *lex, legis* law]

priv·i·leged (priv′ə·lijd) *adj.* Having or enjoying a privilege.

priv·i·ly (priv′ə·lē) *adv.* Privately; secretly.

priv·i·ty (priv′ə·tē) *n. pl.* **·ties 1.** Private or secret knowledge shared with another or others and usually implying consent or concurrence. **2.** *Law* **a** A mutual or successive relationship to the same rights of property. **b** The relation between privies (def. 1). [< OF *privite* < L *privus* one's own]

priv·y (priv′ē) *adj.* **1.** Participating with another or others in the knowledge of a secret transaction: with *to: privy* to the plot. **2.** *Archaic* Removed from publicity; clandestine; secret. **3.** Designed for private use, as of a monarch; personal. — *n. pl.* **priv·ies 1.** *Law* One who is concerned with another in a matter affecting the interests of both: *privies* in contract; *privies* in estate. **2.** A small toilet or outhouse. [< F *privé* < L *privatus*. Doublet of PRIVATE.]

privy council Any body of advisers or counselors, as appointed by a sovereign for his personal use.

Privy Council 1. In Great Britain, the sovereign's personal council whose duties have been largely assumed by the cabinet. **2.** In Canada, a body, including the federal cabinet, that advises the Governor General. Abbr. *P.C.* — **Privy Councillor**

privy seal In Great Britain, the seal used by the sovereign on papers that later pass under the great seal or do not demand the great seal. Abbr. *P.S.*

prix fixe (prē fēks′) **1.** A complete meal in a restaurant or hotel, the price of which meal is the same no matter which entrée or accompanying dishes one chooses. Compare À LA CARTE, TABLE D'HOTE. **2.** The price of such a meal. [< F, fixed price]

prize¹ (prīz) *n.* **1.** That which is offered or won as an honor and reward for superiority or success, as in a contest; an award. **2.** Anything to be striven for. **3.** Anything offered or won, as in a lottery, etc. — *adj.* **1.** Offered or awarded as a prize: a *prize* medal. **2.** Having drawn a prize; entitled to a prize. **3.** Highly valued or esteemed. — *v.t.* **prized, priz·ing 1.** To value highly; regard as very valuable; treasure. **2.** To estimate the value of; appraise. [Var. of PRICE.]

prize² (prīz) *n.* **1.** In international law, property, as a vessel and cargo, captured by a belligerent at sea in conformity with the laws of war. **2.** The act of capturing; also, the person or thing captured. **3.** *Dial.* A lever or pry: also spelled *prise*. — *v.t.* **prized, priz·ing 1.** To seize as a prize, as a ship. **2.** To raise or force with a lever; pry: also spelled *prise*. [< F *prise* something taken, booty, orig. fem. of pp. of *prendre* to take < L *praehendere* to seize]

prize court A court sitting for the adjudication of prizes taken at sea in wartime.

prize fight A fight between professional boxers for a prize, a certain sum of money, etc., generally limited to a specified number of rounds. — **prize fighter** — **prize fighting**

prize money The proceeds of the sale of a maritime prize, distributable among the officers and crew of the vessel making the capture, abolished in the United States in 1899.

priz·er (prī′zər) *n.* **1.** An appraiser. **2.** *Archaic* A contestant for a prize, as in athletics.

prize ring A roped enclosure within which boxers fight. — **the prize ring** Professional boxing.

pro¹ (prō) *n. pl.* **pros 1.** An argument or vote in favor of something: in the phrase *pros and cons*. **2.** *Usually pl.* One who votes for or favors a proposal. — *adv.* In behalf of; in favor of; for: to argue *pro* and con. Abbr. *p.* [< L, for]

pro² (prō) *n. pl.* **pros** *Informal* **1.** A professional athlete. **2.** An expert in any field.

pro-¹ *prefix* **1.** Forward; to or toward the front from a position behind; forth: *produce*, to lead forth; *project*, to throw forth. **2.** Forth from its place; away: *profugate*, to flee away. **3.** To the front of; forward and down: *prolapse*, to slip forward and down. **4.** Forward in time or direction: *proceed*, to go forward. **5.** In front of: *proexhibit*, to hold in front of. **6.** In behalf of: *prolocutor*. **7.** In place of; substituted for: *procathedral*, *proconsul*. **8.** In favor of: *pro-Russian*. [< L *pro-* < *pro* before, forward, for]

pro-² *prefix* **1.** Prior; occurring earlier in time: *prognosis*. **2.** Situated in front; forward; before: *proboscis*. [< Gk. *pro-* < *pro* before, in front]

PRO or **P.R.O.** Public Relations Officer.

pro·a (prō′ə) *n.* A swift Malaysian vessel, sailing equally well in either direction, having a single outrigger, and a lateen sail. Also called *prahu*. [< Malay *prāū*]

prob. 1. Probable; probably. **2.** Problem.

prob·a·bil·ism (prob′ə·bəl·iz′əm) *n. Philos.* **1.** The doctrine that certainty is unattainable, but that belief and action must be governed by probability. **2.** The doctrine that as long as the lawfulness or unlawfulness of an action remains doubtful, one may follow his own inclination. [< L *probabilis*] — **prob′a·bil·ist** *n.* — **prob′a·bil·is′tic** *adj.*

prob·a·bil·i·ty (prob′ə·bil′ə·tē) *n. pl.* **·ties 1.** The state or quality of being probable; likelihood. **2.** A probable event, statement, condition, etc. **3.** *Stat.* The ratio of the chances favoring an event to the total number of chances for and against it. [< F *probabilité* < L *probabilitas, -tatis* < *probabilis.* See PROBABLE.]

prob·a·ble (prob′ə·bəl) *adj.* **1.** Having more evidence than the contrary, but not proof; likely to be true or to happen, but leaving room for doubt. **2.** That renders something worthy of belief, but falls short of demonstration: *probable* evidence. Abbr. *prob.* [< OF < L *probabilis* < *probare* to prove, test]
— **Syn. 1.** *Probable*, *likely*, and *possible* relate to the magnitude of a probability. Something *probable* has a chance of being or occurring greater than one half; *likely* has much the same meaning, but suggests a judgment based on less precise estimation. A *possible* thing may occur, but our expectation is less than one half. See APPARENT. — **Ant.** improbable, unlikely.

probable cause A state of facts that warrants the belief that an accused person is guilty.

prob·a·bly (prob′ə·blē) *adv.* In all probability; so far as the evidence shows; presumably. Abbr. *prob.*

pro·bang (prō′bang) *n. Surg.* A slender, flexible rod used for operations on the esophagus or larynx. [Earlier *provang*; origin unknown]

pro·bate (prō′bāt) *adj.* **1.** Of or pertaining to a probate court. **2.** Pertaining to making proof. — *n.* **1.** Formal, legal proof, as of a will. **2.** The right or jurisdiction of proving wills. — *v.t.* **·bat·ed, ·bat·ing** To obtain probate of, as a will. [< L *probatus*, pp. of *probare* to prove]

probate court A court having jurisdiction of the proof of wills, of guardianships, and of the settlement of estates.

pro·ba·tion (prō·bā′shən) *n.* **1.** *Law* A method of allowing a person convicted of a minor offense to go at large under suspension of sentence, but usually under the supervision of a probation officer. **2.** A proceeding or period designed to test character, qualifications, etc., as of a new employee. **3.** The status or condition of one being tried out, or free under suspension of sentence: to be on *probation*. **4.** The act of proving; also, proof. [< OF *probacion* < L *probatio, -onis*] — **pro·ba′tion·al, pro·ba′tion·ar′y** *adj.*

pro·ba·tion·er (prō·bā′shən·ər) *n.* One on probation.

probation officer A person delegated by a court to supervise an offender on suspended sentence.

pro·ba·tive (prō′bə·tiv) *adj.* **1.** Serving to prove or test. **2.** Pertaining to probation; proving. Also **pro·ba·to·ry** (prō′bə·tôr′ē, -tō′rē). [< L *probativus*]

probe (prōb) *v.* **probed, prob·ing** *v.t.* **1.** To explore with a probe. **2.** To investigate or examine thoroughly. — *v.i.* **3.** To penetrate; search. — *n.* **1.** *Surg.* An instrument for exploring cavities, wounds, etc. **2.** That which proves or tests. **3.** *U.S.* A searching investigation or inquiry, especially into crime or wrongdoing. **4.** A space probe (which see). [< LL *proba* proof < *probare.* Doublet of PROVE.] — **prob′er** *n.*

pro·bi·ty (prō′bə·tē, prob′ə-) *n.* Virtue or integrity tested and confirmed; strict honesty. [< F *probité* < L *probitas* < *probus* good, honest]

prob·lem (prob′ləm) *n.* **1.** A perplexing question or situation, especially when difficult or uncertain of solution. **2.** Any puzzling or difficult circumstance or person. **3.** *Math.* A proposition in which some operation or construction is required, as to bisect an angle. Abbr. *prob.* — **Syn.** See PUZZLE. — *adj.* **1.** Presenting and dealing with a problem:

problem drama. **2.** Being a problem, especially in point of behavior, maladjustment, etc.: a *problem* child. [< OF *probleme* < L *problema* < Gk. *problēma* something thrown forward (for discussion) < *pro-* forward + *ballein* to throw]

prob·lem·at·ic (prob′ləm·at′ik) *adj.* Constituting or involving a problem; questionable; contingent. Also **prob′·lem·at′i·cal.** [< MF *problématique* < LL *problematicus* < Gk. *problēmatikos* < *problēma.* See PROBLEM.] — **prob′·lem·at′i·cal·ly** *adv.*

pro bo·no pub·li·co (prō bō′nō pub′li·kō) *Latin* For the public good; for the benefit of the public.

pro·bos·cid·i·an (prō′bə·sid′ē·ən) *adj.* **1.** Of or belonging to an order (*Proboscidea*) of ungulates with columnar legs and a proboscis, as the elephants and the extinct mammoth, mastodon, etc. **2.** Of, having, or pertaining to a proboscis. — *n.* Any member of this group.

pro·bos·cis (prō·bos′is) *n. pl.* **·bos·cis·es** or **·bos·ci·des** (-bos′ə·dēz) **1.** *Zool* **a** A long flexible snout, as of the tapir. **b** The trunk of an elephant. **2.** *Entomol.* Any of various tubular feeding structures of certain insects, as bees and mosquitoes. **3.** A human nose, especially when unusually large or prominent: a humorous term. [< L < Gk. *proboskis* < *pro-* before + *boskein* to feed]

proc. **1.** Proceedings. **2.** Procedure. **3.** Process.

pro·caine (prō·kān′, prō′kān) *n.* A white crystalline compound, $C_{13}H_{20}O_2N_2$, used chiefly in its hydrochloride form as a local anesthetic. [< PRO-¹ + (CO)CAINE]

pro·cam·bi·um (prō·kam′bē·əm) *n. Bot.* The embryonic tissue giving rise to the vascular bundle of plants. [< NL < PRO-¹ + CAMBIUM] — **pro·cam′bi·al** *adj.*

pro·carp (prō′kärp) *n. Bot.* A one- or several-celled female sexual organ in certain algae, that on fertilization becomes a sporocarp. [< PRO-¹ + -CARP]

pro·ca·the·dral (prō′kə·thē′drəl) *n.* A church or edifice used temporarily as a cathedral. [< PRO¹ + CATHEDRAL]

pro·ce·dure (prə·sē′jər) *n.* **1.** A manner of proceeding or acting in any course of action. **2.** The methods or forms of conducting a business, parliamentary affairs, etc. **3.** *Law* The methods of conducting judicial proceedings as distinguished from the legal definition and recognition of rights. **4.** A course of action; a proceeding. Abbr. *proc.* [< F *procédure* < *procéder* to proceed] — **pro·ce′du·ral** *adj.*

pro·ceed (prə·sēd′) *v.i.* **1.** To go on or forward, especially after a stop or interruption. **2.** To begin and carry on an action or process. **3.** To issue or come, as from some cause, source, or origin: with *from.* **4.** *Law* To institute and carry on legal proceedings. [< OF *proceder* < L *procedere* to go forward < *pro-* forward + *cedere* to go] — **pro·ceed′er** *n.*

pro·ceed·ing (prə·sē′ding) *n.* **1.** An act or course of action; also, a particular act or course of action. **2.** The act of one who or that which proceeds. **3.** *pl.* The records or minutes of the meetings of a society, etc. Abbr. *proc.* **4.** *Law* **a** Any action instituted in a court. **b** Any of the various steps taken in a cause: a *proceeding* by writ of error.

pro·ceeds (prō′sēdz) *n.pl.* **1.** The useful or material results of an action or course; also, that which accrues therefrom. **2.** The amount derived from the disposal of goods, work, or the use of capital; return; yield.

proc·ess (pros′es, *esp. Brit.* prō′ses) *n.* **1.** A course or method of operations in the production of something: a metallurgical *process.* **2.** A series of continuous actions that bring about a particular result, end, or condition: the *process* of growth. **3.** A forward movement; progressive or continuous proceeding; passage; advance; course. **4.** *Law* **a** Any judicial writ or order issued at the commencement or during the progress of an action. **b** A writ issued to bring a defendant into court. **c** The whole course of proceedings in a cause, civil or criminal, from beginning to end. **5.** *Biol.* An accessory outgrowth or prominence of an organism or any of its parts: vertebral *process.* **6.** *Physiol.* The fibrous prolongation from the body of the nerve cell that carries the nervous impulse; an axon or dendrite. **7.** In patent law, a means of effecting a result otherwise than by mechanism, as by chemical action. **8.** *Photog.* Any of the modern methods of producing relief printing surfaces by photography and mechanical or chemical means. — *adj.* **1.** Produced by a special method: *process* butter; *process* cheese. **2.** Pertaining to, for, or made by a mechanical or chemical photographic process: a *process* illustration. — *v.t.* **1.** To subject to a routine procedure: to *process* an application. **2.** To treat or prepare by a special method. **3.** *Law* **a** To issue or serve a process on. **b** To proceed against. Abbr. *proc.* [< OF *proces* < L *processus* progress, orig. pp. of *procedere.* See PROCEED.] — **proc′es·sor** or **proc′ess·er** *n.*

proc·ess·ing tax (pros′es·ing) A tax imposed by the government on the processing of various farm products.

pro·ces·sion (prə·sesh′ən prō-) *n.* **1.** An array, as of persons or vehicles, arranged in succession and moving in a formal manner; a parade: a funeral *procession*; also, any continuous course: the *procession* of the stars. **2.** The act of proceeding or issuing forth: the *procession* of the Holy Ghost from the Father. **3.** A hymn sung by persons moving in orderly array. — *v.i.* To march in procession. [< OF < L *processio, -onis* < *procedere.* See PROCEED.]

pro·ces·sion·al (prə·sesh′ən·əl) *adj.* Of, pertaining to, or moving in a procession. — *n.* **1.** A book containing the services in a religious procession. **2.** The music played or sung during a procession. — **pro·ces′sion·al·ly** *adv.*

process printing Color printing from halftone plates, each of which carries one of the primary colors, red, yellow, and blue, with sometimes a fourth plate for black.

process server A person, as a deputy sheriff, who serves summonses or processes.

pro·cès-ver·bal (prȯ·se′ver·bȧl′) *n. pl.* **·baux** (-bō′) In French law, a detailed statement in writing made by an official relating to a crime within his jurisdiction; also, any official report. [< F, lit., verbal process]

pro·chein (prō′shen) *adj. Law* Nearest in time, relation, or degree. Also **pro·chain** (prō′shän, *Fr.* prȯ·shań′). [< F *prochain* < L *propius,* compar. of *prope* near]

pro·claim (prō·klām′) *v.t.* **1.** To announce or make known publicly or officially; declare. **2.** To make plain; manifest: His manner *proclaimed* his innocence. **3.** To outlaw, prohibit, or restrict by proclamation. [< L *proclamare* < *pro-* before + *clamare* to call] — **pro·claim′er** *n.*

proc·la·ma·tion (prok′lə·mā′shən) *n.* **1.** The act of proclaiming. **2.** That which is proclaimed; a public authoritative announcement. [< OF *proclamacion* < L *proclamatio, -onis* < *proclamare.* See PROCLAIM.]

pro·clit·ic (prō·klit′ik) *adj.* Having no independent accent, but pronounced as part of the word that follows, as English *it* in '*tis,* French *je* in *j'ai.* — *n.* A proclitic word. [< NL *procliticus* < Gk. *proklinein* < *pro-* forward + *klinein* to lean; after Gk. *enklitikos* enclitic]

pro·cliv·i·ty (prō·kliv′ə·tē) *n. pl.* **·ties** Natural disposition or tendency; propensity: usually with *to:* a *proclivity* to grumble. [< L *proclivitas* < *proclivis* downward < *pro-* before + *clivus* slope]

Pro·clos (prō′klȯs, prok′lȯs) See PROCULUS.

Proc·ne (prok′nē) In Greek mythology, an Athenian princess whom the gods transformed into a swallow after she killed her son.

pro·con·sul (prō·kon′səl, prō′kon′-) *n.* **1.** In ancient Rome, an official, usually an ex-consul, who exercised consular authority over a province or an army. **2.** A governor of a dependency, especially a British one; a viceroy. [< L] — **pro·con′su·lar** (-sə·lər, -syə-) *adj.* — **pro·con′su·late** (-sə·lit, -syə-), **pro·con′sul·ship** *n.*

Pro·con·sul (prō·kon′səl, prō′kon′-) *n. Paleontol.* Any of various primates (genus *Proconsul*) of the Miocene epoch, considered by some scientists to be ancestral to apes and man.

Pro·co·pi·us (prō·kō′pē·əs), 490?–565?, Byzantine historian.

pro·cras·ti·nate (prō·kras′tə·nāt) *v.* **·nat·ed, ·nat·ing** *v.i.* **1.** To put off taking action until a future time; be dilatory. — *v.t.* **2.** To defer or postpone. [< L *procrastinatus,* pp. of *procrastinare* < *pro-* forward + *crastinus* pertaining to the morrow < *cras* tomorrow] — **pro·cras′ti·na′tor** *n.*

pro·cras·ti·na·tion (prō·kras′tə·nā′shən) *n.* The act, tendency, or habit of procrastinating; dilatoriness; delay.

pro·cre·ant (prō′krē·ənt) *adj.* Effecting, conducive to, or connected with procreation; generating; fruitful. [< L *procreans, -antis,* ppr. of *procreare.* See PROCREATE.]

pro·cre·ate (prō′krē·āt) *v.t.* **·at·ed, ·at·ing** **1.** To engender or beget (offspring). **2.** To originate; produce. [< L *procreatus,* pp. of *procreare* < *pro-* before + *creare* to create] — **pro′cre·a′tion** *n.* — **pro′cre·a′tor** *n.*

pro·cre·a·tive (prō′krē·ā′tiv) *adj.* **1.** Possessed of generative power; reproductive. **2.** Pertaining to procreation.

Pro·crus·te·an (prō·krus′tē·ən) *adj.* **1.** Pertaining to or characteristic of Procrustes. **2.** Ruthlessly or violently bringing about conformity.

Pro·crus·tes (prō·krus′tēz) In Greek mythology, a giant of Attica, who tied travelers to an iron bed and amputated or stretched their limbs until they fitted it. [< L < Gk. *Prokroustēs* < *prokrouein* to stretch out < *pro-* thoroughly + *krouein* to beat]

procto- *combining form Med.* Related to or affecting the rectum or anus: *proctology.* Also, before vowels, **proct-.** [< Gk. *proktos* anus]

proc·tol·o·gy (prok·tol′ə·jē) *n.* The branch of medicine that treats of the anatomy, physiology, and diseases of the rectum. [< PROCTO- + -LOGY] — **proc·to·log′i·cal** (prok′tə·loj′i·kəl) *adj.* — **proc·tol′o·gist** *n.*

proc·tor (prok′tər) *n.* **1.** An agent acting for another; attorney; proxy; especially, a practitioner in an admiralty, ecclesiastical, or probate court. **2.** A university or college official charged with maintaining order, supervising examinations. etc. — *v.t.* and *v.i.* To supervise (an examination). [ME *proketour, procutour,* contr. of L *procurator.* See PROCURATOR.] — **proc·to·ri·al** (prok·tȯr′ē·əl, -tō′rē-) *adj.* — **proc′tor·ship** *n.*

proc·to·scope (prok′tə·skōp) *n.* An instrument for examining the interior of the rectum. — **proc·tos·co·py** (prok·tos′kə·pē) *n.*

Proc·u·lus (prok′yə·ləs), 410?–485, Greek Neo-Platonic philosopher; opposed Christianity. Also *Proclos.*

pro·cum·bent (prō·kum′bənt) *adj.* **1.** *Bot.* Lying on the ground; trailing, as certain vines and plants. **2.** Leaning forward or lying down or on the face; prone; prostrate. [< L *procumbens, -entis,* ppr. of *procumbere* to lean forward < *pro-* forward + *cumbere* to lie down]

pro·cur·a·ble (prō-kyŏŏr′ə-bəl) *adj.* That can be procured.

proc·u·ra·cy (prok′yər·ə·sē) *n. pl.* **·cies** The act, office, or service of a procurator or proctor.

pro·cur·ance (prō-kyŏŏr′əns) *n.* The process of procuring. Also **pro·cur′al.**

proc·u·ra·tion (prok′yə·rā′shən) *n.* **1.** The act of procuring. **2.** *Law* **a** The function of an attorney; an agency; a proxy. **b** A power of attorney. [< OF < L *procuratio, -onis* < *procurare.* See PROCURE.] — **proc′u·ra·to·ry** (-rə-tôr′ē, -tō′rē) *adj.*

proc·u·ra·tor (prok′yə·rā′tər) *n.* **1.** A person authorized and employed to act for and manage the affairs of another. **2.** In ancient Rome, one who had charge of the imperial revenues or, in a province, was an administrator or viceroy. **3.** The public magistrate of some Italian cities. [< L *procurare.* See PROCURE.] — **proc′u·ra·to′ri·al** (-rə-tôr′ē·əl, -tō′rē-) *adj.* — **proc′u·ra′tor·ship** *n.*

pro·cure (prō·kyŏŏr′) *v.* **·cured, ·cur·ing** *v.t.* **1.** To obtain by some effort or means; acquire. **2.** To bring about; cause. **3.** To obtain (women) for the gratification of the lust of others. — *v.i.* **4.** To be a procurer or procuress. — **Syn.** See GET. [< OF *procurer* < L *procurare* to look after < *pro-* on behalf of + *curare* to attend to < *cura* care]

pro·cure·ment (prō-kyŏŏr′mənt) *n.* **1.** The act of procuring; obtainment; attainment. **2.** The act of effecting or causing to be effected.

pro·cur·er (prō·kyŏŏr′ər) *n.* One who procures for another, as to gratify lust; a pimp. [< AF *procurour* < L *procurator.* See PROCURATOR.] — **pro·cur′ess** *n.fem.*

Pro·cy·on (prō′sē·on) *n.* One of the 20 brightest stars, 0.38 magnitude; Alpha in the constellation Canis Minor. See table at STAR. [< L < Gk. *Prokyōn* < *pro-* before + *kyōn* dog]

prod (prod) *v.t.* **prod·ded, prod·ding 1.** To punch or poke with or as with a pointed instrument. **2.** To arouse mentally; urge; goad. — *n.* **1.** Any pointed instrument used for prodding; a goad. **2.** A thrust or punch with or as with a prod; a poke. **3.** A reminder. [Origin unknown] — **prod′der** *n.*

prod. 1. Produce(d). **2.** Product.

prod·i·gal (prod′ə·gəl) *adj.* **1.** Addicted to wasteful expenditure, as of money, time, or strength; extravagant. **2.** Yielding in profusion; bountiful. **3.** Lavish; profuse. — *n.* One who is wasteful or profligate; a spendthrift. [< L *prodigus* wasteful < *prodigere* to drive forth, get rid of < *pro-* forward + *agere* to drive] — **prod′i·gal·ly** *adv.*

prod·i·gal·i·ty (prod′ə·gal′ə·tē) *n. pl.* **·ties 1.** Extravagance; wastefulness. **2.** Great abundance; lavishness. **3.** Extreme generosity; bounteousness. [< OF *prodigalite* < Med.L *prodigalitas* < L *prodigus.* See PRODIGAL.]

pro·di·gious (prə·dij′əs) *adj.* **1.** Enormous or extraordinary in size, quantity, or degree; vast. **2.** Marvelous; amazing. **3.** *Obs.* Of the nature of a prodigy. [< L *prodigiosus* < *prodigium* omen] — **pro·dig′ious·ly** *adv.* — **pro·dig′ious·ness** *n.*

prod·i·gy (prod′ə·jē) *n. pl.* **·gies 1.** A person having remarkable qualities or powers, especially a young child so gifted: a musical *prodigy.* **2.** Something that excites wonder and admiration. **3.** Something out of the ordinary course of nature; a monstrosity. **4.** *Archaic* A portent. [< L *prodigium*]

pro·drome (prō′drōm) *n. Pathol.* A sign of approaching disease; a premonitory symptom. [< F < L *prodromus* < Gk. *prodromos* forerunner < *pro-* before + *dromos* running] — **prod·ro·mal** (prod′rə·məl) *adj.*

pro·duce (*v.* prə·dōōs′, -dyōōs′; *n.* prod′ōōs, -yōōs, prō′dōōs, -dyōōs) *v.* **·duced, ·duc·ing** *v.t.* **1.** To bring forth or bear; yield, as young or a natural product. **2.** To bring forth by mental effort; compose, write, etc.: to *produce* a book. **3.** To bring about; cause to happen or be: His words *produced* a violent reaction. **4.** To bring to view; exhibit; show: to *produce* evidence. **5.** To manufacture; make. **6.** To bring to performance before the public, as a play. **7.** To extend or lengthen, as a line. **8.** *Econ.* To create (anything with exchangeable value). — *v.i.* **9.** To yield or generate an appropriate product or result. — *n.* That which is produced; a product; especially, farm products collectively. Abbr. *prod.* [< L *producere* < *pro-* forward + *ducere* to lead] — **pro·duc′i·ble** *adj.*
— **Syn. 1.** engender, generate, propagate. **2.** create, originate.

pro·duc·er (prə·dōō′sər, -dyōō′-) *n.* **1.** One who produces. **2.** One who cultivates or makes things for sale and use. **3.** One who finances and generally controls the production of a play, concert, motion picture, etc. **4.** That which produces or generates. **5.** An apparatus for manufacturing producer gas.

producer gas A combustible gas formed by driving air and steam over burning coke, used for heating or for driving engines: also called *air gas.*

producer goods *Econ.* Goods having indirect use, as tools or raw materials used in making other goods. Also **producers' goods.**

prod·uct (prod′əkt, -ukt) *n.* **1.** Anything produced or obtained as a result of some operation or work, as by generation, growth, labor, study, or skill. **2.** A result: Crime is often a *product* of poverty. **3.** *Math.* The result obtained by multiplication. **4.** Any substance resulting from chemical change: distinguished from *educt.* Abbr. *prod.* [< L *productus,* pp. of *producere.* See PRODUCE.]

pro·duc·tion (prə·duk′shən) *n.* **1.** The act or process of producing. **2.** That which is produced. **3.** Any tangible result of industrial, artistic, or literary effort. **4.** *Econ.* A producing for use, involving the creation or increase of wealth. [< F < L *productio, -onis* prolongation < *producere.* See PRODUCE.]

pro·duc·tive (prə·duk′tiv) *adj.* **1.** Producing or tending to produce; fertile; creative, as of artistic things. **2.** Producing or tending to produce profits or increase in quantity, quality, or value: *productive* labor. **3.** Causing; resulting in: with *of.* [< Med.L *productivus*] — **pro·duc′tive·ly** *adv.* — **pro·duc·tiv·i·ty** (prō′duk·tiv′ə·tē), **pro·duc′tive·ness** *n.*

pro·em (prō′əm) *n.* An introductory statement; preface; prelude. [< OF *proeme* < L *prooemium* < Gk. *prooimion* overture < *pro-* before + *oimē* song, lay] — **pro·e·mi·al** (prō·ē′mē·əl) *adj.*

pro et con (prō′ et kon′) *Latin* For and against.

pro·ette (prō·et′) *n.* A woman professional athlete, such as a tennis player or golfer.

prof (prof) *n. Informal* Professor.

Prof. or **prof.** Professor.

prof·a·na·tion (prof′ə·nā′shən) *n.* **1.** The act of profaning; abuse or dishonoring of sacred things; desecration; also, an instance of it. **2.** Abusive or improper treatment of anything; misuse. [< MF < LL *profanatio, -onis* < L *profanare.* See PROFANE.]
— **Syn. 1.** *Profanation, desecration,* and *sacrilege* signify the violation of sacred things. *Profanation* is relatively mild, usually indicating a lack of proper respect; the entry of a man wearing a hat into a Christian church is a *profanation. Desecration* is defilement by improper use, and points often to a conscious or intentional act; the stabling of horses in a cathedral would be a *desecration. Sacrilege* is the strongest of these words; it suggests a contemptuous violation of the sacred character of an object, person, or place.

pro·fane (prə·fān′, prō-) *v.t.* **·faned, ·fan·ing 1.** To treat (something sacred) with irreverence or abuse; desecrate; pollute. **2.** To put to an unworthy or degrading use; debase. — *adj.* **1.** Manifesting irreverence, disrespect, or undue familiarity toward the Deity or sacred things; blasphemous. **2.** Not religious or concerned with religious things; secular: opposed to *sacred.* **3.** Not initiated into the inner mysteries. **4.** Vulgar; common; coarse: *profane* language. [< F *profaner* < L *profanare* < *profanus* before or outside the temple, hence, unsacred < *pro-* before + *fanum* temple] — **pro·fan·a·to·ry** (prə·fan′ə·tôr′ē, -tō′rē) *adj.* — **pro·fane′ly** *adv.* — **pro·fan′er** *n.*

pro·fan·i·ty (prə·fan′ə·tē) *n. pl.* **·ties 1.** The state of being profane. **2.** Profane speech or action. Also **pro·fane′ness** (-fān′nis).
— **Syn. 2.** *Profanity, blasphemy, cursing,* and *swearing* are compared as they denote irreverence or impiety in speech. *Profanity* is the most general of these words; it may refer to irreverent use of a sacred name, as well as to the use of words considered lewd or coarse. *Blasphemy* is a much stronger word; *profanity* may be thoughtless or careless speech, but *blasphemy* denotes a degree of malicious insult to sacred things so great as to be sometimes considered a crime in common law. *Cursing* and *swearing* are types of *profanity; cursing* involves the uttering of imprecations in the name of God, generally as an expression of rage or frustration, while *swearing* is the uttering of rash or empty oaths.

pro·fess (prə·fes′) *v.t.* **1.** To declare openly; avow; affirm. **2.** To assert, usually insincerely; make a pretense of: to *profess* remorse. **3.** To declare or affirm faith in: to *profess* Taoism. **4.** To claim skill or learning in; have as one's profession: to *profess* the law. **5.** To receive into a religious order. — *v.i.* **6.** To make open declaration; avow; offer public affirmation. **7.** To take the vows of a religious order. [< L *professus,* pp. of *profiteri* to avow, confess < *pro-* before + *fateri* to confess]

pro·fess·ed·ly (prə·fes′id·lē) *adv.* **1.** By open profession; avowedly. **2.** Pretendedly.

pro·fes·sion (prə·fesh′ən) *n.* **1.** An occupation that properly involves a liberal, scientific, or artistic education or its equivalent, and usually mental rather than manual labor; especially, one of the **three learned professions,** law, medicine, or theology. **2.** The collective body of those following such occupations. **3.** The act of professing or declaring; declaration; avowal: *professions* of good will. **4.** That which is avowed or professed; a declaration.

5. The act of binding oneself to a religious order; also, the condition of being so bound. — **Syn.** See OCCUPATION. [< OF < L *professio, -onis* < *profiteri*. See PROFESS.]

pro·fes·sion·al (prə·fesh′ən·əl) *adj.* **1.** Connected with, preparing for, engaged in, appropriate to, or conforming to a profession: *professional* courtesy; a *professional* soldier; a *professional* job. **2.** Of or pertaining to an occupation pursued for gain: a *professional* ball game or player. — *n.* **1.** One who pursues as a business some vocation or occupation. **2.** One who engages for money to compete in sports; an athlete without amateur standing. **3.** One skilled in a profession, craft, or art. — **pro·fes′sion·al·ly** *adv.*

pro·fes·sion·al·ism (prə·fesh′ən·əl·iz′əm) *n.* **1.** The methods, manner, or spirit of a profession; also, its practitioners. **2.** The practice of some profession as a business.

pro·fes·sor (prə·fes′ər) *n.* **1.** A teacher of the highest rank in a university or college, or in an institution where professional or technical studies are pursued: sometimes called *full professor*; also, an associate professor or assistant professor (which see). ◆ *Professor* may be abbreviated *Prof.* before the full name but is usually written out before the surname, as *Professor Smith*. The clipped word *prof* does not take a period. **2.** One who professes skill and offers instruction in some sport or art. **3.** One who makes open declaration of his opinions or sentiments; especially, one who avows a religious faith. [< L, public teacher < *professus*. See PROFESS.]

pro·fes·sor·ate (prə·fes′ər·it) *n.* The position of a professor.

pro·fes·so·ri·al (prō′fə·sôr′ē·əl, -sō′rē- prof′ə-) *adj.* Of, pertaining to, or characteristic of a professor; pedagogic; academic. — **pro′fes·so′ri·al·ly** *adv.*

pro·fes·so·ri·ate (prō′fə·sôr′ē·it, -sō′rē-, prof′ə-) *n.* Professors collectively; also, a professorship.

pro·fes·sor·ship (prə·fes′ər·ship) *n.* **1.** The office and duties of a professor. **2.** The state of being a professor.

prof·fer (prof′ər) *v.t.* To offer for acceptance. — *n.* The act of proffering, or that which is proffered. [< AF *proffrir,* OF *poroffrir* < *por-* (< L *pro-*) in behalf of < *offrir* (< L *offere*) to offer] — **prof′fer·er** *n.*

pro·fi·cien·cy (prə·fish′ən·sē) *n.* *pl.* **·cies** A high state of attainment in some knowledge, art, or skill; expertness.

pro·fi·cient (prə·fish′ənt) *adj.* Thoroughly versed, as in an art or science; skilled; expert. — **Syn.** See SKILLFUL. — *n.* An expert. [< L *proficiens, -entis,* ppr. of *proficere* to make progress < *pro-* forward + *facere* to do] — **pro·fi′cient·ly** *adv.*

pro·file (prō′fīl, *esp. Brit.* prō′fēl) *n.* **1.** The outline of a human face or figure as seen from the side; also, a drawing of this outline. **2.** Any outline or contour or drawing of it. **3.** A short biographical sketch vividly presenting the most striking characteristics of a personality. **4.** A graphic or numerical representation of various characteristics of a person or thing indicated on or as on a set of parallel linear scales: a personality *profile*. **5.** *Archit.* The outline of a perpendicular section of a building, etc., or the contour of an architectural member. **6.** *Geol.* A vertical section of the earth's crust. — *v.t.* **·filed, ·fil·ing 1.** To draw a profile of; outline. **2.** To write or make a profile of. [< Ital. *profilo, proffilo* outline < *proffilare* to draw in outline < L *pro-* forward + *filum* thread, line]

profile drag *Aeron.* The part of the total drag of a wing caused by skin friction and the profile shape of the airfoil.

prof·it (prof′it) *n.* **1.** Any advantage or gain; benefit; return. **2.** *Often pl.* Excess of returns over outlay or expenditure: a business yielding fair *profits.* **3.** The return from the employment of capital after deducting the amount paid for raw material and for wages, real or estimated rent, interest, insurance, etc. **4.** That part of the amount received for goods which exceeds the sum originally paid for them with or without all secondary expenses involved. **5.** The income of invested property without counting its increased value by any actual rise in the market. **6.** In invested capital, the ratio of the increment to the actual amount of capital for a given year. — **gross profit** The excess of receipts from sales over expenditures for production or purchase. — **net profit** The surplus remaining after all necessary deductions, as for interest, transportation, bad debts, etc. — **Syn.** See ADVANTAGE. — *v.i.* **1.** To be of advantage or benefit. **2.** To derive gain or benefit. — *v.t.* **3.** To be of profit or advantage to. [< OF < L *profectus,* pp. of *proficere* to go forward. See PROFICIENT.]

prof·it·a·ble (prof′it·ə·bəl) *adj.* Bringing profit or gain; remunerative; advantageous. — **prof′it·a·ble·ness** *n.* — **prof′it·a·bly** *adv.*

profit and loss In bookkeeping, an account of the profits and losses, in which the profits are entered on the creditor side and losses on the debtor side. — **prof′it-and-loss′** (prof′it·ənd·lôs′, -los′) *adj.*

prof·i·teer (prof′ə·tir′) *v.i.* To seek or obtain excessive profits. — *n.* One who is given to making excessive profits, especially to the detriment of others. — **prof′it·eer′ing** *n.*

prof·it·less (prof′it·lis) *adj.* Resulting in no gain or benefit; unprofitable.

profit sharing A system of remuneration by which work-

men are given a share of the net profits of a business. — **prof′it-shar·ing** (prof′it·shâr′ing) *adj.*

prof·li·ga·cy (prof′lə·gə·sē) *n.* *pl.* **·cies** The state or quality of being profligate.

prof·li·gate (prof′lə·git, -gāt) *adj.* **1.** Lost or insensible to principle, virtue, or decency. **2.** Recklessly extravagant; in great profusion. — *n.* **1.** A depraved or dissolute person. **2.** A reckless spendthrift. [< L *profligatus,* pp. of *profligare* to strike to the ground, destroy < *pro-* forward + *fligere* to dash] — **prof′li·gate·ly** *adv.* — **prof′li·gate·ness** (-git·nis, -gāt′nis) *n.*

prof·lu·ent (prof′lōō·ənt) *adj.* Flowing smoothly or plentifully. [< L *profluens, -entis,* ppr. of *profluere* to flow along < *pro-* before + *fluere* to flow] — **prof′lu·ence** *n.*

pro for·ma (prō fôr′mə) *Latin* As a matter of form.

pro·found (prə·found′, prō-) *adj.* **1.** Intellectually deep or penetrating: *profound* learning. **2.** Reaching to, arising from, or affecting the depth of one's nature: *profound* respect. **3.** Situated far below the surface; deep; unfathomable. **4.** Deep. **5.** Thorough; exhaustive: *profound* changes. — *n.* **1.** A fathomless depth; an abyss. **2.** The ocean; the deep. [< OF *profond* < L *profundus* < *pro-* very + *fundus* deep] — **pro·found′ly** *adv.* — **pro·found′ness** *n.*

pro·fun·di·ty (prə·fun′də·tē, prō-) *n.* *pl.* **·ties 1.** The state or quality of being profound, in any sense; depth. **2.** A deep place or thing. **3.** A profound or abstruse statement, theory, or the like. [< OF *profundite* < LL *profunditas* < L *profundus.* See PROFOUND.]

pro·fuse (prə·fyōōs′, prō-) *adj.* **1.** Giving or given forth lavishly; liberal; extravagant; prodigal. **2.** Copious; overflowing; abundant: *profuse* vegetation. [< L *profusus,* pp. of *profundere* to pour forth < *pro-* forward + *fundere* to pour] — **pro·fuse′ly** *adv.* — **pro·fuse′ness** *n.*

pro·fu·sion (prə·fyōō′zhən, prō-) *n.* **1.** A lavish supply or condition: a *profusion* of ornaments. **2.** The act of pouring forth or supplying in great abundance; prodigality. [< MF < L *profusio, -onis* < *profundere.* See PROFUSE.]

prog (prog) *Dial. v.i.* **progged, prog·ging** To prowl about for food or plunder. — *n.* Food obtained by begging. [Origin unknown] — **prog′ger** *n.*

Prog. Progressive.

pro·gen·i·tor (prō·jen′ə·tər) *n.* A forefather or parent. — **Syn.** See ANCESTOR. [< F < L < *progenitus,* pp. of *progignere* to beget < *pro-* forth + *gignere* to beget] — **pro·gen′i·tor·ship′** *n.*

prog·e·ny (proj′ə·nē) *n.* *pl.* **·nies** Offspring. [< F < L *progenies* < *progignere.* See PROGENITOR.]

pro·ges·ta·tion·al (prō′jes·tā′shən·əl) *adj. Med.* **1.** Promoting gestation. **2.** Designating those substances and processes active in the menstrual cycle or during pregnancy.

pro·ges·ter·one (prō·jes′tə·rōn) *n. Biochem.* A female hormone, isolated from the corpus luteum as a white, crystalline compound, $C_{21}H_{30}O_2$, and also made synthetically. It is active in preparing the uterus for reception of the fertilized ovum. Also **pro·ges·tin** (prō·jes′tin). [< PRO-[1] + GE(STATION) + STER(OL) + -ONE]

pro·glot·tid (prō·glot′id) *n.* *pl.* **·glot·ti·des** (-glot′ə·dēz) *Zool.* One of the segments or joints of a tapeworm, in each of which a full set of reproductive organs develops. Also **pro·glot·tis** (-glot′is). [< NL *proglottis, proglottidis* < Gk. *proglōssis* tip of the tongue < *pro-* forward + *glōtta* tongue; from their shape] — **pro·glot′tic** *adj.*

prog·na·thous (prog′nə·thəs, prog·nā′thəs) *adj.* Having abnormally projecting jaws: opposed to *opisthognathous.* Also **prog·nath·ic** (prog·nath′ik). [< PRO-[2] + -GNATHOUS] — **prog·na·thism** (prog′nə·thiz′əm), **prog·na·thy** (prog′nə·thē) *n.*

prog·no·sis (prog·nō′sis) *n.* *pl.* **·ses** (-sēz) **1.** *Med.* **a** A prediction or conclusion regarding the course of a disease and the probability of recovery. **b** Likelihood of recovery: The *prognosis* is excellent. **2.** Any prediction or forecast. [< NL < Gk. *prognōsis* < *pro-* before + *gignōskein* to know]

prog·nos·tic (prog·nos′tik) *adj.* **1.** Of, pertaining to, or serving as a prognosis. **2.** Predicting or foretelling. — *n.* **1.** A sign of some future occurrence; an omen. **2.** *Med.* A symptom indicative of the course of a disease. [< F *prognostique* < Med.L *prognosticus* omen < Gk. *prognōstikon* < *prognōsis.* See PROGNOSIS.]

prog·nos·ti·cate (prog·nos′tə·kāt) *v.t.* **·cat·ed, ·cat·ing 1.** To foretell (future events, etc.) by present indications. **2.** To indicate beforehand; foreshadow. — **Syn.** See AUGUR. [< Med.L *prognosticatus,* pp. of *prognosticare* < L *prognosticus.* See PROGNOSTIC.] — **prog·nos′ti·ca′tor** *n.*

prog·nos·ti·ca·tion (prog·nos′tə·kā′shən) *n.* **1.** The act of prognosticating; prediction. **2.** A prediction or prophecy.

pro·gram (prō′gram, -grəm) *n.* **1.** A performance or show, especially one given at a scheduled time on television or radio. **2.** A printed announcement or schedule of events, especially one for a theatrical performance. **3.** Any prearranged, proposed, or desired plan or course of proceedings. **4.** A set of ordered questions, etc., used in programed instruction. **5.** *Electronics* A sequence of instructions set up on the control panels of an electronic computer as guides in the performance of a desired operation or group of operations. **6.** A preface or prefatory statement. **7.** *Obs.* A public proclamation; official edict or decree. Also *Brit.* **pro′. gramme.** —*v.t.* **·gramed** or **·grammed**, **·gram·ing** or **·gram·ming 1.** To arrange or include in a program. **2.** To work out or make up a program for (a radio station, a computer, etc.). [< LL *programma* public announcement < Gk. < *programhein* to write in public < *pro-* before + *graphein* to write; Brit. spelling infl. by F. *programme*] — **pro·gram·mat·ic** (prō/grə·mat/ik) or **pro′gram·at′ic** *adj.*

programed instruction Instruction in which the learner responds to a prearranged series of questions, items, or statements, using various printed texts, audio-visual means, or a teaching machine. Also **programmed instruction.**

pro·gram·mer (prō/gram·ər) *n.* One who programs, especially one who makes up a computer program. Also **pro′. gram·er.**

program music See under MUSIC.

prog·ress (*n.* prog/res, *esp. Brit.* prō/gres; *v.* prə·gres/) *n.* **1.** A moving forward in space; movement forward nearer a goal. **2.** Advancement toward maturity or completion; gradual development, as of mankind or civilization; improvement. **3.** A journey of state, as of a monarch through his realm. —*v.i.* **1.** To move forward or onward. **2.** To advance toward completion or fuller development. [< L *progressus,* pp. of *progredi* to go forward < *pro-* forward + *gradi* to walk]

— **Syn.** (noun) **1, 2.** *Progress, advance, development,* and *growth* are compared as they relate to change of position or condition. Both *progress* and *advance* are used of physical movement forward: he made slow *progress* in the mud, the *advance* of the flood isolated several towns. The sense of continuous motion is stronger in *progress,* while *advance* stresses the discrete steps or stages of motion: hence, *progress* suggests a preexisting course, sequence, or cycle, and *advance,* an isolated step: the rapid *progress* of science in the 19th century, the discovery of antibiotics was a great *advance* in the war against disease. Both *progress* and *advance* have come to imply improvement. *Development* and *growth* denote progressive change in size, character, condition, etc., rather than motion. *Development* is the gradual unfolding of character, or the passing through stages, determined by the very nature of a thing: the *development* of the human embryo. *Growth* points more specifically to a gradual enlargement or accretion which is governed both by innate structure and by external influence: the *growth* of a crop, the *growth* of popular resentment against a ruler.

pro·gres·sion (prə·gresh/ən) *n.* **1.** The act of progressing; advancement. **2.** *Math.* A sequence of numbers or quantities, each of which is derived from the preceding by a constant relationship. **3.** *Music* **a** A movement from one tone or chord to another. **b** A succession of tones, chords, etc. **4.** Course or lapse of time; passage. [< MF < L *progressio, -onis* < *progredi.* See PROGRESS.] — **pro·gres′. sion·al** *adj.* — **pro·gres′sion·ism** *n.*

pro·gres·sion·ist (prə·gresh/ən·ist) *n.* **1.** One who believes that society is progressing. **2.** An evolutionist.

prog·ress·ist (prog/res·ist, prō/gres-) *n.* **1.** A progressionist. **2.** A member of any party held to be progressive.

pro·gres·sive (prə·gres/iv) *adj.* **1.** Moving forward; advancing. **2.** Proceeding gradually or step by step: the *progressive* disintegration of an empire. **3.** Aiming at or characterized by progress. **4.** Spreading from one part to others; increasing: said of a disease: *progressive* paralysis. **5.** Striving for or favoring progress or reform, especially social, political, educational, or religious: a *progressive* party; *progressive* schools. **6.** Denoting or pertaining to a tax or taxes in which the tax rate increases as the amount taxed increases. **7.** *Gram.* Designating an aspect of the verb that expresses the action as being in progress at some time in the past, present, or future: formed with any tense of the auxiliary *be* and the present participle; as, He *is speaking;* he *had been speaking;* he *was to have been speaking;* he *will be speaking.* — **Syn.** See LIBERAL. — *n.* **1.** One who believes in progress or in progressive methods; especially, one who favors or promotes reforms or changes, as in politics or religion. Abbr. *Prog.* **2.** *Gram.* A progressive verb form. [< OF *progressif*] — **pro·gres′sive·ly** *adv.* — **pro·gres′sive·ness** *n.* — **pro·gres′siv·ism** *n.* — **pro·gres′siv·ist** *n.*

Pro·gres·sive-Con·ser·va·tive Party (prə·gres/iv·kən·sûr/və·tiv) In Canada, one of the principal political parties, formerly called the Conservative Party.

Progressive Party 1. A political party formed under the leadership of Theodore Roosevelt in 1912, that sought political reforms and social security legislation: also called *Bull Moose Party.* **2.** A political party seeking labor and agricultural reforms, formed in 1924 under the leadership of Robert M. LaFollette. **3.** A political party formed in 1948, which nominated Henry A. Wallace for president.

pro·hib·it (prō·hib/it) *v.t.* **1.** To forbid, especially by authority or law; interdict. **2.** To prevent or hinder. [< L *prohibitus,* pp. of *prohibere* < *pro-* before + *habere* to have] — **pro·hib′it·er** *n.*

— **Syn. 1.** *Prohibit, forbid, interdict, ban,* and *debar* mean to declare that something must not be done. Legal authority *prohibits; forbid* points to a more personal authority and relationship: walking on the grass in the park is *prohibited,* a mother *forbids* her child to leave the house. Ecclesiastical authority *interdicts;* so may civil authority: transport of certain growing plants between states is *interdicted. Ban* frequently implies moral condemnation: literature considered obscene is *banned* from the mails. *Debar* suggests exclusion, as by the erection of a barrier against: his plea of insanity is *debarred* by his own admissions. — **Ant.** permit, sanction.

pro·hi·bi·tion (prō/ə·bish/ən) *n.* **1.** The act of prohibiting, preventing, or stopping; also, a decree or order forbidding anything. **2.** The forbidding of the manufacture, transportation, and sale of alcoholic liquors as beverages. [< OF < L *prohibitio, -onis* < *prohibere.* See PROHIBIT.]

Prohibition Amendment The Eighteenth Amendment (which see).

pro·hi·bi·tion·ist (prō/ə·bish/ən·ist) *n.* **1.** One who favors legal prohibition of the manufacture and sale of alcoholic liquors. **2.** *Often cap.* A member of the Prohibition Party.

Prohibition Party A political party advocating the prohibition by law of the manufacture and sale of alcoholic liquors as beverages.

pro·hib·i·tive (prō·hib/ə·tiv) *adj.* **1.** Prohibiting or tending to prohibit. **2.** Preventing the sale, purchase, etc., of something: *prohibitive* costs. Also **pro·hib′i·to·ry** (-tôr/ē, -tō/rē). — **pro·hib′i·tive·ly** *adv.*

proj·ect (*n.* proj/ekt; *v.* prə·jekt/) *n.* **1.** Something proposed or mapped out in the mind, as a course of action; a plan. **2.** In schools, a problem, task, or piece of work given to a student or group of students. **3.** A housing project (which see). —*v.t.* **1.** To cause to extend forward or out. **2.** To throw forth or forward, as missiles. **3.** To visualize as an external reality: to *project* an image of one's destiny. **4.** To cause (an image, shadow, etc.) to fall on a surface. **5.** To propose or plan. **6.** *Math.* **a** To make a projection of (a solid, etc.) on a plane. **b** To reproduce (a figure) by drawing lines from a vertex through every point (of the figure) to the corresponding point of the reproduction. **7.** To use or produce (one's voice, words, etc.) so as to be heard clearly and at a distance. —*v.i.* **8.** To extend forward or out; protrude. **9.** *Psychol.* To attribute one's own ideas, impulses, etc., to others. **10.** To speak or sing so as to be heard clearly and at a distance. [< L *projectus,* pp. of *projicere* to throw out, cause to protrude < *pro-* before + *jacere* to throw]

pro·jec·tile (prə·jek/təl, *esp. Brit.* -tīl) *adj.* **1.** Projecting, or impelling forward. **2.** Capable of being or intended to be projected or shot forth. **3.** Protrusile. —*n.* **1.** A body projected or thrown forth by force. **2.** *Mil.* A missile for discharge from a gun or cannon. [< NL *projectilis* < L *projectus.* See PROJECT.]

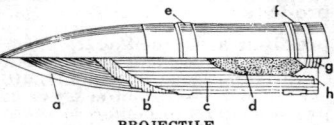

PROJECTILE
a Windshield. *b* Armor-piercing cap. *c* Body. *d* Bursting charge. *e* Bourrelet. *f* Copper rotating band. *g* Fuse. *h* Plug.

pro·jec·tion (prə·jek/shən) *n.* **1.** The act of projecting; a jutting, throwing, or shooting out or forth. **2.** That which projects; a projecting part; prominence. **3.** A scheme; project. **4.** A system of lines drawn on a given fixed plane, as in a map, representing point for point a given terrestrial or celestial surface. **5.** *Psychol.* **a** The unconscious process of attributing one's own feelings, attitudes, etc., to others, especially as a defense against guilt or feelings of inferiority. **b** An instance of this process. **6.** *Photog.* **a** The process of exhibiting motion pictures or slides on a screen. **b** The representation thus produced. [< OF < L *projectio, -onis* < *projicere.* See PROJECT.] — **pro·jec′tion·al** *adj.*

pro·jec·tion·ist (prə·jek/shən·ist) *n.* One who operates a motion-picture projector.

projection printing *Photog.* The process of enlarging a photograph by projecting the negative onto sensitized paper.

pro·jec·tive (prə·jek/tiv) *adj.* Of, pertaining to, or made by projection. — **pro·jec′tive·ly** *adv.*

projective geometry A branch of geometry that investigates the properties of figures by means of projections in two or three dimensions.

projective test *Psychol.* Any of various tests for the determination of hidden personality traits and motivations, as by theatricals, response to pictures, etc.

pro·jec·tor (prə·jek/tər) *n.* **1.** An apparatus for throwing illuminated images or motion pictures upon a screen. **2.** A mirror or combination of lenses for projecting a beam of light. **3.** One who devises projects; schemer; promoter.

pro·jet (prô·zhe/) *n. French* A plan or outline; especially, a draft of a proposed treaty or law.

Pro·kof·iev (prô·kôf/yəf), **Sergei Sergeyevich,** 1891–1953, Soviet composer. Also **Pro·kof′ieff.**

Pro·kop·yevsk (pro-kôpy'′yifsk) A city in the southern R.S.F.S.R., in the Kuznetsk Basin; pop. 275,000 (1970). Also **Pro·kop′′yevsk.**

pro·lac·tin (prō-lak′tin) n. Biochem. A hormone from the anterior lobe of the pituitary gland, active in initiating lactation in mammals and stimulating the crop glands of birds. [< PRO-¹ + LACT- + -IN]

pro·la·mine (prō′lə-mēn, -min) n. Biochem. Any of a group of simple proteins that are insoluble in pure water or absolute alcohol, as gliadin from wheat. Also **pro′la·min** (-min). [< PROL(INE) + AM(MONIA) + -INE²]

pro·lapse (prō-laps′) Pathol. v.i. **·lapsed, ·laps·ing** To fall out of place, as an organ or part. — n. The falling down of an organ or part, as the uterus, from its normal position. Also **pro·lap·sus** (prō-lap′səs). [< L prolabi to fall forward < pro- forward + labi to glide, fall]

pro·late (prō′lāt) adj. **1.** Extended lengthwise. **2.** Lengthened toward the poles, as a spheroid generated by the revolution of an ellipse around its long axis: opposed to oblate. [< L prolatus, pp. of proferre to extend, carry forward < pro- forward + ferre to carry]

pro·leg (prō′leg) n. Entomol. One of the abdominal legs of insect larvae, as of caterpillars. [< PRO-¹ + LEG]

pro·le·gom·e·non (prō′lə-gom′ə-non) n. pl. **·na** (-nə) Often pl. An introductory remark or remarks; a preface. [< Gk., neut. passive ppr. of prolegein to say beforehand < pro- before + legein to say] — **pro′le·gom′e·nous** adj.

pro·lep·sis (prō-lep′sis) n. pl. **·ses** (-sēz) **1.** Anticipation. **2.** A rhetorical figure consisting in the anticipation, and answering or nullifying beforehand, of objections or opposing arguments. **3.** The use of an adjective or a noun as an objective predicate in anticipation of the result of the verbal action, as in the phrase to shoot a person dead. **4.** An error by which a date earlier than the true date is assigned to an event. [< L < Gk. prolēpsis anticipation < prolambanein to take beforehand < pro- before + lambanein to seize, take] — **pro·lep′tic** (-tik) or **·ti·cal** adj.

pro·le·tar·i·an (prō′lə-târ′ē-ən) adj. Of or pertaining to the proletariat. — n. A member of the proletariat. [< L proletarius < proles offspring: so called because, being without property, they served the Roman state only by having children] — **pro′le·tar′i·an·ism** n.

pro·le·tar·i·at (prō′lə-târ′ē-ət) n. **1.** Wageworkers collectively; the working class: a term used especially in Marxism. **2.** In ancient Rome, the propertyless and lowest class of the state. [< F prolétariat. See PROLETARIAN.]

pro·le·tar·y (prō′lə-ter′ē) n. pl. **·tar·ies** In ancient Rome, a member of the proletariat.

pro·lif·er·ate (prō-lif′ə-rāt) v.t. & v.i. **·at·ed, ·at·ing** To produce, reproduce, or grow, especially with rapidity, as cells in tissue formation. [< PROLIFER(OUS) + -ATE¹] — **pro·lif′er·a′tion** n. — **pro·lif′er·a′tive** adj.

pro·lif·er·ous (prō-lif′ər·əs) adj. **1.** Producing offspring freely. **2.** Bot. **a** Developing buds, branches, and flowers from unusual places. **b** Bearing progeny in the way of offshoots, buds, etc. [< Med.L prolifer < L proles, prolis offspring + ferre to bear]

pro·lif·ic (prō-lif′ik) adj. **1.** Producing abundantly, as offspring or fruit; fertile. **2.** Producing results abundantly: a prolific writer. [< F prolifique < Med.L prolificus < L proles, prolis offspring + stem of facere to make] — **pro·lif′i·ca·cy** (-i-kə-sē), **pro·lif′ic·ness** n. — **pro·lif′i·cal·ly** adv. — **Syn. 1.** fruitful, fecund. **2.** productive.

pro·line (prō′lēn, -lin) n. Biochem. An amino acid, $C_5H_9O_2N$, found in proteins. [Contr. of pyrroline < PYRROLE + -INE²]

pro·lix (prō′liks, prō-liks′) adj. **1.** Unduly long and verbose, as an address. **2.** Indulging in long and wordy discourse; tedious: a prolix orator. [< F prolixe < L prolixus extended < pro- before + stem of liquere to flow] — **pro·lix·i·ty** (prō-lik′sə-tē), **pro′lix·ness** n. — **pro′lix·ly** adv.

pro·loc·u·tor (prō-lok′yə-tər) n. **1.** One who speaks for another; a spokesman or advocate. **2.** The presiding officer of a convocation; especially, the speaker or chairman of the lower house of convocation in the Church of England. [< L < prolocutus, pp. of proloqui to declare, speak for < pro- in behalf of + loqui to talk]

pro·logue (prō′lôg, -log) n. **1.** A prefatory statement to a poem, discourse, or performance; especially, an introduction, often in verse, spoken or sung before a play or opera. **2.** Any anticipatory act or event. — v.t. To introduce with a prologue or preface. Also **pro′log.** [< OF prologue < L prologus < Gk. prologos < pro- before + logos discourse]

pro·logu·ize (prō′lôg-īz, -log-) v.i. **·ized, ·iz·ing** To make or utter a prologue. Also **pro′log·ize.** — **pro′logu·iz′er** n.

pro·long (pra-lông′, -long′) v.t. **1.** To extend in time or space; continue; lengthen. — **Syn.** See INCREASE. Also **pro·lon′-gate** (-lông′gāt, -long′-). [< OF prolonguer < LL prolongare < L pro- forth + longus long] — **pro·long′er** n. — **pro·long′ment** n.

pro·lon·ga·tion (prō′lông-gā′shən, -long-) n. **1.** The act of prolonging. **2.** That by which anything is increased; an extension. [< F < LL prolongare. See PROLONG.]

pro·longe (prō-lonj′, Fr. prô-lôňzh′) n. Mil. A rope having

a hook at one end and a toggle at the other, used for drawing a gun carriage: also called trail rope. [< F < prolonger < OF prolonguer. See PROLONG.]

pro·lu·sion (prō-lōō′zhən) n. **1.** That which is introductory to the principal effort or performance; a prologue. **2.** An essay written as a preliminary to a more elaborate treatise. [< L prolusio, -onis prelude < prolusus, pp. of proludere to play beforehand < pro- before + ludere to play]

prom (prom) n. U.S. Informal A formal college or school dance or ball. [Short for promenade]

prom. 1. Promenade. **2.** Promontory.

prom·e·nade (prom′ə-nād′, -näd′) n. **1.** A walk for amusement or exercise, or as part of a formal or social entertainment. **2.** A ceremonious parade on horseback or in a vehicle. **3.** A place for promenading. **4.** A concert or ball opened with a formal march; also, the march. Abbr. prom. — v. **·nad·ed, ·nad·ing** v.i. **1.** To take a promenade. — v.t. **2.** To take a promenade through or along. **3.** To take or exhibit on or as on a promenade; parade. [< MF < promener to take for a walk < LL prominare to drive forward < pro- before + minare to drive (cattle)] — **prom′e·nad′er** n.

promenade deck The upper deck of a passenger ship or a space on such a deck for passengers to promenade.

pro·me·the·a moth (pra-mē′thē-ə, prō-) A large moth common in eastern North America (Callosoma promethea) that emerges from a suspended cocoon, the adult having a black and dull red body: also called spicebush silkworm. For illustration see COCOON.

Pro·me·the·an (pra-mē′thē-ən) adj. **1.** Of, pertaining to, or like Prometheus. **2.** Creative or life-bringing. — n. One who is Promethean in manner or deed.

Pro·me·theus (pra-mē′thyōōs, -thē-əs) In Greek mythology, a Titan who stole fire from heaven for mankind and as a punishment was chained to a rock, where an eagle daily devoured his liver, which was made whole again at night. He was released by Hercules. [< L < Gk. Promētheus]

pro·me·thi·um (pra-mē′thē-əm) n. A rare radioactive element (symbol Pm), separated from uranium fission products and belonging to the lanthanide series: formerly called illinium. See ELEMENT. [< NL < PROMETHEUS]

prom·i·nence (prom′ə-nəns) n. **1.** The state or quality of being prominent. **2.** That which is prominent; a protuberance. **3.** Astron. One of the great tongues of flame shooting out from the sun's surface, seen during total eclipses. Also **prom′i·nen·cy.** [< F < L prominentia]

prom·i·nent (prom′ə-nənt) adj. **1.** Jutting out; projecting; protuberant. **2.** Conspicuous in position, character, or importance. **3.** Well-known; eminent. [< L prominens, -entis, ppr. of prominere to project] — **prom′i·nent·ly** adv.

pro·mis·cu·i·ty (prō′mis-kyōō′ə-tē, prom′is-) n. **1.** The state of being promiscuous. **2.** Promiscuous sexual union. **3.** An indiscriminate or confused mixture.

pro·mis·cu·ous (pra-mis′kyōō-əs) adj. **1.** Composed of individuals or things confusedly or indiscriminately mingled. **2.** Indiscriminate, especially in sexual relations. **3.** Informal Lacking plan or purpose; casual; irregular. [< L promiscuus mixed < pro- thoroughly + stem of miscere to mix] — **pro·mis′cu·ous·ly** adv. — **pro·mis′cu·ous·ness** n.

prom·ise (prom′is) n. **1.** An assurance given by one person to another that the former will or will not perform a specified act. **2.** Reasonable ground for hope or expectation, especially of future excellence or satisfaction. **3.** Something promised. — v. **·ised, ·is·ing** v.t. **1.** To engage or pledge by a promise: used with the infinitive or a clause: He promised that he would do it. **2.** To make a promise of (something) to someone. **3.** To give reason for expecting: The sky promised rain. **4.** Informal To assure (someone). — v.i. **5.** To make a promise. **6.** To give reason for expectation: often with well or fair. [< L promissum, pp. of promittere to send forward < pro- forth + mittere to send] — **prom′is·er** n.

Promised Land 1. Canaan, promised to Abraham by God. Gen. xv 18. **2.** Any longed-for place of happiness or improvement. **3.** Heaven; paradise. Also Land of Promise.

prom·is·ee (prom′is-ē′) n. Law One to whom a promise is made.

prom·is·ing (prom′is-ing) adj. Giving promise of good results or development: a promising sign; a promising student. — **prom′is·ing·ly** adv.

prom·is·or (prom′is-ôr) n. Law One who makes a promise. [< L promissor < promittere. See PROMISE.]

prom·is·so·ry (prom′ə-sôr′ē, -sō′rē) adj. **1.** Containing or of the nature of a promise. **2.** Indicating what is to be required or to take place after the signing of an insurance contract. [< Med.L promissorius < L promissor. See PROMISOR.]

promissory note A written promise by one party to pay another party a certain sum of money at a specified time, or upon demand: also called note of hand. Abbr. P/n, p.n.

prom·on·to·ry (prom′ən-tôr′ē, -tō′rē) n. pl. **·ries 1.** A high point of land extending into the sea; headland. **2.** Anat. A rounded projection or part. Abbr. prom. [< Med.L promontorium < L promunturium, ? < prominere to project]

pro·mote (pra-mōt′) v.t. **·mot·ed, ·mot·ing 1.** To contribute to the progress, development, or growth of; further; encourage. **2.** To advance to a higher position, grade, or honor: opposed to *demote*. **3.** To work in behalf of; advocate actively: to *promote* social reforms. **4.** In education, to advance (a pupil) to the next higher school grade. **5.** To seek to make (a commercial product, business venture, etc.) popular or successful, as by securing capital or by advertising. [< L *promotus*, pp. of *promovere* to move forward < *pro-* forward + *movere* to move]

pro·mot·er (prə·mō′tər) *n.* **1.** One who or that which promotes. **2.** One who assists in promoting a financial or commercial enterprise, as by securing capital.

pro·mo·tion (prə·mō′shən) *n.* **1.** Advancement or preferment in honor, dignity, rank, or grade. **2.** Furtherance; encouragement. **3.** The act of promoting, or the state of being promoted. [< OF < L *promotio, -onis* < *promovere*. See PROMOTE.] — **pro·mo′tion·al** *adj.*

pro·mo·tive (prə·mō′tiv) *adj.* Tending to promote.

prompt (prompt) *v.t.* **1.** To incite to action; instigate. **2.** To suggest or inspire (an act, thought, etc.). **3.** To remind of something forgotten or next in order; give a cue to. — *v.i.* **4.** To give help or suggestions. — *adj.* **1.** Acting or ready to act at the moment; quick to respond; punctual. **2.** Done or rendered with readiness or alacrity; taking place at the appointed time. — *n.* **1.** A term of credit allowed for the payment of a debt as stated in a prompt note. **2.** An act of prompting. **3.** The information imparted by prompting; a reminder. [< OF < L *promptus* brought forth, pp. of *promere* < *pro-* forth + *emere* to take] — **prompt′ness** *n.* — **Syn.** (verb) **1.** arouse, stimulate, animate, excite.

prompt·book (prompt′bŏŏk′) *n.* An annotated script of a play used by a prompter or director.

prompt·er (promp′tər) **1.** In a theater, one who follows the lines and prompts the actors. Abbr. *P.* **2.** One who or that which prompts.

promp·ti·tude (promp′tə·tōōd, -tyōōd) *n.* The quality, habit, or fact of being prompt; promptness. [< MF, or < LL *promptitudo*]

prompt·ly (prompt′lē) *adv.* In a prompt manner; at once; directly. — **Syn.** See IMMEDIATELY.

prompt note In commerce, a note delivered to a purchaser of merchandise as a reminder, and containing a statement of the sum due, day of payment, etc.

pro·mul·gate (prō·mul′gāt, prom′əl·gāt) *v.t.* **·gat·ed, ·gat·ing** To make known or announce officially and formally; put into effect by public proclamation, as a law or dogma. [< L *promulgatus*, pp. of *promulgare* to make known, prob. alter. of *provulgare* < *pro-* forth + *vulgus* people] — **pro·mul·ga·tion** (prō′mul·gā′shən, prom′əl-) *n.* — **pro·mul·ga·tor** (prō′mul′gā·tər, prom′əl-) *n.* — **Syn.** proclaim, publish, declare.

pro·mulge (prō·mulj′) *v.t.* **·mulged, ·mulg·ing** *Archaic* To promulgate. [< L *promulgare*. See PROMULGATE.]

pro·my·ce·li·um (prō′mī·sē′lē·əm) *n. pl.* **·li·a** (-lē-ə) *Bot.* A short-jointed filament that develops on the germination of certain smut or rust spores and gives rise to sporidia. — **pro′my·ce′li·al** *adj.*

pron. 1. Pronominal. **2.** Pronoun. **3.** Pronounce(d); pronunciation.

pro·nate (prō′nāt) *v.t.* **·nat·ed, ·nat·ing** To place in a position of pronation. [< L *pronatus*, pp. of *pronare* to bow < *pronus* prone]

pro·na·tion (prō·nā′shən) *n. Physiol.* **1.** The act or movement of turning the palm of the hand, or the corresponding surface of the forelimb, downward or backward. **2.** The position of a limb so turned: opposed to *supination*.

pro·na·tor (prō·nā′tər) *n. pl.* **·na·to·res** (prō′nə·tôr′ēz, -tō′rēz) *Anat.* A muscle of the forearm by which pronation is effected. [< Med.L < L *pronare*. See PRONATE.]

prone (prōn) *adj.* **1.** Lying flat, especially with the face, front, or palm downward; prostrate. **2.** Leaning forward or downward; also, moving or sloping sharply downward. **3.** Mentally inclined or predisposed: with *to*. [< L *pronus* prostrate < *pro-* before] — **prone′ly** *adv.* — **prone′ness** *n.* — **Syn. 3.** given, subject. Compare ADDICTED.

pro·neph·ros (prō·nef′ros) *n. Biol.* The anterior of three similar tubular organs found in connection with the genitourinary apparatus of the vertebrate embryo. [< NL < Gk. *pro-* before + *nephros* kidney] — **pro·neph′ric** *adj.*

prong (prông, prong) *n.* **1.** A pointed end of an instrument, as the tine of a fork. **2.** Any pointed, projecting part, as the end of an antler. — *v.t.* To prick or stab with or as with a prong. [Cf. LG *prange* pointed stick, Du. *prangen* to pinch]

prong·horn (prông′hôrn′, prong′-) *n. pl.* **·horns** or **·horn** A ruminant (*Antilocapra americana*) of western North America, resembling an antelope, with deciduous branched horns.

pro·nom·i·nal (prō·nom′ə·nəl) *adj.* Of, pertaining to, or of the nature of a pronoun. Abbr. *pron.* [< LL *pronominalis* < L *pronomen*. See PRONOUN.] — **pro·nom′i·nal·ly** *adv.*

pronominal adjective The possessive case of a personal pronoun used attributively, as *my, your, his, her*, etc.

pro·noun (prō′noun) *n. Gram.* A word that may be used in-

stead of a noun or noun phrase (personal, relative, demonstrative, indefinite, and reflexive pronouns), or as an adjective (adjective pronoun), or to introduce a question (interrogative pronoun). Abbr. *pr., pron.* [< OF *pronom* < L *pronomen* < *pro-* in place of + *nomen* name, noun]

pro·nounce (prə·nouns′) *v.* **·nounced, ·nounc·ing** *v.t.* **1.** To utter or deliver officially or solemnly; proclaim: to *pronounce* judgment. **2.** To assert; declare, especially as one's judgment: The judge *pronounced* her guilty. **3.** To enunciate or articulate (sounds). **4.** To utter the constituent sounds of (a word or phrase) in a particular sequence or with a particular accentual pattern. **5.** To utter (the sound of a letter): to *pronounce* the *t* in *often*. — *v.i.* **6.** To make a judgment or pronouncement. **7.** To articulate words; speak. Abbr. *pron.* [< OF *pronuncier* < LL *pronunciare* < L *pronuntiare* to proclaim < *pro-* forth + *nuntiare* to announce] — **pro·nounce′a·ble** *adj.* — **pro·nounc′er** *n.*

pro·nounced (prə·nounst′) *adj.* Of marked or clearly indicated character; decided. — **pro·nounc·ed·ly** (prə·noun′sid·lē) *adv.*

pro·nounce·ment (prə·nouns′mənt) *n.* **1.** The act of pronouncing. **2.** A formal declaration or announcement.

pron·to (pron′tō) *adv. U.S. Informal* Quickly; promptly; instantly. [< Sp. < L *promptus*. See PROMPT.]

pro·nu·cle·us (prō·nōō′klē·əs, -nyōō′-) *n. pl.* **·cle·i** (-klē·ī) *Biol.* The nucleus of either the male or female gamete, the union of which forms the nucleus of the fertilized ovum. [< NL < Gk. *pro-* before + L *nucleus* kernel]

pronun. Pronunciation.

pro·nun·ci·a·men·to (prə·nun′sē·ə·men′tō, -shē-ə-) *n. pl.* **·tos** A public announcement; proclamation; manifesto. [< Sp. *pronunciamiento*, lit., pronouncement < L *pronuntiare*. See PRONOUNCE.]

pro·nun·ci·a·tion (prə·nun′sē·ā′shən) *n.* **1.** The act or manner of uttering words. **2.** Articulation. Abbr. *pron., pronun.* [< F < L *pronunciatio, -onis* < *pronuntiatus*, pp. of *pronuntiare*. See PRONOUNCE.]

proof (prōōf) *n.* **1.** The act or process of proving; especially, the establishment of a fact by evidence or a truth by other truths. **2.** A trial of strength, truth, fact, or excellence, etc.; a test. **3.** Evidence and argument sufficient to induce belief. **4.** *Law* Anything that serves to convince the mind of the truth or falsity of a fact or proposition, including evidence, presumptions either of fact or of law, and citations of law. **5.** The state or quality of having successfully undergone a test. **6.** Impenetrability; also, impenetrable armor. **7.** The standard of strength of alcoholic liquors. See PROOF SPIRIT. **8.** *Printing* A printed trial sheet showing the contents or condition of matter in type or of a plate, or the like, either with or without marked corrections. **9.** In engraving and etching, a trial impression taken from an engraved plate, stone, or block; also, a perfect impression from such a plate, etc., when finished. **10.** *Photog.* A trial print from a negative. **11.** *Math.* A process to check a computation by using its result; also, a demonstration. **12.** Anything proved true; experience. **13.** In philately, an experimental printing of a stamp. — *adj.* **1.** Employed in or connected with proving or correcting. **2.** Capable of resisting successfully; firm; impenetrable: with *against*: *proof* against bribes. **3.** Of standard alcoholic strength, as liquors. [< OF *prueve* < LL *proba* < *probare*. See PROVE.]

-proof *combining form* **1.** Impervious to; able to withstand; not damaged by: *waterproof, bombproof*. **2.** Protected against: *mothproof*. **3.** As strong as: *armorproof*. **4.** Resisting; showing no effects of: *panicproof*. Adjectives formed with *-proof* may also be used as verbs. [< PROOF, adj.]

proof·read (prōōf′rēd′) *v.t. & v.i.* **·read** (-red′), **·read·ing** (-rē′ding) To read and correct (printers' proofs).

proof·read·er (prōōf′rē′dər) *n.* One who reads and marks the errors in printers' proofs. — **proof′read′ing** *n.*

proof spirit An alcoholic liquor that contains a standard amount of alcohol. In the United States 100 proof indicates a liquor half of whose volume is ethyl alcohol having a specific gravity of 0.7939 at 60° F.

prop¹ (prop) *n.* **1.** A rigid object, as a beam or pole, that bolsters or sustains an incumbent weight. **2.** One who gives support to an institution, organization, etc. — *v.t.* **propped, prop·ping 1.** To support or keep from falling with or as with a prop. **2.** To lean or place: usually with *against*. **3.** To support; sustain. [< MDu. *proppe* a support] — **Syn.** (verb) **1.** bolster, brace, buttress, shore, stay.

prop² (prop) *n.* A property (def. 8).

prop³ (prop) *n. Informal* A propeller.

prop. 1. Proper(ly). **2.** Property. **3.** Proposition. **4.** Proprietor. **5.** Proprietary.

pro·pae·deu·tic (prō′pə·dōō′tik, -dyōō′-) *adj.* **1.** Pertaining to or of the nature of preliminary instruction. **2.** Relating to or introductory to an art or science. Also **pro′pae·deu′ti·cal.** — *n.* A preparatory or introductory subject or course. [< Gk. *propaideuein* < *pro-* before + *paideuein* to educate < *pais, paidos* child]

---

pro·pae·deu·tics (prō/pə·dōō/tiks, -dyōō/-) *n.pl.* (*construed as sing.*) The body of principles or rules introductory to an art or science.

prop·a·ga·ble (prop/ə·gə·bəl) *adj.* Capable of being propagated. [< L *propagare* (See PROPAGATE) + -ABLE]

prop·a·gan·da (prop/ə·gan/də) *n.* **1.** A systematic effort to persuade a body of people to support or adopt a particular opinion, attitude, or course of action. **2.** Any selection of facts, ideas, or allegations forming the basis of such an effort. **3.** An institution or scheme for propagating a doctrine or system. ◆ *Propaganda* is now often used in a disparaging sense, as of a body of distortions and half-truths calculated to bias one's judgment or opinions. [< PROPAGANDA]

Prop·a·gan·da (prop/ə·gan/də) *n.* In the Roman Catholic Church, a society of cardinals charged with overseeing the foreign missions, originated by Pope Gregory XV in 1622 as the **Con·gre·ga·ti·o de Prop·a·gan·da Fi·de** (kon·gra·gā/shē·ō dē prop·ə·gan/də fī/dē) (Congregation for the Propagation of the Faith): with *the*. [< NL (*congregatio de*) *propaganda* (*fide*) (the council for) propagating (the faith) < L, gerundive of *propagare*. See PROPAGATE.]

prop·a·gan·dism (prop/ə·gan/diz·əm) *n.* The art, practice, or system of using propaganda.

prop·a·gan·dist (prop/ə·gan/dist) *n.* One who supports a doctrine, etc., by means of propaganda. — *adj.* Of, pertaining to, or of the nature of propaganda.

prop·a·gan·dize (prop/ə·gan/dīz) *v.* **·dized, ·diz·ing** *v.t.* **1.** To spread by means of propaganda. **2.** To subject to propaganda. — *v.i.* **3.** To carry on or spread propaganda.

prop·a·gate (prop/ə·gāt) *v.* **·gat·ed, ·gat·ing** *v.t.* **1.** To cause (animals, plants, etc.) to multiply by natural reproduction; breed. **2.** To spread from person to person, as a doctrine or belief; promulgate; disseminate. **3.** To transmit through a medium; extend the action of: to *propagate* heat. **4.** To reproduce (itself), as a species of plant or animal. **5.** To pass on (traits, qualities, etc.) to one's offspring. **6.** *Obs.* To increase. — *v.i.* **7.** To multiply by natural reproduction; have offspring; breed. [< L *propagatus*, pp. of *propagare* to reproduce by slips < *propago* slip, shoot < *pro-* forth + *pag-*, root of *pangere* to fasten] — **prop/a·ga/tive** *adj.* — **prop/a·ga/tor** *n.*
— **Syn.** **1.** beget, generate, procreate. **4.** increase, multiply.

prop·a·ga·tion (prop/ə·gā/shən) *n.* **1.** The act of propagating, or the state of being propagated; reproduction. **2.** Dissemination; diffusion.

prop·a·gule (prop/ə·gyōōl) *n. Bot.* A bud, shoot, or other plant part that vegetatively propagates the species. Also **pro·pag·u·lum** (prō·pag/yə·ləm). [< NL *propagulum*, dim. of L *propago*. See PROPAGATE.]

pro·pane (prō/pān) *n. Chem.* A gaseous hydrocarbon of the methane series, C_3H_8, obtained from petroleum and sometimes used as a fuel gas. [< PROP(YL) + (METH)ANE]

pro·pane·di·ol (prō/pān·dī/ol) *n. Chem.* **1.** Propylene glycol. **2.** Trimethylene glycol.

pro·par·ox·y·tone (prō/pə·rok/sə·tōn) *adj.* Having an acute accent on the antepenult. — *n.* A proparoxytone word. [< Gk. *proparoxytonos* < *pro-* before + *paroxytonos* paroxytone]

pro pa·tri·a (prō pā/trē·ə) *Latin* For one's country.

pro·pel (prə·pel/) *v.t.* **·pelled, ·pel·ling** To cause to move forward or ahead; drive or urge forward. [< L *propellere* to drive before < *pro-* forward + *pellere* to drive]
— **Syn.** push, impel.

pro·pel·lant (prə·pel/ənt) *n.* **1.** One who or that which propels. **2.** *Mil.* An explosive that upon ignition propels a projectile from a gun. **3.** A solid or liquid fuel that serves to propel a rocket, guided missile, etc.: also spelled *propellent*.

pro·pel·lent (prə·pel/ənt) *adj.* Able to propel; propelling. — *n.* See PROPELLANT. [< L *propellens, -entis,* ppr. of *propellere.* See PROPEL.]

pro·pel·ler (prə·pel/ər) *n.* **1.** One who or that which propels. **2.** Any device for propelling a craft through water or air; especially, one having blades mounted at an angle on a power-driven shaft and producing a thrust by their rotary action on the medium.

pro·pend (prō·pend/) *v.i. Obs.* To be disposed in favor; tend. [< L *propendere* to hang forward, be inclined < *pro-* forward + *pendere* to hang]

pro·pene (prō/pēn) *n.* Propylene. [< PROP(YL) + -ENE]

pro·pe·no·ic acid (prō/pə·nō/ik) *Chem.* Acrylic acid (which see). [< PROPEN(E) + (BENZ)OIC]

pro·pen·si·ty (prə·pen/sə·tē) *n. pl.* **·ties 1.** A natural disposition or tendency; bent. **2.** *Obs.* A liking for; partiality. [< L *propensus,* pp. of *propendere.* See PROPEND.]

prop·er (prop/ər) *adj.* **1.** Specially suited or adapted for some end; fit; appropriate: the *proper* medicine. **2.** Conforming to a prevalent standard of conduct or manners; correct; fitting. **3.** Understood in a strict or literal sense: usually following the noun modified: part of the book *proper.* **4.** Naturally belonging to a particular person, thing, or class; peculiarly suitable: Crying is *proper* to babies. **5.** Modest; decent. **6.** *Gram.* Designating a particular person, place, or the like: a *proper* name. **7.** *Brit. Informal* Thorough or thoroughgoing; unmitigated: a *proper* bore. **8.** *Eccl.* Appointed for special use: the *proper* psalms for Christmas. **9.** *Heraldry* Represented in the natural color. **10.** *Archaic* Belonging to or affecting oneself; own. **11.** *Archaic* Handsome. **12.** *Archaic* Good; excellent; pleasant. **13.** *Obs.* Respectable; worthy; honest. — **Syn.** See APPROPRIATE. — *n. Sometimes cap. Eccl.* The portion of the breviary, missal, or Mass containing the prayers and collects suitable to special occasions or feasts: with *the:* distinguished from *ordinary.* Abbr. *prop.* [< OF *propre* < L *proprius* one's own] — **prop/er·ness** *n.*

proper fraction *Math.* A fraction in which the numerator is less than the denominator.

prop·er·ly (prop/ər·lē) *adv.* In a proper manner; suitably; rightly. Abbr. *prop.*

proper noun *Gram.* A noun that names a particular person, place, or thing, and is always capitalized, as *Paul, Venice, U.S.S. Nautilus:* distinguished from *common noun.*

prop·er·tied (prop/ər·tēd) *adj.* Owning property.

Pro·per·tius (prō·pûr/shəs), **Sextus,** 50?–16? B.C., Roman poet.

prop·er·ty (prop/ər·tē) *n. pl.* **·ties 1.** Any object of value that a person may lawfully acquire and hold; that which may be owned, as stocks, land, etc.; any possession. **2.** The legal right to the possession, use, enjoyment, and disposal of a thing; ownership or dominion. **3.** Holdings, land, etc., owned; wealth. **4.** A parcel of land. **5.** Any of the qualities or characteristics that together make up the nature or basic structure of a thing; a constituent part or element. **6.** A quality or feature that belongs distinctively to a particular object or class; a peculiarity. **7.** An attribute of a body or substance under stated conditions, especially as perceived by the senses, as color, odor, hardness, density, etc. **8.** In the theater, any portable article used in a performance other than scenery and the costumes, as books, dishes, etc.: also called *prop.* **9.** Something considered as being owned or available to a group of people or to the public: common *property.* **10.** *Logic* That which is not a part of the essence of a thing but is necessarily connected with the essence. Abbr. *prop.* [< OF *propriete* < L *proprietas, -tatis* < *proprius* one's own. Doublet of PROPRIETY.] — **prop/er·ty·less** *adj.*
— **Syn.** **3.** chattels, goods, estate. **6.** See CHARACTERISTIC. **7.** See ATTRIBUTE.

pro·phase (prō/fāz) *n. Biol.* The first stage in the mitosis of the cell, during which the chromatin of the nucleus is formed into longitudinally split chromosomes. [< Gk. *pro-* before + PHASE]

proph·e·cy (prof/ə·sē) *n. pl.* **·cies 1.** A prediction made under divine influence and direction. **2.** Any prediction. **3.** Discourse delivered by a prophet under divine inspiration. **4.** A book of prophecies. **5.** *Obs.* Public interpretation of Scripture; preaching. [< OF *profecie* < LL *prophetia* < Gk. *prophēteia* < *prophētēs* < *pro* before + *phanai* to speak]

proph·e·sy (prof/ə·sī) *v.* **·sied, ·sy·ing** *v.t.* **1.** To utter or foretell with or as with divine inspiration. **2.** To predict (a future event). **3.** To point out beforehand. — *v.i.* **4.** To speak by divine influence, or as a medium between God and man. **5.** To foretell the future; make predictions. **6.** To explain or teach religious subjects; preach. [< OF *prophecier* < *profecie.* See PROPHECY.] — **proph/e·si/er** *n.*
— **Syn.** **1.** *Prophesy* and *foretell* are often interchangeable, but in Scriptural sense *prophesy* refers to the uttering of religious truths under divine inspiration, and does not necessarily include the prediction of future events. *Foretell* always bears the latter sense. Compare AUGUR.

proph·et (prof/it) *n.* **1.** One who delivers divine messages or interprets the divine will. **2.** One who foretells the future; especially, an inspired predictor. **3.** A religious leader. **4.** An interpreter or spokesman for any cause. **5.** A mantis. **6.** In Christian Science, a spiritual seer. — **the Prophet** According to Islam, Mohammed. — **the Prophets** The second of the three ancient divisions of the Old Testament, containing all those books not found in the Pentateuch or the Hagiographa. The Prophets consist of the following books (names in the Douai Bible, when different, are given in parentheses): Joshua, Judges, I Samuel (I Kings), II Samuel (II Kings), I Kings (III Kings), II Kings (IV Kings), Isaiah (Isaias), Jeremiah (Jeremias), Ezekiel (Ezechiel), Hosea (Osee), Joel, Amos, Obadiah (Abdias), Jonah (Jonas), Micah (Micheas), Nahum, Habakkuk (Habacuc), Zephaniah (Sophonias), Haggai (Aggeus), Zechariah (Zacharias), Malachi (Malachias). [< OF *prophete* < LL *propheta* < Gk. *prophētēs* < *pro-* before + *phanai* to speak] — **proph/et·ess** *n.fem.*

proph·et·hood *n.*

pro·phet·ic (prə·fet/ik) *adj.* **1.** Of or pertaining to a prophet or prophecy; vatic. **2.** Pertaining to or involving prediction or presentiment; predictive. Also **pro·phet/i·cal.** — **pro·phet/i·cal·ly** *adv.* — **pro·phet/i·cal·ness** *n.*

proph·y·lac·tic (prō/fə·lak/tik, prof/ə-) *adj.* Tending to protect against or ward off something, especially disease; preventive. — *n.* A prophylactic medicine or appliance. [< Gk. *prophylaktikos* < *prophylassein* < *pro-* before + *phylassein* to guard]

pro·phy·lax·is (prō/fə·lak/sis, prof/ə-) *n.* Preventive treatment for disease. [< NL < Gk. *pro-* before + *phylaxis* guarding]

pro·pine (prō·pīn′) *Scot. v.t.* ·**pined**, ·**pin·ing** To offer, as a gift; propose. — *n.* An offering; pledge. [< L *propinare* < Gk. *propinein* < *pro-* before + *pinein* to drink]

pro·pin·qui·ty (prō·ping′kwə·tē) *n.* **1.** Nearness in place or time. **2.** Kinship. — **Syn.** See APPROXIMATION. [< L *propinquitas*, *-tatis* < *propinquus* < *prope* near]

pro·pi·o·nate (prō′pē·ə·nāt′) *n. Chem.* A salt or ester of propionic acid.

pro·pi·on·ic acid (prō′pē·on′ik, -ō′nik) *Chem.* A colorless, liquid, fatty acid, $C_3H_6O_2$, occurring in nature, as in molasses from the beet root, and produced by synthesis. [< PRO(TO) + Gk. *piōn* fat + -IC]

pro·pi·ti·ate (prō·pish′ē·āt) *v.t.* ·**at·ed**, ·**at·ing** To cause to be favorably disposed; appease; conciliate. [< L *propitiatus*, pp. of *propitiare* to propitiate < *propitius.* See PROPITIOUS.] — **pro·pi·ti·a·ble** (-ē·ə·bəl) *adj.* — **pro·pi′ti·at′ing·ly** *adv.* — **pro·pi′ti·a′tive** *adj.* — **pro·pi′ti·a′tor** *n.*

pro·pi·ti·a·tion (prō·pish′ē·ā′shən) *n.* **1.** The act of propitiating. **2.** That which propitiates. — **Syn. 1.** *Propitiation, appeasement, atonement,* and *expiation* are compared as they relate to the placating of some ruling power. *Propitiation* is any action which makes such a power more lenient toward the offender; the gift of candy to an injured or angry sweetheart is an act of *propitiation. Appeasement* mollifies by making concession to demands, and often suggests weakness, cowardice, or bad judgment. *Atonement* originally meant reconciliation, but now denotes an offering or sacrifice sufficient to win forgiveness for an offense. The word suggests some degree of equality between the injury suffered and the reparation for it. *Expiation* is more legalistic, and refers to the enduring of the full penalty for a wrong.

pro·pi·ti·a·to·ry (prō·pish′ē·ə·tôr′ē, -tō′rē) *adj.* Pertaining to or causing propitiation. — *n. pl.* ·**ries** The mercy seat.

pro·pi·tious (prō·pish′əs) *adj.* **1.** Attended by favorable circumstances; auspicious. **2.** Kindly disposed; gracious. [< OF *propicius* < L *propitius* favorable, ? < *pro-* before + *petere* to seek] — **pro·pi′tious·ly** *adv.* — **pro·pi′tious·ness** *n.* — **Syn. 1.** *Propitious* and *auspicious* may both be applied to circumstances that appear to favor a project or bode well for the future. But *propitious* may also be applied to persons, while *auspicious* is not so used.

prop·jet (prop′jet′) *n. Aeron.* A turboprop. [< PROP(ELLER) + JET]

prop·o·lis (prop′ə·lis) *n.* A resinous, adhesive substance collected by bees to serve as a cementing material. [< L < Gk. < *pro-* before + *polis* city]

pro·pone (prə·pōn′) *v.t.* ·**poned**, ·**pon·ing** *Scot.* To propose or propound; put forward.

pro·po·nent (prə·pō′nənt) *n.* **1.** One who makes a proposal or puts forward a proposition; one who propounds a thing. **2.** *Law* One who presents a will for probate. **3.** One who advocates or supports a cause or doctrine. [< L *proponens*, *-entis*, ppr. of *proponere* < *pro-* forth + *ponere* to put]

Pro·pon·tis (prə·pon′tis) The ancient name for the (Sea of) MARMARA.

pro·por·tion (prə·pôr′shən, -pōr′-) *n.* **1.** Relative magnitude, number, or degree, as existing between parts, a part and a whole, or different things. **2.** Fitness and harmony; symmetry. **3.** A proportionate or proper share; any share or part. **4.** An equality or identity between ratios. **5.** *Math.* **a** The relationship among four terms such that the product of the second and third terms is equal to the product of the first and fourth. **b** The rule of three. **6.** *pl.* Size; dimensions: a picture of large *proportions.* — *v.t.* **1.** To adjust properly as to relative magnitude, amount, or degree: to *proportion* one's expenses to one's means. **2.** To form with a harmonious relation of parts. [< OF *proporcion* < L *proportio*, *-onis* < *pro-* for + *portio*, *-onis* share] — **pro·por′tion·a·ble** *adj.* — **pro·por′tion·a·bly** *adv.* — **pro·por′tion·er** *n.*

pro·por·tion·al (prə·pôr′shən·əl, -pōr′-) *adj.* **1.** Of, pertaining to, or being in proportion. **2.** *Math.* **a** Constituting the terms of a proportion. **b** Varying so that corresponding values form a proportion. — *n.* Any quantity or number in proportion to another or others. — **pro·por′tion·al·ly** *adv.* — **pro·por′tion·al′i·ty** (-al′ə·tē) *n.*

proportional representation A system of election by which political parties secure legislative representation in a government in proportion to voting strength. *Abbr. P.R.*

pro·por·tion·ate (*adj.* prə·pôr′shən·it, -pōr′-; *v.* prə·pôr′shən·āt, -pōr′-) *adj.* Being in due proportion; proportional. — *v.t.* ·**at·ed**, ·**at·ing** To make proportionate. — **pro·por′tion·ate·ly** *adv.* — **pro·por′tion·ate·ness** *n.*

pro·por·tion·ment (prə·pôr′shən·mənt, -pōr′-) *n.* The act of placing or putting things in proportion.

pro·po·sal (prə·pō′zəl) *n.* **1.** An offer proposing something to be accepted or adopted. **2.** An offer of marriage. **3.** Something proposed, as a scheme or plan. — **Syn.** *Proposal, proposition, bid,* and *overture* are compared as they signify something said as a basis for discussion. *Proposal* most clearly implies an effort to ascertain the views of another, especially as to some suggested action. *Proposition* is used spe-

cifically in mathematics to denote a statement asserted as a truth to be argued and proved, if possible; in all contexts, it implies a concrete, often detailed, statement, while a *proposal* may be vague. A *bid* is usually commercial, an offer of an amount to be paid for goods, services, or privilege. An *overture* may be a *proposal,* or may precede its act as an offer to enter into discussion or negotiation.

pro·pose (prə·pōz′) *v.* ·**posed**, ·**pos·ing** *v.t.* **1.** To put forward for acceptance or consideration. **2.** To nominate, as for admission or appointment. **3.** To intend; purpose. **4.** To suggest the drinking of (a toast or health). — *v.i.* **5.** To form or announce a plan or design. **6.** To make an offer, as of marriage. [< OF *proposer* < *pro-* forth (< L) + *poser.* See POSE[1].] — **pro·pos′er** *n.* — **Syn. 3.** In strict usage, *propose* and *purpose* are distinct in the sense of intend. What we *propose* to do, even when we keep the intention unknown to others, is subject to further consideration. What we *purpose* to do is settled; the word suggests that the mind has been made up, and is not subject to change.

prop·o·si·tion (prop′ə·zish′ən) *n.* **1.** A scheme or proposal offered for consideration or acceptance. **2.** *U.S. Informal* Any matter or person to be dealt with: a tough *proposition.* **3.** *Informal* An indecent or immodest proposal. **4.** A subject or statement presented for discussion. **5.** *Logic* **a** A statement in which something (the *subject*) is affirmed or denied in terms of something else (the *predicate*), the two being related usually by a copula. **b** That which is expressed in a sentence, as distinguished from the way it is expressed. **6.** *Math.* A statement of a truth to be demonstrated (a *theorem*) or of an operation to be performed (a *problem*). *Abbr. prop.* — **Syn.** See PROPOSAL. — *v.t. Informal* To make an improper suggestion to. [< OF < L *propositio*, *-onis* a setting forth < *proponere.* See PROPONENT.] — **prop′o·si′tion·al** *adj.* — **prop′o·si′tion·al·ly** *adv.*

pro·pos·i·tus (prō·poz′i·təs) *n. pl.* ·**ti** (-tī) *Law* The person from whom a line of descent is reckoned. [< L, pp. of *proponere.* See PROPONENT.]

pro·pound (prə·pound′) *v.t.* To put forward for consideration, solution, etc.; suggest; submit. [Earlier *propone* < L *proponere* to set forth. See PROPONENT.] — **pro·pound′er** *n.*

pro·pre·tor (prō·prē′tər) *n.* In ancient Rome, an officer, especially a governor of a province, having the authority of a pretor without pretorian rank. Also **pro·prae′tor.** [< L *propraetor* < *pro-* on behalf of + *praetor* pretor]

pro·pri·e·tar·y (prə·prī′ə·ter′ē) *adj.* **1.** Pertaining or belonging to a proprietor. **2.** Subject to exclusive ownership. **3.** Designating an article, as a medicine, protected as to name, composition, or process of manufacture by copyright, patent, secrecy, etc. — *n. pl.* ·**tar·ies 1.** A proprietor or proprietors collectively. **2.** Proprietorship; ownership. *Abbr. prop.* [< LL *proprietarius* < *proprietas.* See PROPERTY.]

proprietary colony An early American colony, as Maryland, Pennsylvania, and Delaware, organized by Great Britain under a royal grant of territory with full administrative powers to a private person or persons.

pro·pri·e·tor (prə·prī′ə·tər) *n.* A person having the exclusive title to anything. *Abbr. prop.* [< PROPRIETARY] — **pro·pri′e·tor·ship′** *n.* — **pro·pri′e·tress** *n.fem.*

pro·pri·e·ty (prə·prī′ə·tē) *n. pl.* ·**ties 1.** The character or quality of being proper; especially, accordance with recognized usage, custom, or principles. **2.** *Obs.* An exclusive right of possession; also, a possession or property owned. — **the proprieties** The methods or standards of good society. [< OF *propriete.* Doublet of PROPERTY.]

pro·pri·o·cep·tive (prō′prē·ə·sep′tiv) *adj.* Of, pertaining to, or being stimuli that arise within the organism.

pro·pri·o·cep·tor (prō′prē·ə·sep′tər) *n. Physiol.* One of the sensory receptors situated within the body that are responsive to internal stimuli. Compare EXTEROCEPTOR, INTEROCEPTOR. [< NL < L *proprius* one's own + (RE)CEPTOR]

prop root *Bot.* The supporting root of a plant, growing into the soil from above ground, as in corn.

prop·to·sis (prop·tō′sis) *n. pl.* ·**ses** (-sēz) *Med.* A forward displacement; bulging, as of the eyeball. [< LL < Gk. *proptōsis* a falling forward < *propiptein* < *pro-* before + *piptein* to fall]

pro·pul·sion (prə·pul′shən) *n.* **1.** The act or operation of propelling. **2.** A propelling force. [< L *propulsus*, pp. of *propellere.* See PROPEL.] — **pro·pul′sive** (-siv) *adj.*

pro·pyl (prō′pil) *n. Chem.* The univalent radical, C_3H_7, derived from propane. [< PROP(IONIC) + -YL]

prop·y·lae·um (prop′ə·lē′əm) *n. pl.* ·**lae·a** (-lē′ə) *Usually pl. Archit.* **1.** A structure forming an imposing entrance or gateway before an ancient temple. **2.** A porch or vestibule. [< L < Gk. *propylaion* < *pro-* before + *pylē* gate]

pro·pyl·ene (prō′pil·lēn) *n. Chem.* A gaseous hydrocarbon, C_3H_6, obtained from propane and as a by-product in petroleum refining: also called *propene.*

propylene glycol *Chem.* An organic compound, $C_3H_8O_2$, derived from propylene and glycerol, used as an antifreeze mixture and solvent: also called *propanediol.*

prop·y·lite (prop'ə·līt) *n.* A variety of andesite that has been altered by the action of hot water. [< Gk. *propylon* PROPYLON + -ITE¹]

prop·y·lon (prop'ə·lon) *n. pl.* **·la** (-lə) A monumental gateway placed before the principal entrance of an important building or temple, as in ancient Egypt. [< L < Gk. < *pro-* before + *pylē* gate]

pro ra·ta (prō rā'tə, rat'ə, rä'tə) In proportion: The loss was shared *pro rata*. [< L *pro rata* (*parte*) according to the calculated (share)]

pro·rate (prō·rāt', prō'rāt') *v.t. & v.i.* **·rat·ed, ·rat·ing** To distribute or divide proportionately. [< PRO RATA] — **pro·rat'a·ble** *adj.* — **pro·ra'tion** *n.*

pro·ro·ga·tion (prō'rə·gā'shən) *n.* 1. The act of proroguing. 2. The act of prolonging or extending in time; also, continuance; prolongation. [< OF *prorogacion* < L *prorogatio, -onis* < *progorare*. See PROROGUE.]

PROPYLON OF PTOLEMY EUERGETES AT KARNAK

pro·rogue (prō·rōg') *v.t.* **·rogued, ·ro·guing** 1. To discontinue a session of (an assembly, especially the British Parliament). 2. *Obs.* To put off or postpone. 3. *Obs.* To protract or prolong. [< MF *proroguer* < L *prorogare* to prolong < *pro-* forward + *rogare* to ask]

pros. Prosody.

pro·sa·ic (prō·zā'ik) *adj.* 1. Lacking in those qualities that impart animation or interest; unimaginative; commonplace; dull. 2. Pertaining to or like prose. Also **pro·sa'i·cal.** [< LL *prosaicus* < L *prosa* prose] — **pro·sa'i·cal·ly** *adv.* — **pro·sa'ic·ness** *n.*

pro·sa·ism (prō'zā·iz'əm) *n.* A prosaic expression, phrase, or style. [< F *prosaïsme*]

pro·sce·ni·um (prō·sē'nē·əm) *n. pl.* **·ni·a** (-nē·ə) 1. In a modern theater or similar building, the part of the stage in front of the curtain, sometimes including the curtain and its arch. 2. In the ancient theater, the wall that formed a background for the actors. [< L < Gk. *proskēnion* < *pro-* before + *skēnē* stage, tent]

pro·sciut·to (prō·shoo'tō) *n.* A spicy, cured ham. [< Ital.]

pro·scribe (prō·skrīb') *v.t.* **·scribed, ·scrib·ing** 1. To denounce or condemn; prohibit; interdict. 2. To outlaw or banish. 3. In ancient Rome, to publish the name of (one condemned or exiled). [< L *proscribere* to write publicly < *pro-* before + *scribere* to write] — **pro·scrib'er** *n.*

pro·scrip·tion (prō·skrip'shən) *n.* 1. The act of proscribing, or the state of being proscribed. 2. Interdiction; ostracism; outlawry. [< L *proscriptio, -onis* < *proscribere*. See PROSCRIBE.] — **pro·scrip'tive** *adj.* — **pro·scrip'tive·ly** *adv.* — **pro·scrip'tive·ness** *n.*

prose (prōz) *n.* 1. Speech or writing without metrical structure: distinguished from *verse.* 2. Commonplace or tedious discourse. 3. *Eccl.* A hymn of irregular meter sometimes sung in the Eucharistic liturgy after the gradual. 4. A proser. — *adj.* 1. Of or pertaining to prose. 2. Tedious; tiresome. — *v.t. & v.i.* **prosed, pros·ing** To write or speak in prose. [< OF < L *prosa* (*oratio*) straightforward (discourse) < *prorsus* < *provertere* < *pro-* forward + *vertere* to turn]

pro·sect (prō·sekt') *v.t.* To dissect for purposes of anatomical demonstration and instruction. [Back formation < *prosector* an anatomist < L *prosecare* < *pro-* for + *secare* to cut] — **pro·sec'tion** (-sek'shən) *n.* — **pro·sec'tor** *n.*

pros·e·cute (pros'ə·kyoot) *v.* **·cut·ed, ·cut·ing** *v.t.* 1. To go on with so as to complete; pursue to the end. 2. To carry on or engage in, as a trade or profession. 3. *Law* a To bring suit against for redress of wrong or punishment of crime. b To seek to enforce or obtain, as a claim or right, by legal process. — *v.i.* 4. To begin and carry on a legal proceeding. — **Syn.** See PUSH. [< L *prosecutus,* pp. of *prosequi* to pursue < *pro-* forward + *sequi* to follow]

prosecuting attorney The attorney empowered to act in behalf of the state, county, or national government in prosecuting for penal offenses. Compare DISTRICT ATTORNEY.

pros·e·cu·tion (pros'ə·kyoo'shən) *n.* 1. The act or process of prosecuting. 2. *Law* a The instituting and carrying forward of a judicial proceeding to obtain some right or to redress and punish some wrong. b The institution and continuance of a criminal proceeding. c The party instituting and conducting it.

pros·e·cu·tor (pros'ə·kyoo'tər) *n.* 1. One who prosecutes. 2. *Law* a One who institutes and carries on a suit, especially a criminal suit. b A prosecuting attorney.

pros·e·lyte (pros'ə·līt) *n.* One who has been brought over to any opinion, belief, sect, or party, especially from one religious belief to another. — **Syn.** See CONVERT. — *v.t. & v.i.* **·lyt·ed, ·lyt·ing** To proselytize. [< LL *proselytus* < Gk. *prosēlytos,* orig., a newcomer < *pros* toward + *elyth-* stem of *erchesthai* to come]

pros·e·lyt·ism (pros'ə·lə·tiz'əm, -līt'iz·əm) *n.* The making of converts to a religion, sect, or party, or the state of being thus converted.

pros·e·lyt·ize (pros'ə·lit·īz') *v.* **·ized, ·iz·ing** *v.i.* 1. To make proselytes. — *v.t.* 2. To make a convert of. Also *proselyte.*

pros·en·ceph·a·lon (pros'en·sef'ə·lon) *n. Anat.* The anterior segment of the three divisions of the brain in embryos, developing into the cerebrum and the optic thalamus, with related structures: also called *forebrain.* [< NL < Gk. *pros* toward + *encephalon* brain. See ENCEPHALON.] — **pros'en·ce·phal'ic** (-sə·fal'ik) *adj.*

pros·en·chy·ma (pros·eng'ki·mə) *n. Bot.* Plant tissue composed of elongated, pointed, typically thick-walled cells, as distinguished from the parenchyma. [< NL < Gk. *pros-* toward, near + *enchyma* infusion < *en* in + *chyma* fluid < *cheein* to pour] — **pros·en·chym·a·tous** (pros'eng·kim'ə·təs) *adj.*

prose poem A prose work that resembles poetry either in style, structure, or emotional content.

pros·er (prō'zər) *n.* A dull or tedious writer or talker; a bore.

Pros·er·pine (pros'ər·pīn, prō·sûr'pə·nē) In Roman mythology, the daughter of Ceres and wife of Pluto: identified with the Greek *Persephone.* Also **Pro·ser·pi·na** (prō·sûr'pə·nə).

pro·sim·i·an (prō·sim'ē·ən) *adj. Zool.* Designating any of a suborder or group (*Prosimii*) of widely distributed early primates, as lemurs, indris, lorises, and tarsiers, characterized by small size and primitive brain development. — *n.* A prosimian animal. [< NL < PRO-¹ + L *simia* ape]

pro·sit (prō'sit, *Ger.* prō'zit) *interj.* To your good health: used as a drinking toast, especially by the Germans. Also **prost** (prōst). [< L, lit., may it benefit]

pro·slav·er·y (prō·slā'vər·ē, -slāv'rē) *adj.* In United States history, advocating Negro slavery or the policy of noninterference with it. — *n.* The advocacy of slavery.

pro·sod·ic (prō·sod'ik) *adj.* 1. Of or pertaining to prosody. Also **pro·sod'i·cal.** 2. *Phonet.* Pertaining to those features of speech that are independent of the articulation of a speech sound, as stress, pitch, and quantity; suprasegmental. — **pro·sod'i·cal·ly** *adv.*

prosodic symbols In the scansion of verse, those signs used to indicate the various kinds of syllables, stresses, feet, etc.: these include the breve (◡), macron (—), acute ('), caesura (‖), and vertical bar (|).

pros·o·dist (pros'ə·dist) *n.* One adept in prosody.

pros·o·dy (pros'ə·dē) *n.* The science of poetical forms, including quantity and accent of syllables, meter, versification, and metrical composition. Abbr. *pros.* [< L *prosodia* the accent of a syllable < Gk. *prosōidia* a song sung to music, variation in pitch < *pros-* to + *ōidē* a song] — **pro·so·di·ac** (prō·sō'dē·ak), **pro·so·di·al** (prō·sō'dē·əl) *adj.*

pro·so·po·pe·ia (prō·sō'pə·pē'ə) *n.* 1. A rhetorical figure in which the speaker impersonates another. 2. Personification (def. 1). Also **pro·so'po·poe'ia.** [< L < Gk. *prosōpopoiia* < *prosōpon* face, person + *poieein* to make]

pros·pect (pros'pekt) *n.* 1. A future probability based on present indications; especially, often in the plural, the chance for future success. 2. A scene spread out before one's eyes; an extended view. 3. The direction in which anything faces; an exposure; outlook. 4. A prospective buyer. 5. The act of observing; sight; survey. 6. *Mining* a An indication of the presence of mineral ore. b A place giving such indications. c The sample of metal or mineral obtained by washing a portion of ore or dirt. — *v.t. & v.i.* To explore (a region) for gold, oil, etc. [< L *prospectus* view < *prospicere* < *pro-* forward + *specere* to look]

pro·spec·tive (prə·spek'tiv) *adj.* 1. Being still in the future; anticipated. 2. Looking forward or concerned with the future; anticipatory. — **pro·spec'tive·ly** *adv.*

pros·pec·tor (pros'pek·tər) *n.* One who searches or examines a region for mineral deposits or precious stones.

pro·spec·tus (prə·spek'təs) *n. pl.* **·tus·es** 1. A paper containing information of a proposed literary, commercial, or industrial undertaking. 2. A summary; outline. [< L. See PROSPECT.]

pros·per (pros'pər) *v.i.* 1. To be prosperous; thrive; flourish. — *v.t.* 2. *Archaic* To render prosperous. [< OF *prosperer* < L *prosperare* to cause to succeed < *prosper, prosperus* favorable, prosperous. ?Akin to *sperare* to hope.]

pros·per·i·ty (pros·per'ə·tē) *n. pl.* **·ties** The state of being prosperous; material well-being. [< F *prospérité* < L *prosperitas*]

Pros·per·o (pros'pər·ō) In Shakespeare's *Tempest,* the banished Duke of Milan.

pros·per·ous (pros'pər·əs) *adj.* 1. Successful; flourishing. 2. Favoring or tending to success; auspicious. 3. Promising; favorable. [< MF *prospereus* < L *prosperus* favorable] — **pros'per·ous·ly** *adv.* — **pros'per·ous·ness** *n.*

pros·tate (pros'tāt) *Anat. adj.* Designating or pertaining to the prostate gland. — *n.* The prostate gland. [< NL < Gk. *prostatēs* stander before < *proistanai* < *pro-* before + *histanai* to set]

pros·ta·tec·to·my (pros'tə·tek'tə·mē) *n. pl.* **·mies** *Surg.* Excision of the prostate gland. [< PROSTAT(O)- + -ECTOMY]

prostate gland *Anat.* A partly muscular gland at the base of the bladder and surrounding the urethra in male mammals, providing some of the chemicals necessary to maintain the sperm for reproduction. — **pro·stat·ic** (prō·stat'ik) *adj.*

prostato- *combining form Med.* The prostate gland; of or related to the prostate: *prostatotomy.* Also, before vowels, **prostat-.** [< Gk. *prostatēs.* See PROSTATE.]

pros·ta·tot·o·my (pros/tə-tot/ə-mē) n. pl. ·mies Surg. An incision into the prostate gland. [< PROSTATO- + -TOMY]

pros·the·sis (pros/thə-sis) n. pl. ·ses (-sēz) **1.** Surg. The fitting of artificial parts to the body. **2.** A part so fitted, as an artificial limb, false tooth, etc. **3.** Ling. Prothesis. [< L < Gk., addition < prostithenai to add < pros- to + tithenai to put] — **pros·thet·ic** (pros-thet/ik) adj.

pros·thet·ics (pros-thet/iks) n.pl. (construed as sing.) The branch of surgery that specializes in artificial parts. [< Gk. prosthetikos additional < prosthetos put on < prostithenai. See PROSTHESIS.] — **pros·the·tist** (pros/thə-tist) n.

pros·tho·don·tics (pros/thə-don/tiks) n. (construed as sing. or pl.) The branch of dentistry concerned with the making of crowns, bridges, dentures, and artificial teeth; dental prosthetics. Also **pros·tho·don·ti·a** (pros/thə-don/shē-ə, -shə). [< NL < Gk. prosthesis addition + odous, odontos tooth] — **pros·tho·don·tist** (pros/thə-don/tist) n.

pros·ti·tute (pros/tə-tōōt, -tyōōt) n. **1.** A woman who offers her body for hire for purposes of sexual intercourse; a harlot; whore. **2.** One who offers his services solely for financial gain or for unworthy purposes. — v.t. ·tut·ed, ·tut·ing **1.** To apply to base or unworthy purposes: to prostitute one's talent. **2.** To offer (oneself or another) for lewd purposes, especially for hire. [< L prostitutus, pp. of prostituere < pro- forward + statuere to place] — **pros/ti·tu/tor** n. — **Syn.** (noun) **1.** courtesan, strumpet, streetwalker, slut. — (verb) **1.** defame, defile, maltreat, pervert.

pros·ti·tu·tion (pros/tə-tōō/shən, -tyōō/-) n. **1.** The act or business of prostituting. **2.** The act of hiring or devoting to base purposes, as one's honor, talents, resources, etc.

pros·trate (pros/trāt) adj. **1.** Lying prone, or with the face to the ground. **2.** Brought low in mind or spirit. **3.** Lying at the mercy of another; defenseless. **4.** Bot. Trailing along the ground; procumbent. — v.t. ·trat·ed, ·trat·ing **1.** To bow or cast (oneself) down, as in adoration or pleading. **2.** To throw flat; lay on the ground. **3.** To overthrow or overcome; make helpless. [< L prostratus, pp. of prosternere < pro- before + sternere to stretch out] — **pros/tra·tor** n.

pros·tra·tion (pros-trā/shən) n. **1.** The act of prostrating. **2.** Exhaustion of body or mind; great dejection or depression.

pro·style (prō/stīl) adj. Archit. Having a range of detached columns in front, but no columns on the sides or back of the building; also, constituting such a portico. [< L prostylus < Gk. prostylos < pro- before + stylos a pillar]

pros·y (prō/zē) adj. pros·i·er, pros·i·est **1.** Like prose; prosaic. **2.** Dull; tedious; commonplace. — **pros/i·ly** adv. — **pros/i·ness** n.

prot- Var. of PROTO-.

Prot. Protestant.

pro·tac·tin·i·um (prō/tak·tin/ē-əm) n. A radioactive metallic element (symbol Pa) of the actinide series, intermediate between thorium and uranium: also called protoactinium. See ELEMENT. [< PROT- + ACTINIUM]

pro·tag·o·nist (prō-tag/ə-nist) n. **1.** The actor who played the chief part in a Greek drama. **2.** Any leading character, contender, etc. [< Gk. prōtagōnistēs < prōtos first + agōnistēs contestant, actor < agōn contest]

Pro·tag·o·ras (prō-tag/ər-əs), 481?–411? B.C., Greek Sophist philosopher.

pro·ta·mine (prō/tə-mēn, -min) n. Biochem. One of a class of strongly basic, simple proteins, uncoagulable by heat, soluble in ammonia, and yielding a few amino acids when hydrolyzed. Also **pro/ta·min** (-min). [< PROT- + -AMINE]

pro·ta·nop·i·a (prō/tə-nō/pē-ə) n. Pathol. Color blindness marked by inability to distinguish red. [< PROT- + AN-¹ + -OPIA] — **pro·ta·nope** (prō/tə-nōp) n.

prot·a·sis (prot/ə-sis) n. **1.** In a conditional sentence, the clause that contains the condition: distinguished from apodosis. **2.** In classical drama, the introductory part of a play. [< LL < Gk., proposition < pro before + teinein to stretch]

pro·te·an (prō/tē-ən, prō-tē/ən) adj. Readily assuming different forms or various aspects; changeable. [< PROTEUS]

pro·te·ase (prō/tē-ās) n. Biochem. An enzyme that digests proteins. [< PROTE(IN) + -ASE]

pro·tect (prə-tekt/) v.t. **1.** To shield or defend from attack, harm, or injury; guard; defend. **2.** Econ. To assist (domestic industry) by means of protective tariffs. **3.** In commerce, to provide funds to guarantee payment of (a draft, etc.). [< L protectus, pp. of protegere to protect < pro- before + tegere to cover] — **pro·tect/ing·ly** adv. — **Syn.** **1.** keep, preserve, shelter, harbor.

pro·tec·tion (prə-tek/shən) n. **1.** The act of protecting, or the state of being protected. **2.** That which protects. **3.** Econ. A system aiming to protect the industries of a country by governmental action, as by imposing duties. See PROTECTIVE TARIFF. **4.** A safe-conduct; passport. **5.** U.S. Slang Security purchased under threat of violence from racketeers; also, the money so paid.

pro·tec·tion·ism (prə-tek/shən·iz/əm) n. The economic doctrine or system of protection. — **pro·tec/tion·ist** n.

pro·tec·tive (prə-tek/tiv) adj. **1.** Affording or suitable for protection; sheltering; defensive. **2.** Econ. Insuring or intended to insure protection to home industries: a protective tariff. **3.** Providing or alleging to provide protection: protective custody. — n. **1.** Something that protects. **2.** Med. An aseptic covering for a wound. — **pro·tec/tive·ly** adv. — **pro·tec/tive·ness** n.

protective tariff A tariff that is intended to insure protection of domestic industries against foreign competition. Compare FREE TRADE.

pro·tec·tor (prə-tek/tər) n. **1.** One who protects; a defender. **2.** In English history, one appointed as a regent of the kingdom during minority or incapacity of the sovereign. Also **pro·tect/er.** — **pro·tec/tress** n.fem.

Pro·tec·tor (prə-tek/tər) n. The official title of the chief ruler during the Protectorate: in full, Lord Protector. The title was borne by Oliver Cromwell, 1653–58, and by Richard Cromwell, his son, 1658–59.

pro·tec·tor·ate (prə-tek/tər-it) n. **1.** A relation of protection and partial control by a strong nation over a weaker power. **2.** A country or region under the protection of another. **3.** The office, or period of office, of a protector of a kingdom. Also **pro·tec/tor·ship.**

Pro·tec·tor·ate (prə-tek/tər-it) n. The English government during the rule of the Cromwells, 1653–59. See COMMON-WEALTH OF ENGLAND.

pro·tec·to·ry (prə-tek/tər-ē) n. pl. ·to·ries An institution for the care and education of homeless or destitute children.

pro·té·gé (prō/tə-zhā, Fr. prô·tā·zhā/) n. One who is under the special care of a usually older person of superior position and experience to be guided in the development of a talent or career. [< F, pp. of protéger to protect < L protegere] — **pro/té·gée** n.fem.

pro·te·in (prō/tē-in, -tēn) n. Biochem. Any of a class of highly complex nitrogenous organic compounds originally synthesized by plants, and after hydrolysis by enzymes, into amino acids, forming an essential constituent in the processes of animal metabolism. Also **pro/te·id** (-id). [< G < Gk. prōtetos primary < prōtos first; so called because a chief constituent of living matter]

pro·te·in·ase (prō/tē·in·ās, -āz) n. Biochem. A proteolytic enzyme, as rennin, that breaks down proteins.

pro tem·po·re (prō tem/pə·rē) Latin For the time being; temporary. Abbr. pro tem., p.t.

pro·ten·si·ty (prō·ten/sə·tē) n. Psychol. The temporal attribute of a sensation or other mental phenomenon. Compare EXTENSITY. [< L protensus, pp. of protendere < pro- forth + tendere to stretch] See — **pro·ten/sive** adj.

pro·te·ol·y·sis (prō/tē·ol/ə·sis) n. Biochem. The change or splitting up of proteins into simpler products during digestion. [< NL < proteo- (< PROTEIN) + Gk. lysis a loosening < lyein to loosen] — **pro·te·o·lyt·ic** (-ə·lit/ik) adj.

pro·te·ose (prō/tē·ōs) n. Biochem. Any of a group of proteins formed naturally in the process of digestion. [< PRO-TE(IN) + -OSE²]

Prot·er·o·zo·ic (prot/ər·ə·zō/ik) Geol. adj. Of or designating the geological era following the Archeozoic and succeeded by the Paleozoic. See chart for GEOLOGY. — n. The Proterozoic era. [< protero- (< Gk. proteros former) + ZOIC]

pro·test (n. prō/test; v. prə·test/) n. **1.** A solemn or formal objection or declaration. **2.** A public expression of dissent, especially if organized. **3.** A formal notarial certificate attesting the fact that a note or bill of exchange has been presented for acceptance or payment and that it has been refused. **4.** In maritime law, a written declaration by the master of a vessel stating that an injury to the vessel or the cargo was not owing to the neglect or misconduct of the master. **5.** A formal statement in writing made by a person called upon to pay a sum of money, as an import duty or a tax, in which he declares that he does not concede the legality of the claim. **6.** The act of protesting. — adj. Of or relating to public protest: protest demonstrations. — v.t. **1.** To assert earnestly or positively; state formally, especially against opposition or doubt. **2.** U.S. To make a protest against; object to: I protested his actions. **3.** To declare formally that payment of (a promissory note, etc.) has been duly submitted and refused. — v.i. **4.** To make solemn affirmation. **5.** To make a protest; object. [< OF protester < L protestari < pro- forth + testari to testify < testis a witness] — **pro·test/er** n. — **pro·test/ing·ly** adv.

prot·es·tant (prot/is·tənt, prə·tes/-) n. One who makes a protest. — adj. Protesting. [< MF < L protestans, -antis, ppr. of protestari. See PROTEST.] — **Syn.** (noun) **1.** dissent, disagreement, disaffection.

Prot·es·tant (prot/is·tənt) n. **1.** A member of one of those bodies of Christians that adhere to Protestantism, as distinguished from Roman Catholicism. **2.** In the 17th century, a Lutheran or Anglican. **3.** Originally, one of those German princes who, at the second Diet of Spires, April 19, 1529, protested against the decree of the majority representing the Roman Catholic states that involved a virtual submission to the authority of the Roman Catholic Church. — *adj.* Pertaining to Protestants or Protestantism. Abbr. *Prot.*

Protestant Episcopal Church A religious body in the United States that is descended from the Church of England, but has been organized as a separate and independent body since 1789: also called *Episcopal Church.*

Protestant ethic Rules of conduct that stress hard work, personal responsibility, frugality, and strict adherence to the law, regarded as characteristic of early capitalism in northern Europe.

Prot·es·tant·ism (prot′is·tənt·iz′əm) *n.* 1. The principles and common system of doctrines of the Protestants. 2. The ecclesiastical system founded upon this faith; also, Protestants, collectively. 3. The state of being a Protestant.

prot·es·ta·tion (prot′is·tā′shən) *n.* 1. The act of protesting; also, that which is protested. 2. A formal declaration of dissent. 3. Any solemn or urgent avowal.

Pro·test·er (prə·tes′tər) *n.* A Scotsman who protested against the union of the Presbyterians and the Royalists in 1650. Also **Pro·tes′tor.**

Pro·te·us (prō′tē·əs, -tyo͞os) In Greek mythology, a sea god who could assume different forms. — **Pro′te·an** *adj.*

pro·tha·la·mi·on (prō′thə·lā′mē·on, -ən) *n. pl.* **·mi·a** (-mē·ə) A song celebrating a marriage; an epithalamium. Also **pro′. tha·la′mi·um** (-mē·əm). [< NL < Gk. *pro* before + *thalamos* bridal chamber; coined by Spenser on analogy with *epithalamion*]

pro·thal·li·um (prō·thal′ē·əm) *n. pl.* **·li·a** (-lē·ə) *Bot.* The gametophyte formed on the germination of the asexually produced spores in ferns. Also **pro·thal′lus.** [< NL < Gk. *pro* before + *thallion*, dim. of *thallos* shoot] — **pro·thal′li·al** *adj.* — **pro·thal′line** (-thal′īn, -in) *adj.*

proth·e·sis (proth′ə·sis) *n. pl.* **·ses** (-sēz) 1. *Ling.* The development of a new sound at the beginning of a word, as *e* in Spanish *escriber* (to write) from Latin *scribere:* also called *prosthesis.* 2. In the Greek Orthodox Church, the preparation of the elements for consecration in the Eucharist. [< LL < Gk., a placing before < *protithenai* < *pro-* before + *tithenai* to place] — **pro·thet·ic** (prō·thet′ik) *adj.* — **pro·thet′i·cal·ly** *adv.*

pro·thon·o·tar·y (prō·thon′ə·ter′ē, prō′thə·nō′tər·ē) *n. pl.* **·tar·ies** 1. A chief clerk. 2. In the Roman Catholic Church, one of the seven ecclesiastics at Rome who keep the registry of important pontifical proceedings, or one having the title and some of the associated privileges. 3. In some States of the United States, a probate officer. Also called *protonotary.* [< LL *protonotarius* < Gk. *prōtos* first + L *notarius.* See NOTARY.] — **pro·thon′o·tar′i·al** (-tär′ē·əl) *adj.*

prothonotary warbler A North American warbler (*Protonotaria citrea*), the male of which is noted for the brilliant yellow to orange coloring of its head and under parts.

pro·tho·rax (prō·thôr′aks, -thō′raks) *n. pl.* **·rax·es** or **·tho·ra·ces** (-thôr′ə·sēz, -thō′rə-) *Entomol.* The anterior segment of the thorax of an insect, bearing the first pair of legs. [< NL < Gk. *pro-* in front + *thorax* thorax] — **pro·tho·rac·ic** (prō′thô·ras′ik, -thō-) *adj.*

pro·throm·bin (prō·throm′bin) *n. Biochem.* A blood-clotting factor that reacts with calcium ions to produce thrombin. [< NL < Gk. *pro-* before + *thrombos* clot]

Pro·tić (prō′tich), **Stojan,** 1857–1923, Serbian statesman; one of the founders of Yugoslavia; first prime minister 1918–1919.

pro·tist (prō′tist) *n. Biol.* Any member of a large division or kingdom (*Protista*) of one-celled or noncellular plants and animals, including bacteria, flagellates, rhizopods, and ciliates. [< NL *protista* < Gk. *prōtistos,* superl. of *prōtos* first] — **pro·tis′tan** *adj. & n.* — **pro·tis′tic** *adj.*

pro·ti·um (prō′tē·əm) *n. Chem.* The hydrogen isotope of atomic mass 1 (symbol H^1). [< NL < Gk. *prōtos* first]

proto- *combining form* 1. First in rank or time; chief; typical: *protomartyr.* 2. Primitive; original: *prototype.* 3. *Chem.* Designating the first or lowest member of a series; having the least amount (of an element or radical): *protoxide.* Also, before vowels, *prot-.* [< Gk. *prōtos* first]

pro·to·ac·tin·i·um (prō′tō·ak·tin′ē·əm) *n.* Protactinium.

pro·to·chor·date (prō′tō·kôr′dāt) *n. Zool.* Any chordate animal lacking a true spinal cord or brain, as a lancelet or tunicate.

pro·to·col (prō′tə·kôl, -kol) *n.* 1. The rules of diplomatic and state etiquette and ceremony. 2. The preliminary draft of an official document, as a treaty. 3. The preliminary draft or report of the negotiations and conclusions arrived at by a diplomatic conference, having the force of a treaty when ratified. — *v.i.* **·coled** or **·colled.** **·col·ing** or **·col·ling** To write or form protocols. [< OF *prothocole* < Med.L *protocollum* < LGk. *prōtokollon* the first sheet glued to a papyrus roll < *prōtos* first + *kolla* glue]

pro·to·derm (prō′tə·dûrm) *n. Bot.* Dermatogen.

pro·to·hu·man (prō′tō·hyo͞o′mən) *Paleontol. adj.* Of, pertaining to, or describing any of several hominoid primates regarded as being at an earlier stage of development than *Homo sapiens.* — *n.* Any primate antedating modern man.

pro·to·mar·tyr (prō′tō·mär′tər) *n.* The first martyr or victim in any cause. [< OF *prothomartir* < Med.L *protomartyr* < Gk. *prōtos* first + *martyr* a witness]

pro·to·mor·phic (prō′tō·môr′fik) *adj. Biol.* Of, pertaining to, or having the most primitive or elementary form or structure. — **pro′to·morph** *n.*

pro·ton (prō′ton) *n. Physics* One of the elementary particles in the nucleus of an atom, having a unitary positive charge and a mass of approximately 1.672×10^{-24} gram. The atomic number of an element is equivalent to the number of protons in its nucleus. [< NL < Gk. *prōton,* neut. of *prōtos* first]

pro·to·ne·ma (prō′tə·nē′mə) *n. pl.* **·ne·ma·ta** (-nē′mə·tə) *Bot.* A green filamentous structure developed from the spore in mosses, on which the leafy plant arises as a lateral or terminal shoot. Also **pro′to·neme.** (-nēm). [< NL < Gk. *prōtos* first + *nēma* thread]

pro·ton·o·tar·y (prō·ton′ə·ter′ē, prō′tə·nō′tər·ē) *n. pl.* **·tar·ies** A prothonotary.

pro·ton-pro·ton reaction (prō′ton·prō′ton) *Physics* A thermonuclear chain reaction assumed to provide stellar energy by the fusion of 4 protons to make a helium nucleus.

pro·to·path·ic (prō′tə·path′ik) *adj. Physiol.* Pertaining to or designating cutaneous sensibility assumed to be responsive only to gross, typically painful stimuli: distinguished from *epicritic.* [< PROTO- + -PATHIC]

pro·to·phyte (prō′tə·fīt) *n. Bot.* 1. Any single-celled plant. 2. A member of a former division (*Protophyta*) embracing only the lowest and simplest plants. [< NL *protophytum* < Gk. *prōtos* first + *phyton* plant]

pro·to·plasm (prō′tə·plaz′əm) *n. Biol.* 1. The physicochemical basis of living matter, a viscid, grayish, translucent, colloidal substance of granular structure and complex composition that forms the essential part of plant and animal cells. 2. Formerly, the cytoplasm of the cell. [< G *protoplasma* < Gk. *prōtos* first + *plasma* form] — **pro′to·plas′. mic** or **plas′mal** or **·plas·mat′ic** *adj.*

pro·to·plast (prō′tə·plast) *n.* 1. That which is formed first. 2. *Biol.* **a** The original or primordial cell. **b** Formerly, a plastid (def. 1). [< F *protoplaste* < LL *protoplastus* < Gk. *protoplastos* < *prōtos* first + *plastos* formed < *plassein* to form] — **pro′to·plas′tic** *adj.*

pro·to·ste·le (prō′tə·stē′lē, -stēl) *n. Bot.* The dense central cylinder of roots and young stems. [< PROTO- + STELE²] — **pro′to·ste′lic** *adj.*

pro·to·troph·ic (prō′tə·trof′ik, -trō′fik) *adj. Biol.* Capable of assimilating only simple inorganic substances: said of the earliest forms of life, as plants and certain bacteria. [< PROTO- + -TROPHIC]

pro·to·type (prō′tə·tīp) *n.* 1. *Biol.* A primitive or ancestral organism; an archetype: opposed to *ectype.* 2. An original model on which subsequent forms are to be based. 3. A standard to which all others must conform. — **Syn.** See IDEAL. [< F < NL *prototypon* < Gk. *prototypon* < *prōtos* first + *typos* form] — **pro′to·typ′al** (-tī′pəl), **pro′to·typ′ic** (-tip′ik), **pro′to·typ′i·cal** *adj.*

pro·tox·ide (prō·tok′sīd, -sid) *n. Chem.* An oxide having the lowest proportion of oxygen for a given series. Compare PEROXIDE. Also **pro·tox′id** (-sid).

pro·to·zo·an (prō′tə·zō′ən) *n.* Any of a subkingdom or phylum (*Protozoa*) of animals embracing microscopic, single-celled organisms, largely aquatic and including many parasitic forms, reproducing typically by binary fission. Also **pro′to·zo′on.** [< NL < Gk. *prōtos* first + *zōion* animal] — **pro′to·zo′an** *adj.* — **pro′to·zo′ic** *adj.*

pro·to·zo·ol·o·gy (prō′tō·zō·ol′ə·jē) *n.* The study or science of unicellular organisms. — **pro′to·zo′o·log′i·cal** (-zō′ə·loj′i·kəl) *adj.* — **pro′to·zo·ol′o·gist** *n.*

pro·tract (prō·trakt′) *v.t.* 1. To extend in time; prolong. 2. In surveying, to draw or map by means of a scale and protractor; plot. 3. *Anat.* To protrude or extend. [< L *protractus,* pp. of *protrahere* < *pro-* forward + *trahere* to draw] — **pro·trac′tive** *adj.*

pro·tract·er (prō·trak′tər) *n.* 1. One who or that which protracts. 2. See PROTRACTOR.

pro·trac·tile (prō·trak′til) *adj.* Capable of being protracted or protruded; protrusile.

pro·trac·tion (prō·trak′shən) *n.* 1. The act of protracting. 2. In prosody, the irregular lengthening of a syllable ordinarily short.

pro·trac·tor (prō·trak′tər) *n.* 1. An instrument for measuring and laying off angles. 2. A tailor's adjustable pattern. 3. *Anat.* A muscle that extends a limb or moves it forward. Also spelled *protracter.*

pro·trude (prō·tro͞od′) *v.t. & v.i.* **·trud·ed, ·trud·ing** To push or thrust out; project outward. [< L *protrudere* < *pro-* forward + *trudere* to thrust]

pro·tru·sile (prō·tro͞o′sil) *adj.* Adapted to being thrust out, often rapidly, as the tongue of an anteater. Also **pro·tru′sible.** [< L *protrusus,* pp. of *protrudere* to protrude + -ILE. See PROTRUDE.]

pro·tru·sion (prō·tro͞o′zhən) *n.* 1. The act of protruding, or the state of being protruded. 2. The part or object protruded. [< F < L *protrusus.* See PROTRUSILE.]

pro·tru·sive (prō·tro͞o′siv) *adj.* 1. Tending to protrude; protruding. 2. Pushing or driving forward. — **pro·tru′sive·ly** *adv.* — **pro·tru′sive·ness** *n.*

pro·tu·ber·ance (prō-tōō′bər-əns, -tyōō′-) *n.* **1.** Something that protrudes; a knob; prominence. **2.** The state of being protuberant. Also **pro·tu′ber·an·cy, pro·tu′ber·a′tion.**

pro·tu·ber·ant (prō-tōō′bər-ənt, -tyōō′-) *adj.* Swelling out beyond the surrounding surface; bulging. [< LL *protuberans, -antis,* ppr. of *protuberare* to bulge out < L *pro-* forth + *tuber* a swelling] — **pro·tu′ber·ant·ly** *adv.*

pro·tu·ber·ate (prō-tōō′bə-rāt, -tyōō′-) *v.i.* **·at·ed, ·at·ing** To be protuberant; bulge out. [< LL *protuberatus,* pp. of *protuberare.* See PROTUBERANT.]

pro·tyle (prō′tīl, -til) *n.* The hypothetical primitive substance of the universe, of which all existing elements are supposed to be modifications. Also **pro′tyl** (-til). [< Gk. *prōtos* first + *hylē* wood, material]

proud (proud) *adj.* **1.** Actuated by, possessing, or manifesting pride; arrogant; haughty; also, self-respecting. **2.** Sensible of honor and personal elation: generally followed by *of* or by a verb in the infinitive. **3.** High-mettled, as a horse; spirited. **4.** Proceeding from or inspired by pride. **5.** Being a cause of honorable pride, as a distinction: a *proud* achievement. **6.** Splendid; stately; glorious. **7.** *Obs.* Bold; fearless. — **to do oneself proud** To do extremely well. [OE *prūd* < OF *prud, prod,* prob. ult. < L *prodesse* to be useful < *pro* for + *esse* to be] — **proud′ly** *adv.* — **Syn. 1.** vain, conceited, cocky, overweening.

proud flesh *Pathol.* A granulated growth resembling flesh in a wound or sore. [So called from its swelling up]

Proud·hon (prōō-dôṅ′), **Pierre Joseph,** 1809–65, French socialist and political philosopher; one of the founders of anarchism.

Proust (prōōst), **Marcel,** 1871–1922, French novelist.

proust·ite (prōōs′tīt) *n.* An adamantine ruby-red sulfide of silver and arsenic, crystallizing in the rhombohedral system. [< F, after Joseph Louis *Proust,* 1754–1826, French chemist, its discoverer]

prov. 1. Province; provincial. **2.** Provisional. **3.** Provost.

Prov. 1. Provençal. **2.** Proverbs.

prove (prōōv) *v.* **proved, proved** or **prov·en, prov·ing** *v.t.* **1.** To show to be true or genuine, as by evidence or argument. **2.** To determine the quality or genuineness of; test: to *prove* a gun. **3.** To establish the authenticity or validity of, as a will. **4.** *Math.* To verify the accuracy of (a calculation or demonstration) by an independent process. **5.** *Printing* To take a proof of or from. **6.** *Archaic* To learn by experience; undergo. — *v.i.* **7.** To be shown to be by the result or outcome; turn out to be: His hopes *proved* vain. **8.** *Archaic* To make trial. — **Syn.** See CONFIRM. [< OF *prouver* < L *probare* to test, find good < *probus* upright. Doublet of PROBE.] — **prov′a·ble** *adj.* — **prov′er** *n.*

pro·vec·tion (prō-vek′shən) *n. Ling.* A transfer of the final consonant of one word to the beginning of the next word, as in a *newt* for *an ewt.* [< LL *provectio, -onis* < L *provehere* to advance < *pro-* forward + *vehere* to carry]

prov·en (prōō′vən) Alternative past participle of PROVE: the less common form. — *adj.* Proved; established; verified.

prov·e·nance (prov′ə-nəns) *n.* Provenience; origin. [< F *provenant,* ppr. of *provenir* to come forth]

Pro·ven·çal (prō′vən-säl′, *Fr.* prō-väṅ-säl′) *n.* **1.** A native or resident of Provence, France. **2.** The Romance language of Provence, developed from *langue d'oc,* and used especially in the 12th and 13th centuries in the lyric literature of the troubadours. — *adj.* Of or pertaining to Provence, its inhabitants, or their language. Abbr. *Pr., Prov.*

Pro·vence (prō-väṅs′) A region and former province of SE France.

prov·en·der (prov′ən-dər) *n.* **1.** Food for cattle; especially, dry food, as hay. **2.** *Rare* Provisions generally. — **Syn.** See FEED. — *v.t.* To provide with food, as cattle. [< OF *provende < LL *praebenda.* See PREBEND.]

pro·ve·ni·ence (prō-vē′nē-əns, -vēn′yəns) *n.* The origin or source of a thing. [< L *proveniens, -entis,* ppr. of *provenire* < *pro-* forth + *venire* to come]

prov·erb (prov′ərb) *n.* **1.** A pithy saying, especially one condensing the wisdom of experience; adage; saw; maxim. **2.** An enigmatic saying: to speak in a *proverb.* **3.** Something proverbial; a typical example; byword. [< OF *proverbe* < L *proverbium < pro-* before + *verbum* word] — **Syn. 1.** *Proverb, adage, saw, saying, maxim, precept, aphorism,* and *apothegm* denote a brief expression of what is supposed to be a general truth. A *proverb* is usually a homely illustration of a general truth, as: A rolling stone gathers no moss. An *adage* is a time-honored and generally accepted *proverb,* as: A man is known by the company he keeps. Any ancient and hackneyed *adage* is a *saw,* as: All that glitters is not gold. Anything much repeated is a *saying*; this includes cliché phrases as well as sentences: he is drunk as a lord, as the *saying* goes. A *maxim* is a practical rule of conduct

or action, as: Lend every man thine ear, but few thy purse. An ethical *maxim* is a *precept*; as: A gentleman never offends unintentionally. *Precept* is also extended to any instruction in behavior, whether or not in the form of a *maxim* or *adage*: to teach by example rather than by *precept. Aphorism* and *apothegm* differ from the other words in that their authorship is usually known. An *aphorism* is an epigrammatic *saying,* as: Eternal vigilance is the price of liberty. An *apothegm* is generally a startling or paradoxical assertion, as: Property is theft.

pro·ver·bi·al (prə-vûr′bē-əl) *adj.* **1.** Of the nature of, pertaining to, or like a proverb: *proverbial* brevity. **2.** Being the object of general remark, as a typical case; well-known; notorious. — **pro·ver′bi·al·ly** *adv.*

Prov·erbs (prov′ərbz) *n.pl.* (*construed as sing.*) An Old Testament book of moral sayings. Abbr. *Prov.*

pro·vide (prə-vīd′) *v.* **·vid·ed, ·vid·ing** *v.t.* **1.** To supply or furnish. **2.** To afford; yield. **3.** To prepare, make ready, or procure beforehand. **4.** To set down as a condition; stipulate. — *v.i.* **5.** To take measures in advance: with *for* or *against.* **6.** To furnish means of subsistence: usually with *for.* **7.** To make a stipulation. [< L *providere* to foresee < *pro-* before + *videre* to see. Doublet of PURVEY.] — **Syn. 1.** procure, purvey, cater. **2.** render, produce. **3.** arrange, contrive, devise.

pro·vid·ed (prə-vī′did) *conj.* On condition; if: with *that* expressed or understood: He will get the loan *provided* he offers good security. [Orig. pp. of PROVIDE]

prov·i·dence (prov′ə-dəns) *n.* **1.** The care exercised by God over the universe. **2.** An event or circumstances ascribable to divine interposition. **3.** The exercise of foresight and care for the future; prudent economy. [< OF < L *providentia < providens, -entis,* ppr. of *providere.* See PROVIDE.] — **Syn. 3.** judiciousness, wisdom.

Prov·i·dence (prov′ə-dəns) God; the Deity.

Prov·i·dence (prov′ə-dəns) The capital of Rhode Island, in the NE part, a port on Narragansett Bay; pop. 179,213.

prov·i·dent (prov′ə-dənt) *adj.* Anticipating and making ready for future wants or emergencies; exercising foresight. — **prov′i·dent·ly** *adv.*

prov·i·den·tial (prov′ə-den′shəl) *adj.* Resulting from or exhibiting the action of God's providence. — **Syn.** See FORTUNATE. — **prov′i·den′tial·ly** *adv.*

pro·vid·er (prə-vī′dər) *n.* One whose income supports a family: He's a good *provider.*

pro·vid·ing (prə-vī′ding) *conj.* On condition; provided.

prov·ince (prov′ins) *n.* **1.** A considerable country incorporated with a kingdom or empire and subject to the central administration without having itself any voice in that administration. **2.** Any large administrative division of a country with a permanent local government: the *provinces* of the Roman Empire. **3.** *pl.* Regions lying at a distance from the capital or most populous part of a country. **4.** A comprehensive department or sphere of knowledge or activity: the *province* of chemistry. **5.** A definite sphere of action, especially one authoritatively assigned or properly belonging to a person. **6.** *Ecol.* A zoogeographic area less than a region, having its own special flora, fauna, and types of mankind. Abbr. *prov.* [< OF < L *provincia* province]

Prov·ince·town (prov′ins-toun′) A resort town in SE Massachusetts, on the northern tip of Cape Cod; pop. 2,911.

pro·vin·cial (prə-vin′shəl) *adj.* **1.** Of or pertaining to a province. **2.** Confined to a province; rustic; local. **3.** Narrow; uncultured; illiberal. — *n.* **1.** A native or inhabitant of a province. **2.** One who is provincial. Abbr. *prov.* — **pro·vin′ci·al′i·ty** (-shē-al′ə-tē) *n.* — **pro·vin′cial·ly** *adv.*

pro·vin·cial·ism (prə-vin′shəl-iz′əm) *n.* **1.** The quality of being provincial. **2.** A provincial custom or peculiarity, especially of speech.

provincial park In Canada, a tract of land provided and maintained by a Province for conservation and recreation.

provincial parliament In Canada, the legislative assembly of a Province.

proving ground A site used for testing new weapons, equipment, scientific theories, etc.

pro·vi·sion (prə-vizh′ən) *n.* **1.** The act of providing, or the state of being provided. **2.** Measures taken or means made ready in advance. **3.** *pl.* Food or a supply of food; victuals. **4.** Something provided or prepared, as against future need. **5.** The part of an agreement, instrument, etc., referring to one specific thing; a stipulation or agreement. **6.** Appointment to a see or benefice not yet vacant, including designation, institution, and installation, especially by a pope. **7.** *pl.* Medieval English statutes by which certain important matters were provided for. — *v.t.* To provide with food or provisions. [< OF < L *provisio, -onis* a foreseeing < *videre.* See PROVIDE.] — **pro·vi′sion·er** *n.* — **Syn. 3.** stores, stock, provender. **5.** condition, proviso. — (*verb*) furnish, cater, purvey.

pro·vi·sion·al (prə-vizh′ən-əl) *adj.* **1.** Provided for a present service or temporary necessity: a *provisional* army. **2.** Adopted tentatively or for lack of something better. Also **pro·vi′sion·ar′y.** Abbr. *prov.* — **pro·vi′sion·al·ly** *adv.*

pro·vi·so (prə·vī′zō) *n.* *pl.* **·sos** or **·soes** A stipulation or clause, as in a contract or statute, limiting, modifying, or rendering conditional its operation. [< Med.L *proviso* it being provided, ablative of pp. of L *providere*. See PROVIDE.]

pro·vi·so·ry (prə·vī′zər·ē) *adj.* **1.** Containing or made dependent on a proviso; conditional. **2.** Provisional. — **pro·vi′so·ri·ly** *adv.*

pro·vi·ta·min (prō·vī′tə·min) *n. Biochem.* Any of various substances believed to promote the formation of vitamins, as carotene (**provitamin A**) or ergosterol.

Pro·vo (prō′vō) A city in north central Utah, on the Provo River; pop. 53,131.

prov·o·ca·tion (prov′ə·kā′shən) *n.* **1.** The act of provoking. **2.** An incitement to action; stimulus. [< OF < L *provocatio, -onis* < *provocare*. See PROVOKE.]

pro·voc·a·tive (prə·vok′ə·tiv) *adj.* Serving to provoke; stimulating. — *n.* That which provokes or tends to provoke. — **pro·voc′a·tive·ly** *adv.* — **pro·voc′a·tive·ness** *n.*

pro·voke (prə·vōk′) *v.t.* **·voked, ·vok·ing 1.** To stir to anger or resentment; irritate; vex. **2.** To arouse or stimulate to some action. **3.** To stir up or bring about: to *provoke* a quarrel. **4.** To induce or cause; elicit: to *provoke* a smile. **5.** *Obs.* To call forth; summon. [< OF *provoquer* < L *provocare* to challenge < *pro-* forth + *vocare* to call] — **pro·vok′ing·ly** *adv.* — **pro·vok′ing·ness** *n.*

— **Syn. 1.** See IRRITATE. **2.** excite. **3.** foment, induce.

prov·ost (prov′əst *for defs.* 1, 2, 3, 4; prō′vō *for def.* 5) *n.* **1.** A person having charge or authority over others. **2.** The chief magistrate of a Scottish city, corresponding to the English mayor. **3.** In some English and American colleges, the head of the faculty. **4.** The head of a collegiate chapter or a cathedral; a dean. **5.** Provost marshal (which see). *Abbr.* **prov.** [< OE *profost* and OF *provost*, both < LL *propositus*, var. of L *praepositus* chief < *prae-* before + pp. of *ponere* to place] — **prov′ost·ship** *n.*

pro·vost court (prō′vō) A military court for trying civilians and soldiers charged with minor offenses committed within areas occupied by the army.

pro·vost guard (prō′vō) A company of soldiers detailed for police duty under a provost marshal.

pro·vost marshal (prō′vō) A military or naval officer exercising police functions: also called *provost*. *Abbr.* PM, P.M.

pro·vost sergeant (prō′vō) A noncommissioned officer who supervises the work and duties of the military police.

prow[1] (prou) *n.* **1.** The fore part of the hull of a vessel; the bow. **2.** Any pointed projection. **3.** *Poetic* A ship. [< MF *proue* < L *prora* < Gk. *prōira*]

prow[2] (prou) *adj. Archaic* Brave; valiant: a *prow* knight. [< OF *prou* brave < LL *prode* (*esse*) (to be) useful < L *prodesse* < *pro-* for + *esse* to be]

prow·ess (prou′is) *n.* **1.** Strength, skill, and courage, especially in battle. **2.** A daring and valiant deed. [< OF *prouesse, proece* < *prou*. See PROW[2].]

— **Syn. 1.** bravery, gallantry, heroism, valor.

prowl (proul) *v.t.* & *v.i.* To roam about stealthily, as in search of prey or plunder. — *n.* The act of prowling. [ME *prollen* to search; ult. origin uncertain] — **prowl′er** *n.*

prowl car *U.S.* A police patrol car.

prox·i·mal (prok′sə·məl) *adj.* **1.** *Anat.* Relatively nearer the central portion of the body or point of origin: opposed to *distal.* **2.** Proximate. — **prox′i·mal·ly** *adv.*

prox·i·mate (prok′sə·mit) *adj.* Being in immediate relation with something else; next: also *proximal.* [< LL *proximatus*, pp. of *proximare* to come near < L *proximus*, superl. of *prope* near] — **prox′i·mate·ly** *adv.*

— **Syn.** contiguous, touching, bordering.

prox·im·i·ty (prok·sim′ə·tē) *n.* The state or fact of being near or next; nearness. [< MF *proximité* < L *proximitas* < *proximus.* See PROXIMATE.]

proximity fuse A fuse in a projectile, usually activated by an electronic device, that detonates by simple proximity to the target: also called *VT fuse.* For illustration see FUSE[1].

prox·i·mo (prok′sə·mō) *adv. Archaic* In or of the next or coming month: distinguished from *instant, ultimo. Abbr.* **prox.** [< L *proximo* (*mense*) in the next (month), ablative of *proximus.* See PROXIMATE.]

prox·y (prok′sē) *n. pl.* **prox·ies 1.** A person empowered by another to act for him. **2.** The office or right to so act, or the instrument conferring it. — **Syn.** See DELEGATE. [ME *prokecie*, contr. of *procuracie* procuracy]

prs. Pairs.

prude (prood) *n.* A person who makes an affected display of modesty and propriety, especially in matters relating to sex. [< F *preude* (*femme*) strong, hence, modest (woman) < *preu* var. of *prou.* See PROW[2].]

pru·dence (prood′ns) *n.* The quality or state of being prudent; sagacity; discretion.

pru·dent (prood′nt) *adj.* **1.** Careful to avoid errors and follow the most politic and profitable course; cautious; worldly-wise. **2.** Exercising sound judgment; sagacious; judicious. **3.** Characterized by practical wisdom or discretion; not extravagant. **4.** Decorously discreet: a *prudent* maiden. [< OF < L *prudens, -entis* knowing, foreseeing, contr. of *providens.* See PROVIDENCE.] — **pru′dent·ly** *adv.*

— **Syn. 1.** discreet, circumspect, wary. **3.** thrifty, economical, frugal. — **Ant.** imprudent, indiscreet, rash, reckless.

pru·den·tial (proo·den′shəl) *adj.* **1.** Proceeding from or marked by prudence. **2.** Exercising prudence and wisdom. — **pru·den′tial·ly** *adv.*

prud·er·y (proo′dər·ē) *n. pl.* **·er·ies 1.** Extreme priggishness; primness. **2.** Prudish action or language.

prud·ish (proo′dish) *adj.* Showing prudery; prim. — **prud′ish·ly** *adv.* — **prud′ish·ness** *n.*

pru·i·nose (proo′i·nōs) *adj. Biol.* Having the surface covered by a powdery secretion, as the bloom on a cabbage leaf. [< L *pruinosus* frosty < *pruina* hoarfrost]

prune[1] (proon) *n.* **1.** The dried fruit of any of several varieties of plum. **2.** Any of various plums that may be dried without spoiling. **3.** *Slang* A stupid or uninteresting person. [< OF < LL *pruna* < L *prunum* < Gk. *proumnon* plum. Doublet of PLUM[1].]

prune[2] (proon) *v.t.* & *v.i.* **pruned, prun·ing 1.** To trim or cut branches or parts (from) so as to improve growth, appearance, etc. **2.** To cut off (branches or parts). [< OF *proöignier, proignier,* ? < *provaignier* to cut < *provain* slip < L *propago*; prob. infl. in form by *rooignier* to cut off, ult. < L *rotundus* round] — **prun′er** *n.*

prune[3] (proon) *v.t.* & *v.i.* **pruned, prun·ing** *Archaic* To dress up; preen. [< OF *poroindre* to anoint < *por-* (< L *pro* before) + *oindre* to anoint < L *ungere*]

pru·nel·la (proo·nel′ə) *n.* **1.** A strong woolen cloth used for the uppers of shoes. **2.** A similar twilled heavy dress fabric. **3.** *pl.* Shoes made partly of prunella. Also **pru·nel′lo** (-nel′ō). [< F *prunelle* sloe-colored, dim. of *prune.* See PRUNE[1].]

pru·nelle (proo·nel′) *n.* **1.** A small yellow prune, usually packed with the stone and skin removed. **2.** A plum-flavored liqueur. [< F, dim. of *prune.* See PRUNE[1].]

pru·ri·ent (proor′ē·ənt) *adj.* **1.** Impure in thought and desire; lewd. **2.** Having lustful cravings or desires. **3.** Longing; desirous. [< L *pruriens, -entis,* ppr. of *prurire* to itch] — **pru·ri·ence, pru·ri·en·cy** *n.* — **pru·ri·ent·ly** *adv.*

pru·ri·go (proo·rī′gō) *n. Pathol.* A chronic inflammatory skin disease marked by eruption and itching. [< L, an itching < *prurire* to itch] — **pru·rig′i·nous** (-rij′ə·nəs) *adj.*

pru·ri·tus (proo·rī′təs) *n. Pathol.* Intense itching. [< L < *prurire* to itch] — **pru·rit·ic** (-rit′ik) *adj.*

Prus. or **Pruss.** Prussia; Prussian.

Pru·sa (proo′sä) An ancient name for BRUSA.

Prus·sia (prush′ə) A former state, the largest and most important, of northern Germany; formally dissolved, Feb. 1947; territory divided among East and West Germany, Poland, and the Soviet Union: German *Preussen.*

Prus·sian (prush′ən) *adj.* **1.** Of or pertaining to Prussia, its inhabitants, or their language. **2.** Characteristic of the Junkers of Prussia; militaristic; overbearing. — *n.* **1.** A native or inhabitant of Prussia. **2.** The old language of Prussia, belonging to the Balto-Slavic branch of the Balto-Slavic subfamily of Indo-European languages, extinct since the 17th century: also called *Borussian:* also **Old Prussian.**

Prussian blue 1. *Chem.* Any one of a group of cyanogen compounds containing chiefly ferric ferrocyanide, formerly much used in dyeing. **2.** A deep, strong, blue pigment with a coppery sheen, obtained from these compounds: also called *Berlin blue, Chinese blue, Paris blue.* [So called because discovered in Berlin]

Prus·sian·ism (prush′ən·iz′əm) *n.* The practices or policies of the Prussian ruling class during its leadership of Germany, characterized by militarism.

prus·si·ate (prush′ē·āt, -it, prus′-) *n. Chem.* **1.** A salt of hydrocyanic acid; also, a cyanide. **2.** A ferrocyanide or a ferricyanide.

prus·sic acid (prus′ik) Hydrocyanic acid (which see).

Prut (proot) A river forming the boundary between the SW Soviet Union and Rumania, and flowing 530 miles SW to the Danube. Formerly also **Pruth.**

pry[1] (prī) *v.i.* **pried, pry·ing** To look or peer carefully, curiously, or slyly; snoop. — *n. pl.* **pries 1.** A sly and searching inspection. **2.** One who pries; an inquisitive, prying person. [ME *prien;* ult. origin unknown] — **pry′ing·ly** *adv.*

pry[2] (prī) *v.t.* **pried, pry·ing** *Chiefly U.S.* **1.** To raise, move, or open by means of a lever; prize. **2.** To obtain by effort. — *n.* A lever, as a bar, stick, or beam; also, leverage. [Back formation < PRIZE[1] (def. 3)]

pry·er (prī′ər) See PRIER.

Prze·myśl (pshe′mish·l) A city in SE Poland near the Ukrainian border; scene of several battles in World War I, 1915; pop. 41,100 (est. 1958).

ps. Pieces.

Ps. Psalms.

P.S. 1. Passenger Steamer. **2.** Postscript: also **p.s. 3.** Privy Seal. **4.** Prompt side (theater). **5.** Public sale. **6.** Public School.

psalm (säm) *n.* **1.** *Often cap.* A sacred song or lyric contained in the Old Testament Book of Psalms. **2.** Any sacred song. — *v.t.* To celebrate or praise in psalms. [OE *psealm* < LL *psalma* < Gk. *psalmos* song accompanied by a harp, orig., a plucking of strings < *psallein* to pluck]

psalm·ist (sä′mist) *n.* A maker or composer of psalms. — **the Psalmist** King David, as the traditional author of many of the Scriptural psalms.

psalm·o·dy (sä′mə·dē, sal′-) *n. pl.* **·dies** 1. The use of psalms in divine worship; psalm-singing. 2. A collection of psalms. [< OF *psalmodie* < LL *psalmodia* < Gk. *psalmōidia* singing accompanied on the harp < *psalmos* psalm + *aeidein* to sing] — **psalm′o·dist** *n.*

Psalms (sämz) A lyrical book of the Old Testament, containing 150 hymns. Also **Book of Psalms.**

psal·ter (sôl′tər) *n.* 1. The psalms appointed to be read or sung at any given service. 2. In the Roman Catholic Church, a rosary of 150 beads, equaling the number of the Psalms. [OE *psaltere* < L *psalterium*. See PSALTERY.] — **psal·te·ri·an** (sôl·tir′ē·ən, sal-) *adj.*

Psal·ter (sôl′tər) *n.* 1. The Book of Psalms; especially, the version of Psalms in the Book of Common Prayer. 2. The Latin version of Psalms used in the Roman Catholic breviary. Also **Psal′ter·y.**

psal·te·ri·um (sôl·tir′ē·əm, sal-) *n. pl.* **·te·ri·a** (-tir′ē·ə) The omasum; so called because its many folds make it resemble the instrument. — **psal·te′ri·al** *adj.*

psal·ter·y (sôl′tər·ē) *n. pl.* **·ter·ies** An ancient stringed musical instrument, similar to a dulcimer but played by plucking with the fingers or a plectrum. [< OF *psalterie* < L *psalterium* < Gk. *psaltērion* < *psallein* to pluck]

psam·mite (sam′īt) *n. Geol.* Fine-grained sandstone. [< F < Gk. *psammos* sand + -ITE¹] — **psam·mit·ic** (sa·mit′ik) *adj.*

pse·phite (sē′fīt) *n. Geol.* A conglomeration of small pebbles; fragmental rock. [< Gk. *psēphos* a pebble + -ITE¹] — **pse·phit′ic** (-fit′ik) *adj.*

pseph·ol·o·gy (sef·ol′ə·jē) *n.* The study and statistical analysis of elections. [< Gk. *psephos* vote, lit., pebble (used as a counter) + -LOGY] — **pseph·ol′o·gist** *n.*

pseud- Pseudonym.

pseu·dax·is (soo·dak′sis) *n.* A sympodium. [< PSEUD(O)- + AXIS]

pseu·de·pig·ra·pha (soo′də·pig′rə·fə) *n.pl.* Spurious writing; especially, spurious religious writings falsely ascribed to Scriptural characters or times. [< Gk., neut. pl. of *pseudepigraphos* with a false title < *pseudēs* false + *epigraphein.* See EPIGRAPH.] — **pseu·dep·i·graph·ic** (soo′dep·i·graf′ik) or **·i·cal, pseu′de·pig′ra·phous** *adj.*

pseu·do (soo′dō) *adj.* Pretended; sham.

pseudo- *combining form* 1. False; pretended: *pseudonym.* 2. Counterfeit; not genuine: *pseudepigrapha.* 3. Closely resembling: *pseudopodium.* 4. Illusory; apparent: *pseudoaquatic.* 5. Abnormal; erratic: *pseudocarp.* Also, before vowels, **pseud-.** [< Gk. < *pseudēs* false]

pseu·do·a·quat·ic (soo′dō·ə·kwat′ik, -kwot′-) *adj.* Not really aquatic, but native to or found in wet places.

pseu·do·carp (soo′dō·kärp) *n. Bot.* A fruit that includes other parts besides the pericarp and seeds, as the apple, checkerberry, and mulberry. — **pseu·do·car′pous** *adj.*

pseu·do·clas·sic (soo′dō·klas′ik) *adj.* Emulating or pretending to be classic.

pseu·do·morph (soo′dō·môrf) *n.* 1. An irregular or false form. 2. *Mineral.* A mineral having the external crystalline form of another mineral. — **pseu′do·mor′phic** *adj.* — **pseu′·do·mor′phism** *n.* — **pseu′do·mor′phous** *adj.*

pseu·do·nym (soo′də·nim) *n.* A fictitious name; pen name. Abbr. *pseud.* [< F < Gk. *pseudonymos* having a false name < *pseudēs* false + *onoma* name] — **pseu·don·y·mous** (soo·don′ə·məs) *adj.* — **pseu·don′y·mous·ly** *adv.* — **pseu·don′y·mous·ness, pseu·do·nym′i·ty** *n.*

— **Syn.** *Pseudonym, alias, pen name, nom de plume, allonym,* and *nom de guerre* denote an assumed name. *Pseudonym* is the general term, including all the others. An *alias* is a name taken to conceal one's true identity, most often for some wrongful purpose. *Pen name* and *nom de plume* refer to a fictitious name signed to a book or other literary work, by its author. An *allonym* is the name of one person assumed by another, while a *nom de guerre* is a name assumed by one who must conceal his true identity to retain freedom of action: Tito was the *nom de guerre* of Josip Broz. Compare NICKNAME.

pseu·do·Pin·dar·ic ode (soo′dō·pin·dar′ik) An ode lacking the formal stanzaic structure and unity of the Pindaric ode: also called *Cowleian ode, irregular ode.*

pseu·do·pod (soo′də·pod) *n.* 1. A pseudopodium. 2. An organism with pseudopodia; a rhizopod. — **pseu·dop·o·dal** (soo·dop′ə·dəl) *adj.*

pseu·do·po·di·um (soo′də·pō′dē·əm) *n. pl.* **·di·a** (-dē·ə) 1. *Zool.* A process formed by the temporary extension of the protoplasm of a cell or a protozoan, used for taking in food, locomotion, etc. 2. *Bot.* A false pedicel in certain mosses. Also *pseudopod:* also **pseu′do·pode** (-pōd). [< NL < PSEUDO- + -PODIUM]

p.s.f. or **psf** Pounds per square foot.

pshaw (shô) *interj.* An exclamation of annoyance, disapproval, disgust, or impatience. — *v.t. & v.i.* To exclaim *pshaw* at (a person or thing).

psi (sī, psī, psē) *n.* The twenty-third letter in the Greek alphabet (Ψ, ψ): equivalent to English *ps.* See ALPHABET.

p.s.i. or **psi** Pounds per square inch.

psi·lan·thro·py (sī·lan′thrə·pē) *n.* The doctrine of the mere humanity of Christ. Also **psi·lan′thro·pism.** [< LGk. *psilanthrōpos* merely human < *psilos* mere, bare + *anthrōpos* man] — **psi·lan·throp·ic** (sī′lan·throp′ik) *adj.*

psi·lom·e·lane (sī·lom′ə·lān) *n.* A black to steel-gray hydrous oxide of manganese, found in masses. [< Gk. *psilos* bare + *melan,* neut. of *melas* black]

Psi·lo·ri·ti (psē′lô·rē′tē) See IDA.

psi·lo·sis (sī·lō′sis) *n. Pathol.* Sprue². [< NL < Gk. *psilōsis* a stripping bare < *psiloein* to strip bare] — **psi·lot′ic** (-lot′ik) *adj.*

psit·ta·cine (sit′ə·sīn, -sin) *adj.* Of or pertaining to parrots.

psit·ta·co·sis (sit′ə·kō′sis) *n.* An acute, infectious virus disease of parrots and related birds, transmissible to man, in whom it causes fever and nausea, with complications resembling influenza and typhoid fever: also called *parrot fever.* [< NL < Gk. *psittakos* parrot + -OSIS]

Pskov (pskôf) A city in the NW R.S.F.S.R. on the southern end of **Lake Pskov,** *Russian* Pskov′sko·ye O′ze·ro (-skȧ·yə ô′zyi·rə), the southern part of Lake Peipus; pop. 127,000 (est. 1970).

pso·as (sō′əs) *n. Anat.* Either of two muscles of the interior of the pelvis, arising from the spine and constituting the loin. [< NL < Gk., accusative pl. of *psoa* muscle of the loins]

pso·ra·le·a (sə·rā′lē·ə) *n.* Any of a genus (*Psoralea*) of scented herbs or shrubs of the bean family, especially the common breadroot. [< NL < Gk. *psōraleos* scabby]

pso·ri·a·sis (sə·rī′ə·sis) *n. Pathol.* A noncontagious, inflammatory skin disease, chronic or acute, characterized by reddish patches and white scales. [< NL < Gk. *psōra* an itch] — **pso·ri·at·ic** (sôr′ē·at′ik, sō′rē-) *adj.*

P.S.S. or **p.s.s.** Postscripts.

PST or **P.S.T.** or **p.s.t.** Pacific Standard time.

psych- Var. of PSYCHO-.

psych. Psychological; psychologist; psychology.

psy·che (sī′kē) *n.* 1. The human soul; the mind; the intelligence. 2. *Psychoanal.* The aggregate of the mental components of an individual, including both conscious and unconscious states, and often regarded as an entity functioning apart from or independently of the body. [< Gk. *psyche* soul, breath of life < *psychein* to breathe. Cf. SPIRIT.]

Psy·che (sī′kē) In Greek and Roman mythology, a maiden who, after many tribulations caused by the jealousy of Aphrodite, is united with her lover, Eros, and accorded a place among the gods as a personification of the soul.

psy·che·del·ic (sī′kə·del′ik) *adj.* Causing or having to do with an abnormal stimulation of consciousness or perception: *psychedelic drugs;* a *psychedelic experience.* [< Gk. *psychē* soul + *del(os)* manifest, evident + -IC]

Psyche knot A knot of hair coiled at the back of the head in imitation of an ancient Greek style of dressing the hair.

psy·chi·a·trist (sī·kī′ə·trist, si-) *n.* A physician specializing in the practice of psychiatry. Also **psy·chi′a·ter.**

psy·chi·a·try (sī·kī′ə·trē, si-) *n.* The branch of medicine that deals with the diagnosis, treatment, and prevention of mental disorders. [< PSYCH- + -IATRY] — **psy·chi·at·ric** (sī′kē·at′rik) or **·ri·cal** *adj.*

psy·chic (sī′kik) *adj.* 1. Pertaining to the mind or soul; mental, as distinguished from physical and physiological. 2. Pertaining to or designating those mental phenomena that are or appear to be independent of normal sensory stimuli, as clairvoyance, telepathy, and extrasensory perception. 3. Caused by, proceeding from, or attributed to a nonmaterial or occult agency. 4. Sensitive to mental or occult phenomena. Also **psy′chi·cal.** — *n.* 1. One sensitive to extrasensory phenomena. 2. A spiritualistic medium. 3. The field of extrasensory phenomena: with *the.* [< Gk. *psychikos* < *psyche.* See PSYCHE.] — **psy′chi·cal·ly** *adv.*

psy·chic-en·er·giz·er drug (sī′kik·en′ər·jī′zər) A drug used to combat severe mental depression.

psycho- *combining form* Mind; soul; spirit: *psychosomatic.* Also, before vowels, *psych-.* [< Gk. *psychē.* See PSYCHE.]

psy·cho·a·cous·tics (sī′kō·ə·koos′tiks) *n.pl.* (*construed as sing.*) The study of sound with reference to its physiological basis and effects. — **psy′cho·a·cous′tic** or **·ti·cal** *adj.*

psychoanal. Psychoanalysis.

psy·cho·a·nal·y·sis (sī′kō·ə·nal′ə·sis) *n.* 1. A body of doctrine concerned with the study and interpretation of mental states in terms of the dynamic interplay of conflicting drives and processes originating in the unconscious. 2. A system of psychotherapy developed by Sigmund Freud that seeks to alleviate neuroses and other mental disorders by the systematic technical analysis of unconscious factors as revealed in dreams, free association, lapses of memory, etc. Also **psych′·a·nal′y·sis.** — **psy′cho·an′a·lyt′ic** (-an′ə·lit′ik) or **·i·cal** *adj.* — **psy′cho·an′a·lyt′i·cal·ly** *adv.*

PSALTERY

psy·cho·an·a·lyst (sī'kō·an'ə·list) *n.* One who practices psychoanalysis.

psy·cho·an·a·lyze (sī'kō·an'ə·līz) *v.t.* **·lyzed**, **·lyz·ing** To treat by psychoanalysis. Also *Brit.* **psy'cho·an'a·lyse.**

psy·cho·bi·ol·o·gy (sī'kō·bī·ol'ə·jē) *n.* **1.** The study of the mind and mental processes in relation to anatomy, physiology, and the nervous system. **2.** Psychology in its biological aspects. Also called *biopsychology.* — **psy'cho·bi'o·log'i·cal** (-bī'ə·loj'i·kəl) *adj.* — **psy'cho·bi·ol'o·gist** *n.*

psy·cho·chem·i·cal (sī'kō·kem'i·kəl) *n. Chem.* Any of various drugs and compounds capable of acting directly on the brain and affecting consciousness and behavior. — *adj.* Consisting or of the nature of a psychochemical.

psy·cho·dra·ma (sī'kō·drä'mə, -dram'ə) *n.* A form of psychotherapy in which the patient acts out, occasionally before an audience, situations involving his problems.

psy·cho·dy·nam·ics (sī'kō·dī·nam'iks) *n.pl.* (*construed as sing.*) The study of mental processes in action. — **psy'cho·dy·nam'ic** *adj.*

psy·cho·gen·e·sis (sī'kō·jen'ə·sis) *n.* Genesis or development due to the action of the mind or psyche, as distinguished from external influences. Also **psy·chog·e·ny** (sī·koj'ə·nē). — **psy'cho·ge·net'ic** (-jə·net'ik) *adj.* — **psy'cho·ge·net'i·cal·ly** *adv.*

psy·cho·gen·ic (sī'kō·jen'ik) *adj.* Having mental origin, or being affected by mental actions and states.

psy·chog·no·sis (sī'kog·nō'sis) *n.* The study of mental states. [< PSYCHO- + -GNOSIS] — **psy'chog·nos'tic** (nos'tik) *adj.*

psy·cho·graph (sī'kə·graf, -gräf) *n.* **1.** *Psychol.* A chart graphically representing the personality traits of an individual: also **psy'cho·gram** (-gram). **2.** A description of the personality traits of an individual. — **psy'cho·graph'ic** *adj.*

psy·cho·his·to·ry (sī'kō·his'tə·rē) *n.* History that stresses psychology, especially that of great persons. — **psy'cho·his·tor'i·cal** (-his·tôr'i·kəl) *adj.* — **psy'cho·his·tor'i·cal·ly** *adv.*

psy·cho·ki·ne·sis (sī'kō·ki·nē'sis) *n.* The alleged power of controlling the behavior of physical objects, as cards, dice, etc., by mental influence upon them. Abbr. *PK*

psy·chol. Psychological; psychologist; psychology.

psy·cho·log·i·cal (sī'kə·loj'i·kəl) *adj.* **1.** Of or pertaining to psychology. **2.** Of or in the mind. **3.** Suitable for or affecting the mind. Also **psy'cho·log'ic.** Abbr. *psych.*, *psychol.* — **psy'cho·log'i·cal·ly** *adv.*

psychological warfare The use of brainwashing, propaganda, etc., to demoralize an enemy or opponent.

psy·chol·o·gist (sī·kol'ə·jist) *n.* A student of or a specialist in psychology. Abbr. *psych.*, *psychol.*

psy·chol·o·gize (sī·kol'ə·jīz) *v.i.* **·gized**, **·giz·ing** **1.** To study psychology. **2.** To theorize on psychology.

psy·chol·o·gy (sī·kol'ə·jē) *n. pl.* **·gies 1.** The science of the human mind in any of its aspects, operations, powers, or functions. **2.** The systematic investigation of mental phenomena, especially those associated with consciousness, behavior, and the problems of adjustment to the environment. **3.** The aggregate of the emotions, traits, and behavior patterns regarded as characteristic of an individual, type, period, group, particular experience, etc.: the *psychology* of the fanatic. **4.** A work on psychology. Abbr. *psych.*, *psychol.*

psy·chom·e·try (sī·kom'ə·trē) *n.* **1.** The science of the measurement of psychophysical processes; mental testing: also **psy·cho·met·rics** (sī·kō·met'riks). **2.** Divination by physical contact or proximity of the properties of things touched or approached. — **psy·chom'e·trist** *n.*

psy·cho·mo·tor (sī'kō·mō'tər) *adj. Physiol.* Of or pertaining to muscular movements resulting from or caused by mental processes.

psy·cho·neu·ro·sis (sī'kō·nŏŏ·rō'sis, -nyŏŏ-) *n. pl.* **·ses** (-sēz) *Psychiatry* Neurosis (which see). — **psy'cho·neu·rot'ic** (-rot'ik) *adj. & n.*

psy·cho·path (sī'kō·path) *n.* One who is mentally unstable, especially in a criminal or antisocial manner.

psy·cho·path·ic (sī'kō·path'ik) *adj.* Of or characterized by psychopathy.

psy·cho·pa·thol·o·gy (sī'kō·pə·thol'ə·jē) *n.* The pathology of the mind. — **psy'cho·path'o·log'i·cal** (-path'ə·loj'i·kəl) *adj.* — **psy'cho·pa·thol'o·gist** *n.*

psy·chop·a·thy (sī·kop'ə·thē) *n.* Mental disorder, especially as apart from disease of the brain.

psy·cho·phar·ma·col·o·gy (sī'kō·fär'mə·kol'ə·jē) *n.* The branch of pharmacology dealing with drugs that affect the mind. — **psy'cho·phar'ma·co·log'ic** (-kə·loj'ik) *adj.*

psy·cho·phys·ics (sī'kō·fiz'iks) *n.pl.* (*construed as sing.*) The science of the relations between mental and physical phenomena. — **psy'cho·phys'i·cal** *adj.* — **psy'cho·phys'i·cist** *n.*

psy·cho·phys·i·ol·o·gy (sī'kō·fiz'ē·ol'ə·jē) *n.* The physiology of mental processes.

psy·cho·sis (sī·kō'sis) *n. pl.* **·ses** (-sēz) *Psychiatry* A mental disorder, severe in character, often involving disorganization of the total personality, with or without organic disease: also, *Obs.*, *neuropsychosis.* [< NL < Gk. *psychōsis* giving of life < *psychoein* to animate < *psuchē* soul]

psy·cho·so·mat·ic (sī'kō·sō·mat'ik) *adj.* **1.** Of or pertaining to the interrelationships of mind and body, with special reference to disease. **2.** Designating a branch of medicine that investigates the reciprocal influences of body and mind in the cause, prevention, treatment, and cure of disease.

psy·cho·sur·ger·y (sī'kō·sûr'jər·ē) *n.* The branch of surgery concerned with the operative relief of mental disorders. — **psy'cho·sur'gi·cal** *adj.*

psy·cho·tech·nics (sī'kō·tek'niks) *n.pl.* (*construed as sing.*) The direct application of psychological principles and methods to practical ends. — **psy'cho·tech'ni·cal** *adj.* — **psy'·cho·tech·ni'cian** (-tek·nish'ən) *n.*

psy·cho·ther·a·py (sī'kō·ther'ə·pē) *n. pl.* **·pies** The treatment of nervous and mental disorders by psychological methods, as hypnosis, re-education, psychoanalysis, etc. Also **psy'cho·ther'a·peu'tics** (-ther'·ə·pyŏŏ'tiks). — **psy'·cho·ther'a·peu'tic** *adj.* — **psy'cho·ther'a·pist** *n.*

psy·chot·ic (sī·kot'ik) *n.* One suffering from a psychosis. — *adj.* Of or characterized by a psychosis.

psy·chot·o·gen·ic (sī·kot'ō·jen'ik) *adj.* Capable of inducing a psychosis or a psychotic condition, as certain drugs.

psy·chot·o·mi·met·ic (sī·kot'ō·mi·met'ik, -mī·met'ik) *adj.* Designating a group of drugs capable of inducing altered states of consciousness and having possible therapeutic value.

psy·cho·trop·ic (sī'kō·trop'ik, -trō'pik) *adj.* Capable of modifying mental activity, as opiates, tranquilizers, etc.

psychro- *combining form* Cold: *psychrophobia.* [< Gk. *psychros* cold]

psy·chrom·e·ter (sī·krom'ə·tər) *n.* An instrument for determining the dew point and relative humidity, consisting of a dry-bulb and wet-bulb thermometer so connected that they may be ventilated by whirling in the air as a unit. — **psy·chro·met'ric.** [< PSYCHRO- + -METER]

psy·chro·ther·a·py (sī'krō·ther'ə·pē) *n. pl.* **·pies** *Med.* Cryotherapy (which see).

pt. **1.** Part. **2.** Payment. **3.** Pint(s). **4.** Point(s). **5.** Port. **6.** Preterit.

p.t. For the time being (L *pro tempore*).

Pt *Chem.* Platinum.

P.T. **1.** Pacific Time. **2.** Physical Training.

PTA or **P.T.A.** Parent-Teacher Association.

Ptah (ptä, ptäkh) In ancient Egyptian religion, the chief divinity of Memphis, the creator of gods and men.

ptar·mi·gan (tär'mə·gən) *n. pl.* **·gans** or **·gan** A grouse (genus *Lagopus*) of the northern hemisphere, having winter plumage chiefly pure white, and with feathered toes; especially, the **willow ptarmigan** (*L. lagopus*) of the Arctic, and the **white-tailed ptarmigan** (*L. leucurus*) of the Rocky Mountains. [< Scottish Gaelic *tarmachan*]

ptas. Pesetas.

PT boat A patrol torpedo boat (which see).

pter·i·dol·o·gy (ter'i·dol'ə·jē) *n.* The branch of botany that treats of ferns. [< Gk. *pteris*, *pteridos* fern + -LOGY] — **pter'i·do·log'i·cal** (-dō·loj'i·kəl) *adj.* — **pter'i·dol'o·gist** *n.*

pter·i·do·phyte (ter'i·dō·fīt') *n.* Any of a major division (*Pteridophyta*) of flowerless, seedless plants comprising the ferns, clubmosses, and horsetails. [< NL < Gk. *pteris*, *pteridos* fern + *phyton* plant] — **pter'i·do·phyt'ic** (-fit'ik), **pter'i·doph'y·tous** (-dof'ə·təs) *adj.*

ptero- *combining form* Wing; feather; winglike: *pterodactyl.* Also, before vowels, **pter-.** [< Gk. *pteron* wing]

pter·o·dac·tyl (ter'ə·dak'til) *n. Paleontol.* Any of a genus (*Pterodactylus*) of extinct pterosaurian flying reptiles of the Jurassic period, characterized by a birdlike skull, long jaws, and wing membranes supported by the fourth finger. [< NL < Gk. *pteron* wing + *daktylos* finger]

pter·o·pod (ter'ə·pod) *n.* Any of a subclass or order (*Pteropoda*) of gastropods with the middle region of the foot expanded into winglike lobes or fins: also called *sea butterfly.* — *adj.* **1.** Having the foot expanded into lobes. **2.** Of or pertaining to the *Pteropoda*: also **pte·rop·o·dan** (tə·rop'ə·dən). [< NL *pteropoda* < Gk. *pteron* wing + *pous* foot]

pter·o·sau·ri·an (ter'ə·sôr'ē·ən) *n. Paleontol.* Any of an extinct order (*Pterosauria*) of flying reptiles, including pterodactyls, of the Mesozoic, with long external digits developed to support a flying membrane. Also **pter'o·saur.** — *adj.* Of or pertaining to the Pterosauria. [< NL *pterosaurus* < Gk. *pteron* wing + *saura* lizard]

-pterous *combining form* Having (a specified number or kind of) wings: *dipterous.* [< Gk. *pteron* wing]

pter·y·goid (ter'ə·goid) *adj.* Having the form of a wing; winglike. Also **pter'y·goi'dal**, **pter'y·goi'de·an.** [< Gk. *pteryx*, *pterygos* wing + -OID]

ptg. Printing.

ptis·an (tiz'ən) *n.* **1.** A tea or infusion of herbs or barley: also called *tisane.* **2.** The juice of grapes drained off without pressure. [< OF (p)tisane < LL *ptisana* barley gruel < Gk *ptisane* peeled barley < *ptissein* to peel]

P.T.O. or **p.t.o.** Please turn over (page).

Ptol·e·ma·ic (tol'ə·mā'ik) *adj.* Of or pertaining to Ptolemy, the astronomer, or to the dynasty of Egyptian kings of Macedonian descent that began with Ptolemy I. [< Gk. *Ptolemaïkos*]

Ptolemaic system The ancient astronomical system of

Ptolemy. It assumed that the earth was the central body around which the sun, planets, and celestial bodies revolved.

Ptol·e·ma·is (tol′ə·mā′is) The New Testament name for ACRE.

Ptol·e·ma·ist (tol′ə·mā′ist) *n.* A believer in or adherent of the Ptolemaic system.

Ptol·e·my (tol′ə·mē) Second-century Greek astronomer, mathematician, and geographer in Alexandria: full name **Claudius Ptol·e·mae·us** (tol′ə·mē′əs).

Ptol·e·my I (tol′ə·mē), 367?–285 B.C., king of Egypt 305–285; general under Alexander the Great; founded the Ptolemaic dynasty: called **So·ter** (sō′tər) (Savior).

Ptolemy II, 309–246 B.C., king of Egypt 285–46; patron of the arts: called **Phil·a·del·phus** (fil′ə·del′fəs) (Lover of his sister).

Ptolemy III, 282?–221 B.C., king of Egypt 246–21: called **Eu·er·ge·tes** (yoō·ûr′jə·tēz) (Benefactor).

pto·maine (tō′mān, tō·mān′) *n. Biochem.* Any of a class of basic nitrogenous compounds, some of which are poisonous, derived from decomposing or putrefying animal or vegetable protein. Also **pto′main**. [< Ital. *ptomaina* < Gk. *ptōma* corpse < *piptein* to fall]

ptomaine poisoning An erroneous term for food poisoning.

pto·sis (tō′sis) *n. Pathol.* The permanent drooping of the upper eyelid, due to nerve paralysis. [< NL < Gk. *ptōsis* falling < *piptein* to fall] — **pto·tic** (tō′tik) *adj.*

pts. 1. Parts. 2. Payments. 3. Pints. 4. Points. 5. Ports.

pty·a·lin (tī′ə·lin) *n. Biochem.* An enzyme, contained in saliva, that converts starch into dextrin and maltose. [< Gk. *ptyalon* saliva < *ptuein* to spit + -IN]

pty·a·lism (tī′ə·liz′əm) *n.* Abnormal flow of saliva; salivation. [< Gk. *ptyalon* saliva + -ISM]

Pu *Chem.* Plutonium.

pub (pub) *n. Brit. Informal* A public house; inn; tavern.

pub. 1. Public. 2. Publication. 3. Published; publisher; publishing.

pu·ber·ty (pyoō′bər·tē) *n. pl.* **·ties** The period during which an individual becomes physiologically capable of reproduction. [< L *pubertas* < *pubes*, *puberis* an adult]

pu·bes (pyoō′bēz) *n.* 1. *Anat.* The part of the lower hypogastric region that is covered with hair in the adult; the pubic region. 2. The hair that appears at puberty on the pubic region. 3. *Biol.* Pubescence. [< L, pubic hair]

pu·bes·cence (pyoō·bes′əns) *n.* 1. The state or quality of being pubescent. 2. *Biol.* A growth of fine hairs or down, especially that upon certain plants: also called *pubes*.

pu·bes·cent (pyoō·bes′ənt) *adj.* 1. Arriving or having arrived at puberty. 2. *Biol.* Exhibiting pubescence. [< MF < L *pubescens*, *-entis*, ppr. of *pubescere* to grow hair, attain puberty < *pubes*. See PUBES.]

pu·bic (pyoō′bik) *adj.* Of or pertaining to the region in the lower part of the abdomen: the *pubic* bones.

public defender *U.S.* An attorney assigned by a court to defend a person accused of a criminal offense who is unable to afford legal representation.

pu·bis (pyoō′bis) *n. pl.* **·bes** (-bēz) *Anat.* Either of the two bones that join with a third to form an arch on either ventral side of the pelvis. [< NL < L (*os*) *pubis* pubic bone < *pubes*. See PUBES.]

pub·lic (pub′lik) *adj.* 1. Of, pertaining to, or affecting the people at large or the community. 2. Maintained by or for the public; open to all: *public* parks. 3. Participated in by the people: a *public* demonstration. 4. For the use of the public; especially, for hire: a *public* cab, hall, etc. 5. Done or made in public or without concealment; well-known; open; notorious: a *public* scandal. 6. Occupying an official or professional position; acting before or for the community: a *public* speaker. — *n.* 1. Those who may be grouped together for any given purpose: the church-going *public*. 2. An audience; especially, the admirers of an actor or other celebrity. — **the public** The people of a locality or nation. Abbr. *pub.* [< MF < L *publicus*. Prob. akin to L *populus* the people.] — **pub′lic·ness** *n.*

pub·lic-ad·dress system (pub′lik·ə·dres′) An apparatus for the amplification of speech, music, etc., in public places. Abbr. *PA*

pub·li·can (pub′lə·kən) *n.* 1. In England, the keeper of a public house. 2. In ancient Rome, one who farmed or collected the public revenues. [< OF *publicain* < L *publicanus* < *publicum* public revenue, orig. neut. of *publicus*. See PUBLIC.]

pub·li·ca·tion (pub′lə·kā′shən) *n.* 1. The act of publishing or offering to public notice. 2. Any printed work placed on sale or otherwise distributed or offered for distribution. 3. Notification to people at large orally or by writing or print; promulgation; proclamation. 4. *Law* The communication of a defamation to a third person. Abbr. *pub.* [< OF *publicacion* < L *publicatio*, *-onis* < *publicatus*, pp. of *publicare*. See PUBLISH.]

public domain Lands owned by a state or national government; public lands. — **in the public domain** Available

for unrestricted use: said of material on which copyright or patent right has expired.

public enemy 1. A person, especially a criminal, regarded as a menace to the public. 2. An enemy state.

Public Health Service *U.S.* A Federal agency under the Surgeon General, which, as a constituent organization of the Department of Health, Education, and Welfare, is responsible for protecting and improving the health of the nation. Abbr. *PHS*

public house 1. An inn, tavern, or hotel. 2. In England, a place licensed to sell intoxicating liquors; a saloon.

pub·li·cist (pub′lə·sist) *n.* 1. A writer on international law or on topics of public interest. 2. A public-relations man or publicity agent.

pub·lic·i·ty (pub·lis′ə·tē) *n.* 1. Information or personal news intended to promote the interests of individuals, institutions, etc. 2. The state of being public, or the act of making or becoming public; exposure; notoriety. 3. The attention or interest of the public gained by any method.

pub·li·cize (pub′lə·sīz) *v.t.* **·cized**, **·ciz·ing** To give publicity to; advertise.

public land Land owned by a government, usually a national government.

public library 1. A library maintained for the use of the public. 2. The building in which it is contained.

pub·lic·ly (pub′lik·lē) *adv.* 1. In an open or public manner; openly. 2. In the name or with the consent and concurrence of the public.

public opinion The prevailing ideas, beliefs, and aims of the people, collectively.

public relations 1. The activities and techniques used by organizations and individuals to establish favorable attitudes and responses in their behalf on the part of the general public or of special groups; also, the occupation of establishing such attitudes and responses. 2. The public conduct of the affairs of an organization with regard to its reputation and standing and to public opinion. 3. The state of the relationship between the general public and an institution of any kind. Abbr. *PR*

public school 1. *U.S.* A school maintained by public funds for the free education of the children of the community, usually covering elementary and secondary grades: distinguished from *private school*. 2. *Brit.* A private or endowed school not run for profit, especially one preparing students for the universities, as Eton, Harrow, etc. Abbr. *P.S.*

public servant A government official.

public service 1. Government employment, especially in the civil departments. 2. The radio or television broadcasting of noncommercial announcements of civic interest.

pub·lic-ser·vice corporation (pub′lik·sûr′vis) Any corporation operating a public utility, as a railroad, gas, electric, or water company.

public spirit Active, enlightened interest in and concern for matters that affect the welfare of the community. — **pub·lic-spir·it·ed** (pub′lik·spir′it·id) *adj.*

public utility A business organization or industry that supplies water, electricity, gas, etc., to the public and is subject to governmental regulations; public-service corporation.

public works Architectural or engineering works or improvements built with public money, as parks, roads, etc.

pub·lish (pub′lish) *v.t.* 1. To print and issue (a book, magazine, map, etc.) to the public. 2. To make known or announce publicly; promulgate. 3. *Law* To communicate (a defamation) to a third person. 4. To print and issue the work of: to *publish* Hemingway. — *v.i.* 5. To engage in the business of publishing. 6. To have one's work published. [< OF *publier*, *puplier* < L *publicare* to make public < *publicus*. See PUBLIC.] — **pub′lish·a·ble** *adj.*

pub·lish·er (pub′lish·ər) *n.* One who publishes; especially, one whose business is publishing books, etc. Abbr. *pub.*

Puc·ci·ni (poōt·chē′nē), **Giacomo**, 1858–1924, Italian operatic composer: full name **Giacomo Antonio Domenico Michele Secundo Maria Puccini**.

puc·coon (pə·koōn′) *n.* 1. Any of several North American herbs (genus *Lithospermum*) of the borage family, yielding a red or yellow dye; especially, the **hoary puccoon** (*L. canescens*), with orange-yellow flowers: also called *alkanet*. 2. The pigment or dye made from these plants. 3. The bloodroot. [< Algonquian (Virginian) *puccoon*, *pakon* < *pak* blood]

puce (pyoōs) *adj.* Of a dark brown or purplish brown. [< F, flea color, flea < L *pulex*, *-icis* flea]

puck[1] (puk) *n.* An evil sprite or hobgoblin. [OE *pūca*]

puck[2] (puk) *n.* The black, hard, rubber disk used in playing ice hockey. [? < dial. E, to strike. Akin to POKE[1].]

Puck (puk) In English folklore, a mischievous elf or goblin, as in Shakespeare's *A Midsummer Night's Dream*: identified with *Robin Goodfellow*. [< PUCK[1]]

puck·a (puk′ə) See PUKKA.

puck-car·ri·er (puk′kar′ē·ər) *n.* In hockey, the player in possession of the puck.

puck·er (puk′ər) *v.t.* & *v.i.* To gather or draw up into small folds or wrinkles. — *n.* 1. A wrinkle or group of wrinkles. 2. *Informal* Agitation; perplexity; confusion. [Appar. freq. of POKE²] **—puck′er·y** *adj.*

puck·ish (puk′ish) *adj.* Mischievous; impish.

pud·ding (pŏŏd′ing) *n.* 1. A sweetened and flavored dessert of soft food, usually made of milk, flavoring, a thickening agent, etc. 2. A sausage of seasoned minced meat, blood, or the like, usually boiled or broiled: also called *puddle.* [ME *poding,* orig., sausage, black pudding, prob. < OF *bodin, boudin*]

pud·dle (pud′l) *n.* 1. A small pool of water, especially dirty water. 2. A small pool of any liquid. 3. A pudding (def. 2). — *v.t.* **·dled, ·dling** 1. *Metall.* To convert (molten pig iron) into wrought iron by melting and stirring in the presence of oxidizing substances. 2. To mix (clay, etc.) with water so as to obtain a watertight paste. 3. To make muddy; stir up. [ME *podel,* dim. of OE *pudd* ditch] **—pud′dly** *adj.*

pud·dle·ball (pud′l·bôl′) *n. Metall.* A ball of iron reduced to a pasty condition in the puddling furnace and ready for hammering or rolling: also called *loop.*

pud·dle·bar (pud′l·bär′) *n.* A bar into which a puddleball is rolled or hammered.

pud·dler (pud′lər) *n.* 1. One who puddles. 2. A device for stirring fused metal. 3. A puddling furnace (which see).

pud·dling (pud′ling) *n.* 1. *Metall.* The operation or business of making wrought iron from pig iron in a puddling furnace. 2. Puddled clay for lining the banks of canals, etc. 3. The operation of lining a canal with such clay.

puddling furnace A reverberatory furnace for puddling pig iron: also called *hearth, puddler.*

pu·den·cy (pyōō′dən·sē) *n.* Shame; modesty; also, prudishness. [< LL *pudentia* < L *pudens, -entis,* ppr. of *pudere* to be ashamed]

pu·den·dum (pyōō·den′dəm) *n. pl.* **·da** (-də) 1. The external genital parts of the female; vulva. 2. *pl.* The external genitals of either sex. [< L, neut. of *pudendus,* gerundive of *pudere* to be ashamed] **—pu′dic, pu·den′dal** *adj.*

pudg·y (puj′ē) *adj.* **pudg·i·er, pudg·i·est** Short and fat; dumpy; chubby: also *podgy.* [< Scot.]

Pue·bla (pwä′blä) A State in southern Mexico; 13,124 sq. mi.; 2,483,770 (1970); capital, **Puebla,** pop. 521,885 (1970).

pueb·lo (pweb′lō *for def. 1;* pwä′blō *for defs. 2 and 3*) *n. pl.* **·los** 1. A communal adobe or stone building or group of buildings of the Indians of the SW United States. 2. A town or village of Indians or Spanish Americans, as in Mexico. 3. In the Philippines, a municipality. [< Sp., village < L *populus* people]

Pueb·lo (pweb′lō) *n.* A member of one of the Indian tribes of Mexico and the SW United States, as a Zuñi, Hopi, etc.

Pueb·lo (pweb′lō) A city in south central Colorado; pop. 97,453.

pu·er·ile (pyōō′ər·il, pyōō′rəl, -rīl, pwer′əl, -īl) *adj.* 1. Pertaining to or characteristic of childhood; juvenile. 2. Immature; weak; silly: a *puerile* suggestion. [< L *puerilis* < *puer, pueri* boy] **—pu′er·ile·ly** *adv.* **—pu′er·ile·ness** *n.*

pu·er·il·ism (pyōō′ər·il·iz′əm, -ī·liz′-, pyōō′rəl-, pwer′əl-) *n.* Childishness, especially as indicative of mental disorder.

pu·er·il·i·ty (pyōō′ə·ril′ə·tē, pyōō·ril′-, pwer·il′-) *n. pl.* **·ties** 1. Puerile state; childishness. 2. A childish act or expression.

pu·er·per·al (pyōō·ûr′pər·əl) *adj. Med.* Pertaining to, resulting from, or following childbirth. [< L *puerpera* woman in childbirth < *puer* child + *parere* to bear]

Puer·to Ri·co (pwer′tō rē′kō, pôr′-; *Sp.* pwär′tō) The easternmost island of the Greater Antilles, ceded to the United States by Spain in 1898; since 1952 a Commonwealth; 3,423 sq. mi.; pop. 2,689,930 (est. 1970); capital, San Juan; former official name, *Porto Rico.* Abbr. *P.R.* **—Puer′to Ri′can** *adj.* & *n.*

puff (puf) *n.* 1. A breath emitted suddenly and with force; a sudden emission, as of air, smoke, or steam; a whiff. 2. A light, air-filled piece of pastry: a cream *puff.* 3. A light ball, tuft, wad, or pad for dusting powder on the hair or skin; a powder puff. 4. A loose roll of hair in a coiffure, or a light cushion over which it is rolled. 5. A quilted bed coverlet, usually filled with cotton, wool, or down; a comforter. 6. In dressmaking, a part of a fabric so gathered as to produce a loose, fluffy distention. 7. A public expression of fulsome praise, as in a newspaper or advertisement. 8. A puffball. — *v.i.* 1. To blow in puffs, as the wind. 2. To breathe hard, as after violent exertion. 3. To emit smoke, steam, etc., in puffs. 4. To smoke a cigar, etc., with puffs. 5. To move, act, or exert oneself while emitting puffs: with *away, up,* etc. 6. To swell, as with air or pride; dilate: often with *up* or *out.* — *v.t.* 7. To send forth or emit with short puffs or breaths. 8. To move, impel, or stir up with or in puffs. 9. To smoke, as a pipe or cigar, with puffs. 10. To swell or distend. 11. To praise excessively. 12. To arrange (hair, etc.) in a puff. [ME *puf* < *puffen,* OE *pyffan;* ult. imit.]

puff adder A large, sluggish, venomous African viper

(*Bitis arietans*), with variously colored chevron and crescent markings and a habit of violently puffing out its breath.

puff·ball (puf′bôl′) *n.* Any of various globular fungi (genus *Lycoperdon*) that puff out dustlike spores when broken open.

puff·er (puf′ər) *n.* 1. One who or that which puffs. 2. A globefish or similar fish.

puff·er·y (puf′ər·ē) *n. pl.* **·er·ies** Excessive public praise or publicity.

puf·fin (puf′in) *n.* A sea bird (family *Alcidae*) allied to the auk and murre, with a deep, compressed bill; especially, the **common puffin** (*Fratercula arctica*) of the North Atlantic, and the **tufted puffin** (*Lunda cirrhata*) of the Pacific coast. [ME *poffin,* prob. < PUFF; with ref. to its large beak or the plumpness of its young]

PUFFIN (About 12 inches long; wingspread to 24 inches)

puff paste A rich paste used to make flaky pastry.

puff·y (puf′ē) *adj.* **puff·i·er, puff·i·est** 1. Swollen with or as with air, etc.; bloated. 2. Inflated in manner; bombastic. 3. Blowing in puffs. **—puff′i·ly** *adv.* **—puff′i·ness** *n.*

pug¹ (pug) *n.* 1. Clay ground and worked with water, for molding pottery or bricks. 2. A machine in which clay is ground and mixed or tempered: also **pug mill.** — *v.t.* **pugged, pug·ging** 1. To knead or work (clay) with water, as in brickmaking. 2. To fill in with clay, etc. 3. To fill in or cover with mortar, felt, etc., so as to deaden sound. [Origin unknown]

pug² (pug) *n.* 1. A breed of dog characterized by a short square body, upturned nose, curled tail, and short smooth coat. 2. A pug nose. [Prob. alter. of PUCK]

pug³ (pug) *n. Anglo-Indian* An animal's footprint; trail. — *v.t.* **pugged, pug·ging** To track, as game, by pugs; trail. [< Hind. *pag* foot]

pug⁴ (pug) *n. Slang* A professional pugilist. [Short for PUGILIST]

Pu·get Sound (pyōō′jit) An inlet of the Pacific in NW Washington, extending about 100 miles south from Juan del Fuca Strait to Olympia.

pugh (pyōō, pōō) *interj.* An exclamation of contempt or disgust.

pu·gi·lism (pyōō′jə·liz′əm) *n.* The art or practice of boxing or fighting with the fists. [< L *pugil* boxer. Akin to *pugnus* fist.]

pu·gi·list (pyōō′jə·list) *n.* One who fights with his fists; especially, a prize fighter. **—pu′gi·lis′tic** *adj.*

Pu·glia (pōō′lyä) The Italian name for APULIA.

pug·na·cious (pug·nā′shəs) *adj.* Disposed or inclined to fight; quarrelsome. [< L *pugnax, -acis* < *pugnare* to fight < *pugnus* fist] **—pug·na′cious·ly** *adv.*

pug·nac·i·ty (pug·nas′ə·tē) *n. pl.* **·ties** The quality of being pugnacious; quarrelsome disposition; combativeness. Also **pug·na′cious·ness** (-nā′shəs·nis). [< L *pugnacitas*]

pug nose A short nose tilted upward at the end. [< PUG²] **—pug-nosed** (pug′nōzd′) *adj.*

pug·ree (pug′rē) *n. Anglo-Indian* 1. A light scarf wound round a hat to keep off the sun. 2. A turban worn by natives of India. Also **pug·ga·ree** (pug′ə·rē), **pug′gree, pug′gry.** [< Hind. *pagri* turban]

puis·ne (pyōō′nē) *adj. Law* Junior as to rank; younger; inferior: a *puisne* judge. — *n.* One who is of inferior rank or younger; a junior associate. [< OF *puisne* < *puis* afterwards (< L *postea* < *post* after) + *né* born < L *natus*]

pu·is·sance (pyōō′ə·səns, pyōō·is′əns, pwis′əns) *n.* The power to accomplish or achieve; potency. [< OF]

pu·is·sant (pyōō′ə·sənt, pyōō·is′ənt, pwis′ənt) *adj.* Powerful; mighty. [< OF < L *posse* to be able] **—pu′is·sant·ly** *adv.*

—Syn. forceful, potent, strong.

puke (pyōōk) *v.t.* & *v.i.* **puked, puk·ing** To vomit or cause to vomit. — *n.* Vomit, or the act of vomiting. [Origin unknown]

puk·ka (puk′ə) *adj. Anglo-Indian* 1. Made of good materials; substantial. 2. Genuine; superior. Also spelled *pucka.* [< Hind. *pakkā* substantial, cooked, ripe]

Pu·la (pōō′lä) A port city in NW Croatia, Yugoslavia; formerly in Italy; pop. 40,000 (est. 1963): Italian *Pola.* Formerly **Pulj** (pōōly′).

Pu·las·ki (pōō·las′kē, pə-; *Polish* pōō·läs′kē), **Casimir,** 1748?–79, Polish general in the American Revolution.

pul·chri·tude (pul′krə·tōōd, -tyōōd) *n.* Beauty; grace; physical charm. [< L *pulchritudo, -inis* < *pulcher* beautiful]

pul·chri·tu·di·nous (pul′krə·tōō′də·nəs, -tyōō′-) *adj.* Beautiful; lovely; especially, having physical beauty.

pule (pyōōl) *v.i.* **puled, pul·ing** To cry plaintively, as a child; whimper; whine. [Prob. imit.] **—pul′er** *n.*

pu·li·cene (pyōō′lə·sēn) *adj.* Of, pertaining to, or infested with fleas. [< L *pulex, -icis* flea]

pul·ing (pyōō′ling) *n.* A plaintive cry; whining. — *adj.* Whimpering; whining. **—pul′ing·ly** *adv.*

Pul·itz·er (pyōō′lit·sər, pool′it-), **Joseph,** 1847–1911, U.S. journalist and newspaper publisher born in Hungary.

Pulitzer Prize One of several annual awards for outstanding work in American journalism, letters, music, and art, established by Joseph Pulitzer.

pull (pŏŏl) *v.t.* **1.** To apply force to so as to cause motion toward or in the direction of the person or thing exerting force; drag; tug. **2.** To draw or remove from a natural or fixed place: to *pull* a tooth. **3.** To give a pull or tug to. **4.** To pluck, as a fowl. **5.** To rip; tear; rend: to *pull* to pieces. **6.** To strain so as to cause injury: to *pull* a ligament. **7.** In golf, etc., to strike (the ball) so that it curves obliquely from the direction in which the striker faces. **8.** In baseball, to hit (the ball) to the field that the batter faces on completing his swing. **9.** *Slang* To put into effect; carry out: often with *off*. **10.** *Slang* To make a raid on; arrest. **11.** *Slang* To draw out so as to use: to *pull* a knife. **12.** *Printing* To make or obtain by impression from type: to *pull* a proof. **13.** In boxing, to deliver (a punch, etc.) with less than one's full strength. **14.** In horse racing, to rein in or otherwise restrain (a horse) so as to prevent its winning. **15.** In rowing: **a** To operate (an oar) by drawing toward one. **b** To propel or transport by rowing. **c** To be propelled by: The gig *pulls* four oars. — *v.i.* **16.** To use force in hauling, dragging, moving, etc. **17.** To move: with *out*, *in*, *away*, *ahead*, etc. **18.** To drink or inhale deeply: to *pull* at a cigar. **19.** To propel a boat with oars; row. — **to pull for 1.** To strive in behalf of. **2.** *Informal* To declare one's allegiance to. — **to pull oneself together** To regain one's composure. — **to pull out** To withdraw, as from established position. — **to pull through** To manage to succeed, recover, etc. — **to pull up 1.** To move ahead. **2.** To remove by or as by the roots: to *pull up* roots. **3.** To come to a halt. — **to pull up with** To advance to a position even with. — *n.* **1.** The act of pulling; the exertion of force to draw something toward one. **2.** Something pulled, as the handle of a drawer, cabinet, etc. **3.** An impression made by pulling the lever of a hand press. **4.** A long swallow, or a deep puff, as on a pipe or cigar. **5.** Exercise in rowing: a *pull* on the river. **6.** The exertion expended in climbing a mountain. **7.** Any steady, continuous effort. **8.** *Slang* A means of influencing those in power; influence to one's advantage: political *pull*. **9.** Attraction; appeal: These ads have *pull*. **10.** The action of restraining a horse by pulling on the reins; especially, in horse racing, the checking of a horse so that he may be defeated. **11.** In baseball, golf, etc., the act of pulling the ball. **12.** The amount of resistance met in drawing a bowstring, pulling a trigger, or the like. [OE *pullian* to pluck] — **pull′er** *n.*

pull·back (pŏŏl′bak′) *n.* **1.** That which keeps or holds back; a restraint or drawback. **2.** A device for drawing or holding something back, as part of a dress, or a window.

pul·let (pŏŏl′it) *n.* A young hen, or one not fully grown. [< OF *polete*, *poulet*, dim. of *poule* hen < L *pullus* chicken, young animal]

pul·ley (pŏŏl′ē) *n. pl.* **·leys 1.** A wheel grooved to receive a rope, and usually mounted in a block, used to increase the mechanical advantage of an applied force and to transmit or change the direction of power by means of a flexible belt or rope. **2.** A block with its pulleys or tackle. **3.** *Mech.* A flat or flanged wheel driving, carrying, or being driven by a flat belt, used in a system for transmitting power. [< OF *polie* < Med.L *poleia*, prob. ult. < Gk. *polos* pivot, axis]

PULLEYS

a Single fixed. *b* Single runner. *c* Fixed and runner. *d* First system. *e* Second system.

Pull·man (pŏŏl′mən) *n.* A sleeping car or chair car on a passenger train: a trade name. Also **Pullman car**. [after George M. *Pullman*, 1831–97, U.S. inventor]

pul·lo·rum disease (pə·lôr′əm, -lō′rəm) A highly destructive bacterial disease afflicting the young of domestic fowl and other birds, transmitted chiefly by the egg. [< L *pullorum*, genitive pl. of *pullus* chicken, young animal]

pull·out (pŏŏl′out′) *n.* **1.** A withdrawal, as of troops. **2.** *Aeron.* The maneuver of an airplane in passing from a dive to horizontal flight.

pull·o·ver (pŏŏl′ō′vər) *adj.* Put on by being drawn over the head. — *n.* A garment so put on, as a sweater or shirt.

pull strap A loop or strap at the back of a shoe, to help in drawing on the shoe. For illustration see SHOE.

pul·lu·late (pul′yə·lāt) *v.i.* **·lat·ed**, **·lat·ing 1.** To germinate; bud. **2.** To breed in abundance; swarm; teem. [< L *pullulatus*, pp. of *pullulare* to sprout < *pullulus*, dim. of *pullus* young animal] — **pul′lu·la′tion** *n.* — **pul′lu·la′tive** *adj.* — **pul′lu·la′tive·ly** *adv.*

pulmo- *combining form* Lung. [< L *pulmo* -*onis* lung]

pul·mo·nar·y (pul′mə·ner′ē, pŏŏl′-) *adj.* **1.** Of, pertaining to, or affecting the lungs: also *pneumonic*. **2.** Having lunglike organs. [< L *pulmonarius* < *pulmo*, -*onis* lung]

pulmonary artery *Anat.* An artery that conveys venous blood from the right ventricle of the heart to the lungs.

pulmonary tuberculosis Tuberculosis (def. 2).

pulmonary vein *Anat.* One of four veins that return arterial blood from the lungs to the left atrium of the heart.

pul·mo·nate (pul′mə·nāt, -nit) *adj.* **1.** Having lunglike organs. **2.** Of or belonging to an order of gastropods (*Pulmonata*), including most land snails, slugs, and freshwater snails, that have lunglike organs. — *n.* One of the *Pulmonata*. [< NL *pulmonatus* < L *pulmo*, -*onis* lung]

pul·mon·ic (pul·mon′ik) *adj.* Pertaining to or affecting the lungs. [< MF *pulmonique* < L *pulmo*, -*onis* lung]

Pul·mo·tor (pul′mō′tər, pŏŏl′-) *n.* An apparatus for producing artificial respiration by forcing oxygen into the lungs: a trade name. Also **pul′mo′tor**. [< PUL(MO)- + MOTOR]

pulp (pulp) *n.* **1.** A moist, soft, slightly cohering mass of matter, as the succulent part of fruit. **2.** A mixture of wood fibers or rags reduced to a pulpy consistency and forming the substance of paper. **3.** *Often pl.* A magazine printed on rough, unglazed paper, and usually having contents of a cheap, sensational nature: distinguished from *slick*. **4.** Powdered ore mixed with water. **5.** A pulplike organ or part. **6.** *Dent.* The soft tissue of vessels and nerves that fills the central cavity of a tooth. — *v.t.* **1.** To reduce to pulp. **2.** To remove the pulp or envelope from. — *v.i.* **3.** To be or become of a pulpy consistency. [< MF *poulpe* < L *pulpa* flesh, pulp of fruit, pith] — **pulp′less** *adj.*

pul·pit (pŏŏl′pit) *n.* **1.** An elevated stand or desk for a preacher in a church. **2.** The office or work of preaching. **3.** The clergy as a class. **4.** An elevated platform usually boxed in and variously used: the harpooner's *pulpit* on a whaling vessel. — *adj.* Of or pertaining to the pulpit: *pulpit* oratory. [< L *pulpitum* scaffold, stage, platform]

pulp·wood (pulp′wŏŏd′) *n.* The soft wood of certain trees, as the spruce, used in the manufacture of paper.

pulp·y (pul′pē) *adj.* **pulp·i·er**, **pulp·i·est 1.** Consisting of or resembling pulp. **2.** Of a soft, juicy consistency. Also **pul′pous** (-pəs). — **pulp′i·ly** *adv.* — **pulp′i·ness** *n.*

pul·que (pul′kē, pŏŏl′-; *Sp.* pŏŏl′kä) *n.* A fermented drink made from the juice of various species of agave, as the maguey. [< Am. Sp.; prob. of Nahuatl origin]

pul·sar (pul′sär) *n.* An astronomical object that emits radio waves in pulses whose repetition rate is extremely uniform. [< *puls*(ating) + (st)*ar*]

pul·sate (pul′sāt) *v.i.* **·sat·ed**, **·sat·ing 1.** To move or throb with rhythmical impulses, as the pulse or heart. **2.** To vibrate; quiver. [< L *pulsatus*, pp. of *pulsare*, freq. of *pellere* (pp. *pulsus*) to beat]

pul·sa·tile (pul′sə·til) *adj.* **1.** Pulsatory; pulsating. **2.** Sounding when struck; percussive.

pul·sa·tion (pul·sā′shən) *n.* **1.** The act or process of pulsating. **2.** A rhythmical impulse or throb, as a heartbeat.

pul·sa·tive (pul′sə·tiv) *adj.* Pulsating; throbbing; pulsatile. — **pul′sa·tive·ly** *adv.*

pul·sa·tor (pul·sā′tər) *n.* A machine or device that operates by pulsation.

pul·sa·to·ry (pul′sə·tôr′ē, -tō′rē) *adj.* Of or pertaining to pulsation; having rhythmical movement; throbbing.

pulse¹ (puls) *n.* **1.** *Physiol.* The rhythmical beating of the arteries resulting from the successive contractions of the heart, especially as felt in the radial artery at the wrist. ◆ Collateral adjectives: *sphygmic*, *sphygmoid*. **2.** Any throbbing characterized by a short, quick, regular stroke or motion; pulsation. **3.** *Telecom.* A brief surge of electrical or electromagnetic energy, usually transmitted as a signal in communication. **4.** An indication of general opinion or sentiment. — *v.i.* **pulsed**, **puls·ing** To pulsate; throb. [< OF *pous* < L *pulsus* (*venarum*) the beating (of the veins), orig. pp. of *pellere* to beat] — **pulse′less** *adj.*

pulse² (puls) *n.* Leguminous plants collectively, as peas, beans, etc.; also, their edible seeds. [< OF *pols* < L *puls* pottage of meal or pulse]

pulse-jet (puls′jet′) *n.* *Aeron.* A jet engine having movable vanes that intermittently take in air to develop power in rapid bursts: also *resojet*. Also **pul′so·jet′** (-sō·jet′).

pulse repeater *Telecom.* A transponder.

pul·sim·e·ter (pul·sim′ə·tər) *n.* An instrument for indicating and registering the frequency, force, and variations of the pulse: also called *pulsometer*. [< L *pulsus* (See PULSE¹) + -METER]

pul·som·e·ter (pul·som′ə·tər) *n.* **1.** A device for pumping liquids by steam pressure, consisting of two pear-shaped chambers connected by valves: also called *vacuum pump*. **2.** A pulsimeter. [< L *pulsus* (See PULSE¹) + -METER]

pul·ver·a·ble (pul′vər·ə·bəl) *adj.* Capable of being pulverized; pulverizable.

pul·ver·ize (pul′və·rīz) *v.* **·ized**, **·iz·ing** *v.t.* **1.** To reduce to powder or dust, as by crushing. **2.** To demolish; annihilate. — *v.i.* **3.** To become reduced to powder or dust. Also *Brit.* **pul′ver·ise.** [< MF *pulveriser* < LL *pulverizare* < L *pulvis, pulveris* powder, dust] — **pul′ver·iz′a·ble** *adj.* — **pul′ver·i·za′tion** *n.* — **pul′ver·iz′er** *n.*

pul·ver·u·lent (pul·ver′yə·lənt) *adj.* **1.** Consisting of, reducible to, or reduced to fine powder or dust. **2.** Dusty; powdery. [< L *pulverulentus* dusty < *pulvis, pulveris* powder, dust] — **pul·ver′u·lence** *n.*

pul·vil·lus (pul·vil′əs) *n. pl.* **·vil·li** (-vil′ī) *Entomol.* One of a pair of adhesive pads between the claws of an insect's foot, as the paired cushions of a fly's foot. [< L, contr. of *pulvinulus*, dim. of *pulvinus* cushion]

pul·vi·nate (pul′və·nāt) *adj.* **1.** Cushion-shaped. **2.** Having a pulvinus. Also **pul′vi·nar, pul′vi·nat′ed.** [< L *pulvinatus* < *pulvinus* cushion]

pul·vi·nus (pul·vī′nəs) *n. pl.* **·ni** (-nī) *Bot.* The enlargement or swelling at the base of the leaves and leaflets of many plants. [< L, cushion]

pu·ma (pyōō′mə) *n.* A reddish tawny American carnivore (*Felis concolor*) of the cat family, ranging from Canada to Patagonia: also called *cougar, mountain cat, mountain lion.* [< Sp. < Peruvian]

pum·ice (pum′is) *n.* Spongy or cellular volcanic lava, used as an abrasive and polishing material, especially when powdered. Also **pumice stone.** — *v.t.* **·iced, ·ic·ing** To smooth, polish, or clean with pumice. [< OF *pomis, pumis* < L *pumex, pumicis*] — **pu·mi·ceous** (pyōō·mish′əs) *adj.*

pum·mel (pum′əl) *v.t.* **·meled** or **·melled, ·mel·ing** or **·mel·ling** To pommel. — *n.* a pommel.

pump[1] (pump) *n.* A mechanical device for raising, circulating, exhausting, or compressing a liquid or gas by drawing or pressing it through openings and pipes. — *v.t.* **1.** To raise with a pump, as water or other liquid. **2.** To remove the water, etc., from. **3.** To inflate with air by means of a pump. **4.** To propel, discharge, force, etc., from or as if from a pump: The heart *pumps* blood. **5.** To cause to operate in the manner of a pump or pump handle. **6.** To question or obtain information from persistently or subtly: to *pump* a witness. **7.** To obtain (information) in such a manner. — *v.i.* **8.** To work a pump; raise water or other liquid with a pump. **9.** To move up and down like a pump or pump handle. [Prob. < MDu. *pompe*, prob. < Sp. *bomba*] — **pump′er** *n.*

pump[2] (pump) *n.* A low-cut shoe without a fastening, having either a high or a low heel. [Origin uncertain]

pum·per·nick·el (pum′pər·nik′əl) *n.* A coarse, dark, sour bread made from unsifted rye. [< G, Westphalian rye bread, orig., lout, peasant]

pump·kin (pump′kin, pung′-) *n.* **1.** A large, round, edible, yellow-orange fruit borne by a coarse trailing vine (*Cucurbita pepo*) with heart-shaped leaves. **2.** The vine. **3.** Any of several related European plants. [Earlier *pompion* < MF *pompon, popon* < L *pepo, peponis* < Gk. *pepon* melon, lit., ripe, cooked by the sun]

pump·kin·seed (pump′kin·sēd′, pung′-) *n.* **1.** The seed of a pumpkin. **2.** A small fresh-water sunfish (*Lepomis gibbosus*) of eastern North America.

pump priming **1.** Any device or method for priming a pump. **2.** Government spending for the purpose of stimulating business.

pun (pun) *n.* The humorous use of two words having the same or similar sounds but different meanings, or of two different, more or less incongruous meanings of the same word: also called *paronomasia.* — *v.* **punned, pun·ning** *v.i.* **1.** To make a pun or puns. — *v.t.* **2.** To affect in a specified manner by puns. [Origin uncertain] — **pun′ning·ly** *adv.*

pu·na[1] (pōō′nä) *n.* The poon, a tree.

pu·na[2] (pōō′nä) *n.* **1.** A cold, arid region at high altitudes, as in the Andes. **2.** An illness caused by rarefaction of the air; mountain sickness. [< Peruvian]

punch[1] (punch) *n.* **1.** A tool for perforating or indenting, or for driving out or in an object inserted in a hole, as a bolt or pin. **2.** A machine for impressing a design or stamping a die. — *v.t.* To perforate, shape, indent, etc., with a punch. [Prob. short for PUNCHEON[1]]

PUNCHES
a Blacksmith's square. *b* Center. *c* Revolving belt. *d* Ticket. *e, g* Stamping. *f, h, i* Cutting.

punch[2] (punch) *v.t.* **1.** To strike sharply, especially with the fist. **2.** To poke with a stick; prod. **3.** To operate; work; use: to *punch* a time clock. **4.** *U.S.* In the West, to drive (cattle). — *n.* **1.** A swift blow with the fist; also, a thrust or nudge. **2.** *Slang* Vitality; force. — **Syn.** See BLOW[2]. [Prob. var. of POUNCE[2]] — **punch′er** *n.*

punch[3] (punch) *n.* A beverage having wine or spirits, milk, tea, or fruit juices as a basic ingredient, sweetened, sometimes spiced, and diluted with water. [? < Hind. *pānch* < Skt. *pañchan* five; from the five original ingredients: arrack, tea, sugar, water, and lemon]

Punch (punch) The quarrelsome, grotesque hero of a comic

puppet show, **Punch and Judy**, who habitually fights with his wife, Judy. — **pleased as Punch** Extremely pleased; highly gratified. [Short for PUNCHINELLO]

punch bowl A large bowl for serving punch.

punch card In data processing, a card having a well-defined arrangement of positions by means of which information can be stored by the presence or absence of punched holes. Also **punched card** (puncht).

punch-drunk (punch′drungk′) *adj.* **1.** Suffering from the effects of repeated blows to the head so as to be groggy, slow in movement, speech, etc. **2.** Confused; dazed. Also *Slang* **punch′y** (punch′ē).

pun·cheon[1] (pun′chən) *n.* **1.** An upright supporting timber. **2.** A punch or perforating tool, especially one for chipping stone or for stamping figures on plate or other material. **3.** A broad, heavy piece of roughly dressed timber, having one flat, hewed side. [< OF *ponçon, poinchon* a punch, ult. < L *punctus*, pp. of *pungere* to prick]

pun·cheon[2] (pun′chən) *n.* **1.** A liquor cask of variable capacity, from 72 to 120 gallons. **2.** A liquor measure of varying amount, usually of wine; in England, 84 gallons. [< OF *ponçon, poinchon.* See PUNCHEON[1].]

Pun·chi·nel·lo (pun′chə·nel′ō) *n. pl.* **·los** or **·loes** **1.** A character in an Italian burlesque or puppet show, the original of the English Punch. **2.** Any comic or grotesque character; buffoon. [Earlier *polichinello* < dial. Ital. (Neapolitan) *Polcenella*] Also **pun′chi·nel′lo.**

punch·ing bag (pun′ching) An inflated or stuffed ball, usually suspended, that is punched with the fists for exercise.

punch line *U.S. Informal* The last line or element of a joke, story, speech, etc., that gives it humor and force.

punch press A machine equipped with dies for cutting or forming metal.

punc·tate (pungk′tāt) *adj.* Covered or studded with dots, points, or minute depressions; dotted. Also **punc′tat·ed.** [< NL *punctatus* < L *punctum* point] — **punc·ta′tion** *n.*

punc·til·i·o (pungk·til′ē·ō) *n. pl.* **·i·os** A fine point of etiquette, procedure, or ceremony. [< Sp. *puntillo*, dim. of *punto* point < Ital. *puntiglio* < L *punctum*]

punc·til·i·ous (pungk·til′ē·əs) *adj.* **1.** Very careful or exact in the observance of forms of etiquette, etc. **2.** Of or pertaining to precise etiquette. — **Syn.** See METICULOUS. — **punc·til′i·ous·ly** *adv.* — **punc·til′i·ous·ness** *n.*

punc·tu·al (pungk′chōō·əl) *adj.* **1.** Acting or arriving promptly. **2.** Done or made precisely at an appointed time, as a payment. **3.** Punctilious; exact. **4.** Consisting of or confined to a point as related to space. [< Med.L *punctualis* < L *punctus* pricking, point] — **punc′tu·al·ly** *adv.*

punc·tu·al·i·ty (pungk′chōō·al′ə·tē) *n. pl.* **·ties** The quality, characteristic, or act of being punctual.

punc·tu·ate (pungk′chōō·āt) *v.* **·at·ed, ·at·ing** *v.t.* **1.** To divide or mark with punctuation. **2.** To interrupt at intervals. **3.** To emphasize; stress. — *v.i.* **4.** To use punctuation. [< Med.L *punctuatus*, pp. of *punctuare* < L *punctus* point] — **punc′tu·a′tor** *n.*

punc·tu·a·tion (pungk′chōō·ā′shən) *n.* The use of points or marks in written or printed matter to indicate the separation of the words into sentences, clauses, and phrases, and to aid in the better comprehension of the meaning and grammatical relation of the words; also, the marks so used (**punctuation marks**). [< Med.L *punctuatio, -onis*] — **punc′tu·a′tive** *adj.* The chief punctuation marks are:

period	.	exclamation mark	!
colon	:	parentheses	( )
semicolon	;	brackets	[ ]
comma	,	dash	—
question mark	?	hyphen	-
(interrogation point)		quotation marks	" "

punc·ture (pungk′chər) *v.* **·tured, ·tur·ing** *v.t.* **1.** To pierce with a sharp point. **2.** To make by pricking, as a hole. **3.** To cause to collapse: to *puncture* a reputation. — *v.i.* **4.** To be pierced or punctured. — *n.* **1.** A small hole, as in a pneumatic tire, made by piercing with a sharp point. **2.** A minute depression; pit. **3.** The act of puncturing. [< L *punctura* prick < *punctus*, pp. of *pungere* to prick]

pun·dit (pun′dit) *n.* **1.** A learned Brahman, especially one versed in Sanskrit lore and in the science, laws, and religion of the Hindus. **2.** Any learned man. [< Hind. *pandit* < Skt. *pandita*, lit., learned, skilled]

pung (pung) *n. U.S. Dial.* A low box sled for one horse. [Short for *tom pung*, prob. alter. of TOBOGGAN]

pun·gent (pun′jənt) *adj.* **1.** Causing a sharp pricking, piercing, or acrid effect on the sense of taste or smell; keen; penetrating: a *pungent* odor. **2.** Affecting the mind or feelings as by sharp points, so as to cause pain; piercing. **3.** Caustic; biting; racy: *pungent* sarcasm. **4.** Ending in a hard sharp point, as a pine needle. — **Syn.** See RACY. [< L *pungens, -entis*, ppr. of *pungere* to prick] — **pun′gence** (-jəns), **pun′gen·cy** *n.* — **pun′gent·ly** *adv.*

Pu·nic (pyōō′nik) *adj.* **1.** Of or pertaining to ancient Carthage or the Carthaginians, who were regarded by the Romans as treacherous. **2.** Faithless; untrustworthy. — *n.* The Northwest Semitic language of the Carthaginians, a dialect of Phoenician. [< L *punicus* < *poenicus* < *Poenus* Carthaginian, Phoenician < Gk. *Phoinix, -ikos*]

Punic Wars See table for WAR.

pun·ish (pun′ish) *v.t.* **1.** To subject to pain, confinement, or other penalty for a crime or fault. **2.** To subject the perpetrator of (an offense) to a penalty: to *punish* forgery. **3.** To use roughly; injure; hurt. **4.** To make heavy inroads upon; deplete, as a stock of food. [< OF *puniss-*, stem of *punir* < L *punire* to punish < *poenire* < *poena* punishment, penalty, fine] — **pun′ish·er** *n.*

pun·ish·a·ble (pun′ish·ə·bəl) *adj.* Deserving of or liable to punishment, as offenders or offenses: a crime *punishable* by death. — **pun′ish·a·bil′i·ty** *n.*

pun·ish·ment (pun′ish·mənt) *n.* **1.** A penalty imposed, as for transgression of law. ◆ Collateral adjective: *penal.* **2.** Any ill suffered in consequence of wrongdoing. **3.** The act of punishing. **4.** *Informal* Rough handling, as in a prize fight, a naval engagement, etc.

pu·ni·tive (pyōō′nə·tiv) *adj.* **1.** Pertaining to or inflicting punishment: One must often resort to *punitive* measures. **2.** *Law* Of a character to punish or vindicate. Also **pu′ni·to·ry** (-tôr′ē, -tō′rē). [< Med.L *punitivus* or MF *punitif* < L *punitus*, pp. of *punire*. See PUNISH.] — **pu′ni·tive·ly** *adv.* — **pu′ni·tive·ness** *n.*

Pun·jab (pun′jäb, pun·jäb′) **1.** A region of NW India and West Pakistan. **2.** A former province of British India, divided in 1947 between Punjab State, India, and West Pakistan. **3.** A State of India; 47,456 sq. mi.; pop. 13,935,000 (est. 1971); capital, Chandigarh.

Punjab Hill States A former political agency under British rule in NW India, consisting of 22 princely states that came to be part of India.

Pun·ja·bi (pun·jä′bē) *n.* **1.** A native of the Punjab. **2.** The Sanskritic language of the Punjab: also spelled *Panjabi.*

Punjab States A former political agency under British rule in NW India, consisting of 14 princely states and also, after 1936, the Punjab Hill States.

punk[1] (pungk) *n.* **1.** Wood decayed through the action of a fungus, useful as tinder: also called *spunk, touchwood.* **2.** An artificial preparation used to repel insects, etc. [< Algonquian. Cf. Lenape *punk* ashes.]

punk[2] (pungk) *n.* **1.** *U.S. Slang* Rubbish; nonsense. **2.** *U.S. Slang* A petty hoodlum. **3.** *U.S. Slang* A young, inexperienced boy or man: a contemptuous term. **4.** *Obs.* A prostitute. — *adj. U.S. Slang* **1.** Worthless; poor; inferior. **2.** Not in good health; unwell. [Origin uncertain]

pun·ka (pung′kə) *n.* A fan; especially, a rectangular strip of cloth, etc., swung from the ceiling and moved by a servant or by machinery. Also **pun′kah.** [< Hind. *pankhā* fan < Skt. *pakshaka* < *paksha* wing]

pun·ky (pung′kē) *n. pl.* **·kies** A minute, annoying, blood-sucking gnat or midge (genus *Culicoides*). Also **pun′key, pun′kie.** [< Du. *punki* < Algonquian (Lenape) *punk, ponk,* orig., fine ashes]

pun·ster (pun′stər) *n.* One addicted to punning. Also **pun′ner.**

punt[1] (punt) *n.* A flat-bottomed, square-ended boat, often propelled by a pole and usually having a seat in the middle and a well or seat at one or both ends, used in shallow waters. — *v.t.* **1.** To propel (a boat) by pushing with a pole against the bottom of a shallow stream, lake, etc. **2.** To convey in a punt. — *v.i.* **3.** To go or hunt in a punt. [OE < L *ponto, -onis* punt, pontoon < *pons, pontis* bridge] — **punt′er** *n.*

PUNT

punt[2] (punt) *v.i.* To gamble or bet, especially against a bank, as at faro, roulette, or baccarat. [< F *ponter* < *ponte* point < Sp. *punto* < L *punctum*] — **punt′er** *n.*

punt[3] (punt) *n.* In football, a kick made by dropping the ball from the hands and kicking it before it strikes the ground. — *v.t. & v.i.* In football, to propel (the ball) with a punt. [? Var. of BUNT] — **punt′er** *n.*

Pun·ta A·re·nas (pōōn′tä ä·rā′näs) The southernmost city in the world, a port in Chile on the Strait of Magellan; pop. 64,958 (est. 1970): also *Magallanes.*

pun·to (pun′tō) *n.* A hit or thrust in fencing. [< Ital. or Sp., point < L *punctum*]

pun·ty (pun′tē) *n. pl.* **·ties** An iron rod used in glassmaking to handle the hot glass: also called *pontil.* [< F *pontil* < LL *pontilis* bridgelike < L *pons* bridge]

pu·ny (pyōō′nē) *adj.* **·ni·er, ·ni·est** **1.** Of small and feeble development or importance; weak and insignificant. **2.** *Obs.* Puisne: born later; younger. [< OF *puisne.* See PUISNE.] — **pu′ni·ly** *adv.* — **pu′ni·ness** *n.*

pup (pup) *n.* **1.** A puppy (def. 1). **2.** The young of the seal, the shark, and certain other animals. — *v.i.* **pupped, pupping** To bring forth pups. [Short for PUPPY]

pu·pa (pyōō′pə) *n. pl.* **·pae** (-pē) **1.** *Entomol.* **a** The quiescent stage in the development of an insect, following the larval and preceding the adult stage. **b** An insect in such a

stage. **2.** *Zool.* A developmental state in some echinoderms. [< NL < L, girl, doll, puppet] — **pu′pal** *adj.*

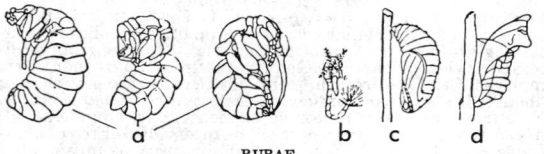

PUPAE

a Three pupal stages of a bumblebee. *b* Aquatic pupa of a gnat. *c* Suspended pupa of a butterfly. *d* Girdled pupa of a butterfly.

pu·pate (pyōō′pāt) *v.i.* **·pat·ed, ·pat·ing** To enter upon or undergo the pupal condition. — **pu·pa′tion** *n.*

pu·pil[1] (pyōō′pəl) *n.* **1.** A person of any age under the care of a teacher; learner. **2.** In civil law, a minor who is under the age of puberty and has a guardian. — **Syn.** See STUDENT. [< OF *pupille*, orig., orphan, ward < L *pupillus*, dim. of *pupus* boy and *pupilla*, dim. of *pupa* girl]

pu·pil[2] (pyōō′pəl) *n. Anat.* The contractile opening in the iris of the eye, through which light reaches the retina. [< OF *pupille* < L *pupilla* figure reflected in the eye, pupil of the eye, dim. of *pupa*]

pu·pil·age (pyōō′pəl·ij) *n.* The state or period of being a pupil. Also **pu′pil·lage.**

pu·pi·lar·i·ty (pyōō′pə·lar′ə·tē) *n.* In Scots law, the interval between birth and the age of 14 in males and 12 in females. Also **pu′pil·lar′i·ty.** [< OF *pupillarite* < L *pupillaris* pertaining to an orphan]

pu·pil·lar·y[1] (pyōō′pə·ler′ē) *adj.* Of or pertaining to a pupil or a ward. [< MF *pupillaire* or < L *pupillaris*] Also **pu′pi·lar·y.**

pu·pil·lar·y[2] (pyōō′pə·ler′ē) *adj.* Of or pertaining to the pupil of the eye.

Pu·pin (pyōō·pēn′, *Hungarian* pōō·pēn′), **Michael Idvorsky,** 1858–1935, U.S. physicist and inventor born in Hungary.

pu·pip·a·rous (pyōō·pip′ər·əs) *adj.* Of or pertaining to a division (*Pupipara*) of dipterous insects in which the young are born ready to pupate, as bat ticks, sheep ticks, etc. [< NL *pupiparus* < *pupa* + L *parere* to bring forth]

pup·pet (pup′it) *n.* **1.** A small figure of a person, animal, etc., usually with a cloth body and solid head fitting over and animated by the hand. **2.** A marionette. **3.** One slavishly subject to the will of another; a tool. **4.** A toy in the form of a person; doll. — *adj.* **1.** Of or pertaining to puppets. **2.** Not autonomous: a *puppet* state. [< OF *poupette* < L *pupa* girl, doll, puppet]

pup·pet·eer (pup′i·tir′) *n.* One who manipulates puppets.

pup·pet·ry (pup′it·rē) *n.* The performances of puppets or the manipulation of puppets; mummery.

puppet show A drama with puppets for the actors.

Pup·pis (pup′is) *n.* A constellation, the Poop (of a ship). See CONSTELLATION. [< L]

pup·py (pup′ē) *n. pl.* **·pies** **1.** A young dog: also called *pup.* **2.** A pup (def. 2). **3.** A conceited young man. [< OF *poupee, popee* < L *pupa* girl, doll] — **pup′py·ish** *adj.*

puppy love Sentimental, adolescent love or infatuation.

pup tent A shelter tent (which see).

pur (pûr) See PURR.

Pu·ra·na (pōō·rä′nə) *n.* Any of a number of Hindu scriptures in the form of verse dialogues, coming next after the Vedas and dealing especially with the god Vishnu and his incarnations. [< Skt. *purāna*, lit., ancient < *purā* of old]

pur·blind (pûr′blind′) *adj.* **1.** Afflicted with dimness of vision. **2.** Having little or no insight or understanding. **3.** *Obs.* Totally blind. [ME *purblind* < *pur* (< OF, plain) + *blind* blind] — **pur′blind′ly** *adv.* — **pur′blind′ness** *n.*

Pur·cell (pûr′sal), **Henry,** 1658?–95, English composer.

Pur·chas (pûr′chəs), **Samuel,** 1575?–1626, English clergyman, traveler, and writer.

pur·chas·a·ble (pûr′chəs·ə·bəl) *adj.* **1.** That can be purchased. **2.** Venal; corrupt. — **pur′chas·a·bil′i·ty** *n.*

pur·chase (pûr′chəs) *v.t.* **·chased, ·chas·ing** **1.** To acquire by paying money or its equivalent; buy. **2.** To obtain by exertion, sacrifice, flattery, etc. **3.** *Law* To acquire (property) by lawful means other than descent or inheritance. **4.** To move, hoist, or hold by a mechanical purchase. — *n.* **1.** Something purchased: especially, that which is bought with money. **2.** The act of purchasing. **3.** A mechanical hold or grip. **4.** A device that gives a mechanical advantage, as a tackle or lever; also, leverage. **5.** Any means of increasing influence or advantage. **6.** *Law* The act of acquiring property by payment of a price or value. **b** Any lawful mode of acquiring property other than by inheritance or descent or by the mere operation of law. **7.** Value; worth. [< AF *purchacer*, OF *porchacier* to seek for < *pur-*, *por-* for (< L *pro-*) + *chacier* to chase] — **pur′chas·er** *n.*

pur·dah (pûr′də) *n.* *Anglo-Indian* **1.** A curtain or screen used to seclude women. **2.** The state or system of such seclusion. [< Urdu and Persian *pardah*]

pure (pyŏŏr) *adj.* **pur·er, pur·est 1.** Free from mixture or contact with that which weakens, impairs, or pollutes; containing no foreign or vitiating material. **2.** Free from adulteration; clear; clean. **3.** Genuine; stainless: *pure food; pure motives.* **4.** Free from moral defilement; innocent; chaste; unsullied; also, free from coarseness; refined: a *pure* life. **5.** Free from foreign or imported elements, as a language. **6.** *Music* **a** Mathematically correct, as intervals. **b** Free of overtones: *pure* tones. **7.** Free of harsh qualities, as music; also, correct in form or style; finished. **8.** *Philos.* Considered apart from its attributes or from concrete experience; abstract; also, a priori. **9.** *Phonet.* Having a single, unvarying tone or sound; monophthongal: said of vowels. **10.** Concerned with fundamental research, as distinguished from practical application; theoretical: said of sciences. **11.** *Genetics* Breeding true with respect to one or more characters; homozygous. **12.** Nothing but; sheer: *pure* luck. [< OF *pur* < L *purus* clean, pure] — **pure′ness** *n.*
— **Syn. 1, 2.** unblemished, spotless, immaculate. **4.** continent, undefiled, virtuous. **5.** *Pure* and *absolute*, as here compared, denote freedom from anything extraneous. *Pure* suggests the absence of any element felt to be alien or nonessential: *pure* lyric poetry, *pure* French. *Absolute* is usually applied to abstract terms or ideas considered as altogether independent of external objects or relationships: *absolute* motion. — **Ant.** impure, mixed, tarnished, tainted, polluted, corrupt, immoral.

pure·bred (*adj.* pyŏŏr′bred′; *n.* pyŏŏr′bred′) *adj.* *Biol.* Bred from stock having had no admixture for many generations: said especially of livestock. — *n.* A purebred animal.

pure culture *Bacteriol.* A nutrient medium for the isolation and cultivation of microorganisms of a particular kind.

pu·rée (pyŏŏ·rā′, pyŏŏr′ā; *Fr.* pü·rā′) *n.* A thick pulp, usually of vegetables, boiled and strained. — *v.t.* **·réed ·rée·ing** To put (cooked or soft food) through a sieve, blender, etc.: to *purée* vegetables. [< F < OF, pp. fem. of *purer* to strain < L *purare* to purify < *purus* pure]

pure line *Genetics* A strain of plants or animals that through self-fertilization, continued inbreeding, or other means, exhibits a high degree of genetic stability.

pure·ly (pyŏŏr′lē) *adv.* **1.** So as to be free from admixture, taint, or any harmful substance. **2.** Chastely; innocently. **3.** Completely; totally. **4.** Merely; simply.

pur·fle (pûr′fəl) *v.t.* **·fled, ·fling** To decorate, as with a wrought or flowered border: also *purl.* — *n.* A richly ornamented border: also **pur′fling.** [< OF *profiler, pourfiler < por-, pour-* for (< L *pro-*) + *fil* thread (< L *filum*)]

pur·ga·tion (pûr·gā′shən) *n.* The act of purging; catharsis. [< OF *purgacion* < L *purgatio, -onis < purgatus*, pp. of *purgare.* See PURGE.]

pur·ga·tive (pûr′gə·tiv) *adj.* Tending to purge; especially, precipitating a bowel movement. — *n.* A purgative agent; a cathartic.

pur·ga·to·ri·al (pûr′gə·tôr′ē·əl, -tō′rē-) *adj.* **1.** Pertaining to purgatory. **2.** Tending to purge from sin.

pur·ga·to·ry (pûr′gə·tôr′ē, -tō′rē) *n.* *pl.* **·ries 1.** In Roman Catholic theology, a state or place where the souls of those who have died penitent are made fit for paradise by expiating venial sins and undergoing any punishment remaining for previously forgiven sins. **2.** Any place or state of temporary banishment, suffering, or punishment. [< AF *purgatorie*, OF *purgatoire* < Med.L *purgatorium* < LL *purgatorius* cleansing < *purgare.* See PURGE.]

purge (pûrj) *v.* **purged, purg·ing** *v.t.* **1.** To cleanse of what is impure or extraneous; purify. **2.** To remove (impurities, etc.) in cleansing: with *away, off,* or *out.* **3.** To rid (a group, nation, etc.) of elements regarded as undesirable or inimical, especially by killing. **4.** To remove or kill (a person or persons) in such a manner. **5.** To cleanse or rid of sin, fault, or defilement. **6.** *Med.* **a** To cause evacuation of (the bowels, etc.). **b** To induce evacuation of the bowels of. **7.** *Law* To clear of accusation, suspicion, or guilt. — *v.i.* **8.** To become clean or pure. **9.** *Med.* To have or induce evacuation of the bowels, etc. — *n.* **1.** The act or process of purging. **2.** That which purges; especially, a medicine causing evacuation of the bowels. [< OF *purgier* < L *purgare* to cleanse < *purigare < purus* pure] — **purg′er** *n.* — **purg′ing** *n.*

Pu·ri (pōō′rē) A port town and Hindu pilgrimage center on the Bay of Bengal in SW Orissa, India; pop. about 49,000. See JUGGERNAUT.

pu·ri·fi·ca·tion (pyŏŏr′ə·fə·kā′shən) *n.* The act or operation of purifying. ◆ Collateral adjective: *lustral.* [< OF, or < L *purificatio, -onis < purificare.* See PURIFY.]

pu·ri·fy (pyŏŏr′ə·fī) *v.* **·fied, ·fy·ing** *v.t.* **1.** To make pure or clean; rid of extraneous or noxious matter. **2.** To free from sin or defilement. **3.** To free of foreign or debasing elements, as a language. — *v.i.* **4.** To become pure. [< OF *purifier* < L *purificare < purus* pure + *facere* to make] — **pu·rif·i·ca·to·ry** (pyŏŏ·rif′ə·kə·tôr′ē, -tō′rē) *adj.* — **pu′ri·fi′er** *n.*
— **Syn. 1.** cleanse, wash, filter. **3.** refine. — **Ant.** contaminate, taint, pollute, defile, corrupt.

Pu·rim (pŏŏr′im, pyŏŏr′im; *Hebrew* pōō·rēm′) *n.* A Jewish festival commemorating the defeat of Haman's plot to massacre the Jews (*Esth.* ix 26), observed about the first of March. [< Hebrew *pūrīm,* pl. of *pūr* lot]

pu·rine (pyŏŏr′ēn, -in) *n.* *Biochem.* A white, crystalline compound, C₅H₄N₄, derived from uric acid. Also **pu·rin** (pyŏŏr′in). [< G *purin* < L *purus* pure + NL *uricum* uric acid + *-in* -ine²]

purine group *Biochem.* An important group of organic compounds widely distributed in nature and related to purine, as caffeine, xanthine, uric acid, etc.

pur·ist (pyŏŏr′ist) *n.* **1.** One who believes in or practices exact or meticulous usage, as of a language, style, etc. **2.** One who practices or advocates an art form in which primary stress is placed on structural discipline, as in works of a geometric nature. — **pur′ism** *n.* — **pu·ris′tic** *adj.*

pu·ri·tan (pyŏŏr′ə·tən) *n. Sometimes cap.* One who is scrupulously strict or exacting in his religious or moral life: often used disparagingly. — *adj.* Of or pertaining to a puritan or puritans; puritanical.

Pu·ri·tan (pyŏŏr′ə·tən) *n.* One of a group of English Protestants who in the 16th and 17th centuries advocated simpler forms of creed and ritual in the Church of England. — *adj.* Of or pertaining to the Puritans or to their beliefs or customs. [< LL *puritas* purity < L *purus* pure] — **Pu′ri·tan·ism** *n.*

pu·ri·tan·i·cal (pyŏŏr′ə·tan′i·kəl) *adj.* **1.** Rigidly scrupulous or exacting in religious observance or morals; strict. **2.** *Often cap.* Of or characteristic of the Puritans. Also **pu′ri·tan′ic.** — **pu′ri·tan′i·cal·ly** *adv.* — **pu′ri·tan′i·cal·ness** *n.*

pu·ri·tan·ism (pyŏŏr′ə·tən·iz′əm) *n. Sometimes cap.* Strictness in religious conduct or morals: often used disparagingly.

pu·ri·ty (pyŏŏr′ə·tē) *n.* **1.** The quality or state of being pure. **2.** Freedom from dirt or foreign or adulterating matter; cleanness. **3.** Freedom from sinister or improper design; innocence. **4.** Absence of admixture. **5.** Saturation: said of a color. **6.** The use of no foreign words, phrases, or idioms; also, precise or accepted usage of words.

Pur·kin·je (pŏŏr′kin·ye), **Johannes Evangelista,** 1787–1869, Czech physiologist, patriot, and poet.

purl¹ (pûrl) *v.i.* **1.** To whirl; turn. **2.** To flow with a bubbling sound; ripple. **3.** To move in eddies. — *n.* **1.** A circling movement of water; an eddy. **2.** A gentle, continued murmur, as of a rippling stream. [Cf. Norw. *purla* to gush out, bubble up]

purl² (pûrl) *v.t.* **1.** In knitting, to make (a stitch) backward. **2.** To edge with lace, embroidery, etc. Also spelled *pearl.* **3.** To purfle. — *v.i.* **4.** To do edging with lace, etc.: also spelled *pearl.* — *n.* **1.** An edge of lace, embroidery, etc. **2.** In knitting, the inversion of the knit stitch, giving a horizontal rib effect. Also spelled *pearl.* **3.** A spiral of gold or silver wire used in lacework. [Earlier *pyrle,* orig. twisted gold or silver thread < *pyrl* twist; ult. origin unknown]

pur·lieu (pûr′lōō) *n.* **1.** *pl.* The outlying districts or outskirts of any place. **2.** A place in which one is free to come and go; a haunt. **3.** Formerly, ground unlawfully taken from a royal forest, but afterward disafforested and restored to its rightful owners. [< AF *puralee* < OF < *puraler* to go through < *pur-* through (< L *per-*) + *aler* to go; infl. in form by MF *lieu* place]

pur·lin (pûr′lin) *n.* One of several horizontal timbers supporting rafters. Also **pur′line** (-lin). For illustration see ROOF. [ME *purlyn,* prob. < OF]

pur·loin (pûr·loin′) *v.t. & v.i.* To steal; filch. — **Syn.** See STEAL. [< AF *purloignier,* OF *porloignier* to remove, put far off < *pur-, por-* for (< L *pro-*) + *loing, loin* far (< L *longe*)] — **pur·loin′er** *n.*

pur·ple (pûr′pəl) *n.* **1.** A color of mingled red and blue, between crimson and violet. **2.** Cloth or a garment of this color, worn formerly by sovereigns. **3.** Royal power or dignity; preeminence in rank or wealth: usually in the phrase *born to the purple.* **4.** The office of a cardinal, from the official red hat and robes. **5.** The office of a bishop. — *v.t. & v.i.* **·pled, ·pling** To make or become purple. — *adj.* **1.** Of the color of purple. **2.** Imperial; regal. **3.** Ornate; flowery: a *purple* passage of prose. [OE (Northumbrian), var. of OE *purpure* < OF *purpre* < L *purpura,* orig., shellfish yielding Tyrian purple dye, or cloth dyed with it < Gk. *porphyra*]

pur·ple-fringed orchid (pûr′pəl·frinjd′) A terrestrial orchid of North America (genus *Habenaria*) with fragrant purplish or white flowers.

purple gallinule A gallinule (*Porphyrula martinica*) of tropical America, having purple, green, blue, or white plumage, a yellow bill, and yellow legs.

Purple Heart A decoration of honor of the **Order of the Purple Heart** established by George Washington in 1782 and revived in 1932, awarded to members of the armed forces or to citizens of the United States honorably wounded in action against the enemy. See DECORATION. Abbr. *PH*

purple martin See under MARTIN.
purple medic Alfalfa.
purple osier Red osier (which see).
pur·plish (pûr′plish) *adj.* Somewhat purple.

pur·port (pûr′pôrt, -pōrt; *for v., also* pər·pôrt′) *v.t.* **1.** To have or bear as its meaning; signify; imply. **2.** To claim or profess (to be), especially falsely. — *n.* **1.** That which is conveyed or suggested to the mind as the meaning or intention; import; significance. **2.** The substance of a statement, etc., given in other than the exact words. [< AF or OF *purporter* to extend < *pur-* forth (< L *pro-*) + *porter* to carry (< L *portare*)] — **pur·port′ed·ly** *adv.* — **Syn.** (verb) **1.** suggest, intimate. **2.** pretend.

pur·pose (pûr′pəs) *n.* **1.** An idea or ideal kept before the mind as an end of effort or action; plan; design; aim. **2.** A particular thing to be effected or attained. **3.** Practical advantage or result; consequence; use: words to little *purpose.* **4.** Settled resolution; determination; constancy. **5.** Purport; intent, as of spoken or written language. **6.** A proposition; proposal; question at issue. — **on purpose** Intentionally. — *v.t. & v.i.* **·posed, ·pos·ing** To have the intention of doing or accomplishing (something); intend; aim. [< OF *purpos* < *porposer*, var. of *proposer*. See PROPOSE.] — **Syn.** (noun) **1.** *Purpose, intent, intention, aim, goal, design, end, object,* and *objective* describe what one hopes to effect for a plan or course of action. *Purpose* is perhaps the strongest of these words; it implies a fixed determination and a clear exercise of the will: his *purpose* in coming was to crush the revolt. *Intent* is like *purpose,* but shows somewhat less determination; it is now largely restricted to legal usage: assault with deadly *intent. Intention* is even weaker, denoting chiefly what one has decided on: I have no *intention* of reading his novel. *Aim* and *goal* are metaphors from archery and racing; they agree in connoting that toward which one's efforts are directed: his *goal* was to be the head of his class. *Design* stresses the careful planning and arranging of details that are often required for the successful achievement of a *purpose; end* refers to the final step or stage of a *design Object* and *objective* are sometimes interchanged with *end,* but they are also used to indicate a secondary *purpose,* or an intermediate step in a *design; objective* is the more concrete word, and is frequently used in military or quasi-military contexts: capture of the fort was the army's next *objective.* See REASON. — (verb) See PROPOSE.

pur·pose·ful (pûr′pəs-fəl) *adj.* Having or marked by purpose; intentional; important; significant. — **pur′pose·ful·ly** *adv.* — **pur′pose·ful·ness** *n.*

pur·pose·less (pûr′pəs-lis) *adj.* Having no definite purpose; aimless. — **pur′pose·less·ly** *adv.*

pur·pose·ly (pûr′pəs-lē) *adv.* For a purpose; intentionally; deliberately; on purpose.

pur·po·sive (pûr′pə-siv) *adj.* **1.** Pertaining to, having, or indicating purpose. **2.** Functional; useful. — **pur′po·sive·ly** *adv.* — **pur′po·sive·ness** *n.*

pur·pu·ra (pûr′pyŏŏ-rə) *n. Pathol.* A disease characterized by livid or purple spots on the skin caused by extravasated blood. [< L. See PURPLE.]

pur·pure (pûr′pyŏŏr) *n. Heraldry* Purple, one of the colors or tinctures used in heraldic description. [OE]

pur·pu·ric (pûr-pyŏŏr′ik) *adj.* **1.** Of or pertaining to a purple tint. **2.** Relating to or resembling purpura.

pur·pu·rin (pûr′pyŏŏ-rin) *n. Chem.* A red crystalline dyestuff and staining agent, $C_{14}H_8O_5$, contained in madder, and prepared synthetically. Also **pur′pu·rine** (-rēn). [< L *purpura* purple + -IN]

purr (pûr) *n.* A murmuring sound, such as a cat makes when pleased. — *v.i.* **1.** To make such a sound. — *v.t.* **2.** To express by or as by purring. Also spelled *pur.* [Imit.]

purse (pûrs) *n.* **1.** A small bag or pouch, especially one for carrying money. **2.** Anything used for carrying money on the person. **3.** Available resources or means; treasury: the public *purse.* **4.** A sum of money offered as a prize. — *v.t.* **pursed, purs·ing** **1.** To contract into wrinkles or folds; pucker: to *purse* the lips. **2.** *Rare* To place in a purse. [OE *purs* < LL *bursa* < Gk. *byrsa* skin, hide. Doublet of BURSE.]

purs·er (pûr′sər) *n.* **1.** An officer having charge of the accounts, etc., of a vessel. **2.** Formerly, a naval paymaster.

purse seine A type of large, circular seine that is pulled by two boats so that it completely surrounds a school of fish. Its bottom is then drawn shut, thus capturing the fish.

purs·lane (pûrs′lin, -lān) *n.* A common garden herb (*Portulaca oleracea*) with reddish green stem and leaves and small yellow flowers, used as a salad: also called *pussley.* [< OF *porcelaine* < L *porcilaca* < *portulaca*]

pur·su·ance (pər-sōō′əns) *n.* The act of pursuing; a following up; prosecution: usually in the phrase **in pursuance of.**

pur·su·ant (pər-sōō′ənt) *adj.* Done in accordance with or by reason of something; conformable. — *adv.* In accordance; agreeably: usually with *to:* also **pur·su′ant·ly.** [< OF *poursuiant,* ppr. of *poursuir*]

pur·sue (pər-sōō′) *v.* **·sued, ·su·ing** *v.t.* **1.** To follow in an attempt to overtake or capture; chase. **2.** To seek or attain: to *pursue* fame. **3.** To advance along the course of; keep to the direction or provisions of, as a path, plan, or system. **4.** To apply one's energies to or have as one's profession or chief interest: to *pursue* one's studies. **5.** To follow persistently; harass; worry. — *v.i.* **6.** To follow; chase. **7.** To continue; persist. [< AF *pursuer,* OF *porsievre* < LL *prosequere* < L *prosequi < pro-* forth + *sequi* to follow] — **pur·su′a·ble** *adj.* — **pur·su′er** *n.*

pur·suit (pər-sōōt′) *n.* **1.** The act of pursuing; a chase. **2.** That which is followed as a continued employment, pastime, etc. — **Syn.** See OCCUPATION. [< AF *purseute,* OF *porsieute, poursuite < porsievre.* See PURSUE.]

pursuit plane *Mil.* A fighter plane (which see).

pur·sui·vant (pûr′swi·vənt) *n.* **1.** An attendant upon a herald, an officer of the Herald's College. **2.** *Obs.* A follower; especially, a military attendant of the king. [< OF *porsivant,* ppr. of *porsievre.* See PURSUE.]

purs·y (pûr′sē) *adj.* **purs·i·er, purs·i·est** **1.** Short-breathed; asthmatic. **2.** Fat; hefty. [Earlier *pursive* < AF *pursif,* OF *polsif < polser* to pant, gasp] — **purs′i·ness** *n.*

pur·te·nance (pûr′tə·nəns) *n. Obs.* **1.** Appurtenance. **2.** The inner organs of an animal. [< AF *purtinaunt,* OF *partenant.* See PERTINENT.]

pu·ru·lent (pyŏŏr′ə·lənt, -yə·lənt) *adj.* Consisting of or secreting pus; suppurating. [< L *purulentus < pus, puris* pus] — **pu′ru·lence** or **·len·cy** *n.* — **pu′ru·lent·ly** *adv.*

Pu·rus (pŏō·rōōs′) A river in SE Peru and western Brazil, flowing about 2,100 miles NE to the Amazon.

pur·vey (pər-vā′) *v.t. & v.i.* To furnish (provisions, etc.). [< AF *purveier* < L *providere.* Doublet of PROVIDE.]

pur·vey·ance (pər-vā′əns) *n.* **1.** The act of purveying. **2.** That which is purveyed or supplied; provisions. [< OF *purveance* < L *providentia.* See PROVIDENCE.]

pur·vey·or (pər-vā′ər) *n.* **1.** One who furnishes supplies, especially food. **2.** Formerly, an officer who made provision for the king's household.

pur·view (pûr′vyŏō) *n.* **1.** Extent, sphere, or scope of anything, as of official authority. **2.** Range of view, experience, or understanding; outlook. **3.** *Law* The body or the scope or limit of a statute. [< AF *purveu* provided, OF *porveu,* pp. of *porveier.* See PURVEY. Orig. in AF legal phrases *purveu est* it is provided and *purveu que* provided that.]

pus (pus) *n.* A viscid, yellowish secretion from inflamed or suppurating tissues, as in healing wounds. [< L]

Pu·san (pōō·sän) A port city in SE South Korea, on Korea Strait; pop. 1,425,703 (1966): Japanese *Fusan.*

Pu·sey (pyŏō′zē), **Edward Bouverie,** 1800–82, English theologian; one of the leaders of the Oxford movement.

Pu·sey·ism (pyŏō′zē·iz′əm) *n.* Tractarianism. [after E. B. *Pusey*] — **Pu′sey·ite** *n.*

push (pŏŏsh) *v.t.* **1.** To exert force upon or against (an object) for the purpose of moving. **2.** To force (one's way), as through a crowd, jungle, etc. **3.** To press forward, prosecute, or develop with vigor and persistence: to *push* trade with South America. **4.** To urge, advocate, or promote vigorously and persistently: to *push* a new product. **5.** To bear hard upon; distress; harass: I am *pushed* for time. **6.** *Slang* To sell (narcotic drugs) illegally. — *v.i.* **7.** To exert steady pressure against something so as to move it. **8.** To move or advance vigorously or persistently: to *push* through a crowd. **9.** To exert great effort. **10.** To project; extend; reach: The island *pushed* far out into the sea. — *n.* **1.** The act of pushing; a shove. **2.** *Informal* An extremity; exigency: at a *push* for money. **3.** Determined activity; energy. **4.** Anything pushed to cause action. **5.** *Slang* A number of friends or associates; crowd. **6.** An influential clique. **7.** *Austral. Slang* A group of ruffians. [< OF *poulser* < L *pulsare.* See PULSATE.]

push·ball (pŏŏsh′bôl′) *n.* A game, played with a ball 6 feet in diameter and weighing 48 pounds, in which each of two sides tries to push the ball across the opponent's goal.

push·but·ton (pŏŏsh′but′n) *adj.* Activated or carried on by or as if by push buttons: *push-button* warfare.

push button A button or knob that on being pushed opens or closes a circuit in an electric system.

push·cart (pŏŏsh′kärt′) *n.* A two- or four-wheeled cart pushed by hand, used by fruit venders, peddlers, etc.

push·er (pŏŏsh′ər) *n.* **1.** One who or that which pushes; especially, an active, energetic person. **2.** *Aeron.* An airplane with the propeller in the rear of the wings. **3.** *U.S. Slang* One who illegally sells narcotics to addicts.

push·ing (pŏŏsh′ing) *adj.* **1.** Possessing enterprise and energy. **2.** Aggressive; impertinent. — **push′ing·ly** *adv.*

Push·kin (pŏŏsh′kin), **Aleksander Sergeyevich,** 1799–1837, Russian poet.

push·o·ver (pŏŏsh′ō′vər) *n. Slang* **1.** One who is easily defeated, overcome, taken advantage of, etc.; an easy mark. **2.** Anything that can be done with little or no effort.

push·pin (pŏŏsh′pin′) *n.* A sharp pin with a large head, used for mounting and holding in place papers, drawings, etc.

push-pull (pŏŏsh′pŏŏl′) *adj. Electronics* Designating a circuit or system that uses two similar components operating in opposite phase.

Push·tu (push′tŏō) *n.* Pashto.

push-up (pŏŏsh′up′) *n.* A type of exercise in which, while lying prone, one pushes the body up from the floor with the arms, the toes remaining on the floor.

push·y (pŏŏsh′ē) *adj.* **·i·er, ·i·est** *Informal* Offensively aggressive; bossy. — **push′i·ly** *adv.* — **push′i·ness** *n.*

pu·sil·la·nim·i·ty (pyōō/sə·lə·nim/ə·tē) *n.* The state of being pusillanimous; cowardice.   [< OF *pusillanimite* < LL *pusillanimitas*]

pu·sil·lan·i·mous (pyōō/sə·lan/ə·məs) *adj.* **1.** Lacking strength of mind, courage, or spirit; cowardly. **2.** Characterized by weakness of purpose or lack of courage. [< LL *pusillanimis* < L *pusillus* very little + *animus* soul] — **pu·sil·lan/i·mous·ly** *adv.* — **pu·sil·lan/i·mous·ness** *n.*
— **Syn. 1.** timorous, faint-hearted, spiritless, recreant, dastardly. — **Ant.** brave, spirited.

puss[1] (pŏŏs) *n. Informal* **1.** A cat. **2.** A child or young woman: a term of affection. [Cf. Du. *poes*, LG *puus*, name for a cat]

puss[2] (pŏŏs) *n. Slang* The mouth; face.   [< Irish *pus* mouth, lips]

puss·ley (pus/lē) *n.* Purslane. Also **puss/ly.** [Alter. of PURSLANE]

pus·sy[1] (pŏŏs/ē) *n. pl.* **·sies** *Informal* **1.** A cat. **2.** A fuzzy catkin, as of a willow, birch, etc. [Dim. of PUSS[1]]

pus·sy[2] (pus/ē) *adj.* **pus·si·er, pus·si·est** Full of pus.

pus·sy·foot (pŏŏs/ē·fŏŏt/) *v.i.* **1.** To move softly and stealthily, as a cat does. **2.** To act or proceed without committing oneself or revealing one's intentions.

pus·sy willow (pŏŏs/ē) **1.** A small American willow (*Salix discolor*) with silky catkins in early spring: also called *glaucous willow.* **2.** Any of various similar willows.

pus·tu·lant (pus/chŏŏ·lənt) *adj.* Causing pustules. — *n.* A medicine that causes pustules. [< LL *pustulans, -antis*, ppr. of L *pustulare.* See PUSTULATE.]

pus·tu·lar (pus/chŏŏ·lər) *adj.* **1.** Proceeding from or marked by pustules: a *pustular* eruption. **2.** Resembling pustules. Also **pus/tu·lous.** [< NL *pustularis*]

PUSSY WILLOW

pus·tu·late (pus/chŏŏ·lāt; *for adj., also* pus/chŏŏ·lit) *v.t. & v.i.* **·lat·ed, ·lat·ing** To form into or become pustules. — *adj.* Covered with pustules or pustulelike elevations. [< L *pustulatus*, pp. of *pustulare* to blister < *pustula* pustule]

pus·tu·la·tion (pus/chŏŏ·lā/shən) *n.* The formation or eruption of pustules; also, a pustule. [< LL *pustulatio, -onis*]

pus·tule (pus/chŏŏl) *n.* **1.** *Pathol.* A small elevation of the skin with an inflamed base containing pus. **2.** Any elevation resembling a pimple or a blister. [< L *pustula*]

put (pŏŏt) *v.* **put, put·ting** *v.t.* **1.** To bring into or set in a specified or implied place or position; lay: *Put* the book on the table. **2.** To bring into a specified state, condition, or relation: to *put* a prisoner to death. **3.** To bring to bear; apply: *Put* your back into it! **4.** To impose: to *put* a tariff on bicycles. **5.** To ascribe or attribute, as the wrong interpretation on a remark. **6.** To place according to one's estimation: I *put* the time at five o'clock. **7.** To throw with a pushing motion of the arm: to *put* the shot. **8.** To incite; prompt: Who *put* him up to it? **9.** To bring forward for debate, answer, consideration, etc.: to *put* a question. **10.** To subject: Let's *put* it to a vote. **11.** To express in words; state: That's *putting* it mildly. **12.** To risk; bet: I'll *put* six dollars on that horse. — *v.i.* **13.** To go; proceed: to *put* to sea. — **to put about** *Naut.* To change to the opposite tack; change direction. — **to put aside (or away or by) 1.** To place in reserve; save. **2.** To thrust aside; discard. — **to put down 1.** To repress; crush. **2.** To degrade; demote. **3.** To write down; record. **4.** *Slang* To humble or deflate; disparage. — **to put forth 1.** To extend, as the arm or hand. **2.** To grow, as shoots or buds. **3.** To exert. **4.** To set out; leave port. — **to put forward** To advance; urge, as a claim. — **to put in** *Naut.* To enter a harbor or place of shelter. **2.** To interpolate; interpose. **3.** *Informal* To devote; expend, as time. **4.** To advance (a claim, etc.). **5.** To submit, as an application. — **to put off 1.** To delay; postpone. **2.** To discard. — **to put on 1.** To don. **2.** To bring into action; turn on. **3.** To simulate; pretend. **4.** To give a representation of; stage. **5.** *Slang* To deceive; mock. — **to put out 1.** To extinguish. **2.** To expel; eject. **3.** To disconcert; embarrass. **4.** To inconvenience. **5.** To put forth. **6.** In baseball, to retire (a batter or base runner). — **to put over 1.** To place in command or charge. **2.** *Informal* To accomplish successfully. — **to put one (or something) over on** *Informal* To deceive or dupe. — **to put through 1.** To bring to successful completion. **2.** To cause to undergo. — **to put up 1.** To erect; build. **2.** To preserve or can. **3.** To wager; bet. **4.** To provide (money, capital, etc.). **5.** To sheathe, as a weapon. — **to put upon** To take advantage of; deceive. — **to put up with** To endure; tolerate. — *n.* **1.** The act of putting, as a cast or throw. **2.** In the securities trade, a contract by which one person, in consideration of money paid to another, acquires the privilege of selling or delivering to the latter within a certain time stock or other commodities at a stipulated price. Compare CALL, STRADDLE. — *adj. Informal* Fixed; settled: My hat won't stay *put.* [Fusion of OE *pūtian* to instigate, *potian* to push, and *pȳtan* to put out]
— **Syn. 1.** set, situate, deposit.

pu·ta·men (pyōō·tā/min) *n. pl.* **·tam·i·na** (-tam/ə·nə) *Bot.* The hard stone of certain fruits, as the cherry.   [< L, waste, a husk < *putare* to cleanse, prune] — **pu·tam/i·nous** *adj.*

pu·ta·tive (pyōō/tə·tiv) *adj.* Supposed; reported; reputed. [< MF *putatif* or LL *putativus* < L *putatus*, pp. of *putare* to think] — **pu/ta·tive·ly** *adv.*

put·log (pŏŏt/lôg, -log, put/-) *n.* A crosspiece in a scaffolding, its inner end resting in a hole in the wall and its outer end on a ledger. [Earlier *putlock* < *put*, pp. of PUT]

Put·nam (put/nəm), Israel, 1718–90, American Revolutionary general.

put-off (pŏŏt/ôf/, -of/) *n.* An evasion; excuse.

put-on (pŏŏt/on/) *n. Slang* A hoax or deception.

put-out (pŏŏt/out/) *n.* In baseball, the act of causing an out, as of a batter or base runner. Abbr. *po, p.o.*

put-put (put/put/) *n. Slang* A gasoline engine, especially one used in propelling a small boat. [Imit.]

pu·tre·fac·tion (pyōō/trə·fak/shən) *n.* **1.** The progressive chemical decomposition of organic matter, with the production of foul-smelling compounds. **2.** The state of being putrefied. **3.** Putrescent or putrefied matter.   [< OF < L *putrefactio, -onis* < *putrefacere.* See PUTREFY.]

pu·tre·fac·tive (pyōō/trə·fak/tiv) *adj.* **1.** Of or pertaining to putrefaction. **2.** Producing putrefaction.

pu·tre·fy (pyōō/trə·fī) *v.t. & v.i.* **·fied, ·fy·ing 1.** To decay or cause to decay with a fetid odor; rot; decompose. **2.** To make or become gangrenous — **Syn.** See DECAY.   [< F *putréfier* < L *putrefacere* < *putrere* to decay (< *puter* rotten) + *facere* to make] — **pu/tre·fi·er** *n.*

pu·tres·cence (pyōō·tres/əns) *n.* **1.** The state of undergoing putrefaction. **2.** Something putrescent.

pu·tres·cent (pyōō·tres/ənt) *adj.* **1.** Becoming putrid; undergoing putrefaction. **2.** Pertaining to putrefaction.   [< L *putrescens, -entis*, ppr. of *putrescere* to grow rotten, inceptive of *putrere.* See PUTREFY.]

pu·tres·ci·ble (pyōō·tres/ə·bəl) *adj.* Liable to putrefy. — *n.* A substance that putrefies. — **pu·tres/ci·bil/i·ty** *n.*

pu·tres·cine (pyōō·tres/ēn, -in) *n. Biochem.* A colorless, foul-smelling ptomaine, $C_4H_{12}N_2$, resulting from the decomposition of animal tissues.

pu·trid (pyōō/trid) *adj.* **1.** Being in a state of putrefaction; decomposed or decomposing; rotten: *putrid* meat. **2.** Indicating or produced by putrefaction: a *putrid* smell. **3.** Rotten; corrupt.   [< L *putridus* < *putrere.* See PUTREFY.] — **pu/trid·i·ty** *n.*

Putsch (pŏŏch) *n.* An outbreak or rebellion; an attempted *coup d'état.*   [< G < dial. G (Swiss), lit., push, blow]

putt (put) *n.* In golf, a light stroke made on a putting green to place the ball in or near the hole. — *v.t. & v.i.* To strike (the ball) with such a stroke. [Var. of PUT]

put·tee (put/ē, pu·tē/) *n.* A strip of cloth wound spirally about the leg from knee to ankle, used by soldiers, sportsmen, etc.; also, a leather gaiter strapped around the leg. Also **put/ty.** [< Hind. *paṭṭī* bandage < Skt. *paṭṭa* strip of cloth]

put·ter[1] (put/ər) *n.* **1.** In golf, one who putts. **2.** An upright, stiff-shafted golf club used on the putting green.

put·ter[2] (put/ər) *v.i.* **1.** To act, work, or proceed in a dawdling or ineffectual manner. — *v.t.* **2.** To waste or spend (time, etc.) in dawdling or puttering. [Var. of POTTER[1]]

put·ti·er (put/ē·ər) *n.* One who putties; a glazier.   [< PUTTY]

put·ting green (put/ing) In golf: **a** Green (*n.* def. 5). **b** A place set aside for putting practice.

put·ty (put/ē) *n.* **1.** Whiting mixed with linseed oil to the consistency of dough, used for filling holes or cracks in wood surfaces, securing panes of glass in the sash, etc. **2.** Any of various similar substances, as red and white lead, used in pipe joints. **3.** Fine lime mortar for filling cracks, finishing, etc. — *v.t.* **·tied, ·ty·ing** To fill, stop, fasten, etc., with putty. [< OF *potée* calcined tin, lit., potful < *pot* pot]

putty knife A knife with a broad blade, used to apply putty.

putty powder Tin oxide, or tin and lead oxide, used for polishing glass, metals, etc.

put·ty·root (put/ē·rōōt/, -rŏŏt/) *n.* An American orchid (*Aplectrum hyemale*) bearing a loose raceme of brownish flowers produced yearly: also called *Adam-and-Eve.* [So called from a sticky substance found in its bulbs]

Pu·tu·ma·yo (pōō/tōō·mä/yō) A river forming part of the boundary between Colombia and Peru, flowing about 1,000 miles SE to the Amazon: Portuguese (Brazilian) *Içá.*

put-up (pŏŏt/up/) *adj. Informal* Prearranged or contrived in an artful manner: a *put-up* job.

Pu·vis de Cha·vannes (pü·vēs/ də shä·vän/), Pierre, 1824–1898, French painter.

Puy-de-Dôme (pwē·də·dōm/) An extinct volcano in central France; site of an observatory and a ruined temple of Mercury; 4,806 ft.

Pu-yi (pōō/yē/), 1906–1967, emperor of China 1908–1912; last of the Manchu dynasty; abdicated; puppet emperor of Manchukuo, 1934–45: called **Henry Pu-yi.**

puz·zle (puz/əl) *v.* **·zled, ·zling** *v.t.* **1.** To confuse or perplex; mystify. **2.** To solve by investigation and study, as something perplexing: with *out.* — *v.i.* **3.** To be perplexed or confused. — **to puzzle over** To attempt to understand or solve. — *n.* **1.** Something that puzzles; a problem; enig-

ma. **2.** A toy, word game, etc., designed to test one's ingenuity or patience. **3.** The state of being puzzled; a quandary; perplexity. [Origin unknown]
— **Syn.** (verb) **1.** confound, bewilder, baffle, daze. — (noun) **1.** *Puzzle, problem, enigma, conundrum, riddle,* and *mystery* signify broadly any difficult or perplexing matter. A *puzzle* is usually intricate but can be solved by ingenuity and patience; many *puzzles* are made for amusement. A *problem* usually demands special knowledge and good judgment; formal *problems* are given to students to test their learning and skill. An *enigma* is something said or written whose meaning is hidden and can only be inferred from clues. A *conundrum* is a baffling question, the answer to which depends upon some trick of words. *Conundrums* are also called *riddles,* but a *riddle* is usually less playful in character: the *riddle* of the Sphinx. A *mystery* was originally something beyond human comprehension, but the word is now freely applied to perplexing situations, some elements of which are unknown.

puz·zle·ment (puz′əl·mənt) *n.* The state of being puzzled; perplexity.

puz·zler (puz′lər) *n.* One who or that which puzzles.

Pvt. *Mil.* Private.

pwt. Pennyweight.

PX *Mil.* Post exchange.

pxt. He (or she) painted (L *pinxit*).

py- Var. of PYO-.

pyc·nid·i·um (pik·nid′ē·əm) *n.* *pl.* **·nid·i·a** (-nid′ē·ə) *Bot.* A spore-bearing receptacle found in certain fungi. [< NL < Gk. *pyknos* dense, thick + *-idion,* dim. suffix] — **pyc·nid′i·al** *adj.*

pyc·nom·e·ter (pik·nom′ə·tər) *n.* A bottle or flask used in determining the specific gravity or density of a substance. [< Gk. *pyknos* dense, thick + *-METER*]

Pyd·na (pid′nə) An ancient city in south central Macedonia, Greece; scene of the final Roman victory over Macedonia, 168 B.C.

pye (pī) See PIE⁴.

py·e·li·tis (pī′ə·lī′tis) *n.* *Pathol.* Inflammation of the pelvis or the kidney. [< NL < Gk. *pyelos* pelvis + *-itis* inflammation of] — **py′e·lit′ic** (-lit′ik) *adj.*

pyelo- *combining form* Pelvis: *pyelography.* Also, before vowels, **pyel-.** [< Gk. *pyelos* pelvis, trough]

py·e·lo·gram (pī′ə·lō·gram′) *n.* A picture taken by pyelography. [< PYELO- + -GRAM]

py·e·log·ra·phy (pī′ə·log′ra·fē) *n.* The technique of making X-rays of the ureter and the kidney by the use of a radiopaque dye. [< PYELO- + -GRAPHY] — **py′e·lo·graph′ic** (-lō·graf′ik) *adj.*

py·e·mi·a (pī·ē′mē·ə) *n.* *Pathol.* General septicemia with metastatic abscesses, marked by chills, fever, and sometimes jaundice. Also **py·ae′mi·a.** [< NL < Gk. *pyon* pus + *haima* blood] — **py·e′mic** *adj.*

Pyg·ma·li·on (pig·mā′lē·ən, -māl′yən) In Greek mythology, a sculptor of Cyprus who fell in love with his statue, Galatea, which Aphrodite later brought to life.

pyg·my (pig′mē) *adj.* **1.** Diminutive; dwarfish. **2.** Trivial; unimportant. — *n.* *pl.* **·mies** A small person or thing regarded as insignificant. Also spelled *pigmy.* [< L *pygmaeus* < Gk. *pygmaios* dwarfish, dwarf < *pygmē* the length from elbow to knuckles]

Pyg·my (pig′mē) *n.* *pl.* **·mies** **1.** A member of a Negroid people of equatorial Africa, ranging in height from four to five feet. **2.** Any of the Negrito peoples of the Philippines, Andaman Islands, and Malaya. **3.** In Greek legend, one of a race of dwarfs. Compare DWARF, MIDGET. [< L *pygmaeus.* See PYGMY.]

pygmy rattlesnake A small rattlesnake (*Sistrurus miliarius*) of the SE United States: also called *ground rattlesnake, massasauga.*

py·ic (pī′ik) *adj.* Of or pertaining to pus; purulent. [< PY(O)- + -IC]

py·in (pī′in) *n.* *Biochem.* A protein compound contained in pus. [< PY(O)- + -IN]

py·ja·mas (pə·jä′məz, -jam′əz) See PAJAMAS.

pyk·nic (pik′nik) *adj.* Denoting a physical type characterized by plump contours and a broad, stocky build. — *n.* A person of the pyknic type. [< Gk. *pyknos* thick, compact]

Pyle (pīl), Howard, 1853–1911, U.S. artist and writer.

py·lon (pī′lon) *n.* **1.** *Archit.* A monumental structure constituting an entrance to an Egyptian temple or other large edifice, consisting of a central gateway, flanked on each side by a truncated pyramidal tower. **2.** A stake marking the course in an airport or turning point in an air race. **3.** One of the steel towers supporting a high-tension electric power line. **4.** *Surg.* An artificial leg, usually temporary. [< Gk. *pylōn* gateway < *pylē* gate]

py·lo·rec·to·my (pī′lə·rek′tə·mē) *n* *pl.* **·mies** *Surg.* Excision of the pylorus. [< PYLOR(US) + -ECTOMY]

py·lo·rus (pī·lôr′əs, -lō′rəs, pi-) *n.* *pl.* **·ri** (-rī) *Anat.* The opening between the stomach and the duodenum, surrounded by a sphincter. [< LL < Gk. *pylōros* gatekeeper < *pylē* gate + *ouros* watcher] — **py·lor′ic** (-lôr′ik, -lor′ik) *adj.*

Pym (pim), **John,** 1584–1643, English Roundhead statesman and orator: called **King Pym.**

pyo- *combining form* Pus; of or related to pus: *pyorrhea.* Also, before vowels, **py-.** [< Gk. *pyon* pus]

py·o·gen·e·sis (pī′ō·jen′ə·sis) *n.* *Pathol.* The formation or secretion of pus; suppuration. — **py′o·gen′ic** *adj.*

py·oid (pī′oid) *adj.* Resembling pus; purulent.

Pyong·yang (pyông·yäng) The capital of North Korea, in the western part; pop. 800,000 (est. 1965).

py·or·rhe·a (pī′ə·rē′ə) *n.* *Pathol.* A continuous discharge of pus; especially, pyorrhea alveolaris. Also **py′or·rhoe′a.** [< NL < Gk. *pyon* pus + *rheein* to flow] — **py′or·rhe′al** *adj.*

pyorrhea al·ve·o·la·ris (al·vē′ō·lâr′is) *Pathol.* A disease marked by inflammation of the gum tissues and the loosening of the teeth: also called *Riggs's disease.*

py·o·sis (pī·ō′sis) *n.* *Pathol.* The formation of pus; suppuration. [< NL < Gk. *pyōsis*]

pyr- Var. of PYRO-.

py·ra·can·tha (pī′rə·kan′thə, pir′ə-) *n.* An evergreen, typically thorny shrub (genus *Pyracantha*) of the rose family, bearing white flowers and a scarlet or orange fruit, and used as an ornamental hedge: also called *firethorn.* [< L < Gk. *pyrakantha* < *pyr, pyros* fire + *akantha, -ēs* thorn]

pyr·a·mid (pir′ə·mid) *n.* **1.** *Archit.* A structure of masonry typically having a square base and triangular sides meeting in an apex, sometimes vast in size. Such structures were used as tombs, as in ancient Egypt, or as temples. **2.** Something pyramidal in form. **3.** *Geom.* A solid consisting of a polygonal base and triangular sides, the apices of the triangles coming together at the vertex. **4.** *Mineral.* A crystal form consisting of three or more similar planes having a common point of intersection. **5.** *Anat.* Any of various pyramidal or conical structures found in animal organisms. For illustration see KIDNEY. **6.** Any tree trained in pyramidal form. **7.** The operations involved in pyramiding stock. — *v.t. & v.i.* **1.** To arrange or form in the shape of a pyramid. **2.** To buy or sell (stock) with paper profits, and to continue so buying or selling. [ME *piramis* (pl. *pyramids*) and later borrowing of F *pyramide,* both < L *pyramis, -idis* < Gk. *pyramis, -idos,* ? < *pyr, pyros* fire, or < *pyros* grain]

PYRAMIDS AT GIZA

py·ram·i·dal (pi·ram′i·dəl) *adj.* Of or shaped like a pyramid. Also **pyr·a·mid·ic** (pir′ə·mid′ik) or **·i·cal.** — **py·ram′i·dal·ly** *adv.*

Pyr·a·mus and This·be (pir′ə·məs; thiz′bē) In classical legend, two Babylonian lovers. Believing Thisbe slain by a lion, Pyramus killed himself, and Thisbe, finding his body, took her own life.

py·ran (pī′ran, pī·ran′) *n.* *Chem.* Either of two isomeric cyclic compounds, C_5H_6O, each having in its ring 5 carbon atoms, the parent forms of certain physiologically active substances. [< PYRONE]

py·rar·gy·rite (pī·rär′jə·rīt) *n.* A metallic, black sulfide of antimony and silver, crystallizing in the rhombohedral system. [< PYR- + Gk. *argyros* silver + -ITE¹]

pyre (pīr) *n.* **1.** A heap of combustibles arranged for burning a dead body. **2.** Any pile or heap of combustible material. [< L *pyra* hearth, funeral pile < Gk. < *pyr* fire]

py·rene¹ (pī′rēn) *n.* *Chem.* A cyclic hydrocarbon, $C_{16}H_{10}$, contained in that portion of coal-tar oil boiling above 360° C. [< PYR- + -ENE]

py·rene² (pī′rēn) *n.* *Bot.* The stone of a drupe; nutlet; putamen. [< NL *pyrena* < Gk. *pyrēn* fruit stone]

Pyr·e·nees (pir′ə·nēz) A mountain chain between France and Spain, from the Bay of Biscay to the Mediterranean; highest point, Pico de Aneto, 11,168 ft. — **Pyr·e·ne·an** (pir′ə·nē′ən) *adj.*

py·reth·rum (pī·reth′rəm, -rē′thrəm) *n.* **1.** The powdered flowers of a chrysanthemum (*Chrysanthemum cinerariaefolium*), used medically as an ointment, and as an insecticide. **2.** The dried and powdered roots of the pellitory, used in medicine. [< L. feverfew < Gk. *pyrethron*]

py·ret·ic (pī·ret′ik) *adj.* **1.** Affected with or relating to fever; feverish. **2.** Remedial in fevers. [< NL *pyreticus* < Gk. *pyretos* fever < *pyr* fire]

pyr·e·tol·o·gy (pir′ə·tol′ə·jē, pī′rə-) *n.* The branch of medicine that treats of fevers. [< Gk. *pyretos* fever + -LOGY]

pyr·e·to·ther·a·py (pir′ə·tō·ther′ə·pē, pī′rə-) *n.* Medical treatment by the artificial induction of fever: also called *fever therapy.* [< Gk. *pyretos* fever + THERAPY]

Py·rex (pī′reks) *n.* A type of heat-resisting glass having a high silica content, with additions of soda, aluminum, and boron: a trade name. Also **py′rex.**

py·rex·i·a (pī·rek′sē·ə) *n.* *Pathol.* Fever (def. 1). [< NL < Gk. *pyrexis < pyressein* to be feverish < *pyretos.* See PYRETIC.] — **py·rex′i·al** *adj.* — **py·rex′ic** *adj.*

pyr·he·li·om·e·ter (pĭr-hē/lē-om/ə-tər, pir-) *n. Astron.* An instrument for measuring the quantity and rate of solar radiation by its thermal effects on a silvered disk or other sensitive surface. [< PYR- + HELIO- + -METER]

Pyr·i·ben·za·mine (pir/ə-ben/zə-mēn, -min) *n.* Proprietary name of an antihistamine drug, used to treat allergies.

pyr·i·dine (pir/ə-dēn, -din) *n. Chem.* A colorless, liquid compound, C_5H_5N, with a pungent odor, obtained from coal tar and bone oil and also made synthetically, used in organic syntheses and in medicine. [< PYR(ROLE) + -ID(E) + -INE²] — **py·rid·ic** (pĭ-rid/ik) *adj.*

pyr·i·dox·ine (pir/ə-dok/sēn, -sin) *n. Biochem.* Vitamin B_6, a water-soluble compound, $C_8H_{10}NO_3$, occurring in cereal grains, vegetable oils, legumes, yeast, meats, and fish, and also made synthetically, known to prevent dermatitis in rats. [PYRID(INE) + OX(Y)-² + -INE²]

pyr·i·form (pir/ə-fôrm) *adj.* Pear-shaped. [< NL *pyriformis* < Med.L *pyrum* pear (< L *pirum*) + L *forma* form]

py·rim·i·dine (pĭ-rim/ə-dēn, -din, pir/ə-mə-dēn/, -din/) *n. Biochem.* An organic compound, $C_4H_4N_2$, resulting from the acid hydrolysis of a nucleic acid and forming the base of many products of metabolism. Also **py·rim/i·din** (-din). [< G *pyrimidin* < *pyridin* pyridine]

py·rite (pī/rīt) *n. pl.* **py·ri·tes** (pī-rī/tēz) A metallic, pale yellow iron disulfide, FeS_2, a source of sulfuric acid: also called *fool's gold, iron pyrites.* [< L *pyrites* < Gk. *pyritēs* flint < *pyritēs* (*lithos*) fire (stone) < *pyr* fire] — **py·rit/ic** (-rit/ik) or **-i·cal** *adj.*

py·ri·tes (pī-rī/tēz) *n.pl.* Any of various metallic sulfides.

pyro- *combining form* 1. Fire; heat: *pyromania.* 2. *Chem.* **a** Denoting actual or hypothetical derivation by the action of heat. **b** In certain inorganic acids, indicating derivation from two molecules of an ordinary (ortho) acid by the elimination of one molecule of water, as $2H_3AsO_4$ (arsenic acid) $+ H_2O \rightarrow H_4As_2O_7$ (*pyroarsenic* acid). 3. *Geol.* Resulting from the action of fire or heat: *pyrolusite.* Also, before vowels, *pyr-.* [< Gk. *pyr, pyros* fire]

py·ro·cat·e·chol (pī/rə-kat/ə-kōl, -chōl, -kol, pir/ə-) *n. Chem.* A white crystalline phenol compound, $C_6H_6O_2$, originally obtained from catecha, used in photography as a developer and in medicine: also called *catechol.* Also **py/ro·cat/e·chin** (-kin, -chin). [< PYRO- + CATECH(U) + (PHEN)OL]

py·ro·chem·i·cal (pī/rə-kem/i-kəl) *adj.* Pertaining to chemical changes induced or effected by high temperature.

py·ro·clas·tic (pī/rə-klas/tik) *adj. Geol.* Formed from or consisting of fragmentary or comminuted material, chiefly of volcanic origin. [< PYRO- + CLASTIC]

py·ro·con·duc·tiv·i·ty (pī/rə-kon/duk-tiv/ə-tē) *n.* Conductivity of an electric current dependent upon or improved by heat. — **py/ro·con·duc/tive** (-kən-duk/tiv) *adj.*

py·ro·crys·tal·line (pī/rə-kris/tə-lin, -līn, pir/ə-) *adj.* Crystallized from materials in a state of fusion.

py·ro·e·lec·tric (pī/rō-i-lek/trik, pir/ō-) *adj.* Of, pertaining to, or manifesting pyroelectricity; developing poles when heated. — *n.* A pyroelectric substance.

py·ro·e·lec·tric·i·ty (pī/rō-i-lek/tris/ə-tē, -ē/lek-, pir/ō-) *n.* Electrification or electric polarity developed in certain minerals by a change in temperature.

py·ro·gal·late (pī/rə-gal/āt, pir/ə-) *n.* A salt of pyrogallol.

py·ro·gal·lic (pī/rə-gal/ik, pir/ə-) *adj. Chem.* 1. Of, pertaining to, or derived by heat from gallic acid. 2. Pertaining to or designating pyrogallol.

py·ro·gal·lol (pī/rə-gal/ōl, -ol, -gə-lōl/, pir/ə-) *n. Chem.* A white, crystalline compound, $C_6H_3(OH)_3$, obtained by heating gallic acid, used as a photographic developer, as a dye, and in certain medical preparations. Also **pyrogallic acid.** [< PYRO- + GALL(IC) + (PHEN)OL]

py·ro·gen (pī/rə-jən) *n. Biochem.* A pyrotoxin.

py·ro·gen·ic (pī/rə-jen/ik, pir/ə-) *adj.* 1. Causing or produced by heat. 2. Caused by or inducing fever. 3. *Geol.* Igneous. Also **py·rog·e·nous** (pī-roj/ə-nəs, pi-).

py·rog·nos·tics (pī/rag-nos/tiks, pir/əg-) *n.pl.* (*usually construed as sing.*) The characteristics of a mineral as shown by heat of varying intensity produced with a blowpipe. [< PYRO- + Gk. *gnōstikos* knowing]

py·rog·ra·phy (pī-rog/rə-fē, pi-) *n.* The art or process of producing a design, as on wood or leather, by a red-hot point or fine flame. — **py·ro·graph** (pī/rə-graf, -gräf, pir/ə-) *n.* — **py·rog/ra·pher** *n.* — **py·ro·graph/ic** *adj.*

py·ro·lig·ne·ous (pī/rə-lig/nē-əs, pir/ə-) *adj.* Pertaining to that which is derived from wood by heat, especially by dry distillation. [< PYRO- + LIGNEOUS]

pyroligneous acid Crude acetic acid as derived from wood by distillation: also called *wood vinegar.*

py·rol·o·gy (pī-rol/ə-jē) *n.* The scientific examination of materials by heat; blowpipe analysis. [< PYRO- + -LOGY] — **py·ro·log·i·cal** (pī/rə-loj/i-kəl, pir/ə-) *adj.*

py·ro·lu·site (pī/rə-loo/sīt, pī/rol/yə-sīt) *n.* A soft, metallic, black or steel-gray manganese dioxide, MnO_2, a principal ore of manganese, widely used in glassmaking and as a depolarizer of dry-cell batteries. [< Gk. *pyr, pyros* fire + *lousis* washing (< *louein* to wash) + -ITE¹]

py·rol·y·sis (pī-rol/ə-sis) *n. Chem.* Decomposition of organic compounds or other substances by the action of heat.

[< NL < Gk. *pyr, pyros* fire + *lysis* loosing < *lyein* to loosen] — **py·ro·lit·ic** (pī/rə-lit/ik, pir/ə-) *adj.*

py·ro·mag·net·ic (pī/rō-mag-net/ik, pir/ō-) *adj.* Of, pertaining to, or produced by changes in magnetic properties caused by change of temperature.

py·ro·man·cy (pī/rə-man/sē, pir/ə-) *n.* Divination by fire. [< PYRO- + -MANCY]

py·ro·ma·ni·a (pī/rə-mā/nē-ə, -mān/yə, pir/ə-) *n.* A compulsion to set things on fire. — **py/ro·ma/ni·ac** (-ak) *adj. & n.* — **py·ro·ma·ni·a·cal** (pī/rō-mə-nī/ə-kəl, pir/ō-) *adj.*

py·ro·met·al·lur·gy (pī/rō-met/ə-lûr/jē, pir/ə-) *n.* The practice of heating ores during refining in order to hasten chemical reactions, melt the metal, etc.

py·rom·e·ter (pī-rom/ə-tər) *n.* An instrument for measuring high degrees of heat. — **py·ro·met·ric** (pī/rə-met/rik, pir/ə-) or **-ri·cal** *adj.* — **py·rom/e·try** *n.*

py·ro·mor·phite (pī/rə-môr/fīt, pir/ə-) *n.* A resinous phosphate and chloride of lead, found in masses or crystals of a green, brown, or yellow color: also called *green lead ore.* [< Gk. *pyr, pyros* fire + *morphos* form + -ITE¹]

py·rone (pī/rōn, pī-rōn/) *n. Chem.* A cyclic compound, $C_5H_4O_2$, existing in two isomeric forms, yielding yellow dyestuffs. [< G *pyron*]

py·rope (pī/rōp) *n.* A variety of deep red garnet: also called *precious garnet.* [< OF *pirope* < L *pyropus* gold bronze < Gk. *pyrōpos,* lit., fiery-eyed < *pyr, pyros* fire + *ōps, ōpos* eye, face]

py·ro·phor·ic (pī/rə-fôr/ik, -for/ik) *adj.* Spontaneously combustible, as certain materials that are easily and quickly flammable. [< NL *pyrophorus* < Gk. *pyrophoros* < *pyr, pyros* fire + *pherein* to carry] — **py/ro·phore** (-fôr, -fōr) *n.*

py·ro·phos·phate (pī/rə-fos/fāt, pir/ə-) *n.* A salt of pyrophosphoric acid.

py·ro·phos·phor·ic acid (pī/rō-fos-fôr/ik, -for/ik, pir/ō-) *Chem.* An acid, $H_4P_2O_7$, obtained by removing one molecule of water from two molecules of orthophosphoric acid.

py·ro·pho·tom·e·ter (pī/rō-fō-tom/ə-tər, pir/ō-) *n.* A pyrometer used to determine high temperatures by means of the luminosity of a substance.

py·ro·phyl·lite (pī/rə-fil/īt, pir/ə-) *n.* A compact, variously colored, hydrous aluminum silicate, used in making slate pencils. [< PYRO- + PHYLL(O)- + -ITE¹]

py·ro·sis (pī-rō/sis) *n. Pathol.* Heartburn. [< NL < Gk. *pyrōsis* a burning < *pyroun* to set on fire < *pyr* fire]

py·ro·stat (pī/rə-stat, pir/ə-) *n.* A thermostat especially adapted for higher temperatures. [< PYRO- + -STAT]

py·ro·sul·fate (pī/rə-sul/fāt, pir/ə-) *n.* A salt of pyrosulfuric acid: also called *disulfate.*

py·ro·sul·fu·ric acid (pī/rō-sul-fyoor/ik, pir/ō-) *Chem.* A brown, fuming liquid, $H_2SO_4SO_3$, obtained by adding liquid sulfuric oxide to sulfuric acid: also called *disulfuric acid.*

py·ro·tech·nic (pī/rə-tek/nik, pir/ə-) *adj.* Pertaining to fireworks or their manufacture. Also **py/ro·tech/ni·cal.**

py·ro·tech·nics (pī/rə-tek/niks, pir/ə-) *n.pl.* (*construed as sing. in defs. 1, 4*) 1. The art of making or using fireworks. Also **py·ro·tech·ny** (pī/rə-tek/nē, pir/ə-) 2. A display of fireworks. 3. An ostentatious display, as of oratory. 4. *Mil.* Rockets, flares, or the like, that produce flame or smoke for signaling, lighting, screening, etc. [< MF *pyrotechnie* < Gk. *pyr, pyros* fire + *technē* art] — **py/ro·tech/nist** *n.*

py·ro·tox·in (pī/rə-tok/sin, pir/ə-) *n. Biochem.* Any of various toxins found in the body and inducing a rise of bodily temperature or symptoms of fever: also called *pyrogen.*

py·rox·ene (pī/rok-sēn) *n.* Any of a large group of monoclinic minerals, composed principally of the silicates of calcium, magnesium, iron, and other elements, a frequent component of igneous rocks. [< F *pyroxène* < Gk. *pyr, pyros* fire + *xenos* stranger; because at first considered alien to igneous rocks] — **py·rox·en·ic** (pī/rok-sen/ik) *adj.*

py·rox·e·nite (pī/rok/sə-nīt) *n.* An igneous rock composed mostly of pyroxene, but without olivine.

py·rox·y·lin (pī-rok/sə-lin) *n. Chem.* A cellulose nitrate mixture, less explosive than guncotton, and widely used in making Celluloid, collodion, lacquers, adhesives, etc. Also **py·rox/y·line** (-lin, -lin). [< F *pyroxyline* < Gk. *pyr, pyros* fire + *xylon* wood + F -*in* -in]

Pyr·rha (pir/ə) In Greek mythology, the daughter of Epimetheus and wife of Deucalion.

pyr·rhic¹ (pir/ik) *n.* In prosody, a metrical foot consisting of two short or unaccented syllables. — *adj.* Of or pertaining to pyrrhics. [< L (*pes*) *pyrrhicius.* See PYRRHIC².]

pyr·rhic² (pir/ik) *adj.* In Greek antiquity, pertaining to a martial dance imitating the movements of combat. — *n.* The pyrrhic dance. [< L *pyrrhicius* < Gk. *pyrrichios* < *pyrriche* war dance < *Pyrrichos* Pyrrhichus, a Greek said to have invented it]

Pyr·rhic victory (pir/ik) A victory gained at a ruinous loss, such as that of Pyrrhus over the Romans in 279 B.C. at Asculum Apulum (now Ascoli Satriano in SW Italy). [after *Pyrrhus* king of Epirus]

Pyr·rho·nism (pir/ə-niz/əm) *n.* A system of skeptic philosophy taught by **Pyr·rho of E·lis** (pir/ō; ē/lis), 360?–270? B.C. [< F < L *Pyrrhonius* pertaining to Pyrrho < Gk. *Pyrrōn* Pyrrho]

pyr·rho·tite (pir′ə-tīt) *n.* A metallic, bronze-colored, slightly magnetic iron sulfide, FeS. Also **pyr′rho·lite** (-līt), **pyr′rho·tine** (-tīn). [< Gk. *pyrrotēs* redness (< *pyrros* flame-colored < *pyr* fire) + -ITE¹]

pyr·rhu·lox·i·a (pir′ə-lok′sē-ə) *n.* A grosbeak (*Pyrrhuloxia sinuata*) of the western United States, with a slender gray and red body and a parrotlike bill. [< NL < *Pyrrhula* genus of birds (< Gk. *pyrrhos* fiery < *pyr* fire) + *Loxia* genus of the crossbills < Gk. *loxos* oblique]

Pyr·rhus (pir′əs), 318?–272 B.C., king of Epirus; fought against the Romans.

Pyr·rhus (pir′əs) In Greek legend, Neoptolemus.

pyr·role (pi·rōl′, pir′ōl) *n. Chem.* A five-membered, cyclic nitrogenous compound, C_4H_4NH, having an odor of chloroform, obtained by synthesis, and occurring in many natural substances, as chlorophyll and hemoglobin: also called *azole*. [< *C pyrrol* (< Gk. *pyrros* reddish < *pyr* fire) + -*ol* -ole¹]

pyr·rol·i·dine (pi·rol′ə-dēn, -din) *n. Chem.* A colorless compound, C_4H_9N, with a mild ammonia odor, found in tobacco and carrot leaves. [< PYRROL(E) + -ID(E) + -INE²]

py·ru·vic acid (pi·rōō′vik, pi-) *Biochem.* A colorless to pale yellow ketone, $C_3H_4O_3$, formed during glycolysis and in other metabolic processes and made synthetically by the distillation of tartaric acid. [< PYR- + L *uva* grape + -IC]

Py·thag·o·ras (pi·thag′ər-əs) Sixth-century B.C. Greek philosopher and mathematician. — **Py·thag·o·re′an** (pi·thag′-ə·rē′ən) *adj. & n.*

Py·thag·o·re·an·ism (pi·thag′ə·rē′ən·iz′əm) *n.* The mystical philosophy taught by Pythagoras, including the doctrine of metempsychosis and the idea that number is the essence of all things. [< L *Pythagoreus* < Gk. *Pythagoreios* < *Pythagoras* Pythagoras]

Pythagorean theorem *Geom.* The theorem that the sum of the squares of the legs of a right triangle is equal to the square of the hypotenuse.

Pyth·i·a (pith′ē-ə) In ancient Greece, the priestess of Apollo at Delphi, who was believed to be inspired by the god when seated on a tripod over the rock sacred to him, and to utter his oracles. — **Pyth′ic** *adj.*

Pyth·i·ad (pith′ē·ad) *n.* In ancient Greece, the period from one celebration of the Pythian games to the next. [< Gk. *Pythias, -ados* < (*hiera*) *Pythia* Pythian (games), neut. pl. of *Pythios* Pythian]

Pyth·i·an (pith′ē-ən) *adj.* 1. Relating to Delphi, to Apollo's temple there, its oracle, or its priestess. 2. Relating to the

Pythian games. — *n.* 1. A native or inhabitant of Delphi. 2. The priestess of Apollo. 3. An epithet of the Delphic Apollo. [< L *Pythius* < Gk. *Pythios*]

Pythian games In ancient Greece, games held every four years at Delphi as a pan-Hellenic festival in honor of Apollo.

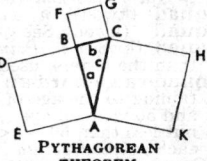

PYTHAGOREAN THEOREM
Sum of squares ABDE and BCGF equals square ACHK
$(a^2 + b^2 = c^2)$

Pyth·i·as (pith′ē·əs) See DAMON AND PYTHIAS.

py·thon (pī′thon, -thən) *n.* 1. A large, nonvenomous serpent (genus *Python*) that crushes its prey. 2. Any nonvenomous constrictor. 3. A soothsayer or soothsaying spirit: from the tradition that the Python delivered oracles at Delphi. [< L < Gk. *Python* Python]

Py·thon (pī′thon, -thən) In Greek mythology, a monstrous serpent that haunted the caves of Parnassus and was killed by Apollo near Delphi.

py·tho·ness (pī′thə·nis, pith′ə-) *n.* 1. The priestess of the Delphic oracle. 2. Any woman supposed to be possessed of the spirit of prophecy; a witch. [< OF *phitonise* < Med.L *phitonissa* < LL *pythonissa* < Gk. *Python* Python]

py·thon·ic (pī·thon′ik, pi-) *adj.* 1. Of, pertaining to, or resembling pythons or a python. 2. Inspired; prophetic.

py·u·ri·a (pī·yōōr′ē·ə) *n. Pathol.* The presence of pus in the urine. [< NL < Gk. *pyon* pus + *ouron* urine]

pyx (piks) *n. Eccl.* 1. A vessel or casket, usually of precious metal, in which the Host is preserved. 2. A receptacle for coins selected for trial at the British mint: also **pyx chest**. [< L *pyxis* box < Gk. < *pyxos* box tree. Doublet of BOX.]

pyx·id·i·um (pik·sid′ē·əm) *n.* pl. **·i·a** (-ē·ə) *Bot.* A seed vessel with transverse dehiscence, the upper portion separating as a lid: also *pyxis*. For illustration see FRUIT.

pyx·ie (pik′sē) *n.* A trailing evergreen shrub (*Pyxidanthera barbulata*) of the eastern United States, with solitary white or rose-colored flowers. [Prob. short for NL *Pyxidanthera*, the genus name < Gk. *pyxos* box tree + *antheros* flowery]

pyx·is (pik′sis) *n.* pl. **pyx·i·des** (pik′sə·dēz) 1. A box or pyx; especially, an ancient form of ornamental jewel case or toilet box. 2. An emollient ointment. 3. *Bot.* A pyxidium. [< L. See PYX.]

Pyx·is (pik′sis) *n.* A constellation, the Box. See CONSTELLATION. [< L]

Q

q, Q (kyōō) *n.* pl. **q's** or **qs, Q's** or **Qs, cues** (kyōōz) 1. The 17th letter of the English alphabet. The 17th letter of the Phoenician letter *qoph* was adopted in some early Greek alphabets as *koppa* and became Roman Q. Also *cue*. 2. The sound represented by the letter *q*. In English *q* is always followed by *u* and represents (kw), as in *quack, quest, quote, equal,* etc. In some words borrowed from French, however, English follows the French pronunciation with (k) alone, as in *appliqué, conquer, coquette, pique.* Final *-que* always represents (k), as in *antique, oblique, physique, unique,* etc.

q. 1. Farthing (L *quadrans*). 2. Quart(s). 3. Quarter(ly). 4. Quarto. 5. Quasi. 6. Query. 7. Question. 8. Quetzal. 9. Quintal. 10. Quire.

Q Queen (chess).

Q. (pl. **Qq.**) Quarto. 2. Quebec (unofficial). 3. Queen. 4. Question.

Qair·wan (kīr·wän′) See KAIROUAN.

Qan·da·har (kän′də·här′) See KANDAHAR.

Qa·tar (kä′tär) An emirate formerly under British protection, comprising the **Qatar Peninsula** on the western coast of the Persian Gulf; about 8,500 sq. mi.; pop. 90,000 (est. 1975); capital, Doha. See map of SAUDI ARABIA.

q.b. or **qb** Quarterback.

QB Queen's bishop (chess).

Q.B. *Brit.* Queen's Bench.

QBP Queen's bishop's pawn (chess).

Q.C. Queen's Counsel.

Q.E.D. Which was to be demonstrated (L *quod erat demonstrandum*).

Q.E.F. Which was to be done (L *quod erat faciendum*).

Qishm (kish′m) An island of Iran in the Strait of Hormuz; about 500 sq. mi. Also **Qeshm** (kesh′m).

QKt Queen's knight (chess).

QKtP Queen's knight's pawn (chess).

ql. Quintal.

QM Quartermaster.

QMC Quartermaster Corps.

QMG Quartermaster General.

QP Queen's pawn (chess).

q.pl. or **Q.P.** As much as you please (L *quantum placet*).

Qq. Quartos.

qq.v. Which see (L *quae vide*).

qr. (pl. **qrs.**) 1. Farthing (L *quadrans*). 2. Quarter(ly). 3. Quire.

QR Queen's rook (chess).

QRP Queen's rook's pawn (chess).

q.s. 1. As much as suffices (L *quantum sufficit*). 2. Quarter section.

qt. 1. Quantity. 2. Quart(s).

q.t. or **Q.T.** *Slang* Quiet: chiefly in the phrase **on the q.t.**

qto. Quarto.

qu. 1. Quart. 2. Quarter(ly). 3. Queen. 4. Query. 5. Question.

qua (kwā, kwä) *adv.* In the capacity of; by virtue of being; insofar as. [< L, ablative sing. fem. of *qui* who]

quack¹ (kwak) *v.i.* To utter a harsh, croaking cry, as a duck. — *n.* The sound made by a duck, or a similar croaking noise. [Imit.]

quack² (kwak) *n.* 1. A pretender to medical knowledge or skill. 2. One who falsely poses as an expert; a charlatan. — *adj.* Of or pertaining to quacks or quackery; ignorantly or falsely pretending to cure. — *v.i.* To play the quack. [Short for QUACKSALVER] — **quack′ish** *adj.* — **quack′ish·ly** *adv.* — Syn. 2. humbug, faker, impostor.

quack·er·y (kwak′ər·ē) *n.* pl. **·er·ies** Ignorant or fraudulent practice. Also **quack′hood** (-hŏŏd), **quack′ism.**

quack grass _U.S._ Couch grass (which see). [? < G _quecke_]

quack·sal·ver (kwak′sal′vər) _n._ A medical quack. [< MDu. < _quacken_ quack¹ + _salf_ salve]

quad¹ (kwod) _n._ Informal A quadrangle, as of a college.

quad² (kwod) See QUOD.

quad³ (kwod) _n._ _Printing_ A piece of type metal of less height than the letters, used for spacing: also called _quadrat_.

quad·ra·ge·nar·i·an (kwod′rə·jə·nâr′ē·ən) _adj._ Of or pertaining to the age of 40 years, or to the decade between 40 and 50 years of age. — _n._ One who is 40 or more years old but less than 50. [< L _quadragenarius_ < _quadrageni_ forty each < _quadraginta_ forty]

Quad·ra·ges·i·ma (kwod′rə·jes′ə·mə) _n._ _Obs._ The forty fast days before Easter; Lent. [< L, fortieth]

quad·ra·ges·i·mal (kwod′rə·jes′ə·məl) _adj._ 1. Of or pertaining to the number forty, especially to the forty days of Lent. 2. Used during or appropriate to Lent; Lenten.

Quadragesima Sunday The first Sunday of Lent.

quad·ran·gle (kwod′rang·gəl) _n._ 1. _Geom._ A plane figure having four sides and four angles. 2. A court, either square or oblong, as within a public building; also, the building or buildings that surround such a court. 3. A tract of land as represented by the United States Geological Survey on one of its atlas sheets. [< OF < LL _quadrangulum_ < _quattuor_ four + _angulus_ angle]

quad·ran·gu·lar (kwod′rang′gyə·lər) _adj._ Having four angles and four sides.

quad·rant (kwod′rənt) _n._ 1. A quarter section of a circle, subtending an arc of 90°; also, the arc subtended. 2. An instrument having a graduated arc of 90°, with a movable radius for measuring angles on it, used in navigation, surveying, and astronomy for measuring altitudes. 3. _Geom._ In a Cartesian coordinate system, any of the four sections formed by the intersection of the _X_- and _Y_-axes. Moving counterclockwise from the upper right-hand quadrant, they are called the **first, second, third,** and **fourth quadrants.** 4. Anything resembling the shape of a quarter section of a circle, as certain machine parts. [< L _quadrans, -antis_ a fourth part < _quattuor_ four] — **quad·ran·tal** (kwod·ran′təl) _adj._

quad·ra·phon·ic (kwod′rə·fon′ik) _adj._ _Electronics_ 1. Designating a system of sound reproduction in which four receivers or loudspeakers are so placed as to give the effect of hearing the sound from all directions. 2. Designating a technique of recording or broadcasting that permits the use of such a system. Compare STEREOPHONIC.

quad·rat (kwod′rət) _n._ 1. _Printing_ A quad³. 2. _Ecol._ A square area of varying size laid down to estimate the number of plants enclosed, or to determine the character of successful changes. [See QUADRATE.]

quad·rate (kwod′rāt; _for n._, _also_ kwod′rit) _n._ 1. _Anat._ A bone or cartilaginous element suspending the lower jaw in certain of the lower vertebrates. 2. In astrology, an aspect of two heavenly bodies in which they are distant from each other 90°. 3. A cubical or square object, or an object resembling a cube. — _adj._ 1. Square; four-sided, as a muscle. 2. Distant from each other 90°: said of two heavenly bodies. 3. Of or pertaining to the quadrate bone or cartilage. — _v._ **·rat·ed, ·rat·ing** _v.i._ 1. To correspond or agree: with _with_. — _v.t._ 2. To cause to conform; bring in accordance with. [< L _quadratus_, pp. of _quadrare_ to square < _quattuor_ four]

quad·rat·ic (kwod·rat′ik) _adj._ 1. Square. 2. _Math._ Pertaining to an equation, curve, surface, etc., of the second degree. — _n._ _Math._ A quadratic equation, curve, etc.

quad·rat·ics (kwod·rat′iks) _n.pl._ (_construed as sing._) _Rare_ The branch of algebra dealing with quadratic equations.

quad·ra·ture (kwod′rə·chər) _n._ 1. The act or process of squaring. 2. _Math._ The determination of the area of a surface. 3. _Astron._ **a** The relative position of two heavenly bodies that are 90° apart as viewed from the center of a third body. **b** Either of two points in an orbit midway between conjunction and opposition. **c** A half-moon.

quad·ren·ni·al (kwod·ren′ē·əl) _adj._ 1. Occurring once in four years. 2. Lasting four years. — **quad·ren′ni·al·ly** _adv._

quad·ren·ni·um (kwod·ren′ē·əm) _n._ _pl._ **·ren·ni·ums** or **·ren·ni·a** (-ren′ē·ə) A space or period of four years. Also **quad·ri·en·ni·um** (kwod′rē·en′ē·əm). [< L]

quadri- _combining form_ Four: _quadrilateral_. Also _quadru-_: also _quadr-_ (before vowels). [< L _quattuor_ four]

quad·ric (kwod′rik) _adj._ _Math._ Of the second degree. — _n._ A quantic of the second degree. [< L _quadra_ square]

quad·ri·cen·ten·ni·al (kwod′ri·sen·ten′ē·əl) _n._ A four-hundredth anniversary. — _adj._ Of or pertaining to such an anniversary.

quad·ri·ceps (kwod′rə·seps) _n._ _Anat._ The extensor muscle of the leg. [< QUADRI- + L _caput_ head] — **quad·ri·cip′i·tal** (-sip′ə·təl) _adj._

quad·ri·fid (kwod′rə·fid) _adj._ _Bot._ Divided into four segments, as a flower petal. [< L _quadrifidus_ < _quadri-_ + root of _findere_ to cleave]

quad·ri·ga (kwod·rī′gə) _n._ _pl._ **·gae** (-jē) In ancient Rome, a two-wheeled chariot to which four horses were harnessed abreast. [< L < _quattuor_ four + _jugum_ yoke]

quad·ri·lat·er·al (kwod′rə·lat′ər·əl) _adj._ Formed or bounded by four lines; four-sided. — _n._ 1. _Geom._ **a** A figure bounded by four straight lines terminated at four angles. **b** A figure formed of four straight lines, having six intersections. 2. A space or area defended by four enclosing fortresses. [< L _quadrilaterus_ < _quattuor_ four + _latus, lateris_ side]

quad·ri·lin·gual (kwod′rə·ling′gwəl) _adj._ Written, expressed in, or using four languages.

qua·drille¹ (kwa·dril′) _n._ 1. A square dance for four couples, having five figures. 2. Music for or in the manner of this dance, alternately in 6/8 and 2/4 meter. [< F < Sp. _cuadrilla_ band, troop < _cuadra_ square < L _quadrum_ < _quattuor_ four]

qua·drille² (kwa·dril′) _n._ A card game for four persons, played with a deck of 40 cards, popular in the 18th century. [< F < Ital. _quadriglio_ or Sp. _cuartillo_]

quad·ril·lion (kwod·ril′yən) _n._ 1. _U.S._ A thousand trillions, written as 1 followed by fifteen zeros: a cardinal number. 2. _Brit._ A million trillions (def. 2), written as 1 followed by twenty-four zeros: a cardinal number. — _adj._ Being a quadrillion in number. [< MF < _quadri-_ four + (_mi_)_llion_ million]

quad·ril·lionth (kwod·ril′yənth) _adj._ 1. Having the number one quadrillion: the ordinal of _quadrillion_. 2. Being one of a quadrillion equal parts. — _n._ 1. One of a quadrillion equal parts. 2. That which is numbered one quadrillion.

quad·ri·no·mi·al (kwod′rə·nō′mē·əl) _n._ _Math._ An algebraic expression having four terms.

quad·ri·par·tite (kwod′rə·pär′tīt) _adj._ 1. Consisting of or embracing four parts. 2. Having four parties, as an agreement or contract. [< L _quadripartitus_ < _quattuor_ four + _partitus_ divided] — **quad′ri·par·ti′tion** (-tish′ən) _n._

quad·ri·syl·la·ble (kwod′rə·sil′ə·bəl) _n._ A word of four syllables. — **quad′ri·syl·lab′ic** (-sə·lab′ik) _adj._

quad·ri·va·lent (kwod′rə·vā′lənt) _adj._ _Chem._ Having a valence of four, as carbon: also _tetratomic, tetravalent_. [< QUADRI- + L _valens, -entis_, ppr. of _valere_ to be worth] — **quad′ri·va′lence, quad′ri·va′len·cy** _n._

quad·riv·i·al (kwod·riv′ē·əl) _adj._ 1. Having four roads radiating ways. 2. Leading to or going in four directions: _quadrivial_ streets. [< L _quadrivius_ < _quattuor_ four + _via_ way]

quad·riv·i·um (kwod·riv′ē·əm) _n._ _pl._ **·i·a** (-ē·ə) In medieval times, the four sciences, geometry, astronomy, arithmetic, and music, that composed the higher group of the seven liberal arts. Compare TRIVIUM. [< L, place where four roads meet]

quad·roon (kwod·rōōn′) _n._ A person having one Negro and three white grandparents. [< Sp. _cuarteron_ < _cuarto_ fourth]

quadru- Var. of QUADRI-.

quad·ru·ma·nous (kwod·rōō′mə·nəs) _adj._ 1. Having four feet resembling hands, as certain primates; four-handed. 2. Of or pertaining to a former order (_Quadrumana_) of mammals now classed with man under the primates. [< QUADRU- + L _manus_ hand] — **quad·ru·mane** (kwod′rōō·mān) _n._

quad·ru·ped (kwod′rōō·ped) _n._ An animal having four feet; especially, a four-footed mammal. — _adj._ Having four feet. [< L _quadrupes, -pedis_ < _quattuor_ four + _pes_ foot] — **quad·ru·pe·dal** (kwod·rōō′pə·dəl, kwod′rōō·ped′l) _adj._

quad·ru·ple (kwod′rōō·pəl, kwod·rōō′pəl) _v.t._ & _v.i._ **·pled, ·pling** To multiply by four; make or become four times larger. — _adj._ 1. Consisting of four; having four parts or members; fourfold. 2. Multiplied by four. — _n._ A number or sum four times as great as another. — _adv._ So as to make four times larger; fourfold. [< L < L _quadruplus_]

quadruple meter _Music_ See under METER².

quad·ru·plet (kwod′rōō·plit, kwod·rōō′-) _n._ 1. A compound or combination of four things or objects. 2. One of four offspring born of the same mother at one birth.

quad·ru·plex (kwod′rōō·pleks, kwod·rōō′-) _adj._ 1. Consisting of four; fourfold. 2. Pertaining to or designating a telegraph system in which four messages, two in each direction, may be sent simultaneously over one wire. — _n._ A sending instrument used in quadruplex telegraphy. [< L < _quattuor_ four + stem of _plicare_ to fold]

quad·ru·pli·cate (kwod·rōō′plə·kāt; _for adj._ & _n._, _also_ kwod·rōō′plə·kit) _adj._ 1. Quadruple; fourfold. 2. Raised to the fourth power. — _v.t._ **·cat·ed, ·cat·ing** To multiply by four; quadruple. — _n._ One of four like things. [< L _quadruplicatus_, pp. of _quadruplicare_ < _quadruplex_. See QUADRUPLEX.] — **quad·ru′pli·ca′tion** _n._

quae·re (kwē′rē) _n._ A question or query to signify that a point is open to inquiry. [< L. See QUERY.]

quaes·tor (kwes′tər, kwēs′-) _n._ In ancient Rome: **a** Originally, one of two magistrates who inquired into and punished capital crimes. **b** Later, one who took charge of the public treasury and expenditure. Also spelled _questor_. [< L < _quaerere_ to seek, inquire] — **quaes·to·ri·al** (kwes·tôr′ē·əl, -tō′rē-, kwēs-) _adj._ — **quaes′tor·ship** _n._

quaff (kwaf, kwof, kwôf) _v.t._ & _v.i._ To drink, especially copiously or with relish. — _n._ A drink; swallow. [Origin uncertain] — **quaff′er** _n._

quag (kwag, kwog) _n._ A marshy place or quagmire. [< obs. _quag_ to shake; ult. origin unknown]

quag·ga (kwag′ə) _n._ 1. A South African equine mammal (_Equus quagga_), now extinct. 2. A zebra: an erroneous use. [< native Hottentot name]

quag·gy (kwag′ē, kwog′ē) *adj.* **·gi·er, ·gi·est** Yielding to or quaking under the foot, as soft, wet earth; boggy.

quag·mire (kwag′mīr′, kwog′-) *n.* 1. Marshy ground that gives way under the foot; bog. 2. A difficult situation. [< QUAG + MIRE] — **quag′mired′, quag′·mir′y** *adj.*

qua·hog (kwô′hôg, -hog, kwə·hôg′, -hog′) *n.* An edible clam (*Venus mercenaria*) of the Atlantic coast of North America: also called *cohog, hard-shelled clam, round clam.* Also **qua′haug.** [< Algonquian (Narraganset) *poquauhock*]

QUAGGA
(About 3½ feet high at withers)

Quai d' Or·say (kā dôr·sā′) 1. A quay on the left bank of the Seine in Paris, on which the French Foreign Office is situated. 2. The French Foreign Office.

quaigh (kwākh) *n. Scot.* A small cup or drinking vessel. Also **quaich.**

quail¹ (kwāl) *n.* 1. An Old World game bird (*Coturnix coturnix*) similar to the partridge, having a very short tail. 2. Any of various small American game birds (family *Perdicidae*) related to the partridge; especially, the bobwhite. 3. *Obs.* A prostitute. [< OF *quaille*, prob. of Gmc. origin]

quail² (kwāl) *v.i.* To shrink with fear; lose heart or courage. [ME *quailen*; origin uncertain]

quaint (kwānt) *adj.* 1. Combining an antique appearance with a pleasing oddity, fancifulness, or whimsicalness. 2. Pleasingly odd or old-fashioned; fanciful. 3. *Obs.* Curiously wrought; also, ornamental. 4. *Obs.* Crafty. — **Syn.** See ANTIQUE. [< OF *cointe* < L *cognitus*, pp. of *cognoscere* to ascertain] — **quaint′ly** *adv.* — **quaint′ness** *n.*

quake (kwāk) *v.i.* **quaked, quak·ing** 1. To shake, as with violent emotion or cold. 2. To shake or tremble, as earth during an earthquake. — **Syn.** See SHAKE. — *n.* 1. The act of quaking. 2. An earthquake. [OE *cwacian* to shake]

Quak·er (kwā′kər) *n.* A member of the Society of Friends: originally a term of derision. [< QUAKE, v.; with ref. to their founder's admonition to tremble at the word of the Lord] — **Quak′er·ess** *n.fem.* — **Quak′er·ish** *adj.* — **Quak′er·ish·ly** *adv.*

quaker bonnet Either of two lupines of the United States, the **eastern quaker bonnet** (*Lupinus perennis*) of New England, with vivid blue flowers, or the **Texas quaker bonnet** (*L. subcarnosus*), the State flower of Texas.

quaker buttons The dried, ripe seeds of nux vomica.

Quaker City A nickname of PHILADELPHIA.

Quaker gun A dummy gun, as one made of wood. [from the Friends' doctrine of nonviolent resistance]

Quak·er·ism (kwā′kə·riz′əm) *n.* The beliefs or practices of the Quakers.

quak·er-la·dies (kwā′kər·lā′dēz) *n.pl.* The bluet, a flower.

Quak·er·ly (kwā′kər·lē) *adj.* Like the Quakers. — *adv.* After the manner of the Quakers.

Quaker meeting 1. Any meeting of the Society of Friends for worship, in which, following their usage, they remain silent until the Inner Light moves some member to speak or pray aloud. 2. Any gathering at which silence prevails.

Quaker State Nickname of PENNSYLVANIA.

quak·y (kwā′kē) *adj.* **quak·i·er, quak·i·est** Shaky; tremulous. — **quak′i·ly** *adv.* — **quak′i·ness** *n.*

qual·i·fi·ca·tion (kwol′ə·fə·kā′shən) *n.* 1. The act of qualifying, or the state of being qualified. 2. Any ability, training, attribute, or accomplishment that fits a person for a specific office, role, position, profession, etc. 3. A restriction; mitigation: to accept without *qualification.*

qual·i·fied (kwol′ə·fīd) *adj.* 1. Competent or fit, as for public office. 2. Restricted or modified in some way. — **Syn.** See ABLE. — **qual′i·fied′ly** *adv.*

qual·i·fy (kwol′ə·fī) *v.* **·fied, ·fy·ing** *v.t.* 1. To make fit or capable, as for an office, occupation, or privilege. 2. To make legally capable, as by the administration of an oath. 3. To limit or restrict, as by conditions or exceptions. 4. To attribute a quality to; describe; characterize or name. 5. To make less strong or extreme; soften; moderate. 6. To change the strength or flavor of. 7. *Gram.* To modify. — *v.i.* 8. To be or become qualified or fit; meet the requirements, as for entering a race. [< MF *qualifier* < Med.L *qualificare* to define, limit < L *qualis* of such a kind + *facere* to make] — **qual′i·fi′a·ble** *adj.* — **qual′i·fi′er** *n.* — **Syn.** 1. form, train. 3. restrict, delimit. 5. temper, modulate, mitigate, restrain.

qual·i·ta·tive (kwol′ə·tā′tiv) *adj.* Of or pertaining to quality: distinguished from *quantitative.* [< LL *qualitativus* < L *qualitas.* See QUALITY.] — **qual′i·ta·tive·ly** *adv.*

qualitative analysis *Chem.* The process of determining the kind and number of ingredients present in a substance.

qual·i·ty (kwol′ə·tē) *n. pl.* **·ties** 1. That which makes something such as it is; a distinguishing element or characteristic. 2. The basic or essential character, nature, etc., of something: the *quality* of summer. 3. Excellence: to aim for

quality rather than quantity. 4. The degree of excellence; relative goodness; grade: the high *quality* of these fabrics. 5. A moral or personality trait or characteristic: He has many good *qualities.* 6. *Logic* The character of a proposition or judgment in regard to its being either negative or affirmative. 7. *Music* The timbre of a voice or musical instrument. 8. *Phonet.* The character of a vowel sound as determined by the size and shape of the oral cavity and pharynx acting as resonance chambers. 9. *Archaic* High or superior social rank or birth: a lady of *quality*; also, persons of superior rank collectively. — **Syn.** See ATTRIBUTE. [< F *qualité* < L *qualitas* < *qualis* of such a kind]

qualm (kwäm, kwôm) *n.* 1. A feeling of sickness. 2. A twinge of conscience; moral scruple. 3. A sensation of fear or misgiving. [? OE *cwealm* death. Akin to G *qualm* black smoke, MHG *twalm* stupor.]

qualm·ish (kwä′mish, kwô′-) *adj.* 1. Feeling or affected with qualms. 2. Likely to produce qualms. Also **qualm′y.** — **qualm′ish·ly** *adv.* — **qualm′ish·ness** *n.*

quam·ash (kwom′ash, kwə·mash′) *n.* Camass, a plant.

quan·da·ry (kwon′dər·ē, -drē) *n. pl.* **·da·ries** A state of hesitation or perplexity; predicament. — **Syn.** See PREDICAMENT. [Origin uncertain]

quand même (kän mem′) *French* Notwithstanding; even though; nevertheless.

quan·dong (kwon′dong) *n.* 1. A small Australian tree (*Fusanus acuminatus*) of the sandalwood family. 2. Its edible drupaceous fruit, used as a preserve. Also **quan′dang** (-dong). [< native Australian name]

quant (kwant, kwont) *n. Brit.* A punting pole with a flange at the end to prevent its sinking in the mud. — *v.t. & v.i.* To propel or be propelled with a quant. [? < L *contus* boat pole]

quan·ta (kwon′tə) Plural of QUANTUM.

quan·tic (kwon′tik) *n. Math.* A rational homogeneous function of two or more variables, usually containing only positive integers. [< L *quantus* how much]

quan·ti·fy (kwon′tə·fī) *v.t.* **·fied, ·fy·ing** 1. To determine the quantity of. 2. *Logic* To express the quantity of explicitly, as by using *all, some,* or *none.* [< Med.L *quantificare* < L *quantus* how great + *facere* to make] — **quan′ti·fi·ca′·tion** *n.* — **quan′ti·fi′er** *n.*

quan·tim·e·ter (kwon·tim′ə·tər) *n. Med.* A dosimeter (which see).

quan·ti·ta·tive (kwon′tə·tā′tiv) *adj.* 1. Of or pertaining to quantity. 2. Having to do with quantities only: distinguished from *qualitative.* 3. In classical prosody, or pertaining to syllables that are classified as long or short rather than accented or unaccented. — **quan′ti·ta′tive·ly** *adv.* — **quan′ti·ta′tive·ness** *n.*

quantitative analysis *Chem.* The process of finding the amount or percentage of each element or ingredient present in a material or compound.

quan·ti·ty (kwon′tə·tē) *n. pl.* **·ties** 1. A specified or indefinite number, amount, weight, etc. 2. The property of a thing that admits of exact measurement. 3. *Often pl.* A large amount; profusion; abundance: *quantities* of food. 4. Measure; amount: *quantity* rather than quality. 5. *Math.* An entity regarded as possessing a certain determinable magnitude, as of length, size, volume, or number. 6. In prosody and phonetics, the relative period of time in which the articulators remain in the position required for the production of a given sound; length; duration. 7. *Logic* The extent of a general term or proposition as applying to the whole or to a part of a class. 8. *Music* The duration of a tone. 9. *Electr.* The magnitude or amount of current, expressed in coulombs or amperes. Abbr. *qt.* [< OF *quantite* < L *quantitas, -tatis* < *quantus* how much]

quan·tize (kwon′tīz) *v.t.* **·tized, ·tiz·ing** *Physics* 1. To restrict the possible values of (an observable quantity or magnitude) to a discrete set: always used in the passive. 2. To determine the allowed discrete values of (a dynamic system) by quantum mechanics. 3. To express as multiples of a given quantity or quantum. — **quan′ti·za′tion** *n.*

quan·tum (kwon′təm) *n. pl.* **·ta** (-tə) 1. An object that has quantity or is concrete. 2. A certain amount; also, a prescribed or a sufficient quantity. 3. *Physics* A fundamental unit of energy or action as provided for in the quantum theory. [< L, neuter of *quantus* how much]

quantum mechanics The branch of physics that investigates the motions of dynamic systems, especially in the atomic and subatomic range, by application of quantum theory

quantum number *Physics* A number indicating any of the energy levels possible in an atom under specified conditions.

quantum theory *Physics* The theory that energy is not a smoothly flowing continuum but is manifested by the emission from radiating bodies of discrete particles or *quanta,* the values of which are expressed as the product of Planck's constant multiplied by the frequency of the given radiation.

Qua·paw (kwä′pô) *n.* One of a tribe of North American Indians of Siouan stock, formerly living in Arkansas, now in Oklahoma: also called *Arkansas*.

quar·an·tine (kwŏr'ən·tēn, kwor'-) *n.* **1.** The enforced isolation for a fixed period of time of persons, ships, or goods arriving from places infected with or exposed to contagious disease. **2.** A place designated for the enforcement of such interdiction. **3.** The enforced isolation of any person or place infected with contagious disease. **4.** Any enforced isolation. **5.** A period of forty days. — *v.t.* **·tined, ·tin·ing** To subject to or retain in quarantine; isolate by or as by quarantine. [< Ital. *quarantina* ult. < L *quadraginta* forty]

quark (kwärk) *n. Physics* Any of a group of three types of hypothetical fundamental particles, carrying fractional electric charge and fractional baryon number, proposed as the entities of which all other strongly interacting particles are composed. [Coined by Murray Gell-Mann, born 1929, U.S. physicist, appar. after use by James Joyce in *Finnegans Wake*]

Quarles (kwôrlz, kwärlz), **Francis**, 1592–1644, English poet.

quar·rel¹ (kwôr'əl, kwor'-) *n.* **1.** An unfriendly, angry, or violent dispute. **2.** A falling out or contention; breach of amity. **3.** The cause for dispute. — *v.i.* **quar·reled** or **·relled, quar·rel·ing** or **·rel·ling 1.** To engage in a quarrel; dispute; contend; fight. **2.** To break off a mutual friendship; fall out; disagree. **3.** To find fault; cavil. [< F *que-relle* < L *querela* complaint < *queri* to complain] — **quar'·rel·er** or **quar'rel·ler** *n.*

— **Syn.** (noun) **1.** *Quarrel, wrangle, bicker, squabble, spat,* and *tiff* are compared as they denote a verbal dispute. *Quarrel* is the most extreme in its implication of anger, violence, and estrangement. *Wrangle* implies a prolonged and stubborn argument. *Bicker* suggests childish contradiction and recrimination, while *squabble* refers to a dispute over some petty matter, often without heat or ill feeling. A *spat* is sudden and short, arising often from ill temper, while a *tiff* is a mild *spat*, often caused by hurt feelings. Compare ROW³.

quar·rel² (kwôr'əl, kwor'-) *n.* **1.** A dart or arrow with a four-edged head, formerly used with a crossbow. **2.** A tool having a point with several edges, as a stonemason's chisel. [< OF < Med.L *quadrellum* < L *quadrum* square < *quattuor* four]

quar·rel·some (kwôr'əl·səm, kwor'-) *adj.* Inclined to quarrel. — **quar'rel·some·ly** *adv.* — **quar'rel·some·ness** *n.*

quar·ry¹ (kwôr'ē, kwor'ē) *n. pl.* **·ries 1.** A beast or bird hunted, seized, or killed, as in the chase; game; prey. **2.** Anything hunted, slaughtered, or eagerly pursued. **3.** *Obs.* A heap of slaughtered game. [< OF *cuiree* < L *corium* hide]

quar·ry² (kwôr'ē, kwor'ē) *n. pl.* **·ries** An excavation from which stone is taken by cutting, blasting, or the like. — *v.t.* **·ried, ·ry·ing 1.** To cut, dig, or take from or as from a quarry. **2.** To establish a quarry in. [< OF *quarriere* < L *quadrum* a square (stone) < *quadrus* square < *quattuor* four] — **quar·ri·er** (kwôr'ē·ər, kwor'-) *n.*

quar·ry³ (kwôr'ē, kwor'ē) *n. pl.* **·ries 1.** A square or lozenge. **2.** A small square or lozenge-shaped pane of glass, tile, etc. **3.** Quarrel² (def. 1). [Var. of QUARREL²]

quart¹ (kwôrt) *n.* **1.** A measure of capacity, the fourth part of a gallon, or two pints. In the U.S. the dry quart is equal to 1.10 liters and the liquid quart is equal to 0.946 liter. Abbr. *q., qt., qu.* See table inside back cover. **2.** A container having such a capacity. [< OF *quarte* < L *quartus* fourth]

quart² (kärt) *n.* **1.** In fencing, a quarte. **2.** In piquet, a sequence of four cards of the same suit, called **quart major** if they are the highest four. [< F *quarte*. See QUART¹]

quar·tan (kwôr'tən) *adj.* Pertaining to the fourth in a series; especially, occurring every fourth day. — *n. Pathol.* A malarial fever caused by the parasite *Plasmodium malariae*, in which the paroxysms recur every fourth day, or 72 hours, reckoning inclusively. [< OF *quartaine* < L *quartanus* < *quartus* fourth]

quarte (kärt, *Fr.* kȧrt) *n.* In fencing, a thrust or parry, the fourth regular position: also spelled *carte*. [< F]

quar·ter (kwôr'tər) *n.* **1.** One of four equal parts into which anything is or may be divided. **2.** In the United States and Canada, a coin having the value of 25 cents. **3.** Fifteen minutes or the fourth of an hour; also, the moment such a period begins or ends. **4.** Three months or a fourth of a year. **5.** A term of school, usually one fourth of a year. **6.** *Astron.* **a** A fourth part of the moon's revolution about the earth. **b** Either of two phases of the moon, as the **first quarter**, between the new and full moon, and the **third** or **last quarter** between the full moon and the new. For illustration see MOON. **7.** One of the four periods into which a game, as football, is divided. **8.** One fourth of a hundredweight or 25 pounds; in Great Britain, 28 pounds. **9.** One fourth of a yard; a span. **10.** One fourth of a pound. **11.** One fourth of a mile. **12.** One fourth of a ton of grain. **13.** *Music* A quarter note (which see). **14.** One of the four principal points or divisions of the compass or divisions of the horizon; also, a point or direction of the compass. **15.** A particular division, district, or locality, as of a city: the native *quarter*. **16.** A place, origin, or source from which something comes: on authority of the highest *quarter*. **17.** *Usually pl.* Proper or assigned station, position, or place, as of officers and crew on a

warship. **18.** *pl.* A place of lodging or residence. **19.** Mercy shown to a vanquished enemy; clemency. **20.** Either of the four limbs of a quadruped, together with the adjacent parts. **21.** A haunch of venison. **22.** The side of a horse's hoof, just in front of the heel. **23.** In shoemaking, that part of a boot or shoe from the middle of the heel to the line of the ankle bone. **24.** *Naut.* **a** The upper part of a vessel's side, near the stern and similar in length to the quarterdeck. **b** That part of a yard outside the slings. **25.** *Heraldry* **a** Any of four equal divisions into which a shield is divided. **b** An ordinary occupying such a division. Abbr. *q., qr., qu.* — **at close quarters** Close by; at close range. — *adj.* **1.** Being one of four equal parts. **2.** Having one fourth of a standard value. — *v.t.* **1.** To divide into four equal parts. **2.** To divide into a number of parts or pieces. **3.** To cut the body of (an executed person) into four parts: He was hanged, drawn, and *quartered.* **4.** To range from one side to the other of (a field, etc.) while advancing. **5.** To furnish with quarters or shelter; lodge. **6.** *Heraldry* **a** To divide (a shield) into quarters by vertical and horizontal lines. **b** To bear or arrange (coats of arms) quarterly, as upon a shield. **7.** *Mech.* To mark or place at intervals of a quarter, especially of a quarter of a circle. — *v.i.* **8.** To be stationed or lodged. **9.** To range from side to side of an area, as dogs in hunting. **10.** *Naut.* To blow on a ship's quarter: said of the wind. [< OF *quartier* < L *quartarius* < *quartus* fourth]

quar·ter·age (kwôr'tər·ij) *n.* **1.** A quarterly allowance or payment. **2.** Board and lodging, especially for troops, a work gang, etc.; also, the cost of such lodging.

quar·ter·back (kwôr'tər·bak') *n.* In American football, one of the backfield, who often calls the signals; also, the position played by this player. Abbr. *qb, q.b.*

quarter crack *Vet.* A crack on the inner quarter of a horse's forehoof. Compare SAND CRACK.

quarter day Any of the days of the year when quarterly payments are due. Quarter days for the U.S. government are the first days of January, April, July, and October, and in Great Britain they are Lady Day (March 25), Midsummer Day (June 24), Michaelmas (September 29), and Christmas (December 25).

quar·ter·deck (kwôr'tər·dek') *n. Naut.* The rear part of a ship's upper deck, reserved for officers.

quar·ter·fi·nal (kwôr'tər·fī'nəl) *n.* A competition immediately preceding the semifinal in sporting events. — *adj.* Next to the semifinal. — **quar'ter·fi'nal·ist** *n.*

quar·ter·foil (kwôr'tər·foil') *n.* Quatrefoil.

quarter horse One of a breed of horses now used as ranch horses or cow ponies, originally used as racers over quarter-of-a-mile courses by early settlers of Virginia.

quar·ter·hour (kwôr'tər·our') *n.* Fifteen minutes; also, a point, as on the face of a clock, fifteen minutes before or after the hour. — **quar'ter·hour'ly** *adj. & adv.*

quar·ter·ing (kwôr'tər·ing) *adj.* **1.** *Naut.* **a** Blowing against or on the quarter. **b** Sailing so as to have the wind on the quarter. **2.** Set or being at right angles. — *n.* **1.** A dividing or marking off into quarters. **2.** *Heraldry* **a** The division of a shield into quarters. **b** Any of the coats that are quartered on the shield, or the quarter containing it. **3.** Quarters, or the assigning of quarters, as for soldiers.

quar·ter·ly (kwôr'tər·lē) *adj.* **1.** Containing or being a fourth part. **2.** Occurring at intervals of three months. — *n. pl.* **·lies** A publication issued once every three months. — *adv.* **1.** Once in a quarter of a year. **2.** In or by quarters. Abbr. *q., qr., qu.*

quar·ter·mas·ter (kwôr'tər·mas'tər, -mäs'-) *n.* **1.** *Usually cap. Mil.* An officer responsible for the supply of food, fuel, clothing, etc. **2.** On shipboard, a petty officer responsible for steering and related functions. Abbr. *QM*

Quartermaster Corps A branch of the U.S. Army that is responsible for the supply of food, fuel, clothing, and related items, and for providing certain services. Abbr. *QMC*

Quartermaster General In the U.S. Army, the major general who heads the Quartermaster Corps. Abbr. *QMG*

quar·tern (kwôr'tərn) *n.* **1.** A fourth part of certain measures or weights, as of a peck or pound. **2.** *Chiefly Brit.* A four-pound loaf of bread. [< OF *quartron* < L *quaterni* four each < *quater* four times < *quartus* fourth]

quar·ter·ni·on (kwôr·tûr'nē·ən) *n. Printing* A gathering of four sheets, each folded into pages, usually four to a sheet, to make a section of a book, pamphlet, etc.

quarter note *Music* A note having one fourth the time value of a whole note: also *crotchet.* For illustration see NOTE.

quar·ter·phase (kwôr'tər·fāz') *adj. Electr.* Diphase.

quar·ter·saw (kwôr'tər·sô') *v.t.* **·sawed, ·sawed** or **·sawn, ·saw·ing** To saw (a log) lengthwise into quarters so that each face corresponds with one of the log's radii.

quarter section In the system of land surveying adopted by the governments of the United States and Canada, a tract of land half a mile square, containing one fourth of a square mile, or 160 acres. Abbr. *q.s.*

quarter sessions A court held quarterly.

quar·ter·staff (kwôr'tər·staf', -stäf') *n. pl.* **·staves** (-stāvz') A stout, iron-tipped staff about 6½ feet long, formerly used in England as a weapon; also, the use of the quarterstaff.

quarter tone *Music* Half of a semitone. Also **quar·ter·tone** (kwôr′tər·tōn′).

quar·tet (kwôr·tet′) *n.* **1.** A composition for four voices or instruments. **2.** The four persons who perform such compositions. **3.** Any group or set of four things of a kind. Also **quar·tette**. [< F *quartette* < Ital.]

quar·tic (kwôr′tik) *Math. adj.* Denoting a quantic function of the fourth degree. — *n.* Such a function.

quar·tile (kwôr′tīl, -til) *n.* **1.** In astrology, a quadrate. **2.** *Stat.* The portion of a frequency distribution comprising a fourth of the total observed cases. — *adj.* Of or pertaining to a quartile. [< LL *quartilis* < L *quartus* fourth]

quar·to (kwôr′tō) *adj.* Having four leaves or eight pages to the sheet: a *quarto* book. — *n. pl.* **·tos** A book or pamphlet having pages the size of a fourth of a sheet: often written **4to** or **4°.** *Abbr. q., Q., qto.* [< L (*in*) *quarto* (in) fourth]

quartz (kwôrts) *n.* Silicon dioxide, SiO_2, a hard, vitreous, widely distributed mineral occurring in many varieties, sometimes massive, as jasper and chalcedony, or sometimes in colorless and transparent or diversely colored forms crystallizing in the hexagonal system. [< G *quarz*]

quartz crystal A thin section of pure quartz, accurately ground and polished for use in certain optical instruments and as a high-frequency oscillator in some electron tubes; a piezoelectric oscillator. Also **quartz plate.**

quartz·if·er·ous (kwôrt·sif′ər·əs) *adj.* Consisting of or containing quartz.

quartz·ite (kwôrt′sīt) *n.* A massive metamorphic rock formed by the hardening of sandstone through the deposition of quartz about each grain.

qua·sar (kwā′zär, -sär) *n. Astron.* Any of a class of very distant, celestial objects that are strong radio sources, have unusual light spectra, show large red shifts, and have a vast, unexplained energy output. [< QUAS(I) + (STELL)AR (RADIO SOURCES)]

quash[1] (kwosh) *v.t. Law* To make void or set aside, as an indictment; annul. — **Syn.** See ANNUL. [< OF *quasser* < L *quassare* to shatter; meaning infl. by LL *cassare* to annul]

quash[2] (kwosh) *v.t.* To put down or suppress forcibly or summarily: to *quash* a rebellion. [< OF *quasser* < L *quassare* to shatter; meaning infl. by SQUASH[1]]

qua·si (kwā′zē, -sē, kwä′zī, -sī) *adj.* Resembling in some particulars but not exactly of the same kind: *quasi* fascists. — *adv.* Seemingly; nearly; almost. [< L, as if, nearly]

quasi- *prefix* **1.** (With nouns) Resembling; not genuine, as in:

quasi-accident	quasi-injury
quasi-adult	quasi-insight
quasi-approval	quasi-integrity
quasi-artist	quasi-invasion
quasi-attack	quasi-kindred
quasi-authority	quasi-lament
quasi-bargain	quasi-liberal
quasi-blunder	quasi-luxury
quasi-certificate	quasi-market
quasi-characteristic	quasi-method
quasi-comprehension	quasi-miracle
quasi-conquest	quasi-neutrality
quasi-conservative	quasi-owner
quasi-consultation	quasi-pleasure
quasi-critic	quasi-poem
quasi-dependence	quasi-protection
quasi-despair	quasi-purity
quasi-development	quasi-reality
quasi-difference	quasi-recreation
quasi-distress	quasi-refusal
quasi-endorsement	quasi-remedy
quasi-escape	quasi-repair
quasi-faith	quasi-scholar
quasi-farmer	quasi-tradition
quasi-friend	quasi-triumph
quasi-guarantee	quasi-victory
quasi-handicap	quasi-worship
quasi-illness	quasi-zeal

2. (With adjectives) Nearly; almost, as in:

quasi-absolute	quasi-hereditary
quasi-amiable	quasi-human
quasi-beneficial	quasi-humorous
quasi-classic	quasi-important
quasi-colloquial	quasi-infinite
quasi-comic	quasi-internal
quasi-complex	quasi-jocose
quasi-continuous	quasi-lexicographic
quasi-converted	quasi-medical
quasi-devoted	quasi-natural
quasi-eligible	quasi-normal
quasi-equal	quasi-official
quasi-evil	quasi-practical
quasi-exempt	quasi-private
quasi-explicit	quasi-probable
quasi-financial	quasi-religious
quasi-forgotten	quasi-righteous
quasi-formidable	quasi-scientific
quasi-genteel	quasi-similar
quasi-grateful	quasi-spiritual

quasi-stylish	quasi-typica
quasi-sufficient	quasi-valid
quasi-tangible	quasi-vital
quasi-theatrical	quasi-willing

3. *Law* Superficially resembling but intrinsically different, as in:

quasi-corporation	quasi-entail
quasi-delict	quasi-legislative
quasi-deposit	quasi-partner

[< L, as if, nearly]

qua·si-con·tract (kwä′sī·kon′trakt, -zī-, kwä′sē-) *n. Law* An obligation to do something, enforceable by a contract remedy, but imposed by operation of law regardless of the consent of the defendant.

qua·si-ju·di·cial (kwä′sī·jōō·dish′əl, -zī-, kwä′sē-) *adj.* Exercising functions of a judicial nature as a guide for official action, as a committee investigating facts and drawing conclusions from them.

quass (kväs, kvas) See KVASS.

quas·si·a (kwosh′ē·ə, kwosh′ə) *n.* **1.** The wood of either of two tropical American trees (*Picrasma excelsa* or *Quassia amara*) typical of a family (*Simarubaceae*), yielding a variety of economic products. **2.** The bitter principle of this wood, used in medicine. **3.** The tree itself. [< NL, after Graman *Quassi* who discovered its use in 1730]

quatch grass (kwoch) Couch grass (which see).

quate (kwāt) *adj. Scot.* Quiet.

qua·ter·na·ry (kwä′tər·ner·ē) *adj.* **1.** Consisting of four. **2.** Fourth in order. — *n. pl.* **·ries 1.** The number four; a group of four things. **2.** *Math.* A quantic function having four variables. [< L *quaternarius* < *quaterni* by fours]

Qua·ter·na·ry (kwə·tûr′nə·rē) *adj. Geol.* Of, pertaining to, or designating a geological period and system of the Cenozoic era, following the Tertiary and still continuing. See chart for GEOLOGY. — *n.* The Quaternary system or period.

qua·ter·ni·on (kwə·tûr′nē·ən) *n.* **1.** A set, system, or file of four. **2.** *Math.* **a** An operator or factor that changes one vector into another: so called because expressible as the sum of four quantities. **b** The form of the calculus of vectors based on and making use of the quaternion operator. [< LL *quaternio, -onis* < *quattuor* four < L *quattor*]

Quath·lam·ba (kwät·läm′bä) See DRAKENSBERG.

quat·rain (kwot′rān) *n.* A stanza or poem of four lines. [< F < *quatre* four]

qua·tre (kä′tər, *Fr.* kȧ′tr′) *n.* **1.** A card, domino, etc., marked with four spots or pips. **2.** The number four. [< F]

Qua·tre-Bras (kä′tr′·brä′) A village in Belgium; scene of English victory over the French prior to Waterloo, 1815.

quat·re·foil (kat′ər·foil′, kat′rə-) *n.* **1.** A leaf, etc., having four leaflets. **2.** *Archit.* An ornament with four foils or lobes. Also **quarterfoil.** [< OF *quatre* four + *foil* leaf]

quat·tro·cen·to (kwat′trō·chen′tō) *n.* The 15th century as connected with the revival of art and literature, especially in Italy. — *adj.* Of or pertaining to the quattrocento. [< Ital.]

QUATREFOILS

qua·ver (kwā′vər) *v.i.* **1.** To tremble or shake: said usually of the voice. **2.** To produce trills or quavers in singing or in playing a musical instrument. — *v.t.* **3.** To utter or sing in a tremulous voice. — *n.* **1.** A quivering or tremulous motion. **2.** A shake or trill, as in singing. **3.** *Music Chiefly Brit.* An eighth note. [Freq. of obs. *quave*, ME *cwafian* to tremble. Cf. dial. Sw. *kuabba*, G *quabbeln*.] — **qua′ver·y** *adj.*

quay (kē) *n.* A wharf or artificial landing place where vessels may load or unload. [< OF *cai* hedge, wall, embankment < Celtic]

quay·age (kē′ij) *n.* **1.** Charge or dues for using a quay. **2.** Space on a quay. **3.** Quays collectively.

Que. Quebec (unofficial).

quean (kwēn) *n.* **1.** A brazen or ill-behaved woman; harlot; prostitute. **2.** *Scot.* A young or unmarried woman; a girl. [OE *cwene* prostitute]

quea·sy (kwē′zē) *adj.* **quea·si·er, quea·si·est 1.** Sick at the stomach. **2.** Nauseating; also, caused by nausea. **3.** Easily nauseated. **4.** Fastidious; squeamish. **5.** Requiring to be carefully treated; delicate; ticklish. **6.** Uncertain; hazardous. [ME *coisy*; origin unknown] — **quea′si·ly** *adv.* — **quea′si·ness** *n.*

Que·bec (kwi·bek′) A Province of eastern Canada; 594,860 sq. mi.; pop. 6,030,000; capital, **Quebec,** a port on the St. Lawrence River, pop. 182,418; formerly *Lower Canada. Abbr. P.Q.* — **Que·beck′er** or **Que·bec′er** *n.*

Quebec heater *Canadian* A type of space heater.

Quebec highlander *Canadian Slang* A French Canadian priest.

que·bra·cho (kā·brä′chō) *n. pl.* **·chos 1.** Any of several tropical American trees; especially, the **white quebracho** (*Aspidosperma quebracho-blanco*), a Chilean tree whose bark is used as a febrifuge and for respiratory diseases, and the **red quebracho** (*Schinopsis lorentzii*), a tree whose heartwood is rich in tannin. **2.** The wood or bark of any of these trees. [< Sp., var. of *quiebrahacha*, lit., ax breaker]

Quech·ua (kech'wä) *n.* **1.** One of a tribe of South American Indians that dominated the Inca empire prior to the Spanish conquest. **2.** The language of the Quechuas, still spoken as a mother tongue in parts of Peru and Ecuador: also called *Incan*. Also spelled *Kechua*.

Quech·uan (kech'wən) *adj.* Of or pertaining to the Quechua or their language. — *n.* Quechua. Also spelled *Kechuan*.

queen (kwēn) *n.* **1.** The wife of a king. **2.** A female sovereign or monarch. **3.** A woman preeminent in a given sphere. **4.** In chess, the most powerful piece, capable of moving any number of squares in a straight line. Abbr. *Q* **5.** A playing card bearing a conventional picture of a queen. Also *Archaic* **Queene.** **6.** *Entomol.* The single fully developed female in a colony of social insects, as bees, ants, etc. Abbr. *Q.*, *qu.* — *v.t.* **1.** To make a queen of. **2.** In chess, to make a queen of (a pawn) by moving it to the eighth row. — *v.i.* **3.** To reign as or play the part of a queen. — **to queen it** To act in a domineering, queenly manner. [OE *cwēn* woman, queen. Cf. ON *kvān* wife, queen, Gk. *gunē* woman.]

Queen Anne's lace The wild carrot.

Queen Anne style **1.** *Archit.* A style prevalent in England in the early 18th century, or a style similar to it used in the United States in the latter part of the 19th century, characterized by the use of red brickwork on which relief ornaments are carved, and by plain, unpretentious design. **2.** A type of furniture characterized by much upholstery and marquetry.

Queen Anne's War See WAR OF THE SPANISH SUCCESSION in table for WAR.

Queen Char·lotte Sound (shär'lət) A bay of the Pacific in British Columbia between Vancouver Island and the **Queen Charlotte Islands,** an archipelago (3,970 sq. mi.) of British Columbia.

queen consort The wife of a reigning king, who does not share his sovereignty.

queen dowager The widow of a king.

queen·ly (kwēn'lē) *adj.* **queen·li·er, queen·li·est** **1.** Of, pertaining to, or like a queen. **2.** Fit for a queen. — *adv.* In the manner of a queen. — **queen'li·ness** *n.*

Queen Maud Mountains (môd) A range extending south of the Ross Shelf Ice, Antarctica; rising over 13,000 ft.

queen mother A queen dowager who is mother of a reigning sovereign.

queen of the prairie A tall perennial herb (*Filipendula rubra*) common to American meadows and prairies.

queen olive A large variety of Spanish olive.

queen post One of two upright suspending or sustaining posts of compression members, as in a roof truss.

queen regent **1.** A queen who rules in behalf of another. **2.** A queen who rules in her own right: also **queen regnant.**

Queens (kwēnz) The easternmost borough of New York City, located on Long Island; 113 sq. mi.; pop. 1,987,174.

Queen's Bench Court of Queen's Bench. See under COURT OF KING'S BENCH.

Queens·ber·ry Rules (kwēnz'ber·ē) See MARQUIS OF QUEENSBERRY RULES.

Queen's Counsel See under KING'S COUNSEL.

queen's-de·light (kwēnz'di·līt') *n.* A smooth, erect perennial (*Stillingia sylvatica*) of the spurge family, with alternate leaves and a medicinal root.

queen's English King's English (which see).

queen's evidence See under KING'S EVIDENCE.

queen's highway See under KING'S HIGHWAY.

Queens·land (kwēnz'lənd) A State of NE Australia; about 667,000 sq. mi.; pop. 1,810,000 (est. 1970, excluding aborigines); capital, Brisbane.

queen's metal An alloy of tin, antimony, copper, and zinc, softer than Britannia metal, used for ornamental purposes.

Queen's Scout See under KING'S SCOUT.

Queens·town (kwēnz'toun) A former name for CÓBH.

queer (kwir) *adj.* **1.** Being out of the usual course of events; singular; odd. **2.** Of questionable character; open to suspicion. **3.** *Slang* Counterfeit. **4.** *Slang* Homosexual. — *n. Slang* **1.** Counterfeit money. **2.** A homosexual person. — *v.t.* *U.S. Slang* To jeopardize or spoil. [Origin unknown. Cf. G *quer* oblique.] — **queer'ly** *adv.* — **queer'·ness** *n.*

— **Syn.** (adj.) **1.** strange, peculiar, eccentric, erratic. Compare ODD, FANTASTIC. — **Ant.** ordinary, familiar, normal, natural.

quell (kwel) *v.t.* **1.** To put down or suppress by force; extinguish. **2.** To quiet; allay, as pain. [OE *cwellan* to kill] — **quell'er** *n.*

— **Syn. 1.** subdue, crush. **2.** soothe, still.

Quel·part (kwel'pärt) A former name for CHEJU.

quel·que chose (kel'kə shōz') *French* A trifle; something.

Que·moy Islands (ki·moi') *n. pl.* Two fortified islands of the Republic of China in Formosa Strait near the China mainland; 54 sq. mi.

quench (kwench) *v.t.* **1.** To put out or extinguish, as a fire. **2.** To put an end to; cause to cease. **3.** To slake or satisfy (thirst). **4.** To suppress or repress, as emotions. **5.** To cool, as heated iron or steel, by thrusting into water or other liquid. [OE *-cwencan*, causative of *cwincan* to grow less, disappear] — **quench'a·ble** *adj.* — **quench'er** *n.*

quench·less (kwench'lis) *adj.* Incapable of being quenched; insatiable. — **quench'less·ly** *adv.* — **quench'less·ness** *n.*

que·nelle (kə·nel') *n. French* A ball of savory paste made of minced meat, as chicken, veal, or fish, with bread crumbs and egg, usually poached.

quer·ce·tin (kwûr'sə·tin) *n. Biochem.* A yellow crystalline compound, $C_{15}H_{10}O_7$, found in the bark of the American oak and in the rind of certain fruits, used as a base for dyestuffs. [< L *quercus* oak + -IN] — **quer·cet·ic** (kwər·set'ik, -sē'tik) *adj.*

quer·cine (kwûr'sin, -sīn) *adj.* Of or pertaining to oaks. [< L *quercinus* < L *quercus* oak]

quer·cit·ron (kwûr'sit·ron) *n.* **1.** The crushed and powdered inner bark of the American black oak (*Quercus velutina*), used in dyeing and tanning. **2.** The yellow dye made from this bark. **3.** The dyer's oak (*Q. coccinea*). [< L *uquercs* oak + CITRON]

Quer·cus (kwûr'kəs) *n.* A genus of hardwood trees and shrubs, the oaks, of the beech family, widely distributed in north temperate regions. [< NL < L, an oak]

que·ri·da (kā·rē'dä) *n. SW U.S.* A beloved girl or woman; a darling. [< Sp.]

que·rist (kwir'ist) *n.* An inquirer; questioner.

quern (kwûrn) *n.* **1.** An old form of hand mill for grinding grain. **2.** A small hand mill for grinding spices. [OE *cweorn*]

quer·u·lous (kwer'ə·ləs, -yə·ləs) *adj.* **1.** Disposed to complain or be fretful; captious. **2.** Indicating or expressing a complaining or whining disposition. [< LL *querulosus* < *queri* to complain] — **quer'u·lous·ly** *adv.* — **quer'u·lous·ness** *n.*

que·ry (kwir'ē) *v.* **·ried, ·ry·ing** *v.t.* **1.** To inquire into; ask about. **2.** To ask questions of; interrogate. **3.** To express doubt concerning the correctness or truth of, especially, as in printing, by marking with a query. — *v.i.* **4.** To have or express doubt; question. — **Syn.** See ASK. — *n. pl.* **·ries** **1.** An inquiry, or a memorandum of an inquiry, to be answered; a question. **2.** A doubt; interrogation: often indicated, as in printing, by the question mark (?). Abbr. *q.*, *qu.*, *qy.* [< L *quaere*, imperative sing. of *quaerere* to ask]

ques. Question.

Ques·nay (ke·nā'), **François,** 1694–1774, French physician and political economist; founder of physiocracy.

quest (kwest) *n.* **1.** The act of seeking or looking for something; a search. **2.** An adventure or expedition, as in medieval romance. **3.** The person or persons engaged in a quest. **4.** *Rare* An inquest. — *v.i.* **1.** To go on a quest. **2.** To make a search. **3.** To search for game. **4.** To bay on the trail of game: said of hunting dogs. — *v.t.* **5.** To search for; seek. [< OF *queste* < L *quaesitus*, pp. of *quaerere* to ask, seek] — **quest'er** *n.*

ques·tion (kwes'chən) *n.* **1.** An interrogative sentence calling for an answer; an inquiry. **2.** A subject of inquiry or debate; a matter to be decided; problem. **3.** A subject of dispute; a controversy; disagreement. **4.** A proposition under discussion in a deliberative assembly. **5.** Possibility of disagreement or dispute; doubt: no *question* about it. **6.** The act of asking or inquiring. Abbr. *q.*, *Q.*, *qu.*, *ques.* — **beside the question** Irrelevant; not pertinent. — **beyond (all) question** Not open to dispute; settled. — **in question** Under discussion or consideration. — **out of the question** Not to be thought of; impossible. — *v.t.* **1.** To put a question or questions to; interrogate. **2.** To be uncertain of; doubt. **3.** To make objection to; challenge; dispute. — *v.i.* **4.** To ask a question or questions. — **Syn.** See ASK. [< OF < L *quaestio, -onis* < *quaerere* to ask] — **ques'tion·er** *n.*

ques·tion·a·ble (kwes'chən·ə·bəl) *adj.* **1.** Characterized by doubtful integrity, honesty, respectability, etc.: a *questionable* reputation. **2.** Liable to be called in question; debatable. **3.** Uncertain; difficult to decide. **4.** *Obs.* Capable of being questioned or inquired of. — **ques'tion·a·bil'i·ty, ques'·tion·a·ble·ness** *n.* — **ques'tion·a·bly** *adv.*

ques·tion·ar·y (kwes'chən·er'ē) *adj.* Of the nature of an examination. — *n. pl.* **·ar·ies** A questionnaire.

ques·tion·less (kwes'chən·lis) *adj.* Unquestionable; indubitable; also, unquestioning. — *adv.* Beyond or without question.

question mark A mark of punctuation (?) indicating that the sentence it closes is a direct question: also called *interrogation point.*

ques·tion·naire (kwes'chə·nâr') *n.* A written or printed form comprising a series of questions submitted to a number of persons to obtain data for a survey or report. [< F]

ques·tor (kwes'tər) See QUAESTOR.

Quet·ta (kwet'ə) A city in western West Pakistan; capital of the former Baluchistan; pop. 106,633 (1961).

quet·zal (ket·säl') *n. pl.* **·zals** or **·za·les** (-sä'lās) **1.** A bird (*Pharomacrus mocinno*) of brilliant plumage, the national symbol of Guatemala, regarded as a deity by the Mayas, whose chiefs alone were permitted to wear cloaks decorated with its plumes. **2.** The standard monetary unit of Guatemala, equivalent to 100 centavos. Also **que·zal** (kā·säl′). Abbr. *q.* [< Sp. < Nahuatl]

Quet·zal·co·a·tl (ket-säl′kō·ä′tl) A traditional god and heroic figure of the Aztecs.

queue (kyōō) *n.* **1.** A pendent braid of hair on the back of the head; pigtail. **2.** A line of persons or vehicles. — *v.i.* **queued, queu·ing** *Brit.* To form a line: usually with *up.* Also **cue.** [< MF < L *cauda* a tail]

quey (kwā) *n. Scot.* A young cow; heifer. [< ON *kviga*]

Que·zon (kā′zon, *Sp.* kā′sôn, -thôn), **Manuel Luis,** 1878–1944, Philippine statesman; first president 1935–44: full name **Manuel Luis Quezon y Mo·li·na** (ē mō·lē′nä).

Que·zon City (kā′sôn, -thôn) The capital of the Philippines, on southern Luzon; pop. 780,700 (est. 1971).

quib·ble (kwib′əl) *n.* **1.** An evasion of a point or question. **2.** A trivial distinction or objection; cavil. **3.** *Rare* A pun. — *v.i.* **·bled, ·bling** To evade the truth or the point in question, as by raising trivial objections. **4.** [< obs. *quib* < L *quibus,* ablative pl. of *qui* who, which; with ref. to its use in legal documents] — **quib′bler** *n.*

QUETZAL
(About 4 feet long overall)

Qui·be·ron (kēb·rôn′) A peninsula of Brittany, France, nearly enclosing **Quiberon Bay,** scene of a British naval victory over the French, 1759.

Qui·ché (kē·chā′) *n.* **1.** An Indian of a tribe of Mayan stock of Guatemala. **2.** The Mayan language of this tribe.

quick (kwik) *adj.* **1.** Done or occurring in a short time; rapid; swift. **2.** Responding readily or eagerly to impressions or instruction: a *quick* mind. **3.** Alert; sensitive; perceptive: a *quick* ear. **4.** Easily aroused or excited; hasty: a *quick* temper. **5.** Characterized by rapidity or readiness of movement or action; nimble: *quick* fingers. **6.** Pregnant; with child. **7.** Refreshing; bracing. **8.** Burning briskly; fiery. **9.** *Archaic* Having life; living. — **Syn.** See SWIFT[1]. — *n.* **1.** Those who are alive: chiefly in the phrase **the quick and the dead. 2.** The living flesh, especially the tender flesh under a fingernail. **3.** The feelings: cut to the *quick.* **4.** A plant suitable for hedges. — *adv.* Quickly; rapidly. [OE *cwic* alive. Cf. OS *quik,* OHG *queck.* Akin to L *vivus* alive.] — **quick′ness** *n.*

quick assets Assets readily convertible to cash; liquid assets.

quick bread Any bread, biscuits, etc., whose leavening agent makes immediate baking possible.

quick·en (kwik′ən) *v.t.* **1.** To cause to move more rapidly; hasten or accelerate. **2.** To make alive; give or restore life to. **3.** To excite or arouse; stimulate: to *quicken* the appetite. — *v.i.* **4.** To move or act more quickly; become more rapid. **5.** To come or return to life; revive. **6.** To reach the stage of pregnancy at which the motions of the fetus first become perceptible: said of the mother. **7.** To begin to manifest signs of life: said of the fetus. — **quick′en·er** *n.*

— **Syn.** 1, 4. *Quicken, accelerate, speed, hasten,* and *hurry* mean to move or to cause to move faster. *Quicken* suggests greater animation in the performance of an action, as well as a shorter time required for its completion; it is close in sense to *accelerate,* which denotes an increase in the rate of movement, growth, progress, etc. of a thing: the dancers *quickened* their steps, neglect has *accelerated* this building's decay. *Speed* differs from *quicken* and *accelerate* in that it always implies rapidity of movement: the auto *sped* along the road. *Hasten* indicates urgency, or sometimes a sudden and premature result: the storm's approach *hastened* our departure. *Hurry* is similar to *hasten,* but suggests agitation precipitous or confused motion: the late arrivals were *hurried* to their seats. — **Ant.** retard, slow, slacken, deaden.

quick fire The firing of quick successive shots, used chiefly against moving or bobbing targets.

quick-fir·ing (kwik′fīr′ing) *adj.* Firing or able to fire shots rapidly and continuously. Also **quick′-fire′.**

quick-freeze (kwik′frēz′) *v.t.* **·froze, ·fro·zen, ·freez·ing** To subject (food) to rapid refrigeration for storing at or below freezing temperatures.

quick grass Couch grass (which see).

quick·hatch (kwik′hach′) *n. Canadian* Wolverine.

quick·ie (kwik′ē) *n. U.S. Slang* Anything done hastily, as by short cuts or makeshift methods.

quick·lime (kwik′līm′) *n.* See under LIME[1].

quick·ly (kwik′lē) *adv.* In a quick manner; rapidly; soon.

quick march A march in quick time; quickstep.

quick·sand (kwik′sand′) *n.* A bed of sand, often of considerable depth, so water-soaked as to engulf any object, person, or animal resting or moving upon it.

quick·set (kwik′set′) *n.* **1.** A plant suitable for hedges, especially hawthorn. **2.** A hedge made of it. — *adj.* Composed of quickset.

quick·sil·ver (kwik′sil′vər) *n.* **1.** Mercury in its liquid

form. **2.** An amalgam of tin, used for the backs of mirrors. [OE *cwicseolfor.* Trans. of L *argentum vivum.*]

quick-step (kwik′step′) *n.* A march or dance written in a rapid tempo; also, a quick march.

quick-tem·pered (kwik′tem′pərd) *adj.* Easily angered.

quick time A marching step of 120 paces a minute, each pace of 30 inches, used in military drills and ceremonies.

quick·wa·ter (kwik′wô′tər, -wot′ər) *n.* A stream or that part of a stream having a decided current.

quick-wit·ted (kwik′wit′id) *adj.* Having a ready wit or quick discernment; keen; alert. — **quick′-wit′ted·ly** *adv.* — **quick′-wit′ted·ness** *n.*

quid[1] (kwid) *n.* **1.** A small portion of chewing tobacco. **2.** A cud; a portion of a cow. [OE *cwudu.* Var. of CUD.]

quid[2] (kwid) *n. pl.* **quid** *Brit. Slang* A pound sterling, or a sovereign. [? Suggested by L QUID PRO QUO]

Quid·de (kvid′ə), **Ludwig,** 1858–1941, German politician, author, and pacifist.

quid·di·ty (kwid′ə·tē) *n. pl.* **·ties 1.** The essence of a thing. **2.** A subtle or trifling distinction or objection; cavil. [< LL *quidditas, -tatis* < L *quid* which, what, neut. of *quis* who]

quid·nunc (kwid′nungk′) *n.* One who seeks to know all that is going on; a busybody. [< L *quid nunc* what now]

quid pro quo (kwid′ prō kwō′) *Latin* **1.** Something for something; an equivalent in return. **2.** Formerly, one medicine used in place of another. **3.** A substitution.

qui·en sa·be (kyen sä′vä) *Spanish* Who knows?

qui·es·cent (kwī·es′ənt) *adj.* **1.** Being in a state of repose or inaction; quiet; still. **2.** Resting free from anxiety, emotion, or agitation. **3.** *Phonet.* In the Semitic languages, denoting a letter or vowel point having no phonetic value; silent; aphonic. [< L *quiescens, -entis,* ppr. of *quiescere* to be quiet] — **qui·es′cence** *n.* — **qui·es′cent·ly** *adv.*

qui·et (kwī′ət) *adj.* **1.** Making little or no noise. **2.** Having little or no motion; still; calm. **3.** Characterized by silence; also, retired or secluded: a *quiet* nook. **4.** Free from excessive activity, turmoil, or vexation; restful; tranquil: a *quiet* day at the office. **5.** Free from undue emotion, excitement, or impatience; gentle; mild: a *quiet* temperament. **6.** Restful to the eye; reposeful: a *quiet* scene. **7.** Not showy or pretentious; modest: *quiet* decorations. **8.** Not loud or brash; reserved; subdued: a *quiet* sense of humor. **9.** In commerce, not busy or active. — **Syn.** See CALM. — *n.* **1.** The quality or condition of being quiet. **2.** Peace; tranquillity; calmness. — *v.t.* & *v.i.* To make or become quiet: often with *down.* — *adv.* In a quiet or peaceful manner. [< OF *quiete* < L *quies, quietis* rest, repose. Doublet of COY.] — **qui′et·ly** *adv.* — **qui′et·ness** *n.*

qui·et·ism (kwī′ə·tiz′əm) *n.* **1.** A form of religious mysticism, prominent in 17th-century Europe, in which the will and the intellect remain profoundly indifferent to worldly or outward activities, even to virtue, and instead fix themselves in a passive contemplation of God. **2.** A state of quiet. **qui·et·ist** (kwī′ə·tist) *n.* An advocate of quietism.

qui·e·tude (kwī′ə·tōod, -tyōod) *n.* A state or condition of calm or tranquillity; repose; rest.

qui·e·tus (kwī·ē′təs) *n.* **1.** A silencing or suppressing, as of a rumor. **2.** Anything that kills, as a blow. **3.** A final discharge, as of a debt. [< L *quietus est* he is quit]

quill (kwil) *n.* **1.** *Ornithol.* One of the large, strong flight feathers or tail feathers of a bird. For illustration see FEATHER. **2.** A pen made from a feather; also, any pen. **3.** The hollow, horny stem of a feather; a calamus. **4.** Such a stem used for a receptacle or measure, as for a drug, or as a plectrum for playing a stringed instrument. **5.** *Zool.* One of the large, sharp spines of a porcupine or hedgehog. **6.** A piece of cane or reed used as a musical pipe. **7.** A slow-burning fuse made formerly of the quill of a feather filled with powder. **8.** A piece of bark rolled into cylindrical form: a cinnamon *quill.* **9.** A quill toothpick. **10.** *Mech.* A hollow shaft, with or without openings, designed to revolve on a solid shaft when the clutches are engaged. **11.** In weaving, a spindle or bobbin. **12.** A fluted ridge, or cylindrical fold, as in a ruff or ruffle. — *v.t.* **1.** To make or iron (a garment or fabric) with rounded plaits or ridges. **2.** To wind (thread or yarn) on a quill or quills. — *v.i.* **3.** To wind thread or yarn on a quill or quills. [ME *quil;* ult. origin uncertain. Akin to MHG *kil.*]

quil·lai (ki·lī′) *n.* A Chilean evergreen tree (*Quillaja saponaria*) of the rose family, whose alkaline inner bark, soapbark, is used as medicine and as a substitute for soap: also spelled *cullay.* [< Sp. < Araucanian]

quill·back (kwil′bak′) *n.* A carplike fish (*Carpiodes cyprinus*) common in the Mississippi Valley.

Quil·ler-Couch (kwil′ər·kōoch′), **Sir Arthur Thomas,** 1863–1944, English man of letters: pseudonym **Q.**

quil·let (kwil′it) *n. Obs.* A quibble; subtlety. [? Abbreviation of *quillity,* var. of QUIDDITY]

quill·wort (kwil′wûrt′) *n.* A small plant (genus *Isoetes*), found in marshes, pond edges, etc., consisting of a cormlike stem sending up a tuft of quill-like leaves.

---

quilt (kwilt) *n.* **1.** A bedcover made by stitching together firmly two layers of cloth or patchwork with some soft and warm substance (as wool or cotton) between them. **2.** Any bedcover, especially if thick. **3.** A quilted skirt or other quilted article. **4.** *Obs.* A mattress. — *v.t.* **1.** To stitch together (two pieces of material) with a soft substance between. **2.** To stitch in ornamental patterns or crossing lines. **3.** To sew up or secure between two layers. **4.** To pad or line with something soft. — *v.i.* **5.** To make a quilt or quilted work. [< OF *cuilte* < L *culcita* bed, cushion]

quilt·ing (kwil′ting) *n.* **1.** The act or process of making a quilt, or of stitching as in making a quilt. **2.** Material for quiltwork. **3.** A quilting bee or party.

quilting bee A social gathering of women for working on a quilt or quilts. Also **quilting frolic, quilting party.**

quin·a·crine (kwin′ə-krēn) *n. Chem.* A bright yellow, crystalline compound, C₂₃H₃₀ClN₃O·2HCl, used in medicine as an antimalarial drug. [< QUIN(INE) + ACR(ID) + -INE]

qui·na·ry (kwī′nər·ē) *adj.* Consisting of or containing five parts or elements; arranged by fives, or in sets or groups of five. — *n. pl.* **·ries** A number, body, group, or system of five; something composed of five similar parts. [< L *quinarius* < *quini* five each. Akin to L *quinque* five.]

qui·nate (kwī′nāt, kwin′āt) *adj.* **1.** Arranged in five. **2.** *Bot.* Having five similar parts together, as the five leaflets of the Virginia creeper. [< L *quini* five each]

quince (kwins) *n.* **1.** The hard, acid, applelike, yellowish fruit of a small deciduous tree (*Cydonia oblonga*) of the rose family, used for preserves. **2.** The tree. [< MF *quynes*, pl. of *quyne* < OF *cooin* < L *cotoneum* < Gk. *kydónion* (*malon*) Cydonian (fruit), quince < *Kydonia* town in Crete]

quin·cun·cial (kwin·kun′shəl) *adj.* **1.** Arranged in a quincunx. **2.** *Bot.* Arranged in a set of five, as leaves. Also **quin·cunx′ial** (-kungk′shəl) — **quin·cun′cial·ly** *adv.*

quin·cunx (kwin′kungks) *n.* **1.** An arrangement of five things, as trees, in a square having one in each corner and one in the center. **2.** A disposition of such squares repeated indefinitely. **3.** A quincuncial arrangement, as of flower parts. [< L *quincunx* five twelfths < *quinque* five + *uncia* twelfth part]

Quin·cy (kwin′zē for def. 1; kwin′sē for def. 2) **1.** A city in eastern Massachusetts, near Boston; pop. 87,966. **2.** A city in western Illinois, on the Mississippi; pop. 45,288.

Quin·cy (kwin′sē), **Josiah,** 1744–75, American Revolutionary statesman.

quin·dec·a·gon (kwin·dek′ə·gon) *n. Geom.* A polygon having fifteen sides and fifteen angles. [< L *quindecim* fifteen + Gk. *gōnia* angle]

quin·de·cen·ni·al (kwin′di·sen′ē·əl) *n.* A fifteenth anniversary. — *adj.* **1.** Of or pertaining to the fifteenth anniversary. **2.** Lasting for or occurring every fifteen years. [< L *quindecim* fifteen + *annus* year]

qui·nel·la (kwi·nel′ə, kē-) *n.* In horse racing, a single bet won by choosing the first two horses in a race without specifying their order of finish. [< Am. Sp. *quiniela*]

quin·ic (kwin′ik) *adj.* Of, pertaining to, or derived from quinine.

quinic acid *Chem.* A white crystalline compound, C₇H₁₂O₆, contained in cinchona bark, coffee beans, etc.

quin·i·dine (kwin′ə·dēn, -din) *n. Chem.* A white crystalline alkaloid, C₂₀H₂₄N₂O₂, isomeric with quinine, contained in certain cinchona barks, the sulfate of which is used in medicine to regulate the heartbeat and to treat malaria.

qui·nine (kwī′nīn, *esp. Brit.* kwi·nēn′) *n. Chem.* A white, amorphous or slightly crystalline, very bitter alkaloid, C₂₀H₂₄N₂O₂, contained in cinchona barks, the salts of which are used in medicine for their tonic and antipyretic qualities and in the treatment of malaria. Also **quin·in** (kwin′in). [< Sp. *quina* cinchona bark and its extract (< Quechua) + -INE²]

quinine water A carbonated beverage flavored with quinine: also called *tonic.*

quin·nat (kwin′at) *n. U.S. & Canadian* The chinook salmon. [< Chinook]

quin·oid (kwin′oid) *adj. Chem.* Having a quinone nucleus.

qui·noi·dine (kwi·noi′dēn, -din) *n. Chem.* A resinous substance, consisting chiefly of products of cinchona bark, used as a cheap substitute for quinine. Also **qui·noi′din** (-din).

quin·o·line (kwin′ə·lēn, -lin) *n. Chem.* **1.** A colorless liquid compound, C₉H₇N, having a tarry odor, obtained from coal tar, used as a preservative and solvent. **2.** Any of a class of quinoline derivatives. Also **quin′o·lin** (-lin).

qui·none (kwi·nōn′, kwin′ōn) *n. Chem.* One of various cyclic hydrocarbon compounds obtained from benzene and its homologues; especially, a crystalline compound, C₆H₄O₂, having a pungent odor, formed variously, as by the oxidation of aniline and glycerol, used in organic syntheses.

quin·o·noid (kwin′ə·noid) *adj.* Of, resembling, or like quinone.

quin·qua·ge·nar·i·an (kwin′kwə·jə·nâr′ē·ən) *adj.* Of or pertaining to the age of 50 years, or to the decade between 50 and 60 years of age. — *n.* One who is 50 or more years old but less than 60.

Quin·qua·ges·i·ma Sunday (kwin′kwə·jes′ə·mə) The fifti-

eth day before Easter; the Sunday before Ash Wednesday: also called *Shrove Sunday.* [< L *quinquagesima* (*dies*) fiftieth (day)]

quinque- *combining form* Five: quinquefoliate. Also, before vowels, **quinqu-.** [< L *quinque* five]

quin·que·fo·li·ate (kwin′kwə·fō′lē·it, -āt) *adj. Bot.* Five-leaved. Also **quin′que·fo′li·o·late** (-fō′lē·ə·lāt′). [< QUINQUE- + L *foliatus* < *folium* leaf]

quin·quen·ni·al (kwin·kwen′ē·əl) *adj.* Occurring every five years, or once in five years; also, lasting five years. — *n.* **1.** A fifth anniversary or its celebration. **2.** A quinquennium. [< L *quinque* five + *annus* year]

quin·quen·ni·um (kwin·kwen′ē·əm) *n. pl.* **·quen·ni·ums** or **·quen·ni·a** (-kwen′ē·ə) A period of five years. [< L]

quin·que·va·lent (kwin′kwə·vā′lənt) *adj. Chem.* Pentavalent (which see). — **quin′que·va′lence** *n.*

quin·sy (kwin′zē) *n. Pathol.* A suppurative inflammation of the tonsils. [< Med.L *quinancia* < Gk. *kynanché* dog's collar < *kyōn* dog + *anchein* to squeeze]

quint (kwint) *n.* **1.** A fifth. **2.** A set of five. **3.** *Informal* A quintuplet. **4.** In piquet, a sequence of five of the same suit: if of the five highest cards, called a **quint major. 5.** An organ stop adding tones a fifth above those of the keys that are pressed. [< L *quintus* fifth]

quin·tain (kwin′tin) *n. Obs.* An object set up to be tilted at; also, the game or place of tilting at a quintain. [< OF *quintaine* < L *quintana* street in a camp separating the fifth multiple from the sixth, orig. fem. of *quintanus* of the fifth rank < *quintus* fifth]

quin·tal (kwin′təl) *n.* **1.** A measure of weight, a hundredweight. **2.** In the metric system, 100 kilograms. *Abbr. q., ql.* [< MF < Med.L *quintale* < Arabic *quintar* < LL *centarium* one hundred pieces of gold < L *centum* one hundred]

quin·tan (kwin′tən) *adj.* Recurring on every fifth day, the counting to include both days of consecutive occurrence: a *quintan fever.* — *n.* Trench fever. [< L *quintanus* of the fifth < *quintus* fifth]

quin·tes·sence (kwin·tes′əns) *n.* **1.** An extract from anything, containing in concentrated form its most essential principle. **2.** The purest and most essential part of anything. **3.** *Philos.* In the doctrine of the Pythagoreans, the fifth or celestial essence, ether, above the four elements of earth, air, fire, and water. [< F < Med.L *quinta essentia* fifth essence] — **quin·tes·sen·tial** (kwin′tə·sen′shəl) *adj.*

quin·tet (kwin·tet′) *n.* **1.** A musical composition for five voices or instruments; also, the five persons performing it. **2.** Any group of five persons or things. Also **quin·tette′.** [< F *quintette* < Ital. *quintetto,* dim. of *quinto* fifth]

quin·tic (kwin′tik) *Math. adj.* Denoting an algebraic function of the fifth degree. — *n.* Such a function.

quin·tile (kwin′til) *n.* **1.** In astrology, the aspect of planets separated by 72°, or by the fifth part of the zodiac. **2.** *Stat.* That part of a frequency distribution containing one fifth of the total observations or cases. [< L *quintus* fifth + -ILE]

Quin·til·i·an (kwin·til′ē·ən, -til′yən), 35?–95?, Latin rhetorician: full name **Marcus Fabius Quin·til·i·a′nus** (-ā′nəs).

quin·til·lion (kwin·til′yən) *n.* **1.** *U.S.* A thousand quadrillions, written as 1 followed by 18 zeros: a cardinal number. **2.** *Brit.* A million quadrillions (def. 2), written as 1 followed by 30 zeros: a cardinal number. — *adj.* Being a quintillion in number. [< *quinti-* five + (*mi*)*llion*]

quin·til·lionth (kwin·til′yənth) *adj.* **1.** Having the number one quintillion: the ordinal of *quintillion.* **2.** Being one of a quintillion equal parts. — *n.* **1.** One of a quintillion equal parts. **2.** That which is numbered one quintillion.

quin·tin (kwin′tin) *n. Rare* A fine linen fabric. Also **quin′tain** (-tin). [after *Quintin,* town in Brittany]

quin·tu·ple (kwin′tŏŏ·pəl, -tyŏŏ-, kwin·tŏŏ′pəl, -tyŏŏ′-) *v.t. & v.i.* **·pled, ·pling** To multiply by five; make or become five times as much or as large. — *adj.* **1.** Consisting of five things united or of five parts. **2.** Multiplied by five. — *n.* A number or a sum five times as great as another. [< F < LL *quintuplex* fivefold < *quintus* fifth + *plic-,* stem of *plicare* to fold]

quintuple meter *Music* See under METER².

quin·tu·plet (kwin′tŏŏ·plit, -tyŏŏ-, kwin·tŏŏ′plit, -tyŏŏ′-, -tup′lit) *n.* **1.** Five things of a kind used or occurring together. **2.** One of five born of the same mother at one birth.

quin·tu·pli·cate (*adj.* kwin·tŏŏ′plə·kit, -tyŏŏ′-; *v.* kwin·tŏŏ′plə·kāt, -tyŏŏ′-) *adj.* **1.** Fivefold. **2.** Raised to the fifth power. — *v.t. & v.i.* **·cat·ed, ·cat·ing** To multiply by five; quintuple. — *n.* One of five identical things. — **in quintuplicate** So as to have five identical copies. — **quin·tu′pli·cate·ly** *adv.* — **quin·tu′pli·ca′tion** *n.*

quip (kwip) *n.* **1.** A sarcastic or sharp jest, remark, or retort; gibe. **2.** A clever or witty sally without sarcasm. **3.** A quibble. **4.** An odd, fantastic action or object. — **Syn.** See JEST. — *v.i.* quipped, quip·ping To make a witty remark; jest. [Prob. < L *quippe* indeed] — **quip′pish** *adj.*

quip·ster (kwip′stər) *n.* One who makes quips.

qui·pu (kē′pŏŏ, kwip′ŏŏ) *n.* An aboriginal Peruvian device for recording and conveying information, consisting of a series of varicolored and knotted strings tied at one end to a thicker cord. Also **quip'pu.** [< Quechua *quipu* knot]

quire[1] (kwīr) *n.* **1.** The twentieth part of a ream of paper; 24 (or 25) sheets. **2.** A set of all the sheets necessary to make a book. Abbr. *q., qr.* — *v.t.* **quired, quir·ing** To fold or separate into quires. [< OF *quaer,* ult. <L *quaterni* a set of four < *quater* four times]

quire[2] (kwīr) *Archaic* Choir.

Qui·ri·nal (kwir'ə·nəl) *n.* **1.** One of the Seven Hills of Rome, containing the **Quirinal palace,** formerly a papal residence but after 1870 the official residence of the kings of Italy. **2.** The monarchical or civil government of Italy: distinguished from the *Vatican.* — *adj.* Pertaining to or situated on the Quirinal.

Qui·ri·no (kē·rē'nō), **Elpidio,** 1890–1956, Philippine statesman; president 1948–54.

Qui·ri·nus (kwi·rī'nəs) An ancient Italic god of war: ultimately identified with the deified *Romulus.*

Qui·ri·tes (kwi·rī'tēz) *n.pl.* The citizens of ancient Rome in their civil as distinguished from their military or political capacity. [< L]

quirk (kwûrk) *n.* **1.** A personal peculiarity, mannerism, or caprice. **2.** An evasion or subterfuge; quibble. **3.** A short or sharp turn or twist. **4.** A sudden curve or flourish, as in writing. **5.** A bright retort; quip. **6.** *Archit.* **a** A small groove in, beside, or between moldings or beads. **b** A molding or bead having a groove on one or both edges. [Origin uncertain] — **quirk'y** *adj.*

quirt (kwûrt) *n.* A short-handled riding whip with a braided rawhide lash. — *v.t.* To strike with a quirt. [< Am. Sp. *cuarta*]

qui s'ex·cuse s'ac·cuse (kē seks·küz' sȧ·küz') *French* He who excuses himself accuses himself.

quis·ling (kwiz'ling) *n.* One who betrays his country to the enemy and is then given political power by the conquerers. [after Vidkun *Quisling,* 1887–1945, Norwegian Nazi party leader and traitor] — **quis'ling·ism** *n.*

quit (kwit) *v.* **quit** or **quit·ted, quit·ting** *v.t.* **1.** To cease or desist from; discontinue. **2.** To give up; renounce; relinquish. **3.** To go away from; leave. **4.** To let go of (something held). **5.** *Archaic* To acquit (oneself). — *v.i.* **6.** To stop; cease; discontinue. **7.** To leave; depart. **8.** *Informal* To resign from a position, etc. — *adj.* Released, relieved, or absolved from something, as a duty, obligation, encumbrance, or debt; clear; free; rid. — *n.* The act of quitting. — **to be quits** To be even (with another). — **to cry quits** To declare (oneself) willing to stop competing. [< OF *quitter,* < Med.L *quitare,* ult. < L *quietus* at rest]

quitch grass (kwich) Couch grass (which see). Also **quitch.** [OE *cwice* + GRASS]

quit·claim (kwit'klām') *n. Law* A full release and acquittance given by one to another in regard to a certain demand, suit, or right of action. Also **quit'claim'ance** (-əns). — *v.t.* To relinquish or give up claim or title to; release from a claim. [< MF *quite clamer* to declare quit or free]

quite (kwīt) *adv.* **1.** To the fullest extent; totally: *quite* dead. **2.** Really; truly. **3.** *Informal* To a great or considerable extent; noticeably; very; *quite* ill. ◆ The phrase *quite a* is used in many idioms to indicate considerable but indefinite number, size, quantity, etc., as in *quite a lot* (a good deal), *quite a few* (many), *quite a while* (a long while). It is also used in informal expressions with the sense of "wonderful, great, outstanding, or unusual," as in *quite a guy, quite an athlete, quite a character.* [ME; var. of QUIT, adj.]

Qui·to (kē'tō) The capital of Ecuador, in the north central part; pop. 314,000 (est. 1960).

quit·rent (kwit'rent') *n.* A fixed rent formerly paid by a freeholder, whereby he was released from feudal services.

quit·tance (kwit'ns) *n.* **1.** Discharge or release, as from a debt or obligation. **2.** A document or receipt certifying this. **3.** Something given or tendered by way of requital; repayment. [< OF < *quittant,* ppr. of *quitter* to quit]

quit·ter (kwit'ər) *n.* One who quits needlessly; a shirker.

quit·tor (kwit'ər) *n. Vet.* A fistulous sore on the hoof of a horse or any solid-hoofed animal: also **quit'ter, quit'ter·bone'** (-bōn'). [? < OF *quiture* cooking]

qui va là? (kē vȧ lä') *French* Who goes there?

quiv·er[1] (kwiv'ər) *v.i.* To shake with a slight, tremulous motion; vibrate; tremble. — *n.* The act or fact of quivering; a trembling or shaking. [Var. of QUAVER]

quiv·er[2] (kwiv'ər) *n.* A portable case for arrows; also, its contents. [< AF *quivier,* OF *cuivre* < OHG *kochar*]

quiv·er[3] (kwiv'ər) *adj. Obs.* Brisk; active; nimble. [OE *cwifer,* found in *cwiferlice* zealously]

qui vive? (kē vēv') *French* Who goes there?; literally, Who lives?: used by French sentinels. — **to be on the qui vive** To be on the lookout; be wide-awake.

quix·ot·ic (kwik·sot'ik) *adj.* **1.** Of, pertaining to, or like Don Quixote. **2.** Ridiculously chivalrous or romantic; having high but impractical sentiments, aims, etc. — **quix·ot'i·cal·ly** *adv.* — **quix·ot·ism** (kwik'sə·tiz'əm) *n.*

quiz (kwiz) *n.* **1.** The act of questioning; especially, an informal oral or written examination of a class or individual. **2.** Something or someone odd or ridiculous; an eccentric. **3.** One given to quizzing. **4.** A hoax; practical joke. — *v.t.* **quizzed, quiz·zing** **1.** To examine by asking questions; question. **2.** *Brit.* To make fun of; ridicule. — **Syn.** See ASK. [Origin unknown] — **quiz'zer** *n.*

quiz program A television or radio program in which selected contestants or a panel of experts try to answer questions presented by the master of ceremonies.

quiz·zi·cal (kwiz'i·kəl) *adj.* **1.** Given to chaffing or bantering. **2.** Queer; odd. **3.** Questioning; puzzled: a *quizzical* smile. — **quiz'zi·cal·ly** *adv.*

quizzing glass A monocle or single eyeglass.

quo' (kwō) *v.t. Scot.* Quoth.

quod (kwod) *n. Brit. Slang* A prison: also spelled *quad.*

quod e·rat de·mon·stran·dum (kwod er'at dem'ən·stran'· dəm) *Latin* Which was to be proved or demonstrated. Abbr. *Q.E.D.*

quod e·rat fa·ci·en·dum (kwod er'at fā'shē·en'dəm) *Latin* Which was to be done. Abbr. *Q.E.F.*

quod vi·de (kwod vī'dē) *Latin* Which see: usually abbreviated to *q.v.* and used in parentheses after a word by way of reference.

quoin (koin, kwoin) *n.* **1.** An external angle or corner of a building. **2.** A stone or stones forming such an angle. **3.** A wedge or wedgelike piece, as one of the stones in an arch. **4.** *Printing* A wedge or pair of wedges for locking type in a chase or galley. — *v.t.* To provide, secure, or support with a quoin or quoins. [Var. of COIN]

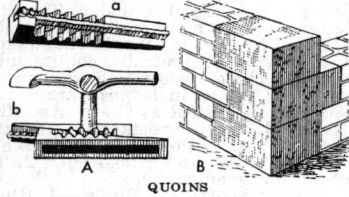

QUOINS
A Printer's: *a* Single quoin, *b* Pair ready for locking with key.
B Quoins of dressed stone.

quoit (kwoit, *esp. Brit.* koit) *n.* **1.** A disk of iron or other material with a round hole in the center to be thrown in a game at a short stake, either encircling it or coming as close to it as possible. **2.** *pl.* (*construed as sing.*) The game so played. — *v.t.* To pitch as a quoit. [< MF *coite,* ? flat stone < OF *cuilte.* See QUILT.]

quo ju·re (kwō jŏŏr'ē) *Latin* By what right? By what law?

quo·mo·do (kwō·mō'dō) *Latin adv.* In what manner? how? — *n.* The means; manner.

quon·dam (kwon'dəm) *adj.* Having been formerly; former. [< L]

Quon·set hut (kwon'sit) A prefabricated, metal structure the roof of which is half of a cylinder cut lengthwise and resting on the ground, designed for use by the U.S. armed services: a trade name. [after *Quonset,* Rhode Island, where first made]

quo·rum (kwôr'əm, kwō'rəm) *n.* **1.** The number of members of any deliberative or corporate body as is necessary for the legal transaction of business, commonly, a majority. **2.** Formerly, in England, certain designated justices of the peace whose presence was required before the court could act. **3.** A select or chosen body. [< L, genitive plural of *qui* who]

quo·ta (kwō'tə) *n.* A proportional part or share required from each person, group, state, etc., for making up a certain number or quantity. [< Med.L *quota* (*pars*) how great (a part) < L *quotus* how many < *quot*]

quot·a·ble (kwō'tə·bəl) *adj.* Suitable for quotation. — **quot'a·bil'i·ty** *n.*

Quo Tai·chi (gwō' tī'chē'), 1889?–1952, Chinese diplomat.

quo·ta·tion (kwō·tā'shən) *n.* **1.** The act of quoting. **2.** The words quoted or cited. **3.** A price quoted or current, as of securities, etc.: the *quotations* for wheat. Abbr. *quot.* [< Med.L *quotatio, -onis* < *quotare.* See QUOTE.] — **quo·ta'tion·al** *adj.* — **quo·ta'tion·al·ly** *adv.* — **quo·ta'tion·ist** *n.*

quotation mark Either of the marks placed at the beginning and end of a quoted word or passage. In English usage, one or two inverted commas (' ") mark the beginning of a quotation, and correspondingly, one or two apostrophes (' ") the close, the single marks usually being used to set off a quotation within a quotation.

quote (kwōt) *v.* **quot·ed, quot·ing** *v.t.* **1.** To reproduce the words of. **2.** To repeat or cite (a rule, author, etc.), as for authority or illustration. **3.** In commerce: **a** To state (a price). **b** To give the current or market price of. **4.** *Printing* To enclose within quotation marks. — *v.i.* **5.** To make a quotation, as from a book. — *n.* **1.** Loosely, a quotation. **2.** A quotation mark. [< Med.L *quotare* to distinguish by number < L *quot* how many] — **quot'a·ble** *adj.* — **quot'er** *n.* — **quote'wor'thy** (-wûr'thē) *adj.* — **quot'ing·ly** *adv.*

quoth (kwōth) *v.t.* Said or spoke; uttered: the imperfect tense of the obsolete verb *queth*, used only in the first and third persons, the subject always following the verb: *quoth he*. [OE *cwæth*, pt. of *cwethan* to say]

quo·tha (kwō′thə) *interj.* *Archaic* Indeed! forsooth!: usually uttered in slight contempt. [< *quoth he*]

quo·tid·i·an (kwō·tĭd′ē·ən) *adj.* Recurring or occurring every day. —*n.* A fever whose paroxysms return every day. [< L *quotidianus* daily]

quo·tient (kwō′shənt) *n.* *Math.* The result obtained by division; a number indicating how many times one quantity

is contained in another. [< L *quotiens* how often < *quot* how many]

quo war·ran·to (kwō wô·ran′tō, wo-) *Law* **1.** Formerly, a judicial writ commanding a person to show by what authority he exercises an office or franchise. **2.** A proceeding, usually criminal in form but in substance civil, by which a government or sovereign seeks to recover an office or franchise. [< L, by what warrant]

q.v. Which see. (L *quod vide*).

qy. Query.

R

r, R (är) *n.* *pl.* **r's** or **rs, R's** or **Rs, ars** (ärz) **1.** The 18th letter of the English alphabet. The shape of the Phoenician letter *resh* was adopted by the Greeks as *rho* and became Roman *R*. Also *ar.* **2.** The sound represented by the letter *r*, usually a voiced retroflex continuant but without phonetic value in those areas where preconsonantal (r), as in *park*, and final (r), as in *manner*, are not used in the standard speech. —*symbol* **1.** *Chem.* An alkyl group. **2.** *Math.* Ratio. **3.** *Electr.* Resistance. —**the three R's 1.** Reading, writing, and arithmetic (regarded humorously as spelled *reading, 'riting,* and *'rithmetic*). **2.** The essential elements of a primary education.

r 1. Roentgen(s). **2.** Ruble. **3.** Rupee.

r or **r.** Run(s) (baseball).

r. 1. Radius. **2.** Rare. **3.** Received. **4.** Recipe. **5.** Residence; resides. **6.** Retired. **7.** Right-hand page (L *recto*). **8.** Rises. **9.** Rod. **10.** Rubber. **11.** Ruble.

R 1. *Chem.* Gas constant. **2.** Radius. **3.** Ratio. **4.** *Eccl.* Respond or response. **5.** Rook (chess). **6.** Rupee.

R. 1. Rabbi. **2.** Radical. **3.** Railroad. **4.** Réaumur. **5.** Rector. **6.** Redactor. **7.** Regina. **8.** Republican. **9.** Response. **10.** Rex. **11.** Right (theater). **12.** River. **13.** Road. **14.** Royal.

Ra (rä) The supreme deity of ancient Egypt: also *Re*.

Ra *Chem.* Radium.

RA *Mil.* Regular Army.

R.A. 1. *Mil.* Rear Admiral. **2.** *Astron.* Right ascension. **3.** Royal Academy.

Raab (räb) The German name for GYÖR.

RAAF or **R.A.A.F.** Royal Australian Air Force.

Ra·bat (rä·bät′) The capital of Morocco, a port in the northern part on the Atlantic; pop. 435,-000 (1969).

ra·ba·to (rə·bā′tō, -bä′-) See REBATO.

Ra·baul (rə·boul′, rä′boul) The chief city of New Britain; formerly the administrative center of the Territory of New Guinea; pop. about 8,400.

Rab·bath Am·mon (rab′əth am′ən) The Old Testament name for AMMAN.

rab·bet (rab′it) *n.* **1.** A recess or groove in or near the edge of one piece of wood, etc., cut so as to receive the edge of another piece. **2.** A joint so made. —*v.* **·bet·ed, ·bet·ing** *v.t.* **1.** To cut a rabbet in. **2.** To unite in a rabbet. —*v.i.* **3.** To be jointed by a rabbet. Also *rebate*. [< OF *rabat* < *rabattre* to beat down. See REBATE.]

RABBET JOINTS

rab·bi (rab′ī) *n.* *pl.* **·bis** or **·bies** In Judaism: **a** The spiritual head of a Jewish community, authorized to perform various religious duties. **b** Master; teacher: a title for one learned in the Law. **c** Formerly, one declared qualified to make decisions in Jewish law. Also **rab′bin** (-in). *Abbr.* **R.** [< Hebrew *rabbi* my master < *rabh* great, master + *-i* my]

rab·bin·ate (rab′in·āt) *n.* **1.** The office or term of office of a rabbi. **2.** Rabbis collectively.

Rab·bin·ic (rə·bin′ik) *n.* The language or dialect of the rabbis; especially, the Hebrew language as used in Biblical and Talmudic exegesis by Jewish scholars of the late ancient and early medieval periods.

rab·bin·i·cal (rə·bin′i·kəl) *adj.* Pertaining to the rabbis or to their opinions, languages, or writings. Also **rab·bin′ic.** —**rab·bin′i·cal·ly** *adv.*

rab·bin·ism (rab′in·iz′əm) *n.* **1.** The teachings or doctrines of the rabbis. **2.** A rabbinical phrase, expression, or idiom.

rab·bin·ist (rab′in·ist) *n.* A Jew adhering to the Talmud and the traditions of the rabbis. Also **rab′bin·ite** (-īt). —**rab·bin·is′tic** or **·ti·cal, rab′bin·it′ic** (-it′ik) *adj.* —**rab′bin·is′ti·cal·ly** *adv.*

rab·bit (rab′it) *n.* **1.** Any of a family (*Leporidae*) of various

small, long-eared mammals allied to but smaller than the hare, as the common American cottontail. **2.** The pelt of a rabbit or hare. **3.** Welsh rabbit. —*v.i.* To hunt rabbits. [Akin to Walloon *robett*, Flemish *robbe*] —**rab′bit·er** *n.*

rabbit fever Tularemia.

rabbit foot 1. A common clover (*Trifolium arvense*) having soft, hairy flower heads supposed to resemble rabbits' paws: also **rab·bit's-foot clover** (rab′its·foŏt′). **2.** The left hind foot of a rabbit, carried as a good-luck charm. Also **rab·bit's foot.**

rabbit hutch A coop in which domestic rabbits are bred.

rabbit punch A short chopping blow at the base of the skull or back of the neck.

rab·bit·ry (rab′it·rē) *n.* *pl.* **·ries** A place where rabbits are kept; also, a group of rabbit hutches.

rab·ble[1] (rab′əl) *n.* A disorderly crowd or mob. —**the rabble** The common people; hoi polloi: a contemptuous term. —*adj.* Of, suited to, or characteristic of a rabble; disorderly. —*v.t.* **·bled, ·bling** To mob. [? < RABBLE[3]]

rab·ble[2] (rab′əl) *n.* *Metall.* An iron implement for stirring or skimming melted iron in puddling. Also **rab′bler.** —*v.t.* **·bled, ·bling** To stir or skim with a rabble. [< F *râble* < L *rutabulum* poker < *ruere* to overturn]

rab·ble[3] (rab′əl) *v.t. & v.i.* **·bled, ·bling** *Scot. & Brit. Dial.* To speak or utter in an incoherent or disconnected manner; gabble. [Cf. Du. *rabbelen* to speak indistinctly]

rab·ble·ment (rab′əl·mənt) *n.* **1.** An uproar. **2.** A rabble.

rab·ble-rous·er (rab′əl·rou′zər) *n.* One who tries to incite mobs by arousing prejudices and passions; a demagogue.

rab·bo·ni (ra·bō′nē) *n.* My great master: a former or Biblical term of address. [< Hebrew < Aramaic]

rab·do·man·cy (rab′də·man′sē) See RHABDOMANCY.

Rab·e·lais (rab′ə·lā, *Fr.* rȧ·ble′), **François,** 1494?–1553?, French humorist and satirist: pseudonym **Al·co·fri·bas Na·sier** (ȧl·kô·frē·bȧs′ nȧ·zyā′).

Rab·e·lai·si·an (rab′ə·lā′zē·ən, -zhən) *adj.* **1.** Of, pertaining to, or resembling Rabelais or his works. **2.** Bawdy and boisterous. —*n.* A student or imitator of Rabelais. —**Rab′e·lai′si·an·ism, Rab′e·la′ism** *n.*

Ra·bi (rä′bē), **Isidor Isaac,** born 1898, U.S. physicist born in Austria.

Ra·bi·a (rä·bē′ä) *n.* Either of two months of the Moslem year. See (Moslem) CALENDAR.

rab·id (rab′id) *adj.* **1.** Affected with, arising from, or pertaining to rabies; mad. **2.** Unreasonably zealous; fanatical; violent. **3.** Furious; raging. Also **rab′ic.** [< L *rabidus* < *rabere* to be mad] —**rab′id·ly** *adv.* —**rab′id·ness** *n.*

ra·bies (rā′bēz, -bi·ēz) *n.* An acute, infectious, usually fatal disease of certain animals, especially of dogs, caused by a virus that attacks the brain and central nervous system, readily transmissible to man by the bite of an affected animal: also called *hydrophobia, lyssa.* [< L, madness < *rabere* to rave. See RAGE.] —**ra′bi·et′ic** (-et/ik) *adj.*

rac·coon (ra·kōōn′) *n.* **1.** A North American nocturnal carnivore (*Procyon lotor*), grayish brown with a black cheek patch and a black-and-white-ringed bushy tail. **2.** The fur of this animal. Also spelled *racoon.* [Alter. of Algonquian *arakunem* hand-scratcher]

raccoon dog A wild dog (*Nyctereutes procyonoides*) of Japan and northeastern Asia, with long, loose fur, short ears, and a long bushy tail.

RACCOON
(To 30 inches long; tail to 10 inches)

race[1] (rās) *n.* **1.** One of the major zoological subdivisions of mankind, regarded as having a common origin and exhibiting a relatively constant set of genetically determined physical traits. On the basis of the more commonly used criteria such as pigmentation, hair form, epicanthic folds, facial and bodily proportions, mankind has been divided into primary stocks or races, each of which is regarded as including a varying number of ethnic groups. According to some, the primary stocks are the Caucasoid, the Mongoloid, and the Negroid. A number of groups, such as the Polynesian, are of doubtful classification. **2.** Any group of people or any grouping of peoples having, or assumed to have, common characteristics, habits, appearance, etc. **3.** A nation: the German *race*. **4.** A genealogical or family stock; clan: the *race* of MacGregor. **5.** Pedigree; lineage: a noble *race*. **6.** Any class of beings having characteristics uniting them, or differentiating them from others: the human *race*; the *race* of lawyers. **7.** *Biol.* A group of plants or animals, having characteristics clearly differentiating it from other groups within the same species, and which breeds true except for minor variations; a variety: a *race* of wheat. **8.** A stock, breed, or strain of domestic animals or plants. **9.** A quality or aggregate of qualities by which origin is determined; especially, the characteristic flavor or taste of wine. — **Syn.** See PEOPLE. [< MF < Ital. *razza*; origin uncertain]

race² (rās) *n.* **1.** A contest to determine the relative speed of the contestants. **2.** Any contest. **3.** Movement or progression, especially when regular or swift. **4.** Duration of life; course; career. **5.** A swift current of water or its channel. **6.** A swift current or heavy sea resulting from the meeting of two tides: the Portland *Race*. **7.** A sluice or channel by which to conduct water to or from a water wheel or around a dam. **8.** Any groove or channel along which some part of a machine slides or is guided. — *v.* **raced**, **rac·ing** *v.i.* **1.** To take part in a contest of speed. **2.** To move at great or top speed. **3.** To move at an accelerated or too great speed, usually because of decreased resistance: said of machinery. — *v.t.* **4.** To contend against in a race. **5.** To cause to race. [< ON *rās*. Akin to OE *ræs* a rushing.]

race³ (rās) *n.* A root; especially, a root of ginger. [< OF *rais* < L *radix* root]

Race (rās), **Cape** The southeasternmost point of Newfoundland.

race·a·bout (rās′ə·bout′) *n. Naut.* A sloop-rigged racing boat having a short bowsprit. Compare KNOCKABOUT.

race·course (rās′kôrs′, -kōrs′) *n.* A racetrack.

race·horse (rās′hôrs′) *n.* A horse bred and trained for contests of speed.

ra·ceme (rā·sēm′, rə-) *n.* **1.** *Bot.* An inflorescence in which the flowers are arranged singly on distinct, nearly equal pedicels at intervals on a common axis. For illustration see INFLORESCENCE. **2.** *Chem.* A racemic compound. [< L *racemus* cluster] — **rac·e·mif·er·ous** (ras′ə·mif′ər·əs) *adj.*

ra·ce·mic (rā·sē′mik, -sem′ik, rə-) *adj.* **1.** *Bot.* Of, pertaining to, or contained in racemes. **2.** *Chem.* Indicating or relating to any compound that is optically inactive, but separable into equal quantities of two isomers, one dextrorotatory, the other levorotatory. Also **rac·e·moid** (ras′ə·moid).

racemic acid *Chem.* A white, crystalline, optically inactive compound contained with tartaric acid in certain grapes and separable into dextrorotatory and levorotatory forms.

rac·e·mism (ras′ə·miz′əm, rā·sē′miz·əm) *n. Chem.* The quality or condition of being racemic.

rac·e·mize (ras′ə·mīz, rā·sē′mīz) *v.t.* **·mized**, **·miz·ing** *Chem.* To change (an optically active compound) into an optically inactive compound or isomer. — **rac′e·mi·za′tion** *n.*

rac·e·mose (ras′ə·mōs) *adj.* **1.** Like a raceme in form or nature. **2.** Arranged in or as in clusters or racemes: a *racemose* gland. Also *botryose*. Also **rac′e·mous** (-məs). [< L *racemosus*] — **rac′e·mose·ly** *adv.*

rac·er (rā′sər) *n.* **1.** One who races. **2.** Anything designed or used for racing, as a car, yacht, etc. **3.** One of various colubrine snakes, as the blacksnake.

race riot A violent conflict between groups in the same community, based on differences of color or creed.

race suicide The slow reduction in numbers of a people through voluntary failure on the part of individuals to maintain the birth rate at or above the level of the death rate.

race·track (rās′trak′) *n.* A track or course over which a horse race, dog race, etc., is run: also called *racecourse*.

race·way (rās′wā′) *n.* **1.** A channel for conducting water. **2.** A tube for protecting wires, as in a subway. **3.** *U.S.* A racetrack for trotting horses.

Ra·chel (rā′chəl) The wife of Jacob; mother of Joseph and Benjamin. *Gen.* xxix 6. [< Hebrew, lit., ewe]

Ra·chel (rà·shel′) Pseudonym of **Élisa Fé·lix** (fā·lēks′), 1821?–58, French actress born in Switzerland.

ra·chis (rā′kis) *n. pl.* **ra·chi·des** (rā′kə·dēz) or **·chis·es** **1.** *Bot.* The axis of an inflorescence. **2.** *Ornithol.* The shaft of a feather, especially the part filled with pith, which bears the barbs. **3.** *Anat.* The spinal column. Also spelled *rhachis*. [< NL < Gk. *rhachis* spine] — **ra·chi·al** (rā′kē·al) *adj.*

ra·chi·tis (rə·kī′tis) *n. Pathol.* Rickets. [< NL < Gk. *rhachitis* spinal inflammation < *rachis* spine] — **ra·chit′ic** (-kit′ik) *adj.*

Rach·ma·ni·noff (räkh·mä′ni·nôf), **Sergei Vassilievich**, 1873–1943, Russian pianist and composer.

ra·cial (rā′shəl) *adj.* Of, pertaining to, or characteristic of a race, races, or descent. — **ra′cial·ly** *adv.*

Ra·ci·bórz (rä·chē′bŏŏsh) See RATIBOR.

Ra·cine (rə·sēn′) A port city in SE Wisconsin, on Lake Michigan; pop. 95,162.

Ra·cine (rà·sēn′), **Jean Baptiste**, 1639–99, French dramatist.

ra·cism (rā′siz·əm) *n.* **1.** A belief that people differ significantly and systematically, as in ability, intellect, etc., because of racial differences. **2.** A belief in or advocacy of the superiority or inferiority of a particular group on the basis of supposed racial differences; racial prejudice. Also **ra·cial·ism** (rā′shəl·iz′əm) — **ra′cist** *n., adj.*

rack¹ (rak) *n.* **1.** An open grating, framework, or the like, in or on which articles may be placed. **2.** A framework to hold fodder for horses, cattle, etc. **3.** A triangular frame for arranging the balls on a billiard table. **4.** A container or framework in an airplane for carrying bombs. **5.** *Mech.* A bar or the like having teeth that engage with those of a gearwheel, pinion, or worm gear. **6.** A machine for stretching or making tense; especially, an instrument of torture that stretches the limbs of victims. **7.** Torture or punishment as by the rack; also, intense mental or physical suffering. **8.** A wrenching or straining, as from a storm. — *v.t.* **1.** To place or arrange in or on a rack. **2.** To torture on the rack. **3.** To cause suffering to; torment. **4.** To strain, as with the effort of thinking: to *rack* one's brains. **5.** To raise (rents) excessively: see RACK-RENT. — **to rack up** *U.S. Informal* To achieve; post: to *rack up* a perfect score. [< MDu. *rec* framework < *recken* to stretch] — **rack′er** *n.*

rack² (rak) *n.* The single-foot. — *v.i.* To proceed or move with this gait. [Origin uncertain]

rack³ (rak) *n.* **1.** Thin, flying, or broken clouds. **2.** Any floating vapor. — *v.i.* To move rapidly; send, as clouds before the wind. Also spelled *wrack*. [< Scand. Cf. dial. ON *rak* drifting wreckage, *reka* to drive.]

rack⁴ (rak) *n.* Destruction; wreck; demolition: now usually in the phrase **rack and ruin**. — **to rack up** *U.S. Slang* To wreck. [Var. of WRACK²]

rack⁵ *v.t.* To draw off from the lees, as liquor. [< Provençal *arracar* < *raca* refuse of grapes]

rack and pinion *Mech.* A machine movement in which a toothed rack and a pinion mesh together, for converting rotary motion into linear motion or vice versa.

rack·et¹ (rak′it) *n.* **1.** A nearly elliptical hoop of bent wood, usually strung with catgut or nylon, and having a handle, used in striking a tennis ball, etc. **2.** A large wooden sole or shoe to support the weight of a man or horse on swampy ground. **3.** A snowshoe. **4.** An organ stop. **5.** *Often pl.* A game resembling court tennis, played in a court with four walls. Often spelled *racquet*. [< MF *raquette* < Arabic *rāha* palm of the hand]

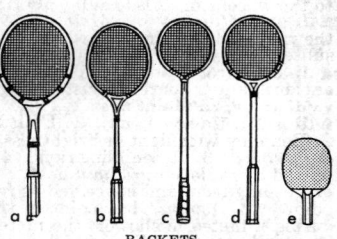

RACKETS

a Tennis. *b* Badminton. *c, d* Squash. *e* Table tennis.

rack·et² (rak′it) *n.* **1.** A clattering, vociferous, or confused noise; fuss; commotion. **2.** *Informal* A scheme for getting money or other benefits by fraud, intimidation, or other illegitimate means. **3.** *Slang* Any business or occupation: the retailing *racket*. **4.** Social activity or excitement. — *v.i.* **1.** To make a loud, clattering noise. **2.** To indulge in noisy sport or diversion; carouse. [Prob. imit.]

rack·et·eer (rak′ə·tir′) *n.* **1.** One engaged in a racket. **2.** Formerly, a bootlegger or rumrunner. — **rack′et·eer′ing** *n.*

rack·et·y (rak′it·ē) *adj.* Making a racket; noisy.

Rack·ham (rak′əm), **Arthur**, 1867–1939, English painter and illustrator.

rack·le (rak′əl) *adj. Brit. Dial. & Scot.* **1.** Hasty or rough in action. **2.** Strong; vigorous.

rack railway A cog railway (which see).

rack-rent (rak′rent′) *n.* An exorbitant rent. — *v.t.* To exact rack-rent from or for. [< RACK¹ + RENT¹] — **rack′-rent′er** *n.*

rack·work (rak′wûrk′) *n.* A mechanism with a rack or a rack and pinion as the leading characteristic.

rac·on·teur (rak′on·tûr′, *Fr.* rà·kôn̄·tœr′) *n.* A skilled storyteller.

ra·coon (ra·kōōn′) See RACCOON.

rac·quet (rak′it) See RACKET¹.

rac·y (rā′sē) *adj.* **rac·i·er**, **rac·i·est** **1.** Having a spirited or pungent interest; spicy; piquant. **2.** Having a characteristic flavor assumed to be indicative of origin, as wine; rich, fresh, or fragrant. **3.** Suggestive; slightly immodest: a *racy* story. [< RACE¹] — **rac′i·ly** *adv.* — **rac′i·ness** *n.*

— **Syn.** *Racy, pungent, spicy,* and *piquant* signify sharp in smell or taste, and all are extended to mean stimulating to the mind. *Racy* is used in its literal sense to describe the pleasant flavor of some wines; in extension, strong or lusty writing is described as *racy.* Anything acrid or prickly to the senses is said to be *pungent*; *pungent* writing is colorful, sarcastic, or sardonic. *Spicy* and *piquant* mean pleasantly sharp in taste; *spicy* stories are sensational or scandalous, while a *piquant* account of some event arouses worthy interest by its liveliness, vividness, etc. **— Ant.** bland, insipid, flat, vapid.

rad² (rad) *n. Physics* A unit of nuclear radiation equivalent to 100 ergs of absorbed energy per gram of absorbing material. Compare REM. [< R(ADIATION) A(BSORBED) D(OSE)]

Rad. Radnorshire.

ra·dar (rā′där) *n. Telecom.* An electronic device that locates objects by beaming radio-frequency impulses that are reflected back from the object, and determines its distance by a measurement of the time elapsed between transmission and reception of the impulses. [< ra(dio) d(etection) a(nd) r(anging)]

radar beacon *Telecom.* The part of a radar that transmits radio-frequency waves. Also **ra·con** (rā′kon).

ra·dar·scope (rā′där·skōp) *n. Telecom.* The oscilloscope of a radar set.

Rad·cliffe (rad′klif), **Ann,** 1764–1823, *née* Ward, English novelist.

rad·dle¹ (rad′l) See REDDLE, RUDDLE.

rad·dle² (rad′l) *v.t.* **·dled, ·dling** To intertwine or weave together. [< OF *reddale* stout stick < MHG *reidel*]

Ra·dek (rä′dek), **Karl,** 1885–1939, Soviet revolutionist born in Austria: original name **Karl So·bel·sohn** (zō′bəl·sōn).

Ra·detz·ky (rä·dets′kē), **Count Joseph Wenzel,** 1766–1858, Austrian field marshal.

Rad·ford (rad′fərd), **Arthur William,** 1896–1973, U.S. admiral; chairman of joint chiefs of staff 1953–57.

ra·di·al (rā′dē·əl) *adj.* **1.** Pertaining to, consisting of, or resembling a ray or radius. **2.** Extending from a center in the manner of rays. **3.** Of or pertaining to the radius or a radiating part. **4.** *Anat.* Denoting the radius. **5.** Developing uniformly on all sides. **— n.** A radiating part. **— ra′di·al·ly** *adv.*

radial engine A multicylinder internal-combustion engine having its cylinders arranged like the spokes in a wheel.

radial tire An automotive tire having cords perpendicular to the wheel rim. Also **radial-ply tire.**

ra·di·an (rā′dē·ən) *n. Math.* **1.** An arc equal in length to the radius of the circle of which it is a part. **2.** The angle subtended by such an arc, equal to 57° 17′ 44.80625″ +.

ra·di·ance (rā′dē·əns) *n.* The quality or state of being radiant; brilliant or sparkling luster; brightness; effulgence. Also **ra′di·an·cy, ra′di·ant·ness.**

ra·di·ant (rā′dē·ənt) *adj.* **1.** Emitting rays of light or heat. **2.** Beaming with light or brightness, kindness, or love: a *radiant* smile. **3.** Resembling rays. **4.** Consisting of or transmitted by radiation: *radiant* heat. **— n. 1.** A straight line proceeding from and conceived as revolving around a given point. **2.** *Astron.* That point in the heavens from which, during a meteoric shower, the meteors seem to shoot. **3.** The luminous point from which light proceeds or is made to radiate. **4.** That which radiates. [< L *radians, -antis,* ppr. of *radiare* to emit rays < *radius* ray] **— ra′di·ant·ly** *adv.*

radiant energy *Physics* The energy associated with and transmitted in the form of waves, especially those of electromagnetic frequencies, as heat, light, radio waves, X-rays, gamma rays, etc.

radiant flux *Physics* The time rate of flow of radiant energy, expressed in various units.

radiant heating A system of heating a house, room, etc., in which the warmth is diffused by radiation from panels or the floor: also called *panel heating.*

ra·di·ate (*v.* rā′dē·āt; *adj. & n.* rā′dē·it) *v.* **·at·ed, ·at·ing** *v.i.* **1.** To emit rays or radiation; be radiant. **2.** To issue forth in rays, as light from the sun. **3.** To spread out from a center, as the spokes of a wheel. **— v.t. 4.** To send out or emit in rays. **5.** To cause to spread as if from a center; diffuse; disseminate. **6.** To show as if shining with: to *radiate* joy. **— adj. 1.** Divided or separated into rays; having rays; radiating. **2.** *Bot.* Bearing rays or ray flowers. **3.** *Zool.* Characterized by radial symmetry, as echinoderms and coelenterates. **4.** Adorned with rays, as a head on a coin; radiated. **— n. 1.** An organism having radial symmetry, as a starfish. **2.** A ray or raylike projection. [< L *radiatus,* pp. of *radiare* to emit rays. See RADIANT.] **— ra′di·a′tive** *adj.*

ra·di·a·tion (rā′dē·ā′shən) *n.* **1.** The act of radiating, or the state of being radiated. **2.** *Physics* **a** The emission and propagation of radiant energy, especially by radioactive substances capable of affecting living tissue. **b** The stages of emission, absorption, and transmission involved in such propagation. **3.** *Biol.* Adaptive radiation (which see).

radiation absorbed dose *Physics* The rad.

radiation pressure *Physics* The force exerted upon an exposed surface by radiant energy, as from light waves.

radiation sickness *Pathol.* A diseased condition due to the body's absorption of excess radiation and marked by fatigue, nausea, vomiting, internal hemorrhage, and progressive tissue breakdown.

ra·di·a·tor (rā′dē·ā′tər) *n.* **1.** That which radiates. **2.** A chamber, coil, or flat hollow vessel, through which is passed steam or hot water for warming a building or apartment. **3.** In engines, a nest of tubes for cooling water flowing through them. **4.** *Physics* Any source of radiant energy, whether in the form of particles or of electromagnetic waves. **— ra′di·a·to′ry** (-ə·tôr′ē, -tō′rē) *adj.*

rad·i·cal (rad′i·kəl) *adj.* **1.** Of, proceeding from, or pertaining to the root or foundation; essential; fundamental; inherent; basic. **2.** Thoroughgoing; unsparing; extreme: a *radical* operation; *radical* measures. **3.** *Math.* Pertaining to the root or roots of a number. **4.** In etymology, belonging or referring to a root or a root syllable; underived. **5.** *Bot.* Springing from, belonging, or relating to the root: *radical* leaves. **6.** *Chem.* Pertaining to a radical. **7.** Of or pertaining to political radicals. **— Syn.** See FUNDAMENTAL, LIBERAL. **— n. 1.** One who carries his theories or convictions to their furthest application; an extremist. **2.** In politics, one who advocates widespread governmental changes and reforms at the earliest opportunity. **3.** The primitive or underived part of a word; a primitive word or syllable; a root; etymon. **4.** *Math.* **a** A quantity that is the root of another quantity. **b** The radical sign. **5.** *Chem.* A group of atoms that acts as a unit in a compound and may pass unchanged through a series of reactions: also spelled *radicle.* Abbr. *R.* (for n. def. 5) symbol *R* [< LL *radicalis* having roots < L *radix, -icis* root] **— rad′i·cal·ness** *n.*

radical empiricism *Philos.* A branch of empiricism that holds all knowledge to be reducible to sensations: also called *sensationalism, sensualism.*

rad·i·cal·ism (rad′i·kəl·iz′əm) *n.* **1.** The state of being radical. **2.** Advocacy of radical measures.

rad·i·cal·ly (rad′ik·lē) *adv.* **1.** Completely; thoroughly; fundamentally. **2.** With reference to root or origin; originally; primitively. **3.** In a radical, extreme manner.

radical sign *Math.* The symbol √ placed before a quantity to indicate that a designated root is to be taken: a modification of the letter *r* (Latin *radix* root).

rad·i·cand (rad′i·kand) *n. Math.* The quantity under the radical sign: $x + 1$ is the *radicand* of $\sqrt{x + 1}$. [< L *radicandus,* gerundive of *radicare* to root]

rad·i·cel (rad′i·sel) *n.* A rootlet. [< NL *radicella,* dim. of L *radix, -icis* root]

rad·i·cle (rad′i·kəl) *n.* **1.** *Bot.* **a** The embryonic root below the cotyledon of a plant. **b** A small root or rootlet. **2.** *Anat.* A rootlike part, as the initial fiber of a nerve. **3.** *Chem.* A radical. [< L *radicula,* dim. of *radix, -icis* root]

ra·di·i (rā′dē·ī) Plural of RADIUS.

ra·di·o (rā′dē·ō) *n. pl.* **·os 1.** The propagation, transmission, and detection of radio waves that have been modulated to carry information either in the form of sound or of a code; also, the process or occupation of, or techniques for doing this. **2.** A radio program or broadcast; also, the combined operations for its production. **3.** A receiver, transmitter, transceiver, or other radio apparatus. **4.** A radio message or radiogram. **5.** The radio business and industry. **— adj.** Of, pertaining to, designating, employing, or produced by radiant energy, especially in the form of electromagnetic waves: a *radio* beam. **— v.t. & v.i.** **ra·di·oed, ra·di·o·ing** To transmit (a message, etc.) or communicate with (someone) by radio. Also, *Brit., wireless.* [< RADIO(TELEGRAPHY)]

radio- *combining form* **1.** Radial. **2.** Radio; produced or obtained by or related to radio: *radiogram.* **3.** Radioactive. **4.** Radium: *radiotherapy.* **5.** Radiation. [< L *radius* ray]

ra·di·o·ac·tive (rā′dē·ō·ak′tiv) *adj.* Pertaining to, exhibiting, caused by, or characteristic of radioactivity.

radioactive series *Physics* The sequence of disintegration products through which a radioactive element passes before reaching a stable form as an isotope of lead. The three principal series are those of uranium, thorium, and actinium.

ra·di·o·ac·tiv·i·ty (rā′dē·ō·ak·tiv′ə·tē) *n. Physics* The spontaneous nuclear disintegration of certain elements and isotopes, with the emission of nucleons or of electromagnetic radiation; also, a particular form of such disintegration.

radio astronomy The branch of astronomy and astrophysics that studies celestial objects by the analysis of radio waves intercepted by radio telescopes.

ra·di·o·au·tog·ra·phy (rā′dē·ō·ô·tog′rə·fē) *n.* Autoradiography. [< RADIO- + AUTOGRAPH + -Y²]

ra·di·o·au·to·gram (rā′dē·ō·ô′tə·gram) *n.* Autoradiograph. Also **ra′di·o·au′to·graph** (-graf, -gräf).

radio beacon A stationary radio transmitter that sends out characteristic signals for the guidance of ships and aircraft.

radio beam A beam (def. 10).

ra·di·o·bi·ol·o·gy (rā′dē·ō·bī·ol′ə·jē) *n.* The study of the effects of radiation upon living organisms.

ra·di·o·broad·cast (rā′dē·ō·brôd′kast′, -käst′) *v.t. & v.i.* **·cast** or **·cast·ed, ·cast·ing** To broadcast by radio. **— n.** A broadcast. **— ra′di·o·broad′cast′er** *n.* **— ra′di·o·broad′cast′ing** *n.*

ra·di·o·car·bon (rā′dē·ō·kär′bən) *n. Physics* The radioactive isotope of carbon of mass 14 with a half life of about 5570 years, much used in the dating of fossils, artifacts, and certain kinds of geological formations: also called *carbon 14.*

ra·di·o·chem·is·try (rā′dē·ō·kem′is·trē) *n.* That branch of chemistry dealing with the properties and reactions of radioactive substances, as radium and thorium.

radio compass *Aeron.* A directional radio receiver that indicates the bearing of a radio transmitting station.

radio control Control by radio signals.

ra·di·o·el·e·ment (rā′dē·ō·el′ə·mənt) *n. Physics* Any isotope or element exhibiting radioactivity.

ra·di·o·dat·ing (rā′dē·ō·dā′ting) *n.* The technique of dating objects by measuring their radioactivity.

radio fix The position of an aircraft, ship, or radio transmitter, as determined by use of radio signals.

radio frequency Any wave frequency lying between about 10 kilocycles and about 30,000 megacycles. *Abbr. r.f.*

ra·di·o·gram (rā′dē·ō·gram′) *n.* **1.** A message sent by wireless telegraphy. **2.** A radiographic negative or print.

ra·di·o·graph (rā′dē·ō·graf′, -gräf′) *n.* A picture made by means of radioactivity; an X-ray photograph. — *v.t.* To make a radiograph of. — **ra·di·og·ra·pher** (-og′rə·fər) *n.* — **ra′di·o·graph′ic** or **·i·cal** *adj.* — **ra′di·og′ra·phy** *n.*

ra·di·o·i·so·tope (rā′dē·ō·ī′sə·tōp) *n. Physics* A radioactive isotope, usually one produced artificially from a normally stable element, used in biological and physical research and in medicine for diagnostic and therapeutic purposes.

ra·di·o·lar·i·an (rā′dē·ō·lâr′ē·ən) *n.* Any member of an order (*Radiolaria*) of marine protozoans having typically a siliceous skeleton enclosing a perforated membrane. [< NL *Radiolaria* < *radiolus*, dim. of L *radius* ray]

ra·di·o·lo·ca·tion (rā′dē·ō·lō·kā′shən) *n.* The use of radar to locate objects.

ra·di·ol·o·gy (rā′dē·ol′ə·jē) *n.* The branch of science that relates to radiant energy and its applications, especially in the diagnosis and treatment of disease. — **ra′di·o·log′i·cal** (rā′dē·ō·loj′i·kəl) or **ra′di·o·log′ic** *adj.* — **ra′di·ol′o·gist** *n.*

ra·di·o·lu·cent (rā′dē·ō·loo′sənt) *adj.* Permeable to X-rays and other forms of electromagnetic radiation.

ra·di·o·lu·mi·nes·cence (rā′dē·ō·loo′mə·nes′əns) *n.* Luminescence produced by, or resulting from, any form of radiant energy. — **ra′di·o·lu′mi·nes′cent** *adj.*

ra·di·o·me·te·or·o·graph (rā′dē·ō·mē′tē·ər·ə·graf′, -gräf′, -mē′tē·ôr′ə·, -or′ə·) *n.* A radiosonde.

ra·di·om·e·ter (rā′dē·om′ə·tər) *n.* An instrument for detecting and measuring radiant energy by converting it into mechanical energy, as by the rotation of blackened vanes suspended in a vacuum and exposed to sunlight. — **ra′di·o·met′ric** (-ō·met′rik) *adj.* — **ra′di·om′e·try** *n.*

ra·di·o·mi·crom·e·ter (rā′dē·ō·mī·krom′ə·tər) *n.* An instrument, consisting primarily of an extremely sensitive thermoelectric couple suspended in a magnetic field, for measuring minute variations of heat.

ra·di·o·paque (rā′dē·ō·pāk′) *adj.* Impermeable to X-rays or other forms of electromagnetic radiation. [< RADIO- + (O)PAQUE]

ra·di·o·phone (rā′dē·ō·fōn′) *n.* **1.** Any device for the production or transmission of sound by radiant energy. **2.** A radiotelephone. — **ra′di·o·phon′ic** (-fon′ik) *adj.* — **ra′di·oph′o·ny** (-of′ə·nē) *n.*

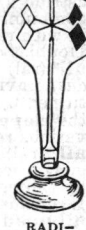

RADI-OMETER

ra·di·o·pho·tog·ra·phy (rā′dē·ō·fə·tog′rə·fē) *n.* The transmission of a photograph by radio waves. — **ra′di·o·pho′to·graph** (-fō′tə·graf, -gräf) *n.*

radio pill *Med.* A tiny radio transmitter that can be introduced into the body to transmit physiological data.

radio receiver A receiver (def. 7b).

ra·di·o·scope (rā′dē·ō·skōp′) *n.* An apparatus for detecting radioactivity or X-rays.

ra·di·os·co·py (rā′dē·os′kə·pē) *n.* Examination of opaque bodies with the aid of X-rays or some other form of radiant energy. [< RADIO- + -SCOPY] — **ra′di·o·scop′ic** (-skop′ik) or **·i·cal** *adj.*

ra·di·o·sen·si·tive (rā′dē·ō·sen′sə·tiv) *adj. Med.* Reducible or destructible by X-rays, as certain tumors.

ra·di·o·sonde (rā′dē·ō·sond′) *n. Meteorol.* An airborne device, usually attached to a balloon, that radios meteorological data to the ground: also called *radiometeorograph.* [< F < *radio* radio + *sonde* sounding. Cf. ME *sonde* messenger.]

radio spectrum The full range of frequencies pertaining to and associated with radiant energy; especially, the radio frequencies.

radio star Any of a large number of stars that may be identified and studied by means of the characteristically large proportion of radio waves they emit.

radio station An installation of all the equipment needed for effective radio broadcasting,

RADIO-SONDE

a Instrument box.

especially when used for commercial or educational purposes and licensed to employ an assigned frequency and power.

ra·di·o·stron·tium (rā′dē·ō·stron′shəm, -tē·əm) *n. Physics* Strontium 90.

ra·di·o·tel·e·gram (rā′dē·ō·tel′ə·gram) *n.* A message sent by radiotelegraphy.

ra·di·o·te·leg·ra·phy (rā′dē·ō·tə·leg′rə·fē) *n.* Telegraphic communication by means of radio waves. — **ra′di·o·tel′e·graph′ic** (-tel′ə·graf′ik) *adj.* — **ra′di·o·tel′e·graph** (-graf, -gräf) *n.*

ra·di·o·tel·e·phone (rā′dē·ō·tel′ə·fōn) *n.* A telephone that operates by means of radio waves. — **ra′di·o·tel′e·phon′ic** (-tel′ə·fon′ik) *adj.* — **ra′di·o·te·leph′o·ny** (-tə·lef′ə·nē) *n.*

radio telescope *Astron.* A highly sensitive radio receiver, designed to receive radio waves from outer space.

ra·di·o·ther·a·py (rā′dē·ō·ther′ə·pē) *n. Med.* The use of X-rays and other forms of radioactivity in the treatment of disease.

ra·di·o·ther·my (rā′dē·ō·thûr′mē) *n. Med.* The therapeutic use of radiant heat, as in diathermy.

ra·di·o·tho·ri·um (rā′dē·ō·thôr′ē·əm, -thō′rē·əm) *n.* A radioactive isotope of thorium, with a half life of 1.9 years.

ra·di·o·tox·ic (rā′dē·ō·tok′sik) *adj. Med.* Of or pertaining to the toxic effect of radioactive materials, especially radioisotopes. — **ra′di·o·tox·ic′i·ty** (-tok·sis′ə·tē) *n.*

radio tube An electron tube for radio.

radio wave Any electromagnetic wave having a radio frequency; a Hertzian wave. Compare MICROWAVE.

rad·ish (rad′ish) *n.* **1.** The pungent, edible root of a tall, branching herb (*Raphanus sativus*) of the mustard family. **2.** The herb yielding this root. [OE *rædic*, later infl. by F *radis* or Ital. *radice*, all < L *radix, radicis* root. Doublet of RADIX.]

ra·di·um (rā′dē·əm) *n.* A powerfully radioactive metallic element (symbol Ra), obtained principally as a disintegration product of the uranium series. It has a half life of about 1,600 years and its atoms undergo spontaneous disintegration, emitting alpha and beta particles and gamma rays in a succession of stages beginning with radon and continuing from radium A to radium G, a stable isotope of lead. See ELEMENT. [< NL < L *radius* ray + -IUM]

radium therapy The treatment of diseases, especially cancer, by means of radium.

ra·di·us (rā′dē·əs) *n. pl.* **·di·i** (-dē·ī) or **·di·us·es** **1.** A straight line from the center of a circle or sphere to the circumference or surface. *Abbr. R* **2.** *Anat.* The thicker and shorter bone of the forearm, on the same side as the thumb. For illustration see ULNA. **3.** *Zool.* A similar bone in the forelimb of other vertebrates. **4.** *Bot.* A ray floret of a composite flower; also, a branch of an umbel. **5.** A ray or radiating part. **6.** In a sextant, quadrant, etc., a pivoted arm, mounted so as to move radially, as on a graduated arc or circle. **7.** *Mech.* A wheel spoke; a rod or bar that with others extends from a common point. **8.** A circular area or boundary measured by the length of its radius. **9.** Sphere, scope, or limit, as of activity. **10.** A fixed limit of travel or operation: the cruising *radius* of a ship. *Abbr. r.* [< L, orig. rod, hence spoke of a wheel, ray of light. Doublet of RAY]

radius vector *pl.* **radius vectors** or **ra·di·i vec·to·res** (rā′dē·ī vek·tôr′ēz, -tō′rēz) **1.** *Math.* **a** The straight-line distance from a fixed origin to any point of a curve. **b** The distance from a point to the pole in the polar coordinate system. **2.** *Astron.* A line from a center of attraction to a body describing an orbit about it, as from the sun to any of the planets.

ra·dix (rā′diks) *n. pl.* **rad·i·ces** (rad′ə·sēz, rā′də-) or **ra·dix·es** **1.** *Math.* A number or symbol used as the basis of a scale of enumeration: 10 is the *radix* of the common system of logarithms. **2.** *Bot.* The root of a plant. **3.** An original word from which others are derived; radical; root; etymon. [< L, root. Doublet of RADISH.]

RAdm. *Mil.* Rear Admiral.

Rad·nor·shire (rad′nər·shir) A former county of central Wales; 471 sq. mi.; pop. 18,262 (1971); county seat, Presteigne. Also **Rad′nor.**

Ra·dom (rä′dôm) A city in east central Poland; pop. 148,400 (est. 1968).

ra·dome (rā′dōm) *n.* A protective housing for the antenna of a radar assembly. [< RA(DAR) + DOME]

ra·don (rā′don) *n.* A heavy, gaseous, radioactive element (symbol Rn), an emanation of radium with a half life of about 4 days: formerly called *niton.* See ELEMENT. [< RAD(IUM) + -ON]

rad·u·la (raj′oo·lə) *n. pl.* **·lae** (-lē) *Zool.* A narrow, tongue-like organ in the mouth of many mollusks, set with rows of horny teeth for rasping food. [< L, scraper < *radere* to scrape] — **rad′u·lar** *adj.*

Rae·burn (rā′bərn), **Sir Henry,** 1756–1823, Scottish painter.

Rae·der (rā′dər), **Erich,** 1876–1960, German admiral in World War II.

Rae·mae·kers (rä′mä·kərz), **Louis,** 1869–1956, Dutch political cartoonist.

RAF or **R.A.F.** Royal Air Force.

raff (raf) *n.* **1.** The rabble; riffraff. **2.** *Scot. & Brit. Dial.* A disorderly collection. [< dial. *raff* to rake < OF *rafler* < *rafle*. See RAFFLE.]

raf·fi·a (raf'ē·ə) *n.* **1.** A cultivated palm (*Raphia peduncu-lata*) of Madagascar, the leafstalks of which furnish fiber for making hats, mats, baskets, etc. **2.** Its fiber. Also spelled *raphia*. [< Malagasy *rafia*]

raf·fi·nose (raf'ə·nōs) *n. Biochem.* A crystalline trisaccha-ride, $C_{18}H_{32}O_{16}\cdot5H_2O$, having a mildly sweetish taste, found in cottonseed and in the molasses of the sugar beet. [< F *raffiner* to refine + -OSE²]

raff·ish (raf'ish) *adj.* **1.** Tawdry; gaudy; flashy. **2.** Dis-reputable. [< RAFF + -ISH¹]

raf·fle¹ (raf'əl) *n.* A form of lottery in which one buys a chance on an object. — *v.* **·fled**, **·fling** *v.t.* **1.** To dispose of by a raffle: often with *off*. — *v.i.* **2.** To take part in a raffle. [< OF *rafle* a game of dice < Du. *rafelen*] — **raf'fler** *n.*

raf·fle² (raf'əl) *n. Naut.* A jumble of rubbish; tangle. [Prob. < RAFF]

raf·fle·si·a (ra·flē'zhē·ə, -zē·ə) *n.* Any of a genus (*Rafflesia*) of parasitic plants found in Malaya, and having huge, stem-less, malodorous flowers. [< NL, after Sir T. S. *Raffles*, 1781–1826, British governor in Sumatra, who discovered it]

raft¹ (raft, räft) *n.* **1.** A float of logs, planks, etc., fastened together for transportation by water. **2.** A life raft (which see). — *v.t.* **1.** To transport on a raft. **2.** To form into a raft. — *v.i.* **3.** To travel by, be employed on, or manage a raft. [< ON *raptr* rafter]

raft² (raft, räft) *n. Informal* A large number or indiscrimi-nate collection of any kind. [< RAFF]

raft·er (raf'tər, räf'-) *n.* A beam giving form, slope, and support to a roof. For illustration see ROOF. [OE *ræfter*]

rafts·man (rafts'mən, räfts'-) *n. pl.* **·men** (-mən) One who manages or works on a raft.

rag¹ (rag) *v.t.* **ragged**, **rag·ging** *Slang* **1.** To tease or irri-tate. **2.** To scold. **3.** *Brit.* To play a practical joke on. — *n. Brit.* A ragging. [Origin uncertain]

rag² (rag) *n.* **1.** A torn or discarded piece of cloth. **2.** A small cloth used for washing, cleaning, etc. **3.** A fragment of anything. **4.** *pl.* Cotton or linen textile remnants used in the making of rag paper. **5.** *pl.* Tattered or shabby cloth-ing. **6.** Any clothing: a jocular usage. **7.** Anything re-sembling a rag in appearance or worth: used humorously or in disparagement. **8.** In citrus fruits, the axis and carpel-lary walls. — **glad rags** *Slang* One's best clothes. — **to chew the rag** *Slang* To talk or argue at great length. [OE *ragg*, as in *raggig* raggy, < ON *rögg* tuft]

rag³ (rag) *n.* **1.** A roofing slate rough on one side, and meas-uring 2 x 3 feet. **2.** *Brit.* Any hard rock of cellular or coarse-ly granular texture. [Prob. var. of RAG²]

rag⁴ (rag) *v.t.* **ragged**, **rag·ging** To compose or play in rag-time. — *n.* Ragtime.

rag·a·muf·fin (rag'ə·muf'in) *n.* Anyone, especially a child, wearing very ragged clothes. [after *Ragamoffyn*, demon in William Langland's *Piers Plowman*, 1393]

rag bag A bag in which rags or scraps of cloth are kept.

rag doll A cloth doll stuffed with rags or cotton.

rage (rāj) *n.* **1.** Violent anger; wrath; fury. **2.** Any great violence or intensity, as of a fever or a storm. **3.** Extreme eagerness or emotion; ardent desire; great enthusiasm. **4.** Something popular or in demand; a fad; fashion. — **Syn.** See ANGER. — *v.i.* **raged**, **rag·ing 1.** To speak, act, or move with unrestrained anger; feel or show violent anger. **2.** To act or proceed with great violence: The storm *raged*. **3.** To spread or prevail uncontrolled, as an epidemic. [< OF < LL *rabia* < L *rabies* madness < *rabere* to rage] — **rag'-ing·ly** *adv.*

rag·ged (rag'id) *adj.* **1.** Rent or worn into rags; frayed: a *ragged* coat. **2.** Wearing worn, frayed, or shabby garments. **3.** Of rough, broken, or uneven character or aspect. **4.** Nat-urally of a rough or shaggy appearance. — **rag'ged·ly** *adv.* — **rag'ged·ness** *n.* — **Syn. 1.** threadbare, tattered, shabby.

ragged edge *Informal* The extreme or precarious edge; the verge: the *ragged* edge of starvation. — **on the ragged edge** Dangerously near to losing one's self-control, sanity, etc.

ragged robin A perennial European herb (*Lychnis floscu-culi*) having red or pink flowers in panicles: also called *cuckoo-flower*.

rag·i (rag'ē, rä'gē) *n.* A cereal grass (*Eleusine coracona*) of the East Indies. Also **rag'ee, rag'gy**. [< Hind. *rāgī*]

rag·lan (rag'lən) *n.* An overcoat or topcoat, the sleeves of which extend in one piece up to the collar. — *adj.* Denoting a garment with such sleeves. [after Lord *Raglan*]

Rag·lan (rag'lən), **Lord,** 1788–1855, Fitzroy James Henry Somerset, English field marshal in the Crimean War.

rag·man (rag'man', -mən) *n. pl.* **·men** (-men', -mən) One who buys and sells old rags and other waste; a ragpicker.

Rag·na·rök (räg'nä·rœk) In Norse mythology, the twilight of the gods, and the doomsday of the world, preceding its re-generation. Also **Rag'na·rok** (-rok). [< ON < *ragna* of the gods (genitive pl. of *regin*) + *rök* judgment]

ra·gout (ra·gōō') *n.* A highly seasoned dish of stewed meat and vegetables. — *v.t.* **ra·gouted** (-gōōd'), **ra·gout·ing** (-gōō'ing) To make into a ragout. [< F]

rag·pick·er (rag'pik'ər) *n.* One who picks up rags and other junk for a livelihood.

rag rug A rug made of rags.

rag·tag (rag'tag') *n.* Ragged people; the rabble. Also **rag and tag, ragtag and bobtail, rag, tag, and bobtail.**

rag·time (rag'tīm') *n.* **1.** A kind of American dance music, developed from about 1890 to 1920, characterized by highly syncopated rhythm in fast time. **2.** The rhythm of this music. Also called *rag*. [< *ragged time*]

Ra·gu·sa (rä·gōō'sä) **1.** The Italian name for DUBROVNIK. **2.** A commune in SE Sicily; pop. 55,274 (1961).

rag·weed (rag'wēd') *n.* **1.** A coarse, very common annual or perennial herb (genus *Ambrosia*), the pollen of which in-duces hay fever; especially, the **common ragweed** (*A. ar-temisifolia*), and the **great ragweed** (*A. trifida*), with stout hairy stem 5 to 15 feet high: also called *blackweed, hogweed, stickweed*. **2.** *Brit.* The ragwort.

rag·wort (rag'wûrt') *n.* Any of several herbs (genus *Sene-cio*) of the composite family, as the **European ragwort** (*S. jacobaea*), with bright yellow flowers, and the **golden rag-wort** (*S. aureus*) of North America.

rah (rä) *interj.* Hurrah: a cheer used chiefly in college yells.

Rah·way (rô'wā) A city in NE New Jersey, near Elizabeth; pop. 29,114.

ra·ia (rä'yə, rī'ə) See RAYAH.

raid (rād) *n.* **1.** A hostile or predatory incursion by a rapid-ly moving body of troops or an armed vessel; a foray. **2.** An air raid (which see). **3.** Any sudden invasion, capture, or seizure: a police *raid*. **4.** An attempt by speculators to lower stock prices. — *v.t.* To make a raid on. — *v.i.* To participate in a raid. [< Scottish form of OE *rād* a riding. Var. of ROAD.] — **raid'er** *n.*

rail¹ (rāl) *n.* **1.** A bar of wood, metal, etc., resting on sup-ports, as in a fence, at the side of a stair-way, or capping the bulwarks of a ship; a railing. **2.** One of a series of parallel bars of iron or steel, resting upon crossties and forming a support and guide for wheels, as of a railroad. **3.** A railroad considered as a means of transportation: to ship by *rail*. — **to go by rail** To travel by train. — **to ride (someone) on a rail** To put (a person) astride a rail and carry around or beyond the limits of a community, as a punishment. — *v.t.* To furnish or shut in with rails; fence. [< OF *reille* < L *regula* wooden ruler. Doublet of RULE.]

RAIL FENCE

rail² (rāl) *n.* **1.** Any of numerous marsh birds (family *Ralli-dae*), having very short wings, long legs and toes, and a short turned-up tail; especially, the **Virginia rail** (*Rallus limicola*), the **clapper rail** (*R. longirostris*), and the sora. **2.** Any of various related birds, as the corn crake. [< OF *raale*]

rail³ (rāl) *v.i.* **1.** To use scornful, insolent, or abusive lan-guage; scold: with *at* or *against*. — *v.t.* **2.** To drive or force by railing. [< MF *railler* < Provençal *ralhar* to jest at < L *ragulare* to brag] — **rail'er** *n.*

rail·head (rāl'hed') *n.* **1.** A railroad terminus. **2.** On an incompleted railroad, the farthest point to which rails have been laid. **3.** The point on a railroad from which a military unit draws its supplies.

rail·ing (rā'ling) *n.* **1.** A bar, as along a stairway, or a barrier, made up of one or more rails resting on supports. **2.** Rails, or the material from which rails are made.

rail·ler·y (rā'lər·ē) *n. pl.* **·ler·ies** Merry jesting or teasing; banter. — **Syn.** See BANTER. [< F *raillerie* jesting]

rail·road (rāl'rōd') *n.* **1.** A graded road having metal rails supported by ties or sleepers, for the passage of trains or roll-ing stock drawn by locomotives. **2.** The system of tracks, stations, rolling stock, etc., used in transportation by rail. Abbr. **R., RR, R.R. 3.** The corporation or persons owning or operating such a system. — *v.t.* **1.** To transport by rail-road. **2.** *U.S. Informal* To rush or force with great speed or without deliberation: to *railroad* a bill through Congress. **3.** *U.S. Slang* To cause to be imprisoned on false charges or without fair trial. — *v.i.* **4.** To work on a railroad.

rail·road·er (rāl'rō'dər) *n.* One who works on a railroad.

rail·road·ing (rāl'rō'ding) *n.* The construction, operation, or business of a railroad.

rail·split·ter (rāl'split'ər) *n.* One who splits logs into fence rails. — **the Rail-Splitter** Abraham Lincoln.

rail·way (rāl'wā') *n.* **1.** *Chiefly Brit.* A railroad. **2.** Rails similar to but lighter or smaller than those of a railroad, as for streetcars. **3.** A track or set of rails, as in a warehouse or factory, for handling heavy articles, etc. Abbr. *Ry.*

rai·ment (rā'mənt) *n. Archaic* Wearing apparel; clothing; garb. [Aphetic var. of *arrayment* < ARRAY + -MENT]

rain (rān) *n.* **1.** The condensed water vapor of the atmos-phere falling in drops. ◆ Collateral adjective: *pluvial*. **2.** The fall of such drops. **3.** A fall or shower of anything in the manner of rain: a *rain* of bombs. **4.** A rainstorm; shower. **5.** *pl.* The rainy season, as in a tropical country. — **rain or shine** Whether it rains or not; in any weather. — *v.i.* **1.** To fall from the clouds in drops of water: usually with *it* as the subject. **2.** To fall like rain, as tears. **3.** To send or pour down rain, as clouds. — *v.t.* **4.** To send down like rain; shower. — **to rain out** To cause (a game, outdoor event, etc.) to be canceled or postponed because of rain. [OE *regn.* Akin to OHG *regan,* ON *regn.*]

rain·band (rān′band′) *n. Astron.* A dark band in the solar spectrum, caused by the presence of water vapor in the atmosphere.

rain·bow (rān′bō′) *n.* **1.** An arch of prismatic colors formed in the sky opposite the sun and caused by refraction, reflection, and dispersion of light in raindrops falling through the air. **2.** Any similar display of color. [OE *regnboga.*]

Rainbow Bridge National Monument A region in southern Utah, site of a natural bridge; 160 acres; established, 1910.

rainbow cactus A cactus (*Echinocereus rigidissimus*) of the SW United States, having red and white spines and red flowers.

rainbow chaser One who pursues imaginary or impossible goals; a visionary.

rainbow trout See under TROUT.

rain check *U.S.* **1.** The stub of a ticket to an outdoor event, as a baseball game, entitling the holder to admission at a future date if for any reason the event is called off. **2.** A postponed invitation. — **to take a rain check** To defer the acceptance of an invitation.

rain·coat (rān′kōt′) *n.* A coat, often waterproof, intended to be worn in rainy weather. Also, *Brit., waterproof.*

rain crow Any of various birds thought by farmers to be a sign of rain, as the yellow-billed cuckoo.

rain·drop (rān′drop′) *n.* A drop of rain.

rain·fall (rān′fôl′) *n.* **1.** A fall of rain. **2.** *Meteorol.* The amount of water, measured in inches, precipitated in a given region over a stated time, as rain, hail, snow, or the like.

rain gauge An instrument for measuring the amount of rainfall at a given place or during a given time: also called *pluviometer, udometer.* Also **rain gage.**

Rai·nier (rā·nir′, rā′nir), **Mount** An extinct volcano in the Cascade Range, SW Washington; 14,408 feet; in Mount Rainier National Park.

rain·mak·er (rān′mā′kər) *n.* One reputedly able to cause rain; especially, among certain American Indians, one who uses incantations to produce rain. — **rain′mak′ing** *n.*

rain·out (rān′out′) *n. Physics* Precipitation of radioactive water droplets following an underwater nuclear explosion.

rain·proof (rān′proof′) *adj.* Shedding rain, as garments.

rain shadow *Meteorol.* An area of relatively small average rainfall on the leeward side of mountains.

rain·storm (rān′stôrm′) *n.* A storm accompanied by rain.

rain·wa·ter (rān′wô′tər, -wot′-) *n.* Water that falls or has fallen in the form of rain. Also **rain water.**

rain·y (rā′nē) *adj.* **rain·i·er, rain·i·est** Characterized by, abounding in, or bringing rain. — **rain′i·ly** *adv.* — **rain′i·ness** *n.*

rainy day A time of need; hard times.

raise (rāz) *v.* **raised, rais·ing** *v.t.* **1.** To cause to move upward or to a higher level; lift; elevate. **2.** To place erect; set up. **3.** To construct or build; erect. **4.** To make greater in amount, size, or value: to *raise* the price of corn. **5.** To advance or elevate in rank, estimation, etc. **6.** To increase the strength, intensity, or degree of. **7.** To breed; grow: to raise chickens or tomatoes. **8.** *U.S.* To rear (children, a family, etc.). **9.** To give utterance to; cause to be heard: to *raise* a hue and cry. **10.** To cause; occasion, as a smile or laugh. **11.** To stir to action or emotion; arouse. **12.** To waken; animate or reanimate: to *raise* the dead. **13.** To gather together; obtain or collect, as an army, capital, etc. **14.** To bring up for consideration, as a question. **15.** To cause to swell or become lighter; leaven. **16.** To put an end to, as a siege. **17.** In poker, to bet more than. **18.** *Naut.* To cause to appear above the horizon, as land or a ship, by approaching nearer. **19.** *Scot.* To madden; enrage. — *v.i.* **20.** *Informal* To cough up phlegm. **21.** *Dial.* To rise or arise. **22.** In poker, to make a raise. — **Syn.** See ELEVATE. — **to raise the devil** (or **the dickens, hell, the roof, a rumpus,** etc.) *Informal* To make a great disturbance; stir up commotion. — **to raise steam** To get or produce steam, as in a boiler, for the purpose of starting up a steam engine. — *n.* **1.** The act of raising. **2.** An increase, as of wages or a bet. ◆ In British usage, a *rise* is an increase in wages. **3.** *Brit. Dial.* Something raised; an ascent; mound. [< ON *reisa* causative of *risa* to rise. Akin to OE *ræran* to rear, causative of *rīsan* to rise.] — **rais′er** *n.*

raised (rāzd) *adj.* **1.** Elevated in low relief. **2.** Made with yeast or leaven.

rai·sin (rā′zən) *n.* A grape of a special sort dried in the sun or in an oven, used in cookery, as a dessert, etc. [< OF *raizin* < L *racemus* bunch of grapes.]

rais·ing (rā′zing) *n.* **1.** The act or process of causing to rise. **2.** *U.S.* A gathering of persons for the purpose of erecting the frame of a building: also **raising bee.**

rai·son d'é·tat (re·zôn′ dā·tà′) *French* Political motive; literally, reason of state.

rai·son d'ê·tre (re·zôn′ de′tr′) *French* Reason or excuse for existing; literally, reason for being.

rai·son·né (re·zô·nā′) *adj. French* Arranged analytically or systematically; logical: a catalogue *raisonné.*

raj (räj) *n.* In India, sovereignty; rule. [< Hind. *rāj*]

Raj·ab (ruj′əb) *n.* The seventh month of the Moslem year. See (Moslem) CALENDAR.

ra·jah (rä′jə) *n.* A Hindu prince or chief of a tribal state in India; also, a Malay or Javanese ruler: often used as a courtesy title. Also **ra·ja.** [< Hind. *rājā* < Skt. *rājan* king. Cf. L *rex* king.]

Ra·ja·sthan (rä′jə·stän) A State of NW India, formed by the merger of most of the Rajputana States (1948–50) and the former state of Ajmer (1956); 132,077 sq. mi.; pop. 25,-724,600 (est. 1971); capital, Jaipur. Also **Ra′ja·stan.**

Raj·put (räj′poot) *n.* One of a powerful and warlike Hindu caste. Also **Raj·poot.** [< Hind. *rājpūt* prince < Skt. *rāja-putra* < *rājan* king + *putra* son]

Raj·pu·ta·na (räj′poo·tä′nə) A region in NW India.

rake[1] (rāk) *n.* A toothed implement for drawing together loose material, loosening the surface of the soil, etc. — *v.* **raked, rak·ing** *v.t.* **1.** To scrape or gather together with or as with a rake. **2.** To smooth, clean, or prepare with a rake: to *rake* a lawn. **3.** To gather by diligent effort; scrape together. **4.** To search or examine carefully. **5.** To direct heavy gunfire along the length of, as a ship or column of troops; enfilade. — *v.i.* **6.** To use a rake. **7.** To scrape or pass roughly or violently: with *across, over,* etc. **8.** To make a search. — **to rake in** *Informal* To earn or acquire (money, etc.) in large quantities. [OE *raca.* Cf. OHG *rehho,* ON *reka.*] — **rak′er** *n.*

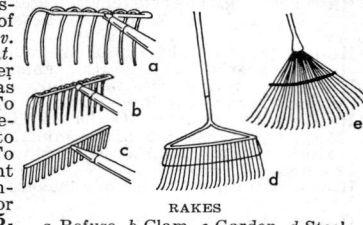

RAKES

a Refuse. *b* Clam. *c* Garden. *d* Steel lawn. *e* Broom lawn.

rake[2] (rāk) *v.* **raked, rak·ing** *v.i.* **1.** To lean from the perpendicular, as a ship's masts. — *v.t.* **2.** To cause to lean; incline. — *n.* Inclination from the perpendicular or horizontal, as of the edge of a cutting tool. [Origin uncertain]

rake[3] (rāk) *n.* A dissolute, lewd man; a roué. — *v.i.* **raked, rak·ing** *Archaic* To play the rake; live a lewd, dissolute life: with *it.* [Short for RAKEHELL]

rake[4] (rāk) *v.i.* **raked, rak·ing** **1.** To hunt by following a scent with the nose to the ground, as a hunting dog. **2.** To fly after game, as a hawk; also, to fly wide of the game. [OE *racian* to speed forward]

rake·hell (rāk′hel′) *Archaic adj.* Recklessly abandoned and dissolute: also **rake′hel′ly.** — *n.* A rake; libertine. [ME *rakel* rash, wild; refashioned after RAKE[1] + HELL]

rake-off (rāk′ôf′, -of′) *n. U.S. Slang* **1.** A share, as of profits; commission. **2.** A rebate, usually illegitimate.

rak·i (rak′ē, rä′kē) *n.* A Turkish liquor distilled from grain, etc., and often aromatically flavored. Also **rak′ee.** [< Turkish *rāqi* < Arabic *'araq.* Akin to ARRACK.]

rak·ish[1] (rā′kish) *adj.* **1.** Dashing; jaunty; smart. **2.** *Naut.* Having the masts unusually inclined, so as to suggest speed. [< RAKE[2]; def. 1 infl. by RAKISH[2]] — **rak′ish·ly** *adv.* — **rak′ish·ness** *n.*

rak·ish[2] (rā′kish) *adj.* Characteristic of a rake; dissolute; profligate. — **rak′ish·ly** *adv.* — **rak′ish·ness** *n.*

râle (räl) *n. Pathol.* A sound additional to that of normal respiration, heard on auscultation of the chest and indicative of the presence, nature, or stage of a disease. [< F, rattle]

Ra·leigh (rô′lē) The capital of North Carolina, in the central part; pop. 121,577.

Ra·leigh (rô′lē), **Sir Walter,** 1552?–1618. English courtier, colonizer, admiral, and poet; beheaded. Also *Brit.* **Ra′legh.**

rall. Rallentando.

ral·len·tan·do (ral′ən·tan′dō, *Ital.* räl′len·tän′dō) *Music adj. & adv.* Gradually slower. — *n. pl.* **·dos** A gradual slowing down. [< Ital.]

ral·li·form (ral′ə·fôrm) *adj. Ornithol.* Pertaining to or like the rails. [< NL *rallus* rail[2] + -FORM]

ral·line (ral′īn, -in) *adj.* Of, pertaining, or belonging to the rail family (*Rallidae*) or subfamily (*Rallinae*) of birds. [< NL *rallus* rail[2]]

ral·ly[1] (ral′ē) *n. pl.* **·lies** **1.** A meeting or assembly of persons for a common purpose. **2.** A rapid recovery of a normal condition as after exhaustion, depression, etc. **3.** A return, as of scattered troops, to order or action. **4.** In tennis, the interchange of several strokes before one side wins the point. **5.** A driving competition or procession over a fixed, often extensive course, as for sports cars, antique automobiles, etc.

— *v.* **·lied, ·ly·ing** *v.t.* **1.** To bring together and restore to effective discipline: to *rally* fleeing troops. **2.** To summon up or revive: to *rally* one's spirits. **3.** To bring together for common action. — *v.i.* **4.** To return to effective discipline or action: The enemy *rallied*. **5.** To unite for common action. **6.** To make a partial or complete return to a normal condition; improve. **7.** In tennis, to engage in a rally. [< F *rallier* to reunite < *re-* again + *allier* to join. See ALLY.] — **ral′li·er** *n.*

ral·ly² (ral′ē) *v.t. & v.i.* **·lied, ·ly·ing** To mock or tease with raillery; banter. [< F *railler* to banter] — **ral′li·er** *n.*

ram (ram) *n.* **1.** A male sheep. **2.** A device for driving, forcing, or crushing by heavy blows or thrusts, as: **a** A battering-ram (which see). **b** The striking weight of a pile driver or steam hammer. **c** The plunger of a force pump. **3.** Formerly, a projection or beak on the bow of a warship, for crushing or cutting into an opposing vessel; also, a warship constructed with such a beak. **4.** *Mech.* A hydraulic ram (which see). — *v.t.* **rammed, ram·ming 1.** To strike with or as with a ram; dash against. **2.** To drive or force down or into something. **3.** To cram; stuff. [OE *ramm*. Cf. ON *ramr* very strong.] — **ram′mer** *n.*

Ram (ram) *n.* The constellation and sign of the zodiac Aries.

R.A.M. 1. Royal Academy of Music. **2.** Royal Arch Mason.

Ra·ma (rä′mə) In Hindu mythology, the name of three heroes, especially that of Ramachandra.

Ra·ma·chan·dra (rä′mə·chun′drə) The seventh avatar of Vishnu, hero of the *Ramayana*.

Ram·a·dan (ram′ə·dän′) *n.* **1.** The ninth month of the Moslem year, the time of the annual fast of thirty days. See (Moslem) CALENDAR. **2.** The fast itself. Also **Ram′a·dhan′, Ram′a·zan′** (-zän′).

Ra·man (rä′mən), **Sir Chandrasekhara (Venkata)**, 1888–1970, Indian physicist.

Ra·ma·ya·na (rä·mä′yə·nə) One of the two great epics of ancient India, recounting the adventures of Rama. Compare MAHABHARATA.

ram·ble (ram′bəl) *v.i.* **·bled, ·bling 1.** To walk about freely and aimlessly; roam. **2.** To write or talk aimlessly or without sequence of ideas. **3.** To proceed with turns and twists; meander. — **Syn.** See WANDER. — *n.* **1.** The act of rambling; an aimless or leisurely stroll. **2.** A meandering path; maze. [? ME *romblen*, freq. of *romen* to roam]

ram·bler (ram′blər) *n.* **1.** One who or that which rambles. **2.** Any of several varieties of climbing roses, as the **crimson rambler** (*Rosa barbierana*), with clusters of deep red flowers.

ram·bling (ram′bling) *adj.* Lacking plan or system; aimless; wandering. — **ram′bling·ly** *adv.*

Ram·bouil·let (ram′bŏŏ-lā, *Fr.* rän·bŏŏ-ye′) *n.* A variety of merino sheep bred in France for meat and wool. [after *Rambouillet*, town in northern France]

ram·bunc·tious (ram-bungk′shəs) *adj. U.S. Informal* Rude and boisterous; rough. [Prob. var. of ROBUSTIOUS]

ram·bu·tan (ram-bŏŏ′tən) *n.* **1.** The spiny, bright red, pleasantly acid fruit of an East Indian and Malayan tree (*Nephelium lappaceum*). **2.** The tree that bears it. [< Malay < *rambut* hair]

ram·e·kin (ram′ə·kin) *n.* **1.** A seasoned dish of bread crumbs with eggs and cheese, baked and served in a shallow dish. **2.** A dish, usually with a handle, in which ramekins are baked. **3.** Any dish used both for baking and serving. Also **ram′e·quin.** [< F *ramequin* < Du. Cf. G *rahm* cream]

ra·men·tum (rə·men′təm) *n.* *pl.* **·ta** (-tə) *Bot.* A thin, membranous, chaffy scale, formed on the surface of leaves, the stems of ferns, etc. [< L *scraping* < *radere* to scrape] — **ram·en·ta·ceous** (ram′ən·tā′shəs) *adj.*

Ram·e·ses II (ram′ə·sēz) 1292–1225 B.C., Egyptian king; allegedly the pharaoh who oppressed the Israelites. Also *Ramses II.*

ram·ie (ram′ē) *n.* **1.** A shrubby Chinese and East Indian perennial (*Boehmeria nivea*) of the nettle family, with numerous rodlike stems and large heart-shaped leaves. **2.** The fiber yielded by its stem, used for cordage and certain textiles. Also **ram′ee.** [< Malay *rami*]

ram·i·fi·ca·tion (ram′ə·fə·kā′shən) *n.* **1.** The act or process of ramifying. **2.** An offshoot or subdivision. **3.** A result, consequence, etc., stemming from a main source. **4.** *Bot.* The arrangement of branches or parts, as on a plant, also, one of the parts.

ram·i·form (ram′ə·fôrm) *adj.* **1.** Branch-shaped. **2.** Branched. [< L *ramus* branch + -FORM]

ram·i·fy (ram′ə·fī) *v.t. & v.i.* **·fied, ·fy·ing 1.** To divide or spread out into branches. **2.** To divide into various divisions or categories. [< F *ramifier* < Med.L *ramificare* < L *ramus* branch + *facere* to make]

ram·il·lie (ram′ə·lē) *n.* A type of wig with a plaited tail, worn in 18th-century England. Also **ram′i·lie, ram′i·lies, ram′il·lies.** [after the battle of *Ramillies*]

Ram·il·lies (ram′ə·lēz, *Fr.* rȧ·mē·yē′) A village in central Belgium; scene of Marlborough's victory over French forces, 1706. Also **Ra·mil·lies-Of·fus** (rȧ·mē·yē′ô·fü′).

ram·jet engine (ram′jet′) A jet engine in which the forward motion of the plane rather than a system of turbines is used to collect and compress air for the combustion process. Such engines are useful only at high speeds.

ram·mish (ram′ish) *adj.* Resembling or characteristic of a ram. Also **ram′my** (-mē). — **ram′mish·ness** *n.*

ra·mose (rā′mōs, rə·mōs′) *adj.* **1.** Branching. **2.** Consisting of or having branches. [< L *ramosus* < *ramus* branch]

ra·mous (rā′məs) *adj.* **1.** Of, pertaining to, or like branches. **2.** Ramose. [See RAMOSE]

ramp¹ (ramp) *n.* **1.** An inclined passageway or roadway, as between floors or different levels of a building. **2.** A movable stairway by which passengers enter or leave an airplane. **3.** In building, a concave part at the top or cap of a railing, wall, or coping. [< F *rampe* < *ramper*. See RAMP².]

ramp² (ramp) *v.i.* **1.** To rear up on the hind legs and stretch out the forelegs, as a quadruped. **2.** *Heraldry* To be in a rampant or threatening position. **3.** To act in a violent or threatening manner; storm; rampage. — *n.* The act of ramping. [< OF *ramper* to climb < Gmc.]

ram·page (*n.* ram′pāj; *v.* ram·pāj′) *n.* Boisterous agitation or excitement; a dashing about with anger or violence. — *v.i.* **·paged, ·pag·ing 1.** To rush or act violently. **2.** To storm; rage. [Orig. Scot., ? < RAMP²] — **ram·pag′er** *n.*

ram·pa·geous (ram-pā′jəs) *adj.* Violent; boisterous. — **ram·pa′geous·ly** *adv.* — **ram·pa′geous·ness** *n.*

ram·pan·cy (ram′pən·sē) *n.* The condition or quality of being rampant.

ram·pant (ram′pənt) *adj.* **1.** Exceeding all bounds; unrestrained; wild. **2.** Widespread or unchecked, as an erroneous belief or superstition. **3.** Standing on the hind legs; rearing: said of a quadruped. **4.** *Heraldry* Standing on the sinister hind leg, with both forelegs elevated, the dexter above the sinister, and the head in profile: said of a beast of prey. **5.** *Archit.* Springing from points on an inclined plane, as an arch. [< OF, ppr. of *ramper.* See RAMP².] — **ram′pant·ly** *adv.*

ram·part (ram′pärt, -pərt) *n.* **1.** The embankment surrounding a fort, on which the parapet is raised, and sometimes including the parapet. **2.** A bulwark or defense. — *v.t.* To supply with or as with ramparts; fortify. — **Syn.** See BULWARK. [< F *rempart* < *remparer* to fortify < *re-* again + *emparer* < Provençal *amparar*, ult. < L *ante* before + *parare* to prepare]

ram·pike (ram′pīk′) *n. Canadian* The bleached skeleton of a tree killed by fire: also *ranpike.* Also **ram′pole** (-pōl).

ram·pi·on (ram′pē·ən) *n.* **1.** A European perennial (*Campanula rapunculus*) having an edible root eaten as a salad. **2.** One of various similar plants, as the **horned rampion** (genus *Phyteuma*), bearing spikes of blue flowers. [Prob. < Fr. *raiponce* < Ital. *raponzolo* < L *rapum* turnip]

Ram·pur (räm′pŏŏr) A city in north central Uttar Pradesh, India; capital of the former state of Rampur; pop. 136,350 (est. 1971).

ram·rod (ram′rod′) *n.* **1.** A rod used to drive home the charge of a muzzleloading gun or pistol. **2.** A similar rod used for cleaning the barrel of a rifle, etc.

Ram·say (ram′zē), **Allan**, 1686–1758, Scottish poet. — **James Andrew** See (Marquis of) DALHOUSIE. — **Sir William**, 1852–1916, British chemist.

Ram·ses II (ram′sēz) See RAMESES II.

Rams·gate (ramz′gāt, *Brit.* -git) A municipal borough in eastern Kent, England; a port and resort; pop. 39,140 (1969).

ram·shack·le (ram′shak′əl) *adj.* Likely to go to pieces, as from age or neglect; shaky; unsteady. [< *ransackled*, pp. of *ransackle*, freq. of RANSACK]

ram's horn A shofar.

ram·son (ram′zən, -sən) *n.* A species of broad-leaved garlic (*Allium ursinum*) whose root is used as a relish and for salads. [OE *hramsan*, pl. of *hramsa*]

ram·stam (ram′stam′, räm′stäm′) *Brit. Dial. & Scot. adj.* Rash; thoughtless; precipitate. — *adv.* Rashly; heedlessly.

ram·til seed (ram′til) Niger seed (which see). [< Hind.]

ram·u·lose (ram′yə·lōs) *adj. Bot.* Bearing many small branches. [< L *ramulosus* < *ramulus*, dim. of *ramus* branch]

ra·mus (rā′məs) *n. pl.* **·mi** (-mī) A branchlike division of a forked structure, as of a nerve, bone, plant, etc.

ran (ran) Past tense of RUN.

Ran (rän) In Norse mythology, the goddess of the sea.

RAN or **R.A.N.** Royal Australian Navy.

rance (rans) *n.* A kind of dull red marble with blue and white markings: also called *Belgian marble.* [< F]

ranch (ranch) *n.* **1.** An establishment for raising or grazing cattle, sheep, horses, etc., in large herds. **2.** The buildings, personnel, and lands connected with it. **3.** A large farm: a fruit *ranch.* — *v.i.* To manage or work on a ranch. [< Sp. *rancho* soldiers' mess]

ranch·er (ran′chər) *n.* **1.** The owner of a ranch. **2.** One who works on a ranch; a cowboy.

ran·che·ro (ran·châr′ō) *n. pl.* **·ros** *SW U.S.* A rancher. [< Sp.]

ranch house 1. The main building of a ranch. **2.** *U.S.* A one-story house usually having a low-pitched roof with a wide overhang.

ranch·man (ranch′mən) *n. pl.* **·men** (-mən) **1.** A herdsman on a ranch. **2.** The owner of a ranch; a rancher.

ran·cho (ran′chō, rän′-) *n. pl.* **·chos** *SW U.S.* **1.** A hut or group of huts in which ranchmen lodge. **2.** A stock farm; ranch. [< Sp.]

ran·cid (ran′sid) *adj.* Having the unpleasant taste or smell of oily substances that have begun to spoil; rank; sour. [< L *rancidus* < *rancere* to be rank]

ran·cid·i·ty (ran·sid′ə·tē) *n.* **1.** The quality or state of being rancid. **2.** A rancid smell or taste. Also **ran·cid·ness.**

ran·cor (rang′kər) *n.* Bitter and vindictive enmity; malice; spitefulness. Also *Brit.* **ran′cour.** — **Syn.** See ENMITY. [< OF < LL < L *rancere* to be rank] — **ran′cor·ous** *adj.* — **ran′cor·ous·ly** *adv.* — **ran′cor·ous·ness** *n.*

rand[1] (rand) *n.* **1.** In shoe manufacturing, a strip of leather at the heel of a shoe to which the lifts are attached. **2.** *Brit. Dial. & Scot.* A grassy border, as of a field or river bank. [OE, edge, shield, boss. Prob. akin to RIM.]

rand[2] (rand, ränd) *n.* The monetary unit of South Africa, Lesotho, and Botswana, equivalent to 100 cents. [< The Rand]

Rand (rand), **The** See WITWATERSRAND.

ran·dan (ran′dan, ran·dan′) *n.* **1.** A boat rowed by three persons, the one amidships having two oars and the others one each. **2.** This style of rowing. [Origin uncertain]

Ran·dolph (ran′dolf), **John,** 1773–1833, American statesman and orator: called **John Randolph of Roanoke.** — **Peyton,** 1721?–75, American patriot; president of first Continental Congress 1774.

ran·dom (ran′dəm) *n.* Lack of definite aim or intention: now chiefly in the phrase **at random,** without definite purpose or aim; haphazardly. — *adj.* Done or chosen without definite aim or deliberate purpose; chance; casual. [< OF *randon* rapidity, impetuosity < Gmc.] — **ran′dom·ly** *adv.*

ran·dom·ize (ran′dəm·īz) *v.t.* **·ized, ·iz·ing** To make random; especially, to arrange or distribute (individual items) in a deliberately chance order as a means of reducing error in statistical analysis. — **ran′dom·i·za′tion** *n.*

random sample *Stat.* A limited group of individuals, cases, or observations, so assembled from a total array as to be representative of the whole. Also **random selection.**

ran·dy (ran′dē) *adj.* **1.** *Scot.* Disorderly; riotous; also, coarse. **2.** Lewd; lustful. — *n. pl.* **·dies** *Scot.* **1.** An impudent beggar. **2.** A boisterous, coarse, or loose woman.

ra·nee (rä′nē) See RANI.

rang (rang) Past tense of RING[2].

range (rānj) *n.* **1.** The area over which anything moves, operates, or is distributed. **2.** *U.S.* An extensive tract of land over which cattle, sheep, etc., roam and graze. **3.** *U.S.* Pasturage; grazing ground. **4.** *Biol.* The geographical area throughout which a specific plant or animal exists. **5.** The extent or scope of something: the whole *range* of politics. **6.** The extent to which any power can be made effective: *range* of vision; *range* of influence. **7.** The extent of variation of anything: the temperature *range.* **8.** The extent of possible variation in pitch: said of musical instruments or the voice. **9.** A line, row, or series, as of mountains. **10.** *U.S.* A single series or row of townships, numbered east or west from a base meridian, each township being further numbered as north or south of the survey base line. **11.** The maximum distance that an aircraft, ship, vehicle, etc., can travel before its fuel is exhausted; also, the maximum distance at which a weapon, transmitter, etc., is effective. **12.** A place for shooting at a mark: a rifle *range.* **13.** A large cooking stove made for preparing several dishes, courses, etc., at one time. **14.** *Stat.* The inclusive difference between the extreme values in any series of variable data. — *adj.* Of or pertaining to a range. — *v.* **ranged, rang·ing** *v.t.* **1.** To place or arrange in definite order, as in rows or lines. **2.** To assign to a class, division, or category; classify; rank. **3.** To move about or over (a region, etc.), as in exploration. **4.** To put (cattle) to graze on a range. **5.** *Mil.* **a** To obtain the range of (a target) by firing alternately above and below it. **b** To be capable of achieving a specified range (def. 11). **6.** To place in position; adjust or train, as a telescope or gun. **7.** *Naut.* To lay out (the anchor cable) on deck so that the anchor may descend without hindrance. — *v.i.* **8.** To move over an area in a thorough, systematic manner. **9.** To rove; roam. **10.** To occur; be found: said of plants and animals. **11.** To extend or proceed: The shot *ranged* to the right. **12.** To exhibit variation within specified limits. **13.** To lie in the same direction, line, etc. [< OF < *ranger* to set in line < *ranc* row < Gmc. Doublet of RANK[1].]

range finder An instrument for determining the distance of an object from a given point.

rang·er (rān′jər) *n.* **1.** One who or that which ranges; a rover. **2.** One of an armed band, usually mounted, designed to protect large tracts of country. **3.** One of a herd of cattle that feeds on a range. **4.** *Brit.* A government official in charge of a royal forest or park. **5.** *U.S.* A warden employed in patrolling forest tracts. — **rang′er·ship** *n.*

Rang·er (rān′jər) *n.* One of a select group of U.S. soldiers trained for raiding action on enemy territory.

ranging figures *Printing Brit.* Lining figures (which see).

Ran·goon (rang·gōn′) The capital of Burma. a port in lower Burma; pop. 1,927,000 (est. 1971, with suburbs).

rang·y (rān′jē) *adj.* **rang·i·er, rang·i·est** **1.** Disposed to roam, or adapted for roving, as cattle. **2.** Having long, slender limbs, as an animal or person. **3.** Affording wide range; roomy. **4.** Resembling a mountain range.

ra·ni (rä′nē) *n.* **1.** The wife of a rajah or prince. **2.** A reigning Hindu queen or princess. Also spelled *ranee.* [< Hind. < Skt. *rājnī,* fem. of *rajan* king]

rank[1] (rangk) *n.* **1.** A series of objects ranged in a line or row; a range. **2.** Degree of official standing, especially in the armed forces. See table for GRADE. **3.** A line of soldiers drawn up side by side in close order: distinguished from *file.* **4.** *pl.* An army; also, the mass of soldiery; the order of private soldiers: The colonel rose from the *ranks.* **5.** A row of eight squares on a chessboard extending from the left of the player to the right. **6.** Relative position in a scale of dignity or of life; degree; grade: the *rank* of baronet; the *rank* of a plant or animal organism. **7.** High degree or position; especially, the state of being a member of a titled nobility: a lady of *rank.* **8.** Degree of worth or excellence; relative status. — **Syn.** See CLASS. — **to pull rank** *U.S. Slang* To attempt to dominate or exploit others by reason of one's superior rank or status. — *v.t.* **1.** To place or arrange in a rank or ranks. **2.** To place in a class, order, etc.; assign to a position or classification. **3.** To take precedence of; outrank: Sergeants *rank* corporals. — *v.i.* **4.** To hold a specified place or rank: to *rank* high. **5.** To have the highest rank or grade. [< OF *ranc* < Gmc. Doublet of RANGE.]

rank[2] (rangk) *adj.* **1.** Very vigorous and flourishing in growth, as vegetation. **2.** Strong and disagreeable to the taste or smell. **3.** Utter; complete: used pejoratively: *rank* injustice. **4.** Producing a luxuriant growth; fertile. **5.** *Law* Inequitable; excessive. **6.** *Obs.* Lustful. — **Syn.** See FLAGRANT. [OE *ranc* strong] — **rank′ly** *adv.* — **rank′ness** *n.*

rank and file **1.** The common soldiers of an army, including all from the corporals downward. **2.** Those who form the bulk of any organization, as distinct from officers or leaders.

Ran·ke (räng′kə), **Leopold von,** 1795–1886, German historian.

rank·er (rangk′ər) *n. Brit.* **1.** One who serves in the ranks. **2.** A commissioned officer who has risen from the ranks.

Rankin (rangk′in), **Jeannette,** 1880–1973, first woman U.S. Representative; from Montana 1917–19, 1941–43.

rank·ing (rangk′ing) *adj.* Superior in rank; taking precedence over others in the same category: a *ranking* senator.

ran·kle (rang′kəl) *v.* **·kled, ·kling** *v.i.* **1.** To cause continued resentment, sense of injury, etc.: The defeat *rankles* in his breast. **2.** To become irritated or inflamed; fester. — *v.t.* **3.** To irritate; embitter. [< OF *rancler* to fester < Med.L *dracunculus* abscess < L, dim. of *draco* dragon]

ran·pike (ran′pīk′) *n.* A rampike (which see).

ran·sack (ran′sak) *v.t.* **1.** To search through every part of. **2.** To search throughout for plunder; pillage. [< ON *rannsaka* to search a house < *rann* house + *sækja* to seek] — **ran′sack·er** *n.*

ran·som (ran′səm) *v.t.* **1.** To secure the release of (a person, property, etc.) for a required price, as from captivity or detention. **2.** To set free on payment of ransom. **3.** To redeem from sin or its consequences. — *n.* **1.** The payment given or demanded for the release of a person or property captured or detained. **2.** Release by ransoming. [< OF *rançon* < L *redemptio, -onis* redemption < *redimere* < *re-* back + *emere* to buy. Doublet of REDEMPTION.] — **ran′som·er** *n.*

rant (rant) *v.i.* **1.** To speak in loud, violent, or extravagant language; declaim vehemently; rave. **2.** *Scot. & Brit. Dial.* To frolic noisily; be uproariously jolly. — *v.t.* **3.** To exclaim or utter in a ranting manner. — *n.* **1.** Declamatory and bombastic talk. **2.** *Scot. & Brit. Dial.* Wild gaiety; a boisterous revel. [< MDu. *ranten* to rave] — **rant′er** *n.*

ra·nun·cu·la·ceous (rə·nung′kyə·lā′shəs) *adj. Bot.* Belonging or pertaining to the crowfoot family (*Ranunculaceae*) of plants including the buttercup, larkspur, peony, etc.

ra·nun·cu·lus (rə·nung′kyə·ləs) *n. pl.* **·lus·es** or **·li** (-lī) Any of a genus (*Ranunculus*) of herbaceous annuals or perennials typical of the crowfoot family. [< L, a medicinal plant, orig. dim. of *rana* frog]

rap[1] (rap) *v.* **rapped, rap·ping** *v.t.* **1.** To strike sharply and quickly; hit. **2.** To utter in a sharp manner: with *out:* to *rap* out an oath. — *v.i.* **3.** To strike sharp, quick blows. **4.** *Slang* To converse; speak. — *n.* **1.** A sharp blow. **2.** A sound caused by or as by knocking; especially, such a sound ascribed to the agency of spirits. **3.** *Slang* A charge of wrongdoing; blame. — **to beat the rap** *Slang* **1.** To escape punishment or blame. **2.** To be acquitted of a criminal charge. — **to take the rap** *Slang* To accept the punishment or responsibility for a crime, especially without being guilty. [ME, prob. imit. Cf. Dan. *rap,* Sw, *rapp.*]

rap[2] (rap) *v.t.* **rapt** or **rapped, rap·ping** **1.** *Obs.* To snatch. **2.** *Archaic* To seize or transport as with ecstasy; carry away:

now current only in the past participle *rapt*. [Back formation < RAPT]

rap³ (rap) *n.* **1.** A counterfeit coin used as a halfpenny in Ireland in the 18th century. **2.** The least bit: I don't care a *rap*. [Origin uncertain. Cf. G. *rappe* a small coin.]

ra·pa·cious (rə·pā′shəs) *adj.* **1.** Given to plunder or rapine. **2.** Grasping; greedy. **3.** Predatory; subsisting on prey seized alive, as hawks, etc. [< L *rapax, -acis* < *rapere* to seize] — **ra·pa′cious·ly** *adv.* — **ra·pa′cious·ness** *n.*

ra·pac·i·ty (rə·pas′ə·tē) *n.* The quality or character of being rapacious.

Ra·pal·lo (rä·päl′lō) A port in NW Italy, at the head of the **Gulf of Rapallo**, an inlet of the Gulf of Genoa; pop. about 12,000.

Ra·pa Nu·i (rä′pä noo′ē) The native name for EASTER ISLAND.

rape¹ (rāp) *v.* **raped, rap·ing** *v.t.* **1.** To commit rape upon; ravish. **2.** To plunder or sack (a city, etc.). **3.** *Archaic* To carry off by force. — *v.i.* **4.** To commit rape. — *n.* **1.** The act of forcing a woman to have sexual intercourse; especially, in law, the forcible and unlawful carnal knowledge of a woman against her will. **2.** *Archaic* A capturing or snatching away by force; abduction. [< AF < L *rapere* to seize]

rape² (rāp) *n.* An Old World annual (*Brassica napus*) related to the cabbage, grown as a forage crop for sheep and hogs, and having seeds that yield rape oil. [< L *rapum* turnip]

rape³ (rāp) *n. Sometimes pl.* In winemaking, refuse stalks and skins of grapes. [< F *râpe* < Med.L *raspa* seeded grapes, ? < Gmc. *raspon* to grate.]

rape oil An oil obtained from rapeseed, and used as a lubricant and in the manufacture of rubber substitutes, soft soaps, etc.: also called *colza oil*.

rape·seed (rāp′sēd′) *n.* **1.** The seed of the rape. **2.** The plant.

Raph·a·el (raf′ē·əl, rā′fē·əl) One of the archangels.

Raphael, 1483–1520. Italian painter: full name Raphael (or **Raffaello) San·zio** (sän′tsyō).

Raph·a·el·esque (raf′ē·əl·esk′) *adj.* Characteristic of, or executed in the style of Raphael. — **Raph′a·el·ism** *n.* — **Raph′a·el·ite′** *n.*

ra·phe (rā′fē) *n. pl.* **·phae** (-fē) **1.** *Anat.* A seamlike appearance along the median line joining two halves of a symmetrical organ or part. **2.** *Bot.* The fibrovascular cord that connects the hilum of plant ovules with the chalaza. **3.** A line or rib connecting the nodules on the valve of a diatom. Also spelled *rhaphe*. [< NL < Gk. *rhaphē* seam < *rhaptein* to stitch together]

ra·phi·a (rā′fē·ə) See RAFFIA.

ra·phide (rā′fid) *n. pl.* **raph·i·des** (raf′ə·dēz) *Bot.* One of the needle-shaped crystals of oxalate of lime found in many plant cells Also **ra′phis** (-fis). [< NL < Gk. *rhaphis, rhaphidos* needle]

rap·id (rap′id) *adj.* **1.** Having or moving with great speed; swift. **2.** Bearing the marks of or characterized by rapidity: a *rapid* style. **3.** Done or completed in a short time; advancing speedily to a termination: *rapid* growth. — **Syn.** See SWIFT¹. — *n. Usually pl.* A part of a river where the bed slopes down and the current is fast and often agitated. [< L *rapidus* < *rapere* to seize, rush] — **rap′id·ly** *adv.*

Rap·i·dan River (rap′ə·dan′) A river of northern Virginia, flowing about 90 miles, generally east, to the Rappahannock.

Rapid City A city in SW South Dakota, near the site of a U.S. Air Force Base; pop. 43,836.

rap·id-fire (rap′id·fīr′) *adj.* **1.** Firing shots rapidly. **2.** Designating single-barreled, breechloading guns larger than small arms, designed for the discharge of projectiles in rapid succession. Abbr. *r.f.* **3.** Characterized by speed: *rapid-fire* repartee. Also **rap′id-fir′ing.**

rapid fire A rate of gunfire lower than that of quick fire.

ra·pid·i·ty (rə·pid′ə·tē) *n.* The quality or state of being rapid; swiftness. Also **rap·id·ness** (rap′id·nis).

rapid transit The local transportation of passengers in a city by means of the elevated or subway.

ra·pi·er (rā′pē·ər, rāp′yər) *n.* **1.** A long, straight, two-edged sword with a large cup hilt, used in the 16th and 17th centuries for dueling, chiefly for thrusting. **2.** The French small sword of the 18th century, a shorter straight sword without cutting edge and therefore used for thrusting only. [< MF *rapière*; ult. origin uncertain. Cf. F. *raspière* poker.]

RAPIER

rap·ine (rap′in) *n.* The taking of property by force, as in war; spoliation; pillage. [< OF < L *rapina* < *rapere* to seize. Doublet of RAVEN², RAVINE.]

rap·ist (rā′pist) *n.* One who commits rape.

Rap·pa·han·nock River (rap′ə·han′ək) A river in northern Virginia, flowing 212 miles generally SE, to Chesapeake Bay.

rap·pa·ree (rap′ə·rē′) *n.* **1.** An Irish guerrilla of the 17th century. **2.** *Rare* A freebooter or bandit. [< Irish *rapaire* short pike]

rap·pee (ra·pē′) *n.* A dark, coarse, strong snuff. [< F *râpé* grated, pp. of *râper* to scrape]

rap·pel (ra·pel′) *v.i.* **·pelled, ·pel·ling** In mountaineering, to descend from a precipitous height by means of a rope. — *n.* Descent of a cliff or mountainside using a rope. [< F]

rap·per (rap′ər) *n.* **1.** One who raps. **2.** A knocker, as on a door.

rap·port (rə·pôr′, -pōr′) *n.* Harmony or sympathy of relation; agreement; accord: to be in *rapport* with someone. — **en rapport** (än rà·pôr′) *French* In close accord. [< F < *rapporter* to bring back]

rap·proche·ment (rà·prôsh·män′) *n. French* A state of harmony or reconciliation; restoration of cordial relations, as between nations.

ras·cal·lion (ras·skal′yən) *n.* A rogue; scamp; rascal. [< earlier *rascallion*, extension of RASCAL]

rapt (rapt) *adj.* **1.** Carried away with lofty emotion; enraptured; transported. **2.** Engrossed; intent; deeply engaged. [< L *raptus*, pp. of *rapere* to seize]

rap·to·ri·al (rap·tôr′ē·əl, -tō′rē-) *adj.* **1.** Seizing and devouring living prey; predatory. **2.** Having talons or claws adapted for seizing and holding prey: said especially of hawks, vultures, eagles, owls, and other carnivorous birds. [< L *raptor* snatcher < *rapere* to seize]

rap·ture (rap′chər) *n.* **1.** The state of being rapt or transported; ecstatic joy; ecstasy. **2.** *Rare* The act of transferring a person from one place to another. **3.** *Often pl.* An act or expression of excessive delight. **4.** *Obs.* A snatching away; violent seizure. — **Syn.** See PLEASURE. — *v.t.* **·tured, ·turing** *Poetic* To enrapture; transport with ecstasy. [< RAPT]

rap·tur·ous (rap′chər·əs) *adj.* Experiencing, expressing, or characterized by rapture. — **rap′tur·ous·ly** *adv.* — **rap′tur·ous·ness** *n.*

ra·ra a·vis (râr′ə ā′vis) *pl.* **ra·rae a·ves** (râr′ē ā′vēz) *Latin* An unusual or rare person or thing; literally, a rare bird.

rare¹ (râr) *adj.* **rar·er, rar·est** **1.** Infrequent in occurrence, distribution, etc. **2.** Highly esteemed because of infrequency or uncommonness; valuable; choice. **3.** Rarefied: now said chiefly of the atmosphere, gases, etc. **4.** *Obs.* Dispersed. Abbr. *r.* [< L *rarus* rare] — **Syn.** **1.** scarce, unusual, exceptional. See OBSOLETE.

rare² (râr) *adj.* **rar·er, rar·est** Not thoroughly cooked, as roasted or broiled meat retaining its redness and juices. [OE *hrēre*]

rare·bit (râr′bit) *n.* Welsh rabbit. [Alter. of (WELSH) RABBIT]

rare earth *Chem.* Any of the metallic oxides of the lanthanide series of elements.

rare-earth element (râr′ûrth′) *Chem.* Any of a group of metallic elements constituting the lanthanide series. Also **rare-earth metal.**

rar·ee show (râr′ē) **1.** A show carried or contained in a box; a peepshow. **2.** A street show. [Alter. of *rare show*]

rar·e·fac·tion (râr′ə·fak′shən) *n.* The process or act of making rare or less dense. Also **rar′e·fi·ca′tion.** [< L *rarefactus*, pp. of *rarefacere*. See RAREFY.] — **rar′e·fac′tive** *adj.*

rar·e·fy (râr′ə·fī) *v.* **·fied, ·fy·ing** *v.t.* **1.** To make rare, thin, less solid, or less dense; expand by dispersion of the particles. **2.** To refine or purify. — *v.i.* **3.** To become rare, thin, less solid. **4.** To become more pure. [< F *raréfier* < L *rarefacere* < *rarus* rare + *facere* to make] — **rar′e·fi′a·ble** *adj.*

rare·ly (râr′lē) *adv.* **1.** Not often; infrequently. **2.** With unusual excellence or effect; finely. **3.** Exceptionally; extremely; in an unusual degree.

rare·ness (râr′nis) *n.* The condition or quality of being rare in any sense.

rare-ripe (râr′rīp′) *adj.* Ripening early. — *n.* A fruit that ripens early, as some varieties of peaches. [OE *hrathe* early, soon + RIPE]

rar·ing (râr′ing) *adj. U.S. Informal* Extremely eager or enthusiastic. [< Pres. part. of *rare*, dial. of REAR²]

rar·i·ty (râr′ə·tē) *n. pl.* **·ties** **1.** The quality or state of being rare, uncommon, or infrequent; infrequency. **2.** That which is exceptionally valued because of scarceness. **3.** The state of being rare, thin, or tenuous.

Ra·ro·ton·ga (rä′rō·tông′gə) The largest and southwestern-most of the Cook Islands; 26 sq. mi.

ras (räs) *n.* An Ethiopian prince. [< Arabic *ra's* head]

ras·bo·ra (raz·bôr′ə, -bō′rə) *n.* Any of a genus (*Rasbora*) of small tropical fish frequently kept in aquariums.

ras·cal (ras′kəl) *n.* **1.** An unprincipled fellow; rogue; knave: sometimes used playfully. **2.** *Obs.* One of low birth or station. — **Syn.** See SCOUNDREL. — *adj. Obs.* Pertaining to the rabble; contemptible; base; mean. [< OF *rascaille* rabble < *rasche* scurf, ult. < L *radere* to scratch]

ras·cal·i·ty (ras·kal′ə·tē) *n. pl.* **·ties** **1.** The quality of being rascally. **2.** A rascally act.

ras·cal·ly (ras′kəl·ē) *adj.* Typical of a rascal; knavish; base. — *adv.* In the manner of a rascal.

rase (rāz) *v.t.* **rased, ras·ing** To raze. [Var. of RAZE]

rash¹ (rash) *adj.* **1.** Acting without due caution or regard of consequences; reckless. **2.** Exhibiting recklessness or precipitancy. **3.** *Obs.* Quick, speedy. [Prob. < MLG *rasch* < OHG *rasc* lively] **— rash′ly** *adv.*

rash² (rash) *n.* A superficial eruption of the skin, often localized. [< OF *rasche.* See RASCAL.]

rash³ (rash) *n. Scot.* A rush; bulrush.

rash·er¹ (rash′ər) *n.* A thin slice of meat, especially bacon. [? < obs. *rash* to cut, slash]

rash·er² (rash′ər) *n.* A vermilion rockfish (*Sebastodes miniatus*) of California. [? < Sp. *rascacio*]

rash·ness (rash′nis) *n.* The state or quality of being rash. **— Syn.** See TEMERITY.

Rask (räsk), **Rasmus Christian,** 1787–1832, Danish philologist and writer.

Ras·mus·sen (räs′mŏos·ən), **Knud Johan Victor,** 1879–1933, Danish Arctic explorer and ethnologist.

ra·so·ri·al (ra·sôr′ē·əl, -sō′rē-) *adj.* Habitually scratching the ground for food, as domestic fowl and other gallinaceous birds. [< NL *Rasores*, lit., scratchers < L *rasum*, pp. of *radere* to scratch]

rasp (rasp, räsp) *n.* **1.** A file having coarse pyramidal projections for abrasion. **2.** The act or sound of rasping. **—** *v.t.* **1.** To scrape with or as with a rasp. **2.** To scrape or rub roughly. **3.** To affect unpleasantly; irritate. **4.** To utter in a rough voice. **—** *v.i.* **5.** To grate; scrape. **6.** To make a rough, harsh sound. [< OF *raspe* < *rasper* to scrape, prob. < Gmc. Cf. OHG *raspon* to grate.] **— rasp′er** *n.*

rasp·ber·ry (raz′ber′ē, -bər·ē, räz′-) *n. pl.* **·ries 1.** The round fruit of certain brambles (genus *Rubus*) of the rose family, composed of drupes clustered around a fleshy receptacle. **2.** Any plant yielding this fruit, as the European **red raspberry** (*R. idaeus*), with many varieties, and the native American **black raspberry** (*R. occidentalis*), or blackcap. **3.** *Slang* A Bronx cheer: also spelled *razzberry.* [< earlier *raspis* (berry) < *raspis* wine, prob. < OF (*vin*) *raspé*, ? < *rasper* to scrape]

rasped (raspt, räspt) *adj.* Rough or roughened with or as with a coarse file: said of uncut book edges.

rasp·ing (ras′ping, räs′-) *adj.* Harsh or irritating in sound or effect.

Ras·pu·tin (ras·pyŏo′tin, *Russ.* räs·pōo′tin), **Grigori Yefimovich,** 1871–1916, Russian monk; favorite of Nicholas II and his wife; assassinated.

ras·py (ras′pē, räs′-) *adj.* **rasp·i·er, rasp·i·est** Inclined to rasp; rough; grating.

Ras·se·las (ras′ə·ləs) The hero of a philosophical romance (1759) of this name by Samuel Johnson.

rat (rat) *n.* **1.** A destructive and injurious rodent (family *Muridae*) of world-wide distribution, larger and more aggressive than the mouse; especially, the **Norway rat** (*Rattus norvegicus*) and the smaller **roof** or **black rat** (*R. rattus*), both of which are carriers of bubonic plague and endemic typhus. **2.** Any of various similar or related animals. **3.** *Slang* A cowardly or selfish person who deserts or betrays his associates. **4.** A cushion or pad over which a woman's hair is combed to give a coiffure body or volume. **— to smell a rat** To suspect that something is wrong. **—** *v.i.* **rat·ted, rat·ting 1.** To hunt rats. **2.** *Slang* To desert one's party, etc., especially for one's own safety or advantage. **3.** *Slang* To inform; betray: with *on.* [OE *ræt*]

rat·a·ble (rā′tə·bəl) *adj.* **1.** *Brit.* Subject to assessment; legally liable to taxation. **2.** Estimated proportionally; pro rata: a *ratable* distribution. **3.** That may be rated or valued. Also **rate′a·ble. — rat′a·bil′i·ty, rat′a·ble·ness** *n.* **— rat′a·bly** *adv.*

rat·a·fi·a (rat′ə·fē′ə) *n.* **1.** A cordial flavored with almonds, peach kernels, or the like. **2.** A sweet, almond-flavored biscuit. Also **rat′a·fee′** (-fē′). [< F]

ra·tal (rāt′l) *n.* An amount on which rates are assessed. [< RATE + -AL¹]

ra·tan (ra·tan′) See RATTAN.

rat·a·ny (rat′ə·nē) See RHATANY.

rat·a·plan (rat′ə·plan′) *n.* A rapidly repeated sound, as of the beating of a drum. **—** *v.t. & v.i.* **·planned, ·plan·ning** To sound a rataplan (on). [< F; imit. of drumming]

rat-a-tat-tat (rat′ə·tat′tat′) *n.* A quick, sharp rapping sound, as a knock at a door. Also **rat′-a-tat′.** [Imit.]

rat·bite fever (rat′bīt′) *Pathol.* An infectious disease caused by the bite of a rat infested with certain bacteria, and characterized by ulcerations, muscular pains, and fever. Also **ratbite disease.**

ratch (rach) *n.* A ratchet. [< RATCHET]

ratch·et (rach′it) *n.* **1.** A mechanism consisting of a notched wheel, the teeth of which engage with a pawl, permitting motion of the wheel in one direction only. **2.** The pawl or the wheel thus used. For illustration see MACHINE. Also **ratchet wheel.** [< F *rochet* bobbin < Gmc.]

rate¹ (rāt) *n.* **1.** The measure of a thing by its relation to a standard; proportional or comparative amount or degree: a high *rate* of speed. **2.** Degree of value; price; also, the unit cost of a commodity or service: the *rate* for electricity,

gas, etc. **3.** Comparative rank or class; condition. **4.** The amount of variation of a timepiece; gain or loss in seconds. **5.** A ratio for the assessment of property taxes. **6.** *Brit.* A local tax on property. **7.** Proportion, as of an incidence or occurrence, to the total of relevant cases involved: the death *rate.* **8.** A fixed allowance or amount. **9.** *Obs.* Degree; estimation. **— at any rate** In any case; under any circumstances; anyhow. **—** *v.* **rat·ed, rat·ing 1.** To estimate the value or worth of; appraise. **2.** To place in a certain rank or grade. **3.** To fix the amount of tax or liability on. **4.** To consider; regard: He is *rated* as a great statesman. **5.** To fix the rate for the transportation of (goods), as by rail, water, or air. **6.** *Informal* To deserve; be worthy of: He *rates* a promotion. **—** *v.i.* **7.** To have rank, rating, or value. **8.** *Informal* To stand in comparison with others: How does he *rate*? [< OF < L *rata* (*pars*) calculated (part), fem. of *ratus*, pp. of *reri* to calculate]

rate² (rāt) *v.t. & v.i.* **rat·ed, rat·ing** To reprove with vehemence; rail at; scold. [? < OF *areter* to accuse < L *reputare* to impute. Cf. Sw. *rata* to find fault.]

ra·tel (rā′təl, rä′-) *n.* A nocturnal carnivore (genus *Mellivora*) of Africa and India, related to the badger. [< Afrikaans *rateldas* < Du. *raat* honeycomb + *das* badger]

rate of exchange The value of one currency as stated in terms of another; also, the ratio or percentage of one currency value in relation to the value of another.

rate·pay·er (rāt′pā′ər) *n. Brit. & Canadian* One who pays local property taxes or rates.

rat·er¹ (rā′tər) *n.* One who or that which rates or estimates.

rat·er² (rā′tər) *n.* One who scolds or berates.

Rat·haus (rät′hous′) *n. German* A government or municipal building; a town hall.

rathe (rāth) *adj. Obs.* **1.** Occurring, arriving, etc., in the early part of a year, season, etc. **2.** Swift; quick; soon. Also **rath** (rath). [OE *hrathe* quickly, *hræth* quick]

Ra·the·nau (rä′tə·nou), **Walther,** 1867–1922, German statesman and industrialist; assassinated.

rath·er (rath′ər, rä′thər) *adv.* **1.** With preference for one of two things or courses; more willingly. **2.** With more reason, justice, wisdom, etc. **3.** More precisely, strictly, or accurately. **4.** Somewhat; in a greater or less degree; to a certain extent: *rather* cold. **5.** On the contrary. **6.** *Brit.* Yes indeed! **7.** *Obs.* Sooner; earlier; more quickly. ◆ Both *had rather* and *would rather* are acceptable forms. [OE *hrathor* sooner, compar. of *hrathe* soon, quickly]

raths·kel·ler (rath′skel·ər, räts′kel·ər) *n.* **1.** In Germany, the cellar of a city hall, often used as a beer hall or restaurant. **2.** Any beer hall or similar restaurant. [< G < *rat* council, town hall + *keller* cellar]

Ra·ti·bor (rä′tē·bôr) A port city in southern Poland, on the Oder; pop. about 30,000: Polish *Racibórz.*

rat·i·fi·ca·tion (rat′ə·fə·kā′shən) *n.* The act of ratifying, or the state of being ratified.

rat·i·fy (rat′ə·fī) *v.t.* **·fied, ·fy·ing** To give sanction to, especially official or authoritative sanction; make valid by approving; confirm. [< OF *ratifier* < Med.L *ratificare* < L *ratus* fixed, calculated + *facere* to make] **— rat′i·fi′er** *n.* **— Syn.** *Ratify, confirm, validate, sanction,* and *endorse* mean to make legal or effective by approving. The U.S. Senate *ratifies* a proposed treaty; Congress *confirms* Presidential appointments; notarization *validates* a bill of sale. These words are chiefly used of governmental process. *Sanction* and *endorse* are mostly used in more general senses: Public opinion *sanctioned* a more liberal view about divorce; Local officials have *endorsed* changes intended to modernize the building code. **— Ant.** disapprove, reject, rescind. Compare ANNUL.

rat·i·né (rat·ə·nā′) *n.* A heavy, loosely woven fabric with a nubby surface. [< F, pp. of *ratiner* to frieze, make nubby]

rat·ing¹ (rā′ting) *n.* **1.** Classification according to a standard; grade; rank; status. **2.** The classification of a vessel. **3.** An evaluation of the financial standing of a business firm or an individual. **4.** The designation of the operating capacity of a piece of machinery, as expressed in horsepower, kilowatts, etc. **5.** Any specialist grade held by an enlisted man or officer: the *rating* of pilot in the Air Force. **6.** *Brit.* An enlisted man in the Royal Navy.

rat·ing² (rā′ting) *n.* A harsh rebuke; scolding. [< RATE²]

ra·tio (rā′shō, -shē·ō) *n. pl.* **·tios 1.** Relation of degree, number, etc.; proportion; rate. **2.** The relation of two quantities, especially the quotient of the first divided by the second. A ratio of 3 to 5 is expressed as 3 : 5 or ⅗. Abbr. *R* **3.** Formerly, the relation expressed by subtracting one quantity from the other. **4.** *Obs.* A portion; ration. [< L, account < *ratus*, pp. of *reri* to think. Doublet of RATION, REASON.]

ra·ti·oc·i·nate (rash′ē·os′ə·nāt) *v.i.* **·nat·ed, ·nat·ing** To make a deduction from premises; reason. [< L *ratiocinatus*, pp. of *ratiocinari* to calculate, deliberate < *ratio* counting. See REASON.] **— ra′ti·oc′i·na′tor** *n.*

ra·ti·oc·i·na·tion (rash′ē·os′ə·nā′shən) *n.* The deduction of conclusions from premises; reasoning.

---

ra·ti·oc·i·na·tive (rash/ē·os/ə·nā/tiv) *adj.* **1.** Of or pertaining to the act or process of reasoning. **2.** Given to or characterized by ratiocination.

ra·tion (rash/ən, rā/shən) *n.* **1.** A portion; share. **2.** A fixed allowance or portion of food, etc., allotted in time of scarcity. **3.** *Mil.* Food for one person for one day. — *v.t.* **1.** To provide with rations; issue rations to, as an army. **2.** To give out or allot in rations. **3.** To restrict to limited rations. — **Syn.** See APPORTION. [< F < L *ratio, -onis.* Doublet of RATIO, REASON.] — **ra/tion·ing** *n.*

ra·tion·al (rash/ən·əl) *adj.* **1.** Possessing the faculty of reasoning. **2.** Having full possession of one's mental faculties; sane. **3.** Conformable to reason; judicious; sensible. **4.** Pertaining to reason; attained by reasoning. **5.** Pertaining to rationalism. **6.** *Math.* **a** Pertaining to a rational number. **b** Denoting an algebraic expression containing no variables within irreducible radicals. **7.** In Greek and Latin prosody, denoting the measurement of metrical units; capable of being measured in metrical units. [< L *rationalis* < *ratio, -onis.* See RATIO.] — **ra/tion·al·ly** *adv.* — **ra/tion·al·ness** *n.*
— **Syn.** (adj.) **1, 2, 3, 4.** *Rational* and *reasonable* refer to the power of reasoning. We call man a *rational* being because he possesses this power. When we call a particular man *rational,* we may mean that he is not insane, or that he is being guided by his intellect rather than by his emotions. A *rational* proposition is one that is derived logically from facts, data, or circumstances. *Rational* indicates only that human reason is at work; *reasonable* goes further and says that it is working well. A *reasonable* man bases his views or actions on good reasons; a reasonable proposition is not only logical, but also displays good judgment, sagacity, practicality, etc. — **Ant.** irrational, insane; unreasonable, absurd.

ra·tion·ale (rash/ən·al/, -ä/lē, -ā/lē) *n.* **1.** The rational or logical basis of something. **2.** A rational exposition of principles. [< L, neut. of *rationalis.* See RATIONAL.]

ra·tion·al·ism (rash/ən·əl·iz/əm) *n.* **1.** The formation of opinions by relying upon reason alone, independently of authority or of revelation. **2.** *Philos.* **a** The theory of a priori ideas, that truth and knowledge are attainable through reason rather than by empirical means. **b** The theory that reason itself is a source of knowledge independent of sense perception. — **ra/tion·al·ist** *n.* — **ra/tion·al·is/tic** or **·ti·cal** *adj.* — **ra/tion·al·is/ti·cal·ly** *adv.*

ra·tion·al·i·ty (rash/ən·al/ə·tē) *n. pl.* **·ties 1.** The quality or condition of being rational; reasonableness. **2.** The cause or reason; rationale. **3.** Something rational, as an act, belief, practice, etc.

ra·tion·al·i·za·tion (rash/ən·əl·ə·zā/shən, -ī·zā/shən) *n.* The act or process of rationalizing; also, an instance of it.

ra·tion·al·ize (rash/ən·əl·īz/) *v.* **·ized, ·iz·ing** *v.t.* **1.** *Psychol.* To explain or base (one's behavior) on grounds ostensibly rational but not in accord with the actual or unconscious motives. **2.** To explain or treat from a rationalistic point of view. **3.** To make rational or reasonable. **4.** *Chiefly Brit.* To reorganize (an industry, etc.) in accordance with up-to-date methods and practices. **5.** *Math.* To remove the radicals containing variables from (an expression or equation); also, to alter the radicals so as to change (the expression) into more workable form. — *v.i.* **6.** To think in a rational or rationalistic manner. Also *Brit.* **ra/tion·al·ise/.** — **ra/tion·al·iz/er** *n.*

rational number *Math.* A number that can be expressed as an integer or as a quotient of integers.

Rat·is·bon (rat/is·bon, -iz-) See REGENSBURG.

rat·ite (rat/īt) *adj.* Designating a group of flightless birds including ostriches, cassowaries, kiwis, emus, etc., having undeveloped wings and a breastbone without a keel. — *n.* A ratite bird. [< L *ratis* raft + -ITE[1]]

rat·line (rat/lin) *n. Naut.* **1.** One of the small ropes fastened across the shrouds of a ship, used as a ladder for going aloft or descending. For illustration see SHROUD[2]. **2.** The rope so used. Also **rat/lin** (-lin). [Origin unknown]

RA·TO (rā/tō) *n.* An airplane takeoff assisted by an auxiliary rocket motor or unit; also, the rocket motor or unit used. Also **ra/to.** [< *r(ocket)* + *a(ssisted)* + *t(ake)o(ff)*]

ra·toon (ra·tōōn/) *n.* A new shoot from the root of a cropped plant, as a sugar cane. — *v.i.* To sprout from a root planted the previous year. Also spelled **rattoon.** [< Sp. *retono;* ult. origin uncertain]

rat race *Slang* A frantic, usually fruitless, struggle; a wearisome hustle.

rats·bane (rats/bān/) *n.* Rat poison; especially, arsenous oxide, As_2O_3.

rat's nest *Informal* A cluttered and messy place or situation.

rat·tail (rat/tāl/) *adj.* Resembling a rat's tail in form. Also **rat/-tailed/** (-tāld/).

rat·tan (ra·tan/) *n.* **1.** The long, tough, flexible stem of various tropical palms (genera *Calamus* and *Daemonorops*), used in making wickerwork, light furniture, etc. **2.** The palm itself. **3.** A cane or switch of rattan. Also spelled **ratan.** [< Malay *rotan*]

rat·teen (ra·tēn/) *n. Obs.* A thick woolen twilled cloth. [< F *ratine*]

rat·ten (rat/n) *v.t. Brit.* To persecute or harass (an employer or employee). [Origin uncertain] — **rat/ten·er** *n.*

rat·ter (rat/ər) *n.* **1.** A dog or cat that catches rats. **2.** *Slang* A deserter; traitor.

rat·tish (rat/ish) *adj.* Characteristic of or resembling a rat.

rat·tle[1] (rat/l) *v.* **·tled, ·tling** *v.i.* **1.** To make a series of sharp noises in rapid succession, as of hard objects striking one another. **2.** To move or act with such noises; also, to make a gurgling sound in the throat. **3.** To talk rapidly and foolishly; chatter. — *v.t.* **4.** To cause to rattle: to *rattle* pennies in a tin cup. **5.** To utter or perform rapidly or noisily. **6.** *Informal* To confuse; disconcert; agitate. — **Syn.** See EMBARRASS. — *n.* **1.** A series of short, sharp sounds in rapid succession, as from the collision of small, hard objects. **2.** A plaything, implement, etc., made to produce a rattling noise. **3.** Any of the jointed horny rings in the tail of a rattlesnake; also, the noise produced by their vibration. **4.** Rapid and noisy talk; chatter. **5.** One who talks fast and foolishly. **6.** The death rattle (which see). [Imit. Akin to MHG *razzeln.*]

rat·tle[2] (rat/l) *v.t.* **·tled, ·tling** *Naut.* To fit with ratlines: used chiefly in the phrase **to rattle down the rigging.** [< RATLINE]

rat·tle·box (rat/l·boks/) *n.* **1.** Any of several leguminous plants (genus *Crotalaria*) having seeds that rattle loosely in inflated pods. **2.** The bladder campion.

rat·tle·brain (rat/l·brān/) *n.* A talkative, flighty person; foolish chatterer. Also **rat/tle·head/** (-hed/), **rat/tle·pate/** (-pāt/). — **rat/tle·brained/** *adj.*

rat·tler (rat/lər) *n.* **1.** One who or that which rattles. **2.** A rattlesnake.

rat·tle·snake (rat/l·snāk/) *n.* Any of several venomous American snakes (genera *Crotalus* and *Sistrurus*) with a tail ending in a series of horny, loosely connected, modified joints, that make a rattling noise when the tail is vibrated.

RATTLESNAKE
(To 8 feet long)

rattlesnake plantain Any of several small orchids (genus *Goodyera*) having leaves mottled or striped with white and dark green.

rattlesnake root 1. Any of several erect perennial herbs (genus *Prenanthes*) of the composite family, with thick, tuberous, bitter roots. **2.** The root or tuber of these plants. **3.** Any of various plants having roots considered a cure for rattlesnake bite, as the Seneca snakeroot (which see).

rattlesnake weed 1. A species of hawkweed (*Hieracium venosum*) of the northern United States. **2.** Button snakeroot (def. 2).

rat·tle·trap (rat/l·trap/) *n.* **1.** Any clattering or worn-out vehicle or article. **2.** *Slang* A loquacious person.

rat·tling (rat/ling) *adj.* **1.** Making a clatter. **2.** *Informal* Brisk; sprightly; lively. **3.** Extraordinary; good. — *adv. Informal* Extraordinarily; very: a *rattling* good time.

rat·tly (rat/lē) *adj.* **1.** Inclined to rattle. **2.** Clattering.

rat·ton (rat/n) *n. Scot. & Brit. Dial.* A rat.

rat·toon (ra·tōōn/) See RATOON.

rat·trap (rat/trap/) *n.* **1.** A trap for catching rats. **2.** Any hopeless or involved predicament.

rat·ty (rat/ē) *adj.* **·ti·er, ·ti·est 1.** Ratlike. **2.** Abounding in rats. **3.** *Slang* Disreputable; shabby.

rau·cous (rô/kəs) *adj.* **1.** Rough in sound; hoarse; harsh. **2.** Boisterous; unruly; disorderly. [< L *raucus*] — **rau/ci·ty** (-sə·tē), **rau/cous·ness** *n.* — **rau/cous·ly** *adv.*

raun·chy (rôn/chē, rän/-) *adj.* **·chi·er, ·chi·est** *U.S. Slang* **1.** Risqué or obscene. **2.** Lustful; lecherous. **3.** Having a poor quality or low standard. [Origin unknown]

rau·wol·fi·a (rou·wōōl/fē·ə) *n.* **1.** Any of a genus (*Rauwolfia*) of tropical trees or shrubs of the dogbane family, several of which contain alkaloids having valuable medicinal properties. **2.** The powdered root of *R. serpentina,* a species of rauwolfia of India from which reserpine was first prepared. Also called *snakeroot.* [after Leonard *Rauwolf,* 17th c. German botanist]

rav·age (rav/ij) *v.* **·aged, ·ag·ing** *v.t.* **1.** To lay waste, as by pillaging or burning; despoil. — *v.i.* **2.** To wreak havoc; be destructive. — *n.* Violent and destructive action, or its result; ruin. [< MF < *ravir.* See RAVISH.] — **rav/ag·er** *n.*

rave[1] (rāv) *v.* **raved, rav·ing** *v.i.* **1.** To speak wildly or incoherently. **2.** To speak with extravagant enthusiasm. **3.** To make a wild, roaring sound; rage. — *v.t.* **4.** To utter wildly or incoherently. — *n.* The act or state of raving; a frenzy. — *adj. Informal* Extravagantly enthusiastic: *rave* reviews. [< OF *raver* to wander, to be delirious]

rave[2] (rāv) *n.* A vertical sidepiece in a wagon body or sleigh. [Var. of ME *rathe;* origin unknown]

rav·el (rav/əl) *v.* **rav·eled** or **·elled, rav·el·ing** or **·el·ling** *v.t.* **1.** To separate the threads or fibers of; unravel. **2.** To make clear or plain; explain: often with *out.* **3.** *Archaic* To tangle; confuse. — *v.i.* **4.** To become separated, as threads or fibers; unravel; fray. **5.** *Archaic* To become tangled or confused. — *n.* **1.** A broken or rejected thread. **2.** A raveling. [< MDu. *ravelen* to tangle] — **rav/el·er** or **rav/el·ler** *n.*

Ra·vel (rȧ·vel/), **Maurice Joseph,** 1875-1937, French composer.

rave·lin (rav′lin) *n. Mil.* An outwork with two faces forming a salient angle at the front. [< F < Ital. *ravellino*]

rav·el·ing (rav′əl·ing) *n.* 1. A thread or threads raveled from a fabric. 2. The act of one who or that which ravels. Also **rav′el·ling**.

rav·el·ment (rav′əl·mənt) *n.* A ravel; tangle; confusion.

ra·ven[1] (rā′vən) *n.* A large, omnivorous, widely distributed corvine bird (*Corvus corax*), having lustrous black plumage with the feathers of the throat elongated. — *adj.* Black and shining, like the plumage of a raven. [OE *hræfn.* Akin to OHG *hraban*, ON *hrafn.*]

rav·en[2] (rav′ən) *v.t.* 1. To devour hungrily or greedily. 2. To take by force; ravage. — *v.i.* 3. To search for or take prey or plunder. 4. To eat voraciously; be ravenous. — *n.* The act of plundering; spoliation; pillage. Also spelled *ravin.* [< OF *raviner* < *ravine* rapine < L *rapina* < *rapere* to seize. Doublet of RAPINE.] — **rav′en·er** *n.*

Ra·ven (rā′vən) *n.* The constellation Corvus.

rav·en·ing (rav′ən·ing) *adj.* 1. Seeking eagerly for prey; rapacious. 2. Devouring; voracious. 3. Mad; rabid. — *n.* 1. Propensity for prey or booty; rapacity. 2. The prey seized. [ppr. of RAVEN[2]] — **rav′en·ing·ly** *adv.*

Ra·ven·na (rä·ven′nä) A commune in north central Italy; capital of the Western Roman Empire 402–476; pop. 128,900 (est. 1967).

rav·en·ous (rav′ən·əs) *adj.* 1. Violently voracious or hungry. 2. Extremely eager for gratification. [< OF *ravinos* < *ravine.* See RAVEN[2].] — **rav′en·ous·ly** *adv.* — **rav′en·ous·ness** *n.*

Ra·vi (rä′vē) A river in NW India and West Pakistan, flowing about 475 miles, generally SW, to the Chenab river: ancient *Hydraotes.*

rav·in (rav′ən) See RAVEN[2].

ra·vine (rə·vēn′) *n.* A long, narrow, and deep cleft or valley between heights, especially one worn by a flow of water. [< F. Doublet of RAVEN[2], RAPINE.]

rav·ing (rā′ving) *adj.* 1. Furious; delirious; frenzied. 2. *Informal* Outstandingly attractive: a *raving* beauty. — *n.* Furious, incoherent, or irrational utterance.

ra·vi·o·li (rä·vyō′lē, rä′vē·ō′lē, rav′ē-) *n.pl.* Little envelopes of dough for encasing seasoned meat or cheese, boiled, and often served in a tomato sauce. [< Ital. pl. of *raviolo* little turnip < L *rapa*]

rav·ish (rav′ish) *v.t.* 1. To fill with strong emotion, especially delight; enrapture. 2. To commit a rape upon. 3. *Obs.* To carry off (a woman) by force. 4. *Archaic* To seize and carry off by violence. [< OF *raviss-*, stem of *ravir* to carry off < L *rapere* to seize. Akin to RAPE, RAPTURE.] — **rav′ish·er** *n.*

rav·ish·ing (rav′ish·ing) *adj.* Filling with delight; enchanting. — **rav′ish·ing·ly** *adv.*

rav·ish·ment (rav′ish·mənt) *n.* 1. The act of ravishing, or the state of being ravished. 2. Ecstasy; delight.

raw (rô) *adj.* 1. Not changed or prepared by cooking; uncooked. 2. Having the skin irritated or abraded. 3. Bleak; chilling: a *raw* wind. 4. In a natural state; crude; unrefined or untreated. 5. Unblended or untempered, as colors. 6. Newly done; fresh: *raw* paint, *raw* work. 7. Inexperienced; undisciplined: a *raw* recruit. 8. Obscene; coarse; off-color: a *raw* joke. 9. Harshly unfair; ruthless; cruel. — *n.* A sore or abraded spot: with *the.* — **in the raw** 1. In a raw, unrefined, or untempered state: nature *in the raw.* 2. *U.S. Informal* Naked; nude. [OE *hrēaw.*] — **raw′ly** *adv.* — **raw′ness** *n.*

Ra·wal·pin·di (rä′wəl·pin′dē, rôl·pin′dē) A city in northern Pakistan; former capital; pop. 432,100 (1968).

raw·boned (rô′bōnd′) *adj.* Having prominent bones and little flesh; bony; gaunt.

raw deal *Slang* Harsh or unfair treatment.

raw·hide (rô′hīd′) *n.* 1. A hide dressed without tanning. 2. A whip made of such hide.

raw·ish (rô′ish) *adj.* Somewhat raw.

Raw·lin·son (rô′lin·sən), **George,** 1812–1902, English Orientalist and historian. — **Sir Henry Creswicke,** 1810–1895, English Assyriologist and diplomat; brother of the preceding.

raw material Unprocessed material used in manufacturing, as contrasted with finished products.

raw silk 1. Silk fibers as unwound from the silkworm cocoon, still coated with a gummy substance. 2. A fabric woven from such fibers.

rax (raks) *v.t. & v.i. Scot.* To stretch out; reach. [OE *raxan*]

ray[1] (rā) *n.* 1. A narrow beam of light. 2. Anything representing or suggesting this. 3. A slight manifestation; glimmer; hint. 4. *Geom.* One of several straight lines emerging from a point and unlimited in one direction. 5. A streak or line; a straight row. 6. *Zool.* **a** One of the rods supporting the membrane of a fish's fin. **b** One of the radiating parts of a radiate animal, as a starfish. 7. *Bot.* **a** A ray flower (which see). **b** One of the pedicels or flower

stalks of an umbel. 8. *Physics* **a** A line of propagation of any form of radiant energy. **b** A stream of particles spontaneously emitted by a radioactive substance. — *v.i.* 1. To emit rays; shine. 2. To issue forth as rays; radiate. — *v.t.* 3. To send forth as rays. 4. To mark with rays or radiating lines. 5. To irradiate. 6. To treat with or expose to X-rays, etc. [< OF *rai* < L *radius.* Doublet of RADIUS.]

ray[2] (rā) *n.* Any of various elasmobranch fishes (order *Selachii*) having a cartilaginous skeleton, a flattened body with expanded pectoral fins, and gill openings on the lower surface. [< OF *raie* < L *raia*]

Ray (rā), **Cape** A promontory at the SW extremity of Newfoundland.

ra·yah (rä′yə, rī′ə) *n.* A non-Moslem inhabitant of Turkey: sometimes spelled *raia.* Also **ra′ya.** [Turkish < Arabic *ra′iyah* flock, herd]

Ray·burn (rā′bûrn), **Sam**(**uel Taliaferro**), 1882–1961, U.S. legislator; Speaker of the House of Representatives 1940–61: called **Mr. Sam.**

ray flower *Bot.* Any of the flat marginal flowers surrounding the disk in various flowers of the composite family, as the daisy or sunflower. Also **ray floret.**

ray·grass (rā′gras′, -gräs′) *n.* Rye grass (which see).

Ray·leigh (rā′lē), **Lord,** 1842–1919, John William Strutt, English physicist.

ray·less (rā′lis) *adj.* 1. Having no light rays. 2. Extremely dark. 3. Having no rays, as the flowers of certain composite plants. — **ray′less·ly** *adv.* — **ray′less·ness** *n.*

ray·on (rā′on) *n.* 1. A synthetic fiber produced from cellulose, the viscous material being forced through fine spinnerets to produce threadlike filaments. 2. A fabric made from such fibers. [Coined from RAY[1]; prob. infl. by F *rayon* ray]

raze (rāz) *v.t.* **razed, raz·ing** 1. To level to the ground; demolish, as a building. 2. *Rare* To scrape or shave off. 3. *Obs.* To wound slightly; graze. Also spelled *rase.* — *Syn.* See DEMOLISH. [< OF *raser* < L *rasum*, pp. of *radere* to scrape]

ra·zee (rā·zē′) *v.t.* **·zeed, ·zee·ing** To make (a ship) lower by removing the upper deck or decks. — *n.* A vessel that has been reduced by cutting away the upper deck or decks. [Var. of RAZE]

ra·zor (rā′zər) *n.* A sharp cutting implement used for shaving off the beard or hair, etc. Compare ELECTRIC SHAVER, SAFETY RAZOR. [< OF *rasor* < LL *rasorium* scraper < *radere* to scrape]

ra·zor·back (rā′zər·bak′) *n.* 1. The rorqual, a whale. 2. A lean, long-legged, half-wild hog, common in the southeastern United States. 3. A hill with a sharp, narrow ridge.

ra·zor-billed auk (rā′zər·bild′) See under AUK.

razor blade A thin, metal blade, having either one or two sharpened edges, inserted in a safety razor or used for cutting or scraping.

razor clam Any of various clams (family *Solenidae*) having a long, narrow, slightly curved shell.

razz (raz) *Slang n.* A Bronx cheer. — *v.t.* To heckle; deride. [< RAZZBERRY]

razz·ber·ry (raz′ber′ē, -bər·ē. räz′-) *n.* *pl.* **·ries** *U.S. Slang* A Bronx cheer. [< RASPBERRY]

raz·zle-daz·zle (raz′əl·daz′əl) *n. U.S. Slang* Bewildering, exciting, or dazzling activity or performance. Also **razz·ma·tazz** (raz′mə·taz′). [Varied reduplication of DAZZLE]

Rb *Chem.* Rubidium.

R.B.A. Royal Society of British Artists.

RBI or **r.b.i.** or **rbi** Run(s) batted in (baseball).

R.C. 1. Red Cross. 2. Reserve Corps. 3. Roman Catholic.

RCAF or **R.C.A.F.** Royal Canadian Air Force.

R.C.Ch. Roman Catholic Church.

rcd. Received.

R.C.M.P. Royal Canadian Mounted Police.

RCN or **R.C.N.** Royal Canadian Navy.

r-col·ored (är′kul·ərd) *adj. Phonetics* Articulated with a retroflexion of the tip of the tongue toward the hard palate: said of certain vowels. — **r′-col′or·ing** *n.*

Rct. *Mil.* Recruit.

rd. 1. Road. 2. Rod(s). 3. Round.

Rd. 1. Rix-dollar. 2. Road.

R.D. Rural Delivery.

re[1] (rā) *n. Music* The second of the syllables used in solmization; the second degree of a major scale; also, the tone D. [< L *re*(*sonare*). See GAMUT.]

re[2] (rē) *prep.* Concerning; about; in the matter of: used in business letters, law, etc. [< L, ablative of *res* thing]

r.e. or **re** Right end.

re- *prefix* 1. Back: *rebound, remit.* 2. Again; anew; again and again. [< L *re-*, *red-* back, again]

◆ Sense 2 of *re-* is freely used in forming words, particularly verbs or words derived from verbs. Some words thus formed are hyphenated to prevent confusion with similarly spelled words, as *recoil*, to spring back, and *re-coil*, to coil again, but in current usage most other words using *re-* as a prefix are written solid. However, many writers still prefer to hyphenate some combinations of *re-* and a word beginning with a vowel, especially *e.*

A list of self-explanatory words containing the prefix *re-* (def. 2) appears below.

Re (rā) See RA.

Re *Chem.* Rhenium.

Re. or **re.** Rupee.

R.E. **1.** Real estate. **2.** Reformed Episcopal. **3.** Right Excellent. **4.** Royal Engineers.

REA Rural Electrification Administration.

reach (rēch) *v.t.* **1.** To stretch out or forth, as the hand; extend. **2.** To present by means of or as by means of the outstretched hand; hand over. **3.** To extend as far as; be able to touch or grasp, as with the hand: Can you *reach* the top shelf? **4.** To arrive at or come to by motion or progress. **5.** To achieve communication with; gain access to. **6.** To amount to; total. **7.** To strike or hit, as with a blow or missile. — *v.i.* **8.** To stretch the hand, foot, etc., out or forth. **9.** To make a motion of attempting to touch or grasp something: He *reached* for his wallet. **10.** To have extent in space, time, etc.: The ladder *reached* to the ceiling. **11.** *Naut.* To sail on a tack with the wind on or forward of the beam. — *n.* **1.** The act or power of reaching. **2.** The distance one is able to reach, as with the hand, an instrument, or missile. **3.** Extent of thought, influence, etc.; scope; range. **4.** An unbroken stretch, as of a stream; a vista or expanse. **5.** A pole or bar connecting the rear axle, truck, or runners of a vehicle with some part at the forward end. **6.** *Naut.* The sailing, or the distance sailed, by a vessel on one tack. [OE *ræcan.* Cf. G *reichen* to reach.] — **reach′er** *n.*

reach·less (rēch′lis) *adj.* Unreachable; unattainable.

reach-me-down (rēch′mē-doun′) *Brit. Informal adj.* Passed on to another person, as a garment; secondhand. — *n. Usually pl.* Secondhand clothing; hand-me-down.

re·act (rē-akt′) *v.i.* **1.** To act in response, as to a stimulus. **2.** To act in a manner contrary to some preceding act; come into or tend toward a former or opposite state. **3.** *Physics* To exert an opposite and equal force on an acting or impinging body. **4.** *Chem.* To enter into or undergo a reacton.

re-act (rē-akt′) *v.t.* To act again.

re·ac·tance (rē-ak′tans) *n. Electr.* In a circuit, the opposition to an alternating current caused by inductance and capacitance, equal to the difference between capacitive and inductive reactance (which see).

re·ac·tion (rē-ak′shən) *n.* **1.** Responsive action, attitude, etc. **2.** Tendency toward a former or reversed state of things; especially, a trend toward an earlier social, political, or economic policy or condition. **3.** The action of a muscle, nerve, organ, etc., in response to a stimulus; reflex action. **4.** *Psychol.* A response to an experience, situation, influence, etc. **5.** *Physics* **a** The equal and opposite force exerted on an agent by the body acted upon. **b** A nuclear reaction (which see). **6.** *Chem.* The reciprocal action of substances subjected to chemical change, or some distinctive result of such action. **7.** *Med.* The effect upon an organism or any of its parts of any foreign substance introduced for therapeutic purposes, or for testing, immunizing, etc.

re·ac·tion·ar·y (rē-ak′shən-er′ē) *adj.* Pertaining to, favoring, or characterized by reaction (def. 2). — *n. pl.* **·ar·ies** One who favors political or social reaction; one hostile toward change or progress. Also **re·ac′tion·ist.**

reaction engine An engine using the reactive thrust of a stream of matter forcibly expelled, as in jet propulsion.

reaction formation *Psychoanal.* The development of character traits, attitudes, and forms of behavior in direct opposition to unconscious trends.

reaction time *Physiol.* The time required for a response

to a sensory stimulus, especially one applied for experimental or testing purposes.

re·ac·ti·vate (rē-ak′tə-vāt) *v.t.* **·vat·ed, ·vat·ing** To make active or effective again. — **re·ac′ti·va′tion** *n.*

re·ac·tive (rē-ak′tiv) *adj.* **1.** Reacting or tending to react. **2.** Resulting from reaction. **3.** Responsive to a stimulus.

re·ac·tiv·i·ty (rē′ak-tiv′ə-tē) *n.* **1.** The state or quality of being reactive. **2.** *Chem.* The relative tendency of an element to enter into chemical reactions.

re·ac·tor (rē-ak′tər) *n.* **1.** One who or that which reacts. **2.** *Electr.* A device for introducing reactance into a circuit, as for starting motors, controlling current, etc. **3.** *Biol.* An animal or person giving a positive reaction to a specified bacteriological or medical test. **4.** *Physics* Any of various assemblies for the generation and control of atomic energy, consisting essentially of fissionable material used as fuel, moderators, reflectors, and auxiliary equipment: formerly called *pile.*

read (*v. & n.* rēd; *adj.* red) *v.* **read** (red), **read·ing** (rē′ding) *v.t.* **1.** To apprehend the meaning of (a book, writing, etc.) by perceiving the form and relation of the printed or written characters. **2.** To utter aloud (something printed or written); to speak the words represented by the written forms of (a letter, book, etc.). **3.** To understand the significance, intent, etc., of as if by reading: to *read* the sky; to *read* someone's mind. **4.** To apprehend the meaning of something printed or written in (a foreign language). **5.** To make a study of; also, to obtain knowledge of: to *read* law. **6.** To discover the true nature of (a person, character, etc.) by observation or scrutiny. **7.** To interpret (something read) in a specified manner. **8.** To take as the meaning of something read. **9.** To have as its wording: The passage *reads* "principal," not "principle." **10.** To indicate or register, as an instrument or device: The meter *reads* zero. **11.** To bring into a specified condition by reading: I *read* her to sleep. — *v.i.* **12.** To apprehend written or printed characters, as of words, music, etc. **13.** To utter aloud the words or contents of a book, etc.; to speak the words represented by written forms. **14.** To gain information by reading: with *of* or *about.* **15.** To learn by means of books; study. **16.** To have a specified wording: How does the contract *read*? **17.** To admit of being read in a specified manner: The first verse *reads* well. **18.** To have the quality of a specified style or manner of writing: His work *reads* like poetry. **19.** To give a public reading or recital. — **to read between the lines** To perceive or infer what is not expressed or obvious, as a hidden or true meaning, implication, or motive. — **to read into** To discern (implicit meanings or implications) in a statement or position: Don't *read* anything *into* my decision not to run for office. — **to read up** (or **up on**) To learn by reading. — *adj.* Informed by books or reading; acquainted with books or literature: well *read.* — *n. Informal* A reading; a period spent in reading. [OE *rædan* to advise, read]

Read (red), **Sir Herbert (Edward)**, 1893–1968, English writer and art critic.

read·a·ble (rē′də-bəl) *adj.* **1.** Legible. **2.** Interesting or enjoyable to read. — **read′a·bil′i·ty, read′a·ble·ness** *n.* — **read′a·bly** *adv.*

Reade (rēd), **Charles**, 1814–84, English novelist.

read·er (rē′dər) *n.* **1.** One who reads. **2.** A professional reciter or elocutionist. **3.** One who reads and criticizes manuscripts offered to publishers. **4.** A proofreader (which see). **5.** A textbook containing matter for exercises in reading. **6.** *Eccl.* A layman or minor church functionary authorized to read the lessons in church services. **7.** *Brit.* A university or college lecturer.

read·er·ship (rē′dər·ship) *n.* **1.** The readers, collectively,

reabandon	reascend	rebury	reconsecrate	redivide	reenjoyment
reabsorb	reascension	recarry	reconsolidate	redivision	reenkindle
reabsorption	reascent	recelebrate	reconvene	redo	reenlist
reaccept	reassemble	rechallenge	recopy	redraw	reenlistment
reaccommodate	reassembly	rechange	recoronation	redrive	reenslave
reaccompany	reassert	recharge	recross	redry	reerect
reaccuse	reassertion	recharter	recrown	redye	reestablish
reacquire	reassign	recheck	recrystallization	reecho	reestablishment
readapt	reassimilate	rechoose	recrystallize	reedit	reexchange
readdress	reassimilation	rechristen	recultivate	reelect	reexhibit
readjourn	reassociate	recircle	recultivation	reelection	reexpel
readjournment	reassume	recirculate	rededicate	reelevate	reexperience
readopt	reassumption	reclasp	rededication	reembark	reexpulsion
readorn	reattach	reclean	redefeat	reembody	reface
readvance	reattack	reclothe	redefine	reembrace	refashion
realign	reattain	recoin	redemonstrate	reemerge	refasten
realignment	reattempt	recoinage	redeny	reemergence	refertilize
reannex	reavow	recolonize	redeposit	reemigrate	refire
reanoint	reawake	recolor	redescend	reenact	reflow
reappear	reawaken	recombine	redescent	reenaction	reflower
reappearance	rebaptism	recombination	redescribe	reenactment	refold
reapply	rebaptize	recommence	redetermine	reencourage	reforge
reappoint	rebind	recommission	redigest	reencouragement	reformulate
reappointment	rebloom	recondense	rediscover	reendow	refortification
reapportion	reblossom	reconduct	rediscovery	reengage	refortify
reapportionment	reboil	reconfirm	redissolve	reengagement	reframe
reargue	rebuild	reconquer	redistill	reengrave	refreeze
reargument	rebuilt	reconquest	redistribute	reenjoy	refurnish

of a publication or type of publication. **2.** The office or condition of a reader.

read·i·ly (red′ə·lē) *adv.* **1.** In a ready manner; promptly; easily. **2.** Willingly; without reluctance.

read·i·ness (red′ē·nis) *n.* **1.** The quality or state of being ready. **2.** The quality of being quick or prompt; facility; aptitude. **3.** A disposition for prompt compliance; willingness. — **Syn.** See EASE.

read·ing (rē′ding) *n.* **1.** The act or practice of one who reads. **2.** A public or formal recital of something written, as a will, piece of proposed legislation, etc. **3.** Literary research; study; scholarship. **4.** Matter that is read or is designed to be read. **5.** The indication of a meter, dial, graduated instrument, etc. **6.** The form in which any passage or word appears in any copy of a work. **7.** An interpretation, as of something with an obscure or hidden meaning; rendering. — *adj.* **1.** Pertaining to or suitable for reading. **2.** Of or pertaining to a reader or readers.

Read·ing (red′ing) **1.** The county seat of Berkshire, England, a county borough in the central part of the county; pop. 127,530 (est. 1969). **2.** A city in SE Pennsylvania, on the Schuylkill River; pop. 87,643.

Read·ing (red′ing), **Marquis of,** 1860–1935, Rufus Daniel Isaacs, British statesman and jurist.

reading desk A desk adapted to hold books, manuscripts, etc., for a speaker or reader, as in church services; a lectern.

reading room A room provided with periodicals, books, etc., as in a library or club, and set aside for readers.

re·ad·just (rē′ə·just′) *v.t. & v.i.* To adjust again or anew; rearrange. — **re′ad·just′er** *n.*

re·ad·just·ment (rē′ə·just′mənt) *n.* **1.** The act or process of readjusting, or the state of being readjusted. **2.** The reorganization of a company or corporation, usually voluntary.

re·ad·mit (rē′əd·mit′) *v.t.* **-mit·ted, -mit·ting** To admit again. — **re′ad·mis′sion** (-əd·mish′ən), **re′ad·mit′tance** *n.*

read·y (red′ē) *adj.* **read·i·er, read·i·est** **1.** Prepared for use or action. **2.** Prepared in mind; willing. **3.** Likely or liable: with *to*: *ready* to sink. **4.** Quick to act, follow, occur, or appear; prompt. **5.** Immediately available or at hand; convenient; handy. **6.** Designating the standard position in which a rifle is held just before aiming. **7.** Quick to perceive or understand; alert; facile: a *ready* wit. **8.** *Obs.* Here; present: used in answering a roll call. — *n.* **1.** The state of being ready. **2.** The position in which a rifle is held before aiming. **3.** *Informal* Cash: with *the*. — *v.t.* **read·ied, read·y·ing** To make ready; prepare. [ME < OE *ræde, geræde + ig,* suffix of adverbs]

read·y-made (red′ē·mād′) *adj.* **1.** Not made to order; prepared or kept on hand for general demand: said especially of clothing. **2.** Prepared beforehand; not impromptu. **3.** Lacking in originality; borrowed; trite.

read·y-mix (red′ē·miks) *adj. U.S.* Ready to use after adding and mixing some liquid: *ready-mix* pancake flour.

ready money Money on hand; cash.

read·y-to-wear (red′ē·tə·wâr′) *adj.* Ready-made: said of clothing.

read·y-wit·ted (red′ē·wit′id) *adj.* Quick to apprehend or learn; alert.

re·af·firm (rē′ə·fûrm′) *v.t.* To affirm again, as for emphasis. — **re′af·firm′ance, re·af·fir·ma·tion** (rē′af·ər·mā′shən) *n.*

re·a·gent (rē·ā′jənt) *n. Chem.* Any substance used to ascertain the nature or composition of another by means of their reciprocal chemical action. [< RE- + AGENT]

real¹ (rēl, rē′əl) *adj.* **1.** Having existence or actuality as a thing or state; not imaginary: a *real* event. **2.** Being in accordance with appearance or claim; genuine; not artificial or counterfeit. **3.** Representing the true or actual, as opposed to the apparent or ostensible: the *real* reason. **4.** Unaffected; unpretentious: a *real* person. **5.** *Philos.* Having actual existence, and not merely possible, apparent, or imaginary. **6.** *Law* **a** Pertaining to property regarded as immovable or permanent, as land or tenements: distinguished from *personal.* **b** Pertaining to things, as distinguished from persons. — *adv. Informal* Very; extremely: to be *real* glad. [< OF < LL *realis* < L *res* thing.] — **real′ness** *n.*

re·al² (rē′əl, *Sp.* rä·äl′) *n. pl.* **re·als** or **re·a·les** (rä·ä′läs) *for def. 1,* **reis** (rās) *for def. 2* **1.** A former small silver coin of Spain and various Latin-American countries, also formerly current in the United States, where it was called a *bit.* **2.** A former Portuguese and Brazilian coin, one thousandth of a milreis. [< Sp., lit., royal < L *regalis*]

real estate Land, including whatever is made part of or attached to it by man or nature, as trees, houses, etc. Abbr. *R.E.* — **real-es·tate** (rel′ə·stāt′, rē′əl-) *adj.*

real focus See under FOCUS.

re·al·gar (rē·al′gər) *n.* An orange-red arsenic sulfide, As_2S_2, used in fireworks and formerly as a pigment. [< Med.L, ult. < Arabic *rahj al-ghār* powder of the cave]

real image See under IMAGE.

re·al·ism (rē′əl·iz′əm) *n.* **1.** The tendency to be concerned with and act in accordance with actual facts rather than ideals, feelings, etc. **2.** In literature and art, the treatment of subject matter in conformance with nature or real life and without idealization: opposed to *idealism.* **3.** *Philos.* **a** The doctrine that abstract concepts have objective existence and are more real than concrete objects: opposed to *nominalism.* **b** The doctrine that things have reality apart from the conscious perception of them: opposed to *idealism.*

re·al·ist (rē′əl·ist) *n.* **1.** An adherent of the doctrine of realism in any of its forms, as in literature, art, etc. **2.** One who is devoted to or concerned with what is real or practical rather than what is imaginary, theoretical, or ideal.

re·al·is·tic (rē′əl·is′tik) *adj.* **1.** Pertaining to, dealing with, or emphasizing what is real, factual, or practical, rather than what is theoretical or imaginary. **2.** Showing or characterizing objects, existence, etc., in a lifelike or objective manner, as in art or literature. **3.** Of or pertaining to the philosophic doctrine of realism. — **re·al·is′ti·cal·ly** *adv.*

re·al·i·ty (rē·al′ə·tē) *n. pl.* **·ties** **1.** The fact, state, or quality of being real or genuine. **2.** That which is real; an actual thing, situation, or event. **3.** The sum or totality of real things. **4.** That which exists, as contrasted with what is fictitious or merely conceived of. **5.** *Philos.* The absolute or ultimate, as contrasted with phenomena or the apparent. [< Med.L *realitas, -tatis* < L *realis* real]

reality principle *Psychoanal.* The adjustment of the ego to meet the requirements of the external world. Compare PLEASURE PRINCIPLE.

re·al·i·za·tion (rē′əl·i·zā′shən, -ī·zā′-) *n.* **1.** The act of realizing. **2.** The state of being realized. **3.** A product or instance of realizing. **4.** The conversion into fact or action of plans, ambitions, fears, etc.

regather	reinfection	rekindle	renomination	requicken	restring
regear	reinflame	relabel	renotify	reradiate	restrive
regerminate	reinform	relace	renumber	reread	restudy
regermination	reinfuse	relaunch	reobtain	rerecord	resubject
regild	reinhabit	relaunder	reobtainable	rerise	resummon
reglaze	reinoculate	relearn	reoccupation	reroll	resummons
reglorify	reinoculation	relight	reoccupy	reroute	resupply
reglue	reinscribe	reline	reoccur	resaddle	resurvey
regrade	reinsert	reliquidate	reoccurrence	resail	reteach
regraft	reinsertion	reliquidation	reoppose	resalute	retest
regrant	reinspect	reload	reordain	reseal	retie
regroup	reinspection	reloan	reordination	reseed	retranslate
rehandle	reinspire	relocate	repacify	reseek	retraverse
rehearing	reinstruct	relocation	repack	resegregate	retrim
reheel	reintegrate	remade	repaint	reseize	retype
rehire	reintegration	remake	repaper	reseizure	reuse
reignite	reinter	remanufacture	repave	resettle	reutilize
reimplant	reinterment	remeasure	repenalize	resettlement	reutter
reimpose	reinterrogate	remelt	replant	reshape	revarnish
reimposition	reintrench	remerge	replantation	resharpen	reverification
reimpregnate	reintroduce	remigrate	replay	reshuffle	reverify
reimpress	reintroduction	remigration	repledge	resift	revictual
reimprint	reinundate	remilitarization	replunge	resolder	revictualment
reimprison	reinvent	remilitarize	repolish	resolidify	revindicate
reimprisonment	reinvestigate	remix	repopulate	resow	revindication
reinaugurate	reinvestigation	remodification	repopulation	respread	rewarm
reincite	reinvigorate	remodify	repour	restack	rewash
reincorporate	reinvigoration	remold	reproclaim	restipulate	reweigh
reincur	reinvite	rename	repurchase	restipulation	rewin
reinduce	reinvolve	renavigate	repurify	restrengthen	rewind
reinfect	rejudge	renominate	repursue	restrike	rework

re·al·ize (rē′əl·īz) v. **·ized**, **·iz·ing** v.t. **1.** To understand or appreciate fully. **2.** To make real or concrete. **3.** To cause to appear real. **4.** To obtain as a profit or return. **5.** To obtain money in return for: He *realized* his holdings for a profit. **6.** To bring as a profit or return: said of property. — v.i. **7.** To sell property for cash. Also *Brit.* **re′al·ise**. — **re′al·iz′a·ble** adj. — **re′al·iz′er** n.

re·al·iz·ing (rē′əl·īz′ing) adj. **1.** Conceiving of or able to visualize as real. — **re′al·iz′ing·ly** adv.

re·al-life (rē′əl·līf′, rēl′-) adj. *U.S. Informal* Actual; true, as distinguished from fictional or imaginative.

real·ly (rē′ə·lē, rēl′ē) adv. **1.** In reality; as a matter of fact; actually; indeed. **2.** Honestly; truly: used for emphasis.

re·al·ly (rē′ə·lī′) v.t. & v.i. **·al·lied**, **·al·ly·ing** To ally again. — **re′·al·li′ance** n.

realm (relm) n. **1.** A kingdom or domain. **2.** The scope or range of any power or influence: the *realm* of imagination. **3.** A primary zoogeographical division of the globe: the Nearctic *realm*: also called *region*. [< OF *realme* < LL *regalimen* < L *regalis*. See REGAL.]

real number *Math.* Any rational or irrational number that does not contain an even root of a negative number.

Re·al·po·li·tik (rā′äl·pō′li·tēk′) n. *German* Literally, practical or realistic politics: often used to mean the attainment of political ends by the use or threatened use of force.

real-time (rēl′tīm′, rē′əl-) adj. Designating a computer inquiry or task that can be processed in the length of time taken by the other necessary operations. — **real time** n.

Re·al·tor (rē′əl·tər, -tôr) n. *U.S.* A person engaged in the real estate business, as a broker, appraiser, etc., who is a member of the National Association of Real Estate Boards: a trade name. Also **re′al·tor**. [< REALTY¹ + -OR¹]

re·al·ty¹ (rē′əl·tē) n. pl. **·ties** *U.S. Law* Real estate or real property in any form. [< REAL¹ (def. 6) + -TY¹]

re·al·ty² (rē′əl·tē) n. *Obs.* **1.** Fealty. **2.** Royalty. [< OF *realte*]

real wages Wages evaluated in terms of purchasing power: distinguished from *nominal wages*.

ream¹ (rēm) n. **1.** A unit of quantity for sheets of paper consisting of twenty quires or 480 sheets (**short ream**), 500 sheets (**long ream**), or 516 sheets (**printer's** or **perfect ream**). *Abbr.* **rm.** **2.** pl. *Informal* A prodigious amount of printed, written, or spoken material: *reams* of footnotes. [< OF *reyme* < Sp. *resma* < Arabic *rizmah* bundle]

ream² (rēm) v.t. **1.** To increase the size of (a hole). **2.** To enlarge or taper (a hole) with a rotating cutter or reamer. **3.** To get rid of (a defect) by reaming. [? OE *ryman* to enlarge < *rum* space, room]

ream³ (rēm) n. *Scot. & Brit. Dial.* Cream; froth; foam. — v.t. To skim, as cream. [Cf. G *rahm*]

ream·er (rē′mər) n. **1.** One who or that which reams. **2.** A finishing tool with a rotating cutting edge for reaming: sometimes called *rimmer*. **3.** A device with a ridged cone for extracting juice from citrus fruits.

REAMERS (With cross-sections)
a Fluted. *b* Smooth with cutting tip. *c,d* Broaches or flat-sided.

re·an·i·mate (rē·an′ə·māt) v.t. **·mat·ed**, **·mat·ing** **1.** To bring back to life; resuscitate. **2.** To give renewed strength or vigor to; revive. — **re·an′i·ma′tion** n.

reap (rēp) v.t. **1.** To cut and gather (grain); harvest or gather (a crop) with a scythe, reaper, etc. **2.** To cut the growth from or gather the fruit of, as a field. **3.** To obtain as the result of action or effort; receive as a return or result. — v.i. **4.** To harvest grain, etc. **5.** To receive a return or result. [OE *rēopan*, *ripan*. Akin to RIPE.] — **reap′a·ble** adj.

reap·er (rē′pər) n. **1.** One who reaps. **2.** A reaping machine.

reaping machine (rē′ping) A machine for harvesting standing grain: also called *harvester*.

re·ap·pear (rē·ə·pir′) v.i. To appear again.

rear¹ (rir) n. **1.** The back or hind part. **2.** A place or position at the back of or behind any person or thing. **3.** The portion of a military force that is last or farthest from the front: opposed to *van*. — adj. Being in the rear.

rear² (rir) v.t. **1.** To place upright; raise. **2.** To build; erect. **3.** To care for and bring to maturity. **4.** To breed or grow. — v.i. **5.** To rise upon the hind legs, as a horse. **6.** To rise high; tower, as a mountain. — Syn. See ELEVATE. [OE *rǣran*, causative of *rīsan* to rise] — **rear′er** n.

rear admiral *Naval* A commissioned officer ranking next below a vice admiral. Also *Brit. & Canadian* **rear-ad·mi·ral** (rir′ad′mər·əl). See tables at GRADE. *Abbr.* **R.A., RAdm.**

rear guard A body of troops to protect the rear of an army.

re·arm (rē·ärm′) v.t. & v.i. **1.** To arm again. **2.** To arm with more modern weapons.

rear·ma·ment (rē·ärm′ə·mənt) n. The act or process of rearming, or the state of being rearmed: said of a nation.

rear·most (rir′mōst′) adj. Coming or stationed last.

rear·mouse (rir′mous′) See REREMOUSE.

re·ar·range (rē·ə·rānj′) v.t. & v.i. **·ranged**, **·rang·ing** To arrange again or in some new way. — **re·ar·range′ment** n.

rear sight The sight of a gun that is nearest the breech.

rear·view mirror (rir′vyoo′) In motor vehicles, a mirror so placed that the driver can see to the rear. Also **rear·vi·sion mirror** (rir′vizh′ən).

rear·ward¹ (rir′wərd) adj. Coming last or toward the rear; hindward. — adv. Toward or at the rear; backward: also **rear′wards**. — n. Hindward position; the rear; end.

rear·ward² (rir′wôrd′) n. *Obs.* A rear guard.

rea·son (rē′zən) n. **1.** A motive or cause for an action, belief, thought, etc. **2.** An explanation for or defense of an action, belief, etc.; justification. **3.** The faculty of thinking logically; power of drawing conclusions or making inferences. **4.** Good judgment; common sense. **5.** A normal state of mind; sanity. **6.** *Logic* One of the premises of an argument, especially the minor premise. — **by reason of** Because of. — **in reason** In accordance with reason or good sense. — **it stands to reason** It is logical or reasonable. — **with reason** Justifiably; properly. — v.i. **1.** To think logically; obtain inferences or conclusions from known or presumed facts. **2.** To talk or argue logically. — v.t. **3.** To think out carefully and logically; analyze: with *out*. **4.** To influence by means of reason; persuade or dissuade. **5.** To argue; debate. [< OF *raison* < L *ratio*, *-onis* < *ratus*, pp. of *reri* to think, reckon. Doublet of RATION, RATIO.] — **rea′son·er** n.

— **Syn.** (noun) *Reason, purpose, motive, ground,* and *argument* are compared as they denote the basis of a human action. A *reason* seeks to explain or justify an action by citing facts, circumstances, inducement, and the like, together with the workings of the mind upon them. *Reasons* may include *purpose* and *motive* as internal or subjective elements, and also *grounds* and *arguments* that are external or objective. The *purpose* of an action is the effect that it is intended to produce; its *motive* is the inner impulse that sets it in motion and guides it. *Grounds* are the facts, data, etc., that the mind weighs in reaching a decision; and *argument* is the logical demonstration of how these facts and data determine the decision. **2.** See CAUSE. **3.** See INTELLECT.

rea·son·a·ble (rē′zən·ə·bəl) adj. **1.** Conformable to reason; sensible. **2.** Having the faculty of reason; rational. **3.** Governed by reason in acting or thinking. **4.** Moderate, as in price; fair. — **Syn.** See RATIONAL. [< OF *raisonable*; after L *rationabilis*] — **rea′son·a·bil′i·ty, rea′son·a·ble·ness** n. — **rea′son·a·bly** adv.

rea·soned (rē′zənd) adj. Founded upon or characterized by reason; premeditated or studied.

rea·son·ing (rē′zən·ing) n. **1.** The mental process of drawing conclusions from known or presumed facts. **2.** The proofs, data, etc., employed in or resulting from this process.

rea·son·less (rē′zən·lis) adj. **1.** Devoid of the faculty of reason. **2.** Not conformable to reason.

re·as·sure (rē·ə·shoor′) v.t. **·sured**, **·sur·ing** **1.** To restore to courage or confidence. **2.** To assure again. **3.** To reinsure. — **re·as·sur′ance** n. — **re·as·sur′ing·ly** adv.

Réaum. Réaumur.

Ré·au·mur scale (rā′ə·myoor′, rā′ə·myoor′; *Fr.* rā·ō·mür′) The thermometric scale in which the zero point corresponds to the temperature of melting ice, and 80° to the temperature of boiling water. Also **Ré′au·mur′.** *Abbr.* **R., Réaum.** For illustration see THERMOMETER. [after René Antoine Ferchault de *Réaumur*, 1683–1757, French biologist]

reave (rēv) v.t. **reaved** or **reft**, **reav·ing** *Archaic* **1.** To carry off as spoil or booty. **2.** To deprive of something; bereave. **3.** To tear up or apart; strip. [OE *rēafian* to rob]

reav·er (rē′vər) n. *Archaic* One who plunders or carries off by force; robber: also spelled *reiver, riever.*

Reb (reb) n. A Yiddish title of respect or address, used with the given name. [< RABBI]

re·bate¹ (rē′bāt, ri·bāt′) v.t. **·bat·ed**, **·bat·ing** **1.** To allow as a deduction. **2.** To make a deduction from. **3.** *Obs.* To blunt, as an edge. — n. A deduction from a gross amount; discount: also **re·bate′ment.** [< OF *rabattre* to beat down < *re-* again + *abattre*. See ABATE.] — **re′bat·er** n.

re·bate² (rē′bāt, rab′it) See RABBET.

re·ba·to (rə·bä′tō) n. pl. **·tos** A collar turned down and falling over the shoulders, worn in the 15th and 16th centuries: also *rabato*. [< MF *rabat* < *rabattre*. See REBATE.]

re·bec (rē′bek) n. An early bowed string instrument, possibly an ancestor of the violin. Also **re′beck.** [< F, alter. of OF *rebebe* < Arabic *rabāb*]

Re·bec·ca (ri·bek′ə) In the Bible, the wife of Isaac, and mother of Esau and Jacob. *Gen.* xxiv 15.

re·bel (v. ri·bel′; n. & adj. reb′əl) v.i. **·belled**, **·bel·ling** **1.** To rise in armed resistance against the established government or ruler of one's land. **2.** To resist any authority or established usage. **3.** To react with violent aversion: usually with *at*. — n. One who rebels. — adj. Rebellious; refractory. [< OF *rebeller* < L *rebellare* < *re-* again + *bellare* to make war < *bellum* war. Doublet of REVEL.]

reb·el·dom (reb′əl·dəm) n. **1.** The domain of rebels; also, rebels collectively. **2.** Rebellious behavior.

REBEC

re·bel·lion (ri·bel′yən) n. **1.** The act of rebelling. **2.** Organized resistance to a lawful government or authority. — **the Rebellion** The American Civil War.

— **Syn. 2.** *Rebellion, revolution, revolt, insurrection, uprising,* and *mutiny* denote an organized effort to defy or overthrow a ruling power. *Rebellion* is armed resistance against a government, usually on a large scale, and usually unsuccessful. A *rebellion,* if successful, becomes a *revolution,* the actual overthrow or change of government, social order, economic institutions, or the like. In its early stages, a *rebellion* may be called a *revolt, insurrection,* or *uprising. Revolt* stresses the effort to escape oppression; *insurrection,* the effort to seize power. *Uprising* is a broad term that might include all the other words, but it is usually confined to a small-scale *revolt,* or to one whose character is not yet clear. A *mutiny* is a *revolt* against military authority, as by soldiers or sailors.

re·bel·lious (ri·bel′yəs) *adj.* **1.** Being in a state of rebellion; insubordinate. **2.** Of or pertaining to a rebel or rebellion. **3.** Resisting control; refractory: *rebellious* curls. — **re·bel′lious·ly** *adv.* — **re·bel′lious·ness** *n.*

re·bill (rē·bil′) *v.t.* To render another bill to; bill again.

re·birth (rē·bûrth′, rē′bûrth′) *n.* **1.** A new birth. **2.** A revival or renaissance.

reb·o·ant (reb′ō·ənt) *adj.* Bellowing back; resounding loudly. [< L *reboans, -antis,* ppr. of *reboare* to resound < *re-* again + *boare* to roar]

re·born (rē·bôrn′) *adj.* Born again; having undergone emotional or mental regeneration.

re·bound (ri·bound′; *for n., also* rē′bound′) *v.i.* To bound back; recoil. — *v.t.* To cause to rebound. — *n.* **1.** Recoil; elasticity. **2.** Something that rebounds or resounds; an echo. **3.** *Informal* Reaction of feeling or emotion after a disappointment: to fall in love on the *rebound.* [< F *rebondir* < *re-* back + *bondir* to bound]

re·bo·zo (rā·bō′sō) *n. Spanish* A long scarf, often embroidered, worn wrapped about the head and shoulders by women in Spain and Spanish America.

re·broad·cast (rē·brôd′kast′, -käst′) *v.t.* **·cast** or **·cast·ed, ·cast·ing 1.** To broadcast (the same program) more than once from the same station. **2.** To broadcast (a program received from another station). — *n.* A program so transmitted.

re·buff (ri·buf′) *v.t.* **1.** To reject or refuse abruptly or rudely. **2.** To drive or beat back; repel. — *n.* **1.** A sudden repulse; curt denial. **2.** A sudden check; defeat. **3.** A beating back. [< MF *rebuffer* < Ital. *ribuffare* to reprimand]

re·buff (rē·buf′) *v.t.* To buff again.

re·buke (ri·byōōk′) *v.t.* **·buked, ·buk·ing 1.** To reprove sharply; reprimand. **2.** *Obs.* To check or restrain by a command. — *n.* A strong and authoritative expression of disapproval. — **Syn.** See REPROOF. [< AF *rebuker,* OF *rebuchier* < *re-* back + *buchier* to beat] — **re·buk′a·ble** *adj.* — **re·buk′er** *n.*

re·bus (rē′bəs) *n. pl.* **·bus·es** A puzzle representing a word, phrase, sentence, etc., by letters, numerals, pictures, etc., whose names have the same sounds as the words represented. [< L, ablative pl. of *res* thing]

re·but (ri·but′) *v.t.* **·but·ted, ·but·ting 1.** To refute by contrary evidence or proof, as in formal argument; disprove. **2.** *Obs.* To drive back. — **Syn.** See REFUTE. [< OF *rebouter* to repulse < *re-* back + *bouter, boter.* See BUTT¹.]

re·but·tal (ri·but′l) *n.* The act of rebutting; refutation.

re·but·ter (ri·but′ər) *n.* **1.** One who or that which rebuts. **2.** In common-law pleading, a defendant's answer to the plaintiff's surrejoinder.

rec. 1. Receipt. **2.** Received. **3.** Recipe. **4.** Record; recorded; recorder; recording.

re·cal·ci·trant (ri·kal′sə·trənt) *adj.* Not complying; obstinate; disobedient; refractory. — *n.* One who is recalcitrant. [< L *recalcitrans, -antis,* ppr. of *recalcitrare* < *re-* back + *calcitrare* to kick < *calx, calcis* heel] — **re·cal′ci·trance, re·cal′ci·tran·cy** *n.*

re·cal·ci·trate (ri·kal′sə·trāt) *v.i.* **·trat·ed, ·trat·ing** To refuse compliance; be recalcitrant. — **re·cal′ci·tra′tion** *n.*

re·ca·lesce (rē′kə·les′) *v.i.* **·lesced, ·lesc·ing** To exhibit recalescence. [< L *recalescere* < *re-* again + *calescere* to grow warm < *calere* to be warm]

re·ca·les·cence (rē′kə·les′əns) *n.* **1.** A glowing again. **2.** *Physics* A phenomenon peculiar to heated iron or steel of glowing more brightly when certain temperatures are reached in the process of cooling from a state of high incandescence: opposed to *decalescence.* — **re′ca·les′cent** *adj.*

re·call (ri·kôl′; *for n., also* rē′kôl) *v.t.* **1.** To call back; order or summon to return. **2.** To summon back in awareness or attention. **3.** To recollect; remember. **4.** To take back; revoke. **5.** *Poetic* To revive; restore. — **Syn.** See REMEMBER. — *n.* **1.** A calling back or to mind. **2.** A signal to call back soldiers, etc., as by a bugle call. **3.** Revocation, as of an order. **4.** In certain States, a system whereby officials may be removed from office by popular vote.

Ré·ca·mier (rā·kà·myā′), **Madame,** 1777–1849, French society leader and patroness of literature: original name **Jeanne Françoise Julie Adélaïde Ber·nard** (ber·nàr′).

re·cant (ri·kant′) *v.t.* **1.** To withdraw formally one's belief in (something previously believed or maintained). — *v.i.* **2.** To disavow an opinion or belief previously held. — **Syn.** See RENOUNCE. [< L *recantare* < *re-* back + *cantare* to sing] — **re·can·ta·tion** (rē′kan·tā′shən) *n.* — **re·cant′er** *n.*

re·cap¹ (*v.* rē′kap′, rē·kap′; *n.* rē′kap′) *v.t.* **·capped, ·cap·ping** To recondition (an automobile tire) by vulcanizing new rubber onto the surface that comes in contact with the road. — *n.* A tire that has been recapped. [< RE- + CAP]

re·cap² (rē′kap) *Informal v.t. & v.i.* **·capped, ·cap·ping** To recapitulate. — *n.* A summary or recapitulation.

re·cap·i·tal·ize (rē·kap′ə·təl·īz′) *v.t.* **·ized, ·iz·ing** To capitalize again or differently. — **re·cap′i·tal·i·za′tion** *n.*

re·ca·pit·u·late (rē′kə·pich′ōō·lāt) *v.t. & v.i.* **·lat·ed, ·lat·ing 1.** To review briefly; sum up. **2.** *Zool.* To reproduce (typical ancestral forms) in the course of embryonic development. [< LL *recapitulare* to number again < *re-* again + *capitulare.* See CAPITULATE.] — **re′ca·pit′u·la′tion** *n.* — **re′ca·pit′u·la·tive** (-lā′tiv), **re′ca·pit′u·la·to·ry** (-lə·tôr′ē, -tō′rē) *adj.*

re·cap·ture (rē·kap′chər) *v.t.* **·tured, ·tur·ing 1.** To capture again; obtain by recapture. **2.** To recall; remember. — *n.* **1.** The act of retaking; especially, in war, the forcible recovery of booty or goods. **2.** A prize retaken; anything recaptured. **3.** The taking by the public of the earnings of a public service corporation over and above a stated profit.

re·cast (*v.* rē·kast′, -käst′; *n.* rē′kast′, -käst′) *v.t.* **·cast, ·cast·ing 1.** To form anew; cast again. **2.** To fashion anew by changing style, arrangement, etc., as a discourse. **3.** To calculate anew. — *n.* Something that has been recast.

recd. Received.

re·cede (ri·sēd′) *v.i.* **·ced·ed, ·ced·ing 1.** To move back; withdraw, as flood waters. **2.** To withdraw, as from an assertion, position, agreement, etc. **3.** To slope backward: a *receding* forehead. **4.** To become more distant; move or fade away. [< L *recedere* < *re-* back + *cedere* to go]

re·cede (rē·sēd′) *v.t.* **·ced·ed, ·ced·ing** To cede back; grant or yield to a former owner. [< RE- + CEDE]

re·ceipt (ri·sēt′) *n.* **1.** The act or state of receiving anything. **2.** *Usually pl.* That which is received: cash *receipts.* **3.** A written acknowledgment of the payment of money, of the delivery of goods, etc. **4.** A recipe. — *v.t.* **1.** To give a receipt for the payment of. **2.** To write acknowledgment of payment on, as a bill. — *v.i.* **3.** To give a receipt, as for money paid. Abbr. *rec., rect., rec't* [< OF *recete* < L *recepta,* pp. of *recipere.* See RECEIVE.]

re·ceipt·or (ri·sē′tər) *n. Law* One who gives a receipt; especially, one who gives a receipt for goods that have been attached.

re·ceiv·a·ble (ri·sē′və·bəl) *adj.* **1.** Capable of being received; fit to be received, as legal tender. **2.** Maturing for payment: said of a bill. — *n. pl.* Outstanding accounts listed among the assets of a business.

re·ceive (ri·sēv′) *v.* **·ceived, ·ceiv·ing** *v.t.* **1.** To take into one's hand or possession (something given, offered, delivered, etc.); acquire; accept. **2.** To gain knowledge or information of: He *received* the news at breakfast. **3.** To take from another by hearing or listening: The king *received* his oath of fealty. **4.** To bear; support: These columns *receive* the weight of the building. **5.** To experience; meet with: to *receive* abuse. **6.** To undergo; suffer: He *received* a wound in his arm. **7.** To intercept or encounter the force of (a blow, etc.). **8.** To contain; hold. **9.** To allow entrance to; admit to one's presence; greet. **10.** To perceive mentally; understand. — *v.i.* **11.** To accept as true, proven, authoritative, etc. — *v.i.* **12.** To be a recipient; get, obtain, or acquire something. **13.** To welcome visitors or callers. **14.** To partake of the Eucharist. **15.** *Telecom.* To convert radio waves into some useful form by means of a receiver. [< OF *receivre* < L *recipere* < *re-* back + *capere* to take]

— **Syn. 1.** *Receive, acquire, get, accept,* and *admit* are compared as they refer to a giving over into custody or possession. *Receive* has no close synonym; he who *receives* takes what is given or what comes entirely passively. *Acquire* implies an active role, or some effort to obtain; the same is true of *get,* for the most part, but this word is broad enough to include some of the sense of *receive:* to *get* (or *acquire*) a rare manuscript for a collection, to *get* (or *receive*) presents on one's birthday. *Accept* and *admit* imply an exercise of choice, and the possibility of rejecting, as *receive* does not.

Received Standard English *Brit.* The dialect of highest prestige in England, used by public-school graduates, members of the Establishment, etc.

re·ceiv·er (ri·sē′vər) *n.* **1.** One who receives; a recipient. **2.** An official assigned to receive money due. **3.** *Law* A person appointed by a court to take into his custody, control, and management the property or funds of another pending judicial action concerning them. **4.** One who buys or receives stolen or embezzled goods, knowing them to be stolen. **5.** Something that receives; a receptacle. **6.** A vessel considered as a receptacle for a fluid, as a jar for re-

ceiving and condensing a liquid that has been distilled.
7. *Telecom.* **a** An instrument in an electric circuit serving to receive and reproduce signals transmitted from another part of the circuit: a telephone *receiver.* **b** Any of various electronic devices that convert radio waves into audio signals, video signals, etc., or into forms useful as a basis for observation, as in radio telescopes or radar: also **receiving set. 8.** The troughlike part of a gun, directly behind the breech, that guides the round into the chamber.

re·ceiv·er·ship (ri·sē′vər·ship) *n.* **1.** The office and functions pertaining to a receiver under appointment of a court. **2.** The state of being in the hands of a receiver.

receiving line At formal parties, balls, wedding receptions, etc., a group of persons including the hosts, guests of honor, etc., who stand at the entrance to greet guests.

re·cen·sion (ri·sen′shən) *n.* **1.** The editing of a text, especially of an early writer, so as to incorporate the most plausible readings found in varying manuscripts. **2.** The textual version thus established. [< L *recensio, -onis* enumeration < *recensere* to examine, survey < *re-* thoroughly + *censere* to estimate, value]

re·cent (rē′sənt) *adj.* Pertaining to, or formed, developed, or created in time not long past; modern; fresh; new. — **Syn.** See MODERN. [< MF *récent* < L *recens, -entis*] — **re′cent·ly** *adv.* — **re′cen·cy, re′cent·ness** *n.*

Re·cent (rē′sənt) *adj. Geol.* Pertaining to or designating the present geological epoch, succeeding the Pleistocene. See chart for GEOLOGY.

re·cept (rē′sept) *n. Psychol.* A mental image formed by the repetition of related percepts, with reinforcement of common characteristics. [< RE- + *-cept* as in CONCEPT.]

re·cep·ta·cle (ri·sep′tə·kəl) *n.* **1.** Anything that serves to contain or hold something else. **2.** *Bot.* The base to which the parts of the flower, fruit, or seeds are fixed. For illustration see FLOWER. [< L *receptaculum* < *receptare,* freq. of *recipere.* See RECEIVE.]
— **Syn.** 1. container, repository, vessel.

re·cep·tion (ri·sep′shən) *n.* **1.** The act of receiving, or the state of being received. **2.** A formal social entertainment of guests: a wedding *reception.* **3.** The manner of receiving a person or persons: a warm *reception.* **4.** Mental acceptance, as of a proposition. **5.** *Telecom.* The act or process of receiving, or the quality of reproduction achieved. [< OF, or < L *receptio, -onis* < *recipere.* See RECEIVE.]

re·cep·tion·ist (ri·sep′shən·ist) *n.* One employed to receive callers at the entrance to an office.

reception room 1. A room for callers in a private house. **2.** A waiting room in a hospital, or adjoining a doctor's, dentist's, or lawyer's office.

re·cep·tive (ri·sep′tiv) *adj.* **1.** Able or inclined to receive, as truths or impressions. **2.** Able to take in or hold. — **re·cep′tive·ly** *adv.* — **re·cep·tiv·i·ty** (rē′sep·tiv′ə·tē), **re·cep′tive·ness** *n.*

re·cep·tor (ri·sep′tər) *n. Anat.* The terminal structure of an afferent neuron, specialized to receive external and internal stimuli and transmit them to the spinal cord and brain. [< OF or L, receiver]

re·cess (*n.* ri·ses′, rē′ses; *for def. 2, usually* rē′ses; *v.* ri·ses′) *n.* **1.** A depression or indentation in any otherwise continuous line or surface, especially in a wall; niche; alcove; cavity. **2.** A time of cessation from employment or occupation: The school took a *recess.* **3.** *Usually pl.* A quiet and secluded spot; withdrawn or inner place: the *recesses* of the mind. — *v.t.* **1.** To place in or as in a recess. **2.** To make a recess in, as a wall. **3.** To interrupt or dismiss for a recess: to *recess* a court. — *v.i.* **4.** To take a recess. [< L *recessus* a receding, pp. of *recedere.* See RECEDE.]

re·ces·sion (ri·sesh′ən) *n.* **1.** The act of receding; a withdrawal. **2.** The procession of the clergy, choir, etc., as they leave the chancel after a church service. **3.** An economic setback in commercial and industrial activity, especially one occurring as a downward turn during a period of generally rising prosperity; a slight depression. [< L *recessio, -onis* < *recedere.* See RECEDE.]

re·ces·sion (rē·sesh′ən) *n.* The act of ceding again; a giving back.

re·ces·sion·al (ri·sesh′ən·el) *adj.* Of or pertaining to recession. — *n.* A hymn sung as the choir or clergy leave the chancel after service.

re·ces·sive (ri·ses′iv) *adj.* **1.** Having a tendency to recede or go back; receding. **2.** *Genetics* Designating one of a pair of hereditary characters that, appearing in a hybrid offspring, is masked by a contrasting character. — *n. Genetics* A recessive character. — **re·ces′sive·ly** *adv.*

ré·chauf·fé (rā·shō·fā′) *n. French* **1.** Food reheated. **2.** Reworked or "warmed over" literary work; rehash.

re·cher·ché (rə·sher·shā′) *adj. French* **1.** Rare and exquisite; choice. **2.** Elegant and refined; also, overrefined; precious. **3.** Far-fetched.

re·cid·i·vism (rə·sid′ə·viz′əm) *n.* The tendency of an offender to repeat criminal acts and patterns of antisocial behavior. Also **rec·i·div·i·ty** (res′ə·div′ə·tē). [< L *recidivus* relapsing < *recidere* < *re-* back + *cadere* to fall] — **re·cid′i·vist** *n.* — **re·cid′i·vis′tic, re·cid′i·vous** *adj.*

Re·ci·fe (rä·sē′fə) The capital of Pernambuco State, NE Brazil, a port on the Atlantic; pop. 1,100,404 (1968): also *Pernambuco.*

rec·i·pe (res′ə·pē) *n.* **1.** A formula or list of ingredients of a mixture, giving the exact proportions together with proper directions for compounding, cooking, etc. **2.** A medical prescription: so called from its opening word: usually abbreviated to ℞. **3.** A method prescribed for attaining a desired result. Abbr. *r., rec.* [< L, take, imperative of *recipere.* See RECEIVE.]

re·cip·i·ence (ri·sip′ē·əns) *n.* **1.** The process or act of receiving. **2.** Receptivity. Also **re·cip′i·en·cy.**

re·cip·i·ent (ri·sip′ē·ənt) *adj.* Receiving or ready to receive; receptive. — *n.* One who or that which receives; a receiver. [< L *recipiens, -entis,* ppr. of *recipere.* See RECEIVE.]

re·cip·ro·cal (ri·sip′rə·kəl) *adj.* **1.** Done or given by each of two to the other, or existing in both; mutual: *reciprocal* affection. **2.** Done or given in return: a *reciprocal* favor. **3.** Mutually interchangeable or corresponding: *reciprocal* diplomatic inquiries. **4.** *Gram.* Expressive of mutual relationship or action: used of certain pronouns and verbs or their meaning. **5.** *Math.* Of or pertaining to reciprocals; inverse. — *n.* **1.** That which is reciprocal. **2.** *Math.* The quotient obtained by dividing unity by a number or expression, as $1/x$ is the *reciprocal* of *x.* In a fraction, the numerator and denominator are reversed, as $3/2$ is the *reciprocal* of $2/3$. — **Syn.** See MUTUAL. [< L *reciprocus*] — **re·cip′ro·cal·i·ty** (-kal′ə·tē), **re·cip′ro·cal·ness** *n.* — **re·cip′ro·cal·ly** *adv.*

reciprocal pronouns *Gram.* Pronouns or pronominal phrases denoting reciprocal action or relation, as *each other, one another.*

re·cip·ro·cate (ri·sip′rə·kāt) *v.* **·cat·ed, ·cat·ing** *v.t.* **1.** To cause to move backward and forward alternately. **2.** To give and receive mutually, as favors or gifts; interchange. **3.** To give, feel, do, etc., in return; requite, as an emotion. — *v.i.* **4.** To move backward and forward. **5.** To make a return in kind. **6.** To give and receive favors, gifts, etc., mutually. **7.** To correspond; be equivalent. [< L *reciprocatus,* pp. of *reciprocare* < *reciprocus* reciprocal] — **re·cip′ro·ca′tive** *adj.* — **re·cip′ro·ca′tor** *n.*

reciprocating engine *Mech.* An engine having a piston or pistons that move to and fro.

re·cip·ro·ca·tion (ri·sip′rə·kā′shən) *n.* **1.** The act of reciprocating; a mutual giving and returning. **2.** Alternation; alternate motion.

re·cip·ro·ca·to·ry (ri·sip′rə·kə·tôr′ē, -tō′rē) *adj.* Alternating in direction or movement; reciprocating.

rec·i·proc·i·ty (res′ə·pros′ə·tē) *n.* **1.** Reciprocal obligation, action, or relation. **2.** A trade relation or policy between two countries by which each makes concessions favoring the importation of the products of the other. [< F *réciprocité*]

re·ci·sion (ri·sizh′ən) *n.* The act of rescinding or annulling. [< L *recisio, -onis* < *recidere* < *re-* back + *caedere* to cut]

recit. Recitative.

re·cit·al (ri·sīt′l) *n.* **1.** A telling over in detail, or that which is thus told; a narration. **2.** A public delivery of something previously memorized. **3.** A musical program performed usually by one person or several appearing as soloists. **4.** A detailed statement.

rec·i·ta·tion (res′ə·tā′shən) *n.* **1.** The act of repeating from memory; especially, the reciting of a memorized piece before an audience: a program of songs and *recitations.* **2.** The meeting of a class, as for the reciting of a lesson. **3.** That which is recited. [< L *recitatio, -onis* < *recitare.* See RECITE.]

rec·i·ta·tive[1] (res′ə·tā′tiv, ri·sī′tə·tiv) *adj.* Of the nature of a recital, as of facts or details; narrative.

rec·i·ta·tive[2] (res′ə·tə·tēv′, rə·sit′ə·tiv) *n. Music* **1.** Language uttered in the rhythm and phrasing of ordinary speech, but set to music. **2.** This style of singing, or a vocal passage so rendered. Also *Italian* **re·ci·ta·ti·vo** (rā′chē·tä·tē′vō). — *adj.* Of the nature of a recitative. [< Ital. *recitativo*]

re·cite (ri·sīt′) *v.* **·cit·ed, ·cit·ing** *v.t.* **1.** To declaim or say from memory, especially formally, as a lesson in class. **2.** To tell in particular detail; relate. **3.** To enumerate. — *v.i.* **4.** To declaim or speak something from memory. **5.** To repeat or be examined in a lesson or part of a lesson in class. [< OF *reciter* < L *recitare* < *re-* again + *citare.* See CITE.] — **re·cit′er** *n.*
— **Syn.** 1. repeat. 2. recount, narrate, recapitulate.

re-cite (rē·sīt′) *v.t. & v.i.* **·cit·ed, ·cit·ing** To cite again. [< RE- + CITE]

reck (rek) *v.t. & v.i. Archaic* **1.** To have a care or thought (for); heed; mind. **2.** To be of concern or interest (to): It *recks* me not. [OE *reccan*]

reck·less (rek′lis) *adj.* **1.** Foolishly heedless of danger; rash. **2.** Proceeding from carelessness or rashness: *reckless* driving. [OE *recceléas*] — **reck′less·ly** *adv.*

reck·less·ness (rek′lis·nis) *n.* The state or quality of being reckless. — **Syn.** See TEMERITY.

Reck·ling·hau·sen (rek′ling·hou′zən) A city in NW North Rhine–Westphalia, West Germany; pop. 125,523 (est. 1970).

reck·on (rek′ən) *v.t.* 1. To count; compute; calculate. 2. To look upon as being; regard: They *reckon* him a fool. — *v.i.* 3. To make computation; count up. 4. To rely or depend: with *on* or *upon*: to *reckon* on help. 5. *Informal* or *Dial.* To suppose; guess. — **Syn.** See CALCULATE, CONSIDER. — **to reckon for** To pay for; receive the penalty of. — **to reckon with** 1. To settle accounts with. 2. To take into consideration; bear in mind; consider. [OE *recenian* to explain. Akin to RECK and to MHG *rechnen* to count.]

reck·on·er (rek′ən·ər) *n.* 1. One who reckons. 2. A book of mathematical tables or a device for aiding one to compute.

reck·on·ing (rek′ən·ing) *n.* 1. The act of counting; computation; a settlement of accounts. 2. Account; score; bill, as at a hotel. 3. *Naut.* Dead reckoning (which see).

re·claim (ri·klām′) *v.t.* 1. To bring (swamp, desert, etc.) into a condition to support cultivation or life, as by draining or irrigating. 2. To obtain (a substance) from used or waste products: to *reclaim* rubber. 3. To cause to return from wrong or sinful ways of life; reform. 4. *Obs.* To tame, as a hawk. — *n.* The act of reclaiming, or state of being reclaimed. [< OF *reclamer* to call back < L *reclamare* < *re-* back + *clamare* to cry out] — **re·claim′a·ble** *adj.* — **re·claim′ant, re·claim′er** *n.*

re·claim (rē·klām′) *v.t.* To claim again.

rec·la·ma·tion (rek′lə·mā′shən) *n.* 1. The act or process of reclaiming. 2. Restoration, as to ownership, cultivation, usefulness, or a moral life.

ré·clame (rā·kläm′) *n. French* Publicity; advertising.

re·cline (ri·klīn′) *v.* ·clined, ·clin·ing *v.i.* 1. To assume a recumbent position; lie down or back. — *v.t.* 2. To cause to assume a recumbent position; lay down or back. [< L *reclinare* < *re-* back + *clinare* to lean] — **rec·li·na·tion** (rek′lə·nā′shən) *n.* — **re·clin′er** *n.* — **Syn.** 1. lean, repose.

rec·luse (ri·klōōs′; *for n.*, *also* rek′lōōs) *n.* 1. One who lives in retirement or seclusion. 2. A religious devotee who lives voluntarily shut up in a cell and practices exceptional austerities. — *adj.* Secluded or retired from the world; solitary. [< OF *reclus*, orig. pp. of *reclure* < L *recludere* < *re-* back + *claudere* to shut] — **re·clu′sive** *adj.* — **Syn.** (noun) 2. hermit, anchorite, eremite.

re·clu·sion (ri·klōō′zhən) *n.* 1. The state of being a recluse. 2. The condition of being in solitary confinement.

rec·og·ni·tion (rek′əg·nish′ən) *n.* 1. The act of recognizing, or the state of being recognized. 2. Acknowledgment of a fact or claim. 3. Friendly notice; salutation; attention. 4. Acknowledgment and acceptance on the part of one government of the independence of another. [< L *recognitio*, *-onis* < *recognoscere*. See RECOGNIZANCE.] — **re·cog·ni·to·ry** (ri·kog′nə·tôr′ē, -tō′rē), **re·cog′ni·tive** *adj.*

re·cog·ni·zance (ri·kog′nə·zəns, -kon′ə-) *n.* 1. *Law* a An acknowledgment or obligation of record, with condition to do some particular act, as to appear and answer, or to keep the peace. b A sum of money deposited as surety for fulfillment of such act or obligation, and forfeited by its nonperformance. 2. Recognition. [< OF *reconoissance* < *reconoistre* < L *recognoscere* to recall < *re-* again + *cognoscere*. See COGNITION. Doublet of RECONNAISSANCE.] — **re·cog′ni·zant** *adj.*

rec·og·nize (rek′əg·nīz) *v.t.* ·nized, ·niz·ing 1. To know again; perceive as identical with someone or something previously known. 2. To identify or know, as by previous experience or knowledge: I *recognize* poor poetry when I see it. 3. To perceive as true; realize: to *recognize* the facts in a case. 4. To acknowledge the independence and validity of, as a newly constituted government. 5. To indicate appreciation or approval of: to *recognize* merit. 6. To approve formally; regard as valid or genuine: to *recognize* a claim. 7. To give (someone) permission to speak, as in a legislative body. 8. To admit the acquaintance of. 9. *Law* To bind by a recognizance. Also *esp. Brit.* **rec′og·nise.** [Back formation < RECOGNIZANCE] — **rec·og·niz·a·ble** (rek′əg·nī′zə·bəl) *adj.* — **rec′og·niz′a·bly** *adv.* — **rec′og·niz′er** *n.*

re·coil (ri·koil′, *for n.*, *also* rē′koil) *v.i.* 1. To start back, as in fear or loathing; shrink: He *recoiled* at the sight. 2. To spring back, as from force of discharge or impact. 3. To return to the source; react: with *on* or *upon*: Crime *recoils* upon its perpetrator. 4. To move or draw back; retreat. — *n.* 1. A backward movement or impulse, as of a gun at the moment of firing; rebound; also, a shrinking. 2. The condition existing as the result of a recoil. [< OF *reculer* < *re-* backwards + *cul* backside < L *culus*] — **re·coil′er** *n.*

re·coil (rē′koil′) *v.t. & v.i.* To coil again.

re·coil·less (rē′koil·lis) *adj.* 1. Having no recoil. 2. *Mil.* Equipped with rear-facing pets or ports for the escape of gases to counteract recoil: said of certain weapons.

rec·ol·lect (rek′ə·lekt′) *v.t.* 1. To call back to the mind; revive in the memory; remember. — *v.i.* 2. To have a recollection of something. — **Syn.** See REMEMBER. [< L *recollectus*, pp. of *recolligere* to gather again < *re-* again + *colligere*. See COLLECT.]

re·col·lect (rē′kə·lekt′) *v.t.* 1. To collect again, as things scattered. 2. To collect or compose (one's thoughts or nerves); compose or recover (oneself). — **re′col·lec′tion** *n.*

rec·ol·lec·tion (rek′ə·lek′shən) *n.* 1. The act or power of recollecting or remembering; remembrance. 2. Something remembered; reminiscence; memory. 3. A state or condition of inner tranquillity or prayerfulness. — **Syn.** See MEMORY. — **rec′ol·lec′tive** *adj.* — **rec′ol·lec′tive·ly** *adv.*

recombinant DNA research *Genetics* Work that produces or tries to produce new strains of organisms by combining DNA strands.

re·com·bi·na·tion (rē′kom·bə·nā′shən) *n. Genetics.* 1. A crossing over. 2. A combining again. — **re·com′bi·nant** *adj.*

rec·om·mend (rek′ə·mend′) *v.t.* 1. To commend with favorable representations; praise as desirable, worthy, etc. 2. To make attractive or acceptable: His sagacity *recommends* him. 3. To advise; urge. 4. To give in charge; commend. [< Med.L *recommendare* < L *re-* again + *commendare*. See COMMEND.] — **rec′om·mend′er** *n.*

rec·om·men·da·tion (rek′ə·men·dā′shən) *n.* 1. The act of recommending, or of being recommended. 2. A letter recommending a person.

rec·om·mend·a·to·ry (rek′ə·men′də·tôr′ē, -tō′rē) *adj.* 1. Serving to recommend. 2. In praise; recommending.

re·com·mit (rē′kə·mit′) *v.t.* ·mit·ted, ·mit·ting 1. To commit again. 2. To refer back to a committee, as a bill.

rec·om·pense (rek′əm·pens) *v.t.* ·pensed, ·pens·ing 1. To give compensation to; pay or repay; reward; requite. 2. To give compensation for; make up for, as a loss. — *n.* 1. An equivalent for anything given or done; payment. 2. Compensation. 3. Reward. [< OF *recompenser* < LL *recompensare* < L *re-* again + *compensare*. See COMPENSATE.] — **Syn.** (verb) 1. remunerate, reimburse. 2. indemnify. — (noun) See SALARY.

re·com·pose (rē′kəm·pōz′) *v.t.* ·posed, ·pos·ing 1. To restore the composure of; tranquilize. 2. To compose or form anew; rearrange; reconstitute; recombine. — **re·com·po·si·tion** (rē′kom·pə·zish′ən) *n.*

rec·on·cil·a·ble (rek′ən·sī′lə·bəl) *adj.* 1. Capable of being reconciled or of renewing friendship. 2. Capable of being adjusted or harmonized. — **rec′on·cil′a·bil′i·ty, rec′on·cil′a·ble·ness** *n.* — **rec′on·cil′a·bly** *adv.*

rec·on·cile (rek′ən·sīl) *v.t.* ·ciled, ·cil·ing 1. To bring back to friendship after estrangement. 2. To settle or adjust, as a quarrel. 3. To bring to acquiescence, content, or submission: to *reconcile* one to his lot. 4. To make or show to be consistent or congruous; harmonize: often with *to* or *with*: Can he *reconcile* his statement with his conduct? — **Syn.** See ADAPT. [< OF *reconciler* < L *reconciliare* < *re-* again + *conciliare* to unite. See CONCILIATE.] — **rec′on·cile′ment** *n.* — **rec′on·cil′er** *n.*

rec·on·cil·i·a·tion (rek′ən·sil′ē·ā′shən) *n.* 1. The act of reconciling, or the state of being reconciled. 2. The process of making consistent or congruous. — **rec′on·cil′i·a·to·ry** (-sil′ē·ə·tôr′ē, -tō′rē) *adj.*

rec·on·dite (rek′ən·dīt, ri·kon′dīt) *adj.* 1. Remote from ordinary or easy perception; abstruse; secret. 2. Dealing in abstruse matters. 3. Hidden; not readily observed. [< L *reconditus*, pp. of *recondere* to hide < *re-* back + *condere* to store < *con* together + *dare* to put] — **rec′on·dite′ly** *adv.* — **rec′on·dite′ness** *n.*

re·con·di·tion (rē′kən·di′shən) *v.t.* To put into good or working condition, as by making repairs; overhaul.

re·con·nais·sance (ri·kon′ə·səns, -säns) *n.* 1. A reconnoitering; a preliminary examination or survey. 2. *Mil.* The act of obtaining information, especially regarding the position, strength, and movement of enemy forces. Also **re·con′nois·sance.** [< F. Doublet of RECOGNIZANCE.]

re·con·noi·ter (rē′kə·noi′tər, rek′ə-) *v.t.* To examine or survey, as for military or engineering purposes. — *v.i.* To make a reconnaissance. Also *Brit.* **re′con·noi′tre.** [< OF *reconoistre*. See RECOGNIZANCE.] — **re′con·noi′ter·er** *n.*

re·con·sid·er (rē′kən·sid′ər) *v.t.* 1. To consider again, especially with a view to a reversal of previous action. 2. In parliamentary usage, to bring before the house for renewed action (a matter previously decided). — *v.i.* 3. To consider again a matter or decision. — **re·con·sid·er·a′tion** *n.*

re·con·sign (rē′kən·sīn′) *v.t.* To consign again; especially, to consign (goods) to a different place or person while still in transit. — **re′con·sign′ment** *n.*

re·con·sti·tute (rē·kon′stə·tōōt, -tyōōt) *v.t.* ·tut·ed, ·tut·ing To constitute again; make over. — **re·con′sti·tu′tion** *n.*

re·con·struct (rē′kən·strukt′) *v.t.* To construct again.

re·con·struc·tion (rē′kən·struk′shən) *n.* 1. The act of reconstructing, or the state of being reconstructed. **2.** *Often cap.* The restoration of the seceded States as members of the Union under the **Reconstruction Acts** of March 2 and 23, 1867. **— re′con·struc′tive** *adj.*

Re·con·struc·tion·ism (rē′kən-struk′shən-iz′əm) *n.* A movement of 20th-century American Judaism that stresses the cultural heritage common to all Jews as the basis for a viable religious civilization for all Jews. **— Re′con·struc′· tion·ist** *n.*

Reconstruction period *U.S.* The period following the Civil War during which the seceded Southern States were reorganized in accordance with the Congressional program.

re·con·vert (rē′kən-vûrt′) *v.t.* **1.** To change back to a state or form previously possessed. **2.** To convert back to a previously held religious belief. **3.** *Logic* To transpose again (the subject and predicate of a proposition). **4.** *Law* To change again into something of equivalent worth. **— re′· con·ver′sion** *n.*

re·con·vey (rē′kən-vā′) *v.t.* To convey back to an original owner or place. **— re′con·vey′ance** *n.*

rec·ord (*n. & adj.* rek′ərd; *v.* ri·kôrd′) *n.* **1.** An account in written or other permanent form serving as a memorial or authentic evidence of a fact or event. **2.** Something on which such an account is made, as a document or monument. **3.** Information on facts or events, preserved and handed down: the heaviest rainfall on *record.* **4.** The known career or performance of a person, animal, organization, etc., regarded as a series of things done or achieved: a good *record* in politics. **5.** The best listed achievement, as in a competitive sport: to beat the world's *record.* **6.** *Law* **a** A written account of an act, statement, or transaction made by an officer acting under authority of law, and intended as permanent evidence thereon. **b** An official written account of a judicial or legislative proceeding, including the judgments or enactments and an official copy of all related documents. **7.** A phonograph record. **— off the record** **1.** Unofficial or unofficially. **2.** Not for quotation or publication, or not from a source to be identified. **—** *adj.* Surpassing any previously recorded achievement or performance of its kind: a *record* turnout. **—** *v.t.* **1.** To write down or otherwise inscribe, as for preserving an authentic account, evidence, etc. **2.** To indicate; register, especially in permanent form, as a cardiograph does. **3.** To make a tape or phonograph record of. **—** *v.i.* **4.** To record something. Abbr. *rec.* [< OF, memory < *recorder* < L *recordari* to remember < *re-* again + *cor, cordis* heart, mind] **— Syn.** (noun) **1.** note, memorandum, register, roll, catalogue, inventory, archives, muniments. Compare HISTORY.

record changer A device on some record players that automatically feeds successive records onto the turntable.

re·cord·er (ri·kôr′dər) *n.* **1.** One who records. **2.** A magistrate having criminal jurisdiction in a city or borough. **3.** A registering apparatus. **4.** Any of a group of fipple flutes having eight finger holes, and various ranges. **5.** A tape or wire recorder. Abbr. *rec* **— re·cord′er·ship** *n.*

TREBLE RECORDER

re·cord·ing (ri·kôr′ding) *n.* **1.** *Telecom.* The process of registering a relatively permanent physical record of sounds or other communicable signals. **2.** A phonograph record. Abbr. *rec.*

record player A motor-driven turntable with a pickup attachment and auxiliary equipment for the playing of phonograph records: also called *gramophone, phonograph.*

re·count (ri·kount′) *v.t.* **1.** To relate the particulars of; narrate in detail. **2.** To enumerate; recite. [< OF *re-conter* to relate]

re·count (rē-kount′; *for n.,* also rē′kount′) *v.t.* To count again. **—** *n.* A repetition of a count; especially, a second count of votes cast.

re·count·al (ri·koun′təl) *n.* A recounting.

re·coup (ri·kōōp′) *v.t.* **1.** To recover or obtain an equivalent for; make up, as a loss. **2.** To reimburse for a loss; indemnify. **3.** *Law* To keep back (something due) in order to make good a counterclaim. **—** *n.* The act or process of recouping. [< OF *recouper* < *re-* back + *couper* to cut. See COUP.] **— re·coup′a·ble** *adj.* **— re·coup′ment** *n.*

re·cou·pé (rə-kōō′pā′) *adj.* *Heraldry* Divided a second time, as an escutcheon. [< F]

re·course (rē′kôrs, -kōrs, ri·kôrs′, -kōrs′) *n.* **1.** Resort to or application for help or security. **2.** *Law* The right to exact payment from a party secondarily liable, where the first party liable has failed to pay. **3.** One who or that which is resorted to for help or supply. **4.** *Obs.* Admission; entrance. **— without recourse** A restricted or qualified endorsement of a promissory note or transfer that signifies that the endorser merely transfers the instrument, but disclaims liability upon it. [< OF *recours* < L *recursus* a running back, pp. of *recurrere.* See RECUR.]

re·cov·er (ri·kuv′ər) *v.t.* **1.** To obtain again after losing; regain. **2.** To make up for; retrieve, as a loss. **3.** To restore (oneself) to natural balance, health, etc. **4.** In sports, to regain (one's position of guard, balance, etc.). **5.** To re-

claim, as land. **6.** *Law* **a** To gain in judicial proceedings: to *recover* judgment. **b** To gain or regain by legal process. **—** *v.i.* **7.** To regain health, composure, etc. **8.** *Law* To succeed in a lawsuit. **9.** In sport, to regain one's balance or position of guard. [< OF *recovrer* < L *recuperare.* See RECUPERATE.] **— re·cov′er·a·ble** *adj.* **— re·cov′er·er** *n.*

re·cov·er (rē·kuv′ər) *v.t.* To cover again.

re·cov·er·y (ri·kuv′ər·ē) *n.* *pl.* **·er·ies** **1.** The act of recovering. **2.** The state of being or having recovered. **3.** Restoration from sickness or from a condition of evil. **4.** In boating, the forward movement of an oarsman, after having finished one stroke, to take the next. **5.** In fencing and sparring, the act of regaining a defensive position after attack. **6.** The extraction of valuable substances and materials from original sources, by-products, waste, etc. **— final recovery** *U.S. Law* The final verdict in an action.

recovery room A hospital room for patients who have just undergone an operation.

rec·re·ant (rek′rē·ənt) *adj.* **1.** Unfaithful to a cause or pledge; apostate; false. **2.** Craven; cowardly. **—** *n.* A cowardly or faithless person; also, a deserter; an apostate. [< OF, ppr. of *recreire* to surrender allegiance < Med.L *recredere* < L *re-* back + *credere* to believe] **— rec′re·ance, rec′re·an·cy** *n.* **— rec′re·ant·ly** *adv.*

rec·re·ate (rek′rē·āt) *v.* **·at·ed, ·at·ing** *v.t.* **1.** To impart fresh vigor to; refresh, especially after toil, by some form of relaxation or entertainment. **—** *v.i.* **2.** To take recreation. **— Syn.** See ENTERTAIN. [< L *recreatus,* pp. of *recreare* < *re-* again + *creare* to create] **— rec′re·a′tive** *adj.*

re-cre·ate (rē′krē·āt′) *v.t.* **·at·ed, ·at·ing** To create anew. **— re′cre·a′tion** *n.*

rec·re·a·tion (rek′rē·ā′shən) *n.* **1.** Refreshment of body or mind; diversion; amusement. **2.** Any pleasurable exercise or occupation. **— rec′re·a′tion·al** *adj.*

rec·re·ment (rek′rə·mənt) *n.* **1.** *Physiol.* A secretion reabsorbed by the body after having performed its function, as gastric juice, saliva, etc. **2.** Waste material; dross; refuse. [< L *recrementum* < *re-* back + *cretum,* pp. of *cernere* to separate] **— rec′re·men′tal** (-men′təl) *adj.* **— rec′re·men·ti′tial** (-men·tish′əl), **rec′re·men·ti′tious** *adj.*

re·crim·i·nate (ri·krim′ə·nāt) *v.* **·nat·ed, ·nat·ing** *v.t.* **1.** To accuse in return. **—** *v.i.* **2.** To repel one accusation by making another in return. [< Med.L *recriminatus,* pp. of *recriminare* < L *re-* again + *criminare.* See CRIMINATE.] **— re·crim′i·na·tive, re·crim′i·na·to·ry** (ri·krim′ə·nə·tôr′ē, -tō′rē) *adj.* **— re·crim′i·na′tor** *n.*

re·crim·i·na·tion (ri·krim′ə·nā′shən) *n.* **1.** The act of recriminating. **2.** A countercharge.

re·cru·desce (rē′krōō·des′) *v.i.* **·desced, ·desc·ing** To break out afresh, as a disease. [< L *recrudescere* < *re-* again + *crudescere* to become raw < *crudus* bleeding]

re·cru·des·cence (rē′krōō·des′əns) *n.* **1.** A breaking out afresh, as of a disease or sore. **2.** A reappearance; return. **— re′cru·des′cent** *adj.*

re·cruit (ri·krōōt′) *v.t.* **1.** To enlist (men) for military or naval service. **2.** To muster; raise, as an army, by enlistment. **3.** To supply with recruits. **4.** To regain or revive (lost health, strength, etc.). **5.** *Rare* To replenish. **—** *v.i.* **6.** To enlist new men for military or naval service. **7.** To regain lost health or strength. **8.** To gain or raise new supplies of anything lost or needed. **—** *n.* A newly enlisted member of an organization, especially of the armed forces; especially, the lowest grade of enlisted man in the U.S. Army and Navy. See tables at GRADE. Abbr. *Rct.* [< F *recrute* < OF *recreü,* pp. of *recroistre* < L *recrescere* < *re-* again + *crescere* to grow] **— re·cruit′er** *n.* **— re·cruit′ment** *n.*

rec. sec. Recording secretary.

rect. **1.** Receipt: also **rec′t.** **2.** Rector. **3.** Rectory.

rec·tal (rek′təl) *adj.* *Anat.* Relating to, involving, or in the region of the rectum.

rec·tan·gle (rek′tang′gəl) *n.* A parallelogram with all its angles right angles. [< F < LL *rectangulum* < L *rectus* straight + *angulus* angle]

rec·tan·gu·lar (rek·tang′gyə·lər) *adj.* **1.** Having one or more right angles. **2.** Resembling a rectangle in shape. **— rec·tan′gu·lar′i·ty** (-lar′ə·tē) *n.* **— rec·tan′gu·lar·ly** *adv.*

rectangular coordinate system The Cartesian coordinate system (which see).

recti- *combining form* Straight: *rectilinear.* Also, before vowels, **rect-.** [< L *rectus* straight < *regere* to guide]

rec·ti·fi·er (rek′tə·fī′ər) *n.* **1.** One who or that which rectifies. **2.** *Electr.* A device, usually with two terminals, that conducts far more easily in one direction than in the other. **3.** A refiner or compounder of spirituous liquors.

rec·ti·fy (rek′tə·fī) *v.t.* **·fied, ·fy·ing** **1.** To make right; correct; amend. **2.** *Chem.* To refine, as a liquid, by repeated distillations until a desired degree of purity is obtained. **3.** *Electr.* To change (an alternating current) into a direct current. **4.** *Math.* To determine the length of (a curve or arc). **5.** To allow for errors or inaccuracies in, as a compass reading. **6.** To adjust for accurate calculations: to *rectify* a globe. **— Syn.** See AMEND. [< MF *rectifier* < LL *rectificare* < L *rectus* straight < *regere* to guide) + *facere* to make] **— rec′ti·fi·a·ble** *adj.* **— rec·ti·fi·ca·tion** (rek′tə·fə·kā′shən) *n.*

rec·ti·lin·e·ar (rek′tə·lin′ē·ər) *adj*. Pertaining to, consisting of, moving in, or bounded by a straight line or lines; straight. Also **rec′ti·lin′e·al** (-ē·əl). **— rec′ti·lin′e·ar·ly** *adv*.

rec·ti·tude (rek′tə·tood, -tyood) *n*. 1. Uprightness in principles and conduct. 2. Correctness, as of judgment. 3. *Obs*. Straightness. [< F < LL *rectitudo* < L *rectus* straight]

rec·to (rek′tō) *n*. *pl*. **·tos** A right-hand page, as of a book: opposed to *verso*. Abbr. *r* [< L *recto (folio)* on the right (page)]

recto- *combining form* Rectal; pertaining to the rectum. Also, before vowels, **rect-**. [See RECTUM.]

rec·tor (rek′tər) *n*. 1. In the Church of England, a priest who has full charge of a parish, and receives the parochial tithes. 2. In the Protestant Episcopal Church, a priest in charge of a parish. 3. In the Roman Catholic Church: **a** A priest in charge of a congregation or church, especially one not having parochial status. **b** The head of a seminary or religious house. 4. In certain universities, colleges, and schools, the head or chief officer. Abbr. *R.*, *rect*. [< L *regere* to guide, rule] **— rec′tor·ate** (-it) *n*. **— rec·to·ri·al** (rek·tôr′ē·əl, -tō′rē-) *adj*.

rec·to·ry (rek′tər·ē) *n*. *pl*. **·ries** 1. A rector's dwelling. 2. In England, a parish domain with its buildings, revenue, etc. Abbr. *rect*.

rec·tum (rek′təm) *n*. *pl*. **·ta** (-tə) *Anat*. The terminal portion of the large intestine, connecting the colon with the anus. [< NL *rectum* (*intestinum*) straight (intestine)]

rec·tus (rek′təs) *n*. *pl*. **·ti** (-tī) *Anat*. A straight muscle, as of the eye, the abdomen, etc. [< NL < L, straight]

re·cum·ben·cy (ri·kum′bən·sē) *n*. *pl*. **·cies** A recumbent position. Also **re·cum′bence**.

re·cum·bent (ri·kum′bənt) *adj*. 1. Lying down, wholly or partly; reclining; leaning. 2. *Biol*. Tending to rest upon or extend from a surface, as certain plant or animal organs. [< L *recumbens*, *-entis*, ppr. of *recumbere* < *re-* back + *-cumbere* < *cubare* to lie down] **— re·cum′bent·ly** *adv*.

re·cu·per·ate (ri·koo′pə·rāt, -kyoo′-) *v*. **·at·ed**, **·at·ing** *v.i*. 1. To regain health or strength. 2. To recover from loss, as of money. **— v.t.** 3. To obtain again after loss; recover. 4. To restore to vigor and health. **— Syn.** See RECOVER. [< L *recuperatus*, pp. of *recuperare* to get back < *re-* back + *capere* to take] **— re·cu′per·a′tion** *n*.

re·cu·per·a·tive (ri·koo′pə·rā′tiv, -pər·ə·tiv, -kyoo′-) *adj*. Tending, assisting, or pertaining to recovery; restorative. Also **re·cu′per·a·to′ry** (-pər·ə·tôr′ē, -tō′rē).

re·cu·per·a·tor (ri·koo′pə·rā′tər, -kyoo′-) *n*. 1. One who or that which recuperates. 2. *Mech*. A device, operated by springs or compressed air, for restoring a gun to firing position after the recoil. 3. *Chem*. An apparatus for the recovery of heat from hot gases.

re·cur (ri·kûr′) *v.i*. **·curred**, **·cur·ring** 1. To happen again or repeatedly, especially at regular intervals: a disease that *recurs*. 2. To come back or return; especially, to return to the mind or in recollection. 3. *Rare* To turn for aid; have recourse. [< L *recurrere* < *re-* back + *currere* to run]

re·cur·rence (ri·kûr′əns) *n*. The act or fact of recurring; recourse. Also **re·cur′ren·cy**.

re·cur·rent (ri·kûr′ənt) *adj*. 1. Happening or appearing again or repeatedly; recurring. 2. *Anat*. Running back: said of arteries and nerves. **— re·cur′rent·ly** *adv*.

recurrent fever Relapsing fever (which see).

recurring decimal A repeating decimal (which see).

re·cur·vant (ri·kûr′vənt) *adj*. *Heraldry* Coiled with the head raised to strike: said of a serpent.

re·cur·vate (ri·kûr′vit, -vāt) *adj*. Bent back. **— re·cur′va·ture** (-və·chər) *n*.

re·curve (ri·kûrv′) *v.t. & v.i*. **·curved**, **·curv·ing** To curve or bend back or down. [< L *recurvare* < *re-* back + *curvus* curved] **— re·cur·va·tion** (rē′kûr·vā′shən) *n*.

rec·u·sant (rek′yə·zənt, ri·kyoo′zənt) *adj*. 1. Persistently refusing to conform. 2. In English history, refusing to attend services of the Anglican Church. **— n.** One of a recusant character, position, or party; a noncomformist. [< L *recusans*, *-antis*, ppr. of *recusare*. See RECUSE.] **— rec·u·san·cy** (rek′yə·zən·sē, ri·kyoo′zən·sē) *n*.

re·cuse (ri·kyooz′) *v.t.* **·cused**, **·cus·ing** *Rare* In law, to object to, protest, or challenge (a judge, juror, etc.). [< F *recuser* < L *recusare* < *re-* against + *causa* cause, case]

re·cy·cle (rē′sī′kəl) *v.t.* **·cy·cled**, **·cy·cling** 1. To set or institute a different cycle in (a machine, process, etc.). 2. To reset or reinstitute a cycle in (a machine, process, etc.). 3. To reclaim materials such as paper, glass, and metals by salvage and reprocessing.

red[1] (red) *adj.* **red·der**, **red·dest** 1. Being of or having a bright color resembling that of blood; of the same hue as that color of the spectrum farthest from the violet. 2. Communistic. **— n.** 1. One of the primary colors, occurring at the opposite end of the spectrum from violet; the color of blood. 2. Any pigment or dye having or giving this color. 3. An ultraradical in political views, especially a communist.

4. A red object considered with reference to its color: the *red* (ball) in billiards. **— in the red** *Informal* Operating at a loss; owing money: from the practice of making entries in the debit column of an account book in red ink: distinguished from *in the black*. **— to see red** *Informal* To be very angry. [OE *rēad*. Cf. OHG *rōt*, ON *rauthr*, L *rufus*.] **— red′ly** *adv.* **— red′ness** *n.*

red[2] (red) See REDD.

Red (red) *n.* 1. A member of the Communist party of Russia. 2. A member of the Communist party of any country. 3. Any person who supports or approves of the aims of the Communist party. 4. An ultraradical; anarchist. [< RED[1]; from the color of their flags and banners]

re·dact (ri·dakt′) *v.t.* 1. To prepare, as for publication; edit; revise. 2. To draw up or frame, as a message or edict. [< L *redactus*, pp. of *redigere* to reduce to order < *re-* back + *agere* to drive] **— re·dac′tor** *n.*

re·dac·tion (ri·dak′shən) *n.* 1. The act of reducing or shaping, as literary matter, into proper form and condition for publication; editing. 2. Literary matter so edited or revised.

red algae Any of a class (*Rhodophyceae*) of algae of a red, brownish red, or purplish color.

re·dan (ri·dan′) *n.* A fortification with two parapets meeting at a salient angle. [< F < OF *redent* < *re-* back + *dent* tooth; from its appearance]

Red Army The army of the Soviet Union.

red-bait·ing (red′bā′ting) *n.* The practice of denouncing groups or individuals as communist or sympathetic to communism, often with little evidence. **— red′bait′er** *n.*

red·bay (red′bā′) *n.* A tree of the laurel family (*Persea borbonia*) of eastern North America, yielding a black fruit.

red·bird (red′bûrd′) *n.* 1. The cardinal (def. 2). 2. The scarlet tanager.

red-blood·ed (red′blud′id) *adj.* Having vitality and vigor.

red·breast (red′brest′) *n.* 1. A bird having a red breast, as the American or European robin. 2. A fresh-water sunfish (*Lepomis auritus*) of the eastern United States.

red·brick university (red′brik′) *Brit.* One of the urban universities, as distinct from Oxford and Cambridge.

red·bud (red′bud′) *n.* The Judas tree.

red·bug (red′bug′) *n.* A chigger.

red·cap (red′kap′) *n.* 1. *U.S.* A porter for carrying bags, as in a railroad station. 2. The European goldfinch. See under GOLDFINCH. 3. *Brit. Informal* A military policeman.

red cedar 1. An American juniper tree (genus *Juniperus*) of the cypress family, having a fine-grained, durable wood of a bright or dark red color resembling cedar; especially, the **eastern** (*J. virginiana*) and the **western** (*J. scopulorum*) **red cedar**. 2. A giant arborvitae (*Thuja plicata*) of the western United States, having a light, brittle but durable heartwood. 3. The wood of any of these trees.

red cent A United States copper one-cent piece. **— not worth a red cent** *U.S. Informal* Worthless.

Red Chamber The Senate chamber at Ottawa.

Red China *Informal* The People's Republic of China.

red·coat (red′kōt′) *n.* A British soldier of the period when a red coat was part of the uniform, especially during the American Revolution and the War of 1812.

Red Crescent In Turkey, an organization similar to the Red Cross and having a red crescent as its symbol.

red cross The cross of St. George, the emblem of England.

Red Cross An international organization for the care of the sick and wounded in war, formed in accordance with the international convention signed at Geneva in 1864, the members wearing a red Geneva cross as a badge of neutrality. These societies are now national organizations, as the **American Red Cross**, and continue their activities in times of peace, as in fighting disease, etc. Abbr *R.C.*

Red Cross Convention The Geneva Convention.

redd (red) *v.t. Dial.* 1. To put in order; make ready: usually with *up*. 2. To empty. 3. To adjust, as a quarrel. Also spelled *red*. [OE *rǣdan* to arrange; infl. by OE *hreddan* to free from] **— redd′er** *n.*

red deer 1. The common European and Asian stag (*Cervus elaphus*). 2. The white-tailed deer in its rufous summer coat.

red·den (red′n) *v.t.* 1. To make red. **— v.i.** 2. To grow red; flush; blush.

red·dish (red′ish) *adj.* Mixed with or somewhat red. **— red′dish·ly** *adv.* **— red′dish·ness** *n.*

red·dle (red′l) *n.* Red ocher or red chalk, used for marking sheep. **— v.t.** **·dled**, **·dling** To mark or stain with reddle. Also spelled *raddle*. [Var. of RUDDLE]

red·dle·man (red′l·mən) *n.* *pl.* **·men** (-mən) One who deals in reddle: also called *ruddleman*.

red-dog (red′dôg′, -dog′) *v.t.* **-dogged**, **-dog·ging** In football, to attack (the opposing quarterback) by rushing through the gap between two linemen: also *blitz*.

red drum A large drumfish (*Sciaenops ocellata*) of the Atlantic coast, esteemed as a food fish. Also **red drumfish**.

rede (rēd) *Scot.* or *Obs. v.t.* 1. To advise; counsel. 2. To explain; interpret. — *n.* **1.** Advice; counsel. **2.** A plan or scheme. **3.** A narrative; also, interpretation. [OE *rǣdan*]

re·dec·o·rate (ri-dek′ə-rāt) *v.t. & v.i.* **·rat·ed, ·rat·ing** To renovate or remodel, as an apartment. — **re′dec′o·ra′tion** *n.*

re·deem (ri-dēm′) *v.t.* **1.** To regain possession of by paying a price; especially, to recover, as mortgaged property. **2.** To pay off; receive back and satisfy, as a promissory note. **3.** To set free; rescue; ransom. **4.** *Theol.* To rescue from sin and its penalties. **5.** To fulfill, as an oath or promise. **6.** To make amends for; compensate for: The play was *redeemed* by its acting. [< MF *rédimer* < L *redimere* < *re-* back + *emere* to buy]

re·deem·a·ble (ri-dē′mə-bəl) *adj.* **1.** Capable of being redeemed. **2.** That is to be redeemed, as a bond, etc. Also **re·demp·ti·ble** (ri-demp′tə-bəl).

re·deem·er (ri-dē′mər) *n.* One who redeems. — **The Redeemer** Jesus Christ.

re·deem·ing (ri-dē′ming) *adj.* Compensating for faults, lacks, poor quality, etc.: the *redeeming* feature.

re·de·liv·er (rē′di-liv′ər) *v.t.* **1.** To deliver again, as a message or a speech. **2.** To give back; return; restore. — **re′·de·liv′er·ance, re′de·liv′er·y** *n.*

re·de·mand (rē′di-mand′, -mänd′) *v.t.* **1.** To demand again. **2.** To demand or ask the return of.

re·demp·tion (ri-demp′shən) *n.* **1.** The act of redeeming, or the state of being redeemed. **2.** The recovery of what is mortgaged or pledged. **3.** The payment of a debt or obligation; especially, the paying of the value of its notes, warrants, etc., by a government. **4.** *Theol.* Salvation from sin through the atonement of Christ. [< OF < L *redemptio, -onis* < *redimere* to redeem. Doublet of RANSOM.]

re·demp·tion·er (ri-demp′shən-ər) *n.* In Colonial days, an emigrant who redeemed himself by service in the new country in payment of passage money.

re·demp·tive (ri-demp′tiv) *adj.* Serving to redeem, or connected with redemption. Also **re·demp′to·ry** (-tər-ē). [< L *redemptus,* pp. of *redimere.* See REDEEM.]

Re·demp·tor·ist (ri-demp′tər-ist) *n.* A member of a religious order, the **Congregation of the Most Holy Redeemer,** founded in 1732 by St. Alphonsus de Liguori.

Red Ensign The Canadian flag, bearing both the Union Jack and the arms of Canada.

re·de·vel·op (rē′di-vel′əp) *v.t.* **1.** To develop again. **2.** *Photog.* To intensify with chemicals and put through a second developing process. — *v.i.* **3.** To develop again. Also **re′de·vel′ope.** — **re′de·vel′op·er** *n.* — **re′de·vel′op·ment** *n.*

red·eye (red′ī′) *n.* **1.** *U.S. Informal* The danger signal in a railroad semaphore system. **2.** *U.S. Slang* Inferior whisky. **3.** *Canadian Slang* Beer and tomato juice. **4.** The rudd.

red·fin (red′fin′) *n.* *pl.* **·fins** or **·fin** One of various cyprinoid fishes; especially, the common shiner (*Notropis cornutus*) of eastern North America.

red fir **1.** Any of various pinaceous trees, especially the **California red fir** (*Abies magnifica*), the largest of the genus. **2.** The wood of any of these trees. **3.** Douglas fir.

red fire A mixture of easily combustible ingredients, especially strontium salts, that burns with a red light, used in flares, pyrotechnic displays, etc.

red fox See under FOX.

red grouper See under GROUPER.

red grouse See under GROUSE¹.

red gum *Pathol.* Strophulus.

red-hand·ed (red′han′did) *adj.* **1.** Having just committed any crime. **2.** Caught in the act of doing some particular thing. — **red′-hand′ed·ly** *adv.* — **red′-hand′ed·ness** *n.*

red·head (red′hed′) *n.* **1.** A person with red hair. **2.** An American duck (*Aythya americana*), similar to the European pochard and sometimes mistaken for the canvasback.

red·head·ed woodpecker (red′hed′id) See under WOODPECKER.

red heat **1.** The state of being red-hot. **2.** The temperature at which a metal is red-hot.

red herring **1.** Herring dried and smoked to a reddish color. **2.** A diverting of attention from the main subject by introducing some irrelevant topic: from the use of a red herring in training hunting dogs to follow a scent.

red hind A serranoid fish (*Epinephelus guttatus*) of the West Indies and southward.

red-hot (red′hot′) *adj.* **1.** Heated to redness. **2.** New, as if just from the fire: *red-hot* news. **3.** Heated; excited: *red-hot* argument. **4.** Extreme.

red Indian A North American Indian.

red·in·gote (red′ing-gōt) *n.* An outer coat with long full skirts. [< F *rédingote,* alter. of E *riding coat*]

red·in·te·grate (red·in′tə-grāt) *v.t.* **·grat·ed, ·grat·ing** To restore to a perfect state; make complete; renew. — *adj.* Restored; renewed. [< L *redintegratus,* pp. of *redintegrare* < *red-* again + *integrare.* See INTEGRATE.]

red·in·te·gra·tion (red·in′tə-grā′shən) *n.* **1.** The act or process of restoration to a whole or sound state. **2.** *Psychol.* The tendency to complete the whole of a complex mental state, upon the renewal of any part of it.

re·di·rect¹ (rē′di-rekt′) *v.t.* To direct again or anew: to *redirect* a letter. — **re′di·rec′tion** *n.*

re·di·rect² (rē′di-rekt′) *adj. Law* Designating the examination of a witness, after cross-examination, by the party who first examined him.

re·dis·count (rē-dis′kount) *n.* **1.** A second (or any subsequent) discount on a sum. **2.** *Usually pl.* Commercial paper that has been rediscounted. — *v.t.* To discount again.

re·dis·trict (rē-dis′trikt) *v.t.* To district again; especially, to redraw the boundaries of the election districts of.

red·i·vi·vus (red′ə-vī′vəs) *adj.* Come or brought into existence again; revived; restored. [< LL < *redivivus* renewed]

Red·lands (red′ləndz) A city in SW California, near San Bernardino; pop. 36,355.

red lead (led) Minium.

red lead ore Crocoite.

red-letter day (red′let′ər) A memorable occasion: from the use on calendars of red letters to indicate holidays.

red light A red traffic or signal light meaning "stop."

red-light district (red′līt′) A part of a city or town in which brothels, often marked by a red light, are numerous.

red lobelia The cardinal flower.

red man An American Indian.

red maple A maple (*Acer rubrum*) of North America, widely used as a shade tree in parks, etc.: also called *swamp maple.*

Red·mond (red′mənd), **John Edward,** 1851–1918, Irish statesman.

red mullet A goatfish.

red·neck (red′nek′) *n.* In the rural South, a poor, uneducated person, especially one having violently anti-Negro sentiments. Also **red-neck.**

red oak **1.** Any of several oaks having a dense, cross-grained wood, as the **northern red oak** (*Quercus borealis*). **2.** The wood of any of these oaks.

red ocher A variety of ocher containing a large proportion of iron oxide.

red·o·lent (red′ə-lənt) *adj.* Full of or diffusing a pleasant fragrance; odorous. [< OF < L *redolens, -entis,* ppr. of *redolere* to emit a smell < *red-* thoroughly + *olere* to smell] — **red′o·lence, red′o·len·cy** *n.* — **red′o·lent·ly** *adv.*

Re·don (rə-dôn′), **Odilon,** 1840–1916, French painter.

Re·don·da (rə-don′də) See ANTIGUA.

Re·don·do Beach (rē′don′dō) A resort city in SW California, near Los Angeles; pop. 56,075.

red osier **1.** A willow (*Salix purpurea*) whose red-tinted twigs are used in making baskets: also called *purple osier.* **2.** The red-brier dogwood: see under DOGWOOD.

re·dou·ble (rē-dub′əl) *v.t. & v.i.* **·led, ·ling** **1.** To make or become double. **2.** To increase greatly. **3.** To echo or re-echo. **4.** To fold or turn back. **5.** In bridge, to double (an opponent's double). — *n.* In bridge, the doubling of an opponent's double.

re·doubt (ri-dout′) *n.* **1.** An enclosed fortification, especially a temporary one of any form. **2.** An earthwork or simple fortification placed within the main rampart line of a permanent fortification. [< F *redoute* < Ital. *ridotto* < Med.L < L *reductus* secret place, pp. of *reducere.* See REDUCE.]

re·doubt·a·ble (ri-dou′tə-bəl) *adj.* **1.** Inspiring fear; formidable. **2.** Deserving respect or deference. Also **re·doubt′ed** (-dou′tid). [< F *redoutable* < *redouter* to fear, dread, ult. < L *re-* thoroughly + *dubitare* to doubt] — **re·doubt′a·ble·ness** *n.* — **re·doubt′a·bly** *adv.*

re·dound (ri-dound′) *v.i.* **1.** To have an effect, as by reaction, to the credit, discredit, advantage, etc., of the original agent; return; react; accrue. **2.** *Obs.* To surge or flow back. **3.** *Obs.* To overflow. — *n.* A return by way of consequence; result; requital. [< F *redonder* < L *redundare* to overflow < *red-* back + *undare* to surge < *unda* wave]

re·do·wa (red′ə-wə, -və) *n.* Either of two Bohemian dances, one in ¾ time, resembling a mazurka, the other in ¾ time, like a polka. [< F < Czechoslovakian *rejdovati* to turn]

red pepper A species of capsicum (*Capsicum frutescens*), cultivated in many varieties and used as a condiment: also called *cayenne pepper.*

red·poll (red′pōl′) *n.* Any of various small finches (genus *Acanthis*) of northern regions, having a reddish crown.

Red Poll One of an English breed of hornless, reddish dairy cattle. Also **Red Polled.**

re·draft (*n.* rē′draft′, -dräft′; *v.* rē-draft′, -dräft′) *n.* **1.** A second draft or copy. **2.** A bill of exchange drawn by the holder of a protested bill on the drawer or endorsers for the reimbursement of the amount of the original bill with costs and charges. — *v.t. & v.i.* To make a redraft (of).

re·dress (ri-dres′; *for n.,* also rē′dres) *v.t.* **1.** To set right, as a wrong, by compensation or by punishment of the wrongdoer; make reparation for. **2.** To make reparation to; compensate. **3.** To remedy; correct. **4.** To adjust, as balances. — *n.* **1.** Satisfaction for wrong done; reparation; amends. **2.** A restoration; reformation; correction. [< F *redresser* to straighten < *re-* again (< L) + *dresser.* See DRESS.] — **re·dress′er** or **re·dres′sor** *n.*

re-dress (rē-dres′) *v.t. & v.i.* To dress again.

Red River **1.** A river in Texas, Arkansas, and Louisiana, flowing 1,018 miles east to the Mississippi. **2.** A river in the United States and Canada, flowing about 540 miles north from NW Minnesota through Manitoba to Lake Winnipeg: also **Red River of the North. 3.** The longest river of North Vietnam, flowing about 730 miles SE from Yünnan Province, China, to the Gulf of Tonkin: Annamese *Song Coi*.

Red River cart *Canadian* A stout two-wheeled horse- or ox-drawn cart used in the settlement of the West.

red·root (red′rōōt′, -rŏŏt′) *n.* **1.** An herb (*Lachnanthes tinctoria*) with sword-shaped, fleshy leaves and fibrous red root, found in swamps along the Atlantic coast of the United States. **2.** The tormentil. **3.** An American amaranth (*Amaranthus retroflexus*) bearing green flowers: also called *pigweed*.

red salmon The sockeye.

Red Sea A sea between Egypt and Arabia; 1,450 mi. long; about 170,000 sq. mi.

red·shank (red′shangk′) *n.* **1.** A Scottish Highlander: so called in allusion to the kilt. **2.** A common Old World shore bird (*Totanus totanus*): also called *tattler*.

red shift *Astron.* An optical Doppler effect involving the displacement of characteristic spectrum lines in the light from a celestial body toward red, caused by an increase in the light wavelengths as the body recedes at high velocity.

red·skin (red′skin′) *n.* A North American Indian.

red snapper The pargo, a fish.

red squirrel See under SQUIRREL.

red·start (red′stärt′) *n.* **1.** A small singing bird (genus *Phoenicura*) allied to the warblers; especially, the common European redstart (*P. phoenicura*), dark gray, with a black throat, white forehead, and rust-red breast, sides, and tail: also called *brantail*. **2.** A small fly-catching warbler (*Setophaga ruticella*) of eastern North America, with bright orange-red patches against black and white. [< RED¹ + START²]

red stick 1. A stick painted red as a war symbol of the Indian chief, Tecumseh. **2.** An Indian who carried one of Tecumseh's red sticks. **3.** Formerly, any Indian hostile to the United States.

red-tailed buzzard (red′tāld′) See under BUZZARD.

red tape Rigid official procedure involving delay or inaction: from the tying of public documents with red tape.

red tide A reddish coloration of the sea due to the presence of great numbers of red protozoan flagellates.

red·top (red′tŏp′) *n.* A species of bent grass (*Agrostis alba*): also called *herd's-grass*. [from its reddish panicle]

re·duce (ri·dōōs′, -dyōōs′) *v.* **·duced, ·duc·ing** *v.t.* **1.** To make less in size, amount, number, intensity, etc.; diminish. **2.** To bring from a higher to a lower condition; lower; degrade. **3.** To bring to submission; subdue; conquer. **4.** To bring to a specified condition or state: with *to*: to *reduce* rock to powder; to *reduce* a person to desperation. **5.** To thin (paint, etc.) with oil or turpentine. **6.** *Math.* To change (an expression) to a more elementary form. **7.** *Surg.* To restore (displaced parts) to normal position. **8.** *Chem.* **a** To decrease the valence of (an atom or group of atoms) by adding electrons. **b** To remove oxygen from (a compound): opposed to *oxidize*. **c** To extract (a metal) from a combined state, as in an ore. **9.** *Photog.* To diminish the density of (a photographic negative). **10.** *Biol.* To effect or cause to undergo meiosis. — *v.i.* **11.** To become less in any way. **12.** To decrease one's weight, as by dieting. — **Syn.** See DECREASE. [< L *reducere* < *re-* back + *ducere* to lead] — **re·duc′i·bil′i·ty** *n.* — **re·duc′i·ble** *adj.* — **re·duc′i·bly** *adv.*

re·duc·er (ri·dōō′sər, -dyōō′-) *n.* **1.** One who or that which reduces. **2.** *Photog.* A chemical solution for reducing.

reducing agent *Chem.* A substance that effects reduction, while increasing its valence and becoming oxidized.

reducing glass A concave lens that gives a reduced image.

reducing valve *Mech.* An automatic valve for maintaining uniform reduced pressure of a fluid, as steam or gas.

re·duc·tase (ri·duk′tās) *n.* *Biochem.* Any of a class of enzymes that promote the reduction of compounds to simpler forms. [< REDUCT(ION) + -ASE]

re·duc·ti·o ad ab·sur·dum (ri·duk′shē·ō ad ab·sûr′dəm) *Latin* Reduction to an absurdity; disposal of a proposition by showing that its logical conclusion is absurd.

re·duc·tion (ri·duk′shən) *n.* **1.** The act or process of reducing, or its results. **2.** *Biol.* The halving of the total number of chromosomes during meiotic cell division. **3.** *Chem.* **a** The process of depriving a compound of oxygen. **b** The process by which atoms gain valence electrons or cease to share them with a more electronegative element; a decrease in positive valence. **4.** *Math.* **a** Any formula by which trigonometric functions of angles greater than 90° can be reduced to functions of angles less than 90°. **b** The process of expressing a fraction in decimal terms. — **re·duc′tion·al** *adj.* — **re·duc′tive** (-tiv) *adj.*

re·dun·dance (ri·dun′dəns) *n.* **1.** The condition or quality of being redundant. **2.** That which is redundant. **3.** Excess; surplus.

re·dun·dan·cy (ri·dun′dən·sē) *n.* *pl.* **·cies 1.** Redundance. **2.** In information theory, the extent to which a signal repeats the same message, reducing the probability of error and reducing the effective capacity of the channel.

re·dun·dant (ri·dun′dənt) *adj.* **1.** Being more than is required; constituting an excess. **2.** Unnecessarily verbose; tautological. [< L *redundans, -antis*, ppr. of *redundare*. See REDOUND.] — **re·dun′dant·ly** *adv.*

re·dupl. Reduplicated; reduplication.

re·du·pli·cate (*v.* ri·dōō′plə·kāt, -dyōō′-; *adj.* ri·dōō′plə·kit, -dyōō′-) *v.* **·cat·ed, ·cat·ing** *v.t.* **1.** To repeat again and again; redouble; iterate. **2.** *Ling.* To affix a reduplication to. — *v.i.* **3.** To undergo reduplication. — *adj.* **1.** Repeated again and again; duplicated; doubled. **2.** *Bot.* Valvate with the margins reflexed. [< L *reduplicatus*, pp. of *reduplicare* < *re-* again + *duplicare*. See DUPLICATE.]

re·du·pli·ca·tion (ri·dōō′plə·kā′shən, -dyōō′-) *n.* **1.** The act of reduplicating, or the state of being reduplicated; a redoubling. **2.** A rhetorical figure in which the ending of a sentence, line, or clause is repeated and emphasized at the beginning of the next. **3.** *Ling.* **a** The repetition of an initial element or elements in a word. In the verbs of some Indo-European languages, repetition of some part of the root, usually with vowel modification, serves as a mark of the perfect, as in Greek *bebeka* I have walked, Latin *dedidi* I have given. **b** The doubling of all or part of a word, often with vowel or consonant change, as in *fiddle-faddle*, *razzle-dazzle*. **c** The sound or syllable thus repeated.

re·du·pli·ca·tive (ri·dōō′plə·kā′tiv, -dyōō′-) *adj.* **1.** Tending to reduplicate. **2.** Of or formed by reduplication. **3.** *Bot.* Reduplicate.

red·vein maple (red′vān′) The flowering maple (which see).

red·ware (red′wâr′) *n.* A large brown seaweed (*Laminaria digitata*) of the New England coast, sometimes used for food.

red·wing (red′wing′) *n.* **1.** An American blackbird (*Agelaius phoeniceus*) with bright scarlet patches on the wings of the male. Also **red-/winged/ blackbird** (-wingd′). **2.** An Old World red-winged thrush (*Turdus musicus*), bright reddish orange on the sides and the underwing coverts.

red·wood (red′wŏŏd′) *n.* **1.** A sequoia (def. 1). **2.** Its durable reddish wood. **3.** Any of various other trees having a reddish wood, or the wood itself, yielding a red dye.

Redwood City A city in western California; pop. 55,686.

red-yel·low (red′yel′ō) *n.* Orange.

re·ech·o (ri·ek′ō) *v.t.* **1.** To echo back, as a sound. **2.** To echo again; repeat, as an opinion. — *v.i.* **3.** To echo again; reverberate. — *n.* That which is reechoed.

reed (rēd) *n.* **1.** The slender, frequently jointed stem of certain tall grasses growing in wet places, or the grasses themselves. **2.** A thin, elastic plate of reed, wood, or metal nearly closing an opening, as in a pipe, used in reed organs, reed pipes, oboes, clarinets, etc., to produce a musical tone. **3.** A musical pipe made of the hollow stem of a plant; a shepherd's pipe. **4.** *Archit.* A semicylindrical ornamental molding or bead. **5.** The part of a loom that drives the filling against the woven fabric, consisting of two horizontal parallel bars near together and connected by numerous thin parallel slips. **6.** An arrow. **7.** An ancient Hebrew measure of length; six cubits. **8.** The abomasum. — *v.t.* **1.** To fashion into or decorate with reeds. **2.** To thatch with reeds. [OE *hrēod*]

Reed (rēd), **John,** 1887–1920, U.S. radical journalist and poet. — **Walter,** 1851–1902, U.S. army surgeon; proved the transmission of yellow fever by mosquitoes.

reed·bird (rēd′bûrd′) *n.* *Southern U.S.* The bobolink.

reed·buck (rēd′buk′) *n.* An antelope (*Redunca arundineum*) of southern Africa that frequents reedy places: also called *reitbok*.

reed bunting A European black-headed bunting (*Emberiza schoeniclus*), having a white collar, found in marshes.

reed·ing (rē′ding) *n.* **1.** Beading or semicylindrical moldings collectively. **2.** Ornamentation by such moldings. **3.** A molding of this kind. Compare FLUTING. **4.** The knurling on the edge of a coin, as distinguished from milling.

reed·ling (rēd′ling) *n.* The European bearded titmouse (*Panurus biarmicus*), common in reedy places. The male has a black tuft of feathers on each side of the chin.

reed-mace (rēd′mās′) *n.* The cattail. Also **reed mace.**

reed organ A keyboard musical instrument sounding by means of free reeds vibrated by air currents.

reed pipe An organ pipe having a reed whose vibrations set in motion the air column. Compare FLUE PIPE.

reed stop An organ stop controlling a set of reed pipes.

re·ed·u·cate (rē·ej′ŏŏ·kāt) *v.t.* **·cat·ed, ·cat·ing 1.** To educate again. **2.** To rehabilitate, as a criminal, by education. — **re′-ed·u·ca′tion** *n.*

reed warbler A small warbler (*Acrocephalus scirpaceus*) found in marshy places in most parts of the Old World.

reed·y (rē′dē) *adj.* **reed·i·er, reed·i·est 1.** Full of reeds. **2.** Like a reed. **3.** Having a thin, sharp tone, like a reed instrument. — **reed′i·ness** *n.*

reef¹ (rēf) *n.* **1.** A ridge of sand or rocks, or especially of coral, at or near the surface of the water. **2.** A lode, vein, or ledge. Compare SHOAL¹. — **Syn.** See BANK¹. [< ON *rif* reef] — **reef′y** *adj.*

reef² (rēf) *Naut.* *n.* **1.** The part of a sail that is folded and secured or untied and let out in regulating its size on the mast. **2.** The tuck taken in a sail when reefed. — *v.t.* **1.** To reduce (a sail) by folding a part and fastening it to a yard or boom. **2.** To shorten or lower, as a topmast by taking part of it in. [< ON *rif* rib]

reef band *Naut.* A strip of canvas used to give strength to sails along the lines where the reef points are attached.

reef·er¹ (rē'fər) *n.* **1.** One who reefs. **2.** A close-fitting, often double-breasted coat or jacket of heavy material.

reef·er² (rē'fər) *n.* *U.S. Slang* A marijuana cigarette. [? from its resemblance to the reef of a sail]

reef knot A square knot (which see).

reef point *Naut.* One of a series of short lines attached by their centers to the eyelets of a reef band, and used to fasten the sail in reefing.

reek (rēk) *v.i.* **1.** To give off smoke, vapor, etc. **2.** To give off a strong, offensive smell. **3.** To be pervaded with anything offensive. — *v.t.* **4.** To expose to smoke or its action. **5.** To give off or emit (fumes, an odor, etc.). — *n.* **1.** A strong or offensive odor. **2.** *Chiefly Scot.* Smoke; vapor. [OE *rēocan* to smoke] — **reek'er** *n.*

reek·y (rēk'ē) *adj.* **reek·i·er, reek·i·est** Emitting or full of fumes or effensive odor.

reel¹ (rēl) *n.* **1.** A rotary device or frame for winding rope, film, or other flexible substance. **2.** Motion picture film wound on one reel, used as a unit of length. **3.** A wooden spool for wire, thread, etc. **4.** Material, as thread, paper, etc., wound on a reel. — *v.t.* **1.** To wind on a reel or bobbin, as a line. **2.** To pull by reeling a line: with *in:* to *reel* a fish in. **3.** To say, do, etc., easily and fluently: with *off.* [OE *hrēol*] — **reel'a·ble** *adj.* — **reel'er** *n.*

reel² (rēl) *v.i.* **1.** To stagger, sway, or lurch, as when giddy or drunk. **2.** To whirl round and round. **3.** To have a sensation of giddiness or whirling: My head *reels.* **4.** To waver or fall back, as attacking troops. — *v.t.* **5.** To cause to reel. — *n.* A staggering motion; giddiness. [< REEL¹] — **reel'er** *n.*

reel³ (rēl) *n.* A lively dance, chiefly Scottish or Irish; also, the music for this dance. [? < REEL¹]

re·en·force (rē'en·fôrs', -fōrs'), **re·en·force·ment** (rē'en·fôrs'mənt), etc. See REINFORCE, etc.

re·en·ter (rē·en'tər) *v.i.* **1.** To enter or come in again. — *v.t.* **2.** To record again, as on a list. — **re·en'trance** (-trans) *n.*

re·en·ter·ing (rē·en'tər·ing) *adj.* **1.** Entering again. **2.** Extending inward, as an angle.

reentering angle An angle that is turned inward, as in a figure or structure.

re·en·trant (rē·en'trant) *adj.* Reentering; extending inward. — *n.* **1.** One who or that which reenters. **2.** A reentering angle, as in a fortification wall.

re·en·try (rē·en'trē) *n.* *pl.* **·tries 1.** The act of entering again. **2.** *Law* The act of resuming possession of lands or tenements. **3.** In whist and bridge, an entry. **4.** *Aerospace* The return of a rocket or other object to the atmosphere of the earth after travel to very high altitudes.

reest¹ (rēst) *v.t. & v.i. Scot. & Brit. Dial.* To check; balk. [Var. of REST¹ or aphetic var. of ARREST]

reest² (rēst) *v.t. & v.i. Scot.* To dry or cure (meat, fish, etc.) by smoking.

re·e·val·u·ate (rē'i·val'yōō·āt) *v.t.* **·at·ed, ·at·ing** To evaluate or consider anew. — **re'e·val'u·a'tion** *n.*

reeve¹ (rēv) *v.t.* **reeved** or **rove, reev·ing** *Naut.* **1.** To pass, as a rope or rod, through a hole, block, or aperture. **2.** To fasten in such manner. **3.** To pass a rope, etc., through (a block or pulley). [Origin uncertain]

reeve² (rēv) *n.* **1.** In Canada, the elected head of a rural municipal council. **2.** In medieval England: **a** A high administrative officer formerly holding authority over landed areas. **b** A bailiff; overseer; steward. [OE *gerēfa*]

reeve³ (rēv) *n.* The female of the ruff, a sandpiper.

re·ex·am·ine (rē'ig·zam'in) *v.t.* **1.** To examine again. **2.** To go over again; review. **3.** *Law* To question (a witness) again after a cross-examination. — **re'ex·am'i·na'tion** *n.*

re·ex·port (*v.* rē'iks·pôrt', -pōrt', ri·eks'pôrt, -pōrt; *n.* ri·eks'pôrt, -pōrt) *v.t.* To export again. — *n.* **1.** The act of exporting again. **2.** That which is reexported. — **re'ex·por·ta'tion** *n.*

ref. 1. Referee. **2.** Reference. **3.** Referred. **4.** Reformation; reformed. **5.** Refunding.

Ref. Ch. Reformed Church.

re·fect (ri·fekt') *v.t. Obs.* To refresh with food or drink.

re·fec·tion (ri·fek'shən) *n.* **1.** Refreshment with food and drink. **2.** A light meal. **3.** *Med.* Spontaneous recovery from symptoms of vitamin deficiency. [< OF < L *refectio, -onis* < *reficere,* pp. of *reficere* < *re-* again + *facere* to make]

re·fec·to·ry (ri·fek'tər·ē) *n.* *pl.* **·ries** A room or hall for eating, especially in a religious house or college. [< Med.L *refectorium* < L *refectus.* See REFECTION.]

re·fer (ri·fûr') *v.* **·ferred, ·fer·ring** *v.t.* **1.** To direct or send for information, assistance, etc. **2.** To hand over or submit for consideration, settlement, etc. **3.** To assign or attribute to a source, cause, class, period, etc. — *v.i.* **4.** To make

reference; allude. **5.** To turn, as for information, help, or authority: to *refer* to the dictionary. — **Syn.** See ATTRIBUTE. [< OF *referer* < L *referre* < *re-* back + *ferre* to carry] — **ref·er·a·ble** (ref'ər·ə·bəl), **re·fer'ra·ble** or **re·fer'ri·ble** *adj.* — **re·fer'ral** *n.* — **re·fer'rer** *n.*

ref·er·ee (ref'ə·rē') *n.* **1.** A person to whom something is referred, especially for settlement or arbitration. **2.** In certain sports, as football, a supervisory official. **3.** *Law* A person to whom a case is sent by order of court for investigation and report; an arbitrator. Abbr. *ref.* — **Syn.** See JUDGE. — *v.t. & v.i.* **·reed, ·ree·ing** To judge as a referee.

ref·er·ence (ref'ər·əns, ref'rəns) *n.* **1.** The act of referring. **2.** An incidental allusion or direction of the attention: *reference* to a recent event. **3.** A note or other indication in a book, referring to some other book or passage. Compare CROSS-REFERENCE. **4.** One who or that which is or may be referred to. **5.** The state of being referred or related: used in the phrases **with** (or **in**) **reference to. 6.** *Law* The act or process of submitting a matter to a referee; also, the proceedings of and before a referee. **7.** The person or persons to whom one seeking employment may refer for recommendation; also, a written statement or testimonial, as of character or dependability. Abbr. *ref.* — **ref'er·enc·er** *n.*

reference mark Any mark or symbol used in printing or writing to indicate a reference, as *, †, ‡, §, ¶, ‖, #.

ref·er·en·dum (ref'ə·ren'dəm) *n.* *pl.* **·dums** or **·da** (-də) **1.** The submission of a proposed public measure or law that has been passed upon by a legislature or convention to a vote of the people for ratification or rejection. **2.** The vote in such a procedure. Compare INITIATIVE. [< L, gerund of *referre.* See REFER.]

ref·er·ent (ref'ər·ent) *n.* The object, concept, etc., to which reference is made in a statement or its symbolic equivalent. [< L *referens, -entis,* ppr. of *referre.* See REFER.]

re·fill (*v.* rē·fil'; *n.* rē'fil') *v.t.* To fill again. — *n.* Any commodity packaged to fit and fill a container originally containing that commodity: a *refill* for a lipstick case.

re·fine (ri·fīn') *v.* **·fined, ·fin·ing** *v.t.* **1.** To make fine or pure; free from impurities or extraneous matter. **2.** To make polished or cultured. **3.** To improve or change by subtle or precise alterations. — *v.i.* **4.** To become fine or pure. **5.** To become more polished or cultured. **6.** To make fine distinctions; use subtlety in thought or speech. [< RE- + FINE¹, *v.*] — **re·fin'er** *n.*

re·fined (ri·fīnd') *adj.* **1.** Characterized by refinement; cultivated; polished. **2.** Free from impurity; purified. **3.** Exceedingly precise or exact; subtle.

re·fine·ment (ri·fīn'mənt) *n.* **1.** Fineness of thought, taste, language, etc.; freedom from coarseness or vulgarity; delicacy; culture. **2.** The act, effect, or process of refining; purification. **3.** A nice distinction; subtlety. **4.** Fastidiousness.

— **Syn. 1.** *Refinement, cultivation, culture,* and *breeding* denote a quality we attribute to persons regarded as superior in intellect, sensitivity, taste, or manners. *Refinement* is perhaps the strongest word, implying not only the elimination of vulgarity and grossness but also the development of delicate perception and understanding. *Cultivation* is the self-discipline, study, and exercise that bring urbanity, learning, esthetic taste, etc. *Culture* primarily contrasts the enlightenment of the civilized man with that of a savage or a child; *breeding* suggests the training that manifests itself in good manners, tact, and consideration for others. — **Ant.** coarseness, grossness, vulgarity.

re·fin·er·y (ri·fī'nər·ē) *n.* *pl.* **·er·ies** A place where some crude material, as sugar or petroleum, is purified.

re·fit (rē·fit') *v.t. & v.i.* **·fit·ted, ·fit·ting** To make or be made fit or ready again, as by making repairs, replacing equipment, etc. — *n.* The repair of damages or wear, especially of a ship.

refl. 1. Reflection. **2.** Reflective(ly). **3.** Reflex. **4.** Reflexive.

re·flate (rē·flāt') *v.t.* **·flat·ed, ·flat·ing** To inflate again. [< RE- + (IN)FLATE]

re·flect (ri·flekt') *v.t.* **1.** To turn or throw back, as waves of light, heat, or sound. **2.** To give back an image of; mirror. **3.** To cause as a result of one's actions, character, etc.; cast: He *reflects* credit on his teacher. **4.** To manifest as a result of influence, imitation, etc.: to *reflect* another's opinions. **5.** *Obs.* To bend or fold back. — *v.i.* **6.** To send back rays, as of light or heat. **7.** To shine back. **8.** To give back an image; be mirrored. **9.** To think carefully; ponder. **10.** To bring blame, discredit, etc.: with *on* or *upon.* **11.** *Anat.* To fold back upon itself, as a membrane or tissue. — **Syn.** See DELIBERATE. [< OF *reflecter* < L *reflectere* < *re-* back + *flectere* to bend]

re·flec·tance (ri·flek'təns) *n.* *Physics* The ratio of the radiant or luminous flux reflected from a given surface to the total light falling upon it: also called *reflectivity.*

re·flect·ing telescope (ri·flek'ting) See under TELESCOPE.

re·flec·tion (ri·flek'shən) *n.* **1.** The act of reflecting, or the state of being reflected. **2.** *Physics* The throwing off or back from a surface of impinging light, heat, sound, or any form of radiant energy. **3.** The result of reflecting; reflected rays or an image thrown by reflection. **4.** Meditation; careful consideration; thought. **5.** An imputation of blame or censure.

6. *Anat.* The folding of a part upon itself. Also **re·flex′ion.** Abbr. *refl.* — **re·flec′tion·al** or **re·flex′ion·al** *adj.*
— **Syn. 4.** rumination, reverie, thought. **5.** aspersion, animadversion.

re·flec·tive (ri-flek′tiv) *adj.* **1.** Given to reflection or thought. **2.** Of, pertaining to, or caused by reflection. **3.** Having the quality of throwing back light, heat, sound, etc. Abbr. *refl.* — **re·flec′tive·ly** *adv.* — **re·flec′tive·ness** *n.*

re·flec·tiv·i·ty (rē′flek·tiv′ə·tē) *n. pl.* **·ties 1.** The state or quality of being reflective. **2.** *Physics* Reflectance.

re·flec·tor (ri-flek′tər) *n.* **1.** That which reflects. **2.** A polished surface for reflecting light, heat, sound, etc. **3.** A telescope that transmits an image from a reflecting surface to the eyepiece. **4.** *Physics* A substance placed around the core of a nuclear reactor for the purpose of reducing neutron leakage and maintaining the level of the chain reaction: sometimes called *tamper.* **5.** *Telecom.* Any surface or object that reflects or redirects radio-frequency energy, especially in a directional antenna assembly.

re·flet (rə-fle′) *n.* Iridescence of surface, especially on pottery. [< F, reflection]

re·flex (*adj. & n.* rē′fleks; *v.* ri·fleks′) *adj.* **1.** *Physiol.* Of, pertaining to, or produced by involuntary response to a stimulus. **2.** Turned, thrown, or directed backward or in the opposite direction. **3.** Bent back; reflexed. **4.** *Telecom.* Designating a radio receiving circuit in which a single electron tube serves for the simultaneous amplification of two different frequencies. — *n.* **1.** *Physiol.* An involuntary movement or response to a stimulus, as in winking, sneezing, shivering, etc.: also **reflex action.** **2.** Reflection, or an image produced by reflection, as from a mirror or like surface. **3.** Light reflected from an illuminated surface to a shady one. — *v.t.* To bend back; turn back or reflect. Abbr. *refl.* [< L *reflexus* reflected, pp. of *reflectere.* See REFLECT.]

reflex angle *Geom.* An angle greater than a straight angle.

reflex arc *Physiol.* The entire path of a nerve impulse from the point of origin in the receptors to the nerve center, and thence outwards to the effectors.

reflex camera A camera in which a mirror reflects the lens image into a viewer for focusing by means of a device coupled to the lens.

re·flex·ive (ri-flek′siv) *adj.* **1.** *Gram.* **a** Of verbs, having an object that is identical with the subject, as "dresses" in the sentence "He dresses himself." **b** Of pronouns in the objective case, being identical with the subject, as "herself" in the sentence "She hurt herself." **2.** Of or pertaining to a reflex or reflection. — *n. Gram.* A reflexive verb or pronoun. Abbr. *refl.* — **re·flex′ive·ly** *adv.* — **re·flex′ive·ness, re·flex·iv·i·ty** (rē′flek·siv′ə·tē) *n.*

ref·lu·ent (ref′lōō-ənt) *adj.* Flowing back; ebbing, as the tide. [< L *refluens, -entis,* ppr. of *refluere* to flow back < *re-* back + *fluere* to flow] — **ref′lu·ence** *n.*

re·flux (rē′fluks′) *n.* A flowing back; ebb: the flux and *reflux* of fortune. [< L *refluxus,* pp. of *refluere.* See REFLUENT.]

re·for·est (rē-fôr′ist, -for′-) *v.t. & v.i.* To replant (an area) with trees. — **re′for·es·ta′tion** *n.*

re·form (ri-fôrm′) *v.t.* **1.** To make better by removing abuses, altering, etc.; restore to a better condition. **2.** To improve morally; persuade or educate to a better life. **3.** To put an end to; stop (an abuse, malpractice, etc.). — *v.i.* **4.** To give up sin or error; become better. — *n.* **1.** An act or result of reformation; change for the better, especially in administration; correction of evils or abuses. **2.** Improvement in one's personal life, especially by abandonment of bad habits. [< OF *reformer* < L *reformare* < *re-* again + *formare* to form] — **re·form′a·tive** *adj.* — **re·form′er, re·form′ist** *n.*
— **Syn.** (verb) **1.** improve, reclaim. Compare AMEND.

re-form (rē′fôrm′) *v.t. & v.i.* To form again [< RE- + FORM] — **re′-for·ma′tion** *n.*

ref·or·ma·tion (ref′ər-mā′shən) *n.* The act of reforming, or the state of being reformed; especially, moral improvement. Abbr. *ref.*

Ref·or·ma·tion (ref′ər-mā′shən) *n.* The religious revolution of the 16th century in Europe that began as a movement to reform Catholicism and ended with the establishment of Protestantism.

re·form·a·to·ry (ri-fôr′mə·tôr′ē, -tō′rē) — *n. pl.* **·ries** An institution for the reformation of juvenile offenders. Also **reform school.** — *adj.* Tending or aiming to reform.

Reform Bill The bill passed by the British Parliament in 1832 for the correction and extension of the suffrage.

re·formed (ri-fôrmd′) *adj.* **1.** Restored to a better state. **2.** Improved in conduct, habits, etc. Abbr. *ref.*

Re·formed (ri-fôrmd′) *adj.* **1.** Designating the Protestant churches following the teachings of Calvin and Zwingli, that separated from the Lutherans in the 16th century. **2.** Of or pertaining to Reform Judaism.

Reform Judaism The branch of Judaism that does not accept in entirety the Mosaic Laws, the Talmud, and rabbinical interpretations as binding in the changed conditions

of today and placesm ore stress on traditional religious and moral values than on ceremonial and ritual details.

re·fract (ri-frakt′) *v.t.* **1.** To deflect (a ray) by refraction. **2.** *Optics* To determine the degree of refraction of (an eye or lens). [< L *refractus,* pp. of *refringere* to turn aside < *re-* back + *frangere* to break]

re·fract·ing telescope (ri-frak′ting) See under TELESCOPE.

re·frac·tion (ri-frak′shən) *n.* **1.** *Physics* The change of direction of a ray, as of light or heat, in passage from one medium to another of different density, or in traversing a medium whose density is not uniform. **2.** *Optics* The refracting of light rays by the eye so as to form an image upon the retina. — **double refraction** The property possessed by certain types of crystals of breaking up a beam of light into two differently refracted and polarized rays. — **re·frac′tive** *adj.* — **re·frac′tive·ly** *adv.* — **re·frac′tive·ness, re·frac·tiv·i·ty** (rē′frak·tiv′ə·tē) *n.*

LIGHT REFRACTION

refractive index *Optics* The ratio of the velocity of a specific radiation in a vacuum to its velocity in a given medium: also called *index of refraction.*

re·frac·tom·e·ter (rē′frak·tom′ə·tər) *n.* Any instrument for measuring refractive indices. [< REFRACT + -METER]

re·frac·tor (ri-frak′tər) *n.* **1.** That which refracts. **2.** A refracting telescope. See under TELESCOPE.

re·frac·to·ry (ri-frak′tər·ē) *adj.* **1.** Not amenable to control; unmanageable; obstinate. **2.** Resisting heat or ordinary methods of reduction, as an ore. **3.** Resisting treatment, as a disease. — *n. pl.* **·ries 1.** One who or that which is refractory. **2.** Any of various materials highly resistant to the action of great heat, as fire clay. [Alter. of obs. *refractary* < L *refractarius* < *refractus.* See REFRACT.] — **re·frac′to·ri·ly** *adv.* — **re·frac′to·ri·ness** *n.*

re·frain[1] (ri-frān′) *v.i.* **1.** To keep oneself back; abstain from action; forbear. — *v.t.* **2.** *Obs.* To restrain; curb. [< OF *refrener* < L *refrenare* to curb < *re-* back + *frenum* bridle] — **re·frain′er** *n.*
— **Syn.** *Refrain, abstain,* and *forbear* mean to check oneself from performing an action. *Refrain* may indicate mere nonperformance, or may imply a positive subjugation of an impulse or inclination: to *refrain* from voting, to *refrain* from making an angry retort. *Abstain* indicates a considered policy, usually of self-denial: to *abstain* from hard liquor. *Forbear* suggests patience, kindness, or leniency: to *forbear* from punishing an offender.

re·frain[2] (ri-frān′) *n.* **1.** A phrase or strain in a poem or song repeated at intervals, especially at the end of each stanza. **2.** Any saying that is repeated over and over. [< OF < *refraindre* to break off < L *refringere.* See REFRACT.]

re·fran·gi·ble (ri-fran′jə·bəl) *adj.* Capable of being refracted, as light. [< RE- + L *frangere* to break + -IBLE] — **re·fran′gi·bil′i·ty, re·fran′gi·ble·ness** *n.*

re·fresh (ri-fresh′) *v.t.* **1.** To make fresh or vigorous again, as by food or rest; reinvigorate; revive. **2.** To make fresh, clean, cool, etc. **3.** To stimulate, as the memory. **4.** To renew or replenish with or as with new supplies. — *v.i.* **5.** To become fresh again; revive. **6.** To take refreshment. [< OF *refreschier* < *re-* again (< L) + *fres* fresh. See FRESHEN.]
— **Syn. 1.** brace, strengthen, reanimate. **2.** restore, freshen.

re·fresh·er (ri-fresh′ər) *adj.* Serving to reacquaint one with the material of subjects previously studied: a *refresher* course. — *n.* **1.** One who or that which refreshes. **2.** *Brit. Law* An additional fee paid to a lawyer when a case is adjourned or unduly prolonged.

re·fresh·ing (ri-fresh′ing) *adj.* **1.** Serving to refresh. **2.** Enjoyably novel or unusual. — **re·fresh′ing·ly** *adv.*

re·fresh·ment (ri-fresh′mənt) *n.* **1.** The act of refreshing, or the state of being refreshed; restoration of vigor or liveliness. **2.** That which refreshes, as food or drink. **3.** *pl.* Food, or food and drink, served as a light meal.

refrig. Refrigeration.

re·frig·er·ant (ri-frij′ər·ənt) *adj.* **1.** Cooling or freezing. **2.** Allaying bodily heat or fever. — *n.* **1.** Any medicine or material, as ice, that reduces abnormal heat of the body. **2.** A substance used for obtaining and maintaining a low temperature, as frozen carbon dioxide or ammonia.

re·frig·er·ate (ri-frij′ə·rāt) *v.t.* **·at·ed, ·at·ing 1.** To keep or make cold. **2.** To freeze or chill (foodstuffs, etc.) for preservative purposes. [< L *refrigeratus,* pp. of *refrigerare* < *re-* thoroughly + *frigerare* to cool < *frigere* to be cold < *frigus* cold] — **re·frig′er·a′tion** *n.* — **re·frig′er·a′tive** *adj. & n.* — **re·frig′er·a·to·ry** (-tôr′ē, -tō′rē) *adj.*

re·frig·er·a·tor (ri-frij′ə·rā′tər) *n.* **1.** A box, cabinet, room, railroad car, etc., equipped with apparatus for preserving the freshness of perishable foods, etc., by means of ice or other refrigerant. **2.** That which refrigerates.

re·frin·gen·cy (ri-frin′jən·sē) *n. pl.* **·cies** Power to refract. Also **re·frin′gence.** [< L *refringere.* See REFRACT.] — **re·frin′gent** *adj.*

Ref. Sp. Reformed Spelling.

reft (reft) Past tense and past participle of REAVE.

re·fu·el (rē-fyōō′əl, -fyōōl′) v. ·eled or ·elled, ·el·ing or ·el·ling v.t. **1.** To replenish with fuel. — v.i. **2.** To take on a fresh supply of fuel.

ref·uge (ref′yōōj) n. **1.** Shelter or protection, as from danger or distress. **2.** One who or that which shelters or protects. **3.** A safe place; asylum. **4.** Brit. A safety area for the use of pedestrians at busy street crossings. — v.t. & v.i. ·uged, ·ug·ing Obs. To give or take refuge. [< OF < L refugium < refugere < re- back + fugere to flee] — **Syn.** (noun) **3.** sanctuary, retreat, haven.

ref·u·gee (ref′yōō-jē′, ref′yōō-jē′) n. **1.** One who flees to a refuge. **2.** One who flees from invasion, persecution, or political danger.

re·ful·gence (ri-ful′jəns) n. Splendor; brilliant radiance. Also **re·ful′gen·cy.**

re·ful·gent (ri-ful′jənt) adj. Shining brilliantly; radiant. [< L refulgens, -entis, ppr. of refulgere to reflect light < re- back + fulgere to shine] — **re·ful′gent·ly** adv.

re·fund[1] (v. ri-fund′; n. rē′fund) v.t. **1.** To give or pay back (money, etc.). **2.** To repay; reimburse. **3.** Obs. To pour back. — v.i. **4.** To make repayment. — n. A repayment; also, the amount repaid. [< OF refunder < L refundere < re- back + fundere to pour] — **re·fund′er** n.

re·fund[2] (rē-fund′) v.t. To fund anew; replace (an old loan) by issuing new securities.

re·fur·bish (re-fûr′bish) v.t. To furbish again; renovate or freshen; polish up; brighten.

re·fus·al (ri-fyōō′zəl) n. **1.** The act of refusing; declination. **2.** The privilege of accepting or rejecting; option.

re·fuse[1] (ri-fyōōz′) v. ·fused, ·fus·ing v.t. **1.** To decline to do, permit, take, or yield. **2.** Mil. To turn back (the wing of a line of troops), so that it stands at an angle with the main body. **3.** To decline to jump over: said of a horse at a ditch, hedge, etc. **4.** Obs. To disown; renounce; resign. — v.i. **5.** To decline to do, permit, take, or yield something. [< OF refuser < L refusus, pp. of refundere. See REFUND[1].]

ref·use[2] (ref′yōōs) n. Anything worthless; rubbish. — adj. Rejected as worthless. [< OF refus, pp. of refuser. See REFUSE[1].]

re-fuse (rē-fyōōz′) v.t. & v.i. ·fused, ·fus·ing To fuse again.

ref·u·ta·tion (ref′yōō-tā′shən) n. **1.** The act of refuting a statement, charge, etc. **2.** Disproof. Also **re·fu·tal** (ri-fyōōt′l).

re·fute (ri-fyōōt′) v.t. ·fut·ed, ·fut·ing **1.** To prove the incorrectness or falsity of (a statement). **2.** To prove (a person) to be in error; confute. [< L refutare to repulse] — **re·fut′a·bil·i·ty** n. — **re·fut′a·ble** adj. — **re·fut′a·bly** adv. — **re·fut′er** n. — **Syn. 1.** Refute, disprove, rebut, and confute mean to show to be incorrect or fallacious. Refute emphasizes the fact of opposing a statement or argument; disprove emphasizes the result of such opposition. To rebut is to refute in formal debate, while to confute is to disprove, overthrow, or put to confusion; confute may include the use of ridicule, as well as of logical argument.

reg. 1. Regent. **2.** Regiment. **3.** Region. **4.** Register(ed). **5.** Registrar. **6.** Registry. **7.** Regular(ly). **8.** Regulation. **9.** Regulator.

re·gain (ri-gān′) v.t. **1.** To get possession of again, as something lost; recover. **2.** To reach again; get back to: He regained the street. [< MF regaigner] — **re·gain′er** n.

re·gal (rē′gəl) adj. **1.** Belonging to or fit for a king; royal. **2.** Stately. — **Syn.** See KINGLY. [< OF < L regalis < rex, regis king. Doublet of ROYAL.] — **re′gal·ly** adv.

re·gale (ri-gāl′) v. ·galed, ·gal·ing v.t. **1.** To give unusual pleasure to; delight: He regaled us with stories. **2.** To entertain sumptuously; feast. — v.i. **3.** To feast. — n. Obs. **1.** A sumptuous feast. **2.** Refreshment. **3.** A choice dish. [< F régaler < ré- again + OF gale pleasure] — **re·gale′ment** n.

re·ga·li·a (ri-gā′lē-ə, -gāl′yə) n.pl. **1.** The insignia and emblems of royalty, as the crown, scepter, etc. **2.** The distinctive symbols, insignia, etc., of any society, order, or rank. **3.** Fine clothes; fancy trappings. [< L, neut. pl. of regalis. See REGAL.]

re·gal·i·ty (ri-gal′ə-tē) n. pl. ·ties **1.** Sovereign jurisdiction; royalty. **2.** A territorial jurisdiction conferred by the crown on a subject. **3.** A country subject to royal authority; a kingdom. [< OF regalite]

Re·gan (rē′gən) In Shakespeare's King Lear, one of Lear's two ungrateful daughters.

re·gard (ri-gärd′) v.t. **1.** To look at or observe closely or attentively. **2.** To look on or think of in a certain or specified manner; consider: I regard him as a friend. **3.** To take into account; consider. **4.** To have relation or pertinence to; concern. **5.** Obs. To care for. — v.i. **6.** To pay attention. **7.** To gaze or look. — **Syn.** See ADMIRE, CONSIDER. — n. **1.** Careful attention or notice; heed; consideration. **2.** Esteem; respect. **3.** Reference; relation: in regard to this matter. **4.** A look or aspect. **5.** Usually pl. Good wishes; affection: My kindest regards to your family. — **Syn.** See DEFERENCE. [< OF regarder to look at < re- again + garder to guard, heed < Gmc. Akin to REWARD.]

re·gard·ant (ri-gär′dənt) adj. Heraldry Looking backward. [< F, ppr. of regarder to look at]

re·gard·ful (ri-gärd′fəl) adj. **1.** Having or showing regard; heedful. **2.** Respectful; deferential. — **re·gard′ful·ly** adv. — **re·gard′ful·ness** n.

re·gard·ing (ri-gär′ding) prep. In reference to; concerning.

re·gard·less (ri-gärd′lis) adj. Having no regard or consideration; heedless; negligent: often with of. — adv. Informal In spite of everything. — **re·gard′less·ly** adv.

re·gat·ta (ri-gat′ə, -gä′tə) n. **1.** A boat race, or a series of such races. **2.** Originally, a gondola race. [< Ital.]

re·ge·late (rē′jə-lāt) v.i. ·lat·ed, ·lat·ing To refreeze, as melting ice, as a result of reduced pressure that raises the melting point. [< RE- + L gelatus, pp. of gelare to freeze] — **re′ge·la′tion** n.

re·gen·cy (rē′jən-sē) n. pl. ·cies **1.** The government or office of a regent or body of regents. **2.** The period during which a regent or body of regents governs. **3.** A body of regents. **4.** The district under the rule of a regent. Also **re′gent·ship.** — **the Regency 1.** In English history, the years 1811–20. **2.** In French history, the years 1715–23. [< LL regentia < L regens, -entis. See REGENT.]

re·gen·er·a·cy (ri-jen′ər-ə-sē) n. The state of being regenerate.

re·gen·er·ate (v. ri-jen′ə-rāt; adj. ri-jen′ər-it) v. ·at·ed, ·at·ing v.t. **1.** To cause complete moral and spiritual reformation or regeneration in. **2.** To produce or form anew; re-create; reproduce. **3.** To make use of (heat or other energy that might otherwise be wasted) by means of various devices. **4.** Biol. To grow or form by regeneration. **5.** Telecom. To amplify (signal strength) by regeneration. — v.i. **6.** To form anew; be reproduced. **7.** To become spiritually regenerate. **8.** To effect regeneration. — adj. **1.** Having new life; restored. **2.** Spiritually renewed; regenerated. [< L regeneratus, pp. of regenerare < re- again + generare to generate] — **re·gen′er·a·tive** (ri·jen′ə·rā′tiv, -ər-ə-tiv) adj. — **re·gen′er·a·tive·ly** adv.

re·gen·er·a·tion (ri-jen′ə-rā′shən) n. **1.** The act of regenerating, or the state of being regenerated. **2.** The imparting of spiritual life by divine grace. **3.** Biol. **a** The reproduction of a lost part or organ, as in lizards. **b** The renewal or reproduction of cells, tissues, etc., in the ordinary vital processes. **4.** Any of various processes by which heat or other forms of energy are saved and reutilized. **5.** Telecom. The amplification of electromagnetic signal strength by returning part of the output of an amplifier to the input as a result of feedback: compare DEGENERATION. [< OF]

re·gen·er·a·tor (ri-jen′ə-rā′tər) n. **1.** One who or that which regenerates. **2.** Mech. **a** A device in a furnace, gas burner, or similar apparatus by which the waste heat of escaping gases is used to heat the gas and air just entering. **b** A furnace containing such a device.

Re·gens·burg (rā′gənz-bŏŏrkh) A port city in eastern Bavaria, West Germany, on the Danube; pop. 128,083 (1970): also English **Ratisbon.**

re·gent (rē′jənt) n. **1.** One who rules in the name and place of a sovereign. **2.** Any ruler or governor. **3.** A resident master who takes part in the government of a university or college. **4.** One of various officers having charge of the higher education, as of a state. **5.** Usually cap. A style of cutting gems: also called Pitt. For illustration see DIAMOND. — adj. **1.** Exercising authority in another's place. **2.** Governing; ruling. Abbr. reg., Regt. [< OF < L regens, -entis, ppr. of regere to rule]

Reg·gio di Ca·la·bri·a (rād′jō dē kä·lä′brē·ä) A port commune in southern Italy, on the Strait of Messina; pop. 150,334 (1961). Also **Reggio Calabria.**

Reg·gio nell'E·mi·lia (nel·ā·mē′lyä) A commune in north central Italy; pop. 116,515 (1961). Also **Reggio Emilia.**

reg·i·cide (rej′ə-sīd) n. **1.** The killing of a king or sovereign. **2.** One who has killed a king or sovereign. [< L rex, regis king + -CIDE] — **reg′i·ci′dal** adj.

re·gime (ri-zhēm′) n. **1.** System of government or administration. **2.** A social system. **3.** Regimen (def. 1). Also **ré·gime** (rā-zhēm′). [< F régime < L regimen < regere to rule, guide. Doublet of REGIMEN.]

reg·i·men (rej′ə-mən) n. **1.** A systematized course of living, as to food, clothing, etc.: also called regime. **2.** Government; control. **3.** Gram. The influence of one word in determining the form of another connected with it. [< L regimen < regere to rule. Doublet of REGIME.]

reg·i·ment (rej′ə-mənt; v. rej′ə-ment) n. **1.** Mil. An administrative and tactical unit of infantry, artillery, etc., larger than a battalion and smaller than a division, usually commanded by a colonel. Abbr. reg., Regt. **2.** Any large body of persons. **3.** Obs. Government over a people or country. — v.t. **1.** To form into a regiment or regiments; organize. **2.** To assign to a regiment. **3.** To form into well-defined or specific units or groups; systematize. **4.** To make uniform at the expense of individual differences. [< OF < LL regimentum < L regere to rule] — **reg′i·men′tal** adj.

reg·i·men·tals (rej′ə-men′təlz) n.pl. **1.** A military uniform. **2.** The uniform worn by a regiment.

reg·i·men·ta·tion (rej′ə-men·tā′shən) n. **1.** The act of regimenting. **2.** Organization into disciplined, uniform groups.

Re·gin (rā′gin) In Germanic mythology, a dwarf, foster father of Sigurd, by whom he was slain. Also **Re′ginn.**

re·gi·na (ri-jī′nə) *n. Latin* Queen. Abbr. *R.*

Re·gi·na (ri-jī′nə) The capital of Saskatchewan. Canada, in the southern part of the Province; pop. 137,759.

re·gi·nal (ri-jī′nəl) *adj.* Pertaining to a queen; queenly; also, supporting or favoring a queen. [< *Med.*L *reginalis* < L *regina* queen]

re·gion (rē′jən) *n.* **1.** An indefinite portion of territory or space, usually of considerable extent; a country or district. **2.** A particular area or place: the delta *region* of the Nile. **3.** General area; scope; province: in the *region* of literature. **4.** *Ecol.* An area of land or water distinguished by its animal or plant life. **5.** A portion of the body arbitrarily circumscribed for anatomical and medical purposes: the abdominal *region.* **6.** A realm (def. 3). Abbr. *reg.* [< AF *regiun,* OF *region* < L *regio, -onis* < *regere* to rule]

re·gion·al (rē′jən-əl) *adj.* **1.** Of or pertaining to a particular region; sectional; local: *regional* planning. **2.** Of or pertaining to an entire region or section, especially a geographic one: *regional* features. — **re′gion·al·ly** *adv.*

reg·is·ter (rej′is-tər) *n.* **1.** A formal or official record or account, as of names or transactions; also, a book containing such a record. **2.** An individual entry or listing in a register. **3** Any of various mechanical or electrical devices for counting or recording: a cash *register.* **4.** A keeper of records, especially one officially or legally designated; registrar. **5.** *Music* **a** A portion of the compass of a voice or instrument produced in a specific manner and having tones of a relatively homogeneous timbre. **b** A full set of organ pipes or harpsichord strings controlled by a single stop. **6.** A device by which heated or cooled air is admitted to a room: also called *regulator.* **7.** *Photog.* Proper correspondence of position between the sensitive plate or film and the focusing screen. **8.** *Printing* **a** Exact correspondence of the lines and margins on the opposite sides of a printed sheet. **b** Correct relation of the colors in color printing. **9.** The act of recording or registering; registry. — *v.t.* **1.** To enter in or as in a register; record officially or exactly. **2.** To indicate, as on a scale. **3.** To express; show: His face *registered* shock. **4.** To cause (mail) to be recorded, on payment of a fee, when deposited with the postal system, so as to insure delivery. **5.** *Printing* To effect the exact correspondence of; put in register. — *v.i.* **6.** To enter one's name in a register. **7.** To cause one's name to be included on a list of eligible voters by fulfilling certain legal and procedural requirements. **8.** *Informal* To have effect; make an impression. **9.** *Printing* To be in register. Abbr. *reg.* [< OF *registre* < Med.L *registrum* < LL *regesta* < L *regerere* to record < *re-* back + *gerere* to carry] — **reg·is·tra·ble** (rej′is-trə-bəl) *adj.*

reg·is·tered (rej′is-tərd) *adj.* **1.** Recorded, as a birth, a voter, an animal's pedigree, etc. **2.** Having a required or official certificate, as a nurse. Abbr. *reg.*

registered nurse A graduate nurse licensed to practice by the appropriate State authority and entitled to add R.N. after her name. Compare PRACTICAL NURSE.

register ton See under TON[1] (def. 4).

reg·is·trant (rej′is-trənt) *n.* **1.** One who registers, as a voter. **2.** One who registers a trademark or patent. [< F]

reg·is·trar (rej′is-trär, rej/is-trär′) *n.* An authorized keeper of a register or of records; especially, a college or university officer who records the enrollment of students, their grades, etc.: also called *register.* Abbr. *reg.* [< Med.L *registrarius*]

reg·is·tra·tion (rej′is-trā′shən) *n.* **1.** The act of entering in a registry; also, such an entry. **2.** The registering of voters; also, the number of voters registered. **3.** Enrollment in a school, college, or university. **4.** *Music* The combination of stops used in playing a composition on the organ. [< Med.L *registratio, -onis*]

reg·is·try (rej′is-trē) *n. pl.* **·tries** **1.** The act of registering; registration. **2.** A register, or the place where it is kept. **3.** The condition of being registered. Abbr. *reg.*

re·gi·us (rē′jē-əs) *adj. Latin* Royal: a designation of certain English and Scottish university professorships founded by the crown, or of their incumbents.

reg·let (reg′lit) *n.* **1.** A flat, narrow molding. **2.** *Printing* A thin wooden strip used for making space between lines of type, as in posters; also, the strips collectively or the material of which they are made. [< OF, dim. of *regle* < L *regula.* See RULE.]

reg·ma (reg′mə) *n. pl.* **·ma·ta** (-mə·tə) *Bot.* A capsular fruit made up of two or more carpels, each of which dehisces at maturity. [< NL < Gk. *rhēgma* fracture < *rhēgnynai* to break]

reg·nal (reg′nəl) *adj.* Of or pertaining to a reign, a king, or a kingdom. [< Med.L *regnalis* < L *regnum* reign]

reg·nant (reg′nənt) *adj.* **1.** Reigning in one's own right. **2.** Dominant; commanding. [< L *regnans, -antis,* ppr. of *regnare* to reign < *regnum* reign] — **reg′nan·cy** *n.*

reg·nat pop·u·li (reg′nət pop′yŏŏ·lī) *Latin* The people rule: motto of Arkansas.

re·gorge (ri-gôrj′) *v.* **·gorged, ·gorg·ing** *v.t.* **1.** To vomit up; disgorge. — *v.i.* **2.** To gush or flow back. [< F *regorger* < *re-* again + *gorger* to gorge < *gorge* throat < L *gurges* whirlpool. Akin to REGURGITATE.]

re·grade (ri-grād′) *v.t.* **·grad·ed, ·grad·ing** To grade again.

re·grate (ri-grāt′) *v.t.* **·grat·ed, ·grat·ing** **1.** To buy up, as provisions, for the purpose of selling at a higher price in or near the same market. **2.** To retail, as provisions. [< OF *regrater* < Gmc. Akin to REGRET.]

re·gress (*n.* rē′gres; *v.* ri-gres′) *n.* **1.** Passage back; return. **2.** The power or right of passing back or returning. **3.** Withdrawal; retrogression. — *v.i.* **1.** To go back; move backward; return. **2.** *Stat.* To return to the mean value of a series of observations. [< L *regressus,* pp. of *regredi* to go back < *re-* back + *gradi* to walk] — **re·gres′sor** *n.*

re·gres·sion (ri-gresh′ən) *n.* **1.** The act of regressing. **2.** *Psychoanal.* A retreat of the libido to earlier and less mature forms of behavior. **3.** *Stat.* The return to a mean or average value. **4.** *Med.* The subsidence of a disease.

re·gres·sive (ri-gres′iv) *adj.* **1.** Tending to regress. **2.** Of or marked by regression. **3.** Denoting or pertaining to a tax or taxes in which the tax rate decreases as the amount taxed increases. — **re·gres′sive·ly** *adv.*

re·gret (ri-gret′) *v.t.* **·gret·ted, ·gret·ting** **1.** To look back upon with a feeling of distress or loss. **2.** To feel sorrow or grief concerning. — **Syn.** See MOURN. — *n.* **1.** Distress of mind in recalling some past event; a wish that something had or had not happened. **2.** Remorseful sorrow; compunction. **3.** An expression of sorrow or disappointment. **4.** *pl.* A polite refusal in response to an invitation. [< OF *regreter* < Gmc. Cf. ON *grāta* to weep, OE *grētan.*] — **re·gret′ta·ble** *adj.* — **re·gret′ta·bly** *adv.* — **re·gret′ter** *n.*

re·gret·ful (ri-gret′fəl) *adj.* Feeling, expressive of, or full of regret. — **re·gret′ful·ly** *adv.* — **re·gret′ful·ness** *n.*

Regt. **1.** Regent. **2.** Regiment.

reg·u·lar (reg′yə-lər) *adj.* **1.** Made according to rule; symmetrical; normal. **2.** Acting according to rule; recurring without fail; methodical; orderly: *regular* habits. **3.** Constituted, appointed, or conducted in the proper manner; duly authorized: a *regular* meeting. **4.** *Gram.* Undergoing the inflection that is normal or most common to the class of words to which it belongs: said especially of weak verbs. **5.** *Bot.* Having all the parts or organs of the same kind uniform in structure or shape and size: said mainly of flowers. **6.** *Eccl.* Bound by a religious rule; pertaining or belonging to a religious order: the *regular* clergy. **7.** *Mil.* Pertaining or belonging to the permanent military services. **8.** In politics, adhering loyally to a party organization or platform; also, nominated by the official party organization: said of a candidate. **9.** *Geom.* Having equal sides and angles. **10.** *Math.* Controlled or governed by one law or operation throughout: a *regular* equation. **11.** *Informal* Thorough; unmitigated; absolute. **12.** *U.S.* Designating the component of the armed services that consists of persons in continuous service on active duty in both peace and war: the *regular* Army. — **Syn.** See NORMAL. — *n.* **1.** A soldier belonging to a standing army, as distinguished from a volunteer, draftee, or member or a reserve unit. **2.** *Informal* One regularly employed or engaged; also, a habitual customer. **3.** *Eccl.* A member of a religious or monastic order. **4.** A person loyal to a certain political party. Abbr. *reg.* [< OF *reguler* < L *regularis* < *regula.* See RULE.] — **reg′u·lar·ness** *n.*

reg·u·lar·i·ty (reg′yə-lar′ə-tē) *n. pl.* **·ties** The state, quality, or character of being regular; also, an instance of this.

reg·u·lar·ize (reg′yə-lə-rīz′) *v.t.* **·ized, ·iz·ing** To make regular. Also *Brit.* **reg′u·lar·ise′.** — **reg′u·lar·i·za′tion** *n.*

reg·u·lar·ly (reg′yə-lər-lē) *adv.* In a regular manner; according to the usual method or order. Abbr. *reg.*

regular ode Pindaric ode (which see).

reg·u·late (reg′yə-lāt) *v.t.* **·lat·ed, ·lat·ing** **1.** To direct, manage, or control according to certain rules, principles, etc. **2.** To adjust according to a standard, degree, etc.: to *regulate* currency. **3.** To adjust to accurate operation. **4.** To put in order; set right. [< LL *regulatus,* pp. of *regulare* to rule < L *regula.* See RULE.] — **reg′u·la′tive** *adj.* — **Syn.** **1.** rule, govern, conduct. **4.** correct, rectify.

reg·u·la·tion (reg′yə-lā′shən) *n.* **1.** The act of regulating, or the state of being regulated. **2.** A rule prescribed for conduct: army *regulations.* Abbr. *reg.* — **Syn.** See LAW[1].

reg·u·la·tor (reg′yə-lā′tər) *n.* **1.** One who or that which regulates. **2.** A clock used as a standard; also, an index arm for regulating the rate of a watch. **3.** *Mech.* A contrivance for regulating or equalizing motion or flow, as the governor of a steam engine. **4.** A register (def. 6). **5.** *Electr.* A device for keeping at constant strength the current produced by a dynamo. Abbr. *reg.* — **reg′u·la′tor·ship** *n.*

reg·u·la·to·ry (reg′yə-lə-tôr′ē, -tō′rē) *adj.* Tending or serving to regulate. Also **reg′u·la·tive.**

reg·u·lus (reg′yə-ləs) *n. pl.* **·li** (-lī) *Metall.* **1.** The metallic mass that sinks with the slag to the bottom of the vessel in which ore is being treated. **2.** An intermediate product obtained in smelting ores of various metals. [< L, lit., king-let, dim. of *rex, regis* king] — **reg·u·line** (-lin, -līn) *adj.*

Reg·u·lus (reg′yə·ləs) A white star, one of the 20 brightest, 1.36 magnitude; Alpha in the constellation Leo. [< L]

Reg·u·lus (reg′yə·ləs), **Marcus Atilius**, died 250 B.C., Roman general; fought the Carthaginians.

re·gur·gi·tate (ri·gûr′jə·tāt) *v.* **·tat·ed, ·tat·ing** *v.i.* **1.** To rush, pour, or surge back. — *v.t.* **2.** To cause to surge back, as partially digested food; vomit. [< Med.L *regurgitatus,* pp. of *regurgitare* < *re-* back + LL *gurgitare* to swallow, en-gulf < L *gurges, gurgites* whirlpool] — **re·gur′gi·tant** *adj.*

re·gur·gi·ta·tion (ri·gûr′jə·tā′shən) *n.* **1.** The act of rush-ing back or reswallowing. **2.** *Physiol.* The backward rush of blood into the heart due to defective valves.

re·ha·bil·i·tate (rē′hə·bil′ə·tāt) *v.t.* **·tat·ed, ·tat·ing 1.** To restore to a former state, capacity, privilege, rank, etc.; rein-state. **2.** To restore to a state of health, useful activity, etc., through training, therapy, guidance. [< Med.L *rehabilita-tus,* pp. of *rehabilitare* < *re-* back + *habilitare*. See HABILI-TATE.] — **re·ha·bil′i·ta′tion** *n.*

re·hash (*v.* rē·hash′; *n.* rē′hash′) *v.t.* To work into a new form; go over again. — *n.* Something hashed over, or made or served up from something used before.

re·hear (rē·hir′) *v.t.* **·heard** (hûrd), **·hear·ing** To hear (a case, etc.) again.

re·hear·ing (rē·hir′ing) *n.* A new hearing, as in court.

re·hears·al (ri·hûr′səl) *n.* **1.** A practice session or perform-ance of a play, etc., held in preparation for a formal per-formance. **2.** The act of reciting or telling over again.

re·hearse (ri·hûrs′) *v.* **·hearsed, ·hears·ing** *v.t.* **1.** To per-form privately in preparation for public performance, as a play or song. **2.** To cause to perform or recite by way of preparation; instruct by rehearsal. **3.** To say over again; repeat aloud; recite. **4.** To give an account of; relate. — *v.i.* **5.** To rehearse a play, song, dance, etc. [< OF *rehercier* < *re-* again + *hercier* to harrow < *herce*. See HEARSE.] — **re·hears′er** *n.*

re·heat (rē·hēt′) *v.t.* To heat again or anew. — **re·heat′er** *n.*

Rehn·quist (ren′kwist), **William Hubbs**, born 1924, U.S. lawyer; associate justice of the Supreme Court 1971–.

rei (rā) *n.* Erroneous English form for Portuguese *real*. See REAL² (def. 2).

Reich (rīkh) *n.* Germany or its government. — **First Reich** The Holy Roman Empire from its establishment in the ninth century to its collapse in 1806. — **Second Reich** The Ger-man Empire, 1871–1919, or the Weimar Republic, 1919–1933, or both German governments in the period 1871–1933. — **Third Reich** The Nazi state under Adolf Hitler, 1933–45. [< G, realm]

Reich (rīkh), **Wilhelm**, 1897–1957, U.S. psychotherapist and natural scientist, born in Germany.

Reichs·bank (rīkhs′bängk) *n.* The state or national bank of Germany, founded in 1876. [< G]

reichs·mark (rīkhs′märk′) *n.* A former standard monetary unit of Germany, equivalent to 100 reichspfennigs and worth about 24 U.S. cents. See MARK². Abbr. *r.m., Rm., RM, R.M.*

reichs·pfen·nig (rīkhs′pfen′ikh) *n. pl.* **·pfen·nigs** or **·pfen-ni·ge** (-pfen′i·gə) A former bronze coin of Germany, equiva-lent to one-hundredth of a reichsmark. Compare PFENNIG.

Reichs·rat (rīkhs′rät) *n.* **1.** The former parliament of the Austrian Empire. **2.** The council of the Reich under the Weimar Republic. Also **Reichs′rath**. [< G]

Reichs·tag (rīkhs′täkh) *n.* The former legislative assembly of Germany. [< G]

Reid (rēd), **Whitelaw**, 1837–1912, U.S. journalist and diplo-mat.

reif (rēf) *n. Scot.* Robbery; plunder. [OE *rēaf*]

re·i·fy (rē′ə·fī) *v.t.* **·fied, ·fy·ing** To make real or concrete; materialize: to *reify* an idea. [< L *res, rei* thing + -FY] — **re′i·fi·ca′tion** *n.* — **re′i·fi′er** *n.*

reign (rān) *n.* **1.** The possession or exercise of supreme power, especially royal power; sovereignty; dominion. **2.** The time or duration of a sovereign's rule. — *v.i.* **1.** To hold and exercise sovereign power; be the head of a mon-archy. **2.** To hold sway; be predominant; prevail: Winter *reigns*. [< F *règne* < L *regnum* rule < *rex, regis* king]

Reign of Terror The period of the French Revolution from May, 1793, to August, 1794, during which thousands were guillotined, including Louis XVI and Marie Antoinette.

re·im·burse (rē′im·bûrs′) *v.t.* **·bursed, ·burs·ing 1.** To pay back (a person) an equivalent for what has been spent or lost; recompense; indemnify. **2.** To pay back; refund. [< RE- + obs. *imburse,* ult. < L *in-* in + *bursa* purse; infl. by F *rembourser*] — **re′im·burs′a·ble** *adj.* — **re′im·burse′ment** *n.* — **re′im·burs′er** *n.*

re·im·port (*v.* rē′im·pôrt′, -pōrt′, rē·im′pôrt, -pōrt; *n.* rē·im′-pôrt, -pōrt) *v.t.* To import (goods, etc., previously export-ed) again. — *n.* **1.** The act of importing again. **2.** That which is reimported. — **re′im·por·ta′tion** *n.*

re·im·pres·sion (rē′im·presh′ən) *n.* **1.** A new or second im-pression. **2.** A reprint of a book without editorial change.

Reims (rēmz, *Fr.* raṅs) A city in NE France; its cathedral is the former coronation place of the French kings; pop. 151,-988 (1968): also *Rheims.*

rein (rān) *n.* **1.** *Usually pl.* A strap attached to the bit to control a horse or other draft animal. **2.** Any means of re-straint or control; a check. — *v.t.* **1.** To guide, check, or halt with or as with reins. **2.** To furnish with reins. — *v.i.* **3.** To check or halt a horse by means of reins: with *in* or *up*. **4.** *Archaic* To obey the reins. [< AF *redne,* OF *resne* < L *retinere*. See RETAIN.]

Rei·nach (re·näk′), **Salomon**, 1858–1932, French archeolo-gist.

re·in·car·nate (rē′in·kär′nāt) *v.t.* **·nat·ed, ·nat·ing** To cause to undergo reincarnation.

re·in·car·na·tion (rē′in·kär·nā′shən) *n.* **1.** A rebirth of the soul in successive bodies; also, the belief in such rebirth. **2.** In Vedic religions, the becoming of an avatar again, one of the series in the transmigrations of souls. — **re′in·car·na′-tion·ist** *n.*

rein·deer (rān′dir′) *n. pl.* **·deer** A deer (genus *Rangifer*) of northern regions, having branched antlers in both sexes, long domesticated for its milk, hide, and flesh, and used as a pack animal. [< ON *hreindȳri* < *hreinn* reindeer + *dȳr* deer. Akin to OE *hrān.*]

Rein·deer Lake (rān′dir′) A lake in northern Saskatch-ewan and Manitoba, Canada; 2,444 sq. mi.

reindeer moss A gray, branched lichen (*Cladonia rangi-ferina*) found as far as the extreme limits of arctic vegeta-tion, and furnishing food for reindeer and sometimes man.

re·in·force (rē′in·fôrs′, -fōrs′) *v.t.* **·forced, ·forc·ing 1.** To give new force or strength to. **2.** *Mil.* To strengthen with ad-ditional personnel or equipment. **3.** To add some strength-ening part or material to; thicken; strengthen; support. **4.** *Psychol.* To strengthen (a response) by the addition of another stimulus, as a reward. — *n.* That which reinforces. Also spelled *reenforce*. [< RE- + *inforce,* var. of ENFORCE]

reinforced concrete Concrete containing metal bars, rods, or netting disposed through the mass to increase its tensile strength and durability: also called *ferro-concrete*.

re·in·force·ment (rē′in·fôrs′mənt, -fōrs′-) *n.* **1.** The act of reinforcing. **2.** *Often pl. Mil.* A fresh body of troops or addi-tional vessels. **3.** Any increase in force. Also spelled *reen-forcement*.

Rein·hardt (rīn′härt), **Max**, 1873–1943, Austrian theatrical director and producer active in Germany and the United States: original name **Max Gold·mann** (gōlt′män).

reins (rānz) *n.pl. Archaic* **1.** The kidneys. **2.** The region near the kidneys. **3.** The loins, considered as the seat of the affections and passions. [< OF < L *renes,* pl. of *ren*]

re·in·stall (rē′in·stôl′) *v.t.* To install again. — **re·in·stal-la·tion** (rē′in·stə·lā′shən) *n.* — **re′in·stal′ment** or **re′in·stall′-ment** *n.*

re·in·state (rē′in·stāt′) *v.t.* **·stat·ed, ·stat·ing** To restore to a former state, position, etc. — **re′in·state′ment** *n.*

re·in·sure (rē′in·shoŏr′) *v.t.* **·sured, ·sur·ing 1.** To protect (the risk on a policy already issued) by obtaining insurance from a second insurer: said of a first insurer. **2.** To insure anew. — **re′in·sur′ance** *n.* — **re′in·sur′er** *n.*

re·in·vest (rē′in·vest′) *v.t.* To invest (money) again; espe-cially, to invest earnings from previous investments. — **re′-in·vest′ment** *n.*

reis (rēs) Plural of REAL² (def. 2).

re·is·sue (rē·ish′oō) *n.* **1.** A second or subsequent issue, as of a publication changed in form or price. **2.** A second print-ing of postage stamps from the same plates. — *v.t.* **·sued, ·su·ing** To issue again.

reit·bok (rīt′bok) *n.* The reedbuck [< Du. *rietbok*]

re·it·er·ate (rē·it′ə·rāt) *v.t.* **·at·ed, ·at·ing** To say or do again and again; repeat. [< L *reiteratus,* pp. of *reiterare* < *re-* again + *iterare*. See ITERATE.] — **re·it′er·a′tion** *n.*

re·it·er·a·tive (rē·it′ə·rā′tiv) *adj.* Characterized by reitera-tion. — *n.* A word or syllable repeated, usually with some slight change; also, the word so formed, as *tittle-tattle*. — **re·it′er·a′tive·ly** *adv.*

reiv·er (rē′vər) See REAVER.

Ré·jane (rā·zhän′) Pseudonym of **Gabrielle Charlotte Ré-ju** (rā·zhü′), 1857–1920, French actress, manager, and co-medienne.

re·ject (*v.* ri·jekt′; *n.* rē′jekt) *v.t.* **1.** To refuse to accept, rec-ognize, believe, etc. **2.** To refuse to grant; deny, as a peti-tion. **3.** To refuse (a person) recognition, acceptance, etc. **4.** To expel, as from the mouth; vomit. **5.** To cast away as worthless; discard. — *n.* One who or that which has been rejected. [< L *rejectus,* pp. of *reicere* < *re-* back + *jacere* to throw] — **re·ject′er** or **re·jec′tor** *n.*

— **Syn. 1.** disbelieve. **2.** repudiate, disallow. **3.** repulse, ex-clude.

re·jec·ta·men·ta (ri·jek′tə·men′tə) *n.pl.* **1.** Things thrown away. **2.** Things rejected from a living organism; excre-ment. [< NL, pl. of *rejectamentum* < L *rejectare,* freq. of *reicere* to fling back]

re·jec·tion (ri·jek′shən) *n.* **1.** The act of rejecting or state of being rejected. **2.** That which is rejected.

rejection slip The printed slip or other notice sent by pub-lishers to the authors of rejected stories, articles, etc.

re·joice (ri·jois′) *v.* **·joiced, ·joic·ing** *v.i.* **1.** To feel joyful; be glad. — *v.t.* **2.** To fill with joy; gladden. [< OF *resjoir*

< *re*- again (< L) + *esjoir* < L *ex*- thoroughly + *gaudere* to be joyous] — **re·joic′er** *n.*

re·joic·ing (ri·joi′sing) *adj.* Pertaining to or characterized by joyfulness. — *n.* The feeling or expression of joy. — **Syn.** (noun) exultation, delight, jubilation.

re·join[1] (ri·join′) *v.t.* **1.** To say in reply; answer. — *v.i.* **2.** To answer; respond. **3.** *Law* To make answer to a plaintiff's replication. [< F *rejoindre* < *re*- again (< L) + *joindre*. See JOIN.]

re·join[2] (rē′join′) *v.t.* **1.** To come again into company with. **2.** To join together again; reunite. — *v.i.* **3.** To come together again. [< RE- + JOIN]

re·join·der (ri·join′dər) *n.* **1.** An answer to a reply; also, any reply or retort. **2.** *Law* The answer filed by a defendant to a plaintiff's replication. — **Syn.** See ANSWER. [< F *rejoindre* to answer, reply]

re·ju·ve·nate (ri·jōō′və·nāt) *v.t.* **·nat·ed**, **·nat·ing** **1.** To give new vigor or youthfulness to; make young. **2.** *Geog.* To restore (a mature or old river) to its youthful condition by the development of lakes, etc. Also **re·ju′ve·nize**. [< RE- + L *juvenis* young + -ATE[1]] — **re·ju′ve·na′tion** *n.*

re·ju·ve·nes·cence (ri·jōō′və·nes′əns) *n.* A renewal of youth. [< L *rejuvenescens*, ppr. of *rejuvenescere* < *re*- again + *juvenescere* to grow young < *juvenis* young] — **re·ju′ve·nes′cent** *adj.*

rel. **1.** Relating. **2.** Relative(ly). **3.** Released. **4.** Religion; religious.

re·lapse (ri·laps′; *for n., also* rē′laps) *v.i.* **·lapsed**, **·laps·ing** **1.** To lapse back, as into disease after partial recovery. **2.** To return to bad habits or ways; backslide. — *n.* The act or condition of relapsing. [< L *relapsus*, pp. of *relabi* < *re*- back + *labi* to slide] — **re·laps′er** *n.*

relapsing fever *Pathol.* An acute infectious disease due to certain spirochetes transmitted by lice and ticks, and marked by recurrent attacks of fever: also called *recurrent fever.*

re·late (ri·lāt′) *v.* **·lat·ed**, **·lat·ing** *v.t.* **1.** To tell the events or the particulars of; narrate. **2.** To bring into connection or relation. — *v.i.* **3.** To have relation: with *to*. **4.** To have reference: with *to*. [< F *relater* < L *relatus*, pp. of *referre*. See REFER.] — **re·lat′er** *n.*
— **Syn.** **1.** report, recount, recite, rehearse, state. **2.** connect, link, join, associate. **3.** pertain, apply.

re·lat·ed (ri·lā′tid) *adj.* **1.** Standing in relation; connected. **2.** Connected by blood or marriage; of common ancestry; akin. **3.** Narrated; told. — **re·lat′ed·ness** *n.*

re·la·tion (ri·lā′shən) *n.* **1.** The fact or condition of being related or connected in some way, either objectively or in the mind. **2.** Connection by blood or marriage; kinship. **3.** A person connected by blood or marriage; kinsman. **4.** *Law* **a** The statement of the grounds of a complaint or grievance by a relator. **b** Retroactive application of an act or judicial decree. **5.** Reference; regard; allusion: in *relation* to that matter. **6.** The position of one person with respect to another: the *relation* of ruler to subject. **7.** *pl.* Conditions or connections in general that bring an individual in touch with his fellows; also, any conditions or connections by or in which one country may come into contact with another politically and commercially. **8.** The act of narrating or relating; also, that which is narrated or told. [< F < L *relatio, -onis* < *referre*. See REFER.]

re·la·tion·al (ri·lā′shən·əl) *adj.* **1.** Pertaining to or expressing relation, as certain parts of speech. **2.** Having relation or kinship.

re·la·tion·ship (ri·lā′shən·ship) *n.* The state of being related; connection.
— **Syn.** *Relationship, kinship, consanguinity,* and *affinity* are compared as they apply to persons of the same descent or family. *Relationship* is the most general term, embracing all the others and also the connection between things. *Kinship* is *relationship* by blood or marriage, and suggests mutual regard and affection. *Consanguinity* is *relationship* by blood only, and *affinity, relationship* by marriage only.

rel·a·tive (rel′ə·tiv) *adj.* **1.** Having connection; pertinent: an inquiry *relative* to one's health. **2.** Resulting from or depending upon relation; comparative: a *relative* truth. **3.** Intelligible only in relation to each other: the *relative* terms "father" and "son." **4.** Referring to, relating to, or qualifying an antecedent term: a *relative* pronoun. **5.** *Music* Having the same key signature, as major and minor keys and scales. — *n.* **1.** One who is related; a kinsman. **2.** A relative word or term; especially, a relative pronoun. Abbr. *rel.* [< OF *relatif* < Med.L *relativus* < L *relatus*] — **rel′a·tive·ly** *adv.* — **rel′a·tive·ness** *n.*
— **Syn.** **1.** referential, connective, germane. **2.** approximative, proportionate.

relative clause *Gram.* An adjective clause (which see).

relative pronoun *Gram.* A pronoun that relates to an antecedent and introduces a qualifying clause, as *who* in *We found a boatman who ferried us.* Abbr. *rel. pron.*

rel·a·tiv·ism (rel′ə·tiv·iz′əm) *n.* *Philos.* The theory that truths are relative and may vary according to the individual, place, or time. — **rel′a·tiv·ist** *n.* — **rel′a·tiv·is′tic** *adj.*

re·la·tiv·i·ty (rel′ə·tiv′ə·tē) *n.* **1.** The quality or condition of being relative; relativeness. **2.** *Philos.* Existence only as an object of, or in relation to, a thinking mind. **3.** A condition of dependence or of close relation, as of the solar system on the sun. **4.** *Physics* The principle of the interdependence of matter, energy, space, and time, as mathematically formulated by Albert Einstein. The **special theory of relativity** (1905) states that the velocity of light is the maximum velocity possible in the universe, that it is constant and independent of the motion of its source, that motion itself is a meaningless concept except as between two physical systems or material bodies moving relatively to each other, and that energy and mass are interconvertible in accordance with the equation *energy = mass* $\times$ *the square of the speed of light* or $E = mc^2$. The **general theory of relativity** (1915) extends these principles to the law of gravitation and the motions of the heavenly bodies.

relativity of knowledge *Philos.* The theory that knowledge of what things really are is impossible, since knowledge itself is dependent upon the subjective nature of the mind.

re·la·tor (ri·lā′tər) *n.* **1.** One who relates; a relater. **2.** *Law* One who institutes a special proceeding by relation or by information. [< L]

re·lax (ri·laks′) *v.t.* **1.** To make lax or loose; make less tight or firm. **2.** To make less stringent or severe, as discipline. **3.** To abate; slacken, as efforts. **4.** To relieve from strain or effort: to *relax* the eyes. — *v.i.* **5.** To become lax or loose; loosen. **6.** To become less stringent or severe. **7.** To rest; repose. **8.** To become less formal; unbend. [< L *relaxare* < *re*- again + *laxare* to loosen < *laxus* loose. Doublet of RELEASE.] — **re·lax′a·ble** *adj.* — **re·lax′er** *n.*
— **Syn.** **1.** loosen. **2.** ease, mitigate, soften. **3.** remit, lessen, relent. **6.** ease, mitigate, soften. **7.** divert, recreate.

re·lax·ant (ri·laks′ənt) *n.* A drug, therapy, etc., that relaxes the muscles or reduces nervous tension. — *adj.* Of or causing relaxation.

re·lax·a·tion (rē′lak·sā′shən) *n.* **1.** The act of relaxing or the state of being relaxed. **2.** Indulgence in diversion, or the diversion itself; entertainment. [< L *relaxatio, -onis*] — **re·lax·a·tive** (ri·lak′sə·tiv) *adj. & n.*

re·lay (rē′lā, ri·lā′) *n.* **1.** A fresh set, as of men, horses, or dogs, to replace or relieve a tired set. **2.** A supply of anything kept in store for anticipated use or need. **3.** A relay race, or one of its laps or legs. **4.** *Electr.* **a** A device that utilizes variations in the condition or strength of a current in a circuit to effect the operation of similar devices in the same or another circuit: a telegraph *relay*. **b** An electrically operated device that opens and closes an electrical circuit. — *v.t.* **1.** To send onward by or as by relays. **2.** To provide with relays. **3.** *Electr.* To operate or retransmit by means of a relay. [< MF *relai* < *relaier* release < L *relaxare* to loosen again. See RELAX.]

re·lay (rē·lā′) *v.t.* **-laid**, **-lay·ing** To lay again.

relay race A race between teams each member of which races a set part of the course and is relieved by a teammate.

re·lease (ri·lēs′) *v.t.* **·leased**, **·leas·ing** **1.** To set free; liberate. **2.** To deliver from worry, pain, obligation, etc. **3.** To free from something that holds, binds, etc. **4.** To permit the circulation, sale, performance, etc., of, as a motion picture, phonograph record, or news item. — *n.* **1.** The act of releasing or the state of being released; liberation from restraint of any kind. **2.** A deliverance or final relief, as from anything grievous or oppressive. **3.** A discharge from responsibility or penalty, as from a debt. **4.** *Law* An instrument of conveyance by which one of two persons having a mutual interest in lands surrenders and relinquishes all his interest and estate to the other; quitclaim. **5.** Anything formally released to the public, as news, a motion picture, etc. **6.** Exhaust of motive fluid in a steam engine; also, the point at which such exhaust begins. **7.** *Mech.* Any catch or device to hold and release a mechanism, weights, etc. [< OF *relaissier* to let free < L *relaxare*. Doublet of RELAX.] — **re·leas′er** *n.*
— **Syn.** (verb) **1.** emancipate. **3.** disengage, discharge.

re·lease (rē′lēs′) *v.t.* **-leased**, **-leas·ing** To lease again.

released time *U.S.* A period during which the children in some school systems are released from classes to receive religious instruction.

rel·e·gate (rel′ə·gāt) *v.t.* **·gat·ed**, **·gat·ing** **1.** To send off or consign, as to an obscure position or place. **2.** To assign, as to a particular class or sphere. **3.** To refer (a matter) to someone for decision. **4.** To banish; exile. [< L *relegatus*, pp. of *relegare* to send away < *re*- back + *legare* to send] — **rel′e·ga′tion** *n.*

re·lent (ri·lent′) *v.i.* **1.** To soften in temper; become more gentle or compassionate. — *v.t.* **2.** *Obs.* To cause to relent. [< L *relentescere* to grow soft < *re*- again + *lentus* soft]

re·lent·less (ri·lent′lis) *adj.* **1.** Unremitting; continuous. **2.** Pitiless. — **re·lent′less·ly** *adv.* — **re·lent′less·ness** *n.*
— **Syn.** **1.** incessant, uninterrupted. **2.** unfeeling, unmerciful, ruthless.

rel·e·vant (rel′ə·vənt) *adj.* **1.** Fitting or suiting given requirements; pertinent; applicable: usually with *to.* **2.** *Ling.* Designating those features of a phoneme that function to distinguish it from other phonemes in a language, as place of articulation in English consonants: also *distinctive.* — *Syn.* See APPROPRIATE. [< Med.L *relevans, -antis,* ppr. of *relevare* to bear upon < L, to raise up. See RELIEVE.] — **rel′e·vance, rel′e·van·cy** *n.* — **rel′e·vant·ly** *adv.*

re·li·a·ble (ri·lī′ə·bəl) *adj.* **1.** That may be relied upon; worthy of confidence; trustworthy. **2.** *Stat.* Exhibiting a reasonable consistency in results obtained, as in a group of repeated tests: distinguished from *valid.* — **re·li′a·bil′i·ty, re·li′a·ble·ness** *n.* — **re·li′a·bly** *adv.*
— *Syn.* *Reliable, dependable, trustworthy,* and *trusty* characterize that in which we have great confidence. A *reliable* person acts rightly, competently, or consistently; a *reliable* thing is adequate, serviceable, or true; we may say that a reference book is *reliable* if the information it presents is accurate, or that a man is a *reliable* judge of horses if his opinions are sound. *Dependable* is akin to *reliable,* but a little more subjective; we go to a *dependable* person or thing confident of receiving loyalty, support, or aid. *Trustworthy* is stronger than either of the foregoing words, implying that our confidence is complete and profound: a *trustworthy* servant. That which has been found *reliable* in the past is *trusty,* though it may not merit as much confidence as something *trustworthy:* a *trusty* sword. — *Ant.* dubious, questionable.

re·li·ance (ri·lī′əns) *n.* **1.** The act of relying, or the condition of being reliant; confidence; trust; dependence. **2.** That upon which one relies; a ground of confidence.

re·li·ant (ri·lī′ənt) *adj.* Manifesting reliance, especially upon oneself. — **re·li′ant·ly** *adv.*

rel·ic (rel′ik) *n.* **1.** Some remaining portion or fragment of that which has vanished or been destroyed: a *relic* of barbarism. **2.** Something cherished in memory of a person, place, or event; a keepsake or memento. **3.** The body or part of the body of a saint, or an object connected with a saint or his tomb; a sacred memento. **4.** Any outworn custom, institution, etc. **5.** *pl. Obs.* A corpse; remains. Also, *Archaic, relique.* [< OF *relique* < L *reliquiae* remains, leavings < relinquere to leave. See RELINQUISH.]

rel·ict (*n.* rel′ikt; *adj.* ri·likt′) *n.* **1.** *Ecol.* A plant or animal species persisting in a given area as a survival from an earlier period or type. **2.** *Rare* A widow or widower. — *adj. Geol.* Left by gradual erosion; residual. [< L *relicta* widow, fem. of *relictus,* pp. of *relinquere* to leave behind. See RELINQUISH.]

re·lief (ri·lēf′) *n.* **1.** The act of relieving, or the state of being relieved. **2.** That which relieves. **3.** Charitable aid in the form of money, food, clothing, etc., given to the needy. **4.** The release, as of a sentinel or guard, from his post or duty, and the substitution of another or others; also, the person or persons so substituted. **5.** In architecture and sculpture, the projection of a figure, ornament, etc., from a surface: also, any such figure: also called *relievo.* **6.** In painting, the apparent projection of forms and masses from the plane of a picture: also called *relievo.* **7.** In feudal law, a fee paid to the lord by the heir of a deceased vassal for the right of assuming the lapsed tenancy. **8.** *Geog.* **a** The elevations and unevenness of land surface. **b** The parts of a map that portray the configuration of the district represented; contour lines. — **on relief** Receiving money, food, clothing, etc., from a local or other government because of need. [< OF < relever. See RELIEVE.]

re·li·er (ri·lī′ər) *n.* One who or that which relies.

re·lieve (ri·lēv′) *v.t.* **·lieved, ·liev·ing 1.** To free wholly or partly from pain, embarrassment, etc. **2.** To lessen or alleviate, as pain or anxiety. **3.** To give aid or assistance to. **4.** To free from obligation, injustice, etc. **5.** To release from duty, as a sentinel, by providing or serving as a substitute. **6.** To make less monotonous, harsh, or unpleasant; vary. **7.** To bring into relief or prominence; display by contrast. **8.** To rid (oneself) of urine or excrement. — **to relieve of** To take from: to *relieve* someone *of* his money. — *Syn.* See ALLEVIATE. [< OF *relever* to raise again < L *relevare* to lift up < *re-* again + *levare* to lift, raise < *levis* light] — **re·liev′a·ble** *adj.* — **re·liev′er** *n.*

re·lie·vo (ri·lē′vō) *n. pl.* **·vos** Relief (defs. 5 and 6). [< Ital. < rilevare to emphasize, elevate < L relevare. See RELIEVE.]

re·li·gieuse (rə·lē·zhyœz′) *n. pl.* **·gieuses** (-zhyœz′) *French* A nun.

re·li·gieux (rə·lē·zhyœ′) *n. French* A monk.

re·li·gion (ri·lij′ən) *n.* **1.** The beliefs, attitudes, emotions, behavior, etc., constituting man's relationship with the powers and principles of the universe, especially with a deity or deities; also, any particular system of such beliefs, attitudes, etc. **2.** An essential part or a practical test of the spiritual life. **3.** An object of conscientious devotion or scrupulous care. **4.** *Obs.* Religious practice or belief. Abbr. *rel.* [< OF < L *religio, -onis* < religare < re- back + ligare to bind] — *Syn.* **1.** *Religion, faith, cult, denomination, church,* and *sect* denote a particular system of religious beliefs or the persons that adhere to it. *Religion* is the general name for all such systems, from earliest recorded history to the present day. A *faith* is a clearly formulated system of religious beliefs and worship. A *cult* is an agglomeration of practices, not necessarily theistic; the word is often applied to forms of religious worship which are regarded with suspicion or disfavor. A *denomination* is a group of persons adhering to a particular creed under a distinctive name; Baptists, Methodists, and Presbyterians are separate Christian *denominations.* *Church* is interchangeable with *denomination* in this sense. A *sect* is a smaller group within a *denomination,* especially one that differs from the larger body in a particular matter of faith or worship. *Sect* is also used derogatorily of a *denomination,* to stress its separateness or particularity.

re·lig·ion·ism (ri·lij′ən·iz′əm) *n.* The practice of or adherence to religion: used derogatorily to imply affectation and insincerity. — **re·lig′ion·ist** *n.*

re·lig·i·os·i·ty (ri·lij′ē·os′ə·tē) *n. pl.* **·ties** Religiousness; also, pious sentimentality. [< Med.L *religiositas*]

re·lig·ious (ri·lij′əs) *adj.* **1.** Feeling and manifesting religion; devout; pious. **2.** Of or pertaining to religion: a *religious* teacher. **3.** Having thorough and genuine fidelity; strict in performance; conscientious: a *religious* loyalty. **4.** Belonging to the monastic life; bound by monastic vows. — *n. pl.* **·ious** A person or people devoted to a life of piety and devotion; a monk or nun. Abbr. *rel.* [< OF *religious* < Med.L *religiosus*] — **re·lig′ious·ly** *adv.* — **re·lig′ious·ness** *n.*

re·lin·quish (ri·ling′kwish) *v.t.* **1.** To give up; abandon; surrender. **2.** To cease to demand; renounce: to *relinquish* a claim. **3.** To let go (a hold, etc.). [< OF *relinquiss-,* stem of *relinquir* < L *relinquere* < re- back, from + *linquere* to leave] — **re·lin′quish·er** *n.* — **re·lin′quish·ment** *n.*
— *Syn.* **1.** *Relinquish, abandon, surrender, yield, cede,* and *waive* mean to let go from one's possession or control. *Relinquish* is the most neutral term, indicating no more than the release of one's grasp: he *relinquished* the oars. *Abandon* is the most extreme in the sense of voluntary and complete withdrawal from control: the crew *abandoned* the ship. *Surrender* implies external compulsion: he *surrendered* his account books to the court. *Yield* is close to *surrender,* but implies milder compulsion, as of our own good nature: he *yielded* the floor to his opponent. *Cede* is used chiefly of the transfer of territory: France *ceded* Alsace-Lorraine to Germany. We *waive* rights, privileges, claims, and the like, but not material objects. — *Ant.* keep, retain.

rel·i·quar·y (rel′ə·kwer′ē) *n. pl.* **·quar·ies** A repository for relics, as a casket, coffer, or shrine. [< F *reliquaire* < L *reliquiae* remains. See RELIC.]

rel·ique (rel′ik, ri·lēk′) See RELIC.

re·liq·ui·ae (ri·lik′wi·ē) *n.pl. Latin* Fossil organisms; relics; organic remains.

rel·ish (rel′ish) *n.* **1.** Appetite; appreciation; liking: a *relish* for excitement. **2.** The flavor, especially when agreeable, in food and drink. **3.** The quality in anything that lends spice or zest: Danger gives *relish* to adventure. **4.** Something taken with food to lend it flavor or zest, as chopped pickles and spices. **5.** A small but important characteristic; flavoring: no *relish* of nature in his poetry. — *v.t.* **1.** To like the taste or savor of; enjoy: to *relish* a dinner or a joke. **2.** To give pleasant flavor to. — *v.i.* **3.** To have an agreeable flavor; afford gratification. [ME *reles* < OF *reles,* var. of *relais* remainder < *relaissier* to leave behind. See RELEASE.] — **rel·ish·a·ble** *adj.*
— *Syn.* (noun) **1.** gusto, zest.

re·live (rē·liv′) *v.* **·lived, ·liv·ing** *v.t.* **1.** To experience anew (a sensation, emotion, etc.). — *v.i.* **2.** To live again.

re·lo·cate (rē·lō′kāt) *v.t. & v.i.* **·cat·ed, ·cat·ing** To locate again or anew.

rel. pron. Relative pronoun.

re·lu·cent (ri·loō′sənt) *adj.* Shining back; reflecting light; gleaming. [< L *relucens, -entis,* ppr. of *relucere* < re- back + *lucere* to shine. See LUCENT.]

re·luct (ri·lukt′) *v.i. Archaic* **1.** To show reluctance; hesitate. **2.** To make opposition; rebel. [< L *reluctari.* See RELUCTANT.]

re·luc·tance (ri·luk′təns) *n.* **1.** The state of being reluctant. **2.** *Electr.* Capacity for opposing magnetic induction: the reciprocal of *permeance.* **3.** *Obs.* Resistance; opposition. Also **re·luc′tan·cy.** [< RELUCTANT]
— *Syn.* **1.** disinclination, unwillingness.

re·luc·tant (ri·luk′tənt) *adj.* **1.** Marked by unwillingness or rendered unwillingly. **2.** Disinclined to yield to some requirement. **3.** *Obs.* Struggling; offering opposition. [< L *reluctans, -antis,* ppr. of *reluctari* < re- back + *luctari* to fight] — **re·luc′tant·ly** *adv.*
— *Syn.* **1.** averse, hesitant, indisposed, loath.

re·luc·tiv·i·ty (rel′ək·tiv′ə·tē) *n. pl.* **·ties** *Electr.* The specific electrical reluctance, or the resistance to magnetization, of a given substance per unit of length or cross section: the reciprocal of *permeability.*

re·lume (ri·loōm′) *v.t.* **·lumed, ·lum·ing 1.** To light again; rekindle. **2.** To illuminate again. Also **re·lu·mine** (ri·loō′min). [< RE- + (IL)LUME]

re·ly (ri·lī′) *v.i.* **·lied, ·ly·ing** To place trust or confidence: with *on* or *upon.* [< OF *relier* to bind (together), adhere to < L *religare* < re- again + *ligare* to bind]

rem (rem) *n. Physics.* The quantity of absorbed ionizing radiation that has the same biological effect as one roentgen of high-voltage X-ray radiation. [< R(OENTGEN) + E(QUIVALENT) + M(AN)]

re·main (ri·mān′) *v.i.* **1.** To stay or be left behind after the removal, departure, or destruction of other persons or things. **2.** To continue in one place, condition, or character: He *remained* in office. **3.** To be left as something to be done, dealt with, etc.: It *remains* to be proved. **4.** To endure or last; abide. **— Syn.** See ABIDE. [< OF *remaindre* < L *remanere* < *re-* back + *manere* to stay, remain]

re·main·der (ri-mān′dər) *n.* **1.** That which remains; something left after a subtraction, expenditure, or passing over of a part; a residue; remnant. **2.** *Math.* The quantity left after subtraction or division. **3.** *Law* An estate in expectancy, but not in actual possession and enjoyment; the remnant or residue of interest that, on the creation of a particular prior estate, is by the same instrument limited to another to be enjoyed on the termination of that estate. **4.** In philately, an obsolete issue of stamps, demonetized by the government and generally sold at a large discount. **5.** A copy or part of an edition of a book remaining with a publisher after sales have ceased. **—** *adj.* Left over; remaining. **—** *v.t.* To sell (books, etc.) as a remainder. [< AF < OF *remaindre*. See REMAIN.]

re·main·der·man (ri-mān′dər-mən) *n. pl.* **·men** (-mən) *Law* One who is entitled to the remainder of an estate.

re·mains (ri-mānz′) *n.pl.* **1.** That which is left after a part has been removed or destroyed; remnants. **2.** The body of a deceased person; a corpse. **3.** Writings of an author published after his death. **4.** Survivals of the past, as fossils, monuments, etc.: the *remains* of ancient Troy.

re·man (rē-man′) *v.t.* **·manned, ·man·ning 1.** To furnish with a fresh complement of men. **2.** To instill courage or manliness into.

re·mand (ri-mand′, -mänd′) *v.t.* **1.** To order or send back: to *remand* a soldier to his post. **2.** *Law* **a** To recommit to custody, as an accused person after a preliminary examination. **b** To send back to a lower court, as a case improperly brought before the court so ordering. **—** *n.* **1.** The act of remanding, or the state of being remanded. **2.** A remanded person. [< OF *remander* < LL *remandare* < L *re-* back + *mandare* to order] **— re·mand′ment** *n.*

rem·a·nence (rem′ə-nəns) *n.* **1.** The state or quality of remaining; also, that which remains. **2.** *Electr.* That part of magnetic induction remaining in a material after the removal of an applied magnetomotive force. [< L *remanens, -entis,* ppr. of *remanere* to remain] **— rem′a·nent** *adj.*

re·mark (ri-märk′) *n.* **1.** An oral or written comment or saying; a casual observation. **2.** Conversational speech in general: I enjoyed his *remarks*. **3.** The act of observing or noticing; observation; notice. **4.** See REMARQUE. **—** *v.t.* **1.** To say or write by way of comment. **2.** To take particular notice of. **3.** *Obs.* To mark; distinguish. **—** *v.i.* **4.** To make remarks: with *on* or *upon*. [< F *remarque* < *remarquer* to notice < *re-* again + *marquer* to mark < Gmc. Akin to MARK¹.] **— re·mark′er** *n.*

— Syn. (noun) **1.** *Remark, observation, comment,* and *note* signify a brief statement of fact or opinion. A *remark* or *observation* may concern a subject under discussion, or be independent of it. A *remark* is a casual utterance; an *observation* is a considered statement. *Comments* and *notes* seek to clarify something said or written, or that has happened. A *comment* includes some opinion of the speaker, while a *note* is usually confined to supplementary facts.

re·mark·a·ble (ri-mär′kə-bəl) *adj.* **1.** Worthy of notice. **2.** Extraordinary; unusual; conspicuous; distinguished. **— re·mark′a·ble·ness** *n.* **— re·mark′a·bly** *adv.*

re·marque (ri-märk′) *n.* **1.** A small picture or other mark on an engraved plate, appearing on the engraved surface or in the margin, to indicate a stage in its progress before completion. **2.** A print from an engraved or etched plate bearing such a mark. Also spelled *remark.* [< F]

Re·marque (rə-märk′), **Erich Maria,** 1897–1970, U.S. novelist born in Germany: original name **Erich Paul Kra·mer** (krä′mər).

re·mar·ry (rē-mar′ē) *v.t. & v.i.* **·ried, ·ry·ing** To marry again. **— re·mar′riage** (-mar′ij) *n.*

re·match (*v.* rē-mach′; *n.* rē′mach) *v.t. & v.i.* To match again. **—** *n.* A contest between two opponents previously matched.

Rem·brandt (rem′brant, *Du.* rem′bränt), 1606–69, Dutch painter and etcher: full name **Rembrandt Harmenszoon van Rijn** (vän rīn) or **van Ryn.**

re·me·di·a·ble (ri-mē′dē·ə·bəl) *adj.* Capable of being cured or remedied. [< MF *remédiable* < L *remediabilis*] **— re·me′di·a·ble·ness** *n.* **— re·me′di·a·bly** *adv.*

re·me·di·al (ri-mē′dē·əl) *adj.* Of the nature of or adapted to be used as a remedy: *remedial* measures. [< L *remedialis* < *remediare* to remedy] **— re·me′di·al·ly** *adv.*

rem·e·di·less (rem′ə-dē-lis) *adj.* Without remedy; incurable; irreparable.

rem·e·dy (rem′ə·dē) *n. pl.* **·dies 1.** That which cures or affords relief to bodily disease or ailment; a medicine; also, remedial treatment. **2.** A means of counteracting or removing an error, evil, etc. **3.** *Law* A legal mode for enforcing a right or redressing or preventing a wrong. **4.** Tolerance

(def. 5). **—** *v.t.* **·died, ·dy·ing 1.** To cure or heal, as by medicinal treatment. **2.** To make right; repair; correct. **3.** To overcome or remove (an evil, defect, etc.). [< AF < OF *remede* < L *remedium* < *re-* again + *mederi* to heal] **— Syn.** (noun) **1.** cure, restorative. **—** (verb) **2.** redress, restore. **3.** counteract, relieve.

re·mem·ber (ri-mem′bər) *v.t.* **1.** To bring back or recall again to the mind or memory. **2.** To bear in mind carefully, as for a purpose. **3.** To bear in mind with affection, awe, etc. **4.** To bear in mind as worthy of a reward, gift, etc.: She *remembered* me in her will. **5.** To reward; tip: *Remember* the steward. **6.** *Obs.* To remind. **—** *v.i.* **7.** To have or use one's memory. **— to remember (one) to** To inform a person of the regard of: *Remember* me *to* your wife. [< OF *remembrer* < LL *rememorari* < L *re-* again + *memorare* to bring to mind < *memor* mindful] **— re·mem′ber·er** *n.*

— Syn. *Remember, recall,* and *recollect* mean to bring to mind something stored in the memory; they differ in the implied degree of effort. *Remember* suggests something stored in the memory for future use; frequently there is little or no effort of recall implied: to *remember* an address. *Recall* implies the slight effort of bringing to conscious attention what is quickly available: to *recall* one's wedding day. *Recollect* implies the strongest effort, since it suggests many details that must be gathered into a whole. Compare MEMORY. **— Ant.** forget, overlook.

re·mem·brance (ri-mem′brəns) *n.* **1.** The act or power of remembering, or the state of being remembered; memory. **2.** The period within which one can remember. **3.** That which is remembered; a reminiscence. **4.** *Often pl.* A memento; keepsake; also, a token or message of friendship. **5.** Mindful regard. **— Syn.** See MEMORY. [< OF]

Remembrance Day In Canada, November 11, set apart to honor those killed in World Wars I and II.

re·mem·branc·er (ri-mem′brən·sər) *n. Chiefly Brit.* **1.** One who or that which causes one to remember; a reminder. **2.** *Cap.* One of the recording officers of the Exchequer in England, as the **King's** or **Queen's Remembrancer,** an officer of the Supreme Court responsible for collecting debts due to the sovereign.

re·mex (rē′meks) *n. pl.* **rem·i·ges** (rem′ə·jēz) *Usually pl. Ornithol.* One of the quill feathers of a bird's wing. [< L, oarsman < *remus* oar] **— re·mig·i·al** (ri-mij′ē·əl) *adj.*

re·mind (ri-mīnd′) *v.t.* To bring to (someone's) mind; cause to remember. [< RE- + MIND] **— re·mind′er** *n.*

re·mind·ful (ri-mīnd′fəl) *adj.* **1.** Serving as a reminder: said of things. **2.** Mindful: said of persons.

Rem·ing·ton (rem′ing·tən), **Frederic,** 1861–1909, U.S. painter and sculptor.

rem·i·nisce (rem′ə·nis′) *v.i.* **·nisced, ·nisc·ing** *Chiefly U.S.* To recall incidents or events of the past; indulge in reminiscences. [Back formation < REMINISCENCE]

rem·i·nis·cence (rem′ə·nis′əns) *n.* **1.** The recalling to mind of past incidents and events. **2.** The narration of past experiences. **3.** An expression, fact, or feature serving as a reminder of something else. **— Syn.** See MEMORY. [< MF *réminiscence* or LL *reminiscentia*]

rem·i·nis·cent (rem′ə·nis′ənt) *adj.* **1.** Of the nature of or possessing reminiscence. **2.** Recalling or dwelling upon the past. **3.** Inducing a reminiscence of a person or thing; suggestive. [< L *reminiscens, -entis,* ppr. of *reminisci* < *re-* again + *memini* to remember] **— rem′i·nis′cent·ly** *adv.*

re·mise (ri-mīz′) *v.t.* **·mised, ·mis·ing** *Law* To give; surrender; release; relinquish. **—** *n.* The act of remising. [< F, fem. of *remis,* pp. of *remettre* < L *remittere.* See REMIT.]

re·miss (ri-mis′) *adj.* **1.** Slack or careless in matters requiring attention; dilatory; negligent. **2.** Lacking in earnestness or energy. [< L *remissus,* pp. of *remittere* to send back, relax. See REMIT.] **— re·miss′ness** *n.*

re·mis·si·ble (ri-mis′ə·bəl) *adj.* Capable of being remitted or pardoned, as sins. [< F *rémissible*] **— re·mis′si·bil′i·ty** *n.*

re·mis·sion (ri-mish′ən) *n.* **1.** The act of remitting, or the state of being remitted. **2.** Discharge from penalty; pardon; deliverance, as from a debt or obligation. **3.** Abatement, as of a fine erroneously imposed. **4.** Relaxation, as from work or study. **5.** *Med.* Temporary abatement of a disease or pain. **6.** The act of sending a remittance. Also **re·mit·tal** (ri-mit′l).

re·mit (ri-mit′) *v.* **·mit·ted, ·mit·ting** *v.t.* **1.** To send, as money in payment for goods; transmit. **2.** To refrain from exacting or inflicting, as a penalty. **3.** To pardon; forgive, as a sin or crime. **4.** To abate; relax, as vigilance. **5.** To restore; replace. **6.** To put off; postpone. **7.** To refer or submit for judgment, settlement, etc., as to one in authority. **8.** *Law* To refer (a legal proceeding) to a lower court for further consideration. **9.** *Rare* To send back, as to prison. **10.** *Obs.* To resign; renounce. **11.** *Obs.* To free; release. **—** *v.i.* **12.** To send money, as in payment. **13.** To diminish; abate. **—** *n.* The act of remitting; especially, the sending of a legal cause from one tribunal to another. **— Syn.** See PARDON. [< L *remittere* to send back < *re-* back + *mittere* to send] **— re·mit′ta·ble** *adj.* **— re·mit′ter** or **re·mit′tor** *n.*

re·mit·tance (ri-mit′əns) *n.* The act of sending or transmitting money or credit; also, the money or credit so sent or transmitted.

remittance man A ne'er-do-well living outside his home country on money sent by friends or relatives.

re·mit·tent (ri-mit′ənt) *adj.* **1.** Having remissions. **2.** Having partial, irregular, or temporary diminutions of energy or action, as a fever. — *n.* A remittent fever. [< L *remittens, -entis,* ppr. or *remittere.* See REMIT.] — **re·mit′tence, re·mit′ten·cy** *n.* — **re·mit′tent·ly** *adv.*

rem·nant (rem′nənt) *n.* **1.** That which remains of anything. **2.** The piece of cloth, silk, etc., left over after the last cutting. **3.** A remaining trace or vestige of anything, suggestive of former condition, use, or belief. **4.** Any small piece or quantity. **5.** A small remaining number of people. — *adj.* Like a remnant; remaining. [< OF *remenant,* ppr. of *remenoir.* See REMAIN.] — **Syn.** **1.** scrap, part. **4.** fragment, relic.

re·mod·el (rē-mod′l) *v.t.* ·eled or ·elled, ·el·ing or ·el·ling **1.** To model again. **2.** To make over or anew.

re·mon·e·tize (ri-mon′ə-tīz) *v.t.* ·tized, ·tiz·ing To reinstate (especially silver) as lawful money. — **re·mon′e·ti·za′tion** *n.*

re·mon·strance (ri-mon′strəns) *n.* **1.** The act of remonstrating; protest; expostulation. **2.** Expostulatory counsel or reproof. [< OF]

Re·mon·strance (ri-mon′strəns) *n.* The document formulating the five points of Arminian dissent from strict Calvinism, presented to the states of Holland and Friesland in 1610. — **Re·mon′strant** *n.*

re·mon·strant (ri-mon′strənt) *adj.* Having the character of a remonstrance; expostulatory. — *n.* One who presents or signs a remonstrance. [< Med.L *remonstrans, -antis,* ppr. of *remonstrare.* See REMONSTRATE.]

re·mon·strate (ri-mon′strāt) *v.* ·strat·ed, ·strat·ing *v.t.* **1.** To say or plead in protest or opposition. **2.** *Obs.* To point out; demonstrate. — *v.i.* **3.** To urge strong reasons against any course or action; protest; object. [< Med.L *remonstratus,* pp. of *remonstrare* to demonstrate < L *re-* again + *monstrare* to show] — **re·mon·stra·tion** (rē′mon-strā′shən, rem′ən-) *n.* — **re·mon′stra·tive** (-strə·tiv) *adj.* — **re·mon′stra·tor** (-strā·tər) *n.*

re·mon·tant (ri-mon′tənt) *adj. Bot.* Ascending or blooming more than once in a season, as certain roses. — *n.* A remontant rose. [< F, ppr. of *remonter.* See REMOUNT.]

rem·on·toir (rem′ən-twär′, *Fr.* rə-môn̄-twàr′) *n. Mech.* An apparatus that impels the pendulum of a clock at regular intervals. [< F]

rem·o·ra (rem′ər-ə) *n.* **1.** Any of a genus (*Remora*) of fish having on its head an oval suctorial disk by means of which it attaches itself to sharks, other fishes, or floating objects: also called *suckfish.* **2.** Any delay or impediment. [< L, hindrance < *re-* back + *mora* delay]

re·morse (ri-môrs′) *n.* **1.** The keen or hopeless anguish caused by a sense of guilt; distressing self-reproach. **2.** *Obs.* Compassion; pity. — **Syn.** See REPENTANCE. [< OF *remors* < LL *remorsus* a biting back < L *remordere* to keep biting < *re-* again + *mordere* to bite] — **re·morse′ful** *adj.* — **re·morse′ful·ly** *adv.* — **re·morse′ful·ness** *n.*

re·morse·less (ri-môrs′lis) *adj.* Having no compassion; pitiless; cruel. — **re·morse′less·ly** *adv.* — **re·morse′less·ness** *n.*

re·mote (ri-mōt′) *adj.* ·mot·er, ·mot·est **1.** Located far from a specified place: *remote* regions. **2.** Removed far from present time; distant in time: the *remote* future. **3.** Having slight relation or connection; separated; foreign; distant: a *remote* cousin. **4.** Not obvious; slight: a *remote* likeness. **5.** Abstracted; absent-minded. **6.** Distant in manner; aloof. [< L *remotus,* pp. of *removere* to remove < *re-* again + *movere* to move] — **re·mote′ly** *adv.* — **re·mote′ness** *n.*

remote control Control from a distance by electrical or radio circuits, as in the operation of a machine, aircraft, guided missile, etc.

re·mo·tion (ri-mō′shən) *n.* **1.** The act of removing; removal. **2.** *Obs.* Departure. [< OF]

ré·mou·lade (rā′mə-läd′, *Fr.* rā-mōō-làd′) *n.* A sharp sauce made of hard-boiled egg yolks, oil, vinegar, and seasoning. [< F < Ital. *remolata,* lit., vigorously stirred]

re·mount (*v.* rē·mount′; *n.* rē′mount′) *v.t. & v.i.* To mount again or anew. — *n.* **1.** A new setting or framing. **2.** A fresh riding horse. [< OF *remonter* < *re-* again (< L) + *monter* to climb]

re·mov·a·ble (ri-mōō′və-bəl) *adj.* **1.** Capable of being removed; movable. **2.** Capable of being displaced, dismissed, or obliterated: *removable* stains. — **re·mov′a·bil′i·ty, re·mov′a·ble·ness** *n.* — **re·mov′a·bly** *adv.*

re·mov·al (ri-mōō′vəl) *n.* **1.** The act of removing, or the state of being removed. **2.** Dismissal, as from office. **3.** Changing of place, as of residence or business.

re·move (ri-mōōv′) *v.* ·moved, ·mov·ing *v.t.* **1.** To take or move away, as from one place to another. **2.** To take off; doff, as a hat. **3.** To get rid of; do away with: to *remove* abuses. **4.** To kill; assassinate. **5.** To displace or dismiss, as from office. **6.** To take out; extract: with *from.* — *v.i.*

7. To change one's place of residence or business; move. **8.** *Poetic* To go away; depart. — *n.* **1.** The act of removing, as one's business or belongings; a removal. **2.** The space moved over in changing an object from one position to another. **3.** A degree of difference; step; interval: He is only one *remove* from a fool. **4.** *Brit.* A dish or course at dinner removed to give place to another. **5.** *Obs.* A period of absence. [< OF *remouvoir* < L *removere* < *re-* again + *movere* to move] — **re·mov′er** *n.* — **Syn.** (verb) **1.** transfer, transplant, transpose. **3.** eliminate, eradicate. **5.** depose, disestablish.

re·moved (ri-mōōvd′) *adj.* **1.** Separated, as by intervening space, time, or relationship; or by difference in kind: a cousin twice *removed.* **2.** Taken away; transferred. — **re·mov·ed·ness** (ri-mōō′vid·nis) *n.*

Rem·scheid (rem′shīt) A city in central North Rhine-Westphalia, West Germany; pop. 124,200 (est. 1960).

Rem·sen (rem′sən) Ira, 1846–1927, U.S. chemist and educator.

re·mu·da (rā-mōō′dä) *n. SW U.S.* The extra mounts or saddle horses of each cowboy herded together; also, in the Northwest, *saddle band.* [< Sp. < *re-* again + *mudar* to change < L *mutare*]

re·mu·ner·ate (ri-myōō′nə-rāt) *v.t.* ·at·ed, ·at·ing To make just or adequate return to or for; pay or pay for; compensate. [< L *remuneratus,* pp. of *remunerari* to reward < *re-* again + *munus, muneris* gift] — **re·mu′ner·a·bil′i·ty** *n.* — **re·mu′ner·a·ble** *adj.* — **re·mu′ner·a·tor** (-tər) *n.* — **Syn.** requite, reward.

re·mu·ner·a·tion (ri-myōō′nə-rā′shən) *n.* **1.** The act or fact of remunerating. **2.** That which remunerates; pay; compensation; recompense.

re·mu·ner·a·tive (ri-myōō′nə-rā′tiv, -nər-ə-tiv) *adj.* **1.** Profitable; lucrative. **2.** Serving to pay or remunerate: *remunerative* justice. — **re·mu′ner·a′tive·ly** *adv.* — **re·mu′ner·a′tive·ness** *n.*

Re·mus (rē′məs) In Roman mythology, the twin brother of Romulus. See ROMULUS.

Remus (rē′məs), **Uncle** See UNCLE REMUS.

ren- Var. of RENI-.

ren·ais·sance (ren′ə-säns′, -zäns′, ri-nā′səns; *Fr.* rə-ne-säns′) *n.* A new birth; resurrection; renascence. [< F < L *renascens, -entis,* ppr. of *renasci.* See RENASCENCE.]

Ren·ais·sance (ren′ə-säns′, -zäns′, ri-nā′səns; *Fr.* rə-ne-säns′) *n.* **1.** The revival of letters and art in Europe, marking the transition from medieval to modern history. It began in Italy in the 14th century and gradually spread to other countries. **2.** The period of this revival, roughly from the 14th through the 16th century. **3.** The style of art, literature, etc., marked by a classical influence, that was developed in and characteristic of this period. Also *Renascence.* — *adj.* **1.** Of, pertaining to, or characteristic of the Renaissance. **2.** Pertaining to a style of architecture developed in Italy in the 15th century, and based on the classic Roman style.

RENAISSANCE ARCHITECTURE (Church of the Redentore, Venice, 1578–80)

re·nal (rē′nəl) *adj.* Of, pertaining to, affecting, or near the kidneys. [< F *rénal* < LL *renalis* < L *renes* kidneys]

renal gland The adrenal gland (which see). Also **renal capsule.**

Re·nan (rə-nän′), (Joseph) **Ernest,** 1823–92, French historian, philologist, and critic.

Ren·ard (ren′ərd) See REYNARD.

re·nas·cence (ri-nas′əns) *n.* A new birth or rebirth; a renaissance; revival. [< L *renascens, -entis,* ppr. of *renasci* < *re-* again + *nasci* to be born] — **re·nas′cent** *adj.*

Re·nas·cence (ri-nas′əns) *n.* The Renaissance.

ren·con·tre (rän-kôn′tr′) *n. French* A rencounter.

ren·coun·ter (ren-koun′tər) *n.* **1.** An unexpected encounter, as of travelers. **2.** A contest or debate. **3.** *Obs.* A sudden hostile collision, as with an enemy. — *v.t. & v.i. Obs.* To meet unexpectedly or by surprise. [< F *rencontrer.* See RE- and ENCOUNTER.]

rend (rend) *v.* **rent** or **rend·ed, rend·ing** *v.t.* **1.** To tear apart forcibly; split; break. **2.** To pull or remove forcibly: with *away, from, off,* etc. **3.** To pass through (the air) violently and noisily. **4.** To distress (the heart, etc.), as with grief or despair. — *v.i.* **5.** To split; part. [OE *rendan* to tear, cut down] — **rend′er** *n.* — **Syn.** **1.** rip, rive, cleave, sunder.

ren·der (ren′dər) *v.t.* **1.** To give, present, or submit for action, approval, payment, etc. **2.** To provide or furnish; give: to *render* aid to the poor. **3.** To give as due: to *render* obedience. **4.** To perform; do: to *render* great service. **5.** To give or state formally: to *render* judgment. **6.** To give by way of requital or retribution: to *render* double for one's sins. **7.** To represent or depict, as in music or painting. **8.** To cause to be or become: to *render* a ship seaworthy. **9.** To express in another language; translate. **10.** To melt and clarify, as lard. **11.** To give back; return: often with *back*. **12.** To surrender; give up: to *render* a fortress. — *n.* **1.** A payment, as for rent. **2.** A coat of plaster applied without intervening lathing. [< F *rendre* < LL *rendere* < L *reddere* < *re-* back + *dare* to give] — **ren'der·a·ble** *adj.* — **ren'der·er** *n.*

ren·dez·vous (rän'dā·vōō, -də-; *Fr.* räṅ·dā·vōō') *n. pl.* **·vous** (-vōōz, *Fr.* -vōō') **1.** An appointed place of meeting. **2.** A meeting or an appointment to meet. **3.** *Mil.* A planned meeting or joining of forces at a specified time and place. **4.** *Obs.* A resort; refuge. — *v.t. & v.i.* **·voused** (-vōōd), **·vous·ing** (-vōō'ing) To assemble or cause to assemble at a certain place or time. [< F *rendez-vous*, lit., betake yourself < *se rendre* to betake oneself] — **Syn.** (noun) **2.** tryst, assignation, date.

ren·di·tion (ren·dish'ən) *n.* **1.** The interpretation of a text; a translation. **2.** Artistic, dramatic, or musical interpretation; also, the performance or execution of a dramatic or musical composition. **3.** A surrendering, especially of a person. **4.** The act of rendering; also, that which is rendered. [< obs. F < *rendre* to render]

ren·e·gade (ren'ə·gād) *n.* **1.** One who forsakes his faith, etc.; an apostate. **2.** A traitor; deserter. Also **ren'e·ga'do** (-gä'dō). — *adj.* Of or characteristic of a renegade; traitorous. [< Sp. *renegado*, pp. of *renegar* to deny < Med.L *renegare* < L *re-* again + *negare* to deny]

re·nege (ri·nig', -neg', -nēg') *v.i.* **·neged, ·neg·ing 1.** In card games, to fail to follow suit when able and required by the rules to do so; revoke. **2.** *Informal* To fail to fulfill a promise. **3.** *Obs.* To renounce; deny. [< Med.L *renegare*. See RENEGADE.] — **re·neg'er** *n.*

re·new (ri·nōō', -nyōō') *v.t.* **1.** To make new or as if new again; restore to a former or sound condition. **2.** To begin again; resume: to *renew* an argument. **3.** To repeat: to *renew* an oath of loyalty. **4.** To acquire again; regain (vigor, strength, etc.). **5.** To cause to continue in effect; extend: to *renew* a subscription. **6.** To revive; reestablish. **7.** To replenish or replace, as provisions. — *v.i.* **8.** To become new again. **9.** To begin or commence again. [< RE- + NEW] — **re·new'a·ble** *adj.* — **Syn. 1.** refresh, restore. **6.** regenerate, re-create.

re·new·al (ri·nōō'əl, -nyōō'-) *n.* The act of renewing, or the state of being renewed.

re·new·ed·ly (ri·nōō'id·lē, -nyōō'-) *adv.* Anew; repeatedly.

Renf. Renfrew.

Ren·frew (ren'frōō) A county in SW Scotland; 240 sq. mi.; pop. 359,090 (est. 1969); county seat, **Renfrew**, pop. 19,114 (est. 1969). Also **Ren'frew·shire** (-shir).

Re·ni (rā'nē), **Guido**, 1575–1642, Italian painter.

reni- *combining form* Kidney; of or related to the kidneys: *reniform.* Also *ren-* (before vowels): also *reno-.* [< L *ren, renis* kidney]

ren·i·form (ren'ə·fôrm, rē'nə-) *adj.* Kidney-shaped. [< RENI- + -FORM]

ren·in (ren'in) *n. Biochem.* A protein substance secreted by an ischemic kidney or by a blood vessel and supposed to be responsible for a rise in blood pressure. [< L *ren* kidney]

re·ni·tent (ri·nī'tənt, ren'ə·tənt) *adj.* **1.** Offering resistance to any influence or force; continuously reluctant; recalcitrant. **2.** Presenting elastic resistance to pressure. [< L *renitens, -entis*, ppr. of *reniti* to resist < *re-* back + *niti* to struggle] — **re·ni·tence** (ri·nī'təns, ren'ə·təns) or **·ten·cy** *n.*

Rennes (ren) A city in NW France; pop. 176,024 (1968).

ren·net (ren'it) *n.* **1.** The dried stomach of certain young, hoofed animals. **2.** The mucous membrane lining the fourth stomach of a suckling calf or sheep. **3.** *Biochem.* A substance that yields rennin, obtained from the stomach of such an animal. **4.** An extract or preparation containing rennin. [ME *rennen* to cause to run]

ren·nin (ren'in) *n. Biochem.* A milk-curdling enzyme present in rennet: also called *chymosin.* [< RENN(ET) + -IN]

Re·no (rē'nō) A city in western Nevada; pop. 72,863.

Re·noir (rə·nwär'), **Pierre Auguste**, 1840–1919, French Impressionist painter.

re·nounce (ri·nouns') *v.* **·nounced, ·nounc·ing** *v.t.* **1.** To give up, especially by formal statement. **2.** To disown; repudiate. **3.** In card games, to indicate inability to follow (a suit led) by playing a card of another suit. — *v.i.* **4.** In card games, to renounce the suit led. [< F *renoncer* < L *renuntiare* to protest against, announce < *re-* back, against + *nuntiare* to report < *nuntius* messenger] — **re·nounce'· ment** *n.* — **re·nounc'er** *n.* — **Syn. 1.** *Renounce, abjure, forswear, recant,* and *retract* are compared as they mean to take back something said. *Renounce, abjure,* and *forswear* originally meant to repudiate solemnly, under oath, but the first two are now often used in the general sense of put aside or abandon: to *renounce* one's citizenship, to *abjure* vice. *Forswear* has acquired an implication of perjury, which is explicit

in the reflexive form: he *forswore* himself, that is, he swore falsely. We *recant* our professed beliefs, principles, theories, and the like, and we *retract* assertions, accusations, etc., that have proven to be in error. — **Ant.** maintain, avow, uphold, acknowledge, own.

ren·o·vate (ren'ə·vāt) *v.t.* **·vat·ed, ·vat·ing 1.** To make as good as new; repair. **2.** To renew; refresh; reinvigorate. — *adj. Archaic* Renovated. [< L *renovatus*, pp. of *renovare* < *re-* again + *novare* to make new < *novus* new] — **ren'o·va'tion** *n.* — **ren'o·va'tor** *n.*

re·nown (ri·noun') *n.* **1.** Exalted reputation; celebrity; fame. **2.** *Obs.* Rumor; report. — **Syn.** See FAME. — *v.t. Obs.* To spread the fame of; render famous. [< AF *renoun* < OF *renon* < *renomer* to name again, make famous < L *re-* again + *nominare* to name < *nomen* name]

re·nowned (ri·nound') *adj.* Having renown; famous. — **Syn.** distinguished, illustrious, notable.

rens·se·laer·ite (ren'sə·lə·rīt', ren'sə·lär'īt) *n.* A light-colored, waxlike variety of talc. [after Stephen Van *Rensselaer*, 1764–1839, U.S. soldier and politician]

rent[1] (rent) *n.* **1.** Compensation made in any form by a tenant to a landlord or owner for the use of land, buildings, etc., especially when paid in money at regular or specified intervals. **2.** Similar payment for the use of any property, movable or fixed. **3.** *Econ.* **a** Income derived by the owner from the use of his land or property. **b** The return afforded by cultivated land in excess of the costs, as of labor or materials. **c** That which is yielded by land in excess of the yield of the poorest land cultivated under equal conditions: also called **economic rent. d** A return derived from a similar advantage, as in a monopoly of natural resources. **4.** *Obs.* **a** Landed or other property affording revenue. **b** Income or revenue. — **for rent** Available for use or occupancy by the paying of rent. — *v.t.* **1.** To obtain temporary possession and use of for a compensation, usually made at fixed intervals. **2.** To grant the temporary possession and use of for a rent. — *v.i.* **3.** To be let for rent. [< OF *rente* < LL *rendita*, L *reddita* what is given back or paid, fem. pp. of *reddere.* See RENDER.] — **rent'a·ble** *adj.*

rent[2] (rent) Alternative past tense and past participle of REND. — *n.* **1.** A hole or slit made by rending or tearing; rip; fissure. **2.** A violent separation; schism.

rent·al (ren'tal) *n.* **1.** The revenue derived from rented property. **2.** A schedule of rents. — *adj.* Of or pertaining to rent. [< AF]

rente (ränt) *n. French* **1.** *pl.* The bonds and other securities representing the government indebtedness of France; also, the sums paid as interest on this indebtedness: also **rentes sur l'É·tat** (ränt sür lā·tà'). **2.** Income or revenue in general; annuity.

rent·er (ren'tər) *n.* **1.** One who leases property by paying rent. **2.** One who lets property in exchange for rent.

ren·tier (rän·tyä') *n. French* One who owns or derives a fixed income from invested capital or lands.

re·nun·ci·a·tion (ri·nun'sē·ā'shən, -shē-) *n.* **1.** The act of renouncing or disclaiming; repudiation. **2.** A declaration or statement in which something is renounced. — **Syn.** See SELF-ABNEGATION. [< L *renuntiatio, -onis* proclamation] — **re·nun'ci·a·tive** *adj.* — **re·nun·ci·a·to·ry** (ri·nun'sē·ə·tôr'ē, -tō'rē, -shē-) *adj.*

re·o·pen (rē·ō'pən) *v.t. & v.i.* **1.** To open again. **2.** To begin again; resume.

re·or·der (rē·ôr'dər) *v.t.* **1.** To order (goods) again. **2.** To put back into order. **3.** To give a different order to; rearrange. — *n.* Goods ordered again.

re·or·gan·i·za·tion (rē'ôr·gən·ə·zā'shən, -ī·zā'-) *n.* **1.** The act of reorganizing, or the condition of being reorganized. **2.** The legal reconstruction of a corporation, usually after or to avert a failure. Also *Brit.* **re'or·gan·i·sa'tion.**

re·or·gan·ize (rē·ôr'gən·īz) *v.t. & v.i.* **·ized, ·iz·ing** To organize anew. Also *Brit.* **re·or'gan·ise.** — **re·or'gan·iz'er** *n.*

re·o·ri·ent (rē·ôr'ē·ənt -ō'rē-) *v.t. & v.i.* To orient again. — *adj. Rare* Rising again.

rep[1] (rep) *n.* A silk, cotton, rayon, or wool fabric having a crosswise rib: also spelled *repp.* [< F *reps*, prob. < E *ribs*]

rep[2] (rep) *n. Slang* Reputation.

rep[3] (rep) *n. Slang* A representative.

rep[4] (rep) *n. Physics* A unit of ionizing nuclear radiation equivalent to the absorption of from 83 to 97 ergs per gram of absorbing material. Compare RAD[2]. [< R(OENTGEN) + E(QUIVALENT) + P(HYSICAL)]

rep. 1. Report; reporter. **2.** Representative. **3.** Republic.

Rep. 1. Representative. **2.** Republic. **3.** Republican.

re·pair[1] (ri·pâr') *v.t.* **1.** To restore to sound or good condition after damage, injury, decay, etc.; mend. **2.** To make amends for (an injury); remedy. **3.** To make up, as a loss; compensate for. — *n.* **1.** The act or process of repairing. **2.** Condition after use or after repairing: in good *repair.* [< OF *reparer* < L *reparare* < *re-* again + *parare* to prepare, make ready] — **re·pair'er** *n.*

re·pair[2] (ri·pâr') *v.i.* **1.** To betake oneself; go: to *repair* to the garden. **2.** *Archaic* To return. — *n.* **1.** The act of repairing, or the place to which one repairs; a haunt. **2.** *Scot.* A concourse of people to a certain spot. [< OF *repairer* < LL *repatriare*. See REPATRIATE.]

re·pair·man (ri·pâr'man', -mən) *n. pl.* **·men** (-men', -mən) A man whose work is to make repairs.

re·pand (ri·pand') *adj. Bot.* Having a wavy or uneven outline: said of leaves. [< L *repandus* bent back < *re-* back + *pandus*, pp. of *pandare* to bend]

rep·a·ra·ble (rep'ər·ə·bəl) *adj.* Capable of being repaired. Also **re·pair·a·ble** (ri·pâr'ə·bəl). [< F *réparable* < L *reparabilis*] — **rep'a·ra·bil'i·ty** *n.* — **rep'a·ra·bly** *adv.*

rep·a·ra·tion (rep'ə·rā'shən) *n.* **1.** The act of making amends; atonement. **2.** That which is done by way of amends or satisfaction. **3.** The act of repairing, or the state of being repaired. **4.** *pl.* Indemnities paid by defeated countries for acts of war. [< OF < LL *reparatio, -onis* < L *parare*. See REPAIR.[1]] — **re·par·a·tive** (ri·par'ə·tiv) *adj.*

rep·ar·tee (rep'ər·tē', -âr-, -tā') *n.* **1.** Conversation marked by quick and witty replies. **2.** Skill or quickness in such conversation. **3.** A witty or quick reply; a sharp rejoinder. [< OF *repartie*, fem. pp. of *repartir* to depart again, reply < *re-* again (< L) + *partir* to divide, depart]

re·par·ti·tion (rē'pär·tish'ən) *n.* **1.** Distribution; allotment. **2.** The act of partitioning anew; redistribution.

re·pass (rē·pas', -päs') *v.t. & v.i.* To pass again; pass back.

re·pas·sage (rē·pas'ij) *n.* The right to repass, as across territory.

re·past (ri·past', -päst') *n.* **1.** Food taken at a meal. **2.** A meal. **3.** Food in general. [< OF < Med.L *repastum* meal < LL *repascere* < L *re-* again + *pascere* to feed]

re·pa·tri·ate (v. rē·pā'trē·āt; n. rē·pā'trē·it) *v.t.* **·at·ed, ·at·ing** To send back to one's own country or to the place of citizenship, as a captured soldier. — *n.* One who has been repatriated. [< LL *repatriatus*, pp. of *repatriare* < L *re-* again + *patria* native land] — **re·pa'tri·a'tion** *n.*

re·pay (ri·pā') *v.* **·paid, ·pay·ing** *v.t.* **1.** To replace or refund. **2.** To pay back or refund something to. **3.** To give a reward or inflict a penalty for; recompense or retaliate for. — *v.i.* **4.** To make repayment or requital. [< OF *repaier*] — **re·pay'a·ble** *adj.* — **re·pay'ment** *n.*

re·peal (ri·pēl') *v.t.* **1.** To rescind, as a law; revoke. **2.** *Obs.* To summon back, as from exile. — **Syn.** See ANNUL. — *n.* **1.** The act of repealing; revocation; rescission. **2.** *Obs.* Recall, as from exile. [< OF *rapeler* < *re-* back, again + *apeler* to call, summon. See APPEAL.] — **re·peal'a·ble** *adj.* — **re·peal'er** *n.*

re·peat (ri·pēt') *v.t.* **1.** To say again; iterate: to *repeat* a question. **2.** To recite from memory. **3.** To say (what another has just said). **4.** To tell, as a secret, to another. **5.** To do, make, or experience again. — *v.i.* **6.** To say or do something again. **7.** *U.S.* To vote more than once at the same election. — *n.* **1.** The act of repeating; a repetition. **2.** *Music* A passage, phrase, section, etc., that is repeated; also, any of the various notations indicating this, as double bar lines with vertical rows of dots. **3.** Anything repeated, as a supply of goods. [< OF *repeter* < L *repetere* < *re-* again + *petere* to seek, attack, demand]

re·peat·ed (ri·pē'tid) *adj.* Occurring or spoken again and again; reiterated. — **re·peat'ed·ly** *adv.*

re·peat·er (ri·pē'tər) *n.* **1.** One who or that which repeats. **2.** A watch that will strike again the hour last struck when a spring is pressed. **3.** A repeating firearm. **4.** *Telecom.* An instrument for automatically retransmitting electromagnetic signals: a telegraph *repeater.* **5.** *U.S.* One who votes, or attempts to vote, more than once at the same election. **6.** One who has been repeatedly imprisoned.

re·peat·ing decimal (ri·pē'ting) A decimal number in which a series of digits is repeated indefinitely, as 0.16353535 . . .: also called *circulating decimal, recurring decimal.*

repeating firearm A gun, rifle, or pistol capable of shooting several bullets without reloading.

re·pel (ri·pel') *v.* **·pelled, ·pel·ling** *v.t.* **1.** To force or drive back; repulse. **2.** To reject; refuse, as a suggestion. **3.** To cause to feel distaste or aversion: His manner *repels* me. **4.** To refuse to mix with or adhere to. **5.** To push or keep away, especially with invisible force: Like magnetic poles *repel* each other. — *v.i.* **6.** To act so as to drive something back or away. **7.** To cause distaste or aversion. [< L *repellere* < *re-* back + *pellere* to drive] — **re·pel'ler** *n.*

re·pel·lent (ri·pel'ənt) *adj.* **1.** Serving, tending, or having power to repel. **2.** Resistant to water; waterproof. **3.** Repugnant; repulsive. — *n.* **1.** A waterproof cloth. **2.** A remedial application that tends to repel fluids from a swollen part. **3.** A chemical compound intended to repel insects and other vermin. — **re·pel'lence, re·pel'len·cy** *n.*

re·pent[1] (ri·pent') *v.i.* **1.** To feel remorse or regret, as for something one has done or failed to do; be contrite. **2.** To change one's mind concerning past action because of disappointment, failure, etc.: with *of*: He *repented* of his generosity. **3.** *Theol.* To feel such sorrow for one's sins as to reform. — *v.t.* **4.** To feel remorse or regret for (an action, sin, etc.). **5.** To change one's mind concerning (a past action). [< OF *repentir* < L *re-* again + *poenitere* to cause to repent < *poena* punishment] — **re·pent'er** *n.*

re·pent[2] (rē'pənt) *adj.* **1.** *Bot.* Lying flat and rooting, as certain plants; procumbent. **2.** *Zool.* Reptant. [< L *repens, repentis*, ppr. or *repere* to creep]

re·pen·tance (ri·pen'təns) *n.* **1.** The act of turning with sorrow from a past course or action. **2.** The condition of being penitent. **3.** Regret; contrition.

— **Syn.** *Repentance, penitence, remorse, compunction, contrition,* and *attrition* are sorrow for sin or wrongdoing. *Repentance* and *penitence* both denote sorrow for past faults, and a sincere desire to avoid them in the future. *Repentance* often stresses a sense of self-condemnation; *penitence* points more often to the outward expressions of this inward feeling. *Remorse* and *compunction* suggest the sting of a guilty conscience. *Remorse,* the stronger word, is a prolonged or recurrent feeling of guilt over something said or done; *compunction* is often no more than a momentary regret for some past, present, or contemplated action: to feel *remorse* over past indecision and failure to act, to ignore a social obligation without *compunction. Contrition* and *attrition* are theological terms; *contrition* is *repentance* arising from love of God, while *attrition* is such *repentance* arising from less worthy motives, such as fear of punishment. *Contrition* is also used in a general sense as a close synonym of *penitence.* Compare SORROW.

re·pen·tant (ri·pen'tənt) *adj.* Showing, feeling, or characterized by repentance. [< OF] — **re·pen'tant·ly** *adv.*

re·peo·ple (rē·pē'pəl) *v.t.* **·pled, ·pling** **1.** To people anew. **2.** To provide again with animals; restock.

re·per·cus·sion (rē'pər·kush'ən) *n.* **1.** The act of driving or throwing back, or the state of being driven back; repulse. **2.** Echo; reverberation. **3.** A stroke or blow given in return; also, the recoil after impact. **4.** The indirect result of something; aftereffect. [< L *repercussio, -onis* < *repercussus*, pp. of *repercutere* to rebound < *re-* again + *percutere* to strike. See PERCUSS.] — **re·per·cus·sive** (rē'pər·kus'iv) *adj.*

rep·er·toire (rep'ər·twär, -twôr) *n.* A list of songs, plays, operas, or the like, that a person or company is prepared to perform; also, such pieces collectively: also called *repertory.* [< F *répertoire* < LL *repertorium.* See REPERTORY.]

rep·er·to·ry (rep'ər·tôr'ē, -tō'rē) *n. pl.* **·ries** **1.** Repertoire. **2.** A place where things are gathered together; a repository. **3.** The things so gathered; a collection. [< LL *repertorium* inventory < L *repertus*, pp. of *reperire* to discover < *re-* again + *parire* to produce, invent]

repertory company A theatrical group having a repertoire of productions, each typically running for a few weeks, and usually having some acting personnel continuing from one production to the next. Also called **repertory theater.**

rep·e·tend (rep'ə·tend, rep'ə·tend') *n.* **1.** *Math.* The part of a repeating decimal that is repeated indefinitely. **2.** Something repeated or to be repeated. [< L *repentendus* to be repeated, gerundive of *repetere.* See REPEAT.]

rep·e·ti·tion (rep'ə·tish'ən) *n.* **1.** The act of repeating; the doing, making, or saying of something again. **2.** Recital from memory. **3.** That which is repeated. [< F *répétition* < L *repetitio, -onis* < *repetere* to attack or seek again]

rep·e·ti·tious (rep'ə·tish'əs) *adj.* Characterized by or containing repetition, especially useless or tedious repetition. — **rep'e·ti'tious·ly** *adv.* — **rep'e·ti'tious·ness** *n.*

re·pet·i·tive (ri·pet'ə·tiv) *adj.* Pertaining to, marked by, or like repetition. — **re·pet·i·tive·ly** *adv.*

re·phrase (rē·frāz') *v.t.* **·phrased, ·phras·ing** To phrase again; especially, to express in a new way.

re·pine (ri·pīn') *v.i.* **·pined, ·pin·ing** To be discontented or fretful; complain; murmur. [< RE- + PINE[2]] — **re·pin'er** *n.*

re·place (ri·plās') *v.t.* **·placed, ·plac·ing** **1.** To put back in place. **2.** To take or fill the place of; supersede. **3.** To refund; repay. — **re·place'a·ble** *adj.* — **re·plac'er** *n.*

re·place·ment (ri·plās'mənt) *n.* **1.** That which takes the place of anything discarded, worn out, or obsolete. **2.** One who takes the place of someone or something; a substitute. **3.** A soldier available to fill a vacancy. **4.** *Mineral.* **a** The formation of a new crystal face that obliterates an edge or angle. **b** The development in an old mineral of a new one that differs from it wholly or partly in chemical composition.

re·plead·er (ri·plē'dər) *n. Law* **1.** An order of court directing the parties to file new pleadings in order to present a better issue for trial. **2.** The right of pleading again. [< RE- + obs. *pleader* pleading in court]

re·plen·ish (ri·plen'ish) *v.t.* **1.** To fill again, as something that has been wholly or partially emptied. **2.** To bring back to fullness or completeness, as supplies. **3.** To repeople; restock. [< OF *repleniss-*, stem of *replenir* < L *re-* again + *plenus* full] — **re·plen'ish·er** *n.* — **re·plen'ish·ment** *n.*

re·plete (ri·plēt') *adj.* **1.** Full to the uttermost. **2.** Gorged with food or drink; sated. **3.** Abundantly supplied or stocked; abounding. [< OF *replet* < L *repletus*, pp. of *re·plere* to fill again < *re-* again + *plere* to fill]

re·ple·tion (ri·plē'shən) *n.* **1.** The state of being replete; excessive fullness; surfeit. **2.** The satisfaction of a want.

re·plev·in (ri·plev'in) *Law* **1.** An action to regain possession of personal property unlawfully retained, on giving security to try the title and respond to the judgment; also, recovery of property by such action. **2.** The writ or process by which such proceedings are instituted. Also called *replevy.* — *v.t.* To replevy. [< AF *replevine* < OF *replevir* to warrant, pledge < *re-* back + *plevir* to pledge < Gmc.]

re·plev·y (ri-plev′ē) *Law v.t.* **·plev·ied, ·plev·y·ing 1.** To recover possession of (chattels) by proceedings in replevin. **2.** To admit to bail or give bail for. Also *replevin.* — **n.** Replevin. [< OF *replevir.* See REPLEVIN.] — **re·plev′i·a·ble, re·plev′is·a·ble** (-ə·sə·bəl) *adj.*

rep·li·ca (rep′lə·kə) *n.* **1.** A duplicate of a picture, etc., executed by the original artist. **2.** Any close copy or reproduction. — **Syn.** See DUPLICATE. [< Ital. < L *replicare* to reply, answer to. See REPLY.]

rep·li·cate (*adj.* rep′lə·kit; *v.* rep′lə·kāt) *adj.* Folded backward, as a leaf. Also **rep′li·cat′ed** (-kā′tid). — *v.t.* **·cat·ed, ·cat·ing 1.** To fold over. **2.** To make a replica of; reproduce. **3.** To answer; reply. — *v.i.* **4.** To reproduce itself or oneself. [< L *replicatus,* pp. of *replicare* to answer to.]

rep·li·ca·tion (rep′lə·kā′shən) *n.* **1.** A reply; response. **2.** *Law* A plaintiff's reply to a defendant's plea or answer. **3.** A repetition or copy. **4.** A methodical or systematic doubling over of a surface. **5.** The sending back again of sound; reverberation; echo. [< OF < L *replicatio, -onis* < *replicare* to answer to. See REPLY.] — **rep′li·ca′tive** *adj.*

re·ply (ri-plī′) *v.* **·plied, ·ply·ing** *v.i.* **1.** To give an answer orally or in writing. **2.** To respond by some act, gesture, etc.: He *replied* with a blow. **3.** To bounce back, as a sound; echo. **4.** *Law* To file a pleading in answer to the statement of the defense. — *v.t.* **5.** To say in answer: often with a clause as object: She *replied* that she would do it. — *n.* *pl.* **·plies** Something said, written, or done by way of answer. — **Syn.** See ANSWER. [< OF *replier* < L *replicare* to fold back, answer to < *re-* back + *plicare* to fold] — **re·pli′er** *n.*

ré·pon·dez s'il vous plaît (rā·pôn·dā′ sēl voo ple′) *French* Please reply: used on invitations. *Abbr.* **r.s.v.p., R.S.V.P.**

re·port (ri·pôrt′, -pōrt′) *v.t.* **1.** To make or give an account of, often formally: to *report* the minutes of a meeting. **2.** To relate, as information obtained by investigation: Please *report* your findings. **3.** To bear back or repeat to another, as an answer. **4.** To complain about, especially to a superior: I'll *report* you to the manager. **5.** To state the result of consideration concerning: The committee *reported* the bill. — *v.i.* **6.** To make a report. **7.** To act as a reporter. **8.** To present oneself, as for duty. — *n.* **1.** That which is reported; an announcement, statement, or account. **2.** The formal statement of the result of an investigation: a medical *report.* **3.** Common talk; rumor: *reports* grossly untrue. **4.** Fame, reputation, or character: a person of good *report.* **5.** A record with more or less detail of the transactions of a deliberative body. **6.** An account of any occurrence prepared for publication through the press. **7.** *Usually pl. Law* A published narration (usually official) of a case or series of cases judicially considered. **8.** An explosive sound. — **Syn.** See ACCOUNT. *Abbr.* **rep., rp.** [< OF *reporter* < L *reportare* < *re-* back + *portare* to carry] — **re·port′a·ble** *adj.*

re·port·age (ri·pôr′tij, -pōr′-, rep′ər·täzh′) *n.* **1.** The act, process, or style of reporting news. **2.** Articles, reports, etc., written in journalistic form. [< F]

report card *U.S.* A periodic statement of a pupil's scholastic record, which is presented to the parents or guardian.

re·port·ed·ly (ri·pôr′tid·lē, -pōr′-) *adv.* According to report.

re·port·er (ri·pôr′tər, -pōr′-) *n.* **1.** One who reports; especially, one who is employed by a newspaper, magazine, etc., to report news. **2.** One who edits reports of important cases in court for official publication. *Abbr.* **rep.** [< OF *reporteur*] — **rep·or·to·ri·al** (rep′ər·tôr′ē·əl, -tō′rē-) *adj.*

re·pose¹ (ri·pōz′) *n.* **1.** The act of taking rest or the state of being at rest; especially, rest in a recumbent posture. **2.** Freedom from excitement or anxiety; composure. **3.** Ease of manner; graceful and dignified calmness. **4.** That which conduces to rest or calm. — *v.* **·posed, ·pos·ing** *v.t.* **1.** To lay or place in a position of rest: to *repose* oneself on a bed. — *v.i.* **2.** To lie at rest. **3.** To rely; depend: with *on, upon,* or *in.* [< F *reposer* < LL *repausare* < *re-* again + *pausare* to pause] — **re·pos′al** *n.* — **re·pos′er** *n.*

re·pose² (ri·pōz′) *v.t.* **·posed, ·pos·ing 1.** To place, as confidence or hope: with *in.* **2.** *Rare* To deposit. [ME *reposen* < L *repositus,* pp. of *reponere* to put back, on analogy with *depose, oppose,* etc. See REPOSITORY.] — **re·pos′al** *n.*

re·pose·ful (ri·pōz′fəl) *adj.* Full of repose; restful.

re·pos·it (ri·poz′it) *v.t.* To put in some secure and proper place; deposit. [< L *repositus.* See REPOSITORY.] — **re·po·si·tion** (rē′pə·zish′ən, rep′ə-) *n.*

re·pos·i·to·ry (ri·poz′ə·tôr′ē, -tō′rē) *n. pl.* **·ries 1.** A place in which goods are or may be stored; a depository. **2.** A person to whom a secret is entrusted. **3.** A building used as a place of exhibition and sale. **4.** A burial vault. **5.** A sepulcher (def. 2). [< L *repositorium* < *repositus,* pp. of *reponere* < *re-* back, again + *ponere* to place]

re·pos·sess (rē′pə·zes′) *v.t.* **1.** To have possession of again. **2.** To give back possession or ownership to. **3.** *Scot.* To reinstate: with *in.* — **re·pos·ses′sion** (-zesh′ən) *n.*

re·pous·sé (rə·pōō·sā′) *adj.* **1.** Formed in relief, as a design in metal. **2.** Adorned with such designs. [< F]

repp (rep) See REP¹.

Rep·plier (rep′lir), **Agnes,** 1855–1950, U.S. essayist.

repr. 1. Representing. **2.** Reprinted.

rep·re·hend (rep′ri·hend′) *v.t.* To criticize sharply; find fault with; blame. [< L *reprehendere* < *re-* back + *prehendere* to hold] — **Syn.** censure, rebuke, animadvert, denounce.

rep·re·hen·si·ble (rep′ri·hen′sə·bəl) *adj.* Deserving blame or censure. [< LL *reprehensibilis* < *reprehendere.* See REPREHEND.] — **rep′re·hen′si·bil′i·ty, rep′re·hen′si·ble·ness** *n.* — **rep′re·hen′si·bly** *adv.*

rep·re·hen·sion (rep′ri·hen′shən) *n.* The act of reprehending; also, an expression of blame; a rebuke. — **rep′re·hen′sive** *adj.* — **rep′re·hen′si·bly** *adv.*

rep·re·hen·so·ry (rep′ri·hen′sər·ē) *adj.* Censorious.

rep·re·sent (rep′ri·zent′) *v.t.* **1.** To serve as the symbol, expression, or designation of; symbolize: The letters of the alphabet *represent* the sounds of speech. **2.** To express or symbolize in this manner: to *represent* royal power with a scepter. **3.** To set forth a likeness or image of; depict; portray, as in painting or sculpture. **4.** To produce on the stage, as an opera. **5.** To act the part of; impersonate. **6.** To serve as or be the delegate, agent, etc., of. **7.** To describe as being of a specified character or condition: They *represented* him as a genius. **8.** To set forth in words; state; explain: He *represented* the circumstances of his case. **9.** To bring before the mind; present clearly. **10.** To serve as an example, specimen, type, etc., of; typify. [< OF *representer* < L *repraesentare* < *re-* again + *praesentare.* See PRESENT².] — **rep′re·sent′a·ble** *adj.* — **rep′re·sent′a·bil′i·ty** *n.*

re-pre·sent (rē′pri·zent′) *v.t.* To present again. — **re′-pre′·sen·ta′tion** *n.*

rep·re·sen·ta·tion (rep′ri·zen·tā′shən) *n.* **1.** The act of representing or the state of being represented. **2.** Anything that represents, as a verbal description, a picture, a statue, etc. **3.** A dramatic performance. **4.** The right of acting authoritatively for others, especially in a legislative body. **5.** The system of electing delegates to act for a constituency. **6.** Representatives collectively. **7.** *Law* The authorized acting for or in the stead of another in regard to that other's affairs. **8.** A setting forth by statement or account; especially, an argument against some object or proposal. [< OF]

rep·re·sen·ta·tion·al (rep′ri·zen·tā′shən·əl) *adj.* **1.** Serving to represent; especially, denoting a style of art that seeks to represent objects. **2.** Of, pertaining to, or of the nature of representation.

rep·re·sen·ta·tive (rep′ri·zen′tə·tiv) *adj.* **1.** Typifying or typical of a group or class. **2.** Acting, having the power or authority to act, or qualified to act, as an agent. **3.** Made up of representatives. **4.** Based on or pertaining to the political principle of representation. **5.** Presenting, portraying, or representing, or capable of so doing. — *n.* **1.** One who or that which is fit to stand as a type; a typical instance. **2.** One who is a qualified agent of any kind. **3.** A member of a deliberative or legislative body chosen by vote of the people; especially, in the United States, a member of the lower house of Congress or of a State legislature. *Abbr.* **rep., Rep.** — **Syn.** See DELEGATE. — **rep′re·sen·ta·tive·ly** *adv.* — **rep′re·sen·ta·tive·ness** *n.*

re·press (ri·pres′) *v.t.* **1.** To keep under restraint or control. **2.** To put down; quell, as a rebellion. **3.** *Psychoanal.* To effect the repression of, as fears, impulses, etc. [< L *repressus,* pp. of *reprimere* < *re-* back + *premere* to press] — **re·press′er** or **re·pres′sor** *n.* — **re·press′i·ble** *adj.* — **Syn. 1.** check, curb, rein, restrain, subdue, suppress.

re-press (rē′pres′) *v.t. & v.i.* To press again.

re·pres·sion (ri·presh′ən) *n.* **1.** The act of repressing or the condition of being repressed. **2.** That which holds in check; a restraint. **3.** *Psychoanal.* The exclusion from consciousness of painful, unpleasant, or unacceptable memories, desires, and impulses.

re·pres·sive (ri·pres′iv) *adj.* **1.** Tending to repress. **2.** Capable of repressing. — **re·pres′sive·ly** *adv.* — **re·pres′sive·ness** *n.*

re·prieve (ri·prēv′) *v.t.* **·prieved, ·priev·ing 1.** To suspend temporarily the execution of a sentence upon. **2.** To relieve for a time from suffering, danger, or trouble. **3.** To postpone or delay. — *n.* **1.** The temporary suspension of a sentence, or the instrument ordering such a suspension. **2.** Temporary relief or cessation of pain or ill. **3.** The act of reprieving or the state of being reprieved. [< earlier *repry* < F *repris,* pp. of *reprendre* to take back; infl. in form by ME *repreven* < OF *reprover* to reprove] — **re·priev′a·ble** *adj.*

rep·ri·mand (rep′rə·mand, -mänd) *v.t.* To reprove sharply or formally. — *n.* Severe reproof or formal censure, public or private. — **Syn.** See REPROOF. [< F *réprimande* < L *reprimenda,* fem. of *reprimendus,* gerundive of *reprimere.* See REPRESS.]

re·print (*n.* rē′print′; *v.* rē·print′) *n.* An edition of a printed work that is a verbatim copy of the original; especially, a copy of matter already printed, as in another country. — *v.t.* To print a new edition or copy of. — **re·print′er** *n.*

re·pri·sal (ri·prī′zəl) *n.* **1.** Forcible seizure of anything from an enemy by way of retaliation or indemnity. **2.** Anything taken from an enemy as indemnification or in retaliation. **3.** Any act of retaliation. **4.** *Mil.* The application of force or violence by one nation against another in retaliation for acts committed or to compel compliance. **5.** *Obs.* A prize seized or gained. — **Syn.** See REVENGE. [< OF *reprisaille* < *repris*, pp. of *reprendre* to take back < L *reprehendere*. See REPREHEND.]

re·prise (ri·prīz′ *for def. 1;* rə·prēz′, -prīz′ *for def. 2*) *n.* **1.** *pl. Brit. Law* Deductions and payments (as for annuities) out of lands: a manor's yearly value over and above *reprises*. **2.** *Music* A repeated phrase; especially, the repetition of or return to the subject after an intermediate movement. [< OF, fem. of *repris.* See REPRISAL.]

re·proach (ri·prōch′) *v.t.* **1.** To charge with or blame for something wrong; rebuke; censure. **2.** To bring discredit and disgrace upon; to disgrace. — *n.* **1.** The act of reproaching, or the words of one who reproaches; censure; reproof; rebuke. **2.** A cause of blame or disgrace. **3.** Disgrace; discredit. — **Syn.** See REPROOF. [< F *reprocher*; ult. origin uncertain.] — **re·proach′a·ble** *adj.* — **re·proach′a·ble·ness** *n.* — **re·proach′a·bly** *adv.* — **re·proach′er** *n.*

re·proach·ful (ri·prōch′fəl) *adj.* **1.** Containing or full of reproach; expressing reproach. **2.** *Obs.* Disgraceful. — **re·proach′ful·ly** *adv.* — **re·proach′ful·ness** *n.*

rep·ro·bate (rep′rə·bāt) *adj.* **1.** Having lost all sense of duty; depraved; profligate. **2.** Abandoned to punishment; condemned. **3.** *Obs.* Not enduring proof or trial; inferior or base. — *n.* A depraved or profligate person. — *v.t.* **·bat·ed, ·bat·ing 1.** To disapprove of heartily; condemn. **2.** *Theol.* To abandon, condemn, or foreordain to damnation. [< LL *reprobatus,* pp. of *reprobare.* See REPROVE.]

rep·ro·ba·tion (rep′rə·bā′shən) *n.* **1.** The act of reprobating or the condition of being reprobated; censure. **2.** *Theol.* Rejection or condemnation by God.
— **Syn. 1.** reprehension, denunciation, animadversion.

rep·ro·ba·tive (rep′rə·bā′tiv) *adj.* Of, pertaining to, or expressing reprobation. — **rep′ro·ba·tive·ly** *adv.*

re·proc·ess (rē·pros′es) *v.t.* To process again.

re·proc·essed wool (rē·pros′est) Woven or knitted wool fibers, never used by a consumer, that are unraveled, spun, and rewoven into fabric.

re·pro·duce (rē′prə·d͞oos′, -dy͞oos′) *v.* **·duced, ·duc·ing** *v.t.* **1.** To make a copy, image, or reproduction of. **2.** *Biol.* **a** To give rise to (offspring) by sexual or asexual generation. **b** To replace (a lost part or organ) by regeneration. **3.** To cause the reproduction of (plant life, etc.). **4.** To produce again; bring forward or exhibit anew. **5.** To bring into existence again; re-create. **6.** To recall to the mind; visualize again. — *v.i.* **7.** To produce offspring. **8.** To undergo copying, reproduction, etc. — **re′pro·duc′i·ble** *adj.*

re·pro·duc·er (rē′prə·d͞oos′ər, -dy͞oo′-) *n.* One who or that which reproduces.

re·pro·duc·tion (rē′prə·duk′shən) *n.* **1.** The act or power of reproducing. **2.** *Biol.* The process by which an animal or plant gives rise to another of its kind. **3.** That which is reproduced, as a revival of a play or a copy of a picture.

re·pro·duc·tive (rē′prə·duk′tiv) *adj.* Pertaining to, employed in, or tending to reproduction. — **re′pro·duc′tive·ly** *adv.* — **re′pro·duc′tive·ness** *n.*

re·proof (ri·pro͞of′) *n.* **1.** The act of reproving; rebuke; blame; censure. **2.** *Obs.* Ignominy; reproach. Also **re·prov·al** (ri·pro͞o′vəl). [< OF *reprove* < *reprover.* See REPROVE.]
— **Syn. 1.** *Reproof, rebuke, censure, reprimand, reproach,* and *admonition* denote disapproval and blame directed at a person to chasten him. *Reproof* may be mild and friendly; *rebuke* is sharper; *censure* is the most severe. *Reprimand* is formal *reproof,* as for carelessness or poor judgment. *Reproach* expresses personal hurt or displeasure, as at thoughtlessness or selfishness. *Admonition* is warning or counsel, looking to future conduct rather than to past misdeeds. Compare ANIMADVERSION.

re·prove (ri′pro͞ov′) *v.t.* **·proved, ·prov·ing 1.** To censure, as for a fault; rebuke. **2.** To express disapproval of (an act). **3.** *Obs.* To convince; convict. [< OF *reprover* < LL *reprobare* < *re-* again (< L) + *probare* to test < *probus* upright] — **re·prov′a·ble** *adj.* — **re·prov′er** *n.* — **re·prov′ing·ly** *adv.*
— **Syn. 1.** chide, upbraid, reprimand. Compare REPROOF.

re·prove (rē·pro͞ov′) *v.t.* **·proved, ·prov·ing** To prove (a theory, assertion, etc.) anew.

rep·tant (rep′tənt) *adj. Zool.* Creeping; crawling: also **re·pent.** [< L *reptans, -antis,* ppr. of *reptare,* intens. of *repere* to creep. Cf. REPTILE.]

rep·tile (rep′til, -tīl) *n.* **1.** Any of a class (*Reptilia*) of cold-blooded, air-breathing vertebrates, including the snakes, crocodiles, lizards, and turtles, having fully ossified skeletons and bodies usually covered with horny plates or scales. **2.** A groveling, abject person. — *adj.* **1.** Crawling on the belly. **2.** Groveling morally; sly and base; treacherous. **3.** Of, pertaining to, or resembling a reptile. [< LL, neut. sing. of *reptilis* crawling < *reptus,* pp. of *repere* to creep]

rep·til·i·an (rep·til′ē·ən) *adj.* Of, pertaining to, or characteristic of a reptile or reptiles. — *n.* Any reptile.

Repub. **1.** Republic. **2.** Republican.

re·pub·lic (ri·pub′lik) *n.* **1.** A state in which the sovereignty resides in the people or a certain portion of the people, and the legislative and administrative powers are lodged in officers elected by and representing the people; a representative democracy. Compare DEMOCRACY. **2.** A community of persons working freely in or devoted to the same cause: the *republic* of letters. Abbr. *rep., Rep., Repub.* — **the Republic 1.** The United States. **2.** A dialogue on government written by Plato. [< F *république* < L *respublica* co nmonwealth < *res* thing + *publica,* fem. of *publicus* public]

Re·pú·bli·ca Do·mi·ni·ca·na (rä·po͞o′blē·kä dō·mē′nē·kä′nä) The Spanish name for the DOMINICAN REPUBLIC.

re·pub·li·can (ri·pub′li·kən) *adj.* **1.** Of, pertaining to, like, or suitable for a republic. **2.** Of or pertaining to any party supporting republican government. — *n.* One who advocates or upholds a republican form of government or belongs to a party upholding republican government.

Re·pub·li·can (ri·pub′li·kən) *adj.* Pertaining to or belonging to the Republican Party of the United States, or to any political group that calls itself by this name. — *n.* A member of the Republican Party. Abbr. *R., Rep., Repub.*

Republican calendar See under CALENDAR.

re·pub·li·can·ism (ri·pub′li·kən·iz′əm) *n.* **1.** The theory or principles of republican government. **2.** Advocacy of or adherence to republican principles.

Re·pub·li·can·ism (ri·pub′li·kən·iz′əm) *n.* The policy and principles of the Republican Party of the United States.

re·pub·li·can·ize (ri·pub′li·kən·īz′) *v.t.* **·ized, ·iz·ing** To make republican. — **re·pub′li·can·i·za′tion** *n.*

Republican Party 1. One of the two major political parties of the United States, founded in 1854 in opposition to the extension of slavery. **2.** The political party founded by Thomas Jefferson in 1792: full name, **Democratic-Republican Party.** One of its several factions became, in 1828, the present Democratic Party. **3.** One of various political parties of foreign countries, devoted to the overthrow of monarchy or to the establishment of democratic ideals.

Republican River A river in Colorado, Nebraska, and Kansas, flowing 445 miles, generally east, to the Kansas River.

re·pub·li·ca·tion (rē′pub·lə·kā′shən) *n.* The act of republishing, or that which is republished.

Ré·pu·blique Cen·tra·fri·caine (rä′pü·blēk′ säṅ·trà′frē·ken′) The French name for the CENTRAL AFRICAN REPUBLIC.

République de Gui·née (də gē·nā′) The French name for the (Republic of) GUINEA.

République de Haute-Vol·ta (ōt′vòl·tà′) The French name for the (Republic of) UPPER VOLTA.

République du Con·go (kôṅ·gō′). **1.** The French name for the (Republic of the) CONGO (BRAZZAVILLE). **2.** The French name for the (Republic of the) CONGO (LEOPOLDVILLE).

République du Côte d'I·voire (dü kōt dē·vwàr′) The French name for the (Republic of the) IVORY COAST.

République du Dahomey The French name for DAHOMEY.

République du Ma·li (mà′lē′) The French name for the (Republic of) MALI.

République du Ni·ger (nē·zhâr′) The French name for the (Republic of) NIGER.

République du Sé·né·gal (sā·nā·gàl′) The French name for the (Republic of) SENEGAL.

République du Tchad (chàd) The French name for CHAD.

République Ga·bo·naise (gà·bô·nez′) The French name for the (Republic of) GABON.

République Is·la·mique de Mau·ri·ta·nie (ēs·là·mēk′ də mô·rē·tà·nē′) The French name for the (Islamic Republic of) MAURITANIA.

République Mal·gache (màl·gàsh′) The French name for the MALAGASY REPUBLIC.

République To·go·laise (tô·gô·lez′) The French name for TOGO.

re·pub·lish (rē·pub′lish) *v.t.* **1.** To publish again. **2.** *Law* To revive, as a canceled will, by executing anew. — **re·pub′lish·er** *n.*

re·pu·di·ate (ri·pyo͞o′dē·āt) *v.t.* **·at·ed, ·at·ing 1.** To refuse to accept as valid or binding; reject. **2.** To refuse to acknowledge or pay. **3.** To cast off; disown, as a son. **4.** *Obs.* To divorce (a wife). [< L *repudiatus,* pp. of *repudiare* to divorce < *repudium* divorce, separation, ? < *re-* back + *pudere* to feel shame] — **re·pu′di·a′tive** *adj.* — **re·pu′di·a′tor** *n.*

re·pu·di·a·tion (ri·pyo͞o′dē·ā′shən) *n.* **1.** The act of repudiating or the state of being repudiated. **2.** The disowning of a contract, debt, or obligation, as by a government.

re·pugn (ri·pyo͞on′) *v.t. & v.i. Obs.* To oppose; resist. [< OF *repugner* < L *repugnare* < *re-* back + *pugnare* to fight]

re·pug·nance (ri·pug′nəns) *n.* **1.** The state of feeling aversion and resistance. **2.** *Logic* The relation of contradictories; inconsistency. **3.** *Obs.* Opposition. Also **re·pug′nan·cy.**
— **Syn. 1.** antagonism, antipathy, detestation.

re·pug·nant (ri·pug′nənt) *adj.* **1.** Offensive to taste or feeling; exciting aversion or repulsion. **2.** Being inconsistent or opposed; antagonistic. **3.** Hostile; resisting. [< OF < L *repugnans, -antis,* ppr. of *repugnare.* See REPUGN.]

re·pulse (ri·puls′) *v.t.* **·pulsed, ·puls·ing** **1.** To drive back; repel, as an attacking force. **2.** To repel by coldness, discourtesy, etc.; reject; rebuff. **— n. 1.** The act of repulsing or the state of being repulsed. **2.** Rejection; refusal. [< L *repulsus,* pp. of *repellere.* See REPEL.] **— re·puls′er** *n.*

re·pul·sion (ri·pul′shən) *n.* **1.** The act of repelling or repulsing, or the state of being repelled or repulsed. **2.** Aversion; repugnance. **3.** *Physics* The mutual action of two bodies that tends to drive them apart.

re·pul·sive (ri·pul′siv) *adj.* **1.** Exciting feelings of dislike, disgust, or horror; grossly offensive. **2.** Such as to forbid approach or familiarity; forbidding. **3.** Acting by repulsion: *repulsive* forces. **— re·pul′sive·ly** *adv.* **— re·pul′sive·ness** *n.*

rep·u·ta·ble (rep′yə·tə·bəl) *adj.* **1.** Having a good reputation; estimable; honorable. **2.** Consistent with proper usage, as words. **— rep·u·ta·bil′i·ty** *n.* **— rep′u·ta·bly** *adv.*

rep·u·ta·tion (rep′yə·tā′shən) *n.* **1.** The general estimation in which a person or thing is held by others, especially by a community; repute. **2.** The state of being in high regard or esteem; good repute: to ruin one's *reputation.* **3.** A particular credit or character ascribed to a person or thing: a *reputation* for honesty. **— Syn.** See FAME. [< L *reputatio, -onis* < *reputare,* pp. of *reputare.* See REPUTE.]

re·pute (ri·pyōōt′) *v.t.* **·put·ed, ·put·ing** To regard or consider to be as specified; esteem: usually in the passive: They are *reputed* to be an intelligent people. **— n. 1.** Reputation (defs. 1 and 2). **2.** Public opinion; general report. **— Syn.** See FAME. [< OF *reputer* or L *reputare* to reckon, be reputed < *re-* again + *putare* to think, count]

re·put·ed (ri·pyōō′tid) *adj.* Generally thought or supposed: a *reputed* criminal. **— re·put′ed·ly** *adv.*

req. 1. Required. **2.** Requisition.

re·quest (ri·kwest′) *v.t.* **1.** To express a desire for, especially politely; ask for; solicit. **2.** To ask (a person) to do a favor, answer an inquiry, etc. **— Syn.** See ASK. **— n. 1.** The act of requesting; petition. **2.** That which is requested. **3.** The state of being so esteemed as to be in demand; demand: in *request.* **4.** Having been asked for; in response to a request: a *request* program. [< OF *requeste* < Med.L *requisita* < L *requisitus,* pp. of *requirere* to seek again. See REQUIRE.]

re·qui·em (rē′kwē·əm, rek′wē-) *n.* **1.** Any musical hymn, composition, or service for the dead. **2.** *Often cap. Eccl.* In the Roman Catholic Church, a solemn mass sung for the repose of the souls of the dead: also **Requiem mass. 3.** *Often cap.* A musical setting for such a mass; also, a similar piece of music using different words. [< L *Requiem* (*aeternam dona eis, Domine*) rest (eternal give unto them, O Lord), the opening words of the introit of this mass]

req·ui·es·cat (rek′wē·es′kat) *n.* A prayer for the repose of the dead. [< L, first word of REQUIESCAT IN PACE]

req·ui·es·cat in pa·ce (rek′wē·es′kat in pā′sē) May he rest in peace. *Abbr. R.I.P.* [< L]

re·quire (ri·kwīr′) *v.* **·quired, ·quir·ing** *v.t.* **1.** To have need of; find necessary. **2.** To demand authoritatively; insist upon: to *require* absolute silence. **3.** To command; order: He *requires* us to be punctual. **— v.i. 4.** To make demand or request. **— Syn.** See DEMAND. [< OF *requerre* < L *requirere* < *re-* again + *quaerere* to ask, seek] **— re·quir′a·ble** *adj.* **— re·quir′er** *n.*

re·quire·ment (ri·kwīr′mənt) *n.* **1.** That which is required; a requisite. **2.** The act of requiring. **3.** A demand.

req·ui·site (rek′wə·zit) *adj.* Required by the nature of things or by circumstances; indispensable. **— Syn.** See NECESSARY. **— n.** That which cannot be dispensed with; a necessity; requirement. [< L *requisitus,* pp. of *requirere.* See REQUEST.] **— req′ui·site·ly** *adv.* **— req′ui·site·ness** *n.*

req·ui·si·tion (rek′wə·zish′ən) *n.* **1.** A formal request, summons, or demand, as by a government. **2.** A necessity or requirement. **3.** The state of being required. **4.** A demand for the surrender of a fugitive from justice made by the governing official of one state or country upon another. **— v.t.** To make a requisition for or upon; demand or take upon requisition. *Abbr. req.* [< L *requisitio, -onis* < *requisitus,* pp. of *requirere.* See REQUIRE.]

re·quit·al (ri·kwīt′l) *n.* **1.** The act of requiting. **2.** That which requites; reward or retaliation.

re·quite (ri·kwīt′) *v.t.* **·quit·ed, ·quit·ing** **1.** To make equivalent return for, as kindness, service, or injury; make up for. **2.** To make return to; compensate or repay in kind. **3.** To give or do in return. [< RE- + *quite,* obs. var. of QUIT] **— re·quit′a·ble** *adj.* **— re·quit′er** *n.*

re·ra·di·a·tion (rē′rā′dē·ā′shən) *n. Physics* Secondary emission.

rere·dos (rir′dos) *Chiefly Brit. n.* **1.** An ornamental screen behind an altar. **2.** The back of an open fire hearth. In old armor, a backplate. [< AF < *rere* rear (ult. < L *retro*) + *dos* back < L *dorsum*]

rere·mouse (rir′mous) *n. pl.* **·mice** (-mīs) *Brit. Dial.* A bat: also spelled *rearmouse.* [OE *hrēremūs,* prob. < *hrēran* to move + *mus* mouse]

re·run (*n.* rē′run; *v.* rē·run′) *n.* **1.** The presenting of a motion picture, play, etc., after its original run is over; also, the motion picture, play, etc., so presented. **2.** The act or process of running again or a second time. **— v.t. ·ran, ·run, ·run·ning 1.** To present as a rerun. **2.** To run again or a second time.

res. 1. Research. **2.** Reserve. **3.** Residence. **4.** Resides. **5.** Residue. **6.** Resigned. **7.** Resolution.

Re·sa·ca de la Pal·ma (rā·sä′kä dā lä päl′mä) A locality in southern Texas north of Brownsville; scene of an American victory over the Mexicans, 1846.

res ad·ju·di·ca·ta (rēz a·jōō′də·kā′tə) See RES JUDICATA.

re·sale (rē′sāl, rē·sāl′) *n.* The act of selling again.

re·scind (ri·sind′) *v.t.* To make void, as an act; abrogate; repeal: to *rescind* a resolution. **— Syn.** See ANNUL. [< L *rescindere* < *re-* back + *scindere* to cut] **— re·scind′a·ble** *adj.* **— re·scind′er** *n.*

re·scis·si·ble (ri·sis′ə·bəl) *adj.* Capable of being rescinded.

re·scis·sion (ri·sizh′ən) *n.* The act of rescinding or abrogating.

re·scis·so·ry (ri·sis′ər·ē, -siz′-) *adj.* Having power to rescind; rescinding; revoking. [< LL *rescissorius* < L *rescissus,* pp. of *rescindere.* See RESCIND.]

re·script (rē′skript) *n.* **1.** In ancient Rome, an imperial decree, consisting of the emperor's answer to questions on matters of state or law. **2.** Any decree, edict, order, or formal announcement. **3.** A formal, written reply by the Pope to a petition or question of morality or canon law submitted to him. **4.** Something written over again, as a facsimile. [< L *rescriptum,* orig. neut. pp. of *rescribere* to write in reply < *re-* back + *scribere* to write]

res·cue (res′kyōō) *v.t.* **·cued, ·cu·ing 1.** To save or free from danger, captivity, evil, etc.; deliver. **2.** *Law* To take or remove forcibly from the custody of the law. **— n.** The act of rescuing; deliverance. [< OF *rescourre* < *re-* back (< L) + *escorre* to move, shake < L *excutere* < *ex-* out of + *quatere* to shake] **— res′cu·a·ble** *adj.* **— res′cu·er** *n.*

re·search (ri·sûrch′, rē′sûrch) *n.* **1.** Diligent, protracted investigation; studious inquiry. **2.** A systematic investigation of some phenomenon or series of phenomena by the experimental method. **— v.i.** To undertake research; investigate. *Abbr. res.* [< F *recherche* < *re-* back (< L) + *chercher* to seek. See SEARCH.] **— re·search′er** *n.*

re-search (rē·sûrch′) *v.t. & v.i.* To search again or anew.

re·seat (rē·sēt′) *v.t.* **1.** To seat again. **2.** To put a new seat or seats in or on.

ré·seau (rā·zō′) *n. pl.* **·seaux** (-zō′) **1.** In textile work, a netted ground or meshed foundation. **2.** *Astron.* The small lines forming squares cut upon a glass plate, used in mapping out the heavens by photography. **3.** *Meteorol.* A group of weather stations operating in the same territory or under common direction. **4.** *Photog.* A sensitive filter screen for making color films. [< F, dim. of OF *roiz* net < L *rete*]

re·sect (ri·sekt′) *v.t. Surg.* To cut or pare off. [< L *resectus,* pp. of *resecare* < *re-* back + *secare* to cut]

re·sec·tion (ri·sek′shən) *n.* **1.** *Surg.* The operation of cutting out part of a bone, organ, etc. **2.** The determination of a position with reference to points of known location, whether on the ground or on a map or chart.

re·se·da (ri·sē′də) *n.* **1.** Any of a genus (*Reseda*) of herbs that include the mignonette. **2.** A light yellowish or grayish green: also called *mignonette.* [< L, prob. < *resedare* assuage; because once used as part of a healing charm]

res·e·da·ceous (res′ə·dā′shəs) *adj. Bot.* Designating a family (*Resedaceae*) of annual or perennial herbs of which the mignonette is typical.

re·sell (rē·sel′) *v.t.* **·sold, ·sell·ing** To sell anew or again. **— re·sell′er** *n.*

re·sem·blance (ri·zem′bləns) *n.* **1.** The quality of similarity in nature, form, etc.; relative identity; likeness. **2.** That which resembles; a semblance or likeness of a person or thing. **3.** *Obs.* A characteristic quality or attribute. **4.** *Obs.* Probability or likelihood. **— Syn.** See ANALOGY.

re·sem·ble (ri·zem′bəl) *v.t.* **·bled, ·bling 1.** To be similar to in appearance, quality, or character. **2.** *Obs.* To compare; liken. [< OF *resembler* < *re-* again (< L) + *sembler* to seem < L *simulare.* See SIMULATE.] **— re·sem′bler** *n.*

re·send (rē·send′) *v.t. & v.i.* **·sent, ·send·ing** To send again or send back.

re·sent (ri·zent′) *v.t.* To feel or show resentment at; be indignant at, as an injury or insult. [< F *ressentir* < *re-* again + *sentir* to feel < L *sentire*]

re·sent·ful (ri·zent′fəl) *adj.* Full of or characterized by resentment; disposed to resent. **— re·sent′ful·ly** *adv.* **— re·sent′ful·ness** *n.*

re·sent·ment (ri·zent′mənt) *n.* Anger and ill will in view of real or fancied wrong or injury. **— Syn.** See ANGER.

re·ser·pine (ri·sûr′pēn, -pin, res′ər-) *n.* A drug originally prepared from alkaloids found in rauwolfia, used as a tranquilizer. [Prob. < *reserp-* < NL *Rauwolfia serpentina,* genus name + -INE]

res·er·va·tion (rez'ər-vā'shən) *n.* **1.** The act of reserving. **2.** That which is reserved, kept back, or withheld. **3.** A qualification or condition, as to an opinion or commitment: The president had one *reservation* about the bill. **4.** An agreement by which a seat on a train, hotel room, etc., is reserved in advance for a scheduled time or date. **5.** A tract of government land reserved for a special purpose, as for the use and occupancy of an Indian tribe, or for the preservation of forests, wildlife, etc. [< OF < LL *reservatio, -onis*]

re·serve (ri-zûrv') *v.t.* **·served, ·serv·ing 1.** To hold back or set aside for special or future use; store up. **2.** To keep as one's own; retain: He *reserves* that privilege for himself. **3.** To arrange for ahead of time; have set aside for one's use: I *reserved* two tickets on the train. **4.** *Eccl.* To set aside (a portion of the consecrated elements of the Eucharist) for communion of the sick. — **Syn.** See RETAIN. — *n.* **1.** Something stored up for future use or set apart for a particular purpose. **2.** A reservation of land. **3.** In banking, the amount of funds reserved from investment, in order promptly to meet regular or emergent demands. **4.** The act of reserving; reservation. **5.** Silence or reticence as to one's feelings, opinions, or affairs; also, absence of exaggeration. **6.** A fighting force held back from action to meet possible emergencies or demands. **7.** The component of a branch of the armed forces composed of persons trained for military service or assignment and subject to call to active duty in emergencies. — *adj.* Held in reserve; constituting a reserve: a *reserve* supply of money. Abbr. *res.* [< OF *reserver* < L *reservare* < *re-* back + *servare* to keep] — **re·serv'a·ble** *adj.* — **re·serv'er** *n.*

re·serve (rē-sûrv') *v.t. & v.i.* **-served, -serv·ing** To serve again.

reserve bank A member of the Federal Reserve System.

re·served (ri-zûrvd') *adj.* **1.** Characterized by reserve of manner; distant; undemonstrative. **2.** Retained; kept back. — **re·serv·ed·ly** (ri-zûr'vid-lē) *adv.* — **re·serv'ed·ness** *n.* — **Syn. 1.** reticent, uncommunicative. See TACITURN. — **Ant.** outgoing, expansive, affable.

Reserve Officers' Training Corps In the United States, a military corps engaged in training students at certain colleges and universities to qualify as officers in a reserve. Abbr. *ROTC, R.O.T.C.*

re·serv·ist (ri-zûr'vist) *n.* A member of a military reserve.

res·er·voir (rez'ər-vwôr, -vwär, -vôr) *n.* **1.** A basin, either natural or artificial, for collecting and containing a supply of water, as for use in a city or for water power. **2.** A receptacle where some material, especially a liquid or gas, may be stored. **3.** An attachment to a stove, machine, or instrument, for containing a fluid to be used in its operation. **4.** An extra supply; a store of anything. [< F *réservoir*]

re·set (*v.* rē-set'; *n.* rē'set') *v.t.* **·set, ·set·ting** To set again. — *n.* **1.** The act of resetting, or that which is reset. **2.** A resetting of type. — **re·set'ter** *n.*

res ges·tae (rēz jes'tē) *n.pl. Latin* Achievements; things accomplished.

resh (resh) *n.* The twentieth letter in the Hebrew alphabet. See ALPHABET.

re·ship (rē-ship') *v.* **·shipped, ·ship·ping** *v.t.* **1.** To ship again. **2.** To transfer (oneself) to another vessel. — *v.i.* **3.** To go on a vessel again. **4.** To sign for another voyage as a crew member or a passenger.

re·ship·ment (rē-ship'mənt) *n.* **1.** The act of reshipping. **2.** The thing reshipped.

Resht (resht) A city in northern Iran, near the Caspian Sea; pop. 143,557 (1966).

re·side (ri-zīd') *v.i.* **·sid·ed, ·sid·ing 1.** To dwell for a considerable time; make one's home; live. **2.** To exist as an attribute or quality: with *in.* **3.** To be vested: with *in.* — **Syn.** See LIVE. [< F *résider* < L *residere* to abide < *re-* back + *sedere* to sit] — **re·sid'er** *n.*

res·i·dence (rez'ə-dəns) *n.* **1.** The place or the house where one resides. **2.** The act of residing. **3.** Inherence in a thing, as of an attribute in a subject. **4.** The fact of being officially present, especially in the phrase **in residence:** the poet *in residence.* **5.** The seat or place of power of government. **6.** The length of time one resides in a place. Also *residency.* Abbr. *r., res.* — **Syn.** See HOME. [< OF < LL *residentia*]

res·i·den·cy (rez'ə-dən-sē) *n. pl.* **·cies 1.** Residence. **2.** In the East Indies, the official abode of the representative of the governor general, as at a court in one of the Indian States. **3.** *Med.* The period of clinical training served by a physician in his chosen specialty.

res·i·dent (rez'ə-dənt) *n.* **1.** One who resides or dwells in a place. **2.** A diplomatic representative residing at a foreign court or seat of government. **3.** An agent in a protectorate. **4.** *Med.* One serving a residency. Also *residentiary.* — *adj.* **1.** Having a residence; residing. **2.** Abiding in a place in connection with one's official work: a *resident* physician. **3.** Inherent: Pungency is *resident* in pepper. **4.** Not migratory: said of certain birds. [< L *residens, -entis,* ppr. of *residere* to settle]

res·i·den·tial (rez'ə-den'shəl) *adj.* **1.** Of, pertaining to, or resulting from residence; having residence. **2.** Of, consisting of, or suitable for residences or living quarters.

res·i·den·ti·ar·y (rez'ə-den'shē-er'ē, -shər-ē) *adj.* **1.** Having or maintaining a residence, especially an official residence. **2.** Pertaining to residence. — *n. pl.* **·ar·ies** A resident.

re·sid·u·al (ri-zij'ōō-əl) *adj.* **1.** Pertaining to or having the nature of a residue or remainder. **2.** Left over as a residue. — *n.* **1.** Something left over from a total mass, magnitude, or quantity that has been acted upon in any specified way; a remainder or remnant. **2.** *Stat.* **a** The difference between observed results and those obtained by computation according to formula. **b** The difference between the value of a given observation and the mean of a series to which it belongs.

re·sid·u·ar·y (ri-zij'ōō-er'ē) *adj.* Of or pertaining to a residuum or remainder; residual.

res·i·due (rez'ə-dōō, -dyōō) *n.* **1.** A remainder or surplus after a part has been separated or otherwise treated. **2.** *Chem.* **a** Insoluble matter left after filtration or separation from a liquid. **b** An atom or radical separated from a molecule of a substance. **c** A residuum. **3.** *Law* The portion of an estate that remains after all charges, debts, and particular bequests have been satisfied: also called *residuum.* Abbr. *res.* [< OF < L *residuum < residere.* See RESIDE.]

re·sid·u·um (ri-zij'ōō-əm) *n. pl.* **·u·a** (-ōō-ə) **1.** That which remains after any process of subtraction; a residue. **2.** *Chem.* A residual product: the *residuum* from the distillation of coal tar: also called *residue.* **3.** *Law* Residue (def. 3). [< L]

re·sign (ri-zīn') *v.t.* **1.** To give up, as a position, office, or trust. **2.** To relinquish (a privilege, claim, etc.). **3.** To give over (oneself, one's mind, etc.), as to fate. — *v.i.* **4.** To resign a position, etc. [< OF *resigner* < L *resignare* to annul, unseal < *re-* back + *signare* to seal] — **re·sign'er** *n.*

re·sign (rē-sīn') *v.t.* To sign again.

res·ig·na·tion (rez'ig-nā'shən) *n.* **1.** The act of resigning, as a position or office. **2.** A written statement declaring one's intention to resign or recording the fact of having resigned. **3.** The quality of being submissive; unresisting acquiescence. [< F *résignation* < Med.L *resignationem* < *resignatus*]

re·signed (ri-zīnd') *adj.* Disposed to accept without resistance; submissive: *resigned* to a life of little leisure. — **re·sign·ed·ly** (ri-zī'nid-lē) *adv.* — **re·sign'ed·ness** *n.*

re·sile (ri-zīl') *v.i.* **·siled, ·sil·ing 1.** To spring back; recoil. **2.** To resume original shape or position after being stretched or compressed. [< MF *resiler* < L *resilire* < *re-* back + *salire* to leap]

re·sil·ience (ri-zil'yəns) *n.* The quality or power of being resilient; elasticity; rebound. Also **re·sil'ien·cy.**

re·sil·ient (ri-zil'yənt) *adj.* **1.** Springing back to a former shape or position. **2.** Capable of recoiling from pressure or shock unchanged or undamaged. **3.** Elastic; buoyant. — **Syn.** See ELASTIC. [< L *resiliens, -entis,* ppr. of *resilire.* See RESILE.] — **re·sil'ient·ly** *adv.*

res·in (rez'in) *n.* **1.** An amorphous organic substance exuded from plants, especially from fir or pine trees, yellowish or dark in color and usually translucent or transparent. It is soluble in alcohol and ether, and is a nonconductor of electricity. **2.** Any of a class of similar substances made by chemical synthesis, especially those used in the making of plastics. **3.** A resinous precipitate obtained from a vegetable tincture by treatment with water, used in pharmacy. **4.** Rosin (def. 1). — *v.t.* To apply resin to. [< OF *resine* < L *resina* < Gk. *rhētinē*] — **res·i·na·ceous** (rez'ə-nā'shəs) *adj.*

res·in·ate (rez'ən-āt) *v.t.* **·at·ed, ·at·ing** To infuse or impregnate with resin.

res·in·if·er·ous (rez'ən-if'ər-əs) *adj.* Producing resin.

res·in·oid (rez'ən-oid) *adj.* Resembling resin. — *n.* **1.** A substance either wholly or partially of a resinous nature. **2.** Any of a class of thermosetting synthetic resins.

res·in·ous (rez'ə-nəs) *adj.* **1.** Of the nature of resins, or containing resin as an ingredient. **2.** Obtained from resin: *resinous* electricity. Also **res·in·y** (rez'ən-ē).

re·sist (ri-zist') *v.t.* **1.** To strive against; act counter to for the purpose of stopping, preventing, defeating, etc. **2.** To be proof against; withstand; defeat. **3.** To refrain from: I can't *resist* teasing him. — *v.i.* **4.** To offer opposition. — **Syn.** See OPPOSE. — *n.* Any substance applied to a surface to protect it from corrosion, etc. [< OF *resister* < L *resistere* to withstand < *re-* back + *sistere,* causative of *stare* to stand] — **re·sist'er** *n.*

re·sis·tance (ri-zis'təns) *n.* **1.** The act of resisting. **2.** Any force tending to hinder motion. **3.** *Electr.* **a** The opposition that a conductor offers to the passage of a current, resulting from the conversion of energy into heat, light, etc., radiated away from the circuit, expressed in ohms: the reciprocal of *conductance:* also **true resistance. b** A resistor. **c** Impedance: also **apparent resistance.** Abbr. *r, R.* **4.** *Psychoanal.* The action of the ego in preventing the return to consciousness of unpleasant incidents and experiences. **5.** The underground and guerrilla movement opposing an occupying power. [< F *résistance* < LL *resistentia*]

re·sis·tant (ri-zis'tənt) *adj.* Offering or tending to produce resistance; resisting. — *n.* One who or that which resists. [< F *résistant*]

re·sist·i·ble (ri-zis'tə-bəl) *adj.* Capable of being resisted. — **re·sist'i·bil'i·ty** *n.* — **re·sist'i·bly** *adv.*

re·sis·tive (ri-zis′tiv) *adj.* Having or exercising the power of resistance. **— re·sis′tive·ly** *adv.*

re·sis·tiv·i·ty (rē′zis-tiv′ə-tē) *n.* **1.** The capacity to resist, or the degree of that capacity. **2.** *Electr.* Specific resistance to electric or magnetic force of a substance as tested in a cube measuring one centimeter: the reciprocal of *conductivity.*

re·sist·less (ri-zist′lis) *adj.* **1.** Incapable of resisting; irresistible. **2.** Offering no resistance; powerless. **— re·sist′less·ly** *adv.* **— re·sist′less·ness** *n.*

re·sis·tor (ri-zis′tər) *n. Electr.* A device, as a coil of wire, for introducing resistance into an electrical circuit: also called *resistance.*

res ju·di·ca·ta (rēz jōō′də-kā′tə) *Latin* Literally, a matter decided; an issue or point of law that has been previously decided by a court of authoritative or competent jurisdiction and that when pleaded is conclusive of the matter in controversy: also *res adjudicata.*

res·na·tron (rez′nə-tron) *n. Electronics* A tetrode electron tube operating on the resonance principle and capable of generating large power at high frequency and maximum efficiency. [< RES(O)NA(TOR) + -TRON]

re·so·jet (rez′ō-jet′) *n. Aeron.* A pulsejet (which see). [< RESO(NANCE) + JET]

re·sole (rē-sōl′) *v.t.* **·soled, ·sol·ing** To sole (a shoe, etc.) again.

res·o·lu·ble (rez′ə-lōō-bəl, ri-zol′yə-bəl) *adj.* Capable of being resolved; soluble. [< LL *resolubilis* < *resolvere*] **— res′·o·lu·bil′i·ty, res′o·lu·ble·ness** *n.*

res·o·lute (rez′ə-lōōt) *adj.* **1.** Having a fixed purpose; determined; constant; steady. **2.** Bold; unflinching. [< L *resolutus*, pp. of *resolvere.* See RESOLVE.] **— res′o·lute·ly** *adv.* **— res′o·lute·ness** *n.*

res·o·lu·tion (rez′ə-lōō′shən) *n.* **1.** The act of resolving or of reducing to a simpler form. **2.** The state of being resolute; active fortitude; resoluteness. **3.** The making of a resolve; also, the purpose or course resolved upon; a resolve; determination. **4.** The separation of anything into component parts. **5.** A proposition offered to or adopted by an assembly. **6.** *Law* A judgment or decision of a court. **7.** *Med.* The termination of an abnormal condition. **8.** *Music* **a** The succession of a dissonant tone by another tone, usually in stepwise fashion; also, the replacement of a dissonant chord so that its most obviously dissonant tones proceed stepwise. **b** The tone or chord replacing the original dissonant tone or chord. *Abbr. res.* **— Syn.** See DETERMINATION, FORTITUDE. [< L *resolutio, -onis* < *resolutus.* See RESOLUTE.] **— res′o·lu′tion·er, res′o·lu′tion·ist** *n.*
— Syn. 2. pluck, backbone, guts, grit, sand. See FORTITUDE. **— Ant.** faint-heartedness, pusillanimity.

re·solv·a·ble (ri-zol′və-bəl) *adj.* Capable of being resolved, analyzed, or solved. **— re·solv′a·bil′i·ty, re·solv′a·ble·ness** *n.*

re·solve (ri-zolv′) *v.* **·solved, ·solv·ing** *v.t.* **1.** To decide or determine (to do something). **2.** To cause to decide or determine. **3.** To separate or break down into constituent parts; analyze. **4.** To make clear; explain or solve, as a problem. **5.** To explain away; remove (doubts, etc.). **6.** To state or decide by vote, as in a legislative assembly. **7.** To transform; convert: He *resolves* his anger into pride. **8.** *Music* To cause (a tone or chord) to undergo resolution. **9.** *Chem.* To separate (a racemic compound) into its optically active components. **10.** *Optics* To make distinguishable the structure or parts of, as in a microscope or telescope. **11.** *Med.* To cause to disperse or be absorbed without the formation of pus. **12.** *Obs.* To melt; dissolve. **13.** *Obs.* To inform. **—** *v.i.* **14.** To make up one's mind; arrive at a decision: with *on* or *upon.* **15.** To become separated into constituent parts. **16.** *Music* To undergo resolution. **—** *n.* **1.** Fixity of purpose; resolution. **2.** A fixed determination; a resolution. **3.** The action of a deliberative body expressing formally its intention or purpose. [< L *resolvere* < *re-* again + *solvere* to loosen] **— re·solv′er** *n.*

re·solve (rē-solv′) *v.t.* **·solved, ·solv·ing** To solve anew or again.

re·solved (ri-zolvd′) *adj.* **1.** Fixed or set in purpose; determined. **2.** Having formed a resolve. **— re·solv·ed·ly** (ri-zol′vid-lē) *adv.*

re·solv·ent (ri-zol′vənt) *adj.* Having the power to cause the dissolution or resolution of a thing into its elements. **—** *n.* **1.** A resolvent substance; a solvent. **2.** *Med.* A preparation that has the property of reducing or dispersing a swelling. [< L *resolvens, -entis*, ppr. of *resolvere.* See RESOLVE.]

res·o·nance (rez′ə-nəns) *n.* **1.** The state or quality of being resonant. **2.** *Physics* **a** The property whereby any vibratory system responds with maximum amplitude to an applied force having a frequency equal or nearly equal to its own. **b** The reinforcement and prolongation of sound caused by standing waves built up in a tuned cavity or other vibratory system. **3.** *Chem.* That property of a molecule by virtue of which it assumes an electronic structure intermediate between two other theoretically possible structures. **4.** *Electr.* The condition of an electric circuit in which maximum flow of current is obtained by impressing an electromotive force of given frequency.

res·o·nant (rez′ə-nənt) *adj.* **1.** Sending back or having the quality of sending back or prolonging sound. **2.** Resounding. **3.** Having resonance. [< L *resonans, -antis*, ppr. of *resonare* to echo < *re-* again + *sonare* to sound] **— res′·o·nant·ly** *adv.*

res·o·nate (rez′ə-nāt) *v.i.* **·nat·ed, ·nat·ing 1.** To exhibit resonance. **2.** To manifest sympathetic vibration, as a resonator. [< L *resonatus*, pp. of *resonare.* See RESONANT.]

res·o·na·tor (rez′ə-nā′tər) *n.* **1.** That which resounds. **2.** *Electronics* Any device used to exhibit or utilize the effects of resonance, especially one used in connection with a waveguide. **3.** *Physics* A set or cluster of electrons that absorb electromagnetic waves of certain frequencies. **4.** In acoustics, an object having a specific period of vibration used to reinforce or isolate sound of a particular pitch. [< NL]

re·sorb (ri-sôrb′) *v.t.* To absorb again; reabsorb. [< L *resorbere* < *re-* back + *sorbere* to suck up] **— re·sorp·tion** (ri-sôrp′shən) *n.*

re·sor·cin·ol (ri-zôr′sin-ōl, -ol) *n. Chem.* A colorless crystalline compound, $C_6H_6O_2$, used as an antiseptic and in the making of dyes. Also **re·sor′cin.** [< RES(IN) + ORCINOL] **— re·sor′cin·al** *adj.*

re·sort (ri-zôrt′) *v.i.* **1.** To go frequently or habitually; repair. **2.** To have recourse; apply or betake oneself for relief or aid: with *to.* **—** *n.* **1.** A place frequented for recreation or rest: summer *resort;* health *resort.* **2.** The use of something as a means; a recourse; refuge. **3.** The act of frequenting a place. [< OF *resortir* < *re-* again + *sortir* to go out] **— re·sort′er** *n.*

re·sort (rē-sôrt′) *v.t. & v.i.* To sort anew or again.

re·sound (ri-zound′) *v.i.* **1.** To be filled with sound; echo; reverberate. **2.** To make a loud, prolonged, or echoing sound. **3.** To ring; echo: said of sounds. **4.** *Poetic* To be famed or extolled. **—** *v.t.* **5.** To give back (a sound, etc.); re-echo. **6.** *Poetic* To extol. **7.** *Rare* To utter loudly. [ME *resounen* < OF *resoner* < L *resonare.* See RESONANT.]

re·sound (rē-sound′) *v.t. & v.i.* To sound again.

re·source (ri-sôrs′, -zôrs′, -sōrs′, rē′sôrs, -sōrs) *n.* **1.** That which is resorted to for aid or support; resort. **2.** *pl.* Available means or property; a supply that can be drawn on; any natural advantages or products: natural *resources.* **3.** Capacity for finding or adapting means; power of achievement. **4.** Fertility in expedients; skill or ingenuity in meeting any situation; resourcefulness. [< OF *ressource* < *resourdre* < *re-* (< L) again + *sourdre* < L *surgere* to rise]

re·source·ful (ri-sôrs′fəl, -sōrs′-, -zôrs′-) *adj.* **1.** Fertile in resources or expedients. **2.** Full of resources. **— re·source′·ful·ly** *adv.* **— re·source′ful·ness** *n.*

resp. 1. Respective(ly). **2.** Respondent.

re·spect (ri-spekt′) *v.t.* **1.** To have deferential regard for; esteem. **2.** To treat with propriety or consideration. **3.** To regard as inviolable; avoid intruding upon. **4.** To have relation or reference to; concern. **— Syn.** See ADMIRE. **—** *n.* **1.** Regard for and appreciation of worth; honor and esteem: I have great *respect* for the man. **2.** Demeanor or deportment indicating deference; courteous regard: to have *respect* for one's elders. **3.** *pl.* Expressions of consideration or esteem; compliments: to pay one's *respects.* **4.** Conformity to duty or obligation; compliance or observance: *respect* for the law. **5.** The condition of being honored or respected: to be held in *respect.* **6.** A specific aspect or feature; detail: In what *respect* is he wanting? **7.** Reference or relation: usually with *to:* with *respect* to profits. **8.** *Rare* Undue inclination or bias of mind. **9.** *Obs.* Consideration. **— Syn.** See DEFERENCE. [< L *respectus*, pp. of *respicere* to look back, consider < *re-* again + *specere* to look]

re·spect·a·bil·i·ty (ri-spek′tə-bil′ə-tē) *n. pl.* **·ties 1.** The characteristic or quality of being respectable; honorable social standing; good repute. **2.** The respectable people of a community collectively. **3.** *pl.* Certain conventions and other features of conduct presumed to be signs of gentility, social position, morality, etc. Also **re·spect′a·ble·ness.**

re·spect·a·ble (ri-spek′tə-bəl) *adj.* **1.** Deserving of respect; being of good name or repute; also, respected. **2.** Being of moderate excellence; fairly good; average. **3.** Considerable in number, quantity, size, quality, etc. **4.** Having a good appearance; presentable. **5.** Conventionally correct or socially acceptable in conduct. **— re·spect′a·bly** *adv.*

re·spect·er (ri-spek′tər) *n.* One who respects. **— respecter of persons** One who is influenced by the social standing, etc., of others.

re·spect·ful (ri-spekt′fəl) *adj.* Marked by or manifesting respect; deferential. **— re·spect′ful·ly** *adv.* **— re·spect′ful·ness** *n.*

re·spect·ing (ri-spek′ting) *prep.* In relation to; regarding.

re·spec·tive (ri-spek′tiv) *adj.* **1.** Pertaining or relating severally to each of those under consideration; several; particular. **2.** *Obs.* Attentive. *Abbr. resp.*

re·spec·tive·ly (ri-spek′tiv-lē) *adv.* As singly or severally considered; singly in the order designated: The first three go to John, James, and William *respectively*. Abbr. *resp.*

re·spell (rē-spel′) *v.t.* To spell again, especially in a system whereby pronunciation is indicated.

Re·spi·ghi (rā-spē′gē), **Ottorino**, 1879–1936, Italian composer.

re·spir·a·ble (ri-spīr′ə-bəl, res′pər-ə-bəl) *adj.* **1.** Capable of being respired or breathed; fit for respiration. **2.** Able to breathe or respire. [< F] — **re·spir′a·bil′i·ty** *n.*

res·pi·ra·tion (res′pə-rā′shən) *n.* **1.** The act of inhaling and exhaling; breathing. **2.** The process by which a plant or animal takes in oxygen from the air and gives off carbon dioxide and other products of oxidation. [< L *respiratio, -onis*]

res·pi·ra·tor (res′pə-rā′tər) *n.* **1.** A screen, as of fine gauze, worn over the mouth or nose, as a protection against dust, etc. **2.** A device worn over the nose and mouth for the inhalation of medicated vapors, or to warm or sift the air for lung patients. **3.** *Brit.* A gas mask. **4.** An apparatus for artificial respiration. [< L *respiratus*, pp. of *respirare*. See RESPIRE.]

re·spir·a·to·ry (ri-spīr′ə-tôr′ē, -tō′rē, res′pər-ə-) *adj.* Of, pertaining to, used in, or caused by respiration.

re·spire (ri-spīr′) *v.* **·spired**, **·spir·ing** *v.i.* **1.** To inhale and exhale air; breathe. **2.** To breathe again; recover vitality, hope, etc. — *v.t.* **3.** To inhale and exhale; breathe. **4.** *Rare* To breathe or give forth; exhale. [< MF *respirer* < L *respirare* < *re-* again + *spirare* to breathe]

res·pite (res′pit) *n.* **1.** Postponement; delay. **2.** Temporary intermission of labor or effort; an interval of rest. **3.** *Law* Temporary suspension of the execution of a sentence for a capital offense; reprieve. — *v.t.* **·pit·ed**, **·pit·ing 1.** To relieve by a pause or rest. **2.** To grant delay in the execution of (a penalty, sentence, etc.). **3.** To postpone. [< OF *respit* < L *respectus* regard, refuge < *respicere*. See RESPECT.]

re·splen·dence (ri-splen′dəns) *n.* The state or quality of being resplendent; brilliant luster; splendor. Also **re·splen′den·cy.**

re·splen·dent (ri-splen′dənt) *adj.* Shining with brilliant luster; vividly bright; splendid; gorgeous. [< L *resplendens, -entis*, ppr. of *resplendere* to glitter < *re-* back + *splendere* to shine] — **re·splen′dent·ly** *adv.*

re·spond (ri-spond′) *v.i.* **1.** To give an answer; reply. **2.** To act in reply or return; react. **3.** *Law* To be liable or answerable. — *v.t.* **4.** To say in answer; reply. — *n.* **1.** *Archit.* A pilaster or similar feature placed against a wall, to receive an arch. **2.** *Eccl.* A response (def. 2). [< L *respondere* to undertake in return < *re-* back + *spondere* to pledge]

re·spon·dence (ri-spon′dəns) *n.* **1.** The character or condition of being respondent. **2.** The act of responding. Also **re·spon′den·cy.**

re·spon·dent (ri-spon′dənt) *adj.* **1.** Giving response, or given as a response; answering; responsive. **2.** *Law* Occupying the position of defendant. **3.** *Obs.* Correspondent. — *n.* **1.** One who responds or answers. **2.** *Law* The party called upon to answer an appeal or petition; a defendant, especially in a suit in equity, admiralty, or divorce. Abbr. *resp.* [< L *respondens, -entis*, ppr. of *respondere*. See RESPOND.]

re·spon·der (ri-spon′dər) *n.* **1.** One who responds or answers. **2.** *Telecom.* The part of a transponder that sends signals in response to an interrogator.

re·sponse (ri-spons′) *n.* **1.** The act of responding, or that which is responded; words or acts evoked by the words or acts of another or others; an answer; reply; reaction. **2.** *Eccl.* **a** A portion of a liturgy or church service said or sung by the congregation or choir in reply to the officiating priest. **b** An anthem sung or said during or after a reading. Also called *respond*. Abbr. *R, R.* **3.** *Biol.* The behavior of an organism resulting from a stimulus or influence; a reaction. **4.** In bridge, the play of a high or low card in following suit, as a signal to one's partner. — **Syn.** See ANSWER. [< OF < L *responsum*, pp. neut. of *respondere*. See RESPOND.]

re·spon·ser (ri-spon′sər) *n. Telecom.* A radio or radar receiver, used in connection with an interrogator, that receives and displays answering signals from a transponder.

re·spon·si·bil·i·ty (ri-spon′sə-bil′ə-tē) *n. pl.* **·ties 1.** The state of being responsible or accountable. **2.** That for which one is answerable; a duty or trust. **3.** Ability to meet obligations or to act without superior authority or guidance. Also **re·spon′si·ble·ness.**

re·spon·si·ble (ri-spon′sə-bəl) *adj.* **1.** Answerable legally or morally for the discharge of a duty, trust, or debt. **2.** Having capacity to perceive the distinctions of right and wrong; having ethical discrimination. **3.** Able to meet legitimate claims; having sufficient property or means for the payment of debts. **4.** Involving accountability or obligation. **5.** Denoting the status of a cabinet or ministry with respect to the legislative body to which it is answerable. [< MF < L *responsus*, pp. of *respondere*. See RESPOND.] — **re·spon′si·bly** *adv.*

re·spon·sion (ri-spon′shən) *n.* **1.** *Rare* A response; reply. **2.** *pl.* At Oxford University, the first of three examinations for a B.A. degree. [< L *responsio, -onis*]

re·spon·sive (ri-spon′siv) *adj.* **1.** Inclined or ready to respond; being or reacting in accord, sympathy, or harmony;

responding. **2.** Constituting, or of the nature of, response or reply. **3.** Characterized by or containing responses. — **re·spon′sive·ly** *adv.* — **re·spon′sive·ness** *n.*

re·spon·so·ry (ri-spon′sər-ē) *n. pl.* **·ries** *Eccl.* **1.** A response sung between readings. **2.** A response of the people or congregation to the officiating priest or clergyman. [< Med.L *responsorium*]

res pub·li·ca (rēz pub′li·kə) *pl.* **·cae** (-sē) *Latin* **1.** The commonwealth; the republic. **2.** *pl.* Things that belong to the state.

rest[1] (rest) *v.i.* **1.** To cease working, exerting oneself, etc., so as to refresh oneself. **2.** To cease from effort or activity for a time. **3.** To seek or obtain ease or refreshment by lying down, sleeping, etc. **4.** To sleep. **5.** To be at peace; be tranquil. **6.** To lie in death; be dead. **7.** To remain unchanged: And there the matter *rests*. **8.** To be supported; stand, lean, lie, or sit: with *against, on*, or *upon*. **9.** To be founded or based: with *on* or *upon*. **10.** To rely; depend: with *on* or *upon*: Our hopes *rest* on you. **11.** To be placed as a burden or responsibility: with *on* or *upon*. **12.** To be or lie in a specified place: The blame *rests* with me. **13.** To be directed; remain, as the gaze or eyes, on something. **14.** *Law* To cease presenting evidence in a case. **15.** *Agric.* To lie fallow. — *v.t.* **16.** To give rest to; refresh by rest. **17.** To put, lay, lean, etc., as for support or rest. **18.** To found; base. **19.** To direct (the gaze, eyes, etc.). **20.** *Law* To cease presenting evidence in (a case). — *n.* **1.** The act or state of resting; cessation from labor, exertion, action, or motion; repose; quiet. **2.** Freedom from disturbance or disquiet; peace; tranquillity. **3.** Sleep; also, death. **4.** That on which anything rests; a support; basis. **5.** In billiards and pool, a support for a cue; a bridge. **6.** A place of repose or quiet; a stopping place; abode. **7.** *Music* A pause or interval of silence that corresponds to the time value of a note; also, the character indicating such a pause. For illustration see NOTE. **8.** In prosody, a pause in a verse; caesura. **9.** *Obs.* Restored or renewed strength. **10.** *Mil.* A command given troops, allowing them to relax. — **at rest 1.** In a state of repose, as in sleep or death. **2.** Not in motion; undisturbed; still: a body *at rest*. **3.** Free from anxiety or worry: to set one's mind *at rest*. [OE *restan*] — **rest′er** *n.*

rest[2] (rest) *n.* **1.** That which remains or is left over; a remainder. **2.** (*construed as pl.*) Those remaining or not enumerated; the others. **3.** A balance, as of resources. — *v.i.* **1.** To be and remain; continue; stay: *Rest* content. **2.** *Obs.* To be left: Nothing *rests* but hope. — *v.t.* **3.** *Obs.* To cause to stay: God *rest* you merry. [< OF *reste* < *rester* to remain < L *restare* to stop, stand < *re-* back + *stare* to stand]

rest[3] (rest) *n.* On medieval armor, a support for a lance.

re·state (rē-stāt′) *v.t.* **·stat·ed**, **·stat·ing** To state again or anew. — **re·state′ment** *n.*

res·tau·rant (res′tər-ənt, -tə-ränt) *n.* A place where refreshments or meals are provided; a public dining room. Abbr. *restr.* [< F, lit., restoring, ppr. of *restaurer* < OF *restorer*. See RESTORE.]

res·tau·ra·teur (res′tər-ə-tûr′, *Fr.* res-tō-rà-tœr′) *n.* The proprietor or keeper of a restaurant. [< F]

rest cure A treatment, as of nervous disorders, prescribing seclusion and quiet, generous diet, massage, etc.

rest·ful (rest′fəl) *adj.* **1.** Full of or giving rest; affording freedom from disturbance, work, or trouble. **2.** Being at rest or in repose; quiet. — **rest′ful·ly** *adv.* — **rest′ful·ness** *n.*

rest·har·row (rest′har′ō) *n.* A low European undershrub (*Ononis hircina*) of the bean family, with pink and white flowers. [< ARREST + HARROW]

res·ti·form (res′tə-fôrm) *adj. Anat.* Ropelike; twisted. [< L *restis* cord + -FORM]

restiform bodies *Anat.* Two ropelike bundles of nerve fibers of the medulla oblongata that pass upward to the cerebellum.

rest·ing (res′ting) *adj.* **1.** In a state of rest; reposing; also, dead. **2.** *Bot.* Dormant: a *resting* spore.

res·ti·tu·tion (res′tə-tōō′shən, -tyōō′-) *n.* **1.** The act of restoring something that has been taken away or lost. **2.** The act of making good or rendering an equivalent for injury or loss; indemnification. **3.** Restoration to, return to, or recovery of a former position or condition. **4.** *Physics* The tendency of elastic bodies to recover their shape after compression. **5.** Establishment of the true nature or position of objects distorted in an aerial photograph. [< OF < L *restitutio, -onis* < *restituere* to restore < *re-* again + *statuere* to set up]

res·tive (res′tiv) *adj.* **1.** Impatient of control; unruly. **2.** Restless; fidgety. [< F *restif* < *rester* to remain < L *restare*. See REST[2].] — **res′tive·ly** *adv.* — **res′tive·ness** *n.* — **Syn. 1.** fractious, intractable. Compare REBELLIOUS. **2.** uneasy, nervous, fretful, skittish, jittery.

rest·less (rest′lis) *adj.* **1.** Having no rest; never quiet; unresting: the *restless* waves. **2.** Unable or disinclined to rest. **3.** Constantly seeking change; uneasy; discontented. **4.** Obtaining no rest or sleep; sleepless. — **rest′less·ly** *adv.* — **rest′less·ness** *n.*

re·stock (rē-stok′) *v.t.* To stock again or anew.

res·to·ra·tion (res′tə-rā′shən) *n.* **1.** The act of restoring a person or thing to a former place or condition. **2.** The state of being restored; rehabilitation; renewal. **3.** The reconstruction or repair of something so as to restore it to its original or former state; also, an object that has been so restored, as a building or sculpture, a fossil skeleton, etc. — **the Restoration 1.** The return of Charles II to the English throne in 1660, after the overthrow of the Protectorate; also, the following period until 1685. **2.** The return of the Bourbons to power in 1814 under Louis XVIII; also, the period following. **3.** The return of the Jews to Palestine after the Babylonian captivity. [< OF *restauration* < LL *restauratio, -onis* < L *restaurare*. See RESTORE.]

re·sto·ra·tive (ri-stôr′ə-tiv, -stō′rə-) *adj.* **1.** Tending or able to restore. **2.** Pertaining to restoration. — *n.* That which restores; especially, something to restore consciousness after a fainting fit.

re·store (ri-stôr′, -stōr′) *v.t.* **·stored, ·stor·ing 1.** To bring into existence or effect again: to *restore* peace. **2.** To bring back to a former or original condition, appearance, etc.: to *restore* a great painting. **3.** To put back in a former place or position; reinstate, as a deposed monarch. **4.** To bring back to health and vigor. **5.** To give back (something lost or taken away); return. [< OF *restorer* < L *restaurare* < *re-* again + *-staurare* to make firm] — **re·stor′er** *n.*

re·store (rē-stôr′, -stōr′) *v.t.* **-stored, -stor·ing** To store again or anew.

restr. Restaurant.

re·strain (ri-strān′) *v.t.* **1.** To hold back from acting, proceeding, or advancing; keep in check; repress. **2.** To deprive of freedom or liberty, as by placing in a prison or asylum. **3.** To restrict or limit. [< OF *restraindre* < L *restringere* < *re-* back + *stringere* to draw tight] — **re·strain′a·ble** *adj.* — **re·strain′ed·ly** *adv.* — **Syn. 1.** curb, bridle, inhibit. Compare REPRESS. — **Ant.** release, free; impel, incite.

re·strain·er (ri-strā′nər) *n.* **1.** One who or that which restrains. **2.** *Photog.* A chemical agent used to retard the action of the developer.

re·straint (ri-strānt′) *n.* **1.** The act of restraining. **2.** The state of being restrained; abridgment of liberty; confinement. **3.** That which restrains; a restriction. **4.** Self-repression; constraint. [< OF *restrainte* < *restraindre*. See RESTRAIN.]

restraint of trade Interference with the free flow of goods or with fair competition, as by price fixing.

re·strict (ri-strikt′) *v.t.* To hold or keep within limits or bounds; confine. [< L *restrictus*, pp. or *restringere*. See RESTRAIN.]

re·strict·ed (ri-strik′tid) *adj.* **1.** Limited; confined. **2.** Not available or open to the general public; limited to a specific group or class: *restricted* information. **3.** Excluding people of certain races, religions, or nationalities: a *restricted* housing development. — **re·strict′ed·ly** *adv.*

re·stric·tion (ri-strik′shən) *n.* **1.** The act of restricting, or the state of being restricted; limitation. **2.** That which restricts; a restraint.

re·stric·tive (ri-strik′tiv) *adj.* **1.** Serving, tending, or operating to restrict. **2.** *Logic* Limiting in thought, expression, or application. **3.** *Gram.* Denoting a word or word group, especially an adjective clause, that limits the identity of its antecedent and is therefore essential to the meaning of the sentence, as *who votes for Jones* in *Any man who votes for Jones is a fool.* Compare NONRESTRICTIVE. — **re·stric′tive·ly** *adv.*

rest room A toilet and washroom in a public building.

re·sult (ri-zult′) *n.* **1.** The outcome of an action, course, process, or agency; consequence; effect; conclusion. **2.** *Math.* A quantity or value ascertained by calculation. **3.** The final determination of a deliberative assembly. — **Syn.** See EFFECT. — *v.i.* **1.** To be a result or outcome; be a physical or logical consequent; follow: with *from.* **2.** To have an issue; terminate; end: with *in.* [< L *resultare* to recoil < *re-* back + *saltare*, freq. of *salire* to leap]

re·sul·tant (ri-zul′tənt) *adj.* Arising or following as a result. — *n.* **1.** That which results; a consequence. **2.** *Physics* A force, velocity, or other vector quantity, resulting from and equivalent in effect to the action of two or more quantities of the same kind, as in the composition of forces. [< L *resultans, -antis*, ppr. of *resultare*. See RESULT.]

re·sume (ri-zoōm′) *v.* **·sumed, ·sum·ing** *v.t.* **1.** To take up again after cessation or interruption; begin again. **2.** To take or occupy again: *Resume* your places. **3.** To take for oneself again: to *resume* a title. — *v.i.* **4.** To continue after cessation or interruption. [< MF *résumer* < L *resumere* to take up again < *re-* again + *sumere* to take] — **re·sum′a·ble** *adj.* — **re·sum′er** *n.*

rés·u·mé (rez′oō-mā′, rez′oō-mā) *n.* A summary, as of one's employment record. [< F]

re·sump·tion (ri-zump′shən) *n.* The act of resuming. [< L *resumptio, -onis* < *resumere.* See RESUME.]

re·su·pi·nate (ri-soō′pə-nāt) *adj.* *Bot.* Seeming to be up-

side down; inverted; reversed, as the flowers of orchids. [< L *resupinatus*, pp. of *resupinare* to bend back < *resupinus.* See RESUPINE.] — **re·su′pi·na′tion** *n.*

re·su·pine (rē′soō-pīn′) *adj.* Lying on the back; supine. [< L *resupinus* < *re-* again + *supinus* on the back]

re·sur·face (rē-sûr′fis) *v.t.* **·faced, ·fac·ing 1.** To provide with a new surface. **2.** To come back to the surface of a body of water, as a submarine.

re·surge (ri-sûrj′) *v.i.* **·surged, ·surg·ing 1.** To rise again; be resurrected. **2.** To surge or sweep back again, as the tide. [< L *resurgere* < *re-* again + *surgere* to rise]

re·sur·gence (ri-sûr′jəns) *n.* A rising again.

re·sur·gent (ri-sûr′jənt) *adj.* **1.** Rising again. **2.** Surging back or again. [< L *resurgens, -entis*, ppr. of *resurgere.* See RESURGE.]

res·ur·rect (rez′ə-rekt′) *v.t.* **1.** To bring back to life; raise from the dead. **2.** To bring back into use or to notice. — *v.i.* **3.** To rise again from the dead. [Back formation < RESURRECTION]

res·ur·rec·tion (rez′ə-rek′shən) *n.* **1.** A rising again from the dead. **2.** The state of those who have risen from the dead. **3.** Any revival or renewal, as of a practice or custom, after disuse, decay, etc.; restoration; rebirth. **4.** In Christian Science, material belief yielding to spiritual understanding. — **the Resurrection** *Theol.* **1.** The rising of Christ from the dead. **2.** The rising again of all the dead at the day of final judgment. [< L *resurrectio, -onis* < *resurgere.* See RESURGE.] — **res′ur·rec′tion·al** *adj.*

res·ur·rec·tion·ar·y (rez′ə-rek′shən·er′ē) *adj.* **1.** Of or pertaining to resurrection. **2.** Of or pertaining to the exhuming of dead bodies.

res·ur·rec·tion·ist (rez′ə-rek′shən·ist) *n.* **1.** A body snatcher. **2.** One who resurrects something. **3.** A believer in the rising again of the dead. — **res′ur·rec′tion·ism** *n.*

resurrection plant The rose of Jericho.

re·sus·ci·tate (ri-sus′ə-tāt) *v.t. & v.i.* **·tat·ed, ·tat·ing** To bring or come back to life; revive from unconsciousness or apparent death. [< L *resuscitatus*, pp. of *resuscitare* < *re-* again + *suscitare* to revive < *sub-* under + *citare* to call. See CITE.] — **re·sus′ci·ta′tive** *adj.* — **re·sus′ci·ta′tor** *n.*

re·sus·ci·ta·tion (ri-sus′ə-tā′shən) *n.* The act of resuscitating, or the state of being resuscitated; revivification.

Resz·ke (resh′ke), **Édouard de,** 1855–1917, Polish basso. — **Jean de,** 1850–1925, Polish tenor; brother of the preceding: original name **Jan Mieczyslaw de Reszke.**

ret (ret) *v.t.* **ret·ted, ret·ting** To steep or soak, as flax, to separate the fibers: also *rot.* [ME *reten* < MDu. *reten*]

ret. 1. Retain. **2.** Retired. **3.** Return(ed).

re·ta·ble (ri-tā′bəl) *n.* **1.** A shelf or ledge raised above the back of an altar to support ornaments, lights, etc. **2.** A panel containing a picture or bas-relief of subjects from sacred history. [< F < OF *rere-table* < Med.L *retrotabulum* < L *retro-* behind + *tabula* plank]

re·tail (*n. & adj.* rē′tāl; *v.* ri·tāl′) *n.* The selling of goods in small quantities, especially to the ultimate consumer: distinguished from *wholesale.* — *adj.* Pertaining to, involving, or engaged in the sale of goods at retail. — *v.t.* **1.** To sell at retail. **2.** To repeat, as gossip. — *v.i.* **3.** To be sold at retail. [< OF < *retailler* to cut up < *re-* back (< L) + *tailler* to cut < LL *taliare* < L *talea* stake]

re·tail·er (rē′tāl·ər) *n.* One who sells to the consumer.

re·tain (ri-tān′) *v.t.* **1.** To keep or continue to keep in one's possession; hold. **2.** To maintain in use, practice, etc.: to *retain* one's standards. **3.** To keep in a fixed condition or place. **4.** To keep in mind; remember. **5.** To hire; also, to engage (an attorney or other representative) by paying a retainer. Abbr. *ret.* [< OF *retenir* < L *retinere* < *re-* back + *tenere* to hold] — **re·tain′a·ble** *adj.* — **Syn. 1.** *Retain, keep, hold, withhold, detain,* and *reserve* are compared as they mean to maintain in one's possession or custody. The sense of *retain* is chiefly negative, denoting a failure to give or put away. *Keep* is a very broad word, sometimes equivalent to *retain,* but more often implying some effort to possess and defend, and capable of expressing the utmost resolution: I will *keep* this place, come what may. We may *hold* something merely by having it in our custody, or by resisting another's effort to take it; the latter sense is explicit in *withhold.* To *detain* is to *keep* from continuing in progress: a prisoner or a ship may be *detained.* To *reserve* is to set aside for future use, that is, to *withhold* from present use. — **Ant.** relinquish.

re·tained object (ri-tānd′) See under OBJECT.

re·tain·er¹ (ri-tā′nər) *n.* **1.** A servant. **2.** One who retains or keeps. **3.** *Mech.* A device for holding the parts of ball or roller bearings in place.

re·tain·er² (ri-tā′nər) *n.* **1.** The fee paid, or the agreement made, to employ an attorney to serve in a suit; a retaining fee. **2.** A similar fee paid to anyone to retain his services. [< OF *retenir* to hold back, used as noun]

re·tain·ing wall (ri-tā′ning) A wall to prevent the material of an embankment or cut from sliding, as a revetment.

re·take (*v.* rē-tāk′; *n.* rē′tāk′) *v.t.* **·took, ·tak·en, ·tak·ing 1.** To take back; receive again. **2.** To recapture. **3.** To photograph again. — *n.* A motion-picture or television scene, part of a musical or other recording, etc., done again.

re·tal·i·ate (ri·tal′ē·āt) *v.* **·at·ed, ·at·ing** *v.i.* **1.** To return like for like; especially, to repay evil with evil. — *v.t.* **2.** To repay (an injury, wrong, etc.) in kind; revenge. [< L *retaliatus,* pp. of *retaliare* < *re-* back + *talio* punishment in kind] — **re·tal′i·a·tive** *adj.*

re·tal·i·a·tion (ri·tal′ē·ā′shən) *n.* The act of retaliating; reprisal; requital. — **Syn.** See REVENGE.

re·tal·i·a·to·ry (ri·tal′ē·ə·tôr′ē, -tō′rē) *adj.* Of, pertaining to, or of the nature of retaliation.

re·tard (ri·tärd′) *v.t.* **1.** To cause to move or proceed slowly; hinder the advance or course of; impede; delay. — *v.i.* **2.** To be delayed. — **Syn.** See HINDER¹. — *n.* The act of retarding; delay. [< MF *retarder* < L *retardare* < *re-* back + *tardare* to make slow < *tardus* slow] — **re·tard′a·tive** (-ə·tiv) *adj. & n.*

re·tard·ant (ri·tär′dənt) *n.* Something that retards. — *adj.* Tending to retard.

re·tar·date (ri·tär′dāt) *n. U.S.* A person who is mentally retarded.

re·tar·da·tion (rē′tär·dā′shən) *n.* **1.** The act of retarding, or the state of being retarded. **2.** A lessening of velocity, gain, or progress; a delaying. **3.** The amount of delay or hindrance. **4.** That which retards; a hindrance. **5.** *Music* A slackening of the tempo. [< L *retardatio, -onis*]

re·tard·ed (ri·tär′did) *adj. Psychol.* Slowed down or backward in mental development or school achievement.

re·tard·er (ri·tär′dər) *n.* **1.** One who or that which retards. **2.** *Chem.* A substance that slows the rate of a chemical reaction: compare CATALYST.

retch (rech) *v.i.* To make an effort to vomit; strain; heave. [OE *hrǣcan* to clear one's throat. Akin to OE *hrāca* spittle.]

retd. 1. Retained. **2.** Returned.

re·te (rē′tē) *n. pl.* **·ti·a** (-shē·ə, -tē·ə) *Anat.* An interlacing arrangement, as of nerves; network. [< L, net]

re·tell (rē·tel′) *v.t.* **·told, ·tell·ing** To count or relate again.

re·tem (rē′təm) *n.* A desert shrub (genus *Retama*) of Arabia and Syria, with small white flowers, the Old Testament juniper. [< Arabic *ratam,* pl. of *ratamah*]

ret·ene (ret′ēn, rē′tēn) *n. Chem.* A colorless crystalline compound, C₁₈H₁₈, contained in resinous pine wood, certain fossil stems, etc. [< Gk. *rhētinē* resin]

re·ten·tion (ri·ten′shən) *n.* **1.** The act of retaining or the state of being retained. **2.** The ability to remember; memory. **3.** The capacity or ability to retain. **4.** *Med.* A retaining within the body of materials normally excreted, as urine. [< OF < L *retentio, -onis* < *retiner.* See RETAIN.]

re·ten·tive (ri·ten′tiv) *adj.* Having the power or tendency to retain; retaining. — **re·ten′tive·ness** *n.*

re·ten·tiv·i·ty (rē′ten·tiv′ə·tē) *n. pl.* **·ties 1.** The state or quality of being retentive. **2.** *Physics* The capacity of a material to retain magnetism after the withdrawal of the magnetizing force.

Re·thondes (rə·tôṅd′) A village near Compiègne, northern France; armistice to suspend hostilities of World War I signed here, Nov. 11, 1918; during World War II, armistice to suspend hostilities between Germany and France signed here, June 22, 1940.

re·ti·ar·i·us (rē′shē·âr′ē·əs) *n. pl.* **·ar·i·i** (-âr′ē·ī) In ancient Rome, a gladiator armed with a net to enmesh his adversary, and a trident to dispatch him. [< L < *rete* net]

re·ti·ar·y (rē′shē·er′ē) *adj.* Of, pertaining to, or furnished with a net or networks. [< L *rete, retis* net + -ARY¹]

ret·i·cence (ret′ə·sens) *n.* The quality of being reticent; taciturnity. Also **ret′i·cen·cy.**

ret·i·cent (ret′ə·sent) *adj.* **1.** Not given to speaking freely; secretive; uncommunicative. **2.** Quiet and reserved in manner, appearance, style, etc.: the *reticent* decorations of the room. [< L *reticens, -entis,* ppr. of *reticere* to keep silent < *re-* again + *tacere* to be silent] — **ret′i·cent·ly** *adv.*

ret·i·cle (ret′i·kəl) *n. Optics* The network of fine threads or lines in the focal plane of a telescope or other optical instrument, serving to determine the position of an observed object: also called *reticule.* [< L *reticulum.* See RETICULUM.]

re·tic·u·lar (ri·tik′yə·lər) *adj.* Like a network; reticulate; intricate. Also **re·tic′u·lar·y.** [< NL *reticularis* < L *reticulum.* See RETICULUM.]

re·tic·u·late (ri·tik′yə·lāt; *for adj.,* also ri·tik′yə·lit) *v.* **·lat·ed, ·lat·ing** *v.t.* **1.** To make a network of. **2.** To cover with or as with lines of network. — *v.i.* **3.** To form a network. — *adj.* **1.** Having the form or appearance of a network. **2.** *Bot.* Having lines or veins crossing: also **re·tic′u·lat·ed.** [< L *reticulatus* < *reticulum.* See RETICULUM.] — **re·tic·u·la′tion** *n.*

ret·i·cule (ret′ə·kyōōl) *n.* **1.** A small bag formerly used by women for carrying personal articles., etc. **2.** *Optics* A reticle. [< F *réticule* < L *reticulum.* See RETICULUM.]

re·tic·u·lum (ri·tik′yə·ləm) *n. pl.* **·la** (-lə) **1.** A netlike structure; network. **2.** *Anat.* A protoplasmic network of cells or cellular tissue. **3.** *Zool.* The second stomach of a ruminant. [< L, dim. of *rete* net]

Re·tic·u·lum (ri·tik′yə·ləm) *n.* A constellation, the Net. See CONSTELLATION. [< NL]

re·ti·form (rē′tə·fôrm, ret′ə-) *adj.* Arranged like a net; reticulate. [< NL *retiformis* < L *rete* net + *forma* form]

ret·i·na (ret′ə·nə, ret′nə) *n. pl.* **·nas** or **·nae** (-nē) *Anat.* The inner membrane at the back of the eyeball, containing light-sensitive rods and cones that transmit the image to the optic nerve. For illustration see EYE. [< Med.L < L *rete* net] — **ret′i·nal** *adj.*

ret·in·ene (ret′ən·ēn) *n. Biochem.* The carotenoid pigment in the retina, that combines with a protein to form visual yellow. [< RETIN(A) + -ENE]

ret·i·nite (ret′ə·nīt) *n.* A hard, brittle, fossil resin obtained from lignite. [< Gk. *rhētinē* resin + -ITE¹]

ret·i·ni·tis (ret′ə·nī′tis) *n. Pathol.* Inflammation of the retina.

ret·i·nol (ret′ə·nōl, -nol) *n.* A yellowish liquid hydrocarbon obtained by the distillation of various resins, used as a solvent and antiseptic: also called *rosin oil.* [< Gk. *rhētinē* resin + -OL²]

ret·i·nos·co·py (ret′ə·nos′kə·pē) *n.* Skiascopy. [< RETIN(A) + -SCOPY] — **ret′i·no·scop′ic** (-nō·skop′ik) *adj.*

ret·i·nue (ret′ə·nōō, -nyōō) *n.* The body of retainers attending a person of rank; an escort; cortège. [< F *retenue* < *retenir.* See RETAIN.]

re·tire (ri·tīr′) *v.* **·tired, ·tir·ing** *v.i.* **1.** To go away or withdraw, as for privacy, shelter, or rest. **2.** To go to bed. **3.** To withdraw oneself from business, public life, or active service. **4.** To fall back; retreat, as troops under attack. **5.** To move back; recede or appear to recede. — *v.t.* **6.** To remove from active service, as an officer of the army or navy. **7.** To pay off and withdraw from circulation: to *retire* bonds. **8.** To withdraw (troops, etc.) from action. **9.** In baseball, etc., to put out (a batter or side). [< MF *retirer* < *re-* back + *tirer* to draw]

re·tired (ri·tīrd′) *adj.* **1.** Withdrawn from public view; existing or passed in seclusion; solitary; secluded: a *retired* life. **2.** Withdrawn from active service, business, office, etc.: a *retired* sea captain. **3.** Due to or received by a person withdrawn from active service: *retired* pay. Abbr. *r., ret.*

re·tire·ment (ri·tīr′mənt) *n.* **1.** The act of retiring, or the state of being retired. **2.** A secluded place; a retreat.

re·tir·ing (ri·tīr′ing) *adj.* **1.** Shy; modest; reserved; unobtrusive. **2.** Pertaining to retirement: a *retiring* pension.

re·tort¹ (ri·tôrt′) *v.t.* **1.** To direct (a word or deed) back upon the originator. **2.** To reply to, as an accusation or argument, by a similar accusation, etc. — *v.i.* **3.** To make answer, especially sharply. — *n.* **1.** A keen rejoinder or retaliatory speech; caustic repartee. **2.** The act of retorting. — **Syn.** See ANSWER. [< L *retortus,* pp. of *retorquere* < *re-* back + *torquere* to twist] — **re·tort′er** *n.*

re·tort² (ri·tôrt′) *n.* **1.** *Chem.* A vessel with a bent tube, for the heating of substances, or for distillation. **2.** *Metall.* A vessel in which ore may be heated for the removal of its metal content. [< L *re·tortus* bent back. See RETORT¹.]

re·tor·tion (ri·tôr′shən) *n.* **1.** The act of retorting. **2.** A bending, turning, or twisting back. **3.** Retaliation; especially, in international law, the infliction by one nation upon the subjects of another of the same ill-treatment that its own citizens have received from the latter government: also **re·tor′sion.** [< Med.L *retortio, -onis*]

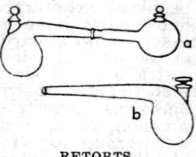

RETORTS

a Retort with receiver. *b* Common retort.

re·touch (rē·tuch′; *for n.,* also rē′tuch) *v.t.* **1.** To add new touches to; modify; revise. **2.** *Photog.* To change or improve, as a print, usually with a hard, sharp pencil or a fine brush. — *n.* An additional touch, as to a picture, model, or other work of art. [< F *retoucher*] — **re·touch′er** *n.*

re·trace (ri·trās′) *v.t.* **·traced, ·trac·ing 1.** To go back over; follow backward, as a path. **2.** To trace the whole story of, from the beginning. **3.** To go back over with the eyes or mind. [< F *retracer*] — **re·trace′a·ble** *adj.*

re·trace (rē·trās′) *v.t.* **·traced, ·trac·ing** To trace again, as an engraving, drawing, or map.

re·tract (ri·trakt′) *v.t. & v.i.* **1.** To take back (an assertion, accusation, admission, etc.); make a disavowal (of); recant. **2.** To draw back or in, as the claws of a cat. **3.** *Phonet.* To produce (a sound) with the tongue drawn back from a given position. — **Syn.** See RENOUNCE. [< L *rétracter* < L *retractare* < *re-* again + *tractare* to handle, freq. of *trahere* to draw] — **re·tract′a·ble** or **·i·ble** *adj.* — **re·trac·ta·tion** (rē′trak·tā′shən) *n.*

re·trac·tile (ri·trak′til) *adj. Zool.* Capable of being drawn back or in, as a cat's claws or the head of a tortoise. [< F *rétractile*] — **re·trac·til·i·ty** (rē′trak·til′ə·tē) *n.*

re·trac·tion (ri·trak′shən) *n.* The act of retracting, or the state of being retracted.

re·trac·tive (ri·trak′tiv) *adj.* Having the power or tendency to retract; retracting.

re·trac·tor (ri·trak′tər) *n.* **1.** One who or that which retracts. **2.** *Surg.* An instrument used to hold apart the edges of a wound, incision, etc.

re·tread (*n.* rē′tred′; *v.* rē·tred′) *n.* A pneumatic tire furnished with a new tread. — *v.t.* **·tread·ed**, **·tread·ing** To fit or furnish (an automobile tire) with a new tread.

re·tread (rē·tred′) *v.t.* **-trod, -trod·den, -tread·ing** To tread again.

re·treat (ri·trēt′) *v.i.* **1.** To go back or backward; withdraw; retire. **2.** To curve or slope backward. — *v.t.* **3.** In chess, to move (a piece) back. — *n.* **1.** The act of retreating. **2.** The retirement of a military force from a position of danger or from an enemy; also, a signal for retreating, made by a trumpet or drum. **3.** *Mil.* A signal, as by bugle, for the lowering of the flag at sunset. **4.** Retirement; seclusion; solitude. **5.** A place of retirement, quiet, or security; a refuge; haunt. **6.** Religious retirement; also, the time spent in religious retirement. **7.** An establishment for the mentally ill, for alcoholics, etc. — **to beat a retreat 1.** To give a signal for retreat, as by the beat of drums. **2.** To turn back; flee. [< OF *retraite*, orig. fem. of pp. of *retraire* < L *retrahere* < *re-* back + *trahere* to draw]

re·trench (ri·trench′) *v.t.* **1.** To cut down or reduce; curtail (expenditures). **2.** To cut off or away; remove; omit. — *v.i.* **3.** To make retrenchments; economize. [< MF *retrencher* < *re-* back + *trencher* to cut. See TRENCH.]

re·trench·ment (ri·trench′mənt) *n.* **1.** The act of retrenching. **2.** Reduction, as of expenses, for the sake of economy. **3.** *Mil.* An interior fortification from which the enemy can be resisted should the outer line be taken.

re·tri·al (rē·trī′əl) *n.* A second or succeeding trial, as of a judicial case.

ret·ri·bu·tion (ret′rə·byoō′shən) *n.* **1.** The act of requiting; especially, impartial infliction of punishment. **2.** That which is done or given in requital, as a reward or punishment. — **Syn.** See REVENGE. [< OF < L *retributio, -onis* < *retribuere* to pay back < *re-* back + *tribuere* to divide (among the tribes), grant < *tribus* tribe]

re·trib·u·tive (ri·trib′yə·tiv) *adj.* Tending to reward or punish. Also **re·trib′u·to·ry** (-tôr′ē, -tō′rē).

re·triev·al (ri·trē′vəl) *n.* The act or process of retrieving. **2.** Possibility of restoration or recovery.

re·trieve (ri·trēv′) *v.* **trieved, triev·ing** *v.t.* **1.** To get back; regain. **2.** To restore; revive, as flagging spirits. **3.** To make up for; remedy the consequences of. **4.** To call to mind; remember. **5.** To find and bring in (wounded or dead game): said of dogs. **6.** *Electronics* To obtain or extract (specific information) from the storage unit of an electronic computer. — *v.i.* **7.** To retrieve game. — *n.* The act of retrieving; retrieval; recovery. [ME *retreve* < OF *retrouver* < *re-* again + *trouver* to find] — **re·triev′a·bil′i·ty** *n.* — **re·triev′a·ble** *adj.* — **re·triev′a·bly** *adv.*

re·triev·er (ri·trē′vər) *n.* **1.** A sporting dog variously bred and specifically trained to retrieve game. **2.** One who retrieves.

retro- *prefix* **1.** Back; backward: *retroflex*, *retrograde*. **2.** Behind: *retrolental*. [< L *retro* back, backward]

ret·ro·act (ret′rō·akt′, rē′trō-) *v.i.* **1.** To act reciprocally or in return; react. **2.** *Law* To affect past acts, obligations, or penalties. [Back formation < RETROACTIVE] — **ret′ro·ac′tion** *n.*

ret·ro·ac·tive (ret′rō·ak′tiv, rē′trō-) *adj.* Taking effect at a (usually specified) time prior to its enactment, ratification, etc., as a provision in a law or contract; applying retrospectively. — **ret′ro·ac′tive·ly** *adv.* — **ret′ro·ac·tiv′i·ty** *n.*

ret·ro·cede (ret′rō·sēd′) *v.* **·ced·ed, ·ced·ing** *v.t.* **1.** To cede, grant, or give back. — *v.i.* **2.** To go back; recede. [< L *retrocedere* < *retro-* back + *cedere* to go]

ret·ro·ces·sion (ret′rō·sesh′ən) *n.* **1.** The act of retroceding. **2.** *Anat.* A backward displacement of the uterus. **3.** *Law* The conveyance of an estate to a former owner. [< LL *retrocessio, -onis* < *retrocedere*. See RETROCEDE.]

ret·ro·choir (ret′rə·kwīr) *n.* The part of a church interior that is east of or beyond the altar. [< RETRO- + CHOIR]

ret·ro·fire (ret′rə·fīr) *n.* *Aerospace* The operation or moment of firing a retrorocket.

ret·ro·flex (ret′rə·fleks) *adj.* **1.** Bent backward; reflexed. **2.** *Phonet.* Cacuminal. Also **ret·ro·flexed** (ret′rə·flexst). [< LL *retroflexus*, pp. of *retroflectere* < L *retro-* back + *flectere* to bend]

ret·ro·flex·ion (ret′rə·flek′shən) *n.* **1.** A bending or being bent backward. **2.** *Anat.* A position of the uterus in which its body is bent back at an angle with the cervix. Also **ret′ro·flec′tion**.

ret·ro·grade (ret′rə·grād) *adj.* **1.** Going or tending backward; contrary; reversed. **2.** Declining to or toward a worse state or character. **3.** *Astron.* Apparently moving from east to west relative to the fixed stars. **4.** Reversed; inverted. **5.** *Obs.* Opposed; contrary. — *v.* **grad·ed, ·grad·ing** *v.i.* **1.** To move or appear to move backward; recede. **2.** To grow worse; degenerate. **3.** *Astron.* To have a retrograde motion. — *v.t.* **4.** To cause to move backward; reverse. [< L *retrogradus* < *retrogradi*. See RETROGRESS.] — **ret′ro·gra·da′tion** (-grā·dā′shən) *n.*

ret·ro·gress (ret′rə·gres) *v.i.* To go back to an earlier or worse condition. [< L *retrogressus*, pp. of *retrogradi* < *retro-* backward + *gradi* to walk] — **Syn.** *Retrogress* and *degenerate* are synonymous only in their extended senses; a moral backslider may be said to *retrogress* or to *degenerate*. In stricter usage, *retrogress* suggests a return to a former place or condition, while *degenerate* implies a passing into a worse condition.

ret·ro·gres·sion (ret′rə·gresh′ən) *n.* **1.** The act or process of retrogressing. **2.** *Biol.* Return to or toward a less complex or less perfect structure.

ret·ro·gres·sive (ret′rə·gres′iv) *adj.* **1.** Tending to retrogress. **2.** *Biol.* Exhibiting retrogression; degenerating.

ret·ro·len·tal (ret′rō·len′təl) *adj.* Behind the lens of the eye. [< RETRO- + NL *lens, lent(is)* lens + -AL¹]

ret·ro·rock·et (ret′rō·rok′it) *n.* *Aerospace* An auxiliary rocket whose reverse thrust lessens the velocity of a rocket or spaceship.

ret·rorse (ri·trôrs′) *adj.* Turned or directed backward. [< L *retrorsus*, contraction of *retroversus* < *retro-* backward + *versus*, pp. of *vertere* to turn] — **re·trorse′ly** *adv.*

ret·ro·spect (ret′rə·spekt) *n.* A view or contemplation of something past. — **Syn.** See MEMORY. — *v.i. Rare* **1.** To think about the past. **2.** To look or refer back. — *v.t.* **3.** *Rare* To consider or think about in retrospect. [< L *retrospectus*, pp. of *retrospicere* < *retro-* back + *specere* to look]

ret·ro·spec·tion (ret′rə·spek′shən) *n.* A looking back upon or recollection of the past; a remembering.

ret·ro·spec·tive (ret′rə·spek′tiv) *adj.* **1.** Looking back on the past. **2.** Looking or facing backward. **3.** Applying retroactively, as legislation. **4.** Characterized by retrospection. — *n.* A retrospective show. — **ret′ro·spec′tive·ly** *adv.*

retrospective show An art exhibition that presents the work of an artist, school, etc., covering a period of years.

ret·rous·sé (ret′roō·sā′, *Fr.* rə·troō·sā′) *adj.* Turned up at the end: said of a nose. [< F, pp. of *retrousser* to turn up]

ret·ro·ver·sion (ret′rə·vûr′zhən, -shən) *n.* **1.** A tipping or bending backward. **2.** The act of looking or turning back. **3.** *Anat.* The backward displacement of the entire uterus in relation to the pelvic axis.

ret·ro·vert (ret′rə·vûrt) *v.t. Obs.* To turn back. [< L *retro-* back + *vertere* to turn]

re·try (rē·trī′) *v.t.* **tried, ·try·ing** To try again, as a judicial case.

re·turn (ri·tûrn′) *v.i.* **1.** To come or go back, as to or toward a former place or condition. **2.** To come back or revert in thought or speech. **3.** To revert to a former owner. **4.** To answer; respond. — *v.t.* **5.** To bring, carry, send, or put back; restore; replace. **6.** To give in return for something. **7.** To repay or requite, especially with an equivalent: to *return* a compliment. **8.** To yield or produce, as a profit or interest. **9.** To send back; reflect, as light or sound. **10.** To render (a verdict, etc.). **11.** To submit, as a report or writ, to one in authority. **12.** To report or announce officially. **13.** To replace (a weapon, etc.) in its holder. **14.** In card games, to lead (a suit previously led by one's partner). — *n.* **1.** The act, process, state, or result of coming back or returning. **2.** That which is returned. **3.** That which accrues, as from investments, labor, or use; profit. **4.** A coming back, reappearance, or recurrence, as of a periodical event. **5.** A report, list, etc.; especially, a formal or official report. **6.** *pl.* A set of tabulated statistics: election *returns*. **7.** *Archit.* A continuation of a dripstone, molding, etc., to form a termination having a different direction from the main part. **b** A part or face of a building at an angle with the main part of the façade. **8.** *Law* The sending back by a sheriff or other officer of a writ to the court from which it was issued; also, a report on such a writ by the officer to whom it was issued. **9.** In card games, a lead in a suit formerly led, especially by one's partner. **10.** In tennis, etc., the act of returning a ball to one's opponent; also, the ball, etc., so returned. — *adj.* **1.** Of, pertaining to, or for a return: a *return* ticket. **2.** Given, taken, or done in return: a *return* visit. **3.** Occurring or presented a second time or again: a *return* showing. **4.** Reversing direction; doubling back, as a U-shaped bend. *Abbr. ret.* [< OF *retorner* < *re-* back (< L) + *torner* to turn < L *tornare*. See TURN.] — **re·turn′er** *n.*

re·turn (rē′tûrn′) *v.t. & v.i.* To turn or fold back again.

re·turn·a·ble (ri·tûr′nə·bəl) *adj.* **1.** Capable of being or suitable to be returned. **2.** Required to be returned.

re·turned man (ri·tûrnd′) *Canadian* A war veteran.

re·turn·ing officer (ri·tûr′ning) In Canada, an official responsible for conducting an election.

return ticket A round-trip ticket.

re·tuse (ri·toōs′, -tyoōs′) *adj. Bot.* Having a rounded apex with a slight depression or notch: said of leaves. [< L *retusus*, pp. of *retundere* < *re-* back + *tundere* to beat]

Retz (rets), **Cardinal de**, 1614–79, Jean François Paul de Gondi, French ecclesiastic and author.

Reu·ben (rōō′bin) In the Old Testament, the eldest son of Jacob and Leah. *Gen.* xxix 32. — *n.* The tribe of Israel descended from Reuben.

Reuch·lin (roikh′lēn, roikh·lēn′), **Johann,** 1455–1522, German humanist and Hebraist. — **Reuch·lin′i·an** *adj.* — **Reuch′lin·ism** *n.*

re·u·ni·fy (rē-yōō′nə·fī) *v.t.* To unify again.

re·un·ion (rē-yōōn′yən) *n.* **1.** The act of reuniting; renewed harmony. **2.** A gathering of persons who have been separated: a family *reunion.*

Ré·un·ion (rē-yōōn′yən, *Fr.* rā·ü·nyôn′) A French Overseas Department comprising an island east of Madagascar; 970 sq. mi.; pop. 436,000 (est. 1969); capital, Saint-Denis; formerly *Bourbon Island.*

re·un·ion·ism (rē-yōōn′yən·iz·əm) *n.* Advocacy of reunion, especially of the various Christian churches. — **re·un′ion·ist** *n.* — **re·un′ion·is′tic** *adj.*

re·u·nite (rē-yōō·nīt′) *v.t. & v.i.* ·nit·ed, ·nit·ing To unite, cohere, or combine again after separation. — **re′u·nit′er** *n.*

Reu·ter (roi′tər), **Baron Paul Julius von,** 1816–99, British news agency pioneer born in Germany: original name **Israel Beer Jo·sa·phat** (yō′zä·fät).

Reu·ter·dahl (roi′tər·däl), **Henry,** 1871–1925, U.S. painter born in Sweden.

Reu·ters (roi′tərz) *n.* A British organization for collecting news and distributing it to member newspapers. Also **Reuter's News Agency.** [after Baron P. J. von *Reuter*]

Reu·ther (rōō′thər), **Walter Philip,** 1907–70, U.S. labor leader.

rev (rev) *n.* A revolution, as of a motor or machine part. — *v.t. & v.i.* **revved, rev·ving** To alter the speed of (a motor): with *up.* [Short for REVOLUTION]

rev. 1. Revenue. **2.** Reverse(d). **3.** Review(ed). **4.** Revise(d); revision. **5.** Revolution. **6.** Revolving.

Rev. 1. Revelation. **2.** Reverend.

Re·val (rā′väl) The German name for TALLINN. Also **Re·vel** (rā′vəl).

re·val·u·ate (rē·val′yōō·āt) *v.t.* ·at·ed, ·at·ing To place a different value on, as currency; value anew.

re·val·ue (rē·val′yōō) *v.t.* ·ued, ·u·ing To value differently or anew; reevaluate.

re·vamp (rē·vamp′) *v.t.* **1.** To patch up; make over; renovate. **2.** To vamp (a boot or shoe) anew. — *n.* Something revamped. [< RE- + VAMP]

re·vanch·ism (rē-vanch′iz·əm) *n.* The advocacy of war or violence for the purpose of revenge. [< F *revanche* revenge] — **re·vanch′ist** *n.*

re·veal (ri·vēl′) *v.t.* **1.** To make known; disclose; divulge. **2.** To make visible; expose to view; exhibit; show. — *n. Archit.* The vertical side of an aperture or opening in a wall; especially, the portion of the side of a door or window between the line where the window frame or door frame stops and the outer edge of the opening. [< OF *reveler* < L *revelare* to unveil < *re-* back + *velum* veil] — **re·veal′a·ble** *adj.* — **re·veal′er** *n.*

re·veal·ment (ri·vēl′mənt) *n.* The act of revealing or the state of being revealed; revelation.

rev·eil·le (rev′i·le) *n.* **1.** A morning signal by drum or bugle, notifying soldiers or sailors to rise. **2.** The hour at which this signal is sounded. [< F *reveillez-vous,* imperative of *se reveiller* to wake up < *re-* (< L) again + *veiller,* ult. < L *vigilare* to keep watch]

rev·el (rev′əl) *v.i.* **rev·eled** or **·elled, rev·el·ing** or **·el·ling 1.** To take delight; indulge freely: with *in:* He *revels* in his freedom. **2.** To engage in boisterous festivities; make merry. — *n.* **1.** Merrymaking; carousing; noisy festivity. **2.** *Often pl.* An occasion of boisterous festivity; a celebration. [< OF *reveler* to make an uproar < L *rebellare.* Doublet of REBEL.] — **rev′el·er** or **rev′el·ler** *n.* — **Syn.** (noun) 1. revelry, carousal, carnival, jollification.

rev·e·la·tion (rev′ə·lā′shən) *n.* **1.** The act or process of revealing, or the state of being revealed. **2.** That which is or has been revealed. **3.** *Theol.* **a** The act of revealing or communicating divine truth, especially by divine agency or supernatural means. **b** That which has been so revealed, as concerning God in his relations to man. **c** That which is revealed in the Bible; also, the Bible itself. [< OF < LL *revelatio, -onis* < L *revelare.* See REVEAL.]

Rev·e·la·tion (rev′ə·lā′shən) *n. Often pl.* The Apocalypse, or book of Revelation, the last book of the New Testament, attributed to Saint John: in full, **The Revelation of Saint John the Divine.** Abbr. *Rev.*

rev·e·la·tion·ist (rev′ə·lā′shən·ist) *n.* One who believes that God has made a supernatural revelation of himself and his will.

rev·e·la·tor (rev′ə·lā′tər) *n.* One who reveals. [< LL]

rev·el·ry (rev′əl·rē) *n. pl.* ·ries Noisy or boisterous merriment. — **rev′el·rous** *adj.*

rev·e·nant (rev′ə·nənt) *n.* **1.** One who or that which returns. **2.** A ghost or apparition. — **Syn.** See GHOST. [< F, ppr. of *revenir* to come back]

re·venge (ri·venj′) *v.* **venged, veng·ing** *v.t.* **1.** To inflict punishment, injury, or loss in return for; to take vengeance for; avenge. **2.** To take or seek vengeance in behalf of.

— *v.i.* **3.** *Obs.* To take vengeance. — *n.* **1.** The act of revenging; retaliation. **2.** A mode or means of avenging oneself or others. **3.** A desire for vengeance. [< OF *revengier* < *re-* (< L) again + *vengier* to take vengeance < L *vindicare.* See VINDICATE.] — **re·veng′er** *n.*

— **Syn.** (verb) See AVENGE. — (noun) 1. *Revenge, vengeance, retaliation, reprisal,* and *retribution* denote the infliction of punishment or injury for a wrong. *Revenge* stresses personal bitterness that seeks relief in harming or humiliating an enemy. *Vengeance,* originally the indignant vindication of justice, is now applied to any furious and thoroughgoing *revenge. Retaliation* suggests the repayment of an act by a like act. *Reprisal* denotes any calculated *retaliation,* as by one nation against another. *Reprisals* are usually undertaken to obtain redress of a wrong, or to force a change of policy. *Retribution* is punishment for a wrong, but not necessarily by its victim; thus, a misfortune suffered by a wrongdoer may be regarded as the *retribution* of fate or providence.

re·venge·ful (ri·venj′fəl) *adj.* Disposed to or full of revenge; vindictive. — **re·venge′ful·ly** *adv.* — **re·venge′ful·ness** *n.*

rev·e·nue (rev′ə·nyōō, -nōō) *n.* **1.** Total current income of a government, except duties on imports: also called *internal revenue.* **2.** Income from any form of property. **3.** The department of government or civil service that collects the national funds. **4.** A source or an item of income. Abbr. *rev.* [< F *revenu,* pp. of *revenir* < L *revenire* < *re-* back + *venire* to come]

revenue cutter ·An armed vessel in the government revenue service used to enforce customs regulations and prevent smuggling.

rev·e·nu·er (rev′ə·nyōō·ər, -nōō-) *n. U.S. Informal* A revenue officer or cutter.

revenue stamp A stamp affixed to a commodity to show that the tax on it has been paid.

re·ver·ber·ant (ri·vûr′bər·ənt) *adj.* Resounding; reverberating. [< L *reverberans, -antis,* ppr. of *reverberare.* See REVERBERATE.]

re·ver·ber·ate (ri·vûr′bə·rāt) *v.* ·at·ed, ·at·ing *v.i.* **1.** To resound or re-echo. **2.** To be reflected or repelled. **3.** To bend back, as flames in a reverberatory furnace. **4.** To rebound or recoil. — *v.t.* **5.** To echo back (a sound); re-echo. **6.** To reflect. **7.** To cause to bend back, as flames in a reverberatory furnace; deflect. **8.** To expose to heat in a reverberatory furnace. [< L *reverberatus,* pp. of *reverberare* to repel < *re-* back + *verberare* to beat]

re·ver·ber·a·tion (ri·vûr′bə·rā′shən) *n.* **1.** The act or process of reverberating. **2.** That which is reverberated. **3.** The rebound or reflection of light, heat, or sound waves. — **re·ver′ber·a′tive** *adj.*

re·ver·ber·a·tor (ri·vûr′bə·rā′tər) *n.* **1.** One who or that which causes reverberation. **2.** A reflecting lamp, or a reverberatory mirror.

re·ver·ber·a·to·ry (ri·vûr′bər·ə·tôr′ē, -tō′rē) *adj.* Producing or intended to produce reverberation; reverberative. — *n. pl.* ·ries A reverberatory furnace (which see).

reverberatory furnace A furnace having a vaulted ceiling that deflects the flame and heat downward toward the upper surface of the substance to be treated: also called *reverberatory.*

re·vere (ri·vir′) *v.t.* **vered, ·ver·ing** To regard with reverence; venerate. — **Syn.** See VENERATE. [< L *revereri* to feel awe of < *re-* again + *vereri* to fear] — **re·ver′er** *n.*

Re·vere (ri·vir′) A resort city in eastern Massachusetts, near Boston; pop. 43,159.

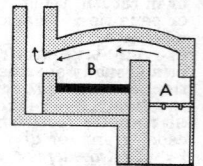

REVERBERATORY FURNACE
A Flames and gases.
B Bed of molten iron.

Re·vere (ri·vir′), **Paul,** 1735–1818, American Revolutionary patriot and silversmith; famous for his midnight ride from Charlestown to Lexington, Mass., the night of April 17–18, 1775, to warn the colonists of the approach of British troops.

rev·er·ence (rev′ər·əns) *n.* **1.** A feeling of profound respect often mingled with awe and affection; veneration. **2.** An act of respect; an obeisance. **3.** The quality or character that commands respect. — *v.t.* **·enced, ·enc·ing** To regard with reverence. — **Syn.** See VENERATE. [< OF < L *reverentia* < *revereri.* See REVERE.]

Rev·er·ence (rev′ər·əns) *n.* A title or form of address for clergymen: often preceded by *His, Your,* etc.

rev·er·end (rev′ər·ənd) *adj.* **1.** Worthy of reverence. **2.** *Often cap.* A title of respect often used with the name of a clergyman. **3.** Of or pertaining to the clergy or the clerical office. — *n. Informal* A clergyman; minister. Abbr. *Rev.* [< L *reverendus,* gerundive of *revereri.* See REVERE.]

rev·er·ent (rev′ər·ənt) *adj.* **1.** Impressed with or feeling reverence. **2.** Expressing reverence. [< L *reverens, -entis,* ppr. of *revereri.* See REVERE.] — **rev′er·ent·ly** *adv.*

rev·er·en·tial (rev′ə·ren′shəl) *adj.* Proceeding from or expressing reverence. — **rev′er·en′tial·ly** *adv.*

rev·er·ie (rev′ər·ē) *n. pl.* ·er·ies **1.** Abstracted musing; dreaming. **2.** A product of such musing in written or musical composition. Also **rev′er·y.** [< F *rêverie* < MF

resverie delirium < *resver* to be delirious, dream < L *rabere* to rage]

re·vers (rə·vir′, -vâr′) *n. pl.* **·vers** (-virz′, -vârz′) **1.** A part of a garment folded over to show the inside, as the lapel of a coat. **2.** Material used to cover such a part. Also **re·vere′**. [< OF. See REVERSE.]

re·vers·al (ri·vûr′səl) *n.* **1.** The act of reversing, or the state of being reversed. **2.** *Law* An annulling or setting aside: the *reversal* of a decree.

re·verse (ri·vûrs′) *adj.* **1.** Having a contrary or opposite direction, character, order, etc.; turned backward. **2.** On the other side; backward; inverted. **3.** Causing backward motion: the *reverse* gear of an automobile. — *n.* **1.** That which is directly opposite or contrary: The *reverse* of what you say is true. **2.** The back, rear, or secondary side of anything: distinguished from *obverse*. **3.** A change to an opposite position, direction, or state; reversal. **4.** A change for the worse; a check or partial defeat; setback. **5.** *Mech.* A reversing gear or movement. — *v.* **·versed**, **·vers·ing** *v.t.* **1.** To turn upside down or inside out; invert or overturn. **2.** To turn in an opposite direction. **3.** To transpose; exchange. **4.** To change into something different or opposite; alter: to *reverse* policy. **5.** To set aside; annul: to *reverse* a decree. **6.** *Mech.* To cause to have an opposite motion or effect. — *v.i.* **7.** To move or turn in the opposite direction, as in dancing. **8.** To reverse its action, as an engine. Abbr. **rev.** [< OF *revers* < L *reversus*, pp. of *revertere*. See REVERT.] — **re·verse′ly** *adv.* — **re·vers′er** *n.*

reverse fault *Geol.* A thrust fault (which see).

re·vers·i·ble (ri·vûr′sə·bəl) *adj.* **1.** Capable of being reversed in direction or position. **2.** Capable of going either forward or backward, as a chemical reaction or physiological process. **3.** Capable of being used or worn inside out or backward, as a coat. **4.** Having the finish on both sides, as a fabric. — *n.* A reversible coat. — **re·vers′·i·bil′i·ty, re·vers′i·ble·ness** *n.* — **re·vers′i·bly** *adv.*

re·ver·sion (ri·vûr′zhən, -shən) *n.* **1.** A return to or toward some former state or condition. **2.** The act of reversing, or the state of being reversed. **3.** A return, as to a former practice or belief. **4.** *Biol.* **a** The reappearance of ancestral characteristics that had not been latent for two or more generations. **b** A return to an earlier or primitive type. Also called *atavism*. **5.** *Law* **a** The return of an estate to the grantor or his heirs after the expiration of the grant. **b** The estate so returning. **c** The right of succession to an estate. [< OF < L *reversio, -onis*. See REVERT.]

re·ver·sion·ar·y (ri·vûr′zhən·er′ē, -shən-) *adj.* Of, pertaining to, characterized by, or involving reversion. Also **re·ver′sion·al** (-əl).

re·ver·sion·er (ri·vûr′zhən·ər, -shən-) *n. Law* One entitled to an estate in reversion.

re·ver·so (ri·vûr′sō) *n. pl.* **·sos** Verso (which see). [< Ital. *riverso* reverse]

re·vert (ri·vûrt′) *v.i.* **1.** To go or turn back to a former place, condition, attitude, etc. **2.** *Biol.* To return to or show characteristics of an earlier, primitive type. **3.** *Law* To return to the former owner or to his heirs. — *n.* **1.** One who is reconverted to a former faith. **2.** That which reverts. [< OF *revertir* < L *revertere* to turn back < *re-* back + *vertere* to turn] — **re·vert′i·ble** *adj.* — **re·ver′tive** *adj.*

re·vest (rē·vest′) *v.t.* **1.** To vest or invest again, as with rank, authority, or ownership. **2.** To vest again, as office or powers. — *v.i.* **3.** To take effect again, as a title reverting to a former owner. [< OF *revestir* < LL *revestire* < L *re-* again + *vestire* to clothe < *vestis* garment]

re·vet (ri·vet′) *v.* **·vet·ted**, **·vet·ting** *v.t.* **1.** To face, as an embankment, with masonry. — *v.i.* **2.** To construct revetments. [< F *revêtir* to clothe < OF *revestire*. See REVEST.]

re·vet·ment (ri·vet′mənt) *n.* **1.** A facing or sheathing, as of masonry, for protecting earthworks, river banks, etc.; a retaining wall. **2.** A protective wall of earth or sandbags. [< F *revêtement*]

re·view¹ (ri·vyōō′) *v.t.* **1.** To go over or examine again; look at or study again. **2.** To look back upon, as in memory; think of retrospectively. **3.** To go over, as a manuscript, so as to correct defects. **4.** To make an inspection of, especially formally. **5.** To write or make a critical review of, as a new book. **6.** *Law* To examine (something done or adjudged by a lower court) so as to determine its legality or correctness. — *v.i.* **7.** To write a review or reviews, as for a magazine. [< RE- + VIEW; modeled on F *revoir* to look at again]

re·view² (ri·vyōō′) *n.* **1.** A second, repeated, or new view, examination, consideration, or study of something; a retrospective survey. **2.** A lesson studied or recited again. **3.** Critical study or examination. **4.** An article or essay containing a critical examination, discussion, or notice of some work; a criticism; critique. **5.** A periodical devoted to essays in criticism and on general subjects. **6.** A formal or official inspection or view, as of troops. **7.** *Law* A judicial

revision by a superior court of the order or decree of a subordinate court. **8.** A revision, as of a work by its author; examination with a view to correction or improvement. **9.** See REVUE. Abbr. **rev.** [< MF *reveue* < pp. of *reveoir* < L *revidere* < *re-* again + *videre* to see]

re·view·al (ri·vyōō′əl) *n.* The act of reviewing; a review.

re·view·er (ri·vyōō′ər) *n.* One who reviews; especially, one who critically reviews new books, plays, movies, etc.

re·vile (ri·vīl′) *v.* **·viled**, **·vil·ing** *v.t.* **1.** To assail with abusive or contemptuous language; vilify; abuse. — *v.i.* **2.** To use abusive or contemptuous language. — **Syn.** See SCOLD. [< OF *reviler* to despise < *re-* + *vil* vile] — **re·vile′ment** *n.* — **re·vil′er** *n.* — **re·vil′ing·ly** *adv.*

re·vis·al (ri·vī′zəl) *n.* The act of revising; revision.

re·vise (ri·vīz′) *v.t.* **·vised**, **·vis·ing** **1.** To read or read over so as to correct errors, suggest or make changes, etc.: to *revise* a manuscript. **2.** To change; alter: He has *revised* his opinions. — **Syn.** See AMEND. — *n.* **1.** The act or result of revising or reviewing; a revision. **2.** A corrected proof after revision. Abbr. **rev.** [< MF *reviser* < L *revisere* < *re-* again + *visere* to scrutinize, freq. of *videre* to see] — **re·vis′er** or **re·vi′sor** *n.*

Revised Standard Version See under KING JAMES BIBLE.

Revised Version See under KING JAMES BIBLE.

re·vi·sion (ri·vizh′ən) *n.* **1.** The act or process of revising. **2.** A product of revising; something revised, as a new version of a book. Abbr. **rev.** — **re·vi′sion·al, re·vi′sion·ar′y** *adj.*

re·vi·sion·ist (ri·vizh′ən·ist) *n.* **1.** One who advocates revision, as of a policy, dogma, political philosophy, etc. **2.** One who revises. — *adj.* Of or pertaining to revisionists or to their doctrines. — **re·vi′sion·ism** (-iz′əm) *n.*

re·vis·it (rē·viz′it) *v.t.* To visit again. — *n.* A return visit. — **re·vis·i·ta′tion** *n.*

re·vi·so·ry (ri·vī′zər·ē) *adj.* Effecting, or capable of effecting, revision; revising: *revisory* powers.

re·vi·tal·ize (rē·vī′təl·īz) *v.t.* **·ized**, **·iz·ing** To restore vitality to; bring back to life; revive. — **re·vi′tal·i·za′tion** *n.*

re·viv·al (ri·vī′vəl) *n.* **1.** The act of reviving, or the state of being revived. **2.** A recovery, as from depression. **3.** A restoration or renewal of interest after neglect, oblivion, or obscurity: the *revival* of letters. **4.** A renewed interest in religious matters or duties. **5.** A series of highly emotional religious meetings or services to reawaken faith. — **Revival of Learning** The Renaissance.

re·viv·al·ism (ri·vī′vəl·iz′əm) *n.* **1.** The spirit and methods of religious revivals or revivalists. **2.** A tendency to restore former conditions or principles.

re·viv·al·ist (ri·vī′vəl·ist) *n.* A preacher or leader in a religious revival movement.

re·vive (ri·vīv′) *v.* **·vived**, **·viv·ing** *v.t.* **1.** To bring back to life or restore to consciousness. **2.** To give new vigor, health, etc., to. **3.** To bring back into use or currency. **4.** To make effective or operative again. **5.** To renew in the mind or memory; refresh; reawaken. **6.** To produce again, as an old play. — *v.i.* **7.** To come back to life again; return to consciousness. **8.** To assume new vigor, health, etc. **9.** To come back into use or currency. **10.** To become effective or operative again. [< MF *revivre* < L *revivere* < *re-* again + *vivere* to live] — **re·viv′er** *n.*

re·viv·i·fy (ri·viv′ə·fī) *v.t.* **·fied**, **·fy·ing** To give new life to; revive. [< L *revivificare* < *re-* again + *vivificare* to vivify < *vivus* alive + *facere* to make] — **re·viv′i·fi·ca′tion** *n.*

re·vi·vis·cence (rev′ə·vis′əns) *n.* A renewal of life or vigor; restoration; revival. Also **rev′i·vis′cen·cy**. [< L *reviviscens, -entis*, ppr. of *reviviscere* < *re-* again + *viviscere* to come to life, freq. of *vivere* to live] — **rev′i·vis′cent** *adj.*

rev·o·ca·ble (rev′ə·kə·bəl) *adj.* Capable of being revoked. Also **re·vok·a·ble** (ri·vō′kə·bəl). [< F *révocable*] — **rev′o·ca·bil′i·ty** *n.* — **rev′o·ca·bly** *adv.*

rev·o·ca·tion (rev′ə·kā′shən) *n.* **1.** The act of revoking, or the state of being revoked; repeal; reversal. **2.** *Law* The annulment or cancellation of an instrument, act, or promise. [< OF *revocacion*] — **rev·o·ca·to·ry** (rev′ə·kə·tôr′ē, -tō′rē) *adj.*

re·voice (rē·vois′) *v.t.* **·voiced**, **·voic·ing** **1.** To restore or give the proper quality of tone to: to *revoice* an organ pipe. **2.** To voice again or in return; echo.

re·voke (ri·vōk′) *v.* **·voked**, **·vok·ing** *v.t.* **1.** To annul or make void by recalling; cancel; rescind. **2.** *Obs.* To call or summon back; recall. — *v.i.* **3.** In card games, to fail to follow suit when possible and when required by the rules. — **Syn.** See ANNUL. — *n.* In card games, neglect to follow suit; a renege. [< OF *revoquer* < L *revocare* < *re-* back + *vocare* to call] — **re·vok′er** *n.*

re·volt (ri·vōlt′) *n.* **1.** An uprising against authority; a rebellion or mutiny; insurrection. **2.** An act of protest, refusal, revulsion, or disgust. **3.** The state of a person or persons who revolt: to be in *revolt*. — *v.i.* **1.** To rise in rebellion against constituted authority; renounce allegiance; mutiny; rebel. **2.** To turn away in disgust or abhorrence; be shocked or repelled: with *against, at,* or *from*. — *v.t.* **3.** To cause to feel disgust or revulsion; repel. [< MF *révolte* < *révolter* < Ital. *rivoltare* < L *revoltus* < *revolvere*. See RE-VOLVE.] — **re·volt′er** *n.*

re·volt·ing (ri·vōl′ting) *adj.* Abhorrent; loathsome; nauseating. — **re·volt′ing·ly** *adv.*

rev·o·lute (rev′ə·lōōt) *adj. Bot.* Rolled backward or downward from the margins upon the under surface, as certain leaves. [< L *revolutus.* See REVOLT.]

rev·o·lu·tion (rev′ə·lōō′shən) *n.* **1.** The act or state of revolving. **2.** A motion in a closed curve around a center, or a complete circuit made by a body in such a course. **3.** *Mech.* **a** Rotation about an axis. **b** Any winding or turning about an axis, as in a spiral or other bend, so as to come to a point corresponding to the starting point. **4.** *Astron.* **a** The movement of a planet around the sun or of any celestial body around a center of attraction. **b** Apparent movement around the earth. **5.** A round or cycle of successive events or changes. **6.** The overthrow and replacement of a government or political system by those governed. **7.** An extensive or drastic change in a condition, method, idea, etc.: a *revolution* in industry. Abbr. *rev.* — **Syn.** See RE-BELLION. [< OF < LL *revolutio, -onis* < L *revolvere.* See REVOLVE.]

— **American Revolution** The war for independence carried on by the thirteen American colonies against Great Britain, 1775–83. Also *Revolutionary War.* See table for WAR.

— **Chinese Revolution** The events in China during the years 1911–12, inspired by Sun Yat-sen, that overthrew the authority of the Manchu Empire and resulted in the establishment of a republic.

— **English Revolution** The course of events in England in 1642–89 that brought about the execution of Charles I, the rise of the Commonwealth, the dethronement of James II, and the establishment of a constitutional government under William III and Mary: called in England **The Revolution,** sometimes with reference to the events of 1688.

— **French Revolution** The revolution that began in France in 1789, overthrew the French monarchy, and culminated in the start of the Napoleonic era in 1799.

— **Russian Revolution** The conflict (1917–22), beginning in a Petrograd uprising on March 12, 1917, that resulted in a provisional moderate government and the abdicaton of Nicholas II. On November 6 (October 24, Old Style), the Bolsheviks under Lenin overthrew this government (the **October Revolution**), and after resisting counterrevolution and libertarian revolution until December, 1922, united the soviet states in the Union of Soviet Socialist Republics under Communist (Bolshevik) control.

rev·o·lu·tion·ar·y (rev′ə·lōō′shən·er′ē) *adj.* **1.** Pertaining to or of the nature of revolution, especially political; causing or tending to produce revolution. **2.** Rotating; revolving. — *n. pl.* **·ar·ies** A revolutionist.

Revolutionary calendar See (Republican) CALENDAR.

Revolutionary War The American Revolution. See under REVOLUTION.

rev·o·lu·tion·ist (rev′ə·lōō′shən·ist) *n.* One who takes part in a revolution: also called *revolutionary.*

rev·o·lu·tion·ize (rev′ə·lōō′shən·īz) *v.t.* **·ized, ·iz·ing** To effect a radical or entire change in the character, operation, or affairs of: to *revolutionize* an industry.

re·volve (ri·volv′) *v.* **·volved, ·volv·ing** *v.i.* **1.** To move in an orbit about a center; move in a circular path. **2.** To spin around on an axis; rotate. **3.** To move in cycles; recur periodically. — *v.t.* **4.** To cause to move in a circle or orbit. **5.** To cause to rotate. **6.** To turn over mentally; consider; ponder. [< L *revolvere* to turn around < *re-* back + *volvere* to roll] — **re·volv′a·ble** *adj.*

— **Syn. 1.** *Revolve, rotate,* and *roll* describe three different circular motions, though they are frequently interchanged. A body *revolves* around a center outside itself: the earth *revolves* around the sun. A body *rotates* around its own axis or center. A body *rolls* on a plane or other surface, with which its circumference is in continuous contact: a wagon wheel *rolls* on the ground, while it *rotates* on its axle.

re·volv·er (ri·vol′vər) *n.* **1.** A type of pistol having a revolving cylinder in the breech chambered to hold several cartridges that may be fired in succession without reloading. **2.** One who or that which revolves.

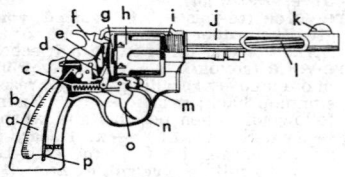

REVOLVER

a Stock. *b* Frame. *c* Trigger spring. *d* Sear. *e* Bolt. *f* Hammer. *g* Extractor. *h* Cylinder. *i* Barrel pin. *j* Barrel. *k* Front sight. *l* Rifling. *m* Cylinder stop. *n* Trigger guard. *o* Trigger. *p* Mainspring.

revolving door A door rotating like a turnstile about a central post and consisting of three or four adjustable leaves so encased in a doorway as to exclude drafts of air.

revolving fund A fund set up to finance loans or operations that yield returns that are placed in the fund for re-use.

re·vue (ri·vyōō′) *n.* A kind of musical comedy without plot, typically consisting of songs, dances, and skits that lampoon or burlesque contemporary people and events: also spelled *review.* [< F. See REVIEW².]

re·vul·sion (ri·vul′shən) *n.* **1.** A sudden change of or strong reaction in feeling. **2.** The drawing back from something; violent withdrawal or recoil. **3.** *Med.* A turning or diverting of any disease from one part of the body to another, as by counterirritation. [< OF < L *revulsio, -onis* < *revulsus,* pp. of *revellere* to pluck away < *re-* back + *vellere* to pluck, pull] — **re·vul′sive** (-siv) *adj.*

Rev. Ver. Revised Version (of the Bible).

re·ward (ri·wôrd′) *n.* **1.** Something given or done in return; especially, a gift, prize, or recompense for merit, service, or achievement. **2.** Money offered for information, for the return of lost goods, the apprehension of criminals, etc. **3.** Profit; return. — *v.t.* **1.** To give a reward to or for; requite; recompense. **2.** To be a reward for. [< OF *rewarder,* var. of *regarder* to look at < *re-* back (< L) + *warder* to guard < Gmc. Akin to REGARD.] — **re·ward′er** *n.*

re·ward·ing (ri·wôr′ding) *adj.* Yielding intangible rewards; worthwhile; satisfying: a *rewarding* career.

re·wind (rē·wīnd′) *v.t.* **·wound, ·wind·ing** To wind anew.

re·wire (rē·wīr′) *v.t.* **·wired, ·wir·ing** To wire again, as a house or a machine.

re·word (rē·wûrd′) *v.t.* **1.** To say again in other words; express differently. **2.** To utter or say again in the same words.

re·write (*v.* rē·rīt′; *n.* rē′rīt′) *v.t.* **·wrote, ·writ·ten, ·writ·ing** **1.** To write over again. **2.** In American journalism, to put into publishable form (a story submitted by a reporter). — *n.* A news item written in this manner.

rewrite man *U.S.* On a newspaper, a writer or editor who receives, transcribes, and rewrites news reports.

rex (reks) *n. pl.* **re·ges** (rē′jēs) *Usually cap. Latin* King. Abbr. *R.*

Rey·kja·vik (rā′kyə·vik) The capital of Iceland, a port on the SW coast; pop. 81,476 (1969). *Icelandic* **Rey·kja·vík** (rā′kyä·vēk′).

Rey·nard (ren′ərd, rā′närd) *n.* The fox, especially as the personification of cunning: also spelled *Renard.* [< MDu. < OHG *Reginhard* personal name; name of fox in the medieval beast-epic *Roman de Reynard*]

Rey·naud (rā·nō′), **Paul,** 1878–1966, French statesman, premier, 1940.

Rey·nolds (ren′əldz), **Sir Joshua,** 1723–92, English painter.

rf. Right fielder (baseball).

r.f. **1.** Radio frequency. **2.** Rapid-fire.

R.F. French Republic (F *République française*).

RFC Royal Flying Corps.

RFD or **R.F.D.** Rural Free Delivery.

r.g. or **rg** Right guard.

r.h. **1.** Relative humidity. **2.** Right hand.

r.h. or **rh** Right halfback.

Rh **1.** *Chem.* Rhodium. **2.** *Biochem.* See RH FACTOR.

R.H. Royal Highness.

rhab·do·man·cy (rab′də·man′sē) *n.* Divination by means of a divining rod: also spelled *rabdomancy.* [< LL *rhabdomantia* < Gk. *rhabdomanteia* < *rhabdos* rod + *manteia* divination] — **rhab′do·man′tist** *n.*

rha·chis (rā′kis) See RACHIS.

Rhad·a·man·thus (rad′ə·man′thəs) In Greek mythology, a son of Zeus and Europa who was noted for justice during his lifetime, and in the afterworld was made a judge, together with Minos and Aeacus. Also **Rhad′a·man′thys.** — **Rhad′a·man′thine** (-thin) *adj.*

Rhae·ti·a (rē′shē·ə) An ancient Roman province, including part of modern Tirol and the Grisons, and later extended to the Danube. Also **Rhæ′ti·a.** — **Rhae·tian** (rē′shən) *adj. & n.*

Rhaetian Alps A division of the central Alps on the Italo-Swiss and Swiss-Austrian borders; highest peak, Piz Bernina, 13,300 ft.

Rhae·tic (rē′tik) *adj.* **1.** *Geol.* Of or pertaining to a group of rock strata representing the upper division of the Triassic system in England and western Europe. **2.** Of or pertaining to the Rhaetian Alps. Also **Rhe′tic.** [< L *Rhaeticus*]

Rhae·to·Ro·man·ic (rē′tō·rō·man′ik) *adj.* Of or pertaining to the peoples of SE Switzerland, northern Italy, and Tirol, or to their Romance dialects known as Ladin, Romansch, and Friulian. — *n.* These dialects as a group.

-rhage, -rhagia, -rhagy See -RRHAGIA.

rham·na·ceous (ram·nā′shəs) *adj. Bot.* Of, pertaining to, or designating the buckthorn family (*Rhamnaceae*) of spiny shrubs and small trees, having simple leaves and regular flowers in cymes. [< LL < Gk. *rhamnos* prickly shrub]

rha·phe (rā′fē) See RAPHE.

-rhaphy See -RRHAPHY.

rhap·so·dist (rap′sə·dist) *n.* **1.** Among the ancient Greeks, a wandering minstrel who recited epic poems; especially, one who declaimed the Homeric poems. Also **rhap′sode** (-sōd). **2.** One who rhapsodizes.

rhap·so·dize (rap′sə·dīz) *v.t. & v.i.* **·dized, ·diz·ing** To express or recite rhapsodically.

rhap·so·dy (rap′sə·dē) *n. pl.* **·dies** **1.** A series of disconnected and often extravagant sentences, extracts, or utterances, gathered or composed under excitement; rapt or rapturous utterance. **2.** In ancient Greece, an epic poem, or a part of such a poem, especially from the *Odyssey* or *Iliad*, recited by a rhapsodist; also, the recitation itself. **3.** *Music* An instrumental composition of irregular form, often suggestive of improvisation. **4.** A miscellaneous collection; a medley. [< L *rhapsodia* < Gk. *rhapsōidia* < *rhapsōidos* rhapsodist < *rhaptein* to stitch together + *ōidē* song] — **rhap·sod·ic** (rap·sod′ik) or **·i·cal** *adj.* — **rhap·sod′i·cal·ly** *adv.*

rhat·a·ny (rat′ə·nē) *n.* *pl.* **·nies 1.** Either of two perennial, shrubby South American leguminous plants (genus *Krameria*), the **Peruvian rhatany** (*K. triandra*), or the **Brazilian rhatany** (*K. argentea*). **2.** The dried roots of these plants, or medicinal substances prepared from them. Also spelled *ratany.* [< NL < Sp. *ratania* < Quechua]

r.h.b. or **rhb** Right halfback.

rhe·a (rē′ə) *n.* A ratite bird (genus *Rhea*) of the plains of South America, smaller than true ostriches, and having three toes: also called *ostrich.* [< NL < L < Gk.]

Rhe·a (rē′ə) In Greek mythology, the daughter of Uranus and Gaea, wife of her brother Kronos, and mother of Zeus, Poseidon, Hades, Hera, Demeter, and Hestia: identified with the Phrygian *Cybele* and the Roman *Ops.* See CRONUS.

-rhea See -RRHEA.

Rhea Sylvia In Roman mythology, a vestal, the mother by Mars of Romulus and Remus.

Rhee (rē), **Syngman,** 1875–1965, Korean statesman; president of the Republic of Korea 1948–60.

Rheims (rēmz, *Fr.* raṅs) See REIMS.

Rhein (rīn) See RHINE.

Rhein·gold (rīn′gōlt), **Das** *German* The gold of the Rhine, title of a music drama by Richard Wagner. See RING OF THE NIBELUNG.

Rhein·land (rīn′länt) See RHINELAND.

Rhein·land-Pfalz (rīn′länt-pfälts′) The German name for the RHINELAND-PALATINATE.

rhe·mat·ic (ri·mat′ik) *adj.* **1.** Relating to or derived from a verb. **2.** Pertaining to the formation of words. [< Gk. *rhēmatikos* < *rhēma* word, verb]

Rhen·ish (ren′ish) *adj.* Pertaining to the river Rhine, or to the adjacent lands. —*n.* Rhine wine. [< L *Rhenus* Rhine]

Rhenish Prussia See RHINE PROVINCE.

rhe·ni·um (rē′nē·əm) *n.* A heavy, lustrous, rare metallic element (symbol Re) of the manganese group. See ELEMENT. [< NL < L *Rhenus* Rhine]

Rhe·nus (rē′nəs) The ancient name for the RHINE.

rheo- *combining form* Current or flow, as of water or electricity: *rheostat.* [< Gk. *rheos* a current]

rheo. Rheostat(s).

rhe·o·base (rē′ə·bās) *n.* *Physiol.* The minimum electrical voltage required to stimulate a nerve or muscle. Compare CHRONAXY.

rhe·ol·o·gy (rē·ol′ə·jē) *n.* The study of the properties and behavior of matter in the fluid state. — **rhe·ol′o·gist** *n.*

rhe·om·e·ter (rē·om′ə·tər) *n.* A device for indicating the force or velocity of fluid flow, especially of blood.

rhe·o·scope (rē′ə·skōp) *n.* A galvanoscope (which see). — **rhe·o·scop′ic** (-skop′ik) *adj.*

rhe·o·stat (rē′ə·stat) *n.* *Electr.* A variable resistor used to control current and voltage strength in a circuit. [< RHEO- + Gk. *statos* standing] — **rhe·o·stat′ic** *adj.*

rhe·o·tax·is (rē′ə·tak′sis) *n.* *Biol.* The movement of an organism in response to the influence of a current of water. — **rhe′o·tac′tic** (-tak′tik) *adj.*

rhe·ot·ro·pism (rē·ot′rə·piz′əm) *n.* *Biol.* Growth or response of an organism under the influence of a current of water. — **rhe·o·trop·ic** (rē′ə·trop′ik) *adj.*

rhe·sus (rē′səs) *n.* A macaque (*Macaca mulatta*) with a short tail, common throughout India and widely used in biological and medical research. [< NL < Gk. *Rhēsos* Rhesus]

Rhe·sus (rē′səs) In the *Iliad*, a king of Thrace and ally of the Trojans, killed by Odysseus the night of his arrival before Troy.

Rhesus factor (rē′səs) Rh factor (which see).

rhet. Rhetoric(al).

rhe·tor (rē′tər) *n.* **1.** Formerly, one who taught rhetoric. **2.** An orator. [< L < Gk. *rhētōr*]

rhet·o·ric (ret′ə·rik) *n.* **1.** The art of discourse, both written and spoken. **2.** The study of the techniques used in literature and public address, as figures of speech, diction, rhythms, and structure. **3.** The power of pleasing or persuading. **4.** Affected and exaggerated display in the use of language; ornamentation in composition. **5.** Language without honest meaning or intention: mere *rhetoric.* **6.** The art of prose as distinct from verse. **7.** Historically, oratory or declamation, including persuasive speech. Abbr. *rhet.*

[< MF *rhetorique* < Gk. *rhētorikē* (*technē*) rhetorical (art) < *rhētōr* public speaker. Akin to Gk. *rhēma* word]

rhe·tor·i·cal (ri·tôr′i·kəl, -tor′-) *adj.* **1.** Pertaining to rhetoric; oratorical. **2.** Designed for showy oratorical effect. Abbr. *rhet.* — **rhe·tor′i·cal·ly** *adv.* — **rhe·tor′i·cal·ness** *n.*

— **Syn. 2.** *Rhetorical, bombastic, flowery, euphuistic, magniloquent,* and *grandiloquent* characterize an ornate style of speech or writing. *Rhetorical* implies the careful choice of words or phrases to emphasize the ideas, and may be complimentary or neutral. The other words are all pejorative. *Bombastic* speech is verbose, extravagant, and exaggerated, while *flowery* speech is overloaded with similes, metaphors, and other figures. *Euphuistic* characterizes writing that strains for verbal effects, to the detriment of the subject. *Magniloquent* and *grandiloquent* describe writing that attempts to raise a banal or commonplace subject to grandeur by pompous words and expressions.

rhetorical question A question put only for oratorical or literary effect, the answer being implied in the question.

rhet·o·ri·cian (ret′ə·rish′ən) *n.* **1.** A master or teacher of rhetoric. **2.** One who writes or speaks eloquently.

rheum (rōōm) *n.* *Pathol.* A thin, watery catarrhal discharge from the nose and eyes. **2.** A cold; catarrh. [< OF *reume* < L *rheuma* < Gk. *rheuma* stream < *rheein* to flow] — **rheum′y** *adj.*

rheu·mat·ic (rōō·mat′ik) *adj.* **1.** Of or relating to rheumatism. **2.** Affected with rheumatism. —*n.* **1.** One affected with rheumatism. **2.** *pl. Informal* Rheumatic pains. [< OF *reumatique* < L *rheumaticus* < Gk. *rheumatikos* < *rheuma.* See RHEUM.]

rheumatic fever *Pathol.* A severe, probably infectious disease chiefly affecting children and young adults, characterized by painful inflammation around the joints, typically intermittent fever, and inflammation of the pericardium and valves of the heart: sometimes called *rheumatism.*

rheu·ma·tism (rōō′mə·tiz′əm) *n.* *Pathol.* **1.** A painful inflammation and stiffness of the muscles, joints, etc. **2.** Rheumatic fever. **3.** Rheumatoid arthritis. [< L *rheumatismus* < Gk. *rheumatismos* < *rheuma.* See RHEUM.]

rheu·ma·toid (rōō′mə·toid) *adj.* *Pathol.* **1.** Resembling rheumatism: *rheumatoid* arthritis. **2.** Rheumatic. Also **rheu′ma·toi′dal** (-toid′l). — **rheu′ma·toi′dal·ly** *adv.*

rheumatoid arthritis *Pathol.* A persisting inflammatory disease of the joints, marked by atrophy, rarefaction of the bones, and deformities: also called *rheumatism.*

Rheydt (rīt) A city in western North Rhine–Westphalia, West Germany; pop. 100,650 (est. 1970).

Rh factor *Biochem.* An agglutinogen present in the blood of most persons (who are said to be **Rh positive**) and that may cause hemolytic reactions under certain conditions, as during pregnancy or following transfusions with persons lacking this factor (who are said to be **Rh negative**): also called *Rhesus factor.* [< *Rh(esus)*, because first discovered in the blood of rhesus monkeys]

rhig·o·lene (rig′ə·lēn) *n.* *Chem.* A colorless, volatile, flammable liquid distillate of petroleum, used in medicine as a local freezing anesthetic for minor surgery. [< Gk. *rhigos* cold + L *oleum* oil]

rhin- Var. of RHINO-.

rhi·nal (rī′nəl) *adj.* Of or pertaining to the nose; nasal. [< RHIN- + -AL]

Rhine (rīn) A river in west central Europe, flowing 810 miles, generally north, from SE Switzerland, through Germany and the Netherlands, to the North Sea. It forms several branches and a large delta with the Meuse in the Netherlands. Ancient *Rhenus*: German *Rhein*: Dutch *Rijn.* French **Rhin** (raṅ).

Rhine·gold (rīn′gōld′) The hoard of the Nibelungs, secreted in the Rhine. Compare RHEINGOLD.

Rhine·land (rīn′land′, -lənd) **1.** The part of Germany west of the Rhine. **2.** The Rhine Province. German *Rheinland.*

Rhine·land-Pa·lat·i·nate (rīn′land′pə·lat′ə·nāt) A state of western West Germany; 7,654 square miles; pop. 3,671,300 (est. 1970); capital, Mainz. German **Rhein·land-Pfalz** (rīn′länt-pfälts′).

rhi·nen·ceph·a·lon (rī′nen·sef′ə·lon) *n.* *pl.* **·la** (-lə) *Anat.* The portion of the brain consisting of the olfactory structures. [< RHIN- + ENCEPHALON] — **rhi·nen·ce·phal·ic** (rī′nen·sə·fal′ik) *adj.*

Rhine Palatinate See PALATINATE.

Rhine Province A former Prussian province in western Germany, since 1945 divided between North Rhine–Westphalia and Rhineland-Palatinate: also *Rhenish Prussia.*

rhine·stone (rīn′stōn′) *n.* A highly refractive, colorless glass or paste, used as an imitation gemstone. [Trans. of F *caillou du Rhin*; so called because orig. made at Strasbourg]

Rhine wine 1. Wine made from grapes grown in the neighborhood of the Rhine: also called *Rhenish.* **2.** Any of various white, dry, still wines.

rhi·ni·tis (rī·nī′tis) *n.* *Pathol.* Inflammation of the mucous membranes of the nose. [< RHIN- + -ITIS]

rhi·no¹ (rī′nō) *n.* *pl.* **·nos** A rhinoceros.

rhi·no² (rī′nō) *n.* *Slang* Money; cash. [Origin unknown]

RHEOSTAT

a Sliding contact. *b* Resistance coil. *c* Lug.

rhino- *combining form* Nose; nasal: *rhinoplasty*. Also, before vowels, **rhin-**. [< Gk. *rhis, rhinos* nose]

rhi·noc·e·ros (rī-nos′ər-əs) *n.* *pl.* **·ros·es** or **·ros** A large, herbivorous, odd-toed mammal (family *Rhinocerotidae*) of Africa and Asia, having one or two horns on the snout, a very thick hide, and the upper lip protruded and prehensile. [< LL < Gk. *rhinokerōs < rhis, rhinos* nose + *keras* horn]

RHINOCEROSES

a African (about 4½ feet high at shoulder). *b* Indian (about 6 feet high at shoulder).

rhi·nol·o·gy (rī-nol′ə-jē) *n.* The branch of medicine that relates to the nose and its diseases. — **rhi·nol′o·gist** *n.*

rhi·no·plas·ty (rī′nō-plas′tē) *n.* Plastic surgery of the nose. — **rhi′no·plas′tic** *adj.*

rhi·no·scope (rī′nə-skōp) *n.* *Med.* An instrument for inspecting the nasal cavities.

rhi·nos·co·py (rī-nos′kə-pē) *n.* *pl.* **·pies** *Med.* Inspection of the nasal passages.

rhizo- *combining form* Root; pertaining to a root or roots: *rhizogenic*. Also, before vowels, **rhiz-**. [< Gk. *rhiza* root]

rhi·zo·bi·um (rī-zō′bē-əm) *n.* *pl.* **·bi·a** (-bē-ə) *Bacteriol.* One of a genus (*Rhizobium*) of rod-shaped, nitrogen-fixing bacteria causing nodules on the roots of leguminous plants. [< NL < RHIZO- + Gk. *bios* life]

rhi·zo·car·pous (rī′zō-kär′pəs) *adj.* *Bot.* Having annual stems and growing from perennial roots: said of perennial plants. Also **rhi′zo·car′pic**.

rhi·zo·ceph·a·lous (rī′zō-sef′ə-ləs) *adj.* *Zool.* Belonging or pertaining to a suborder (*Rhizocephala*) of hermaphroditic crustaceans parasitic on crabs.

rhi·zo·gen·ic (rī′zō-jen′ik) *adj.* *Bot.* Producing roots, as certain cells at the periphery of the central cylinder of a root. Also **rhi·zog·e·nous** (rī-zoj′ə-nəs).

rhi·zoid (rī′zoid) *adj.* Rootlike; similar to or resembling a root. — *n.* *Bot.* A delicate, hairlike, branching organ by which mosses and liverworts obtain nourishment and support. — **rhi·zoi·dal** (rī-zoid′l) *adj.*

rhi·zome (rī′zōm) *n.* *Bot.* A procumbent subterranean rootlike stem, producing roots from its lower surface and leaves or shoots from its upper surface: also called *rootstalk, rootstock*. Also **rhi·zo·ma** (rī-zō′mə). [< NL *rhizoma* < Gk. *rhizōma*, ult. < *rhiza* root] — **rhi·zom·a·tous** (rī-zom′ə-təs, -zō′mə-) *adj.*

rhi·zo·mor·phous (rī′zō-môr′fəs) *adj.* *Bot.* Branching out or shaped like a root. [< RHIZO- + -MORPHOUS]

rhi·zoph·a·gous (rī-zof′ə-gəs) *adj.* Feeding on roots. [< RHIZO- + -PHAGOUS]

rhi·zo·pod (rī′zə-pod) *n.* Any of a class or subclass (*Rhizopoda*) of protozoans with pseudopodia for locomotion and the ingestion of food, including the ameba. — **rhi·zop·o·dan** (rī-zop′ə-dən) *adj.* & *n.* — **rhi·zop′o·dous** *adj.*

rhi·zo·pus (rī′zō-pəs) *n.* Any of a genus (*Rhizopus*) of mold fungi, especially one (*R. nigricans*) producing bread mold.

rhi·zot·o·my (rī-zot′ə-mē) *n.* *pl.* **·mies** *Surg.* The cutting of the roots of the spinal nerves, for the relief of pain or spastic paralysis. [< RHIZO- + -TOMY]

Rh negative See under RH FACTOR.

rho (rō) *n.* The seventeenth letter in the Greek alphabet (P, ρ), corresponding to the English *r* aspirated. See ALPHABET. [< Gk. *rhō*]

rho·da·mine (rō′də-mēn, -min) *n.* *Chem.* Any of various red or pink dyestuffs obtained by condensing an amino derivative of phenol with phthalic anhydride. Also **rho′da·min** (-min). [< Gk. *rhodon* rose + AMINE]

Rhode Island (rōd) A southern New England State of the United States; 1,214 sq. mi.; pop. 949,723; capital, Providence; entered the Union May 29, 1790, one of the original thirteen States; the smallest State in the Union; nickname *Little Rhody.* Abbr. *R.I.* — **Rhode Islander.**

Rhode Island Red An American breed of domestic fowls, reddish and black in color, with yellow smooth legs.

Rhodes (rōdz) **1.** The largest island of the Dodecanese group; 545 sq. mi. **2.** Its chief city, capital of the Dodecanese Islands; pop. about 24,000. See COLOSSUS OF RHODES.

Rhodes (rōdz), **Cecil John**, 1853–1902, British colonial statesman, financier, and philanthropist active in South Africa. — **James Ford**, 1848–1927, U.S. historian.

Rho·de·sia (rō-dē′zhə, -zhē-ə) **1.** Formerly, a region of south central Africa divided by the Zambesi river into **Northern Rhodesia**, a British Protectorate, and **Southern Rhodesia**, a British Colony. See ZAMBIA. **2.** A British Colony in south central Africa consisting of the former Southern Rhodesia; unilaterally declared its independence in 1965; 150,333 sq. mi.; pop. 5,310,000 (est. 1970): capital, Salisbury. — **Rho·de′sian** *adj.* & *n.*

Rhodesia and Nyasaland, Federation of From 1953–63, a political association of Northern and Southern Rhodesia and Nyasaland, formed in 1953; capital, Salisbury, Southern Rhodesia. See map of SOUTH AFRICA.

Rhodesian man *Anthropol.* An African forerunner (*Homo rhodesiensis*) of Neanderthal man, represented by the massive upper jaw and cranium of a skull discovered in 1921 at Broken Hill, Rhodesia.

Rhodes scholarships One of a number of scholarships at Oxford University, provided for in the will of Cecil Rhodes, for selected scholars (**Rhodes scholars**) from the United States and the British dominions and colonies.

Rho·di·an (rō′dē-ən) *adj.* Of or pertaining to the island of Rhodes. — *n.* A native of Rhodes.

rho·dic (rō′dik) *adj.* *Chem.* Of, pertaining to, or derived from rhodium, especially in its higher valence.

rho·di·um (rō′dē-əm) *n.* A whitish gray, metallic element (symbol Rh) of the platinum group, whose salts are for the most part rose-colored, used in electroplating to prevent corrosion. See ELEMENT. [< NL < Gk. *rhodon* rose]

rho·do·chro·site (rō′də-krō′sīt) *n.* A vitreous manganese carbonate, $MnCO_3$, usually rose red in color. [< G *rhodochrosit* < Gk. *rhodochrōs* rose-colored < *rhodon* rose + *chrōs* color]

rho·do·den·dron (rō′də-den′drən) *n.* Any of a genus (*Rhododendron*) of evergreen shrubs or small trees of the heath family, with clusters of white, pink, or purple flowers; especially, the pink rhododendron (which see), and the **great** or **rosebay rhododendron** (*R. maximum*), the State flower of West Virginia. [< L < Gk. < *rhodon* rose + *dendron* tree]

rho·do·lite (rō′də-līt) *n.* A pale rose-colored garnet, used as a gem. [< Gk. *rhodon* rose + -LITE]

rho·do·nite (rō′də-nīt) *n.* A vitreous, red or pink manganese silicate, $MnSiO_3$, often used as an ornamental stone. [< Gk. *rhodon* rose + ITE¹]

Rhod·o·pe Mountains (rod′ə·pē) A mountain chain of the Balkan Peninsula, dividing Bulgaria from Thrace and Macedonia; highest peak, Musala, 9,596 ft.

rho·dop·sin (rō-dop′sin) *n.* *Biochem.* Visual purple. [< Gk. *rhodon* rose + *opsis* appearance]

rho·do·ra (rō-dôr′ə, -dō′rə) *n.* A handsome North American shrub (*Rhododendron canadense*), from 1 to 3 feet high, having terminal clusters of pale purple flowers that develop before the leaves. [< L *rhodora* kind of plant]

-rhoea See -RRHEA.

rhomb (rom, romb) *n.* A rhombus. [< F *rhombe*]

rhom·ben·ceph·a·lon (rom′ben-sef′ə-lon) *n.* *Anat.* One of the three vesicles of the embryonic brain, that divides into the metencephalon and myelencephalon and includes the pons Varolii, medulla oblongata, and cerebellum: also called *hindbrain*. [< NL]

rhom·bic (rom′bik) *adj.* **1.** Pertaining to or having the shape of a rhombus. **2.** Orthorhombic. Also **rhom′bi·cal.**

rhom·bo·he·dron (rom′bə-hē′drən) *n.* *pl.* **·drons** or **·dra** (-drə) *Geom.* A prismatic form having six equal rhombic faces. — **rhom′bo·he′dral** *adj.*

rhom·boid (rom′boid) *n.* *Geom.* **1.** A parallelogram having opposite sides and opposite angles equal but having no right angle. For illustration see PARALLELOGRAM. **2.** A solid bounded by such parallelograms. — *adj.* **1.** Having the character or shape of a rhomboid. **2.** Having a shape approaching that of a rhombus. [< F *rhomboïde*] — **rhom·boi·dal** (rom-boid′l) *adj.*

rhom·bus (rom′bəs) *n.* *pl.* **·bus·es** or **·bi** (-bī) *Geom.* **1.** An equilateral parallelogram having the angles usually, but not necessarily, oblique. For illustration see PARALLELOGRAM. **2.** A rhombohedron. [< L < Gk. *rhombos* spinning top. Akin to *rhembein* to whirl.]

rhon·chus (rong′kəs) *n.* *pl.* **·chi** (-kī) *Pathol.* A rattling or whistling sound in respiration, especially when it resembles snoring; a râle. [< L < Gk. *rhonchos*] — **rhon′chal** (-kəl), **rhon′chi·al** (-kē-əl) *adj.*

Rhond·da (ron′thə) An urban district of Mid Glamorgan, SE Wales; pop. 87,100 (1976): also *Ystradyfodwg.*

Rhône (rōn) A river in Switzerland and SE France, flowing 504 miles, generally SW, to the Mediterranean. Also **Rhone.**

rho·ta·cism (rō′tə-siz-əm) *n.* The inability to articulate (r) correctly. [< L *rhotacismus* < Gk. *rhotakismos* < *rhotakizein* to display rhotacism < *rho* r] — **rho′ta·cist** *n.* & *adj.*

Rh positive See under RH FACTOR.

rhu·barb (rōō′bärb) *n.* **1.** A stout, coarse, perennial herb (genus *Rheum*) of the buckwheat family, having large leaves and small clusters of flowers on tall stalks; especially, the common rhubarb (*R. rhaponticum*), whose acid leafstalks are used in cooking. **2.** The dried roots of the medicinal rhubarb (*R. officinale* and *R. palmatum*), used as a cathartic and bitter tonic. **3.** *U.S. Slang* A heated argument or quarrel. [< MF *reubarbe* < LL *rhabarbarum* < Gk. *rha rhubarb*, ? < *Rha* the Volga + L *barbarus* < Gk. *barbaros* foreign]

rhumb (rum, rumb) *n.* *Naut.* **1.** One of the 32 points of the mariners' compass, separated by arcs of 11° 15′. **2.** One of these arcs or divisions. [< OF *rumb*]

rhum·ba (rum′bə) See RUMBA.

rhumb line A line or course along the surface of a sphere crossing successive meridians at the same angle: also called *loxodromic curve.*

rhyme (rīm) *n.* **1.** A correspondence of sounds in two or more words, especially at the ends of lines of poetry. See

NEAR RHYME, INTERNAL RHYME, TERMINAL RHYME. **2.** A verse whose lines have a correspondence of sounds in the end words. **3.** A word corresponding in sound with another. **4.** Poetry; verse. — *v.* **rhymed, rhym·ing** *v.i.* **1.** To make rhymes or verses. **2.** To correspond in sound or in terminal sounds. — *v.t.* **3.** To put or write in rhyme or verse. **4.** To use as a rhyme. **5.** To cause to correspond in sound. Also spelled *rime*. [< OF *rime*, either < L *rhythmus* (see RHYTHM) or < Gmc. Cf. OE *rīm* number, sequence.]

rhym·er (rī′mər) *n.* One who makes rhyming verse, especially inferior verse: also spelled *rimer*.

rhyme royal A stanza of seven lines in iambic pentameter, rhymed *ababbcc*, first used in Chaucer's *Complaint unto Pity*.

rhyme scheme The pattern of rhymes in a stanza or poem, usually represented by letters, as *ababbcc*.

rhyme·ster (rīm′stər) *n.* A rhymer: also spelled *rimester*.

rhyn·cho·ce·pha·li·an (ring′kō-sə-fā′lē-ən) *adj.* Pertaining to or designating a nearly extinct order of lizardlike reptiles (*Rhynchocephalia*), now represented by the sphenodon of New Zealand. — *n.* A rhynchocephalian lizard. [< NL *Rhynchocephalia* < Gk. *rhynchos* snout + *kephalē* head]

rhy·o·lite (rī′ə-līt) *n.* A highly acidic, variously colored volcanic rock. [< Gk. *rhyax* stream + -LITE]

rhythm (rith′əm) *n.* **1.** The recurrence or repetition of stress, beat, sound, accent, motion, etc., usually occurring in a regular or harmonious pattern or manner. **2.** *Music* **a** The relative duration and accent of musical sounds. **b** Any specific arrangement of the accents or durations of musical sounds. **3.** In poetry, the cadenced flow of sound as determined by the succession of long and short syllables (**classical rhythm**), or accented and unaccented syllables (**modern rhythm**). When definitely measured by feet or bars or periods, which make lines or verses, it becomes *meter*. **4.** A metrical foot or measure. **5.** Verse or rhyme. **6.** In painting, sculpture, etc., a regular or harmonious succession of lines, forms, colors, etc. [< MF *rhythme* < L *rhythmus* < Gk. *rhythmos*. Akin to *rheein* to flow]
— **Syn.** *Rhythm, meter,* and *cadence* relate to the regularly recurring accent in poetry and music. *Rhythm* is applied to broad, prevailing accentual patterns: the *rhythm* of the waltz, the *rhythm* of the Alexandrine hexameter. *Meter* refers to the measure of the elements of *rhythm*: the *meter* of successive lines, stanzas, or bars may be different within a single rhythmic scheme. *Cadence* was originally a falling, and this sense is preserved in music where a *cadence* is the approach to the closing chord of a composition or one of its sections. *Cadence* is also sometimes substituted for *rhythm* in poetry, and sometimes denotes the rise and fall (and other modulation) of the voice in recitation and singing.

rhyth·mi·cal (rith′mə-kəl) *adj.* Of, pertaining to, or possessing rhythm. Also **rhyth·mic** (rith′mik). — **rhyth′mi·cal·ly** *adv.*

rhyth·mics (rith′miks) *n.pl.* (construed as sing.) The science of rhythm.

rhyth·mist (rith′mist) *n.* A master of rhythmical composition; also, one versed in rhythm.

rhythm method A means of birth control based upon sexual abstinence during the woman's estimated monthly period of fertility.

R.I. **1.** King and Emperor (L *Rex et Imperator*). **2.** Queen and Empress (L *Regina et Imperatrix*). **3.** Rhode Island.

ri·al (rī′al) *n.* The monetary unit of Iran (equivalent to 100 dinars), of Oman (equivalent to 100 baizas), and of Yemen (equivalent to 100 fils). [< OF *rial, real* royal]

ri·al·to (rē·al′tō) *n.* *pl.* **·tos** A market or place of exchange.

Ri·al·to (rē·al′tō, *Ital.* rē·äl′tō) **1.** An island comprising the ancient business quarter of Venice. **2.** A bridge over the Grand Canal connecting the old Rialto with the island of San Marco at Venice, Italy: short for **Pon·te del Rialto** (pôn′tā del). **3.** In New York City, the theater district.

ri·ant (rī′ənt) *adj.* Laughing. [< F, ppr. of *rier* to laugh] — **ri′ant·ly** *adv.*

ri·a·ta (rē·ä′tə) *n.* A lasso; lariat. [< Sp. *reata*]

rib (rib) *n.* **1.** *Anat.* One of the series of bony rods attached to the spine of most vertebrates, and nearly encircling the thoracic cavity. In man there are twelve ribs on each side, forming the walls of the thorax. For illustration see SKELETON, THORAX. ◆ Collateral adjective: *costal*. **2.** Something likened to the rib of an animal; a ridge, strip, or band. **3.** A curved side timber bending away from the keel in a boat or ship. **4.** A raised wale or stripe in cloth or knit goods. **5.** *Aeron.* A structural member in an airfoil, extending from the leading edge to the trailing edge and crossing the wing spars, to hold the covering in shape. **6.** *Bot.* A vein of a leaf, especially a central one; any ridge on a plant. **7.** A cut of meat including one or more ribs. **8.** *Archit.* A projecting band or strip covering a transverse or diagonal arch of a vault, as in Gothic architecture. **9.** A wife: in jocular allusion to *Gen.* ii 22. **10.** *Slang* A practical joke. — *v.t.* **ribbed, rib·bing** **1.** To make with ridges: to *rib* a piece of knitting. **2.** To strengthen or protect by or enclose within ribs. **3.** *Slang* To make fun of; tease. [OE. Cf. OHG *rippa,* ON *rif*.]

R.I.B.A. Royal Institute of British Architects.

rib·ald (rib′əld) *adj.* Pertaining to or indulging in coarse or offensive language or vulgar jokes; coarsely jocular. — *n.* One who uses coarse or abusive language. [< OF *ribauld* < *riber* to be wanton < OHG *riban* to be amorous, orig., to rub]

rib·ald·ry (rib′əl·drē) *n.* *pl.* **·ries** Ribald language. [< OF *ribauderie*]

rib·band (rib′band′, rib′ənd, -ən) *n.* *Naut.* A lengthwise strip following a vessel's curves and bolted to its ribs to hold them in place until they receive the planking or plating. Also **rib′-band′**. [< RIB + BAND¹]

Rib·ben·trop (rib′ən-trôp), **Joachim von,** 1893–1946, German Nazi diplomat; executed.

rib·bing (rib′ing) *n.* An arrangement or collection of ribs, as in ribbed cloth, etc.

rib·bon (rib′ən) *n.* **1.** A narrow strip of fine fabric, usually silk or satin, having finished edges and made in a variety of weaves, used as trimming. **2.** Something shaped like or suggesting a ribbon, as a watch spring. **3.** *Often pl.* A narrow strip; a shred: torn to *ribbons*. **4.** An ink-bearing strip of cloth for giving the impression in a typewriter or similar device. **5.** A ribband. **6.** *pl. Informal* Driving reins. **7.** A colored strip of cloth worn to signify membership in an order, the award of a prize, etc.; also, a similar strip of cloth worn on the left breast of a military or naval uniform to indicate campaigns served in, medals won, etc. — *v.t.* To ornament with ribbons; also, to form or tear into ribbons. — *adj.* **1.** Made of or like ribbon. **2.** Having parallel bands or streaks, as certain minerals: *ribbon* jasper. **3.** Of a standard to receive a prize in a competitive show: a *ribbon* hog. Also *Archaic* **rib·and** (rib′ənd). [< MF *riban* < Gmc]

rib·bon·fish (rib′ən·fish′) *n.* *pl.* **·fish** or **·fish·es** Any of several marine fishes (family *Trachipteridae*) of Atlantic and Pacific waters, having a ribbonlike body, as a dealfish.

ribbon worm *Zool.* A nemertean.

Ri·be·ra (rē·vā′rä), **José,** 1588–1656, Spanish painter: called **Spa·gno·let·to** (spä′nyō-lāt′tō) (Little Spaniard).

ri·bo·fla·vin (rī′bō-flā′vin) *n.* *Biochem.* A member of the vitamin B complex, vitamin B_2, an orange-yellow, crystalline compound, $C_{17}H_{22}N_4O_9PNa2H_2O$, found in milk, leafy vegetables, egg yolk, and meats, and also made synthetically: formerly called *lactoflavin, vitamin G*. [< RIBO(SE) + FLAVIN]

ri·bo·nu·cle·ase (rī′bō-nōō′klē-ās, -nyōō-, -āz) *n.* *Biochem.* A pancreatic enzyme that splits ribonucleic acid.

ri·bo·nu·cle·ic acid (rī′bō-nōō-klē′ik, -nyōō-) *Biochem.* A nucleic acid of high molecular weight found in the cytoplasm and nuclei of cells and serving to promote the synthesis of cell proteins. Abbr. *RNA*

ri·bose (rī′bōs) *n.* *Chem.* A sugar, $C_5H_{10}O_5$, derived from pentose and occurring in certain nucleic acids. [< G *ribonsäure*, arbitrary alteration of ARABINOSE + -*säure* acid]

ri·bo·some (rī′bə·sōm) *n.* *Biol.* One of a class of minute protein particles found in the cytoplasm of plant and animal cells, associated with ribonucleic acid in the transmission of genetic characteristics. — **ri·bo·so·mal** (rī′bə·sō′məl) *adj.*

rib·wort (rib′wûrt′) *n.* **1.** The English plantain (*Plantago lanceolata*). **2.** Any of several related plantains.

-ric *combining form* Realm or jurisdiction of: *bishopric*. [OE *rīce* kingdom, realm]

Ri·car·do (ri·kär′dō), **David,** 1772–1823, English political economist. — **Ri·car′di·an** (-dē-ən) *adj. & n.*

Ric·cio (rēt′chō), **David** See RIZZIO.

rice (rīs) *n.* **1.** The edible seeds of an annual cereal grass (*Oryza sativa*), rich in carbohydrates and, in polished or unpolished condition, forming a staple food throughout the world. **2.** The grass itself, cultivated in many varieties in warm climates. — *v.t.* **riced, ric·ing** To press (potatoes or other vegetables) through a ricer. [< OF *ris* < Ital. *riso* < L < Gk. *oryza*]

Rice (rīs), **Elmer L.,** 1892–1967, U.S. dramatist. — **Grant·land,** 1880–1954, U.S. sports journalist.

rice·bird (rīs′bûrd′) *n.* **1.** Any bird frequenting rice fields; especially, in the southern United States, the bobolink: also **rice bunting. 2.** The Javanese sparrow.

rice paper **1.** Paper made from rice straw. **2.** A delicate vegetable paper made from the pith of a Chinese shrub, the **rice-paper plant** (*Tetrapanax papyriferus*), pared into thin rolls and flattened into sheets.

ric·er (rī′sər) *n.* A kitchen utensil consisting of a container perforated with small holes through which potatoes and other vegetables are pressed.

rice weevil A small brown weevil (*Sitophilus* or *Calandra oryza*) destructive to growing rice and the stored grain. For illustration see INSECTS (injurious).

rich (rich) *adj.* **1.** Having large possessions, as of money, goods, or lands; wealthy; opulent. **2.** Composed of rare or precious materials; valuable; costly: *rich* fabrics. **3.** Having in a high degree qualities pleasing to the senses; luscious to the taste, often implying an unwholesome excess of butter, fats, flavoring, etc. **4.** Full, satisfying, and pleasing, as a tone, voice, color, etc. **5.** Luxuriant; abundant: *rich* hair;

rich crops. **6.** Yielding abundant returns; fruitful. **7.** Abundantly supplied: often with *in* or *with*. **8.** Abounding in desirable qualities; of full strength, as blood. **9.** *Informal* Exceedingly humorous; amusing or ridiculous: a *rich* joke. **10.** Of a fuel-air mixture, containing a relatively high ratio of fuel to air. [Fusion of OE *rīce* powerful, rich and OF *riche* < Gmc.] — **rich'ness** *n.*

Rich·ard I (rich'ərd), 1157–99, king of England 1189–99; went on Third Crusade: called **the Lion-Hearted** (lī'ən-här'tid). Also called *Coeur de Lion.*

Richard II, 1367–1400, king of England 1377–99, overthrown by Henry IV; deposed by Parliament.

Richard III, 1452–85, duke of Gloucester, king of England 1483–85; usurped the throne; killed at Bosworth Field: called **Crouch·back** (krouch'bak').

Rich·ards (rich'ərdz), **Ivor Armstrong,** born 1893, English literary critic. — **Theodore William,** 1868–1928, U.S. chemist.

Rich·ard·son (rich'ərd·sən), **Henry Handel** Pseudonym of **Henrietta Richardson,** 1870–1946, British novelist born in Australia. — **Henry Hobson,** 1838–86, U.S. architect. — **Owen Willans,** 1879–1959, English physicist. — **Samuel,** 1689–1761, English novelist.

Ri·che·lieu (rē'shə·lyœ'), **Duc de,** 1585–1642, Armand Jean du Plessis, French cardinal; prime minister of Louis XIII, 1624–42: called **E·mi·nence Rouge** (ā·mē·näns' rōōzh').

Ri·che·lieu River (rē·shə·lyœ', rish'ə·lōō) A river in southern Quebec, flowing about 75 miles north from Lake Champlain to the Saint Lawrence.

rich·es (rich'iz) *n.pl.* **1.** Abundant possessions; wealth. **2.** Abundance of whatever is precious. [< OF *richesse* wealth, power < *riche* < Gmc.]

Ri·chet (rē·she'), **Charles Robert,** 1850–1935, French physiologist.

Rich·field (rich'fēld) A village in eastern Minnesota, a suburb of Minneapolis: pop. 47,231.

rich·ly (rich'lē) *adj.* **1.** In a rich manner. **2.** Fully, amply.

Rich·mond (rich'mənd) **1.** The capital of Virginia, in the east central part, a port city on the James River; capital of the Confederacy 1861–65; pop. 249,621. **2.** A city in western California, on San Francisco Bay; pop. 79,043. **3.** A city in eastern Indiana; pop. 43,999. **4.** A borough of New York City; pop. 295,443. **5.** A municipal borough in southern England, part of greater London; pop. 41,002 (1961).

Rich·ter (rikh'tər), **Jean Paul Friedrich,** 1763–1825, German author and humorist: pseudonym **Jean Paul.**

Richter scale A scale for measuring the strength and magnitude of earthquakes, based on deviations from the horizontal of a standard seismograph record. It runs from 0 to 8.9, each whole number representing a tenfold increase in the magnitude of the earthquake. [After C. F. Richter, born 1900, U.S. seismologist]

Richt·ho·fen (rikht'hō·fən), **Baron Manfred von,** 1892–1918, German aviator in World War I, killed in action.

ri·cin (rī'sin, ris'in) *n. Chem.* A highly toxic protein isolated from the castor bean in the form of a white powder, used to agglutinate red blood corpuscles. [< L *ricinus* castor bean]

ric·in·o·le·ic acid (ris'in·ō·lē'ik, ris'ə·nō'lē·ik) *Chem.* An unsaturated fatty acid, $C_{18}H_{34}O_3$, present in castor oil.

ric·in·o·le·in (ris'in·ō'lē·in) *n. Chem.* The glycerol ester of ricinoleic acid, the principal constituent of castor oil. [< L *ricinus* castor bean + *oleum* oil + -IN]

rick (rik) *n.* A stack, as of hay, having the top rounded and thatched or covered to protect the interior from rain. — *v.t.* To pile in ricks. [OE *hrēac*]

Rick·en·back·er (rik'ən·bak'ər), **Edward Vernon,** born 1890, U.S. aviation executive; aviator in World War I.

rick·ets (rik'its) *n. Pathol.* A disease of early childhood, chiefly due to a deficiency of calcium salts or vitamin D, characterized by softening of the bones and consequent deformity: also called *rachitis.* [? Alter. of Gk. *rachitis* inflammation of the spine < *rachis* spine]

rick·ett·si·a (rik·et'sē·ə) *n. pl.* **·si·ae** (-sī·ē) Any of a genus (*Rickettsia*) of microorganisms typically parasitic in the bodies of certain ticks and lice, the causative agent of typhus, Rocky Mountain spotted fever, etc. [after Howard T. *Ricketts*, 1871–1910, U.S. pathologist]

rick·ett·si·al (rik·et'sē·əl) *adj.* Of or caused by rickettsia.

rick·et·y (rik'it·ē) *adj.* **·et·i·er, ·et·i·est 1.** Ready to fall; tottering. **2.** Affected with or like rickets. **3.** Irregular, as motion. **4.** Feeble. — **rick'et·i·ly** *adv.* — **rick'et·i·ness** *n.*

rick·ey (rik'ē) *n. pl.* **·eys** A cooling drink of liquor, lime juice, and carbonated water. [Said to be after a Colonel *Rickey*]

rick·rack (rik'rak') *n.* Flat braid made in zigzag form, used as a trimming. Also **ric'rac'.** [Reduplication of RACK[1]]

rick·shaw (rik'shô) *n.* A jinriksha. Also **rick'sha.** [Short for JINRIKSHA]

ric·o·chet (rik'ə·shā', -shet') *v.i.* **·cheted** (-shād') or **·chet·ted** (-shet'id), **·chet·ing** (-shā'ing) or **·chet·ting** (-shet'ing) To glance from a surface, as a stone thrown over the water; make a series of skips or bounds. — *n.* **1.** A bounding, as of a projectile over or off a surface. **2.** The method of firing by which a projectile is made to rebound. **3.** A projectile so rebounding. [< F; origin uncertain]

ric·tus (rik'təs) *n.* **1.** The expanse of the open mouth; a gaping. **2.** A fissure or cleft. [< L *ringi* to open the mouth wide] — **ric'tal** *adj.*

rid[1] (rid) *v.t.* **rid** or **rid·ded, rid·ding 1.** To free, as from a burden or annoyance; clear: usually with *of*: to *rid* a house of vermin. **2.** *Obs.* To rescue; deliver. **3.** *Obs.* To drive away. — *adj.* Free; clear; quit: with *of*: We are well *rid* of him. [< ON *rythja* to clear land. Cf. OE *āryddan* to strip.]

rid[2] (rid) Obsolete past tense and past participle of RIDE.

rid·a·ble (rī'də·bəl) *adj.* That may be ridden on, through, or over, as an animal or a road.

rid·dance (rid'ns) *n.* A ridding of something undesirable, or the state of being rid. — **good riddance** A welcome deliverance from something undesirable.

rid·den (rid'n) Past participle of RIDE.

rid·dle[1] (rid'l) *v.t.* **·dled, ·dling 1.** To perforate in numerous places, as with shot. **2.** To sift through a coarse sieve. **3.** To damage, injure; criticize, etc., as if by perforating: to *riddle* a theory. — *n.* **1.** A coarse sieve, such as one used in a foundry or in washing for gold. **2.** A board set with pins, used for straightening wire. [OE *hriddel* sieve] — **rid'dler** *n.*

rid·dle[2] (rid'l) *n.* **1.** A puzzling question stated as a problem to be solved by clever ingenuity; a conundrum. **2.** Any puzzling or mysterious object or person. — **Syn.** See PUZZLE. — *v.* **·dled, ·dling** *v.t.* **1.** To solve; explain. — *v.i.* **2.** To utter or solve riddles; speak in riddles. [OE *rædels* advice, interpretation < *rædan* to counsel. Akin to READ.]

ride (rīd) *v.* **rode** (*Archaic* **rid**), **rid·den** (*Archaic* **rid**), **rid·ing** *v.i.* **1.** To sit on and be borne along by a horse or other animal, especially while guiding or controlling its motion. **2.** To be borne along as if on horseback. **3.** To travel or be carried on or in a vehicle or other conveyance. **4.** To be supported in moving: The wheel *rides* on the shaft. **5.** To move; be borne; float: The ship *rides* on the waves. **6.** To support and carry a rider in a specified manner: This car *rides* easily. **7.** To seem to float in space, as a star. **8.** *Naut.* To lie at anchor, as a ship. **9.** To overlap or overlie, as broken bones. **10.** To work or move upward out of place: with *up*: His sleeve has *ridden* up. **11.** *Slang* To continue unchanged: Let it *ride.* — *v.t.* **12.** To sit on and control the motion of (a horse, bicycle, etc.). **13.** To move or be borne or supported upon. **14.** To overlap or overlie. **15.** To travel or traverse (an area, etc.) on horseback, in an automobile, etc. **16.** To control imperiously or oppressively: usually in the past participle: a king-*ridden* people. **17.** To accomplish by riding: to *ride* a race. **18.** To cause to ride. **19.** To place (someone) astride something and carry him, especially as a punishment: They *rode* him out of town on a rail. **20.** *Naut.* To keep at anchor. **21.** *Informal* To tease or harass by ridicule or petty criticisms; tyrannize. — **to ride out** To survive; endure successfully. — *n.* **1.** An excursion by any means of conveyance, as on horseback, by car, etc. **2.** A road intended for riding. [OE *rīdan.* Cf. OHG *rītan*, G *reiten*, ON *ritha*]

Ri·deau Hall (rē'dō) In Canada, the residence of the Governor General in Ottawa.

ri·dent (rī'dənt) *adj.* Laughing; smiling; grinning. [< L *ridens, -entis*, ppr. of *ridere* to laugh]

rid·er (rī'dər) *n.* **1.** One who or that which rides, as a horseman or a bicyclist. **2.** One who breaks in horses. **3.** Any device that rides upon or weighs down something else. **4.** A separate piece of writing or print added to a document, record, or the like. **5.** An addition or proposed addition to a legislative bill, adding to or modifying its original purport. **6.** A metallic weight for use astride the graduated beam of a delicate balance. **7.** The top rail of a rail fence.

ridge (rij) *n.* **1.** An elevation or protuberance long in proportion to its width and height and generally having sloping sides; a raised strip. **2.** A long, relatively narrow elevation of land; a long hill, or range of hills. **3.** That part of a roof where the rafters meet the ridge pole. **4.** Any raised strip, as on fabric, etc. **5.** The back or backbone of an animal, especially of a whale. **6.** *Meteorol.* A relatively narrow band of high pressure between two cyclone areas, as shown on a weather map. — **Syn.** See BANK[1]. — *v.* **ridged, ridg·ing** *v.t.* **1.** To mark with ridges. **2.** To form into ridges. — *v.i.* **3.** To form ridges. [OE *hrycg*]

ridge·pole (rij'pōl') *n.* A horizontal timber at the ridge of a roof, to which the upper ends of the rafters are nailed. Also **ridge beam, ridge piece, ridge plate.** For illustration see ROOF.

Ridg·way (rij'wā), **Matthew Bunker,** born 1895, U.S. general in World War II, chief of staff 1953–55.

Ridge·wood (rij'wŏŏd) A village in NE New Jersey, near Paterson; pop. 27,547.

ridg·y (rij'ē) *adj.* **ridg·i·er, ridg·i·est** Having ridges; raised in a ridge; ridged.

rid·i·cule (rid'ə·kyōōl) *n.* **1.** Language or actions calculated to make a person or thing the object of contemptuous or humorous derision or mockery. **2.** An object of mocking merriment; butt. **3.** *Obs.* Ridiculousness. — *v.t.* **·culed, ·cul·ing** To make fun of; hold up as a laughingstock; deride. [< OF < L *ridiculum* a joke, ult. < *ridere* to laugh] — **rid'i·cul'er** *n.*

ri·dic·u·lous (ri·dik'yə·ləs) *adj.* Exciting or calculated to excite ridicule; absurd and unworthy of consideration. — **Syn.** See ABSURD. [< L *ridiculus*] — **ri·dic′u·lous·ly** *adv.* — **ri·dic′u·lous·ness** *n.*

rid·ing (rī′ding) *n.* The act of one who rides; a ride. — *adj.* **1.** Suitable for riding. **2.** To be used while riding: *riding* boots. **3.** For use while at anchor: a *riding* light.

rid·ing² (rī′ding) *n.* **1.** One of the three administrative divisions of Yorkshire, England, North Riding, East Riding, and West Riding. **2.** Any similar administrative division. **3.** In Canada, a political division represented by a member of parliament; constituency. [OE *thrithing* < ON *thrithjungr* third part < *thrithi* third; initial *-th* absorbed by *-t* or *-th* in *North, West,* or *East Riding*]

riding habit   Apparel worn by horseback riders, consisting usually of a jacket and breeches or jodhpurs.

riding school   An establishment where the art of riding on horseback is taught.

Rid·ley (rid′lē)   A township in SE Pennsylvania, near Philadelphia; pop. 39,085.

Rid·ley (rid′lē), **Nicholas,** 1500?–55, English Anglican bishop, reformer, and martyr.

ri·dot·to (ri-dot′ō) *n. pl.* **·tos** A public musical and dancing entertainment much in vogue in England in the 18th century. [< Ital., a retreat, meeting place. See REDOUBT.]

Rid·path (rid′path, -päth), **John Clark,** 1840–1900, U.S. educator and historian.

Rieg·ger (rē′gər), **Wallingford,** 1885–1961, U.S. composer.

ri·el (rē-el′) *n.* The monetary unit of Cambodia, equivalent to 100 sen.

Rie·mann (rē′män), **Georg Friedrich Bernhard,** 1826–66, German mathematician.

Ri·en·zi (rē-en′zē), **Cola di,** 1313?–54, Italian patriot, reformer, and orator: original name **Niccolo Ga·bri·ni** (gä-brē′nē). Also **Ri·en′zo** (-zō).

riev·er (rē′vər)   See REAVER.

Rif (rif)   A mountain range bordering the northern coast of Morocco; highest point, Tidiguin Peak, 8,060 ft. Also **Riff.**

ri·fa·ci·men·to (rē-fä′chē-men′tō) *n. pl.* **·ti** (-tē) *Italian* A remaking; recasting: said of literary or musical adaptations.

rife (rīf) *adj.* **1.** Great in number or quantity; plentiful; abundant. **2.** Prevalent; current. **3.** Containing in abundance: followed by *with.* [OE *rȳfe*]

riff (rif) *n.* In jazz music, a melodic phrase or motif, played repeatedly as background or used as the main theme. [? Back formation < RIFFLE¹, or ? < REFRAIN]

Riff (rif) *n.* One of a Berber tribe inhabiting the mountainous region of northern Morocco. — **Rif′fi·an** *adj. & n.*

rif·fle (rif′əl) *n.* **1.** *U.S.* A shoal or rocky obstruction lying beneath the surface of a river or other stream. **2.** A stretch of shallow, choppy water caused by such a shoal. **3.** The act or a way of shuffling cards. — *v.t. & v.i.* **·fled, ·fling 1.** To cause or form a rapid. **2.** To shuffle (cards) by bending up adjacent corners of two halves of the pack, and permitting the cards to slip together as they are released. **3.** To thumb through (the pages of a book). [? Alter. of RUFFLE]

rif·fle² (rif′əl) *n.* *Mining* **1.** A transversely grooved lining set in the bottom of an inclined trough or sluice, for arresting gold contained in sands or gravels. **2.** One of the cross ridges or slats rising above the bottom of such a sluice: also **riffle bar, riffle block.** [Prob. < RIFFLE¹]

riff·raff (rif′raf′) *n.* **1.** The populace; rabble. **2.** Miscellaneous rubbish. [ME *riff and raff* one and all < OF *rif et raf*]

ri·fle¹ (rī′fəl) *n.* **1.** A firearm having a rifled or spirally grooved bore for imparting rotation and, thus, greater range and accuracy to the bullet, designed to be fired from the shoulder. Compare MUSKET. **2.** An artillery piece having a rifled bore. **3.** *Archaic* One of the spiral grooves of such a bore. **4.** *U.S. Mil.* M–1 rifle (which see). **5.** *pl.* A body of soldiers equipped with rifles. — **riflemen.** — *v.t.* **·fled, ·fling** To cut a spirally grooved bore in (a firearm, etc.). [< *rifled gun* < OF *rifler* to file]

ri·fle² (rī′fəl) *v.t.* **·fled, ·fling 1.** To search through and rob, as a safe. **2.** To search and rob (a person). **3.** To seize and take away by force. [< OF *rifler* to plunder < OHG *riffilōn* to tear by rubbing]

rifle grenade   A grenade to be discharged from a rifle.

ri·fle·man (rī′fəl-mən) *n. pl.* **·men** (-mən) One armed or skilled with the rifle.

rifle pit   A trench, the earth from which is thrown up in front, as a protection for riflemen.

U.S. RIFLES
A Springfield, 1903. *B* Garand semiautomatic, World War II.
C M–14 automatic, 1958.

ri·fler (rī′flər) *n.* A robber.

rifle range   An area used for shooting rifles at a target.

ri·fling (rī′fling) *n.* **1.** The operation of forming the grooves in a rifle. **2.** The grooves of a rifle collectively: shallow or deep *rifling.* For illustration see REVOLVER. [< RIFLE¹]

rift¹ (rift) *n.* **1.** An opening made by riving or splitting; a cleft; fissure. **2.** Any disagreement or lack of harmony, as between friends, nations, etc. — *v.t. & v.i.* To rive; burst open; split. [< Scand. Cf. Dan. *rift,* ON *rifa.*]

rift² (rift) *n.* **1.** A shallow place in a stream. **2.** The wash up the beach after a wave has broken. [? Alter. of *riff,* obs. var. of REEF¹]

Rift Valley   See GREAT RIFT VALLEY.

rig¹ (rig) *v.t.* **rigged, rig·ging 1.** To fit out; equip. **2.** *Naut.* **a** To fit, as a ship, with rigging. **b** To fit (sails, stays, etc.) to masts, yards, etc. **3.** *Informal* To dress; clothe, especially in finery. **4.** To make or construct hurriedly or by makeshifts: often with *up:* to *rig* up a door from old boards. — *n.* **1.** *Naut.* The arrangement of sails, rigging, spars, etc., on a vessel. **2.** *Informal* A style of dress; costume. **3.** *U.S. Informal* A horse or horses and vehicle. **4.** Any apparatus, gear, or tackle: an oil-well *rig.* **5.** Fishing tackle. [< Scand. Cf. Norwegian and Sw. *rigga.*]

rig² (rig) *v.t.* **rigged, rig·ging** To control fraudulently; manipulate: to *rig* an election. — **to rig the market** To manipulate the exchange market by raising or lowering prices without regard to the value of the security or commodity traded in, in order to derive a profit. — *n.* **1.** A practical joke; a trick; jest. **2.** A tumult; frolic. [Origin uncertain]

rig³ (rig) *n. Scot. & Brit. Dial.* A ridge or strip of ground. [Var. of RIDGE]

Ri·ga (rē′gə)   The capital of the Latvian S.S.R., a port on the **Gulf of Riga,** an inlet of the Baltic Sea; pop. 733,000 (est. 1970).

rig·a·doon (rig′ə-dōōn′) *n.* **1.** A gay, quick dance for two, originating probably in Provence. **2.** Music for or in the manner of this dance, in rapid duple meter. Also **ri·gau·don** (rē-gō-dôn′). [< F; origin uncertain]

Ri·gel (rī′jəl, -gəl)   One of the 20 brightest stars, 0.14 magnitude; Beta in the constellation Orion. See STAR. [< Arabic *rijl* foot]

rig·ger (rig′ər) *n.* **1.** One who rigs. **2.** One who fits the rigging of ships. **3.** One who assembles and aligns the major parts of an aircraft. **4.** One skilled in the use of cables, pulleys, and other gear used in cranes, scaffolds, slings, etc.

rig·ging (rig′ing) *n.* **1.** *Naut.* The entire cordage system of a vessel. **2.** Tackle used in logging. **3.** The act of one who or that which rigs.

Riggs's disease (rig′ziz) *Pathol.* Pyorrhea alveolaris. [after J. M. *Riggs,* 1810–85, U.S. dentist]

Ri·ghi (rē′gē)   See RIGI.

right (rīt) *adj.* **1.** Done in accordance with or conformable to moral law or to some standard of rightness; equitable; just; righteous. **2.** Conformable to truth or fact; correct; true; accurate. **3.** Conformable to a standard of propriety or to the conditions of the case; proper; fit; suitable. **4.** Most desirable or preferable; also, fortunate. **5.** Pertaining to, designating, or situated on the side of the body that is toward the south when one faces east, and usually having the stronger and more dominant hand. **6.** Holding one direction, as a line; straight; direct. **7.** Properly placed, disposed, or adjusted; well-regulated; orderly. **8.** Sound in mind or body; healthy; well. **9.** *Geom.* Formed with reference to a line or plane perpendicular to another line or plane: a *right* angle. **10.** Designed to be worn outward or when in use placed toward an observer: the *right* side of cloth. **11.** *Law* Rightful; legal. **12.** *Sometimes cap.* Designating a person, party, faction, etc., having absolutely or relatively conservative or reactionary views and policies. **13.** *Obs.* Real or genuine in character; not spurious. — **Syn.** See CORRECT. — **to rights** In a proper or orderly condition: to put a room to *rights.* — *adv.* **1.** In accordance with justice or moral principle. **2.** According to the fact or truth; correctly. **3.** In a straight line; directly. **4.** Very: used dialectally or in some titles: a *right* good time, *Right* Reverend. **5.** Suitably; properly. **6.** Precisely; just; also, immediately. **7.** Without delay or evasion. **8.** Toward the right. **9.** Completely or quite: The house burned *right* to the ground. — *n.* **1.** That which is right; moral rightness; also, justice. **2.** *Often pl.* A just and proper claim or title to anything, or that which may be claimed on just, moral, legal, or customary grounds. **3.** *Law* A claim or title to, or interest in, anything whatsoever that is enforceable by law. **4.** The right hand, side, or direction. **5.** Anything adapted for right-hand use or position. **6.** *Often cap.* A group, party, etc., whose views and policies are right (adj. def. 12); especially, in Europe, such parties whose members sit to the presiding officer's right in a deliberative assembly. **7.** The outside or front side of a thing. **8.** In boxing, a blow delivered with the right hand. **9.** A stockholder's privilege to purchase new stock in a corporation at a special price, usually at par.

— **natural rights** Rights with which mankind is supposedly endowed by nature. — *v.t.* **1.** To restore to an upright or normal position. **2.** To put in order; set right. **3.** To make correct or in accord with facts. **4.** To make reparation for; redress or avenge: to *right* a wrong. **5.** To make reparation to (a person); do justice to. — *v.i.* **6.** To regain an upright or normal position. Abbr. *R.*, *rt.* [OE *riht.* Akin to G *recht*, ON *rēttr*, L *rectus* straight.] — **right'er** *n.*

right·a·bout (rīt'ə·bout') *n.* **1.** The opposite direction. **2.** A turning in or to the opposite direction.

right angle *Geom.* An angle whose sides are perpendicular to each other; an angle of 90°.

right-an·gled (rīt'ang'gəld) *adj.* Forming or containing a right angle or angles: a *right-angled* triangle.

right ascension *Astron.* The angular distance of a celestial body from the vernal equinox, measured eastward along the celestial equator to the hour circle and reckoned in hours, minutes, and seconds from 0 to 24 hours. Abbr. *R.A.*

right away At once; immediately.

right·eous (rī'chəs) *adj.* **1.** Conforming in disposition and conduct to a standard of right and justice; upright; virtuous. **2.** Morally right; equitable: a *righteous* act. [OE *rihtwīs < riht* right + *wīs* wise] — **right'eous·ly** *adv.*

right·eous·ness (rī'chəs·nis) *n.* **1.** The quality or character of being righteous; uprightness; rectitude. **2.** A righteous act or quality. **3.** Rightfulness; justice.

right face In military drill, a 90-degree pivot to the right, using the ball of the left foot and the heel of the right.

right·ful (rīt'fəl) *adj.* **1.** Characterized by or conforming to a right or just claim; also, owned or held by just claim: *rightful* heritage. **2.** Consonant with moral right or with justice and truth. **3.** Proper. **4.** Upright; just. [OE *rihtful*] — **right'ful·ly** *adv.* — **right'ful·ness** *n.*

right-hand (rīt'hand') *adj.* **1.** Of, for, pertaining to, or situated on the right side or right hand. **2.** Chiefly depended on: *right-hand* man. **3.** Turning, opening, or swinging to the right.

right-hand·ed (rīt'han'did) *adj.* **1.** Using the right hand habitually or more easily than the left. **2.** Done with the right hand. **3.** Turning or moving from left to right, as the hands of a clock. **4.** Adapted or intended for use by the right hand. **5.** In conchology, having the spirals rising from left to right. — *adv.* With the right hand. — **right'-hand'ed·ly** *adv.* — **right'-hand'ed·ness** *n.*

right-hand rope Rope that is plain-laid.

right·ist (rī'tist) *n.* One whose views and policies are right (adj. def. 12). — *adj.* Right (adj. def. 12). — **right'ism** *n.*

right·ly (rīt'lē) *adv.* **1.** Correctly. **2.** Honestly; uprightly. **3.** Properly; aptly.

right-mind·ed (rīt'mīn'did) *adj.* Having right opinions.

right·ness (rīt'nis) *n.* **1.** The quality or condition of being right. **2.** Rectitude. **3.** Correctness. **4.** Straightness.

right·o (rī'tō) *interj.* *Brit. Informal* Right! All right!

right of asylum In international law, the right to protection from arrest by taking refuge in a place recognized by law or custom, as in a foreign embassy.

right off Right away.

right of search In international law, the right of a belligerent vessel in time of war to verify the nationality of a vessel and to ascertain, if neutral, whether it carries contraband goods. Also **right of visit and search.**

right of way **1.** *Law* The right of a person to pass over the land of another; also, the path or piece of land over which passage is made. **2.** The strip of land over which a railroad lays its tracks, on which a public highway is built, or above which a high-tension power line is built. **3.** The legal or customary precedence which allows one vehicle or vessel to cross in front of another. Also **right-of-way** (rīt'əv·wā).

right shoulder arms The position in which the rifle is held at an angle of 45 degrees on the right shoulder.

right-to-work law (rīt'tōō·wûrk') *U.S.* A statute outlawing the closed shop. Also **right-to-work legislation.**

right triangle A triangle containing one right angle.

right whale Any of several whales (genus *Balaena*); especially, *B. mysticetus* of polar seas, having a large head and elastic whalebone plates in its mouth: also called *bowhead.*

RIGHT WHALE
(About 60 feet long)

right wing **1.** *Sometimes cap.* A party, group, faction, etc., having rightist policies. **2.** The wing, division, part, etc., on the right side. — **right-wing** (rīt'wing') *adj.* — **right'-wing'er** *n.*

Ri·gi (rē'gē) A mountain between Lakes Lucerne and Zug, central Switzerland; highest peak, Kulm, 5,908 ft.: also *Righi.*

rig·id (rij'id) *adj.* **1.** Resisting change of form; stiff. **2.** Rigorous; inflexible; severe. **3.** Not moving; fixed. **4.** Strict; exact, as reasoning. **5.** *Aeron.* Designating a dirigible whose cells are enclosed within a rigid framework. [< L *rigidus < rigere* to be stiff] — **rig'id·ly** *adv.* — **rig'id·ness** *n.*

ri·gid·i·ty (ri·jid'ə·tē) *n.* *pl.* **·ties** **1.** The state, condition, or quality of being rigid; also, an instance of this. **2.** *Physiol.* A strong, often persisting muscular contraction.

Rig·il Ken·tau·rus (rij'il ken·tôr'əs) *n.* One of the 20 brightest stars, −0.27 magnitude; Alpha in the constellation Centaurus. See STAR.

rig·ma·role (rig'mə·rōl, rig'ə·mə-) *n.* **1.** Confused or nonsensical statements; incoherent talk or writing. **2.** A pointless or needlessly complicated procedure. Also **rig'a·ma·role'** (-ə·mə-). [Alter. of *ragman roll* deed on parchment < ME *rageman* document; ult. origin uncertain]

rig·or (rig'ər) *n.* **1.** The condition of being stiff or rigid. **2.** Stiffness of opinion or temper; harshness. **3.** Exactness without allowance or indulgence; inflexibility; strictness; severity. **4.** Inclemency, as of the weather; hardship. **5.** A severe, harsh, or cruel act. **6.** *Med.* **a** A violent chill from cold or nervous shock. **b** The trembling observed in the chill preceding a fever. **7.** *Physiol.* Rigidity. Also *Brit.* **rig'our.** [< OF *rigour* < L < *rigere* to be stiff]

rig·or·ism (rig'ə·riz'əm) *n.* **1.** Stiffness in opinion or conduct. **2.** Austerity or severity in style or living, etc. Also *Brit.* **rig'our·ism.** — **rig'or·ist** *n.* — **rig'or·is'tic** *adj.*

rig·or mor·tis (rig'ər môr'tis, rī'gôr) The muscular rigidity that ensues shortly after death. [< L, stiffness of death]

rig·or·ous (rig'ər·əs) *adj.* **1.** Marked by or acting with rigor; uncompromising; severe. **2.** Logically accurate; exact; strict. **3.** Inclement; severe: a *rigorous* climate. [< OF *rigoureux*] — **rig'or·ous·ly** *adv.* — **rig'or·ous·ness** *n.*

Rigs·dag (rēks'däg) *n.* The two chambers that form the Danish parliament, consisting of the Landsting and the Folketing. [< Dan. < *rige* kingdom + *dag* session, lit., day. See REICHSTAG.]

rigs·da·ler (rēks'dä'lər) *n.* A rix-dollar. Also **rijks·daal·der** (rēks'däl'dər).

Rig-Ve·da (rig·vā'də, -vē'-) The oldest collection of hymns and verses in Hindu sacred literature, supposedly dating from 2000 B.C. See VEDA. [< Skt. *Rigveda < ric* praise, hymn + *veda* knowledge]

rig·wid·die (rig·wid'ē) *adj.* *Scot.* Bony; sapless; scrawny. Also **rig·wood·ie** (-wōōd'ē).

Riis (rēs), **Jacob August,** 1849–1914, U.S. journalist, social reformer, and author born in Denmark.

Ri·je·ka (rē·ye'kä) A port city in NW Croatia, Yugoslavia, including its SE suburb and officially called **Ri·je·ka-Su'šak** (-sōō'shäk); pop. 108,000 (est. 1968): Italian *Fiume.*

Rijn (rīn) The Dutch name for the RHINE.

Rijs·wijk (rīs'wīk) The Dutch name for RYSWICK.

Riks·mål (rēks'môl) *n.* One of the two official forms of Norwegian, based on literary Danish: also called *Dano-Norwegian.* Also *Danish* **Rigs·mål** (rēks'môl). Compare LANDS-MÅL. [< Norw., speech of the kingdom]

rile (rīl) *v.t.* **riled, ril·ing** *Informal* or *Dial.* **1.** To vex; irritate. **2.** To make (a liquid) muddy or unsettled. Also *roil.* [Var. of ROIL]

ri·ley (rī'lē) *adj.* *U.S. Informal* Riled.

Ri·ley (rī'lē), **James Whitcomb,** 1849–1916, U.S. poet: called **the Hoosier Poet.**

ri·lie·vo (rē·lyä'vō) *n.* *pl.* **·vi** (-vē) Relief (defs. 5 and 6). [< Ital.]

Ril·ke (ril'kə), **Rainer Maria,** 1875–1926, Austrian poet born in Prague.

rill (ril) *n.* **1.** A small stream; rivulet. **2.** A long, narrow, and generally straight valley on the face of the moon: also **rille.** [Prob. < LG *rille*]

rill·et (ril'it) *n.* A little rill (def. 1).

rim (rim) *n.* **1.** The edge of an object, usually of a circular object; a margin; border. **2.** The peripheral part of a wheel, connected to the hub by spokes. **3.** Formerly, the detachable band on an automobile wheel, over which the tire fitted. **4.** The frame of a pair of spectacles, surrounding the lenses. — *v.t.* **rimmed, rim·ming** **1.** To provide with a rim; border. **2.** In sports, to roll around the edge of (the basket, cup, etc.) without falling in: The ball *rimmed* the cup. [OE *rima*]

Rim·baud (ran·bō'), **Arthur,** 1854–91, French poet: full name **Jean Nicholas Arthur Rimbaud.**

rime¹ (rīm) See RHYME.

rime² (rīm) *n.* **1.** A milky white, granular deposit of ice formed on objects by fog or water vapor that has frozen. **2.** Frost. — *v.i.* & *v.t.* **rimed, rim·ing** To cover with or congeal into rime. [OE *hrīm* frost]

rim·er (rī'mər) See RHYMER.

rime riche (rēm rēsh') *French* In prosody, rhyme involving words identical in sound but of different meaning.

rime·ster (rīm'stər) See RHYMESTER.

Rim·i·ni (rim'i·nē, *Ital.* rē'mē·nē) A port city in north central Italy, on the Adriatic; pop. about 53,000: ancient *Ariminum.*

rim·mer (rim'ər) *n.* A reamer (def. 2).

ri·mose (rī'mōs, rī·mōs') *adj.* Full of fissures or cracks; chinky. Also **ri'mous** (-məs). [< L *rimosus < rima* a crack] — **ri·mose'ly** *adv.* — **ri·mos·i·ty** (rī·mos'ə·tē) *n.*

rim·ple (rim'pəl) *n.* A fold or wrinkle. — *v.t.* & *v.i.* **·pled, ·pling** To wrinkle; rumple. [OE *hrympel.* Akin to MLG or MDu. *rimpel* wrinkle]

Rim·sky-Kor·sa·kov (rim'skē·kôr'sə·kôf, *Russ.* rēm'skē·kor'sä·kôf), **Nicholas Andreievich,** 1844–1908, Russian composer.

rim·y (rī′mē) *adj.* **1.** White with rime. **2.** Cold; frosty.

rin (rin) *v.t. & v.i.* **ran, rin·ning** *Scot.* To run or melt.

rind[1] (rīnd) *n.* The skin or outer coat that may be peeled or taken off, as of bacon, fruit, cheese, etc. [OE *rind* bark, crust]

rind[2] (rind, rīnd) See RYND.

rin·der·pest (rin′dər·pest) *n. Vet.* An acute intestinal virus disease of cattle and sometimes of sheep. [< G < *rinder* cattle + *pest* plague]

rin·for·zan·do (rēn′fôr·tsän′dō) *Music. n.* A sudden stress applied to a tone or chord. — *adj.* Of or pertaining to a tone or chord so played. [< Ital., ppr. of *rinforzare* to reinforce]

ring[1] (ring) *n.* **1.** Any circular object, line, mark, etc., having an opening of nearly its own diameter. **2.** A circular band, usually of precious metal, worn on a finger. **3.** Any metal or wooden band used for holding or carrying something: a napkin *ring*; also, a hoop. **4.** A group of persons or things in a circle; also, a circular course or movement, as in dancing. **5.** A combination of persons, often for corrupt or mercenary cooperation, as in business or politics; a clique. **6.** A place where the bark has been cut away around a branch or tree trunk. **7.** One of a series of concentric layers of wood in the trunk of a tree, formed by annual growth. **8.** An area or arena, usually square, as that in which boxers fight; prize fighting in general; also, a circular racecourse or track, as of a circus or horse show. **9.** The field of competition or rivalry: He tossed his hat into the *ring*. **10.** The area set apart for bookmakers and other betters at a racetrack; also, bookmakers collectively. **11.** *Chem.* An arrangement of atoms in a closed chain: the benzene *ring*. **12.** The space between two concentric circles. — **to run rings around** *Informal* To be superior to in some way. — *v.* **ringed, ring·ing** *v.t.* **1.** To surround with a ring; encircle. **2.** To form into a ring or rings. **3.** To provide or decorate with a ring or rings. **4.** To cut a ring of bark from (a branch or tree); girdle. **5.** To put a ring in the nose of (a pig, bull, etc.). **6.** To hem in (cattle, etc.) by riding in a circle around them. **7.** In certain games, to cast a ring over (a peg or pin). — *v.i.* **8.** To form a ring or rings. **9.** To move or fly in rings or spirals; circle. [OE *hring*]

ring[2] (ring) *v.* **rang** (*Archaic* or *Dial.* **rung**), **rung, ring·ing** *v.i.* **1.** To give forth a resonant, sonorous sound, as a bell when struck. **2.** To sound loudly or be filled with sound and resonance; reverberate; resound. **3.** To cause a bell or bells to sound. **4.** To have or suggest a sound expressive of a specified quality: His story *rings* true. **5.** To have a continued sensation of ringing or buzzing: My ears *ring*. — *v.t.* **6.** To cause (a bell, etc.) to ring. **7.** To produce, as a sound, by or as by ringing. **8.** To announce or proclaim by ringing: to *ring* the hour. **9.** To summon, escort, usher, etc., in this manner: with *in* or *out*: to *ring* out the old year. **10.** To strike (coins, etc.) on something so as to test their quality by the sound produced. **11.** To call on the telephone: often with *up*. — *n.* **1.** The sound produced by a bell or other vibrating, sonorous body. **2.** The act of sounding a bell. **3.** A telephone call. **4.** Any reverberating sound, as of acclamation. **5.** Characteristic sound or impression; stamp; seal: the *ring* of truth. **6.** A set, chime, or peal of bells. [OE *hringan*; imit.]

ring-billed (ring′bild′) *adj.* Having a ring of color around the beak: said of certain birds.

ring·bolt (ring′bōlt′) *n.* A bolt having a ring through an eye in its head.

ring·bone (ring′bōn′) *n.* A bony enlargement of the pastern bones of a horse, usually causing lameness.

ring·dove (ring′duv′) *n.* **1.** The cushat. **2.** One of several other pigeons as *Streptopelia risoria* of southeastern Europe, having a black ring partially surrounding the neck.

ringed (ringd) *adj.* **1.** Having a wedding ring; lawfully married. **2.** Encircled by raised or depressed lines or bands, as the stems or roots of some plants. **3.** Marked by a ring or rings. **4.** Composed of rings.

rin·gent (rin′jənt) *adj. Biol.* Gaping, as a corolla in which the lips are widely separated, or as the valves of certain bivalve mollusks. [< L *ringens, -entis,* ppr. of *ringi* to gape]

ring·er[1] (ring′ər) *n.* **1.** One who or that which rings (a bell or chime). **2.** *Slang* An athlete, horse, etc., illegally entered in a contest by concealing disqualifying facts, as age, professional status, etc. **3.** *Slang* A person who bears a marked resemblance to another: You are a *ringer* for Jones.

ring·er[2] (ring′ər) *n.* **1.** One who or that which rings. **2.** A quoit or horseshoe that falls around one of the posts.

Ring·er's solution (ring′ərz) *Med.* A physiologically balanced solution of the chlorides of sodium, potassium, and calcium, used in medicine to correct all forms of dehydration. [after Sidney *Ringer,* 1835–1910, English physiologist]

ring finger The third finger (next to the little finger) of the left hand, on which the marriage ring is worn.

ring·git (ring′git) *n.* The monetary unit of Malaysia, equivalent to 100 sen.

ring·hals (ring′hals) *n. pl.* **·hals·es** The spitting snake. [< *Afrikaans,* lit., ringneck]

ring·lead·er (ring′lē′dər) *n.* A leader or organizer of any undertaking, especially of an unlawful one, as a riot.

ring·let (ring′lit) *n.* **1.** A curl. **2.** A small ring.

ring·mas·ter (ring′mas′tər, -mäs′-) *n.* One who has charge of a circus ring and of the performances in it.

ring·neck (ring′nek′) *n.* **1.** The ring snake. **2.** Any of various ring-necked birds, as the ring-necked duck, etc.

ring-necked (ring′nekt′) *adj.* Having a ring of color around the neck: said of certain birds and animals.

ring-necked duck A North American duck (*Aythya collaris*), blackish with a chestnut collar about the neck.

ring-necked pheasant See under PHEASANT.

Ring of the Ni·be·lung (nē′bə·lŏŏng) In Germanic legend, a ring from the Nibelungen hoard. In his tetralogy of music dramas, *Das Rheingold, Die Walküre, Siegfried,* and *Die Götterdämmerung,* which collectively bear this title, Richard Wagner traces the story of the ring. Also German *Der Ring des Ni·be·lung·en* (der ring des nē′bə·lŏŏng′ən).

ring plover Any of certain small plovers (genus *Charadrius*) marked with a black band around the breast.

ring·side (ring′sīd′) *n.* The space or seats immediately surrounding a ring, as at a prize fight.

ring snake A small, harmless, grayish green snake of North America (*Diadophis punctatus*) having a bright yellow ring around the neck: also called *ringneck.*

ring-streaked (ring′strēkt′) *adj.* Streaked with rings, as an animal. Also *Archaic* **ring′straked′** (-strākt′).

ring·worm (ring′wûrm′) *n. Pathol.* Any of several contagious skin diseases, caused by certain fungi, and marked by the appearance of discolored, scaly patches on the skin.

rink (ringk) *n.* **1.** A smooth, artificial surface of ice, used for ice-skating or hockey. **2.** A smooth floor, used for roller-skating. **3.** A building containing a surface smoothed and prepared for ice-skating or roller-skating. **4.** An area on a field of ice marked off for the game of curling. **5.** The part of a bowling green occupied by one side. **6.** In bowling, quoits, and curling, the players on one side. [< Scot., course, race < OF *renc* ring]

rink rat *Canadian* A boy who does chores around a hockey rink in return for use of the rink, tickets to games, etc.

rinse (rins) *v.t.* **rinsed, rins·ing** **1.** To remove soap from by putting through clear water. **2.** To wash lightly, as by dipping in water or by running water over or into. **3.** To remove (dirt, etc.) by this process. — *n.* The act of rinsing, or the solution in which something is rinsed. [< OF *rincer, recincier,* ult. < L *recens* fresh] — **rins′er** *n.*

rins·ing (rin′sing) *n.* **1.** A rinse. **2.** The liquid in which anything is rinsed. **3.** That which is removed by rinsing.

Río Bra·vo (rē′ō brä′vō) The Mexican name for the RIO GRANDE. Also **Río Bravo del Nor·te** (thel nôr′tä).

Rí·o de Ja·nei·ro (rē′ō dē zhə·nâr′ō, zhə·nâr′ō; *Pg.* rē′ŏŏ thə zhə·nā′rŏŏ) A port city in SE Brazil, the second largest city and former capital of Brazil; pop. 4,261,000 (est. 1969). Also **Rí·o.** An inhabitant of the city is known as a *Carioca.*

Rí·o de la Pla·ta (rē′ō thä lä plä′tä) The estuary of the Paraná and Uruguay rivers between Argentina and Uruguay, extending 170 miles SE to the Atlantic: also, *Brit., River Plate.*

Rí·o de O·ro (rē′ō thä ō′rō) A territory of Spanish Sahara; 73,362 sq. mi.; pop. about 157,000; capital, Villa Cisneros.

Rí·o Grande (rē′ō grand′) **1.** A river flowing 1,800 miles, generally SE, from the Rocky Mountains to the Gulf of Mexico and forming the boundary between Texas and Mexico: Mexican Spanish *Río Bravo, Río Bravo del Norte.* **2.** See RIO GRANDE DO SUL.

Rí·o Gran·de do Nor·te (rē′ŏŏ gränn′də thŏŏ nôr′tə) A state of NE Brazil; 20,482 sq. mi.; pop. 1,271,000 (est. 1967); capital, Natal.

Rio Grande do Sul (thŏŏ sŏŏl′) **1.** A state in southern Brazil; 109,037 sq. mi.; pop. 6,397,000 (est. 1967); capital, Pôrto Alegre. **2.** A port city in Rio Grande do Sul; pop. 117,500 (1968); formerly *São Pedro de Rio Grande do Sul:* also *Rio Grande.*

Rí·o Mu·ni (rē′ō mŏŏ′nē) The mainland province that with the island of Fernando Po comprises the Republic of Equatorial Guinea, in western Africa; formerly an overseas province and colony of Spain; 10,039 sq. mi.; pop. 222,000 (est. 1970). See map of (Gulf of) GUINEA.

Rí·o Ne·gro (rē′ŏŏ nā′grŏŏ) A river in NW Brazil, flowing about 1,400 miles, generally SE, to the Amazon. See map of AMAZON.

Rí·o Ne·gro (rē′ō nā′grŏ) A river in southern Argentine Republic, flowing 400 miles east and SE to the Atlantic.

Rí·o Sa·la·do (rē′ō sä·lä′thō) **1.** A river in north central Argentina, flowing 1,250 miles generally SE to the Paraná: also **Río Salado del Nor·te** (ᵺel nôr′tā). **2.** A river in eastern Argentina, flowing 400 miles SE to the Río de la Plata.

ri·ot (rī′ət) *n.* **1.** A disturbance consisting of wild and turbulent conduct of a large number of persons, as a mob; uproar; tumult. **2.** *Law* A tumultuous disturbance of the public peace by three or more assembled persons who, in the execution of some private object, do an act, lawful or unlawful, in a manner calculated to terrorize the people. **3.** A brilliant or sometimes confusing display: *The garden was a riot of color.* **4.** Boisterous festivity; revelry. **5.** Loose or profligate living or activity. **6.** *U.S. Slang* An uproariously amusing person, thing, or performance. — **to run riot 1.** To act or move wildly and without restraint. **2.** To grow profusely or luxuriantly, as vines. — *v.i.* **1.** To take part in a riot or public disorder. **2.** To live a life of feasting, drinking, etc.; revel. — *v.t.* **3.** To spend (time, money, etc.) in riot or revelry. [< OF *riote* < *rioter* to quarrel, ult. < L *rugire* to roar] — **ri′ot·er** *n.*

riot act Any forceful or vigorous warning or reprimand. — **to read the riot act to** To reprimand bluntly and severely.

Riot Act English statute of George I (1715), providing that if any twelve persons or more are unlawfully assembled and disturbing the peace, they may be commanded to disperse, and that if they refuse to obey they are guilty of felony.

riot gun A short-barreled shotgun.

Rí·o·tin·to (rē′ō·tēn′tō) See MINAS DE RÍOTINTO.

ri·ot·ous (rī′ət·əs) *adj.* **1.** Of, pertaining to, or like a riot. **2.** Engaged in or inciting to riot. **3.** Loud; uproarious: *riotous laughs.* **4.** Indulging in revelry; also, profligate: *riotous spending.* — **ri′ot·ous·ly** *adv.* — **ri′ot·ous·ness** *n.*

riot squad A group of policemen specially trained, armed, and equipped to deal with riots.

rip¹ (rip) *v.* **ripped, rip·ping** *v.t.* **1.** To tear or cut apart roughly or violently; slash. **2.** To tear or cut from something else in a rough or violent manner: with *off, away, out,* etc. **3.** To saw or split (wood) in the direction of the grain. — *v.i.* **4.** To be torn or cut apart; split. **5.** *Informal* To utter with vehemence: with *out.* **6.** *Informal* To rush headlong. — *n.* A place torn or ripped open, especially along a seam; a tear. **2.** A ripsaw (which see). [Cf. MLG *reppen,* MDu. *rippen.*]

rip² (rip) *n.* **1.** A ripple; a rapid in a river. **2.** A riptide (which see). [? < RIP¹]

R.I.P. May he (she, or they) rest in peace (L *requiescat,* or *requiescant, in pace*)

ri·par·i·an (ri·pâr′ē·ən, rī-) *adj.* **1.** Pertaining to the bank of a river: *riparian* rights. **2.** Growing naturally in the sides or banks of watercourses, ponds, etc. [< L *riparius* < *ripa* river bank]

ri·par·i·ous (ri·pâr′ē·əs, rī-) *adj.* Growing or living along the banks of streams, as an animal or a plant.

rip·cord (rip′kôrd′) *n. Aeron.* **1.** The cord, together with the handle and fastening pins, that when pulled releases a parachute from its pack. **2.** A cord attached to the rip panel of a balloon, that when pulled frees the panel and allows gas to escape and the balloon to descend.

ripe¹ (rip) *adj.* **1.** Grown to maturity and fit for food, as fruit or grain. **2.** Brought by keeping and care to a condition for use, as wine or cheese. **3.** Fully developed; matured. **4.** Advanced in years. **5.** In full readiness to do or try; prepared; ready: *The men are ripe for mutiny.* **6.** Fit; opportune: *The times are ripe for war.* **7.** Resembling ripe fruit; rosy; luscious. **8.** *Surg.* Ready for an operation of removal or opening, as an appendix or an abscess. [OE *rīpe.* Akin to REAP.] — **ripe′ly** *adv.* — **ripe′ness** *n.*

ripe² (rīp) *v.t.* **riped, rip·ing** *Scot. & Brit. Dial.* **1.** To cleanse. **2.** To examine thoroughly. **3.** To search. [OE *rȳpan*]

rip·en (rīp′ən) *v.t. & v.i.* To make or become ripe; mature. — **rip′en·er** *n.*

Rip·ley (rip′lē), **William Zebina,** 1867–1941, U.S. economist.

rip·off (rip′ôf′) *U.S. Slang n.* An instance of theft. — **to rip off** To steal or steal from.

ri·poste (ri·pōst′) *n.* **1.** A return thrust, as in fencing. **2.** A quick, clever reply; repartee. — *v.i.* **·post·ed, ·post·ing 1.** To make a riposte. **2.** To reply quickly. Also **ri·post′.** [< F < Ital. *risposta* reply]

rip panel *Aeron.* A segment of the fabric in a balloon or airship that may be ripped open for quick deflation.

rip·per (rip′ər) *n.* **1.** One who or that which rips. **2.** A tool for ripping, as a ripsaw. **3.** A double-ripper (which see). **4.** *Brit. Slang* A thoroughgoing or efficient person or thing; something or someone extremely good.

rip·ping (rip′ing) *Brit. Slang adj.* Splendid; excellent. — *adv.* Very; extraordinarily: *a ripping good time.*

rip·ple¹ (rip′əl) *v.* **·pled, ·pling** *v.i.* **1.** To become slightly agitated on the surface, as water running over a rough, pebbly surface or blown on by a light breeze; form small waves or undulations. **2.** To flow with small waves or undulations on the surface. **3.** To make a sound like water flowing in small waves. — *v.t.* **4.** To cause to form ripples.

— *n.* **1.** One of the wavelets on the surface of water; a ruffle, or slight curling wave. **2.** Any sound like that made by rippling. **3.** Any appearance like a wavelet. [? Fusion of RIFFLE + RIP²] — **rip′pler** *n.* — **rip′ply** *adj.*

rip·ple² (rip′əl) *n.* A toothed tool, especially a comblike instrument for cleaning flax fiber or broomcorn. — *v.t.* **·pled, ·pling** To cleanse, as flax or hemp, with a ripple. [< MLG or MDu. Cf. MDu. *repelen.*]

rip·rap (rip′rap′) *n.* **1.** Broken stones loosely thrown together for a foundation, as in deep water or on a soft bottom; also, the stones used, or the foundation so made. **2.** *pl.* Artificial islands in Chesapeake Bay. — *v.t.* **·rapped, ·rap·ping** To make a riprap in or upon; strengthen with ripraps. [Imit. reduplication of RAP]

rip-roar·ing (rip′rôr′ing, -rōr′-) *adj. U.S. Slang* Good and lively; boisterous.

rip-roar·i·ous (rip-rôr′ē·əs, -rōr′-) *adj. U.S. Slang* Uproarious; boisterous; violent. — **rip-roar′i·ous·ly** *adv.*

rip·saw (rip′sô′) *n.* A coarse-toothed saw used for cutting wood in the direction of the grain: also called *rip.*

rip·snort·er (rip′snôr′tər) *n. Archaic Slang* **1.** Any person or thing excessively noisy, violent, or striking. **2.** A violent windstorm.

rip·tide (rip′tīd′) *n.* Water agitated and made dangerous for swimmers by conflicting tides or currents: also called *rip, tiderip.*

Ri·pu·ar·i·an (rip′yōō·âr′ē·ən) *adj.* Designating or pertaining to a branch of the Frankish people that dwelt on both sides of the Rhine, near Cologne, in the fourth century. — *n.* A Ripuarian Frank. [< Med.L *ripuarius,* prob. < L *ripa* river bank]

Rip Van Win·kle (rip van wing′kəl) In Washington Irving's tale by that name in *The Sketch Book,* a Dutch villager, who, while out hunting in the Catskills, falls asleep for twenty years, and awakes to find his world changed and himself forgotten.

rise (riz) *v.* **rose, ris·en, ris·ing** *v.i.* **1.** To move upward; go from a lower to a higher position. **2.** To slope gradually upward: *The ground rises here.* **3.** To have height or elevation; extend upward: *The city rises above the plain.* **4.** To gain elevation in rank, status, fortune, or reputation. **5.** To swell up: *Dough rises.* **6.** To become greater in force, intensity, height, etc.; also, to become higher in pitch, as the voice. **7.** To become greater in amount, value, etc. **8.** To become erect after lying down, sitting, etc.; stand up. **9.** To get out of bed. **10.** To return to life. **11.** To revolt; rebel: *The people rose against the tyrant.* **12.** To adjourn: *The House passed the bill before rising.* **13.** To appear above the horizon: said of heavenly bodies. **14.** To come to the surface, as a fish after a lure. **15.** To have origin; begin: *The river rises in the mountains.* **16.** To become perceptible to the mind or senses. **17.** To occur; happen. **18.** To be able to cope with an emergency, danger, etc.: *Will he rise to the occasion?* — *v.t.* **19.** To cause to rise. **20.** *Naut.* To cause (a ship) to appear above the horizon by drawing nearer to it. — **to rise above** To prove superior to; show oneself indifferent to. — *n.* **1.** The act of rising; ascent. **2.** Degree of ascent; elevation; also, an ascending course. **3.** The act of beginning to be or appear, as from a source: *the rise of a stream.* **4.** An elevated place; a small hill. **5.** The act of appearing above the horizon. **6.** Increase or advance, as in price or value. **7.** Advance or elevation, as in rank, prosperity, or importance. **8.** The spring or height of an arch above the impost level. **9.** The height of a stair step. **10.** Ascent in a musical scale; also, increase in volume of tone. **11.** The ascent of a fish to food or bait; also, the flying up of a game bird. **12.** *Informal* An emotional reaction; a response or retort. **13.** *Brit.* An increase in salary. [OE *rīsan.* Akin to ON *rīsa.*]

ris·en (riz′ən) Past participle of RISE.

ris·er (rī′zər) *n.* **1.** One who rises or gets up, as from bed: *He is an early riser.* **2.** The vertical part of a step or stair. **3.** A vertical pipe within a building, especially one used to convey steam for heating an interior.

ris·i·bil·i·ty (riz′ə·bil′ə·tē) *n. pl.* **·ties 1.** A tendency to laughter. **2.** *pl.* Impulses to laughter; appreciation of what seems laughable: also **ris′i·bles** (-bəlz).

ris·i·ble (riz′ə·bəl) *adj.* **1.** Having the power of laughing. **2.** Of a nature to excite laughter. **3.** Pertaining to laughter. [< F < LL *risibilis* < L *ridere* to laugh] — **ris′i·bly** *adv.*

ris·ing (rī′zing) *adj.* **1.** Increasing in wealth, power, or distinction. **2.** Ascending; also, sloping upward: *a rising hill.* **3.** Advancing to adult years or to a state of vigor and activity; growing: *the rising generation.* — *n.* **1.** The act of one who or that which rises. **2.** That which rises above the surrounding surface; an eminence or projection. **3.** An insurrection or revolt. **4.** Yeast or leaven used to make dough rise. **5.** *Dial.* A boil or abscess.

risk (risk) *n.* **1.** A chance of encountering harm or loss; hazard; danger. **2.** In insurance, hazard of loss, as of a ship or cargo, or of goods or other property; also, degree of exposure to loss or injury. **3.** An obligation or contract of insurance on the part of the insurer: *to take a risk on a cargo.* **4.** An applicant for an insurance policy considered with regard to the advisability of placing insurance upon him. — **Syn.** See DANGER. — *v.t.* **1.** To expose to a chance of injury or loss; hazard. **2.** To incur the risk of. [< F *risque* < Ital. *risico*; ult. origin uncertain] — **risk'er** *n.*

risk·y (ris'kē) *adj.* **risk·i·er, risk·i·est** Attended with risk; hazardous; dangerous.
— **Syn.** perilous, precarious, chancy. Compare DANGER.

Ri·sor·gi·men·to (rē·sôr'jē·men'tō) *n.* The movement for the liberation and unification of Italy from about 1750 to 1870. [< Ital., resurgence < L *resurgere*]

ri·sot·to (rē·sôt'tō) *n.* Rice cooked in broth and served with meat, cheese, and various condiments. [< Ital. < *riso* rice]

ris·qué (ris·kā', Fr. rēs·kā') *adj.* Bordering on or suggestive of impropriety; bold; daring; off-color: a *risqué* story or play. [< F, pp. of *risquer* to risk]
— **Syn.** racy, ribald, suggestive.

ris·sole (ris'ōl, Fr. rē·sôl') *n.* In cookery, a sausagelike roll consisting of minced meat or fish, enclosed in a thin puff paste and fried. [< F, ult. < LL *russeolus* reddish < *russus* red]

ris·so·lé (rē·sō·lā') *adj. French* Browned by frying.

ri·sus (rī'səs) *n.* A grin or laugh. [< L]

risus sar·do·ni·cus (sär·don'i·kəs) The twisted, grinning expression caused by spasm of the facial muscles, as in tetanus.

rit. or **ritard.** *Music* Ritardando.

ri·tar·dan·do (rē'tär·dän'dō) *Music adj.* Slackening in tempo gradually; retarding. — *n. pl.* **·dos** A gradual slackening of tempo. [< Ital.]

rite (rīt) *n.* **1.** A solemn or religious ceremony performed in an established or prescribed manner, or the words or acts constituting or accompanying it. **2.** Any formal practice or custom. [< L *ritus*]

Rit·ter (rit'ər) *n. German* A knight; one of the lowest of the noble orders in Austria and Germany.

rit·u·al (rich'ōō·əl) *n.* **1.** A prescribed form or method for the performance of a religious or solemn ceremony; any body of rites or ceremonies. **2.** A book setting forth such a system of rites or observances. — *adj.* Of, pertaining to, or practiced as a rite or rites. [< L *ritualis* < *ritus* rite] — **rit'u·al·ly** *adv.*

rit·u·al·ism (rich'ōō·əl·iz'əm) *n.* **1.** Insistence upon ritual; adherence to ritual. **2.** The study of religious ritual. **3.** A love of ritual.

rit·u·al·ist (rich'ōō·əl·ist) *n.* One who practices or advocates ritualism. — *adj.* Ritualistic.

rit·u·al·is·tic (rich'ōō·əl·is'tik) *adj.* **1.** Of or pertaining to ritual or ritualism. **2.** Advocating or adhering to ritualism. — **rit'u·al·is'ti·cal·ly** *adv.*

ritz·y (rit'sē) *adj.* **ritz·i·er, ritz·i·est** *U.S. Slang* Smart; elegant; classy. [< the *Ritz*-Carlton Hotel, New York; after César *Ritz*, 1850–1918, who founded it]

riv. River.

riv·age (riv'ij) *n. Archaic* A shore; coast; bank. [< OF < *rive* < L *ripa* shore]

ri·val (rī'vəl) *n.* **1.** One who strives to equal or excel another, or is in pursuit of the same object as another; a competitor. **2.** One equaling or nearly equaling another, in any respect. **3.** *Obs.* An associate, or companion in office. — **Syn.** See ENEMY. — *v.* **ri·valed** or **·valled, ri·val·ing** or **·val·ling** *v.t.* **1.** To strive to equal or excel; compete with. **2.** To be the equal of or a match for. — *v.i.* **3.** *Archaic* To be a competitor. — *adj.* Being a rival; competing. [< L *rivalis*, pl. *rivales* those living near the same stream, hence those on opposite banks < *rivus* river]

ri·val·ry (rī'vəl·rē) *n. pl.* **·ries 1.** The act of rivaling. **2.** The state of being a rival or rivals; competition.

rive (rīv) *v.* **rived, rived** or **riv·en, riv·ing** *v.t.* **1.** To split asunder by force; cleave. **2.** To break (the heart, etc.). — *v.i.* **3.** To become split. [< ON *rifa*] — **riv·er** (rī'vər) *n.*

riv·en (riv'ən) Alternative past participle of RIVE. — *adj.* Rent; torn apart; split; cleaved.

riv·er (riv'ər) *n.* **1.** A large, natural stream of water, usually fed by converging tributaries along its course and discharging into a larger body of water, as into the ocean, a lake, or another stream. ◆ Collateral adjective: *fluvial.* **2.** A large stream of any kind; copious flow. Abbr. R., riv. — **to sell down the river** To betray the trust of; deceive: from the former selling of slaves to the severe conditions on the plantations of the lower Mississippi. — **to send up the river** To send to the penitentiary: from the fact that Sing Sing is up the Hudson from New York. [< OF *rivière,* ult. < L *riparius.* See RIPARIAN.]

Ri·ve·ra (rē·vā'rä), **Diego,** 1886–1957, Mexican painter.

Ri·ve·ra y Or·ba·ne·ja (rē·vā'rä ē ôr'vä·nā'hä), **Miguel Primo de,** 1870–1930, Marqués de Estella, Spanish general, chief of state 1923–30.

river basin *Geog.* An extensive area of land drained by a river and its branches.

river fever Tsutsugamushi disease.

riv·er·head (riv'ər·hed') *n.* The source of a river.

river horse A hippopotamus.

River Indians Formerly, those Indians collectively who lived on the upper Connecticut River, as distinguished from the coastal tribes.

riv·er·ine (riv'ə·rīn, -ər·in) *adj.* Pertaining to or like a river; riparian.

Riv·ers (riv'ərz), **William Halse,** 1864–1922, English physiologist and anthropologist.

riv·er·side (riv'ər·sīd') *n.* The space alongside of or adjacent to a river.

Riv·er·side (riv'ər·sīd') A city in southwestern California; pop. 140,089.

riv·er·weed (riv'ər·wēd') *n.* A small aquatic plant (*Podostemon ceratophyllum*) resembling a seaweed, found in the eastern and southern United States.

riv·et (riv'it) *n.* A short, soft metal bolt, having a head on one end, used to join objects, as metal plates, by passing the shank through holes and forming a new head by flattening out the other end. — *v.t.* **1.** To fasten with or as with a rivet. **2.** To batter the headless end of (a bolt, etc.) so as to make fast. **3.** To fasten firmly. **4.** To engross or attract (the eyes, attention, etc.). [< OF < *river* to clench, prob. < MDu. *wriven* to cause to turn. Cf. MDu. *rivet* rivet.] — **riv'et·er** *n.*

Ri·vi·er·a (riv'ē·âr'ə, *Ital.* rē·vyä'rä) The coastal strip between the southernmost Alpine ranges and the Mediterranean, extending from Hyères, France, about 230 miles to La Spezia, Italy.

ri·vière (rē·vyâr') *n. French* A necklace of diamonds or other gems, usually in several strings.

riv·u·let (riv'yə·lit) *n.* A small stream or brook: also called *streamlet.* [< Ital. *rivoletto,* dim. of *rivolo* < L *rivulus,* dim. of *rivus* stream]

rix·dol·lar (riks'dol'ər) *n.* Any one of several small silver coins formerly current in the Scandinavian countries and the Netherlands; also *rigsdaler, rijksdaalder.* Abbr. *Rd.* [< Du. *rijksdaler* dollar of the realm]

Ri·yadh (rē·yäd') One of the capitals of Saudi Arabia, in the eastern part; pop. 400,000 (est. 1971). Also **Ri·yad'.**

ri·yal (rē·yôl') *n.* The monetary unit of Saudi Arabia (equivalent to 100 hallalas), and of Qatar (equivalent to 100 dirhams).

Ri·zal (rē·säl'), **José,** 1861–96, Philippine patriot and author, shot by the Spanish.

Rizal Day A holiday observed on December 30 in the Philippines in memory of José Rizal.

Ri·za Shah Pah·la·vi (ri·zä' shä' pä'lə·vē), 1877–1944, shah of Iran 1925–41; abdicated. Also **Pah'le·vi.**

Riz·zi·o (rēt'tsyō), **David,** 1533?–66. Italian musician and courtier; secretary to Mary, Queen of Scots; assassinated. Also **Ric'cio.**

rm. (*pl.* **rms.**). **1.** Ream. **2.** Room.

RM or **R.M., Rm.,** or **r.m.** Reichsmark(s).

rms or **r.m.s.** Root mean square.

R.M.S. 1. Railway Mail Service. **2.** Royal Mail Service. **3.** Royal Mail Steamship.

Rn *Chem.* Radon.

R.N. 1. Registered nurse. **2.** Royal Navy.

RNA *Biochem.* Ribonucleic acid.

R.N.A.S. Royal Naval Air Service.

R.N.R. Royal Naval Reserve.

R.N.V.R. Royal Naval Volunteer Reserve.

R.N.W.M.P. Royal Northwest Mounted Police.

roach[1] (rōch) *n.* **1.** A European fresh-water fish (*Rutilus rutilus*) of the carp family, with a greenish back. **2.** Any of various other related cyprinoid fishes, as a fresh-water sunfish. [< OF *roche*; ult. origin uncertain]

roach[2] (rōch) *n.* A cockroach (which see).

road (rōd) *n.* **1.** An open way for public passage, especially from one city, town, or village to another; a highway. **2.** Any way of advancing or progressing: the *road* to fame. **3.** *Usually pl.* A roadstead: Hampton *Roads.* **4.** *U.S.A* railroad. Abbr. **R., rd., Rd. — on the road 1.** On tour: said of circuses, theatrical companies, etc. **2.** Traveling, as a canvasser or salesman. **3.** Living the life of a tramp or hobo. [OE *rād* journey < *rīdan* to ride. Akin to RIDE.]
— **Syn. 1.** *Road, highroad, turnpike, lane,* and *thoroughfare* are compared as they denote ways for interurban or rural travel. *Road* is the general word. A *highroad* is one adapted for fast travel, as by the elimination of steep hills, sharp curves, frequent intersections, and the like. A *turnpike* is a road on which a toll is collected. A *lane* is a private road giving access to a public *thoroughfare,* or it may be any narrow road. A *thoroughfare* is a road accessible at both ends; this word is now rare in specific names, but survives in the phrase "No *thoroughfare.*"

road allowance *Canadian* Public land reserved for or bordering a road.

road·bed (rōd'bed') *n.* **1.** The graded foundation of gravel, etc., on which the ties, rails, etc., of a railroad are laid. **2.** The graded foundation or surface of a road.

road·block (rōd′blok′) *n.* **1.** An obstruction in a road. **2.** Any arrangement of men and materials for blocking passage, as of enemy troops.

road hog A driver who keeps his vehicle in or near the middle of a road, making it difficult for other drivers to pass.

road·house (rōd′hous′) *n.* A restaurant, dance hall, etc., located at the side of a road in a rural area.

road metal Broken stone or the like, used for making or repairing roads.

road runner A long-tailed ground cuckoo (*Geococcyx californianus*) inhabiting open regions of southwestern North America, and running with great swiftness: also called *chaparral cock, chaparral hen*.

road·side (rōd′sīd′) *n.* The area along the side of a road. — *adj.* Situated on the side of a road.

road·stead (rōd′sted) *n. Naut.* A sheltered place of anchorage offshore, but less sheltered than a harbor. [< ROAD + STEAD (def. 4)]

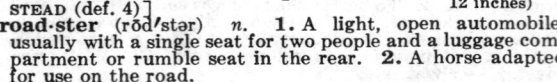

ROAD RUNNER
(Body to 24 inches; tail 12 inches)

road·ster (rōd′stər) *n.* **1.** A light, open automobile, usually with a single seat for two people and a luggage compartment or rumble seat in the rear. **2.** A horse adapted for use on the road.

road·way (rōd′wā′) *n.* A road, especially that part over which vehicles pass.

road·work (rōd′wûrk′) *n. U.S.* Outdoor running as a form of physical exercise or conditioning.

roam (rōm) *v.i.* **1.** To move about purposelessly from place to place; wander; rove. — *v.t.* **2.** To wander over; range: to *roam* the fields. — *n.* The act of roaming; a ramble. [ME *romen*; origin unknown] — **roam′er** *n.*

roan (rōn) *adj.* **1.** Of a horse, having a color consisting of bay, sorrel, or chestnut, thickly interspersed with gray or white. **2.** Made of roan leather. — *n.* **1.** A roan color. **2.** An animal of a roan color. **3.** A soft sheepskin leather, tanned to a roan color and used in bookbinding: also **roan leather.** [< MF < Sp. *roano,* ? ult. < L *ravus* grey, tawny]

Ro·a·noke (rō′ə·nōk) A city in western Virginia; pop. 92,115.

Roanoke Island An island off the coast of NE North Carolina; settlements attempted by Raleigh in 1585 and 1587 failed; 12 mi. long, 3 mi. wide.

Roanoke River A river in Virginia and North Carolina, flowing 410 miles, generally SE, to Albemarle Sound.

roar (rôr, rōr) *v.i.* **1.** To utter a deep, prolonged cry, as of rage or distress. **2.** To make a loud noise or din, as the sea or a cannon. **3.** To laugh loudly. **4.** To move, proceed, or function with a roar, as an automobile. **5.** To make a labored, rasping sound in breathing, as a horse. — *v.t.* **6.** To utter or express by roaring: The crowd *roared* its disapproval. — *n.* **1.** A full, deep, resonant cry, as of a beast, or of a human being in pain, grief, anger, etc. **2.** Any loud, prolonged sound, as of wind or waves. [OE *rārian*; ult. imit.] — **roar′er** *n.*
— **Syn.** (noun) **1.** bellow, boom, bray. Compare CRY.

roar·ing (rôr′ing, rōr′ing) *adj.* **1.** Emitting or uttering roars; bellowing. **2.** *Informal* Very prosperous or brisk: a *roaring* business. — *n.* A loud, deep, continued sound, as of some animals, or of the waves.

roast (rōst) *v.t.* **1.** To cook (meat, etc.) by subjecting to the action of heat, as in an oven. **2.** To cook before an open fire, or by placing in hot ashes, embers, etc. **3.** To heat excessively, or to an extreme degree. **4.** To dry and parch under the action of heat: to *roast* coffee. **5.** *Metall.* To heat (ores) with access of air for the purpose of dehydration, purification, or oxidation. **6.** *Informal* To criticize or ridicule severely. — *v.i.* **7.** To roast food in an oven, etc. **8.** To be cooked or prepared by this method. **9.** To be uncomfortably hot. — *n.* **1.** Something roasted; especially, a piece of roasted meat. **2.** A piece of meat adapted or prepared for roasting. **3.** The act of roasting. — *adj.* Roasted. [< OF *rostir* < Gmc.]

roast·er (rōs′tər) *n.* **1.** One who or that which roasts. **2.** A pan or contrivance for roasting something. **3.** Something suitable for roasting, especially a pig.

rob (rob) *v.* **robbed, rob·bing** *v.t.* **1.** To seize and carry off the property of by unlawful violence or threat of violence; commit robbery upon. **2.** To deprive of something belonging or due; defraud. **3.** To plunder; rifle, as a house. **4.** To steal. — *v.i.* **5.** To commit robbery. [< OF *rober* < *robe* booty < Gmc. Akin to REAVE, ROBE.]
— **Syn. 3.** loot, pillage, burglarize. Compare STEAL.

rob·a·lo (rob′ə·lō, rō′bə-) *n. pl.* **·los** or **·lo** Any of a family (*Centropomidae*) of perchlike fishes of tropical American seas, as the snook. [< Sp. *róbalo* < Catalan *elobarro,* ult. < L *lupus* wolf]

rob·and (rob′ənd) *n. Naut.* A piece of spun yarn for fastening the head of a sail to a spar: also called *rope band.* Also **rob·bin** (rob′ən). [Earlier *raband,* ult. < Du. *raband* or ON *rābenda* to bend a sail on a yard < *ra* sail yard + *benda* to bend, bind]

rob·ber (rob′ər) *n.* One who robs.

robber baron **1.** A feudal lord who subsisted by raiding and robbing travelers, etc. **2.** *U.S.* One of the powerful and unscrupulous financial adventurers of the late 19th century, as Jay Gould, James J. Hill, etc.

robber fly The assassin fly (which see).

rob·ber·y (rob′ər·ē) *n. pl.* **·ber·ies** The act of one who robs; the taking away of the property of another unlawfully, by force or fear. — **Syn.** See THEFT.

Rob·bia (rôb′byä), **Andrea della,** 1435–1525, and his uncle, **Luca della,** 1400?–82, Florentine sculptors and ceramists.

robe (rōb) *n.* **1.** A long, loose, flowing garment, worn over other dress; a gown. **2.** A bathrobe (which see). **3.** *pl.* Such a garment worn as a badge of office or rank. **4.** Anything that covers in the manner of a robe. **5.** *U.S.* A blanket or covering, as for use in a carriage or automobile: lap *robe.* — **the robe** *Brit.* The legal profession: also **the long robe.** — *v.* **robed, rob·ing** *v.t.* **1.** To put a robe upon; clothe; dress. — *v.i.* **2.** To put on robes. [< OF, orig. booty < Gmc. Akin to ROB.]

robe de cham·bre (rôb′ də shän′br′) *French* A dressing gown. Also **robe′-de-cham′bre.**

Rob·ert I (rob′ərt), died 1035, duke of Normandy 1028–35; father of William the Conqueror: called **Robert the Devil.**

Robert II, 1056?–1134, duke of Normandy 1087–1134; son of William the Conqueror.

Rob·erts (rob′ərts), **Frederick Sleigh,** 1832–1914, first Earl Roberts of Kandahar, Pretoria, and Waterford, British field marshal born in India: called **Bobs Ba·ha·dur** (bobz bə·hä′door). — **Joseph Jenkins,** 1809–76, Liberian statesman born in the United States; first president 1847. — **Kenneth (Lewis),** 1885–1957, U.S. novelist. — **Owen Josephus,** 1875–1955, U.S. jurist; associate justice of the Supreme Court 1930–45.

Rob·ert·son (rob′ərt·sən), **William,** 1721–93, Scottish historian and clergyman. — **Sir William Robert,** 1860–1933, English field marshal; chief of staff 1915–18.

Robe·son (rōb′sən), **Paul,** 1898–1976, U.S. singer and actor.

Robes·pierre (rōbz′pē·âr, -pir; *Fr.* rô·bəs·pyâr′), 1758–94, French Revolutionary leader; guillotined: full name **Maximilien François Marie Isidore de Robespierre:** called **the Incorruptible.**

rob·in (rob′in) *n.* **1.** A large North American thrush (*Turdus migratorius*) with black head and tail, grayish wings and sides, and reddish brown breast and underparts. **2.** A small European bird (*Erithacus rubecula*) of the thrush family, especially common in Great Britain, with the forehead, cheeks, and breast yellowish red. Also **robin redbreast.** [< OF *Robin,* dim. of *Robert*]

Rob·in Good·fel·low (rob′in good′fel′ō) In English folklore, a mischievous sprite: identified with *Puck.*

Robin Hood A legendary medieval outlaw of England, famed for his chivalry and daring, who lived in Sherwood Forest and robbed from the rich to relieve the poor.

rob·in's-egg blue (rob′inz·eg′) A light greenish blue.

Rob·in·son (rob′in·sən), **Edwin Arlington,** 1869–1935, U.S. poet. — **James Harvey,** 1863–1936, U.S. historian. — **Sir Robert,** 1886–1975, English biochemist.

Rob·in·son Cru·soe (rob′in·sən kroo′sō) The hero of Defoe's *Robinson Crusoe* (1719), a sailor shipwrecked on a tropical island, where, by ingenious devices, he maintained himself until rescued.

ro·ble (rō′blā) *n.* Any of several oaks; especially, a very tall white oak (*Quercus lobata*) of California. [< Sp. < L *robur* oak]

rob·o·rant (rob′ər·ənt) *adj.* Restoring strength; strengthening. — *n.* A tonic. [< L *roborans, -antis,* ppr. of *roborare* to strengthen < *robur, -oris* oak]

ro·bot (rō′bət, -bot′, rob′ət) *n.* **1.** A mechanical man constructed to perform work in the place of human beings. **2.** One who works mechanically; automaton. **3.** Any mechanism or device that operates automatically or is remotely controlled. [after a creation in *R.U.R.* (*Rossum's Universal Robots*), play by Karel Čapek; ult. < Czechoslovakian *robota* forced labor] — **ro′bot·ism, ro′bot·ry** *n.* — **ro·bot·is′tic** or **·ti·cal** *adj.*

robot bomb A high-explosive bomb provided with a jet engine or rocket permitting it to travel under its own power after being launched on the target, as the German V-1 of World War II: also called *buzz bomb.*

robot pilot An automatic pilot (which see).

Rob·son (rob′sən), **Mount** The highest peak in the Canadian Rockies, in eastern British Columbia; 12,972 ft.

ro·bust (rō·bust′, rō′bust) *adj.* **1.** Possessing or characterized by great strength or endurance; rugged; healthy. **2.** Requiring strength. **3.** Violent; rude. **4.** Rich, as in flavor: a *robust* soup. [< L *robustus* < *robur* oak, hence strength] — **ro·bust′ly** *adv.* — **ro·bust′ness** *n.*

ro·bus·tious (rō·bus′chəs) *adj. Archaic* Of a robust character; also, rough: now often a humorous term. — **ro·bus′tious·ly** *adv.* — **ro·bus′tious·ness** *n.*

roc (rok) *n.* In Arabian and Persian legend, an enormous and powerful bird of prey. [< Arabic *rokh* < Persian *rukh*]

Ro·ca (rō′kä), **Cape** A cape near Lisbon, Portugal; westernmost point of continental Europe.

roc·am·bole (rok′əm·bōl) *n.* A European perennial (*Allium scorodoprasum*), allied to the leek, with cloves resembling those of garlic. [< F < G *rokenbolle* rye bulb]

Ro·cham·beau (rō·shän·bō′), **Comte de**, 1725–1807, Jean Baptiste Donatien de Vimeure, French marshal in the American Revolution.

Roch·dale (roch′dāl) A county borough in Greater Manchester, England; headquarters of the **Rochdale Pioneers**, a cooperative movement founded 1844; pop. 210,600 (1976).

Rochdale principles The traditional rules and policies of cooperatives, governing the rights of members, sharing of proceeds, etc. [after *Rochdale*]

Ro·chelle powder (rō·shel′) Seidlitz powder (which see).

Rochelle salt A white crystalline tartrate of potassium and sodium $KNaC_4H_4O_6 \cdot 4H_2O$, used as a cathartic. [after La *Rochelle*]

roches mou·ton·nées (rosh′ mōō·tô·nā′, rôsh′) Rounded knobs of rock ground down and smoothed by glacial action: so called because smooth and rounded like a sheep's back: also *sheepbacks*. [< F, sheep-shaped rocks]

Roch·es·ter (roch′es·tər) 1. A city in western New York, near Lake Ontario; pop. 296,233. 2. A city in SE Minnesota; site of the Mayo Clinic; pop. 53,766. 3. A municipal borough in Kent, England; pop. 55,810 (1969).

Roch·es·ter (roch′es·tər, -is-), **Earl of**, 1647–80, John Wilmot, English courtier, wit, and poet.

roch·et (roch′it) *n.* A ceremonial garment similar to a surplice, but with closer sleeves or without sleeves, worn by bishops and other high churchmen. [< OF, dim. of cloak < Med.L *rochetum* < Gmc. Cf. OHG or MHG *roc* cloak.]

Ro·ci·nan·te (rō′thē·nän′tā) The raw-boned steed of Don Quixote. — *n.* Any broken-down riding horse: also spelled *Rosinante*. [< Sp. *rocin* nag]

rock¹ (rok) *n.* 1. A large mass of stone or stony material, usually forming a cliff. 2. A fragment of rock small enough to be thrown; stone. 3. *Geol.* The consolidated material forming the essential part of the earth's crust, consisting principally of minerals in various states of aggregation and classified according to mode of formation, as igneous or sedimentary. 4. Something resembling or suggesting a rock, as a firm support, source of strength, etc. 5. A rock dove (which see). 6. The striped bass. 7. *U.S. Slang* A gemstone, especially a large diamond. 8. *Chiefly Brit.* A hard candy of various flavors. 9. *Usually pl. U.S. Slang* A piece of money. — **on the rocks** *U.S. Informal* 1. Ruined; also, destitute or bankrupt. 2. Served with ice cubes but without soda or water: said of whisky or other liquors. — *adj.* Made of or composed of rock. [< OF *roque, roche*; ult. origin uncertain]

rock² (rok) *v.i.* 1. To move backward and forward or from side to side; sway. 2. To sway, reel, or stagger, as from a blow; shake. 3. *Mining* To be washed in a cradle, as ores. — *v.t.* 4. To move backward and forward or from side to side, especially so as to soothe or put to sleep. 5. To cause to sway or reel. 6. *Mining* To wash (ores) in a cradle. 7. In mezzotint engraving, to prepare (a plate) by roughing its surface with a rocker (def. 8). — *n.* The act of rocking; a rocking motion. [OE *roccian*]

rock·a·by (rok′ə·bī) *interj.* Go to sleep: from a nursery song intended to lull a child to slumber. — *n.* A lullaby. Also **rock′a·bye, rock′-a·bye.**

rock-and-roll (rok′ən·rōl′) *adj.* Denoting a form of popular music derived from hillbilly styles, characterized by repetitious melody and rhythm and exaggerated vocal mannerisms. — *n.* Rock-and-roll music. Also **rock 'n' roll.**

rock·a·way (rok′ə·wā) *n.* A four-wheeled, two-seated pleasure carriage with standing top. [after *Rockaway*, New Jersey]

rock bass A fresh-water food fish (*Ambloplites rupestris*) common in eastern North America.

rock bottom The very bottom; the lowest possible level: Prices hit *rock bottom*. — **rock-bot·tom** (rok′bot′əm) *adj.*

rock-bound (rok′bound′) *adj.* Encircled by or bordered with rocks.

rock candy Large crystals of sugar.

rock cod A rockfish (*Sebastodes mystinus*) of American Pacific waters.

rock cork A variety of asbestos: also called *rock leather*.

Rock Cornish hen A variety of domestic fowl obtained by crossbreeding Cornish and white Plymouth Rock fowls, used especially as small roasting chickens.

rock crystal Colorless transparent quartz.

rock dove The wild pigeon (*Columba livia*) of Europe, the parent of domestic varieties: also called *rock*.

Rock·e·fel·ler (rok′ə·fel′ər) A family prominent in American industry and philanthropy, notably **John D(avison)**, 1839–1937, his son, **John D(avison)**, **Jr.**, 1874–1960, and his grandsons, **John Davison III**, born 1906, **Nelson Aldrich**, born 1908, vice president of the United States 1974–77, **Laurance S.**, born 1910, **Winthrop**, 1912–73, governor of Arkansas 1967–71, and **David**, born 1915, banker.

rock·er (rok′ər) *n.* 1. One who rocks, as a cradle or rocking chair. 2. One of the curved pieces on which a rocking chair or a cradle rocks. 3. A rocking chair. 4. A rock shaft. 5. A rocking horse. 6. *Mining* A cradle. 7. An ice skate having a curved runner. 8. A small steel plate with a serrated edge for preparing a copper plate for a mezzotint. — **off one's rocker** *Slang* Mentally unbalanced; nuts.

rocker arm *Mech.* An arm on a rock shaft, as in the valve mechanism of a steam engine.

rocker cam A cam on a rock shaft.

rock·er·thon (rok′ər·thon) *n. Canadian* An endurance rocking contest in rocking chairs, popular in Quebec.

rocker shaft A rock shaft (which see).

rock·er·y (rok′ər·ē) *n. pl.* **·er·ies** A rock garden.

rock·et¹ (rok′it) *n.* 1. A firework, projectile, missile, or other device, usually cylindrical in form, that is propelled by the reaction of escaping gases produced during flight. 2. A type of vehicle operated by rocket propulsion and designed for space travel. — *v.i.* 1. To move like a rocket. 2. To fly straight up into the air, as a bird when alarmed. — *v.t.* 3. To propel by means of a rocket. [< Ital. *rocchetta*, dim. of *rocca* distaff < Gmc.; from its resemblance to a distaff]

rock·et² (rok′it) *n.* 1. Any of several ornamental Old World herbs (genus *Hesperis*), especially the dameworт. 2. An annual (*Eruca sativa*), used in southern Europe as a salad. [< MF *roquette*, ult. < L *eruca* colewort]

rocket bomb A bomb delivered to its target by means of a rocket, as the German V-2 of World War II.

rock·et·eer (rok′ə·tir′) *n.* One who designs or launches rockets; a student of rocket flight.

rocket engine A reaction engine fueled by a liquid or solid propellant containing its own oxidizing agent.

rocket gun Any gunlike device used for the discharge of rocket projectiles, as a bazooka.

rocket launcher A device for aiming and discharging rockets.

rocket propulsion Propulsion obtained from a rocket engine.

rock·et·ry (rok′it·rē) *n.* The science, art, and technology of rocket flight, design, construction, etc.

rock·et·sonde (rok′it·sond′) *n. Meteorol.* A radiosonde adapted for use on high-altitude rockets.

rock·fish (rok′fish′) *n. pl.* **·fish** or **·fish·es** 1. A fish living about rocks. 2. Any of several scorpaenoid fishes (genus *Sebastodes* and related genera) of the Pacific coast of North America, as the **brown rockfish** (*S. auriculatus*) and the rock cod. 3. Any of various other fishes, as the striped bass.

rock flour Finely pulverized rock produced by the grinding action of glacier ice: also called *glacier meal*.

Rock·ford (rok′fərd) A city in northern Illinois; pop. 147,370.

rock garden A garden with flowers and plants growing in rocky ground or among rocks.

Rock Hill A city in northern South Carolina; pop. 33,846.

Rock·ies (rok′ēz) See ROCKY MOUNTAINS.

rocking chair A chair having the legs set on rockers.

Rock·ing·ham (rok′ing·əm). **Marquis de**, 1730–82, Charles Watson–Wentworth, English statesman; prime minister 1765–66, 1782.

rocking horse A toy horse mounted on rockers, large enough to be ridden by a child: also called *hobbyhorse*.

Rock Island A city in NW Illinois, on the Mississippi River; pop. 50,166.

rock leather Rock cork (which see).

rock lobster The spiny lobster (which see).

rock maple The sugar maple (which see).

rock music A form of popular music derived from rock-and-roll that has retained its heavy beat but has eliminated the repetitious melody and rhythm. Also **rock, hard rock.** See **rock and roll.**

Rock·ne (rok′nē), **Knute (Kenneth)**, 1888–1931, U.S. football coach, born in Norway.

rock oil Petroleum.

rock·oon (rok·ōōn′) *n.* A small rocket equipped with various meteorological recording devices and attached to a balloon, from which it is released at predetermined altitudes. [< ROCK(ET)¹ + (BALL)OON]

rock-ribbed (rok′ribd′) *adj.* 1. Having rocky ridges. 2. Unyielding; inflexible.

rock-rose (rok′rōz′) *n.* Any of several plants (genera *Cistus, Helianthemum* and *Crocanthemum*) typical of a family (*Cistaceae*) of flowering herbs and shrubs.

rock salt Halite (which see).

rock·shaft (rok′shaft′, -shäft′) A shaft made to rock on its bearings; also called *rocker, rocker shaft.*

FIREWORKS ROCKET
a Head. *b* Bursting charge. *c* Composition. *d* Clay choke. *e* Fuse. *f* Gas exhaust. *g* Stick.

Rock·ville (rok′vil) A town in western Maryland; pop. 41,564.

Rockville Centre A village in SE New York on Long Island, a suburb of New York City; pop. 27,444.

rock·weed (rok′wēd′) *n.* Any of various coarse seaweeds (genera *Fucus* and *Ascophyllum*) growing on rocks.

rock wool Mineral wool (which see).

rock·y[1] (rok′ē) *adj.* **rock·i·er, rock·i·est** **1.** Consisting of, abounding in, or resembling rocks. **2.** Tough; unfeeling; hard. — **rock′i·ness** *n.*

rock·y[2] (rok′ē) *adj.* **rock·i·er, rock·i·est** **1.** Inclined to rock or shake; unsteady. **2.** *Informal* Dizzy or weak, as from dissipation. — **rock′i·ness** *n.*

Rocky Mount A city in east central North Carolina; pop. 34,284.

Rocky Mountain goat A goatlike, shaggy white ruminant (*Oreamnos americanus*), with short black horns, found in the mountains of NW North America: also called *mountain goat*.

Rocky Mountain National Park A mountainous region in northern Colorado; 395 sq. mi.; established, 1915.

Rocky Mountains The major mountain system of western North America, extending from the Arctic to Mexico; highest peak, Mount McKinley, 20,300 feet: also *Rockies.*

Rocky Mountain sheep The bighorn.

Rocky Mountain spotted fever *Pathol.* An acute infectious disease caused by a microorganism (*Rickettsia rickettsii*) transmitted by the bite of certain ticks, and marked by fever, chills, skin eruptions, headache, and diffuse pains: also called *spotted fever.*

ro·co·co (rə·kō′kō, rō′kə·kō′) *n.* **1.** A style of art that developed in France in the 18th century and spread throughout Europe; especially, architecture and ornament characterized by curvilinear designs, often delicately imitating shells, foliage, and scrolls in asymmetrical arrangements. **2.** *Music* The elegant, formal style of European music from about 1726 to 1775, immediately following the baroque. **3.** Florid, fantastic, or odd style, as in literature. — *adj.* **1.** In the rococo style. **2.** Overelaborate; florid. [< F, fanciful alter. of *rocaille* shellwork < *roc* rock]

rod (rod) *n.* **1.** A straight, slim piece of wood, metal, or other material. **2.** A shoot or cane of any woody plant. **3.** A switch or several switches together, used as an instrument of punishment. **4.** Discipline; correction: with *the:* Spare the *rod* and spoil the child. **5.** A scepter or badge of office; a wand. **6.** Dominion; power. **7.** A bar, typically of metal, forming part of a machine: a connecting *rod.* **8.** A light pole used to suspend and manipulate a fishing line. **9.** A measure of length, equal to 5.5 yards, 16.5 feet, or 5.03 meters; also, a square rod: sometimes called *perch, pole.* Abbr. *rd., r.* See table inside back cover. **10.** A measuring rule. **11.** A rodlike body of the retina sensitive to faint light. **12.** A rod-shaped bacterium. **13.** In the Bible, a line of family descent. **14.** A lightning rod (which see). **15.** *U.S. Slang* A pistol. **16.** *U.S. Slang* A hot rod (which see). — **to ride the rods** *U.S. Slang* To steal a ride by getting on the metal framework underneath a freight train. [OE *rodd.* Akin to ROOD.]

rode (rōd) Past tense of RIDE.

ro·dent (rōd′nt) *n.* Any of a large cosmopolitan order (*Rodentia*) of gnawing mammals, having in each jaw two (rarely four) incisors growing continually from persistent pulps, and no canine teeth, as a squirrel, beaver, or rat. — *adj.* **1.** Gnawing; corroding. **2.** Of or pertaining to a rodent or rodents. [< L *rodens, -entis,* ppr. of *rodere* to gnaw]

rodent ulcer *Pathol.* A malignant ulcer that progressively destroys soft tissues and bones, especially of the face.

ro·de·o (rō′dē·ō, rō·dā′ō) *n. pl.* **·os** **1.** The driving of cattle together to be branded, counted, inspected, etc.; a roundup. **2.** A public spectacle in which the more exciting features of a roundup are presented, as the riding of broncos, branding, lariat throwing, etc. **3.** An enclosure for cattle. [< Sp. < *rodear* to go around < *rueda* wheel < L *rota*]

Rod·gers (roj′ərz), **Richard,** born 1902, U.S. composer.

Ro·din (rō·dañ′), **Auguste,** 1840–1917, French sculptor.

rod·man (rod′mən) *n. pl.* **·men** (-mən) One who uses or carries a surveyor's leveling rod. Also **rods′man.**

Rod·ney (rod′nē), **George Brydges,** 1718–92, first Baron Rodney, English admiral.

rod·o·mon·tade (rod′ə·mon·tād′, -täd′) *n.* Vainglorious boasting; bluster. — *adj.* Bragging; boastful. — *v.i.* **tad·ed, ·tad·ing** To boast; bluster; brag. [< F < Ital. *rodomontata* < *Rodomonte,* a boastful Saracen king in Boiardo's *Orlando Innamorato* and Ariosto's *Orlando Furioso*]

ROCKY MOUNTAIN GOAT
(About 3½ feet high at shoulder)

roe[1] (rō) *n.* **1.** The spawn or eggs of female fish. **2.** The milt of male fish. **3.** The eggs of crustaceans. [Var. of dial. *roan,* appar. < ON *hrogn* or MDu. *roch*]

roe[2] (rō) *n.* A small, graceful deer (genus *Capreolus*) of Europe and western Asia. Also **roe deer.** [OE *rā*]

Roeb·ling (rōb′ling), **John Augustus,** 1806–69, U.S. civil engineer born in Germany. — **Washington Augustus,** 1837–1926, U.S. civil engineer; son of the preceding.

roe·buck (rō′buk′) *n.* The male of the roe deer.

roent·gen (rent′gən, runt′-; *Ger.* rœnt′gən) *n.* The international unit of ionizing radiation, as gamma or X-rays, being the quantity of radiation that will produce 1 electrostatic unit of positive or negative electricity in 1 cubic centimeter of air at normal temperature and pressure: also spelled *röntgen.* Abbr. *r* [after Wilhelm Konrad *Roentgen*]

Roent·gen (rent′gən, runt′-; *Ger.* rœnt′gən), **Wilhelm Konrad,** 1845–1923, German physicist, discoverer of X-rays. Also *Röntgen.*

roent·gen·ize (rent′gən·īz, runt′-) *v.t.* **·ized, ·iz·ing** To subject to the action of X-rays. — **roent·gen·i·za′tion** *n.*

roentgeno- *combining form* X-rays; using, produced by, or producing X-rays: *roentgenogram.* Also, before vowels, **roentgen-.** [< ROENTGEN]

roent·gen·o·gram (rent′gən·ə·gram′, runt′-) *n.* An X-ray photograph, especially one taken for medical or therapeutic purposes. Also **roent′gen·o·graph′** (-graf′, -gräf′).

roent·gen·og·ra·phy (rent′gən·og′rə·rē, runt′-) *n. Med.* Photography by means of X-rays; radiography. — **roent′gen·o·graph′ic** (-ə·graf′ik) *adj.* — **roent′gen·o·graph′i·cal·ly** *adv.*

roent·gen·ol·o·gy (rent′gən·ol′ə·jē, runt′-) *n.* The science that treats of the properties, action, and effects of X-rays. — **roent′gen·ol′o·gist** *n.*

roent·gen·o·paque (rent′gən·ō·pāk′, runt′-) *adj.* Impervious to X-rays.

roent·gen·o·ther·a·py (rent′gən·ō·ther′ə·pē′, runt′-) *n. Med.* Treatment of disease by means of X-rays.

Roentgen rays X-rays (which see).

Roer·ich (rœr′ikh), **Nicholas Konstantin,** 1874–1947, Russian painter and archeologist active in the United States.

Ro·gal·lo wing (rō·gal′ō) *Aeron.* A kitelike triangular flexible wing that can be used on simple aircraft, as a kite, or as a type of parachute: also called *flex wing.* [after F. M. *Rogallo,* U.S. engineer, the inventor]

ro·ga·tion (rō·gā′shən) *n.* **1.** In ancient Rome, the submission of a proposed law by the consul or tribune to the people, requesting its adoption; also, a law submitted in this manner and accepted. **2.** *Often pl.* Litany; supplication, especially as part of the rites of the Rogation Days. [< L *rogatio, -onis* < *rogatus,* pp. of *rogare* to ask]

Rogation Days *Eccl.* The three days immediately preceding Ascension Day, observed as days of special supplication.

ro·ga·to·ry (rō′gə·tôr′ē, -tō′rē) *adj. Rare* Requesting or seeking information: letters *rogatory.* [< F *rogatoire* < Med.L *rogatorius*]

rog·er (roj′ər) *interj.* **1.** *Often cap.* Message received: used in radio communication. **2.** *Informal* All right; O.K. [after *Roger,* personal name representing *r* in telecommunication]

Rog·ers (roj′ərz), **Will,** 1879–1935, U.S. actor and humorist: full name **William Penn Adair Rogers.**

Ro·get (rō·zhā′), **Peter Mark,** 1779–1869, English physician and philologist.

rogue (rōg) *n.* **1.** A dishonest and unprincipled person; trickster; rascal. **2.** One who is innocently mischievous or playful. **3.** *Biol.* A variation from a standard. **4.** A fierce and dangerous animal, as an elephant, separated from the herd. **5.** *Archaic* A roving beggar; a vagrant. — **Syn.** See SCOUNDREL. — *v.* **rogued, ro·guing** *v.t.* **1.** To practice roguery upon; defraud. **2.** *Bot.* To eliminate (inferior individuals) from a plot of plants undergoing selection. — *v.i.* **3.** *Rare* To live or act like a rogue. [Origin uncertain]

ro·guer·y (rō′gər·ē) *n. pl.* **·guer·ies** **1.** Conduct characteristic of a rogue; trickery. **2.** A roguish act.

rogues' gallery A collection of photographs of criminals taken to aid the police in identification.

ro·guish (rō′gish) *adj.* **1.** Playfully mischievous. **2.** Knavish; dishonest. — **ro′guish·ly** *adv.* — **ro′guish·ness** *n.*

roil (roil) *v.t.* **1.** To make muddy or turbid, as by stirring up sediment. **2.** To vex; irritate; rile. [< F *rouiller, ruiler*]

roil·y (roi′lē) *adj.* **roil·i·er, roil·i·est** Turbid; muddy.

Roi So·leil (rwä sô·lā′), **le** See LOUIS XIV.

roist·er (rois′tər) *v.i.* **1.** To act in a blustery manner; swagger. **2.** To engage in tumultuous merrymaking; revel. [earlier *roister* loud bully < OF *ruistre* < L *rusticus.* See RUSTIC.] — **roist′er·er** *n.*

ROK (rok) *n.* **1.** The Republic of Korea (South Korea). **2.** A soldier in the South Korean army.

Ro·kos·sov·sky (ro·kə·sôf′skē), **Konstantin,** 1896–1968, Soviet field marshal and politician born in Poland.

Ro·land (rō′lənd, *Fr.* rô·läñ′) Legendary nephew of Charlemagne and hero of the medieval French epic *Chanson de Roland,* in which he dies fighting the Saracens at Roncesvalles. — **a Roland for an Oliver** Something in return or retaliation for that which was said or done by another; an eye for an eye.

role (rōl) *n.* **1.** A part or character taken by an actor. **2.** Any assumed character or function. Also **rôle.** [< F *rôle*]

Rolfe (rolf), **John,** 1585–1622, English colonist in Virginia; husband of Pocahontas.

roll (rōl) *v.i.* **1.** To move forward on a surface by turning round and round, as a ball or wheel. **2.** To move or be moved on wheels or rollers: The cart *rolled* down the hill. **3.** To move or appear to move in undulations or swells, as waves. **4.** To assume the shape of a ball or cylinder by turning over and over upon itself, as a ball of yarn. **5.** To pass; elapse: with *on* or *by*: Months *rolled* by. **6.** Of sounds: **a** To make a deep, prolonged sound; rumble, as thunder. **b** To trill, as a bird. **c** To produce a roll, as on a drum. **7.** To rotate wholly or partially: Their eyes *rolled*. **8.** To sway or move from side to side, as a ship: to pitch and *roll*. **9.** To wander or travel about. **10.** To walk with a swaying motion; swagger; also, to stagger. **11.** To become spread or flat because of pressure applied by a roller, etc.: The metal *rolls* easily. **12.** To perform a periodic revolution or cycle, as the seasons. **13.** To move ahead; progress. — *v.t.* **14.** To cause to move along a surface by turning round and round, as a ball, log, etc. **15.** To move, push forward, etc. on wheels or rollers. **16.** To wrap round and round upon itself or on an axis: often with *up*: He *rolled* the carpet up. **17.** To cause to assume the shape of a ball or cylinder by means of rotation and pressure: to *roll* a cigarette. **18.** To impel or cause to move onward with a steady, surging motion: The ocean *rolls* its waves upon the shore. **19.** To spread or make flat by pressing with a roller or rollers, as dough. **20.** To impart a swaying motion to. **21.** To wrap or envelop in or as in a covering. **22.** To rotate, as the eyes. **23.** Of sounds: **a** To utter with a trilling sound: to *roll* one's r's. **b** To emit in a full and swelling manner. **c** To beat a roll upon (a drum, etc.). **24.** To cast (dice) in the game of craps. **25.** *Printing* To apply ink to (a form) by means of a roller or rollers. **26.** *U.S. Slang* To rob (a drunk or a person who is asleep). — **Syn.** See REVOLVE. — **to roll back** In commerce, to cause (prices, wages, etc.) to return to a previous, lower level, as by government direction. — **to roll in** *Informal* **1.** To arrive, especially in numbers; congregate. **2.** To wallow; luxuriate: to *roll in* money. — **to roll up** *Informal* **1.** To accumulate; amass, as profits. **2.** To arrive, as an automobile. — *n.* **1.** Anything rolled up in cylindrical form: a *roll* of toilet paper. **2.** A register or list of names. **3.** A roller; especially, a cylinder in fixed bearings used as a roller. **4.** A strip of material, as of ribbon or carpeting, that is rolled upon itself or upon a core, often of an agreed length for use as a measure. **5.** Any food rolled up in preparation for use; also, a small, individually shaped portion of bread. **6.** A rolling gait or movement, as of a ship. **7.** Of sounds: **a** reverberation, as of thunder. **b** A rapid sustained series of short sounds: a drum *roll*. **c** A trill, as of a bird. **8.** A swell or undulation of a surface, as of land or water. **9.** *U.S. Slang* **a** A wad of paper money. **b** Money in general. **10.** The act of rolling, or the state of being rolled. **11.** *Aeron.* **a** A complete rotation of an airplane about its longitudinal axis without change in the direction of flight. **b** The rapid movement of an airplane along the ground, as after a landing. **12.** A strip of leather or other material fitted with pockets to hold tools, toilet articles, etc., around which it is rolled and fastened. [< OF *roller* < L *rotula* < *rota* wheel]

Rol·land (rô·län′), **Romain,** 1868–1944, French novelist and dramatist.

roll·a·way (rōl′ə·wā′) *adj.* Mounted on rollers for easy movement into storage: a *rollaway* bed.

roll·back (rōl′bak′) *n.* A return, as by government direction, to a previous, lower price or wage level.

roll call 1. The act of calling a roll or list of the names of a number of persons, as soldiers, to determine which are present. **2.** The time of or signal for calling the roll.

roll·er (rō′lər) *n.* **1.** One who or that which rolls. **2.** Any of various cylindrical devices that roll or rotate. **3.** The wheel of a caster or roller skate. **4.** A rod on which a window shade, towel, map, etc., is rolled. **5.** A heavy cylinder for rolling, smoothing, or crushing something: a steam *roller*. **6.** *Printing* A cylindrical device, often of hard rubber, used to spread ink on a form before impressing on paper. **7.** *U.S.* A hollow cylinder of plastic, wire mesh, etc., around which a lock of hair is wrapped to produce a soft, wide curl or wave. **8.** *Surg.* A long rolled bandage. **9.** One of a series of long, swelling waves that break on a coast, especially after a storm. **10.** *Ornithol.* **a** Any of various nonpasserine birds (family *Coraciidae*) of Europe having gaudy colors and remarkable for their rolling and tumbling flight; especially, the **common roller** (*Coracias garrulus*). **b** A canary having a trilling song.

·oller bearing A bearing employing steel rollers to lessen friction between the parts of a mechanism.

roller coaster *U.S.* A railway with small, open cars run over a route of steep inclines and sharp turns, common at amusement parks.

roll·er-skate (rō′lər·skāt′) *v.i.* **-skat·ed, -skat·ing** To go on roller skates.

roller skate A skate having wheels instead of a runner, used on wooden floors in rinks and outdoors, as on sidewalks.

roller towel A long towel with the ends joined to form a continuous strip, for use on a roller: also called *jack towel.*

rol·lick (rol′ik) *v.i.* To move or behave in a careless, frolicsome manner. [? Blend of ROLL and FROLIC]

rol·lick·ing (rol′ik·ing) *adj.* **1.** Acting in a carefree, swaggering manner. **2.** Jovial; light-hearted; merry. Also **rol′·lick·some** (-səm), **rol′lick·y.**

roll·ing (rō′ling) *adj.* **1.** Turning round and round, especially so as to move forward on a surface. **2.** Having a succession of sloping elevations and depressions; undulating: *rolling* hills. **3.** Turning on or as if on wheels; rotating. **4.** Turned back or down as if over a roll: a *rolling* collar. **5.** Surging in puffs, billows, or waves, as smoke, clouds, water, etc. **6.** Of sounds: **a** Trilled: a *rolling* note. **b** Resounding; reverberating: *rolling* thunder. **7.** Swaying from side to side: a *rolling* gait. **8.** Recurring; elapsing. — *n.* The act of one who or that which rolls or is rolled.

rolling hitch A knot having one or more intermediate turns between the first and last hitch. For illustration see HITCH.

rolling mill 1. An establishment in which metal is rolled into sheets, bars, etc. **2.** A machine used to roll metal.

rolling pin A cylindrical device, usually of wood and with a handle at each end, for rolling out dough, etc.

rolling stock The wheeled transportation equipment of a railroad, as locomotives and passenger cars.

Rol·lo (rol′ō), died 930?, Viking leader; first duke of Normandy: also called *Hrolf.*

roll-top (rōl′top′) *adj.* Designating a type of desk having a flexible, slatted cover that rolls back out of the way.

roll·way (rōl′wā′) *n.* An inclined way, natural or artificial, down which logs, etc., may be rolled or shot; chute.

Röl·vaag (rœl′väg), **Ole Edvart,** 1876–1931, U.S. educator and novelist born in Norway.

ro·ly-po·ly (rō′lē·pō′lē) *adj.* Short and fat; pudgy; dumpy. — *n. pl.* **-po·lies 1.** A roly-poly person or thing. **2.** *Chiefly Brit.* A pudding made of pastry dough spread with fruit, preserves, etc., rolled up and cooked. [Reduplication of ROLL]

rom. *Printing* Roman (type).

Rom. 1. Roman. **2.** Romance. **3.** Romans.

Ro·ma (rō′mä) The Italian and Latin name for ROME.

Ro·ma·gna (rō·mä′nyä) A region and former province of the Papal States in north central Italy.

Ro·ma·ic (rō·mā′ik) *adj.* Pertaining to or characteristic of the language or people of modern Greece. — *n.* Modern Greek, especially the popular spoken form. [< LL *Romaicus* < Gk. *Rhōmaikos* Roman < *Rhōmē* Rome]

ro·maine (rō·mān′) *n.* A variety of lettuce (*Lactuca sativa longifolia*) characterized by long, crisp leaves. [< F, fem. of *romain* Roman < L *Romanus*]

Ro·mains (rô·maṅ′), **Jules** Pseudonym of **Louis Fa·ri·goule** (fà·rē·gōōl′), born 1885, French novelist.

ro·man[1] (rō′mən) *Sometimes cap. n.* A common style of type or lettering characterized chiefly by serifs, perpendicularity, and thicker vertical strokes than horizontal strokes: This line is set in roman. — *adj.* Pertaining to, designating, or printed in roman. Compare ITALIC. Abbr. *rom.* [< ROMAN]

ro·man[2] (rô·mäṅ′) *n. French* **1.** A type of metrical narrative, especially common in Old French literature, developed from the ancient chansons de geste. **2.** A romantic novel.

Ro·man (rō′mən) *adj.* **1.** Of, pertaining to, or characteristic of modern or ancient Rome or its people. **2.** Of or belonging to the Roman Catholic Church. **3.** Of, pertaining to, or characteristic of the language of ancient Rome; Latin. **4.** Pertaining to a style of architecture characterized by massive, round arches and vaults and the use of Greek embellishments. **5.** Of or pertaining to the Holy Roman Empire. — *n.* **1.** A native, resident, or citizen of ancient or modern Rome. **2.** The Italian spoken in Rome. **3.** The language of ancient Rome; Latin. **4.** *Informal* A Roman Catholic. [< OF *romain* < L *Romanus* < *Roma* Rome]

ro·man à clef (rô·mäṅ′ à klef′) *French* A novel in which actual persons and places appear under fictitious names; literally, novel with a key.

Roman alphabet The Latin alphabet (which see).

Roman calendar See under CALENDAR.

Roman candle A firework consisting of a tube filled with a composition that discharges colored balls and sparks of fire.

Roman Catholic A member of the Roman Catholic Church. Abbr. *R.C.*

Roman Catholicism The doctrine, system, and practice of the Roman Catholic Church.

Roman Catholic Church The Christian church that recognizes the Pope as its supreme head: also called *Catholic Church, Church of Rome.* Abbr. *R.C.Ch.*

ro·mance (rō·mans′; *for n., also* rō′mans) *n.* **1.** A love affair. **2.** A kind of love between the sexes, usually youthful and nonmarital, characterized by high ideals of purity and devotion, strong ardor, etc. **3.** Adventurous, heroic, or picturesque character or nature; strange and fascinating appeal: the *romance* of faraway places. **4.** A disposition or tendency toward the mysterious or adventurous. **5.** A long narrative, sometimes in verse, based on medieval legends, presenting chivalrous ideals and usually involving heroes in strange adventures and affairs of love. **6.** Any long fictitious narrative embodying scenes and events remote from common life and filled with extravagant adventures. **7.** The class of literature consisting of romances (defs. 5 and 6). **8.** An extravagant or fanciful falsehood. **9.** *Music* A simple, lyrical song or instrumental piece. — *v.* **·manced, ·manc·ing** *v.i.* **1.** To tell or write romances. **2.** To think or act in a romantic manner. **3.** *Informal* To make love. — *v.t.* **4.** *Informal* To make love to; woo. [< OF *romans* story written in French < L *Romanice* in Roman style < *Romanicus* Roman] — **ro·manc'er** *n.*

Ro·mance (rō·mans', rō'mans) *adj.* Pertaining or belonging to one or more, or all, of the languages that have developed from Vulgar Latin and that exist now as French, Italian, Spanish, Portuguese, Catalan, Provençal, Rhaeto-Romanic, and Rumanian. — *n.* One or all collectively, of the Romance languages. Abbr. *Rom.*

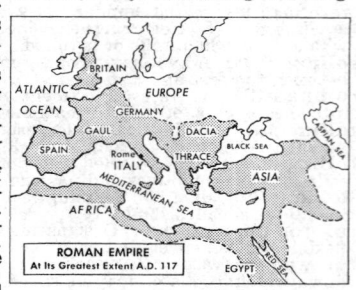

ROMAN EMPIRE
At Its Greatest Extent A.D. 117

Roman collar A clerical collar (which see).
Roman de la Rose (rō·mäN' də lä rôz') *French* An allegorical Old French verse romance, begun about the middle of the 13th century, and completed in satirical tone toward the end of the century.
Roman Empire The empire of ancient Rome, established by Augustus in 27 B.C. and continuing until the reign of Theodosius I in A.D. 395, when it was divided into the Eastern Roman Empire and the Western Roman Empire.
ro·man·esque (rō'mən·esk') *adj.* Romantic; extravagant; fanciful. [< F < Ital. *romanesco* < Med.L *romaniscus* < L *romanus* Roman]
Ro·man·esque (rō'mən·esk') *adj.* **1.** Of, pertaining to, or designating a style of Western architecture that developed from Roman principles, reached its height from about the 11th to 13th centuries, and was characterized by rounded arches, often placed in tiers, general massiveness, and elaborate ornamentation. **2.** Of, pertaining to, or designating corresponding styles in art and sculpture. **3.** Pertaining to or characterized by the Romance languages, especially Provençal. — *n.* **1.** The Romanesque style of art, architecture, or sculpture. **2.** The vernacular of Languedoc and other provinces in Southern France.

ROMANESQUE ARCHITECTURE
(Notre Dame de la Grande, Poitiers, France, 11th century)

ro·man-fleuve (rō·mäN'flœv') *n. pl.* **ro·mans-fleuves** (rō·mäN'flœv') *French* A saga novel (which see).
Ro·mâ·nia (rō·män'yə, *Rumanian* rô·mœ'nyä) The Rumanian name for RUMANIA.
Ro·man·ic (rō·man'ik) *adj.* **1.** Roman. **2.** Romance. [< L *Romanicus* < *Romanus*]
Ro·man·ism (rō'mən·iz'əm) *n.* The dogmas, forms, etc., of the Roman Catholic Church: often used disparagingly.
Ro·man·ist (rō'mən·ist) *n.* **1.** An adherent of Roman Catholicism: often used disparagingly. **2.** An authority on Roman law, language, or culture. **3.** A student of or expert in Romance languages.
Ro·man·ize (rō'mən·īz) *v.t. & v.i.* **·ized, ·iz·ing** **1.** To make or become Roman or Roman Catholic. **2.** To write in the Roman style, language, etc. — **Ro'man·i·za'tion** *n.*
Roman law The system of jurisprudence of the Roman Empire, codified in the reign of Justinian, and constituting the basis of the legal systems in many European countries today: also called *civil law.*
Roman mile See under MILE.
Roman nose A nose that is somewhat aquiline.
Roman numerals The letters used by the ancient Romans as symbols in arithmetical notation. The basic letters are I(1), V(5), X(10), L(50), C(100), D(500), and M(1000), and intermediate and higher numbers are formed as follows: Any symbol following another of equal or greater value adds to its value, as II = 2, XI = 11; any symbol preceding one of greater value subtracts from its value, as IV = 4, IX = 9, XC = 90. When a symbol stands between two of greater

value, it is subtracted from the second and the remainder added to the first, as XIV = 14, LIX = 59.
Ro·man·o (rō·mä'nō) See GIULIO ROMANO.
Ro·man·o (rō·mä'nō) *n.* A hard, sharp cheese, usually grated to be sprinkled on spaghetti. [< Ital., of Rome]
Ro·ma·nov (rō'mə·nôf, *Russian* rô·mä'nôf) A Russian dynasty founded by Czar Michael in 1613, and ended in 1918 with the execution of Nicholas II. Also **Ro'ma·noff.**
Roman punch A flavored ice consisting of beaten egg whites blended with lemon juice and rum.
Ro·mans (rō'mənz) *n.pl.* (construed as sing.) One of the books of the New Testament, a letter from the apostle Paul to the Christians at Rome: in full **Epistle to the Romans.** Abbr. *Rom.*
Ro·mansch (rō·mansh', -mänsh') *n.* **1.** A Rhaeto-Romanic dialect spoken in the canton of Grisons, Switzerland. **2.** The Rhaeto-Romanic dialects as a group. Also **Ro·mansh'.** [< L *Romanicus* < *Romanus*]
ro·man·tic (rō·man'tik) *adj.* **1.** Of, pertaining to, characterized by, or of the nature of romance. **2.** Characterized by or given to feelings or thoughts of love or romance: a *romantic* girl. **3.** Suitable for or conducive to love or amorousness: a *romantic* setting. **4.** Visionary; impractical: a *romantic* scheme. **5.** Not based on fact; imaginary; fictitious. **6.** Of or pertaining to romanticism in art, literature, and music. — **Syn.** See SENTIMENTAL. — *n.* **1.** One who is romantic. **2.** An adherent of romanticism in art, literature, or music. **3.** *pl.* Romantic ideas, behavior, etc. [< F *romantique* < *romant, roman* romance, novel] — **ro·man'ti·cal·ly** *adv.*
ro·man·ti·cism (rō·man'tə·siz'əm) *n.* **1.** *Usually cap.* A movement in art, music, and literature originating in Europe in the late 18th century, characterized by a strong interest in nature, a revolt against the neoclassic adherence to rules, forms, and traditions, an exalting of the feelings and senses, and a marked preference for individualism, lyricism, and the supernatural and strange: distinguished from *classicism.* Also **Romantic Movement. 2.** Romantic quality. — **ro·man'ti·cist** *n.*
ro·man·ti·cize (rō·man'tə·sīz) *v.* **·cized, ·ciz·ing** *v.t.* **1.** To regard or interpret in a romantic manner. — *v.i.* **2.** To act or think romantically.
Rom·a·ny (rom'ə·nē, rō'mə-) *n. pl.* **·nies 1.** A Gypsy (def. 1). **2.** The Indic language of the Gypsies, containing elements of the language of each country in which they live: also called *Gypsy.* — *adj.* Of or pertaining to the Gypsies or their language. Also **Rom'ma·ny** (rom'ə·nē). [< Romany *romani* < *rom* man]
ro·maunt (rō·mänt', -mônt') *n. Archaic* A romance, usually in verse. [< OF *romant*, var. of *romans*. See ROMANCE.]
Rom·berg (rom'bûrg), Sigmund, 1887-1951, U.S. composer born in Hungary.
Rome (rōm) **1.** The capital of Italy, in the western part on the Tiber; site of the Vatican City; capital of the former Roman republic, the Roman Empire, and the States of the Church; pop. 2,630,500 (1967): Italian and Latin *Roma.* **2.** The Roman Catholic Church. **3.** A city in central New York; pop. 50,148. **4.** A city in NW Georgia; pop. 30,759.
Ro·me·o (rō'mē·ō) The hero of Shakespeare's *Romeo and Juliet.*
Rom·ish (rō'mish) *adj.* Of or pertaining to the Roman Catholic Church: often used disparagingly.
Rom·mel (rum'əl, *Ger.* rôm'əl), Erwin, 1891-1944, German field marshal in World War II: called **the Desert Fox.**
Rom·ney (rom'nē, rum'-), George, 1734-1802, English painter.
romp (romp) *v.i.* **1.** To play boisterously. **2.** To win easily. — *n.* **1.** One who romps, especially a girl. **2.** Noisy, exciting frolic or play. **3.** *Informal* An easy win. [? Var. of RAMP[2]]
romp·er (rom'pər) *n.* **1.** One who romps. **2.** *pl.* A garment combining a waist and bloomers, worn by young children.
romp·ish (rom'pish) *adj.* Inclined toward boisterousness in play. — **romp'ish·ly** *adv.* — **romp'ish·ness** *n.*
Rom·u·lo (rom'yoō·lō), Carlos Pena, born 1899, Philippine statesman, general, and writer.
Rom·u·lus (rom'yə·ləs) In Roman mythology, a son of Mars and founder of Rome, later deified as *Quirinus,* who with his twin brother Remus, was reared by a she-wolf. Later Romulus slew his brother to become the first ruler of Rome.
Ron·ces·val·les (ron'sə·valz, *Sp.* rôn'thes·vä'lyes) A village in the Pyrenees, northern Spain; nearby **Roncesvalles Pass** was the scene of Roland's death and the defeat of Charlemagne's rear guard, 778. *French* **Ronce·vaux** (rôNs·vō').
ron·deau (ron'dō, ron·dō') *n. pl.* **·deaux** (-dōz, -dōz') A poem of French origin, consisting of thirteen (or sometimes ten) lines with only two rhymes, and in which the opening words are repeated in two places as an unrhymed refrain. [< F < *rondel* < *rond* round]
ron·del (ron'dəl, -del) *n.* A form of French verse consisting of 13 or 14 lines, in two stanzas of four and one of five or six lines, the first two lines being repeated, as a refrain, in the seventh and eighth lines, and again in the thirteenth and fourteenth. [< F. See RONDEAU.]

ron·de·let (ron′də·let) *n.* A brief French verse form with a refrain that generally consists of two or more words of the first line. [< OF, dim. of *rondel.* See RONDEAU.]
ron·do (ron′dō, ron·dō′) *n.* **1.** *Music* A composition or movement having a main theme and several contrasting episodes, the main theme being repeated after each subordinate theme. **2.** The musical setting of a rondeau. [< Ital. < F *rondeau.* See RONDEAU.]
ron·dure (ron′jər) *n.* *Poetic* Anything circular or spherical; a curve or swell. [< F *rondeur* roundness]
ron·ion (run′yən) *n. Obs.* A mangy or scabby animal or person. Also **ron′yon.** [? < F *rogne* scab]
Ron·sard (rôn·sàr′), **Pierre de**, 1524–85, French poet.
rönt·gen (rent′gən, runt′-) See ROENTGEN.
Rönt·gen (rent′gən, runt′-; *Ger.* rœnt′gən), **Wilhelm Konrad.** See ROENTGEN.
rood (rōod) *n.* **1.** A cross or crucifix; especially, a large crucifix or representation of the Crucifixion over the altar screen of a church. **2.** A linear measure varying locally between six and eight yards. **3.** A land measure equivalent to one-fourth of an acre, or 40 square rods: also **square rood.** [OE *rōd* rod, measure of land, cross. Akin to ROD.]
rood beam A beam over the entrance to a choir for supporting a cross or crucifix.
rood loft A gallery or platform on top of the rood screen: also called *jube.*
rood screen An embellished screen, usually surmounted by a rood, separating the choir presbytery from the nave.
roof (rōof) *n.* **1.** The exterior upper covering of a building. For other illustrations see GABLE ROOF, GAMBREL ROOF. **2.** Any top covering, as of a car or oven. **3.** A house; home. **4.** The most elevated part of anything; top; summit. — *v.t.* To cover with or as with a roof. [OE *hrōf*]
roof·er (rōo′fər, rōof′-ər) *n.* One who makes or repairs roofs.

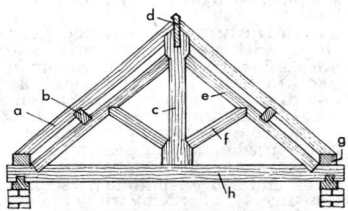

ROOF, KINGPOST TYPE
a Common rafter. *b* Purlin. *c* Kingpost. *d* Ridge pole. *e* Principal rafter. *f* Strut. *g* Pole plate. *h* Tie beam.

roof garden **1.** A garden on the roof of a building. **2.** A space on a roof including a garden and used as a restaurant, recreation area, etc.
roof·ing (rōo′fing, rōof′ing) *n.* **1.** The act of covering with a roof. **2.** Material for roofs. **3.** Roofs collectively. **4.** A roof; covering.
roof·less (rōof′lis, rōof′-) *adj.* **1.** Having no roof. **2.** Destitute of shelter; homeless.
roof·tree (rōof′trē′, rōof′-) *n.* **1.** The ridgepole of a roof; also, the roof itself. **2.** A home or dwelling.
rook[1] (rook) *n.* **1.** An Old World corvine bird (*Corvus frugilegus*), noted for its gregariousness and marked in the adult state by a bare, whitish face patch. **2.** A trickster or cheat; a sharper. — *v.t. & v.i.* To cheat; defraud. [OE *hrōc*]
rook[2] (rook) *n.* One of a pair of castle-shaped chessmen that can move any number of unoccupied squares parallel to the sides of the board: also called *castle.* Abbr. *R* [< OF *roc* ult. < Persian *rukh*; orig. meaning unknown]
rook·er·y (rook′ər·ē) *n. pl.* **·er·ies** **1.** A colony or breeding place of rooks. **2.** A breeding place of sea birds, seals, etc. **3.** An old, densely populated tenement.
rook·ie (rook′ē) *n. Slang* **1.** A raw recruit in the army, police, or any other service. **2.** Any novice, as in professional baseball. [Prob. alter. of RECRUIT]
rook·y (rook′ē) *adj.* **1.** Pertaining to rooks and their habits. **2.** Abounding in rooks.
room (rōom, room) *n.* **1.** An extent of space used for some implied or specified purpose; free or open space. **2.** A space for occupancy or use enclosed on all sides, as in a building; an apartment; chamber. **3.** *pl.* Lodgings. **4.** Suitable or warrantable occasion; opportunity: *room* for doubt. — *v.i.* To occupy a room; lodge. Abbr. **rm.** — **to room in** To live in the house where one works as a servant. [OE *rūm* space]
room and board Lodging and meals.
room divider Something used to partition a room or rooms into separate areas, as a set of book shelves.
room·er (rōo′mər, room′ər) *n.* A lodger; especially, one who rents a room and eats elsewhere.
room·ette (rōo·met′, room·et′) *n.* A small compartment in a railroad sleeping car furnished with a folding bed.
room·ful (rōom′fool′, room′-) *n. pl.* **·fuls** **1.** As many or as much as a room will hold. **2.** A number of persons present in a room.
rooming house *U.S.* A house for roomers; also called *lodging house.*

room·mate (rōom′māt′, room′-) *n.* *U.S.* One who shares lodgings with another or others.
room·y (rōo′mē, room′ē) *adj.* **room·i·er, room·i·est** Having abundant room; spacious. — **room′i·ly** *adv.* — **room′i·ness** *n.*
roor·back (rōor′bak) *n.* *U.S.* A fictitious report circulated for political purposes. [after *Roorback,* purported author of a (nonexistent) book of travel that was cited as authority for certain defamatory charges made against President Polk in the 1844 campaign]
roose (rōoz, rooz) *Scot. v.t.* **roosed, roos·ing** To praise. — *n.* Praise. [< ON *hrōsa*] — **roos′er** *n.*
Roo·se·velt (rō′zə·velt, rōz′velt, -vəlt), **(Anna) Eleanor,** 1884–1962, *née* Roosevelt, U.S. lecturer, writer, and diplomat; wife of Franklin Delano. — **Franklin Delano,** 1882–1945, U.S. statesman, 32nd president of the United States 1933–45; only president to hold a third and fourth term. — **Theodore,** 1858–1919, U.S. army officer and statesman; 26th president of the United States 1901–09.
Roosevelt Dam A dam in the Salt River, central Arizona; 280 ft. high; 1,125 ft. long; completed 1911.
roost (rōost) *n.* **1.** A perch upon which fowls rest at night; also, any place where birds resort to spend the night. **2.** Any temporary resting place. — *v.i.* **1.** To sit or perch upon a roost. **2.** To come to rest; settle. [OE *hrōst*]
roost·er (rōos′tər) *n.* The male of the chicken; cock. [< ROOST + -ER[1]]
root[1] (rōot, root) *n.* **1.** The underground portion or descending axis of a plant, that absorbs moisture, obtains or stores nourishment, and provides support. **2.** Any underground growth, as a tuber or bulb. **3.** Any of certain growths serving to attach or support, as in the ivy or mistletoe. **4.** That from which anything derives origin, growth, or life and vigor: Money is the *root* of evil. **5.** An antecedent; ancestor. **6.** The condition or feeling of belonging to a society, place, tradition etc. **7.** A rootlike part of an organ or structure: the *root* of a tooth or nerve. **8.** *Ling.* **a** In etymology, the minimum unreducible base common to all cognate forms; etymon; radical. **b** In morphology, a base to which affixes and thematic vowels may be added to form words, as *know* in *unknown, knowable* and *unknowingly.* See STEM. **9.** *Math.* A quantity that, multiplied by itself a specified number of times, will give a given quantity: 3 is the square *root* of 9 and the cube *root* of 27. **10.** *Music* **a** The tone of a triad that contains the other two tones in its first six harmonics. **b** The tone of any chord that occupies a similar predominant position; a fundamental. — *v.i.* **1.** To put forth roots and begin to grow; take root. **2.** To be or become firmly fixed or established. — *v.t.* **3.** To fix or implant by or as by roots. **4.** To pull, dig, or tear up by or as by the roots; extirpate: with *up* or *out.* [OE *rōt* < ON]
root[2] (rōot, root) *v.t.* **1.** To turn up or dig with the snout or nose, as swine. — *v.i.* **2.** To turn up the earth with the snout. **3.** To search for something; rummage. **4.** To work hard; toil. [OE *wrōtan* to root up]
root[3] (rōot, root) *v.i.* *U.S. Informal* To cheer for or encourage a contestant, team, etc., with *for.* [Prob. var. of ROUT[2]]
Root (rōot, root), **Elihu,** 1845–1937, U.S. lawyer and statesman.
root beer A beverage made with yeast and the extracts of several roots.
root canal The cavity within the root of a tooth, occupied by the pulp of the tooth.
root climber Any plant that climbs by means of adventitious roots developed from stems.
root·er[1] (rōo′tər, root′ər) *n.* One who or that which takes root.
root·er[2] (rōo′tər, root′ər) *n.* One who or that which roots, as a swine, or tears up as by rooting.
root·er[3] (rōo′tər, root′ər) *n.* *U.S. Informal* One who gives encouragement, as by applauding.
root hair *Bot.* Hairlike outgrowths of plant roots, having an absorbent and protective function.
root·less (rōot′lis, root′-) *adj.* Without roots. — **root′less·ness** *n.*
root·let (rōot′lit, root′-) *n.* A small root.
root sheath The tough membrane covering the root portion of a hair. For illustration see HAIR.
root·stalk (rōot′stôk′, root′-) *n. Bot.* A rhizome.
root·stock (rōot′stok′, root′-) *n.* **1.** Original source; origin. **2.** *Bot.* A rhizome.
root·y (rōo′tē, root′ē) *adj.* **root·i·er, root·i·est** **1.** Full of or consisting of roots. **2.** Resembling roots. — **root′i·ness** *n.*
rope (rōp) *n.* **1.** A construction of twisted fibers, as of hemp, cotton, flax, etc., so intertwined in several strands as to form a thick cord. **2.** A collection of things plaited or united in a line. **3.** A slimy or glutinous filament or thread. **4.** A cord or halter used in hanging. **5.** Execution or death by strangling or hanging: to die by the *rope.* **6.** *U.S.* A lasso. — **to give (one) plenty of rope** To allow (a person) to pursue unchecked a course that is considered foolish. — **to know the**

ropes *Informal* 1. To be familiar with all the elements of a sphere of activity. 2. To be sophisticated in the ways of the world. — *v.* **roped, rop·ing** *v.t.* 1. To tie or fasten with or as with rope. 2. To enclose, border, or divide with a rope: usually with *off*: He *roped* off the arena. 3. *U.S.* To catch with a lasso. 4. *Informal* To take in; deceive: with *in*. — *v.i.* 5. To become drawn out or extended into a filament or thread. [OE *rāp*]

rope band Roband (which see).

rope·danc·er (rōp′dan/sər, -dän′-) *n.* A tightrope walker, especially when skilled at dancing on a tightrope. — **rope′danc′ing** *n.*

rope ladder A ladder made of ropes or having rope sides.

rope·walk (rōp′wôk′) *n.* A long alley or building used for the spinning of rope yarn.

rope·walk·er (rōp′wô/kər) *n.* One who performs on the tightrope; a tightrope walker.

rop·y (rō′pē) *adj.* **rop·i·er, rop·i·est** 1. That may be drawn into threads, as a glutinous substance; stringy. 2. Resembling ropes or cordage. — **rop′i·ly** *adv.* — **rop′i·ness** *n.*

roque (rōk) *n.* A form of croquet requiring more skill than the ordinary game. [Aphetic alter. of CROQUET]

Roque·fort (rōk′fərt, *Fr.* rôk·fôr′) A village in south central France. Also **Roquefort-sur-Soul·zon** (-sûr·sool·zôn′).

Roquefort cheese A strong cheese with a blue mold (*Penicillium roqueforti*), made from ewe's and goat's milk in the town of Roquefort, France.

roqu·e·laure (rok′ə-lôr, rok′lôr, -lōr) *n.* A type of short cloak worn by men in the 18th century. [after Duc de *Roquelaure*, 1656–1738, French nobleman]

ro·quet (rō·kā′) *v.t. & v.i.* **·queted** (-kād′) **, ·quet·ing** (-kā′ing) In croquet, to cause one's own ball to strike (another player's ball). — *n.* The act of roqueting. [See ROQUE.]

Ro·rer (rôr′ər, rō′rər), **Sarah Tyson**, 1849–1937, *née* Heston, U.S. home economist and writer.

ror·qual (rôr′kwəl) *n.* Any of a genus (*Balaenoptera*) of whalebone whales of the Atlantic and Pacific oceans: also called *finback, razorback*. [< F < Norw. *röyrkval*]

Ror·schach test (rôr′shäk, -shäkh, rōr′-) *Psychol.* A test of personality and intelligence based upon the subject's interpretation of a series of standard inkblot patterns. [after Hermann *Rorschach*, 1884–1922, Swiss psychiatrist]

Ros. Roscommon.

Ro·sa (rô′zä), **Saint**, 1586–1617, Peruvian Dominican nun; first saint born in the Americas: original name **Isabel Flo·res** (flō′räs): called **Rose of Lima**.

Ro·sa (rô′zä), **Salvator**, 1615?–73, Italian painter.

ro·sa·ceous (rō·zā′shəs) *adj.* 1. *Bot.* Of, pertaining to, or designating the rose family (*Rosaceae*) of trees, shrubs, and herbs. 2. Resembling a rose. [< L *rosaceus* < *rosa* rose]

Ros·a·lind (roz′ə-lind) In Shakespeare's *As You Like It*, the heroine, daughter of the banished duke, who assumes male attire.

ro·san·i·line (rō·zan′ə-lin, -lēn) *n. Chem.* A crystalline compound, $C_{20}H_{21}ON_3$, obtained from aniline, used as a red dye and as a base for other dyes. [< ROSE¹ + ANILINE]

Ro·sa·rio (rō·sä′ryō) A port city in east central Argentina, on the Paraná; pop. 671,852 (1960).

ro·sa·ry (rō′zə-rē) *n. pl.* **·ries** 1. *Eccl.* A series of prayers, consisting in its common form (**Dominican rosary**) of fifteen decades, each containing ten Aves preceded by a paternoster and followed by the Gloria Patri, and each related to a mystery or event in the life of Christ or the Virgin Mary that is contemplated during its recitation. **b** A string of beads for keeping count of the prayers thus recited. 2. A garden or bed of roses. 3. A chaplet or garland. 4. A collection of literary selections. [< L *rosarium* rose garden < L *rosa* rose]

Ros·coe (ros′kō), **Sir Henry** (**Enfield**), 1833–1915, English chemist.

Ros·com·mon (ros·kom′ən) A county of central Ireland; 951 sq. mi.; county town, **Roscommon**. *Abbr. Ros.*

rose¹ (rōz) *n.* 1. Any of a large genus (*Rosa*) of hardy, erect or climbing shrubs grown in many varieties, with rodlike, prickly stems: the national flower of England and the State flower of New York, North Dakota, and Iowa. The rose family (*Rosaceae*) includes such important fruit plants as the apple, pear, peach, cherry, and strawberry. 2. The flower of such a shrub, usually having five sepals and exhibiting a wide range of colors, principally white, yellow, pink, or red. 3. Any of various other plants or flowers likened to the true rose. 4. A light pinkish red, like the color of many roses. 5. An ornamental knot, as of ribbon or lace; a rosette. 6. A perforated cap, plate, or nozzle at the end of a pipe, for throwing water in a fine spray. 7. A form in which gems, especially diamonds, are often cut, characterized by a flat base with a hemispherical upper surface covered with small facets; also, a diamond so cut. For illustration see DIAMOND. — **bed of roses** A peaceful or carefree time, place, or condition. — *v.t.* **rosed, ros·ing** To cause to blush; redden; flush. [OE < L *rosa*, prob. < Gk. *rhodea*]

rose² (rōz) Past tense of RISE.

rose acacia A locust tree (*Robinia hispida*) of the SE United States, bearing racemes of large rose or purplish flowers.

ro·se·ate (rō′zē-it, -āt) *adj.* 1. Of a rose color. 2. Rosy;

rose-colored. 3. Cheerful; optimistic. [< L *roseus*] — **ro′se·ate·ly** *adv.*

roseate spoonbill A tropical American wading bird (*Ajaia ajaja*) having a bare head and throat and pink plumage.

rose-bay (rōz′bā′) *n.* Any rhododendron.

rose beetle The rose chafer (which see).

Rose·ber·y (rōz′bər-ē), **Earl of**, 1847–1929, Archibald Philip Primrose, English statesman and author.

rose-breast·ed grosbeak (rōz′bres′tid) A North American finchlike bird (*Pheucticus ludovicianus*), of which the male has a black head, black and white wings and a bright rose breast.

rose-bud (rōz′bud′) *n.* 1. The bud of a rose. 2. A young girl, as a debutante.

rose-bush (rōz′boosh′) *n.* A rose-bearing shrub or vine.

rose campion An herbaceous plant (*Lychnis coronaria*), cultivated for its pink or crimson flowers. 2. The corncockle.

rose chafer A hairy, fawn-colored beetle (*Macrodactylus subspinosus*) injurious to roses: also called *rose beetle*. Also **rose bug**. For illustration see INSECTS (injurious).

rose-col·ored (rōz′kul/ərd) *adj.* Pink or crimson, as a rose. — **to see through rose-colored glasses** To see things in an unduly favorable light; to look too much or only on the bright side.

Rose·crans (rōz′kranz), **William Starke**, 1819–1898, Union general in the Civil War.

rose fever *Pathol.* A variety of hay fever, assumed to be caused by rose pollen. Also **rose cold**.

rose-fish (rōz′fish′) *n. pl.* **-fish** or **-fish·es** An orange-red scorpaenoid food fish (*Sebastes marinus*) of the North Atlantic.

rose geranium A cultivated geranium (*Pelargonium capitatum*) with rose-scented leaves and dense clusters of rose-purple flowers, grown extensively in South Africa.

rose mallow 1. The hibiscus. 2. The hollyhock.

rose-mar·y (rōz′mâr′ē) *n. pl.* **·mar·ies** An evergreen, fragrant Old World shrub (*Rosmarinus officinalis*) of the mint family, commonly with blue flowers, cultivated for an essential oil used in making perfume and in cookery. [ME *rosmarine* < L *rosmarinus* < *ros* dew + *marinus* of the sea; infl. by ROSE¹ and *Mary* feminine personal name]

rose moss A garden variety of portulaca (*Portulaca grandiflora*).

Ro·sen·wald (rō′zən·wôld), **Julius**, 1862–1932, U.S. businessman and philanthropist.

rose of Jericho A small annual plant (*Anastatica hierochuntica*) of the mustard family growing in desert places. It rolls up when dry and expands again when moist. Also called *resurrection plant, Jericho rose*.

rose of Sharon 1. A flower mentioned in the Bible (*Canticles* ii 1), perhaps the autumn crocus or the narcissus. 2. A hardy shrub (*Hibiscus syriacus*) of the mallow family: also called *shrub althea*. 3. A species (*Hypericum calycinum*) of St. Johnswort having large, yellow flowers.

ro·se·o·la (rō·zē′ə-lə) *n. Pathol.* A rose-colored rash appearing on the skin. Also **rose rash**. [< NL < L *roseus* rosy]

rose quartz A semitransparent variety of quartz, pink or rose in color and often used for ornament and as a gemstone.

ros·et (roz′it) *n. Scot.* Resin.

Ro·set·ta stone (rō·zet′ə) A tablet of basalt containing an inscription in two forms of Egyptian hieroglyphics (demotic and hieratic) and in Greek, found near Rosetta, Egypt, in 1799. It supplied Champollion with the key to the ancient inscriptions of Egypt.

ro·sette (rō·zet′) *n.* 1. An ornament or badge having some resemblance to a rose; especially, a painted or sculptured architectural ornament with parts circularly arranged. 2. A ribbon badge worn in the lapel buttonhole of civilian clothes to indicate possession of a certain military decoration. 3. A ribbon decoration shaped like a full-blown or double rose and made of gathered or pleated silk, lace, etc. 4. A flowerlike cluster of leaves, organs, or markings, arranged in circles, as in certain plants. [< F, dim. of *rose*]

Rose·ville (rōz′vil) A city in SE Michigan; pop. 60,529.

rose-wa·ter (rōz′wô/tər, -wot/ər) *adj.* 1. Made with or resembling rose water, as in fragrance. 2. Extremely or affectedly delicate or sentimental.

rose water A fragrant preparation made variously by the distillation of rose petals or rose oil with water, used as a toilet water and in cooking.

rose window A circular window filled with tracery, often radiating from the center like spokes.

rose-wood (rōz′wood′) *n.* 1. A hard, close-grained, dark-colored, fragrant wood yielded by certain tropical American trees (genus *Dalbergia*): also called *granadillo*. 2. Any of various other woods resembling true rosewood. 3. Any tree yielding such a wood.

Rosh Ha·sha·na (rosh hə-shä′nə, rōsh) The Jewish New Year, celebrated on Tishri 1st and 2nd (September–early October). Also **Rosh Ha·sho′nah** (-shō′-). [< Hebrew *rōsh* head + *hash-shānāh* of the year]

Ro·si·cru·cian (rō′zə-kroo′shən, roz′ə-) *n.* One who is a member of an international fraternity devoted to the practical application of an occult philosophy to human affairs.

— *adj.* Of or pertaining to this society, its members, or its doctrines. [< L *rosa* rose + *crucis* of the cross, Latinized form of Christian *Rosenkreuz*, 1387–1484, an Austrian who allegedly founded this order] — **Ro·si·cru′cian·ism** *n.*

ros·in (roz′in) *n.* **1.** The hard, amber-colored resin forming the residue after the distillation of oil of turpentine from crude turpentine: also called *colophony, resin.* **2.** Resin (defs. 1, 2, & 3). — *v.t.* To apply rosin to. [Alter. of RESIN] — **ros′in·y** *adj.*

Ros·i·nan·te (roz′ə-nan′tē) See ROCINANTE.

rosin oil Retinol.

ros·in·weed (roz′in-wēd′) *n.* **1.** A coarse perennial herb (genus *Silphium*) of the composite family, with copious resinous juice, growing in the central and western United States: also called *cup plant.* **2.** The compass plant (def. 1).

ro·so·lio (rō-zō′lyō) *n.* A cordial made from raisins and brandy, drunk chiefly in the Mediterranean countries. [< Ital. < Med.L *ros solis* (< L *ros* dew + *solis* of the sun) sundew, from which it was once extracted]

Ross (rôs) A township in SW Pennsylvania; pop. 32,892.

Ross (rôs), **Betsy**, 1752–1836, *née* Griscom, American patriot; reputed to have made the first American flag. — **Sir James Clark**, 1800–62, English Arctic and Antarctic explorer; discovered north magnetic pole 1831. — **Sir John**, 1777–1856, British Arctic explorer; uncle of Sir James Clark Ross. — **Sir Ronald**, 1857–1932, British physician born in India; pioneer in study of malaria-bearing mosquitoes.

Ross and Crom·ar·ty (krom′ər-tē, krum′-) A county of NW Scotland; 3,089 sq. mi.; pop. 56,650 (1969); county seat, Dingwall.

Ross Dependency A region of Antarctica claimed by New Zealand; 175,000 sq. mi.

Ros·set·ti (rō-set′ē, -zet′ē), **Christina Georgina**, 1830–94, English poet; sister of Dante Gabriel: pseudonym **Ellen Alleyn.** — **Dante Gabriel**, 1828–82, English poet and painter.

Ros·si (rôs′sē), **Bruno**, born 1905, Italian physicist.

Ros·si·ni (rôs-sē′nē), **Gioacchino Antonio**, 1792–1868, Italian composer.

Ros·si·ya (ros-syē′yə) The Russian name for RUSSIA.

Ross Sea An inlet of the Pacific in Antarctica south of New Zealand.

Ross Shelf Ice An area of shelf ice in Antarctica, occupying the southern part of the Ross Sea; about 400 mi. wide on its seaward side. Also **Ross Barrier.**

Ros·tand (rôs′tän′), **Edmond**, 1864–1918, French dramatist and poet.

ros·tel·late (ros′tə-lāt, -lit) *adj.* Having a small beak or rostellum. [< NL *rostellatus*]

ros·tel·lum (ros-tel′əm) *n.* *pl.* **·tel·la** (-tel′ə) **1.** *Bot.* A small, beaklike structure developed from the stigma of an orchid. **2.** *Zool.* The hooked prominence surrounding the head of a tapeworm. [< L, dim. of *rostrum* beak]

ros·ter (ros′tər) *n.* **1.** A list of officers and men enrolled for duty; also, a list of active military organizations. **2.** Any list of names. [< Du. *rooster* list, lit. gridiron]

Ros·tock (ros′tok, Ger. rôs′tôk) A port city in northern East Germany, on the Baltic; pop. 190,275 (est. 1968).

Ros·tov-on-Don (ros′tov-on-don′) A city in the SW R.S.F. S.R.; pop. 789,000 (1970). *Russian* **Ros·tov-na-Do·nu** (ros-tôf′nä-dô-nōō′). Also **Ros′tov.**

Ros·tov·tzeff (ro-stôf′tsəf), **Michael Ivanovich**, 1870–1952, U.S. historian and archeologist born in Russia.

ros·tral (ros′trəl) *adj.* **1.** Of or pertaining to a rostrum. **2.** Having a rostrum, or beaklike process. Also **ros′trate** (-trāt). [< LL *rostralis* < L *rostrum* beak]

ros·trum (ros′trəm) *n.* *pl.* **·trums** or **·tra** (-trə) *for defs. 1 & 3,* **·tra** *for def. 2* **1.** A pulpit or platform. **2.** In ancient Rome: **a** A beaklike part on the prow of a ship, especially of a war galley, used for ramming. **b** The orators' platform in the Roman forum, embellished with such parts captured from enemy ships. **3.** *Biol.* A beaklike process or part. [< L *rostrum* beak]

ROSTRUM (def. 2a)

Ros·well (roz′wəl) A city in SE New Mexico, near a U.S. Air Force Base; pop. 33,908.

ros·y (rō′zē) *adj.* **ros·i·er, ros·i·est 1.** Like a rose; rose red; blushing. **2.** Bright, pleasing, or flattering. **3.** Made of or ornamented with roses. **4.** Auguring success; optimistic: *rosy predictions.* — **ros′i·ly** *adv.* — **ros′i·ness** *n.*

rosy finch A finch (*Leucosticte tephrosis*) of the NW United States, having a chestnut-brown body and a yellow bill.

rot (rot) *v.* **rot·ted, rot·ting** *v.i.* **1.** To undergo decomposition; decompose; decay. **2.** To fall or pass by decaying: with *away, off,* etc. **3.** To become morally rotten. — *v.t.* **4.** To cause to decompose; decay. **5.** To ret. — **Syn.** See DECAY. — *n.* **1.** The process of rotting or the state of being rotten. **2.** That which is rotten. **3.** A wasting disease, as of the lungs. **4.** A parasitic disease affecting sheep and other domestic animals. **5.** A form of decay in

plants, caused by fungi and bacteria. **6.** *Informal* Trashy and nonsensical opinions or expressions; twaddle; bosh. — *interj.* Nonsense; bosh. [OE *rotian*]

ro·ta (rō′tə) *n.* *Chiefly Brit.* **1.** A roll of names, giving order of duty. **2.** A round, as of duties. [< L, wheel]

Ro·ta (rō′tə) *n.* In the Roman Catholic Church, an ecclesiastical court composed of ten prelates or auditors, subject only to papal authority, and serving as a court of final appeal: in full **Sa·cra Ro·man·a Rota** (sā′krə rō-man′ə).

Ro·tar·i·an (rō-târ′ē-ən) *n.* A member of a Rotary Club. — *adj.* Of or pertaining to Rotary Clubs or their members. — **Ro·tar′i·an·ism** *n.*

ro·ta·ry (rō′tər-ē) *adj.* **1.** Turning or designed to turn around its axis, like a wheel. **2.** Having some part that turns on its axis: a *rotary* press. **3.** Characterized by movement around an axis; rotatory: *rotary* motion. — *n.* *pl.* **·ries 1.** A rotary device or part. **2.** *U.S. & Canadian* A traffic circle. [< LL *rotarius* < L *rota* wheel]

Rotary Club A club belonging to an international association of clubs, **Rotary International**, whose aim is to improve civic service.

rotary engine *Mech.* **1.** An engine in which rotary motion is directly produced, as in a turbine. **2.** In internal-combustion engines, a radial engine revolving about a fixed crankshaft.

rotary harrow *Agric.* A harrow with many spikes set along the rim of a wheel that turns on a horizontal axis as it is pulled along the ground.

rotary plow *Agric.* A set of plowshares arranged on the rim of a rotating, power-driven shaft.

rotary press A printing press using curved type plates that revolve against the paper.

rotary snowplow A snowplow that throws snow out to the side with a rapidly spinning rotor.

ro·tate (rō′tāt) *v.t.* & *v.i.* **·tat·ed, ·tat·ing 1.** To turn or cause to turn on or as on its axis. **2.** To alternate in a definite order or succession. — *adj.* *Bot.* Wheel-shaped; circular, as the corollas of certain flowers. [< L *rotatus,* pp. of *rotare* to turn < *rota* wheel] — **ro′tat·a·ble** *adj.*

— **Syn.** (verb) **1.** spin, whirl, twirl, turn, gyrate. See REVOLVE.

ro·ta·tion (rō-tā′shən) *n.* **1.** The act or state of rotating; rotary motion. **2.** Change or alternation in a particular sequence; regular variation: *rotation* of crops. **3.** *Astron.* The movement of the earth or other planet, satellite, etc. around its axis. [< L *rotatio, -onis*] — **ro·ta′tion·al** *adj.*

ro·ta·tive (rō′tə-tiv) *adj.* Pertaining to or causing rotation; turning. — **ro′ta·tive·ly** *adv.*

ro·ta·tor (rō′tā-tər) *n.* **1.** One who or that which rotates or causes rotation. **2.** *pl.* **ro·ta·to·res** (rō′tə-tôr′ēz, -tō′rēz) *Anat.* A muscle that rolls or rotates a part upon its axis. [< L]

ro·ta·to·ry (rō′tə-tôr′ē, -tō′rē) *adj.* **1.** Having, pertaining to, or producing rotation. **2.** Following in succession. **3.** Alternating or recurring.

ROTC or **R.O.T.C.** Reserve Officers' Training Corps.

rotche (roch) *n.* The dovekie (def. 1), a bird. Also **rotch.** [Earlier *rotge*; ult. origin uncertain]

rote[1] (rōt) *n.* **1.** Mechanical routine. **2.** Repetition of words as a means of learning them, with slight attention to the sense. — **by rote** Mechanically, without intelligent attention: to learn *by rote.* [ME; origin uncertain]

rote[2] (rōt) *n.* *Rare* The roar of the surf. [Cf. ON *rōt* breaking of waves]

ro·te·none (rō′tə-nōn) *n.* *Chem.* A crystalline heterocyclic compound, $C_{23}H_{22}O_6$, the effective principle in insecticides and fish poisons, obtained from the roots of various plants, especially a tropical tree (genus *Lonchocarpus*). [Origin unknown]

rot·gut (rot′gut′) *U.S.* An inferior raw whisky.

Roth·er·ham (roth′ər-əm) A county borough in South Yorkshire, England; pop. 248,100 (1976).

Roth·schild (rôth′child, Ger. rōt′shilt) A family of European bankers prominent in international finance, notably **Mayer Anselm**, 1743–1812, founder of the worldwide banking enterprise (**House of Rothschild**) at Frankfort on the Main, Germany, and his sons who opened branches: **Solomon**, 1774–1855, at Vienna; **Nathan Mayer**, 1777–1836, at London; **Charles Mayer**, 1780–1855, at Naples; **Jacob**, 1792–1868, at Paris.

ro·ti·fer (rō′tə-fər) *n.* One of a division (*Rotifera*) of many-celled, microscopic, aquatic organisms usually found in stagnant fresh water, having rings of cilia that in motion resemble revolving wheels: also called *wheel animalcule.* [< NL < L *rota* wheel + *ferre* to bear] — **ro·tif·er·al** (rō-tif′ər-əl), **ro·tif′er·ous** *adj.*

ro·ti·form (rō′tə-fôrm) *adj.* Shaped like a wheel; rotate. [< L *rota* wheel + -FORM]

ro·tis·se·rie (rō-tis′ər-ē) *n.* **1.** A restaurant where patrons select uncooked food and have it roasted and served. **2.** A shop where food is roasted and sold. **3.** A rotating device for roasting meat, etc. [< F < *rôtir* to roast]

rot·l (rot′l) *n. pl.* **ar·tal** (är′täl) A unit of weight in Moslem countries, varying in different localities between one and five pounds. [< Arabic *raṭl*]

ro·to·gra·vure (rō′tə·grə·vyoŏr′, -grāv′yər) *n.* **1.** The process of printing photographs, letters, etc., from cylinders etched from photographic plates and run through a rotary press. **2.** A picture printed by this process. **3.** The section of a newspaper containing such pictures. [< L *rota* wheel + GRAVURE]

ro·tor (rō′tər) *n.* **1.** *Electr.* The rotating section of an alternating-current motor. **2.** *Mech.* The revolving portion of a dynamo, turbine, or other power generator: distinguished from *stator*. **3.** *Aeron.* The horizontally rotating unit of a helicopter or autogiro, consisting of the airfoils and hub. [Contraction of ROTATOR]

rotor ship A vessel propelled by rotors operated by wind power but fitted with auxiliary power.

rot·ten (rot′n) *adj.* **1.** Decomposed by natural process; putrid. **2.** Untrustworthy; treacherous. **3.** Corrupt; venal. **4.** Afflicted with the rot, as sheep. **5.** Liable to break; unsound. **6.** *Informal* Worthless. [< ON *rotinn*. Akin to OE *rotian* to rot.] — **rot′ten·ly** *adv.* — **rot′ten·ness** *n.*
— **Syn. 1.** decayed, putrefied, putrescent, carious, fetid. Compare DECAY. — **Ant.** fresh, sweet, sound, wholesome, healthy.

rotten borough **1.** Any English borough prior to 1832 having few voters, yet entitled to send a member to Parliament. **2.** Any election district or political unit no longer having sufficient population to justify the representation allotted to it.

rot·ten·stone (rot′n·stōn′) *n.* A soft, friable rock, consisting largely of siliceous particles, used for polishing: also called *tripoli*.

rot·ter (rot′ər) *n. Chiefly Brit. Slang* A worthless or objectionable person; scoundrel. — **Syn.** See SCOUNDREL.

Rot·ter·dam (rot′ər·dam) A port city in the western Netherlands; pop. 686,580 (est. 1970).

ro·tund (rō·tund′) *adj.* **1.** Rounded out; spherical; plump. **2.** Full-toned, as a voice or utterance; sonorous. [< L *rotundus*. Akin to *rota* wheel. Doublet of ROUND.] — **ro·tund′ly** *adv.* — **ro·tund′ness** *n.*

ro·tun·da (rō·tun′də) *n.* **1.** A circular building or an interior hall, surmounted with a dome. **2.** *Canadian* A large room having a high ceiling, as a hotel lobby; foyer. [< Ital. *rotonda* < L *rotunda*, fem. of *rotundus*. See ROTUND.]

ro·tun·di·ty (rō·tun′də·tē) *n. pl.* **·ties 1.** The condition of being rotund. **2.** A rotund object or protuberance.

ro·tu·rier (rō·tü·ryā′) *n. French* A plebeian or peasant.

Rou·ault (roō·ō′), **Georges,** 1871–1958, French painter.

Rou·baix (roō·be′) A city in extreme northern France; pop. 114,239 (1968).

rou·ble (roō′bəl) See RUBLE.

rouche (roōsh) See RUCHE.

rou·é (roō·ā′) *n.* A sensualist; debauchee. [< F, jaded, orig. pp. of *rouer* to break on the wheel, beat severely]

Rou·en (roō·än′) A city in northern France, on the Seine; site of a famous cathedral; scene of the burning of Joan of Arc; pop. 118,323 (1968).

rouge (roōzh) *n.* **1.** Any cosmetic used for coloring the cheeks or lips pink or red. **2.** A ferric oxide used in polishing metals and glass. **3.** *Canadian* In football, a point scored by a team that kicks the ball into the opponent's end zone and prevents its being returned to the field of play. — *v.* **rouged, roug·ing** *v.t.* **1.** To color, as the face, with rouge. **2.** *Canadian* To tackle (a player) and score a rouge. — *v.i.* **3.** To apply rouge. **4.** *Canadian* To score a rouge. [< F, red < L *rubeus* ruby]

rouge et noir (roōzh′ ā nwär′) A gambling game played with cards on a table having four diamond-shaped figures, two red and two black. [< F, red and black]

Rou·get de Lisle (roō·zhe′ də lēl′), **Claude Joseph,** 1760–1836, French army officer and composer; wrote the *Marseillaise*, 1792. Also **Rouget de Lisle.**

rough (ruf) *adj.* **1.** Having an uneven surface; not smooth or polished. **2.** Coarse in texture; shabby: a *rough* suit. **3.** Disordered or ragged; shaggy: a *rough* shock of hair. **4.** Having the surface broken; uneven: a *rough* country. **5.** Characterized by rude or violent action: *rough* sports. **6.** Boisterous or tempestuous; stormy: a *rough* passage. **7.** Characterized by harshness of spirit; brutal. **8.** Lacking the finish and polish bestowed by art or culture; unpolished; crude. **9.** Done or made hastily and without attention to details, as a drawing. **10.** In classical Greek, uttered with aspiration; aspirated. **11.** Harsh to the ear; grating; inharmonious. **12.** Approximate: a *rough* estimate. — *n.* **1.** A low, rude, and violent fellow; a ruffian; a rowdy. **2.** A crude, incomplete, or unpolished object, material, or condition. **3.** Any part of a golf course on which tall grass, bushes, etc., grow. **4.** A spike for insertion in a horseshoe, to prevent slipping. — **in the rough** In a crude or unpolished state. — *v.t.* **1.** To make rough; roughen. **2.** To treat roughly; especially, in football, to treat (a player) with needless and intentional violence. **3.** To make, cut, or sketch roughly: with *in* or *out*: to *rough* in the details of a plan. — *v.i.* **4.** To

become rough. **5.** To behave roughly. — **to rough it 1.** To live under rough, hard, or impoverished conditions. **2.** To camp out or travel in a rough manner. — **to rough out** *Informal* To make a sketchy preliminary version of. — **to rough up** *Informal* To subject to physical abuse; manhandle. — *adv.* In a rude manner; roughly [OE *rūh*] — **rough′ly** *adv.* — **rough′ness** *n.*
— **Syn.** (adj.) **1.** uneven, rugged, jagged, craggy. — **Ant.** even, level, smooth, sleek.

rough·age (ruf′ij) *n.* **1.** Any coarse or tough substance. **2.** Food material containing a high percentage of indigestible constituents, as cellulose.

rough-and-read·y (ruf′ən·red′ē) *adj.* **1.** Characterized by or acting with rude but effective promptness. **2.** Unpolished but good enough.

rough-and-tum·ble (ruf′ən·tum′bel) *adj.* **1.** Marked by the disregard of all rules, as a fight. **2.** Scrambling; disorderly. — *n.* **1.** A rough-and-tumble fight or scuffle. **2.** Rough or adventurous existence.

rough breathing In classical Greek: **a** An aspirate sound equivalent to our letter *h.* **b** The symbol (‘) placed over an initial vowel to indicate this sound. Also called *asper, spiritus asper*.

rough·cast (ruf′kast, -käst′) *v.t.* **·cast, ·cast·ing 1.** To shape or prepare in a preliminary or incomplete form. **2.** To roughen the surface of (pottery) before firing. **3.** To coat, as a wall, with coarse plaster, and cover with thin mortar by dashing it on. — *n.* **1.** Very coarse plaster for the outside of buildings. **2.** A form or model of something in its first rough stage. — **rough′cast′er** *n.*

rough·draw (ruf′drô′) *v.t.* **·drew, ·drawn, ·draw·ing** To sketch hastily or crudely.

rough·dry (ruf′drī′) *v.t.* **·dried, ·dry·ing** To dry without ironing, as washed clothes.

rough·en (ruf′ən) *v.t. & v.i.* To make or become rough.

rough·er (ruf′ər) *n.* One who makes things in the rough.

rough·hew (ruf′hyoō′) *v.t.* **·hewed, ·hewed** or **·hewn, ·hew·ing 1.** To hew or shape roughly or irregularly. **2.** To make crudely; roughcast.

rough·house (ruf′hous′) *n. Slang.* **n.** A noisy, boisterous or violent game; rough play. — *v.* **·housed, ·hous·ing** *v.i.* To make a disturbance; engage in horseplay or violence. — *v.t.* To handle or treat roughly but without hostile intent.

rough·ish (ruf′ish) *adj.* Somewhat rough.

rough·neck (ruf′nek′) *n. U.S. Slang* **1.** A rowdy. **2.** A member of a rotary drilling crew in the oil fields.

rough·rid·er (ruf′rī′dər) *n. U.S.* **1.** One skilled in breaking broncos or performing dangerous feats in horsemanship. **2.** A western cowboy.

Rough Riders The 1st U.S. Volunteer Cavalry in the Spanish-American War of 1898, mainly organized and subsequently commanded by Theodore Roosevelt.

rough·shod (ruf′shod′) *adj.* Shod with rough shoes to prevent slipping, as a horse. — **to ride roughshod (over)** To act overbearingly; domineer without consideration.

rou·lade (roō·läd′) *n.* **1.** In singing, a run of short notes on one syllable; also, a roll or flourish, as on a drum. **2.** A slice of meat rolled around a filling and cooked. [< F < *rouler* to roll]

rou·leau (roō·lō′) *n. pl.* **·leaux** (-lōz) or **·leaus 1.** A roll of coins in paper. **2.** *Usually pl.* In millinery, a roll of ribbon used for piping. [< F < OF *rolel*, dim. of *role* roll]

Rou·lers (roō·lâr′) A town in western Belgium; scene of several battles of World War I; pop. 40,077 (est. 1967).

rou·lette (roō·let′) *n.* **1.** A game played at a table divided into spaces numbered and colored red and black, and having in the center a rotating disk (**roulette wheel**) on which a ball is rolled until it drops into one of 37 or 38 correspondingly numbered and colored spaces, a player winning if he has staked his money on that space or its color or on a combination including it. **2.** An engraver's disk of tempered steel, as for tracing points on a copperplate; also, a draftsman's wheel for making dotted lines. **3.** In philately, a series of incisions, made in any of several shapes, without removal of paper. Compare PERFORATION. — *v.t.* **·let·ted, ·let·ting** To perforate or mark with a roulette. [< F, dim. of *rouelle*, dim. of *roue* wheel < L *rota*]

Roum (roōm) See RUM.

Rou·ma·ni·a (roō·mā′nē·ə, -mān′yə), **Rou·ma·ni·an** (roō·mā′ne·ən, -mān′yə) See RUMANIA, etc.

Rou·me·li·a (roō·mē′lē·ə) See RUMELIA.

round[1] (round) *adj.* **1.** Having a contour that is circular or approximately so; spherical, ring-shaped, or cylindrical. **2.** Having a curved contour or surface; not angular or flat; convex or concave. **3.** Liberal; ample; large: a good *round* fee. **4.** Easy and free, as in motion; brisk: a *round* pace. **5.** Of full cadence; well-balanced; full-toned: a *round* tone. **6.** Made without reserve; bold; outspoken: a *round* assertion. **7.** Open; just; honorable. **8.** Formed or moving in rotation or a circle: a *round* dance. **9.** Returning to the point of departure, usually by the same means of transportation: a *round* trip. **10.** Passing through the same or a like series of mutations: the *round* year. **11.** Of a number, increased or decreased by a relatively small amount for the sake of

convenience or simplicity: 3,992 is 4,000 in *round* numbers. **12.** Semicircular: a *round* arch. **13.** Characterized by the round arch: the *round* style. **14.** Full; complete: a *round* dozen. **15.** *Phonet.* Labialized; rounded. — *n.* **1.** Something round, as a globe, ring, or cylinder, a rung of a ladder, a crossbar connecting the legs of a chair, a portion of the thigh of a beef, etc. **2.** *Often pl.* A circular course or range; circuit; beat. **3.** A single revolution; also revolving motion. **4.** A series of recurrent movements; routine; order: the daily *round* of life. **5.** One of a series of concerted actions performed in succession by a number of persons: a *round* of applause. **6.** One of the divisions of a boxing match; a bout. **7.** In archery, the total number of arrows shot; the sum of all arrows in two or three ranges. **8.** In golf, a number of holes or an interval of play in a match. **9.** *Music* A short canon in the octave or unison, in which each voice enters in turn and returns to the beginning upon reaching the end. **10.** A firing by a company or squad in which each soldier fires once; volley. **11.** A single shot or complete unit of ammunition. **12.** A round dance (which see). **13.** The state of being carved out on all sides: sculpture in the *round*. **14.** The state or condition of being circular; roundness. **15.** A thick slice from a haunch: a *round* of beef. — **to go** (or **make**) **the rounds 1.** To take a usual walk or tour, as of inspection. **2.** To pass from mouth to mouth or person to person of a certain group. — *v.t.* **1.** To make round. **2.** To bring to completion; perfect: usually with *off* or *out*. **3.** To free of angularity; fill out to fullness of form. **4.** *Phonet.* To utter (a vowel) with the lips in a rounded position; labialize. **5.** To travel or go around; make a circuit of. **6.** *Archaic* To encircle; surround. — *v.i.* **7.** To become round. **8.** To come to completeness or perfection. **9.** To fill out; become plump. **10.** To make a circuit; travel a circular course. **11.** To turn around. — **to round off 1.** To make round or rounded. **2.** To make into a round number. — **to round up 1.** To collect (cattle, etc.) in a herd, as for driving to market. **2.** *Informal* To gather together; assemble. — *adv.* **1.** On all sides; in such a manner as to encircle: A crowd gathered *round*. **2.** With a circular or rotating motion: The wheel turns *round*. **3.** Through a circle or circuit, as from person to person or point to point: provisions enough to go *round*. **4.** So as to form a complete circuit or cycle of time: Will summer ever come *round* again? **5.** In circumference: a log 3 feet *round*. **6.** From one view or position to another; hither and yon; to and fro. **7.** In the vicinity: to hang *round*. — *prep.* **1.** Enclosing; encircling: a belt *round* his waist. **2.** On every side of, or from every side toward; surrounding. **3.** Toward every side from; about: He peered *round* him. **4.** To the people or places of: to distribute books *round* the school. Abbr. *rd.* [< OF *roonde*, fem. of *roond* < L *rotundus*. Doublet of ROTUND.] — **round′ness** *n.*
Round may appear as a combining form in solid or hyphenated words:

round-arched	round-edged	round-pointed
round-armed	round-faced	round-ribbed
round-backed	round-fenced	round-rooted
round-barreled	round-footed	round-sided
round-bellied	round-furrowed	round-skirted
round-billed	round-handed	round-spun
round-bodied	roundheaded	round-stalked
round-boned	round-hoofed	round-tailed
round-bottomed	round-horned	round-toed
round-bowled	round-leaved	round-topped
round-celled	round-limbed	round-trussed
round-cornered	round-lobed	round-visaged
round-crested	round-mouthed	round-winged
round-eared	roundnosed	round-wombed

round[2] (round) *v.t. & v.i. Obs.* To whisper (to). [OE *rūnian*]

round·a·bout (round′ə-bout′) *adj.* **1.** Circuitous; indirect. **2.** Covering the whole field; ample. **3.** Encircling. — *n.* **1.** An outer garment reaching to the waist; a jacket. **2.** *Brit.* A merry-go-round. **3.** *Brit.* A traffic circle.

round clam The quahog.

round dance 1. A country dance in which the dancers form a circle. **2.** A dance with a revolving motion, as a waltz, performed by couples. Also called *round*.

round·ed (roun′did) *adj.* **1.** Round or spherical. **2.** *Phonet.* Formed or uttered with the lips rounded; labialized.

roun·del (roun′dəl) *n.* **1.** A roundelay (def. 3). **2.** In prosody, a modification of the rondeau, written in three stanzas of three lines each, with a refrain after the first and third. **3.** *Archit.* A semicircular recess, small round window, etc. [< OF *rondel* roundelay < *rond* round]

roun·de·lay (roun′də-lā) *n.* **1.** A simple melody. **2.** A musical setting of a poem with a recurrent refrain. **3.** A dance performed in a circle: also called *roundel*. [< OF *rondelet*, dim. of *rondel*. See ROUNDEL.]

round·er (roun′dər) *n.* **1.** A tool for rounding. **2.** *U.S. Slang* A drunkard, drifter, or petty criminal. **3.** *pl.* (*construed as sing.*) An old English game of ball somewhat resembling baseball.

Round·head (round′hed′) *n.* A member of the parliamentary party in England in the civil war of 1642–49: a contemptuous term applied by the Royalists because of their close cropped hair. Compare CAVALIER.

round·house (round′hous′) *n.* **1.** A cabin on the after part of the quarter-deck of a vessel. **2.** A round building with a turntable in the center for housing and switching locomotives. **3.** In pinochle, a meld of four kings and four queens: also called *round trip*. **4.** In baseball, a pitch thrown so as to make a wide curve. **5.** *U.S. Informal* A punch, swing, etc., done with a wide, sweeping arm movement.

round·ish (roun′dish) *adj.* Somewhat round. — **round′ish·ness** *n.*

round·let (round′lit) *n.* A little circle. [< F *rondelet*. See ROUNDELAY.]

round·ly (round′lē) *adv.* **1.** In a round manner or form; circularly; spherically. **2.** Severely; vigorously: to be *roundly* denounced. **3.** Frankly; bluntly. **4.** Thoroughly.

round·nose (round′nōz′) *adj.* Designating a kind of pliers whose gripping surfaces meet in a round, tapering point. For illustration see PLIERS.

round number A number expressed to the nearest ten, hundred, thousand, etc. Also **round figure**.

round robin 1. A tournament, as in tennis or chess, in which each player meets every other player. **2.** A letter circulated among the members of a group, and to which each person usually adds a comment. **3.** A number of signatures, as to a petition, written in a circle so as to avoid giving prominence to any one name; also, a paper so signed.

round scad The cigar fish.

round-shoul·dered (round′shōl′dərd) *adj.* Having the back rounded or the shoulders stooping.

rounds·man (roundz′mən) *n. pl.* **·men** (-mən) A police officer having charge of a group of patrolmen.

round table 1. A meeting place for conference or discussion. **2.** Any discussion group. — **round-ta·ble** (round′-tā′bəl) *adj.*

Round Table 1. The table of King Arthur, made exactly circular so as to avoid any question of precedence among his knights. **2.** King Arthur and his knights.

round-the-clock (round′thə-klok′) *adj.* Through all twenty-four hours of the day.

round trip 1. A trip to a place and back again; a two-way trip. **2.** A roundhouse (def. 3). — **round′-trip′** *adj.*

round·up (round′up′) *n. U.S.* **1.** The bringing together of cattle scattered over a range, as for inspection or branding. **2.** The cowboys, horses, etc., employed in this work. **3.** *Informal* A bringing together of persons or things.

round·worm (round′wûrm′) *n.* A nematode worm, especially one (*Ascaris lumbricoides*), parasitic in the human intestines.

roup[1] (rōōp) *n. Vet.* An infectious respiratory and catarrhal disease affecting poultry. [Origin unknown]

roup[2] (roup, rōōp) *Scot. n.* An auction. — *v.t.* To auction. [Akin to OE *hrōpan* to cry out]

roup·et (rōō′pit, rou′pit) *adj. Scot.* Roupy.

roup·y (rōō′pē) *adj.* **1.** Pertaining to, like, or affected with roup. **2.** *Scot.* Hoarse.

rouse[1] (rouz) *v.* **roused, rous·ing** *v.t.* **1.** To cause to awaken from slumber, repose, unconsciousness, etc. **2.** To excite to vigorous thought or action; stir up. **3.** To startle or drive (game) from cover. — *v.i.* **4.** To awaken from sleep or unconsciousness. **5.** To become active. **6.** To start from cover: said of game. — *n.* **1.** The act of rousing. **2.** *Brit.* Reveille. [Orig. technical term in hawking and hunting; origin uncertain.] — **rous′er** *n.*

rouse[2] (rouz) *n.* **1.** *Archaic* A full draft of liquor; a bumper. **2.** Noisy mirth; carousal. [Aphetic form of CAROUSE]

rouse[3] (rouz) *v.t. & v.i.* **roused, rous·ing** *Naut.* To pull together and with vigor. [? < ROUSE[1]]

rous·ing (rou′zing) *adj.* **1.** Able to rouse or excite: a *rousing* speech. **2.** Lively; active; vigorous: a *rousing* trade. **3.** *Informal* Outrageous; astonishing: a *rousing* lie.

Rous·seau (rōō-sō′), **Henri,** 1844–1910, French painter: called **le Dou·an·ier** (lə dwä-nyä′) (the customs officer). — **Jean Jacques,** 1712–78, French philosopher and author born in Switzerland. — **Théodore,** 1812–67, French painter: full name **Pierre Étienne Théodore Rousseau.**

rous·seau (rōō-sō′) *n. Canadian* Fried pemmican.

Rous·sil·lon (rōō-sē-yôn′) A region and former province of southern France, on the Spanish border.

roust (roust) *v.t. & v.i. Informal* To arouse and drive (a person or thing); stir up: usually with *out*. [< ROUSE[1]]

roust·a·bout (roust′ə-bout′) *n.* **1.** A laborer on river craft or on the waterfront. **2.** One who is employed for casual work; especially, a transient laborer on a cattle ranch, etc. **3.** A laborer in a circus.

rout[1] (rout) *n.* **1.** A disorderly and overwhelming defeat or flight. **2.** A boisterous and disorderly assemblage; the rabble. **3.** An entourage; a retinue. **4.** *Law* A disturbance of the peace by three or more persons with riotous intent.

5. *Archaic* A large and festive evening social gathering. **6.** *Archaic* Any assembly; a throng. — *v.t.* To defeat disastrously; put to flight. [< OF *route* < L *rupta*, fem. of *ruptus*, pp. of *rumpere* to break]

rout² (rout) *v.i.* **1.** To root, as swine. **2.** To search; rummage. — *v.t.* **3.** To dig or turn up with the snout. **4.** To turn up as if with the snout; disclose to view: with *out*. **5.** To hollow, gouge, or scrape, as with a scoop. **6.** To drive or force out. [Var. of ROOT²]

rout³ (rout, rōōt) *v.i. Scot.* or *Obs.* To make a loud noise. — *n. Obs.* **1.** Snoring. **2.** An uproar. [OE *hrūtan*]

route (rōōt, rout) *n.* **1.** A course, road, or way taken in traveling from one point to another. **2.** The specific course over which mail is sent. **3.** The territory covered by a newsboy, milkman, etc. — *v.t.* **rout·ed, rout·ing** To dispatch or send by a certain way, as passengers, goods, etc. [< OF < L *rupta (via)* broken (road), fem. of *ruptus*. See ROUT¹.]

route march *Mil.* A troop marching in which the men are permitted to break step, talk, etc. Also **route step.**

rout·er (rou′tər) *n.* **1.** One who scoops or routs. **2.** A tool for routing. **3.** A plane devised for working a molding around a circular sash. [< ROUT²]

routh (rōōth, routh) *Scot. adj.* Abundant. — *n.* Plenty; abundance. Also spelled *rowth.*

rou·tine (rōō·tēn′) *n.* **1.** A detailed method of procedure, regularly followed: an official *routine.* **2.** Habitual methods of action induced by circumstances. — *adj.* Customary; habitual. [< F < *route* way, road] — **rou·tine′ly** *adv.*

rou·tin·ism (rōō·tē′niz·əm) *n.* Adherence to routine or routine methods in general. — **rou·tin′ist** *n.*

rou·tin·ize (rōō·tē′nīz) *v.t.* **·ized, ·i·zing** To reduce or fit to a routine.

roux (rōō) *n. French* Butter and an equal portion of flour mixed and browned together, used for sauces, etc.

rove¹ (rōv) *v.* **roved, rov·ing** *v.i.* **1.** To wander from place to place; go or move without any definite destination. — *v.t.* **2.** To roam over, through, or about. — *n.* The act of roving; a ramble. [ME *roven*]

rove² (rōv) *v.t.* **roved, rov·ing 1.** To join and elongate, as slivers of fabric from a carding machine, by passing between rollers. **2.** To pass through an eye. **3.** To draw into thread; ravel out. **4.** To reduce the diameter of with a hooked, flat tool: to *rove* a grindstone. — *n.* **1.** A slightly twisted sliver of wool, cotton, flax, jute, or silk. **2.** A metal ring or washer for use in clinching a nail in boatbuilding. [Origin uncertain]

rove³ (rōv) Alternate past tense and past participle of REEVE¹.

rove beetle Any of a family (*Staphylinidae*) of beetles, mainly scavengers, having elongated bodies with very short elytra. For illustration see INSECTS (beneficial).

rove-o·ver (rōv′ō′vər) *adj.* In prosody, designating a verse in sprung rhythm in which a foot is begun at the end of the line and completed at the beginning of the next. — *n.* A rove-over verse.

rov·er¹ (rō′vər) *n.* **1.** One who roves; a wanderer. **2.** A pirate, or pirate vessel. **3.** A croquet ball that has been sent through all the arches and has only to strike the final stake to go out. [< M.Du., robber < *roven* to rob. Akin to OE *rēafian* to reave.]

rov·er² (rō′vər) *n.* **1.** One who roves fabrics, especially on a machine. **2.** A machine for roving fabrics.

rov·er³ (rō′vər) *n.* In archery, any object, usually distant, chosen as a mark. Also **roving mark.** [Origin unknown]

row¹ (rō) *n.* **1.** An arrangement or series of persons or things in a continued line; a rank; file. **2.** A street lined with houses on both sides. **3.** A line of seats, as in a theater. — **a long row to hoe** A hard task or undertaking. — *v.t.* To arrange in a row: with *up*. [OE *rāw*, var. of *rǣw* line]

row² (rō) *v.i.* **1.** To use oars, etc., in propelling a boat. — *v.t.* **2.** To propel across the surface of the water with oars, as a boat. **3.** To transport by rowing. **4.** To be propelled by (a specific number of oars): said of boats. **5.** To make use of (oars or rowers), especially in a race. **6.** To row against in a race. — *n.* **1.** The act of rowing. **2.** A turn at the oars. **3.** A trip in a rowboat. [OE *rōwan*]

row³ (rou) *n.* **1.** A noisy disturbance or quarrel; a brawl. **2.** Any dispute or disturbance. — *v.t. & v.i.* To engage in a row or brawl. [Origin uncertain]

— **Syn.** (noun) *Row, rumpus, fracas, melee, brawl,* and *scrap* are much alike in denoting a noisy altercation. *Row* emphasizes the noise, *rumpus* the tumult, *fracas* the physical violence, and *melee* the confusion. *Brawl* is applied to any noisy free-for-all, even (humorously) to an amicable social party. A *scrap* is a physical fight, sometimes in friendly exercise.

row⁴ (rō) *Scot. n.* A roll, as of wool. — *v.t. & v.i.* To roll.

row·an (rō′ən, rou′-) A small tree (*Sorbus aucuparia*) native to Europe, having pinnate leaves and clusters of bright orange berries: also called *mountain ash.*

row·boat (rō′bōt′) *n. U.S.* A boat propelled by oars.

row·dy (rou′dē) *n. pl.* **·dies** One inclined to create disturbances; a rough, disorderly person. — *adj.* **·di·er, ·di·est** Rough and loud; disorderly. [Origin unknown] — **row′dy·ish** *adj.* — **row′dy·ism, row′di·ness** *n.*

Rowe (rō), **Nicholas,** 1674–1718, English poet and dramatist; poet laureate 1715–18.

row·el (rou′əl) *n.* **1.** A spiked or toothed wheel, as on a spur. **2.** *Vet.* A hair or silk thread passed through a horse's skin, to facilitate the discharge of pus. — *v.t.* **row·eled** or **·elled, row·el·ing** or **·el·ling 1.** To prick with a rowel; spur. **2.** *Vet.* To apply a rowel to. [< OF *roele* < L *rota* wheel]

row·en (rou′ən) *n.* A second growth of grass or hay; aftermath. [< OF *regain*]

Row·land·son (rō′lənd·sən), **Thomas,** 1756–1827, English painter and caricaturist.

row·lock (rō′lok′) *n. Brit.* An oarlock (which see). [Alter. of OARLOCK; infl. by *row²*]

rowth (rōōth, routh) See ROUTH.

Ro·xas y A·cu·ña (rō′häs ē ä·kōō′nyä), **Manuel,** 1892–1948, Philippine statesman; president 1946–48.

Rox·burgh (roks′bûr·ə) A county in southern Scotland; 666 sq. mi.; pop. 42,619 (1969); county seat, Jedburgh. Also **Rox·burgh·shire** (roks′bûr·ə·shir′).

roy·al (roi′əl) *adj.* **1.** Pertaining to a monarch; kingly. **2.** Under the patronage or authority of a king, or connected with a monarchical form of government: a *royal* governor. **3.** Like or befitting a king; regal. **4.** Of superior quality or size: *royal* octavo. **5.** *Informal* Extraordinarily good, large, impressive, etc.: a *royal* view of the scene. — **Syn.** See KINGLY. — *n.* **1.** A size of paper, 19 x 24 inches for writing, 20 x 25 inches for printing. **2.** *Naut.* A sail next above the topgallant, and set in a light breeze. For illustration see SHIP. Abbr. *R.* [< OF *roial* < L *regalis* kingly < *rex* king. Doublet of REGAL.] — **roy′al·ly** *adv.*

Royal Academy A society established in 1768 by George III of England for the advancement of painting, sculpture, and design: in full **Royal Academy of Arts.** Abbr. *R.A.*

Royal Air Force The air force of Great Britain. Abbr. *RAF, R.A.F.*

Royal Australian Air Force The air force of Australia. Abbr. *RAAF, R.A.A.F.*

Royal Australian Navy The navy of Australia. Abbr. *RAN, R.A.N.*

royal blue A brilliant blue, often with reddish overtones.

Royal Canadian Air Force The air force of Canada. Abbr. *RCAF, R.C.A.F.*

Royal Canadian Mounted Police The federal police force of Canada: formerly called *North West Mounted Police.* Abbr. *R.C.M.P.*

Royal Canadian Navy The navy of Canada. Abbr. *RCN, R.C.N.*

royal commission *Brit. & Canadian* A person or persons appointed by the Crown to investigate and report, with recommendations, upon some matter; also, the investigation.

royal fern A deep-rooted fern (*Osmunda regalis*) of Asia, Africa, and America, having branched stems with oval or elliptical leaflets.

royal flush See under FLUSH³.

roy·al·ism (roi′əl·iz′əm) *n.* Adherence to the principles or cause of royalty.

roy·al·ist (roi′əl·ist) *n.* A supporter of a royal dynasty. — *adj.* Of or pertaining to royalists: also **roy′al·is′tic.**

Roy·al·ist (roi′əl·ist) *n.* **1.** In English history, a Cavalier or adherent of King Charles I, as against the Parliament, in the middle of the 17th century. **2.** In French history, a supporter of the Bourbon or Orléans claims to the throne since 1793. **3.** In the American Revolution, a supporter of the king; Loyalist; Tory.

royal jelly *Entomol.* A white, highly concentrated food produced in the stomachs of worker honey bees. Larvae that eat it for only three days become workers, while the larvae that become queens eat it throughout their whole development.

roy·al·mast (roi′əl·mast′, -mäst′) *n. Naut.* The section of a mast next above the topgallant mast.

Royal Navy The naval forces of Great Britain. Abbr. *R.N.*

Royal Oak A city in SE Michigan; a suburb of Detroit; pop. 85,499.

royal palm Any of a genus (*Roystanea*) of feather palms native to tropical America, noted for their height and striking appearance, especially a Cuban species (*R. regia*).

royal purple 1. A very deep violet color verging toward blue. **2.** Originally, a rich crimson.

Royal Society A society founded about 1660 in London, concerned with the advancement of science.

royal tine The tine of an antler projecting away from the bez tine: also called *trez tine.* For illustration see ANTLER.

roy·al·ty (roi′əl·tē) *n. pl.* **·ties 1.** Royal rank, birth, or lineage; kingly nature or quality; kingliness; regal authority; sovereignty. **2.** A royal personage; also, royal persons collectively. **3.** A share of proceeds paid to a proprietor, author, or inventor, by those doing business under some right belonging to him. **4.** A tax or seigniorage paid to the crown on the produce of royal mines, or on gold and silver coinage. **5.** A royal possession or domain. **6.** Any domain or province. [< OF *roialte*]

Royce (rois), **Josiah,** 1855–1916, U.S. philosopher and psychologist.

R.P. 1. Reformed Presbyterian. 2. Regius Professor.
R.P.D. Doctor of Political Science (L *Rerum Politicarum Doctor*).
rpm or **r.p.m.** Revolutions per minute.
rps or **r.p.s.** Revolutions per second.
rpt. Report.
R.R. 1. Railroad: also **RR** 2. Right Reverend. 3. Rural route.
-rrhagia *combining form Pathol.* An abnormal or violent discharge or flow; an eruption: *metrorrhagia*: also *-rhage, -rhagia, -rhagy.* Also **-rrhage, -rrhagy.** Corresponding adjectives are formed with **-rrhagic.** [< Gk. < *rrhag-*, root of *rrhēgnynai* to burst]
-rrhaphy *combining form* A sewing together; a suture: *neurorrhaphy*, the suturing of a nerve. Also spelled *-rhaphy.* [< F *-rrhaphie* < Gk. *rhaptein* to sew together]
-rrhea *combining form Pathol.* An abnormal or excessive flow or discharge: *diarrhea*: also spelled *-rhea, -rhoea.* Also **-rrhoea.** [< Gk. *-rrhoia* < *rheein* to flow]
RR Ly·rae variable (lī′rē) *Astron.* A Cepheid variable with a very short period, from 1½ to 29 hours.
R.S.A. or **RSA** Republic of South Africa.
R.S.F.S.R. or **RSFSR** Russian Soviet Federated Socialist Republic (Russian *Rossiyskaya Sovetskaya Federativnaya Sotsialisticheskaya Respublika*).
RSV or **R.S.V.** Revised Standard Version (of the Bible).
R.S.V.P. or **r.s.v.p.** Répondez s'il vous plaît.
rt. Right.
r.t. or **rt** Right tackle.
Rt. Hon. Right Honorable.
Rt. Rev. Right Reverend.
Ru *Chem.* Ruthenium.
Ru·an·da (rōō-än′də) See RWANDA.
Ru·an·da-U·run·di (rōō-än′də-ōō-rōōn′dē) A former UN Trust Territory in central Africa, administered by Belgium. See BURUNDI, RWANDA.
rub (rub) *v.* **rubbed, rub·bing** *v.t.* **1.** To move or pass over the surface of with pressure and friction. **2.** To cause (something) to move or pass with friction; scrape; grate. **3.** To cause to become frayed, worn, or sore from friction: This collar *rubs* my neck. **4.** To clean, shine, burnish, etc., by means of pressure and friction, or by means of a substance so applied. **5.** To apply or spread with pressure and friction: to *rub* polish on a table. **6.** To force by rubbing: with *in* or *into*: to *rub* oil into wood. **7.** To remove or erase by friction: with *off* or *out.* — *v.i.* **8.** To move along a surface with friction; scrape. **9.** To exert pressure and friction. **10.** To become frayed, worn, or sore from friction; chafe. **11.** To undergo rubbing or removal by rubbing: with *off, out*, etc. — **to rub it in** *Slang* To harp on someone's errors, faults, etc. — **to rub out** *Slang* To kill. — **to rub the wrong way** *Slang* To irritate; annoy. — *n.* **1.** A subjection to frictional pressure; rubbing: Give it a *rub.* **2.** That which renders progress difficult; a hindrance or a doubt: There's the *rub.* **3.** Something that rubs or is rough to the feelings; a sarcasm. **4.** A roughness or unevenness of surface, quality, or character. [ME *rubben*, prob. < LG]
rub·a·boo (rub′ə-bōō) *n. Canadian* Soup made of pemmican. Also **rub′ba·boo.**
ru·bái·yát (rōō′bī-yät, -bē-) *n.pl.* In Persian poetry, four-lined stanzas; quatrains. — **The Rubáiyát** A poem by Omar Khayyám and an English translation of it by Edward FitzGerald. [< Arabic *rubā'iyāt*, pl. of *rubā'iyah* quatrain, fem. of *rubā'i* fourfold < *rubā* four]
Rub al Kha·li (rōōb′ äl khä′lē) The desert region of southern Arabia; 250,000 sq. mi.: also *Empty Quarter, Ar Rimal.*
ru·basse (rōō-bas′, -bäs′) *n.* A crystalline variety of quartz stained a ruby red by spangles of hematite. Also **ru·bace′.** [< F *rubace* < *rubi.* See RUBY.]
ru·ba·to (rōō-bä′tō) *Music adj.* Denoting the lengthening of one note at the expense of another. — *n. pl.* **·tos** A rubato modification. — *adv.* In a rubato manner. [< Ital., robbed]
rub·ber¹ (rub′ər) *n.* **1.** A resinous elastic material obtained by coagulating the milky latex of certain tropical plants, especially the tree *Hevea brasiliensis.* When purified, crude rubber is a white polymerized isoprene, that may be treated with various vulcanizing agents, fillers, and pigments and molded into the desired form: also called *India rubber.* **2.** Anything used for rubbing, erasing, polishing, etc. **3.** An article made of rubber. **4.** In baseball, the pitcher's plate. **5.** *Slang* A condom. **6.** One who or that which rubs. — *adj.* Made of rubber. [< RUB]
rub·ber² (rub′ər) *n.* In bridge, whist, and other card games, a series of two or three games terminated when one side has won two games; also, the odd game that breaks a tie between the players. Abbr. *r.* [Origin unknown]
rubber cement An adhesive composed of unvulcanized rubber and a solvent.
rubber check *U.S. Slang* A check returned by a bank as worthless; a check that bounces.

rub·ber·ize (rub′ər-īz) *v.t.* **·ized, ·iz·ing** To coat, impregnate, or cover, as silk, with a preparation of rubber.
rub·ber·neck (rub′ər-nek′) *U.S. Slang n.* One who cranes his neck in order to see something; a sightseer; tourist. — *v.i.* To stretch or crane one's neck; gape.
rubber plant 1. Any of several plants yielding rubber. **2.** An East Indian tree (*Ficus elastica*) of the mulberry family, having large, glossy, leathery leaves, much cultivated as a house plant.
rub·ber-stamp (rub′ər·stamp′) *v.t.* **1.** To endorse, initial, or approve with the mark made by a rubber stamping device. **2.** *Informal* To pass or approve as a matter of course or routine.
rub·ber·y (rub′ər-ē) *adj.* Resembling rubber, as in elasticity; tough.
rub·bish (rub′ish) *n.* **1.** Waste refuse, or broken matter; trash. **2.** Nonsense; rot. [ME *rubbous, robys*; origin uncertain]
rub·bish·y (rub′ish-ē) *adj.* Without value; worthless.
rub·ble (rub′əl; *for def. 3, also* rōō′bəl) *n.* **1.** Rough, irregular pieces of broken stone. **2.** The debris to which buildings of brick, stone, etc., are reduced by violent actions, as by earthquakes or bombings. **3.** In quarrying, the weathered or friable surface layer of rock. **4.** Rough pieces of stone for use in construction, especially in residences; also, masonry composed of such pieces. [Origin uncertain. Prob. akin to RUBBISH.] — **rub′bly** *adj.*
rub·ble-work (rub′əl-wûrk′) *n.* Masonry composed of irregular or broken stone.
rub·down (rub′doun′) *n.* A type of massage.
rube (rōōb) *n. Slang* A farmer; rustic. [Abbreviation of *Reuben*, a personal name]
ru·be·fa·cient (rōō′bə-fā′shənt) *adj.* Causing redness, as of the skin. — *n.* A medicament for producing irritation of the skin. [< L *rubefaciens, -entis* < *rubefacere* to redden < *rubeus* red + *facere* to make] — **ru·be·fa′cience** *n.* **ru′be·fac′tion** (-fak′shən) *n.*
ru·bel·la (rōō-bel′ə) *n. Pathol.* German measles. [< NL, neut. pl. of L *rubellus* reddish, dim. of *ruber* red]
ru·bel·lite (rōō′bə-līt) *n.* A red, usually transparent, tourmaline, used as a gem. [< L *rubellus.* See RUBELLA.]
Ru·bens (rōō′bənz, *Flemish* rü′bəns), **Peter Paul**, 1577–1640, Flemish painter.
ru·be·o·la (rōō-bē′ə-lə) *n. Pathol.* **1.** Measles (def. 1). **2.** German measles. [< NL, neut. pl. dim. of L *rubeus* red] — **ru·be′o·lar** *adj.*
ru·bes·cent (rōō-bes′ənt) *adj.* Becoming red; reddening. [< L *rubescens, -entis*, ppr. of *rubescere* to grow red, inceptive of *rubere* < *rubeus* red] — **ru·bes′cence** *n.*
ru·bi·a·ceous (rōō′bē-ā′shəs) *adj. Bot.* Belonging or pertaining to the madder family of plants. [< NL *Rubiaceae* < L *rubia* madder]
Ru·bi·con (rōō′bi-kon) A river in north central Italy, flowing 15 miles NE to the Adriatic: *Italian* **Ru·bi·co·ne** (rōō-bē-cô′nä). It formed the boundary separating Caesar's province of Gaul from Italy, and by crossing it under arms in 49 B.C. he committed himself to a civil war with Pompey. — **to cross the Rubicon** To be committed definitely to some course of action; make an irrevocable move.
ru·bi·cund (rōō′bə-kənd) *adj.* Red, or inclined to redness; rosy. [< L *rubicundus* red] — **ru′bi·cun′di·ty** *n.*
ru·bid·i·um (rōō-bid′ē-əm) *n.* A soft, rare, silvery white, metallic element (symbol Rb) resembling potassium. See ELEMENT. [< NL < L *rubidus* red]
ru·big·i·nous (rōō-bij′ə-nəs) *adj.* Having a rusty or brownish red color: rubiginous plants. Also **ru·big′i·nose** (-nōs). [< LL *rubiginosus* < L *rubigo, rubiginis* rust]
ru·bi·go (rōō-bī′gō, -bē′-) *n.* Red iron oxide, used as a polishing powder and pigment. [< L, rust]
Ru·bin·stein (rōō′bin-stīn), **Anton Gregor**, 1829–94, Russian pianist and composer. — **Artur**, born 1886, U.S. pianist born in Poland.
ru·bi·ous (rōō′bē-əs) *adj.* Red; ruby-colored. [< RUBY]
ru·ble (rōō′bəl) *n.* **1.** A standard monetary unit of the U.S.S.R., equivalent to 100 kopecks: also spelled *rouble.* **2.** Formerly, a Russian silver coin of this denomination. Abbr. *r, r.*
ru·bric (rōō′brik) *n.* **1.** A part of an early manuscript or a book that appears in red or in some distinctive type, used to indicate initial letters, caption words, headings, etc. **2.** The heading or title of a statute or of a section in a code of law, formerly written in red. **3.** *Eccl.* A direction or rule printed in devotional or liturgical office, as in a prayer book, missal, or breviary; also, such rules collectively. **4.** A division, group, or category. **5.** The color red. **6.** *Obs.* Red ochre or chalk; reddle. **7.** Any direction or rule of conduct. **8.** A distinguishing flourish or mark after a person's signature. — *adj.* **1.** Red or reddish. **2.** Written or printed in red. [< F *rubrique* or < L *rubrica* red earth < *ruber* red] — **ru′bri·cal** *adj.* — **ru′bri·cal·ly** *adv.*
ru·bri·cate (rōō′brə-kāt) *v.t.* **·cat·ed, ·cat·ing 1.** To mark

or tint with red; illuminate with red, as a book. **2.** To furnish with a rubric or rubrics; arrange in permanent form. — *adj.* Marked, written, or printed in red. [< L *rubricatus,* pp. of *rubricare* to redden < *rubrica.* See RUBRIC.] — **ru′bri·ca′tion** *n.* — **ru′bri·ca′tor** *n.*

ru·bri·cian (rōo·brish′ən) *n.* One versed in the knowledge of rubrics.

ru·by (rōo′bē) *n. pl.* **·bies 1.** A translucent, deep purplish red variety of corundum, highly valued as a gemstone: also called *Oriental ruby.* **2.** A rich red color like that of a ruby. **3.** Something like a ruby in color, as red wine or a carbuncle. **4.** Something made of a ruby; especially, in watchmaking, a bearing or roller made of a ruby or similar material. **5.** In England, a size of type (5½ points) equivalent to agate in the United States. — *adj.* Pertaining to or like a ruby; being of a rich crimson: *ruby* lips. — *v.t.* **·bied, ·by·ing** To tint with the color of a ruby; redden. [< OF *rubi,* ult. < L *rubeus* red]

ru·by-crowned kinglet (rōo′bē·kround′) See under KINGLET.

ruby spinel See under SPINEL.

ru·by-throat·ed hummingbird (rōo′bē·thrō′tid) See under HUMMINGBIRD.

ru·cer·vine (rōo·sûr′vēn, -vin) *adj.* **1.** Of or pertaining to a genus (*Rucervus*) of large deer native in SE Asia. **2.** Denoting the antlers characteristic of such deer. For illustration see ANTLER. [< NL *Rucervus,* name of the genus]

ruche (rōosh) *n.* A quilted or ruffled strip of fine fabric, worn about the neck or wrists of a woman's costume: also spelled *rouche.* [< F, beehive, frill < Med.L *rusca* tree bark, ? of Celtic origin]

ruch·ing (rōo′shing) *n.* Material for ruches; ruches collectively.

ruck¹ (ruk) *n.* **1.** The common run; a crowd. **2.** Trash; rubbish. [ME < Scand. Cf. Norw. *ruka* heap, crowd.]

ruck² (ruk) *v.t. & v.i.* **1.** To wrinkle, rumple, crease, etc. **2.** To annoy; ruffle: usually with *up.* — *n.* A wrinkle, crease, or ridge, as in paper. [< ON *hrukka* wrinkle]

ruck·sack (ruk′sak′, rŏok′-) *n.* A canvas knapsack. [< G < *rucken,* var. of *rücken* back + *sack* sack]

ruck·us (ruk′əs) *n. U.S. Slang* An uproar; commotion; rumpus. [Prob. blend of RUMPUS and RUCTION]

ruc·tion (ruk′shən) *n. Informal* A riotous outbreak; quarrel; uproar. [Prob. alter. of INSURRECTION]

ruc·tious (ruk′shəs) *adj. Slang* Difficult; quarrelsome. [< RUCTION]

rud·beck·i·a (rud·bek′ē·ə) *n.* Any of a genus (*Rudbeckia*) of North American herbs of the composite family, having showy yellow heads; especially, the black-eyed Susan: also called *coneflower.* [after Olaus *Rudbeck,* 1630–1702, Swedish botanist]

rudd (rud) *n.* A European fresh-water cyprinoid fish (*Scardinius erythrophthalmus*), olive brown with red fins: also called *redeye.* [? < OE *rudu* red color]

rud·der (rud′ər) *n.* **1.** *Naut.* A broad, flat, movable device hinged vertically at the stern of a vessel to direct its course. **2.** Anything that guides or directs a course. **3.** *Aeron.* A hinged or pivoted surface, used to control the position of an aircraft about its vertical axis. [OE *rōthor* oar, scull] — **rud′der·less** *adj.*

rudder bar *Aeron.* A foot-operated rod in some airplanes by which the pilot controls the rudder.

rud·der·head (rud′ər·hed′) *n. Naut.* The extension of the rudderstock to which the tiller is attached.

rud·der·stock (rud′ər·stok′) *n.* The vertical shaft to which the rudder of a ship or boat is attached, having at its upper portion a yoke (**rudder crosshead**) or tiller by which it may be turned. Also **rud′der·post′.**

RUDDERS
A Sailboat. *B* Motor-boat. *r* Rudder. *s* Screw.

rud·dle (rud′l) *n.* A variety of red ocherous iron ore; reddle. — *v.t.* **·dled, ·dling** To color or stain with red ocher. Also spelled *raddle.* [OE *rudu* red color]

rud·dle·man (rud′l·mən) *n. pl.* **·men** (-mən) A reddleman (which see).

rud·dock (rud′ək) *n.* The European robin (*Erithacus rubicola*). [OE *rudduc* robin]

rud·dy (rud′ē) *adj.* **·di·er, ·di·est 1.** Tinged with red. **2.** Having a healthy glow; rosy: a *ruddy* complexion. **3.** *Brit. Slang* Bloody: a euphemism. [OE *rudig*] — **rud′di·ly** *adv.* — **rud′di·ness** *n.*

ruddy duck A small North American duck (*Oxyura jamaicensis rubida*) having stiffened tail feathers and, in the adult male, a bright chestnut-colored body: also called *blatherskite, paddywhack, pintail.*

rude (rōod) *adj.* **rud·er, rud·est 1.** Offensively blunt or uncivil; rough or abrupt; impudent. **2.** Characterized by lack of polish or refinement; uncultivated; uncouth. **3.** Unskillfully made or done; lacking in skill or training; crude; rough: *rude* workmanship. **4.** Characterized by robust vigor; strong: *rude* health. **5.** Barbarous; savage. **6.** Humble;

lowly; rustic. **7.** Severe; harsh; tempestuous: a *rude* storm. [< OF, or < L *rudis* rough] — **rude′ly** *adv.* — **rude′ness** *n.*

rudes·by (rōodz′bē) *n. Archaic* An ill-bred boor.

ru·di·ment (rōo′də·mənt) *n.* **1.** A first principle, step, stage, or condition. **2.** That which is as yet undeveloped or only partially developed. **3.** *Biol.* **a** An organ or part in an early, embryonic, or incomplete stage of development. **b** An organ or part that has become aborted and functionless; a vestige. [< F < L *rudimentum* first attempt < *rudis* rough]

ru·di·men·ta·ry (rōo′də·men′tər·ē) *adj.* **1.** Pertaining to or of the nature of a rudiment or first principle; elementary: *rudimentary* knowledge. **2.** Being or remaining in an imperfectly developed state; vestigial; abortive. Also **ru′di·men′-tal.** — **ru′di·men′ta·ri·ly** *adv.* — **ru′di·men′ta·ri·ness** *n.*

Rudolf (rōo′dolf), **Lake** A lake in NW Kenya, extending into Ethiopia on the north; about 3,500 sq. mi.

Ru·dolf I (rōo′dolf), 1218–91, Holy Roman Emperor 1273–1291; founded the Hapsburg dynasty.

Rudolph II, 1552–1612, Holy Roman Emperor 1576–1612.

Rudolph of Hapsburg, 1858–89, crown prince of Austria; son of Franz Josef; committed suicide.

rue¹ (rōo) *v.* **rued, ru·ing** *v.t.* **1.** To feel sorrow or remorse for; regret extremely. — *v.i.* **2.** To feel sorrow or remorse; be regretful. — **Syn.** See MOURN. — *n.* **1.** Sorrowful remembrance; regret. **2.** *Scot.* Repentance. [OE *hrēowan* to be sorry] — **ru′er** *n.*

rue² (rōo) *n.* **1.** A small, bushy herb (*Ruta graveolens*) with bitter, acrid leaves, formerly much used in medicine, typical of a family (*Rutaceae*) that includes the citrus fruits. **2.** An infusion made from this plant. **3.** Any bitter draft. [< L *ruta* < Gk. *rhytē*]

rue anemone A delicate American woodland perennial (*Anemonella thalictroides*), having white flowers in the spring.

rue·ful (rōo′fəl) *adj.* **1.** Feeling or causing sorrow, regret, or pity; deplorable; sorrowful. **2.** Expressing sorrow or pity. — **rue′ful·ly** *adv.* — **rue′ful·ness** *n.*

ru·fes·cent (rōo·fes′ənt) *adj.* Inclining to reddishness; somewhat reddish or rufous. [< L *rufescens, -entis,* ppr. of *rufescere* to redden < *rufus* reddish] — **ru·fes′cence** *n.*

ruff¹ (ruf) *n.* **1.** A pleated, round, heavily starched collar popular in the 16th century. **2.** Ruffle¹ (defs. 1 and 2). **3.** A natural collar of projecting feathers or hair around the neck of a bird or mammal. **4.** An Old World sandpiper (*Philomachus pugnax*) of which the male in the breeding season has an erectile frill of elongated feathers about the neck. The female is called a *reeve.* [Short for RUFFLE¹]

ruff² (ruf) *n.* **1.** The playing of a trump upon another suit when one has no cards of that suit. **2.** An old card game, the predecessor of whist. — *v.t. & v.i.* To trump when unable to follow suit. [< OF *roffle, rouffle, ronfle,* ? aphetic alter. of *triomphe* triumph. Cf. Ital. *ronfa* a card game < *trionfo* triumph. Akin to TRUMP¹.]

ruff³ (ruf) *n.* A small perchlike fish (*Acerina cernua*) of European fresh waters. Also **ruffe.** [? < ROUGH]

ruffed (ruft) *adj.* Having a ruff, ruffle, or frill; ruffled.

ruffed grouse A North American grouse (*Bonasa umbellus*): called *partridge* in the northern and *pheasant* in the southern United States.

ruf·fi·an (ruf′ē·ən, ruf′yən) *n.* A lawless, brutal, cruel fellow; a tough. — *adj.* Lawlessly or recklessly brutal or cruel. [< OF *ruffian;* ult. origin uncertain] — **ruf′fi·an·ism** *n.* — **ruf′fi·an·ly** *adj.* — **Syn.** (noun) roughneck, rowdy, thug, desperado, gangster.

ruf·fle¹ (ruf′əl) *n.* **1.** A pleated strip; frill, as for trim or ornament. **2.** Anything resembling such a strip. Also called *ruff.* **3.** A temporary discomposure. **4.** A slight disturbance, as a ripple. — *v.* **·fled, ·fling** *v.t.* **1.** To disturb or destroy the smoothness or regularity of: The wind *ruffles* the lake. **2.** To draw into folds or pleats; gather. **3.** To furnish with ruffles. **4.** To erect (the feathers) in a ruff, as a bird when frightened. **5.** To disturb or irritate; upset. **6.** To riffle (the pages of a book). **7.** To shuffle (cards). — *v.i.* **8.** To be or become rumpled or disordered. **9.** To become disturbed or irritated. [< RUFFLE²]

RUFFED GROUSE
(Length of body to 19 inches; tail to 7 inches)

ruf·fle² (ruf′əl) *n.* A low, continuous beat of a drum, not as loud as a roll. — *v.t.* **·fled, ·fling** To beat a ruffle upon, as a drum. [Cf. *earlier ruff;* prob. imit.]

ruf·fle³ (ruf′əl) *v.i.* **·fled, ·fling** To act in a rough or turbulent manner; swagger; bluster. [Cf. LG *ruffelen* to crumple, curl and ON *hrufla* to scratch.] — **ruf′fler** *n.*

ru·fous (rōo′fəs) *adj.* Dull red; rust-colored. [< L *rufus* red]

rufous hummingbird See under HUMMINGBIRD.

rug¹ (rug) *n.* **1.** A heavy textile fabric, made in one piece, to cover a portion of a floor. **2.** A covering made from the skins of animals. **3.** *Chiefly Brit.* A heavy coverlet or lap robe. [< Scand. Cf. Norw. *rugga* coarse coverlet, *skinrugga* skin rug and ON *rögg* long, rough fleece.]

rug² (rug) *v.t.* **rugged, rug·ging** *Scot. & Brit. Dial.* To tug or tear roughly.

ru·ga (rōō′gə)   *n.*   *pl.* **·gae** (-jē) A fold, wrinkle, or crease. [< L]

ru·gate (rōō′gāt, -git)   *adj.* Covered with or having rugae; corrugated; wrinkled. [< L *rugatus*, pp. of *rugare* to wrinkle < *ruga* wrinkle]

Rug·by (rug′bē) A municipal borough in eastern Warwickshire, England: site of a boys' school founded in 1567; pop. 57,700 (est. 1969).

rugby football   **1.** *Usually cap. Brit.* A form of football played between two teams of fifteen men each, in which the ball is propelled toward the opponents' goal by kicking or carrying, but in which no player of the side in possession of the ball may be ahead of the ball while it is in play.   **2.** *Canadian* Football (def. 3).

rug·ged (rug′id)   *adj.*   **1.** Having a surface of abrupt inequalities; broken into irregular points or crags; steep and rocky; rough; uneven.   **2.** Shaggy; unkempt; disordered; ragged.   **3.** Rough in temper, character, or action; harsh; stern.   **4.** Having strongly marked features; wrinkled; frowning.   **5.** Lacking culture or refinement; rude.   **6.** Rough to the ear; grating.   **7.** Robust; sturdy; hale.   **8.** Tempestuous; stormy. [< Scand. Cf. Sw. *rugga* to roughen. Prob. akin to RUG[1].]   — **rug′ged·ly** *adv.*   — **rug′ged·ness** *n.*

ru·gose (rōō′gōs)   *adj.*   **1.** Covered with or full of wrinkles; rugate.   **2.** *Bot.* Having a rough or wrinkled surface, as some strongly veined leaves. Also **ru′gous** (-gəs). [< L *rugosus* < *ruga* wrinkle]   — **ru·gos·i·ty** (rōō·gos′ə·tē) *n.*

Ruhm·korff coil (rōōm′kôrf) *Electr.* An induction coil with a circuit breaker for use with direct and constant current. [after H. D. *Ruhmkorff*, 1803–77, German inventor]

Ruhr (rōōr)   **1.** A river of western West Germany, flowing 142 miles west to the Rhine.   **2.** The region south of which the Ruhr river flows, an industrial and coal-mining district; about 2000 sq. mi.; included in North Rhine–Westphalia, West Germany.

ru·in (rōō′in)   *n.*   **1.** Total destruction of value or usefulness.   **2.** Loss of honor, position, wealth, etc.; degradation.   **3.** *Often pl.* That which remains of something demolished, destroyed, or decayed.   **4.** A condition of desolation or destruction.   **5.** That which causes destruction, downfall, decay, or injury.   **6.** The act of falling down; collapse.   — *v.t.*   **1.** To bring to ruin; destroy; demolish.   **2.** To bring to bankruptcy or poverty.   **3.** To deprive of chastity; seduce.   — *v.i.*   **4.** To fall into ruin.   — **Syn.** See DEMOLISH. [< OF *ruine* < L *ruina* < *ruere* to fall]   — **ru′in·a·ble** *adj.*   — **ru′in·er** *n.*

ru·in·ate (rōō′in·āt)   *Rare v.t.* **·at·ed, ·at·ing** To ruin.   — *adj.* Ruined. [< Med.L *ruinatus*, pp. of *ruinare* to ruin < *ruina*. See RUIN.]

ru·in·a·tion (rōō′in·ā′shən)   *n.*   **1.** The act of ruining, or the state of being ruined.   **2.** Something that ruins.

ru·in·ous (rōō′in·əs)   *adj.*   **1.** Causing or tending to ruin.   **2.** Falling to ruin; decayed; dilapidated; ruined. [< OF *ruineux* < L *ruinosus*]   — **ru′in·ous·ly** *adv.*   — **ru′in·ous·ness** *n.*

Ruis·dael (rois′däl, *Du.* rœis′däl) See RUYSDAEL.

rule (rōōl)   *n.*   **1.** Controlling power, or its possession and exercise; government; dominion; authority.   **2.** A method or principle of action; common or regular course of procedure, or customary standard or form: I make early rising my *rule*.   **3.** An authoritative direction or enactment respecting the doing or method of doing something, as a regulation of a legislative body for the government of its own proceedings, or a regulation to be observed in playing a given game.   **4.** A regulation for the conduct of religious services or for the government of life; especially, the body of directions laid down by or for a religious order: the *rule* of St. Francis.   **5.** A prescribed form, method, or set of instructions for solving a given class of mathematical problems.   **6.** An established usage or law, fixing the form or use of words or the construction of sentences: a *rule* for forming the plural.   **7.** Something belonging to the ordinary course of events or condition of things: In some communities illiteracy is the *rule*.   **8.** Regular or proper method; propriety, as of conduct; regularity.   **9.** *Law* **a** A formal regulation prescribed by authority touching a certain matter: a *rule* of court. **b** A judicial decision on some motion or special application: a *rule* to show cause.   **10.** A straight-edged instrument for use in measuring, or as a guide in drawing lines, usually marked in inches, feet, etc.; a ruler.   **11.** *Printing* A strip of type-high metal for handling type or for printing a rule or line.   **12.** A ruled line.   — **as a rule** Ordinarily; usually.   — **rule of court** *Law* An order made by a court, as for regulating the practice of the court (**general rule**) or for sending a case before a referee (**special rule**).   — *v.* **ruled, rul·ing** *v.t.*   **1.** To have authority or control over; govern.   **2.** To influence greatly; dominate: Greed has *ruled* his life.   **3.** To decide or determine judicially or authoritatively.   **4.** To restrain; keep in check: *Rule* your temper.   **5.** To mark with straight, parallel lines.   **6.** To make (a straight line) with or as with a ruler.   — *v.i.*   **7.** To have authority or control; be in command.   **8.** To maintain a stand-

ard of rates: Prices *ruled* high.   **9.** To form and express a decision.   — **to rule out**   **1.** To dismiss from consideration: They *ruled out* a strike as impractical.   **2.** To preclude; prevent. [< OF *reule* < *regula* ruler, rule < *regere* to lead straight, direct. Doublet of RAIL[1].]   — **rul′a·ble** *adj.*

rule of three   *Math.* The rule for finding one of the four terms of a proportion when three terms are given. It states that the product of the second and third terms is equal to the product of the first and fourth terms of a proportion: sometimes called *proportion*.

rule of thumb   **1.** Measurement by the thumb.   **2.** Roughly practical rather than scientifically accurate measure.

rul·er (rōō′lər)   *n.*   **1.** One who rules or governs, as a sovereign.   **2.** A straight-edged strip for guiding a marking implement.   **3.** One who rules lines, as on paper.

rul·ing (rōō′ling)   *adj.* Exercising dominion; controlling; predominant.   — *n.*   **1.** The act of one who rules or governs.   **2.** A decision, as of a judge or presiding officer.   **3.** The act of making ruled lines, or the lines so made.

ruling elder   A presbyter (def. 3b).

rum[1] (rum)   *n.*   **1.** An alcoholic liquor distilled from fermented molasses or cane juice.   **2.** Any alcoholic liquor: demon *rum*. [Origin uncertain; ? short for obs. *rumbullion* rum, alter. of *Rambouillet*, town in France]

rum[2] (rum)   *adj. Brit. Slang* Queer; strange; peculiar. [? < Romany *rom* man]

Rum (rōōm)   The Arabic name for the BYZANTINE EMPIRE: also *Roum*.

Rum.   Rumania; Rumanian.

Ru·ma·ni·a (rōō·mā′nē·ə, -mān′yə)   A Republic in SE Europe; 91,671 sq. mi.; pop. 20,394,000 (est. 1970); capital, Bucharest: also *Romania*, *Roumania*. Rumanian *România*. See map of BLACK SEA.

Ru·ma·ni·an (rōō·mā′nē·ən, -mān′yən)   *adj.* Of Rumania, its people, or their language.   — *n.*   **1.** A native or inhabitant of Rumania.   **2.** The Romance language of the Rumanians. Also *Romanian*, *Roumanian*.

rum·ba (rum′bə, *Sp.* rōōm′bä)   *n.*   **1.** A dance having its origin among Cuban Negroes.   **2.** A modern ballroom dance based on this; also, music for or in the manner of such a dance. Also spelled *rhumba*. [< Am.Sp.]

rum·ble (rum′bəl)   *v.* **·bled, ·bling** *v.i.*   **1.** To make a low, heavy, rolling sound, as thunder.   **2.** To move or proceed with such a sound.   — *v.t.*   **3.** To cause to make a low, heavy, rolling sound.   **4.** To utter with such a sound.   **5.** To subject to the action of a tumbling box.   — *n.*   **1.** A continuous low, heavy, rolling sound; a muffled roar.   **2.** A tumbling box.   **3.** A seat or baggage compartment in the rear of a carriage.   **4.** A folding seat in the back of a coupé or roadster: in full **rumble seat**.   **5.** *U.S. Slang* A gang fight, usually involving a group of teen-agers. [ME *romblen*. Akin to MDu. *rommelen*.]   — **rum′bling·ly** *adv.*   — **rum′bly** *adj.*

rum·bler (rum′blər)   *n.*   **1.** One who or that which rumbles.   **2.** A tumbling box.

Ru·me·li·a (rōō·mē′lē·ə)   The possessions of the former Ottoman Empire in the Balkan Peninsula, including Macedonia, Thrace, and Albania: also *Roumelia*.

ru·men (rōō′men)   *n.*   *pl.* **ru·mi·na** (rōō′mə·nə)   **1.** The first stomach of a ruminant.   **2.** The cud of a ruminant. [< L *gullet*]

Rum·ford (rum′fərd), **Count**, 1753–1814, Benjamin Thompson, scientist, born in America, active in Germany, England, and France.

ru·mi·nant (rōō′mə·nənt)   *n.* One of a division or suborder (*Ruminantia*) of even-toed, cud-chewing ungulates, as the deer, antelope, sheep, goat, cow, bison, camel, giraffe, etc., having a stomach with four complete cavities, the rumen, reticulum, omasum, and abomasum.   — *adj.*   **1.** Chewing the cud.   **2.** Of or pertaining to the *Ruminantia*.   **3.** Meditative or contemplative; thoughtful; quiet. [< L *ruminans*, *-antis*, ppr. of *ruminare* to chew over < *rumen* gullet]

ru·mi·nate (rōō′mə·nāt)   *v.t. & v.i.* **·nat·ed, ·nat·ing**   **1.** To chew (food previously swallowed and regurgitated) over again; chew (the cud).   **2.** To meditate or reflect (upon); ponder. [< L *ruminatus*, pp. of *ruminare*. See RUMINANT.]   — **ru′mi·nat·ing·ly** *adv.*   — **ru′mi·na·tive** *adj.*   — **ru′mi·na′tive·ly** *adv.*   — **ru′mi·na′tor** *n.*

ru·mi·na·tion (rōō′mə·nā′shən)   *n.*   **1.** The act, process, or characteristic of chewing the cud.   **2.** The act of meditating; thoughtfulness.

rum·mage (rum′ij)   *v.* **·maged, ·mag·ing** *v.t.*   **1.** To search through (a place, box, etc.) by turning over and disarranging the contents; ransack.   **2.** To find or bring out by searching: with *out* or *up*.   — *v.i.*   **3.** To make a thorough search.   — *n.*   **1.** Any act of rummaging; especially, disarranging things by searching thoroughly.   **2.** An upheaval or stirring up; bustle.   **3.** A rummage sale. [< MF *arrumage* < *arrumer* to stow cargo < *rum* ship's hold < Gmc.]   — **rum′mag·er** *n.*

rummage sale   **1.** A sale of second-hand objects to obtain money for some charitable purpose.   **2.** A sale of unclaimed articles, or a sale for clearing out articles prior to restocking.

rum·mer (rum′ər) *n.* A glass or cup for drinking; especially, a tall stemless glass; also, its contents. [< Du. *roemer* < *roemen* to praise; from its use in drinking toasts]

rum·my[1] (rum′ē) *n.* A card game in which each player in turn draws a card and discards another card, the object being to combine or get rid of one's hand in sequences of three cards or more of the same suit. [? < Brit. slang *rummy, rum queer*]

rum·my[2] (rum′ē) *n. pl.* **·mies** *Slang* A drunkard. — *adj.* **·mi·er, ·mi·est** 1. Of or resembling rum: a *rummy* flavor. 2. Affected by rum; befuddled; drunk.

ru·mor (rōō′mər) *n.* 1. An unverified or unfounded report, story, etc., circulating from person to person. 2. Common gossip; hearsay. 3. *Archaic* A confused or tumultuous sound; loud murmur. 4. *Obs.* Fame, reputation. — *v.t.* To tell or spread as a rumor; noise about. Also *Brit.* **ru′mour.** [< OF < L]

rump (rump) *n.* 1. The rounded or fleshy upper part of the hind quarters of an animal. 2. The analogous region in man; the buttocks. 3. A cut of beef between the loin and the round. For illustration see MEAT. 4. A legislative group, representative body, etc., having only a remnant of its original membership, and therefore regarded as unauthoritative. 5. A last, often undesirable remnant. [ME *rumpe* < Scand.]

Rum·pel·stilts·kin (rum′pəl·stilt′skin, *Ger.* rōōm′pəl·shtilts′kin) In German folklore, a dwarf who saves the life of a girl who has married a king, by spinning for her a fabulous quantity of flax, demanding in return her first child. The dwarf releases her from her promise when she guesses his name. Also **Rum·pel·stilts·chen** (rōōm′pəl·shtilts′khən)

rum·ple (rum′pəl) *v.t. & v.i.* **·pled, ·pling** To form into creases or folds; wrinkle; ruffle. — *n.* 1. An irregular fold; untidy wrinkling. 2. The condition of being rumpled. [< MDu. *rumpelen*]

Rump Parliament See LONG PARLIAMENT under PARLIAMENT.

rum·pus (rum′pəs) *n. Informal* A row; wrangle; to-do. — **Syn.** See ROW[3]. [Origin uncertain]

rumpus room A room for games, informal gatherings, etc.

rum·run·ner (rum′run′ər) *n.* One who illicitly transports or smuggles alcoholic liquors across a border; also, a vessel employed in illegal liquor traffic.

run (run) *v.* **ran** (*Archaic* or *Dial.* **run**), **run, run·ning** *v.i.* 1. To move by rapid steps, faster than walking, in such a manner that both feet are off the ground for a portion of each step. 2. To move rapidly; go swiftly. 3. To flee; take flight. 4. To make a brief or rapid journey: We *ran* over to Staten Island. 5. To make regular trips; ply: This steamer *runs* between New York and Liverpool. 6. To take part in a race; also, to be a candidate or contestant: to *run* for dogcatcher. 7. To finish a race in a specified position: I *ran* a poor last. 8. To move or pass easily: The rope *runs* through the block. 9. To pass continuously and rapidly; elapse: The hours *run* by. 10. To proceed in direction or extent: This road *runs* north. 11. To move in or as in a stream; flow. 12. To become liquid and flow, as wax; also, to spread or mingle confusedly, as colors when wet. 13. To move or pass into a specified condition: to *run* into trouble; a ship that has *run* aground. 14. To climb or grow in long shoots, as vines. 15. To become torn by unraveling longitudinally, as a knitted fabric. 16. To give forth a discharge or flow; suppurate. 17. To leak. 18. To continue or proceed without restraint: The conversation *ran* on and on. 19. To be in operation; be operative; work: Will the engine *run*? 20. To continue in existence or effect; extend in time: Genius *runs* in her family. 21. To be reported or expressed: The story *runs* as follows. 22. To migrate, as salmon from the sea to spawn. 23. To occur or return, as to the mind: An idea *ran* through his head; also, to occur with specified variation of size, quality, etc.: The corn is *running* small this year. 24. To incline; tend: Her taste *runs* to luxuries. 25. To be performed or repeated in continuous succession: The play *ran* for forty nights. 26. To make a rapid succession of demands for payment, as on a bank. 27. To continue unexpired or unpaid, as a debt; become payable. — *v.t.* 28. To go along by running, as a route, course, or path. 29. To make one's way over, through, or past: to *run* rapids. 30. To perform or accomplish by or as by running: to *run* a race or an errand. 31. To compete against in or as in a race. 32. To enter (a horse, etc.) for a race. 33. To present and support as a candidate. 34. To hunt or chase, as game. 35. To bring to a specified condition by or as by running: to *run* oneself out of breath. 36. To drive or force: with *out of, off, into, through*, etc. 37. To cause (a vessel) to move rapidly or freely: They *ran* the ship into port. 38. To move (the eye, hand, etc.) quickly or lightly: He *ran* his hand over the table. 39. To cause to move, slide, etc., as into a specified position: to *run* up a flag. 40. To cause to go or ply: to *run* a train between New York and Washington. 41. To transport or convey in a vessel or vehicle. 42. To smuggle. 43. To cause to flow: to *run* water into a pot. 44. To give forth a flow of; emit: Her eyes *ran* tears. 45. To mold, as from melted metal; found. 46. To sew or stitch in a continuous line. 47. To maintain or control the motion or operation of, as a machine.

48. To direct or control; manage; oversee. 49. To allow to continue or mount up, as a bill: often with *up*. 50. To become liable to; incur: to *run* a risk. 51. In games, to make (a number of points, strokes, etc.) successively. 52. To publish in a magazine or newspaper: to *run* an ad. 53. To mark, set down, or trace, as a boundary line. 54. To suffer from (a fever, etc.). — **to run across** To meet by chance. — **to run down** 1. To pursue and overtake, as a fugitive. 2. To strike down while moving. 3. To exhaust, damage, lessen in worth, vigor, etc., as by abuse or overwork. 4. To speak of disparagingly; decry. — **to run in** 1. To insert; include. 2. *Printing* To print without a paragraph or break. 3. *Slang* To arrest and place in confinement. 4. To adapt or accustom to use by an initial period of operation, as an engine. — **to run in** 1. To meet by chance. 2. To collide with. — **to run off** 1. To produce on a typewriter, printing press, etc. 2. To decide (a tied race, game, etc.) by the outcome of another, subsequent race, game, etc. 3. To flee or escape; elope. — **to run out** To come to an end; be exhausted, as supplies. — **to run out of** To exhaust one's supply of. — **to run over** 1. To ride or drive over; run down. 2. To overflow. 3. To go over or examine hastily or quickly; rehearse. — **to run through** 1. To spend wastefully; squander. 2. To stab or pierce. 3. To run over (def. 3). — *n.* 1. An act or instance of running or going rapidly. 2. The movement or gait of running: to break into a *run*. 3. A distance covered by running. 4. A distance traveled between two points, as by a train or vessel: the *run* from New York to Albany. 5. A rapid journey; short, quick trip. 6. A course or route followed, as in accomplishing a purpose or reaching a destination. 7. The privilege of free use or access: to have the *run* of the place. 8. A series, succession, or sequence, as of playing cards in consecutive order, successful shots in billiards, etc. 9. A continuous spell of a specified condition: a *run* of luck. 10. A continuous period of consecutive performances, as of a theatrical production. 11. A trend or tendency: the *run* of the market. 12. A broadly inclusive category, type, or class: the general *run* of readers. 13. A period of continuous operation, as of a machine or factory. 14. The output during such a period. 15. A continuous length or extent of something: a *run* of pipe. 16. A lengthwise rip in knitted fabric, caused by broken threads or dropped stitches. 17. Characteristic direction, tendency, or linear form: the *run* of the grain in wood. 18. Flowing movement, as of a stream or liquid. 19. The period of such flow. 20. A swift stream or current. 21. Mass migration or movement of animals, especially of fish to their spawning grounds. 22. A trail, burrow, or terrain frequented by a specific kind of animal. 23. An enclosure for animals or poultry, allowing considerable freedom of action. 24. A steep course or runway, as for skiing or sledding. 25. An unusually large number of demands for payment, as on a bank. 26. Any great sustained demand, as for a commodity. 27. *Music* A rapid succession of tones; roulade. 28. In baseball, the scoring of a point by a player's making a complete circuit of the bases; also, a point so scored. Abbr. *r, r.* 29. In football, the ball carrier's attempt to run through or around the line of the opposing team: an end *run*. 30. In cricket, the scoring of a point by both batsmen successfully reaching opposite popping creases after a hit. 31. *Naut.* The after part of a ship's bottom where it narrows off from the floor timbers to the sternpost. 32. *Mining* A vein of ore or rock. 33. An approach to a target made by a bombing plane: also *bomb run.* — **a run for one's money** A successful or satisfactory instance of activity, especially in competition. — **in the long run** As the ultimate outcome of any train of circumstances. — **on the run** 1. Almost without pausing while doing something else; hastily: to eat *on the run*. 2. In full retreat. 3. While running. — *adj.* 1. Made liquid; melted. 2. Made by a process of melting and casting or molding: *run* metal; *run* butter. 3. Extracted or drained: *run* honey. 4. Smuggled; contraband: *run* liquor. [OE *rinnan*]

run·a·bout (run′ə·bout′) *n.* 1. A small, open automobile. 2. A light, open wagon. 3. A small motorboat.

run·a·gate (run′ə·gāt) *n. Archaic* 1. A deserter; renegade. 2. A vagabond; homeless wanderer. [Alter. of RENEGADE; infl. by *run*, dial. *agate* on the way]

run·a·round (run′ə·round′) *n.* 1. *Slang* Artful deception; evasion. 2. *Printing* Type set narrower than the body of the text, as around illustrations.

run·a·way (run′ə·wā′) *adj.* 1. Escaping or escaped from restraint or control; fugitive. 2. Brought about by running away: a *runaway* marriage. 3. Easily won: said of a horse race. 4. Decisive; one-sided. 5. Of, pertaining to, or characterized by a rapid price rise. — *n.* 1. One who or that which runs away or flees; also, a horse of which the driver has lost control. 2. An act of running away. 3. *Informal* An easily won victory, as in a race.

run·ci·ble spoon (run′sə·bəl) A fork with three broad tines, one with a sharp edge. [< RUNC(INATE) + -IBLE]

run·ci·nate (run′sə·nāt, -nit) *adj. Bot.* Saw-toothed, with the incisions or teeth inclined backward: said of leaves. [< L *runcinatus*, pp. of *runcinare* to plane off < *runcina* plane]

run·dle (run′dəl) *n.* 1. A rung, as of a ladder. 2. Something that rotates about an axis, as the drum of a capstan. [Var. of ROUNDEL]

rund·let (rund/lit) *n.* A small barrel, or the measure of wine it contains, about 18 wine gallons: also *runlet.* [< OF *rondelet*, dim. of *rondelle* small barrel]

run·down (run/doun/) *n.* 1. A summary; resumé. 2. In baseball, a play in which a base runner is put out when trapped between two bases.

run-down (run/doun/) *adj.* 1. Debilitated; physically weak; tired out. 2. Dilapidated; shabby. 3. Stopped because not wound: said of a timepiece.

Rund·stedt (rōont/shtet), **Karl Rudolf Gerd von**, 1875–1953, German field marshal in World War II.

rune (rōōn) *n.* 1. Any of the characters in the runic alphabet. 2. A Finnish poem or one of its cantos. 3. *pl.* Old Norse lore expressed in or as in runes. 4. Rhymes or poetry in general. 5. Any obscure or mystic song, poem, verse, or saying. [< OE and ON *rūn* mystery, secret conversation] — **ru/nic** *adj.*

RUNES
(Tomb inscription, Sweden, 11th century)

Ru·ne·berg (rōō/nə·ber/y'), **Johan Ludvig**, 1804–77, Finnish poet.

rung[1] (rung) *n.* 1. A round crosspiece forming one of the steps of a ladder. 2. A crosspiece used in chairs to strengthen or support the legs or back. 3. The spoke of a wheel. 4. *Naut.* a One of the handles on the rim of a ship's tiller. b A floor timber of a ship. 5. *Scot. & Brit. Dial.* A heavy club or staff; cudgel. [OE *hrung* staff, pole]

rung[2] (rung) Past participle of RING[2].

runic alphabet An old Germanic alphabet, probably originating in both the Latin and Greek, consisting originally of 24 characters, or runes, later reduced to 16 in Scandinavian writings, the earliest inscriptions of which are of the second or third century A.D.: also called *futhark.*

run-in (*n.* run/in/; *adj.* run/in/) *n.* 1. A quarrel; bicker. 2. *Printing* Inserted or added matter. — *adj. Printing* Inserted or added.

Run·jeet Singh (run/jēt sin/hə) See RANJIT SINGH.

run·kle (rung/kəl) *Scot. n.* A wrinkle. — *v.t. & v.i.* **·kled, ·kling** To wrinkle. [< Scand.]

run·let[1] (run/lit) *n.* A little stream; rivulet; runnel.

run·let[2] (run/lit) See RUNDLET.

run·nel (run/əl) *n.* A rivulet. [OE *rynel* < *rinnan* to run]

run·ner (run/ər) *n.* 1. One who or that which runs; especially, one who runs a race; also, a fugitive or deserter. 2. One who operates or manages anything; especially, the driver of a locomotive. 3. One who runs errands or goes about on any kind of business; especially, one who drums up or solicits patronage or business, as for a hotel. 4. That part on which an object runs or slides: the *runner* of a skate. 5. *Mech.* A device to assist sliding motion. 6. Any of various carangoid fishes of warm and temperate seas; especially, the **blue runner** (*Caranx crysos*) of the Atlantic from Brazil to Cape Cod. 7. *Bot.* a A slender, procumbent stem rooting at the end and nodes, as in the strawberry; also, sometimes, the plant itself. b Any of various twining plants: the scarlet *runner.* 8. A smuggler. 9. A long, narrow rug or carpeting, used in hallways, etc. 10. A narrow strip of cloth, usually of fine quality, used on tables, dressers, etc.

run·ner-up (run/ər·up/) *n.* A contestant or team finishing in second place.

run·ning (run/ing) *adj.* 1. Moving or going rapidly. 2. Inclined or trained to run rather than to pace or trot: said of horses. 3. Creeping or clinging, as a plant. 4. Flowing: *running* water. 5. Slipping or untying easily: a *running* knot. 6. Moving or pulling easily and freely: a *running* rope. 7. Being or able to be in operation: a *running* engine. 8. Cursive: a *running* handwriting. 9. Liquid or fluid. 10. Discharging, as pus from a sore. 11. In a straight line: said of measurements: three feet *running.* 12. Current, as an account. 13. Continuous; repeated: a *running* design. 14. Kept up continuously. 15. Passing; cursory: a *running* glance. 16. Following one another without intermission; successive: He talked three hours *running.* 17. Accomplished or performed with a run. 18. Of or pertaining to a trip or run: the train's *running* time. — *n.* 1. The act of one who or that which runs. 2. That which runs or flows. 3. The amount or quantity that runs. 4. Ability or power to run. 5. Competition or race: He is out of the *running.*

running board A footboard on the side of a locomotive, street car, automobile, etc.

running gear 1. *Mech.* The wheels and axles of any vehicle and their immediate attachments, as distinguished from the body that they support. 2. *Naut.* The movable ropes and wires on a boat or ship by which sails, etc., are raised, lowered, and trimmed.

running hand Writing done with a continuous easy motion without lifting the pen from the paper between letters, and usually having the letters slanted forward.

running knot A knot made so as to slip along a noose and tighten when pulled upon: also called *slipknot.*

running light 1. *Naut.* A sidelight (which see). 2. *Aeron.* A navigation light (which see).

running mate 1. A horse that is teammate for another; also, a horse entered to set the pace for another entered to run in a horse race. 2. The candidate for the lesser of two offices closely linked by constitutional provisions, as the vice-presidency with the presidency.

running title *Printing* A title or headline repeated at the head of every page or every other page throughout a book or chapter. Also **running head.**

Run·ny·mede (run/i·mēd) A meadow in Surrey, England, on the Thames west of London, where King John is said to have met his barons to sign the Magna Carta.

run·off (run/ôf/, -of/) *n.* 1. The part of the rainfall that is not absorbed directly by the soil but is drained off in rills or streams. 2. A special contest held to break a tie.

run-of-the-mill (run/əv·thə·mil/) *adj.* Not special in any way; average; ordinary. Also **run-of-the-mine.**

run-on (run/on/, -ôn/) *n. Printing* Added matter.

run·out (run/out/) *n.* That portion of a motion-picture film immediately following the last frame of the picture itself.

run·o·ver (run/ō·vər) *adj.* 1. Extended beyond what is normal or designated. 2. Worn down, as the heels of shoes.

runt (runt) *n.* 1. An unusually small, weak, or stunted animal or plant. 2. A small person: often a contemptuous term. [< Scot. *runt* old cow. Akin to MDu. *runt* cow] — **runt·y** (run/tē) *adj.* **runt·i·er, runt·i·est** Dwarfish; stunted. — **runt/i·ness** *n.*

run·way (run/wā/) *n.* 1. A way or path over or through which something runs. 2. A pathway extending from a stage into the audience, used for certain types of theatrical entertainment. 3. The channel or bed of a stream. 4. In lumbering, the incline down which logs are slid; a chute. 5. Any track specially laid for wheeled vehicles. 6. *Aeron.* An improved or unimproved roadlike surface, used for the take-off and landing of aircraft: compare LANDING STRIP.

Run·yon (run/yən), (**Alfred**) **Damon**, 1884–1946, U.S. journalist and writer.

ru·pee (rōō·pē/) *n.* 1. The monetary unit of India and Pakistan, equivalent to 100 naye paise. 2. The monetary unit of Mauritius (equivalent to 100 cents), of Nepal (equivalent to 100 paise), of the Republic of Maldives (equivalent to 100 laris), of Seychelles (equivalent to 100 cents), and of Sri Lanka (equivalent to 100 cents). Abbr. *r, R, re., Re.* [< Hind. *rupīya* < Skt. *rūpya* coined silver < *rupya* shape]

Ru·pert (rōō/pərt), **Prince**, 1619–82, duke of Bavaria, English Royalist general born in Prague.

ru·pi·ah (rōō·pē/ä) *n.* The standard monetary unit of Indonesia, equivalent to 100 sen.

rup·ture (rup/chər) *n.* 1. The act of breaking apart, or the state of being broken apart. 2. *Pathol.* Hernia. 3. Breach of friendship or concord between individuals or nations. — *v.t. & v.i.* **·tured, ·tur·ing** 1. To break apart; separate into parts. 2. To affect with or suffer a rupture. [< Med.L *ruptura* < *rumpere* to break] — **rup/tur·a·ble** *adj.*

ru·ral (rōōr/əl) *adj.* 1. Of or pertaining to the country as distinguished from the city or the town; rustic. 2. Of or pertaining to farming or agriculture. [< MF < L *ruralis* < *rus, ruris* country] — **ru/ral·ism** *n.* — **ru/ral·ist** *n.* — **ru/ral·ly** *adv.*

— **Syn.** 1. *Rural, rustic, pastoral,* and *bucolic* refer to life in the open country as contrasted with that in urban districts. *Rural* means of the country, without further implication: a *rural* community. *Rustic* contrasts the simplicity and rudeness of the country with the sophistication and refinement of the town: the *rustic* outlook of the farmer. *Pastoral*, referring originally to the life of a shepherd, dwells on the idealized beauty and serenity of country life: the *pastoral* paintings of Watteau. *Bucolic*, originally closely akin to *pastoral*, now chiefly emphasizes the provincial attitude of the untutored countryman: *bucolic* tastes. — **Ant.** urban.

rural dean A dean (def. 4).

rural free delivery A government service of house-to-house free mail delivery in rural districts: in addresses abbreviated *RFD, R.F.D.* Often shortened to *R.D.*

ru·ral·i·ty (rōō·ral/ə·tē) *n. pl.* **·ties** 1. The condition or quality of being rural. 2. A rural characteristic or peculiarity.

ru·ral·ize (rōōr/əl·īz) *v.* **·ized, ·iz·ing** *v.t.* 1. To make rural. — *v.i.* 2. To go into or live in the country; rusticate. — **ru/ral·i·za/tion** *n.*

rural route A rural mail route. Abbr. *R.R.*

Ru·rik (rōō/rik), died 879, Viking conqueror; reputed founder of the Russian monarchy, the **House of Rurik,** that lasted from 862? to 1598.

ruse (rōōz) *n.* An action intended to mislead or deceive; a stratagem; trick. — **Syn.** See ARTIFICE. [< MF < *ruser* to turn aside. See RUSH¹.]

rush¹ (rush) *v.i.* **1.** To move or go swiftly or with violence. **2.** To make an attack; charge: with *on* or *upon*. **3.** To proceed recklessly or rashly; plunge: with *in* or *into*. **4.** To come, surge, flow, etc., suddenly. — *v.t.* **5.** To drive or push with haste or violence; hurry. **6.** To do or perform hastily or hurriedly: to *rush* one's work. **7.** To make a sudden assault upon; also, to capture by such an assault. **8.** *Slang* To seek the favor of with assiduous attentions. **9.** In football, to move (the ball) toward the goal of the other team by a rush or rushes. **10.** *U.S.* To consider for membership in a fraternity or sorority, usually by entertaining. — *n.* **1.** The act of rushing; a sudden turbulent movement, drive, or onset. **2.** A state of pressed or impatient activity; hurry. **3.** A sudden surge, flow, or outpouring. **4.** A sudden pressing demand; run: a *rush* on foreign bonds. **5.** A sudden or urgent press of traffic, business, etc. **6.** A sudden flocking of people to a new region, especially to an area rumored to be rich in a precious mineral: a gold *rush*. **7.** *U.S.* A general contest or scrimmage between students from different classes, as between sophomores and freshmen. **8.** In football, an attempt to take the ball through the opposing linemen and toward the goal. **9.** *pl.* In motion pictures, the first film prints of a scene or series of scenes, before editing or selection. — *adj.* **1.** Requiring urgency or haste: a *rush* order. **2.** Characterized by much traffic, business, etc.: the *rush* hours. **3.** *U.S.* Denoting a time or function set aside for fraternity or sorority members to meet new students to consider them for membership: *rush* week. [< AF *russher* < OF *ruser*, *reuser* to push back < L *recusare* to refuse. See RECUSE.]

rush² (rush) *n.* **1.** Any one of various grasslike, usually aquatic herbs (family *Juncaceae*), growing in marshy ground and having pliant, cylindrical, leafless stems, often used for making mats, seats of chairs, etc. **2.** A thing of little or no value. **3.** A rushlight. [OE *risc*]

Rush (rush), **Benjamin**, 1745–1813, American physician and patriot; signer of the Declaration of Independence.

rush·er (rush′ər) *n.* **1.** One who rushes. **2.** In football, a lineman.

rush hour A time when traffic or business is at its height. — **rush-hour** (rush′our′) *adj.*

rush·light (rush′līt′) *n.* A candle made by dipping a rush in tallow. Also **rush candle**.

rush line Formerly, in football, the linemen collectively.

Rush·more (rush′môr), **Mount** A mountain in the Black Hills of western South Dakota, on the side of which are carved gigantic faces of Washington, Jefferson, Lincoln, and Theodore Roosevelt; part of **Mount Rushmore National Memorial**; 1,220 acres; established 1929.

rush·y (rush′ē) *adj.* **rush·i·er**, **rush·i·est** **1.** Abounding in, covered with, or made of rushes. **2.** Like a rush.

ru·sine (roō′sin, -sīn) *adj.* Of or pertaining to a genus (*Rusa*) of deer native in the East Indies. [< Malay *rūsa* deer]

rusine antler An antler having a simple brow tine and a simple fork at the tip of the beam. For illustration see ANTLER.

rus in ur·be (rus′ in ûr′bē) *Latin* The country in the city.

rusk (rusk) *n.* **1.** A light, sweetened bread or biscuit. **2.** Bread or cake that has been crisped and browned in an oven. [< Sp. *rosca*, twisted loaf of bread]

Rus·kin (rus′kin), **John**, 1819–1900, English art critic and author.

Russ (rus) *adj. & n.* Russian.

Russ. Russia; Russian.

Russell diagram The Hertzsprung-Russell diagram (which see).

Rus·sell (rus′əl), **Bertrand** (**Arthur William**), 1872–1970, third Earl Russell, English mathematician and philosopher. — **Charles Taze**, 1852–1916, U.S. religious leader; founder of Jehovah's Witnesses: called **Pastor Russell**. — **Elizabeth Mary**, 1866–1941, Countess von Arnim, British novelist born in Australia: original name **Mary Beau·champ** (bē′chəm): pseudonym **Elizabeth**. — **George William**, 1867–1935, Irish poet and artist: pseudonym **Æ**. — **Lord John**, 1792–1878, first Earl Russell, English statesman, orator, and author: called **Finality John**. — **Lillian**, 1861–1922, U.S. soprano: original name **Helen Louise Leon·ard** (len′ərd).

rus·set (rus′it) *n.* **1.** A reddish or yellowish brown. **2.** Coarse homespun cloth or clothing of this color. **3.** Russet leather. **4.** A winter apple of greenish color, mottled with brown. — *adj.* **1.** Of a reddish or yellowish brown color. **2.** Made of russet cloth; also, coarse; homespun; rustic. **3.** Finished, but not blacked: said of leather: *russet* shoes. [< OF *rousset*, dim. of *rous* < L *russus* red]

Rus·sia (rush′ə) **1.** Before 1917, an empire of eastern Europe and northern Asia: capital, Saint Petersburg (Petrograd). **2.** The Russian Soviet Federated Socialist Republic. **3.** Loosely, the Soviet Union. Russian *Rossiya*.

Rus·sian (rush′ən) *adj.* Of or pertaining to Russia, its people, or their language. — *n.* **1.** A native or citizen of the Soviet Union or the former Russian Empire; especially, a Great Russian, Ukrainian, or Byelorussian. **2.** The East Slavic language of Russia, including Great Russian, Ukrainian, and Byelorussian.

Russian dressing Mayonnaise dressing to which chili sauce, pimientos, chopped pickles, etc., have been added.

Rus·sian·ize (rush′ən-īz) *v.t.* **·ized**, **·iz·ing** To make Russian in manner, character, etc.

Russian leather A smooth, well-tanned, high-grade leather of calfskin or light cattle hide, dressed with birch oil and having a characteristic odor.

Russian Orthodox Church An autonomous branch of the Eastern Orthodox Church in the Soviet Union, under the patriarch of Moscow.

Russian Revolution See under REVOLUTION.

Russian roulette A suicidal stunt in which one spins the cylinder of a revolver containing one cartridge, aims at one's head, and pulls the trigger, with one chance in six of being shot.

Russian Soviet Federated Socialist Republic The largest constituent Republic of the Soviet Union, occupying 76 per cent of the total area and extending across northern Eurasia; 6,592,800 sq. mi.; pop. 130,090,000 (1970); capital, Moscow; also (*Soviet*) *Russia*. Also **Russian S.F.S.R.** Abbr. *R.S.F.S.R.*

Russian Turkestan See under TURKESTAN.

Russian wolfhound The borzoi.

Russo- *combining form* Russia; pertaining to the Russians: *Russophobia*.

Russo-Japanese War (rus′ō-jap′ə-nēz′, -nēs′) See table for WAR.

Rus·so·phile (rus′ə-fīl, -fil) *n.* One who favors Russia, or its people, culture, government, etc.

Rus·so·pho·bi·a (rus′ə-fō′bē-ə) *n.* Fear of the policy or influence of Russia. — **Rus′so·phobe** *n.*

rust (rust) *n.* **1.** The reddish or yellow coating formed on iron and steel by exposure to air and moisture, consisting of ferric hydroxide, $Fe(OH)_3$, and ferric oxide, Fe_2O_3. **2.** Any film formed on the surface of a metal by oxidation. **3.** Any of the parasitic fungi of the order *Uredinales*, living on the tissues of higher plants. **4.** The disease caused by such fungi, characterized by the appearance of orange or reddish brown spots on the host plant. **5.** Any coating or accretion formed by a corrosive or degenerative process: *rust* on salted meat. **6.** A condition or tendency that destroys or weakens energy or active qualities: the *rust* of idleness. **7.** Any of several shades of reddish brown, somewhat like the color of rust, but containing more orange. — *v.t. & v.i.* **1.** To become or cause to become rusty; undergo or cause to undergo oxidation. **2.** To contract or cause to contract rust. **3.** To become or cause to become weakened or impaired because of inactivity or disuse: to allow one's powers to *rust*. **4.** To make or become rust-colored. [OE *rūst*. Akin to RED.]

rus·tic (rus′tik) *adj.* **1.** Typical of or appropriate to simple country life. **2.** Plain; simple; homely: *rustic* garments. **3.** Uncultured; rude; awkward: *rustic* manners. **4.** Unaffected; artless: *rustic* simplicity. **5.** Of or pertaining to any irregular style of work or decoration appropriate to the country; also, of or pertaining to work in natural, unpolished wood. — **Syn.** See RURAL. — *n.* **1.** One who lives in the country. **2.** A country person of simple manners or character; also, a coarse or clownish person. **3.** Rusticwork (which see). **4.** Country dialect. [< L *rusticus* < *rus* country] — **rus′ti·cal·ly** *adv.*

rus·ti·cate (rus′tə-kāt) *v.* **·cat·ed**, **·cat·ing** *v.i.* **1.** To go to the country. **2.** To stay or live in the country. — *v.t.* **3.** To send or banish to the country. **4.** *Brit.* To suspend (a student) and send away temporarily, as from a college. **5.** To make rustic. **6.** To construct (masonry) with rusticwork. [< L *rusticatus*, pp. of *rusticari* < *rusticus*. See RUSTIC.] — **rus′ti·ca′tion** *n.* — **rus′ti·ca′tor** *n.*

rus·tic·i·ty (rus·tis′ə-tē) *n.* *pl.* **·ties** **1.** Rustic condition, character, or manners; simplicity; homeliness; awkwardness. **2.** A rustic trait or peculiarity. [< F *rusticité* < L *rusticitas*, *-tatis*]

rus·tic·work (rus′tik-wûrk′) *n.* **1.** Ashlar masonry having rough surfaces, and often deeply sunk grooves at the joints. **2.** Furniture, etc., made of the natural limbs and roots of trees. Also **rustic work**.

rus·tle¹ (rus′əl) *v.t. & v.i.* **·tled**, **·tling** To fall, move, or cause to move with a quick succession of small, light, rubbing sounds, as dry leaves or sheets of paper. — *n.* A rustling sound. [ME *rustel*, alter. of OE *hrūxlian* to make a noise] — **rus′tler** *n.* — **rus′tling·ly** *adv.*

rus·tle² (rus′əl) *v.t. & v.i.* **·tled**, **·tling** **1.** *Informal* To act with or obtain by energetic or vigorous action. **2.** *U.S. Informal* To steal (cattle, etc.). [Blend of RUSH and HUSTLE]

rus·tler (rus′lər) *n.* *U.S. Informal* **1.** A cattle or horse thief. **2.** A pushing, energetic person.

rust·y¹ (rus′tē) *adj.* **rust·i·er**, **rust·i·est** **1.** Covered or affected with rust. **2.** Consisting of or produced by rust. **3.** Having the reddish or yellowish appearance of rust: said often of salted fish or meat that has become rancid. **4.** Impaired by inaction or want of exercise; also, lacking nimbleness; stiff. **5.** Ineffective or weakened through neglect: My tennis game is *rusty*; also, having lost skill for want of practice: He is *rusty* in math. **6.** *Biol.* Appearing as if covered with rust; brownish red. [OE *rūstig* < *rūst* rust] **— rust′i·ly** *adv.* **— rust′i·ness** *n.*

rust·y² (rus′tē) *adj. Brit. Dial.* Cross; stubborn; obstinate.

rut¹ (rut) *n.* **1.** A sunken track worn by a wheel, as in a road; also, a groove forming a path for anything. **2.** A settled habit or course of procedure; routine. **— v.t. rut·ted, rut·ting** To wear or make a rut or ruts in. [Var. of ROUTE]

rut² (rut) *n.* **1.** The sexual excitement of various animals, especially of deer and other ruminants; estrus. **2.** The period during which this excitement lasts. **3.** A roaring or uproar made by an animal in this condition. **— v. rut·ted, rut·ting** *v.i.* **1.** To be in rut. **2.** *Rare* To unite with in copulation. [< MF < L *rugitus* bellowing < *rugire* to roar]

Rut. or **Rutd.** or **Rutl.** Rutland; Rutlandshire.

ru·ta·ba·ga (rōō′tə·bā′gə) *n.* **1.** A cultivated plant (*Brassica napobrassica*) allied to the turnip. **2.** Its edible root. Also called *Swedish turnip.* [< dial. Sw. *rotabagge*]

ru·ta·ceous (rōō·tā′shəs) *adj. Bot.* Of or pertaining to the rue family. [< L *rutaceus* < *ruta* rue < Gk. *rhytē*]

ruth (rōōth) *n. Archaic* **1.** Compassion; pity. **2.** Grief; repentance; regret. [ME *reuthe, reowthe* < OE *hrēow* sad]

Ruth (rōōth) A widow of Moab who left her own people and went with her mother-in-law Naomi to Bethlehem, where she married Boaz. *— n.* The book of the Old Testament in which this story is told.

Ruth (rōōth), **George Herman,** 1895–1948, U.S. baseball player: called **Babe Ruth.**

Ru·the·ni·a (rōō·thē′nē·ə) A former province of eastern Czechoslovakia, now in the Ukrainian S.S.R. See TRANS-CARPATHIAN OBLAST.

Ru·the·ni·an (rōō·thē′nē·ən) *n.* **1.** One of a group of Ukrainians living in eastern Czechoslovakia and the Transcarpathian Oblast, formerly Ruthenia. **2.** The Ukrainian language. *— adj.* Of or pertaining to the Ruthenians or their language.

ru·then·ic (rōō·then′ik) *adj. Chem.* Of, pertaining to, or derived from ruthenium, especially in its higher valence.

ru·the·ni·ous (rōō·thē′nē·əs) *adj. Chem.* Of, pertaining to, or derived from ruthenium, especially in its lower valence.

ru·the·ni·um (rōō·thē′nē·əm) *n.* A gray, brittle, rare metallic element (symbol Ru) of the platinum group. See ELEMENT. [< NL, from *Ruthenia*]

ruth·er·ford (ruth′ər·fərd) *n.* A unit of radioactivity, equal to a million nuclear disintegrations per second. [after Sir Ernest *Rutherford*]

Ruth·er·ford (ruth′ər·fərd), **Sir Ernest,** 1871–1937, first Baron Rutherford, British physicist born in New Zealand. **— Joseph Franklin,** 1869–1942, U.S. religious leader of Jehovah's Witnesses: called **Judge Rutherford.**

ruth·ful (rōōth′fəl) *adj. Archaic* **1.** Full of sorrow or pity; sorrowful; merciful. **2.** Causing sorrow. **— ruth′ful·ly** *adv.* **— ruth′ful·ness** *n.*

ruth·less (rōōth′lis) *adj.* Having no compassion; merciless. [< RUTH] **— ruth′less·ly** *adv.* **— ruth′less·ness** *n.*

ru·ti·lant (rōō′tə·lənt) *adj.* Of a shining red color. [< L *rutilans, -antis,* ppr. of *rutilare* to turn red < *rutilus*. See RUTILE.]

ru·ti·lat·ed (rōō′tə·lā′tid) *adj.* Enclosing rutile needles, as quartz.

ru·tile (rōō′til, -tēl, -tīl) *n.* An adamantine, reddish brown, transparent to opaque titanium dioxide, TiO_2, usually containing a quantity of iron. [< F < G *rutil* < L *rutilus* golden red]

Rut·land·shire (rut′lənd·shir) A former county of eastern England; 152 sq. mi.; pop. 27,463 (1971); county seat, Oakham. Also **Rut′land.**

Rut·ledge (rut′lij), **Ann,** 1816–35, reputed fiancée of Abraham Lincoln. **— Edward,** 1749–1800, American patriot; signer of the Declaration of Independence. **— John,** 1739–1800, American jurist and statesman; brother of the preceding.

rut·tish (rut′ish) *adj.* Disposed to rut; lustful; libidinous.

rut·ty (rut′ē) *adj.* **·ti·er, ·ti·est** Full of ruts. **— rut′ti·ness** *n.*

Ru·wen·zo·ri (rōō′wən·zôr′ē, -zō′rē) A mountain group in Africa on the boundary between the Republic of Zaire and Uganda, identified with the "Mountains of the Moon" of ancient writers; highest peak, Mt. Stanley, 16,795 ft.

Ruys·dael (rois′däl, *Du.* rœis′däl), **Jacob van,** 1625?–82, Dutch painter. Also *Ruisdael.*

Ruy·ter (roi′tər), **Michel Adriaanszoon de,** 1607–76, Dutch admiral.

RV or **R.V.** Revised Version (of the Bible).

R.W. **1.** Right Worshipful. **2.** Right Worthy.

Rwan·da (rwän′dä, rōō·än′dä) A Republic in central equatorial Africa. part of the former UN Trust Territory of Ruanda-Urundi; 10,169 sq. mi.; pop. 4,052,000 (est. 1973); capital, Kigali: also *Ruanda.* See BURUNDI.

-ry Var. of -ERY.

Ry. Railway.

Rya·zan (rē·ə·zän′, *Russ.* ryä·zäny′) A city in the western R.S.F.S.R., near the Oka river; pop. 213,000 (1959). Also *Rya·zan′.*

Ry·binsk (ri′byinsk) A city in the NW R.S.F.S.R., on the Volga; pop. 181,000 (1959): from 1946–59 *Shcherbakov.*

Rybinsk Reservoir An artificial lake in the NW R.S.F.S.R., on the Volga; 1,800 sq. mi. Also **Rybinsk Sea.**

Ry·der (ri′dər), **Albert Pinkham,** 1847–1917, U.S. painter.

rye¹ (ri) *n.* **1.** The grain or seeds of a hardy cereal grass (*Secale cereale*) closely allied to wheat, used in the making of flour and whisky, and as a feed for livestock. **2.** The plant. **3.** Whisky distilled from rye or partly from rye. [OE *ryge*]

rye² (ri) *n.* In Gypsy dialect, a gentleman. [< Romany *rei, rai.* Cf. Skt. *rajah* king.]

rye grass Darnel: sometimes called *raygrass.*

ryke (rīk, rēk) *v.i.* **ryked, ryk·ing** *Scot.* To reach.

rynd (rind, rīnd) *n.* An iron piece for the support of an upper millstone: also spelled *rind.* [Prob. < MDu. *rijn*]

ry·ot (rī′ət) *n.* In India, a tenant or tiller of the soil; peasant. [< Hind. *raiyat* < Arabic *ra'īyah* flock]

Rys·wick (riz′wik) A village in the southern Netherlands, near The Hague; site of the signing of a treaty by France, Germany, the Netherlands, England, and Spain, 1697; pop. 37,504 (1960): Dutch *Rijswijk.*

Ryu·kyu Islands (ryōō·kyōō) An archipelago between Kyushu and Taiwan, constituting a Japanese prefecture; seized by the U.S. in 1945; the islands north of Okinawa were returned to Japan in 1953; in 1972 the remaining islands were returned; chief island, Okinawa; 848 sq. mi.; pop. about 1,000,000 (1972).

S

s, S (es) *n. pl.* **s's** or **ss, S's** or **Ss, ess·es** (es′iz) **1.** The 19th letter of the English alphabet: the shape of the Phoenician letter *shin* was adopted by the Greeks as *sigma* and became Roman *S.* Also *ess.* **2.** The sound represented by the letter *s,* usually a voiceless sibilant, but often voiced in intervocalic position, as in *easy. — symbol* **1.** Anything shaped like an S. **2.** *Chem.* Sulfur (symbol S).

s- *Chem.* Symmetrical.

s. **1.** *Anat.* Sacral. **2.** Second. **3.** Section. **4.** See. **5.** Semi-. **6.** Shilling. **7.** Singular. **8.** Sire. **9.** Son. **10.** South; southern. **11.** Stem; stem of. **12.** Substantive. **13.** Sun. **14.** Surplus.

-s¹ A variant of -es¹, inflectional ending of the plurals of nouns, attached to nouns not ending in a sibilant or an affricate: *books, words, cars.* It represents (s) after a voiceless consonant, and (z) after a voiced consonant or a vowel. Compare -ES¹.

-s² An inflectional ending used to form the third person singular present indicative of verbs not ending in a sibilant, affricate, or vowel: *reads, walks, sings.* Compare -ES².

-s³ *suffix* On; of a; at: often used in adverbs without appreciable force: *nights, Mondays, always, towards.* [OE *-es,* forming adverbial genitives]

-'s¹ An inflectional ending used to form the possessive of nouns not ending in -s or -es: a *man's* world; *women's* fashions. With plural nouns ending in -s or -es, the possessive is formed by adding a simple apostrophe: the *churches'* towers; the various *girls'* schools. With singular nouns ending in -s or -es, the possessive is formed either with -'s or simply with -': *Dickens's* novels or *Dickens'* novels. Modern practice, however, seems to favor using only -' with proper nouns, as in *Charles'* book, while using -'s with common nouns, as in The *dress's* color faded.

-'s² Contraction of: **a** Is: *He's* here. **b** Has: *She's* left. **c** Us: *Let's* go.

S **1.** In chess, a knight (G *springer*). **2.** Saxon. **3.** South; southern.

S. **1.** Fellow (L *Socius*). **2.** Sabbath. **3.** Saint. **4.** Saturday. **5.** Saxon. **6.** School. **7.** Sea. **8.** Senate. **9.** September. **10.** Signor. **11.** South; southern. **12.** Sunday.

PRONUNCIATION KEY: add, āce, câre, pälm; end, ēven; it, īce; odd, ōpen, ôrder; tŏŏk, pōōl; up, bûrn; ə = a in *above,* e in *sicken,* i in *flexible,* o in *melon,* u in *focus;* yōō = u in *fuse;* oil; pout; check; go; ring; thin; this; zh, vision. For å, œ, ü, kh, ṅ, see inside front cover.

Sa *Chem.* Samarium.

Saa·di (säʹdē), **Muslih-ud-Din,** 1184?–1291?, Persian poet. Also *Sadi.*

Saar (zär) A river in NE France and western Germany, flowing 152 miles north to the Moselle.

Saar (zär), **The** A State of western West Germany, in the Saar valley; 989 sq. mi.; pop. 1,127,400 (est. 1970); capital, **Saar·brück·en** (zärʹbrük·ən) in the SW part, pop. 130,765 (est. 1970): French *Sarre.* German **Saar·landt** (zärʹlänt). Also **Saar Basin, Saar Territory.**

Saa·re (säʹrā) An island of the Estonian S.S.R., at the mouth of the Gulf of Riga; 1,046 sq. mi.: also *Sarema.* Also **Saa·re·maa** (säʹre·mä).

Saa·ri·nen (säʹri·nen), **Eero,** 1910–61, U.S. architect. — **Eliel,** 1873–1950, U.S. architect born in Finland; father of the preceding.

sab (sab) *Scot.* *n.* A sob. — *v.t. & v.i.* **sabbed, sab·bing** To sob.

Sab. Sabbath.

Sa·ba (säʹbä) The Arabic name for SHEBA.

sab·a·dil·la (sab/ə·dilʹə) *n.* **1.** The acrid seeds of a Mexican and Central American bulbous plant (*Schoenocaulon officinale*), used in medicine. **2.** The plant yielding these seeds. Also *cebadilla, cevadilla.* [< Sp. *cebadilla,* dim. of *cebada* barley, ult. < L *cibus* food]

Sa·bah (säʹbä) The new name of NORTH BORNEO. See under BORNEO.

Sa·ba·ism (säʹbə·iz/əm) *n.* The worship of stars. [< Hebrew *tsābhā* host, army + -ISM] — **Sa·ba·ist** *n.*

Sab·a·oth (sabʹə·oth, sə·bāʹōth) *n.pl.* Armies; hosts: chiefly in the phrase **the Lord of Sabaoth.** *Rom.* ix 29, *James* v 4. [< LL < Gk. *Sabaōth* < Hebrew *tsebhāōth,* pl. of *tsābhā* host, army]

Sa·ba·tier (sà·bà·tyāʹ), **Paul,** 1854–1941, French chemist.

sab·bat (sabʹət) *n.* The witches' Sabbath. Also **Sab/bat.** [< OF. See SABBATH.]

Sab·ba·tar·i·an (sab/ə·târʹē·ən) *adj.* Pertaining to the Sabbath or its strict observance. — *n.* **1.** A Christian who observes Sunday strictly. **2.** A Christian who observes the seventh day as the Sabbath. [< L *sabbatarius* < *sabbatum.* See SABBATH.] — **Sab·ba·tar/i·an·ism** *n.*

Sab·bath (sabʹəth) *n.* **1.** The seventh day of the week, appointed in the Decalogue as a day of rest to be obs'rved by the Jews; now, Saturday. **2.** The first day of the week as observed by Christians; Sunday. **3.** The institution or observance of a day of rest; a time of rest, peace, or quiet. **4.** The sabbatical year of the Jews. *Lev.* xxv 4. Abbr. S., *Sab.* [Fusion of OE *sabat* and OF *sabbat, sabat,* both < L *sabbatum* < Gk. *sabbaton* < Hebrew *shabbāth* < *shābath* to rest] — **Sab·bat/ic** or **·i·cal** *adj.* — **Sab·bat/i·cal·ly** *adv.*
   — **Syn.** **2.** *Sabbath, Sunday, the Lord's Day,* and *First Day* denote the day of rest observed within the Christian community. *Sabbath* emphasizes the sacred character of this day, but is ambiguous in that it may refer either to the first or the seventh day of the week. *Sunday* is explicitly the first day of the week, but the name has no necessary religious significance. Frequently this difficulty has been met by calling *Sunday* the *Lord's Day.* Among certain groups, notably the Society of Friends, *Sunday* is called *First Day.*

Sabbath law A blue law (def. 2).

Sabbath school A Sunday school (which see).

sab·bat·i·cal (sə·batʹi·kəl) *adj.* Of the nature of the Sabbath as a day of rest; offering rest at regular intervals. Also **sab·bat/ic** — *n.* A sabbatical year.

sabbatical year 1. In the ancient Jewish economy, every seventh year, in which the people were required to refrain from tillage. **2.** A year's vacation awarded to teachers in some American educational institutions every seven years.

sa·be (säʹbē) *SW U.S.* *v.i.* **sa·bed** (-bēd), **sa·be·ing** To understand; know; savvy. — *n.* Understanding; savvy. [< Sp. *saber* to know < L *sapere*]

Sa·be·an (sə·bēʹən) *adj.* Of or pertaining to ancient Sheba, its people, or their language. — *n.* **1.** One of an ancient, wealthy, commercial people of the kingdom of Sheba in SW Arabia in the first millennium B.C. **2.** The Southwest Semitic language of these people. Also **Sa·bae/an.**

Sa·bel·li·an (sə·belʹē·ən) *n.* A branch of the Italic subfamily of Indo-European languages, including the ancient Aequian, Marsian, Sabine, and Volscian.

sa·ber (säʹbər) *n.* **1.** A heavy one-edged cavalry sword, with a thick-backed blade, often curved. **2.** In fencing, a light swordlike instrument, used for both thrusting and slashing, hits being scored with the point or either edge. — *v.t.* To strike, wound, or kill with a saber. Also, *Brit.,* **sabre.** [< F *sabre* < G *sabel,* prob. < Hung. *szablya* < *szabni* to cut]

saber rattling A threat of war or a threatening display of military power.

sa·ber-toothed tiger (säʹbər·tōͦthtʹ)

SABER-TOOTHED TIGER
(About 3 feet high at shoulder)

Paleontol. A large, extinct carnivore (subfamily *Machaerodontinae*), characterized by long, trenchant upper canine teeth; especially, *Smilodon californicus,* common in the western hemisphere until its extinction in the Pleistocene.

sa·bin (sāʹbin) *Physics* A measure of sound absorption, equivalent to one square foot of a completely absorbing substance. [after W. C. W. *Sabine,* 1868–1919, U.S. physicist]

Sa·bin (sāʹbin), **Albert Bruce,** born 1906, U.S. virologist born in Russia, developed an oral vaccine for polio.

sab·ine (sabʹin) *n.* Savin.

Sa·bine (sāʹbīn) *n.* **1.** One of an ancient central Italian people, conquered and absorbed by Rome in 290 B.C. **2.** The language of these people, belonging to the Sabellian branch of the Italic languages. — *adj.* Of or pertaining to the Sabines or to their language.

Sabine River (sə·bēnʹ) A river in eastern Texas and western Louisiana, flowing 578 miles, generally SE, passing through **Sabine Lake** (about 17 mi. long) and entering the Gulf of Mexico through **Sabine Pass** (about 7 mi. long).

sa·bir (sa·bērʹ) *n.* Lingua franca (def. 2). [< *Si ti sabir,* jargon phrase for "if you know" in Molière's *Le Bourgeois Gentilhomme* < Sp. *saber* to know]

sa·ble (sāʹbəl) *n.* **1.** A carnivore (*Martes zibellina*), of northern Asia and Europe, related to the marten and prized for its valuable fur. ◆ Collateral adjective: *zibeline.* **2.** The dressed fur of a sable, especially of the Asian sable. **3.** *pl.* Garments made wholly or partly of this fur. **4.** The color black; also, mourning or a mourning garment. **5.** *Heraldry* Black, represented, when uncolored, by crosshatching. — *adj.* **1.** Black, especially as the color of mourning. **2.** Made of or having the color of sable fur; dark brown. [< OF *sable* < Med.L *sabelum* < Slavic]

Sable, Cape 1. The southernmost point of the United States, at the SW tip of Florida. **2.** The southernmost extremity of Nova Scotia, on an islet just south of **Cape Sable Island** (7 mi. long, 3 mi. wide).

sable antelope A large, black, African antelope (*Hippotragus niger*) having long, curved horns.

sa·ble·fish (sāʹbəl·fish/) *n.* *pl.* **·fish** or **·fish·es** A fish (*Anoplopoma fimbria*) of the Pacific coast of the United States.

Sable Island An island SW of Nova Scotia; 30 mi. by 2 mi.

sa·bot (sabʹō, *Fr.* sà·bōʹ) *n.* **1.** A wooden shoe. **2.** A shoe having a wooden sole but flexible shank. **3.** A casing formerly attached to a projectile to hold it in the bore, or to take the rifling, of a gun. [< F < OF *savate,* ult. < Arabic *sabbat* sandal; infl. in form by *bot* boot]

sab·o·tage (sab/ə·täzh, *Fr.* sà·bô·tàzhʹ) *n.* An act of malicious damage or destruction, as one intended to obstruct the production of war materiel by the enemy. — *v.* **·taged, ·tag·ing** *v.i.* **1.** To engage in sabotage. — *v.t.* **2.** To damage or destroy by sabotage. [< F < *saboter* to damage < *sabot* sabot; with ref. to damage done to machinery with sabots]

sab·o·teur (sab/ə·tûrʹ, *Fr.* sà·bô·tœrʹ) *n.* One who engages in sabotage. [< F]

sa·bra (säʹbrə) *n.* A native Israeli. [< Hebrew *sābrāh* cactus; because tough outside and soft inside]

sa·bre (sāʹbər) See SABER.

sa·bre·tache (sāʹbər·tash, sabʹər-) *n.* A leather pocket hung from the sword belt of a cavalryman. [< F < G *säbeltasche* < *säbel* saber + *tasche* pocket]

sab·u·lous (sabʹyə·ləs) *adj.* Gritty, like sand. Also **sab·u·lose** (-lōs) [< L *sabulosus* < *sabulum* sand]

sac (sak) *n.* *Biol.* A membranous pouch or receptacle in an animal or plant, as for containing a liquid: the ink *sac* of a squid. [< F < L *saccus.* See SACK[1].]

Sac (sak, sôk) See SAUK.

SAC Strategic Air Command.

sac·a·ton (sak/ə·tōnʹ) *n.* A perennial grass (*Sporobolus wrighti*) of the United States and Mexico, yielding hay. [< Am. Sp. *zacatón* < *zacate* coarse grass < Nahuatl *çacatl*]

sac·cate (sakʹit, -āt) *adj.* **1.** Sac-shaped. **2.** Having a sac or pouch. [< Med.L *saccatus* < L *saccus.* See SACK[1].]

sac·cha·rate (sak/ə·rāt) *n.* *Chem.* **1.** A salt of saccharic acid. **2.** A compound of a saccharide with a metallic oxide.

sac·char·ic acid (sə·karʹik) *adj.* *Chem.* A dibasic acid, $C_6H_{10}O_8$, obtained by the oxidation of glucose.

sac·cha·ride (sak/ə·rīd, -rid) *n.* *Chem.* Any of a large group of carbohydrates containing sugar, usually classified as *monosaccharide, disaccharide,* etc.

sac·char·i·fy (sə·kar/ə·fī, sak/ər·ə·fī) *v.t.* **·fied, ·fy·ing** To convert, as starches, into sugar; impregnate with sugar.

sac·cha·rim·e·ter (sak/ə·rimʹə·tər) *n.* A polariscope for detecting the concentration of sugar in a solution.

sac·cha·rin (sak/ə·rin) *n.* *Chem.* A white crystalline compound, $C_7H_5O_3NS$, derived from toluene and 300 to 500 times sweeter than cane sugar, used as a noncaloric sweetening agent. [< L *saccharon* type of sugar < Gk. *sakcharon,* ult. < Skt. *sharkarā* grit, gravel, sugar) + -IN]

sac·cha·rine (sak/ər·in, -ə·rīn) *adj.* **1.** Of, pertaining to, or of the nature of sugar; sweet. **2.** Cloyingly sweet: a *sac-*

charine manner. — *n.* Saccharin. [< SACCHAR(O)- + -INE¹] — **sac′cha·rine·ly** *adv.* — **sac′cha·rin′i·ty** *n.*

sac·cha·rize (sak′ə·rīz) *v.t.* ·**rized**, ·**riz·ing** *Chem.* To convert into sugar; ferment. — **sac′cha·ri·za′tion** *n.*

saccharo- *combining form* Sugar; of or pertaining to sugar: *saccharometer.* Also, before vowels, **racchar-**. [< Gk. *sakcharon.* See SACCHARIN.]

sac·cha·roid (sak′ə·roid) *adj.* **1.** Resembling sugar. **2.** *Geol.* Having crystalline granular structure like that of loaf sugar: *saccharoid* marble. Also **sac′cha·roi′dal** (-roid′l).

sac·cha·rom·e·ter (sak′ə·rom′ə·tər) *n.* A hydrometer for determining the amount of sugar in a solution.

sac·cha·ro·my·cete (sak′ə·rō·mī′sēt) *n.* Any of a genus (*Saccharomyces*) of fungi of the yeast family, most of which ferment sugar to ethyl alcohol and carbon dioxide. [< SACCHARO- + MYCETE] — **sac′cha·ro·my·ce′tic** (-sē′tik), **sac′cha·ro·my′cous** (-sē′təs) *adj.*

sac·cha·rose (sak′ə·rōs) *n.* Sucrose.

Sac·co (sak′ō, *Ital.* säk′kō), **Nicola**, 1891–1927, and his friend, **Bartolomeo Vanzetti**, 1888–1927, philosophical anarchists in the United States; convicted of murder in connection with a robbery in Massachusetts, and executed. Their trial, the **Sacco-Vanzetti Case**, aroused national and international protest because it was thought to have been influenced by political considerations.

sac·cu·late (sak′yə·lāt) *adj.* Formed into a series of saclike expansions; dilated and constricted alternately. Also **sac′cu·lat′ed**. [< SACCUL(US) + -ATE¹]

sac·cule (sak′yōol) *n.* **1.** A little sac. Also **sac′cu·lus** (·yə·ləs). **2.** *Anat.* Part of the membranous labyrinth of the inner ear. [< L *sacculus*, dim. of *saccus*. See SACK.]

sac·er·do·tal (sas′ər·dōt′l) *adj.* **1.** Pertaining to a priest or priesthood; priestly. **2.** Believing in the divine authority of the priesthood. [< MF < L *sacerdotalis* < *sacerdos*, *-dotis* priest < *sacer* sacred + *do-*, stem of *dare* to give] — **sac′er·do′tal·ly** *adv.*

sac·er·do·tal·ism (sas′ər·dōt′l·iz′əm) *n.* **1.** The character and methods of the priesthood; priestcraft. **2.** Zeal for priestly things.

sa·chem (sā′chəm) *n.* **1.** A North American Indian hereditary chief. **2.** Any chief or head of a political party; especially, one of the leaders of Tammany in New York. [< Algonquian (Narraganset). Akin to SAGAMORE.]

sa·chet (sa·shā′, *esp. Brit.* sash′ā) *n.* A small ornamental bag for perfumed powder. [< MF, dim. of *sac* < L *saccus* sack]

Sachs (zäks), **Hans**, 1494–1576, German Meistersinger and shoemaker, hero of Wagner's *Die Meistersinger.*

Sach·sen (zäkh′sən) The German name for SAXONY.

sack¹ (sak) *n.* **1.** A bag for holding bulky articles. **2.** A measure or weight of varying amount. **3.** A loose jacket-like garment, worn by women and babies: also **sacque**. **4.** *Slang* Dismissal: especially in the phrases **to get the sack, to give (someone) the sack. 5.** In baseball slang, a base. **6.** *U.S. Slang* A bed; mattress. — **to be left holding the sack** *U.S. Informal* To be left to take the consequences of a bad situation. — **to hit the sack** *U.S. Slang* To go to bed. — **to sack out** *U.S. Slang* To go to bed. — *v.t.* **1.** To put into a sack or sacks. **2.** To dismiss, as a servant. *Informal sk.* [OE *sacc* < L *saccus* < Gk. *sakkos* < Hebrew *saq* sack, sackcloth]

sack² (sak) *v.t.* To plunder or pillage (a town or city) after capturing. — *n.* **1.** The pillaging of a captured town or city. **2.** Loot or booty obtained by pillage. [< MF *sac* < Ital. *sacco*, orig., plunder < Med.L *saccare* to pillage < L *saccus* sack; from the use of sacks in carrying off plunder] — **sack′er** *n.*

sack³ (sak) *n.* Light-colored Spanish dry wine; also, any strong white wine from southern Europe. [Earlier (*wyne*) *seck* < F (*vin*) *sec* dry (wine) < L *siccus* dry]

sack·but (sak′but) *n.* **1.** An early instrument resembling the trombone. **2.** In the Bible, a stringed instrument. [< MF *saquebute*, orig., a hooked lance for horseback fighting < OF *saquer* to draw + *bouter* to push]

sack·cloth (sak′klôth′, -kloth′) *n.* **1.** A coarse cloth used for making sacks. **2.** Coarse cloth or haircloth worn in penance. — **in sackcloth and ashes 1.** In the Bible, wearing garments of sackcloth and sprinkling ashes on one's head as marks of penance or sorrow. **2.** In any state of sorrow, penance, or self-abasement.

sack coat A short, loose-fitting coat with no waist seam.

sack·ful (sak′fŏŏl′) *n. pl.* ·**fuls** Enough to fill a sack.

sack·ing (sak′ing) *n.* A coarse cloth made of hemp or flax and used for sacks; bagging.

sack race A race run with the feet in a sack.

Sack·ville (sak′vil), **Thomas**, 1536–1608, first Earl of Dorset and Baron Buckhurst, English poet and diplomat.

Sack·ville-West (sak′vil·west′), **V**(**ictoria Mary**), 1892–1962, English novelist and poet.

sa·cral¹ (sā′krəl) *adj.* Of, pertaining to, or situated near the sacrum. — *n.* A sacral vertebra or nerve. *Abbr. s.* [< NL *sacralis* < *sacrum*. See SACRUM.]

sa·cral² (sā′krəl) *adj.* Pertaining to sacred rites. [< L *sacrum* rite < *sacer* sacred]

sac·ra·ment (sak′rə·mənt) *n.* **1.** *Eccl.* A rite ordained by Christ or by the church as an outward and visible sign of an inward and spiritual grace. Traditionally in the Greek, Roman Catholic, and some other churches, they are seven in number (baptism, the Eucharist, confirmation, matrimony, orders, penance, and unction); since the Reformation only two of these (baptism and the Eucharist) are recognized by most Protestant churches. **2.** *Often cap. Eccl.* **a** The Eucharist; the Lord's Supper. **b** The consecrated bread and wine of the Eucharist: often with *the*. See BLESSED SACRAMENT. **3.** Any sign or token of a solemn covenant or pledge. **4.** Anything considered to have a secret or mysterious meaning. [< OF *sacrement* < L *sacramentum* oath, pledge < *sacrare* to consecrate]

sac·ra·men·tal (sak′rə·men′tal) *n.* **1.** One of certain rites, such as the use of holy water, oil, or salt, employed as adjuncts to sacraments, or regarded as analogous to a sacrament. **2.** *pl.* The objects, words, or ceremonies used in administering a sacrament. — *adj.* **1.** Of or pertaining to a sacrament. **2.** Constituting or composing a sacrament. **3.** Having the influence or efficacy of a sacrament. **4.** Consecrated, as by sacred vows: the *sacramental* host of God's elect. — **sac′ra·men′tal·ism** *n.* — **sac′ra·men′tal·ist** *n.* — **sac′ra·men′tal·ly** *adv.*

sac·ra·men·tar·i·an (sak′rə·men·târ′ē·ən) *n.* One who regards the sacraments as channels of divine grace. Also **sac·ra·men′ta·rist, sac·ra·ment·er** (sak′rə·men′tər). — *adj.* Of or pertaining to a sacrament or sacraments, or to sacramentarians. — **sac′ra·men·tar′i·an·ism** *n.*

Sac·ra·men·tar·i·an (sak′rə·men·târ′ē·ən) *n.* One who regards the sacraments as simply symbols or signs: the name given to Calvinists and followers of Zwingli.

sac·ra·men·ta·ry (sak′rə·men′tər·ē) *n. pl.* ·**ries** Any of various early books containing the ritual for mass, the sacraments, and various other rites.

Sac·ra·men·to (sak′rə·men′tō) The capital of California, in the north central part; pop. 254,413; on the **Sacramento River**, that flows 382 miles, generally south, through Central Valley to Suisun Bay.

sa·crar·i·um (sə·krâr′ē·əm) *n. pl.* ·**i·a** (-ē·ə) **1.** Any sacred or secluded place or shrine of the ancient Romans where venerated things were deposited. **2.** The sanctuary of a church. **3.** A piscina. [< L *sacer* sacred]

sa·cred (sā′krid) *adj.* **1.** Set apart or dedicated to religious use; hallowed: a *sacred* edifice: opposed to *profane*. **2.** Pertaining or related to deity, religion, or hallowed places or things. **3.** Consecrated or dedicated to a person or purpose. **4.** Entitled to reverence or respect; not to be profaned; inviolable. **5.** *Rare* Set apart for evil; accursed. — **Syn.** See HOLY. [< OF *sacrer* < L *sacrare* to treat as sacred < *sacer*, *sacris* dedicated to divinity, hence either holy or accursed] — **sa′cred·ly** *adv.* — **sa′cred·ness** *n.*

Sacred College The College of Cardinals (which see).

sacred cow 1. *U.S. Informal* Something or someone regarded as above criticism or reproach. **2.** A cow when considered sacred, as by the Hindus.

sac·ri·fice (sak′rə·fīs) *n.* **1.** The act of making an offering to a deity, in worship or atonement; also, that which is so offered. **2.** A giving up of some cherished or desired object, person, idea, etc., usually for the sake of something else; also, that which is so given up. **3.** Loss incurred or suffered without return; destruction, as of life. **4.** A reduction of price that leaves little or no profit or involves loss. **5.** In baseball, a sacrifice hit (which see). — *v.* ·**ficed**, ·**fic·ing** *v.t.* **1.** To make an offering or sacrifice of, as to a god or deity in propitiation, supplication, etc. **2.** To give up, yield, permit injury to, or relinquish (something valued) for the sake of something else, as a person, thing, or idea. **3.** To sell at a reduced price; part with at a loss. **4.** In baseball, to advance (one or more runners) by means of a sacrifice hit. — *v.i.* **5.** To make a sacrifice. **6.** To make a sacrifice hit. [< OF < L *sacrificium* < *sacrum* religious act (< *sacer* sacred) + *facere* to perform, do] — **sac′ri·fic′er** *n.* — **sac′ri·fic′ing·ly** *adv.*

sacrifice fly In baseball, a fly ball hit with less than two out that enables a runner on third base to score after the catch, not counted as an official time at bat.

sacrifice hit In baseball, a bunt made with less than two out that enables a runner or runners to advance a base while the batter is being retired, not counted as an official time at bat. Also **sacrifice bunt**.

sac·ri·fi·cial (sak′rə·fish′əl) *adj.* Of, pertaining to, performing, or like a sacrifice. — **sac′ri·fi′cial·ly** *adv.*

sac·ri·lege (sak′rə·lij) *n.* The act of violating or profaning anything sacred, including sacramental vows. — **Syn.** See PROFANATION. [< OF < L *sacrilegium* < *sacrilegus* temple robber < *sacer*, *sacris* sacred + *legere* to gather, steal] — **sac′ri·le′gist** (-lē′jist) *n.*

sac·ri·le·gious (sak′rə·lij′əs, -lē′jəs) *adj.* **1.** Having committed sacrilege; impious. **2.** Of, pertaining to, or like sacrilege. — **sac·ri·le′gious·ly** *adv.* — **sac′ri·le′gious·ness** *n.*

sa·cring bell (sā′kring) *Eccl.* **1.** The tolling of the church bell during the elevation of the Host at Mass. **2.** The Sanctus bell (which see). [ME *sacring*, ppr. of *sacre* to consecrate]

sa·crist (sā′krist) *n.* **1.** A sacristan or sexton. **2.** A person who takes charge of choir books and copy music. [< ML *sacrista* < L *sacer, sacris* sacred]

sac·ris·tan (sak′ris·tən) *n.* An officer having charge of the sacristy of a church or house. [< Med.L *sacristanus* < *sacrista.* See SACRIST. Doublet of SEXTON.]

sac·ris·ty (sak′ris·tē) *n. pl.* **·ties** A room in a religious house for the sacred vessels and vestments; vestry. [< Med.L *sacristia, sacrista.* See SACRIST.]

sacro- *combining form Med.* Near, or related to the sacrum: *sacrosciatic.* [< L (*os*) *sacrum* the sacral (bone)]

sac·ro·il·i·ac (sak′rō·il′ē·ak) *adj. Anat.* Pertaining to the sacrum and the ilium and to the joints or ligaments connecting them. [< SACRO- + ILIAC]

sac·ro·sanct (sak′rō·sangkt) *adj.* Peculiarly and exceedingly sacred; inviolable: sometimes used ironically. [< L *sacrosanctus* < *sacro*, ablative of *sacrum* rite (< *sacer* sacred) + *sanctus*, pp. of *sancire* to make holy, inviolable] — **sac·ro·sanc·ti·ty** (sak′rō·sangk′tə·tē) *n.*

sa·cro·sci·at·ic (sā′krō·sī·at′ik) *adj. Anat.* Of or pertaining to the sacrum and the ischium: *sacrosciatic* ligaments.

sa·crum (sā′krəm) *n. pl.* **·cra** (-krə) *Anat.* A composite bone formed by the union of the five vertebrae between the lumbar and caudal regions, constituting the dorsal part of the pelvis. For illustration see PELVIS. [< NL < L (*os*) *sacrum* sacred (bone); from its use in sacrifices]

sad (sad) *adj.* **sad·der, sad·dest** **1.** Sorrowful or depressed in spirits; expressing or bearing an appearance of grief or sorrow; unhappy; mournful; gloomy. **2.** Causing sorrow or pity; distressing; unfortunate. **3.** *Dial.* Heavy; soggy: said of food. **4.** *Informal* Pitifully inadequate; bad; contemptible: a pretty *sad* effort. **5.** Dark-hued; somber. [OE *sæd*, orig., sated] — **sad′ly** *adv.* — **sad′ness** *n.*
— **Syn. 1.** dejected, depressed, desolate, despondent, disconsolate, dismal, doleful, downcast, dreary, lugubrious, melancholy, miserable, sorrowful, woebegone, woeful. — **Ant.** happy, joyous.

sad·den (sad′n) *v.t. & v.i.* To make or become sad.

sad·dle (sad′l) *n.* **1.** A seat or pad for a rider, as on the back of a horse or on a bicycle. **2.** A padded cushion for a horse's back, used as part of a harness or to support a pack, etc. **3.** A part of an animal that is similar to a saddle in shape, position, etc.; especially, the lower part of the back of a fowl. For illustration see FOWL. **4.** The two hindquarters of a carcass, as of mutton, veal, or venison; also, the undivided loins of such a carcass. **5.** A col. **6.** Something resembling a saddle in form or position, as a bearing for a car axle. — **in the saddle** In control. — *v.* **·dled, ·dling** *v.t.* **1.** To put a saddle on: to *saddle* a horse. **2.** To load, as with a burden. **3.** To place as a burden or responsibility: with *upon*. — *v.i.* **4.** To get into a saddle. [OE *sadol*. Prob. ult. akin to SIT.]

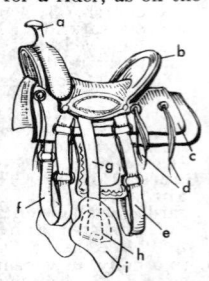

AMERICAN STOCK OR RANGE SADDLE
a Pommel or horn. *b* Cantle. *c* Saddle. *d* Saddle strings. *e* Back cinch. *f* Front cinch. *g* Stirrup strap or leather. *h* Stirrup. *i* Stirrup hood or tapadera.

sad·dle·back (sad′l·bak) *n.* Something that is saddlebacked.

sad·dle·backed (sad′l·bakt) *adj.* **1.** Concave, as a saddle, in the back or upper part. **2.** Having a saddlelike mark, as some birds.

sad·dle·bag (sad′l·bag) *n.* One of a pair of pouches connected by a strap or band and slung over an animal's back or attached to a saddle.

saddle band *U.S.* A remuda.

saddle block *Surg.* A type of spinal anesthesia affecting the buttocks, the inner thighs, and the perineum.

sad·dle·bow (sad′l·bō′) *n.* The arched front upper part of a saddletree.

sad·dle·cloth (sad′l·klôth′, -kloth′) *n.* A cloth placed under and attached to a saddle.

saddle horse A horse used with or trained for the saddle.

sad·dler (sad′lər) *n.* **1.** A maker of saddles, harness, etc. **2.** A saddle horse.

saddle roof A ridge roof having two gables.

sad·dler·y (sad′lər·ē) *n. pl.* **·dler·ies** **1.** Saddles, harnesses, etc., collectively. **2.** A shop where such articles are sold. **3.** The craft or business of a saddler.

saddle shoe A white sport shoe having a dark band of leather across the instep.

saddle soap A softening and preserving soap for leather, containing pure white soap, as Castile, and neat's-foot oil.

sad·dle·tree (sad′l·trē′) *n.* **1.** The frame of a saddle. **2.** The tuliptree.

Sad·du·cee (saj′oo·sē, sad′yoo·sē) *n.* A member of an ancient Jewish sect that adhered to the Mosaic law but repudiated the oral traditions associated with it, rejecting the resurrection of the body, the existence of angels, etc. Compare PHARISEE. [Appar. ult. after *Zadok*, a high priest (*Ezek.* xl 46)] — **Sad′du·ce′an, Sad′du·cae′an** *adj.* — **Sad′du·cee′ism** *n.*

sa·de (sä·dā′) *n.* The eighteenth letter in the Hebrew alphabet: also spelled *tsade.* Also **sa·dhe′.** See ALPHABET.

Sade (säd), *Comte Donatien Alphonse François de*, 1740–1814, French novelist and libertine: called **Marquis de Sade.**

sa·dhu (sä′doo) *n.* A Hindu holy man. [< Skt. *sādhu* straight]

Sa·di (sä·dē′) See SAADI.

sad·i·ron (sad′ī′ərn) *n.* An iron for pressing clothes, pointed at both ends and having a removable handle. [< SAD, in obs. sense "heavy" + IRON]

sad·ism (sä′diz·əm, sad′iz·əm) *n.* **1.** *Psychol.* A condition in which sexual gratification depends largely on the infliction of pain upon others. **2.** A tendency to take delight in being cruel. Compare MASOCHISM. [after Comte Donatien de *Sade*, who described such sexual aberrations in his writings] — **sad·ist** (sä′dist, sad′ist) *n. & adj.* — **sa·dis′tic** (sə·dis′tik, sä-) *adj.* — **sa·dis′ti·cal·ly** *adv.*

Sa·do·va (sä′dô·vä) A town in southern Bohemia, Czechoslovakia; scene of a defeat of the Austrians by Prussian forces, 1866; pop. about 20,000. German **Sa′do·wa.**

sad sack *U.S. Slang* A blundering, pitiable person. [< SAD + SACK; because ruefully regarded as a sack of excrement]

sae (sā) *adv. Scot.* So. [OE *swa*]

SAE or **S.A.E.** Society of Automotive Engineers.

SAE number A number representing the viscosity of a lubricant according to standards established by the Society of Automotive Engineers, by which SAE 10, SAE 20, SAE 30, and SAE 40 designate increasingly thick oils.

sa·fa·ri (sə·fä′rē) *n. pl.* **·ris** **1.** An expedition or journey, often on foot, as for hunting. **2.** The hunters, attendants, and animals employed in such an expedition. Also spelled *suffari.* [< Swahili < Arabic *safara* to travel]

safe (sāf) *adj.* **saf·er, saf·est** **1.** Free or freed from danger or evil. **2.** Having escaped injury or damage; unharmed. **3.** Not hazardous; not involving risk or loss. **4.** Conferring safety. **5.** Prudent or trustworthy: a *safe* guide. **6.** Not likely to disappoint; free from doubt or error. **7.** Not likely to cause or do harm or injury. **8.** In politics, adhering to party principles; to be depended on to support certain interests or to vote for a certain candidate. **9.** In baseball, having reached base without being retired. — *n.* **1.** A strong metal receptacle, usually fireproof, for protecting valuables. **2.** Any place of safe storage, as a room or box, for preserving perishable articles or foods. [< OF *sauf* < L *salvus* whole, healthy] — **safe′ly** *adv.* — **safe′ness** *n.*

safe·blow·ing (sāf′blō′ing) *n.* The act of using explosives to open a safe to be robbed. — **safe′blow′er** *n.*

safe·break·er (sāf′brā′kər) *n.* A safecracker (which see).

safe·con·duct (*n.* sāf′kon′dukt; *v.* sāf′kən·dukt′) *n.* **1.** An official document assuring protection on a journey or voyage, as in time of war; a passport. **2.** The act of conducting in safety. — *v.t.* **1.** To convoy in safety. **2.** To provide with a safe-conduct.

safe·crack·er (sāf′krak′ər) *n.* One who breaks into safes to rob them. — **safe′crack′ing** *n.*

safe deposit A room, vault, or other fireproof storage place for valuables.

safe-de·pos·it box (sāf′di·poz′it) A box, safe, drawer, or other fireproof receptacle for valuable jewelry, papers, etc., generally in a bank.

safe·guard (sāf′gärd′) *n.* **1.** One who or that which guards or keeps in safety, as an escort, guard, or safe-conduct. **2.** A mechanical device designed to prevent accident or injury. — *v.t.* To defend; protect; guard.

safe hit A base hit (which see).

safe·keep·ing (sāf′kē′ping) *n.* The act or state of keeping or being kept in safety; protection.

safe·light (sāf′līt′) *n.* A dim, usually red lamp that permits limited vision in a photographic darkroom without affecting film.

safe·ty (sāf′tē) *n. pl.* **·ties** **1.** Freedom from danger or risk. **2.** Freedom from injury. **3.** A device or catch designed as a safeguard, as in a firearm. **4.** In football, the act or play of touching the ball to the ground behind the player's own goal line when the impetus that sent the ball over the goal line was given to it by one of his own side. Also **safe′ty·touch′down′** (-tuch′doun′). **5.** In baseball, a base hit. — *adj.* Giving, contributing to, or concerned with safety. [< OF *salvete* < Med.L *salvus* sound]

safety belt **1.** A strap or strip of strong belting encircling the user and fastened to a fixed object, worn by linemen, window cleaners, etc., as a safeguard against falling. **2.** A strap fixed to the seat of an aircraft or vehicle, by which the occupant is secured against sudden shocks or turning movements: also called *seat belt.*

safety glass Two sheets of glass having a film of transparent, adhesive plastic tightly pressed between them: also called *shatterproof glass.*

safety lamp 1. A miner's lamp having the flame surrounded by fine wire gauze that prevents the ignition of explosive gases: also called *davy*. 2. A specially protected incandescent electric lamp.

safety match A match that will ignite only when struck upon a chemically prepared surface.

safety pin 1. A pin whose point springs into place within a protecting sheath. For illustration see PIN. 2. A pin that prevents the premature detonation of a grenade, bomb, etc.

safety play In bridge, a play that sacrifices an available trick to insure against the loss of several tricks.

safety razor A razor provided with a guard or guards for the blade to prevent accidental gashing of the skin.

safety valve 1. *Mech.* A valve in a steam boiler, etc., for automatically relieving excessive pressure. 2. Any outlet for pent-up energy or emotion.

saf·flow·er (saf′lou′ər) *n.* 1. A thistlelike herb (*Carthamus tinctorius*) about 2 feet high, with spiny heads of orange-red flowers. 2. The dried flower heads of this plant, used as a red dyestuff and in medicine in the treatment of malnutrition. [< Du. *saffloer* < OF *saffleur, safour* < Ital. *saffiore*; infl. in form by FLOWER]

saf·fron (saf′rən) *n.* 1. An autumn-flowering species of crocus (*Crocus sativus*). 2. The dried orange-colored stigmas of this plant, used for coloring confectionery, varnishes, etc., and as a flavoring in cookery. 3. A deep yellow-orange: also **saffron yellow**. — *adj.* Having the orange color of saffron. [< OF *safran* < Med.L *safranum* < Arabic *za′farān*]

S.Afr. South Africa; South African.

saf·ra·nine (saf′rə-nēn, -nin) *n. Chem.* Any of a class of compounds derived from phenazine, whose salts form important dyes. Also **saf′ra·nin** (-nin). [< F or G *safran* + -INE²]

saf·role (saf′rōl) *n. Chem.* A yellowish liquid, $C_{10}H_{10}O_2$, found in the oil of sassafras, etc., used in medicine and perfumery. Also **saf′rol**. [< F or G *safran* saffron + -OLE¹]

sag (sag) *v.* **sagged, sag·ging** *v.i.* 1. To bend or sink downward from weight or pressure, especially in the middle. 2. To hang unevenly. 3. To lose firmness or determination; weaken, as from exhaustion, age, etc. 4. To decline, as in price or value. 5. *Naut.* To drift. — *v.t.* 6. To cause to sag. — *n.* 1. A sagging; also, its extent or degree. 2. A sagging place or part, as of a roof. 3. *Naut.* A sidewise drift, as of a vessel. 4. A depressed or sunken place in flat land; a marsh. [ME *saggen*. Cf. MLG–LG *sacken*.]

SAG or **S.A.G.** Screen Actors Guild.

sa·ga (sä′gə) *n.* 1. A medieval Scandinavian (especially Icelandic) prose narrative dealing with legendary or historical exploits, usually of a single hero or a single family. 2. A long story, sometimes poetic, often chronicling the history of a family. [< ON. Akin to *segja* to say.]

sa·ga·cious (sə-gā′shəs) *adj.* 1. Characterized by discernment, shrewdness, and wisdom. 2. Ready and apt to apprehend and to decide on a course. 3. Quick of scent, as a hound. — **Syn.** See ASTUTE. [< L *sagax, sagacis.* Akin to *sagire* to perceive acutely.] — **sa·ga′cious·ly** *adv.* — **sa·ga′cious·ness** *n.*

sa·gac·i·ty (sə-gas′ə-tē) *n.* The quality of being sagacious; discernment and judgment; shrewdness. — **Syn.** See SENSE. [< MF *sagacité* < L *sagax* sagacious]

sa·ga·man (sä′gə-man′, -mən) *n. pl.* **·men** (-mən) The author, singer, or narrator of a saga; a Scandinavian poet or bard. [Trans. of ON *sögumathr*]

sag·a·more (sag′ə-môr, -mōr) *n.* A tribal or lesser chief among the Algonquian Indians of North America, usually inferior to sachem. [< Algonquian (Penobscot) *sagamo* he prevails. Akin to SACHEM.]

sag·a·nash (sag′ə-nash) *n.* A white man: an Algonquian Indian term. [< Algonquian *sagannash*]

saga novel A long, multivolume, originally French form of the novel that usually chronicles the history of several generations of a family: also called *roman-fleuve*.

sage¹ (sāj) *n.* A venerable man of recognized experience, prudence, and foresight; a profoundly wise counselor or philosopher. — *adj.* **sag·er, sag·est** 1. Characterized by or proceeding from calm, far-seeing wisdom and prudence. 2. Befitting a sage; profound; learned. 3. *Obs.* Grave; serious. — **Syn.** See WISE¹. [< OF, ult. < LL *sapius* prudent, wise < L, pleasant tasting < *sapere* to taste, to have good taste. Akin to SAVORY.] — **sage′ly** *adv.* — **sage′ness** *n.*

sage² (sāj) *n.* 1. Any of a genus (*Salvia*) of herbs and shrubs of the mint family; especially, the **garden sage** (*S. officinalis*) having gray-green leaves and purple, blue, or white flowers, used for flavoring meats, and the **scarlet sage** (*S. splendens*), having scarlet flowers. 2. The leaves of these plants. 3. The sagebrush. [< F *sauge* < L *salvia* < *salvus* safe; from its reputed medicinal properties]

Sage (sāj), Russell, 1816–1906, U.S. financier.

sage·brush (sāj′brush′) *n.* An aromatic, bitter, typically perennial herb or small shrub (genus *Artemisia*) of the composite family, widely distributed on the alkali plains of the western United States; especially, *A. tridentata*, the State flower of Nevada. Compare WORMWOOD.

Sagebrush State Nickname of NEVADA.

sage hen 1. A large grouse (*Centrocercus urophasianus*) of the western United States. 2. *Usually cap.* A native of Nevada: a nickname.

sage sparrow A small, pale gray, finchlike bird (*Amphispiza nevadensis*) of the western United States.

sag·gar (sag′ər) *n.* 1. A vessel of baked fireproof clay in which are fired delicate pieces of pottery that would be injured by direct exposure to the heat. 2. Clay used for making saggars. Also called *seggar*. Also **sag′gard** (-ərd). — *v.t.* To place or treat in a saggar, as pottery. Also **sag′ger**. [Contraction of SAFEGUARD]

Sa·ghal·ien (sə-gäl′yən) See SAKHALIN.

Sag·i·naw (sag′ə-nô) A port city in east central Michigan, on the Saginaw River; pop. 91,849.

Saginaw Bay A SW inlet of Lake Huron, extending about 60 miles into eastern Michigan.

Sa·git·ta (sə-jit′ə) *n.* A constellation, the Arrow. See CONSTELLATION. [< L]

sag·it·tal (saj′ə-təl) *adj.* 1. Of, pertaining to, or resembling an arrow or arrowhead. 2. *Anat.* **a** Denoting the suture between the two parietal bones of the skull. **b** Of or pertaining to the longitudinal plane dividing an animal into right and left halves. [< L *sagitta* arrow] — **sag′it·tal·ly** *adv.*

Sag·it·ta·ri·us (saj′ə-târ′ē·əs) *n.* A constellation, the Archer; also, the ninth sign of the zodiac. See CONSTELLATION, ZODIAC. [< L < *sagitta* arrow]

sag·it·tate (saj′ə-tāt) *adj. Bot.* Shaped like an arrowhead, as certain leaves. See illustration of LEAF. Also **sag′it·tat′ed, sa·git·ti·form** (sə-jit′ə-fôrm). [< L *sagitta* arrow]

sa·go (sä′gō) *n. pl.* **·gos** 1. Any of several varieties of East Indian palm (genus *Metroxylon*). 2. The dried, powdered pith of this palm, used as a thickening agent in puddings, etc. [< Malay *sāgū*]

Sa·guache (sə·wach′) See SAWATCH RANGE.

sa·gua·ro (sə·gwä′rō, -wä′-) *n. pl.* **·ros** A large desert cactus (*Cereus giganteus*) of the SW United States, with an erect, columnar trunk, sometimes branching, many ribs, strong spines, and flowering tops: its blossom is the State flower of Arizona: also called *giant cactus*. Also **sa·hua′ro** (-wä′-). [< Sp. < Piman]

Sag·ue·nay River (sag′ə-nā′) A river in southern Quebec province, Canada, flowing about 475 miles, generally SE, through Lake St. John to the St. Lawrence River.

sa·gum (sā′gəm) *n. pl.* **·ga** (-gə) The ancient Roman soldiers' military cloak, a symbol of war, as the toga was of peace. [< L < Celtic]

Sa·gun·to (sä-gōōn′tō) An ancient town in eastern Spain; destroyed by Hannibal, 219 B.C.; pop. 26,978 (est. 1959): formerly *Murviedro*. Ancient **Sa·gun·tum** (sə-gun′təm).

sag·y (sā′jē) *adj.* **sag·i·er, sag·i·est** Flavored or seasoned with sage.

Sa·hap·tan (sä-hap′tən) *n.* Shahaptian.

Sa·har·a (sə-har′ə, -hâr′ə, -hä′rə) The world's largest desert area, extending across most of northern Africa; about 3 million sq. mi. Also **Sahara Desert**.

Sa·ha·ran·pur (sə-hä′rən-pŏŏr) A city in northern Uttar Pradesh, India; pop. 223,460 (est. 1971).

Sa·hib (sä′ib) *n.* Master; Mr.; sir: used in India and Pakistan for people of rank and, especially formerly, for Europeans. Also **Sa′heb**. [< Urdu *sāhib* < Arabic *şāhib* lord, companion]

saice (sīs) See SYCE.

said¹ (sed) Past tense and past participle of SAY¹. — *adj. Law* Previously mentioned; aforesaid.

sa·id² (sä′vid, sī′id) See SAYID.

Sa·i·da (sä·ē·dä) A port city in SW Lebanon, on the Mediterranean; pop. 32,200 (est. 1961): ancient *Sidon*: also *Sayida*.

sai·ga (sī′gə) *n.* An antelope (*Saiga tartarica*) of the Siberian steppes, resembling a sheep. [< Russian *saiga*]

Sai·gon (sī·gon′, *Fr.* sá·ē·gôn′) The capital of South Vietnam, in the southern part; pop. 1,706,869 (est. 1969, including suburbs).

sail (sāl) *n. pl.* **sails;** *for def. 3, often* **sail** 1. *Naut.* A piece of canvas, dacron, or other material, attached to a vessel so that it may be spread to the wind and aid in the vessel's propulsion and by adjustment assist in its maneuvering. 2. Sails collectively: *full sail*. 3. A sailing vessel or craft: *30 sail in sight*. 4. A trip or passage in a sailing vessel, or in any watercraft. 5. Anything resembling a sail in form or use; as: **a** The broad part of the arm of a windmill. **b** The fairing conning tower of a modern submarine. **c** A bird's wing. — **to make sail** 1. To unfurl a sail or sails. 2. To set out on a voyage. — **to set sail** To begin a

SAILS
A Fore-and-aft. B Square. *a* Head. *b* Foot. *c* Leech. *d* Luff. *e* Clew.

voyage; get under way. **— under sail** Sailing; with sails spread and driven by the wind. **— v.i.** 1. To move across the surface of water by the action of wind or mechanical power. 2. To travel over water in a ship or boat. 3. To begin a voyage; set sail. 4. To manage a sailing craft: Can you *sail?* 5. To move, glide, or float in the air; soar. 6. To move along in a stately or dignified manner. 7. *Informal* To pass rapidly. 8. *Informal* To proceed boldly into action: with *in*. **— v.t.** 9. To move or travel across the surface of (a body of water) in a ship or boat. 10. To navigate (a ship, etc.). **— to sail into** 1. To begin with energy. 2. To attack violently. [OE *segl*] **— sail'a·ble** *adj.*

sail·boat (sāl'bōt/) *n.* *U.S.* A small boat propelled by a sail or sails.

sail·cloth (sāl'klôth/, -kloth/) *n.* A very strong, firmly woven cotton canvas suitable for sails.

sail·er (sā'lər) *n.* A vessel that sails; a ship having a specified sailing power: a fast *sailer*.

sail·fish (sāl'fish/) *n.* *pl.* **·fish** or **·fish·es** Any of a genus (*Istiophorus*) of marine fishes allied to the spearfish, having a large or conspicuous dorsal fin likened to a sail.

sail·ing (sā'ling) *n.* 1. The act of one who or that which sails. 2. The art and method of determining the direction and distance sailed by a ship at sea, the point reached, and the course to be taken; navigation. 3. The departure of a vessel beginning a voyage; especially, the time of departure.

sailing orders Instructions given to a ship's captain, covering all details of a voyage.

sail loft A room where sails are cut out and sewed.

sail·or (sā'lər) *n.* 1. A seaman; mariner. 2. A sailor hat (which see). **— sail'or·ly** *adj.*

— Syn. 1. *Sailor, mariner, seaman, tar, bluejacket,* and *gob* denote a man who works aboard a ship at sea. *Sailor* is a broad term applied to any member of a ship's crew, from the captain down, or specifically to one skilled in managing boats or ships under sail. *Mariner* may be equally broad, or may mean specifically an officer skilled in navigation. *Seaman* is chiefly applied to a professional *sailor* who is not an officer, and *tar* is used of a veteran *seaman*. A *bluejacket* is an enlisted man in the British or U.S. Navy, and *gob* is the U.S. slang equivalent of *bluejacket*.

sailor collar A large collar, square in back and V-shaped in the front.

sailor hat A low-crowned, flat-topped straw hat with a brim, worn by both sexes: also called *sailor*.

sail·or's-choice (sā'lərz-chois/) *n.* 1. Any of various fishes common off the Atlantic coast of the United States, as the pigfish and pinfish. 2. A species of grunt (*Haemulon parra*) of South Atlantic waters from Florida to Brazil.

sain (sān) *v.t.* *Scot.* or *Archaic* To sign or bless with the sign of the cross to preserve against malign influence: also spelled *sane*. [OE *segnian* < L *signare* < *signum* sign]

sain·foin (sān'foin) *n.* An Old World leguminous cloverlike herb (*Onobrychis viciaefolia*), having variegated flowers and cultivated for forage. Also **saint'foin** (sānt'-). [< F < *sain* healthy (< L *sanus*) + *foin* hay < L *faenum*]

saint (sānt) *n.* 1. A holy or godly person. 2. In certain churches, such a person who has died and been canonized. For individual canonized saints, see specific name, as (Saint) AMBROSE. 3. Any one of the blessed in heaven. 4. An angel. 5. In the New Testament, any Christian believer. *Eph.* i 1. 6. A very patient, unselfish person. **— v.t.** To canonize; venerate as a saint. **— adj.** Holy; canonized. *Abbr.* S., St. [< OF *saint* < L *sanctus* holy < *sancire* to make sacred]

Saint For entries not found under *Saint*, see under St.

Saint (sānt) *n.* A member of one of the religious bodies known as **Saints:** Latter-day *Saint*.

Saint Bernard A working dog of great size and strength, characterized by a massive head, and a thick, white, red, or brindled coat, formerly used to rescue travelers by the hospice at Great St. Bernard Pass in the Swiss Alps.

Saint-Cloud (sän·klōō/) A town in northern France near Paris; former residence of French monarchs; pop. 28,016 (1968).

SAINT BERNARD
(About 27 inches high at shoulder)

Saint-Cyr (sän·sēr/), **Marquis Laurent de Gouvion,** 1764–1830, French marshal.

Saint-Cyr-l'É·cole (sän·sēr·lā·kôl/) A town in north central France near Versailles; site of a national military academy; pop. about 10,000.

Saint-De·nis (sän·də·nē/) 1. A city in northern France, near Paris; burial place of many French kings; pop. 99,027 (1968). 2. The capital of Réunion; pop. 37,050 (est. 1967).

Sainte-Beuve (sänt·bœv/), **Charles Augustin,** 1804–69, French poet, critic, and historian.

saint·ed (sān'tid) *adj.* 1. Canonized. 2. Of holy character; saintly.

Saint-É·tienne (sänt·tā·tyen/) A city in SE central France, near Lyon; pop. 212,843 (1968).

Saint-Ex·u·pé·ry (sän·teg·zü·pā·rē/), **Antoine de,** 1900–44, French writer and aviator.

Saint-Gau·dens (sānt·gô/dənz), **Augustus,** 1848–1907, U.S. sculptor born in Ireland.

Saint-Ger·main (sän·zher·man/) A city in north central France, near Paris; scene of the signing of the peace treaty between France and Austria, 1919; pop. 36,251 (1968). Also **Saint-Germain-en-Laye** (-än·lā/).

saint·hood (sānt/hŏŏd) *n.* 1. The character or condition of being a saint. 2. Saints collectively.

Saint-Jean Bap·tiste Societies (sän·jän/bà·tēst/) In French Canada, organizations for the fostering and preservation of French-Canadian language and culture.

Saint-Just (sän·zhüst/), **Louis Antoine Léon de,** 1767–94, French revolutionist; guillotined.

Saint-Lô (sän·lō/) A town in NW France; partially destroyed during World War II; pop. 17,347 (1968).

Saint-Lou·is (sän·lōō·ē/) A city in NW Senegal, at the mouth of the Senegal river; pop. 50,000 (est. 1965).

saint·ly (sānt/lē) *adj.* **·li·er, ·li·est** Like, concerned with, or suitable for a saint. **— saint'li·ness** *n.*

Saint-Ma·lo (sän·mà·lō/) A port city in NW France, on the **Gulf of Saint-Malo,** an inlet of the English Channel; pop. 40,252 (1968).

Saint-Mi·hiel (sän·mē·yel/) A town in NE France on the Meuse; scene of an American victory of World War I, 1918.

Saint-Na·zaire (sän·nà·zâr/) A port city in western France, at the mouth of the Loire; pop. 60,696 (1968).

Saint Patrick's Day March 17, a day traditionally celebrated by the Irish in honor of their patron saint.

Saint·paul·i·a (sānt·pô/lē·ə) *n.* The African violet. [< NL, after Baron Walter von *Saint Paul,* German botanist]

Saint-Pierre (sän·pyâr/), **Jacques Henri Bernardin de,** 1737–1814, French author.

Saint-Quen·tin (sän·kän·tan/) A city in northern France, on the Somme; pop. 63,932 (1968).

Saint-Saëns (sän·säns/), **Charles Camille,** 1835–1921, French composer.

Saints·bur·y (sānts/ber·ē), **George Edward Bateman,** 1845–1933, English literary critic and historian.

saint·ship (sānt/ship) *n.* Sainthood.

Saint-Si·mon (sän·sē·môn/), **Comte Claude Henri de,** 1760–1825, French philosopher and socialist. **— Duc de,** 1675–1755, Louis de Rouvroy, French author and diplomat.

Saint-Vaast-la-Hogue (sän·väst/là·ôg/) A port town in NW France, on the Cotentin Peninsula; site of a French naval defeat by English and Dutch forces, 1692: also *La Hogue, La Hougue.*

Saint Valentine's Day February 14, the anniversary of the beheading of St. Valentine by the Romans, and also a day when valentines are exchanged.

Sai·pan (sī·pän/, -pan/, sī/pan) One of the Mariana Islands; 47 sq. mi.; captured from Japan by U.S. forces in World War II, 1944.

Sa·ïs (sā/is) An ancient city of Lower Egypt on the Rosetta branch of the Nile; an ancient capital of Lower Egypt. **— Sa·ite** (sā/īt) *n.* **— Sa·it·ic** (sā·it/ik) *adj.*

saith (seth) *Archaic* Present indicative third person singular of SAY[1].

sai·yid (sī/id, sä/yid) See SAYID.

sa·jou (sə·jōō/) *n.* A capuchin (def. 2). [Var. of SAPAJOU]

Sa·kai (sä·kī) A city on southern Honshu, Japan, on Osaka Bay; pop. 544,000 (est. 1968).

sake[1] (sāk) *n.* 1. Purpose of obtaining or accomplishing: to speak slowly for the *sake* of clarity. 2. Affectionate or reverent consideration; interest; account; advantage: for your own *sake*. [OE *sacu* strife, lawsuit]

— Syn. 2. *Sake* and *behalf* are akin in reference to a person; something done for the *sake* of such a person, or on his *behalf*, is intended to promote his welfare. But *sake* suggests the benevolence of a parent or friend, while *behalf* suggests a somewhat less personal relationship, as that of an attorney, agent, or patron.

sa·ke[2] (sä/kē) *n.* A fermented liquor made in Japan from rice. Also **sa/ki.** [< Japanese]

Sa·kel (zä/kəl), **Manfred,** 1906–57, Austrian psychiatrist active in the United States; originator of insulin shock therapy.

sa·ker (sā/kər) *n.* A large Old World falcon (*Falco cherrug* or *F. sacer*), used in falconry. [< OF *sacre* < Sp. *sacro* < Arabic *saqr*]

Sa·kha·lin (sak/ə·lēn/, *Russ.* sə·khä·lyēn/) An island of the SE R.S.F.S.R., comprising the **Sakhalin Oblast** (also **Sakhalin Region,** *Russian* **Sa·kha·lin/ska·ya Oblast** (-ska·ya); 29,700 sq. mi.; pop. 600,000 (est. 1967); center, Yuzhno-Sakhalinsk. The southern part of the island (13,930 sq. mi.), known as *Karafuto*, was ceded to Japan by the Treaty of Portsmouth, but was reoccupied after World War II. Formerly *Saghalien*.

Sa·ki (sä/kē) Pseudonym of *Hector Hugh Munro,* 1870–1916, British satirical writer.

Sak·ti (säk/tē, sak/-; *Sanskrit* shuk/tē) See SHAKTI.

Sa·kun·ta·la (sə·kŏŏn/tə·lä, shə-) The heroine of a famous Sanskrit play of this name by Kalidasa. Also *Shakuntala*.

sal (sal) *n.* Salt. [< L]

sa·laam (sə·läm/) *n.* An oriental salutation or obeisance made with a low bow, the palm of the right hand being held to the forehead; also, a respectful or ceremonious verbal greeting. **— v.t. & v.i.** To greet with or make a salaam. [< Arabic *salām* peace, a salutation < *aslama* to submit]

sal·a·ble (sā′lə·bəl) *adj.* Such as can be sold; marketable: also spelled *saleable.* **—sal′a·bil′i·ty, sal′a·ble·ness** *n.* **—sal′a·bly** *adv.*

sa·la·cious (sə·lā′shəs) *adj.* **1.** Lustful; lewd. **2.** Obscene: a *salacious* joke. [< L *salax, salacis* < *salire* to leap] **—sa·la′cious·ly** *adv.* **—sa·la′cious·ness, sa·lac′i·ty** (-lăs′ə·tē) *n.*

sal·ad (sal′əd) *n.* **1.** Green herbs or vegetables, usually uncooked and served with a dressing, sometimes mixed with chopped cold meat, fish, etc.; also, a similar dish made with fruit. **2.** The course consisting of such a dish. [< OF *salade* < Provençal *salada* < *salar* to salt < L *sal* salt]

sa·la·dang (sə·lä′däng) *n.* The East Indian ox (*Bos gaurus*): also called *gaur*: also spelled *seladang.* [Var. of *seladang* < Malay *sĕladañ*]

salad days Days of youth, freshness, and inexperience.

salad dressing A savory sauce used on salads, as mayonnaise, or a mixture of salt, oil, and vinegar, etc.

Sal·a·din (sal′ə·din) 1137?–93, sultan of Egypt and Syria, 1174?–93; defended Acre against Crusaders: full name **Sa·lah·al-Din Yusuf ibn-Ayyud** (sä·lä′ä·dēn′).

Sal·a·man·ca (sal′ə·mang′kə, *Sp.* sä′lä·mäng′kä) A city in west central Spain; scene of a victory of Wellington over the French, 1812; pop. 89,085 (est. 1960).

sal·a·man·der (sal′ə·man′dər) *n.* **1.** Any of an order (*Caudata*) of tailed, lizardlike amphibians having a smooth, moist skin and two pairs of limbs, as the American **spotted salamander** (*Ambystoma punctatum*). **2.** A mythical lizard or other creature fabled to live in fire. **3.** Any person or thing that can stand great heat. **4.** A large poker or other implement used around or in fire, or when red-hot. **5.** A mass of hardened metal or slag left in the hearth of a furnace after the fires are drawn: also called *shadrach.* [< OF *salamandre* < L *salamandra* < Gk] **—sal′a·man′drine** (-drin) *adj.*

SPOTTED SALAMANDER (To 7¾ inches long)

Sa·lam·bri·a (sä′läm·brē′ä, *Greek* säl′äm·brē·ä′) The former name for the PENEUS.

sa·la·mi (sə·lä′mē) *n.* A salted, spiced sausage, originally Italian. [< Ital., pl., ult. < L *sal* salt]

Sal·a·mis (sal′ə·mis) **1.** An ancient ruined city on eastern Cyprus. **2.** An island of Greece in the Aegean; 39 sq. mi.; containing the Bay of Salamis, site of a Greek naval victory over the Persians, 480 B.C.

sal ammoniac Ammonium chloride. [< L *sal Ammoniacum*, lit., salt of Ammon; so called because orig. made from camel's dung near the shrine of Jupiter *Ammon* in Libya]

sal·a·ried (sal′ər·ēd, sal′rēd) *adj.* **1.** In receipt of a salary. **2.** Yielding a salary.

sal·a·ry (sal′ər·ē, sal′rē) *n. pl.* **·ries** A periodic, fixed payment for services, especially for official or professional services as distinguished from manual or menial labor. **—v.t. ·ried, ·ry·ing** To pay or allot a salary to. [< AF *salarie* < L *salarium* money paid Roman soldiers for their salt < *salarius* of salt < *sal* salt]

—Syn. (noun) Salary, *stipend, wage, pay, compensation, recompense, emolument, fee,* and *honorarium* denote money paid for work or services; all but the last two imply periodic payment. *Salary* is applied to trained and skilled workers, as those in professional, management, and white-collar positions; *salary* is paid weekly, monthly, or at longer intervals. *Stipend* is sometimes (chiefly in Britain) substituted for *salary,* or applied specifically to a clergyman's *salary.* A *wage,* or *wages,* is paid to manual and unskilled workers, usually weekly. *Pay* is often interchanged with *wages,* and is preferred in speaking of the *salary* or *wages* of persons in military or naval service. *Compensation* and *recompense* come into comparison here only because they are used euphemistically for *salary* or *wages,* to emphasize the arduousness of the work done. *Emolument* is a bookish term for all the advantages of a salaried position—gifts, prestige, and the like, as well as *salary.* A *fee* is a single sum paid for service to one otherwise self-employed, as a doctor or lawyer. An *honorarium* is a gift for services when an agreed *fee* or *salary* is prohibited by law or propriety; the word is also used humorously for *wage.*

Sa·la·zar (sä′lə·zär′), Antonio de Oliveira, 1889–1970, Portuguese statesman, prime minister 1932–68.

sale (sāl) *n.* **1.** The act of selling; the exchange or transfer of property of any kind for money or its equivalent. **2.** An auction. **3.** The selling of something at bargain prices. **4.** Opportunity of selling; demand by purchasers; market: Stocks find no *sale.* **—for sale** (or **on sale**) Offered or ready for sale. [OE *sala* < ON. Akin to SELL.]

sale·a·ble (sā′lə·bəl) See SALABLE.

Sa·lem (sā′ləm) **1.** A port city in NE Massachusetts; pop. 40,556. **2.** The capital of Oregon, in the NW part, on the Willamette River; pop. 68,296. **3.** An Old Testament name for JERUSALEM. **4.** A city in central Madras, India; pop. 297,160 (est. 1971).

sal·ep (sal′ep) *n.* A farinaceous meal obtained from the dry tubers of various orchids, used as food and formerly as medicine. [< F or Sp. < Arabic *saḥlab,* contraction of *khuṣa al-tha′lab* fox's testicles]

sal·e·ra·tus (sal′ə·rā′təs) *n.* Sodium bicarbonate, for use in cookery; baking soda. [< NL *sal aëratus* aerated salt]

Sa·ler·no (sä·ler′nō) A port commune in SW Italy, on the Gulf of Salerno, an inlet of the Tyrrhenian Sea; scene of fierce fighting in World War II between Germans and Allied landing forces, 1943; pop. 118,171 (1961). Ancient **Sa·ler·num** (sə·lûr′nəm).

sales·clerk (sālz′klûrk′) *n. U.S.* A clerk who sells goods in a store.

sales·girl (sālz′gûrl′) *n. U.S.* A woman or girl hired to sell merchandise, especially in a store.

sales·la·dy (sālz′lā′dē) *n. pl.* **·dies** *Informal* A woman or girl hired to sell merchandise, especially in a store.

sales·man (sālz′mən) *n. pl.* **·men** (-mən) A man hired to sell goods, stock, etc., in a store or by canvassing.

sales·man·ship (sālz′mən·ship) *n.* **1.** The work or profession of a salesman. **2.** Ability or skill in selling.

sales·peo·ple (sālz′pē′pəl) *n.pl.* Salespersons.

sales·per·son (sālz′pûr′sən) *n.* A person hired to sell merchandise, especially in a store.

sales resistance The ability to resist any attempts to induce one to buy certain goods or services.

sales·room (sālz′rōom′, -rŏŏm′) *n.* A room where merchandise is displayed for sale.

sales tax A tax on money received from sales of goods.

sales·wom·an (sālz′wŏŏm′ən) *n. pl.* **·wom·en** (-wim′in) A woman or girl hired to sell merchandise, especially in a store.

Sal·ford (sôl′fərd) A county borough in Greater Manchester, England; pop. 273,600 (1976).

Sa·li·an (sā′lē·ən) *adj.* Of or pertaining to the Sal·i·i (sal′ē·ī), a tribe of Franks who, in the fourth century A.D., settled on both sides of the lower Rhine, near the Zuyder Zee. **—n.** One of the Salii. Also **Salian Frank.**

sal·ic (sal′ik) *adj. Geol.* Belonging to a group of igneous rocks composed chiefly of silica and alumina, as the feldspars, quartz, etc. [< S(ILICA) + AL(UMINUM) + -IC]

Sal·ic (sal′ik) *adj.* **1.** Of or pertaining to the Salic Law. **2.** Of or pertaining to the Salian Franks. Also spelled *Salique.* [< MF *Salique* < Med.L *Salicus* < LL *Salii* the Salii]

sal·i·ca·ceous (sal′ə·kā′shəs) *adj. Bot.* Of or pertaining to the willow family (*Salicaceae*) of shrubs and trees. [< NL *salicaceus* < L *salix, -icis* willow]

sal·i·cin (sal′ə·sin) *n. Chem.* A white, crystalline, bitter glycoside, $C_{13}H_{18}O_7$, contained in the bark of certain willows and poplars, and made synthetically, used in medicine for arthritis and as an antiperiodic. Also **sal′i·cine** (-sēn, -sin). [< F *salicine* < L *salix, -icis* willow + F *-ine -ine²*]

Salic Law 1. A law derived from Germanic sources in the fifth century and providing that males only could inherit land. **2.** A similar law prohibiting women from succeeding to the thrones of France or Spain. Also spelled *Salique Law.*

sal·i·cyl·ate (sal′ə·sil′āt, sə·lis′ə·lāt) *n. Chem.* A salt or ester of salicylic acid.

sal·i·cyl·ic acid (sal′ə·sil′ik) *Chem.* A white crystalline compound, $C_7H_6O_3$, occurring in many plants and also made synthetically, the salts of which are used for treating arthritis. [< SALIC(IN) + -YL + -IC]

sa·li·ence (sā′lē·əns) *n.* **1.** The condition of being salient. **2.** A protruding feature or detail. Also **sa′li·en·cy.**

sa·li·ent (sā′lē·ənt) *adj.* **1.** Standing out prominently; striking; conspicuous: a *salient* feature. **2.** Extending beyond the general line; projecting. **3.** Leaping; springing. **—n.** The part of a fortification, trench, etc., that most protrudes towards the enemy. For illustration see BASTION. [< L *saliens, -entis,* ppr. of *salire* to leap] **—sa′li·ent·ly** *adv.* **—sa′li·ent·ness** *n.*

sa·li·en·ti·an (sā′lē·en′shē·ən) *n.* Any of an order (*Salientia*) of tailless amphibians characterized by broad, stocky bodies and hind legs adapted for leaping, including the frogs and toads. **—adj.** Belonging or pertaining to the *Salientia.* [< NL *Salientia* < L *saliens.* See SALIENT.]

sa·lif·er·ous (sə·lif′ər·əs) *adj.* Containing a considerable proportion of salt in beds or as brine: *saliferous* rocks. [< L *sal, salis* salt + -FEROUS]

sal·i·fy (sal′ə·fī) *v.t.* **·fied, ·fy·ing 1.** To combine or impregnate with a salt. **2.** To form into a salt, as with an acid. [< F *salifier* < L *sal, salis* salt + *facere* to make] **—sal′i·fi′a·ble** *adj.* **—sal′i·fi·ca′tion** *n.*

sa·li·na (sə·lī′nə) *n.* **1.** A pool, pond, or marsh containing salt water diked in from the sea; also, a salt spring. **2.** A saltworks or salt mine. [< Sp. < L *salinae* salt pits < *sal, salis* salt]

Sa·li·na (sə·lī′nə) A city in central Kansas, on the Smoky Hill River; pop. 37,714.

Sa·li·nas (sə·lē′nəs) A city in western California; pop. 58,896.

sa·line (sā′lēn, -līn) *adj.* **1.** Of, composing, or characteristic of salt. **2.** Containing salt; salty. **—n. 1.** A metallic salt. **2.** A salt solution used in the investigation of biological and physiological processes, and also in medicine. [< F *salin* < LL (assumed) *salinus* < L *sal, salis* salt]

sa·lin·i·ty (sə·lin′ə·tē) *n.* **1.** The state or degree of being salt or saline. **2.** A measure of the total amount of salt per kilogram of a saline solution. Compare CHLORINITY.

sal·i·nom·e·ter (sal′ə·nom′ə·tər) *n.* A hydrometer graduated to show the percentage of salt in a solution. [< *salino-* (< SALINE) + -METER] — **sal′i·nom′e·try** *n.*

Sa·lique (sə·lēk′, sal′ik, sā′lik) See SALIC, SALIC LAW.

Salis·bur·y (sôlz′ber·ē, -brē) **1.** The chief city of Wiltshire, England, a municipal borough in the southeastern part of the county; pop. 101,105 (1976): also *New Sarum.* **2.** The capital of Rhodesia, in the northeastern part; pop. 385,530 (est. 1970).

Salis·bur·y (sôlz′ber·ē, -brē), **Marquis of,** 1830–1903, Robert Arthur Talbot Gascoyne-Cecil. English statesman.

Salisbury Plain An undulating chalk plateau in southern Wiltshire, England; 300 sq. mi.; site of Stonehenge.

Salisbury steak Hamburger (def. 2).

Sa·lish (sā′lish) *n.* **1.** A North American Indian of Salishan stock: commonly called *Flathead.* **2.** Any of the languages of the Salishan Indians.

Sa·lish·an (sā′lish·ən, sal′ish-) *adj.* Of or pertaining to a stock of North American Indians, formerly inhabiting Oregon, Washington, British Columbia, and Montana. — *n.* Any of the Salishan languages. Also **Sa′lish.**

sa·li·va (sə·lī′və) *n. Physiol.* The slightly alkaline fluid containing ptyalin and secreted by the glands of the mouth, considered a promoter of digestion. [< L] — **sal′i·var·y** (sal′ə·ver′ē) *adj.*

sal·i·vate (sal′ə·vāt) *v.* **·vat·ed, ·vat·ing** *v.i.* To secrete saliva. — *v.t.* To produce salivation in. [< L *salivatus,* pp. of L *salivare* < *saliva* saliva]

sal·i·va·tion (sal′ə·vā′shən) *n.* **1.** The act or process of salivating. **2.** An abnormally increased flow of saliva, especially when due to the effect of drugs, as mercury.

Salk (sôk, sôlk), **Jonas Edward,** born 1914, U.S. bacteriologist; developed injected vaccine for poliomyelitis.

salle à man·ger (sal à män·zhā′) *French* A dining room.

sal·let (sal′it) *n.* A rounded, 15th-century helmet extending over the back of the neck. [< OF *salade* < Ital. *celata* < L *caelata* (*cassis*) engraved (helmet) < *caelare* to engrave]

sal·low[1] (sal′ō) *adj.* Of an unhealthy yellowish color: said chiefly of the human skin. [OE *salu*] — **sal′low·ish** *adj.* — **sal′low·ly** *adv.* — **sal′low·ness** *n.*

sal·low[2] (sal′ō) *n.* A willow: especially, the **great sallow** (*Salix caprea*) of Europe. [OE *sealh.* Akin to L *salix.*]

sal·low·y (sal′ō·ē) *adj.* Fringed with or abounding in sallows.

Sal·lust (sal′əst), 86?–34? B.C., Roman historian: full name **Gaius Sallustius Cris·pus** (kris′pus).

sal·ly (sal′ē) *v.i.* **·lied, ·ly·ing 1.** To rush out suddenly. **2.** To set out energetically. **3.** To go out, as from a room or building. — *n. pl.* **·lies 1.** A rushing forth, as of troops against besiegers; sortie. **2.** Any sudden rushing forth. **3.** A going forth, as on a walk. **4.** A bantering remark or witticism. [< OF *saillie* < *saillir* < L *salire* to leap]

sal·ly lunn (sal′ē lun) A raised and sweetened, muffinlike teacake. [after *Sally Lunn,* 18th c. pastry cook, of Bath, England]

sal·ma·gun·di (sal′mə·gun′dē) *n.* **1.** A saladlike dish of chopped meat, anchovies, eggs, onions, oil, etc. **2.** Any medley or mixture. Also **sal′ma·gun′dy.** [< F *salmigondis.* ? Cf. Ital. *salame* salt meat and *condire* to pickle.]

Sal·ma·gun·di (sal′mə·gun′dē) A series of humorous and satirical papers published periodically in 1807–08 by Washington Irving and others.

sal·mi (sal′mē) *n.* A spiced dish of birds or game roasted, minced, and stewed in wine; a ragout. Also **sal·mis** (sal′mē, *Fr.* sàl·mē′). [< F, prob. contraction of *salmigondis.* See SALMAGUNDI.]

salm·on (sam′ən) *n.* **1.** Any of various food fishes (family *Salmonidae*); especially, the **Atlantic salmon** (*Salmo salar*), inhabiting the North Atlantic coastal waters and ascending to the headwaters of adjacent rivers to spawn, having a brownish color above, silvery sides, black spots, and a delicate pink flesh. **2.** Any of various other salmonoid fishes, especially the quinnat and the sockeye. **3.** A reddish or pinkish orange color: also **salmon pink.** — *adj.* Having a salmon color. [< OF *saumon* < L *salmo, -onis,* prob. akin to *salire* to leap]

salm·on·ber·ry (sam′ən·ber′ē) *n. pl.* **·ries 1.** A hardy raspberry (*Rubus spectabilis*) of the Pacific coast. **2.** The cloudberry (which see). **3.** A raspberry (*R. parviflorus*) of the United States, having a white blossom.

sal·mo·nel·la (sal′mə·nel′ə) *n. pl.* **·la** or **·lae** (-lē) or **·las** Any of a genus (*Salmonella*) of aerobic, rodlike, preponderantly motile bacteria causing food poisoning and other disorders in man. [< NL, after Daniel Elmer *Salmon,* U.S. pathologist, 1850–1914]

Sal·mo·ne·us (sal·mō′nē·əs) In Greek mythology, a son of Aeolus and king of Elis who was destroyed by thunderbolts for claiming to be the equal of Zeus.

sal·mo·noid (sal′mə·noid) *adj.* **1.** Resembling a salmon. **2.** Belonging to the salmon family. — *n.* A salmonoid fish.

salmon trout 1. The European brown trout (*Salmo trutta*).

2. The lake trout (which see). **3.** The steelhead.

sal·ol (sal′ōl, -ol) *n. Chem.* A colorless crystalline compound, $C_{13}H_{10}O_3$, derived from salicylic acid, used in medicine. [< SAL(ICYLIC ACID) + -OL[1]]

Sa·lo·me (sə·lō′mē) The daughter of Herodias, who asked Herod for the head of John the Baptist in return for her dancing. *Matt.* xiv 8.

Sal·o·mon (sal′ō·mən), **Haym,** 1740?–85, American patriot born in Poland; helped finance the American Revolution.

sa·lon (sa·lon′, *Fr.* sà·lôn′) *n.* **1.** A room in which guests are received; a drawing room. **2.** The periodic gathering or reception of noted persons, under the auspices of some distinguished woman, especially in Paris in the 17th and 18th centuries. **3.** A hall or gallery used for exhibiting works of art. **4.** An exhibition of works of art. **5.** An establishment devoted to some specific purpose: a beauty *salon.* [< F < Ital. *salone* < *sala* hall < Gmc.]

Sa·lon (sa·lon′, *Fr.* sà·lôn′) *n.* An annual exhibition of works by living artists, held in Paris.

Sa·lo·ni·ka (sā′lô·nē′kä) A port city in NE Greece, on the **Gulf of Salonika,** an inlet of the Aegean; pop. 448,000 (1961): ancient *Therma.* Greek *Thessalonike.* Also **Sa′lo·ni′ki** (-kē), **Sa′lo·ni′ca.**

sa·loon (sə·lōōn′) *n.* **1.** *U.S.* A place where alcoholic drinks are sold; a bar. **2.** *Brit.* In a public house, a section of the bar set aside for patrons of a higher social status than those in the public bar. **3.** A large apartment or room for assemblies, public entertainment, exhibitions, etc. **4.** The main cabin of a passenger ship, used by the passengers in general. **5.** *Brit.* A sedan (def. 1). [< F *salon* salon. See SALON.]

sa·loon·keep·er (sə·lōōn′kē′pər) *n.* One who owns or manages a saloon (def. 1).

sa·loop (sə·lōōp′) *n. Brit.* An infusion of sassafras chips, salep, or similar aromatic herbs, formerly used largely as a beverage, as a cure for rheumatism, etc. [Var. of SALEP]

Sal·op (sal′əp) A county in western England; 1,347 sq. mi.; pop. 354,400 (1976); county seat, Shrewsbury. Also *Shropshire.*

sal·pa (sal′pə) *n.* Any of a genus (*Salpa*) of free-swimming, transparent, cylindrical tunicates found in warm seas. Also **sal′pi·an** (-pē-ən), **sal′pid** (-pid). [< NL < L < Gk. *salpē,* a sea fish] — **sal′pi·form** (-pə·fôrm). *adj.*

sal·pin·gec·to·my (sal′pin·jek′tə·mē) *n. pl.* **·mies** *Surg.* The excision of a Fallopian tube; sterilization of women. [< NL *salpinx, salpingos* Fallopian tube (< Gk., trumpet) + -ECTOMY]

sal·pinx (sal′pingks) *n. pl.* **sal·pin·ges** (sal·pin′jēz) *Anat.* A tube in man and other mammals, especially the Eustachian or Fallopian tube. [< NL < Gk., trumpet]

sal·si·fy (sal′sə·fē, -fī) *n. pl.* **·fies 1.** An Old World plant (*Tragopogon porrifolius*) of the composite family, with a white, edible root and an oysterlike flavor: also called *oyster plant, vegetable oyster.* **2.** The goatsbeard (def. 1). [< F *salsifis* < Ital. *sassefrica*]

sal·sil·la (sal·sil′ə) *n.* Any of several tropical American plants (genus *Bomarea*) of the amaryllis family, yielding edible tubers. [< NL *salsillus* salty < L *sal* salt]

sal soda Sodium carbonate.

salt (sôlt) *n.* **1.** Sodium chloride, NaCl, a widely distributed compound found in sea water and as a mineral, used as a seasoning and as a preservative. ◆ Collateral adjective: *saline.* **2.** *Chem.* Any compound consisting of the cation of a base and the anion of an acid, combined in proportions that give a balance of electropositive and electronegative charges. **3.** *pl.* A salt used as a laxative or cathartic; also, smelling salts (which see). **4.** Piquant humor; dry wit; repartee: Attic *salt.* **5.** That which preserves, corrects, or purifies; seasoning: the salt of criticism. **6.** *Informal* A sailor: an old *salt.* **7.** A saltcellar. — **below the salt** In inferior, subordinate, or servile position. — **to take with a grain of salt** To allow for exaggeration; have doubts about. — *adj.* **1.** Flavored with salt: salty; briny. **2.** Cured or preserved with salt. **3.** Containing, or growing or living in or near. salt water. **4.** *Obs.* Salacious; licentious; gross. — *v.t.* **1.** To season with salt. **2.** To preserve or cure with salt. **3.** To furnish with salt: to *salt* cattle. **4.** To season as if with salt; add zest or piquancy to. **5.** To add something to so as to increase the value fraudulently: to *salt* a mine with gold. — **to salt away 1.** To pack in salt for preserving. **2.** *Informal* To store up; save. — **to salt out** To separate (coal-tar colors) by adding salt to solutions containing them. [OE *sealt*]

sal·tant (sal′tənt) *adj.* Leaping; jumping; saltatory. [< L *saltans, -antis,* ppr. of *saltare,* freq. of *salire* to leap]

sal·ta·rel·lo (sal′tə·rel′ō, Ital. säl′tä·rel′lō) *n. pl.* **·rel·li** (-rel′ē, Ital. -rel′lē) **1.** A quick Italian dance, diversified by skips. **2.** Music for or in the manner of this dance. [< Ital. < *saltare* to leap < L. See SALTANT.]

sal·ta·tion (sal·tā′shən) *n.* **1.** A leap, as in a dance. **2.** A throbbing or palpitation, as of a blood vessel. **3.** *Biol.* An abrupt variation or mutation, especially as a factor in speciation. [< L *saltatio, -onis* < *saltare.* See SALTANT.]

sal·ta·to·ri·al (sal′tə·tôr′ē·əl, -tō′rē-) *adj.* **1.** Built or adapted for leaping. **2.** *Zool.* Adapted for or characterized by leaping. [< SALTATORY]

sal·ta·to·ry (sal′tə·tôr′ē, -tō′rē) *adj.* **1.** Of or pertaining to leaping or dancing. **2.** Moving by leaps or hops, as certain birds. [< L *saltatorius* < *saltare*. See SALTANT.]

salt·box (sôlt′boks′) *n.* *U.S.* A small two-story house of square plan having a gable roof with a steeper and shorter pitch at the front of the house than at the back.

salt cake Crude sodium sulfate, especially as obtained by the action of sulfuric acid on sodium chloride.

salt·cel·lar (sôlt′sel′ər) *n.* A small receptacle for salt; a saltshaker. [ME *salt saler* < *salt* + F *salière* saltcellar < L *sal*]

salt chuck *U.S. & Canadian* In the Pacific Northwest, the sea.

salt·ed (sôl′tid) *adj.* **1.** Treated with or as with salt; preserved. **2.** *Informal* Experienced in some occupation.

salt·er (sôl′tər) *n.* **1.** One who applies salt to cure fish, meat, etc. **2.** One who manufactures or deals in salt. [OE *sealtere*]

salt·ern (sôl′tərn) *n.* A place or building where salt is manufactured. [OE *sealtern*]

salt grass Any of certain grasses found growing on salt marshes or on alkaline western plains.

salt hay Hay made from salt grass.

sal·tie (sôl′tē) See SALTY (def. 4).

sal·ti·grade (sal′tə·grād) *adj.* Adapted for leaping: said especially of certain insects, as grasshoppers. [< L *saltus* leap + *gradi* to step]

Sal·til·lo (säl·tē′yō) The capital of Coahuila, NE Mexico; pop. 191,879 (1970).

sal·tine (sôl·tēn′) *n.* A crisp, salty cracker.

sal·tire (sal′tir) *n.* *Heraldry* An ordinary formed by a bend and a bend sinister crossing as in St. Andrew's cross: also called *sautoir*. Also **sal′tier.** [< OF *sauteoir* < Med.L *saltatorium* stirrup < L *saltatorius*. See SALTATORY.]

salt·ish (sôl′tish) *adj.* Somewhat salty.

Salt Lake See GREAT SALT LAKE.

Salt Lake City The capital and largest city of Utah, SE of Great Salt Lake; center of Mormonism; pop. 175,885.

salt lick A place to which animals go to lick salt from superficial deposits; a salt spring or dried salt pond.

salt marsh Low coastal land frequently overflowed by the tide, usually covered with coarse grass. Also **salt meadow.**

salt of the earth The fundamentally fine people of the world; those who add value to mankind. *Matt.* v 13.

Sal·ton Sink (sôl′tən) A depression in southern California; lowest part, 280 ft. below sea level; in 1905 and 1906 became **Salton Sea,** a shallow, saline lake, by an overflow of the Colorado River; originally about 450 sq. mi., reduced to about 300 sq. mi. by evaporation.

salt·pan (sôlt′pan′) *n.* **1.** A vessel in which salt is made by evaporating saline water. **2.** A pond or basin from which salt is obtained by natural evaporation.

salt·pe·ter (sôlt′pē′tər) *n.* Potassium nitrate. — **Chile saltpeter** Mineral sodium nitrate, found chiefly in Chile. Also *Brit.* **salt′pe′tre.** [< OF *salpetre* < Med.L *sal petrae* rock salt < L *sal* salt + *petra* a rock < Gk.]

salt rheum *Pathol.* One of various skin eruptions, as eczema.

salt-ris·ing (sôlt′rī′zing) *n.* Salted batter used as leaven, or bread made from it.

Salt River **1.** A river in central Arizona, flowing about 200 miles, generally west, to the Gila River. **2.** A river in NE Missouri, flowing 200 miles to the Mississippi.

salt·shak·er (sôlt′shā′kər) *n.* A container with small holes for sprinkling table salt.

salt spring A flow of salt water from the earth.

salt-wa·ter (sôlt′wô′tər, -wot′ər) *adj.* Of, composed of, or living in salty water. Also **salt′wa′ter.**

salt well A well from which brine is obtained.

salt·works (sôlt′wûrks′) *n.* *pl.* **·works** An establishment where salt is made on a commercial scale. Also *esp. Brit.* **salt′work.**

salt·wort (sôlt′wûrt′) *n.* **1.** Any of various maritime plants (genus *Salsola*), of the goosefoot family; especially, the common saltwort (*S. kali*), used in making soda ash. **2.** Any of various glassworts.

salt·y (sôl′tē) *adj.* **salt·i·er, salt·i·est** **1.** Of, containing, or tasting like salt. **2.** Reminiscent of the sea; smelling of the sea. **3.** Piquant; sharp; pungent, as literature or speech. **4.** *U.S. & Canadian Informal* A deep-sea vessel sailing the Great Lakes: also spelled *saltie.* — **salt′i·ly** *adv.* — **salt′i·ness** *n.*

sa·lu·bri·ous (sə·lōō′brē·əs) *adj.* Conducive to health; healthful; wholesome. [< L *salubris* < *salus* health] — **sa·lu′bri·ous·ly** *adv.* — **sa·lu′bri·ous·ness, sa·lu′bri·ty** *n.*

sa·lu·ki (sə·lōō′kē) *n.* A very old breed of hound, having feathered ears, tail, and legs, and a gray body. [< Arabic *salūḳi* < *Salūq* an ancient Arabian city]

Sa·lus (sā′ləs) In Roman mythology, goddess of health and prosperity. [< L *salus*, health]

sal·u·tar·y (sal′yə·ter′ē) *adj.* **1.** Calculated to bring about a sound condition by correcting evil or promoting good; beneficial. **2.** Salubrious; wholesome. [< F *salutaire* < L *salutaris* < *salus, salutis* health] — **sal′u·tar′i·ly** *adv.* — **sal′u·tar′i·ness** *n.*

sal·u·ta·tion (sal′yə·tā′shən, -yōō-) *n.* **1.** The act of saluting. **2.** Any form of greeting. **3.** The opening words of a letter, as *Dear Sir.* [< MF < L *salutatio, -onis* < *salutare*. See SALUTE.]

sa·lu·ta·to·ri·an (sə·lōō′tə·tôr′ē·ən, -tō′rē-) *n.* *U.S.* In colleges and schools, the graduating student, usually receiving second highest honors, who delivers the salutatory at commencement. [< SALUTATORY]

sa·lu·ta·to·ry (sə·lōō′tə·tôr′ē, -tō′rē) *n.* *pl.* **·ries** An opening oration, as at a college commencement. — *adj.* Pertaining to or consisting in greeting or welcome; especially, relating to a salutatory address. [< L *salutatorius* pertaining to salutation < *salutare*. See SALUTE.]

sa·lute (sə·lōōt′) *n.* **1.** A greeting by display of military, naval, or other official honors, as by presenting arms, firing cannon, etc. **2.** The act or attitude assumed in giving a military salute. **3.** A gesture of greeting, compliment, respect, or the like, as a bow, kiss, etc. — *v.* **·lut·ed, ·lut·ing** *v.t.* **1.** To greet with an expression or sign of welcome, respect, etc. **2.** To honor in some prescribed way, as by raising the hand to the cap, presenting arms, firing cannon, etc. — *v.i.* **3.** To make a salute. — *Syn.* See GREET. [< F < L *salutare* < *salus, salutis* health] — **sa·lut′er** *n.*

Salv. Salvador.

sal·va·ble (sal′və·bəl) *adj.* Capable of being saved or salvaged. [< LL *salvare*. See SAVE[1].] — **sal′va·bly** *adv.*

Sal·va·dor (sal′və·dôr′; *Sp.* säl′vä·thôr′; *Pg.* säl′və·thôr′) **1.** See EL SALVADOR. **2.** The capital of Bahia state, Brazil; pop. 892,392 (est. 1968): formerly *Bahia, São Salvador.*

Sal·va·do·ri·an (sal′və·dôr′ē·ən, -dō′rē-) *adj.* Relating to El Salvador or its people. — *n.* A native or inhabitant of El Salvador. Also **Sal′va·do′ran.**

sal·vage (sal′vij) *v.t.* **·vaged, ·vag·ing** To save, as a ship or its cargo, from wreck, capture, etc. — *n.* **1.** The saving of a ship, cargo, etc., from loss. **2.** Any act of saving property. **3.** Compensation to persons by whose voluntary exertions a vessel, her cargo, or the lives of those belonging to her are saved from danger or loss. **4.** That which is saved from a wrecked or abandoned vessel or from a fire. **5.** Anything saved from destruction. [< MF < Med.L *salvagium* < L *salvus* safe] — **sal′vage·a·ble** *adj.* — **sal′vag·er** *n.*

sal·va·gee (sal′və·jē′) *n.* In maritime law, a person in whose favor or behalf salvage has been effected.

Sal·var·san (sal′vər·san) *n.* Proprietary name for a brand of arsphenamine. Also **sal′var·san.** [< G < LL *salvare* to save + G *arsen* arsenic]

sal·va·tion (sal·vā′shən) *n.* **1.** The process or state of being saved; preservation from impending evil. **2.** *Theol.* Deliverance from sin and penalty, realized in a future state; redemption. **3.** Any means of deliverance from danger, evil, or ruin. **4.** In Christian Science, Life, Truth, and Love understood and demonstrated as supreme over all. [< OF < LL *salvatio, -onis* < L *salvus* safe]

Salvation Army A religious and charitable organization on semimilitary lines, founded by William Booth in England in 1865: called the *Christian Mission* before 1878.

Sal·va·tion·ist (sal·vā′shən·ist) *n.* A member of the Salvation Army.

salve[1] (sav, säv) *n.* **1.** A thick, adhesive ointment for local ailments. **2.** Anything that heals, soothes, or mollifies. **3.** Praise or flattery. — *v.t.* **salved, salv·ing** **1.** To dress with salve or ointment. **2.** To soothe; appease, as conscience, pride, etc. [OE *sealf*]

salve[2] (salv) *v.t.* **salved, salv·ing** To save from loss; salvage. [< Med.L *salvare*]

sal·ve[3] (sal′vē) *interj.* Hail. [< L, imperative of *salvere* to be well]

Sal·ve·mi·ni (säl·vā′mē·nē), **Gaetano,** 1873–1957, Italian historian active in the United States.

sal·ver (sal′vər) *n.* A tray, as of silver. [< OF *salve* < Sp. *salva,* the foretasting of food, as for a king < *salvar* to taste, save < LL *salvare*. See SAVE[1].]

sal·vi·a (sal′vē·ə) *n.* Any of a genus (*Salvia*) of ornamental plants of the mint family, as the sage. [< L. See SAGE[2].]

Sal·vi·ni (säl·vē′nē), **Tommaso,** 1829–1915, Italian actor.

sal·vo[1] (sal′vō) *n.* *pl.* **·vos** or **·voes** **1.** A simultaneous discharge of artillery, or of two or more bombs from an aircraft. **2.** A salute given by firing all the guns. **3.** Any salute or simultaneous outburst: a *salvo* of applause. **4.** The concentrated fire of many pieces, as in a naval engagement. [< Ital. *salva* salute < L *salve*. See SALVE[3].]

sal·vo[2] (sal′vō) *n.* *pl.* **·vos** **1.** A saving clause; proviso. **2.** An evasion, reservation, or bad excuse. [< L *salvo* (*jure*) (right) being reserved, ablative of *salvus* safe]

sal·vo·lat·i·le (sal vō·lat′ə·lē) Ammonium carbonate; also, an aromatic solution of ammonium carbonate, used as smelling salts. [< NL, volatile salt < L]

sal·vor (sal′vər) n. A person or ship that helps to salvage a vessel or cargo at sea. Also **salv′er**. [< SALVE² + -OR]

Sal·ween (sal′wēn′) A river of Tibet, SW China, and Burma, flowing about 1,750 miles, generally south, to the Andaman Sea. Also **Sal′win′**.

Salz·burg (zälts′bŏŏrkh) A city in western Austria; the birthplace of Mozart; pop. 120,200 (est. 1968).

SAM (sam) Surface-to-air missile.

Sam. Samuel.

S.Am. South America; South American.

Sa·ma·ni (sä·mä′nē) n.pl. A Persian dynasty ruling from A.D. 874–1005, noted for its encouragement of the arts.

Sa·mar (sä′mär) One of the Visayan Islands, third largest of the Philippines; 5,050 sq. mi.

sam·a·ra (sam′ər·ə, sə·mâr′ə) n. Bot. A one-seeded indehiscent fruit, as of the elm, ash, or maple, provided with a membrane or wing; also called key fruit. [< L, elm seed]

Sa·ma·ra (sä·mä′rä) The former name for KUIBYSHEV.

Sa·ma·rang (sä·mä′räng) See SEMARANG.

Sa·mar·i·a (sə·mâr′ē·ə) 1. In the Bible, a city of Palestine, capital of the northern kingdom of Israel, or the hill on which it was built. 2. In the Bible, the territory occupied by the kingdom of Israel, or, later, a restricted portion of central Palestine west of the Jordan occupied by the Samaritans.

Sa·mar·i·tan (sə·mar′ə·tən) n. 1. One of the people of Samaria, a mixed population. II Kings xvii. 2. The Northwest Semitic language of this people. 3. Good Samaritan (which see). — adj. Of or pertaining to Samaria.

sa·mar·i·um (sə·mâr′ē·əm) n. A hard, brittle, yellowish gray, metallic element (symbol Sm) of the lanthanide series. See ELEMENT. Abbr. Sa [< NL < SAMAR(SKITE); so called because first identified in the spectrum of samarskite]

Sam·ar·kand (sam′ər·kand′, Russ. sə·mär·känt′) A city in the eastern Uzbek S.S.R., the former capital; ancient capital of Tamerlane's empire and site of his tomb; pop. 267,000 (est. 1970): ancient Maracanda.

sa·mar·skite (sə·mär′skīt) n. An orthorhombic, vitreous, black mineral, source of several rare-earth elements, as samarium, etc. [< G samarskit, after Col. Samarski, 19th c. Russian mining official]

Sa·ma-Ve·da (sä′mə·vā′də, -vē′də) See under VEDA.

sam·ba (sam′bə, säm′bä) n. 1. A popular dance of Brazilian origin. 2. Music for or in the manner of this dance, in duple meter. — v.i. To dance the samba. [< Pg. < native African name]

sam·bo (sam′bō) n. pl. ·bos A Latin American having one Negro and one American Indian or mulatto parent. [< Am. Sp. zambo; ? of African origin]

Sam·bre (sän′br′) A river in northern France and SW Belgium, flowing 120 miles NE to the Meuse.

Sam Browne belt (sam′ broun′) A military belt worn by officers, with a shoulder strap running diagonally across the chest, used to carry a pistol or a sword. [after Sir Samuel J. Browne, 1824–1901, British general who designed it]

sam·bu·ca (sam·byōō′kə) n. An ancient, triangular stringed instrument of Asian origin. Also **sam·buke** (sam′byōōk). [< L < Gk. sambykē, prob. < Aramaic sabbĕkhā]

sam·bur (sam′bər, säm′-) n. A rusine deer, especially Cervus aristotelis, of hilly districts in India, Burma, and China. Also **sam′bar**. [< Hind. sābar < Skt. shambara]

same (sām) adj. 1. Having individual or specific identity or quality; identical; equal: with the. 2. Similar in kind or quality. 3. Similar in quantity or measure; equivalent. 4. Aforesaid; identical: said of a person or thing just mentioned or held in mind. 5. Equal in degree of preference; indifferent. 6. Unchanged; monotonous. — all the same 1. Nevertheless; yet. 2. Equally acceptable or unacceptable. — just the same 1. Nevertheless; yet. 2. Exactly identical or corresponding; unchanged. — Syn. See IDENTICAL. — pron. The identical person, thing, event, etc. — adv. In like manner; equally: with the. [< ON samr. Akin to OE same equally.]

sa·mek (sä′mek) n. The fifteenth letter in the Hebrew alphabet. Also **sa′mech** (-mekh), **sa′mekh**. See ALPHABET.

same·ness (sām′nis) n. 1. Lack of change or variety; monotony. 2. Close similarity; likeness. 3. Identity; unity.

S.Amer. South America; South American.

Sam Hill (sam′ hil′) U.S. Slang Hell: a euphemism.

sam·iel (sam′yel) n. Meteorol. The simoom. [< Turkish samyel < sam poison + yel wind]

S.Am.Ind. South American Indian.

sam·i·sen (sam′i·sen) n. A Japanese guitarlike instrument with three strings, played with a plectrum. [< Japanese < Chinese san hsien three strings]

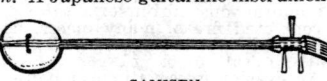
SAMISEN

sa·mite (sä′mīt, sam′-it) n. A fabric of silk, often interwoven with gold or silver. [< OF samit < Med.L samitum, var. of examitum < Med.Gk. hexamiton < hexamitos, < Gk. hex six + mitos thread]

sam·let (sam′lit) n. A young salmon; a parr. [Contracted dim. of SALMON]

Sam·nite (sam′nīt) n. 1. One of an ancient people who inhabited Samnium in central Italy, and who were descended from the Sabines. 2. The Italic language of these people. Compare OSCAN. — adj. Of or pertaining to Samnium, the Samnites, or their language.

Sam·ni·um (sam′nē·əm) An ancient country of central Italy, on the Adriatic, conquered by the Romans.

Sa·mo·a (sə·mō′ə) An island group in the SW Pacific; 1,209 sq. mi.; divided into **American** (or **Eastern**) **Samoa**, an unincorporated territory of the United States; 76 sq. mi.; pop. 32,000 (est. 1969); capital Pago Pago; and **Western Samoa**, an independent State, formerly a UN Trust Territory administered by New Zealand; 1,133 sq. mi.; pop. 141,000 (est. 1969); capital, Apia.

Sa·mo·an (sə·mō′ən) adj. Of or pertaining to Samoa, to its aboriginal Polynesian inhabitants, or to their language. — n. 1. A native of the Samoan islands. 2. The Polynesian language of the Samoans.

Sa·mos (sā′mos, Greek sä′môs) An island of Greece in the Aegean; 194 sq. mi. — **Sa·mi·an** (sā′mē·ən) adj. & n.

Sam·o·thrace (sam′ə·thrās) An island of Greece in the NE Aegean; 71 sq. mi. Greek **Sa·mo·thra·ke** (sä′mô·thrä′kē). — **Sam′o·thra′cian** (-thrā′shən) adj. & n.

sam·o·var (sam′ə·vär, sam′ə·vär′) n. A metal urn for heating water, as for making tea. [< Russian, lit., self-boiler]

Sam·o·yed (sam′ə·yed′) n. 1. One of a Mongoloid people inhabiting the Arctic coasts of Siberia. 2. A large dog having a thick white coat of long hair, originally bred by the Samoyeds as a sled dog and for herding reindeer. — adj. Of the Samoyeds or their language; Samoyedic. Also **Sam′o·yede** (-yed′). [< Russian, lit., self-eater]

Sam·o·yed·ic (sam′ə·yed′ik) adj. Of or pertaining to the Samoyeds or their language. — n. A subfamily of the Uralic languages, including the language of the Samoyeds.

samp (samp) n. Coarse, hulled Indian corn; also, a porridge made of it. [< Algonquian (Narraganset) nasaump softened with water]

sam·pan (sam′pan) n. A small flat-bottomed boat or skiff used along rivers and coasts of China and Japan. [< Chinese san three + pan board, plank]

SAMPAN

sam·phire (sam′fīr) n. 1. A European herb (Crithmum maritimum) of the parsley family, having fleshy leaves. 2. A species of glasswort (Salicornia europaea). [Alter. of F l'herbe de Saint Pierre St. Peter's herb]

sam·ple (sam′pəl) n. A portion, part, or piece taken or shown as a representative of the whole. — v.t. **·pled**, **·pling** To test or examine by means of a portion or sample. [< OF essample. See EXAMPLE.]

sam·pler¹ (sam′plər) n. 1. One who tests by sampling or exhibits samples. 2. A device for removing a portion of a substance for testing. [< SAMPLE]

sam·pler² (sam′plər) n. A piece of needlework, originally designed to show a beginner's skill. [Aphetic var. of OF essamplaire < LL exemplarium < L exemplum. See EXAMPLE.]

sample room A room in which various types or samples of merchandise are stored or kept on display.

sam·pling (sam′pling) n. 1. A small part of something or a number of items from a group selected for examination or analysis in order to estimate the quality or nature of the whole. 2. The act or process of making such a selection.

Samp·son (samp′sən), **William Thomas**, 1840–1902, U.S. admiral.

sam·sa·ra (sən·sä′rə) n. 1. In Buddhism, the course of mundane existence; the endless cycle of birth, death and rebirth. 2. Transmigration; metempsychosis. [< Skt. samsāra, lit., passing through]

sam·shu (sam′shōō′) n. 1. Alcoholic liquor distilled in China from rice or millet. 2. Loosely, any kind of spirits. [? < Chinese sao chiu spirits that will burn]

Sam·son (sam′sən) A Hebrew judge of great strength, betrayed to the Philistines by Delilah. Judges xii-xvi.

Sam·u·el (sam′yōō·əl) A Hebrew judge and prophet. — n. Either of two historical books, I and II Samuel, of the Old Testament. Abbr. Sam.

sam·u·rai (sam′ŏŏ·rī) n. pl. ·rai Under the Japanese feudal system, a member of the soldier class of the lower nobility, acting as a military retainer of the daimios; also, the class itself. [< Japanese]

San (sän) A river in SE Poland, flowing 247 miles, generally NW, to the Vistula.

Sa·naa (sä·nä′) The capital of Yemen, in the central part; pop. 100,000 (1964). Also **Sa·na′**, **San′a′** (sän·ä′), **San′a′**.

San An·ge·lo (san an′jə·lō) A resort city in west central Texas; near a U.S. Air Force Base; pop. 63,884.

San An·to·ni·o (san an·tō′nē·ō) A city in south central Texas; site of the Alamo; pop. 654,153.

san·a·tive (san′ə·tiv) adj. Healing; sanatory; health-giving. [< OF sanatif < Med.L sanativus < L sanare to heal]

san·a·to·ri·um (san′ə·tôr′ē·əm, -tō′rē-) *n. pl.* **·ri·ums** or **·ri·a** (-tôr′ē·ə, -tō′rē·ə) **1.** An institution for the treatment and care of invalids and convalescents. **2.** A health resort. Also called *sanitarium.* ◆ A *sanitarium* is sometimes said to be more of a hospital and less of a resort than a *sanatorium*, but the words are often used interchangeably. [< NL < LL *sanatorius* < L *sanatus*, pp. of *sanare* to heal]

san·be·ni·to (san′bə·nē′tō) *n. pl.* **·tos** A black garment worn by a condemned heretic or a yellow cloak worn by a penitent under the Inquisition. [< Sp. *sambenito* < *San Benito* Saint Benedict; so called from its resemblance to a Benedictine's cloak.]

San Ber·nar·di·no (san bûr′nər·dē′nō) A city in SW California; near a U.S. Air Force Base; pop. 104,251.

San Bernardino Mountain A peak in the San Bernardino Mountains; 10,630 ft.

San Bernardino Mountains A range in SE California south of the Mojave Desert; highest peak, San Gorgonio Mountain, 11,485.

San Ber·nar·di·no Pass (san bûr′nər·dē′nō) A pass in the Lepontine Alps, SE Switzerland; elevation, 6,770 ft.

San Bru·no (san brōō′nō) A city in western California, near San Francisco; pop. 36,254.

San Bue·na·ven·tu·ra (san bwā·nə·ven·tōō′rə) A port city in SW California; pop. 55,797: also *Ventura*.

San·cho Pan·za (san′chō pan′zə, *Sp.* sän′chō pän′thä) The credulous squire of Don Quixote.

sanc·ti·fied (sangk′tə·fīd) *adj.* **1.** Made holy; freed from sin; consecrated. **2.** Sanctimonious; self-righteous.

sanc·ti·fy (sangk′tə·fī) *v.t.* **·fied, ·fy·ing 1.** To set apart as holy or for holy purposes; consecrate. **2.** To free of sin; purify or make holy. **3.** To give religious sanction to; render sacred or inviolable, as a vow. **4.** To render productive of or conducive to holiness or spiritual blessing. [< OF *sanctifier* < LL *sanctificare* < L *sanctus* holy + *facere* to make] — **sanc′ti·fi·ca′tion** *n.* — **sanc′ti·fi′er** *n.*

sanc·ti·mo·ni·ous (sangk′tə·mō′nē·əs) *adj.* **1.** Making an ostentatious display or pretense of sanctity. **2.** *Obs.* Saintly. — **sanc′ti·mo′ni·ous·ly** *adv.*

sanc·ti·mo·ni·ous·ness (sangk′tə·mō′nē·əs·nəs) *n.* The state or quality of being sanctimonious. — **Syn.** See HYPOCRISY.

sanc·ti·mo·ny (sangk′tə·mō′nē) *n.* Assumed or outward sanctity; a show of holiness or devoutness; exaggerated gravity or solemnity. — **Syn.** See HYPOCRISY. [< OF *sanctimonie* < L *sanctimonia* holiness < *sanctus* holy]

sanc·tion (sangk′shən) *n.* **1.** To approve authoritatively; confirm; ratify. **2.** To countenance; allow. — **Syn.** See ALLOW, RATIFY. — *n.* **1.** Final and authoritative confirmation; justification or ratification. **2.** A formal decree. **3.** A provision for securing conformity to law, as by the enactment of rewards or penalties or both; a reward or penalty. **4.** *usually pl.* In international law, coercive measures adopted, usually by several nations at the same time, to force a nation that is violating international law to desist or yield to adjudication. **5.** In ethics, that which makes virtue morally obligatory, or which furnishes a motive for man to seek it. [< L *sanctio, -onis* decree, sanction < *sancire* to hallow]

sanc·ti·ty (sangk′tə·tē) *n. pl.* **·ties 1.** The state of being sanctified; holiness. **2.** Sacredness; solemnity. [< L *sanctitas, -tatis* < *sanctus* holy]

sanc·tu·ar·y (sangk′chōo·er·ē) *n. pl.* **·ar·ies 1.** A holy or sacred place; especially, a building or space, as a church, mosque, or temple. **2.** The most sacred part of a place in a sacred structure; especially: **a** The part of a church where the principal altar is situated. **b** In Scripture, the holy of holies of the Jewish tabernacle and temple. **c** The adytum of an ancient Greek or Roman temple. **3.** A place of refuge; asylum; also, immunity. [< OF *saintuarie* < LL *sanctuarium* < L *sanctus* holy]

sanc·tum (sangk′təm) *n. pl.* **·tums** or **·ta** (-tə) **1.** A sacred place. **2.** A private room where one is not to be disturbed.

sanc·tum sanc·to·rum (sangk′təm sangk·tôr′əm, -tō′rəm) **1.** The holy of holies. **2.** A place of great privacy: often used humorously. [< L < Gk. trans. of Hebrew *godhesh haggodhoshim*]

Sanc·tus (sangk′təs) *n. Eccl.* **1.** An ascription of praise to God, occurring at the end of the Preface in many eucharistic liturgies. **2.** A musical setting for this. [< L *sanctus* holy, its opening word]

Sanctus bell *Eccl.* A bell rung at the singing of the Sanctus, the elevation of the Host, etc.: also called *sacring bell.*

sand (sand) *n.* **1.** A hard, granular, comminuted rock material finer than gravel and coarser than dust. **2.** *pl.* Stretches of sandy beach, desert, etc. **3.** *pl.* Sandy grains in an hourglass. **4.** *pl.* Moments of time or life. **5.** *Slang* Grit; courage. **6.** A reddish yellow color. — *v.t.* **1.** To sprinkle or cover with sand. **2.** To smooth or abrade with sand or sandpaper. **3.** To mix sand with. **4.** To fill with sand. [OE. Ult. akin to L *sabulum* sand]

Sand (sand, *Fr.* säṅd), **George** Pseudonym of **Amandine**

Aurore Lucie Du·pin (dü·paṅ′), 1804–76, Baroness Dudevant, French novelist.

san·dal¹ (san′dəl) *n.* **1.** A foot covering, consisting usually of a sole only, held to the foot by thongs. **2.** A light slipper. **3.** An overshoe of rubber, cut very low. **4.** A strap or latchet for fastening a low shoe on the foot. **5.** Sendal. [< OF *sandale* < *sandalium* < Gk. *sandalion*, dim. of *sandalon*] — **san′daled, san′dalled** *adj.*

san·dal² (san′dəl) *n.* Sandalwood. [< Med.L *sandalum*, ult. < Skt. *çandana*]

sandal tree The santol.

san·dal·wood (san′dəl·wŏŏd′) *n.* **1.** The fine-grained, dense, fragrant wood of any of several East Indian trees (genus *Santalum*), especially the **white sandalwood** (*S. alba*) of India. **2.** The similar wood of other trees, as the East Indian **red sandalwood** (*Pterocarpus santalinus*), whose dark red wood is used as a dyestuff. Also called *sandal.* [< SANDAL² + WOOD]

Sandalwood Island A former name for SUMBA.

san·da·rac (san′də·rak) *n.* A pale yellow aromatic gum resin that exudes from the sandarac tree, used as a lacquer and as an incense. Also **san′da·rach.** [< L *sandaraca* < Gk. *sandarakē*, prob. akin to Skt. *çandana* sandal-wood]

sandarac tree A North African tree (*Tetraclinis articulata*), yielding sandarac gum and a hard, dark-colored, fragrant wood susceptible of a high polish and used in ornamental work. Also **sandarach tree.**

sand·bag (sand′bag′) *n.* **1.** A bag filled with or intended for holding sand, used for building fortifications, for ballast, etc. **2.** A long, narrow bag filled with sand and used as a club or weapon. — *v.t.* **·bagged, ·bag·ging 1.** To fill or surround with sandbags. **2.** To strike or attack with or as with a sandbag. — **sand′bag′ger** *n.*

sand·bar (sand′bär′) *n.* A ridge of silt or sand in rivers, along beaches, etc., formed by the action of currents or tides. — **Syn.** See BANK¹.

sand·blast (sand′blast′, -bläst′) *n.* **1.** A fine jet of sand, propelled under steam or air pressure and used to clean, grind, or decorate hard surfaces. **2.** The apparatus used in applying this blast. **3.** A wind that carries sand along. — *v.t.* To clean or engrave by means of a sandblast.

sand·blind (sand′blīnd′) *adj.* Partially blind. [ME, prob. < OE *samblind* < *sam-* half + *blind*] — **sand blindness**

sand·box (sand′boks′) *n.* **1.** A box on a locomotive or streetcar filled with sand to be poured on the rail treads to prevent slipping. **2.** A box of sand for children to play in.

sandbox tree A tropical American tree (*Hura crepitans*), often cultivated for its grooved, roundish woody capsules that burst with a loud report when ripe.

sand·bur (sand′bûr′) *n.* **1.** A pernicious weed (*Solanum rostratum*) of the great plains of the western United States, having prickly foliage. **2.** A shrubby weed (*Franseria acanthicarpa*) of western North America. Also **sand′burr′.**

Sand·burg (sand′bûrg, san′-), **Carl,** 1878–1967, U.S. poet and biographer.

sand·cast (sand′kast′, -käst′) *v.t.* **·cast, ·cast·ing** To make (a casting) by pouring metal into a mold of sand.

sand crack *Vet.* A crack running from the top of a horse's hoof: also called *toe crack.* Compare QUARTER CRACK.

sand dab See under DAB¹.

sand dollar Any small, flat sea urchin (genus *Echinarachnius*) having a circular shell, found on sandy bottoms from New Jersey to Labrador and on the Pacific coast.

sand·ed (san′did) *adj.* **1.** Filled, covered, or clogged with sand. **2.** Of a sandy color; minutely speckled. **3.** Smoothed with sand or sandpaper.

sand eel The sand lance.

sand·er (san′dər) *n.* One who or that which sands.

san·der·ling (san′dər·ling) *n.* A small, widely distributed shore bird (*Crocethia alba*) of arctic breeding habits, gray and white in winter but largely chestnut-colored in summer. [Prob. < SAND + OE *yrthling* a small bird, farmer, lit., earthling]

sand flea 1. A sand-dwelling flea, as the chigoe. **2.** A beach flea.

sand fly Any of various minute hairy flies (family *Psychodidae*) found near the seashore and in damp places. Some of the bloodsucking genus *Phlebotamus* are carriers of various animal and human diseases, including leishmaniasis.

sand grouse An Old World bird (family *Pteroclidae*) of pigeonlike form, having long pointed wings and short feathered legs, and inhabiting sandy tracts.

san·dhi (san′dē, sän′-) *n. Ling.* **1.** The process of phonetic modification that takes place in word groups, generally affecting the initial and final sounds of the constituent words, as the assimilative change of (d) and (y) to (j) in "Did you"

SANDALS

a Egyptian. *b* Greek. *c* Roman. *d* Japanese.

spoken as (dij′ōō) or the interchange of allomorphs in *a house* but *an apple.* **2.** The syntactic environment in which such modification occurs: "Did you" becomes (dij′ōō) in *sandhi.* [< Skt. *samdhi* a placing together < *sam* together + *dadhāti* he places]

sand·hill crane (sand′hil′) See under CRANE.

sand·hog (sand′hôg′, -hog′) *n.* One who works under air pressure, as in caisson sinking, tunnel building, etc.

sand hopper A beach flea.

Sand·hurst (sand′hûrst) A village in Berkshire, England; seat of the Royal Military College; pop. about 3,700.

San Di·e·go (san dē·ā′gō) A port city in SW California; site of a U.S. naval base; pop. 696,769; on **San Diego Bay,** a sheltered inlet of the Pacific.

sand lance One of a family (*Ammodytidae*) of small marine fishes with elongate bodies: also called *launce, sand eel.* Also **sand launce.**

sand lily A low-growing herb (*Leucocrinum montanum*) of the lily family, with fragrant white flowers, native in western and Pacific States: also *star lily.*

sand-lot (sand′lot′) *adj.* Of or in a vacant lot in or near an urban area: *sand-lot* baseball.

sand·man (sand′man′) *n.* In nursery lore, a mythical person supposed to make children sleepy by casting sand in their eyes: sometimes called *dustman.*

sand martin The bank swallow. See under SWALLOW².

sand painting A form of painting by the American Indians, especially the Navaho, in which pigments of fine sand are trickled on a ground base of neutral-colored sand.

sand·pa·per (sand′pā′pər) *n.* Heavy paper coated with sand for smoothing or polishing. — *v.t.* To rub or polish with sandpaper.

sand pine The smooth-barked pine (*Pinus clausa*) of sandy areas of the southern United States, especially common along the Gulf Coast of Florida.

sand·pi·per (sand′pī′pər) *n.* Any of certain small wading birds (family *Scolopacidae*), mostly frequenting seashores in flocks; especially, the **common sandpiper** (*Actitis hypoleuca*) of Europe, the **spotted sandpiper** (*A. macularia*) of North America, and the small **least sandpiper** or pewit (*Erolia minutilla*). Also **sand/peep/** (-pēp′).

San·dro·cot·tus (san′drō·kot′əs) See CHANDRAGUPTA I.

sand·stone (sand′stōn′) *n.* A rock consisting chiefly of quartz sand cemented with silica, feldspar, lime, or clay.

sand·storm (sand′stôrm′) *n.* A high wind by which sand or dust is carried along.

San·dus·ky (san·dus′kē) A port city in northern Ohio, on Lake Erie; pop. 32,674.

sand verbena A trailing plant (genus *Abronia*) of the four o'clock family, with vivid red, yellow, or white flowers, native in deserts of the western United States.

sand viper 1. The hognose. **2.** The horned viper (which see).

sand·wich (sand′wich, san′-) *n.* **1.** Two thin slices of bread, having between them meat, cheese, etc. **2.** Any combination of alternating dissimilar things pressed together. — *v.t.* **1.** To place between two layers or objects; press; squeeze: *sandwiched* between two suitcases. **2.** To insert between dissimilar things. [after John Montagu, fourth Earl of *Sandwich,* 1718–92, who originated it in order to eat without leaving the gaming table]

Sand·wich (sand′wich) A municipal borough in eastern Kent, England; the most ancient of the Cinque Ports; pop. 4,234 (1961).

Sandwich Islands A former name for the HAWAIIAN ISLANDS.

sandwich man *n.* *pl.* **men** *Informal* A man carrying advertising boards slung in front and behind.

sand·wort (sand′wûrt′) *n.* Any of a genus (*Arenaria*) of low, usually tufted herbs, with small white flowers.

sand·y (san′dē) *adj.* **sand·i·er, sand·i·est 1.** Consisting of or characterized by sand; containing, covered with, or full of sand. **2.** Yellowish red: a *sandy* beard. — **sand/i·ness** *n.*

Sandy Hook A peninsula extending north from eastern New Jersey, at the entrance to New York Bay.

sane¹ (sān) *adj.* **1.** Mentally sound; not deranged. **2.** Proceeding from a sound mind. [< L *sanus* whole, healthy] — **sane/ly** *adv.* — **sane/ness** *n.*
— **Syn. 1.** lucid, rational. **2.** prudent, judicious, sensible.

sane² (sān) See SAIN.

SANE Committee for a Sane Nuclear Policy.

San·ford (san′fərd), **Mount** The highest peak of the Wrangell Mountains in southern Alaska; 16,208 ft.

San·for·ize (san′fə·rīz) *v.t.* **·ized, ·iz·ing** To treat (cloth) by a special mechanical process so as to prevent more than slight shrinkage: a trade name. Also **san′for·ize.** [after Sanford L. Cluett, born 1874, U.S. inventor of the process.]

San Fran·cis·co (san′frən·sis′kō) The second largest city in California, a port on **San Francisco Bay,** an inlet of the Pacific; pop. 715,674. — **San/ Fran·cis/can** *n.* & *adj.*

San Francisco Mountain The highest of the **San Francisco Peaks,** three peaks of an extinct eroded volcano in northern Arizona, and the highest point in the State; 12,655 ft. Also *Humphreys Peak.*

sang (sang) Past tense of SING.

San·gal·lo (sän·gäl′lō), **Giuliano da,** 1445–1516, Florentine architect and sculptor.

sang·ar (sang′ər, sung′ər) *n.* A shelter, breastwork, or rifle pit for two or three men. Also **sang′er, san′ga.** [< Hind.]

san·ga·ree (sang′gə·rē′) *n.* A tropical drink of wine or brandy and water, spiced and sweetened. [< Sp. *sangria,* lit., bleeding < *sangre* blood < L *sanguis*]

Sang·er (sang′ər), **Margaret,** 1883–1966, *née* Higgins, U.S. nurse, leader in birth-control education.

San Ger·ma·no (san jûr·man′ō, *Ital.* sän zhär·mä′nō) The former name for CASSINO.

sang-froid (sän·frwä′) *n.* Calmness amid trying circumstances; coolness; composure. [< F, lit., cold blood]

San·gre·al (sang′grē·əl) *n.* The Grail. Also **San·graal** (sang·gräl′). [< OF *Saint Graal* < *saint* holy (< L *sanctus*) + *graal.* See GRAIL.]

San·gre de Cris·to Mountains (säng′grä dā krēs′to) The southernmost range of the Rocky Mountains, in Colorado; highest point, Blanca Peak, 14,363 ft.

sangui- *combining form* Blood: *sanguiferous.* [< L *sanguis* blood]

san·guic·o·lous (sang·gwik′ə·ləs) *adj.* Inhabiting the blood, as a parasite. [< SANGUI- + L *colere* to inhabit]

san·guif·er·ous (sang·gwif′ər·əs) *adj.* Conducting blood, as the organs of circulation. [< SANGUI- + -FEROUS]

san·gui·nar·i·a (sang′gwə·nâr′ē·ə) *n.* **1.** The bloodroot. **2.** An emetic prepared from the bloodroot. [< NL < L (*herba*) *sanguinaria,* fem. of *sanguinarius.* See SANGUINARY.]

san·gui·nar·y (sang′gwə·ner′ē) *adj.* **1.** Attended with bloodshed. **2.** Bloodthirsty. **3.** Consisting of blood. — **Syn.** See BLOODY. [< L *sanguinarius* < *sanguis, -inis* blood] — **san/gui·nar/i·ly** *adv.* — **san/gui·nar/i·ness** *n.*

san·guine (sang′gwin) *adj.* **1.** Of buoyant disposition; hopeful; confident; cheerful. **2.** Ruddy; robust. **3.** Having the color of blood; of, like, or full of blood. **4.** *Obs.* Bloodthirsty; sanguinary. [< OF *sanguin* < L *sanguineus* < *sanguis, -inis* blood] — **san/guine·ly** *adv.* — **san/guine·ness** *n.*

san·guin·e·ous (sang·gwin′ē·əs) *adj.* **1.** Pertaining to, consisting of, or forming blood. **2.** Full-blooded; sanguine; hopeful. **3.** Of the color of blood. [< L *sanguineus.* See SANGUINE.]

San·he·drin (san′hi·drin, san′i-, san·hē′drin, -hed′rin) *n.* **1.** In ancient times, the supreme council and highest court of the Jewish nation. Also **Great Sanhedrin. 2.** Any council or assembly. Also *Synedrion, Synedrium.* Also **San′he·drim** (-drim). [< Hebrew < Gk. *synedrion* assembly < *syn-* together + *hedra* a sitting]

san·i·cle (san′i·kəl) *n.* Any of a genus (*Sanicula*) of herbs of the parsley family, reputed to have medicinal roots: also called *selfheal.* [< OF < Med.L *sanicula* < L *sanus* healthy]

sa·ni·es (sā′ni·ēz) *n. Pathol.* A serous, greenish, blood-tinged fluid discharged from ulcers. [< NL < L]

San Il·de·fon·so (san ēl′thä·fōn′sō) A town in central Spain, NW of Madrid; site of royal palace; scene of the signing of a treaty by Spain, France, and England, 1796; pop. about 3,000.

sa·ni·ous (sā′nē·əs) *adj.* **1.** Of or like sanies; watery and blood-tinged. **2.** Producing or discharging sanies.

san·i·tar·i·an (san′ə·târ′ē·ən) *adj.* Of or relating to sanitation or health. — *n.* An expert in sanitation or public health.

san·i·tar·i·um (san′ə·târ′ē·əm) *n. pl.* **·tar·i·ums** or **·tar·i·a** (-târ′ē·ə) A sanatorium. ◆ See note under SANATORIUM. [< NL < L *sanitas* health]

san·i·tar·y (san′ə·ter′ē) *adj.* **1.** Relating to the preservation of health. **2.** Favorable to health; cleanly. — *n. pl.* **·tar·ies** A public watercloset or urinal. [< F *sanitaire* < L *sanitas* health < *sanus* healthy] — **san/i·tar/i·ly** *adv.*

sanitary belt A belt, usually made of elastic, that has tabs to which a sanitary napkin may be attached.

sanitary cordon A cordon sanitaire (which see).

sanitary napkin An absorbent pad worn by women during menstruation.

san·i·tate (san′ə·tāt) *v.t.* **·tat·ed, ·tat·ing** To apply sanitary measures to.

san·i·ta·tion (san′ə·tā′shən) *n.* The use and practical application of sanitary measures; the removal or neutralization of elements injurious to health.

san·i·tize (san′ə·tīz) *v.t.* **·tized, ·tiz·ing** To make sanitary, as by sterilizing.

san·i·ty (san′ə·tē) *n. pl.* **·ties 1.** The state of being sane; soundness of mind; mental health. **2.** Sane moderation or reasonableness. [< L *sanitas* health < *sanus* healthy]

San Ja·cin·to (san′ jə·sin′tō) A locality in eastern Texas, scene of a Texan victory against Mexico, 1836; at the mouth of the **San Jacinto River,** that flows about 115 miles, generally south, to Galveston Bay.

san·jak (sän′jäk) *n.* Formerly, an administrative subdivision of a Turkish vilayet. [< Turkish *sanjāq,* lit., banner]

San Joa·quin River (san′wô·kēn′, wä·kēn′) A river of

south central California, flowing 317 miles, generally NW, through Central Valley to the Sacramento River.

San Jo·sé (sän′ hō·zā′, *Sp.* sän hō·zā′) **1.** The capital of Costa Rica in the central part; pop. 182,961 (1966). **2.** A city in western California, on the Coyote and Guadalupe rivers; pop. 445,779.

San Jo·sé scale (sän′ hō·zā′) A scale insect (*Quadraspidiotus perniciosus*) destructive to various fruit trees, first appeared in the United States at San José, California. For illustration see INSECTS (injurious).

San Juan (sän hwän′) **1.** The capital of Puerto Rico, a port in the NE part; pop. 444,952 (1970). **2.** A Province of west central Argentina; 33,249 sq. mi.; pop. 352,461 (1960); capital, **San Juan**; pop. 106,746 (1960).

San Juan de la Cruz (thä lä krōōth′) See JOHN OF THE CROSS.

San Juan Hill A hill near Santiago de Cuba; captured by United States troops in the Spanish-American War.

San Juan Islands An island group of NW Washington, near SE Vancouver Island at the northern end of Puget Sound.

San Juan Mountains A range of the Rocky Mountains in SW Colorado; highest point, Uncompahgre Peak, 14,306 ft.

sank (sangk) Past tense of SINK.

San·khya (säng′kyə) *n.* The oldest system of Indian philosophy, professing dualism. [< Skt. *Sāṁkhya* < *saṁkhyā* enumeration]

San Le·an·dro (san lē·an′drō) A city in western California, near Oakland; pop. 68,698.

San Lu·is Po·to·sí (sän lōō·ēs′ pō′tō·sē′) A State in central Mexico; 24,415 sq. mi.; pop. 1,257,028 (1970); capital, **San Luis Potosí**; pop. 274,320 (1970).

San Ma·ri·no (mä·rē′nō) A Republic, an enclave in NE Italy; 23 sq. mi.; pop. 16,000 (est. 1962); capital, **San Marino**. See map at ENCLAVE.

San Mar·tín (mär·tēn′), **José Francisco de**, 1778–1850, South American general and revolutionary leader born in Argentina.

San Ma·te·o (san mə·tā′ō) A city in western California, on San Francisco Bay; pop. 78,991.

san·nup (san′up) *n.* A married male American Indian. Also **san′nop.** [< Algonquian (Narraganset) *sannop*]

San Pa·blo Bay (san′ pä′blō) The northern part of San Francisco Bay, California.

San Re·mo (sän rā′mō) A port and resort town in NW Italy, on the Gulf of Genoa; pop. about 30,000.

sans (sanz, *Fr.* säṅ) *prep.* Without. [< OF *sanz*, alter. of L *absentia* absence, infl. by *sine* without]

San Sal·va·dor (san sal′və·dôr, *Sp.* sän säl′vä·thôr′) The capital of El Salvador, in the southern part, on the Pacific; pop. 349,725 (est. 1969).

San Salvador Island An island in the central Bahamas, the first landing place of Columbus in the New World, 1492: also *Watling Island*.

san·sar (sän′sər) *n.* A sarsar (which see).

sans-cu·lotte (sanz′kyōō·lot′, *Fr.* säṅ·kü·lôt′) *n.* **1.** A revolutionary: originally a term of contempt applied by the aristocrats to the French revolutionaries in 1789, later a popular name for one of a revolutionary mob; a Jacobin. **2.** Any revolutionary or radical. [< F, lit., without knee breeches] — **sans-cu·lot′tic** *adj.* — **sans′-cu·lot′tism** *n.*

sans-cu·lot·tides (sanz′kyōō·lot′idz, *Fr.* säṅ′kü·lô·tēd′) *n.pl.* The supplementary days at the end of the last month in the Republican calendar. See (Republican) CALENDAR.

sans doute (säṅ dōōt′) *French* Without doubt; certainly.

San Se·bas·tián (san sə·bas′chən, *Sp.* sän sä·väs·tyän′) A port city in northern Spain, on the Bay of Biscay; pop. 135,149 (1960).

San·sei (sän·sā) *n.* *pl.* **·sei** or **·seis** An American citizen of Japanese descent whose grandparents settled in the United States; a third-generation Japanese American. [< Japanese, third generation]

san·se·vi·e·ri·a (san′sə·vi·ir′ē·ə) *n.* Any of a genus (*Sansevieria*) of erect perennial herbs of the lily family, native in Africa but sometimes cultivated in the United States as an ornamental plant. [< NL, after the Prince of *Sanseviero*, 1710–71, a Neapolitan scholar]

San·skrit (san′skrit) *n.* The ancient and classical language of the Hindus of India, belonging to the Indic branch of the Indo-Iranian subfamily of Indo-European languages. It includes **Vedic Sanskrit**, the language of the Vedas, and the later **classical Sanskrit** of India's great religious, philosophical, and poetic literature, still used for sacred or learned writings. Compare PRAKRIT. Also **San′scrit.** Abbr. *Skr., Skt.* [< Skt. *saṁskrita* artificial, highly cultivated < *sam-* together + *kṛ* to make, do] — **San′skrit·ist** *n.*

San·skrit·ic (san·skrit′ik) *adj.* **1.** Of, pertaining to, or written in Sanskrit. **2.** Designating a group of some 30 to 40 ancient and modern languages and dialects of India, embracing Sanskrit, Prakrit, Pali, Assamese, Bengali, Eastern and Western Hindi, Punjabi, Singhalese, Romany, etc.

San·so·vi·no (sän′sō·vē′nō), 1479–1570, Florentine sculptor and architect: original name **Jacopo Tat·ti** (tät′tē).

sans pa·reil (säṅ pä·rā′y′) *French* Without equal.

sans peur et sans re·proche (säṅ pœr ā säṅ rə·prôsh′) *French* Without fear and without reproach.

sans ser·if (sanz ser′if) *Printing* A type face without serifs: also called *gothic*.

sans sou·ci (säṅ sōō·sē′) *French* Without care.

San Ste·fa·no (sän stā′fä·nō) A village in NW Turkey, near Istanbul; scene of the signing of a Russo-Turkish treaty, 1878. Turkish *Yeşilköy*.

San·ta An·a (san′tə an′ə, *Sp.* sän′tä ä′nä) **1.** A city in NW El Salvador; a coffee center; pop. 102,301 (est. 1969). **2.** A city in SW California; pop. 156,601.

San·ta An·na (sän′tä ä′nä), **Antonio López de**, 1795–1876, Mexican general; president 1833–35, 1841–47, 1853–55; massacred the survivors of the Alamo, 1836; defeated by Zachary Taylor, 1847. Also *San′ta A′na*.

San·ta Bar·ba·ra (san′tə bär′bər·ə) A resort city in SW California; pop. 70,215; on **Santa Barbara Channel**, a strait between the mainland and the **Santa Barbara Islands**, an offshore island chain; about 150 mi. long.

San·ta Cat·a·li·na (san′tə kat′ə·lē′nə) One of the Santa Barbara Islands; a tourist resort; 70 sq. mi.: also *Catalina Island*.

San·ta Clar·a (san′tə clar′ə, *Sp.* sän′tä clä′rä) **1.** A city in central Cuba; pop. 137,700 (est. 1967). **2.** A city in western California; pop. 87,717.

San·ta Claus (san′tə klôz′) In nursery lore, a fat, jolly old man with a white beard who brings presents at Christmas time, often identified with Saint Nicholas. [< Du. *Sant Nikolaas* Saint Nicholas]

San·ta Cruz (san′tə krōōz′, *Sp.* sän′tä krōōth′) **1.** See ST. CROIX. **2.** A northern island of the Santa Barbara Islands; 23 mi. long. **3.** A city in western California, on Monterey Bay; pop. 32,076.

Santa Cruz de Ten·er·ife (də ten′ə·rif′, *Sp.* thä tä′nä·rē′fä) A port city on NE Tenerife, in the Canary Islands; pop. 133,100 (1960).

San·ta Fe (san′tə fā′) The capital of New Mexico, in the northern part; pop. 41,167.

San·ta Fé (sän′tä fä′) A Province of NE central Argentina; 51,341 sq. mi.; pop. 2,106,200 (est. 1960); capital, **Santa Fé**, pop. 259,560 (1960).

Santa Fe Trail The trade route, important from 1821–80, between Independence, Missouri, and Santa Fe, New Mexico.

san·ta·la·ceous (san′tə·lā′shəs) *adj.* *Bot.* Of or pertaining to the sandalwood family (*Santalaceae*) of apetalous shrubs, herbs, and some trees. [< NL < *Santalum*, genus name < Med.L, sandalwood]

san·tal·ic (san·tal′ik) *adj.* Of, pertaining to, or derived from sandalwood.

San·ta Ma·ri·a (san′tə mə·rē′ə, *Sp.* sän′tä mä·rē′ä) One of the three ships of Columbus on his maiden voyage to America. For illustration see CARAVEL.

San·ta Ma·ri·a (sän′tä mä·rē′ä) An active volcano in SW Guatemala; 12,362 ft.

Santa Maria del·la Ro·tun·da (del′lä rô·tōōn′dä) See PANTHEON.

San·ta Mau·ra (sän′tä mou′rä) The Italian name for LEVKAS.

San·ta Mon·i·ca (san′tə mon′i·kə) A city in SW California, a suburb of Los Angeles; pop. 88,289.

San·tan·der (sän′tän·der′) A port city in northern Spain, on the Bay of Biscay; pop. 118,435 (1960).

San·ta Ro·sa (san′tə rō′zə) A city in western California; pop. 50,006.

San·ta·ya·na (sän′tä·yä′nä), **George**, 1863–1952, U.S. philosopher and author born in Spain.

San·tee River (san·tē′) A river in east central South Carolina, flowing 143 miles SE to the Atlantic.

San·ti·a·go (sän′tē·ä′gō) **1.** The capital of Chile, in the central part; pop. 2,596,929 (1970). Also **Santiago de Chi·le** (thä chē′lä). **2.** Santiago de Compostela.

Santiago de Com·po·ste·la (thä kōm′pō·stä′lä) A city and pilgrimage center in NW Spain; pop. 37,916 (1960). Also *Santiago*.

Santiago de Cu·ba (thä cōō′bä) **1.** The capital of Oriente Province, SE Cuba, a port on the southern coast; pop. 259,000 (est. 1970). **2.** The former name for ORIENTE.

San·to Do·min·go (sän′tō dō·ming′gō) **1.** The capital of the Dominican Republic, in the southern part on the Caribbean; pop. 671,400 (1970): from 1936–62 *Ciudad Trujillo*. **2.** The former name for the DOMINICAN REPUBLIC.

san·tol (sän·tōl′) *n.* A tropical, evergreen tree (*Sandoricum koetjape*), having an edible berry: also called *sandal tree*.

san·ton·i·ca (san·ton′i·kə) *n.* **1.** A wormwood (*Artemisia maritima*), especially one native in Iran and Turkestan. **2.** The flower heads of this plant, used as a vermifuge. [< NL < L (*herba*) *Santonica* < *Santoni* a people of Aquitania]

san·to·nin (săn′tə·nĭn) *n. Chem.* A colorless crystalline compound, $C_{15}H_{18}O_3$, contained in santonica, used in medicine as a vermifuge. Also **san·to·nine** (-nēn, -nĭn). [< F *santonine* < NL *santon(ica)* + F *-ine* -INE²]

San·tos (săn′tōōs) A port city in SE Brazil; pop. 253,629 (est. 1955).

San·tos-Du·mont (săn′tŏoz·dü·môń′), **Alberto,** 1873–1932, Brazilian aeronautical pioneer.

São Fran·cis·co (souń frän·sēs′kōō) A river of eastern Brazil, flowing 1,800 miles, generally east, to the Atlantic.

São Lu·ís (souń lōō·ēs′) The capital of Maranhão State, NE Brazil, a port on the Atlantic; pop. 218,780 (est. 1968). Formerly **São Luis do Ma·ra·nhão** (thōō mä′rə·nyouń′). Also **São Luiz.**

São Mi·guel (souń mē·gel′) An island in the eastern Azores; 288 sq. mi.

Saône (sōn) A river in eastern France, flowing 268 miles south to the Rhône.

São Pau·lo (souń pou′lōō) A State of SE Brazil; 95,428 sq. mi.; pop. 16,081,000 (est. 1967); capital, **São Paulo,** the largest city in Brazil, pop. 5,684,706 (est. 1970).

São Paulo de Lo·an·da (thə lō·än′də) A former name for LUANDA.

São Pe·dro de Ri·o Gran·de do Sul (souń pä′thrōō thə rē′ōō graṅ′də thōō sōōl′) A former name for the port of RIO GRANDE DO SUL.

Saor·stat Eir·eann (sâr′stät âr′ən) *Irish Gaelic* Irish Free State, a former name for IRELAND.

São Sal·va·dor (souń säl′və·thôr′) The former name for SALVADOR.

São To·mé e Prin·ci·pe (souń tōō·me′ e prēń′sē·pə) An independent Republic off west central Africa in the Gulf of Guinea, comprising the islands of **São Tomé** (also **São Thomé**), 320 sq. mi., and **Principe,** 62 sq. mi.; pop. 66,000 (est. 1969); capital, **São Tomé,** pop. 7,364 (1960).

sap¹ (sap) *n.* **1.** The aqueous juices of plants, that contain and transport the materials necessary to vegetable growth. **2.** Any vital fluid; vitality. **3.** Sapwood (which see). **4.** *Slang* A foolish, gullible, or ineffectual person. [OE *sæp*]

sap² (sap) *v.* **sapped, sap·ping** *v.t.* **1.** To weaken or destroy gradually and insidiously; enervate; exhaust. **2.** To approach or undermine (an enemy fortification) by digging a sap or saps. — *v.i.* **3.** To dig a sap or saps. — *n.* A deep, narrow trench or tunnel dug to approach or undermine a fortification. [< MF *saper* < *sape* < Ital. *zappa* spade, goat]

sap·a·jou (sap′ə·jōō, *Fr.* sȧ·pȧ·zhōō′) *n.* A capuchin (def. 2). [< F < Tupi]

sa·pan·wood (sə·pan′wŏod′) *n.* **1.** The brownish red dye wood obtained from an East Indian leguminous tree (*Caesalpinia sappan*). **2.** The tree yielding this wood. Also spelled *sappanwood*: also called *brazil.* [Trans. of Du. *sapanhout* < Malay *sapang*]

Sa·phar (sä·fär′) *n.* The second month of the Moslem year. See (Moslem) CALENDAR.

sap·head (sap′hed′) *n. Slang* A soft-headed person; simpleton; sap. [< SAP¹ (def. 4) + HEAD] — **sap′head′ed** *adj.*

sa·phe·na (sə·fē′nə) *n. pl.* **·nae** (-nē) *Anat.* One of the two large superficial veins of the leg. [< Med.L < Arabic *ṣāfīn*] — **sa·phe′nous** *adj.*

sap·id (sap′id) *adj.* **1.** Pleasant to the taste; savory. **2.** Interesting and agreeable. [< L *sapidus* < *sapere* to taste] — **sa·pid′i·ty, sap′id·ness** *n.*

sa·pi·ence (sā′pē·əns) *n.* Wisdom; learning: often used ironically. Also **sa′pi·en·cy.** [< OF < L *sapientia* < *sapiens, -entis.* See SAPIENT.]

sa·pi·ent (sā′pē·ənt) *adj.* Wise; sagacious: often used ironically. [< OF < L *sapiens, -entis,* ppr. of *sapere* to have good taste] — **sa′pi·ent·ly** *adv.*

sa·pi·en·tial (sā′pē·en′shəl) *adj.* Of, marked by, or expounding wisdom. — **sa′pi·en′tial·ly** *adv.*

sap·in·da·ceous (sap′in·dā′shəs) *adj. Bot.* Of or pertaining to the soapberry family (Sapindaceae). [< NL < *Sapindus,* genus name < L *sapo* soap + *Indicus* Indian]

sap·less (sap′lis) *adj.* **1.** Destitute of sap; withered. **2.** Wanting vitality, spirit, or vivacity; insipid; dull.

sap·ling (sap′ling) *n.* **1.** A young tree. **2.** A youth. [Dim. of SAP¹]

sap·o·dil·la (sap′ə·dil′ə) *n.* **1.** A large evergreen tree (*Achras zapota*) of the West Indies and tropical America. **2.** Its edible, apple-shaped fruit, a source of chicle: also **sapodilla plum.** Also called *naseberry.* Also **sa·po·ta** (sə·pō′tə), **sap′a·dil′lo, sap′o·dil′lo.** [< Sp. *zapotille,* dim of *zapota* < Nahuatl *tzapotl*]

sap·o·na·ceous (sap′ə·nā′shəs) *adj.* Of the nature of soap; soapy. [< NL *saponaceus* < L *sapo, saponis* soap]

sa·pon·i·fy (sə·pon′ə·fī) *v.t.* **·fied, ·fy·ing** *Chem.* **1.** To convert (a fat or oil) into soap by the action of an alkali. **2.** To decompose (an ester) into an acid and an alcohol. [< F *saponifier* < L *sapo, saponis* soap + *facere* to make] — **sa·pon′i·fi·a·ble** *adj.* — **sa·pon′i·fi·ca·tion** (sə·pon′ə·fə·kā′shən) *n.* — **sa·pon′i·fi′er** *n.*

sap·o·nin (sap′ə·nĭn) *n. Biochem.* Any of several nearly white amorphous glycosides contained in various plants and

characterized by their ability to form emulsions and soapy lathers. Also **sap′o·nine** (-nēn, -nĭn). [< F *saponine* < L *sapo, saponis* soap + F *-ine.* See -INE².]

sap·o·nite (sap′ə·nīt) *n.* A soft, hydrous silicate of magnesium and aluminum, found as an amorphous soaplike mass in rock cavities. [< Sw. *saponit* < L *sapo, saponis* soap + -ITE¹]

sa·por (sā′pər, -pôr) *n.* That quality of a substance affecting the sense of taste; flavor; taste. Also *Brit.* **sa′pour.** [< L, taste < *sapere* to taste, know] — **sap·o·rif·ic** (sap′ə·rif′ik), **sap′o·rous** *adj.*

sap·o·ta·ceous (sap′ə·tā′shəs) *adj. Bot.* Of or pertaining to a family (Sapotaceae) of trees and shrubs yielding a milky juice and also some edible fruits, as the sapodilla. [< NL < *sapota* < Sp. *zapota.* See SAPODILLA.]

sap·pan·wood (sə·pan′wŏod′) See SAPANWOOD.

sap·per (sap′ər) *n.* **1.** One who or that which saps. **2.** A soldier employed in making a sap². [< SAP² + -ER]

Sap·phic (saf′ik) *adj.* **1.** Pertaining to or in the manner of Sappho. **2.** In prosody, denoting a meter or verse form used by Sappho, especially a stanza of three Sapphics followed by an Adonic. — *n.* In prosody, a line of trochaic pentameter with a dactyl in the third foot, much used by Sappho. [< L *Sapphicus* < Gk. *Sapphikos* < *Sapphō* Sappho]

Sapphic ode Horatian ode (which see).

sap·phire (saf′īr) *n.* **1.** Any of the hard, translucent, colored varieties of corundum other than the red variety, that when cut are used as gems; especially, a deep blue corundum. **2.** A deep, pure blue. — *adj.* Having a deep, pure blue color. [< OF *safir* < L *sapphirus* < Gk. *sappheiros,* ult. < Skt. *śanipriya* dear to Saturn]

sap·phi·rine (saf′ər·in, -ə·rēn) *adj.* Consisting of or like sapphire. — *n.* **1.** A vitreous pale blue or green silicate of aluminum and magnesium, crystallizing in the monoclinic system. **2.** A blue variety of spinel.

Sap·pho (saf′ō) Sixth-century B.C. Greek lyric poetess.

Sap·po·ro (säp·pō·rō) A city on western Hokkaido island, Japan, on Otaru Bay; pop. 523,837 (1960).

sap·py (sap′ē) *adj.* **·pi·er, ·pi·est** **1.** Full of sap; juicy. **2.** Vital; strong. **3.** *Slang* Immature; silly. — **sap′pi·ly** *adv.* — **sap′pi·ness** *n.*

sa·pre·mi·a (sə·prē′mē·ə) *n. Pathol.* Intoxication of the blood by the products of putrefaction. Also **sa·prae′mi·a.** [< NL < SAPR(O)- + -EMIA] — **sa·pre′mic** *adj.*

sapro- *combining form* **1.** Decomposition or putrefaction: *saprogenic.* **2.** Saprophytic: *saproplankton.* [< Gk. *sapros* rotten]

sap·ro·gen·ic (sap′rə·jen′ik) *adj.* **1.** Productive of putrefaction. **2.** Developing in or living upon putrefying matter. Also **sa·prog·e·nous** (sə·proj′ə·nəs). [< SAPRO- + -GENIC]

sap·ro·lite (sap′rə·līt) *n. Geol.* Thoroughly decomposed, earthy rock, lying in its original place. [< SAPRO- + -LITE] — **sap′ro·lit′ic** (-lit′ik) *adj.*

sa·proph·a·gous (sə·prof′ə·gəs) *adj.* Feeding on decaying substances.

sap·ro·phyte (sap′rə·fīt) *n.* A vegetable organism that lives on dead or decaying organic matter, as certain funguses or other plants, various bacteria, etc. — **sap′ro·phyt′ic** (-fit′ik) *adj.*

sap·ro·plank·ton (sap′rə·plangk′tən) *n.* Plankton found on the surface of stagnant water. [< SAPRO- + PLANKTON]

sap·sa·go (sap·sā′gō, sap′sə·gō) *n.* A hard, green Swiss cheese flavored with melilot, used chiefly in cooking. [< G *schabzieger* < *schaben* to scrape + *zieger* whey]

sap·suck·er (sap′suk′ər) *n.* Any of various small black and white woodpeckers (genus *Sphyrapicus*); especially, the **yellow-bellied sapsucker** (*S. varius*), that damages orchard trees by exposing and drinking the sap.

sap·wood (sap′wŏod′) *n. Bot.* The new wood next to the bark of an exogenous tree: also called *alburnum, sap.* For illustration see EXOGEN.

Sar. Sardinia.

S.A.R. **1.** Sons of the American Revolution: also **SAR** **2.** South African Republic.

sar·a·band (sar′ə·band) *n.* **1.** A slow, stately dance of the 17th and 18th centuries, derived from a faster dance. **2.** Music for or in the manner of this dance, in triple meter, commonly used in the baroque suite, sometimes in its faster form. Also **sar′a·bande.** [< F *sarabande* < Sp. *zarabanda,* ult. < Persian *sarband* a kind of dance and song]

Sar·a·cen (sar′ə·sən) *n.* **1.** Originally, a nomad Arab of the Syrian-Arabian desert, who harassed the frontiers of the Roman Empire. **2.** A Moslem, especially during the Crusades. **3.** Any Arab. [< LL *Saracenus* < LGk. *Sarakēnos*] — **Sar′a·cen′ic** (-sen′ik) or **·i·cal** *adj.*

Sar·a·gos·sa (sar′ə·gos′ə) A city in NE Spain, on the Ebro; capital of former Aragon; pop. 326,316 (1960): Spanish *Zaragoza.*

Sar·ah (sâr′ə) The wife of Abraham. *Gen.* xvii 15.

YELLOW-
BELLIED
SAPSUCKER
(About 8 inches
long)

Sa·ra·je·vo (sä′rä′ye·vô) The capital of Bosnia and Herzegovina, central Yugoslavia; scene of the assassination of Archduke Franz Ferdinand, June 28, 1914; pop. 223,000 (est. 1968): also *Serajevo, Serayevo.* Also **Sa′ra′ye·vo.**

sa·ran (sə·ran′) *n.* Any of a class of synthetic fibers and textile materials obtained by the polymerization of vinyl chloride. [Coined by Dow Chemical Co.]

Sar·a·nac Lake (sar′ə·nak) A village in NE New York, near lower Saranac Lake; a health resort; pop. 6,086.

Saranac Lakes Three lakes in NE New York, in the Adirondack Mountains, **Upper Saranac, Middle Saranac,** and **Lower Saranac,** joined by the **Saranac River** that flows about 50 miles, generally NE, to Lake Champlain.

sa·ra·pe (sə·räp′ē) *n.* A blanketlike outer garment, usually having a slit in the middle to fit over the head, worn in Latin America, especially in Mexico: also spelled *serape.* [< Mexican Sp.]

Sar·a·so·ta (sar′ə·sō′tə) A port city in SW Florida, on **Sarasota Bay,** a lagoon connected with Tampa Bay and the Gulf of Mexico; pop. 40,237.

Sar·a·to·ga (sar′ə·tō′gə) A former name for SCHUYLERVILLE.

Saratoga Springs A resort city in eastern New York; site of a mineral springs and racetrack; pop. 18,845.

Saratoga trunk A very large traveling trunk used formerly by ladies. [after *Saratoga* Springs]

Sa·ra·tov (sä·rä′təf) A city in the SW R.S.F.S.R., on the Volga; pop. 758,000 (est. 1970).

Sa·ra·wak (sä·rä′wäk, -wä) A part of Malaysia on NW Borneo; 47,071 sq. mi.; pop. 950,000 (est. 1969); capital, Kuching. See maps of INDONESIA, THAILAND. — **Sa·ra′·wak·ese′** (-ēz′, -ēs′) *adj. & n.*

sar·casm (sär′kaz·əm) *n.* **1.** An ironical or scornful utterance; contemptuous and taunting language. **2.** The use of biting gibes or cutting rebukes. [< LL *sarcasmus* < Gk. *sarkasmos* < *sarkazein* to tear flesh, sneer < *sarx, sarkos* flesh]
— **Syn. 1.** *Sarcasm* and *irony* are two methods that may be used, among others, in satire. Both differ from the mere expression of scorn, as in derision, by their witty exposure of the weakness of their victims. *Sarcasm* may describe a man's weakness in subtly pejorative terms, or may show the vanity of his pretensions, or his absurdity. *Irony* is more limited, and is sometimes regarded as one of the methods of *sarcasm*; it consists of the assertion of the opposite of what is really meant.

sar·cas·tic (sär·kas′tik) *adj.* **1.** Characterized by or of the nature of sarcasm; taunting. **2.** Given to the use of sarcasm. Also **sar·cas′ti·cal.** — **sar·cas′ti·cal·ly** *adv.*
— **Syn. 1.** *Sarcastic* and *sardonic* speech are both derisive, but *sarcastic* refers to the choice of words, and *sardonic* to the intent to ridicule.

sarce·net (särs′nit) See SARSENET.

sarco- *combining form* Flesh; of or related to flesh: *sarcogenic.* Also, before vowels, **sarc-.** [< Gk. *sarx, sarkos* flesh]

sar·co·carp (sär′kō·kärp) *n. Bot.* The succulent part of a drupaceous fruit, as the fleshy edible part of a plum or peach. [< SARCO- + -CARP]

sar·co·gen·ic (sär′kō·jen′ik) *adj.* Flesh-producing. Also **sar·cog·e·nous** (sär·koj′ə·nəs).

sar·co·lem·ma (sär′kō·lem′ə) *n. Anat.* The elastic membrane that encloses striated muscular fibers. [< NL < Gk. *sarx, sarkos* flesh + *lemma* husk]

sar·co·ma (sär·kō′mə) *n. pl.* **·ma·ta** (-mə·tə) *Pathol.* A tumor, often highly malignant, made up of cells resembling those of embryonic connective tissue. [< Gk. *sarkōma* < *sarx, sarkos* flesh] — **sar·co′ma·toid, sar·co′ma·tous** (-kō′-mə·təs, -kom′ə-) *adj.*

sar·co·ma·to·sis (sär·kō′mə·tō′sis) *n. Pathol.* The excessive formation of sarcomatous growths in the body.

sar·coph·a·gus (sär·kof′ə·gəs) *n. pl.* **·gi** (-jī) **1.** A stone coffin or tomb. **2.** A large ornamental coffin of marble or other stone placed in a crypt or exposed to view. **3.** A kind of limestone, used by the Greeks for coffins and said to reduce flesh to dust. [< L < Gk. *sarkophagos* flesh-eating]

sar·cous (sär′kəs) *adj.* Of, pertaining to, or composed of flesh or muscle. [< Gk. *sarx, sarkos* flesh]

sard (särd) *n.* The deep brownish red, translucent variety of chalcedony, used as a gem. Also called *sardine, sardius.* [< OF *sarde* < L *sarda* < Gk. *sardios* Sardian]

sar·dine[1] (sär·dēn′) *n.* **1.** A small, herringlike fish commonly preserved in oil as a food delicacy, especially the pilchard of European waters. **2.** Any of various related fishes similarly preserved, as the **Pacific** or **California sardine** (*Sardinops sagax*) and the **Spanish sardine** (*Sardinella anchovis*). [< OF < L < Gk. *sardēnē*, ? < *Sardo* Sardinia]

sar·dine[2] (sär′din) *n.* Sard.

Sar·din·i·a (sär·din′ē·ə) **1.** An island in the Mediterranean, comprising with adjacent islands a Region of Italy; 9,298 sq. mi.; pop. 1,413,239 (1961); capital, Cagliari. *Italian* **Sar·de·gna** (sär·dā′nyä). **2.** A former kingdom of northern Italy, including Sardinia with Savoy and Piedmont. — **Sar·din′·i·an** *adj. & n.*

Sar·dis (sär′dis) An ancient city of Asia Minor, capital of Lydia; destroyed by Tamerlane. Also **Sar′des.**

sar·di·us (sär′dē·əs) *n.* **1.** A sard. **2.** A stone in the breastplate of the Hebrew high priest. *Ex.* xxviii 17. [< LL < Gk. *sardios, sardion* < *Sardeis* Sardis]

sar·don·ic (sär·don′ik) *adj.* Scornful or derisive; sneering; mocking; cynical. — **Syn.** See SARCASTIC. [< F *sardonique* < L *sardonius* < Gk. *sardonios* < *sardanios* bitter, scornful; infl. in form by *Sardō* Sardinia, because thought to be < *sardanē*, a bitter plant of Sardinia causing fatal, laughterlike convulsions] — **sar·don′i·cal·ly** *adv.* — **sar·don′i·cism** *n.*

sar·do·nyx (sär′də·niks) *n.* A variety of chalcedony in bands varying from light to reddish brown, with other colors. [< L < Gk., appar. < *sardios* sardius + *onyx* onyx]

Sar·dou (sár·dōō′), **Victorien,** 1831–1908, French dramatist.

Sa·re·ma (sä′re·mä, *Russ.* sä′ryi·mə) See SAARE.

sar·gas·so (sär·gas′ō) *n.* An olive-brown seaweed (genus *Sargassum*) having small air bladders on its stalks, native in tropical American waters: also called *gulfweed.* Also **sar·gas′sum.** [< Pg. *sargaço* < *sarga,* ? < L *salicastrum*]

Sargasso Sea A part of the North Atlantic, extending from the West Indies to the Azores, known for its relatively still water and its large amounts of floating seaweed.

Sar·gent (sär′jənt), **John Singer,** 1856–1925, U.S. painter born in Italy.

Sar·gon II (sär′gon), died 705 B.C., king of Assyria 722–705 B.C.; consolidated the Assyrian empire.

sa·ri (sä′rē) *n. pl.* **·ris** A long piece of cotton or silk cloth, constituting the principal garment of Hindu women, worn round the waist, one end falling to the feet, and the other crossed over the bosom and shoulder, and sometimes over the head. Also **sa′ree.** [< Hind. *sarī* < Skt. *śāṭī*]

sark (särk) *n. Scot.* A shirt or chemise. [OE *serc*]

Sar·ma·ti·a (sär·mā′shē·ə, -shə) An ancient name for a region of Poland and the Soviet Union between the Vistula and the Volga. — **Sar·ma′tian** *adj. & n.* — **Sar·mat′ic** (-mat′ik) *adj.*

sar·men·tose (sär·men′tōs) *adj. Bot.* Having or producing sarmenta. Also **sar·men·ta·ceous** (sär′men·tā′shəs), **sar·men′tous.** [< L *sarmentosus* full of twigs < *sarmentum.* See SARMENTUM.]

sar·men·tum (sär·men′təm) *n. pl.* **·ta** (-tə) *Bot.* The slender runner of a plant, as in a vine. Also **sar′ment.** [< NL < L, lopped-off twig < *sarpere* to prune (trees)]

sa·rong (sə·rong′) *n.* **1.** A skirtlike garment of colored silk or cotton cloth worn by both sexes in the Malay Archipelago, etc. **2.** The material used for this garment. [< Malay *sārung,* prob. < Skt. *sāraṅga* variegated]

Sa·ron·ic Gulf (sə·ron′ik) An inlet of the Aegean in Greece, separating Attica from the Peloponnesus; 50 mi. long, 30 mi. wide: also *Gulf of Aegina.*

Sa·ros (sä′rôs), **Gulf of** An arm of the Aegean in NW Turkey, north of the Gallipoli Peninsula; 37 mi. long, 22 mi. wide.

Sa·roy·an (sə·roi′ən), **William,** born 1908, U.S. novelist and playwright.

Sar·pe·don (sär·pē′dən) In Greek mythology: **a** A son of Zeus and Europa who was allowed to live for three generations. **b** A Lycian prince and warrior killed by Patroclus in the Trojan War.

sar·ra·ce·ni·a (sar′ə·sē′nē·ə) *n.* Any of a genus (*Sarracenia*) of North American marsh plants, having pitcher-shaped leaves by which insects are entrapped and then digested; a pitcher plant. [< NL, after Dr. D. *Sarrazin,* 1659–1734, Quebec physician] — **sar′ra·ce′ni·a′ceous** (-sē′nē·ā′shəs) *adj.*

Sarre (sár) The French name for THE SAAR.

sar·sa·pa·ril·la (sas′pə·ril′ə, sär′sə·pə·ril′ə) *n.* **1.** The dried roots of certain tropical American climbing plants (genus *Smilax*) of the lily family. **2.** A medicinal preparation or a beverage made from such roots. **3.** Any of various plants resembling true sarsaparilla, as the **wild sarsaparilla** (*Aralia nudicaulis*) of North America. [< Sp. *zarzaparilla* < *zarza* bramble + *parilla,* dim. of *parra* vine]

sar·sar (sär′sər) *n. Meteorol.* A cold, whistling wind of Moslem lands: also called *sansar.* [< Arabic *ṣarṣar* a cold wind]

sarse·net (särs′nit) *n.* A fine, thin silk, used for linings: also spelled *sarcenet.* [< AF *sarzinet,* dim. of ME *sarzin* Saracen; prob. infl. by OF *drap sarrasinois,* lit., Saracen cloth < Med.L *pannus saracenicus*]

Sar·to (sär′tō), **Andrea del,** 1486–1531, Florentine painter: original name **Andrea d'Angelo di Fran·ces·co** (frän·ches′kō).

sar·tor (sar′tər) *n.* A tailor: a humorous or literary term. [< L, patcher, mender < *sarcire* to mend]

sar·to·ri·al (sär·tôr′ē·əl) *adj.* **1.** Pertaining to a tailor or his work. **2.** Pertaining to men's clothes. **3.** *Anat.* Relating to the sartorius. — **sar·to′ri·al·ly** *adv.*

sar·to·ri·us (sär·tôr′ē·əs, -tō′rē·əs) *n. Anat.* A flat, narrow muscle of the thigh, the longest muscle in the human body, extending obliquely from the hip to the inner side of the tibia. [< NL < L < *sartor* tailor]

Sar·tre (sär′tr′), **Jean Paul,** born 1905, French philosopher, novelist, and dramatist.

S.A.S. Fellow of the Society of Antiquaries (L *Societatis Antiquariorum Socius*).

Sa·se·bo (sä·se·bō) A port city on NW Kyushu island, Japan; pop. 262,488 (1960).

Sa·se·no (sä′se·nô) An island of Albania at the entrance to the bay of Valona; 2 sq. mi.

sash[1] (sash) *n.* An ornamental band or scarf, worn as a girdle, or around the waist or over the shoulder, often as part of a uniform or as a badge of distinction. [Orig. *shash* < Arabic *shāsh* muslin, turban]

sash[2] (sash) *n.* A frame, as of a window, in which glass is set. —*v.t.* To furnish with a sash. [Alter. of CHASSIS, taken as a pl.]

sa·shay (sa·shā′) *v.i. U.S. Informal* 1. To dance the chassé, as in a square dance. 2. To move with a swinging or gliding motion. [Alter. of CHASSÉ]

sa·sin (sā′sin) *n.* The black buck. [< Nepalese]

Sask. Saskatchewan.

Sas·katch·e·wan (sas·kach′ə·won) A Province of west central Canada; 251,700 sq. mi.; pop. 928,000; capital, Regina. **Sas·katch′e·wan′i·an** *n. & adj.*

Saskatchewan River A river of west central Canada, flowing 340 miles east to Lake Winnipeg.

sas·ka·toon (sas′kə·tōōn′) *n. Chiefly Canadian* A shadbush (*Amelanchier alnifolia*) of western North America, having thick leaves and a globular purple fruit. [< Algonquian (Cree) *misaskwatomin* < *misāskwat* shadbush + *min* fruit, berry]

Sas·ka·toon (sas′kə·tōōn′) A city in south central Saskatchewan, Canada; pop. 125,079.

sass (sas) *Informal n.* Impudence; back talk. —*v.t.* To talk to impudently or disrespectfully. [Dial. alter. of SAUCE]

sas·sa·by (sas′ə·bē) *n. pl.* **·bies** A large, dark red South African antelope (genus *Damaliscus*), having a blackish back and face. [< Bantu *tsessébe, tsessábi*]

sas·sa·fras (sas′ə·fras) *n.* 1. An aromatic, deciduous tree (genus *Sassafras*) of the laurel family. 2. The root bark of a North American species (*S. albidum*) of this tree, used for flavoring, and yielding a volatile oil containing safrol and camphor. [< Sp. *sasafrás*, prob. < N. Am. Ind. name; infl. in form by Sp. *saxafrax* saxifrage]

Sas·sa·nid (sas′ə·nid) *n. pl.* **Sas·sa·nids** or **Sas·san·i·dae** (sa·san′ə·dē) A member of the last national dynasty of ancient Persia (226–651). —*adj.* Of or pertaining to the Sassanids. Also **Sas·sa·ni·an** (sa·sā′nē·ən), **Sas′sa·nide**.

Sas·se·nach (sas′ə·nakh) *n. Scot. & Irish* A person of Saxon blood; an Englishman; a Protestant. [< Irish *sasa-nach*, Scottish Gaelic *Sasunnach* < Gaelic *Sasunn* Saxon]

Sas·soon (sa·sōōn′), **Siegfried (Lorraine),** 1886–1967, English poet and author.

sas·sy[1] (sas′ē) *adj.* **·si·er, ·si·est** *U.S. Dial.* Saucy; impertinent; cheeky.

sas·sy[2] (sas′ē) *n.* A West African tree (*Erythrophleum guineense*) having a bark that yields a poisonous alkaloid. Also **sas′sy·bark′** (-bärk′), **sas′sy·wood′** (-wōōd′). [< native W. African name]

sas·tru·ga (sas·trōō′gə) See ZASTRUGA.

sat (sat) Past tense of SIT.

Sat. 1. Saturday. 2. Saturn.

Sa·tan (sā′tən) *n.* In the Bible, the great adversary of God and tempter of mankind; the Devil: identified with *Lucifer. Luke* iv 5–8; *Rev.* xii 7–9. Also **Sa′than** (sā′tən), **Sath·a·nas** (sath′ə·nas). [< Hebrew *sātān* enemy < *sātan* to oppose, plot against]

sa·tang (sä·tang′) *n. pl.* **sa·tang** A bronze coin and money of account in Thailand, equivalent to one hundredth of a baht. [< Thai *satān*]

sa·tan·ic (sā·tan′ik) *adj.* Devilish; infernal; wicked. Also **sa·tan′i·cal.** —**sa·tan′i·cal·ly** *adv.*

Sa·tan·ism (sā′tən·iz′əm) *n.* Satan worship; especially, a cult addicted to profane mockeries of the holy rites of Christian worship. —**Sa′tan·ist** *n.*

sat·a·ra (sat′ər·ə, sə·tä′rə) *n.* A lustrous ribbed woolen fabric. [after *Satara*, a town about 100 miles from Bombay, India]

satch·el (sach′əl) *n.* A small handbag or suitcase. [< OF *sachel* < L *saccellus*, dim. of *saccus* sack]

sate[1] (sāt) *v.t.* **sat·ed, sat·ing** To satisfy the appetite of; satiate. [Appar. alter. of obs. *sade* to sate, OE *sadian*; refashioned after L *sat, satis* enough]

sate[2] (sāt) Archaic past tense of SIT.

sa·teen (sa·tēn′) *n.* A cotton fabric woven so as to give it a satin surface. [Alter. of SATIN; infl. in form by VELVETEEN]

sat·el·lite (sat′ə·līt) *n.* 1. *Astron.* A smaller body attending upon and revolving round a larger one; a moon. 2. One who attends upon a person in power. 3. Any obsequious attendant. 4. A small nation that is politically, economically, or militarily dependent on a great power. 5. A town or community whose activities are largely determined by those of a neighboring metropolis. 6. An airfield, base, etc., dependent upon a larger one. 7. Any manmade object launched from and revolving around the earth, as the sputnik. [< F < L *satelles, satellitis* attendant, guard]

satem languages (sä′təm, sā′-) Those Indo-European languages, including the Indo-Iranian, Armenian, Albanian, and Balto-Slavic subfamilies, in which the velar stop (k) of primitive Indo-European is typically sibilated, as in Avestan *satem* "hundred." Compare CENTUM LANGUAGES.

sa·ti·a·ble (sā′shē·ə·bəl, -shə·bəl) *adj.* Capable of being satiated. —**sa′ti·a·bil′i·ty, sa′ti·a·ble·ness** *n.* —**sa′ti·a·bly** *adv.*

sa·ti·ate (sā′shē·āt) *v.t.* **·at·ed, ·at·ing** 1. To satisfy the appetite or desire of; gratify. 2. To fill or gratify beyond natural desire; glut; surfeit. —*Syn.* See SATISFY. —*adj.* Filled to satiety; satiated. [< L *satiatus*, pp. of *satiare* to fill < *satis* enough] —**sa′ti·a′tion** *n.*

Sa·tie (sà·tē′), **Erik,** 1866–1925, French composer: full name **Alfred Erik Leslie Satie.**

sa·ti·e·ty (sə·tī′ə·tē) *n. pl.* **·ties** The state of being satiated; repletion; surfeit. [< F *satieté* < L *satietas, -tatis* < *satis* enough]

sat·in (sat′ən) *n.* A silk, cotton, rayon, or acetate fabric of thick texture, with glossy face and dull back. —*adj.* Of or resembling satin; glossy; smooth. [< OF < Med.L *satinus, setinus*, ult. < L *seta* silk]

sat·i·net (sat′ə·net′) *n.* 1. A strong fabric with cotton warp and woolen filling. 2. A thin satin. Also **sat′i·nette′.** [< F, dim. of *satin* satin]

sat·in·flow·er (sat′ən·flou′ər) *n.* The honesty. Also **sat′in·pod′** (-pod′).

sat·in·wood (sat′ən·wōōd′) *n.* 1. The satinlike wood of an East Indian tree (*Chloroxylon swietenia*) of the mahogany family. 2. The tree yielding this wood. 3. A West Indian tree (*Zanthoxylum flavum*) of the rue family, having a fine-textured, golden yellow wood used in cabinetwork.

sat·in·y (sat′ən·ē) *adj.* Glossy or smooth, like satin.

sat·ire (sat′īr) *n.* 1. Sarcasm, irony, or wit used to expose abuses or follies; ridicule. 2. A written composition in which vice, folly, etc., is held up to ridicule; also, a branch of literature composed of or dealing with such compositions. [< MF < L *satira, satura* satire, earlier, a discursive verse composition on a number of subjects, orig. medley < (*lanx*) *satura* fruit salad, lit., full (dish), fem. of *satur* full] —*Syn.* 1. chaff, raillery, mockery, derision. Compare SARCASM, BANTER, CARICATURE, LAMPOON.

sa·tir·ic (sə·tir′ik) *adj.* Of, pertaining to, or resembling satire, especially literary satire: *satiric* verse. Also *satirical.*

sa·tir·i·cal (sə·tir′i·kəl) *adj.* 1. Given to or characterized by satire: a *satirical* writer. 2. Severely sarcastic; biting; caustic: a *satirical* laugh. 3. Satiric. —**sa·tir′i·cal·ly** *adv.* —**sa·tir′i·cal·ness** *n.*

sat·i·rist (sat′ə·rist) *n.* 1. A writer of satire. 2. A satirical person.

sat·i·rize (sat′ə·rīz) *v.t.* **·rized, ·riz·ing** To subject to or criticize by means of satire. —**sat′i·riz′er** *n.*

sat·is·fac·tion (sat′is·fak′shən) *n.* 1. The act of satisfying or the state of being satisfied; gratification. 2. The making of amends, reparation, or payment, as of a claim or obligation. 3. That which satisfies; atonement; compensation. [< OF *satisfactiun* < L *satisfactio, -onis* < *satisfactus*, pp. of *satisfacere.* Compare SATISFY.] —*Syn.* 1. comfort, content, contentment, complacency, gratification. Compare SATISFY. —*Ant.* dissatisfaction, discontent.

sat·is·fac·to·ry (sat′is·fak′tər·ē) *adj.* 1. Giving satisfaction; answering fully all desires, expectations, or requirements; sufficient. 2. Making satisfaction; atoning; expiatory. —*Syn.* See ADEQUATE. —**sat′is·fac′to·ri·ly** *adv.* —**sat′is·fac′to·ri·ness** *n.*

sat·is·fy (sat′is·fī) *v.* **·fied, ·fy·ing** *v.t.* 1. To supply fully with what is desired, expected, or needed; cause to have enough; gratify. 2. To free from doubt or anxiety; assure; convince. 3. To give what is due to. 4. To pay or discharge (a debt, obligation, etc.). 5. To answer sufficiently or convincingly, as a question or objection. 6. To fulfill the conditions or requirements of, as an equation. 7. To make reparation for; expiate. —*v.i.* 8. To give satisfaction. [< OF *satisfier* < L *satisfacere* < *satis* enough + *facere* to do] —**sat′is·fi′er** *n.* —**sat′is·fy′ing·ly** *adv.* —*Syn.* 1. Satisfy, gratify, and satiate, meaning to give what is wanted or needed, have diverged in connotation. *Satisfy* suggests the giving of just enough, and no more, and a state of mind that is merely content. To *gratify* is to please, hence to give liberally, while *satiate* is now chiefly used to indicate an excess or oversupply. —*Ant.* disappoint, deny, stint, tantalize.

sa·to·ri (sä·tôr′ē) *n.* The illumination of spirit sought by Zen Buddhists. [< Japanese]

sa·trap (sā′trap, sat′rap) *n.* 1. A governor of a province in ancient Persia. 2. A subordinate, often despotic, ruler or governor. [< L *satrapes* < Gk. *satrapēs* < OPersian *shathraparan*, lit., protector of a province]

sa·trap·y (sā′trə·pē, sat′rə·pē) *n. pl.* **·trap·ies** The territory or the jurisdiction of a satrap. Also **sa·trap·ate** (sā′trə·pit, sat′rə-).

Sa·tsu·ma (sä·tsōō·mä) A former province of southern Kyushu island, Japan.

Satsuma ware A kind of yellow pottery, originally made at Satsuma.

sat·u·rant (sach′ər·ənt) *adj.* That saturates. — *n.* A substance that fully neutralizes another. [< L *saturans, -antis,* ppr. of *saturare.* See SATURATE.]

sat·u·rate (sach′ə·rāt; *for adj., also* sach′ə·rit) *v.t.* ·rat·ed, ·rat·ing 1. To soak or imbue thoroughly. 2. To fill, impregnate, or charge, as a solution or by chemical action or magnetism. — **Syn.** See PERMEATE. — *adj.* 1. Filled to repletion; saturated. 2. Very intense; deep: said of colors. [< L *saturatus,* pp. of *saturare* to fill up < *satur* full] — **sat·u·ra·ble** (sach′ər·ə·bəl) *adj.* — **sat′u·ra′ter** *or* ·tor *n.*

sat·u·rat·ed (sach′ə·rā′tid) *adj.* 1. Incapable of holding more of a substance or material; completely satisfied; replete: *saturated* vapor. 2. *Chem.* Designating an organic compound, as paraffin or methane, having no free valences and without double or triple bonds. 3. Designating a color or hue exhibiting high saturation.

sat·u·ra·tion (sach′ə·rā′shən) *n.* 1. The act of saturating, or the state of being saturated; full impregnation. 2. The impregnation of one substance with another till no more can be received, as by solution or by chemical combination. 3. *Meteorol.* The filling of the atmosphere with any vapor to the point of condensation. 4. The maximum magnetization of which a body is capable. 5. The degree of vividness or purity of a color, as indicated by its freedom from admixture with white.

Sat·ur·day (sat′ər·dē, -dā) *n.* The seventh or last day of the week; the Jewish Sabbath. Abbr. *S., Sat.* [OE *Sæterdæg, Sæternsdæg,* trans. of L *Saturni dies* Saturn's day]

Sat·urn (sat′ərn) In Roman mythology, the god of agriculture: identified with the Greek *Cronus.* — *n.* The second largest planet of the solar system and sixth in order from the sun. See PLANET. Abbr. *Sat.* [< L *Saturnus.* ? Akin to *satus,* pp. of *serere* to sow.]

sat·ur·na·li·a (sat′ər·nā′lē·ə) *n.pl.* (*Usually construed as sing.*) Any season or period of general license or revelry. [< L. See SATURNALIA.]

Sat·ur·na·li·a (sat′ər·nā′lē·ə) *n.pl.* The feast of Saturn held at Rome in mid-December, celebrating the winter solstice, and marked by wild reveling and licentious abandon. [< L, orig. neut. pl. of *Saturnalis* of Saturn < *Saturnus* Saturn] — **Sat′ur·na′li·an** *adj.*

Sa·tur·ni·an (sə·tûr′nē·ən) *adj.* 1. Of or pertaining to the god Saturn, especially to a fabled golden age in his reign, marked by simplicity, virtue, and happiness. 2. Of or pertaining to the planet Saturn.

sa·tur·ni·id (sə·tûr′nē·id) *n.* Any of a family (*Saturniidae*) of large, hairy, brightly colored moths, widely distributed in most temperate regions. — *adj.* Of or pertaining to the *Saturniidae.* [< NL < *Saturnia* genus name < L *Saturnius* of Saturn < *Saturnus* Saturn]

sat·ur·nine (sat′ər·nīn) *adj.* 1. Having a grave, gloomy, or morose disposition or character; heavy; dull. 2. In old chemistry, pertaining to lead. 3. *Pathol.* Pertaining to or produced by lead. [< OF *saturnin* of Saturn, of lead, heavy < Med.L *Saturnus* lead, Saturn < L, Saturn]

Sat·ur·nine (sat′ər·nīn) *adj.* 1. Of or pertaining to the planet Saturn. 2. Born or being under the influence of the planet Saturn. 3. Gloomy; heavy.

sat·urn·ism (sat′ərn·iz′əm) *n. Pathol.* Lead poisoning. [< Med.L *Saturnus.* See SATURNINE.]

Sat·ya·gra·ha (sut′yə·gru′hə) *n.* A movement characterized by nonviolent resistance and noncooperation, adopted in India, 1919, by the followers of M. K. Gandhi in protest against certain civil and religious abuses. [< Hind., truth-force, lit., a grasping for truth]

sat·yr (sat′ər, sā′tər) *n.* 1. In Greek mythology, a woodland deity in human form, having pointed ears, goat's legs, and budding horns, and of wanton nature. 2. A very lascivious man. 3. Any butterfly of the family *Agapetidae,* commonly brown and gray with eyelike spots. [< L *satyrus* < Gk. *satyros*] — **sa·tyr·ic** (sə·tir′ik) *or* ·i·cal *adj.*

sat·y·ri·a·sis (sat′ə·rī′ə·sis) *n. Psychiatry* An excessive and uncontrollable sexual desire in men. [< NL < Gk. *satyriaein* to suffer from satyriasis < *satyros* satyr]

sauce (sôs) *n.* 1. An appetizing dressing or liquid relish for food. 2. Any appetizing garnish of a meal. 3. Formerly, any condiment, as salt or pepper. 4. A dish of fruit pulp stewed and sweetened: cranberry *sauce.* 5. *Informal* Table vegetables, as roots or greens. Also **garden sauce.** 6. *Informal* Pert or impudent language. — *v.t.* **sauced, sauc·ing** 1. To flavor with sauce; season. 2. To give zest or piquancy to. 3. *Informal* To be saucy to. [< OF < LL *salsa,* orig. fem. of L *salsus* salted, pp. of *salire* to salt < *sal* salt]

sauce·box (sôs′boks′) *n. Informal* A saucy person.

sauce·pan (sôs′pan′) *n.* A metal or enamel pan with projecting handle, for cooking food.

sau·cer (sô′sər) *n.* 1. A small dish for holding a cup. 2. Any small, round, shallow vessel of similar shape. [< OF *saussier* < *sauce* sauce]

sau·cy (sô′sē) *adj.* ·ci·er, ·ci·est 1. Disrespectful to superiors; impudent. 2. Piquant; sprightly; amusing. — **sau′ci·ly** *adv.* — **sau′ci·ness** *n.*

Sa·ud (sä·ōōd′), **King,** 1902–1969, king of Saudi Arabia 1953–1964, son of Ibn Saud: full name **Ibn Abdul Aziz al Saud.**

Sa·u·di Arabia (sä·ōō′dē) A kingdom in the northern and central part of Arabia; 927,000 sq. mi.; pop. 7.2 million (est. 1969); capitals, Mecca and Riyadh.

sauer·bra·ten (sour′-brätn, *Ger.* zou′ər·brä′tən) *n.* Beef marinated in vinegar before being braised. [< G < *sauer* sour + *braten* to roast]

sauer·kraut (sour′-krout′) *n.* Shredded and salted cabbage fermented in its own juice: also called *kraut:* also spelled *sourcrout.* [< G < *sauer* sour + *kraut* cabbage, vegetable, plant]

sau·ger (sô′gər) *n.* A percoid fish (*Stizostidion canadense*), resembling the walleye: a pike perch. [? < N. Am. Ind.]

saugh (sôkh) *n. Scot.* The sallow; the willow. — **saugh′y** *adj.*

Sauk (sôk) *n.* One of a tribe of North American Indians of Algonquian stock, formerly occupying Michigan, later Wisconsin and the Mississippi valley, now on reservations in Oklahoma, Iowa, and Kansas. Also spelled *Sac.*

saul (sôl) *n. Scot.* Soul; mettle.

Saul (sôl) 1. The first king of Israel. I *Sam.* ix 2. 2. The Hebrew name of the Apostle Paul (*Acts* xiii 9): also **Saul of Tarsus.**

sault (sōō, sō) *n. Chiefly Canadian* A waterfall or rapids. [< dial. F (Canadian) < F, leap]

Sault Sainte Ma·rie (sōō′sānt′mə·rē′) 1. A port city in northern Michigan, on St. Marys River; pop. 15,136. 2. A city opposite it in south central Ontario; pop. 74,858. Also **Sault Ste. Marie.**

Sault Sainte Marie Canals Three ship canals that circumvent the rapids in the St. Marys River, connecting Lake Superior with Lake Huron. Also, *Informal,* **Soo Canals.**

sau·na (sou′nə) *n.* A room or house for taking steam baths by the Finnish method, in steam produced by throwing water on hot stones; also, such a steam bath, often ended with a brisk run out into the snow and cold. [< Finnish]

saun·ter (sôn′tər) *v.i.* To walk in a leisurely or lounging way; stroll. — *n.* 1. A slow, aimless manner of walking. 2. An idle stroll. [ME *santren* to muse, meditate; ult. origin unknown]

sau·rel (sôr′əl) *n.* A carangoid marine fish (*Trachurus symmetricus*) of America and Europe: also called *scad.* [< F < L. *sauros* horse mackerel]

sau·ri·an (sôr′ē·ən) *n.* One of a suborder (*Sauria*) of reptiles, including the lizards, geckos, and chameleons. — *adj.* Pertaining to the *Sauria.* [< NL < Gk. *sauros* lizard]

sau·ris·chi·an (sô·ris′kē·ən) *adj. Paleontol.* Of, pertaining to, or belonging to an order (*Saurischia*) of dinosaurs that flourished through most of the Mesozoic era, including the large carnivorous types. — *n.* A member of this order. [< NL < Gk. *sauros* lizard + *ischion* hip]

sauro- combining form Lizard: *sauropod.* Also, before vowels, **saur-.** [< Gk. *sauros* lizard]

sau·ro·pod (sôr′ə·pod) *n. Paleontol.* One of a suborder (*Sauropoda*) of long-necked, long-tailed, four-footed saurischian dinosaurs of herbivorous habits. — *adj.* Of or pertaining to the *Sauropoda.* [< NL < Gk. *sauros* lizard + *pous, podos* foot] — **sau·rop·o·dous** (sô·rop′ə·dəs) *adj.*

-saurus combining form *Zool.* Lizard: used to form genus names: *Brontosaurus, Plesiosaurus.* [< Gk. *sauros* lizard]

sau·ry (sôr′ē) *n. pl.* ·ries 1. An edible fish (*Scomberesox saurus*) of the Atlantic, having the jaws developed into a slim beak. 2. A related fish of the Pacific (*Cololabis saira*). Also called *skipper:* also **saury pike.** [< NL *saurus* < Gk. *sauros* lizard]

sau·sage (sô′sij) *n.* 1. Finely chopped and highly seasoned meat, commonly stuffed into the cleaned and prepared entrails of some animal or into artificial casings. 2. *Aeron.* A type of barrage or observation balloon, shaped like a sausage. [< AF *saussiche* < LL *salsicia,* ult. < L *salsus.* See SAUCE.]

sau·té (sō·tā′, sô-) *adj.* Fried quickly with little grease. — *v.t.* **·téed**, **·té·ing** To fry quickly in a little fat. [< F, pp. of *sauter* to leap < L *saltare*]

sau·terne (sō·tûrn′, sô-; *Fr.* sō·tern′) *n.* A sweet, white French wine. Also **sau·ternes′**. [after *Sauternes*, district in SW France]

sau·toir (sō·twàr′) *n. Heraldry* A saltire. Also **sau·toire′**. [< F. SALTIRE.]

sauve qui peut (sōv kē pœ′) *French* A stampede; rout; literally, save himself who can.

Sa·va (sä′vä) A river of northern Yugoslavia, flowing about 583 miles east to the Danube. See map of DANUBE.

sav·age (sav′ij) *adj.* **1.** Having a wild and untamed nature; not domesticated. **2.** Ferocious; fierce. **3.** Living in or belonging to a primitive condition of human life and society; uncivilized: *savage* tribes. **4.** Vicious; cruel; furious: a *savage* attack. **5.** Rude; uncultivated; rough. **6.** *Obs.* Remote from human abode; belonging to the wilderness: a *savage* trail. — **Syn.** See BARBAROUS. — *n.* **1.** A primitive or uncivilized human being. **2.** A brutal, fierce, and cruel person; a barbarian. — *v.t.* **·aged**, **·ag·ing** To attack savagely, especially with the teeth. [< OF *salvage*, *sauvage* < L *salvaticus*, *silvaticus* < *silva* a wood] — **sav′·age·ly** *adv.* — **sav′age·ness** *n.*

Sav·age (sav′ij) **Richard**, 1697?–1743, English poet.

Savage Island See NIUE.

sav·age·ry (sav′ij·rē) *n. pl.* **·ries** **1.** The state of being savage. **2.** Cruelty in disposition or action; a cruel or savage act. **3.** Savages collectively: also **sav′age·dom** (-dəm). Also **sav′ag·ism**.

Sa·vai·i (sä·vī′ē) The largest island of Western Samoa; about 700 sq. mi.

sa·van·na (sə·van′ə) *n.* **1.** A tract of level land covered with low vegetation. **2.** Any large area of tropical or subtropical grassland, covered in part with trees and spiny shrubs. Also **sa·van′nah**. [Earlier *zavana* < Sp. < Carib]

Sa·van·nah (sə·van′ə) A port city in eastern Georgia; pop. 118,349; at the mouth of the **Savannah River**, that flows 314 miles SE to the Atlantic and forms most of the boundary between Georgia and South Carolina.

sa·vant (sə·vänt′, sav′ənt; *Fr.* sà·vän′) *n.* A man of exceptional learning. [< F, orig. ppr. of *savoir* to know]

save¹ (sāv) *v.* **saved**, **sav·ing** *v.t.* **1.** To preserve or rescue from danger, harm, etc. **2.** To keep from being spent, expended, or lost; avoid the loss or waste of. **3.** To set aside for future use; accumulate: often with *up*. **4.** To treat carefully so as to avoid fatigue, harm, etc.: to *save* one's eyes. **5.** To avoid the need or trouble of; prevent by timely action: A stitch in time *saves* nine. **6.** *Theol.* To deliver from spiritual death or the consequences of sin; redeem. — *v.i.* **7.** To avoid waste; be economical. **8.** To preserve something from danger, harm, etc. **9.** To admit of preservation, as food. [< OF *salver*, *sauver* < LL *salvare* to save < L *salvus* safe] — **sav′a·ble** or **save′a·ble** *adj.* — **sav′a·ble·ness** *n.* — **sav′er** *n.*

save² (sāv) *prep.* Except; but. — *conj.* **1.** Except; but: usually with *that*. **2.** *Archaic* Unless. [< OF *sauf* being excepted, orig., safe < L *salvus*]

save-all (sāv′ôl′) *n.* **1.** A contrivance for preventing waste; anything that saves fragments. **2.** A child's savings bank. **3.** An overall or pinafore.

sav·e·loy (sav′ə·loi) *n.* A kind of highly seasoned, dried sausage made of salted pork. [Alter. of F *cervelas* < Ital. *cervellata* < *cervello* brain < L *cerebellum*. See CEREBELLUM.]

sav·in (sav′in) *n.* **1.** A bushy shrub or small tree (*Juniperus sabina*) of the cypress family. **2.** The young shoots of this plant, yielding **savin oil**, an acrid volatile oil used in medicine. Also called *sabine*. [OE *safine* and OF *savine* < L (*herba*) *Sabina* Sabine (herb), fem. of *Sabinus*]

sav·ing (sā′ving) *adj.* **1.** That saves; preserving, as from destruction. **2.** Redeeming; delivering. **3.** Avoiding needless waste or expense; economical; frugal. **4.** Incurring no loss, if not gainful: a *saving* investment. **5.** Holding in reserve; making an exception; qualifying: a *saving* clause. — *n.* **1.** Preservation from loss or danger. **2.** Avoidance of waste; economy. **3.** The extent of something saved; reduction in cost: a *saving* of 16 percent. **4.** *pl.* Sums of money not expended. **5.** That which is saved. **6.** *Law* Reservation; exception. — *prep.* **1.** With the exception of; save. **2.** With due respect for: *saving* your presence. — *conj.* Save; but. — **sav′ing·ly** *adv.* — **sav′ing·ness** *n.*

savings account An account drawing interest at a bank.

savings bank **1.** A bank whose chief functions are receiving and investing savings and paying interest on deposits. **2.** A container with a slot for depositing coins.

sav·ior (sāv′yər) *n.* One who saves. Also *Brit.* **sav′iour**. [< OF *saveour* < LL *salvator*, *-oris* < L *salvare*. See SAVE.]

Sav·iour (sāv′yər) *n.* A title sometimes applied directly to God, but chiefly to Jesus Christ, as the Redeemer: usually with *the*. Also **Sav′ior**.

sa·voir-faire (sà·vwàr·fâr′) *French* Ability to say and do the right thing; tact; literally, to know how to act.

sa·voir-vi·vre (sà·vwàr·vē′vr′) *French* Good breeding; good social manners; literally, to know how to live.

Sa·vo·na·ro·la (sav′ə·nə·rō′lə, *Ital.* sä′vō·nä·rō′lä), **Girolamo**, 1452–98, Italian Dominican monk; political and religious reformer; burned as a heretic.

sa·vor (sā′vər) *n.* **1.** The quality of a thing that affects the sense of taste or smell, or both; flavor; odor. **2.** Specific or characteristic quality or approach to a quality; flavor. **3.** Relish; zest: The conversation had *savor*. **4.** *Archaic* Character; reputation. — **Syn.** See SMELL. — *v.i.* **1.** To have a specified savor; taste or smell: with *of*. **2.** To have a specified quality or character: with *of*. — *v.t.* **3.** To give flavor to; season. **4.** To taste or enjoy with pleasure; relish. **5.** To have the savor or character of. Also *Brit.* **sa′vour**. [< OF *savour* < L *sapor* taste < *sapere* to taste, know] — **sa′vor·er** *n.* — **sa′vor·ous** *adj.*

sa·vor·less (sā′vər·lis) *adj.* Tasteless; insipid.

sa·vor·y¹ (sā′vər·ē) *adj.* **1.** Of an agreeable taste and odor; appetizing. **2.** Piquant to the taste. **3.** In good repute; respectable. — *n. Brit.* A small, hot serving of food eaten at the end or beginning of a dinner. Also *Brit.* **sa′vour·y**. [< OF *savouré*, pp. of OF *savourer* to taste < *savour* < L SAVOR.] — **sa′vor·i·ly** *adv.* — **sa′vor·i·ness** *n.* — **Syn.** (adj.) **1.** flavorous, palatable, relishable, sapid, tasty, toothsome. Compare DELICIOUS.

sa·vor·y² (sā′vər·ē) *n.* A hardy, annual, aromatic herb (*Satureia hortensis*) of the mint family, used for seasoning. Also **summer savory**. [OE *sætherie* < L *satureia*; infl. in form by OF *savour* to savor]

sa·voy (sə·voi′) *n.* A variety of cabbage with wrinkled leaves and a compact head. [< F (*chou de*) *Savoie* (cabbage of) Savoy]

Sa·voy (sə·voi′) A region and former duchy of the kingdom of Sardinia, between Italy and France; ceded to France in 1860. *French* **Sa·voie** (sà·vwà′).

Sa·voy (sə·voi′), **House of** A family of French nobles, reigning in Italy from 1861–1946.

Sa·voy·ard (sə·voi′ərd, *Fr.* sà·vwà·yàr′) *n.* **1.** A native or inhabitant of Savoy, France. **2.** An actor or actress in the Gilbert and Sullivan operas, most of which were originally produced at the Savoy Theatre in London. **3.** An admirer or producer of these operas. — *adj.* **1.** Of or pertaining to Savoy, France. **2.** Of the Savoy Theatre, London. [< F < *Savoie* Savoy]

sav·vy (sav′ē) *Slang v.i.* **·vied**, **·vy·ing** To understand; comprehend. — *n.* Understanding; good sense. [Alter. of Sp. ¿ *Sabe* (*usted*)? Do (you) know? < *saber* < L *sapere* to know, taste]

saw¹ (sô) *n.* **1.** A cutting instrument with pointed teeth arranged continuously along the edge of the blade, used to cut or divide wood, bone, metal, etc. **2.** A machine for operating a saw or gang of saws. **3.** Any tool or instrument without teeth used like a saw, as a steel disk for cutting armor plate, etc. — **circular saw** A disk having saw teeth in or on its periphery, and mounted on an arbor, with which it is rotated, usually at high speed. — *v.* **sawed**, **sawed** or **sawn**, **saw·ing** *v.t.* **1.** To cut or divide with a saw. **2.** To shape or fashion with a saw. **3.** To cut or slice (the air, etc.) as if using a saw. **4.** To cause to move with a to-and-fro motion like that of a saw. — *v.i.* **5.** To use a saw. **6.** To cut: said of a saw. **7.** To be cut with a saw: This wood *saws* easily. [OE *sagu*. Akin to L *secare* to cut.] — **saw′er** *n.*

saw² (sô) *n.* A proverbial or familiar saying; old maxim. — **Syn.** See PROVERB. [OE *sagu*. Akin to SAGA.]

saw³ (sô) Past tense of SEE¹.

Sa·watch Range (sə·woch′) A range of the Rocky Mountains in central Colorado; highest peak, Mt. Elbert, 14,431 ft.: also *Saguache*.

saw·bill (sô′bil′) *n.* The motmot, a bird.

saw·bones (sô′bōnz′) *n. Slang* A surgeon.

saw·buck (sô′buk′) *n.* **1.** A sawhorse consisting of two X-shaped ends joined by a connecting bar or bars. **2.** *U.S. Slang* A ten-dollar bill: so called from the resemblance of X, Roman numeral ten, to the ends of a sawbuck. [Trans. of Du. *zaagbok*]

SAWBUCK

a Sawbuck with bucksaw (*b*). *c* Sawhorse.

saw·dust (sô′dust′) *n.* Small particles of wood produced by the action of sawing.

sawed-off (sôd′ôf′, -of′) *adj.* **1.** Having one end sawed off, as a shotgun. **2.** *U.S. Slang* Short; not of average height.

saw·fish (sô′fish′) *n. pl.* **·fish** or **·fish·es** Any of various elongate, sharklike tropical fish (genus *Pristis*) with the snout prolonged into a flat blade with teeth on each side.

saw·fly (sô′flī′) *n. pl.* **·flies** Any of various hymenopterous insects (family *Tenthredinidae*) having in the female a sawlike ovipositor for piercing plants, soft wood, etc.

saw grass Any of various sedges having leaves with minutely toothed edges; especially, the **Jamaica saw grass** (*Cladium jamaicense*) growing in swamps in tropical and subtropical North America.

saw·horse (sô′hôrs′) *n.* A frame on which to rest wood, etc., for sawing, usually consisting of a long wooden bar or plank supported by four extended legs.

saw log A log of suitable size for sawing.

saw·mill (sô′mil′) *n.* 1. An establishment for sawing logs with power-driven machinery. 2. A large sawing machine.

sawn (sôn) Alternative past participle of SAW[1].

saw palmetto Any of various palmettos having spiny leafstalks; especially, *Serenoa repens* and *Paurotis wrighti* of the southern United States and the West Indies.

saw pit A pit over which a timber is laid to be sawed by two sawyers, one standing in the pit.

saw screw A screw with a special bolt, used to fasten the blade of a saw to the handle. For illustration see SCREW.

saw set An instrument to give set to, or bend slightly outward, the teeth of a saw.

saw-toothed (sô′tōōtht′) *adj.* Serrate; having teeth or toothlike processes similar to those of a saw.

saw·yer (sô′yər) *n.* 1. One whose occupation is the sawing of wood, as in lumbering or in a sawmill. 2. Any of various longicorn beetles having larvae that bore into wood, as the **pine sawyer** (genus *Monochamus*). [Alter. of SAWER]

sax[1] (saks) *n.* A chopping tool for trimming edges of roofing slates. [OE *seax* knife]

sax[2] (saks) *n. Informal* A saxophone.

Sax. 1. Saxon. 2. Saxony.

sax·a·tile (sak′sə-til) *adj. Ecol.* Saxicoline. [< L *saxatilis* < *saxum* rock]

Saxe (saks) The French name for SAXONY.

Saxe (saks), **Comte Maurice de**, 1696–1750, French marshal.

Saxe-Al·ten·burg (saks′äl′tən-bûrg) A former duchy in central Germany.

Saxe-Co·burg (saks′kō′bûrg) A former duchy in central Germany; united in 1826 with **Saxe-Go·tha** (-gō′thə) to form the duchy of **Saxe-Coburg-Gotha**, which was divided between Thuringia and Bavaria in 1918.

Saxe-Co·burg-Go·tha (saks′kō′bûrg-gō′thə) Former name of the British royal family. See WINDSOR.

Saxe-Mei·ning·en (saks′mī′ning-ən) A former duchy in central Germany.

Saxe-Wei·mar (saks′vī′mär) A former grand duchy in central Germany; became the duchy of **Saxe-Weimar-Ei·se·nach** (ī′zə-näkh) in 1741.

sax·horn (saks′hôrn′) *n.* Any of a family of valved brass instruments resembling the bugle, made in a wide series of ranges. [after the inventor, Antoine Joseph *Sax* (called Adolphe), 1814–94, Belgian instrument maker + HORN]

sax·ic·o·line (sak·sik′ə-lin, -lin) *adj. Ecol.* Living or growing among rocks: also *saxatile*. Also **sax·ic′o·lous**. [< NL *saxicola* < L *saxum* rock + *colere* to inhabit]

sax·i·fra·ga·ceous (sak′sə-frə-gā′shəs) *adj. Bot.* Belonging to the saxifrage family. [< NL < L *saxifraga*. See SAXIFRAGE.]

sax·i·frage (sak′sə-frij) *n.* Any of a large, widely distributed genus (*Saxifraga*) of herbaceous plants growing in rocky places. It is typical of a family (*Saxifragaceae*) that includes currants, gooseberries, and alumroot. [< OF < L (*herba*) *saxifraga*, lit., stone-breaking (herb)]

Sax·o Gram·mat·i·cus (sak′sō grə-mat′i-kəs) 1150?–1220?, Danish historian.

Sax·on (sak′sən) *n.* 1. A member of a Germanic tribal group formerly inhabiting what is now Schleswig-Holstein. 2. A member of any of the offshoots of this group, as those who, with the Angles and Jutes, invaded England in the fifth and sixth centuries A.D. 3. An Anglo-Saxon (def. 2). 4. An inhabitant of Saxony. 5. The modern High German dialect of Saxony. Abbr. *S, S., Sax.* — **Old Saxon** The dialect of Low German current in the valley of the lower Elbe in the early Middle Ages. Abbr. *OS, OS., O.S.* — *adj.* 1. Of or pertaining to the Saxons or to their language. 2. Anglo-Saxon; English. 3. Of or pertaining to Saxony, Germany. [< F < L *Saxo, Saxonis* < WGmc.]

Sax·on·ism (sak′sən-iz′əm) *n.* A word, phrase, etc., of English, especially Anglo-Saxon, origin.

Sax·o·ny (sak′sə-nē) *n. pl.* **-nies** 1. A fabric originally made from wool raised in Saxony, central Germany. 2. A variety of fine woolen knitting yarn.

Sax·o·ny (sak′sə-nē) 1. A former duchy, electorate, and kingdom of central Germany. 2. A former Prussian province of central Germany, constituted in 1816, largely from the territories of the kingdom of Saxony. 3. A former state of east central Germany, 1918–45. 4. A former state of SE East Germany, 1949–52. German *Sachsen*, French *Saxe*.

Sax·o·ny-An·halt (sak′sə-nē-än′hält) A former state of central East Germany.

sax·o·phone (sak′sə-fōn) *n.* Any of a family of metal wind instruments having a single reed and conical bore, made in a wide series of ranges. [after A. J. *Sax* (see SAXHORN) + -PHONE] — **sax′o·phon′ist** *n.*

sax·tu·ba (saks′tōō′bə, -tyōō′-) *n.* A bass or contrabass saxhorn. [< SAX(HORN) + TUBA]

say[1] (sā) *v.* **said, say·ing** *v.t.* 1. To pronounce or utter;

speak. 2. To declare or express in words; tell; state. 3. To state positively or as an opinion: *Say* which you prefer. 4. To recite; repeat: to *say* one's prayers. 5. To report; allege. 6. To assume; suppose: Let us *say* that this statement is true. — *v.i.* 7. To make a statement; speak. — **that is to say** In other words. — *adv.* 1. Approximately; at a guess: He is worth, *say*, a million. 2. For example: Choose a number, *say*, ten. — *n.* 1. What one has said or has to say; testimony; word. 2. Right or turn to speak or choose: to have one's *say*. 3. Authority: to have the *say*. — *interj. U.S. Informal* A hail or an exclamation to command attention: also *Brit.* **I say.** Compare LISTEN. [OE *secgan*] — **say′er** *n.*

say[2] (sā) *n.* A fine, thin serge used in the 16th century. [< OF *saie* < L *saga*, pl. of *sagum* military cloak]

Sa·yan Mountains (sä-yän′) A mountain system in the southern R.S.F.S.R.; highest peak, Munku Sardik, 11,453 ft.

Say·ers (sā′ərz, sârz), **Dorothy L(eigh)**, 1893–1957, English author.

say·id (sī′id, sä′yid) *n.* Lord: a title applied to supposed descendants of Mohammed through his elder grandson, Husain: also *said, saiyid*. Also **say′yid**. [< Arabic *sayyid*]

Sa·yi·da (sä′yə-dä) See SAIDA.

say·ing (sā′ing) *n.* 1. A maxim; adage. 2. Something said; an utterance. — **Syn.** See PROVERB.

says (sez) Third person singular, present indicative of SAY[1].

say-so (sā′sō′) *n. Informal* 1. An unsupported assertion or decision. 2. Right or power to make decisions.

Saz·e·rac (saz′ə-rak′) *n. U.S.* A drink made of bourbon, absinthe- or anise-flavored liqueur, bitters, and sugar. [Origin uncertain]

sb. Substantive.

s.b. or **sb** Stolen base(s).

Sb *Chem.* Antimony (L *stibium*).

S.B. Bachelor of Science (L *Scientiae Baccalaureus*).

SbE South by east.

'sblood (zblud) *interj. Archaic* God's blood: an oath.

SbW South by west.

sc. 1. He (or she) carved or engraved it (L *sculpsit*). 2. Namely (L *scilicet*). 3. Scale. 4. Scene. 5. Science(s).

s.c. 1. *Printing* Small capitals. 2. Supercalendered.

Sc 1. *Chem.* Scandium. 2. Stratocumulus.

Sc. Scotch; Scotland; Scottish.

SC Security Council (of the United Nations).

S.C. South Carolina.

scab (skab) *n.* 1. A crust formed on the surface of a wound or sore. 2. *Vet.* Scabies. 3. Any of certain plant diseases characterized by a roughened or warty appearance. 4. *Slang* A mean, contemptible fellow. 5. *Informal* A workman who will not join or act with a labor union; especially, one who replaces a striker at his work; a strikebreaker. — *v.i.* **scabbed, scab·bing** 1. To form or become covered with a scab. 2. *Informal* To take the job of a striker; act as a scab. [Fusion of ON *skabb* (assumed) and OE *sceabb*; infl. in meaning by L *scabies*. See SCABIES.]

scab·bard (skab′ərd) *n.* A sheath for a weapon, as for a bayonet or a sword. — *v.t.* To sheathe in or furnish with a scabbard. [< OF *escalberc*, prob. < OHG *scar* sword + *bergan* to hide, protect]

scabbard fish 1. Any of various food fish (genus *Lepidopus*) having a long, slender silvery body. 2. The cutlass fish.

scab·ble (skab′əl) *v.t.* **·bled, ·bling** In stoneworking, to dress or shape roughly. [Earlier *scapple* < OF *escapeler* to dress timber]

scab·by (skab′ē) *adj.* **·bi·er, ·bi·est** 1. Having, consisting of, or resembling a scab or scabs. 2. Having scabies. 3. *Informal* Contemptible. — **scab′bi·ly** *adv.* — **scab′bi·ness** *n.*

sca·bi·es (skā′bi·ēz, -bēz) *n.* 1. A skin disease caused by the itch mite; itch. 2. *Vet.* A similar skin disease of sheep: also called *scab*. [< L, roughness, an itch < *scabere* to scratch, scrape. Akin to SHAVE.] — **sca·bi·et·ic** (skā′bē·et′ik) *adj.*

sca·bi·ous[1] (skā′bē·əs) *adj.* 1. Pertaining to or resembling scabies. 2. Having scabs. [< L *scabiosus* < *scabies*. See SCABIES.]

sca·bi·ous[2] (skā′bē·əs) *n.* Any of a genus (*Scabiosa*) of herbs allied to the teasel, with involucrate heads of variously colored flowers, as the **sweet scabious** (*S. atropurpurea*). Also **sca/bi·o′sa** (-ō′sə). [< NL < Med.L (*herba*) *scabiosa*, fem. sing. of *scabiosus*. See SCABIOUS[1].]

sca·brous (skab′rəs, skā′brəs) *adj.* 1. Roughened with minute points; scurfy. 2. Off-color; risqué. 3. Difficult to handle tactfully; knotty. [< LL *scabrosus* < *scabere* to scratch] — **sca′brous·ly** *adv.* — **sca′brous·ness** *n.*

scad (skad) *n. pl.* **scad** or **scads** The saurel, a fish. [Origin uncertain]

scads (skadz) *n.pl. Informal* A large amount or quantity. [? Var. of dial E *scald* a large amount, great number]

Sca·fell Pike (skô·fel′) A mountain in southern Cumberland, England, the highest peak in England; 3,210 ft.

scaf·fold (skaf′əld, -ōld) *n.* 1. A temporary elevated structure for the support of workmen, materials, etc., as in building. 2. Any raised wooden framework, as for drying tobacco, fish, etc. **3.** A platform for the execution of criminals. **4.** A stage, as for exhibition purposes. — *v.t.* **1.** To furnish or support with a scaffold. **2.** To place on a scaffold. [< OF (*e*)*schaffaut, escadafaut.* Akin to CATAFALQUE.]

scaf·fold·ing (skaf′əl-ding) *n.* A scaffold, or system of scaffolds, or the materials for constructing them.

scag·li·o·la (skal-yō′lə) *n.* Plasterwork imitating marble, granite, or other stone, made of powdered gypsum and glue. [< Ital. *scagliuola,* dim. of *scaglia* scale, chip]

scal·a·ble (skā′lə-bəl) *adj.* Capable of being scaled, as a wall, cliff, etc. — **scal′a·ble·ness** *n.* — **scal′a·bly** *adv.*

sca·lade (skə-lād′) *n.* An escalade. Also **sca·la·do** (skə-lä′dō). [< Ital. *scalada < scalare* to scale < *scala* ladder < L. See SCALE².]

scal·age (skā′lij) *n.* **1.** A percentage by which something is scaled down to allow for shrinkage. **2.** The amount of lumber estimated to be in a log or logs being scaled.

sca·lar (skā′lər) *Math. adj.* Definable by a number on a line or scale: said of a quantity having magnitude only, as a volume or mass. — *n.* A quantity representing only magnitude: distinguished from *vector.* [< L *scalaris* of a ladder < *scala* ladder. See SCALE².]

sca·la·re (ska-lä′rē, -lä′rā) *n.* A cichlid fish (genus *Pterophyllum*) of South American rivers, having vertical black and silver bands, and popular as an aquarium fish: also called *angelfish.* [< NL < L *scalaris* of a ladder; from the bands]

sca·lar·i·form (skə-lar′ə-fôrm) *adj. Biol.* Ladderlike: said of cells or vessels. [< NL *scalariformis* < L *scalaris* of a ladder + *forma* form]

scal·a·wag (skal′ə-wag) *n.* **1.** *Informal* A worthless fellow. **2.** *U.S.* A native Southern white who became or remained a Republican during the Reconstruction period: compare CARPETBAGGER (def. 1). Also called *scallywag:* also spelled *scallawag.* — **Syn.** See SCOUNDREL. [Origin uncertain]

scald¹ (skôld) *v.t.* **1.** To burn with or as with hot liquid or steam. **2.** To cleanse or treat with boiling water. **3.** To heat (a liquid) to a point just short of boiling. — *v.i.* **4.** To be or become scalded. — **Syn.** see BURN¹. — *n.* **1.** A burn or injury to the skin by a hot fluid, as steam or water. **2.** An act of scalding. **3.** A destructive parasitic disease of plants, especially cranberries. **4.** A discoloration of plant tissue due to improper conditions of growth, storage, etc.: *apple scald.* [< AF *escalder* < LL *excaldare* to wash with hot water < *ex-* very + *calidus* hot]

scald² (skôld, skäld) See SKALD.

scald³ (skäld, skôld) *v.t. & v.i. Scot.* To scold.

scald⁴ (skôld) *n.* Scall, a skin eruption.

scale¹ (skāl) *n.* **1.** One of the thin, flat, horny, membranous or bony outgrowths of the skin of various vertebrates, as most fishes, usually overlapping and forming a nearly complete covering. **2.** Any similar thin, flat formation, piece, or part. **3.** A scab. **4.** A scale insect. **5.** *Bot.* A rudimentary or metamorphosed leaf, as of a pine cone. **6.** *Metall.* The coating of oxide that forms on heated iron, etc. **7.** An incrustation formed on the inside of boilers, etc. — *v.* **scaled, scal·ing** *v.t.* **1.** To strip or clear of scale or scales. **2.** To form scales on; cover with scales. **3.** To take off in layers or scales. **4.** To throw (a thin, flat object) so that it moves through the air edgewise or skips along the surface of water. — *v.i.* **5.** To come off in layers or scales; peel. **6.** To shed scales. **7.** To become incrusted with scales. [< OF *escale* husk < Gmc.; infl. in meaning by OF *escaille* fish scale, oyster shell < Med.L *scalia* < Gmc.] — **scal′er** *n.*

scale² (skāl) *n.* **1.** Any instrument bearing accurately spaced lines or gradations for use in measurement. **2.** The series of marks so used. **3.** Any system of designating units of measurement: the Fahrenheit *scale.* **4.** A fixed proportion used in determining measurements or dimensions: a *scale* of one inch to the mile. **5.** Any progressive or graded classification: wage *scale;* social *scale.* **6.** Relative proportion, degree, scope, etc.: with *on:* on a grand *scale.* **7.** *Math.* A system of notation in which the successive places determine the value of the figures: the decimal *scale.* **8.** *Music* An arrangement of tones in ascending or descending order through the interval of an octave: a diatonic *scale;* a pentatonic *scale.* Compare MODE. **9.** *Obs.* A ladder or staircase. *Abbr. sc.* — **major scale** *Music* A scale having semitones between the third and fourth and the seventh and eighth steps and whole tones between all the others. — **minor scale** A scale having semitones between the second and third and the fifth and sixth steps (the natural form), or between the second and third, fifth and sixth, and seventh and eighth steps (the harmonic form), or between the second and third and seventh and eighth steps ascending and the sixth and fifth and third and second descending (the melodic form), all the other intervals being whole tones. — *v.* **scaled, scal·ing** *v.t.* **1.**

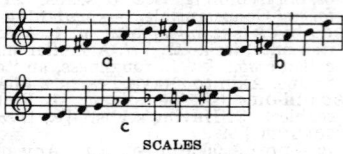

SCALES
a Major. *b* Pentatonic.
c Constructed.

To climb to the top of; go up by or as by means of a ladder· **2.** To make according to a scale. **3.** To regulate or adjust according to a scale or ratio: with *up, down,* etc. **4.** To measure (logs) or estimate the amount of lumber in (standing timber). — *v.i.* **5.** To climb; ascend. **6.** To rise in steps or stages. [< Ital. *scala* ladder < L < *scandere* to climb] — **scal′er** *n.*

scale³ (skāl) *n.* **1.** Any weighing machine or device. **2.** A pan, scoop, platform, etc., that holds the object or material to be weighed in a weighing instrument or balance. **3.** *Usually pl.* A balance (defs. 1 & 2). — **to turn the scales** To determine; decide. — *v.* **scaled, scal·ing** *v.t.* **1.** To weigh in scales. **2.** To amount to in weight. — *v.i.* **3.** To be weighed in scales. [< ON *skál* bowl, in pl., a weighing balance. Akin to SHALE, SHELL.]

scale·board (skāl′bôrd′, -bōrd′) **1.** A thin piece of board, as for the back of a picture. **2.** *Printing* A narrow strip of wood used in justifying a line of type. [< SCALE¹ + BOARD]

scale insect One of numerous small, hemipterous insects (family *Coccidae*) that feed on plants.

scale moss A liverwort (def. 1).

sca·lene (skā′lēn, skā-lēn′) *adj.* **1.** *Geom.* Designating a triangle having no two sides equal. **2.** *Anat.* Designating one of several muscles attached to the cervical vertebrae and first two ribs and acting to bend the neck. Also **sca·le·nous** (skā-lē′nəs). [< LL *scalenus* < Gk. *skalēnos* uneven]

sca·le·nus (skə-lē′nəs) *n.* A scalene muscle. [< NL (*musculus*) *scalenus* < L. See SCALENE.]

Scales (skālz) *n.pl.* The constellation and sign of the zodiac Libra.

Scal·i·ger (skal′ə-jər), **Joseph Justus,** 1540–1609, French philologist. — **Julius Caesar,** 1484–1558, French philologist and physician born in Italy; father of the preceding.

scall (skôl) *n. Pathol.* A scabby or scaly skin eruption: sometimes called *scald.* [< ON *skalle* bald head]

scal·la·wag (skal′ə-wag) See SCALAWAG.

scal·lion (skal′yən) *n.* **1.** An onion with a narrow bulb and a long thick neck, as a shallot or leek. **2.** A green onion (which see). [< AF *scalun,* OF *eschalogne,* ult. < L (*caepa*) *Ascalonia* (onion) of Ashkelon < *Ascalon* Ashkelon, a Palestinian seaport]

scal·lop (skal′əp, skol′-) *n.* **1.** A bivalve mollusk (genus *Pecten*), having a rounded, ridged shell whose valves are snapped together in swimming. **2.** The edible adductor muscle of certain species of this mollusk. **3.** The shell of a scallop, formerly worn as a pilgrim's badge. **4.** A scallop shell, or similarly shaped dish, in which seafood is cooked or served. **5.** One of a series of semicircular curves along an edge, as for ornament. — *v.t.* **1.** To shape the edge of with scallops; ornament with scallops. **2.** To bake (food) in a casserole with a sauce, often topped with bread crumbs. Also spelled *escallop, scollop.* [< OF *escalope* < Gmc. Akin to SCALE¹.] — **scal′lop·er** *n.*

SCALLOP SHELL

scal·ly·wag (skal′ē-wag) *n.* A scalawag.

scal·op·pi·ne (skal′ə-pē′nē, skä′lə-) *n. pl.* Meat, especially veal, that has been thinly sliced and cooked in a wine sauce with herbs. [< Ital. *scaloppine,* pl. of *scaloppina,* dim. of *scaloppa* thin slice of meat]

scalp (skalp) *n.* **1.** The skin of the top and back of the human skull, usually covered with hair. **2.** A portion of this, formerly cut or torn away as a war trophy among certain North American Indians. **3.** A trophy or symbol of victory. **4.** A piece of hide from the head of a wild animal, taken as evidence that it has been killed for the collection of a bounty. **5.** A small profit taken by a speculator. — *v.t.* **1.** To cut or tear the scalp from. **2.** *Informal* To buy and resell (tickets) at prices exceeding the established rate **3.** *Informal* To buy and sell again quickly in order to make a small profit. **4.** *Informal* To defeat utterly, as in an athletic contest. — *v.i.* **5.** *Informal* To scalp bonds, tickets, etc. [ME, prob. < Scand. Cf. ON *skálpr* sheath.] — **scalp′er** *n.*

scal·pel (skal′pəl) *n.* A small pointed knife with a very sharp, thin blade, used in dissections and in surgery. [< L *scalpellum,* dim. of *scalprum* knife < *scalpere* to cut]

scalp lock A long lock of hair left on the crown of the head by certain North American Indians as a defiant gesture.

scal·y (skā′lē) *adj.* **scal·i·er, scal·i·est 1.** Having a covering of scales. **2.** Resembling or of the nature of a scale or scales. **3.** Incrusted with a scalelike or scurfy substance. **4.** *Slang* Mean; dishonorable. [< SCALE¹ + -Y¹] — **scal′i·ness** *n.*

scaly anteater A pangolin.

Sca·man·der (skə-man′dər) The ancient name for the MENDERES (def. 2).

scam·mo·ny (skam′ə-nē) *n. pl.* **·nies 1.** A climbing plant (*Convolvulus scammonia*) of the morning-glory family, native in Asia Minor. **2.** The dried resin of scammony roots, used as a cathartic. [< L *scammonia* < Gk. *skammōnia*]

scamp¹ (skamp) *n.* A confirmed rogue; good-for-nothing fellow; rascal. — **Syn.** See SCOUNDREL. [< obs. verb *scamp* to roam, contraction of SCAMPER.] — **scamp′ish** *adj.*

scamp² (skamp) *v.t.* To perform (work) carelessly or dishonestly. [Orig. dial. E, ? < ON *skemma* to shorten < *skammr* short. Akin to SCANT, SKIMP.] — **scamp′er** *n.*

scam·per (skam′pər) *v.i.* To run quickly or hastily, as from danger; hurry away. — *n.* A hurried run or departure. [? < obs. Du. *schampen* to run away < AF *escamper*, OF *eschamper* to decamp, run off hurriedly, escape, ult. < L *ex* out from + *campus* plain, battlefield] — **scam′per·er** *n.*

scam·pi (skam′pē) *n. pl.* Large shrimp or prawns, especially those used in Italian cooking. [< Ital.]

scan (skan) *v.* **scanned, scan·ning** *v.t.* **1.** To examine in detail; scrutinize closely. **2.** To pass the eyes over quickly; glance at; read hastily. **3.** To separate (verse) into metrical feet; ascertain or indicate the rhythm of. **4.** *Telecom.* To pass a beam of light or electrons rapidly over every point of (a surface, image, etc.) for television, facsimile, or other reproduction. — *v.i.* **5.** To scan verse. **6.** To conform to metrical rules: said of verse. **7.** *Telecom.* To scan a surface, image, etc. — **Syn.** See SEE¹. [< LL *scandere* to scan verses < L, climb] — **scan′na·ble** *adj.* — **scan′ner** *n.*

Scand. **1.** Scandinavia: also **Scan.** **2.** Scandinavian.

scan·dal (skan′dəl) *n.* **1.** Heedless or malicious gossip or repetition of reports of a disreputable or damaging character. **2.** Disgrace or reproach caused by outrageous or improper conduct. **3.** A discreditable circumstance, event, or action; cause of reproach. **4.** Censure or open disapproval, as of improper or unconventional conduct. **5.** One whose conduct results in disgrace or censure. [< AF *escandle* < L *scandalum* cause of stumbling < Gk. *skandalon* snare; refashioned after MF *scandale*. Doublet of SLANDER.]

scan·dal·ize (skan′dəl·īz) *v.t.* **·ized, ·iz·ing** To shock the moral feelings of, as by improper, frivolous, or offensive conduct; outrage. — **scan′dal·i·za′tion** *n.* — **scan′dal·iz′er** *n.*

scan·dal·mong·er (skan′dəl·mung′gər, -mong′-) *n.* One who spreads or repeats scandal.

scan·dal·ous (skan′dəl·əs) *adj.* **1.** Causing or tending to cause scandal; disgraceful. **2.** Consisting of or spreading scandal. — **scan′dal·ous·ly** *adv.* — **scan′dal·ous·ness** *n.*

scan·dent (skan′dənt) *adj.* Climbing, as a plant. [< L *scandens, -entis*, ppr. of *scandere* to climb]

Scan·der·beg (skan′dər·beg), 1403–68, Albanian nobleman and national hero: original name *George Castriota.*

scan·di·a (skan′dē·ə) *n. Chem.* Scandium oxide, Sc₂O₃, a white powder soluble in acids. [< NL < SCANDIUM]

Scan·di·an (skan′dē·ən) *adj.* Scandinavian. [< L *Scandia*]

scan·dic (skan′dik) *adj. Chem.* Pertaining to or derived from scandium.

Scan·di·na·vi·a (skan′də·nā′vē·ə) The region of NW Europe occupied by Sweden, Norway, and Denmark, sometimes including Finland, Iceland, and the Faroe Islands. Ancient **Scan·di·a** (skan′dē·ə).

Scan·di·na·vi·an (skan′də·nā′vē·ən) *adj.* Of or pertaining to Scandinavia, its people, or their languages. — *n.* **1.** A native or inhabitant of Scandinavia. **2.** The North Germanic group of languages: see under GERMANIC. Also *Norse.* Abbr. *Scand.* — **Old Scandinavian** Old Norse. See under NORSE. [< L *Scandinavia*, var. of *Scadinavia* < Gmc.]

Scandinavian Peninsula The peninsula of NW Europe containing Norway and Sweden.

scan·di·um (skan′dē·əm) *n.* A metallic element (symbol Sc) of the lanthanide series. See ELEMENT. [< NL < L *Scandia* Scandinavia]

scan·sion (skan′shən) *n.* The division or analysis of lines of verse according to a metrical pattern. Compare METER² (def. 1). [< F < LL *scansio, -onis* < L *scandere.* See SCAN.]

scan·so·ri·al (skan·sôr′ē·əl, -sō′rē-) *adj. Zool.* Pertaining to or adapted for climbing. [< L *scansorius* < *scansus,* pp. of *scandere* to climb]

scant (skant) *adj.* **1.** Scarcely enough; meager in measure or quantity. **2.** Being just short of the measure specified: often with the indefinite article even with a plural noun: a *scant* half-hour; a *scant* five yards. **3.** Insufficiently supplied with: with *of:* We were *scant* of breath. — *v.t.* **1.** To restrict or limit in supply; stint. **2.** To treat briefly or inadequately. — *adv. Dial.* Scarcely; barely. [< ON *skamt,* neut. of *skammr* short] — **scant′ly** *adv.* — **scant′ness** *n.*

scant·ling (skant′ling) *n.* **1.** A piece of lumber of small or moderate cross section, used for studding, etc. **2.** Such lumber collectively. **3.** The dimensions of a timber in thickness and width or those of a building stone in length, breadth, and thickness. **4.** A small quantity or part; sample. [Alter. of obs. *scantillon* < OF *eschantillon* specimen, cornerpiece, chip; ? infl. in meaning by SCANT]

scant·y (skan′tē) *adj.* **scant·i·er, scant·i·est** **1.** Restricted in quantity or amount; scarcely sufficient; meager. **2.** Limited in extent; small; close; cramped. **3.** Sparing; stingy. [< SCANT] — **scant′i·ly** *adv.* — **scant′i·ness** *n.*

Sca·pa Flow (skä′pə flō′, skap′ə) A sea basin and British naval base in the Orkney Islands, Scotland; 50 sq. mi.

scape¹ (skāp) *n.* **1.** *Bot.* A long, leafless stalk rising from the ground, as in the dandelion. **2.** *Zool.* **a** A stemlike part, as of an insect antenna. **b** The shaft of a feather. **3.** *Archit.* **a** The shaft of a column. **b** An apophyge. [< L *scapus* < dial. Gk. (Doric) *scapos.* Akin to SCEPTER.]

scape² (skāp) *n.* A scene, as of land, sea, clouds, etc. [Back formation < LANDSCAPE]

scape³ (skāp) *Archaic v.t. & v.i.* To escape. — *n.* An escape or means of escape. Also **'scape.**

scape·goat (skāp′gōt′) *n.* **1.** In the Bible, the goat upon whose head Aaron symbolically laid the sins of the people on the day of atonement, after which it was led away into the wilderness. *Lev.* xvi. **2.** An animal, person, or group chosen to bear symbolically or suffer for the bad luck or sins of an individual or group. **3.** Any person bearing blame for others. [< SCAPE³, n. + GOAT]

scape·grace (skāp′grās′) *n.* A mischievous or incorrigible person; rogue. [< SCAPE³ + GRACE (def. 9)]

scape wheel An escape wheel (which see).

scaph·oid (skaf′oid) *n. Anat.* The navicular, a bone. — *adj.* Boat-shaped. [< NL *scaphoides* < Gk. *skaphoeidēs* < *skaphē* boat + *eidos* form]

scapi- *combining form* A stalk, stem, or shaft: *scapiform.* [< L *scapus* stalk]

scap·i·form (skap′ə·fôrm) *adj. Biol.* Resembling a scape.

scap·o·lite (skap′ə·līt) *n.* Any of a group of grayish white silicates, chiefly of aluminum, calcium, and sodium, found massive or in crystals: also called *wernerite.* [< G *skapolith* < Gk. *skapos* rod + *lithos* stone]

sca·pose (skā′pōs) *adj. Biol.* Bearing, consisting of, or resembling a scape. [< SCAPE¹ + -OSE]

s.caps. *Printing* Small capitals.

scap·u·la (skap′yə·lə) *n. pl.* **·lae** (-lē) *Anat.* Either of a pair of large, flat, triangular bones in the back of the shoulder in man and having an analogous position in the skeleton of vertebrates: also called *shoulder blade.* For illustration see THORAX. [< LL, shoulder < L *scapulae* shoulder blades]

scap·u·lar (skap′yə·lər) *n.* **1.** An outer garment consisting of two strips of cloth joined across the shoulders, worn by members of certain religious orders. **2.** A badge or sign of devotion worn about the neck by members of certain religious orders and groups. **3.** *pl. Ornithol.* The shoulder feathers of a bird. — *adj.* Of or pertaining to the scapula or shoulder. [< Med.L *scapulare* < LL *scapula.* See SCAPULA.]

scap·u·lar·y (skap′yə·ler′ē) *n. pl.* **·ries** A scapular. — *adj.* Scapular.

scar¹ (skär) *n.* **1.** The mark left on the skin after the healing of a wound or sore; a cicatrix. **2.** Any mark, damage, or lasting effect resulting from past injury, stress, etc. **3.** A mark left on a stem, branch, etc., as by separation of a leaf. **4.** An indentation or mark made by use, motion, or contact. — *v.t. & v.i.* **scarred, scar·ring** To mark or become marked with a scar. [< OF *escare* < LL *eschara* scab < Gk.]

scar² (skär) *n.* **1.** A bare rock standing alone. **2.** A cliff or rocky place on the side of a hill or mountain. Also, *Scot., scaur.* [< ON *sker*]

scar·ab (skar′əb) *n.* **1.** A scarabaeid beetle; especially, a large, black dung beetle (*Scarabaeus sacer*), held sacred by the ancient Egyptians as the symbol of resurrection and fertility. **2.** A gem or ornament representing this beetle, used in ancient Egypt as an amulet. [< MF *scarabée* < L *scarabaeus*]

scar·a·bae·id (skar′ə·bē′id) *adj.* Of or pertaining to a large family (*Scarabaeidae*) of beetles, including cockchafers, June beetles, and dung beetles. — *n.* A scarabaeid beetle. Also **scar′a·bae′oid.** [< NL < L *scarabaeus* scarab]

scar·a·bae·us (skar′ə·bē′əs) *n. pl.* **·bae·us·es** or **·bae·i** (-bē′ī) A scarab. [< L]

scar·a·boid (skar′ə·boid) *adj.* Resembling or of the nature of a scarab or scarabaeid. — *n.* A scarab or scarabaeid.

scar·a·mouch (skar′ə·mouch, -mōōsh) *n.* A swaggering rascal. [< *Scaramouch*]

Scar·a·mouch (skar′ə·mouch, -mōōsh) In old Italian comedy, a stock character represented as a boastful, cowardly buffoon. [< F *Scaramouche* < Ital. *Scaramuccia,* lit., skirmish]

Scar·bor·ough (skär′bûr·ə) A municipal borough and resort in North Yorkshire, England, on the North Sea; pop. 97,310 (1976).

scarce (skârs) *adj.* **scarc·er, scarc·est** **1.** Rarely seen or found; infrequent. **2.** Not plentiful; scant; insufficient. — **to make oneself scarce** *Informal* To go away or stay away. [< AF *scars, escars,* OF *eschars* scanty, insufficient, ult. < L *excerptus.* See EXCERPT.] — **scarce′ness** *n.*

scarce·ly (skârs′lē) *adv.* **1.** Only just; barely. **2.** Not quite; hardly. ◆ See note under HARDLY.

scarce·ment (skârs′mənt) *n.* A ledge or projection in a wall, etc. [Appar. < obs. verb *scarce* to lessen + -MENT]

scar·ci·ty (skâr′sə·tē) *n. pl.* **·ties** **1.** Inadequate supply; insufficiency; dearth. **2.** Infrequency of occurrence; rarity.

scare (skâr) *v.* **scared, scar·ing** *v.t.* **1.** To strike with sudden fear; frighten. **2.** To drive or force by frightening: with *off* or *away:* to *scare* away an intruder. — *v.i.* **3.** To take fright; become scared. — **Syn.** See FRIGHTEN. — **to scare up** *Informal* To get together or produce hurriedly or on the spur of the moment: to *scare up* a meal. — *n.* **1.** Sudden fright, especially from slight or imaginary cause. **2.** A state of apprehensive alarm; panic. [< ON *skiarr* to frighten < *skiarr* shy] **— scar'er** *n.* **— scar'ing·ly** *adv.*

scare·crow (skâr'krō') *n.* **1.** Any effigy set up to scare crows and other birds away from growing crops. **2.** Something frightening but not dangerous. **3.** A person of ragged or disreputable appearance.

scare·head (skâr'hed') *n. Informal* An exceptionally large newspaper headline giving news of sensational interest.

scare·mon·ger (skâr'mung'gər, -mong'-) *n.* One who spreads an alarming rumor; an alarmist.

scarf[1] (skärf) *n. pl.* **scarfs** or **scarves** (skärvz) **1.** A band or square of cloth worn about the head, neck, etc., for warmth or protection, or as a decorative accessory. **2.** A necktie, cravat, kerchief, etc. **3.** A runner for a bureau or dresser. **4.** An official sash denoting rank. **5.** A fur neckpiece, tippet, etc. **—** *v.t.* **1.** To cover or decorate with or as with a scarf. **2.** To use as a scarf; wrap loosely around one. [< AF *escarpe*, OF *escharpe*, ? < *escreppe* wallet, scrip]

scarf[2] (skärf) *n. pl.* **scarfs 1.** In carpentry, a lapped joint made by notching two timbers at the ends and joining them so as to form one continuous piece. Also **scarf joint. 2.** The notched end of a timber so cut. **3.** An incision made in the blubber of a whale as an aid in removing it. **—** *v.t.* **1.** To unite with a scarf joint. **2.** To cut a scarf in. [? < ON *skarfr* notch in a timber]

scarf-skin (skärf'skin') *n.* The epidermis. [< SCARF[2] + SKIN]

SCARF JOINTS

scar·i·fi·ca·tor (skar'ə-fə-kā'tər) *n.* A surgical instrument for scarifying.

scar·i·fy (skar'ə-fī) *v.t.* **·fied, ·fy·ing 1.** To scratch or make slight incisions in, as the skin in surgery. **2.** To criticize severely; make cutting comments on. **3.** To stir or break up the surface of, as soil. **4.** To cut or soften the outer covering of (seeds) to hasten germination. [< MF *scarifier* < LL *scarificare* < L *scarifare* < Gk. *skariphasthai* to scratch an outline, sketch < *skariphos* stylus] **— scar'i·fi'er** *n.* **— scar'i·fi·ca'tion** *n.*

scar·i·ous (skâr'ē-əs) *adj. Bot.* Thin, dry, and membranous, as a bract. Also **scar'i·ose** (-ōs). [< F *scarieux* < NL *scariosus* < L *scaria* thorny shrub]

scar·la·ti·na (skär'lə-tē'nə) *n. Pathol.* **1.** Scarlet fever. **2.** A mild form of scarlet fever. [< NL < Ital. *scarlattina*, fem. dim. of *scarlatto* < Med.L *scarlatum*. See SCARLET.]

scar·la·ti·noid (skär'lə-tē'noid, skär-lat'ə-noid) *adj.* Resembling scarlet fever.

Scar·lat·ti (skär-lät'tē), **Alessandro,** 1659–1725, and his son, **Domenico,** 1685–1757, Italian composers.

scar·let (skär'lit) *n.* **1.** A brilliant red, inclining to orange. **2.** Cloth or clothing of this color. **—** *adj.* **1.** Being scarlet in color. **2.** Unchaste; whorish. [< OF *escarlate* < Med.L *scarlatum*, prob. < Arabic *siqillāt* < Persian *saqalāt* a rich, scarlet cloth]

scarlet fever *Pathol.* An acute infectious fever caused by hemolytic streptococci and characterized by a diffused scarlet rash followed by scaling of the skin: also called *scarlatina*.

scarlet letter A scarlet "A," a badge of shame that women convicted of adultery were once compelled to wear.

scarlet runner A tall climbing bean (*Phaseolus coccineus*) of tropical America, having vivid red flowers and long seed pods, widely cultivated as an ornamental plant.

scarlet tanager An American tanager (*Piranga olivacea*), the male of which has brilliant red plumage with black wings and tail: also called *redbird*.

Scarlet Woman An unholy woman described in the New Testament (*Rev.* xvii 4–6), and later an abusive epithet first applied to pagan Rome and later to the Roman Catholic Church.

scarp (skärp) *n.* **1.** A steep slope; abrupt declivity. **2.** An embankment or wall at the outer part of a fortification; escarpment. For illustration see BASTION. **—** *v.t.* To cut or form to a steep slope. [< AF *escarpe* < Ital. *scarpa*]

Scar·ron (skȧ-rôn'), **Paul,** 1610–60, French poet and dramatist.

scart (skärt) *Scot. n.* Scratch; scrape. **—** *v.i. & v.t.* To scratch; scrape. [ME *scratte*; origin uncertain]

scarves (skärvz) Alternative plural of SCARF[1].

scar·y (skâr'ē) *adj.* **scar·i·er, scar·i·est** *Informal* **1.** Easily scared; timid. **2.** Causing fear or alarm; frightening.

scat[1] (skat) *v.i.* **scat·ted, scat·ting** *Informal* To go away; depart: usually in the imperative. [? < SCATTER]

scat[2] (skat) *Slang* A type of jazz singing in which meaningless syllables are improvised on the melody. **—** *v.i.* **scat·ted, scat·ting** To sing in this manner. [Prob. < SCAT[1]]

scathe (skāth) *v.t.* **scathed, scath·ing 1.** To criticize severely; assail verbally. **2.** To injure severely; harm; blast. **—** *n.* Severe injury; harm; loss. [< ON *skatha* < *skathi* to harm. Akin to OE *sceatha* malefactor, injury.] **— scathe'ful** *adj.*

scathe·less (skāth'lis) *adj.* Free from harm.

scath·ing (skā'thing) *adj.* **1.** Mercilessly severe; blasting;

withering: a *scathing* rebuke. **2.** Harshly damaging or painful: a *scathing* experience. **— scath'ing·ly** *adv.*

scato- *combining form* Dung; excrement: *scatology*. Also, before vowels, **scat-**. [< Gk. *skōr, skatos* dung]

scat·o·log·i·cal (skat'ə-loj'i·kəl) *adj.* Of or pertaining to scatology; obscene. Also **scat'o·log'ic.**

sca·tol·o·gy (skə-tol'ə-jē) *n.* **1.** The study of excrement, as in paleontology, medicine, and psychiatry. **2.** Preoccupation with excrement, excretory functions, etc., in literature. [< SCATO- + -LOGY] **— sca·tol'o·gist** *n.*

scat·ter (skat'ər) *v.t.* **1.** To throw about in various places; sprinkle; strew. **2.** To separate and drive away in different directions; disperse; rout. **3.** *Physics* To reflect, refract, or deflect (radiant energy) irregularly. **—** *v.i.* **4.** To separate and go in different directions; disperse; dissipate. [ME *scateren* to squander. ? Akin to SHATTER.] **— scat'ter·er** *n.*

scat·ter·brain (skat'ər-brān') *n.* One lacking powers of mental concentration or organization; a flighty or forgetful person. **— scat'ter·brained'** *adj.*

scat·ter·good (skat'ər-good') *n.* A wastrel; spendthrift.

scat·ter·ing (skat'ər-ing) *n.* **1.** A sparse, random occurrence or distribution over an area, as of votes for a candidate. **2.** Dispersion. **3.** *Physics* The random distribution of a system of particles, waves, and the like upon collision with another system or with any obstacle preventing continuous propagation in the original direction. **—** *adj.* Placed at intervals or at a distance apart. **— scat'ter·ing·ly** *adv.*

scatter rug A small rug used to cover only part of a floor.

sca·tu·ri·ent (skə-choor'ē-ənt) *adj. Rare* Gushing forth, as a fountain. [< L *scaturiens, -entis*, ppr. of *scaturire* < *scatere* to flow out]

scaup[1] (skôp) *n.* A sea duck (genus *Aythya*) of northern regions, related to the canvasback, having the head and neck black in the male; especially, the **greater scaup** (*A. marila*) and the **lesser scaup** (*A. affinis*): also called *bluebill, shuffler*. Also **scaup duck.** [< SCAUP[2]]

scaup[2] (skôp) *n. Obs. & Scot.* **1.** The scalp; skull. **2.** A mussel bed. [Var. of SCALP]

scaur (skär, skôr) See SCAR[2].

scav·enge (skav'inj) *v.* **·enged, ·eng·ing** *v.t.* **1.** To remove filth, rubbish, and refuse from, as streets. **2.** To remove exhaust gases from (the cylinder of an internal-combustion engine). **3.** *Metall.* To remove impurities from (a metal or alloy). **—** *v.i.* **4.** To act as a scavenger. **5.** To search or rummage, as for food. [Back formation < SCAVENGER]

scav·en·ger (skav'in·jər) *n.* **1.** An animal that feeds on carrion, as the buzzard. **2.** One who searches refuse, garbage, etc., for usable material. **3.** A street cleaner. [ME *scavager* < AF *scawager* < *scawage* inspection < *escauwer* to inspect < Flemish *scauwen* to see]

Sc.B. Bachelor of Science (L *Scientiae Baccalaureus*).

Sc.D. Doctor of Science (L *Scientiae Doctor*).

sce·nar·i·o (si-nâr'ē·ō, -nä'rē·ō) *n. pl.* **·nar·i·os 1.** A summary or outline of the plot of a dramatic work. **2.** The written plot and arrangement of incidents of a motion picture. **3.** A possible course of action or events as described for criticism in making plans. [< Ital. < LL *scenarius* of stage scenes < L *scena*. See SCENE.]

sce·nar·ist (si-nâr'ist, -nä'rist) *n.* One who writes scenarios.

scend (send) *Naut. v.i.* To heave upward, as a vessel on a wave. **—** *n.* The act of rising or moving upward, as a ship: opposed to *pitch*. Also spelled *send*. **— pitch and scend** The longitudinal rocking of a vessel. [Var. of SEND[2]; infl. in form by ASCEND]

scene (sēn) *n.* **1.** A locality or area and all connected with it, as presented to view; a landscape. **2.** The place in which the action of a drama is supposed to occur; setting; locale. **3.** The place and surroundings of any event, real or imagined: the *scene* of the crime. **4.** A division of an act of a play; one comprehensive event in a play. **5.** Any incident or episode that may serve as the subject of a description. **6.** The painted canvas screen or screens for the background for a play. **7.** Any striking exhibition or display; especially, a display of passion or excited feeling. Abbr. *sc.* **— behind the scenes 1.** Out of sight of a theater audience; backstage. **2.** Privately; in secret. **— to make the scene** *U.S. Slang* To visit or appear at a place. [< OF < L *scena, scaena* < Gk. *skēnē* tent, stage]

scen·er·y (sē'nər·ē) *n. pl.* **·er·ies 1.** The appearance or visible aspects of a landscape, locality, etc.; especially, the pleasing appearance of natural features of a countryside. **2.** The settings, backdrops, etc., of a theatrical production. [< Ital. *scenario*. See SCENARIO.]

sce·nic (sē'nik, sen'ik) *adj.* **1.** Of or pertaining to natural scenery; picturesque. **2.** Relating to stage scenery. Also **sce'ni·cal. — sce'ni·cal·ly** *adv.*

sce·nog·ra·phy (sē-nog'rə-fē) *n.* **1.** The art of representing objects in perspective. **2.** The use of this art in painting stage scenery. [< F *scénographie* < L *scaenographia* < Gk. *skēnographia* < *skēnē* scene, tent + *graphein* to write] **— scen·o·graph·ic** (sē'nə-graf'ik, sē'nə-), **scen/o·graph/i·cal** *adj.*

scent (sent) *n.* **1.** A distinctive odor, especially a pleasant one. **2.** A residual odor by which an animal can be tracked. **3.** A trail, trace, or clue aiding pursuit or investigation. **4.**

An extract from flowers or other fragrant substances; perfume. **5.** The sense of smell. **— Syn.** See SMELL. — *v.t.* **1.** To perceive by the sense of smell. **2.** To form a suspicion of. **3.** To cause to be fragrant; perfume. — *v.i.* **4.** To hunt by the sense of smell: said of hounds. [< OF *sentir* to discern by the senses, feel < L *sentire*] **— scent′less** *adj.*

scep·ter (sep′tər) *n.* **1.** A staff or wand carried as the badge of command or sovereignty. **2.** Kingly office or power. — *v.t.* To confer the scepter on; invest with royal power. Also *esp. Brit.* **scep′tre** (-tər). [< OF *ceptre, sceptre* < L *sceptrum* < Gk. *skēptron* staff < *skēplesthai* to prop oneself, lean on]

scep·tic (skep′tik), **scep·ti·cal,** etc. See SKEPTIC, etc.

Schacht (shäkht), **Hjalmar,** 1877–1970, German financier and economic adviser: full name **Horace Greeley Hjalmar Schacht.**

Scha·den·freu·de (shä′dən-froi′də) *n. German* Malicious, gloating pleasure.

Schaff·hau·sen (shäf′hou′zən) A town in northern Switzerland, on the Rhine; pop. about 26,000.

Scharn·horst (shärn′hôrst), **Gerhard Johann David von,** 1755–1813, Prussian general and military writer.

schat·chen (shät′khən) *n.* A Jewish marriage broker. Also **schad′chan.** [< Yiddish < Hebrew *shadhkhān*]

Schaum·burg-Lip·pe (shoum′bŏŏrkh·lip′ə) A former state of NW Germany, included in Lower Saxony 1945.

sched·ule (skej′ŏŏl, -əl, -ōō·əl; *Brit.* shed′yōōl) *n.* **1.** A written or printed statement, usually in tabular form, specifying the details of some matter, and often annexed to statutes, petitions, etc. **2.** A list; catalogue; inventory. **3.** A timetable, as for a transportation service. **4.** A detailed and timed plan for any procedure; program. — *v.t.* **·uled, ·ul·ing** **1.** To place in or on a schedule. **2.** To make a schedule of. **3.** To appoint or plan for a specified time or date: He *scheduled* his appearance for five o'clock. [Alter. of ME *sedule* < OF *cedule* < LL *scedula,* dim. of L *scida, scheda* leaf of paper < Gk. *schidē* wood splinter < *schizein* to split; infl. in form by Med.L *schedula*]

Schee·le (shā′lə), **Karl Wilhelm,** 1742–86, Swedish chemist.

schee·lite (shē′līt) *n.* A vitreous, variously colored, crystalline calcium tungstate. [after K. W. *Scheele*]

Sche·her·e·za·de (shə·her′ə·zä′də, -zäd′) In the *Arabian Nights,* the bride of a murderous sultan, who tricks him into sparing her life by telling him an exciting story each night. Also **Sche·her′a·za′de.**

Scheldt (skelt) A river in northern France, Belgium, and the Netherlands, flowing 270 miles, generally NE, to the North Sea: French *Escaut.* *Flemish & Dutch* **Schel·de** (skhel′də).

Schel·ling (shel′ing), **Friedrich Wilhelm Joseph von,** 1775–1854, German philosopher. **— Schel·lin·gi·an** (she·lin′jē·ən) *adj.*

sche·ma (skē′mə) *n. pl.* **·ma·ta** (-mə·tə) **1.** A scheme, synopsis, or summary. **2.** An abstract representation, as a diagram, of a process, organization, etc. [< Gk. See SCHEME.] **— sche·mat·ic** (skē·mat′ik) or **·i·cal** *adj.* **— sche·mat′i·cal·ly** *adv.*

sche·ma·tism (skē′mə·tiz′əm) *n.* **1.** A particular form or disposition of anything. **2.** Orderly arrangement of parts, as in a philosophic system.

sche·ma·tize (skē′mə·tīz) *v.t.* **·tized, ·tiz·ing** To form into or arrange according to a scheme or schema. [< Gk. *schēmatizein* < *schēma, -atos* a form] **— sche′ma·ti·za′tion** *n.*

scheme (skēm) *n.* **1.** A plan of something to be done; a plot or device for the accomplishment of an object. **2.** A systematic arrangement, plan, or design. **3.** A secret or underhand plot or plan. **4.** A visionary or impractical plan. **5.** An outline drawing or sketch; diagram. **6.** In astrology, a plan representing the aspects of the heavenly bodies at any given time. — *v.* **schemed, schem·ing** *v.t.* **1.** To make a scheme for; devise; plan. **2.** To plan or plot in an underhand manner. — *v.i.* **3.** To make schemes; plan or plot; connive. [< L *schema* a shape, figure of speech < Gk. *schēma,* also a form, plan] **— schem′er** *n.*

Sche·nec·ta·dy (skə·nek′tə·dē) A city in eastern New York, on the Mohawk River; pop. 77,859.

scher·zan·do (sker·tsän′dō) *Music adv.* In a sportive or playful manner. — *adj.* Sportive; playful. [< Ital., ppr. of *scherzare* to play < *scherzo.* See SCHERZO.]

scher·zo (sker′tsō) *n. pl.* **·zos** or **·zi** (-tsē) *Music* A playful or satirical movement, often following a slow movement, as in a symphony or sonata. [< Ital., a jest < G *scherz*]

Sche·ven·ing·en (skhā′vən·ing′ən) A resort town in the western Netherlands, a suburb of the Hague on the North Sea; scene of a British naval victory over the Dutch, 1653.

Schia·pa·rel·li (skyä′pä·rel′lē), **Giovanni Virginio,** 1835–1910, Italian astronomer.

Schick (shik), **Béla,** 1877–1967, Austrian pediatrician born in Hungary and active in the United States.

Schick test A test to determine the susceptibility of a person to diphtheria by the subcutaneous injection of a diluted diphtheria toxin, nonimmunity being indicated by a reddening of the skin. [after Dr. Béla *Schick,* who devised it]

schil·ler (shil′ər) *n. Mineral.* A bronzelike luster or iridescence due to the reflection of particles dispersed in certain minerals. [< G, play of colors < *schillern* to change color]

Schil·ler (shil′ər), **Johann Christoph Friedrich von,** 1759–1805, German poet and dramatist.

schil·ler·ize (shil′ə·rīz) *v.t.* **·ized, ·iz·ing** To impart schiller to (a mineral or crystal). **— schil′ler·i·za′tion** *n.*

schil·ling (shil′ing) *n.* **1.** The standard monetary unit of Austria, equivalent to 100 groschen; also, a coin of this value. **2.** Formerly, a minor coin of Germany. [< G]

schip·per·ke (skip′ər·kē) *n.* A Belgian breed of black, usually tailless dogs, used as watchdogs and sometimes for hunting. [< dial. Du., little boatman, dim. of Du. *schipper*; so called because orig. used as watchdogs on boats]

schism (siz′əm, skiz′-) *n.* **1.** A division of a church or other organized body into factions. **2.** The offense of causing division in a church or other body. **3.** Any group, especially an ecclesiastical one, separated from a larger or older body. [< OF *cisme, scisme* < LL *schisma* < Gk., split < *schizein* to split]

schis·mat·ic (siz·mat′ik) *adj.* Relating to, having the character of, implying, or promoting schism. Also **schis·mat′i·cal.** — *n.* One who makes or participates in a schism. **— Syn.** See HERETIC. [< OF *cismatique, scismatique* < LL *schismaticus* < LGk. *schismatikos* < Gk. *schisma, -atos.* See SCHISM.] **— schis·mat′i·cal·ly** *adv.* **— schis·mat′i·cal·ness** *n.*

schist (shist) *n. Geol.* Any rock, especially a metamorphic rock, that readily splits or cleaves into parallel layers: also spelled *shist.* [< F *schiste* < L *schistos* readily split < Gk. < *schizein* to split] **— schist′ous, schist·ose** (shis′tōs) *adj.*

schisto- *combining form* Split: *schistosome.* Also, before vowels, **schist-.** [< Gk. *schistos* split]

schis·to·some (shis′tə·sōm) *n.* Any of a genus (*Schistosoma*) of trematode worms, including certain flukes parasitic in the blood of man and other mammals. [< NL < Gk. *schistos* split (< *schizein* to split) + *sōma* body]

schis·to·so·mi·a·sis (shis′tə·sō·mī′ə·sis) *n. Pathol.* A disease, usually found in tropical countries, caused by infestation with schistosomes: also called *bilharziasis.* [< SCHISTOSOM(E) + -IASIS]

schiz (skits, skiz) *n. Slang* A schizophrenic or schizoid.

schizo- *combining form* Split: *schizophrenia.* Also, before vowels, **schiz-.** [< Gk. *schizein* to split]

schiz·o·carp (skiz′ə·kärp) *n. Bot.* A pericarp splitting at maturity into two or more one-seeded indehiscent portions. For illustration see FRUIT. **— schiz′o·car′pous, schiz′o·car′pic** *adj.*

schiz·o·gen·e·sis (skiz′ō·jen′ə·sis) *n. Biol.* Reproduction by fission.

schiz·oid (skit′soid, skiz′oid) *Psychiatry n.* One who is abnormally shy and withdrawn. — *adj.* **1.** Of, pertaining to, or like a schizoid. **2.** Loosely, of or pertaining to schizophrenia. [< SCHIZ(OPHRENIA) + -OID]

schiz·o·my·cete (skiz′ō·mī·sēt′) *n.* One of a class (*Schizomycetes*) of widely distributed, minute, unicellular plants reproducing by fission and allied to the fungi. [< NL < Gk. *schizein* to split + *mykēs, -ētos* mushroom] **— schiz′o·my·ce′tous** *adj.*

schiz·o·my·co·sis (skiz′ō·mī·kō′sis) *n. Pathol.* Any disease due to the presence of schizomycetes. [< NL]

schiz·o·phre·ni·a (skit′sō·frē′nē·ə, skiz′ō-) *n. Psychiatry* Any of a group of psychotic disorders characterized by delusional formations, a retreat from reality, conflicting emotions, and deterioration of the personality: formerly called *dementia precox.* [< NL < Gk. *schizein* to split + *phrēn* mind] **— schiz′o·phren′ic** (-fren′ik) *adj. & n.*

schiz·o·phyte (skiz′ə·fīt) *n.* One of a division (*Schizophyta*) of unicellular or simple multicellular plants that reproduce by fission, including the bacteria and the blue-green algae. [< NL < Gk. *schizein* to split + *phyton* plant] **— schiz′o·phyt′ic** (-fit′ik) *adj.*

schiz·o·pod (skiz′ə·pod) *n.* Any of a former order (*Schizopoda*) of crustaceans having a soft carapace and resembling the shrimp, now included in the subclass *Malacostraca.* [< NL < Gk. *schizopous, -podos* having parted toes < *schizein* to split + *pous, podos* foot]

schiz·o·thy·mi·a (skit′sō·thī′mē·ə, skiz′ō-) *n. Psychiatry* A schizoid condition marked by introversion and a withdrawing from the world, but milder than schizophrenia. [< NL < Gk. *schizein* to split + *thymos* spirit] **— schiz′o·thyme** *n.* **— schiz′o·thy′mic** *adj.*

Schle·gel (shlā′gəl), **August Wilhelm von,** 1767–1845, German philologist, poet, and critic. **— Friedrich von,** 1772–1829, German author and critic; brother of the preceding.

Schlei·er·ma·cher (shlī′ər·mäkh′ər), **Friedrich Ernst Daniel,** 1768–1834, German theologian and philosopher.

schle·miel (shlə·mēl′) *n. Slang* An inept, easily duped person; a bungler; dolt. Also **schle·mihl′.** [< Yiddish, an unlucky person < Hebrew *Shelumiēl,* a personal name; also, influenced by Peter *Schlemihl,* title character in a popular novel by Adelbert von Chamisso, 1814]

Schle·si·en (shlä′zē·ən) The German name for SILESIA.

Schles·wig (shläs′vikh) **1.** A city in NE West Germany; former capital of Schleswig-Holstein; pop. 33,317 (est. 1970). **2.** The southern part of the Jutland Peninsula, divided between Germany and Denmark: Danish *Slesvig.*

Schles·wig-Hol·stein (shläs′vikh-hōl′shtīn) A state of NE West Germany; 6,052 sq. mi.; pop. 2,557,200 (est. 1970); capital, Kiel.

Schlie·mann (shlē′män), **Heinrich,** 1822–90, German merchant and archeologist.

schlie·ren (shlē′rən) *n.* **1.** *Geol.* In an igneous rock, irregular portions differing in composition or texture from the general mass. **2.** *Physics* Any disturbance in the light path of an interferometer that alters the density of the air and thus changes the interference pattern of the light waves. [< G, pl. of *schliere,* lit., streak]

schlock (shlok) *U.S. Slang n.* Anything that is cheap or of inferior quality. — *adj.* Cheap or inferior. [< Yiddish, damaged goods < G *schlag* a blow]

schmaltz (shmälts) *n. Slang* **1.** Anything overly sentimental. **2.** Extreme sentimentalism. [< Yiddish < G *schmalz,* lit., rendered fat] — **schmaltz′y** *adj.*

schmel·ze (shmel′tsē, -tse) *n.* Any of various kinds of decorative glass, especially one colored red with a metallic salt and used to flash white glass. [< G *schmelz* enamel]

Schmidt telescope (shmit) A reflecting telescope equipped with the **Schmidt objective,** a lens system that corrects the aberration of a spherical mirror without introducing blurring, and yields undistorted images of a very wide field. [after B. *Schmidt,* died 1935, German optical designer]

schmo (shmō) *n. U.S. Slang* **1.** A naive, pitiable person. **2.** A person one does not like. Also **schmoe.** [< Yiddish]

schmoose (shmōōz, shmōōs) *v.i.* **schmoosed, schmoos·ing** *U.S. Slang* To chat, converse idly. — *n.* A chat. Also **schmooze.** [< Yiddish *shmuesen < schmues* chat, gossip < Hebrew *shmuāh* report]

schmuck (shmuk) *n. U.S. Slang* A foolish or clumsy person. [< Yiddish *schmuck* penis < G *schmuck* jewel, ornament]

Schna·bel (shnä′bəl), **Artur,** 1882–1951, U.S. pianist and composer born in Austria.

schnap·per (shnap′ər, snap′-) *n.* A snapper (def. 4).

schnapps (shnäps, shnaps) *n. pl.* **schnapps** Any strong, spiritous liquor, especially Hollands. Also **schnaps.** [< G, dram, nip < Du. *snaps,* lit., gulp, mouthful]

schnau·zer (shnou′zər) *n.* A terrier originally developed in Germany, having a wiry, black or pepper-and-salt coat. [< G, lit., growler < *schnauzen* to growl, snarl]

Schnitz·ler (shnits′lər), **Arthur,** 1862–1931, Austrian playwright and novelist.

schnook (shnŏŏk) *n. U.S. Slang* A person who is unimportant or easily deceived. [Origin uncertain]

schnor·rer (shnôr′ər) *n.* A professional or habitual beggar. [< Yiddish < G *schnurrer* < slang *schnurren* to go begging, orig., whirr, purr; with ref. to musical instruments carried by beggars]

schnoz·zle (shnoz′əl) *n. Slang* Nose. [< Yiddish < G *schnauze.* Akin to SNOUT.]

Scho·field (skō′fēld), **John McAllister,** 1831–1906, U.S. general.

scho·la can·to·rum (skō′lə kan·tôr′əm, -tōr′-) *pl.* **·lae** (-lē) **1.** A choir school. **2.** A building or section of a church for a choir or choir school. [< Med. L, school of singers]

schol·ar (skol′ər) *n.* **1.** A person eminent for learning, especially in the humanities. **2.** A learned person; especially, a university teacher in the humanities who does authoritative research and writing in some special field: a Renaissance *scholar.* **3.** The holder of a scholarship. **4.** *Rare* A pupil. — **Syn.** See STUDENT. [Prob. fusion of OE *scolere* and OF *escoler,* both < LL *scholaris* < L *schola.* See SCHOOL[1].]

schol·arch (skol′ärk) *n.* **1.** In Greek antiquity, the head of a school of philosophy in Athens. **2.** The head of any school. [< Gk. *scholarchē < scholē* school + *archein* to rule]

schol·ar·ly (skol′ər·lē) *adj.* **1.** Of or befitting a scholar: *scholarly* methods. **2.** Having the qualities of a scholar. — *adv.* After the manner of a scholar.

schol·ar·ship (skol′ər·ship) *n.* **1.** The mental attainments of a scholar; learning; erudition; also, scholarly character or qualities. **2.** Scholarly inquiry or research. **3.** Maintenance or a stipend for a student, awarded by an educational institution: also, the position of such a student.

scho·las·tic (skə·las′tik, skō-) *adj.* **1.** Pertaining to or characteristic of scholars, education, or schools. **2.** Pertaining to or characteristic of the medieval schoolmen. **3.** Precise; pedantic. Also **scho·las′ti·cal.** — *n.* **1.** A student; pupil. **2.** *Often cap.* A schoolman; an advocate of scholasticism. **3.** A pedant. [< L *scholasticus* < Gk. *scholastikos < scholazein* to be at leisure, devote leisure to study < *scholē.* See SCHOOL[1].] — **scho·las′ti·cal·ly** *adv.*

scho·las·ti·cate (skə·las′tə·kāt, skə-) *n.* A general house of higher studies for Jesuit scholastics. [< NL *scholasticatus* < L *scholasticus.* See SCHOLASTIC.]

scho·las·ti·cism (skō·las′tə·siz′əm, skə-) *n.* **1.** *Often cap.* The systematized Christian logic, philosophy, and theology of medieval scholars from the 10th to the 15th centuries, based on Aristotle's *Logic* and *Metaphysics* and the writings of the early Christian fathers. Compare HUMANISM. **2.** Any system of teaching that insists on traditional doctrines, etc.

scho·li·ast (skō′lē·ast) *n.* A commentator; especially, an ancient grammarian or annotator of classical texts. [< L *scholiasta* < Gk. *scholiastēs < scholion* commentary < *scholē* school] — **scho′li·as′tic** *adj.*

scho·li·um (skō′lē·əm) *n. pl.* **·li·ums** or **·li·a** (-lē·ə) **1.** An explanatory marginal note, as on a classical text by an ancient grammarian. **2.** An observation or note amplifying a mathematical proof. [< LL *scholium* < Gk. *scholion.*] See SCHOLIAST.]

Schön·berg (shœn′berkh), **Arnold,** 1874–1951, Austrian composer and conductor active in the United States.

Schon·gau·er (shōn′gou·ər), **Martin,** 1446?–88, German painter and engraver.

school[1] (skōōl) *n.* **1.** Any institution devoted primarily to imparting knowledge or to developing certain skills or talents; especially, an educational institution for children. **2.** A place where formal instruction is given; also, the instruction itself. **3.** A period or session of an educational institution; a course of study at a school: *School* begins tomorrow. **4.** The pupils in an educational institution. **5.** A subdivision of a university devoted to a special branch of higher education: the *school* of medicine. **6.** The prescribed drill, duties, instruction, and training of any branch of the army or navy; also, the manual of such instruction. **7.** A body of disciples of a teacher or system; also, the system, methods, or opinions characteristic of those thus associated: a painting of the Flemish *school.* **8.** A general style of life, manners, etc.: a gentleman of the old *school.* **9.** In medieval times, a seminary of logic, metaphysics, and theology. **10.** *pl.* The seats of the scholastic philosophy. **11.** Any sphere or means of instruction: the *school* of hard knocks. Abbr. S. — *v.t.* **1.** To instruct in or as in a school; train; educate. **2.** To subject to rule or discipline. — **Syn.** See TEACH. [OE *scōl* < L *schola* < Gk. *scholē* leisure or that which is done during leisure time, school]

school[2] (skōōl) *n.* A large number of fish, whales, etc., swimming together; shoal. — *v.i.* To swim together in a school. [< Du., a crowd, school of fishes. Akin to SHOAL[2].]

school board A board of education.

school·book (skōōl′bŏŏk′) *n.* A book for use in school.

school·boy (skōōl′boi′) *n.* A boy attending school.

school·fel·low (skōōl′fel′ō) *n.* A schoolmate.

school·girl (skōōl′gûrl′) *n.* A girl attending school.

school·house (skōōl′hous′) *n.* A building in which a school is conducted.

school·ing (skōōl′ing) *n.* **1.** Instruction given at school. **2.** The process of teaching or being taught in a school.

school·man (skōōl′mən) *n. pl.* **·men** (-mən) One of the theologians of the Middle Ages; a scholastic.

school·marm (skōōl′märm′) *n. Informal* A woman schoolteacher, especially one considered to be prudish, spinsterish, or strict. Also **school′ma′am′** (-mäm′).

school·mas·ter (skōōl′mas′tər, -mäs′-) *n.* **1.** A man who teaches in or directs a school. **2.** Anything that instructs or disciplines: Necessity was his *schoolmaster.* **3.** A Caribbean fish (*Lutjanus apodus*) of the snapper family.

school·mate (skōōl′māt′) *n.* A fellow pupil.

school·mis·tress (skōōl′mis′tris) *n.* A woman teacher.

school·room (skōōl′rōōm′, -rŏŏm′) *n.* A room in which classes are held or instruction is given.

school·teach·er (skōōl′tē′chər) *n.* One who gives instruction in a school below the college level.

school·yard (skōōl′yärd′) *n.* The grounds about a school.

school year The part of the year during which a school or the schools of an educational system are in session.

schoon·er (skōō′nər) *n.* **1.** A fore-and-aft rigged vessel having two or more masts. **2.** A large beer glass, holding usually about a pint or more. [Appar. coined in New England < dial. *scoon* to skim on water, prob. < Scand.]

Scho·pen·hau·er (shō′pən·hou′ər), **Arthur,** 1788–1860, German philosopher. — **Scho′pen·hau′er·i·an** *adj.*

Scho·pen·hau·er·ism (shō′pən·hou′-ə·riz′əm) *n.* The philosophy of Arthur Schopenhauer, who taught that life is evil and the will to perpetuate it should be overcome.

schorl (shôrl) *n.* Tourmaline, especially the black variety: also spelled **shorl.** [< G *schörl*] — **schor·la·ceous** (shôr·lā′shəs) *adj.*

schot·tische (shot′ish) *n.* **1.** A round dance similar to the polka, but somewhat slower. **2.** Music for or in the manner of this dance, in duple meter. [< G (*der*) *schottische* (*tanz*) (the) Scottish (dance)]

Schreck·lich·keit (shrek′likh·kīt) *n. German* Terror and atrocity, especially as a policy of state.

STANDARD SCHNAUZER (18–20 inches high at shoulder)

SCHOONER
a Jib topsail. *b* Flying jib. *c* Jib. *d* Foresail. *e* Fore club topsail. *f* Maintopmast staysail. *g* Main club topsail. *h* Mainsail.

schrik (skhrik) *n.* *Afrikaans* Panic or sudden fright.
Schrö·ding·er (shrœ′ding·ər), **Erwin,** 1887–1961, Austrian physicist.
schtick (shtik) See SHTICK.
Schu·bert (shōō′bərt, *Ger.* shōō′bert), **Franz Peter,** 1797–1828, Austrian composer.
schuit (skoit) *n.* A sloop-rigged Dutch vessel used in rivers and canals. [< Du. *schuit, schuyt* < M.Du. *schute*]
Schu·man (shü·män′), **Robert,** 1886–1963, French political leader born in Luxembourg.
Schu·mann (shōō′män), **Robert,** 1810–56, German composer.
Schu·mann-Heink (shōō′män·hīngk′), **Ernestine,** 1861–1936, *née* Rössler, U.S. contralto born in Austria.
Schur·man (shûr′mən), **Jacob Gould,** 1854–1942, U.S. philosopher, diplomat, and educator born in Canada.
Schurz (shŏorts), **Carl,** 1829–1906, U.S. statesman, journalist, and general born in Germany.
Schusch·nigg (shōōsh′nik), **Kurt von,** born 1897, Austrian statesman.
schuss (shŏos) *v.i.* To ski down a steep slope at high speed. — *n.* **1.** A straight, steep ski course. **2.** The act of skiing such a course. [< G, lit., a shot]
Schutz·staf·fel (shŏots′shtä′fäl) *n.* *pl.* **-feln** (-fäln) *German* In Nazi Germany: **a** Hitler's personal bodyguard, known as the Black Shirts. **b** A section of the militia used to maintain order in Germany and occupied countries. Abbr. *SS., SS*
Schuy·ler (skī′lər), **Philip John,** 1733–1804, American Revolutionary general and statesman.
Schuy·ler·ville (skī′lər·vil) A village in eastern New York; scene of the Battle of Saratoga and General Burgoyne's surrender, October 17, 1777, in the American Revolution; pop. 1,402; formerly *Saratoga.*
Schuyl·kill River (skōōl′kil, skōō′kəl) A river in SE Pennsylvania, flowing 130 miles SE to the Delaware River.
schwa (shwä, shvä) *n.* **1.** *Phonet.* A weak, neutral vowel sound occurring in most of the unstressed syllables in English speech, as the *a* in *alone,* the *e* in *happen,* or the *u* in *circus:* written ə. **2.** In Hebrew, the obscure vowel sound: written : and often transliterated by *e.* [< G < Hebrew *shewa*]
Schwab (shwäb), **Charles Michael,** 1862–1939, U.S. industrialist.
Schwa·ben (shvä′bən) The German name for SWABIA.
Schwann (shvän), **Theodor,** 1810–82, German physiologist.
schwan·pan (shwän′pän′) See SWANPAN.
Schwarz·wald (shvärts′vält) The German name for the BLACK FOREST.
Schwein·furt (shvīn′fŏort) A city in NW Bavaria, West Germany; pop. 59,293 (est. 1970).
Schweit·zer (shvī′tsər), **Albert,** 1875–1965, French (Alsatian) clergyman, physician, missionary, philosopher, and musicologist; founder and director of the hospital at Lambaréné, Gabonese Republic.
Schweiz (shvīts) The German name for SWITZERLAND.
Schwe·rin (shve·rēn′) A city in East Germany, capital of the former state of Mecklenburg; pop. 92,356 (est. 1966).
Schwyz (shvēts) A canton of east central Switzerland bordering on Lake Lucerne; 350 sq. mi.; pop. 84,800 (1965); capital, *Schwyz.*
sci. Science; scientific.
sci·ae·noid (sī·ē′noid) *adj.* Of or pertaining to a family (*Sciaenidae*) of spiny-finned, carnivorous, chiefly marine fishes having air bladders enabling them to make grunting or drumming noises, as drumfishes. — *n.* A sciaenoid fish. Also **sci·ae·nid** (-ē′nid). [< NL < L *sciaena* < Gk. *skiaina,* a kind of fish]
sci·am·a·chy (sī·am′ə·kē) *n.* *pl.* **·chies** A struggle with a shadow or with an imaginary foe; useless combat: also spelled *sciomachy.* [< Gk. *skiamachia* < *skia* shadow + *machein* to fight]
sci·at·ic (sī·at′ik) *adj.* Pertaining to or affecting the hip or its nerves. — *n.* A sciatic nerve or part. [< MF *sciatique* < Med.L *sciaticus,* alter. of L *ischiadicus* < Gk. *ischiadikos* < *ischion* hip, hip joint]
sci·at·i·ca (sī·at′i·kə) *n.* *Pathol.* **1.** Neuralgia affecting the sciatic nerve traversing the hip and thigh. **2.** Any painful affection of the hip or adjoining areas. [< Med.L *sciatica* (*passio*) (the) sciatic (disease), fem. of *sciaticus.* See SCIATIC.]
sci·ence (sī′əns) *n.* **1.** Any department of knowledge in which the results of investigation have been logically arranged and systematized in the form of hypotheses and general laws subject to verification. **2.** Knowledge of facts, phenomena, laws, and proximate causes, gained and verified by exact observation, organized experiment, and ordered thinking. **3.** An orderly presentation of facts, reasonings, doctrines, and beliefs concerning some subject or group of subjects: the *science* of theology. **4.** Systematic knowledge in general. **5.** Expertness, skill, or proficiency resulting from knowledge. Abbr. *sc., sci.* [< OF < L *scientia* < *sciens, -entis,* ppr. of *scire* to know]

science fiction Fiction in which facts or theories of contemporary science are employed as elements of plot or background, often fantastic or dealing with the future.
sci·en·tial (sī·en′shəl) *adj.* **1.** Of, characterized by, or producing knowledge or science. **2.** Skillful; knowing.
sci·en·tif·ic (sī′ən·tif′ik) *adj.* **1.** Of, pertaining to, discovered by, derived from, or used in science. **2.** Agreeing with the rules, principles, or methods of science; accurate; systematic; exact. **3.** Versed in science or a science; eminently learned or skillful. Also **sci·en·tif′i·cal.** Abbr. *sci.* [< LL *scientificus* < *scientia* knowledge + *facere* to make; orig. trans. of Gk. *epistēmonikos* pertaining to knowledge, science] — **sci·en·tif′i·cal·ly** *adv.*
scientific method A method of inquiry depending upon the reciprocal interplay of observable data and generalizations. It consists typically of the statement of a problem and the accumulation and analysis of relevant data that may lead to the construction of a hypothesis, in turn tested by the reliability and accuracy of deductions from it and by its consistency with other hypotheses and observed data.
sci·en·tism (sī′ən·tiz′əm) *n.* **1.** Adherence to or belief in the aims and methods of scientists. **2.** Uncritical or unsuitable application of scientific concepts and terms.
sci·en·tist (sī′ən·tist) *n.* One versed in science or devoted to scientific study or investigation.
Sci·en·tist (sī′ən·tist) *n.* A Christian Scientist (which see).
sci-fi (sī′fī′) *adj., n.* Science fiction.
scil·i·cet (sil′ə·set) *adv.* Namely; to wit: introducing a word to be supplied, or an explanation. Abbr. *scil., sc.,* or *ss.* [< L, contr. of *scire licet* it is permitted to know]
Scil·la (sil′ə, *Ital.* shēl′lä) A town at the NE end of the Strait of Messina, southern Italy, on a small promontory supposed to be the site of the cave of the legendary Scylla.
Scil·ly Islands (sil′ē) An archipelago off the SW coast of Cornwall, England; 6.3 sq. mi.
scim·i·tar (sim′ə·tər) *n.* **1.** A curved Oriental sword or saber. **2.** A billhook of somewhat similar form. Sometimes spelled *similar.* Also **scim′e·tar, scim′i·ter.** [< MF *cimeterre;* infl. in form by Ital. *scimitarra;* both ? < Persian *shamshīr*]
scin·coid (sing′koid) *adj.* Of or belonging to a family (*Scincidae*) of lizardlike viviparous reptiles with typically smooth scales, as a skink. — *n.* A scincoid reptile. Also **scin·coi·di·an** (sing·koi′dē·ən). [< NL *scincoides* < L *scincus* skink]
scin·til·la (sin·til′ə) *n.* A spark; trace; iota: a *scintilla* of truth. [< L]
scin·til·lant (sin′tə·lənt) *adj.* Emitting sparks; scintillating.
scin·til·late (sin′tə·lāt) *v.* **·lat·ed, ·lat·ing** *v.i.* **1.** To give off sparks. **2.** To sparkle; glitter. **3.** To twinkle, as a star. — *v.t.* **4.** To give off as a spark or sparks. — **Syn.** See SHINE. [< L *scintillatus,* pp. of *scintillare* < *scintilla* spark] — **scin′til·lat′ing·ly** *adv.*
scin·til·la·tion (sin·tə·lā′shən) *n.* **1.** The act or state of scintillating; a sparkling, tremulous flashing or twinkling. **2.** A spark or sparkle. **3.** The twinkling of the stars.
scintillation counter *Physics* An instrument for detecting ionizing radiation, including gamma rays. Also **scintillation detector.**
sci·o·lism (sī′ə·liz′əm) *n.* Superficial knowledge; charlatanism. [< LL *sciolus* a smatterer, dim. of L *scius* knowing < *scire* to know] — **sci′o·list** *n.* — **sci′o·lis′tic** *adj.*
sci·om·a·chy (sī·om′ə·kē) *n.* Sciamachy.
sci·on (sī′ən) *n.* **1.** A child or descendant. **2.** See CION. [< OF *cion,* prob. blend of *scier* to saw and L *sectio, -onis* a cutting, both < L *secare* to cut]
Sci·o·to River (sī·ō′tə, -tō) A river in central and southern Ohio, flowing about 237 miles south to the Ohio River.
Scip·i·o (sip′ē·ō) A family prominent in Roman history, notably Scipio the Elder, 236?–183? B.C., general who defeated Hannibal at Zama 202 B.C.: full name **Publius Cornelius Scipio Af·ri·ca·nus** (af′rə·kā′nəs); and his grandson by adoption, Scipio the Younger, 183?–129 B.C., general who captured Carthage 146 B.C.: full name **Publius Cornelius Scipio Aemilianus Africanus Nu·man·ti·nus** (nōō′mən·tē′nəs).
sci·re fa·ci·as (sī′rē fā′shē·əs) *Law* **a** A writ commanding the party against whom it is issued to show cause why the plaintiff should not have advantage of or execution on a judicial record, or why a nonjudicial record should not be repealed or annulled. **b** The proceeding under such a writ. Abbr. *sci. fa., s.f.* [< L, that you cause to know]
scir·rhus (skir′əs, sir′-) *n.* *pl.* **scir·rhi** (skir′ī, sir′-) or **scir·rhus·es** *Pathol.* A hard tumor; especially, a cancerous tumor involving connective tissue. [< NL < L *scirros* < Gk. *skirrhos* tumor < *skiros* hard] — **scir·rhos·i·ty** (ski·ros′ə·tē, si-) *n.* — **scir′rhous, scir′rhoid** (-roid) *adj.*

SCIMITAR

scis·sile (sis′il) *adj.* Capable of being cut or split easily and evenly. [< L *scissilis* < *scissus*, pp. of *scindere* to cut]

scis·sion (sizh′ən, sish′-) *n.* **1.** The act of cutting or splitting, or the state of being cut. **2.** Any division. [< OF < LL *scissio*, *-onis* < *scissus*, pp. of *scindere* to cut]

scis·sor (siz′ər) *v.t. & v.i.* To cut with scissors.

scis·sors (siz′ərz) *n.pl.* (construed as *sing. in defs. 2 & 3*) **1.** A cutting implement with handles and a pair of blades pivoted face to face so that the opposed edges may be brought together on the object to be cut. Also **pair of scissors**. **2.** In wrestling, a hold secured by clasping the legs about the body or head of the opponent. **3.** A gymnastic feat in which the movement of the legs suggests the opening and closing of scissors. [< OF *cisoires* < LL *cisoria*, pl. of *cisorium* cutting instrument < *caedere* to cut; infl. in form by L *scissor* one who cuts < *scindere* to cut]

scissors kick In swimming, a kick performed usually with the side stroke, in which both legs are thrust apart, the upper leg bent at the knee while the lower is kept straight, then brought sharply together.

scis·sor·tail (siz′ər·tāl′) *n.* A flycatcher (*Muscivora forficata*) of the SW United States and Mexico, having a scissorlike tail.

scis·sure (sizh′ər, sish′-) *n.* **1.** A lengthwise cut; fissure. **2.** Any division, rupture, or schism. [< MF < L *scissura* < *scissus*. See SCISSION.]

sci·u·rine (sī′yŏŏ·rĭn, -rĭn) *adj.* Belonging or pertaining to a family (*Sciuridae*) of rodents, including squirrels, chipmunks, woodchucks, marmots, etc.: also *sciuroid*. — *n.* A sciurine rodent. [< L *sciurus* squirrel < Gk. *skiouros* < *skia* shadow + *oura* tail + -INE¹]

sci·u·roid (sī·yŏŏr′oid) *adj.* **1.** Sciurine. **2.** *Bot.* Resembling a squirrel's tail, as the tufted spikes of certain cereal grasses. [< NL < L *sciurus* squirrel + Gk. *eidos* form]

sclaff (sklaf) *v.i.* **1.** In golf, to strike the ground with the club before hitting the ball. — *v.t.* **2.** In golf: **a** To strike (the ball) or make (a stroke) after hitting the ground with the club. **b** To drag (the club) in such a manner. — *n.* **1.** A slight slap or blow; also, the noise so made. **2.** A light shoe; a slipper. **3.** A golf stroke made by sclaffing. [< dial. E (Scottish) *sclaf* slap, shuffle; ult. imit.]

Sclav (skläv), **Sclav·ic** (sklä′vik), etc. Obsolete forms of SLAV, etc.

scle·ra (sklir′ə) *n. Anat.* The hard, white, fibrous outer coat of the eyeball, continuous with the cornea. Also **scle·rot·i·ca** (sklə·rot′i·kə). For illustration see EYE. [< NL < Gk. *sklēros* hard]

scle·ren·chy·ma (sklə·reng′kə·mə) *n. Bot.* A tough, thick-walled tissue that protects and supports plants. [< NL < Gk. *sklēros* hard + *enchyma* infusion] — **scle·ren·chym·a·tous** (sklir′eng·kim′ə·təs) *adj.*

scle·rite (sklir′īt) *n. Zool.* **1.** One of the definite hard pieces of the integument of an arthropod. **2.** A hard element in the integument of a polyp. [< Gk. *sklēros* hard + -ITE¹] — **scle·rit·ic** (sklə·rit′ik) *adj.*

scle·ri·tis (sklə·rī′tis) *n. Pathol.* Inflammation of the sclera: also called *sclerotitis*. [< SCLER(A) + -ITIS]

sclero- *combining form* Hardness; hard: *scleroderma*. Also, before vowels, **scler-**. [< Gk. *sklēros* hard]

scle·ro·der·ma (sklir′ō·dûr′mə, skler′-) *n. Pathol.* A disease of the skin characterized by thickening, hardening, and pigmented patches. [< NL < Gk. *sklēros* hard + *derma* skin]

scle·ro·der·ma·tous (sklir′ō·dûr′mə·təs, skler′-) *adj. Zool.* Provided with a horny or bony covering, as an armadillo. [< Gk. *sklēros* hard + *derma*, *-atos* skin]

scle·roid (sklir′oid) *adj. Biol.* Hard; sclerous; hard in texture, as the shells of nuts, etc. [< Gk. *sklēroeidēs* < *sklēros* hard + *eidos* form]

scle·ro·ma (sklə·rō′mə) *n. pl. ·ma·ta* (-mə·tə) *Pathol.* A hardened patch of cellular tissue. [< NL < Gk. *sklērōma* < *sklēroein* to harden < *sklēros* hard]

scle·rom·e·ter (sklə·rom′ə·tər) *n.* An instrument for determining the degree of hardness of a substance, especially of a mineral.

scle·rosed (sklə·rōst′) *adj.* Affected with sclerosis; grown abnormally hard. [< SCLEROS(IS) + -ED³]

scle·ro·sis (sklə·rō′sis) *n. pl. ·ses* (-sēz) **1.** *Pathol.* The thickening and hardening of a tissue or part. **2.** *Bot.* The hardening of a plant cell wall by the formation of lignin in it. [< Med.L *sclirosis* < Gk. *sklērōsis* < *sklēroein* to harden < *sklēros* hard] — **scle·ro′sal** *adj.*

scle·rot·ic (sklə·rot′ik) *adj.* **1.** Dense; hard, as the sclera. **2.** Of or pertaining to the sclera. **3.** *Pathol.* Pertaining to or affected with sclerosis. [< NL *scleroticus* < Gk. *sklērotēs* hardness < *sklēros* hard. See SCLEROMA.] — **scle·ro·tit·ic** (sklir′ō·tit′ik, skler′-) *adj.*

scle·ro·ti·tis (sklir′ō·tī′tis, skler′-) *n. Pathol.* Scleritis. — **scle·ro·tit·ic** (sklir′ō·tit′ik) *adj.*

scle·ro·ti·um (sklə·rō′shē·əm) *n. pl. ·ti·a* (-shē·ə) *Bot.* A compact horny, dormant mass of mycelia, found in certain higher fungi. [< NL < Gk. *sklēros* hard] — **scle·ro′ti·oid** (-shē·oid), **scle·ro′tial** (-shəl) *adj.*

scle·rot·o·my (sklə·rot′ə·mē) *n. pl. ·mies* *Surg.* Incision of the sclera. [< SCLER(A) + -TOMY]

scle·rous (sklir′əs) *adj.* Hard or indurated; bony. [< SCLER(O)- + -OUS]

Sc.M. Master of Science (L *Scientiae Magister*).

scoff (skôf, skof) *v.i.* **1.** To speak with contempt or derision; jeer: often with *at*. — *v.t.* **2.** To deride; mock. — *n.* An expression or an object of contempt or derision. [ME *scof*, prob. < Scand. Cf. Dan. *skof* jest, mockery.] — **scoff′er** *n.* — **scoff′ing·ly** *adv.*
— **Syn.** (verb) **1.** sneer, gibe, flout.

scoff·law (skôf′lô′, skof′-) *n.* One who scoffs at or flouts the law; especially, a habitual or deliberate violator of traffic, safety, or public-health regulations.

scold (skōld) *v.t.* **1.** To find fault with harshly. — *v.i.* **2.** To find fault harshly or continuously. — *n.* One who scolds, especially a shrewish woman. [Appar. < ON *skáld* poet, satirist] — **scold′er** *n.* — **scold′ing·ly** *adv.*
— **Syn.** (verb) berate, revile, abuse. Compare REPROVE, CHASTEN, ASPERSE.

scol·e·cite (skol′ə·sīt, skō′lə-) *n.* A vitreous or silky, colorless, hydrous silicate of calcium and aluminum; a zeolite. [< G < Gk. *skōlēx*, *-ēkos* worm; so called because it sometimes curls up when heated]

sco·lex (skō′leks) *n. pl.* **sco·le·ces** (skō·lē′sēz) or **scol·i·ces** (skol′ə·sēz, skō′lə-) *Zool.* The knoblike head of a tapeworm, equipped with a circular disk of hooks and a group of two or four suckers. [< NL < Gk. *skōlēx* worm]

sco·li·o·sis (skō′lē·ō′sis, skol′ē-) *n. Pathol.* Abnormal curvature of the spine, especially a lateral curvature. Also **sco′li·o′ma**. [< NL < Gk. *skoliōsis* < *skolios* curved] — **scol·i·ot·ic** (-ot′ik) *adj.*

scol·lop (skol′əp), etc. See SCALLOP, etc.

scol·o·pen·drid (skol′ə·pen′drid) *n.* One of a family of chilopods (*Scolopendridae*) including the typical centipedes. [< NL < L *scolopendra* < Gk. *skolopendra* milliped] — **scol′o·pen′drine** (-drīn, -drin) *adj.*

scom·broid (skom′broid) *adj.* Of or pertaining to a widely distributed family (*Scombridae*) of teleost fishes, including mackerels. — *n.* A scombroid fish. [< NL < L *scomber* mackerel < Gk. *skombros*]

sconce¹ (skons) *n.* **1.** A small earthwork or fort. **2.** A protective shelter, covering, or screen. [< Du. *schanz* fortress, wicker basket; infl. in form by SCONCE²]

sconce² (skons) *n.* An ornamental wall bracket for holding a candle or other light. [< OF *esconse* dark lantern, hiding place < Med.L *sconsa*, short for L *absconsa*, pp. fem. of *abscondere* to hide]

sconce³ (skons) *n. Informal* **1.** The head or skull. **2.** Brains; wit. [? Special use of SCONCE¹]

sconce⁴ (skons) *Brit.* Among university students, a light fine or penalty. — *v.t.* **sconced**, **sconc·ing** To fine; mulct. [? < SCONCE³]

scone (skōn, skon) *n.* **1.** A round tea cake or biscuit usually eaten with butter. **2.** *Scot.* Originally, a thin oatmeal cake baked on a griddle. [? < MDu. *schoonbrot* fine bread]

Scone (skōōn, skon) A village in SE Perthshire, Scotland; coronation place of Scottish kings, 1153 to 1488; pop. about 3,000. — **the Stone of Scone** The stone on which early Scottish kings were crowned, brought to England by Edward I and placed under the seat of the coronation chair in Westminster Abbey.

scoop (skōōp) *n.* **1.** A shovellike instrument or large shovel with high sides. **2.** A small shovellike implement or ladle used by grocers, druggists, etc. **3.** An implement for bailing, as water from a boat. **4.** A spoon-shaped instrument for using in a cavity: a surgeons' *scoop*. **5.** An implement for dispensing uniform, spherical portions of ice cream, etc.; also, a portion thus dispensed. **6.** An act of scooping; a scooping movement. **7.** *Informal* A large gain, especially in speculation: He made a big *scoop* on that deal. **8.** A bowl-shaped cavity; hollow excavation. **9.** *Slang* In journalism, a news story obtained and published ahead of rival papers. **10.** *Slang* Any item of recent news: What's the *scoop*? — *v.t.* **1.** To take or dip out with or as with a scoop. **2.** To hollow out, as with a scoop; excavate. **3.** To empty with a scoop. **4.** *Informal* To heap up or gather in or as in scoopfuls; amass. **5.** *Slang* In journalism, to obtain and publish a news story before (a rival). [Fusion of MDu. *schope* vessel for bailing out water, and *schoppe* shovel] — **scoop′er** *n.*

scoot (skōōt) *Informal v.i.* To go quickly; dart off. — *n.* The act of scooting; a hurried darting off. [Prob. < Scand. Cf. ON *skióta* to shoot. Akin to SHOOT.]

scoot·er (skōō′tər) *n.* **1.** A child's vehicle consisting of a footboard mounted between two tandem wheels and steered by means of a long handle attached to the front axle. **2.** A motor scooter (which see). **3.** A sailboat with runners that may be used in water and on ice.

scop (skop) *n. Obs.* A bard, minstrel, or poet. — **Syn.** See BARD. [OE]

Sco·pas (skō′pəs) Fourth-century B.C. Greek sculptor and architect.

scope (skōp) *n.* **1.** Room for the exercise of faculties or function; capacity for achievement or effectiveness. **2.** Range of view or activity; outlook: a mind of limited *scope*.

3. The area or sphere in which any activity takes place: the *scope* of a scientific work. **4.** *Naut.* The length or sweep of a cable at which a ship rides at anchor. **5.** *Informal* Any of various optical or detecting instruments, as a telescope, microscope. **6.** *Rare* Purpose; aim. [< Ital. *scopo* < L *scopus* < Gk. *skopos* watcher < *skopeein* to look at]

-scope *combining form* An instrument for viewing, observing, or indicating: *telescope*. [< Gk. *skopos* watcher < *skopeein* to watch]

Scopes (skōps), **John T**(**homas**), 1901-1970, U.S. teacher; convicted and fined for teaching the theory of organic evolution in Tennessee.

sco·pol·a·mine (skō·pol′ə·mēn, -min, skō′pə·lam′ēn, -in) *n. Chem.* An alkaloid, $C_{17}H_{21}O_4N$, extracted from the dried rhizomes of certain solanaceous plants (genus *Scopolia*), the salts of which are used in medicine as a mydriatic, hypnotic, and sedative: also called *hyoscine*. [< G *scopolamin* < NL *Scopolia*, genus name of plants from which it is obtained, after G. A. *Scopoli*, 1723–88, Italian naturalist]

sco·po·line (skō′pə·lēn, -lin) *n. Chem.* A crystalline derivative of scopolamine, $C_8H_{13}NO_2$. [< SCOPOL(AMINE) + -INE[2]]

scop·u·late (skop′yə·lit, -lāt) *adj. Zool.* Broom-shaped. [< L *scopulae* little broom, pl. of *scopula* broom twig, dim. of *scopa* twig, broom]

Sco·pus (skō′pəs), **Mount** A peak in central Palestine, NE of Jerusalem; 2,736 ft.

-scopy *combining form* Observation; viewing: *microscopy*. [< Gk. -*skopia* < *skopeein* to watch]

scor·bu·tic (skôr·byōō′tik) *adj.* Relating to, characteristic of, or affected with scurvy: also **scor·bu′ti·cal**. [< NL *scorbuticus* < Med.L *scorbutus* scurvy, appar. < M Du. *scheurbuik* < *scheuren* to break, lacerate + *buik* belly] — **scor·bu′ti·cal·ly** *adv.*

scorch (skôrch) *v.t.* **1.** To change the color, taste, etc., of by slight burning; char the surface of. **2.** To wither or shrivel by heat. **3.** To criticize severely. —*v.i.* **4.** To become scorched. **5.** *Informal* To go at high speed. — **Syn.** See BURN[1]. —*n.* **1.** A superficial burn. **2.** A mark caused by heat, as a slight burn. [Prob. akin to ME *skorken* < ON *skorpna* to dry up, shrivel; infl. in form by OF *escorchier* to flay < L *excorticare* < *ex-* off + *cortex*, -*icis* bark] — **scorch′ing** *adj.* — **scorch′ing·ly** *adv.*

scorched-earth policy (skôrcht′ûrth′) The military policy of destroying all crops, industrial equipment, dwellings, etc., so as to leave nothing for the use of the enemy.

scorch·er (skôr′chər) *n.* **1.** One who or that which scorches. **2.** *Informal* An extremely hot day. **3.** *Informal* Severe or caustic criticism. **4.** *Informal* One who or that which moves at great speed.

score (skôr, skōr) *n.* **1.** The record of the winning points in a competition or game; also, the total of such points made by a player or a team. **2.** *Psychol.* A quantitative value assigned to an individual or group response to a test or series of tests, as of intelligence or performance. **3.** Grade or rating in a test or examination. **4.** Any record, especially of indebtedness. **5.** A notch or groove cut in something for keeping a tally. **6.** Something charged or laid up against one; a grudge: to settle old *scores*. **7.** A set of twenty: a *score* of years ago. **8.** *pl.* An indefinitely large number. **9.** *Music* The complete notation for a composition, showing the various instrumental or vocal parts on two or more staffs arranged one above another. — **to know the score** *Informal* To be aware of the real facts of a situation. —*v.* **scored, scor·ing** *v.t.* **1.** To mark with notches, cuts, or lines. **2.** To mark with cuts or lines for the purpose of keeping a tally or record. **3.** To obliterate or cross out by means of a line drawn through: with *out*. **4.** To make or gain, as points, runs, etc. **5.** To count for a score of, as in games: A touchdown *scores* six points. **6.** To rate or grade, as an examination paper; evaluate. **7.** *Music* **a** To orchestrate. **b** To arrange or adapt for an instrument. **8.** *Informal* To criticize severely; scourge. **9.** In cooking, to make superficial cuts in (meat, etc.). —*v.i.* **10.** To make points, runs, etc., as in a game. **11.** To keep score. **12.** To make notches, cuts, etc. **13.** To win an advantage or success. [OE *scoru* < ON *skor* notch, tally] — **scor′er** *n.*

sco·ri·a (skôr′ē·ə, skō′rē·ə) *n., pl.* **·ri·ae** (-ri·ē) **1.** Refuse or slag remaining after metal has been smelted. **2.** Loose, clinkerlike pieces of lava. [< L < Gk. *skōria* refuse < *skōr* dung] — **sco′ri·a′ceous** (-ā′shəs) *adj.*

sco·ri·fy (skôr′ə·fī, skō′rə-) *v.t.* **·fied, ·fy·ing** *Metall.* **1.** To separate, as gold or silver, from an ore by smelting with lead, borax, etc. **2.** To reduce to scoria or dross. [< SCORI(A) + -FY] — **sco′ri·fi·ca′tion** *n.*

scorn (skôrn) *n.* **1.** A feeling of contempt or loathing, as for someone or something deemed inferior or unworthy of attention; disdain. **2.** Behavior characterized by such a feeling; derision. **3.** An expression of contempt or disdain. **4.** An object of scorn. —*v.t.* **1.** To hold in or treat with contempt; despise. **2.** To reject with scorn; disdain;

spurn. —*v.i.* **3.** *Obs.* To mock; jeer. [< OF *escarn* < *escarnir* < Gmc.] — **scorn′er** *n.* — **scorn′ful** *adj.* — **scorn′ful·ly** *adv.* — **scorn′ful·ness** *n.*

— **Syn.** (noun) **1.** *Scorn, disdain,* and *contempt* denote feelings directed toward that which we regard as base or repellent. *Disdain* is the mildest term; it may be shown simply by avoidance of the unworthy. *Scorn* suggests a more overt expression and is often shown by a loud and haughty rejection of that which offends. We may show *scorn* or *disdain* toward something we find repellent or uninteresting; *contempt* always implies the passing of a adverse moral judgment upon another person or thing. — **Ant.** regard, approval, appreciation.

scor·pae·noid (skôr·pē′noid) *adj.* Belonging to a family (*Scorpaenidae*) of spiny-finned marine fishes including the rockfishes. —*n.* A scorpaenoid fish: also **scor·pae′nid** (-nid). [< NL < L *scorpaena* a kind of fish (< Gk. *skōrpaina*) + -OID]

Scor·pi·o (skôr′pē·ō) *n.* A constellation, the **Scorpion**, containing the bright star Antares; also, the eighth sign of the zodiac. Also **Scor′pi·us** (-əs). See CONSTELLATION, ZODIAC. [< L]

scor·pi·oid (skôr′pē·oid) *adj.* **1.** Resembling a scorpion; scorpionlike. **2.** Rolled or curled like the tail of a scorpion. See illustration of INFLORESCENCE. [< Gk. *skorpioeidēs* < *skorpios* scorpion + *eidos* form]

scor·pi·on (skôr′pē·ən) *n.* **1.** One of an order (*Scorpionida*) of arachnids found chiefly in warmer regions, having an elongated, lobsterlike body and a segmented tail that bears a venomous sting. **2.** An instrument of chastisement; a whip or scourge. I *Kings* xii 11. [< OF < L *scorpio, -onis* < Gk. *skorpios*]

SCORPION
s Stinger.
(To about 3
in. long)

scorpion fish Any of various scorpaenoid fishes (*Scorpaena* and related genera) having poisonous dorsal spines, as the **California scorpion fish** (*S. guttata*), or sculpin.

scorpion fly A mecopterous insect (genus *Panorpa*) in which the end of the abdomen of the male is upcurved like a scorpion's sting. For illustration see INSECTS (beneficial).

scot (skot) *n.* An assessment or tax. [Fusion of ON *skot* and OF *escot*; infl. by OE *scot* payment]

Scot (skot) *n.* **1.** A native of Scotland: also called *Scotsman*. **2.** Formerly, a Gaelic Highlander. **3.** One of a Gaelic people who migrated in the fifth century to northwestern Britain from Ireland. [OE *Scottas*, pl., the Irish < LL *Scotus, Scoti*]

Scot. Scotch; Scotland; Scottish.

scot and lot An assessment in Great Britain formerly laid on all of a borough, according to their ability to pay. — **to pay scot and lot** To pay in full.

scotch[1] (skoch) *v.t.* **1.** To cut; scratch. **2.** To wound so as to maim or cripple. **3.** To put down; crush or suppress. —*n.* **1.** A superficial cut; a scratch; notch. **2.** A line traced on the ground, as for hopscotch. [Origin uncertain]

scotch[2] (skoch) *v.t.* To block, as a wheel or log, with a chock or wedge to prevent moving or slipping. —*n.* A block put behind or under something, as a wheel, to prevent rolling or sliding. [Origin unknown]

Scotch (skoch) *n.* **1.** The people of Scotland collectively: with *the*. **2.** One or all of the dialects spoken by the people of Scotland. **3.** Scotch whisky. —*adj.* Of or pertaining to Scotland, its inhabitants, or their language; Scottish; Scots. Abbr. *Sc., Scot.*

♦ **Scotch, Scots, Scottish** Of these three proper adjectives, the form *Scotch* developed in the dialects of the Midland and southern England, and is accepted even in Scotland as applying to *Scotch* plaid, *Scotch* whisky, etc. In Scotland and in northern England, however, the forms *Scots* and *Scottish* (earlier *Scottis*) prevailed, and are preferred as applying to the people, culture, and institutions of Scotland: *Scots* or *Scottish* English, the *Scottish* church. This distinction is now widely accepted.

Scotch broom See under BROOM.

Scotch elm The wych-elm (which see).

Scotch·man (skoch′mən) *n., pl.* **·men** (-mən) A Scot; Scotsman. ♦ These forms are preferred to *Scotchman*.

Scotch tape A rolled strip of transparent cellulose tape having an adhesive on one side: a trade name.

Scotch terrier A Scottish terrier (which see).

Scotch whisky Whisky made in Scotland from malted barley and having rather a smoky flavor.

Scotch woodcock Eggs cooked and served on toast or crackers spread with anchovy paste.

sco·ter (skō′tər) *n.* Any of several dark sea ducks (genera *Oidemia* and *Melanitta*) of northern regions, having the bill gibbous or swollen at the base, especially the **common scoter** (*O. nigra*): also, loosely, *coot*. [? < dial. E *scote*, var. of SCOOT.]

scot-free (skot′frē′) *adj.* **1.** Without injury or loss; unharmed; whole. **2.** Free from scot; untaxed.

sco·ti·a (skō′shē·ə, -shə) *n. Archit.* A concave molding common in the bases of classical columns. For illustration see MOLDING. [< L < Gk. *skotia* < *skotos* darkness; so called from the darkness in its concavity]

Sco·tism (skō′tiz·əm) *n.* The scholastic system and metaphysical doctrines of the Scottish philosopher John Duns Scotus. — **Sco′tist** *n.* — **Sco·tis′tic** *adj.*

Scot·land (skot′lənd) A political division and the northern part of Great Britain; a separate kingdom until its legislative union with England, 1707; 30,405 sq. mi.; pop. 5,194,700 (1969); capital, Edinburgh. *Medieval Latin* **Sco·tia** (skō′shə).

Scotland Yard 1. The headquarters of the London Metropolitan Police and of the London Criminal Investigation Department, since 1890 located at the **New Scotland Yard** on the Thames Embankment. **2.** Formerly, the headquarters of the London police, situated in Great Scotland Yard, a short street in central London.

scoto- *combining form* Darkness: *scotophobia.* Also, before vowels, **scot-.** [< Gk. *skotos* darkness]

sco·to·ma (skə·tō′mə) *n. pl.* **·ma·ta** (-mə·tə) *Pathol.* A defect or blind spot in the field of vision. [< LL < Gk. *skotōma* dizziness < *skotoein* to darken < *skotos* darkness]

Scots (skots) *adj.* Scottish. — *n.* The Scottish dialect of English. ◆ See note at SCOTCH. [Earlier *Scottis*, var. of SCOTTISH]

Scots·man (skots′mən) *n. pl.* **·men** (-mən) A Scot.

Scott (skot), **Dred**, 1795?–1858, U.S. Negro; noted as the central figure in a Supreme Court decision. — **Sir George Gilbert**, 1811–78, English architect. — **Robert**, 1811–87, English lexicographer and classicist. — **Robert Falcon**, 1868–1912, English naval officer and Antarctic explorer; reached South Pole, Jan. 17, 1912; perished on return journey. — **Sir Walter**, 1771–1832, Scottish novelist and poet. — **Winfield**, 1786–1866, U.S. general; commander in chief in the Mexican War; occupied Mexico City 1847.

Scot·ti·cism (skot′ə·siz′əm) *n.* A form of expression or an idiom peculiar to the Scottish people.

Scot·tish (skot′ish) *adj.* Pertaining to or characteristic of Scotland, its inhabitants, or their language: also *Scots.* — *n.* **1.** The dialect of English spoken in Scotland, especially in the Lowlands; Scots. **2.** The people of Scotland collectively: with *the.* Abbr. *Sc., Scot.* ◆ See note at SCOTCH. [OE *Scottisc* < *Scotta* Scot]

Scottish Gaelic The Goidelic language of the Scottish Highlands: also called *Erse.*

Scottish terrier A small, short-legged terrier originating in Scotland, having a large head and a wiry coat: also *Scotch terrier.* Also *Informal* **Scot·tie** (scot′ē), **Scot′ty.**

scoun·drel (skoun′drəl) *n.* A mean, unprincipled rascal; a rogue; villain. — *adj.* Of or characteristic of a scoundrel. [? < AF *escoundre*, OF *escoundre* to abscond]

— **Syn.** *Scoundrel, knave, cad, rotter, rascal, rogue, scamp,* and *scalawag* are, in American English, somewhat archaic terms of opprobrium for a base fellow. They differ in that they suggest different vices or kinds of turpitude. A *scoundrel* is utterly dishonest, a *knave* is deceitful and two-faced, and a *cad* behaves in a manner not befitting a gentleman. *Rotter* points to immorality, and *rascal* and *rogue* connote corruption and lawlessness respectively. A *scamp* is tricky and roguish, while a *scalawag* is completely unscrupulous. The last four synonyms are often used in good-natured derogation between friends. All these words may be used in formal contexts except *scalawag,* which is informal, and *rotter,* which is slang. Compare HEEL¹, BASTARD.

scoun·drel·ly (skoun′drəl·ē) *adj.* **1.** Having the character of a scoundrel. **2.** Pertaining to or characteristic of a scoundrel; rascally.

scour¹ (skour) *v.t.* **1.** To clean or brighten by thorough washing and rubbing, as with sand or steel wool. **2.** To remove dirt, etc., from; clean: to *scour* wool. **3.** To remove by or as by rubbing away. **4.** To clear by means of a strong current of water; flush. **5.** To purge the bowels of. **6.** To clean (wheat) before milling. — *v.i.* **7.** To rub something vigorously so as to clean or brighten it. **8.** To become bright or clean by rubbing. — *n.* **1.** The act of scouring. **2.** A place scoured, as by running water. **3.** A cleanser used in cleaning wool. **4.** *Usually pl.* A watery diarrhea in cattle. [Prob. < MDu. *schuren* < OF *escurer*, ult. < L *ex-* out + *curare* to take care of < *cura* care]

scour² (skour) *v.t.* **1.** To range over or through, as in making a search. **2.** To move or run swiftly over or along. — *v.i.* **3.** To range about, as in making a search. **4.** To move swiftly. [ME *scoure.* Cf. ON *skura* to rush, run.]

scour·er¹ (skour′ər) *n.* **1.** One who or that which cleanses, removes stains, etc. **2.** A purgative. [< SCOUR¹]

scour·er² (skour′ər) *n.* One who prowls about the streets by night; a vagabond. [< SCOUR²]

scourge (skûrj) *n.* **1.** A whip for inflicting suffering or punishment. **2.** Any instrumentality or means for causing suffering or death. **3.** Severe punishment. **4.** A cause of suffering or trouble. — *v.t.* **scourged, scourg·ing 1.** To whip severely; lash; flog. **2.** To punish severely; chastise; afflict. [< AF *escorge* < LL *excoriare* to flay < L *ex-* off + *corium* hide] — **scourg′er** *n.*

Scourge of God See ATTILA.

scour·ing rush (skour′ing) Any species of horsetail,

formerly much used for polishing wood and metal: also called *scrub grass.*

scour·ings (skour′ingz) *n.pl.* **1.** The residue after scouring grain. **2.** Dirt or other residue left after any scouring.

scouse (skous) *n.* A sailor's dish of sea biscuit and vegetables with or without meat. [Short for LOBSCOUSE]

scout¹ (skout) *n.* **1.** One who or that which is engaged in scouting; especially, a person sent out to observe and get information, as of a war enemy, rival team in sports, etc. **2.** The act of scouting. **3.** At Oxford University, an undergraduate's manservant. **4.** *Slang* A fellow or friend. **5.** A boy or girl scout. — **Syn.** See SPY. — *v.t.* **1.** To observe or spy upon for the purpose of gaining information; reconnoiter. — *v.i.* **2.** To go or act as a scout. — **to scout around** To go in search. [< OF *escoute* listener, listening < *escouter* to listen < L *auscultare*] — **scout′er** *n.*

scout² (skout) *v.t. & v.i.* To reject with disdain; mock; jeer. [< Scand. Cf. ON *skuta* taunt.]

scout car An armored motor car for reconnaissance work.

scouth (skooth) *n. Scot.* Room for movement; scope.

scouth·er (skō′thər, skoo′-) *v.t. Scot.* To toast over a gridiron; scorch; singe. Also **scowd·er** (skoo′dər).

scout·ing (skout′ing) *n.* The activities of a scout, especially of a Boy Scout or Girl Scout.

scout·mas·ter (skout′mas′tər, -mäs′-) *n.* The leader of a troop of Boy Scouts.

scow (skou) *n.* A large boat with a flat bottom and square ends, chiefly used for freight and usually towed. [< Du. *schouw* boat propelled by a pole < MDu. *schoude*]

scowl (skoul) *n.* **1.** A lowering of the brows, as in anger, disapproval, or sullenness. **2.** Gloomy aspect. — *v.i.* **1.** To lower and contract the brows in anger, sullenness, or disapproval. **2.** To look threatening; lower. — *v.t.* **3.** To affect or express by scowling. [ME *skoul,* prob. < Scand. Cf. Dan. *skule.*] — **scowl′er** *n.* — **scowl′ing·ly** *adv.*

scr. Scruple (weight).

scrab·ble (skrab′əl) *v.* **·bled, ·bling** *v.i.* **1.** To scratch, scrape, or paw, as with the hands. **2.** To make irregular or meaningless marks; scribble. **3.** To struggle or strive. — *v.t.* **4.** To make meaningless marks on; scribble on. **5.** To gather hurriedly; scrape together. — *n.* **1.** The act of scrabbling or scrambling. **2.** A scrawling character, mark, etc.; scribble. **3.** A sparse growth, as of underbrush. **4.** The game of Scrabble. [< Du. *schrabbelen,* freq. of *schrabben* to scratch]

Scrab·ble (skrab′əl) *n.* A game resembling anagrams, played with letters printed on small, flat wooden blocks: a trade name. Also *scrabble.*

scrag (skrag) *v.t.* **scragged, scrag·ging** *Informal* To use roughly; wring the neck of; especially, to kill by hanging; garrote. — *n.* **1.** Something thin or lean, as a person. **2.** *Slang* The human neck. **3.** A lean or bony piece of meat. **4.** A small bush or hedge. [? < Scand. Cf. Norw. *skragg* lean, feeble person.]

scrag·gly (skrag′lē) *adj.* **·gli·er, ·gli·est** Unkempt; shaggy; irregular; jagged. [Prob. < SCRAGG(Y) + -LY]

scrag·gy (skrag′ē) *adj.* **·gi·er, ·gi·est 1.** Rough. **2.** Lean; scrawny; bony. [< SCRAG + -Y¹] — **scrag′gi·ly** *adv.* — **scrag′gi·ness** *n.*

scraich (skrākh) *Scot. v.i.* To screech, as a fowl. — *n.* A shrill cry; screech. Also **scraigh.**

scram (skram) *v.i.* **scrammed, scram·ming** *U.S. Slang* To go away; leave quickly. [Prob. short for SCRAMBLE]

scram·ble (skram′bəl) *v.* **·bled, ·bling** *v.i.* **1.** To move by clambering or crawling on hands and feet. **2.** To struggle with others in a disorderly manner; scuffle; also, to strive for something in such a manner. **3.** *Aeron.* To put interceptor aircraft into the air hurriedly to meet enemy aircraft. — *v.t.* **4.** To mix together haphazardly or confusedly. **5.** To gather or collect hurriedly or confusedly. **6.** To fry (eggs) with the yolks and whites stirred together. **7.** *Telecom.* To alter or garble (a signal) so that a special receiving apparatus is needed to render it comprehensible. — *n.* **1.** The act of scrambling. **2.** A disorderly performance or struggle. **3.** A difficult climb or trek, as over rocks or rough terrain. [Prob. nasalized var. of SCRABBLE]

scram·bler (skram′blər) *n.* One who or that which scrambles.

scran·nel (skran′əl) *Archaic adj.* **1.** Thin; lean; slight. **2.** Harsh, as sound. — *n.* A lean person. [Prob. < Scand. Cf. Norw. *skrann* lean.]

Scran·ton (skran′tən) A city in NE Pennsylvania; an anthracite and manufacturing center; pop. 103,564.

scrap¹ (skrap) *n.* **1.** A small piece cut or broken from something; fragment. **2.** A brief, printed or written extract. **3.** *pl.* Pieces of crisp fat tissue after the oil has been expressed by cooking; also, any bits of food. **4.** Old or refuse metal. — *v.t.* **scrapped, scrap·ping 1.** To break up into scrap; make scrap of. **2.** To discard; throw away. — *adj.* Having the form of scraps; discarded after use. [< ON *skrap* scrapings, scraps < *skrapa* to scrape. Akin to SCRAPE.]

scrap² (skrap) *v.i.* **scrapped, scrap·ping** *Slang* To fight; quarrel. — *n.* A quarrel, fight, or disagreement. — **Syn.** See ROW³. [< SCRAPE (*n.* def. 2)] — **scrap′per** *n.*

scrap·book (skrap'bŏŏk') *n.* **1.** A blank book in which to paste pictures, cuttings from periodicals, etc. **2.** A personal notebook.

scrape (skrāp) *v.* **scraped, scrap·ing** *v.t.* **1.** To rub, as with something rough or sharp, so as to abrade or to remove an outer layer or adherent matter. **2.** To remove thus: with *off, away,* etc. **3.** To rub (a rough or sharp object) across a surface. **4.** To rub roughly across or against (a surface). **5.** To dig or form by scratching or scraping. **6.** To gather or accumulate with effort or difficulty: usually with *up* or *together.* —*v.i.* **7.** To scrape something. **8.** To rub with a grating noise. **9.** To emit or produce a grating noise. **10.** To draw the foot backward along the ground in bowing: to bow and *scrape.* **11.** To manage or get along with difficulty. **12.** To be very or overly economical. —**to scrape acquaintance** To make acquaintance without an introduction. —*n.* **1.** The act or effect of scraping; also, the noise made by scraping. **2.** A difficult situation; predicament. **3.** A scraping or drawing back of the foot in bowing. —**Syn.** See PREDICAMENT. [Prob. fusion of OE *scrapian* and ON *skrapa* to scrape, erase]

scrap·er (skrā'pər) *n.* **1.** One who or that which scrapes. **2.** Any instrument used for scraping.

scrap·ing (skrā'ping) *n.* **1.** The act of someone or something that scrapes. **2.** The sound so produced. **3.** *Often pl.* That which is scraped off or together.

scrap iron Old pieces of iron suitable for reworking.

scrap·ple (skrap'əl) *n.* A mixture of meal or flour boiled with scraps of pork, seasoned, and allowed to set, usually cooked by frying. [Dim. of SCRAP¹]

scrap·py¹ (skrap'ē) *adj.* **·pi·er, ·pi·est** Composed of scraps; disconnected; fragmentary. [< SCRAP¹ + -Y¹] —**scrap'pi·ly** *adv.* —**scrap'pi·ness** *n.*

scrap·py² (skrap'ē) *adj.* **·pi·er, ·pi·est** Pugnacious; given to picking fights. [< SCRAP² + -Y¹] —**scrap'pi·ly** *adv.* —**scrap'pi·ness** *n.*

scratch (skrach) *v.t.* **1.** To tear or mark the surface of with something sharp or rough. **2.** To scrape or dig with something sharp or rough, as the claws or nails. **3.** To scrape lightly with the nails, etc., as to relieve itching. **4.** To rub with a grating sound; scrape. **5.** To write or draw awkwardly or hurriedly. **6.** To erase or cancel by or as by scratches or marks. **7.** To erase or cancel the name of (a candidate) from a political ticket, while supporting the rest of the ticket; also, to bolt (a ticket or party) in this way. **8.** To withdraw (an entry) from a race, game, etc. —*v.i.* **9.** To use the nails or claws, as in fighting or digging. **10.** To scrape the skin, etc., lightly, as to relieve itching. **11.** To make a harsh, grating noise. **12.** To manage or get along with difficulty. **13.** To withdraw from a game, race, etc. **14.** In billiards and pool, to make a scratch. —*n.* **1.** A mark or incision made on a surface by scratching; also, a quick mark or scribble, as made by a pencil. **2.** A slight flesh wound or cut. **3.** A harsh, grating sound. **4.** The act of scratching. **5.** The line from which contestants start, as in racing. **6.** The contestant who competes against an allowance. **7.** Formerly in pugilism, a line across a prize ring at which fighters began each round. **8.** In billiards, a chance shot; also, a fluke; in billiards and pool, a shot resulting in a penalty. —**from scratch** From the beginning; from nothing. —**up to scratch** *Informal* Meeting the standard or requirement in courage, stamina, or performance; in proper or fit condition. —*adj.* **1.** Done by chance; haphazard. **2.** In sports, without handicap or allowance. **3.** Used for quick notes, a memorandum, etc.: a *scratch* pad. **4.** Chosen at random or by chance: a *scratch* team. [Prob. blend of ME *scratte* to scratch (prob. < Scand.; cf. Sw. *kratta* to rake) and *cracchen* to scratch < MDu. *cratsen*] —**scratch'er** *n.*

scratch sheet *U.S. Slang* A dope sheet (which see).

scratch test *Med.* A test to determine the substances to which a person is allergic by rubbing allergens in small scratches made in his skin.

scratch·y (skrach'ē) *adj.* **scratch·i·er, scratch·i·est** **1.** Characterized by or covered with scratches. **2.** Making a scratching noise. **3.** Straggling; shaggy; rough. **4.** That scratches or irritates. —**scratch'i·ly** *adv.* —**scratch'i·ness** *n.*

scrawl (skrôl) *v.t. & v.i.* To write hastily or illegibly. —*n.* Irregular or careless writing. [? < dial. E, var. of CRAWL; ? infl. in meaning by SCRIBBLE, etc.] —**scrawl'er** *n.*

scrawl·y (skrô'lē) *adj.* **scrawl·i·er, scrawl·i·est** Consisting of or characterized by ill-formed or irregular characters.

scraw·ny (skrô'nē) *adj.* **·ni·er, ·ni·est** Lean and bony; skinny; thin. [< dial. E *scranny,* var. of SCRANNEL] —**scraw'ni·ness** *n.*

screak (skrēk) *v.i.* To creak; screech. —*n.* A screech; also, a creak. [< ON *skrækja*]

scream (skrēm) *v.i.* **1.** To utter a prolonged, piercing cry, as of pain, terror, or surprise. **2.** To make a prolonged, piercing sound. **3.** To laugh loudly or immoderately. **4.** To use heated, hysterical language. **5.** To have an odd or startling effect, as of screaming. —*v.t.* **6.** To utter with a scream. —*n.* **1.** A loud, shrill, prolonged cry or sound, generally denoting fear or pain. **2.** *U.S. Slang* A person or situation arousing great mirth. [ME *scraemen,* ? < ON *skraema* to scare]

scream·er (skrē'mər) *n.* **1.** One who or that which screams. **2.** Any of various birds of South America related to the ducks (family *Anhimidae* or *Palamedidae*) including the **horned screamer** (*Anhima* or *Palamedea cornuta*) and the **crested screamer** (genus *Chauna*). **3.** *U.S. Slang* Something calculated to call forth screams of admiration, astonishment, etc. **4.** *U.S. Slang* A sensational headline in a newspaper.

scream·ing (skrē'ming) *adj.* **1.** Uttering or emitting screams. **2.** Provocative of screams or of laughter: a *screaming* farce. **3.** Like a scream. —**scream'ing·ly** *adv.*

scree (skrē) *n.* A sloping mass of debris of stones and rock fragments at the foot of a cliff or steep, rocky face. See TALUS. [Back formation < *screes,* earlier *screethes* < ON *skridha* landslide]

screech (skrēch) *n.* **1.** A shrill, harsh cry; shriek. **2.** *Canadian Slang* Cheap rum or wine. —*v.t.* **1.** To utter with or as with a screech. —*v.i.* **2.** To make a prolonged, harsh, piercing sound. [Var. of obs. *scritch,* prob. < Scand. Cf. ON *skrækja;* prob. imit.] —**screech'er** *n.* —**screech'y** *adj.*

screech owl **1.** Any of various owls (genus *Otus*) common from Canada to Brazil; especially, the small, gray *O. asio* of the eastern United States. **2.** The barn owl of England.

screed (skrēd) *n.* **1.** A prolonged tirade; harangue. **2.** A long piece of discursive prose. **3.** A wooden strip or a strip of mortar laid on a wall at intervals, to gauge the thickness of the plastering. **4.** *Scot.* A tearing; rent; tear; also, a drinking spree. —*v.t.* **1.** To rend or tear into shreds. **2.** *Scot.* To repeat glibly. [Var. of SHRED]

screen (skrēn) *n.* **1.** That which separates or cuts off, shelters, or protects, as a light partition. **2.** A sieve or riddle for sifting. **3.** A smooth surface, on which motion pictures, etc., may be shown. **4.** A motion picture or motion pictures collectively. **5.** A plate of glass bearing very finely ruled lines, placed between the object and the camera in photographing for reproduction by the halftone process. **6.** *Mil. & Naval* A force or detachment interposed between the main body and the enemy to prevent hostile observation or interference. **7.** *Physics* Any of various devices for confining the action of a physical agency or instrument to a definite area: a magnetic *screen.* **8.** *Psychoanal.* One who or that which serves to conceal; especially, a person who stands for someone else, as in a dream. —*v.t.* **1.** To shield from observation or annoyance with or as with a screen. **2.** To cause to pass through a screen or sieve; sift. **3.** To show or exhibit on a screen, as a motion picture. **4.** To determine the competence or eligibility of (an individual) for a specified task. —*v.i.* **5.** To be shown or be suitable for showing on a motion-picture screen. [Prob. < OF *escren, escrin,* prob. < OHG *skirm*] —**screen'a·ble** *adj.* —**screen'er** *n.*

screen·ings (skrē'ningz) *n.pl.* The residue of anything passed through a sieve, as coal or defective grains; siftings.

screen·play (skrēn'plā') *n.* The script for a motion picture, consisting of dialogue and descriptions of the settings, action, and camera work.

screw (skrōō) *n.* **1.** A device resembling a nail but having a slotted head and a tapering grooved spiral for driving into wood with a screwdriver. **2.** A similar device of cylindrical form, for insertion into a corresponding grooved part: also **male** or **external** screw. **3.** A cylindrical socket with a spiral groove: also **female** or **internal** screw. **4.** Anything having the form of a screw. **5.** A screw propeller. **6.** A turn of or as of a screw. **7.** Pressure; force. **8.** *Brit. Slang* Salary; pay. **9.** *Slang* A prison guard. **10.** A haggler over prices; a crafty bargainer. **11.** *Brit.* A worthless horse. **12.** *Brit.* A small packet of tobacco. —**to have a screw loose** *Slang* To be mentally deranged, eccentric, etc. —**to put the screws on** (or **to**) *Slang* To exert pressure or force upon. —*v.t.* **1.** To tighten, fasten, attach, etc., by or as by a screw or screws. **2.** To turn or twist. **3.** To force as if by the pressure of a screw; urge: to *screw* one's courage to the sticking point. **4.** To twist out of shape; contort, as one's features. **5.** To practice oppression or extortion on; defraud. **6.** To obtain by extortion. **7.** *Slang* To copulate with. —*v.i.* **8.** To turn or admit of being turned as a screw. **9.** To be attached or become detached by means of a screw or screws: with *on, off,* etc. **10.** To have turns like those of a screw. **11.** To practice oppression or extortion. Abbr. *sc.* [Appar. < OF *escroue* nut, female screw, ? < L *scrofa* sow; infl. in OF by L *scrobis* vulva] —**screw'er** *n.*

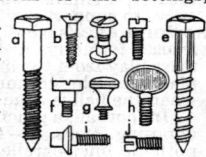

SCREWS

a Lag. *b* Wood. *c* Saw. *d* Fillister. *e* Skein. *f* Shoulder. *g,h* Thumbscrews. *i* Collar. *j* Slotted.

screw·ball (skrōō'bôl') *n.* **1.** In baseball, a pitch thrown with a wrist motion opposite to that used for the outcurve, and breaking sharply and often unpredictably. **2.** *U.S. Slang* An unconventional or erratic person.

screw bean **1.** A tree or shrub (*Strombocarpa* or *Prosopis odorata*) of the mimosa family bearing spiral pods used as fodder. **2.** The pod of this tree. Also called *mesquite.*

screw·driv·er (skrōō'drī'vər) *n.* **1.** A tool with a flattened metal end that fits into the slot of a screw in order to turn it. **2.** A cocktail consisting of vodka and orange juice.

screwed (skrōōd) *adj.* **1.** Having screw threads. **2.** *Brit. Slang* Intoxicated.

screw eye A screw having a head in the form of a ring.

screw jack A jackscrew.

screw log A patent log (which see).

screw·pile (skrōō'pīl') *n.* A pile having a strong metal base with a screw thread to ensure firm penetration of hard ground or bedrock.

screw pine A pandanus.

screw propeller A mechanism consisting of a revolving shaft with radiating blades set at an angle to produce a spiral action, used in propelling ships, etc.

screw thread **1.** The projecting spiral ridge of uniform pitch on the outer or inner surface of a screw or nut. **2.** A complete revolution of any point on this ridge.

screw·worm fly (skrōō'wûrm') A large, shiny, blue-green blowfly (genus *Cochliomyia*), whose larvae breed in living flesh; especially, a destructive cattle pest (*C. americana*) of the southern and western United States.

screw·y (skrōō'ē) *adj.* **screw·i·er, screw·i·est** *Slang* Extremely irrational; crazy.

Scria·bin (skryä'bĕn), **Aleksandr Nikolayevich,** 1872–1915, Russian composer.

scrib·ble (skrĭb'əl) *v.* **·bled, ·bling** *v.t.* **1.** To write hastily and carelessly. **2.** To cover with careless or illegible writing or marks. — *v.i.* **3.** To write in a careless or hasty manner. **4.** To make illegible or meaningless marks. — *n.* **1.** Hasty, careless writing. **2.** Meaningless lines and marks; any scrawl. [< Med.L *scribillare*, freq. of L *scribere* to write]

scrib·bler (skrĭb'lər) *n.* **1.** One who scribbles. **2.** A writer of no reputation; a petty or inferior author.

scribe (skrīb) *n.* **1.** One who writes or copies manuscripts. **2.** A clerk, public writer, or amanuensis. **3.** An author, penman, or journalist: used humorously. **4.** An ancient Jewish teacher, interpreter, or writer of the Mosaic law. **5.** A pointed instrument for marking wood, bricks, etc. — *v.* **scribed, scrib·ing** *v.t.* **1.** To mark or scratch with a pointed instrument. **2.** To write, inscribe, or engrave. **3.** In carpentry, to mark and fit closely. — *v.i.* **4.** *Rare* To write; work as a scribe. [< L *scriba* < *scribere* to write] — **scrib'al** *adj.*

Scribe (skrēb), **Augustin Eugène,** 1791–1861, French dramatist.

scrib·er (skrī'bər) *n.* Any sharp-pointed tool used in scribing on wood, etc.

scrieve (skrēv) *v.i.* **scrieved, scriev·ing** *Scot.* To glide swiftly along.

scrim (skrĭm) *n.* **1.** A lightweight, open-mesh, cotton fabric, usually white or ecru, used for draperies, etc. **2.** In the theater, a similar fabric, often painted, used as a transparency, to support artificial foliage, etc. [Origin unknown]

scrim·mage (skrĭm'ĭj) *n.* **1.** A rough-and-tumble contest; fracas; formerly, a skirmish. **2.** In American football, a mass play from the line of scrimmage after the ball has been placed on the ground and snapped back, the play ending when the ball is dead. **3.** In Rugby football, a scrummage. **4.** In football, a practice session or unofficial game played by opposing teams. — **line of scrimmage** In football, the hypothetic line, parallel to the goal lines, on which the ball rests and along which the opposing linemen take position at the start of play. — *v.t. & v.i.* **·maged, ·mag·ing** To engage in a scrimmage. Also *scrummage.* [Alter. of *scrimish*, var. of SKIRMISH]

scrimp (skrĭmp) *v.i.* **1.** To be very or overly economical. — *v.t.* **2.** To be overly sparing with, skimp. **3.** To cut too small, narrow, etc. — *adj.* Scanty; scrimpy. [Prob. akin to OE *scrimman* to shrink, shrivel]

scrimp·it (skrĭmp'ĭt) *adj.* *Scot.* Niggardly; scanty.

scrimp·y (skrĭmp'ē) *adj.* **·i·er, ·i·est** **1.** Scanty; skimpy; short. **2.** Tending to scrimp; niggardly. — **scrimp'i·ness** *n.*

scrim·shaw (skrĭm'shô) *v.t. & v.i.* To perform meticulous mechanical work; especially, to ornament (ivory, whale's teeth, etc.) by cutting or carving: a sailor's term. — *n.* A scrimshawed article, ornamented with fanciful carving. [? < *Scrimshaw*, a surname]

scrip[1] (skrĭp) *n.* **1.** A scrap of paper, especially one containing writing. **2.** A writing; a certificate, schedule, or written list. **3.** A piece of paper money less than a dollar, formerly issued in the United States: also called *shinplaster.* [< SCRIPT; prob. infl. in form by SCRAP]

scrip[2] (skrĭp) *n.* A provisional document (or documents collectively) certifying that the holder is entitled to receive something else, as shares of stock or land. [Short for obs. *subscription receipt*]

scrip[3] (skrĭp) *n.* A wallet or small bag. [Prob. fusion of ON *skreppa* a bag and OF *escrepe*, in phrase *escrepe et bordon* wallet and staff]

scrip dividend A distribution of surplus to stockholders in the form of scrip or promises to pay the amount of the dividend at a certain time.

Scripps (skrĭps), **Edward Wyllis,** 1854–1926, U.S. newspaper publisher and philanthropist.

scrip·sit (skrĭp'sĭt) *Latin* He (or she) wrote (it): used after an author's name on manuscripts, etc.

script (skrĭpt) *n.* **1.** Writing of the ordinary cursive form. **2.** Type, or printed or engraved matter, in imitation of handwriting. *This line is in script.* **3.** *Law* A writing, especially an original; in English practice, a will; codicil. **4.** A piece of writing; especially, a prepared copy of a play or dramatic role, for the use of actors. **5.** Alphabet; writing system: Greek *script*; phonetic *script*. — *v.t. & v.i.* *U.S. Informal* To prepare a script for (a radio, television, or theatrical performance). [< OF *escript* < L *scriptum*, neut. of pp. of *scribere* to write]

Script. Scriptural; Scripture(s).

scrip·to·ri·um (skrĭp·tôr'ē·əm, -tō'rē-) *n.* *pl.* **·ri·ums** or **·ri·a** (-rē·ə) The writing room of a monastery, where records, annals, and manuscripts were written, copied, or illuminated. [< Med.L < L *scriptus*, pp. of *scribere* to write]

scrip·tur·al (skrĭp'chər·əl) *adj.* Relating to writing; written. — **scrip'tur·al·ly** *adv.* — **scrip'tur·al·ness** *n.*

Scrip·tur·al (skrĭp'chər·əl) *adj.* Pertaining to, contained in, quoted from, or in accordance with the Scriptures. *Abbr. Script.* — **Scrip'tur·al·ly** *adv.* — **Scrip'tur·al·ness** *n.*

Scrip·ture (skrĭp'chər) *n.* **1.** The books of the Old and New Testaments, including often the Apocrypha. **2.** A text or passage from the Bible. *Abbr. Script.*

◆ Both the singular and plural forms of this word, taking singular and plural verbs respectively, are used to refer to the Bible. There is no difference in meaning, but the plural requires the definite article. *Scripture is* often quoted. *The Scriptures are* often quoted.

script·writ·er (skrĭpt'rī'tər) *n.* A writer who prepares copy for the use of an actor or announcer.

scrive (skrīv) *v.t.* **scrived, scriv·ing** **1.** To engrave. **2.** *Obs.* To write; scribe. [? < OF *escrivre* to write < L *scribere*]

scri·vel·lo (skri·vĕl'ō) *n.* *pl.* **·loes** or **·los** An elephant's tusk. [< Pg. *escrevelho*, ? var. of *escaravelho* pin, peg]

scriv·en·er (skrĭv'ən·ər, skrĭv'nər) *n.* *Archaic* **1.** One who prepares deeds, contracts, and other writings; a clerk or scribe. **2.** A notary. [< obs. *scrivein* < OF *escrivain* < Ital. *scrivano* < L *scribere* to write]

scro·bic·u·late (skrō·bĭk'yə·lĭt, -lāt) *adj.* *Biol.* Marked with many small depressions or pits. Also **scro·bic'u·lat'ed** (-lā'tĭd). [< L *scrobiculus*, dim. of *scrobis* trench]

scrod (skrŏd) *n.* A young codfish, especially when split and prepared for broiling. [? < MDu. *schrode* piece cut off. Akin to SHRED.]

scrof·u·la (skrŏf'yə·lə) *n.* *Pathol.* A tuberculous condition of the lymphatic glands, characterized by enlargement, suppurating abscesses, and cheeselike degeneration: also called *evil, king's evil, struma.* [Orig. pl. < LL *scrofulae*, dim. pl. of *scrofa* breeding sow; so called because sows were supposed to be subject to the disease]

scrof·u·lous (skrŏf'yə·ləs) *adj.* **1.** Pertaining to, affected with, or of the nature of scrofula. **2.** Morally corrupt; degraded. — **scrof'u·lous·ly** *adv.* — **scrof'u·lous·ness** *n.*

scrog·gy (skrŏg'ē) *adj.* **·gi·er, ·gi·est** *Scot. & Brit. Dial.* Stunted; dwarfed; shriveled; also, abounding with brushwood. [Prob. < Scand. Cf. Dan. *skrog* lean carcass.]

scroll (skrōl) *n.* **1.** A roll of parchment, paper, or the like, especially one containing or intended for writing; also, the writing on such a roll. **2.** Anything resembling or suggestive of a parchment roll; especially, a convoluted ornament or an ornamental space or tablet on sculptured work. **3.** The curved head of a violin or similar instrument. For illustration see VIOLIN. **4.** *Heraldry* A ribbon bearing a motto. [Earlier *scrowle*, alter. of obs. *scrow* < AF *escrowe* scroll; prob. infl. in form by ME *rowle* roll]

scroll saw A narrow-bladed hand or power saw for doing curved or irregular work.

scroll·work (skrōl'wûrk') *n.* Ornamental work of scroll-like pattern; especially, fanciful designs cut from thin material by means of scroll saws.

Scrooge (skrōōj), **Ebenezer** In Dickens's *A Christmas Carol*, a miser whose hard nature is transformed on Christmas Eve.

scroop (skrōōp) *v.i.* To give a harsh, scraping sound; grate. — *n.* A harsh, grating sound. [Imit.; infl. by SCRAPE]

scroph·u·lar·i·a·ceous (skrŏf'yə·lâr'ē·ā'shəs) *adj.* *Bot.* Of or pertaining to the figwort family (*Scrophulariaceae*) of herbs, shrubs, and trees. [< NL *Scrophularia*, type genus + -(A)CEOUS; so called from its supposed power to cure scrofula]

scro·tum (skrō'təm) *n.* *pl.* **·ta** (-tə), **·tums** *Anat.* The pouch of skin that contains the testicles in most mammals. [< L] — **scro'tal** *adj.*

scrouge (skrōōj, skrouj) *v.t.* **scrouged, scroug·ing** *Informal* or *Dial.* To squeeze; crowd; press. [Earlier *scruze*, prob. a blend of SCREW and SQUEEZE]

scrounge (skrounj) *v.t. & v.i.* **scrounged, scroung·ing** *Slang* **1.** To hunt about in order to take (something); pilfer. **2.** To mooch; sponge; beg. — *n.* One who scrounges: also **scroung'·er.** [? < dial. E *scrunge* to steal, var. of SCROUGE]

scrub[1] (skrub) *v.* **scrubbed, scrub·bing** *v.t.* **1.** To rub vigorously, as with the hand or a brush, in washing. **2.** To remove (dirt, etc.) by such action. **3.** To cleanse (a gas). **4.** *U.S. Slang* To cancel; call off. — *v.i.* **5.** To rub something vigorously, as in washing. — *n.* The act of scrubbing. [? < Scand. Cf. Dan. *skrubbe,* MDu. *shrubben.*]

scrub[2] (skrub) *n.* **1.** A stunted tree; also, such trees collectively. **2.** A thicket or tract of stunted trees or shrubs. **3.** A domestic animal of inferior breed. **4.** A poor, insignificant person. **5.** In sports, a player not on the varsity or regular team. **6.** A game, as of baseball, contrived hastily by a few players. — *adj.* **1.** Undersized or stunted-looking; inferior. **2.** Consisting of or participated in by untrained players or scrubs: *scrub* team; *scrub* game. [Dial. var. of SHRUB[1]]

scrub·ber (skrub'ər) *n.* **1.** One who or that which scrubs. **2.** Any apparatus that removes undesired material or impurities, especially from a gas.

scrub·by (skrub'ē) *adj.* **·bi·er, ·bi·est 1.** Of stunted growth. **2.** Covered with or consisting of scrub or underbrush. [< SCRUB[2]] — **scrub'bi·ness** *n.*

scrub grass The scouring rush.

scrub·land (skrub'land') *n.* Land covered with scrub.

scrub oak Any of various dwarf oaks of the United States.

scrub pine Any of several American pines having a tendency toward stunted or crowded growth.

scrub typhus *Pathol.* Tsutsugamushi disease.

scruff (skruf) *n.* The nape or outer back part of the neck. [Earlier *scuff,* ? < ON *skopt* hair; infl. in form by *scruff,* var. of SCURF]

scrum (skrum) *n. Brit. Informal* A scrummage.

scrum·mage (skrum'ij) *v.t. & v.i.* **·maged, ·mag·ing** To scrimmage. — *n.* **1.** A scrimmage. **2.** In Rugby football, a formation around the ball, out of which the ball is kicked to begin play. [Var. of SCRIMMAGE] — **scrum'mag·er** *n.*

scrump·tious (skrump'shəs) *adj. Slang* Elegant or stylish; fine; delightful; splendid. [Prob. alter. of SUMPTUOUS]

scrunch (skrunch) *v.t. & v.i.* To crush; squeeze; crunch. — *n.* A crunch. [Imit. alter. of CRUNCH]

scru·ple (skrōō'pəl) *n.* **1.** Doubt or uncertainty regarding a question of moral right or duty; reluctance arising from conscientious disapproval. **2.** An apothecaries' weight of twenty grains, or 1.296 grams (symbol: ℈). Abbr. *sc., scr.* See table inside back cover. **3.** A minute quantity. **4.** An ancient Roman coin. — *v.t. & v.i.* **·pled, ·pling** To have scruples (about); hesitate (to do) from motives of conscience. [< OF *scrupule* < L *scrupulus* small sharp stone]

scru·pu·lous (skrōō'pyə·ləs) *adj.* **1.** Cautious in action because of a wish to do right; nicely conscientious. **2.** Resulting from the exercise of scruples; exact; careful. — **Syn.** See METICULOUS. [< L *scrupulosus*] — **scru'pu·lous·ly** *adv.* — **scru'pu·los·i·ty** (-los'ə·tē), **scru'pu·lous·ness** *n.*

scru·ti·neer (skrōō'tə·nir') *n. Canadian* A party representative assigned to insure the fair conduct of a poll.

scru·ti·nize (skrōō'tə·nīz) *v.t.* **·nized, ·niz·ing** To observe carefully; examine in detail. Also *Brit.* **scru'ti·nise.** — **scru'ti·niz'er** *n.* — **scru'ti·niz'ing·ly** *adv.*

scru·ti·ny (skrōō'tə·nē) *n. pl.* **·nies 1.** The act of scrutinizing; close examination or investigation. **2.** A method of electing a pope by secret ballot. **3.** An official examination of votes after an election. [< OF *scrutinie* < LL *scrutinium* < L *scrutari* to examine]

scu·ba (skōō'bə, skyōō'-) *n. Sometimes cap.* An underwater breathing apparatus equipped with compressed-air tanks and needing no connection with the surface, worn by free divers. Also called *Aqua-Lung, aqualung.* [< *s(elf)-c(on-tained)* *u(nderwater)* *b(reathing)* *a(pparatus)*]

scud (skud) *v.i.* **scud·ded, scud·ding 1.** To move, run, or fly swiftly. **2.** *Naut.* To run rapidly before the wind; especially, to run before a gale with little or no sail set. — *n.* **1.** The act of scudding or moving swiftly. **2.** Light clouds driven rapidly before the wind; a misty rain. **3.** *Brit. Slang* A swift runner. [Prob. < Scand.; ? infl. in meaning by *scut,* in earlier sense of "hare"; ult. origin uncertain]

Scu·dé·ry (skü·dā·rē′), **Madeleine de,** 1607–1701, French novelist.

scu·do (skōō'dō) *n. pl.* **scu·di** (skōō'dē) A former Italian and Sicilian silver or gold coin. [< Ital. < L *scutum* shield]

scuff (skuf) *v.i.* **1.** To walk with a dragging movement of the feet; shuffle. — *v.t.* **2.** To scrape (the floor, ground, etc.) with the feet. **3.** To roughen or wear down the surface of by rubbing or scraping. — *n.* **1.** The act of scuffing; also, the noise so made. **2.** A flat slipper having no covering for the heel. [Prob. < ON *skúfa* to shove]

scuf·fle[1] (skuf'əl) *v.i.* **·fled, ·fling 1.** To struggle roughly or confusedly. **2.** To drag one's feet; shuffle. — *n.* A disorderly struggle; confused fracas. [Prob. freq. of SCUFF] — **scuf'fler** *n.*

scuf·fle[2] (skuf'əl) *n.* A form of hoe used by pushing in the manner of a spade. Also **scuffle hoe.** For illustration see HOE. [< Du. *schoffel* weeding hoe]

scul·dud·der·y (skul·dud'ər·ē) *n. pl.* **·der·ies** *Scot.* Obscenity.

scull[1] (skul) *n.* **1.** A long oar worked from side to side over the stern of a boat. **2.** A light, short-handled oar, used in pairs by one person. **3.** A small boat for sculling. — *v.t. & v.i.* To propel (a boat) by a scull or sculls. [ME *sculle, skulle;* origin unknown] — **scull'er** *n.*

scull[2] (skul) *n. Scot.* A large, shallow wicker basket.

scul·ler·y (skul'ər·ē) *n. pl.* **·ler·ies** A room where kitchen utensils are kept and cleaned; a back kitchen. [< OF *escuelerie* care of dishes < *escuelle* dish < L *scutella* tray]

scul·lion (skul'yən) *n. Archaic* **1.** A servant who washes and scours dishes, pots, and kettles. **2.** A base, contemptible person. [< OF *escouillon* mop < *escouve* broom < L *scopae* bundle of twigs, pl. of *scopa* twig]

sculp. or **sculpt. 1.** He (or she) carved it (L *sculpsit*). **2.** Sculptor; sculpture.

scul·pin (skul'pin) *n. pl.* **·pins** or **·pin 1.** One of several broad-mouthed fishes (family *Cottidae*), with a large, spiny head; especially, the **Arctic sculpin** (*Myoxocephalus scorpioides*), a common North Atlantic species. **2.** The California scorpion fish. See under SCORPION FISH. **3.** A worthless or contemptible fellow. [Prob. alter. of F *escorpene* < L *scorpaena* scorpionlike fish < Gk. *skorpaina* < *skorpios* scorpion]

sculp·sit (skulp'sit) *Latin* He (or she) sculptured (it). Abbr. *sc., sculp., sculpt.*

sculpt (skulpt) *v.t. & v.i. Informal* To sculpture. Also **sculp** (skulp). [Short for SCULPTURE]

sculp·tor (skulp'tər) *n.* One who creates sculpture by carving wood, modeling clay or plastics, working metal, or chiseling stone, etc. Abbr. *sculp., sculpt.* [< L < *sculpere* to sculpture] — **sculp'tress** (-tris) *n.fem.*

Sculp·tor (skulp'tər) *n.* A constellation, the **Sculptor's Workshop.** See CONSTELLATION.

sculp·ture (skulp'chər) *n.* **1.** The art of fashioning figures of wood, clay, plastics, metal, or stone. **2.** Figures or groups carved, cut, hewn, cast, or modeled in such materials. **3.** Raised or incised lines or markings, as upon a shell. — *v.t.* **·tured, ·tur·ing 1.** To fashion, as statuary, by modeling, carving, casting, or welding. **2.** To represent or portray in sculpture. **3.** To embellish with sculpture. **4.** To change, as the face of a valley or canyon, by erosion and deposition. Abbr. *sculp., sculpt.* [< L *sculptura* < *sculptus,* pp. of *sculpere* to carve in stone < *scalpere* to cut] — **sculp'tur·al** *adj.*

sculp·tur·esque (skulp'chə·resk') *adj.* Resembling sculpture; coldly, calmly, or grandly beautiful; statuesque. — **sculp'tur·esque'ly** *adv.* — **sculp'tur·esque'ness** *n.*

scum (skum) *n.* **1.** Impure or extraneous matter that rises to the surface of boiling or fermenting liquids. **2.** Minute vegetation on stagnant water. **3.** Scoria or dross of molten metals. **4.** Worthless element; refuse. **5.** A vile or worthless person or group of persons: often in the phrase **the scum of the earth.** — *v.* **scummed, scum·ming** *v.t.* **1.** To take scum from; skim. — *v.i.* **2.** To become covered with or form scum. [< MDu. *schuum*] — **scum'mer** *n.*

scum·ble (skum'bəl) *v.t.* **·bled, ·bling** In drawing and painting, to soften the outlines or blend the colors of by rubbing, as with comparatively dry or opaque color. **2.** To soften. **1.** The softening or blending of colors so produced. **2.** The material used in scumbling. [Freq. of SCUM]

scum·my (skum'ē) *adj.* **·mi·er, ·mi·est 1.** Covered with, containing, or resembling scum. **2.** Mean, vile; contemptible.

scun·ner (skun'ər) *Scot. v.i.* To feel loathing or disgust. — *n.* Loathing; abhorrence.

Scun·thorpe (skun'thôrp) A municipal borough in Humberside, England; pop. 70,880 (est. 1971). Formerly **Scunthorpe** and **Frod·ing·ham** (frod'ing·əm).

scup (skup) *n. pl.* **scup** or **scups** A sparoid food fish (*Stenotomus chrysops*) of the eastern coast of the United States: also called *porgy.* Also **scup·paug** (skup'ôg, skə·pôg'). [< Algonquian (Narraganset) *mishcup* < *mishe* large + *cuppi* scale]

scup·per[1] (skup'ər) *n. Naut.* A hole or gutter along the side of a ship's deck, to let water run off. [? Short for *scupper hole* < OF *escope* bailing scoop < Gmc. Akin to SCOOP.]

SCUP
(About 12 inches long)

scup·per[2] (skup'ər) *v.t. Brit. Slang* To massacre in a surprise attack; overwhelm and annihilate. [? < SCUPPER[1]]

scup·per·nong (skup'ər·nông, -nong) *n.* **1.** A variety of muscadine grape grown in the southern United States. **2.** A sweet, straw-colored wine made from this grape. [after the *Scuppernong* River in North Carolina]

scurf (skûrf) *n.* **1.** Loose outer skin thrown off in minute scales, as in dandruff. **2.** Any scaly matter adhering to a surface. [OE, alter. of *sceorf*; prob. < Scand. Cf. Dan. *skurv.*]

scurf·y (skûrf′ē) *adj.* **scurf·i·er, scurf·i·est** Covered with or resembling scurf. — **scurf′i·ness** *n.*

scur·ril·i·ty (skə-ril′ə-tē) *n. pl.* **·ties 1.** A scurrilous remark. **2.** The quality of being obscenely jocular. [< MF *scurrilité* < L *scurrilitas* < *scurrilis*. See SCURRILOUS.]

scur·ri·lous (skûr′ə·ləs) *adj.* **1.** Grossly and offensively abusive. **2.** Expressed with or given to coarse jocularity. Also **scur·rile** (skûr′il), **scur′ril.** [Earlier *scurrile* < L *scurrilis* buffoonlike < *scurra* buffoon] — **scur′ri·lous·ly** *adv.* — **scur′ri·lous·ness** *n.*

scur·ry (skûr′ē) *v.i.* **·ried, ·ry·ing** To move or go hurriedly; scamper. — *n. pl.* **·ries 1.** The act or sound of scurrying. **2.** A flurry, as of snow. **3.** A short, fast run or race on horseback. [Short for HURRY–SCURRY]

S-curve (es′kûrv′) *n.* A curve shaped like the letter S.

scur·vy (skûr′vē) *adj.* **·vi·er, ·vi·est 1.** Meanly low or contemptible; base. **2.** *Obs.* Scurfy; scabby. — *n. Pathol.* A disease caused by lack of vitamin C in the diet, and characterized by swollen and bleeding gums, and great prostration. ◆ Collateral adjective: *scorbutic.* [< SCURF] — **scur′vi·ly** *adv.* — **scur′vi·ness** *n.*

scurvy grass A biennial herb (*Cochlearia officinalis*), formerly believed to be a remedy for scurvy.

scut (skut) *n.* A short tail, as of a rabbit or deer. [ME, tail, hare, prob. < Scand. Cf. Icelandic *skott* fox's tail.]

scu·tage (skyoo′tij) *n.* In the feudal period, a tax exacted from knights in lieu of personal military service. [< Med.L *scutagium* < L *scutum* shield]

Scu·ta·ri (skoo′tä·rē) **1.** Üsküdar. **2.** A city in NW Albania (pop. about 41,000), at the SE end of **Lake Scutari,** a lake on the Albanian-Yugoslav border.

scu·tate (skyoo′tāt) *adj.* **1.** *Zool.* Covered with horny, shieldlike plates or large scales. **2.** *Bot.* Shaped like a shield. [< L *scutatus* provided with a shield < *scutum* shield]

scutch (skuch) *v.t.* **1.** To dress (textile fiber) by beating. **2.** To separate the woody parts from the valuable fiber of (flax, etc.) by beating. — *n.* An implement for scutching hemp and flax. [< OF *escousser* to shake] — **scutch′er** *n.*

scutch·eon (skuch′ən) *n.* **1.** An escutcheon. **2.** *Zool.* A scute. [Aphetic var. of ESCUTCHEON]

scute (skyoot) *n. Zool.* A horny plate or scale, as of a reptile. [< L *scutum* shield]

scu·tel·late (skyoo′tel·it, skyoo′tə·lāt) *adj. Zool.* **1.** Platterlike; shield-shaped. **2.** Covered with transverse scales; scutate. Also **scu′tel·lat·ed** (·tə-lā′tid). [< NL *scutellatus* < L *scutella* platter, dim. of *scutra* tray; infl. in meaning by L *scutum* shield]

scu·tel·la·tion (skyoo′tel·ə-lā′shən) *n. Zool.* The presence or arrangement of scales, as on a bird's tarsus and toes.

scu·tel·lum (skyoo·tel′əm) *n. pl.* **·la** (-lə) *Biol.* A small, shieldlike organ or part, as on the leg of a bird. [< NL, dim. of L *scutum* shield] — **scu·tel′lar** *adj.*

scu·ti·form (skyoo′tə-fôrm) *adj.* Shield-shaped. [< NL *scutiformis* < L *scutum* shield + *forma* form]

scut·ter (skut′ər) *Chiefly Brit. & Scot. v.i.* To scurry; scuttle. — *n.* A hasty running. [< SCUTT(LE)³ + -ER⁴]

scut·tle¹ (skut′l) *n.* **1.** A small opening or hatchway with a movable lid or cover, especially in the deck or side of a ship. **2.** The lid closing such an opening. **3.** A sea cock in the bottom of a ship. — *v.t.* **·tled, ·tling** To sink (a ship) by making holes in the bottom or by opening the sea cocks. [< MF *escoutille* hatchway < Sp. *escotilla*, prob. < Gmc.]

scut·tle² (skut′l) *n.* **1.** A metal vessel or hod for coal. **2.** A large, shallow basket for carrying grain, vegetables, etc. [OE *scutel* dish, platter < L *scutella*]

scut·tle³ (skut′l) *v.i.* **·tled, ·tling** To run in haste; scurry. — *n.* A hurried run or departure. [? Var. of *scuddle*, freq. of SCUD]

scut·tle·butt (skut′l·but) *n.* **1.** A drinking fountain aboard ship. **2.** Formerly, a cask containing the day's drinking water. **3.** *U.S. Slang* Rumor; gossip. [Orig. *scuttled butt* = a lidded cask for drinking water]

scu·tum (skyoo′təm) *n. pl.* **·ta** (-tə) **1.** *Zool.* A platelike piece or part, as in a turtle, fish, etc.; a large scale. **2.** In ancient Rome, the large oval or rectangular shield of the legionaries. [< L]

Scu·tum (skyoo′təm) *n.* A constellation, the Shield. See CONSTELLATION. [< L]

S.C.V. Sons of Confederate Veterans.

Scyl·la (sil′ə) In Greek mythology, a six-headed sea monster who dwelt in a cave on the Italian coast opposite the whirlpool Charybdis. See SCILLA. — **between Scylla and Charybdis** Between two dangers, where one cannot be avoided without incurring equally great peril from the other.

scy·phi·form (si′fi-fôrm) *adj. Biol.* Cup-shaped. [< SCYPHI- + FORM]

scypho- *combining form* Cup; vessel: also, before vowels, **scyph-.** Also **scyphi-.** [< L *scyphus* and Gk. *scyphos* cup]

scy·pho·zo·an (si′fə-zō′ən) *adj.* Of or pertaining to a class (*Scyphozoa*) of marine coelenterates including the medusa and jellyfish. — *n.* A scyphozoan coelenterate. [< NL < Gk. *skyphos* cup + *zoōn* animal]

Scy·ros (si′rəs) The Latin name for SKYROS.

scythe (sīth, *sometimes* sī) *n.* An implement used for mow-

ing, reaping, etc., consisting of a long, curved blade fixed at an angle to a long bent handle, or snath. — *v.t.* **scythed, scyth·ing** To cut or mow with or as with a scythe. [OE *sīthe*]

Scyth·i·a (sith′ē·ə) An ancient region of southern Europe, generally considered as lying north of the Black Sea.

Scyth·i·an (sith′ē·ən) *n.* **1.** One of an ancient nomadic people dwelling along the north shore of the Black Sea. **2.** The Iranian language of the Scythians. — *adj.* Of or pertaining to the Scythians, their land, or their language. [< L *Scythia* < Gk. *Skythia* < *Skythēs* Scythian]

sd. Sound.

s.d. Sine die.

S.D. 1. Doctor of Science (L *Scientiae Doctor*). **2.** *Stat.* Standard deviation: also **s.d.**

S.Dak. South Dakota: also **S.D.** (unofficial).

'sdeath (zdeth) *interj. Archaic* God's death: an imprecation.

Sdot Yam (sdôt yäm) A settlement in NW Israel, on the site of ancient Caesarea.

Se *Chem.* Selenium.

SDR or **S.D.R.** Special drawing rights (which see).

SE or **se, S.E.,** or **s.e.** Southeast; southeastern.

sea (sē) *n.* **1.** The great body of salt water covering the larger portion of the earth's surface; the ocean. **2.** A large or considerable body of oceanic water partly or almost entirely enclosed by land: the Adriatic *Sea.* **3.** A large inland body of water, salt or fresh: the Dead *Sea*; the *Sea* of Galilee. **4.** The swell of the ocean; the course, flow, or set of the waves. **5.** Anything that resembles or suggests the sea, as something vast, boundless, or widespread. Abbr. **S.** — **at sea 1.** On the ocean. **2.** At a loss; bewildered. — **to follow the sea** To follow the occupation of a sailor. — **to go to sea 1.** To become a sailor. **2.** To take an ocean voyage. — **to put to sea** To start on a voyage, as a ship. [OE *sæ*]

sea anchor A large canvas bag or sail dragged from the stern of a ship to reduce yawing, as in a gale: also called *drag anchor, drift anchor, drogue.*

sea anemone Any of various marine coelenterates (class *Anthozoa*), that attach themselves to rocks, etc., suggesting flowers by their coloring and outspread tentacles.

sea bag A cylindrical canvas bag, fastened with a drawstring, in which sailors stow their clothes.

sea bass 1. Any of various serranoid food fishes (genus *Centropristes* and related genera) of Atlantic waters; especially, the **black sea bass** (*C. striatus*), or blackfish. **2.** Any of various similar or related fishes, as the **giant sea bass** (*Stereolepis gigas*), and the **white sea bass** (*Cynoscion nobilis*) of Pacific waters.

SEA ANEMONE (3 to 5 inches high) *a* Tentacles contracted. *b* Tentacles extended.

Sea·bee (sē′bē′) *n.* A member of the Construction Battalions of the U.S. Navy, organized to build base facilities, airfields, etc. [< C(*onstruction*) B(*attalion*)]

sea bird Any of various birds frequenting the ocean or seacoast.

sea biscuit Hardtack.

sea·board (sē′bôrd′, -bōrd′) *n.* The seashore or seacoast; also, the land or region bordering the sea. — *adj.* Bordering on the sea. [ME < SEA + *board* border, OE *bord*]

Sea·borg (sē′bôrg), **Glenn Theodore,** born 1912, U.S. chemist; codiscoverer of plutonium.

sea bread An unsalted hard biscuit used at sea; hardtack.

sea bream Any of several sparoid food fishes, especially *Pagellus centrodontus,* a common Old World species.

sea breeze A cool breeze blowing from the ocean toward the land.

sea butterfly A pteropod.

sea calf The harbor seal.

sea captain The captain of a seagoing vessel.

sea·coast (sē′kōst′) *n.* The seashore; seaboard.

sea cock A cock or valve controlling connection with the water through a vessel's hull.

sea coconut The very large and heavy bilobate seed of a palm (*Lodoicea maldivica*) native to islands of the Indian Ocean.

sea cow 1. Any sirenian, as the manatee or the dugong. **2.** The walrus.

sea cucumber Any of a group of marine echinoderms (genera *Cucumaria* and *Thyone*) shaped like a cucumber.

sea·dog (sē′dôg′) *n.* A fogdog (which see).

sea dog 1. The harbor seal. **2.** The sea lion. **3.** An old or experienced sailor.

sea·drome (sē′drōm′) *n. Aeron.* An airport established at sea for the accommodation and servicing of aircraft making overseas flights. [< SEA + -DROME]

sea duck Any of various diving ducks, especially the eider.

sea eagle Any of various eagles that live principally on fish; especially, the **gray sea eagle** (*Haliaeetus albicilla*): sometimes called *erne.*

sea fan A coral (*Gorgonia flabellum*) of Florida and the West Indies, with fanlike branches.

sea·far·er (sē′fâr′ər) *n.* A seaman; a mariner. [< SEA + FARER]

sea·far·ing (sē′fâr′ing) *adj.* **1.** Following the sea as a calling. **2.** Traveling by sea. — *n.* **1.** Travel by sea. **2.** The calling of a seaman.

sea fight A conflict between vessels on the high seas.

sea·flow·er (sē′flou′ər) *n.* A sea anemone or related anthozoan.

sea foam **1.** Foam of the ocean. **2.** Meerschaum. **3.** A fluffy candy made of spun sugar.

sea·food (sē′fōod′) *n.* *U.S.* Edible fish, shellfish, etc. Also **sea food.**

sea·fowl (sē′foul′) *n.* A sea bird, or sea birds collectively.

sea front Land that borders on the sea; buildings, etc., that face the sea.

sea·girt (sē′gûrt′) *adj.* Surrounded by waters of the sea or ocean. [< SEA + GIRT²]

sea·go·ing (sē′gō′ing) *adj.* **1.** Adapted for use on the ocean. **2.** Seafaring.

sea green A deep bluish green, like the color of sea water.

sea gull Any gull or large tern.

sea hog A porpoise.

sea holly A European coarse herb (*Eryngium maritimum*) of the parsley family.

sea horse **1.** A marine fish (genus *Hippocampus*), having a prehensile tail and a head resembling that of a horse. **2.** A walrus. **3.** A fabulous animal, half horse and half fish, driven by Neptune. **4.** A large, white-crested wave.

Sea Island cotton A valuable long-staple variety of cotton (*Gossypium barbadense*) formerly grown on the Sea Islands, now also cultivated elsewhere.

Sea Islands A chain of small islands off the coast of South Carolina, Georgia, and northern Florida.

sea kale A hardy perennial herb (*Crambe maritima*) of the mustard family, cultivated for its edible young shoots.

sea king A viking pirate king of the Middle Ages.

seal¹ (sēl) *n.* **1.** An instrument or device used for making an impression upon some plastic substance, as wax or a wafer; also, the impression made. **2.** The wax, wafer, or similar token affixed to a document as a proof of authenticity; also, an impression, scroll, or mark on the paper. **3.** A substance employed to secure a letter, door, lid, wrapper, joint, etc., firmly. **4.** Anything that confirms or ratifies; a pledge; authentication. **5.** Any instrumentality that keeps something close, secret, or unknown. **6.** *Mech.* The fluid filling the trap of a drainage pipe and preventing the upward flow of gas. **7.** An ornamental stamp for packages, etc. — **under seal** Fastened or secured with an authoritative seal. — *v.t.* **1.** To affix a seal to, as to prove authenticity or prevent tampering. **2.** To stamp or impress a seal upon in order to attest to weight, quality, etc. **3.** To fasten or close with or as with a seal: to *seal* a letter; to *seal* a glass jar. **4.** To grant or assign under seal. **5.** To establish or settle finally; determine. **6.** In Mormon usage, to solemnize forever, as a marriage or the adoption of a child. **7.** To sign with the cross; also, to baptize or confirm. **8.** To secure, set, or fill up, as with plaster. **9.** *Mech.* To supply with a device or trap for preventing a return flow of gas or air. [< OF *seel* < L *sigillum* small picture, seal, dim. of *signum* sign] — **seal′a·ble** *adj.*

seal² (sēl) *n.* **1.** Any of a suborder (*Pinnipedia*) of aquatic carnivorous mammals mostly of northern latitudes, divided into the eared or fur seals, and the hair seals (which see). ◆ Collateral adjective: *phocine.* **2.** The fur of a fur seal; sealskin. **3.** Leather made from the hide of a seal. **4.** Any fur prepared so as to look like sealskin. — *v.i.* To hunt seals. [< OE *seolh*]

sea lavender Any of a genus (*Limonium*) of mostly Old World marine herbs bearing lavender-colored flowers.

sea lawyer *Informal* A sailor given to criticizing and querying at every opportunity.

seal brown A dark, slightly reddish brown color.

sealed orders Orders given under seal, as to the master of a ship, with instructions to open at a given time or place under specified conditions.

sea legs *Informal* The ability to walk aboard ship, especially in rough seas, without losing one's balance.

seal·er¹ (sē′lər) *n.* **1.** One who or that which seals. **2.** An officer who certifies weights, materials, etc. [< SEAL¹]

seal·er² (sē′lər) *n.* A person or ship employed in hunting seals. [< SEAL²]

seal·er·y (sē′lər·ē) *n. pl.* **·er·ies** **1.** The occupation of hunting seals. **2.** A place where seals are regularly hunted.

sea lettuce A green seaweed (genus *Ulva*) often used for food.

sea level **1.** The assumed mean level of the ocean surface, especially as used in determining elevation on maps, etc. **2.**

The actual mean level of the ocean surface as determined at a given point.

sea lily A crinoid resembling a flower.

sealing wax A mixture of shellac and resin with turpentine and pigment that is fluid when heated but becomes solid as it cools, used for sealing papers, packages, etc.

sea lion Any of various large, eared seals (family *Otariidae*); especially, the **California sea lion** (*Zalophus californianus*): also called *sea dog.*

seal ring A finger ring containing an engraved stone or signet: also called *signet ring.*

seal·skin (sēl′skin′) *n.* **1.** The under fur of the fur seal when prepared for use by removing the long hairs and dyeing dark brown or black. **2.** A coat, etc., made of this fur. — *adj.* Made of this fur.

Sea·ly·ham terrier (sē′lē·ham, -əm) A breed of terrier first developed at Sealyham, Wales, having short legs and a wiry, usually white coat.

seam (sēm) *n.* **1.** A visible line of junction between parts, especially the edges of two pieces of cloth sewn together. **2.** A crack; fissure. **3.** A ridge made in joining two pieces or left by a mold upon a casting. **4.** A scar or cicatrix; also, a wrinkle. **5.** A thin stratum of rock. **6.** A suture. — *v.t.* **1.** To unite by means of a seam. **2.** To mark with a cut, furrow, wrinkle, etc. **3.** In knitting, to give the appearance of a seam to; purl. — *v.i.* **4.** To crack open; become fissured. **5.** In knitting, to form seams. [OE *seam*] — **seam′er** *n.*

SEALYHAM TERRIER
(About 10½ inches high at shoulder)

sea-maid·en (sē′mād′n) *n.* *Poetic* A sea nymph or a mermaid. Also **sea′-maid′** (-mād′).

sea·man (sē′mən) *n. pl.* **·men** (-mən) **1.** One skilled in the work of a ship and the ways of the sea; a mariner; sailor: distinguished from *landsman.* **2.** *Naval* An enlisted man of any of the lowest grades, with a general apprenticeship in the broadest occupational area concerned with working and fighting on a ship. See tables at GRADE. — **sea′man·like** (-līk′) *adj.* — **sea′man·ly** *adj. & adv.*

sea·man·ship (sē′mən·ship) *n.* The skill and ability of a seaman in the operation and handling of a boat or ship.

sea·mark (sē′märk′) *n.* Any landmark that serves as a guide in navigation, as a beacon or lighthouse.

sea mew A gull, especially the common gull of Europe.

sea milkwort A succulent aquatic herb (*Glaux maritima*) of the primrose family, with small, whitish flowers.

seam·less (sēm′lis) *adj.* Having no seam.

sea monster **1.** Any huge, terrifying, or strange marine creature, as a devilfish or giant squid. **2.** A fabulous or mythical man-eating monster of the sea.

sea·mount (sē′mount′) *n.* *Geol.* A submarine mountain.

sea mouse Any of a genus (*Aphrodite*) of segmented marine worms with iridescent hairlike setae.

seam·stress (sēm′stris, *Brit.* sem′-) *n.* A woman skilled in needlework, especially one whose occupation is sewing. Also *sempstress.* [< OE *sēamestre* seamster + -ESS]

seam·y (sē′mē) *adj.* **seam·i·er, seam·i·est** **1.** Full of seams, as the wrong side of a garment. **2.** Showing the worst aspect: the *seamy* side. — **seam′i·ness** *n.*

Sean·ad Eir·eann (san′ad âr′ən) The Senate, or upper house, of the Irish parliament.

sé·ance (sā′äns, *Fr.* sā·äns′) *n.* **1.** A session or sitting. **2.** A meeting of persons seeking spiritualistic manifestations. [< F < OF *seoir* to sit < L *sedere*]

sea oat A tall, oatlike grass (*Uniola paniculata*) that grows along the coast in the southern United States.

Sea of, etc. See specific name, as (Sea of) AZOV.

sea onion Squill¹ (def. 1).

sea otter A large, nearly extinct otter (*Enhydra lutris*) of the North Pacific coast, having a valuable dark brown fur.

sea pen Any of various coelenterates (*Pennatula* and related genera) having a rodlike base with the polyps borne on lateral pinnae, giving the appearance of a feather.

sea·plane (sē′plān′) *n.* An airplane equipped with floats or a boatlike understructure to enable it to land on or take off from the water: also called *hydroplane.*

sea·port (sē′pôrt′, -pōrt′) *n.* **1.** A harbor or port on a coast accessible to seagoing ships. **2.** A town located on such a harbor. *Abbr.* spt.

sea power **1.** A nation of great naval importance. **2.** The naval strength of a nation.

sea purse *Zool.* The horny capsule enclosing the eggs of certain sharks, skates, and rays.

sea·quake (sē′kwāk′) *n.* A seismic disturbance of the ocean floor.

SEA PURSE
(Partially cut away to show embryo)

sear¹ (sir) *v.t.* **1.** To wither; dry up. **2.** To burn the surface of; scorch. **3.** To burn or cauterize, as with a hot iron; brand. **4.** To make callous; harden. — *v.i.* **5.** *Obs.*

SEA HORSE
(2 to 12 inches long)

To become withered; dry up. — *adj. Poetic* Dried or blasted; withered. — *n.* A scar or brand. Also spelled *sere.* [OE *sēarian* to wither < *sēar* dry]

sear² (sir) *n.* The pawl in a gunlock that holds the hammer at half or full cock. For illustration see REVOLVER. [< OF *serre* grasp < *serrer* to close, press < LL *serrare* to bolt, bar < L *serare* to bolt, bar < *sera* lock; infl. in LL by L *serrare* to saw]

sea raven A large marine sculpin (*Hemitripterus americanus*) of the North American Atlantic coast.

search (sûrch) *n.* **1.** The act of seeking or looking diligently. **2.** Investigation; inquiry. **3.** A critical examination or scrutiny. **4.** *Law* Right of search. — *v.t.* **1.** To look through or explore thoroughly in order to find something; go over or through in making a search. **2.** To subject (a person) to an examination of his clothing or personal effects, as for concealed weapons, etc. **3.** To examine with close attention; probe. **4.** To penetrate or pierce. **5.** To learn by examination or investigation: with *out.* — *v.i.* **6.** To make a search. [< OF *cercher* < L *circare* to go round, explore < *circus* ring] — **search'a·ble** *adj.* — **search'er** *n.*

search·ing (sûr'ching) *adj.* **1.** Investigating minutely. **2.** Keenly penetrating; observant: a *searching* gaze. — **search'·ing·ly** *adv.* — **search'ing·ness** *n.*

search·light (sûrch'līt') *n.* **1.** An apparatus containing a reflector and an intensely brilliant light that may be thrown in various directions for search or signaling. **2.** The beam of light from this apparatus.

search warrant A warrant authorizing an officer to search a house or other specified place for things alleged to be unlawfully concealed there.

sea risk Danger or hazard at sea in traveling or transporting cargo.

sea robin A fish, one of various gurnards, especially the American brown-finned species (*Prionotus evolans*).

sea room Sufficient space for a vessel to be maneuvered.

sea·scape (sē'skāp') *n.* **1.** An ocean view. **2.** A picture presenting a marine view. [< SEA + (LAND)SCAPE]

sea·scout·ing (sē'skou'ting) *n.* Training in seamanship given to older Boy Scouts, called **Sea Scouts.**

sea serpent An imaginary snakelike animal, of monstrous size, believed by many to inhabit the ocean.

sea·shell (sē'shel') *n.* The shell of any marine mollusk.

sea·shore (sē'shôr', -shōr') *n.* **1.** Land adjacent to or bordering on the ocean. **2.** *Law* The ground between high- and low-water marks.

sea·sick (sē'sik') *adj.* Suffering from seasickness.

sea·sick·ness (sē'sik'nis) *n.* Nausea, dizziness, and prostration caused by the motion of a vessel at sea.

sea·side (sē'sīd') *n.* The seashore, especially as a place of resort. — *adj.* Of or pertaining to the seashore.

sea snake Any of several venomous fish-eating snakes (subfamily *Hydrophinae*) of tropical seas.

sea·son (sē'zən) *n.* **1.** A division of the year as determined by the earth's position with respect to the sun, and as marked by the temperature, moisture, vegetation, etc. **2.** A period of time. **3.** Any of the periods into which the Christian year is divided. **4.** A period of special activity: usually with the definite article: the hunting *season.* **5.** A fit or suitable time. **6.** That which imparts relish; seasoning. — **in season 1.** In condition and obtainable for use: Clams are *in season* during the summer. **2.** In good or sufficient time; opportunely. **3.** Legally permitted to be killed or taken, as game. **4.** Ready to mate or breed: said of animals. — *v.t.* **1.** To increase the flavor or zest of (food), as by adding spices, etc. **2.** To add zest or piquancy to. **3.** To render more suitable for use, especially by drying or hardening, as timber. **4.** To make accustomed or inured; harden: to *season* troops. **5.** To mitigate or soften; moderate. — *v.i.* **6.** To become seasoned. [< OF *seson* < LL *satio, -onis* sowing time < L, a sowing < *satus,* pp. of *serere* to sow] — **sea'son·er** *n.*

sea·son·a·ble (sē'zən·ə·bəl) *adj.* **1.** Being in keeping with the season. **2.** Done at the proper time. — **sea'son·a·ble·ness** *n.* — **sea'son·a·bly** *adv.*

sea·son·al (sē'zən·əl) *adj.* Characteristic of, affected by, or occurring at a certain season. — **sea'son·al·ly** *adv.*

sea·son·er (sē'zən·ər) *n. U.S.* One engaged to serve for the season on a fishing vessel.

sea·son·ing (sē'zən·ing) *n.* **1.** The act or process by which something, as lumber, is rendered fit for use. **2.** Something added to food to give relish; especially, a condiment. **3.** Something added to increase enjoyment, zest, etc.

season ticket A ticket or pass, usually at a reduced rate, entitling the holder to daily trips on a train for a certain period or to admission to a series of sporting events, etc.

sea squirt An ascidian.

seat (sēt) *n.* **1.** That on which one sits, as a chair, bench, or stool. **2.** The part of a thing upon which one rests in sitting, or upon which an object or another part rests. **3.** The buttocks; also, the portion of a garment covering them. **4.** The place where anything is situated, settled, or established: the *seat* of pain; the *seat* of a government. **5.** A place of abode; an estate or mansion, especially a country estate. **6.** The privilege or right of membership in a legislative

body, stock exchange, etc. **7.** The manner of sitting, as on horseback. **8.** A surface or part upon which the base of anything rests. **9.** A position in a legislature or an office. — *v.t.* **1.** To place on a seat or seats; cause to sit down. **2.** To have seats for; furnish with seats: The theater *seats* only 299 people. **3.** To put a seat on or in; renew or repair the seat of. **4.** To locate, settle, or center: usually in the passive: The French government is *seated* in Paris. **5.** To fix or set firmly or in place. [< ON *sǣti.* Akin to SIT.]

sea tangle Any of various large brown seaweeds (genus *Laminaria*) of the temperate zones.

seat belt A safety belt (def. 2).

seat·ing (sē'ting) *n.* **1.** The act of providing with seats. **2.** Fabric for upholstering seats. **3.** The arrangement of seats, as in a room, auditorium, etc.

SEATO (sē'tō) Southeast Asia Treaty Organization.

sea train A sea-going ship equipped to carry railroad cars.

sea trout 1. A trout that descends to the sea after spawning. **2.** Any of several fishes (genus *Cynoscion*) of the drum family, frequenting coastal waters of the eastern United States: also called *squeteague.*

seat·stone (sēt'stōn') *n.* Underclay.

Se·at·tle (sē·at'l) A port city in west central Washington, on Puget Sound; pop. 538,831.

sea urchin Any echinoderm (class *Echinoidea*) having a soft rounded body covered with a shell bearing numerous movable spines: also called *echinus.*

sea wall A wall or an embankment to prevent the encroachments of the sea, the erosion of the shore, etc.

sea walnut Any of various ctenophores having an ovate body, especially of the genus *Pleurobrachia.*

sea·wan (sē'wən) *n.* An oblong bead made from shell, used by the Algonquian Indians of North America as money; wampum: also spelled *sewan.* Also **sea'want** (-wənt). [< Algonquian (Narraganset) *seawohn* scattered, i.e., unstrung (shell beads)]

sea·ward (sē'wərd) *adj.* **1.** Going toward the sea. **2.** Blowing, as wind, from the sea. — *adv.* In the direction of the sea: also **sea'wards** (-wərdz).

sea·ware (sē'wâr') *n.* Seaweed, especially that used as fertilizer. [OE *sǣwār* < *sǣ* sea + *wār* alga]

sea·way (sē'wā') *n.* **1.** A way or lane over the sea. **2.** An inland waterway that receives ocean shipping. **3.** The headway made by a ship. **4.** A rough sea: usually in *in a seaway.*

sea·weed (sē'wēd') *n.* **1.** Any of a widely distributed class (*Algae*) of plants growing in the sea, including the kelps, rockweeds, dulse, etc. **2.** Any marine plant.

sea·wor·thy (sē'wûr'thē) *adj.* In fit condition for a voyage: said of a vessel. — **sea'wor'thi·ness** *n.*

sea wrack Seaweed, especially a kelp or other large species.

se·ba·ceous (si·bā'shəs) *adj. Physiol.* **1.** Pertaining to, like, or having the nature of fat. **2.** Secreting fat. [< NL *sebaceus* < L *sebum* tallow]

sebaceous glands Any of the glands in the corium of the skin that secrete sebum.

se·bac·ic acid (si·bas'ik, -bā'sik) A white crystalline acid, $C_{10}H_{18}O_4$, obtained from castor oil and used in the manufacture of synthetic resins. [< SEBAC(EOUS) + -IC]

Se·bas·to·pol (si·bas'tə·pōl) See SEVASTOPOL.

Se·bat (shi·bät') See SHEBAT.

sebi- *combining form* Fat; fatty matter: *sebiferous:* also, before vowels, **seb-.** Also **sebo-.** [< L *sebum* tallow]

se·bif·er·ous (si·bif'ər·əs) *adj.* Secreting or producing fat or fatty matter: *sebaceous:* also *sebiferous* glands. Also **se·bip·a·rous** (si·bip'ər·əs). [< SEBI- + -FEROUS]

seb·or·rhe·a (seb'ə·rē'ə) *n. Pathol.* An abnormal increase of secretion from the sebaceous glands. Also **seb'or·rhoe'a.** [< L *sebum* tallow + -RRHEA]

se·bum (sē'bəm) *n. Physiol.* A fatty matter secreted by the sebaceous glands. [< L, tallow]

sec (sek) *adj. French* Dry: said of wines. Also *Italian* **sec·co** (sek'kō).

sec. 1. According to (L *secundum*). **2.** Secant. **3.** Second(s). **4.** Secondary. **5.** Secretary. **6.** Section(s). **7.** Sector.

SEC or S.E.C. Securities and Exchange Commission.

se·cant (sē'kənt, -kant) *adj.* Cutting, especially into two parts; intersecting. — *n.* **1.** *Geom.* **a** A straight line intersecting a given curve. **b** A line drawn from the center of a circle through one extremity of an arc to the tangent drawn from the other extremity of the same arc. **2.** *Trig.* A function of an acute angle, equal to the ratio of the hypotenuse to the side adjacent to the angle when the angle is included in a right triangle; also, a function of any angle, equal to the distance of a point from the origin divided by the abscissa of the point when the point is plotted on Cartesian coordinates and the point is on the line forming the angle with the X-axis. For illustration see TRIGONOMETRIC FUNCTIONS. Abbr. *sec.* [< L *secans, -antis,* ppr. of *secare* to cut]

se·cede (si·sēd') *v.i.* **·ced·ed, ·ced·ing** To withdraw formally from a union, fellowship, or association, especially from a political or religious organization. [< L *secedere* < *se-* apart + *cedere* to go] — **se·ced'er** *n.*

se·cern (si-sûrn′) *v.t.* **1.** To discriminate or distinguish. **2.** *Physiol.* To secrete: said of a gland or follicle. [< L *secernere* < *se-* apart + *cernere* to separate]

se·ces·sion (si-sesh′ən) *n.* **1.** The act of seceding; withdrawal from fellowship, especially from political or religious association. **2.** *Usually cap. U.S.* The withdrawal of the Southern States from the Union in 1860–61. [< L *secessio, -onis* < *secedere*. See SECEDE.] — **se·ces′sion·al** *adj.*

se·ces·sion·ism (si-sesh′ən-iz′əm) *n. U.S.* During the Civil War, the principles and doctrines of those who favored the withdrawal of the Southern States from the Union. — **se·ces′sion·ist** *adj. & n.*

Seck·el (sek′əl, sik′əl) *n.* A variety of small, sweet pear: sometimes called *sickle pear.* [after the Pennsylvania farmer who introduced it]

se·clude (si-klōōd′) *v.t.* **·clud·ed, ·clud·ing 1.** To remove and keep apart from the company or society of others; isolate. **2.** To screen or shut off, as from view. [< L *secludere* < *se-* apart + *claudere* to shut]

se·clud·ed (si-klōō′did) *adj.* **1.** Separated; withdrawn; living apart from others. **2.** Protected or screened. — **se·clud′ed·ly** *adv.* — **se·clud′ed·ness** *n.*

se·clu·sion (si-klōō′zhən) *n.* **1.** The act of secluding, or the state or condition of being secluded; solitude; retirement. **2.** A secluded place. [< Med.L *seclusio, -onis* < L *secludere*. See SECLUDE.]

se·clu·sive (si-klōō′siv) *adj.* Having a tendency to seclusion. — **se·clu′sive·ly** *adv.* — **se·clu′sive·ness** *n.*

sec·ond¹ (sek′ənd) *n.* **1.** A unit of time, ⅟₆₀ of a minute. **2.** *Geom.* A unit of angular measure, ⅟₆₀ of a minute of arc. Symbol: ″. Abbr. *s., sec.* [< OF *seconde* < Med.L *seconda,* fem. of L *secundus.* See SECOND².]

sec·ond² (sek′ənd) *adj.* **1.** Next in order, authority, responsibility, etc., after the first: the ordinal of *two.* **2.** Ranking next to or below the first or best; of inferior quality or value; secondary; subordinate. **3.** Identical in character with another or preceding one; another; other. **4.** *Music* Designating one of two parts for like instruments or voices, usually the one lower in pitch or in some manner subordinate. **5.** *Mech.* Pertaining to the forward gears with the second highest ratio in an automobile transmission. — *n.* **1.** The one next after the first in position, rank, importance, or quality. **2.** An attendant who supports or aids another, as in a duel. **3.** *pl.* Articles of merchandise of imperfect manufacture, of second grade, or of inferior quality. **4.** *Music* **a** The interval between any note and the next above or below in the diatonic scale. For illustration see INTERVAL. **b** A note separated by this interval from any other. **c** Two notes at this interval written or sounded together. **d** The resulting dissonance. **e** A second or subordinate part, instrument, or voice. **5.** In parliamentary law, an utterance whereby a motion is seconded: Do I hear a *second?* **6.** *Mech.* The forward gears with the second highest ratio in an automobile transmission. — *v.t.* **1.** To act as a supporter or assistant of; promote; encourage. **2.** In deliberative bodies, to support formally, as a motion, resolution, etc., as a prerequisite to discussion or adoption. — *adv.* In the second order, place, or rank: also, in formal discourse, **sec′ond·ly.** [< OF < L *secundus* following < *sequi* to follow]

Second Advent The expected second coming of Christ. Also **Second Coming.** — **Second Adventist.**

sec·on·dar·y (sek′ən-der′ē) *adj.* **1.** Of second rank, grade, or influence; subordinate; auxiliary; subsequent; resultant. **2.** Depending on what is primary or original: *secondary* sources. **3.** *Ornithol.* Of or pertaining to the secondaries of a bird's wings. **4.** *Electr.* Of, pertaining to, or noting an induced current or its circuit, especially in an induction coil. **5.** *Chem.* Formed by replacement of atoms or radicals in the molecules of certain organic compounds: a *secondary* alcohol. **6.** *Geol.* Subsequent in origin; involving some chemical or physical change of the original mineral. **7.** Pertaining to instruction in a secondary school. — *n. pl.* **·dar·ies 1.** One who acts in a secondary or subordinate capacity; an assistant; a deputy or delegate. **2.** Anything of secondary size, position, or importance. **3.** *Ornithol.* One of the feathers that grow on the second joint or forearm of a bird's wing. See illustrations under BIRD, FOWL. **4.** *Entomol.* One of the hind wings of an insect. **5.** In football, the defensive backfield. Abbr. *sec.* — **sec′on·dar′i·ly** *adv.*

secondary accent See under ACCENT.

secondary cell *Electr.* A type of cell that can be recharged by the passage of direct current in reverse direction through the electrolyte: also called *storage cell.*

secondary color A color obtained by mixing certain primary colors together in equal proportions.

secondary education High school or preparatory school education between the elementary and college levels.

secondary emission *Physics* The emission of electrons from a substance exposed to direct impact of electrons or ions, as by X-rays, etc.: also called *reradiation.* Also **secondary radiation.**

secondary school A high school or preparatory school intermediate between the elementary school and college.

second base In baseball, the base situated between first and third base. See illustration at BASEBALL.

second base·man (bās′mən) *n. pl.* **·men** (-mən) A baseball player stationed at or near second base.

sec·ond-best (sek′ənd-best′) *adj.* Next to the best.

second childhood Senility; dotage.

sec·ond-class (sek′ənd-klas′, -kläs′) *adj.* **1.** Ranking next below the first or best; inferior; mediocre. **2.** Of or pertaining to travel accommodations ranking between first class and third class. **3.** Of or pertaining to a class of mail including all printed periodicals. — *adv.* By second-class ticket or by using second-class conveniences.

se·conde (si-kond′, *Fr.* sə-gônd′) *n.* The second of eight positions in fencing. [< F]

second estate The nobility.

second fiddle 1. The part played by the second violin or violins in an orchestral composition, string quartet, etc. **2.** Any secondary status; a substitute. — **to be** (or **play**) **second fiddle** To be of secondary importance in an undertaking or in the affections of another.

sec·ond-guess (sek′ənd-ges′) *v.t.* **1.** To judge or conjecture about (something) after it has occurred. **2.** To make subsequent conjectures or judgments about the actions, decisions, etc., of. — *v.i.* To form opinions, etc., after the event. — **sec′ond-guess′er** *n.*

sec·ond·hand (sek′ənd-hand′) *adj.* **1.** Having been previously owned, worn, or used by another; not new. **2.** Received from another; not direct from the original source: *secondhand* information. **3.** Handling or dealing in merchandise that is not new: *secondhand* furniture dealer.

second hand The hand that marks the seconds on a clock or a watch.

sec·on·dine (sek′ən-dīn, -din) See SECUNDINE.

second lieutenant *Mil.* The lowest grade of commissioned officer, ranking below first lieutenant.

second mortgage A mortgage given next after and subordinate to a first mortgage.

second nature A disposition or character that is acquired and not innate; deep-seated habits that have become fixed.

second papers A popular name for a certificate of naturalization.

sec·ond-rate (sek′ənd-rāt′) *adj.* Second in quality, size, rank, importance, etc.; second-class. — **sec′ond-rat′er** *n.*

Second Reader In Christian Science services, a person chosen to assist the First Reader by reading aloud selections from the Bible.

Second Republic The republic established in France in 1848 on the abdication of Louis Philippe when Louis Napoleon was elected president, and succeeded in 1852 by the Second Empire under Napoleon III.

second sight The alleged power of seeing events occurring at distant places, in the future, etc.; clairvoyance.

second sound *Physics* A vibratory motion resembling that of sound waves, associated with a superfluid.

sec·ond-sto·ry man (sek′ənd-stôr′ē, -stō′rē) *U.S. Slang* A burglar.

second-string (sek′ənd-string′) *adj. U.S. Informal* **1.** In sports, ranking next to the regular or starting player or team. **2.** Second-rate.

Second World War See WORLD WAR II in table for WAR.

sec·par (sek′pär) *n. Astron.* Parsec (which see). [< *sec(ond)* of) *par(allax)*]

se·cre·cy (sē′krə-sē) *n. pl.* **·cies 1.** The condition or quality of being secret or hidden; concealment. **2.** The character of being secretive; secretiveness. **3.** Privacy; retirement; solitude. Also **se·cret·ness** (sē′krit-nis). [ME *secretee*; refashioned after *primacy, lunacy,* etc.]

se·cret (sē′krit) *adj.* **1.** Kept separate or hidden from view or knowledge, or from all persons except the individuals concerned; concealed; hidden. **2.** Beyond normal comprehension; obscure; recondite. **3.** Known or revealed only to the initiated; mystic: *secret* rites. **4.** Affording privacy; secluded. **5.** Good at keeping secrets; close-mouthed. **6.** Unrevealed or unavowed as such: a *secret* partner. **7.** *U.S. Mil.* Denoting the second highest category of security classification. Compare TOP-SECRET, CONFIDENTIAL. — *n.* **1.** Something not to be told. **2.** A thing undiscovered or unknown. **3.** An underlying reason; that which, when known, explains; key. **4.** A secret contrivance. **5.** Secrecy. — **in secret** In privacy; in a hidden place. [< OF *secret* < L *secretus,* pp. of *secernere* < *se-* apart + *cernere* to separate] — **se′cret·ly** *adv.*

sec·re·tar·i·at (sek′rə-târ′ē-it, -at) *n.* **1.** A secretary's position. **2.** The place where a secretary transacts his business and preserves his official records. **3.** The executive department of a governmental organization, especially of the United Nations. Also **sec′re·tar′i·ate.** [< F *secrétariat* < Med.L *secretariatus* the office of secretary < *secretarius.* See SECRETARY.]

sec·re·tar·y (sek′rə·ter′ē) *n. pl.* **·tar·ies** **1.** A person employed to deal with correspondence, keep records, and handle clerical business for an individual, business, committee, etc. **2.** An executive officer presiding over and managing a department of government. **3.** A writing desk with a bookcase or cabinet with pigeonholes on top. Abbr. *sec.,* *secy,* *sec′y* [< Med.L *secretarius* < L *secretum* secret, neut. of *secretus*] — **sec′re·tar′i·al** (-târ′ē·əl) *adj.*

secretary bird A South African bird (*Sagittarius serpentarius*) that feeds largely on reptiles and has long legs and a crested head: so named from the resemblance of its crest to quill pens stuck behind the ear.

secretary general *pl.* **secretaries general** A chief secretary; an assistant to a governor general. — **sec′re·tar′y-gen′er·al·cy** (-jen′ər·əl·sē) *n.*

sec·re·tar·y·ship (sek′rə·ter′ē·ship) *n.* The work or position of a secretary.

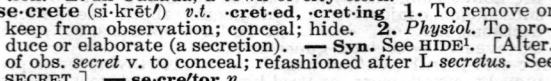

sec·re·tar·y-treas·ur·er (sek′rə·ter′ē·trezh′ər·ər) *n.* **1.** One who performs the combined duties of secretary and treasurer; especially, an official in an organization. **2.** In Canada, a town or city clerk.

SECRETARY BIRD
(About 4 feet high)

se·crete (si·krēt′) *v.t.* **·cret·ed, ·cret·ing** **1.** To remove or keep from observation; conceal; hide. **2.** *Physiol.* To produce or elaborate (a secretion). — **Syn.** See HIDE¹. [Alter. of obs. *secret* v. to conceal; refashioned after L *secretus.* See SECRET.] — **se·cre′tor** *n.*

se·cre·tin (si·krē′tin) *n. Biochem.* A hormone produced in the lining of the small intestine and serving to stimulate the flow of pancreatic juice. [< SECRET(ION) + -IN]

se·cre·tion (si·krē′shən) *n. Physiol.* **1.** The process, generally a glandular function, by which materials are separated from the blood and elaborated into new substances, as bile, milk, etc. **2.** The substance secreted. [< OF *secretion* < L *secretio, -onis* < *secernere.* See SECRET.]

se·cre·tive (si·krē′tiv; *for def. 1, also* sē′krə·tiv) *adj.* **1.** Inclined to secrecy; reticent. **2.** *Physiol.* Producing or causing secretion. — **Syn.** See TACITURN. — **se·cre′tive·ly** *adv.* — **se·cre′tive·ness** *n.*

se·cre·to·ry (si·krē′tər·ē) *adj.* **1.** Pertaining to secretion. **2.** Performing the function of secretion. — *n. pl.* **·ries** A secreting organ or gland.

secret police A police force working clandestinely, especially to detect and repress activities against the state.

secret service **1.** Investigation conducted secretly for a government. **2.** The secret or espionage work of various government agencies in time of war.

Secret Service A section of the Department of the Treasury concerned with the suppression of counterfeiting, the protection of the President of the United States, etc.

secret society A society or association that uses secret signs, oaths, rites, or symbols.

sect (sekt) *n.* **1.** A body of persons distinguished by peculiarities of faith and practice from other bodies adhering to the same general system; especially, the adherents collectively of a particular religious creed or confession; a denomination. **2.** Adherents of a particular philosophical system or teacher. **3.** Any number of persons united in opinion or interest, as in the state or in society; a party or faction; an order. **4.** A cutting in horticulture. — **Syn.** See RELIGION. [< OF *secte* < L *secta* < *sequi* to follow. Doublet of SET.]

-sect *combining form* To cut; divide (in a specified manner or number of parts): *vivisect, bisect.* [< L *sectus,* pp. of *secare* to cut]

sect. Section; sectional.

sec·tar·i·an (sek·târ′ē·ən) *adj.* **1.** Pertaining to or belonging to a particular sect. **2.** Adhering or confined to a specific group, party, etc.; partisan. — *n.* A member of a sect, especially if bigoted.

sec·tar·i·an·ism (sek·târ′ē·ən·iz′əm) *n.* Sectarian character or tendency; excessive devotion to or zeal for a particular sect, group, party, etc.

sec·tar·i·an·ize (sek·târ′ē·ən·īz′) *v.t.* **·ized, ·iz·ing** To make sectarian.

sec·ta·ry (sek′tər·ē) *n. pl.* **·ries** **1.** A sectarian. **2.** A dissenter from an established church; a nonconformist. **3.** *Obs.* A religious sect. Also **sec′ta·rist.** [< MF *sectaire* or Med.L *sectarius* < L *secta.* See SECT.]

sec·tile (sek′til) *adj.* Capable of being cut or severed smoothly. [< F < L *sectilis* < *secare* to cut] — **sec·til·i·ty** (sek·til′ə·tē) *n.*

sec·tion (sek′shən) *n.* **1.** A separate part or division; as: **a** A portion of a book, treatise, or writing. **b** A subdivision of a chapter. **c** A division of law. **2.** A distinct part of a country, community, etc. **3.** *U.S.* An area of public land one mile square, containing 640 acres and constituting ¹⁄₃₆ of a township. **4.** A portion of a railway company's tracks under the care of a particular set of men. **5.** In a sleeping car, a space containing two berths. **6.** *Mil.* A tactical unit of the U.S. Army, smaller than a platoon and larger than a squad. **7.** *Naval* A tactical unit of ships within a division. **8.** A

representation, picture, or drawing of a building, machine, geological formation, etc., as if cut by an intersecting plane; also, the thing so cut or viewed. **9.** *Biol.* A very thin slice of anything, especially for microscopic examination. **10.** The character §, indicating a subdivision: used also as a reference mark. **11.** The act of cutting; division by cutting, as in surgical operations. **12.** *Geom.* The figure formed by the intersection of a plane or other surface with a solid. — **Syn.** See PORTION. — *v.t.* **1.** To cut or divide into sections. **2.** To shade (a drawing) so as to designate a section or sections. Abbr. *s., sec., sect.* [< MF or L *sectio, -onis* < *secare* to cut]

-section *combining form* The act or process of cutting or dividing: *vivisection.* [< L. See SECTION.]

sec·tion·al (sek′shən·əl) *adj.* **1.** Pertaining to a section, as of a country; local; characteristic of the people of a certain section or area; regional: a *sectional* dialect. **2.** Dividing or alienating one section from another: *sectional* problems. **3.** Made up of sections. — *n. U.S.* A long sofa or divan composed of several units that also may be used separately. Abbr. *sect.* — **sec′tion·al·ly** *adv.*

sec·tion·al·ism (sek′shən·əl·iz′əm) *n.* Regard for a particular section of the country rather than the whole; sectional feeling; intense consciousness of sectional differences. — **sec′tion·al·ist** *n.*

sec·tion·al·ize (sek′shən·əl·īz′) *v.t.* **·ized, ·iz·ing** **1.** To make sectional. **2.** To divide into sections. — **sec′tion·al·i·za′tion** *n.*

section boss The foreman in charge of a section gang.

section gang *U.S.* A railroad work crew.

sec·tor (sek′tər) *n.* **1.** *Geom.* A part of a circle or ellipse bounded by two radii and the arc subtended by them. **2.** A mathematical instrument consisting of two arms marked with various scales and hinged together at one end. **3.** *Mil.* A defined area for which a unit is responsible. **4.** A special interest group: business *sector.* Abbr. *sec.* — **Syn.** See PORTION. — *v.t.* To divide into sectors. [< LL < L, cutter < *sectus,* pp. of *secare* to cut]

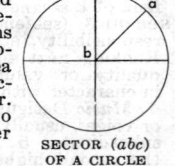

SECTOR (*abc*) OF A CIRCLE

sec·to·ri·al (sek·tôr′ē·əl, -tō′rē-) *adj.* **1.** Of or pertaining to a sector. **2.** *Zool.* Adapted for cutting; carnassial, as the front teeth of some carnivores.

sec·u·lar (sek′yə·lər) *adj.* **1.** Of or pertaining to this world or the present life; temporal; worldly: distinguished from *spiritual.* **2.** Not under the control of the church; civil; not ecclesiastical. **3.** Not concerned with religion; not sacred: *secular* art. **4.** Not bound by monastic vows: opposed to *regular:* the *secular* clergy. **5.** Occurring or observed but once in an age or century. **6.** Lasting for ages. — *n.* **1.** One in holy orders who is not bound by monastic vows. **2.** A layman. [< OF *seculer* < LL *saecularis* < L *saeculum* generation, an age; defs. 5 & 6 directly < L]

sec·u·lar·ism (sek′yə·lə·riz′əm) *n.* **1.** The belief that morality should be based on the well-being of mankind without any consideration of religious systems and forms of worship. **2.** The point of view that religion should not be introduced into public education or civil affairs.

sec·u·lar·ist (sek′yə·lə·rist) *n.* An adherent or advocate of secularism.

sec·u·lar·i·ty (sek′yə·lar′ə·tē) *n. pl.* **·ties** **1.** Secularism. **2.** Worldliness. **3.** A secular matter or concern.

sec·u·lar·ize (sek′yə·lə·rīz′) *v.t.* **·ized, ·iz·ing** **1.** To make secular; convert from sacred to secular uses. **2.** To make worldly. **3.** To change from a monastic or regular to a secular, as a monk. — **sec′u·lar·i·za′tion** *n.*

se·cund (sē′kund, sek′und) *adj. Biol.* Having the parts or organs arranged on one side only; unilateral. [< L *secundus* following. See SECOND².]

Se·cun·der·a·bad (si·kun′dər·ə·bäd′) A northern suburb of Hyderabad, Andhra Pradesh, India, where Sir Ronald Ross discovered that mosquitoes transmit malaria, 1898.

se·cun·dine (sek′ən·dīn, -din) *n.* **1.** *Bot.* The inner, first-developed coat or integument of an ovule. **2.** *pl. Physiol.* The afterbirth. Also spelled *secondine.* [< LL *secundinae,* pl., the afterbirth < L *secundus* following. See SECOND².]

se·cun·dum (si·kun′dəm) *adv. Latin* According to.

se·cure (si·kyōōr′) *adj.* **1.** Guarded against or not likely to be exposed to danger; safe. **2.** Free from fear, apprehension, etc. **3.** Fixed or holding firmly in place. **4.** So strong or well-made as to render loss, escape, or failure impossible. **5.** Assured; certain; guaranteed. **6.** *Archaic* Too confident; careless. — *v.* **·cured, ·cur·ing** *v.t.* **1.** To make secure; protect. **2.** To make firm, tight, or fast; fasten. **3.** To make sure or certain; ensure. **4.** To obtain possession of; get. — *v.i.* **5.** To be or become secure; take precautions: with *against,* etc. [< L *securus* < *se-* without + *cura* care. Doublet of SURE.] — **se·cur′a·ble** *adj.* — **se·cure′ly** *adv.* — **se·cure′ment** *n.* — **se·cure′ness** *n.* — **se·cur′er** *n.*

Securities and Exchange Commission An agency of the U.S. government that supervises the registration of security issues, prosecutes fraudulent stock manipulations, and regulates transactions in securities. Abbr. *SEC, S.E.C.*

se·cur·i·ty (si·kyŏŏr′ə·tē) *n. pl.* **·ties** **1.** The state of being secure; freedom from danger, poverty, or apprehension. **2.** One who or that which secures or guarantees. **3.** Something deposited or pledged as a guarantee for payment of money, etc. **4.** *pl.* Stocks, bonds, notes, etc.: used in financial transactions. **5.** Methods adopted for ensuring freedom or secrecy of action, communications, etc., as in wartime; also, the protection afforded by such methods.
— **Syn. 2., 3.** *Security, surety, bond, collateral, pledge,* and *bail* denote something given into custody of another as a guarantee of performance, appearance, payment, etc. Both *security* and *surety* may mean the property so given or the person who gives it, but *security* is chiefly used in the first sense, and *surety* in the second. A *bond* is a written promise to pay compensation for loss, damage, failure to perform, etc. *Collateral,* short for *collateral security,* is property of intrinsic value, as stocks, bonds, or merchandise, which may be seized in case of default. A *pledge* is similar; it is personal property or chattels, chiefly of sentimental value, which may also be seized in case of default. *Bail* is specifically the *security* given to guarantee a person's appearance before a court.

Security Council A permanent organ of the United Nations charged with the maintenance of international peace and security, having as its five permanent members the People's Republic of China, France, the U.S.S.R., the United Kingdom, and the United States, and having ten elected members, who serve two-year terms. Abbr. *SC*

security risk *U.S.* A person regarded as unfit for employment in government or in a job connected with national defense because of membership in proscribed organizations, poor character, dubious associations, criminal record, etc.

secy Secretary: also **sec′y.**

se·dan (si·dan′) *n.* **1.** A closed automobile having two or four doors and a front and back seat, capable of seating four to six persons including the driver: also, *Brit.,* **saloon.** **2.** A sedan chair. [? < Ital. *sedere* to sit < L]

Se·dan (si·dan′, *Fr.* sa·däN′) A city in NE France, on the Meuse; scene of the decisive French defeat in the Franco-Prussian War, 1870; pop. 22,998 (1968).

sedan chair A portable, enclosed chair, usually for one passenger, carried by means of poles at the front and back.

se·date (si·dāt′) *adj.* **1.** Characterized by habitual composure; unhurried; calm. **2.** Sober and decorous. — *v.t.* To place under sedation. [< L *sedatus,* pp. of *sedare* to make calm, settle < *sedere* to sit] — **se·date′ly** *adv.* — **se·date′ness** *n.*
— **Syn.** *Sedate, staid, grave,* and *solemn* characterize persons, deportment, and occasions that are calm and serious. The *sedate* person is not easily excited or disconcerted; a *sedate* occasion is decorous. The *staid* person is settled in habit and manner, and often unemotional and undemonstrative. The *grave* person verges on being somber, as though weighed down by cares or responsibilities. A *solemn* occasion is awe-inspiring; a *solemn* person behaves with the dignified restraint appropriate to a *solemn* occasion. Compare SERIOUS. — **Ant.** excited, agitated, flurried.

se·da·tion (si·dā′shən) *n. Med.* The act or process of reducing distress, irritation, excitement, etc., by administering sedatives.

sed·a·tive (sed′ə·tiv) *adj.* **1.** Having a soothing effect. **2.** *Med.* Allaying irritation; assuaging pain. — *n.* Any means, as a medicine, of soothing distress or allaying pain.

sed·en·tar·y (sed′ən·ter′ē) *adj.* **1.** Characterized by, done with, or requiring much sitting or a habitual sitting posture. **2.** Settled in one place, as certain tribes; sluggish; inactive. **3.** Accustomed to sitting. **4.** Resulting from much or long sitting. **5.** *Zool.* Remaining in one place; attached or fixed to an object. [< L *sedentarius* < *sedens, -entis,* ppr. of *sedere* to sit] — **sed′en·tar′i·ly** *adv.* — **sed′en·tar′i·ness** *n.*

Se·der (sā′dər) *n. pl.* **Se·ders** or **Se·dar·im** (sə·där′im) In Judaism, the feast commemorating the departure of the Israelites from Egypt, celebrated on the eve of the first day of Passover, and by Orthodox and Conservative Jews again on the eve of the second day. [< Hebrew *sedher* service]

sedge (sej) *n.* **1.** Any of various grasslike herbs (genus *Carex*), typical of a family (*Cyperaceae*) of plants widely distributed in marshy places. **2.** Any plant of this family. [OE *secg*] — **sedg′y** *adj.*

Sedge·moor (sej′mŏŏr) A tract in Somersetshire, England; scene of the victory of James II over the Duke of Monmouth, 1685.

se·dile (si·dī′lē) *n. pl.* **·dil·i·a** (-dil′ē·ə) A seat near the altar in the chancel of a church, for officiating clergy. Also **se·dil′i·um** (-dil′ē·əm). [< L, seat < *sedere* to sit]

sed·i·ment (sed′ə·mənt) *n.* **1.** Matter that settles to the bottom of a liquid; settlings; dregs; lees. **2.** *Geol.* Fragmentary material deposited by water or air. — **Syn.** See WASTE. [< MF *sédiment* < L *sedimentum* a settling < *sedere* to sit, settle]

sed·i·men·ta·ry (sed′ə·men′tər·ē) *adj.* **1.** Pertaining to or having the character of sediment. **2.** *Geol.* Designating rocks and other inorganic materials formed from sediment deposited after transportation from its original position. Also **sed′i·men′tal.**

sed·i·men·ta·tion (sed′ə·men·tā′shən) *n.* **1.** The accumulation or depositing of sediment. **2.** The depositing of an insoluble material.

sedimentation rate *Med.* A measure of the speed with which erythrocytes are deposited in a given volume of citrated fresh blood.

se·di·tion (si·dish′ən) *n.* **1.** Language or conduct directed against public order and the tranquillity of the state. **2.** The incitement of such disorder, tending toward treason, but lacking an overt act. **3.** Dissension; revolt. [< OF < L *seditio, -onis* < *sed-* aside + *itio, -onis* a going < *ire* to go]

se·di·tion·ar·y (si·dish′ən·er′ē) *adj.* Seditious. — *n. pl.* **·ar·ies** One who promotes sedition: also **se·di′tion·ist.**

se·di·tious (si·dish′əs) *adj.* **1.** Pertaining to, promoting, or having the character of sedition. **2.** Inclined to, taking part in, or guilty of sedition. [< OF *seditieux* < L *seditiosus* < *seditio, -onis.* See SEDITION.] — **se·di′tious·ly** *adv.* — **se·di′tious·ness** *n.*

se·duce (si·dōos′, -dyōos′) *v.t.* **·duced, ·duc·ing** **1.** To lead astray; entice into wrong, disloyalty, etc.; tempt. **2.** To induce to engage in illicit sexual intercourse, especially for the first time. [< L *seducere* < *se-* apart + *ducere* to lead] — **se·duc′er** *n.* — **se·duc′i·ble** or **se·duce′a·ble** *adj.*

se·duc·tion (si·duk′shən) *n.* **1.** The act of seducing. **2.** Something that seduces; an enticement. Also **se·duce·ment** (si·dōos′mənt, -dyōos′-). [< MF *séduction* < L *seductio, -onis* < *seducere.* See SEDUCE.]

se·duc·tive (si·duk′tiv) *adj.* Tending to seduce; enticing. — **se·duc′tive·ly** *adv.* — **se·duc′tive·ness** *n.*

se·duc·tress (si·duk′tris) *n.* A female seducer.

se·du·li·ty (si·dōo′lə·tē, -dyōo′-) *n.* The state or character of being sedulous.

sed·u·lous (sej′ŏŏ·ləs) *adj.* Constant in application or attention; assiduous. [< L *sedulus* careful, appar. < *sedulo* sincerely] — **sed′u·lous·ly** *adv.* — **sed′u·lous·ness** *n.*
— **Syn.** diligent, persevering. Compare BUSY.

se·dum (sē′dəm) *n.* Any of a large genus (*Sedum*) of chiefly perennial plants of the orpine family, having very thick leaves and chiefly white, yellow, or pink flowers. Compare STONECROP. [< L, houseleek]

see¹ (sē) *v.* **saw, seen, see·ing** *v.t.* **1.** To perceive with the eyes; gain knowledge or awareness of by means of one's vision. **2.** To perceive with the mind; understand. **3.** To find out or ascertain: *See* who is at the door. **4.** To have experience or knowledge of: We have *seen* worse times. **5.** To encounter; chance to meet: I *saw* your husband today. **6.** To have a meeting or interview with; visit or receive as a guest, visitor, etc.: The doctor will *see* you now. **7.** To attend as a spectator; view. **8.** To accompany; escort. **9.** To take care; be sure: with a clause as object: *See* that you do it! **10.** In poker, to accept (a bet) or equal the bet of (a player) by betting an equal sum. — *v.i.* **11.** To have or exercise the power of sight. **12.** To find out; inquire: I will go and *see.* **13.** To understand; comprehend. **14.** To think; consider. **15.** To gain certain knowledge, as by awaiting an outcome: We will *see* if you are right or wrong. Abbr. *s.* — **to see about 1.** To inquire into the facts, causes, etc., of. **2.** To take care of; attend to. — **to see (someone) off** To accompany to a point of departure, as for a journey. — **to see (someone) out** To accompany to a point of exit: *See* him to the door. — **to see (someone) through** To aid or protect, as throughout a period of difficulty or danger. — **to see (something) through** or **out** To work or wait until an undertaking, ordeal, etc., is finished. — **to see through** To penetrate, as a disguise or deception. — **to see to** To be responsible for; give one's attention to. [OE *sēon*]
— **Syn. 1.** *See, behold, contemplate, observe, survey,* and *scan* mean to perceive with the eyes. *See* is the most neutral term, implying neither effort nor thoroughness. *Behold* is also passive, but is more emphatic. *See* may be used of mental images: the pictures *seen* with the mind's eye; but *behold* is used only of physical sight. The other terms imply some degree of positive action. To *contemplate* is to look at in a prolonged but leisurely way. To *observe* is to give heed or attention to what we *see,* and *survey* and *scan* imply complete, detailed examination. Compare DISCERN, EXAMINE, LOOK.

see² (sē) *n.* **1.** The local seat from which a bishop, archbishop, or pope exercises jurisdiction. **2.** Episcopal or papal jurisdiction, authority, or rank; a bishop's or pope's office. **3.** *Obs.* A seat, especially of dignity or power. — **Holy See** The Pope's jurisdiction, court, or office: also **See of Rome.** [< OF *se, sie, sed* < L *sedes* seat]

See·beck effect (zā′bek, sē-) *Physics* The current produced in an electric circuit when junctions of dissimilar metals are kept at different temperatures, as in thermocouples. Compare PELTIER EFFECT. [after Thomas Johann *Seebeck,* 1780–1831, German physicist]

see·catch (sē′kach′) *n. pl.* **·catch·ie** (-kach′ē) An adult male fur seal. [< Russian *sekach*]

seed (sēd) *n.* **1.** The ovule from which a plant may be reproduced; the fertilized ovule containing an embryo. **2.** That from which anything springs; source. **3.** Offspring; children. **4.** The male fertilizing element; semen; milt. **5.** Any small, usually hard fruit; also, any part of a plant from which it may be propagated, as bulbs, tubers, etc. **6.** Seeds collectively. **7.** The seed-bearing stage. **8.** Ancestry; stock. **9.** A young oyster fit for transplanting. **10.** *U.S. Dial.* An animal or animals used for breeding. **— to go to seed 1.** To develop and shed seed. **2.** To become shabby, useless, etc.; deteriorate. **—** *v.t.* **1.** To sow with seed. **2.** To sow (seed). **3.** To remove the seeds from: to *seed* raisins. **4.** In sports: **a** To arrange (the drawing for positions in a tournament, etc.) so that the more skilled competitors meet only in the later events. **b** To rank (a skilled competitor) thus. **5.** To intersperse (clouds) with particles of silver iodide or other substances in order to produce rainfall. **—** *v.i.* **6.** To sow seed. **7.** To grow to maturity and produce or shed seed. [OE *sǣd*] **— seed′less** *adj.*

seed bud *Bot.* The germ within a seed; also, the ovule.
seed cake 1. A sweet cake containing aromatic seeds, as caraway. **2.** Cottonseed-oil cake.
seed capsule *Bot.* A testa (def. 1).
seed·case (sēd′kās′) *n. Bot.* A pericarp.
seed coat *Bot.* The integument of a seed, usually the outer one: also called *tunic.*
seed coral Small pieces of coral used in jewelry and ornaments.
seed corn Corn of high quality used or intended for seed.
seed·er (sē′dər) *n.* **1.** One who or that which sows seed, as a machine. **2.** A device for removing seeds from fruit.
seed leaf *Bot.* A cotyledon.
seed·ling (sēd′ling) *n.* **1.** *Bot.* A plant grown from seed, as distinguished from one propagated by grafting. **2.** A very small or young tree or plant.
seed oyster A young oyster, especially one transplanted to another bed: also *oyster seed.*
seed pearl A small pearl, used in jewelry, embroidery, etc.
seeds·man (sēdz′mən) *n. pl.* **·men** (-mən) **1.** A dealer in seeds. **2.** A sower. Also **seed′man.**
seed·time (sēd′tīm′) *n.* The season for sowing seed.
seed vessel *Bot.* A pericarp.
seed·y (sē′dē) *adj.* **seed·i·er, seed·i·est 1.** Full of seeds. **2.** Gone to seed. **3.** Poor and ragged; shabby. **4.** *Informal* Feeling or looking wretched. **— seed′i·ly** *adv.* **— seed′i·ness** *n.*
see·ing (sē′ing) *n.* The act of seeing; vision; sight. **—** *conj.* Taking into consideration; since; in view of the fact.
Seeing Eye A philanthropic organization located near Morristown, New Jersey, that trains and supplies dogs (**Seeing Eye dogs**) as guides and companions to the blind.
seek (sēk) *v.* **sought, seek·ing** *v.t.* **1.** To go in search of; look for. **2.** To strive for; try to get or obtain. **3.** To endeavor or try: with an infinitive as object: He *seeks* to mislead me. **4.** To ask or inquire for; request: to *seek* information. **5.** To go to; betake oneself to: to *seek* a warmer climate. **6.** *Obs.* or *Dial.* To search or explore. **—** *v.i.* **7.** To make a search or inquiry. [OE *sēcan*] **— seek′er** *n.*
See·land (zā′länt) The German name for ZEALAND.
seem (sēm) *v.i.* **1.** To give the impression of being; appear. **2.** To appear to oneself: followed by the infinitive: I seem to hear strange voices. **3.** To appear to exist: There *seems* no reason for hesitating. **4.** To be evident or apparent: It *seems* to be raining. [ME *sēmen* < ON *sœma* to conform to. Cf. OE *sēman* to reconcile.] **— seem′er** *n.*
seem·ing (sē′ming) *adj.* Having the appearance of reality; apparent but not necessarily actual. **— Syn.** See APPARENT. **—** *n.* Appearance; semblance; especially, false show. **— seem′ing·ly** *adv.*
seem·ly (sēm′lē) *adj.* **·li·er, ·li·est** Befitting the proprieties; proper; decorous. **— Syn.** See BECOMING. **—** *adv.* Becomingly; decently; appropriately. [< ON *sœmiligr* honorable < *sœmr* fitting] **— seem′li·ness** *n.*
seen (sēn) Past participle of SEE.
seep (sēp) *v.i.* To soak though pores or small interstices; percolate; ooze. **—** *n.* A small spring or a place out of which water, oil, or other liquid oozes. [Alter. of OE *sypian* to soak]
seep·age (sē′pij) *n.* **1.** The act or process of seeping or oozing. **2.** The fluid or moisture that oozes.
seer[1] (sē′ər *for def. 1; also* sir *for defs. 2 and 3*) *n.* **1.** One who sees. **2.** One who foretells events; a prophet. **3.** One believed to have second sight. [< SEE[1] + -ER] **— seer′ess** *n.fem.*
seer[2] (sir) *n.* A unit of weight used in different parts of India, and having varying local values: also spelled *ser.* [< Hind. *ser*]
seer·suck·er (sir′suk′ər) *n.* A thin fabric of cotton, rayon, nylon, etc., usually striped in colors, with a crinkled surface. [< Hind. *shirshaker* < Persian *shir o shakkar*, lit., milk and sugar]
see·saw (sē′sô′) *n.* **1.** A balanced plank or board made to move alternately up and down by persons seated or standing at opposite ends: also called *teeter, teeter board, teeter-totter.* **2.** The action or diversion of balancing on such a board. **3.** Any up-and-down or to-and-fro movement. **—** *v.t. & v.i.* **1.** To move or cause to move on or as if on a seesaw. **2.** To alternate; fluctuate. **—** *adj.* Moving to and fro; vacillating. [Reduplication of SAW[1]]

seethe (sēth) *v.* **seethed** (*Obs.* **sod**), **seethed** (*Obs.* **sod·den**, **sod**), **seeth·ing** *v.i.* **1.** To boil. **2.** To foam or bubble as if boiling. **3.** To be agitated or excited, as by rage **—** *v.t.* **4.** To soak in liquid; steep. **5.** *Archaic* To boil. **—** *n.* The act or condition of seething; turmoil. [OE *sēothan*]
seg·gar (seg′ər) *n.* A saggar.
seg·ment (seg′mənt) *n.* **1.** A part cut off or divided from the other parts of anything; a section. **2.** *Geom.* **a** A part of a figure cut off by a line or plane; especially, the part of a circle included within a chord and its arc. **b** A finite part of a line. **3.** *Zool* **a** One of the serial divisions of an animal; somite; metamere. **b** The portion of a limb between two joints. **— Syn.** See PORTION. **—** *v.t. & v.i.* To divide into segments. [< L *segmentum* < *secare* to cut] **— seg·men·tar·y** (seg′mən·ter′ē) *adj.*
seg·men·tal (seg·men′təl) *adj.* **1.** Of or pertaining to a segment or segments. **2.** Divided into segments. **3.** *Ling.* Denoting speech sounds that follow one another in the stream of speech; linear: distinguished from *suprasegmental.* **— seg·men′tal·ly** *adv.*
seg·men·ta·tion (seg′mən·tā′shən) *n.* **1.** The act of cutting or dividing into segments. **2.** The state of being so divided. **3.** *Biol.* The cleavage of a cell.
segmentation cavity *Biol.* A blastocele.
seg·no (sā′nyō) *n. pl.* **·gni** (-nyē) *Music* A sign; especially, the musical sign 𝄋 or 𝄌, indicating the beginning or end of a repeat. [< Ital. < L *signum*]
se·go (sē′gō) *n. pl.* **·gos 1.** A perennial herb (*Calochortus nuttalli*) of the lily family, having white flowers: the State flower of Utah. **2.** Its edible bulb. Also **sego lily.** [< Shoshonean (Ute) *sīgo*]
Se·go·via (sā·gō′vyä) A city in central Spain; remarkable for its architecture, and a Roman aqueduct still supplying the city; pop. 33,360 (1960).
Se·go·via (sā·gō′vyä), **Andrés,** born 1894, Spanish classical guitarist.
seg·re·gate (seg′rə·gāt; *for adj. also* seg′rə·git) *v.* **·gat·ed, ·gat·ing** *v.t.* **1.** To place apart from others or the rest; isolate. **2.** To subject to segregation (def. 3). **—** *v.i.* **3.** To separate from a mass and gather about nuclei or along lines of fracture, as in crystallization or solidification. **4.** To undergo segregation. **—** *adj.* Set apart from others. [< L *segregatus,* pp. of *segregare* to separate < *se-* apart + *grex, gregis* flock] **— seg′re·ga′tive** *adj.* **— seg′re·ga′tor** *n.*
seg·re·ga·tion (seg′rə·gā′shən) *n.* **1.** The act or process of segregating. **2.** *Genetics* The separation of paired hereditary characters in the process of meiosis, without loss of individuality of either in subsequent transmission by the offspring. **3.** The practice of requiring separate facilities, as in housing, schools, and transportation, for use by whites and nonwhites, especially Negroes.
seg·re·ga·tion·ist (seg′rə·gā′shən·ist) *n.* One who practices or advocates racial segregation.
se·gui·di·lla (sā′gē·dē′lyä) *n. Spanish* **1.** A lively Spanish dance. **2.** The music of such a dance in triple meter, or its movement, based on a stanza of four to seven short lines, partly assonant. **3.** *pl.* An air to which the dancers sing a group of these stanzas.
sei·cen·to (sā·chen′tō) *n.* The 17th century considered with reference to Italian art and literature. [< Ital., short for *mil seicento* one thousand six hundred]
seiche (sāsh) *n.* An occasional rhythmic oscillation of water above and below the mean level of lakes or landlocked seas, lasting from a few minutes to an hour or more. [< dial. F (Swiss), ? ult. < L *siccus* dry]
Seid·litz powder (sed′lits) An aperient consisting of two separate parts, tartaric acid, and sodium bicarbonate mixed with Rochelle salt, used by dissolving separately, mixing the solutions, and drinking while the mixture is effervescing: also called *Rochelle powder.* [after *Seidlitz,* a Czech village, site of a medicinal spring]
seign·ior (sēn′yər) *n.* **1.** A lord; noble. **2.** A title of respect equivalent to *Sir.* **3.** In French Canada, one granted a seigniory; landholder. **4.** Formerly, a feudal lord. **sei·gneur** (sēn·yûr′). [< AF *segnour,* OF *seignor* < L *senior* older] **— sei·gnio·ri·al** (sēn·yôr′ē·əl, -yō′rē-) *adj.*
seign·ior·age (sēn′yər·ij) *n.* **1.** Something charged or claimed by a superior as a prerogative. **2.** A charge made by a government for coining bullion; also, the difference between the cost of bullion and the face value of coin made from it. Compare BRASSAGE.
seign·ior·y (sēn′yər·ē) *n. pl.* **·ies 1.** The territory or jurisdiction of a seignior; a manor. **2.** Right or priority belonging to feudal superiority. **3.** In French Canada, land or an estate granted originally by the King of France. Also spelled *signory.* Also **sei′gneur·y.**
seine (sān) *n.* A long fishnet hanging vertically in the water and having floats at the top edge and weights at the bottom. **—** *v.t. & v.i.* **seined, sein·ing** To fish or catch with a seine. [OE *segne* < L *sagena* < Gk. *sagēnē* fishnet]

Seine (sān, *Fr.* sen) A river of NE France, flowing 482 miles NW to the English Channel.

sein·er (sān′ər) *n.* One who fishes with or a boat that uses a seine. Also **seine-net·ter** (sān′net′ər).

seise (sēz) **sei·sin** (sē′zin) See SEIZE (def. 8), SEIZIN.

seism (sī′zəm, -səm) *n.* An earthquake. [< Gk. *seismos.* See SEISMIC.]

seis·mic (sīz′mik, sīs′-) *adj.* Pertaining to, characteristic of, or produced by earthquakes. Also **seis′mal, seis′mi·cal, seis·mat·i·cal** (sīz·mat′ə·kəl, sīs-). [< Gk. *seismos* earthquake < *seiein* to shake]

seismic sea wave A large and often destructive wave caused by a submarine earthquake; a tsunami.

seis·mism (sīz′miz·əm, sīs′-) *n.* The processes or phenomena involved in earth movements.

seismo- *combining form* Earthquake: *seismograph.* Also, before vowels, **seism-.** [< Gk. *seismos* earthquake]

seis·mo·gram (sīz′mə·gram, sīs′-) *n.* The record of an earthquake or earth tremor made by a seismograph.

seis·mo·graph (sīz′mə·graf, -gräf, sīs′-) *n.* An instrument for recording automatically the intensity, direction, and duration of an earthquake shock. — **seis′mo·graph′ic** *adj.* — **seis·mog·ra·pher** (sīz·mog′rə·fər, sīs-).

seis·mog·ra·phy (sīz·mog′rə·fē, sīs-) *n.* The study and recording of earthquake phenomena. [< SEISMO- + -GRAPHY]

seis·mol·o·gy (sīz·mol′ə·jē, sīs-) *n.* The science of earthquake phenomena. [< SEISMO- + -LOGY] — **seis·mo·log·ic** (sīz′mə·loj′ik, sīs′-) or **·i·cal** *adj.* — **seis·mo·log′i·cal·ly** *adv.* — **seis·mol′o·gist** *n.*

seis·mom·e·ter (sīz·mom′ə·tər, sīs-) *n.* A seismograph. — **seis·mo·met·ric** (sīz′mō·met′rik, sīs-) or **·ri·cal** *adj.*

SEISMOGRAPH
(Vertical motion type)

a Concrete base. *b* Clock. *c* Seismogram. *d* Stylus. *e* Weight. *f* Spring suspension.

seize (sēz) *v.* **seized, seiz·ing** *v.t.* **1.** To take hold of suddenly and forcibly; clutch; grasp. **2.** To grasp mentally; comprehend; understand. **3.** To take possession of by authority or right. **4.** To take possession of by or as by force: The usurper *seized* the throne. **5.** To take prisoner; capture; arrest. **6.** To act upon with sudden and powerful effect; attack; strike: Terror *seized* the enemy. **7.** To take advantage of immediately, as an opportunity. **8.** *Law* To put into legal possession: usually spelled *seise.* **9.** *Naut.* To fasten or bind by turns of cord, line, or small rope; lash. — *v.i.* **10.** To take a sudden or forcible hold. — **Syn.** See CATCH. [< OF *saisir, seisir* < Med.L (*ad propriam*) *sacire* to take (into one's own possession), prob. < Gmc.] — **seiz′a·ble** *adj.*

seiz·er (sē′zər) *n.* **1.** One who seizes. **2.** *Law* One who takes livery of seizin: also **seiz′or, seis′or.**

sei·zin (sē′zin) *n.* *Law* **1.** The possession of land under a claim of freehold. **2.** That which is possessed; property. **3.** The act of taking possession. — **livery of seizin** The delivery of corporeal possession of lands and tenements of freehold. Also spelled *seisin.* [< OF *saisine* < *saisir.* See SEIZE.]

seiz·ing (sē′zing) *n.* **1.** The act of grasping or taking forcible possession. **2.** The process of fastening or binding together with turns of cord. **3.** A small cord used in making such fastenings. **4.** The fastening itself.

sei·zure (sē′zhər) *n.* **1.** The act of seizing. **2.** A sudden or violent attack, as of epilepsy; fit; spell.

se·jant (sē′jənt) *adj.* *Heraldry* Sitting with the fore limbs erect, as a lion. Also **se′jeant.** [< AF *sejant,* OF *seant,* ppr. of AF *seier,* OF *seoir* to sit < L *sedere*]

Se·ja·nus (si·jā′nəs), **Lucius Aelius,** died A.D. 31, Roman courtier; favorite of Tiberius; executed.

Sejm (sām) *n. Polish* An assembly or diet having legislative power; especially, the former Constituent Assembly of the Polish Republic.

sel (sel) *n. Scot.* Self.

se·la·chi·an (si·lā′kē·ən) *adj.* Of or belonging to an order or subclass (*Selachii*) of elasmobranch fishes including the sharks, skates, dogfishes, and rays. — *n.* A selachian fish. [< NL < Gk. *selachos* shark]

se·la·dang (sə·lä′däng) See SALADANG.

sel·a·gi·nel·la (sel′ə·ji·nel′ə) *n.* One of a widely distributed genus (*Selaginella*) of flowerless herbs with scalelike leaves. [< NL, dim. of L *selago, -inis,* a plant like the savin]

se·lah (sē′lə) A word of unknown meaning occurring often at the end of a verse in the Psalms, usually considered as a direction to readers or musicians. [< Hebrew *selāh*]

se·lam·lik (si·läm′lik) *n.* The men's quarters in a Turkish house, where guests are received. [< Turkish *selāmliq* < Arabic *salām* health, peace]

Se·lan·gor (se·läng′gôr, -gōr) A State in western Malaya, on the Strait of Malacca; 3,167 sq. mi.; pop. 1,339,142 (est. 1966); capital, Kuala Lumpur.

Sel·den (sel′dən), **John,** 1584–1654, English jurist and antiquary.

sel·dom (sel′dəm) *adv.* At widely separated intervals, as of time or space; infrequently. Also *Archaic* **sel′dom·ly.** [OE *seldum, seldan*]

se·lect (si·lekt′) *v.t.* **1.** To take in preference to another or others; pick out; choose. — *v.i.* **2.** To make a choice; choose. — **Syn.** See CHOOSE. — *adj.* **1.** Chosen in preference to others; taken as being most fit or desirable; choice. **2.** Exclusive. **3.** Very particular in selecting. [< L *selectus,* pp. of *seligere* < *se-* apart + *legere* to choose] — **se·lect′ness** *n.*

se·lec·tee (si·lek′tē′) *n.* One selected; especially, one drafted for military or naval service.

se·lec·tion (si·lek′shən) *n.* **1.** The act of selecting; choice. **2.** Anything selected. **3.** A thing or collection of things chosen with care. **4.** *Biol.* The process by which certain organisms, or any of their characteristics, are favored in the struggle for survival and perpetuation. — **Syn.** See ALTERNATIVE.

se·lec·tive (si·lek′tiv) *adj.* **1.** Pertaining to selection; tending to select. **2.** Having or characterized by good selectivity.

selective service Compulsory military service according to specified conditions of age, fitness, etc.

selective transmission *Mech.* A transmission for motor vehicles effected by a single lever that directly changes the gear from one speed to another.

se·lec·tiv·i·ty (si·lek′tiv′ə·tē) *n.* **1.** The state or quality of being selective. Also **se·lec′tive·ness.** **2.** *Telecom.* That characteristic of a radio or television receiver, electrical circuit, etc., by which certain frequencies can be received to the exclusion of others.

se·lect·man (si·lekt′mən) *n. pl.* **·men** (-mən) In New England, one of a board of town officers, elected annually to exercise executive authority in local affairs.

select meeting In the Society of Friends, a meeting composed of ministers and elders.

se·lec·tor (si·lek′tər) *n.* One who or that which selects; especially, a valve, switch, or similar device in a machine or apparatus for the selection and control of a desired action.

sel·e·nate (sel′ə·nāt) *n. Chem.* A salt or ester of selenic acid. [< SELEN(IC) + -ATE³]

Se·le·ne (si·lē′nē) In Greek mythology, goddess of the moon: identified with the Roman *Luna.* Also **Se·le′na** (-nə). [< Gk. *Selēnē,* lit., the moon]

se·len·ic (si·len′ik, -lē′nik) *adj. Chem.* Of, pertaining to, or derived from selenium, especially in its higher valence. [< SELEN(IUM) + -IC]

selenic acid *Chem.* A strongly corrosive acid, H_2SeO_4, analogous to sulfuric acid.

se·le·ni·ous (si·lē′nē·əs) *adj. Chem.* Of, pertaining to, or derived from selenium, especially in its lower valence.

sel·e·nite¹ (sel′ə·nīt) *n.* A pearly, usually transparent variety of gypsum. [< L *selenites* < Gk. *selēnītēs* (*lithos*), lit., moonstone < *selēnē* the moon; so called because it was thought to wax and wane with the moon]

sel·e·nite² (sel′ə·nīt) *n.* A salt of selenious acid. [< SELEN(IUM) + -ITE²]

se·le·ni·um (si·lē′nē·əm) *n.* A gray, crystalline, nonmetallic element (symbol Se) of the sulfur group, varying greatly in electrical resistance under the influence of light. See ELEMENT. [< NL < Gk. *selēnē* the moon]

selenium cell A photoelectric cell in which plates of selenium respond to the action of light upon them.

seleno- *combining form* Moon; pertaining to the moon; lunar: *selenography.* Also, before vowels, **selen-.** [< Gk. *selēnē* the moon]

se·le·nog·ra·phy (sel′ə·nog′rə·fē) *n.* The science or study of the moon's surface. [< SELENO- + -GRAPHY] — **se·le·nog′ra·pher** *n.* — **sel′e·no·graph′ic** (-nō·graf′ik) or **·i·cal** *adj.*

se·le·nol·o·gy (sel′ə·nol′ə·jē) *n.* The branch of astronomy that treats of the moon. [< SELENO- + -LOGY] — **se·le·no·log·i·cal** (sel′ə·nə·loj′i·kəl) *adj.* — **sel′e·nol′o·gist** *n.*

Se·leu·cia (si·lōō′shə) **1.** An ancient city on the NE Mediterranean, in extreme southern Turkey; formerly the port of Antioch. Also **Seleucia Pi·e·ri·a** (pī·ir′ē·ə). **2.** An ancient city of Mesopotamia, on the Tigris, near Baghdad, Iraq.

Se·leu·cid (si·lōō′sid) *adj.* Pertaining to the Seleucids: also **Se·leu′ci·dan, Se·leu·cid·i·an** (sē′lōō·sid′ē·ən). — *n.* One of the Seleucids. [< L *Seleucides* < Gk. *Seleukidēs,* descendant of Seleucus < *Seleukos* Seleucus]

Se·leu·cids (si·lōō′sids) *n.pl.* The members of the dynasty that ruled Syria from 312 B.C. till the Roman conquest, 64 B.C. Also **Se·leu′ci·dae** (-dē).

Se·leu·cus (si·lōō′kəs) Name of six kings of the Seleucid dynasty; especially, **Seleucus I,** 358?–280 B.C., Macedonian general under Alexander the Great, and founder of the dynasty: also called **Seleucus Ni·ca·tor** (nī·kā′tər) (the Conqueror).

self (self)   *n.*   *pl.* **selves** **1.** An individual known or considered as the subject of his own consciousness. **2.** Anything considered as having a distinct personality. **3.** Personal interest or advantage. **4.** Any thing, class, or attribute that, abstractly considered, maintains a distinct and characteristic individuality or identity. — *adj.* **1.** Being of the same color, substance, etc., throughout; uniform; unmixed. **2.** Of a part, accessory, etc., made of the same material as that with which it is used. **3.** Same; identical: obsolete except in *selfsame.* [OE]

◆ *Self* may appear as a combining form with various meanings as shown in the following list.

1. Of the self (the object of the root word); as in:

self-abandonment	self-expansion
self-abasing	self-expatriation
self-abhorrence	self-exploiting
self-accusation	self-exposure
self-adaptive	self-extermination
self-admiration	self-fearing
self-admission	self-flatterer
self-adornment	self-flattering
self-adulation	self-flattery
self-advancement	self-folding
self-advertisement	self-forgetful
self-advertising	self-formation
self-affliction	self-glorification
self-aggrandizement	self-gratification
self-analysis	self-guidance
self-annihilation	self-harming
self-applause	self-helpful
self-appreciation	self-humbling
self-approbation	self-humiliation
self-approval	self-hypnosis
self-asserting	self-hypnotism
self-awareness	self-hypnotized
self-bedizenment	self-idolatry
self-betrayal	self-idolizing
self-blame	self-ignorance
self-castigation	self-ignorant
self-chastisement	self-imitation
self-cognizance	self-immolation
self-commendation	self-immurement
self-committal	self-impairment
self-comparison	self-indignation
self-comprehending	self-indulging
self-condemnation	self-inspection
self-condemning	self-instruction
self-conditioning	self-insurer
self-confinement	self-integration
self-confounding	self-intensifying
self-congratulatory	self-interrogation
self-conquest	self-introduction
self-conservative	self-judgment
self-conserving	self-justification
self-consideration	self-justifying
self-consoling	self-laudatory
self-consuming	self-limitation
self-contempt	self-limiting
self-contradicting	self-loss
self-conviction	self-maceration
self-correction	self-maintenance
self-corruption	self-martyrdom
self-creation	self-mastery
self-criticism	self-mistrust
self-cure	self-mortification
self-damnation	self-murder
self-debasement	self-murderer
self-deceit	self-mutilation
self-deceiving	self-neglect
self-dedication	self-neglectful
self-defeating	self-nourishment
self-deflation	self-observation
self-degradation	self-offense
self-deifying	self-opinion
self-dejection	self-painter
self-delusion	self-paying
self-deprecating	self-perceiving
self-depreciation	self-perceptive
self-depreciative	self-perfecting
self-destroying	self-perfection
self-destruction	self-perpetuating
self-destructive	self-perpetuation
self-direction	self-persuasion
self-disapproval	self-pleasing
self-disclosure	self-praise
self-discovery	self-praising
self-disgrace	self-preparation
self-disparagement	self-presentation
self-display	self-preserving
self-disposal	self-projection
self-disquieting	self-protecting
self-dissolution	self-protection
self-doubt	self-punishment
self-easing	self-raising
self-enriching	self-recollection
self-estimate	self-reconstruction
self-evacuation	self-reduction
self-exalting	self-regulation
self-exculpation	self-representation
self-excuse	self-repressing

self-repression	self-surrender
self-reproach	self-suspicious
self-reproachful	self-taxation
self-restriction	self-teacher
self-revealing	self-terminating
self-revelation	self-tolerant
self-ruin	self-torment
self-satirist	self-torture
self-scrutinizing	self-treatment
self-scrutiny	self-trust
self-searching	self-trusting
self-slaughter	self-undoing
self-soothing	self-upbraiding
self-study	self-valuing
self-subjection	self-vaunting
self-subordination	self-vindication
self-suppression	self-worship

2. By oneself or itself; by one's own effort (the agent of the root word); as in:

self-abandoned	self-doomed	self-named
self-administered	self-elaborated	self-offered
self-approved	self-elected	self-ordained
self-authorized	self-explained	self-paid
self-balanced	self-exposed	self-pampered
self-beguiled	self-furnished	self-performed
self-betrayed	self-generated	self-perpetuated
self-blinded	self-honored	self-perplexed
self-caused	self-idolized	self-planted
self-chosen	self-illumined	self-posed
self-condemned	self-imposed	self-powered
self-conducted	self-incurred	self-proclaimed
self-constituted	self-initiated	self-professed
self-convicted	self-instructed	self-punished
self-corrupted	self-invited	self-renounced
self-declared	self-judged	self-repressed
self-defended	self-justified	self-restrained
self-deluded	self-kindled	self-revealed
self-deprived	self-limited	self-schooled
self-destroyed	self-maimed	self-sown
self-determined	self-matured	self-subdued
self-devised	self-misused	self-sustained
self-divided	self-mortified	self-tempted

3. To, toward, in, for, on, or with oneself; as in:

self-absorbed	self-desire	self-permission
self-aid	self-despair	self-pictured
self-aim	self-directed	self-pleased
self-amusement	self-direction	self-preference
self-application	self-disdain	self-prescribed
self-applied	self-disgust	self-pride
self-assumed	self-dislike	self-procured
self-assuming	self-dissatisfied	self-produced
self-benefit	self-elation	self-profit
self-care	self-enamored	self-purifying
self-comment	self-enclosed	self-reflection
self-communing	self-exultation	self-relation
self-compassion	self-focusing	self-relying
self-complacence	self-gain	self-repellent
self-complacency	self-helpfulness	self-repose
self-complacent	self-injurious	self-reproof
self-conflict	self-injury	self-repulsive
self-consistency	self-kindness	self-resentment
self-consistent	self-liking	self-resigned
self-content	self-loathing	self-respectful
self-contented	self-oblivious	self-rigorous
self-delight	self-occupied	self-sent
self-dependence	self-panegyrical	self-tenderness
self-dependent	self-penetration	self-vexation

4. From oneself or itself; from one's own nature or power; as in:

self-apparent	self-fruition	self-poise
self-arising	self-healing	self-poised
self-born	self-inclusive	self-refuting
self-coherence	self-initiative	self-renewing
self-complete	self-intelligible	self-resourceful
self-defining	self-issuing	self-resplendent
self-derived	self-luminous	self-restoring
self-desirable	self-manifestation	self-reward
self-developing	self-moving	self-rewarding
self-effort	self-operative	self-sprung
self-evolving	self-opinionated	self-stability
self-explaining	self-originating	self-stimulated
self-forbidden	self-perfect	self-warranting

5. Independent; as in:

self-agency	self-dominance	self-existence
self-authority	self-dominion	self-ownership
self-credit	self-entity	self-sovereignty

6. In technology, automatic or automatically; as in:

self-acting	self-cocking	self-lubricating
self-adapting	self-cooled	self-moving
self-adjustable	self-defrosting	self-oiling
self-adjusting	self-emptying	self-primer
self-aligning	self-feed	self-priming
self-burning	self-feeder	self-recording
self-changing	self-feeding	self-registering
self-charging	self-filling	self-regulated
self-checking	self-inking	self-regulating
self-cleaning	self-lighting	self-righting
self-closing	self-locking	self-setting

self·a·base·ment (self′ə·bās′mənt)   *n.*   Abasement or degradation of oneself.

self·ab·ne·ga·tion (self′ab′ni·gā′shən)   *n.*   The complete putting aside of oneself and one's own claims for the sake of some other person or object; self-sacrifice. — **Syn. 1.** *Self-abnegation, self-denial, renunciation,* and *self-sacrifice* refer to the voluntary giving up of something desired or prized. *Self-abnegation* implies the valuation of another's welfare above one's own; we speak of a mother's *self-abnegation* in nursing a sick child at the expense of her own comfort or health. *Self-denial* emphasizes conscious deprivation to achieve some purpose or personal advantage: to practice *self-denial* of food to avoid overweight. Prolonged *self-denial* becomes *renunciation*: to gain inner peace by the *renunciation* of worldly ambitions. The strongest of these words is *self-sacrifice*; it implies the surrender of something dearly prized, and may extend to the giving up of life itself for another. — **Ant.** self-indulgence, self-gratification.

self-ab·sorp·tion (self′ab·sôrp′shən, -zôrp′-) *n.* Absorption in or concentration on one's own affairs, work, interests, etc.

self-a·buse (self′ə·byŏŏs′) *n.* **1.** The disparagement of one's own person or powers. **2.** Masturbation.

self-ad·dressed (self′ə·drest′) *adj.* Addressed to oneself.

self-ap·point·ed (self′ə·poin′təd) *adj.* Appointed or designated by oneself rather than by others: a *self-appointed* boss.

self-as·ser·tion (self′ə·sûr′shən) *n.* The asserting or putting forward of oneself, one's opinions, claims, or rights. — **self′-as·ser′tive** *adj.* — **self′-as·ser′tive·ly** *adv.*

self-as·sured (self′ə·shŏŏrd′) *adj.* Confident in one's own abilities; self-reliant. — **self′-as·sur′ance** *n.*

self-cen·tered (self′sen′tərd) *adj.* Concerned chiefly with one's own affairs and interests, often with a lack of consideration for others. Also *Brit.* **self′-cen′tred.** — **self-cen′tered·ness** *n.* — **self-cen′tered·ly** *adv.*

self-col·ored (self′kul′ərd) *adj.* **1.** Having the natural color. **2.** Of but one color or tint. Also *Brit.* **self′-col′oured.**

self-com·mand (self′kə·mand′, -mänd′) *n.* The state of having all the faculties and powers fully at command.

self-com·posed (self′kəm·pōzd′) *adj.* Controlling one's emotions; calm.

self-con·ceit (self′kən·sēt′) *n.* An unduly high opinion of oneself or one's abilities, acquirements, etc.; vanity. — **self′-con·ceit′ed** *adj.*

self-con·fi·dence (self′kon′fə·dəns) *n.* Confidence in oneself or in one's own unaided powers, judgment, etc. — **self′-con′fi·dent** *adj.* — **self′-con′fi·dent·ly** *adv.*

self-con·scious (self′kon′shəs) *adj.* **1.** Unduly conscious that one is observed by others; embarrassed by inability to forget oneself; ill at ease. **2.** Manifesting such consciousness or embarrassment. **3.** Conscious of one's existence. — **self′-con′scious·ly** *adv.* — **self′-con′scious·ness** *n.*

self-con·tained (self′kən·tānd′) *adj.* **1.** Keeping one's thoughts and feelings to oneself; uncommunicative; impassive. **2.** Exercising self-control. **3.** Complete and independent; self-sustaining. **4.** Having all parts needed for working order, as a machine bearing its own motor.

self-con·tra·dic·tion (self′kon′trə·dik′shən) *n.* **1.** The act or state of contradicting oneself or itself. **2.** That which contradicts itself. — **self′-con′tra·dic′to·ry** *adj.*

self-con·trol (self′kən·trōl′) *n.* The act, power, or habit of having one's faculties or energies under control of the will.

self-de·fense (self′di·fens′) *n.* Defense of oneself, one's property, or one's reputation. Also *Brit.* **self′-de·fence′.** — **self′-de·fen′sive** *adj.*

self-de·ni·al (self′di·nī′əl) *n.* The act or power of denying oneself gratification; passive self-sacrifice. — **Syn.** See AB-STINENCE, SELF-ABNEGATION. — **self′-de·ny′ing** *adj.* — **self′-de·ny′ing·ly** *adv.*

self-de·ter·mi·na·tion (self′di·tûr′mə·nā′shən) *n.* **1.** The principle of free will; decision by oneself. **2.** Decision by the people of a country or section as to its future political status. — **self′-de·ter′min·ing** *adj. & n.*

self-de·vo·tion (self′di·vō′shən) *n.* Devotion of oneself, with one's claims, wishes, or interests, to the service of a person or a cause. — **self′-de·vo′tion·al** *adj.*

self-dis·ci·pline (self′dis′ə·plin) *n.* The discipline or training of oneself, often for improvement.

self-dis·trust (self′dis·trust′) *n.* Doubting of one's own abilities, judgment, etc.; lack of self-confidence. — **self′-dis·trust′ful** *adj.* — **self′-dis·trust′ful·ly** *adv.*

self-driv·en (self′driv′ən) *adj.* Driven by itself.

self-ed·u·cat·ed (self′ej′ŏŏ·kā′tid) *adj.* **1.** Educated through one's own efforts without the aid of instructors. **2.** Educated at one's own expense. — **self′-ed′u·ca′tion** *n.*

self-ef·face·ment (self′i·fās′mənt) *n.* The keeping of oneself in the background through modesty, timidity, etc.

self-em·ployed (self′im·ploid′) *adj.* Earning one's livelihood from one's own business, skills, or profession; being one's own employer. — **self′-em·ploy′ment** *n.*

self-es·teem (self′ə·stēm′) *n.* A good opinion of oneself; an overestimate of oneself. — **Syn.** See EGOTISM, PRIDE.

self-ev·i·dent (self′ev′ə·dənt) *adj.* Carrying its evidence or proof in itself; requiring no proof of its truth. — **self′-ev′i·dence** *n.* — **self′-ev′i·dent·ly** *adv.*

self-ex·am·i·na·tion (self′ig·zam′ə·nā′shən) *n.* Examination of one's own motives, desires, habits, etc.

self-ex·e·cut·ing (self′ek′sə·kyŏŏ′ting) *adj.* Containing provisions for its own execution independent of legislation: said of a law, etc.

self-ex·ist·ence (self′ig·zis′təns) *n.* Inherent, underived, independent existence. — **self′-ex·ist′ent** *adj.*

self-ex·plan·a·to·ry (self′ik·splan′ə·tôr′ē, -tō′rē) *adj.* Easily comprehended without explanation; evident; plain; obvious.

self-ex·pres·sion (self′ik·spresh′ən) *n.* Expression of one's own temperament or emotions, as in art.

self-fer·til·i·za·tion (self′fûr′təl·ə·zā′shən, -ī·zā′shən) *n. Biol.* Fertilization of an ovum by sperm from the same animal or of a plant ovule by its own pollen.

self-gov·ern·ment (self′guv′ərn·mənt, -ər·mənt) *n.* **1.** Government of a country or region by its own people; self-rule. **2.** The state of being so governed. **3.** *Archaic* Self-control. — **self′-gov′erned, self′-gov′ern·ing** *adj.*

self-hard·en·ing (self′här′də·ning) *adj.* Pertaining to or designating materials that will harden properly without further special treatment. Also **self′-hard′ened.**

self-heal (self′hēl′) *n.* **1.** Any of various weedy, perennial herbs (genus *Prunella*) with violet or purple flowers, formerly reputed to cure disease, as the **common self·heal** (*P. vulgaris*) of North America: also called *bluecurls, heal-all.* **2.** One of various similar plants, as the sanicle.

self-help (self′help′) *n.* The act or condition of getting along by one's own efforts without the aid of others.

self·hood (self′hŏŏd) *n.* **1.** The state of being an individual, or that which constitutes such a state; personality. **2.** Selfishness; self-centeredness.

self-i·den·ti·ty (self′ī·den′tə·tē) *n.* **1.** The identity of a thing with itself. **2.** That state of consciousness by or through which the self recognizes itself as one and the same.

self-im·por·tance (self′im·pôr′təns) *n.* Pompous self-conceit. — **self′-im·por′tant** *adj.*

self-im·prove·ment (self′im·prŏŏv′mənt) *n.* Improvement of one's abilities or condition through one's own efforts.

self-in·duced (self′in·dŏŏst′, -dyŏŏst′) *adj.* **1.** Induced by oneself or itself. **2.** *Electr.* Produced by self-induction.

self-in·duc·tion (self′in·duk′shən) *n. Electr.* Induction within the same circuit, causing it to resist any change in the amount of current flowing in it. — **self′-in·duc′tive** *adj.*

self-in·dul·gence (self′in·dul′jəns) *n.* The indulgence or gratification of one's own desires, weaknesses, etc. — **self′-in·dul′gent** *adj.* — **self′-in·dul′gent·ly** *adv.*

self-in·flict·ed (self′in·flik′tid) *adj.* Inflicted on oneself by oneself: a *self-inflicted* wound. — **self′-in·flic′tion** *n.*

self-in·sur·ance (self′in·shŏŏr′əns) *n.* The practice of setting aside money to cover possible loss rather than seeking coverage by an insurance company.

self-in·ter·est (self′in′tər·ist, -in′trist) *n.* Personal interest or advantage, or the pursuit of it; selfishness. — **self′-in′ter·est·ed** *adj.*

self-ish (sel′fish) *adj.* **1.** Caring chiefly for oneself or one's own interests or comfort, especially to the point of disregarding the welfare or wishes of others. **2.** Proceeding from or characterized by undue love of self. — **self′ish·ly** *adv.*

self·ish·ness (sel′fish·nis) *n.* The quality of being selfish. — **Syn.** self-seeking, self-love. See EGOTISM.

self-knowl·edge (self′nol′ij) *n.* Knowledge of one's own character, motives, limitations, etc.

self·less (self′lis) *adj.* Regardless of self; unselfish. — **self′less·ly** *adv.* — **self′less·ness** *n.*

self-lim·it·ed (self′lim′it·id) *adj.* **1.** Independent of or unaffected by external influences. **2.** *Med.* Running a definite course, as certain diseases.

self-liq·ui·dat·ing (self′lik′wə·dā′ting) *adj.* Designating a business transaction in which goods in great demand are converted into cash over a short period; also, paying back by means of dividends, etc., the money originally invested.

self-load·ing (self′lō′ding) *adj.* Of firearms, utilizing a portion of the force of the exploding gas or of recoil to extract and eject the empty case and chamber the next round.

self-love (self′luv′) *n.* The desire or tendency that leads one to seek his own well-being. — **self′-lov′ing** *adj.*

self-made (self′mād′) *adj.* **1.** Having attained honor, wealth, etc., by one's own efforts. **2.** Made by oneself.

self-per·cep·tion (self′pər·sep′shən) *n.* Perception of one's own existence or mental states; introspection.

self-pit·y (self′pit′ē) *n.* The act or state of pitying oneself. — **self′-pit′y·ing** *adj.* — **self′-pit′y·ing·ly** *adv.*

self-pol·li·na·tion (self′pol′ə·nā′shən) *n. Bot.* The transfer of pollen from stamens to pistils of the same flower. — **self′-pol′li·nat·ed** *adj.*

self-por·trait (self′pôr′trit, -pōr′-, -trāt) *n.* A portrait or portrayal of oneself; especially, a likeness of himself executed by a painter or sculptor.

self-pos·ses·sion (self′pə·zesh′ən) *n.* **1.** The full possession or control of one's powers or faculties; freedom from perturbation, perplexity, or excitement. **2.** Presence of mind; self-command. — **self′-pos·sessed′** *adj.*

self-pres·er·va·tion (self′prez′ər·vā′shən) *n.* **1.** The protection of oneself from destruction. **2.** The urge to protect oneself, regarded as an instinct.

self-prof·it (self′prof′it) *n.* Advantage to oneself.

self-pro·nounc·ing (self′prə·noun′sing) *adj.* Having marks of pronunciation and stress applied to a word without phonetic alteration of the spelling.

self-pro·pelled (self′prə·peld′) *adj.* **1.** Able to propel itself. **2.** Having the means of propulsion contained within itself, as an automobile.

self-re·al·i·za·tion (self′rē′əl·i·zā′shən, -ī-) *n.* Full development of one's potential abilities or of one's personality.

self-re·gard (self′ri·gärd′) *n.* **1.** Regard or consideration for oneself or one's own interests. **2.** Estimation of self.

self-re·li·ance (self′ri·lī′əns) *n.* Reliance on one's own abilities, resources, or judgment. — **self′-re′li′ant** *adj.*

self-re·nun·ci·a·tion (self′ri·nun′sē·ā′shən) *n.* Renunciation of one's own rights, privileges, or claims. — **self′-re·nun′ci·a·to·ry** (-sē·ə·tôr′ē, -tō′rē) *adj.*

self-re·spect (self′ri·spekt′) *n.* Regard or respect for oneself and one's own character; rational self-esteem. — **self′-re·spect′ing** *adj.*

self-re·straint (self′ri·strānt′) *n.* Restraint, as of the passions, by the force of one's own will; self-control.

self-right·eous (self′rī′chəs) *adj.* Righteous in one's own estimation; pharisaic. — **self′-right′eous·ly** *adv.* — **self′-right′eous·ness** *n.*

self-ris·ing (self′rī′zing) *adj.* **1.** That rises of itself. **2.** Having the leaven already added, as some flours.

self-rule (self′rōōl′) *n.* **1.** Rule or power over oneself. **2.** Self-government (defs. 1 & 2).

self-sac·ri·fice (self′sak′rə·fīs) *n.* The sacrifice or subordination of one's self or one's personal welfare or wishes, for the sake of duty or for the good of others. — **Syn.** See SELF-ABNEGATION. — **self′-sac′ri·fic′ing** *adj.*

self·same (self′sām′) *adj.* Exactly the same; identical. — **Syn.** See IDENTICAL. — **self′same′ness** *n.*

self-sat·is·fac·tion (self′sat′is·fak′shən) *n.* Satisfaction with one's own actions and characteristics; conceit; complacency. — **self′-sat′is·fied** *adj.* — **self′-sat′is·fy′ing** *adj.*

self-seek·ing (self′sē′king) *adj.* Exclusively seeking one's own interests or gain. — *n.* Actions, motives, etc., characteristic of a self-seeking person. — **self′-seek′er** *n.*

self-ser·vice (self′sûr′vis) *adj.* Designating a restaurant, store, etc., where patrons serve themselves.

self-ser·ving (self′sûr′ving) *adj.* Tending to advance one's own interests, often in disregard of facts or at the expense of others.

self-start·er (self′stär′tər) *n.* A starter (def. 3).

self-styled (self′stīld′) *adj.* Characterized (as such) by oneself: a *self-styled* gentleman.

self-suf·fi·cient (self′sə·fish′ənt) *adj.* **1.** Able to support or maintain oneself without aid or cooperation from others. **2.** Having overweening confidence in oneself. Also **self′-suf·fic′ing** (-sə·fī′sing). — **self′-suf·fi′cien·cy** *n.*

self-sup·port (self′sə·pôrt′, -pōrt′) *n.* The act or state of supporting oneself entirely by one's own efforts. — **self′-sup·port′ed, self′-sup·port′ing** *adj.*

self-sus·tain·ing (self′sə·stān′ing) *adj.* Sustaining oneself or itself without outside help; self-supporting.

self-taught (self′tôt′) *adj.* Taught by oneself or through one's own efforts, without the aid of formal instruction.

self-will (self′wil′) *n.* Strong or tenacious adherence to one's own will or wish, especially with disregard of the wishes of others; obstinacy. — **self′-willed′** *adj.*

self-wind·ing (self′wīn′ding) *adj. Mech.* Having a magnetic, electrical, or other device that automatically winds a clock or other mechanism.

self-wrong (self′rông′, -rong′) *n.* Injury done to one's self.

Sel·juk (sel·jōōk′) *n.* A member of one of several Turkish dynasties that reigned over a large part of central and western Asia from the 11th to the 13th centuries. — *adj.* Pertaining to a Seljuk. Also **Sel·ju·ki·an** (sel·jōō′kē·ən). [< Turkish *seljūq*, after *Seljūq*, a Turkish chieftain, reputed ancestor of the Seljuk dynasties]

Selk. Selkirk.

Sel·kirk (sel′kûrk) A county of SE Scotland; 267 sq. mi.; pop. 20,273 (est. 1969); county seat, **Selkirk**, pop. 5,527 (est. 1969). Also **Sel′kirk·shire** (-shir).

Sel·kirk (sel′kûrk), **Alexander**, 1676–1721, Scottish sailor; his adventures while marooned on Juan Fernandez Island, Pacific Ocean, for four years, are said to have suggested Defoe's *Robinson Crusoe*.

Selkirk Mountains A range of the Rocky Mountains in SE British Columbia; highest peak, Mt. Sir Sanford, 11,590 ft.

sell[1] (sel) *v.* **sold, sell·ing** *v.t.* **1.** To transfer (property) to another for money or for some other consideration; dispose of by sale. **2.** To deal in; offer for sale. **3.** To deliver, surrender, or betray for a price or reward: to *sell* one's honor. **4.** To promote or influence the sale of: Good advertising *sells* many products. **5.** *Informal* To cause to accept or approve something: with *on*: They *sold* him on the scheme. **6.** *Informal* To cause the acceptance or approval of: He

always *sold* himself well. **7.** *Slang* To deceive; cheat. — *v.i.* **8.** To transfer ownership for money, etc.; engage in selling. **9.** To be on sale; be sold. **10.** *Informal* To attract buyers: This item *sells* well. **11.** *Informal* To gain acceptance or approval: Will his plan *sell?* — **to sell off** To get rid of by selling. — **to sell out 1.** To sell all one's merchandise, possessions, etc. **2.** *Slang* To betray through a secret bargain or agreement. — **to sell up** *Chiefly Brit.* **1.** To sell all of one's goods, possessions, etc. **2.** To dispose of the goods of (a bankrupt person, etc.) so as to satisfy creditors: to *sell* him *up*. — *n.* **1.** On the stock exchange, a stock that ought to be sold. **2.** *Slang* A trick; joke; swindle. [OE *sellan* to give]

sell[2] (sel) *n. Obs.* **1.** An elevated seat; also, any seat. **2.** An honorable place. **3.** A saddle. [< OF *selle* < L *sella* seat, ult. < *sedere* to sit]

sell·er (sel′ər) *n.* **1.** One who sells. **2.** Something with a measure of salability: This book is a good *seller*.

sell·ing-plat·er (sel′ing·plā′tər) *n.* A horse that runs in a selling race.

selling race *Brit.* A horse race in which the entrants may be claimed for a set price, and the winning horse must be offered at auction. Compare CLAIMING RACE. Also **sell′ing·er**.

sell·out (sel′out′) *n.* **1.** An act of selling out. **2.** *Informal* A performance for which all seats have been sold. **3.** *Slang* A betrayal through a secret bargain or agreement.

Sel·ma (sel′mə) A city in south central Alabama, on the Alabama River; pop. 27,379.

Sel·syn (sel′sin) *n.* A remote-control apparatus of the synchro type: a trade name.

Selt·zer (selt′sər) *n.* An effervescing mineral water. Also **Seltzer water.** [Alter. of G *Selterser*, from *Nieder Selters*, a village in SW Prussia, its place of origin]

sel·vage (sel′vij) *n.* **1.** The edge of a woven fabric so finished that it will not ravel. **2.** Any similar edge. **3.** The edge plate of a lock having an opening for a bolt. Also **sel′vedge**. [< SELF + EDGE, trans. of MDu. *selfegghe*]

selves (selvz) Plural of SELF.

Sem. **1.** Seminary. **2.** Semitic.

se·man·tic (si·man′tik) *adj.* **1.** Of or pertaining to meaning. **2.** Of or relating to semantics. [< Gk. *sēmantikos* < *sēmainein* to signify]

se·man·ti·cist (si·man′tə·sist) *n.* A specialist in semantics.

se·man·tics (si·man′tiks) *n.pl.* (construed as *singular*) **1.** *Ling.* The study of the meanings of speech forms, especially of the development and changes in meaning of words and word groups. **2.** *Logic* The relation between signs or symbols and what they signify or denote: also called *semasiology, semiotics.* **3.** Loosely, verbal trickery.

sem·a·phore (sem′ə·fôr, -fōr) *n.* An apparatus for making signals, as with movable arms, disks, flags, or lanterns. — *v.t.* To send by semaphore. [< F *sémaphore* < Gk. *sēma* a sign + -PHORE] — **sem′a·phor′ic** (-fôr′ik, -for′ik) or **-i·cal** *adj.*

Se·ma·rang (sə·mä′räng) A port city on northern Java, Indonesia; pop. 487,006 (1961): also *Samarang*.

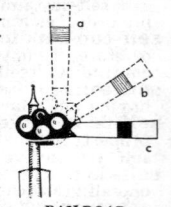

RAILROAD SEMAPHORE

a Clear. *b* Approach. *c* Stop.

se·ma·si·ol·o·gy (si·mā′sē·ol′ə·jē, -zē-) *n. pl.* **·gies** Semantics (def. 2). [< Gk. *sēmasia* the signification of a word < *sēma* sign + -LOGY] — **se·ma·si·o·log·i·cal** (si·mā′sē·ə·loj′i·kəl, -zē-) *adj.* — **se·ma·si·ol′o·gist** *n.*

se·mat·ic (si·mat′ik) *adj.* **1.** Of the nature of a sign; significant; warning. **2.** *Biol.* In animal coloration, serving to distinguish as a means of recognition or warning. [< Gk. *sēma, -atos* a sign]

sem·bla·ble (sem′blə·bəl) *adj.* **1.** Resembling; similar. **2.** Apparent: not real. — *n.* A thing resembling another thing. Also **sem′bla·tive**. [< OF < *sembler*. See SEMBLANCE.] — **sem′bla·bly** *adv.*

sem·blance (sem′bləns) *n.* **1.** A mere show without reality; pretense. **2.** Outward appearance; look; aspect. **3.** A likeness or resemblance. [< OF < *sembler* to seem < L *simulare, similare* to simulate < *similis* like]

se·mé (sə·mā′, *Fr.* sə·mā′) *adj. Heraldry* Strewn or scattered over with small bearings, as fleurs-de-lis; powdered. [< OF, pp. of *semer* to sow < L *seminare* < *semen* seed]

se·mei·ol·o·gy (sē′mī·ol′ə·jē, sē′mē-), **se·mei·ot·ic** (sē′mī·ot′ik, sē′mē-), etc. See SEMIOLOGY, SEMIOTIC, etc.

Sem·e·le (sem′ə·lē) In Greek mythology, the mother of Dionysus by Zeus. She was destroyed by lightning when she asked to see Zeus as he appeared to the gods.

se·meme (sē′mēm) *n. Ling.* The meaning of a morpheme. [< Gk. *sēma* sign; on analogy with *phoneme*]

se·men (sē′mən) *n.* The impregnating fluid of male animals that contains spermatozoa; seed. [< L < *serere* to sow]

se·mes·ter (si·mes′tər) *n.* **1.** A college half year. **2.** In U.S. colleges and universities, a period of instruction, usually lasting 17 or 18 weeks. [< G < L (*cursus*) *semestris* (a period) of six months < *sex* six + *mensis* month] — **se·mes′tral** *adj.*

sem·i (sem′ī) 1. *U.S. Informal* A semitrailer. 2. *Canadian Slang* An American: so called from the occasional U.S. pronunciation (sem′ī).

semi- *prefix* 1. Not fully; partially; partly: *semiautomatic, semicivilized.* 2. Exactly half: *semicircle.* 3. Occurring twice (in the period specified): *semiweekly.* Abbr. *s.* [< L] ◆ *Semi-* (def. 1) appears as a prefix in many words, as in the following words and in the list below. It is pronounced sem′ē, sem′ə, or sometimes sem′ī.

sem·i·an·nu·al (sem′ē-an′yōō-əl) *adj.* Issued or occurring twice a year; half-yearly. — *n.* A publication issued twice a year. — **sem·i·an′nu·al·ly** *adv.*

sem·i·a·quat·ic (sem′ē-ə-kwat′ik, -kwot′ik) *adj. Biol.* Adapted for living or growing near water, as certain types of plants and animals.

sem·i·au·to·mat·ic (sem′ē-ô′tə-mat′ik) *adj.* 1. Partly automatic. 2. Of firearms, self-loading but firing once at each pull on the trigger: compare AUTOMATIC (def. 5).

sem·i·breve (sem′ē-brēv′, -brev′) *n. Chiefly Brit. Music* A whole note.

sem·i·cen·ten·ni·al (sem′ē-sen-ten′ē-əl) *adj.* Occurring or celebrated at the end of fifty years from some event. — *n.* A semicentennial anniversary.

sem·i·cir·cle (sem′ē-sûr′kəl) *n.* 1. A half-circle; an arc or a segment of 180°. 2. Anything formed or arranged in a half-circle. — **sem′i·cir′cu·lar** (-kyə-lər) *adj.*

semicircular canal *Anat.* One of the three tubular structures in the labyrinth of the ear, serving as the organ of equilibrium. For illustration see EAR.

sem·i·cir·cum·fer·ence (sem′ē-sər-kum′fər-əns, -frəns) *n.* One half of a circumference.

sem·i·civ·i·lized (sem′ē-siv′ə-līzd) *adj.* Partly civilized.

sem·i·co·lon (sem′ē-kō′lən, sem′ə-) *n.* A mark (;) of punctuation, indicating a greater degree of separation than the comma.

sem·i·con·duc·tor (sem′ē-kən-duk′tər) *n. Physics* One of a class of substances, as germanium, silicon, and lead sulfide, whose electronic conductivity at ordinary temperatures is between that of a metal and an insulator, used in the manufacture of transistors.

sem·i·con·scious (sem′ē-kon′shəs) *adj.* Partly conscious; half-conscious.

sem·i·de·tached (sem′ē-di-tacht′) *adj.* Joined to another on one side only; especially, designating a house having one wall in common with another house.

sem·i·di·am·e·ter (sem′ē-dī-am′ə-tər) *n.* A half of a diameter; a radius.

sem·i·di·ur·nal (sem′ē-dī-ûr′nəl) *adj.* 1. Pertaining to or continuing during a half-day. 2. Occurring or accomplished in a half-day, or once each half-day. 3. Designating either half of the arc described by a heavenly body during its rising or setting.

sem·i·dome (sem′ē-dōm′) *n. Archit.* A roof structure resembling half of a dome divided vertically.

sem·i·el·lip·ti·cal (sem′ē-i-lip′ti-kəl) *adj.* Having the form of half of an ellipse, especially one that has been divided along the major axis.

sem·i·fi·nal (sem′ē-fī′nəl) *n.* 1. In sports, a competition that precedes the final event. 2. One of two competitions in a tournament, the winners of each meeting in the final. — *adj.* Next before the final. — **sem′i·fi′nal·ist** *n.*

sem·i·flu·id (sem′ē-flōō′id) *adj.* Fluid, but thick and viscous. — *n.* A thick, viscous fluid.

sem·i·for·mal (sem′ē-fôr′məl) *adj.* Partly but not altogether formal, as a social event. — *n.* Something semiformal in character. — **sem′i·for′mal·ly** *adv.*

sem·i·liq·uid (sem′ē-lik′wid) *adj.* Half liquid. — *n.* A partly liquid substance.

sem·i·lu·nar (sem′ē-lōō′nər) *adj.* Resembling or shaped like a half-moon; crescentic. Also **sem′i·lu′nate** (-nāt).

semilunar bone *Anat.* The middle bone in the upper row of wrist bones.

semilunar valve *Anat.* One of the crescent-shaped pockets at the entrances to the aorta and the pulmonary artery, whose function is to prevent the backward flow of blood to the left and the right ventricles, respectively, of the heart.

SEMIDOME

sem·i·month·ly (sem′ē-munth′lē) *adj.* Taking place twice a month. — *n. pl.* **·lies** A publication issued twice a month. — *adv.* At half-monthly intervals.

sem·i·nal (sem′ə-nəl) *adj.* 1. Of, pertaining to, or containing seeds or semen. 2. Having productive power; germinal; propagative. 3. Not developed; embryonic; rudimentary. Also *seminary.* [< OF < L *seminalis* < *semen, seminis* semen, seed] — **sem′i·nal·ly** *adv.*

sem·i·nar (sem′ə-när) *n.* 1. A group of advanced students at a college or university, meeting regularly and informally with a professor for discussion of research problems. 2. The course thus conducted. Also called *seminary.* [< G < L *seminarium.* See SEMINARY.]

sem·i·nar·i·an (sem′ə-ner′ē-ən) *n.* A student at a seminary.

sem·i·nar·y (sem′ə-ner′ē) *n. pl.* **·nar·ies** 1. A special school, especially one for the training of priests, ministers, or rabbis. 2. A school, especially an academy for girls. 3. The place where anything is nurtured. 4. A seminar. — *adj.* 1. Seminal. 2. Pertaining to a seminary. Abbr. *Sem.* [< L *seminarium* seed plot, orig. neut. of *seminarius* seminal < *semen, seminis* seed, semen]

sem·i·na·tion (sem′ə-nā′shən) *n.* 1. The act of sowing or spreading; dispersion of seeds. 2. Propagation; reproduction. [< L *seminatio, -onis* < *seminare* to sow < *semen* seed]

sem·i·nif·er·ous (sem′ə-nif′ər-əs) *adj.* 1. Carrying or producing semen. 2. Bearing a seed or seeds.

sem·i·niv·o·rous (sem′ə-niv′ər-əs) *adj.* Feeding on seeds.

Sem·i·nole (sem′ə-nōl) *n.* One of a Florida tribe of North American Indians of Muskhogean stock, an offshoot of the Creeks, now chiefly in Oklahoma. [< Muskhogean (Creek) *Simanóle,* lit., separatist, runaway]

sem·i·of·fi·cial (sem′ē-ə-fish′əl) *adj.* Having some official authority or sanction; official to a certain extent.

se·mi·ol·o·gy (sē′mē-ol′ə-jē, sē′mī-) *n.* 1. The science that relates to sign language. 2. Symptomatology. 3. The use of signs in signaling. Also spelled *semeiology.* [< Gk. *sēmeion,* dim. of *sēma* mark + -LOGY]

sem·i·o·paque (sem′ē-ō-pāk′) *adj.* Translucent but not transparent; partly opaque.

se·mi·ot·ic (sē′mē-ot′ik, sē′mī-) *adj.* 1. Of or pertaining to semantics (def. 2). 2. Relating to symptomatology. Also spelled *semeiotic.* Also **se′mi·ot′i·cal.** [< Gk. *sēmeiōtikos* < *sēmeion.* See SEMIOLOGY.]

semiacquaintance	semi-Christian	semidivine	semihobo	semiovoid	semisacred
semiadherent	semiclerical	semidomestic	semihostile	semipagan	semisatiric
semiaffectionate	semiclosed	semidomesticated	semihumanitarian	semipanic	semisatirical
semiagricultural	semiclosure	semidry	semihumorous	semiparallel	semiscientific
semialcoholic	semicoagulated	semi-Empire	semi-idle	semiparalysis	semisecrecy
semiallegiance	semicollapsible	semienclosed	semi-idleness	semipastoral	semisecret
semianarchist	semicolonial	semierect	semi-incandescent	semipeace	semiserious
semiangular	semicoma	semieremitical	semi-independence	semiperfect	semiseriousness
semianimal	semicomplete	semiexposed	semi-independent	semiperishable	semisocial
semianimated	semiconceal	semiextinction	semi-intoxicated	semipermanent	semisocialism
semiarborescent	semiconfident	semifailure	semi-intoxication	semiperspicuous	semisoft
semiarchitectural	semiconfinement	semifatalistic	semi-invalid	semipinnate	semispontaneity
semiarid	semiconformist	semifeudalism	semileafless	semiplastic	semispontaneous
semiatheist	semiconnection	semifictional	semilegendary	semipolitical	semistagnant
semiattached	semiconservative	semifinished	semiliberal	semipolitician	semistagnation
semiautonomous	semiconversion	semifit	semilined	semiporous	semistarvation
semiautonomy	semicooperation	semifitting	semiliterate	semipublic	semistarved
semibald	semicooperative	semifixed	semilucent	semiradical	semisuccess
semibarbarian	semicured	semiflexed	semimilitary	semiraw	semisuccessful
semibarbaric	semicylindrical	semifluctuating	semimobile	semireactionary	semisuspension
semibarbarism	semidangerous	semiforeign	semimodern	semirebellion	semisymmetric
semibarbarous	semidarkness	semifriable	semimonastic	semireligious	semisymmetrical
semibarren	semideaf	semifrontier	semimonopoly	semiresolute	semitailored
semibleached	semidelirious	semifunctional	semimute	semirespectability	semitechnical
semiblind	semidenatured	semigala	semimystical	semirespectable	semitrained
semiblunt	semidependent	semigenuflection	seminecessary	semiretirement	semitruth
semiboiled	semidestructive	semi-Gothic	seminervous	semiriddle	semivirtue
semibourgeois	semideveloped	semigranulate	semioblivious	semi-Romanesque	semivital
semichannel	semidiaphanous	semihard	semiobscurity	semi-Romanized	semivoluntary
semichaotic	semidigested	semihigh	semiopened	semiroyal	semiwarfare
semichivalrous	semidirect	semihistorical	semiorganized	semirustic	semiwild

se·mi·ot·ics (sē'mē·ot'iks, sē'mī-) *n.pl.* (*construed as singular*) **1.** Semantics (def. 2). **2.** Symptomatology. Also spelled *semeiotics*.

Se·mi·pa·la·tinsk (syi·myi·pə·lä'tyinsk) A city in the eastern Kazakh S.S.R., on the Irtysh; pop. 236,000 (1970).

sem·i·pal·mate (sem'ē·pal'māt, -mit) *adj. Ornithol.* Having the toes connected by webs for less than half their length, as many shore birds. Also **sem'i·pal'mat·ed.**

sem·i·par·a·sit·ic (sem'ē·par'ə·sit'ik) *adj. Biol.* Partly parasitic, as certain bacteria.

sem·i·per·me·a·ble (sem'ē·pûr'mē·ə·bəl) *adj.* Partially permeable, as membranes that separate a solvent from the dissolved substance.

sem·i·por·ce·lain (sem'ē·pôr'sə·lin, -pōr'-, -pôrs'lin, -pōrs'-) *n.* **1.** A grade of porcelain having little or no translucency. **2.** Earthenware resembling porcelain.

sem·i·post·al (sem'ē·pōs'təl) *adj.* Designating a postage stamp or series of stamps sold by postal authorities for more than the franking value, the additional proceeds usually going to a philanthropic purpose. — *n.* A semipostal stamp.

sem·i·pre·cious (sem'ē·presh'əs) *adj.* Of, pertaining to, or designating gemstones, as jade, garnet, opal, amethyst, etc., that are somewhat less rare or valuable than precious stones.

sem·i·pri·vate (sem'ē·prī'vit) *adj.* Partly but not wholly private, as a hospital room for two or several patients.

sem·i·pro·fes·sion·al (sem'ē·prə·fesh'ən·əl) *adj.* **1.** Engaged in a sport for profit, but not as a full-time occupation. **2.** Of or pertaining to organizations, teams, etc., composed of semiprofessional persons. **3.** Resembling a profession in some respects but not in others. — *n.* **1.** A semiprofessional athlete. **2.** One whose occupation resembles a profession in some respects. Also (for adj. & n. def. 1) *Informal* **sem'i·pro'** (-prō'). — **sem'i·pro·fes'sion·al·ly** *adv.*

sem·i·qua·ver (sem'ē·kwā'vər) *n. Chiefly Brit. Music* A sixteenth note.

Se·mir·a·mis (si·mir'ə·mis) In Assyrian legend, the beautiful and wise wife of Ninus and founder of Babylon.

sem·i·rig·id (sem'ē·rij'id) *adj. Aeron.* Partly rigid, as an airship in which an exterior stiffener supports the load. — *n.* A semirigid airship.

sem·i·round (sem'ē·round') *adj.* Having one side round and the other flat. — *n.* A semiround object.

sem·i·skilled (sem'ē·skild') *adj.* Partly skilled, but not enough to perform specialized work.

sem·i·sol·id (sem'ē·sol'id) *adj.* Nearly solid; partly solid.

Sem·ite (sem'īt, sē'mīt) *n.* **1.** One of a people of Caucasian stock, now represented by the Jews and Arabs, but originally including the ancient Babylonians, Assyrians, Arameans, Phoenicians. etc. **2.** A person believed to be or considered as a descendant of Shem. Also *Shemite.* [< NL *Semita* < LL *Sem* Shem < Gk. *Sēm* < Hebrew *Shēm*]

Se·mit·ic (sə·mit'ik) *adj.* Of or pertaining to the Semites, or to any of their languages. — *n.* A subfamily of the Hamito-Semitic family of languages, divided into three groups, **East Semitic** (Akkadian), **Northwest Semitic** (Phoenician, Hebrew, Aramaic, etc.), and **Southwest Semitic** (Arabic, Ethiopic, Amharic, etc.). Abbr. *Sem.*

Se·mit·ics (sə·mit'iks) *n.pl.* (*construed as sing.*) The scientific study of the history, language, and literature of the Semitic peoples.

Sem·i·tism (sem'ə·tiz'əm) *n.* **1.** A Semitic word or idiom. **2.** Semitic practices, opinions, or customs collectively. **3.** Any political or economic policy favoring or thought to favor the Jews.

sem·i·tone (sem'ē·tōn') *n. Music* The smallest interval of the chromatic scale; a minor second: also called *half step, half tone.* — **sem'i·ton'ic** (-ton'ik) *adj.*

sem·i·trail·er (sem'ē·trā'lər) *n.* A trailer having wheels only at the rear, the front end resting on the tractor or towing vehicle: also, *U.S. Informal, semi.*

sem·i·trans·lu·cent (sem'ē·trans·lōō'sənt, -tranz-) *adj.* Half or partly translucent.

sem·i·trans·par·ent (sem'ē·trans·par'ənt, -tranz-) *adj.* Half or partly transparent.

sem·i·trop·i·cal (sem'ē·trop'i·kəl) *adj.* Partly tropical.

sem·i·vit·ri·fied (sem'ē·vit'rə·fīd) *adj.* Partly vitrified.

sem·i·vo·cal (sem'ē·vō'kəl) *adj. Phonet.* Of or pertaining to a semivowel. Also **sem'i·vo·cal'ic** (-kal'ik).

sem·i·vow·el (sem'ē·vou'əl) *n. Phonet.* A vowellike sound used as a consonant, as (w), (y), and (r): also called *glide.*

sem·i·week·ly (sem'ē·wēk'lē) *adj.* Issued or occurring twice a week. — *n. pl.* **·lies** A publication issued twice a week. — *adv.* At half-weekly intervals.

sem·i·year·ly (sem'ē·yir'lē) *adj.* Issued or occurring twice a year. — *n. pl.* **·lies** A semiyearly occurrence. — *adv.* At half-yearly intervals.

Semmes (semz), **Raphael,** 1809–77, American Confederate naval officer.

sem·o·li·na (sem'ə·lē'nə) *n.* The gritty or grainlike portions of wheat retained in the bolting machine after the fine flour has been passed through. [Alter. of Ital. *semolino,* dim. of *semola* bran < L *simila* fine flour]

Sem·pach (zem'päkh) A town in central Switzerland; scene of a Swiss victory over the Austrians, 1386; pop. about 1,500.

sem·per fi·de·lis (sem'pər fi·dē'lis, fi·dā'lis) *Latin* Always faithful: motto of the U.S. Marine Corps.

sem·per pa·ra·tus (sem'pər pə·rā'təs) *Latin* Always prepared: motto of the U.S. Coast Guard.

sem·pi·ter·nal (sem'pə·tûr'nəl) *adj.* Eternal; everlasting. [< OF *sempiternel* or LL *sempiternalis* < L *sempiternus* everlasting < *semper* always] — **sem'pi·ter'ni·ty** *n.*

sem·pli·ce (sem'plē·chā) *adj. Music* Simple; unaffected: a direction to performers. [< Ital. < L *simplex, simplicis*]

sem·pre (sem'prā) *adv. Music* Always; throughout: *sempre legato.* [< Ital. < L *semper*]

semp·stress (semp'stris, sem'-) *n.* A seamstress.

sen (sen) *n. pl.* **sen** **1.** A former monetary unit and coin of Japan, equal to one hundredth of a yen. **2.** A monetary unit and coin of Indonesia, equal to one hundredth of a rupiah.

-sen A descendant of: Amund*sen*: a patronymic suffix commonly used in Norwegian and Danish surnames, equivalent to the English *-son.*

Sen. or **sen.** **1.** Senate; senator. **2.** Senior.

sen·a·ry (sen'ər·ē) *adj.* Of or pertaining to six; containing six units. [< L *senarius* < *seni* six each < *sex* six]

sen·ate (sen'it) *n.* **1.** The governing body of some universities and institutions of learning. **2.** An advisory body of members of the faculty and representative students in a school or college. **3.** A body of distinguished or venerable men; council; legislative body. [< OF *senat* < L *senatus,* lit., council of old men < *senex, senis* old]

Sen·ate (sen'it) *n.* **1.** The upper branch of national or state legislative bodies of the United States, Canada, France, and other governments. The **United States Senate** is composed of two Senators elected by popular vote from each State. **2.** In ancient Rome, the state council, whose extensive powers were curtailed under the empire. Abbr. *S., sen., Sen.*

sen·a·tor (sen'ə·tər) *n. Often cap.* A member of a senate. Abbr. *sen., Sen.* [< OF *senateur* < L *senator* < *senex, senis* old man, old] — **sen'a·tor·ship'** *n.*

sen·a·to·ri·al (sen'ə·tôr'ē·əl, -tō'rē-) *adj.* **1.** Of, pertaining to, or befitting a senator or senate. **2.** Composed of senators. **3.** Entitled to elect a senator. — **sen'a·to'ri·al·ly** *adv.*

Senatorial district In Canada, the constituency of each Senator from Quebec.

se·na·tus con·sul·tum (sə·nā'təs kən·sul'təm) *Latin* A decree of the ancient Roman Senate, pronounced upon some matter of law or public policy. Also **se·na'tus con·sult'.**

send[1] (send) *v.* **sent, send·ing** *v.t.* **1.** To cause or direct (a person or persons) to go; dispatch. **2.** To cause to be taken or directed to another place; transmit; forward: sometimes with *off:* to *send* a present; to *send* a radio message. **3.** To cause to issue; emit or discharge, as heat, light, smoke, etc.: with *forth. out,* etc. **4.** To throw or drive by force; impel. **5.** To cause to come, happen, etc.; grant: God *send* us peace. **6.** To bring into a specified state or condition; drive: The decision *sent* him into bankruptcy. **7.** *U.S. Slang* To make rapturous with joy. — *v.i.* **8.** To dispatch an agent, messenger, or message. — **to send (someone) about his** (or **her**) **business** To dismiss with reproach or warning. — **to send down** *Brit.* To expel from a university. — **to send flying** **1.** To scatter or knock violently away. **2.** To cause to flee. — **to send for** To summon by a message or messenger. — **to send packing** To dismiss quickly and forcefully. — **to send to the showers** *U.S. Informal* To expel or dismiss from or as from a baseball game or other game. — **to send up** *Informal* To sentence to prison. [OE *sendan*] — **send'er** *n.*

send[2] (send) *Naut.* *n.* **1.** The flow or impulse of the waves. **2.** See SCEND. — *v.i.* **sent, send·ing** **1.** To move by the force of waves. **2.** See SCEND. [< SEND[1]; prob. infl. in meaning by ASCEND]

Sen·dai (sen·dī) A city on NE Honshu island, Japan; pop. 425,250 (1960).

sen·dal (sen'dəl) *n.* A light, thin, silken fabric much used for dresses, etc., in the Middle Ages. Also called *sandal.* [< OF *cendal, sendal,* prob. ult. < Gk. *sidōn* fine linen]

send-off (send'ôf', -of') *n.* **1.** The act of sending off; a start. **2.** A farewell dinner or other celebration or demonstration at parting. **3.** Encouragement, as in starting a career.

Sen·e·ca (sen'ə·kə) *n.* One of a tribe of North American Indians of Iroquoian stock formerly inhabiting western New York, the largest tribe of the confederation of Five Nations. [< Du. *Sennacaas* the Five Nations < Algonquian (Mohegan) *A'sinnika,* trans. of Iroquoian *Oneñiute,* short for *oneñiute' roñ non* Oneida, lit., people of the standing rock]

Sen·e·ca (sen'ə·ka), **Lucius Annaeus,** 4? B.C.–A.D. 65, Roman Stoic philosopher, statesman, and dramatist: called **Seneca the Younger.**

Sen·e·ca Lake (sen'ə·kə) One of the Finger Lakes in west central New York, extending about 35 miles north and south; about 67 sq. mi.

sen·e·ga snakeroot (sen'ə·gə) **1.** A plant (*Polygala senega*) of the milkwort family, whose dried root is used as an expectorant: also called *rattlesnake root.* Also **Seneca snakeroot.** **2.** The dried root of this plant: also **senega.** [< NL, alter. of SENECA; so called because identified with the Seneca Indians, who used it to treat snakebites + SNAKEROOT]

Sen·e·gal (sen′ə·gal, -gôl) A river in NW Africa forming part of the boundary between the Republics of Senegal and Mauritania, and flowing about 1,000 miles, generally west, to the Atlantic. *French* **Sé·né·gal** (sā·nā·gàl′).

Sen·e·gal (sen′ə·gal, -gôl), **Republic of** A Republic of the French Community in NW Africa; 76,084 sq. mi.; pop. 3,780,000 (est. 1969); capital, Dakar: French *République du Sénégal*. — **Sen′e·ga·lese′** (-gə·lēz′, -lēs) *adj. & n.*

Sen·e·gam·bi·a (sen′ə·gam′bē·ə) The former name for the territory between the Senegal and Gambia rivers, now part of Mali and Senegal. — **Sen′e·gam′bi·an** *adj. & n.*

se·nes·cent (si·nes′ənt) *adj.* **1.** Growing old. **2.** Characteristic of old age. [< L *senescens, -entis,* ppr. of *senescere* to grow old < *senex* old] — **se·nes′cence** *n.*

sen·e·schal (sen′ə·shəl) *n.* **1.** An official in the household of a medieval prince or noble, having charge of feasts, etc.; a steward or major-domo. **2.** *Brit.* A cathedral official. [< OF < Gmc. Cf. OHG *siniskalk* old servant.]

se·nile (sē′nīl, -nil, sen′īl) *adj.* **1.** Pertaining to, proceeding from, or characteristic of old age. **2.** Infirm; weak; doting. **3.** *Geog.* Almost worn away to base level: a *senile* continent. [< L *senilis* < *senex* old] — **se′nile·ly** *adv.*

senile dementia *Psychiatry* The progressive deterioration of cerebral functions and mental faculties as a concomitant of old age: also called *dementia senilis.* Also **senile psychosis.**

se·nil·i·ty (si·nil′ə·tē) *n.* Mental and physical infirmity due to old age; old age accompanied by infirmity.

sen·ior (sēn′yər) *adj.* **1.** Older in years or higher in rank. **2.** Denoting the older of two: opposed to *junior.* ◆ The form used to distinguish a father from a son of the same name is usually written *Albert Jones, Sr.* or *Albert Jones, senior.* **3.** Belonging to maturity or later life. **4.** Earlier in effect or longer in tenure: the *senior* senator from Ohio. **5.** Pertaining to the last year of a high-school or collegiate course of four years. — *n.* **1.** The older of two. **2.** One longer in service or higher in standing. **3.** A student in the fourth or senior year of a high-school, college, or university course. *Abbr. sr., Sr., sen., Sen.* [< L, comparative of *senex* old]

senior citizen *U.S. & Canadian* An elderly person.

senior high school A high school, in the United States typically comprising grades 10, 11, and 12.

sen·ior·i·ty (sēn·yôr′ə·tē, -yor′-) *n.* *pl.* **·ties 1.** The state of being senior; priority of age or rank. **2.** Precedence or priority due to length of service.

Sen·lac (sen′lak) A hill near Hastings, in Sussex, England; scene of the battle of Hastings, 1066.

sen·na (sen′ə) *n.* **1.** The dried leaflets of any of several leguminous plants (genus *Cassia*), used medicinally as purgatives, as the **Alexandria senna** (*C. acutifolia*), and the **Congo** or **Indian senna** (*C. angustifolia*). **2.** Any plant yielding senna or a similar product. [< NL < Arabic *sanā*]

Sen·nach·er·ib (si·nak′ər·ib), died 681 B.C.; king of Assyria 705–681 B.C.

Sen·nar (sen·när′) An ancient city in the Sudan between the White Nile and the Blue Nile, capital of a large native kingdom, 15th to 19th centuries. Also **Sen·naar′.**

sen·net (sen′it) *n.* A signal of exit or entrance sounded on a horn, used as a stage direction in Elizabethan plays. [< OF *senet, sinet, signet.* Doublet of SIGNET.]

sen·night (sen′īt, -it) *n.* *Archaic* A week: also called *sevennight.* Also **se′n′night.** [OE *seofan nihta* < *seofan* seven + *nihta,* pl. of *niht* night]

sen·nit (sen′it) *n.* **1.** Plaited cordage of from 3 to 9 strands, used for gaskets on ships. **2.** Plaited grass or straw for hatmaking. [Earlier *sinnet;* origin uncertain]

se·ñor (sā·nyôr′) *n.* *pl.* **·ño·res** (-nyō′rās) *Spanish* **1.** A gentleman. **2.** Sir; Mr.: used alone or as a title of address prefixed to the name. *Abbr. Sr.*

se·ño·ra (sā·nyō′rä) *n.* *Spanish* **1.** A lady. **2.** Mrs.; madam. *Abbr. Sra.*

se·ño·ri·ta (sā′nyō·rē′tä) *n.* *Spanish* **1.** A young, unmarried lady. **2.** Miss. *Abbr. Srta.*

sen·sate (sen′sāt) *adj.* Perceived by the senses. Also **sen′sat·ed.** — *v.t.* **·sat·ed, ·sat·ing** To perceive by the senses. [< LL *sensatus* gifted with sense < L *sensus* sense]

sen·sa·tion (sen·sā′shən) *n.* **1.** The aspect of consciousness resulting from the stimulation of any of the sense organs, as hearing, taste, touch, smell, or sight. **2.** *Physiol.* The capacity to respond to such stimulation. **3.** That which produces great interest or excitement: The news was a *sensation.* **4.** An excited condition: to cause a *sensation.* [< Med.L *sensatio, -onis* < LL *sensatus.* See SENSATE.]

— **Syn. 1.** *Sensation, percept,* and *perception* refer to a stimulus conveyed to the brain through the nervous system. A *sensation* may originate within or without the body: recollection brought a *sensation* of sadness; a *sensation* of warmth caused by a stove. A *percept* is always external in origin, and arises from the excitation of a sense organ. *Perception* involves interpretation of a stimulus, and the recognition of the external object that has produced a *sensation.* **2.** irritability, sensitivity. Compare SENSIBILITY.

sen·sa·tion·al (sen·sā′shən·əl) *adj.* **1.** Pertaining to emotional excitement. **2.** Of or pertaining to physical sensation. **3.** Causing excitement; startling. **4.** Causing unnatural emotional excitement; melodramatic: a *sensational* story. — **sen·sa′tion·al·ly** *adv.*

sen·sa·tion·al·ism (sen·sā′shən·əl·iz′əm) *n.* **1.** *Philos.* Radical empiricism. **2.** The use of melodramatic methods. **3.** The theory that feeling is the only criterion of good. — **sen·sa′tion·al·ist** *n.* — **sen·sa′tion·al·is′tic** *adj.*

sense (sens) *n.* **1.** The faculty of sensation; sense perception. **2.** Any of certain agencies by or through which an individual receives impressions of the external world, as through taste, touch, hearing, smell, or sight. **3.** *Physiol.* Any receptor, or group of receptors, specialized for the perception of external objects or internal bodily changes. **4.** Rational perception accompanied by feeling; realization; discriminating cognition: a *sense* of wrong. **5.** *Often pl.* Normal power of mind or understanding; sound or natural judgment: The fellow has no *sense*; She is coming to her senses. **6.** Signification; import; meaning. **7.** Opinion, view, or judgment of the majority: The *sense* of the meeting was manifest. **8.** That which commends itself to the understanding as being in accordance with reason and good judgment: to talk *sense.* **9.** Capacity to perceive or appreciate: a *sense* of color. — *v.t.* **sensed, sens·ing 1.** To become aware of through the senses. **2.** *Informal* To comprehend; understand. [< F *sens* < L *sensus* perception < *sentire* to feel]

— **Syn. 5.** *Sense, discernment, judgment, discretion, sagacity,* and *wisdom* relate to the ability to understand situations, to make sound decisions, and to anticipate consequences. *Sense,* the most general of these words, is the ability to act effectively in a given situation, and may be a characteristic of men or of animals. The other words describe human qualities only. *Discernment* is analytic *sense,* the ability to see things clearly and to perceive relationships. *Judgment* and *discretion* refer to the practical use of *sense. Judgment* is *sense* applied to the making of sound and correct decisions and so depends to some degree upon *discernment; discretion* adds a note of caution or shrewdness to *judgment* and suggests the making of decisions that are safe as well as sound and correct. *Sagacity* and *wisdom* may be considered the highest development of *sense.* Both words suggest native ability, enhanced by training and experience. *Sagacity* is habitual good *sense* and sound judgment; *wisdom* is a unique quality implying, in addition to wide learning and experience, a trained intellect and the capacity for profound thought and insight.

sense datum *Psychol.* Something that is directly experienced as a result of the stimulation of a sense organ.

sense·less (sens′lis) *adj.* **1.** Devoid of sense; making no sense; irrational. **2.** Deprived of consciousness; unconscious. **3.** Incapable of feeling or perception; insensate. — **sense′less·ly** *adv.* — **sense′less·ness** *n.*

sense organ A structure specialized to receive sense impressions, as the eye, nose, ear, etc.

sense perception Direct knowledge or perception of things through the senses.

sen·si·bil·i·ty (sen′sə·bil′ə·tē) *n.* *pl.* **·ties 1.** The capability of sensation; power to perceive or feel. **2.** The capacity of sensation and rational emotion, as distinguished from intellect and will. **3.** *Often pl.* Susceptibility or sensitiveness to outside influences or mental impressions; also, abnormal sensitiveness. **4.** Appreciation accompanying mental apprehension; discerning judgment. **5.** Delicacy or sensitiveness of an instrument. **6.** Responsiveness to pathos or to artistic or esthetic values. **7.** *Archaic* Sentimentality.

— **Syn. 1, 3.** *Sensibility, sensitivity, susceptibility,* and *feeling* relate to the capacity to perceive and feel. *Sensibility* may be used of mere physical sensation, but more often denotes qualities of mind: *sensibility* to heat and cold, the *sensibility* of the artist to beauty. *Sensitivity* suggests great *sensibility,* and the readiness to be excited by small cause: the *sensitivity* of the heliotrope to light, the *sensitivity* of the politician to public opinion. *Susceptibility* is the capacity to receive, contain, or be influenced: *susceptibility* to magnetization, *susceptibility* to colds. *Feeling* specifically refers to the tactile sense, but is also used in the sense of emotional response as a general, but less precise, substitute for the other words.

sen·si·ble (sen′sə·bəl) *adj.* **1.** Possessed of good practical judgment; exhibiting sound sense and understanding; discreet; judicious. **2.** Capable of physical sensation; sensitive: *sensible* to pain. **3.** Perceptible or appreciable through the senses: *sensible* heat. **4.** Emotionally or mentally sensitive. **5.** Having a perception or cognition; fully aware; persuaded. **6.** Great enough to be perceived; appreciable. **7.** *Obs.* Sensitive to minute changes. — *n.* **1.** A substance capable of being felt or observed. **2.** A sentient being. **3.** *Music* The leading note; the seventh of a scale: also **sensible note** (or **tone**). [< OF < L *sensibilis* < *sensus,* pp. of *sentire* to feel, perceive] — **sen′si·ble·ness** *n.* — **sen′si·bly** *adv.*

sensible horizon See under HORIZON.

sen·si·tive (sen′sə·tiv) *adj.* **1.** Easily affected by outside operations or influences; excitable or impressionable; touchy; easily offended. **2.** Reacting readily to external agents or forces: paper *sensitive* to light. **3.** Pertaining to or depending on the senses or sensation: *sensitive* motions. **4.** Closing or moving when touched or irritated, as certain plants. **5.** Liable to fluctuation. **6.** *Obs.* Wise; sensible. **7.** Capable of indicating minute changes or differences; delicate. [< OF *sensitif* < Med.L *sensitivus* < L *sensus.* See SENSIBLE.] — **sen·si·tive·ly** *adv.* — **sen·si·tive·ness** *n.*

sensitive plant 1. A shrubby tropical herb (*Mimosa pudica*), whose leaves close at a touch. **2.** Any of various similar or related plants, as the **wild sensitive plant** (*Cassia nictitans*) of eastern North America. **3.** A sensitive person.

sen·si·tiv·i·ty (sen′sə-tiv′ə-tē) *n. pl.* **·ties 1.** The state or degree of being sensitive; sensitiveness. **2.** *Physiol.* The degree of acuteness with which sensations are discriminated; irritability, as of organs. **3.** *Electr.* The degree of responsiveness to an electric current or to radio waves. **4.** *Photog.* Sensitiveness to light. — **Syn.** See SENSIBILITY.

sen·si·tize (sen′sə-tīz) *v.t.* **·tized, ·tiz·ing 1.** To render sensitive. **2.** *Photog.* To make sensitive to light, as a plate or film. **3.** *Med.* To make susceptible or hypersensitive to the action of a substance, as a drug. [< SENSIT(IVE) + -IZE] — **sen′si·ti·za′tion** *n.* — **sen′si·tiz′er** *n.*

sen·si·tom·e·ter (sen′sə-tom′ə-tər) *n. Photog.* An apparatus for testing the sensitiveness to light of a film by means of a set of carefully exposed photographic plates. [< SENSIT(IVE) + METER]

sen·sor (sen′sər) *n.* That which receives and responds to a stimulus or signal; especially, an instrument or device, as an antenna, gyroscope, photoelectric cell, etc., designed to detect and respond to some force, change, or radiation for purposes of information or control. — *adj.* Sensory: applied to nerves and nerve organs.

sen·so·ri·mo·tor (sen′sə-ri-mō′tər) *adj. Physiol.* Of or pertaining to muscular and nervous responses induced by sensory stimuli. [< SENSORY + MOTOR]

sen·so·ri·um (sen-sôr′ē-əm, -sō′rē-) *n. pl.* **·ri·a** (-rē-ə) **1.** *Anat.* The nervous system, including the cerebrum, as the collective organ of sensation. **2.** *Biol.* The entire sensory apparatus. [< LL < L *sensus.* See SENSIBLE.]

sen·so·ry (sen′sər-ē) *adj.* **1.** Of or pertaining to sensation. **2.** Conveying or producing sense impulses. **3.** Pertaining to the sensorium. Also **sen·so·ri·al** (sen-sôr′ē-əl, -sō′rē-). [< LL *sensorium* sensorium]

sen·su·al (sen′shōō-əl) *adj.* **1.** Unduly indulging the appetites or sexual pleasure; lewd. **2.** Pertaining to the body or to the physical senses; carnal. **3.** Pertaining to sensualism (def. 4). ◆ See note under SENSUOUS. [< MF *sensuel* < LL *sensualis* < L *sensus.* See SENSE.] — **sen′su·al·ly** *adv.*

sen·su·al·ism (sen′shōō-əl-iz′əm) *n.* **1.** Sensuality. **2.** *Philos.* Radical empiricism. **3.** A system of ethics predicating the pleasures of sense to be the highest good. **4.** Emphasis on the sensuous elements of beauty, rather than the ideal. — **sen′su·al·ist** *n.* — **sen′su·al·is′tic** *adj.*

sen·su·al·i·ty (sen′shōō-al′ə-tē) *n. pl.* **·ties 1.** The state of being sensual, or sensual acts collectively. **2.** Sensual indulgence. Also called *sensualism:* also **sen′su·al·ness.**

sen·su·al·ize (sen′shōō-əl-īz′) *v.t.* **·ized, ·iz·ing** To make sensual. Also *Brit.* **sen′su·al·ise′.** — **sen′su·al·i·za′tion** *n.*

sen·su·ous (sen′shōō-əs) *adj.* **1.** Pertaining or appealing to or derived from the senses: used in a higher and purer signification than *sensual.* **2.** Keenly appreciative of and aroused by beauty, refinement, or luxury. **3.** Resembling imagery that appeals to the senses: a *sensuous* portrayal. [< L *sensus* +-OUS] — **sen′su·ous·ly** *adv.* — **sen′su·ous·ness** *n.* ◆ **sensuous, sensual** *Sensuous* refers not only to the physical senses but to any means of feeling, as intellectual or esthetic sensitivity, intuition, etc.: the *sensuous* pleasure of walking in the rain. *Sensual* is generally restricted to bodily sensations and to the satisfaction of physical appetites.

sent (sent) Past tense and past participle of SEND.

sen·tence (sen′təns) *n.* **1.** *Gram.* A group of words containing a subject and a predicate, as declarative, interrogative, imperative, and exclamatory sentences, or a single word in the case of the simple imperative. In English speech a spoken sentence generally ends with a drop in pitch, while level or rising pitches within an utterance signalize the presence of clausal or phrasal constructions. An utterance ending with a falling pitch, but lacking the grammatical requisites of a sentence, may be termed a **sentence fragment.** — **simple sentence** A sentence consisting of a subject and a predicate without any subordinate clauses. — **compound sentence** A sentence consisting of two or more independent clauses, usually connected by a semicolon or a coordinating conjunction or both. — **complex sentence** A sentence consisting of an independent clause and one or more subordinate clauses. **2.** *Law* A penalty pronounced upon a person convicted. **3.** A determination or opinion, especially as expressed formally. **4.** *Archaic* An instructive saying; a maxim. — *v.t.* **·tenced, ·tenc·ing** To pass sentence upon; condemn to punishment. [< OF < L *sententia* opinion < *sentire* to feel, be of opinion] — **sen·ten′tial** (sen-ten′shəl) *adj.*

sen·tenc·er (sen′tən-sər) *n.* One who pronounces sentence. **sentence stress** The variation in emphasis given to words in a sentence. Also **sentence accent.**

sen·ten·tious (sen-ten′shəs) *adj.* **1.** Abounding in or giving terse expression to thought; axiomatic. **2.** Habitually

using terse, laconic, or aphoristic language. **3.** Pompously formal; moralizing. [< L *sententiosus* < *sententia.* See SENTENCE.] — **sen·ten′tious·ly** *adv.* — **sen·ten·ti·os·i·ty** (sen-ten′shē-os′ə-tē), **sen·ten′tious·ness** *n.*

sen·ti·ence (sen′shē-əns, -shəns) *n.* **1.** The state of being sentient or conscious. **2.** Capacity for sensation or sense perception. **3.** Sensation as immediate experience, distinguished from thought or perception. Also **sen′ti·en·cy.**

sen·ti·ent (sen′shē-ənt, -shənt) *adj.* Possessing powers of sense or sense perception; having sensation or feeling. — *n.* **1.** A sentient person or thing. **2.** The mind. [< L *sentiens, -entis,* ppr. of *sentire* to feel] — **sen′ti·ent·ly** *adv.*

sen·ti·ment (sen′tə-mənt) *n.* **1.** Noble, tender, or artistic feeling, or susceptibility to such feeling; sensibility. **2.** A verbal expression of such feeling. **3.** A mental attitude or response to a person, object, or idea, based on feeling instead of reason. **4.** An exaggerated emotional reaction. **5.** Idealistic, personal, or esthetic reaction as distinguished from intellectual or practical. **6.** *Often pl.* An opinion or judgment. **7.** An expressive thought or idea in appropriate language. — **Syn.** See OPINION. [< OF *sentement* < Med.L *sentimentum* < L *sentire* to feel]

sen·ti·men·tal (sen′tə-men′təl) *adj.* **1.** Characterized by sentiment or emotion. **2.** Experiencing, displaying, or given to sentiment, often in an extravagant or mawkish manner: a *sentimental* novel. — **sen′ti·men′tal·ly** *adv.* — **Syn. 2.** *Sentimental, romantic, mawkish,* and *maudlin* refer to an excessive or unwarranted display of emotion. *Sentimental* may be used in a good sense to indicate the presence of elevated or noble feelings, but more frequently it is derogatory and suggests undue or artificial emotion. *Romantic* refers to an exaggerated or unrealistic emotional response arising from an idealized view of people or events; the word usually implies innocence and lack of experience. *Mawkish* suggests emotion that is repellent because of its obvious pretense and exaggeration, while *maudlin* points to a lack of self-control in the expression of sorrow, regret, or the like.

sen·ti·men·tal·i·ty (sen′tə-men-tal′ə-tē) *n. pl.* **·ties 1.** The state or quality of being mawkishly sentimental. **2.** Any expression of sentiment. Also **sen′ti·men′tal·ism** (-men′-təl·iz′əm). — **sen′ti·men′tal·ist** *n.*

sen·ti·men·tal·ize (sen′tə-men′təl-īz) *v.* **·ized, ·iz·ing** *v.t.* **1.** To make sentimental. **2.** To cherish sentimentally. — *v.i.* **3.** To behave sentimentally. Also *Brit.* **sen′ti·men′tal·ise.**

sen·ti·nel (sen′tə-nəl) *n.* **1.** A sentry. **2.** Any watcher or guard. — *v.t.* **·neled** or **·nelled, ·nel·ing** or **·nel·ling 1.** To watch over as a sentinel. **2.** To protect or furnish with sentinels. **3.** To station or appoint as a sentinel. [< OF *sentinelle* < Ital. *sentinella* < LL *sentinare* to avoid danger < *sentire* to feel, perceive]

sen·try (sen′trē) *n. pl.* **·tries 1.** A soldier placed on guard to see that only authorized persons pass his post and to warn of danger. **2.** The watch or guard kept by a sentry. [? Short for obs. *centrenel,* var. of SENTINEL]

sentry box A small shelter or cabin to protect a sentry from the weather.

Se·nus·si (se-nōō′sē) *n.pl.* A belligerent Moslem religious sect of northern Africa and Arabia, founded about 1842 by **Sidi Mohammed Ibn Ali el Senussi,** 1791–1851. Also **Se·nu′si, Se·nus′sites** (-sīts). — **Se·nus′si·an** *adj.*

Se·oul (sā-ōōl′, sōl; *Korean* syœ-ōōl) The capital of the Republic of Korea (South Korea), in the NW part; pop. 2,444,-883 (1960): also *Kyongsong: Japanese Keijo.*

sep. 1. Sepal(s). **2.** Separate.

Sep. 1. September. **2.** Septuagint.

se·pal (sē′pəl) *n. Bot.* One of the individual leaves of a calyx. For illustration see FLOWER. Abbr. *sep.* [< F *sépale* < NL *sepalum* < L *sep(aratus)* separate + (*pet*)*alum* petal] — **sep·a·line** (sep′ə-lin, -līn), **sep′a·lous** *adj.*

sep·a·ra·ble (sep′ər·ə·bəl, sep′rə-) *adj.* Capable of being separated. [< F *séparable* or L *separabilis* < *separare* to separate] — **sep′a·ra·bil′i·ty, sep′a·ra·ble·ness** *n.* — **sep′a·ra·bly** *adv.*

sep·a·rate (*v.* sep′ə-rāt; *adj.* sep′ər·it, sep′rit) *v.* **·rat·ed, ·rat·ing** *v.t.* **1.** To set asunder; disunite or disjoin; sever. **2.** To occupy a position between; serve to keep apart: The Hudson River *separates* New York from New Jersey. **3.** To divide into components, parts, etc. **4.** To isolate or obtain from a compound, mixture, etc. **5.** To consider separately; distinguish between. **6.** *Law* To part by separation. — *v.i.* **7.** To become divided or disconnected; draw apart. **8.** To part company; withdraw from association or combination. — *adj.* **1.** Existing or considered apart from others; distinct; individual: *separate* rooms. **2.** Disunited from the body; disembodied. **3.** Separated; disjoined. Abbr. *sep.* [< L *separatus,* pp. of *separare* < *se-* apart + *parare* to prepare] — **sep′a·rate·ly** *adv.* — **sep′a·rate·ness** *n.*

separate school *Canadian* A private school; especially, a Roman Catholic parochial school.

sep·a·ra·tion (sep′ə-rā′shən) *n.* **1.** The act or process of separating; division. **2.** The state of being disconnected or apart. **3.** A dividing line. **4.** *Law* Relinquishment of cohabitation between husband and wife by mutual consent: distinguished from *divorce.*

separation center A central army or navy point that handles the discharging and releasing of personnel.

sep·a·ra·tist (sep'ər·ə·tist, sep'rə-) *n.* One who advocates or upholds separation; especially, a seceder. Also **sep'a·ra'·tion·ist.** — **sep'a·ra·tism** *n.*

sep·a·ra·tive (sep'ə·rā'tiv, -rə·tiv) *adj.* Tending to or inducing separation; useful in separating. Also **sep·a·ra·to·ry** (sep'ər·ə·tôr'ē, -tō'rē, sep'rə-).

sep·a·ra·tor (sep'ə·rā'tər) *n.* **1.** Any device, implement, or apparatus for dividing or separating things into their component parts, as chaff from grain, cream from milk, etc. **2.** One who separates.

Se·phar·dim (si·fär'dim) *n.pl.* The Spanish and Portuguese Jews or their descendants: distinguished from the *Ashkenazim.* Also **Se·phar'a·dim** (-ə·dim). [< Hebrew *sephārādhīm* < *Sephārad,* country mentioned in *Obad.* iii 20, identified by the rabbis with Spain, but prob. orig. in Asia Minor] — **Se·phar'dic** *adj.*

se·pi·a (sē'pē·ə) *n.* **1.** A reddish brown pigment prepared from the inky secretion of the cuttlefish. **2.** The color of this pigment. **3.** A picture done in this pigment. **4.** Any of a genus (*Sepia*) of decapod mollusks having an internal shell; especially, the common cuttlefish (*S. officinalis*) of European waters. — *adj.* Executed in or colored like sepia; dark brown with a tinge of red. [< L < Gk. *sēpia* cuttlefish]

se·pi·o·lite (sē'pē·ə·līt') *n.* Meerschaum (def. 1). [< G *sepiolith* < NL *sepium* cuttlebone (< Gk. *sēpion,* dim. of *sēpia* cuttlefish) + Gk. *lithos* stone]

se·poy (sē'poi) *n.* A native Indian soldier outfitted and trained in European style; especially, one employed in the former British Indian Army. [< Pg. *sipae* < Urdu *sipāhī* soldier < Persian *sipāh* army]

Sepoy Mutiny The Indian Mutiny (which see). Also **Sepoy Rebellion.**

sep·pu·ku (sep·poo·koo) *n. Japanese* Hara-kiri.

sep·sis (sep'sis) *n. Pathol.* Infection of the blood by material containing pathogenic microorganisms. [< NL < Gk. *sēpsis* < *sēpein* to make putrid]

sept (sept) *n.* **1.** A division of a tribe ruled by a hereditary chief, especially in ancient and medieval Ireland. **2.** Any similar social unit or group descended from a common ancestor. [Prob. < OF *septe,* var. of *secte* sect] — **sep'tal** *adj.*

sept-1 Var. of SEPTI-1.

sept-2 Var. of SEPTI-2.

Sept. **1.** September. **2.** Septuagint.

sep·ta (sep'tə) Plural of SEPTUM.

sep·tar·i·um (sep·târ'ē·əm) *n. pl.* **·tar·i·a** (-târ'ē·ə) *Geol.* A rock nodule or concretion, having a compact crust and an internal mass broken up by intersecting cracks filled with calcite or some other material: also called *turtlestone.* [< NL < L *septum* enclosure, wall] — **sep·tar'i·an** *adj.*

sep·tate (sep'tāt) *adj.* Divided by or provided with a partition or partitions; having a septum or septa. [< NL *septatus* < LL, surrounded < L *septum* enclosure, wall]

Sep·tem·ber (sep·tem'bər) The ninth month of the year, containing 30 days; the seventh month in the old Roman calendar. Abbr. *S., Sep., Sept.* — **massacre of September** The massacre in Paris in September, 1792, when 10,000 persons were put to death in prison by order of Danton: also **September massacre** or **massacres.** [< L *septem* seven]

Sep·tem·brist (sep·tem'brist) *n.* **1.** A member of the Parisian mob that massacred political prisoners in the massacre of September 2 to 6, 1792. **2.** A cruel and bloodthirsty person; a butcher; murderer.

sep·te·nar·y (sep'tə·ner'ē) *adj.* **1.** Consisting of, pertaining to, or being seven. **2.** Septennial. **3.** Septuple. — *n. pl.* **·nar·ies** **1.** The number seven; heptad. **2.** Anything that has some definite relation to the number seven, as a group of seven things. **3.** A verse containing seven feet. Also **sep'·te·nar'i·us** (sep'tə·nâr'ē·əs). [< L *septenarius* < *septeni* seven each < *septem* seven]

sep·ten·ni·al (sep·ten'ē·əl) *adj.* **1.** Recurring every seven years. **2.** Continuing or capable of lasting seven years. Also **septenary.** [< L *septennium* period of seven years < *septem* seven + *annus* year] — **sep·ten'ni·al·ly** *adv.*

Sep·ten·tri·o (sep·ten'trē·ō) The constellation Ursa Major. Also **Sep·ten'tri·on** (-on). [< L, sing. of *septentriones,* orig. *septem triones* the seven stars of the Big Dipper < *septem* seven + *triones,* pl. of *trio* plow ox]

sep·ten·tri·on (sep·ten'trē·on) *n. Archaic* The north; northern regions. [< L *septentrionalis* < *septentrio.* See SEPTENTRIO.]

sep·ten·tri·o·nal (sep·ten'trē·ə·nəl) *adj.* Of, pertaining to, or coming from the north; boreal. [< L *septentrionalis*]

sep·tet (sep·tet') *n.* **1.** A group of seven singers, players, or other persons, things, or parts. **2.** *Music* A composition for seven singers or instrumentalists. Also **sep'tette'.** [< G < L *septem* seven]

septi-1 *combining form* Seven: *septilateral.* Also, before vowels, *sept-.* [< L *septem* seven]

septi-2 *combining form* **1.** A partition; fence: *septicidal.* **2.**

Med. The nasal septum. Also, before vowels, *sept-.* Also **septo-.** [< L *septum* enclosure, wall]

sep·tic (sep'tik) *adj.* **1.** Of, pertaining to, or caused by sepsis. **2.** Producing sepsis; infective. Also **sep'ti·cal.** — *n.* Any agent producing sepsis. [< LL *septicus* < Gk. *sēptikos* < *sēpein* to putrefy] — **sep·tic·i·ty** (sep·tis'ə·tē) *n.*

sep·ti·ce·mi·a (sep'tə·sē'mē·ə) *n. Pathol.* An infection of the blood by pathogenic microorganisms; blood poisoning. Also **sep'ti·cae'mi·a.** [< NL < Gk. *sēptikos* putrefactive + *haima* blood] — **sep'ti·ce'mic** (-sē'mik) *adj.*

sep·ti·ci·dal (sep'tə·sīd'l) *adj. Bot.* Dividing at the partitions or the septa: said of the dehiscence of a plant capsule. Also **sep'ti·cide.** [< SEPTI-2 + L *caedere* to cut] — **sep'ti·ci'dal·ly** *adv.*

septic tank A tank in which sewage is allowed to remain until purified by the action of anaerobic bacteria.

sep·tif·ra·gal (sep·tif'rə·gəl) *adj. Bot.* Breaking away from the partitions: said of a form of dehiscence in plants. [< SEPTI-2 + L *frangere* to break]

sep·ti·lat·er·al (sep'tə·lat'ər·əl) *adj.* Seven-sided. [< SEPTI-1 + LATERAL]

sep·til·lion (sep·til'yən) *n.* **1.** *U.S.* A thousand sextillions, written as 1 followed by twenty-four zeros: a cardinal number. **2.** *Brit.* A million sextillions (def. 2), written as 1 followed by forty-two zeros: a cardinal number. — *adj.* Being a septillion in number. [< MF < *septi-* seven + (*mi*)*llion* million]

sep·til·lionth (sep·til'yenth) *adj.* **1.** Having the number one septillion: the ordinal of *septillion.* **2.** Being one of a septillion equal parts. — *n.* **1.** One of a septillion equal parts. **2.** That which is numbered one septillion.

sep·time (sep'tēm) *n.* The seventh position of a swordsman in fencing. [< L *septimus* seventh < *septem* seven]

sep·tu·a·ge·nar·i·an (sep'choo·ə·jə·nâr'ē·ən, sep'too-) *n.* A person 70 years old, or between 70 and 80. — *adj.* **1.** Seventy years old, or between 70 and 80. **2.** Of or pertaining to a septuagenarian. [< L *septuagenarius* < *septuaginta* seventy]

sep·tu·ag·e·nar·y (sep'choo·aj'ə·ner'ē, sep'too-) *adj.* **1.** Of or pertaining to the number 70; progressing by seventies. **2.** Septuagenarian. — *n. pl.* **·nar·ies** A septuagenarian.

Sep·tu·a·ges·i·ma (sep'choo·ə·jes'ə·mə, sep'too-) *n.* The third Sunday before Lent. Also **Septuagesima Sunday.** [< L, seventieth, on analogy with *Quadragesima, Quinquagesima*]

Sep·tu·a·gint (sep'choo·ə·jint', sep'too-) *n.* An old Greek version of the Old Testament Scriptures, made in Alexandria between 280 and 130 B.C., and used by the early Eastern Church. Abbr. *Sep., Sept.* [< L *septuaginta* seventy; from a tradition that it was produced for Ptolemy II in 70 days by a group of 72 scholars] — **Sep'tu·a·gin'tal** *adj.*

sep·tum (sep'təm) *n. pl.* **·ta** (-tə) *Biol.* **1.** A dividing wall between two cavities: the nasal septum. **2.** A partition, as in coral or in a spore. [< L < *sepire* to enclose < *sepes* hedge] — **sep'tal** *adj.*

sep·tu·ple (sep'too·pəl, -tyoo, sep·too'-, -tyoo'-) *adj.* **1.** Consisting of seven; sevenfold. **2.** Multiplied by seven; seven times repeated. Also **septenary.** — *v.t. & v.i.* **·pled, ·pling** To multiply by seven; make or become septuple. — *n.* A number or sum seven times as great as another. [< L *septuplus* < *septem* seven]

septuple meter See under METER2.

sep·tu·pli·cate (sep·too'plə·kit, -tyoo'-) *adj.* Sevenfold; septuple. [< L *septuplus,* on analogy with *duplicate, triplicate,* etc.]

sep·ul·cher (sep'əl·kər) *n.* **1.** A burial place, especially one found or made in a rock or solidly built of stone; tomb; vault. **2.** A receptacle for relics, especially in an altar slab: also called *repository.* — **the Holy Sepulcher** The rock-hewn tomb in which the body of Jesus was buried. — *v.t.* **·chered** or **·chred, ·cher·ing** or **·chring** To place in a sepulcher; bury. Also *Brit.* **sep'ul·chre** (-kər). [< OF *sepulcre* < L *sepulcrum* burial place, tomb < *sepultus,* pp. of *sepelire* to bury]

se·pul·chral (si·pul'krəl) *adj.* **1.** Pertaining to a sepulcher. **2.** Suggestive of burial or the grave; dismal; gloomy. **3.** Unnaturally low and hollow in tone, as a voice. — **se·pul'chral·ly** *adv.*

sep·ul·ture (sep'əl·chər) *n.* **1.** The act of entombing; burial. **2.** *Archaic* A sepulcher. [< OF < L *sepultura* burial < *sepultus.* See SEPULCHER.]

seq. **1.** Sequel. **2.** The following (one) (L *sequens*).

seqq. The following (ones) (L *sequentia*).

se·qua·cious (si·kwā'shəs) *adj.* **1.** Disposed to follow slavishly; servile; attendant. **2.** Logically consecutive. [< L *sequax, -acis* following, pursuing < *sequi* to attend, follow] — **se·qua'cious·ly** *adv.* — **se·quac·i·ty** (si·kwas'ə·tē) *n.*

se·quel (sē'kwəl) *n.* **1.** Something that follows and serves as a continuation; a development from what went before. **2.** A narrative discourse that, though complete in itself, develops from a preceding one. **3.** A consequence; upshot; result. Abbr. *seq.* [< OF *sequelle* < L *sequela* < *sequi* to follow]

se·que·la (si·kwē′lə) *n. pl.* **·lae** (-lē) **1.** That which follows; a consequence. **2.** *Pathol.* An abnormal condition resulting from a preceding disease. [< L, sequel]

se·quence (sē′kwəns) *n.* **1.** The process or fact of following in space, time, or thought; succession or order: also **se′quen·cy. 2.** Order of succession; arrangement. **3.** A number of things following one another, considered collectively; a series. **4.** An effect or consequence. **5.** *Music* A regular succession of similar melodic or harmonic units at different pitches. **6.** *Eccl.* In the Roman Catholic Church, a prose or hymn sung immediately after the gradual and before the gospel. **7.** In card games, a set of three or more cards next each other in value. **8.** A section of motion-picture film presenting a single episode, without time lapses or interruptions. **9.** *Math.* An ordered succession of quantities, as 2x, 4x², 8x³, 16x⁴. Abbr. *sq.* [< L *sequentia* < *sequens, -entis*, ppr. of *sequi* to follow]

sequence of tenses See under TENSE².

se·quenc·er (sē′kwən·sər) *n.* A person or thing that determines a sequence.

se·quent (sē′kwənt) *n.* That which follows; a consequence; result. — *adj.* **1.** Following in the order of time; succeeding. **2.** Consequent; resultant. [< OF < L *sequens.* See SEQUENCE.]

se·quen·tial (si·kwen′shəl) *adj.* **1.** Characterized by or forming a sequence, as of parts. **2.** Sequent. — **se·quen·ti·al·i·ty** (si·kwen′shē·al′ə·tē) *n.* — **se·quen′tial·ly** *adv.*

se·ques·ter (si·kwes′tər) *v.t.* **1.** To place apart; separate; segregate. **2.** To seclude; withdraw: often used reflexively. **3.** *Law* To take (property) into custody until a controversy, claim, etc., is settled or satisfied. **4.** In international law, to confiscate and control (enemy property) by preemption. **5.** *Chem.* To render inactive, as by the process of chelation. [< OF *sequestrer* < LL *sequestrare* to remove, lay aside < *sequester* trustee] — **se·ques′tra·ble** *adj.*

se·ques·tered (si·kwes′tərd) *adj.* Retired; secluded.

se·ques·trant (si·kwes′trənt) *n. Chem.* A chelating agent or substance.

se·ques·trate (si·kwes′trāt) *v.t.* **·trat·ed, ·trat·ing** **1.** To seize, especially for the use of the government; confiscate. **2.** To take possession of for a time, with a view to the just settlement of the claims of creditors. **3.** To seclude; sequester. [< LL *sequestratus*, pp. of *sequestrare.* See SEQUESTER.] — **se·ques·tra·tion** (sē′kwes·trā′shən, sek′wes-) *n.* — **se·ques·tra·tor** (sē′kwes·trā′tər, si·kwes′trā·tər) *n.*

se·ques·trum (si·kwes′trəm) *n. pl.* **·tra** (-trə) *Pathol.* A piece of dead bone remaining in its place, but separated from the living bone. [< NL < L, something separated, orig. neut. of *sequester* standing apart]

se·quin (sē′kwin) *n.* **1.** A small coinlike ornament sewn on clothing. **2.** An obsolete gold coin of the Venetian republic, later introduced into Turkey: also called *zecchino.* [< F < Ital. *zecchino* < *zecca* the mint < Arabic *sikka* coining-die]

se·quoi·a (si·kwoi′ə) *n.* **1.** A gigantic evergreen tree (*Sequoia sempervirens*) of the western United States, with spreading, lanceolate leaves and small cones: also called *redwood.* **2.** A closely related tree (*Sequoiadendron giganteum* or *Sequoia gigantea*) of the Sierra Nevada mountains of California, sometimes reaching a height of 300 feet: also called *big tree.* [< NL, after *Sequoyah*, 1770?–1843, a half-breed Cherokee Indian who invented the Cherokee alphabet]

Sequoia National Park An area in east central California including Mount Whitney and containing many giant sequoias and redwoods; 602 sq. mi.; established 1890.

ser (sir) See SEER².

ser- Var. of SERO-.

ser. 1. Serial. **2.** Series. **3.** Sermon.

se·ra (sir′ə) Plural of SERUM.

sé·rac (sā·rák′) *n. Geol.* A large block or tower-shaped form into which glacier ice breaks in passing down steep inclines. [< dial. F (Swiss), a cheese put up in cubes]

se·ra·glio (si·ral′yō, -räl′-) *n.* **1.** The portion of a Moslem house reserved for the wives and concubines; a harem. **2.** Any residence of a sultan. Also **se·rail.** [< Ital. *serraglio* enclosure, ult. < LL *serrare*, var. of L *serare* to lock up < *sera* lock; used to render Turkish *serai* palace, lodging, because of similarity of sound.]

se·ra·i (se·rä′ē) *n.* **1.** In the Orient, an inn or caravansary. **2.** A Turkish palace. [< Persian *serāī*]

Se·ra·je·vo, Se·ra·ye·vo (se·rä·yā′vō) See SARAJEVO.

Se·rang (sā′räng, sə·räng′) See CERAM.

se·ra·pe (se·rä′pē) *n.* See SARAPE.

ser·aph (ser′əf) *n. pl.* **ser·aphs** or **ser·a·phim** (ser′ə·fim) **1.** A celestial being having three pairs of wings. *Isa.* vi 2. **2.** *pl. Theol.* The highest of the nine orders of angels. See ANGEL. [Back formation < *Seraphim*, pl. < LL < Hebrew *serāphīm*, ? ult. < *sāraph* to burn] — **se·raph·ic** (si·raf′ik), **se·raph′i·cal** *adj.* — **se·raph′i·cal·ly** *adv.*

ser·a·phim (ser′ə·fim) *n.* **1.** Plural of SERAPH: also **ser′a·phin** (-fin). **2.** *pl.* **·phims** A seraph: an erroneous usage.

Se·ra·pis (si·rā′pis) In Egyptian mythology, a god of the lower world in the form of the dead Apis. — **Se·ra′pic** *adj.*

Ser·bi·a (sûr′bē·ə) A constituent Republic of eastern Yugoslavia, formerly an independent kingdom; 34,107 sq. mi.; pop. 7,637,800 (1965); capital, Belgrade: formerly *Servia.* Serbo-Croatian *Srbija.* — **Serb, Ser′bi·an** *adj. & n.*

Ser·bo-Cro·a·tian (sûr′bō·krō·ā′shən) *n.* **1.** The South Slavic language of Yugoslavia, including all the old languages and dialects of Serbia, Montenegro, Bosnia, Herzegovina, Croatia, Slavonia, and Dalmatia. **2.** One whose native tongue is Serbo-Croatian. Also *Servo-Croatian.* Also **Ser′bo-Cro′at** (-krō′at, -ət). — *adj.* Of or pertaining to the Serbo-Croatian language or to those who speak it.

Ser·bo·ni·an (sûr·bō′nē·ən) *adj.* Designating a large marshy tract (the **Serbonian Bog** or **Lake**) that once existed in Lower Egypt, and in which according to Herodotus whole armies were engulfed: also spelled *Sirbonian.*

Serbs, Croats, and Slovenes, Kingdom of the See YUGOSLAVIA.

ser·dab (sûr′dab, sûr·däb′) *n.* A secret cell within an ancient Egyptian tomb in which images of the deceased were deposited. [< Arabic *serdāb* cellar < Persian, icehouse, grotto]

sere¹ (sir) See SEAR¹.

sere² (sir) *n. Ecol.* The series of changes found in a given plant formation from the initial to the ultimate stage. [Back formation < SERIES] — **ser′al** *adj.*

se·rein (sə·rań′) *n. Meteorol.* A fine rain that falls sometimes from an apparently clear sky, especially in the tropics after sunset. [< F; ult. < L *sera* (hora) late]

ser·e·nade (ser′ə·nād′) *n.* **1.** An evening song, usually that of a lover beneath his sweetheart's window. **2.** Music performed in honor of some person in front of his residence in the open air at night. **3.** The music for such a song. **4.** *Music* A form of instrumental music similar to the suite, having a number of movements of various types and usually including a march and a minuet: also called *serenata.* — *v.t. & v.i.* **·nad·ed, ·nad·ing** To entertain with a serenade. [< F *sérénade* < Ital. *serenata* < *sereno* serene, open air < L *serenus* clear, serene; infl. in meaning by L *sera* (hora) the evening (hour), fem. of *serus* late] — **ser′e·nad′er** *n.*

ser·e·na·ta (ser′ə·nä′tə) *n. pl.* **·tas, ·te** (tā) *Music* **1.** A dramatic cantata. **2.** A serenade. [< Ital. See SERENADE.]

ser·en·dip·i·ty (ser′ən·dip′ə·tē) *n.* The faculty of happening upon fortunate discoveries when not in search of them. [Coined by Horace Walpole (1754), in *The Three Princes of Serendip* (Ceylon), the heroes of which make such discoveries] — **ser′en·dip′i·tous** *adj.*

se·rene (si·rēn′) *adj.* **1.** Clear; fair; calm: a *serene* sky. **2.** Marked by peaceful repose; tranquil; unruffled; placid: a *serene* spirit. **3.** Of exalted rank: chiefly in the titles of certain European princes: His *Serene* Highness. — **Syn.** See CALM. — *n. Rare* or *Poetic* **1.** Clearness, or a serene or clear region. **2.** Calmness; placidity. [< L *serenus*] — **se·rene′ly** *adv.* — **se·rene′ness** *n.*

se·ren·i·ty (si·ren′ə·tē) *n. pl.* **·ties** **1.** The state or quality of being serene; peacefulness; repose. **2.** Clearness; brightness. **3.** *Usually Cap.* A title of honor given to certain members of royal families: preceded by *His, Your*, etc.

Se·reth (zā′ret) See SIRET.

serf (sûrf) *n.* **1.** In feudal times, a person bound in servitude on an estate. **2.** Anyone in servile subjection. **3.** *Obs.* A slave. — **Syn.** See SLAVE. [< OF < L *servus* slave] — **serf′age, serf′dom, serf′hood** *n.*

serge (sûrj) *n.* **1.** A strong twilled fabric made of wool yarns and characterized by a diagonal rib on both sides of the cloth. **2.** In the Middle Ages, a coarse woolen cloth. **3.** A rayon lining fabric. [< OF *sarge, serge* < L *serica* (*lana*) (wool) of the Seres < *Seres* the Seres, an eastern Asian people]

ser·geant (sär′jənt) *n.* **1.** *Mil.* Any of several noncommissioned officer grades. See tables at GRADE. **2.** A police officer ranking next below a captain (sometimes lieutenant) in the United States, and next below an inspector in England. **3.** *Brit.* Formerly, one who held land of the king by tenure of military service; also, a gentleman of less than knightly rank. **4.** A sergeant at arms (which see). **5.** A sergeant at law (which see). **6.** A constable or bailiff. **7.** The sergeant fish (def. 1). Also, *esp. Brit.*, *serjeant.* Abbr. **Sgt.** [< OF *sergent, serjant* < L *serviens, -entis*, ppr. of *servire* to serve] — **ser′gean·cy, ser′geant·cy, ser′geant·ship** *n.*

sergeant at arms **1.** An executive officer in a legislative body who enforces order. **2.** The title of certain court or city officials who have ceremonial duties.

sergeant at law Formerly, a barrister of high rank having social but not professional precedence of king's counsel.

sergeant fish **1.** A large, dusky fish (*Rachycentron canadus*) of warm seas, with a broad black band suggesting a chevron on the sides: also called *cobia, sergeant.* **2.** The snook.

sergeant major A noncommissioned officer in the highest enlisted grade of the U.S. Army and Marine Corps. See table at GRADE. Abbr. *SMaj.*

Sergeant Major of the Army The highest enlisted rank in the U.S. Army. See table at GRADE.

SEQUOIA
(To over 300 feet high)

se·ri·al (sir′ē-əl) *adj.* **1.** Of the nature of a series. **2.** Published in a series at regular intervals. **3.** Arranged in rows or ranks; successive: also **se·ri·ate** (sir′ē-it, -āt). **4.** *Music* **a** Of or pertaining to the technique of composing with tone rows. **b** Composed in this technique. — *n.* **1.** A novel or other story regularly presented in successive installments, as in a magazine, on radio or television, or in motion pictures. **2.** *Brit.* A periodical. *Abbr.* **ser.** [< NL *serialis* < L *series* row, order] — **se′ri·al·ly** *adv.*

se·ri·al·ism (sir′ē-əl-iz′əm) *n. Music* The method or practice of composing with tone rows. Also **serial technique.**

se·ri·al·ist (sir′ē-əl-ist) *n.* **1.** A writer of serials. **2.** *Music* A composer who practices serialism.

se·ri·al·ize (sir′ē-əl-īz′) *v.t.* **·ized, ·iz·ing** To arrange or publish in serial form. — **se′ri·al·i·za′tion** *n.*

serial number A number assigned to a person, object, item of merchandise, etc., as a means of identification.

se·ri·a·tim (sir′ē-ā′tim, ser′ē-) *adv.* One after another; serially. [< Med.L < L *series*, on analogy with *gradatim*]

se·ri·a·tion (sir′ē-ā′shən) *n.* The arrangement of unorganized material or data in an orderly series.

se·ri·ceous (si-rish′əs) *adj.* **1.** Lustrous like silk; silky. **2.** *Bot.* Having fine, soft, appressed hairs, as the leaves of certain plants. [< L *sericeus* < *sericum* silk, orig. neut. of *sericus* silken, belonging to the Seres. See SERGE.]

ser·i·cin (ser′ə-sin) *n. Biochem.* A viscous substance formed on the surface of raw silk fiber and usually removed by boiling in soapy water. [< L *sericus* silken + -IN]

ser·i·cul·ture (ser′ə-kul′chər) *n.* The raising and care of silkworms for the production of silk. [Contraction of F *sériciculture* < L *sericum* silk + *cultura* a raising, culture] — **ser′i·cul′tur·al** *adj.* — **ser′i·cul′tur·ist** *n.*

ser·i·e·ma (ser′i-ē′mə, -ā′mə) *n.* **1.** A long-legged, crested bird (*Cariama cristata*) of the plains of Brazil and Paraguay. **2.** A smaller related bird (*Chunga burmeisteri*) of Argentina. [< NL *seriema, cariama* < Tupi *siriema, sariama* crested]

se·ries (sir′ēz) *n. pl.* **se·ries 1.** An arrangement of one thing after another; a connected succession of persons, things, data, etc. on the basis of like relationships. **2.** *Math.* An ordered arrangement of terms the sum of which is indicated. **3.** *Electr.* A connection of electrical circuit elements in which the same current flows through each in turn. **4.** *Gram.* A group of successive coordinate elements of a sentence. *Abbr.* **ser.** [< L < *serere* to join, weave together]

series winding *Electr.* The winding of a dynamo or an electric motor in such a way that the field circuit is connected in series with the armature circuit. — **se·ries-wound** (sir′ēz·wound′) *adj.*

ser·if (ser′if) *n. Printing* A light line or stroke crossing or projecting from the end of a main line or stroke in a letter: also spelled **ceriph.** [< Du. *schreef* stroke, line < *schrijve* to write < L *scribere*]

ser·i·graph (ser′ə-graf, -gräf) *n.* **1.** An artist's color print made by serigraphy. **2.** A device for testing the tensile strength and elasticity of textile fabrics, paper, leather, etc., under specified conditions. [< L *sericum* silk + -GRAPH]

se·rig·ra·phy (si-rig′rə-fē) *n.* An adaptation of the silkscreen process in which handmade prints are made on any desired surface by the use of stencils, one stencil to each color. — **se·rig′ra·pher** *n.* — **ser·i·graph·ic** (ser′ə-graf′ik) *adj.*

ser·in (ser′in) *n.* A greenish finch (*Serinus canarius*), related to the wild canary. [< F; ult. origin unknown]

ser·ine (ser′ēn, -in) *n. Biochem.* A white crystalline amino acid, C₃H₇NO₃, originally isolated from sericin. Also **ser′in** (-in). [< L *sericus* silken + -INE²]

se·rin·ga (si-ring′gə) *n.* Any of several Brazilian trees (genus *Hevea*) yielding rubber. [< Pg. < L *syringa* syringa]

Se·rin·ga·pa·tam (sə-ring′gə-pə-tam′) A town in southern Mysore, India; former seat of the sultans of Mysore; pop. about 8,000.

se·ri·o·com·ic (sir′ē-ō-kom′ik) *adj.* Mingling the serious with the comic. Also **se′ri·o·com′i·cal.** [< *serio-* partly serious (< SERIOUS) + COMIC]

se·ri·ous (sir′ē-əs) *adj.* **1.** Grave and earnest in quality, feeling, or disposition; thoughtful; sober. **2.** Said, planned, or done with full practical intent; being or done in earnest. **3.** Of grave importance; weighty: a *serious* problem. **4.** Attended with considerable danger or loss: a *serious* accident. [< MF *sérieux* < LL *seriosus* < L *serius*] — **se′ri·ous·ly** *adv.* — **se′ri·ous·ness** *n.*

— **Syn. 1.** *Serious, earnest,* and *sober* are compared as they characterize persons. A *serious* person is not frivolous, but diligent in work, and always mindful of his responsibilities as a parent, citizen, employee, etc. *Earnest* adds a note of zeal, sincerity, and perseverance to *serious,* and so is generally a stronger word. The *sober* person is calm and composed, and not easily excited; *sober* may imply a phlegmatic disposition, or may be used to indicate a person engaged in some important matter.

ser·jeant (sär′jənt) See SERGEANT.

ser·mon (sûr′mən) *n.* **1.** A discourse based on a passage or text of the Bible, delivered as part of a church service. **2.** Any discourse intended for the pulpit. **3.** Any speech of a serious or solemn kind, as a formal reproof or exhortation. *Abbr.* **ser.** — *Syn.* See SPEECH. [< AF *sermun,* OF *sermon* < L *sermo, -onis* talk]

ser·mon·ic (sər-mon′ik) *adj.* Pertaining to or of the nature of a sermon or sermonizing; didactic. Also **ser·mon′i·cal.**

ser·mon·ize (sûr′mən-īz) *v.t. & v.i.* **·ized, ·iz·ing 1.** To compose or deliver a sermon or sermons (to). **2.** To address at length in a moralizing manner. — **ser′mon·iz′er** *n.*

Sermon on the Mount The discourse of Jesus found recorded in *Matt.* v, vi, vii: properly distinguished from the **Sermon on the Plain,** *Luke* vi 20–49.

sero- *combining form* Connected with or related to serum: *serology.* Also, before vowels, **ser-.** [< L *serum* whey]

se·rol·o·gy (si-rol′ə-jē) *n.* The science of serums and their actions. [SERO- + -LOGY] — **se·ro·log·ic** (sir′ə-loj′ik) or **-i·cal** *adj.*

se·ro·tine¹ (ser′ə-tin, -tīn) *n.* A moderately large, insectivorous European bat (*Eptesicus serotinus*) related to the common brown bats.

se·ro·tine² (ser′ə-tin, -tīn) *adj.* Serotinous.

se·rot·i·nous (si-rot′ə-nəs) *adj.* Produced, blossoming, or developing relatively late in the season: also *serotine.* Also **se·rot′i·nal.** [< L *serotinus* < *serus* late]

se·ro·to·nin (ser′ə-tō′nin) *n. Biochem.* A crystalline protein found in many body tissues but chiefly in the brain and blood, a powerful vasoconstrictor. [< SERO- + TON- + -IN]

se·rous (sir′əs) *adj.* Pertaining to, producing, or resembling serum. [< F *séreux* < L *serosus* < *serum* serum, whey]

serous fluid Any of the thin, watery fluids secreted by the serous membranes.

serous membrane *Anat.* A tissue of endothelial cells lining the large cavities of the body, as the peritoneum.

ser·ow (ser′ō) *n.* Any of a genus (*Capricornis*) of antelopes ranging from the Himalayas to Japan; especially, the large goat antelope (*C. bubalinus*). [< Tibetan]

Ser·pens (sûr′penz) *n.* A constellation, the **Serpent.** See CONSTELLATION. [< L]

ser·pent (sûr′pənt) *n.* **1.** A scaly, limbless reptile; a snake. **2.** Anything of serpentine form or appearance. **3.** An obsolete musical wind instrument, bent several times in serpentine form. **4.** An insinuating and treacherous person. **5.** Satan; the devil. [< OF < L *serpens, -entis* serpent, creeping thing, orig. ppr. of *serpere* to creep]

Ser·pent-hold·er (sûr′pənt-hōl′dər) *n.* The constellation Ophiuchus.

ser·pen·tine (sûr′pən-tēn, -tīn) *adj.* **1.** Pertaining to or like a serpent; sinuous. **2.** Subtle; cunning. — *n.* A mottled green or yellow hydrous magnesium silicate, used as a source of asbestos, and as architecturally decorative stonework. [< OF *serpentin* < L *serpentinus* < *serpens.* See SERPENT]

ser·pi·go (sər-pī′gō) *n. Pathol.* An eruption on the skin, as spreading ringworm. [< Med.L < L *serpere* to creep] — **ser·pig·i·nous** (sər-pij′ə-nəs) *adj.*

Ser·ra (ser′rä), **Junipero,** 1713–84, Spanish Franciscan missionary in California: original name **Miguel José Serra.**

ser·ra·noid (ser′ə-noid) *adj.* Pertaining or belonging to a family (*Serranidae*) of chiefly marine fishes, including the sea basses and groupers. — *n.* A serranoid fish. [< NL < *Serranus,* genus name (< L *serra* saw) + Gk. *eidos* form]

ser·rate (ser′āt, -it) *adj.* **1.** Toothed or notched like a saw. **2.** *Bot.* Having notched edges, as certain leaves. See illustration of LEAF. Also **ser′rat·ed.** [< L *serratus,* ult. < *serra* saw]

ser·ra·tion (se-rā′shən) *n.* **1.** The state of being serrated. **2.** One of the projections of a serrate formation, or a series of such projections. Also **ser·ra·ture** (ser′ə-chər). [< NL *serratio, -onis* < L *serrare* to saw < *serra* saw]

ser·ried (ser′ēd) *adj.* Compacted in rows or ranks, as soldiers in company formation. [pp. of obs. *serry* to press close together in ranks < MF *serré,* pp. of *serrer* to tighten]

ser·ri·form (ser′ə-fôrm) *adj.* Formed like a saw; sawtoothed. [< L *serra* saw + -FORM]

ser·ru·late (ser′ə-lit, -lāt, ser′yə-) *adj.* Having small, fine teeth. Also **ser′ru·lat′ed** (-lā′tid). [< L *serrula,* dim. of *serra* saw + -ATE¹]

ser·ru·la·tion (ser′ə-lā′shən, ser′yə-) *n.* **1.** The state of being serrulate. **2.** One of the teeth of a serrulate margin, as of a leaf.

Ser·to·ri·us (sər-tôr′ē-əs, -tō′rē-), **Quintus,** died 72 B.C., Roman general; assassinated.

ser·tu·lar·i·an (sûr′chŏŏ-lâr′ē-ən) *n. Zool.* One of a genus (*Sertularia*) of branching colonial hydroids common between tide lines. [< NL < L *sertula,* dim. of *serta* garland]

se·rum (sir′əm) *n. pl.* **se·rums** or **se·ra** (sir′ə) **1.** The clear, slightly yellow portion of an animal liquid after separation from its solid constituents, especially that formed by the clotting of blood. **2.** Loosely, an antiserum. **3.** Serum of milk; whey. **4.** Any similar secretion. [< L, whey, watery fluid]

ser·val (sûr′vəl) *n.* An African wildcat (*Felis serval*), yellow with black spots and having a ringed tail and long legs: also called *tiger cat.* [< F < Pg. *lobo cerval* lynx < *lobo* wolf (< L *lupus*) + *cerval* stag < L *cervus*]

ser·vant (sûr′vənt) *n.* **1.** A person hired to assist in domestic matters, sometimes living within the employer's house; hired help. **2.** A person employed to work for another; an employee. **3.** A slave or bondman. **4.** A public servant (which see). [< OF, orig. ppr. of *servir.* See SERVE.]

serve (sûrv) *v.* **served, serv·ing** *v.t.* **1.** To work for, especially as a servant; be in the service of. **2.** To be of service to; wait on. **3.** To promote the interests of; aid; help: to *serve* one's country. **4.** To obey and give homage to: to *serve* God. **5.** To satisfy the requirements of; suffice for. **6.** To perform the duties connected with, as a public office. **7.** To go through (a period of enlistment, term of punishment, etc.). **8.** To furnish or provide, as with a regular supply. **9.** To offer or bring food or drink to (a guest, etc.); wait on at table. **10.** To bring and place on the table or distribute among guests, as food or drink. **11.** To operate or handle; tend: to *serve* a cannon. **12.** To copulate with: said of male animals. **13.** In tennis, etc., to put (the ball) in play by hitting it to one's opponent. **14.** *Law* **a** To deliver (a summons or writ) to a person. **b** To deliver a summons or writ to. **15.** *Naut.* To wrap (a rope, stay, etc.), as with marlin or spun yarn, so as to strengthen or protect. — *v.i.* **16.** To work as or perform the functions of a servant. **17.** To wait at table; distribute food or drink. **18.** To perform the duties of any employment, office, etc. **19.** To go through a term of service, as in the army or navy. **20.** To be suitable or usable, as for a purpose; perform a function. **21.** To be favorable, as weather. **22.** In tennis, etc., to put the ball in play. — *n.* **1.** In tennis, etc., the delivering of the ball by striking it toward an opponent. **2.** The turn of the server. [< OF *servir* < L *servire* < *servus* slave]

serv·er (sûr′vər) *n.* **1.** One who serves. **2.** *Eccl.* An attendant aiding a priest at low mass. **3.** That which is used in serving, as a tray. **4.** The male of any domestic animal used for breeding. **5.** The player who serves the ball in certain games, as in tennis, badminton, etc.

Ser·ve·tus (sər·vē′təs), **Michael,** Latinized name of **Miguel Ser·ve·to** (sär·vā′tō), 1511–53, Spanish physician and theologian; burned as a heretic.

Ser·vi·a (sûr′vē·ə) A former name for SERBIA.

ser·vice (sûr′vis) *n.* **1.** Assistance or benefit afforded another: to render a *service.* **2.** A useful result or product of labor that is not a tangible commodity. **3.** *pl.* Such products collectively, as distinguished from goods. **4.** The manner in which one is waited on or served: The *service* in this restaurant is only fair. **5.** A system of labor and material aids used to accomplish some regular work or accommodation for the public or a portion of it: telephone *service.* **6.** A division of public employment devoted to a particular function: the diplomatic *service.* **7.** Employment as a public servant in government. **8.** A public duty or function: jury *service.* **9.** Any branch of the armed forces: to enter the *service.* **10.** Military duty or assignment: to volunteer for foreign *service.* **11.** Devotion to God, as demonstrated by obedience and good works. **12.** A formal and public exercise of worship: to attend Sunday *service.* **13.** A ritual prescribed for a particular ministration or observance: a marriage *service.* **14.** The music for a liturgical office or rite. **15.** The state or position of a servant, especially a domestic servant. **16.** A set of tableware for a specific purpose: a tea *service.* **17.** Installation, maintenance, and repair of an article provided a buyer by a seller. **18.** In tennis, etc., the act of serving; also, a player's turn at serving. **19.** *Law* **a** The legal communication of a writ or process to a designated person. **b** Duty or work rendered by one person for another. **c** A duty rendered by a feudal tenant as recompense to his lord. **20.** *Naut.* The protective cordage wrapped around a rope. **21.** In animal husbandry, the copulation or covering of a female. — *adj.* **1.** Pertaining to or for service. **2.** For the use of servants or tradespeople: a *service* entrance. **3.** Of, pertaining to, or belonging to a military service. **4.** Worn during active military service: a *service* cap. — *v.t.* **·viced, ·vic·ing 1.** To maintain or repair: to *service* a car. **2.** To supply service to. [< OF *servise* < L *servitium* < *servus* slave]

Ser·vice (sûr′vis), **Robert William,** 1874–1958, Canadian writer.

serv·ice·a·ble (sûr′vis·ə·bəl) *adj.* **1.** That can be made of service; beneficial; usable. **2.** Capable of rendering long service; durable. **3.** *Obs.* Obliging; attentive. — **serv′ice·a·bil′i·ty, serv′ice·a·ble·ness** *n.* — **serv′ice·a·bly** *adv.*

serv·ice·ber·ry (sûr′vis·ber′ē) *n.* *pl.* **·ries 1.** A small tree (*Amelanchier canadensis*), bearing racemes of white flowers and purple edible berries: also called *service tree, shadbush.* **2.** A berry from this tree. Also called *Juneberry, shadberry.*

service cap A military uniform cap with a visor.

service club 1. An organization to promote community welfare and further the interests of its members. **2.** A recreational area for military personnel.

serv·ice·man (sûr′vis·man′) *n.* *pl.* **·men** (-men′) **1.** A member of one of the armed forces. **2.** A man who performs services of maintenance, supply, repair, etc. Also **service man.** — **ser′vice·wom′an** (-wōom′ən) *n.fem.*

service station 1. A place for supplying automobiles, trucks, etc., with gasoline, oil, water, etc. **2.** A place where adjustments and repairs can be made and parts obtained for electrical or mechanical devices.

service stripe A stripe worn on the sleeve of a uniform to denote years of service or employment, as in an army.

service tree 1. Either of two deciduous trees (genus *Sorbus*) of Europe, having alternate pinnate leaves and panicled cream-colored flowers; especially, *S. domestica*, with an edible berrylike fruit, and the **wild service tree** (*S. torminalis*): also called *checker tree.* **2.** The serviceberry (def. 1).

ser·vi·ette (sûr′vē·et′, -vyet′) *n. Brit. & Canadian* A table napkin. [< MF, prob. < *servir.* See SERVE.]

ser·vile (sûr′vīl, -vil) *adj.* **1.** Having the spirit of a slave; slavish; abject: a *servile* flatterer. **2.** Pertaining to or appropriate for slaves or servants: *servile* employment. **3.** Being of a subject class; existing in a condition of servitude. **4.** Obedient; subject: with *to.* [< L *servilis* < *servus* slave] — **ser′vile·ly** *adv.* — **ser′vile·ness, ser·vil′i·ty** (sûr·vil′ə·tē) *n.*

serv·ing (sûr′ving) *n.* A portion of food for one person.

ser·vi·tor (sûr′və·tər) *n.* One who waits upon and serves another; an attendant; servant. [< OF < LL < L *servire.* See SERVE.] — **ser′vi·tor·ship′** *n.*

ser·vi·tude (sûr′və·tōōd, -tyōōd) *n.* **1.** The condition of a slave; slavery; bondage. **2.** Enforced service as a punishment for crime: penal *servitude.* **3.** A state of subjection to a person or thing: *servitude* to vice. **4.** The condition or duties of a servant; menial service. **5.** *Law* A right that one man may have to use the land of another for a special purpose; an easement. [< MF < L *servitudo* < *servus* slave]

ser·vo (sûr′vō) *n.* *pl.* **·vos** Any of various relay devices used in the automatic control of a complex machine, instrument, operation, or process: also called *monitor.* Also **ser′vo·mech′a·nism** (-mek′ə·niz′əm). [< L *servus* slave]

servo- *combining form* In technical use, auxiliary: *servomotor.* [< L *servus* slave]

Ser·vo-Cro·a·tian (sûr′vō·krō·ā′shən) See SERBO–CROATIAN.

ser·vo·mo·tor (sûr′vō·mō′tər) *n.* An electric motor connected with and supplying power for a servo.

ses·a·me (ses′ə·mē) *n.* **1.** An East Indian plant (*Sesamum indicum*): also called *benne.* **2.** The seeds of this plant, used as food and as a source of the pale yellow **sesame oil,** an emollient: also called *gingeley.* [< F *sésame* < L *sesamum, sesama* < Gk. *sēsamon, sēsamē,* prob. < an Oriental source]

ses·a·moid (ses′ə·moid) *adj. Anat.* Shaped like a sesame seed; obovate, as certain bones and cartilages. [< L *sesamoides* < Gk. *sēsamoeidēs* < *sēsamon* sesame + *eidos* form]

sesqui- *prefix* **1.** One and a half; one-half more; one and a half times: *sesquicentennial.* **2.** *Chem.* Indicating the presence of three atoms of one element and two of another in a compound, as chromium sesquioxide, Cr_2O_3. [< L *sesqui-* one-half more < *semis* half + *que* and]

ses·qui·cen·ten·ni·al (ses′kwi·sen·ten′ē·əl) *adj.* Of or pertaining to a century and a half. — *n.* A 150th anniversary, or its celebration.

ses·qui·pe·da·li·an (ses′kwi·pi·dā′lē·ən) *adj.* **1.** Long and ponderous, as polysyllabic words. **2.** Using or characterized by very long words: a *sesquipedalian* style. **3.** Measuring a foot and a half. Also **ses·quip·e·dal** (ses·kwip′ə·dəl, ses′kwi·pēd′l). — *n.* **1.** One who or that which characteristically uses very long words. **2.** A very long word. [< *sesquipedalis* < *sesqui-* more by a half + *pes, pedis* foot] — **ses′qui·pe·dal′i·an·ism** *n.*

ses·sile (ses′il) *adj.* **1.** *Bot.* Attached by its base, without a stalk, as a leaf. **2.** *Zool.* Firmly or permanently attached; fixed; sedentary. [< L *sessilis* sitting down, stunted < *sessus,* pp. of *sedere* to sit] — **ses·sil′i·ty** *n.*

ses·sion (sesh′ən) *n.* **1.** The sitting together of a legislative assembly, court, etc., for the transaction of business. **2.** A single meeting or series of meetings of a group of persons, convened for a specific purpose or activity: a jam *session.* **3.** A division of a school year; term: summer *session.* **4.** A part of a day during which classes meet in a school. **5.** *Law* The term for which a court or legislative body sits continuously for the transaction of business. **6.** *pl.* The sitting of a certain court: the quarter *sessions.* **7.** In the United States, a court of criminal jurisdiction: the Court of Sessions. **8.** The governing body of a Presbyterian Church congregation. **9.** Any one of certain courts, especially in England: general *sessions.* **10.** *Obs.* The act of sitting, or the state of one who is seated. [< F < L *sessio, -onis* < *sedere* to sit] — **ses′sion·al** *adj.* — **ses′sion·al·ly** *adv.*

sessional indemnity *Canadian* The stipend of a member of Parliament.

sess·pool (ses′pōol′) See CESSPOOL.

ses·terce (ses′tûrs) *n. pl.* **·ter·ces** (ses·tûr′sēz) A coin of ancient Rome equal to ¼ denarius, originally of silver, later of bronze. Also **ses·ter·ti·us** (-shē·əs). [< L *sestertius* that is two and a half < *semis* half + *tertius* third; so called because worth two and a half asses]

ses·ter·ti·um (ses-tûr′shē-əm) *n.* *pl.* **·ti·a** (-shē-ə) An ancient Roman money of account equivalent to 1,000 sesterces. [< L, short for (*mille*) *sestertium* (a thousand) sesterces, gen. pl. of *sestertius* sesterce]

ses·tet (ses-tet′) *n.* **1.** The last six lines of a sonnet; also, any six-line stanza. **2.** *Music* See SEXTET (def. 1). [< Ital. *sestetto* < *sesto* sixth (< L *sextus*) + -*etto*, dim. suffix]

ses·ti·na (ses-tē′nə) *n.* A verse form consisting of six stanzas of six generally unrhymed lines and a three-line envoy. The end words of the first stanza are progressively changed in order in the remaining five, and appear medially and terminally in the envoy. Also **ses′tine** (-tin). [< Ital. < *sesto* sixth < L *sextus*]

Ses·tos (ses′tos) A ruined town in NE Turkey, on the Dardanelles. See ABYDOS.

set¹ (set) *v.* **set, set·ting** *v.t.* **1.** To put in a certain place or position; place. **2.** To put into a fixed or immovable position, condition, or state: to *set* brick; to *set* one's jaw. **3.** To bring to a specified condition or state: *Set* your mind at ease; to *set* a boat adrift. **4.** To restore to proper position for healing, as a broken bone. **5.** To place in readiness for operation or use: to *set* a trap. **6.** To adjust according to a standard: to *set* a clock. **7.** To adjust (an instrument, dial, etc.) to a particular calibration or position. **8.** To place knives, forks, etc., on (a table) in preparing for a meal. **9.** To bend the teeth of (a saw) to either side alternately. **10.** To appoint or establish; prescribe: to *set* a time. **11.** To fix or establish a time for: We *set* our departure for noon. **12.** To assign for performance, completion, etc.; allot: to *set* a task. **13.** To assign to some specific duty or function; appoint; station: to *set* a guard. **14.** To cause to sit. **15.** To present or perform so as to be copied or emulated: to *set* a bad example. **16.** To give a specified direction to; direct: He *set* his course for the Azores. **17.** To put in place so as to catch the wind: to *set* the jib. **18.** To place in a mounting or frame, as a gem. **19.** To stud or adorn with gems: to *set* a crown with rubies. **20.** To arrange (hair) in waves, curls, etc., while moist. **21.** To place (a hen) on eggs to hatch them. **22.** To place (eggs) under a fowl or in an incubator for hatching. **23.** To place (a price or value): with *by* or *on*: to *set* a price on an outlaw's head. **24.** To point (game): said of hunting dogs. **25.** *Printing* **a** To arrange (type) for printing; compose. **b** To put into type, as a sentence, manuscript, etc. **26.** *Music* **a** To arrange (music) for words. **b** To write (words) to accompany music. **27.** To describe (a scene) as taking place: to *set* the scene in Monaco. **28.** In the theater, to arrange (a stage) so as to depict a scene. **29.** In some games, as bridge, to defeat. **30.** *Dial.* or *Illit.* To sit. — *v.i.* **31.** To go or pass below the horizon, as the sun. **32.** To wane; decline. **33.** To sit on eggs, as fowl. **34.** To become hard or firm; solidify; congeal. **35.** To begin a journey; start: with *forth, out, off,* etc. **36.** To have a specified direction; tend. **37.** To hang or fit, as clothes. **38.** To point game: said of hunting dogs. **39.** *Bot.* To begin development or growth, as a rudimentary fruit. **40.** *Dial.* or *Illit.* To sit. — **to set about** To start doing; begin. — **to set against 1.** To balance; compare. **2.** To make unfriendly to; prejudice against. — **to set aside 1.** To place apart or to one side. **2.** To reject; dismiss. **3.** To declare null and void. — **to set back 1.** To hinder or delay. **2.** To reverse: to *set back* a clock. — **to set down 1.** To place on a surface. **2.** To write; record. **3.** To judge or consider. **4.** To attribute; ascribe. — **to set forth 1.** To state or express. **2.** To start, as a journey. — **to set in 1.** To begin to occur: Rigor mortis *set in.* **2.** To blow or flow toward shore, as wind or tide. — **to set off 1.** To put apart by itself. **2.** To serve as a contrast or foil for; enhance. **3.** To cause to explode. — **to set on** To incite or instigate; urge. — **to set out 1.** To present to view; display; exhibit. **2.** To lay out or plan (a garden, etc.). **3.** To establish the limits or boundaries of, as a town. **4.** To plant. **5.** To start a journey. **6.** To begin any enterprise. — **to set to 1.** To start; begin. **2.** To start fighting. — **to set up 1.** To place in an upright position. **2.** To raise. **3.** To place in power, authority, etc. **4.** To construct or build; put together; assemble. **5.** To found; establish. **6.** To provide with the means to start a new business. **7.** To cause to be heard: to *set up* a cry. **8.** To propose or put forward (a theory, etc.). **9.** To cause. **10.** *Informal* **a** To pay for the drinks, etc., of; treat. **b** To pay for (drinks, etc.). **11.** *Informal* To encourage; exhilarate. — *adj.* **1.** Established by authority or agreement; prescribed; appointed: a *set* time; a *set* method. **2.** Customary; conventional: a *set* phrase. **3.** Deliberately and systematically conceived; formal: a *set* speech. **4.** Fixed and motionless; rigid. **5.** Fixed in opinion or disposition; obstinate. **6.** Formed; built; made: with a qualifying adverb: deep-*set* eyes. **7.** Ready; prepared: to get *set.* — *n.* **1.** The act or condition of setting. **2.** Permanent change of form, as by chemical action, cooling, pressure, strain, etc. **3.** The arrangement, tilt, or hang of a garment, hat, sail, etc. **4.** Carriage or bearing: the *set* of his shoulders.

5. The sinking of a heavenly body below the horizon. **6.** The direction of a current or wind. **7.** A young plant for setting out; a cutting, slip, or seedling. **8.** *Mech.* The spread in opposite directions given to the alternate teeth of certain saws. **9.** *Psychol.* A condition, temporary or recurrent, preparing an individual for a particular kind of action or response. **10.** A group of games constituting a division of a tennis match. [OE *settan* to cause to sit. Akin to SIT.]

set² (set) *n.* **1.** A number of persons regarded as associated through status, common interests, etc.: a new *set* of customers. **2.** A social group having some exclusive character; coterie; clique: the fast *set.* **3.** A number of things belonging together and customarily used together: a *set* of instruments; a *set* of dishes. **4.** A number of specific things so grouped as to form a whole: a *set* of lyrics; a *set* of motives; a *set* of features. **5.** A group of volumes issued together and related by common authorship or subject. **6.** The number of couples needed for a square dance or country dance. **7.** The group of movements that compose a square dance. **8.** In motion pictures, television, etc., the complete assembly of properties, structures, etc., required in a scene. **9.** Radio or television receiving equipment assembled for use. **10.** *Math.* An array of objects, quantities, magnitudes, etc., arranged in some particular way: the *set* of integers. — **Syn.** See CLIQUE. [< OF *sette* < L *secta* sect; infl. by SET¹. Doublet of SECT.]

Set (set) In Egyptian mythology, the animal-headed god of darkness, night, and evil; slayer of Osiris: also called *Seth.*

se·ta (sē′tə) *n.* *pl.* **·tae** (-tē) *Biol.* **1.** A bristle, or slender, bristlelike part or process of an organism. **2.** A slender spine or prickle. **3.** A coarse, rigid hair. [< L]

se·ta·ceous (si-tā′shəs) *adj.* **1.** Bristly; more or less covered with bristles. **2.** Of the nature or form of setae. Also **se′tal** (sēt′l). [< NL *setaceus* < L *seta* bristle]

set·back (set′bak′) *n.* **1.** An unexpected reverse or relapse. **2.** A countercurrent; eddy. **3.** *Archit.* In tall buildings, the stepping of upper sections so that they progressively recede from the street line.

Seth (seth) **1.** The third son of Adam. *Gen.* v 3. **2.** The Egyptian god Set.

SET

set hammer A hammer the head of which may be easily removed from the handle. For illustration see HAMMER.

seti- *combining form* A bristle: *setiferous.* Also, before vowels, **set-.** [< L *seta* bristle]

se·tif·er·ous (si-tif′ər-əs) *adj.* Bearing setae; bristly.

se·ti·form (sē′tə-fôrm) *adj.* Having the form of a seta.

set·off (set′ôf′, -of′) *n.* **1.** That which offsets or counterbalances; a counterpoise. **2.** A decorative contrast or setting. **3.** A counterclaim or the discharge of a debt by a counterclaim. **4.** *Archit.* A ledge; offset.

se·ton (sē′tən) *n.* *Surg.* A bristle, or a few threads, passed through a fold of the skin to produce an issue. [< Med.L *seto, -onis,* appar. < *seta* silk < L, bristle]

Se·ton (sē′tən), **Ernest Thompson,** 1860–1946, U.S. naturalist and writer born in England.

se·tose (sē′tōs) *adj.* Setaceous; bristly. Also **se′tous** (-təs). [< L *setosus* < *seta* bristle]

set·screw (set′skrōō′) *n.* A screw used as a clamp, especially one used to screw through one part and slightly into another to bind the parts tightly.

set·tee¹ (se-tē′, set·tē′) *n.* **1.** A long wooden seat with a high back. **2.** A sofa suitable for two or three people. [< SET¹ or SET (TLE), n. + -*ee*, dim. suffix; infl. in meaning by SEAT]

set·tee² (se-tē′) *n.* A Mediterranean vessel with long prow. [< Ital. *saettia,* prob. < *saetta* arrow < L *sagitta*]

set·ter (set′ər) *n.* **1.** One who or that which sets. **2.** One of a breed of medium-sized, silky-coated, lithe hunting dogs trained to indicate the presence of game birds by standing rigid. See ENGLISH SETTER, GORDON SETTER, IRISH SETTER.

set·ting (set′ing) *n.* **1.** The act of anything that sets. **2.** An insertion. **3.** That in which something is set; a frame; environment. **4.** The act of indicating game like a setter. **5.** A number of eggs placed together for hatching. **6.** The music adapted to a song or poem. **7.** The scene or background of a play, movie, or narrative. **8.** The apparent sinking of the sun, etc., below the horizon. **9.** The tableware set out for one person.

set·tle (set′l) *v.* **·tled, ·tling** *v.t.* **1.** To put in order; set to rights: to *settle* affairs. **2.** To put firmly in place; establish or fix permanently or as if permanently: He *settled* himself on the couch. **3.** To free of agitation or disturbance; calm; quiet: to *settle* one's nerves. **4.** To cause (sediment or dregs) to sink to the bottom. **5.** To cause to subside or come to rest; make firm or compact: to *settle* dust or ashes. **6.** To make clear or transparent, as by causing sediment or dregs to sink. **7.** *Informal* To make quiet or orderly: One blow *settled* him. **8.** To decide or determine finally, as an argument or difference. **9.** To pay, as a debt; satisfy, as a claim.

---

10. To establish residents or residence in (a country, town, etc.). **11.** To establish as residents. **12.** To establish in a permanent occupation, home, etc. **13.** To decide (a suit at law) by agreement between the litigants. **14.** *Law* To make over or assign (property) by legal act: with *on* or *upon*. — *v.i.* **15.** To come to rest, as after moving about or flying. **16.** To sink gradually; subside. **17.** To sink or come to rest, as dust or sediment. **18.** To become more firm or compact. **19.** To become clear or transparent, as by the sinking of sediment. **20.** To take up residence; establish one's abode or home. **21.** To come to a decision; determine; resolve: with *on*, *upon*, or *with*. **22.** To pay a bill, etc. — **to settle down 1.** To start living a regular, orderly life, especially after a period of wandering or irresponsibility. **2.** To apply steady effort or attention. — *n.* **1.** A long seat or bench, generally of wood, with a high back, often with arms and sometimes having a chest from seat to floor. **2.** A wide step; platform. **3.** *Obs.* A ledge. [OE *setl* seat, *setlan* to seat]

set·tle·ment (set′l-mənt) *n.* **1.** The act of settling, or the state of being settled; especially, an adjustment of affairs by public authority. **2.** The settling of a new region; colonization. **3.** An area of country newly occupied by those who intend to live and labor there; a colony. **4.** A collection of frontier dwellings forming a community. **5.** The settling down or subsidence of a structure, or its effect. **6.** *Brit.* A regular or settled place of living; one's dwelling place. **7.** An accounting; adjustment; liquidation in regard to amounts. **8.** The conveyance of property in such form as to provide for some future object, especially the support of members of the settler's family; also, the property so settled. **9.** A religious community. **10.** Formerly, Negro quarters on a southern plantation. **11.** A welfare institution established in a congested part of a city, having a resident staff of workers to conduct educational and recreational activities for the community: also called *social settlement:* also **settlement house.**

set·tler (set′lər) *n.* **1.** One who settles; especially, one who establishes himself in a colony or new country; a colonist. **2.** One who or that which settles or decides something.

set·tling (set′ling) *n.* **1.** The act of one who or that which settles or sinks. **2.** *pl.* Dregs; sediment.

set-to (set′tōō′) *n. pl.* **-tos** A bout at fighting, fencing, arguing, or any other mode of contest. [< SET TO. See under SET[1]]

set·u·lose (sech′ŏŏ-lōs) *adj.* Clothed or covered with setae or bristles. [< NL, dim. of L *seta* bristle]

set·up (set′up′) *n.* **1.** *U.S. Informal* The overall scheme or pattern of organization or construction; the salient elements of a situation; circumstances. **2.** *U.S. Slang* A contest or match arranged to result in an easy victory. **3.** *U.S. Informal* Ice, soda water, etc., provided for use in alcoholic drinks. **4.** *U.S. Informal* The napkin, silverware, etc., set for a customer in a restaurant. **5.** Physique; physical build; make-up. **6.** Carriage of the body; bearing.

Seu·rat (sœ·rà′), **Georges Pierre**, 1859–91, French painter.

Se·van (syi·vän′) **Lake** A lake in the eastern Armenian S.S.R.; 546 sq. mi.

Se·vas·to·pol (sə·vas′tə·pōl, sev′əs·tō′pəl; *Russ.* syi·vəs·tô′pəly′) A port city and naval base in the southern Crimea; pop. 229,000 (1970): formerly, in English, *Sebastopol.* Also **Se·vas·to′pol′.**

sev·en (sev′ən) *n.* **1.** The sum of six and one: a cardinal number. **2.** Any symbol of this number, as 7, vii, VII. **3.** Anything consisting of or representing seven units, as a playing card, team, etc. — *adj.* Being one more than six. [OE *seofon*]

Seven against Thebes In Greek legend, the seven heroes (Adrastus, Amphiaraus, Capaneus, Hippomedon, Parthenopaeus, Polynices, and Tydeus) who unsuccessfully marched on Thebes to restore Polynices to the throne, which had been usurped by his brother Eteocles.

seven deadly sins *Often cap.* Pride, lust, envy, anger, covetousness, gluttony, and sloth: also called *cardinal sins.*

Seven Hills of Rome The seven hills on and around which the city of Rome was built: the Palatine, Caelian, Esquiline, Capitoline, Quirinal, Viminal, and Aventine.

seven liberal arts The three subjects of the trivium (grammar, logic, and rhetoric), plus the four subjects of the quadrivium (geometry, astronomy, arithmetic, and music).

sev·en·night (sev′ən·nīt′) *n.* Sennight (which see).

Seven Pines See FAIR OAKS.

seven seas All the oceans of the world, now considered to be the North and South Atlantic, the North and South Pacific, the Indian, the Arctic, and the Antarctic oceans.

sev·en·teen (sev′ən·tēn′) *n.* **1.** The sum of sixteen and one: a cardinal number. **2.** Any symbol of this number, as 17, xvii, XVII. **3.** Anything consisting of or representing seventeen units, as an organization, game token, etc. — *adj.* Being one more than sixteen. [OE *seofontīene*]

sev·en·teenth (sev′ən·tēnth′) *adj.* **1.** Next after the sixteenth: the ordinal of *seventeen.* **2.** Being one of seventeen equal parts. — *n.* **1.** One of seventeen equal parts. **2.** That which follows the sixteenth.

sev·en·teen-year locust (sev′ən·tēn′yir′) A dark-bodied, wedge-shaped cicada (*Magicicada septemdecim*) native to the

eastern United States, having an underground nymphal stage of from 13 to 17 years.

sev·enth (sev′ənth) *adj.* **1.** Next after the sixth: the ordinal of *seven.* **2.** Being one of seven equal parts. — *n.* **1.** One of seven equal parts. **2.** That which follows the sixth. **3.** *Music* **a** The interval between any tone and the seventh tone above it in the diatonic scale, counting the starting point as one. **b** A tone separated by this interval from any other, considered with reference to that other; especially, the seventh above the tonic. See INTERVAL (def. 6). — *adv.* In the seventh order, place, or rank: also, in formal discourse, **sev′enth·ly.** [ME *seventhe* < *seven* + -TH, replacing OE *seofotha*]

sev·enth-day (sev′ənth·dā′) *adj.* **1.** Pertaining to the seventh day of the week. **2.** *Often cap.* Advocating the observance of the seventh day as the Sabbath: a *Seventh-Day* Adventist.

seventh day Saturday: a Quaker term.

Seventh-Day Adventist See under ADVENTIST.

seventh heaven 1. A condition of great happiness. **2.** The highest heaven according to various ancient systems of astronomy or in certain theologies.

sev·en·ti·eth (sev′ən·tē·ith) *adj.* **1.** Tenth in order after the sixtieth: the ordinal of *seventy.* **2.** Being one of seventy equal parts. — *n.* **1.** One of seventy equal parts. **2.** That which is tenth in order after the sixtieth.

sev·en·ty (sev′ən·tē) *n. pl.* **-ties 1.** The sum of sixty and ten: a cardinal number. **2.** Any symbol of this number, as 70, lxx, LXX. **3.** Anything consisting of or representing seventy units, as an organization, game token, etc. — *adj.* Being ten more than sixty. [OE (*hund-*) *seofontig*]

Sev·en·ty-Six (sev′ən·tē·siks′) Short for 1776, the year of the Declaration of Independence.

sev·en-up (sev′ən·up′) *n.* A game of cards: originally so called from the number of points required to win: also called *all fours, old sledge, pitch.*

Seven Wonders of the World The seven works of man considered the most remarkable in the ancient world: the Egyptian pyramids, the hanging gardens of Babylon, the temple of Diana at Ephesus, the statue of Zeus by Phidias at Olympia, the mausoleum of King Mausolos at Halicarnassus, the Colossus of Rhodes, and the pharos or lighthouse of Alexandria.

Seven Years' War See table for WAR.

sev·er (sev′ər) *v.t.* **1.** To put or keep apart; separate. **2.** To cut or break into two or more parts. **3.** To break off; dissolve, as a relationship or tie. — *v.i.* **4.** To come or break apart or into pieces. **5.** To go away or apart; separate. [< AF *severer*, OF *sevrer* < L *separare.* See SEPARATE.]

sev·er·a·ble (sev′ər·ə·bəl) *adj.* **1.** Capable of being severed. **2.** *Law* That can be severed from something of which it forms part; especially, denoting a contract that is not invalidated by nonfulfillment of one of its obligations.

sev·er·al (sev′ər·əl, sev′rəl) *adj.* **1.** Being of an indefinite number, more than two, yet not large; divers. **2.** Considered individually; pertaining to an individual; single; separate. **3.** *Law* Pertaining individually and separately to each tenant or party to a bond: a joint and *several* note. **4.** Individually different; various or diverse. [< AF < Med.L *separalis* < L *separ* separate, distinct]
— **Syn. 1.** *Several, various, divers,* and *sundry* indicate some indefinite number less than many. All these words originally meant miscellaneous or different, a meaning still occasionally found in *several:* voting lists were sent to the *several* districts. More frequently, *several* refers to a few like things: *several* eggs, *several* books; and *various* is used to stress difference or dissimilarity: a collection of poems in *various* meters. *Divers* and *sundry* are both somewhat archaic; *divers* is vaguest in number, and may suggest a great many, while *sundry* implies dissimilarity: *divers* opinions have been expressed on this question in *sundry* times and places. Compare MANY.

sev·er·al·ly (sev′ər·əl·ē, sev′rəl·ē) *adv.* **1.** Individually; separately. **2.** Respectively.

sev·er·al·ty (sev′ər·əl·tē, sev′rəl-) *n. pl.* **-ties 1.** *Law* The holding of land in one's own right without participation; a sole tenancy. **2.** The character of being several or distinct.

sev·er·ance (sev′ər·əns, sev′rəns) *n.* **1.** The act of severing, or the condition of being severed. **2.** Separation; partition.

se·vere (si·vir′) *adj.* **·ver·er, ·ver·est 1.** Rigorous in the treatment of others; unsparing. **2.** Conforming to rigid rules; marked by pure and simple excellence; accurate. **3.** Serious and austere in disposition or manner; austerely plain. **4.** Causing extreme anguish: a *severe* pain. **5.** Causing extreme hardship; harsh: a *severe* snowstorm. [< MF *sévère* < L *severus*] — **se·vere′ly** *adv.* — **se·vere′ness** *n.*
— **Syn. 1.** onerous, oppressive. **2.** stern, strict, exacting, unrelenting. **5.** hard, arduous.

se·ver·i·ty (si·ver′ə·tē) *n. pl.* **-ties 1.** The quality of being severe. **2.** Harshness or cruelty of disposition or treatment. **3.** Extreme strictness; rigor; exactness. **4.** Seriousness; austerity. **5.** Strict conformity to truth or law.

Sev·ern (sev′ərn) A river of northern Wales and western England, flowing 210 miles to the Bristol Channel.

Se·ver·na·ya Dvi·na (sye′vyir·nə·yə dvyē′nə) The Russian name for the DVINA (def. 1).

Se·ver·na·ya Zem·lya (sye'vyir·nə·yə zyim·lyä') An archipelago in the Arctic Ocean in the northern R.S.F.S.R.; 14,300 sq. mi.

Se·ver·sky (si·ver'skē), **Alexander Prokofieff de,** born 1894, U.S. airplane designer and manufacturer born in Russia.

Se·ve·rus (si·vir'əs), **Lucius Septimius,** 146–211, Roman emperor 193–211, rebuilt Hadrian's Wall across England.

Sé·vi·gné (sā·vē·nyā'), **Madame de,** 1626–96, Marie de Rabutin-Chantal, French writer.

Se·ville (sə·vil') A city in SW Spain; pop. 442,890 (1960). *Spanish* **Se·vil·la** (sā·vēl'lyä).

Sè·vres (se'vr') *n.* A fine porcelain originally made at Sèvres, France. Also **Sèvres ware.**

Sè·vres (se'vr') A city in France, on the Seine near Paris; pop. 20,025 (1968).

sew (sō) *v.* **sewed, sewed** or **sewn, sew·ing** *v.t.* **1.** To make, mend, or fasten with needle and thread. **2.** To affect by sewing: often with *up.* —*v.i.* **3.** To work with needle and thread. —**to sew up** *U.S. Informal* To conclude (a deal, etc.) successfully. [OE *siwian, sēowan*]

sew·age (sōō'ij) *n.* The waste matter from domestic, commercial, and industrial establishments carried off in sewers: also called *sewerage.* [< SEW(ER) + -AGE]

Sew·all (sōō'al), **Samuel,** 1652–1730, English jurist and diarist in Massachusetts.

se·wan (sōō'ən) See SEAWAN.

Sew·ard (sōō'ərd), **William Henry,** 1801–72, U.S. statesman; negotiated the purchase of Alaska from Russia, 1867.

Sew·ard Peninsula (sōō'ərd) The westernmost part of Alaska, extending 210 miles west to Cape Prince of Wales.

sew·er[1] (sōō'ər) *n.* **1.** A conduit, usually laid underground, to carry off drainage and excrement. ◆ Collateral adjective: *cloacal.* **2.** Any large public drain. [< OF *seuwiere* channel from a fish pond, ult. < L *ex-* off + *aqua* water]

sew·er[2] (sōō'ər) *n.* Formerly, in England, an attendant who supervised the serving of meals and seating of guests. Also **sew'ar.** [< AF *asseour,* OF *asseoir* to cause to sit < L *assidere* < *ad-* to + *sedere* to sit]

sew·er[3] (sō'ər) *n.* One who or that which sews.

sew·er·age (sōō'ər·ij) *n.* **1.** A system of sewers. **2.** Systematic draining by sewers. **3.** Sewage.

sew·ing (sō'ing) *n.* **1.** The act, business, or occupation of one who sews. **2.** That which is sewed; needlework.

sewing circle **1.** A group of women, meeting periodically to sew, usually for some charitable purpose. **2.** A meeting of such a group. Also **sewing society.**

sewing machine A machine for stitching or sewing.

sewn (sōn) Alternative past participle of SEW.

sex (seks) *n.* **1.** Either of two divisions, male and female, by which organisms are distinguished with reference to the reproductive functions. **2.** Males or females collectively. **3.** The character of being male or female. **4.** The activity or phenomena of life concerned with sexual desire or reproduction. **5.** *Informal* Sexual gratification. —*v.t.* To ascertain the sex of (very young chickens). [< OF *sexe* < L *sexus,* prob. orig. < *secare* to divide]

sex- *combining form* Six: *sexpartite:* also *sexi-.* [< L *sex* six]

sex·a·ge·nar·i·an (sek'sə·jə·nâr'ē·ən) *n.* A person between sixty and seventy years of age. —*adj.* **1.** Sixty years old, or between sixty and seventy. **2.** Of or pertaining to a sexagenarian. [< SEXAGENARY]

sex·ag·e·nar·y (seks·aj'ə·ner'ē) *adj.* **1.** Of or pertaining to the number sixty; progressing by sixties. **2.** Sexagenarian. —*n. pl.* **·nar·ies** A sexagenarian. [< L *sexagenarius* < *sexageni* sixty each < *sexaginta* sixty]

Sex·a·ges·i·ma (sek'sə·jes'ə·mə) *n.* The second Sunday before Lent. Also **Sexagesima Sunday.** [< L *sexagesima* (*dies*) sixtieth (day)]

sex·a·ges·i·mal (sek'sə·jes'ə·məl) *adj.* Pertaining to or founded on the number sixty. [< Med.L *sexagesimalis* < L *sexagesimus* sixtieth < *sexaginta* sixty]

sex appeal A quality that attracts sexual interest.

sex cell A gamete; a sperm or ovum.

sex·cen·te·nar·y (seks·sen'tə·ner'ē, seks'sen·ten'ər·ē) *adj.* Pertaining to or consisting of six hundred, especially six hundred years. —*n. pl.* **·nar·ies 1.** A period of six hundred years or a collection of six hundred units. **2.** A six-hundredth anniversary. [< L *sexcenti* six hundred each < *sexcenti* six hundred < *sex* six + *centum* hundred]

sex chromosome *Genetics* A chromosome whose presence in the reproductive cells of certain plants and animals is associated with the determination of the sex of offspring. In mammals the ovum carries two X-chromosomes and the sperm carries an X- and a Y-chromosome. In the fertilized ovum, females are produced by a paired XX and males by a paired XY.

sex·en·ni·al (seks·en'ē·əl) *adj.* Happening once every six years, or lasting six years. —*n.* A sixth anniversary. [< L *sexennis, sexennium* < *sex* six + *annus* year] —**sex·en'ni·al·ly** *adv.*

sex gland A gonad; either of the testes or ovaries.

sex hygiene Hygiene that deals with sexual conduct.

sexi- Var. of SEX-.

sex·ism (sek'siz·əm) *n.* Sexual prejudice against women. [< SEX + -ISM, an analogy with *racism*] —**sex'ist** *adj., n.*

sex·less (seks'lis) *adj.* **1.** Having or appearing to have no sex; neuter. **2.** Provoking or showing little sexual desire. —**sex'less·ly** *adv.* —**sex'less·ness** *n.*

sex linkage *Biol.* That type of inheritance that is associated with the transmission of genes attached to the sex chromosomes. —**sex-linked** (seks' lingkt') *adj.*

sex·ol·o·gy (seks·ol'ə·jē) *n.* The study of human sexual behavior. [< SEX + -(O)LOGY] —**sex·o·log·ic** (sek'sə·loj'ik) or **·i·cal** *adj.* —**sex·ol'o·gist** *n.*

sex·par·tite (seks·pär'tīt) *adj.* Divided into or made up of six parts, as a groined arch or other structure. [< NL *sexpartitus* < L *sexus* six + *partitus.* See PARTITE.]

sex·ploi·ta·tion (sek'sploi·tā'shən) *n. Informal* The commercial exploitation of interest in sex, as by means of pornography [Blend of SEX and EXPLOITATION]

sex ratio *Sociol.* The ratio of males to females in a given population, usually expressed as the number of males per 100 females.

sext (sekst) *n. Often cap. Eccl.* **1.** Prescribed prayers constituting the fourth of the seven canonical hours, originally recited at noon, or the sixth hour by ancient Roman reckoning. **2.** The sixth book of the decretals, added by Pope Boniface VIII. [< LL *sexta* < L *sexta* (*hora*) the sixth (hour), fem. of *sextus* sixth < *sex* six]

sex·tan (seks'tan) *adj.* Occurring or returning at intervals of six days. —*n.* A fever returning at intervals of six days. [< NL *sextana* (*febris*) sextan (fever) < L *sextus.* See SEXT.]

Sex·tans (seks'tanz) *n.* A constellation, the **Sextant.** See CONSTELLATION. [< L]

sex·tant (seks'tənt) *n.* **1.** An instrument for measuring angular distance between two objects, as a heavenly body and the horizon, by a double reflection from two mirrors, used especially in determining latitude at sea. **2.** The sixth part of a circle; an arc of 60 degrees. [< L *sextans, -antis* sixth part < *sextus* sixth]

sex·tar·i·us (seks·târ'ē·əs) *n. pl.* **·tar·i·i** (-târ'ē·ī) An ancient Roman liquid measure; one sixth of a congius. [< L, sixth part < *sextus* sixth < *sex* six]

sex·tet (seks·tet') *n.* **1.** *Music* A group of six singers or players; also, a musical composition for six performers: also called *sestet.* **2.** Any collection of six persons or things. Also **sex·tette'.** [Alter. of SESTET; refashioned after L *sex* six]

sex·tile (seks'til) *adj.* Indicated or measured by a distance of 60 degrees. —*n.* **1.** *Astron.* The aspect of two planets at a distance of 60 degrees from each other. **2.** *Stat.* One of the divisions of a frequency distribution containing exactly one sixth of the total number of cases or observations included. [< L *sextilis* (*mensis*) the sixth (month), i.e., August < *sextus* sixth]

sex·til·lion (seks·til'yən) *n.* **1.** *U.S.* A thousand quintillions, written as 1 followed by twenty-one zeros: a cardinal number. **2.** *Brit.* A million quintillions (def. 2), written as 1 followed by thirty-six zeros: a cardinal number. —*adj.* Being a sextillion in number. [< MF < *sexti* six + (*mi*)*llion* million]

sex·til·lionth (seks·til'yənth) *adj.* **1.** Having the number one sextillion: the ordinal of *sextillion.* **2.** Being one of a sextillion equal parts. —*n.* **1.** One of a sextillion equal parts. **2.** That which is numbered one sextillion.

sex·to·dec·i·mo (seks'tō·des'ə·mō) *n. pl.* **·mos 1.** A page size made from a printer's sheet folded so as to have 16 leaves, usually measuring 4½ x 6⅞ inches. **2.** A book or pamphlet having pages this size. —*adj.* Having or consisting of pages this size. Also *sixteenmo.* Also written **16 mo., 16°.** [< L, ablative of *sextusdecimus* sixteenth < *sextus* sixth < *decimus* tenth]

sex·ton (seks'tən) *n.* **1.** A janitor of a church having charge also of ringing the bell, overseeing burials, etc.; also, formerly, a gravedigger. **2.** Any of certain carrion beetles (genus *Necrophorus*) that bury small dead animals by excavating the ground beneath or near them: also called *burying beetle.* [< AF *segertaine,* OF *secretain* < Med.L *sacristanus.* Doublet of SACRISTAN.] —**sex'ton·ship** *n.*

sex·tu·ple (seks'tōō·pəl, -tyōō-, seks·tōō'-, -tyōō'-) *v.t.* **·pled, ·pling** To multiply by six. —*adj.* **1.** Consisting of six or of six parts. **2.** Multiplied by six. **3.** *Music* Having six beats to the measure. —*n.* A number or sum six times as great as another. [< L *sextus* sixth < *sex* six, formed on analogy with *quadruple, quintuple,* etc.] —**sex'tu·ply** *adv.*

SEXTANT

a Scale. *b* Clamp screw. *c* Tangent screw. *d* Reading lens. *e* Glass shades. *f* Horizon glass. *g* Index glass. *h* Telescope. *i* Movable arm. *j* Handle.

sex·tu·plet (seks′tōō·plit, -tyōō-, seks·tōō′-, -tyōō′-) *n.* **1.** A set of six similar things. **2.** One of six offspring produced at a single birth. [< SEXTUPLE on analogy with *triplet*]

sex·tu·pli·cate (*adj., n.* seks·tōō′plə·kit, -tyōō′-; *v.* seks·tōō′-plə·kāt, -tyōō′-) *adj.* **1.** Sixfold. **2.** Raised to the sixth power. — *v.t.* **·cat·ed, ·cat·ing** To multiply by six; sextuple. — *n.* One of six like things. [< Med.L *sextuplicatus*, pp. of *sextuplicare* < *sextuplex* multiplied by six < *sex* six] — **sex·tu′pli·cate·ly** *adv.* — **sex·tu′pli·ca′tion** *n.*

sex·u·al (sek′shōō·əl) *adj.* **1.** Of, pertaining to or characteristic of sex, the sexes, or the organs or functions of sex. **2.** Characterized by or having sex. **3.** *Biol.* Designating a type of reproduction involving both sexes. [< LL *sexualis* < L *sexus* sex] — **sex′u·al·ly** *adv.*

sex·u·al·i·ty (sek′shōō·al′ə·tē) *n.* **1.** The state of having, or of being distinguished by, sex. **2.** Preoccupation with sex. **3.** Possession of sexual power.

sexual selection *Biol.* A phase of natural selection whereby characters considered as especially attractive to the opposite sex, tend to become perpetuated or enhanced.

sex·y (sek′sē) *adj.* **sex·i·er, sex·i·est** *Informal* **1.** Provocative of sexual desire: a *sexy* dress; a *sexy* woman. **2.** Concerned in large or excessive degree with sex: a *sexy* novel.

Sey·chelles (sā·shel′, -shelz′) An independent Republic comprising an archipelago in the western Indian Ocean; 100 sq. mi.; pop. 60,000 (est. 1974); capital, Victoria.

Sey·mour (sē′môr, -mōr), **Jane**, 1510?–37, third wife of Henry VIII of England; mother of Edward VI.

sf or **sf.**, **sfz**, or **sfz.** *Music* With emphasis (Ital. *sforzando*, *sforzato*).

Sfax (sfäks) A port city in eastern Tunisia, on the Gulf of Gabès; pop. 65,635 (1956).

SFC *Mil.* Sergeant First Class.

sfer·ics (sfir′iks, sfer′-) *n.pl.* (*construed as sing.*) *Meteorol.* **1.** An electronic device for the detection and plotting of electrical discharges in the atmosphere. **2.** Atmospherics (which see). [Short for ATMOSPHERICS]

Sfor·za (sfôr′tsä) A Milanese ducal family prominent in Italian Renaissance history, notably **Giacomuzzo**, 1369–1424, his son, **Francesco**, 1401–66, and his grandson, **Lodovico**, 1451–1508: called **Il Mo·ro** (ēl mô′rō) (the Moor). — **Count Carlo**, 1873–1952, Italian statesman and historian.

sfor·zan·do (sfôr·tsän′dō) *Music adj.* Accented more forcibly than the rhythm requires; especially, sounded, as a chord, with sudden explosive force. — *adv.* In a sforzando manner. — *n.* *pl.* **·dos** The playing of a tone or chord in this manner; also, the notation for it. Also *forzando.* Also **sfor·za′to** (-tsä′tō). [< Ital., forcing < *sforzare* to force]

S.F.S.R. or **SFSR** Soviet Federated Socialist Republic (Russian *Sovetskaya Federativnaya Sotsialisticheskaya Respublika*).

s.g. Specific gravity.

sgd. Signed.

'sGra·ven·ha·ge (skhrä′vən·hä′khə) The Dutch name for THE HAGUE.

Sgt. *Mil.* Sergeant.

sh. **1.** Share(s). **2.** Sheep. **3.** Sheet. **4.** Shilling(s).

Shaa·ban (shä·bän′) *n.* The eighth month of the Moslem year. See (Moslem) CALENDAR.

shab·by (shab′ē) *adj.* **·bi·er, ·bi·est.** **1.** Threadbare; ragged. **2.** Wearing worn or seedy garments. **3.** Mean; paltry. [OE *sceabb* scab + -Y¹] — **shab′bi·ly** *adv.* — **shab′bi·ness** *n.*

Sha·bu·oth (shä·vōō′ōth, shə·vōō′əs) *n.pl.* The Jewish festival of Pentecost. [< Hebrew *shebuōth*, lit., weeks]

shack (shak) *n.* *U.S. & Canadian Informal* A rude cabin, as of logs. — **to shack up** *Slang* **1.** To spend the night. **2.** To cohabit. — *Syn.* See HUT. [? < dial. Sp. (Mexican) *jacal* wooden hut < Nahuatl *xacalli*; prob. infl. by RAM-SHACKLE]

shack·le (shak′əl) *n.* **1.** A ring, clasp, or braceletlike fastening for encircling and fettering a limb; fetter. **2.** Impediment or restraint. **3.** One of various forms of fastenings, as the bow of a padlock, a clevis, etc. — *v.t.* **·led, ·ling** **1.** To restrain or confine with shackles; fetter. **2.** To keep or restrain from free action or speech. **3.** To connect or fasten with a shackle. [OE *sceacul*] — **shack′ler** *n.*

shackle bolt **1.** A bolt having on its end a shackle or clevis, or a bolt that is passed through the eyes of a shackle. **2.** The shackle of a padlock, chain, etc. **3.** *Heraldry* Shackle and padlock, used as a bearing.

Shack·le·ton (shak′əl·tən), **Sir Ernest Henry**, 1874–1922, British Antarctic explorer born in Ireland.

shack·o (shak′ō) See SHAKO.

shad (shad) *n.* *pl.* **shad** A deep-bodied fish (genus *Alosa*) related to the herring; especially the common or American shad (*A. sapidissima*) of the Atlantic coast, highly esteemed as food. [OE *sceadd*]

shad·ber·ry (shad′ber′ē) *n.* *pl.* **·ries** The serviceberry (which see). [< SHAD(BUSH) + BERRY]

shad·bush (shad′bŏŏsh′) *n.* **1.** The serviceberry (def. 1). **2.** Any of various other plants of the same genus (*Amelanchier*), as the saskatoon. Also **shad′blow′** (-blō′). [< SHAD + BUSH¹; so called because it flowers when the shad appear in U.S. rivers]

shad·dock (shad′ək) *n.* **1.** The large, pale, yellow fruit of a tropical tree (*Citrus grandis*), varying in size from the smaller grapefruit to the pompelmous. **2.** The tree bearing this fruit. [after Capt. *Shaddock*, who brought the seed to the West Indies from the East Indies in 1696]

shade (shād) *v.* **shad·ed, shad·ing** *v.t.* **1.** To screen from light by intercepting its rays; put in shade. **2.** To make dim with or as with shade; darken; overcast. **3.** To screen or protect with or as with a shade. **4.** To cause to change, pass, blend, or soften, by gradations. **5.** In graphic arts: **a** To represent (degrees of shade, colors, etc.) by gradations of light or dark lines or shading. **b** To represent varying shades, colors, etc., in (a picture or painting) thus. **6.** To make slightly lower, as a price. — *v.i.* **7.** To change or vary by degrees. — *n.* **1.** Relative obscurity due to interception of the rays of light; gloom; darkness. **2.** The state of being outshone; obscurity. **3.** A shady place; secluded retreat. **4.** *U.S.* A screen that shuts off light, heat, air, dust, etc. **5.** A gradation of color; also, slight degree; minute difference. **6.** The unilluminated part of a picture, drawing, or engraving. **7.** A disembodied spirit; ghost; something unreal. — *Syn.* See GHOST. — **the shades** The abode of departed spirits; Hades. [OE *sceadu*] — **shade′less** *adj.*

shade grass Pachysandra.

shad·ing (shā′ding) *n.* **1.** Protection against light or heat. **2.** The lines, dots, etc., by which degrees of darkness, color, or depth are represented in a picture or painting. **3.** A slight difference or variation.

sha·doof (shä·dōōf′) *n.* A water-raising device, operating on the principle of a well sweep, used in Egypt and in the Orient for irrigation, etc. Also **sha·duf′.** [< Arabic *shādūf*]

shad·ow (shad′ō) *n.* **1.** A comparative darkness within an illuminated area, especially that caused by the interception of light by a body or object. **2.** The dark figure or image thus produced on a surface and representing the approximate shape of the intercepting body: the *shadow* of a man. **3.** The shaded or dark portion of a picture. **4.** A mirrored image: to see one's *shadow* in a pool. **5.** A delusive image or semblance; anything unreal or unsubstantial. **6.** A phantom; ghost; shade. **7.** A faint representation or indication; a symbol. **8.** A remnant; vestige: *shadows* of his former glory. **9.** An insignificant trace or portion: not a *shadow* of evidence. **10.** *Archaic* Shelter; protection. **11.** Gloom; a saddening influence. **12.** An inseparable companion. **13.** One who trails or follows another, as a detective or spy. — *v.t.* **1.** To cast a shadow upon; overspread with shadow; shade. **2.** To darken or cloud; make gloomy. **3.** To represent or foreshow dimly or vaguely: with *forth* or *out.* **4.** To follow closely or secretly; spy on. **5.** To shade in painting, drawing, etc. **6.** *Archaic* To screen; shelter. [OE *sceadwe*, genitive and dative of *sceadu* shade] — **shad′ow·er** *n.*

shad·ow·box (shad′ō·boks′) *v.i.* To spar with an imaginary opponent as a form of exercise. — **shad′ow·box′ing** *n.*

shad·ow·graph (shad′ō·graf, -gräf) *n.* **1.** A pictorial image formed by casting a shadow, usually of the hands, upon a lighted surface or screen. **2.** A drama produced by a series of these images. Also **shadow play.** **3.** Any X-ray photograph, as a radiograph.

shad·ow·y (shad′ō·ē) *adj.* **·ow·i·er, ·ow·i·est** **1.** Full of or affording shadow; dark; shady. **2.** Like shadows in indistinctness; vague; dim. **3.** Unsubstantial or illusory; unreal; ghostly. — *Syn.* See DARK. — **shad′ow·i·ness** *n.*

sha·drach (shad′rak, shā′drak) *n.* A salamander (def. 5).

Sha·drach (shā′drak, shad′rak) A Hebrew captive in Babylon, who, with Meshach and Abednego, was cast into a fiery furnace by Nebuchadnezzar. *Dan.* i 7; iii 1–30.

Shad·well (shad′wel), **Thomas**, 1640?–92, English dramatist; poet laureate 1688.

shad·y (shā′dē) *adj.* **shad·i·er, shad·i·est** **1.** Full of shade; casting a shade. **2.** Shaded or sheltered. **3.** *Informal* Questionable as to honesty or legality; dubious. **4.** Quiet; hidden. — *Syn.* See DARK. — **to keep shady** **1.** To stay in hiding; keep out of the way. **2.** To hide and protect (another). — **on the shady side of** Older than; past the age of. — **shad′i·ly** *adv.* — **shad′i·ness** *n.*

SHAEF (shāf) In World War II, Supreme Headquarters Allied Expeditionary Forces.

shaft¹ (shaft, shäft) *n.* **1.** The long narrow rod of an arrow, spear, etc. **2.** An arrow. **3.** Anything resembling a missile in appearance or effect: *shafts* of ridicule. **4.** A beam or streak of light. **5.** A long handle, as of a hammer, ax, etc. **6.** *Mech.* A long and usually cylindrical bar, especially if rotating and transmitting motive power. **7.** *Archit.* **a** The portion of a column between capital and base. **b** A slender column. **8.** An obelisk or memorial column. **9.** The vertical part of a cross. **10.** The stem of a feather. For illustration see FEATHER. **11.** *Anat.* **a** A long slender portion, as the diaphysis of a bone. **b** The portion of a hair from the root to the end. **12.** On a loom, one of the long laths at the ends of the heddles. **13.** One of two poles by which a horse is harnessed to a vehicle; a thill. **14.** *U.S. Slang* The penis. — **to get the shaft** *U.S. Slang* To be tricked, cheated, etc. — *v.t.* **shaft·ed, shaft·ing** *U.S. Slang* To treat harshly or unfairly; trick; cheat. [OE *sceaft*]

shaft² (shaft, shäft) *n.* **1.** A narrow, vertical or inclined, excavation connected with a mine; also, a passage for light or air. **2.** The tunnel of a blast furnace. **3.** An opening through the floors of a building, as for an elevator. [< LG *schacht* rod, shaft; infl. by SHAFT¹]

Shaftes·bur·y (shafts/bər·ē, shäfts/-), **Earl of**, 1621–83, Anthony Ashley Cooper, English statesman; opponent of Roman Catholics.

shaft·ing (shaf/ting, shäf/-) *n.* **1.** A system of shafts or rods, as in pulleys or gearwheels, for communicating power. **2.** Material from which to make shafts.

shag¹ (shag) *n.* **1.** A rough coat or mass, as of hair. **2.** A wild growth, as of weeds. **3.** A long nap on cloth. **4.** Cloth having a rough or long nap; formerly, a silk or worsted cloth having a velvet nap. **5.** The cormorant (def. 1), a bird. **6.** A coarse, strong tobacco: also **shag tobacco**. — *v.* **shagged**, **shag·ging** *v.t.* **1.** To make shaggy or hairy; roughen. **2.** In baseball, to catch (flies) in practice. — *v.i.* **3.** To become shaggy or rough. — *adj.* Shaggy: also **shag·ged** (shag/id). [OE *sceacga* rough hair, wool]

shag² (shag) *n.* A dance of the late 1930's, consisting of hopping quickly on alternate feet. — *v.i.* **shagged**, **shag·ging** To dance the shag.

shag·a·nap·pi (shag/ə·nap/ē) *n. Canadian* A rawhide cord or thong.

shag·bark (shag/bärk/) *n.* **1.** A rough-barked hickory (*Carya ovata*), yielding high-grade, light-colored nuts. **2.** Its tough, durable wood. Also called *shellbark*.

shag·gy (shag/ē) *adj.* **·gi·er**, **·gi·est 1.** Having, consisting of, or resembling rough hair or wool; rugged; rough. **2.** Covered with any rough, tangled growth; fuzzy; scrubby. **3.** Unkempt. — **shag/gi·ly** *adv.* — **shag/gi·ness** *n.*

shag·gy-dog story (shag/ē·dôg/, -dog) A joke, often long, whose humor lies in an absurd, low-keyed punch line: so called from a story about a shaggy dog.

sha·green (shə·grēn/) *n.* **1.** The rough skin of various sharks and rays, used for polishing. **2.** A rough-grained Russian or Oriental leather or parchment, usually dyed green, or a pressed leather made in imitaton of it. [< F *chagrin* < Turkish *sāghrī* horse's hide]

shah (shä) *n.* An eastern king or ruler, especially of Iran. [< Persian *shāh*, short for *pādshāh*. See PADISHAH.]

Sha·hap·ti·an (shä·hap/tē·ən) *n.* **1.** A stock of North American Indians of which the Nez Percés were the chief tribe, formerly occupying the upper Columbia River valley, now on reservations in Oregon. **2.** Their language. Also *Sahaptin*.

Shah·ja·han·pur (shä·jə·hän/pŏŏr) A city in central Uttar Pradesh, India; pop. 117,225 (1961).

Shah Je·han (shä jə·hän/), 1592?–1666, Mogul emperor 1628–58; founded Delhi; built the Taj Mahal. Also **Shah Ja·han/**.

shaird (shârd) *n. Scot.* **1.** A shard. **2.** A fragment. [OE *sceard*]

shairn (shârn) *n. Scot.* Sharn.

Shairp (shärp, shärp), **John Campbell**, 1819–85, British literary critic, poet, and educator.

shai·tan (shī·tän/) *n.* **1.** In Moslem countries, the devil. **2.** Any evil spirit; an evilly disposed person. **3.** In India, a dust storm. Also spelled *sheitan*. [< Arabic *shaiṭān* < Hebrew *śāṭān*. See SATAN.]

shake (shāk) *v.* **shook**, **shak·en**, **shak·ing** *v.t.* **1.** To cause to move to-and-fro or up and down with short, rapid movements. **2.** To affect in a specified manner by or as by vigorous action: with *off, out, from*, etc.: to *shake* out a sail; to *shake* off a tackler. **3.** To cause to tremble or quiver; jolt; vibrate: The blows *shook* the door. **4.** To cause to stagger or totter. **5.** To weaken or disturb; unsettle: I could not *shake* his determination. **6.** To agitate or rouse; stir: often with *up*. **7.** *Slang* To get rid of or away from. **8.** *Music* To trill. **9.** In dice games, to mix (the dice) before casting. — *v.i.* **10.** To move to-and-fro or up and down in short, rapid movements. **11.** To be affected in a specified way by vigorous action: with *off, out, from*, etc. **12.** To tremble or quiver; as from cold or fear. **13.** To become unsteady; totter. **14.** *Music* To trill on a note, etc. — **to shake a leg** *Informal* To hurry; make haste. — **to shake down 1.** To cause to fall by shaking; bring down. **2.** To cause to settle; make compact. **3.** *Slang* To extort money from. — **to shake hands** To clasp hands as a form of greeting, agreement, etc. — **to shake off** To rid oneself of by or as by shaking. — **to shake up 1.** To shake, mix, or stir. **2.** *U.S. Informal* To shock or jar mentally or physically. — *n.* **1.** A shaking; concussion; agitation; vibration; shock; jolt. **2.** The state of being shaken. **3.** *pl. Informal* The chill or ague of intermittent fever. **4.** A rough, unshaved shingle used to cover barns and shanties. **5.** A frost or wind crack in timber; also, a tight fissure in rock. **6.** An earthquake. **7.** *Slang* An instant; a jiffy. **8.** *Music* A trill. **9.** A unit of time equal to one hundredth of a millionth of a second: used in nuclear physics. — **no great shakes** *Informal* Of no

great importance; mediocre. — **to get a good** (or **fair**) **shake** *U.S. Slang* To receive fair treatment. — **U.S. Slang to give** (**someone**) **the shake** To get rid of (someone). [OE *scacan*] — **shak/a·ble**, **shake/a·ble** *adj.*

— **Syn.** (verb) **3.** rattle, rock. Compare JOLT. **10.** swing, flutter, flap, shimmy. Compare FLUCTUATE. **12.** shiver, shudder, quake, quaver. **13.** sway, waver. Compare TOTTER.

shake·down (shāk/doun/) *n.* **1.** Any makeshift bed, as blankets or straw spread on the floor. **2.** *U.S. Slang* A swindle; extortion. — *adj. U.S. Informal* For the purpose of adjusting mechanical parts or habituating people: a *shake-down* cruise.

shak·er (shā/kər) *n.* **1.** One who or that which shakes. **2.** A container for shaking something: cocktail *shaker*. **3.** A container with a perforated top for pouring something: a *saltshaker*. **4.** One who shivers or shakes; a totterer.

Shak·er (shā/kər) *n.* One of a sect practicing celibacy and communal living: so called from their characteristic bodily movements during religious meetings. Their official name is *The United Society of Believers in Christ's Second Appearing.* — **Shak/er·ism** *n.*

Shaker Heights A city in northern Ohio; a suburb of Cleveland; pop. 36,306.

Shake·speare (shāk/spir), **William**, 1564–1616, English poet and dramatist. Also **Shake/spere, Shak/speare, Shak/spere**.

Shake·spear·e·an (shāk·spir/ē·ən) *adj.* Of, pertaining to, or characteristic of Shakespeare, his work, or his style. — *n.* A specialist on Shakespeare or his writings. Also **Shake·spear/i·an**.

Shake·spear·e·an·ism (shāk·spir/ē·ən·iz/əm) *n.* **1.** An expression peculiar to Shakespeare. **2.** Shakespearean style.

Shakespearean sonnet A sonnet having the rhyme scheme *ababcdcdefefgg*: also called *Elizabethan sonnet, English sonnet*.

shake-up (shāk/up/) *n.* A radical change of personnel or organization, as in a business office, etc.

Shakh·ty (shäkh/ti) A city in the SW R.S.F.S.R.; pop. 205,000 (est. 1970).

shaking palsy *Pathol.* Parkinson's disease.

shak·o (shak/ō) *n. pl.* **·os** A kind of high, stiff military headdress, originally of fur, having a peak and an upright plume: also spelled *shacko*. [< F *schako* < Hungarian *csákó*]

SHAKO

Shak·ti (shuk/tē) In Hinduism, the consort and female energy of Siva, an aspect of Devi worshiped under various forms. Also spelled *Sakti*. [< Skt. *śakti* power] — **Shak/tism** *n.*

Sha·kun·ta·la (shə·kŏŏn/tə·lə) See SAKUNTALA.

shak·y (shā/kē) *adj.* **shak·i·er**, **shak·i·est 1.** Habitually shaking or tremulous; tottering; weak; unsound. **2.** Wavering; unreliable. — **shak/i·ly** *adv.* — **shak/i·ness** *n.*

shale¹ (shāl) *n.* A fissile argillaceous rock resembling slate, with fragile, uneven laminae. [Origin uncertain] — **shal/y** *adj.*

shale² (shāl) *n.* Shell or husk. [OE *scealu*] — **shaled** *adj.*

shale oil Petroleum obtained by the distillation of bituminous shales.

shall (shal) *v.* Present *3rd person sing.* **shall**; past **should** A defective verb having a past tense that is now used only as an auxiliary followed by the infinitive without *to*, or elliptically without the infinitive, to express: **1.** In the first person, simple futurity, with a matter-of-fact attitude toward the action or state projected: We *shall* take only the usual precautions. (But see usage note below.) **2.** In the second and third persons, futurity combined with a mood or feeling of: **a** Determination: They *shall* not pass. **b** Promise: You *shall* have whatever you need. **c** Threat: You *shall* pay for this. **d** Command: No one *shall* twice be put in jeopardy. **e** Inevitability: When earthly time *shall* end, will life survive? **3.** In all persons, indefinite future time in conditional statements: If and when you or we or the divers *shall* locate the treasure, it will (or, in legal use, the mandatory *shall*) be shared out according to the agreement. **4.** In all persons, futurity involving ideal certainty, in clauses following expressions of anxiety, demand, or desire: They are anxious that you or I or both of us *shall* go, rather than any outsider. [OE *sceal* I am obliged, 1st person sing.]

◆ **shall, will** The formal view on the use of *shall* and *will* is that to indicate simple futurity *shall* is used in the first person, *will* in the second and third; their roles are reversed to express determination, command, inevitability, etc., while in questions the choice depends on the form expected in the answer. These rules apply to American usage only at the most formal level. In general usage in the United States today *will*, in all persons, is used to express futurity and usually to express determination, etc., as well. Occasionally *shall* is used simply as an elegant variation on *will*, but not by careful writers. *Shall we* is regularly used as a polite substitute for *let's: Shall we go in?*

shal·loon (sha·lōōn′) *n.* A light, woven woolen fabric used for linings. [< F *chalon*, after *Châlons*-sur-Marne, France]
shal·lop (shal′əp) *n.* An open boat propelled by oars or sails. [< F *chaloupe* < Du. *sloep.* See SLOOP.]
shal·lot (shə·lot′) *n.* **1.** An onionlike culinary vegetable (*Allium ascalonicum*) allied to garlic but having milder bulbs that are used in seasoning and for pickles. **2.** A small onion. Also called *eschalot.* [< OF *eschalotte*, alter. of *eschaloigne.* See SCALLION.]
shal·low (shal′ō) *adj.* **1.** Having the bottom not far below the surface or top; lacking depth. **2.** Lacking intellectual depth; not wise or profound; superficial. — *n.* A shallow place in a body of water; shoal. — *v.t. & v.i.* To make or become shallow. [ME *schalowe.* Prob. akin to OE *sceald*] — **shal′low·ly** *adv.* — **shal′low·ness** *n.*
shalt (shalt) Archaic or poetic second person singular, present tense of SHALL: used with *thou.*
sham (sham) *v.* **shammed, sham·ming** *v.t.* **1.** To assume or present the appearance of; counterfeit; feign. **2.** To represent oneself as; pretend to be. **3.** *Obs.* To delude; deceive. — *v.i.* **4.** To make false pretenses; feign something. — *adj.* False; pretended; counterfeit. — *n.* **1.** A pretense; imposture; deception. **2.** One who affects or simulates a certain character; a pretender: also *sham′mer.* **3.** A deceptive imitation; counterfeit. **4.** A bordered strip simulating the edge of a sheet on a made-up bed; an embroidered covering simulating a pillow cover. [Prob. dial. var. of SHAME]
sha·man (shä′mən, shā′-, sham′ən) *n.* **1.** A priest of Shamanism; a magician. **2.** Among certain northwestern North American Indians, a tribal medicine man or wizard. — *adj.* Of or pertaining to a shaman: also **sha·man·ic** (shə·man′ik). [< Russian < Tungusic *samān* < Skt. *śamaṇa* ascetic]
Sha·man·ism (shä′mən·iz′əm, shā′-, sham′ən-) *n.* **1.** A primitive religion of NE Asia and Europe holding that gods, demons, ancestral spirits, etc., work for the good or ill of mankind through the sole medium of the shamans. **2.** Any similar religion, as of certain Indians of the American Northwest. — **Sha′man·ist** *adj. & n.* — **Sha′man·is′tic** *adj.*
Sha·mash (shä′mäsh) In Assyro-Babylonian religion, the sun god regarded as the deity controlling crops and personifying righteousness.
sham·a·teur·ism (sham′ə·tŏŏr′iz·əm, -ə·tər·iz′-) *n.* The practice in some sports of offering amateur athletes large fees, ostensibly for expenses, but actually as an inducement to participate. [< SHAM + AMATEURISM]
sham·ble (sham′bəl) *v.i.* **·bled, ·bling** To walk with shuffling or unsteady gait. — *n.* A shambling walk; shuffling gait. [Origin uncertain]
sham·bles (sham′bəlz) *n.pl.* (*usually construed as sing.*) **1.** A place where butchers kill animals; slaughterhouse. **2.** Any place of carnage or execution. **3.** A place marked by great destruction or disorder. **4.** *Brit. Dial.* A meat market; in the singular, a table or stall in such a market. [OE *scamol* bench, stool < L *scamellum*, dim. of *scamnum* bench, stool]
shame (shām) *n.* **1.** A painful sense of guilt or degradation caused by consciousness of guilt or of anything degrading, unworthy, or immodest. **2.** Sensitiveness or susceptibility to such feelings. **3.** One who or that which brings reproach or disgrace. **4.** A state or condition of regret, dishonor, or disgrace. — **to put to shame 1.** To disgrace; make ashamed. **2.** To surpass or eclipse. — *v.t.* **shamed, sham·ing 1.** To make ashamed; cause to feel shame. **2.** To bring shame upon; disgrace. **3.** To impel by a sense of shame: with *into* or *out of.* [OE *scamu*]
shame·faced (shām′fāst′) *adj.* Easily abashed; showing shame or bashfulness in one's face; modest; bashful. [Alter. of ME *shamefast*, OE *scamfæst* abashed] — **shame′fac·ed·ly** (shām′fā′sid·lē, shām′fāst′lē) *adv.* — **shame′fac′ed·ness** *n.*
shame·ful (shām′fəl) *adj.* **1.** Deserving or bringing shame or disgrace; disgraceful; scandalous. **2.** Exciting shame; indecent. — **shame′ful·ly** *adv.* — **shame′ful·ness** *n.*
shame·less (shām′lis) *adj.* **1.** Impudent; brazen; immodest. **2.** Done without shame; indicating a want of pride or decency. — **shame′less·ly** *adv.* — **shame′less·ness** *n.*
sham·mes (shom′əs) *n.* *pl.* **sham·mo·sim** (shom·os′əm, -ēm) **1.** A minor official in a synagogue: also called *beadle.* **2.** The candle in the Hanukkah Menorah with which the others are lit. Also **sha′mes, sham′mas, sham′mash, sham′mos.** [< Hebrew *shammāsh* servant]
sham·my (sham′ē), **sham·ois** (sham′ē) See CHAMOIS.
sham·poo (sham·pōō′) *n.* **1.** Any of various liquid preparations of soap, chemical solvents, etc., used to cleanse the hair and scalp. **2.** The act or process of shampooing. — *v.t.* To cleanse (the hair and scalp) with a shampoo. [< Hind. *chāmpnā* to press] — **sham·poo′er** *n.*
sham·rock (sham′rok) *n.* Any of several trifoliate plants, accepted as the national emblem of Ireland, variously identified as oxalis, the white clover, and the black medic. [< Irish *seamrōg*, dim. of *seamar* trefoil]
sham·us (shom′əs, shä′-) *U.S. Slang* **1.** A policeman. **2.** A private detective. [< SHAMMES, prob. infl. in form and pronun. by the Irish given name *Seamus* (shā′məs)]
Shan (shan, shän) *n.* **1.** One of a group of Mongoloid tribes of southern China, Assam, Burma, and Thailand. **2.** The

Thai language of these tribes. — *adj.* Of or pertaining to the Shan people or their language.
shan·dry·dan (shan′drē·dan) *n.* *Irish* **1.** A two-wheeled cart or hooded chaise: also **shan′da·ra·dan′, shan′der·y·dan′.** **2.** An old-fashioned or rickety vehicle. [Origin unknown]
shan·dy·gaff (shan′dē·gaf) *n.* An alcoholic drink, usually ale or beer and ginger beer. [Origin unknown]
shang·hai (shang′hī, shang·hī′) *v.t.* **·haied, ·hai·ing 1.** To drug or render unconscious and kidnap for service aboard a ship. **2.** To cause to do something by force or deception. [after *Shanghai*, China]
Shang·hai (shang′hī′) *n.* One of a former large breed of domestic fowls, with long legs and feathered shanks, said to have originated in Shanghai, China.
Shang·hai (shang′hī′, *Chinese* shäng′hī′) A port city in eastern China; pop. 10,000,000 (est. 1970).
Shan·gri-la (shang′grē·lä′) *n.* Any imaginary hidden utopia or paradise. [after the locale of *Lost Horizon*, a novel by James Hilton, 1900-54, English author]
Shan·hai·kwan (shän′hī′gwän′) A city in NE Hopeh Province, China, at the eastern end of the Great Wall; pop. about 25,000. Formerly called **Lin·yü** (lin′yōō′).
shank (shangk) *n.* **1.** The part of the leg between the knee and the ankle. **2.** A cut of meat from the leg of an animal; the shin. **3.** The tarsus of a bird. For illustration see FOWL. **4.** Something resembling a leg. **5.** The part of a tool connecting the handle with the working part, as the stem of a drill. **6.** The projecting piece or loop by which some forms of buttons are attached. **7.** The stem of an anchor. **8.** The stem of a key between the bow and the bit. **9.** The straight part of a hook. **10.** The narrow part of a spoon handle. **11.** A continuation of the tang of a tool or instrument. **12.** *Printing* The body of a type. **13.** The narrow part of a shoe sole. For illustration see SHOE. **14.** *Bot.* A pedicel. **15.** *Rare* The remaining part of a thing: the *shank* of the evening. — *v.i. Scot.* To travel on foot. [OE *scanca*]
Shan·ka·ra (shung′kə·rä) Ninth-century Hindu religious reformer, teacher, and writer; foremost exponent of Vedanta philosophy; considered an incarnation of Siva. Also **Shan·ka·ra·char·ya** (shung′kə·rä·chär′yə).
shanks′ mare (shangks) *Informal* One's own legs as a means of conveyance.
Shan·non (shan′ən) The chief river of Ireland, in the central part, flowing 224 miles south and west to the Atlantic.
Shan·si (shän′sē′) A Province of NE China; 60,000 sq. mi.; pop. 15,960,000 (est. 1957).
Shan States (shän, shan) A constituent State of eastern Upper Burma, comprising the **Northern Shan State** and the **Southern Shan State;** 61,090 sq. mi.; pop. 1,987,000 (est. 1956). Also **Shan State.**
sha′nt (shant, shänt) Shall not. Also **shan′t.**
shan·tey (shan′tē) See CHANTEY.
shan·tung (shan′tung, shan·tung′) *n.* A silk fabric similar to pongee and having the same rough, nubby surface, originally made in China of wild silk, now often made of rayon combined with cotton. [< SHANTUNG]
Shan·tung (shan′tung′, *Chinese* shän′dŏŏng′) A Province of NE China; 55,000 sq. mi.; pop. 54,030,000 (est. 1957); capital, Tsinan.
shan·ty¹ (shan′tē) *n.* *pl.* **·ties** A hastily built shack or cabin; a ramshackle or rickety dwelling. — **Syn.** See HUT. [< F (Canadian) *chantier* lumberer's shack]
shan·ty² (shan′tē) See CHANTEY.
shan·ty·man (shan′tē·mən) *n.* *pl.* **·men** (-mən) One who lives in a shanty; especially, a woodcutter or lumberman.
shan·ty·town (shan′tē·toun′) *n.* **1.** The section of a city or town composed of ramshackle or hastily constructed shacks. **2.** The inhabitants collectively of such a section.
Shao·hing (shou′shing′) A city in northern Chekiang Province, China; pop. 225,000 (est. 1970). Also **Shao′-hsing′.**
shape (shāp) *n.* **1.** Outward form or construction; configuration; contour. **2.** A developed expression or definite formulation; realization or application; embodiment; cast: to put an idea into *shape.* **3.** A being, image, or appearance considered with reference to its form, generally incorporeal; phantom. **4.** The character or form in which a thing appears; guise; aspect. **5.** Something that gives or determines form; a pattern or mold; in millinery, a stiff frame. **6.** The lines of a person's body; figure. **7.** Manner of execution. **8.** Condition: Everything is in good *shape.* — **to take shape** To have or assume a definite form. — *v.* **shaped, shaped** (*Rare* **shap·en**), **shap·ing** *v.t.* **1.** To give shape to; mold; form. **2.** To adjust or adapt; modify. **3.** To devise; prepare. **4.** To give direction or character to: to *shape* one's course of action. **5.** To put into or express in words. **6.** *Obs.* To appoint; ordain. — *v.i.* **7.** To take shape; develop; form: often with *up* or *into.* **8.** *Rare* To become adapted; conform. **9.** *Rare* To happen; come about. — **to shape up** *Informal* **1.** To proceed satisfactorily or favorably. **2.** To develop proper form. [OE *gesceap* creation, *scieppan* to create] — **shap′er** *n.*
SHAPE Supreme Headquarters Allied Powers Europe.
shaped (shāpt) *adj.* **1.** Formed. **2.** Resembling in shape: used in compounds: leaf-*shaped.*

shaped charge An explosive charge so shaped within its container as to concentrate and direct the effect, used especially in armor-piercing projectiles.

shape·less (shāp′lĭs) *adj.* Having no definite shape; lacking symmetry. **— shape′less·ly** *adv.* **— shape′less·ness** *n.*

shape·ly (shāp′lē) *adj.* **·li·er, ·li·est** Having a pleasing shape; well-formed; graceful. **— shape′li·ness** *n.*

shape-up (shāp′up′) *n.* The selection of a work crew by an employer representative, a labor union deputy, or other agent, who chooses from among a number of workers, especially longshoremen, assembled for a work shift.

Shap·ley (shap′lē), **Harlow**, born 1885, U.S. astronomer.

shard (shärd) *n.* **1.** A broken piece of a brittle substance, as of an earthen vessel; a potsherd; a fragment: also called *sherd.* **2.** *Zool.* A hard, thin shell, or a wing cover, of an insect. [OE *sceard.* Related to SHEAR.]

share[1] (shâr) *n.* **1.** A portion; allotted or equitable part. **2.** One of the equal parts into which the capital stock of a company or corporation is divided. **3.** An equitable part of something enjoyed or suffered in common. **— to go shares** To partake equally, as in an enterprise. *Abbr. sh.* **— v. shared, shar·ing** *v.t.* **1.** To divide and give out in shares or portions; apportion. **2.** To enjoy or endure in common; participate in. **3.** *Chem.* Of atoms, to arrange (valence electrons) with another atom so that the electrons resonate between them, the resulting configuration being more stable than either atom alone. *— v.i.* **4.** To have a part; participate: with *in.* [OE *scearu < scieran* to shear. Related to SHEAR.] **— shar′er** *n.*

share[2] (shâr) *n.* A plowshare (which see).

share·crop·per (shâr′krop′ər) *n.* A tenant farmer who pays a share of his crop as rent for his land.

share·hold·er (shâr′hōl′dər) *n.* An owner of a share or shares of a company's stock; a stockholder.

Sha·ri (shä′rē) A river in the northern Central African Republic and western Chad, flowing about 500 miles NW to Lake Chad: also *Chari.*

shark[1] (shärk) *n.* One of a group of elasmobranch fishes (order *Selachii*), mostly marine, of medium to large size, having dun-colored bodies covered with placoid scales. Some species, as the **great white shark** or **man-eater** (*Carcharodon carcharias*), are dangerous to man. *— v.i.* To fish for sharks. [Origin uncertain]

shark[2] (shärk) *n.* **1.** A bold and dishonest person; a rapacious swindler. **2.** *Slang* A person of exceptional skill or ability in some special line. Also **shark′er.** *— v.t.* **1.** *Archaic* To obtain by unscrupulous or deceitful means. *— v.i.* **2.** To live by trickery. [Prob. < G *schürke* scoundrel; infl. by SHARK[1]]

shark·skin (shärk′skin′) *n.* **1.** The skin of a shark. **2.** A fabric with a smooth, almost shiny surface, made of acetate rayon and used for sports clothes.

sharn (shärn) *n. Scot.* Cow dung: also *shairn.* [OE *scearn*] **— sharn′y** *adj.*

Shar·on (shar′ən) A city in western Pennsylvania, near the Ohio border; pop. 22,653.

Shar·on (shar′ən), **Plain of** A part of the coastal plain of western Israel, extending about 50 miles between the Hills of Ephraim and the Mediterranean.

sharp (shärp) *adj.* **1.** Having a keen edge or an acute point; capable of cutting or piercing. **2.** Coming to an acute angle; not obtuse; abrupt: a *sharp* peak. **3.** Keen of perception or discernment; also, shrewd in bargaining; artful; overreaching. **4.** Ardent; eager; keen, as the appetite; impetuous or fiery, as a combat or debate; vigilant or attentive. **5.** Affecting the mind or senses, as if by cutting or piercing; poignant; acrimonious. **6.** Shrill. **7.** Pinching; cutting, as cold. **8.** Having an acrid or pungent taste. **9.** Distinct, as an outline; not blurred. **10.** *Music* **a** Raised in pitch by a semitone. **b** Above the right, true pitch. **c** Having sharps in the key signature. **11.** Hard and rough; gritty, as sand. **12.** *Phonet.* Of consonants, voiceless: opposed to *flat.* **13.** *U.S. Slang* Excellent, as in dress, mental perception, etc. **— Syn.** See ASTUTE. *— adv.* **1.** In a sharp manner; sharply. **2.** Promptly; exactly: at 4 o'clock *sharp.* **3.** *Music* Above the proper pitch. *— n.* **1.** *Music* A sign (♯) placed before a note to indicate that the note is raised a semitone from its normal pitch; also, the note so altered. **2.** A sewing needle of long, slender shape. **3.** A cheating rogue; sharper: a *card-sharp.* **4.** *Obs.* A dueling sword; rapier. **— sharps and flats** *Music* Loosely, the black keys on a keyboard. *— v.t.* **1.** *Music* To raise in pitch, as by a half step. *— v.i.* **2.** *Music* To sing, play, or sound above the right pitch. [OE *scearp*] **— sharp′ly** *adv.* **— sharp′ness** *n.*

Sharp (shärp), **William**, 1855–1905, Scottish poet, critic, and editor: pseudonym *Fiona Macleod.*

sharp·en (shär′pən) *v.t. & v.i.* To make or become sharp. **— sharp′en·er** *n.*

sharp·er (shär′pər) *n.* A swindler; cheat.

sharp-eyed (shärp′īd′) *adj.* **1.** Having acute eyesight. **2.** Keenly observant; alert.

sharp·ie (shär′pē) *n.* A long, sharp, flat-bottomed sailboat having a centerboard and one or two masts, each having a triangular sail, originally used in the oyster and scallop fisheries. [< SHARP; in allusion to its outline]

Sharps·burg (shärps′bûrg) A village in NW Maryland; site of the battle of Antietam, 1862, in the Civil War; pop. 833.

sharp-set (shärp′set′) *adj.* **1.** Set at a sharp angle; prepared like a saw for cutting. **2.** Keen; eager; fierce. **3.** Ravenous; hungry; thin and hungry-looking.

sharp-shinned hawk (shärp′shind′) *n.* A small hawk (*Accipiter striatus*) of North America, with short rounded wings and a long square tail.

sharp-shoot·er (shärp′shoo′tər) *n.* **1.** A skilled marksman, especially in the use of the rifle. **2.** *Mil.* **a** In the U.S. Army, the second grade of skill in the use of small arms. **b** A soldier having this qualification. Compare EXPERT, MARKSMAN. **— sharp′shoot′ing** *n.*

sharp-sight·ed (shärp′sī′tid) *adj.* Having keen vision. **— sharp′-sight′ed·ness** *n.*

sharp-tongued (shärp′tungd′) *adj.* Bitter or caustic in speech.

sharp-wit·ted (shärp′wit′id) *adj.* Acute; intelligent. **— sharp′-wit′ted·ness** *n.*

Shas·ta (shas′tə), **Mount** An extinct volcano in the Cascade Range of northern California; 14,162 ft.

Shasta daisy A cultivated variety of a short-lived perennial (*Chrysanthemum maximum*) having large, white-rayed flowers.

Shatt-el-Ar·ab (shat′al-ar′əb) A river in SE Iraq, formed by the Tigris and Euphrates, flowing about 120 miles SE to the Persian Gulf, and forming part of the Iran-Iraq border.

shat·ter (shat′ər) *v.t.* **1.** To break into pieces suddenly, as by a blow. **2.** To break the health or tone of, as the body or mind; disorder; damage. **3.** *Obs.* To scatter. *— v.i.* **4.** To break into pieces; burst. **— Syn.** See BREAK. *— n. Obs.* **1.** A shattered fragment; a splinter: a tree rent into *shatters.* **2.** A shattered or disordered condition: His nerves are in a *shatter.* [ME *schateren.* ? Akin to SCATTER.]

shat·ter·proof glass (shat′ər-proof′) Safety glass (which see).

shaul (shôl) See SHOAL[1].

shave (shāv) *v.* **shaved, shaved** or **shav·en, shav·ing** *v.t.* **1.** To cut hair or beard close to the skin with a razor. *— v.t.* **2.** To remove hair or beard from (the face, head, etc.) with a razor. **3.** To cut (hair or beard) close to the skin with a razor: often with *off.* **4.** To trim closely as if with a razor: to *shave* a lawn. **5.** To cut thin slices from, as in preparing the surface; pare; plane. **6.** To cut into thin slices: to *shave* ice. **7.** To touch or scrape in passing; graze; come close to. **8.** *U.S.* To buy (commercial paper) at a reduction greater than the bank discount. *— n.* **1.** The act or operation of cutting off the beard with a razor. **2.** A knife or blade, mounted between two handles, as for shaving wood: also **draw shave, spoke shave.** **3.** A shaving; thin slice. **4.** An extra or exorbitant discount paid for cashing a note or draft, as a premium given for an extension of time. **5.** *Informal* The act of barely grazing something; a narrow escape: a close *shave.* **6.** One who drives hard bargains. [OE *scafan* to shave]

shave·ling (shāv′ling) *n.* **1.** One who is shaven; opprobriously, a monk or priest. **2.** A youth.

shav·en (shā′vən) Alternative past participle of SHAVE. *— adj.* **1.** Shaved; also, tonsured. **2.** Trimmed closely.

shav·er (shā′vər) *n.* **1.** One who shaves. **2.** *Informal* A lad.

shave·tail (shāv′tāl′) *n. U.S. Slang* **1.** A second lieutenant, especially one recently commissioned. **2.** An untrained or intractable mule. **3.** A tenderfoot [Formerly in allusion to young, unbroken army mules with their tails bobbed]

Sha·vi·an (shā′vē-ən) *n.* An admirer of George Bernard Shaw, his books, or his theories. *— adj.* Of, pertaining to, or like George Bernard Shaw, or his style and methods.

shav·ie (shā′vē) *n. Scot.* A deceptive trick.

shav·ing (shā′ving) *n.* **1.** The act of one who or that which shaves. **2.** A thin paring shaved from anything, as a board.

shaw[1] (shô) *v.t. Scot.* To show.

shaw[2] (shô) *n. Brit.* **1.** A thicket; copse: also **shaugh.** **2.** *Usually pl.* The leaves and tops of vegetables. [OE *sceaga* copse]

Shaw (shô), **George Bernard**, 1856–1950, British dramatist, critic, and novelist born in Ireland. **— Henry Wheeler,** 1818–85, U.S. humorist: pseudonym *Josh Billings.*

shawl (shôl) *n.* A wrap, as a square cloth, or large broad scarf, worn over the upper part of the body. [< Persian *shāl*]

shawm (shôm) *n.* Any of a class of ancient, double-reed instruments; the forerunner of the modern oboe family. [< OF *chalemie* pipe < LL *calamellus*, dim. of L *calamus* reed]

PRONUNCIATION KEY: add, āce, câre, pälm; end, ēven; it, īce; odd, ōpen, ôrder; tōōk, pōōl; up, bûrn; ə = a in *above,* e in *sicken,* i in *flexible,* o in *melon,* u in *focus*; yōō = u in *fuse*; oil; pout; check; go; ring; thin; this; zh, vision. For à, œ, ü, kh, ṅ, see inside front cover.

Shaw·nee (shô·nē′) *n.* One of a tribe of North American Indians of Algonquian stock, formerly living in Tennessee and South Carolina: now in Oklahoma. [< Algonquian (Shawnee) *Shawunogi* southerners < *shawun* south]

Shaw·wal (shô·wäl′) *n.* The tenth month of the Moslem year. See (Moslem) CALENDAR.

shay (shā) *n. Dial.* A chaise. [Back formation due to mistaking *chaise* for a plural]

Shays (shāz), **Daniel**, 1747?–1825, American Revolutionary officer, leader of **Shays' Rebellion**, 1786–87, a popular insurrection in western Massachusetts, caused by economic distress. — **Shays′ite** *n.*

Shcher·ba·kov (shchir·bə·kôf′) See RYBINSK.

she (shē) *pron., possessive* **her** or **hers**, *objective* **her**; *pl. nominative* **they**, *possessive* **their** or **theirs**, *objective* **them** **1.** The nominative singular pronoun of the third person, used of the female person or being previously mentioned or understood, or of things conventionally regarded as feminine, as ships, machines, etc. **2.** That woman or female; any woman: *She* who listens learns. — *n. pl.* **shes** A female person or being. [ME *sche*, *scho* < OE *sēo*, *sīo*, fem. of *sē* the, replacing *hēo* she]

she- *combining form* Female; feminine: in hyphenated compounds: a *she-lion*; *she-devil*.

shea (shē) *n.* A large tree (*Butyrospermum parki*) growing only in western tropical Africa and yielding the **shea butter**, used for food, and making soap, etc. [< Mandingo *si*, *se*]

sheaf[1] (shēf) *n. pl.* **sheaves** (shēvz) **1.** A quantity of the stalks of cut grain or the like, bound together; a bundle of straw. **2.** Any collection of things, as papers, tied together. **3.** The quiverful of arrows carried by an archer, usually 24. — *v.t.* To bind in a sheaf; sheave. [OE *scēaf*]

sheaf[2] (shēf) See SHEAVE[2].

sheal[1] (shēl) *n. Scot. & Brit. Dial.* A shealing.

sheal[2] (shēl) *n. Brit.* A pod or shell. [Var. of SHELL]

sheal·ing (shē′ling) *n.* **1.** *Brit. Dial.* A hut or cabin for the use of shepherds or sportsmen in the hills, for fishermen at the shore, etc.: also spelled *shieling*. **2.** *Scot.* A shed for sheltering sheep at night in the hills. Also called *sheal*.

shealing hill *Scot.* A hill upon which grain is winnowed by the wind: also spelled *sheeling hill*.

shear (shir) *n.* **1.** A two-bladed cutting instrument: obsolete except in the plural. See SHEARS. **2.** *Physics* A deformation of a solid body, equivalent to a sliding over each other of adjacent laminar elements, with a progressive relative displacement: also **shearing stress. 3.** The act or result of shearing. **4.** A plowshare. **5.** *Naut.* Sweep; sheer. — **Syn.** See STRESS. — *v.* **sheared** (*Archaic* **shore**), **sheared** or **shorn, shear·ing** *v.t.* **1.** To cut the hair, fleece, etc., from. **2.** To remove by cutting or clipping: to *shear* wool. **3.** To deprive; strip, as of power or wealth. **4.** To cut or clip with or as with shears: to *shear* a cable. **5.** *Dial.* To reap, as grain, with a sickle. — *v.i.* **6.** To use shears or a similar instrument. **7.** To slide or break from a shear (def. 2). **8.** To proceed by or as by cutting a way: with *through*. **9.** *Dial.* To reap with a sickle. [OE *scēarra* scissors < *scieran* to shear. Akin to SHARD, SHARE.] — **shear′er** *n.*

shear·ling (shir′ling) *n.* **1.** The fleece from the second shearing of a sheep. **2.** The sheep from which one fleece has been cut.

shears (shirz) *n.pl.* **1.** Any large cutting or clipping instrument worked by the crossing of cutting edges. Also **pair of shears. 2.** The ways or guides, as of a lathe. **3.** An apparatus for hoisting and moving heavy objects, consisting of two or more spars with lower ends spread out and upper ends jointed to receive the tackle: also **shear legs:** sometimes spelled *sheers*. [See SHEAR]

shear·wa·ter (shir′wô′tər, -wot′ər) *n.* Any of a genus (*Puffinus*) of far-ranging sea birds related to the fulmars and petrels: so called because they skim close to the water: also called *haqdon*.

sheat·fish (shēt′fish′) *n. pl.* **·fish** or **·fish·es** A large catfish (*Siluris glanis*) of the fresh waters of central and eastern Europe, sometimes weighing as much as 400 pounds. [OE *sceota* trout + FISH]

sheath (shēth) *n. pl.* **sheaths** (shēthz, shēths) **1.** An envelope or case, as for a sword; scabbard. **2.** *Bot.* A case enclosing the lower part of the leaves in grasses. **3.** *Zool.* Any covering in animals that resembles a sheath. **4.** A close-fitting dress having a straight, narrow skirt. — *v.t.* To sheathe. [OE *scæth*] — **sheath′less** *adj.*

sheath·bill (shēth′bil′) *n.* Either of two sea birds (genus *Chionis*), natives of the Antarctic islands, having white plumage and a horny sheath at the base of the bill.

sheathe (shēth) *v.t.* **sheathed, sheath·ing 1.** To put into a sheath. **2.** To plunge (a sword, etc.) into flesh, as if into a sheath. **3.** To encase or protect with a covering, as the hull of a ship with metal. **4.** To draw in, as claws. [< SHEATH]

sheath·ing (shē′thing) *n.* **1.** A protective covering, as of a ship's hull; that which sheathes; also, the material used. **2.** The act of one who sheathes. **3.** The covering or waterproof material on outside walls or roofs.

sheath knife A large case knife carried in a sheath attached to a belt, worn by sailors and riggers.

sheave[1] (shēv) *v.t.* **sheaved, sheav·ing** To gather into sheaves; collect. [< SHEAF]

sheave[2] (shēv) *n.* **1.** A grooved pulley wheel; also, a pulley wheel and its block. **2.** An eccentric, or its disk. **3.** *Scot.* A slice or cut. Also spelled *sheaf, sheeve*. [Var. of SHIVE[1]]

sheaves (shēvz) Plural of SHEAF[1].

She·ba (shē′bə) The Old Testament name for a region of the SW Arabian peninsula, corresponding to modern Yemen: Arabic *Saba*.

She·ba (shē′bə), **Queen of** A queen who visited Solomon to test his wisdom. I *Kings* x 1–3. Also, in the Koran, called *Balkis*.

she·bang (shi·bang′) *n. U.S. Slang* **1.** A building, vehicle, etc. **2.** Matter; affair: tired of the whole *shebang*. [Var. of SHEBEEN]

She·bat (shi·bät′) *n.* The fifth month of the Hebrew year. Also spelled *Sebat*. See (Hebrew) CALENDAR.

she·been (shi·bēn′) *n. Irish & Scot.* **1.** A groggery; especially, a place where liquor is sold without a license. **2.** Weak ale or beer. [< Irish *sibīn* little mug]

She·boy·gan (shə·boi′gən) A port city in eastern Wisconsin, on Lake Michigan; pop. 48,484.

She·chem (shē′kem) The ancient name for NABLUS.

shed[1] (shed) *v.* **shed, shed·ding** *v.t.* **1.** To pour forth in drops; emit, as tears or blood. **2.** To cause to pour forth. **3.** To send forth or abroad; diffuse; radiate, as light. **4.** To throw off without allowing to penetrate, as rain; repel. **5.** To cast off by natural process, as hair, skin, etc. **6.** To rid oneself of. — *v.i.* **7.** To cast off or lose hair, skin, etc., by natural process. **8.** To fall or drop, as leaves or seed. — **to shed blood** To kill. — *n.* **1.** That which sheds, as a sloping surface or watershed. **2.** That which has been shed. **3.** A separation or division: applied technically to the opening in the warp through which the shuttle is thrown in weaving, and in parts of Great Britain to the parting of the hair. **4.** The slope of a hill. [OE *scēadan* to separate, part]

shed[2] (shed) *n.* **1.** A small low building, often with front or sides open; also, a lean-to: a wagon *shed*. **2.** *Brit.* A storehouse; barn. **3.** A temporary covering. **4.** A hangar. **5.** *Physics* A unit of the cross section of an atomic nucleus, equal to 10^{-24} barn or 10^{-48} square centimeter. [Var. of SHADE]

she'd (shēd) **1.** She had. **2.** She would.

shed·der (shed′ər) *n.* **1.** One who sheds. **2.** An animal that sheds or has lately shed its skin, as a snake.

she-dev·il (shē′dev′əl) *n.* **1.** A bad-tempered and spiteful woman. **2.** A female demon.

sheel·ing hill (shē′ling) See SHEALING HILL.

sheen (shēn) *n.* **1.** A glistening brightness, as if from reflection. **2.** Bright, shining attire. — *adj.* Shining; radiant; beautiful. — *v.i.* To shine; gleam; glisten. [OE *sciene* beautiful; infl. in meaning by SHINE. Akin to G *schön* beautiful.] — **sheen′y** *adj.*

sheep (shēp) *n. pl.* **sheep 1.** A medium-sized, domesticated, even-toed ruminant (genus *Ovis*, family *Bovidae*), bred in many varieties for its flesh, wool, and skin. ◆ Collateral adjective: *ovine*. **2.** Sheepskin (def. 1). **3.** A meek, bashful, or timid person. Abbr. (for defs. 1, 2) sh. [OE *scēap*]

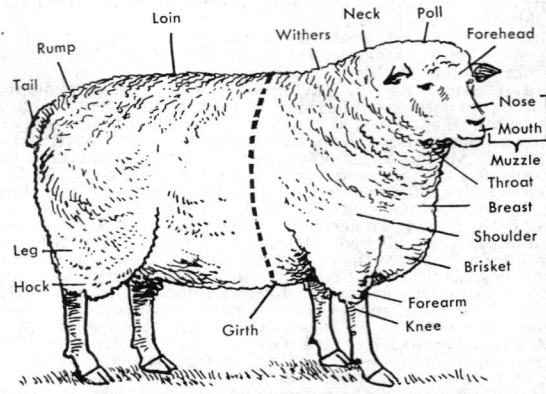

SHEEP (Anatomical nomenclature)

sheep·backs (shēp′baks′) *n.pl.* Roches moutonnées.

sheep·ber·ry (shēp′ber′ē) *n. pl.* **·ries** **1.** A tree (*Viburnum lentago*), bearing black, oval, edible drupes. **2.** The drupe of this tree.

sheep·cote (shēp′kōt′) *n.* A small enclosure for the protection of sheep; a sheepfold. Also **sheep′cot′** (-kot′).

sheep dip Any of several liquid disinfectants containing creosote, nicotine, arsenic, etc., used for dipping sheep.

sheep dog **1.** A dog trained to guard and control sheep, often a collie, but also an **old English sheep dog**, a rough-coated, heavy, bobtailed dog much used by drovers in England: also called *shepherd dog, shepherd's dog.* **2.** A chaperon.

sheep·fold (shēp′fōld′) *n.* A place where sheep are enclosed at night; a pen for sheep.

sheep·herd·er (shēp′hûr′dər) *n.* A herder of sheep. — **sheep′herd′ing** *n.*

sheep·ish (shē′pish) *adj.* Foolish, as a sheep; awkwardly diffident; abashed. — **sheep′ish·ly** *adv.* — **sheep′ish·ness** *n.*

sheep laurel Lambkill.

sheep ranch A ranch and range where sheep are bred and raised. Also *Brit.* **sheep·walk** (shēp′wôk′), *Austral.* **sheep run.**

sheep's eyes (shēps) Bashful, or amorous glances.

sheeps·head (shēps′hed′) *n.* **1.** A common deep-bodied sparoid food fish (*Archosargus probatocephalus*) of the Atlantic coast of the United States. **2.** The drumfish (def. 2). **3.** A black or rose-colored food fish of California waters (*Pimelometopon pulchrum*). **4.** A foolish or silly person.

sheep·shear·ing (shēp′shir′ing) *n.* **1.** The act of shearing sheep. **2.** The shearing season; also, a feast given at an occasion at which sheep are shorn. — **sheep′shear′er** *n.*

sheep·skin (shēp′skin′) *n.* **1.** The skin of a sheep, tanned or untanned, or anything made from it, as leather or parchment. **2.** A document written on parchment, as an academic diploma.

sheep sorrel An herb (*Rumex acetosella*) of the buckwheat family, widely distributed in dry places, and having leaves of an acrid taste.

sheer¹ (shir) *v.i.* To swerve from a course; turn aside. — *v.t.* To cause to swerve or deviate. — *n.* **1.** *Naut.* **a** The rise, or the amount of rise from a level, of the lengthwise lines of a vessel's hull. **b** A position of a vessel that enables it to swing clear of a single anchor. **2.** A swerving or curving course. [< SHEAR]

sheer² (shir) *adj.* **1.** Having no modifying conditions; unmitigated; absolute; downright; utter: *sheer folly.* **2.** Exceedingly thin and fine: said of fabrics. **3.** Perpendicular; steep; ascending vertically: a *sheer* precipice. **4.** Pure; pellucid. **5.** *Obs.* Bright; shining. — **Syn.** See STEEP¹. — *n.* Any very thin fabric used for clothes. — *adv.* Steeply; perpendicularly [ME *schere.* Cf. ON *skærr* clear, bright and OE *scīr* bright, shining.] — **sheer′ness** *n.* — **sheer′ly** *adv.*

sheers (shirz) See SHEARS (def. 3).

sheet (shēt) *n.* **1.** A very thin and broad piece of any substance; as: **a** A large rectangular piece of bed linen. **b** A piece of paper, especially one of a regular size, as a leaf of a book. **c** A newspaper, especially a tabloid. **d** A piece of metal or other substance hammered, rolled, fused, or cut very thin. **2.** A broad, flat surface; superficial expanse: a *sheet* of water. **3.** *Naut.* **a** A rope or chain from a lower corner of a sail to extend it or move it. **b** *pl.* In an open boat, the space at the bow and stern not occupied by the thwarts. The former is termed the **fore sheets** and the latter the **stern sheets. 4.** A sail: a literary use. **5.** *Geol.* **a** An originally horizontal or moderately inclined layer of igneous rock of small thickness as compared with its lateral extent. **b** Any superficial deposit, as of gravel left by a glacier, or of soil or ice. **6.** The large, unseparated block of stamps printed by one impression of a plate. *Abbr.* **sh.** — **three sheets in the wind** *Slang* Tipsy; drunk. — *v.t.* **1.** To stretch by hauling on a sheet: used only in the expression **to sheet home,** to stretch the clews of a sail to the extremities of the next lower yard. **2.** To cover with or wrap in a sheet. **3.** To furnish with sheets. — *v.i.* **4.** To extend in a particular direction: said of the sheets of a sail. [OE *scȳte* linen cloth]

sheet anchor 1. One of two anchors for use only in emergency; formerly, the main anchor. **2.** One who or that which can be depended upon in danger or an emergency.

sheet bend *Naut.* A knot used to join two ropes' ends, made by passing one end through a loop of the other rope, carrying it around the loop, and slipping it under its own running part: also called **weaver's hitch, weaver's knot.**

sheet·ing (shē′ting) *n.* **1.** The act of sheeting, in any sense. **2.** Cotton, muslin, etc., used for making sheets for beds.

sheet lightning Lightning appearing in sheetlike form as a momentary and broadly diffused radiance in the sky, caused by the reflection of a distant lightning flash.

sheet metal Metal rolled and pressed into sheets.

sheet music Music printed on unbound sheets of paper; especially, music for popular songs.

sheeve (shēv) See SHEAVE².

Shef·field (shef′ēld) A county borough in South Yorkshire, England; pop. 561,500 (1976).

sheik (shēk, *Brit.* shāk) *n.* **1.** A Moslem high priest or a venerable man; also, the chief or head of an Arab tribe or family. **2.** *Archaic Slang* A man who fascinates women; a lady-killer. Also **sheikh.** [< Arabic *sheikh, shaykh,* lit., an elder, chief < *shakha* to grow old]

sheik·dom (shēk′dəm) *n.* The land ruled by a sheik. Also **sheikh′dom.**

shei·tan (shī·tän′) See SHAITAN.

shek·el (shek′əl) *n.* **1.** An Assyrian, Babylonian, and, later, Hebrew unit of weight and money; also, a coin having this weight. **2.** *pl. Slang* Money; riches. [< Hebrew *sheqel* < *shāqal* to weigh]

She·ki·nah (shi·kī′na) *n.* A cloud of glory that accompanied the tabernacle of the Jews, a symbol and manifestation of the divine presence. [< Hebrew *shekhinah,* lit., dwelling place < *shākhan* to dwell]

Shel·by (shel′bē), **Joseph Orville,** 1830–97, American Confederate general.

shel·drake (shel′drāk′) *n.* **1.** A large Old World duck (genera *Tadorna* or *Casarca,* as the common sheldrake (*T. tadorna*), or the **ruddy sheldrake** (*C. rutila*) of southeastern Europe and North Africa. **2.** A merganser, especially the **salt-water sheldrake** (*Mergus serrator*). [< dial. E *sheld* piebald, dappled + DRAKE]

shelf (shelf) *n. pl.* **shelves** (shelvz) **1.** A board or slab set horizontally into or against a wall to support articles, as books; also, one of the boards in a bookcase or closet. **2.** Contents of a shelf. **3.** Any flat projecting ledge, as of rock. **4.** A steep-sided bank or shallow place in a body of water; a reef; shoal. **5.** The stratum of bedrock met in sinking a shaft. — **on the shelf** No longer in use; discarded. [< LG *schelf* set of shelves]

shell (shel) *n.* **1.** Any of various hard structures encasing an animal, as a mollusk or other shellfish. **2.** The hard, relatively fragile outer coat of an egg. **3.** The carapace of a turtle. **4.** The relatively hard, tough outermost covering of a fruit, seed, or nut. **5.** The material composing a shell. **6.** A hollow structure or vessel, generally thin and weak; also, a framework with its interior removed or destroyed, or one to be filled out or built upon. **7.** A very light, long, and narrow racing rowboat. **8.** A hollow metallic projectile filled with an explosive or chemical; especially, an artillery projectile filled with high explosive. **9.** The plates, etc., constituting the framework of a steam boiler or the like. **10.** A metallic or paper cartridge case for small arms; also, any case used to contain the explosives of fireworks. For illustration see CARTRIDGE. **11.** *Physics* One of the orbits in which the electrons of an atom are assumed to function, each orbit representing a different energy level. **12.** A shape or outline that merely simulates a reality; hollow form; external semblance. **13.** The external ear; auricle. **14.** The lyre: originally a stringed tortoise shell. **15.** A reserved or impersonal attitude: to come out of one's *shell.* — *v.t.* **1.** To divest of or remove from a shell; strip from the husk, pod, or shell. **2.** To separate from the cob, as corn. **3.** To bombard with shells, as a fort. **4.** To cover with shells. — *v.i.* **5.** To shed or become freed from the shell or pod. **6.** To fall off, as a shell or scale. — **to shell out** *Informal* To hand over, as money. [OE *sciell* shell] — **shell′er** *n.* — **shell′y** *adj.*

she'll (shēl) She will.

shel·lac (sha·lak′) *n.* **1.** A purified lac in the form of thin plates, extensively used in varnish, sealing wax, insulators, etc. **2.** A varnishlike solution of flake shellac dissolved in methylated spirit, used for coating floors, woodwork, etc. — *v.t.* **·lacked, ·lack·ing 1.** To cover or varnish with shellac. **2.** *Slang* To belabor; beat. **3.** *Slang* To defeat utterly. Also **shell′·lac′, shel·lack′.** [< SHELL + LAC¹, trans. of F *laque en écailles* lac in thin plates]

shel·lack·ing (sha·lak′ing) *n. U.S. Slang* **1.** A beating; assault. **2.** A thorough defeat.

shellac varnish Any of several varnishes containing dissolved shellac and giving a thin, hard, sometimes glossy coat.

shell·back (shel′bak′) *n.* A veteran sailor; an old salt; especially, one who has crossed the equator. [Prob. with reference to the shell of the sea turtle.]

shell·bark (shel′bärk′) *n.* The shagbark or one of its nuts.

shell bean Any of various beans cultivated for their edible mature seeds.

Shel·ley (shel′ē), **Mary Wollstonecraft,** 1797–1851, *née* Godwin, English novelist; wife of Percy Bysshe. — **Percy Bysshe,** 1792–1822, English poet.

shell·fire (shel′fir′) *n.* The firing of artillery shells.

shell·fish (shel′fish′) *n. pl.* **·fish** or **·fish·es** Any aquatic animal having a shell, as a mollusk.

shell game 1. A swindling game in which the victim bets on the location of a pea covered by one of three nutshells; thimblerig. **2.** Any game in which the victim cannot win.

shell·heap (shel′hēp′) *n.* A kitchen midden. Also **shell′·mound′** (-mound′).

shell hole A hole made by an exploding shell; especially, a craterlike depression in the ground. Also **shell crater.**

shell jacket A snugly fitted jacket, short at the back, worn in place of the tuxedo in tropical countries.

shell·proof (shel′prōof′) *adj.* Built to resist the destructive effect of projectiles and bombs.

shell shock *Psychiatry* Combat fatigue. — **shell-shocked** (shel′shokt′) *adj.*

shel·ter (shel′tər) *n.* **1.** That which covers or shields from exposure or danger; a place of safety. **2.** The state of being sheltered or protected. **3.** A cover from the weather. **4.** One who protects; a guardian. — *v.t.* **1.** To provide protection or shelter for; shield, as from danger or inclement weather. — *v.i.* **2.** To take shelter. [? Alter. of ME *sheltrum* < OE *sceld-truma* a body of men armed with shields, phalanx, protection] — **shel′ter·er** *n.* — **shel′ter·less** *adj.* — **Syn.** (verb) house, lodge; shield, protect. — (noun) **1.** cover, asylum. Compare REFUGE, DEFENSE.

shelter tent *Mil.* A tent for two men, divided into two sections, each of which, called a **shelter half,** is carried as part of a soldier's field equipment: also called *pup tent.*

shelt·ie (shel′tē) *n. Scot.* A Shetland pony. Also **shelt′y.**

shelve (shelv) *v.* **shelved, shelv·ing** *v.t.* **1.** To place on a shelf. **2.** To postpone indefinitely; put aside. **3.** To retire. **4.** To provide or fit with shelves. — *v.i.* **5.** To incline gradually; slope. [< SHELF] — **shelv′y** *adj.*

shelves (shelvz) Plural of SHELF.

shelv·ing (shel′ving) *n.* **1.** Shelves collectively. **2.** Material for shelves. **3.** The act of putting away on shelves; also, putting aside; dismissing. **4.** A slight inclining.

Shem (shem) The eldest son of Noah. *Gen.* v 32.

Shem·ite (shem′īt) See SEMITE.

Shen·an·do·ah (shen′an·dō′ə) A river in Virginia and West Virginia, flowing 55 miles. generally NE. to the Potomac. The **Shenandoah Valley,** the part of the Great Appalachian Valley drained by this river, was the scene of several Confederate victories in the Civil War, March–June, 1862, and Union victories in 1864.

Shenandoah National Park A region in the Blue Ridge Mountains of NW Virginia; 302 sq. mi.; established 1935.

she·nan·i·gan (shi·nan′ə·gən) *n. Often pl. Informal* Trickery; foolery; nonsense; also, treacherous action or a treacherous act. [? < Irish *sionnach* fox]

shend (shend) *v.t.* **shent, shend·ing** *Archaic* **1.** To bring to shame; disgrace. **2.** To chide; scold. **3.** To defeat; destroy. [OE *scendan* to put to shame]

Shen·si (shen′sē′) A Province of NW central China; 75,598 sq. mi.; pop. 18,130,000 (est. 1957); capital, Sian.

Shen·stone (shen′stən, -stōn), **William,** 1714–63, English poet.

Shen·yang (shun′yäng′) The capital of Liaoning Province, China, in the central part of the Province; capital of former Manchuria; pop. 2,450,000 (est. 1968): formerly *Fengtien, Mukden.*

she·ol (shē′ōl) *n.* Hell. [< Hebrew *she′ōl* cave < *shā′al* to dig]

She·ol (shē′ōl) In the Old Testament, a place under the earth where the departed spirits were believed to go.

Shep·ard (shep′ərd), **Alan B., Jr.,** born 1923, U.S. naval officer; first U.S. astronaut to make a rocket flight into space and first astronaut to control the space vehicle himself, May 5, 1961.

shep·herd (shep′ərd) *n.* **1.** A keeper or herder of sheep. **2.** A pastor, leader, or guide. — *v.t.* To watch and tend as a shepherd. [OE *sceaphyrde*] — **shep′herd·ess** (-is) *n.fem.*

shepherd dog A sheep dog (def. 1). Also **shepherd's dog.**

Shepherd Kings The Hyksos.

shep·herd's-nee·dle (shep′ərdz·nēd′l) *n.* A plant, venus's-comb.

shep·herd's-purse (shep′ərdz·pûrs′) *n.* A common herbaceous weed (*Capsella bursa-pastoris*) bearing small white flowers and notched triangular parts.

Sher·a·ton (sher′ə·tən) *adj.* Denoting the graceful, straight-lined, classically chaste style of English furniture developed by Thomas Sheraton.

Sher·a·ton (sher′ə·tən), **Thomas,** 1751–1806, English furniture maker and designer.

sher·bet (shûr′bit) *n.* **1.** A flavored water ice. **2.** *Brit.* An Oriental drink, made of sweetened fruit juice diluted with water. [< Turkish *sherbet,* ult. < Arabic *sharbah* drink < *shariba* to drink. Doublet of SYRUP.]

Sher·brooke (shûr′brŏŏk) A city in southern Quebec, Canada; pop. 80,457.

sherd (shûrd) *n.* A fragment of pottery: often in combination: *potsherd:* also called *shard.* [Var. of SHARD.]

Sher·i·dan (sher′ə·dən), **Philip Henry,** 1831–88, Union general in the Civil War. — **Richard Brinsley,** 1751–1816, British dramatist, orator, and statesman born in Ireland.

she·rif (she·rēf′) *n.* **1.** A member of a princely Moslem family descended from Mohammed through his daughter Fatima. **2.** The chief magistrate of Mecca: also **grand sherif. 3.** An Arab chief. Also **she·reef′.** [< Arabic *sharīf* noble]

sher·iff (sher′if) *n.* The chief administrative officer of a county, who executes the mandates of courts, enforces order, etc. [OE *scīr-gerēfa* shire reeve] — **sher′iff·dom** *n.*

Sher·lock (shûr′lok) *n. Slang* A detective. [after Sherlock Holmes]

Sher·lock Holmes (shûr′lok hōmz′) A fictitious English detective, the central character of numerous stories by Arthur Conan Doyle.

Sher·man (shûr′mən), **Forrest Percival,** 1896–1951, U.S. admiral in World War II. — **John,** 1823–1900, U.S. statesman. — **Roger,** 1721–93, American Revolutionary patriot

and statesman; signed the Declaration of Independence. — **William Tecumseh,** 1820–91, Union general in the Civil War; led the march from Atlanta to the sea, 1864.

she·root (shə·rōōt′) See CHEROOT.

Sher·pa (shûr′pə) *n.* One of a Tibetan tribe living on the southern slopes of the Himalayas in Nepal, and famous as mountaineering guides and porters.

Sher·riff (sher′if), **Robert Cedric,** born 1896, English writer.

Sher·ring·ton (sher′ing·tən), **Sir Charles Scott,** 1861–1952, English physiologist.

sher·ry (sher′ē) *n. pl.* **·ries** The fortified wines of Jerez (formerly Xerez), Spain, or a wine made in imitation of these, as in California. [after *Xerez,* Spain]

sherry cobbler A beverage of sherry, lemon, sugar, water, and ice.

's Her·to·gen·bosch (ser′tō·khan·bôs′) The capital of North Brabant Province, Netherlands, in the central part of the Province; pop. 72,684 (1961): French *Bois-le-Duc.*

Sher·wood (shûr′wŏŏd), **Robert Emmet,** 1896–1955, U.S. playwright.

Sherwood Forest A forest, chiefly in Nottinghamshire, England, known as the home of Robin Hood and his men.

she's (shēz) **1.** She is. **2.** She has.

Shet. Shetland (Islands).

Shet·land Islands (shet′lənd) An island group NE of the Orkney Islands, comprising **Shetland** (also *Zetland*), a county of Scotland; 551 sq. mi.; pop. 17,809 (1961); county seat, Lerwick.

Shetland pony A small, hardy, shaggy breed of pony originally bred on the Shetland Islands.

Shetland wool Thin, very loosely twisted yarn from the wool of Shetland sheep; also, the wool.

sheuch (shŭkh) *n. Scot.* A ditch or open drain. Also **sheugh.**

shew (shō) *v.t. & v.i.* **shewed, shewn, shew·ing** *Chiefly Brit. & Archaic* To show. — **shew′er** *n.*

shew·bread (shō′bred′) *n.* Unleavened bread formerly displayed in the Jewish temple: also spelled *showbread.*

she-wolf (shē′wŏŏlf′) *n. pl.* **-wolves** (-wŏŏlvz′) A female wolf.

SHF or **shf** Superhigh frequency. Also **S.H.F., s.h.f.**

Shi·ah (shē′ə) *n.* **1.** One of the two great sects of Islam, consisting of followers of Ali, the cousin and son-in-law of Mohammed, who maintain that Ali was the first Imam and true Successor to the Prophet. Compare SUNNI. **2.** A Shiite. [< Arabic *shi′i* follower, sect]

shib·bo·leth (shib′ə·leth) *n.* **1.** A test word or pet phrase of a party; a watchword: from the Hebrew word *shibboleth,* given by Jephthah (*Judges* xii 4–6) as a test to distinguish his own men from the Ephraimites, who used the pronunciation *sibboleth.* **2.** A custom or use of language regarded as distinctive of a particular social class, profession, etc. [< Hebrew *shibbōleth* ear of grain]

Shi·de·ha·ra (shē·de·hä·rä), **Baron Kijuro,** 1872–1951, Japanese diplomat and statesman.

shied (shīd) Past tense and past participle of SHY.

shield (shēld) *n.* **1.** A broad piece of defensive armor, commonly carried on the left arm; a large buckler. **2.** Something that protects or defends; a defender; shelter. **3.** Any device for covering or protecting something. **4.** *Mil.* A screen of steel attached to a gun to protect the men who are serving it. **5.** *Mining* A framework or screen of wood or iron protecting the workers. **6.** *Heraldry* An escutcheon. **7.** *Zool.* A platelike protective part, as the carapace of a crustacean. **8.** A conventional figure having an oval bottom and a cusp at the top, used in flags, emblems, etc.; also, anything shaped like this, as an escutcheon or a policeman's badge. **9.** *Physics* A mass of material, as of cement or lead, enclosing a nuclear reactor and designed to reduce the amount of radiation escaping into the surrounding area. — *v.t.* **1.** To protect from danger as with a shield; defend; guard. **2.** *Archaic* To avert; forbid. — *v.i.* **3.** To act as a shield or safeguard. [OE *scild*] — **shield′er** *n.* — **shield′-bear′er** (-bâr′ər) *n.* — **shield′-shaped′** (-shāpt′) *adj.*

SHIELD (def. 8)

shield·fern (shēld′fûrn′) *n.* A fern (genus *Dryopteris*), so called from its shield-shaped sporangia.

shield·ing (shēl′ding) *n.* Material used to prevent nuclear reactors, radioactive substances, electron tubes or circuits, electric wires or cables, etc., from spreading or receiving undesired radiation or fields; also, a structure made of such material.

shield of David The mogen David (which see).

shiel·ing (shē′ling) See SHEALING.

shi·er (shī′ər) Comparative of SHY. — *n.* A horse in the habit of shying. Also spelled *shyer.*

shift (shift) *v.t.* **1.** To change or move from one position, place, etc., to another. **2.** To change for another or others of the same class. **3.** To change (gears) from one arrangement to another. **4.** *Ling.* To alter as part of a systematic change. — *v.i.* **5.** To change position, place, etc. **6.** To evade; equivocate. **7.** To shift gears: The car *shifts* automatically. — **to shift for oneself** To do the best one can to provide for one's needs. — *n.* **1.** The act of shifting. **2.** A recourse or contrivance adopted in the absence of direct means; a dodge; artifice; trick; evasion; expedient: We made *shift* to get along. **3.** *Archaic* or *Dial.* An undergarment; chemise. **4.** A straight, loosely hanging woman's garment, as a dress. **5.** *Rare* A change of clothes. **6.** A change of place, direction, or form: a *shift* in the wind. **7.** Transfer, as of a burden. **8.** A change of the position of the hand when playing on the fingerboard of an instrument of the viol class. **9.** A relay of workers; also, the working time of each group. **10.** *Physics* Any of various displacements of spectral lines caused by velocity of the light source, gravitational effect, etc. See DOPPLER EFFECT. **11.** *Geol.* The relative displacement of areas on opposite sides of a rock fault and outside of the zone of dislocation. **12.** *Ling.* **a** A patterned phonetic or phonemic change, as the consonant *shift* described in Grimm's Law. **b** Functional shift (which see). [OE *sciftan* to divide] — **shift'er** *n.*

shift·less (shift'lis) *adj.* **1.** Unable or unwilling to shift for oneself; inefficient or lazy. **2.** Showing lack of energy or resource. — **shift'less·ly** *adv.* — **shift'less·ness** *n.*

shift·y (shif'tē) *adj.* **shift·i·er, shift·i·est 1.** Artful; tricky; fickle. **2.** Full of expedients; alert; capable. — **shift'i·ly** *adv.* — **shift'i·ness** *n.*

Shi·ge·mi·tsu (shē·ge·mē·tsōō), **Mamoru,** 1887–1957, Japanese diplomat.

Shi·ism (shē'iz·əm) *n.* The doctrine held by the Shiah or Persian branch of Moslems, showing traces of the earlier Persian faith. See SHIAH.

Shi·ite (shē'īt) *n.* A Moslem of the Shiah sect: distinguished from *Sunnite:* also *Shiah.* Also **Shi·e'ite, Shi'ite.** — **Shi·it'ic** (-it'ik) *adj.*

shi·kar (shi·kär') *Anglo-Indian v.t.* To hunt. — *n.* Hunting; sport; the chase. [< Urdu < Persian]

shi·ka·ree (shi·kä'rē) *n.* A hunter or sportsman; especially, a native attendant and guide in the chase. Also **shi·kar'ree, shi·ka'ri.** [< Urdu *shikari*]

Shi·ko·ku (shē·kō·kōō) An island of SW Japan, east of Kyushu; 7,248 sq. mi.

shill¹ (shil) *adj. Scot.* Shrill.

shill² (shil) *n. Slang* The assistant of a sidewalk peddler or gambler, who makes a purchase or bet to encourage onlookers to buy or bet; a capper. [Origin unknown]

shil·le·lagh (shi·lā'lə, -lē) *n.* In Ireland, a stout cudgel made of oak or blackthorn. Also **shil·la'la, shil·la'lah, shil·lea'lah, shil·le'lah.** [after *Shillelagh,* a town in Ireland famed for its oaks]

shil·ling (shil'ing) *n.* **1.** A former British monetary unit, since the Norman Conquest equivalent to 12 pence or 1/20 pound; also, a coin of this value. **2.** The monetary unit of Kenya, Tanzania, and Uganda, equivalent to 100 cents, and of Somalia, equivalent to 100 centesimi. **3.** A former monetary unit in different States of the United States. *Abbr.* **s., sh.** — **King's shilling** A British shilling formerly handed to a recruit on his joining the military service, considered binding as a contract: also called *press money:* also **Queen's shilling.** [OE *scilling*]

Shil·long (shi·lông') The capital of Assam State, India; pop. about 54,000.

shil·ly-shal·ly (shil'ē-shal'ē) *v.i.* **·lied, ·ly·ing 1.** To act with indecision; be irresolute; vacillate. **2.** To trifle. — *adj.* Weak; hesitating. — *n.* Weak or foolish vacillation; irresolution. — *adv.* In an irresolute manner. [Dissimilated reduplication of *shall I?*] — **shil'ly-shal'li·er** *n.*

Shi·loh (shī'lō) **1.** An ancient Israelite sanctuary in central Palestine, NW of the Dead Sea. **2.** A national military park in SW Tennessee; scene of a Union victory in the Civil War, 1862; 6 sq. mi.; established 1894.

shil·pit (shil'pit) *adj. Scot.* **1.** Watery and insipid; weak: *shilpit* drink. **2.** Sickly; puny: a *shilpit* girl.

shi·ly (shī'lē) See SHYLY.

shim (shim) *n.* In machinery, stoneworking, and railroading, a piece of metal or other material used to fill out space, as where joints are worn loose, or between something and its support. — *v.t.* **shimmed, shim·ming** To wedge up or fill out by inserting a shim. [Origin unknown]

shim·mer (shim'ər) *v.i.* To shine faintly; give off or emit a tremulous light; glimmer. — **Syn.** See SHINE. — *n.* A tremulous shining or gleaming; glimmer; gleam. [OE *scimerian*] — **shim'mer·y** *adj.*

shim·my (shim'ē) *n. pl.* **·mies** *U.S.* **1.** *Informal* A chemise. **2.** A jazz dance accompanied by shaking movements: also **shimmy shake. 3.** Unusual vibration, as in automobile wheels. — *v.i.* **·mied, ·my·ing 1.** To vibrate or wobble. **2.** To dance the shimmy. [Alter. of CHEMISE]

Shim·o·no·se·ki (shē·mō·nō·sā·kē) A port city on SW Honshu island, Japan, on Shimonoseki Strait, connecting the Sea of Japan with the Inland Sea; pop. 246,939.

shin¹ (shin) *n.* **1.** The front part of the leg below the knee; also, the shinbone. **2.** The lower foreleg: a *shin* of beef. — *v.t. & v.i.* **shinned, shin·ning 1.** To climb (a pole) by gripping with the hands or arms and the shins or legs: usually

with *up.* **2.** To kick (someone) in the shins. [OE *scinu*]

shin² (shēn) *n.* The twenty-first letter in the Hebrew alphabet. See ALPHABET.

Shi·nar (shī'när) An ancient country along the lower Tigris and Euphrates. *Gen.* x 10.

shin·bone (shin'bōn') *n.* The tibia.

shin·dig (shin'dig) *n. U.S. Slang* A dance or noisy party. [< SHINDY, by folk etymology, suggesting *a dig on the shin*]

shin·dy (shin'dē) *n. pl.* **·dies 1.** *Slang* A quarrel; row. **2.** A shindig. [Var. of SHINNY]

shine (shīn) *v.i.* **shone** or (*esp. for def. 5*) **shined, shin·ing 1.** To emit light; beam; glow. **2.** To gleam, as by reflected light. **3.** To excel or be conspicuous in splendor, beauty, or intellectual brilliance; be preeminent. — *v.t.* **4.** To cause to shine. **5.** To brighten by rubbing or polishing. — **to shine up to** *Slang* To try to please. — *n.* **1.** The state or quality of being bright or shining; radiance; luster; sheen. **2.** Fair weather; sunshine. **3.** *U.S. Informal* A liking or fancy. **4.** *U.S. Informal* A smart trick or prank. **5.** A gloss or polish on shoes. — **to take a shine to** *U.S. Informal* To become fond of. [OE *scīnan*] — **Syn.** (verb) **1, 2.** *Shine, glow, glare, twinkle, flash, sparkle, scintillate, glitter, glisten, glister, coruscate, gleam, glint, glimmer,* and *shimmer* mean to give out light. A body may *shine* with its own, or with some reflected bright and steady light. *Glow* usually implies a reddish light caused by heat, and hence self-luminosity. *Glare* suggests a dazzling brightness. To *twinkle* is to give out light intermittently, as distant stars appear to do. *Flash* describes a sudden, brief burst of light; *sparkle* and *scintillate* mean to *flash* continually or repeatedly, like a gem when it is turned. *Glitter, glisten, glister,* and *coruscate* refer to or suggest the bright and variable reflections of polished metal. *Gleam* and *glint* refer to fainter or less brilliant reflections from a metallic surface. *Glimmer* and *shimmer* are used of any faint or flickering light.

shin·er (shī'nər) *n.* **1.** One who or that which shines or causes to shine. **2.** A bright or gold coin. **3.** One of various silvery cyprinoid fresh-water fishes (genus *Notropis*) related to the minnows and chubs, common in North America. **4.** A silverfish, an insect. **5.** *Slang* A black eye from a blow.

shin·gle¹ (shing'gəl) *n.* **1.** A thin, tapering, oblong piece of wood or other material, laid in rows to cover roofs, with each higher row overlapping the next lower. **2.** A small sign board, as a wooden or brass plate, bearing the name of a doctor, lawyer, etc., and placed outside his office. **3.** A short haircut. — *v.t.* **·gled, ·gling 1.** To cover (a roof, building, etc.) with or as with shingles. **2.** To cut (the hair) short all over the head. [ME *schingle* < L *scindula,* var. of *scandula* shingle] — **shin'gler** *n.*

shin·gle² (shing'gəl) *n.* **1.** Rounded, waterworn detritus, coarser than gravel, found on the seashore. **2.** A place strewn with shingle, as a beach. [Cf. Norw. *singl* coarse gravel] — **shin'gly** *adj.*

shin·gle³ (shing'gəl) *v.t.* **·gled, ·gling** *Metall.* To drive out impurities from (puddled iron) by heavy blows or pressure. [Origin unknown]

shin·gles (shing'gəlz) *n.pl.* (*construed as sing.* or *pl.*) *Pathol.* An acute inflammatory virus disease characterized by skin vesicles along the course of the affected nerve ganglia and accompanied by pain: also called *herpes zoster.* [Alter. of Med.L *cingulus* < L *cingulum* girdle < *cingere* to gird]

shin·ing (shī'ning) *adj.* **1.** Emitting or reflecting a continuous light; gleaming; luminous. **2.** Of unusual brilliance or excellence; conspicuous. — **shin'ing·ly** *adv.*

shin·leaf (shin'lēf') *n.* **1.** A low perennial herb (*Pyrola elliptica*), with rounded evergreen leaves and white flowers, common in the woods of the northern United States: sometimes called *wintergreen.* **2.** *U.S.* Wintergreen (def. 2). [From the use of its leaves for shinplasters]

shin·ny¹ (shin'ē) *n.* **1.** A game resembling hockey; also, one of the sticks or clubs used by the players. **2.** *Canadian* Pond hockey. Also **shin'ney.** [< *shin ye,* a cry used in the game]

shin·ny² (shin'ē) *v.i.* **·nied, ·ny·ing** *U.S. Informal* To climb by holding on alternately with the arms and legs while moving up the free limbs: usually with *up.*

shin·plas·ter (shin'plas'tər, -pläs'-) *n.* **1.** *U.S.* Fractional currency issued by other than the constituted authorities. **2.** Any scrip or paper money issued by private enterprises. **3.** A plaster for a sore shin.

shin·ti·yan (shin'tē-yan) *n.pl.* Wide loose trousers worn by Moslem women. [< Arabic < Turkish *chintiyan*]

Shin·to (shin'tō) *n.* A religion of Japan, consisting chiefly in ancestor worship, nature worship, and the worship of many ethnic divinities, from the chief of whom the Emperor was thought to be descended. Also **Shin'to·ism.** [< Japanese, way of the gods < Chinese *shin* god + *tao* way or law] — **Shin'to·ist** *n.*

shin·y (shī'nē) *adj.* **shin·i·er, shin·i·est 1.** Glistening; glossy; polished. **2.** Bright; clear.

ship (ship) *n.* **1.** Any vessel suitable for deep-water navigation; also, its personnel. **2.** A large seagoing sailing vessel with at least three masts, carrying square-rigged sails on all three. **3.** An airship or airplane. — **when one's ship**

comes in (or **home**) When one's fortune has been made or hopes realized. — *v.* **shipped, ship·ping** *v.t.* **1.** To transport by ship or other mode of conveyance. **2.** To send by any established mode of transportation, as by rail. **3.** To hire and receive for service on board a vessel, as sailors. **4.** *Naut.* To receive over the side, as in rough weather: to *ship* a wave. **5.** *Informal* To get rid of. **6.** To set or fit in a prepared place on a boat or vessel, as a mast, or a rudder; also, to draw (oars) inside a boat from rowlocks. — *v.i.* **7.** To go on board ship; embark. **8.** To undergo shipment: Raspberries do not *ship* well. **9.** To enlist as a seaman: usually with *out*. [OE *scip*]

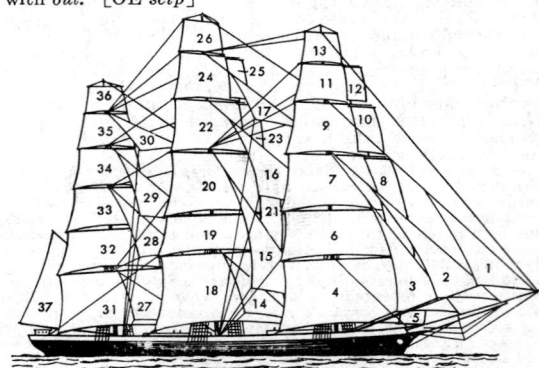

FULL-RIGGED SHIP

1. Flying jib. 2. Jib. 3. Foretopmast staysail. 4. Foresail. 5. Lower studdingsail. 6. Lower foretopsail. 7. Upper foretopsail. 8. Foretopmast staysail. 9. Foretopgallant sail. 10. Foretopgallant studdingsail. 11. Fore royal. 12. Fore royal studdingsail. 13. Fore skysail. 14. Main staysail. 15. Maintopmast staysail. 16. Maintopgallant staysail. 17. Main royal staysail. 18. Mainsail. 19. Lower maintopsail. 20. Upper maintopsail. 21. Maintopmast studdingsail. 22. Maintopgallant. 23. Maintopgallant studdingsail. 24. Main royal. 25. Main royal studdingsail. 26. Main skysail. 27. Mizzen staysail. 28. Mizzen topmast staysail. 29. Mizzen topgallant staysail. 30. Mizzen royal staysail. 31. Mizzen sail. 32. Lower mizzen topsail. 33. Upper mizzen topsail. 34. Mizzen topgallant sail. 35. Mizzen royal. 36. Mizzen skysail. 37. Spanker.
(Only port studdingsails are shown here; normally they are rigged port and starboard. No studdingsails are rigged to the mizzenmast.)

-ship *suffix of nouns* **1.** The state, condition, or quality of: *friendship*. **2.** Office, rank, or dignity of: *kingship*. **3.** The art or skill of: *marksmanship*. [OE *-scipe*]

ship biscuit Hardtack.

ship·board (ship'bôrd', -bōrd') *n.* **1.** The side or deck of a ship. **2.** A vessel: used only in the phrase **on shipboard**.

ship·build·er (ship'bil'dər) *n.* One who designs, superintends, contracts for, or works at the building of vessels. — **ship'build'ing** *n.*

ship canal A waterway deep enough for seagoing vessels.

ship chandler One who deals in supplies for vessels.

Ship·ka Pass (shep'kä) A pass in the central Balkan Mountains, Bulgaria; elevation, 4,166 ft.; scene of a defeat of the Turks by the Bulgarians, 1877.

ship·load (ship'lōd') *n.* The quantity that a ship carries or can carry; a cargo.

ship·man (ship'mən) *n.* *pl.* **·men** (-mən) *Archaic* A sailor on or a master of a ship.

ship·mas·ter (ship'mas'tər, -mäs'-) *n.* The captain or master of a merchant ship.

ship·mate (ship'māt') *n.* A fellow sailor.

ship·ment (ship'mənt) *n.* **1.** The act of shipping. **2.** That which is shipped. Abbr. **shpt.**

ship money A tax levied on English maritime towns and counties, for providing and arming a fleet of warships, declared illegal in 1640.

ship of the line Formerly, a man-of-war large enough to take a position in a line of battle.

ship·own·er (ship'ō'nər) *n.* A person owning a ship, ships, or shares in them.

ship·pa·ble (ship'ə·bəl) *adj.* That can be shipped or transported.

ship·pen (ship'ən) *n.* *Scot.* A cow shed; barn. Also **ship'-pon.** [OE *scipen*]

ship·per (ship'ər) *n.* One who ships goods.

ship·ping (ship'ing) *n.* **1.** Ships collectively; the body of vessels belonging to a country or port; also, tonnage. **2.** The act of shipping. **3.** *Obs.* A voyage.

shipping clerk A clerk who has charge of shipments.

shipping room A room or office in a business establishment where goods are made ready and sent for shipping.

ship-rigged (ship'rigd') *adj.* *Naut.* Rigged as a ship, with three or more masts and square sails.

ship·shape (ship'shāp') *adj.* Well arranged, orderly, and neat, as on a ship. — *adv.* In an orderly manner; neatly.

ship's papers The documents required by international law to be carried by a ship.

ship·way (ship'wā') *n.* **1.** The structure on which a ship is built, launched, or examined. **2.** A ship canal.

ship·worm (ship'wûrm') *n.* One of a family (*Teredinidae*) of marine bivalves, resembling worms, especially *Teredo navalis*, that burrows into the timbers of ships, piers, wharfs, etc.: also called *borer*.

ship·wreck (ship'rek') *n.* **1.** The partial or total destruction of a ship at sea. **2.** Utter or practical destruction; ruin. **3.** Scattered remnants, as of a wrecked ship; wreckage. — *v.t.* **1.** To wreck, as a vessel. **2.** To bring to disaster; ruin.

ship·wright (ship'rit') *n.* One who helps build or repair ships.

ship·yard (ship'yärd') *n.* A place where ships are built or repaired.

Shi·raz (shē·räz') A city in SW Iran; pop. 269,865 (1966).

shire (shīr) *n.* A territorial division of Great Britain; a county. [OE *scīr*]

Shi·re (shē'rā) A river of southern Nyasaland and central Mozambique, flowing about 250 miles south from Lake Nyasa to the Zambezi. Also **Shi·ré.**

shire horse One of a breed of large draft horses originating in the shires or midland counties of England.

shire·town (shīr'toun') *n.* *Canadian* In Nova Scotia, a county seat.

shire town A county town (which see).

shirk (shûrk) *v.t.* **1.** To avoid the doing of; evade doing (something that should be done). **2.** *Obs.* To obtain by trickery. — *v.i.* **3.** To avoid work or evade obligation. — *n.* One who shirks: also **shirk'er.** [? < G *schürke* rascal. Akin to SHARK².]

Shir·ley (shûr'lē), **James,** 1596–1666, English dramatist.

shirr (shûr) *v.t.* **1.** To draw (material) into three or more parallel rows of gathers. **2.** To bake with crumbs in a buttered dish, as eggs. — *n.* **1.** A drawing of material into three or more parallel rows of gathers. **2.** A rubber thread woven into a fabric to make it elastic. [Origin unknown]

shirt (shûrt) *n.* **1.** A garment for the upper part of the body, usually having collar and cuffs and a front closing. **2.** A closely fitting undergarment for the upper part of the body. **3.** A shirtwaist. — **to keep one's shirt on** *Slang* To remain calm; keep one's temper. — **to lose one's shirt** *Slang* To lose everything. [OE *scyrte* shirt, short garment. Akin to SKIRT.] — **shirt'less** *adj.*

shirt·ing (shûr'ting) *n.* Closely woven material of cotton, linen, silk, etc., used for making shirts, blouses, dresses, etc.

shirt·waist (shûrt'wāst') *n.* **1.** A woman's tailored, sleeved blouse or shirt, usually worn tucked in under a skirt or slacks. **2.** A woman's tailored dress having a bodice like a shirtwaist: also **shirtwaist dress.**

shish ke·bab (shish'kə·bob') Meat roasted or broiled in small pieces on skewers and served with condiments: also called *cabob, kabob*. [< Turkish *shish* skewer + *kebap* roast meat]

shist (shist) See SCHIST.

shit·tim wood (shit'im) *n.* In the Bible, a yellowish brown wood of the **shit·tah** (shit'ə) tree, a species of acacia, used in making the ark of the covenant and some furniture of the Jewish tabernacle. [< Hebrew *shittīm*, pl. of *shittāh*]

shiv (shiv) *n.* *Slang* A knife or razor, especially a switchblade knife. [Origin uncertain]

shiv·a (shiv'ə) *n.* In Judaism, a seven-day period of mourning for a close relative. — **to sit shiva** To observe a seven-day period of mourning. [< Hebrew *shib'āh* seven]

Shi·va (shē'və) Siva, a Hindu god.

shiv·a·ree (shiv'ə·rē') *n.* *U.S.* A charivari. [Alter. of CHARIVARI]

shive¹ (shīv) *n.* *Brit.* **1.** *Dial.* A short flat cork or bung. **2.** A slice cut off, as of bread. [Cf. ON *skifa* slice]

shive² (shīv) *n.* **1.** A thin fragment; sliver. **2.** A woody fragment separated from flax. [Cf. Flemish *schif*.]

shiv·er¹ (shiv'ər) *v.i.* **1.** To tremble, as with cold or fear; shake; vibrate; quiver. — *v.t.* **2.** *Naut.* To cause to flutter in the wind, as a sail. — *n.* The act of shivering; a tremble. [ME *chivere*; origin uncertain]

shiv·er² (shiv'ər) *v.t. & v.i.* To break suddenly into fragments; shatter. — **Syn.** See BREAK. — *n.* A splinter; sliver. [ME *schivere*. Cf. MDu. *scheveren*.]

shiv·er·y¹ (shiv'ər·ē) *adj.* **1.** Resembling a shiver or shivering. **2.** Inclined to shiver. **3.** Causing shivering.

shiv·er·y² (shiv'ər·ē) *adj.* Easily shivered; brittle.

Shi·zu·o·ka (shē·zoō·ō·kä) A city on central Honshu island, Japan; pop. 328,820 (1960).

shoal¹ (shōl) *n.* **1.** A shallow place in any body of water. **2.** A sandbank or bar, especially one seen at low water. Compare REEF¹. — **Syn.** See BANK¹. — *v.i.* **1.** To become shallow. — *v.t.* **2.** To make shallow. **3.** To sail into a lesser depth of (water): said of a ship. — *adj.* Of little depth; shallow. Also, *Scot.*, **shaul.** [OE *sceald* shallow]

shoal² (shōl) *n.* **1.** An assemblage or multitude; throng. **2.** A school of fish. — *v.i.* **1.** To throng in shoals or multitudes. **2.** To school: said of fish. [OE *scolu* troop, multitude. Akin to SCHOOL².]

shoal·y (shō′lē) *adj.* **shoal·i·er, shoal·i·est** Abounding in shoals. — **shoal′i·ness** *n.*

shoat (shōt) *n.* A young hog that has been weaned: also spelled *shote*. [Cf. West Flemish *schote* young pig]

shock¹ (shok) *n.* **1.** A violent collision or concussion; impact; blow. **2.** A sudden and violent sensation, as if causing one to shake or tremble; a stroke: a *shock* of paralysis. **3.** A sudden and severe agitation of the mind or emotions, as in horror or great sorrow. **4.** *Pathol.* Prostration of bodily functions, as from sudden injury. **5.** The physical reactions produced by the passage of a strong electric current through the body, as involuntary muscular contractions. — *v.t.* **1.** To shake by sudden collision; jar. **2.** To disturb the emotions or mind of; horrify; disgust. **3.** To give an electric shock to. — *v.i.* **4.** *Archaic* To come into violent contact; collide. [< F *choc* < *choquer* < Gmc. Cf. MDu. *schokken* to collide.]

shock² (shok) *n.* A number of sheaves of grain, stalks of maize, or the like, stacked for drying upright in a field. — *v.t. & v.i.* To gather (grain) into a shock or shocks. [ME *schokke* < Gmc. Cf. MLG *schok*.] — **shock′er** *n.*

shock³ (shok) *adj.* Shaggy; bushy. — *n.* **1.** A coarse, tangled mass, as of hair. **2.** A dog with a woolly coat. [Back formation < *shock dog* a shaggy or woolly dog]

shock absorber *Mech.* A device designed to absorb the energy of sudden impacts or of abrupt changes in velocity, as the springs of an automobile, or an airplane landing gear.

shock action *Mil.* The effect of a sudden, violent attack by mobile and massed military units.

shock·er (shok′ər) *n.* **1.** One who or that which shocks or startles. **2.** A sensational novel, motion picture, etc.

shock·head·ed (shok′hed′id) *adj.* Having thick, bushy hair. Also **shock′head.**

shock·ing (shok′ing) *adj.* **1.** Causing a mental or emotional shock, as with horror or disgust. **2.** *Informal* Terrible; awful. — **shock′ing·ly** *adv.* — **shock′ing·ness** *n.*

shock therapy *Psychiatry* The treatment of certain psychotic disorders by the subcutaneous injection of drugs, as insulin, Metrazol, etc., or by electrical shocks, both methods inducing coma, with or without convulsions.

shock troops *Mil.* Seasoned men selected to lead an attack.

shock wave *Physics* A compression wave following a sudden and violent disturbance of the transmitting medium, through which it is propagated with a velocity equal to or greater than that of sound.

shod (shod) Past tense and alternative past participle of SHOE.

shod·dy (shod′ē) *n.* *pl.* **·dies 1.** Wool obtained by shredding discarded woolens or worsteds. **2.** Fiber or cloth manufactured of reclaimed wool or any inferior material. **3.** Any inferior goods made to resemble those of better quality. **4.** Refuse; waste. — *adj.* **shod·di·er, shod·di·est 1.** Made of or containing shoddy. **2.** Sham; inferior. [Origin uncertain] — **shod′di·ly** *adv.* — **shod′di·ness** *n.*

shoe (shōo) *n.* *pl.* **shoes** (*Obs.* **shoon**) **1.** An outer covering, usually of leather, for the human foot, sometimes limited to those coverings that do not reach above the ankle, as distinguished from boots. **2.** Something resembling a shoe in position or use. **3.** A rim or plate of iron to protect the hoof of an animal from wear or injury. **4.** A strip of iron, steel, etc., fitted under a sleigh or sledge runner to receive friction. **5.** A drag of iron or wood placed under the wheel of a vehicle to retard its motion. **6.** The part of the brake that presses upon a wheel or drum and causes the friction necessary for retarding motion. **7.** An iron socket or ferrule for protecting the point of a spike, pole, or staff. **8.** The tread or outer covering of a pneumatic tire, as for an automobile. **9.** The part of a bridge on which the superstructure rests. **10.** The sliding contact plate on an electric car or locomotive by which it obtains current from the third rail. — *v.t.* **shod, shod** or **shod·den, shoe·ing 1.** To furnish with shoes or the like. **2.** To furnish with a guard of metal, wood, etc., for protection, as against wear. [OE *scōh*]

SHOE
a Tongue. *b* Top. *c* Lace. *d* Eyelet. *e* Vamp. *f* Toe cap. *g* Outsole. *h* Slipsole. *i* Insole. *j* Shank. *k* Heel. *l* Counter. *m* Backstay. *n* Pull strap.

shoe·bill (shōo′bil′) *n.* A large, storklike bird (*Balaeniceps rex*) of central Africa, having a vaulted and hooked bill.

shoe·black (shōo′blak′) *n.* One who cleans or polishes shoes as an occupation.

shoe·horn (shōo′hôrn′) *n.* A smooth curved implement of horn, metal, etc., used to help put on a shoe.

shoe·lace (shōo′lās′) *n.* A lace or cord for fastening shoes.

shoe·mak·er (shōo′mā′kər) *n.* One who makes or repairs shoes, boots, etc. — **shoe′mak′ing** *n.*

sho·er (shōo′ər) *n.* One who supplies or fits shoes; especially, a blacksmith.

shoe·shine (shōo′shīn′) *n.* **1.** The waxing and polishing of a pair of shoes. **2.** The polished look of shined shoes.

shoe·string (shōo′string′) *n.* A shoelace (which see). — **on a shoestring** With a small sum of money with which to begin a business, etc.

shoe·tree (shōo′trē′) *n.* A form for inserting in a shoe to preserve its shape or to stretch it: also called *boot tree.*

sho·far (shō′fär) *n.* A ram's horn used in Jewish ritual, sounded on solemn occasions and in war. It is still blown on Rosh Hashana and on Yom Kippur: also spelled *shophar*. [< Hebrew *shōphār*]

sho·gun (shō′gun, -gōon) *n.* **1.** The hereditary commander in chief of the Japanese army until 1868: known to foreigners as the *tycoon*. **2.** Any of the hereditary military dictators who ruled Japan until the 19th century and under whom the emperor was merely a figurehead. [< Japanese < Chinese *chiang-chün* leader of an army] — **sho′gun·ate** (-it, -āt) *n.*

sho·ji (shō′jē) *n.* A translucent paper screen forming a partition, door, etc., in a Japanese house. Also **shoji screen.** [< Japanese]

Sho·la·pur (shō′lə·pŏor) A city in central Maharashtra, India; pop. 337,544 (1961).

Sho·lo·khov (shō′lə·khôf), **Mikhail Aleksandrovich,** born 1905, Soviet novelist.

shone (shōn, shon) Past tense and past participle of SHINE.

shoo (shōo) *interj.* Begone! be off! away!: used in driving away fowls, etc. — *v.t.* **1.** To drive away, as by crying "shoo." — *v.i.* **2.** To cry "shoo." [Imit.]

shoo·fly (shōo′flī) *n.* *pl.* **·flies** *U.S.* **1.** A shuffling dance; also, the music for it. **2.** An enclosed child's rocker with sides representing horses, swans, etc. **3.** A kind of pie with a syrupy filling made with molasses and brown sugar: also **shoofly pie. 4.** In railroading, a temporary track circumventing an obstructed regular line.

shoo-in (shōo′in′) *U.S. Informal n.* **1.** A race or contest easily won. **2.** A contestant, candidate, etc., who is certain to win. — *adj.* Certain or easy to win.

shook¹ (shŏok) Past tense of SHAKE.

shook² (shŏok) *n.* **1.** A collection of barrel staves, shaped, chamfered, and arranged for assembling. **2.** A set of boards arranged for nailing together into a packing box. **3.** A shock of sheaves. [? Var. of SHOCK²]

shool (shōol) *n. Scot.* A shovel.

shoon (shōon) Obsolete plural of SHOE.

shoot (shōot) *v.* **shot, shoot·ing** *v.t.* **1.** To hit, wound, or kill with a missile discharged from a weapon. **2.** To discharge (a missile) from a bow, rifle, etc. **3.** To discharge (a weapon): often with *off*: to *shoot* a cannon. **4.** To take the altitude of with a sextant, etc.: to *shoot* the sun. **5.** To send forth as if from a weapon, as questions, glances, etc. **6.** To pass over or through swiftly: to *shoot* rapids. **7.** To go over (an area) in hunting game. **8.** To emit, as rays of light. **9.** To photograph; film. **10.** To cause to stick out or protrude; extend. **11.** To put forth in growth; send forth (buds, leaves, etc.). **12.** To push into or out of the fastening, as the bolt of a door. **13.** To propel, discharge, or dump, as down a chute or from a container. **14.** To variegate, as with streaks of color: usually in the past participle: His paintings are *shot* with pink and brown. **15.** In games: **a** To score (a goal, point, etc.) by kicking or otherwise forcing the ball, etc., to the objective. **b** To play (golf, craps, pool, etc.). **c** To propel (a marble) from between the thumb and forefinger; play (marbles). **d** To cast (the dice). — *v.i.* **16.** To discharge a missile from a bow, firearm, etc. **17.** To go off; discharge. **18.** To move swiftly; dart. **19.** To hunt game. **20.** To jut out; extend or project. **21.** To put forth buds, leaves, etc.; germinate; sprout. **22.** To take a photograph. **23.** To start the cameras, as in motion pictures. **24.** In games, to make a play by propelling the ball, puck, etc., in a certain manner. — **to shoot at** (or **for**) *Informal* To strive for; attempt to attain or obtain. — **to shoot down** To bring to earth by shooting. — **to shoot off one's mouth** *Slang* To talk too freely or too much. — **to shoot up 1.** To move or grow upward quickly. **2.** To strike with several or many shots. **3.** *SW U.S.* To ride through (a town, etc.) shooting recklessly in all directions. — *n.* **1.** A young branch or sucker of a plant; offshoot. **2.** A narrow passage in a stream; a rapid. **3.** An inclined passage down which anything may be shot; a chute. **4.** The act of shooting; a shot. **5.** A shooting match, hunting party, etc. **6.** *U.S. Informal* A rocket or missile launching. **7.** The thrust of an arch. **8.** Any new growth, as a new antler. **9.** Shooting distance. **10.** A thrusting movement. **11.** In rowing, the interval between strokes. [OE *scēotan*] — **shoot′er** *n.*

shoot·ing (shōo′ting) *n.* The act of one who or that which shoots.

shooting box A small house in a game district, furnishing accommodation for sportsmen. Also **shooting lodge.**

shooting gallery A place, usually enclosed, where one can shoot at targets.

shooting iron *U.S. Slang* A firearm.

shooting star 1. A meteor. 2. Any of certain small perennial herbs (genus *Dodecatheon*); especially *D. meadia*, having oblong leaves and clusters of white, rose, or crimson flowers.

shop (shop) *n.* 1. A place for the sale of goods at retail. Also **shoppe.** 2. A place for making or repairing any article, or the carrying on of any artisan craft: a blacksmith's *shop*. 3. One's own craft or business as a subject of conversation: to talk *shop*. — *v.i.* **shopped, shop·ping** To visit shops or stores to purchase or look at goods. [OE *sceoppa* booth]
— **Syn.** (noun) 1. *Shop, store, emporium,* and *bazaar* denote a place for the retail sale of goods. In the United States, *shop* is generally restricted to a place dealing in a limited class of goods: a millinery *shop*, a pastry *shop*. *Store* is the all-inclusive U.S. term; where distinguished from *shop*, it implies a large and miscellaneous stock: a grocery *store*, a department *store*. *Emporium* was formerly used as a pretentious substitute for *store*, but is now chiefly humorous. *Bazaar* is applied chiefly to the sale at one time of collected miscellaneous articles: a charity *bazaar*.

shop·boy (shop'boi') *n.* A boy who works in a shop.

shop·girl (shop'gûrl') *n.* A girl who works in a shop.

sho·phar (shō'fär) See SHOFAR.

shop·keep·er (shop'kē'pər) *n.* One who runs a shop or store; a tradesman.

shop·lift·er (shop'lif'tər) *n.* One who steals goods exposed for sale in a shop. — **shop'lift'ing** *n.*

shop·man (shop'mən) *n. pl.* **·men** 1. One who sells goods in a shop; salesman. 2. A shopkeeper.

shop·per (shop'ər) *n.* 1. One who shops. 2. An employee of a store who compares the merchandise of competitors as to quality, price, etc. — **shop'ping** *n.*

shopping center A group of retail shops or stores comprising an architectural unit, usually serving a suburban area.

shop steward A union worker chosen by fellow workers to represent them to management in seeking redress of grievances, etc. Also **shop chairman.**

shop·talk (shop'tôk') *n.* Conversation limited to one's job or profession.

shop·walk·er (shop'wô'kər) *n. Brit.* A floorwalker (which see).

shop·worn (shop'wôrn', -wōrn') *adj.* 1. Soiled or otherwise deteriorated from having been handled or on display in a shop. 2. Worn out, as from overuse; not fresh or original; stale: a *shopworn* melody.

sho·ran (shôr'an, shō'ran) *n.* A high-precision electronic navigation system that transmits pulses, usually from an aircraft or ship, to ground stations whose positions are determined by the time between emission and return of the pulses. [< SHO(RT) RA(NGE) N(AVIGATION)]

shore¹ (shôr, shōr) *n.* 1. The coast or land adjacent to an ocean, sea, lake, or large river. ◆ Collateral adjective: *littoral*. 2. *Law* Land: to be on *shore*. 3. *Law* The ground between the ordinary high-water mark and low-water mark. — **in shore** Near or toward the shore. — *v.t.* **shored, shor·ing** 1. To set on shore. 2. To surround as with a shore. [ME *schore*. Cf. MLG *schore*.]
— **Syn.** (noun) 1. *Shore, strand, coast, beach,* and *bank* denote the land adjacent to a body of water. *Shore* is the general term; we speak of the *shore* of the sea, of a lake, or of a river. *Strand* is a poetical word for *shore*, or specifically for the *shore* of the sea between high-water and low-water marks. *Coast* is the ocean *shore*, especially along a great extent of land: the *coast* of Florida. *Beach* and *bank* denote particular formations of land at the *shore*. A *beach* is a low, gently sloping expanse of sand or gravel; a *bank* is a more or less steep slope: the *banks* of the Red River.

shore² (shôr, shōr) *v.t.* **shored, shor·ing** To prop, as a wall, by a vertical or sloping timber: usually with *up*. — *n.* A beam set endwise as a prop or temporary support against the side of a building, a ship in drydock, etc. [Cf. Du. *schoor* prop, ON *skortha* stay]

shore³ (shôr, shōr) Archaic past tense of SHEAR.

Shore (shôr, shōr), **Jane**, 1445?–1527, mistress of Edward IV of England.

shore bird Any of various birds (suborder *Charadrii*) that frequent beaches and also the shores of inland waters, including the snipe, sandpiper, and plover.

shore·less (shôr'lis, shōr'-) *adj.* 1. Having no shore. 2. Boundless.

shore·line (shôr'līn', shōr'-) *n.* The line or contour of a shore.

shore patrol A detail of the U.S. Navy, Coast Guard, or Marine Corps assigned to police duties ashore. Abbr. *SP*

shore·ward (shôr'wərd, shōr'-) *adj. & adv.* Toward the shore. Also **shore'wards** (-wərdz).

shor·ing (shôr'ing, shō'ring) *n.* 1. The operation of propping, as with shores. 2. Shores, collectively.

shorl (shôrl) See SCHORL.

shorn (shôrn, shōrn) Alternative past participle of SHEAR.

short (shôrt) *adj.* 1. Having little linear extension; not long; of no great distance. 2. Being below the average stature; not tall. 3. Having little extension in time; of lim-

ited duration; brief. 4. Abrupt in manner or spirit; curt; petulant; cross. 5. Not reaching or attaining a requirement, result, or mark; deficient; inadequate: often with *of*. 6. Having a scant or insufficient amount: followed by *on*: *short* on supplies. 7. Having little scope or breadth; narrow: a *short* view. 8. In commerce: a Not having in possession when selling, but having to procure in time to deliver as contracted. b Of or pertaining to stocks or commodities not in possession of the seller: *short* sales. 9. Not comprehensive or retentive; at fault; in error: a *short* memory. 10. Breaking easily; friable; crisp. 11. *Phonet.* a Relatively brief in articulation: said of vowels. b Denoting the vowel sounds of *Dan, den, din, don, duck,* as contrasted with those of *Dane, dean, dine, dome, dune*. 12. In classical prosody, requiring a relatively short time to pronounce: said of syllables. 13. In English prosody, unaccented. 14. Less than: with *of*. 15. Concise; compressed. — *n.* 1. Anything that is short. 2. A deficiency; as in a payment. 3. A short syllable or vowel. 4. A short contract or sale; one who has sold short; a bear. 5. *pl.* Bran mixed with coarse meal or flour. 6. *pl.* Trousers with legs extending part way to the knees. 7. *pl.* A man's undergarment covering the loins and often a portion of the legs. 8. In baseball slang, shortstop. 9. *pl.* Clippings, scraps, etc., left over in the manufacture of different products and used to make an inferior quality of the product. 10. *Electr.* A short circuit. 11. A short subject (which see). — **for short** For brevity: Edward was called Ed *for short*. — **in short** In a word; briefly. — *adv.* 1. Abruptly: to stop *short*. 2. Curtly; crossly. 3. So as not to reach or extend to a certain point, condition, etc.: to fall *short*. 4. Without having in actual possession that which is sold: to sell *short*. — *v.t. & v.i.* To short-circuit. [OE *sort*] — **short'ness** *n.*

Short (shôrt), **Walter Campbell,** 1880–1949, U.S. general.

short account 1. The account of a person who sells short on the stock market. 2. The total open short sales in the market or of a specific commodity.

short·age (shôr'tij) *n.* 1. An insufficient supply or amount; lack: a national shortage of pennies. 2. The amount by which anything is short; deficiency.

short·bread (shôrt'bred') *n.* A rich, dry cake or cooky made with shortening.

short·cake (shôrt'kāk') *n.* 1. A cake made short and crisp with butter or other shortening. 2. Cake or biscuit served with fruit: strawberry *shortcake*.

short·change (shôrt'chānj') *v.t.* **·changed, ·chang·ing** *Informal* To give less change than is due; also, to cheat or swindle. — **short'chang'er** *n.*

short-cir·cuit (shôrt'sûr'kit) *v.t. & v.i.* To make a short circuit (in).

short circuit *Electr.* A path of relatively low resistance between two points of differing voltage in an electric circuit, effectively bypassing the load and often allowing excessive current flow.

short·com·ing (shôrt'kum'ing) *n.* A failure or deficiency in character, action, etc.

short commons A scanty supply of food.

short covering The buying of stocks or securities to close out a short sale.

short-cut (shôrt'kut') *v.t. & v.i.* **-cut, -cut·ting** To take a short cut (in).

short cut 1. A byway or path between two places that is shorter than the regular way. 2. Any means or method that saves distance or time.

short·en (shôr'tən) *v.t.* 1. To make short or shorter; curtail. 2. To reduce; diminish; lessen. 3. To furl or reef (a sail) so that less canvas is exposed to the wind. 4. To make brittle or crisp, as pastry, by adding shortening. — *v.i.* 5. To become short or shorter. — **short'en·er** *n.*

short·en·ing (shôr'tən·ing) *n.* 1. A fat, such as lard or butter, used to make pastry crisp. 2. An abbreviation. 3. The act of one who shortens.

short·hand (shôrt'hand') *n.* Any system of rapid writing, usually employing symbols other than letters, words, etc.: distinguished from *longhand*. — *adj.* 1. Written in shorthand. 2. Using shorthand.

short·hand·ed (shôrt'han'did) *adj.* Not having a sufficient or the usual number of assistants, workmen, etc.

short·horn (shôrt'hôrn') *n.* One of a breed of cattle with short horns, originally from northern England.

shor·ti·a (shôr'tē·ə) *n.* Any of a genus (*Shortia*) of perennial evergreen herbs having bell-shaped, nodding, white flowers, especially *S. galacifolia* of North and South Carolina. [after C. W. *Short*, 1794–1863, U.S. botanist]

short·ish (shôr'tish) *adj.* Rather short.

short-lived (shôrt'līvd', -livd') *adj.* Living or lasting but a short time.

short·ly (shôrt'lē) *adv.* 1. In a short time; quickly; soon. 2. In few words; briefly. 3. Curtly; abruptly.

short order Food requiring little time to prepare. — **in short order** Without any delay; quickly; abruptly. — **short·or·der** (shôrt'ôr'dər) *adj.*

short sale A sale for future delivery of goods or stocks not in possession at time of sale.

short shrift 1. A short time in which to confess before dying. 2. Little or no mercy or delay, as in dealing with a person. — **to make short shrift of** To dispose of quickly.
short·sight·ed (shôrt/sī/tid) *adj.* 1. Unable to see clearly at a distance; myopic; nearsighted. 2. Lacking foresight. 3. Resulting from or characterized by lack of foresight. — **short/sight/ed·ly** *adv.* — **short/sight/ed·ness** *n.*
short-spo·ken (shôrt/spō/kən) *adj.* Characterized by shortness or curtness of speech or manner; abrupt; gruff.
short·stop (shôrt/stop/) *n.* In baseball, an infielder stationed between second and third bases; also, the position he occupies.
short story A narrative prose story presenting a central theme, impression, or characterization and shorter than a novel or novelette, usually under 10,000 words.
short subject A motion picture of relatively short duration, often displayed between showings of the feature attraction on a program: also called *short.*
short-tem·pered (shôrt/tem/pərd) *adj.* Easily angered.
short-term (shôrt/tûrm/) *adj.* In finance, due or payable within a short time, usually one year: said of loans, etc.
short ton See under TON[1].
short waves Electromagnetic waves that are 60 meters or less in length. — **short-wave** (shôrt/wāv/) *adj.*
short-wind·ed (shôrt/win/did) *adj.* Affected with difficulty of breathing; becoming easily out of breath.
Sho·sho·ne (shō-shō/nē) *n.* 1. One of a large tribe of North American Indians of northern Shoshonean stock of the Uto-Aztecan family, formerly occupying parts of Wyoming, Idaho, Nevada, and Utah. 2. The Shoshonean language of this tribe. Also **Sho·sho/ni.**
Sho·sho·ne·an (shō-shō/nē-ən, shō/shə-nē/ən) *n.* The largest branch of the Uto-Aztecan family of North American Indians, including the Comanche, Paiute, Ute, and Shoshone plateau tribes, and the Hopi Indians. — *adj.* Of or pertaining to this linguistic branch. Also **Sho·sho/ni·an.**
Shoshone Cavern A national monument in NW Wyoming, on the Shoshone River; 212.4 acres; established 1909.
Shoshone Dam The former name for BUFFALO BILL DAM.
Shoshone Falls A cascade in the Snake River, southern Idaho; over 200 ft. high.
Shoshone River A river in NW Wyoming, flowing 100 miles NE to the Bighorn River.
Shos·ta·ko·vich (shos/tə-kô/vich), **Dimitri**, 1906–75, Soviet composer.
shot[1] (shot) *n. pl.* **shots;** *for def. 1* **shot** 1. A solid missile, as a ball of iron, or a bullet or pellet of lead, to be discharged from a firearm; also, such spherules or pellets collectively. For illustration see CARTRIDGE. 2. The act of shooting; any stroke, hit, or blow. 3. One who shoots; a marksman. 4. The distance traversed or that can be traversed by a projectile; reach; range. 5. *U.S. Informal* The firing of a rocket, etc., that is directed toward a specific target: a moon *shot.* 6. A blast, as in mining. 7. A stroke, especially in certain games, as in billiards. 8. A conjecture; guess. 9. An attempted performance or try. 10. A metal sphere that a competitor puts, pushes, or slings, in a distance contest. 11. *Informal* A hypodermic injection of a drug. 12. *Informal* A drink of liquor. 13. A single action or scene recorded on motion-picture or television film or tape; also, a specific angle, distance, or manner in or at which a scene is shot. 14. A picture taken with a camera; a photograph or a snapshot. 15. *Naut.* A unit of chain length: in the United States, 15 fathoms; in Great Britain, 12½ fathoms. 16. *Obs.* Any projectile. — *v.t.* **shot·ted, shot·ting** 1. To load or weight with shot. 2. To clean, as bottles, by partially filling with shot and shaking. [OE *scot*]
shot[2] (shot) Past tense and past participle of SHOOT. — *adj.* 1. Of changeable color, as when warp and weft are of different colors; also, streaked or mixed irregularly with other colors: a sky *shot* with pink. 2. *Slang* More or less intoxicated. 3. *Informal* Completely done for; ruined; also, worn out; completely broken.
shot[3] (shot) *n. Brit. & Canadian* A reckoning or charge, or a share of it, as in a restaurant or bar. [Var. of SCOT]
shote (shōt) See SHOAT.
shot effect *Electronics* The background noise resembling the patter of small shot, developed in an electron tube by the fluctuating emission of electrons from the heated filament. Also **shot noise.**
shot·gun (shot/gun/) *n.* A light, smoothbore gun, either single or double barreled, adapted for the discharge of shot at short range. — *adj.* 1. Having a clear passageway straight through: a *shotgun* house. 2. Coerced with, or as with, a shotgun: a *shotgun* wedding.

SHOTGUNS
a Double-barrel hammerless. *b* Repeating.

shot-put (shot/pŏŏt/) *n.* 1. An athletic contest in which a shot is thrown, or put, for distance. 2. A single put of the shot. — **shot/-put/ter** *n.*
shot·ten (shot/n) *adj.* Having spawned: said of a fish, especially a herring. [Obs. pp. of SHOOT]
shot tower A tall structure from which droplets of molten lead were formerly let fall into water to form shot.
Shot·well (shot/wel/), **James Thomson**, 1874–1965, U.S. historian born in Canada.
should (shŏŏd) Past tense of SHALL, but rarely a true past, rather chiefly used as a modal auxiliary that, while conveying varying shades of present and future time, expresses a wide range of subtly discriminated feelings and attitudes: 1. Obligation or propriety in varying degrees, but milder than *ought:* You *should* write that letter; *Should* we tell him the truth about his condition?; His father thought that he *should* go. 2. Condition: **a** Simple contingency, but involving less probability than *shall* or the present with future sense: If I *should* die before I wake . . .; If I *should* go, he would go too. **b** Assumption: *Should (Assuming that)* the space platform prove practicable, as seems almost certain, a trip to the moon will be easy. 3. Surprise at an unexpected event in the past: When I reached the station, whom *should* I run into but the detective! 4. Expectation: I *should* be at home by noon. ("I said that I *should* be home by noon" implies expectation, whereas "I said that I *would* be home by noon" implies intention.) 5. *U.S. Informal* Irony, in positive statement with negative force: He'll be pitied heavily, but with all his money he *should* (*need not*) worry! — **Syn.** See OUGHT[1]. ◆ In American usage the first person may be followed by either *should* or *would* in such expressions as I *should/would* be glad to see you. *Should* is sometimes felt to convey a slightly greater degree of politeness. [OE *scolde,* pt. of *sculan* to owe]
shoul·der (shōl/dər) *n.* 1. The part of the trunk between the neck and the free portion of the arm or forelimb; also, the joint connecting the arm or forelimb with the body. 2. Anything that supports, bears up, or projects like a shoulder. 3. The forequarter of various animals. 4. An enlargement, projection, or offset, as for keeping something in place, or preventing movement past the projection. 5. *Printing* The top of the shank of a type when extending above or below the face of the letter. 6. Either edge of a road or highway. 7. The angle of a bastion included between a face and the adjacent flank: also **shoulder angle.** — **shoulder to shoulder** 1. Side by side and close together. 2. With united effort; in cooperation. — **straight from the shoulder** *Informal* Candidly; straightforwardly. — **to cry on (one's) shoulder** To seek sympathy and understanding from (one). — **to give the cold shoulder to** 1. To treat with scorn, contempt, or coldness. 2. To ignore, shun, or avoid. — **to put (one's) shoulder to the wheel** To work with great vigor and purpose. — **to rub shoulders with** To mingle with (famous or influential people, etc.). — *v.t.* 1. To assume as something to be borne; sustain; bear. 2. To push with or as with the shoulder or shoulders. 3. To fashion with a shoulder or abutment; make a shoulder on. — *v.i.* 4. To push with the shoulder or shoulders. — **to shoulder arms** To rest a rifle against the shoulder, holding the butt with the hand on the same side, the arm being held bent and close to the side. [OE *sculdor*]
shoulder blade *Anat.* The scapula.
shoulder patch A cloth insignia worn on the upper part of the sleeve of a uniform to indicate one's branch or unit.
shoulder screw A screw having a shoulder, as for limiting the depth to which it may be sunk. For illustration see SCREW.
shoulder strap 1. A strap worn on or over the shoulder to support an article of dress. 2. A strap of cloth marked with insignia of rank, worn by army and navy officers: also **shoulder loop.**
should·na (shŏŏd/nə) *Scot.* Should not.
should·n't (shŏŏd/nt) Should not.
shouldst (shŏŏdst) Archaic second person singular, past tense of SHALL: used with *thou.* Also **should·est** (shŏŏd/ist).
shout (shout) *n.* A sudden and loud outcry, often expressing joy, exultation, anger, etc., or used as a call or command. — *v.t.* 1. To utter with a shout; say or express loudly. — *v.i.* 2. To utter a shout; cry out loudly. [Cf. ON *skūta* a taunt] — **shout/er** *n.*
shove (shuv) *v.t. & v.i.* **shoved, shov·ing** 1. To push, as along a surface: to *shove* a boat with a pole. 2. To press forcibly (against); jostle. — **to shove off** 1. To push along or away, as a boat. 2. *Informal* To depart. — *n.* The act of pushing or shoving. [OE *scūfan*] — **shov/er** *n.*
shov·el (shuv/əl) *n.* 1. A somewhat flattened scoop with a handle, as for digging, lifting earth, rock, snow, etc.; also, any large, usually toothed device for extensive, heavy digging. 2. *Informal* A shovel hat (which see). — *v.* **shov·eled** or **·elled, shov·el·ing** or **·el·ling** *v.t.* 1. To take up and move or gather with a shovel. 2. To toss hastily or in large

quantities as if with a shovel. **3.** To clear with a shovel, as a path. *— v.i.* **4.** To work with a shovel. [OE *scoft*]

shov·el·er (shuv′əl-ər, shuv′lər) *n.* **1.** One who or that which shovels. **2.** A large river duck (genus *Spatula*) with spatulate bill; especially, the **common shoveler** (*S. clypeata*) of the northern hemisphere: also called *spoonbill*: also **shov·el·bill** (shuv′əl-bil′). Also **shov·el·ler.**

shovel hat A hat with broad brim turned up at the sides and projecting in front.

shov·el·head (shuv′əl-hed′) *n.* **1.** A shark (*Sphyrna tiburo*) resembling the hammerhead, about 5 feet long. **2.** The shovelnose (def. 1).

shov·el·nose (shuv′əl-nōz′) *n.* **1.** A sturgeon (*Scaphirhynchus platyrhynchus*), common in the Mississippi valley, having a broad, shovel-shaped snout. **2.** Any of several varieties of shark with a shovellike nose; especially, a cow shark (*Hexanchus griseus*), found on the Pacific coast of the United States.

shov·el·nosed (shuv′əl-nōzd′) *adj.* Having a broad, flattened snout or beak.

show (shō) *v.* **showed, shown** or, sometimes, **showed, show·ing** *v.t.* **1.** To cause or permit to be seen; present to view; exhibit; manifest; display. **2.** To give in a marked or open manner; confer; bestow: to *show* favor. **3.** To cause or allow (something) to be understood or known; explain; reveal; tell. **4.** To cause (someone) to understand or see; explain something to; convince; teach. **5.** *Law* To advance an allegation; plead: to *show* cause. **6.** To make evident by logical process; prove; demonstrate. **7.** To guide; lead; introduce, as into a room or building: with *in* or *up*: to *show* a caller in. **8.** To indicate: The thermometer *shows* the temperature. **9.** To enter in a show or exhibition. *— v.i.* **10.** To become visible or known; be manifested or displayed. **11.** To appear; seem. **12.** To make one's or its appearance; be present. **13.** *Informal* To give a theatrical performance; appear: to *show* in Newark. **14.** In racing, to finish third: distinguished from *place, win.* Also, *Archaic,* **shew. — to show off 1.** To exhibit proudly or ostentatiously. **2.** To make an ostentatious display of oneself, or of one's accomplishments. **— to show up 1.** To expose or be exposed, as faults. **2.** To be evident or prominent. **3.** To attend; arrive; make an appearance. **4.** *Informal* To be better than; outdo. *— n.* **1.** An entertainment or performance: a TV *show;* a Broadway *show.* **2.** Anything shown or manifested: a *show* of stupidity. **3.** An elaborate display: a *show* of wealth. **4.** A pretense or semblance: a *show* of piety. **5.** Any public exhibition, contest, etc.: a dog *show;* an art *show.* **6.** An appearance: a bad *show.* **7.** An indication; promise: a *show* of ore. **8.** *Informal* An opportunity or chance. **9.** The third position among the first three winners of a race. **10.** The act of showing. **— show of hands** A display of raised hands indicating the vote of a group. [OE *scēawian*] **— show′er** *n.*

show bill A poster announcing a play or show.

show biz (biz) *U.S. Slang* Show business.

show·boat (shō′bōt′) *n.* A boat, such as the old sternwheelers on the Mississippi, on which a traveling troupe gives a theatrical performance.

show·bread (shō′bred′) See SHEWBREAD.

show business The entertainment arts, especially the theater, motion pictures, television, etc., collectively considered as an industry or profession.

show·case (shō′kās′) *n.* **1.** A glass case for exhibiting and protecting articles for sale. **2.** Something on display, especially a model specimen used for publicity or propaganda.

show·down (shō′doun′) *n.* **1.** In poker, the play in which the hands are laid on the table face up. **2.** Any action or disclosure that brings an issue to a head.

show·er (shou′ər) *n.* **1.** A fall of rain, hail, or sleet, especially heavy rain of short duration within a local area. **2.** A copious fall, as of tears, sparks, or other small objects. **3.** A shower bath (which see). **4.** An abundance or profusion of something. **5.** A variety of fireworks for simulating a shower of stars. **6.** A party for the bestowal of gifts, as to a bride; also, the gifts. *— v.t.* **1.** To sprinkle or wet with or as with showers. **2.** To discharge in a shower; pour out. **3.** To bestow with liberality. *— v.i.* **4.** To fall as in a shower. **5.** To take a shower bath. [OE *scūr*] **— show′er·y** *adj.*

shower bath A bath in which water is sprayed on the body from an overhead, perforated nozzle; also, the area or room in which this is done.

show·ing (shō′ing) *n.* **1.** A show or display: a *showing* of the latest fashions. **2.** A presentation or statement, as of a subject, case, etc.

show·man (shō′mən) *n. pl.* **·men** (-mən) **1.** One who is characteristically concerned with and adept at getting and holding the attention of others, often by dramatic means. **2.** One who exhibits or owns a show.

show·man·ship (shō′mən-ship) *n.* The ability to present or show something in a very dramatic or favorable manner.

Show Me State Nickname of MISSOURI.

shown (shōn) Past participle of SHOW.

show-off (shō′ôf′, -of′) *n. Informal* **1.** The act of showing off; ostentatious display. **2.** One who shows off.

show·piece (shō′pēs′) *n.* **1.** A prized object considered worthy of special exhibit. **2.** An object on display.

show place A place exhibited for its beauty, historic interest, etc.

show room A room in which things, as merchandise, are displayed for sale or advertising.

show·y (shō′ē) *adj.* **show·i·er, show·i·est** **1.** Making a great or brilliant display. **2.** Given to cheap display; gaudy; ostentatious. **— show′i·ly** *adv.* **— show′i·ness** *n.*

shpt. Shipment.

shrank (shrangk) Past tense of SHRINK.

shrap·nel (shrap′nəl) *n. pl.* **·nel** *Mil.* **1.** A field artillery projectile for use against personnel, containing a quantity of metal balls and a time fuse and base charge that expel the balls in mid-air. **2.** Shell fragments. [after Henry *Shrapnel,* 1761–1842, British artillery officer]

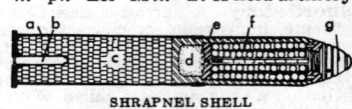

SHRAPNEL SHELL
a Brass casing. *b* Percussion primer. *c* Smokeless powder. *d* Black powder. *e* Steel shell body. *f* Shrapnel balls. *g* Time fuse.

shred (shred) *n.* **1.** A small irregular strip torn or cut off. **2.** A bit; fragment; particle. *— v.t.* **shred·ded** or **shred, shred·ding 1.** To tear or cut into shreds. **2.** *Brit. Dial.* To lop off; trim. [OE *scrēade*] **— shred′der** *n.*

Shreve·port (shrēv′pôrt, -pōrt) A city in NW Louisiana, on the Red River; pop. 182,064.

shrew (shrōō) *n.* **1.** Any of numerous diminutive, chiefly insectivorous mammals (family *Soricidae*) having a long pointed snout and soft fur, as the **long-tailed shrew** (*Sorex longicauda*) of North America. Also **shrew′mouse** (-mous′). ◆ Collateral adjective: *soricine.* **2.** A woman of vexatious, scolding, or nagging disposition. [OE *scrēawa*] **— Syn. 2.** scold, vixen, termagant, virago.

shrewd (shrōōd) *adj.* **1.** Sharp or wise; sagacious. **2.** Artful; sly. **3.** *Obs.* Keen or sharp; biting. **4.** *Obs.* Shrewish; also, vexatious; vicious; dangerous. **— Syn.** See ASTUTE. [ME *shrewed,* pp. of *shrewen* to curse < *shrew* malicious person] **— shrewd′ly** *adv.* **— shrewd′ness** *n.*

shrew·ish (shrōō′ish) *adj.* Like a shrew; ill-tempered; nagging. **— shrew′ish·ly** *adv.* **— shrew′ish·ness** *n.*

Shrews·bur·y (shrōōz′ber·ē, -bər·ē; *Brit.* shrōz′brē) The county seat of Salop, England, in the central part of the county; pop. 83,900 (1976).

shriek (shrēk) *n.* A sharp shrill outcry or scream. *— v.i.* **1.** To utter a shriek. *— v.t.* **2.** To utter with or in a shriek. [ME. Akin to ON *skrækja.*] **— shriek′er** *n.*

shriev·al·ty (shrē′vəl·tē) *n. pl.* **·ties** The office, term, or jurisdiction of a sheriff. **— shriev′al** *adj.*

shrieve (shrēv) *n. Obs.* A sheriff.

shrift (shrift) *n.* **1.** The act of shriving. **2.** Confession or absolution, as to or from a priest. [OE *scrift*]

shrike (shrīk) *n.* Any of numerous predatory birds (family *Laniidae*) with hooked bill, short wings, and long tail; especially, the **loggerhead shrike** (*Lanius ludovicianus*) of the southern Atlantic coast: also called *mousebird.* [OE *scrīc* thrush]

shrill (shril) *adj.* **1.** Having a high-pitched and piercing tone quality. **2.** Emitting a sharp, piercing sound. **3.** *Poetic* Sharp to other senses than that of hearing; keen. *— v.t.* **1.** To cause to utter a shrill sound. *— v.i.* **2.** To make a shrill sound. *— adv.* Shrilly. [< Gmc. Cf. LG *schrell* having a sharp tone.] **— shrill′ness** *n.*

shril·ly (shril′ē; *adv.* shril′lē) *adj. Poetic* Shrill, or somewhat shrill. *— adv.* In a shrill manner.

shrimp (shrimp) *n.* **1.** Any of numerous small, long-tailed, principally marine decapods, (*Crago* and allied genera), especially the common edible shrimp (*C. vulgaris*) of the northern hemisphere. **2.** *Slang* A small or unimportant person. [Akin to OE *scrimman* to shrink, G *schrimpfen*]

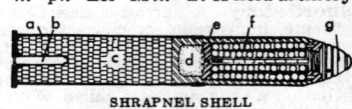

SHRIMP
a Cephalothorax. *b* Abdomen. *c* Tail. *t* Telson.

shrine (shrīn) *n.* **1.** A receptacle for sacred relics. **2.** A place, as a tomb or a chapel, sacred to some holy personage, or considered as sanctified by the remains or presence of such. **3.** A thing or spot made sacred by historic or other association. *— v.t.* **shrined, shrin·ing** *Rare & Poetic* To enshrine. [OE *scrīn* < L *scrinium* case, chest]

Shrine (shrīn) *n.* A secret fraternal order established in the United States in 1872: officially called **Ancient Arabic Order of Nobles of the Mystic Shrine. — Shrin′er** *n.*

shrink (shringk) *v.* **shrank** or **shrunk, shrunk** or, sometimes, **shrunk·en, shrink·ing** *v.i.* **1.** To draw together; contract, as from heat, cold, etc. **2.** To diminish; become less or smaller. **3.** To draw back, as from disgust, horror, or timidity; withdraw; recoil: with *from.* **4.** To flinch; wince. *— v.t.* **5.** To cause to shrink, contract, or draw together. *— n.* **1.** The act of shrinking; shrinkage; contraction. **2.** *Slang* A psychiatrist or psychoanalyst. [OE *scrincan*] **— shrink′a·ble** *adj.* **— shrink′er** *n.*

shrink·age (shringk′ij) *n.* **1.** The act or fact of shrinking; contraction. **2.** The amount lost by such shrinking. **3.** Decrease in value; depreciation.

shrinking violet *Informal* A shy or reclusive person; especially, one who avoids public recognition.

shrive (shrīv) *v.* **shrove** or **shrived, shriv·en** or **shrived, shriv·ing** *v.t.* **1.** To receive the confession of and give absolution to. **2.** To obtain absolution for (oneself) by confessing one's sins and doing penance. — *v.i.* **3.** To make confession. **4.** To hear confession. [OE *scrīfan,* ult. < L *scribere* to write, prescribe] — **shriv′er** *n.*

shriv·el (shriv′əl) *v.t. & v.i.* **shriv·eled** or **·elled, shriv·el·ing** or **·el·ling 1.** To contract into wrinkles; shrink and wrinkle: often with *up.* **2.** To make or become impotent; wither. [Origin uncertain. Cf. Sw. *skryvla.*]

shriv·en (shriv′ən) Alternative past participle of SHRIVE.

shroff (shrof) *n.* **1.** In China and Japan, an expert detector of counterfeit money or base coin. **2.** In India, a money-changer. [< Hind. *sarrāf* < Arabic]

Shrop·shire (shrop′shir, -shər) See SALOP.

Shrop·shire (shrop′shir, -shər) *n.* A breed of black-faced, hornless sheep, noted for heavy fleece and superior mutton, originating in Shropshire.

shroud[1] (shroud) *n.* **1.** A dress or garment for the dead; winding sheet. **2.** Something that envelops or conceals like a garment: the *shroud* of night. — *v.t.* **1.** To dress for the grave; clothe in a shroud. **2.** To envelop, as with a garment. **3.** *Archaic* To shelter. — *v.i.* **4.** *Obs.* To take shelter; go under cover; also, to gather together, as beasts, for warmth. [OE *scrūd* garment] — **shroud′less** *adj.*

shroud[2] (shroud) *n.* **1.** *Naut.* One of a set of ropes, often of wire, stretched from a masthead to the sides of a ship, serving as means of ascent and as a support for the masts. **2.** *Usually pl.* A guy, as a support for a smokestack. **3.** One of the supporting ropes attached to the edges of a parachute canopy. [< SHROUD[1]]

shroud-laid (shroud′lād) *adj.* Made of four strands twisted around a core: said of rope.

shrove (shrōv) Alternative past tense of SHRIVE.

Shrove·tide (shrōv′tīd′) *n.* The three days immediately preceding Ash Wednesday, **Shrove Sunday** (Quinquagesima Sunday), **Shrove Monday, Shrove Tuesday,** on which confession is made in preparation for Lent. [ME *schroftide* < stem of SHRIVE + TIDE[1], n. (def. 4)]

shrub[1] (shrub) *n.* A woody perennial plant of low stature, characterized by persistent stems and branches springing from the base. [OE *scrybb* brushwood]

shrub[2] (shrub) *n.* A beverage of sweetened fruit juice, sometimes made with an alcoholic liquor. [< Arabic *sharāb.* See SHERBET.]

shrub althea The rose of Sharon.

shrub·ber·y (shrub′ər·ē) *n. pl.* **·ber·ies 1.** Shrubs collectively. **2.** A collection of shrubs, as in a garden.

shrub·by (shrub′ē) *adj.* **·bi·er, ·bi·est 1.** Containing many shrubs; covered with shrubs. **2.** Of, pertaining to, or like a shrub. — **shrub′bi·ness** *n.*

shrug (shrug) *v.t. & v.i.* **shrugged, shrug·ging** To draw up (the shoulders), as in displeasure, doubt, surprise, etc. — *n.* **1.** The act of shrugging the shoulders. **2.** A short jacket, open in front. [ME *schrugge;* origin uncertain]

shrunk (shrungk) Alternative past tense and past participle of SHRINK.

shrunk·en (shrungk′ən) Alternative past participle of SHRINK. — *adj.* Contracted and atrophied.

shtick (shtik) *n. U.S. Slang* An artificial or contrived device, mannerism, special area of knowledge, etc., intended to make one appear distinctive or unique; a gimmick: also spelled *schtick.* [< Yiddish < G *stück* piece, bit]

shuck (shuk) *n.* **1.** A husk, shell, or pod. **2.** A shell of an oyster or a clam. **3.** *Usually pl. U.S. Informal* Something of little or no value: not worth *shucks.* — *v.t.* **1.** To remove the shucks or from; remove the husk or shell from (corn, oysters, etc.). **2.** *Informal* To take off or cast off, as clothes. [Origin unknown] — **shuck′er** *n.*

shuck·ing (shuk′ing) *n. U.S. Informal* **1.** A husking bee. **2.** The removing of shucks, especially from corn.

shucks (shuks) *interj. U.S. Informal* A mild ejaculation expressing annoyance, disgust, etc.

shud·der (shud′ər) *v.i.* To tremble or shake, as from fright or cold; shiver; quake. — *n.* The act of shuddering; a convulsive shiver, as from horror or fear; tremor. [ME *shodder.* Akin to LG *schuddern.*]

shuf·fle (shuf′əl) *n.* **1.** A mixing or changing of the order of things, as of cards in a pack before each deal. **2.** A hesitating, evasive, or tricky action; artifice. **3.** A scraping

of the feet, as in walking; a slow, dragging gait. **4.** A dance, or the step used in it, where the dancer pushes his foot along the floor at each step. — *v.* **fled,** **·fling** *v.t.* **1.** To shift this way and that; mix; confuse; disorder; especially, to change the order of by mixing, as cards in a pack. **2.** To move (the feet) along the ground or floor with a dragging gait. **3.** To change from one place to another. **4.** To make up or remove fraudulently or hastily; also, to put aside carelessly: with *up, off,* or *out.* — *v.i.* **5.** To change position; shift ground. **6.** To resort to indirect methods; prevaricate. **7.** To dance the shuffle. **8.** To scrape the feet along. **9.** To scrape or struggle along awkwardly. [Prob. < LG *schuffeln* to move with dragging feet, mix cards, etc.]

shuf·fle·board (shuf′əl·bôrd′, -bōrd′) *n.* **1.** A game in which wooden or composition disks are slid by means of a pronged cue along a smooth surface toward numbered spaces. **2.** The board or surface on which the game is played. Also called *shovelboard.*

shuf·fler (shuf′lər) *n.* **1.** One who shuffles. **2.** The scaup.

Shu·fu (shoō′foō′) The Chinese name for KASHGAR.

shul (shoōl) *n.* A synagogue. [< Yiddish]

Shu·lam·ite (shoō′ləm·īt) *n.* The chief female character in the Song of Solomon. *Cant.* vi 13.

shun (shun) *v.t.* **shunned, shun·ning 1.** To keep clear of; avoid; refrain from. **2.** *Obs.* To escape; evade. **3.** *Obs.* To abhor. — *Syn.* See ESCAPE. [OE *scunian*] — **shun′ner** *n.*

shunt (shunt) *n.* **1.** The act of shunting. **2.** A railroad switch. **3.** *Electr.* A conductor joining two points in a circuit and serving to divert part of the current to an auxiliary circuit: also called *by-pass.* — *v.t.* **1.** To turn aside. **2.** To switch, as a train or car, from one track to another. **3.** *Electr.* To distribute by means of shunts. **4.** To evade by turning away from; put off on someone else, as a task. — *v.i.* **5.** To move to one side. **6.** *Electr.* To be diverted by a shunt: said of current. **7.** To shift or transfer one's views or course. [ME *schunten;* origin uncertain] — **shunt′er** *n.*

shunt-wound (shunt′wound′) *adj. Electr.* Designating a type of direct current motor in which the armature circuit and field circuit are connected in parallel.

shure (shūr) *Scot.* Past tense of SHEAR.

shush (shush) *v.t.* To quiet; hush up, as by making the sound "sh." — *n.* Such a sound used to command quiet. [Imit.]

Shu·shan (shoō′shan) The Old Testament name for SUSA.

shut (shut) *v.* **shut, shut·ting** *v.t.* **1.** To bring into such position as to close an opening or aperture; close, as a door, lid, or valve. **2.** To close (an opening, aperture, etc.) so as to prevent ingress or egress. **3.** To close and fasten securely, as with a latch or lock. **4.** To forbid entrance into or exit from. **5.** To keep from entering or leaving; confine or exclude; bar: with *in, out, from,* etc. **6.** To close, fold, or bring together, as extended, expanded, or unfolded parts: to *shut* an umbrella. **7.** To hide from view; obscure. — *v.i.* **8.** To be or become closed or in a closed position. — **to shut down 1.** To cease from operating, as a factory or mine; close up; stop work. **2.** To lower; come down close: The fog *shut down.* **3.** *Informal* To suppress: with *on.* — **to shut one's eyes to** To ignore. — **to shut out** In sports, to keep (an opponent) from scoring during the course of a game. — **to shut up 1.** *Informal* To stop talking or cause to stop talking. **2.** *Informal* To become exhausted and stop running, as a horse in a race. **3.** To close all the entrances to, as a house. **4.** To imprison; confine. — *adj.* **1.** Made fast or closed. **2.** Not sonorous; dull: said of sound. — *n.* **1.** The act of shutting; also, the time of shutting, closing, or ending. **2.** The place of shutting or closing together; especially, the connection or line of connection between welded pieces of metal. [OE *scyttan*]

shut·down (shut′doun′) *n.* The closing of or ceasing of work in a mine, mill, factory, or other industrial plant.

Shute (shoōt), Nevil, 1899–1960, English aeronautical engineer and writer: full name **Nevil Shute Nor·way** (nôr′wā).

shut·eye (shut′ī) *n. Slang* Sleep.

shut-in (shut′in′) *n.* An invalid unable to go out. — *adj.* **1.** Obliged to stay at home. **2.** Inclined to avoid people.

shut·off (shut′ôf′, -of′) *n. Mech.* A device for shutting something off.

shut·out (shut′out′) *n.* **1.** A shutting out; especially, a lockout (which see). **2.** In sports, a game in which one side is prevented from scoring.

shut·ter (shut′ər) *n.* **1.** One who or that which shuts. **2.** That which shuts out or excludes; especially, a cover or screen, usually hinged, for closing a window. **3.** *Photog.* Any of various mechanisms for momentarily admitting light through a camera lens to the film or plate. — *v.t.* To furnish, close, or divide off with shutters.

shut·ter·bug (shut′ər·bug′) *n. U.S. Slang* A photography enthusiast. [< SHUTTER + BUG[1] (def. 5)]

shut·tle (shut′l) *n.* **1.** A device used in weaving to carry the weft to and fro between the warp threads. **2.** A similar rotating or other device in a sewing machine, or one used in tatting, knitting, etc. **3.** A transport system operating be-

SHROUDS

a Chain plates.
b Shrouds.
c Swifter.
d Deadeyes.
e Lanyards.
f Ratlines.
g Topmast backstays.

tween two nearby points. — *v.t. & v.i.* **·tled, ·tling** To move to and fro, like a shuttle. [OE *scytel* missile; so called because shot to and fro in weaving]

shut·tle·cock (shut/l·kok/) *n.* A rounded piece of cork, with a crown of feathers, used in badminton and battledore; also, the game of battledore. — *v.t.* To send or knock back and forth like a shuttlecock. [< SHUTTLE + COCK[1]]

shwan·pan (shwän/pän/) See SWANPAN.

shy[1] (shī) *v.i.* **shied, shy·ing** **1.** To start suddenly aside, as in fear: said of a horse. **2.** To draw back, as from doubt or caution: with *off* or *away.* — *adj.* **shi·er** or **shy·er, shi·est** or **shy·est** **1.** Easily frightened or startled; timorous. **2.** Bashful; reserved; coy. **3.** Circumspect, as from motives of caution; watchful; wary: with *of.* **4.** Not easy to perceive, seize, or secure; elusive. **5.** Not prolific: said of plants, trees, or, rarely, birds. **6.** *Informal* Having less money than is called for or required: originally a term used in poker: to be *shy* a dollar in the pool. **7.** *Informal* Short; lacking: often with *on.* — *n.* A starting aside, as in fear. [OE *scēoh* timid. Akin to ESCHEW.] — **shy/ness** *n.*

shy[2] (shī) *v.t. & v.i.* **shied, shy·ing** To throw with a swift sidelong motion. — *n.* *pl.* **shies** **1.** A careless throw or fling. **2.** A verbal fling; sneer. **3.** A trial; experiment. [Origin unknown]

shy·er (shī/ər) *n.* One who shies. See SHIER.

Shy·lock (shī/lok) In Shakespeare's *Merchant of Venice*, a revengeful usurer who endeavors to exact a pound of flesh from Antonio's body as a forfeit for nonpayment of a debt. — *n.* *Slang* Any relentless creditor.

shy·ly (shī/lē) *adv.* In a shy manner: also spelled *shily.*

shy·ster (shīs/tər) *n.* *Slang* Anyone, especially a lawyer, who conducts his business in an unscrupulous or tricky manner. [Origin uncertain]

si[1] (sē) *n.* *Music* Ti[1].

si[2] (sē) *adv.* Italian, Portuguese, Spanish, and sometimes French, for "yes." [< L *sic* thus]

Si *Chem.* Silicon.

S.I. **1.** Sandwich Islands. **2.** Staten Island.

si·al (sī/al) *n.* *Geol.* A rock formation rich in silica and alumina, that underlies sedimentary rock in continental land masses. — **si·al/ic** *adj.* [< SI(LICA) + AL(UMINA)]

Si·al·kot (sē·äl/kōt) A city in NE West Pakistan; pop. 167,543 (1961).

sialo- *combining form* Saliva; pertaining to saliva: *sialogogue.* Also, before vowels, **sial-.** [< Gk. *sialon* saliva]

si·al·o·gogue (sī·al/ə·gog) *n.* Any agent exciting a flow of saliva. Also **si·al/a·gogue.** [< F, or < NL *sialogogum*] — **si·a·lo·gog·ic** (sī/ə·lō·goj/ik) *adj. & n.*

si·a·loid (sī/ə·loid) *adj.* Resembling saliva.

Si·am (sī·am/) See THAILAND.

Siam, Gulf of A part of the South China Sea, separating the Malay Peninsula from Indochina; 300 to 350 mi. wide, 450 mi. long.

si·a·mang (sē/ə·mang) *n.* A large black gibbon (genus *Symphalangus*) found in Sumatra. [< Malay *siaman* < *iaman* black]

si·a·mese (sī/ə·mēz/) *adj.* Of, pertaining to, or having a pipe joint in the form of a Y that permits connection of two pipes or hoses to a larger pipe. — *n.* A siamese joint or pipe. [< SIAMESE (TWINS)]

Si·a·mese (sī/ə·mēz/, -mēs/) *adj.* **1.** Pertaining to Thailand (Siam), its people, or their language. **2.** Closely connected; twin. — *n.* **1.** *pl.* **mese** A native of Siam, belonging to the Thai stock. **2.** The Thai language of the people of Siam, now officially called *Thai.*

Siamese cat A breed of short-haired cat, typically fawn-colored, with dark-tipped ears, tail, feet, and face, and blue, gently slanting eyes.

Siamese twins Any twins joined together at birth. [after the two Chinese males, Eng and Chang, 1811–74, born in Siam, whose bodies were joined by a fleshy band]

Si·an (sē/än/, shē/-) The capital of Shensi Province, China; pop. 1,900,000 (est. 1970): formerly *Singan.*

Siang·tan (syäng/tän/, shyäng/-) A city in east central Hunan Province, China; pop. 300,000 (est. 1970).

sib (sib) *Rare* *n.* **1.** A blood relation; kinsman. **2.** Kinsmen collectively; relatives. — *adj.* **1.** Related by blood; akin. **2.** Related; similar. Also **sibb.** [OE *sibb*]

Sib. Siberia; Siberian.

sib·bo·leth (sib/ə·leth) See SHIBBOLETH.

Si·be·li·us (si·bā/lē·əs, -bäl/yəs; *Finnish* si·bā/lyŏŏs), **Jean,** 1865–1957, Finnish composer.

Si·be·ri·a (sī·bir/ē·ə) A region roughly comprising the part of the R.S.F.S.R. east of the Ural Mountains; about 5 million sq. mi. *Russian* **Si·bir, Si·bir′** (syi·byēry′/). — **Si·be/ri·an** *adj. & n.*

sib·i·lant (sib/ə·lant) *adj.* **1.** Hissing. **2.** *Phonet.* Denoting those consonants produced by the fricative passage of breath through a very narrow orifice, in the front part of the mouth, as (s), (z), (sh), and (zh). — *n.* *Phonet.* A sibilant consonant. [< L *sibilans, -antis,* ppr. of *sibilare* to hiss] — **sib/i·lance, sib/i·lan·cy** *n.* — **sib/i·lant·ly** *adv.*

sib·i·late (sib/ə·lāt) *v.t.* **·lat·ed, ·lat·ing** To give a hissing sound to, or change to a hissing sound. [< L *sibilatus,* pp. of *sibilare* to hiss] — **sib/i·la/tion** *n.*

Si·biu (si·byŏŏ/) A city in central Rumania; pop. 97,211 (est. 1960): German *Hermannstadt.*

sib·ling (sib/ling) *n.* A brother or sister. [OE, a relative]

sib·yl (sib/əl) *n.* **1.** In ancient Greece and Rome, any of several women who prophesied under the supposed inspiration of some deity. **2.** A fortuneteller; sorceress. [< F *sibile* < L *sibylla* < Gk.]

sib·yl·line (sib/əl·īn, -ēn, -in) *adj.* **1.** Of, pertaining to, or characteristic of the sibyls. **2.** Prophetic; oracular; occult. **3.** Exorbitant; excessive. Also **si·byl·ic** (si·bil/ik), **si·byl/lic.**

Sibylline Books A collection of nine books reputedly bought from the Cumaean sibyl by Tarquin the Proud and supposed to reveal the destiny of Rome.

sic[1] (sik) *adv.* So; thus: inserted in brackets after a quotation to indicate that it is accurately reproduced even though it may seem questionable or incorrect. [< L]

sic[2] (sik) *adj.* *Scot.* Such. Also **sic/can** (-ən).

sic[3] (sik) *v.t.* **sicked, sick·ing** To sick. See SICK[2].

Sic. Sicilian; Sicily.

Si·ca·ni·an (si·kā/nē·ən) *adj.* Sicilian.

sic·ca·tive (sik/ə·tiv) *adj.* Causing to dry; drying. — *n.* Something that causes drying, as an additive to paint, or certain medicines. [< LL *siccativus* < L *siccatus,* pp. of *siccare* to dry < *siccus* dry]

sice (sīs) See SYCE.

Sicilian Vespers A general massacre of the French in Sicily (1282) by Sicilians rising against the French rule, so called because the bell for vespers gave the signal for attack.

Sic·i·lies (sis/ə·lēz), **The Two** See (The) TWO SICILIES.

Sic·i·ly (sis/ə·lē) An island of Italy in the Mediterranean (9,831 sq. mi.), constituting with small neighboring islands an autonomous Region; 9,926 sq. mi.; pop. 4,711,783 (1961); capital, Palermo: ancient *Trinacria.* *Italian* **Si·ci·lia** (sē·chē/lyä). — **Si·cil/i·an** (si·sil/ē·ən, -sil/yən) *adj. & n.*

sick[1] (sik) *adj.* **1.** Affected with disease; ill; ailing. **2.** Of or used by ill persons: often used in combination: *sickroom.* **3.** Affected by nausea; desiring to vomit. **4.** Expressive of or experiencing disgust or unpleasant emotion. **5.** Impaired or unsound from any cause. **6.** Mentally unsound. **7.** Pallid; wan. **8.** Depressed and longing; languishing: *sick* for the sea. **9.** Disinclined by reason of satiety or disgust; surfeited: with *of: sick* of music. **10.** Sadistic or macabre in some way; morbid: *sick* jokes. **11.** *Agric.* Of soil: **a** Exhausted; unable to produce a profitable yield. **b** Diseased. — *n.* Sick people collectively: with *the.* [OE *sēoc*]
— **Syn.** **1, 3.** *Sick, ill, ailing, unwell,* and *indisposed* mean afflicted by a disease or ailment. In U.S. usage, *sick* is the general term, and may refer to a slight ailment or the most severe illness; it may also mean nauseated, the sense it always bears in British usage. *Ill* and *unwell* are close synonyms of *sick; ill* is sometimes felt to be affected, while *unwell* is frequently avoided because of its popular euphemistic use. *Ailing* and *indisposed* refer to slight illnesses. *Ailing* implies a minor, but chronic, condition; *indisposed* suggests a trivial or temporary illness that prevents normal social or business activity. Compare DISEASE.

sick[2] (sik) *v.t.* **1.** To attack: used in the imperative as an order to a dog. **2.** To urge to attack: I'll *sick* the dog on you. Also spelled *sic.* [Var. of SEEK]

sick·bay (sik/bā/) *n.* That part of a ship or of a naval base set aside for the care of the sick.

sick·bed (sik/bed/) *n.* The bed a sick person lies on.

sick call *Mil.* **1.** The daily period during which all nonhospitalized sick or injured personnel report to the medical officer. **2.** The call or signal that announces this.

sick·en (sik/ən) *v.t. & v.i.* To make or become sick or disgusted. — **sick/en·er** *n.*

sick·en·ing (sik/ən·ing) *adj.* Disgusting; revolting; nauseating. — **sick/en·ing·ly** *adv.*

sick·er[1] (sik/ər) *adj.* Comparative of SICK[1].

sick·er[2] (sik/ər) *adj.* *Scot. & Brit. Dial.* Safe; sure; also, cautious. — *adv.* Surely; securely. Also spelled *siker.* [OE *sicor* < L *securus* safe]

sick headache Headache accompanied by nausea; especially, migraine.

sick·ish (sik/ish) *adj.* **1.** Somewhat sick. **2.** Slightly nauseating. — **sick/ish·ly** *adv.* — **sick/ish·ness** *n.*

sick·le (sik/əl) *n.* An implement with a curved or crescent-shaped blade mounted on a short handle, used for cutting tall grass, grains, etc. — *v.t.* **·led, ·ling** To cut with a sickle, as grass. [OE *sicol* < L *secula* < *secare* to cut]

Sick·le (sik/əl) *n.* A sickle-shaped group of stars in the constellation Leo.

sick·le·bill (sik/əl·bil/) *n.* Any of several birds having a strongly curved bill, as a hummingbird or curlew.

sickle cell A crescent-shaped red blood corpuscle containing a genetically transmitted type of hemoglobin in which the oxygen concentration is below normal, and causing an anemia (**sickle cell anemia**) occurring chiefly among Negroes.

SIAMESE CAT
(About 11 inches high at shoulder)

sickle feather One of the long curved feathers in the tail of a domestic cock. For illustration see FOWL.

sick·le·mi·a (sik/əl·ē/mē·ə, si·klē/-) *n. Pathol.* The presence of sickle cells in the blood.

sickle pear Loosely, a Seckel pear.

sick list A list of those incapacitated by illness, as in the army or navy.

sick·ly (sik/lē) *adj.* **·li·er, ·li·est 1.** Habitually indisposed; ailing; unhealthy: a *sickly* child. **2.** Marked by the prevalence of sickness: a *sickly* summer. **3.** Nauseating; disgusting. **4.** Pertaining to or characteristic of the sick or sickness: a *sickly* appearance. **5.** Weak; faint. **6.** Mawkish; insipid: *sickly* sentimentality. — *adv.* In a sick manner; poorly: also **sick/li·ly.** — *v.t.* **·lied, ·ly·ing** To make sickly, as in color or complexion. — **sick/li·ness** *n.*

sick·ness (sik/nis) *n.* **1.** The state of being sick. **2.** A particular form of disease. **3.** Nausea. **4.** Any disordered, disturbed, or morbid state.

sick·room (sik/room/, -room/) *n.* A room in which a sick person lies or stays.

sic pas·sim (sik pas/im) *Latin* Thus everywhere (as throughout a book).

Sic·y·on (sish/ē·on) An ancient city in the Peloponnesus, Greece: Greek *Sikyon.*

Sid·dons (sid/nz), **Sarah,** 1755–1831, *née* Kemble, British actress.

sid·dur (sid/ŏŏr) *n.* The Jewish prayer book, containing the year's prayers for weekdays, Sabbaths, fast days, and holy days. [< Hebrew *siddūr* arrangement]

side¹ (sīd) *n.* **1.** Any one of the bounding lines of a surface or of the bounding surfaces of a solid object; also, a particular line or surface other than top or bottom: the *side* of a mountain. **2.** A lateral part of a surface or object, usually designated as *right* or *left.* **3.** Either of the two surfaces of a piece of paper, cloth, etc.; also, a specific surface of something: the rough *side* of sandpaper. **4.** One of two or more contrasted directions, parts, or places: the east *side* of town. **5.** A distinct party or body of competitors or partisans; a faction. **6.** An opinion, aspect, or point of view: my *side* of the question. **7.** Family connection, especially by descent through one parent: my grandfather on my father's *side.* **8.** The lateral half of a slaughtered animal or of a tanned skin or hide. **9.** Either half of the human body as divided by the median plane. **10.** The space beside someone. **11.** A page of written or printed paper. **12.** *Naut.* The part of a ship's hull from stem to stern above the water line. **13.** In billiards, a lateral spin given to the cue ball. **14.** In sports, a team. **15.** *Brit. Slang* Superciliousness of manner; pretentiousness. — **side by side** Beside or next to each other. — **to take sides** To support or be in favor of a particular opinion, point of view, etc. — **Syn.** See PHASE. — *adj.* **1.** Situated at or on one side; lateral: a *side* window. **2.** Being or viewed as if from one side; oblique: a *side* glance. **3.** Directed towards one side: a *side* blow. **4.** Not primary; subordinate; incidental: a *side* issue. — *v.t.* **sid·ed, sid·ing 1.** To provide with sides, as a building. **2.** To cut into sides, as a carcass. **3.** To thrust aside. — **to side with** To support or take the part of. [OE *sīde*]

side² (sīd) *adj.* **1.** *Scot. & Brit. Dial.* Relatively long or wide; large: said of garments. **2.** *Scot.* Far; distant.

side-arm (sīd/ärm/) *adj.* Executed with the hand level with the elbow, as a pitch. — *adv.* In a sidearm manner.

side arms Weapons worn at the side, as swords, pistols, bayonets, etc.

side·band (sīd/band/) *n. Telecom.* One of the two frequency bands immediately higher or lower than the carrier-wave frequency, and defined by and corresponding to the frequency of the modulating wave. Also **side band.**

side·board (sīd/bôrd/, -bōrd/) *n.* **1.** A piece of dining-room furniture for holding tableware. **2.** A board at the side of something, as on sailing canoes.

side·burns (sīd/bûrnz/) *n.pl. Chiefly U.S.* The hair growing on the sides of a man's face below the hairline, especially when worn as whiskers with the rest of the beard shaved off. [Alter. of BURNSIDES]

side·car (sīd/kär/) *n.* **1.** A small, one-wheeled passenger car attached to the side of a motorcycle. **2.** A cocktail containing equal parts of lemon juice, brandy, and curaçao or Cointreau. **3.** A jaunting car (which see).

sid·ed (sī/did) *adj.* Having or characterized by (a specified kind or number of) sides: used in combination: *one-sided.*

side dish A portion of food served in addition to the main dish of a course; also, the dish in which it is served.

side effect A secondary, often injurious effect: the *side effect* of taking certain medicines.

side·kick (sīd/kik/) *n. U.S. Slang* A close friend; buddy.

side·light (sīd/līt/) *n.* **1.** A side window. **2.** A light coming from the side. **3.** Incidental facts or information. **4.** *Naut.* **a** One of the colored lights, red on the port side and green on the starboard, displayed on the sides of ships at night: also called *running light.* **b** A night light in the gangway of a war vessel.

side·line (sīd/līn/) *n.* **1.** An auxiliary line of goods sold by a store or a commercial traveler. **2.** Any additional or secondary work differing from one's main job. **3.** A track or road, especially of a railroad, branching off from the main line. **4.** In sports: **a** One of the lines bounding the two sides of a football field, tennis court, etc. **b** *Often pl.* The area just outside these lines. **5.** The point of view of an outsider or nonparticipant. Also **side line.** — *v.t.* **·lined, ·lin·ing** To prevent or remove (someone) from active participation.

side·ling (sīd/ling) *adj.* Having a slanting or oblique position or motion; indirect. — *adv.* Sidewise; obliquely.

side·long (sīd/lông, -long/) *adj.* **1.** Inclining, tending or directed to one side. **2.** Steeply inclined. — *adv.* In a lateral or oblique direction.

side·man (sīd/man/) *n. pl.* **·men** (-men/) *U.S.* A member of a jazz band, other than the leader.

side meat *U.S. Dial.* Salt pork or bacon.

side·piece (sīd/pēs/) *n.* A piece at or forming the side of anything.

si·de·re·al (sī·dir/ē·əl) *adj.* **1.** Of or pertaining to stars. **2.** Measured by means of the stars: *sidereal* year. [< L *sidereus* < *sidus, sideris* star] — **si·de/re·al·ly** *adv.*

sidereal day The period of one complete rotation of the earth with reference to the vernal equinox.

sidereal hour The twenty-fourth part of a sidereal day.

sidereal time Time based upon the rotation of the earth with reference to the vernal equinox.

sidereal year The period of 365 days, 6 hours, 9 minutes, and 9 seconds in which the sun apparently returns to the same position among the stars. It is longer than the astronomical year, owing to the precession of the equinoxes.

sid·er·ite (sid/ə·rīt) *n.* **1.** A vitreous iron carbonate, $FeCO_3$, generally found in brownish masses: also called *chalybite.* **2.** An iron meteorite. [< F < L *siderites* < Gk. *siderītēs* of iron < *sideros* iron] — **sid/er·it/ic** (-rit/ik) *adj.*

sidero-¹ *combining form* Iron; of or pertaining to iron: *siderolite.* Also, before vowels, **sider-.** [< Gk. *sideros* iron]

sidero-² *combining form* Star; stellar: *siderostat.* Also, before vowels, **sider-.** [< L *sidus, sideris* star]

sid·er·o·lite (sid/ər·ə·līt/) *n.* A meteorite consisting of iron containing embedded grains of certain minerals, as chrysolite. [< SIDERO-¹ + -LITE]

sid·er·o·sis (sid/ə·rō/sis) *n. Pathol.* A lung disease caused by the inhalation of iron or other metallic dust.

sid·er·o·stat (sid/ər·ə·stat/) *n. Astron.* A mirror turning by clock motion so as constantly to reflect the light of a star into a fixed telescope or other astronomical instrument. [< SIDERO-² + -STAT] — **sid/er·o·stat/ic** *adj.*

side·sad·dle (sīd/sad/l) *n.* A woman's saddle having one stirrup and designed so that both legs of the rider are on the same side of the horse. — *adv.* On or as on a sidesaddle.

side show 1. A small show incidental to but connected with a larger or more important one: a circus *side show.* **2.** Any subordinate issue or attraction.

side·slip (sīd/slip/) *v.i.* **·slipped, ·slip·ping** To slip or skid sideways. — *n.* **1.** A lateral skid, as of an automobile. **2.** *Aeron.* A downward, sideways slipping of an airplane along the lateral axis, executed to lose altitude without a gain in forward speed.

side·split·ting (sīd/split/ing) *adj.* **1.** Hearty and uproarious, as laughter. **2.** Causing great laughter or hilarity.

side·step (sīd/step/) *v.* **stepped, ·step·ping** *v.i.* **1.** To step to one side. **2.** To avoid responsibility, conflict, etc. — *v.t.* **3.** To avoid, as an issue, or postpone, as a decision; evade. — **side/step/per** *n.*

side step 1. A step or movement to one side, as of a pugilist. **2.** *Usually pl.* One of a series of steps at the side of a building, etc.

side stroke In swimming, a stroke made while lying on the side, the arms being thrust forward alternately, and the legs executing a scissors kick.

side·swipe (sīd/swīp/) *n.* A sweeping blow along the side. — *v.t. & v.i.* **swiped, ·swip·ing** To strike or collide with such a blow.

side·track (sīd/trak/) *v.t. & v.i.* **1.** To move to a siding, as a railroad train. **2.** To divert or distract from the main issue or subject. — *n.* A railroad siding; also, a branch line.

side·walk (sīd/wôk/) *n. U.S.* A path or pavement at the side of the street, for the use of pedestrians.

sidewalk superintendent *U.S. Informal* A pedestrian watching the construction or demolition of a building, etc.

side wall *U.S.* One of the side surfaces of a tire.

side·ward (sīd/wərd) *adj.* Directed or moving toward or from the side; lateral. — *adv.* Toward or from the side; laterally: also **side/wards** (-wərdz).

side·ways (sīd/wāz/) *adv.* **1.** From one side. **2.** So as to incline toward one side, or with the side forward: Hold it *sideways.* **3.** Toward one side; obliquely. — *adj.* Moving to or from one side. Also **side/way/, side/wise/** (-wīz/).

side wheel A wheel at the side; especially, one of two paddle wheels on either side of a steamboat. **— side-wheel** (sīd′hwēl′) *adj.* **— side′-wheel′er** *n*.

side·wind·er (sīd′wīn′dər) *n.* **1.** A small rattlesnake (*Crotalus cerastes*) found in the SW United States, so called because of its characteristic lateral motion. **2.** A heavy, swinging, sideways blow with the fist.

MARY POWELL

SIDE WHEEL

Sidewinder *n. U.S.* An air-to-air missile using a heat homing system.

sid·ing (sī′ding) *n.* **1.** A railway track by the side of the main track. **2.** The boarding that covers the side of a wooden house, etc.

si·dle (sīd′l) *v.i.* **·dled, ·dling** To move sideways, especially in a cautious or stealthy manner. **—** *n.* A sideways step or movement. [Back formation < obs. *sidling* sidelong] **— si′dler** *n.*

Sid·ney (sid′nē), **Sir Philip,** 1554–86, English courtier, poet, and statesman. Also *Sydney*.

Si·don (sī′dn) The capital of ancient Phoenicia, on the site of modern Saida. **— Si·do·ni·an** (sī·dō′nē·ən) *adj. & n.*

Sid·ra (sid′rə), **Gulf of** An inlet of the Mediterranean in the coast of Libya; 275 mi. wide: ancient *Syrtis Major*.

siè·cle (sye′kl′) *n. French* Century; age; period.

Sieg·bahn (sēg′bän), **Karl Manne Georg,** born 1886, Swedish physicist.

siege (sēj) *n.* **1.** The act of surrounding a town or any fortified area with the intention of capturing it. **2.** A steady attempt to win something; also, the protracted period spent in the effort. **3.** The time during which one undergoes a protracted illness or difficulty. **4.** *Obs.* A seat; chair; throne. **5.** *Obs.* Rank; station. **— to lay siege to** To attempt to capture or gain; besiege. **—** *v.t.* **sieged, sieg·ing** To try to capture, win, or gain (something); besiege. [< OF < L *sedes* seat < *sedere* to sit]

Siege Perilous A seat at King Arthur's Round Table, fatal to all occupants except Sir Galahad.

Sieg·fried (sēg′frēd, *Ger.* zēkh′frēt) **1.** The hero of the *Nibelungenlied* and other Germanic legends. He corresponds to Sigurd, the hero of the *Volsunga Saga*. **2.** A music drama by Richard Wagner. See RING OF THE NIBELUNG.

Siegfried Line In World War II, a system of German fortifications facing the Maginot Line: also called *Westwall*.

Sieg Heil (zēkh′ hīl′) *German* Hail to victory: a Nazi salute.

Sieg·mund (sēg′mŏond, *Ger.* zēkh′mŏond) The father of Siegfried in the *Nibelungenlied*. He corresponds to Sigmund in the *Volsunga Saga*.

Sie·mens (sē′mənz, *Ger.* zē′məns), **Sir William,** 1823–83, British engineer and inventor born in Germany: original name **Karl Wilhelm Siemens.**

Si·en·a (sē·en′ə, *Ital.* syä′nä) A commune in Tuscany, central Italy; pop. 62,215 (1961). **— Si·en·ese** (sē′ən·ēz′, -ēs′) *adj. & n.*

si·en·ite (sī′ən·īt) See SYENITE.

Sien·kie·wicz (shen·kye′vich), **Henryk,** 1846–1916, Polish novelist.

si·en·na (sē·en′ə) *n.* **1.** A brownish yellow clay containing oxides of iron and manganese, used as a pigment. **2.** The brownish yellow color of this pigment. **3.** Burnt sienna (which see). [< Ital. (*terra di*) *Siena* (earth of) Siena]

si·er·ra (sē·er′ə) *n.* **1.** A mountain range or chain, especially one having a jagged outline. **2.** Any of several large mackerellike fishes, as the cero. [< Sp. < L *serra* saw]

Si·er·ra Le·o·ne (sē·er′ə lē·ō′nē, lē·ōn′) An independent member of the Commonwealth of Nations on the west coast of Africa; 27,925 sq. mi.; pop. 2,512,000 (est. 1969); capital, Freetown. See map of (Gulf of) GUINEA.

Si·er·ra Ma·dre (sē·er′ə mä′drä, mad′rē; *Sp.* sē·er′rä mä′thrä) A mountain chain bordering the central plateau of Mexico; highest point, Pico de Orizaba, 18,700 ft.

Si·er·ra Ne·vad·a (sē·er′ə nə·vad′ə, -vä′də; *Sp.* sē·er′rä nä·vä′thä) **1.** A mountain range of eastern California, extending 400 miles north and south; highest point, Mt. Whitney, 14,495 ft. **2.** A mountain range in southern Spain; highest peak, Mulhacén, 11,411 ft.

si·es·ta (sē·es′tə) *n.* A midday or afternoon nap. [< Sp. < L *sexta* (*hora*) sixth (hour), noon < *sex* six]

sieur (syœr) *n.* Sir; master: a former French title of respect. [< F < L *senior* older]

sieve (siv) *n.* **1.** A utensil or apparatus for straining or sifting, consisting of a frame provided with a bottom of wire mesh, etc. **2.** One who spreads gossip, reveals secrets, etc. **—** *v.t. & v.i.* **sieved, siev·ing** To pass through a sieve. [OE *sife* sieve]

sieve cell *Bot.* A thin-walled, elongated cell having perforations (**sieve pores**) arranged in **sieve plates** that permit communication between contiguous cells.

Sie·vers (sē′vərz, *Ger.* zē′fərs), **Georg Eduard,** 1850–1932, German philologist.

sieve tube *Bot.* An arrangement of sieve cells by means of which conduction is accomplished.

Sie·yès (syä·yes′), **Emmanuel Joseph,** 1748–1836, French Revolutionary statesman: called Abbé Sieyès.

sif·fleur (sē·flœr′) *n. Canadian* The hoary marmot. See under MARMOT. [< dial. F (Canadian), whistler]

sift (sift) *v.t.* **1.** To pass through a sieve in order to separate the fine parts from the coarse. **2.** To scatter by or as by a sieve. **3.** To examine carefully. **4.** To separate as if with a sieve; distinguish: to *sift* fact from fiction. **—** *v.i.* **5.** To use a sieve; sift something. **6.** To fall or pass through or as through a sieve. [OE *siftan*] **— sift′er** *n.*

sift·ings (sif′tingz) *n.pl.* Things removed or separated by or as by a sieve.

Sig. or **sig. 1.** Signature. **2.** Signor; signore; signori.

SigC *Mil.* Signal Corps.

sigh (sī) *v.i.* **1.** To draw in and exhale a deep, audible breath, as in expressing sorrow, weariness, pain, etc. **2.** To make a sound suggestive of a sigh, as the wind. **3.** To yearn; long. **—** *v.t.* **4.** To express with a sigh. **5.** *Archaic* To lament with sighs. **—** *n.* The act or sound of or as of sighing. [Back formation < ME *sighte*, pt. of *siken* < OE *sīcan* to sigh]

sight (sīt) *n.* **1.** The act or fact of seeing. **2.** That which is seen; a view. **3.** *pl.* Things worth seeing: the *sights* of the town. **4.** The faculty of seeing; vision. **5.** The range or scope of vision; limit of eyesight. **6.** A mental point of view; estimation. **7.** An opportunity for investigation or study. **8.** A device to assist aim, as on a gun, leveling instrument, etc. **9.** An aim or observation taken with a telescope or other sighting instrument. **10.** *Informal* Something unusual or ugly to look at: He was a *sight*. **11.** *Dial.* A great quantity or number: a *sight* of people. **— at** (or on) **sight 1.** As soon as seen: to read or shoot *at sight*. **2.** On presentation for payment: said of drafts, bills, etc. **— not by a long sight 1.** Never; not at all. **2.** Not nearly. **— sight unseen** Without ever having seen the object in question. **—** *v.t.* **1.** To perceive with the eyes; observe: to *sight* a whale. **2.** To take a sight of; look at through a telescope or similar instrument. **3.** To furnish with sights, or adjust the sights of, as a gun. **4.** To give the proper aim or elevation to, as a gun; take aim with. **5.** To present, as a bill to its drawee. **—** *v.i.* **6.** To take aim. **7.** To make an observation or sight. [OE *gesiht*]

sight draft A draft or bill payable on presentation. Also **sight bill.**

sight·ed (sī′tid) *adj.* **1.** Having sight. **2.** Having or characterized by (a specified kind of) sight: used in combination: *nearsighted*.

sight·hole (sīt′hōl′) *n.* A hole to look through; peephole.

sight·less (sīt′lis) *adj.* **1.** Lacking sight; blind. **2.** Invisible. **— sight′less·ly** *adv.* **— sight′less·ness** *n.*

sight·ly (sīt′lē) *adj.* **·li·er, ·li·est 1.** Pleasant to the view; comely. **2.** Affording a fine view. **— sight′li·ness** *n.*

sight-read (sīt′rēd′) *v.t. & v.i.* **-read** (red) **-read·ing** (-rē′ding) To read or perform at sight, as music. **— sight′-read′er** *n.*

sight-see·ing (sīt′sē′ing) *n.* The visiting of places of interest. **— sight′seer** *n.*

sig·il (sij′il) *n.* **1.** A seal or signet. **2.** A mark or sign supposed to exercise occult power. [< L *sigillum* seal]

Sig·is·mund (sij′əs·mənd, sig′-), 1368–1437, Holy Roman Emperor 1411–37.

sig·ma (sig′mə) *n.* **1.** The 18th letter in the Greek alphabet, written Σ (capital), σ (small initial or medial), or ς (small final), and corresponding to English s in *so*. See ALPHABET. **2.** *Math.* The symbol Σ, signifying that the sum is to be taken of a series or sequence following. **3.** Something shaped like a sigma. [< Gk.]

sig·mate (sig′māt) *adj.* Having the shape of the letter S or of sigma.

sig·moid (sig′moid) *adj.* **1.** Shaped like the Greek capital letter sigma (Σ), or like the letter S. **2.** Pertaining to the sigmoid flexure. Also **sig·moi·dal** (sig·moid′l). [< Gk. *sigmoeidēs*]

sigmoid flexure *Anat.* An S-shaped bend in the colon just above the rectum.

Sig·mund (sig′mŏond) In the *Volsunga Saga*, the father of Sigurd. He corresponds to Siegmund in the *Nibelungenlied*.

sign (sīn) *n.* **1.** A motion or action indicating a thought, desire, command, etc. **2.** A board, placard, or representation of any sort, generally bearing an inscription conveying information of some kind: a street *sign*; an advertising *sign*. **3.** Any arbitrary mark, symbol, or token used to indicate a word, etc., or having its own specific meaning: a *sign* of mourning. **4.** Any indication, trace, or evidence of a state, condition, etc.: *signs* of poverty. **5.** Any evidence of a recent presence; a vestige; trace. **6.** *Music* Any mark used in musical notation, as a flat or sharp. **7.** *Math.* A conventional mark to indicate an operation or relation. **8.** Any indicative or significant object, event, or condition: a *sign* of the times. **9.** Any omen, portent, or miraculous occurrence. **10.** One of the twelve equal divisions of the zodiac, named from the constellations that formerly occupied them. **11.** In hunting, a trace left by an animal; spoor. **12.** *Med.* Any objective symptom or other indication of a disease. **— Syn.** See EMBLEM. **—** *v.t.* **1.** To write one's signature or initials on. **2.** *Law* To acknowledge an instrument by affixing a mark or seal to. **3.** To indicate or represent by a sign; stand for. **4.** To mark or consecrate with a sign, especially with a cross. **5.** To engage by obtaining the signature of to a contract: to *sign* a baseball player; also, to hire (oneself) out for work: often with *on*. **6.** To dispose of or transfer title to by signature: with *off*, *over*, or *away*. **7.** To express or indicate with a sign. — *v.i.* **8.** To make signs or signals. **9.** To write one's signature or initials. — **to sign off** *Telecom.* To announce the close of a program from a broadcasting station and stop transmission. — **to sign up** To enlist, as in a branch of military service. [< OF *signe* < L *signum*] — **sign′er** *n.*

sig·nal (sig′nəl) *n.* **1.** A sign or means of communication agreed upon or understood, and used to convey information, a command, etc. **2.** *Telecom.* An electromagnetic impulse that transmits information, whether direct or in code. **3.** Anything that incites to action or movement. **4.** In some card games, a lead or play that conveys certain information to one's partner. **5.** In communication theory, the physical embodiment of a message. — *adj.* **1.** Distinguished by some outstanding characteristic; notable; conspicuous. **2.** Used to signal: a *signal* fire. — *v.* **sig·naled** or **·nalled**, **sig·nal·ing** or **·nal·ling** *v.t.* **1.** To make signals to; inform or notify by signals. **2.** To communicate by signals. — *v.i* **3.** To make a signal or signals. [< F < L *signalis* < *signum* sign] — **sig′nal·er** or **sig′nal·ler** *n.*

Signal Corps A branch of the U.S. Army responsible for the development and operation of communications equipment and systems, photography, electronic reconnaissance devices, and related matters. Abbr. *SigC*

sig·nal·ize (sig′nəl·īz) *v.t.* **·ized**, **·iz·ing** **1.** To render noteworthy. **2.** To point out with care.

sig·nal·ly (sig′nəl·ē) *adv.* In a signal manner; eminently.

sig·nal·man (sig′nəl·mən) *n. pl.* **·men** (-mən) One who makes or interprets signals; especially, one who operates a railroad signal.

sig·nal·ment (sig′nəl·mənt) *n.* A description of a person, as a criminal, for identification. [< F *signalement*]

sig·na·to·ry (sig′nə·tôr′ē, -tō′rē) *adj.* Bound by the terms of a signed document; having signed: *signatory* powers. — *n.* One who has signed or is bound by a document; especially, a nation so bound. [< L *signatorius* < *signatus*, pp. of *signare* to sign < *signum* sign]

sig·na·ture (sig′nə·chər) *n.* **1.** The name of a person, or something representing his name, written, stamped, or inscribed by himself or by deputy, as a sign of agreement or acknowledgment; also, the act of signing one's name. **2.** A distinctive mark, characteristic, etc. **3.** *Printing* **a** A distinguishing mark, letter, or number on the first page of each form or sheet of a book, as a guide to the binder. **b** The form or sheet on which this mark is placed. **c** A large printed sheet that, when folded, forms four, or a multiple of four, pages of a book. **4.** *Music* A symbol or group of symbols at the beginning of a staff, indicating meter or key. **5.** *Telecom.* The musical number or sound effect that introduces or closes a program. **6.** *Med.* The part of a prescription that indicates how the medicine is to be taken, usually preceded by *S.* or *Sig.* Abbr. *sig.*, *Sig.* [< F < Med.L *signatura* < L *signatus.* See SIGNATORY.]

sign·board (sīn′bôrd′, -bōrd′) *n.* A board on which a sign, direction, or advertisement is displayed.

signed number *Math.* A directed number (which see).

sig·net (sig′nit) *n.* **1.** A seal, especially one used to authenticate documents, personal papers, etc. **2.** An impression made by or as by a seal. — *v.t.* To mark or make official with a signet or seal. [< F, dim. of *signe* sign < L *signum.* Doublet of SENNET.]

signet ring A seal ring (which see).

sig·nif·i·cance (sig·nif′ə·kəns) *n.* **1.** The character or state of being significant. **2.** That which is signified or intended to be expressed; meaning. **3.** Importance; consequence. Also **sig·nif′i·can·cy.**

sig·nif·i·cant (sig·nif′ə·kənt) *adj.* **1.** Having or expressing a meaning; bearing or embodying a meaning. **2.** Conveying or having some covert meaning: a *significant* look. **3.** Important; weighty; momentous. — *n.* Something having meaning, as a symbol or token. [< L *significans*, *-antis*, ppr. of *significare* to make a sign, mean < *signum* sign + *facere* to do, make] — **sig·nif′i·cant·ly** *adv.*

sig·ni·fi·ca·tion (sig′nə·fə·kā′shən) *n.* **1.** That which is signified; meaning; sense; import. **2.** The act of signifying; communication.

sig·nif·i·ca·tive (sig·nif′ə·kā′tiv, -kə·tiv) *adj.* **1.** Representing, as a sign; symbolical. **2.** Conveying or tending to convey a meaning; significant.

sig·ni·fy (sig′nə·fī) *v.* **·fied**, **·fy·ing** *v.t.* **1.** To make known by signs or words; express; communicate; announce. **2.** To betoken in any way; import. **3.** To amount to; mean. **4.** To denote (medical use) by signature or markings. — *v.i.* **5.** To have some meaning or importance; matter. — **sig′·ni·fi′er** *n.*

sign language A system of communication by means of signs, largely manual, as the system used by the Plains Indians to communicate with tribes speaking other languages.

sign manual *pl.* **signs manual** A personal signature, especially of a sovereign, as at the top of state papers.

si·gnor (sēn′yôr) *n.* An Anglicized form of the Italian title *signore.* Also **si′gnior.** Abbr. *S.*, *sig.*, *Sig.*

si·gno·ra (sē·nyō′rä) *n. pl.* **·re** (-rā) *Italian* The Italian title of courtesy for a married woman, equivalent to *Mrs.*, *Madam.*

si·gno·re (sē·nyō′rā) *n. pl.* **·ri** (-rē) The Italian title of courtesy for a man, equivalent to *Mr.*, *sir.*

Si·gno·rel·li (sē′nyō·rel′lē), **Luca**, 1441–1523, Italian painter: full name **Luca di Egidio di Ventura de′ Signorelli.**

si·gno·ri·na (sē′nyō·rē′nä) *n. pl.* **·ne** (-nä) The Italian title of courtesy for an unmarried woman, equivalent to the English *Miss.*

si·gno·ri·no (sē′nyō·rē′nō) *n. pl.* **·ni** (-nē) The Italian title of courtesy for a young man, equivalent to *Master.*

si·gno·ry (sēn′yə·rē) See SEIGNIORY.

sign·post (sīn′pōst′) *n.* **1.** A post bearing a sign. **2.** Any sign, clue, or indication.

Sig·urd (sig′ŏŏrd) In Germanic mythology, the hero who slays Fafnir. He corresponds to Siegfried, the hero of the *Nibelungenlied.*

sike (sīk, sik) *n. Scot & Brit. Dial.* A small stream; a rill; also, a gutter: also spelled *syke.* [OE *sīc* streamlet]

sik·er (sik′ər) See SICKER[2].

Sikh (sēk) *n.* One of a religious and military sect founded in India early in the 16th century. — *adj.* Of or pertaining to the Sikhs. [< Hind., lit., disciple]

Sikh·ism (sēk′iz·əm) *n.* The creed and practices of the Sikhs, a monotheistic system that rejects caste and enjoins purity of life and toleration.

Sik·kim (sik′im) An Indian Protectorate in the eastern Himalayas; 2,818 sq. mi.; pop. 191,000 (1971); capital, Gangtok.

Si·kor·sky (si·kôr′skē), **Igor Ivanovich**, 1889–1972, U.S. engineer born in Russia; pioneered the helicopter.

Sik·y·on (sik′ē·on) The Greek name for SICYON.

si·lage (sī′lij) *n.* Ensilage. [< ENSILAGE]

si·le·na·ceous (sī′lə·nā′shəs) *adj.* Caryophyllaceous (def. 1). [< NL *Silene*, a genus of plants < L *Silenus* Silenus + -ACEOUS]

si·lence (sī′ləns) *n.* **1.** The state or quality of being silent; abstinence from speech or noise. **2.** Absence of sound or noise; stillness. **3.** A failure to mention or take note of something. **4.** Oblivion. **5.** Secrecy. **6.** *Music* A rest. — *v.t.* **·lenced**, **·lenc·ing** **1.** To make silent; take away the authority to speak or the power of reply from. **2.** To stop the motion or activity of; quiet. **3.** To force (guns, etc.) to cease firing, as by return fire, bombing, or the like. — *interj.* Be silent. [< F < L *silentium* < *silere* to be silent]

si·lenc·er (sī′lən·sər) *n.* **1.** A tubular device attached to the muzzle of a firearm to reduce the sound of the report. **2.** *Chiefly Brit.* A muffler (def. 1). **3.** One who or that which silences.

si·lent (sī′lənt) *adj.* **1.** Not making any sound or noise; noiseless; still; mute. **2.** Not given to speech; taciturn. **3.** Making no mention or allusion; passing by without notice or record. **4.** Unspoken or unuttered: *silent* grief. **5.** Free from activity, motion, or disturbance; calm; quiet: a *silent* retreat. **6.** Written, but not having phonetic value; not representing a sound; aphonic: said of a letter, as the *b* in *debt.* — **Syn.** See TACITURN. [< L *silens*, *-entis*, ppr. of *silere* to be silent] — **si′lent·ly** *adv.* — **si′lent·ness** *n.*

silent butler A small receptacle with a handle and hinged lid, used for collecting refuse from ashtrays, etc.

silent partner One who has invested money in a business but does not participate in its management or its affairs.

si·le·nus (sī·lē′nəs) *n. pl.* **·ni** (-nī) In Greek mythology, any woodland deity resembling a satyr.

Si·le·nus (sī·lē′nəs) In Greek mythology, the foster father and teacher of Bacchus and leader of the satyrs, traditionally represented as a fat, drunken old satyr riding on an ass. [< L < Gk. *Seilēnos* Silenus]

si·le·sia (si·lē′shə, sī-) *n.* **1.** A glazed linen cloth first made in Silesia. **2.** A thin, twilled cotton fabric for linings.

Si·le·sia (si·lē′shə, sī-) A region of east central Europe divided between Czechoslovakia and Poland; formerly a province of Prussia and a crownland of Austria; about 20,000 sq. mi.: German *Schlesien*, Polish *Śląsk*, Czech *Slezsko.* — **Si·le′sian** *adj. & n.*

si·lex (sī′leks) *n.* **1.** Silica. **2.** Glass that is resistant to heat. [< L, flint]

Si·lex (sī′leks) *n.* A vacuum coffee maker: a trade name. Also **si′lex.**

MAXIM SILENCER
a Socket for attaching to gun. *b* Vortex chamber for gases. *c* Passage groove for bullet.

sil·hou·ette (sil′ōō·et′) *n.* **1.** A profile drawing or portrait having its outline filled in with uniform color, commonly black, and often cut out of paper, etc. **2.** The figure or likeness cast by a shadow; also, the outline of a solid figure. — *v.t.* **·et·ted, ·et·ting** To cause to appear in silhouette; outline; make a silhouette profile of. [after Étienne de *Silhouette*, 1709–67, French minister of finance; in mockery of the petty economies for which he was notorious]

silic- Var. of SILICO-.

sil·i·ca (sil′i·kə) *n.* A white or colorless, very hard, crystalline silicon dioxide, SiO₂, the principal constituent of quartz and sand: also called *silex*. [< NL < L *silex, silicis* flint]

silica gel (jel) A highly adsorbent colloidal silica, used for deodorizing and cleaning air, purifying blast-furnace gases, etc.

sil·i·cate (sil′i·kit) *n. Chem.* A salt or ester of silicic acid.

si·li·ceous (si·lish′əs) *adj.* **1.** Pertaining to, resembling, or containing silica. **2.** Growing or living on soil rich in silica. Also **si·li′cious**. [< L *siliceus* < *silex, silicis* flint]

si·lic·ic (si·lis′ik) *adj.* Of, pertaining to, or derived from silica or silicon. [< SILIC- + -IC]

silicic acid *Chem.* Any of several gelatinous and easily decomposed compounds of silica and water; especially, the ortho form, H₄SiO₄, associated in the formation of many metallic silicates.

sil·i·cide (sil′ə·sīd) *n. Chem.* A binary compound of silicon with a metal.

sil·i·cif·er·ous (sil′ə·sif′ər·əs) *adj.* Containing, producing, or united partially with silica. [< SILIC- + -FEROUS]

si·lic·i·fied wood (si·lis′ə·fīd) Wood that has become quartz but still retains the original form and structure of the wood.

si·lic·i·fy (si·lis′ə·fī) *v.* **·fied, ·fy·ing** *v.t.* **1.** To convert into silica, as wood. — *v.i.* **2.** To become silica, or become impregnated with it. [< SILIC- + -FY] — **si·lic′i·fi·ca′tion** *n.*

sil·i·cle (sil′i·kəl) *n. Bot.* A very short, flat silique. [< L *silicula*, dim. of *siliqua* pod]

silico- *combining form* Silicon; of, related to, or containing silicon. Also, before vowels, *silic-*, as in *silicosis*. [< L *silex, silicis* flint]

sil·i·con (sil′ə·kən, -kon) *n.* A widely distributed nonmetallic element (symbol Si) prepared as a dull brown amorphous powder, as shining metallic scales, or as a steel-gray crystalline mass. See ELEMENT. [< L *silex, silicis* flint]

sil·i·cone (sil′ə·kōn) *n. Chem.* Any of various compounds containing a silicon-carbon bond. Their great physical, chemical, and electrical stability adapts them for many industrial uses as lubricants, greases, insulating resins, waterproofing materials, etc. [< SILICON]

sil·i·co·sis (sil′ə·kō′sis) *n. Pathol.* A pulmonary disease caused by the inhalation of finely powdered silica or quartz.

si·lic·u·lose (si·lik′yə·lōs) *adj.* Siliquose. Also **si·lic′u·lous** (-ləs). [< SILIQUOSE]

si·lique (si·lēk′, sil′ik) *n. Bot.* A narrow, dry, two-valved pod or fruit characteristic of plants of the mustard family. Also **sil·i·qua** (sil′ə·kwə). [< F < L *siliqua* pod]

sil·i·quose (sil′ə·kwōs) *adj.* **1.** Having siliques. **2.** Of, pertaining to, or resembling a silique: also *siliculose*. Also **sil′i·quous** (-kwəs). [< NL *siliquosus* < L *siliqua* pod]

silk (silk) *n.* **1.** The strong, glossy, very fine natural fiber produced by silkworms, the larvae of certain moths, to form cocoons. **2.** A similar filamentous material spun by other insects or arachnids. **3.** Cloth, thread, or garments made of silk. **4.** Anything resembling or suggestive of silk, as the fine soft styles of an ear of corn. — **to hit the silk** *Slang* To descend from an aircraft by parachute. — *adj.* **1.** Consisting of silk. **2.** Resembling silk. **3.** Of or pertaining to silk. — *v.t.* **1.** To clothe or cover with silk: *grand ladies plumed and silked.* — *v.i.* **2.** To produce the portion of the flower called silk: said of corn. [OE *seolc*, ult. < L *sericus* silken, lit., pertaining to the Seres (Chinese), from whom silk was bought. Related to SERGE.]

silk·a·line (sil′kə·lēn′) *n.* A soft and thin mercerized cotton fabric resembling silk. Also **silk′a·lene′**.

silk cotton The silky seed covering of various species of a genus (*Bombax*) of tropical American trees; especially, kapok fiber.

silk-cot·ton tree (silk′kot′n) Any tree producing silk cotton; especially, the kapok tree (which see).

silk·en (sil′kən) *adj.* **1.** Made of silk. **2.** Like silk; glossy; delicate; smooth. **3.** Dressed in silk. **4.** Luxurious.

silk hat A high cylindrical hat covered with fine silk plush, worn by men in dress clothes.

silk-screen process (silk′skrēn′) A stencil process that forces ink through the open meshes of a silk screen on which the desired pattern or design has been imposed, with those parts not to be printed stopped by an impermeable coating.

silk-stock·ing (silk′stok′ing) *adj.* **1.** Wearing silk stockings. **2.** Wealthy; luxurious. — *n.* **1.** One who wears silk stockings; a member of the wealthy class. **2.** A supporter of a branch of the Whig party in the United States in the early 19th century.

silk·weed (silk′wēd′) *n.* Any of several varieties of milkweed.

silk·worm (silk′wûrm′) *n.* The caterpillar of certain moths that spin a dense silken cocoon; especially, the **common silkworm** (*Bombyx mori*), yielding commercial silk.

silk·y (sil′kē) *adj.* **silk·i·er, silk·i·est** **1.** Like silk in any way; soft; lustrous. **2.** Made of or consisting of silk; silken. **3.** Long and fine, as hairs, or covered with such hairs, as leaves. **4.** Gentle or insinuating in manner, usually implying insincerity. — **silk′i·ly** *adv.* — **silk′i·ness** *n.*

silky oak Lacewood.

sill (sil) *n.* **1.** *Archit.* A horizontal, lower member of something, as the bottom of a door or window casing. **2.** A timber in the frame of the floor of a railroad car: end *sill*; side *sill*. **3.** *Geol.* A stratum of igneous rock intruded between level or gently inclined beds of other rock. [OE *syll*]

sil·la·bub (sil′ə·bub) *n.* A dish made by combining milk or cream with wine or cider, which is then whipped into a froth, or made solid by boiling. Also spelled *syllabub*. [Alter. of obs. *sillibouk*]

Sil·lan·pää (sil′län·pa), **Frans Eemil**, 1888–1964, Finnish novelist.

sil·ler (sil′ər) *adj. & n. Scot.* Silver.

Sil·li·man (sil′i·mən), **Benjamin**, 1779–1864, U.S. chemist and geologist.

sil·ly (sil′ē) *adj.* **·li·er, ·li·est** **1.** Destitute of ordinary good sense; foolish; fatuous. **2.** Characterized by or resulting from stupidity; absurd: *silly* talk. **3.** *Rare* Simple; plain; rustic. **4.** *Informal* Stunned; dazed, as by a blow. **5.** *Obs.* or *Brit. Dial.* Frail; feeble; weak. **6.** *Scot.* Idiotic; moronic. **7.** *Obs.* Scanty; meager. — *n. pl.* **·lies** *Informal* A silly person. [OE *sælig* happy] — **sil′li·ly** *adv.* — **sil′li·ness** *n.*

si·lo (sī′lō) *n. pl.* **·los** **1.** A structure, usually a cylindrical pit or tower, in which fodder, grain, or other food is stored green to be fermented and used as feed for cattle, etc. See ENSILAGE. **2.** A similar structure, built underground, for the housing or launching of rockets, guided missiles and the like. — *v.t.* **·loed, ·lo·ing** To put or preserve in a silo; turn into ensilage. [< Sp. < L *sirus* < Gk. *siros* pit for corn]

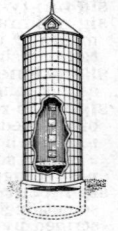

SILO
(Showing interior and pit)

Si·lo·am (si·lō′əm, sī-) A spring and pool outside Jerusalem. *John* ix 7.

silt (silt) *n.* An earthy sediment consisting of fine particles of rock and soil suspended in and carried by water. — *v.i.* **1.** To become filled or choked with silt: usually with *up.* **2.** To ooze; drift. — *v.t.* **3.** To fill or choke with silt or mud: usually with *up.* [ME *cylte*. Cf. Dan. *sylt* salt marsh, Norw. *sylta* coastland washed by the sea.] — **silt′y** *adj.*

Sil·u·res (sil′yə·rēz) *n.pl.* The pre-Celtic inhabitants of ancient Britain, occupying what is now SE Wales, described by Tacitus as of Iberian origin. [< L]

Si·lu·ri·an (si·lŏŏr′ē·ən, sī-) *adj.* **1.** *Geol.* Of or pertaining to the period or rock system of the Paleozoic era following the Ordovician and preceding the Devonian. See chart for GEOLOGY. **2.** Of or pertaining to the Silures. — *n. Geol.* The Silurian period or system.

si·lu·rid (si·lŏŏr′id, sī-) *adj.* Of or pertaining to a large family of fishes (*Siluridae*), the catfishes, including many freshwater food fishes of the United States. — *n.* A silurid fish. Also **si·lu′roid**. [< NL *Siluridae*, name of the family < L *silurus* river fish < Gk. *silouros*]

sil·va (sil′və) *n.pl.* **·vas**, etc. See SYLVA, etc.

Sil·va·nus (sil·vā′nəs) In Roman mythology, a god of woods and farming: also *Sylvanus*. [< L < *silva* forest]

sil·ver (sil′vər) *n.* **1.** A white, ductile, and very malleable metallic element (symbol Ag) of high electric conductivity, crystallizing in the isometric system, found native as well as in combination, and having many uses in medicine, industry, and the arts: also called *argentum*. See ELEMENT. Abbr. *Ar., arg.* **2.** Silver regarded as a commodity or as a standard of currency. **3.** Silver coin; cash or change; money in general. **4.** Articles for domestic use, as tableware, made of silver or silver plate; silverware. **5.** A lustrous, pale gray color characteristic of or resembling that of silver. **6.** *Photog.* Silver nitrate or one of the other salts of silver, used for sensitizing paper. — *adj.* **1.** Made of or coated with silver. **2.** Pertaining to, containing, or producing silver. **3.** Having a silvery lustre. **4.** Having the soft, clear tones of a silver bell. **5.** Persuasive; eloquent: a *silver* tongue. **6.** White or hoary, as the hair or beard. **7.** Favoring the use of silver as a monetary standard. — *v.t.* **1.** To coat or plate with silver. **2.** To coat with some substance having a resemblance to silver; especially, to coat with an amalgam of tin and mercury, as a mirror. **3.** To make silvery; cause to glitter like silver. **4.** To coat, as photographic paper, with a film of a silver salt. — *v.i.* **5.** To become silver or white, as with age; to become silvery. [OE *seolfor*] — **sil′ver·er** *n.*

silver age In classical mythology, the age of Jupiter's rule, succeeding that of Kronos or Saturn.

silver anniversary A 25th anniversary.

silver bell A small tree (*Halesia carolina*) of the southern United States, having bell-shaped white flowers: sometimes called *snowdrop tree*. Also **sil·ver-bell tree** (sil′vər·bel′).

sil·ver·ber·ry (sil′vər·ber′ē) *n. pl.* **·ries** A shrub (*Elaeagnus commutata*) of the northwestern United States, having silvery foliage.

silver bromide *Chem.* A photosensitive compound, AgBr, used in photography.

silver certificate *U.S.* Paper currency representing one dollar in silver bullion on deposit in the U.S. treasury.

silver chloride *Chem.* A white precipitate, AgCl, made by treating silver salts with chloride solutions, used in photography for developing and printing.

sil·ver·fish (sil′vər·fish′) *n. pl.* **·fish** or **·fish·es** 1. A silvery-white goldfish. 2. Any of various fish of silvery appearance, as the tarpon. 3. Any of numerous primitive, wingless insects (genus *Lepisma*), that damage books, papers, etc.: often called *bristletail*. 4. Any of several related insects.

silver fox 1. A color phase of the red fox of North America, having fur that is interspersed with white-tipped hairs. See under FOX. 2. The fur of this animal.

silver gray A light, slightly bluish gray, the color of silver.

sil·ver·ing (sil′vər·ing) *n.* 1. A plating or covering of silver or a similar substance. 2. The art or process of coating surfaces with or as with silver.

silver iodide A pale-yellow powder, AgI, which is insoluble in water and darkens upon exposure to light, used in photography, medicine, and in seeding clouds to produce rain.

sil·ver·ly (sil′vər·lē) *adv.* In silvery tone or manner.

silver maple The white maple (which see).

sil·vern (sil′vərn) *adj. Archaic* or *Poetic* Made of or resembling silver.

silver nitrate *Chem.* A white, crystalline, poisonous compound, AgNO₃, obtained by treating silver with nitric acid, widely used in industry, photography, and medicine.

silver plate Articles, as table utensils, made of silver or metal plated with silver.

silver poplar The white poplar (which see).

sil·ver·sides (sil′vər·sīdz′) *n.* Any of certain small fishes (family *Atherinidae*) related to the mullets, having a silver band along each side of the body; especially, the **Atlantic silversides** (*Menidia notata*) of the coast of the eastern United States: also called *silverfish*. Also **sil′ver·side′**.

sil·ver·smith (sil′vər·smith′) *n.* A worker in silver.

Silver Spring An unincorporated place in western Maryland, near Washington, D.C.; pop. 77,496.

silver standard A monetary standard or system based on silver.

Silver Star A U.S. military decoration, first issued in 1932, awarded for gallantry in action. See DECORATION.

Silver State Nickname of Nevada.

silver thaw *Canadian* A storm of freezing rain; also, glitter ice.

sil·ver-tongued (sil′vər-tungd′) *adj.* Eloquent.

sil·ver·ware (sil′vər-wâr′) *n.* 1. Articles, especially for table use, made of or plated with silver. 2. Table utensils; knives, spoons, and forks.

sil·ver·weed (sil′vər-wēd′) *n.* A perennial herb (*Potentilla anserina*) of the rose family, having leaves silvery on the underside: also called *goosegrass*.

sil·ver·y (sil′vər·ē) *adj.* 1. Containing or adorned with silver. 2. Resembling silver, as in luster or hue. 3. Soft and clear in sound. — **sil′ver·i·ness** *n.*

sil·vi·cul·ture (sil′vi·kul′chər) *n.* The art or process of producing and tending a forest and forest trees. [< F < L *silva* forest + CULTURE] — **sil′vi·cul′tur·al** *adj.* — **sil′vi·cul′tur·al·ly** *adv.* — **sil′vi·cul′tur·ist** *n.*

s'il vous plaît (sēl vōō plě′) *French* If you please; please.

si·ma (sī′mə) *n. Geol.* An igneous rock rich in silica and magnesium underlying sill formations in continental land masses. [< SI(LICA) + MA(GNESIUM)]

si·mar (si·mär′) *n.* A light, flowing robe formerly worn by women: also spelled *cymar*. [< F *simarre* < Ital. *cimarra* < Arabic *simmū̄r* sable]

sim·a·ru·ba (sim′ə·rōō′bə) *n.* Any of a genus (*Simaruba*) of tropical American trees of the quassia family, as *S. amara*, the bark of which is used in pharmacy. Also **sim′a·rou′ba**. [< NL < native Carib name] — **sim′a·ru·ba′ceous** or **sim′a·rou·ba′ceous** *adj.*

Sim·chath To·rah (sim′khäs tō′rə) A Jewish holiday that falls on the 23rd of Tishri and closes the feast of Sukkoth; literally, the rejoicing over the Law. Also **Sim′hath To′rah**.

Sim·e·on (sim′ē·ən) 1. In the New Testament, a devout man who, on seeing Jesus Christ as an infant, spoke the words of the Nunc Dimittis. *Luke* ii 25–32. 2. In the Old Testament, a son of Jacob and Leah. *Gen.* xxix 33. — *n.* The tribe of Israel descended from him.

Simeon Sty·li·tes (stī·lī′tēz), **Saint**, 390?–459, Syrian ascetic; first of the stylites.

Sim·fer·o·pol (syim·fyir-ô′pəly′) The center of the Crimea (Crimean Oblast), in the southern Ukrainian S.S.R.; pop. 250,000 (est. 1970). Also **Simferopol′**.

sim·i·an (sim′ē·ən) *adj.* Pertaining to, resembling, or characteristic of apes and monkeys. — *n.* An ape or monkey. [< L *simia* ape]

sim·i·lar (sim′ə·lər) *adj.* 1. Bearing resemblance to one another or to something else; like, but not completely identical. 2. Of like characteristics, nature, or degree; of the same scope, order, or purpose. 3. *Geom.* Shaped alike, as figures that may become congruent by the alteration of linear dimensions, the angles remaining unchanged. [< F *similaire* < L *similis* like] — **sim′i·lar·ly** *adv.*

sim·i·lar·i·ty (sim′ə·lar′ə·tē) *n. pl.* **·ties** 1. The quality or state of being similar. 2. The point in which the objects being compared are similar. 3. *pl.* Things that coincide with or resemble each other. — **Syn.** See ANALOGY.

sim·i·le (sim′ə·lē) *n.* A figure of speech expressing comparison or likeness by the use of such terms as *like*, *as*, *so*, etc.: distinguished from *metaphor*. [< L, neut. of *similis* similar] — **Syn.** *Simile*, *metaphor*, *comparison*, and *analogy* denote an expression that likens one thing with another. *Simile* is a literary device to conjure up a vivid picture; "an Alpine peak like a frosted cake" is a *simile*. A *metaphor* differs from a *simile* only in omitting "like" or "as", the words of comparison; "the silver pepper of the stars" is a *metaphor*. Both *simile* and *metaphor* assert a common attribute in things otherwise quite dissimilar, whereas a *comparison* brings together things of the same kind or class; "the Hudson River is much like the Rhine" is a *comparison*. The purpose of an *analogy* is to explain, rather than to make vivid; it compares dynamic rather than visual aspects; "an electric current is like the flow of a river, with voltage corresponding to force, volume of water to amperage, etc." is an example of an *analogy*.

si·mil·i·tude (si·mil′ə·tōōd, -tyōōd) *n.* 1. Similarity. 2. One who or that which is similar; a counterpart or likeness. 3. *Rare* A simile; also, a parable. — **Syn.** See ANALOGY. [< OF < L *similitudo* < *similis* like]

sim·i·ous (sim′ē·əs) *adj.* Simian. Also **sim′i·oid**. [See SIMIAN.]

sim·i·tar (sim′ə·tər) See SCIMITAR.

Sim·la (sim′lə) The capital of Himachal Pradesh, India, in a small enclave of Punjab located within the Territory; formerly, summer capital of India; pop. 42,600 (est. 1971).

sim·lin (sim′lin) See CYMLIN.

sim·mer (sim′ər) *v.i.* 1. To boil gently or with a subdued sound; be or stay at or just below the boiling point. 2. To be on the point of breaking forth, as with rage. — *v.t.* 3. To keep at or just below the boiling point. — **to simmer down** 1. To reduce in quantity or liquid content by boiling gently. 2. *Informal* To subside from a state of anger or excitement; become calm. — *n.* The state or process of simmering. [< obs. *simper* to boil; origin unknown; prob. imit.]

Simms (simz), **William Gilmore**, 1806–70, U.S. novelist and poet.

sim·nel (sim′nəl) *n. Brit.* 1. A brittle cake or bread made of fine flour. 2. A rich cake eaten at Easter, Christmas, etc. [< OF *simenel* < LL *siminellus* < L *simila* fine wheat flour, prob. < Gk. *semidalis*, ult. < Babylonian *samidu* fine flour]

si·mo·le·on (si·mō′lē·ən) *n. U.S. Slang* A dollar. [Origin unknown]

Si·mon (sī′mən), **Sir John Allsebrook**, 1873–1954, first viscount Simon, English lawyer and statesman.

si·mo·ni·ac (si·mō′nē·ak) *n.* One who is guilty of simony. [< OF < Med.L *simoniacus*. See SIMONY.] — **sim·o·ni·a·cal** (sim′ə·nī′ə·kəl) *adj.* — **sim′o·ni·a·cal·ly** *adv.*

Si·mo·ni·an (si·mō′nē·ən, sī-) *adj.* Of or pertaining to Simon Magus or his followers. — *n.* One of an early sect that held Simon Magus to be the Messiah.

Si·mon·i·des of Ceos (sī·mon′ə·dēz), 556?–469? B.C., Greek poet.

Simon Le·gree (li·grē′) 1. A cruel overseer of slaves in Harriet Beecher Stowe's *Uncle Tom's Cabin*. 2. Any brutal master.

Simon Ma·gus (mā′gəs) First-century Samarian magician; founder of the Simonians.

Simon Peter See PETER.

si·mon-pure (sī′mən·pyŏŏr′) *adj.* Real; genuine; authentic. [after *Simon Pure*, a character in the comedy *A Bold Stroke for a Wife* (1718), who is impersonated by a rival]

si·mo·ny (sī′mə·nē, sim′ə-) *n.* Traffic in sacred things; the purchase or sale of ecclesiastical preferment. [< Med.L *simonia* < *Simon* (*Magus*), who offered Peter money for the gift of the Holy Spirit] — **si′mon·ist** *n.*

Simon Ze·lo·tes (zē·lō′tēz) One of the twelve apostles: called Simon the Cananaite, Saint Simon.

si·moom (si·mōōm′, sī-) *n. Meteorol.* A hot dry, desert wind full of sand in north Africa, Arabia, etc.: also *samiel*. Also **si·moon′** (-mōōn′). [< Arabic *samūm* < *samma* poison]

simp (simp) *n. U.S. Slang* A simpleton.

sim·pat·i·co (sim·pat′i·kō) *adj. U.S. Informal* 1. Charming; pleasant; congenial. 2. Compatible; sympathetic. [< Ital.]

sim·per (sim′pər) *v.i.* 1. To smile in a silly, self-conscious manner; smirk. — *v.t.* 2. To say with a simper. — *n.* A silly, self-conscious smile; smirk. — **Syn.** See SMILE. [Prob. < Scand. Cf. Sw. and Norw. *semper* affected, coy.] — **sim′per·er** *n.* — **sim′per·ing·ly** *adv.*

SILVER STAR

sim·ple (sim′pəl) *adj.* **·pler, ·plest** **1.** Consisting of one thing; single; uncombined. **2.** Not complex or complicated; easy. **3.** Without embellishment; plain; unadorned. **4.** Free from affectation; sincere; artless. **5.** Of humble rank or condition; lowly. **6.** Of weak intellect; silly; feeble-minded. **7.** Insignificant; trifling. **8.** Lacking luxury; frugal. **9.** Having nothing added; mere: the *simple* truth. **10.** *Chem.* That cannot be or has not been decomposed; elementary; also, unmixed. **11.** *Bot.* Not divided or subdivided; entire: a *simple* leaf. **— Syn.** See INGENUOUS. **—** *n.* **1.** That which is simple; an unartificial, uncomplex, or natural thing. **2.** *Archaic* A medicinal plant, or the medicine extracted from it. **3.** A simpleton. **4.** *Archaic* A person of humble position or birth. [< OF < L *simplex* or *simplus*]
simple fraction *Math.* A fraction in which both numerator and denominator are integers.
simple fracture See under FRACTURE.
simple fruit *Bot.* A fruit produced by the ripening of a single pistil, as the tomato, banana, etc.
simple interest Interest computed on the original principal alone.
simple machine Any of certain elementary mechanical contrivances, as the lever, the wedge, the inclined plane, the screw, the wheel and axle, and the pulley.
sim·ple-mind·ed (sim′pəl·mīn′did) *adj.* **1.** Artless or unsophisticated. **2.** Mentally defective. **3.** Stupid; foolish. **— sim′ple-mind′ed·ly** *adv.* **— sim′ple-mind′ed·ness** *n.*
simple sentence See under SENTENCE.
Simple Simon A foolish fellow in an old English nursery rhyme. **—** *n.* A simpleton.
sim·ple·ton (sim′pəl·tən) *n.* A weak-minded or silly person.
simple vow In the Roman Catholic Church, a vow, as of poverty, chastity, or obedience, taken by a religious for a certain length of time and then renewed. Dispensation from a simple vow can be had without Papal sanction.
sim·plex (sim′pleks) *adj.* **1.** Simple. **2.** Pertaining to or denoting a form of telegraphy in which only one message is sent over a wire at a time. [< L, simple]
simplici- *combining form* Simple. Also, before vowels, **simplic-.** [< L *simplex, simplicis* simple]
sim·pli·ci·den·tate (sim′plə·si·den′tāt) *adj.* Pertaining or belonging to a former suborder (*Simplicidentata*) of rodents having a single pair of upper incisors, as mice, squirrels, etc.
sim·plic·i·ty (sim·plis′ə·tē) *n. pl.* **·ties** **1.** The state of being simple; freedom from admixture, ornament, formality, ostentation, subtlety, or difficulty. **2.** Sincerity; unaffectedness. **3.** Deficiency of intelligence or good sense. [< OF *simplicite* < L *simplicitas, -tatis*]
sim·pli·fy (sim′plə·fī) *v.t.* **·fied, ·fy·ing** To make more simple or less complex. [< F *simplifier* < Med.L *simplificare* < L *simplex* simple + *facere* to make] **— sim′pli·fi·ca′tion** *n.* **— sim′pli·fi′er** *n.*
sim·plism (sim′pliz·əm) *n.* The quality of being simplistic.
sim·plis·tic (sim·plis′tik) *adj.* Tending to ignore or overlook underlying questions, complications, or details; overly simple: *simplistic* attitudes. **— sim·plis′ti·cal·ly** *adv.*
Sim·plon Pass (sim′plon, *Fr.* saṅ·plôṅ′) A pass over the Alps in SW Switzerland; elevation, 6,592 ft.; traversed by a road built by Napoleon; near the **Simplon Tunnel** connecting Switzerland and Italy; length, 12.3 mi.
sim·ply (sim′plē) *adv.* **1.** In a simple manner; intelligibly. **2.** Without ostentation or extravagance. **3.** Without subtlety or affectation; unassumingly **4.** Merely. **5.** Without sense or discretion; foolishly. **6.** Really; absolutely: *simply* charming: sometimes used ironically.
sim·u·la·cre (sim′yə·lā′kər) *n. Obs.* An image.
sim·u·la·crum (sim′yə·lā′krəm) *n. pl.* **·cra** (-krə) **1.** An image. **2.** An imaginary, visionary, or shadowy semblance. **3.** A sham. [< L, image < *simulare*. See SIMULATE.]
sim·u·lant (sim′yə·lənt) *adj.* Simulating. **—** *n.* One who or that which simulates. [< L *simulans, -antis*, ppr. of *simulare*. See SIMULATE.]
sim·u·lar (sim′yə·lər) *n.* One who simulates; a pretender. **—** *adj.* Imitative; counterfeit.
sim·u·late (*v.* sim′yə·lāt; *for adj., also* -lit) *v.t.* **·lat·ed, ·lat·ing** **1.** To assume or have the appearance or form of, without the reality; counterfeit; imitate. **2.** To make a pretense of. **—** *adj.* Simulated; pretended. [< L *simulatus*, pp. of *simulare* to imitate < *similis* like] **— sim′u·la′tor** *n.*
sim·u·la·tion (sim′yə·lā′shən) *n.* **1.** The act of simulating; counterfeit; sham. **2.** The taking on of a particular aspect or form. **— sim′u·la′tive, sim′u·la·to′ry** (-lə·tôr′ē, -tō′rē) *adj.* **— sim′u·la′tive·ly** *adv.*
si·mul·cast (sī′məl·kast′, -käst′) *v.t.* **·cast, ·cast·ing** To broadcast by radio and television simultaneously. **—** *n.* A broadcast transmitted by radio and television simultaneously. [< SIMUL(TANEOUS) + (BROAD)CAST]
si·mul·ta·ne·ous (sī′məl·tā′nē·əs, sim′əl-) *adj.* Occurring, done, or existing at the same time. [< LL *simultaneus* < L *simul* at the same time] **— si′mul·ta·ne·ous·ly** *adv.* **— si′mul·ta·ne·ous·ness, si·mul·ta·ne′i·ty** (-tə·nē′ə·tē) *n.*
simultaneous equations *Math.* A group of algebraic equations such that each is satisfied by the same values of the variables.

sin[1] (sin) *n.* **1.** A transgression, especially when deliberate, of a law having divine authority. **2.** A particular instance of such transgression. **3.** Any fault or error; an offense against a standard: a literary *sin*. **— Syn.** See OFFENSE. **—** *v.* **sinned, sin·ning** *v.i.* **1.** To commit sin; transgress, neglect, or disregard the divine law. **2.** To violate any requirement of right, duty, or propriety; do wrong. **—** *v.t.* **3.** To commit or do wrongfully: to *sin* a great sin. **4.** To effect, cause to have a specified result, etc., by sin. [OE *synn*]
sin[2] (sin) *adv., prep., & conj. Scot. & Brit. Dial.* Since.
sin[3] (sēn) *n.* The twenty-first letter in the Hebrew alphabet. See ALPHABET.
sin *Trig.* Sine.
Si·nai (sī′nī, -nē·ī′) A peninsula between the Mediterranean and the Red Sea, the easternmost part of Egypt. Also **Si·naitic Peninsula.** See map of SUEZ CANAL.
Si·nai (sī′nī, -nē·ī′), **Mount** The mountain where Moses received the law from God, generally identified with a mountain in the southern part of Sinai. *Ex.* xix.
Si·na·lo·a (sē′nä·lō′ä) A State in western Mexico, on the Gulf of California; 22,580 sq. mi.; pop. 1,273,228 (1970); capital, Culiacán.
Sin·an·thro·pus (sin·an′thrə·pəs, sī′nan·thrō′pəs) *n. Paleontol.* A genus of extinct hominid primates identified from fossil remains discovered in the Pleistocene deposits of a cave near Peking, China, and considered by some authorities to be closely related to Pithecanthropus. Also called *Peking man.* [< NL < Gk. *Sinai* Chinese + *anthropos* man]
sin·a·pism (sin′ə·piz′əm) *n.* A mustard plaster. [< L *sinapismus* < Gk. *sinapismos* < *sinapi* mustard]
Sin·ar·quist (sin′är·kwist) *n.* A member of an armed fascist group (*Union Nacional Sinarquista*), formed about 1937 in Mexico with the purpose of establishing an authoritarian clerical state. [< Sp. *sinarquista* < *sinarquismo* < *sin-* (< L *sine*) without + *anarquismo* anarchism] **— Sin′ar·quism** *n.* **— Sin′ar·quis′tic** *adj.*
Sin·bad (sin′bad) See SINDBAD THE SAILOR.
sin bin *Canadian Slang* In hockey, the penalty box.
since (sins) *adv.* **1.** From a past time, mentioned or referred to, up to the present. **2.** At some time between a certain past time or event and the present: He was willing at first, but has *since* refused. **3.** In time before the present; ago; before now. **—** *prep.* **1.** During or within the time after or later than: *since* you left. **2.** Continuously throughout the time after: *since* noon. **—** *conj.* **1.** During or within the time after which. **2.** Continuously from the time when: She has been ill *since* she arrived. **3.** Because of or following upon the fact that; inasmuch as. [ME *sithens* < OE *siththan* afterwards + -*s* (adverbial termination)]
sin·cere (sin·sir′) *adj.* **·cer·er, ·cer·est** **1.** Being in reality as it is in appearance; real; genuine: *sincere* regret. **2.** Free from hypocrisy; honest; faithful: a *sincere* friend. **3.** *Obs.* Being without admixture; pure. **4.** *Obs.* Sound; whole. [< L *sincerus* uncorrupted < *sin-* without + stem of *caries* decay] **— sin·cere′ly** *adv.*
sin·cer·i·ty (sin·ser′ə·tē) *n. pl.* **·ties** The state or quality of being sincere; honesty of purpose or character; freedom from hypocrisy, deceit, or simulation. Also **sin·cere′ness.**
sin·ci·put (sin′si·put) *n. Anat.* The top of the head, especially the anterior portion. [< L < *semi-* half + *caput* head] **— sin·cip·i·tal** (sin·sip′ə·təl) *adj.*
Sin·clair (sin·klâr′), **Upton** (Beall), 1878–1968, U.S. author and socialist: pseudonym **Charles Fitch.**
Sind (sind) A former province of West Pakistan, incorporated into West Pakistan Province, 1955.
Sind·bad the Sailor (sind′bad) In the *Arabian Nights*, a merchant of Baghdad, who relates the marvelous adventures that befell him on his seven voyages. Also called *Sinbad.*
sine[1] (sīn) *n. Trig.* A function of an acute angle, equal to the ratio of the side opposite the angle to the hypotenuse when the angle is included in a right triangle; also, a function of any angle, equal to the ordinate of a point divided by its distance from the origin when the angle is plotted on Cartesian coordinates and the point is on the line forming the angle with the X-axis. For illustration see TRIGONOMETRIC FUNCTIONS. Abbr. *sin* [< L *sinus* a bend (trans. of Arabic *jayb* bosom of a garment, sine). Doublet of SINUS.]
si·ne[2] (sī′nē) *prep. Latin* Without.
si·ne·cure (sī′nə·kyŏŏr, sin′ə-) *n.* **1.** An office or position for which recompense is received, but involving few or no duties. **2.** *Eccl.* A benefice without cure of souls. [< L *sine* without + *cura* care] **— si′ne·cur·ism** *n.* **— si′ne·cur·ist** *n.*
sine curve *Math.* The plane curve of the equation $y = \sin x$: also called *sinusoid.*
si·ne di·e (sī′nē dī′ē) *Latin* Without setting a day for reassembling; literally, without a day. Abbr. *s.d.*
si·ne pro·le (sī′nē prō′lē) *Latin* Without offspring: used in genealogical tables. Abbr. *s.p.*
si·ne qua non (sī′nē kwā non′) *Latin* That which is indispensable; an essential; literally, without which not.
sin·ew (sin′yōō) *n.* **1.** A tendon or similar fibrous cord. **2.** Strength, or that which supplies strength. **—** *v.t.* To strengthen or knit together, as with sinews; supply with sinews. [OE *seono*]

sin·ew·less (sin′yōō·lis) *adj.* **1.** Lacking sinews. **2.** Lacking strength or vigor.

sin·ew·y (sin′yōō·ē) *adj.* **1.** Characteristic or consisting of a sinew or sinews. **2.** Well supplied with sinews; strong; brawny. **3.** Forceful; vigorous: a *sinewy* style.

sin·fo·ni·a (sin·fō′nē·ə, *Ital.* sēn′fō·nē′ä) *n.* **1.** A symphony. **2.** In the Baroque period, an orchestral piece introducing an opera, cantata, etc. [< Ital.]

sin·ful (sin′fəl) *adj.* Characterized by, suggestive of, or tainted with sin; wicked; immoral. [OE *synfull*] — **sin′·ful·ly** *adv.* — **sin′ful·ness** *n.*

sing (sing) *v.* **sang** or (*less commonly*) **sung**, **sung**, **sing·ing** *v.i.* **1.** To produce word sounds that differ from speech in that vowels are lengthened, pitches are clearly defined, and voiceless consonants are minimized. **2.** To use the voice in this manner for musical rendition or performance. **3.** To produce melodious sounds, as a bird. **4.** To produce music with the nuances of fine singing: the violin *sings.* **5.** To make a melodious sound suggestive of singing, as a teakettle, the wind, etc. **6.** To buzz or hum; ring. **7.** To be suitable for singing. **8.** To relate something in verse; compose poetry. **9.** *Slang* To confess the details of a crime, and so implicate others. — *v.t.* **10.** To produce (a tone or tones) with the voice. **11.** To render (a song, etc.) by singing. **12.** To chant, intone, or utter in a songlike manner. **13.** To produce (music) with the nuances of fine singing, as a musical instrument. **14.** To bring to a specified condition by singing: *Sing* me to sleep. **15.** To accompany or escort with songs. **16.** To relate in or as in song; acclaim: they *sing* his fame. — **to sing out** *Informal* To call out loudly; shout. — *n.* **1.** A humming sound, as of a bullet in flight. **2.** *Informal* A gathering for general participation in singing: a community *sing.* [OE *singan*] — **sing′a·ble** *adj.*

sing. Singular.

Si·ngan (sē′ngän′) A former name for SIAN.

Sin·ga·pore (sing′ə·pôr, sing′gə-) An island south of the Malay Peninsula, comprising with adjacent islands an independent member of the British Commonwealth; 225 sq. mi.; pop. about 2 million (est. 1969); capital **Singapore**, a port on **Singapore Strait**.

singe (sinj) *v.t.* **singed**, **singe·ing** **1.** To burn slightly or superficially; discolor by burning; scorch. **2.** To remove bristles or feathers from by passing through flame. **3.** To burn the ends of (hair, etc.). — **Syn.** See BURN[1]. — *n.* **1.** The act of singeing, especially as performed by a barber. **2.** A superficial burn; scorch. [OE *sengan* to scorch, hiss, causative of *singan* sing; from the hissing sound produced]

sing·er[1] (sing′ər) *n.* **1.** One who sings, especially as a profession. **2.** That which produces a songlike utterance, as a songbird. **3.** A poet.

sing·er[2] (sin′jər) *n.* One who or that which singes.

Sing·er (sing′ər) **Isaac Merritt**, 1811–75, U.S. inventor; devised a sewing machine.

Sin·gha·lese (sing′gə·lēz′, -lēs′) *adj.* Of or pertaining to Ceylon, to a people constituting the majority of the inhabitants of Ceylon, or to their language. — *n.* **1.** One of the Singhalese people. **2.** The language of the Singhalese, belonging to the Indic branch of the Indo-Iranian languages, but containing many Dravidian words. Also *Sinhalese.* [< Skt. *Sinhala* Ceylon]

sin·gle (sing′gəl) *adj.* **1.** Consisting of one only; separate; individual. **2.** Having no companion or assistant; alone. **3.** Unmarried. **4.** Pertaining to the unmarried state. **5.** Consisting of only one part; simple; uncompounded. **6.** Unswerving in purpose, intention, etc.; sincere. **7.** Designed for use by only one person or individual: a *single* bed. **8.** Engaged in by individuals in opposition to one another: *single* combat. **9.** *Bot.* **a** Solitary, as a flower when it is the only one on a stem. **b** Having only one row of petals. **10.** *Brit.* Of medium strength; mild; not strong, as ale. — *n.* **1.** One who or that which is single; a unit; individual. **2.** In baseball, a base hit that enables the batter to reach first base. **3.** A hotel room for one person. **4.** A golf match between two players only: opposed to *foursome.* **5.** In cricket, a hit that scores one run. **6.** *pl.* In tennis, etc., a game having one player on each side. — *v.* **·gled**, **·gling** *v.t.* **1.** To choose or select (one) from others: usually with *out.* — *v.i.* **2.** To single-foot, as a horse. **3.** In baseball, to make a one-base hit. [< OF < L *singulus*]

sin·gle-act·ing (sing′gəl·ak′ting) *adj.* Doing effective work in only one direction, as a reciprocating engine or motor.

sin·gle-ac·tion (sing′gəl·ak′shən) *adj.* Designating a type of firearm that must be cocked by a separate action prior to firing.

single bed A bed wide enough for one person.

single blessedness Celibacy.

sin·gle-breast·ed (sing′gəl·bres′tid) *adj.* Having only one thickness of cloth over the breast and fastening in front with a single set of buttons, loops, etc., as a coat or jacket.

sin·gle-cross (sing′gəl·krôs′, -kros′) *n. Genetics* The first generation of a cross between two inbred lines.

single entry A method of bookkeeping in which the daybook and ledger are the essential books, transactions being carried to a single account only. — **sin·gle-en·try** (sing′gəl·en′trē) *adj.*

single file A line of people, animals, etc., disposed one behind the other, with no two abreast.

sin·gle-foot (sing′gəl·fŏŏt′) *n.* The gait of a horse in which the footfall sequence is right hind, right fore, left hind, left fore, the body supported alternately upon one foot and two feet. — *v.i.* To go at this gait. Also *rack.*

sin·gle-hand·ed (sing′gəl·han′did) *adj.* **1.** Having no assistance; unaided. **2.** Having or using but one hand. **3.** Capable of being used with a single hand. **4.** Having only one workman. — **sin′gle-hand′ed·ly** *adv.*

sin·gle-heart·ed (sing′gəl·här′tid) *adj.* Sincere; straightforward; loyal. — **sin′gle-heart′ed·ly** *adv.*

sin·gle man A checker that may be moved only forward.

sin·gle-mind·ed (sing′gəl·mīn′did) *adj.* **1.** Having but one purpose or aim. **2.** Free from duplicity; ingenuous; sincere. — **sin′gle-mind′ed·ly** *adv.* — **sin′gle-mind′ed·ness** *n.*

sin·gle·ness (sing′gəl·nis) *n.* The condition, state, or quality of being single.

sin·gle-phase (sing′gəl·fāz′) *adj. Electr.* Designating an alternating-current circuit having one phase at any given instant. Abbr. *s.p.*

single sideband *Telecom.* Any of several systems of transmission using only one sideband, and thus permitting more channels within a given range of frequencies.

sin·gle·stick (sing′gəl·stik′) *n.* **1.** A cudgel. **2.** A stick with a basket-shaped hilt, used in fencing. **3.** The art or practice of fencing with singlesticks.

sin·gle-stick·er (sing′gəl·stik′ər) *n. Informal* A sloop.

sin·glet (sing′glit) *n. Chiefly Brit.* A woolen or cotton undershirt or jersey.

single tax A tax to be obtained from a single source, especially from a levy on land and natural resources, as a substitute for all other forms of taxation.

sin·gle·ton (sing′gəl·tən) *n.* **1.** In a hand of cards dealt to one player, a single card of a suit. **2.** Any single thing or individual, as distinguished from a pair or larger group.

sin·gle·tree (sing′gəl·trē′) *n.* A whiffletree (which see).

sin·gly (sing′glē) *adv.* **1.** Without companions or associates; alone; unaided, as an individual. **2.** One by one; one at a time. **3.** *Obs.* Sincerely; honestly.

Sing Sing (sing′ sing′) **1.** A State prison near Ossining, New York. **2.** The former name of OSSINING.

sing·song (sing′sông′, -song′) *n.* **1.** Monotonous cadence in speaking or reading. **2.** Inferior verse; doggerel. — *adj.* Monotonous; droning, as verse, speech, etc.

sing·spiel (sing′spēl, *Ger.* zing′shpēl) *n.* **1.** A drama, etc., in which dialogue and song alternate. **2.** Opera in which music is subordinated to words. [< G, lit., sing-play]

sin·gu·lar (sing′gyə·lər) *adj.* **1.** Extraordinary; remarkable; uncommon. **2.** Odd; unconventional; peculiar; not customary or usual. **3.** Representing the only one of its type; unique: a *singular* instance. **4.** *Gram.* Of or designating a word form that denotes one person or thing, or a class considered as a unit: distinguished from *dual, plural.* **5.** *Logic* Embodying something specific or individual; not general: a *singular* idea. — *n. Gram.* The singular number, or a word form having this number. Abbr. (for adj. def. 4, and n.) s., *sing.* [< OF *singuler* < L *singularis* < *singulus* single] — **sin′gu·lar·ly** *adv.* — **sin′gu·lar·ness** *n.*

sin·gu·lar·i·ty (sing′gyə·lar′ə·tē) *n. pl.* **·ties** **1.** The state or quality of being singular. **2.** Something by which a person or thing is distinguished from all or many others; a peculiarity. **3.** Something uncommon or remarkable.

sin·gu·lar·ize (sing′gyə·lə·rīz′) *v.t.* **·ized**, **·iz·ing** To make or designate as singular.

Sin·ha·lese (sin′hə·lēz′, -lēs′) *adj. & n.* Singhalese.

Sin·i·cism (sin′ə·siz′əm) *n.* A custom, usage, etc., peculiar to the Chinese. [< LL *Sinae* the Chinese]

Si·ning (sē′ning′) The capital of Tsinghai Province, China; pop. 250,000 (est. 1970).

sin·is·ter (sin′is·tər) *adj.* **1.** Underhandedly or suspiciously wrong or wicked. **2.** Malevolent; evil. **3.** Boding, tending toward, or attended with disaster; unlucky: often with *to.* **4.** *Rare* Situated on the left side or hand. **5.** *Heraldry* Being on the wearer's left, and hence on the observer's right: opposed to *dexter:* see illustration of ESCUTCHEON. [< F *sinistre* < L *sinister* left] — **sin′is·ter·ly** *adv.* — **sin′is·ter·ness** *n.*

sin·is·tral (sin′is·trəl) *adj.* **1.** Of, pertaining to, or turned toward the left side. **2.** Left-handed. [< OF] — **sin′is·tral·ly** *adv.*

sin·is·trorse (sin′is·trôrs, sin′is·trôrs′) *adj. Bot.* Twining spirally toward the left, as certain climbing plants: opposed to *dextrorse.* Also **sin·is·tror′sal.** [< L *sinistrorsus,* contraction of *sinistroversus* turned toward the left side < *sinister* left + *versum* turned, pp. of *vertere* to turn] — **sin′is·tror′sal·ly** *adv.*

sin·is·trous (sin′is·trəs) *adj.* **1.** Of, pertaining to, or directed toward the left; sinistral. **2.** Sinister; unpropitious; ill-omened. [< L *sinister* left] — **sin′is·trous·ly** *adv.*

sink (singk) *v.* **sank** or (*less commonly*) **sunk, sunk** (*Obs.* **sunk·en**), **sink·ing** *v.i.* **1.** To go beneath the surface or to the bottom, as of a liquid. **2.** To descend to a lower level; go down, especially slowly or by degrees. **3.** To descend toward or below the horizon, as the sun. **4.** To incline downward; slope, as land. **5.** To pass into a specified state: to *sink* into a coma. **6.** To fail, as from ill health or lack of strength; approach death: He's *sinking* fast. **7.** To become less in force, volume, or degree: His voice *sank* to a whisper. **8.** To become less in value, price, etc. **9.** To decline in moral level, prestige, wealth, etc.: to *sink* into vice. **10.** To permeate: The oil *sank* into the wood. **11.** To become hollow; cave in, as the cheeks. **12.** To be impressed or fixed, as in the mind: with *in:* I think that lesson will *sink* in. — *v.t.* **13.** To cause to go beneath the surface or to the bottom. **14.** To cause to fall or drop; lower. **15.** To force or drive into place: to *sink* a fence post. **16.** To make (a mine shaft, well, etc.) by digging or excavating. **17.** To reduce in force, volume, or degree. **18.** To debase or degrade, as one's character or honor. **19.** To suppress, hide, or omit. **20.** To defeat; ruin. **21.** To invest. **22.** To invest and subsequently lose: I *sank* a million in that deal. — *n.* **1.** A box-shaped or basinlike porcelain or metal receptacle with a drainpipe and usually with a water supply. **2.** A cesspool, etc. **3.** A place of corruption and vice. **4.** A natural pool, marsh, or basin in which a river terminates by evaporation or percolation. [OE *sincan*] — **sink′a·ble** *adj.*

sink·er (singk′ər) *n.* **1.** One who or that which sinks, or causes to sink. **2.** A weight for sinking a fishing or sounding line. **3.** In baseball, a pitch that curves sharply downward as it approaches home plate. **4.** *U.S. Slang* A doughnut.

sink·hole (singk′hōl′) *n.* A natural cavity, especially a drainage cavity, as a hole worn by water through a rock along a joint or fracture.

Sin·kiang-Ui·gur Autonomous Region (shin′jyäng′wē′-gŏr′) The westernmost division of China; 635,829 sq. mi.; pop. 5,640,000 (est. 1957); capital, Urumchi (Tihwa): also *Chinese Turkestan.* Formerly **Sinkiang.**

sinking fund A fund established and invested so that its gradual accumulations will wipe out a debt.

sin·less (sin′lis) *adj.* Having no sin; guiltless; innocent. — **sin′less·ly** *adv.* — **sin′less·ness** *n.*

sin·ner (sin′ər) *n.* One who has sinned; especially, one who has transgressed against religious laws or moral principles.

Sinn Fein (shin fān) An Irish political society that originated about 1905, having as its aims both independence and the cultural development of the Irish people. [< Irish, we ourselves] — **Sinn Fein′er** — **Sinn Fein′ism**

Sino- *combining form* Chinese; of or pertaining to the Chinese people, language, etc. Compare CHINO-. [< LL *Sinae* the Chinese]

Sin·o·logue (sin′ə·lôg, -log, sī′nə-) *n.* One who is versed in Sinology. Also **Sin′o·log.** [< SINO- + Gk. *logos* discourse]

Si·nol·o·gy (si·nol′ə·jē, sī-) *n.* The study of the Chinese people, their language, literature, history, culture, etc. — **Sin·o·log·i·cal** (sin′ə·loj′i·kəl, sī′nə-) *adj.* — **Si·nol′o·gist** *n.*

Si·no-Ti·bet·an (sī′nō-ti·bet′n) *n.* A putative family of languages spoken over a wide area in central and SE Asia, comprising the two established subfamilies **Sino-Thai** (sī′nō-tī′) and **Tibeto-Burman:** also called *Indochinese.* — *adj.* Of these languages or the people who speak them.

sin·syne (sin′sīn) *adv. Scot.* Since; ago.

sin·ter (sin′tər) *n.* **1.** Calcareous or siliceous material deposited by springs. **2.** *Metall.* Metal particles made cohesive by sintering. — *v.t. & v.i. Metall.* To make or become cohesive by the combined action of heat and pressure. [< G, dross of iron]

Sint Eu·sta·ti·us (sint ū·stä′tē·ŏŏs) The Dutch name for ST. EUSTATIUS.

Sint Maar·ten (sint mär′tən) The Dutch name for ST. MARTIN.

sin·u·ate (*adj.* sin′yŏŏ·it, -āt; *v.* sin′yŏŏ·āt) *adj.* **1.** Winding in and out; tortuous; sinuous. **2.** *Bot.* Having a wavy or undulating margin: a *sinuate* leaf. Also **sin′u·at·ed.** — *v.i.* **·at·ed, ·at·ing** To curve in and out; turn; wind. [< L *sinuatus,* pp. of *sinuare* to turn, wind < *sinus* curve] — **sin′u·ate·ly** *adv.* — **sin′u·a′tion** *n.*

sin·u·os·i·ty (sin′yŏŏ·os′ə·tē) *n. pl.* **·ties 1.** Sinuous quality. **2.** A bend or series of bends, turns, etc.

sin·u·ous (sin′yŏŏ·əs) *adj.* **1.** Characterized by bends, curves, or folds; winding; undulating. **2.** *Bot.* Sinuate. **3.** Devious; erring. [< L *sinuosus* < *sinus* bend] — **sin′u·ous·ly** *adv.* — **sin′u·ous·ness** *n.*

si·nus (sī′nəs) *n.* **1.** A recess formed by a bending or folding; an opening or cavity. **2.** *Anat.* **a** Any of the air-filled cavities in the cranial bones, communicating with the nostrils. **b** A channel or receptacle for venous blood. **c** A dilated part of a blood vessel. **3.** *Pathol.* Any narrow opening leading to an abscess. **4.** *Bot.* A recess or rounded curve between two projecting lobes or teeth of a leaf. [< L. Doublet of SINE.]

Si·nus Cal·y·do·ni·us (sī′nəs kal′ə·dō′ni·əs, -dōn′yəs) The ancient name for the (Gulf of) PATRAS.

si·nu·si·tis (sī′nə·sī′tis) *n. Pathol.* Inflammation of a sinus or sinuses, especially in the cranial bones. [< SINUS + -ITIS]

si·nu·soid (sī′nyŏŏ·soid, -nə-) *n.* A sine curve. — **si·nu·soi·dal** (sī′nyŏŏ·soid′l, -nə-) *adj.*

sinusoidal projection An equal-area map or map projection in which the parallels and the prime meridian are straight lines and the meridians are sine curves, each with an amplitude proportional to its distance east or west of the prime meridian.

-sion Var. of -TION.

Si·on (sī′ən) See ZION.

Siou·an (sōō′ən) *n.* A large family of North American Indian languages formerly spoken from the west banks of the Mississippi to the Rocky Mountains, and comprising the languages of the Dakota or Sioux tribes proper, as well as those of the Missouri, Winnebago, Crow, etc. — *adj.* Of or pertaining to this family of languages.

Sioux (sōō) *n. pl.* **Sioux** One of a group of North American Indian tribes formerly occupying the Dakotas and parts of Minnesota and Nebraska, and speaking one of the Siouan languages: also called *Dakota.*

Sioux City A port city in western Iowa, on the Missouri River; pop. 85,925.

Sioux Falls A city in SE South Dakota, on the Big Sioux River; pop. 72,488.

sip (sip) *v.* **sipped, sip·ping** *v.t.* **1.** To drink by swallowing small quantities at a time. **2.** To drink from by sips. **3.** To imbibe; absorb. — *v.i.* **4.** To drink in sips. — *n.* **1.** A small amount of liquid swallowed at one time. **2.** The act of sipping. [ME *sippen* < OE *sypian* to absorb]

sipe (sīp) *v.i.* **siped, sip·ing** *Scot.* or *Brit. Dial.* To seep.

si·phon (sī′fən) *n.* **1.** A bent or flexible tube through which liquids may be passed from a higher to a lower level over an intervening elevation by making use of atmospheric pressure. **2.** A siphon bottle. **3.** *Zool.* A tubular structure in certain aquatic animals, as the squid, for drawing in or expelling liquids: for illustration see SQUID. — *v.t.* To draw off or cause to pass through or as through a siphon. — *v.i.* To pass through a siphon. Also spelled *syphon.* [< F < L *sipho, -onis* < Gk. *siphōn*] — **si′phon·al** *adj.*

si·phon·age (sī′fən·ij) *n.* The use or action of a siphon.

siphon bottle A bottle containing aerated or carbonated water that can be expelled by pressure on a valve through a bent tube in the neck of the bottle.

si·pho·no·phore (sī′fə·nə·fôr′, -fōr′, sī·fon′ə-) *n.* Any of an order (*Siphonophora*) of marine organisms consisting of free-swimming colonies of cells, as the Portuguese man-of-war. [< NL *Siphonophora,* name of the order < Gk. *siphōnophoros* tube-carrying < *siphōn* tube + *pherein* to bear]

SIPHON

si·pho·no·stele (sī′fə·nə·stēl′, -stē′lē) *n. Bot.* The hollow, tubular stem of certain plants, as ferns. [< Gk. *siphōn* tube + -STELE]

sip·per (sip′ər) *n.* **1.** One who or that which sips. **2.** A narrow tube of glass, metal, plastic, etc., through which beverages may be drunk.

sip·pet (sip′it) *n.* **1.** A piece of toast or bread used to sop up gravy, sauce, etc. **2.** A very small quantity; bit. [Blend of SIP and SOP in a dim. form]

Si·quei·ros (sē·kā′rōs), **David Alfaro,** born 1898, Mexican painter and muralist.

sir (sûr) *n.* **1.** The conventional term of respectful address to men, used absolutely, and not followed by a proper name. **2.** *Archaic* A title given to a person of rank, an official, a priest, etc.: sometimes used ironically: *sir* herald. **3.** *Obs.* An important or titled person. [< SIRE]

Sir (sûr) *n.* A title of baronets and knights, used before the given name or the full name. Abbr. *Sr.*

Si·ra·cu·sa (sē·rä·kōō′zä) The Italian name for SYRACUSE.

Si·raj-ud-dau·la (sē·räj′ōōd·dou′lə) See SURAJAH DOWLAH.

Sir·bo·ni·an (sər·bō′nē·ən) See SERBONIAN.

sir·dar (sər·där′) *n.* **1.** In India and Oriental countries, a chief or lord. **2.** Formerly, the commander in chief of the army in Egypt. **3.** In India, a head servant, etc. [< Hind. *sardār* leader < *sar* head + *dār* holding]

sire (sīr) *n.* **1.** A father; begetter: sometimes used in combination: *grandsire.* **2.** The male parent of a mammal. **3.** A form of address to a male superior, used in addressing a king or sovereign. **4.** *Obs.* A master; lord; also, a gentleman. — *v.t.* **sired, sir·ing** To beget: now used chiefly of domestic animals. Abbr. *s.* [< OF < L *senior* older. See SENIOR.]

si·ren (sī′rən) *n.* **1.** In Greek legend, one of a group of nymphs living on an island, who lured sailors to destruction by their sweet singing. **2.** A fascinating, dangerous woman.

3. An acoustical device having a perforated rotating disk or disks through which sharp puffs of steam or compressed air are permitted to escape so as to produce a continued musical note or a loud whistle, often used as a warning signal. **4.** *Zool.* Any of a family (*Sirenidae*) of eellike amphibians, as the mud eel. — *adj.* **1.** Of or pertaining to a siren. **2.** Alluring; dangerously fascinating. [< OF < L < Gk. *seirēn*]

si·re·ni·an (sī·rē′nē·ən) *adj.* Of or belonging to an order (*Sirenia*) of fishlike, herbivorous, aquatic mammals, including the manatee, dugong, etc. — *n.* A sirenian mammal: also called *cowfish*. [< NL *Sirenia*, name of the order < L *siren*. See SIREN.]

Si·ret (sē·ret′) A river in west Ukrainian S.S.R. and east Rumania, flowing 270 miles SE to the Danube: also *Sereth*.

Sir·i·us (sir′ē·əs) The brightest star, −1.42 magnitude; Alpha in the constellation Canis Major: also called *Dog Star*. See STAR. [< Gk. *seirios* hot, scorching]

sir·loin (sûr′loin) *n.* A loin of beef, especially the upper portion. [Alter. (after *Sir*, from a legend that the cut was knighted for its excellence) of obs. *surloyn* < OF *surlonge* < *sur-* over, above + *longe* loin < L *lumbus*]

si·roc·co (si·rok′ō) *n.* *pl.* **·cos** *Meteorol.* **1.** A hot, dry, and dusty southerly wind blowing from the African coast to Italy, Sicily, and Spain. **2.** A warm, sultry wind blowing from a warm region toward a center of low barometric pressure. [< Ital. *scirocco* < Arabic *sharq* the east, the rising sun < *sharaqa* to rise]

sir·rah (sir′ə) *n.* *Archaic* Fellow; sir: a term of address expressing contempt or annoyance. [Var. of SIR]

Sir·rah (sir′ə) Alpheratz, a star.

sir-rev·er·ence (sûr·rev′ər·əns) *interj.* *Archaic* Save your reverence; begging your pardon: used as an apology before any unbecoming expression. [Misspelling of *sa' reverence*, contraction of *save (your) reverence*, erroneous trans. of L *salva reverentia* with due regard for decency]

sir·up (sir′əp) See SYRUP.

sir·vente (sêr·vänt′) *n.* A Provençal troubadour lyric that often satirized political and moral themes. [< F < Provençal < L *servens, -entis* ppr. of *servire* to serve]

sis (sis) *n.* *Informal* Sister.

si·sal (sī′səl, sī′zəl, sis′əl, sē′səl) *n.* **1.** A strong fiber obtained from the leaves of an agave (*Agave sisalana*) of the West Indies. **2.** The plant yielding this fiber. Also **sisal grass**, **sisal hemp** [after *Sisal*, town in Yucatán, Mexico]

Sis·er·a (sis′ər·ə) In the Old Testament, a Canaanite chieftain defeated by the Israelites and murdered by Jael. *Judges* iv 2; v 20, 26.

sis·kin (sis′kin) *n.* A finch (genus *Spinus*) related to the goldfinch, as the **European siskin** (*S. spinus*), having green and yellow plumage; also, a pine siskin (which see). [< MDu. *cijsken* < LG *zieske* < Polish *czyżik*, dim. of *czyż* finch]

Sis·ley (sēs·lē′), Alfred, 1830–99, French painter.

Sis·mon·di (sēs·môn·dē′), Jean Charles Léonard Simonde de, 1773–1842, Swiss historian and economist.

sis·si·fied (sis′i·fīd) *adj.* *U.S. Informal* Characteristic of a sissy; effeminate.

sis·sy (sis′ē) *n.* *pl.* **·sies** *U.S. Informal* **1.** An effeminate man or boy; a milksop. **2.** A coward or weakling. [< SIS] — **sis′sy·ish** *adj.*

sis·ter (sis′tər) *n.* **1.** A female having the same parents as another or others of either sex. Daughters of the same parents are **full** or **whole sisters**, while those having only one parent in common are **half sisters**. **2.** A woman or girl allied to another or others by some association: *sisters* in spirit. **3.** Something characterized as female, and closely associated with another of the same kind. **4.** A member of a sisterhood: a nun. **5.** *Brit.* A head nurse in the ward of a hospital; also, popularly, any nurse. *Abbr.* Sr. — *adj.* Bearing the relationship of a sister or one suggestive of sisterhood; sisterly. [OE *sweostor*; infl. by < ON *systir*]

sis·ter-ger·man (sis′tər·jûr′mən) *n.* *pl.* **sis·ters-ger·man** A full sister.

sis·ter·hood (sis′tər·hŏŏd) *n.* **1.** The relationship of or state of being sisters, especially by blood. **2.** A body of women or girls united by some bond of fellowship or sympathy. **3.** A community of women bound by monastic vows or pledged to works of mercy and faith.

sis·ter-in-law (sis′tər·in·lô′) *n.* *pl.* **sis·ters-in-law** **1.** A sister of a husband or wife. **2.** A brother's wife. **3.** The wife of a wife's or husband's brother.

sis·ter·ly (sis′tər·lē) *adj.* Of or characteristic of a sister; affectionate. — *adv.* As a sister. — **sis′ter·li·ness** *n.*

Sis·tine (sis′tēn, -tin) *adj.* Of or pertaining to one of the Popes named Sixtus: also *Sixtine*. [< Ital. *Sistino* < *Sisto* < L *sextus* sixth]

Sistine Chapel The principal chapel in the Vatican Palace at Rome, constructed for Sixtus IV, and decorated with frescoes by Michelangelo and others.

Sistine Madonna The Madonna painted by Raphael for the Church of St. Sixtus in Piacenza, Italy.

sis·troid (sis′troid) *adj.* *Geom.* Included within the convex

sides of two intersecting curves: said of an angle and opposed to *cissoid*. [< SISTR(UM) + -OID]

sis·trum (sis′trəm) *n.* *pl.* **·tra** (-trə) or **·trums** A metal rattle used as a musical instrument in the worship of Isis in ancient Egypt. [< L < Gk. *seistron* < *seiein* to shake]

SISTRUM

Sis·y·phe·an (sis′ə·fē′ən) *adj.* **1.** Of or pertaining to Sisyphus. **2.** Difficult and interminable: a *Sisyphean* task.

Sis·y·phus (sis′ə·fəs) In Greek mythology, a crafty, greedy king of Corinth, condemned in Hades forever to roll uphill a huge stone that always rolled down again.

sit (sit) *v.* **sat** (*Archaic* **sate**), **sat**, **sit·ting** *v.i.* **1.** To rest with the buttocks on a supporting surface, with the body bent at the hips, and the spine nearly vertical. **2.** To occupy a chair, bench, etc., in such a position. **3.** To perch or roost, as a bird; also, to cover eggs so as to give warmth for hatching. **4.** To be or remain in a seated or settled position. **5.** To remain passive or inactive, or in a position of idleness or rest. **6.** To assume an attitude or take a position for a special purpose; pose, as for a portrait. **7.** To meet in assembly for deliberation or business; hold a session. **8.** To occupy or be entitled to a seat in a deliberative body. **9.** To have or exercise judicial authority. **10.** To fit or be adjusted; suit: That hat *sits* well. **11.** To be suffered or borne, as a burden. **12.** To be situated or located; be in some position or direction: The wind *sits* in the east. **13.** To baby-sit; serve as company for someone ill, etc. — *v.t.* **14.** To have or keep a seat or a good seat upon: to *sit* a horse. **15.** To seat (oneself, etc.): *Sit* yourself down. — **to sit in** (on) *U.S.* To join or take part. — **sit on** (or **upon**) **1.** To belong to (a jury, commission, etc.) as a member. **2.** To hold discussions about and look into carefully, as a case. **3.** *Informal* To suppress or squelch. — **to sit out** **1.** To sit or remain quietly till the end of: to *sit out* an entertainment. **2.** To sit aside during: They *sat out* a dance. **3.** To stay longer than. — **to sit tight** *Informal* To wait for the next move; stay put. [OE *sittan*]

si·tar (si·tär′) *n.* A stringed instrument used in Hindu music, somewhat resembling the guitar. [< Hind. *sitār*]

sit-down strike (sit′doun′) A strike during which strikers refuse to leave their place of employment until agreement is reached. Also **sit′-down′**.

site (sīt) *n.* **1.** Place of location. **2.** A plot of ground set apart for some specific use. [< F < L *situs* position]

sith (sith) *adv., prep., & conj.* *Archaic* Since. [OE *sith-than* after]

sit-in (sit′in′) *n.* A demonstration of protest, as by Negroes in the southern United States, in which participants enter and remain seated in a public place, commercial establishment, etc., from which they are customarily excluded.

Sit·ka (sit′kə) A town in SE Alaska, on Baranof Island; site of a U.S. naval base; pop. 3,370.

sito- *combining form* Food. [< Gk. *sitos* food]

si·tos·ter·ol (sī·tos′tə·rōl, -rol) *n.* *Biochem.* Any of a group of sterols found in higher plants and related to cholesterol, especially the *alpha* form, $C_{29}H_{43}O$, from wheat, corn, and beans. [< SITO- + STEROL]

Si·tsang (sē′tsäng′) The Chinese name for TIBET.

sit·ter (sit′ər) *n.* **1.** One who sits. **2.** A baby sitter (which see). **3.** A person posing as a model. **4.** A setting hen.

Sit·ter (sit′ər), **Willem de**, 1872–1934, Dutch astronomer.

sit·ting (sit′ing) *adj.* **1.** Being in a seated position. **2.** Used for sitting: *sitting* room. — *n.* **1.** The act or position of one who sits. **2.** A seat; also, the place of or the right to a seat. **3.** A single period of remaining seated for a specific purpose. **4.** A session or term. **5.** A period of hatching. **6.** The number of eggs on which a bird sits at one incubation.

Sitting Bull, 1834?–90, Sioux Indian chief; defeated Custer at the battle of Little Big Horn, 1876.

sitting duck **1.** A duck resting on water, and therefore an easy target for a hunter. **2.** *Informal* Any easy target.

sitting room A parlor; living room.

sit·u·ate (sich′ŏŏ·āt; *for adj.*, also sich′ŏŏ·it) *v.t.* **·at·ed**, **·at·ing** **1.** To fix a site for; locate. **2.** To place in a certain position or under certain conditions or circumstances. — *adj.* *Archaic* Situated. [< Med.L *situatus*, pp. of *situare* to place < *situs* a place]

sit·u·at·ed (sich′ŏŏ·ā′tid) *adj.* **1.** Having a fixed place or location; placed. **2.** Placed in (usually specified) circumstances or conditions: He is *well* situated.

sit·u·a·tion (sich′ŏŏ·ā′shən) *n.* **1.** Condition as modified or determined by surroundings or attendant circumstances; status. **2.** A combination of circumstances, often leading to a complication, climax, or crisis. **3.** The place in which something is situated; relative local position; locality. **4.** A salaried post of employment, usually subordinate. — *Syn.* See CIRCUMSTANCE. [< MF < Med.L *situatio, onis* < *situare*] — **sit·u·a′tion·al** *adj.*

situation comedy Comedy whose effect arises from the

complex involvement of the characters in a ludicrous situation or predicament.

si·tus (sī′təs) *n. pl.* **·ti** (-tī) **1.** Site; situation; place. **2.** A fitting or natural position, as of a part or organ. [< L]

Sit·well (sit′wel, -wəl) An English literary family, notably **Edith,** 1887–1964, and her brothers, **Sir Osbert,** 1892–1969, and **Sacheverell,** born 1897, poets, critics, and essayists.

sitz bath (sits) **1.** A small bathtub in which one bathes in a sitting posture. **2.** A bath taken in such a tub. Also called *hip bath.* [< G *sitzbad*]

sitz·mark (sits′märk′) *n. Informal* A pit or furrow in the snow left by a skier who has fallen backward. [< G *sitzmarke*]

Si·va (sē′və, shē′-) The Hindu god of destruction and reproduction, forming with Brahma and Vishnu the Hindu trinity: also *Shiva.* [< Hind. *Shiva* < Skt. *śivás* propitious]

Si·va·ism (sē′və-iz′əm, shē′-) *n.* The worship of Siva. — **Si′va·ist** *n.* — **Si′va·is′tic** *adj.*

Si·van (sē-vän′) *n.* The ninth month of the Hebrew year. See (Hebrew) CALENDAR. Also **Si·wan′** (-vän′)

Si·vas (sē-väs′) A city in central Turkey; pop. 108,320 (1965).

si·ver (sī′vər) *n. Scot.* An open drain; sewer.

Si·wash (sī′wosh) *n.* **1.** *U.S. & Canadian* An Indian of the northern Pacific coast: an offensive term. **2.** *U.S. Informal* Any small, rural college having a limited outlook and range of studies: used ironically or contemptuously. [< Chinook jargon < dial. F (Canadian) *sauvage* savage]

six (siks) *n.* **1.** The sum of five and one: a cardinal number. **2.** Any symbol of this number, as 6, vi, VI. **3.** Anything consisting of or representing six units, as a team, playing card, etc. — **at sixes and sevens 1.** In a state of confusion. **2.** At odds; estranged. — **six of one, half-dozen of another** A situation offering no obvious choice; the same on both sides; a toss-up. — *adj.* Being one more than five. [OE]

Six Nations The Five Nations plus the Tuscarora, who joined them in the 18th century. Also **Six Allied Nations.**

six·pence (siks′pəns) *n.* A British silver coin of the value of six pennies, equivalent to half a shilling.

six·pen·ny (siks′pen′ē, -pən·ē) *adj.* **1.** Worth, valued at, or sold for sixpence. **2.** Paltry; trashy. **3.** Denoting a size of nails. See -PENNY.

six-shoot·er (siks′shoo′tər) *n. Informal* A revolver that may be fired six times without reloading.

sixte (sikst) *n.* In fencing, a parry in which the foil is carried to the right at breast level. [< F < L *sextus* sixth]

six·teen (siks′tēn′) *n.* **1.** The sum of fifteen and one: a cardinal number. **2.** Any symbol of this number, as 16, xvi, XVI. **3.** Anything consisting of or representing sixteen units, as an organization, game token, etc. — *adj.* Being one more than fifteen. [OE *sixtȳne*]

six·teen·mo (siks·tēn′mō) *adj. & n.* Sextodecimo. [English reading of *16mo.*]

six·teenth (siks′tēnth′) *adj.* **1.** Next after the fifteenth: the ordinal of *sixteen.* **2.** Being one of sixteen equal parts. — *n.* **1.** One of sixteen equal parts. **2.** That which is numbered sixteen.

sixteenth note *Music* A note having one sixteenth the time value of a whole note: also, *chiefly Brit., semiquaver.* For illustration see NOTE.

sixth (siksth) *adj.* **1.** Next after the fifth: the ordinal of *six.* **2.** Being one of six equal parts. — *n.* **1.** One of six equal parts. **2.** That which follows the fifth. **3.** *Music* **a** The interval between any tone and another tone five steps from it in the diatonic scale. **b** A tone separated by this interval from any other, considered with reference to that other; especially, the sixth above the keynote. For illustration see INTERVAL. — *adv.* In the sixth order, place, or rank: also, in formal discourse, **sixth′ly.** [OE *sixta*: refashioned to conform to *fourth*]

sixth chord *Music* A chord consisting of a triad whose middle tone is played or written as the lowest note.

sixth sense Intuitive perception supposedly independent of the five senses.

six·ti·eth (siks′tē·ith) *adj.* **1.** Tenth in order after the fiftieth: the ordinal of *sixty.* **2.** Being one of sixty equal parts. — *n.* **1.** One of sixty equal parts. **2.** That which is tenth in order after the fiftieth. [OE *sixteogotha*]

Six·tine (siks′tēn, -tin) *adj.* Sistine.

Six·tus IV (siks′təs), 1414–84, pope 1471–84: original name **Francesco del·la Ro·ve·re** (del′lä rō′vā·rä)

Sixtus V, 1521–90, pope 1585–90: original name **Felice Pe·ret·ti** (pā·ret′tē)

six·ty (siks′tē) *n. pl.* **·ties 1.** The sum of fifty and ten: a cardinal number. **2.** Any symbol of this number, as 60, lx, LX. **3.** Anything consisting of or representing sixty units. — *adj.* Being ten more than fifty. [OE *sixtig*]

sixty-four dollar question *U.S. Informal* A very decisive question, upon which much depends.

six·ty-fourth note (siks′tē-fôrth′, -fôrth′) *Music* A note having one sixty-fourth the time value of a whole note: also, *chiefly Brit., hemidemisemiquaver.* For illustration see NOTE.

siz·a·ble (sī′zə-bəl) *adj.* Of comparatively large size. Also **size′a·ble.** — **siz′a·ble·ness** *n.* — **siz′a·bly** *adv.*

siz·ar (sī′zər) *n.* At Cambridge University, England, and Trinity College, Dublin, a student receiving financial assistance from the University, and formerly required to perform menial services. [< SIZE¹ (def. 7)] — **siz′ar·ship** *n.*

size¹ (sīz) *n.* **1.** Measurement or extent of a thing as compared with some standard. **2.** Comparative magnitude or bulk; relative largeness. **3.** One of a series of graded measures, as of hats, shoes, etc. **4.** A standard of measurement; specified quantity. **5.** Mental caliber; importance; character. **6.** *Informal* State of affairs; true situation: That's the *size* of it. **7.** *Obs.* A quantity of provisions, as for a university student. — *v.t.* **sized, siz·ing 1.** To estimate the size of. **2.** To distribute or classify according to size. **3.** To cut or otherwise shape (an article) to the required size. — **to size up** *Informal* **1.** To form an estimate, judgment, or opinion of. **2.** To meet specifications. [< F *assise.* See ASSIZE.]

size² (sīz) *n.* A solution of gelatinous material, usually glue, casein, wax, or clay, used to finish fabrics, glaze paper, coat wall surfaces, etc. — *v.t.* **sized, siz·ing 1.** To treat with size or any similar substance. **2.** To make plastic, as clay. [< OItal. *sisa* painter's glue, aphetic var. of *assisa,* orig., pp. of *assidere* to make sit down < L *assidere.* See ASSIZE.]

sized (sīzd) *adj.* **1.** Being of a definite or specified size: often used in combination: *good-sized.* **2.** Being of a size to fit within or be suitable for: often used in combination: a *pocket-sized* book.

siz·ing (sī′zing) *n.* **1.** Size². **2.** The process of adding or applying size to a fabric, surface, etc.

siz·y (sī′zē) *adj.* **siz·i·er, siz·i·est** Glutinous. [< SIZE²]

siz·zle (siz′əl) *v.i.* **·zled, ·zling 1.** To burn, fry, quench, etc., with or as with a hissing sound; emit a hissing sound under the action of heat. **2.** To be extremely hot. — *n.* A hissing sound as from frying or effervescence. [Imit.]

siz·zler (siz′lər) *n. Informal* Something extremely hot, as a summer day. [< SIZZLE]

S.J. Society of Jesus.

Sjael·land (shel′län) The Danish name for ZEALAND.

sk. Sack.

Ska·gen (skä′gən), **Cape** See (The) SKAW.

Skag·er·rak (skag′ə·rak, *Norw.* skäg′ûr·räk) An inlet of the North Sea between Jutland and Norway; 150 mi. long, 80 to 90 mi. wide. See map of BALTIC SEA.

skald (skôld, skäld) *n.* An ancient Scandinavian poet or minstrel: also spelled *scald.* — **Syn.** See BARD. [< ON] — **skal′dic** *adj.*

skat (skät) *n.* A card game for three players, using thirty-two cards; also, one of the combinations of cards used in this game. [< G, orig. *skart* < Ital. *scartare* to discard]

skate¹ (skāt) *n.* **1.** A boot or shoe fitted with a metal runner to enable the wearer to glide over ice; also, the metal runner and frame secured to the sole of a boot or shoe. **2.** A roller skate (which see). — *v.i.* **skat·ed, skat·ing** To glide or move over ice or some other smooth surface on or as on skates. [< earlier *skates* < Du. *schaats* < OF *escache* stilt < Gmc.]

skate² (skāt) *n.* Any of various rays (genus *Raja*) having large pectoral fins, ventral gill slits, and a pointed snout, as the **barn-door skate** (*R. laevis*) of eastern North America, or the common **gray skate** (*R. batis*) of Europe. [< ON *skata*]

skate³ (skāt) *n. Slang* A fellow. [Origin uncertain]

skat·er (skā′tər) *n.* **1.** One who skates. **2.** The water strider, an insect.

skat·ole (skat′ōl) *n. Chem.* A white, crystalline compound, C_9H_9N, formed in the intestine by the decomposition of proteins. Also **skat′ol.** [< Gk. *skŏr, skatos* dung + -OLE]

Skaw (skô), **The** The northernmost point of Jutland, Denmark: also (*Cape*) *Skagen.*

skean (skēn, skān) *n.* A double-edged dagger or short sword formerly used in Ireland and Scotland. Also **skeen.** [< Irish *sgian* knife]

Skeat (skēt), **W(alter) W(illiam),** 1835–1912, English lexicographer and philologist.

ske·dad·dle (ski-dad′l) *Informal v.i.* **·dled, ·dling** To flee in haste; run away; scamper. — *n.* The act of running away; hasty flight. [Origin unknown]

skee (skē) *n. pl.* **skees** or **skee** A ski. — *v.i.* **skeed, skee·ing** To ski.

skeet (skēt) *n.* A variety of trapshooting in which a succession of targets simulating the flight of birds are fired at from various angles by the shooter. [Ult. < ON *skjota* to shoot]

skeg (skeg) *n. Naut.* **a** The after part of a vessel's keel. **b** A projection on or continuation of it, as for supporting the lower end of the rudder. [< Du. *schegge,* prob. < Scand. Cf. ON *skaga* to project]

skeigh (skekh, skēkh) *Scot. adj.* **1.** Shy. **2.** Proud.

skein (skān) *n.* **1.** A quantity of yarn, thread, etc., wound in a loose, elongated coil. **2.** Something resembling or suggestive of this. **3.** A flight of geese, etc. [< OF *escaigne*]

skein screw A screw with a broad shallow thread. See illustration under SCREW.

skel·e·tal (skel′ə·təl) *adj.* Of, pertaining to, forming, or resembling a skeleton.

skel·e·ton (skel′ə·tən) *n.* **1.** The supporting or protective framework of a human or animal body, consisting of the bones and connective cartilage (endoskeleton) in man and the vertebrates, or of a hard outer structure (exoskeleton), as in crustaceans, insects, etc. **2.** A sketch or outline, as of a written work. **3.** A very thin or emaciated person or animal. **4.** A structure, group, etc., consisting of few parts, reduced numbers, or bare essentials. — **skeleton in the closet** A secret source of shame or discredit. — *adj.* **1.** Consisting merely of a framework, outline, or few parts or members. **2.** Resembling a skeleton in nature or appearance; meager; emaciated. [< NL < Gk. *skeleton* (*sōma*) dried (body), mummy < *skeletos* dried up]

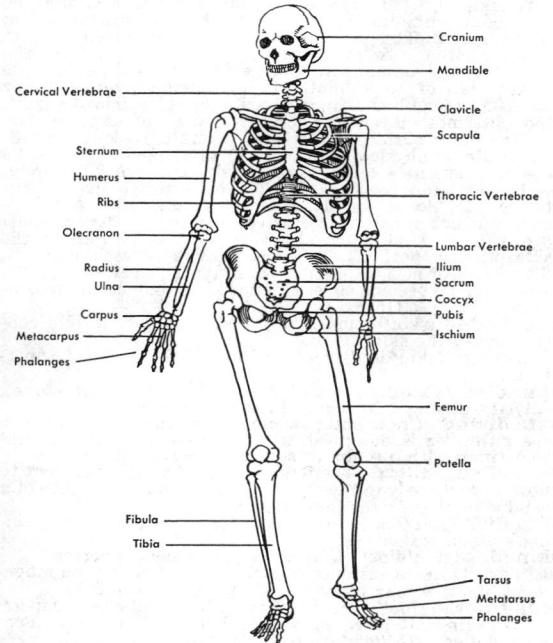

Cervical Vertebrae

Cranium
Mandible
Clavicle
Scapula

Sternum
Humerus
Ribs
Olecranon
Radius
Ulna
Carpus
Metacarpus
Phalanges

Thoracic Vertebrae
Lumbar Vertebrae
Ilium
Sacrum
Coccyx
Pubis
Ischium

Femur

Patella

Fibula
Tibia

Tarsus
Metatarsus
Phalanges

HUMAN SKELETON

skeleton crew   A crew or work force barely sufficient for the job; minimum crew.
skel·e·ton·ize (skel′ə·tən·īz′) *v.t.* **·ized, ·iz·ing 1.** To reduce to a skeleton, framework, or outline by removing soft tissues, extraneous parts, etc. **2.** To reduce greatly in size or numbers. **3.** To draft in outline.
skeleton key   A key filed to a slender shape, and used to open a number of different locks.
skel·lum (skel′əm) *n. Scot.* A scamp.
skelp[1] (skelp) *Brit. Dial. & Scot. v.t.* **1.** To slap with the hand; spank. **2.** To cause to move rapidly. — *v.i.* **3.** To move along quickly. — *n.* A slap.
skelp[2] (skelp) *n.* A strip of iron or steel, especially one from which tubes are made. — *v.t.* To beat out into a skelp, as iron. [Origin unknown]
Skel·ton (skel′tən), **John,** 1460?–1529, English poet, scholar, and clergyman.
skep (skep) *n.* **1.** A beehive, especially one made of straw. **2.** A basket or similar receptacle. [< ON *skeppa* basket]
skep·tic (skep′tik) *n.* **1.** One who doubts, disbelieves, or disagrees with generally accepted conclusions in science, philosophy, etc. **2.** One who by nature doubts or questions what he hears, reads, etc. **3.** One who questions the fundamental doctrines of a religion, especially the Christian religion. **4.** *Sometimes cap.* An adherent of any philosophical school of skepticism. Also spelled *sceptic.* [< F *sceptique* < L *scepticus,* or directly < LGk. *skeptikos* reflective < *skeptesthai* to consider]
  — **Syn.** *Skeptic, freethinker, atheist, unbeliever,* and *agnostic* denote one who denies or doubts some prevailing religious or philosophical creed. *Skeptic* is a general term, and refers to a person who does not feel that the state of human knowledge, or the evidence available, is sufficient to establish the doctrine. A *freethinker* is one who refuses to accept a doctrine, especially a religious doctrine, simply on authority, and demands empiric proof. *Atheist* describes one who denies the existence of God; an *unbeliever* may also lack religious faith, but the word is more often applied to one whose faith is different from that of the speaker. An *agnostic* rejects a doctrine because he believes that human knowledge is, and always will be, incapable of determining its truth or falsity.

Skep·tic (skep′tik) *n.* In ancient Greek philosophy, a member of a school of skepticism, especially that of Pyrrho of Elis. [< SKEPTIC]
skep·ti·cal (skep′ti·kəl) *adj.* **1.** Doubting; questioning; disbelieving. **2.** Of, pertaining to, or characteristic of a skeptic or skepticism. Also spelled *sceptical.* — **skep′ti·cal·ly** *adv.* — **skep′ti·cal·ness** *n.*
skep·ti·cism (skep′tə·siz′əm) *n.* **1.** A doubting or incredulous state of mind; disbelieving attitude. **2.** *Philos.* The doctrine that absolute knowledge is unattainable and that judgments must be continually questioned and doubted in order to attain approximate or relative certainty: opposed to *dogmatism.* Also spelled *scepticism.* — **Syn.** See DOUBT.
sker·ry (sker′ē) *n. pl.* **·ries** *Scot.* An island consisting of a single rock; also, a reef or series of such islands. [< ON *skerr*]
sketch (skech) *n.* **1.** A rapid, incomplete, or hasty delineation or presentation, intended to give a general impression of a work, study, etc., to be completed; an outline. **2.** An artist's rough or rapid drawing or study, often intended for elaboration. **3.** A short, slight, or unpretentious literary or dramatic composition. **4.** A short scene, play, or musical act in a revue, musical comedy, etc. **5.** *Informal* An amusing person; joker. — *v.t.* **1.** To make a sketch or sketches of; outline. — *v.i.* **2.** To make a sketch or sketches. — **to sketch in** To present or explain (details) in a rapid, summary way. — **to sketch out** To present or explain in a rapid, summary way. [< Du. *schets* < Ital. *schizzo* < L *schedium* improvisation < Gk. *schedios*] — **sketch′a·ble** *adj.* — **sketch′er** *n.*
  — **Syn.** (noun) **1.** draft, diagram, plan, skeleton, brief. **2.** cartoon, rough. **4.** skit.
sketch·book (skech′book′) *n.* **1.** A book of paper used for sketching. **2.** A set or collection of literary sketches. Also **sketch book.**
sketch·y (skech′ē) *adj.* **sketch·i·er, sketch·i·est 1.** Resembling or consisting of a sketch; roughly suggested without detail. **2.** Incomplete; superficial; slight. — **sketch′i·ly** *adv.* — **sketch′i·ness** *n.*
skew (skyōō) *v.i.* **1.** To take an oblique direction; move or turn aside; swerve. **2.** To look obliquely or askance; squint. — *v.t.* **3.** To give an oblique position, direction, or form to; make lopsided. **4.** To shift or twist the meaning or significance of; distort. — *adj.* **1.** Placed or turned obliquely; twisted to one side; lopsided. **2.** Distorted in effect or meaning. **3.** Extending further to one side of a median value than to the other; unsymmetrical: a *skew* distribution. — *n.* A deviation from symmetry or straightness; oblique direction or position. [< AF *eskiuer,* OF *eschiuer* to shun < Gmc. Related to ESCHEW.]
skew arch   *Archit.* An arch having its axis in a vertical plane not at right angles with its abutments.
skew·back (skyōō′bak′) *n. Archit.* An abutment with inclined face receiving the thrust of an arch.
skew·bald (skyōō′bôld′) *adj.* Of a horse, etc., having spots of white and another color. [ME *skewed* and *piebald*]
skew·er (skyōō′ər) *n.* **1.** A long pin of wood, or metal, thrust into meat to hold it or keep it in shape while roasting or broiling. **2.** Any of various articles of similar shape or use. — *v.t.* To run through or fasten with or as with a skewer. [Var. of SKIVER]

SKEWBACK (*a*)

skew-gee (skyōō′jē′) *adj. U.S. Dial.* Crooked; lopsided.
skew·ness (skyōō′nis) *n.* **1.** The state of being unsymmetrical or distorted. **2.** *Stat.* **a** The deviation of a frequency distribution curve from a symmetrical form. **b** The amount of such deviation.
ski (skē, *Norw.* shē) *n. pl.* **skis** or **ski** One of a pair of wooden or metal runners about 5 to 7 feet long and 3½ inches wide, with turned-up points, attached to boots or shoes and used in sliding over snow, especially on slopes. — *v.i.* **skied** (skēd), **ski·ing 1.** To glide or travel on skis. **2.** To engage in the sport of gliding over snow-covered inclines on skis. Also spelled *skee.* [< Norw. < ON *skith* snowshoe]
ski·a·gram (skī′ə·gram) *n.* A picture or photograph consisting of shadow forms or outlines; especially, one produced by X-rays. Also **ski′a·graph** (-graf, -gräf). [< Gk. *skia* shadow + -GRAM[1]]
ski·a·scope (skī′ə·skōp) *n. Med.* An instrument for examining the refractive power of the eye by the response of the retina to lights and shadows. [< Gk. *skia* shadow + -SCOPE]
ski·as·co·py (skī·as′kə·pē) *n.* Examination of the eye by the skiascope: also called *retinoscopy.*
skid (skid) *n.* **1.** The act of skidding or slipping. **2.** A small frame or platform upon which merchandise is stacked to be moved about or temporarily stored. **3.** One of a pair of timbers used to support a heavy tilting or rolling object, or a log used as a track in sliding heavy articles about, or forming an inclined plane to ease their descent. **4.** In lum-

bering, one of several logs used to make a skid road or skid-way. **5.** A shoe or drag on a wagon wheel. **6.** *Naut.* Usually *pl.* A fender hung over a vessel's side as protection against rubbing and scraping. **7.** *Aeron.* A runner in an airplane's landing gear. **— on the skids** *U.S. Slang* Rapidly declining in prestige or power. **—** *v.* **skid·ded, skid·ding** *v.i.* **1.** To slide instead of revolving, as a wheel that does not rotate though the vehicle is in motion. **2.** Of a wheel, vehicle, etc., to slide or slip sideways because of loss of traction. **3.** *Aeron.* To move sideways, because of insufficient banking. **—** *v.t.* **4.** To furnish with skids; put, drag, or haul on skids. **5.** To brake or hold back with a skid. [? < ON *skith* piece of wood]

skid·doo (skĭ·dōō′) *interj. Slang* Go away; get out. [< SKEDADDLE]

skid fin *Aeron.* A surface formerly placed above the upper wing of an airplane to improve lateral stability.

skid road **1.** A road or track along which logs are hauled to a skidway, often made of logs laid transversely and spaced about five feet apart. **2.** *U.S. Slang* Skid row.

skid row *U.S. Slang* An urban section inhabited by vagrants and derelicts and consisting mainly of cheap bars, flophouses, etc. [< SKID ROAD; from lumberjack use to indicate a street of bars, brothels, etc.]

skid·way (skĭd′wā′) *n.* A platform or incline made of logs, etc., on which logs are piled before loading.

ski·er (skē′ər) *n.* One who skis.

skiff (skĭf) *n.* A light rowboat or small, open sailing vessel light enough to be rowed with ease. [< F *esquif* < Ital. *schifo* < OHG *scif* ship, boat]

skif·fle (skĭf′əl) *Brit. Slang* n. Folk, jazz, or popular music performed by a group with guitars, one-string upright fiddle-like contrivances, washboards, bottles, and other clangorous devices. **—** *v.i.* **·fled, ·fling** To play skiffle.

ski·ing (skē′ĭng) *n.* The act or sport of one who skis.

ski·jor·ing (skē·jôr′ĭng, -jō′rĭng) *n.* The sport of traveling over ice or snow on skis, towed by a horse or motor vehicle. [< Norw. *skijøring* < *ski* ski + *kjøring* driving]

ski jump **1.** A jump or leap made by a person wearing skis. **2.** A course prepared for making such jumps.

ski lift Any of various devices, usually an endless cable running on towers, with attached bars or chairs, used to transport skiers to the top of a slope or trail.

skill[1] (skĭl) *n.* **1.** Proficiency or technical ability in any art, science, handicraft, etc., demonstrated by ease or expertness in performance, application, etc. **2.** A specific art, trade, or technique. **3.** *Obs.* Understanding. **— Syn.** See ABILITY, DEXTERITY. [< ON *skil* knowledge] **— skill′·less** *adj.*

skill[2] (skĭl) *v.i. Archaic* To matter: usually used impersonally and in the negative. [< ON *skilja* to separate]

skilled (skĭld) *adj.* **1.** Possessing or showing skill; expert; proficient. **2.** Having specialized ability or training, as a worker. **3.** Requiring specialized ability or training, as a job. **— Syn.** See SKILLFUL.

skil·let (skĭl′ĭt) *n.* A frying pan or similar cooking pot having a long handle. [ME *skelet*, ? < OF *esculette* dish or ON *skjóla* pail]

skill·ful (skĭl′fəl) *adj.* **1.** Having skill; clever; dexterous; able. **2.** Characterized by or requiring skill. Also *Brit.* **skil′ful.** **— skill′ful·ly** *adv.* **— skill′ful·ness** *n.*
— Syn. 1. *Skillful, skilled, proficient, adept,* and *expert* mean having the knowledge and experience to do a certain task or type of work well. The *skillful* person owes this ability not only to training, but also to some natural dexterity, ingenuity, or resourcefulness. A *skilled* person has mastered a handicraft or trade; the word generally implies a slightly smaller degree of proficiency than *skillful. Proficient* refers to a high level of competence, especially in some intellectual field: *proficient* in languages. One who is *adept* has a natural gift that has been improved by practice, while *expert* suggests an extraordinary proficiency, combining great skill with thorough knowledge. **— Ant.** unskillful, inept. Compare AWKWARD.

skil·ling (skĭl′ĭng) *n.* A former small copper coin of the Scandinavian countries. [< Dan. and Sw.]

skim (skĭm) *v.* **skimmed, skim·ming** *v.t.* **1.** To remove floating matter from the surface of, as with a ladle: to *skim* milk. **2.** To remove thus: to *skim* cream. **3.** To cover with a thin film, as of ice. **4.** To move lightly and quickly across or over. **5.** To cause to pass swiftly and lightly, as a flat stone across a pond. **6.** To read or glance over hastily or superficially. **—** *v.i.* **7.** To move quickly and lightly across or near a surface; glide. **8.** To make a hasty and superficial perusal; glance: with *over* or *through.* **9.** To become covered with a thin film. **—** *n.* **1.** The act of skimming. **2.** That which has been skimmed, as skim milk. **3.** A thin film or layer. **—** *adj.* Skimmed: *skim* milk. [Var. of SCUM]

skim·ble-scam·ble (skĭm′bəl-skăm′bəl) *adj.* Incoherent; rambling. **—** *n.* Meaningless talk; nonsense. Also **skim′ble-skam′ble.** [Prob. reduplication of dial. *scamble* to scramble]

skim·mer (skĭm′ər) *n.* **1.** A flat ladle or other utensil for skimming. **2.** One who or that which skims. **3.** A ternlike bird (genus *Rhynchops*) having an elongated, bladelike lower mandible with which it skims the surface of the water in feeding, as the **black skimmer** (*R. nigra*) of North America. **4.** A hat having a shallow crown and a wide, round brim.

skim milk Milk from which the cream has been removed: distinguished from *whole milk.*

skim·ming (skĭm′ĭng) *n.* **1.** The act of one who or that which skims. **2.** *Usually pl.* That which is skimmed off.

ski·mo (skē′mō) *n. Canadian Slang* Eskimo

skimp (skĭmp) *v.t. & v.i.* To scrimp or scamp. **—** *adj.* Scant; meager. [Prob. < ON *skemma* to shorten; infl. in meaning by SCRIMP]

skimp·y (skĭm′pē) *adj.* **skimp·i·er, skimp·i·est** **1.** Insufficient in size, amount, etc.; scanty. **2.** Excessively saving or sparing. **— skimp′i·ly** *adv.* **— skimp′i·ness** *n.*

skin (skĭn) *n.* **1.** The membranous tissue covering the body of an animal; the integument. ◆ Collateral adjective: *cutaneous.* **2.** The pelt of a small animal, removed from its body, whether raw or dressed, as distinguished from the hide of a large animal. **3.** A vessel for holding liquids, made of the skin of an animal. **4.** An outside layer, coat, or covering resembling skin, as the rind or epidermis of a fruit, the outermost layer of nacreous matter of a pearl, etc. **5.** The outer surface of a vessel, aircraft, rocket, etc. **6.** One's life or physical existence: to save one's *skin.* **— by the skin of one's teeth** Very closely or narrowly; barely. **— to get under one's skin** **1.** To be provoking or irritating. **2.** To be an obsession. **— under the skin** In a close but not apparent figurative relationship: sisters *under the skin.* **—** *v.* **skinned, skin·ning** *v.t.* **1.** To remove the skin of; flay; peel. **2.** To cover with or as with skin. **3.** To remove or peel off hastily. **4.** *Slang* To cheat or swindle. **—** *v.i.* **5.** To become covered with skin or something resembling skin. [< ON *skinn*]

skin·bound (skĭn′bound′) *adj.* Affected with a rigid contraction of the skin.

skin-deep (skĭn′dēp′) *adj.* Superficial. **—** *adv.* Superficially.

skin-dive (skĭn′dīv′) *v.i.* **-dived** (*U.S. Informal* **-dove**), **-dived, -div·ing** To engage in skin diving.

skin diving Underwater swimming or exploration in which the swimmer is equipped with goggles and flippers, and sometimes with a scuba or snorkel. **— skin diver**

skin effect *Electr.* The tendency of alternating current to flow more densely in the outer layers and on the surface of a conductor than in the inner region.

skin·flick (skĭn′flĭk′) *n. Slang* A motion picture containing nude or sex scenes.

skin·flint (skĭn′flĭnt′) *n.* A miserly, ungenerous person.

skin friction Resistance of air or other fluid to the movement of surfaces in contact with it. Also **skin drag.**

skin·ful (skĭn′fool′) *n. pl.* **-fuls** **1.** The contents or capacity of a skin container. **2.** *Slang* All one can hold, as of alcoholic liquor. **3.** *Slang* All one can endure; bellyful.

skin game **1.** A crooked or rigged gambling game in which the players have no chance. **2.** Any swindle.

skink[1] (skĭngk) *n.* One of a group of lizards (family *Scincidae*) having smooth scales and short limbs, as the **blue-tailed** or **five-lined skink** (*Eumeces fasciatus*) of the United States. [< L *scincos* < Gk. *skinkos* kind of lizard]

skink[2] (skĭngk) *v.t. Brit. Dial.* **1.** To draw or pour out. **2.** To fill with liquor. [< MDu. *schenken*]

skink·er (skĭngk′ər) *n. Brit. Dial.* A bartender or innkeeper. [< SKINK[2]]

skink·ing (skĭngk′ĭng) *adj. Scot.* Thin; watery.

skin·ner (skĭn′ər) *n.* **1.** One who flays or sells the skins of animals. **2.** *U.S. Slang* A mule driver.

Skin·ner (skĭn′ər), *Cornelia Otis,* born 1901, U.S. actress and author. **—** *Otis,* 1858–1942, U.S. actor; father of the preceding.

skin·ny (skĭn′ē) *adj.* **·ni·er, ·ni·est** **1.** Very thin or emaciated; lean. **2.** Consisting of or resembling skin. **— Syn.** See LEAN[2]. **— skin′ni·ness** *n.*

skin·ny-dip (skĭn′ē-dĭp′) *U.S. Slang v.* **-dipped, -dip·ping** *v.i.* To swim in the nude. **—** *n.* A nude swim.

skin·tight (skĭn′tīt′) *adj.* Fitting tightly to the skin, as a garment.

skip (skĭp) *v.* **skipped, skip·ping** *v.i.* **1.** To move with light springing steps; caper. **2.** To bounce over, ricochet from, or skim a surface. **3.** To pass from one point to another omitting or not noticing what lies between. **4.** *Informal* To leave or depart hurriedly; flee. **5.** To be advanced in school beyond the next grade in order. **—** *v.t.* **6.** To leap lightly over. **7.** To cause to skim or ricochet. **8.** To pass over or by; omit. **9.** *Informal* To leave (a place) hurriedly. **—** *n.* **1.** A light bound or spring; especially, a hop alternating between steps in walking. **2.** A passing over without notice. [Prob. < Scand. Cf. Sw. *skuppa* to skip.]

ski pants Long trousers, often with knitted or elasticized cuffs, fitting snugly at the ankles and worn for skiing, etc.

ski patrol Skiers who act as a first-aid and rescue unit.

skip distance *Telecom.* The area within which signals from a radio transmitter are not received, being the distance between the transmitter and the nearest point at which the signals are reflected back to earth.

skip·jack (skĭp′jăk′) *n.* **1.** Any of various fishes that skip along the surface of the water, as the bonito. **2.** One of several tunas (genus *Euthynnus*). **3.** An elaterid beetle.

skip·per[1] (skip'ər) *n.* **1.** One who or that which skips. **2.** Any of a family (*Hesperiidae*) of small butterflies resembling moths in appearance. **3.** The saury, a fish.

skip·per[2] (skip'ər) *n.* **1.** The master or captain of a ship, especially a small vessel. **2.** One in a position of leadership, as the captain of a team, head of an organization, etc. [< Du. *schipper* < *schip* ship]

skip·pet (skip'it) *n.* A round, flat box for containing and protecting the large heavy seal formerly tied to a document. [Dim. of SKEP]

skirl (skûrl, skirl) *Scot. v.i.* **1.** To produce a shrill or shrieking sound, as a bagpipe. — *v.t.* **2.** To play (a bagpipe). — *adj.* Shrill. — *n.* A shrill cry or sound. [Metathetic var. of ME *scrille* < Scand. Cf. Norw. *skrylla*.]

skir·mish (skûr'mish) *v.i.* To fight in a preliminary or desultory way. — *n.* **1.** A light engagement, as between small parties; desultory fighting between opposing forces. **2.** Any encounter or action that evades the main contention or business. — **Syn.** See BATTLE. [< OF *eskermiss-*, stem of *eskermir* to fence, fight < Gmc. Cf. OHG *skirman* to defend < *skirm* shield. Akin to SCRIMMAGE.] — **skir'mish·er** *n.*

skirr (skûr) *v.t.* **1.** To search; scour. **2.** To skim over. — *v.i.* **3.** To move rapidly. — *n.* A whirring sound. [Imit.]

skir·ret (skir'it) *n.* An herb (*Sium sisarum*) of the parsley family, having edible tuberous roots. [ME *skirwhit*, prob. < OF *escheruis* < Arabic *karawya*. Cf. CARAWAY.]

skirt (skûrt) *n.* **1.** The part of a dress, gown, or robe that hangs from the waist downward. **2.** A separate garment hanging from the waist and covering the lower portion of the body. **3.** A margin, border, or outer edge. **4.** *pl.* The border, fringe, or edge of a particular area: on the *skirts* of the town. **5.** One of the flaps or loose, hanging parts of a saddle. **6.** *Slang* A woman or girl. **7.** The diaphragm or midriff of a butchered animal. — *v.t.* **1.** To lie along or form the edge of; to border. **2.** To surround or border: with *with.* **3.** To pass around or about. **4.** To evade or avoid (a subject, issue, etc.) by circumvention. — *v.i.* **5.** To pass or be near the edge or border of something: to *skirt* along the coast. [ON *skyrt* shirt. Akin to SHIRT.]

ski suit An outfit consisting of ski pants and a short, warm jacket, or a similar one-piece garment, worn by skiers, young children, etc.

skit (skit) *n.* **1.** A short, usually humorous dramatic scene or presentation. **2.** A brief, humorous, often satirical piece of writing. **3.** A bantering jest. [< Scand. Cf. ON *skjota* to shoot. akin to SHOOT.]

skite (skīt) *Scot. n.* A quick, sharp slap. — *v.i.* **skit·ed, skit·ing** To glide away quickly; scoot.

ski tow A type of ski lift consisting of an endless rope that skiers cling to as they are hauled up a slope.

skit·ter (skit'ər) *v.i.* **1.** To glide or skim along, touching a surface at intervals. **2.** To fish with a hook twitched along the surface of the water. [Freq. of SKITE]

skit·tish (skit'ish) *adj.* **1.** Easily frightened, as a horse. **2.** Shy; timid. **3.** Capricious; uncertain; unreliable. **4.** Tricky; deceitful. [< dial. E *skit* to caper, as a horse] — **skit'tish·ly** *adv.* — **skit'tish·ness** *n.*

skit·tle (skit'l) *n.* **1.** *pl.* A game of ninepins, in which a flattened ball or thick rounded disk is thrown to knock down the pins. **2.** One of the pins used in this game. — **beer and skittles** Carefree existence; drink and play. [Prob. < Dan *skyttel* a child's earthen ball]

skive[1] (skīv) *v.t.* **skived, skiv·ing** To shave or pare the surface of, as leather. [< ON *skīfa* to slice]

skive[2] (skīv) *n.* A diamond wheel used in cutting gems. [< Du. *schijf*]

skiv·er (skī'vər) *n.* **1.** Thin, split leather, used for bookbinding. **2.** One who skives. **3.** A knife or machine used in skiving. [< SKIVE[1]]

skiv·vy (skiv'ē) *n. pl.* **·vies** *U.S. Slang* **1.** A man's short-sleeved undershirt. Also **skivvy shirt.** **2.** *pl.* Men's underwear. [Origin uncertain]

sklent (sklent) *Scot. v.i.* **1.** To move or be directed slantwise. **2.** To tell a lie. — *n.* **1.** A slant. **2.** A sidelong glance. — *adj.* Slanting.

skoal (skōl) *interj.* To your good health: a toast in drinking, used especially by Scandinavians. [< Scand. Cf. Dan. *skaal* bowl, toast, ON *skāl* bowl.]

Sko·da (skō'dä), **Emil von**, 1839–1900, Czech engineer and industrialist.

Sko·kie (skō'kē) A village in NE Illinois, a suburb of Chicago; pop. 68,627.

skoo·kum (skōō'kəm) *adj. U.S. & Canadian* Large; excellent: used in the Pacific Northwest. [< Chinook jargon]

Skop·lje (skôp'lye) The capital of Macedonia, SE Yugoslavia; pop. 230,000 (est. 1968): Turkish *Üsküb.*

skreigh (skrēkh, skrākh) *Scot. v.i. & v.t.* To shriek; screech. — *n.* A shriek. Also **skreegh.**

Skt. Sanskrit: also **Skr.**

sku·a (skyōō'ə) *n.* A predatory gull-like bird (*Catharacta skua*). [< Faroese *skügver* < ON *skūfr*.]

skul·dug·ger·y (skul·dug'ər·ē) *n. U.S.* Trickery; underhandedness. [Var. of dial. *sculduddery*; origin uncertain]

skulk (skulk) *v.i.* **1.** To move about furtively; lie close or keep hidden. **2.** To shirk; evade work or responsibility. — *n.* **1.** One who skulks. **2.** *Obs.* A group or troop (of foxes). [< Scand. Cf. Dan. *skulke*.] — **skulk'er** *n.*

skull (skul) *n.* **1.** The bony framework of the head of a vertebrate animal; the cranium. **2.** The head considered as the seat of brain; the mind. **3.** A death's-head. [< Scand. Cf. dial. Norw. *skul* shell.]

skull and crossbones A representation of the human skull over two crossed bones, used as a symbol of death, as a warning label on poison, and as an emblem of piracy.

skull·cap (skul'kap') *n.* **1.** A small, snug, brimless cap, often worn indoors. **2.** Any of several herbaceous plants (genus *Scutellaria*) of the mint family, having clusters of bluish violet flowers. **3.** The top of the head.

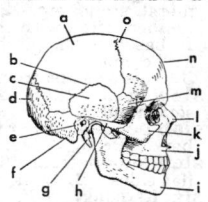

HUMAN SKULL
a Parietal bone. *b* Squamosal suture. *c* Temporal bone. *d* Occipital bone. *e* Ear opening. *f* Mastoid process. *g* Styloid process. *h* Zygomatic arch. *i* Mandible. *j* Maxilla. *k* Malar bone. *l* Nasal bone. *m* Sphenoid bone. *n* Frontal bone. *o* Coronal structure.

skunk (skungk) *n.* **1.** A carnivorous mammal (family *Mustelidae*) of North America, usually black with a white stripe and a bushy tail, and secreting a malodorous liquid ejected at will; especially, the **common** or **striped skunk** (*Mephitis mephitis*), and the **spotted skunk** (genus *Spilogale*) of the United States. **2.** *Informal* A hateful or contemptible person. — *v.t. Slang* To defeat utterly in a game, especially by preventing from scoring. [< Algonquian *seganku*]

skunk cabbage 1. A perennial herb (*Symplocarpus foetidus*) of the arum family, emitting a strong odor, especially when crushed or bruised: also called *swamp cabbage.* **2.** A somewhat similar plant (*Lysichitum americanum*) of western North America. Also **skunk·weed** (skungk'wēd').

sky (skī) *n. pl.* **skies 1.** The region of the upper air seen as a high vault or arch over the earth, on clear days having a characteristic light blue color; the firmament. **2.** *Often pl.* Atmospheric condition or appearance of the upper air: cloudy *skies.* **3.** The celestial regions; heaven. **4.** Climate; weather. **5.** The highest region, range, degree, etc. — *v.t.* **skied, sky·ing** *Informal* **1.** To bat or throw (a ball, etc.) high into the air. **2.** To hang or put (a picture) in a high place [< ON *sky* cloud]

sky blue A blue like the color of the sky. **sky-blue** (skī'blōō') *adj.*

sky·cap (skī'kap') *n. U.S.* A porter for carrying bags at an air terminal.

sky·div·ing (skī'dī'ving) *n.* The sport of parachuting from an airplane.

Skye (skī), **Isle of** The largest of the Inner Hebrides, 670 sq. mi.

Skye terrier A small terrier having a long body, short legs, and long, straight hair.

sky·ey (skī'ē) *adj.* Originating in or resembling the sky.

sky-high (skī'hī') *adj. & adv.* Extremely high.

sky·jack (skī'jak') *v.t. U.S. Slang* To hijack (an airplane) — **sky'jack·ing** *n.*

sky·lark (skī'lärk) *n.* A lark (*Alauda arvensis*) of the Old World that sings as it rises in flight. — *v.i.* To indulge in hilarious or boisterous frolic. — **sky'lark'er** *n.*

sky·light (skī'līt') *n.* A window in a roof or ceiling.

sky·line (skī'līn') *n.* **1.** The line of the visible horizon. **2.** The outline of an object, buildings, etc., against the sky.

sky·man (skī'mən) *n. pl.* **·men** (-mən) *Informal* An aviator.

sky marshal *U.S.* A person employed to ride as a passenger on an airplane to foil any attempt to hijack it.

sky pilot *Slang* A clergyman; especially, a chaplain in the armed forces.

sky·rock·et (skī'rok'it) *n.* A rocket, as in a fireworks display, projected so as to explode high in the air. — *v.i.* To rise rapidly or suddenly.

Sky·ros (skē'ros) An island of Greece, in the Northern Sporades group; 80 sq. mi.: Latin *Scyros.*

sky·sail (skī'səl, -sāl') *n. Naut.* A light sail above the royal in a square-rigged vessel. For illustration see SHIP.

sky·scrap·er (skī'skrā'pər) *n.* A very high building.

sky·ward (skī'wərd) *adv.* Toward the sky. Also **sky'wards.** — *adj.* Moving or directed toward the sky.

sky wave A radio wave that may be reflected back to earth from the ionosphere.

SKUNK
(About 20 inches long; tail 7 inches)

SKYE TERRIER
(10 inches high at shoulder)

sky·way (skī′wā′) *n.* **1.** An air travel route. **2.** An elevated highway.

sky·writ·ing (skī′rī′ting) *n.* **1.** The forming of words in the air by the release of vapor from an airplane. **2.** The words or letters thus formed. — **sky′writ′er** *n.*

s.l. Without place (of publication) (L *sine loco*).

slab[1] (slab) *n.* **1.** A flat plate, piece, mass, or slice, as of metal, stone, etc. **2.** The outside piece of a log sawed for lumber, often with the bark remaining on it. **3.** *U.S. Slang* In baseball, the pitcher's plate. — *v.t.* **slabbed, slab·bing** **1.** To make or form into slabs. **2.** To cover with slabs. **3.** To saw slabs from, as a log. [ME. Origin uncertain.]

slab[2] (slab) *adj.* *Archaic* Thick and viscous. [< ON *slabb* mud]

slab·ber (slab′ər) *v.t. & v.i.* To slobber; drivel. — *n.* Slobber. [Prob. < LG. Cf. Du. *slabberen.*]

slab-sid·ed (slab′sī′did) *adj.* *U.S. Informal* **1.** Having flat sides. **2.** Lanky; gawky; ungainly.

slack[1] (slak) *adj.* **1.** Hanging or extended loosely. **2.** Loose or careless in performance; remiss; slovenly. **3.** Flaccid; loose: a *slack* mouth. **4.** Lacking activity; not busy: a *slack* season. **5.** Listless; limp: a *slack* grip. **6.** Flowing or moving sluggishly, as wind, water between the ebb and flow of the tide, etc. — *v.t.* **1.** To slacken. **2.** To slake, as lime. — *v.i.* **3.** To be or become slack. — **to slack off** To slow down; be less diligent. — *n.* **1.** A part of a rope, sail, etc., that is slack or loose. **2.** Slack condition; looseness. **3.** A period of inactivity, as in a business. **4.** An extent of water where there is no current. — *adv.* In a slack manner. [OE *sleac*] — **slack′ly** *adv.* — **slack′ness** *n.*

slack[2] (slak) *n.* Screenings or small pieces of coal. [Cf. Flemish *slecke*, LG *slacke*]

slack[3] (slak) *n.* *Scot. & Brit. Dial.* **1.** A hollow or dell. **2.** A bog. [< ON *slakki* dip, depression]

slack-baked (slak′bākt′) *adj.* **1.** Not thoroughly cooked; underdone. **2.** Poorly made; imperfect.

slack·en (slak′ən) *v.i.* **1.** To become less active, productive, etc. **2.** To become less tense or tight. **3.** To become slow or less intense. — *v.t.* **4.** To become slow, negligent, or remiss in: to *slacken* one's efforts. **5.** To make slack.

slack·er (slak′ər) *n.* One who shirks his duties or avoids military service in wartime; shirker.

slack-off (slak′ôf′) *n.* *Informal* A slowdown; abatement.

slacks (slaks) *n.pl.* Trousers worn by men or women for casual or sports wear.

slag (slag) *n.* **1.** *Metall.* **a** The fused residue separated in the reduction of metals from their ores. **b** A basic iron silicate that floats on the surface of molten iron. **2.** Volcanic scoria. — *v.t. & v.i.* **slagged, slag·ging** To form into slag. [< MLG *slagge*] — **slag′gy** *adj.*

slag wool Mineral wool (which see).

slain (slān) Past participle of SLAY.

slake (slāk) *v.* **slaked, slak·ing** *v.t.* **1.** To quench or satisfy, as thirst or an appetite. **2.** To lessen the force or intensity of; cause to subside; quell. **3.** To moisten or refresh. **4.** To mix with water or expose to moist air, as in the preparation of slaked lime. **5.** *Obs.* To make loose, slow, or less tense. — *v.i.* **6.** To become disintegrated and hydrated, as lime. **7.** *Rare* To become relaxed, less intense, etc.; slacken. [OE *slacian* to retard < *sleac* slack[1]]

slaked lime See under LIME[1].

sla·lom (slä′lom, slä′-) *n.* In skiing, a race or descent over a winding downhill course laid out between posts and marked with flags. — *v.i.* To ski in such a course. [< Norw.]

slam[1] (slam) *v.* **slammed, slam·ming** *v.t.* **1.** To shut with violence and a loud noise; pull to or push to loudly: to *slam* a door. **2.** To put, dash, throw, etc., violently, often with a loud noise; bang: to *slam* a book down. **3.** *Slang* To hit or strike violently. **4.** *Slang* To disparage or criticize harshly. — *v.i.* **5.** To close, swing, etc., with force and noise. **6.** To make a noisy entrance. — *n.* **1.** A closing or striking with a bang; the act or noise of slamming. **2.** *Slang* Harsh criticism; abuse. [< Scand. Cf. dial. Norw. *slamra* slam.]

slam[2] (slam) *n.* **1.** In bridge, the winning of all (grand slam) or all but one (little or small slam) of the tricks in a round of play; also, a bid to do so. **2.** An old card game.

slam-bang (slam′bang′) *adv.* **1.** Violently; noisily. **2.** Rapidly and recklessly. — *v.i.* To move with noise and violence.

slam·mer (slam′ər) *n.* *Slang* A jail or prison.

slan·der (slan′dər) *n.* **1.** *Law* **a** An oral statement of a false, malicious, or defamatory nature, tending to damage another's reputation, means of livelihood, etc. **b** The utterance of such a statement. Distinguished from *libel*. **2.** A maliciously false tale or report; defamation; calumny. — *v.t.* **1.** To injure by maliciously uttering a false report; defame; calumniate. — *v.i.* **2.** To utter slander. — **Syn.** See ASPERSE. [< AF *esclaundre*, OF *esclandre*, ult. < L *scandalum*. Doublet of SCANDAL.] — **slan′der·er** *n.*

slan·der·ous (slan′dər-əs) *adj.* **1.** Uttering or containing slander. **2.** Characterized by slander; calumnious. — **slan′der·ous·ly** *adv.* — **slan′der·ous·ness** *n.*

slang (slang) *n.* **1.** Language, words, or phrases of a vigorous, colorful, facetious, or taboo nature, invented for specific occasions or uses, or derived from the unconventional use of the standard vocabulary. ◆ The vocabulary of slang, although usually ephemeral, may achieve wide use, and, in the evolution of language, many words originally slang have been adopted by good writers and speakers, and have ultimately taken their place as accepted English. **2.** The special vocabulary of a certain class, group, or profession: college *slang*. **3.** Formerly, the argot or jargon of thieves and vagrants. — **Syn.** See DIALECT. — *v.t.* **1.** To address with slang. **2.** To abuse or talk back to; also, to scold. — *v.i.* **3.** To use slang. [Origin uncertain]

slang·y (slang′ē) *adj.* **slang·i·er, slang·i·est** **1.** Of the nature of or consisting of slang. **2.** Using or characterized by slang. — **slang′i·ly** *adv.* — **slang′i·ness** *n.*

slank (slangk) *Archaic* past tense of SLINK.

slant (slant) *v.t.* **1.** To give an oblique or sloping direction to; turn from the horizontal or vertical; incline. **2.** To write or edit (news or other literary matter) so as to express a special attitude, bias, or opinion. — *v.i.* **3.** To have or take an oblique direction; slope. **4.** To have a certain bias or attitude. — **Syn.** See TIP[1]. — *adj.* Lying at an angle; oblique; sloping. — *n.* **1.** A slanting direction, course, or plane; slope. **2.** A bent, bias, or leaning. **3.** Point of view; attitude. **4.** Glance; look. [< earlier *slent* < Scand. Cf. Norw. *slenta* slope.] — **slant′ing·ly** *adv.*

slant rhyme Near rhyme (which see).

slant·wise (slant′wīz′) *adj.* Slanting; oblique. — *adv.* At a slant or slope; obliquely. Also **slant′ways′** (-wāz′).

slap (slap) *n.* **1.** A blow delivered with the open hand or with something flat. **2.** A sharp rebuke; insult; slur. — **Syn.** See BLOW[2]. — *v.* **slapped, slap·ping** *v.t.* **1.** To hit or strike with the open hand or with something flat. **2.** To rebuff; insult. **3.** To put or place violently or carelessly. — *v.i.* **4.** To strike or beat as if with slaps: The waves *slapped* against the dock. — *adv.* **1.** Suddenly and forcibly; abruptly. **2.** *Informal* Directly; straight: *slap* into his face. [< LG *slapp*] — **slap′per** *n.*

slap·dash (slap′dash′) *adj.* Done or acting in a dashing or reckless way; impetuous; careless. — *n.* Offhand or careless work, behavior, etc. — *adv.* In a careless manner.

slap·hap·py (slap′hap′ē) *adj.* ·pi·er, ·pi·est *Slang* **1.** Dazed or giddy from or as from repeated blows. **2.** Silly; irresponsible. — **slap′hap′pi·ness** *n.*

slap·jack (slap′jak′) *n.* **1.** *U.S.* A griddlecake; flapjack. **2.** A card game played by children.

slap·stick (slap′stik′) *n.* **1.** Boisterous, loud comedy. **2.** A flexible paddle formerly used in farces and pantomimes to make a loud report when an actor was struck with it. — *adj.* Using or suggestive of slapstick: *slapstick* humor.

slash (slash) *v.t.* **1.** To cut by striking violently and without attempt at accuracy; strike violently with or as with an edged instrument. **2.** To strike with long sweeping blows of a whip; lash. **3.** To make long gashes, cuts, or slits in. **4.** To cut slits in, as a garment, so as to expose ornamental material or lining. **5.** To criticize severely; censure harshly. **6.** To cut down wastefully, as timber in a forest. **7.** To curtail sharply, as prices, wages, etc. — *v.i.* **8.** To make sweeping, violent, or haphazard strokes with or as with something sharp. In hockey, to cut with the stick at the body or stick of an opponent. — *n.* **1.** The act or result of slashing. **2.** A sweeping, random cut or stroke, as with a weapon or whip. **3.** A slit or gash. **4.** An ornamental slit or cut in a garment. **5.** An opening or gap left in a forest after logging, a destructive fire, or a high wind. **6.** *Often pl.* A swampy thicket or overgrown bog. **7.** *Printing* A virgule. [? < OF *esclachier* to break] — **slash′er** *n.*

slash·ing (slash′ing) *adj.* **1.** Aggressively or destructively severe; violent: a *slashing* attack. **2.** *Informal* Very fine; splendid. — *n.* **1.** The act of one who or that which slashes. **2.** A slash. — **slash′ing·ly** *adv.*

slash pine **1.** A pine (*Pinus caribaea*) growing in the slashes along the southeastern coast of the United States. **2.** The wood of this tree. **3.** The loblolly pine (which see).

Śląsk (shlônsk) The Polish name for SILESIA.

slat[1] (slat) *n.* **1.** A thin, narrow strip of wood or metal, as one of those in a crate, window blind, etc. **2.** *Aeron.* A movable auxiliary airfoil attached to the leading edge of an airplane wing. — *v.t.* **slat·ted, slat·ting** To provide or make with slats. [< OF *esclat* splinter, chip]

slat[2] (slat) *v.* **slat·ted, slat·ting** *v.t. Dial.* **1.** To throw or dash violently; fling carelessly. **2.** To beat; slap. — *v.i.* **3.** To flap, as sails against yards. — *n. Dial.* A sudden, sharp blow. [? < ON *sletta* to slap]

S.lat. South latitude.

slate[1] (slāt) *n.* **1.** A compact, fine-grained rock that splits readily into thin and even laminae, usually formed by the metamorphosis of shale. **2.** A piece, slab, or plate of slate used for roofing, writing upon, etc. **3.** A record of one's past performance or behavior: a clean *slate*. **4.** A prearranged list, as of political candidates before their nomination or election. **5.** A dull bluish gray color resembling that of slate. — *adj.* **1.** Made of slate. **2.** Having the bluish gray color of slate. — *v.t.* **slat·ed, slat·ing** **1.** To roof with slate. **2.** To put on a political slate or a list of any sort.

3. To designate or mark, as for a specific change in condition. [< OF *esclate*, fem. of *esclat* chip, splinter]

slate[2] (slāt) *v.t.* **slat·ed, slat·ing 1.** To censure or criticize severely. **2.** To punish severely. [? OE *slætan* to bait]

slat·er[1] (slā'tər) *n.* A person whose occupation is to lay slates.

slat·er[2] (slā'tər) *n.* One who censures severely; a caustic critic.

slath·er (slath'ər) *Informal* or *Dial. v.t.* To daub thickly; spend or use profusely; lavish. — *n.pl.* A lot; very much: *slathers* of fun. [Origin uncertain]

slat·ing (slā'ting) *n.* **1.** The act or occupation of laying slates. **2.** Slates or slate collectively. **3.** A liquid for giving a slatelike surface to blackboards, etc.

slat·tern (slat'ərn) *n.* An untidy or slovenly woman. — *adj.* Untidy; slovenly. [< dial. E *slatter* to slop, spill] — **slat'tern·li·ness** *n.* — **slat'tern·ly** *adj. & adv.*

slat·y (slā'tē) *adj.* **slat·i·er, slat·i·est 1.** Consisting of or resembling slate. **2.** Slate-colored.

slaugh·ter (slô'tər) *n.* **1.** The act of killing; especially, the butchering of cattle and other animals for market. **2.** Wanton or savage killing, especially of human beings; massacre; carnage. — **Syn.** See MASSACRE. — *v.t.* **1.** To kill for the market; butcher. **2.** To kill wantonly or savagely, especially in large numbers. [< ON *slātr* butcher's meat. Akin to SLAY.] — **slaugh'ter·er** *n.* — **slaugh'ter·ous** *adj.* — **slaugh'ter·ous·ly** *adv.*

slaugh·ter·house (slô'tər·hous') *n.* A place where animals are butchered; a scene of carnage.

Slav (släv, slav) *n.* A member of any of the Slavic-speaking peoples of northern or eastern Europe, the northern group comprising the Russians, Poles, Czechs, Moravians, Wends, Slovaks, etc., the southeastern group comprising the Bulgarians, Serbians, Croats, and Slovenes. Also, *Obs., Sclav.* [< G *Sklave* < Med.L *Sclavus* < LGk. *Sklabos* < Slavic]

Slav. 1. Slavic. **2.** Slavonian.

slave (slāv) *n.* **1.** One whose person is held as property; a person in slavery; a bondsman; serf. **2.** *Law* A person over whose life, liberty, and property someone has absolute control. **3.** A person in mental or moral subjection to a habit, vice, or influence: a *slave* of tobacco. **4.** One who labors like a slave; a drudge. **5.** A person of slavish disposition; an abject creature. — *v.* **slaved, slav·ing** *v.i.* **1.** To work like a slave; toil; drudge. — *v.t.* **2.** *Rare* To enslave. [< F *esclave* < Med.L *slavus, sclavus,* orig., Slav; because many Slavs were conquered and enslaved] — **Syn.** (noun) **1.** *Slave, bondman, serf, thrall, vassal,* and *peon* denote a person under subjection to another, or under his domination. A *slave* is wholly the property of another; in ancient warfare, captives often became the *slaves* of their conquerors. A *bondman* is bound by a contract to render service to another, but enjoys a degree of liberty denied the *slave*. A *serf* is bound to live and work on a landed estate; he may come under a new master when the estate is sold or inherited. *Thralls* and *vassals* were different types of *bondmen* in the feudal system. *Thralls* were bound to personal service in a household. A *vassal* might be the master of his own business; he owed his lord service in warfare in return for the lord's protection within his domain. *Peon* is usually associated with Spanish-American countries, and refers to a person so ridden by debt or poverty that he is a virtual *serf*. With the passage of slavery in most countries, these words are rarely used in their literal senses, except in historical writing, but they are widely used in extended sense to denote one who is under the dominating influence of another.

slave ant An ant enslaved by members of another species.

Slave Coast The coastal region of Africa extending from the mouths of the Niger to Ghana: named for its former trade in slaves.

slave driver 1. A person hired for or charged with the overseeing of slaves at work. **2.** Any severe or exacting employer.

slave·hold·er (slāv'hōl'dər) *n.* An owner of slaves. — **slave'hold'ing** *adj. & n.*

slav·er[1] (slav'ər) *v.t.* **1.** To dribble saliva over. — *v.i.* **2.** To dribble saliva; drool. — *n.* Saliva issuing or dribbling from the mouth. [Prob. < ON *slafra*] — **slav'er·er** *n.*

slav·er[2] (slā'vər) *n.* **1.** A person or a vessel engaged in the slave trade. **2.** One who procures white slaves.

slav·er·y (slā'vər·ē, slāv'rē) *n.* **1.** Involuntary servitude; especially, the legalized social institution in which human beings are held as property or chattels; complete subjection of one person to another. **2.** Mental, moral, or spiritual bondage. **3.** Slavish toil; drudgery.

slave state Any of the U.S. States where slavery was legal until the end of the Civil War.

slave trade The business of dealing in slaves; especially, the bringing of Negro slaves to America for sale. — **slave trader**

slav·ey (slā'vē, slav'ē) *n. pl.* **slav·eys** *Brit. Informal* A female servant, especially a maid of all work.

Slav·ic (slä'vik, slav'ik) *adj.* Of or pertaining to the Slavs or their languages. — *n.* A branch of the Balto-Slavic

subfamily of the Indo-European language family, consisting of the following groups: **East Slavic** (Russian, including Great Russian, Ukrainian, and Byelorussian); **West Slavic** (Czech, Slovak, Polish, Wendish); **South Slavic** (Serbo-Croatian, Bulgarian, Slovenian, Macedonian). — **Church Slavic** or **Church Slavonic** The liturgical language of the Eastern Orthodox Slavs and of certain Uniats, based largely on South Slavic dialects during the ninth through twelfth centuries: also called *Old Church Slavic, Old Church Slavonic, Old Slavic.* See GLAGOLITIC ALPHABET.

slav·ish (slā'vish) *adj.* **1.** Pertaining to or befitting a slave; servile; base. **2.** Extremely hard or laborious. **3.** Enslaved. — **slav'ish·ly** *adv.* — **slav'ish·ness** *n.*

Slav·ism (slä'viz·əm, slav'iz·əm) *n.* The characteristics or aims of the Slavs, collectively.

Slavo- *combining form* Slavic; of or pertaining to the Slavs: *Slavophobe.* [< SLAV]

slav·oc·ra·cy (släv·ok'rə·sē) *n. pl.* **·cies** Slaveholders or slaveholding interests as a political power, especially for the maintenance of slavery. [< SLAV(E) + -CRACY] — **slav·o·crat** (slä'və·krat) *n.* — **slav'o·crat'ic** *adj.*

Sla·vo·ni·a (slə·vō'nē·ə) A region of Croatia, northern Yugoslavia, between the Sava and Drava rivers. *Serbo-Croatian* **Sla·vo·ni·ja** (slä·vō'nē·yä). — **Sla·vo'ni·an** *adj. & n.*

Sla·von·ic (slə·von'ik) *adj. & n.* Slavic.

slaw (slô) *n.* Cole slaw (which see). [< Du. *sla*, short for *salade* salad]

slay (slā) *v.t.* **slew, slain, slay·ing 1.** To kill, especially by violence; put to death. **2.** *Obs.* To smite; strike. — **Syn.** See KILL[1]. [OE *slēan*] — **slay'er** *n.*

sleave (slēv) *v.t.* **sleaved, sleav·ing** To separate, as a mass of threads; disentangle. — *n.* Something tangled, matted, knotted, or unspun, as silk or thread. [OE *tōslǣfan* to divide]

sleave silk Raw, untwisted silk; floss.

slea·zy (slē'zē, slā'-) *adj.* **·zi·er, ·zi·est 1.** Lacking firmness of texture; poorly made. **2.** Cheap; shoddy; run-down: a *sleazy* waterfront bar. [Origin uncertain] — **slea'zi·ly** *adv.* — **slea'zi·ness** *n.*

sled (sled) *n.* **1.** A vehicle on runners, designed for carrying people or loads over snow and ice; a sledge. **2.** A small, light frame mounted on runners, used especially by children for sliding on snow and ice. — *v.* **sled·ded, sled·ding** *v.t.* **1.** To convey on a sled. — *v.i.* **2.** To ride on or use a sled. [< MLG *sledde*]

sled·der (sled'ər) *n.* **1.** One who rides on or hauls with a sled. **2.** An animal that draws a sled.

sled·ding (sled'ing) *n.* **1.** The condition of roads admitting of the use of sleds. **2.** The act of using a sled; use of sleds in hauling, traveling, etc. **3.** State or circumstances of progress, work, etc.: We have had hard *sledding*.

sledge[1] (slej) *n.* A vehicle mounted on low runners for moving loads; especially, one to be drawn over snow and ice by dogs, horses, or reindeer, or on the ground by draft animals; also, a sled. — *v.t. & v.i.* **sledged, sledg·ing** To travel or convey on a sledge. [< MDu. *sleedse*]

sledge[2] (slej) *n.* A heavy hammer wielded with one or both hands, for blacksmiths' use, or for breaking stone, coal, etc.: also **sledge hammer.** — *v.t.* **sledged, sledg·ing** To hammer, break, or strike with a sledge. [OE *slecg*]

sleek (slēk) *adj.* **1.** Smooth and glossy; polished. **2.** Smooth-spoken; flattering; unctuous; insinuating. — *v.t.* **1.** To make smooth, even, or glossy; polish. **2.** To soothe; mollify; also, to make less disagreeable or offensive. [Var. of SLICK] — **sleek'ly** *adv.* — **sleek'ness** *n.* — **sleek'y** *adj.*

sleek·it (slēk'it) *adj. Scot.* **1.** Sleek. **2.** Deceitful.

sleep (slēp) *n.* **1.** A state or period of reduced physical and nervous activity, accompanied by a suspension of voluntary movements and a complete or partial unconsciousness. **2.** A period of slumber. **3.** Any condition of inactivity, torpor, or rest. — **to go to sleep 1.** To fall asleep. **2.** To become numb, often with a tingling sensation, from retarded circulation of the blood. — *v.* **slept, sleep·ing** *v.i.* **1.** To be or fall asleep; slumber. **2.** To be in a state resembling sleep; to be dormant, inactive or quiet, or to rest in death. **3.** To spin with such velocity as to be without apparent motion, as a top. **4.** *Bot.* To assume a sleeplike appearance during the night, as the petals and leaves of certain plants. — *v.t.* **5.** To rest or repose in: with a cognate object: to *sleep* the sleep of the dead. **6.** To provide with sleeping quarters; lodge: The hotel can *sleep* a hundred guests. — **to sleep away** (or **off** or **out**) To pass or get rid of by or as by sleep: to *sleep off* a hangover. — **to sleep on** To postpone a decision upon. [OE *slǣp*]

sleep·er (slē'pər) *n.* **1.** One who or that which sleeps. **2.** A railroad sleeping car. **3.** A hibernating animal. **4.** In football, a member of the backfield or an end stationed far out at either side before the ball is put in motion. **5.** A heavy beam resting on or in the ground, as a support for a roadway, rails, etc. **6.** *U.S. Informal* A play, motion picture, or book that achieves unexpected and striking success.

sleeping bag A large bag with a warm lining, used for sleeping, especially out of doors.

sleeping car A passenger railroad car with accommodations for sleeping.

sleeping partner *Chiefly Brit.* A silent partner (which see).

sleeping pill *Med.* A sedative; especially, one of the barbiturates taken to relieve acute or persistent insomnia.

sleeping sickness *Pathol.* 1. The final stage of a form of trypanosomiasis prevalent in tropical Africa, marked by nerve degeneration, progressive lethargy, recurrent fever and headaches, terminating in somnolence and death. 2. Encephalitis lethargica.

sleep·less (slēp′lis) *adj.* 1. Unable to sleep. 2. Without sleep; wakeful. — **sleep′less·ly** *adv.* — **sleep′less·ness** *n.*

sleep·walk·ing (slēp′wô′king) *n.* The act or practice of one who walks while asleep. — **sleep′walk′er** *n.*

sleep·y (slē′pē) *adj.* **sleep·i·er, sleep·i·est** 1. Inclined to sleep. 2. Drowsy; sluggish; dull; heavy. 3. Conducive to sleep. — **sleep′i·ly** *adv.* — **sleep′i·ness** *n.*

sleep·y·head (slē′pē·hed′) *n.* A sleepy person. — **sleep′y·head′ed** *adj.*

sleet (slēt) *n.* 1. A mixture of snow or hail and rain. 2. A drizzle or shower of partly frozen rain, or rain that freezes as it falls. 3. A thin coating of ice, as on roads. — *v.i.* To pour or shed sleet. [Akin to MLG *slōte* hail] — **sleet′y** *adj.*

sleeve (slēv) *n.* 1. The part of a garment that serves as a covering for the arm. 2. *Mech.* a A tube surrounding something, as a shaft, for protection or to permit motion of itself or of the shaft. b A short pipe receiving the ends of two other pipes or rods. — **up one's sleeve** Hidden but at hand. — *v.t.* **sleeved, sleev·ing** To furnish or fit with a sleeve or sleeves. [OE *slīefe*] — **sleeve′less** *adj.*

sleigh (slā) *n.* A light vehicle, usually drawn by a horse, with runners for use on snow and ice, used chiefly for pleasure. Compare SLED, SLEDGE[1]. — *v.i.* To ride or travel in a sleigh. [< Du. *slee*, contr. of *slede* sledge] — **sleigh′er** *n.*

SLEIGH

sleigh·ing (slā′ing) *n.* 1. The act of riding in a sleigh. 2. The condition of the snow or ice that admits of using a sleigh.

sleight (slīt) *n.* 1. The quality of being skillful in manipulation; mechanical expertness; skill; dexterity. 2. Craft; cunning. [< ON *slǣgth* slyness]

sleight of hand 1. A juggler's or magician's trick so deftly done that the manner of performance escapes observation: also called *legerdemain.* 2. The performance of such tricks. — **sleight-of-hand** (slīt′ov·hand′) *adj.*

slen·der (slen′dər) *adj.* 1. Having a small diameter or circumference in proportion to the length or height; slim; thin. 2. Having little strength or vigor; feeble; frail; delicate. 3. Having slight basis or foundation; of little validity. 4. Small or inadequate; moderate; insignificant: a *slender* income. 5. Meagerly or insufficiently supplied: a *slender* table. 6. Thin in sound or quality; lacking volume. 7. Formerly, denoting vowels pronounced with a narrow opening above the tongue, as (ē); close. [ME *slendre*, prob. < OF *esclendre*] — **slen′der·ly** *adv.* — **slen′der·ness** *n.*

slen·der·ize (slen′də·rīz) *v.t. & v.i.* **·ized, ·iz·ing** To make or become slender.

slept (slept) Past tense and past participle of SLEEP.

Sle·svig (slās′vikh) The Danish name for SCHLESWIG.

sleuth (slōōth) *n.* 1. *U.S. Informal* A detective. 2. A bloodhound. — *v.t.* 1. To follow; track. — *v.i.* 2. To play the detective. [< ON *slōth* track, trail. Doublet of SLOT[2].]

sleuth·hound (slōōth′hound′) *n.* A bloodhound.

slew[1] (slōō) Past tense of SLAY.

slew[2] (slōō) See SLOUGH[1] (def. 3).

slew[3] (slōō) *n.* *U.S. Informal* A large number, crowd, or amount; a lot: also spelled *slue.* [Cf. Irish *sluagh* crowd]

slew[4] (slōō) See SLUE[1].

Slez·sko (sles′kô) The Czech name for SILESIA.

slice (slīs) *n.* 1. A thin, broad piece cut off from a larger piece: a *slice* of meat. 2. Any of various tools or devices having a broad, flat blade, as for serving fish, removing printing ink, etc. 3. In golf, a stroke that causes the ball to veer to the right; also, the course traveled by the ball. — *v.* **sliced, slic·ing** *v.t.* 1. To cut or remove from a larger piece: often with *off.* 2. To cut into broad, thin pieces; divide; apportion. 3. To sunder, as with a sharp knife; split. 4. To clear out with a slice bar. 5. In golf, to hit (the ball) with a slice. — *v.i.* 6. In golf, to slice a ball. [< OF *esclice* < *esclicer* < OHG *slizan* to slit] — **slic′er** *n.*

slice bar A thin, wide iron tool for cleaning clinkers from the grate bars of a furnace.

slick (slik) *adj.* 1. Smooth; slippery; sleek. 2. Flattering; obsequious; smooth-tongued. 3. *Informal* Dexterously done; cleverly said; specious; tricky. 4. Smart; clever: said of people. 5. Healthy; plump: said of animals. 6. Smooth; oily, as the surface of water. 7. Glazed, as paper; also, printed on glazed paper: *slick* magazines. 8. *Slang* Agreeable; excellent: a *slick* time. — *n.* 1. A smooth place on a surface of water, as from oil; also, a sleek place in the fur or hair of an animal. 2. A broad chisel for paring or slicking: also **slick chisel.** 3. *Usually pl. U.S.* A magazine printed on

glazed paper: distinguished from *pulp.* — *adv. Slang* In a slick or smooth manner; deftly. — *v.t.* 1. To make smooth, trim, glossy, or oily. 2. *Informal* To trim up; make presentable: often with *up.* [ME *slike,* ? < OE *nīgslȳcod* freshly smoothed, glossy]

slick·en·sides (slik′ən·sīdz) *n.pl. Geol.* Polished and scratched or striated rock surfaces, exhibited on the opposed faces of veins or faults where they have moved one upon another. [< *slicken* slick + SIDES] — **slick′en·sid′ed** *adj.* — **slick′en·sid′ing** *n.*

slick·er (slik′ər) *n.* 1. *U.S.* A waterproof overcoat of oilskin, plastic, etc. 2. *Informal* A clever, shifty person. 3. An implement for dressing leather, having a wooden handle.

slide (slīd) *v.* **slid, slid** or **slid·den** (slid′n), **slid·ing** *v.i.* 1. To pass along over a surface with a smooth, slipping movement: to *slide* on ice. 2. To slip off, as scales in shedding. 3. To move easily or smoothly; pass gradually or imperceptibly. 4. To proceed or continue without being acted upon or directed: to let the matter *slide.* 5. *Music* To glide from tone to tone without interrupting the sound. 6. To make a moral slip; err; sin. 7. To lose one's equilibrium or foothold; slip. 8. In baseball, to throw oneself along the ground toward a base, usually feet first, in order to avoid being tagged. — *v.t.* 9. To cause to slide, as over a surface. 10. To move, put, enter, etc., with quietness or dexterity: with *in* or *into.* — *n.* 1. An act of sliding. 2. The slipping of a mass of earth, snow, etc., from a higher to a lower level; avalanche. 3. An inclined plane or channel for sliding, as for children to slide upon, or for sliding goods, etc., to a lower level. 4. A small plate of glass on which a specimen is mounted and examined through a microscope. 5. A small plate of transparent material bearing a single image for projection on a screen. 6. *Photog.* In a camera, the part of a plateholder that covers and uncovers the negative. 7. *Music* a A type of ornament consisting of a series of short notes leading smoothly to a principal note. b A glissando. c In a trumpet or trombone, a U-shaped portion of the tubing that is pushed in and out to vary the pitch. 8. *Mech.* a A sliding part. b A groove, rail, etc., on which something slides. [OE *slīdan*] — **slid′er** *n.*

slide fastener A zipper.

slide·knot (slīd′not′) *n.* A slipknot, particularly one made of two half hitches on a fishing line.

Slide Mountain The highest peak of the Catskill Mountains, in SE New York; 4,204 ft.

slide projector An optical device for projecting magnified images from transparent slides onto a wall or screen: also, *Archaic, magic lantern.*

slide rule A device consisting of a rigid ruler with a central sliding piece, both ruler and slide being graduated in a similar logarithmic scale to permit rapid calculations.

slide trombone See under TROMBONE.

slide valve *Mech.* A valve in the cylinder of a steam engine, regulated to move back and forth over the ports and connect them alternately with the boiler and the exhaust passage, thus imparting reciprocating motion to the piston.

sliding board A children's slide, used in play.

sliding door A door that opens and closes by moving sidewise along grooves or in a track.

sliding scale A schedule affecting imports, prices, or wages, varying under conditions of consumption, demand, or the market price of some article.

sli·er (slī′ər) Alternative comparative of SLY.

sli·est (slī′əst) Alternative superlative of SLY.

slight (slīt) *adj.* 1. Of small importance; trifling. 2. Small in quantity, intensity, or degree; inconsiderable. 3. Slender; frail; delicate; flimsy. 4. Of weak intellect or character. — *v.t.* 1. To manifest neglect of or disregard for; ignore: to *slight* a friend. 2. To omit due care in the doing or performance of; do imperfectly or thoughtlessly; shirk. 3. To treat as trivial or insignificant. — *n.* An act or omission involving failure in courtesy or respect toward another. [ME *slight,* prob. < ON *slettr* smooth < Scand. *sleht-.*] — **slight′ness** *n.* — **Syn.** (verb) 1. *Slight* and *snub* mean to treat discourteously. One *slights* by neglect or omission, but *snubs* by a positive act of disdain. Compare NEGLECT.

slight·ing (slī′ting) *adj.* Conveying, containing, or characterized by a slight: a *slighting* remark. — **slight′ing·ly** *adv.*

slight·ly (slīt′lē) *adv.* 1. In a slight manner; carelessly. 2. To a certain or slight extent; partially.

Sli·go (slī′gō) A county of Connacht Province, NW Ireland; 693 sq. mi.; pop. 53,561 (1966); county seat, **Sligo,** a port on **Sligo Bay,** an inlet of the Atlantic, pop. 13,145 (1966).

sli·ly (slī′lē) See SLYLY.

slim (slim) *adj.* **slim·mer, slim·mest** 1. Small in thickness in proportion to height or length, as a human figure or a tree. 2. Having little logical strength; weak. 3. Constructed unsubstantially; flimsy. 4. Lacking robustness; frail. 5. Insufficient; narrow; meager: a *slim* attendance; a *slim* chance. 6. *Brit. Dial.* Sly; crafty; worthless; bad. — *v.t. & v.i.* **slimmed, slim·ming** To make or become thin or thinner. [< Du. *slim* bad] — **slim′ly** *adv.* — **slim′ness** *n.*

slime (slīm) *n.* 1. Any soft, sticky, or dirty substance. 2. Soft, moist, adhesive mud or earth; muck. 3. A mucous exudation from the bodies of certain animals, as fishes and snails, and certain plants. — *v.* **slimed, slim·ing** *v.t.* **1.** To smear or cover with or as with slime. **2.** To remove slime from, as fishes before canning. [OE *slīm*]

slime mold A myxomycete. Also **slime fungus.**

slim·sy (slim′zē) *adj.* **slim·si·er, slim·si·est** *Informal* Flimsy; frail. Also **slimp·sy** (slimp′sē). [Blend of SLIM and FLIMSY]

slim·y (slī′mē) *adj.* **slim·i·er, slim·i·est 1.** Covered or be-daubed with slime. **2.** Containing slime. **3.** Slimelike; foul. — **slim′i·ly** *adv.* — **slim′i·ness** *n.*

sling[1] (sling) *n.* **1.** A strap or pocket usually with a string attached to each end, for hurling a stone or other missile by whirling the whole and releasing one of the strings. **2.** Any of various ropes, straps, etc., for suspending or hoisting something, as for holding up an injured limb, carrying a rifle, etc. **3.** *Naut.* **a** A rope or chain by which a lower yard or a gaff is suspended. **b** *pl.* The middle portion of a yard. **4.** The act of slinging; a sudden throw; cast; fling. — *v.* **slung, sling·ing** *v.t.* **1.** To fling from or as from a sling; hurl. **2.** To hang loosely by means of a strap or sling. **3.** To move or hoist, as by a rope or tackle. — *v.i.* **4.** To move at an easy gait. [OE *slingan*] — **sling′er** *n.*

sling[2] (sling) *n. U.S.* A drink of brandy, whisky, or gin, with sugar and nutmeg, lemon juice, and ice. [Cf. G *schlingen* to swallow]

sling·shot (sling′shot′) *n.* A weapon or toy consisting of a forked stick with an elastic strap attached to the prongs for catapulting small missiles: also called *catapult.*

slink (slingk) *v.* **slunk** (*Archaic* **slank**), **slunk, slink·ing** *v.i.* **1.** To creep or steal along furtively or stealthily, as in fear. — *v.t.* **2.** To give birth to prematurely; miscarry: said of animals, especially cows. — *adj.* Produced prematurely, as a calf; too immature to be eaten. — *n.* An animal, especially a calf, prematurely born; also, its flesh, too immature to be used as food. [OE *slincan* to creep] — **slink′ing·ly** *adv.*

slink·y (slingk′ē) *adj.* **slink·i·er, slink·i·est 1.** Sneaking; stealthy. **2.** *Slang* Sinuous or feline in movement or form.

slip[1] (slip) *v.* **slipped** or **slipt, slip·ping** *v.t.* **1.** To cause to move smoothly and easily; cause to glide or slide. **2.** To put on or off easily, as a ring or a loose garment. **3.** To convey slyly or secretly. **4.** To free oneself or itself from, as a fetter or bridle. **5.** To let loose; unleash, as hounds. **6.** To release from its fastening and let run out, as a cable. **7.** To give birth to prematurely; slink; cast: said of animals. **8.** To dis-locate, as a bone. **9.** To escape or pass unobserved: It *slipped* my mind. **10.** To overlook; omit negligently: to *slip* an op-portunity. — *v.i.* **11.** To slide accidentally and lose one's footing. **12.** To slide or fall out of place or out of one's grasp. **13.** To fall into an error or fault; err. **14.** To es-cape, as a ship. **15.** To move smoothly and easily; slide; glide. **16.** To get free of restraint; be unleashed. **17.** To go or come stealthily or unnoticed: often with *off, away,* or *from.* — **to let slip** To say without intending to. — **to slip one over on** *Informal* To cheat; hoodwink. — *n.* **1.** An act of slipping; a sudden slide. **2.** A lapse or error in speech, writing, or conduct; a slight mistake. **3.** *U.S.* A narrow space between two wharves. **4.** An artificial pier sloping down to the water, serving as a landing place. **5.** An in-clined plane leading down to the water, on which vessels are repaired or constructed: also called *slipway.* **6.** A woman's undergarment, usually the length of a dress. **7.** A pillow-case: also **pillow slip. 8.** A leash containing a device that permits quick release of the dog. **9.** In cricket, a position on the offside a few yards behind the wicket; also, the player who stands at this position. **10.** *Naut.* **a** The difference be-tween the speed of a screw propeller and that of the ship. **b** The difference between the advance made by a propeller moving in a fluid and the advance it would make if moving against a solid. **11.** *Aeron.* The sideways, and usually down-ward sliding motion of an airplane in certain attitudes. **12.** *Mech.* **a** The relative motion of two surfaces that are meant to be immovable with respect to each other, as a belt on a pulley. **b** Allowance made for slipping or play, as between connected members of a mechanism; slippage. **13.** *Geol.* **a** A joint or fissure where two rock strata have moved upon each other. **b** A small fault. — **to give (someone) the slip** To elude (someone). [< MLG *slippen*]

slip[2] (slip) *n.* **1.** A cutting from a plant for planting or grafting; a cion. **2.** A small, slender person, especially a youthful one. **3.** A small piece of something, as of paper or cloth, rather long relative to its width; a strip. **4.** A small piece of paper for jotting down memoranda, a record, etc. **5.** *U.S.* A narrow pew in a church. — *v.t.* **slipped, slip·ping** To cut off for planting; make a slip or slips of. [< MDu. *slippe < slippen* to cut]

slip[3] (slip) *n.* Liquid potter's clay, used for decorating and coating rough surfaces. [OE *slypa, slyppe*]

slip·cov·er (slip′kuv′ər) *n.* A fitted cloth cover for a chair, sofa, etc., that can be readily removed.

slip·knot (slip′not′) *n.* **1.** A knot having part of the mate-rial drawn through[t] n a loop so that it is easily untied. For illustration see KNOT. **2.** A running knot (which see).

slip-on (slip′on′, -ôn′) *adj.* Easily donned or taken off. — *n.* A slip-on garment, as a blouse.

slip-o·ver (slip′ō′vər) *adj.* Easily donned by drawing over the head: a *slipover* shirt. — *n.* A slipover garment.

slip·page (slip′ij) *n.* **1.** The amount by which or distance through which anything slips, as a screw propeller. **2.** The difference between actual and calculated speed, due to slip-ping. **3.** The act of slipping; slip.

slip·per (slip′ər) *n.* A low, light shoe, chiefly for indoor wear, that is easily slipped on or off the foot. [< SLIP[1] + -ER[2]] — **slip′pered** *adj.*

slip·per·wort (slip′ər·wûrt′) *n.* Calceolaria.

slip·per·y (slip′ər·ē) *adj.* **·per·i·er, ·per·i·est 1.** Having a surface so smooth that objects slip or slide easily on it. **2.** That evades one's grasp; tricky; elusive. **3.** Unreliable; un-dependable; tricky. **4.** *Obs.* Wanton. [< SLIPPER[2] + -Y[3]] — **slip′per·i·ly** *adv.* — **slip′per·i·ness** *n.*

slippery elm A tree (*Ulmus fulva*) of eastern North America. **2.** Its mucilaginous inner bark, used in medicine.

slip ring *Electr.* One of two or more metal rings of an elec-tric machine serving, through contact with stationary brush-es, to deliver or transmit a current.

slip·sheet (slip′shēt′) *Printing n.* A blank piece of paper interleaved between newly printed press sheets to prevent offset. — *v.t.* To insert slipsheets in.

slip·shod (slip′shod′) *adj.* **1.** Carelessly done or wrought; negligent; slovenly: a *slipshod* performance. **2.** Down at the heel; ragged; seedy. [< SLIP[1] + *shod,* pp. of SHOE]

slip-slop (slip′slop′) *n. Informal* **1.** Sloppy victuals; any weak drink; slop. **2.** A blunder, as in speaking.

slip·sole (slip′sōl′) *n.* **1.** A thin insole. **2.** A half sole in-serted between the outsole and the insole to give additional thickness. For illustration see SHOE.

slip·stick (slip′stik′) *n. U.S. Slang* A slide rule.

slip·stream (slip′strēm′) *n. Aeron.* The stream of air driven backwards by the propeller of an aircraft.

slip-up (slip′up′) *n. Informal* A mistake; error.

slip·way (slip′wā′) *n.* Slip[1] (def. 5).

slit (slit) *n.* A cut that is relatively straight and long; also, a long, narrow opening. — *v.t.* **slit, slit·ting 1.** To make a long incision in; slash. **2.** To cut lengthwise into strips. [ME *slitten* to cut. Akin to OE *slītan.*] — **slit′ter** *n.*

slith·er (slith′ər) *v.i.* **1.** To slide; slip, as on a surface where footing is insecure. **2.** To glide, as a snake. — *v.t.* **3.** To cause to slither. [Var. of dial. E *slidder < OE slidrian,* freq. of *slīdan* to slide] — **slith′er·y** *adj.*

slit trench A narrow trench for protection.

sliv·er (sliv′ər) *n.* **1.** A slender piece, as of wood, cut or torn off lengthwise; a splinter. **2.** Corded textile fibers drawn into a fleecy strand. **3.** A piece cut longitudinally from the side of a fish: used as bait; also, a filet. — *v.t. & v.i.* To cut or split into long thin pieces; splinter. [< dial. E *slive* to cleave < OE *tōflīfan*] — **sliv′er·er** *n.*

sli·vo·vitz (sliv′ə·vits) *n.* A white, dry plum brandy, drunk especially in central European countries. [< Serbo-Croatian *šljivovica < šljiva* plum]

slob (slob) *n.* **1.** *Informal* A crude, careless, or unclean person. **2.** *Irish* Mud; mire. [< Irish *slab,* prob. < SLAB[2]]

slob·ber (slob′ər) *v.t.* **1.** To wet and foul with liquids oozing from the mouth. **2.** To shed or spill, as liquid food, in eat-ing. — *v.i.* **3.** To drivel; slaver. **4.** To talk or act gush-ingly. — *n.* **1.** Liquid spilled as from the mouth; slaver. **2.** Gushing, sentimental talk. [Var. of SLABBER] — **slob′-ber·er** *n.* — **slob′ber·y** *adj.*

slob ice *Canadian* Bits of ice floating in masses.

sloe (slō) *n.* **1.** The blackthorn (defs. 1 & 2). **2.** Any of various related plants, as the wild yellow plum (*Prunus americana*). [OE *slāh*]

sloe-eyed (slō′īd′) *adj.* Having dark, velvety eyes.

sloe gin A cordial with a gin base, flavored with sloes.

slog (slog) *v.t. & v.i.* **slogged, slog·ging 1.** To strike hard; slug. **2.** To plod (one's way), as through deep mud. — *n.* A heavy blow. [Var. of SLUG[3]] — **slog′ger** *n.*

slo·gan (slō′gən) *n.* **1.** A battle or rallying cry, originally of the Highland clans. **2.** A catchword or motto adopted by a group, as a political party. [< Scottish Gaelic *sluagh* army + *gairm* yell]

sloid (sloid), **slojd** See SLOYD.

sloop (slōōp) *n. Naut.* A single-masted, fore-and-aft rigged sailing vessel carrying at least one jib, now used principally as a racing vessel. [< Du. *sloep*]

sloop of war 1. Formerly, a vessel rigged either as ship, brig, or schooner, and mount-ing between 18 and 32 guns. **2.** Later, any war vessel larger than a gunboat and carry-ing guns on one deck only.

sloop-rigged (slōōp′rigd′) *adj.* Having rigging like that of a sloop.

SLOOP

slop¹ (slop) *v.* **slopped, slop·ping** *v.i.* **1.** To splash or spill. **2.** To walk or move through slush. — *v.t.* **3.** To cause (a liquid) to spill or splash. **4.** To spill a liquid upon. **5.** *U.S.* To feed (a domestic animal) with slops. — **to slop over 1.** To overflow and splash. **2.** To do or say more than is necessary, because of excess zeal, sentimentality, etc. — *n.* **1.** Slush; watery mud. **2.** A puddle of liquid that has been slopped. **3.** An unappetizing liquid or watery food. **4.** Refuse liquid. **5.** *pl.* Waste food or swill, as from a kitchen, used to feed cattle, pigs, etc. **6.** *pl.* Distiller's mash deprived of its alcohol. [ME *sloppe* < OE *-sloppe*]

slop² (slop) *n.* **1.** *Obs.* A loose outer garment. **2.** *pl.* Articles of clothing, bedding, etc., supplied to sailors on shipboard. **3.** *pl.* Cheap, ready-made clothes. [ME *sloppe* < OE *-slop*]

slope (slōp) *v.* **sloped, slop·ing** *v.i.* **1.** To be inclined from the level or the vertical; slant. **2.** To move on an inclined path; go obliquely. **3.** *Informal* To leave suddenly; run off. — *v.t.* **4.** To cause to slope. — **Syn.** See TIP¹. — *n.* **1.** Any slanting surface or line; a declivity or acclivity. **2.** The degree of inclination of a line or surface from the plane of the horizon. **3.** *Math.* The tangent of the positive angle of less than 180° made by the *x*-axis and a straight line drawn in Cartesian coordinates. [Aphetic var. of *aslope*, OE *āslopen*, ppr. of *āslūpan* to slip away] — **slop'er** *n.*

slop pail A pail for garbage or slops. Also **slop bucket.**

slop·py (slop'ē) *adj.* **·pi·er, ·pi·est 1.** Slushy; splashy; wet. **2.** Watery or pulpy: *sloppy* pudding. **3.** Splashed with liquid or slops. **4.** *Informal* Messy; slovenly; untidy. **5.** *Informal* Slipshod; careless. **6.** *Informal* Maudlin; overly sentimental. — **slop'pi·ly** *adv.* — **slop'pi·ness** *n.*

slop·work (slop'wûrk') *n.* **1.** The manufacture of cheap ready-made clothing; also, the clothing itself. **2.** Any inferior, cheap, slovenly work.

slosh (slosh) *v.t.* **1.** To throw about, as a liquid. — *v.i.* **2.** To splash; flounder: to *slosh* through a pool. — *n.* Slush. [Var. of SLUSH] — **slosh'y** *adj.*

slot¹ (slot) *n.* **1.** A long narrow groove or opening; slit. **2.** A comparatively long, narrow, usually rectangular depression or cavity, cut to receive some corresponding part in a mechanism. **3.** The opening to receive the coin in a slot machine. **4.** *Informal* An opening or position, as a job category or a place in a sequence. **5.** *Aeron.* An opening in an airplane wing to improve the conditions of airflow. — *v.t.* **slot·ted, slot·ting 1.** To adjust in a slot. **2.** To cut a slot in; groove. [< OF *esclot* the hollow between the breasts]

slot² (slot) *n.* The trail of an animal, especially a deer. [< AF *esclot* < ON *slōdh*. Doublet of SLEUTH.]

sloth (slōth, slôth, sloth) *n.* **1.** Disinclination to exertion; habitual indolence; laziness. **2.** A slow-moving, tree-dwelling, edentate mammal (family *Bradypodidae*) of tropical America, as the **three-toed sloth** (genus *Bradypus*), having three toes on each foot, and the **two-toed sloth** (genus *Choloepus*), having two toes on the front and three on the hind feet. **3.** A related fossil edentate (family *Megatheriidae*). [ME *slawthe* < OE *slǣwth*]

THREE-TOED SLOTH
(About 24 inches long)

sloth bear A black bear of India and Ceylon (genus *Melursus*), feeding mainly on honey and fruit: also called *honey bear.*

sloth·ful (slōth'fəl, slôth'-, sloth'-) *adj.* Sluggish; lazy. — **sloth'ful·ly** *adv.* — **sloth'ful·ness** *n.*

slot machine A vending machine or gambling machine having a slot in which a coin is dropped to cause operation.

slot man *U.S. Informal* The chief copy editor of a newspaper: so called because he sits in the slot of a U-shaped desk around which the copy editors are ranged.

slouch (slouch) *v.i.* **1.** To have a downcast or drooping gait, look, or posture. **2.** To hang or droop in a careless manner, as a hat. — *v.t.* **3.** To cause to droop or hang down. — *n.* **1.** A drooping of the head and shoulders caused by sprossion, fatigue, etc. **2.** A drooping of the brim of a hat. **3.** An awkward, heavy, or incompetent person: usually in the negative: He's no *slouch* at baseball. [Origin uncertain] — **slouch'y** *adj.* — **slouch'i·ly** *adv.* — **slouch'i·ness** *n.*

slouch hat A soft hat, usually of felt, with a flexible brim.

slough¹ (slou *for defs. 1 & 4;* slōō *for defs. 2 & 3*) *n.* **1.** A place of deep mud or mire; bog. **2.** A depression in a prairie, often dry but sometimes deeply miry. **3.** A stagnant swamp, backwater, bayou, inlet, or pond in which water backs up: also spelled *slew, slue.* **4.** A state of moral depravity or despair. [OE *slōh*] — **slough'y** *adj.*

slough² (sluf) *n.* **1.** Dead tissue separated and thrown off from the living parts, as in gangrene; also, a scab. **2.** The skin of a serpent that has been or is about to be shed. **3.** Something cast off like dead skin. — *v.t.* **1.** To cast off, as dead from living tissue; shed: with *off.* **2.** To discard; shed, as a habit; get rid of: with *off.* — *v.i.* **3.** To be cast off. **4.** To cast off a slough or tissue. **5.** To drop; decline; slacken: Trade *sloughed* off. [ME *slouh, slughe;* ult. origin uncertain] — **slough'y** *adj.*

slough of despond (slōō) Deep despair or dejection; despondency. [after the *Slough of Despond* in John Bunyan's *Pilgrim's Progress*]

Slo·vak (slō'vak, slō-vak') *n.* **1.** One of a Slavic people of NW Hungary and parts of Moravia, who united with the Czechs to form the Czechoslovak republic in 1918, now in central Czechoslovakia. **2.** The West Slavic language of the Slovaks. — *adj.* Of or pertaining to the Slovaks or to their language. Also **Slo·vak·i·an** (slō-vak'ē-ən, -vä'kē-ən). [< Czech *slovák* Slav]

Slo·vak·i·a (slō-vak'ē-ə, -vä'kē-ə) A region and former province of eastern Czechoslovakia. *Czech* **Slo·ven·sko** (slō'ven·skô).

slov·en (sluv'ən) *n.* One who is careless of dress or of cleanliness; one habitually untidy. [Cf. Flemish *sloef* dirty]

Slo·vene (slō'vēn, slō-vēn') *n.* One of a group of southern Slavs now living in NW Yugoslavia. — *adj.* Of or pertaining to the Slovenes or to their language. [< G *Slovene*]

Slo·ve·ni·a (slō-vē'nē-ə) A constituent Republic of NW Yugoslavia; 7,717 sq. mi.; pop. 1,624,900 (1965); capital, Ljubljana. *Serbo-Croatian, Slovenian* **Slo·ve·ni·ja** (slō'ven/ē-yä).

Slo·ve·ni·an (slō-vē'nē-ən) *adj.* Of or pertaining to Slovenia, its people, or their language. — *n.* The South Slavic language of the Slovenes.

slov·en·ly (sluv'ən-lē) *adj.* **·li·er, ·li·est 1.** Having the habits of a sloven; untidy; careless. **2.** Careless or slipshod in manner or methods of work, etc. — *adv.* In a slovenly manner; untidily. — **slov·en·li·ness** *n.*

slow (slō) *adj.* **1.** Having relatively small velocity; not quick in motion, performance, or occurrence; not advancing or growing rapidly. **2.** Behind the standard time: said of a timepiece. **3.** Taking sufficient time; not precipitate or hasty: *slow* to anger. **4.** Dull or tardy in comprehending; mentally sluggish: a *slow* student. **5.** Lacking promptness, spirit, or liveliness. **6.** *Informal* Dull or tedious in character: a *slow* party; a *slow* town. **7.** Being in a condition that is not conducive to speed: a *slow* track. **8.** Inactive: Business is *slow* today. — *v.t.* **1.** To make slow or slower; cause to go at a slower pace; slacken in speed: often with *up* or *down.* **2.** To retard; delay. — *v.i.* **3.** To go or become slow or slower: often with *up* or *down.* — *adv.* In a slow or cautious manner or speed. [OE *slāw*] — **slow'ly** *adv.* — **slow'ness** *n.*
— **Syn.** (adj.) **1.** See DILATORY. **3.** deliberate, leisurely. — **Ant.** fast.

slow·down (slō'doun') *n.* A slackening of pace, especially when deliberately done by workers or management.

slow loris See under LORIS.

slow match A slowly burning fuse used in firing explosives.

slow motion Action in a motion picture that appears to occur at a slower speed than that at which it was originally filmed.

slow·poke (slō'pōk') *n. Informal* A person who works or moves at an exceedingly slow pace; a laggard.

slow·wit·ted (slō'wit'ed) *adj.* Slow in understanding or discerning; stupid; dull. — **slow'wit'ted·ly** *adv.*

slow·worm (slō'wûrm') *n.* A blindworm (which see).

sloyd (sloid) *n.* A system of elementary manual training in woodworking, etc., originating in Sweden, having exercises graduated from the simplest use of tools to the most complete joinery: also spelled *slojd, slöjd.* [< Sw. *slöjd* skill]

slub (slub) *v.t.* **slubbed, slub·bing** To twist (slivers of wool) slightly in preparation for spinning. — *n.* **1.** A slightly twisted roll of cotton, wool, or silk. **2.** A thick, uneven lump in yarn. [Akin to MDu. *slubbe*]

sludge (sluj) *n.* **1.** Soft, water-soaked mud; mire. **2.** A slush of snow or broken or half-formed ice. **3.** Muddy or pasty refuse of various kinds, as that produced in the purification of sewage. **4.** The sediment in a water tank or boiler. [Earlier *slutch.* ? Akin to SLUSH.] — **sludg'y** *adj.*

slue¹ (slōō) *v.* **slued, slu·ing** *v.t.* **1.** To cause to move sideways, as if some portion were pivoted; swing, slide, or skid to the side. **2.** To cause to twist or turn in its seat or fastenings: said of a boom or mast. — *v.i.* **3.** To move sideways. — *n.* The act of sluing around sideways; a skidding or pivoting about; also, the position of a body that has slued. Also spelled *slew.* [Origin unknown]

slue² (slōō) See SLEW³.

slue³ (slōō) See SLOUGH¹ (def. 3).

slug¹ (slug) *n.* **1.** A bullet or shot of irregular or oblong shape, especially as used in old muskets. **2.** *Printing* **a** A strip of type metal, thicker than a lead and less than type-high, for spacing matter, etc. **b** A metal strip bearing a type-high number, abbreviated title, or the like, used as a compositor's mark. **3.** Any often counterfeit small chunk of metal; especially, one used as a coin in automatic machines, as dial telephones. **4.** *Physics* A unit of mass that, when acted upon by a force of one pound, acquires an acceleration of one foot per second per second. It has the value of about 32.174 pounds or 14.59 kilograms: also called *geepound.* — *v.t.* **slugged, slug·ging** *v.i.* **1.** To take shape to fit the grooves of a rifle, as a bullet. — *v.t.* **2.** To load with slugs. [Origin uncertain. ? Akin to SLAG.]

slug² (slug) *n.* **1.** Any of various gastropods (order *Pulmonata*) related to the snail, having an elongated body and a rudimentary shell concealed in the mantle, especially of the genus *Limax*. ◆ Collateral adjective: *limacine*. **2.** The larva of a sawfly or other insect, resembling a gastropod. **3.** A sluggard. [ME *slugge* sluggard, ? < Scand. Cf. dial. Norw. *slugg* large, heavy object.]

slug³ (slug) *Informal* *n.* **1.** A heavy blow, as with the fist or a baseball bat. **2.** A drink of undiluted liquor. **3.** *pl. Canadian* A teacher's disciplinary whipping of an offender's hand. — *v.t.* **slugged, slug·ging** To strike heavily or brutally, as with the fist or a baseball bat. [Origin uncertain]

slug·ger (slug′ər) *n.* **1.** One who or that which slugs. **2.** In baseball, a strong hitter.

slug·a·bed (slug′ə·bed′) *n.* One who lounges late in bed, because of laziness.

slug·fest (slug′fest′) *n. U.S. Slang* **1.** Vigorous battling; a brawl; free-for-all. **2.** In baseball, a game that is characterized by many hits.

slug·gard (slug′ərd) *n.* A person habitually lazy or idle; a drone. — *adj.* Lazy; sluggish. [< SLUG² + -ARD]

slug·gish (slug′ish) *adj.* **1.** Having little motion or power of motion; slow; inactive; torpid. **2.** Habitually idle and lazy. **3.** Not active; slow; stagnant: a *sluggish* season. — **slug′gish·ly** *adv.* — **slug′gish·ness** *n.*

sluice (slōōs) *n.* **1.** An artificial channel for conducting water, equipped with a valve or gate (**sluice gate**) to regulate the flow. **2.** The body of water so channeled. **3.** Any artificial channel, especially one for excess water. **4.** A trough through which water is run to separate gold ore, to float logs, etc. **5.** That through which anything issues or flows. — *v.* **sluiced, sluic·ing** *v.t.* **1.** To wet or drench, water, or irrigate by or as by means of a sluice. **2.** To wash in or by a sluice. **3.** To draw out or conduct by or through a sluice. **4.** To send (logs) down a sluiceway. — *v.i.* **5.** To flow out or issue from a sluice. [< OF *escluse* < L *exclusa*, pp. fem. of *excludere* to shut out]

sluice·way (slōōs′wā′) *n.* An artificial channel for the passage of water; a sluice.

slum (slum) *n. Often pl.* A squalid, dirty, overcrowded street or section of a city, marked by poverty and poor living conditions. — *v.i.* **slummed, slum·ming** To visit slums or other places considered inferior to one's usual haunts, for amusement or curiosity. [< cant, room; ult. origin unknown] — **slum′mer** *n.*

slum·ber (slum′bər) *v.i.* **1.** To sleep, especially lightly or quietly. **2.** To be inactive; stagnate. — *v.t.* **3.** To spend or pass in sleeping. — *n.* **1.** Sleep. **2.** A state of inactivity or quiescence. [OE *slūma* slumber, *slumere* sleeper] — **slum′ber·er** *n.* — **slum′ber·ing·ly** *adv.* — **slum′ber·less** *adj.*

slum·ber·land (slum′bər·land′) *n.* The region one is imagined to visit during sleep; also, a state of slumber.

slum·ber·ous (slum′bər·əs) *adj.* **1.** Inviting or inducing sleep. **2.** Sleepy; drowsy. **3.** Suggesting or resembling sleep. **4.** Of, pertaining to, or characteristic of sleep. Also **slum′ber·y, slum·brous** (slum′brəs). — **slum′ber·ous·ly** *adv.* — **slum′ber·ous·ness** *n.*

slum clearance The removal and replacement of slums as part of a program of housing improvement.

slum·gul·lion (slum·gul′yən) *n.* **1.** *U.S. Slang* A thin, watery stew of meat and vegetables. **2.** *Brit. Slang* A weak, watery beverage. **3.** A menial servant. **4.** Refuse from fish or blubber processing. **5.** A reddish, muddy deposit in mine sluiceways. [Origin uncertain]

slum·gum (slum′gum′) *n.* The residue of propolis, cocoons, etc., after beeswax is extracted from the honeycomb.

slum·lord (slum′lôrd′) *n. U.S.* The landlord of slum property, especially one who exploits tenants and neglects repairs. [< SLUM + (LAND)LORD]

slum·my (slum′ē) *adj.* **·mi·er, ·mi·est** Consisting of or resembling a slum or slums.

slump (slump) *v.i.* **1.** To break through a crust, as of snow or ice, and sink. **2.** To slide with perceptible motion down a declivity: said of loose earth or rock. **3.** To fall or fail suddenly, as in value or quality. **4.** To stand, walk, or proceed with a stooping posture; slouch. — *n.* **1.** The act of slumping; a collapsing fall. **2.** A collapse or failure; also, a sudden fall of prices: a *slump* in stocks. **3.** A decline, as of interest, excitement, etc. **4.** In sports, a period of inferior playing. [Cf. Norw. *slumpa* to fall, fall upon.]

slung (slung) Past tense and past participle of SLING.

slung·shot (slung′shot′) *n.* A weight attached to a thong or cord, used as a weapon.

slunk (slunk) Past tense and past participle of SLINK.

slur (slûr) *v.t.* **slurred, slur·ring** **1.** To slight; disparage; depreciate. **2.** To pass over lightly or hurriedly; suppress; conceal: to *slur* a fact. **3.** To weaken and elide (speech sounds) by hurried articulation. **4.** *Music* **a** To sing or play as indicated by the slur. **b** To mark with a slur. **5.** To smear; soil; contaminate. — *n.* **1.** A disparaging remark or insinuation. **2.** *Music* **a** A curved line (⌣ or ⌢) indicating that tones so tied are to be sung to the same syllable or performed without a break between them. **b** The legato effect

indicated or produced by this mark. **3.** A blur. **4.** A slurred articulation. [< dial. E, orig., fluid mud. Cf. MDu. *slooren* to drag, trail.]

slurp (slûrp) *v.t. & v.i. Slang* To sip noisily. [< Du. *slurpen* to lap, sip]

slur·ry (slûr′ē) *n. pl.* **·ries** A usually thin mixture of water or other liquid with a finely divided substance, as cement, coal, ore, etc. — *v.t.* **·ried, ·ry·ing** To make a slurry of. [< dial. E *slur* fluid mud]

slush (slush) *n.* **1.** Soft, sloppy material, as melting snow or soft mud. **2.** Greasy material used for lubrication, etc. **3.** The greasy refuse from a ship's galley. **4.** Overly sentimental talk or writing; drivel. — *v.t.* **1.** To cover or daub with slush, as for lubrication. **2.** To fill (spaces in masonry) with mortar: usually with *up*. **3.** To wash by throwing water upon, as a deck. [? Scand. origin. Cf. Dan. *slus*, Norw. *slusk*.] — **slush′y** *adj.*

slush fund *U.S.* **1.** Money collected or spent for corrupt purposes, as bribery, lobbying, etc. **2.** Formerly, on naval vessels, money obtained from the sale of garbage and used to buy small luxuries.

slut (slut) *n.* **1.** A slatternly woman. **2.** A woman of loose character; hussy. **3.** An impudent, brazen girl: a humorous term. **4.** A female dog. [ME *slutte*. Cf. dial. G *schlutte*.]

slut·tish (slut′ish) *adj.* Slatternly; dirty. — **slut′tish·ly** *adv.* — **slut′tish·ness** *n.*

sly (slī) *adj.* **sli·er** or **sly·er, sli·est** or **sly·est** **1.** Artfully dexterous in doing things secretly; cunning in evading notice or detection. **2.** Playfully clever; roguish; mischievous. **3.** Meanly or stealthily clever; crafty. **4.** Done with or marked by artful secrecy: a *sly* trick. **5.** Skillful; possessed of practical ability; wise. — **on the sly** In a stealthy way; with concealment. [< ON *slægr*] — **sly′ness** *n.*

sly·boots (slī′bōōts′) *n.* One who is sly.

sly·ly (slī′lē) *adv.* In a sly manner: also spelled *slily*.

Sm *Chem.* Samarium.

S.M. **1.** Master of Science (L *Scientiae Magister*). **2.** Soldier's Medal.

smack¹ (smak) *n.* **1.** A quick, sharp sound, as of the lips when separated rapidly. **2.** A sounding blow or slap. **3.** The sound of a blow, especially with something flat. **4.** A noisy kiss. — *v.t.* **1.** To make a sharp sound by quickly opening (the lips). **2.** To slap, especially loudly. — *v.i.* **3.** To give or make a smack. [Cf. MDu. *smack* a blow]

smack² (smak) *v.i.* **1.** To have a taste or flavor, especially as tested by smacking: usually with *of*. **2.** To have, keep, or disclose a slight suggestion: with *of*. — *n.* **1.** A suggestive tincture, taste, or flavor. **2.** A mere taste; a little bit; smattering. [OE *smæc* the taste]

smack³ (smak) *n.* A small, decked or half-decked vessel of various rig used chiefly for fishing, especially one having a well for fish in its hold. [< Du. *smak, smacke*]

smack-dab (smak′dab′) *adv. U.S. Slang* Directly; squarely: Fred drove his car *smack-dab* into a tree.

smack·ing (smak′ing) *adj.* Brisk; lively: a *smacking* breeze.

SMaj. *Mil.* Sergeant Major.

small (smôl) *adj.* **1.** Comparatively less in size, quantity, extent, etc.; diminutive. Abbr. *sm.* **2.** Being of slight moment, weight, or importance. **3.** Lacking in moral or mental breadth; narrow; ignoble; mean; paltry. **4.** Lacking in the qualities of greatness; not largely gifted. **5.** Acting or transacting business in a limited way. **6.** Weak in characteristic properties; mildly alcoholic: said of liquors: *small* beer. **7.** Having little body or volume; slender; fine; soft, as a voice. **8.** Of low degree; obscure. **9.** Lacking in power or strength. — **to feel small** To feel humiliated. — *adv.* **1.** In a low or faint tone: to sing *small*. **2.** Into small pieces: to cut *small*. **3.** In a small way; trivially; also, timidly: to talk *small*. — *n.* **1.** A small or slender part: the *small* of the back. **2.** A small thing or quantity. [OE *smæl*] — **small·ness** *n.*

— **Syn.** (adj.) **1.** *Small, little, tiny, wee, diminutive, petite, miniature, minute,* and *microscopic* characterize that which is noticeably less in size, quantity, worth, extent, or the like. *Small* and *little,* the most general words, are used almost interchangeably. *Small* is often preferred when stress is laid on an object's relation to others in its class: a *small* elephant. *Little* is more nearly absolute, suggesting comparison with all other things: a *little* flower. *Little* is also favored when disparagement is implied, or when affection or compassion are indicated: a man of *little* talent, a *little* child. *Tiny* and *wee* are close to this latter use of *little*. *Tiny* emphasizes smallness; *wee* now has a dialectal flavor, and is almost always used endearingly: a *tiny* baby, a *wee* lamb. *Diminutive* means quite, or extremely, *small: diminutive* apples. *Petite* describes a *small,* but well-shaped person, and is almost always applied to girls or women. *Miniature* is used of things that are *tiny,* but perfect in every detail: a *miniature* portrait, a *miniature* chess set. *Minute* and *microscopic* are the strongest of these synonyms. *Minute* describes that which is so *small* as to be seen with difficulty: a *minute* flaw in a fabric. *Microscopic,* in its literal sense, characterizes a thing so *tiny* as to be visible only under a microscope: *microscopic* plants.

small·age (smô′lij) *n.* Celery, especially in the wild state. [< SMALL + F *ache* wild celery < L *apium* parsley]

small arms   Firearms of small caliber, as pistols, rifles, and machine guns.

small beer   **1.** Insipid or weak beer. **2.** *Brit.* An insignificant person or thing.

small calorie   See under CALORIE.

small capital   A capital letter cut slightly larger than the lower-case letters of a specified type size. Abbr. *s.c., s. cap., small cap., sm.c., sm. cap.*

THIS LINE IS IN CAPITAL LETTERS
THIS LINE IS IN SMALL CAPITAL LETTERS
this line is in lower-case letters

small change   **1.** Coins of small denomination. **2.** *U.S.* One who or that which is insignificant or of little value.

small circle   *Geom.* A circle formed on the surface of a sphere by a plane that cuts through the sphere but does not pass through its center. Compare GREAT CIRCLE.

small·clothes (smôl′klōthz′, -klōz′) *n.pl.* Close-fitting knee breeches worn by men in the 18th century: also called *smalls*.

small craft   Small boats or vessels collectively.

small fry   **1.** Small, young fish. **2.** A young child or children. **3.** Small or insignificant people or things.

small hours   The early hours of the morning.

small intestine   See under INTESTINE.

small·ish (smô′lish) *adj.* Somewhat small.

small letter   A lower-case letter, as *a* in *Ra*.

small-mind·ed (smôl′mīn′did) *adj.* **1.** Having a petty mind; interested in trivialities. **2.** Narrow; intolerant; ungenerous. **— small′-mind′ed·ly** *adv.* **— small′-mind′ed·ness** *n.*

small·mouth (smôl′mouth′) *n.* An American black bass (*Micropterus dolomieu*) related to the sunfishes and esteemed as a game and food fish.

small potatoes   *U.S. Informal* Insignificant persons or things.

small·pox (smôl′poks′) *n. Pathol.* An acute, highly contagious disease caused by a virus and characterized by inflammatory fever and the eruption of deep-seated pustules that usually leave permanent scars: also called *variola*.

smalls (smôlz) *n.pl.* **1.** Smallclothes. **2.** *Brit. Informal* The first examination after matriculation; responsions. [< SMALL]

small-scale (smôl′skāl′) *adj.* **1.** Of small size or scope. **2.** Denoting a map giving a relatively small representation of ground features; having a scale on the order of 1 : 500,000 or smaller.

small stores   Small, miscellaneous items, as tobacco, soap, thread, etc., stocked by a ship's store to be sold to the crew.

small·sword (smôl′sôrd, -sōrd) *n.* **1.** A light sword used on dress occasions. **2.** The straight sword of modern fencing.

small talk   Unimportant or trivial conversation.

small-time (smôl′tīm′) *adj. U.S. Slang* Petty; unimportant: a *smalltime* hoodlum.

smalt (smôlt) *n.* A deep blue pigment made of pulverized glass colored with oxide of cobalt. [< F < Ital. *smalto* < Gmc.]

smalt·ite (smôl′tīt) *n.* A white to steel-gray cobalt arsenide, crystallizing in the isometric system. Also **smalt·ine** (smôl′tin, -tēn). [< SMALT]

smal·to (smäl′tō) *n.* *pl.* **·ti** (-tē) *Italian* Colored glass, or a piece of it, employed in mosaics.

smar·agd (smar′agd) *n. Obs.* A green gemstone, as the beryl or the emerald. Also **smar′agde.** [< L *smaragdus* < Gk. *smaragdos.* Doublet of EMERALD.] **— sma·rag·dine** (sma·rag′dēn, -din) *adj.*

sma·rag·dite (sma·rag′dīt) *n.* A thin, foliated, light green variety of amphibole.

smar·my (smär′mē) *adj.* **·mi·er, ·mi·est** *Brit. Informal* Unctuously flattering. [< dial. *smarm, smalm* to smooth out, plaster down]

smart (smärt) *v.i.* **1.** To experience a stinging sensation, generally superficial, either bodily or mental. **2.** To cause a stinging sensation. **3.** To experience remorse. **4.** To have one's feelings hurt. **5.** To suffer a severe penalty. **—** *v.t.* **6.** To cause to smart. **—** *adj.* **1.** Quick in thought or action; bright; acute; clever. **2.** Impertinently witty: often used contemptuously. **3.** Vigorous; emphatic; severe; brisk. **4.** Causing a smarting sensation; stinging; pungent. **5.** Keen or sharp, as at trade; shrewd. **6.** *Dial.* Large; considerable: a *smart* crop of wheat. **7.** Sprucely dressed; showy. **8.** Belonging to the stylish classes; fashionable: a *smart* set. **9.** Making a creditable showing: a *smart* regiment. **—** *n.* **1.** An acute stinging sensation, as from a scratch or an irritant. **2.** Any distress; poignant mental suffering. **3.** *Dial.* A degree, number, or amount: with *right*: a right *smart* of people. [OE *smeortan*] **— smart′ly** *adv.* **— smart′ness** *n.*

smart al·eck (al′ik) *Informal* A cocky, offensively conceited person. **— smart-al·eck·y** (smärt′al′ik·ē) *adj.*

smart·en (smär′tən) *v.t.* **1.** To improve in appearance; make smart, as oneself or one's habitation: with *up.* **2.** To make more alert or clever.

smart money   **1.** *Law* Damages awarded against a defendant because of great aggravation attending the wrong committed. **2.** Money paid for a release from an engagement or from a painful situation. **3.** Money paid by an employer to a workman injured in his service. **4.** *Brit.* Money allowed to soldiers or sailors for injuries received in the service. **5.** *Informal* Money bet by gamblers who are supposedly more shrewd or better informed than most other betters.

smart set   Fashionable society.

smart·weed (smärt′wēd′) *n.* Any of several species of marsh plants (genus *Polygonum*) of the buckwheat family.

smash (smash) *v.t.* **1.** To break in many pieces suddenly, as by a blow, pressure, or collision. **2.** To flatten; crush: to *smash* a hat. **3.** To dash or fling violently so as to crush or break in pieces. **4.** To strike with a sudden, forceful blow. **5.** To make bankrupt. **6.** To destroy, as a theory. **7.** In tennis, etc., to strike (the ball) with a hard, swift, overhand stroke. **—** *v.i.* **8.** To go bankrupt; fail, as a business, etc. **9.** To come into violent contact so as to crush or be crushed; collide. **— Syn.** See BREAK. **— to go to smash** *Informal* To be ruined; fail. **—** *n.* **1.** An act or instance of smashing, or the state of being smashed. **2.** Any disaster or sudden breakup of any kind: a *smash* in business. **3.** A beverage of spirituous liquors, usually brandy, with mint, water, sugar, and ice. **4.** In tennis, etc., a strong overhand shot. **5.** *Informal* Something acclaimed by the public: The film is a box-office *smash*: also **smash hit.** [Prob. imit. Cf. Norw. *smaska.*] **— smash′er** *n.*

smash·ing (smash′ing) *adj. Informal* Extremely impressive; overwhelmingly good: a *smashing* success.

smash-up (smash′up′) *n.* A smash; a disastrous collision.

smat·ter (smat′ər) *v.i.* **1.** To talk of, dabble in, study, or use superficially. **—** *n.* A smattering. [ME *smateren,* ? < Scand. Cf. Sw. *smattra* to crackle, patter.] **— smat′ter·er** *n.*

smat·ter·ing (smat′ər·ing) *n.* **1.** A superficial knowledge of something. **2.** A little bit or a few. **— smat′ter·ing·ly** *adv.*

smaze (smāz) *n. U.S.* A combination of smoke and haze, especially as seen in thickly populated industrial and manufacturing areas. [Blend of SM(OKE) and (H)AZE[1]]

sm.c. or **sm. cap(s).** *Printing* Small capital(s).

smear (smir) *v.t.* **1.** To spread, rub, or cover with grease, paint, dirt, etc.; bedaub. **2.** To spread or apply in a thick layer or coating: to *smear* grease on an axle. **3.** To sully the reputation of; defame; slander. **4.** *U.S. Slang* To defeat utterly. **—** *v.i.* **5.** To be or become smeared. **—** *n.* **1.** A soiled spot; stain. **2.** A small quantity of material, as blood, sputum, etc., placed on a microscope slide or bacterial culture for analysis. **3.** A substance to be smeared on something, as a glaze for pottery. **4.** A slanderous attack; defamation. [OE *smierwan* < *smeoru* grease]

smear·case (smir′kās′) *n. U.S.* Cottage cheese. [< G *schmierkäse*]

smear·y (smir′ē) *adj.* **smear·i·er, smear·i·est** Greasy, viscous, or staining; also, smeared. **— smear′i·ness** *n.*

smed·dum (smed′əm) *n. Scot. & Brit. Dial.* **1.** Powder; especially, ground malt. **2.** Vigor of mind. [OE *smedma*]

smeek (smēk) *Scot. v.t.* To smoke. **—** *n.* Smoke. [OE *smīc*]

smell (smel) *v.* **smelled** or **smelt, smell·ing** *v.t.* **1.** To perceive by means of the nose and its olfactory nerves. **2.** To perceive the odor or perfume of; scent. **3.** To test by odor or smell. **4.** To discover, detect, or seek to know, as if by smelling: often with *out.* **—** *v.i.* **5.** To emit an odor or perfume; give off a particular odor: frequently with *of*; also, to give indications of, as if by odor: to *smell* of treason. **6.** To be malodorous. **7.** To use the sense of smell. **8.** To pry; investigate: with *about.* **—** *n.* **1.** The special sense by means of which odors are perceived. **2.** The sensation excited through the olfactory nerves. **3.** An odor. **4.** A faint suggestion; hint; trace. **5.** An act of smelling. [ME *smellen*]

— Syn. (noun) 3. *Smell, odor, scent, savor, aroma, fragrance, perfume, bouquet, stench,* and *stink* denote that which is perceived by the olfactory sense. *Smell* is the general term, to which *odor* is a close synonym. *Smell,* however, often suggests a strong and slightly unpleasant sensation, and *odor,* a more delicate and pleasing one: the *smell* of a hospital ward, the *odor* of new-mown hay. *Scent* is always delicate: the *scent* of apple blossoms. *Savor* refers to an appetizing sensation that combines both *smell* and taste: the *savor* of roasting meat. *Aroma, fragrance, perfume,* and *bouquet* are pleasant. An *aroma* is delicate and spicy: the *aroma* of coffee. We speak of the *fragrance* or *perfume* of flowers; of the two, *fragrance* is the lighter and more delicate, *perfume* the stronger. *Bouquet,* in this sense, is primarily the *aroma* of a fine wine. *Stench* and *stink* are sickening and unpleasant; a *stench* is putrid or asphyxiating, and a *stink* is fetid: the *stench* of rotten eggs, the *stink* of decaying fish.

smell·er (smel′ər) *n.* **1.** One who smells (anything). **2.** *Slang* The nose.

smelling salts   Pungent or aromatic salts, or mixtures of such, often scented, used as stimulants by smelling.

smell·y (smel′ē) *adj.* **smell·i·er, smell·i·est** *Informal* Having an unpleasant smell; malodorous.

smelt[1] (smelt) *v.t. Metall.* **1.** To reduce (ores) by fusion in a furnace. **2.** To obtain (a metal) from the ore by a process including fusion. **—** *v.i.* **3.** To melt or fuse, as a metal. [< MDu. *smelten* to melt]

smelt[2] (smelt) *n.* *pl.* **smelts** or **smelt** Any of a family (*Osmeridae*) of small silvery food fishes of north Atlantic and

Pacific waters and of the Great Lakes, especially an American species (*Osmerus mordax*). [OE]

smelt³ (smelt) Alternative past tense and past participle of SMELL.

smelt·er (smel′tər) *n.* **1.** One engaged in smelting ore. **2.** An establishment for smelting: also **smelt′er·y**.

Sme·ta·na (sme′tä·nä), **Bedřich**, 1824–84, Czech composer.

Smeth·wick (smeth′wik) A county borough in southern Staffordshire, England; pop. 68,372 (1961).

smew (smyōō) *n.* A small merganser (*Mergus albellus*) of northern parts of the Old World, the male of which is black and white, with a white crest. [Origin unknown. Akin to Frisian *smjunt*.]

smidg·en (smij′ən) *n.* *U.S. Informal* A tiny bit or part; mite; trifle.

Smig·ly-Rydz (shmēg′wē·rēts), **Edward**, 1886–1943?, Polish general; chief of state 1935–39.

smi·la·ceous (smī′lə·kā′shəs) *adj.* *Bot.* Of or pertaining to a former family (*Smilacaceae*) of herbs or woody-stemmed vines that included the smilax. [< NL < L *smilax*. See SMILAX.]

smi·lax (smī′laks) *n.* **1.** Any of various shrubby or herbaceous plants (genus *Smilax*) of the lily family, having thorny stems, flowers in umbels, and globular fruit; especially, *S. aristolochiifolia*, a source of sarsaparilla. **2.** A delicate twining plant (*Asparagus asparagoides*) of the lily family, from South Africa, with greenish flowers, cultivated in greenhouses and used for bouquets, etc. [< L < Gk. *smilax* yew]

smile (smīl) *n.* **1.** A pleased or amused expression of the face, characterized by a raising up of the corners of the mouth. **2.** A pleasant aspect: the *smile* of spring **3.** Propitious or favorable disposition; favor; blessing: the *smile* of fortune. — *v.* **smiled, smil·ing** *v.i.* **1.** To give a smile; wear a cheerful aspect. **2.** To show approval or favor: often with *upon.* — *v.t.* **3.** To express by means of a smile; effect as by a smile. [ME *smilen*, prob. < LG] — **smil′er** *n.* — **smil′ing·ly** *adv.* — **smil′ing·ness** *n.*
— **Syn.** (noun) **1.** *Smile, grin, simper,* and *smirk* denote an expression of pleasure or amusement made by widening the mouth. In a *smile,* the mouth is closed or slightly opened; in a *grin* it is opened wide, displaying the teeth. Otherwise, the words differ chiefly in the state of mind inferred from the expression of the face. A *smile* suggests pleasure, satisfaction, good humor, approval, or amity. A *grin* may denote amusement, triumph, or sudden joy. Self-consciousness, coyness, or affectation are expressed by a *simper,* and a *smirk* may indicate smugness, conceit, or lust. — **Ant.** frown.

Smiles (smīlz), **Samuel**, 1812–1904, Scottish writer and physician.

smirch (smûrch) *v.t.* **1.** To soil, as by contact with grime; smear. **2.** To defame; degrade: to *smirch* a reputation. — *n.* The act of smirching, or the state of being smirched; a smear; a moral stain or defect. [ME *smorchen,* appar. < OF *esmorcher* to hurt, torment]

smirk (smûrk) *v.i.* To smile in a silly, self-complacent, or affected manner. — *n.* An affected or artificial smile. Also *Obs.* **smerk.** — **Syn.** See SMILE. [OE *smearcian*] — **smirk′er** *n.* — **smirk′ing·ly** *adv.*

smite (smīt) *v.* **smote** (*Obs.* **smit**), **smit·ten** or **smit** or **smote**, **smit·ing** *v.t.* **1.** To strike (something). **2.** To strike a blow with (something); cause to strike. **3.** To cut, sever, or break by a blow: usually with *off* or *out.* **4.** To strike with disaster; afflict; destroy by a catastrophe. **5.** To affect powerfully with sudden feeling; in the passive, to affect with love. **6.** To cause to feel regret or remorse: His conscience *smote* him. **7.** To affect as if by a blow; come upon suddenly: The thought *smote* him. **8.** To kill by a sudden blow. — *v.i.* **9.** To come with sudden force; also, to knock against something. [OE *smitan*] — **smit′er** *n.*

smith (smith) *n.* **1.** One who shapes metals by hammering: often used in combination: *goldsmith, tinsmith.* **2.** A blacksmith (which see). [OE]

Smith (smith), **Adam**, 1723–90, Scottish moralist and political economist. — **Alfred E(manuel)**, 1873–1944, U.S. political leader: called **the Happy Warrior.** — **Edmund Kirby**, 1824–93, American Confederate general and educator: also *Edmund Kirby-Smith.* — **Francis Hopkinson**, 1838–1915, U.S. civil engineer, artist, and author. — **Goldwin**, 1823–1910, English historian. — **James**, 1719?–1806, American Revolutionary patriot and statesman; signer of the Declaration of Independence. — **Captain John**, 1580–1631, English adventurer; president of the Virginia colony 1608–09. — **Joseph**, 1805–44, founder and first prophet of the Mormon Church; assassinated. — **Margaret Chase**, born 1898, U.S. legislator. — **Sydney**, 1771–1845, English clergyman and author. — **Walter Bedell**, 1895–1961, U.S. general and diplomat. — **William**, 1769–1839, English geologist. — **Sir William**, 1813–93, English classical scholar. — **William Robertson**, 1846–94, Scottish Biblical scholar and Orientalist.

smith·er·eens (smith′ə·rēnz′) *n.pl.* *Informal* Fragments

produced as by an explosion. Also **smith′ers** (-ərz). [Cf. dial. E (Irish) *smidirin* fragment]

smith·er·y (smith′ər·ē) *n.* *pl.* **·er·ies 1.** The art or trade of a smith. **2.** A smith's shop; a smithy.

Smith·son (smith′sən), **James**, 1765–1829, English chemist and mineralogist.

Smith·so·ni·an Institution (smith·sō′nē·ən) An institution founded in 1846 at Washington, D.C., from funds left by James Smithson "for the increase and diffusion of knowledge among men."

smith·son·ite (smith′sən·īt) *n.* A vitreous zinc carbonate, $ZnCO_3$: also called *dry-bone ore.* [after James *Smithson*]

smith·y (smith′ē, smith′ē) *n.* *pl.* **smith·ies** A blacksmith's shop; a forge. [< ON *smithja*]

smit·ten (smit′n) Alternative past participle of SMITE. — *adj.* **1.** Struck with sudden force; gravely afflicted. **2.** Having the affections suddenly attracted.

smock (smok) *n.* **1.** A loose outer garment of light material worn like a coat to protect one's clothes. **2.** Formerly, a woman's undergarment; chemise. — *v.t.* **1.** To furnish with or clothe in a smock. **2.** To decorate (a garment) with smocking. [OE *smoc*]

smock frock A loose-fitting outer garment or jacket worn by laborers.

smock·ing (smok′ing) *n.* Needlework in which the material is stitched into very small pleats or gathers, forming a kind of honeycomb ornamentation.

smog (smog) *n.* A combination of smoke and fog, especially as seen in thickly populated industrial and manufacturing areas. [Blend of SM(OKE) and (F)OG]

SMOCKING

smoke (smōk) *n.* **1.** The volatilized products of the combustion of organic substances, as coal, wood, etc., forming a colloidal suspension of fine carbon particles in a gas. **2.** Anything transient and unsubstantial; a useless or ephemeral result. **3.** The act of smoking a pipe, cigar, etc. **4.** A period of time during which one smokes tobacco. **5.** *Informal* A cigarette, cigar, or pipeful of tobacco. **6.** A chemical-warfare agent producing a smokelike cloud. **7.** A column of smoke, used as a signal by the North American Indians. **8.** A cheap drink, usually of wood alcohol. — *v.* **smoked, smok·ing** *v.i.* **1.** To emit or give out smoke. **2.** To emit smoke excessively or in an undesired direction, as a stove or lamp. **3.** To raise dust in rapid riding or driving; also, to travel rapidly; speed. **4.** To inhale and exhale the smoke of tobacco, opium, etc. — *v.t.* **5.** To inhale and exhale the smoke of (tobacco, opium, etc.); also, to use (a pipe, etc.) for this purpose. **6.** To cure (meat, fish, etc.) by treating with smoke. **7.** To fumigate (a room, etc.). **8.** To subject to smoke. **9.** To apply smoke to (animals) in order to drive away or expel: with *out.* **10.** To force (a criminal, etc.) out of hiding: with *out.* **11.** To bring forcibly into public view or knowledge: with *out.* **12.** To change the color of (glass, etc.) by darkening with smoke. [OE *smoc*]

smoke drift *U.S. & Canadian* The smoke cloud from a forest fire.

smoke·house (smōk′hous′) *n.* A building or closed room in which meat, fish, hides, etc., are cured by smoke.

smoke·jack (smōk′jak′) *n.* A mechanism by which to turn a roasting spit, operated by the ascending combustion gases in a chimney.

smoke·jump·er (smōk′jum′pər) *n.* *U.S. & Canadian* A firefighter who jumps by parachute into or near a forest fire.

smoke·less (smōk′lis) *adj.* Having or emitting little or no smoke: *smokeless* powder.

smoke·pot (smōk′pot′) *n.* A small container for generating a dense cloud of smoke.

smok·er (smō′kər) *n.* **1.** One who or that which smokes. **2.** A smoking car. **3.** A social gathering of men. **4.** A smoking jacket.

smoke screen A dense cloud of smoke used to prevent enemy observation of a place, force, or operation. Also **smoke blanket, smoke curtain.**

smoke·stack (smōk′stak′) *n.* **1.** An upright pipe, usually of sheet or plate iron, through which combustion gases from a furnace are discharged into the air. **2.** The funnel of a steamboat or locomotive, or the chimney of a factory, etc.

smoke tree 1. An ornamental Old World shrub or tree (*Cotinus coggygria*) with long feathery stalks resembling smoke. **2.** A related American species (*C. americanus*).

smoking car A railroad car in which travelers are permitted to smoke.

smoking jacket A short coat worn instead of a regular suit coat as a lounging jacket.

smok·y (smō′kē) *adj.* **smok·i·er, smok·i·est 1.** Giving forth smoke. **2.** Mixed with or containing smoke: *smoky* air. **3.** Emitting smoke improperly and unpleasantly, as from bad draft. **4.** Discolored with smoke. **5.** Smoke-colored; dark gray. **6.** Covered with mist: said of certain mountains. — **smok′i·ly** *adv.* — **smok′i·ness** *n.*

Smoky Hill River   A river in Colorado and Kansas, flowing 560 miles, generally east, joining the Republican River to form the Kansas River.

Smoky Mountains   See GREAT SMOKY MOUNTAINS.

smoky quartz   Cairngorm.

smol·der (smōl′dər)   *v.i.*   **1.** To burn and smoke with little smoke and no flame.   **2.** To exist in a latent state; to manifest suppressed feeling: His wrath *smoldered.*   — *n.* Smother; smoke.   Also spelled *smoulder.*   [ME *smoldren.* Cf. LG *smölen,* Du. *smeulen.*]

Smo·lensk (smō-lensk′, smo-lyensk′)   A city in the western R.S.F.S.R., on the Dnieper; pop. 211,000 (est. 1971).

Smol·lett (smol′it), **Tobias George,** 1721–71, British novelist and physician.

smolt (smōlt)   *n.* A young salmon on its first descent from the river to the sea.   [? Akin to SMELT[2]]

smooch (smōōch)   *n.*   **1.** *U.S. Slang* A kiss.   **2.** A smear; a smutch.   — *v.t.* **1.** To smear; smudge.   — *v.i.* **2.** *U.S. Slang* To neck.   [Cf. SMUTCH.]

smooth (smōōth)   *adj.*   **1.** Having a surface without irregularities; not rough; continuously even.   **2.** Having no impediments or obstructions; easy; free from shocks or jolts.   **3.** Calm and unruffled; bland; pleasant; mild.   **4.** Flowing melodiously: a *smooth* style.   **5.** Suave, as in speech; flattering: often implying deceit.   **6.** In classical Greek, uttered without aspiration: *smooth* breathing.   **7.** Free from hair; beardless.   **8.** Having no acidulous or astringent taste or quality: said of liquors.   **9.** Without lumps; having the elements perfectly blended: a *smooth* mayonnaise.   **10.** Offering no resistance to a body sliding along its surface; without friction.   **11.** Having projecting parts removed by wear, as the tread of a tire.   — **Syn.** See LEVEL.   — *adv.* Calmly; evenly.   — *v.t.* **1.** To make smooth or even on the surface.   **2.** To make easy or less difficult: to *smooth* one's path.   **3.** To free from obstructions.   **4.** To remove (an obstruction): often with *away*: to *smooth* away a mound.   **5.** To render less harsh or softer and more flowing: to *smooth* one's verses.   **6.** To soften the worst features of; palliate: usually with *over.*   **7.** To make calm; mollify: to *smooth* one's feelings.   — *v.i.* **8.** To become smooth.   — **to smooth (someone's) ruffled feathers** To mollify.   — *n.* **1.** The smooth portion or surface of anything.   **2.** The act of smoothing.   [OE *smōth*]   — **smooth′er** *n.*   — **smooth′ly** *adv.*   — **smooth′ness** *n.*

smooth·bore (smōōth′bôr′, -bōr′)   *n.* A firearm with an unrifled bore.   Also **smooth bore.**   — **smooth′bored′** *adj.*

smooth breathing   In classical Greek: **a** The absence or lack of an aspirated sound.   **b** The symbol (′) placed over a vowel to indicate this.   Also called *lenis, spiritus lenis.*

smooth·en (smōō′thən)   *v.t. & v.i.* To smooth.

smooth-faced (smōōth′fāst′)   *adj.*   **1.** Beardless.   **2.** Of smooth surface, as a wall, etc.   **3.** Bland or mild in expression, especially with deceitful intent.

smooth·ie (smōō′thē)   *n.* *U.S. Informal* One who is suave and persuasive; especially, a man who behaves so towards women.   Also **smooth′y.**

smooth-shod (smōōth′shod′)   *adj.* Shod without sharp projections on the shoes, as a horse.

smör·gås·bord (smôr′gəs-bôrd, *Sw.* smœr′gōs-bōrd)   *n.*   **1.** Scandinavian hors d'oeuvres.   **2.** A buffet supper consisting of such hors d'oeuvres.   **3.** A restaurant serving smörgåsbord.   Also **smor′gas·bord.**   [< Sw.]

smote (smōt)   Past tense of SMITE.

smoth·er (smuth′ər)   *v.t.*   **1.** To prevent the respiration of, as by filling or covering the mouth and nostrils; suffocate; stifle.   **2.** To cover, or cause to smolder, as a fire.   **3.** To hide or suppress: to *smother* one's feelings.   **4.** In cooking, to enclose and cook in a covered dish or under a close mass of some other substance.   — *v.i.* **5.** To suffocate, as from lack of air, from smoke, etc.   **6.** To be covered without vent or air, as a fire.   **7.** To be hidden or suppressed, as wrath.   — *n.* **1.** That which smothers, as stifling vapor or dust.   **2.** The state of being smothered; suppression.   **3.** A smoldering fire.   **4.** A surging of foam or water; a welter.   [Earlier *smorther.* Akin to OE *smorian* to suffocate.]   — **smoth′er·y** *adj.*

smoul·der (smōl′dər)   See SMOLDER.

smudge (smuj)   *v.* smudged, smudg·ing   *v.t.* **1.** To smear; soil.   **2.** To protect (from frost, insects, etc.) by a heavy, smoky pall.   — *v.i.* **3.** To cause a smudge.   **4.** To be smudged.   — *n.* **1.** A soiling, as of dry dirt or soot; smear; stain.   **2.** A smoky fire or its smoke for driving away insects, preventing frost, etc.   [Var. of SMUTCH]

smudge pot   A container for burning oil or other smoky fuels to produce a smudge.

smudg·y (smuj′ē)   *adj.* smudg·i·er, smudg·i·est   Full of or causing smudges.   — **smudg′i·ly** *adv.*   — **smudg′i·ness** *n.*

smug (smug)   *adj.* smug·ger, smug·gest   **1.** Characterized by a self-satisfied or complacent air.   **2.** Trim; spruce.   [Cf. LG *smuk* neat.]   — **smug′ly** *adv.*   — **smug′ness** *n.*

smug-faced (smug′fāst′)   *adj.* Having a prim, self-satisfied face or expression.

smug·gle (smug′əl)   *v.* ·gled, ·gling   *v.t.* **1.** To take (merchandise) into or out of a country without payment of lawful duties.   **2.** To bring in or introduce illicitly.   — *v.i.* **3.** To engage in or practice smuggling.   [< LG *smuggeln*]

smug·gler (smug′lər)   *n.*   **1.** One who smuggles.   **2.** A ship used in smuggling.

smug·gling (smug′ling)   *n.* The offense or practice of fraudulently and illegally importing or exporting merchandise without payment of lawful duties.

smut (smut)   *n.*   **1.** The blackening made by soot, smoke, etc.   **2.** Obscenity; obscene language.   **3.** Any of various fungus diseases of plants, in which the affected parts change into a dusty black powder.   **4.** Any of the fungi (order *Ustiliginales*) causing such a disease.   — *v.* smut·ted, smut·ting   *v.t.* **1.** To blacken or stain, as with soot or smoke.   **2.** To affect with smut, as growing grain.   **3.** To remove the smut from (grain).   **4.** To pollute; defame.   — *v.i.* **5.** To give off smut.   **6.** To be or become stained.   **7.** To be affected with smut, as growing grain.   [< LG *schmutt* dirt]

smutch (smuch)   *v.t.* To smudge; soil.   — *n.* A smear; smudge.   [Cf. MHG *smutzen* to smear]   — **smutch′y** *adj.*

Smuts (smuts), **Jan Christiaan,** 1870–1950, South African general and statesman; prime minister 1919–24, 1939–48.

smut·ty (smut′ē)   *adj.* ·ti·er, ·ti·est   **1.** Soiled with smut; black; stained.   **2.** Affected with smut: *smutty* corn.   **3.** Obscene; coarse; indecent.   — **smut′ti·ly** *adv.*   — **smut′ti·ness** *n.*

Smyr·na (smûr′nə)   The former name of IZMIR.   — **Smyr′ni·ot** (-nē-ot) *adj. & n.*

Smyth (smīth), **Henry De Wolf,** born 1898, U.S. physicist.

Sn   *Chem.* Tin (L *stannum*).

snack (snak)   *n.*   **1.** A sip or bite.   **2.** A slight, hurried meal; also, something eaten between meals.   **3.** A share of something.   [Orig. a verb < MDu. *snacken* to bite, snap]

snack bar   A place where snacks are served.

snaf·fle (snaf′əl)   *n.* A horse's bit without a curb, jointed in the middle.   Also **snaf′fle·bit′** (-bit′).   — *v.t.* ·fled, ·fling To control with a snaffle.   [Cf. Du. *snavel* muzzle]

sna·fu (sna-fōō′, sna′fōō)   *Slang adj.* In a state of utter confusion.   — *v.t.* ·fued, ·fu·ing   To put into a confused or chaotic condition.   — *n. pl.* ·fus   Anything confused or chaotic.   [Acronym for "Situation normal, all fouled up"]

snag (snag)   *n.*   **1.** A jagged or stumpy knot or protuberance, especially the stumpy base of a branch left in pruning.   **2.** The root or remnant of a tooth remaining in the jaw; also, a projecting tooth.   **3.** A branch or point of a deer's antler.   **4.** The trunk of a tree fixed in the bottom of a river, bayou, etc., by which boats are sometimes pierced.   **5.** Any obstacle or difficulty.   — *v.* snagged, snag·ging *v.t.* **1.** To injure, destroy, or impede by or as by a snag.   **2.** To clear of snags.   **3.** *Informal* To block; impede.   — *v.i.* **4.** To run upon a snag: said especially of river craft.   [Prob. < Scand. Cf. dial. Norw. *snag* sharp point, projection.]

snag·gle·tooth (snag′əl-tōōth′)   *n. pl.* ·teeth A tooth that is broken, projecting, or out of alignment with the others.   — **snag′gle·toothed′** (-tōōtht′, -tōōthd′) *adj.*

snag·gy (snag′ē)   *adj.* ·gi·er, ·gi·est   **1.** Full of snags, as a river.   **2.** Full of knots or stubs, as a tree or swamp.   **3.** Like a snag; projecting sharply.

snail (snāl)   *n.*   **1.** Any of a large class (*Gastropoda*) of slow-moving mollusks of aquatic and terrestrial habits and having a spiral shell; especially, the common **garden snail** (*Helix aspersa*) and the **edible snail** (*H. pomatia*).   **2.** A slow or lazy person.   [OE *snægl*]

SNAIL

snail pace   A very slow gait or forward movement.   Also **snail's pace.**   — **snail-paced** (snāl′pāst′) *adj.*

snake (snāk)   *n.*   **1.** Any of numerous species and genera of scaly, legless reptiles (order or suborder *Serpentes*) with long, slim bodies and tapering tails. The bite of most snakes is nonvenomous, but some inject venom into the victim through tubular fangs.   ◆ Collateral adjective *ophidian.*   **2.** A treacherous or unreliable person.   **3.** A flexible, resilient wire used to clean clogged drains, etc.   — *v.* snaked, snak·ing *v.t.* **1.** To drag by seizing an end and pulling forcibly, as a log along the ground.   **2.** To pull with jerks.   — *v.i.* **3.** To crawl or move like a snake.   [OE *snaca*]

snake·bird (snāk′bûrd′)   *n.* Any of several birds (genus *Anhinga*), having very long slender necks, frequenting southern swamps and feeding upon fish: also called *anhinga, darter, water turkey.*

snake·bite (snāk′bīt′)   *n.*   **1.** The bite of a snake.   **2.** Poisoning caused by the venom of a snake.

snake charmer   An entertainer who charms venomous snakes by rhythmic motions of his body and by music.

snake dance   **1.** A ceremonial dance of the Hopi Indians of Arizona in which live rattlesnakes are carried in the mouths of the dancers.   **2.** A procession of persons moving in a winding or zigzag line to celebrate an athletic victory, etc.

snake eyes   In craps, a cast of two.

snake fence   A variety of worm fence (which see).

snake hawk   The swallow-tailed kite (*Elanoides forficatus*) of North and South America.

snake·head (snāk′hed′)   *n.* The turtlehead (which see).

snake·mouth (snāk′mouth′)   *n.* A terrestrial orchid (*Pogonia ophioglossoides*) native in eastern North America, with fragrant pink flowers.

Snake River A river flowing 1,083 miles from NW Wyoming, through Idaho, forming parts of the Idaho-Oregon and Idaho-Washington borders, and joining the Columbia River in SE Washington. See map of COLUMBIA RIVER.

snake·root (snāk′rōōt′, -rŏŏt′) *n.* **1.** Any of various plants having roots reputed to be effective against snakebite; especially, the **Virginia snakeroot** (*Aristolochia serpentaria*), with purplish brown flowers and fibrous roots, the **white snakeroot** (*Eupatorium rugosum*) of Europe and the United States, and the senega snakeroot (which see). **2.** The root of any of these plants. **3.** Rauwolfia.

snake·skin (snāk′skin′) *n.* **1.** The skin of a snake. **2.** Leather made from this.

snake·weed (snāk′wēd′) *n.* The bistort.

snak·y (snā′kē) *adj.* **snak·i·er, snak·i·est 1.** Of or like a snake; serpentine; winding. **2.** Insinuating; cunning; treacherous. **3.** Full of snakes. — **snak′i·ly** *adv.* — **snak′i·ness** *n.*

snap (snap) *v.* **snapped, snap·ping** *v.i.* **1.** To make a sharp, quick sound, as of percussion. **2.** To break suddenly with a cracking noise; part with a snap. **3.** To fly off or give way quickly, as when tension is suddenly relaxed. **4.** To make the jaws come suddenly together in an effort to bite: often with *up* or *at.* **5.** To seize or snatch suddenly: often with *up* or *at.* **6.** To speak sharply, harshly, or irritably: often with *at.* **7.** To emit, or seem to emit, a spark or flash of light: said of the eyes. **8.** To close, fasten, etc., with a click or snapping sound, as a lock. **9.** To move or act with sudden, neat gestures: He *snapped* to attention. — *v.t.* **10.** To seize suddenly or eagerly, with or as with the teeth; snatch: often with *up.* **11.** To sever with a snapping sound. **12.** To utter, address, or interrupt harshly, abruptly, or irritably: often with *out.* **13.** To cause to make a sharp, quick sound: to *snap* one's fingers. **14.** To close, fasten, etc., with a snapping sound. **15.** To strike, flourish, etc., with a snap: to *snap* a whip. **16.** To cause to move suddenly, neatly, etc. **17.** To photograph instantaneously with a camera. **18.** In football, to put in play: said of the ball when sent to a back by the center. — **to snap one's fingers at** To be unimpressed or unintimidated by. — **to snap out of it** *Informal* **1.** To recover quickly, as from a state of depression. **2.** To change one's attitude. — *n.* **1.** The act of snapping, or a sharp, quick sound produced by it. **2.** A sudden breaking of anything, or the sound so produced. **3.** Any catch, fastener, or other device that closes or springs into place with a snapping sound. **4.** A sudden seizing or effort to seize with or as with the teeth. **5.** A quick blow of the thumb sprung from the finger or of the finger from the thumb. **6.** The sudden release of the tension of a spring or elastic cord. **7.** A small, thin, crisp cake or cooky. **8.** Brisk energy; vigor; vim; zip. **9.** A brief spell; a sudden turn: said chiefly of cold weather. **10.** *Informal* Any task or duty easy to perform: often in the phrase **a soft snap. 11.** A bit: It is not worth a *snap.* **12.** The instantaneous taking of a photograph; also, the photograph so taken; a snapshot. **13.** A snap bean. **14.** *Canadian* A center in football: an obsolescent term. — *adj.* **1.** Made or done suddenly and without consideration; offhand. **2.** Fastening with a snap. **3.** *Informal* Easy; requiring little work: a *snap* course. — *adv.* With a snap; quickly. [< MDu. *snappen* to bite at]

snap·back (snap′bak′) *n.* **1.** Formerly, in football, the center. **2.** The act of snapping back.

snap bean *Southern U.S.* A bean with an edible pod, especially the string bean.

snap-brim hat (snap′brim′) A hat whose brim can be turned up or down, and is usually turned down in the front.

snap·drag·on (snap′drag′ən) *n.* **1.** A plant (genus *Antirrhinum*) of the figwort family; especially, the **common snapdragon** (*A. majus*) having solitary axillary flowers likened to dragons' heads. **2.** An old game in which raisins, etc., are snatched from burning brandy; also, anything so snatched: also called *flapdragon.*

snap·per (snap′ər) *n.* **1.** One who or that which snaps. **2.** A large food fish (genus *Lutianus*) of the Gulf Coast, as the **red snapper** (*L. blackfordii*). **3.** A snapping turtle. **4.** A sparoid food fish (*Pagrosomus auratus*) of Australia and New Zealand, reddish with blue bars or spots: also called *schnapper.*

snapping beetle A click beetle (which see).

snapping turtle A large voracious turtle (*Chelydra serpentina*) of North America, much used as food.

snap·pish (snap′ish) *adj.* **1.** Apt to speak crossly or tartly. **2.** Disposed to snap, as a dog. — **snap′pish·ly** *adv.* — **snap′pish·ness** *n.*

snap·py (snap′ē) *adj.* **·pi·er, ·pi·est 1.** *Informal* Brisk; energetic; vivacious. **2.** *Informal* Smart or stylish in appearance. **3.** Snappish. — **make it snappy** *Informal* Hurry up! — **snap′pi·ly** *adv.* — **snap′pi·ness** *n.*

snap·shot (snap′shot′) *n.* **1.** A photograph taken with a small camera without timing. **2.** A shot made without aim.

snap·weed (snap′wēd′) *n.* The jewelweed (which see).

snare[1] (snâr) *n.* **1.** A device, as a noose, for catching birds or other animals; a trap. **2.** Anything by which one is entangled or entrapped; an allurement. **3.** *Surg.* A loop of wire used to remove tumors and other growths from the body. — *v.t.* **snared, snar·ing 1.** To catch with a snare; ensnare; entrap. **2.** To capture by trickery; entice; inveigle. [OE *sneare* < ON *snara.* Akin to SNARE².] — **snar′er** *n.*

snare[2] (snâr) *n.* **1.** One of the cords or wires stretched across one of the heads of a snare drum to increase the resonance. **2.** A snare drum. [< MDu., a string. Akin to SNARE¹.]

snare drum A small drum having snares on one head. For illustration see DRUM¹.

snark (snärk) *n.* A mysterious imaginary creature in Lewis Carroll's nonsense poem *The Hunting of the Snark.*

snarl[1] (snärl) *n.* A sharp, harsh, angry growl; harsh or quarrelsome utterance. — *v.i.* **1.** To growl harshly, as a dog. **2.** To speak angrily and resentfully. — *v.t.* **3.** To utter or express with a snarl. [Freq. of obs. *snar* to growl] — **snarl′er** *n.* — **snarl′ing·ly** *adv.* — **snarl′y** *adj.*

snarl[2] (snärl) *n.* **1.** A tangle, as of hair or yarn. **2.** Any complication or entanglement. **3.** *Informal* A wrangle; quarrel. **4.** A knot or gnarl in wood. — *v.i.* **1.** To get into a snarl or tangle; become entangled. — *v.t.* **2.** To put into a snarl or tangle. **3.** To confuse; entangle mentally; embarrass. **4.** To emboss or flute (thin metalware). [< SNARE¹] — **snarl′er** *n.* — **snarl′y** *adj.*

snash (snash, snäsh) *n. Scot.* Impertinent, abusive, or sneering language.

snatch (snach) *v.t.* **1.** To seize or lay hold of suddenly, hastily, or eagerly. **2.** To take or remove suddenly. **3.** To take or obtain as the opportunity arises: to *snatch* a few hours of sleep. **4.** *Slang* To kidnap. — *v.i.* **5.** To attempt to seize swiftly and suddenly: with *at.* **6.** To be eager to accept: with *at.* — **Syn.** See GRASP, STEAL. — *n.* **1.** An act of snatching; a hasty grab or grasp: usually with *at.* **2.** A brief period: a *snatch* of rest. **3.** A small amount; fragment: *snatches* of a conversation. **4.** *Slang* A kidnaping. **5.** In weightlifting, a bringing of the weight from the floor to above the head in one motion. [ME *snacchen.* ? Akin to SNACK.] — **snatch′er** *n.*

snatch block *Naut.* A single block having an opening in one cheek to receive a rope, and usually having a swivel hook. For illustration see BLOCK¹.

snatch·y (snach′ē) *adj.* **snatch·i·er, snatch·i·est** Interrupted; spasmodic.

snath (snath) *n.* The long curved handle of a scythe. Also **snathe** (snāth). [Var. of dial. E *snead* < OE *snæd*]

snaw (snô, snä) *Scot. n.* Snow. — *v.i. & v.t.* To snow.

sneak (snēk) *v.i.* **1.** To move or go in a stealthy manner. **2.** To act with covert cowardice or servility. — *v.t.* **3.** To put, give, transfer, move, etc., secretly or stealthily. **4.** *Informal* To pilfer. — *n.* **1.** One who sneaks; a mean, cowardly fellow. **2.** *pl. Informal* Sneakers. **3.** A stealthy movement. — *adj.* Stealthy; covert: a *sneak* attack. [Akin to OE *snīcan* to creep]

sneak·er (snē′kər) *n.* **1.** One who sneaks; a sneak. **2.** *pl. U.S. Informal* Rubber-soled canvas shoes worn especially for sports.

sneak·ing (snē′king) *adj.* **1.** Acting in an underhand way. **2.** Secret; unavowed: a *sneaking* suspicion. — **sneak′ing·ly** *adv.*

sneak preview *U.S.* The showing of a new motion picture before its date of release, in order to test its reception by an audience.

sneak thief One who steals small miscellaneous articles, without violence, by sneaking in through unfastened doors or windows.

sneak·y (snē′kē) *adj.* **sneak·i·er, sneak·i·est** Like a sneak; sneaking. — **sneak′i·ly** *adv.* — **sneak′i·ness** *n.*

sned (sned) *v.t.* **sned·ded, sned·ding** *Scot.* To trim; lop off.

sneer (snir) *n.* **1.** A grimace of contempt or derision made by slightly raising the upper lip. **2.** A mean or contemptuous insinuation. — *v.i.* **1.** To make or show a sneer. **2.** To express derision or contempt in speech, writing, etc. — *v.t.* **3.** To utter with a sneer or in a sneering manner. [ME *sneren*; ult. origin uncertain] — **sneer′er** *n.* — **sneer′ing·ly** *adv.*

sneesh (snēsh) *n. Scot.* Snuff. Also **sneesh′ing.**

sneeze (snēz) *sneezed, sneez·ing* *v.i.* To drive air forcibly and audibly out of the mouth and nose by a spasmodic involuntary action caused by irritation of the mucus membranes. — **not to be sneezed at** *Informal* Worthy of consideration. — *n.* An act of sneezing. [Alter. of ME *fnese*, OE *fnēosan* to sneeze] — **sneezer** *n.* — **sneez′y** *adj.*

sneeze·weed (snēz′wēd′) *n.* Any of a genus (*Helenium*) of plants of the composite family; especially, *H. autumnale*, the leaves and flowers of which are said to cause sneezing: also called *bitterweed.*

sneeze·wort (snēz′wûrt′) *n.* A perennial composite plant (*Achillea ptarmica*), native to Europe and Asia, whose powdered dry leaves produce sneezing.

snell¹ (snel) *n.* A short line of gut, horsehair, etc., bearing a fish hook, to be attached to a longer line. [Origin unknown]

snell² (snel) *adj.* **1.** *Scot.* Sharp; keen; piercing. **2.** Austere; severe. **3.** Nimble; quick. [OE]

snick (snik) *n.* **1.** A small cut; nick; snip. **2.** A knot in thread or the like. **3.** In cricket, a glancing hit. — *v.t.* **1.** To cut a nick in. **2.** To hit (a ball) a glancing blow. [Back formation < *snick or snee.* See SNICKERSNEE.]

snick·er (snik′ər) *n.* A half-suppressed or smothered laugh, often in derision. — *v.i.* **1.** To utter a snicker; laugh slyly and foolishly with audible catches of the voice; giggle. — *v.t.* **2.** To utter or express with a snicker. [Imit.]

snick·er·snee (snik′ər·snē′) *n.* **1.** A swordlike knife. **2.** *Archaic* A fight with knives. Also **snick′-a-snee, snick′-or-snee′.** [Alter. of earlier *snick or snee* to thrust or cut, ult. < Du. *steken* to thrust + *snijen* to cut]

snide (snīd) *adj.* Malicious or derogatory; nasty: *snide* comments. [Origin unknown]

sniff (snif) *v.i.* **1.** To breathe through the nose in short, quick, audible inhalations. **2.** To express contempt, etc., by or as by sniffing: often with *at.* **3.** To inhale a scent in sniffs. — *v.t.* **4.** To breathe in through the nose; inhale. **5.** To smell or attempt to smell with sniffs. **6.** To perceive as if by sniffs: to *sniff* peril. **7.** To express (contempt) by sniffs. — *n.* **1.** An act or the sound of sniffing. **2.** Perception by or as by sniffing. **3.** That which is inhaled by sniffing. [Appar. back formation < SNIVEL]

snif·fle (snif′əl) *v.i.* **·fled, ·fling 1.** To breathe through the nose noisily, as when it is obstructed with mucus. **2.** To snivel or whimper. — *n.* A snuffle. — **the sniffles** *Informal* The condition of sniffling, as when one has a cold in the head: also *the snuffles.* [Freq. of SNIFF]

snif·fy (snif′ē) *adj.* **·fi·er, ·fi·est** *Informal* Disposed to sniff or be disdainful or scornful.

snif·ter (snif′tər) *n.* **1.** A pear-shaped liquor glass with a small opening to concentrate the aroma of brandy, etc. **2.** *U.S. Slang* A small drink of liquor, usually a dram. [< *snift,* var. of SNIFF]

snig·ger (snig′ər) *n.* A snicker. — *v.t. & v.i.* To snicker. [Var. of SNICKER]

snig·gle (snig′əl) *v.* **·gled, ·gling** *Brit. v.i.* **1.** To fish for eels by thrusting the bait into their hiding places. — *v.t.* **2.** To catch (eels) in this manner. [< dial. E *snig* eel]

snip (snip) *v.* **snipped, snip·ping** *v.t.* **1.** To clip, remove, or cut with a short, light stroke or strokes of scissors or shears: often with *off.* — *v.i.* **2.** To cut with small, quick strokes. — *n.* **1.** An act of snipping. **2.** A small piece snipped off. **3.** *U.S. Informal* A small or insignificant person or thing. **4.** *pl.* Small shears for cutting metal. [< Du. *snippen*]

snipe (snīp) *n.* *pl.* **snipe** or **snipes 1.** Any of various long-billed shore or marsh birds (genus *Capella* or related genera), allied to the woodcock and much sought as a game bird; especially, the **common snipe** (*C. gallinago*), and **Wilson's snipe** (*C. gallinago delicata*). **2.** The jacksnipe (which see). **3.** A shot from a hiding place. **4.** *U.S. Slang* A cigarette or cigar butt. — *v.i.* **sniped, snip·ing 1.** To hunt or shoot snipe. **2.** To shoot at or pick off individual enemies from hiding. **3.** *U.S. Slang* To hunt for cigarette or cigar butts. [< ON *snipa*]

snip·er (snī′pər) *n.* One who shoots an enemy from hiding.

snip·pet (snip′it) *n.* **1.** A small piece snipped off. **2.** A small portion or share.

snip·py (snip′ē) *adj.* **·pi·er, ·pi·est** *Informal* **1.** Pert; impertinent. **2.** Fragmentary; scrappy. Also **snip′pet·y** (-it-ē).

snit (snit) *n. Informal* A state of irritation, anger, or flurry: to be in a *snit.* [Origin unknown]

snitch (snich) *Slang v.t.* **1.** To grab quickly; steal; swipe. — **Syn.** See STEAL. — *v.i.* **2.** To turn informer: usually with *on.* [Origin unknown]

sniv·el (sniv′əl) *v.* **·eled** or **·elled, ·el·ing** or **·el·ling** *v.i.* **1.** To cry in a snuffling manner. **2.** To make tearful complaints; whine. **3.** To run at the nose. — *v.t.* **4.** To utter with sniveling or sniffing. — *n.* **1.** The act of sniveling. **2.** Nasal mucus. [OE (assumed) *snyflan* < *snyflung* mucus from the nose] — **sniv′el·er** or **sniv′el·ler** *n.*

snob (snob) *n.* **1.** One who makes birth, wealth, education, or intelligence the sole criterion of worth. **2.** One who is cringing to superiors and overbearing with inferiors. **3.** Any pretender to gentility. **4.** *Obs. Brit.* A common or vulgar person. [Origin uncertain] — **snob′ber·y** *n.*

snob·bish (snob′ish) *adj.* Characteristic of or befitting a snob or snobs. — **snob′bish·ly** *adv.* — **snob′bish·ness** *n.*

Sno·cat (snō′kat′) *n.* A trucklike vehicle having steerable runners at the front and broad caterpillar treads at the rear, used for traveling in arctic conditions: a trade name. Also **sno′cat.** [< SNO(W) + CAT(ERPILLAR)]

snood (snōōd) *n.* **1.** A small, meshlike cap or bag, worn by women to keep the hair in place. **2.** *Scot.* A fillet formerly worn about the hair by an unmarried woman. — *v.t.* To bind (hair) with a snood. [OE *snōd*]

snook¹ (snōōk, snook) *v.i.* **1.** *Scot.* To sniff. **2.** To lurk. — *n.* **1.** A smell; sniff; a bite. **2.** *Slang* An informer.

snook² (snōōk, snook) *n.* *pl.* **snook** or **snooks** Any of various percoid fishes of the genus *Centropomus;* especially,

C. undecimalis, of Southern Atlantic waters: also called *robalo, sergeant fish.* [< Du. *snoek* pike]

snook³ (snōōk, snook) *n.* A derisive gesture, as in **to cock a snook,** to thumb one's nose. [Origin unknown]

snool (snōōl) *Scot. v.i.* **1.** To yield submissively. — *v.t.* **2.** To browbeat; cow. — *n.* One who is meanly subservient.

snoop (snōōp) *Informal v.i.* To look or pry into things with which one has no business. — *n.* One who snoops: also **snoop′er.** [< Du. *snoepen* to eat goodies on the sly]

snoop·y (snōō′pē) *adj.* **snoop·i·er, snoop·i·est** *Informal* Given to snooping.

snoot (snōōt) *n. Informal* **1.** The nose or face. **2.** A wry face; a grimace. [Var. of SNOUT]

snoot·y (snōō′tē) *adj.* **snoot·i·er, snoot·i·est** *U.S. Informal* Conceited or supercilious.

snooze (snōōz) *Informal v.i.* **snoozed, snooz·ing** To sleep lightly; doze. — *n.* A short nap. [Origin uncertain]

Sno·qual·mie Falls (snō·kwol′mē) A waterfall (height, 270 ft.) in the **Snoqualmie River,** a river flowing about 45 miles west and NW in central Washington.

snore (snôr, snōr) *v.i.* **snored, snor·ing** To breathe in sleep through the nose and open mouth with a hoarse, rough noise and rattling vibrations of the soft palate. — *n.* An act or the noise of snoring. [ME *snoren.* Akin to MLG *snorren* to hum, drone.] — **snor′er** *n.*

snor·kel (snôr′kəl) *n.* **1.** A mouth tube permitting a skin diver to breathe while swimming on the surface with his face under water. **2.** An apparatus for the ventilation of a submerged submarine, consisting of retractable tubes for the intake of fresh air and the removal of toxic gases. — *v.i.* **·keled, ·kel·ing** To use a snorkel underwater. [< G *schnörkel,* lit., spiral]

Snor·ri Stur·lu·son (snôr′ē stûr′lə·sən, stōōr′-), 1179–1241, Icelandic historian and poet; assassinated.

snort (snôrt) *v.i.* **1.** To force air violently and noisily through the nostrils, as a horse. **2.** To express indignation, ridicule, etc., by a snort. **3.** *Informal* To laugh with a boisterous outburst. — *v.t.* **4.** To utter or express by snorting. **5.** To expel by or as by a snort. — *n.* **1.** The act or sound of snorting. **2.** *Slang* A small drink, usually taken quickly. [ME *snorten.* ? Akin to SNORE.] — **snort′er** *n.*

snot (snot) *n.* **1.** Mucus from or in the nose: a vulgar term. **2.** *Slang* A low or mean fellow. [OE *gesnot*]

snot·ty (snot′ē) *adj.* **·ti·er, ·ti·est 1.** Dirtied with snot: a vulgar term. **2.** *Slang* Contemptible; mean; paltry. **3.** *Slang* Impudent; proudly conceited; saucy.

snout (snout) *n.* **1.** The forward projecting part of a beast's head, especially of a swine's; proboscis; muzzle. **2.** Some similar anterior prolongation of the head, as in certain gastropods and beetles. **3.** Something resembling a hog's snout. **4.** A person's nose: a contemptuous or humorous term. — *v.t.* To provide with a snout or nozzle. [ME *snūte.* Akin to OE *snytan* to blow the nose.]

snout beetle The curculio.

snout·ed (snout′id) *adj.* **1.** Having a snout. **2.** Having or characterized by a (specified kind of) snout: used in combination: *long-snouted.*

snow (snō) *n.* **1.** Water vapor in the air precipitated in the form of minute ice crystals when the temperature is below 32° F., and usually falling in irregular masses or flakes. ◆ Collateral adjective: *nival.* **2.** Anything resembling snow in being white or composed of flakes: a *snow* of blossoms. **3.** A fall of snow; snowstorm. **4.** A winter. **5.** *Slang* Heroin or cocaine. **6.** The pattern of snowlike flecks appearing on a television screen as a result of weakened signals in a receiver. — *v.i.* **1.** To fall as snow: usually used impersonally: It is *snowing.* — *v.t.* **2.** To scatter or cause to fall as or like snow. **3.** To cover, enclose, or obstruct with snow: with *in, over, under,* or *up.* **4.** *U.S. Slang* To subject to a snow job. [OE *snāw*]

Snow may appear as a combining form, or as the first element in two-word phrases; as in:

snow-beaten	snow-colored	snowless
snow bed	snow-covered	snowlike
snow blast	snow-crested	snow-lined
snow-blown	snow-driven	snow peak
snow-bright	snow field	snowscape
snow cloud	snow-haired	snow-tipped
snow-cold	snowland	snow-topped

snow apple A variety of apple, the Fameuse.

snow·ball (snō′bôl′) *n.* **1.** A small round mass of snow compressed to be thrown, as in sport. **2.** The guelder-rose: also **snowball bush** or **tree.** — *v.i.* **1.** To throw snowballs. **2.** To gain in size, importance, etc., as a snowball that rolls over snow. — *v.t.* **3.** To throw snowballs at.

snow·bank (snō′bangk′) *n.* A large mound of snow.

snow·bell (snō′bel′) *n.* Any of a genus (*Styrax*) of trees and shrubs of warm regions, bearing showy white flowers in racemes; especially, *S. americana* of the SE United States.

snow·ber·ry (snō′ber′ē) *n. pl.* **·ries** A bushy American shrub (*Symphoricarpos albus*) having white berries: also called *waxberry.*

snow·bird (snō′bûrd′) *n.* **1.** The junco. **2.** The snow bunting. **3.** *Slang* A cocaine or heroin addict.

snow blindness A temporary dimming of the sight caused by ultraviolet light reflected by snow. **— snow-blind** (snō′-blīnd′) *adj.*

snow-blink (snō′blingk′) *n.* The glare of light reflected from a field of ice or snow: also, *Canadian, snowshine.*

snow-blow-er (snō′blō′ər) *n.* *U.S.* A small snowplow for use on driveways, sidewalks, etc.: also called *snowthrower.*

snow-bound (snō′bound′) *adj.* Hemmed in or forced to remain in a place because of heavy snow; snowed in.

snow-broth (snō′brôth′, -broth′) *n.* 1. Melted snow or snow and water mixed. 2. Any very cold liquid.

snow bunting Any of various fringilline birds (genus *Plectrophenax*); especially, *P. nivalis* of northern regions, the male of which in the breeding season is snow-white with black markings: also called *snowbird, snowflake.*

snow-bush (snō′bŏŏsh′) *n.* Any of various California shrubs (genus *Ceanothus*) of the buckthorn family, as *C. cordulatus,* that bears numerous small white flowers.

snow-cap (snō′kap′) *n.* A crest of snow, as on a mountain peak. **— snow′-capped′** *adj.*

snow-clad (snō′klad′) *adj.* Covered with snow.

Snow-don (snōd′n) A mountain in Caernarvonshire, the highest point in Wales; 3,560 ft.

snow-drift (snō′drift′) *n.* A snowbank made by the wind.

snow-drop (snō′drop′) *n.* A low, European, early-blooming bulbous plant (*Galanthus nivalis*) of the amaryllis family, bearing a single, white, drooping flower.

snowdrop tree The silver bell.

snow eater The chinook (def. 2).

snow-fall (snō′fôl′) *n.* 1. A fall of snow. 2. The amount of snow that falls in a given period.

snow fence *U.S. & Canadian* Portable fencing of thin, closely placed slats, used to prevent the drifting of snow.

snow-flake (snō′flāk′) *n.* 1. One of the small, feathery masses in which snow falls. 2. The snow bunting. 3. Any of certain plants (genus *Leucojum*) allied to and resembling the snowdrop; especially, the **spring snowflake** (*L. vernum*), the **summer snowflake** (*L. aestivum*), and the **autumn snowflake** (*L. autumnale*).

snow goose Any of certain North American geese (genus *Chen*) that breed in the Arctic, having snow-white plumage with black primary feathers; especially, *C. hyperborea atlantica* of the North Atlantic and *C. hyperborea hyperborea* of the West: also called *wavey, white brant.*

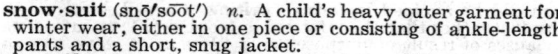

SNOWFLAKES

snow job *U.S. Slang* An elaborate, insincere speech contrived to impress or persuade.

snow leopard A large, carnivorous, feline mammal (*Panthera uncia*) of Central Asia, having long, spotted fur: also called *ounce.*

snow line 1. The limit of perpetual snow on the sides of mountains, varying with the latitude, the season, and the climate. 2. Either of the imaginary lines north and south of the equator within which snow never falls. Also **snow limit.**

snow-man (snō′man′, -mən) *n.* *pl.* **-men** (-men′, -mən) A rough image of a man, made of snow.

snow-mo-bile (snō′mō′bēl) *n.* Any of various enclosed vehicles, often with caterpillar treads and steerable front runners, used for traveling over snow or ice. [< SNOW + (AUTO)MOBILE]

snow pellets Snowlike particles sometimes precipitated from a cloud during showers.

snow plant A blood-red saprophytic herb (*Sarcodes sanguinea*) found in the mountain forests in southern California, frequently covered with snow in its blooming season.

snow-plow (snō′plou′) *n.* 1. Any plowlike device for turning fallen snow aside from a road or railroad, or for the removal of snow from surfaces. 2. *Skiing* The act of slowing or stopping by bringing the front points of the skis toward each other. Also **snow′plough′.**

snow pudding A pudding containing gelatin, sugar, and white of egg whipped into a snowlike foam.

snow-shed (snō′shed′) *n.* *U.S. & Canadian* A timber structure, as one built over portions of a railway, as a protection from snowslides.

snow-shine (snō′shīn′) *n. Canadian* Snowblink.

snow-shoe (snō′shŏŏ′) *n.* A device, usually a network of thongs in a wooden frame, fastened on the foot by a strap across the toes, and worn as a support in walking over snow. **— v.i. -shoed, -shoe-ing** To walk on snowshoes. **— snow′sho′er** (-shŏŏ′-ər) *n.*

SNOWSHOES
a Sioux Indian.
b Iroquois Indian.

snow-slide (snō′slīd′) *n.* An avalanche of snow.

snow squall A flurry of wind and snow.

snow-storm (snō′stôrm′) *n.* A storm with a fall of snow.

snow-suit (snō′sŏŏt′) *n.* A child's heavy outer garment for winter wear, either in one piece or consisting of ankle-length pants and a short, snug jacket.

snow-throw-er (snō′thrō′ər) *n.* A snowblower.

snow tire A tire with a heavy tread of knobs and ridges to provide traction on snow and ice.

snow-white (snō′hwīt′) *adj.* White as snow.

snow-y (snō′ē) *adj.* **snow-i-er, snow-i-est** 1. Abounding in or full of snow. 2. Snow-white. 3. Pure; unblemished; spotless: *snowy linen.* **— snow′i-ly** *adv.* **— snow′i-ness** *n.*

snowy egret See under EGRET.

snub (snub) *v.t.* **snubbed, snub-bing** 1. To treat with contempt or disdain, especially by ignoring; slight. 2. To rebuke or check with a sharp or cutting remark. 3. To stop or check, as a rope in running out, by taking a turn about a post, etc.; also, to make fast (a boat, etc.) thus. 4. *Obs.* To clip; stunt; nip. **— Syn.** See SLIGHT. **— adj.** Short; pug: said of the nose. **— n.** 1. An act of snubbing; deliberate slight. 2. A sudden checking, as of a running rope or cable. 3. A snub nose. [< ON *snubba* to snub] **— snub′ber** *n.*

snub-nosed (snub′nōzd′) *adj.* Having a pug or snub nose.

snuff¹ (snuf) *v.t.* 1. To draw in (air, etc.) through the nose. 2. To catch the scent of; smell; sniff; also, to examine by smelling. **— v.i.** 3. To snort; sniff. 4. To inhale in disdain or anger. **— n.** An act of snuffing; sniff. [< MDu. *snuffen*]

snuff² (snuf) *n.* The charred portion of a wick. **— v.t.** 1. To put out or extinguish: with *out.* 2. To crop the snuff from (a wick). **— to snuff out** *Informal* To end by or as if by death. [Cf. G *schnuppe* snuff of a candle]

snuff³ (snuf) *n.* 1. Pulverized tobacco to be inhaled into the nostrils. 2. The quantity of it taken at one time. 3. Any medicinal powder to be drawn into the nostrils. **— up to snuff** *Informal* 1. Meeting the usual standard, as in quality, health, etc. 2. Not easily deceived; sharp-witted. **— v.i.** To take or use snuff. [< Du. *snuf,* appar. short for *snuiftabak,* lit., tobacco to be inhaled]

snuff-box (snuf′boks′) *n.* A small box for carrying snuff.

snuf-fer¹ (snuf′ər) *n.* One who snuffs or sniffs.

snuf-fer² (snuf′ər) *n.* 1. One who or that which snuffs (a candle). 2. *pl.* A scissorslike instrument for extinguishing candles or removing the snuff.

snuf-fle (snuf′əl) *v.* **-fled, -fling** *v.i.* 1. To sniffle. 2. To breathe noisily, as a dog following a scent. 3. To talk through the nose; snivel. **— v.t.** 4. To utter in a nasal tone. **— n.** 1. An act of snuffling, or the sound made by it. 2. An affected nasal or emotional voice or twang. 3. *Rare* Cant; hypocrisy. **— the snuffles** *Informal* The sniffles. [Freq. of SNUFF¹] **— snuf′fler** *n.* **— snuf′fly** *adj.*

snuff-y (snuf′ē) *adj.* **snuf-fi-er, snuf-fi-est** 1. Pertaining to or like snuff. 2. Soiled with or smelling of snuff. 3. Dingy; unattractive. **— snuf′fi-ly** *adv.* **— snuf′fi-ness** *adj.*

snug (snug) *adj.* **snug-ger, snug-gest** 1. Closely and comfortably sheltered, covered, or situated. 2. Close or compact; having room enough, but not too much; comfortable; cozy. 3. Having everything closely secured; trim: said of a ship. 4. Fitting closely but comfortably. **— v. snugged, snug-ging** *v.t.* 1. To make snug. **— v.i.** 2. To snuggle; move close. **— to snug down** To make a vessel ready for a storm by reducing sail, etc. **— n.** *Brit. Informal* The bar parlor of a public house or inn. [Prob. < LG. Cf. Du. *snugger* clean, smooth.] **— snug′ly** *adv.* **— snug′ness** *n.*

snug-ger-y (snug′ər-ē) *n.* *pl.* **-ger-ies** 1. A cozy and comfortable place or room. 2. A snug.

snug-gle (snug′əl) *v.t. & v.i.* **-gled, -gling** To lie or draw close; nestle; cuddle: often with *up* or *together.* [Freq. of SNUG, v.]

snye (snī) *n. Canadian* A side channel in a river or creek.

so¹ (sō) *adv.* 1. To this or that or such a degree; to this or that extent; in such quantity or proportion. 2. In this, that, or such a manner; in like or corresponding manner; in the same way: often following a clause beginning with *as,* or preceding one beginning with *that:* As the twig is bent, *so* is the tree inclined; I'm sure he's right, even if you don't think *so.* 3. Just as said, directed, suggested or implied: Do it *so;* I will do *so.* 4. According to fact: That is not *so.* 5. *Informal* To an extreme degree; very. 6. About as many or as much stated; thereabouts: I shall stay a day or *so.* 7. According to the truth of what is sworn or averred: *So* help me God. 8. To such an extent: used elliptically for *so much:* I love him *so!* 9. Too: used in emphatic contradiction of a negative statement: You can *so!* 10. Consequently; thus; therefore. 11. *Informal* It seems that; can it be that; apparently: used to indicate surprise, disapproval, inquiry, etc.: *So* you don't like it here! 12. Let it be that way; very well. **— conj.** 1. With the purpose that: usually with *that:* They left early *so* that they would avoid meeting him. 2. As a consequence of which: He consented, *so* they left. **— interj.** 1. Is that so! Indeed! 2. Hold still! Steady! [OE *swā*]

◆ As an intensive, *so,* as in "He's *so* handsome!" (adv. def. 5) gives an impression of schoolgirl breathlessness and should be avoided in formal writing. Careful writers use *so that* rather than the informal *so* (conj. def. 1) to introduce clauses of result or purpose, as in "I want to leave now *so that* I won't be late."

so² (sō) *n. Music* Sol.

s.o. or **so** Struck out; strike-out.

So. South; southern.

soak (sōk) *v.t.* **1.** To place in liquid till thoroughly saturated; steep. **2.** To wet thoroughly; drench: The rain *soaks* the earth. **3.** To take in through or as through pores or interstices; suck up; absorb: with *in* or *up*. **4.** To become imbued with; take in eagerly or readily: with *up*: to *soak up* knowledge. **5.** *Informal* To drink, especially to excess. **6.** *U.S. Slang* To charge exorbitantly; mulct. **7.** *U.S. Slang* To strike hard; beat. — *v.i.* **8.** To remain or be placed in liquid till saturated. **9.** To penetrate; pass: with *in* or *into*. **10.** *U.S. Slang* To drink to excess. — *n.* **1.** The act of soaking, or state of being soaked. **2.** Liquid in which something is soaked. **3.** *Slang* A hard drinker. [OE *socian*. Akin to SUCK.] — **soak′er** *n.*

soak·age (sō′kij) *n.* **1.** The act of soaking, or the state of being soaked. **2.** The quantity of liquid that soaks in or through, or seeps out.

soak·ers (sō′kerz) *n.pl.* Short pants of absorbent material, usually wool, worn by babies over diapers.

so-and-so (sō′ən·sō′) *n.* **1.** An unnamed or undetermined person or thing. **2.** *Informal* A euphemism for many offensive epithets.

soap (sōp) *n.* **1.** A cleansing agent consisting of sodium or potassium salts of fatty acids, made by decomposing the glyceryl esters of fats and oils with alkalis. **2.** A metallic salt of one of the fatty acids. **3.** *U.S. Slang* Money used for bribery. — **no soap** *U.S. Slang* **1.** No; not a chance: George wanted to go, but we told him *no soap*. **2.** Futile; fruitless: We tried, but it was *no soap*. — *v.t.* To rub or treat with soap. [OE *sāpe*]
— **Syn.** (noun) **1.** *Soap* and *detergent* are cleansing agents. *Soap* is specifically the alkali salt of a fatty acid, and is one of various agents called *detergents*. However, in technical usage, *detergent* is often intended to exclude *soap*, and refers to surface-active sulfonated compounds, fatty alcohols as well as acids.

soap·bark (sōp′bärk′) *n.* **1.** The bark of the quillai. **2.** The bark of a tropical American shrub (genus *Pithecellobium*) used as a substitute for soap. Also **soapbark tree.**

soap·ber·ry (sōp′ber′ē) *n. pl.* **·ries 1.** The fruit of any of several trees or shrubs (genus *Sapindus*) typical of a large family (*Sapindaceae*) of mostly tropical plants. It is used as a substitute for soap. **2.** A tree or shrub bearing this fruit, especially *S. saponaria.*

soap·box (sōp′boks′) *n.* **1.** A box or crate for soap. **2.** Any box or crate used as a platform by street orators. Also **soap box.** — **soapbox oratory** Impromptu or crude oratory, marked by vigor rather than logic.

soapbox derby *U.S.* A race among unpowered model racing cars, steered down a slope by the boys who have built them.

soap·box·er (sōp′bok′sər) *n. Informal* A loud and ranting speaker; street-corner orator; a tub thumper.

soap bubble 1. An inflated bubble of soapsuds, forming a hollow globule. **2.** Anything attractive but unsubstantial.

soap opera A daytime television or radio serial drama usually dealing with domestic themes of a highly emotional character: so called from sponsorship by soap companies.

soap·stone (sōp′stōn′) *n.* Steatite.

soap·suds (sōp′sudz′) *n. pl.* Suds of water and soap.

soap·wort (sōp′wûrt′) *n.* A perennial herb (*Saponaria officinalis*) of the pink family, having clusters of pink or whitish, often double, flowers, and leaves that produce lather when crushed in water: also called *bouncing Bet.*

soap·y (sō′pē) *adj.* **soap·i·er, soap·i·est 1.** Resembling, containing, or consisting of soap. **2.** Smeared with soap. **3.** *Slang* Flattering; unctuous.

soar (sôr, sōr) *v.i.* **1.** To rise high into the air, as a bird flying. **2.** To sail through the air without perceptibly moving the wings, as a hawk or vulture. **3.** *Aeron.* To fly without power while gaining or holding altitude. **4.** To rise sharply above the usual level: Prices *soared.* **5.** To attain or approach a lofty or exalted state: the imagination *soars.* — **Syn.** See FLY. — *n.* The act of soaring; also, the height or range reached in soaring. [< F *essorer* < L *ex* out + *aura* breeze, air] — **soar′er** *n.*

sob (sob) *v.* **sobbed, sob·bing** *v.i.* **1.** To weep with audible, convulsive catches of the breath. **2.** To make a sound like a sob, as the wind. — *v.t.* **3.** To utter with sobs. **4.** To bring to a specified condition by sobbing: to *sob* oneself to sleep. — *n.* The act of sobbing; an audible, convulsive catch of the breath. [ME *sobben.* Cf. Frisian *sobje.*] — **sob′bing·ly** *adv.*

so·be·it (sō·bē′it) *conj. Archaic* If so; if only; provided.

so·ber (sō′bər) *adj.* **1.** Possessing or characterized by properly controlled faculties; well-balanced. **2.** Grave, sedate. **3.** Not under the influence of an intoxicant; not drunk. **4.** Moderate or abstinent, especially in the use of intoxicating drink. **5.** Subdued or modest in color, manner of dress, etc. — **Syn.** See SERIOUS. — *v.t. & v.i.* To make

or become sober. [< OF *sobre* < L *sobrius*] — **so′ber·ly** *adv.* — **so′ber·ness** *n.*

So·bies·ki (sô·byes′kē), **John** See JOHN III.

So·bran·je (sō·brän′yə) *n.* The national assembly of Bulgaria. Also **So·bran·i·ye** (sə·brän′i·yə), **So·bran′ye.**

so·bri·e·ty (sō·brī′ə·tē) *n. pl.* **·ties 1.** The state or quality of being sober. **2.** Moderateness in temper or conduct; sedateness; seriousness. **3.** Abstinence from intoxicating drink. — **Syn.** See ABSTINENCE. [< F *sobriété* or L *sobrietas, -tatis* < *sobrius* sober]

so·bri·quet (sō′bri·kā) *n.* A fanciful or humorous appellation; a nickname: also *soubriquet.* — **Syn.** See NICKNAME. [< F, orig., a tap under the chin]

sob sister *U.S. Slang* A woman journalist who writes mawkishly sentimental news stories.

sob story *Slang* A sad personal narrative told to elicit pity.

soc. **1.** Socialist. **2.** Society.

soc·age (sok′ij) *n.* **1.** The feudal tenure of land by certain determinate services other than knight service. **2.** Later, tenure by any fixed service other than military. [< *soc,* var. of SOKE] — **soc′ag·er** *n.*

so-called (sō′kôld′) *adj.* Called as stated; generally styled thus: often implying a doubtful or incorrect designation.

soc·cer (sok′ər) *n.* A form of football in which the ball is propelled toward the opponents' goal by kicking or by striking with the body or head, the goalkeepers being the only players allowed to touch the ball with the hands or forearms: officially called *association football.* [Alter. of ASSOCIATION]

So·che (sō′che′) The Chinese name for YARKAND.

so·cia·bil·i·ty (sō′shə·bil′ə·tē) *n.* The quality or character of being sociable; also, an instance of it.

so·cia·ble (sō′shə·bəl) *adj.* **1.** Inclined to seek company; social. **2.** Agreeable in company; genial. **3.** Characterized by or affording occasion for agreeable conversation and friendliness. — *n.* *U.S.* An informal social gathering, especially for members of a church: also called *social.* [< F < L *sociabilis* < *socius* friend] — **so′cia·ble·ness** *n.* — **so′cia·bly** *adv.*

so·cial (sō′shəl) *adj.* **1.** Of or pertaining to society or its organization; relating to persons as living in society or to the public as an aggregate body: *social* life, *social* questions. **2.** Disposed to hold friendly intercourse with others; sociable; also, devoted to or promoting friendly intercourse: a *social* club. **3.** Constituted or disposed to live in society: *social* beings. **4.** Of or pertaining to public welfare: *social* insurance. **5.** Of, pertaining to, or characteristic of persons considered aristocratic, fashionable, etc.: *social* register. **6.** Of animals or insects, living in communities. **7.** *Bot.* Of plants, growing compactly or in clumps. **8.** Venereal: *social* disease. **9.** Pertaining to or between allies or confederates, as the wars waged by Rome in 90–89 B.C. — **Syn.** See FRIENDLY, GOOD. — *n.* A sociable. [< L *socialis* < *socius* ally]

social climber One who attempts to become friendly with prominent or wealthy people.

social contract The theory of Hobbes, Locke, Rousseau, etc., that society evolved from associations of individuals for their mutual protection, and that the surrender of their individual sovereignty was made not through force but by mutual consent. Also **social compact.**

Social Credit Party A political party of Canada.

social dancing A type of dancing performed by groups or by couples for recreation.

social democrat A socialist; especially, a socialist who emphasizes gradual reform. — **so′cial-dem′o·crat′ic** (sō′shəl·dem′ə·krat′ik) *adj.*

Social Democrat 1. A member of the Social Democratic Party of Germany, founded by Bebel and Liebknecht in 1869 and based on Marxian principles. **2.** A member of a similar party in other countries. — **So′cial-Dem′o·crat′ic** *adj.*

social distance *Sociol.* The constraint or reserve in social interactions between individuals belonging to groups having marked cultural differences or to groups regarded as inferior or superior.

social insurance Government insurance designed to protect wage earners against unemployment, illness, accident, or the like, and not always requiring the payment of a premium on the part of the insured.

so·cial·ism (sō′shəl·iz′əm) *n.* **1.** Public collective ownership or control of the basic means of production, distribution, and exchange, with the avowed aim of operating for use rather than for profit, and of assuring to each member of society an equitable share of goods, services, and welfare benefits. **2.** The doctrines, practices, etc., of those advocating this system.

so·cial·ist (sō′shəl·ist) *n.* An advocate of socialism. Abbr. *soc.* — *adj.* Socialistic.

so·cial·is·tic (sō′shəl·is′tik) *adj.* **1.** Of, pertaining to, or practicing socialism. **2.** Like or tending toward socialism.

Socialist Labor Party A U.S. political party formed in 1876 as the **Workingmen's Party of the United States,** changed to **Socialistic Labor Party** in 1877, and renamed in 1890.

Socialist Party The U.S. political party of socialism, formed in 1901 under the leadership of Eugene V. Debs by a merger of several older groups. In some States it is named the **Social Democratic Party,** and in 1957 it officially changed its title to **Socialist Party-Social Democratic Federation.**

so·cial·ite (sō′shəl-īt) *n. Informal* One who is prominent in fashionable society.

so·ci·al·i·ty (sō′shē-al′ə-tē) *n. pl.* **·ties 1.** The state or character of being social; sociability. **2.** The instinct or tendency that is the basis of social organization.

so·cial·ize (sō′shəl-īz) *v.* **·ized, ·iz·ing** *v.t.* **1.** To place under group or government control; especially, to regulate according to socialist principles. **2.** To convert from an antisocial to a social attitude; make friendly, cooperative, or sociable. **3.** To convert or adapt to the needs of a social group. — *v.i.* **4.** *Informal* To take part in social activities. Also *Brit.* **so′cial·ise.** — **so′cial·i·za′tion** *n.*

socialized medicine A system proposing to supply the public with medical care at nominal cost, by regulating services and fees, by government subsidies to physicians and medical projects, or by cooperative projects.

so·cial·ly (sō′shəl-ē) *adv.* **1.** In a social manner: *socially pleasant.* **2.** By social standards: *socially* acceptable. **3.** In or by society: *socially* prominent.

social register A directory of persons prominent in fashionable society.

social science 1. The body of knowledge that relates to man as a member of society, or of a component of society, as the state, family, or any systematized human institution. **2.** Any field of knowledge dealing with human society, as economics, history, sociology, education, politics, ethics, etc.

social security 1. Any system that provides welfare services for members of the group who are in need. **2.** *U.S.* A Federal program of old-age and unemployment insurance, public assistance to the blind, disabled, and dependent, and maternal and child welfare services, administered by the **Social Security Administration** (abbr. *SSA, S.S.A.*).

social service Organized activity intended to advance human welfare. — **so·cial-ser·vice** (sō′shəl-sûr′vis) *adj.*

social settlement A settlement (def. 11).

social studies *U.S.* In elementary and secondary schools, a course or unit of study based upon the social sciences.

social work Any clinical, social, or recreational service for improving community welfare, as through health clinics, recreational facilities, aid to the poor and the aged, etc.

so·ci·e·ty (sə·sī′ə·tē) *n. pl.* **·ties 1.** The system of community life in which individuals form a continuous and regulatory association for their mutual benefit and protection. **2.** The body of persons composing such a community; also, all people collectively, regarded as having certain common characteristics and relationships. **3.** A number of persons in a community regarded as forming a class having certain common interests, similar status, etc. **4.** The fashionable or aristocratic portion of a community, considered as a class; also, their activities, manner of life, etc. **5.** A body of persons associated for a common purpose or object; an association: a medical *society.* **6.** *U.S.* In some States, an incorporated religious congregation. **7.** A club or fraternity. **8.** Association based on friendship or intimacy; companionship; also, one's friends or associates. **9.** *Ecol.* A group of plants or animals living together under the same physiographic conditions and influences. Abbr. *soc.* [< OF *societe* < L *societas, -tatis* < *socius* friend] — **so·ci′e·tal** *adj.*

Society Islands An island group of French Polynesia, south of the Tuamotu Islands; about 650 sq. mi.; divided administratively into the **Windward Islands** and the **Leeward Islands;** total pop. 81,500 (est. 1967); capital, Papeete on Tahiti.

Society of Friends A Christian religious group founded in England by George Fox about 1650, and characterized by the doctrine of "waiting upon the Spirit" for direct guidance and the repudiation of ritual, formal sacraments, a separate clergy, oaths, and violence: commonly known as *Quakers.*

Society of Jesus The religious organization of the Jesuits. Abbr. *S.J.*

So·cin·i·an (sō·sin′ē·ən) *adj.* Pertaining to either or both of the Italian theologians named Socinus or to their religious doctrines, which stressed denial of the Trinity, the natural depravity of man, and the efficacy of sacraments. — *n.* A believer in the Socinian theory. — **So·cin′i·an·ism** *n*

So·ci·nus (sō·sī′nəs), **Faustus,** 1539–1604, Italian theologian and reformer: original name **Fausto Soz·zi·ni** (sō·tsē′nē). — **Laelius,** 1525–1562, Italian theologian; uncle of the preceding: original name **Lelio Sozzini.**

socio- *combining form* **1.** Society; social: *sociology.* **2.** Sociology; sociological: *sociometry.* [< F < L *socius* companion]

so·ci·o·e·co·nom·ic (sō′sē·ō·ek′ə·nom′ik, sō′shē-, -ē′kə-) *adj.* Social and economic: considered as a unit based upon the interrelationship of social and economic factors: an upper

socioeconomic group. — **so′ci·o·ec′o·nom′i·cal·ly** *adv.*

sociol. Sociological; sociology.

so·ci·o·lin·guis·tics (sō′sē·ō·ling·gwis′tiks, sō′shē-) *n. pl.* (construed as sing.) The branch of linguistics that studies language as it relates to society; especially, the study of dialect distinctions related to social class.

so·ci·ol·o·gy (sō′sē·ol′ə·jē, sō′shē-) *n.* The science that treats of the origin and evolution of human society and social phenomena, the progress of civilization, and the laws controlling human institutions and functions. Abbr. *sociol.* — **so·ci·o·log·ic** (sō′sē·ə·loj′ik) or **·i·cal** *adj.* — **so′ci·o·log′i·cal·ly** *adv.* — **so′ci·ol′o·gist** *n.*

so·ci·om·e·try (sō′sē·om′ə·trē, sō′shē-) *n.* The study of the interrelationships of individuals within a community or social group, especially as expressed by attitudes of acceptance or rejection. — **so′ci·o·met′ric** (-ə·met′rik) *adj.*

sock[1] (sok) *n. pl.* **socks;** *for def. 1 also* **sox 1.** A short stocking reaching above the ankle or just below the knee. **2.** The light shoe worn by comic actors in the Greek and Roman drama. Compare BUSKIN. **3.** A windsock (which see). — **to be socked in** *U.S. Informal* Having weather conditions that prohibit air traffic: said of an airport. [OE *socc* < L *soccus* slipper]

sock[2] (sok) *Slang v.t.* To strike or hit, especially with the fist; to punch. — *n.* A hard blow. [Origin unknown]

sock·dol·a·ger (sok·dol′ə·jər) *n. Archaic U.S. Slang* **1.** A decisive blow. **2.** Something of great size, force, etc.; a rouser. Also **sock·dol′o·ger.** [Alter. of DOXOLOGY]

sock·et (sok′it) *n.* **1.** *Mech.* A cavity or an opening adapted to receive and hold some corresponding piece or fixture: the *socket* for an electric-light bulb. **2.** *Anat.* A cavity or hollowed depression for the reception of an organ or part. — *v.t.* To furnish with, hold by, or put into a socket. [< AF *soket,* dim. of OF *soc* plowshare < Celtic]

socket wrench A wrench having a socket to fit over the nut or bolt, and often a square stud or another socket to make it interchangeable on a handle or other turning device.

sock·eye (sok′ī′) *n.* A salmon (*Oncorhynchus nerka*) of the Pacific coast, highly valued as a food fish: also called *kokanee, red salmon.* [Alter. of Salishan *sukkegh*]

so·cle (sō′kəl) *n. Archit.* **1.** A square block, higher than a plinth, supporting a statue or other work of art. **2.** A base supporting a wall or a range of ornaments. [< F < Ital. *zoccolo* pedestal, shoe < L *socculus,* dim. of *soccus* shoe]

soc·man (sok′mən) *n. pl.* **·men** (-mən) In old English law, one who holds land in socage: often spelled *sokeman.* Also **soc′man.**

So·co·tra (sō·kō′trə) An island of South Yemen near the entrance of the Gulf of Aden; 1,400 sq. mi.; pop. about 12,-000; capital, Tamarida: also *Sokotra, Soqotra.*

Soc·ra·tes (sok′rə·tēz), 469?–399 B.C., Greek philosopher; chief character in the dialogues of Plato.

So·crat·ic (sō·krat′ik) *adj.* Pertaining to or characteristic of Socrates: also **So·crat′i·cal.** — *n.* A disciple of Socrates. — **So·crat′i·cal·ly** *adv.* — **Soc′ra·tist** *n.*

Socratic irony A pretense of ignorance assumed in argument to expose the errors in an opponent's reasoning.

Socratic method The dialectic method of instruction by questions and answers, as used by Socrates.

So·cred (sō′cred′) *n. Canadian* **1.** The Social Credit Party. **2.** A member of the Social Credit Party.

sod[1] (sod) *n.* **1.** A piece of grassy surface soil held together by the matted roots of grass and weeds; a turf or divot. **2.** The surface of the earth, especially that covered with grass. — **the Old Sod** Ireland. — *v.t.* **sod·ded, sod·ding** To cover with sod. [< MDu. *sode* piece of turf]

sod[2] (sod) Obsolete past tense of SEETHE.

so·da (sō′də) *n.* **1.** Any of several white, alkaline compounds widely used in medicine, industry, and the arts, especially sodium carbonate, sodium bicarbonate, and sodium hydroxide. **2.** Soda water; also, a soft drink containing carbonated water and flavoring: also **soda pop.** **3.** A drink made from carbonated water, ice cream, and, sometimes, flavoring. **4.** In faro, the first card to appear face up in the dealing box. [< Med.L, ? < Ital. *soda* (*cenere*) solid (ash) < L *solidus*]

soda ash The anhydrous form of sodium carbonate, a white powder widely used in the manufacture of glass, soaps, paper, etc., and in photography.

soda biscuit 1. A biscuit leavened with sodium bicarbonate. **2.** A soda cracker.

soda cracker A thin, crisp cracker made with yeast-leavened dough containing soda.

soda fountain 1. An apparatus from which soda water is drawn, usually containing receptacles for syrups, ice cream, etc. **2.** A counter at which soft drinks, etc., are dispensed.

soda jerk *U.S. Slang* A clerk at a soda fountain.

soda lime A mixture of sodium hydroxide and calcium oxide that yields ammonia when heated with a nitrogenous compound.

so·da·lite (sō′də·līt) *n.* A vitreous, crystalline or massive

silicate of sodium and aluminum, with some chlorine.
[< SODA + -LITE]

so·dal·i·ty (sō-dăl′ə-tē) *n. pl.* **·ties 1.** Companionship. **2.** A society; association. **3.** In the Roman Catholic Church, a society organized for devotional and charitable purposes. [< L *sodalitas, -tatis* < *sodalis* companion]

soda water 1. An effervescent drink consisting of water charged under pressure with purified carbon dioxide gas. **2.** Formerly, a solution of water, bicarbonate of soda, and acid.

sod·den (sod′n) *adj.* **1.** Soaked with moisture: *sodden* ground. **2.** Doughy; soggy, as bread, biscuits, etc. **3.** Flabby and pale; flaccid, especially from dissipation: said of persons or their features. **4.** Dull; dreary. — *v.t. & v.i.* To make or become sodden. [ME *soden,* orig. pp. of SEETHE] — **sod′den·ly** *adv.* — **sod′den·ness** *n.*

Sod·dy (sod′ē), **Frederick,** 1877–1956, English chemist and physicist.

Sö·der·blom (sœ′dər-blŏōm), **Nathan,** 1866–1931, Swedish Protestant theologian.

sod house A dwelling having sod or turf walls, and often a wooden roof, used by early settlers on the prairies.

so·di·um (sō′dē-əm) *n.* A silver-white, highly reactive, alkaline, metallic element (symbol Na) that is soft and malleable, and forms many compounds: also called *natrium.* See ELEMENT. [< NL < SODA]

sodium benzoate *Chem.* A white, odorless, amorphous, granular or crystalline powder, $NaC_7H_5O_2$, used in medicine and as a food preservative: also called *benzoate of soda.*

sodium bicarbonate *Chem.* A white crystalline compound, $NaHCO_3$, of alkaline taste, used in medicine and cookery: also called *baking soda, bicarbonate of soda.*

sodium carbonate *Chem.* A strongly alkaline compound, Na_2CO_3, that in crystalline hydrated form is known as washing soda, and in the anhydrous form as soda ash: also called *sal soda.*

sodium chloride Common salt, NaCl.

sodium dichromate *Chem.* A red crystalline compound, $Na_2Cr_2O_7 \cdot 2H_2O$, used as a dye and in making inks.

sodium hydroxide *Chem.* A strongly basic fusible compound, NaOH, used as a bleaching agent, etc.: also called *caustic soda.*

sodium hyposulfite *Chem.* **1.** Sodium thiosulfate (which see). **2.** A colorless crystalline salt, Na_2SO_3.

sodium nitrate *Chem.* A white compound, $NaNO_3$, used as a fertilizer and in explosives, occurring naturally as Chile saltpeter. See under SALTPETER.

sodium Pen·to·thal (pen′tə-thôl, -thal) Proprietary name for a brand of thiopental sodium: also called *Pentothal Sodium.* Also **sodium pent′o·thal.**

sodium propionate *Chem.* A colorless, crystalline, water-soluble compound, $NaC_3H_5O_2$, used in medicine as a fungicide and to retard bacterial and mold growth in foods.

sodium silicate Any of various soluble silicate preparations used in industry; especially, an aqueous solution used in preserving eggs, as a facing for walls, etc.: also called *soluble glass, water glass.*

sodium sulfate *Chem.* A compound, Na_2SO_4, made by the action of sulfuric acid on common salt or on Chile saltpeter, used in glassmaking, in medicine, etc.

sodium thiosulfate *Chem.* A crystalline salt, $Na_2S_2O_3$, used industrially and medicinally and in photography as a fixing agent: also called *hypo, sodium hyposulfite.*

Sod·om (sod′əm) In the Bible, a city on the Dead Sea, destroyed with the neighboring city of Gomorrah because of the wickedness of the people. *Gen.* xiii 10.

sod·om·ite (sod′əm-īt) *n.* One guilty of sodomy.

Sod·om·ite (sod′əm-īt) *n.* One of the people of Sodom.

sod·om·y (sod′əm-ē) *n.* Unnatural sexual relations, especially between male persons or between a human being and an animal. [< OF *sodomie* < LL *Sodoma* Sodom, to whose people this practice was imputed]

Soe·kar·no (sōō-kär′nō) See SUKARNO.

Soem·ba (sōōm′bä) The Dutch name for SUMBA.

Soem·ba·wa (sōōm-bä′wä) The Dutch name for SUMBAWA.

Soe·ra·ba·ja (sōō′rä-bä′yä) The Dutch name for SURABAYA.

so·ev·er (sō-ev′ər) *adv.* To or in some conceivable degree: used in generalizing and emphasizing what follows: a word often added to *who, which, what, where, when, how,* etc., to form the compounds *whosoever,* etc., giving them specific force. Often used separately: *how* great *soever* he might be.

so·fa (sō′fə) *n.* A wide seat, upholstered and having a back and raised ends. [< F < Arabic *soffah* a part of a floor raised to form a seat]

sofa bed A sofa that may be opened up to form a large bed: also, *Canadian, bed chesterfield, chesterbed.*

sof·fit (sof′ĭt) *n. Archit.* The under side of a staircase, entablature, lintel, archway, or cornice. [< F *soffite* < Ital. *soffita* < L *suffixus.* Doublet of SUFFIX.]

So·fi·a (sō′fē-ə, sō-fē′ə) The capital of Bulgaria; in the western part; pop. 840,110 (est. 1968). *Bulgarian* **So·fi·ya** (sō′fĭ·yä).

S. of Sol. Song of Solomon.

soft (sôft, soft) *adj.* **1.** Being or composed of a substance whose shape is changed easily by pressure, but without fracture; pliable, or malleable; easily worked: *soft* opposed to *hard.* **2.** Smooth and delicate to the touch: *soft* skin. **3.** Gentle in its effect upon the ear; not loud or harsh. **4.** Mild in any mode of physical action; gentle; bland: a *soft* breeze. **5.** Of subdued coloring or delicate shading; not glaring or abrupt. **6.** Expressing mildness, sympathy, etc.; gentle; conciliatory; courteous: *soft* words. **7.** Giving or enjoying rest; placid: *soft* sleep. **8.** Easily or too easily touched in feeling; tender; sympathetic: a *soft* heart. **9.** Incapable of bearing hardship, strain, etc.; delicate: *soft* muscles. **10.** Of yielding character; weak; effeminate. **11.** *Informal* Involving little effort; easy: a *soft* job. **12.** Free from mineral salts that prevent the detergent action of soap: said of water. **13.** Bituminous, as opposed to anthracite: said of coal. **14.** *Phonet.* **a** Describing *c* and *g* when articulated fricatively as in *cent* and *gibe:* opposed to *hard.* **b** Voiced and weakly articulated. **c** Palatalized, as certain consonants in the Slavic languages: traditional and popular usage. **15.** *Scot. & Brit. Dial.* Characterized by moisture or thawing: said of the weather. **16.** *Physics* Having relatively weak penetrating power: *soft* X-rays. — *n.* **1.** That which is soft; softness; a soft part or material. **2.** *Informal* One who is soft or foolish; a softy. — *adv.* **1.** Softly. **2.** Quietly; gently. — *interj. Archaic* Proceed softly; be quiet or slow. [OE *sōfte*] — **soft′ly** *adv. & interj.* — **soft′ness** *n.*

sof·ta (sof′tə) *n. Turkish* A student at a Moslem mosque.

soft·ball (sôft′bôl′, soft′-) *n.* **1.** A variation of baseball, requiring a larger ball. **2.** The ball used in this game.

soft-boiled (sôft′boild′) *adj.* **1.** Boiled, as an egg, to an extent of incomplete coagulation of the albumen. **2.** *Informal* Mild in disposition; lenient.

soft chancre A chancroid (which see).

soft clam The common long clam (*Mya arenaria*) of the north Atlantic coast.

soft coal Bituminous coal (which see).

soft drink A nonalcoholic beverage, as sweetened soda water, ginger ale, etc.

sof·ten (sôf′ən, sof′-) *v.t. & v.i.* To make or become soft or softer. — **soft′en·er** *n.*

soft-finned (sôft′fĭnd′, soft′-) *adj. Zool.* Having fins whose membrane is supported on flexible or jointed rays: opposed to *spiny-finned.*

soft focus *Photog.* A slightly blurred effect obtained by an imperfect focusing of the lens upon a scene or object.

soft goods Textiles and textile products.

soft hail Graupel.

soft·head (sôft′hed′, soft′-) *n.* A foolish or simple person. — **soft′-head′ed** *adj.*

soft-heart·ed (sôft′här′tĭd, soft′-) *adj.* Tender-hearted; merciful. — **soft′heart′ed·ly** *adv.* — **soft′heart′ed·ness** *n.*

soft landing The landing of a space vehicle at a low velocity without damage to its equipment.

soft-ped·al (sôft′ped′l, soft′-) *v.t.* **·aled** or **·alled, ·al·ing** or **·al·ling 1.** To mute the tone of by depressing the soft pedal. **2.** *Informal* To make less emphatic; tone down.

soft pedal A pedal that mutes the tone, as in a piano.

soft sell *U.S. Informal* Subtle and indirect selling or advertising: distinguished from *hard sell.*

soft-shell (sôft′shel′, soft′-) *adj.* Having a soft shell, as certain clams, or a crab or lobster after shedding its shell: also **soft′-shelled′** (-sheld′). — *n.* A soft-shelled crab.

soft-shelled crab A crab, especially the **blue crab** (*Callinectes sapidus*) of North America, after it has molted: before molting it is known as a *hard-shelled crab.*

soft-shelled turtle Any member of a family (*Trionychidae*) of turtles having a long snout and a soft, leathery shell, especially *Trionyx* (or *Amyda*) *spinifera,* common from the Gulf States to the St. Lawrence River.

soft-soap (sôft′sōp′, soft′-) *v.t.* **1.** To apply soft soap to. **2.** *Informal* To flatter; cajole. — **soft′-soap′er** *n.*

soft soap 1. Fluid or semifluid soap. **2.** *Informal* Flattery; cajolery.

soft-spo·ken (sôft′spō′kən) *adj.* **1.** Speaking with a soft, low voice. **2.** Ingratiating; suave: said of speech.

soft·ware (sôft′wâr′, soft′-) *n.* In a digital computer, any of the programs designed to control various aspects of the operation of the machine, such as input and output operations: distinguished from *hardware* (def. 4).

soft water Water free of the salts of calcium and magnesium, as rain water and that of sandstone districts.

soft·wood (sôft′wŏŏd′, soft′-) *n.* **1.** A coniferous tree or its wood. **2.** Any soft wood, or any tree with soft wood.

soft·y (sôft′tē, soft′-) *n. pl.* **soft·ies** *Informal* **1.** An extremely sentimental person. **2.** A sissy.

Sog·di·an (sog′dē-ən) *n.* **1.** A member of an ancient Iranian people inhabiting Sogdiana. **2.** Their extinct Iranian language.

Sog·di·a·na (sog′dē-ā′nə) An ancient region of central Asia comprising part of the Persian Empire; capital, Samarkand: also *Transoxiana.*

sog·gy (sog′ē) *adj.* **·gi·er, ·gi·est 1.** Saturated with water or moisture; wet and heavy; soaked. **2.** Heavy: said of pastry. **3.** Soft; boggy: said of land. Also **sog·ged** (sog′-

id). [< dial. E *sog* a swamp, bog < Scand. Cf. dial. Norw. *soggjast* to get wet.] **— sog'gi·ly** *adv.* **— sog'gi·ness** *n.*

So·ho (sō'hō, sō·hō') The foreign quarter of London, noted for its restaurants; also, an artists' quarter south of Houston Street in New York.

soi-di·sant (swä·dē·zäṅ') *adj.* *French* Self-styled; pretended: usually a disparaging term.

soi·gné (swä·nyā') *adj.* *French* Cared for; well-groomed.

soil[1] (soil) *n.* **1.** Finely divided rock mixed with vegetable or animal matter, constituting that portion of the surface of the earth in which plants grow. **2.** Land; country: native *soil.* **3.** A particular kind of earth: rocky *soil.* **4.** A medium for development or growth: Slums are fertile *soil* for disease. [< OF *soile, sueil* < L *solium* a seat, mistaken for *solum* the ground]

soil[2] (soil) *v.t.* **1.** To make dirty; smudge. **2.** To disgrace; defile. **— v.i. 3.** To become dirty. **— n. 1.** The act of soiling, or the state of being soiled. **2.** A spot or stain. **3.** Filth; sewage. **4.** Manure used as fertilizer. [< OF *soillier*, ult. < L *suculus*, dim. of *sus* pig]

soil[3] (soil) *v.t.* **1.** To feed and fatten (livestock) with soilage. **2.** To purge with green food. [? < OF *saoler, saouler* to fill < L *satullare* < *satullus*, dim. of *satur* sated]

soil·age (soil'lij) *n.* Green crops for feeding animals.

soil·ure (soil'yər) *n.* Soiling, or the condition of being soiled.

soi·ree (swä·rā', *Fr.* swä·rā') *n.* A party or reception given in the evening. Also **soi·rée'.** [< F < *soir* evening]

Sois·sons (swä·sôṅ') A city in NE France on the Aisne; pop. 25,409 (1968).

so·ja (sō'jə, sō'yə) *n.* The soybean. [< NL < Du. *soya*]

so·journ (*v.* sō'jûrn, sō·jûrn'; *n.* sō'jûrn) *v.i.* To stay or dwell temporarily; abide for a time. **— Syn.** See LIVE. **— n.** A temporary residence or stay, as of one in a foreign land. [< OF *sojorner, sojourner*, ult. < L *sub-* under + *diurnus* daily] **— so'journ·er** *n.*

soke (sōk) *n.* **1.** In feudal law, a franchise or privilege to administer justice within a certain territory, as a manor. **2.** The district within which such privilege was exercised. [< Med.L *soca* < OE *sōcn* jurisdiction]

soke·man (sōk'mən) See SOCMAN.

Soke of Peterborough An administrative county in NE Northamptonshire, England; 83 sq. mi.; pop. 74,442 (1961); county seat, Peterborough.

So·ko·tra (sō·kō'trə) See SOCOTRA.

sol[1] (sōl) *n.* *Music* The fifth of the syllables used in solmization; the fifth tone of a major scale; also, the tone G: also *so.* [See GAMUT]

sol[2] (sol) *n.* A former French silver coin, equivalent to 12 deniers. [< OF < LL *solidus* a gold coin < L, solid]

sol[3] (sōl) *n.* *pl.* **so·les** (sō'lās) The monetary unit of Peru, equivalent to 100 centavos; also, a coin of this value. Also **sol de o·ro** (thä ō'rō). [< Sp., sun]

sol[4] (sol, sōl) *n.* A colloidal suspension of a solid in a liquid: also called *soliquid.* [< (HYDRO)SOL]

sol. 1. Soluble. **2.** Solution.

Sol (sol) **1.** The sun. **2.** In Roman mythology, the god of the sun. [< L]

Sol. 1. Solicitor. **2.** Solomon.

so·la (sō'lə) See SOLUS.

sol·ace (sol'is) *n.* Comfort in grief, trouble, or calamity; also, that which supplies such comfort: also **sol'ace·ment.** **— v.t. ·aced, ·ac·ing 1.** To comfort or cheer in trouble, grief, or calamity; console. **2.** To alleviate, as grief; soothe; assuage; mitigate. **— Syn.** See CONSOLE[1]. [< OF *solacier*, *solasier* < *solas* comfort < L *solacium*] **— sol'ac·er** *n.*

so·lan (sō'lən) *n.* The gannet, a bird. Also **so'land** (-lənd, -lən), **solan goose.** [< ON *súla* gannet]

sol·a·na·ceous (sol'ə·nā'shəs) *adj.* *Bot.* Pertaining or belonging to the nightshade family (*Solanaceae*) of plants, some of which have narcotic or poisonous properties, and including belladonna, tobacco, eggplant, stramonium, and the potato. [< NL < L *solanum* nightshade]

so·la·no (sō·lä'nō) *n.* *pl.* **·nos** A hot, violent, southeasterly wind of the Mediterranean. [< Sp. < L *sol* sun]

so·la·num (sō·lā'nəm) *n.* Any of a genus (*Solanum*) of herbs and shrubs of the nightshade family, especially the potato. [< NL < L, nightshade]

so·lar (sō'lər) *adj.* **1.** Pertaining to, proceeding from, or connected with the sun. **2.** Affected, determined, or measured by the sun. **3.** Operated by the action of the sun's rays: a *solar* engine. [< L *solaris* < *sol* sun]

solar battery An assembly of photovoltaic cells for the direct conversion of solar energy into electricity.

solar constant The amount of solar energy falling on the earth, equal to approximately 1.94 calories per square centimeter per minute.

so·lar·im·e·ter (sō'lə·rim'ə·tər) *n.* An instrument for determining the intensity of solar radiation.

so·lar·ism (sō'lə·riz'əm) *n.* The belief that folk tales symbolizing solar phenomena presuppose sun worship.

so·lar·i·um (sō·lâr'ē·əm) *n.* *pl.* **·i·a** (-ē·ə) or **·i·ums** A room or enclosed porch exposed to the sun's rays, as in a sanatorium. [< L]

so·lar·i·za·tion (sō'lər·ə·zā'shən, -ī·zā'-) *n.* **1.** Exposure to the sun's rays. **2.** *Photog.* Injury to a sensitized film, as from overexposure to light, or from overprinting.

so·lar·ize (sō'lə·rīz) *v.* **·ized, ·iz·ing** *v.t.* **1.** To affect or injure by the action of the sun's rays. **2.** *Photog.* To overexpose. **— v.i. 3.** *Photog.* To be overexposed.

solar month See under MONTH.

solar plexus 1. *Anat.* The large network of the sympathetic nervous system, found behind the stomach, and containing important ganglia serving the abdominal viscera. **2.** *Informal* The pit of the stomach.

solar system The sun together with the heavenly bodies that revolve about it.

solar wind The streams of charged particles emanating outward in all directions from the surface of the sun.

solar year An astronomical year (which see).

so·la·ti·um (sō·lā'shē·əm) *n.* *pl.* **·ti·a** (-shē·ə) **1.** Compensation; solace. **2.** *Law* Compensation for injury to the feelings, as distinguished from pecuniary loss or physical suffering. [< L, var. of *solacium* solace]

sold (sōld) Past tense and past participle of SELL.

sol·dan (sol'dən) *n.* *Archaic* A ruler or sovereign of a Moslem country, especially Egypt: also *suldan, soudan.* [< OF *soudan* < Arabic *sultān* king, sovereign]

sol·der (sod'ər) *n.* **1.** A fusible metal or alloy used for joining metallic surfaces or margins, applied in a melted state, as a **hard solder,** melting at a red heat, or as a **soft solder,** melting below a red heat. **2.** Anything that unites or cements. **— v.t. 1.** To unite or repair with solder. **2.** To join together. **— v.i. 3.** To work with solder. **4.** To be united by or as by solder. [< OF *soudure* < *souder* to make hard < L *solidare* < *solidus* firm, hard] **— sol'der·er** *n.*

sol·dier (sōl'jər) *n.* **1.** A person serving in an army. **2.** An enlisted man, as distinguished from a commissioned officer. **3.** A brave, skillful, or experienced warrior. **4.** One who serves loyally in any cause. **5.** *Archaic Informal* One who makes a show of working but does little; a shirker; malingerer. **6.** *Entomol.* An asexual form of a termite or of certain ants, in which the head and jaws are largely developed to defend the colony. **— v.i. 1.** To be a soldier; perform military service. **2.** *Archaic Informal* To make a show of working; malinger. **— v.i.** To be a soldier; perform military service. **2.** *Archaic Informal* To make a show of working; malinger. **— v.i.** To soldier pay, wages < LL *solidus.* See SOL[2].] **— sol·dier·ly** (sōl'jər·lē) *adj.*

soldier of fortune An adventurous, restless person who is willing to serve wherever his services are well paid.

Soldier's Medal A U.S. military decoration awarded to any member of the army, or of a military organization connected with it, for heroism not involving actual conflict with the enemy. See DECORATION. Abbr. *S.M.*

sol·dier·y (sōl'jər·ē) *n.* *pl.* **·dier·ies 1.** Soldiers collectively. **2.** Military service.

sol·do (sol'dō, *Ital.* sôl'dō) *n.* *pl.* **·di** (-dē) A small Italian copper coin worth, generally, one twentieth of a lira. [< Ital. < LL *solidus,* a gold coin < L, solid]

sole[1] (sōl) *n.* **1.** The bottom surface of the foot. ◆ Collateral adjectives: *plantar, volar*[2]. **2.** The bottom surface of a shoe, boot, etc. **3.** The lower part of a thing, or the part on which it rests when standing; especially, the bottom part of a plowshare. **4.** The bottom part of the head of a golf club. **— v.t. soled, sol·ing 1.** To furnish with a sole; resole, as a shoe. **2.** In golf, to allow (the clubhead) to rest flat on the ground, just behind the ball. [< OF < Med.L *sola,* var. of L *solea* sandal]

sole[2] (sōl) *n.* **1.** Any of a family (*Soleidae*) of flatfishes allied to the flounders, having a small mouth; especially, the common **European sole** (*Solea solea*), highly esteemed as food, and the **American sole** (genus *Achirus*), common on the Atlantic coast of the United States. **2.** One of various flounders, as *Psettichthys melanostictus,* a food fish of the Pacific coast of the United States. [< OF < L *solea*]

sole[3] (sōl) *adj.* **1.** Being alone or the only one; existing or acting without another; only; individual. **2.** Being several of many or of a group: They were the *sole* survivors. **3.** Limited to one person, group, etc.; exclusive; absolute: to have *sole* rights to something. **4.** *Law* Unmarried; single: feme sole (an unmarried woman). **5.** *Archaic* Solitary. [< OF *sol* < L *solus* alone]

sol·e·cism (sol'ə·siz'əm) *n.* **1.** A violation of grammatical rules or of the approved idiomatic usage of language. **2.** Any impropriety or incongruity. [< L *soloecismus* < Gk. *soloikismos* < *soloikos* speaking incorrectly < *Soloi,* a Cilician town whose people spoke a substandard Attic dialect] **— sol'e·cist** *n.* **— sol'e·cis'tic** or **·ti·cal** *adj.*

sol·e·cize (sol'ə·sīz) *v.i.* **·cized, ·ciz·ing** *Rare* To use solecisms. Also *Brit.* **sol'e·cise.**

sole·ly (sōl'lē) *adv.* **1.** By oneself or itself alone; singly. **2.** Completely; entirely. **3.** Without exception; exclusively.

sol·emn (sol'əm) *adj.* **1.** Characterized by majesty, mystery, or power; exciting grave or serious thought; impressive; awe-inspiring. **2.** Marked by gravity; serious; earnest. **3.** Characterized by ceremonial observances; religious; sacred. **4.** *Law* Done in due form of law; executed formally: a *solemn* protest. **5.** *Obs.* Of great reputation, dignity, or importance. **6.** *Obs.* Somber; sober: said of color. — **Syn.** See SEDATE. [< OF *solemne* < L *solemnis*] — **sol′em·ness, sol′emn·ness** *n.* — **sol′emn·ly** *adv.*

so·lem·ni·ty (sə·lem′nə·tē) *n. pl.* **·ties 1.** The state or quality of being solemn; solemn feeling; gravity; reverence. **2.** A rite expressive of religious reverence; also, any ceremonious observance. **3.** A thing of a solemn or serious nature. **4.** *Law* A formality to be seriously observed and requisite to the validity or legality of an act.

sol·em·nize (sol′əm·nīz) *v.t.* **·nized, ·niz·ing 1.** To perform as a ceremony or solemn rite, or according to legal or ritual forms: to *solemnize* a marriage. **2.** To dignify, as with a ceremony; celebrate. **3.** To make solemn, grave, or serious. Also *Brit.* **sol′em·nise.** — **Syn.** See CELEBRATE. — **sol′em·ni·za′tion** *n.* — **sol′em·niz′er** *n.*

Solemn League and Covenant See under COVENANT.

solemn vow In the Roman Catholic Church, a vow, as of poverty, chastity, or obedience, taken by a religious for life. Dispensation from a solemn vow is reserved exclusively to the Holy See.

so·le·noid (sō′lə·noid) *n. Electr.* A conducting wire in the form of a helix, capable of setting up a magnetic field by the passage through it of an electric current. [< F < Gk. *sōlēn* a channel + -OID] — **so·le·noi′dal** *adj.* — **so′le·noi′dal·ly** *adv.*

SOLENOID

So·lent (sō′lənt), **The** A strait between the Isle of Wight and Southampton, England; ¾–5 mi. wide, 15 mi. long.

sol·er·et (sol′ə·ret′) See SOLLERET.

sole trader A feme-sole trader (which see).

So·leure (sô·lœr′) The French name for SOLOTHURN.

sol·fa (sōl′fä′) *n.* Tonic sol-fa (which see). [< SOL¹ + FA]

sol·fa·ta·ra (sōl′fä·tä′rä) *n. Geol.* An area or phase of volcanic action characterized by the escape of steam, various gases, and sublimates. [< Ital., a solfatara near Naples, Italy < *solfo* sulfur] — **sol′fa·ta′ric** *adj.*

sol·feg·gio (sōl·fej′ō) *n. pl.* **·feg·gi** (-fej′ē) or **·feg·gios** *Music* **1.** A singing exercise of runs, etc., sung either to different syllables or all to the same syllable or vowel. **2.** Solmization. [< Ital. < *solfa* the gamut. See GAMUT.]

so·lic·it (sə·lis′it) *v.t.* **1.** To ask for earnestly; seek to obtain by persuasion or entreaty. **2.** To beg or entreat (a person) persistently. **3.** To influence to action; tempt; especially, to entice (one) to an unlawful or immoral act. — *v.i.* **4.** To make petition or solicitation. — **Syn.** See ASK. [< OF *solliciter* < L *sollicitare* to agitate]

so·lic·i·ta·tion (sə·lis′ə·tā′shən) *n.* **1.** Importunity; the act of soliciting. **2.** An attempt to entice.

so·lic·i·tor (sə·lis′ə·tər) *n.* **1.** A person who does any kind of soliciting; especially, one who solicits gifts of money or subscriptions to magazines. **2.** The legal advisor to certain branches of the public service. In England, a lawyer who may advise clients or prepare cases for presentation in court, but who may appear as an advocate in the lower courts only: distinguished from *barrister.* Also **so·lic′i·ter.** Abbr. *Sol.* — **so·lic′i·tor·ship′** *n.*

Solicitor General *pl.* **Solicitors General 1.** In the United States, an officer who ranks after the Attorney General, and, in the absence of the latter, acts in his place. **2.** The principal law officer in some States, corresponding to the Attorney General in others. **3.** In England, a law officer of the Crown, ranking next after the Attorney General.

so·lic·i·tous (sə·lis′ə·təs) *adj.* **1.** Full of anxiety or concern, as for the attainment of something: *solicitous* of our good will. **2.** Full of eager desire; willing. — **so·lic′i·tous·ly** *adv.* — **so·lic′i·tous·ness** *n.*

so·lic·i·tude (sə·lis′ə·tood, -tyood) *n.* **1.** The state of being solicitous; anxiety or concern. **2.** *Usually pl.* That which makes one solicitous. — **Syn.** See CARE.

sol·id (sol′id) *adj.* **1.** Having definite shape and volume; not fluid. **2.** Substantial; firm and stable. **3.** Filling the whole of; not hollow. **4.** Having no aperture or crevice; compact. **5.** Manifesting strength and firmness; not weak or sickly; sound. **6.** Characterized by reality; substantial or satisfactory. **7.** Exhibiting united and unbroken characteristics, opinions, etc.; being or acting in unison; unanimous: a *solid* vote. **8.** Financially sound or safe. **9.** *U.S. Informal* Certain and safe in approval and support: They were *solid* with the boss. **10.** Having or relating to the three dimensions of length, breadth, and thickness: *solid* geometry. **11.** Written without a hyphen: said of a compound word. **12.** Cubic in shape: a *solid* yard. **13.** Unadulterated; unalloyed: *solid* gold. **14.** Carrying weight or conviction: a *solid* argument. **15.** Serious; reliable; exhibiting sound judgment: a *solid* citizen. **16.** Continuous; unbroken: a *solid* hour. **17.** *Printing* Having no leads or slugs between the lines; not open. — *n.* **1.** A state of matter characterized by definite shape and volume. **2.** A magnitude that has length, breadth, and thickness, as a cone, cube, pyramid,

prism, or sphere. [< F *solide* < L *solidus*] — **sol′id·ly** *adv.* — **sol′id·ness** *n.*

sol·i·da·go (sol′ə·dā′gō) *n. pl.* **·gos** Any of a large North American genus (*Solidago*) of perennial plants of the composite family; a goldenrod. [< NL < L *solidare* to strengthen; with ref. to its alleged curative powers]

solid angle *Geom.* The angle formed at the vertex of a cone or subtended at the point of intersection of three or more planes. Compare POLYHEDRAL ANGLE.

sol·i·dar·i·ty (sol′ə·dar′ə·tē) *n. pl.* **·ties** Coherence and oneness in nature, relations, or interests, as of a class.

sol·i·dar·y (sol′ə·der′ē) *adj.* United in nature or interests.

solid fuel *Aerospace* A rocket fuel in solid, rather than liquid or gaseous, form. Also **solid propellant.**

solid geometry The geometry that includes all three dimensions of space in its reasoning.

so·lid·i·fy (sə·lid′ə·fī) *v.t. & v.i.* **·fied, ·fy·ing 1.** To make or become solid, hard, firm, or compact. **2.** To bring or come together in unity. — **so·lid′i·fi·ca′tion** *n.*

so·lid·i·ty (sə·lid′ə·tē) *n. pl.* **·ties 1.** The quality or state of being solid; the property of occupying space; extension in the three dimensions of space. **2.** Mental, moral, or financial soundness; substantial or reliable character or quality; firm standing; stability. **3.** *Aeron.* The ratio of the total blade area of a rotor or propeller to the area swept by the blades. **4.** *Geom.* Cubic contents; volume.

Solid South *U.S.* The Southern States regarded as traditionally supporting the Democratic Party.

solid state physics The branch of physics that deals with the properties of solids, especially at the atomic and molecular levels.

sol·i·dus (sol′ə·dəs) *n. pl.* **·di** (-dī) **1.** A gold coin of the Byzantine Empire, first issued under Constantine and remaining the standard unit of currency during the Middle Ages, when it was called a *bezant.* **2.** A medieval money of account, equal to 12 denarii. **3.** The sign (/) used to divide shillings from pence: 10/6 (10s. 6d.), being originally the long *f* written for shilling: sometimes also used instead of a horizontal line to express fractions: 3/4. [< LL]

so·li·fid·i·an (sol′ə·fid′ē·ən) *n. Theol.* One who maintains that faith alone, without works, is the one requisite to salvation. [< L *solus* alone + *fides* faith]

so·lil·o·quize (sə·lil′ə·kwīz) *v.i.* **·quized, ·quiz·ing** To talk to oneself; utter a soliloquy. Also *Brit.* **so·lil′o·quise.**

so·lil·o·quy (sə·lil′ə·kwē) *n. pl.* **·quies** A talking or discourse to oneself, as in a drama; a monologue. [< LL *soliloquium* < L *solus* alone + *loqui* to talk]

So·li·mões (sō′lē·moinzh′) The upper reaches of the Amazon river, extending from the Peruvian border to the Río Negro.

So·ling·en (zō′ling·ən) A city in North Rhine-Westphalia, West Germany; pop. 175,895 (est. 1970).

sol·i·on (sol′ī′ən) *n. Physics* A small electrochemical cell so constructed that the movement of the ions indicates the kind and amount of changes in external conditions, used as an electronic control device. [< SOL(UTION) + ION]

sol·ip·sism (sol′ip·siz′əm) *n. Philos.* The theory that the self is the only thing really existent and therefore that reality is subjective: opposed to *objectivism.* [< L *solus* alone + *ipse* self] — **sol′ip·sist** *n.*

so·liq·uid (sol′i·kwid) *n.* A sol⁴.

sol·i·taire (sol′ə·târ′) *n.* **1.** A diamond or other gem set alone. **2.** *Chiefly U.S.* One of many games, especially of cards, played by one person: also, *Brit., patience.* **3.** An extinct bird (*Pezophaps solitarius*) somewhat resembling the dodo but more slender and graceful. **4.** *Brit.* Pegboard. [< F < L *solitarius* solitary]

sol·i·tar·y (sol′ə·ter′ē) *adj.* **1.** Living, being, or going alone. **2.** Made, done, or passed alone: a *solitary* life. **3.** Unfrequented by human beings; secluded; lonely; desolate. **4.** Lonesome; lonely. **5.** Single; one; sole: Not a *solitary* soul was there. — *n. pl.* **·tar·ies 1.** One who lives alone; a hermit; recluse. **2.** *Informal* Solitary confinement. [< L *solitarius* < *solus* alone] — **sol′i·tar′i·ly** *adv.* — **sol′i·tar′i·ness** *n.*

solitary confinement A form of imprisonment in which the prisoner is confined completely apart from other prisoners, usually as a form of punishment.

sol·i·tude (sol′ə·tood, -tyood) *n.* **1.** The state of being solitary or remote from others; seclusion. **2.** A deserted or lonely place. [< OF < L *solitudo* < *solus* alone]

sol·ler·et (sol′ə·ret′) *n.* In medieval armor, a mounted warrior's steel shoe or one of its overlapping splints: also spelled *soleret.* [< OF, dim. of *soller, soler* a shoe < L *solea* sole of the foot]

sol·mi·za·tion (sol′mə·zā′shən) *n. Music* The use of syllables, most commonly do, re, mi, fa, sol, la, ti (si), as names for the tones of a major scale, with vowel changes to indicate chromatic tones. *Do* may either be fixed at C or movable. [< SOL¹ + MI]

so·lo (sō′lō) *n. pl.* **·los** or **·li** (lē) **1.** A musical composition or passage for a single voice or instrument, with or without accompaniment. **2.** Any of several card games of the whist group, especially one in which one player may play alone against the other three. **3.** Any performance accomplished alone or without assistance. — *adj.* **1.** Composed or written for, or executed by, a single voice or instrument; performed as a solo. **2.** Done by a single person alone: a *solo* flight. — *adv.* Without another person; alone: to fly *solo*. — *v.i.* **·loed, ·lo·ing** To fly an airplane alone, especially for the first time. [< Ital. < L *solus* alone]

So·lo (sō′lō) See SURAKARTA.

so·lo·ist (sō′lō·ist) *n.* One who performs a solo or solos.

Sol·o·mon (sol′ə·mən) Tenth-century B.C. king of Israel; son of David and Bathsheba; noted for his wisdom and magnificence; built the first Temple. Abbr. *Sol.*

Solomon Islands An archipelago in the SW Pacific; about 16,500 sq. mi.; including the **British Solomon Islands**, a Protectorate; about 11,500 sq. mi.; pop. 161,500 (est. 1969); capital, Honiara; and several islands in the NW part included in Papua, New Guinea.

Sol·o·mon's-seal (sol′ə·mənz·sēl′) *n.* Any of several rather large perennial herbs (genus *Polygonatum*) of the lily family, having tubular flowers and rootstocks marked at intervals by circular scars.

Solomon's seal A six-pointed star in the form of a hexagram, believed to possess mystical properties and sometimes used as a talisman. Compare MOGEN DAVID. For illustration see HEXAGRAM.

So·lon (sō′lən, -lon) 638?–559? B.C., Athenian lawmaker. — *n.* Any wise lawmaker. — **So·lo·ni·an** (sə·lō′nē·ən) *adj.*

so long *Informal* Good-by.

So·lo·thurn (zō′lō·tŏŏrn) A canton in NW Switzerland; 305 sq. mi.; pop. 220,000 (est. 1965); capital, Solothurn. French *Soleure.*

sol·stice (sol′stis) *n.* **1.** *Astron.* The time of year when the sun is at its greatest distance from the celestial equator, and seems to pause before returning on its course; either the **summer solstice**, about June 22 in the northern hemisphere, or the **winter solstice**, about December 22. **2.** Either of the two points on the ecliptic marking these distances. **3.** A culminating or high point; epoch; limit. [< F < L *solsititium* < *sol* sun + *sistere* to cause to stand] — **sol·sti·tial** (sol·stish′əl) *adj.*

sol·u·bil·i·ty (sol′yə·bil′ə·tē) *n. pl.* **·ties** The state of being soluble; capability of being dissolved. Also **sol′u·ble·ness.**

sol·u·ble (sol′yə·bəl) *adj.* **1.** Capable of being dissolved in a liquid: Sugar is *soluble* in water. **2.** Susceptible of being solved or explained. Abbr. *sol.* [< OF < L *solubilis* < *solvere* to solve, dissolve] — **sol′u·bly** *adv.*

soluble glass Sodium silicate.

so·lus (sō′ləs) *adj. Latin* Alone; by oneself: used especially in stage directions. — **so·la** (sō′lə) *adj. fem.*

sol·ute (sol′yŏŏt, sō′lŏŏt) *n.* The substance dissolved in a solution, as distinguished from the solvent. — *adj.* **1.** Dissolved; in solution. **2.** *Bot.* Separate; not adhering.

so·lu·tion (sə·lŏŏ′shən) *n.* **1.** A homogeneous mixture formed by dissolving one or more substances, whether solid, liquid, or gaseous, in another substance, and whose composition may undergo continuous variation within certain limits. **2.** The act or process by which such a mixture is made. **3.** The act or process of explaining, settling, or disposing, as of a difficulty, problem, or doubt. **4.** *Law* Payment or satisfaction of a claim or debt. **5.** The termination or crisis of a disease. **6.** The answer to a problem; also, the method of finding the answer. **7.** Separation; disruption. Abbr. *sol.* [< OF < L *solutio, -onis* < *solutus,* pp. of *solvere* to dissolve]

So·lu·tre·an (sə·lŏŏ′trē·ən) *adj. Anthropol.* Pertaining to or characteristic of an Upper Paleolithic culture preceding the Magdalenian and typified by a skilled technique in the making of flint implements. Also **So·lu′tri·an.** [after *Solutré*, a village in central France, where remains were found]

solv·a·ble (sol′və·bəl) *adj.* **1.** That may be solved. **2.** That may be dissolved. — **solv′a·bil′i·ty, solv′a·ble·ness** *n.*

Sol·vay process (sol′vā) A process of making soda by passing carbon dioxide through a concentrated solution of common salt saturated with ammonia, yielding sodium bicarbonate that is converted into soda by heat. [after Ernst *Solvay,* 1888–1922, Belgian chemist]

solve (solv) *v.t.* **solved, solv·ing** To arrive at or work out the correct explanation or solution of; find the answer to; resolve. [< L *solvere* to solve, loosen] — **solv′er** *n.*

sol·ven·cy (sol′vən·sē) *n.* The condition of being solvent.

sol·vent (sol′vənt) *adj.* **1.** Having means sufficient to pay all debts; having more assets than liabilities. **2.** Having the power of dissolving. — *n.* **1.** That which solves. **2.** A substance, generally a liquid, capable of dissolving other substances. [< L *solvens, -entis,* ppr. of *solvere* to solve, loosen]

Sol·way Firth (sol′wā) An inlet of the Irish Sea on the boundary between England and Scotland; about 40 mi. long.

Sol·y·man the Magnificent (sol′i·mən) See SULEIMAN THE MAGNIFICENT.

Solzh·e·nit·syn (sōlzh′ə·nit′sin), **Aleksandr Isayevich,** born 1918, Russian novelist.

Som. **1.** Somaliland. **2.** Somerset; Somersetshire.

so·ma (sō′mə) *n. pl.* **·ma·ta** (-mə·tə) *Biol.* The body of any organism, excluding germ plasm. [< Gk. *sōma* body]

-soma See -SOME[2].

So·ma·li (sō·mä′lē) *n.* **1.** A member of one of certain Hamitic tribes of Somalia, Kenya, Ethiopia, and the French Territory of the Afars and Issas. **2.** The Hamitic language of the Somalis. Also **So·mal** (sō·mal′).

So·ma·li·a (sō·mä′lyə, -lē·ə) A Republic in eastern Africa, on the Indian Ocean, comprising the former British Somaliland and Italian Somaliland; 246,000 sq. mi.; pop. about 2,997,000 (est. 1973); capital, Mogadishu.

So·ma·li·land (sō·mä′lē·land) See BRITISH SOMALILAND, FRENCH SOMALILAND, ITALIAN SOMALILAND.

so·mat·ic (sō·mat′ik) *adj. Biol.* **1.** Of or relating to the body; physical; corporeal. **2.** Of or pertaining to the framework or walls of a body. **3.** Of or relating to the soma. [< Gk. *sōmatikos* < *sōma* body]

somatic cell *Biol.* Any of the cells composing the tissues, organs, etc., of the body and whose function is to assist with the maintenance of the body rather than with the reproduction of the species: distinguished from *germ cell.*

somato- *combining form* Body; of, pertaining to, or denoting the body: *somatology.* Also, before vowels, **somat-.** [< Gk. *sōma, sōmatos* the body]

so·ma·tol·o·gy (sō′mə·tol′ə·jē) *n.* **1.** The science of the human body, embracing anatomy and physiology. **2.** The branch of anthropology dealing with the physical nature of man. [< SOMATO- + -LOGY] — **so′ma·to·log′ic** (-tō·loj′ik) or **·i·cal** *adj.* — **so′ma·to·log′i·cal·ly** *adv.* — **so·ma·tol′o·gist** *n.*

som·ber (som′bər) *adj.* **1.** Partially deprived of light or brightness; dusky; murky; gloomy. **2.** Somewhat melancholy; producing or denoting gloomy feelings; depressing. Also *Brit.* **som′bre,** *Archaic* **som′brous.** [< F *sombre;* ult. origin uncertain] — **som′ber·ly** *adv.* — **som′ber·ness** *n.*

som·bre·ro (som·brâr′ō) *n. pl.* **·ros** A broad-brimmed hat, usually of felt, much worn in Spain, Latin America, and the southwestern United States. [< Sp. < *sombra* shade]

some (sum) *adj.* **1.** Of indeterminate quantity, number, or amount. **2.** Limited in degree or amount; moderate. **3.** Conceived or thought of, but not definitely known: *some* person. **4.** *Logic* Part (at least one) but not all of a class. **5.** *U.S. Informal* Worthy of notice; extraordinary: That was *some* cake. — *pron.* **1.** A certain undetermined quantity or part; a portion. **2.** Certain particular ones not definitely known or not specifically designated. — *adv.* **1.** In an approximate degree; as nearly as may be estimated: about: *Some* eighty people were present. **2.** *Informal* or *Dial.* Somewhat. [OE *sum*]

-some[1] *suffix of adjectives* Characterized by, or tending to be (what is indicated by the main element): *blithesome, frolicsome, darksome.* [OE *-sum* like, resembling]

-some[2] *suffix of nouns* A body: *chromosome.* Also spelled **-soma.** [< Gk. *sōma* a body]

-some[3] *suffix of nouns* A group consisting of (a specified number): *twosome, foursome.* [< SOME]

some·bod·y (sum′bod′ē, -bəd·ē) *pron.* A person unknown or unnamed. — *n. pl.* **·bod·ies** A person of consequence or importance: She thinks herself a *somebody.*

some·day (sum′dā′) *adv. U.S.* At some future time.

some·deal (sum′dēl′) *adv. Archaic* Somewhat.

some·how (sum′hou′) *adv.* In some way or in some manner not explained.

some·one (sum′wun′, -wən) *pron.* Some person; somebody. — *n.* A somebody.

some·place (sum′plās′) *adv. Informal* Somewhere.

som·er·sault (sum′ər·sôlt) *n.* **1.** An acrobatic stunt in which a person either leaps or rolls from a sitting posture, turning heels over head. **2.** A complete reversal of opinion, attitude, etc. — *v.i.* To perform a somersault. Also called *summerset:* also spelled *summersault.* Also **som′er·set** (-set). [< OF *sombresault,* alter. of *sobresault,* ult. < L *supra* above + *saltus* leap]

Som·er·set (sum′ər·set) A county in SW England; 1,613 sq. mi.; pop. 400,420 (1976); county seat, Taunton. Also **Som′er·set·shire** (-shir′).

Som·er·vell (sum′ər·vel), **Brehon Burke,** 1892–1955, U.S. general in World War II.

Som·er·ville (sum′ər·vil) A city in eastern Massachusetts, near Boston; pop. 88,779.

some·thing (sum′thing) *n.* **1.** A particular thing indefinitely conceived or stated. **2.** Some portion or quantity. **3.** A person or thing of importance. — *adv.* Somewhat: now only in the phrase **something like.**

some·time (sum′tīm′) *adv.* **1.** At some future time not precisely stated; eventually. **2.** At some indeterminate time or occasion. — *adj.* Former; quondam: a *sometime* student.

some·times (sum′tīmz′) *adv.* **1.** At times; occasionally. **2.** *Obs.* Formerly; once.

some·way (sum′wā′) *adv.* In some way or other; somehow. Also **some way, some′ways′** (-wāz′).

some·what (sum'hwot', -hwət) *n.* **1.** An uncertain quantity or degree; something. **2.** An individual or thing of consequence. — *adv.* In some degree.

some·where (sum'hwâr') *adv.* **1.** In, at, or to some place unspecified or unknown. **2.** In one place or another. **3.** In or to some existent place. **4.** Approximately: with *about*: She is *somewhere* about forty. — *n.* An unspecified or unknown place.

some·wheres (sum'hwârz') *adv. Chiefly Dial.* Somewhere.

some·whith·er (sum'hwith'ər) *adv. Archaic* To some indefinite or unknown place; somewhere.

some·wise (sum'wīz') *adv.* In some way or other: now only in the phrase **in somewise**.

so·mite (sō'mīt) *n. Biol.* A serial segment of the body of certain animals: also called *metamere*. [< Gk. *sōma* body + -ITE¹] — **so·mi·tal** (sō'mə·təl), **so·mit·ic** (sō·mit'ik) *adj.*

Somme (sôm) A river in northern France, flowing 150 miles to the English Channel; scene of battles in World War I (1916, 1918), and in World War II (1940, 1944).

som·me·lier (sô·me·lyā') *n. French* A wine steward.

som·nam·bu·late (som·nam'byə·lāt) *v.* **·lat·ed, ·lat·ing** *v.i.* **1.** To walk or wander about while asleep. — *v.t.* **2.** To walk over or through while asleep. [< L *somnus* sleep + AMBULATE]

som·nam·bu·lism (som·nam'byə·liz'əm) *n.* The act or state of walking during sleep; sleepwalking. Also **som·nam'·bu·la'tion.** — **som·nam'bu·lant** (-lənt) *adj.* — **som·nam'·bu·list** *n.* — **som·nam'bu·lis'tic** *adj.*

somni- *combining form* Sleep; of or pertaining to sleep: *somniferous*. [< L *somnus* sleep]

som·nif·er·ous (som·nif'ər·əs) *adj.* Tending to produce sleep; soporiferous; narcotic. Also **som·nif'ic.** [< SOMNI- + -FEROUS]

som·nil·o·quy (som·nil'ə·kwē) *n.* **1.** The act or habit of talking when asleep. **2.** The words so spoken. [< SOMNI- + L *loqui* to speak] — **som·nil'o·quist** *n.*

som·no·lence (som'nə·ləns) *n.* Oppressive drowsiness or inclination to sleep. Also **som'no·len·cy.**

som·no·lent (som'nə·lənt) *adj.* **1.** Inclined to sleep; drowsy. **2.** Tending to induce drowsiness. [< F < L *somnolentus* < *somnus* sleep] — **som'no·lent·ly** *adv.*

Som·nus (som'nəs) In Roman mythology, the god of sleep: identified with the Greek *Hypnos*.

son (sun) *n.* **1.** A male child considered with reference to either parent or to both parents. **2.** Any male descendant. **3.** One who occupies the place of a son, as by adoption, marriage, or regard. **4.** A person regarded as a native of a particular country or place. **5.** A male person characterized or influenced by some quality or thing or representing some quality or character: a *son* of liberty. Abbr. *s.* [OE *sunu*]

-son A descendant of: English and Scandinavian patronymic suffix: *Anderson.*

Son (sun) Jesus Christ; the second person of the Trinity.

so·nance (sō'nəns) *n.* **1.** A sound, as of music; also, a tune or air. **2.** The state or quality of being sonant.

so·nant (sō'nənt) *adj.* **1.** Sounding; resonant. **2.** *Phonet.* Voiced. — *n. Phonet.* **1.** A voiced speech sound. **2.** A syllabic sound; in the Indo-European languages, a sonorant. [< L *sonans, -antis,* ppr. of *sonare* to resound]

so·nar (sō'när) *n.* A device using underwater sound waves for navigation, range finding, detection of submerged objects, communication, etc. — *adj.* Of, or pertaining to this device. [< SO(UND) NA(VIGATION AND) R(ANGING)]

so·na·ta (sə·nä'tä) *n. Music* A composition for one, two, or in older music, three or more instruments. [< Ital. < *sonare* to sound]

sonata form *Music* The outline upon which a movement, especially the first, of a sonata, quartet, symphony, etc., is based. A movement in sonata form has three main sections, called *exposition, development,* and *recapitulation,* often ending in a coda.

so·na·ti·na (son'ə·tē'nə) *n. pl.* **·ti·nas** or **·ti·ne** (-tē'nä) *Music* A short or easy sonata. [< Ital., dim. of SONATA]

son·der (zon'dər) *n. Naut.* A class of small yachts, of which the sum of the water-line length, extreme beam, and extreme draft must not be greater than thirty-two feet. Also **son'der·class** (-klas', -kläs'). [Short for G *sonderklasse* < *sonder* particular + *klasse* class]

sone (sōn) *n. Physics* A unit of loudness, equivalent to a simple tone having a frequency of 1,000 cycles per second at 40 decibels above the listener's threshold of hearing. [< L *sonus* sound]

song (sông, song) *n.* **1.** A musical composition for one or more voices. **2.** The rendering of vocal music; more widely, any melodious utterance, as of a bird. **3.** A short poem whether intended to be sung or not; a lyric or ballad. **4.** Poetry; verse. — **for a song** At a very low price. [OE] — **song'less** *adj.*

song and dance **1.** A short theatrical act consisting of a song and dance, as in vaudeville. **2.** *U.S. Informal* A long explanation or alibi, especially one to evoke sympathy or serve as an excuse. **3.** *U.S. Informal* Nonsense; bunk.

song·bird (sông'bûrd', song'-) *n.* A bird that utters a musical call.

Song Coi (sông' koi') The Annamese name for the RED RIVER.

song·ful (sông'fəl, song'-) *adj.* Full of song or melody.

Song of Solomon A book of the Old Testament consisting of a Hebrew dramatic love poem attributed to Solomon: also, in the Douai Bible, *Canticle of Canticles.* Also **Song of Songs.** Abbr. *S. of Sol.*

song sparrow A common sparrow (*Melospiza melodia*) of the eastern United States, noted for its song.

song·ster (sông'stər, song'-) *n.* **1.** A person or bird given to singing. **2.** A poet.

song·stress (sông'stris, song'-) *n.* A female songster.

song thrush A bird (*Turdus ericetorum*) of the thrush family, native to Europe and having brown wings and a spotted breast: also called *mavis, throstle.*

song·writ·er (sông'rī'tər) *n.* One who writes music or lyrics, or both, for songs, especially popular songs. Also **song writer.**

son·ic (son'ik) *adj.* **1.** Of, pertaining to, determined or affected by sound: *sonic* vibrations. **2.** Having a speed approaching that of sound. [< L *sonicus* < *sonus* sound]

sonic barrier *Aeron.* The transonic barrier (which see).

sonic boom A shock wave generated by an airplane traveling at supersonic speed, heard as a sudden boom and sometimes causing concussion damage.

so·nif·er·ous (sō·nif'ər·əs) *adj.* Producing or conducting sound. [< L *sonus* sound + -FEROUS]

son-in-law (sun'in·lô') *n. pl.* **sons-in-law** The husband of one's daughter.

son·net (son'it) *n.* A poem of fourteen decasyllabic or (rarely) octosyllabic lines, originally composed of an octave and a sestet, properly expressing two successive phases of a single thought or idea. See PETRARCHAN SONNET, SHAKESPEAREAN SONNET. — *v.t.* **1.** To celebrate in sonnets. — *v.i.* **2.** To compose sonnets. [< F < Ital. *sonnetto* < Provençal *sonet,* dim. of *son* sound < L *sonus*]

son·net·eer (son'ə·tir') *n.* A composer of sonnets. — *v.i.* To compose sonnets.

son·ny (sun'ē) *n. Informal* Youngster: a familiar form of address to boys.

So·no·ra (sō·nō'rä) A State in NW Mexico; 70,465 sq. mi.; pop. 1,092,458 (1970); capital, Hermosillo.

so·no·rant (sə·nôr'ənt, -nō'rənt) *n. Phonet.* A voiced consonant of relatively high sonority, as (l), (r), (m), and (n), capable of constituting a syllable.

so·nor·i·ty (sə·nôr'ə·tē, -nor'-) *n. pl.* **·ties** **1.** Sonorous quality or state; resonance; carrying power; audibility: also **so·no'rous·ness.** **2.** A sound.

so·no·rous (sə·nôr'əs, -nō'rəs, son'ər·əs) *adj.* **1.** Productive or capable of sound vibrations; sounding. **2.** Loud and full-sounding; resonant. **3.** *Phonet.* Sonant. **4.** Noble, lofty, or impressive, as in quality, effect, style, etc. [< L *sonorus* < *sonare* to resound] — **so·no'rous·ly** *adv.*

son·ship (sun'ship) *n.* The state or relation of being a son.

Sons of Liberty The various patriotic societies, or members thereof, organized to oppose British rule in the American colonies.

son·sy (son'sē) *adj. Scot. & Brit. Dial.* Having sweet, engaging looks; happy; jolly; well-conditioned. Also **son'sie.** [< Scottish Gaelic *sonas* good fortune]

Soo Canals (sōō) An informal name for the SAULT SAINTE MARIE CANALS.

soo·chong (sōō'chong', -jong') See SOUCHONG.

soon (sōōn) *adv.* **1.** At a future or subsequent time not long distant; shortly. **2.** Without delay; in a speedy manner. **3.** With ease; readily. **4.** With willingness or readiness: usually preceded by *would as, had as,* etc. **5.** In good season; early. **6.** *Obs.* Immediately. [OE *sōna* immediately]

soon·er (sōō'nər) *n. U.S. Slang* **1.** A person who goes before the appointed time to take up free public land, and thus obtains one of the most desirable sites. **2.** One who makes an unfair and premature start.

Soon·er (sōō'nər) *n. U.S.* A nickname for a native of Oklahoma.

Sooner State Nickname for OKLAHOMA.

Soong (sōōng) A Chinese family prominent in public affairs, notably Tse-ven, 1894–1971, statesman and financier: called **T. V. Soong;** and his sisters, **Ai-ling,** born 1888, wife of Hsiang-hsi Kung, **Ching-ling,** born 1890, widow of Sun Yat-sen, and **Mei-ling,** born 1896, wife of Chiang Kai-shek.

soot (sōōt, soot) *n.* A black substance, essentially carbon from the incomplete combustion of wood, coal, natural gas, etc., as deposited on the inside of chimneys and other surfaces in contact with smoke. — *v.t.* To soil or cover with soot. [OE *sōt*]

sooth (sōōth) *Archaic adj.* **1.** True; real. **2.** Soothing; smooth. — *n.* **1.** Truth. Also *soth.* — **in sooth** In truth. [OE *sōth*] — **sooth'ly** *adv.*

soothe (sōōth) *v.* **soothed, sooth·ing** *v.t.* **1.** To restore to a quiet or normal state; calm. **2.** To mitigate, soften, or relieve, as pain or grief. — *v.i.* **3.** To afford relief; have a calming or relieving effect. [OE *sōthian* to verify < *sōth* truth] — **sooth'er** *n.*

sooth·fast (sōōth'fast', -fäst') *adj. Archaic* **1.** Truthful;

also, steadfast; loyal. **2.** Real; true. [OE *sōthfast*] — **sooth'fast'ly** *adv.* — **sooth'fast'ness** *n.*

sooth·ing (sōō'*th*ing) *adj.* Calming; quieting, as a sedative; pacifying. — **sooth'ing·ly** *adv.*

sooth·say (sōōth'sā') *v.i.* **·said, ·say·ing** To announce the future, as a soothsayer. — **sooth'say'ing** *n.*

sooth·say·er (sōōth'sā'ər) *n.* One who claims to have supernatural insight and to be able to foretell events.

soot·y (sōōt'ē, sōō'tē) *adj.* **soot·i·er, soot·i·est 1.** Blackened or stained by soot. **2.** Producing or consisting of soot. **3.** Black like soot. — **soot'i·ly** *adv.* — **soot'i·ness** *n.*

sooty grouse A blue grouse (which see).

sop (sop) *v.* **sopped, sop·ping** *v.t.* **1.** To dip or soak in a liquid. **2.** To drench. **3.** To take up by absorption: often with *up.* — *v.i.* **4.** To be absorbed; soak in. **5.** To be or become saturated or drenched. — *n.* **1.** Anything softened in liquid, as bread. **2.** Anything given to pacify, as a bribe. **3.** Any soggy mass. [OE *sopp*] — **sop'py** *adj.*

sop. *Music* Soprano.

SOP or **S.O.P.** *Mil.* Standard operating procedure.

soph·ism (sof'iz·əm) *n.* **1.** A false argument intentionally used to deceive. **2.** The doctrine or method of the sophists. [< F *sophime* or L *sophisma* < Gk., ult. < *sophos* wise]

soph·ist (sof'ist) *n.* **1.** A philosopher; a learned man; a thinker. **2.** One who argues cleverly but fallaciously or unnecessarily minutely. — *adj.* Pertaining to the art or method of sophists, or to sophistry. [< L *sophista* < Gk. *sophistēs*, ult. < *sophos* wise]

Soph·ist (sof'ist) *n.* **1.** A member of a school of early Greek philosophy, preceding the Socratic school. **2.** One of the later Greek teachers of philosophy and rhetoric, who showed great skill in subtle disputation under logical forms.

soph·is·ter (sof'is·tər) *n.* **1.** In certain English universities, as Cambridge, a student in his second year (**junior sophister**) or in his third year (**senior sophister**). **2.** A sophist or a sophister.

so·phis·tic (sə·fis'tik) *adj.* Pertaining to a Sophist, sophists, or sophistry. — *n.* The art or method of the Sophists. Also **so·phis'ti·cal.** — **so·phis'ti·cal·ly** *adv.* — **so·phis'ti·cal·ness** *n.*

so·phis·ti·cate (*v.* sə·fis'tə·kāt; *n.* sə·fis'tə·kit, -kāt) *v.* **·cat·ed, ·cat·ing** *v.t.* **1.** To make less simple or ingenuous in mind or manner; render worldly-wise. **2.** *Rare* To mislead or corrupt (a person). **3.** To increase the complexity and capability of. **4.** *Rare* To adulterate. **5.** *Rare* To falsify (a text, statement, etc.) by unauthorized or deceptive alterations. — *v.i.* **6.** To indulge in sophistry; be sophistic. — *n.* A sophisticated person. [< Med.L *sophisticatus*, pp. of *sophisticare* < *sophisticus* sophistic] — **so·phis'ti·ca'tor** *n.*

so·phis·ti·cat·ed (sə·fis'tə·kā'tid) *adj.* **1.** Having fine or subtle perceptions; cultured. **2.** Appealing to the intellect; not suited to popular tastes; complex: a *sophisticated* novel. **3.** Worldly-wise; deprived of natural simplicity: a *sophisticated* child. **4.** Very complicated in design, capabilities, etc.: said of mechanical and electronic devices. **5.** Pretentiously wise; possessing superficial information.

so·phis·ti·ca·tion (sə·fis'tə·kā'shən) *n.* **1.** Sophisticated ideas, attitudes, etc., derived from education and culture. **2.** The act of sophisticating. **3.** Adulteration; falsification.

soph·is·try (sof'is·trē) *n.* *pl.* **·tries 1.** Subtly fallacious reasoning or disputation. **2.** The art or methods of the Greek Sophists. — **Syn.** See FALLACY.

Soph·o·cles (sof'ə·klēz), 496?–406 B.C., Athenian tragic poet. — **Soph'o·cle'an** *adj.*

soph·o·more (sof'ə·môr, -mōr) *n.* In American high schools, colleges, and universities having a four-year course, a second-year student. [Earlier *sophumer* one who uses sophisms; later infl. in meaning by Gk. *sophos* wise + *mōros* fool]

soph·o·mor·ic (sof'ə·môr'ik, -mōr'-) *adj.* **1.** Of, pertaining to, or like a sophomore. **2.** Marked by a shallow assumption of learning or by empty grandiloquence; immature; callow. Also **soph'o·mor'i·cal.** — **soph'o·mor'i·cal·ly** *adv.*

Soph·o·ni·as (sof'ə·nī'əs) *n.* The Douai Bible name for ZEPHANIAH.

So·phy (sō'fē) *n. Obs.* A title of kings of Persia. Also **So'phi.** [< Persian *Safawi*, a Persian royal family]

-sophy *combining form* Knowledge pertaining to a (specified) field: *theosophy.* [< Gk. *sophia* wisdom]

so·por (sō'pər) *n.* Abnormally deep sleep. [< L]

so·po·rif·er·ous (sō'pə·rif'ər·əs, sop'ə-) *adj.* Bringing sleep. — **so'po·rif'er·ous·ly** *adv.* — **so'po·rif'er·ous·ness** *n.*

so·po·rif·ic (sō'pə·rif'ik, sop'ə-) *adj.* **1.** Causing or tending to cause sleep. **2.** Drowsy; sleepy. — *n.* A medicine that produces sleep.

sop·ping (sop'ing) *adj.* Wet through; drenched; soaking.

sop·py (sop'ē) *adj.* **·pi·er, ·pi·est 1.** Saturated and softened with moisture; very wet. **2.** Rainy. **3.** *Brit. Slang* Mawkish; sentimental.

so·pra·ni·no (sō'prə·nē'nō) *n.* An instrument that is higher in pitch than a soprano instrument. — *adj.* Of or pertaining to such an instrument or a part written for it. [< Ital., dim. of SOPRANO]

so·pran·o (sə·pran'ō, -prä'nō) *n. pl.* **so·pran·os** or **so·pra·ni** (sə·prä'nē) **1.** A voice of the highest range, usually extending from middle C upward about two octaves; also, an instrument having about this range. **2.** The music intended for such a voice or instrument. **3.** A person having a treble or high-range voice, or singing such a part. — *adj.* Of or pertaining to a soprano voice, instrument, or part. Abbr. *sop.* [< Ital. < *sopra* above < L *supra.* Akin to SOVEREIGN.]

soprano clef *Music* The C clef as used to locate middle C on the lowest line of the staff. For illustration see CLEF.

So·qo·tra (sō·kō'trə) See SOCOTRA.

so·ra (sôr'ə, sō'rə) *n.* A small grayish brown North American rail (*Porzana carolina*), esteemed as food: also called *ortolan.* Also **sora rail.** [? < N.Am.Ind.]

So·ra·ta (sô·rä'tä) See ILLAMPU.

sorb (sôrb) *n.* **1.** The service tree, or the rowan. **2.** The fruit of either of these. [< F *sorbe* < L *sorbus* service tree]

Sorb (sôrb) *n.* A Wend.

sorb apple The fruit of the service tree.

sor·be·fa·cient (sôr'bə·fā'shənt) *adj.* Conducive to absorption; absorptive. — *n.* A medicine that promotes absorption. [< L *sorbere* to absorb + -FACIENT]

Sorb·i·an (sôr'bē·ən) *adj.* Of or pertaining to the Sorbs or Wends or to their language. — *n.* **1.** A Sorb or Wend. **2.** The West Slavic language of the Sorbs; Wendish.

sor·bi·tol (sôr'bə·tōl, -tol) *n. Chem.* A white, sweetish, crystalline alcohol, $C_6H_{14}O_6$, found in mountain-ash berries and some other fruits, used as a moistening agent and in the manufacture of ascorbic acid. [< SORB + -IT(E)[1] + -OL[1]]

Sor·bon·ist (sôr'bən·ist) *n.* A doctor of or student at the Sorbonne.

Sor·bonne (sôr·bon') **1.** The faculties of literature and science of the University of Paris. **2.** A former theological college founded in Paris, 1255–59. [after Robert de *Sorbon*, 1201–74, founder of the college]

sor·bose (sôr'bōs) *n.* A monosaccharide, $C_6H_{12}O_6$, obtained from sorbitol by bacterial action and important in the synthesis of vitamin C. [< SORB(ITOL) + -OSE[2]]

sor·cer·er (sôr'sər·ər) *n.* A wizard; conjurer; magician. — **sor'cer·ess** *n.fem.*

sor·cer·y (sôr'sər·ē) *n. pl.* **·cer·ies 1.** Alleged employment of supernatural agencies; magic; witchcraft. **2.** Any remarkable or inexplicable means of accomplishment; witchery. — **Syn.** See MAGIC. [< OF *sorcerie* < *sorcier* < L *sors* fate] — **sor'cer·ous** *adj.* — **sor'cer·ous·ly** *adv.*

Sor·del·lo (sôr·del'ō, *Ital.* sôr·del'lō), 1180?–1255?, Provençal troubadour.

sor·did (sôr'did) *adj.* **1.** Filthy; dirty. **2.** Of, pertaining to, or actuated by a low desire for gain; mercenary. **3.** Of degraded character; vile; base. — **Syn.** See MEAN[2]. [< L *sordidus* squalid < *sordes* filth] — **sor'did·ly** *adv.* — **sor'did·ness** *n.*

sor·dine (sôr'dēn, sôr·dēn') *n.* A mute for a musical instrument. Also **sor·di·no** (sôr·dē'nō).

sore (sôr, sōr) *adj.* **sor·er, sor·est 1.** Painful or tender to the touch as an inflamed or injured part of the body. **2.** Grieved; distressed: a *sore* heart. **3.** Arousing painful feelings; irritating: a *sore* point. **4.** Extreme or severe: *sore* need. **5.** *Informal* Offended; aggrieved. — *n.* **1.** A place on the body where the skin or flesh is bruised, broken, or inflamed. **2.** A painful memory; grief. — *adv. Archaic* Sorely. [OE *sār*] — **sore'ness** *n.*

sore·head (sôr'hed', sōr-) *n. U.S. Slang* A disgruntled or offended person. — **sore'head·ed** *adj.*

sor·el (sôr'əl, sor-) See SORREL[2].

sore·ly (sôr'lē, sōr'-) *adv.* **1.** Grievously; distressingly. **2.** Greatly; in high degree: His aid was *sorely* needed.

sore spot *Informal* A point or matter about which one is particularly irritable or sensitive.

sor·ghum (sôr'gəm) *n.* **1.** Any of a genus (*Sorghum*) of stout, canelike tropical grasses cultivated for their saccharine juices and as fodder, especially any of the varieties of *S. vulgare.* **2.** Syrup prepared from the sweet juices of the plant. [< NL < Ital. *sorgo*, ult. < L *Syricus* of Syria, where originally grown]

sor·go (sôr'gō) *n. pl.* **·gos** *Spanish* Any variety of sorghum cultivated for its sweet juices and for forage. Also **sor'gho.**

so·ri (sô'rī, sō'rī) Plural of SORUS.

sor·i·cine (sôr'ə·sīn, -sin, sor'-) *adj.* Of, pertaining to, or resembling the shrews. [< NL < L *sorex, soricis* shrew]

so·ri·tes (sə·rī'tēz, sor'-) *n. pl.* **·tes** *Logic* A form of compound syllogism made up of successive coordinate members: Bucephalus is a horse; a horse is a quadruped; a quadruped is an animal; therefore Bucephalus is an animal. [< L < Gk. *sōreitēs* < *sōros* heap] — **so·rit'i·cal** (-rit'i·kəl) *adj.*

sorn (sôrn) *v.i. Scot.* To force oneself on others for food and lodging. — **sorn'er** *n.*

so·ro·che (sō·rō'chā) *n. Spanish* Mountain sickness.

So·ro·kin (sə·rō′kən), **Pitirim Alexandrovich,** 1889–1968, U.S. sociologist born in Russia.

So·rol·la y Bas·ti·da (sō·rō′lyä ē väs·tē′thä), **Joaquín,** 1863–1923, Spanish painter.

so·ror·ate (sôr′ə·rāt, sō′rə·rāt) *n. Anthropol.* The marriage of a man with the sister or sisters of his wife. Compare LEVIRATE. [< L *soror* sister]

so·ror·i·cide (sə·rôr′ə·sīd) *n.* **1.** The killing of one's sister. **2.** One who has killed his sister. [< LL *sororicidium* < L *sororicida* < *soror* sister + *caedere* to kill]

so·ror·i·ty (sə·rôr′ə·tē, -ror′-) *n. pl.* **·ties** A sisterhood; especially, a women's national or local association having chapters in a secondary school, college, or university. [< Med.L *sororitas, -tatis* < L *soror* sister]

so·ro·sis[1] (sə·rō′sis) *n. pl.* **·ses** *Bot.* A type of multiple fruit consisting of a fleshy mass formed by the merging of many flowers, as in the mulberry. [< NL < Gk. *sōros* heap]

so·ro·sis[2] (sə·rō′sis) *n. pl.* **·ses** *U.S.* A women's club or society.

sorp·tion (sôrp′shən) *n.* Any process by which one substance takes up and holds the molecules of another substance, as by absorption or adsorption. [< NL *sorptio, -onis* < L *sorbere*]

sor·rel[1] (sôr′əl, sor′-) *n.* **1.** Any of several low perennial herbs (genus *Rumex*) of the buckwheat family, with acid leaves, especially the common sorrel (*R. acetosa*). **2.** The oxalis, or wood sorrel. [< F *surele* < *sur* < OHG. *sour*]

sor·rel[2] (sôr′əl, sor′-) *n.* **1.** A reddish or yellowish brown color. **2.** An animal of this color. **3.** A male deer in its third year. Also spelled *sorel.* [< OF *sorel* < *sor* hawk with red plumage]

sorrel tree An American tree (*Oxydendrum arboreum*) of the heath family, with drooping clusters of white flowers and sour evergreen leaves.

Sor·ren·to (sôr·ren′tō) A port city in SW Italy, on the Bay of Naples, pop. about 8,000.

sor·row (sôr′ō, sor′ō) *n.* **1.** Pain or distress of mind because of loss, injury, or misfortune. **2.** An event that causes pain or distress of mind; affliction; misfortune; woe. **3.** The expression of grief; lamentation; mourning. — *v.i.* To feel sorrow; grieve; lament; be sad. [OE *sorg*] — **sor′row·er** *n.*
— **Syn.** (noun) **1.** *Sorrow, grief, anguish,* and *woe* denote a distressed state of mind *Sorrow* combines sadness with regret, and may be aroused by our own misfortune or that of a friend; it sobers, but rarely cows the spirit: to feel *sorrow* at the passing of summer. *Grief* is more acute, more distressing, and usually less enduring than sorrow: to feel *grief* at parting from a friend. The extreme of *grief* is *anguish,* which tortures or terrifies the spirit, while *woe* is prolonged and inconsolable *sorrow.* — **Ant.** joy, gladness.

sor·row·ful (sor′ə·fəl, sôr′-) *adj.* Sad; unhappy; mournful. — **sor′row·ful·ly** *adv.* — **sor′row·ful·ness** *n.*

sor·ry (sor′ē, sôr′ē) *adj.* **·ri·er, ·ri·est 1.** Grieved or pained; affected by sorrow from any cause. **2.** Causing sorrow; dismal. **3.** Pitiable or worthless; paltry. **4.** Painful; grievous. [OE *sārig* < *sār* sore] — **sor′ri·ly** *adv.* — **sor′ri·ness** *n.*

sort (sôrt) *n.* **1.** Any number or collection of persons or things characterized by the same or similar qualities; a kind; species; class; set. **2.** Form of being or acting; character; nature; quality; also, manner; style. ◆ See note under KIND. **3.** *Usually pl. Printing* A character or type considered as a portion of a font. **4.** *Obs.* Social rank, especially high rank. **5.** *Obs.* A lot; destiny. — **of sorts** Originally, of various or different kinds; now, of a poor or unsatisfactory kind: used disparagingly: an actor *of sorts.* — **out of sorts 1.** *Informal* In an ill humor; irritable. **2.** *Printing* Having some sorts of type in short supply or out of stock. — **sort of** *Informal* Somewhat. — *v.t.* **1.** To arrange or separate into grades, kinds, or sizes; classify; assort. — *v.i.* **2.** To agree; correspond. **3.** To associate; consort. [< OF *sorte* < L *sors, sortis* lot, condition] — **sort′a·ble** *adj.* — **sort′a·bly** *adv.* — **sort′er** *n.*

sor·tie (sôr′tē) *n. Mil.* **1.** A sally of troops from a besieged place to attack the besiegers. **2.** A single trip of an aircraft on a military or naval mission. [< F < *sortir* to go forth]

sor·ti·lege (sôr′tə·lij) *n.* **1.** The act or practice of drawing lots; divination by lot. **2.** Sorcery. [< OF *sortilege* < LL *sortilegus* diviner < L *sors, sortis* lot + *legere* to pick, choose]

so·rus (sôr′əs, sō′rəs) *n. pl.* **so·ri** (sôr′ī, sō′rī) *Bot.* In ferns and fernlike plants, a cluster of sporangia. [< NL < Gk. *sōros* a heap]

sos. or **sost.** or **sosten.** Sostenuto.

S O S (es′ō′es′) **1.** The code signal of distress adopted by the Radiotelegraphic Convention in 1912, and used by airplanes, ships, etc. **2.** Any call for assistance.

So·sno·wiec (sô·snô′vyets) A city in SW Poland; pop. 131,-600 (est. 1960).

so-so (sō′sō′) *adj.* Passable; neither very good nor very bad; mediocre. — *adv.* Indifferently; tolerably.

sos·te·nu·to (sôs′te·nōō′tō) *Music adj.* Sustained or continuous in tone; prolonged or held. — *adv.* In a sostenuto manner. — *n. pl.* **·tos** or **·ti** (-tē) A sostenuto manner of playing or singing. Also **sos′ti·nen′to** (-tē·nen′tō), **sos′te·nen′do** (-te·nen′dō). [< Ital., pp. of *sostenere* to sustain]

sot (sot) *n.* A habitual drunkard. [OE < OF < LL *sottus* drunkard]

so·te·ri·ol·o·gy (sə·tir′ē·ol′ə·jē) *n. Theol.* The doctrine of salvation by Jesus Christ. [< Gk. *sōtērios* < *sōtēr* savior + -LOGY] — **so·te′ri·o·log′ic** (-ə·loj′ik) or **·i·cal** *adj.*

soth (sōth) *adj. & n.* Sooth.

So·thic cycle (sō′thik, soth′ik) A period of 1460 Sothic years. Also **Sothic period.**

Sothic year The fixed solar year of the ancient Egyptians, consisting of 365 days and 6 hours, so called because determined by the heliacal rising of Sothis.

So·this (sō′this) *n.* Sirius, the Dog Star. [< Gk. < Egyptian] — **So′thic** *adj.*

So·tho (sō′thō) *n.* A Bantu language of southern Africa.

so·tol (sō′tōl) *n.* Any of a genus (*Dasylirion*) of plants allied to the yucca, found in the SW United States. [< Am. Sp. < Nahuatl *tzotolli*]

sot·tish (sot′ish) *adj.* **1.** Stupefied with drink. **2.** Prone to drink excessively. **3.** Stupid; doltish. — **sot′tish·ly** *adv.*

sot·to vo·ce (sot′ō vō′chē, *Ital.* sōt′tō vō′chä) Softly; in an undertone; privately. [< Ital., under the (normal) voice]

sou (sōō) *n.* A former French coin of varying value. [< F < LL *solidus* a gold coin]

sou·a·ri (sōō·ä′rē) *n.* Any of several tropical American trees (genus *Caryocar*), yielding a durable timber known as **souari wood,** and edible nuts called **souari nuts** or butternuts; especially, *C. nuciferum.* [< F *saouari* < native name]

sou·bise (sōō·bēz′) *n. French* A sauce of onions, butter, and white sauce. Also **soubise sauce.** [after Prince Charles Soubise, 1715–87, marshal of France]

sou·brette (sōō·bret′) *n.* **1.** In light opera or comedy, the role of a pert, intriguing lady's maid. **2.** An actress playing such a role. **3.** Any frivolous or coquettish young woman character. [< F < Provençal *soubreto* < *soubret* shy, coy] — **sou·bret′ish** *adj.*

sou·bri·quet (sōō′bri·kā) *n.* A sobriquet.

sou·car (sou·kär′) *n. Anglo-Indian* A native banker: also spelled *sowcar.*

sou·chong (sōō′chong′, -shong′) *n.* A variety of black tea made from large leaves: spelled *soochong.* [< F < Chinese *siao* small + *chung* plant]

Sou·dan (sōō′dän′) See (Republic of) MALI.

souf·fle (sōō′fəl) *n. Pathol.* A low whispering or blowing sound heard on auscultation. [< F < *souffler* to blow]

souf·flé (sōō·flā′) *adj.* Made light and frothy, and fixed in that condition by heat: also **souf·fléed′** (-flād′). — *n.* A light, baked dish made fluffy with beaten egg whites combined with the yolks, and often with cheese, mushrooms, or other ingredients. [< F, orig. pp. of *souffler* to blow < L *sufflare* < *sub-* under + *flare* to blow]

Sou·fri·ère (sōō·frē·âr′) **1.** A dormant volcano on Montserrat, West Indies; 3,002 ft. **2.** A dormant volcano on Basse-Terre, Guadeloupe, French West Indies; 4,869 ft.

sough (suf, sou) *v.i.* To make a sighing sound. — *n.* A deep, murmuring sound. [OE *swōgan* to sound, roar, rustle]

sought (sôt) Past tense and past participle of SEEK.

soul (sōl) *n.* **1.** The rational, emotional, and volitional faculties in man, conceived of as forming an entity distinct from the body. **2.** *Theol.* **a** The divine principle of life in man. **b** The moral or spiritual part of man as related to God, considered as surviving death and liable to joy or misery in a future state. **3.** The emotional faculty of man as distinguished from the intellect: He puts his *soul* into his acting. **4.** Fervor; emotional force; heartiness; vitality: His music lacks *soul.* **5.** The animating principle of a thing; an essential or vital element: Justice is the *soul* of law. **6.** The leading figure or inspirer of a cause, movement, party, etc.: Lee was the *soul* of the Confederacy. **7.** A person considered as the embodiment of a quality or attribute: He is the *soul* of generosity. **8.** A living person; a human being: Every *soul* trembled at the sight. **9.** The disembodied spirit of one who has died; a ghost. **10.** In Christian Science, the divine Principle; God. **11.** *U.S.* A feeling of racial pride and culture among Negroes. — *adj. U.S.* Of or pertaining to Negro pride or culture: *soul* music. [OE *sāwol*] — **souled** *adj.*

soul·ful (sōl′fəl) *adj.* Full or expressive of deep feeling: a *soulful* gaze. — **soul′ful·ly** *adv.* — **soul′ful·ness** *n.*

soul·less (sōl′lis) *adj.* **1.** Heartless; unemotional. **2.** Having no soul. — **soul′less·ly** *adv.* — **soul′less·ness** *n.*

soul-searching (sōl′sûr′ching) *n.* Deep self-examination of one's motives, principles, convictions, desires, etc.

Soult (sōōlt), **Nicolas Jean de Dieu,** 1769–1851, Duke of Dalmatia, French marshal under Napoleon.

sou mar·qué (sōō mär·kā′) *French* **1.** An 18th-century copper coin of France. **2.** Something of little value; a trifle. Also **sou mar·kee′** (-kē′), **sou mar·quee′** (-kē′).

sound[1] (sound) *n.* **1.** Any of a class of waves consisting of mechanical disturbances, as varying pressure or alternating movement, in an elastic system, especially in air. **2.** The auditory stimulation produced by waves of this type having frequencies between about 20 and 20,000 cycles per second. Abbr. *sd.* **3.** An instance of this stimulation: the *sound* of a car; a shrill *sound.* **4.** A speech sound (which see). **5.** Significance; implication: *The story has a sinister sound.* **6.** Sounding or hearing distance; earshot: *within sound of battle.* **7.** Noise: *full of sound and fury.* **8.** *Obs.* Rumor. — *v.i.* **1.** To give forth a sound or sounds. **2.** To give a specified impression; seem: *The story sounds true.* — *v.t.* **3.** To cause to give forth sound. **4.** To give a signal or order for or announcement of: *to sound retreat.* **5.** To utter audibly; pronounce. **6.** To articulate (the sound represented by) a letter: *to sound the r in park.* **7.** To make known or celebrated: *to sound a hero's fame.* **8.** To test or examine by sound; auscultate. — **to sound in tort** *Law* To act as or have the nature of a tort. [< OF *son* < L *sonus*] — **Syn.** (noun) **3.** *Sound, tone,* and *noise* designate sensations excited in the ear. *Sound* is the general term, embracing sensations of all qualities. A *tone* is a *sound* of definite pitch, caused by vibrations predominantly of one frequency. *Noise* is a *sound* lacking pitch, caused by vibrations of different and dissonant frequencies.

sound² (sound) *adj.* **1.** Having all the organs or faculties complete and in normal action and relation; healthy. **2.** Free from injury, flaw, mutilation, defect, or decay: *sound timber.* **3.** Founded in truth; valid; legal. **4.** Correct in views or processes of thought. **5.** Solvent. **6.** Profound, as rest; deep; unbroken. **7.** Complete and effectual; thorough. **8.** Solid; stable; firm; safe; also, trustworthy. **9.** Based on good judgment. [OE *gesund*] — **sound′ly** *adv.* — **sound′ness** *n.*

sound³ (sound) *n.* **1.** A long and narrow body of water, more extensive than a strait, connecting larger bodies. Abbr. **sd. 2.** The air bladder of a fish. [Fusion of OE *sund* sea, swimming and ON *sund* strait, swimming]

sound⁴ (sound) *v.t.* **1.** To test the depth of (water, etc.), especially by means of a lead weight at the end of a line. **2.** To measure (depth) thus. **3.** To explore or examine (the bottom of the sea, etc.) by means of a sounding lead adapted for bringing up adhering particles. **4.** To discover or try to discover the views and attitudes of (a person) by means of conversation and roundabout questions: usually with *out.* **5.** To try to ascertain or determine (beliefs, attitudes, etc.) in such a manner. **6.** *Surg.* To search or examine, as with a sound. — *v.i.* **7.** To measure depth, as with a sounding lead. **8.** To dive down suddenly and deeply, as a whale when harpooned. **9.** To make investigation; inquire. — *n. Surg.* An instrument for exploring a cavity. [< L *sonder,* ? < L *sub-* under + *unda* a wave] — **sound′a·ble** *adj.*

Sound (sound), **The** See ÖRESUND.

sound barrier *Aeron.* The transonic barrier (which see).

sound·board (sound′bôrd′, -bōrd′) *n.* A thin board, as in a piano or violin, often forming the upper plate of a resonant box: also called *belly, sounding board.*

sound box The hollow part of a stringed instrument, designed to provide a resonance cavity for the sound.

sound change *Ling.* A change in the articulation of a whole class of sounds in a given language at a given time, as umlaut in Old English.

sound effects In motion pictures, radio, etc., the incidental and often mechanically produced sounds, as of rain, hoofbeats, explosions, etc., used to give the illusion of reality.

sound·er (soun′dər) *n.* **1.** One who or that which sounds or gives a sound. **2.** An apparatus for taking soundings, as at sea. **3.** A probe. **4.** A telegraphic device for converting electromagnetic code impulses into sound.

sound film A motion picture with spoken words, music, sound effects, etc.: also *talking picture, talkie.*

sound·ing¹ (soun′ding) *adj.* **1.** Giving forth a full sound; sonorous. **2.** Having much sound with little significance.

sound·ing² (soun′ding) *n.* **1.** The act of one who or that which sounds. **2.** Measurement of the depth of water. **3.** *pl.* The depth of water as sounded; also, water of such depth that the bottom may be reached by sounding.

sounding balloon See under BALLOON.

sounding board **1.** A structure or suspended dome over a pulpit or speaker's platform to amplify and clarify the speaker's voice. **2.** Soundboard (which see).

sounding lead The lead or other weight on a sounding line.

sounding line A weighted line marked at fathom intervals, used for determining the depth of water.

sound·less (sound′lis) *adj.* Having or making no sound; silent. — **sound′less·ly** *adv.* — **sound′less·ness** *n.*

sound·proof (sound′proof′) *adj.* Resistant to the penetration or spread of sound. — *v.t.* To make soundproof.

sound ranging A method of locating the point of origin of a sound by checking time intervals as recorded from microphones of known position.

sound spectrograph See under SPECTROGRAPH.

sound track The portion along the edge of a motion-picture film that carries the sound record.

sound truck A truck with a mounted loudspeaker.

soup (soop) *n.* **1.** Liquid food made by boiling meat, vegetables, etc., in water: distinguished from *broth,* that is usually strained. **2.** *Photog.* A developer. **3.** *Slang* A thick overcast or fog. **4.** *U.S. Slang* Nitroglycerin. — **in the**

soup *U.S. Slang* In difficulties; in a quandary. — **to soup up** *U.S. Slang* To supercharge or otherwise modify (an automobile) for high speed. [< F *soupe* < Gmc.]

soup·çon (soop-sôn′) *n. French* A minute quantity; a taste.

soup kitchen A place where soup, etc., is served to the needy either free or at very low cost.

soup·spoon (soop′spoon′) *n.* A spoon used in eating soup.

soup·y (soo′pē) *adj.* **soup·i·er, soup·i·est 1.** Like soup in appearance or consistency. **2.** *U.S. Informal* Sentimental.

sour (sour) *adj.* **1.** Sharp to the taste; acid; tart, like vinegar. **2.** Having an acid or rancid taste as the result of fermentation; also, pertaining to fermentation. **3.** Having a rancid, acid smell or vapor; dank. **4.** Misanthropic and crabbed; cross; morose: *a sour person; a sour smile.* **5.** Cold and wet; unpleasant: *sour weather.* **6.** Acid; harsh to crops: said of land. **7.** Containing sulfur compounds: said of gasoline. — *v.t. & v.i.* To become or make sour. — *n.* **1.** Something sour or distasteful. **2.** An acid solution used in bleaching or in curing skins. **3.** A treatment with such a solution. **4.** A sour or acid beverage: *a whisky sour.* [OE *sūr*] — **sour′ly** *adv.* — **sour′ness** *n.*

— **Syn.** (adj.) *Sour, acid, bitter, acrid,* and *tart* all mean harsh or sharp in taste. *Sour* and *acid* refer to the taste of vinegar, but *acid* stresses natural composition and *sour* the result of fermentation or decay. *Bitter* suggests the taste of quinine or gall; *acrid* is sharply *bitter* or pungent, and is always unpleasant. *Tart* is usually pleasant, and describes that which is somewhat *acid* and piquant.

source (sôrs, sōrs) *n.* **1.** That from which any act, movement, or effect proceeds; an originator; creator; origin. **2.** A place where something is found or whence it is taken or derived. **3.** The spring or fountain from which a stream of water proceeds; a fountainhead; fountain. **4.** A person, writing, or agency from which information is obtained. **5.** The initiator of a payment, dividend, etc. — **Syn.** See BEGINNING. [< OF, orig. pp. of *sourdre* to rise < L *surgere*]

sour cherry See under CHERRY.

sour cream A commercial food product made of cream to which a culture of lactic acid bacteria has been added.

sour·crout (sour′krout′) See SAUERKRAUT.

sour·dine (soor-dēn′) *n.* **1.** A mute, especially a trumpet mute. **2.** A stop on the harmonium producing a soft effect. **3.** An obsolete, double-reed, woodwind instrument. **4.** In telegraphy, a silencer. [< F < Ital. *sordino* < *sordo* < L *surdus* deaf]

sour·dough (sour′dō′) *n.* **1.** *Dial.* Fermented dough for use as leaven in making bread. **2.** *U.S. & Canadian Slang* A pioneer or prospector, especially in Alaska or Canada.

sour gourd **1.** A large Australian tree (*Adansonia gregorii*) having a huge trunk and woody gourdlike fruit. **2.** The acid fruit of this tree.

sour grapes The attitude of affecting to despise something one cannot do or have: an allusion to a fable of Aesop.

sour gum The black gum (which see).

sour·puss (sour′poos′) *n. Slang* A person with a sullen, peevish expression or character.

sour·sop (sour′sop′) *n.* **1.** A tree (*Annona muricata*) of tropical America. **2.** The pulpy, acid fruit of this tree.

Sou·sa (soo′zə, -sə) **John Philip,** 1854–1932, U.S. bandmaster and composer.

sou·sa·phone (soo′zə-fōn, -sə-) *n.* A large circular tuba with a bell that flares in the direction faced by the player, used chiefly in military bands. [after John P. *Sousa*]

souse¹ (sous) *v.t. & v.i.* **soused, sous·ing 1.** To dip or steep in a liquid. **2.** To pickle. **3.** *Slang* To make or get drunk. — *n.* **1.** The act of sousing. **2.** Something steeped in pickle, especially the feet and ears of a pig. **3.** Formerly, any salt pickle. **4.** A liquid used in pickling; brine. **5.** *Slang* A drunkard. [< OF *sous* < OHG *sulza* brine]

souse² (sous) *Archaic v.* **soused, sous·ing** *v.t.* **1.** To pounce upon. — *v.i.* **2.** To swoop suddenly, as a hawk: with *on* or *upon.* — *n.* A swoop, as of a hawk on its prey; a downright blow or stroke. — *adv.* Suddenly; with a plunge or swoop. [Var. of SOURCE, in earlier sense of "a rising"]

sou·tache (soo-tâsh′) *n. French* **1.** A narrow, flat braid in a herringbone effect. **2.** Mohair or silk rounded braid.

sou·tane (soo-tän′) *n.* A Roman Catholic priest's cassock. [< F < Ital. *sottana* < *sotto* under < L *subtus*]

south (south) *n.* **1.** The direction along a meridian that falls to the right of an observer on earth facing the sun at sunrise. **2.** One of the four cardinal points of the compass, directly opposite *north* and 90° clockwise from *east.* See COMPASS CARD. **3.** Any direction near this point. **4.** *Sometimes cap.* Any region south of a specified point. — **the South** In the United States: **a** The population or territory of the southern or southeastern States; especially, the region south of the Mason-Dixon line, and east and south of the western and northern borders of Missouri. **b** The Confederacy. — *adj.* **1.** To, toward, facing, or in the south; southern. **2.** Coming from the south: *the south wind.* — *adv.* In or toward the south; southward. Abbr. *s.,* S, S., So. [OE *sūth*]

South Africa, Republic of A Republic, formerly a member of the Commonwealth of Nations, situated at the southern tip of Africa; 472,359 sq. mi.; pop. 21,282,000 (est. 1970); seat of government, Pretoria; seat of legislature, Capetown. Formerly **Union of South Africa**.

South African 1. Pertaining to South Africa, especially to the Republic of South Africa. **2.** A native of the Republic of South Africa, especially one of European descent; an Afrikander. Abbr. *S.Afr.*

South African Dutch Afrikaans.

South African Republic A former state of South Africa, coextensive with the Transvaal.

South African War The Boer War (which see).

South America The southern continent of the Western Hemisphere; about 6.9 million sq. mi.; pop. 186 million (est. 1969). — **South American**

South·amp·ton (south·hamp′tən, sou·thamp′-) **1.** An administrative county, the mainland part of Hampshire, southern England; 1,503 sq. mi.; pop. 1,551,900 (1969); county seat, Winchester. **2.** A county borough and port in southern Southampton, England, at the head of **Southampton Water**, an inlet of the Solent; pop. 210,000 (est. 1969).

South Australia A State of southern Australia; 380,070 sq. mi.; pop. 1,169,600 (1970, excluding aborigines); capital, Adelaide.

South Bend A city in northern Indiana; pop. 125,580.

south·bound (south′bound′) *adj.* Going southward. Also **south′-bound′.**

south by east A point on the mariner's compass, 15 points or 168° 45′ clockwise from due north. See COMPASS CARD. Abbr. *SbE*

south by west A point on the mariner's compass, 17 points or 191° 15′ clockwise from due north. See COMPASS CARD. Abbr. *SbW*

South Carolina A SE State of the United States, on the Atlantic; 31,055 sq. mi.; pop. 2,590,516; capital, Columbia; entered the Union May 23,1788; one of the thirteen original States; nickname *Palmetto State*: abbr. *S.C.* — **South Carolinian**

South China Sea The part of the Pacific between the SE Asian mainland and the Malay Archipelago.

South Dakota A State in the north central United States; 77,047 sq. mi.; pop. 666,257; capital, Pierre; entered the Union Nov. 2, 1889; nickname *Coyote State*. Abbr. *S. Dak.* — **South Dakotan**

South·down (south′doun′) *n.* One of an English breed of hornless sheep with brown legs and faces, originally bred in the South Downs, England.

South Downs A range of hills in southern England, chiefly in Sussex.

south·east (south′ēst′, *Naut.* sou′ēst′) *n.* **1.** The direction midway between south and east. **2.** A point on the mariner's compass, 12 points or 135° clockwise from due north. See COMPASS CARD. **3.** Any region lying in or toward this point. — *adj.* **1.** To, toward, facing, or in the southeast. **2.** Coming from the southeast. — *adv.* In or toward the southeast. Abbr. *se, s.e.,* SE, S.E. — **south′east′ern** *adj.*

Southeast Asia Treaty Organization A regional security pact between Australia, France, New Zealand, Pakistan, the Philippines, Thailand, the United Kingdom, and the United States, implemented by the **Southeast Asia Collective Defense Treaty** signed at Baguio, Philippines, Sept. 8, 1954. Abbr. *SEATO*

southeast by east A point on the mariner's compass, 11 points or 123° 45′ clockwise from due north. See COMPASS CARD.

southeast by south A point on the mariner's compass, 13 points or 146° 15′ clockwise from due north. See COMPASS CARD.

south·east·er (south′ēs′tər, *Naut.* sou′ēs′tər) *n.* A gale or storm from the southeast.

south·east·er·ly (south′ēs′tər·lē, *Naut.* sou′ēs′tər·lē) *adj.* **1.** In, of, or toward the southeast. **2.** From the southeast, as a wind. — *adv.* Toward or from the southeast. — *n. pl.* **·lies** A wind or storm from the southeast.

south·east·ward (south′ēst′wərd, *Naut.* sou′ēst′wərd) *adv.* Toward the southeast. Also **south′east′wards.** — *adj.* To, toward, facing, or in the southeast. — *n.* Southeast.

south·east·ward·ly (south′ēst′wərd·lē, *Naut.* sou′ēst′wərd·lē) *adj. & adv.* Toward or from the southeast.

South·end-on-Sea (south′end′on·sē′) A county borough and resort in SE Essex, England; pop. 164,976 (1961).

south·er (sou′thər) *n.* A gale or storm from the south.

south·er·ly (suth′ər·lē) *adj.* **1.** In, of, toward, or pertaining to the south. **2.** From the south, as a wind. — *adv.* Toward or from the south. — *n. pl.* **·lies** A wind or storm from the south. — **south′er·li·ness** *n.*

south·ern (suth′ərn) *adj.* **1.** To, toward, or in the south. **2.** Native to or inhabiting the south. **3.** *Sometimes cap.* Of, pertaining to, or characteristic of the south or South. **4.** From the south, as a wind. **5.** *Astron.* South of the celestial equator. Abbr. *s., S, S., So.* [OE *sútherne*]

Southern Alps A mountain range in west central South Island, New Zealand; highest peak Mt. Cook, 12,349 ft.

Southern Cross A southern constellation having four bright stars in the form of a cross. See CONSTELLATION.

Southern Crown The constellation Corona Australis.

south·ern·er (suth′ərn·ər) *n.* **1.** One who is native to or lives in the south. **2.** *Usually cap.* One who lives in or comes from the southern United States.

Southern Fish The constellation Piscis Austrinus.

Southern Hemisphere See under HEMISPHERE.

Southern Kar·roo (ka·rōō′) A plateau region in SW Cape of Good Hope Province, South Africa.

southern lights The aurora australis.

south·ern·most (suth′ərn·mōst′) *adj.* Farthest south.

Southern Protectorate of Morocco A former Spanish protectorate in NW Africa; since 1958 a part of Morocco.

Southern Rhodesia See under RHODESIA.

south·ern·wood (suth′ərn·wood′) *n.* A European plant (*Artemisia abrotanum*) allied to wormwood.

Southern Yemen See SOUTH YEMEN.

South Eu·clid (yōō′klid) A city in NE Ohio, a suburb of Cleveland; pop. 29,579.

South·ey (sou′thē, suth′ē), **Robert,** 1774–1843, English poet; poet laureate 1813–43.

South·field (south′fēld) A city in SE Michigan; pop. 69,285.

South·gate (south′gāt) A city in SE Michigan, near Wyandotte; pop. 33,909.

South Gate A city in SW California; a suburb of Los Angeles; pop. 56,909.

South Georgia An island included in the Falkland Islands; 1,600 sq. mi.

South Glamorgan A county in SE Wales; 160 sq. mi.; pop. 391,100 (1976); county seat, Cardiff.

South Holland A Province of the western Netherlands; 1,085 sq. mi.; pop. 2,968,670 (1960); capital, The Hague.

south·ing (sou′thing) *n.* **1.** *Chiefly Naut.* **a** Difference in latitude between two positions resulting from a northward movement. **b** Deviation or progression toward the south. **2.** *Astron.* South declination. See DECLINATION.

South Island The larger of the two main islands of New Zealand; 58,093 sq. mi.

South Korea See under KOREA.

south·land (south′land′) *n. Sometimes cap.* A land or region in the south or South. — **south′land′er** *n.*

south·paw (south′pô′) *Informal n.* **1.** In baseball, a left-handed pitcher. **2.** Any left-handed person or player. — *adj.* Left-handed.

South Platte River A river in Colorado and Nebraska, flowing 450 miles east and NE to join the North Platte, forming the Platte River.

South Pole The southern extremity of the earth's axis.

South·port (south′pôrt, -pōrt) A county borough and port in SW Lancashire, England, on the Irish Sea; pop. 79,430 (est. 1969).

south·ron (suth′rən, south′-) *Chiefly Scot. adj.* Southern. — *n. Often cap.* One who lives in the south; especially, an Englishman. [Alter. of dial. *E southren*, var. of SOUTHERN; infl. in form by *Saxon, Briton*, etc.]

South San Francisco A city in western California, a suburb of San Francisco; pop. 46,646.

South San Ga·bri·el (san gā′brē·əl) An unincorporated place in SW California; pop. 29,176.

South Sea Islands The islands of the South Pacific; Oceania.

South Seas 1. The South Pacific Ocean. **2.** The seas of the world south of the Equator.

South Shields A county borough and port in NE Durham, England, at the mouth of the Tyne; pop. 109,533 (1961).

South Slavic See under SLAVIC.

south·south·east (south′south′ēst′, *Naut.* sou′sou′ēst′) *n.* **1.** The direction midway between south and southeast. **2.** A point on the mariner's compass, 14 points or 157° 30′ clockwise from due north. See COMPASS CARD. — *adj. & adv.* In, toward, or from the south-southeast. Abbr. *sse, s.s.e.,* SSE, S.S.E.

south·south·west (south′south′west′, *Naut.* sou′sou′west′) *n.* **1.** The direction midway between south and southwest. **2.** A point on the mariner's compass, 18 points or 202° 30′ clockwise from due north. See COMPASS CARD. — *adj. & adv.* In, toward, or from the south-southwest. Abbr. *ssw, s.s.w.,* SSW, S.S.W.

South Vietnam See under VIETNAM.

south·ward (south′wərd, *Naut.* suth′ərd) *adv.* Toward the south. Also **south′wards.** — *adj.* To, toward, facing, or in the south. — *n.* A southward direction or point; also, a southern part or region.

south·ward·ly (south′wərd·lē, *Naut.* suth′ərd·lē) *adj.* & *adv.* **1.** Toward the south. **2.** Coming from the south.

South·wark (suth′ərk) A borough of London, England, on the south bank of the Thames; pop. 86,175 (1961).

south·west (south′west′, *Naut.* sou′west′) *n.* **1.** The direction midway between south and west. **2.** A point on the mariner's compass, 20 points or 225° clockwise from due north. See COMPASS CARD. **3.** Any region lying in or toward this point. — *adj.* **1.** To, toward, facing, or in the southwest. **2.** Coming from the southwest: a *southwest* wind. — *adv.* In or toward the southwest. Abbr. *sw, s.w., SW, S.W.* — **south′west′ern** *adj.*

South-West Africa A mandated Territory in SW Africa, on the Atlantic, administered by the Republic of South Africa; 317,877 sq. mi.; pop. 615,000 (1969); capital, Windhoek; formerly *German Southwest Africa:* official UN name *Namibia.* Also **South West Africa.** See map of SOUTH AFRICA.

southwest by south A point on the mariner's compass, 19 points or 213° 45′ clockwise from due north. See COMPASS CARD.

southwest by west A point on the mariner's compass, 21 points or 236° 15′ clockwise from due north. See COMPASS CARD.

south·west·er (south′wes′tər, *Naut.* sou′wes′tər) *n.* **1.** A gale or storm from the southwest. **2.** A waterproof hat with a broad brim to protect the neck. Also **sou′west′er.**

south·west·er·ly (south′wes′tər·lē, *Naut.* sou′wes′tər·lē) *adj.* **1.** In, of, or toward the southwest. **2.** From the southwest, as a wind. — *adv.* Toward or from the southwest. — *n. pl.* **·lies** A wind or storm from the southwest.

Southwest Semitic See under SEMITIC.

south·west·ward (south′west′wərd, *Naut.* sou′west′wərd) *adv.* Toward the southwest. Also **south′west′wards.** — *adj.* To, toward, facing, or in the southwest. — *n.* Southwest. — **south′west′ward·ly** *adj., adv.*

South Yemen A republic on the Arabian peninsula, containing most of the territory of the former Aden and Aden Protectorate; area about 110,000 sq. mi.; pop. 1,300,000 (est. 1970); capital, Medina al-Eshaab: also *Southern Yemen.* Officially, **People's Democratic Republic of Yemen.**

South Yorkshire A county in north central England; 602 sq. mi.; pop. 1,317,200 (1976); county seat, Barnsley.

sou·ve·nir (sōō′və·nir′, sōō′və·nir) *n.* A token of remembrance; memento. [< F *se souvenir* to remember < L *subvenire* to come to mind]

sov·er·eign (sov′rən, suv′-) *n.* **1.** One in whom the supreme power of a state or nation is vested; monarch; ruler. **2.** An individual, governing body, etc., having supreme authority. **3.** An English gold coin equivalent to one pound sterling or twenty shillings. — *adj.* **1.** Exercising or possessing supreme authority, jurisdiction, or power. **2.** Free, independent, and in no way limited by external authority or influence: a *sovereign* state. **3.** Possessing supreme excellence or greatness; preeminent; paramount. **4.** Superior in efficacy; potent: a *sovereign* remedy. [< OF *soverain,* ult. < L *super* above. Akin to SOPRANO.] — **sov′er·eign·ly** *adv.*

sov·er·eign·ty (sov′rən·tē, suv′-) *n. pl.* **·ties 1.** The state of being sovereign; supreme authority. **2.** The ultimate, supreme power in a state. **3.** A sovereign state or similar political entity. **4.** The status or dominion of a sovereign. — **popular sovereignty** The political doctrine that sovereignty belongs to the body of the people.

so·vi·et (sō′vē·et, -ət, sō′vē·et′) *n.* **1.** In the Soviet Union, any of the legislative bodies existing at various governmental levels. See SUPREME SOVIET. **2.** Any of various similar legislative bodies. [< Russian *sovyet* council]

So·vi·et (sō′vē·et, -ət, sō′vē·et′) *adj.* Of or pertaining to the Union of Soviet Socialist Republics.

Soviet Central Asia The region of Kazakh, Kirghiz, Tadzhik, Turkmen, and Uzbek S.S.R.: also *Central Asia.*

so·vi·et·ism (sō′vē·ə·tiz′əm) *n.* The policies of or government by soviets, especially as practiced in the Soviet Union. — **so′vi·et·ist** *n.* — **so′vi·et·is′tic** *adj.*

Soviet Russia 1. See RUSSIAN SOVIET FEDERATED SOCIALIST REPUBLIC. **2.** The Soviet Union.

Soviet Union The Union of Soviet Socialist Republics.

sov·ran (sov′rən, suv′-) *adj. & n. Chiefly Poetic* Sovereign. — **sov′ran·ly** *adv.* — **sov′ran·ty** *n.*

sow[1] (sō) *v.* **sowed, sown** or **sowed, sow·ing** *v.t.* **1.** To scatter (seed) over land for growth. **2.** To scatter seed over (land). **3.** To spread abroad; disseminate; implant: to *sow* the seeds of distrust. **4.** To cover or sprinkle. — *v.i.* **5.** To scatter seed. [OE *sāwan*] — **sow′er** *n.*

sow[2] (sou) *n.* **1.** A female hog. **2.** *Metall.* **a** The connection between pieces of pig iron before breaking up. **b** The conduit into the pig bed for molten metal. [OE *sū, sugu*]

so·war (sō·wär′, -wôr′) *n. Anglo-Indian* Formerly, in the British-Indian army, a mounted native trooper. [< Persian *sawar* horseman]

sow·bel·ly (sou′bel′ē) *n. U.S. Dial.* Salt pork.

sow·bread (sou′bred) *n.* The cyclamen, a plant.

sow bug (sou) A small, terrestrial isopod (family *Oniscidae*) found under logs and stones: also called *wood louse.*

sow·car (sou·kär′) See SOUCAR.

sow·ens (sō′ənz) *n. Scot.* Sour porridge made from husks of oatmeal.

sow thistle (sou) Any of a genus (*Sonchus*) of spiny plants of the composite family; especially, the **common sow thistle** (*S. oleraceus*), a coarse weed with yellow flowers.

soy (soi) **1.** The soybean. **2.** An Asian sauce prepared from soybeans fermented and steeped in brine: also **soy sauce.** [< Japanese *soy, shoy,* short for *shōyū*]

soy·bean (soi′bēn′) *n.* **1.** An erect, leguminous herb (*Glycine max*) native to China and India, and cultivated for forage. **2.** Its bean, a source of oil, flour, and other products. Also called *soy:* also **soy·a** (soi′ə). [< SOY + BEAN]

So·yuz So·vet·skikh So·tsi·a·lis·ti·ches·kikh Res·pub·lik (so·yōōz′ so·vyet′skyikh sə·tsyi·ə·lyis·tyē′chis·kyikh ryis·pōōb′lyik) The Russian name for the UNION OF SOVIET SOCIALIST REPUBLICS. Abbr. in the Russian alphabet CCCP

so·zin (sō′zin) *n. Biochem.* Any protein normally contained in the body of an animal and forming a protection against germs. Also **so′zine.** [< Gk. *sōzein* to save + -IN]

sp. 1. Special. **2.** Species. **3.** Specific. **4.** Specimen. **5.** Spelling. **6.** Spirit(s).

s.p. 1. Sine prole (L, without issue). **2.** Single phase.

Sp. Spain; Spaniard; Spanish.

SP *Naval* Shore patrol (or police).

spa (spä) *n.* **1.** Any locality frequented for its mineral springs. **2.** A mineral spring. [from SPA]

Spa (spä) A resort town in east Belgium; pop. about 9.000.

Spaak (späk), **Paul Henri,** 1899–1972, Belgian statesman.

Spaatz (späts), **Carl,** 1891–1974, U.S. general.

space (spās) *n.* **1.** That which is characterized by dimensions extending indefinitely in all directions from any given point, and within which all material bodies are located. **2.** An interval or area between or within points or objects. **3.** Area, room, or extent, as for some purpose or use: parking *space.* **4.** Outer space (which see). **5.** An interval of time; period; while. **6.** An occasion or opportunity. **7.** *Printing* A piece of type metal, less than type-high, used for spacing between words; especially, one less than one en in width. **8.** A part of a musical staff included between two lines. **9.** One of the intervals during the transmission of a telegraph message when the key is open or not in contact. **10.** Reserved accommodations, as on a train or airplane. **11.** Pages, linage, broadcasting time, etc., available for advertisements. **12.** *Math.* A system of continuous, unlimited points in a series; an ordered set of infinite numbers. — *v.t.* **spaced, spac·ing 1.** To separate by spaces. **2.** To divide into spaces. [< OF *espace* < L *spatium*] — **space′less** *adj.* — **spac′er** *n.*

Space, meaning of, pertaining to, for, or concerned with outer space, may appear as a combining form or in two-word phrases, as in:

space age	space fiction	space rocket
space capsule	space flight	space suit
space crew	space patrol	space travel
space environment	space program	space vehicle

space bar A bar at the bottom of a typewriter keyboard, pressed to produce a space rather than a letter or symbol.

space·craft (spās′kraft′, -kräft′) *n. Aerospace* Any vehicle, manned or unmanned, designed for research, exploration, or travel in outer space. Also **space·ship** (spās′ship′).

space heater *U.S.* A stove or other heating unit designed to warm an enclosed area, as a room, loft, garage, etc.

space lattice *Physics* The arrangement of the atoms or structural units in a crystal, such that corresponding units are separated by constant intervals along any straight line drawn through their centers.

space·man (spās′mən) *n. pl.* **·men** (-mən) *Aerospace* One who travels in outer space; an astronaut. — **space′man·ship** *n.*

space medicine *Aerospace* medicine (which see).

space platform *Aerospace* An artificial earth satellite designed as a base for research or for launching other spacecraft. Also **space station.**

space·port (spās′pôrt′, -pōrt′) *n. Aerospace* A base for rockets and other spacecraft, including the equipment necessary for their testing, storage, maintenance, launching, etc.

space probe *Aerospace* An artificial satellite or other spacecraft designed and equipped to obtain knowledge of phenomena and conditions in outer space.

space shuttle *Aerospace* A rocket controllable like an airplane, designed for flights to and from space platforms.

SPACE LATTICE

space-time (spās′tīm′) *n.* A four-dimensional continuum within which any event may be precisely located. It consists of three spatial coordinates and one coordinate of time. Also **space-time continuum.**

space·walk (spās′wôk′) *n.* The maneuvers of an astronaut who leaves his vehicle while traveling through space, remaining attached to it by an umbilical.

spa·cial (spā′shəl) See SPATIAL.

spac·ing (spā′sing) *n.* **1.** The act, process, or result of arrangement by spaces. **2.** A space or spaces, as in print.

spa·cious (spā′shəs) *adj.* **1.** Of indefinite or vast extent. **2.** Capacious. — **spa′cious·ly** *adv.* — **spa′cious·ness** *n.*

spack·le (spak′əl) *n.* A plasterlike powder mixed to form a paste used for filling cracks and holes in walls, ceilings, etc., before painting or decorating. Also **Spackle.** — *v.t.* **·led, ·ling** To apply spackle to. [< *Spackle,* a trade name]

spade[1] (spād) *n.* **1.** An implement used for digging, cutting turf, etc., heavier than a shovel and having a flatter blade. **2.** Any of various tools or implements resembling a spade, as a large chiselike implement for flensing whales. **3.** A heavy piece of metal at the end of a gun-carriage trail that helps to keep the carriage in position when the gun recoils. — **to call a spade a spade** To call a thing by its right name; speak the plain, uncompromising truth. — *v.t.* **spad·ed, spad·ing** To dig or cut with a spade. [OE *spadu*] — **spad′er** *n.*

spade[2] (spād) *n.* **1.** A figure on playing cards, resembling a heart with a stalk or handle at the juncture of the lobes. **2.** A card so marked. **3.** *Usually pl.* The suit of cards so marked. [< Sp. *espada* sword < L *spatha* < Gk. *spathē*]

spade·fish (spād′fish′) *n.* *pl.* **·fish** or **·fish·es 1.** A spiny-finned food fish (*Chaetodipterus faber*) of the Atlantic coast from Massachusetts to the West Indies. **2.** A related species (*C. zonatus*) of Pacific waters.

spade·work (spād′wûrk′) *n.* **1.** Work done with a spade. **2.** Preliminary work necessary to get a project under way.

spa·di·ceous (spā-dish′əs) *adj.* **1.** Of or like a spadix. **2.** Of a clear brown or bay color.

spa·dix (spā′diks) *n.* *pl.* **spa·di·ces** (spā-dī′sēz) *Bot.* A spike or head of flowers with a fleshy axis, usually enclosed within a spathe. [< Gk. *spadix* < *spaein* to break]

spae (spā) *v.t.* **spaed, spae·ing** *Scot.* To foretell.

spa·ghet·ti (spə-get′ē) *n.* **1.** A food consisting of cordlike strands of flour paste, between macaroni and vermicelli in thickness. **2.** Insulated tubing through which wire is passed, as in a radio circuit. [< Ital., pl. dim. of *spago* cord]

spa·gyr·ic (spə-jir′ik) *adj.* Of or pertaining to alchemy. Also **spa·gyr′i·cal.** [< NL *spagyricus;* prob. coined by Paracelsus]

spa·hi (spä′hē) *n.* *pl.* **spa·his** (-hēz) **1.** Formerly, a member of a Turkish corps of irregular cavalry. **2.** Formerly, one of an Algerian cavalry corps in the French service. Also **spa′-hee.** [< Turkish *sipahi* < Persian *sipāh* army. Cf. SEPOY.]

Spain (spān) A monarchy in SW Europe, occupying the Iberian Peninsula, and including the Balearic and Canary Islands: 194,368 sq. mi.; pop. 35,470,000 (est. 1975); capital, Madrid: Spanish *España.*

spake (spāk) *Archaic* past tense of SPEAK.

Spa·la·to (spä′lä·tō) The Italian name for SPLIT.

spale (spāl) *n.* *Scot.* or *Brit. Dial.* A lath, chip, or shaving. Also **spail.**

spall (spôl) *v.t.* **1.** To break up or chip, especially so as to prepare for sorting, as ore. — *v.i.* **2.** To chip at the edges, as a stone under pressure. — *n.* A chip, splinter, or flake, as from a stone. [ME *spalle*; ult. origin unknown]

Spal·lan·za·ni (späl′län·dzä′nē) **Lazzaro,** 1729–99, Italian biologist; challenged the theory of spontaneous generation.

spal·la·tion (spə·lā′shən) *n.* *Physics* The splitting of an atomic nucleus into its component nuclides. [< SPALL + -ATION]

spal·peen (spal·pēn′, spal′pēn) *n.* *Irish* A scamp; good-for-nothing. [< Irish *spailpīn* laborer]

Sp. Am. Spanish American.

span[1] (span) *v.t.* **spanned, span·ning 1.** To measure, especially with the hand with the thumb and little finger extended. **2.** To encircle or grasp with the hand, as in measuring. **3.** To stretch across; extend over or from side to side of: This road *spans* the continent. **4.** To provide with something that stretches across or extends over. — *n.* **1.** The extreme space over which the hand can be expanded, usually considered as nine inches. **2.** Distance or extent between any two extremities. **3.** Any small interval or distance. **4.** *Archit.* The space or distance between the supports of an arch, abutments of a bridge, etc. **5.** That which spans, as a bridge. **6.** *Aeron.* The maximum lateral distance from tip to tip of airplane wings. [OE *spann*] — **span′less** *adj.*

span[2] (span) *v.* **spanned, span·ning** *v.t.* To bind; make fast; fetter. — *n.* **1.** *Naut.* A rope or chain used as a fastening. **2.** A pair of matched horses or oxen. **3.** Especially in South Africa, a team of two or more oxen or bullocks. [< MDu. *spannen* to fasten, draw together]

span[3] (span) *Archaic* past tense of SPIN.

span·drel (span′drəl) *n.* *Archit.* **a** The triangular space between the outer curve of an arch and the rectangular figure formed by the moldings or framework surrounding it. **b** The

space between the shoulders of two adjoining arches. For illustration see ARCH. Also **span/dril.** [Dim. of AF *spaundre,* prob. < OF *espandre* to expand]

spang (spang) *adv.* *U.S. Informal* Directly; exactly; straight: He ran *spang* into the wall. [Origin uncertain]

span·gle (spang′gəl) *n.* **1.** A small bit of sparkling metal, plastic, etc., used for decoration in dress, as in theatrical costume. **2.** Any small sparkling object. — *v.* **·gled, ·gling** *v.t.* **1.** To adorn with or as with spangles; cause to glitter. — *v.i.* **2.** To sparkle as spangles; glitter. [Dim. of MDu. *spang* clasp, brooch] — **span′gly** *adj.*

Span·iard (span′yərd) *n.* A native or citizen of Spain. Abbr. *Sp.*

span·iel (span′yəl) *n.* **1.** Any of various breeds of small or medium-sized dogs having large pendulous ears and usually long silky hair. **2.** One who follows like a dog; an obsequious follower. [< OF *espaignol* Spanish (dog)]

Span·ish (span′ish) *adj.* Of or pertaining to Spain, its people, or their language. — *n.* **1.** The Romance language of Spain, Spanish America, and the Philippine Islands. **2.** The inhabitants of Spain collectively: with *the.* Abbr. *Sp.*

Spanish America The parts of the western hemisphere in which Spanish is the common language, consisting of Mexico, Central America excluding British Honduras, South America excluding Brazil and the Guianas, and most of the Caribbean islands.

Span·ish-A·mer·i·can (span′ish-ə-mer′ə-kən) *adj.* **1.** Of or pertaining to Spanish America. **2.** Designating or pertaining to the war between the United States and Spain, 1898. — *n.* One of Spanish origin living in America, especially Central or South America; a citizen of a Spanish-American country.

Spanish-American War See table for WAR.

Spanish Armada See under ARMADA.

Spanish cedar A tree (*Cedrela odorata*) of the mahogany family from whose wood cigar boxes are made.

Spanish dagger Any of various species of yucca, with sword-shaped leaves. Also **Spanish bayonet.**

Spanish Equatorial Region The part of western Africa which up to 1968 comprised the Spanish Overseas Provinces of Río Muni and Fernando Po: also called **Spanish Guinea.** See *Equatorial Guinea.*

Spanish fly 1. A bright green blister beetle (*Lytta vesicatoria*) of the Mediterranean region, used in the preparation of cantharides. For illustration see INSECTS (beneficial). **2.** Cantharides.

Spanish Inquisition See under INQUISITION.

Spanish mackerel A large, spotted fish (*Scomberomorus maculatus*) of warmer American waters.

Spanish Main 1. The mainland of Spanish America, especially the coastal region of South America between Panama and the Orinoco. **2.** Loosely, the part of the Caribbean through which Spanish merchant vessels frequently sailed.

Spanish Morocco A former Spanish protectorate on the coastal strip of northern Morocco; incorporated into Morocco, 1956.

Spanish moss A long, pendent, epiphytic plant (*Tillandsia usneoides*) that grows on trees of the southern United States near the seacoast: sometimes called *long moss, Florida moss.* Also **Spanish beard.**

Spanish needles 1. A smooth annual plant (*Bidens bipinnata*) of the composite family, having bipinnate leaves and spiny achenia: also called *agrimony.* **2.** The barbed, prickly fruit of this plant.

Spanish onion A large, fleshy variety of onion, usually having a mild flavor.

Spanish paprika A cultivated variety of paprika, widely used as a condiment.

Spanish Sahara A Spanish Overseas Province on the coast of NW Africa; 105,409 sq. mi.; pop. 63,000 (est. 1969).

Spanish West Africa The part of NW Africa comprising Spanish Sahara and Ifni.

spank (spangk) *v.t.* **1.** To slap or strike, especially on the buttocks with the open hand as a punishment. — *v.i.* **2.** To move briskly. — *n.* A smack on the buttocks; a spanking. [Imit.]

spank·er (spangk′ər) *n.* **1.** One who or that which spanks. **2.** *Naut.* A fore-and-aft sail extended by a boom and a gaff from the mizzenmast of a ship or boat. For illustration see SHIP. **3.** Any person or thing uncommonly large or fine. **4.** One who or that which proceeds rapidly.

spank·ing (spangk′ing) *adj.* **1.** Moving or blowing rapidly; swift; dashing; lively; strong. **2.** *Brit. Informal* Uncommonly large or fine. — *n.* A series of slaps on the buttocks; also, the act of administering such punishment.

span·ner (span′ər) *n.* **1.** One who or that which spans. **2.** *Brit.* A hand tool used to turn nuts, bolts, etc., a form of wrench. **3.** A measuring worm. [def. 2 < G]

span-new (span′nōō′, -nyōō′) *adj. Dial.* Really or freshly new. [< ON *span-nýr* < *spánn* chip + *nýr* new]

span·worm (span′wûrm′) *n.* A measuring worm (which see).

spar[1] (spär) *n.* **1.** *Naut.* A heavy, round wooden or metal piece, as a mast, yard, boom, gaff, or the like, used to support rigging. **2.** Any similar long, heavy pole. **3.** *Aeron.* Any principal longitudinal member of an airplane wing. **4.** *Naut.* A spar buoy: see under BUOY. — *v.t.* **sparred, spar·ring 1.** To furnish with spars. **2.** *Archaic* To fasten, as with a bolt. [Cf. ON *sparri*, MDu. *sparre* beam]

spar² (spär) *v.i.* **sparred, spar·ring 1.** To box, especially with care and adroitness. **2.** To bandy words; wrangle. **3.** To fight, as cocks, by striking with spurs. — *n.* The act or practice of boxing; a boxing match. [? < OF *esparer* < Ital. *sparare* to kick < L *parare* to prepare]

spar³ (spär) *n.* A vitreous, crystalline, easily cleavable, lustrous mineral of varied composition. [< MDu. Akin to OE *spæren* gypsum.]

Spar (spär) *n.* A member of the women's reserve of the United States Coast Guard. Also **SPAR.** [< L *s(emper) par(atus)* always ready, the motto of the U.S. Coast Guard]

spar·a·ble (spar'ə-bəl) *n.* A kind of small headless nail used by shoemakers in soling boots: also called *sparrow bill*. [Alter. of *sparrow bill*; so called from resemblance in shape]

spar buoy See under BUOY.

spar deck *Naut.* The light upper deck of a vessel, extending from bow to stern.

spare (spâr) *v.* **spared, spar·ing** *v.t.* **1.** To refrain from injuring, molesting, or killing; treat with mercy or lenience. **2.** To free or relieve (someone) from (pain, expense, etc.): *Spare* us the sight. **3.** To refrain from using or exercising; use frugally. **4.** To part with; do without: Can you *spare* a dime? — *v.i.* **5.** To be frugal; live or act economically. **6.** To be lenient or forgiving; show mercy. — *adj.* **spar·er, spar·est 1.** That can be spared or used at will; disposable; available. **2.** Held in reserve; additional; extra. **3.** Having little flesh; thin; lean. **4.** Not lavish or abundant; scanty. **5.** Economical; chary; stingy; parsimonious. — **Syn.** See LEAN². — *n.* **1.** That which has been saved or stored away; something unused. **2.** A duplicate item kept as a substitute in case the original breaks down, as an automobile tire or a mechanical part. **3.** In bowling, the knocking down by a player of all the pins with the two bowls in any frame; also, the score so made: distinguished from *strike*. [OE *sparian*] — **spare'ly** *adv.* — **spare'ness** *n.* — **spar'er** *n.*

spare·rib (spâr'rib') *n.* A cut of meat, especially pork, consisting of ribs somewhat closely trimmed. [? Alter. of MLG *ribbespēr*]

sparge (spärj) *v.t. & v.i.* **sparged, sparg·ing** To scatter; sprinkle; shower. — *n.* A sprinkling. [< OF *espargier* < L *spargere* to sprinkle] — **sparg'er** *n.*

spar·ing (spâr'ing) *adj.* **1.** Scanty; slight. **2.** Frugal; stingy. **3.** Merciful; forbearing. — **Syn.** See FRUGAL. — **spar'ing·ly** *adv.* — **spar'ing·ness** *n.*

spark¹ (spärk) *n.* **1.** An incandescent particle thrown off from a red-hot or burning substance or struck from a flint. **2.** Any glistening or brilliant point or transient luminous particle. **3.** Anything that kindles or animates. **4.** *Electr.* **a** The luminous effect of a disruptive electric discharge, or the discharge itself. **b** A small transient arc or an incandescent particle thrown off from such an arc. **5.** A small diamond or bit of diamond, as for cutting glass. **6.** A small trace or indication. — *v.i.* **1.** To give off sparks; sparkle; scintillate. **2.** In an internal-combustion engine, to have the ignition operating. — *v.t.* **3.** To bring into action or being; activate or cause: to *spark* a revolution. [OE *spearca*]

spark² (spärk) *n.* **1.** A man fond of gallantry. **2.** A lover; suitor; gallant. — *v.t. & v.i.* To play the spark (to); woo; court. [Special use of SPARK¹]

spark arrester 1. A sievelike device for catching sparks thrown from an open fire. **2.** *Electr.* An apparatus to prevent injurious sparking at the opening of a circuit made and broken frequently: also called *sparker*.

spark chamber *Physics* A detecting device in which the ionization path of a subatomic particle can be seen as a luminous trail of sparks between sets of charged metal plates in a neon-filled chamber.

spark coil *Electr.* An induction coil used with an internal-combustion engine, wireless telegraph equipment, etc., to produce sparking.

spark·er (spär'kər) *n.* **1.** One who or that which sparks. **2.** A spark arrester (which see).

spark gap *Electr.* **1.** An arrangement of two electrodes between which a disruptive electric charge may pass. **2.** The space so covered.

spark generator *Electr.* Any device capable of generating a sufficiently high voltage to discharge across a spark gap.

spark·ish (spär'kish) *adj.* **1.** Jaunty; sprightly; airy; gay. **2.** Showy; fine; well-dressed.

spark killer *Electr.* A device for reducing harmful sparking at frequently interrupted points in a circuit. Also **spark suppressor.**

spar·kle (spär'kəl) *v.i.* **·kled, ·kling 1.** To give off flashes of light; scintillate; glitter. **2.** To emit sparks. **3.** To bubble; effervesce. **4.** To be brilliant or vivacious. — **Syn.** See SHINE. — *n.* A spark; gleam. [Freq. of SPARK¹]

spar·kler (spär'klər) *n.* **1.** Something that sparkles. **2.** A sparkling gem. **3.** A thin, rodlike firework that emits sparks. **4.** A person who shines with spirit or vivacity.

spar·kling (spär'kling) *adj.* **1.** Giving out sparks or flashes; glittering. **2.** Brilliant; vivacious. — **spar'kling·ly** *adv.* — **spar'kling·ness** *n.*

spark·plug (spärk'plug') *v.t.* **·plugged, ·plug·ging** To lead, inspire, or animate (a group, undertaking, etc.).

spark plug 1. An electrical device for igniting the explosive gases in an internal-combustion engine by means of a spark passing between two terminals. Also *Brit.* **spark'ing plug. 2.** *Informal* One who leads a group or undertaking.

sparks (spärks) *n. Sometimes cap.* A ship's radio officer or operator.

Sparks (spärks), **Jared,** 1789–1866, U.S. editor and historian.

spark transmitter *Telecom.* A type of radio transmitter that utilizes an oscillatory discharge through a spark gap as a source of radio-frequency signals.

spar·ling (spär'ling) *n.* **1.** A smelt, parr, or other young fish. **2.** A young herring. [< OF *esperlinge* < Gmc.]

spar·oid (spâr'oid, spar'-) *adj.* Of or pertaining to a family (*Sparidae*) of spiny-finned marine fishes allied to the grunts and including the porgy, sheepshead, etc. — *n.* A sparoid fish. [< L *sparus* < Gk. *sparos* gilthead + -OID]

spar·row (spar'ō) *n.* **1.** A small hardy bird (*Passer domesticus*) related to the finches, grosbeaks, and buntings, introduced from Europe into the United States, where it is known as the **English sparrow:** also called *house sparrow*. **2.** Any of various Old World weaverbirds. **3.** Any of several North American fringilline birds, as the chipping sparrow, field sparrow, or song sparrow. [OE *spearwa*]

sparrow bill A sparable.

spar·row·grass (spar'ō-gras', -gräs') *n. Dial.* Asparagus. Also **spar'ry·grass'** (spar'ē-).

sparrow hawk 1. A small American falcon (*Falco sparverius*) that preys on other birds, mice, insects, etc. **2.** A small European hawk (*Accipiter nisus*) that preys on birds.

spar·ry (spär'ē) *adj.* **·ri·er, ·ri·est** Of, abounding in, or like the mineral spar.

sparse (spärs) *adj.* Scattered at considerable distances apart; thinly diffused; not dense. [< L *sparsus*, pp. of *spargere* to sprinkle, scatter] — **sparse'ly** *adv.* — **sparse'ness, spar·si·ty** (spär'sə-tē) *n.*

Spar·ta (spär'tə) An ancient city in the Peloponnesus, southern Greece; capital of ancient Laconia: also *Lacedaemon.* See map of ATTICA.

Spar·ta·cus (spär'tə-kəs), died 71 B.C., Thracian gladiator; led a slave rebellion against Rome 73–71 B.C.

Spar·tan (spär'tən) *adj.* **1.** Of or pertaining to Sparta or the Spartans. **2.** Resembling the Spartans in character; courageous, hardy, austere, stoical, and rigorous. — *n.* **1.** A native or citizen of Sparta. **2.** A person of Spartan character. — **Spar'tan·ism** *n.*

Spar·tan·burg (spär'tən-bûrg) A city in NW South Carolina; pop. 44,546.

spar·te·ine (spär'ti·ēn, -tē·in) *n.* A colorless, oily alkaloid, $C_{15}H_{26}N_2$, contained in the Scotch broom and used in medicine. [< L *spartium* < Gk. *spartos* broom + -INE²]

S.P.A.S. Fellow of the American Philosophical Society (L *Societatis Philosophiae Americanae Socius*).

spasm (spaz'əm) *n.* **1.** Any sudden, transient burst of energy or activity. **2.** *Pathol.* Any involuntary convulsive muscular contraction. When manifested by alternate contractions and relaxations it is a *clonic spasm*; when persistent and steady, it is a *tonic spasm*. [< L *spasma*, *spasmus* < Gk. *spasmos* < *span* to draw, pull]

spas·mod·ic (spaz·mod'ik) *adj.* **1.** Of the nature of a spasm; convulsive. **2.** Violent, or impulsive and transitory. Also **spas·mod'i·cal.** — **spas·mod'i·cal·ly** *adv.*

spas·tic (spas'tik) *adj.* Of, pertaining to, or characterized by spasms; spasmodic. — *n.* A person afflicted with cerebral palsy. [< L *spasticus* < Gk. *spastikos* < *span* to draw, pull] — **spas'ti·cal·ly** *adv.*

spat¹ (spat) Past tense and past participle of SPIT¹.

spat² (spat) *n.* **1.** Spawn of shellfish; especially, spawn of the oyster. **2.** A young oyster, or young oysters collectively. — *v.i.* **spat·ted, spat·ting** To spawn, as oysters. [? Akin to SPIT¹]

spat³ (spat) *n.* **1.** A slight blow; slap. **2.** A splash, as of rain; spatter. **3.** A petty dispute. — **Syn.** See QUARREL.¹ — *v.* **spat·ted, spat·ting** *v.i.* **1.** To strike with a slight sound; slap. **2.** To engage in a petty quarrel. — *v.t.* **3.** To slap. [Prob. imit.]

spat⁴ (spat) *n. Usually pl.* A short gaiter worn over a shoe and fastened underneath with a strap. [Short for SPATTERDASH]

spate (spāt) *n.* **1.** *Chiefly Brit.* A freshet; overflow. **2.** *Chiefly Brit.* A sudden, violent rainstorm; also, a waterspout. **3.** A sudden or vigorous outpouring, as of words, feeling, etc. Also **spait.** [Origin uncertain]

spa·tha·ceous (spə-thā′shəs) *adj.* *Bot.* Bearing or of the nature of a spathe. Also **spa·thal** (spā′thəl).

spathe (spāth) *n.* *Bot.* A large bract or pair of bracts sheathing a flower cluster, spadix, etc. [< L *spatha* < Gk. *spathē* broadsword] — **spa·those** (spā′thōs, spath′ōs) *adj.*

spath·ic (spath′ik) *adj.* *Mineral.* Of, pertaining to, or resembling spar. Also **spath·ose** (spath′ōs). [< G *spath* spar]

spa·tial (spā′shəl) *adj.* Pertaining to, involving, or having the nature of space. Also spelled *spacial.* [< L *spatium* space] — **spa·ti·al·i·ty** (spā′shē·al′ə·tē) *n.* — **spa′tial·ly** *adv.*

spa·ti·o·tem·po·ral (spā′shē·ō·tem′pər·əl) *adj.* Of or pertaining to both space and time.

spat·ter (spat′ər) *v.t.* **1.** To scatter in drops or splashes, as mud or paint. **2.** To splash with such drops; bespatter. **3.** To defame; slander. — *v.i.* **4.** To throw off drops or splashes; sputter. **5.** To fall in a shower, as raindrops. — *n.* **1.** The act of spattering, or the matter spattered; a splash. **2.** A pattering noise, as of falling rain. [Cf. Frisian *spatterje,* Du. *spatten* to spatter]

spat·ter·dash (spat′ər·dash′) *n.* A legging or puttee.

spat·ter·dock (spat′ər·dok′) *n.* The yellow pond lily. See under POND LILY.

spat·u·la (spach′ŏŏ·lə) *n.* **1.** A knifelike instrument with a flat, flexible blade, used to spread plaster, cake icing, etc. **2.** *Med.* An instrument used to press the tongue down or aside, as in examinations. [< L, dim. of *spatha.* See SPATHE.] — **spat′u·lar** *adj.*

spat·u·late (spach′ŏŏ·lit, -lāt) *adj.* **1.** Shaped like a spatula. **2.** *Bot.* Oblong, with an attenuated base, as many leaves. For illustration see LEAF.

spav·in (spav′in) *n.* *Vet.* A disease of the hock joint of horses, occurring either as an infusion of lymph within the joint (**bog spavin**) or as an bony deposit stiffening the joint (**bone spavin**). Also *Scot.* **spa·vie** (spā′vē, spav′ē). [< OF *espavain, esparvain*; ult. origin uncertain] — **spav′ined,** *Scot.* **spa·viet** (spā′vit, spav′it) *adj.*

spawn (spôn) *n.* **1.** *Zool.* The eggs of fishes, amphibians, mollusks, etc., especially in masses. **2.** The offspring of any animal. **3.** Outcome or results; product; yield. **4.** The spat of the oyster. **5.** Very small fish; fry. **6.** *Bot.* The mycelium of mushrooms or other fungi. — *v.i.* **1.** To produce spawn; deposit eggs or roe. **2.** To come forth as or like spawn. — *v.t.* **3.** To produce (spawn). **4.** To give rise to; originate. **5.** To bring forth abundantly or in great quantity. **6.** To plant with spawn or mycelium. [< AF *espaundre,* OF *espendre* < L *expandere.* Doublet of EXPAND.]

spay (spā) *v.t.* To remove the ovaries from (a female animal). [< AF *espeier,* OF *espeer* to cut with a sword < *espee* sword < L *spatha*]

SPC South Pacific Commission.

S.P.C.A. Society for the Prevention of Cruelty to Animals.

S.P.C.C. Society for the Prevention of Cruelty to Children.

speak (spēk) *v.* **spoke** (*Archaic* **spake**), **spo·ken** (*Archaic* **spoke**), **speak·ing** *v.i.* **1.** To employ the vocal organs in ordinary speech; utter words. **2.** To express or convey ideas, opinions, etc., in or as in speech: to *speak* about a matter. **3.** To make a speech; deliver an address. **4.** To talk together; converse. **5.** To make a sound; also, to bark, as a dog. — *v.t.* **6.** To express or make known in or as in speech. **7.** To utter in speech: to *speak* words of love. **8.** To use or be capable of using (a language) in conversation. **9.** To speak to. **10.** *Naut.* To hail and exchange communications with (a vessel) at sea. — **Syn.** See TALK. — **to speak daggers** To express hatred. — **to speak for 1.** To speak in behalf of; represent officially. **2.** To lay claim to; bespeak; engage. [OE *specan, sprecan*]

speak·a·ble (spē′kə·bəl) *adj.* That may, or may properly, be spoken.

speak·eas·y (spēk′ē′zē) *n.* *pl.* **·eas·ies** *Slang* A saloon where liquor is sold illegally.

speak·er (spē′kər) *n.* **1.** One who speaks. **2.** The presiding officer in any one of various legislative bodies. **3.** A volume of oratorical selections, for declamation. **4.** A loudspeaker (which see). — **speak′er·ship** *n.*

speak·ing (spē′king) *adj.* **1.** Having the power of effective speech; uttering speech. **2.** Expressive; vivid; telling; lifelike. — *n.* **1.** The act of utterance; vocal expression. **2.** Oratory; public declamation. — **speak′ing·ly** *adv.*

spean (spēn) *v.t. Brit. Dial.* To wean. [< MDu. *spene* teat]

spear (spir) *n.* **1.** A weapon consisting of a pointed head on a long shaft. **2.** A similar instrument, barbed and usually forked, as for use in spearing fish; a fishgig. **3.** A spearman. **4.** A leaf or slender stalk, as of grass. — *v.t.* **1.** To pierce or capture with a spear. — *v.i.* **2.** To pierce as a spear does. **3.** To send forth spears or spires, as a plant. **4.** In hockey, to check a puck-carrier by stabbing with the stick. **5.** In football, to block an opponent with the helmet rather than the body. [OE *spere* spear] — **spear′er** *n.* — **Syn.** (noun) **1.** pike, lance, javelin, harpoon, spontoon.

spear·fish (spir′fish′) *n.* *pl.* **·fish** or **·fish·es** Any of several powerful marine fish (genus *Tetrapturus*) with a long, sword-shaped snout, related to the swordfish.

spear gun A weapon that discharges a spear on a length of line, and is used for catching fish.

spear·head (spir′hed′) *n.* **1.** The point of a spear. **2.** One who or that which leads, influences, or directs an action, etc.; especially, a military force leading an attack on enemy positions. — *v.t.* To be in the lead of (an attack, etc.).

spear man (spir′mən) *n.* *pl.* **·men** (-mən) A man armed with a spear. Also **spears′man** (spirz′-).

spear·mint (spir′mint′) *n.* An aromatic herb (*Mentha spicata*) similar to peppermint.

spear side *Archaic* The male branch of a family: opposed to *distaff* side. Also **spear half.**

spear·wort (spir′wûrt′) *n.* Any of several species of crowfoot having lance-shaped or linear leaves.

spec. **1.** Special. **2.** Specification. **3.** Speculation.

spe·cial (spesh′əl) *adj.* **1.** Having some peculiar or distinguishing characteristic or characteristics; out of the ordinary; uncommon; particular. **2.** Designed for or assigned to a specific purpose; limited or specific in range, aim, or purpose. **3.** Of, pertaining to, constituting, or designating a species; specific; distinguishing; differential. **4.** Unique; singular; exceptional. **5.** Extra or additional, as a dividend. **6.** Intimate; esteemed; beloved. ◆ See note at ESPECIAL. — *n.* **1.** A person or thing made, detailed for, or appropriated to a specific service or occasion, as a train, a newspaper edition, etc. **2.** A featured dish or course in a restaurant or cafeteria. **3.** A temporary sale. **4.** A television show produced for a single presentation. Abbr. *sp., spec.* [< OF *especial* or L *specialis* < *species* kind, species] — **spe′cial·ly** *adv.* — **spe′cial·ness** *n.*

special delivery *U.S.* Mail delivery in advance of regular delivery, a service obtained for an additional fee.

special drawing rights An international reserve currency system created in 1969 by the International Monetary Fund to provide the first international legal tender, known as *paper gold.* Abbr. *SDR, S.D.R.*

spe·cial·ism (spesh′əl·iz′əm) *n.* The confining of oneself to a particular line of study or work; a special field of work.

spe·cial·ist (spesh′əl·ist) *n.* **1.** A person devoted to some one line of study, occupation, or professional work; especially, a physician who restricts his practice to one branch of medicine. **2.** In the U.S. Army, an enlisted person in a technical or administrative position, with pay equal to that of a noncommissioned officer in the same grade. See table at GRADE. — **spe′cial·is′tic** *adj.*

spe·ci·al·i·ty (spesh′ē·al′ə·tē) *n.* *pl.* **·ties** **1.** A specific or individual characteristic; peculiarity. **2.** Specialty (defs. 3, 4, 5). ◆ In British usage, this form is preferred to *specialty.*

spe·cial·i·za·tion (spesh′əl·ə·zā′shən, -ī·zā′-) *n.* **1.** The act or process of specializing; also, the state of being or becoming specialized. **2.** *Biol.* The development of a plant or animal organ or part in adaptation to environmental influences or for a special function.

spe·cial·ize (spesh′əl·īz) *v.* **·ized, ·iz·ing** *v.i.* **1.** To concentrate on one particular activity or subject; engage in a specialty. **2.** *Biol.* To take on a special form or forms by specialization. — *v.t.* **3.** To adapt for some special use or purpose. **4.** *Biol.* To modify or adapt by specialization. **5.** To endorse, as a check, to a particular payee. **6.** To mention specifically; particularize. Also *Brit.* **spe′cial·ise.**

special pleading **1.** *Law* The allegation of new or special matter in reply to the opposing party's averments, rather than a direct denial. **2.** A presentation of the favorable aspects of an argument while suppressing the unfavorable.

spe·cial·ty (spesh′əl·tē) *n.* *pl.* **·ties** **1.** A special occupation, craft, or study. **2.** The state of being special or of having peculiar characteristics. **3.** An individual characteristic or peculiarity; distinguishing mark. **4.** An article dealt in exclusively or chiefly, or having a special quality or character. **5.** *Law* A sealed contract; deed. — **specialty of the house** A featured dish or course in a restaurant.

spe·ci·a·tion (spē′shē·ā′shən) *n.* *Biol.* The formation of a species by the action of evolutionary processes.

spe·cie (spē′shē) *n.* Coined money; coin. — **Syn.** See MONEY. — **in specie** **1.** In coin. **2.** *Law* In kind; in the shape mentioned; in sort. [< L (*in*) *specie* (in) kind]

spe·cies (spē′shēz, -shiz, -sēz; *Lat.* spē′shi·ēz) *n.* *pl.* **·cies** **1.** *Biol.* A category of animals or plants subordinate to a genus but above a breed, race, strain, or variety. See GENUS (def. 1). **2.** A group of individuals or objects agreeing in some common attribute or attributes and designated by a common name. **3.** *Eccl.* **a** The visible form of bread or of wine retained by the eucharistic elements after consecration. **b** The consecrated elements of the Eucharist. **4.** A kind, sort, or variety. **5.** An image, form, or appearance. **6.** *Obs.* Specie; coin. Abbr. *sp.* [< L, form, kind. Doublet of SPICE.]

specif. Specifically.

spec·i·fi·a·ble (spes′ə·fī′ə·bəl) *adj.* Such as can be specified.

spe·cif·ic (spi-sif′ik) *adj.* **1.** Distinctly and plainly set forth; definite or determinate; particular; explicit. **2.** *Biol.* Of, pertaining to, or distinguishing a species: a *specific* name of an animal. **3.** Peculiar or special, as characteristics, qualities, etc. **4.** Characteristic of or proper to a given substance or phenomenon, especially in relation to some arbitrary but constant standard of comparison: *specific* gravity; *specific* heat. **5.** *Med.* **a** Curing or alleviating a special disease or pathological condition: said of a remedy or medicine. **b** Caused by a particular condition, germ, etc.: said of a disease. **6.** Denoting a customs duty chargeable upon imported merchandise by quantity, weight, or number, without regard to value. Also *Rare* **spe·cif'i·cal.** — *n.* **1.** Anything specific or adapted to effect a specific result. **2.** A medicine specially indicated to cure or prevent some particular disease. **3.** *Usually pl. U.S. Informal* A particular; item; instance. Abbr. *sp.* [< L *specificus* < *species* kind, class + *facere* to make] — **spec·i·fic'i·ty** (spes'ə·fis'ə·tē) *n.*

spe·cif·i·cal·ly (spi·sif'ik·lē) *adv.* **1.** In a specific manner; explicitly; particularly; definitely. **2.** As to or in respect to species. **3.** In a particular sense or case. Abbr. *specif.*

spec·i·fi·ca·tion (spes'ə·fə·kā'shən) *n.* **1.** The act of specifying. **2.** Something specified, as in a contract, plans, etc.; also, one detail in such a statement. **3.** In patent law, the detailed statement of the nature of an invention and the method of constructing and applying it. **4.** *Usually pl.* A specific description of certain dimensions, types of material, etc., to be used in a manufacturing, construction, or engineering project. Abbr. *spec.*

specific gravity *Physics* The ratio of the mass of a body to that of an equal volume of some standard substance, water in the case of solids and liquids, and air or hydrogen in the case of gases; a measure of density. Abbr. *s.g., s.p. gr.*

specific heat *Physics* The amount of heat required to raise the temperature of one gram of a given substance 1° C, measured in calories.

specific impulse *Aerospace* The thrust in pounds produced in one second by the burning with its oxidizer of one pound of a specified fuel, as in a rocket motor or jet engine.

spec·i·fy (spes'ə·fī) *v.t.* **·fied, ·fy·ing** **1.** To mention specifically; state in full and explicit terms. **2.** To embody in a specification. [< OF *specifier* < L *specificare* < *species* kind, species + *facere* to make]

spec·i·men (spes'ə·mən) *n.* **1.** One of a class of persons or things regarded as representative of the class; an example; sample. **2.** *Biol.* A plant or animal, entire or in part, prepared and kept as an example to illustrate a species or variety. **3.** *Med.* A sample of body tissue or exudates taken for analysis and diagnosis. **4.** *Informal* A person of pronounced or curious type; a character. Abbr. *sp.* [< L < *specere* to look at]

spe·ci·os·i·ty (spē'shē·os'ə·tē) *n. pl.* **·ties** **1.** One who or that which is specious and plausible at first view. **2.** *Obs.* The state of being beautiful.

spe·cious (spē'shəs) *adj.* **1.** Apparently good or right, but actually not so; plausible: *specious* reasoning. **2.** Pleasing or attractive in appearance, but deceptive: a *specious* promise. **3.** Beguiling, but lacking in sincerity. **4.** *Archaic* Pleasing to the eye; showy. [< L *speciosus* fair] — **spe'·cious·ly** *adv.* — **spe'cious·ness** *n.*

speck (spek) *n.* **1.** A small spot, stain, or discoloration. **2.** Any very small thing; a particle. — *v.t.* To mark with spots or specks; speckle. [OE *specca*]

speck·le (spek'əl) *v.t.* **·led, ·ling** To mark with specks or speckles. — *n.* A small spot; speck.

speck·led (spek'əld) *adj.* **1.** Dotted with specks or spots. **2.** Of motley appearance or mixed character.

specs (speks) *n.pl. Informal* **1.** Eyeglasses; spectacles. Also **specks.** **2.** Specifications (def. 4).

spec·ta·cle (spek'tə·kəl) *n.* **1.** That which is exhibited to public view, especially something grand or showy. **2.** An unwelcome or deplorable exhibition; a painful sight. **3.** *pl.* A pair of eyeglasses. **4.** *pl.* Something suggesting a pair of eyeglasses in shape, use, etc. [< F < L *spectaculum* < *spectare*, freq. of *specere* to see]

spec·ta·cled (spek'tə·kəld) *adj.* **1.** Wearing spectacles. **2.** Having markings resembling a pair of spectacles: the *spectacled* cobra.

spec·tac·u·lar (spek·tak'yə·lər) *adj.* **1.** Characterized by or displaying unusual, exciting, or unexpected qualities, conditions, etc.: a *spectacular* rescue. **2.** Of, pertaining to, or like a spectacle. — *n.* **1.** An imposing exhibition. **2.** In television, a lavish dramatic or musical production. **3.** An elaborate, illuminated sign. — **spec·tac'u·lar·ly** *adv.* — **spec·tac'u·lar'i·ty** (-lar'ə·tē) *n.*

spec·ta·tor (spek'tā·tər, spek·tā'-) *n.* **1.** One who beholds; eyewitness; onlooker. **2.** One who is present at and views a show, game, spectacle, etc. [< L < *spectare* to look at]

Spectator, The An English periodical, conducted by Joseph Addison and Richard Steele from March, 1711, to Dec., 1712; revived by Addison, June–Dec., 1714.

spectator sport *U.S.* A sport, as baseball, football, horse racing, etc., enjoyed by many spectators who do not themselves take part in it.

spec·ter (spek'tər) *n.* **1.** A ghost or apparition. **2.** Anything of a fearful or horrible nature. Also *Brit.* **spec'tre.** — **Syn.** See GHOST. [< F *spectre* < L *spectrum* vision]

spec·tra (spek'trə) Plural of SPECTRUM.

spec·tral (spek'trəl) *adj.* **1.** Of, pertaining to, or like a

specter; ghostly. **2.** Pertaining to a spectrum or spectra. — **spec·tral'i·ty** (spek·tral'ə·tē) *n.* — **spec'tral·ly** *adv.*

spectro- *combining form* **1.** Radiant energy, as exhibited in the spectrum: *spectroscope*. **2.** Spectroscope; spectroscopic: *spectrobolometer*. [< SPECTRUM]

spec·tro·bo·lom·e·ter (spek'trō·bō·lom'ə·tər) *n.* A bolometer combined with a spectroscope for measuring the heat of different parts of the spectrum.

spec·tro·gram (spek'trə·gram) *n.* A photograph made by a spectrograph.

spec·tro·graph (spek'trə·graf, -gräf) *n.* **1.** An apparatus for photographing or forming a representation of the spectrum: also called *photospectroscope*. **2.** A spectrogram. — **sound spectrograph** An electronic instrument designed to record the acoustic characteristics of speech sounds.

spec·tro·he·li·o·gram (spek'trō·hē'lē·ə·gram') *n.* A photograph of the sun made by the spectroheliograph.

spec·tro·he·li·o·graph (spek'trō·hē'lē·ə·graf', -gräf') *n.* An instrument for photographing the sun and its prominences by means of monochromatic light.

spec·trom·e·ter (spek·trom'ə·tər) *n.* **1.** An instrument by means of which the angular deviation or the wavelength of a ray of light can be determined. **2.** A spectroscope provided with such an instrument. — **spec·tro·met·ric** (spek'trō·met'rik) *adj.*

spec·tro·pho·tom·e·ter (spek'trō·fō·tom'ə·tər) *n.* An instrument for determining the relative intensity of two spectra or of the corresponding bands of color in two spectra.

spec·tro·scope (spek'trə·skōp) *n.* An optical instrument for forming and analyzing the spectrum emitted by bodies or substances. — **spec'·tro·scop'ic** (-skop'ik) or **·i·cal** *adj.* — **spec'·tro·scop'i·cal·ly** *adv.*

spectros·co·py (spek·tros'kə·pē) *n.* The study and analysis of the phenomena observed with the spectroscope. — **spec·tros'co·pist** *n.*

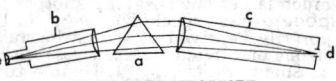

SIMPLE SPECTROSCOPE

a Prism. *b* Telescope for viewing prism through eyepiece (*e*). *c* Collimator with slit (*d*).

spec·trum (spek'trəm) *n. pl.* **·tra** (-trə) **1.** *Physics* **a** The band of color observed when a beam of white light is passed through a prism or diffraction grating that separates each component of the light according to wavelengths, comprising, from longest to shortest, red, orange, yellow, green, blue, indigo, and violet. **b** An image formed by radiant energy directed through a spectroscope and brought to a focus, and in which each wavelength corresponds to a specific band or line in a progressive series characteristic of the emitting source. **2.** Any range of characteristics, values, activities, etc.: His emotional *spectrum* is limited. **3.** An afterimage. [< L, vision]

spectrum analysis The investigation or qualitative analysis of bodies or substances by means of their spectra.

spec·u·la (spek'yə·lə) Plural of SPECULUM.

spec·u·lar (spek'yə·lər) *adj.* Of, pertaining to, or like a speculum or mirror. [< L *specularis* < *speculum* mirror]

spec·u·late (spek'yə·lāt) *v.i.* **·lat·ed, ·lat·ing** **1.** To form conjectures regarding anything without experiment; theorize; conjecture. **2.** To make an investment involving a risk, but with hope of gain. [< L *speculatus*, pp. of *speculari* to look at, examine < *specere* to see]

spec·u·la·tion (spek'yə·lā'shən) *n.* **1.** The act of theorizing or conjecturing; speculating. **2.** A theory or conjecture. **3.** A conclusion reached by or based upon conjecture. **4.** An investment involving risk with hope of large profit. **5.** The act of engaging in risky business transactions that offer a possibility of large profit. Abbr. *spec.*

spec·u·la·tive (spek'yə·lā'tiv, -lə·tiv) *adj.* **1.** Of, pertaining to, engaged in, or given to speculation, meditation, conjecture, etc. **2.** Strictly theoretical or purely scientific. **3.** Engaging in or involving financial speculation. **4.** Risky. — **spec'u·la·tive·ly** *adv.* — **spec'u·la·tive·ness** *n.*

spec·u·la·tor (spek'yə·lā'tər) *n.* One who speculates. — **spec'u·la·to'ry** (-lə·tôr'ē, -tō'rē) *adj.*

spec·u·lum (spek'yə·ləm) *n. pl.* **·la** (-lə) or **·lums** **1.** A mirror of polished metal or of glass coated with a metal film, used for telescope reflectors, etc. **2.** *Med.* An instrument that dilates a passage of the body for examination. **3.** *Ornithol.* A specially colored, typically iridescent area on the wings of certain birds, as ducks. [< L, mirror < *specere* to see]

sped (sped) Alternative past tense and past participle of SPEED.

Spee (shpā), **Count Maximilian von,** 1861–1914, German admiral in World War I.

speech (spēch) *n.* **1.** The faculty of expressing thought and emotion by spoken words; the power of speaking. **2.** The act of speaking, involving the production of meaningful combinations of distinctive speech sounds. **3.** That which is spoken; conversation; talk; a saying or remark. **4.** A public

address or talk. **5.** A characteristic manner of speaking: His *speech* is loud and unpleasant. **6.** A particular language, idiom, or dialect: American *speech*. **7.** Any audible or visible method of communication, including cries, gestures, and sign language. **8.** The study of oral communication, including the physiology of articulation, the nature of speech sounds, and the techniques of effective expression. [OE *spǣc*, *sprǣc* < *specan*, *sprecan* to speak]
— **Syn. 4.** *Speech, address, talk, oration, harangue, lecture, discourse, sermon,* and *homily* denote something said to an audience. Any public speaking may be called a *speech*. An *address* is a formal *speech*, as on a ceremonial occasion. *Talk*, on the other hand, suggests informality. An *oration* is an eloquent *address* that appeals to the emotions, while a *harangue* is a vehement *speech*, appealing to the emotions and often intended to spur the audience to action of some sort. A *lecture* is directed to the listener's intellect; it gives information, explanation, or counsel. Any carefully prepared *speech* or writing is a *discourse*. *Sermon* and *homily* are concerned with religious instruction; a *sermon* is usually an interpretation of Scripture, and a *homily* gives ethical guidance.

speech clinic A place where speech disorders are treated.
speech community All the speakers of a given language or dialect in both contiguous and dispersed areas.
speech disorder Disorganization or impairment of speech caused either by physical defect or by mental disorder.
speech habits The characteristic articulatory and vocal behavior of an individual.
speech·i·fy (spē′chə·fī) *v.i.* **·fied, ·fy·ing** To make speeches: a derisive or dialectal term. — **speech′i·fi′er** *n.*
speech island A small speech community surrounded by a much larger one speaking another language or dialect.
speech·less (spēch′lis) *adj.* **1.** Unable to speak or temporarily deprived of speech because of physical weakness, strong emotion, etc.: *speechless* with rage. **2.** Mute; dumb. **3.** Silent; reticent. **4.** Unable to be expressed in words: *speechless* joy. — **speech′less·ly** *adv.* — **speech′less·ness** *n.*
speech·mak·er (spēch′mā′kər) *n.* One who delivers a speech or speeches. — **speech′mak′ing** *n.*
speech mechanism The apparatus of articulation and of vocal production; organs of speech.
speech organ Any of the parts of the body used in speaking, as the larynx, tongue, or lips.
speech pattern **1.** The speech habits of an individual conceived as a functioning unit. **2.** Any phonological or linguistic system.
speech sound An articulation that functions in oral communication; a phone, allophone, or phoneme.
speed (spēd) *n.* **1.** The act or state of moving or progressing swiftly; rapidity of motion; swiftness. **2.** Rate of motion, especially in physics, as considered without reference to direction. **3.** Rate of performance, as shown by the ratio of work done to time spent. **4.** *Mech.* A transmission gear in a motor vehicle. **5.** *Photog.* In a camera lens, the minimum time required for an effective exposure. **6.** *Archaic* Good luck; success; prosperity. — *v.* **sped** or **speed·ed, speed·ing** *v.i.* **1.** To move or go with speed. **2.** To exceed a speed limit. **3.** *Obs.* To prosper. **4.** *Obs.* To fare in a specified manner. — *v.t.* **5.** To promote the forward progress of; cause to move or go with speed. **6.** To promote the success of. **7.** To wish Godspeed to: *Speed* the parting guest. — **Syn.** See QUICKEN. — **to speed up** To accelerate in speed or action. — *adj.* Having, pertaining to, characterized by, regulating, or indicating speed: used chiefly in compounds:

speed gauge	speed lathe	speed recorder
speed gear	speed light	speed reducer
speed indicator	speed pulley	speed test

[OE *spēd* prosperity, power]
speed·boat (spēd′bōt′) *n.* A high-speed motorboat.
speed·er (spē′dər) *n.* One who or that which speeds.
speed·ing (spē′ding) *adj.* Moving with speed. — *n.* Travel at high speed; especially, travel at an unsafe or reckless speed or above a specified speed limit.
speed·light (spēd′līt′) A strobe light (which see).
speed limit A legally set maximum speed at which vehicles may travel on certain roads or through specified districts.
speed·om·e·ter (spi·dom′ə·tər) *n.* A device for indicating the speed of a vehicle, often combined with an odometer.
speed·ster (spēd′stər) *n.* **1.** A speeder. **2.** An automobile, usually having two seats, designed for speed.
speed trap *U.S.* A village, section of highway, etc., often with ambiguous speed-limit signs and electronic and other recording devices, very closely watched by the police to catch speeding drivers.
speed·up (spēd′up′) *n.* An acceleration in work, output, movement, etc.
speed·way (spēd′wā′) *n.* A specially reserved or prepared road for vehicles traveling at high speed.
speed·well (spēd′wel) *n.* One of various low herbs (genus *Veronica*) of the figwort family, bearing blue or white flowers; especially, the **common speedwell** (*V. arvensis*) and the **germander speedwell** (*V. chamaedrys*) or bird's-eye, having bright blue flowers: also called *veronica*.
speed·y (spē′dē) *adj.* **speed·i·er, speed·i·est 1.** Characterized by speed; rapid. **2.** Without delay; prompt. — **Syn.** See SWIFT. — **speed′i·ly** *adv.* — **speed′i·ness** *n.*

speel (spēl) *v.t. & v.i. Scot.* To climb.
speer (spir) *v.t. & v.i. Scot.* To inquire; ask: also spelled *spier*. — **to speer at** To question. [OE *spyrian*]
speer·ing (spir′ing) *n. Scot.* Inquiry; news; information.
speiss (spīs) *n. Metall.* A mixture of the arsenides of certain metals, as copper, iron, and nickel, obtained during the smelting of certain ores. Also *Ger.* **spei·se** (shpī′zə). [< G *speise* amalgam, lit., food < L *expensa*]
spe·le·an (spi·lē′ən) *adj.* **1.** Dwelling in a cave or caves. **2.** Of, pertaining to, or like a cave or caverns. Also **spe·lae′an.** [< L *spelaeum* < Gk. *spēlaion* cave]
speleo- *combining form* Cave: *speleology.* [< L *spelaeum* cave < Gk. *spēlaion*]
spe·le·ol·o·gy (spē′lē·ol′ə·jē) *n.* **1.** The scientific study of caves in their physical, geological, and biological aspects. **2.** The exploration of caves as a sport or profession. [< SPELEO- + -LOGY] — **spe′le·o·log′i·cal** (-ə·loj′i·kəl) *adj.* — **spe′le·ol′o·gist** *n.*
spell¹ (spel) *v.* **spelled** or **spelt, spell·ing** *v.t.* **1.** To name or write the letters of (a word); especially, to do so correctly. **2.** To form or be the letters of: C-a-t *spells* cat. **3.** To compose; make up. **4.** To signify; mean: Extravagance *spells* disaster. — *v.i.* **5.** To form words out of letters, especially correctly. — **to spell out 1.** To read with difficulty. **2.** To puzzle out and learn. **3.** To make clear and explicit: to *spell out* our objectives. [< OF *espeler* < Gmc. Akin to SPELL².]
spell² (spel) *n.* **1.** A word formula used as a charm; incantation; charm. **2.** An irresistible fascination or attraction; overpowering charm. — *v.t.* **spelled, spell·ing** To cast a spell upon. [OE, story, statement. Akin to SPELL¹.]
spell³ (spel) *n.* **1.** A period of time, usually of short length. **2.** *Informal* A continuous period characterized by a certain type of weather. **3.** *Informal* A short distance. **4.** *Informal* A fit of illness, debility, etc. **5.** A turn of duty in relief of another. **6.** A period of work or employment. **7.** *Austral.* A period of relaxation; rest. — *v.t.* **1.** To relieve temporarily from some work or duty. **2.** *Chiefly Austral.* To give a rest to, as a horse. — *v.i.* **3.** To take a rest. [OE *gespelia* substitute, one who spells another]
spell·bind (spel′bīnd′) *v.t.* **·bound, ·bind·ing** To bind or enthrall, as if by a spell.
spell·bind·er (spel′bīn′dər) *n.* One who casts a spell over others; especially, a political orator.
spell·bound (spel′bound′) *adj.* Bound as by a spell; fascinated; enchanted; bewitched.
spell·er (spel′ər) *n.* **1.** One who spells. **2.** A spelling book.
spell·ing (spel′ing) *n.* **1.** The act of one who spells. **2.** The art of correct spelling; orthography. **3.** The way in which a word is spelled. Abbr. *sp.*
spelling bee A gathering at which contestants engage in spelling words, those who spell wrongly usually being retired until only one remains.
spelling book A book of exercises for teaching spelling.
spelling pronunciation A pronunciation based on the presumed phonetic values of the letters in a word, as (ôf′tən) for *often.*
Spell·man (spel′mən), **Francis Joseph,** 1889–1967, U.S. cardinal; archbishop of New York.
spelt¹ (spelt) Alternative past tense and past participle of SPELL¹.
spelt² (spelt) *n.* A species of wheat (*Triticum spelta*) or any of its winter or spring varieties. [OE]
spel·ter (spel′tər) *n.* Zinc in the form of plates, slabs, and ingots. [Var. of PEWTER]
spe·lunk·er (spē·lung′kər) *n.* An enthusiast in the exploration and study of caves; a speleologist. [< L *spelunca* cave]
spe·lunk·ing (spē·lung′king) *n.* The process or hobby of exploring and charting caves.
spence (spens) *n. Brit. Dial.* **1.** A pantry or larder. **2.** The parlor of a cottage. [< OF *despense* < L *dispendere.* See DISPENSE.]
spen·cer¹ (spen′sər) *n.* A trysail.
spen·cer² (spen′sər) *n.* **1.** A man's short jacket of the early 19th century. **2.** A similar garment for women. [after 2nd Earl *Spencer*, 1758–1834, English nobleman]
Spen·cer (spen′sər), **Herbert,** 1820–1903, English philosopher.
Spen·ce·ri·an (spen·sir′ē·ən) *adj.* **1.** Pertaining to Herbert Spencer, or to his doctrine. **2.** Pertaining to a system of penmanship employing rounded, slanting letters. — *n.* A follower of Herbert Spencer and his system.
Spen·cer·ism (spen′sə·riz′əm) *n.* The doctrine of Herbert Spencer that the universe has evolved through mechanical forces from relative simplicity to relative complexity: also called *synthetic philosophy.* Also **Spen·ce·ri·an·ism** (spen·sir′ē·ən·iz′əm).
spend (spend) *v.* **spent, spend·ing** *v.t.* **1.** To pay out or disburse (money). **2.** To expend by degrees; use up. **3.** To apply or devote, as thought or effort, to some activity, purpose, etc. **4.** To pass: to *spend* one's life in jail. **5.** To lose: now chiefly in the nautical phrase **to spend a mast. 6.** To emit, as milt or spawn. — *v.i.* **7.** To pay out or disburse money, etc. **8.** *Obs.* To be wasted or exhausted. [OE *aspendan* < L *expendere.* See EXPEND.] — **spend′er** *n.*

Spen·der (spen'dər), **Stephen (Harold)**, born 1909, English poet and critic.
spending money Money used for small, personal purchases or expenses.
spend·thrift (spend'thrift') *n.* One who spends money lavishly or wastefully. — *adj.* Excessively lavish; prodigal.
Speng·ler (speng'glər, *Ger.* shpeng'lər), **Oswald**, 1880–1936, German philosopher and historian.
Spen·ser (spen'sər), **Edmund**, 1552?–99, English poet.
Spen·se·ri·an (spen-sir'ē-ən) *adj.* Of or pertaining to Edmund Spenser or to his style.
Spenserian stanza A nine-line stanza consisting of eight lines of ten syllables and a final line of twelve syllables and rhyming *ababbcbcc*, used by Edmund Spenser in *The Faerie Queene*.
spent (spent) Past tense and part participle of SPEND. — *adj.* 1. Worn out or exhausted. 2. Deprived of force: a *spent* bullet.
sperm[1] (spûrm) *n.* 1. The male fertilizing fluid; semen. 2. A male reproductive cell; spermatozoon. [< OF *esperme* or L *sperma* < Gk. *sperma* seed < *speirein* to sow]
sperm[2] (spûrm) *n.* 1. A sperm whale. 2. Spermaceti. 3. Sperm oil. [Short for SPERMACETI]
-sperm *combining form Bot.* A seed (of a specified kind): *gymnosperm*. [< Gk. *sperma, spermatos* seed]
sper·ma·ce·ti (spûr'mə-sē'tē, -set'ē) *n.* A white, waxy substance separated from the oil contained in the head of the sperm whale, used for making candles, ointments, etc. [< L *sperma ceti* seed of a whale]
sper·ma·ry (spûr'mər-ē) *n. pl.* ·ries The gland of the male that generates sperm; testis.
sper·mat·ic (spûr·mat'ik) *adj.* 1. Of, pertaining to, or like sperm; generative. 2. Of or pertaining to a spermary.
spermatic cord *Anat.* The cord, made up of the vas deferens and its accompanying arteries, veins, and nerves, that suspends each testicle within the scrotum and passes into the abdominal cavity.
spermatic fluid *Physiol.* Semen.
sper·ma·ti·um (spûr·mā'shē-əm) *n. pl.* ·ti·a (-shē-ə) *Bot.* The nonmotile male gamete of red algae that unites with the carpogonium in fertilization. [< NL < Gk. *spermation*, dim. of *sperma* seed]
spermato- *combining form* 1. Seed; pertaining to seeds: *spermatophyte*. 2. Spermatozoa; of or related to spermatozoa: *spermatophore*. Also *spermo-*. Also, before vowels, **spermat-**. [< Gk. *sperma, spermatos* seed]
sper·ma·to·cyte (spûr'mə-tə-sīt') *n. Biol.* A primary cell developing from a spermatogonium and dividing to produce spermatozoa.
sper·ma·to·gen·e·sis (spûr'mə-tə-jen'ə-sis) *n. Biol.* The development of spermatozoa. — **sper·ma·to·ge·net·ic** (spûr'mə-tō-jə-net'ik) *adj.*
sper·ma·to·go·ni·um (spûr'mə-tə-gō'nē-əm) *n. pl.* ·ni·a (-nē-ə) *Biol.* One of the cells of the seminal tubules that produce the spermatocytes. — **sper·ma·to·go'ni·al** *adj.*
sper·ma·toid (spûr'mə-toid) *adj.* Resembling sperm.
sper·ma·to·phore (spûr'mə-tə-fôr', -fōr') *n. Zool.* A capsule or case containing spermatozoa, as in many mollusks, worms, etc. — **sper·ma·toph'o·ral** (-tof'ər-əl) *adj.*
sper·ma·to·phyte (spûr'mə-tə-fīt') *n. Bot.* Any of a phylum or division (*Spermatophyta*) of the most highly developed plants; a flowering and seed-bearing plant. — **sper'ma·to·phyt'ic** (-fit'ik) *adj.*
sper·ma·to·rrhe·a (spûr'mə-tə-rē'ə) *n. Pathol.* Excessive, involuntary, or frequent seminal discharge. Also **sper'ma·tor·rhoe'a**.
sper·ma·to·zo·id (spûr'mə-tə-zō'id) *adj.* Resembling a spermatozoon. — *n. Bot.* A motile male germ cell generated in the antheridium of plants.
sper·ma·to·zo·on (spûr'mə-tə-zō'on) *n. pl.* ·zo·a (-zō'ə) *Biol.* The male fertilizing element of an animal, usually in the form of a highly motile nucleated cell with a long flagellate process or tail: also called *zoosperm*. [< SPERMATO- + Gk. *zōion* animal] — **sper'ma·to·zo'al, sper'ma·to·zo'ic** *adj.*
sper·mic (spûr'mik) *adj.* Spermatic.
spermo- See SPERMATO-.
sper·mo·go·ni·um (spûr'mə-gō'nē-əm) *n. pl.* ·ni·a (-nē-ə) *Bot.* In certain thallophytes, a cup- or flask-shaped receptacle bearing a great number of spermatia.
sperm oil Oil obtained from the head and blubber cavities of the sperm whale.
sperm·o·phile (spûr'mə-fīl, -fil) *n.* Any of various squirrellike burrowing rodents (*Citellus* and related genera), as the ground squirrel or the suslik.
-spermous *combining form* Having (a specified number or kind of) seeds; seeded: *polyspermous*. Also **-spermal, -spermic**. [< -SPERM + -OUS]
sperm whale A large, toothed whale (*Physeter catodon*) of warm seas, having a huge truncate head containing a reservoir of sperm oil: also called *cachalot*.

Sper·ry (sper'ē), **Elmer Ambrose**, 1860–1930, U.S. engineer and inventor.
sper·ry·lite (sper'i-līt) *n.* A metallic, white platinum arsenide, PtAs$_2$, occurring in small cubic crystals. [after F. L. *Sperry*, Canadian mineralogist + -LITE]

SPERM WHALE
(To 80 feet long)

spew (spyōō) *v.t. & v.i.* To vomit; throw up. — *n.* That which is spewed; vomit. Also spelled *spue*. [OE *spī-wan*]
Spey·er (shpī'ər) A city in the SE Rhineland-Palatinate, West Germany; capital of former Rhine Palatinate; pop. 42,323 (est. 1970). Also *Spires*.
Spe·zia (spe'tsyä) A port commune in NW Italy, on the **Gulf of Spezia**, an inlet of the Gulf of Genoa; pop. 121,191 (1961).
sp. gr. Specific gravity.
sphac·e·late (sfas'ə-lāt) *v.i.* ·lat·ed, ·lat·ing *Pathol.* To become gangrenous; decay; die. [< Gk. *sphakelos* gangrene]
sphag·num (sfag'nəm) *n.* Any of a genus (*Sphagnum*) of whitish gray mosses found in damp places; the bog or peat mosses, used as packing and in surgical dressings. [< L < Gk. *sphágnos*, kind of moss] — **sphag'nous** *adj.*
sphal·er·ite (sfal'ər-īt) *n.* A resinous to adamantine native zinc sulfide, ZnS, with traces of iron and cadmium, generally found massive in a variety of shapes and colors. It is a principal ore of zinc: also called *blende, zinc blende*. [< Gk. *sphaleros* deceptive + -ITE[1]]
sphene (sfēn) *n.* A hard, variously colored silicate of calcium and titanium, crystallizing in the monoclinic system: also called *titanite*. [< F *sphène* < Gk. *sphēn* wedge]
sphe·nic (sfē'nik) *adj.* Wedge-shaped.
spheno- *combining form* 1. Wedge-shaped: *sphenogram*. 2. *Med.* Pertaining to the sphenoid bone. Also, before vowels, **sphen-**. [< Gk. *sphēn, sphēnos* wedge]
sphe·no·don (sfē'nə-don) *n.* A lizardlike reptile (*Sphenodon punctatum*), the sole surviving representative of the order Rhynchocephalia: also called *hatteria, tuatara*. [< NL < Gk. *sphēn, sphēnos* wedge + *odous, odontos* tooth]
sphe·no·gram (sfē'nə-gram) *n.* A cuneiform character.
sphe·noid (sfē'noid) *n.* 1. *Mineral.* A crystal form enclosed by four faces, each of which cuts all three axes. 2. *Anat.* The sphenoid bone. — *adj.* Wedge-shaped. [< SPHEN(O)- + -OID] — **sphe·noi'dal** (sfi-noid'l) *adj.*
sphenoid bone *Anat.* An irregular, compound bone situated at the base of the skull. For illustration see SKULL.
sphe·ra·di·an (sfi-rā'dē-ən) *n.* A steradian.
spher·al (sfir'əl) *adj.* 1. Shaped like a sphere; spherical; rounded; symmetrical. 2. Of or pertaining to a sphere.
sphere (sfir) *n.* 1. The surface described by a semicircle making one complete rotation on its diameter. 2. A solid or hollow figure enclosed by a surface every point of which is equidistant from the center. 3. An approximately globular body; a globe; ball. 4. Compass or field of activity, endeavor, influence, etc.; range; scope; province. 5. A particular social rank or position. 6. One of the heavenly bodies; a planet, sun, or star. 7. The apparent outer dome of the heavens on which the heavenly bodies appear to lie. 8. In old astronomy, one of the concentric and transparent globes believed to revolve about the earth, carrying the various heavenly bodies. — *v.t.* **sphered, spher·ing** 1. To place in or as in a sphere; encircle; encompass. 2. To set among the celestial spheres. 3. To make spherical. [< OF *espere* < L *sphaera* < Gk. *sphaira* ball]
-sphere *combining form* 1. Denoting an enveloping spherical mass: *hydrosphere, atmosphere*. 2. A sphere-shaped body: *oosphere*. 3. Denoting a spherical form: *planisphere*. [< Gk. *sphaira* ball, sphere]
spher·ic (sfir'ik, sfer'-) *adj.* Spherical.
spher·i·cal (sfir'i-kəl, sfer'-) *adj.* 1. Shaped like a sphere; globular. 2. Pertaining to a sphere or spheres. 3. Pertaining to the heavenly bodies; celestial. — **spher'i·cal·ly** *adv.* — **spher'i·cal·ness** *n.*
spherical aberration See under ABERRATION.
spherical angle *Geom.* The angle formed at the intersection of two great circles on a sphere.
spherical sailing Navigation in which calculations are based upon a consideration of the spherical or spheroidal shape of the earth. Compare PLANE SAILING.
spherical triangle *Math.* A spherical polygon the three sides of which are arcs of great circles of a sphere.
sphe·ric·i·ty (sfi-ris'ə-tē) *n. pl.* ·ties The state of being a sphere; spherical form; roundness.
spher·ics (sfir'iks, sfer'-) *n.pl.* (construed as sing.) 1. The geometry and trigonometry of figures on the surface of a sphere. 2. Atmospherics.
sphe·roid (sfir'oid) *n. Geom.* A body having nearly the form of a sphere; an ellipsoid. — **sphe·roi'dal** (sfi-roid'l), **sphe·roi'dic** or **·di·cal** *adj.* — **sphe·roi'dal·ly** *adv.*
sphe·roi·dic·i·ty (sfir'oi-dis'ə-tē) *n.* The state or character of being a spheroid. Also **sphe·roi·dity** (sfi-roi'də-tē).

sphe·rom·e·ter (sfi·rom′ə·tər) *n.* An instrument for measuring curvature or radii of spherical and other curved surfaces. [< SPHERE + -METER]

spher·ule (sfir′ool, sfer′-) *n.* A small or minute sphere; globule. — **spher·u·lar** (sfer′ōō·lər) *adj.*

spher·u·lite (sfir′ŏŏ·līt, sfer′-) *n.* A radiating spherical group of minute crystals common in some igneous rocks. [< SPHERULE + -ITE¹] — **spher′u·lit′ic** (-lit′ik) *adj.*

spher·y (sfir′ē) *adj.* **spher·i·er, spher·i·est** *Poetic* 1. Like a sphere. 2. Of or relating to the celestial spheres.

sphinc·ter (sfingk′tər) *n. Anat.* A ringlike band of muscle that surrounds an opening or tube in the body and serves to close it. [< LL < Gk. *sphinktēr* < *sphingein* to bind fast] — **sphinc′ter·al** *adj.*

sphinx (sfingks) *n.* *pl.* **sphinx·es** or **sphin·ges** (sfin′jēz) 1. In Egyptian mythology, a wingless monster with a lion's body and the head of a man (*androsphinx*, or simply *sphinx*), or of a ram (*criosphinx*), or of a hawk (*hieracosphinx*); also, any monumental representation of such a creature. 2. In Greek mythology, a winged monster with a woman's head and breasts and a lion's body, that destroyed those unable to guess her riddle. 3. A mysterious or enigmatical person. — **the Sphinx** The colossal androsphinx at Gizeh, having the body of a couchant lion, representing Harmachis, the Egyptian god of the morning. [< L < Gk. *sphinx* < *sphingein* to close, strangle]

sphinx moth The hawk moth (which see).

sphra·gis·tics (sfrə·jis′tiks) *n.pl.* (construed as *sing.*) The study of seal rings or engraved seals, including their authenticity, age, history, etc. [< Gk. *sphragistikos* of sealing < *sphragis* seal] — **sphra·gis′tic** *adj.*

sphyg·mic (sfig′mik) *adj. Physiol.* Pertaining to the pulse; pulsatory. [< Gk. *sphygmikos* < *sphygmos* pulse]

sphygmo- *combining form* Pulse; of or related to the pulse: *sphygmogram.* Also, before vowels, **sphygm-.** [< Gk. *sphygmos* pulse]

sphyg·mo·gram (sfig′mə·gram) *n.* The record traced by a sphygmograph.

sphyg·mo·graph (sfig′mə·graf, -gräf) *n.* An instrument that records the rate, force, and variations of the pulse. — **sphyg′mo·graph′ic** *adj.* — **sphyg·mog·ra·phy** (sfig·mog′rə·fē) *n.*

sphyg·moid (sfig′moid) *adj. Physiol.* Pulselike.

sphyg·mo·ma·nom·e·ter (sfig′mō·mə·nom′ə·tər) *n.* An instrument for measuring blood pressure in the arteries.

sphyg·mom·e·ter (sfig·mom′ə·tər) *n.* An instrument for measuring the force and frequency of the pulse.

sphyg·mus (sfig′məs) *n.* The pulse. [< NL < Gk. *sphygmos* pulse]

spi·ca (spī′kə) *n.* *pl.* **·cae** (-sē) 1. An ear of grain; a spike. 2. *Surg.* A bandage having a reversed spiral form, somewhat resembling an ear of wheat. [< L, spike, ear of grain]

Spi·ca (spī′kə) *n.* A spectroscopic binary star, one of the 20 brightest, 0.91 magnitude; Alpha in the constellation Virgo. See STAR.

spi·cate (spī′kāt) *adj.* 1. *Bot.* Arranged in spikes: said of flowers. 2. *Ornithol.* Having a spur, as the legs of some birds. Also **spi′cat·ed.** [< L *spicatus* < *spica* spike]

spic·ca·to (spēk·kä′tō) *Music n.* *pl.* **·tos** A method of producing rapid, detached notes on a stringed instrument, by allowing the bow to rebound slightly from the string. — *adj.* Of or pertaining to this manner of playing. — *adv.* In this manner of playing. [< Ital., pp. of *spicare* to detach]

spice (spīs) *n.* 1. An aromatic, pungent vegetable substance, as cinnamon, cloves, etc., used to flavor food and beverages. 2. Such substances collectively. 3. That which gives zest or adds interest. 4. An aromatic odor; an agreeable perfume. 5. *Obs.* Sort; kind; species; also, a specimen. — *v.t.* **spiced, spic·ing** 1. To season with spice. 2. To add zest or piquancy to. [< OF *espice* < L *species.* Doublet of SPECIES.] — **spic′er** *n.*

spice·ber·ry (spīs′ber′ē) *n.* *pl.* **·ries** 1. A small tree (*Eugenia rhombea*) of the myrtle family, found in the West Indies and Florida. 2. The black or orange fruit of this tree. 3. The wintergreen (def. 1).

spice·bush (spīs′bŏŏsh′) *n.* An aromatic American shrub (*Lindera benzoin*) of the laurel family: also called *benzoin, feverbush, wild allspice.* Also **spice′wood′** (-wŏŏd′).

spicebush silkworm The promethea moth.

Spice Islands A former name for the MOLUCCA ISLANDS.

spic·er·y (spī′sər·ē) *n.* *pl.* **·er·ies** 1. Spices collectively. 2. Spicy quality. 3. *Obs.* A place where spices are kept.

spick (spik) *n. U.S. Slang* A Spanish-speaking person: an offensive term. Also **spic.**

spick-and-span (spik′ən·span′) *adj.* 1. Neat and clean. 2. Perfectly new, or looking as if new. [Prob. < *spick,* var. of SPIKE¹ + SPAN-NEW]

spic·ule (spik′yŏŏl) *n.* 1. A small, slender, sharp-pointed body, as a spikelet. 2. *Zool.* One of the small, needlelike, calcareous growths supporting the soft tissues of certain invertebrates, as sponges, radiolarians, etc. Also **spic·u·la** (spik′yə·lə). [< L *spiculum,* dim. of *spicum* point, spike] — **spic′u·lar, spic′u·late** (-lāt, -lit) *adj.*

spic·u·lum (spik′yə·ləm) *n.* *pl.* **·la** (-lə) 1. A spicule.

2. *Zool.* Any small, dartlike organ, as one of the spines of a sea urchin. [< L]

spic·y (spī′sē) *adj.* **spic·i·er, spic·i·est** 1. Containing, flavored with, or fragrant with spices. 2. Producing spices. 3. Highly flavored; pungent. 4. Having zest or piquancy. 5. Somewhat improper; risqué. — **Syn.** See RACY. — **spic′i·ly** *adv.* — **spic′i·ness** *n.*

spi·der (spī′dər) *n.* 1. Any of a large number of eight-legged wingless arachnids (order *Araneae*) having an unsegmented abdomen and capable of spinning webs for the capture of prey such as flies or other insects. 2. One who or that which resembles a spider in appearance, character, etc. 3. A long-handled iron frying pan, often having legs. 4. A trivet. 5. *Agric.* An apparatus for pulverizing the ground during cultivation. 6. *Electr.* The central part of an armature core. 7. *Naut.* An iron hoop around the mast of a ship for the attachment of shrouds. [OE *spithra* < *spinnan* to spin]

spider crab Any of a genus (*Libinia*) of decapod crustaceans with long legs, especially *L. emarginata,* common on the Atlantic coast of North America.

spi·der·flow·er (spī′dər·flou′ər) *n.* The cleome.

spider monkey An arboreal South American monkey (genus *Ateles*) with very long limbs and a long prehensile tail.

SPIDER CRAB
(To 10 feet in breadth)

spider phaeton A light carriage having a covered seat in front, and a rear seat for a footman or attendant.

spi·der·wort (spī′dər·wûrt′) *n.* 1. Any of a genus (*Tradescantia*) of plants, especially *T. virginiana,* an American perennial with deep blue, three-petaled flowers. 2. Any of various similar or related plants.

spi·der·y (spī′dər·ē) *adj.* 1. Spiderlike. 2. Thin; fine; delicate. 3. Infested with spiders.

spied (spīd) Past tense and past participle of SPY.

spie·gel·ei·sen (spē′gəl·ī′zən) *n.* A white, very hard and brittle cast iron containing manganese. Also **spie′gel.** [< G < *spiegel* mirror + *eisen* iron]

spiel¹ (spēl, shpēl) *U.S. Slang* *v.i.* To talk; orate. — *n.* A speech; especially, a noisy, high-pressure sales talk, as of a pitchman or barker. [< G, game, play < *spielen* to play] — **spiel′er** *n.*

spiel² (spēl) *n.* *Canadian Informal* A bonspiel (which see). Also **'spiel.** — **spiel′er** or **spiel′er** *n.*

spi·er¹ spī′ər) *n.* A spy; scout.

spier² (spir) *See* SPEER.

spif·fy (spif′ē) *adj.* **·fi·er, ·fi·est** *Slang* Smartly dressed; spruce. — **spif′fi·ness** *n.* [< dial. E *spiff* a dandy]

spig·ot (spig′ət, spik′ət) *n.* 1. A faucet. 2. A plug or valve for the bunghole of a cask. 3. A turning plug fitting into a faucet. [ME *spigote.* Prob. akin to SPIKE¹.]

spike¹ (spīk) *n.* 1. A long, thick metal nail. 2. A projecting, pointed piece of metal, or any similar object, as in the soles of shoes to keep the wearer from slipping. 3. A very narrow high heel, used on women's shoes. 4. A steel pin for plugging cannon vents. 5. A straight, unbranched antler, as of a young deer. 6. A young mackerel. — *v.t.* **spiked, spik·ing** 1. To fasten with spikes. 2. To set or provide with spikes. 3. To block the vent of (a cannon) with a spike, rendering it useless. 4. To block; put a stop to. 5. To pierce with or impale on a spike. 6. In baseball, to injure (another player) with the spikes on one's shoes. 7. *Informal* To add alcoholic liquor to. [ME < Scand. Cf. ON *spikr* nail.]

spike² (spīk) *n.* 1. An ear of corn, barley, wheat, or other grain. 2. *Bot.* A flower cluster having numerous flowers arranged closely on an elongated common axis. For illustrations see INFLORESCENCE. [< L *spica* ear of grain]

spike lavender See under LAVENDER.

spike·let (spīk′lit) *n. Bot.* A small spike bearing few flowers and forming the compound inflorescence of cereal grasses and sedges.

spike·nard (spīk′nərd, -närd) *n.* 1. A fragrant and costly ointment of ancient times, supposedly prepared from an East Indian herb (*Nardostachys jatamansi*) of the valerian family: also called *nard.* 2. The plant itself. 3. An American perennial herb (*Aralia racemosa*) of the ginseng family, having an aromatic root. [< L *spica* spike + *nardus* nard]

spik·y (spī′kē) *adj.* **spik·i·er, spik·i·est** 1. Resembling a spike; pointed. 2. Having spikes. — **spik′i·ness** *n.*

spile (spīl) *n.* 1. A post or supporting timber; pile. 2. A wooden pin or plug used as a vent in a cask; a spigot. 3. A spout driven into a sugar maple to lead the sap to a bucket. — *v.t.* **spiled, spil·ing** 1. To pierce for and provide with a spigot. 2. To drive spiles into. [< MDu., skewer, splinter]

spil·i·kin (spil′i·kin) *n.* 1. A jackstraw. 2. *pl.* The game of jackstraws. Also **spil′li·kin.** [Dim. of SPILL²]

spil·ing (spī′ling) *n.* Spiles collectively; piling.

spill¹ (spil) *v.* **spilled** or **spilt, spill·ing** *v.t.* 1. To allow or cause to fall or run out or over, as a liquid or a powder. 2. To shed, as blood. 3. *Naut.* To empty (a sail) of wind. 4. To cause to fall, as from a horse. 5. *Informal* To divulge; make known, as a secret. — *v.i.* 6. To fall or run out or over: said of liquids, etc. — **to spill the beans** *Informal* To divulge information, especially a secret. — *n.* **1.** A fall, as from a horse; tumble. **2.** The act of spilling; also, the amount or substance spilled. [OE *spillan* to destroy] — **spill′er** *n.*

spill² (spil) *n.* **1.** A thin strip of wood or rolled paper, used for lighting lamps, fires, etc. **2.** A slender peg or plug for stopping a hole in a cask; a spile. [Var. of SPILE¹]

spill·age (spil′ij) *n.* That which is spilled.

spill·o·ver (spil′ō′vər) *n.* **1.** The overflowing or excessive part of something that goes beyond its proper or expected limits. **2.** The condition of spilling over.

spill·way (spil′wā′) *n.* A passageway, as in a dam, to release the water in a reservoir.

spilt (spilt) Alternative past tense and past participle of SPILL¹.

spilth (spilth) *n.* That which is spilled or poured out profusely; effusion.

spin (spin) *v.* **spun** (*Archaic* **span**), **spun**, **spin·ning** *v.t.* **1.** To draw out and twist into threads; also, to draw out and twist fiber into (threads, yarn, etc.). **2.** To make or produce as if by spinning. **3.** To form (a web, etc.) from filaments of a viscous substance extruded from the body: said of spiders, silkworms, etc. **4.** To tell, as a story or yarn. **5.** To protract; prolong, as a period of time by delays or a story by additional details: with *out*. **6.** To cause to whirl rapidly: to *spin* a top. — *v.i.* **7.** To make thread or yarn. **8.** To extrude filaments of a viscous substance from the body: said of spiders, etc. **9.** To whirl rapidly; rotate. **10.** To seem to be whirling, as from dizziness. **11.** To move rapidly. **12.** To fish with a spinner. — *n.* **1.** An act or instance of spinning; a rapid whirling: the *spin* of a coin. **2.** Any rapid movement or action. **3.** *Informal* A ride or drive, especially for recreation. **4.** *Aeron.* The descent of an airplane in a helical curve about a vertical axis, with its nose more or less steeply inclined. **5.** *Physics* The angular momentum of an atomic particle or nuclide, commonly given in units of Planck's constant divided by 2π. [OE *spinnan*]

spi·na·ceous (spi-nā′shəs) *adj.* Of, relating to, or resembling spinach or related plants.

spin·ach spin′ich, -ij) *n.* **1.** A potherb (*Spinacia oleracia*) of the goosefoot family. **2.** Its fleshy leaves, used as a vegetable. Also *Dial.* **spin′age**. [< OF *espinage* < LL *spinacia* < Arabic *isbānah*; infl. in form by L *spina* thorn]

spi·nal (spi′nəl) *adj.* **1.** Of or pertaining to the backbone; vertebral. **2.** Resembling a spine, spines, or spinous processes. — *n.* An injection for spinal anesthesia.

spinal anesthesia *Surg.* Anesthesia produced by the injection of an anesthetic into the spinal cord.

spinal canal *Anat.* The tubular cavity on the dorsal side of the spinal column, containing the spinal cord and its membranes.

spinal column *Anat.* The series of articulated vertebrae that enclose and protect the spinal cord and provide dorsal support for the ribs, divided into the cervical, thoracic, lumbar, sacral, and coccygeal regions; the backbone.

spinal cord *Anat.* That portion of the central nervous system enclosed by the spinal column.

spi·nate (spi′nāt) *adj.* Bearing or resembling a spine or thorn.

spin·dle (spin′dəl) *n.* **1.** A rod having a slit or catch in the top and a whorl of wood or metal at its lower end, on which thread is wound from the distaff in hand spinning. **2.** The slender rod in a spinning wheel, containing a spool or bobbin on which the thread is twisted and wound; also, a similar device on a spinning machine or shuttle. **3.** *Mech.* A rotating rod, axis, or shaft, especially when bearing something that rotates: the *spindle* of a lathe. **4.** A needlelike rod mounted on a weighted base, used for impaling bills, checks, etc.: also **spindle file**. **5.** Any narrow, tapering object resembling a spindle. **6.** A small shaft passing through the lock of a door and bearing the knobs or handles. **7.** *Biol.* A structure of elongated achromatic fibers formed during the mitosis of a cell. **8.** A measure of length for yarn, generally 18 hanks, or 15,120 yards. **9.** *Naut.* An iron pile or pipe, surmounted by a lantern or other conspicuous object, placed on a rock or shoal for the guidance of seamen. — *v.* **·dled**, **·dling** *v.i.* **1.** To grow into a long, slender stalk or body; become extremely long and slender. — *v.t.* **2.** To form into or as into a spindle. **3.** To provide with a spindle. [OE *spinel* < *spinnan* to spin]

spin·dle-leg·ged (spin′dəl-leg′id, -legd′) *adj.* Having long, slender legs. Also **spin′dle-shanked′** (-shangkt′).

spindle tree A European shrub or low-spreading tree (*Euonymus europaeus*), used in making spindles, etc.

spin·dling (spind′ling) *adj.* Long and thin; disproportionately slender. — *n.* A spindling person or plant shoot.

spin·dly (spind′lē) *adj.* **·dli·er**, **·dli·est** Of a slender, lanky growth or form, suggesting weakness.

spin·drift (spin′drift) *n.* Blown sea spray: also called *spoon-*

drift. [Alter. of *spoondrift* < *spoon*, var. of SPUME + DRIFT]

spine (spin) *n.* **1.** The spinal column of a vertebrate; backbone. **2.** *Zool.* Any of various hard, pointed outgrowths on the bodies of certain animals, as the fin ray of a fish. **3.** *Bot.* A stiff, pointed woody process on the stems of certain plants; thorn. **4.** The back of a bound book, usually inscribed with the title and name of the author. **5.** A projecting eminence or ridge. **6.** Any slender, thornlike process, as of a vertebra. [< OF *espine* < L *spina* spine, thorn]

spine-finned (spin′find′) *adj.* Spiny-finned.

spi·nel (spi-nel′, spin′əl) *n.* Any of a class of hard, variously colored minerals, consisting chiefly of the oxides of aluminum, magnesium, zinc, or iron, and forming octahedral crystals. Some translucent varieties, as the **ruby spinel**, are used as gemstones. [< F *spinelle* < Ital. *spinella*, dim. of L *spina* spine]

spine·less (spin′lis) *adj.* **1.** Having no spine or backbone; invertebrate. **2.** Lacking spines. **3.** Having a very flexible backbone; limp. **4.** Lacking firmness of will or steadfastness; cowardly. — **spine′less·ness** *n.*

spi·nes·cent (spi-nes′ənt) *adj.* *Biol.* **a** Bearing spines. **b** Terminating in a spine. **c** Tending to become spinous. — **spi·nes′cence** *n.*

spin·et (spin′it) *n.* **1.** A small musical keyboard instrument of the harpsichord class. **2.** A small upright piano. [? after G. *Spinetti*, 16th c. Venetian inventor]

Spin·garn (spin′gärn), **Joel Elias**, 1875–1939, U.S. critic.

spini- *combining form* A spine; thorn: *spiniferous*. [< L *spina* thorn]

spi·nif·er·ous (spi-nif′ər-əs) *adj.* Bearing or producing spines. Also **spi·nig′er·ous** (-nij′ər-əs).

spin·i·fex (spin′i-feks, spi′ni-) *n.* An Australian grass (genus *Spinifex*) having sharp-pointed leaves.

spin·na·ker (spin′ə-kər) *n.* *Naut.* A large, bellying jib sometimes carried on the mainmast of a racing vessel opposite the mainsail, used when sailing before the wind. The foot slides on a spar called the **spinnaker boom**. [? < *spinx*, a mispronunciation of *Sphinx*, the name of the first yacht to carry this kind of sail, 1866]

spin·ner (spin′ər) *n.* **1.** One who or that which spins. **2.** In angling, a whirling spoon bait. **3.** *Aeron.* A streamlined fairing fitted over the boss of an airplane propeller and revolving with it.

spin·ner·et (spin′ə-ret) *n.* **1.** An organ, as of spiders and silkworms, by which a fine silk filament is spun for webs, cocoons, and the like. **2.** A metal plate pierced with holes through which filaments of plastic material are forced, as in the making of rayon fibers.

spin·ner·y (spin′ər-ē) *n.* *pl.* **·ner·ies** A mill or factory devoted to spinning; a spinning mill.

spin·ney (spin′ē) *n.* *pl.* **·neys** *Chiefly Brit.* A small wood or thicket: also spelled **spinny**. [< OF *espinei* < LL *spinetum* < L *spina* thorn]

spin·ning (spin′ing) *n.* The act of one who or that which spins; especially, the activities involved in converting fibers into thread or yarn. — *adj.* **1.** That spins. **2.** Of, belonging to, or used in the process of spinning.

spinning jenny A framed mechanism for spinning more than one strand of yarn at a time: also called *jenny*.

spinning mule Mule¹ (def. 4).

spinning wheel A device used for spinning yarn or thread, consisting of a rotating spindle operated by a treadle and flywheel.

spin·ny (spin′ē) *n.* *pl.* **·nies** A spinney.

spin-off (spin′ôf, -of) *n.* **1.** A new application or incidental result, especially if beneficial; off-shoot or by-product; also, such applications or results considered collectively: commercial *spin-off* from the government's aerospace program: also **spin′off′**. **2.** In commerce, the distribution of stock in new or subsidiary corporations among the stock-holders of the parent corporation.

SPINNING WHEEL

spi·nose (spi′nōs) *adj.* Having many spines. — **spi′nose·ly** *adv.*

spi·nos·i·ty (spi-nos′ə-tē) *n.* *pl.* **·ties** **1.** The state of being spinous or spinose. **2.** A spinous part or thing.

spi·nous (spi′nəs) *adj.* **1.** Spinelike. **2.** Spinose; prickly.

Spi·no·za (spi-nō′zə), **Baruch**, 1632–77, Dutch philosopher. Also **Benedict Spinoza**.

Spi·no·zism (spi-nō′ziz-əm) *n.* *Philos.* The doctrine, developed by Spinoza, that all things and qualities in the universe are aspects of one infinite and universal substance, namely, God. — **Spi·no′zist** *n.* — **Spin·o·zis·tic** (spin′ō-zis′tik) *adj.*

spin·ster (spin′stər) *n.* **1.** A woman who has remained unmarried, especially one no longer young; an old maid. **2.** *Law* In England, any woman who has never married. **3.** A woman who spins; a spinner. [ME < SPIN + -STER] — **spin′ster·hood** *n.* — **spin′ster·ish** *adj.*

spin·thar·i·scope (spin-thar′ə-skōp) *n.* A device for showing the radioactivity of a substance by the scintillations emitted from a minute particle of the substance and thrown against a fluorescent screen. [< Gk. *spintharis* spark + -SCOPE] — **spin·thar'i·scop'ic** (-skop'ik) *adj.*

spi·nule (spī'nyōōl, spin'yōōl) *n.* A small spine; spicule. Also **spin·u·la** (spin'yə-lə). [< L *spinula,* dim. of *spina* spine]

spin·u·lose (spin'yə-lōs, spī'nyə-lōs) *adj.* Having spinules. Also **spin'u·lous** (-ləs).

spin·y (spī'nē) *adj.* **spin·i·er, spin·i·est** 1. Having spines; thorny. 2. Difficult; perplexing. — **spin'i·ness** *n.*

spiny anteater The echidna.

spin·y-finned (spī'nē-find') *adj.* Characterized by fins bearing sharp, unsegmented rays, as the perch, mackerel, etc: opposed to *soft-finned*: also *spine-finned*.

spiny lobster Any of various marine crustaceans (genus *Palinurus*) having spiny shells but lacking large claws; especially, the **California spiny lobster** (*P. interruptus*), valued as a seafood: sometimes called *crayfish, rock lobster*.

spir- Var. of SPIRO-.

spir·a·cle (spir'ə-kəl, spī'rə-) *n.* 1. *Zool.* **a** An aperture or orifice for the passage of air or water in the respiration of various animals, as sharks, rays, tadpoles, and insects. **b** A breathing hole, as the blowhole or nostril of a cetacean. 2. A minute cone formed on a stream of lava by escaping gases. 3. Any opening to admit or expel air; an airhole. [< OF < L *spiraculum* airhole < *spirare* to breathe]

spi·rae·a (spī·rē'ə) *n.* Any of a genus (*Spiraea*) of shrubs of the rose family, having clusters of small, white or pink flowers. Also **spi·re'a**. [< L, meadowsweet < Gk. *speiraia* < *speira* coil]

spi·ral (spī'rəl) *n.* 1. *Geom.* Any plane curve formed by a point that moves around a fixed center and continually increases or decreases its distance from it. 2. A curve winding like a screw thread. 3. Something spirally wound or having a spiral shape, as a spring or a whorled shell. 4. *Aeron.* A flight of an airplane in a spiral path. 5. In football, the motion of a ball rotating on its long axis. — *adj.* 1. Pertaining to or resembling a spiral. 2. Winding and advancing; helical. 3. Winding and rising in a spire, as some springs. — *v.t. & v.i.* **spi·raled** or **·ralled, spi·ral·ing** or **·ral·ling** To take or cause to take a spiral form or course. [< Med.L *spiralis* < L *spira.* See SPIRE².] — **spi'ral·ly** *adv.*

— **Syn.** (noun) 1. *Spiral* and *helix* denote recurrent curves. Strictly speaking, a *spiral* is a plane figure, while a *helix* is three-dimensional. In popular usage, however, *spiral* is often substituted for *helix*: leaves arranged in a *spiral* around a stem.

spiral galaxy *Astron.* An extragalactic system composed of celestial bodies and exhibiting a spiral configuration, as the nebula in Andromeda. Also **spiral nebula**.

spi·rant (spī'rənt) *n. & adj. Phonet.* Fricative.

spire¹ (spīr) *n.* 1. The tapering or pyramidal roof or top of a tower. 2. Any similar high, pointed formation; a pinnacle. 3. A slender stalk or blade. 4. The summit or tapering end of anything, as a steeple. — *v.* **spired, spir·ing** *v.t.* 1. To furnish with a spire or spires. — *v.i.* 2. To shoot or point up in or as in a spire. 3. To put forth a spire or spires; sprout. [OE *spīr* stalk, stem]

spire² (spīr) *n.* 1. A spiral or a single turn of one; whorl; twist. 2. The portion of a spiral formed by a single revolution about the central point. 3. *Zool.* The convoluted portion of a spiral shell. [< F < L *spira* < Gk. *speira* coil]

spired (spīrd) *adj.* Having a spire.

spi·reme (spī'rēm) *n. Biol.* 1. The stage in the mitotic division of a cell during which the chromatin appears like a skein of filaments. 2. One of these filaments. Also **spi'rem** (-rem). [< Gk. *speirēma* coil]

Spires (spīrz) See SPEYER.

Spires, Diet of A diet held at Speyer, Germany, in 1529, at which Lutherans gained further toleration in Catholic states.

spi·rif·er·ous (spī·rif'ər-əs) *adj.* 1. Bearing spiral appendages. 2. Having a spire, as a univalve shell. [< L *spira* coil + -FEROUS]

spi·ril·lum (spī·ril'əm) *n. pl. ·la* (-lə) Any of a genus (*Spirillum*) of rigid, spirally twisted flagellate bacteria. For illustration see BACTERIUM. [< NL, dim. of L *spira* coil]

spir·it (spir'it) *n.* 1. The vital essence or animating force in living organisms, especially man, often considered divine in origin. 2. The part of a human being that is incorporeal and invisible and is characterized by intelligence, personality, self-consciousness, and will; the mind. 3. The substance or universal aspect of reality, regarded as independent of and opposed to matter. 4. *Often cap.* In the Bible, the creative, animating power or divine influence of God. 5. A supernatural or immaterial being, as an angel, demon, elf, fairy, etc. 6. A disembodied soul regarded as manifested to the senses, often as visible: a ghost; specter. 7. A person regarded with reference to any particular activity, characteristic, or temper: a leading *spirit* in the community. 8. *Usually pl.* A state of mind; mood; temper: Success raised his *spirits*. 9. Vivacity or energy; ardor. 10. Ardent loyalty or devotion: school *spirit*. 11. True intent or meaning as opposed to outward, formal observance: the *spirit* of the law. Compare LETTER (def. 4). 12. The emotional faculty of man; the heart: Great poetry stirs the *spirit*. 13. The

the *spirit* of the Reformation. 14. *pl.* Strong alcoholic liquor. 15. *Usually pl. Chem.* The essence or distilled extract of a substance: *spirits* of turpentine. 16. *Often pl.* In pharmacy, a solution of a volatile principle in alcohol: *spirits* of camphor. 17. In dyeing, a solution of a tin salt in acid. 18. In alchemy, one of four substances, mercury, sal ammoniac, sulfur, and arsenic (or orpiment). 19. Any of several fluids formerly supposed to inhere in the body and to control various essential processes, as nutrition, circulation, and motion. 20. *Obs.* The breath. 21. *Usually cap.* In Christian Science, divine substance; God. — **Syn.** See GHOST. — *v.t.* 1. To carry off secretly or mysteriously, as if by the agency of a spirit: with *away, off,* etc. 2. To infuse with spirit or animation; inspirit; encourage: often with *up*. — *adj.* 1. Of or pertaining to ghosts or to the belief in the existence of departed souls; spiritualistic. 2. Operated by the burning of alcohol: a *spirit* lamp. Abbr. *sp.* [< OF *espirit* < L *spiritus* breath, spirit < *spirare* to breathe. Doublet of SPRITE.]

Spir·it (spir'it) *n.* In Christian theology, the Holy Spirit.

spir·it·ed (spir'it·id) *adj.* 1. Full of spirit; animated. 2. Having (a specified kind of) spirit or nature: used in combination: *high-spirited*. — **spir'it·ed·ly** *adv.* — **spir'it·ed·ness** *n.*

spirit gum A quick-drying solution of a gum in ether, used for attaching false whiskers, hair, etc.

spir·it·ing (spir'it·ing) *n.* The activities or work of a spirit.

spir·it·ism (spir'it·iz'əm) *n.* 1. The beliefs or practices of spiritualism. 2. *Rare* Animism (def. 2). — **spir'it·ist** *n.* — **spir'it·is'tic** *adj.*

spir·it·less (spir'it·lis) *adj.* Lacking enthusiasm, energy, etc.; listless. — **spir'it·less·ly** *adv.* — **spir'it·less·ness** *n.*

spirit level An instrument used to determine any deviation from the horizontal or perpendicular by reference to the position of a bubble of air in a tube of liquid.

spi·ri·to·so (spir'i·tō'sō, *Ital.* spē'rē·tō'sō) *Music adj.* Spirited; animated. — *adv.* With spirit. [< Ital.]

spir·it·ous (spir'i·təs) *adj.* 1. Alcoholic; spirituous. 2. *Rare* Distilled or refined, as spirits.

spirits of ammonia A colorless, liquid preparation made from ammonium carbonate and a dilute solution of ammonia, alcohol, water, and various aromatic agents, used as a restorative. Also **aromatic spirits of ammonia**.

spirits of hartshorn An aqueous solution of ammonia: also called *ammonia*.

spirits of turpentine Oil of turpentine. See under TURPENTINE.

spirits of wine Rectified alcohol.

spir·i·tu·al (spir'i·chōō·əl) *adj.* 1. Of, pertaining to, having the nature of, or consisting of spirit, as distinguished from matter; incorporeal. 2. Pertaining to or affecting the immaterial nature or soul of man. 3. Of or pertaining to God, or to the soul as acted upon by the Holy Spirit; holy; pure. 4. Sacred or religious; not lay or temporal; ecclesiastical: *spiritual* authorities: distinguished from *secular.* 5. Marked or characterized by the highest qualities of the human mind; intellectualized. — *n.* 1. A religious folk song originating among the Negroes of the southern United States; also, any song composed in imitation of a Negro spiritual. 2. *Often pl.* That which pertains to sacred matters or to the spirit. [< OF *spirituel* < L *spiritualis* < *spiritus* spirit] — **spir'i·tu·al·ly** *adv.* — **spir'i·tu·al·ness** *n.*

spiritual incest See under INCEST.

spir·i·tu·al·ism (spir'i·chōō·əl·iz'əm) *n.* 1. The belief that the spirits of the dead communicate with and manifest their presence to the living, usually through the agency of a medium; also, the doctrines and practices of those so believing. 2. The doctrine that there are beings that cannot be known by means of the senses, and that are spiritual rather than material in character. 3. *Philos.* A form of idealism that identifies ultimate reality as one universal conscious mind. 4. The state or character of being spiritual. — **spir'i·tu·al·ist** *n.* — **spir'i·tu·al·is'tic** *adj.*

spir·i·tu·al·i·ty (spir'i·chōō·al'ə·tē) *n. pl.* **·ties** 1. The state or quality of being spiritual. 2. That which belongs to the church or to an ecclesiastic.

spir·i·tu·al·ize (spir'i·chōō·əl·īz') *v.t.* **·ized, ·iz·ing** 1. To make spiritual; free of grossness or materialism. 2. To treat as having a spiritual meaning or sense. Also *Brit.* **spir'i·tu·al·ise'**. — **spir'i·tu·al·i·za'tion** *n.* — **spir'i·tu·al·iz'er** *n.*

spir·i·tu·al·ty (spir'i·chōō·əl·te) *n. pl.* **·ties** Ecclesiastical bodies collectively; the clergy.

spir·i·tu·el (spir'i·chōō·el', *Fr.* spē·rē·tü·el') *adj.* Characterized by wit and by the higher and finer qualities of the mind generally. [< F] — **spir'i·tu·elle'** *adj. fem.*

spir·it·u·ous (spir'i·chōō·əs) *adj.* Containing alcohol, as distilled liquors; intoxicating. — **spir'it·u·ous·ness** *n.*

spir·i·tus asper (spir'i·təs) Rough breathing (which see). [< L]

spiritus fru·men·ti (frōō·men'tī) Whisky. [< L, spirit of grain]

spiritus lenis Smooth breathing (which see). [< L]

spirit writing Writing done without the conscious will of the writer, and believed to be supernaturally induced.

spiro-[1] *combining form* Breath; respiration: *spirograph.* Also, before vowels, *spir-.* [< L *spirare* to breathe]

spiro-[2] *combining form* Spiral; coiled; *spirochete.* Also, before vowels, *spir-.* [< Gk. *speira* coil]

spi·ro·chete (spī′rə-kēt) *n.* **1.** Any of a genus (*Spirochaeta*) of motile bacteria having a flexible, corkscrew-like form and commonly found in water and sewage. For illustration see BACTERIUM. **2.** Any of various other similar bacteria of the order *Spirochaetales*, including those that cause syphilis, trench mouth, and yaws. Also **spi′ro·chaete.** [< Gk. *speira* coil + *chaitē* bristle] — **spi′ro·che′tal** *adj.*

spi·ro·che·to·sis (spī′rə-kē-tō′sis) *n.* **1.** *Pathol.* Infection by spirochetes. **2.** *Vet.* An infectious septicemia in chickens caused by a spirochete (*Borrelia anserina*).

spi·ro·graph (spī′rə-graf, -gräf) *n.* An instrument for recording respiratory movements. [< SPIRO-[1] + -GRAPH] — **spi′ro·graph′ic** *adj.* — **spi·rog′ra·phy** (spī-rog′rə-fē) *n.*

spi·ro·gy·ra (spī′rə-jī′rə) *n.* Any of a genus (*Spirogyra*) of bright green, fresh-water algae having chlorophyll bands winding spirally. [< SPIRO-[2] + Gk. *gyros* ring]

spi·roid (spī′roid) *adj.* Resembling a spiral.

spi·rom·e·ter (spī-rom′ə-tər) *n.* An instrument for measuring the capacity of the lungs. [< SPIRO-[1] + -METER] — **spi·ro·met·ric** (spī′rə-met′rik) *adj.* — **spi·rom′e·try** *n.*

spirt (spûrt) See SPURT.

spir·u·la (spir′yə-lə, spir′ōō-) *n. pl.* **·lae** (-lē) Any of a genus (*Spirula*) of cephalopods with an internal spiral shell having whorls partitioned into separate chambers. [< NL < Gk. *speira* coil]

spir·y[1] (spīr′ē) *adj.* **1.** Pertaining to or having the form of a spire. **2.** Abounding in spires, as a city.

spir·y[2] (spīr′ē) *adj.* Having the form of a spiral; coiled.

spit[1] (spit) *v.* **spat** or **spit, spit·ting** *v.t.* **1.** To eject (saliva, etc.) from the mouth. **2.** To eject or utter with violence. **3.** To light, as a fuse. — *v.i.* **4.** To eject saliva, etc., from the mouth. **5.** To make a hissing or sputtering noise. **6.** To fall in scattered drops or flakes, as snow. — *n.* **1.** Spittle; saliva. **2.** An act of spitting or expectorating. **3.** A frothy, spitlike secretion of the spittle insect; also, a spittle insect. **4.** A light, scattered fall or short, driving flurry of snow or rain. **5.** *Informal* Exact likeness; counterpart: because considered so similar as to have been spat out by the original or progenitor. [OE *spittan*] — **spit′ter** *n.*

spit[2] (spit) *n.* **1.** A pointed rod on which meat is turned and roasted before a fire. **2.** A point of low land, or a long, narrow shoal, extending from a shore into the water. — *v.t.* **spit·ted, spit·ting** To transfix or impale with or as with a spit. [OE *spitu*]

spit·al (spit′l) *n. Obs.* A hospital. [Alter. of earlier *spittle* infl. in spelling by HOSPITAL]

spit and image *Informal* An exact likeness; counterpart. Also **spitting image.** [See SPIT[1], n. (def. 5)]

spit and polish *Informal* Formal neatness, order, and cleanliness, especially in military matters.

spit·ball (spit′bôl) *n.* **1.** Paper chewed and shaped into a ball for use as a missile. **2.** In baseball, a pitched ball, now no longer legal, that is wet on one side with saliva, and deviates deceptively in its course. — **spit′ball′er** *n.*

spitch·cock (spich′kok) *v.t.* To split and broil, as a bird or fish. — *n.* An eel split and broiled. [Origin unknown]

spite (spīt) *n.* **1.** Malicious bitterness prompting to vexatious acts; mean hatred; grudge. **2.** That which is done in spite. **3.** *Archaic* Trouble; bad luck: a Shakespearean usage. — **in spite of** (or **spite of**) **1.** Notwithstanding. **2.** Formerly, in contempt of. — *Syn.* See NOTWITHSTANDING. — *v.t.* **spit·ed, spit·ing** **1.** To show one's spite toward; vex maliciously; thwart. **2.** *Obs.* To fill with spite; offend; vex. [Short for DESPITE]

spite·ful (spīt′fəl) *adj.* **1.** Filled with spite. **2.** Prompted by spite. — **spite′ful·ly** *adv.* — **spite′ful·ness** *n.*

spit·fire (spit′fīr′) *n.* A quick-tempered person who is given to saying spiteful things.

Spit·head (spit′hed) A roadstead between the Isle of Wight and southern England, at Portsmouth.

Spits·ber·gen (spits′bûr·gən) A group of Norwegian islands in the Arctic Ocean north of Norway, constituting most of Svalbard; 23,658 sq. mi. Also **Spitz′ber·gen.**

spit·ter (spit′ər) *n.* A young deer whose antlers have emerged, but have not branched.

spitting snake A venomous snake (*Sepedon haemachates*) of South Africa, related to the cobras, that is able to eject its poison for some distance: also called *ringhals.*

spit·tle (spit′l) *n.* **1.** The fluid secreted by the mouth; saliva; spit. **2.** The salivalike matter in which the larvae of spittle insects live. [OE *spātl*; infl. in form by SPIT[1]]

spittle insect A froghopper.

spit·toon (spi-tōōn′) *n.* A receptacle for spit; a cuspidor.

spitz (spits) *n.* One of a breed of small dogs, a variety of Pomeranian, having long silky hair and a tapering muzzle. Also **spitz dog.** [< G, short for *spitzhund* < *spitz* pointed + *hund* dog]

spitz·en·burg (spit′sən-bûrg) *n. Sometimes cap.* A variety of apple, yellow and red in color, prized for its delicate flavor. Also **spitz′en·berg.** [Prob. < Du. *spits* point + *berg* hill; because discovered on an upstate New York hillside]

spiv (spiv) *n. Brit.* **1.** *Slang* A flashy chiseler, sharper, or one who lives by his wits. **2.** In Scotland Yard usage, a low and common thief.

splake (splāk) *n. Canadian* A hybrid fish, a cross between the speckled trout and the lake trout: also called *mendigo.*

splanch·nic (splangk′nik) *adj. Anat.* Pertaining to or supplying the viscera: a *splanchnic* nerve. [< NL < Gk. *splanchnikos* < *splanchnon* entrail]

splanchno- *combining form Anat. & Med.* The viscera; of or related to the viscera. Also, before vowels, **splanchn-.** [< Gk. *splanchnon* entrail]

splash (splash) *v.t.* **1.** To dash or spatter (a liquid, etc.) about. **2.** To spatter, wet, or soil with a liquid dashed about. **3.** To make (one's way) with splashes. **4.** To decorate or mark by or as by splashing. — *v.i.* **5.** To make a splash or splashes. **6.** To move, fall, or strike with a splash or splashes. — *n.* **1.** The act or noise of splashing. **2.** The result of splashing; a spot made by a liquid or color splashed on. **3.** *Informal* A striking or ostentatious impression, action, success, etc.: to make a *splash.* [Var. of PLASH[1]]

splash·board (splash′bôrd′, -bōrd′) *n.* **1.** Any of various devices to protect against splashes, especially on a vehicle. **2.** A board for closing the spillway or sluice of a dam. **3.** A screen to keep water from splashing on the deck of a boat. Also **splash′wing′** (-wing′).

splash·down (splash′doun′) *n.* The setting down of a spacecraft or a part of it in the seas following its flight.

splash·er (splash′ər) *n.* **1.** One who or that which splashes. **2.** A device to protect a surface against splashing.

splash·y (splash′ē) **splash·i·er, splash·i·est** *adj.* **1.** Slushy; wet. **2.** Marked by or as by splashes; blotchy. **3.** *Informal* Sensational; showy: They made a *splashy* appearance.

splat (splat) *n.* A thin, broad piece of wood, as that forming the middle of a chair back. [Origin uncertain]

splat·ter (splat′ər) *v.t. & v.i.* To spatter or splash. — *n.* A spatter; splash. [Blend of SPLASH and SPATTER]

splay (splā) *adj.* **1.** Spread out; broad. **2.** Clumsily formed: a *splay* mouth. **3.** Awkward. **4.** Askew; awry. — *n. Archit.* A slanted surface or beveled edge, as of the sides of a doorway or window, or of a joist. — *v.t.* **1.** To make with a splay; bevel or chamfer away a corner or angle of, as a window opening. **2.** To open to sight; spread; cut open; display. **3.** In farriery, to dislocate. — *v.i.* **4.** To spread out; open. **5.** To slant; slope. [Aphetic var. of DISPLAY]

splay·foot (splā′fŏŏt′) *n. pl.* **·feet** (-fēt′) **1.** Abnormal flatness and turning outward of the feet. **2.** A foot so deformed. — **splay′foot′ed** *adj.*

spleen (splēn) *n. Anat.* **1.** A highly vascular, flattened, ductless organ located on the upper left side of the abdominal cavity, and effecting certain modifications in the blood. **2.** This organ regarded as the seat of various emotions. **3.** Ill temper; spitefulness: to vent one's *spleen.* **4.** *Archaic* Low spirits; melancholy. **5.** *Obs.* Caprice. [< OF *esplen* < L *splen* < Gk. *splēn*] — **spleen′ish, spleen′y** *adj.*

spleen·ful (splēn′fəl) *adj.* Affected with spleen; peevish; ill-tempered. — **spleen′ful·ly** *adv.*

spleen·wort (splēn′wûrt′) *n.* Any of a genus (*Asplenium*) of hardy ferns with simple or compound fronds.

splen·dent (splen′dənt) *adj.* **1.** Shining; lustrous. **2.** Illustrious. [< L *splendens, -entis,* ppr. of *splendere* to shine]

splen·did (splen′did) *adj.* **1.** Magnificent; imposing. **2.** Inspiring to the imagination; glorious; illustrious. **3.** Giving out or reflecting brilliant light; shining. **4.** *Informal* Very good; excellent: a *splendid* offer. [< L *splendidus* < *splendere* to shine] — **splen′did·ly** *adv.* — **splen′did·ness** *n.*

splen·dif·er·ous (splen-dif′ər-əs) *adj. Informal* Exhibiting great splendor; very magnificent: a facetious usage. [< SPLEND(OR) + -FEROUS]

splen·dor (splen′dər) *n.* **1.** Exceeding brilliance from emitted or reflected light. **2.** Magnificence. **3.** Conspicuous greatness of achievement; preeminence. Also *Brit.* **splen′dour.** [< L, brightness < *splendere* to shine] — **splen′dor·ous, splen′drous** *adj.*

sple·nec·to·my (spli-nek′tə-mē) *n. pl.* **·mies** *Surg.* The removal or excision of the spleen.

sple·net·ic (spli-net′ik) *adj.* **1.** Pertaining to the spleen. **2.** Fretfully spiteful; peevish. Also **sple·net′i·cal, splen·i·tive** (splen′ə-tiv). — *n.* A peevish person. — **sple·net′i·cal·ly** *adv.*

splen·ic (splen′ik, splē′nik) *adj.* Of, in, or pertaining to the spleen.

sple·ni·tis (spli-nī′tis) *n. Pathol.* Inflammation of the spleen.

sple·ni·um (splē′nē-əm) *n. pl.* **·ni·a** (-nē-ə) **1.** *Surg.* A compress or bandage. **2.** *Anat.* The rounded posterior end of the corpus callosum. [< NL < Gk. *splēnion* bandage] — **sple′ni·al** *adj.*

sple·ni·us (splē′nē·əs) *n. pl.* **·ni·i** (-nē·ī) *Anat.* A large, thick muscle of the back of the neck, extending in two parts from the skull to the vertebral spines in the cervical and upper thoracic region. [< NL < Gk. *splēnion* bandage]

spleno- *combining form Anat. & Med.* The spleen; of or related to the spleen. Also, before vowels, **splen-**. [< Gk. *splēn, splēnos* spleen]

spleu·chan (sploo′khən) *n. Scot. & Irish* A small bag or wallet to hold tobacco, etc., sometimes used as a purse. [< Irish *spliúcán* leather pouch]

splice (splīs) *v.t.* **spliced, splic·ing 1.** To unite, as by twisting and usually soldering the ends of (wires), intertwining the strands of (rope), gluing the trimmed ends of (film or magnetic tape), etc. **2.** To connect, as timbers, by beveling, scarfing, or overlapping at the ends. **3.** *Slang* To join in marriage: usually in the passive. — *n.* **1.** A union made by splicing. **2.** The place at which two parts are spliced. [< MDu. *splissen*] — **splic′er** *n.*

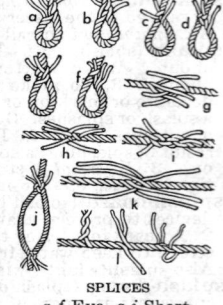

SPLICES
a–f Eye. *g–i* Short.
j Cut. *k,l* Long.

spline (splīn) *n.* **1.** *Mech.* A metal key permanently projecting from a slot in one of two connected rotating mechanical parts, and engaging with a groove cut in the other, thus permitting both parts to rotate as a unit: also called *feather, feather key.* **2.** A long, flexible strip of wood or hard rubber, used by mechanical draftsmen to lay down ship lines, railway curves, or similar work. **3.** A thin strip or tongue of wood or metal used in matching grooved planks, making partitions, filling air spaces, etc. — *v.t.* **splined, splin·ing 1.** To make a slot or groove in for a spline. **2.** To fit with a spline. [? Akin to SPLINT]

splint (splint) *n.* **1.** A thin, flat piece split off; a splinter. **2.** A thin, flexible strip of split wood used for basketmaking, chair bottoms, etc. **3.** In plate armor, one of the flexibly adjusted overlapping laminae. **4.** *Surg.* An appliance, as of wood or metal, used for keeping a fractured limb or other injured part in a fixed or proper position. **5.** A splint bone. **6.** *Vet.* An osseous tumor on the splint bone of a horse. — *v.t.* To confine, support, or brace, as a fractured limb, with or as with splints. [< MDu. *splinte*]

splint bone One of the small rudimentary bones of the metacarpus or metatarsus of the horse and related animals.

splin·ter (splin′tər) *n.* A thin, sharp piece of wood, glass, metal, etc., split or torn off lengthwise; a sliver. — *v.t. & v.i.* To split into thin sharp pieces or fragments; shatter; shiver. — *adj.* Broken away from or independent of an original or main group or body: a *splinter* organization. [< MDu.] — **splin′ter·y** *adj.*

splin·ter·proof (splin′tər·proof′) *adj.* Resistant to the penetration of splinters.

split (split) *v.* **split, split·ting** *v.t.* **1.** To separate into parts by force, especially into two approximately equal parts. **2.** To break or divide lengthwise or along the grain; separate into layers. **3.** To divide into groups or factions; disrupt, as a political party. **4.** To divide and distribute by portions or shares. — *v.i.* **5.** To break apart; divide lengthwise or along the grain. **6.** To become divided or disunited through disagreement, etc. **7.** To share something with others. — **to split hairs** To make fine distinctions; be unnecessarily precise or subtle. — **to split off 1.** To break off by splitting. **2.** To separate by or as by splitting. — **to split the difference** To divide equally a sum in dispute. — **to split up 1.** To separate into parts and distribute. **2.** To cease association; separate. — *n.* **1.** The act of splitting; also, the result of splitting, as a fissure, cleft, or rent. **2.** Separation into factions; rupture; schism: a *split* in the church. **3.** A sliver; splinter. **4.** A share or portion, as of loot or booty. **5.** *Informal* A six-ounce bottle of an alcoholic or carbonated beverage; also, a drink half the usual size. **6.** A split osier, used in certain phases of basketweaving. **7.** A confection made of a split banana, ice cream, syrup, chopped nuts, and whipped cream. **8.** A single thickness of a split skin or hide. **9.** In bowling, the position of two or more pins left standing on such spots so that a spare is nearly impossible. **10.** An acrobatic trick in which the legs are extended upon the floor in a straight line at right angles to the body: also **the splits.** — *adj.* **1.** Cleft, especially longitudinally; fissured. **2.** Dressed and cured after being cleaned: said of fish. **3.** In finance, given in sixteenths, rather than eighths, as a stock quotation: 10¹⁄₁₆ is a *split* quotation. **4.** Divided: a *split* ticket. [< MDu. *splitten*] — **split′ter** *n.*

Split (splēt) A port city in southern Croatia, Yugoslavia, on the Adriatic; pop. 99,462 (1961): Italian *Spalato.*

split infinitive *Gram.* An infinitive in which the sign *to* is separated from the verb, generally by an adverb, as in "to really believe."

split level house A dwelling in which the floors of the several levels are less than a story above or below the adjoining one.

split personality A person or personality showing distinct and incompatible patterns of thought and behavior; also, a schizophrenic person or personality.

split second An extremely brief instant.

split ticket 1. A ballot on which the voter has distributed his vote among candidates of different parties. **2.** A ballot containing names of candidates of more than one party or party faction. Compare STRAIGHT TICKET.

split·ting (split′ing) *adj.* **1.** Acute or extreme in kind or degree: a *splitting* shriek. **2.** That aches severely: a *splitting* head.

splore (splôr, splōr) *n. Scot.* A noisy frolic; carouse.

splotch (sploch) *n.* A discolored spot, as of ink, etc.; a daub; splash; spot. — *v.t.* To soil or mark with a splotch or splotches. [Cf. OE *splott* spot] — **splotch′y** *adj.*

splurge (splûrj) *Informal n.* **1.** An ostentatious display. **2.** An extravagant expenditure. — *v.i.* **splurged, splurg·ing 1.** To show off; be ostentatious. **2.** To spend money lavishly or wastefully. [Origin uncertain] — **splurg′y** *adj.*

splut·ter (splut′ər) *v.i.* **1.** To make a series of slight, explosive sounds, or throw off small particles, as meat frying in fat. **2.** To speak hastily, confusedly, or incoherently, as from surprise or indignation. — *v.t.* **3.** To utter excitedly or confusedly; sputter. **4.** To spatter or bespatter. — *n.* A noise as of spluttering; bustle; confused stir. [Blend of SPLASH and SPUTTER] — **splut′ter·er** *n.*

spode (spōd) *n. Often cap.* Fine porcelain or pottery made originally by Josiah Spode, in Staffordshire, England.

Spode (spōd), **Josiah,** 1754–1827, English potter.

spod·u·mene (spoj′oō·mēn) *n.* A vitreous, transparent to translucent lithium-aluminum silicate, belonging to the pyroxene group and crystallizing in the monoclinic system. [< F *spodomène* < G *spodumen* < Gk. *spodoumenos,* ppr. of *spodoesthai* to be burned to ashes < *spodos* ashes]

spoil (spoil) *v.* **spoiled** or **spoilt, spoil·ing** *v.t.* **1.** To impair or destroy the value, usefulness, or beauty of. **2.** To weaken or impair the character or personality of, especially by overindulgence: to *spoil* a child. **3.** *Obs.* To take property from by force; despoil. **4.** *Obs.* To seize by force. — *v.i.* **5.** To lose normal or useful qualities; especially, to become tainted or decayed, as food. **6.** *Obs.* To plunder; rob. — **Syn.** See DECAY, INJURE. — **to be spoiling for** To long for; crave: He is *spoiling for* a fight. — *n.* **1.** *Often pl.* Plunder seized by violence; booty; loot. **2.** *pl. Chiefly U.S.* The emoluments of public office as the objects of political contests and rewards of political service. **3.** The act of pillaging; spoliation. **4.** An object to be forcibly seized and taken away. **5.** Material removed in digging trenches or excavations. **6.** *Obs.* Ruin; destruction. **7.** *Obs.* Damage; waste. [< OF *espoillier* < L *spoliare* < *spolium* booty]

spoil·age (spoi′lij) *n.* **1.** Spoiled material collectively. **2.** Something that is or has been spoiled. **3.** The process of spoiling. **4.** The state of being spoiled.

spoil·er (spoi′lər) *n.* **1.** One who takes spoil; a robber; despoiler. **2.** One who or that which causes to spoil; a corrupter. **3.** *Aeron.* A small hinged plate on the upper surface of an airplane wing, used to decrease lift.

spoil·five (spoil′fīv′) *n.* A card game played by 2 to 10 persons, in which each player has five cards.

spoils·man (spoilz′mən) *n. pl.* **·men** (-mən) One who advocates the spoils system or works for spoils (def. 2).

spoil·sport (spoil′spôrt′, -spōrt′) *n.* A person whose actions or attitudes spoil the pleasures of others.

spoils system *U.S.* In a political party after a victorious campaign, the system or practice of making public offices the rewards of partisan services.

Spo·kane (spō·kan′) A city in eastern Washington; pop. 170,516.

spoke¹ (spōk) *n.* **1.** One of the rods or bars that serve to support the rim of a wheel by connecting it to the hub. **2.** One of the radial handles of a ship's steering wheel. **3.** A stick or bar for insertion in a wheel to prevent its turning. **4.** A rung of a ladder. — *v.t.* **spoked, spok·ing 1.** To provide with spokes. **2.** To fasten (a wheel) with a stick or spoke to prevent its turning. [OE *spāca*]

spoke² (spōk) Past tense and archaic past participle of SPEAK.

spo·ken (spō′kən) Past participle of SPEAK. — *adj.* **1.** Uttered orally, as opposed to written. **2.** Speaking or having (a specified kind of) speech: *smooth-spoken.*

spoke·shave (spōk′shāv′) *n.* A planing tool having a blade set between two handles, used with a drawing motion in rounding and smoothing wooden surfaces: so called because originally used by wheelwrights in shaping spokes.

spokes·man (spōks′mən) *n. pl.* **·men** (-mən) One who speaks in the name and behalf of another or others. — **spokes′wom′an** (-wŏom′ən) *n.fem.*

spo·li·a·tion (spō′lē·ā′shən) *n.* **1.** The act of despoiling; especially, the authorized seizure of neutral ships by a belligerent. **2.** *Law* Destruction, mutilation, or alteration, especially of a will, bill of exchange, etc. [< L *spoliatio, -onis* < *spoliare* to despoil] — **spo′li·a′tor** *n.*

spo·li·a·tive (spŏ′lē·ā′tiv) *adj.* Tending to abstract from or lessen.

spon·da·ic (spon·dā′ik) *adj.* **1.** Pertaining to or of the nature of a spondee; composed of spondees. **2.** Having a spondee in a position where another kind of metrical foot is usual. Also **spon·da′i·cal.** [< F *spondaïque* < L *spondaicus* < Gk. *spondeiakos* < *spondē.* See SPONDEE.]

spon·dee (spon′dē) *n.* In prosody, a metrical foot consisting of two long syllables or, in English verse, of two accented syllables. [< F *spondée* < L *spondeus* < Gk. *spondeios* (*pous*) libation (meter) < *spondē* libation; because used in the solemn chants accompanying a libation]

spon·du·lics (spon·dōō′liks) *n. Archaic U.S. Slang* Cash money. Also **spon·du′licks, spon·du′lix.**

spon·dy·li·tis (spon′də·lī′tis) *n. Pathol.* Any of various disorders of the vertebrae or spinal column, especially those marked by deformation, rigidity, and inflammation.

spondylo- *combining form Anat. & Med.* A vertebra; of or pertaining to vertebrae. Also, before vowels, **spondyl-.** [< Gk. *spondylos* vertebra]

sponge (spunj) *n.* **1.** Any of a phylum (*Porifera*) of aquatic, usually marine organisms occurring in many forms and sizes, characterized by a highly porous body without specialized internal organs and incapable of free movement. **2.** The skeleton or network of elastic fibers that remains after the removal of the living matter from certain sponges and that readily absorbs liquids, used as an absorbent, for bathing, etc. **3.** Any spongelike device or substance that serves as an absorbent. **4.** Leavened dough, or dough in the process of leavening and before kneading. **5.** A porous, spongelike form assumed by finely divided metals, as iron and platinum. **6.** *Surg.* An absorbent pad, as of sterilized gauze, used in operations, etc., to absorb blood or other fluid matter. **7.** One who consumes or absorbs a great deal. **8.** A sponge bath. **9.** *Informal* One who lives at the expense of another or others; a parasite. **— to throw** (or **toss**) **up** (or **in**) **the sponge** *Informal* To yield; give up; abandon the struggle. **—** *v.* **sponged, spong·ing** *v.t.* **1.** To wipe, wet, or clean with a sponge. **2.** To wipe out; expunge; erase. **3.** To absorb; suck in, as a sponge does. **4.** *Informal* To get without cost or at another's expense. **—** *v.i.* **5.** To be absorbent. **6.** To gather or fish for sponges. **7.** *Informal* To live or get something at the expense of others. [OE < L *spongia*, ult. < Gk. *spongos.* Akin to FUNGUS.]

sponge bath A bath taken by washing oneself with a cloth or sponge rather than in a bathtub or shower.

sponge cake A cake of sugar, eggs, and flour, containing no shortening and beaten very light.

spong·er (spun′jər) *n.* **1.** One who or that which sponges. **2.** A person or ship that gathers sponges. **3.** *Informal* One who sponges on others; parasite.

spon·gi·form (spun′jə·fôrm, spon′-) *adj.* Resembling a sponge in form or structure.

spong·y (spun′jē) *adj.* **spong·i·er, spong·i·est** **1.** Having the nature or character of a sponge; elastic, compressible, and porous. **2.** Having the quality of absorbing and holding fluids. **3.** Porous, as bone. **4.** *Obs.* Wet; soaked. Also **spon·gi·ose** (spun′jē·ōs). **— spong′i·ness** *n.*

spon·sal (spon′səl) *adj.* Relating to marriage or to a spouse. [< L *sponsus*, pp. of *spondere* to promise]

spon·sion (spon′shən) *n.* **1.** The act of becoming surety or sponsor for another. **2.** An engagement or promise made to another. **3.** In international law, an undertaking on behalf of his state by an official not specifically empowered to enter into it.

spon·son (spon′sən) *n.* **1.** A curved projection from the hull of a vessel or seaplane, to give greater stability or increase the surface area. **2.** A similar protuberance on a ship or tank, for storage purposes or for the training of a gun. **3.** An air tank built into the side of a canoe, to improve stability and prevent sinking. [Appar. alter. of EXPANSION]

spon·sor (spon′sər) *n.* **1.** One who makes himself responsible for a statement by, or the debt or duty of, another; a surety. **2.** One who makes the required professions and promises for an infant at baptism and becomes responsible for its religious training; a godfather or godmother. **3.** A business firm or enterprise that assumes all the costs of a radio or television program that advertises its product or service. **—** *v.t.* To act as sponsor for; answer or vouch for. [< L, surety, guarantor < *spondere* to be a security] **— spon·so·ri·al** (spon·sôr′ē·əl, -sō′rē) *adj.* **— spon′sor·ship** *n.*

spon·ta·ne·i·ty (spon′tə·nē′ə·tē) *n. pl.* **·ties** **1.** The quality or fact of being spontaneous. **2.** Spontaneous action or behavior.

spon·ta·ne·ous (spon·tā′nē·əs) *adj.* **1.** Done or resulting from one's own impulse, prompting, or desire; not premeditated; unrestrained. **2.** Arising from inherent qualities without external cause; self-generated: *spontaneous* motion. **3.** *Biol.* Growing or developing without cultivation or labor; wild; indigenous. [< LL *spontaneus* < L *sponte* of free will] **— spon·ta′ne·ous·ly** *adv.* **— spon·ta′ne·ous·ness** *n.*

— Syn. 1. *Spontaneous, impulsive, instinctive,* and *automatic* are here compared as they characterize human actions. A *spontaneous* act seems to be prompted by inner feeling, rather than by external stimulus: a *spontaneous* outburst of applause. An *impulsive* action comes from sudden feeling or inclination, and lacks deliberation: an *impulsive* gesture of welcome. *Instinctive* describes behavior which seems ingrained in the species, and which may conflict with an individual's learned or acquired behavior: *instinctive* fear of darkness. *Automatic* means machinelike, and describes an act that is performed without apparent intervention of the mind: an *automatic* reply to a question.

spontaneous combustion The oxidation of a substance rapidly enough to generate sufficient internal heat to ignite it, as masses of oiled rags, finely powdered ores, coal, etc.

spontaneous generation *Biol.* The doctrine, now no longer held, of the generation of new organisms from putrid or decomposing organic matter assumed to be entirely devoid of life; abiogenesis.

spon·toon (spon·tōōn′) *n.* A half-pike usually armed with a hook, carried by infantry officers in the 18th century. [< F *sponton* < Ital. *spontone* pike < *puntone* point]

spoof (spōōf) *Informal v.t. & v.i.* To deceive or hoax; joke; parody. **—** *n.* Deception; parody; hoax. [after a game invented by Arthur Roberts, 1852–1933, English comedian]

spook (spōōk) *Informal n.* A ghost; an apparition; specter. **— Syn.** See GHOST. **—** *v.t. Informal* To haunt (a person or place). [< Du.] **— spook′ish** *adj.*

spook·y (spōōk′kē) *adj.* **spook·i·er, spook·i·est** *Informal* **1.** Like a ghost; ghostly. **2.** Haunted. **3.** Suggesting the presence or agency of ghosts; eerie. Also **spook′ish.** **— spook′i·ly** *adv.* **— spook′i·ness** *n.*

spool (spōōl) *n.* **1.** A small cylinder, commonly of wood, with a flange at each end and an axial bore, upon which thread or yarn is or may be wound. **2.** The quantity of thread held by a spool; also, the spool and the thread upon it. **3.** Anything resembling a spool in shape or purpose. **—** *v.t.* To wind on a spool. [< MLG *spole*]

spoon (spōōn) *n.* **1.** A utensil having a shallow, generally ovoid bowl and a handle, used in preparing, serving, or eating food. **2.** Something resembling a spoon or its bowl. **3.** A metallic lure attached to a fishing line: also **spoon bait, trolling spoon. 4.** A concave overhanging extension on a torpedo tube to keep the launched torpedo in a straight course. **5.** A wooden golf club with lofted face and comparatively short, stiff shaft, used by some players for approaching. **—** *v.t.* **1.** To lift up or out with a spoon. **2.** To hollow out like the bowl of a spoon. **3.** In certain games, to play or hit (the ball) with little force up into the air; in croquet, to shove or scoop (the ball) with the mallet. **—** *v.i.* **4.** To fish with a spoon. **5.** In certain games, to spoon the ball. **6.** *Informal* To make love, as by caressing or kissing. [OE *spōn* sliver, chip]

spoon·bill (spōōn′bil′) *n.* **1.** Any of the wading birds (genus *Platalea* or *Ajaia*) related to the ibises, having the bill broad and flattened: also called *broadbill.* **2.** The shoveler (def. 2). **3.** The paddlefish. **— spoon′-billed′** *adj.*

spoon·bread (spōōn′bred′) *n.* A quick bread made of cornmeal, eggs, milk, and shortening, baked soft enough to be served with a spoon: also called *batter bread.*

spoon·drift (spōōn′drift′) *n.* Spindrift (which see).

spoon·er·ism (spōō′nə·riz′əm) *n.* The unintentional transposition of sounds or of parts of words in speaking, as in "half-warmed fish" for "half-formed wish." [after William A. *Spooner,* 1844–1930, of New College, Oxford, who was renowned for such slips of the tongue]

spoon-fed (spōōn′fed′) *adj.* **1.** Fed with a spoon. **2.** Pampered; over-indulged. **3.** Not given the opportunity to act or think for oneself.

spoon·ful (spōōn′fŏŏl′) *n. pl.* **·fuls** As much as a spoon will hold.

spoon hook A fish hook with a bright, revolving, spoon-shaped piece of metal attached.

spoon·y (spōō′nē) *Informal adj.* **spoon·i·er, spoon·i·est** Sentimental or silly, as in lovemaking; soft. **—** *n. pl.* **spoon·ies** A foolish, sentimental lover. Also **spoon′ey.**

spoor (spŏŏr) *n.* **1.** A track; trail. **2.** Footprint or other trace of a wild animal. **—** *v.t. & v.i.* To track by or follow a spoor. [< Du.]

Spor·a·des (spŏr′ə·dēz, *Greek* spŏ·rä′thes) **1.** Loosely, all the islands of Greece in the Aegean, exclusive of the Cyclades. **2.** Anciently, the islands of the SE Aegean, off western Asia Minor, including the Dodecanese, Icaria, Samos, and, in some usages, Chios and Lesbos. **3.** Strictly, the **Northern Sporades,** a group of islands of Greece in the western Aegean, off the coasts of Euboea and Thessaly: Greek *Voriai Sporades.*

spo·rad·ic (spô·rad′ik, spō-) *adj.* **1.** Occurring here and there; occasional. **2.** Separate; isolated. **3.** Neither epidemic nor endemic: said of disease. Also **spo·rad′i·cal.** [< Med.L *sporadicus* < Gk. *sporadikos* < *sporas* scattered] **— spo·rad′i·cal·ly** *adv.* **— spo·rad′i·cal·ness** *n.*

spo·ran·gi·um (spô·ran′jē·əm, spō-) *n. pl.* **·gi·a** (-jē·ə) *Bot.*

A sac in which asexual spores are produced, as in certain algae and fungi: also called *spore case*. [< SPOR(O)- + Gk. *angeion* vessel] — **spo·ran/gi·al** *adj.*
spore (spôr, spōr) *n.* **1.** *Bot.* The reproductive body in cryptogams, analogous to the seeds of flowering plants, but capable of developing asexually into an independent organism or individual. **2.** *Bacteriol.* A strongly resistant body developed in certain bacilli and having the property of becoming active under suitable conditions. **3.** *Biol.* Any cell or minute body capable of developing into a new organism; a germ, seed, etc. — *v.i.* **spored, spor·ing** To develop spores: said of plants. [< NL *spora* < Gk. *seed, sowing*] — **spo·ra·ceous** (spô·rā/shəs, spō-) *adj.*
spore case A sporangium.
spo·rif·er·ous (spô·rif/ər·əs, spō-) *adj.* Bearing spores.
sporo- *combining form* Seed; spore: *sporophyte*. Also, before vowels, **spor-**. [< Gk. *spora* seed]
spo·ro·carp (spôr/ə·kärp, spō/rə-) *n. Bot.* In certain cryptogams, a many-celled body bearing or enclosing spores.
spo·ro·cyst (spôr/ə·sist, spō/rə-) *n. Zool.* **1.** An asexual form of a trematode worm that develops directly from the embryo after entry into the intermediate host. **2.** The encysted stage of a protozoan organism that gives rise to spores.
spo·ro·cyte (spôr/ə·sīt, spō/rə-) *n. Biol.* The mother cell from which spores are produced.
spo·ro·gen·e·sis (spôr/ə·jen/ə·sis, spō/rə-) *n. Biol.* **1.** Reproduction by spores. **2.** Sporogony. — **spo·rog·e·nous** (spō·roj/ə·nəs, spō-) *adj.*
spo·rog·o·ny (spō·rog/ə·nē, spō-) *n. Biol.* Spore formation; especially, in sporozoans, the development of spores from a mature zygote. [< SPORO- + -GONY]
spo·ro·phore (spôr/ə·fôr, spō/rə·fôr) *n. Bot.* In fungi, a branch from the thallus that bears the spores.
spo·ro·phyll (spôr/ə·fil, spō/rə-) *n. Bot.* The leaf, or modified leaf, that bears the sporangia. Also **spo/ro·phyl.**
spo·ro·phyte (spôr/ə·fīt, spō/rə-) *n. Bot.* The stage in which spores are produced in certain plants that reproduce by alternation of generations.
spo·ro·tri·cho·sis (spôr/ə·tri·kō/sis, spō/rə-) *n. Pathol.* A chronic disease caused by a fungus (genus *Sporotrichum*) and marked by the formation of ulcerated lesions in the lymph nodes or subcutaneous tissue. [< NL *Sporotrichum*, genus of fungi + -OSIS]
-sporous *combining form* Having (a specified number or kind of) spores: *homosporous*. [< SPOR(O)- + -OUS]
spo·ro·zo·an (spôr/ə·zō/ən, spō/rə-) *adj. Zool.* Designating or belonging to a class (*Sporozoa*) of parasitic protozoans reproducing by sporulation, as the malaria parasite. — *n.* A member of this class. [< SPORO- + Gk. *zōion* animal]
spo·ro·zo·ite (spôr/ə·zō/īt, spō/rə-) *n. Zool.* One of the minute, sickle-shaped bodies formed in the zygote of a sporozoan and constituting the initial phase of the malaria parasite in its host.
spor·ran (spor/ən) *n.* A purse, generally of fur, worn in front of the kilt by Highlanders. For illustration see KILT. [< Scottish Gaelic *sporan* < LL *bursa* purse]
sport (spôrt, spōrt) *n.* **1.** That which amuses in general; diversion; pastime. **2.** A particular game or play pursued for diversion; especially, an outdoor or athletic game, as baseball, football, track, tennis, swimming, etc. **3.** A spirit of jesting or raillery. **4.** That with which one sports; a toy; plaything. **5.** Mockery; an object of derision: to make *sport* of someone; also, a laughingstock; butt. **6.** *Biol.* An animal or plant, or one of its parts, that exhibits sudden and spontaneous variation from the normal type; a mutation. **7.** *Informal* One interested in sports or games that involve gambling. **8.** *Informal* One who lives a fast, gay, or flashy life. **9.** A person characterized by his observance of the rules of fair play, or by his ability to get along with others: a good *sport*. **10.** *Archaic* Amorous fondling; wanton dalliance. — *v.i.* **1.** To amuse oneself; play; frolic. **2.** To participate in games. **3.** To make sport or jest; trifle. **4.** *Biol.* To vary suddenly or spontaneously from the normal type; mutate. **5.** *Archaic & Dial.* To make love in a sportive or trifling manner. — *v.t.* **6.** *Informal* To display or wear ostentatiously; show off. **7.** *Obs.* To amuse; divert. — *adj.* Of, pertaining to, or fitted for sports; also, appropriate for informal wear: a *sport* coat: also **sports.** [Apheptic var. of DISPORT] — **sport/er** *n.* — **sport/ful** *adj.* — **sport/ful·ly** *adv.* — **sport/ful·ness** *n.*
— **Syn.** (noun) **1.** frolic, fun, gambol, play.
sport·ing (spôr/ting, spōr/-) *adj.* **1.** Pertaining to, engaged in, or used in connection with athletic games or field sports. **2.** Characterized by the spirit of sportsmanship; conforming to the codes or standards of sportsmanship. **3.** Interested in or associated with sports for gambling or betting: a *sporting* man. — **sport/ing·ly** *adv.*
sporting chance *Informal* A chance involving the risk of loss or failure.
sporting house A brothel.
spor·tive (spôr/tiv, spōr/-) *adj.* **1.** Relating to or fond of sport or play; frolicsome. **2.** Interested in, active in, or related to sports. **3.** *Obs.* Wanton or amorous. — **spor/tive·ly** *adv.* — **spor/tive·ness** *n.*

sports car A low, rakish automobile, usually seating two persons, and built for high speed and maneuverability.
sports·cast·er (spôrts/kas/tər, -käs/-, spōrts/-) *n. U.S.* One who broadcasts sports events. — **sports/cast/** *n.*
sport shirt A shirt for informal wear, often cut square at the bottom so as to be worn inside or outside slacks. Also **sports shirt.**
sports·man (spôrts/mən, spōrts/-) *n. pl.* **·men** (-mən) **1.** One who pursues field sports, especially hunting and fishing. **2.** A professional gambler; also, one who bets on horse races. **3.** One who abides by a code of fair play in games or in daily practice.
sports·man·like (spôrts/mən·līk/, spōrts/-) *adj.* **1.** Pertaining to sportsmen. **2.** Honorable; generous; conforming to the rules of sportsmanship. Also **sports/man·ly.**
sports·man·ship (spôrts/mən·ship, spōrts/-) *n.* **1.** The art or practice of field sports. **2.** Sportsmanlike conduct.
sports·wear (spôrts/wâr/, spōrts/-) *n.* Clothes made for informal or outdoor activities.
sports·wom·an (spôrts/wŏom/ən, spōrts/-) *n. pl.* **·wom·en** (-wim/in) A woman who participates in sports.
sport·y (spôr/tē, spōr/-) *adj.* **sport·i·er, sport·i·est** *Informal* **1.** Relating to or characteristic of a sport. **2.** Gay, loud, or dissipated. — **sport/i·ly** *adv.* — **sport/i·ness** *n.*
spor·u·late (spôr/yə·lāt, spor/-) *v.i.* **·lat·ed, ·lat·ing** *Biol.* To form spores, especially by multiple cell division after encystment. — **spor·u·la·tion** (spôr/yə·lā/shən) *n.*
spor·ule (spôr/yōol, spor/-) *n.* A spore; especially, a little spore. [< F < NL *sporula*, dim. of *spora* spore]
spot (spot) *n.* **1.** A particular place of small extent; a definite locality. **2.** Any small portion of a surface differing as in color from the rest; blot. **3.** A stain or blemish on character; a fault; a reproach. **4.** A congenital birthmark. **5.** A sciaenoid food fish (*Leiostomus xanthurus*) of the Atlantic coast of the United States, marked with a spot above each pectoral fin. **6.** One of the figures or pips with which a playing card is marked; also, a card having (a certain number of) such marks: the five *spot* of clubs. **7.** *Slang* A currency note having a specified value: a ten *spot*. **8.** *Chiefly Brit.* A portion or bit: a *spot* of tea. **9.** *Slang* Position or situation: He was in a good *spot*. **10.** *U.S. Slang* A spotlight. — **in a spot** *Slang* In a difficult or embarrassing situation; in trouble. — **in spots** Now and then; in some respects: He is bright *in spots*. — **to go to the spot** *Slang* To satisfy a definite need or craving. — **to hit the spot** *Slang* To gratify an appetite or need. — **to hit the high spots** *Informal* To mention only the most important points of a topic, as in a discussion. — **to touch a** (or **one's**) **sore spot** To mention a topic that is painful to one. — **on the spot 1.** At once; immediately. **2.** At the very place. **3.** *Slang* In danger of death. **4.** *Slang* Accountable on or in danger of being held accountable for some action. — *v.* **spot·ted, spot·ting** *v.t.* **1.** To mark or soil with spots. **2.** To decorate with spots; dot. **3.** To place on a designated spot; locate; station. **4.** *Informal* To recognize or detect; see. **5.** *Informal* To yield (an advantage or handicap) to (someone): We *spotted* them five points. — *v.i.* **6.** To become marked or soiled with spots. **7.** To make a stain or discoloration. **8.** *Mil.* To observe the effect of gunfire to obtain data for improving its accuracy. — *adj.* **1.** Being on the place or spot. **2.** Paid or prepared for payment on delivery; also, ready for instant delivery following sale. **3.** Made at random: a *spot* check. [ME < LG. Cf. MDu. *spotte*.] — **spot/ta·ble** *adj.*
spot cash Immediate payment on actual delivery.
spot check An inspection of one or a few typical things out of many, to insure quality, observance of rules, uniformity of product, etc.
spot·less (spot/lis) *adj.* Free from spot, stain, or impurity. — **spot/less·ly** *adv.* — **spot/less·ness** *n.*
spot·light (spot/līt/) *n.* **1.** A circle of powerful light thrown on the stage to bring an actor or actors into clearer view. **2.** The apparatus that produces such a light. **3.** A pivoted automobile lamp for illuminating objects not encompassed by the fixed lights. **4.** Notoriety; publicity.
Spot·syl·va·ni·a (spot/sil·vā/nē·ə) A village in NE Virginia; scene of a 13-day battle in the Civil War, May, 1864. Formerly **Spotsylvania Courthouse.**
spot·ted (spot/id) *adj.* **1.** Discolored in spots; stained; soiled. **2.** Characterized or marked by spots. **3.** Blazed: said of trees, trails, boundary lines, etc.
spotted crake A small European rail (*Porzana porzana*), allied to the American sora: also called *water crake*.
spotted cranebill See under CRANEBILL.
spotted fever *Pathol.* **1.** An epidemic form of cerebrospinal meningitis, due to infection by a bacterium (*Neisseria meningitidis*). **2.** Typhus. **3.** Rocky Mountain spotted fever (which see).
spotted sandpiper See under SANDPIPER.
spot·ter (spot/ər) *n.* **1.** *U.S. Informal* A detective; especially, one employed to discover dishonesty among employees. **2.** In civil defense, one who watches for enemy aircraft. **3.** An observation balloon. **4.** A device on a railroad car that marks irregularities along the track. **5.** In dry cleaning, one who removes spots.

spot·ty (spot′ē) *adj.* **·ti·er, ·ti·est 1.** Having many spots. **2.** Lacking uniformity; unevenly distributed. **— spot′ti·ly** *adv.* **— spot′ti·ness** *n.*

spot-weld (spot′weld′) *v.i. & v.t.* To weld at one point by pressing pointed welding tips or electrodes on each side and applying a high current at a low voltage for a brief period. **— spot′weld′er** *n.*

spot weld A weld made by spot-welding.

spous·al (spou′zəl) *adj.* Pertaining to marriage. **— n.** Often *pl.* Marriage; espousal.

spouse (spouz, spous) *n.* A partner in marriage; one's husband or wife. ◆ Collateral adjective: *sponsal.* **— v.t. spoused, spous·ing** *Obs.* To wed; marry. [< OF *espous, espouse* < L *sponsus,* pp. of *spondere* to promise, betroth]

spout (spout) *v.i.* **1.** To pour out copiously and forcibly, as a liquid under pressure. **2.** To discharge a fluid either continuously or in jets. **3.** *Informal* To speak or orate pompously; declaim. **— v.t. 4.** To cause to pour or shoot forth. **5.** To utter grandiloquently or pompously. **6.** *Brit. Slang* To pawn or pledge. **— n. 1.** A tube, trough, etc., for the discharge of a liquid. **2.** A continuous stream of fluid. **3.** A chute or lift, especially in a pawnbroker's shop. **4.** *Brit. Slang* A pawnbroker's shop. [ME *spoute.* Cf. MD *spoyten.*] **— spout′er** *n.*

spp. Species (plural).

S.P.Q.R. The Senate and People of Rome (L *Senatus Populusque Romanus*).

sprag (sprag) *n.* **1.** A chock or steel bar used to prevent a vehicle from slipping backward on an incline. **2.** *Mining* A wood prop to support a roof or ore. [Origin uncertain]

sprain (sprān) *n.* **1.** A violent straining or twisting of the ligaments surrounding a joint. **2.** The condition due to such strain. **— v.t.** To cause a sprain in; wrench the muscles of (a joint). [? < OF *espreindre* to squeeze < L *exprimere.* See EXPRESS.]

sprang (sprang) Alternative past tense of SPRING.

sprat (sprat) *n.* **1.** A herringlike fish (*Clupea sprattus*) found in shoals on the Atlantic coast of Europe: also called *brisling.* **2.** The young of the herring. [OE *sprott*]

sprat·tle (sprat′l) *Scot. v.i.* **·tled, ·tling** To struggle or scramble. **— n.** A struggle; scramble. [Cf. Sw. *spratta*]

sprawl (sprôl) *v.i.* **1.** To sit or lie with the limbs stretched out ungracefully. **2.** To be stretched out ungracefully, as the limbs. **3.** To move with awkward motions of the limbs. **4.** To spread out in a straggling manner, as handwriting, vines, etc. **— v.t. 5.** To cause to spread or extend awkwardly or irregularly. **— n.** The act or position of sprawling. [OE *spreawlian* to move convulsively] **— sprawl′er** *n.*

spray¹ (sprā) *n.* **1.** Water or other liquid dispersed in fine particles. **2.** An instrument for discharging small particles of liquid; an atomizer. **— v.t. 1.** To disperse (a liquid) in fine particles. **2.** To apply spray to, as with an atomizer. **— v.i. 3.** To send forth or scatter spray. **4.** To go forth in spray. [Akin to MDu. *sprayen* to sprinkle] **— spray′er** *n.*

spray² (sprā) *n.* **1.** A small branch bearing dependent branchlets or flowers. **2.** Any ornament, pattern, etc., having a similar form. [ME; origin uncertain]

spray gun A device resembling a gun that ejects liquids such as paint or insecticides in a fine spray by means of air pressure: also called *squirt gun.*

spread (spred) *v.* **spread, spread·ing** *v.t.* **1.** To open or unfold to full width or extent, as wings, sail, a map, etc. **2.** To distribute over a surface, especially in a thin layer; scatter or smear. **3.** To cover with a layer of something: to *spread* toast with marmalade. **4.** To force apart or farther apart. **5.** To extend over a period of time; prolong: He *spread* the payments over a six-month period. **6.** To make more widely active, active, etc.; promulgate or diffuse: to *spread* a rumor; to *spread* contagion. **7.** To set (a table, etc.), as for a meal. **8.** To arrange or place on a table, etc., as a meal or feast. **9.** To set forth or record in full. **— v.i. 10.** To be extended or expanded; increase in size, width, etc. **11.** To be distributed or dispersed, as over a surface or area; scatter. **12.** To become more widely known, active, etc. **13.** To be forced farther apart; separate. **— n. 1.** The act of spreading: the *spread* of the gospel. **2.** An open extent or expanse. **3.** The limit or extent of expansion of some designated object, as of sail or a bird's wings. **4.** A cloth or covering for a bed, table, or the like. **5.** *Informal* An informal feast or banquet; also, a table with a meal set out on it. **6.** Anything used to spread on bread or crackers: a cheese *spread.* **7.** Two pages of a magazine or newspaper facing each other and covered by related material; also, print spread across two or more columns or on facing pages for advertising or display. **8.** Diffusion; dispersion. **— adj.** Having a broad surface; expanded; outstretched. [OE *sprædan*]

spread-ea·gle (spred′ē′gal) *adj.* **1.** Having the arms and legs outstretched. **2.** *U.S. Informal* Bombastic or extravagant, especially in patriotic oratory. **— v. -ea·gled, -ea·gling** *v.t.* **1.** To lash to the mast or shrouds in spread-eagle

position as a punishment: a former practice. **— v.i. 2.** To deliver an oration in bombastic, patriotic style.

spread eagle 1. The figure of an eagle with extended wings: used as an emblem of the United States. **2.** Any position or movement resembling this, as a figure in skating.

spread·er (spred′ər) *n.* **1.** One who or that which spreads, as a small knife for spreading butter. **2.** A bar of wood, metal, etc., to keep stays or wires apart. **3.** *Agric.* An implement for spreading hay, manure, or the like.

spree (sprē) *n.* **1.** A drinking spell; drunken carousal. **2.** A gay frolic. **3.** Excessive and often unrestrained indulgence in an activity: a buying *spree.* [Origin uncertain]

Spree (sprā, shprā) A river in eastern East Germany, flowing about 250 miles north to the Havel River.

sprig (sprig) *n.* **1.** A shoot or sprout of a tree or plant; an ornament in this form. **2.** A young man; a youth. **3.** One of various small, pointed implements. **4.** A brad without a head. **5.** A small, wedge-shaped piece of metal used to hold glass in a window sash. **— v.t. sprigged, sprig·ging 1.** To ornament with a design of sprigs. **2.** To form (twigs or plants) into sprays. **3.** To fasten with sprigs or brads. [ME *sprigge;* origin uncertain] **— sprig′ger** *n.* **— sprig′gy** *adj.*

spright (sprīt) See SPRITE.

spright·ly (sprīt′lē) *adj.* **·li·er, ·li·est** Full of animation; lively. **— adv.** Spiritedly; briskly; gaily. **— spright′li·ness** *n.*

spring (spring) *v.* **sprang** or **sprung, sprung, spring·ing** *v.i.* **1.** To move or rise suddenly and rapidly; leap; dart: He *sprang* across the creek. **2.** To move suddenly as by elastic reaction; snap together. **3.** To move as if with a leap: An angry retort *sprang* to his lips. **4.** To rise up suddenly, as birds from cover. **5.** To work or snap out of place, as a mechanical part. **6.** To become warped or bent, as boards. **7.** To explode: said of a mine. **8.** To rise above surrounding objects. **9.** To come into being: New towns have *sprung* up. **10.** To originate; proceed, as from a source. **11.** To develop; grow, as a plant. **12.** To be descended: He *springs* from good stock. **13.** *Poetic* To begin to appear, as light or dawn. **— v.t. 14.** To cause to spring or leap. **15.** To cause to act, close, open, etc., unexpectedly or suddenly, as by elastic reaction: to *spring* a trap. **16.** To cause to happen, become known, or appear suddenly: to *spring* a surprise. **17.** To leap over; vault. **18.** To start (game) from cover; flush. **19.** To explode (a mine). **20.** To warp or bend; split. **21.** To cause to snap or work out of place. **22.** To force into place, as a beam or bar. **23.** To undergo (a leak). **24.** *Slang* To obtain the release of (a person) from prison or custody. **— n. 1.** *Mech.* An elastic body or contrivance, as a coiled steel wire, that yields under stress, and returns to its normal form when the stress is removed. **2.** Elastic quality or energy. **3.** The act of flying back from a position of tension; recoil. **4.** An energy or power; a cause of action; impelling motive. **5.** The act of leaping up or forward suddenly; a jump; bound. **6.** The season in which vegetation starts anew, occurring between winter and summer and in the northern hemisphere popularly regarded as including March, April, and May. Astronomically it extends from the vernal equinox to the summer solstice. ◆ Collateral adjective: *vernal.* **7.** A flow or fountain, as of water. **8.** Any source or origin of continued supply. **9.** A crack or break, as of a plank, beam, or spar, or a thing sprung or warped. **10.** *Archit.* The commencement of curvature in an arch. **11.** A spring hinge. **12.** *Scot.* A quick, lively tune. **— adj. 1.** Pertaining to the season of spring. **2.** Acting like or having a spring. **3.** Hung on springs. [OE *springan*]

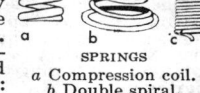
SPRINGS
a Compression coil.
b Double spiral.
c Extension coil.

spring balance A weighing device, often used in classroom experiments, consisting essentially of a spring with a hook at one end to which objects to be weighed may be hung.

spring beauty The claytonia, a plant.

spring·board (spring′bôrd′, -bōrd′) *n.* **1.** A flexible, resilient board used by athletes and acrobats as an aid in leaping or tumbling. **2.** A diving board (which see).

spring·bok (spring′bok′) *n.* A small South African gazelle (*Antidorcas marsupialis*) noted for its ability to leap high in the air: also called *springer.* Also **spring′buck′** (-buk′). [< Afrikaans]

spring chicken 1. A young chicken, 10 weeks to 10 months old, especially tender for cooking: also called *springer.* **2.** *Informal* A young, immature, or unsophisticated person: She's no *spring chicken.*

springe (sprinj) *n.* A snare for catching small game, consisting of a noose tied to a branch that has been bent. **— v. springed** (sprinjd), **springe·ing** or **spring·ing** *v.t.* **1.** To catch with a springe. **— v.i.** To set a springe or springes. [ME *sprenge.* Akin to SPRING.]

SPRINGBOK
(About 2 feet high at shoulder)

PRONUNCIATION KEY: add, āce, câre, pälm; end, ēven; it, īce; odd, ōpen, ôrder; to̅o̅k, po̅o̅l; up, bûrn; ə = a in *above,* e in *sicken,* i in *flexible,* o in *melon,* u in *focus;* yo̅o̅ = u in *fuse;* oil; pout; check; go; ring; thin; this; zh, vision. For ȧ, œ, ü, kh, ṅ, see inside front cover.

spring equinox See under EQUINOX.

spring·er (spring′ər) *n.* **1.** One who or that which springs. **2.** *Archit.* **a** The bottom stone of an arch, lying upon the impost. For illustration see ARCH. **b** A rib in a groined roof or vault. **3.** A springer spaniel. **4.** The springbok. **5.** The grampus (def. 1). **6.** A spring chicken (def. 1).

springer spaniel A large breed of field spaniel used for flushing game.

spring fever The listlessness and restlessness that overtakes many people during the first warm days of spring.

Spring·field (spring′fēld) **1.** The capital of Illinois, in the central part; pop. 91,753. **2.** A city in SW Massachusetts; pop. 163,905. **3.** A city in SW Missouri; pop. 120,096. **4.** A city in west central Ohio; pop. 81,926. **5.** A city in west central Oregon; pop. 27,047.

Springfield rifle A magazine-fed, bolt-action, .30-caliber U.S. Army rifle. Also **Springfield.** [after the U.S. arsenal at *Springfield,* Mass.]

spring·halt (spring′hôlt) *n.* A stringhalt (which see).

spring·head (spring′hed) *n.* A fountainhead; source.

spring hinge A hinge having its leaves connected with a spring to insure automatic closing. For illustration see HINGE.

spring·house (spring′hous) *n.* A small building constructed over a spring, and used for keeping milk, meats, etc., cool.

spring·ing (spring′ing) *n.* **1.** The act of one who or that which springs. **2.** *Archit.* A springer: also **springing line.**

spring·let (spring′lit) *n.* A small spring; streamlet or rill.

spring lock A lock that fastens automatically by a spring.

spring·tail (spring′tāl) *n.* Any of certain very small wingless insects (order *Collembola*) having a pair of springlike appendages beneath the abdomen that enable it to jump.

spring tide **1.** The tide occurring at or shortly after the new or full moon, when the rise and fall are greatest. Compare NEAP TIDE. **2.** Any great wave or flood, as of emotion.

spring·time (spring′tīm) *n.* The season of spring. Also **spring′tide′** (-tīd′).

spring water Water found in or obtained from a spring.

spring·y (spring′ē) *adj.* **spring·i·er, spring·i·est** **1.** Elastic; resilient. **2.** Having many springs of water. — **Syn.** See ELASTIC. — **spring′i·ly** *adv.* — **spring′i·ness** *n.*

sprin·kle (spring′kəl) *v.* **·kled, ·kling** *v.t.* **1.** To scatter in drops or small particles. **2.** To besprinkle; especially, to apply drops of water to, as a form of baptism. — *v.i.* **3.** To fall or rain in scattered drops. — *n.* **1.** A falling in drops or particles, or that which so falls; a sprinkling. **2.** A small quantity. [ME *sprenkelen.* Akin to LG *sprinkeln* to scatter.]

sprin·kler (spring′klər) *n.* **1.** A nozzle or other device for spraying water on lawns. **2.** An outlet in a sprinkler system.

sprinkler system A device for putting out fires, consisting of an arrangement of pipes in the ceiling with outlets that sprinkle water automatically in case of fire.

sprin·kling (spring′kling) *n.* **1.** That which is sprinkled. **2.** A small number or quantity. **3.** A mottling. **4.** The act of scattering drops of liquid.

sprint (sprint) *n.* A short race run at top speed. — *v.i.* To run fast, as in a sprint. [< Scand. Cf. ON *spretta* to run.] — **sprint′er** *n.*

sprit (sprit) *n. Naut.* **1.** A small spar reaching diagonally from a mast to the peak of a fore-and-aft sail. **2.** A bowsprit. [OE *sprēot* pole]

sprite (sprīt) *n.* **1.** A fairy, elf, or goblin. **2.** A disembodied spirit; a ghost. Also spelled *spright.* [< OF *esprit* < L *spiritus.* Doublet of SPIRIT.]

sprit·sail (sprit′səl, sprit′sāl′) *n. Naut.* A sail extended by a sprit.

sprock·et (sprok′it) *n. Mech.* **1.** A projection, as on the rim of a wheel, for engaging with the links of a chain. **2.** A wheel bearing such projections: also **sprocket wheel.** [Origin uncertain]

sprout (sprout) *v.i.* **1.** To put forth shoots; begin to grow; germinate. **2.** To develop or grow rapidly. — *v.t.* **3.** To cause to sprout. **4.** To remove shoots from. — *n* **1.** A new shoot or bud on a plant. **2.** Something like or suggestive of a sprout. **3.** *pl.* Brussels sprouts. [OE *sprūtan*]

sprout·ling (sprout′ling) *n.* A little sprout.

spruce¹ (sproos) *n.* **1.** Any of a genus (*Picea*) of evergreen trees of the pine family, having a pyramidal crown, needleshaped leaves, and pendulous cones; especially, the **black spruce** (*P. mariana*), with deep blue-green foliage, the **Norway spruce** (*P. abies*), the **Englemann spruce** (*P. engelmanni*) of the Pacific coast, and the **white spruce** (*P. glauca*) of Canada and the northern United States. **2.** The wood of these trees. **3.** Any of certain coniferous trees, as the Douglas fir. [Earlier *pruce* Prussian < *Pruce* Prussia < Med.L *Prussia*; so called because first known as native to Prussia]

spruce² (sproos) *adj.* **1.** Having a smart, trim appearance. **2.** Fastidious. — **Syn.** See NEAT¹. — *v.* **spruced, spruc·ing** *v.t.* **1.** To make spruce; dress or arrange neatly: often with *up.* — *v.i.* **2.** To make oneself spruce: usually with *up.* [Special use of SPRUCE¹] — **spruce′ly** *adv.* — **spruce′ness** *n.*

spruce³ (sproos) *n.* A kind of superior Prussian leather. Also **spruce leather.** [See SPRUCE¹]

spruce beer A slightly fermented beverage made by boiling leaves and twigs of spruce with sugar or molasses.

spruce grouse See under GROUSE¹.

sprue¹ (sproo) *n.* In founding, a channel through which the melted metal is poured into the mold. **2.** The waste metal filling this channel; dross. [Origin uncertain]

sprue² (sproo) *n. Pathol.* A chronic disease of tropical regions marked by anemia, emaciation, and gastrointestinal disturbances: also called *psilosis.* [< Du *spruw*]

sprug (sprug) *n. Scot. & Brit. Dial.* The common sparrow.

sprung (sprung) Past participle and alternative past tense of SPRING.

sprung rhythm In prosody, a type of rhythm having feet with a varying number of syllables but of equal time length, the stress usually falling on the first syllable. [Coined by Gerard Manley Hopkins]

spry (sprī) *adj.* **spri·er** or **spry·er, spri·est** or **spry·est** Quick and active; agile. [< dial. E *sprey* < Scand. Cf. Sw. *sprygg* active.] — **spry′ly** *adv.* — **spry′ness** *n.* — **Syn.** brisk, vigorous, energetic. See NIMBLE.

spt. Seaport.

spud (spud) *n.* **1.** A spadelike tool with narrow blade or prongs for removing the roots of weeds by digging or cutting. **2.** *Informal* A potato. — *v.t.* **spud·ded, spud·ding** To remove, as weeds, with a spud. [ME *spudde* < Scand. Cf. Dan. *spyd* spear.]

spud·der (spud′ər) *n.* A tool for removing bark from trees.

Spud Islander *Canadian* A Prince Edward Islander.

spue (spyoo) See SPEW.

spume (spyoom) *n.* Froth, as on an agitated or effervescing liquid; foam; scum. — *v.i.* **spumed, spum·ing** To foam; froth. [< F < L *spuma* foam] — **spu′mous, spum′y** *adj.*

spu·mes·cent (spyoo·mes′ənt) *adj.* Resembling or producing froth or foam; spumy. — **spu·mes′cence** *n.*

spu·mo·ne (spə·mō′nē, *Ital.* spoo·mō′nä) *n. pl.* **·ni** (-nē) A dessert or mousse of ice cream or water ice containing fruit, nuts, or other candied products, in a base of whipped cream. Also **spu·mo′ni.** [< Ital., aug. of *spuma* froth < L *spuma*]

spun (spun) Past tense and past participle of SPIN.

spunk (spungk) *n.* **1.** Punk or other tinder. **2.** A small fire, spark, or flame; also, a match. **3.** *Informal* Mettle; pluck; courage. **4.** To take fire; flare up; kindle. [< Irish *sponnc* tinder < L *spongia* sponge]

spunk·y (spungk′ē) *adj.* **spunk·i·er, spunk·i·est** *Informal* Spirited; courageous; also, touchy. — **spunk′i·ly** *adv.* — **spunk′i·ness** *n.*

spun silk **1.** Short fibers of silk from cocoons that the worms have pierced, and that cannot be reeled. **2.** Yarn or cloth made from these fibers.

spun yarn *Naut.* A two- to four-stranded, left-handed line made from loosely twisted rope yarn, used for seizings, etc.

spur (spûr) *n.* **1.** A pricking or goading instrument worn on a horseman's heel, and bearing a sharp point or a series of points on a rotating wheel. **2.** Anything that incites or urges; instigation; incentive. **3.** A part or attachment projecting like or suggestive of a spur, as a crag or mountain peak. **4.** A stiff, sharp spine, as on the legs of some insects and birds; especially, the spine on the tarsus of the domestic cock. For illustration see FOWL. **5.** *Archit.* **a** A buttress or other offset from a wall. **b** A claw or the like projecting upon the plinth at the four angles of the base of a column. **6.** In carpentry, a brace reinforcing a rafter or post; a strut. **7.** *Bot.* A tubular extension of some part of a flower, as in the columbine and larkspur. **8.** A spur track (which see). **9.** A pointed, curved cutting instrument fastened to each leg of a gamecock during fights; a gaff. — **on the spur of the moment** Hastily; prompted by an impulse. — *v.* **spurred, spur·ring** *v.t.* **1.** To prick or urge with or as with spurs. **2.** To furnish with spurs. **3.** To gash with the spur, as a gamecock. — *v.i.* **4.** To spur one's horse. **5.** To hurry. [OE *spura*] — **spur′rer** *n.*
— **Syn.** (verb) **1.** goad, impel, incite. — **Ant.** (verb) **1.** check, deter, restrain.

spur·gall (spûr′gôl′) *n.* A galled place on a horse's side, caused by the spur. — *v.t.* To injure or gall with a spur.

spurge (spûrj) *n.* A plant, euphorbia. [< OF *espurge* < *espurgier* to purge < L *expurgare* < *ex-* out + *purgare* to cleanse]

spur gear *Mech.* **1.** A spur wheel (which see). **2.** Spur gearing.

spur gearing *Mech.* Gearing composed of spur wheels. Also *spur gear.*

spurge laurel An evergreen shrub of Europe and Asia (*Daphne laureola*), having lance-shaped leaves and yellowish green flowers.

SPUR GEARING

Spur·geon (spûr′jən), **Charles Haddon**, 1834–92, English Baptist preacher and writer.

spu·ri·ous (spyoor′ē·əs) *adj.* **1.** Not proceeding from the source pretended; not genuine; false. **2.** Illegitimate. **3.** *Bot.* Similar in appearance but not in function or structure. [< L *spurius*] — **spu′ri·ous·ly** *adv.* — **spu′ri·ous·ness** *n.*

spurn (spûrn) *v.t.* **1.** To reject with disdain; refuse contemptuously; scorn. **2.** To strike with the foot; kick. — *v.i.* **3.** To reject something with disdain. — *n.* The act of spurning; also, a kick. [OE *spurnan*] — **spurn′er** *n.*

spurred (spûrd) *adj.* **1.** Wearing or having spurs. **2.** Having sharp spikes, claws, or shoots.

spur·ri·er (spûr'ē·ər) *n.* A maker of spurs.

spur·ry (spûr'ē) *n.* *pl.* **·ries** Any of several low annual herbs (genus *Spergula*) of the pink family; especially, the **corn spurry** (*S. arvensis*), a common weed. Also **spur'rey.** [< Du. *spurrie*, ? < Med.L *spergula*]

spurt (spûrt) *n.* **1.** A sudden gush of liquid. **2.** Any sudden outbreak, as of anger. **3.** An extraordinary effort of brief duration. — *v.i.* **1.** To come out in a jet; gush forth. **2.** To make a sudden and extreme effort. — *v.t.* **3.** To force out in a jet; squirt. Also spelled *spirt*. [Var. of earlier *spirt*, metathetic var. of *sprit* < OE *spryttan* to come forth]

spur·tle (spûr'tal) *n.* *Scot.* A stirring stick for porridge.

spur track A short side track connecting with the main track of a railroad: also called *spur*.

spur wheel *Mech.* A wheel having radial teeth on the rim, with their edges parallel to the axis; also called *spur gear*.

sput·nik (sput'nik, spoŏt'-; *Russ.* spoŏt'nyik) *n.* A Soviet artificial earth satellite, the first of which, **Sputnik I,** was launched in 1957. [< Russian, satellite; lit., that which travels with something else]

sput·ter (sput'ər) *v.i.* **1.** To throw off solid or fluid particles in a series of slight explosions. **2.** To emit particles of saliva from the mouth, as when speaking excitedly. **3.** To speak rapidly or confusedly. — *v.t.* **4.** To throw off or emit in small particles. **5.** To utter in a confused or excited manner. — *n.* **1.** The act or sound of sputtering; especially, excited talk; jabbering. **2.** That which is ejected in sputtering. [Akin to Du. *sputteren*] — **sput'ter·er** *n.*

spu·tum (spyoō'təm) *n.* *pl.* **·ta** (-tə) Saliva; spittle; expectorated matter. [< L < *spuere* to spit]

Spuy·ten Duy·vil Creek (spīt'n dī'vəl) A narrow stream in New York City, north of Manhattan, connecting the Hudson and Harlem rivers.

spy (spī) *n.* *pl.* **spies** **1.** A person who, acting clandestinely or on false pretenses, obtains or seeks to obtain information from an enemy or belligerent with the intention of communicating it to the hostile party; secret agent. **2.** One who watches others secretly: often a contemptuous term. **3.** The act of watching secretly. — *v.* **spied, spy·ing** *v.i.* **1.** To keep watch closely or secretly; act as a spy. **2.** To make careful examination; pry: with *into*. — *v.t.* **3.** To observe stealthily and with hostile intent: usually with *out*. **4.** To catch sight of; see; espy. **5.** To discover by careful or secret investigation: with *out*. **6.** To examine or scrutinize carefully. [< OF *espie* < *espier* to espy < Gmc.]

— **Syn.** (noun) **1.** *Spy, secret agent, emissary,* and *scout* denote a person sent to get information for a military force or a government. A *spy* is one who penetrates enemy lines in disguise; if captured in wartime, he is subject to execution. Since *spy* is usually opprobrious, the neutral term *secret agent* is often substituted. An *emissary* was originally a *spy*, but the word is now applied to an avowed diplomatic agent sent on a special mission. *Scout* is a military term for a soldier who lurks in concealment to observe enemy operations; a *scout* is not disguised, so that if captured, he is entitled to be treated as an ordinary prisoner of war.

spy·glass (spī'glas', -gläs') *n.* A small telescope.

sq. **1.** Sequence. **2.** The following one (L *sequens*). **3.** Square.

Sq. Squadron.

sq. ft. Square foot (or feet).

sq. in. Square inch(es).

sq. m. or **sq. mi.** Square mile(s).

sqq. The following ones (L *sequentia*).

squab (skwob) *n.* **1.** A young pigeon, especially when an unfledged nestling. **2.** A fat, short person. **3.** A soft, stuffed cushion. **4.** A sofa; couch. — *adj.* **1.** Fat and short; squat. **2.** Unfledged or recently hatched. [< dial. E < Scand. Cf. dial. Norw. *skvabb* a soft, wet mass.]

squab·ble (skwob'əl) *v.* **·bled, ·bling** *v.i.* **1.** To engage in a petty wrangle or scuffle; quarrel. — *v.t.* **2.** *Printing* To disarrange (composed type) so as to mix the letters or the lines. — *n.* A petty wrangle. — **Syn.** See QUARREL[1]. [Cf. dial. Sw. *skvabbel* to dispute, argue.] — **squab'bler** *n.*

squab·by (skwob'ē) *adj.* **·bi·er, ·bi·est** Short and fat. Also **squab'bish.**

squad (skwod) *n.* **1.** A small group of persons organized for the performance of a specific function. **2.** A small detachment of troops or police; especially, the smallest tactical unit in the infantry of the U.S. Army. **3.** A team: a football *squad*. — *v.t.* **squad·ded, squad·ding** **1.** To form into a squad or squads. **2.** To assign to a squad. [< F *escouade* < OF *esquadre* square < Ital. *squadra* < L *quattuor* four]

squad car An automobile used by police for patrolling, and equipped with radiotelephone for communicating with headquarters: also called *patrol car*.

squad·ron (skwod'rən) *n.* **1.** In the U.S. Navy, two or more divisions of vessels or flights of naval aircraft, usually of the same type. **2.** In the U.S. Air Force, a unit, usually subordinate to a group, composed of two or more flights. **3.** A

subordinate unit of a cavalry regiment. **4.** Any regularly arranged or organized body, as of men. — *v.t.* To arrange in a squadron or squadrons. [< Ital. *squadrone*, aug. of *squadra*. See SQUAD.]

squadron leader In the Royal, Royal Canadian, and other Commonwealth air forces, a commissioned officer ranking next below a wing commander. See table at GRADE.

squal·id (skwol'id) *adj.* Having a foul, mean, or poverty-stricken appearance; dirty, neglected, and wretched. [< L *squalidus* < *squalere* to be foul] — **squal'id·ly** *adv.* — **squal'id·ness, squa·lid·i·ty** (skwo·lid'ə·tē) *n.*

squall[1] (skwôl) *n.* A loud, screaming outcry. — *v.i.* To cry loudly; scream; bawl. [Cf. ON *skvala* to shout, bawl] — **squall'er** *n.*

squall[2] (skwôl) *n.* **1.** A sudden, violent burst of wind, often accompanied by rain or snow. **2.** *Informal* A commotion; disturbance. — *v.i.* To blow a squall; be squally. [Cf. Sw. *skval-regn* sudden rainstorm]

squall cloud A grayish cloud rolling beneath an approaching thunderstorm.

squall line *Meteorol.* A narrow zone characterized by squalls, abrupt wind shifts, sudden pressure rises, and temperature drops, frequently occurring in advance of and generally parallel to a cold front.

squall·y (skwô'lē) *adj.* **squall·i·er, squall·i·est** **1.** Stormy; blustering. **2.** *Informal* Threatening trouble of any kind.

squal·or (skwol'ər) *n.* The state of being squalid; filth and wretched poverty. [< L < *squalere* to be foul]

squa·ma (skwā'mə) *n.* *pl.* **·mae** (-mē) *Biol.* A thin, scalelike structure; a scale. [< L] — **squa'mate** (-māt) *adj.*

squa·ma·tion (skwə·mā'shən) *n.* **1.** The state of being scaly. **2.** The arrangement of epidermal scales on an animal.

squa·mo·sal (skwə·mō'səl) *adj.* **1.** Like a scale; squamous. **2.** *Anat.* Relating to the squamous portion of the temporal bone behind the ear in man, or the analogous bone in other vertebrates. — *n.* A squamosal bone. For illustration see SKULL.

squa·mous (skwā'məs) *adj.* Covered with or formed of squamae or scales; scaly; scalelike. Also **squa'mose** (-mōs). [< L *squamosus* < *squama* scale] — **squa'mous·ly** *adv.* — **squa'mous·ness** *n.*

squam·u·lose (skwam'yə·lōs, skwā'myə-) *adj.* Provided with small bracts or scales, as a plant.

squan·der (skwon'dər) *v.t.* **1.** To spend (money, time, etc.) wastefully; lavish profusely; dissipate. **2.** *Obs.* To scatter. — *n.* Prodigality; wasteful expenditure. [Origin unknown] — **squan'der·er** *n.* — **squan'der·ing·ly** *adv.*

square (skwâr) *n.* **1.** A parallelogram having four equal sides and four right angles. **2.** Any object, part, or surface that has this form, or nearly so, as a pane of glass, or one of the spots on a checkerboard. **3.** An instrument having an L- or T-shape by which to measure or lay out right angles. **4.** An open area in a city or town formed by the intersection of several streets. **5.** An open area in a city or town formed by the intersection of four or more streets, often planted with trees, flowers, etc., and used as a park. **6.** A section in a town bounded on four sides by streets; also, the distance between one street and the next. **7.** *Math.* The product of a number multiplied by itself. **8.** Formerly, a body of troops formed in a four-sided array. **9.** *Obs.* A standard or pattern; rule. **10.** *Slang* One not conversant with the latest trends or fads. — **on the square 1.** At right angles. **2.** On equal terms. **3.** *Informal* In a fair and honest manner. **4.** In Freemasonry, in good standing: said of members. — **out of square 1.** Not at right angles; obliquely. **2.** Incorrectly; askew; out of order. — *adj.* **1.** Having four equal sides and four right angles; also, resembling a square in form. **2.** Formed with or characterized by a right angle; rectangular. **3.** Adapted to forming squares or computing in squares: a *square* measure. **4.** Direct; fair; just; equitable; honest. **5.** Having debit and credit balanced; even; settled. **6.** Absolute; complete; unequivocal. **7.** Having a broad, stocky frame; strong; sturdy. **8.** *Slang* Lacking up-to-date sophistication; conventional. **9.** *Naut.* At right angles to the mast and keel: said of the yards of a square-rigged ship. **10.** Steady: said of a horse's gait. **11.** *Mech.* Having the cylinder bore equal or nearly equal to the piston stroke. — **square meal** A good, satisfying meal. — **square peg in a round hole** A misfit. — *v.* **squared, squar·ing** *v.t.* **1.** To make or form like a square. **2.** To shape or adjust so as to form a right angle, or a right angle with something else. **3.** To mark with or divide into squares. **4.** To test for the purpose of adjusting to a straight line, right angle, or plane surface. **5.** To bring to a position suggestive of a right angle: *Square* your shoulders. **6.** To make satisfactory settlement or adjustment of: to *square* accounts. **7.** To make (the score

SQUARES
a T-square.
b Steel square.
c Try square.

of a game or contest) equal. **8.** To cause to conform; adapt; reconcile: to *square* one's opinions to the times. **9.** *Math.* **a** To multiply (a number) by itself. **b** To determine the area of. — *v.i.* **10.** To be at right angles. **11.** To conform; agree; harmonize. **12.** In golf, to make the scores equal. **13.** *Obs.* To squabble; quarrel. — **to square away 1.** *Naut* To set (the yards) at right angles to the keel. **2.** To square up. — **to square off** To assume a position for attack or defense; prepare to fight. — **to square the circle 1.** To construct a square equal in area to a given circle, an insoluble problem. **2.** To attempt something impossible. — **to square up** To adjust satisfactorily. — *adv.* **1.** So as to be square, or at right angles. **2.** *Informal* Honestly; fairly. **3.** Directly; firmly. Abbr. *sq.* [< OF *esquire, esquarre.* ult. < L *quat-tuor* four] — **square′ness** *n.* — **squar′er** *n.*

Square (skwâr) *n.* The constellation Norma.

square bracket (def. 6).

square-dance (skwâr′dans′) *v.i.* **-danced, -danc·ing** *U.S.* To perform a square dance.

square dance *U.S.* Any dance, as a quadrille, in which the couples form sets in squares.

square deal *Informal* **1.** In card games, an honest deal. **2.** Fair or just treatment.

square·head (skwâr′hed′) *n.* *U.S. Slang* A Scandinavian or German: a contemptuous term.

square knot A common knot, formed of two overhand knots: also called *reef knot.* For illustration see KNOT.

square·ly (skwâr′lē) *adv.* **1.** In a direct or straight manner. **2.** Honestly; fairly. **3.** *U.S.* Plainly; unequivocally. **4.** In a square form. **5.** At right angles (to a line or plane).

square meal *Informal* A full and substantial meal.

square measure A unit or system of units for measuring areas. See also METRIC SYSTEM. See table inside back cover.

square number *Math.* A number, as 1, 4, 9, 16, etc., that is the square of some integer.

square piano An obsolete type of piano, rectangular in shape, with horizontal strings.

square-rigged (skwâr′rigd′) *adj. Naut.* Fitted with square-rigged sails as the principal sails: distinguished from *fore-and-aft-rigged.*

square-rigged sail *Naut.* A four-cornered sail extended by a yard lying horizontally across the mast. Also **square sail.**

square-rig·ger (skwâr′rig′ər) *n.* A square-rigged ship.

square root *Math.* A number that, multiplied by itself, produces the given number: 4 is the *square root* of 16.

square shooter *Informal* An upright person; one who acts honestly and justly.

square-toed (skwâr′tōd′) *adj.* **1.** Having the toes square, as the shoes worn by the Puritans. **2.** Old-fashioned and conservative; prim.

square-toes (skwâr′tōz′) *n.* An old-fashioned, conservative person.

squar·ish (skwâr′ish) *adj.* Somewhat square.

squar·rose (skwar′ōs, skwo·rōs′) *adj.* **1.** *Biol.* Rough with projecting scalelike processes. **2.** *Bot.* Crowded and rigid: *squarrose* leaves. Also **squar·rous** (skwar′əs). [< L *squarrosus* scurfy]

squash¹ (skwosh) *v.t.* **1.** To beat or press into a pulp or soft mass; crush. **2.** To quell or suppress. — *v.i.* **3.** To be smashed or squashed. **4.** To make a splashing or sucking sound. — *n.* **1.** A soft or overripe object; also, a crushed mass. **2.** The sudden fall of a heavy, soft, or bursting body; also, the sound made by such a fall. **3.** The sucking, squelch-ing sound made by walking through ooze or mud. **4.** Either of two games played on an indoor court with rackets and a ball. In **squash rackets** a small firm rubber ball is used, in **squash tennis** an inflated ball slightly smaller than a tennis ball and covered with tight webbing. **5.** A beverage of which one ingredient is a fruit juice: lemon *squash.* — *adv.* With a squelching, oozy sound. [< OF *esquasser,* ult. < L *ex-thoroughly + quassare* to crush] — **squash′er** *n.*

squash² (skwosh) *n.* **1.** The edible fruit of various trailing annuals (genus *Cucurbita*) of the gourd family. **2.** The plant that bears it. [< Algonquian. Cf. Massachuset *askoota-squash,* lit., eaten raw.]

squash bug A large, brownish black, ill-smelling North American hemipterous insect (*Anasa tristis*) that is destructive to squash vines.

squash·y (skwosh′ē) *adj.* **squash·i·er, squash·i·est** Soft and moist; easily squashed. — **squash′i·ly** *adv.* — **squash′i·ness** *n.*

squat (skwot) *v.* **squat·ted** or **squat, squat·ting** *v.i.* **1.** To sit on the heels or hams, or with the legs near the body. **2.** To crouch or cower down, as to avoid being seen. **3.** To settle on a piece of land without title or payment. **4.** To settle on government land in accordance with certain government regulations that will eventually give title. — *v.t.* **5.** To cause (oneself) to squat. — *adj.* **1.** Short and thick; squatty. **2.** Being in a squatting position. — *n.* **1.** A squatting attitude or position. **2.** The act of squatting. [< OF *esquatir* < *es-thoroughly* (< L *ex-*) + *quatir* to press down < L *coactus,* pp. of *cogere* to force < *co-* together + *agere* to drive]

squat·ter (skwot′ər) *n.* **1.** One who or that which squats; especially, one who settles on land without permission or

right, as on public or unimproved land. **2.** In the United States and Australia, one who settles on government land subject to regulations with a view to obtaining title.

squatter sovereignty *U.S.* The political theory that the settlers of a territory had the right to make their own laws.

squat·ty (skwot′ē) *adj.* Disproportionately short and thick.

squaw (skwô) *n.* **1.** An American Indian woman or wife. **2.** *Slang* Any woman or girl. [< Algonquian, woman]

squaw·fish (skwô′fish′) *n. pl.* **·fish** or **·fish·es** A cyprinoid food fish (genus *Ptychocheilus*) found in the rivers of the northern Pacific coast.

squawk (skwôk) *v.i.* **1.** To utter a shrill, harsh cry, as a parrot. **2.** *Slang* To utter loud complaints or protests. — *n.* **1.** The harsh cry of certain birds; also, the act of squawk-ing. **2.** *Slang* A loud protest or complaint. **3.** A night heron (*Nycticorax nycticorax*) of Europe, Asia, and America, having a black crown. [Prob. imit.] — **squawk′er** *n.*

squaw man A white man married to an Indian woman and in possession of tribal rights on that account.

squaw-root (skwô′rōōt′, -rŏŏt′) *n.* A yellowish brown, leafless North American herb (*Conopholis americana*) of the broomrape family, parasitic on roots of trees. **2.** One of cer-tain other plants, as the blue cohosh: see under COHOSH.

squeak (skwēk) *n.* A thin, sharp, penetrating sound. — **narrow** (or **near**) **squeak** *Informal* A narrow escape. — *v.i.* **1.** To make a squeak. **2.** *Informal* To succeed or other-wise progress after narrowly averting failure or reversal: He just managed to *squeak* through. **3.** *Slang* To let out information; squeal. — *v.t.* **4.** To utter or effect with a squeak. **5.** To cause to squeak. [ME *squeke,* prob. < Scand. Cf. *sqväka* to croak.] — **squeak′er** *n.*

squeak·y (skwē′kē) *adj.* **squeak·i·er, squeak·i·est** Making a squeaking noise; tending to squeak. — **squeak′i·ly** *adv.* — **squeak′i·ness** *n.*

squeal (skwēl) *v.i.* **1.** To utter a sharp, shrill, prolonged cry. **2.** *Slang* To turn informer; betray an accom-plice or a plot. — *v.t.* **3.** To utter with a squeal. — *n.* A shrill, prolonged cry, as of a pig. [Imit.] — **squeal′er** *n.*

squeam·ish (skwē′mish) *adj.* **1.** Easily disgusted or shocked; modest; prudish. **2.** Overly fastidious. **3.** Easily nauseated. [< earlier *squaymisch* < AF *escoymous;* ult. ori-gin unknown] — **squeam′ish·ly** *adv.* — **squeam′ish·ness** *n.*

squee·gee (skwē′jē) *n.* **1.** An implement having a stout, straight crosspiece edged with rubber or leather used for re-moving water from decks or floors, window panes, etc. **2.** *Photog.* A smaller similar implement, made in the same way or in the form of a roller, used for pressing a film closer to its mount, or for squeezing the moisture from a print. — *v.t.* **1.** To smooth down, as film, with a squeegee. **2.** To cleanse with a squeegee. Also **squil·gee** (skwil′jē), **skwil·jē′), **squil·la·gee** (skwil′ə·jē). [< *squeege,* var. of SQUEEZE]

squeeze (skwēz) *v.* **squeezed, squeez·ing** *v.t.* **1.** To press hard upon; compress. **2.** To extract something from by pressure: to *squeeze* oranges. **3.** To draw forth by pressure; express: to *squeeze* juice from apples. **4.** To force or push; cram. **5.** To oppress, as with burdensome taxes. **6.** To exert pressure upon (someone) to act as one desires, as by blackmailing. **7.** To make a facsimile impression of. — *v.i.* **8.** To apply pressure. **9.** To force one's way; push: with *in, through,* etc. **10.** To be pressed; yield to pressure. — **to squeeze out** To force out of business, or ruin financially, by unscrupulous methods. — *n.* **1.** The act or process of squeezing; pressure. **2.** A firm grasp of someone's hand; a hearty handclasp; also, an embrace; hug. **3.** Something, as juice, extracted or expressed. **4.** A facsimile, as of a coin or inscription, produced by pressing some soft substance upon it. **5.** *Informal* Pressure exerted for the extortion of money or favors; also, financial pressure. [? < OF *es-* thoroughly (< L *ex-*) + ME *queisen,* OE *cwȳsan* to crush] — **squeez′a·ble** *adj.* — **squeez′er** *n.*

squeeze bottle A container made of soft plastic so that the contents can be squeezed or sprayed out.

squeeze play 1. In baseball, a play in which the batter tries to bunt the ball so that a man on third base may score by starting while the pitcher is about to deliver the ball. **2.** In bridge, any play that compels one's opponent to discard a potentially winning card.

squelch (skwelch) *v.t.* **1.** To crush; squash. **2.** *Informal* To subdue utterly; silence, as with a crushing reply. — *v.i.* **3.** To make a splashing or sucking noise, as when walking in deep mud. **4.** To walk with such a sound. — *n.* **1.** A squelching sound. **2.** A squelched or crushed mass of any-thing. **3.** *Informal* A silencing retort; crushing reply. [Prob. imit.] — **squelch′er** *n.*

sque·teague (skwi·tēg′) *n.* **1.** A sea trout. **2.** A weakfish. [< Algonquian (Narraganset) *pesukwiteaug* they make glue]

squib (skwib) *n.* **1.** A firework to be thrown or rolled swift-ly, finally exploding like a rocket. **2.** A broken firecracker that burns with a spitting sound. **3.** A short speech or writ-ing in a witty or satirical vein; a mild lampoon. **4.** *Obs.* An undistinguished or petty person. — **Syn.** See LAMPOON. — *v.* **squibbed, squib·bing** *v.i.* **1.** To write or use squibs. **2.** To fire a squib. **3.** To explode or sound like a squib. **4.** To move quickly or restlessly. — *v.t.* **5.** To attack with squibs; lampoon. **6.** To fire or use as a squib. [Origin unknown]

squid (skwid) *n.* Any of various ten-armed cephalopods (genera *Loligo* and *Ommastrephes*) having a slender conical body, ink sac, and broad tail flukes, used as food and for bait: also called *calamary.* — *v.i.* Aeron. To assume a narrow, squidlike shape, as a parachute under excess wind or air pressure. [Origin uncertain]

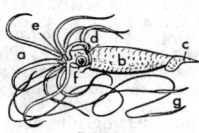

SQUID

a Arm. b Body. c Caudal fin. d Eye. e Mouth. f Siphon. g Tentacles

squid-jigging (skwid′jig′ing) *adj. Canadian* In Newfoundland, catching squid with a jig.

squig·gle (skwig′əl) *Informal n.* A meaningless scrawl. — *v.i.* To wriggle. [Blend of SQUIRM and WRIGGLE]

squig·gly (skwig′lē) *adj.* ·gli·er, ·gli·est Twisty; crooked.

squill (skwil) *n.* **1.** The bulb of a liliaceous plant (*Urginea maritima*) of the Mediterranean region, sliced and dried, used chiefly as an expectorant: also called *sea onion.* **2.** The plant itself. **3.** Any plant of the genus *Scilla,* as the wood hyacinth. [< L *squilla* < Gk. *skilla* sea onion]

squil·la (skwil′ə) *n.* Any of an order (*Stomatopoda*) of burrowing crustaceans having the form and appearance of a mantis: sometimes called *mantis shrimp.* Also **squill** (skwil). [< L *squilla* shrimp]

squinch (skwinch) *n. Archit.* A small stone arch or series of arches, or of projecting courses, across an interior angle of a square tower, to support an oblique side of an octagonal spire or lantern. [Alter. of obs. *scunch,* abbreviation of *scuncheon* < OF *escoinson*]

SQUINCH (Salisbury Cathedral, England)

squint (skwint) *v.i.* **1.** To look with half-closed eyes, as into bright light. **2.** To look with a side glance; look askance. **3.** To be affected with strabismus; to be cross-eyed. **4.** To incline or tend: with *toward,* etc. — *v.t.* **5.** To hold (the eyes) half-shut, as in glaring light. **6.** To cause to squint. — *adj.* **1.** Affected with strabismus; cross-eyed. **2.** Looking obliquely or askance; indirect. — *n.* **1.** *Pathol.* Strabismus. **2.** The act or habit of squinting. **3.** An indirect leaning, tendency, or drift. [Origin uncertain] — **squint′er** *n.*

squint-eyed (skwint′īd′) *adj.* **1.** Affected with strabismus. **2.** Looking sideways; aiming in two directions. **3.** Apt to see awry; prejudiced.

squire (skwīr) *n.* **1.** In England a landed proprietor or country gentleman. **2.** *U.S.* A title often used in small towns and rural areas for justices of the peace, judges, lawyers, etc. **3.** A young aspirant to knighthood serving as an attendant and armorbearer to a knight. **4.** A man who escorts a woman in public; gallant. — *v.t. & v.i.* **squired, squir·ing** To attend or serve (someone) as a squire or escort. [Aphetic var. of ESQUIRE]

squire·ar·chy (skwīr′är·kē) *n. pl.* ·chies **1.** English country gentlemen collectively; also, any body of squires. **2.** Government by squires. Also **squir′ar·chy.**

squire·ling (skwīr′ling) *n.* A petty squire.

squirm (skwûrm) *v.i.* **1.** To bend and twist the body; wriggle; writhe. **2.** To show signs of pain or distress. — *n.* A squirming motion; a wriggle. [Origin uncertain] — **squirm′er** *n.* — **squirm′y** *adj.*

squir·rel (skwûr′əl, *Brit.* skwir′əl) *n.* **1.** Any of various arboreal rodents (family *Sciuridae*) having a long bushy tail and feeding chiefly on nuts, as the **red** (or **pine**) **squirrel** (*Tamiasciurus hudsonicus*), the **gray squirrel** (*Sciurus carolinensis*), and the **fox squirrel** (*S. niger*) of North America. ◆ Collateral adjective: *sciurine.* **2.** Any of various related animals, as the chipmunk, flying squirrel, etc. **3.** The fur of a squirrel. [< OF *esquirel* < LL *scurellus,* dim. of L *sciurus* < Gk. *skiouros* < *skia* shadow + *oura* tail]

GRAY SQUIRREL (To 10 inches long; tail to 8 inches)

squirrel corn A smooth and delicate perennial herb (*Dicentra canadensis*) of the northern United States, having white or cream-colored flowers and yellow grainlike tubers.

squirrel monkey Any of various small, furry monkeys (genus *Saimiri*) of Central and South America, having nonprehensile tails and flesh-colored faces.

squir·rel·y (skwûr′əl·ē) *adj. Slang* Somewhat crazy.

squirt (skwûrt) *v.i.* **1.** To come forth in a thin stream or jet; spurt out. **2.** To eject water, etc., thus. — *v.t.* **3.** To eject (water or other liquid) forcibly in a jet. **4.** To wet or bespatter with a squirt or squirts. — *n.* **1.** The act of squirting or spurting; also, a jet of liquid squirted forth. **2.** A syringe or squirt gun. **3.** *Informal* An impudent or pre-

sumptuous person, especially someone young or small of stature. [Cf. LG *swirtjen.*] — **squirt′er** *n.*

squirt gun 1. A child's toy gun used for squirting water. **2.** A spray gun (which see).

squirting cucumber (skwûrt′ing) The fruit of a procumbent branching herb (*Ecballium elaterium*) of the gourd family, that, when ripe, ejects its seeds and juice.

squish (skwish) *v.t. & v.i. Informal* To squash. — *n.* A squashing sound. [Var. of SQUASH[1]] — **squish′y** *adj.*

sq. yd. Square yard(s).

Sr *Chem.* Strontium.

Sr. 1. Senior. **2.** Señor. **3.** Sir. **4.** Sister.

SR *Mil.* Seaman Recruit.

S.R. Sons of the Revolution.

Sra. Señora.

sra·dha (srä′də) *n.* A Hindu ceremonial offering of rice, flowers, and water to departed ancestors. Also **srad·dha.**

Sr·bi·ja (sûr′bē·jä) The Serbo-Croatian name for SERBIA.

Sri Lank·a (srē·langk′ə) The official name of Ceylon; adopted in May, 1972.

Sri·nag·ar (srē·nug′ər) The capital of Jammu and Kashmir State, NW India; pop. 285,250 (est. 1971).

S.R.O. Standing room only.

Srta. Señorita.

SS or **S.S.** or **S/S** Steamship.

SS. 1. Saints. **2.** The Schutzstaffel: also **SS**

S.S. 1. Sunday School. **2.** Written above (L *supra Scriptum*).

SSA or **S.S.A.** Social Security Act (or Administration).

SSE or **sse, S.S.E.,** or **s.s.e.** South-southeast.

SSM *Mil.* Silver Star Medal.

S.S.R. or **SSR** Soviet Socialist Republic (Russ. *Sovetskaya Sotsialisticheskaya Riespublika*).

SSS Selective Service System.

SST Supersonic transport.

SSW or **ssw, S.S.W.,** or **s.s.w.** South-southwest.

st. 1. Stanza. **2.** Statute(s). **3.** Stere. **4.** Stet. **5.** Stitch. **6.** Stone (weight). **7.** Street. **8.** Strophe.

-st See -EST[2].

St *Meteorol.* Stratus.

St. 1. Saint. **2.** Statute(s). **3.** Strait. **4.** Street.

St. For entries not found under ST., see under SAINT.

sta. 1. Station. **2.** Stationary. **3.** Stator.

Sta. 1. Santa. **2.** Station.

stab (stab) *v.* **stabbed, stab·bing** *v.t.* **1.** To pierce with or as with a pointed weapon; wound. **2.** To thrust (a dagger, etc.), as into a body. **3.** To penetrate; pierce. — *v.i.* **4.** To thrust or lunge with a knife, sword, etc. **5.** To inflict a wound thus. — **to stab in the back** To slander or injure in a treacherous, stealthy manner. — *n.* A thrust made with any pointed weapon. — **to have** (or **make**) **a stab at** To make an attempt at. [? < Scot. & dial. E *stob* to push, thrust, fix a stake < *stob* stake] — **stab′ber** *n.*

Sta·bat Ma·ter (stä′bät mä′tər, stä′bat mä′tər) A 13th-century Latin hymn on the Virgin Mary at the crucifixion, beginning with the words *Stabat Mater.* [< L, The mother was standing]

sta·bile (stā′bil, stä′il) *adj.* **1.** Fixed in one place; stable. **2.** *Med.* **a** Not affected by moderate heat. **b** Pertaining to a method of electrotherapy in which one of the electrodes is kept stationary on a part. — *n.* In art, a piece of stationary abstract sculpture usually made of wire, pieces of metal, wood, etc. Compare MOBILE. [< L *stabilis.* See STABLE[1].]

sta·bil·i·ty (stə·bil′ə·tē) *n. pl.* ·ties **1.** The condition of being stable; steadiness of position. **2.** Steadfastness of purpose or resolution. **3.** Continued existence; permanence. **4.** *Aeron.* The ability of an aircraft to resume equilibrium if displaced. **5.** *Meteorol.* A condition of the atmosphere in which a mass of air resists vertical displacement. **6.** A vow taken by some monks to remain in the same monastery. [< OF *stablete* < L *stabilitas, -tatis* < *stabilis.* See STABLE[1].]

sta·bi·lize (stā′bə·līz) *v.t.* ·lized, ·liz·ing **1.** To make firm or stable. **2.** Keep from changing or fluctuating: to *stabilize* prices. **3.** *Aeron.* To secure or maintain the equilibrium of (an aircraft) by any of several means. Also *esp. Brit.* **sta′bi·lise.** [< L *stabilis* steady + -IZE] — **sta′·bi·li·za′tion** *n.*

sta·bi·liz·er (stā′bə·lī′zər) *n.* **1.** One who or that which stabilizes. **2.** *Aeron.* An airfoil, generally fixed or semifixed, serving to give an aircraft stability in flight. **3.** A device in a ship or boat, as a gyroscope, to keep it from rolling. **4.** *Chem.* A substance that increases the stability of another substance or compound, especially one mixed with an explosive to reduce the danger of its spontaneous combustion.

sta·ble[1] (stā′bəl) *adj.* **1.** Standing firmly in place; not easily moved, shaken, or overthrown; fixed. **2.** Marked by fixity of purpose; steadfast. **3.** Having durability or permanence; abiding. **4.** *Chem.* Not easily decomposed: said of compounds. **5.** *Physics* Resisting forces that tend to change the form or position of a body: *stable* equilibrium. — **Syn.** See PERMANENT. [< F < L *stabilis* < *stare* to stand] — **sta′bly** (-blē) *adv.* — **sta′ble·ness** *n.*

sta·ble² (stā′bəl) *n.* **1.** A building set apart for lodging and feeding horses or cattle; also, the animals lodged there, collectively. **2.** Race horses belonging to a particular establishment; also, the owner and personnel collectively. **3.** *U.S.* A group of writers, artists, athletes, etc., under a single manager. — *v.t. & v.i.* **·bled, ·bling** To put or lodge in a stable. [< OF *estable* < L *stabulum* < *stare* to stand]

sta·ble·boy (stā′bəl·boi′) *n.* A boy employed in a stable.

sta·ble·man (stā′bəl·man′, -mən) *n. pl.* **·men** (-men′, -mən) One who works in a stable; a hostler; groom.

sta·bling (stā′bling) *n.* **1.** The act of one who stables. **2.** Room or accommodation in a stable. **3.** Stables collectively.

stab·lish (stab′lish) *v.t. Archaic* To establish.

stacc. *Music* Staccato.

stac·ca·to (stə·kä′tō) *adj.* **1.** *Music* Having or producing silence through most of the written time value of each note; very short and detached. **2.** Marked by abrupt, sharp emphasis. — *adv.* In a staccato manner. — *n. pl.* **·tos** **1.** *Music* A staccato style or passage. **2.** An abrupt, emphatic manner or sound. [< Ital., pp. of *staccare* to detach]

stack (stak) *n.* **1.** A large, orderly pile of unthreshed grain, hay, or straw, usually conical. **2.** Any systematic pile or heap, as a pile of poker chips purchased or won by a player. **3.** A group of rifles (usually three) set upright and supporting one another. **4.** A case composed of several rows of bookshelves one above the other. **5.** *pl.* That part of a library where most of the books are shelved. **6.** A vertical main smoke flue, especially of a furnace or boiler; a chimney; smokestack; also, a collection of such chimneys or flues. **7.** *Brit.* A measure of fuel (coal or wood), equal to 108 cubic feet or 4 cubic yards. **8.** *Informal* A great amount; plenty. — *v.t.* **1.** To gather or place in a pile; pile up in a stack. **2.** To load (a vehicle, etc.) with stacks of material. — **to stack the cards** (or **deck**) **1.** To arrange cards secretly in the pack in a manner favorable to the dealer. **2.** To have an advantage secured beforehand. [< ON *stakkr*]

stack arms The command to place several rifles upright on the ground against three linked at their swivels.

stacked (stakt) *adj. Slang* Having voluptuous curves; shapely: said of a woman.

stack·er (stak′ər) *n. Agric.* An apparatus for depositing straw from a threshing machine on a wagon or on a stack.

stac·te (stak′tē) *n.* One of the spices anciently used by the Jews in preparing incense. *Ex.* xxx 34. [< L, oil of myrrh < Gk. *staktē* < *stazein* to drip]

stad·dle (stad′l) *n. Brit. Dial.* A foundation or support; especially, a raised platform or frame, to keep a stack of hay or straw dry and free from vermin. [OE *statho*l base]

stad·hold·er (stad′hōl′dər) *n.* **1.** The chief magistrate of the Netherlands, a hereditary office in the family of the princess of Orange. **2.** Formerly, a viceroy or governor of a province or town of the Netherlands as the representative of the sovereign. Also **stadt′hold·er** (stat′-). [< Du. *stadhouder* lieutenant < *stad* place + *houder* holder]

sta·di·a (stā′dē·ə) *n.* **1.** A temporary surveying station. **2.** A graduated rod used with a transit instrument to measure distances in terms of a small angle subtended at the point of observation. **3.** A graduated stick held at arm's length as a simple aid in measuring short distances. — *adj.* Of or pertaining to surveying with a stadia. [Prob. < Ital. *stadia* stage, a measure of length < L *stadium*, see STADIUM.]

sta·di·um (stā′dē·əm) *n. pl.* **·di·a** (-dē·ə), *for def. 2* **·di·ums** **1.** In ancient Greece, a course for foot races, with banked seats for spectators, as at Olympia and Athens, where games were held. **2.** A similar modern structure in which athletic games are played. **3.** An ancient Greek measure of length, equaling 606.75 feet. **4.** A degree of progress or development. **5.** *Med.* A given stage in the course of a disease. [< L < Gk. *stadion*, measure of length]

Staël (stäl), **Madame de,** 1766–1817, Baronne de Staël-Holstein, French essayist and novelist; famous for her salon; daughter of Jacques Necker: original name **Anne Louise Germaine Neck·er** (ne·kâr′).

staff¹ (staf, stäf) *n. pl.* **staffs;** *for defs.* 1, 2 & 3, *also* **staves** (stāvz) **1.** A stick or piece of wood carried for some special purpose, as an aid in walking or climbing, or as a cudgel or weapon, or as an emblem of authority. **2.** A shaft or pole that forms a support or handle: the *staff* of a spear. **3.** A stick used in measuring or testing, as a surveyors' leveling rod. **4.** *Mil.* A body of officers not having command but assigned in an executive or advisory capacity as assistants to the officer in command. See GENERAL STAFF. **5.** A body of persons associated in carrying out some special enterprise under the supervision of a manager or chief: the editorial *staff.* **6.** *Music* The five horizontal lines and four spaces used to represent the pitches of tones: also called *stave.* — *v.t.* To provide (an office, etc.) with a staff. [OE *stæf* stick]

staff² (staf, stäf) *n.* A composition of plaster, fiber, etc., for temporary buildings, statues, etc. [Prob. < G *staffieren* to fill, decorate]

Staf·fa (staf′ə) An islet of the Inner Hebrides, NW Argyll, Scotland; site of Fingal's Cave.

staf·fer (staf′ər) *n. Informal* A member of a staff: an editorial *staffer.*

staff officer **1.** An officer on the staff of a military commander. **2.** In the U.S. Navy, an officer without command or operational functions, as a doctor, dentist, chaplain, etc.

Staf·ford·shire (staf′ərd·shir) A county in central England; 1,153 sq. mi.; pop. 991,100 (1976); county seat, **Stafford,** pop. 114,300 (1976). Also **Stafford.** Shortened form **Staffs.**

stag (stag) *n.* **1.** The male of the red deer (*Cervus elaphus*), especially the matured male. **2.** The male of other large deer, as the caribou. **3.** A swine castrated after maturity. **4.** *Scot.* A colt: also spelled *staig.* **5.** A man who attends a social function unaccompanied by a woman. **6.** A social gathering for men only. — *adj.* Of or for men only: a *stag* party. — *v.i.* **stagged, stag·ging** To attend a social affair unaccompanied by a woman. [OE *stagga*]

stag beetle A large, lamellicorn beetle (family *Lucanidae*), the male of which has mandibles branched like the antlers of a stag: also called *pinchbug.*

stage (stāj) *n.* **1.** A raised platform, with its scenery and mechanical appliances, on which the performance in a theater or hall takes place. **2.** The theater: to write for the *stage.* **3.** The drama; also, the dramatic profession. **4.** The field or plan of action of some notable event: to set the *stage* for war. **5.** A definite portion of a journey. **6.** A step in some development, progress, or process. **7.** *Pathol.* A definite period in the course of a disease, characterized by a certain group of symptoms. **8.** *Biol.* **a** Any of the periods of growth in animals or plants: the larval *stage* of insects. **b** An organism in a specified period of growth. **9.** A water level: The river rose to flood *stage.* **10.** A horizontal section or story of a building. **11.** The horizontal shelf on a microscope that supports the slide or object to be examined. **12.** *Geol.* The stratigraphic subdivision next below a series, composed of deposits occurring during a part of an epoch. **13.** *Aerospace* One of the separate propulsion units of a rocket vehicle, each of which becomes operational after the preceding one reaches burnout and is jettisoned. **14.** An elevated platform or scaffold for the use of workmen. **15.** Any raised platform or floor. **16.** The distance traveled between two stopping points. **17.** One of the regular stopping places on the route of a stagecoach or postrider. **18.** A stagecoach (which see). — **by easy stages** Traveling or acting without hurry and with frequent stops; slowly. — **Syn.** See PHASE. — *v.t.* **staged, stag·ing 1.** To put or exhibit on the stage. **2.** To conduct; carry on: to *stage* an invasion. [< OF *estage,* ult. < L *status,* pp. of *stare* to stand]

stage·coach (stāj′kōch′) *n.* A large, horse-drawn, four-wheeled vehicle having a regular route from town to town.

stage·craft (stāj′kraft′, -kräft′) *n.* Skill in writing or staging plays.

stage door A door to a theater used by actors and stage-hands that leads to the stage or behind the scenes.

stage-door Johnny (stāj′dōor′) *U.S. Slang* A man who frequents stage doors seeking the company of actresses.

stage fright A sudden panic that sometimes attacks those appearing before an audience.

stage·hand (stāj′hand′) *n.* A worker in a theater who handles scenery and props.

stage manager One who superintends the stage during the production of a play.

stag·er (stā′jər) *n.* **1.** One who has had long experience; an old hand: often **old stager.** **2.** *Archaic* An actor.

stage-struck (stāj′struk′) *adj.* Struck with the idea of becoming an actor or an actress; enamored of theatrical life.

stage whisper **1.** Any loud whisper intended to be overheard. **2.** A direction by a prompter in the wings to an actor on the stage, intended not to be heard by the audience.

stag·ey (stā′jē) See STAGY.

stag·fla·tion (stag′flā′shən) *n.* An economic condition marked by simultaneous stagnation and inflation.

stag·gard (stag′ərd) *n.* The male of the red deer in its fourth year. Also **stag′gart** (-ərt). [< STAG + -ARD]

stag·ger (stag′ər) *v.i.* **1.** To walk or run unsteadily; totter; reel. **2.** To begin to give way; become less confident or resolute; waver; hesitate. — *v.t.* **3.** To cause to stagger. **4.** To affect strongly; overwhelm, as with surprise or grief. **5.** To place in alternating rows or groups. **6.** To arrange so as to prevent congestion or confusion, as by distributing: to *stagger* lunch hours. **7.** *Aeron.* To construct (two surfaces, as the wings of a biplane) so that the leading edge of one extends beyond the other. — *n.* **1.** The act of staggering; a reeling motion. **2.** *Aeron.* The amount of advance of the leading edge of one wing of a biplane over that of the other. [< obs. *stacker* < ON *stakra*] — **stag′ger·er** *n.* — **stag′ger·ing·ly** *adv.*

stag·ger·bush (stag′ər·boosh′) *n.* A tall shrub (*Lyonia mariana*) of the heath family, having white or pale red flowers, and poisonous to stock.

stag·gers (stag′ərz) *n.pl.* (*construed as sing.*) **1.** *Vet.* Any of various diseases of domestic animals, as horses, characterized by vertigo, staggering, and sudden falling, due to disorder of the brain and spinal cord: also called *blind staggers.* **2.** A giddy or reeling sensation.

stag·gy (stag′ē) *n. Scot.* A colt. Also **stag′gie.**

stag·hound (stag′hound′) *n.* **1.** One of a breed of large hounds, somewhat resembling the foxhound, formerly used for hunting deer, wolves, etc.   **2.** A deerhound (which see).

stag·ing (stā′jing) *n.* **1.** A scaffolding or temporary platform.   **2.** The act of putting a play upon the stage.   **3.** The business of driving or running stagecoaches; also, traveling by stagecoach.

Sta·gi·ra (stə·jī′rə) A city of ancient Macedonia, on the Chalcidice peninsula, NE Greece; birthplace of Aristotle. Also **Sta·gi·rus** (stə·jī′rəs).

Stag·i·rite (staj′ə·rīt) *n.* A native of Stagira. — **the Stagirite** Aristotle. — *adj.* Of or pertaining to Stagira; also, Aristotelian.

stag line *U.S. Informal* A group of males at a dance who are without partners.

stag·nant (stag′nənt) *adj.* **1.** Standing still; not flowing: said of water or air.   **2.** Foul from long standing, as water.   **3.** Lacking briskness or activity; dull; sluggish.   [< F < L *stagnans, -antis,* pp. of *stagnare* to stagnate < *stagnum* pool] — **stag′nan·cy** *n.* — **stag′nant·ly** *adv.*

stag·nate (stag′nāt) *v.i.* **·nat·ed, ·nat·ing** **1.** To be or become stagnant.   **2.** To become dull or inert; vegetate.   [< L *stagnatus,* pp. of *stagnare.* See STAGNANT.] — **stag·na·tion** (stag·nā′shən) *n.*

St. Ag·nes' Eve (ag′nis) The evening of January 20th, when, by old superstition, a girl might have prevision of her future husband. Also **St. Ag·nes's Eve** (ag′nis·iz).

stag·y (stā′jē) *adj.* **stag·i·er, stag·i·est** Having a theatrical manner; of or suited to the stage: also spelled *stagey.* — **stag′i·ly** *adv.* — **stag′i·ness** *n.*

staid (stād) *adj.* **1.** Steady and sober; sedate; modest.   **2.** Fixed; established. — **Syn.** See SEDATE.   [Orig. pt. and pp. of STAY¹] — **staid′ly** *adv.* — **staid′ness** *n.*

staig (stag) See STAG (def. 4).

stain (stān) *n.* **1.** A discoloration from foreign matter; a spot; smirch; blot.   **2.** The act of discoloring, or the state of being discolored.   **3.** A dye or thin pigment used in staining.   **4.** A chemical reagent for coloring microscopic specimens.   **5.** A moral taint; tarnish. — *v.t.* **1.** To make a stain upon; discolor; soil.   **2.** To color by the use of a dye or stain.   **3.** To bring a moral stain upon; blemish.   **4.** To impregnate, as a microscopic specimen, with a substance whose reaction colors some part without affecting others, thus rendering form or structure visible. — *v.i.* **5.** To take or impart a stain.   [Aphetic var. of DISTAIN] — **stain′a·ble** *adj.* — **stain′er** *n.* — **stain′less** *adj.* — **stain′less·ly** *adv.* — **Syn.** (noun) **1.** See BLEMISH. **5.** stigma, brand. — (verb) **2.** tint, tinge. **3.** sully, dishonor, disgrace.

stained glass (stānd) Glass colored by the addition of pigments in the form of metallic oxides, used in church windows, etc. — **stained-glass** (stānd′glas′, -gläs′) *adj.*

stainless steel A steel alloy made resistant to corrosion and atmospheric influences by the addition of from 10 to 30 percent chromium, and other ingredients.

stair (stâr) *n.* **1.** A step, or one of a series of steps, for mounting or descending from one level to another.   **2.** *Usually pl.* A series of steps.   [OE *stǣger*]

stair·case (stâr′kās′) *n.* A flight or series of flights of stairs, including the supports, balusters, etc.

stair·head (stâr′hed′) *n.* The top of a staircase.

stair·way (stâr′wā′) *n.* A flight of stairs; staircase.

stair·well (stâr′wel′) *n.* A vertical shaft enclosing a staircase.

stake (stāk) *n.* **1.** A stick or post sharpened at one end for driving into the ground, used as a boundary mark, support for a fence, etc.   **2.** A post to which a person is bound to be executed by being burned alive; also, execution in this manner.   **3.** One of a number of uprights set in sockets at the edge of the floor of a vehicle to confine the load.   **4.** Something wagered or risked, as money bet on a race.   **5.** *Often pl.* A prize in a contest.   **6.** An interest in an enterprise.   **7.** An organizational unit of the Mormon Church, consisting of several wards.   **8.** A grubstake (which see). — **at stake** In hazard or jeopardy; in question: My whole future was *at stake.* — **to pull up stakes** To wind up one's business in a place and move on. — *v.t.* **staked, stak·ing** **1.** To fasten or support by means of a stake; tether to a stake.   **2.** To mark the boundaries of with stakes: often with *off* or *out.*   **3.** *Informal* To wager; risk.   **4.** *Informal* To grubstake; also, to supply with working capital; finance.   [OE *staca*]

Staked Plain See LLANO ESTACADO.

Sta·kha·no·vism (stä·khä′no·viz′əm) *n.* In the Soviet Union, a system of increasing production by rewarding workers showing efficiency and initiative.   [after Aleksei G. *Stakhanov,* a Soviet miner who originated it in 1935] — **Sta·kha·no·vite** (stä·khä′no·vīt) *adj. & n.*

sta·lac·ti·form (stə·lak′tə·fôrm) *adj.* Resembling or having the form of a stalactite.

sta·lac·tite (stə·lak′tīt, stal′ək·tīt′) *n.* A long, tapering formation hanging from the roof of a cavern, produced by continuous watery deposits containing certain minerals, especially calcium carbonate.   [< NL *stactites* < Gk. *stalaktos* a

dripping < *stalassein* to trickle, drip] — **stal·ac·tit·ic** (stal′ək·tit′ik) or **·i·cal** *adj.*

sta·lag (stal′ag, *Ger.* shtä′läkh) *n.* A German prisoner-of-war camp.   [< G, contraction of *stammlager* < *stamm* base + *lager* camp]

sta·lag·mite (stə·lag′mīt, stal′əg·mīt) *n.* An incrustation, usually cylindrical or conical, on the floor of a cavern, the counterpart of a stalactite, often fusing with it into a column.   [< NL *stalagmites* < Gk. *stalagmos* a dripping < *stalassein* to drip] — **stal·ag·mit·ic** (stal′əg·mit′ik) or **·i·cal** *adj.*

St. Al·bans (sânt′ ôl′bənz) A municipal borough in southern Hertfordshire, England: scene of a Lancastrian victory in the Wars of the Roses, 1455; pop. 50,276 (1961): Roman *Verulamium.*

STALACTITE (*a*) AND STALAGMITE (*b*)

stale¹ (stāl) *adj.* **stal·er, stal·est** **1.** Having lost freshness; slightly changed or deteriorated, as air, beer, bread, etc.   **2.** Lacking in interest from age or familiarity; worn out; trite: a *stale* joke.   **3.** Being in poor condition from prolonged activity or overstrain.   **4.** Inactive; dull, as after a period of overactivity: said of a stock market.   **5.** *Law* In courts of equity, impaired in legal force, due to long neglect in pressing or asserting a claim or to a change in the condition of the parties. — *v.i.* **staled, stal·ing** To become stale or trite.   [Origin uncertain. Cf. MDu. *stel.*] — **stale′ly** *adv.* — **stale′ness** *n.*

stale² (stāl) *n.* The urine of cattle or horses. — *v.i.* **staled, stal·ing** To urinate: said of cattle and horses.   [Prob. < MLG *stal* horse urine]

stale·mate (stāl′māt′) *n.* **1.** In chess, a draw resulting when a player whose king is not in check can make no move without placing his king in check, or when the distribution of pieces recurs three times in succession.   **2.** Any tie or deadlock. — *v.t.* **·mat·ed, ·mat·ing** **1.** To put into a condition of stalemate.   **2.** To bring to a standstill.   [< AF *estale* fixed position + MATE²]

Sta·lin (stä′lin *Russ.* stä′lyin) **1.** See BRAȘOV.   **2.** See VARNA.

Sta·lin (stä′lin, *Russ.* stä′lyin), **Joseph,** 1879–1953, Soviet statesman; chief of state 1924–53: original name *Iosif Vissarionovich Dzhugashvili.*

Sta·li·na·bad (stə·lyi·nə·bät′) See DYUSHAMBE.

Sta·lin·grad (stä′lin·grad, *Russ.* stə·lyin·grät′) A former name for VOLGOGRAD.

Sta·lin·ism (stä′lin·iz′əm) *n.* The doctrines or practices of Stalin; especially, communism involving a rigid implementation of government policy through coercion, intimidation, and ruthless suppression of opposition, and characterized by ardent patriotism focused upon the Soviet Union and its leader. — **Sta′lin·ist** *n.*

Sta·li·no (stä′lyi·nə) A former name for DONETSK.

Sta·linsk (stä′lyinsk) See NOVO–KUZNETSK.

stalk¹ (stôk) *n.* **1.** The stem or axis of a plant, especially when herbaceous.   **2.** A supporting or connecting part of a plant.   **3.** *Zool.* Any support on which an organ is borne, as a pedicel.   **4.** Any stem or main axis, as of a goblet.   [ME *stalke.* Akin to OSw *stjælke.*] — **stalked** (stôkt) *adj.* — **stalk′less** *adj.*

stalk² (stôk) *v.i.* **1.** To approach game, etc., stealthily.   **2.** To walk in a stiff, dignified manner.   **3.** *Obs.* To go stealthily; creep. — *v.t.* **4.** To approach (game, etc.) stealthily.   **5.** To hover over; pace through: Famine *stalked* the land. — *n.* **1.** The act of stalking game.   **2.** A stately step or walk.   [OE *bestealcian* to move stealthily] — **stalk′er** *n.*

stalk·ing-horse (stô′king-hôrs′) *n.* **1.** Anything serving to conceal one's intention.   **2.** In politics, a candidate put forth to divide the opposition or to hide the candidacy of another person.   **3.** A horse behind which a hunter conceals himself in stalking game.

stalk·y (stô′kē) *adj.* **stalk·i·er, stalk·i·est** **1.** Long and slender, like a stalk.   **2.** Consisting of stalks.

stall (stôl) *n.* **1.** A compartment in which a horse or bovine animal is confined and fed.   **2.** A small booth or compartment in a street, market, etc., for the sale or display of small articles.   **3.** A partially enclosed seat, as in the orchestra of a theater or the choir of a cathedral.   **4.** A working compartment in a coal mine.   **5.** A space set aside for the parking of an automobile.   **6.** A sheath or covering for a finger or thumb; a cot.   **7.** *Aeron.* The condition of an airplane that, from loss of speed or excessive angle of attack, begins to drop.   **8.** *Informal* An evasion or argument made to postpone action or decision. — *v.t.* **1.** To place or keep in a stall.   **2.** To keep in a stall for fattening, as cattle.   **3.** To bring to a standstill; stop the progress or motion of, especially unintentionally.   **4.** To cause to stick fast in mud, snow, etc. — *v.i.* **5.** To come to a standstill; stop, especially unintentionally.   **6.** To stick fast in mud, snow, etc.

7. *Informal* To make delays; be evasive. **8.** To live or be kept in a stall. **9.** *Aeron.* To go into a stall. [OE *steall*]
stall-feed (stôl′fēd′) *v.t.* **-fed, -feed·ing** To feed (cattle) in a stall or stable; fatten. — **stall-fed** (-fed′) *adj.*
stal·lion (stal′yən) *n.* An uncastrated male horse. [< OF *estalon* < OHG *stal* stable]
stall shower A small enclosed place, with a glass door or curtain, for taking a shower bath.
stal·wart (stôl′wərt) *adj.* **1.** Strong and brawny; robust. **2.** Resolute; determined; unwavering. **3.** Brave; courageous. — *n.* **1.** A brave or stalwart person. **2.** An uncompromising partisan, as in politics. [Var. of STALWORTH] — **stal′wart·ly** *adv.* — **stal′wart·ness** *n.*
stal·worth (stôl′wərth) *adj. Obs.* Stalwart. [OE *stǽlwierthe* serviceable < *stǽl* place + *wierthe* worth]
Stam·bul (stäm·bōōl′) **1.** See ISTANBUL. **2.** The old part of Istanbul. Also **Stam·boul′.**
sta·men (stā′mən) *n.* *pl.* **sta·mens** or *Rare* **stam·i·na** (stam′ə·nə) *Bot.* The pollen-bearing organ of a flower, standing inside the floral envelopes and consisting of the filament and the anther. For illustration see FLOWER. [< L, warp, thread < *stare* to stand]
Stam·ford (stam′fərd) A city in SW Connecticut, on Long Island Sound; pop. 108,798.
stam·i·na (stam′ə·nə) *n.* **1.** Physical or moral capacity to endure or withstand hardship or difficulty; vitality; vigor; strength. **2.** The supporting part of a body. [< L, pl. of *stamen* warp, thread. See STAMEN.]
stam·i·nal (stam′ə·nəl) *adj.* **1.** Of or pertaining to a stamen. **2.** Relating to or furnishing stamina.
stam·i·nate (stam′ə·nit, -nāt) *adj. Bot.* **1.** Having stamens. **2.** Having stamens but no pistils.
stamini- *combining form Bot.* Stamen; of or pertaining to stamens: *staminiferous.* Also, before vowels, **stamin-.** [< L *stamen, -inis* fiber, thread]
stam·i·nif·er·ous (stam′ə·nif′ər·əs) *adj.* Bearing stamens.
stam·i·no·di·um (stam′ə·nō′dē·əm) *n.* *pl.* **·di·a** (-dē·ə) *Bot.* An abortive or sterile stamen, or an organ resembling one. Also **stam′i·node** (-nōd). [< NL < L *stamen, -inis* stamen + Gk. *eidos* form]
stam·i·no·dy (stam′ə·nō′dē) *n. Bot.* The conversion of other parts of a flower, as sepals or pistils, into stamens.
stam·mel (stam′əl) *n.* **1.** A dull scarlet color. **2.** *Archaic* A linsey-woolsey of this color. — *adj.* Dull red. [Akin to OF *estamel* < *estamine* < L *stamen* thread]
stam·mer (stam′ər) *v.t. & v.i.* To speak or utter haltingly, with involuntary repetitions or prolongations of a sound or syllable: to *stammer* an apology. — *n.* The act or condition of stammering. [OE *stamerian*] — **stam′mer·er** *n.*
— **Syn.** (verb) *Stammer* and *stutter* agree in meaning to speak jerkily. *Stammer* is applied to broken articulation arising from some temporary condition, as shock, fear, or embarrassment. *Stutter* is used in cases of chronic inability to articulate smoothly, from defect of the vocal organs or the nervous system. *Stutter* denotes specifically, as *stammer* does not, the repetition of the same sound, as in "pu-pu-please."
stamp (stamp) *v.t.* **1.** To strike heavily with the sole of the foot. **2.** To bring down (the foot) heavily and noisily. **3.** To affect in a specified manner by or as by stamping with the foot: to *stamp* a fire out; to *stamp* out opposition. **4.** To make marks or figures upon by means of a die, stamp, etc. **5.** To imprint or impress with a die, stamp, etc. **6.** To fix or imprint permanently: The deed was *stamped* on his memory. **7.** To assign a specified quality to; characterize; brand: to *stamp* a story false. **8.** To affix an official seal, stamp, etc., to. **9.** To crush, break, or pulverize, as ore. — *v.i.* **10.** To strike the foot heavily on the ground. **11.** To walk with heavy, resounding steps. — *n.* **1.** A die or block having a pattern or design for impressing upon a suitable surface: a rubber *stamp.* **2.** The pattern, impression, design, etc., so made. **3.** The weight or block, as in an ore mill, that by its impact crushes the ore; also, the stamping mill itself. **4.** A cutting tool for making articles corresponding to the cutting edges in outline. **5.** Any characteristic mark, as a label or imprint; a brand. **6.** Characteristic quality or form; kind; sort: I dislike men of his *stamp.* **7.** The act of stamping. **8.** A printed device prepared and sold by a government, for attachment to a letter, commodity, etc., as proof that the tax or fee has been paid. [ME *stampen.* Akin to OE *stempan* pound.]
Stamp Act An act of the British Parliament, passed in 1765 and repealed in 1766, requiring the American colonists to affix to various pamphlets, newspapers, etc., a government stamp varying in price from a halfpenny up to £10.
stam·pede (stam·pēd′) *n.* **1.** A sudden starting and rushing off through panic, as a herd of cattle, horses, etc. **2.** Any sudden, impulsive, tumultuous running movement of a crowd or mob. **3.** A movement or rush of people toward a certain region or object. **4.** A sudden unplanned movement to support a candidate at a political convention. **5.** *Canadian* In the West, a rodeo. — *v.* **·ped·ed, ·ped·ing** *v.t.* **1.** To cause a stampede or panic in. — *v.i.* **2.** To rush or flee in a stampede. [< Am. Sp. *estampida* < *estampar* to stamp < Gmc.] — **stam·ped′er** *n.*

stamp·er (stam′pər) *n.* **1.** One who stamps. **2.** One who or that which cancels stamps, as postage stamps. **3.** Any tool or machine for stamping.
stamp·ing ground (stam′ping) **1.** A favorite or habitual gathering place. **2.** A place where horses or other animals gather.
stamp mill A machine for pulverizing rock for the purpose of extracting the ore it contains.
stamp pad A block of ink-soaked material on which to press a rubber stamp.
stance (stans) *n.* **1.** Mode of standing; posture. **2.** In golf, the relative positions of the player's feet and the ball, when making a stroke. **3.** *Scot.* A position; station; site. [< OF *estance* < L *stans, stantis,* ppr. of *stare* to stand]
stanch (stanch, stänch) *v.t.* **1.** To stop or check the flow of (blood, etc.). **2.** To stop the flow of blood from (a wound). **3.** *Obs.* To quench; quell. Also spelled *staunch.* — *adj.* See STAUNCH. [< OF *estanchier* to halt, bring to a stop, make stand, ult. < L *stare* to stand] — **stanch′er** *n.*
♦ The spelling *stanch* is preferred for the verb in both England and the United States, and *staunch* for the adjective, although many writers use one or the other spelling for both.
stan·chion (stan′shən) *n.* **1.** An upright bar forming a principal support. **2.** A vertical bar or pair of bars used to confine cattle in a stall. — *v.t.* **1.** To provide with stanchions. **2.** To support or confine with stanchions. [< OF *estanchon* < *estance* situation, position. See STANCE.]
stand (stand) *v.* **stood, stand·ing** *v.i.* **1.** To assume or maintain an erect position on one's feet. **2.** To be in a vertical position; be erect. **3.** To measure a specified height when standing: He *stands* six feet. **4.** To assume a specified position: to *stand* aside. **5.** To assume or have a definite opinion, position, or attitude: How do you *stand* on civil rights? **6.** To be situated; have position or location; lie. **7.** To remain unimpaired, unchanged, or valid: My decision still *stands.* **8.** To have or be in a specified state, condition, or relation: He *stands* in fear of his life. **9.** To be of a specified rank or class: He *stands* third. **10.** To assume an attitude for defense or offense: *Stand* and fight! **11.** To be or remain firm or resolute, as in determination. **12.** To be consistent; accord; agree. **13.** To collect and remain; also, to be stagnant, as water. **14.** To stop or pause; halt. **15.** To scruple; hesitate. **16.** *Naut.* To take a direction; steer: The brig *stood* into the wind. **17.** To point, as a hunting dog. **18.** *Brit.* To be a candidate, as for election. — *v.t.* **19.** To place upright; set in an erect position. **20.** To put up with; endure; tolerate. **21.** To be subjected to; undergo: He must *stand* trial. **22.** To withstand; resist. **23.** *Informal* To pay for; bear the expense of: to *stand* a treat. — **to stand a chance** (or **show**) To have a chance or likelihood, as of success. — **to stand by 1.** To stay near and be ready to help, operate, or begin. **2.** To help; support. **3.** To abide by; make good. **4.** To remain passive and watch, as when help is needed. **5.** *Telecom.* To wait, as for the completion of an interrupted message. — **to stand clear** To remain at a safe distance. — **to stand down** *Law* To leave the witness stand. — **to stand for 1.** To represent; symbolize. **2.** To put up with; tolerate. — **to stand in** *Informal* To cost. — **to stand in for** To act as a substitute for. — **to stand off** *Informal* **1.** To keep at a distance. **2.** To fail to agree or comply. — **to stand on 1.** To be based on or grounded in; rest. **2.** To insist on or demand observance of: to *stand on* ceremony. **3.** *Naut.* To keep on the same tack or course. — **to stand on one's own (two) feet** (or **legs**) To be independent; manage one's own affairs. — **to stand out 1.** To stick out; project or protrude. **2.** To be prominent; appear in relief or contrast. **3.** To refuse to consent or agree; remain in opposition. — **to stand over 1.** To remain near and watch, as a subordinate. **2.** To be postponed. — **to stand pat 1.** In poker, to play one's hand as dealt, without drawing new cards. **2.** To resist change. — **to stand to reason** To conform to reason. — **to stand up 1.** To stand erect. **2.** To withstand wear, criticism, analysis, etc. **3.** *Slang* To fail, usually intentionally, to keep an appointment with. — **to stand up for** To side with; take the part of. — **to stand up to** To confront courageously; face. — **to stand up with** To be best man or bridesmaid for. — *n.* **1.** The act of standing, especially of standing firmly: to make a *stand* against the enemy. **2.** An opinion, attitude, or position, as in a controversy. **3.** A structure upon which persons or things may stand, or on which articles may be kept or displayed. **4.** A small table on which things may be placed conveniently. **5.** A rack or other piece of furniture on which hats may be hung, or canes, umbrellas, etc., supported. **6.** A stall, counter, or the like, where merchandise is displayed. **7.** A structure upon which persons may sit or stand, as a platform, or a series of raised seats. **8.** A small platform in court from which a witness testifies. **9.** Any place where or in which something stands. **10.** The place of one's customary occupation; an assigned or chosen location. **11.** Cessation from motion or progress; a standstill. **12.** In the theater, a stop made while on tour to give a performance; also, the place where such a stop is made: a one-night *stand.*

13. A tree grown from seed; also, a young tree left when others are cut down. **14.** The growing trees in a forest or in part of a forest. **15.** A growth on the field, as of corn or grass. **16.** A curved metal bar attached to the base of a force pump and serving as a fulcrum for the brake that moves the piston up and down. **17.** A complete set; outfit: chiefly in the phrase **stand of arms**. **18.** *Obs.* A troop; force. **— to take a stand** To have or reveal an opinion or attitude, as on a controversial issue; take sides. [OE *standan*] **— stand'er** *n.*

stan·dard (stan'dərd) *n.* **1.** A flag, ensign, or banner, used as a distinctive emblem of a government, body of men, or special cause. **2.** A figure or an image adopted as the emblem of a nation. **3.** *Mil.* A unit flag. **4.** Any established measure of extent, quantity, quality, or value: a *standard* of weight. **5.** Any type, model, or example for comparison; a criterion of excellence: a *standard* of conduct. **6.** In coinage, the established proportion by weight of fine metal and alloy. **7.** An upright ti ber, post, pole, or beam, especially as a support. **8.** *Bot.* Any tree, shrub, bush, or herb not dwarfed by grafting, and growing on a vigorous upright stem without support of a wall or trellis. **9.** A heavy or stationary article of furniture. **— adj. 1.** Having the accuracy or authority of a standard; serving as a gauge or model: a *standard* weight. **2.** Of recognized excellence or authority: a *standard* book or author. **3.** *Ling.* Designating or belonging to those usages or varieties of a language that have gained literary, cultural, and social acceptance and prestige: *standard* English. Abbr. *std.* [< OF *estandard* banner < G mc.]

stan·dard-bear·er (stan'dərd-bâr'ər) *n.* **1.** The member of a military unit who carries the flag or ensign. **2.** A leader or a candidate for a leading position, as for a presidency.

stan·dard·bred (*n.* stan'dərd·bred'; *adj.* stan'dərd·bred') *n.* A breed of horse notable for its trotters and pacers. **— adj.** Bred so as to be of a required strain, quality, or pedigree, as poultry, horses, etc.

standard candle *Physics* A candle (def. 4).

standard cell *Electr.* A voltaic cell that serves as a standard of electro notive force.

standard deviation *Stat.* The square root of the arithmetic mean of the squares of all the deviations from the mean; the root mean square of the deviations of a set of values. Abbr. *s.d., S.D.*

standard English *Ling.* Those usages in English that have gained literary, cultural, and social acceptance and prestige, and are considered appropriate for educated speakers of the language. See LEVEL OF USAGE. ◆ In this dictionary, words and meanings not considered to be at the level of standard usage are labeled *Slang, Dial.,* or *Illit.* Unlabeled words belong either to the common word stock of English speakers or to formal, literary discourse, while words appropriate for informal or conversational styles are labeled *Informal.*

standard gauge 1. A gauge for determining whether tools, etc., are of a standard size. **2.** A railroad track width of 56½ inches, considered as standard. **3.** A railroad having such a gauge, or a locomotive or car made to run on this gauge. **— stan·dard-gauge** (stan'dərd·gāj') *adj.*

stan·dard·ize (stan'dər·dīz) *v.t.* **·ized, ·iz·ing** To make to or regulate by a standard. **— stan'dard·i·za'tion** *n.* **— stan'dard·iz'er** *n.*

standard lamp 1. Any of several standard lighting units used in photometric determinations. **2.** In the United States: **a** The pentane-burning lamp, equal to 10 international candles. **b** A lamp burning amyl acetate, equal to 0.9 international candle: also called *Hefner lamp.*

standard of living The average quantity and quality of goods, services, luxuries, etc., that a person or group uses or consumes in daily living.

standard pitch See under PITCH².

standard time Time as reckoned from a meridian officially established as standard over a large area. Reckoning from the meridian of Greenwich, each time zone comprises 15 degrees of longitude and represents an interval of one hour, with adjustments to meet various geographic and regional conditions. In the conterminous United States the four standard time zones are the **Eastern** (E.S.T.), **Central** (C.S.T.), **Mountain** (M.S.T.), and **Pacific** (P.S.T.), using respectively the mean local time of the 75th, 90th, 105th, and 120th meridians west of Greenwich, and being 5, 6, 7, and 8 hours slower (or earlier) than Greenwich time. Canada has a fifth zone, the **Atlantic**, based on the local time of the 60th meridian, 4 hours slower than Greenwich time. See TIME ZONE.

stand·by (stand'bī') *n. pl.* **·bys** A person or thing on call for emergency use.

stand·ee (stan·dē') *n. Informal* A person who must stand for lack of chairs or seats, as at a theater or on a train.

stand·fast (stand'fast', -fäst') *n.* That which stands firm and strong; a solid or settled position. **— adj.** Firm; settled.

stand-in (stand'in') *n.* **1.** A position of influence or favor;

a pull. **2.** A person who takes the place of a motion-picture player, as during waiting intervals or in hazardous actions.

stand·ing (stan'ding) *adj.* **1.** Remaining erect; not prostrated or cut down, as grain. **2.** Continuing for regular or permanent use; not special or temporary: a *standing* rule; a *standing* army. **3.** Stagnant; not flowing. **4.** Begun while standing: a *standing* high jump. **5.** Established; permanent. **— n. 1.** Relative position, as in social, commercial, or moral relations; repute; place. **2.** High grade or rank; good reputation: a man of *standing.* **3.** A place to stand in; station. **4.** Time in which something stands or goes on; continuance; duration: a feud of long *standing.* **5.** The act of one who stands; erectness; stance. **— adv.** At or to a sudden stop or standstill: to bring up *standing.*

standing army An army that is prepared at all times for action, especially during peacetime, and that consists of the regular army plus reservists and conscripts.

standing order 1. A relatively permanent military order. **2.** In parliamentary law, a standing rule governing the way in which the business of a body is to be conducted.

standing rigging *Naut.* The ropes or cables that support the masts and fixed spars of a vessel.

standing room Place in which to stand, as in a building, theater, etc., where the seats are all occupied.

standing wave *Physics* A wave whose nodes and peaks remain fixed in space, resulting when a traveling wave is reflected directly back on itself, as in radio antennas, wave guides, acoustic systems, etc.

stand·ish (stan'dish) *n.* A receptacle for pens and ink. [< STAND + DISH]

Stan·dish (stan'dish), **Miles,** 1584?–1656, English colonist; military leader of the Pilgrims; subject of Longfellow's *The Courtship of Miles Standish.*

stand·off (stand'ôf', -of') *n. Informal* **1.** A draw or tie, as in a game. **2.** A counterbalancing or neutralization. **3.** Indifference or coldness; aloofness. **4.** A postponement; delay.

stand·off·ish (stand'ôf'ish, -of-) *adj.* Aloof; coolly reserved. **— stand'off'ish·ness** *n.*

stand oil Linseed or other oil that is thickened and purified by heating, used in varnishes and paints.

stand·out (stand'out') *n.* **1.** Someone or something outstanding, excellent, etc. **2.** *U.S. Informal* One who stubbornly refuses to agree, consent, or cooperate.

stand·pat (stand'pat') *adj.* Characterized by or pertaining to the policy of opposition to change; conservative.

stand·pat·ter (stand'pat'ər) *n.* One who adheres obstinately to a policy or party. **— stand'pat'tism** *n.*

stand·pipe (stand'pīp') *n.* A vertical pipe into which the water is pumped to give it a head; a water tower.

stand·point (stand'point') *n.* A position from which things are viewed or judged; point of view.

St. An·drew's cross (sānt an'drōōz) A cross in the form of the letter X. See SALTIRE. For illustration see CROSS.

St. Andrew's day The last day in November.

stand·still (stand'stil') *n.* A cessation; halt; rest. **— adj.** In a state of rest or inactivity; standing still.

stand·up (stand'up') *adj.* **1.** Having an erect position: a *standup* collar. **2.** Done, consumed, etc., while standing.

stang¹ (stang) *Scot. & Brit. Dial. v.t* **1.** To sting. **— v.i. 2.** To throb with pain. **— n.** A throbbing pain; sting. [< ON *stanga*]

stang² (stang) Obsolete past tense of STING.

stan·hope (stan'hōp) *n.* A light, open, one-seated carriage. [after Fitzroy *Stanhope,* 1787–1864, English clergyman, for whom it was first made]

Sta·ni·slav (stə·nyi·släf') A city in the western Ukrainian S.S.R., formerly in Poland; pop. 66,000 (1959). *German* **Stan·is·lau** (shtän'is·lou), *Polish* **Sta·ni·sła·wów** (stä·nē·swä'vŏof).

Stan·is·lav·sky (stä'ni·släf'skē), **Constantin,** 1863–1938, Russian actor, director, and producer: original name **Konstantin Sergeyevich Al·ek·se·yev** (äl·yek·sye'yev)

stank¹ (stangk) Past tense of STINK.

stank² (stangk) *n. Brit. Dial.* A pool; reservoir; pond; ditch; dam. [< OF *estanc* < L *stagnum* < *stagnare* to stagnate. See STAGNANT.]

Stan·ley (stan'lē), **Sir Henry (Morton),** 1841–1904, British journalist and African explorer; found David Livingstone 1871: original name **John Row·lands** (rō'ləndz). **— Wendell Meredith,** 1901–1971, U.S. biochemist.

Stan·ley (stan'lē), **Mount** The highest peak in the Ruwenzori. See RUWENZORI.

Stanley Cup The trophy awarded to the winner of the post-season playoffs of the National Hockey League, symbolizing the world's professional hockey championship.

Stanley Falls The seven cataracts of the upper Congo river, near the equator; total fall about 200 ft.

Stanley Pool A lakelike expansion of the Congo river between the Republic of the Congo and Zaire; 320 sq. mi.

stan·na·ry (stan'ər·ē) *n. pl.* **·ries** A tin mine or region of tin mines. [< Med.L *stannaria* < L *stannum* tin]

stan·nic (stan′ik) *adj. Chem.* Of, pertaining to, or containing tin, especially in its higher valence.

stannic sulfide *Chem.* A yellow compound, SnS_2, precipitated from a stannic salt solution: also called *mosaic gold.*

stan·nif·er·ous (stə·nif′ər·əs) *adj.* Yielding or containing tin. [< L *stannum* tin + -FEROUS]

stan·nite (stan′īt) *n.* A granular, metallic, steel-gray to black mineral containing tin, copper, iron, sulfur, and sometimes zinc; tin pyrites. [< L *stannum* tin + -ITE¹]

stan·nous (stan′əs) *adj. Chem.* Of, pertaining to, or containing tin, especially in its lower valence.

stan·num (stan′əm) *n.* Tin. [< L]

Stan·o·voi Range (stan′ə·voi) A mountain range in the eastern R.S.F.S.R.; highest peak, Skalisty, 8,143 ft. *Russian* **Sta·no·voi Khre·bet** (stə·no·voi′ khryi·byet′). Also **Stan′o·voy Range, Sta·no·vy Range** (stə·nō′vē).

St. An·tho·ny's cross (sānt an′thə·nēz) The tau cross (which see).

St. Anthony's fire *Pathol.* Erysipelas.

St. Anthony's nut An earthnut (*Conopodium denudatum*), fed to pigs: so called because St. Anthony was once a swineherd: also called *pignut.*

Stan·ton (stan′tən), **Edwin McMasters,** 1814–69, U.S. statesman and jurist; secretary of war in the Civil War. — **Elizabeth Cady,** 1815–1902, U.S. suffragist leader.

stan·za (stan′zə) *n.* A certain number of lines of verse grouped in a definite scheme of meter and sequence; a metrical division of a poem. Abbr. *st.* [< Ital., room, stanza < L *stans, stantis* standing. See STANCE.] — **stan·za·ic** (stan·zā′ik) *adj.*

sta·pe·li·a (stə·pē′lē·ə) *n.* Any of a genus (*Stapelia*) of fleshy African plants of the milkweed family. [< NL, after J. B. van *Stapel*, died 1636, Dutch botanist]

sta·pes (stā′pēz) *n. pl.* **sta·pes** or **sta·pe·des** (stə·pē′dēz) *Anat.* The innermost ossicle of the middle ear of mammals: also called *stirrup bone.* For illustration see EAR. [< LL *stapes* stirrup] — **sta·pe·di·al** (stə·pē′dē·əl) *adj.*

staph (staf) *n. Informal* Staphylococci; also, an infection caused by staphylococci.

staphylo- *combining form* **1.** *Anat.* The uvula: *staphyloplasty.* **2.** *Bacteriol.* Staphylococcus. Also, before vowels, **staphyl-.** [< NL < Gk. *staphylē* bunch of grapes]

staph·y·lo·coc·cus (staf′ə·lō·kok′əs) *n. pl.* **·coc·ci** (-kok′sī) Any of a genus (*Staphylococcus*) of typically pathogenic bacteria occurring singly, in pairs, or in irregular clusters; especially, *S. aureus,* an infective agent in boils and suppurating wounds. For illustration see BACTERIUM. [< NL < Gk. *staphylos* bunch of grapes (< *staphylē*) + *kokkos* berry] — **staph·y·lo·coc·cic** (-kok′sik) *adj.*

staph·y·lo·plas·ty (staf′ə·lō·plas′tē) *n.* Plastic surgery of the soft palate and uvula. — **staph·y·lo·plas′tic** *adj.*

staph·y·lor·rha·phy (staf′ə·lôr′ə·fē, -lor′-) *n. Surg.* The operation of uniting a cleft palate. Also **staph·y·lor′a·phy.** [< STAPHYLO- + -RRHAPHY]

sta·ple¹ (stā′pəl) *n.* **1.** *Usually pl.* A basic food or other ordinary item of household use. **2.** A principal commodity or production of a country or region. **3.** A main constituent of something. **4.** The carded or combed fiber of cotton, wool, or flax. **5.** Raw material. **6.** A store; mart. **7.** A source of supply; storehouse. — *adj.* **1.** Regularly and constantly produced, used, or sold. **2.** Main; chief. **3.** Commercially established; having regular commercial channels; marketable. — *v.t.* **·pled, ·pling** To sort or classify according to length, as wool fiber. [< OF *estaple* market, support < Gmc.]

sta·ple² (stā′pəl) *n.* **1.** A U-shaped piece of metal with pointed ends, driven into a surface to secure a bolt, hook, hasp, etc. **2.** A thin piece of wire usually shaped like a bracket ([), driven into paper, fabrics, etc., to serve as a fastening. — *v.t.* **·pled, ·pling** To fix or fasten by a staple or staples. [OE *stapol* post, prop]

sta·pler¹ (stā′plər) *n.* **1.** A sorter of wool according to its staple. **2.** A merchant who participated in one of the monopolies formerly granted by royal authority.

sta·pler² (stā′plər) *n.* **1.** A small hand device that fastens or binds papers, bags, etc., with a wire staple. **2.** A wire-stitching machine that binds pamphlets, books, etc.

star (stär) *n.* **1.** Any of the heavenly bodies visible from earth on clear nights as apparently fixed points of light. **2.** *Astron.* One of a class of self-luminous celestial bodies, exclusive of comets, meteors, and nebulae, but including the sun. They are classified according to their relative brightness by magnitudes, the first being the brightest and the sixth the faintest visible to the naked eye. The table below gives the names of the principal navigational stars and their apparent magnitudes, with the constellation in which each may be found. ◆ Collateral adjectives: *astral, sidereal, stellar.* **3.** A conventional figure usually having five or more radiating points, used as an emblem or device, as on the shoulder strap of a general. **4.** An actor or actress who plays the leading part. **5.** Anyone who shines prominently in a calling or profession: a sports *star.* **6.** An asterisk (*). **7.** A heavenly body considered as influencing one's fate. **8.** *Often pl.* Fortune; destiny. — **to see stars** *Informal* To see bright spots before the eyes, as from a sharp jolt to the head. — **to thank one's (lucky) stars** To be thankful for one's good fortune. — *v.* **starred, star·ring** *v.t.* **1.** To set or adorn with spangles or stars. **2.** To mark with an asterisk. **3.** To transform into a star. **4.** To present as a star in a play or motion picture. — *v.i.* **5.** To shine brightly as a star; be prominent or brilliant. **6.** To play the leading part; be the star. — *adj.* **1.** Of or pertaining to a star or stars. **2.** Prominent; brilliant: a *star* football player. [OE *steorra*]

TABLE OF PRINCIPAL NAVIGATIONAL STARS

Star	Constellation	Magnitude
Achernar	Eridanus	0.51
Acrux	Crux	0.9
Aldebaran	Taurus	0.86
Alpheratz	Andromeda	2.15
Altair	Aquila	0.77
Antares	Scorpio	0.92
Arcturus	Boötes	−0.06
Betelgeuse	Orion	Var.
Canopus	Carina	−0.72
Capella	Auriga	0.05
Deneb	Cygnus	1.26
Fomalhaut	Piscis Austrinus	1.19
Peacock	Pavo	2.12
Polaris	Ursa Minor	2.12
Pollux	Gemini	1.16
Procyon	Canis Minor	0.38
Regulus	Leo	1.36
Rigel	Orion	0.14
Rigil Kentaurus	Centaurus	−0.27
Sirius	Canis Major	−1.42
Spica	Virgo	0.91
Vega	Lyra	0.04

star apple **1.** A West Indian tree (*Chrysophyllum cainito*) bearing an edible fruit resembling an apple. **2.** Its fruit, which cut open reveals seeds disposed in the shape of a star.

star·board (stär′bərd) *Naut. n.* The right-hand side of a vessel as one faces the front or bow. — *adj.* Being on or toward the starboard. Opposed to *larboard, port.* Abbr. *stbd.* [OE *steorbord* steering side]

starch (stärch) *n.* **1.** *Biochem.* A white, odorless, tasteless, granular carbohydrate $(C_6H_{10}O_5)_n$, found in most plants. It is an important component of vegetable foods, reacting with certain digestive enzymes to produce maltose and dextrin: also called *amylum.* **2.** A preparation of this substance, used for stiffening linen, and for many industrial purposes. **3.** Stiffness or formality; a formal manner. **4.** *U.S. Slang* Energy; vigor. — *v.t.* To apply starch to; stiffen with or as with starch. [ME *sterche* < OE *stercan* (a hypothetical form) to stiffen < *stearc* stiff. Akin to STARK.]

Star Chamber **1.** Formerly, in England, a secret court held by members of the Privy Council with two judges of the courts of common law, and without jury. It was abolished by Parliament in 1641 because of abuses. **2.** Any court engaged in arbitrary or illegal procedure.

starch·y (stär′chē) *adj.* **starch·i·er, starch·i·est** **1.** Stiffened with starch; stiff. Also **starched** (stärcht). **2.** Prim; formal; precise. **3.** Formed of or combined with starch; farinaceous. — **starch′i·ly** *adv.* — **starch′i·ness** *n.*

star-crossed (stär′krôst′, -krost′) *adj.* Astrologically ill-fated; unfortunate; ill-starred.

star·dom (stär′dəm) *n.* The status of a star (defs. 4 & 5).

star drift *Astron.* A common motion of groups and pairs of stars in the same region of the heavens.

stare (stâr) *v.* **stared, star·ing** *v.i.* **1.** To gaze fixedly, often with the eyes wide open, as from admiration, fear, or insolence. **2.** To be conspicuously or unduly apparent; glare. **3.** To stand on end, as hair. — *v.t.* **4.** To stare at. **5.** To affect in a specified manner by staring: to *stare* a person into silence. — **Syn.** See LOOK. — *n.* The act of staring; an intense gaze. [OE *starian*] — **star′er** *n.*

star facet One of eight triangular facets in the crown of a brilliant-cut gem. For illustration see DIAMOND.

star·fish (stär′fish′) *n. pl.* **·fish** or **·fish·es** Any of various radially symmetrical marine echinoderms (class *Asteroidea*), commonly with a star-shaped body having five or more arms.

star·flow·er (stär′flou′ər) *n.* **1.** Any of various plants with conventionally star-shaped flowers; especially, a low perennial (*Trientalis borealis*) with one or more white star-shaped flowers. **2.** The star-of-Bethlehem.

STARFISH

(Ventral view showing tube feet)

star·gaze (stär′gāz′) *v.i.* **·gazed, ·gaz·ing** **1.** To gaze at or study the stars. **2.** To engage in reverie; daydream.

star·gaz·er (stär′gā′zər) *n.* **1.** One who gazes at or studies the stars. **2.** One who habitually daydreams. **3.** Any of a family (*Uranoscopidae*) of carnivorous marine fishes with small eyes near the front of the top of the head.

star·gaz·ing (stär′gā′zing) *adj.* Of or pertaining to one who stargazes. — *n.* **1.** The act or practice of watching or studying the stars. **2.** An absent-minded state.

star grass Any of various grasslike plants (genus *Hypoxis*) of the amaryllis family, with starlike flowers.

stark (stärk) *adj.* **1.** Without ornamentation; blunt; simple: the *stark* truth. **2.** Complete; utter; downright: *stark* misery. **3.** Stiff or rigid, as in death. **4.** Severe; tempestuous, as weather. **5.** Strict or grim, as a person. **6.** Naked: short for *stark naked.* — *adv.* **1.** In a stark manner. **2.** Completely; utterly: *stark* mad. [OE *stearc* stiff. Akin to STARCH.] — **stark'ly** *adv.*

Stark (shtärk), **Johannes,** 1874–1957, German physicist.

Stark (stärk), **John,** 1728–1822, American Revolutionary general. — **Harold R(aynsford),** born 1880, U.S. admiral.

stark naked   Entirely without clothing. [Alter. of ME *stert-naked* < OE *steort* tail + *nacod* naked]

star·less (stär'lis) *adj.* Being without stars or starlight.

star·let (stär'lit) *n.* **1.** A small star. **2.** *U.S. Informal* A young movie or television actress represented as a future star.

star·light (stär'līt') *n.* The light given by a star or stars. — *adj.* Lighted by or only by the stars: also **star'lit'** (-lit').

star·like (stär'līk') *adj.* Like a star; bright; shining.

star lily   The sand lily (which see).

star·ling[1] (stär'ling) *n.* Any of various passerine birds (genus *Sturnus*) native to Europe and naturalized in North America; especially, *S. vulgaris,* dark in color with a metallic purple and green luster. [OE *stærling* < *stær* starling]

star·ling[2] (stär'ling) *n.* **1.** An enclosure of close piling, as around a pier of a bridge for protection. **2.** One of the piles of such an enclosure. [ME *staddling* < OE *statholung* foundation]

star·nose (stär'nōz') *n.* A North American mole (*Condylura cristata*) having a radiate arrangement of fleshy processes around the end of the nose. Also **star-nosed mole.**

star-of-Beth·le·hem (stär'əv-beth'lē-əm, -lə-hem) *n.* A European plant (*Ornithogalum umbellatum*) of the lily family having white stellate flowers, naturalized in the eastern United States: also called *starflower.*

star of Bethlehem   The large star by which the three Magi were guided to Jesus's manger in Bethlehem.

star of David   The mogen David (which see).

starred (stärd) *adj.* **1.** Spangled with stars; marked with stars or a star. **2.** Presented or advertised as the star of a play, motion picture, etc. **3.** Marked with an asterisk. **4.** Affected by astral influence: chiefly in combination: *ill-starred.*

star·ry (stär'ē) *adj.* **·ri·er, ·ri·est** **1.** Set with stars or starlike spots or points; abounding in stars. **2.** Lighted by the stars. **3.** Shining as or like the stars. **4.** Shaped like a star. **5.** Of, pertaining to, proceeding from, or connected with stars. **6.** Consisting of stars; stellar. — **star'ri·ness** *n.*

star·ry-eyed (stär'ē-īd') *adj.* Given to fanciful wishes or yearnings.

Stars and Bars, The   The first flag authorized by the Congress of the Southern Confederacy, consisting of a field of three bars, red, white, and red, and a blue canton with a circle of white stars, one for each State of the Confederacy.

Stars and Stripes, The   The flag of the United States of America, a field of thirteen horizontal stripes, alternately red and white, and a blue union with as many white stars as States.

star sapphire   A sapphire cut en cabochon, with six rays.

star shell   An artillery shell that explodes with a shower of bright light, used for illuminating, signaling, etc.

star-span·gled (stär'spang'gəld) *adj.* Spangled with stars or starlike spots or points: said especially of the United States flag.

Star-Spangled Banner, The **1.** The flag of the United States. **2.** The national anthem of the United States, since 1931. The poem was written by Francis Scott Key in 1814 during the bombardment by the British of Fort McHenry, Md. The music is that of an old English drinking song, *To Anacreon in Heaven.*

start[1] (stärt) *v.i.* **1.** To make a beginning or start; set out. **2.** To begin; commence: The play *starts* at eight o'clock. **3.** To make an involuntary, startled movement, as from fear or surprise. **4.** To move suddenly, as with a spring, leap, or bound; jump. **5.** To seem to bulge or protrude: His eyes *started* from his head. **6.** To be displaced or dislocated; become loose, warped, etc.: The rivets have *started.* — *v.t.* **7.** To set in motion or circulation: to *start* an engine; to *start* a rumor. **8.** To begin; commence: to *start* a lecture. **9.** To set up; establish. **10.** To introduce (a subject) or propound (a question). **11.** To displace or dislocate; loosen, warp, etc.: The collision *started* the ship's seams. **12.** To rouse from cover; cause to take flight; flush, as game. **13.** To draw the contents from; tap, as a cask. **14.** *Archaic* To startle. — **to start in** To begin; undertake. — **to start off** To begin a journey; set out. — **to start out** **1.** To start off. **2.** To make a beginning or start. — **to start up** **1.** To rise or appear suddenly. **2.** To begin or cause to begin operation, as an engine. — **to start with** In the first place; to begin with. — *n.* **1.** A setting out or going forth; beginning. **2.** A quick, startled movement or feeling, as at something unexpected. **3.** A temporary or spasmodic action

or attempt; a brief, intermittent effort: by fits and *starts.* **4.** Advantage or distance in advance at the outset; lead: I had a *start* of five miles in the race. **5.** Impetus at the beginning of motion or course of action: to get a *start* in business. **6.** A loosened place or condition; crack: a *start* in a ship's planking. **7.** *Archaic* A sudden impulse or effusion; sally. [ME *sterten* to start, leap; fusion of ON *sterta* to overturn and OE *styrtan* to start, jump]

start[2] (stärt) *n.* **1.** The sharp point of an antler. **2.** A taillike piece. **3.** The tail of a bird or animal: now obsolete except in compounds: a *redstart.* [OE *steort* tail]

start·er (stär'tər) *n.* **1.** One who or that which starts. **2.** One who sees to it that buses, etc., leave on schedule. **3.** A mechanism for starting an internal combustion engine without manual cranking: also called *self-starter.* **4.** A competitor at the start of a race. **5.** A person who gives the signal for the start of a race.

star thistle **1.** An Old World weed (*Centaurea calcitrapa*) with spiny heads of tubular purple flowers, naturalized in the United States. **2.** Any of a related species (*C. solstitialis*) with yellow flowers.

star·tle (stär'təl) *v.* **·tled, ·tling** *v.t.* **1.** To arouse or excite suddenly; cause to start involuntarily; alarm. — *v.i.* **2.** To be aroused or excited suddenly; take alarm. — **Syn.** See FRIGHTEN. — *n.* A sudden fright or shock; a scare. [OE *steartlian* to kick, struggle] — **star'tler** *n.*

star·tling (stär'ling) *adj.* Rousing sudden surprise, alarm, or the like. — **star'tling·ly** *adv.*

star·va·tion (stär·vā'shən) *n.* The act of starving, or the state of being starved.

starve (stärv) *v.* **starved, starv·ing** *v.i.* **1.** To perish from lack of food. **2.** To suffer from extreme hunger. **3.** To suffer from lack or need: to *starve* for friendship. **4.** *Dial.* To die of cold. **5.** *Obs.* To die. — *v.t.* **6.** To cause to die of hunger; deprive of food. **7.** To bring to a specified condition by starving: to *starve* an enemy into surrender. [OE *steorfan* to die] — **starv'er** *n.*

starve·ling (stärv'ling) *n.* A person or animal that is starving, starved, or emaciated. — *adj.* **1.** Starving; emaciated; hungry. **2.** Failing to meet needs; inadequate.

star·wort (stär'würt') *n.* A stitchwort (which see).

stash (stash) *v.t.* *Slang* To hide or conceal (money, valuables, etc.), for storage and safekeeping: often with *away.* [? Blend of STORE + CACHE]

sta·sis (stā'sis, stas'is) *n.* *pl.* **·ses** (-sēz) **1.** Stoppage in the circulation of any of the body fluids, especially of the blood in the small vessels and capillaries. **2.** Retarded movement of the intestinal contents. **3.** A static state or condition in which there is no movement or progress. [< NL < Gk., a standing < *histanai* to stand]

stat-   Var. of STATO-.

stat. **1.** Immediately (L *statim*). **2.** Static. **3.** Stationary. **4.** Statistics. **5.** Statute (miles). **6.** Statute(s).

-stat *combining form* A device that stops or makes constant: *thermostat; rheostat.* [< Gk. *-statēs* causing to stand < *histanai* to stand]

state (stāt) *n.* **1.** Mode of existence as determined by circumstances, external or internal; nature; condition; situation. **2.** Frame of mind; mood: a *state* of anxiety. **3.** Mode or style of living; station. **4.** Grand and ceremonious style; pomp; formality. **5.** A sovereign political community organized under a distinct government recognized and conformed to by the people as supreme, and having jurisdiction over a given territory; a nation. **6.** *Usually cap.* One of a number of political communities or bodies politic united to form one sovereign state; especially, one of the United States. **7.** *pl.* The legislative bodies of a nation; estates. **8.** The territorial, political, and governmental entity constituting a state or nation; authority of government. **9.** *Obs.* A person of rank; a noble. **10.** *Obs.* An estate; order; class of persons. — **Syn.** See NATION. — **Department of State** An executive department of the U.S. government (established in 1789), headed by the Secretary of State, that supervises the conduct of foreign affairs, directs the activities of all diplomatic and consular representatives, protects national interests abroad, and assists in the formulation of policies in relation to international problems. Also **State Department.** — **the States** *Informal* The continental United States: used chiefly overseas. — **to lie in state** To be placed on public view, with ceremony and honors, before burial. — *adj.* **1.** Of or pertaining to the state, nation, or government: *state* papers. **2.** Intended for use on occasions of ceremony. — *v.t.* **stat·ed, stat·ing** **1.** To set forth explicitly in speech or writing; assert; declare. **2.** To fix; determine; settle. **3.** *Law* To make known specifically; declare as a matter of fact. — **Syn.** See ASSERT. [Aphetic var. of OF *estat* < L *status* condition, state < *stare* to stand. Doublet of STATUS.] — **sta'tal** (stā'tal) *adj.*

state bank **1.** *U.S.* A bank that has a charter from a State government. **2.** Any bank that is owned or controlled by a state, especially one that issues currency.

state·craft (stāt′kraft′, -kräft′) *n.* The art or practice of conducting affairs of state.

stat·ed (stā′tid) *adj.* 1. Announced; specified. 2. Established; regular; fixed. — **stat′ed·ly** *adv.*

State flower A flower or plant adopted as the floral emblem of one of the United States.

State·hood (stāt′hŏŏd) *n.* The condition or status of one of the United States, as distinguished from that of a Territory.

State House A building used for sessions of a State legislature and for other public purposes; State capitol.

state·less (stāt′lis) *adj.* 1. Without nationality: a *stateless* person. 2. Without a state or community of states.

state line In the United States, any boundary between States.

state·ly (stāt′lē) *adj.* ·li·er, ·li·est Dignified; lofty. — *adv.* Loftily: also **state′li·ly** (-lə-lē). — **state′li·ness** *n.*

state·ment (stāt′mənt) *n.* 1. The act of stating. 2. That which is stated. 3. *Law* A formal narration of facts filed as the foundation for judicial proceeding; a pleading. 4. A summary of the assets and liabilities of a bank or firm, showing the balance due. 5. A report sent, usually monthly, to a debtor of a business firm or to a depositor in a bank.

Stat·en Island (stat′n) An island at the entrance to New York Harbor, coextensive with Richmond, New York City; 57 sq. mi. Abbr. *S.I.*

state park *U.S.* A tract of land provided and maintained by a State for conservation and recreation.

State policeman *U.S.* A member of the separate police force of a State; also called *State trooper, trooper.*

State prison A prison built and controlled by a State.

stat·er[1] (stā′tər) *n.* One who makes a statement.

sta·ter[2] (stā′tər) *n.* Any of several ancient Greek coins of various metals and values. [< L < Gk. *statēr*]

state·room (stāt′rŏŏm′, -rŏŏm′) *n.* 1. A private room having sleeping accommodations on a passenger ship. 2. A private sleeping compartment on a railroad car.

State's attorney (stāts) *U.S.* A lawyer appointed by a State to represent it in court.

state's evidence 1. Evidence produced by the State in criminal prosecutions. 2. One who confesses himself guilty of a crime and testifies as a witness against his accomplices. Also, in Great Britain, Canada, Australia, etc., *king's* or *queen's evidence.* — **to turn state's evidence** To become a witness for the state and inculpate one's accomplices.

States-General (stāts′jen′ər·əl) *n.* 1. The legislative assembly of the estates of an entire nation. 2. The Netherlands parliament. 3. The French legislative body before the Revolution: also called *Estates-General.*

state·side (stāt′sīd′) *adj.* Of or in the continental United States. — *adv.* In or to the continental United States.

states·man (stāts′mən) *n.* *pl.* ·men (-mən) 1. One who is skilled in government; a political leader of distinguished ability. 2. One engaged in government, or influential in state affairs. — **states′man·like′, states′man·ly** *adj.* — **states′man·ship** *n.* — **states′wom′an** (-wŏŏm′ən) *n.fem.*

state socialism A political theory advocating government ownership of utilities and industries.

States of the Church A part of central Italy that, before the unification of Italy in 1870, was under the sovereignty of the pope: also called *Papal States.*

States' rights 1. The rights and powers not delegated to the United States by the Constitution nor prohibited by it to the respective States. 2. An interpretation of the Constitution that makes these rights and powers as large as possible. 3. The doctrine that the States have the right to judge and nullify an act of the Federal government. See NULLIFICATION. Also **State rights.**

States' Rights Party A former political party founded during May, 1948, in Jackson, Miss., by Southern Democrats, called Dixiecrats, who were opposed to the civil rights program of the regular Democratic Party.

State trooper *U.S.* A State policeman.

State university A university maintained in and supported by any of the various States of the U.S. and considered as part of that State's public educational system.

state-wide (stāt′wīd′) *adj.* Throughout a state.

stat·ic (stat′ik) *adj.* 1. At rest; quiescent; dormant; not active, moving, or changing. 2. Pertaining to bodies at rest or forces in equilibrium: opposed to *dynamic.* 3. *Physics* Acting as weight, but not moving: *static* pressure. 4. *Electr.* Pertaining to electricity at rest, or to stationary electric charges. 5. Of or pertaining to nonactive elements. 6. Treating of fixed or stable conditions rather than of fluctuations of sales: said of capital or goods. Also **stat′i·cal.** — *n.* *Telecom.* A disturbance of a carrier wave caused by atmospheric or man-made sources; also, the noise caused by this. Abbr. *stat.* [< NL *staticus* < Gk. *statikos* causing to stand < *histanai* to stand] — **stat′i·cal·ly** *adv.*

stat·ics (stat′iks) *n.pl.* (construed as sing.) The branch of mechanics dealing with bodies at rest and with the interaction of forces in equilibrium.

sta·tion (stā′shən) *n.* 1. The headquarters of some official person or body of men: a police *station.* 2. An established building or place serving as a starting point, stage, stopping place, or post; terminal; depot. 3. A place where a person or thing usually stands or is; an assigned location. 4. Social condition; rank; standing. 5. *Mil.* The place to which an individual, unit, or ship is assigned for duty; post. 6. The offices, studios, and technical installations of a radio or television broadcasting unit. 7. *Mining* A recess in a shaft or passage of a mine. 8. *Austral.* A cattle or sheep ranch. 9. In surveying, a point around or from which measurements of angles or distances are made; also, the distance adopted for the standard length. — *v.t.* To assign to a station; place in a post or position. Abbr. *sta.*, *Sta.* [< F < L *statio, -onis* < *stare* to stand]
— **Syn.** (noun) 2. *Station, depot,* and *terminal* are compared as used in railroading. Properly, a train stops at a *station* to take on or discharge passengers or freight. Freight is kept in a *depot,* which is a place of storage. In the early days of railroads, the *station* and the *depot* were often contained in one small building; this was called the *depot,* then regarded as the more elegant term. Today it is regarded as less dignified and has been largely replaced by *station.* A *terminal* is a *station* at the end of a railroad line.

sta·tion·ar·y (stā′shən·er′ē) *adj.* 1. Remaining in one place; fixed. 2. Not portable or not easily portable. 3. Exhibiting no change of character or condition. — *n.* *pl.* ·ar·ies One who or that which is stationary. Abbr. *sta.*, *stat.*

stationary front *Meteorol.* A front between two dissimilar air masses that are not displacing one another.

station break *Telecom.* Any of the regularly scheduled interruptions in a radio or television program in which the call number or letters of the station are announced.

sta·tion·er (stā′shən·ər) *n.* 1. A dealer in stationery and related articles. 2. *Obs.* A bookseller; publisher. [< Med.L *stationarius* stationary, having a fixed location (for business)]

Sta·tion·ers Company (stā′shən·ərz) A London guild of printers, bookbinders, booksellers, etc., incorporated in 1577, and until 1911 exercising a copyright monopoly in England, requiring all publications to be registered at its office, **Stationers' Hall.**

sta·tion·er·y (stā′shən·er′ē) *n.* 1. Writing paper and envelopes. 2. Material used in writing, as pens, pencils, notebooks, etc. [< STATIONER]

station house A police station.

sta·tion·mas·ter (stā′shən·mas′tər, -mäs′-) *n.* The person having charge of a bus or railroad station.

Stations of the Cross The fourteen images or pictures ranged in a church or on church property, representing successive scenes of the Passion of Christ, and before which devotions are performed.

station wagon A large automobile with one or more rows of removable or folding seats and a hinged tailgate.

stat·ism (stā′tiz·əm) *n.* 1. A theory of government holding that the returns from group or individual enterprise are vested in the state. 2. Loosely, adherence to state sovereignty, as in a republic. 3. *Obs.* Statecraft.

stat·ist (stā′tist) *n.* 1. An adherent of statism. 2. A statistician. 3. *Obs.* A statesman; politician. — *adj.* Of, pertaining to, or advocating statism.

sta·tis·tic (stə·tis′tik) *adj.* Statistical. — *n.* 1. Any element entering into a statistical statement or array, as the mean, the standard deviation, number of cases, etc. 2. Statistics (def. 2). [< STATISTICS; n. def. 1 by back formation]

sta·tis·ti·cal (stə·tis′tə·kəl) *adj.* Of, pertaining to, consisting of, or derived from statistics: also *statistic.* — **sta·tis′ti·cal·ly** *adv.*

stat·is·ti·cian (stat′is·tish′ən) *n.* One skilled in collecting and tabulating statistical data. Also called *statist.*

sta·tis·tics (stə·tis′tiks) *n.pl.* (construed as sing. in def. 2) 1. Quantitative data, pertaining to any subject or group, especially when systematically gathered and collated. 2. The science that deals with the collection, tabulation, and systematic classification of quantitative data, especially of occurrence as a basis for inference and induction: also called *statistic.* Abbr. *stat.* [< G *statistik* < Med.L *statisticus* statesmanlike, ult. < L *status.* See STATE.]

Sta·tius (stā′shəs), **Publius Papinius,** 45?–96? A.D. Roman poet.

stato- *combining form* Position: *statoscope.* Also, before vowels, *stat-.* [< Gk. *statos* standing, fixed < *histanai* to stand]

stat·o·cyst (stat′ə·sist) *n.* *Anat.* One of the sacs in the labyrinth of the internal ear, provided with sensitive hairs and otoliths that aid in maintaining body equilibrium.

sta·tor (stā′tər) *n.* *Mech.* The stationary portion of a dynamo, turbine, motor, etc.: distinguished from *rotor.* Abbr. *sta.* [< NL < L, supporter < *status.* See STATE.]

stat·o·scope (stat′ə·skōp) *n.* 1. *Meteorol.* A very sensitive aneroid barometer. 2. *Aeron.* A device that indicates small variations in the altitude of an aircraft. [< STATO- + -SCOPE]

stat·u·ar·y (stach′ŏŏ·er′ē) *n.* *pl.* ·ar·ies 1. Statues collectively. 2. One who makes statues; a sculptor. 3. The art of making statues. — *adj.* Of or suitable for statues. Abbr. *stat.* [< L *statuaria* < *statua* statue. See STATUE.]

stat·ue (stach′ōō) *n.* A representation of a human or animal figure in marble, bronze, etc., especially when nearly life-size or larger, and preserving the proportions in all directions. Abbr. *stat.* [< F < L *statua* < *status*, pp. of *stare* to stand]

sta·tued (stach′ōōd) *adj.* **1.** Adorned with statues. **2.** Sculptured.

Statue of Liberty A giant bronze statue on Liberty Island, depicting a crowned woman holding aloft a burning torch. Created by Frédéric Bartholdi, it was presented to the United States by France and unveiled in 1886. Official name **Liberty Enlightening the World.**

stat·u·esque (stach′ōō·esk′) *adj.* Resembling a statue, as in grace, pose, or dignity. [< STATUE + -ESQUE] — **stat′·u·esque′ly** *adv.* — **stat′u·esque′ness** *n.*

stat·u·ette (stach′ōō·et′) *n.* A small statue. [< F, dim. of *statue*]

stat·ure (stach′ər) *n.* **1.** The natural height of an animal body, especially of a human body. **2.** The height of anything, especially of a tree. **3.** Development; growth: moral *stature.* [< OF < L *statura* < *status.* See STATE.]

sta·tus (stā′təs, stat′əs) *n.* **1.** State, condition, or relation. **2.** Relative position or rank. [< L < *stare* to stand. Doublet of STATE.]

sta·tus quo (stā′təs kwō, stat′əs) The condition or state in which (a person or thing is or has been): often used with *the*: to maintain the *status quo.* Also **status in quo.** [< L]

status quo an·te bel·lum (an′tē bel′əm) *Latin* The state of affairs existing before the war.

stat·u·ta·ble (stach′ōō·tə·bəl) *adj.* Agreeing or conforming with statute; statutory. — **stat′u·ta·bly** *adv.*

stat·ute (stach′ōōt) *n.* **1.** *Law* **a** A legislative enactment duly sanctioned and authenticated by constitutional rule; act of Parliament, Congress, etc. **b** Any authoritatively declared rule, ordinance, decree, or law. **2.** The act of a corporation or its founder, intended as a permanent rule or law: the *statutes* of a university. — **Syn.** See LAW. — *adj.* Consisting of or regulated by statute. Abbr. *st., St., stat.* [< F *statut* < LL *statutum* < *statuere* to set, found, constitute]

statute holiday *Canadian* A federal legal holiday.

statute law The law as set forth in statutes.

statute mile A mile (def. 1).

statute of limitations A statute that imposes time limits upon the right of action in certain cases, as by obliging a creditor to demand payment of a debt within a specified time.

Statute of Westminster The British statute of 1931 that guarantees Canadian sovereignty.

stat·u·to·ry (stach′ə·tôr′ē, -tō′rē) *adj.* **1.** Pertaining to a statute. **2.** Created by or dependent upon legislative enactment.

statutory rape The crime of having sexual relations with a girl who is under the age of consent.

St. Au·gus·tine (sānt ô′gəs·tēn) A city in NE Florida, on the Atlantic; oldest permanent town in the United States; founded by Spain in 1565; pop. 12,352.

staum·rel (stôm′rəl) *Scot. adj.* Half-witted. — *n.* A half-wit. [< *staumer*, dial. var. of STAMMER]

staunch (stônch, stänch) *adj.* **1.** Firm and dependable; constant; loyal: a *staunch* friend. **2.** Having firm constitution or construction; stout: a *staunch* ship. **3.** Strong and vigorous. Also spelled *stanch.* — **Syn.** See FAITHFUL. — *v.t.* See STANCH. ◆ See note under STANCH. [< OF *estanche* watertight, reliable < *estanchier* to make stand. See STANCH.] — **staunch′ly** *adv.* — **staunch′ness** *n.*

stauro- *combining form* Cross: *stauroscope.* [< Gk. *stauros* cross]

stau·ro·lite (stôr′ə·līt) *n.* A brown to black silicate of iron and aluminum, found in prismatic crystals and sometimes used as a gemstone. — **stau·ro·lit·ic** (-lit′ik) *adj.* [< STAURO- + -LITE; from the crosslike twin crystals]

stau·ro·scope (stôr′ə·skōp) *n. Optics* An instrument used to determine the planes of vibration of light in crystals. [< STAURO- + -SCOPE] — **stau·ro·scop·ic** (-skop′ik) *adj.*

Sta·vang·er (stä·väng′ər) A port city in SW Norway; pop. 52,762 (est. 1961).

stave (stāv) *n.* **1.** A curved strip of wood, forming a part of the sides of a barrel, tub, or the like. **2.** Any narrow strip of material used for a like purpose: iron *staves.* **3.** A straight board forming part of a curb, as about a well. **4.** *Music* A staff. **5.** A stanza; verse. **6.** A rod, cudgel, or staff. **7.** A rung of a rack or ladder. — *v.* **staved** or **stove, stav·ing** *v.t.* **1.** To break in the staves or strakes of (a cask or a boat). **2.** To crush the shell or surface of; smash. **3.** To make (a hole) by crushing or collision. **4.** To furnish with staves. **5.** To ward off, as with a staff; keep at a distance: usually with *off*: to *stave* off hunger. — *v.i.* **6.** To be broken in, as a vessel's hull. [Back formation < *staves* (OE *stafas*), pl. of STAFF]

staves (stāvz) **1.** Alternative plural of STAFF. **2.** Plural of STAVE.

staves·a·cre (stāvz′ā′kər) *n.* **1.** A tall larkspur (*Delphinium staphisagria*) of southern Europe. **2.** Its seeds, yielding a poisonous alkaloid formerly used as a purgative and antispasmodic. [< OF *stafisagre* < Med.L *staphis agria* < Gk. *staphis* raisin + *agrios* wild]

Stav·ro·pol (stäv′rə·pəly′) A city in the SW R.S.F.S.R., on the Volga; pop. 198,000 (1970). Also **Stav′ro·pol′**: from 1935–43 *Voroshilovsk.*

staw (stô) *Scot.* Past tense of STEAL.

stay¹ (stā) *v.i.* **1.** To cease motion; stop; halt. **2.** To continue in a specified place, condition, or state: to *stay* indoors; to *stay* healthy. **3.** To remain temporarily as a guest, resident, etc.: Where are you *staying*? **4.** To pause; wait; tarry. **5.** *Informal* To have endurance; stand up; last. **6.** *Informal* To keep pace with a competitor, as in a race. **7.** In poker, to remain in a round by meeting an ante, bet, or raise. **8.** *Archaic* To cease. **9.** *Archaic* To stand firm. — *v.t.* **10.** To bring to a stop; halt; check. **11.** To hinder; delay. **12.** To put off; postpone. **13.** To satisfy the demands of temporarily; quiet; appease: to *stay* the pangs of hunger. **14.** To remain for the duration of: I will *stay* the night. **15.** To remain till or beyond the end of: with *out*: to *stay* out one's welcome. **16.** *Archaic* To quell, as strife. **17.** *Obs.* To wait for. — **to stay put** *U.S. Informal* To remain or hold in spite of everything. — **Syn.** See ABIDE, LIVE. — *n.* **1.** The act or time of staying; continuance in a place; sojourn; visit. **2.** That which checks or stops; especially, a suspension of judicial proceedings. **3.** Staying power; endurance; persistence. **4.** A state of rest; standstill. [< AF *estaier*, OF *ester* < L *stare* to stand] — **stay′er** *n.*

stay² (stā) *v.t.* **1.** To be a support to; prop or hold up. **2.** To support mentally; comfort; sustain. **3.** To cause to depend or rely, as for support: with *on* or *upon*. — *n.* **1.** Anything that props or supports. **2.** A strip of plastic or metal, used to stiffen corsets, girdles, etc. **3.** *pl. Chiefly Brit.* A corset. [< OF *estayer*]

stay³ (stā) *Naut. n.* **1.** A strong rope, often of wire, used to support, steady, or fasten a mast or spar. **2.** Any rope supporting a mast or funnel; a guy rope. — **in stays** In the act of turning about on another tack. — *v.t.* **1.** To support with a stay or stays. **2.** To put (a vessel) on the opposite tack. — *v.i.* **3.** To tack: said of vessels. [OE *stæg*]

stay·ing power (stā′ing) The ability to endure.

stay-in strike (stā′in′) *n. Brit.* A sit-down strike (which see). Also **stay-in.**

stay·sail (stā′səl, -sāl′) *n. Naut.* A sail, usually triangular, extended on a stay. For illustration see SHIP.

S.T.B. **1.** Bachelor of Sacred Theology (L *Sacrae Theologiae Baccalaureus*). **2.** Bachelor of Theology (L *Scientiae Theologicae Baccalaureus*).

stbd. Starboard.

St. Ber·nard Pass (sānt bər·närd′, *Fr.* saṅ ber·nàr′) Either of two passes in the Alps, **Great St. Bernard Pass** between Switzerland and Italy, east of Mont Blanc; elevation 8,120 ft.; site of **St. Bernard hospice** for the rescue of snowbound travelers, or **Little St. Bernard Pass** between France and Italy, south of Mont Blanc; elevation, 7,180 ft.

St. Chris·to·pher Nev·is and An·guil·la (kris′tə·fər nē′vis and ang·gwil′ə, nev′is) A group of islands, formerly British colonies, now members of the West Indies Associated States; comprising **St. Christopher** (68 sq. mi.), **Nevis** (50 sq. mi.), and **Anguilla** (35 sq. mi.); total pop. 60,000 (1971); capital, Basseterre.

St. Clair (klâr), **Lake** A lake between southern Ontario and SE Michigan; 460 sq. mi.; connected with Lake Huron by the **St. Clair River**, that forms part of the boundary between Ontario and Michigan.

St. Clair Shores (shôrz, shōrz) A village in SE Michigan, near Detroit; pop. 88,093. Also **St. Clair.**

St. Cloud (kloud) A city in central Minnesota, on the Mississippi; pop. 39,691.

St. Croix (kroi′) The largest of the Virgin Islands of the United States; 82 sq. mi.: also *Santa Cruz.*

St. Croix River 1. A river forming the boundary between NW Wisconsin and eastern Minnesota and flowing 164 miles SW and south, to the Mississippi River. **2.** A river forming the boundary between Maine and New Brunswick and flowing 75 miles south and east to Passamaquoddy Bay.

std. Standard.

S.T.D. Doctor of Sacred Theology (L *Sacrae Theologiae Doctor*).

Ste. Sainte.

stead (sted) *n.* **1.** Place of another person or thing: preceded by *in*: Serfdom came in the *stead* of slavery. Compare INSTEAD. **2.** Place or attitude of support; use; avail; service: chiefly in the phrase **to stand one in (good) stead. 3.** A steading or farm: used chiefly in compounds: *homestead, Hempstead.* **4.** *Archaic* Position; condition. — *v.t. Archaic* To be of advantage to; help; benefit; support. [OE *stede*]

stead·fast (sted′fast′, -fäst′, -fast) *adj.* **1.** Firmly fixed in faith or devotion to duty; constant; unchanging. **2.** Directed fixedly at one point or to one end, as a gaze or purpose; steady. Also spelled *stedfast.* — **Syn.** See FAITHFUL. [OE *stedefæst*] — **stead′fast′ly** *adv.* — **stead′fast′ness** *n.*

stead·ing (sted′ing) *n. Brit. Dial.* A farmhouse, sheds, and offices; a farmstead.

stead·y (sted′ē) *adj.* **stead·i·er, stead·i·est** **1.** Stable in position; firmly supported; fixed. **2.** Moving or acting with uniform regularity; constant; unfaltering: a *steady* light. **3.** Not readily disturbed or upset: *steady* nerves. **4.** Free from intemperance and dissipation; industrious, sober, and reliable: *steady* habits. **5.** Constant in mind or conduct; not wavering; steadfast. **6.** Regular; reliable: a *steady* customer. **7.** Uninterrupted; continuous: a *steady* flow of conversation. **8.** *Naut.* Having the direction of the ship's head unchanged. — *v.t. & v.i.* **stead·ied, stead·y·ing** To make or become steady. — *interj.* **1.** *Naut.* Keep her steady: an order to a helmsman to keep the ship's head pointed in the same direction. **2.** Not so fast; keep calm: an order enjoining self-control or composure. — *n. Slang* One's regular sweetheart. — **to go steady** *Informal* To date only one person of the opposite sex. [< STEAD + -Y³] — **stead′i·er** *n.* — **stead′i·ly** *adv.* — **stead′i·ness** *n.*

steady-state theory (sted′ē-stāt′) *Astron.* The theory that the universe has no limits and will continue to expand without contraction. Compare BIG-BANG THEORY.

steak (stāk) *n.* **1.** A slice of meat or fish, usually broiled or fried. **2.** Meat chopped for cooking like a steak: hamburger *steak.* [< ON *steik*]

steak·house (stāk′hous′) *n.* A restaurant that offers broiled steaks and chops as its specialty. Also **steak house.**

steal (stēl) *v.* **stole, sto·len, steal·ing** *v.t.* **1.** To take from another without right, authority, or permission, and usually in a secret manner. **2.** To take or obtain in a surreptitious, artful, or subtle manner: He has *stolen* the hearts of the people. **3.** To move, place, or convey stealthily: with *away, from, in, into,* etc. **4.** In baseball, to reach (second base, third base, or home plate) without the aid of a hit, error, passed ball, or wild pitch: said of a baserunner. — *v.i.* **5.** To commit theft. **6.** To move secretly or furtively. **7.** In baseball, to steal a base. — *n.* **1.** The act of stealing. **2.** That which is stolen. **3.** In baseball, the act of stealing a base. **4.** Any financial transaction or other deal that benefits no one but the originators. **5.** *U.S. Slang* A bargain. [OE *stelan*] — **steal′er** *n.*

— **Syn.** (verb) **1.** *Steal, purloin, filch, lift, pilfer, pinch, snitch,* and *swipe* mean to take the property of another unlawfully. *Steal* is the general term; in law, to *steal* is to commit larceny, but in popular usage, *steal* includes embezzle, extort, and plagiarize. *Purloin* is a bookish word for *steal.* To *filch* is to *steal* furtively; *lift* is an informal synonym for *filch.* To *pilfer* is to *steal* by taking a little at a time. *Pinch, snitch,* and *swipe* are slang synonyms denoting petty stealing. Compare THEFT.

steal·age (stē′lij) *n.* **1.** The act of stealing. **2.** Losses suffered from stealing.

stealth (stelth) *n.* **1.** The quality or habit of acting secretly; a concealed manner of acting. **2.** A secret or clandestine act, movement, or proceeding. **3.** *Obs.* Theft, or the thing stolen. [ME *stelthe, stalthe* < OE *stelan* to steal]

stealth·y (stel′thē) *adj.* **stealth·i·er, stealth·i·est** Moving or acting secretly or slyly; done or characterized by stealth; furtive. — **stealth′i·ly** *adv.* — **stealth′i·ness** *n.*

— **Syn.** *Stealthy, furtive, surreptitious, clandestine,* and *underhand* mean done secretly, or characterized by concealment. Anything *stealthy* seeks to avoid notice; it alone of these words may be applied to a worthy act or purpose: the scout made a *stealthy* approach to the enemy position. *Furtive* suggests the actions or manner of a thief; we speak of a *furtive* act, a *furtive* face, a *furtive* method. *Surreptitious* suggests quickness as well as concealment in acting illegally or improperly: a *surreptitious* glance into a neighbor's window. *Clandestine* describes that which is concealed because morally offensive or socially and politically dangerous: a *clandestine* love affair, a *clandestine* rally. *Underhand* adds a note of unfairness, fraud, or corruption to *stealthy:* to win an election by *underhand* means.

steam (stēm) *n.* **1.** Water in the form of vapor. **2.** The gas or vapor into which water is changed by boiling, especially when used under pressure as a source of energy. **3.** The visible mist into which aqueous vapor is condensed by cooling. **4.** Any kind of vaporous exhalation. **5.** *Informal* Vigor; force; speed. — **to let** (or **blow**) **off steam** *Informal* To give expression to pent-up emotions or opinions. — *v.i.* **1.** To give off or emit steam or vapor. **2.** To rise or pass off as steam. **3.** To become covered with condensed water vapor: often with *up.* **4.** To generate steam. **5.** To move or travel by the agency of steam. — *v.t.* **6.** To treat with steam, as in softening, cooking, cleaning, etc. — *adj.* **1.** Of, driven, or operated by steam. **2.** Containing or conveying steam: a *steam* boiler. **3.** Treated by steam. [OE *stēam*]

steam·boat (stēm′bōt′) *n.* A steamship (which see).

steam boiler A closed vessel used in generating steam.

steam chest The box or chest through which steam is delivered from a boiler to an engine cylinder. Also **steam box.**

steam engine An engine that derives its motive force from the action of steam, usually by pressure against a piston sliding within a closed cylinder.

steam·er (stē′mər) *n.* **1.** A ship propelled by steam; steamship. **2.** A vessel in which something is steamed, as for cooking. **3.** A soft-shell clam cooked by steaming. Abbr. *str.*

steamer trunk A trunk small enough to fit under a berth in a ship's cabin.

steam·fit·ter (stēm′fit′ər) *n.* A man who sets up or repairs steam pipes and their fittings. — **steam′fit′ting** *n.*

steam organ A calliope.

steam point *Physics* The boiling point of water at standard atmospheric pressure; 100° C.

steam·rol·ler (stēm′rō′lər) *n.* **1.** A road-rolling machine driven by steam, or now by a gasoline or Diesel engine. **2.** Any force that ruthlessly overcomes opposition. Also **steam roller.** — *v.t.* **1.** To work (a road, etc.) with a steamroller. **2.** To suppress; crush. **3.** To provide a path for by crushing opposition. — *v.i.* **4.** To work with or as with a steamroller. — *adj.* Harsh and aggressive: *steamroller* tactics.

steam·ship (stēm′ship′) *n.* A large vessel used for ocean traffic and usually propelled by one or more screws operated by steam; a steamer. Abbr. *SS, S/S, S.S.*

steam shovel A machine for digging, operated by steam power, or now by a gasoline or Diesel engine.

steam table *U.S.* A long table, as in restaurants, with openings in which containers of food are placed to be kept warm by hot water or steam circulating beneath them.

steam turbine A turbine operated by steam power.

steam·y (stē′mē) *adj.* **steam·i·er, steam·i·est** Consisting of, like, or full of steam. — **steam′i·ly** *adv.* — **steam′i·ness** *n.*

Ste. Anne de Beau·pré (sānt an′ də bō-prā′) A village in southern Quebec, on the St. Lawrence; site of a famous Roman Catholic shrine.

ste·ap·sin (stē-ap′sin) *n. Biochem.* A fat-splitting enzyme contained in pancreatic juice. [< STEA(RIN) + (PE)PSIN]

ste·a·rate (stē′ə-rāt, stir′āt) *n. Chem.* A salt or ester of stearic acid.

ste·ar·ic (stē-ar′ik, stir′ik) *adj. Chem.* Of, pertaining to, or derived from stearin. [< F *stéarique* < Gk. *stear* suet]

stearic acid *Chem.* A white fatty acid, $C_{17}H_{35}COOH$, found in animal fats and in many vegetable oils.

ste·a·rin (stē′ə·rin, stir′in) *n. Chem.* **1.** A white, crystalline ester of glycerol and stearic acid, $(C_{17}H_{35}COO)_3C_3H_5$, obtained from various animal and vegetable fats. **2.** Stearic acid, especially as combined with palmitic acid for making candles, etc. **3.** Fat in solid form. Also **ste′a·rine** (-rin, -rēn). [< F *stéarin* < Gk. *stear* suet]

ste·a·rop·tene (stē′ə·rop′tēn) *n. Chem.* A solid crystalline compound that separates from a volatile oil on standing or exposure to cold: distinguished from *elaeoptene.* [< STEAR-(IC) + (ELAE)OPTENE]

ste·a·tite (stē′ə·tīt) *n.* Massive talc found in extensive beds and quarried for hearths, sink linings, coarse utensils, etc.: also called *soapstone* [< L *steatitis* < Gk. *stear, steatos* suet, tallow] — **ste′a·tit′ic** (-tit′ik) *adj.*

ste·a·to·py·gi·a (stē′ə·tō·pī′jē·ə, -pij′ē·ə) *n.* Abnormal growth of fat on the buttocks, noted especially in women among the Hottentots of Africa. Also **ste′a·to·py′ga** (-pī′gə). [< NL < Gk. *stear, steatos* suet, fat + *pygē* buttock] — **ste′a·to·py′gic** (-pij′ik), **ste′a·to·py′gous** (-pij′gəs) *adj.*

ste·a·tor·rhe·a (stē′ə·tə·rē′ə) *n. Pathol.* Excess fat in fecal discharges. Also **ste′a·tor·rhoe′a.** [< Gk. *stear, steatos* suet + -RRHEA]

Ste·bark (stenm′bärk) The Polish name for TANNENBERG.

sted·fast (sted′fast′, -fäst′, -fəst) See STEADFAST.

steed (stēd) *n.* A horse; especially, a spirited war horse: now chiefly a literary term. [OE *stēda* studhorse]

steek (stēk) *Scot. v.t. & v.i.* To shut; close. — *n.* A stitch.

steel (stēl) *n.* **1.** A tough alloy of iron containing carbon in variable amounts up to about 1.5 percent, malleable under proper conditions, and greatly hardened by sudden cooling. Commercial grades are classified on the basis of carbon content as: **low, mild,** or **soft steel,** with up to about 0.3 percent of carbon; **medium steel,** 0.3 to 0.6 percent of carbon; and **high** or **hard steel,** containing more than 0.6 percent of carbon. The addition of other components, as chromium and nickel, gives a large range of alloys having special properties. **2.** Something made of steel, as a sword. **3.** Hardness of character; steellike nature or quality. **4.** A strip or band of steel, as for stiffening a corset. **5.** The quotation for shares in a steel company. — *adj.* **1.** Made or composed of steel. **2.** Resembling steel, as in hardness. **3.** Adamant; unyielding. — *v.t.* **1.** To cover with steel. **2.** To make hard or strong like steel. **3.** To make unfeeling or unyielding; harden: to *steel* one's heart against misery. [OE *stȳle, stēle*]

steel band A type of percussion band originated in Trinidad that uses as instruments the tops of oil drums hammered out to provide various pitches when struck.

steel blue A color similar to the bluish tinge of certain steels.

steel-die printing (stēl′dī′) Intaglio printing (which see).

Steele (stēl), **Sir Richard,** 1672–1729, British essayist and dramatist born in Ireland: pseudonyms **Isaac Bickerstaffe, Nestor Ironside.**

steel engraving 1. The art and process of engraving on a steel plate. **2.** The impression made from such a plate.

steel gray Any of several shades of gray, like the color of finished steel.

steel·head (stēl′hed′) *n. U.S. & Canadian* The rainbow trout (*Salmo gairdneri*), especially in its migratory stage to and from the sea, highly esteemed as a game fish: also called *salmon trout*.

steel·mak·er (stēl′mā′kər) *n.* A maker of steel; especially, the operator or owner of a steel mill. **— steel′mak′ing** *n.*

steel wool Steel fibers matted together for use as an abrasive, as in cleaning, polishing, etc.

steel·work (stēl′wûrk′) *n.* **1.** Any article or construction of steel. **2.** *pl.* A shop or factory where steel is made or fabricated. **— steel′work′ing** *n.*

steel·work·er (stēl′wûr′kər) *n.* One who works in a steel mill.

steel·y (stē′lē) *adj.* **steel·i·er, steel·i·est 1.** Made of, containing, resembling, or suggesting steel. **2.** Having a steel-like hardness: a *steely* gaze. **— steel′i·ness** *n.*

steel·yard (stēl′yärd′, -yərd, stil′yərd) *n.* A weighing device consisting of a scaled beam, counterpoise, and hooks. The article to be weighed is hung at the short end and the counterpoise weight on the long arm. Also **steel′yards.** [after *Steelyard,* formerly, the London headquarters for Hanseatic traders; a mistranslation of MLG *stalhof* a court where samples of goods are displayed]

Steen (stān), **Jan,** 1626?–79, Dutch painter.

STEELYARDS
a Found at Pompeii.
b Modern.

steen·bok (stān′bok, stēn′-) *n.* A small, fawn-colored African antelope (*Raphicerus campestris*): also called *steinbok, steinbuck.* [< Du. *steenbok* < *steen* stone + *bok* buck]

steep[1] (stēp) *adj.* **1.** Making a large angle with the plane of the horizon; precipitous. **2.** *Informal* Exorbitant; excessive; high, as a price. **—** *n.* A precipitous place, as a cliff or hill. [OE *stēap*] **— steep′ly** *adv.* **— steep′ness** *n.*

— Syn. (adj.) **1.** *Steep, sheer, precipitous,* and *abrupt* mean sloping sharply, as a tract of ground. *Steep* is a relative term; a rise of 100 feet to the mile is *steep* on a railroad, a rise of 500 feet to the mile is *steep* for a horse, a roof or stairway is *steep* if its angle with the horizontal is more than 45°. *Sheer* means vertical or nearly so; *precipitous* is a little less extreme than *sheer. Abrupt* stresses a sudden change of slope or level. **— Ant.** slight, gentle.

steep[2] (stēp) *v.t.* **1.** To soak in a liquid, as for softening, cleansing, extracting an essence, etc.: to *steep* tea; to *steep* cucumbers in brine to make pickles. **2.** To imbue thoroughly; saturate: *steeped* in crime. **—** *v.i.* **3.** To undergo soaking in a liquid. **—** *n.* **1.** The process of steeping, or the state of being steeped. **2.** A liquid or bath for steeping something; especially, a fertilizing liquid for seeds. [ME *stepen,* ? < Scand. Cf. Sw. *stöpa* to steep.] **— steep′er** *n.*

steep·en (stē′pən) *v.t. & v.i.* To make or become steep or steeper.

stee·ple (stē′pəl) *n.* A lofty, usually tapering structure rising above the tower of a church; a spire. [OE *stīpel*]

stee·ple·bush (stē′pəl·boosh′) *n.* An erect shrub (*Spiraea tomentosa*) of the rose family, with dense terminal clusters of rose-colored flowers: also called *hardhack.*

stee·ple·chase (stē′pəl·chās′) *n.* **1.** A race on horseback across country, in which obstacles are to be leaped. **2.** A horse race or foot race over a course artificially prepared, as with hedges, rails, and water jumps. **3.** Any cross-country run. [So called because originally the goal of the racers was a distant church steeple] **— stee′ple·chas′ing** *n.*

stee·ple·chas·er (stē′pəl·chā′sər) *n.* A person or horse that takes part in a steeplechase.

stee·ple·jack (stē′pəl·jak′) *n.* A man whose occupation is to climb steeples and other tall structures to inspect or make repairs. [< STEEPLE + obs. *jack* workman]

steer[1] (stir) *v.t.* **1.** To direct the course of (a vessel or vehicle) by means of a rudder, steering wheel, or other device. **2.** To follow (a course). **3.** To direct; guide; control. **—** *v.i.* **4.** To direct the course of a vessel, vehicle, etc. **5.** To undergo guiding or steering: The car *steers* easily **6.** To follow a course: to *steer* for land. **— to steer clear of** To keep away from; avoid. **—** *n. U.S. Slang* A piece of advice; a tip. [OE *stīeran*] **— steer′a·ble** *adj.* **— steer′er** *n.*

steer[2] (stir) *n.* **1.** A male bovine animal, especially when castrated and from two to four years old. **2.** An ox of any age raised for beef. [OE *stēor*]

steer[3] (stir) *Scot. v.t.* To disturb; molest. **—** *n.* A disturbance; a nudge.

steer·age (stir′ij) *n.* **1.** Formerly, the part of an ocean passenger vessel situated in the forward lower decks, and allotted to passengers paying the lowest fares. **2.** That markedly inferior, overcrowded, third-class accommodations. **3.** The act of steering. **4.** The state of being steered; the effect of the helm on a vessel.

steer·age·way (stir′ij·wā′) *n. Naut.* The lowest speed at which a vessel can be accurately steered.

steer·ing committee (stir′ing) A committee in a legislature or other assemblage that arranges or directs the course of the business to be considered.

steering gear The coordinated mechanism that steers a ship, automotive vehicle, aircraft, bicycle, etc.

steering wheel A wheel turned by the driver or pilot of a vehicle, ship, etc., to change its direction.

steers·man (stirz′mən) *n. pl.* **·men** (-mən) One who steers a boat; a helmsman. **— Syn.** See PILOT.

steeve[1] (stēv) *n.* A derrick or a spar with a block at one end, used in stowing cargo. **—** *v.t.* **steeved, steev·ing 1.** To stow, as cargo in the hold of a vessel, by using a steeve or a jackscrew. **2.** *Scot.* To pack; cram. [< F *estiver* < L *stipare* to compress]

steeve[2] (stēv) *Naut. n.* The angular elevation of a bowsprit from the horizontal: also **steev′ing.** **—** *v.t. & v.i.* **steeved, steev·ing** To set or be set upward at an angle with the horizon. [Origin uncertain. Cf. OE *stīfig* steep.]

Stef·áns·son (stef′ən·sən), **Vilhjálmur,** 1879–1962, U.S. Arctic explorer and anthropologist born in Canada of Icelandic parentage.

Stef·fens (stef′ənz), **(Joseph) Lincoln,** 1866–1936, U.S. journalist.

steg·o·don (steg′ə·don) *n. pl.* **·dons** or **·don** Any of a group of large, extinct mammals of the Pliocene and the Pleistocene, having ridged teeth and related to the mastodons. [< NL < Gk. *stegos* roof + *odous, odontos* tooth]

steg·o·my·ia (steg′ə·mī′ə) *n.* Aedes, a type of mosquito: a former name. [< NL < Gk. *stegos* roof + *myia* fly]

steg·o·sau·rus (steg′ə·sôr′əs) *n. pl.* **·sau·ri** (-sôr′ī) *Paleontol.* Any of a genus (*Stegosaurus*) of herbivorous, ornithiscian dinosaurs of great size that flourished in the western United States during the Upper Jurassic and Lower Cretaceous periods. [< NL < Gk. *stegos* roof + -SAURUS]

Stei·er·mark (shtī′ər·märk) The German name for STYRIA.

stein (stīn) *n.* A beer mug, especially of earthenware. [< G]

Stein (shtīn), **Baron Heinrich Friedrich Karl vom und zum,** 1757–1831, Prussian statesman.

Stein (stīn), **Gertrude,** 1874–1946, U.S. writer active in France.

Stein·am·ang·er (shtīn′äm·äng′ər) See SZOMBATHELY.

Steinbeck (stīn′bek), **John Ernst,** 1902–1968, U.S. writer.

stein·bok (stīn′bok) *n.* A steenbok. Also **stein′buck′** (-buk′).

Stein·metz (stīn′mets), **Charles Proteus,** 1865–1923, U.S. electrical engineer born in Germany.

ste·le[1] (stē′lē) *n. pl.* **·lae** (-lē) or **·les** (-lēz) An upright sculptured slab or tablet of stone, either sepulchral or intended for laws, decrees, treaties, milestones, etc. Also **ste·la** (stē′lə). [< L *stela* < Gk. *stēlē*] **— ste′lar, ste′lene** (-lēn) *adj.*

stele[2] (stēl) *n. Bot.* The central axial cylinder of vascular tissue in plants. [< STELE[1]] **— ste′lic** *adj.*

St. E·li·as (sānt i·lī′əs), **Mount** A peak (18,008 ft.) in the **St. Elias Mountains** in SW Yukon and SE Alaska; filled by an extensive glacier; highest peak, Mt. Logan, 19,850 ft.

stel·lar (stel′ər) *adj.* **1.** Of or pertaining to the stars; astral. **2.** Of or pertaining to a prominent actor or actress or to other persons in the arts: *stellar* attraction. [< LL *stellaris* < L *stella* star]

stel·lar·a·tor (stel′ə·rā′tər) *n. Physics* A device consisting of a series of magnetizing coils surrounding a toroidal glass tube in which a plasma may be briefly heated to thermonuclear temperatures of about 100 million degrees C. [< STELLAR + -ATOR; from the great temperatures developed]

stel·late (stel′it, -āt) *adj.* Star-shaped or starlike; radiating. Also **stel·lat·ed** (stel′ā·tid). [< L *stellatus,* pp. of *stellare* to cover with stars < *stella* star] **— stel′late·ly** *adv.*

stelli- *combining form* Star: *stelliferous.* [< L *stella* star]

stel·lif·er·ous (ste·lif′ər·əs) *adj.* Abounding with stars. [< STELLI- + -FEROUS]

stel·li·form (stel′ə·fôrm) *adj.* Formed like a star; starshaped. [< NL *stelliformis* < L *stella* star + *forma* form]

stel·lu·lar (stel′yə·lər) *adj.* **1.** Bespangled with fine stars. **2.** Shaped like or resembling little stars. [< LL *stellula* little star]

St. El·mo's fire (sānt el′mōz) A luminous charge of atmospheric electricity sometimes appearing on the masts and yardarms of ships, on church steeples, etc.: also called *corposant.* Also **St. Elmo's light.**

stem[1] (stem) *n.* **1.** The ascending axis or stalk of a plant, as distinguished from the root. **2.** The main body or stalk of a tree, shrub, or other plant, rising above the ground or other rooting place. **3.** The relatively slender growth supporting the fruit, flower, or leaf of a plant; a stalk, peduncle, pedicel, or petiole. ◆ Collateral adjective: *cauline.* **4.** A bunch of bananas. **5.** The long, slender, usually cylindrical portion of an instrument: a pipe *stem.* **6.** The slender upright support of a goblet, wineglass, vase, etc. **7.** In a watch, the small, projecting, knobbed rod used for winding the mainspring. **8.** In some locks, the central circular part about which the key turns. **9.** A shaft, as of a hair or feather. **10.** A line of descendants from a particular ancestor. **11.** An ethnic line; race. **12.** *Printing* The upright stroke of a type face or letter. **13.** *Music* The line attached to the head of a written musical note. **14.** *Ling.* A root plus a thematic vowel, as the Latin stem *luci-* ("light") in *lucifer* ("light-bearer"), composed of the root *luc-* plus the thematic vowel *-i-*: also called *theme.* **15.** *Electr.* The sealed, tubular glass section at the base of an incandescent lamp, serving to lead the filaments into the evacuated bulb. For illustration see INCANDESCENT LAMP. — *v.* **stemmed, stem·ming** *v.t.* **1.** To remove the stems of or from. **2.** To supply with stems. — *v.i.* **3.** To be descended or derived: to *stem* from John Alden. Abbr. *s.* [OE *stemn, stefn* stem of a tree, prow of a ship] — **stem′·less** *adj.*

stem² (stem) *n. Naut.* **1.** A nearly upright timber or metal piece uniting the two sides of a vessel at the bow. **2.** The bow or prow of a vessel. — **from stem to stern** From end to end; thoroughly. — *v.* **stemmed, stem·ming** *v.t.* **1.** To resist or make progress against, as a current: said of a vessel. **2.** To stand firm or make progress against (any opposing force): to *stem* the tide. **3.** To strike with the stem (of a vessel). [< STEM¹, in sense "a tree trunk"]

stem³ (stem) *v.t.* **stemmed, stem·ming 1.** To stop, hold back, or dam up, as a current; stanch. **2.** To make tight, as a joint; to plug. [< ON *stemma* to stop]

stem·mer (stem′ər) *n.* **1.** One who removes stems. **2.** A device for stemming fruits, as grapes.

stem·son (stem′sən) *n. Naut.* A curved supporting timber bolted to the stem and keelson of a vessel near the bow. [< STEM² + (KEEL)SON]

stem turn In skiing, a turn made by placing the points of the skis nearly together and the ends wide apart, then placing the weight on the outside ski.

stem·ware (stem′wâr′) *n.* Drinking vessels with stems, as goblets, taken collectively.

stem-wind·er (stem′wīn′dər) *n.* A watch wound by turning the crown of the stem.

stem-wind·ing (stem′wīn′ding) *adj.* Denoting a stem-winder.

stench (stench) *n.* A foul or offensive odor; stink. — Syn. See SMELL. [OE *stenc*]

sten·cil (sten′səl) *n.* **1.** A sheet of paper, etc., in which a pattern is cut by means of spaces or dots, through which applied paint or ink penetrates to a surface beneath. **2.** A decoration or the like produced by stenciling. — *v.t.* **sten·ciled,** or **·cilled, sten·cil·ing** or **·cil·ling** To mark with a stencil. [Prob. ME *stansel* to decorate with many colors < OF *estenceler,* ult. < L *scintilla* spark] — **sten′cil·er** or **sten′cil·ler** *n.*

Sten·dhal (stän·dàl′) Pseudonym of *Marie Henri Beyle,* 1783–1842, French novelist and critic.

sten·gah (steng′gə) *n.* In Malaya, a small whisky and soda. [< Malay *stengah* half]

steno- *combining form* Tight; narrow; contracted: *stenography.* Also, before vowels, **sten-.** [< Gk. *stenos* narrow]

steno. or **stenog.** Stenographer; stenography: also **sten.**

sten·o·graph (sten′ə·graf, -gräf) *n.* **1.** A character or writing in shorthand. **2.** A keyboard machine for printing letters or characters as a means of shorthand.

ste·nog·ra·pher (stə·nog′rə·fər) *n.* One who writes stenography or is skilled in shorthand. Also **ste·nog′ra·phist.** Abbr. *sten., steno., stenog.*

ste·nog·ra·phy (stə·nog′rə·fē) *n.* The art of writing by the use of contractions or arbitrary symbols; shorthand; also, the transcription of shorthand notes. Abbr. *sten., steno., stenog.* [< STENO- + -GRAPHY] — **sten·o·graph·ic** (sten′ə·graf′ik) or **·i·cal** *adj.* — **sten′o·graph′i·cal·ly** *adv.*

sten·o·phyl·lous (sten′ō·fil′əs) *adj. Bot.* Characterized by narrow leaves.

ste·no·sis (sti·nō′sis) *n. Pathol.* Narrowing of a duct or canal in the body. [< NL < Gk. *stenōsis* < *stenos* narrow]

sten·o·trop·ic (sten′ə·trop′ik) *adj. Ecol.* Having a narrow range of adaptability to environmental changes, as a species.

sten·o·type (sten′ə·tīp) *n.* **1.** A letter or combination of letters representing a sound, word, or phrase, especially in shorthand. **2.** A Stenotype.

Sten·o·type (sten′ə·tīp) *n.* A keyboard-operated machine used in stenotypy: a trade name. Also *stenotype.*

sten·o·typ·y (sten′ə·tī′pē) *n.* A system of shorthand employing ordinary letters alone or in various combinations to represent specific sounds, words, or phrases.

sten·tor (sten′tôr) *n.* **1.** One who possesses an uncommonly strong, loud voice. **2.** Any of a genus (*Stentor*) of freshwater, ciliate protozoans having trumpet-shaped bodies capable of attachment by their lower ends. [< *Stentor*]

Sten·tor (sten′tôr) In the *Iliad,* a herald famous for his loud voice.

sten·to·ri·an (sten·tôr′ē·ən, -tō′rē-) *adj.* Extremely loud.

step (step) *n.* **1.** An act of progressive motion that requires one of the supporting limbs of the body to be thrust in the direction of the movement, and to reassume its function of support; a pace. **2.** The distance passed over in making

such a motion. **3.** Any short distance; a space easily traversed. **4.** That which the foot rests upon in ascending or descending, as a stair or ladder rung. **5.** A single action or proceeding regarded as leading to something: a *step* toward emancipation. **6.** An advance or promotion that forms one of a series; grade; degree. **7.** The manner of stepping; walk; gait. **8.** The sound of a footfall. **9.** A footprint; track. **10.** *pl.* Progression by walking; walk. **11.** A combination of foot movements in dancing, forming a pattern that may be repeated, varied, or elaborated: the tango *step.* **12.** *Music* An interval corresponding to one degree of a scale or staff; a major or minor second. **13.** Something resembling a step, as a socket, supporting framework, etc.: the *step* of a mast. **14.** A steplike projection or part, as of the bit of a key. **15.** A break in the contour of a float or hull, as of a seaplane, designed to lessen resistance and improve control. — **in step 1.** Walking, dancing, marching, etc., in accord with the proper rhythm or cadence, or in conformity with others. **2.** *Informal* In agreement or conformity. — **out of step** Not in step. — **to take steps** To adopt measures, as to attain an end. — *v.* **stepped, step·ping** *v.i.* **1.** To move forward or backward by taking a step or steps. **2.** To go by foot; walk a short distance: to *step* across the street. **3.** To move with measured, dignified, or graceful steps. **4.** To move or act quickly or briskly. **5.** To pass into a situation, circumstance, etc., as if in a single step: He *stepped* into a fortune. — *v.t.* **6.** To take (a pace, stride, etc.). **7.** To perform the steps of: to *step* a quadrille. **8.** To place or move (the foot) in taking a step. **9.** To measure by taking steps: often with *off*: to *step* off five yards. **10.** To cut or arrange in steps. **11.** *Naut.* To place the lower end of (a mast) in its step. — **to step down 1.** To decrease gradually, or by steps or degrees. **2.** To resign from an office or position; abdicate. — **to step in** To begin to take part; intervene. — **to step on** (or **upon**) **1.** To put the foot down on; tread upon. **2.** To put the foot on so as to activate, as a brake or treadle. **3.** *Informal* To reprove or subdue. — **to step on it** *Informal* To hurry; hasten. — **to step out 1.** To go outside, especially for a short while. **2.** *Informal* To go out for fun or entertainment. **3.** To quit; resign. **4.** To walk vigorously and with long strides. — **to step up** To increase; raise; accelerate. [OE *stæpe*]

step- *combining form* Related through the previous marriage of a parent or spouse, but not by blood: *stepchild.* [OE *stēop-* < stem of *ástÿpan, ástēpan* to bereave, orphan]

step·broth·er (step′bruth′ər) *n.* The son of one's stepparent by a former marriage.

step·child (step′chīld′) *n.* The child of one's husband or wife by a former marriage.

step·dame (step′dām′) *n. Archaic* A stepmother.

step·daugh·ter (step′dô′tər) *n.* A female stepchild.

step-down (step′doun′) *adj.* **1.** Decreasing by stages. **2.** *Electr.* Converting a current of high voltage into one of low voltage, as a transformer. **3.** *Mech.* Designating a gear that transfers motion at a reduced rate. Opposed to *step-up.*

step·fa·ther (step′fä′thər) *n.* The husband of one's mother, other than one's own father.

Ste·phen (stē′vən), **Saint** The first Christian martyr. *Acts* vii 60.

Ste·phen (stē′vən), **Sir Leslie,** 1832–1904, English biographer, critic, and man of letters.

Stephen I, 975?–1038, first king of Hungary 1000–38: called **Saint Stephen, the Apostle of Hungary.**

Stephen of Blois, 1097?–1154, king of England 1135–54.

Ste·phens (stē′vənz), **Alexander Hamilton,** 1812–83, U.S. legislator and, later, vice president of the Confederacy. — **James,** 1882–1950, Irish poet and novelist.

Ste·phen·son (stē′vən·sən), **George,** 1781–1848, English engineer; perfected the locomotive. — **Robert,** 1803–59, English engineer; devised the tubular bridge; son of the preceding.

step-in (step′in′) *n.* **1.** A woman's brief underpants: also **step′-ins′.** **2.** A pumplike shoe. — *adj.* Put on by being stepped into.

Step·i·nac (step′ē-näts), **Alojzije,** 1898–1960, Yugoslav cardinal; imprisoned 1946–51.

step·lad·der (step′lad′ər) *n.* A set of portable steps with, usually, a hinged frame at the back, that may be extended to support the steps in an upright position.

step·moth·er (step′muth′ər) *n.* The wife of one's father, other than one's own mother.

Step·ney (step′nē) *n.* A metropolitan borough of eastern London, including the districts of Whitechapel and Limehouse; site of the Tower of London; pop. 91,940 (1961).

step·par·ent (step′pâr′ənt) *n.* A stepfather or stepmother.

steppe (step) *n.* A vast plain devoid of forest; especially, one of the extensive plains in Russia and Siberia. — Syn. See PLAIN¹. [< Russian *step′*]

step·per (step′ər) *n.* **1.** One who or that which steps: The horse is a high *stepper.* **2.** *Slang* A dancer.

Steppes (steps), **The** See KIRGHIZ STEPPE.

step·ping·stone (step′ing·stōn′) *n.* **1.** A stone affording a footrest, as for crossing a stream. **2.** A preliminary step or stage in the fulfillment of a goal: *steppingstones* to success.

step·sis·ter (step′sis′tər) *n.* The daughter of one's stepparent by a former marriage.
step·son (step′sun′) *n.* A male stepchild.
step-up (step′up′) *adj.* **1.** Increasing by stages. **2.** *Electr.* Converting a current of low voltage into one of high voltage. **3.** Designating a gear that transfers motion at an increased rate. Opposed to *step-down.*
step·wise (step′wīz′) *adv.* In the manner of steps; step by step.
ster. Sterling.
-ster *suffix of nouns* **1.** One who makes or is occupied with: often pejorative: *songster, prankster.* **2.** One who belongs or is related to: *gangster.* **3.** One who is: *youngster.* [OE *-estre,* fem. suffix expressing the agent]
ste·ra·di·an (sti·rā′dē·ən) *n.* The unit of measurement for solid angles; the solid angle that on a sphere encloses a surface equivalent to the square of a radius: also called *spheradian.* [< Gk. *stereos* solid + RADIAN]
ster·co·ra·ceous (stûr′kə·rā′shəs) *adj.* Consisting of or pertaining to excrement or dung. Also **ster·co·rous** (stûr′kər·əs). [< STERCOR(I)- + -ACEOUS]
stercori- *combining form* Dung; excrement: *stercoricolous:* also, before vowels, **stercor-.** Also **sterco-.** [< L *stercus, stercoris* dung]
ster·co·ric·o·lous (stûr′kə·rik′ə·ləs) *n.* Living in manure, as some insects. [< STERCORI- + -COLOUS]
ster·cu·li·a·ceous (stûr′kyoo′lē·ā′shəs) *adj. Bot.* Designating or belonging to a family (*Sterculiaceae*) of chiefly tropical herbs, shrubs, and trees, including the cacao and the colanut tree. [< NL < L *Sterculius,* the deity of manuring < *stercus* dung]
stere (stir) *n.* In the metric system, a measure of capacity equal to one cubic meter. Abbr. *s., st.* See table inside back cover. [< F *stère* < Gk. *stereos* solid]
ster·e·o (ster′ē·ō, stir′-) *n.* A stereophonic system. —*adj.* Stereophonic.
stereo- *combining form* Solid; firm; hard; three-dimensional: *stereoscope.* Also, before vowels, **stere-.** [< Gk. *stereos* hard]
ster·e·o·bate (ster′ē·ə·bāt′, stir′-) *n. Archit.* A substructure, continuous base, or solid platform without columns. Compare STYLOBATE. [< STEREO- + Gk. *batēs* that which steps] — **ster′e·o·bat′ic** (-bat′ik) *adj.*
ster·e·o·chem·is·try (ster′ē·ō·kem′is·trē, stir′-) *n.* The branch of chemistry that treats of the spatial arrangement of atoms and molecules.
ster·e·o·chrome (ster′ē·ō·krōm′, stir′-) *n.* A picture produced by stereochromy.
ster·e·o·chro·my (ster′ē·ō·krō′mē, stir′-) *n.* The art or process of painting with pigments mixed with waterglass. [< STEREO- + Gk. *chrōma* color] — **ster·e·o·chro′mic** *adj.* — **ster′e·o·chro′mi·cal·ly** *adv.*
ster·e·o·gram (ster′ē·ə·gram′, stir′-) *n.* **1.** A picture or diagram giving the impression of a solid in relief. **2.** A stereograph.
ster·e·o·graph (ster′ē·ə·graf′, -gräf′, stir′-) *n.* **1.** A single or double photograph for viewing through a stereoscope. **2.** An instrument for making projections of solid objects.
ster·e·og·ra·phy (ster′ē·og′rə·fē, stir′-) *n.* **1.** The art of representing solids on a plane by means of lines; perspective. **2.** The branch of geometry that treats of the construction of regularly bounded solids. — **ster′e·o·graph′ic** (-ə·graf′ik) or **·i·cal** *adj.* — **ster′e·o·graph′i·cal·ly** *adv.*
ster·e·o·i·som·er·ism (ster′ē·ō·ī·som′ə·riz′əm, stir′-) *n. Chem.* An isomerism that depends on the spatial arrangement of the atoms or groups in an organic compound. — **ster′e·o·i′so·mer′ic** (-ī′sō·mer′ik), **ster′e·o·mer′ic** *adj.*
ster·e·om·e·try (ster′ē·om′ə·trē, stir′-) *n.* The measurement of the volume of solids. [< STEREO- + -METRY] — **ster′e·o·met′ric** (-ō·met′rik) or **·ri·cal** *adj.* — **ster′e·o·met′ri·cal·ly** *adv.*
ster·e·o·phone (ster′ē·ə·fōn′, stir′-) *n.* Any sound-transmitting system equipped with stereophonic devices.
ster·e·o·phon·ic (ster′ē·ə·fon′ik, stir′-) *adj.* **1.** Pertaining to, designed for, or characterized by the perception of sound by both ears; binaural. **2.** *Electronics* **a** Designating a system of sound reproduction in which two or more receivers or loudspeakers are so placed as to give the effect of hearing the sound from more than one direction: distinguished from *monaural.* **b** Designating a technique of recording or broadcasting that permits the use of such a system: also *binaural.* Also *stereo.* — **ster′e·o·phon′i·cal·ly** *adv.* — **ster·e·o·phon·y** (ster′ē·ə·fō′nē, stir′-, ster′ē·ə·fō′nē, stir′-) *n.* Compare QUADRAPHONIC.
ster·e·op·sis (ster′ē·op′sis, stir′-) *n.* Stereoscopic vision. [< STERE(O)- + -OPSIS]
ster·e·op·ti·con (ster′ē·op′ti·kon, stir′-) *n.* A double slide projector arranged to combine two images of the same object or scene, or used to bring one image after another on the screen. [< STEREO- + Gk. *optikos* of sight]
ster·e·o·scope (ster′ē·ə·skōp′, stir′-) *n.* An instrument for blending into one image two pictures of an object from

slightly different points of view, so as to produce the impression of relief and solidity. [< STEREO- + -SCOPE] — **ster′e·o·scop′ic** (-skop′ik) or **·i·cal** *adj.* — **ster′e·o·scop′i·cal·ly** *adv.*
ster·e·os·co·py (ster′ē·os′kə·pē, stir′-) *n.* **1.** The art of making or using stereoscopes and stereoscopic slides. **2.** The viewing of objects as in three dimensions. — **ster′e·os′co·pist** *n.*

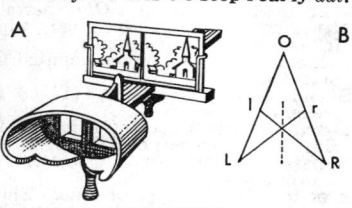

STEREOSCOPE

A Stereoscope. *B* The eyes, looking along *Ll* and *Rr* respectively, combine the images of points *l* and *r* at *O.* A card (represented by the dotted line) blocks the images that would be seen along *Lr* and *Rl.*

ster·e·o·tax·is (ster′ē·ə·tak′sis, stir′-) *n. Biol.* A movement of an organism with reference to a solid object: also called *thigmotaxis.* Also **ster′e·o·tax′y** (-tak′sē). — **ster′e·o·tac′tic** or **·ti·cal** *adj.* — **ster′e·o·tac′ti·cal·ly** *adv.*
ster·e·ot·ro·pism (ster′ē·ot′rə·piz′əm, stir′-) *n. Biol.* Involuntary response of an organism to contact with a foreign body. — **ster′e·o·trop′ic** (-trop′ik) *adj.*
ster·e·o·type (ster′ē·ə·tīp′, stir′-) *n.* **1.** A plate cast in type metal from a matrix, as of papier-maché, and reproducing on its surface the composed type or other material impressed upon the matrix. **2.** Anything made or processed in this way. **3.** Stereotypy. **4.** A conventional or hackneyed expression, custom, mental image, etc. **5.** A person possessing or believed to possess characteristics or qualities that typify a particular group. —*v.t.* **·typed, ·typ·ing 1.** To make a stereotype of. **2.** To fix firmly or unalterably.
ster·e·o·typed (ster′ē·ə·tīpt′, stir′-) *adj.* **1.** Formalized; hackneyed; trite. **2.** Produced from a stereotype.
ster·e·o·typ·er (ster′ē·ə·tī′pər, stir′-) *n.* **1.** One who makes stereotype plates. **2.** A stereotype-making machine for making embossed plates from which printing for the blind is done. Also **ster′e·o·typ′ist.** — **ster′e·o·typ′ic** (-tip′ik), **ster′e·o·typ′i·cal** *adj.*
ster·e·o·typ·y (ster′ē·ə·tī′pē, stir′-) *n.* The art or act of making stereotypes: also called *stereotype.* Also **ster′e·o·typ′er·y** (-tī′pər·ē).
ster·e·o·vi·sion (ster′ē·ō·vizh′ən, stir′-) *n.* Three-dimensional vision.
ster·ic (ster′ik, stir′-) *adj. Chem.* Denoting relative position in space: said of the atoms in a molecule. Also **ster′i·cal.** [< Gk. *stereos* solid]
ster·il·ant (ster′əl·ənt) *n.* That which sterilizes.
ster·ile (ster′əl, *esp. Brit.* -īl) *adj.* **1.** Having no reproductive power; barren. **2.** *Bot.* Producing no pistil or no spores; incapable of germinating. **3.** Lacking productiveness or fertility: *sterile* soil. **4.** Containing no bacteria or other microorganisms; aseptic. **5.** Lacking in vigor or imagination; uninspiring; stale: *sterile* verse. **6.** *Econ.* Unproductive; inactive, as a reserve of gold that is not used for credit. [< L *sterilis* barren] — **ster′ile·ly** *adv.* — **ster′ile·ness** *n.*
ste·ril·i·ty (stə·ril′ə·tē) *n.* The state or quality of being sterile; barrenness.
ster·il·i·za·tion (ster′əl·ə·zā′shən, -ī·zā′-) *n.* **1.** The act or process of making sterile. **2.** The condition of being sterile,
ster·il·ize (ster′əl·īz) *v.t.* **·ized, ·iz·ing 1.** To free from infective or pathogenic microorganisms. **2.** To deprive of reproductive or reproductive power, especially by surgical operation on the Fallopian tubes or on the vas deferens. **3.** To make barren; exhaust the productiveness of. **4.** To make powerless. **5.** *Econ.* To reserve (gold) without using it for credit. Also *Brit.* **ster′il·ise.** — **ster′il·iz′er** *n.*
ster·let (stûr′lit) *n.* A small sturgeon (*Acipenser ruthenus*) found in the Black, Caspian, and Azov seas, yielding superior caviar and isinglass. [< Russian *sterlyad′*]
ster·ling (stûr′ling) *n.* **1.** The official standard of fineness for British coins: for silver, 0.500; for gold, 0.91666. **2.** Sterling silver, 0.925 fine, as used in manufacturing articles, as tableware, etc.; also, an article or articles made of it. **3.** A former silver penny of England and Scotland. —*adj.* **1.** Made of or payable in sterling. **2.** Made of sterling silver. **3.** Having accepted worth; genuine. **4.** Valuable; esteemed: *sterling* qualities. Abbr. *ster., stg.* [Prob. OE *steorra* star + -LING; because a star was stamped on some of the coins]
stern¹ (stûrn) *adj.* **1.** Proceeding from or marked by severity or harshness; unyielding. **2.** Having an austere disposition; strict; severe. **3.** Inspiring fear; awesome. **4.** Resolute; stout: a *stern* resolve. [OE *styrne*] — **stern′ly** *adv.* — **stern′ness** *n.*
stern² (stûrn) *n.* **1.** *Naut.* The back or rear part of a ship, boat, etc. **2.** The hindmost part of any object. —*adj.* Situated at or belonging to the stern. [< ON *stjörn* steering, rudder < *stýra* to steer]

Stern (stûrn), **G**(**ladys**) **B**(**ronwyn**), born 1890, English novelist, dramatist, and short-story writer. — **Otto**, 1888–1969, U.S. physicist born in Germany.

ster·nal (stûr′nəl) *adj.* Of or pertaining to the sternum.

stern chase *Naut.* A chase in which the pursuing vessel follows in the other's course.

stern chaser A cannon mounted in the stern to fire at a pursuing ship.

Sterne (stûrn), **Laurence**, 1713–68, British novelist born in Ireland.

stern·fore·most (stûrn′fôr′mōst′, -məst, -fôr′-) *adv.* **1.** Hind side foremost; backward. **2.** Awkwardly; clumsily.

stern·most (stûrn′mōst′, -məst) *adj.* Farthest to the rear or stern.

sterno- *combining form Anat.* The sternum. Also, before vowels, **stern-**. [< L *sternum* or Gk. *stérnon* breast]

stern·post (stûrn′pōst′) *n. Naut.* The main vertical post of the stern frame of a vessel, to which the rudder is attached.

stern sheets *Naut.* The inside stern portion of a boat; the space in a boat abaft the thwarts.

stern·son (stûrn′sən) *n. Naut.* An inner sternpost attached to the center keelson, to strengthen the stern frame. Also **stern′knee′** (-nē′), **sternson knee.** [< STERN² + (KEEL)SON]

ster·num (stûr′nəm) *n., pl.* **·na** (-nə) or **·nums** *Anat.* The breastbone that forms the ventral support of the ribs in most vertebrates, consisting in man of the manubrium, the gladiolus, and the xiphisternum. For illustration see THORAX. [< L < Gk. *stérnon* breast]

ster·nu·ta·tion (stûr′nyə-tā′shən) *n.* **1.** The act of sneezing. **2.** A sneeze or the noise produced by it. [< L *sternutatio, -onis* < *sternutare*, freq. of *sternuere* to sneeze]

ster·nu·ta·tor (stûr′nyə-tā′tər) *n.* A chemical-warfare agent having a strongly irritant effect upon the nasal and respiratory passages

ster·nu·ta·to·ry (stər-nyōō′tə-tôr′ē, -tō′rē, -nōō′-) *adj.* Causing or tending to cause sneezing: also **ster·nu′ta·tive** (-tə-tiv). — *n., pl.* **·ries** A sternutatory substance.

stern·ward (stûrn′wərd) *adj. & adv.* Toward the stern; astern. Also **stern′wards.**

stern·way (stûrn′wā′) *n. Naut.* Backward movement of a vessel.

stern-wheel·er (stûrn′hwē′lər) *n.* A steamboat of small draft propelled by one large paddle wheel at the stern.

STERN-WHEELER

ster·oid (ster′oid) *n. Biochem.* Any of a large group of fat-soluble organic compounds widely distributed in nature, including the sterols, the bile acids, and the sex hormones. [< STER(OL) + -OID]

ster·ol (ster′ōl, -ol) *n. Biochem.* Any of a class of complex, chiefly unsaturated solid alcohols, widely distributed in plant and animal tissue, as cholesterol. [Contr. of CHOLESTEROL]

Ster·o·pe (ster′ə-pē) In Greek mythology, one of the Pleiades: also called *Asterope.* — *n. Astron.* One of the six visible stars in the Pleiades cluster.

ster·tor (stûr′tər) *n.* A deep snore or snoring. [< NL < L *stertere* to snore]

ster·tor·ous (stûr′tər-əs) *adj.* Characterized by snoring or accompanied by a snoring sound: *stertorous* breathing. — **ster′tor·ous·ly** *adv.* — **ster′tor·ous·ness** *n.*

stet (stet) Let it stand: a direction used in proofreading to indicate that a word, letter, etc., marked for omission or correction is to remain. *Abbr. st.* — *v.t.* **stet·ted, stet·ting** To cancel a former correction or omission of by marking with the word *stet.* Compare DELE. [< L, 3rd person sing. subjunctive of *stare* to stand, stay]

stetho- *combining form* The breast or chest; pectoral: *stethoscope.* Also, before vowels, **steth-.** [< Gk. *stéthos* breast]

ste·thom·e·ter (ste-thom′ə-tər) *n.* An instrument to measure the expansion of the chest in breathing. [< STETHO- + -METER]

steth·o·scope (steth′ə-skōp) *n. Med.* An apparatus for auscultation, adapted for conveying the sounds of the body to the examiner's ear or ears. — **steth′o·scop′ic** (-skop′ik), **steth′o·scop′i·cal** *adj.* — **steth′o·scop′i·cal·ly** *adv.* — **ste·thos·co·py** (ste-thos′kə-pē) *n.*

Stet·son (stet′sən) *n.* A hat; especially, one of felt with high crown and wide brim: a trade name. [after John Batterson *Stetson*, 1830–1906, U.S. hatmaker]

Stet·tin (stet′in, *Ger.* shte-tēn′) A port city in NW Poland, on the Oder; pop. 322,000 (est. 1968): Polish *Szczecin.*

Stet·tin·i·us (stə-tin′ē-əs, -tin′yəs), **Edward Riley**, 1900–49, U.S. industrialist and statesman.

Steu·ben (stōō′bən, *Ger.* shtoi′bən), **Baron Friedrich Wilhelm Ludolph Gerhard Augustin von**, 1730–94, Prussian general; served under Washington in the Revolutionary War.

Steu·ben·ville (stōō′bən-vil) A city in eastern Ohio, on the Ohio River; pop. 30,771.

ste·ve·dore (stē′və-dôr, -dōr) *n.* One whose business is stowing or unloading the holds of vessels. — *v.t. & v.i.* **·dored, ·dor·ing** To load or unload (a vessel). [< Sp. *estivador* < *estivar* to stow < L *stipare* to compress, stuff]

stevedore's knot A knot used by stevedores to prevent unreeving. Also **stevedore knot.**

Ste·vens (stē′vənz), **Thaddeus**, 1792–1868, U.S. statesman; formulated the Reconstruction Acts; introduced impeachment proceedings against President Andrew Johnson. — **Wallace**, 1879–1955, U.S. poet and businessman.

Ste·ven·son (stē′vən-sən), **Adlai Ewing**, 1900–1965, U.S. lawyer and political leader. —**Robert Louis** (**Balfour**), 1850–94, Scottish novelist and essayist active in the United States and Samoa.

STEVE-DORE'S KNOT

stew (stōō, styōō) *v.t. & v.i.* **1.** To boil slowly and gently; seethe; keep or be at the simmering point. **2.** *Informal* To worry. — *n.* **1.** Stewed food, especially a preparation of meat or fish and various vegetables cooked together by stewing. **2.** *Informal* Mental agitation; worry. **3.** *pl. Archaic* A brothel. **4.** *Obs.* A room heated for bathing or drying. [< OF *estuver*, prob. ult. < L *ex-* out + *tufare* < Gk. *typhos* steam, vapor]

stew·ard (stōō′ərd, styōō′-) *n.* **1.** One who is entrusted with the management of property, finances, or other affairs not his own; an administrator. **2.** One who has charge of buying provisions, managing servants, etc., in a private residence or in a club, hotel, etc. **3.** On a ship: **a** One in charge of provisions and usually of the tables. **b** One who administers to the comfort of the guests. **4.** On an airplane or bus, one who waits on the passengers. **5.** One who manages any affair: *steward* of the races. **6.** A shop steward (which see). — **stew′ard·ess** *n.fem.* [OE *stiweard* < *stī* hall, sty + *weard* ward, keeper]

stew·ard·ship (stōō′ərd-ship, styōō′-) *n.* **1.** The office, term, or duties of a steward. **2.** The employment or use of one's time, talents, and possessions.

Stew·art (stōō′ərt, styōō′-), **Dugald**, 1753–1828, Scottish philosopher. — **Potter**, born 1915, U.S. jurist; associate justice of the Supreme Court 1958–.

Stew·art (stōō′ərt, styōō′-) See STUART (the royal family).

Stewart Island An island of New Zealand south of South Island; 670 sq. mi.

stewed (stōōd, styōōd) *adj.* **1.** Cooked by stewing. **2.** *Slang* Drunk.

stew·pan (stōō′pan, styōō′-) *n.* A cooking vessel used for stewing.

stey (stā) *adj. Scot.* **1.** Steep. **2.** Haughty; lofty.

stg. Sterling.

St. Gal·len (sänt gal′ən, *Ger.* zängkt gäl′ən) A Canton in NE Switzerland; 776 sq. mi.; pop. 363,000 (1965); capital, **St. Gallen**, site of a seventh-century Benedictine abbey; pop. 78,900 (1965). Also **St. Gall** (sänt gôl′, *Fr.* saṅ gàl′).

stge. Storage.

St. George's (sänt jôr′jiz) The capital of Grenada, The West Indies; pop. 7,305 (1960). Also **St. George.**

St. George's Channel A strait between Ireland and Wales, connecting the Irish Sea with the Atlantic Ocean; 100 mi. long, 50 to 95 mi. wide.

St. George's cross The cross of St. George, the patron saint of England, the same shape as the Greek cross: also called *red cross.* For illustration see CROSS.

St. Gott·hard (sänt got′ərd, *Ger.* zängkt gôt′härt) A mountain group in south central Switzerland; highest peak, Pizzo Rotondo, 10,483 ft.; site of **St. Gotthard Pass;** elevation 6,929 ft., and **St. Gotthard Tunnel;** length 9.25 mi.; elevation 3,786 ft. Also **St. Got′hard** (*Fr.* saṅ gô-tàr′).

St. He·le·na (sänt hə-lē′nə) An island in the South Atlantic comprising a British Colony with Ascension Island and the Tristan da Cunha group as dependencies; 153 sq. mi.; pop. 4,649 (1966); capital, Jamestown; site of Napoleon's exile, 1815–21.

St. Hel·ens (sänt hel′ənz) A county borough in SW Lancashire, England; pop. 108,348 (1961).

St. Hel·ier (sänt hel′yər) The capital of Jersey, Channel Islands; pop. about 26,000.

sthe·ni·a (sthē′nē-ə, sthi-nī′ə) *n. Med.* Unusual energy or vigor; excited force. [< NL < Gk. *sthenos* strength]

sthen·ic (sthen′ik) *adj.* **1.** Exhibiting activity or energy. **2.** Having or indicating vigor. [< Gk. *sthenos* strength]

Sthe·no (sthē′nō, sthen′ō) One of the Gorgons.

sti·ac·cia·to (styät-chä′tō) *n.* An object in lower relief than bas-relief, as the very low relief used on coins. See RELIEF. [< Ital., crushed, flattened, pp. of *stiacciare*]

stib·ine (stib′ēn, -in) *n. Chem.* A colorless poisonous gas, SbH₃, formed by decomposing antimony compounds in the presence of hydrogen. [< STIB(IUM) + -INE²]

stib·i·um (stib′ē-əm) *n.* Antimony. [< L < Gk. *stibi*] — **stib′i·al** *adj.*

stib·nite (stib′nīt) *n.* A metallic, steel-gray, crystalline antimony sulfide, Sb₂S₃, an important ore of antimony: also called *antimony glance.* [< STIB(I)N(E) + -ITE²]

stich (stik) *n.* **1.** A line of the Bible. **2.** A line of poetry; a verse. [< Gk. *stichos* row]
stich·ic (stik'ik) *adj.* **1.** Relating to or consisting of stichs. **2.** Metrically the same throughout: said of verses.
sti·chom·e·try (sti·kom'ə·trē) *n.* The practice of writing prose in line lengths corresponding to the sense, much used before the adoption of punctuation. [< Gk. *stichos* line + -METRY] — **stich·o·met·ric** (stik'ə·met'rik) or **·ri·cal** *adj.*
sti·chom·y·thy (sti·kom'ə·thē) *n.* The arrangement of a dialogue in alternate lines of verse, characteristic of ancient Greek drama, poetry, and disputation: also spelled *stychomythia*. Also **stich'o·myth'i·a.** [< Gk. *stichos* line + *mythos* speech] — **stich·o·myth·ic** (stik'ə·mith'ik) *adj.*
-stichous *combining form* Having (a specified number of) rows: *tristichous.* [< Gk. *stichos* row, line]
stich·wort (stich'wûrt') See STITCHWORT.
stick (stik) *n.* **1.** A slender piece of wood, as a branch cut from a tree or bush, a baton or wand, etc. **2.** *Brit.* A cane. **3.** Anything resembling a stick in form: a *stick* of candy or dynamite. **4.** *Printing* **a** A composing stick. **b** As much type as a composing stick will hold: also **stick'ful'.** **5.** A piece of wood of any size, cut for fuel, lumber, or timber. **6.** *Aeron.* The control lever of an airplane, that operates the elevators and ailerons. **7.** A poke, stab, or thrust with a stick or pointed instrument. **8.** *Archaic* A difficulty or obstacle; hesitation; stop. **9.** The state of being stuck together; adhesion. **10.** In sports, a baseball bat, hockey stick, racing hurdle, etc. **11.** A timber tree. **12.** *Informal* A stiff, inert, or dull person. **13.** *Slang* Any alcoholic ingredient in an otherwise nonalcoholic drink. **14.** *Informal* The mast of a ship. **15.** *Mil.* A group of bombs released consecutively in a straight line crossing the target area. **16.** A stalk, as of asparagus. **17.** *Informal* A conductor's baton. — **the sticks 1.** A timber forest. **2.** *Informal* An obscure rural district; the backwoods or country. — *v.* **stuck** or (*for defs. 15, 16*) **sticked, stick·ing** *v.t.* **1.** To pierce, stab, or penetrate with a pin, knife, or other pointed object. **2.** To kill or wound by piercing; stab. **3.** To thrust or force, as a sword or pin, into or through something else. **4.** To force the end of (a nail, etc.) into something so as to be fixed in place. **5.** To fasten in place with or as with pins, nails, etc.: to *stick* a ribbon on a dress. **6.** To cover with objects piercing the surface. **7.** To fix on a pointed object; impale; transfix. **8.** To put or thrust: He *stuck* his hand into his pocket. **9.** To fasten to a surface by or as by an adhesive substance. **10.** To bring to a standstill; obstruct; halt: usually in the passive: We were *stuck* in Rome. **11.** *Informal* To smear with something sticky. **12.** *Informal* To baffle; puzzle. **13.** *Slang* To impose upon; cheat. **14.** *Slang* To force great expense, an unpleasant task, responsibility, etc., upon. **15.** To provide with sticks or brush on which to grow, as a vine. **16.** *Printing* To set or compose (type). — *v.i.* **17.** To be or become fixed in place by being thrust in: to *stick* in a cushion. **18.** To become or remain attached or close to something by or as by adhesion; adhere; cling. **19.** To come to a standstill; become blocked or obstructed; stop; halt. **20.** To be baffled or disconcerted. **21.** To hesitate; scruple: with *at* or *to.* **22.** To persist; persevere, as in a task or undertaking: with *at* or *to.* **23.** To remain firm or resolute; be faithful, as to an ideal or bargain. **24.** To be extended; protrude: with *from, out, through, up,* etc. — **to be stuck on** *Informal* To be enamored of. — **to stick around** *Slang* To remain near or near at hand. — **to stick by** To remain faithful to; be loyal to. — **to stick it out** To persevere to the end. — **to stick up** *Slang* To detain and rob. — **to stick up for** *Informal* To take the part of; support; defend. [OE *sticca*]
stick·ball (stik'bôl') *n. U.S.* A form of baseball played in city streets, using a broomstick for a bat.
stick·er (stik'ər) *n.* **1.** A gummed label, sign, etc. **2.** One who or that which fastens with or as with paste. **3.** One who holds tenaciously to anything. **4.** *Informal* Anything that confuses or silences a person; a puzzle. **5.** A prickly stem, thorn, or bur.
stick·ful (stik'fŏŏl) *n. pl.* **·fuls** *Printing* The amount of set type able to be held in a composing stick.
stick·handle (stik'han'dəl) *v.i.* **·dled, ·dling** In hockey, to use the stick to move and retain the puck.
stick Indian *Canadian Slang* In the West, a back-country Indian: an offensive term.
sticking plaster Adhesive tape.
stick insect A walking stick (def. 2).
stick-in-the-mud (stik'in·thə·mud') *n. Informal* A person too sluggish or lacking in initiative to take any progressive action.
stick·it (stik'it) *adj. Scot.* Stuck; unsuccessful.
stick·le (stik'əl) *v.i.* **·led, ·ling 1.** To contend or argue about trifling matters. **2.** To insist or hesitate for petty reasons. [ME *stightlen* to set in order, freq. of OE *stihtan* to arrange, dispose]

stick·le·back (stik'əl·bak') *n.* Any of various small fresh- or salt-water fishes (family *Gasterosteidae*) of northern regions, having sharp dorsal spines.
stick·ler (stik'lər) *n.* **1.** One who contends over or insists upon something: usually with *for*: a *stickler* for details. **2.** Something difficult or puzzling.
stick·pin (stik'pin') *n. U.S.* An ornamental pin for a necktie.
stick·seed (stik'sēd') *n.* Any of a genus (*Lappula*) of coarse weeds, whose prickly seeds stick in clothing.
stick·tight (stik'tīt') *n.* The bur marigold.
stick-to-it·ive (stik·tŏŏ'it·iv) *adj. Informal* Persevering; dogged; pertinacious. — **stick-to'-it·ive·ly** *adv.* — **stick-to'-it·ive·ness** *n.*
stick·up (stik'up') *n. Slang* A robbery or holdup. — **Syn.** See THEFT.
stick·weed (stik'wēd') *n.* Ragweed (which see).
stick·y (stik'ē) *adj.* **stick·i·er, stick·i·est 1.** Adhering to a surface; adhesive. **2.** Covered with something adhesive. **3.** Warm and humid. **4.** *Brit. Informal* Difficult; painful. — **stick'i·ly** *adv.* — **stick'i·ness** *n.*
Stieg·litz (stēg'lits), **Alfred,** 1864–1946, U.S. photographer and art patron.
stiff (stif) *adj.* **1.** Resisting the action of a bending force; not limp or flexible; rigid. **2.** Not easily moved; acting with difficulty or friction: *stiff* brakes; also, moving or functioning painfully or without suppleness: a *stiff* neck. **3.** Not natural, graceful, or easy; constrained and awkward; formal. **4.** Not liquid or fluid; thick; viscous. **5.** Taut; tightly drawn. **6.** Having a strong, steady movement: a *stiff* breeze. **7.** Firm in resistance; obstinate; stubborn. **8.** Difficult to achieve, understand, or accept; harsh; severe: a *stiff* penalty. **9.** High; dear: a *stiff* price. **10.** Firm in prices; strong and steady: a *stiff* market. **11.** *Naut.* Heeling over but little, while carrying much sail; not crank: a *stiff* ship. **12.** *Scot. & Brit. Dial.* Lusty; strong; sturdy. **13.** Dense; not porous, as soil. **14.** Strong or potent, as in alcoholic content: a *stiff* drink. **15.** Difficult; arduous: a *stiff* climb. **16.** *Obs.* Formidable; serious: said of news. — *n. Slang* **1.** A corpse. **2.** An awkward or unresponsive person; especially, a bore. **3.** A man; fellow: working *stiff*; also, a roughneck. **4.** A hobo. **5.** An accomplice in dishonest dealings; also, a prospective victim. [OE *stíf*] — **stiff'ly** *adv.* — **stiff'ness** *n.*
stiff·en (stif'ən) *v.t. & v.i.* To make or become stiff or stiffer.
stiff·en·er (stif'ən·ər) *n.* One who or that which stiffens.
stiff-necked (stif'nekt') *adj.* Not yielding; stubborn.
sti·fle¹ (stī'fəl) *v.* **·fled, ·fling** *v.t.* **1.** To keep back; suppress or repress; check: to *stifle* sobs. **2.** To kill by stopping respiration; suffocate; choke. — *v.i.* **3.** To die of suffocation. **4.** To experience difficulty in breathing, as in a stuffy room. [ME *stufle* < OF *estouffer* to smother; infl. by ON *stífla* to stop up, choke] — **sti'fler** *n.*
sti·fle² (stī'fəl) *n.* **1.** The joint between the tibia and the femur in the hind leg of a horse or dog: also **stifle joint.** For illustration see DOG, HORSE. **2.** Any abnormal condition of the stifle joint. [Origin unknown]
sti·fling (stī'fling) *adj.* Suffocating; oppressive: a *stifling* room. — **sti'fling·ly** *adv.*
stig·ma (stig'mə) *n. pl.* **stig·ma·ta** (stig'mə·tə, stig·mä'tə) or (*for defs. 1–3, usually*) **stig·mas 1.** A mark of infamy, or token of disgrace; blemish; blot, as on one's good name. **2.** A mark indicating a defect or something not normal. **3.** *Bot.* The part of a pistil that receives the pollen. For illustration see FLOWER. **4.** *Biol.* **a** A mark or spot, as on the wings of certain insects. **b** An aperture or opening, as a pore. **5.** A small mark or scar; a birthmark. **6.** *Pathol.* **a** A small red or bleeding spot on the skin caused by nervous tension or by capillary congestion. **b** One of the signs or marks of a disease. **7.** *pl.* The wounds that Christ received during the Passion and Crucifixion; also, marks on the body corresponding to these wounds, said to be miraculously impressed on certain persons. **8.** Formerly, a brand made with a branding iron on slaves and criminals. [< L, mark, brand < Gk., pointed end, mark < *stizein* to prick, brand]
stig·mas·ter·ol (stig·mas'tər·ōl, -ol) *n. Biochem.* A sterol, $C_{29}H_{47}OH$, obtained chiefly from the Calabar bean, and in lesser amounts from soybean oil. [< STIGMA + STEROL]
stig·mat·ic (stig·mat'ik) *adj.* **1.** Of, pertaining to, or marked with a stigma or stigmata. **2.** Anastigmatic. Also **stig·mat'i·cal.** — *n.* One marked with miraculous stigmata: also **stig·ma·tist** (stig'mə·tist).
stig·ma·tism (stig'mə·tiz'əm) *n.* **1.** The state of being affected with stigmas. **2.** *Optics* The quality or condition of a lens or of the cornea of the eye through which rays of light are accurately focused.
stig·ma·tize (stig'mə·tīz) *v.t.* **·tized, ·tiz·ing 1.** To characterize or brand as ignominious. **2.** To mark with a stigma. **3.** To cause stigmata to appear on. Also *Brit.* **stig'ma·tise.**

[< Med. L *stigmatizare* < Gk. *stigmatizein* to mark < *stigma* pointed end, mark] — **stig'ma·ti·za'tion** *n.* **stig'ma·tiz'er** *n.*

stil·bes·trol (stil'bəs·trōl, -trol) *n. Biochem.* Diethylstilbestrol. [< STILB(ENE) + ESTR(ONE) + -OL¹]

stil·bite (stil'bīt) *n.* A vitreous hydrous silicate of aluminum, calcium, and sodium of the zeolite group of minerals, occurring in brown, yellow, reddish or white prismatic crystals. [< Gk. *stilbein* to glitter + -ITE¹]

stile¹ (stīl) *n.* **1.** A step, or series of steps, on each side of a fence or wall to aid in surmounting it. **2.** A turnstile. [OE *stigel* < *stīgan* to climb]

stile² (stīl) *n.* One of the vertical sidepieces in a door or a window sash. [< Du. *stijl* doorpost]

sti·let·to (sti·let'ō) *n. pl.* **·tos** or **·toes** **1.** A small dagger with a slender blade. **2.** A small, sharp-pointed instrument, as of bone, for puncturing eyelets. — *v.t.* **·toed, ·to·ing** To pierce with a stiletto; stab. [< Ital., dim. of *stilo* dagger < L *stilus*. See STYLE¹.]

Stil·i·cho (stil'ə·kō), Flavius, 359?–408, Roman general and statesman; beheaded.

still¹ (stil) *adj.* **1.** Making no sound; silent. **2.** Free from disturbance or agitation; peaceful; tranquil. **3.** Without movement; motionless. **4.** Low in sound; quiet; hushed. **5.** Subdued; soft. **6.** Dead; inanimate. **7.** Having no effervescence: said of wines. **8.** *Photog.* Of or designating a single photograph, as contrasted with a motion picture. — **Syn.** See CALM. — *n.* **1.** *Poetic* Absence of sound or noise; stillness; calm. **2.** A still-life picture. **3.** *Photog.* A still photograph. **4.** A still alarm. — *adv.* **1.** Now as previously; up to this or that time; yet: He is *still* here. **2.** After or in spite of something; all the same; nevertheless. **3.** In increasing degree; even more; even yet: *still* more. **4.** *Poetic & Dial.* Always; constantly. — *conj.* Nevertheless; and yet. — *v.t.* **1.** To cause to be still or calm. **2.** To silence or hush. **3.** To quiet or allay, as fears. — *v.i.* **4.** To become still. [OE *stille*] — **still'ness** *n.*

still² (stil) *n.* **1.** An apparatus in which a substance is vaporized by heat, and the vapor then liquefied in a condenser and collected, used especially for distilling alcoholic liquors. **2.** A distillery. — *v.t. & v.i.* To distill. [< L *stillare* to drip < *stilla* drop]

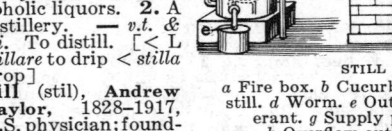

STILL

a Fire box. *b* Cucurbit. *c* Head of still. *d* Worm. *e* Outlet. *f* Refrigerant. *g* Supply pipe for *f*. *h* Overflow outlet for *f*.

Still (stil), Andrew Taylor, 1828–1917, U.S. physician; founder of osteopathy.

still alarm A fire alarm given by telephone or other call without sounding the regular signal apparatus.

still·birth (stil'bûrth') *n.* **1.** The bringing forth or birth of a dead child. **2.** A stillborn child.

still·born (stil'bôrn') *adj.* Dead at birth.

still-hunt (stil'hunt') *v.t. & v.i.* To hunt (game) stealthily; stalk.

still hunt **1.** The hunting of game by stealth. **2.** *Informal* The cautious, guarded pursuit of anything.

stil·li·form (stil'ə·fôrm) *adj.* Drop-shaped. [< NL *stilliformis* < L *stilla* drop + *forma* shape]

still life **1.** In painting, the representation of inanimate objects, as tables, flowers, fruit, etc. **2.** A picture of such a subject.

Still·son wrench (stil'sən) A wrench closely resembling a monkey wrench, but with serrated jaws, one of which is capable of slight angular movement, so that the grip is increased by pressure on the handle: a trade name.

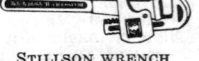

STILLSON WRENCH

still·y (*adj.* stil'ē; *adv.* stil'lē) *adj.* Still; silent; calm. — *adv.* Calmly; quietly; without noise.

stilt (stilt) *n.* **1.** One of a pair of long, slender poles made with a projection to support the foot some distance above the ground in walking. **2.** A tall post or pillar used as a support for something, as for a dock or building. **3.** Any of several long-legged, three-toed, wading birds (genus *Himantopus*) related to the avocet and inhabiting ponds and marshes; especially, the **black-necked stilt** (*H. mexicanus*) of North and South America. **4.** *Scot.* A crutch. — *v.t.* **1.** To raise on stilts. — *v.i.* **2.** *Scot.* To hobble on crutches. [ME *stilte*, ? < LG. Cf. MLG *stelte*.]

stilt·ed (stil'tid) *adj.* **1.** Artificially formal or elevated in manner; pompous. **2.** Raised or built on or as on stilts. — **stilt'ed·ly** *adv.* — **stilt'ed·ness** *n.*

stilted arch *Archit.* An arch whose curve springs from a level some distance above that of the impost.

Stil·ton cheese (stil'tən) A rich cheese permeated when ripe with a blue-green mold, originally made at Stilton, England. Also **Stil'ton.**

Stil·well (stil'wel), Joseph Warren, 1883–1946, U.S. general in World War II: called **Vinegar Joe.**

stime (stīm) *n. Scot.* A glimpse.

Stim·son (stim'sən), Henry Lewis, 1867–1950, U.S. statesman; Secretary of War in World War II.

stim·u·lant (stim'yə·lənt) *n.* **1.** Anything that quickens or promotes the activity of some physiological process, as a drug. **2.** Popularly, an alcoholic beverage. — *adj.* Acting as a stimulant; serving to stimulate. [< L *stimulans, -antis,* ppr. of *stimulare.* See STIMULATE.]

stim·u·late (stim'yə·lāt) *v.* **·lat·ed, ·lat·ing** *v.t.* **1.** To rouse to activity or to quickened action by some agency or motive; spur. **2.** *Physiol.* To excite (an organ or tissue) by applying some form of stimulus: to *stimulate* the skin. **3.** To affect by alcoholic beverages. — *v.i.* **4.** To act as a stimulant. [< L *stimulatus,* pp. of *stimulare* to prick, goad < *stimulus* goad] — **stim·u·lat'er, stim'u·la'tor** *n.* — **stim'u·la'tion** *n.*

stim·u·la·tive (stim'yə·lā'tiv) *adj.* Having the power or tendency to stimulate. — *n.* A stimulus.

stim·u·lus (stim'yə·ləs) *n. pl.* **·li** (-lī) **1.** Anything that rouses the mind or spirits; an incentive. **2.** *Physiol.* Any agent or form of excitation that influences the activity of an organism as a whole or in any of its parts. [< L]

sti·my (stī'mē) See STYMIE.

sting (sting) *v.* **stung** (*Obs.* **stang**), **stung, sting·ing** *v.t.* **1.** To pierce or prick painfully, as with a sharp, sometimes venomous organ. **2.** To cause to suffer sharp, smarting pain from or as from a sting: The blow *stung* his cheek. **3.** To cause to suffer mentally; pain: His heart was *stung* with remorse. **4.** To stimulate or rouse as if with a sting; goad; spur. **5.** *Slang* To impose upon; get the better of; also, to overcharge. — *v.i.* **6.** To have or use a sting, as a bee. **7.** To suffer or cause a sharp, smarting pain. **8.** To suffer or cause mental distress; pain. — *n.* **1.** *Zool.* A sharp, pointed organ, as of a bee or wasp, capable of inflicting a painful and often poisonous wound. **2.** The act of stinging; also, the wound made by a sting, or the pain caused by it. **3.** Any sharp, smarting sensation; stinging quality: the *sting* of remorse. **4.** A keen stimulus; spur; goad. **5.** *Bot.* One of the sharp-pointed hairs of a nettle, charged at the base with an irritating fluid that is emitted when touched: also **stinging hair.** **6.** The point of an epigram. [OE *stingan*] — **sting'ing·ly** *adv.*

sting·a·ree (sting'ə·rē, sting'ə·rē') *n.* A sting ray. [Alter. of STING RAY]

sting·er (sting'ər) *n.* **1.** One who or that which stings. **2.** A plant or animal that stings. **3.** Something that wounds or stings one mentally: that remark was a *stinger.* **4.** *U.S.A* cocktail made of brandy and white crème de menthe.

stin·go (sting'gō) *n. Brit. Slang* **1.** A strong ale or beer. **2.** Zest; vim. [< STING; from the sharpness of the taste]

sting ray Any of a family (*Dasyatidae*) of flat-bodied selachian fishes having broad pectoral fins and a whiplike tail capable of inflicting severe, often poisoned, wounds: also called *stingaree.*

stin·gy¹ (stin'jē) *adj.* **·gi·er, ·gi·est** **1.** Unwilling to spend or give; penurious; miserly. **2.** Scanty; inadequate; meager. [< dial. E *stinge* sting + -Y¹] — **stin'gi·ly** *adv.* — **stin'gi·ness** *n.*
— **Syn.** **1.** niggardly, parsimonious, close, closefisted, tight.

sting·y² (sting'ē) *adj. Informal* Stinging; piercing. — **sting'i·ly** *adv.*

stink (stingk) *n.* A strong, foul odor; stench. — **Syn.** See SMELL. — *v.* **stank** or **stunk, stunk, stink·ing** *v.i.* **1.** To give forth a foul odor. **2.** To be extremely offensive or hateful. **3.** *Informal* To be of extremely bad quality: This novel *stinks.* — *v.t.* **4.** To cause to stink. — **to make** (or **raise**) **a stink** *Slang* To protest vehemently; make a great fuss. — **to stink out** To drive from a den, hideaway, etc., by a foul or suffocating odor. [OE *stincan* to smell] — **stink'ing·ly** *adv.*

stink·ard (stingk'ərd) *n. Rare* A detestable person.

stink·bug (stingk'bug') *n.* Any of a family (*Pentatomidae*) of rather large, broad, flattened bugs that emit a sickening, sweetish odor when disturbed.

stink·er (stingk'ər) *n.* **1.** One who or that which stinks. **2.** The fulmar or other petrel that feeds on carrion. **3.** *Slang* An unpleasant, disgusting, or irritating person.

stink·horn (stingk'hôrn') *n.* Any of an order (*Phallales*) of basidiomycetous, ill-smelling fungi, especially *Phallus impudicus.*

stinking camomile The mayweed.

stinking smut Bunt³ (def. 2).

stink·pot (stingk'pot') *n.* **1.** A jar containing various suffocating, ill-smelling combustibles, formerly used in warfare. **2.** *Slang* Any despised or disliked person.

stink·stone (stingk'stōn') *n.* Any kind of rock that gives off a fetid odor under percussion, as certain limestones containing decayed organic matter.

stink·weed (stingk'wēd') *n.* Any of various plants having a disagreeable odor, as the jimsonweed.

stink·wood (stingk'wood') *n.* **1.** Any of various trees having wood of a disagreeable odor. **2.** The wood of any of these trees.

stint (stint) *v.t.* **1.** To limit, as in amount or share; be stingy with: Don't *stint* yourself. **2.** *Archaic* To stop. **—** *v.i.* **3.** To be frugal or sparing. **4.** *Archaic* To stop. **—** *n.* **1.** A fixed amount, as of work or a task to be performed within a specified time. **2.** A bound; restriction; limit. **3.** A small sandpiper. **4.** *Obs.* A cessation. [ME *stynten* to cause to stop < OE *styntan* to stupefy < *stunt* stupid] **— stint′er** *n.*

stipe (stīp) *n.* **1.** *Zool.* A stalk or support. **2.** *Bot.* A stalklike support or stem, as that supporting the cap of a mushroom, a fern's frond, etc.: also called *stipes*. For illustration see MUSHROOM. [< F < L *stipes* branch]

sti·pel (stī′pəl) *n.* *Bot.* A secondary or small stipule at the base of a leaflet. [< NL *stipella*, dim. of *stipes* branch] **— sti·pel·late** (stī-pel′it, stī′pəl·it, -āt) *adj.*

sti·pend (stī′pend) *n.* An allowance, salary, or pension; especially, a sum of money paid to a student under a scholarship or fellowship. **— Syn.** See SALARY. [< L *stipendium* tax, tribute < *stips* coin, payment in coin + *pendere* to weigh, pay out]

sti·pen·di·ar·y (stī·pen′dē·er′ē) *adj.* **1.** Receiving a stipend. **2.** Performing services for a fixed payment. **3.** Of or like a stipend. **4.** Owing feudal service. **5.** Paid for by a stipend, as services. **—** *n.*, *pl.* **·ar·ies 1.** One who receives a stipend, as a clergyman. **2.** A person owing feudal service. [< L *stipendiarius* < *stipendium*. See STIPEND.]

sti·pes (stī′pēz) *n.* **1.** A stipe. **2.** *Zool.* The central, and usually the largest part of the maxilla of an insect or crustacean. [< L] **— sti′pi·form** (-pə-fôrm′), **stip·i·ti·form** (stip′-ə·tə·fôrm′) *adj.*

stip·i·tate (stip′ə·tāt) *adj.* Having or borne on a stipe; stalked. [< NL *stipitatus* < L *stipes* stock]

stip·ple (stip′əl) *v.t.* **·pled, ·pling** To draw, paint, or engrave with dots or short touches instead of lines. **—** *n.* **1.** In painting, etching, etc., a method of representing light and shade by stippling. **2.** A painting produced by stippling; also the effect of stippling. [< Du. *stippelen* < *stippen* to speckle < *stip* dot] **— stip′pler** *n.*

stip·u·lar (stip′yə·lər) *adj.* *Bot.* **1.** Growing on stipules. **2.** Of, resembling, or pertaining to stalks or stems.

stip·u·late[1] (stip′yə·lāt) *v.* **·lat·ed, ·lat·ing** *v.t.* **1.** To specify as the terms of an agreement, contract, etc. **2.** To specify as a requirement or condition for agreement. **3.** To promise; guarantee. **—** *v.i.* **4.** To demand something as a requirement or condition: with *for*. **5.** To make an agreement. [< L *stipulatus*, pp. of *stipulari* to bargain] **— stip′u·la′tor** *n.*

stip·u·late[2] (stip′yə·lit, -lāt) *adj.* Furnished with stipules. Also **stip′u·lat·ed** (-lā′tid).

stip·u·la·tion (stip′yə·lā′shən) *n.* **1.** The act of stipulating, or the state of being stipulated. **2.** That which is stipulated; a condition. **— stip′u·la·to·ry** (-lə·tôr′ē, -tō′rē) *adj.*

stip·ule (stip′yōōl) *n.* *Bot.* One of a pair of leaflike appendages at the base of the petiole of certain leaves. [< L *stipula* stalk]

stir[1] (stûr) *v.* **stirred, stir·ring** *v.t.* **1.** To agitate so as to alter the relative position of the particles or components of, as soup with a spoon. **2.** To cause to move, especially slightly or irregularly; disturb. **3.** To move vigorously; bestir. **4.** To rouse, as from sleep, indifference, or inactivity; stimulate. **5.** To incite; provoke: often with *up*. **6.** To affect strongly; move with emotion. **—** *v.i.* **7.** To move, especially slightly; the log wouldn't *stir*. **8.** To be active; move about. **9.** To take place; happen: Is anything *stirring* in the news? **10.** To undergo stirring: This molasses *stirs* easily. **—** *n.* **1.** The act of stirring, or state of being stirred; activity. **2.** General interest or commotion. **3.** Any kind of excitement or agitation. **4.** A poke; nudge. [OE *styrian*] **— stir′rer** *n.*

stir[2] (stûr) *n.* *Slang* A jail; prison. **— stir crazy** *Slang* In a nervous or psychotic state as a result of confinement, as in a prison. [Origin uncertain]

Stir. Stirling; Stirlingshire.

stir·a·bout (stûr′ə·bout′) *n.* *Brit.* A porridge made of oatmeal or cornmeal stirred in boiling milk or water.

stirk (stûrk) *n.* **1.** A yearling ox or cow. **2.** *Scot.* A stupid fellow. [OE *stirc* calf < *stēor* steer]

Stir·ling (stûr′ling) A county in central Scotland; 451 sq. mi.: pop. 203,977 (1969); county seat, Stirling, pop. 28,786 (1969). Also **Stir′ling·shire** (-shir).

stir·pi·cul·ture (stûr′pə·kul′chər) *n.* The breeding of special races or strains of animals and plants. [< L *stirps, stirpis* stem, stock + CULTURE] **— stir′pi·cul′tur·al** *adj.* **— stir′pi·cul′tur·ist** *n.*

stirps (stûrps) *n.*, *pl.* **stir·pes** (stûr′pēz) **1.** A family or branch of a family; stock. **2.** *Law* A person from whom a family or family branch descends. [< L]

stir·ring (stûr′ing) *adj.* **1.** Stimulating; inspiring. **2.** Full of activity or stir; lively. **— stir′ring·ly** *adv.*

stir·rup (stûr′əp, stir′-) *n.* **1.** An inverted U-shaped piece of metal or wood with flat footpiece, suspended from either side of a saddle to support the rider's foot in and after mounting. For illustration see SADDLE. **2.** Any similarly shaped loop or piece, as for supporting a beam. **3.** *Naut.* A rope on a ship hanging from a yard and having at its end an eye or thimble to carry a footrope. [OE *stigrāp* mounting rope]

stirrup bone *Anat.* The stapes.

stirrup cup 1. A cup of liquor, as that taken by a mounted horseman on departing. **2.** A farewell drink.

stirrup leather The strap by which the stirrup iron is hung from the saddle. Also **stirrup strap.** For illustration see SADDLE.

stitch[1] (stich) *n.* **1.** A single passage of a threaded needle or other implement through fabric and back again, as in sewing or embroidery, or, in surgery, through skin or flesh. **2.** A single turn of thread or yarn around a needle or other implement, as in knitting or crocheting; also, the link or loop resulting from such a turn. **3.** Any peculiar or individual arrangement of a thread or threads used in sewing, embroidery, or crocheting: a chain *stitch*. **4.** A sharp sudden pain, especially in the back or side. **5.** A ridge between two furrows. **6.** *Informal* A garment: I haven't a *stitch* to wear. **7.** *Informal* The smallest bit or fragment: not a *stitch* of work. **— Syn.** See PAIN. **— to be in stitches** *Informal* To laugh uproariously. **—** *v.t.* **1.** To join together with stitches. **2.** To ornament with stitches. **—** *v.i.* **3.** To make stitches; sew. Abbr. *st.* [OE *stice* a prick, stab] **— stitch′er** *n.*

stitch[2] (stich) *n.* *Brit. Dial.* A space passed over; a span of time; distance. [OE *stycce* piece]

stitch·ing (stich′ing) *n.* A series of stitches.

stitch·wort (stich′wûrt′) *n.* Any of various plants (genus *Stellaria*), especially the common chickweed: also called *starwort, stichwort.* [OE *sticwyrt* < *stice* a prick + *wyrt* plant]

stith·y (stith′ē, stith′ē) *n.*, *pl.* **stith·ies 1.** A smithy or forge. **2.** An anvil. **—** *v.t.* **stith·ied, stith·y·ing** *Archaic* To forge on an anvil. [< ON *stedhi*]

sti·ver (stī′vər) *n.* **1.** A small Dutch coin, ¹⁄₂₀ of a guilder. **2.** Anything of little value. [< Du. *stuiver*]

St. James's (sānt jām′ziz), **Court of** The British royal court.

St. James's Palace The Tudor palace in Pall Mall, London royal residence from Henry VIII to the reign of Victoria.

St. John (sānt jon′) **1.** One of the Virgin Islands of the United States; 19 sq. mi. **2.** A port city in southern New Brunswick, Canada, on the Bay of Fundy; pop. 87,910. **3.** See ST. JOHN'S.

St. John (sānt jon′, sin′jən), **Henry** See (Viscount) BOLINGBROKE.

St. John, Lake A lake in south central Quebec, 375 sq. mi.

St. John River A river flowing 400 miles through northern Maine and western New Brunswick to the Bay of Fundy, forming part of the Maine-New Brunswick boundary.

St. John's (jonz) **1.** The capital of Newfoundland, a port on the SE coast; pop. 86,290. **2.** The capital of Antigua, on the northern coast; pop. 24,367 (1969): also *St. John.*

St. John's bread Carob (def. 2).

St. John's Day June 24, the Newfoundland holiday commemorating the landing of John Cabot in 1497.

St. Johns·wort (sānt jonz′wûrt′) Any of a genus (*Hypericum*) of hardy perennial shrubs and herbs, with deep yellow flowers. Also **St.-John's-wort.**

St. Jo·seph (jō′zif) A city in NW Missouri, on the Missouri River; pop. 72,691.

St. Kitts (kits) See ST. CHRISTOPHER NEVIS AND ANGUILLA.

St. Lau·rent (saṅ lô·rän′), **Louis Stephen,** born 1882, Canadian statesman; prime minister 1948–57.

St. Law·rence River (lôr′əns, lor′-) A river of SE Canada, the outlet of the Great Lakes system, flowing 744 miles NE from Lake Ontario to the **Gulf of St. Lawrence,** an inlet of the North Atlantic between Newfoundland and eastern Canada.

St. Lawrence Seaway A system of ship canals extending 114 miles along the St. Lawrence River above Montreal to Lake Ontario.

ST. LAWRENCE SEAWAY

St. Lou·is (lōō′is, lōō′ē) A port city in Missouri, on the Mississippi below the influx of the Missouri; pop. 622,236.

St. Louis Park A village in eastern Minnesota, a suburb of Minneapolis; pop. 48,883.

St. Lu·ci·a (lōō′shē·ə, lōō·sē′ə, lōō′shə) An island in the Windward group; a former British colony; since 1967 a self-governing member of the West Indies Associated States; 238 sq. mi.; pop. 110,000 (1971); capital, Castries.

St. Mar·y·le·bone (mâr′lə·bōn′) See MARYLEBONE.

St. Mar·ys River (mâr′ēz) A river flowing 63 miles SE from Lake Superior to Lake Huron and forming the boundary between northern Michigan and Ontario.

St. Mo·ritz (sänt môr′its, mō′rits; *Fr.* saṅ mô-rēts′; *Ger.* zängkt mō-rits′) A resort town in SE Switzerland; pop. about 3,000.

sto·a (stō′ə) *n. pl.* **sto·ae** (stō′ē) or **sto·as** In Greek architecture, a covered colonnade or promenade, usually with columns on one side. [< Gk., porch]

stoat (stōt) *n.* The ermine, especially in its brown summer coat. [ME *stote*; origin uncertain]

stob (stob) *Dial. n.* A stake or post; also, the stump of a tree. — *v.t.* **stobbed, stob·bing** To stab. [Var. of STUB]

stoc·ca·do (stə-kä′dō, -kä′-) *n. Archaic* A stabbing or thrusting movement with a rapier. Also **stoc·ca′ta** (-tə). [< Ital. *stoccata* < *stocco* rapier]

sto·chas·tic (stō-kas′tik) *adj.* **1.** Of, pertaining to, or characterized by conjecture; conjectural. **2.** Denoting the process of selecting from among a group of theoretically possible alternatives those factors or elements whose combination will most closely approximate a desired result. [< Gk. *stochastikos* < *stochazesthai* to guess at < *stochos* mark, aim]

stock (stok) *n.* **1.** A quantity of something acquired or kept for future use: to lay in a *stock* of provisions. **2.** The total merchandise or goods that a merchant or other commercial establishment has on hand. **3.** Livestock. **4.** In finance: **a** The capital or fund raised by a corporation through the sale of shares that entitle the holder to interest or dividends and to part ownership of the corporation. **b** The proportional part of this capital credited to an individual stockholder and represented by the number of shares he owns. **c** A certificate showing ownership of a specific number of shares. **5.** The trunk or main stem of a tree or other plant, as distinguished from a branch or root. **6.** A line of familial descent. **7.** The original progenitor of a family line. **8.** An ethnic group; race. **9.** A family of languages. **10.** A related group or family of plants or animals; also, a type of animal or plant from which others are derived. **11.** *Bot.* **a** A rhizome. **b** In horticulture, a stem upon which a graft is made; also, a plant, tree, etc. that provides cuttings and slips. **12.** *Zool.* A zooid. **13.** The broth from boiled meat or fish used in preparing soups, etc. **14.** Raw material: paper *stock.* **15.** *pl.* A timber frame with holes for confining the ankles and often the wrists, formerly used in punishing petty offenders. **16.** *pl.* The timber frame on which a vessel rests during construction. **17.** *pl.* A frame for confining an animal for shoeing or veterinary treatment. **18.** *Naut.* A crosspiece at the end of the shank in an anchor. **19.** The wooden block suspending a bell. **20.** In firearms: **a** The rear wooden portion of a rifle, musket, or shotgun, to which the barrel and mechanisms are secured: also called *gunstock.* **b** The arm on rapidfire guns connecting the shoulder piece to the slide. **c** The handle of a pistol or similar firearm. For illustration see REVOLVER. **d** The member of a gun carriage that usually bears the prolonge and trails along the ground. **21.** The handle of certain instruments, as of a whip or fishing rod. **22.** A theatrical stock company; also, its repertoire. **23.** A broad, stiffened band, formerly worn as a cravat. **24.** *Geol.* A rounded mass of igneous rock rising above ground level. **25.** *Mech.* An adjustable wrench used for grasping and turning thread-cutting dies. **26.** An ornamental garden plant, as the gillyflower. **27.** In card games and dominoes, the part of the pack or group of dominoes that is left on the table and drawn from. — **in stock** On hand and available for sale or use. — **out of stock** Not on hand or available for sale or use, usually only temporarily. — **to take stock 1.** To take an inventory. **2.** To make a careful estimate or appraisal. — **to take stock in** To have trust or belief in; give credence to. — *v.t.* **1.** To furnish with livestock, as a farm, or with merchandise, as a store. **2.** To keep for sale. **3.** To put aside for future use. **4.** To provide with a handle or stock. **5.** *Obs.* To put (a person) in the stocks for punishment. — *v.i.* **6.** To lay in supplies or stock: often with *up.* **7.** To send out new shoots; sprout. — *adj.* **1.** Kept continually ready or constantly brought forth, like old goods: a *stock* joke. **2.** Kept on hand: a *stock* trade. **3.** Banal; commonplace: a *stock* phrase. **4.** Used for breeding purposes: a *stock* mare. **5.** Employed in handling or caring for the stock: a *stock* clerk. **6.** Of, pertaining to, or like a stock theatrical company. — *adv.* Motionlessly; like a stump: used in combination: *stock-still.* Abbr. **stk.** [OE *stocc*]

stock·ade (sto-kād′) *n.* **1.** A line of stout posts, stakes, etc., set upright in the earth to form a fence or barrier; also, the area thus enclosed. **2.** Any similarly enclosed area. — *v.t.* **·ad·ed, ·ad·ing** To surround or fortify with a stockade. [< OF *estocade* < Sp. *estacada* < *estaque* stake < Gmc.]

stock boy A boy or man who unpacks and arranges merchandise in a store.

stock·breed·er (stok′brē′dər) *n.* One who breeds or raises livestock. — **stock′breed′ing** *n.*

stock·bro·ker (stok′brō′kər) *n.* One who buys and sells stocks or securities for others. — **stock′bro′ker·age** (-ij), **stock′bro′king** *n.*

stock car An automobile, often a sedan, modified for racing.

stock certificate See under CERTIFICATE.

stock company 1. An incorporated company that issues

stock. **2.** A more or less permanent dramatic company under one management, that presents a series of plays.

stock dove (duv) The common wild pigeon (*Columba oenas*) of Europe.

stock exchange 1. A place where stocks and bonds are bought and sold. **2.** An association of stockbrokers who transact business in stocks, bonds, etc. Abbr. *St. Ex.*

stock farm A farm that specializes in breeding livestock.

stock·fish (stok′fish′) *n.* Cod, haddock, or the like, cured by splitting and drying in the air, without salt.

stock·hold·er (stok′hōl′dər) *n.* **1.** One who holds certificates of ownership in a company or corporation. **2.** In Australia, an owner of or dealer in livestock. — **stock′hold′ing** *adj. & n.*

Stock·holm (stok′hōm, *Sw.* stôk′hôlm) The capital of Sweden, a port in the SE part, on the Baltic; pop. 756,700 (est. 1969).

stock·i·net (stok′i-net′) *n.* An elastic knitted fabric, machine-made and used for undergarments, stockings, etc. Also **stock′i·nette′.** [Alter. of *stockinget* < STOCKING + -ET]

stock·ing (stok′ing) *n.* **1.** A close-fitting woven or knitted covering for the foot and leg. **2.** Something resembling such a covering. — **in one's stocking feet** Wearing one's stockings or socks, but no shoes. [< STOCK, in obs. sense of "a stocking" + -ING3] — **stock′inged** (-ingd) *adj.* — **stock′ing·less** *adj.*

stock in trade 1. The goods that a storekeeper has for sale. **2.** Resources, either material or spiritual.

stock·ish (stok′ish) *adj.* Like a stock or block of wood; stupid. — **stock′ish·ly** *adv.*

stock·job·ber (stok′job′ər) *n.* **1.** *Brit.* A dealer or speculator in stocks who deals only with stockbrokers. **2.** A stockbroker. — **stock′job′ber·y, stock′job′bing** *n.*

stock·man (stok′mən) *n. pl.* **·men** (-mən) **1.** A man having charge of stock, as on a ranch. **2.** One who raises or owns livestock; a cattleman. **3.** One who works in a stockroom, warehouse, etc.

stock market 1. A stock exchange. **2.** The business transacted in such a place: The *stock market* was active. **3.** The rise and fall of prices of stocks and bonds.

stock·pile (stok′pīl′) *n.* A storage pile of materials or supplies. Also **stock pile.** — *v.t. & v.i.* **·piled, ·pil·ing** To accumulate a supply or stockpile (of).

Stock·port (stok′pôrt, -pōrt) A county borough in Greater Manchester, England; pop. 294,400 (1976).

stock·pot (stok′pot′) *n.* A pot for preparing and keeping soup stock.

stock raising Breeding and raising of various types of livestock. — **stock raiser**

stock·room (stok′rōōm′, -rŏŏm′) *n.* A room where reserve stocks of goods are stored. Also **stock room.**

stock-still (stok′stil′) *adj.* Still as a stock or post; motionless.

Stock·ton (stok′tən) A port city in central California, on a deepwater channel to the San Joaquin River; pop. 107,644.

Stock·ton (stok′tən), **Frank R.,** 1834–1902 U.S. novelist and short-story writer: original name **Francis Richard Stockton.** — **Richard,** 1730–81, American patriot; signer of the Declaration of Independence.

Stock·ton-on-Tees (stok′tən-on-tēz′) A municipal borough and port in Cleveland, England; pop. 162,500 (1976).

stock·y (stok′ē) *adj.* **stock·i·er, stock·i·est** Solidly built, thickset, and usually short. — **stock′i·ly** *adv.* — **stock′i·ness** *n.*

stock·yard (stok′yärd′) *n.* A large yard with pens or stables where cattle, sheep, pigs, etc., are kept ready for shipping or slaughter.

stodge (stoj) *v.* **stodged, stodg·ing** *v.t.* **1.** To render dull and heavy by stuffing with food. — *v.i.* **2.** To become muddy or marshy. [Origin uncertain]

stodg·y (stoj′ē) *adj.* **stodg·i·er, stodg·i·est 1.** Dull, stupid, and commonplace. **2.** Crammed full; distended; bulky. **3.** Indigestible and heavy: said of food. **4.** Thickset; stocky. — **stodg′i·ly** *adv.* — **stodg′i·ness** *n.*

sto·gy (stō′gē) *n. pl.* **·gies 1.** A long, slender, inexpensive cigar. **2.** A stout, heavy boot or shoe. Also **sto′gey, sto′gie.** [Earlier *stoga* < (CONE)STOGA (WAGON), because their drivers wore heavy boots and smoked coarse cigars]

sto·ic (stō′ik) *n.* A person apparently unaffected by pleasure or pain. — *adj.* Indifferent to pleasure or pain; impassive. Also **sto′i·cal.** — **sto′i·cal·ly** *adv.* — **sto′i·cal·ness** *n.*

Sto·ic (stō′ik) *n.* A member of a school of Greek philosophy founded by Zeno about 308 B.C., holding that wisdom lies in being superior to passion, joy, grief, etc., and in unperturbed submission to the divine will. — *adj.* Of or pertaining to the Stoics or Stoicism. [< L *Stoicus* < Gk. *Stoikos* < *Stoa* (*Poikilē*) (Painted) Porch, the colonnade at Athens where Zeno taught]

stoi·chi·ol·o·gy (stoi′kē-ol′ə-jē) *n.* The study of the cellular elements of animal tissues. Also **stoe′chi·ol′o·gy, stoi′chei·ol′o·gy.** [< Gk. *stoicheion* element + -LOGY] — **stoi′chi·o·log′i·cal** (-ə-loj′i-kəl) *adj.*

stoi·chi·om·e·try (stoi′kē-om′ə-trē) *n.* The branch of chemistry that treats of the combining proportions of elements or compounds involved in reactions, and the methods of calculating them. Also **stoe'chi·om'e·try, stoi'chei·om'e·try.** [< Gk. *stoicheion* element + -METRY] — **stoi'chi·o·met'ric** (-ə·met'rik) or **·ri·cal** *adj.*

sto·i·cism (stō'ə·siz'əm) *n.* Indifference to pleasure or pain; stoicalness.

Sto·i·cism (stō'ə·siz'əm) *n.* The doctrines of the Stoics.

stoke (stōk) *v.t. & v.i.* **stoked, stok·ing** To supply (a furnace) with fuel; stir up or tend (a fire or furnace). [Back formation < STOKER]

stoke·hold (stōk'hōld') *n. Naut.* The furnace room of a steamship.

stoke·hole (stōk'hōl') *n.* **1.** The space about the mouth of a furnace or the mouth itself. **2.** A stokehold.

Stoke-on-Trent (stōk'on·trent') A county borough in NW Staffordshire, England; pop. 265,506 (1961). Also **Stoke'-up·on'-Trent'.**

Stoke Po·ges (pō'jis) A village in SE Buckinghamshire, England; generally regarded as the scene of Gray's *Elegy*; pop. about 2,000.

stok·er (stō'kər) *n.* **1.** One who supplies fuel to a furnace; a fireman on a locomotive, etc. **2.** A device for feeding coal to a furnace. [< Du. < *stoken* to stir a fire]

Sto·kow·ski (stə·kôf'skē, -kou'skē), **Leopold (Anton Stanislaw)**, born 1882, U.S. orchestra conductor born in England.

STOL Short takeoff and landing.

stole[1] (stōl) *n.* **1.** *Eccl.* A long, narrow band, usually of decorated silk or linen, worn about the shoulders by priests and bishops, and over the left shoulder only by deacons, when officiating. **2.** A long scarf of fur or fabric, worn about the shoulders by women. **3.** In ancient Rome, a long outer garment worn by matrons. [OE < L *stola* robe < Gk. *stolē* garment] — **stoled** (stōld) *adj.*

stole[2] (stōl) Past tense of STEAL.

sto·len (stō'lən) Past participle of STEAL.

stol·id (stol'id) *adj.* Having or showing little feeling or perception; impassive; dull. [< L *stolidus* dull] — **sto·lid·i·ty** (stə·lid'ə·tē), **stol'id·ness** *n.* — **stol'id·ly** *adv.*

sto·lon (stō'lon) *n.* **1.** *Bot.* **a** A trailing branch that is capable of taking root. **b** A runner or rhizome by which grasses may propagate. **2.** *Zool.* A prolongation of the body of various animals, as in corals, from which new buds and organisms grow. [< NL < L *stolo, stolonis*]

sto·ma (stō'mə) *n. pl.* **sto·ma·ta** (stō'mə·tə, stom'ə·tə) **1.** *Bot.* A minute orifice or pore in the epidermis of plants, especially of leaves and stems. **2.** *Biol.* **a** An aperture in the walls of blood vessels or in serous membranes. **b** A mouthlike opening in nematodes. [< NL < Gk. *stoma* mouth]

-stoma See -STOME.

stom·ach (stum'ək) *n.* **1.** The pouchlike, highly vascular enlargement of the alimentary canal, situated in man and vertebrates between the esophagus and the small intestine, and serving as one of the principal organs of digestion. ◆ Collateral adjective: *gastric.* **2.** Any digestive cavity, as of an invertebrate. **3.** Loosely, the abdomen or belly. **4.** Desire for food; appetite. **5.** Any desire or inclination. **6.** *Obs.* Temper; spirit. **7.** *Obs.* Pride; haughtiness. — *v.t.* **1.** To put up with; endure. **2.** To take into and retain in the stomach; digest. **3.** *Obs.* To resent. [< OF *estomac* < L *stomachus* < Gk. *stomachos* gullet, stomach < *stoma* mouth]

stomach ache Pain in the stomach or abdomen.

stom·ach·er (stum'ək·ər) *n.* A former ornamental article of dress, worn over the breast and stomach.

sto·mach·ic (stō·mak'ik) *adj.* **1.** Pertaining to the stomach. **2.** Beneficial to or stimulating the activity of the stomach. Also **stom·ach·al** (stum'ək·əl), **sto·mach'i·cal.** — *n.* Any medicine strengthening or stimulating the stomach.

stomach pump A device consisting of a flexible tube and a suction pump, used for emptying the stomach of its contents.

stomach tooth Either of the lower canine teeth of infants, so called because their emergence is frequently accompanied by digestive disturbances.

stomach worm Any of various nematode worms, parasitic in the stomachs of man and animals, especially *Haemonchus contortus*, found in sheep.

stom·ach·y (stum'ək·ē) *adj.* **1.** Having a paunch. **2.** *Brit. Dial.* Spirited; haughty; proud; also, choleric; resentful.

sto·ma·ta (stō'mə·tə, stom'ə·tə) Plural of STOMA.

sto·ma·tal (stō'mə·təl, stom'ə-) *adj.* Of, pertaining to, or having a stoma.

sto·mat·ic (stō·mat'ik) *adj.* **1.** Of or pertaining to the mouth. **2.** Stomatal.

sto·ma·ti·tis (stō'mə·tī'tis, stom'ə-) *n. Pathol.* Inflammation of the mouth.

stomato- *combining form* Of, like, or pertaining to the mouth: *stomatoplasty.* Also, before vowels, **stomat-.** [< Gk. *stoma, stomatos* mouth]

sto·ma·tol·o·gy (stō'mə·tol'ə·jē, stom'ə-) *n.* The science treating of the mouth and of its diseases.

sto·ma·to·plas·ty (stō'mə·tə·plas'tē, stom'ə-) *n. pl.* **·ties** Plastic surgery of the mouth.

sto·ma·to·pod (stō'mə·tə·pod', stom'ə-) *n.* Any of an order (*Stomatopoda*) of crustaceans having abdominal gills and legs near the mouth, including the squills. — **sto·ma·top'o·dous** (-top'ə·dəs) *adj.*

sto·ma·tous (stō'mə·təs, stom'ə-) *adj.* Having a stoma or stomata.

-stome *combining form* Mouth; mouthlike opening: *peristome.* Also spelled *-stoma.* [< Gk. *stoma* mouth]

sto·mo·de·um (stō'mə·dē'əm, stom'ə-) *n. pl.* **·de·a** (-dē'ə) *Biol.* The invagination of the ectoderm of the embryo, forming the mouth. Also **sto'mo·dae'um.** [< NL < Gk. *stoma* mouth + *hodaios* on the way < *hodos* way] — **sto'·mo·de'al** or **·dae'al** *adj.*

-stomous *combining form* Having a (specified kind of) mouth: *microstomous.* Also **-stomatous.** [< Gk. *stoma, stomatos* mouth]

stomp (stomp) *v.t. & v.i.* **1.** To tread heavily or violently (upon); press down. **2.** *Dial.* To stamp. — *n.* A dance involving a heavy and lively step. [Var. of STAMP]

-stomy *combining form Surg.* An operation to form an artificial opening for or into (a specified organ or part): *colostomy, ileostomy.* [< Gk. *stoma* mouth]

stone (stōn) *n.* **1.** The hard, nonmetallic mineral or earthy matter of which rock is composed. **2.** A small piece of rock, as a cobble or pebble. **3.** Rock, or a piece of rock that has been hewn or shaped. **4.** A precious stone; gem. **5.** Anything resembling a stone in shape or hardness: a *hailstone.* **6.** A gravestone. **7.** A grindstone or millstone. **8.** *Pathol.* A stony concretion in the bladder, or a disease characterized by such concretions. **9.** *Bot.* The hard covering of the kernel in a fruit. **10.** (*pl.* **stone**) A variable measure of weight; in England, 14 pounds avoirdupois. Abbr. *st.* **11.** *Usually pl.* A testicle. **12.** *Printing* A table having a hard, smooth top, used for composing page forms. — *adj.* **1.** Made of stone: a *stone* ax. **2.** Made of coarse hard earthenware: a *stone* bottle. **3.** Characterized by the use of stone implements: the *Stone* Age. — *v.t.* **stoned, ston·ing 1.** To hurl stones at; pelt or kill with stones. **2.** To remove the stones or pits from. **3.** To furnish or line, as a well, with stone. **4.** To castrate; geld, as a hog. **5.** *Obs.* To make hard or unyielding, as the heart. [OE *stān*] — **ston'er** *n.*

Stone (stōn), **Harlan Fiske,** 1872–1946, U.S. educator and jurist; chief justice of the Supreme Court 1941–46. — **Lucy,** 1818–93, Mrs. Henry Brown Blackwell, U.S. social reformer and suffragist.

Stone Age The earliest known period in the cultural evolution of mankind, marked by the use of stone implements and weapons, preceding the Bronze Age, and subdivided into the Eolithic, Paleolithic, and Neolithic periods.

stone-blind (stōn'blīnd') *adj.* Totally blind.

stone·boat (stōn'bōt') *n. U.S.* A low, flat sled used for transporting rocks or similar heavy objects.

stone-broke (stōn'brōk') *adj. Informal* Without any money; having no funds. Also **ston'y-broke'** (stō'nē-).

stone·chat (stōn'chat') *n.* A small thrushlike European bird (genus *Saxicola*) with upper parts black and breast dark red. [< STONE + CHAT[1], n. (def. 2); from its cry suggesting the knocking together of pebbles]

stone·crop (stōn'krop') *n.* Any of various plants (genus *Sedum*) of the orpine family; especially *S. acre*, having small fleshy leaves and yellow flowers.

stone·cut·ter (stōn'kut'ər) *n.* One who or that which cuts stone; especially, a machine for facing stone.

stoned (stōnd) *adj. U.S. Slang* Intoxicated, as by liquor, narcotics, etc.

stone-deaf (stōn'def') *adj.* Completely deaf.

stone fly A plecopteran.

stone fruit A fruit having a stone; a drupe.

Stone·henge (stōn'henj) A prehistoric megalithic structure on Salisbury Plain, SE Wiltshire, England, consisting primarily of circles of dressed stones, some with lintels, the main structure dating probably from 1500 B.C.

stone lily A fossil sea lily or other crinoid.

STONEHENGE

stone marten 1. An Old World marten (*Martes foina*). **2.** Its fur, marked in white on throat and breast.

stone·ma·son (stōn'mā'sən) *n.* One whose occupation or trade is to prepare and lay stones in building. — **stone'·ma'son·ry** (-rē) *n.*

stone·mint (stōn'mint') *n.* Dittany (def. 1).

Stone Mountain A dome-shaped, granite mountain in NW central Georgia, having a Confederate monument carved on one side; 1,686 ft.

stone parsley An Old World herb (genus *Sium*) of the parsley family, with cream-colored flowers and aromatic seeds: also called *honewort.*

stone roller 1. A fresh-water cyprinoid fish (*Campostoma anomalum*) of North America. **2.** A North American sucker (*Hypentelium nigricans*).

stone sheep *Canadian* A species of bighorn sheep of British Columbia.

Stones River (stōnz) A river in central Tennessee, flowing 39 miles NW to the Cumberland River; scene of a Union victory in the Civil War, 1862–63.

stone's throw 1. The distance a stone may be cast by hand. 2. A short distance.

stone·wall (stōn'wôl') *v.i.* 1. In cricket, to play on the defensive so as to secure a draw: said of batsmen. 2. *Austral.* In politics, to oppose by a policy of obstruction; filibuster. — **stone'wall'er** *n.*

Stone·wall Jackson (stōn'wôl') See (Thomas Jonathan) JACKSON.

stone·ware (stōn'wâr') *n.* A variety of very hard pottery, made from siliceous clay or clay mixed with flint or sand.

stone·work (stōn'wûrk') *n.* 1. Work concerned with cutting or setting stone; work made of stone. 2. *pl.* A place where stone is prepared for masonry; also, a place where stoneware is made. — **stone'work'er** *n.*

stone·wort (stōn'wûrt') *n.* Any of a genus (*Chara*) of green algae growing submerged in fresh or brackish waters and often incrusted with deposits of calcium carbonate.

ston·ish (ston'ish) *v.t. Obs. Dial.* To astonish. [Aphetic var. of ASTONISH] — **ston'ish·ment** *n.*

ston·y (stō'nē) *adj.* **ston·i·er, ston·i·est** 1. Abounding in stone. 2. Made or consisting of stone. 3. Hard as stone. 4. Unfeeling or inflexible. 5. Converting into stone; petrifying; cold and stiff. 6. *Slang* Stone-broke; having no money. — **ston'i·ly** *adv.* — **ston'i·ness** *n.*

stony coral Any coral having a calcareous skeleton.

ston·y·heart·ed (stō'nē·här'tid) *adj.* Hardhearted; pitiless. — **ston'y·heart'ed·ness** *n.*

Stony Point An unincorporated place in SE New York, on the Hudson; scene of an American victory in the Revolutionary War, July, 1779; pop. 8,270.

stood (stŏŏd) Past tense and past participle of STAND.

stooge (stōōj) *Informal n.* 1. An actor placed in the audience to heckle a comedian on the stage. 2. An actor who feeds lines to the principal comedian, acts as a foil for his jokes, etc. 3. Anyone who acts as or is the tool or dupe of another. — *v.i.* **stooged, stoog·ing** To act as a stooge: usually with *for.* — **to stooge around** *Slang* 1. To fly about idly in an airplane. 2. To loiter or idle about. [Origin unknown]

stook (stŏŏk, stŏŏk) *n.* A collection of sheaves set upright in the field; a shock of corn. — *v.t.* To set up in stooks. [Cf. MLG *stuke* bundle.] — **stook'er** *n.*

stool (stōōl) *n.* 1. A backless and armless seat, high or low, for one person. 2. A low bench or portable support for the feet or for the knees in kneeling. 3. A seat used in defecating; a privy. 4. The matter evacuated from the bowels at each movement. 5. *Bot.* **a** A plant from which young plants are produced, as from runners. **b** A stump or root of any kind from which suckers or sprouts shoot up. **c** The shoots from such a root or stump. 6. A decoy, as a bird or likeness of one. — *v.i.* 1. To send up shoots or suckers. 2. To decoy wild fowl with a stool or stools. 3. To void feces. 4. *U.S. Slang* To be a stool pigeon. [OE *stōl*]

stool pigeon 1. A living or artificial pigeon attached to a stool or perch to decoy others. 2. *U.S. Slang* Any decoy, as a person employed to lure others into a gambling house, etc. 3. *U.S. Slang* An informer or spy, especially for the police.

stoop[1] (stōōp) *v.i.* 1. To bend or lean the body forward and down; bow; crouch. 2. To stand or walk with the upper part of the body habitually bent forward; slouch. 3. To bend; lean; sink, as a tree. 4. To lower or degrade oneself: to *stoop* to cheating. 5. To pounce or swoop, as a hawk on prey. 6. *Obs.* To submit; yield. — *v.t.* 7. To bend (one's head, shoulders, etc.) forward. 8. *Obs.* To humble or subdue. — **Syn.** See BEND[1]. — *n.* 1. An act of stooping; a slouch. 2. A habitual forward inclination of the head and shoulders. 3. A decline from dignity or superiority. 4. A swoop, as of a bird of prey. [OE *stūpian*]

stoop[2] (stōōp) *n. U.S.* 1. Originally, a platform at the door of a house approached by steps and having seats. 2. A small porch or platform at the entrance to a house. [< Du. *stoep*]

stoop[3] (stōōp) *n. Brit. Dial.* A post set in the ground; a pillar. [< ON *stolpi*; infl. by MDu. *stupe*]

stoop[4] (stōōp) See STOUP.

stop (stop) *v.* **stopped** or (*Chiefly Poetic*) **stopt, stop·ping** *v.t.* 1. To bring (something in motion) to a halt; arrest the progress of: to *stop* an automobile. 2. To prevent the doing or completion of: to *stop* a revolution. 3. To prevent (a person) from doing something; restrain. 4. To keep back, withhold, or cut off, as wages or supplies. 5. To cease doing; desist from. 6. To intercept in transit, as a letter. 7. To block up, obstruct, or clog (a passage, road, etc.): often with *up.* 8. To fill in, cover over, or otherwise close, as a hole, cavity, etc. 9. To close (a bottle, barrel, etc.) with a cork, plug, or other stopper. 10. To stanch (a wound, etc.). 11. To order a bank not to pay or honor: to *stop* a check. 12. To defeat; also, to kill. 13. *Music* **a** To press down (a

string) on the finger board, or to close (a hole) in order to vary the pitch produced by an instrument; finger. **b** To introduce the hand into the bell of (a brass instrument). 14. To punctuate. 15. In boxing, etc., to parry. — *v.i.* 16. To come to a halt; cease progress or motion. 17. To cease doing something; pause or desist. 18. To come to an end. — **Syn.** See CEASE. — **to stop off** *U.S. Informal* To cease traveling temporarily before reaching one's destination. — **to stop over** *U.S. Informal* 1. To stay at a place temporarily. 2. To interrupt a journey; make a stopover. — *n.* 1. The act of stopping, or the state of being stopped; a halt; pause; end. 2. A place where something stops: a bus *stop.* 3. That which stops or limits the range or time of a movement: a camera *stop.* 4. An obstruction or obstacle. 5. *Music* **a** The stopping of a string or hole of an instrument. **b** Any mechanical aid used in stopping a string or hole. **c** A fret. **d** In an organ or harpsichord, a knob controlling a register of pipes or strings; also the register so controlled. 6. *Brit.* A punctuation mark, as a period. 7. In telegrams and cablegrams, the word *stop* spelled out to indicate a punctuation mark. 8. In joinery, a block, pin, or the like to check sliding motion, as of a drawer. 9. *Naut.* A small line for lashing or fastening anything temporarily. 10. *Phonet.* **a** Complete blockage of the breath stream (implosion), as with the lips or tongue, followed by a sudden release (plosion). **b** A consonant so produced; a plosive: opposed to *continuant.* The stops in English are the bilabials (p) and (b), the alveolars (t) and (d), and the velars (k) and (g). The nasals (m) and (n) may also be included in this category. 11. In dogs, the short incline between the forepart of the skull and the face. For illustration see DOG. [OE *-stoppian*]

stop·cock (stop'kok') *n.* A faucet or short pipe having a valve for stopping or regulating the passage of fluids.

stope (stop) *Mining n.* An excavation from which the ore is removed, either above or below a level in a series of steps. — *v.t. & v.i* **stoped, stop·ing** To excavate in stopes. [Appar. akin to STEP]

stop·gap (stop'gap') *n.* 1. That which stops a gap. 2. Something improvised to fill a need temporarily; an expedient. — *adj.* That serves as a stopgap.

stop·light (stop'lit') *n.* 1. A red light on a traffic sign, directing a motorist or pedestrian to stop. 2. A red light on the rear of a motor vehicle that shines upon application of the brakes.

stop-loss (stop'lôs', -los') *adj.* Intended to prevent further loss, in a brokerage account, from falling prices on financial markets.

stop-motion photography (stop'mō'shən) Time-lapse photography (which see).

stop order An order to an agent or broker to buy or sell a stock at the market only when it reaches a specified price.

stop·o·ver (stop'ō'vər) *n.* 1. The act of staying in a place for a brief period, especially for the night while traveling. 2. The act of interrupting a journey without paying additional fare, as by taking a later train on the same railroad. Also **stop'-off'** (-ôf', -of').

stop·page (stop'ij) *n.* 1. The act of stopping, or the state of being stopped. 2. A deduction from pay to repay something.

stop payment An order to a bank to refuse payment on a certain check.

stop·per (stop'ər) *n.* 1. Something that stops up or closes, as a plug or cork. 2. One who or that which stops or checks a movement, action, etc. — *v.t.* To close with a stopper.

stop·ple (stop'əl) *n.* A stopper, plug, cork, or bung. — *v.t.* **·pled, ·pling** To close with or as with a stopple. [ME *stoppel,* prob. < *stoppen* to stop]

stopt (stopt) Alternative, chiefly poetic, past tense and past participle of STOP.

stop·watch (stop'woch') *n.* A watch that has a hand indicating fractions of a second and that may be instantaneously started, used for timing races, etc.

stor·age (stôr'ij, stō'rij) *n.* 1. The depositing of articles in a warehouse for safekeeping. 2. Space for storing goods. 3. A charge for storing. 4. The charging of a storage battery. 5. *Electronics* The part of an analogue or digital computer designed to hold appropriate items of information and to deliver them when needed in subsequent operations: also called *memory.* Abbr. *stge.*

storage battery One or more secondary cells arranged as a single source of direct current and capable of being recharged on reversal of the current.

storage cell *Electr.* A secondary cell (which see).

sto·rax (stôr'aks, stō'raks) *n.* 1. A fragrant resin obtained from any of several styracaceous

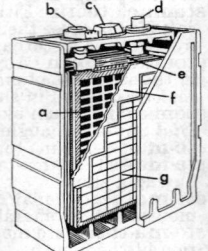

STORAGE BATTERY
a Positive plate.
b Positive terminal.
c Vent cap or plug.
d Negative terminal.
e Electrolyte space.
f Separator.
g Negative plate.

trees or shrubs (genus *Styrax*), especially *S. officinalis*, formerly used in medicine and perfumery. **2.** Any of the trees and shrubs producing this resin. **3.** A liquid balsam obtained from the wood and inner bark of species of liquidambar, especially *Liquidambar orientalis* of Asia Minor, used in medicine, perfumery, etc. [< L < Gk. *styrax*]

store (stôr, stōr) *v.t.* **stored, stor·ing 1.** To put away for future use; accumulate. **2.** To furnish or supply; provide. **3.** To place in a warehouse or other place of deposit for safekeeping. — *n.* **1.** *U.S.* A place where merchandise of any kind is kept for sale; a shop. **2.** That which is stored or laid up against future need. **3.** *pl.* Supplies, as of arms, or clothing. **4.** A large quantity or amount. **5.** A warehouse. — **Syn.** See SHOP. — **in store** Set apart for the future; forthcoming; impending. — **to set store by** To value or esteem; regard. [Aphetic var. of earlier *astore* < OF *estorer* to erect, equip, store < L *instaurare* to restore, erect]

store·house (stôr′hous′, stōr′-) *n.* **1.** A building in which goods are stored; warehouse. **2.** A large or inexhaustible fund; reservoir: a *storehouse* of ideas.

store·keep·er (stôr′kē′pər, stōr′-) *n.* **1.** A person who keeps a retail store or shop; shopkeeper. **2.** One who has charge of receiving and distributing stores; especially, one in charge of naval or military stores.

store·room (stôr′rōōm′, -rŏŏm′, stōr′-) *n.* A room in which things are stored, as supplies.

sto·rey (stôr′ē, stō′rē) See STORY[2].

sto·ried[1] (stôr′ēd, stō′rēd) *adj.* Having or consisting of stories, as a building: usually in compounds: a six-*storied* house. Also **sto′reyed.**

sto·ried[2] (stôr′ēd, stō′rēd) *adj.* **1.** Having a notable history. **2.** Related in a story. **3.** Ornamented with designs representing scenes from history or story.

sto·ri·ette (stôr′ē·et′, stō′rē-) *n.* A short story or tale.

stork (stôrk) *n.* Any of a family (*Ciconiidae*) of large wading birds with long necks and long legs, related to the herons and ibises, especially the Old World **migratory** or **white stork** (*Ciconia ciconia*). [OE *store*]

stork's-bill (stôrks′bil′) *n.* **1.** Any of a genus (*Erodium*) of widely distributed annual or perennial herbs with toothed leaves: also called *heronbill.* **2.** Any species of pelargonium.

storm (stôrm) *n.* **1.** A disturbance of the atmosphere, generally a great whirling motion of the air, accompanied by rain, snow, etc. **2.** *Meteorol.* In the Beaufort scale, a wind force of the 11th degree. See BEAUFORT SCALE. **3.** A furious flight or shower of objects, especially of missiles. **4.** A violent outburst, as of passion or excitement: a *storm* of applause. **5.** *Mil.* A violent and rapid assault on a fortified place. **6.** A violent commotion, as in politics, society, or domestic life. **7.** *U.S. & Canadian Informal* A storm window (which see). — *v.i.* **1.** To blow with violence; rain, snow, hail, etc., heavily: used impersonally: It *stormed* all day. **2.** To be very angry; rage. **3.** To move or rush with violence or rage: He *stormed* about the room. — *v.t.* **4.** *Mil.* To take or try to take by storm. [OE]
Storm may be used as a combining form, as in the following examples:

storm area	storm god	storm-rocked
storm-beaten	storm goddess	storm shutter
storm blast	storm jacket	storm-swept
storm-bound	storm lane	storm-tossed
storm bringer	stormlike	storm-washed
storm coat	storm path	stormwind
	storm-rent	storm-worn

Storm (shtôrm), **Theodor,** 1817–88, German poet and novelist.

storm·belt (stôrm′belt′) *n.* A strip of territory along which storms most frequently move.

storm·bound (stôrm′bound′) *adj.* Delayed, confined, or cut off from communications because of a storm.

storm cellar A cyclone cellar (which see).

storm center 1. *Meteorol.* The center or area of lowest pressure and comparative calm in a cyclonic storm. **2.** The central point of a heated argument; the focus of any trouble.

storm door A strong outer door for added protection during storms and inclement weather.

storm petrel Any of certain small petrels of the North Atlantic; especially *Hydrobates pelagicus*, thought to portend storm; Mother Carey's chicken: also called *stormy petrel.*

storm·proof (stôrm′prŏŏf′) *adj.* Capable of keeping out storms.

storm trooper In Germany, a member of the Nazi party militia unit, the *Sturmabteilung*: also called *Brown Shirt.*

storm warning A signal, as a flag or light, used to warn mariners of coming storm. Also **storm signal.**

storm window An extra window outside the ordinary one as a protection against storms or for greater insulation against cold: also, *Informal,* **storm.**

storm·y (stôr′mē) *adj.* **storm·i·er, storm·i·est 1.** Characterized by or subject to storms; tempestuous. **2.** Characterized by violent emotions or actions: a *stormy* life. [OE *stormig*] — **storm′i·ly** *adv.* — **storm′i·ness** *n.*

stormy petrel 1. The storm petrel (which see). **2.** One who portends trouble or discord, as by rebelling against accepted ideas, practices, etc.

Stor·thing (stôr′ting′, stōr′-) *n.* The Norwegian parliament. Also **Stor′ting′.** [< Norw. < *stor* great + *thing* meeting]

sto·ry[1] (stôr′ē, stō′rē) *n. pl.* **·ries 1.** A narrative or recital of an event or series of events, whether real or fictitious. **2.** A narrative, usually of fictitious events, intended to entertain a reader or hearer. **3.** A short story (which see). **4.** An account or allegation of facts; report. **5.** A news article in a newspaper or magazine; also, the material for such an article. **6.** An anecdote. **7.** *Informal* A lie. **8.** The series of events in a novel, play, etc. **9.** Celebrated or romantic legend or history: to live on in *story.* — **Syn.** See ACCOUNT, LIE[2]. — *v.t.* **·ried, ·ry·ing 1.** To relate as a story. **2.** To adorn with designs representing scenes from history, legend, etc. [< OF *estoire* < L *historia.* Doublet of HISTORY.]

sto·ry[2] (stôr′ē, stō′rē) *n. pl.* **·ries 1.** A horizontal division in a building comprising the space between two successive floors. **2.** Habitable rooms on the same level. **3.** Any of the levels, one above another, into which a building is divided horizontally. Also, *Chiefly Brit.,* **storey.** [Special use of STORY[1]; ? from earlier sense of "a tier of painted windows or sculptures that narrated an event"]

sto·ry·book (stôr′ē·bŏŏk′, stō′rē-) *n.* A book of stories, especially for children. — *adj.* In the style of, or occurring in a storybook; romantic; fantastic.

story line The rough plot of a film, play, novel, etc.

sto·ry·tell·er (stôr′ē·tel′ər, stō′rē-) *n.* **1.** One who relates stories or anecdotes. **2.** *Informal* A prevaricator; liar; fibber. — **sto′ry·tell′ing** *n. & adj.*

stoss (stos, *Ger.* shtōs) *adj. Geol.* Facing the direction toward which a glacier moves: said of a hill, etc. [< G, thrust, push]

sto·tin·ka (stô·ting′kä) *n. pl.* **·ki** (-kē) A small coin of Bulgaria, equivalent to one hundredth of a lev. [< Bulgarian]

stound (stound) *n. Obs.* **1.** A short time. **2.** A sharp pain; pang. — *v.i. Scot.* To ache; hurt. [OE *stund*]

stoup (stōōp) *n.* **1.** *Eccl.* A basin for holy water at the entrance of a church. **2.** *Scot.* A pail, cup, etc.; also, its contents. **3.** A measure for liquids: a pint *stoup.* Also spelled *stoop, stowp.* [< ON *staup* bucket]

stour (stōōr) *n. Archaic or Dial.* **1.** A battle; conflict. **2.** Dust in motion; chaff. Also **stoure.** [< OF *estour* tumult] — **stour′ie, stour′y** *adj.*

stout (stout) *adj.* **1.** Strong or firm of structure or material; sound; tough. **2.** Determined; resolute. **3.** Fat; bulky; thickset. **4.** Substantial; solid: *stout* fare. **5.** Having muscular strength; robust. **6.** Proud; stubborn. — **Syn.** See FAT. — *n.* **1.** A stout person. **2.** A dress or suit made for a stout person. **3.** A strong, very dark porter or ale. [< OF *estout* bold, strong < Gmc. Cf. MDu. *stolt* bold.] — **stout′ly** *adv.* — **stout′ness** *n.*

stout·heart·ed (stout′här′tid) *adj.* Brave; courageous. — **stout′heart′ed·ly** *adv.* — **stout′heart′ed·ness** *n.*

stove[1] (stōv) *n.* **1.** An apparatus, usually of metal, in which gas, oil, electricity, etc., is consumed for heating or cooking. **2.** A drying room or box used in some factories. **3.** A pottery kiln. [OE *stofa* heated room]

stove[2] (stōv) Alternative past tense and past participle of STAVE.

stove·pipe (stōv′pīp′) *n.* **1.** A pipe, usually of thin sheet iron, for conducting the smoke and gases of combustion from a stove to a chimney flue. **2.** *U.S. Informal* A tall silk hat: also **stovepipe hat.**

sto·ver (stō′vər) *n.* Fodder or feed for cattle; cornstalks. [< OF *estover.* See ESTOVERS.]

stow[1] (stō) *v.t.* **1.** To place or arrange compactly; pack. **2.** To fill by packing. **3.** To have room for; hold: said of a room, receptacle, etc. **4.** *Slang* To stop; cease. **5.** *Obs.* To furnish lodging for. — **to stow away 1.** To put in a place of safekeeping, hiding, etc. **2.** To be a stowaway. [ME *stowen* < OE *stōw* place]

stow[2] (stō) *v.t. Scot. & Brit. Dial.* To lop or cut off; crop.

Stow (stō), **John,** 1525?–1605, English historian.

stow·age (stō′ij) *n.* **1.** The act or manner of stowing, or the state of being stowed. **2.** Space for stowing goods; also, the goods stowed. **3.** Charge for stowing goods.

stow·a·way (stō′ə·wā′) *n.* One who conceals himself, as on a vessel, to obtain free passage or evade officials.

Stowe (stō), **Harriet Beecher,** 1811–96, U.S. novelist and humanitarian; wrote *Uncle Tom's Cabin*: original name **Harriet Elizabeth Bee·cher** (bē′chər).

STORM WARNINGS
A Daylight. *B* Night. *a* Small-craft warning. *b* Gale. *c* Whole gale. *d* Hurricane.

Red □ White ■ Black

stown·lins (stoun′linz) *adv. Scot.* Secretly; by stealth.

stowp (stōōp) See STOUP.

St. Paul (sänt pôl′) The capital of Minnesota, in the SE part, on the Mississippi opposite Minneapolis; pop. 309,980.

St. Pe·ters·burg (sänt pē′tərz·bûrg) **1.** A former name for LENINGRAD. **2.** A city in western Florida, on Tampa Bay; pop. 216,232.

St. Pi·erre (sänt pē·âr′, *Fr.* saṅ pyâr′) **1.** A town on southern Réunion Island; pop. 8,752 (est. 1967). **2.** A former town in Martinique, destroyed by the eruption of Mont Pelée, May 8, 1902.

St. Pierre and Mi·que·lon (mik′ə·lon, *Fr.* mē·kə·lôṅ′) Two groups of small islands off the southern coast of Newfoundland comprising a French Overseas Territory; 93 sq. mi.; pop. 5,235 (1967); capital, **St. Pierre.**

str. **1.** Steamer. **2.** Strait. **3.** *Music* String(s).

stra·bis·mus (strə·biz′məs) *n. Pathol.* A condition in which the eyes cannot be simultaneously focused on the same spot. When one or both eyes turn inward (**convergent strabismus**), the patient is *crosseyed*; when outward (**divergent strabismus**), *walleyed* [< NL < Gk. *strabismos* < *strabizein* to squint < *strabos* twisted] — **stra·bis′mal, stra·bis′mic** or **·mi·cal** *adj.*

Stra·bo (strā′bō), 63? B.C.–A.D. 24?, Greek geographer and historian.

stra·bot·o·my (strə·bot′ə·mē) *n. pl.* **·mies** *Surg.* The cutting of the eyeball muscles to correct strabismus. [< Gk. *strabos* squinting + -TOMY]

Stra·chey (strā′chē), John, 1901–63, English politician and writer: full name **Evelyn John St. Loe Strachey.** — **Lytton**, 1880–1932, English biographer and critic: full name **Giles Lytton Strachey.**

strad·dle (strad′l) *v.* **·dled, ·dling** *v.i.* **1.** To stand, walk, or sit with the legs spread apart. **2.** To stand wide apart: said of the legs. **3.** *Informal* To appear to favor both sides of an issue; refuse to commit oneself. — *v.t.* **4.** To stand, walk, or sit with the legs on either side of. **5.** To spread (the legs) wide apart. **6.** *Informal* To appear to favor both sides of (an issue). **7.** *Mil.* To fire shots both beyond and in front of (a target) so as to determine the range. — *n.* **1.** The act of straddling. **2.** The space between the feet or legs of one who straddles. **3.** A noncommittal or vacillating position on any issue. **4.** In the securities trade, a transaction in which the holder obtains the option of either delivering or buying a certain amount of stock or other commodity at a fixed price within a stipulated period: compare CALL, PUT. [Freq. of OE *strǣd-*, var. of *strīdan.* See STRIDE.] — **strad′dler** *n.* — **strad′dling·ly** *adv.*

Stra·di·va·ri (strä′dē·vä′rē), **Antonio**, 1644?–1737, Italian violinmaker. Also **Strad·i·var·i·us** (strad/i·vâr′ē·əs).

Strad·i·var·i·us (strad/i·vâr′ē·əs) *n.* One of the violins produced by Antonio Stradivari, famed for their quality.

strafe (sträf, sträf) *v.t.* **strafed, straf·ing** **1.** To attack (troops, emplacements, etc.) with machine-gun fire from low-flying airplanes. **2.** To bombard or shell heavily. **3.** *Slang* To punish. — *n.* A heavy bombardment. [< G *strafen* to punish] — **straf′er** *n.*

Straf·ford (straf′ərd), **Earl of,** 1593–1641, Thomas Wentworth, English statesman; beheaded.

strag·gle (strag′əl) *v.i.* **·gled, ·gling** **1.** To wander from the road, etc.; stray; especially, to lag behind the main body. **2.** To wander aimlessly about; ramble. **3.** To occur at irregular intervals. [? Freq. of obs. *strake* to move, go about] — **strag′gler** *n.*

strag·gly (strag′lē) *adj.* **·gli·er, ·gli·est** Scattered or spread out irregularly.

straight (strāt) *adj.* **1.** Extending uniformly in one direction without curve or bend: a *straight* road. **2.** Free from kinks; not curly, as hair. **3.** Not stooped or inclined; erect, as in posture. **4.** Not deviating from truth, fairness, or honesty; upright; reliable. **5.** Clear; frank; direct: a *straight* answer. **6.** Free from obstruction; uninterrupted; unbroken. **7.** Correctly kept, ordered, or arranged: Are the facts *straight* in your mind? **8.** Sold without discount for number or quantity taken. **9.** *Informal* Strictly adhering to a particular party or policy: a *straight* Democrat. **10.** In poker, consisting of five cards forming a sequence: a *straight* flush. **11.** Having nothing added; undiluted: *straight* whisky. — *n.* **1.** A straight part or piece. **2.** The part of a racecourse between the winning post and the last turn. **3.** In poker, a numerical sequence of five cards not of the same suit, or a hand containing this. **4.** A straight line. — *adv.* **1.** In a straight line or a direct course. **2.** Closely in line; correspondingly. **3.** At once; straightway. — **to go straight** To reform after a criminal career. [ME *streit, streght* < OE *streht,* pp. of *streccan* to stretch] — **straight′ly** *adv.* — **straight′ness** *n.*

straight angle *Geom.* An angle of 180°, whose sides extend in opposite directions from the vertex: also **flat angle.**

straight-arm (strāt′ärm′) *v.t.* In football, to ward off (a tackler) with an outstretched arm.

straight·a·way (strāt′ə·wā′) *adj.* Having no curve or turn; straightforward. — *n.* A straight course or track. — *adv.* At once; straightway.

straight·edge (strāt′ej′) *n.* A bar of wood or metal having one edge true to a straight line, used for ruling, etc. — **straight′-edged′** *adj.*

straight·en (strāt′n) *v.t.* **1.** To make straight. **2.** To lay out (a corpse). — *v.i.* **3.** To become straight. — **to straighten out** To restore order to; set right; rectify. — **to straighten up** **1.** To free from disorder; make neat; tidy. **2.** To stand in erect posture. **3.** To reform; become honorable after being dishonest. — **straight′en·er** *n.*

straight face A face that betrays no emotion, especially amusement. — **straight-faced** (strāt′fāst′) *adj.*

straight flush See under FLUSH[3].

straight·for·ward (strāt′fôr′wərd) *adj.* **1.** Proceeding in a straight course. **2.** Honest; frank. — *adv.* In a straight course or direct manner: also **straight′for′wards.** — **straight′for′ward·ly** *adv.* — **straight′for′ward·ness** *n.*

straight-line (strāt′līn′) *adj. Mech.* Designating a linkage or similar apparatus intended to copy or generate motion in a straight or nearly straight line.

straight man *U.S. Informal* An entertainer who acts as a foil for a comedian.

straight-out (strāt′out′) *adj. Informal* **1.** Showing the true sentiments or feelings; unreserved. **2.** Real; genuine. **3.** Uncompromising; all-out: a *straight-out* Republican.

straight ticket **1.** A political party ballot or ticket that presents the regular party candidates without addition or change. **2.** A ballot cast for all the candidates of one party.

straight·way (strāt′wā′) *adv.* Immediately; straightaway.

strain[1] (strān) *v.t.* **1.** To exert to the utmost. **2.** To injure by overexertion; sprain; also, to wrench or twist. **3.** To pull or draw tight; stretch. **4.** To stretch beyond the true intent, proper limit, etc.: to *strain* a point. **5.** To pass through a filtering agent or strainer. **6.** To remove by filtration. **7.** To deform in structure or shape as a result of pressure or stress. **8.** To embrace tightly; hug. **9.** *Mech.* To alter in size or shape by applying external force. **10.** *Obs.* To force; constrain. — *v.i.* **11.** To make violent efforts; strive. **12.** To be or become wrenched or twisted. **13.** To filter, trickle, or percolate. — **to strain at** **1.** To push or pull with violent efforts. **2.** To strive for. **3.** To scruple or balk at accepting. — *n.* **1.** An act of straining, or the state of being strained; a violent effort or exertion. **2.** The injury resulting from excessive tension or effort. **3.** Severe mental or emotional tension. **4.** *Mech.* Change of shape or size of a body, especially of a solid, produced by the action of a stress; deformation. — *Syn.* See STRESS. [< OF *estrein-,* stem of *estreindre* < L *stringere* to bind tight]

strain[2] (strān) *n.* **1.** Line of descent, or the individuals, collectively, in that line; race; stock. **2.** Inborn or hereditary tendency; trace; element: to have a heroic *strain* in one's character. **3.** *Biol.* A special line of animals or plants bred from a certain species or variety and maintained at a high standard of perfection by selection. **4.** *Rare* Distinguishing nature or quality; kind; sort. **5.** *Often pl.* A passage of music or other sound when heard. **6.** A passage in a poem. **7.** Prevailing tone, style, or manner; mood. [? Var. of ME *strene,* OE *strēon* offspring]

strained (strānd) *adj.* Not relaxed or natural; forced.

strain·er (strā′nər) *n.* **1.** One who or that which strains. **2.** A utensil or device, containing meshes or porous parts, through which liquids are passed to separate them from coarse particles. **3.** A device used for tightening, strengthening, or stretching.

strain·ing beam (strā′ning) *Archit.* A tie beam receiving a lengthwise pulling stress, and connecting the rafters of a roof with the tops of the queen posts. Also **straining piece.**

strait (strāt) *n.* **1.** *Often pl.* A narrow passage of water connecting two larger bodies of water. Abbr. *St.,* **str. 2.** *Often pl.* A position of perplexity or distress. **3.** *Rare* Any narrow pass or passage. — *adj.* **1.** *Archaic* Of small transverse dimensions; narrow. **2.** Restricted as to space or room; close. **3.** Righteous; strict. [< OF *estreit* < L *strictus,* pp. of *stringere* to bind tight. Doublet of STRICT.] — **strait′ly** *adv.* — **strait′ness** *n.*

strait·en (strāt′n) *v.t.* **1.** To make strait or narrow; contract; restrict. **2.** To embarrass, as in finances; also, to distress. **3.** *Archaic* To keep within narrow limits.

strait·ened (strāt′nd) *adj.* **1.** Contracted; narrowed. **2.** Suffering privation or hardship, as from lack of money.

strait jacket A tight jacket of strong canvas, for confining the arms of violent patients.

strait-laced (strāt′lāst′) *adj.* **1.** Strict, especially in morals or manners. **2.** *Archaic* Encased in tight corsets.

Strait of, etc. See specific name, as (Strait of) MAGELLAN, (Strait of) MALACCA, etc.

Straits (strāts), **The** The Bosporus and the Dardanelles considered as a single passage from the Mediterranean to the Black Sea.

Straits Settlements A former British crown colony comprising Singapore, Penang, Malacca, and Labuan; dissolved, 1946.

strake (strāk) *n. Naut.* A breadth of planking or line of plating on a vessel's hull from stem to stern: also called *streak.* [Appar. akin to STRETCH; infl. in meaning by STREAK]

Stral·sund (shträl′zōŏnt) A port city in northern East Germany, on the Baltic; pop. about 65,000.

stra·min·e·ous (strə-min′ē-əs) adj. 1. Straw-colored. 2. Strawlike; chaffy. [< L stramineus < stramen straw]

stra·mo·ni·um (strə-mō′nē-əm) n. 1. The jimsonweed. 2. A drug prepared from the dried leaves and flowering tops of this plant, used as a sedative and antispasmodic. Also **stram·o·ny** (stram′ə-nē). [< NL < Med.L stramonia, ? ult. < Tartar turman medicine for horses]

strand[1] (strand) n. A shore or beach; especially, that portion of an ocean shore between high and low tides. — Syn. See SHORE[1]. — v.t. & v.i. 1. To drive or run aground. 2. To leave or be left in straits or difficulties: usually in the passive. [OE strand]

strand[2] (strand) n. 1. One of the principal twists or members of a rope. 2. A fiber, hair, or the like. 3. A number of wires twisted into a cable. 4. Anything plaited or twisted. 5. A string of beads or pearls. — v.t. 1. To break a strand of (a rope). 2. To make by twisting strands. [? < OF estran < Gmc.]

strand line A line marking the boundary between the shore and the ocean, especially a line higher than the present one.

strang (strang) adj. Scot. Strong.

strange (strānj) adj. **strang·er**, **strang·est** 1. Previously unknown, unseen, or unheard of; unfamiliar. 2. Not according to the ordinary way; unaccountable; remarkable. 3. Pertaining to another or others; of a different class, character, or kind. 4. Foreign; alien. 5. Distant in manner; reserved; shy. 6. Inexperienced; unskilled; unaccustomed. — adv. In a strange manner. [< OF estrange < L extraneus foreign < extra on the outside. Doublet of EXTRANEOUS.] — **strange·ly** adv. — **strange·ness** n.

stran·ger (strān′jər) n. 1. One who is not an acquaintance. 2. An unfamiliar visitor; guest. 3. A foreigner. 4. One unversed in or unacquainted or unfamiliar with something specified: with to. 5. Law Any person who is neither a party to a transaction nor privy to it. [< OF estrangier < estrange. See STRANGE.]

stran·gle (strang′gəl) v. **·gled**, **·gling** v.t. 1. To choke to death; throttle; suffocate. 2. To repress; suppress: to strangle a sob. 3. To inhibit the action or development of. — v.i. 4. To suffer or die from strangulation. [< F estrangier < L strangulare < Gk. strangalaein < strangalē halter < strangos twisted] — **stran′gler** n.

strangle hold 1. In wrestling, a usually illegal hold that chokes one's opponent. 2. Any influence or power that chokes freedom or progress.

stran·gu·late (strang′gyə-lāt) v.t. **·lat·ed**, **·lat·ing** 1. To strangle. 2. Pathol. To compress, contract, or obstruct, especially so as to cut off circulation of the blood or flow of fluid. — adj. Strangulated. [< L strangulatus, pp. of strangulare. See STRANGLE.]

strangulated hernia Pathol. A form of hernia in which the affected organ is so tightly constricted as to cut off normal circulation of the blood.

stran·gu·la·tion (strang′gyə-lā′shən) n. 1. The act of strangling, or the state of being strangled. 2. Pathol. The constriction of a part, as of the intestine in strangulated hernia, to cut off circulation.

stran·gu·ry (strang′gyə-rē) n. Pathol. Slow and painful urination. [< L stranguria < Gk. strangouria < stranx, strangos drop + ouron urine]

strap (strap) n. 1. A long, narrow, and flexible strip of leather, etc., usually having a buckle or other fastener, for binding about objects. 2. A razor strop. 3. A shoulder strap (which see). 4. Something made of, resembling, or used as a strap. 5. A thin metal band. 6. A loop of metal, leather, etc., suspended overhead, used as a handgrip by standees in buses, trains, etc. — v.t. **strapped**, **strap·ping** 1. To fasten or bind with a strap. 2. To beat with a strap. 3. To embarrass financially. 4. To sharpen or strop. 5. Scot. To hang. [Var. of STROP] — **strap′less** adj.

strap·hang·er (strap′hang·ər) n. A standee on a bus, etc., especially one who holds on to an overhead strap.

strap hinge A hinge having long leaves, designed for attaching to the flat surfaces of a door and jamb. For illustration see HINGE.

strap·pa·do (strə-pā′dō, -pä′dō) n. pl. **·does** 1. A punishment in which one was drawn up by a rope attached usually to the wrists, and let fall to the length of the rope, just short of the ground. 2. The device used. [< Ital. strappata a pulling, orig. fem. pp. of strappare to pull, ? < Gmc.]

strap·per (strap′ər) n. 1. One who uses straps. 2. Informal A strong, tall person. 3. One who grooms horses.

strap·ping (strap′ing) adj. Informal Large and muscular; robust; burly.

Stras·bourg (stras′bûrg, sträz′-; Fr. sträz·bōŏr′) A port city in NE France, on the Rhine; pop. 247,526 (1968). German **Strass·burg** (sträs′bŏŏrkh).

strass (stras) n. Paste[1] (def. 3). [after Josef Strasser, 18th c. German jeweler]

stra·ta (strā′tə, strat′ə) Alternative plural of STRATUM.

strat·a·gem (strat′ə-jəm) n. 1. A maneuver designed to deceive or outwit an enemy in war. 2. A device for obtaining advantage; trick. — Syn. See ARTIFICE. [< F stratagème < L stratagema < Gk. stratēgema piece of generalship < stratēgos general < stratos army + agein to lead]

stra·tal (strāt′l) adj. Of, pertaining to, or characteristic of a stratum or strata.

stra·te·gic (strə-tē′jik) adj. 1. Of or pertaining to strategy. 2. Characterized by, used in, or having relation to strategy. Also **stra·te′gi·cal**, **strat·e·get·ic** (strat′ə-jet′ik) or **·i·cal**. — **stra·te′gi·cal·ly**, **strat′e·get′i·cal·ly** adv.

stra·te·gics (strə-tē′jiks) n.pl. (construed as sing.) The art or science of strategy; generalship.

strat·e·gist (strat′ə-jist) n. One versed in strategy, or skilled in managing affairs.

strat·e·gy (strat′ə-jē) n. pl. **·gies** 1. The science and art of conducting a military campaign on a broad scale: distinguished from tactics. 2. The use of stratagem or artifice, as in business or politics. 3. A plan or technique for achieving some end. [< F stratégie < Gk. strategia < stratēgos general. See STRATAGEM.]

Strat·ford (strat′fərd) A town in SE Connecticut, on Long Island Sound; pop. 49,775.

Strat·ford-on-A·von (strat′fərd·on·ā′von) A town in SW Warwickshire, England, on the Avon; birthplace and burial place of Shakespeare; pop. 19,110 (est. 1969).

strath (strath) n. Scot. A wide, open valley or river course.

Strath·co·na and Mount Royal (strath·kō′nə), **Lord,** 1820–1914, Donald Alexander Smith, British administrator in Canada; helped build Canadian railroads.

strath·spey (strath′spā′, strath′spā′) n. 1. A Scottish dance resembling the reel. 2. The music for this dance.

strati- combining form Stratum; of or pertaining to a stratum or strata: stratiform. Also, before vowels, **strat-**. [< L stratum covering, layer]

strat·i·form (strat′ə-fôrm) adj. 1. Geol. Having the form of or constituting a stratum. 2. Anat. Denoting a fibrous cartilage enclosed in a channel in a bone as a support for tendons. 3. Meteorol. Resembling a stratus cloud. [< STRATI- + -FORM]

strat·i·fy (strat′ə-fī) v. **·fied**, **·fy·ing** v.t. 1. To form or arrange in strata. 2. To preserve (seeds) by spreading in alternating layers of earth and sand. — v.i. 3. To form in strata. 4. Geol. To be formed in strata, as rocks. 5. Sociol. To form social groups at different levels as determined by class, caste, or status. [< F stratifier < Med.L stratificare < L stratum layer + facere to make] — **strat′i·fi·ca′tion** n.

stra·tig·ra·phy (strə-tig′rə-fē) n. Geol. 1. The order and relative position of the strata of the earth's crust. 2. The study or description of such strata. [< STRATI- + -GRAPHY] — **strat·i·graph·ic** (strat′ə-graf′ik) or **·i·cal** adj. — **strat′i·graph′i·cal·ly** adv.

stra·toc·ra·cy (strə-tok′rə-sē) n. pl. **·cies** Government by the armed forces or military class. [< Gk. stratos army + -CRACY] — **strat·o·crat·ic** (strat′ə-krat′ik) adj.

stra·to·cu·mu·lus (strā′tō·kyōō′myə-ləs) n. pl. **·li** (-lī) Meteorol. Large globular masses of cloud (Symbol Sc), gray to black in color, disposed in waves, groups, or bands, and often covering the whole sky: also called cumulostratus. See table for CLOUD. [< strato- (< STRATUS) + CUMULUS]

strat·o·pause (strat′ə-pôz) n. Meteorol. The zone of transition between the stratosphere and the mesosphere.

strat·o·sphere (strat′ə-sfir, strā′tə-) n. Meteorol. That portion of the atmosphere beginning at a height of about seven miles and characterized by a more or less uniform temperature: also called isothermal layer. — **strat′o·spher′ic** (-sfir′ik, -sfer′-) or **·i·cal** adj.

stra·tum (strā′təm, strat′əm) n. pl. **·ta** (-tə) or **·tums** 1. A natural or artificial layer, bed, or thickness. 2. Geol. A more or less homogeneous layer of rock, often in two or more beds, and serving to identify a geological group, system or series. 3. Biol. A sheet or layer of tissue. 4. Something corresponding to a layer, bed, or grade: a low stratum of society. [< L, orig. neut. of stratus, pp. of sternere to spread]

stra·tus (strā′təs, strat′əs) n. pl. **·ti** (-tī) Meteorol. A cloud (Symbol St) of foglike appearance, low-lying and arranged in a uniform layer. See table for CLOUD. [< L, orig. pp. of sternere to spread]

Straus (strous, Ger. shtrous), **Oscar,** 1870–1954, Austrian composer.

Strauss (strous, Ger. shtrous), **David Friedrich,** 1808–74, German theologian and biographer. — **Johann,** 1804–49, Austrian composer. — **Johann,** 1825–99, Austrian composer; son of Johann: called the Waltz King. — **Richard,** 1864–1949, German composer.

stra·vage (strə-vāg′) Irish & Scot. v.i. **·vaged**, **·vag·ing** To stroll; ramble. — n. A stroll. Also **stra·vaig′**, **stra·vague′**. — **stra·vaig′er** n.

STRATUS CLOUD

Stra·vin·sky (strə-vin′skē, *Russ.* strə-vyĕn′skyē), **Igor Fë·dorovich**, 1882–1971, U.S. composer born in Russia.
straw (strô) *n.* **1.** A slender tube of paper, glass, etc., used to suck up a beverage. **2.** Stems or stalks of grain, collectively, after the grain has been thrashed out. **3.** A dry or ripened stalk. **4.** A natural or sometimes artificial strawlike fiber, used in making hats, etc. **5.** Something of little value; a mere trifle. **— the last straw** The final test of patience or endurance: from the phrase **the straw that broke the camel's back**. **— to clutch** (**grasp, catch,** etc.) **at a straw** To try in desperation any solution or expedient. *— adj.* **1.** Like or of straw. **2.** Of no value; worthless; sham. **3.** Made of straw. **4.** Yellowish, as the color of straw. [OE *strēaw*]
straw·ber·ry (strô′ber′ē, -bər·ē) *n. pl.* **·ries 1.** The edible fruit of a stemless perennial herb (genus *Fragaria*) of the rose family. **2.** The plant bearing this fruit. [ME *strauberi* < OE *strēawberige* < *strēaw* straw + *berige* berry]
strawberry bass The calico bass (which see).
strawberry blond A person having reddish blond hair.
strawberry bush The wahoo[1].
strawberry shrub A shrub (genus *Calycanthus*), whose purple or dark red flowers smell like strawberries.
strawberry tomato A variety of ground cherry.
strawberry tree A small evergreen tree (*Arbutus unedo*) of southern Europe, having racemose white flowers and edible fruit resembling strawberries.
straw·board (strô′bôrd′, -bōrd′) *n.* Coarse board, made of straw, used for paper boxes and book covers.
straw boss *U.S. Informal* In construction work, logging, etc., an underforeman.
straw color A pale yellow color, as of clean ripe straw. **— straw-col·ored** (strô′kul′ərd) *adj.*
straw-hat circuit (strô′hat′) *U.S.* A theater or concert circuit of summer resort areas.
straw man A lame or spurious argument, proposition, etc., offered only to gain a victory by its easy refutation.
straw vote An unofficial vote to test the strength of opposing candidates, determine group opinion, etc.
straw wine A sweet wine made from grapes dried on straw.
straw·worm (strô′wûrm′) *n.* The caddis worm. See under CADDIS FLY.
straw·y (strô′ē) *adj.* **straw·i·er, straw·i·est 1.** Of or like straw. **2.** Covered or thatched with straw.
stray (strā) *v.i.* **1.** To wander from the proper course, an area, group, etc.; straggle; roam. **2.** To wander about; rove. **3.** To fail to concentrate; digress. **4.** To deviate from right or goodness; go astray. *— adj.* **1.** Having strayed; straying. **2.** Irregular; occasional; casual; unrelated. *— n.* **1.** A domestic animal that has strayed. **2.** A person who is lost or wanders aimlessly. **3.** The act of straying or wandering. **4.** *pl. Telecom.* Electromagnetic waves, affecting a radio receiver, produced by atmospheric electric discharges and electrical storms. [< OF *estraier* to wander about, ult. < L *extra vagare* to wander outside] **— stray′er** *n.*
streak (strēk) *n.* **1.** A long, narrow, somewhat irregularly shaped mark, line, or stripe: a *streak* of lightning. **2.** A vein or trace; dash: a *streak* of meanness; also, a transient mood; whim. **3.** A period of time; a spell. **4.** *Mineral.* The color of the line of powder left when a mineral is rubbed on an unglazed porcelain plate known as a **streak plate.** **5.** A strake. **6.** A layer or strip: meat with a *streak* of fat. **7.** *Bacteriol.* The application of bacterial or viral material in a thin stripe or line across the surface of a culture medium. *— v.t.* **1.** To mark with a streak; form streaks in or on; stripe. *— v.i.* **2.** To form a streak or streaks. **3.** To move, run, or travel at great speed. [OE *strica.* Akin to STRIKE.] **— streaked** (strēkt) *adj.*
streak·ing *n.* The fad, esp. among college students, of running nude in a public place.
streak·y (strē′kē) *adj.* **streak·i·er, streak·i·est 1.** Marked with or occurring in streaks; streaked. **2.** Of variable quality or character; not uniform. **— streak′i·ly** *adv.* **— streak′i·ness** *n.*
stream (strēm) *n.* **1.** A current or flow of water or other fluid. **2.** Anything continuously flowing, moving, or passing, as people. **3.** A continuous course or advance; drift; current. **4.** Anything issuing out or flowing from a source; a ray. **— on stream** In full commercial production, as an oil refinery, chemical plant, etc. **— to go** (or **drift**) **with the stream** To live or behave as everyone else does; conform. *— v.i.* **1.** To pour forth or issue in a stream. **2.** To pour forth a stream: eyes *streaming* with tears. **3.** To move in continuous succession; proceed uninterruptedly, as a crowd from a hall. **4.** To float with a waving movement, as a flag. **5.** To move with a trail of light, as a meteor. **6.** In mining or dyeing, to wash in running water. *— v.t.* **7.** To emit or exude. **8.** To cause (a flag, etc.) to stretch forth; display. [OE *strēam*] **— stream′y** *adj.*
— Syn. (noun) **1.** watercourse, river, brook, creek, streamlet, rivulet, rill, run, runlet, runnel. **3.** flow, flux, tide.
stream·er (strē′mər) *n.* **1.** An object that streams forth, or hangs extended. **2.** A long, narrow flag or standard. **3.** A shaft of light, such as shoots up from the horizon. **4.** A newspaper headline that runs across the whole page.

stream·let (strēm′lit) *n.* A small stream; rivulet.
stream·line (strēm′līn′) *n.* **1.** *Physics* **a** The course of a fluid in which every particle maintains an identical speed and direction of flow; especially, a course free of turbulence or eddies. **b** The path traversed by one particle in such a course. **2.** Any shape or contour designed to offer minimum resistance to fluid flow. *— adj.* **1.** Streamlined. **2.** Designating an uninterrupted flow or drift. *— v.t.* **·lined, ·lin·ing 1.** To design with a streamlined shape. **2.** To make more simple, efficient, or up to date.
stream·lined (strēm′līnd′) *adj.* **1.** Designed to offer the least resistance to a flow of fluid, as air, etc.: also *streamline.* **2.** Modern; up-to-date. **3.** Simply or efficiently organized.
stream of consciousness *Psychol.* The series of individual conscious states moving continuously on in time.
stream-of-con·scious·ness technique (strēm′əv·kon′shəs·nis) A method of writing fiction in which an author objectifies the characters' inward thoughts, feelings, and sensations to replace dialogue and narrated action.
streek (strēk) *Scot. v.t.* **1.** To stretch or extend. **2.** To lay out, as a corpse. *— n.* Extent; progress.
street (strēt) *n.* **1.** A public way in a city or town, with buildings on one or both sides; also, the roadway for vehicles, between sidewalks. **2.** *Informal* The people living, habitually gathering, or doing business in a street. Abbr. *st., St.* [OE *strǣt* < LL *strata (via)* paved (road)]
Street may appear as a combining form or as the first element in two-word phrases, with the following meanings:
1. Of or pertaining to a street or streets:

street cleaner	street name	street-sprinkling
street-cleaning	street planner	street sweeper
street directory	street planning	street-sweeping
street layer	street sprinkler	street-widening

2. In the streets:

street beggar	street music	street-pacing
street-bred	street musician	street peddler
street fight	street noise	street singer

3. On or abutting a street:

| street corner | street entrance | street gate |
| street door | street floor | street lamp |

street Arab A homeless or outcast child who lives in the streets; a gamin.
street·car (strēt′kär′) *n.* A public passenger car of an electric railway that runs on tracks set into the streets: also called *trolley, trolley car, Brit., tramcar.*
street people People, especially young people, usually without a permanent home and having a life style like that of hippies.
street·walk·er (strēt′wô′kər) *n.* A prostitute who solicits in the streets. **— street′walk′ing** *n. & adj.*
strength (strengkth, strength) *n.* **1.** The quality or property of being strong; muscular force or power. **2.** The capacity of material bodies to sustain the application of force without yielding or breaking; solidity; tenacity; toughness. **3.** Power in general, or a source of power. **4.** Binding force or validity, as of a law. **5.** Vigor or force of intellect, moral power, style, etc. **6.** Available numerical force in a military unit or other organization. **7.** Degree of intensity; vehemence: *strength* of passion. **8.** The degree of intensity or concentration, as of a color, odor, etc. **9.** Potency, as of a drug, chemical, or liquor. **10.** Rising prices; firmness of prices. **11.** One regarded as an embodiment of sustaining or protecting power. **12.** *Archaic & Poetic* A fortress. **— on the strength of** Based on or in reliance or dependence on. [OE *strengthu < strang* strong]
strength·en (strengk′thən, streng′-) *v.t.* **1.** To make strong. **2.** To encourage; hearten; animate. *— v.i.* **3.** To become or grow strong or stronger. **— strength′en·er** *n.*
stren·u·ous (stren′yōō·əs) *adj.* **1.** Necessitating or characterized by strong effort or exertion. **2.** Vigorously active or zealous, as a person. [< L *strenuus.* Akin to Gk. *strēnēs* strong.] **— stren′u·ous·ly** *adv.* **— stren′u·os′i·ty** (-os′ə·tē), **stren′u·ous·ness** *n.*
streph·o·sym·bo·li·a (stref′ō·sim·bō′lē·ə) *n.* A condition in which objects, letters, etc., are seen in reverse, as in a mirror. [< NL < Gk. *strephein* to twist + *symbolon* sign]
strep·i·tous (strep′i·təs) *adj.* Noisy; boisterous. Also **strep′i·tant** (-tənt). [< L *strepitus* din, noise]
strep·to·coc·cus (strep′tə·kok′əs) *n. pl.* **·coc·ci** (-kok′sī) Any of a genus (*Streptococcus*) of Gram-positive, typically nonmotile ovoid or spherical bacteria, grouped in long chains, including species causing many diseases, as scarlet fever, etc. For illustration see BACTERIUM. [< NL < Gk. *streptos* twisted + COCCUS] **— strep′to·coc′cal** (-kok′əl), **strep′to·coc′cic** (-kok′sik) *adj.*
strep·to·my·cin (strep′tō·mī′sin) *n.* A potent antibiotic, $C_{21}H_{39}N_7O_{12}$, isolated from a moldlike organism (*Streptomyces griseus*). [< Gk. *streptos* twisted + *mykēs* fungus]
strep·to·thri·cin (strep′tō·thrī′sin, -thris′in) *n.* An antibiotic isolated from a soil fungus (*Actinomyces lavendulae*). [< NL *Streptothrix* former genus name < Gk. *streptos* twisted + *thrix* hair + -IN]
stress (stres) *n.* **1.** Special weight, importance, or significance: to lay *stress* on the classics. **2.** In prosody, an em-

phasis given to a specific word or syllable to indicate the metrical pattern. **3.** *Music* An accent (def. 7). **4.** *Mech.* **a** Force exerted between contiguous portions of a body or bodies and generally expressed in pounds per square inch; strain; tension. **b** A force or system of forces that tends to produce deformation in a body. **c** The resistance of a body to external forces. **5.** Influence exerted forcibly; pressure; compulsion. **6.** Emotional or intellectual strain or tension. **7.** *Phonet.* The relative force with which a sound, syllable, or word is uttered. — *v.t.* **1.** To subject to mechanical stress. **2.** To put stress or emphasis on; accent, as a syllable. **3.** To put into straits or difficulties; distress. [< OF *estrece* < *estrecier* to constrain < L *strictus*, pp. of *stringere* to draw tight] — **stress′ful** *adj.* — **stress′less** *adj.*

— **Syn.** (noun) **4.** *Stress, strain, pressure, thrust, shear, torsion,* and *tension* are compared as they relate to mechanical forces acting on a body. *Stress* is the measure of such a force; *strain* is the resistance of a body to a force, or the deformation of the body caused by a force. *Pressure* applies to a force distributed uniformly over the surface of a body, tending to squeeze the molecules of the body together; a local *pressure* that tends to displace a body in space is a *thrust. Shear* refers to the action of two forces that are not directly opposed, and that tend to cause sections of a body to slide over each other. *Torsion* refers to a twisting force, while *tension* is a force that tends to pull something apart.

-stress *suffix of nouns* Feminine form of -STER: *songstress.*

stress accent *Phonet.* The prominence given by means of stress to a sound, syllable, or word.

stretch (strech) *v.t.* **1.** To extend or draw out, as to full length or width. **2.** To extend or draw out forcibly, especially beyond normal or proper limits: The weight has *stretched* the cable; to *stretch* the truth. **3.** To cause to reach, as from one place to another or over an area; extend: They *stretched* telegraph wires across the continent. **4.** To put forth, hold out, or extend (the hand, an object, etc.): often with *out*: to *stretch* out the hands in appeal. **5.** To draw tight; tighten. **6.** To strain or exert to the utmost: to *stretch* every nerve. **7.** To cause to be enough; make do with: to *stretch* one's salary with economies. — *v.i.* **8.** To reach or extend over an area or from one place to another: The road *stretches* on and on. **9.** To become extended, especially beyond normal or proper limits. **10.** To extend one's body or limbs, especially to relieve stiffness. **11.** To lie down and extend one's limbs to full length: usually with *out.* — *n.* **1.** The act of stretching, or the state of being stretched. **2.** Extent or reach of that which stretches; scope. **3.** A continuous extent of space or time. **4.** In racing, the part of the track that, being straight, permits the greatest speed; the straightaway. **5.** A particular direction or course. **6.** *Slang* A term of imprisonment. — *adj.* Capable of stretching or of being stretched; elastic: *stretch* pants. [OE *streccan* to stretch] — **stretch′a·ble** *adj.* — **stretch′i·ness** *n.* — **stretch′y** *adj.*

stretch·er (strech′ər) *n.* **1.** One who or that which stretches. **2.** Any device for stretching, as for loosening the fit of gloves or shoes, for drying curtains, etc. **3.** A frame, as of stretched canvas, for carrying the wounded, sick, or dead; a litter. **4.** In masonry, a brick or stone lying lengthwise of a course. **5.** A tie beam in the frame of a building.

stretch·er-bear·er (strech′ər-bâr′ər) *n.* One who carries one end of a stretcher or litter. Also **stretch′er·man′** (-man′).

stretch-out (strech′out′) *n.* **1.** A system of industrial operation in which employees do more work without proportionate increase in pay. **2.** A slowdown practiced by employees so as to make the work last longer.

stretch·pants (strech′pants′) *n. U.S.* Ski pants or slacks made of an elastic fabric, and hence fitting very closely.

stret·to (stret′tō) *n.* *pl.* **·ti** (-tē) or **·tos** *Music* **1.** A portion of a fugue, near the close, in which the answer crowds closely on the subject. **2.** In an oratorio or operatic piece, the portion at the close accelerated in time to produce a climax: also **stret′ta** (-tä). [< Ital., lit., drawn tight < L *strictus.* See STRESS.]

strew (strōō) *v.t.* **strewed, strewed** or **strewn, strew·ing** **1.** To spread about loosely or at random; scatter; sprinkle. **2.** To cover with something scattered or sprinkled. **3.** To be scattered over (a surface). [OE *strewian*]

stri·a (strī′ə) *n.* *pl.* **stri·ae** (strī′ē) **1.** A narrow streak, stripe, or band of distinctive color, structure, or texture, often parallel with others. **2.** *Geol.* A small groove, channel, or ridge on a rock surface, due to the action of glacier ice. **3.** *pl. Mineral.* Minute parallel grooves on the face of a crystal, especially after cleavage. **4.** *pl. Zool.* Concentric or radiating grooves on the surface of certain shells. [< L, groove]

stri·ate (strī′āt) *adj.* **1.** Having fine linear markings; striped or grooved. **2.** Constituting a stria or striae. Also **stri′at·ed.** — *v.t.* **·at·ed, ·at·ing** To mark with striae. [< L *striatus,* pp. of *striare* to groove < *stria* groove]

stri·a·tion (strī-ā′shən) *n.* **1.** The state or condition of being striated; striate form or appearance. **2.** One of a series of parallel striae. Also **stri·a·ture** (strī′ə·chər).

strick (strik) *n.* A bunch of fibers, as flax, hackled or ready for hackling. [ME *stric,* prob. < LG]

strick·en (strik′ən) Alternative past participle of STRIKE. ◆ *Stricken,* obsolete in British, is current in American English in certain senses: *stricken* with grief or with a disease; a remark *stricken* from the record. — *adj.* **1.** Strongly affected or afflicted; overcome, as by calamity or disease. **2.** Wounded, especially by a missile: a *stricken* hare. **3.** Having the contents leveled off even with the top of a container. [OE *stricen,* pp. of *strīcan* to strike]

strick·le (strik′əl) *n.* **1.** A straightedge used for striking off an even measure of grain. **2.** A template or curved piece of wood used in smoothing a sand or loam mold to form a core. **3.** A tool for sharpening scythes. — *v.t.* **·led, ·ling** To shape or smooth with a strickle. [OE *stricel*]

strict (strikt) *adj.* **1.** Observing or enforcing rules exactly; severe. **2.** Containing exact or severe rules or provisions; exacting. **3.** Rigorously enjoined, maintained, and observed. **4.** Exactly defined, distinguished, or applied; not indefinite. **5.** Complete; absolute: *strict* attention. **6.** *Bot.* Close, narrow, and upright, as the panicles of certain plants. **7.** *Archaic* Strait. [< L *strictus,* pp. of *stringere* to draw tight. Doublet of STRAIT.] — **strict′ly** *adv.* — **strict′ness** *n.*

stric·tion (strik′shən) *n. Rare* Constriction. [< L *strictio, -onis* < *strictus.* See STRICT.]

stric·ture (strik′chər) *n.* **1.** Severe criticism. **2.** *Pathol.* An abnormal contraction of some duct or channel. **3.** *Obs.* Strictness. [< L *strictura* < *strictus.* See STRICT.]

stride (strīd) *n.* **1.** A long and sweeping or measured step. **2.** The space passed over by such a step. **3.** A progressive movement by an animal, completed when all the feet are returned to the same relative positions they occupied at the beginning of the movement. **4.** A stage of progress. — **to hit one's stride** To attain one's normal speed. — **to make rapid strides** To make quick progress. — **to take (something) in one's stride** To do or react to (something) without undue effort or disturbance, as if part of one's normal activity. — *v.* **strode, strid·den, strid·ing** *v.i.* **1.** To walk with long steps, as from haste or pride. **2.** *Archaic* To straddle. — *v.t.* **3.** To walk through, along, etc., with long steps. **4.** To pass over with a single stride. **5.** To straddle; bestride. [OE *strīdan*] — **strid′er** *n.*

stri·dent (strīd′nt) *adj.* Having or making a high, harsh sound; shrill; grating. [< L *stridens, -entis,* ppr. of *stridere* to creak] — **stri′dence, stri′den·cy** *n.* — **stri′dent·ly** *adv.*

stri·dor (strī′dər) *n.* **1.** A harsh, shrill, creaking, or grating noise. **2.** *Pathol.* A harsh, grating noise characteristic of respiratory obstruction. [< L]

strid·u·late (strij′oo·lāt) *v.i.* **·lat·ed, ·lat·ing** To make a shrill, creaking noise, as a cicada or cricket. [< NL *stridulatus,* pp. of *stridulare* < *stridulus* rattling < *stridere* to rattle, rasp] — **strid′u·la′tion** *n.* — **strid′u·la·to′ry** (-lə·tôr′ē, -tō′rē) *adj.*

strid·u·lous (strij′oo·ləs) *adj.* Making a shrill, creaking sound. — **strid′u·lous·ly** *adv.* — **strid′u·lous·ness** *n.*

strife (strīf) *n.* **1.** Angry contention; fighting. **2.** Any contest for advantage or superiority; rivalry. **3.** *Rare* The act of striving. [< OF *estrif* < *estriver.* See STRIVE.]

strig·il (strij′il) *n.* **1.** In ancient Greece and Rome, a scraper made of metal, bone, or ivory, and used for scraping the skin, as at the bath. **2.** *Archit.* One of a group of wavy flutings carved on flat or curved surfaces. [< L *strigilis*]

stri·gose (strī′gōs, strī·gōs′) *adj.* **1.** *Bot.* Rough with short, stiff hairs or bristles, as a leaf; hispid. **2.** *Zool.* Marked with narrow stripes or striae. [< NL *strigosus* < L *striga* furrow]

strike (strīk) *v.* **struck, struck** or, sometimes, **strick·en, strik·ing** *v.t.* **1.** To come into violent contact with; hit. **2.** To hit with a blow; deal a blow to; smite. **3.** To deal (a blow, etc.). **4.** To cause to hit forcibly: He *struck* his hand on the table. **5.** To attack; assault: We *struck* the enemy on his left flank. **6.** To remove, separate, or take off by or as by a blow or stroke: with *off, from,* etc.: *Strike* it from the record. **7.** To ignite (a match, etc.); also, to produce (a light, etc.) thus. **8.** To form by stamping, printing, etc.; impress; coin. **9.** To indicate (a specified time) by the sound of a stroke, bell, etc.: The clock *struck* two. **10.** To fall upon; reach; catch: A sound of crying *struck* his ear. **11.** To arrive at; come upon: to *strike* a trail. **12.** To discover; find: to *strike* oil. **13.** To affect suddenly or in a specified manner: He was *struck* speechless. **14.** To come to the mind of; occur to: An idea *strikes* me. **15.** To impress in a specified manner; seem to: He *strikes* me as an honest man. **16.** To attract the attention of; impress: The dress *struck* her fancy. **17.** To assume; take up: to *strike* an attitude. **18.** To cause to enter or penetrate deeply or suddenly: to *strike* dismay into one's heart. **19.** To lower or haul down, as a sail, or a flag in token of surrender. **20.** To cease working at in order to compel compliance to a demand, etc. **21.** In the theater, to dismantle (a set or scene). **22.** To make level (a measure of grain, etc.); strickle. **23.** To make and confirm; as a bargain. **24.** To harpoon (a whale). **25.** To hook (a fish that has taken the lure) by a sharp pull on the line. **26.** To arrive at by reckoning: to *strike* a bal-

ance. — *v.i.* **27.** To come into violent contact; hit. **28.** To deal or aim a blow or blows. **29.** To make an assault or attack. **30.** To make a sound by or as by means of a blow or blows. **31.** To be indicated by the sound of blows or strokes: Noon has just *struck.* **32.** To ignite. **33.** To run aground, as on a reef or shoal: The ship *struck* and heeled over. **34.** To lower a flag in token of surrender or in salute. **35.** To come suddenly or unexpectedly; chance: with *on* or *upon:* to *strike* upon an unknown path. **36.** To take a course; start and proceed: to *strike* for home. **37.** To move quickly; dart. **38.** To cease work in order to enforce demands, etc. **39.** To snatch at or swallow the lure: said of fish. ◆ See note under STRICKEN. **— to strike camp** To take down the tents of a camp. **— to strike down 1.** To fell with a blow. **2.** To affect disastrously; incapacitate completely. **— to strike dumb** To astonish; amaze. **— to strike hands** To clasp hands, especially in confirming a bargain. **— to strike home 1.** To deal an effective blow. **2.** To have telling effect. **— to strike it rich** *Informal* **1.** To find a valuable vein or pocket of ore. **2.** To come into wealth or good fortune. **— to strike off 1.** To remove or take off by or as by a blow or stroke. **2.** To cross out or erase by or as by a stroke of the pen. **3.** To deduct. **— to strike out 1.** To strike off (def. 2). **2.** To aim a blow or blows. **3.** To make a start; begin an undertaking: to *strike out* on one's own. **4.** To originate; hit upon. **5.** In baseball: **a** To put out (the batter) by pitching three strikes. **b** To be put out because of having three strikes counted against one during a single turn at bat. **6.** In bowling, to complete a game by bowling three consecutive strikes. **— to strike up 1.** To begin to play, sing, or sound, as a band or musical instrument. **2.** To start up; begin, as a friendship. — *n.* **1.** An act of striking or hitting; a blow. **2.** In baseball: **a** An unsuccessful attempt by the batter to hit the ball. **b** A pitched ball that passes over home plate not lower than the level of the batter's knees and not above that of his shoulders. **c** A foul bunt or any foul tip held by the catcher. **d** Any ball hit foul except when there have been two strikes. **3.** In bowling, the knocking down by a player of all the pins with the first bowl in any frame; also, the score so made: also called *ten-strike:* distinguished from *spare.* **4.** The quitting of work by a body of workers to enforce some demand. **5.** A new or unexpected discovery, as of oil or ore. **6.** Any unexpected or complete success. **7.** A straight-edged implement for leveling something, as grain in a measure; strickle. **8.** *Geol.* The direction of a line formed by the intersection of a structural feature with a horizontal plane. **9.** The quantity of coin or the number of medals made or struck at one time. **10.** An air attack on a surface target. **11.** The sudden rise and taking of the bait by a fish; a bite. [OE *strīcan* to stroke, move. Akin to STREAK.]
 — Syn. (verb) **1.** *Strike, hit, tap, slap, cuff, clout, swat,* and *smite* mean to aim or deliver a blow to a person or object. *Strike,* the most general of these words, may refer to a gentle or forceful blow delivered with the hand or with some implement; *hit* is freely interchanged with *strike,* but is preferred when the act of aiming or delivering a blow is stressed: to be *struck* (or *hit*) by a snowball, to *hit* (not *strike*) a target with an arrow. *Tap* means to *strike* gently, as with the finger. *Slap,* and the more forceful *cuff,* refer to blows delivered with the hand; one *slaps* with the palm of the hand, and *cuffs* with the open hand. *Clout* is a close synonym for *cuff,* and implies a sudden, angry blow delivered to the head or body. *Swat* suggests a crushing blow delivered with an implement, as a bat, paddle, etc. *Smite,* now chiefly poetic or archaic, is used of a blow so forceful as to cause great injury or death: to *smite* one's foes. Compare BEAT.
strike·bound (strīk′bound′) *adj.* Closed or immobilized by a strike: said of companies, equipment, industries, etc.
strike·break·er (strīk′brā′kər) *n.* One who takes the place of a workman on strike or who supplies workmen to take the place of strikers. **— strike′break′ing** *n.*
strike fault *Geol.* A fault lying parallel with the strike of the rocks through which it cuts.
strike figure *Mineral.* A percussion figure (which see).
strike·out (strīk′out′) *n.* In baseball, an instance of striking out. Abbr. *s.o., so*
strik·er (strī′kər) *n.* **1.** One who or that which strikes. **2.** In certain torpedoes, a plunger that strikes the priming cap and ignites the charge. **3.** An employee who is on strike. **4.** The hammer or clapper of a bell, etc. **5.** In the U.S. Navy, an apprentice in training for a specific technical rating: a radioman *striker.* **6.** In the U.S. Army, a soldier assigned to run errands and do odd jobs for an officer.
strik·ing (strī′king) *adj.* Notable; impressive. **— strik′ing·ly** *adv.* **— strik′ing·ness** *n.*
striking power The troops, materiel, etc., available for a military attack, especially a strong first attack.
Strind·berg (strĭnd′bûrg, *Sw.* strĕn′ber·y′), **August**, 1849–1912, Swedish dramatist and novelist.
string (strĭng) *n.* **1.** A slender line or strip, as of twine, cloth, leather, etc., thinner than a cord and thicker than a thread, used for tying, lacing, etc. **2.** The cord of a bow. **3.** Prepared wire or catgut for musical instruments. **4.** A stringlike organ or formation, as a vegetable fiber or fibers or an animal nerve or tendon. **5.** A thin cord upon which anything is strung; a row or series of things connected by a small cord: a *string* of pearls. **6.** A connected series or succession,

as of things, acts, or events, sometimes implying unusual length: a *string* of lies. **7.** *U.S. Informal* A small collection of animals, especially of racehorses. **8.** *pl.* Stringed instruments, especially those of an orchestra; also, those who play on these. Abbr. *str.* **9.** In billiards: **a** The score. **b** The buttons, strung on a wire, by which the score is kept. **c** The string line. **d** The act of stringing. **10.** *Archit.* **a** A stringcourse. **b** A ramp or sidepiece supporting the steps of a stairway. **11.** In sports, a group of contestants ranked as to skill. **12.** *Usually pl. Informal* A condition, limitation, or restriction attached to a proposition, gift, or donation. **13.** *Ling.* A linear sequence of morphemes, form classes, etc., indicating the syntactic structure of a class of transformationally related sentences. **— to pull strings** To manipulate or influence others to gain some advantage. — *v.* **strung, string-ing** *v.t.* **1.** To thread, as beads, on or as on a string. **2.** To fit with a string or strings, as a guitar. **3.** To cover, drape, or adorn with things attached to a string or strings. **4.** To tune the strings of (a musical instrument). **5.** To brace; strengthen. **6.** To make tense or nervous. **7.** To arrange or extend in a line or series. **8.** To remove the strings from (vegetables). **9.** *U.S. Informal* To hang: usually with *up.* **10.** *Slang* To fool or deceive; hoax: often with *along.* — *v.i.* **11.** To extend, stretch, or proceed in a line or series. **12.** To form into strings. **13.** In billiards, to drive the cue ball from within the string against the farther cushion and back. **— to string along (with)** *Informal* To follow with trust. [OE *streng*]
string bass The double bass (which see).
string bean 1. Any of several varieties of beans (genus *Phaseolus*) cultivated for their edible pods, especially *P. vulgaris.* **2.** The pod itself. Also called *green bean.* **3.** *Informal* A tall, skinny person.
string·board (strĭng′bôrd′, -bōrd′) *n. Archit.* A board serving as a support for the ends of steps in a staircase.
string·course (strĭng′kôrs′, -kōrs′) *n. Archit.* A horizontal molding or ornamental course, as of brick or stone, usually projecting along the face of a building: also called *cordon.*
stringed instrument (strĭngd) A musical instrument that produces its tones by means of one or more vibrating strings; especially, an instrument of the violin or viol family. Also **string instrument.**
strin·gen·cy (strĭn′jən·sē) *n. pl.* **·cies** The quality or condition of being stringent.
strin·gen·do (strĭn·jĕn′dō) *Music adj.* Hastening the tempo as toward a climax; accelerando. — *adv.* In a stringendo manner. — *n. pl.* **·dos** A stringendo passage. [< Ital., ppr. of *stringere* to draw tight < L]
strin·gent (strĭn′jənt) *adj.* **1.** Requiring or compelling adherence to strict requirements; rigid; severe, as regulations. **2.** Hampered by obstructions or scarcity of money; close or tight. **3.** Convincing; forcible. [< L *stringens, -entis,* ppr. of *stringere* to draw tight] **— strin′gent·ly** *adv.*
string·er (strĭng′ər) *n.* **1.** One who or that which strings. **2.** *Archit.* **a** A heavy timber, generally horizontal, supporting other members of a structure, and usually running in the direction of the greatest length of the collection of supported members. **b** A stringcourse or stringpiece. **3.** A lengthwise timber on which rails are laid, as distinguished from a crosstie. **4.** *Informal* One having a specified numerical rank or degree of proficiency, as on a team: a second *stringer.*
string·halt (strĭng′hôlt′) *n. Vet.* A convulsive movement of the hind legs of a horse: also called *springhalt.*
string line In billiards, a line passing across the table, from behind which the cue ball is driven.
string·piece (strĭng′pēs′) *n. Archit.* A heavy supporting timber forming the margin or edge of a framework.
string tie A very narrow necktie, often tied in a bow with the ends hanging loosely.
string·y (strĭng′ē) *adj.* **string·i·er, string·i·est 1.** Containing fibrous strings. **2.** Forming in strings; ropy. **3.** Having tough sinews. **4.** Tall and wiry in build. **— string′i·ly** *adv.* **— string′i·ness** *n.*
strip¹ (strĭp) *n.* **1.** A narrow piece, comparatively long, as of cloth, wood, etc. **2.** A number of stamps attached in a row. **3.** A narrow piece of land. **4.** An airstrip or landing strip (which see). **5.** A comic strip (which see). — *v.t.* **stripped, strip·ping** To cut or tear into strips. [? < MLG *strippe* strap]
strip² (strĭp) *v.* **stripped** (*Rare* **stript**), **strip·ping** *v.t.* **1.** To pull the covering, clothing, etc., from; denude; lay bare. **2.** To pull off (the covering or clothing). **3.** To rob or plunder; spoil. **4.** To make bare or empty. **5.** To remove; take away. **6.** To deprive of something; divest: He was *stripped* of his rank. **7.** To separate the leaves of (tobacco) from the stalks. **8.** To milk (a cow) dry by a downward stroke and compression of the thumb and forefinger. **9.** *Mech.* To damage or break the teeth, thread, etc., of (a gear, bolt, or the like). — *v.i.* **10.** To remove one's clothing; undress. **11.** To undergo stripping. [ME < OE *-strīepan,* as in *bestrīepan* to despoil, plunder]
stripe¹ (strīp) *n.* **1.** A line, band, or strip of different color, material, texture, etc., from the adjacent surface. **2.** Striped cloth. **3.** *pl.* A prison uniform marked with broad, conspicuous stripes. **4.** A piece of material or braid on the

sleeve of a uniform to indicate rank, service, an award, etc.; a chevron. **5.** Kind; sort: a man of his *stripe*. — *v.t.* **striped, strip·ing** To mark with a stripe or stripes. [< MDu.]

stripe² (strīp) *n.* A blow struck with a whip or rod, as in flogging. [Prob. < LG. Cf. Du. *strippen* to whip.]

striped (strīpt, strī′pid) *adj.* Marked with stripes.

striped bass See under BASS¹.

striped mullet See under MULLET.

striped squirrel A chipmunk.

strip·er (strī′pər) *n.* **1.** *U.S. Informal* One wearing (a specified number of) stripes on the sleeve of a uniform: a *one-striper*, or ensign. **2.** A striped bass: see under BASS¹.

strip·ling (strip′ling) *n.* A mere youth. [< STRIP¹ + -LING]

strip mining The mining of coal by stripping off soil, etc.

strip·per (strip′ər) *n.* **1.** One who or that which strips. **2.** *U.S. Slang* A stripteaser.

strip·ping (strip′ing) *n.* **1.** The act or process of one who or that which strips. **2.** *pl.* The milk drawn by stripping.

strip·tease (strip′tēz′) *n.* In burlesque, etc., a gradual disrobing, interspersed with bumps, grinds, etc., by a female performer. Also **strip tease.** — **strip′teas′er** *n.*

strip·y (strī′pē) *adj.* **strip·i·er, strip·i·est** Being in or suggesting stripes or streaks; having or marked with stripes.

strive (strīv) *v.i.* **strove** or (*less commonly*) **strived, striv·en** (striv′ən) or **strived, striv·ing 1.** To make earnest effort. **2.** To engage in strife; contend; fight. **3.** To vie; emulate. [< OF *estriver*, prob. < Gmc.] — **striv′er** *n.*

strobe light (strōb) *Photog. Informal* An electronic tube producing intense, very brief flashes of light: also called *speedlight.* [< STROB(OSCOPE)]

strob·ic (strō′bik) *adj.* Spinning or seeming to spin, as with the motion of a top. [< Gk. *strobos* whirling]

stro·bi·la (strō-bī′lə) *n.* *pl.* **·lae** (-lē) *Zool.* **1.** A stage in the life cycle of some jellyfish, characterized by a series of annular plates each of which separates as a new organism. **2.** The segmented body of a tapeworm. [< NL < Gk. *strobilē* plug of lint shaped like a fir cone < *strobilos* fir cone, anything twisted < *strobos* twisted, ult. < *strephein* to twist]

strob·i·la·ceous (strob′ə-lā′shəs) *adj.* **1.** Pertaining to or resembling a strobile. **2.** Producing strobiles.

strob·i·la·tion (strob′ə-lā′shən) *n.* *Zool.* Asexual reproduction by division into segments, as in jellyfish.

strob·ile (strob′il) *n.* *Bot.* **1.** A cone, as of a pine. **2.** A cone-shaped mass of sporophylls producing spore cases, as in horsetails, club mosses, etc. Also **strob′il.** [See STROBILA.]

strob·o·scope (strob′ə-skōp, strō′bə-) *n.* An instrument for observing the motion of a body or object by rendering it visible only at intervals or at certain points of its path. [< Gk. *strobos* twisting + -SCOPE] — **strob′o·scop′ic** (-skop′ik) or **·i·cal** *adj.* — **strob·os′co·py** (-os′kə-pē) *n.*

strode (strōd) Past tense of STRIDE.

Stro·ga·noff (strō′gə-nôf′, strô′-) *adj.* Cooked in a sauce of sour cream with mushrooms, onions, and seasonings: said of meat. [After Count Paul Stroganoff, 1794–1882, Russian diplomat]

stroke (strōk) *n.* **1.** The act or movement of striking; a knock; impact. **2.** A single movement, as of the hand, arm, or some instrument, by which something is made or done. **3.** A blow or any ill effect caused as if by a blow: a *stroke* of misfortune. **4.** An attack of paralysis or apoplexy. **5.** A blow or the sound of a blow of a striking mechanism, as of a clock. **6.** A sudden or brilliant act; feat; coup: a *stroke* of diplomacy; a *stroke* of wit. **7.** A pulsation, as of the heart. **8.** A mark or dash of a pen or tool. **9.** A light, caressing movement; a stroking. **10.** In tennis, golf, etc., a striking of the ball; also, the form or manner of such striking. **11.** A manner or technique of swimming. **12.** *Informal* A portion or stint, as of work: usually with the negative. **13.** *Mech.* **a** One of a series of alternating linear movements from one extreme position to another, as by the piston of a steam-driven or internal-combustion engine. **b** The distance covered by such a movement. **14.** Stroke oar. — *v.* **stroked, strok·ing** *v.t.* **1.** To pass the hand over gently or caressingly, or with light pressure. **2.** To set the pace for (a rowboat or its crew); act as stroke for. — *v.i.* **3.** To perform strokes, as in tennis, swimming, etc. [ME *strok, strak* < OE *strācian* to strike]

stroke oar 1. The aftmost oar of a boat, whose movement sets the rate of rowing. **2.** The person who rows with this oar: also **strokes·man** (strōks′mən). **3.** The position occupied by such an oarsman.

stroll (strōl) *v.i.* **1.** To walk in a leisurely or idle manner; saunter. **2.** To wander. — *v.t.* **3.** To walk idly over or through. — *n.* A leisurely walk. [Origin uncertain]

stroll·er (strō′lər) *n.* **1.** One who strolls. **2.** A light, often collapsible carriage in which a baby or child may sit upright. **3.** A wandering showman or player. **4.** A tramp.

stro·ma (strō′mə) *n.* *pl.* **·ma·ta** (-mə-tə) *Physiol.* The substance that forms the framework of an organ or cell. [< Gk. *strōma* bed covering] — **stro·mat′ic** (-mat′ik) *adj.*

Strom·bo·li (strŏm′bō-lē) The northernmost of the Lipari Islands; 5 sq. mi.; site of an active volcano, 3,040 ft.

stro·mey·er·ite (strō′mī′ər-īt) *n.* A gray sulfide of copper and silver, crystallizing in the orthorhombic system. [after Friedrich *Stromeyer*, 1786–1835, German chemist]

strong (strông, strong) *adj.* **1.** Powerful in physique; muscular; vigorous. **2.** Healthy; robust: a *strong* constitution. **3.** Morally powerful; firm; resolute; courageous. **4.** Mentally powerful or vigorous. **5.** Especially competent or able in a specified subject or field: *strong* in mathematics. **6.** Abundantly or richly supplied with something: often with *in*: *strong* in literary interest. **7.** Solidly made or constituted; not easily destroyed, injured, or strained: *strong* walls. **8.** Powerful as a rival or combatant: a *strong* team. **9.** Easy to defend or difficult to capture: a *strong* military position. **10.** Having (a specified) numerical force: an army 20,000 *strong*. **11.** Capable of exerting influence, authority, etc.: a *strong* government. **12.** Financially sound: a *strong* bank. **13.** Powerful in effect: *strong* poison, medicine, etc. **14.** Concentrated; not diluted or weak: *strong* coffee. **15.** Containing much alcohol: *strong* drink. **16.** Powerful in flavor or odor; also, rank; unpleasant: a *strong* breath. **17.** Intense in degree or quality; not faint or mild: a *strong* pulse; *strong* light. **18.** Loud and firm: a *strong* voice. **19.** Firm; tenacious: a *strong* grip. **20.** Deeply earnest; fervid: a *strong* desire. **21.** Cogent; convincing: *strong* evidence. **22.** Distinct; marked; definite: a *strong* resemblance. **23.** Extreme; forceful: *strong* measures. **24.** Emphatic; not moderate: *strong* language. **25.** Moving with great force: said of a wind, stream, or tide. **26.** *Meteorol.* Designating a breeze (No. 6) or gale (No. 9) on the Beaufort scale. **27.** Characterized by steady or rising prices: a *strong* market. **28.** *Phonet.* Stressed; accented, as a syllable. **29.** *Gram.* In Germanic languages: **a** Denoting a strong verb (which see). **b** Of nouns and adjectives in German and Old English, showing distinctive declensional endings for case, number, and gender. Compare WEAK (def. 12). — *adv.* In a strong manner; so as to be strong. [OE *strang, strong*] — **strong′ly** *adv.* *Strong* may appear as a combining form, as in the following self-explanatory compounds:

strong-armed	**strong-limbed**	**strong-sounding**
strong-backed	**strong-looking**	**strong-spirited**
strong-bodied	**strong-lunged**	**strong-tasting**
strong-brewed	**strong-made**	**strong-tinted**
strong-built	**strong-natured**	**strong-toned**
strong-colored	**strong-nerved**	**strong-voiced**
strong-growing	**strong point**	**strong-walled**
stronghanded	**strong-seeming**	**strong-winged**
stronghearted	**strong-smelling**	**strong-woven**

strong-arm (strông′ärm′, strong′-) *Informal adj.* Violent; having and depending on physical power. — *v.t.* To use physical force upon; assault.

strong·bark (strông′bärk′, strong′-) *n.* A small tree (*Bourreria ovata*), native to the West Indies and Florida, having brown, hard wood and edible berries.

strong·box (strông′boks′, strong′-) *n.* A strongly built chest or safe for keeping valuables.

strong drink Alcoholic liquors. Also **strong waters.**

strong·hold (strông′hōld′, strong′-) *n.* **1.** A strongly fortified place; fortress. Also **strong·point** (strong′point′). **2.** A place of security or refuge.

strong·man (strong′man′) *n.* *pl.* **·men** (-men′) An important person, especially one who wields great political power.

strong-mind·ed (strông′mīn′did, strong′-) *adj.* Having a determined, vigorous mind. — **strong′-mind′ed·ly** *adv.* — **strong′-mind′ed·ness** *n.*

strong·room (strông′rōom′, -rŏom′, strong′-) *n.* A room especially equipped for the safekeeping of valuables.

strong verb A verb that forms its past tense and past participle by internal vowel change, as *swim, swam, swum.*

strong-willed (strông′wild′, strong′-) *adj.* Having a strong will; decided; obstinate.

stron·gyle (stron′jil) *n.* Any of an order (*Strongyloidea*) of parasitic nematode worms, many of them injurious to man and animals. Also **stron′gyl.** [< Gk. *strongylos* round]

stron·ti·a (stron′shē-ə) *n.* *Chem.* **1.** A grayish white, infusible strontium monoxide, SrO. **2.** Strontium hydroxide, Sr(OH)₂. [< NL < STRONTIUM]

stron·ti·an (stron′shē-ən) *n.* **1.** Strontia. **2.** Strontium.

stron·ti·an·ite (stron′shē-ən-īt′) *n.* A vitreous strontium carbonate, SrCO₃, occurring in various forms and colors.

stron·ti·um (stron′shē-əm, -shəm, -tē-əm) *n.* A hard, yellowish, metallic element (symbol Sr) of the calcium group, known chiefly through its salts, which burn with a red flame and are used largely in pyrotechnics, but also in medicine and ceramics. See ELEMENT. [< NL, from *Strontian*, Argyll, Scotland, where first discovered] — **stron′tic** (-tik) *adj.*

strontium 90 *Physics* A radioactive isotope that emits beta rays and has a half life of about 28 years. Distributed in the fallout of nuclear bombs, it is metabolized by plants and animals along with calcium and constitutes a radiation hazard, especially through progressive concentration in bone tissue. Also called *radiostrontium.*

PRONUNCIATION KEY: add, āce, câre, pälm; end, ēven; it, īce; odd, ōpen, ôrder; tŏok, pōol; up, bûrn; ə = a in *above*, e in *sicken*, i in *flexible*, o in *melon*, u in *focus*; yōo = u in *fuse*; oil; pout; check; go; ring; thin; this; zh, vision. For à, œ, ü, kh, ṅ, see inside front cover.

strontium unit *Physics* A measure of the radiation effect of strontium 90, equal to a millionth of a millionth of a curie per gram of calcium.

strop (strop) *n.* **1.** A strip of leather, canvas, etc., on which to sharpen a razor. **2.** A strap. — *v.t.* **stropped, strop·ping** To sharpen on a strop. [OE < L *struppus* < Gk. *strophos* band, cord]

stro·phan·thin (strō-fan′thin) *n.* A bitter, poisonous, crystalline glycoside contained in certain species of tropical plants (genus *Strophanthus*) and resembling digitalis in its action on the heart. [< NL *Strophanthus* genus name (< Gk. *strophos* cord + *anthos* flower) + -IN]

stro·phe (strō′fē) *n.* **1.** In ancient Greek poetry, the verses sung by the chorus in a play while moving from right to left. **2.** In classical prosody, the lines of an ode constituting a stanza and alternating with the antistrophe. **3.** The first of two alternating metrical systems in a poem. Abbr. *st.* [< Gk. *strophē* turning, twist < *strephein* to turn] — **stroph·ic** (strof′ik, strō′fik) or **·i·cal** *adj.*

stroph·u·lus (strof′yə-ləs) *n. Pathol.* Any of various types of miliaria common in children: also called *tooth rash, red gum.* [< NL, dim. of Gk. *strophos* cord. See STROPHE.]

stroud (stroud) *n.* A coarse, heavy, woolen cloth, or a blanket made from it, formerly used for trading with North American Indians. [after *Stroud*, Gloucestershire, England]

strove (strōv) Past tense of STRIVE.

strow (strō) *v.t.* **strowed, strowed** or **strown, strow·ing** *Archaic* To strew.

struck (struk) Past tense and past participle of STRIKE. — *adj.* Closed down or affected by a strike, as a factory.

struck jury *Law* A jury of twelve selected by a process in which each party strikes twelve names from a list of forty-eight eligible persons, the remaining twenty-four constituting the panel from which the jury is drawn.

struck measure A measure having the contents level with the edge of the container, rather than heaping.

struc·tur·al (struk′chər-əl) *adj.* **1.** Of, pertaining to, possessing, characterized, or caused by structure. **2.** *Geol.* Pertaining to the structure of rocks and other features of the earth's crust. **3.** *Biol.* Morphological. **4.** *Chem.* Pertaining to or denoting the spatial arrangements of atoms in a molecule: a *structural* formula. **5.** Used in or essential to construction. — **struc′tur·al·ly** *adv.*

structural formula See under FORMULA.

structural iron **1.** Iron adapted for use in constructing buildings, bridges, etc. **2.** Iron formed in shapes for this purpose.

struc·tur·al·ism (struk′chər-əl-iz′əm) *n.* The tendency to emphasize structure, or the policy of concentrating upon structure in various fields, including linguistics.

structural linguistics A descriptive study of the systematic arrangement and patterning of the contrastive features of a language, as phonology, morphology, and syntax, considered separately and in their relations to each other.

structural steel **1.** Steel prepared for use in building. **2.** Rolled steel of considerable toughness and strength, especially adapted for use in construction.

struc·ture (struk′chər) *n.* **1.** That which is constructed; a combination of related parts, as a building or machine. **2.** *Biol.* The arrangement and functional union of parts, tissues, and organs of a plant or animal. **3.** *Geol.* **a** The position and arrangement of rock strata in a larger formation. **b** The gross physical characteristics of a rock. **4.** *Chem.* The disposition of atoms within a molecule or of molecules in a compound. **5.** The manner of construction or organization: the social *structure* of a primitive society. **6.** *Archaic* The act of constructing. — *v.t.* **·tured, ·tur·ing** **1.** To form into an organized structure; build. **2.** To conceive or as a structural whole; ideate: He *structured* the plan before proposing it. [< L *structura* < *structus*, pp. of *struere* to build]

stru·del (strōōd′l, *Ger.* shtrōō′dəl) *n.* A kind of pastry made of a thin sheet of dough, spread with fruit or cheese, nuts, etc., rolled, and baked. [< G, lit., eddy]

strug·gle (strug′əl) *n.* **1.** A violent effort or series of efforts; a labored contest. **2.** Conflict; strife; battle. — *v.* **·gled, ·gling** *v.i.* **1.** To contend with an adversary in physical combat; fight. **2.** To put forth violent efforts; strive: to *struggle* against odds. **3.** To make one's way by violent efforts: to *struggle* through mud. — *v.t.* **4.** To accomplish with a struggle. [ME *strogelen*; origin unknown] — **strug′gler** *n.* — **strug′gling·ly** *adv.*

strum (strum) *v.t. & v.i.* **strummed, strum·ming** To play (a stringed instrument, a tune, etc.) idly, monotonously, or without technical skill. — *n.* The act of strumming. [Prob. imit.] — **strum′mer** *n.*

stru·ma (strōō′mə) *n. pl.* **·mae** (-mē) **1.** *Pathol.* **a** Scrofula. **b** Goiter. **2.** *Bot.* A wenlike cushion or swelling on an organ, as at the base of the capsule in certain mosses. [< L < *struere* to build] — **stru·mat·ic** (strōō-mat′ik), **stru′mose** (-mōs), **stru′mous** (-məs) *adj.*

Stru·ma (strōō′mä) A river in SW Bulgaria and NE Greece, flowing 215 miles SE to the Aegean: Greek *Strymon*.

strum·pet (strum′pit) *n.* A whore; harlot. [? Ult. < OF *strupe* concubinage < L *stuprum* dishonor]

strung (strung) Past tense and past participle of STRING.

strunt (strunt) *n. Scot.* A sullen mood; umbrage.

strut (strut) *n.* **1.** A proud or pompous step or walk. **2.** A member in a framework, designed to relieve weight or pressure in the direction of its length. For illustration see ROOF. — *v.* **strut·ted, strut·ting** *v.i.* **1.** To walk pompously, conceitedly, and affectedly. — *v.t.* **2.** To brace or support, as a framing or structure, with or as with struts. [OE *strūtian* to be rigid, stand stiffly] — **strut′ter** *n.* — **strut′ting·ly** *adv.*

stru·thi·ous (strōō′thē-əs) *adj.* Of or pertaining to a family (*Struthionidae*) of large, terrestrial, ratite birds, comprising the ostriches. [< L *struthio* ostrich]

strych·nine (strik′nin, -nēn, -nīn) *n.* A white, crystalline, bitter, extremely poisonous alkaloid, $C_{21}H_{22}N_2O_2$, contained in certain plants (genus *Strychnos*), especially *S. nuxvomica*. Its salts are used in medicine, chiefly as a neural stimulant. Also *Archaic* **strych′nin** (-nē-ə). Also **strych′nin** (-nin). [< F < L *strychnos* < Gk., nightshade]

strych·nin·ism (strik′nin-iz′əm) *n. Pathol.* The diseased condition resulting from the improper usage of strychnine.

Stry·mon (strī′mən) The Greek name for the STRUMA.

St. Swith·in's Day (sānt swith′ənz) July 15th, the day that commemorates Saint Swithin, died 862, a former patron saint of Winchester Cathedral, England. Rain occurring on this day is said to foretell wet weather for the following 40 days. Also **St. Swith′un's Day.**

St. Thom·as (sānt tom′əs) **1.** An island of the Virgin Islands of the United States; 28 sq. mi.; capital, Charlotte Amalie. **2.** The former name for CHARLOTTE AMALIE.

Stu·art (stōō′ərt, styōō′-) The royal family of Scotland, 1371–1603, and of England, 1603–1714. Also *Stewart.* — **Charles Edward,** 1720–88, English prince; grandson of James II; claimant to the English throne: called **Bonnie Prince Charlie:** also called *the Young Pretender.* — **James Francis Edward,** 1688–1766, Prince of Wales; son of James II; father of Charles Edward: called *the Old Pretender.* — **Mary** See MARY, QUEEN OF SCOTS.

Stuart (stōō′ərt, styōō′-), **Gilbert Charles,** 1755–1828, U.S. painter. — **James Ewell Brown,** 1833–64, Confederate cavalry general in the Civil War: called **Jeb Stuart.**

stub (stub) *n.* **1.** Any short projecting part or piece. **2.** The part of a tree trunk, bush, etc., that remains when the main part is cut down. **3.** A short or broken remnant, as of a pencil, cigarette, or broken tooth. **4.** *U.S.* In a checkbook or the like, one of the inner ends upon which a memorandum is entered, and which remains when the check is detached; also, the detachable portion of a theater ticket, etc. **5.** Anything blunt, short, or stumpy, as a pen with a broad point. — *v.t.* **stubbed, stub·bing** **1.** To strike, as the toe, against a low obstruction or projection. **2.** To grub up, as roots; root out. **3.** To clear or remove the stubs or roots from. [OE *stubb*]

stub·bed (stub′id stubd) *adj.* **1.** Made into or resembling a stub. **2.** Full of stubs.

stub·ble (stub′əl) *n.* **1.** The stubs of grain stalks, sugar cane, etc., covering a field after the crop has been cut. **2.** The field itself. **3.** Any surface or growth resembling stubble, as short bristly hair or beard. [< OF *stuble*, ult. < L *stipula* stalk] — **stub′bled** *adj.* — **stub′bly** *adj.*

stub·born (stub′ərn) *adj.* **1.** Inflexible in opinion or intention; unreasonably obstinate. **2.** Difficult to handle, manage, or work with; intractable; resistant. **3.** Characterized by perseverance or persistence: *stubborn* fighting. — **Syn.** See OBSTINATE. [ME, ? < OE *stubb* stump] — **stub′born·ly** *adv.* — **stub′born·ness** *n.*

stub·by (stub′ē) *adj.* **·bi·er, ·bi·est** **1.** Short, stiff, and bristling: a *stubby* beard. **2.** Resembling or of the nature of a stub: a *stubby* pencil. **3.** Stocky; thickset. **4.** Full of stubs. — **stub′bi·ly** *adv.* — **stub′bi·ness** *n.*

stub nail **1.** A short thick nail. **2.** An old horseshoe nail.

stuc·co (stuk′ō) *n. pl.* **·coes** or **·cos** **1.** A fine plaster for walls or their relief ornaments, usually of Portland cement, sand, and a small amount of lime. **2.** Any plaster or cement used for the external coating of buildings. **3.** Ornamental work made from stucco: also **stuc′co·work′** (-wûrk′). — *v.t.* **·coed, ·co·ing** To apply stucco to; decorate with stucco. [< Ital. < Gmc. Akin to OHG *stucchi* crust.] — **stuc′co·er** *n.*

stuck (stuk) Past tense and past participle of STICK.

stuck-up (stuk′up′) *adj. Informal* Conceited; supercilious and arrogant; snobbish.

stud¹ (stud) *n.* **1.** A short intermediate post, as in a building frame; a post to which laths are nailed; a scantling. **2.** A knob, round-headed nail, or small protuberant ornament. **3.** A removable ornamental button used to fasten a shirt front, etc. **4.** A crosspiece in a link, as in a chain cable. **5.** A small pin such as is used in a watch. — *v.t.* **stud·ded, stud·ding** **1.** To set thickly with small points, projections, or knobs. **2.** To be scattered or strewn over. **3.** To support or stiffen by means of studs. [OE *studu* post]

stud² (stud) *n.* **1.** A collection of horses and mares for breeding. **2.** The place where they are kept. **3.** A collection of horses for riding, hunting, or racing. **4.** A studhorse or other male animal used for breeding purposes. **5.** *Slang* A sexually promiscuous man. **6.** Stud poker (which see).

— at stud Of a male animal, used or available for breeding purposes. — *adj.* **1.** Of or pertaining to a stud. **2.** Kept for breeding: a *stud* mare. [OE *stōd*]

stud·book (stud′bŏŏk′) *n.* A record of the pedigree of thoroughbred stock.

stud·die (stud′ē) *n. Scot. & Brit. Dial.* An anvil; a stithy. [Prob. var of STITHY]

stud·ding (stud′ing) *n.* **1.** Studs or joists collectively. **2.** The material from which they are made. **3.** The height of a room from floor to ceiling.

stud·ding·sail (stun′səl, stud′ing·sāl′) *n. Naut.* A light auxiliary sail set out beyond one of the principal sails by extensible booms during a following wind: also called *stunsail*. For illustration see SHIP.

stu·dent (stōōd′nt, styōōd′nt) *n.* **1.** One engaged in a course of study, especially in a secondary school, college or university. **2.** One devoted to study. **3.** One who makes a thorough study of a particular subject. [< OF *estudiant* < L *studens*, *-entis*, ppr. of *studere* to be eager, apply oneself, study]

    — Syn. *Student*, *pupil*, and *scholar* denote a learner. A *student* is one who studies, not necessarily under a teacher: this is the common term for one enrolled in a secondary school or college. A *pupil* is one under close supervision of a teacher; children in elementary schools are called *pupils*, but the term is not synonymous with beginner or tyro. A concert violinist may be called the *pupil* of some great master under whom he has studied. A *scholar* is literally one enrolled in a school. Formerly, a child in elementary school was called a *scholar*, but now the term is rarely used in this sense.

student body All the students attending a school, college, etc.

student lamp An adjustable lamp for use at a desk.

student nurse One who is in training in a hospital school of nursing.

stu·dent·ship (stōōd′nt·ship, styōōd′nt-) *n.* **1.** The condition of being a student. **2.** *Brit.* A scholarship.

student teacher One studying to be a teacher and who serves in a classroom under the supervision of another more experienced teacher.

stud·fish (stud′fish′) *n. pl.* **·fish** or **·fish·es** A killifish (*Fundulus stellifer*) of the Alabama River.

stud·horse (stud′hôrs′) *n.* A stallion kept for breeding. Also **stud horse**.

stud·ied (stud′ēd) *adj.* **1.** Deliberately designed or undertaken; premeditated: a *studied* insult. **2.** Lacking freshness, naturalness, or spontaneity. **3.** *Rare* Learned; versed. — **stud′ied·ly** *adv.* — **stud′ied·ness** *n.*

stu·di·o (stōō′dē·ō, styōō′-) *n. pl.* **·os** **1.** The workroom of an artist, photographer, etc. **2.** A place where motion pictures are filmed. **3.** A room or rooms where radio or television programs are broadcast or recorded. [< Ital., a study < L *studium*. See STUDY.]

studio couch A backless couch with a bed frame underneath that may be drawn out and made level with the couch to form a double bed.

stu·di·ous (stōō′dē·əs, styōō′-) *adj.* **1.** Given to study; devoting oneself to the acquisition of knowledge. **2.** Earnest in effort; assiduous. **3.** Done with deliberation; studied: *studious* politeness. **4.** Used for or favorable to study: *studious* halls. [< L *studiosus* < *studium* zeal. See STUDY.] — **stu′di·ous·ly** *adv.* — **stu′di·ous·ness** *n.*

stud poker A game of poker in which the cards of the first round are dealt face down and the rest face up, betting opening on the second round. [< STUD²]

stud·work (stud′wûrk′) *n.* Work ornamented, set, or supported with studs.

stud·y (stud′ē) *v.* **stud·ied, stud·y·ing** *v.t.* **1.** To apply the mind in acquiring a knowledge of: to *study* physics. **2.** To examine; search into: to study a problem. **3.** To look at attentively; scrutinize: to *study* one's reflection in a mirror. **4.** To endeavor to memorize, as a part in a play. **5.** To give thought and attention to, as something to be done or devised. — *v.i.* **6.** To apply the mind in acquiring knowledge. **7.** To follow a regular course of instruction; be a student. **8.** To muse; meditate. **— to study up on** *Informal* To acquire more complete information concerning, as by investigation. — *n. pl.* **stud·ies** **1.** The act of studying; the process of acquiring information; application of the mind to books, and to art or science, etc. **2.** A particular instance or form of mental work. **3.** Something to be studied; a branch or department of knowledge. **4.** A specific product of or work resulting from studious application. **5.** In art, a first sketch, exercise, etc. **6.** A carefully elaborated literary treatment of a subject. **7.** A room devoted to study, reading, etc. **8.** A state of deep thought or absent-mindedness. **9.** Earnest endeavor; thoughtful attention or care. **10.** Something worthy of close attention. **11.** *Informal* One who studies; especially, an actor with reference to his ability to learn a role: a quick *study*. **12.** *Music* A composition designed to aid development in technical facility; an étude.

[< OF *estudier* < *estudie* study < L *studium* zeal < *studere* to apply oneself, be diligent]

study hall In a school, a room equipped and reserved for study; also, the period of time scheduled for study in such a room.

stuff (stuf) *v.t.* **1.** To fill completely; pack; cram full. **2.** To fill (an opening, etc.) with something forced in; plug. **3.** To obstruct or stop up; choke. **4.** To fill or expand with padding, as a cushion. **5.** To fill (a fowl, roast, etc.) with stuffing. **6.** In taxidermy, to fill the skin of (a bird, animal, etc.) with a material preparatory to mounting. **7.** To fill too full; overload; distend. **8.** To fill or cram with food. **9.** To fill with knowledge, ideas, or attitudes, especially unsystematically: His head is *stuffed* with prejudices. **10.** To force or cram, as into a small space. **11.** To put fraudulent votes into (a ballot box). **12.** To fill the pores of (a skin or pelt) with a preservative of oil and tallow. — *v.i.* **13.** To eat to excess; gluttonize. — *n.* **1.** The material out of which something may be shaped or made; raw or unwrought material. **2.** The fundamental element or basic material of anything, material or abstract: the *stuff* of dreams. **3.** *Informal* Possessions generally, especially household goods. **4.** A worthless collection of things; rubbish. **5.** Worthless ideas: often used as an interjection: *Stuff* and nonsense! **6.** Woven material, especially of wool; also, any textile fabric. **7.** *Informal* Any unspecified or vaguely defined substance, activity, etc. **8.** One of various substances, mixtures, or compounds, prepared for use, as paper pulp, or, in leathermaking, dubbing or stuffing. **9.** A medicinal mixture or potion. **10.** *Slang* Money; means. **11.** *Slang* Skill; ability. [< OF *estoffe*, ? < L *stuppa* tow] — **stuff′er** *n.*

stuffed shirt (stuft) *Informal* A pretentious or pompous person.

stuff·ing (stuf′ing) *n.* **1.** The material with which anything is stuffed. **2.** A mixture, as of bread or cracker crumbs with meat and seasoning, used in stuffing fowls, etc. **3.** The act or process of one who or that which stuffs.

stuffing box *Mech.* A device consisting of a chamber affording passage and motion of a piston rod or shaft, the interior being filled with suitable packing material to prevent leakage of steam or other fluid: also called *packing box*.

stuffing nut The nut tightening or securing a stuffing box.

stuff·y (stuf′ē) *adj.* **stuff·i·er, stuff·i·est** **1.** Badly ventilated. **2.** Impeding respiration. **3.** *Informal* Pompous; smugly self-important. **4.** *Informal* Old-fashioned; stodgy; strait-laced. **5.** *Rare* Angry; sulky. — **stuff′i·ly** *adv.* — **stuff′i·ness** *n.*

Stu·ka (stōō′kə, *Ger.* shtōō′kä) *n.* A German dive bomber. [Contr. of G *Sturzkampfflugzeug*]

stull (stul) *n. Mining* A timber or platform in an excavation, used to support workmen or to protect them from falling stones. [Prob. < G *stollen* post, prop]

stul·ti·fy (stul′tə·fī) *v.t.* **·fied, ·fy·ing** **1.** To cause to appear absurd; give an appearance of foolishness to. **2.** To make worthless or ineffectual; nullify. **3.** *Law* To allege to be of unsound mind. [< LL *stultificare* to make foolish < L *stultus* foolish + *facere* to make] — **stul′ti·fi·ca′tion** *n.* — **stul′ti·fi′er** *n.*

stum (stum) *n.* Unfermented or partly fermented grape juice, sometimes added to wine to produce increased fermentation. — *v.t.* **stummed, stum·ming** To revive (wine), as by adding must. [< Du. *stom* must, lit., silent]

stum·ble (stum′bəl) *v.* **·bled, ·bling** *v.i.* **1.** To miss one's step in walking or running; trip. **2.** To walk or proceed unsteadily or in a blundering manner. **3.** To speak, read, etc., falteringly or unevenly. **4.** To happen upon something by chance: with *across*, *on*, *upon*, etc. **5.** To fall into sin or error. — *v.t.* **6.** To cause to stumble. — *n.* **1.** The act of stumbling. **2.** A blunder; false step. [Cf. Norw. *stumla* to stumble in the dark] — **stum′bler** *n.* — **stum′bling·ly** *dv.*

stum·ble·bum (stum′bəl·bum′) *n. U.S. Slang* One who is blundering and ineffectual as if wandering in a daze.

stumbling block Any obstacle, hindrance, or impediment, as to the achievement of some end.

stump (stump) *n.* **1.** That portion of the trunk of a tree left standing when the tree is felled. **2.** The part of anything, as of a limb, tooth, pencil, etc., that remains when the main part has been removed; a stumplike part; a stub. **3.** *pl. Informal* The legs: chiefly in the phrase **to stir one's stumps**. **4.** A place or platform from which a political speech is made. **5.** *Informal* A challenge; a dare. **6.** In cricket, any one of the three posts (the **off stump**, the **middle stump**, and the **leg stump**) forming the wicket. **7.** A pencil-like soft leather or rubber bar, with conical ends, used to shade drawings of crayon or charcoal or to apply powdered pigments. **8.** A short, thickset person or animal. **9.** A heavy step; a clump; also, the sound made by such a step. **— to be up a stump** To be in trouble or in a dilemma. **— to take the stump** To electioneer in a political campaign. — *adj.* **1.** Being or resembling a stump; stumpy. **2.** Of or pertaining to political oratory or campaigning: a *stump* speaker.

— *v.t.* **1.** To reduce to a stump; truncate; lop. **2.** To remove stumps from (land). **3.** To canvass (a district) by making political speeches: The candidate *stumped* the State. **4.** *Informal* To challenge, as to a contest; dare; defy. **5.** *Informal* To bring to a halt by real or fancied obstacles; nonplus; baffle. **6.** To strike against an obstacle; stub, as one's toe. **7.** To shade (a drawing) by rubbing with a stump (def. 7). — *v.i.* **8.** To go about on or as on stumps; also, to walk heavily, noisily, and stiffly; hobble. **9.** To go about making political speeches. [< MLG] — **stump′er** *n.*

stump·age (stum′pij) *n.* **1.** Standing timber considered with reference to its value for cutting; also, its price. **2.** The right to cut such timber.

stump·y (stum′pē) *adj.* **stump·i·er, stump·i·est 1.** Full of stumps. **2.** Like a stump; short and thick. — **stump′i·ness** *n.*

stun (stun) *v.t.* **stunned, stun·ning 1.** To render unconscious or incapable of action by a blow, fall, etc. **2.** To astonish; astound. **3.** To daze or overwhelm by loud or explosive noise. — *n.* A stupefying blow, shock, or concussion; also, the condition of being stunned. [< OF *estoner* to resound, stun < L *ex-* thoroughly + *tonare* to thunder, crash]

stung (stung) Past tense and past participle of STING.

stunk (stungk) Past participle and alternative past tense of STINK.

stun·ner (stun′ər) *n.* **1.** One who or that which stuns. **2.** *Informal* A person or thing of extraordinary or surprising qualities, such as beauty.

stun·ning (stun′ing) *adj.* **1.** Rendering unconscious. **2.** *Informal* Impressively beautiful, stylish, etc. — **stun′ning·ly** *adv.*

stun·sail (stun′səl) *n. Naut.* A studdingsail (which see). Also **stun′s′le.** [Contr. of STUDDINGSAIL]

stunt[1] (stunt) *v.t.* To check the natural development of; dwarf; cramp. — *n.* **1.** A check in growth, progress, or development. **2.** A stunted animal or thing. [OE *stunt* dull, foolish; prob. infl. in meaning by ON *stuttr* short] — **stunt′ed** *adj.* — **stunt′ed·ness** *n.*

stunt[2] (stunt) *U.S. Informal n.* **1.** A sensational feat, as of bodily skill. **2.** Any thrilling or unusual feat, enterprise, or undertaking. — *v.i.* **1.** To perform a stunt or stunts. — *v.t.* **2.** To perform stunts with (an airplane, etc.). [? < G *stunde* lesson; orig. college slang]

stunt man In motion pictures, a man employed to substitute for an actor in dangerous acts or situations.

stu·pa (stoo′pə) *n.* Tope⁴. [< Skt., heap]

stupe (stoop, styoop) *n. Med.* A hot compress or medicated cloth to be applied to a wound. [< L *stupa, stuppa* tow]

stu·pe·fa·cient (stoo′pə·fā′shənt, styoo′-) *adj.* Having power to stupefy; stupefying: also **stu′pe·fac′tive** (-fak′tiv). — *n.* Anything that stupefies, as a narcotic. [< L *stupefaciens, -entis,* ppr. of *stupefacere* to stun. See STUPEFY.]

stu·pe·fac·tion (stoo′pə·fak′shən, styoo′-) *n.* The act of stupefying or the state of being stupefied.

stu·pe·fy (stoo′pə·fī, styoo′-) *v.t.* **·fied, ·fy·ing 1.** To dull the senses or faculties of; stun. **2.** To amaze; astound. [< F *stupéfier* < L *stupefacere* to stun < *stupere* to be stunned + *facere* to make] — **stu′pe·fied** *adj.* — **stu′pe·fi′er** *n.*

stu·pen·dous (stoo·pen′dəs, styoo′-) *adj.* **1.** Of or characterized by any highly impressive or astonishing feature. **2.** Of prodigious size or bulk. [< L *stupendus* amazed, orig. gerundive of *stupere* to be benumbed, stunned] — **stu·pen′dous·ly** *adv.* — **stu·pen′dous·ness** *n.*

stu·pid (stoo′pid, styoo′-) *adj.* **1.** Very slow of apprehension or understanding; mentally sluggish. **2.** Affected with stupor; stupefied: *stupid* from drink. **3.** Marked by, or resulting from, lack of understanding, reason, or wit; senseless: *stupid* acts. **4.** Tedious; dull; boring. — *n. Informal* A stupid person. [< L *stupidus* struck dumb < *stupere* to be stunned] — **stu′pid·ly** *adv.* — **stu′pid·ness** *n.*
— **Syn. 1.** dense, obtuse, dumb, dull, crass. — **Ant.** bright, clever, intelligent, quick.

stu·pid·i·ty (stoo·pid′ə·tē, styoo′-) *n. pl.* **·ties 1.** The state, quality, or character of being stupid. **2.** Something stupid. [< L *stupiditas, -tatis* < *stupidus.* See STUPID.]

stu·por (stoo′pər, styoo′-) *n.* **1.** A condition in which the senses and faculties are suspended or greatly dulled, as by drugs or liquor. **2.** Mental or moral dullness; gross stupidity. [< L < *stupere* to be stunned] — **stu′por·ous** *adj.*
— **Syn. 1.** *Stupor, lethargy, torpor,* and *coma* are compared as they relate to an impairment of the senses. Though *stupor* may denote unconsciousness, it is usually reserved for a state of partial or complete motor paralysis resulting from fatigue, shock, drugs, or the like. *Lethargy* is a milder state of sluggishness, usually caused by sleepiness. *Torpor* is extreme sluggishness, verging on insensibility; cold-blooded animals fall into *torpor* at low temperatures. *Coma* is complete unconsciousness, usually resulting from serious functional disorder. Compare SYNCOPE.

stur·dy[1] (stûr′dē) *adj.* **·di·er, ·di·est 1.** Possessing rugged health and strength; hardy; vigorous. **2.** Firm and unyielding; resolute: a *sturdy* defense. [< OF *estourdi* dazed, reckless < *estourdir* to stun, amaze < LL *exturdire* to deafen; ult. origin uncertain] — **stur′di·ly** *adv.* — **stur′di·ness** *n.*

stur·dy[2] (stûr′dē) *n. Vet.* The gid, a disease of sheep. [Special use of STURDY[1]] — **stur′died** *adj.*

stur·geon (stûr′jən) *n.* A large, fresh-water and marine ganoid fish of northern regions (family *Acipenseridae*), with coarse, edible flesh. It is valued as a source of isinglass and caviar. [< AF *sturgeon,* OF *sturgiun* < Med.L *sturio, -onis* < OHG *sturjo.* Akin to OE *styria* sturgeon.]

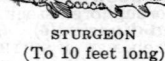

STURGEON
(To 10 feet long)

Stur·lu·son (stûr′lə·sən, stoor′-), **Snorri** See SNORRI STURLUSON.

Sturm·ab·teil·ung (shtoorm′äp·tī′loongk) *n. pl.* **·teil·ung·en** A Nazi political militia, organized to instruct and keep order and noted for acts of violence and terror: also called *Brown Shirts, storm troopers.* [< G, storm detachment]

Sturm und Drang (shtoorm′ oont drängk′) *German* Storm and stress: used to designate the late 18th-century period of German literary romanticism.

stut·ter (stut′ər) *v.t. & v.i.* To utter or speak with spasmodic repetition, blocking, and prolongation of sounds and syllables, especially those in initial position in a word. — *n.* The act or habit of stuttering. — **Syn.** See STAMMER. [Freq. of ME *stutten* to stutter. Akin to Du. *stoteren.*] — **stut′ter·er** *n.* — **stut′ter·ing·ly** *adv.*

Stutt·gart (stut′gärt, *Ger.* shtoot′gärt) The capital of Baden–Württemberg, West Germany; pop. 628,412 (1970).

Stuy·ve·sant (stī′və·sənt), **Peter,** 1592–1672, last Dutch governor of New Amsterdam 1647–64.

St. Vin·cent (sānt vin′sənt) One of the Windward Islands, formerly a British colony; since 1968 a self-governing member of the West Indies Associated States; 133 sq. mi.; pop. 95,000 (est. 1969); capital, Kingstown.

St. Vincent, Cape The SW extremity of Portugal.

St. Vi·tus's dance (sānt vī′təs·iz) *Pathol.* Chorea. Also **St. Vi′tus′ dance, St. Vi·tus dance** (vī′təs).

sty[1] (stī) *n. pl.* **sties 1.** A pen for swine. **2.** Any filthy habitation or place of bestiality or debauchery. — *v.t. & v.i.* **stied, sty·ing** To keep or live in a sty or hovel. [ME < OE *sti, stig*]

sty[2] (stī) *n. pl.* **sties** *Pathol.* A small, inflamed swelling of a sebaceous gland on the edge of the eyelid. Also **stye.** [< obs. *styanye* < OE *stigend,* ppr. of *stigan* to rise + *ye* eye]

stych·o·myth·i·a (stik′ə·mith′ē·ə) See STICHOMYTHY.

Styg·i·an (stij′ē·ən) *adj. Often cap.* **1.** Of or pertaining to the river Styx. **2.** Infernal; dark and gloomy. **3.** Inviolable, as an oath. [< L *Stygius* < Gk. *Stygios* < *Styx* Styx, prob. < *stygein* to hate]

sty·lar (stī′lər) *adj.* Of or resembling a stylus.

style (stīl) *n.* **1.** Manner of expressing thought, in writing or speaking; distinctive or characteristic form of expression: a florid *style*; the *style* of Mark Twain. **2.** A distinctive, characteristic, or suitable mode of expression: His writing lacks *style*. **3.** A particular or characteristic form or mode of composition, construction, or appearance, as in art, music, etc.: the Gothic *style*; the American *style* of automobile. **4.** The manner in which some action or work is performed: The horse ran in fine *style*. **5.** A good or exemplary manner of performing: a team with *style*. **6.** A mode of conduct or behavior; a way of living: to live in makeshift *style*. **7.** A fashionable manner or appearance: to live in *style*. **8.** A particular fashion in clothing. **9.** A particular type or fashion suitable for or agreeable to a person: That coat is not my *style*. **10.** The conventions of typography, design, usage, punctuation, etc., observed by a given publishing house, printing office, or publication. **11.** *Ling.* A manner of speaking or writing suitable for an occasion; especially, a functional variety of standard usage: informal *style*; formal *style*. Compare LEVEL OF USAGE. **12.** The legal or official title or appellation of a person, organization, etc. **13.** A stylus. **14.** The gnomon of a sundial. **15.** *Surg.* A slender probe with a blunt point: also called *stylet*. **16.** *Bot.* The prolongation of a carpel or ovary, bearing the stigma. For illustration see FLOWER. **17.** *Zool.* A stylet. **18.** A system of arranging the length of the calendar years so as to average that of the true solar year. See OLD STYLE, NEW STYLE under CALENDAR. — **Syn.** See NAME. — *v.* **styled, styl·ing** *v.t.* **1.** To name; give a title to. **2.** To make consistent in typography, spelling, punctuation, etc., as copy to be printed. **3.** To give form, fashion, or style to: to *style* clothes. — *v.i.* **4.** In ornamentation, to use a style or stylus. [< OF < L *stilus, stylus* writing instrument] — **styl′er** *n.*

style book A book containing rules of spelling, punctuation, typography, etc., used by printers, editors, etc., in preparing copy and manuscripts.

sty·let (stī′lit) *n.* **1.** Any slender pointed instrument, as a poniard or stiletto. **2.** *Surg.* A style (def. 15). **3.** *Zool.* Any pointed, bristlelike process or appendage. [< F < Ital. *stiletto.* See STILETTO.]

sty·li·form (stī′lə·fôrm) *adj.* Resembling or shaped like a stylus. [< NL *styliformis* < L *stylus* stylus + *forma* form]

styl·ish (stī′lish) *adj.* Having style or fashionableness in clothes, furnishings, manner, etc. — **styl′ish·ly** *adv.* — **styl′ish·ness** *n.*

styl·ist (stī′list) *n.* **1.** One who is a master of literary or rhetorical style. **2.** A designer or adviser of style in clothes, interior decoration, etc. **3.** One who works with or makes consistent the style of printed matter.

sty·lis·tic (stī·lis′tik) *adj.* Of or pertaining to style, especially literary style. — **sty·lis′ti·cal·ly** *adv.*

sty·lite (stī′līt) *n.* One of a class of early religious ascetics who lived without shelter on the tops of pillars. [< Gk. *stylitēs* < *stylos* column]

styl·ize (stī′līz) *v.t.* **·ized, ·iz·ing** To make conform to a distinctive mode or style; conventionalize. Also *Brit.* **styl′ise.** — **styl′i·za′tion** *n.* — **styl′iz·er** *n.*

stylo- *combining form* **1.** A pillar: *stylobate.* **2.** *Bot. & Zool.* A style; of or related to a style: *stylopodium.* **3.** *Anat.* Denoting relationship to a styloid process. Also, before vowels, **styl-.** [< Gk. *stylos* column, pillar]

sty·lo·bate (stī′lə·bāt) *n. Archit.* A continuous base for two or more columns. Compare STEREOBATE. [< L *stylobates* < Gk. *stylobatēs* < *stylos* pillar + *-batēs* treader < *bainein* to walk, step]

sty·lo·graph (stī′lə·graf, -gräf) *n.* A fountain pen from which ink is fed to a conical writing point instead of to a nib. Also **stylographic pen.** — **sty′lo·graph′ic** or **·i·cal** *adj.*

STYLOBATE (a)

sty·log·ra·phy (stī·log′rə·fē) *n.* The art of writing, engraving, etc., with a stylus or other pointed instrument.

sty·loid (stī′loid) *adj.* Resembling a style or peg; styliform.

styloid process *Anat.* One of various bony processes, as at the base of the temporal bone, on the head of the fibula, at the lower extremity of either the radius or the ulna, etc. For illustration see SKULL.

sty·lo·lite (stī′lə·līt) *n. Geol.* A small columnar body of rock of the same composition as the surrounding rock. — **sty′lo·lit′ic** (-lit′ik) *adj.*

sty·lo·po·di·um (stī′lə·pō′dē·əm) *n. pl.* **·di·a** (-dē·ə) *Bot.* The fleshy disk that bears the styles in umbelliferous flowers. [< NL]

sty·lus (stī′ləs) *n. pl.* **·lus·es** (-iz) or **·li** (-lī) **1.** An ancient writing instrument, having one end pointed for writing on wax tablets and the other end blunt for erasure. **2.** A pointed instrument for marking or engraving, as on carbons, stencils, etc. **3.** The needle of a record player or of a recording instrument. Also called *style.* [< L]

sty·mie (stī′mē) *n.* A condition in golf when an opponent's ball lies directly between the player's ball and the hole. — *v.t.* **·mied, ·my·ing** To block or hinder by or as by a stymie. Also spelled *stimy.* Also **sty′my.** [Prob. use of earlier Scot. *styme,* to be unable to see]

styp·sis (stip′sis) *n.* The use or the action of a styptic. [< LL < Gk., contraction < *styphein* to contract]

styp·tic (stip′tik) *adj.* **1:** Causing contraction of tissues, as blood vessels. **2.** Stopping hemorrhage or bleeding; hemostatic. Also **styp′ti·cal.** — *n.* A styptic substance or agent. [< L *stypticus* < Gk. *styptikos* < *stypsis* contraction. See STYPSIS.] — **styp·tic·i·ty** (stip·tis′ə·tē) *n.*

styptic pencil A small stick of styptic substance used to stop bleeding, usually from razor nicks and cuts.

sty·ra·ca·ceous (stī′rə·kā′shəs) *adj. Bot.* Of or pertaining to the storax family (*Styracaceae*) of trees or shrubs yielding resins and gums. [< NL < L *styrax* storax]

sty·rene (stī′rēn) *n. Chem.* A colorless aromatic hydrocarbon, C_8H_8, contained in liquid storax and also obtainable from cinnamic acid. A polymerized form (**styrene resin**) is used in making plastics. [< L *styrax* storax + -ENE]

Styr·i·a (stir′ē·ə) A Province in central and SE Austria; 6,324 sq. mi.; pop. 1,137,460 (1961); capital, Graz: German *Steiermark.*

Sty·ro·foam (stī′rə·fōm′) *n.* A light polystyrene plastic foam, resembling packed snow in appearance and used for decorations, toys, insulation, flotation devices, etc.: a trade name. Also **sty′ro·foam′.**

Styx (stiks) *n.* In Greek mythology, the river of hate, one of the five rivers surrounding Hades.

su·a·ble (sōo′ə·bəl) *adj.* Legally subject to civil process; able to be sued. — **su′a·bil′i·ty** *n.*

sua·sion (swā′zhən) *n.* The act of persuading; persuasion: archaic except in the phrase **moral suasion.** [< L *suasio, -onis* < *suadere* to persuade] — **sua·sive** (swā′siv), **sua·so·ry** (swā′sər·ē) *adj.*

suave (swäv, swāv) *adj.* Smoothly pleasant and ingratiating in manner; blandly polite; urbane. [< F < L *suavis* sweet] — **suave′ly** *adv.* — **suave′ness** *n.*

suav·i·ty (swä′və·tē, swav′ə-) *n. pl.* **·ties 1.** The state or quality of being suave; urbanity. **2.** *pl.* Suave manners or actions. [< F *suavité* < L *suavitas, -tatis* < *suavis* sweet]

sub (sub) *n. Informal* Short for any of various words beginning with *sub-,* as: **a** A substitute. **b** A subordinate or subaltern. **c** A submarine.

sub- *prefix* **1.** Under; beneath; below; as in:

subastral	subcurrent	subsurface
subcoastal	subfloor	subtext

2. *Anat.* Situated under or beneath, or on the ventral side of; as in:

subabdominal	subgenital	subpelvic
subalar	subgingival	subphrenic
subapical	subglottal	subpleural
subaxial	subglottic	subpubic
subcerebellar	subintegumental	subpulmonary
subcostal	subintestinal	subrectal
subcranial	submammary	subretinal
subcuticle	submuscular	subspinal
subcuticular	subnasal	subspinous
subdental	subneural	substernal
subdermal	subnodal	subungual
subdiaphragmatic	subocular	suburethral
subdorsal	suboptic	subvaginal
subepiglottic	suboral	subvertebral

3. Almost; nearly; slightly; imperfectly: chiefly in scientific terms; as in:

subacidulous	subconvex	submetallic
subacrid	subcubical	subnarcotic
subacuminate	subdelirium	suboval
subalkaline	subfebrile	subparallel
subangular	subfluid	subparalytic
subastringent	subhorizontal	subpolar
subaudible	subhumid	subsaline
subcalcareous	subinflammation	subserrate
subcarbureted	sublateral	subsibilant
subcolumnar	sublethal	subtetanic
subconcave	sublinear	subtypical
subconchoidal	subluminous	subvertical
subconical	submedial	subvirile

4. Lower in rank or grade; secondary; subordinate; as in:

subadministration	subeditor	submediator
subadministrator	subelement	submortgage
subassociation	subflavor	subofficer
subcantor	subforeman	suboperation
subcause	subfunction	subpart
subchanter	subholding	subrector
subclass	subidea	subrent
subclerk	sublessee	subsecretary
subcommission	sublessor	subset
subconstellation	sublieutenancy	subtone
subdean	sublieutenant	subvicar
subecho	submeaning	subworker

5. Forming a subdivision; as in:

subarea	subcouncil	subscience
subbranch	subdepartment	subsection
subbureau	subdepot	subsegment
subcategory	subdialect	subseries
subcavity	subdistrict	subshaft
subclass	subheading	subtopic
subclassification	submember	subtype
subcompany	suboffice	subunit
subcorporation	subprovince	subzone

6. *Chem.* **a** Present (in a compound) in less than normal amount: *subchloride, suboxide.* **b** Designating a basic salt compound: *subacetate, subcarbonate.*

Also: *suc-* before *c,* as in *succumb;* *suf-* before *f,* as in *suffer;* *sug-* before *g,* as in *suggest;* *sum-* before *m,* as in *summon;* *sup-* before *p,* as in *support;* *sur-* before *r,* as in *surrogate;* *sus-* before *c, p, t,* as in *susceptible, suspect, sustain.* [< L *sub-* < *sub* under]

sub. **1.** Subaltern. **2.** Subscription. **3.** Substitute. **4.** Suburb; suburban.

sub·ac·id (sub·as′id) *adj.* **1.** Slightly or pleasantly sour or acid, as certain fruits. **2.** Somewhat sharp or biting: a *subacid* remark. — **sub′a·cid′i·ty** (-ə·sid′ə·tē) *n.*

sub·a·cute (sub′ə·kyōot′) *adj.* **1.** Somewhat acute. **2.** *Pathol.* Intermediate between acute and chronic: said of a disease. — **sub′a·cute′ly** *adv.*

sub·a·gent (sub·ā′jənt) *n.* One who works for and is subordinate to an agent. — **sub·a′gen·cy** *n.*

su·bah (sōo′bä) *n.* **1.** A province or governmental district of India. **2.** A subahdar. Also **su′ba.** [< Urdu]

su·bah·dar (sōo′bä·där′) *n.* The native officer of a company of sepoys in the former British Indian Army: also *subah.* Also **su′ba·dar′.** [< Urdu *subahdār* < Persian < Arabic *sūbah* province + Persian *dār* possessor, master]

sub·al·pine (sub·al′pīn, -pin) *adj.* **1.** At or near the foot of the Alps. **2.** Of, pertaining to, or growing in mountainous regions near but below the timber line: also *alpestrine.*

sub·al·tern (sub·ôl′tərn; *for n. def. 3* sub′əl·tûrn′) *adj.* **1.** *Brit. Mil.* Ranking below a captain. **2.** Of inferior rank or position; subordinate, as a species to a genus; or, in logic, as a particular proposition under a universal. — *n.* **1.** A person of subordinate rank or position. **2.** *Brit. Mil.* An officer ranking below a captain. **3.** *Logic* A statement the truth of which is undetermined by the truth or falsity of another, but which cannot be false if the latter is true. Abbr. **sub.** [< LL *subalternus* < L *sub-* under + *alternus* alternate]

sub·al·ter·nate (sub·ôl′tər·nit, -al′-) *adj.* **1.** Succeeding or following by turns; successive. **2.** *Bot.* Alternate, with a tendency to become opposite, as leaves on a stem. — *n.* A particular as opposed to a universal proposition. [< Med.L *subalternatus,* pp. of *subalternare.* See SUBALTERN.] — **sub·al·ter·na·tion** (sub-ôl′tər-nā′shən, -al′-) *n.*

sub·ant·arc·tic (sub′ant-ärk′tik, -är′tik) *adj.* Of or pertaining to the region surrounding the Antarctic Circle.

sub·a·quat·ic (sub′ə-kwat′ik, -ə-kwot′-) *adj.* 1. Partially aquatic. 2. Subaqueous.

sub·a·que·ous (sub-ā′kwē-əs) *adj.* 1. Being, formed, or operating under water; submarine. 2. Occurring or adapted for use under water.

sub·arc·tic (sub-ärk′tik, -är′tik) *adj.* Denoting or pertaining to the region surrounding the Arctic Circle.

sub·ar·cu·ate (sub-är′kyōō-it) *adj.* Moderately arched or bent. Also **sub·ar′cu·at′ed** (-ā′tid).

sub·ar·id (sub-ar′id) *adj.* Partly arid; moderately dry.

sub·as·sem·bly (sub′ə-sem′blē) *n.* An assembled part that is in turn part of a larger assembly; also, the act or process of producing such parts.

sub·a·tom·ic (sub′ə-tom′ik) *adj.* Within the atom: *subatomic* particle.

sub·au·di·tion (sub′ô-dish′ən) *n.* 1. The understanding or supplying of a word or thought not expressed. 2. A word or thought thus understood or supplied.

sub·au·ric·u·lar (sub′ô-rik′yə-lər) *adj.* Situated below the auricle of the ear.

sub·ax·il·lar·y (sub-ak′sə-ler′ē) *adj.* 1. *Bot.* Lying under or beneath the axil. 2. *Anat.* Beneath the armpit.

sub·base (sub′bās′) *n.* *Archit.* The lowest member of a base or pedestal.

sub·base·ment (sub′bās′mənt) *n.* An underground story, or any one of several below the first or true basement.

sub·bass (sub′bās′) *n.* *Music* In an organ, a 16-foot or 32-foot pedal register. Also **sub′base′**.

sub·cal·i·ber (sub·kal′ə-bər) *adj.* *Mil.* 1. Of smaller caliber than the firearm from which it is to be fired: said of a projectile. A tube or disk is used to make up the deficit. 2. Of or pertaining to a subcaliber projectile.

sub·car·ti·lag·i·nous (sub-kär′tə-laj′ə-nəs) *adj.* *Anat.* 1. Beneath cartilage or under tissue. 2. Partly cartilaginous.

sub·ce·les·tial (sub′si-les′chəl) *adj.* 1. Lower than celestial; beneath the heavens. 2. Mundane. 3. Directly beneath the zenith. — *n.* A subcelestial being.

sub·cel·lar (sub′sel′ər) *n.* A cellar under another cellar.

sub·cen·tral (sub-sen′trəl) *adj.* 1. Located beneath a center. 2. Almost or slightly central. — **sub·cen′tral·ly** *adv.*

sub·cla·vi·an (sub-klā′vē-ən) *Anat. adj.* 1. Situated beneath the clavicle. 2. Of or pertaining to a subclavian nerve, vein, muscle, etc. — *n.* A subclavian nerve, vein, muscle, etc. [< NL *subclavius* < L *sub-* under + *clavis* key]

subclavian artery *Anat.* The large main artery that passes under the clavicle to convey blood to the arm.

subclavian groove *Anat.* A groove made by the subclavian artery or vein along each branch of the first rib.

subclavian vein *Anat.* The portion of the main vein of the arm that lies under the clavicle.

sub·cli·max (sub-klī′maks) *n.* *Ecol.* Any stage in the development of a plant or animal community determined by non-climatic agencies, such as a fire or flood, that prevent normal succession. — **sub·cli·mac·tic** (sub′klī-mak′tik) *adj.*

sub·clin·i·cal (sub-klin′i-kəl) *adj.* Having no symptoms apparent in clinical tests, as in the early stages of a disease. — **sub·clin′i·cal·ly** *adv.*

sub·com·mit·tee (sub′kə-mit′ē) *n.* A subordinate committee appointed from the members of the original committee.

sub·con·scious (sub-kon′shəs) *adj.* 1. Not clearly or wholly conscious. 2. *Psychol.* Denoting such phenomena of mental life as are not attended by full consciousness. — *n.* *Psychol.* That portion of mental activity not directly in the focus of consciousness but sometimes susceptible to recall by the proper stimulus. — **sub·con′scious·ly** *adv.* — **sub·con′·scious·ness** *n.*

sub·con·ti·nent (sub-kon′tə-nənt) *n.* *Geog.* A great land mass forming part of a continent but having considerable geographical independence, as India.

sub·con·tract (*n.* sub·kon′trakt; *v.* sub′kən-trakt′) *n.* A contract subordinate to another contract and assigning part of the work to another party. — *v.t. & v.i.* To make a subcontract (for); arrange for part or all of (work) to be performed by another party.

sub·con·trac·tor (sub′kən-trak′tər, -kon′trak-) *n.* One who enters into a contract with a contractor to do work specified in the latter's contract.

sub·cor·tex (sub·kôr′teks) *n. pl.* **·ti·ces** (-tə-sēz) *Anat.* The part of the brain that underlies the cortex. [< NL < L *sub-* under + *cortex* bark]

sub·cor·ti·cal (sub·kor′ti·kəl) *adj.* Of, pertaining to, or constituting nerve centers lying beneath the cortex of the brain. — **sub·cor′ti·cal·ly** *adv.*

sub·crit·i·cal (sub′krit′i·kəl) *adj.* *Physics* Of, pertaining to, or containing fissionable material in a quantity not sufficient to start or sustain a chain reaction: *subcritical* mass.

sub·cul·ture (sub′kul′chər) *n.* 1. *Bacteriol.* A culture of bacteria or other material grown from a preexisting culture. 2. *Sociol.* A group having specific patterns of behavior that set it off from other groups within a culture or society.

sub·cu·ta·ne·ous (sub′kyōō-tā′nē-əs) *adj.* 1. Situated, found, or lying beneath the skin. 2. Introduced or applied beneath the skin, as an injection. [< L *subcutaneus* < L *sub-* under + *cutis* skin] — **sub′cu·ta′ne·ous·ly** *adv.*

sub·dea·con (sub·dē′kən) *n.* A clergyman ranking next below a deacon. [< AF *soudiakene, subdiacne* < Med.L *subdiaconus* (< *sub-* under + *diaconus* deacon), trans. of LGk. *hypodiakonos*]

sub·deb (sub′deb′) *n. Informal* 1. A debutante. 2. Any girl of this age. In a style suitable for girls of this age.

sub·deb·u·tante (sub′deb-yōō-tänt′, -deb′yōō-tant) *n.* A young girl the year before she becomes a debutante.

sub·del·e·gate (*n.* sub·del′ə·gāt, -git; *v.* sub·del′ə·gāt) *n.* One who represents a delegate. — *v.t.* **·gat·ed, ·gat·ing** To appoint as a subdelegate.

sub·di·ac·o·nate (sub′dī·ak′ə-nit, -nāt) *n.* The office, rank, or order of subdeacon. [< Med.L *subdiaconatus* < *subdiaconus*. See SUBDEACON.]

sub·di·vide (sub′di·vīd′) *v.t. & v.i.* **·vid·ed, ·vid·ing** 1. To divide (a part) resulting from a previous division; divide again. 2. To divide (land) into lots for sale or improvement. [< LL *subdividere* < L *sub-* under + *dividere* to separate. See DIVIDE.]

sub·di·vi·sion (sub′di·vizh′ən) *n.* 1. Division following upon division. 2. A part, as of land, resulting from subdividing. 3. An area of land, part of a city, etc., composed of subdivided lots. — **Syn.** See PORTION.

sub·dom·i·nant (sub·dom′ə-nənt) *n. Music* The tone next below the dominant; fourth tone or degree of a major or minor scale.

sub·du·al (sub·dōō′əl, -dyōō′-) *n.* The act of subduing, or the state of being subdued.

sub·duce (sub·dōōs′, -dyōōs′) *v.t.* **·duced, ·duc·ing** *Obs.* To withdraw; take away. Also **sub·duct′** (-dukt′). [< L *subducere* < *sub-* from + *ducere* to lead] — **sub·duc′tion** (-duk′·shən) *n.*

sub·due (sub·dōō′, -dyōō′) *v.t.* **·dued, ·du·ing** 1. To gain dominion over, as by war or force; subjugate; vanquish. 2. To overcome by training, influence, or persuasion; tame. 3. To repress (emotions, impulses, etc.). 4. To reduce the intensity of; soften, as a color or sound. 5. To bring (land) under cultivation. [< OF *soduire* to deceive < L *subducere* to withdraw; infl. in meaning by L *subdere* to overcome] — **sub·du′a·ble** *adj.* — **sub·du′er** *n.*
— **Syn.** 1. conquer. 2. master, control, bridle. 3. check, restrain. 4. moderate, temper.

sub·el·a·phine (sub·el′ə-fin, -fin) *adj. Zool.* Designating a modified form of elaphine antlers. See illustration of ANTLER.

sub·e·qua·to·ri·al (sub·ē′kwə-tôr′ē·əl, -tō′rē-) *adj.* 1. Nearly equatorial. 2. Denoting or belonging to a region adjoining the equatorial region.

su·ber·ic (sōō·ber′ik) *adj.* Of, pertaining to, or derived from cork. Also **su·be·re·ous** (sōō·bir′ē·əs). [< F *subérique* < L *suber* cork]

suberic acid *Chem.* A white crystalline dibasic acid, C₈H₁₄O₄, obtained by the action of nitric acid on cork and on various fatty oils.

su·ber·in (sōō′bər-in) *n.* A waxlike, fatty substance formed in cork cells.

su·ber·i·za·tion (sōō′bər-ə-zā′shən, -ī-zā′-) *n. Bot.* The transformation of plant cell walls into suberin or cork tissue.

su·ber·ize (sōō′bə-rīz) *v.t.* **·ized, ·iz·ing** To make corky, as cell walls.

su·ber·ose (sōō′bər-ōs) *adj.* 1. Corky. 2. Of or pertaining to suberin. Also **su′ber·ous** (-əs).

sub·fam·i·ly (sub·fam′ə·lē, -fam′lē) *n. pl.* **·lies** 1. *Biol.* A division of plants or animals next below a family but above the genus. 2. *Ling.* A division of languages below a family and above a branch.

sub·floor (sub′flôr′) *n.* The rough floor upon which the finished floor is laid; especially, a rough wooden floor nailed diagonally across the floor joists. Also **sub′floor′ing.**

sub·fusc (sub·fusk′) *adj.* Dark or dusky in color. [< L *subfuscus* < *sub-* under + *fuscus* dark, black]

sub·ge·nus (sub·jē′nəs) *n. pl.* **·gen·e·ra** (-jen′ər·ə) or, less commonly, **·ge·nus·es** *Biol.* A primary subdivision of a genus including one or more species with common characters. — **sub·ge·ner′ic** (-ji·ner′ik) *adj.*

sub·gla·cial (sub·glā′shəl) *adj. Geol.* Deposited or formed beneath a glacier. — **sub·gla′cial·ly** *adv.*

sub·group (sub′grōōp′) *n.* 1. A secondary group or division. 2. *Biol.* One of the divisions of an order. 3. *Chem.* A group included within a larger group, as in the periodic table.

sub·head (sub′hed′) *n.* 1. A heading or title of a subdivision. 2. An official next below the head in a college or school.

sub·hu·man (sub·hyōō′mən) *adj.* 1. Less than or imperfectly human. 2. Below the level of the primate type represented by *Homo sapiens.*

sub·in·dex (sub·in′deks) *n. pl.* **·in·dices** (-in′də·sēz) *Math.* A subscript (which see).

sub·in·feu·date (sub·in·fyōō′dāt) *v.t. & v.i.* **·dat·ed, ·dat·ing** To sublet by subinfeudation. Also **sub·in′feud′.**

sub·in·feu·da·tion (sub·in′fyōō-dā′shən) *n.* 1. The granting of part of an estate by a feudal vassal to a tenant who thus assumes all responsibilities. **2.** The tenure or lands so held or established. **— sub·in·feu·da·to·ry** (sub'in-fyōō'də-tôr'ē, -tō'rē) *adj.*

sub·ir·ri·gate (sub·ir'ə·gāt) *v.t.* **·gat·ed, ·gat·ing** To irrigate through underground pipes, etc. **— sub·ir·ri·ga'tion** *n.*

su·bi·to (sōō'bē·tō) *adv. Music* Quickly; suddenly. [< Ital.]

subj. 1. Subject. **2.** Subjective(ly). **3.** Subjunctive.

sub·ja·cent (sub·jā'sənt) *adj.* **1.** Situated directly underneath. **2.** Lower than but not directly below. [< L *subjacens, -entis*, ppr. of *subjacere* < *sub-* under + *jacere* to lie] **— sub·ja'cen·cy** *n.*

sub·ject (*adj., n.* sub'jikt; *v.* səb·jekt') *adj.* **1.** Being under the power of another; owing or yielding obedience to sovereign authority. **2.** Liable to be affected by; exposed to the influence of: with *to: subject to* disease. **3.** Likely to bring about or incur: with *to: subject to* severe criticism. **4.** Dependent on; contingent on the authoritative action of: with *to:* a treaty *subject to* ratification. **— n. 1.** One who is under the governing power of another, as of a ruler or government, especially of a monarch. Compare CITIZEN. **2.** One who or that which is employed or treated in a specified way, as a body for dissection, or a person used in psychological experiments. **3.** A topic or main theme, as of a discussion, written work, etc. **4.** Something represented by or serving as the basic idea for an artistic work. **5.** A branch of learning or course of study. **6.** An originating cause; motive. **7.** *Gram.* The word, phrase, or clause of a sentence about which something is stated or asked in the predicate. **8.** *Music* A melody on which a composition or a part of it is based. **9.** *Philos.* The ego or self; substance; essential being. **10.** *Logic* In a proposition, that term about which something is affirmed or denied. See PROPOSITION. **— Syn.** See MELODY, TOPIC. **—** *v.t.* **1.** To bring under dominion or control; subjugate. **2.** To cause to undergo some experience or action. **3.** To offer for consideration or approval; submit. **4.** To make liable; expose: His inheritance was *subjected* to heavy taxation. **5.** *Obs.* To place beneath. Abbr. *subj.* [< OF *suget, sujet* < L *subjectus*, pp. of *subjicere* < *sub-* under + *jacere* to throw; refashioned after L]

sub·jec·tion (səb·jek'shən) *n.* **1.** The act of making subject. **2.** The state of being subjected.

sub·jec·tive (səb·jek'tiv) *adj.* **1.** Relating to, proceeding from, or taking place within an individual's mind, emotions, etc.: opposed to *objective.* **2.** Originating from or influenced by one's personal interests, prejudices, emotions, etc. **3.** Introspective. **4.** Of the mind or emotions only; fanciful; illusory. **5.** In literature and art, giving prominence to the subject or author as treating of his inner experience and emotion. **6.** Pertaining to the real nature or essence of a person or thing; inherent. **7.** *Gram.* Designating the nominative case in English. Abbr. *subj.* **— sub·jec'tive·ly** *adv.* **— sub·jec'tive·ness, sub·jec·tiv·i·ty** (sub'jek·tiv'ə·tē) *n.*

sub·jec·tiv·ism (səb·jek'tiv·iz'əm) *n. Philos.* **1.** The doctrine that knowledge is merely subjective and relative and is derived from one's own consciousness. **2.** The doctrine that we know directly no external object. **3.** The doctrine that there is no objective standard, test, or measure of truth; relativism. **4.** The doctrine that individual feeling is the standard by which to judge right and wrong. **— sub·jec'tiv·ist** *n.* **— sub·jec'tiv·is'tic** *adj.*

subject matter That which is under consideration, discussion, or inquiry; the subject of thought.

sub·join (sub·join') *v.t.* To add at the end; attach; affix. [< MF *subjoindre* < L *subjungere* < *sub-* in addition + *jungere* to join]

sub·join·der (sub·join'dər) *n.* Something subjoined. [< SUBJOIN, on analogy with *rejoinder*]

sub ju·di·ce (sub jōō'di·sē) *Latin* Under judicial consideration.

sub·ju·gate (sub'jōō·gāt) *v.t.* **·gat·ed, ·gat·ing 1.** To bring under dominion; conquer; subdue. **2.** To make subservient in any way. [< L *subjugatus*, pp. of *subjugare* < *sub-* under + *jugum* yoke] **— sub'ju·ga'tion** *n.* **— sub'ju·ga'tor** *n.*

sub·junc·tion (səb·jungk'shən) *n.* **1.** The act of subjoining, or the state of being subjoined. **2.** That which is subjoined. [< LL *subjunctio, -onis* < L *subjungere.* See SUBJOIN.]

sub·junc·tive (səb·jungk'tiv) *Gram. adj.* Of or pertaining to that mood of the finite verb that is used to express a future contingency, a supposition implying the contrary, a mere supposition with indefinite time, or a wish or desire. ◆ In English the forms of the subjunctive mood are usually introduced by conjunctions of condition, doubt, contingency, possibility, etc., as *if, though, lest, unless, that, till,* or *whether,* but verbs in conditional clauses are not always in the subjunctive mood, for the use of these conjunctions with the indicative is very common. **— n. 1.** The subjunctive mood. **2.** A verb form or construction in this mood. Abbr. *subj.* [< L *subjunctivus* < *subjunctus*, pp. of *subjungere.* See SUBJOIN.]

sub·king·dom (sub·king'dəm) *n. Zool. Obs.* A phylum.

sub·lap·sar·i·an (sub'lap·sâr'ē·ən) *n.* A believer in sublapsarianism. **— adj.** Relating to the sublapsarians or to their tenets. [< NL *sublapsarius* < L *sub-* under + *lapsus* fall]

sub·lap·sar·i·an·ism (sub'lap·sâr'ē·ən·iz'əm) *n. Theol.* The doctrine that God, having permitted the fall of man, elected some fallen men to eternal salvation and provided for their redemption. See INFRALAPSARIANISM, SUPRALAPSARIANISM.

sub·lease (*v.* sub·lēs'; *n.* sub'lēs') *v.t.* **·leased, ·leas·ing** To obtain or let (property) on a sublease. **— n.** A lease of property from a tenant or lessee.

sub·let (sub·let', sub'let') *v.t.* **·let, ·let·ting 1.** To let (property one holds on a lease) to another. **2.** To let (work that one has contracted to do) to a subordinate contractor.

sub·li·mate (sub'lə·māt) *v.* **·mat·ed, ·mat·ing** *v.t.* **1.** *Chem.* To cause (a substance) to convert from the solid to the gaseous state by the application of heat or pressure, and then to solidify again, with no apparent intermediate liquefaction. **2.** To refine; purify. **3.** *Psychol.* To convert the energy of (instinctual drives) unconsciously into acceptable social manifestations. **— v.i. 4.** To undergo sublimation. **— adj.** Sublimated; refined. **— n.** *Chem.* The product of sublimation, especially when regarded as purified by the process. [< L *sublimatus*, pp. of *sublimare* < *sublimis.* See SUBLIME.]

sub·li·ma·tion (sub'lə·mā'shən) *n.* **1.** The act or process of sublimating. **2.** That which has been sublimated. **3.** *Psychol.* The transfer of psychic energy into socially acceptable channels of endeavor.

sub·lime (sə·blīm') *adj.* **1.** Characterized by elevation, nobility, etc.; grand; solemn. **2.** Inspiring awe, deep emotion, etc.; moving. **3.** Being of the highest degree; supreme; utmost. **4.** *Poetic* Of lofty bearing; haughty; proud; elated. **— n.** That which is sublime; height, as of emotion, grandeur, etc.: often with *the.* **— v. ·limed, ·lim·ing** *v.t.* **1.** To make sublime; ennoble. **2.** *Chem.* To sublimate. **— v.i. 3.** To become sublimated. [< L *sublimis* lofty, prob. < *sub-* up to, under + *limen* lintel] **— sub·lime'ly** *adv.* **— sub·lim'er** *n.* **— sub·lim·i·ty** (sə·blim'ə·tē), sub·lime'ness *n.*

Sublime Porte See under PORTE.

sub·lim·i·nal (sub·lim'ə·nəl) *adj. Psychol.* Perceived below the threshold of consciousness, as changes, stimuli, images, etc., of too low an intensity to produce a clear awareness. [< SUB- + L *limen, liminis* threshold, trans. of G *unter der Schwelle (des Bewusstseins)* under the threshold (of consciousness)] **— sub·lim'i·nal·ly** *adv.*

sub·lin·gual (sub·ling'gwəl) *adj.* **1.** Situated beneath the tongue. **2.** Of, pertaining to, or designating the salivary gland situated beneath the tongue.

sub·lit·to·ral (sub·lit'ə·rəl) *adj.* **1.** Close to the seashore. **2.** Pertaining to or designating the area between low-tide mark and a depth of 20 fathoms or of 40 meters.

sub·lu·nar·y (sub·lōō'nər·ē, sub·lōō'nər·ē) *adj.* **1.** Beneath the moon. **2.** Mundane; earthly. Also **sub·lu·nar** (sub·lōō'nər). [< NL *sublunaris* < L *sub-* under + *luna* moon]

sub·ma·chine gun (sub'mə·shēn') A lightweight automatic weapon using pistol ammunition, designed to be fired from the shoulder or hip.

sub·mar·gi·nal (sub·mär'jən·əl) *adj.* **1.** Below the margin. **2.** Of low fertility; unproductive: *submarginal* land. **3.** *Biol.* Situated close to the margin of an organ or structure.

SUBMACHINE GUN
a Stock. *b* Housing. *c* Barrel.
d Trigger. *e* Trigger guard. *f* Clip.

sub·ma·rine (*adj.* sub'mə·rēn'; *n.* sub'mə·rēn) *adj.* **1.** Existing, done, or operating beneath the surface of the sea: a *submarine* mine. **2.** Of or pertaining to submarine boats. **— n.** A ship designed to operate both on and below the surface of the sea. **— sub·mar·i·ner** (sub·mar'ə·nər) *n.*

submarine chaser A small, fast patrol vessel designed and equipped for action against submarines.

sub·max·il·lar·y (sub·mak'sə·ler'ē) *Anat. adj.* **1.** Of, pertaining to, or situated beneath the lower jaw. **2.** Of or pertaining to one of the salivary glands situated on either side of the lower jaw. **— n.** *pl.* **·lar·ies** The lower jaw bone: also **sub·max·il·la** (sub·mak·sil'ə).

sub·me·di·ant (sub·mē'dē·ənt) *n. Music* The sixth tone of a major or minor scale.

sub·men·tal (sub·men'təl) *adj. Anat.* Situated beneath the chin: the *submental* artery.

sub·merge (səb·mûrj') *v.* **·merged, ·merg·ing** *v.t.* **1.** To place under or plunge into water or other liquid. **2.** To cover; hide. **— v.i. 3.** To sink or dive beneath the surface of water, etc. Also **sub·merse'** (-mûrs'). [< L *submergere*, var. of *summergere* < *sub-* under + *mergere* to plunge] **— sub·mer'gence** *n.*

sub·mer·gi·ble (səb·mûr'jə·bəl) *adj.* Submersible. **— sub·mer'gi·bil'i·ty** *n.*

sub·mersed (səb·mûrst′) *adj.* **1.** *Bot.* Growing under water. **2.** Submerged. [< L *submersus*, pp. of *submergere*. See SUBMERGE.]

sub·mers·i·ble (səb·mûr′sə·bəl) *adj.* **1.** Capable of being submerged. **2.** Able to function under water, etc. — *n.* *Archaic* A submarine.

sub·mer·sion (səb·mûr′shən, -zhən) *n.* The act of merging something in a liquid or the state of being submerged. Also **sub·mer′gence** (-jəns).

sub·mi·cron (sub·mī′kron) *n.* A particle of from 50 to 1,000 angstroms in diameter.

sub·mi·cro·scop·ic (sub·mī′krə·skop′ik) *adj.* So small as to be below the limit of vision in a microscope.

sub·min·i·a·ture (sub·min′ē·ə·chŏŏr′) *adj.* Designating something smaller than that termed miniature, as a camera or electronic component.

sub·miss (səb·mis′) *adj.* *Archaic* Submissive; subdued. [< L *submissus*, pp. of *submittere*. See SUBMIT.]

sub·mis·sion (səb·mish′ən) *n.* **1.** The act of submitting or yielding to the power or authority of another. **2.** The state or quality of being submissive. **3.** The act of presenting something for consideration, approval, decision, etc. **4.** *Archaic* Acknowledgment of error.

sub·mis·sive (səb·mis′iv) *adj.* Willing or inclined to submit; yielding; obedient; docile. — **sub·mis′sive·ly** *adv.* — **sub·mis′sive·ness** *n.*

sub·mit (səb·mit′) *v.* **·mit·ted, ·mit·ting** *v.t.* **1.** To place under or yield to the authority, will, or power of another; surrender. **2.** To present for the consideration, decision, or approval of others; refer. **3.** To present as one's opinion; suggest. — *v.i.* **4.** To give up; surrender. **5.** To be obedient or submissive; be acquiescent. — **Syn.** See DEFER[2]. [< L *submittere*, var. of *summittere* < *sub-* underneath + *mittere* to send] — **sub·mit′tal** *n.* — **sub·mit′ter** *n.*

sub·mon·tane (sub·mon′tān) *adj.* **1.** Situated at the foot of a mountain or mountain range. **2.** Beneath a mountain. — **sub·mon′tane·ly** *adv.*

sub·mu·co·sa (sub·myōō·kō′sə) *n. pl.* **·sae** (-sē) *Anat.* The connective tissue situated beneath the mucous membranes. [< SUB- + MUCOSA] — **sub·mu·cous** (-myōō′kəs) *adj.*

sub·mul·ti·ple (sub·mul′tə·pəl) *n.* *Math.* A number or quantity that is contained in another without remainder; an aliquot part. — *adj.* Contained in something an exact number of times. [< LL *submultiplus* < *sub-* opposite of, lesser + *multiplus* multiple]

sub·nor·mal (sub·nôr′məl) *adj.* **1.** Below the normal. **2.** *Psychol.* Less than normal in intelligence or other mental traits. — *n.* A subnormal individual. — **sub·nor·mal·i·ty** (sub′nôr·mal′ə·tē) *n.*

sub·o·ce·an·ic (sub′ō·shē·an′ik) *adj.* Occurring, formed, or happening beneath the ocean or the ocean floor.

sub·or·bi·tal (sub·ôr′bi·təl) *adj.* **1.** *Aerospace* Falling short of a complete revolution around the earth or other celestial body: said of rockets, artificial satellites, and spacecraft. **2.** *Anat.* Situated below the orbital cavities.

sub·or·der (sub′ôr′dər) *n.* **1.** *Biol.* A category of animals or plants next below an order but above a family. **2.** A subordinate architectural order modifying the principal order. — **sub·or·di·nal** (sub·ôr′də·nəl) *adj.*

sub·or·di·nar·y (sub·ôr′də·ner′ē) *n. pl.* **·nar·ies** *Heraldry* A kind of charge usually considered less honorable than an ordinary, including the bordure, orle, tressure, etc.

sub·or·di·nate (*adj.* & *n.* sə·bôr′də·nit; *v.* sə·bôr′də·nāt) *adj.* **1.** Belonging to an inferior or lower order in a classification; secondary; minor. **2.** Subject or subservient to another; inferior in any way. **3.** *Gram.* **a** Of, pertaining to, or designating a clause connected with and dependent upon another clause and functioning as a subject, object, or modifier. **b** Serving to introduce such a clause. — *n.* One who or that which is subordinate. — *v.t.* **·nat·ed, ·nat·ing** **1.** To make subordinate; also, to hold as of less importance. **2.** To make subject or subservient. [< L *subordinatus*, pp. of *subordinare* < *sub-* under + *ordinare* to order] — **sub·or′di·nate·ly** *adv.* — **sub·or′di·nate·ness** *n.* — **sub·or·di·na′tion** *n.* — **sub·or′di·na·tive** *adj.*

subordinate clause *Gram.* A dependent clause. See under CLAUSE.

subordinate conjunction See under CONJUNCTION.

sub·or·di·na·tion·ism (sə·bôr′də·nā′shən·iz′əm) *n.* *Theol.* The doctrine that the second and third persons of the Trinity are inferior to the first person. — **sub·or′di·na′tion·ist** *n.*

sub·orn (sə·bôrn′) *v.t.* **1.** To bribe or procure (someone) to commit perjury. **2.** To incite or instigate to an evil act, especially a criminal act. [< L *subornare* < *sub-* secretly + *ornare* to equip] — **sub·or·na·tion** (sub′ôr·nā′shən) *n.* — **sub·orn′er** *n.*

Su·bo·ti·ca (sōō′bô′tē·tsä) A city in northern Serbia, Yugoslavia; pop. 74,832 (1961): Hungarian *Szabadka*. Also **Su·bo′tit·sa.**

sub·ox·ide (sub·ok′sīd) *n.* *Chem.* An oxide having the minimum amount of oxygen.

sub·phy·lum (sub·fī′ləm) *n. pl.* **·la** (-lə) *Biol.* A primary division of a phylum, superior to the class.

sub·plot (sub′plot′) *n.* A plot subordinate to the principal one in a novel, play, etc.

sub·poe·na (sə·pē′nə, səb-) *n.* A judicial writ requiring a person to appear in court to give testimony. — *v.t.* To notify or summon by writ or subpoena. Also **sub·pe′na.** [< Med.L < L *sub poena* < *sub* under + *poena* penalty]

sub·prin·ci·pal (sub·prin′sə·pəl) *n.* **1.** An assistant principal in a school. **2.** A rafter or brace next to or auxiliary to one of the main timbers of the frame. **3.** *Music* An open diapason subbass in an organ.

sub·re·gion (sub′rē′jən) *n.* A subdivision of a region, especially with reference to the distribution of animals. — **sub·re′gion·al** *adj.*

sub·rep·tion (səb·rep′shən) *n.* **1.** A procuring of some favor or reward, especially ecclesiastical preferment, by suppression of the truth. **2.** Inference resulting from concealment, or misrepresentation of facts. [< L *subreptio*, -*onis* < *subreptus*, pp. of *subripere* < *sub-* secretly + *rapere* to snatch, seize] — **sub·rep·ti·tious** (sub′rep·tish′əs) *adj.*

sub·ro·gate (sub′rō·gāt) *v.t.* **·gat·ed, ·gat·ing** **1.** To substitute (one thing) for another. **2.** To substitute (one person) for another when attributing or assigning rights or appointing to an office. [< L *subrogatus*, pp. of *subrogare* to substitute < *sub-* in place of + *rogare* to ask]

sub·ro·ga·tion (sub′rō·gā′shən) *n.* **1.** The succession or substitution of one person or thing by or for another. **2.** *Law* The putting of a person who (as a surety) has paid the debt of another in the place of the creditor to whom he has paid it.

sub ro·sa (sub rō′zə) *Latin* Confidentially; in secret: literally, under the rose, because the rose was the emblem of the Egyptian god Horus, mistakenly regarded by the Greeks and Romans as the god of silence.

sub·scap·u·lar (sub·skap′yə·lər) *adj.* *Anat.* Situated beneath or under the scapula, as a muscle or artery. — *n.* A subscapular muscle or artery. Also **sub·scap′u·lar′y** (-lər′ē). [< NL *subscapularis* < L *sub-* under + *scapula* shoulder blade]

sub·scribe (səb·skrīb′) *v.* **·scribed, ·scrib·ing** *v.t.* **1.** To write, as one's name, at the end of a document; sign. **2.** To sign one's name to as an expression of assent, acceptance, etc.; attest to by signing. **3.** To promise, especially in writing, to pay or contribute (a sum of money). — *v.i.* **4.** To write one's name at the end of a document. **5.** To give sanction, support, or approval; agree. **6.** To promise to pay or contribute money. **7.** To agree to receive and pay for a specified number of consecutive issues of a newspaper, periodical, etc.: with *to*. [< L *subscribere* < *sub-* underneath + *scribere* to write] — **sub·scrib′er** *n.*

sub·script (sub′skript) *adj.* Written below or lower and to the right or left: distinguished from *adscript*. — *n.* **1.** A subscript character. **2.** *Math.* A subscript character that indicates a specific operation or characteristic: also *subindex, suffix*. Compare SUPERSCRIPT. [< L *subscriptus*, pp. of *subscribere*. See SUBSCRIBE.]

sub·scrip·tion (səb·skrip′shən) *n.* **1.** The act of subscribing; signature. **2.** Consent, confirmation, or agreement. **3.** That which is subscribed; a signed paper or statement. **4.** A signature written at the end of a document. **5.** A signed acceptance of religious articles. **6.** The individual or total sum or number subscribed for any purpose. **7.** A formal agreement or undertaking evinced by signature, as payment of a certain price for the receipt of a magazine, book, ticket, etc. **8.** *Archaic* Submission; obedience. **9.** The part of a doctor's prescription that gives directions for compounding the ingredients. **10.** The sale of books, magazines, tickets, etc., by mail or by personal canvass. *Abbr. sub.* — **to take up a subscription** To collect money (for some special purpose or cause) from a large number of people. — **sub·scrip′tive** *adj.* — **sub·scrip′tive·ly** *adv.*

sub·se·quence (sub′sə·kwəns) *n.* **1.** The condition of being subsequent. **2.** That which is subsequent. Also **sub′se·quen·cy.**

sub·se·quent (sub′sə·kwənt) *adj.* Following in time, place, or order, or as a result. [< L *subsequens*, -*entis*, ppr. of *subsequi* < *sub-* next below + *sequi* to follow] — **sub′se·quent·ly** *adv.* — **sub′se·quent·ness** *n.*

sub·serve (səb·sûrv′) *v.t.* **·served, ·serv·ing** **1.** To be of use or help in furthering (a process, cause, etc.); serve; promote. **2.** To serve as a subordinate to (a person). [< L *subservire* < *sub-* under + *servire*. See SERVE.]

sub·ser·vi·ent (səb·sûr′vē·ənt) *adj.* **1.** Adapted to promote some end or purpose; being of service; useful as a subordinate. **2.** Servile; obsequious; truckling. — *n.* One who or that which subserves. [< L *subserviens*, -*entis*, ppr. of *subservire*. See SUBSERVE.] — **sub·ser′vi·ent·ly** *adv.* — **sub·ser′vi·ent·ness, sub·ser′vi·ence, sub·ser′vi·en·cy** *n.*

sub·shrub (sub′shrub′) *n.* An undershrub or very small shrub.

sub·side (səb·sīd′) *v.i.* **·sid·ed, ·sid·ing** **1.** To become less violent or agitated; become calm or quiet; abate. **2.** To sink to a lower level. **3.** To sink to the bottom, as sediment; settle. — **Syn.** See DECREASE. [< L *subsidere* < *sub-* under + *sidere* to settle < *sedere* to sit]

sub·sid·ence (səb·sīd′ns, sub′sə·dəns) *n.* **1.** The settling of heavy parts to the bottom; precipitation. **2.** The sinking of water or other liquids to a lower or normal level. **3.** A gradual settling into a quiet or inactive state. **4.** A gradual settling of earth structures to a lower level, because of ground movements or underground workings. [< L *subsidentia* sediment < *subsidere*. See SUBSIDE.]

sub·sid·i·ar·y (səb·sid′ē·er′ē) *adj.* **1.** Assisting or functioning in a lesser capacity; supplementary; auxiliary; secondary. **2.** Of, pertaining to, or in the nature of a subsidy; helping by a subsidy. — **Syn.** See AUXILIARY. — *n. pl.* **·ar·ies** **1.** One who or that which furnishes aid or support; an auxiliary. **2.** A subsidiary company. **3.** *Music* A theme subordinate to or dependent on the main theme or subject. [< L *subsidiarius* < *subsidium* < *subsidere*. See SUBSIDE.] — **sub·sid′i·ar′i·ly** *adv.*

subsidiary coin Coin of small denomination, especially when less than the basic monetary unit.

subsidiary company A company controlled by another company that owns the greater part of its shares.

sub·si·dize (sub′sə·dīz) *v.t.* **·dized, ·diz·ing** **1.** To furnish with a subsidy; grant a regular allowance or pecuniary aid to. **2.** To obtain the assistance of by a subsidy: now often implying bribery. Also *Brit.* **sub′si·dise.** — **sub′si·di·za′· tion** *n.* — **sub′si·diz′er** *n.*

sub·si·dy (sub′sə·dē) *n. pl.* **·dies** **1.** Pecuniary aid directly granted by government to an individual or private commercial enterprise deemed beneficial to the public. **2.** Formerly, an aid or tax granted by the House of Commons to the king for urgent needs of the kingdom. **3.** Any financial assistance afforded by one individual or government to another. [< AF *subsidie*, OF *subside* < L *subsidium* auxiliary forces, aid < *subsidere*. See SUBSIDE.]
— **Syn. 1.** *Subsidy, subvention, grant,* and *bounty* denote money given to support an enterprise. A government gives a *subsidy* to support a public service, as an airline. The word *subvention* is sometimes applied to a *subsidy* to a literary or artistic enterprise. A *grant* is given by a government or a private institution on condition that it be spent for a specified purpose: a *grant* for chemical research. A *bounty* is a reward given to individuals, usually by a governmental unit, to encourage the performance of certain acts: a *bounty* on killing wolves, a *bounty* for settling on sparsely populated land.

sub·sist (səb·sist′) *v.i.* **1.** To have existence or reality; continue to exist. **2.** To maintain one's existence; manage to live, often with *on* or *by*: to *subsist* on vegetables. **3.** To continue unchanged; abide. **4.** To have existence in or by virtue of something; inhere. — *v.t. Obs.* **5.** To provide with food and clothing. [< L *subsistere* < *sub-* under + *sistere* to cause to stand < *stare* to stand] — **sub·sist′er** *n.*

sub·sis·tence (səb·sis′təns) *n.* **1.** The act of subsisting. **2.** That on which one subsists; sustenance; means of support; livelihood. **3.** The state of being subsistent; inherent quality. **4.** That which subsists; real being. **5.** A basis; a logical substance; hypostasis. Also **sub·sis′ten·cy.**

sub·sis·tent (səb·sis′tənt) *adj.* **1.** That subsists or is inherent. **2.** Existing; having real being or action. **3.** Having subsistence.

sub·soil (sub′soil′) *n.* The stratum of earth next beneath the surface soil: also called *undersoil.* — *v.t.* To plow so as to turn up the subsoil. — **sub′soil′er** *n.*

sub·so·lar (sub·sō′lər) *adj.* **1.** Situated directly beneath the sun, as at high noon at the equinoxes. **2.** Situated between the tropics. **3.** Mundane; earthly.

sub·son·ic (sub·son′ik) *adj.* **1.** Designating those sound waves beyond the lower limits of human audibility, or with frequencies of less than about 25 cycles per second: also *infrasonic.* **2.** *Aeron.* Having a speed less than that of sound in air or other mediums.

sub·spe·cies (sub′spē′shēz, -shiz, -sēz) *n. pl.* **·cies** *Biol.* A division of a species, especially a geographical subdivision. [< NL < L *sub-* under + *species* appearance, sort] — **sub·spe·cif·ic** (sub′spi·sif′ik) *adj.*

subst. **1.** Substantive. **2.** Substitute.

sub·stance (sub′stəns) *n.* **1.** The material of which anything is made or consists; also, a material object as contrasted with something intangible. **2.** Any type of matter of a specific chemical composition. **3.** Density; body. **4.** A substantial quality; solidity: His ideas have *substance.* **5.** The essential part of anything said or written; the gist or purport. **6.** *Philos.* The essential nature that underlies phenomena; that in which qualities or attributes inhere. **7.** Material wealth; property. **8.** In Christian Science, that which is eternal. [< OF < L *substantia* < *substare* to be present < *sub-* under + *stare* to stand]

sub·stan·dard (sub′stan′dərd) *adj.* **1.** Below the standard. **2.** Lower than the established rate or authorized requirements. **3.** *Ling.* Nonstandard (which see).

substandard English *Ling.* Nonstandard English (which see).

sub·stan·tial (səb·stan′shəl) *adj.* **1.** Solid; strong; firm. **2.** Of real worth and importance; of considerable value. **3.**

Considerable and real: *substantial* progress. **4.** Possessed of wealth and influence. **5.** Of or pertaining to substance; material. **6.** Containing or conforming to the essence of a thing; giving the correct idea; fundamental. **7.** Ample and nourishing. **8.** *Philos.* Having real existence; not immaterial or abstract. — *n.* **1.** That which has substance; a reality. **2.** The more important part. — **sub·stan′ti·al′i·ty** (-shē·al′· ə·tē), **sub·stan′tial·ness** *n.* — **sub·stan′tial·ly** *adv.*

sub·stan·tial·ism (səb·stan′shəl·iz′əm) *n. Philos.* The doctrine that substantial realities underlie all phenomena, and that matter is a real substance. — **sub·stan′tial·ist** *n.*

sub·stan·ti·ate (səb·stan′shē·āt) *v.t.* **·at·ed, ·at·ing** **1.** To establish, as a position or a truth, by substantial evidence; verify. **2.** To give form to; embody. **3.** To make substantial, existent, or real; give substance to. — **Syn.** See CONFIRM. [< NL *substantiatus,* pp. of *substantiare* to establish < L *substantia.* See SUBSTANCE.] — **sub·stan′ti·a′tion** *n.* — **sub·stan′ti·a·tive** *adj.*

sub·stan·tive (sub′stən·tiv) *n.* **1.** A noun or anything that functions as a noun, as a verbal form, phrase, or clause. **2.** One who or that which is independent. — *adj.* **1.** Capable of being used as a noun. **2.** Expressive of or denoting existence. The verb "to be" is called the *substantive* verb. **3.** Having substance or reality; lasting. **4.** Being an essential part or constituent. **5.** Relating to what is essential. **6.** Having distinct individuality. **7.** Independent in resources; self-supporting, as a country. **8.** Of considerable amount; substantial. **9.** In dyeing, not needing a mordant. *Abbr.* **s., sb., subst.** [< OF *substantif* < LL *substantivus* < L *substantia.* See SUBSTANCE.] — **sub′stan·ti′val** (-tī′vəl) *adj.* — **sub′stan·tive·ly** *adv.* — **sub′stan·tive·ness** *n.*

substantive dye A direct dye (which see).

sub·stan·tiv·ize (sub′stən·tiv·īz′) *v.t.* **·ized, ·iz·ing** To treat or use (a phrase, adjective, etc.) as a substantive. Also **sub′stan·tize** (-stən·tīz).

sub·sta·tion (sub′stā′shən) *n.* A subsidiary station, a branch post office, etc.

sub·stit·u·ent (səb·stich′ōō·ənt) *n. Chem.* A radical, atom, or group substituting or replacing another in a chemical reaction. — *adj.* Of a substituting atom or molecule. [< L *substituens, -entis,* ppr. of *substituere.* See SUBSTITUTE.]

sub·sti·tute (sub′stə·tōōt, -tyōōt) *v.* **·tut·ed, ·tut·ing** *v.t.* **1.** To put in the place of another person, constituent, or thing. **2.** *Chem.* To replace as a substituent. — *v.i.* **3.** To act as a substitute. **4.** *Chem.* To act as a substituent. — *n.* **1.** One who or that which takes the place of or serves in lieu of another. **2.** Formerly, one hired to serve in the place of a man drafted into military service. **3.** *Gram.* A word that replaces another word or phrase. *Abbr.* **sub., subst.** — **Syn.** See DELEGATE. [< L *substitutus,* pp. of *substituere* < *sub-* in place of + *statuere* to set up]

sub·sti·tu·tion (sub′stə·tōō′shən, -tyōō′-) *n.* **1.** The act or process of substituting, or the state of being substituted. **2.** Something substituted. — **sub′sti·tu′tion·al** *adj.* — **sub′· sti·tu′tion·al·ly** *adv.*

sub·sti·tu·tive (sub′stə·tōō′tiv, -tyōō′-) *adj.* **1.** Acting or capable of acting as a substitute. **2.** Of or pertaining to substitution.

sub·strate (sub′strāt) *n.* **1.** *Biochem.* The material or substance acted upon by an enzyme or ferment. **2.** A substratum. [< SUBSTRATUM]

sub·stra·tum (sub·strā′təm, -strat′əm) *n. pl.* **·ta** (-tə) or **·tums** **1.** An underlying stratum or layer, as of earth or rock; also, subsoil. **2.** That which forms the foundation or groundwork. **3.** Matter or mind considered as the basis of qualities and phenomena; the substance possessing attributes. **4.** The substance in which something takes root, as vegetable or animal tissue. **5.** *Ling.* A displaced language that influences the form of an adopted language by way of bilingual speakers. [< NL < L, pp. neut. of *substernere* to spread underneath < *sub-* underneath + *sternere* to strew] — **sub·stra′tive** *adj.*

sub·struc·tion (sub·struk′shən) *n.* A foundation. [< F < L *substructio, -onis* < *substruere* < *sub-* underneath + *struere* to build] — **sub·struc′tion·al** *adj.*

sub·struc·ture (sub′struk′chər, sub·struk′-) *n.* **1.** A structure serving as a foundation of a building, etc. **2.** The earthen roadway supporting railroad tracks. — **sub·struc′· tur·al** *adj.*

sub·sume (səb·sōōm′) *v.t.* **·sumed, ·sum·ing** **1.** To place in some particular class; classify. **2.** To include, as the specific or individual in the general. [< NL *subsumere* < L *sub-* underneath + *sumere* to take] — **sub·sum′a·ble** *adj.*

sub·sump·tion (səb·sump′shən) *n.* **1.** The act of subsuming. **2.** That which is subsumed; especially, the minor premise of a syllogism as stated after the major premise. [< NL *subsumptio, -onis* < *subsumere.* See SUBSUME.] — **sub· sump′tive** *adj.*

sub·tan·gent (sub′tan′jənt) *n. Geom.* The portion of the axis of a curve cut off between the tangent to a given point and the ordinate of that point. [< NL *subtangens -entis* < L *sub-* under + *tangens*, ppr. of *tangere* to touch]

sub·tem·per·ate (sub/tem/pər·it) *adj.* Of or pertaining to the colder parts of the Temperate Zone.

sub·ten·ant (sub/ten/ənt) *n.* A person who rents or leases from a tenant: also called *undertenant.* — **sub·ten·an·cy** *n.*

sub·tend (sub·tend/) *v.t.* **1.** *Geom.* To extend under or opposite to, as the chord of an arc or the side of a triangle opposite to an angle. **2.** *Bot.* To enclose in its axil: A leaf *subtends* a bud. [< L *subtendere* < *sub-* underneath + *tendere* to stretch]

subter- *prefix* Under; less than: *subternatural.* [< L *subter* below, beneath]

sub·ter·fuge (sub/tər·fyōōj) *n.* Any stratagem to avoid unpleasantness or difficulty. [< L *subterfugium* < *subterfugere* < *subter-* below, in secret + *fugere* to flee]

sub·ter·nat·u·ral (sub/tər·nach/ər·əl) *adj.* Below the norms of nature.

sub·ter·rane (sub/tə·rān) *n.* An underground room; a cave. [< L *subterraneum* < *sub-* under + *terra* earth]

sub·ter·ra·ne·an (sub/tə·rā/nē·ən) *adj.* **1.** Situated or occurring below the surface of the earth; underground. **2.** Hidden or secret. Also **sub/ter·ra/ne·al, sub/ter·ra/ne·ous.**

sub·ter·res·tri·al (sub/tə·res/trē·əl) *adj.* Subterranean. — *n.* A creature that lives underground.

sub·tile (sut/l, sub/til) *adj.* **1.** Delicate or tenuous in form, character, etc.; ethereal. **2.** Penetrating; pervasive. **3.** Subtle; wily. [< OF *subtil,* alter. of *soutil* subtle; refashioned after L] — **sub/tile·ly** *adv.* — **sub·til·i·ty** (sub·til/ə·tē), **sub/tile·ness** *n.*

sub·ti·lize (sut/l·īz, sub/tə·līz) *v.* **·ized, ·iz·ing** *v.t.* **1.** To make subtle or subtile; refine. **2.** To make acute; sharpen, as the senses. **3.** To discuss or argue subtly. — *v.i.* **4.** To make subtle distinctions; use subtlety. [< Med.L *subtilizare* < L *subtilis.* See SUBTLE.] — **sub/til·i·za/tion** *n.*

sub·til·ty (sut/l·tē, sub/tal·tē) *n. pl.* **·ties** Subtlety.

sub·ti·tle (sub/tīt/l) *n.* **1.** A subordinate or explanatory title, as in a book, play, or document. **2.** A book title repeated, as on top of the first page of text. **3.** In motion pictures: **a** A running written translation of the dialogue from one language into another, usually appearing at the bottom of the screen. **b** A written comment or record of dialogue, as in a silent film.

sub·tle (sut/l) *adj.* **1.** Characterized by cunning, craft, or artifice; wily; crafty. **2.** Keen; penetrative; discriminating: *subtle* humor. **3.** Apt; skillful. **4.** Executed with nice art; ingenious; clever; refined. **5.** Insidious; secretly active. **6.** Hard to understand; abstruse. **7.** Of delicate texture. [< OF *soutil* < L *subtilis* fine, orig., closely woven < *sub-* under + *tela* web] — **sub/tle·ness** *n.* — **sub/tly** *adv.*

sub·tle·ty (sut/l·tē) *n. pl.* **·ties** **1.** The state or quality of being subtle. **2.** The ability to make fine or subtle distinctions. **3.** Something subtle, as a nice distinction. Also spelled *subtilty.*

sub·ton·ic (sub/ton/ik) *n. Music* The tone below the tonic; the seventh tone of a major or minor scale.

sub·tor·rid (sub/tôr/id, -tor/-) *adj.* Subtropical.

sub·tract (səb·trakt/) *v.t. & v.i.* **1.** To take away or deduct, as a portion from the whole, or one quantity from another. **2.** To subject to, undergo, or perform the mathematical process of subtraction. [< L *subtractus,* pp. of *subtrahere* < *sub-* away + *trahere* to draw] — **sub·tract/er** *n.*

sub·trac·tion (səb·trak/shən) *n.* **1.** The act or process of subtracting; a deducting. **2.** Something deducted. **3.** *Math.* The operation, indicated by the minus sign (−), of finding the difference between two quantities.

sub·trac·tive (səb·trak/tiv) *adj.* **1.** Serving or tending to diminish. **2.** *Math.* Having the minus sign; to be subtracted.

sub·tra·hend (sub/trə·hend) *n. Math.* The number to be subtracted from another: opposed to *minuend.* [< L *subtrahendus (numerus)* (the number) to be subtracted, gerundive of *subtrahere.* See SUBTRACT.]

sub·trans·lu·cent (sub/trans·lōō/sənt, -tranz-) *adj.* Not fully translucent, as certain gemstones and other minerals.

sub·treas·ur·y (sub/trezh/ər·ē) *n. pl.* **·ur·ies** A branch of a treasury.

sub·trop·i·cal (sub/trop/i·kəl) *adj.* **1.** Of, pertaining to, or designating regions adjacent to the Torrid Zone. **2.** Having characteristics intermediate between or common to both Torrid and Temperate Zones. Also **sub/trop/ic.**

sub·trop·ics (sub/trop/iks) *n.pl.* Subtropical regions.

su·bu·late (sōō/byə·lāt, -lit) *adj. Biol.* Awl-shaped; slender and tapering to a point. [< NL *subulatus* < L *subula* awl]

sub·urb (sub/ûrb) *n.* **1.** A place adjacent to a city, especially a residential area. **2.** *pl.* Outlying residential districts; outskirts; purlieus. Abbr. *sub.* [< OF *suburbe* < L *surburbium* < *sub-* near to + *urbs, urbis* city]

sub·ur·ban (sə·bûr/bən) *adj.* **1.** Of or pertaining to a suburb. **2.** Dwelling or located in a suburb. — *n.* One who lives in a suburb; suburbanite. Abbr. *sub.*

sub·ur·ban·ite (sə·bûr/bən·īt) *n.* A resident of a suburb.

sub·ur·bi·a (sə·bûr/bē·ə) *n.* **1.** The social and cultural world of suburbanites. **2.** Suburbs or suburbanites collectively.

sub·ur·bi·car·i·an (sə·bûr/bə·kâr/ē·ən) *adj.* Being in the suburbs of Rome; especially, pertaining to or designating any of the six sees that compose the province of the Pope as metropolitan. [< LL *suburbicarius* < L *suburbium.* See SUBURB.]

sub·vene (səb·vēn/) *v.i.* **·vened, ·ven·ing** To come or happen so as to be of aid or support, especially by preventing something; intervene. [< L *subvenire* to come to one's assistance < *sub-* up from under + *venire* to come]

sub·ven·tion (səb·ven/shən) *n.* **1.** The act of subvening; giving of succor; aid. **2.** That which aids; especially, a grant, as of money; subsidy. — **Syn.** See SUBSIDY. [< OF *subvencion* < LL *subventio, -onis* < L *subvenire.* See SUBVENE.] — **sub·ven/tion·ar/y** (-er/ē) *adj.*

sub ver·bo (sub vûr/bō) *Latin* Under the word: used in referring to an entry in a dictionary, index, etc. Also **sub vo·ce** (vō/si). Abbr. *s.v.*

sub·ver·sion (səb·vûr/shən, -zhən) *n.* **1.** The act of subverting, or the state of being subverted; a demolition; overthrow. **2.** A cause of ruin. Also **sub·ver/sal** (-səl). [< OF < LL *subversio, -onis* < L *subvertere.* See SUBVERT.]

sub·ver·sive (səb·vûr/siv) *adj.* Tending to subvert or overthrow, as a legally constituted government. — *n.* One who acts in accordance with subversive principles. — **sub·ver/sive·ly** *adv.*

sub·vert (səb·vûrt/) *v.t.* **1.** To overthrow from the very foundation; destroy utterly. **2.** To undermine the morals, character, or faith of; corrupt. [< OF *subvertir* < L *subvertere* < *sub-* up from under + *vertere* to turn] — **sub·vert/er** *n.* — **sub·vert/i·ble** *adj.*

— **Syn. 1.** uproot, upset, overturn. Compare ABOLISH.

sub·vit·re·ous (sub·vit/rē·əs) *adj.* Having a luster resembling that of glass, but less brilliant.

sub·way (sub/wā) *n.* **1.** *U.S.* An underground railroad, usually electrically operated; also, a tunnel for such a railroad: also, *Brit., underground.* **2.** An artificial underground passage, as for traffic, water mains, electric cables, etc.

suc- Assimilated var. of SUB-.

suc·ce·da·ne·um (suk/si·dā/nē·əm) *n. pl.* **·ne·ums** or **·ne·a** (-nē·ə) A substitute. [< NL < L *succedaneus* < *succedere* to succeed, replace] — **suc/ce·da/ne·ous** *adj.*

suc·ceed (sək·sēd/) *v.i.* **1.** To accomplish what is attempted or intended; be successful. **2.** To come next in order or sequence; follow; ensue. **3.** To come after another into office, ownership, etc.; be the successor: often with *to.* **4.** *Archaic* To achieve an end in a specified manner: They *succeeded* badly. **5.** *Law* To devolve: said of an estate. — *v.t.* **6.** To come after in time or sequence; follow. **7.** To be the successor or heir of. [< OF *succeder* < L *succedere* to follow after < *sub-* under + *cedere* to go] — **suc·ceed/er** *n.*

suc·cen·tor (sək·sen/tər) *n.* A deputy precentor. [< LL < L *succinere* to sing to < *sub-* under + *canere* to sing]

suc·cès d'es·time (sük·se/ des·tēm/) *French* Success marked by the praise of critics but not by widespread popular approval.

suc·cess (sək·ses/) *n.* **1.** A favorable or desired outcome of something attempted; prosperous or advantageous issue. **2.** A successful person, thing, enterprise, etc. **3.** Attainment of wealth, fame, etc. **4.** *Obs.* Any outcome or result. [< L *successus* < *succedere.* See SUCCEED.]

suc·cess·ful (sək·ses/fəl) *adj.* **1.** Obtaining what one desires or intends. **2.** Having reached a high degree of worldly prosperity. **3.** Terminating in or meeting with success; resulting favorably: a *successful* political campaign. — **suc·cess/ful·ly** *adv.* — **suc·cess/ful·ness** *n.*

suc·ces·sion (sək·sesh/ən) *n.* **1.** The act of following in order, or the state of being successive; a following consecutively. **2.** A group of things that succeed in order; a series; sequence. **3.** The act or right of legally or officially coming into a predecessor's office, possessions, etc.; also, that which is so acquired. **4.** The order or plan by which an office, rank, etc., changes hands. **5.** Descendants collectively; issue. — **suc·ces/sion·al** *adj.* — **suc·ces/sion·al·ly** *adv.*

suc·ces·sive (sək·ses/iv) *adj.* Following in sequence; consecutive. — **suc·ces/sive·ly** *adv.* — **suc·ces/sive·ness** *n.*

suc·ces·sor (sək·ses/ər) *n.* One who or that which comes after or succeeds another; especially, a person who succeeds to a throne, property, or office.

suc·ci·nate (suk/si·nāt) *n. Chem.* A salt of succinic acid. [< SUCCIN(IC) + -ATE³]

suc·cinct (sək·singkt/) *adj.* **1.** Consisting of or characterized by brief and meaningful language; terse; concise. **2.** *Entomol.* Supported by an encircling silken thread, as a butterfly chrysalis. **3.** *Archaic* Encircled by or as by a girdle. — **Syn.** See TERSE. [< L *succinctus,* pp. of *succingere* < *sub-* underneath + *cingere* to gird] — **suc·cinct/ly** *adv.* — **suc·cinct/ness** *n.*

suc·cin·ic (sək·sin/ik) *adj.* Derived from or found in amber. [< F *succinique* < L *succinum* amber]

succinic acid *Chem.* A white crystalline compound, $C_4H_6O_4$, contained in amber and also made synthetically, used in organic synthesis and in medicine.

suc·cor (suk/ər) *n.* **1.** Help or relief rendered in danger, difficulty, or distress. **2.** One who or that which affords re-

,ief. — *v.t.* To go to the aid of; help; rescue. Also *Brit.* **suc′-cour.** [< OF *sucurs* < Med.L *succursus* < L *succurrere* < *sub-* up from under + *currere* to run] — **suc′cor·a·ble** *adj.* — **suc′cor·er** *n.*

suc·co·ry (suk′ər·ē) *n.* Chicory. [Alter. of *cicoree, sichorie,* earlier vars. of CHICORY; infl. in form by MDu. *sukerie* chicory]

suc·co·tash (suk′ə·tash) *n.* A dish of corn kernels and beans, usually lima beans, boiled together. [< Algonquian (Narraganset) *misickquatash* ear of corn]

Suc·coth (sŏok′ōth, -ōs, -əs) See SUKKOTH.

suc·cu·ba (suk′yə·bə) *n. pl.* **·bae** (bē) A succubus.

suc·cu·bus (suk′yə·bəs) *n. pl.* **·bus·es** or **·bi** (bī) **1.** In folklore, a female demon that has sexual intercourse with sleeping men. Compare INCUBUS. **2.** Any demon or evil spirit. [< Med.L < LL *succuba* strumpet < L *succubare* < *sub-* underneath + *cubare* to lie]

suc·cu·lent (suk′yə·lənt) *adj.* **1.** Full of juice; juicy. **2.** *Bot.* Juicy; fleshy, as the tissues of certain plants. **3.** Rich or vigorous: a *succulent* theme. [< L *succulentus* < *succus* juice] — **suc′cu·lence, suc′cu·len·cy** *n.* — **suc′cu·lent·ly** *adv.*

suc·cumb (sə·kum′) *v.i.* **1.** To give way; yield, as to force or persuasion. **2.** To die. [< OF *succomber* < L *succumbere* < *sub-* underneath + *cumbere* to lie]

suc·cuss (sə·kus′) *v.t.* **1.** To shake suddenly or forcibly. **2.** *Med.* To shake (a patient) vigorously to detect liquids in the thorax or other cavities of the body. [< L *succussus,* pp. of *succutere* < *sub-* up from under + *quatere* to shake] — **suc·cus′sive** *adj.*

suc·cus·sion (sə·kush′ən) *n.* The act of succussing. Also **suc·cus·sa·tion** (suk′ə·sā′shən). — **suc·cus·sa·to·ry** (sə·kus′ə·tôr′ē, -tō′rē) *adj.*

such (such) *adj.* **1.** Of that kind; of the same or like kind: often with *as* or *that* completing a comparison: *Such* wit as this is rare. **2.** Being the same as what has been mentioned or indicated: *Such* was the king's command. **3.** Being the same in quality: Let the truthful continue *such.* **4.** Being the same as something understood by the speaker or the hearer, or purposely left indefinite: the chief of *such* a clan. **5.** So extreme, unpleasant, or the like: We have come to *such* a pass. — **as such 1.** As being what is indicated or implied: An executive, *as such,* must take responsibility. **2.** In or by itself: Clothes, *as such,* do not make the man. — **such as 1.** For example: Do you have your supplies, *such as* pots and pans and matches? **2.** Of a particular kind or degree: The outcome of the trial was *such as* might be expected. — *pron.* **1.** Such a person or thing, or such persons or things: The friend of *such* as are in trouble. **2.** The same; the aforesaid: I bring good tidings, for *such* the general sent. — *adv. Informal* So: *such* awful manners. ◆ *Such* and *such* a are widely used in informal contexts to intensify the adjective or noun they precede: He was *such* a kind man; He had *such* wisdom. [OE *swelc, swilc, swylc*]

such and such 1. A condition, person, thing, or time, not specifically named. **2.** Being or designating such a condition, person, etc.

such·like (such′līk′) *adj.* Of a like or similar kind. — *pron.* Persons or things of that kind.

Sü·chow (shü′jō′) A city in SW Shantung province, China; pop. 1,500,000 (est. 1970): from 1912–45 *Tungshan:* also *Soochow.*

suck (suk) *v.t.* **1.** To draw into the mouth by means of a partial vacuum created by action of the lips and tongue. **2.** To draw in or take up in a manner resembling this; inhale; absorb: The sponge *sucked* the water up. **3.** To draw liquid or nourishment from with the mouth. **4.** To take into and hold in the mouth. **5.** To consume by licking, or by holding in the mouth: to *suck* candy. **6.** To bring to a specified state or condition by sucking: He *sucked* the lemon dry. — *v.i.* **7.** To draw in liquid, air, etc., by suction. **8.** To suckle. **9.** To draw in air instead of water, as a defective pump does. **10.** To make the characteristic sound of sucking. — **to suck in** *Slang* To take advantage of; cheat. — *n.* **1.** The act of sucking; suction. **2.** That which is sucked or comes by sucking. **3.** A slight draft or drink. **4.** A mother's milk. **5.** A whirlpool or powerful eddy. [OE *sūcan*]

suck·er (suk′ər) *n.* **1.** One who or that which sucks. **2.** A North American fresh-water fish (family *Catostomidae*), related to the cyprinoids, having the mouth usually protractile with thick and fleshy lips adapted for sucking in food. **3.** *Zool.* An organ by which an animal adheres to other bodies by suction. **4.** *U.S. Slang* One who is easily deceived; a foolish or gullible person. **5.** A piston, as of a syringe or a suction pump; a tube or pipe used for suction. **6.** A lollipop. **7.** *Bot.* **a** A shoot or branch originating on a subterranean portion of a stem. **b** A shoot or sprout arising from the root near or remote from the trunk of certain trees. **c** A haustorium. — *v.t.* **1.** To strip of suckers or shoots. — *v.i.* **2.** To form or send out suckers or shoots. [< SUCK]

Sucker State Nickname for ILLINOIS.

suck·fish (suk′fish′) *n. pl.* **·fish** or **·fish·es 1.** A remora

(def. 1). **2.** A clingfish (*Gobiesox maeandricus*) of the Pacific coast, with a ventrally placed sucker by which it attaches itself to stones, shells, etc.

suck·le (suk′əl) *v.* **·led, ·ling** *v.t.* **1.** To allow or cause to take nourishment from the breast by sucking; nurse. **2.** To bring up; nourish. — *v.i.* **3.** To take nourishment at the breast: also *suck.* [ME *sucklen,* prob. back formation < SUCKLING] — **suck′ler** *n.*

suck·ling (suk′ling) *n.* **1.** An unweaned mammal. **2.** An infant or very young child. [ME < *soken* to suck + *-ling* -ling¹]

Suck·ling (suk′ling), **Sir John,** 1609–42?, English poet.

su·cre (sōo′krā) *n.* The standard monetary unit of Ecuador, equivalent to 100 centavos: also, a coin of this value. [< Sp., after Antonio José de *Sucre*]

Su·cre (sōo′krā) The capital of Bolivia, in the south central part; pop. 58,359 (est. 1965). See LA PAZ.

Su·cre (sōo′krā), **Antonio José de,** 1793–1830, South American general born in Venezuela; first president of Bolivia, 1826–28.

su·crose (sōo′krōs) *n. Biochem.* A crystalline disaccharide, $C_{12}H_{22}O_{11}$, forming the greater part of the sugar as obtained from the sugar cane, maple, beet, etc. Also called *saccharose.* [< F *sucre* sugar + *-ose* -ose²]

suc·tion (suk′shən) *n.* **1.** The act or process of sucking. **2.** The production of a partial vacuum in a space connected with a liquid or gas under pressure. **3.** The tendency of a fluid to occupy all or part of a vacuum contiguous with it. [< OF < L *suctio, -onis* < *sugere* to suck]

suction pump A pump operating by suction, consisting of a piston working in a cylinder, both equipped with valves.

suction stop *Phonet.* A click.

suc·to·ri·al (suk·tôr′ē·əl, -tō′rē·əl) *adj.* **1.** Adapted for sucking or for adhesion. **2.** *Zool.* Living by sucking; having organs for sucking.

Su·dan (sōo·dan′) A region extending across Africa from the Atlantic Ocean to the Red Sea, south of the Sahara: formerly *Nigritia.*

Sudan, Republic of the A Republic in NE Africa; 967,500 sq. mi.; pop. 15,312,000 (est. 1970); capital Khartoum: formerly *Anglo-Egyptian Sudan.* See map of NILE.

Sudan durra Feterita, a cereal grass.

Su·da·nese (sōo′də·nēz′, -nēs′) *adj.* Of or pertaining to the Sudan or its people. — *n. pl.* **·nese** A native or inhabitant of the Sudan.

Sudanese Republic See (Republic of) MALI.

Su·dan·ic (sōo·dan′ik) *n.* A family of languages spoken in central Africa from the Atlantic to the Indian oceans, including Dinka, Ewe, Nubian, and Yoruba. — *adj.* Of or pertaining to this family.

su·dar·i·um (sōo·dâr′ē·əm) *n. pl.* **·dar·i·a** (-dâr′ē·ə) **1.** A handkerchief or cloth for removing perspiration; especially, the handkerchief of St. Veronica, said to have been miraculously impressed with the features of Jesus when she wiped his face on his way to Calvary. **2.** Any miraculous picture of Christ; a veronica. **3.** A sudatorium. Also **su·da·ry** (sōo′dər·ē). [< L < *sudor, -oris* sweat]

su·da·tion (sōo·dā′shən) *n. Med.* Abnormal or excessive sweating. [< L *sudatio, -onis* < *sudare* to sweat]

su·da·to·ri·um (sōo′də·tôr′ē·əm, -tō′rē-) *n. pl.* **·i·a** (-ē·ə) A sweating bath; also, a hot-air room, as in a Roman bath. [< L]

su·da·to·ry (sōo′də·tôr′ē, -tō′rē) *adj.* **1.** Producing perspiration; sudorific. **2.** Perspiring. — *n. pl.* **·ries** A sudatorium; a sudatory. **2.** A sudatorium. [< L *sudatorius*]

sudd (sud) *n.* A floating mass of vegetation that frequently obstructs navigation on the White Nile. [< Arabic < *sudd* to obstruct]

sud·den (sud′n) *adj.* **1.** Happening quickly and without warning. **2.** Hurriedly or quickly contrived, used, or done; hasty. **3.** Come upon unexpectedly; causing surprise. **4.** Quick-tempered; precipitate. — **all of a sudden** Without warning; suddenly. [< AF *sodein* < OF *soudain* < L *subitaneus* < *subitus,* pp. of *subire* to come or go stealthily < *sub-* secretly + *ire* to go] — **sud′den·ly** *adv.* — **sud′den·ness** *n.*

sudden death 1. An abrupt or unexpected death. **2.** In sports, a method of settling a tie, whereby the first side to score, win a game, lead at the end of an overtime period, etc., is declared the winner. **3.** Any quick or abrupt way of establishing a winner, as by a flip of a coin.

sudden infant death syndrome See CRIB DEATH.

Su·der·mann (zōo′dər·män), **Hermann,** 1857–1928, German dramatist and novelist.

Su·de·ten·land (sōo·dāt′n·land′, *Ger.* zōo·dā′tən·länt′) The border districts of Bohemia and Moravia, Czechoslovakia.

Su·de·tes (sōo·dē′tēz) A mountainous system along the German-Czechoslovak and Polish-Czechoslovak border; highest peak, Schneekoppe, 5,259 ft. *German* **Su·de·ten** (zōo·dā′tən). *Czech, Polish* **Su·de·ty** (*Czech* sōo′de·tyi, *Polish* sōo·de′ti). Also **Su·det·ic Mountains** (sōo·det′ik).

PRONUNCIATION KEY: add, āce, câre, pälm; end, ēven; it, īce; odd, ōpen, ôrder; tŏok, pōol; up, bûrn; ə = a in *above,* e in *sicken,* i in *flexible,* o in *melon,* u in *focus;* yōo = u in *fuse;* oil; pout; check; go; ring; thin; this; zh, vision. For å, œ, ü, kh, ṅ, see inside front cover.

su·dor (soo'dôr) *n.* Visible perspiration; sweat. [< L] — **su·dor·al** (soo'dər·əl) *adj.*

su·dor·if·er·ous (soo'də·rif'ər·əs) *adj. Med.* Secreting or producing sweat. [< NL *sudoriferus* < L *sudor, -oris* sweat + *ferre* to carry] — **su'dor·if'er·ous·ness** *n.*

su·dor·if·ic (soo'də·rif'ik) *Med. adj.* Causing perspiration. — *n.* A medicine that produces or promotes sweating. [< NL *sudorificus* < L *sudor, -oris* sweat + *facere* to make]

Su·dra (soo'drə) *n.* A member of the fourth and lowest of the Hindu castes.

suds (sudz) *n.pl.* 1. Soapy water, or bubbles and froth on its surface. 2. Foam; lather. 3. *Slang* Beer. [Prob. < MDu. *sudde, sudse* marsh, marsh water]

suds·y (sud'zē) *adj.* **suds·i·er, suds·i·est** Full of or consisting of suds; foamy.

sue (soo) *v.* **sued, su·ing** *v.t.* 1. *Law* **a** To institute proceedings against for the recovery of some right or the redress of some wrong. **b** To prosecute (an action). **c** To seek a grant from (a court). 2. To endeavor to persuade by entreaty; beg; urge; petition. 3. *Archaic* To seek to win in marriage; woo. — *v.i.* 4. To institute legal proceedings. 5. To make entreaty. 6. *Archaic* To pay court; woo. [< AF *suer*, OF *sivre*, ult. < L *sequi* to follow] — **su'er** *n.*

Sue (soo, *Fr.* sü) **Eugène** Pseudonym of **Marie Joseph Sue**, 1804–57, French novelist.

suede (swād) *n.* 1. A leather having a soft napped finish, usually on the flesh side. 2. A woven or knitted fabric finished to resemble this. Also **suède.** [< F *Suède* Sweden, in phrase *gants de Suède* Swedish gloves]

su·et (soo'it) *n.* The fatty tissues about the loins and kidneys of sheep, oxen, etc., used in cookery and to make tallow. [Dim. of AF *sue*, OF *seu* < L *sebum* tallow, fat] — **su'et·y** *adj.*

Sue·to·ni·us (swi·tō'nē·əs) Second-century A.D. Roman biographer and historian: full name **Gaius Suetonius Tran·quil·lus** (trang·kwil'əs).

Su·ez (soo·ez', soo'ez) A port city in NE Egypt, at the northern end of the **Gulf of Suez,** the NW inlet of the Red Sea; pop. 264,500 (1966).

Suez, Isthmus of The neck of land joining Asia and Africa, between the Gulf of Suez and the Mediterranean; traversed by the **Suez Canal,** a ship canal 107 mi. long, 197 ft. wide, constructed (1859–69) by Ferdinand de Lesseps.

suf- Assimilated var. of SUB-.

suf. or **suff.** Suffix.

Suff. 1. Suffolk. 2. Suffragan.

suf·fa·ri (sə·fä'rē) See SAFARI.

suf·fer (suf'ər) *v.i.* 1. To feel pain or distress. 2. To be affected injuriously; experience loss or injury. 3. To undergo punishment; especially, to be put to death. 4. *Archaic* To tolerate or endure pain, injury, etc. — *v.t.* 5. To have inflicted on one; sustain, as an injury or loss. 6. To undergo; pass through, as change. 7. To bear; endure: to *suffer* more pain. 8. To allow; permit: Will he *suffer* us to leave? — **Syn.** See ALLOW. [< AF *suffrir,* OF *sofrir,* ult. < L *sufferre* < *sub-* up from under + *ferre* to bear] — **suf'fer·er** *n.*

suf·fer·a·ble (suf'ər·ə·bəl, suf'rə-) *adj.* Such as can be suffered or endured; tolerable. — **suf'fer·a·bly** *adv.*

suf·fer·ance (suf'ər·əns, suf'rəns) *n.* 1. Permission given or implied by failure to prohibit; passive consent. 2. The act or state of suffering; wretchedness. 3. Power to endure pain or evil. 4. Patience or endurance under suffering; submissiveness. 5. *Rare* Loss; injury; damage. [< AF, OF *sufrance* < LL *sufferentia* < *sufferre.* See SUFFER.]

suf·fer·ing (suf'ər·ing, suf'ring) *n.* 1. The state of anguish or pain of one who suffers. 2. The bearing of pain, injury, or loss. 3. Pain or distress borne or endured; injury. — *adj.* Inured to pain and loss; submissive. — **suf'fer·ing·ly** *adv.*
— **Syn.** 1. *Suffering, distress, misery,* and *anguish* denote a feeling of anguish from pain, injury, loss, etc. *Suffering* is acute bodily or mental pain. *Distress* may be physical, but is more often mental, referring to any deep anxiety, or the external circumstances that may produce it. *Misery* is extreme *suffering* or abject hopelessness, as from sorrow, great loss, poverty, or the like. The mildest of these words is *discomfort,* which denotes little more than the absence of ease and well-being; it may be used, however, in an understatement to imply great *distress.* Compare AGONY, PAIN, SORROW.

suf·fice (sə·fīs') *v.* **·ficed, ·fic·ing** *v.i.* 1. To be sufficient or adequate; meet the requirements or answer the purpose. — *v.t.* 2. To be satisfactory or adequate for; satisfy. [< OF

suffis-, stem of *suffire* < L *sufficere* < *sub-* under + *facere* to make] — **suf·fic'er** *n.*

suf·fi·cien·cy (sə·fish'ən·sē) *n. pl.* **·cies** 1. The state of being sufficient. 2. A sufficient amount to satisfy needs. 3. Adequate pecuniary means or income. 4. Full capability or qualification; efficiency. 5. Conceit; self-sufficiency.

suf·fi·cient (sə·fish'ənt) *adj.* 1. Being all that is needful; adequate; enough. 2. *Archaic* Capable; competent. 3. *Obs.* Financially competent; responsible. — **Syn.** See ADEQUATE, ENOUGH. [< OF < L *sufficiens, -entis,* ppr. of *sufficere.* See SUFFICE.] — **suf·fi'cient·ly** *adv.*

suf·fix (suf'iks, *for v., also* sə·fiks') *n.* 1. *Gram.* A bound form affixed to the end of a base, stem, or root, functioning as a derivative or inflectional element. Compare COMBINING FORM, PREFIX. 2. Any added title. 3. *Math.* A subscript. — *v.t.* To add as a suffix. [< NL *suffixum* < L *suffixus,* pp. of *suffigere* < *sub-* underneath + *figere* to fix. Doublet of SOFFIT.] — **suf·fix·al** *adj.* — **suf·fix·ion** (sə·fik'shən) *n.*

suf·flate (sə·flāt') *v.t.* **·flat·ed, ·flat·ing** *Obs.* To blow up or inflate. [< L *sufflatus,* pp. of *sufflare* < *sub-* up from under + *flare* to blow] — **suf·fla'tion** *n.*

suf·fo·cate (suf'ə·kāt) *v.* **·cat·ed, ·cat·ing** *v.t.* 1. To kill by obstructing respiration in any manner. 2. To obstruct or oppress, as by an inadequate supply of air. 3. To stifle; extinguish; smother, as a fire. — *v.i.* 4. To become choked or stifled; die from suffocation. [< L *suffocatus,* pp. of *suffocare* < *sub-* under + *fauces* throat] — **suf'fo·cat'ing·ly** *adv.* — **suf'fo·ca'tive** *adj.*

suf·fo·ca·tion (suf'ə·kā'shən) The act of suffocating, or the state of being suffocated.

Suf·folk (suf'ək) *n.* 1. A hardy English breed of working horses, with a heavy body and rather short legs. Also **Suffolk punch.** 2. A breed of hornless sheep producing mutton of high quality. [after *Suffolk,* England]

Suf·folk (suf'ək) A county in eastern England; 1,470 sq. mi.; pop. 567,300 (1976); county seat, Ipswich.

Suffr. Suffragan.

suf·fra·gan (suf'rə·gən) *Eccl. n.* An auxiliary or assistant bishop who assists a bishop in the administration of the diocese or is consecrated for service in a limited portion of the diocese. Also **suffragan bishop.** — *adj.* Of or pertaining to a suffragan; assisting; auxiliary. Abbr. *Suff., Suffr.* [< AF, OF < Med.L *suffraganeus* < L *suffragari* to vote for, support] — **suf'fra·gan·ship'** *n.*

suf·frage (suf'rij) *n.* 1. The right or privilege of voting; franchise. 2. The act or process of voting. 3. A vote in support of some measure or candidate. 4. Approbation; assent. 5. *Eccl.* Any short intercessory prayer or petition. [< OF < L *suffragium* voting tablet, vote]

suf·fra·gette (suf'rə·jet') *n.* Formerly, a woman who advocated or agitated for female suffrage. [< SUFFRAGE + -ETTE] — **suf'fra·get'tism** *n.*

suf·fra·gist (suf'rə·jist) *n.* An advocate of some particular form of suffrage, especially of female suffrage.

suf·fru·tex (suf'roo·teks) *n. pl.* **suf·fru·ti·ces** (sə·froo'tə·sēz) *Bot.* 1. An undershrub having a decidedly woody stem. 2. An herb, as the garden sage, having a woody base. [< NL < SUB- + *frutex* fruit]

suf·fru·ti·cose (sə·froo'tə·kōs) *adj. Bot.* Somewhat shrubby; shrubby or woody at the base and herbaceous above. [< NL *suffruticosus* < SUB- nearly + *fruticosus* shrubby]

suf·fu·mi·gate (sə·fyoo'mə·gāt) *v.t.* **·gat·ed, ·gat·ing** To fumigate from or as from underneath. [< L *suffumigatus,* pp. of *suffumigare* < *sub-* up from under + *fumigare.* See FUMIGATE.]

suf·fu·mi·ga·tion (sə·fyoo'mə·gā'shən) *n.* 1. The act of suffumigating. 2. A fume or vapor.

suf·fuse (sə·fyooz') *v.t.* **·fused, ·fus·ing** To overspread, as with a vapor, fluid, or color. [< L *suffusus,* pp. of *suffundere* < *sub-* underneath, up from under + *fundere* to pour] — **suf·fu'sive** (sə·fyoo'siv) *adj.*

suf·fu·sion (sə·fyoo'zhən) *n.* 1. The act of suffusing, or the state of being suffused. 2. That which suffuses, as a blush.

Su·fi (soo'fē) *n.* A follower of a system of Moslem mysticism, especially in Persia. [< Arabic *sufi,* lit., man of wool < *suf* wool] — **Su'fic, Su·fis·tic** (soo·fis'tik) *adj.*

Su·fism (soo'fiz·əm) *n.* The doctrine of the Sufis, that has inspired a body of symbolical religious poetry.

sug- Assimilated var. of SUB-.

sug·ar (shoog'ər) *n.* 1. *Biochem.* **a** A sweet, crystalline carbohydrate, $C_{12}H_{22}O_{11}$, obtained from the juice of various plants, as from the sugar cane, the sugar beet, and the sugar maple. ◆ Collateral adjective: *saccharine.* **b** Any of a large class of similar carbohydrates, widely distributed in plants and animals, and playing an important role in nutrition. 2. Flattering or honeyed words. 3. *Slang* Sweet one: a pet name. — *v.t.* 1. To sweeten, cover, or coat with sugar. 2. To make agreeable or less distasteful, as by flattery. — *v.i.* 3. *Chiefly U.S.* To make maple sugar. 4. To form or produce sugar; granulate. [< OF *sucre* < Med.L *saccarum,* ult. < Arabic *sukkar.* Prob. akin to SACCHARIN.]

sugar apple The sweetsop.

sugar beet A sugar-producing species (*Beta saccharifera*) of the common garden beet.

sug·ar·ber·ry (shŏŏg/ər·ber/ē) *n.* *pl.* ·ries The hackberry (which see).

sugar bowl A small, usually covered container of glass, china, silver, etc., for holding sugar at the table.

sugar·bush (shŏŏg/ər·bŏŏsh/) *n.* A grove of sugar maples.

sugar cane A tall, stout, perennial grass (*Saccharum officinarum*) of tropical regions, having a solid jointed stalk constituting a major source of commercial sugar.

sug·ar·coat (shŏŏg/ər·kōt/) *v.t.* 1. To cover with sugar. 2. To cause to appear attractive or less distasteful, as with euphemisms or flattery.

sugar corn Sweet corn (def. 1).

sug·ar-cured (shŏŏg/ər·kyŏŏrd/) *adj.* Cured by using sugar in the curing process, as ham and pork.

sugar daddy *U.S. Slang* A wealthy old man who gives a young woman presents in return for her favors.

sugar diabetes Diabetes (def. 1).

sug·ared (shŏŏg/ərd) *adj.* 1. Sweetened with sugar; sugarcoated. 2. Honeyed; pleasant; sweetened.

sug·ar·house (shŏŏg/ər·hous/) *n.* 1. A place where sugar is made from the sugar cane, the sugar beet, etc., or from maple sap. 2. A building in which sugar is stored.

su·gar·ing off (shŏŏg/ər·ing) *Chiefly U.S.* 1. The process of making maple sugar by boiling down the maple sap. 2. A social gathering of neighbors at a sugarhouse to help make maple sugar.

sugar loaf 1. A conical mass of hard refined sugar. 2. A conical hat or hill. — **sug·ar-loaf** (shŏŏg/ər·lōf/) *adj.*

Sugar Loaf Mountain A peak in Río de Janeiro, Brazil, at the entrance to Guanabara Bay; 1,296 ft.: Portuguese *Pão de Açúcar.*

sugar maple A maple (*Acer saccharum*) of eastern North America, yielding a sap from which maple sugar is made: also called *hard maple, rock maple, sugar tree.*

sugar of lead Lead acetate.

sugar of milk Lactose.

sugar orchard An orchard of sugar maples.

sugar pine A tall pine (*Pinus lambertiana*) of the Pacific coast, bearing very large cones and having wood much used in construction work.

sug·ar·plum (shŏŏg/ər·plum/) *n.* A small ball or disk of candy; a bonbon.

sugar tree The sugar maple.

sug·ar·y (shŏŏg/ər·ē) *adj.* 1. Composed of or as of sugar; sweet. 2. Insincerely or cloyingly sweet. 3. Consisting of grains; granular. — **sug/ar·i·ness** *n.*

sug·gest (səg·jest/, sə·jest/) *v.t.* 1. To bring or put forward for consideration, action, or approval; propose. 2. To bring to mind by association or connection; connote: Halloween *suggests* witches and black cats. 3. To give a hint or indirect indication of; intimate: The simple house *suggested* a modest income. 4. To act as or provide a motive for; prompt: these events *suggest* a sequel. [< L *suggestus*, pp. of *suggerere* < *sub-* underneath + *gerere* to carry] — **sug·gest/er** *n.*

sug·gest·i·bil·i·ty (səg·jes/tə·bil/ə·tē, sə-) *n.* 1. *Psychol.* Responsiveness to suggestion, especially when heightened or abnormal, as in hypnosis and certain nervous conditions. 2. Readiness to believe and agree without reflection.

sug·gest·i·ble (səg·jes/tə·bəl, sə-) *adj.* 1. That can be suggested. 2. Easily led; yielding: a *suggestible* patient.

sug·ges·tion (səg·jes/chən, sə·jes/-) *n.* 1. The act of suggesting. 2. Something suggested. 3. A hint; insinuation. 4. The spontaneous calling up of an idea in the mind by a connected idea. 5. *Psychol.* **a** The inducing in a person of some idea, impulse, action, or mode of behavior through a stimulus, verbal or other, but without the support of critical argument or rational persuasion. **b** The idea, impulse, etc., so induced.

suggestion box A box in which written ideas or suggestions for improvements may be placed, especially by employees of a firm.

sug·ges·tive (səg·jes/tiv, sə-) *adj.* 1. Fitted or tending to suggest; stimulating to thought or reflection. 2. Hinting at or arousing indecent thoughts; suggesting the improper. — **sug·ges/tive·ly** *adv.* — **sug·ges/tive·ness** *n.*

sugh (sōŏkh) *Scot.* *n.* Sough. — *v.i.* To sough.

su·i·ci·dal (sōō/ə·sīd/l) *adj.* 1. Of, pertaining to, or leading to suicide; self-destructive. 2. Fatal to one's prospects or interests; ruinous. — **su/i·ci/dal·ly** *adv.*

su·i·cide (sōō/ə·sīd) *n.* 1. The intentional taking of one's own life. 2. Self-inflicted political, social, or commercial ruin. 3. One who has taken his own life. — *v.i.* ·cid·ed, ·cid·ing *Informal* To commit suicide. [< NL *suicidium* < L *sui* of oneself + *caedere* to kill]

su·i gen·e·ris (sōō/ī jen/ər·is) *Latin* Forming a kind by itself; unique; literally, of its (his, or her) particular kind.

su·i ju·ris (sōō/ī jŏŏr/is) *Latin* In one's own right; having legal capacity to act for oneself.

su·int (sōō/int, swint) *n.* Natural wool grease from woolwashings, consisting of fatty substances combined with potash salts. [< F < *suer* to sweat < L *sudare*]

Suisse (swēs) The French name for SWITZERLAND.

suit (sōōt) *n.* 1. A set of garments consisting of a coat and trousers or skirt, made of the same fabric. 2. A group of things of like kind or pattern composing a series or set. 3. An outfit or garment for a particular purpose: a bathing *suit*; a space *suit*. 4. In cardplaying, one of the four sets of thirteen cards each that make up a pack, as spades, hearts, diamonds, or clubs. 5. *Law* A proceeding in a court of law or chancery in which a plaintiff demands the recovery of a right or the redress of a wrong. 6. The courting or courtship of a woman. 7. *Archaic* Entreaty; petition; supplication. — **to follow suit** 1. To play a card identical in suit to the card led. 2. To do as somebody or something else has done; follow an example. — *v.t.* 1. To meet the requirements of, or be appropriate to; be in accord with; befit. 2. To please; satisfy. 3. To render appropriate or accordant; accommodate; adapt. 4. *Archaic* To furnish with clothes. — *v.i.* 5. To be befitting; agree; correspond. 6. To be or prove satisfactory. 7. *Obs.* To clothe oneself. [< AF *siwte*, OF *sieute*, ult. < L *sequi* to follow. Doublet of SUITE.]

suit·a·ble (sōō/tə·bəl) *adj.* Appropriate to a particular occasion, condition, etc.; proper. — **Syn.** See APPROPRIATE. — **suit/a·bil/i·ty**, **suit/a·ble·ness** *n.* — **suit/a·bly** *adv.*

suit·case (sōōt/kās/) *n.* A flat, rectangular valise used for carrying clothing, etc.

suite (swēt; *for def. 3, also* sōōt) *n.* 1. A succession of things forming a series and usually intended to go or be used together; a set. 2. A number of connected rooms. 3. A set of furniture designed to be used together in the same room. 4. A company of attendants or followers; retinue. 5. A collection of pictures illustrating consecutive events. 6. *Music* A form of instrumental composition formerly consisting of a series of dances, but now often varying freely in its construction. 7. *Canadian* In the West, an apartment. [< F < OF *sieute*. Doublet of SUIT.]

suit·ing (sōō/ting) *n.* Cloth from which to make suits.

suit·or (sōō/tər) *n.* 1. A man who courts a woman; a wooer. 2. One who institutes a suit in court. 3. One who makes a request; petitioner. [< AF *seutor* < LL *secutor, -oris* < L *secutus*, pp. of *sequi* to follow]

Sui-yü·an (swā/yŏō/än/) A former province of northern China, incorporated in the Inner Mongolian Autonomous Region, 1954.

Su·kar·no (sōō·kär/nō), **Achmed,** 1901–70, Indonesian statesman; first president of Indonesia 1945–67. Also *Soekarno.*

Su·khu·mi (sōō/khōō·mi) The capital of the Abkhaz A.S.S.R., a port on the Black Sea; pop. 64,000 (1959).

su·ki·ya·ki (sōō/kē·yä/kē, -yak/ē; skē-) *n.* A Japanese dish, usually cooked rapidly at the table, made of meat in thin slices, vegetables, and condiments. [< Japanese *suki* spade + *yaki* roast]

Suk·koth (sŏŏk/ōth, -ōs, -əs) *n.* The feast of Tabernacles, a Jewish holiday beginning on the 15th of Tishri (late September–October), originally a harvest festival: also spelled *Succoth.* Also **Suk/kos.** [< Hebrew *sukkōth* tabernacles, booths]

Su·la·we·si (sōō/lä·wä/sē) The Indonesian name for CELEBES.

sul·cate (sul/kāt) *adj.* *Biol.* Having long narrow furrows or channels; grooved; fluted, as a plant stem or horse's hoof. Also **sul/cat·ed.** [< L *sulcatus*, pp. of *sulcare* to plow < *sulcus* furrow] — **sul·ca/tion** *n.*

sul·cus (sul/kəs) *n.* *pl.* ·ci (-sī) 1. A narrow channel or furrow. 2. *Anat.* One of the shallow grooves marking the convolutions of the brain. [< L]

sul·dan (sul/dən) See SOLDAN.

Su·lei·man the Magnificent (sü/lā·män/) 1490?–1566, sultan of Turkey 1520–66; raised the Ottoman Empire to its highest point of power. Also *Solyman the Magnificent.*

sulfa- *combining form Chem.* Sulfur; related to or containing sulfur: also spelled *sulpha-.* Also, before vowels, **sulf-,** as in *sulfarsphenamine.* See also SULFO-. [< SULFUR]

sul·fa·di·a·zine (sul/fə·dī/ə·zēn, -zin) *n.* *Chem.* A white, crystalline derivative of sulfanilamide, $C_{10}H_{10}N_4SO_2$, used in the treatment of infections due to streptococci, pneumococci, and staphylococci: also spelled *sulphadiazine.*

sul·fa drug (sul/fə) *Chem.* Any of a group of organic compounds consisting mainly of substituted sulfanilamide derivatives, effective in the treatment of certain bacterial infections: also spelled *sulpha drug.*

sul·fa·nil·a·mide (sul/fə·nil/ə·mīd, -mid) *n.* *Chem.* A colorless, crystalline sulfonamide, $C_6H_8N_2O_2S$, originally developed and used in the treatment of various bacterial infections: also spelled *sulphanilamide.*

sul·fa·pyr·i·dine (sul/fə·pir/ə·dēn, -din) *n.* *Chem.* A white, crystalline derivative of sulfanilamide, $C_{11}H_{11}N_3O_2S$, now largely replaced by sulfadiazine: also spelled *sulphapyridine.*

sulf·ars·phen·a·mine (sulf/ärs·fen/ə·mēn, -fen·am/in) *n.* *Chem.* A yellow, almost odorless, water-soluble powder containing from 18 to 20 percent arsenic, formerly used in the treatment of syphilis: also spelled *sulpharsphenamine.*

sul·fate (sul'fāt) *n. Chem.* A salt of sulfuric acid. — *v.* ·fat·ed, ·fat·ing *v.t.* **1.** To form a sulfate of; treat with a sulfate or sulfuric acid. **2.** *Electr.* To form a coating of lead sulfate on (the plate of a secondary battery). **3.** To make (red lead) into lead sulfate by the action of sulfuric acid. — *v.i.* **4.** To become sulfated. Also spelled *sulphate.* [< F < NL *sulfas, -atis* sulfate < L *sulfur* sulfur]

sul·fa·thi·a·zole (sul'fə·thī'ə·zōl) *n. Chem.* A sulfanilamide derivative, $C_9H_9N_3O_2S_2$, considered particularly effective in treating certain pneumococcal and staphylococcal infections: also spelled *sulphathiazole.*

sul·fa·tize (sul'fə·tīz) *v.t.* ·tized, ·tiz·ing To turn (ores, etc.) into sulfate, as by roasting: also spelled *sulphatize.*

sul·fide (sul'fīd) *n. Chem.* A compound of sulfur with an element or radical: also called *sulfuret:* also spelled *sulphide, sulphid.* Also **sul'fid** (-fid). [< SULF(A)- + -IDE]

sul·fi·nyl (sul'fə·nil) *n. Chem.* The bivalent sulfur radical OS: also called *thionyl:* also spelled *sulphinyl.* [< *sulfine,* var. of SULFONIUM + -YL]

sul·fite (sul'fīt) *n. Chem.* A salt or ester of sulfurous acid: also spelled *sulphite.* — **sul·fit'ic** (-fit'ik) *adj.*

sulfo- *combining form Chem.* **1.** Sulfur; containing sulfur. **2.** Denoting the replacement of oxygen by sulfur in a compound. **3.** Indicating the presence of the sulfonyl radical. Also spelled *sulpho-.* [< SULFUR]

Sul·fo·nal (sul'fə·nal, sul'fə·nal') *n.* Proprietary name for a brand of sulfonmethane. Also **sul'fo·nal.**

sul·fon·a·mide (sul·fon'ə·mīd, sul·fon·am'īd, -id) *n. Chem.* Any of a class of chemotherapeutic compounds containing the univalent radical SO_2N, especially those derived from sulfanilamide: also spelled *sulphonamide.*

sul·fo·nate (sul'fə·nāt) *v.t.* ·nat·ed, ·nat·ing *Chem.* **1.** To form into a sulfonic acid. **2.** To subject to the treatment of sulfonic acid. — *n.* A salt or ester of sulfonic acid. Also spelled *sulphonate.* — **sul'fo·na'tion** *n.*

sul·fone (sul'fōn) *n. Chem.* Any of several compounds consisting of two organic radicals in combination with the sulfonyl radical: also spelled *sulphone.* [< G *sulfon*] — **sul·fon·ic** (sul·fon'ik) *adj.*

sulfonic acid *Chem.* Any of several compounds having an organic radical in combination with the sulfonic radical SO_2OH, used in organic synthesis: also spelled *sulphonic acid.*

sul·fo·ni·um (sul·fō'nē·əm) *n. Chem.* The positive ion, H_3S, resulting from the addition of a proton to hydrogen sulfide: also spelled *sulphonium.*

sul·fon·meth·ane (sul'fōn·meth'ān) *n. Chem.* A white, crystalline, organic compound, $C_7H_{16}O_4S_2$, used in medicine as a sedative and hypnotic: also spelled *sulphonmethane.*

sul·fo·nyl (sul'fə·nil) *n. Chem.* The bivalent radical SO_2: also called *sulfuryl:* also spelled *sulphonyl.*

sul·fur (sul'fər) *n.* **1.** A pale yellow, nonmetallic element (symbol S), found both free and combined in the native state, and existing in several forms, of which the best known is a crystalline solid that burns with a blue flame and a suffocating odor. It is used for making matches, gunpowder, vulcanized rubber, and medicines. See ELEMENT. **2.** Any one of various yellowish pieridine butterflies, as the common North American **clouded sulfur** (*Colias philodice*) or the **cloudless sulfur** (*Callidryas eubule*). — **flowers of sulfur** A fine yellow powder obtained by the distillation of sulfur. — *v.t.* To treat or fume, as a wine cask or a hive, with sulfur or with sulfurous acid. Also spelled *sulphur.* [< AF *sulfre,* OF *soufre* < L *sulfur, -uris*]

sul·fur-bot·tom (sul'fər·bot'əm) *n.* A whalebone whale (*Sibbaldius musculus*) found in Atlantic and Pacific waters, having a yellowish belly and attaining a length of from 60 to 100 feet: also called *blue whale:* also spelled *sulphur-bottom.*

SULFUR-BOTTOM

sulfur dioxide *Chem.* A colorless, water-soluble, suffocating gas, SO_2, formed by the burning of sulfur and used in the manufacture of sulfuric acid.

sul·fu·re·ous (sul·fyŏŏr'ē·əs) *adj.* Of or like sulfur: also spelled *sulphureous.* [< L *sulfureus* < *sulfur*]

sul·fu·ret (*v.* sul'fyə·ret; *n.* sul'fyə·rit) *v.t.* ·fu·ret·ed or ·ret·ted, ·fu·ret·ing or ·ret·ting To sulfurize. — *n.* A sulfide. [< F *sulfuret* sulfide < NL *sulfuretum* < L *sulfur*]

sul·fu·ric (sul·fyŏŏr'ik) *adj. Chem.* Pertaining to or derived from sulfur, especially in its higher valence: also spelled *sulphuric.*

sulfuric acid *Chem.* A colorless, exceedingly corrosive, oily liquid, H_2SO_4, essentially a combination of sulfur trioxide and water, extensively employed in the manufacture of soda, batteries, guncotton, and in a great variety of industrial operations: formerly called *oil of vitriol, vitriol.*

sul·fur·ize (sul'fyə·rīz) *v.t.* ·ized, ·iz·ing **1.** To impregnate, treat with, or subject to the action of sulfur. **2.** To bleach or fumigate with sulfur. Also *sulfuret:* also spelled *sulphurize.* Also **sul'fu·rate** (-rāt). — **sul'fur·i·za'tion** *n.*

sul·fur·ous (sul'fər·əs, sul·fyŏŏr'əs) *adj.* **1.** Of, pertaining to, derived from, or containing sulfur, especially in its lower valence. **2.** Fiery; hellish. Also spelled *sulphurous.*

sulfurous acid *Chem.* A compound corresponding to the formula H_2SO_3, and known only in solution and by its salts.

sulfur point *Physics* The boiling point of pure liquid sulfur at standard atmospheric pressure, 444.60° C., one of the fixed points of the international temperature scale.

sulfur trioxide *Chem.* A compound, SO_3, formed by the oxidation of sulfur dioxide in the presence of a catalytic agent, and yielding sulfuric acid on the addition of water.

sul·fur·y (sul'fər·ē) *adj.* Resembling or suggesting sulfur; sulfureous: also spelled *sulphury.*

sul·fur·yl (sul'fər·il, -fyə·ril) *n. Chem.* Sulfonyl: also spelled *sulphuryl.*

sulfuryl chloride *Chem.* A colorless, pungent liquid, SO_2Cl_2, used in the manufacture of dyes, drugs, and poison gas.

sulk (sulk) *v.i.* To be sulky or morose. — *n.* **1.** *Often pl.* A sulky mood or humor. **2.** One who sulks. [Back formation < SULKY]

sulk·y¹ (sul'kē) *adj.* sulk·i·er, sulk·i·est **1.** Sullenly cross; doggedly or resentfully ill-humored. **2.** Dismal; gloomy: said of weather. [? OE (*ā*)*solcen* slothful, orig. pp. of (*ā*)*seolcan* to be weak, slothful] — **sulk'i·ly** *adv.* — **sulk'i·ness** *n.*

sulk·y² (sul'kē) *n. pl.* sulk·ies A light, two-wheeled, one-horse vehicle for one person. — *adj.* Resembling a sulky: a *sulky* plow. [< SULKY¹; so called because one rides alone]

Sul·la (sul'ə), 138?–78 B.C., Roman general and dictator 82–79 B.C.: full name **Lucius Cornelius Sulla Fe·lix** (fē'liks).

sul·lage (sul'ij) *n.* **1.** Mud or silt deposited by flowing water. **2.** Refuse; sewage. [< AF *souiller, soillier.* See SOIL²; infl. in form by *sully*]

sul·len (sul'ən) *adj.* **1.** Obstinately and gloomily ill-humored; morose; glum; melancholy. **2.** Depressing; somber: *sullen* clouds. **3.** Slow; sluggish: a *sullen* tread. **4.** Ill-omened; threatening. [Earlier *solein,* appar. < AF < L *solus* alone] — **sul'len·ly** *adv.* — **sul'len·ness** *n.*

Sul·li·van (sul'ə·vən), **Sir Arthur (Seymour),** 1842–1900, English composer; often in collaboration with W. S. Gilbert. — **John,** 1740–95, American Revolutionary general. — **John L(awrence),** 1858–1918, U.S. boxer: called **the Boston Strong Boy.** — **Louis Henri,** 1856–1924, U.S. architect.

sul·ly (sul'ē) *v.* ·lied, ·ly·ing *v.t.* **1.** To mar the brightness or purity of; soil; defile; tarnish. — *v.i.* **2.** To become soiled or tarnished. — *n. pl.* ·lies Anything that tarnishes; a stain; spot; blemish. [< MF *souiller.* See SOIL².]

Sul·ly (sü·lē'), **Duc de,** 1560–1641, Maximilien de Béthune, French Huguenot statesman.

Sul·ly (sul'ē), **Thomas,** 1783–1872, U.S. painter born in England.

Sul·ly-Prud·homme (sü·lē'prü·dôm'), **René François Armand,** 1839–1907, French poet and critic.

sulpha- Var. of SULFA-.

sul·pha·di·a·zine (sul'fə·dī'ə·zēn, -zin), **sulpha drug** (sul'fə), etc. See SULFADIAZINE, etc.

sul·phur (sul'fər), **sul·phu·re·ous** (sul·fyŏŏr'ē·əs), etc. See SULFUR, etc.

sulpho- Var. of SULFO-.

sul·tan (sul'tən) *n.* **1.** The ruler of a Moslem country. **2.** A gallinule (*Porphyrula martinica*) with deep blue or purple plumage and white lower tail coverts. **3.** A small white-crested domestic fowl, originating in Turkey, having heavily feathered legs and feet. **4.** Formerly, any ruler. — **the Sultan** Formerly, the title of the sovereign of Turkey. [< F < Med.L *sultanus* < Arabic *sultān*]

sul·tan·a (sul·tan'ə, -tä'nə) *n.* **1.** A sultan's wife, daughter, sister, or mother. Also **sul·tan·ess** (sul'tən·is). **2.** A royal mistress. **3.** A variety of raisin from around Smyrna, Asia Minor. [< Ital., fem. of *sultano* sultan < Arabic *sultān*]

sul·tan·ate (sul'tən·āt, -it) *n.* The authority or territorial jurisdiction of a sultan. Also **sul'tan·ship.**

sul·try (sul'trē) *adj.* ·tri·er, ·tri·est **1.** Hot, moist, and still; close: said of weather. **2.** Emitting an oppressive heat. **3.** Showing or suggesting passion; sensual. [< obs. *sulter,* var. of SWELTER] — **sul'tri·ly** *adv.* — **sul'tri·ness** *n.*

Su·lu (soo'loo) *n.* **1.** A member of the chief Moro tribe occupying the Sulu Archipelago. **2.** The Indonesian language of this tribe, akin to Tagalog. — **Su·lu'an** *adj. & n.*

Sulu Archipelago An island group north of Borneo, comprising **Sulu Province** of the Philippines; 1,086 sq. mi.; pop. 300,650 (est. 1960); capital, Jolo.

Sulu Sea The part of the Pacific Ocean between the SW Philippines and Borneo.

sum (sum) *n.* **1.** The result obtained by addition. **2.** The entire quantity, number, or substance; the whole; all. **3.** An indefinite amount, as of money. **4.** A problem in arithmetic propounded for solution. **5.** The topmost or highest point; summit; also, the maximum. **6.** The pith or essence; summary. — *v.* summed, sum·ming *v.t.* **1.** To present in brief; recapitulate succinctly: usually with *up:* to *sum up* evidence. **2.** To add into one total; ascertain the sum of: often with *up.* **3.** To ascertain the sum of (the terms of a series). — *v.i.* **4.** To make a summation or recapitulation: usually with *up.* [< AF, OF *summe, somme* < L *summa* (*res*) highest (thing), fem. of *summus* highest]

sum- Var. of SUB-.

su·mac (soo'mak, shoo'-) *n.* **1.** Any of a genus (*Rhus*) of woody, erect, or root-climbing plants, with panicles of small drupaceous fruits, and yielding a resinous or milky juice; especially, the **smooth sumac** (*R. glabra*) used in medicine. **2.** The poison sumac (which see). **3.** The dried and powdered leaves of certain species of sumac, used for tanning and dyeing, especially of **tanner's sumac** (*Rhus coriaria*). Also **su'mach.** [< OF < Med.L *sumach* < Arabic *summāq*]

Su·ma·tra (sŏŏ·mä'trə) An island of Indonesia south of the Malay Peninsula; 163,557 sq. mi. — **Su·ma'tran** *adj. & n.*

Sum·ba (sŏŏm'bä) An island of Nusa Tenggara, Indonesia; 4,300 sq. mi.: formerly *Sandalwood Island*: Dutch *Soemba*.

Sum·ba·wa (sŏŏm·bä'wä) An island of Nusa Tenggara, Indonesia; 5,965 sq. mi.: Dutch *Soembawa*.

Su·mer (sŏŏ'mər) A region and ancient country of Mesopotamia, later the southern division of Babylonia; the sites of its once great cities are in south central Iraq.

Su·me·ri·an (sŏŏ·mir'ē·ən) *adj.* Of or pertaining to ancient Sumer, its people, or their language. — *n.* **1.** One of an ancient non-Semitic people formerly occupying a part of lower Babylonia, culturally important in the Near East from about 3300 to 1800 B.C. **2.** The unclassified language of these people, written in cuneiform characters and preserved on rocks and clay tablets that date from as early as 4000 B.C. Also **Su·mir'i·an.**

sum·less (sum'lis) *adj.* Too great for computation; incalculable; without number.

sum·ma cum lau·de (sum'ə kum lô'dē, sŏŏm'ə kŏŏm lou'də) See under CUM LAUDE.

sum·mand (sum'and) *n.* That which is added; any of the numbers forming part of a sum. [< Med.L *summandus* (*numerus*) (the number) to be added < *summare* to add < L *summa*. See SUM.]

sum·ma·rize (sum'ə·rīz) *v.t.* **·rized,** **·riz·ing** To make a summary of; sum up. Also *Brit.* **sum'ma·rise.** — **sum'ma·rist** (-ər·ist), **sum'ma·riz'er** *n.* — **sum'ma·ri·za'tion** *n.*

sum·ma·ry (sum'ər·ē) *adj.* **1.** Giving the substance or sum; greatly condensed; concise. **2.** Performed without ceremony or delay; instant; offhand. — *n. pl.* **·ries** An abridgment or abstract. [< Med.L *summarius* < L *summarium* < *summa*. See SUM.] — **sum·ma·ri·ly** (sum'ər·ə·lē, emphatic sə·mer'ə·lē) *adv.* — **sum'ma·ri·ness** *n.*

sum·mate (sum·āt') *v.t. & v.i.* **·mat·ed,** **·mat·ing** **1.** To arrive at the sum of (a series). **2.** To sum up. [Back formation < SUMMATION]

sum·ma·tion (sum·ā'shən) *n.* **1.** The act or operation of obtaining a sum; the computation or statement of an aggregate sum or result; addition. **2.** A speech or a portion of a speech summing up the principal points. [< NL *summatio, -onis* < Med.L *summare* to add < *summa*. See SUM.]

sum·mer[1] (sum'ər) *n.* **1.** The warmest season of the year, occurring between spring and autumn and in the northern hemisphere popularly regarded as including June, July, and August. Astronomically it extends from the summer solstice to the autumnal equinox. ◆ Collateral adjective: *estival.* **2.** A year of life, especially of early or happy life. **3.** A bright and prosperous period. — *v.t.* **1.** To keep or care for through the summer. — *v.i.* **2.** To pass the summer. — *adj.* Of, pertaining to, or occurring in summer. [OE *sumor*] — **sum'mer·ly** *adj. & adv.*

sum·mer[2] (sum'ər) *n. Archit.* **1.** A heavy horizontal timber or girder serving as a support for some superstructure in a building, etc.; a lintel. **2.** A large stone, as on a column or pilaster, for supporting one or more arches, or any similar structure. **3.** A horizontal beam resting upon the walls or frame of a building, and supporting the ends of joists: also **summer beam.** [< OF *somier* pack horse, beam < LL *saumarius* < L *sagmarius* < *sagma* pack saddle < Gk.]

summer cottage A house or cottage in the country or on the water, used during the summer: also **summer house.**

summer flounder A flounder (*Paralichthys dentatus*) of the Atlantic coast of North America.

sum·mer·house (sum'ər·hous') *n.* A rustic structure, as in a garden, for rest or shade; gazebo.

sum·mer·sault (sum'ər·sôlt) See SOMERSAULT.

summer school A school, college, or university offering courses during the summer vacation period.

sum·mer·set (sum'ər·set) *n.* A somersault.

summer squash Any garden squash or pumpkin, varieties of *Cucurbita pepo*, as the crookneck.

summer theater *U.S.* The plays, musical shows, etc., performed on the straw-hat circuit. Also **summer stock.**

sum·mer·time (sum'ər·tīm') *n.* Summer; the summer season. Also **sum'mer·tide'.**

sum·mer·y (sum'ər·ē) *adj.* Pertaining to, resembling, or characteristic of summer.

sum·mit (sum'it) *n.* **1.** The highest part; the top; vertex. **2.** The highest degree; maximum. **3.** The highest level or rank, as of government officials: a meeting at the *summit.* **4.** A meeting or discussion among the highest executives of government, especially chiefs of state; also, the place where such a meeting is held. — *adj.* Of, pertaining to, or charac-

terized by diplomacy at the highest level: *summit* talks. [< OF *sommette*, dim. of *som* summit, top < L *summum*, neut. of *summus* highest] — **sum'mit·al** *adj.*
— **Syn.** acme, climax, peak, pinnacle, apex, zenith. — **Ant.** bottom, base, abyss, nadir.

summit meeting A meeting at which the heads of two or more governments discuss international problems and attempt to resolve disagreements. Also **summit conference.**

sum·mit·less (sum'it·lis) *adj.* Being without a summit.

sum·mit·ry (sum'ə·trē) *n.* The practice of conducting diplomacy by means of conferences between the highest executives of government, especially chiefs of state.

sum·mon (sum'ən) *v.t.* **1.** To order to come; send for. **2.** To call together; cause to convene, as a legislative assembly. **3.** To order (a person) to appear in court by a summons. **4.** To call forth or into action; arouse: usually with *up*: to *summon* up courage. **5.** To bid or call on for a specific act: The garrison was *summoned* to surrender. — **Syn.** See CONVOKE. [< AF, OF *somondre* < L *summonere* to suggest, hint < *sub-* secretly + *monere* to warn]

sum·mon·er (sum'ən·ər) *n.* **1.** One who summons. **2.** *Archaic* An officer who summons persons to appear in court.

sum·mons (sum'ənz) *n. pl.* **sum·mon·ses** (sum'ən·zəz) **1.** A call to attend or act at a particular place or time. **2.** *Law* A notice to a defendant summoning him to appear in court, either a judicial writ or process, or a notice signed by the plaintiff or his attorney; any citation issued to a party to an action to appear before a court or judge at chambers. **3.** A notice to a person requiring him to appear in court as a witness or as a juror. **4.** A military demand to surrender. **5.** Any signal or sound that is a peremptory call. [< AF *somonse*, OF *sumunse* < *somondre*. See SUMMON.]

sum·mum bo·num (sum'əm bō'nəm) *Latin* The chief, supreme, or highest good.

Sum·ner (sum'nər), **Charles,** 1811–74, U.S. statesman and abolitionist. — **James Batcheller,** 1887–1955, U.S. biochemist. — **William Graham,** 1840–1910, U.S. sociologist.

su·mo (sŏŏ'mō) *n.* A stylized Japanese form of wrestling in which each of two contestants endeavors to force the other out of the ring or off his feet. [< Japanese]

sump (sump) *n.* **1.** *Mining* A depression at the lowest level in a mine shaft, to receive water and form a pool from which it may be pumped. **2.** *Mech.* The lowest part of the crankcase of an internal-combustion engine, acting as a reservoir for lubricating oil. **3.** A cesspool or other receptacle for drainage. [< MDu. *somp, sump* marsh. Akin to SWAMP.]

sump·ter (sump'tər) *n.* A pack animal; beast of burden. [< OF *sometier* driver of a pack horse, ult. < L *sagma*. See SUMMER[2].]

sump·tu·ar·y (sump'chŏŏ·er'ē) *adj.* Pertaining to expense; limiting or regulating expenditure, as some laws. [< L *sumptuarius* < *sumptus* expenditure < *sumere* to take]

sumptuary law **1.** A law regulating expenditure. **2.** A law regulating private life on moral or religious grounds.

sump·tu·ous (sump'chŏŏ·əs) *adj.* Involving or showing lavish expenditure. **2.** Luxurious; magnificent. [< OF *somptueux* < L *sumptuosus* < *sumptus.* See SUMPTUARY.] — **sump'tu·ous·ly** *adv.* — **sump'tu·ous·ness** *n.*

sump·weed (sump'wēd') *n.* Marsh elder (def. 1).

sun (sun) *n.* **1.** The star that is the center of attraction and the main source of radiant energy in the solar system, with a mean distance from the earth of about 93 million miles, a diameter of 864,000 miles, and a mass 332,000 times that of the earth. ◆ Collateral adjectives: *heliacal, solar.* **2.** Any star, especially one that is the center of a system revolving around it. **3.** The light and heat radiated from the sun; sunshine. **4.** Anything brilliant and magnificent, or that is a source of splendor. **5.** The time of the earth's revolution around the sun; a year. **6.** The daily appearance of the sun; a day; also, the time of its appearance or shining; sunrise. — **a place in the sun 1.** A dominant position in international affairs. **2.** A position in the spotlight; publicity. — *v.* **sunned, sun·ning** *v.t.* **1.** To expose to the light or heat of the sun. **2.** To warm or dry (something) in the sun. — *v.i.* **3.** To bask in the sun; expose oneself to the light or heat of the sun. Abbr. **s.** [OE *sunne*]
Sun may appear as a combining form or as the first element in two-word phrases, with the following meanings:

1. Of the sun; of sunshine:

sun blaze	sunland	sun worship
sun-eclipsing	sun lover	sun worshiper
sun glare	sun-loving	sun-worshiping

2. By or with the sun:

sun-arrayed	sun-browned	sun-heated
sun-bake	sun-cracked	sun-kissed
sun-baked	sun-dappled	sunlit
sun-blanched	sun-dried	sun-scorched
sun-blind	sun-dry	sun-scorching
sun-blinded	sun-filled	sun-streaked
sun-blistered	sun-flooded	sun-warmed
sun-brown	sun-gilt	sun-withered

Sun. or **Sund.** Sunday

sun bath Exposure of the body to the direct rays of the sun.

sun-bathe (sun′bāth́) *v.i.* **-bathed, -bath·ing** To bask in the sun, especially as a method of tanning the skin. — **sun′bath′er** *n.* — **sun′bath′ing** *n.*

sun-beam (sun′bēm′) *n.* A ray or beam of the sun; light from the sun in a visible path.

sun bear Honey bear (def. 1).

sun-bird (sun′bûrd′) *n.* **1.** A brilliantly colored singing bird (family *Nectariniidae*) of Africa and the Far East, resembling the hummingbird. **2.** A sun bittern.

sun bittern Either of two birds (genus *Eurypyga*) of Central and South America, related to the rails and herons, having a slender neck and bill, long wings and tail, and moderately long legs: also called *sunbird.*

sun-bon·net (sun′bon′it) *n.* A bonnet of light material with projecting brim and sometimes a ruffle over the neck.

sun-bow (sun′bō′) *n.* A rainbow formed by the refraction of sunlight passing through spray, as from a cataract or waterfall.

sun-burn (sun′bûrn′) *n.* Discoloration or inflammation of the skin, from exposure to the sun. — *v.t. & v.i.* **·burned** or **·burnt, burn·ing** To affect or be affected with sunburn.

sun-burst (sun′bûrst′) *n.* **1.** A strong burst of sunlight, as through rifted clouds. **2.** A jewelled brooch, ornament, etc., with rays shooting forth in all directions from a central disk.

sun compass A compass serving to establish direction and time from the shadow cast by a fixed pin in sunlight. It is used chiefly in polar regions, where the magnetic compass is unreliable.

sun-cured (sun′kyŏŏrd) *adj.* Cured by the action of the sun, as beef.

sun-dae (sun′dē, -dā) *n.* A refreshment consisting of ice cream topped with crushed fruit, syrup, nuts, etc. [Prob. < SUNDAY; so called because orig. sold only on that day]

Sun-da Islands (sun′də, sŏŏn′də) A former collective name for Borneo, Celebes, Java, Sumatra, the Molucca Islands, and Nusa Tenggara.

sun dance The greatest ceremonial dance of the Plains Indians, usually a summer solstice ceremony.

Sun-da Strait (sun′də, sŏŏn′də) The channel between Java and Sumatra; 16 to 70 mi. wide.

Sun-day (sun′dē, -dā) *n.* The first day of the week; the Christian Sabbath. ◆ Collateral adjective: *dominical.* Abbr. *S., Sun., Sund.* — **Syn.** See SABBATH. [OE *sunnandæg* < *sunnan* of the sun + *dæg* day; trans. of LL *dies solis* day of the sun]

Sun·day (sun′dē, -dā), **Billy,** 1862–1935, U.S. preacher and evangelist: full name **William Ashley Sunday.**

Sun-day-go-to-meet·ing (sun′dē-gô′tə-mē′ting) *adj. Informal* Best: *Sunday-go-to-meeting* clothes.

Sunday law A blue law (which see).

Sunday school A school, generally attached to some church, in which religious instruction is given on Sunday, especially to the young; also, the pupils, or teachers and pupils collectively. Also called *Sabbath school.* Abbr. *S.S.*

sun deck An exposed surface or platform suitable for sunbathing, as on a ship or building; sun roof.

sun-der (sun′dər) *v.t.* **1.** To break apart; disunite; sever. — *v.i.* **2.** To be parted or severed. — *n.* Division into parts; separation. [OE *syndrian, sundrian*] — **sun′der·ance** *n.*

Sun-der-land (sun′dər-lənd) A borough and port in Tyne and Wear, England; pop. 292,600 (1976).

sun-dew (sun′dōō′, -dyōō′) *n.* Any of a genus (*Drosera*) of marsh plants that exude from the tips of hairs on the leaves a sticky liquid by which insects are caught.

sun-di-al (sun′dī′əl) *n.* A device that shows the time of day by the shadow of a gnomon thrown on a dial.

sun disk In Egyptian art (and, in modified forms, in Assyrian and Phoenician representations), the disk symbolizing the sun, usually supported by two uraei and the extended wings of a vulture: also called *winged disk.*

sun-dog (sun′dôg, -dog′) *n. Meteorol.* **1.** A parhelion. **2.** A small rainbow near the horizon.

sun-down (sun′doun′) *n.* **1.** *Chiefly U.S.* Sunset. **2.** A broad-brimmed hat worn by women. [? Contraction of *sun-go-down*]

sun-down·er (sun′dou′nər) *n.* **1.** *Informal* A tramp. **2.** *Austral.* A vagrant who seeks food and lodging at backcountry ranches, often at sundown. **3.** *Slang* **a** Originally, a ship's captain who granted liberty only until sundown. **b** Any strict, rigidly uncompromising ship's officer.

sun-dries (sun′drēz) *n.pl.* Items or things too small or too numerous to be separately specified. [< SUNDRY]

sun-drops (sun′drops′) *n. pl.* **·drops** Any of several American species of evening primrose (genus *Oenothera*), having large yellow flowers, and blooming in the daytime.

sun-dry (sun′drē) *adj.* Of an indefinite small number; various; several; miscellaneous. — **Syn.** See SEVERAL. [OE *syndrig* separate, private]

SUNFED Special United Nations Fund for Economic Development.

sun-fish (sun′fish′) *n. pl.* **·fish** or **·fish·es 1.** Any of various large oceanic plectognath fishes (family *Molidae*) having a deep, compressed body truncated in the rear, and tough, leathery flesh, especially *Mola mola,* of warm seas. **2.** Any of a family (*Centrarchidae*) of North American fresh-water fishes, as the pumpkinseed.

SUNFISH
(def. 1)
(About 8 feet long)

sun-flow·er (sun′flou′ər) *n.* Any of a genus (*Helianthus*) of tall, stout herbs of the composite family, with large leaves and circular heads of bright yellow flowers; especially, the **common sunflower** (*H. annuus*), the source of an edible oil, and the State flower of Kansas.

Sunflower State Nickname of KANSAS.

sung (sung) Past participle and occasional past tense of SING.

Sung (sŏŏng) *n.* A dynasty in Chinese history, 960 to 1280, noted for its achievements in art and philosophy.

Sun·ga·ri (sŏŏng′gä′rē) A river in NE China, flowing 1,150 miles NW to the Amur river. *Chinese* **Sung·hwa** (sŏŏng′hwä′).

Sung·kiang (sŏŏng′jyäng′) A former province of NE China, incorporated in the Inner Mongolian Autonomous Region.

sun-glass (sun′glas′, -gläs′) *n.* A burning glass (which see).

sun-glass·es (sun′glas′iz, -gläs′-) *n.pl.* Glasses with colored lenses to protect the eyes from the glare of the sun.

sun-glow (sun′glō′) *n.* **1.** The rose tint or faint yellow of the sky that precedes sunrise or follows sunset. **2.** The warm glow of the sun.

sun god A god identified with or personifying the sun.

sunk (sungk) Past participle and alternative past tense of SINK.

sunk·en (sung′kən) Obsolete past participle of SINK. — *adj.* **1.** Lying at the bottom of a body of water: a *sunken* ship. **2.** Located beneath a surface. **3.** Lower than the surrounding or usual level: *sunken* gardens. **4.** Deeply depressed or fallen in: *sunken* cheeks.

sun-ket (sung′kit, sŏŏng′-) *n. Scot.* A dainty; tidbit.

sunk fence A ditch having a retaining wall on one side to divide lands; a ha-ha.

sun lamp 1. A lamp radiating ultraviolet rays, used for therapeutic treatments or to acquire a sun tan. **2.** A lamp employing parabolic mirrors to give high-intensity illumination, used in motion-picture studios, etc.

sun-less (sun′lis) *adj.* **1.** Lacking sun or sunlight; overcast; dark. **2.** Cheerless; gloomy. — **sun′less·ness** *n.*

sun-light (sun′līt) *n.* The light of the sun.

sun-lit (sun′lit′) *adj.* Lighted by the sun.

sunn (sun) *n.* An East Indian shrub (*Crotalaria juncea*) of the bean family, with bright yellow flowers and a tough inner bark yielding a fiber used for making cordage, bagging, etc. Also **sunn hemp.** [< Hind. *san* < Skt. *sana*]

Sun-na (sŏŏn′ə) *n.* The part of the orthodox Moslem creed or law based on traditions of Mohammed's words and deeds, a supplement to the Koran. Also **Sun′nah.** [< Arabic *sunnah,* lit., form, way]

Sun-ni (sŏŏn′ē) *n.* One of the two great sects of Islam, consisting of those who acknowledge the first four caliphs as rightful successors of the Prophet, and accept Sunna and the Koran as of equal authority. Compare SHIAH (def. 1).

Sun-nite (sŏŏn′īt) *n.* A Moslem of the Sunni sect: distinguished from *Shiite.*

sun-ny (sun′ē) *adj.* **·ni·er, ·ni·est 1.** Filled with the light and warmth of the sun; also, exposed to the sun. **2.** Of or resembling the sun or sunlight. **3.** Bright; genial; cheery: a *sunny* smile. — **sun′ni·ly** *adv.* — **sun′ni·ness** *n.*

sunny side 1. The side, as of a hill, facing the sun. **2.** The cheerful view of any situation, question, etc.

Sun-ny-vale (sun′ē-vāl) A city in western California; pop. 95,408.

sun parlor A room enclosed in glass and having a sunny exposure. Also **sun porch.**

sun-rise (sun′rīz′) *n.* **1.** The daily first appearance of the sun above the horizon, with the atmospheric phenomena just before and after. **2.** The time at which the sun rises.

sun roof 1. A roof suitable for sun bathing. **2.** A section of an automobile roof that can be slid open.

sun-room (sun′rōōm′, -rŏŏm′) *n.* A room built to admit a great deal of sunlight.

sun-scald (sun′skôld′) *n.* A diseased condition of plants induced by exposure to intense sunlight.

sun-scorch (sun′skôrch′) *n.* A scorched condition of plants.

sun-set (sun′set′) *n.* **1.** The apparent daily descent of the sun below the horizon. **2.** The time when the sun sets;

SUNDIAL
g Gnomon.

SUN DISK

the early evening. **3.** The colors in the sky when the sun sets. **4.** An ending or decline, as of life.

sun·shade (sun′shād′) *n.* Something used as a shade or protection from the sun, as a parasol, an awning, etc.

sun·shine (sun′shīn′) *n.* **1.** The shining light of the sun; the direct rays of the sun. **2.** The warmth of the sun's rays. **3.** The place where the rays fall. **4.** Brightness; cheerfulness. — **sun′shin′y** *adj.*

Sunshine State Nickname of Florida, New Mexico, and South Dakota.

sun·spot (sun′spot′) *n.* **1.** *Astron.* One of many dark irregular spots appearing periodically on the surface of the sun and believed to have connection with terrestrial magnetic storms. **2.** A sun lamp used in color photography.

sun·stone (sun′stōn′) *n.* Aventurine.

sun·stroke (sun′strōk′) *n. Pathol.* A sudden onset of high fever induced by exposure to the sun and often marked by convulsions and coma: also called *insolation.* — **sun′-struck′** (-struk′) *adj.*

sun tan A bronze-colored condition of the skin, produced by exposure to the sun. — **sun′-tanned′** (-tand′) *adj.*

sun tans (tans) A lightweight military uniform having a tan or khaki color. Also **sun·tans** (sun′tans).

sun·up (sun′up′) *n. Chiefly U.S.* Sunrise. [< SUN + UP: on analogy with *sundown*]

Sun Valley A resort village in south central Idaho; pop. 180.

sun·ward (sun′wərd) *adj.* Facing toward the sun. — *adv.* Toward the sun: also **sun′wards.**

sun·wise (sun′wīz′) *adv.* With the sun; in the direction of the sun; clockwise.

Sun Yat-sen (sŏn′ yät′sen′), 1866–1925, Chinese political leader; founder of the Kuomintang 1912.

su·o ju·re (sŏō′ō jŏŏr′ē) *Latin* In one's own right.

su·o lo·co (sŏō′ō lō′kō) *Latin* In its own or proper place.

Su·o·mi (sŏō·ō′mi) The Finnish name for FINLAND.

Su·o·mic (sŏō·ō′mik) *adj.* Of or pertaining to Finland or the Finns. — *n.* The language of the Finns; Finnish.

sup[1] (sup) *v.t. & v.i.* **supped, sup·ping** To take (fluid food) in successive mouthfuls, a little at a time; sip. — *n.* A mouthful or taste of liquid or semiliquid food. [OE *sūpan*]

sup[2] (sup) *v.* **supped, sup·ping** *v.i.* **1.** To eat supper. — *v.t.* **2.** *Obs.* To furnish with or invite to supper. [< OF *soper, super*; ult. origin unknown]

sup- Var. of SUB-.

sup. **1.** Above (L *supra*). **2.** Superior. **3.** Superlative. **4.** Supine. **5.** Supplement; supplementary. **6.** Supply. **7.** Supreme.

supe (sŏōp) *n. Slang* A supernumerary actor. [Short for SUPERNUMERARY]

su·per[1] (sŏō′pər) *n. Informal* A superintendent (def. 2).

su·per[2] (sŏō′pər) *n. Slang* A supernumerary (def. 2).

su·per[3] (sŏō′pər) *n.* **1.** An article of superior size or quality; also, such size or quality. **2.** In bookbinding, a thin, starched cotton fabric used in reinforcement. — *adj. Slang* First-rate; superfine. — *v.t.* To reinforce (a book) with super. [Short for SUPERIOR, SUPERFINE, etc.]

super- *prefix* **1.** Above in position; over: *superstructure.* **2.** *Anat. & Zool.* Situated above, or on the dorsal side of: *superorbital.* **3.** Above or beyond; more than: *supersonic.* **4.** Excessively: *supersaturate.* **5.** *Chem.* Denoting a high proportion of the ingredient indicated (now superseded by PER-, BI-): *superphosphate.* **6.** Greater than or superior to others of its class: *superhighway.* **7.** Extra; additional: *supertax.* [< L *super-* < *super* above, beyond]

In the following list of words *super-* denotes excess or superiority, as *supercritical* excessively critical, *superexcellence* superior excellence.

superabhor	superconformity	superextension	superlenient	superreliance
superabominable	superconfusion	superfecundity	superlie	superremuneration
superabsurd	supercongestion	superfeminine	superlogical	superrespectable
superaccession	superconservative	superfervent	superloyal	superresponsible
superaccommodating	supercontrol	superfoliation	superlucky	superrestriction
superaccomplished	supercordial	superfolly	superluxurious	superreward
superaccumulate	supercritic	superformal	supermagnificently	superrighteous
superachievement	supercritical	superformation	supermanhood	superromantic
superacquisition	supercultivated	superformidable	supermarvelous	supersacrifice
superacute	supercurious	superfriendly	supermasculine	supersafe
superadaptable	supercynical	superfructified	supermechanical	supersagacious
superadequate	superdainty	superfulfillment	supermediocre	supersanguine
superadmiration	superdanger	supergaiety	supermental	supersarcastic
superadorn	superdeclamatory	supergallant	supermentality	supersatisfaction
superaffluence	superdeficit	supergenerosity	supermetropolitan	superscholarly
superagency	superdejection	superglorious	supermishap	superscientific
superaggravation	superdelicate	supergoodness	supermodest	supersensitive
superagitation	superdemand	supergovernment	supermoisten	supersensitiveness
superambitious	superdemonic	supergratification	supermorose	supersensuousness
superangelic	superdesirous	supergravitation	supermundane	supersentimental
superappreciation	superdevelopment	superhandsome	supermystery	superserious
superarbitrary	superdevilish	superhearty	supernecessity	superservere
superarduous	superdevotion	superhero	supernegligent	supersignificant
superarrogant	superdiabolical	superheroic	supernotable	supersimplify
superaspiration	superdifficult	superhistorical	supernumerous	supersmart
superastonish	superdiplomacy	superhypocrite	superobedience	supersolemn
superattachment	superdistribution	superideal	superobese	supersolemnly
superattraction	superdividend	superignorant	superobjectionable	supersolicitation
superattractive	superdonation	superillustrate	superobligation	superspecialize
superbelief	supereconomy	superimpending	superobstinate	superspiritual
superbeloved	supereffective	superimpersonal	superoffensive	superspirituality
superbenefit	supereffluence	superimportant	superofficious	superstimulation
superbenevolent	superelastic	superimprobable	superofficiousness	superstoical
superbenign	superelated	superimproved	superopposition	superstrain
superbias	superelegance	superincentive	superoratorical	superstrenuous
superblessed	supereligible	superinclination	superordinary	superstrict
superblunder	supereloquent	superinclusive	superorganize	superstrong
superbold	superemphasis	superinconsistent	superornamental	superstylish
superbrave	superendorsement	superindependent	superoutput	supersufficient
superbusy	superendow	superindifference	superpatient	supersurprise
supercandid	superenforcement	superindignant	superpatriotic	supersweet
supercapable	superenrollment	superindividualism	superpatriotism	supertension
supercatastrophe	superestablishment	superindividualist	superperfection	superthankful
supercatholic	superesthetic	superindulgence	superpious	superthorough
supercaution	superethical	superindustrious	superplease	supertoleration
superceremonious	superevident	superinference	superpolite	supertragic
superchivalrous	superexacting	superinfinite	superpositive	supertrivial
supercivil	superexalt	superinfirmity	superpraise	superugly
supercivilized	superexaltation	superinfluence	superprecise	superunity
superclassified	superexcellence	superingenious	superpreparation	superurgent
supercolossal	superexcellent	superinitiative	superpressure	supervexation
supercombination	superexcitation	superinjustice	superproduce	supervigilant
supercommendation	superexcited	superinquisitive	superprosperous	supervigorous
supercommercial	superexcitement	superinsistent	superpublicity	supervirulent
supercompetition	superexiguity	superintellectual	superpurge	supervital
supercomplex	superexpansion	superintolerable	superpurgation	supervolume
supercomprehension	superexpectation	superjurisdiction	superradical	superwise
supercompression	superexpenditure	superjustification	superrational	superworldly
superconfident	superexpressive	superknowledge	superrefined	superwrought
superconformist	superexquisiteness	superlaborious	superreform	superzealous

super. **1.** Superfine. **2.** Superintendent. **3.** Superior. **4.** Supernumerary.

su·per·a·ble (soo/pər·ə·bəl) *adj.* That can be surmounted, overcome, or conquered. [< L *superabilis* < *superare* to overcome < *super* over]

su·per·a·bound (soo/pər·ə·bound/) *v.i.* To abound to excess or to an unusual extent. [< LL *superabundare* < L *super-* exceedingly + *abundare* to overflow]

su·per·a·bun·dant (soo/pər·ə·bun/dənt) *adj.* More than sufficient; excessive. [< LL *superabundans, -antis,* ppr. of *superabundare.* See SUPERABOUND.] — **su/per·a·bun/·dance** *n.* — **su/per·a·bun/dant·ly** *adv.*

su·per·add (soo/pər·ad/) *v.t.* To add in addition to something already added; add further. [< LL *superaddere* < *super-* over and above + *addere.* See ADD.] — **su/per·ad·di/·tion** (-ə·dish/ən) *n.*

su·per·an·nu·ate (soo/pər·an/yoo·āt) *v.t.* **·at·ed, ·at·ing** **1.** To permit to retire on a pension on account of age or infirmity. **2.** To set aside or discard as obsolete or too old. [< Med.L *superannuatus* more than a year old (said of cattle) < L *super annum* < *super* beyond + *annus* year]

su·per·an·nu·at·ed (soo/pər·an/yoo·ā/tid) *adj.* **1.** Retired on account of age, especially with a pension. **2.** Too old to be useful or efficient. **3.** Obsolete; outdated.

su·perb (soo·pûrb/, sə-) *adj.* **1.** Having grand, impressive beauty; majestic; imposing: a *superb* edifice. **2.** Luxurious; rich and costly; elegant. **3.** Very good; supremely fine. [< L *superbus* proud < *super-* over] — **su·perb/ly** *adv.* — **su·perb/ness** *n.*

su·per·bomb (soo/pər·bom/) *n.* An awesomely powerful bomb; especially the hydrogen bomb.

su·per·cal·en·der (soo/pər·kal/ən·dər) *n.* A calender having a number of polished rollers for giving a high finish to paper. See CALENDER[1]. — *v.t.* To give a high finish to (paper). — **su/per·cal/en·dered** *adj.*

su·per·car·go (soo/pər·kär/gō) *n. pl.* **·goes** or **·gos** An agent on board ship in charge of the cargo and its sale and purchase. [Alter. of obs. *supracargo* < Sp. *sobrecargo* < *sobre-* over (< L *super-*) + *cargo.* See CARGO.]

su·per·car·ri·er (soo/pər·kar/ē·ər) *n.* An aircraft carrier of exceptional size.

su·per·charge (*v.* soo/pər·chärj/; *n.* soo/pər·chärj/) *v.t.* **·charged, ·charg·ing** **1.** To adapt (an engine) to develop more power by fitting with a supercharger. **2.** To charge to excess; overload. — *n.* **1.** An excess charge. **2.** *Heraldry* One charge or device borne on another.

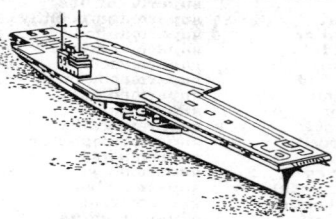

SUPERCARRIER

su·per·charg·er (soo/pər·chär/jər) *n. Mech.* A compressor for supplying air or combustible mixture to an internal-combustion engine at a pressure greater than that developed by the suction of the pistons alone.

su·per·cil·i·ar·y (soo/pər·sil/ē·er/ē) *adj.* **1.** Of or pertaining to the eyebrow. **2.** Situated over the eyebrow; supraorbital. [< NL *superciliaris* < L *supercilium* eyebrow < *super-* above + *cilium* eyelid]

su·per·cil·i·ous (soo/pər·sil/ē·əs) *adj.* Exhibiting haughty contempt or indifference; arrogant. — **Syn.** See ARROGANT. [< L *superciliosus* < *supercilium.* See SUPERCILIARY.] —**su/per·cil/i·ous·ly** *adv.* — **su/per·cil/i·ous·ness** *n.*

su·per·class (soo/pər·klas/, -kläs/) *n. Biol.* A division of plants or animals below a phylum but above a class.

su·per·co·lum·nar (soo/pər·kə·lum/nər) *adj. Archit.* **1.** Erected above a colonnade or another column. **2.** Having one order placed above another.

su·per·con·duc·tiv·i·ty (soo/pər·kon/duk·tiv/ə·tē) *n. Physics.* The property, exhibited by certain metals and alloys, of becoming almost perfect conductors of electricity at temperatures close to absolute zero. — **su/per·con·duc/tive** (-kən·duk/tiv) *adj.* — **su/per·con·duc/tor** *n.*

su·per·cool (soo/pər·kool/) *v.t.* To cool, as a liquid, below the freezing point without solidification. — *v.i.* To become supercooled.

su·per·dom·i·nant (soo/pər·dom/ə·nənt) *n. Music* The tone just above the dominant; the sixth or submediant.

su·per·du·per (soo/pər·doo/pər) *Slang adj.* Superlative; great. — *n.* Anything especially fine. [Reduplication of SUPER[3]]

su·per·e·go (soo/pər·ē/gō, -eg/ō) *n. Psychoanal.* The part of the psyche that acts to secure the conformity of the ego to parental, social, and moral standards.

su·per·em·i·nent (soo/pər·em/ə·nənt) *adj.* Excelling or surpassing others; of a superior or remarkable quality. [< L *supereminens, -entis,* ppr. of *supereminere* to rise above < *super-* above + *eminere* to rise. See EMINENT.] — **su/per·em/i·nence** *n.* — **su/per·em/i·nent·ly** *adv.*

su·per·e·ro·gate (soo/pər·er/ə·gāt) *v.i.* **·gat·ed, ·gat·ing**

To do more than is required or ordered. [< L *supererogatus,* pp. of *supererogare* < *super-* over and above + *erogare* to pay out < *ex-* out + *rogare* to ask]

su·per·er·o·ga·tion (soo/pər·er/ə·gā/shən) *n.* The performance of an act in excess of the demands or requirements of duty. — **works of supererogation** In the Roman Catholic Church, good deeds done by saints in excess of the requirements of divine law; also, voluntary good deeds performed by men over and above God's commandments.

su·per·e·rog·a·to·ry (soo/pər·ə·rog/ə·tôr/ē, -tō/rē) *adj.* **1.** Of, pertaining to, or of the nature of supererogation. **2.** Superfluous; extraneous. Also **su/per·e·rog/a·tive.**

su·per·fam·i·ly (soo/pər·fam/ə·lē, -fam/lē) *n. pl.* **·lies** *Biol.* A division of plants or animals ranking next above the family.

su·per·fe·cun·da·tion (soo/pər·fē/kən·dā/shən, -fek/ən-) *n. Physiol.* The impregnation of two ova within the same menstrual cycle by successive acts of coition.

su·per·fec·ta (soo/pər·fek/tə) *n.* In horse racing, a single bet won by choosing in correct order the first four horses in a specified race.

su·per·fe·male (soo/pər·fē/māl) *n. Genetics* A supersexual organism, characterized in the fruit fly by a ratio of 3 X-chromosomes to 2 sets of autosomes.

su·per·fe·tate (soo/pər·fē/tāt) *v.i.* **·tat·ed, ·tat·ing** *Physiol.* To conceive again prior to the birth of a fetus already conceived. [< L *superfetatus,* pp. of *superfetare* < *super-* over and above + *fetus* foetus]

su·per·fe·ta·tion (soo/pər·fi·tā/shən) *n. Physiol.* **1.** The second impregnation of a female already pregnant. **2.** The progeny from such impregnation. Also **su/per·foe·ta/tion.**

su·per·fi·cial (soo/pər·fish/əl) *adj.* **1.** Of, pertaining to, lying near, or forming the surface; affecting only the surface. **2.** Of or pertaining to only the ordinary and the obvious; not profound; shallow: a *superficial* writer. **3.** Marked by partial knowledge; cursory; hasty; slight: a *superficial* analysis. **4.** Not real or genuine: a *superficial* likeness. **5.** Square: said of measure. [< LL *superficialis* < L *superficies.* See SUPERFICIES.] — **su/per·fi/ci·al·i·ty** (-fish/ē·al/ə·tē), **su/per·fi/cial·ness** *n.* — **su/per·fi/cial·ly** *adv.*

su·per·fi·ci·ar·y (soo/pər·fish/ē·er/ē) *adj.* **1.** Belonging or pertaining to the superficies; superficial. **2.** *Law* Situated on another's land, or resulting from such situation.

su·per·fi·ci·es (soo/pər·fish/i·ēz, -fish/ēz) *n. pl.* **·ci·es** **1.** A surface or its area; superficial area. **2.** External appearance; exterior part. [< L *super-* over + *facies* face]

su·per·fine (soo/pər·fīn/) *adj.* **1.** Of surpassing fineness and delicacy; of the best quality. **2.** Overrefined; unduly elaborate; overnice. *Abbr.* **super.** [< MF *superfin* < *super-* over (< L) + *fin.* See FINE[1].] — **su/per·fine/ness** *n.*

su·per·flu·id (*n.* soo/pər·floo/id; *adj.* soo/pər·floo/id) *n. Physics* Matter, as helium, cooled to within a degree of absolute zero, and characterized by an exceptional heat conductivity, a ready permeation of very dense substances, and the ability to flow upward against gravity. — *adj.* Of or pertaining to such a state.

su·per·flu·i·ty (soo/pər·floo/ə·tē) *n. pl.* **·ties** **1.** The state of being superfluous. **2.** That, or that part, which is superfluous. **3.** Superabundance; plenty. [< OF *superfluite* < Med.L *superfluitas, -tatis* < L *superfluus* excessive < *super-* over + *fluere* to flow]

su·per·flu·ous (soo·pûr/floo·əs) *adj.* **1.** Exceeding what is needed; excessively abundant; surplus. **2.** Unnecessary; uncalled for; irrelevant: a *superfluous* question. **3.** *Music* Augmented: sometimes said of an interval. **4.** *Archaic* Supererogatory; officious. **5.** *Obs.* Overfed, overequipped, or oversupplied. [< L *superfluus.* See SUPERFLUITY.] — **su·per/flu·ous·ly** *adv.* — **su·per/flu·ous·ness** *n.*

su·per·fuse (soo/pər·fyooz/) *v.* **·fused, ·fus·ing** *v.t.* **1.** To pour so as to cover something else. — *v.i.* **2.** To be poured over or on something. [< L *superfusus,* pp. of *superfundere* < *super-* over + *fundere* to pour] — **su/per·fu/sion** (-fyoo/zhən) *n.*

su·per·gla·cial (soo/pər·glā/shəl) *adj. Geol.* Resting upon or deposited from the surface of a glacier.

su·per·heat (*v.* soo/pər·hēt/; *n.* soo/pər·hēt/) *v.t.* **1.** To heat to excess; overheat. **2.** To raise the temperature of (a gas or vapor not in contact with water) above the saturation point for a given pressure. **3.** To heat (a liquid) above the boiling point for a given pressure, but without conversion into vapor. — *n.* The degree to which steam has been superheated, or the heat so imparted.

su·per·heat·er (soo/pər·hē/tər) *n.* A mechanical contrivance for superheating steam.

su·per·het·er·o·dyne (soo/pər·het/ər·ə·dīn/) *adj. Electronics* Pertaining to or designating a type of radio reception using heterodyne circuits between stages of amplification. Also **su/per·het/.** — *n.* A superheterodyne receiver. [< SUPER(SONIC) + HETERODYNE]

su·per·high frequency (soo/pər·hī/) *Telecom.* A band of radio wave frequencies ranging from 3,000 to 30,000 megacycles per second. *Abbr.* **shf, s.h.f., SHF, S.H.F.**

su·per·high·way (soo/pər·hī/wā/) *n.* A highway for high-speed traffic, generally with four or more traffic lanes.

su·per·hu·man (soō'pər·hyoō'mən) *adj.* Above the range of human power or skill; miraculous or divine. **— Syn.** See SUPERNATURAL. **— su'per·hu·man'i·ty** (-hyoō·man'ə·tē) *n.* **— su'per·hu'man·ly** *adv.*

su·per·im·pose (soō'pər·im·pōz') *v.t.* **·posed, ·pos·ing** 1. To lay or impose upon something else. 2. To add to something else. **— su'per·im'po·si'tion** (-im'pə·zish'ən) *n.*

su·per·in·cum·bent (soō'pər·in·kum'bənt) *adj.* Resting or lying on or above something else. [< L *superincumbens, -entis,* ppr. of *superincumbere* < *super-* over + *incumbere* to rest on. See INCUMBENT.] **— su'per·in·cum'bence, su'per·in·cum'ben·cy** *n.*

su·per·in·duce (soō'pər·in·doōs', -dyoōs') *v.t.* **·duced, ·duc·ing** To introduce additionally; bring in or cause as an addition. [< LL *superinducere* to cover over, add < L *super-* over + *inducere.* See INDUCE.] **— su'per·in·duc'·tion** (-duk'shən) *n.*

su·per·in·tend (soō'pər·in·tend') *v.t.* To have the charge and direction of; manage; supervise. [< LL *superintendere* < *super-* over + *intendere* to aim at. See INTEND.]

su·per·in·ten·dence (soō'pər·in·ten'dəns) *n.* Direction and management; guiding and controlling supervision.

su·per·in·ten·den·cy (soō'pər·in·ten'dən·sē) *n. pl.* **·cies** 1. The office or rank of a superintendent. 2. Superintendence; guidance.

su·per·in·ten·dent (soō'pər·in·ten'dənt) *n.* 1. One whose function is to superintend some particular work, office, or undertaking: a school *superintendent.* 2. A person charged with supervising maintenance and repair in an office or apartment building. — *adj.* Of or pertaining to superintendence or a superintendent; superintending. Abbr. *super.,* *supt., Supt.* [< LL *superintendens, -entis,* ppr. of *superintendere* to superintend]

su·pe·ri·or (sə·pir'ē·ər, soō-) *adj.* 1. Surpassing in quantity, quality, or degree; more excellent; preferable. 2. Of great worth or excellence; extraordinary: a *superior* man. 3. Of higher grade, rank, or dignity. 4. Too great or dignified to be influenced; serenely unaffected or indifferent: with *to: superior* to envy. 5. Affecting superiority; supercilious; disdainful: a *superior* smile. 6. Locally higher; more elevated; upper. 7. *Bot.* Situated above or over another organ or part, as an ovary when free from the calyx. 8. *Printing* Set above the level of the line: In C⁴Dⁿ, 4 and n are *superior.* 9. *Logic* Of wider application; generic: said of terms and propositions. 10. *Astron.* a Revolving in an orbit beyond that of the earth: a *superior* planet. b Denoting the conjunction of such a planet with reference to the earth and the sun. — *n.* 1. One who surpasses another in rank or excellence. 2. The ruler of an ecclesiastical order or house, as an abbey, convent, or monastery. 3. *Printing* A superior letter or character. Abbr. *sup., super.* [< OF < L, compar. of *superus* on high, above < *super* above] **— su·pe·ri·or·i·ty** (sə·pir'ē·ôr'ə·tē, -or'-, soō-) *n.* **— su·pe'ri·or·ly** *adv.*

Su·pe·ri·or (sə·pir'ē·ər, soō-) A port city in NW Wisconsin, on Lake Superior; pop. 32,237.

Superior, Lake The largest of the Great Lakes in the United States and Canada; 31,820 sq. mi.

superior court In some States of the United States, a court between the inferior courts and those of last resort.

superiority complex An exaggerated sense of one's own importance and capacities. Compare INFERIORITY COMPLEX.

su·per·ja·cent (soō'pər·jā'sənt) *adj.* Lying or resting immediately upon or above something else; overlying. [< LL *superjacens, -entis,* ppr. of *superjacere* < *super-* above + *jacere* to lie]

superl. Superlative.

su·per·la·tive (sə·pûr'lə·tiv, soō-) *adj.* 1. Elevated to the highest degree; of supreme excellence or eminence; consummate. 2. *Gram.* Expressing or involving the extreme degree: said of a form of comparison of adjectives or adverbs: The *superlative* degree of "wise" is "wisest." — See COMPARISON (def. 3). 3. Excessive. — *n.* 1. That which is of the highest possible excellence or superior to all others. 2. *Gram.* a The highest degree of comparison of the adjective or adverb. b Any word or phrase in the superlative degree. Abbr. *sup., superl.* [< OF *superlatif* < LL *superlativus* < L *superlatif* excessive < *super-* above + *latus,* pp. of *ferre* to carry] **— su·per·la·tive·ly** *adv.* **— su·per'·la·tive·ness** *n.*

su·per·lu·nar (soō'pər·loō'nər) *adj.* Being above or beyond the moon; celestial. Also **su'per·lu'na·ry.**

su·per·male (soō'pər·māl') *n. Genetics* A sterile male having a ratio of 1 X-chromosome to 3 or more sets of autosomes.

su·per·man (soō'pər·man') *n. pl.* **·men** (-men') 1. A hypothetical superior being, characterized by perfection of physique, capacity for power, and a moral nature beyond good and evil; the *Übermensch* of Nietzsche: also called *overman.* 2. A man possessing superhuman powers. [Trans. of G *übermensch*]

su·per·mar·ket (soō'pər·mär'kit) *n.* A large store selling food and household supplies and operating on a self-service, cash-and-carry basis. Also **super market.**

su·per·nal (soō·pûr'nəl) *adj.* 1. Heavenly; celestial. 2. Placed or located above; lofty; overhead; towering. 3. Coming from above or from the sky. [< OF < L *supernus* < *super* over] **— su·per'nal·ly** *adv.*

su·per·na·tant (soō'pər·nā'tənt) *adj.* 1. Floating uppermost, above something, or on the surface. 2. *Chem.* Denoting a liquid from which a precipitate has been thrown down. [< L *supernatans, -antis* < *super-* above + *natare* to swim] **— su'per·na·ta'tion** (-nā·tā'shən) *n.*

su·per·na·tion·al (soō'pər·nash'ən·əl) *adj.* Pertaining to all mankind, rather than to one nation only. **— su'per·na'tion·al·ism** *n.* **— su'per·na'tion·al·ist** *n.*

su·per·nat·u·ral (soō'pər·nach'ər·əl) *adj.* 1. Existing or occurring through some agency beyond the known forces of nature; lying outside the natural order: distinguished from *preternatural.* 2. Believed to be miraculous or caused by the immediate exercise of divine power. 3. Pertaining to the miraculous. — *n.* 1. That which is supernatural. 2. The action or intervention of something supernatural: with *the.* [< Med.L *supernaturalis* < L *super-* above + *natura.* See NATURE.] **— su'per·nat'u·ral·ly** *adv.* **— su·per·nat'u·ral·ness** *n.*

— Syn. (adj.) 1. *Supernatural, preternatural, superhuman,* and *miraculous* are compared as they mean outside of ordinary experience. A *supernatural* event is literally not bound or explainable by known natural laws: a *supernatural* vision, a *supernatural* being. *Preternatural* refers to that which is superlative in degree, but not outside the known realm of nature: to display *preternatural* insight into a situation. *Superhuman* characterizes that which is above human power or experience, though it is often used merely as an intensive: to display *superhuman* strength. Anything *miraculous* is so marvellous or extraordinary that it is usually attributed to divine agency: a *miraculous* recovery from an ordinarily fatal disease.

su·per·nat·u·ral·ism (soō'pər·nach'ər·əl·iz'əm) *n.* 1. The quality of being supernatural. 2. Belief in the doctrine that a supernatural power guides the natural order. **— su'per·nat'u·ral·ist** *adj.* & *n.* **— su'per·nat'u·ral·is'tic** *adj.*

su·per·nor·mal (soō'pər·nôr'məl) *adj. Psychol.* Above the normal in characteristics, properties, or intelligence.

su·per·no·va (soō'pər·nō'və) *n. pl.* **·vae** (-vē) or **·vas** *Astron.* A rare nova that involves the flaring up of most of its stellar material, resulting in its brightness being increased by 10 million to 100 million times.

su·per·nu·mer·ar·y (soō'pər·noō'mə·rer'ē, -nyoō'-) *adj.* 1. Being beyond a fixed or standard number. 2. Beyond a customary or necessary number; superfluous. — *n. pl.* **·ar·ies** 1. A person or thing in excess of the regular, necessary, or customary number. 2. A stage performer, as in mob scenes or processions, without any speaking part: also called *supe, super.* Abbr. *super.* [< LL *supernumerarius* a soldier added to a legion after it is complete < L *super numerum* < *super* over + *numerus* number]

su·per·or·der (soō'pər·ôr'dər) *n. Biol.* A plant or animal division intermediate between a class and an order.

su·per·or·gan·ic (soō'pər·ôr·gan'ik) *adj.* Not affected by the structure or characteristics of the organic.

su·per·phos·phate (soō'pər·fos'fāt) *n. Chem.* 1. An acid phosphate. 2. Any fertilizing material consisting mainly of soluble phosphates.

su·per·phys·i·cal (soō'pər·fiz'i·kəl) *adj.* Beyond or above the physical.

su·per·pose (soō'pər·pōz') *v.t.* **·posed, ·pos·ing** 1. To lay over or upon something else, as one layer upon another. 2. *Geom.* To suppose (one figure) to be placed upon another so that all like parts coincide. 3. *Physics* To combine additively, as forces or wave amplitudes. [< F *superposer* < *super-* over + *poser.* See POSE¹.] **— su'per·pos'a·ble** *adj.* **— su'per·po·si'tion** (-pə·zish'ən) *n.*

su·per·pow·er (soō'pər·pou'ər) *n.* 1. A theoretical entity conceived as having political power over other very powerful states or countries. 2. The United States or the Soviet Union, possessors of decisive numbers of nuclear weapons. 3. The combined sources of electric power in a given area, operating as a connected system.

su·per·sat·u·rate (soō'pər·sach'oō·rāt) *v.t.* **·rat·ed, ·rat·ing** To saturate (a solution) beyond the point normal under given conditions. **— su'per·sat'u·ra'tion** *n.*

su·per·scribe (soō'pər·skrīb') *v.t.* **·scribed, ·scrib·ing** 1. To write or engrave on the outside or upper part of. 2. To inscribe with a name or address, as a letter. [< LL *superscribere* < L *super-* over + *scribere* to write]

su·per·script (soō'pər·skript') *adj.* Written above or overhead. — *n.* 1. A superscript character. 2. *Math.* A character written above and to the right or left of a term to indicate a specific operation or characteristic of the term, as a power or derivative. Compare SUBSCRIPT. [< LL *superscriptus,* pp. of *superscribere.* See SUPERSCRIBE.]

su·per·scrip·tion (soō'pər·skrip'shən) *n.* 1. The act of superscribing an address on a letter. 2. An upper or outer inscription, as a title or a direction; especially, an address on a letter. **3.** The portion of a medical prescription that begins with the word *recipe* (generally abbreviated ℞, and meaning "take"). [< OF < LL *superscriptio, -onis* < *superscribere.* See SUPERSCRIBE.]

su·per·sede (sōō/pər·sēd/) *v.t.* **·sed·ed, ·sed·ing 1.** To take the place of, as by reason of superior worth, right, or appropriateness; replace; supplant. **2.** To put something in the place of; set aside; suspend; annul. [< OF *superceder* < L *supersedere* < *super-* above, over + *sedere* to sit] — **su/per·sed/er** *n.* — **su/per·se/dure** (-sē/jər), **su/per·ses/sion** (-sesh/ən) *n.*

su·per·se·de·as (sōō/pər·sē/dē·əs) *n. Law* A proceeding, as a writ, that operates to supersede or check proceedings. [< L, you shall desist]

su·per·sen·si·ble (sōō/pər·sen/sə·bəl) *adj.* Being above or beyond the range of the senses; supersensual; psychical. — **su/per·sen/si·bly** *adv.*

su·per·sen·su·al (sōō/pər·sen/shōō·əl) *adj.* **1.** Being above the senses; supersensible. **2.** Spiritual; ideal. Also **su/per·sen/so·ry** (-sen/sər·ē).

su·per·ser·vice·a·ble (sōō/pər·sûr/vis·ə·bəl) *adj.* Trying needlessly or disagreeably to be of service; officious. — **su/per·ser/vice·a·bly** *adv.*

su·per·sex (sōō/pər·seks/) *n. Genetics* A sterile organism having a mixture of male and female characteristics due to a disturbed ratio of autosomes to X-chromosomes, as in the fruit fly. — **su/per·sex/u·al** (-sek/shōō·əl) *adj.*

su·per·son·ic (sōō/pər·son/ik) *adj. Aeron.* Of, pertaining to, or characterized by a speed greater than that of sound: distinguished from *ultrasonic.*

su·per·son·ics (sōō/pər·son/iks) *n.pl.* (*construed as sing.*) The science that treats of the phenomena of supersonic speed, with special reference to their practical applications: distinguished from *ultrasonics.*

su·per·state (sōō/pər·stāt/) *n.* A state established as the governing power of a union of subordinate states.

su·per·sti·tion (sōō/pər·stish/ən) *n.* **1.** A belief founded on irrational feelings, especially of fear, and marked by a trust in or reverence for charms, omens, signs, the supernatural, etc.; also, any rite or practice inspired by such belief. **2.** Any unreasonable belief or impression. **3.** *Obs.* Undue scrupulousness. [< OF < L *superstitio, -onis* excessive fear of the gods, amazement, dread < *superstare* < *super-* over + *stare* to stand still]

su·per·sti·tious (sōō/pər·stish/əs) *adj.* **1.** Disposed to believe in or be influenced by superstitions. **2.** Of, pertaining to, or manifesting superstition. — **su/per·sti/tious·ly** *adv.* — **su/per·sti/tious·ness** *n.*

su·per·stra·tum (sōō/pər·strā/təm, -strat/əm) *n.* *pl.* **·stra·ta** (-strā/tə, -strat/ə) A layer superimposed upon or overlying another.

su·per·struct (sōō/pər·strukt/) *v.t.* To build or erect upon a foundation; build over or on something else. [< L *superstructus,* pp. of *superstruere* < *super-* over + *struere* to build] — **su/per·struc/tion** *n.*

su·per·struc·ture (sōō/pər·struk/chər) *n.* **1.** Any structure or part of a structure considered in relation to its foundation. **2.** The sleepers, rails, etc., of a railway, as distinguished from the roadbed. **3.** *Naut.* The parts of a ship's structure, as of a warship, above the main deck.

su·per·sub·tle (sōō/pər·sut/l) *adj.* Extremely subtle; oversubtle.

su·per·tax (sōō/pər·taks/) *n.* An extra tax in addition to the normal tax; especially, a graded additional tax on incomes above certain amounts; a surtax.

su·per·ton·ic (sōō/pər·ton/ik) *n. Music* The tone above the tonic or keynote; the second.

su·per·vene (sōō/pər·vēn/) *v.i.* **·vened, ·ven·ing 1.** To follow closely upon something; come as something extraneous or additional. **2.** To take place; happen. [< L *supervenire* < *super-* over and above + *venire* to come] — **su/per·ven/ient** (-vēn/yənt) *adj.* — **su/per·ven/tion** (-ven/shən) *n.*

su·per·vise (sōō/pər·vīz/) *v.t.* **·vised, vis·ing** To have charge of directing (employees, an operation, etc.); superintend; oversee. [< Med.L *supervisus,* pp. of *supervidere* < L *super-* over + *videre* to see]

su·per·vi·sion (sōō/pər·vizh/ən) *n.* **1.** The act of supervising; superintendence. **2.** The authority to supervise.

su·per·vi·sor (sōō/pər·vī/zər) *n.* **1.** One who supervises or oversees; superintendent; inspector. **2.** *U.S.* **a** A township officer; especially, one of a board of such officers having charge of the business of a county. **b** A borough officer who has charge of road repairs, etc. **3.** A person supervising teachers of special subjects in a school. **4.** *Obs.* A beholder. — **su/per·vi/sor·ship** *n.*

su·per·vi·so·ry (sōō/pər·vī/zər·ē) *adj.* **1.** Of or pertaining to a supervisor or supervision. **2.** Involving or limited to supervision: a *supervisory* position.

su·pi·nate (sōō/pə·nāt) *v.t. & v.i.* **·nat·ed, ·nat·ing 1.** To make or become supine. **2.** To turn, as the hand or forelimb, so that the palm is upward or forward. [< L *supinatus,* pp. of *supinare* to throw (someone) on the back < *supinus.* See SUPINE[1].]

su·pi·na·tion (sōō/pə·nā/shən) *n. Physiol.* **1.** The act of turning the palm of the hand, or the corresponding surface of the forelimb, upward. **2.** The position of a limb so turned: opposed to *pronation.*

su·pi·na·tor (sōō/pə·nā/tər) *n. Anat.* A muscle of the forearm by which supination is effected.

su·pine[1] (sōō·pīn/) *adj.* **1.** Lying on the back, or with the face turned upward. **2.** Having no interest or care; inactive; indolent; listless. **3.** Having an inclined position; sloping, as a hill. [< L *supinus.*] — **su·pine/ly** *adv.* — **su·pine/ness** *n.*

su·pine[2] (sōō/pīn) *n.* In Latin grammar, a part of the verb appearing only in the accusative or ablative form, and generally regarded as a verbal noun, as in *Mirabile dictu!* Wonderful to relate! Abbr. *sup.* [< L *supinum (verbum)* (a) supine (word), neut. of *supinus.* See SUPINE[1].]

supp. or **suppl.** Supplement; supplementary.

sup·per (sup/ər) *n.* **1.** The last meal of the day; the evening meal. **2.** An evening banquet. [< OF *soper, super* to sup]

sup·plant (sə·plant/, -plänt/) *v.t.* **1.** To take the place of; displace. **2.** To take the place of (someone) by scheming, treachery, etc. **3.** To replace (one thing) with another; remove; uproot. [< OF *supplanter* < L *supplantare* to trip up < *sub-* up from below + *planta* the sole of the foot] — **sup·plan·ta·tion** (sup/lan·tā/shən) *n.* — **sup·plant/er** *n.*

sup·ple (sup/əl) *adj.* **sup·pler** (sup/lər), **sup·plest** (sup/ləst) **1.** Easily bent; flexible; pliant: a *supple* bow. **2.** Yielding to the humor or wishes of others; especially, servilely compliant; obsequious. **3.** Showing adaptability of mind; elastic; easily changing. — *v.t. & v.i.* **·pled, ·pling** To make or become supple. [< OF *supple, sople* < L *supplex, -icis* submissive, lit., bending under < *sub-* under + stem of *plicare* to fold] — **sup/ple·ly** *adv.* — **sup/ple·ness** *n.*

sup·ple·jack (sup/əl·jak) *n.* **1.** Any of various woody climbers with tough and lithe stems; especially, a high-climbing vine (*Berchemia scandens*) of the southern United States. **2.** A walking stick made from the wood of such a plant.

sup·ple·ment (*v.* sup/lə·ment; *n.* sup/lə·mənt) *v.t.* To make additions to; provide for what is lacking in. — *n.* **1.** Something that supplements; especially, an addition to a publication. **2.** A supplementary angle (which see). Abbr. *sup., supp., suppl.* — **Syn.** See APPENDAGE. [< L *supplementum* < *supplere.* See SUPPLY[1].]

sup·ple·men·tal (sup/lə·men/təl) *adj.* Like a supplement; additional. Also **sup·ple·to·ry** (sup/lə·tôr/ē, -tō/rē).

sup·ple·men·ta·ry (sup/lə·men/tər·ē) *adj.* Functioning as a supplement; supplemental. Abbr. *sup., supp., suppl.*

supplementary angle *Geom.* Either of two angles whose sum is 180°: also called *supplement.*

sup·pli·ance (sup/lē·əns) *n.* **1.** The act of supplicating. **2.** An urgent petition or prayer.

sup·pli·ant (sup/lē·ənt) *adj.* **1.** Entreating earnestly and humbly; beseeching. **2.** Manifesting entreaty or submissive supplication. — *n.* One who supplicates. [< MF, ppr. of *supplier* < L *supplicare.* See SUPPLICATE.] — **sup/pli·ant·ly** *adv.* — **sup/pli·ant·ness** *n.*

sup·pli·cant (sup/lə·kənt) *n.* One who supplicates; a suppliant. — *adj.* Asking or entreating humbly; beseeching. [< L *supplicans, -antis,* ppr. of *supplicare.* See SUPPLICATE.]

sup·pli·cate (sup/lə·kāt) *v.* **·cat·ed, ·cat·ing** *v.t.* **1.** To ask for humbly or by earnest prayer. **2.** To beg something of; entreat. — *v.i.* **3.** To beg or pray humbly; make an earnest request. — **Syn.** See ENTREAT. [< L *supplicatus,* pp. of *supplicare* to supplicate < *sub-* under + *plicare* to bend, fold] — **sup/pli·ca·to·ry** (-kə·tôr/ē, -tō/rē) *adj.*

sup·pli·ca·tion (sup/lə·kā/shən) *n.* **1.** The act of supplicating. **2.** An earnest prayer or entreaty.

sup·pli·er (sə·plī/ər) *n.* One that supplies.

sup·ply[1] (sə·plī/) *v.* **·plied, ·ply·ing** *v.t.* **1.** To give or furnish (something needful or desirable): to *supply* milk for a city. **2.** To furnish with what is needed: to *supply* an army with ammunition. **3.** To provide for adequately; satisfy: to *supply* a demand. **4.** To make good or compensate for, as a loss or deficiency; make up for. **5.** To fill (the place of another); also, to fill (an office, etc.) or occupy (a pulpit) as a substitute. — *v.i.* **6.** To take the place of another temporarily. — *n.* *pl.* **·plies 1.** That which is or can be supplied. **2.** An amount sufficient for a given use; store or quantity on hand. **3.** *Usually pl.* Accumulated stores reserved for distribution, as for an army or a fleet. **4.** *Econ.* The amount of a commodity offered at a given price or available for meeting a demand. **5.** A substitute or temporary incumbent. **6.** The act of supplying. **7.** *Obs.* Reinforcements for an army or navy. Abbr. *sup.* [< OF *sopleer, soupleier* < L *supplere* < *sub-* up from under + *ple-,* root of *plenus* full]

sup·ply[2] (sup/lē) *adv.* In a supple manner; supplely. [< SUPPLE]

sup·port (sə·pôrt/, -pōrt/) *v.t.* **1.** To bear the weight of,

SUPPLEJACK
a Flower.
b Fruit.

especially from underneath. **2.** To hold in position; keep from falling, sinking, etc. **3.** To bear or sustain (weight, etc.). **4.** To keep (a person, the mind, etc.) from failing or declining; strengthen. **5.** To serve to uphold or corroborate (a statement, theory, etc.); substantiate; verify. **6.** To provide (a person, institution, etc.) with maintenance; provide for. **7.** To give approval or assistance to; uphold; advocate; aid. **8.** To endure or tolerate: I cannot *support* his insolence. **9.** To carry on; keep up; maintain: to *support* a war. **10.** In the theater: **a** To act (a role or part). **b** To act in a subordinate role to. — *n.* **1.** The act of supporting, or the state of being supported. **2.** One who or that which supports. **3.** Subsistence. [< OF *supporter* < L *supportare* to convey < *sub-* up from under + *portare* to carry]

sup·port·a·ble (sə·pôr′tə·bəl, -pōr′-) *adj.* Capable of being supported or endured; bearable; endurable. — **sup·port′· a·ble·ness, sup·port′a·bil′i·ty** *n.* — **sup·port′a·bly** *adv.*

sup·port·er (sə·pôr′tər, -pōr′-) *n.* **1.** One who or that which supports. **2.** One who countenances or supports; an adherent. **3.** *Heraldry* One of a pair representing living objects, standing on the dexter and sinister sides of a shield, as if supporting it. **4.** An elastic or other support for some part of the body. — **Syn.** See ADHERENT.

sup·por·tive (sə·pôr′tiv, -pōr′-) *adj.* Serving to support; providing support.

supportive therapy **1.** *Psychol.* A type of psychotherapy in which the patient receives more or less direct help with his problems and is given advice and encouragement. **2.** *Med.* Therapy for relieving the symptoms of a disturbed condition or disease and for strengthening the patient, as the administration of glucose, blood plasma, etc.: also **supportive care, supportive treatment.**

sup·pos·a·ble (sə·pō′zə·bəl) *adj.* Capable of being supposed or conjectured. — **sup·pos′a·bly** *adv.*

sup·pose (sə·pōz′) *v.* **·posed, ·pos·ing** *v.t.* **1.** To think or imagine to oneself as true. **2.** To believe or believe probable; think; presume. **3.** To assume as true for the sake of argument or illustration: *Suppose* he comes late. **4.** To expect or require: used in the passive: He is *supposed* to be on time. **5.** To imply as cause or consequence; involve as an inference; presuppose. — *v.i.* **6.** To make a supposition; conjecture. [< OF *supposer* < *sup-* under (< L *sub-*) + *poser.* See POSE¹.] — **sup·pos′er** *n.*

— **Syn. 1.** *Suppose, conjecture, surmise,* and *guess* mean to assume as true in the absence of direct knowledge. We *suppose* something to be true in expectation of finding that it is true, or in order to ascertain what follows if it is not true. We *conjecture* or *surmise* when the evidence is admittedly insufficient for certainty: *surmise* suggests slighter grounds for a conclusion than *conjecture.* Also, *conjecture* suggests that the question is one of fact, while *surmise* may refer to questions of interpretation or evaluation: it is *conjectured* that the allies have disagreed on policy, and *surmised* that their joint communiqué is so worded as to conceal this fact. To *guess* is to make a random assumption, with little or no demonstrable basis: to *guess* the number of peas in a jar. — **Ant.** know, ascertain, discover, demonstrate, prove.

sup·posed (sə·pōzd′, -pō′zid) *adj.* Accepted as genuine or true, often erroneously. — **sup·pos·ed·ly** (sə·pō′zid·lē) *adv.*

sup·po·si·tion (sup′ə·zish′ən) *n.* **1.** The act of supposing; conjecture. **2.** That which is supposed or conjectured; hypothesis. — **Syn.** See HYPOTHESIS. [< Med.L *suppositio, -onis* < L, a substitute < *suppositus,* pp. of *supponere* to suppose, substitute < *sub-* under + *ponere* to place] — **sup′po·si′tion·al** *adj.* — **sup′po·si′tion·al·ly** *adv.*

sup·pos·i·ti·tious (sə·poz′ə·tish′əs) *adj.* **1.** Substituted in order to deceive or defraud; spurious. **2.** Supposed or assumed; hypothetical. [< L *suppositus.* See SUPPOSITION.] — **sup·pos′i·ti′tious·ly** *adv.* — **sup·pos′i·ti′tious·ness** *n.*

sup·pos·i·tive (sə·poz′ə·tiv) *adj.* Of the nature of, including, or implying a supposition. — *n. Gram.* A conjunction introducing a supposition, as *if* or *provided.* — **sup·pos′i·tive·ly** *adv.*

sup·pos·i·to·ry (sə·poz′ə·tôr′ē, -tō′rē) *n. pl.* **·ries** *Med.* A solid, readily fusible, medicated preparation for introduction into the rectum, vagina, or urethra. [< LL *suppositorium,* orig. neut. sing. of *suppositorius* placed underneath or up < L *suppositus.* See SUPPOSITION.]

sup·press (sə·pres′) *v.t.* **1.** To put an end or stop to; quell; crush, as a rebellion. **2.** To stop or prohibit the activities of; also, to abolish. **3.** To withhold from knowledge or publication, as a book, news, etc. **4.** To repress, as a groan or sigh. **5.** To check or stop (a hemorrhage, etc.). [< L *suppressus,* pp. of *supprimere* < *sub-* under + *premere* to press] — **sup· press′er** or **sup·pres′sor** *n.* — **sup·press′i·ble** *adj.*

sup·pres·sion (sə·presh′ən) *n.* **1.** The act of suppressing, or the state of being suppressed. **2.** *Psychoanal.* The deliberate exclusion from consciousness and action of an idea, emotion, or desire.

sup·pres·sive (sə·pres′iv) *adj.* Tending to suppress.

sup·pu·rate (sup′yə·rāt) *v.i.* **·rat·ed, ·rat·ing** To form or generate pus; maturate. [< L *suppuratus,* pp. of *suppurare* < *sub-* under + *pus, puris* pus]

sup·pu·ra·tion (sup′yə·rā′shən) *n.* **1.** The act or process of suppurating. **2.** Pus.

sup·pu·ra·tive (sup′yə·rā′tiv) *adj.* Causing or tending to cause suppuration. — *n.* Any drug promoting suppuration.

supr. Supreme.

supra- *prefix* Above; beyond: *supraliminal; suprarenal.* Compare INFRA-. [< L]

su·pra·lap·sar·i·an·ism (soo′prə·lap·sâr′ē·ən·iz·əm) *n. Theol.* The doctrine that before creating man God decreed the fall, and the subsequent salvation of some men and the damnation of others. See INFRALAPSARIANISM, SUBLAPSARIANISM. [< SUPRA- + L *lapsus,* pp. of *labi* to slip, fall + -ARIAN + -ISM] — **su′pra·lap·sar′i·an** *adj. & n.*

su·pra·lim·i·nal (soo′prə·lim′ə·nəl) *adj. Psychol.* Above the threshold of normal consciousness: opposed to *subliminal.*

su·pra·mo·lec·u·lar (soo′prə·mə·lek′yə·lər) *adj.* **1.** Containing more than one molecule. **2.** Of greater complexity than a molecule.

su·pra·na·tion·al (soo′prə·nash′ən·əl) *adj.* Not bound by the political limitations of a nation or nations: *supranational* cooperation.

su·pra·or·bi·tal (soo′prə·ôr′bi·təl) *adj. Anat.* Situated above the orbit of the eye. [< NL *supraorbitalis* < L *supra-* above + *orbita.* See ORBIT.]

su·pra·pro·test (soo′prə·prō′test) *n. Law* Acceptance or payment of a bill of exchange by one not a party to it after protest by the creditor for nonacceptance or nonpayment. Abbr. *s.p.* [< Ital. *sopra protesta* upon protest < *sopra* (< L *supra* above) + *protesta* < L *protestari.* See PROTEST.]

su·pra·re·nal (soo′prə·rē′nəl) *Anat. adj.* **1.** Situated above the kidneys. **2.** Of or pertaining to the suprarenal glands. — *n.* A suprarenal gland. [< NL *suprarenalis* < L *supra-* above + *renalis.* See RENAL.]

suprarenal gland *Anat.* An adrenal gland (which see).

su·pra·seg·men·tal (soo′prə·seg·men′təl) *adj. Ling.* Denoting a feature of spoken or written language that can occur simultaneously with one or more other contrastive features, as the phonemes of stress, pitch, and juncture, or the graphic devices of capitalization and italicization; prosodic: distinguished from *segmental.* — **su′pra·seg·men′tal·ly** *adv.*

su·prem·a·cy (sə·prem′ə·sē, soo-) *n. pl.* **·cies** **1.** The state or quality of being supreme. **2.** Supreme power or authority.

su·preme (sə·prēm′, soo-) *adj.* **1.** Highest in power or authority; dominant. **2.** Highest in degree, importance, quality, etc.; utmost: *supreme* devotion. **3.** Ultimate; last; final. — **Syn.** See ABSOLUTE. Abbr. *sup., supr.* [< L *supremus* highest, superl. of *superus* that is above < *super* above] — **su·preme′ly** *adv.* — **su·preme′ness** *n.*

Supreme Being God.

Supreme Court In the United States and in various States, a court of appellate jurisdiction and, in most cases, of last resort.

supreme sacrifice The sacrifice of one's life.

Supreme Soviet **1.** The highest legislative body of the Soviet Union, consisting of two chambers, the **Soviet of the Union,** elected on the basis of population, and the **Soviet of Nationalities,** elected by the national groups. **2.** The highest legislative body of any of the constituent or autonomous republics of the Soviet Union.

Supt. or **supt.** Superintendent.

sur-¹ *prefix* Above; beyond; over: *surcharge; surcoat.* [< OF *sur-* < L *super-.* See SUPER-.]

sur-² Assimilated var. of SUB-.

sur. **1.** Surcharged. **2.** Surplus.

Sur (soor, sür) A port city of SW Lebanon, on the Mediterranean; site of ancient Tyre; pop. about 12,000: also *Tyre.*

Sur. Surrey.

su·ra (soor′ə) *n.* A chapter or section of the Koran. [< Arabic *surah,* lit., a step, degree]

Su·ra·ba·ya (soo′rä·bä′yä) A port city on NE Java; pop. 989,734 (1961): Dutch *Soerabaja.* Also **Su′ra·ba′ja.**

su·rah (soor′ə) *n.* A soft, usually twilled fabric of silk or silk and rayon. Also **surah silk.** [after *Surat,* India]

Su·ra·jah Dow·lah (sə·rä′jə dou′lə), 1728?–57, nawab of Bengal; imprisoned British soldiers in the Black Hole of Calcutta; defeated by Robert Clive. Also *Siraj-ud-Daula.*

Su·ra·kar·ta (soor′ə·kär′tə) A city on central Java, Indonesia; pop. 363,167 (1961): also *Solo.*

su·ral (soor′əl) *adj. Anat.* Of or pertaining to the calf of the leg. [< NL *suralis* < L *sura* the calf of the leg]

Su·rat (soo·rat′, soor′ət) A port city in northern Gujarat, India; the first British settlement in India, 1612; pop. 288,-167 (1961).

sur·base (sûr′bās′) *n. Archit.* A molding or border above the base of a pedestal, baseboard, etc. [< SUR-¹ + BASE¹]

sur·based (sûr′bāst′) *adj. Archit.* **1.** Having a surbase, as a pedestal. **2.** Flattened; depressed. **3.** Designating an arch having the rise of the curve less than half the span.

sur·cease (sûr·sēs′, sûr′sēs) *Archaic n.* Absolute cessation; end. — *v.t. & v.i.* **·ceased, ·ceas·ing** To cease; end. [< AF *sursise* omission, orig. pp. of *surseoir* to refrain < L *super-sedere.* See SUPERSEDE.]

sur·charge (*n.* sûr′chärj′; *v.* sûr·chärj′) *n.* **1.** An excessive burden, load, or charge. **2.** *Law* The act of surcharging. **3.** An additional or excessive amount charged; overcharge; especially, an unlawful overcharge. **4.** A new valuation or something additional printed on a postage or revenue stamp; also, a stamp so imprinted. — *v.t.* **charged, charg·ing 1.** To charge (a person) too much; overcharge. **2.** *Law* To show an omission of credits in (an account), or of something for which credit should have been allowed. **3.** To overload. **4.** To fill to excess. **5.** To imprint a surcharge on (postage stamps). [< F < *surcharger* < *sur-* over + *charger* < OF *chargier.* See CHARGE.] — **sur·charg′er** *n.*

sur·cin·gle (sûr′sing·gəl) *n.* **1.** A girth or strap encircling the body of a horse, etc., as for holding a saddle. **2.** A girdle, as of a cassock. — *v.t.* **·gled, ·gling** To fasten with a surcingle. [< OF *surcengle* < *sur-* over + L *cingulum* belt]

sur·coat (sûr′kōt′) *n.* **1.** An outer coat or garment. **2.** In the Middle Ages, a loose robe or cloaklike garment worn over armor. [< OF *surcot* < *sur-* over + *cot, cote* coat]

sur·cu·lose (sûr′kyə·lōs) *adj. Bot.* Producing or having suckers: said of plants. [< L *surculosus* < *surculus* twig, sucker, dim. of *surus* twig]

surd (sûrd) *n.* **1.** *Math.* An irrational number, especially an indicated root that can only be approximated, as $\sqrt{2}$. **2.** *Phonet.* A voiceless speech sound. — *adj.* **1.** *Math.* Incapable of being expressed in rational numbers; irrational. **2.** *Phonet.* Voiceless. [< L *surdus* deaf, silent]

sure (shŏŏr) *adj.* **sur·er, sur·est 1.** Free from doubt; certain; positive. **2.** Certain of obtaining, attaining, or retaining something: with *of.* **3.** Not liable to change; firm; stable. **4.** Bound to happen; inevitable. **5.** Not liable to fail or err; infallible. **6.** Fit, proper, or deserving to be depended on; reliable; trustworthy. **7.** *Rare* Secure from danger or harm; safe. — **to be sure** Indeed; certainly. — **to make sure** To be certain; ascertain. — *adv. Informal* Surely; certainly. [< OF *sur* < L *securus.* Doublet of SECURE.] — **sure′ness** *n.*

sure-e·nough (shŏŏr′i·nuf′) *U.S. Informal adj.* Real; genuine. — *adv.* Really; surely.

sure-fire (shŏŏr′fīr′) *adj. Informal* Sure or certain to succeed, win, or meet expectations; unfailing.

sure-foot·ed (shŏŏr′fŏŏt′id) *adj.* **1.** Not liable to fall or stumble. **2.** Not liable to fail or err.

sure·ly (shŏŏr′lē) *adv.* **1.** Without doubt; certainly. **2.** Securely; safely.

sure·ty (shŏŏr′tē, shŏŏr′ə·tē) *n. pl.* **·ties 1.** One who agrees to be responsible for another; a sponsor; especially, one who engages to be responsible for the debt, default, or miscarriage of another. **2.** A pledge or guarantee to secure against loss, damage, default, etc.; security. **3.** That which gives or serves as a basis for security or confidence; a guarantee. **4.** The state of being sure; sureness; certainty. — *Syn.* See SECURITY. [< OF *surte* < L *securitas, -tatis* < *securus.* See SECURE.] — **sure′ty·ship** *n.*

surf (sûrf) *n.* The swell of the sea that breaks upon a shore; also, the foam caused by such a swell. — *v.i.* To ride the surf on a surfboard; engage in surfing. [Earlier *suff,* ? var. of SOUGH] — **surf′y** *adj.*

sur·face (sûr′fis) *n.* **1.** The exterior part or face of anything. **2.** A superficial aspect or view; outward appearance. **3.** That which has length and breadth, but not thickness. — *adj.* **1.** Of, pertaining to, or on a surface. **2.** Superficial; exterior; apparent. — *v.* **faced, fac·ing** *v.t.* **1.** To put a surface on; especially, to make smooth, even, or plain. — *v.i.* **2.** To mine at or near the surface. **3.** To rise to the surface, as a submarine. [< F < *sur-* above + *face.* See FACE.]

sur·face-ac·tive (sûr′fis·ak′tiv) *adj. Chem.* Having the property of reducing the surface tension of a liquid when dissolved in it: said especially of detergents.

surface mail Mail sent by land or sea rather than by air.

surface noise The mechanical noise produced by friction of the needle against the surface of a phonograph record.

surface plate *Mech.* A plate having a precisely flat surface, used for testing other surfaces.

surface tension *Physics* That property of a liquid by virtue of which the surface molecules exhibit a strong inward attraction, thus forming an apparent membrane that tends to contract to the minimum area. Abbr. *T*

sur·fac·tant (sûr·fak′tənt) *n. Chem.* A surface-active agent. [< SURF(ACE)-ACT(IVE) + -ANT]

surf·bird (sûrf′bûrd′) *n.* A ploverlike bird (*Aphriza virgata*) of the Pacific coast of America from Alaska to Chile.

surf·board (sûrf′bôrd′, -bōrd′) *n.* A long, narrow board used in surfing. Compare AQUAPLANE.

surf·boat (sûrf′bōt′) *n.* A boat of extra strength and buoyancy, for launching and landing through surf.

surf·cast·ing (sûrf′kas′ting, -käs′-) *n.* Fishing by casting the line into the surf from the shore. — **surf′cast′er** *n.*

surf duck One of various scoters or sea ducks.

sur·feit (sûr′fit) *v.t.* **1.** To feed or supply to fullness or satiety; satiate. — *v.i.* **2.** To partake of anything to excess; overindulge. — *n.* **1.** The act of surfeiting oneself; excess in eating or drinking; also, the excessive quantity partaken of.

2. The result of such excess; satiety. **3.** The state of being surfeited; oppressive fullness caused by excess in eating or drinking. [< OF *sorfait* < *surfaire* to overdo < *sur-* above + *faire* to make < L *facere*] — **sur′feit·er** *n.*

surf·er (sûrf′ər) *n.* One who engages or is adept in the sport of surfing. Also **surf·rid·er** (sûrf′rī′dər).

surf fish Any of a family (*Embiotocidae*) of viviparous sea fishes, perchlike in form and numerous in shallow waters all along the northern Pacific coast of North America.

surf·ing (sûrf′ing) *n.* A water sport in which a person standing on a surfboard is borne by the surf toward the shore. Also **surf·rid·ing**.

surf scoter A species of North American duck (*Melanitta perspicillata*), the adult male of which is black with a white spot on the forehead and the nape: also called *patchhead, patchhead coot.* Also **surf′er** (sûr′fər).

surg. Surgeon; surgery; surgical.

surge (sûrj) *v.* **surged, surg·ing** *v.i.* **1.** To rise high and roll onward, as waves; swell or heave. **2.** To move or go in a manner suggestive of this. **3.** To increase or vary suddenly, as an electric current. **4.** To slip, as a rope on a windlass. — *v.t.* **5.** To cause to move in surges. **6.** To let go suddenly, as a rope or cable. — *n.* **1.** A large swelling wave; billow; also, such billows collectively. **2.** The act of surging; a heaving and rolling motion, as of great waves. **3.** *Naut.* The tapered drum of a capstan or windlass around which the rope surges. **4.** *Electr.* A sudden fluctuation of voltage. [< OF *sourge-,* stem of *sourdre* to rise < L *surgere*] — **surg′er** *n.* — **surg′y** *adj.*

sur·geon (sûr′jən) *n.* One who practices surgery, as distinguished from a physician. Abbr. *surg.* [< AF *surgien,* var. of OF *cirugien.* See CHIRURGEON.]

sur·geon·cy (sûr′jən·sē) *n. pl.* **·cies** The office, duties, or rank of a surgeon.

surgeon·fish (sûr′jən·fish′) *n. pl.* **·fish** or **·fish·es** A West Indian coral-reef fish (family *Acanthuridae*) having a spiny tail.

Surgeon General *pl.* **Surgeons General** or **Surgeon Generals 1.** The chief officer of the Medical Department in the United States Army or Navy. **2.** The chief medical officer of the United States Public Health Service.

surgeon's knot A knot used in tying ligatures, stitching up wounds, etc. For illustration see KNOT.

sur·ger·y (sûr′jər·ē) *n. pl.* **·ger·ies 1.** The branch of medical science that relates to body injuries, deformities, and diseased conditions requiring treatment by operative procedures, with or without instruments. **2.** A place where surgical treatment is given, as an operating room. **3.** The work of a surgeon. **4.** *Brit.* The office of a doctor. Abbr. *surg.* [< OF *surgerie,* contraction of *serurgerie,* ult. < LL *chirurgia.* See CHIRURGEON.]

sur·gi·cal (sûr′ji·kəl) *adj.* Of, pertaining to, or used in surgery. Abbr. *surg.* — **sur′gi·cal·ly** *adv.*

Su·ri·ba·chi (sōōr′ə·bä′chē), **Mount** An extinct volcano (546 ft.) in southern Iwo Jima; scene of a U.S. victory over the Japanese in World War II, February, 1945.

su·ri·cate (sōōr′ə·kāt) *n.* A small, burrowing carnivore (*Suricata suricata*) of South Africa, allied to the mongoose. [< F *surikate* < Afrikaans, ? < a native South African name]

Su·ri·nam (sōōr′ə·näm′) An autonomous part of the Kingdom of the Netherlands, on the NE coast of South America; 55,129 sq. mi.; pop. 389,000 (est. 1969); capital, Paramaribo: also *Dutch Guiana, Netherlands Guiana. Dutch* **Su·ri·na·me** (sü′rē·nä′mə).

sur·ly (sûr′lē) *adj.* **sur·li·er, sur·li·est 1.** Characterized by or exhibiting rudeness, ill-humor, or gruffness; crabbed; cross. **2.** *Obs.* Haughty. [Earlier *sirly* like a lord < *sir* a lord + *-ly* like] — **sur′li·ly** (-lə·lē) *adv.* — **sur′li·ness** *n.*

sur·mise (sər·mīz′; *for n., also* sûr′mīz) *v.* **·mised, ·mis·ing** *v.t.* To infer on slight evidence; guess. — *v.i.* To make a conjecture. — *Syn.* See SUPPOSE. — *n.* **1.** A conjecture made on slight evidence; supposition. **2.** The act of surmising; conjecture. [< OF, an accusation, pp. fem. of *surmettre* to accuse < *sur-* upon + *mettre* to put < L *mittere* to send]

sur·mount (sər·mount′) *v.t.* **1.** To overcome; prevail over (a difficulty, etc.). **2.** To mount to the top or cross to the other side of; get over, as an obstacle or mountain. **3.** To be or lie over or above. **4.** To place something above or on top of; cap. **5.** *Obs.* To surpass; exceed. [< OF *surmunter* < M.d.L *supermontare* < L *super-* over + *mons, montis* hill, mountain] — **sur·mount′a·ble** *adj.* — **sur·mount′er** *n.*

sur·mul·let (sər·mul′it) *n.* A goatfish.

sur·name (sûr′nām′; *for v., also* sûr·nām′) *n.* **1.** The name of a person's family; the last name of a person: also called *family name.* **2.** A name formerly added to a person's given name and often denoting occupation, locality, etc., or a personally distinctive quality. — *v.t.* **named, nam·ing** To give a surname to; call by a surname. [Alter. of obs. *surnoun* < OF *surnom* < *sur-* above, beyond + *nom* name < L *nomen, -inis;* infl. in form by NAME] — **sur′nam′er** *n.*

sur·pass (sər·pas′, -päs′) *v.t.* **1.** To go beyond or past in degree or amount; excel. **2.** To go beyond the reach or powers of; transcend. — *Syn.* See EXCEED. [< MF *surpasser* < *sur-* above + *passer.* See PASS.] — **sur·pass′a·ble** *adj.*

sur·pass·ing (sər·pas'ing, -päs'-) *adj.* Preeminently excellent; exceeding. — *adv. Poetic* Exceedingly; excellently. — **sur·pass'ing·ly** *adv.* — **sur·pass'ing·ness** *n.*

sur·plice (sûr'plis) *n. Eccl.* A loose white vestment with full sleeves, worn over the cassock by the clergy and choir of the Anglican, Moravian, and Roman Catholic churches. [< *AF surpliz* or *OF sourpeliz* < *Med.L superpellicium* (*vestimentum*) overgarment < *super-* over + *pellicia* fur garment < *pellis* skin]

SURPLICE

sur·plus (sûr'plus) *adj.* Being in excess of what is used or needed. — *n.* **1.** That which remains over and above what has been used or is required; excess; overplus. **2.** Assets in excess of liabilities. **3.** Excess of net assets above the face value of shares of a corporation. **4.** Excess of receipts over expenditures of a government body. *Abbr. s., sur.* [< *OF* < *Med.L superplus* < *super-* over and above + *plus* more]

sur·plus·age (sûr'plus·ij) *n.* **1.** That which is over and above; surplus; overplus. **2.** *Law* Matter in an instrument not necessary to the meaning; irrelevant matter.

sur·print (sûr'print') *v.t.* **1.** To print on or over (matter once printed). **2.** To print (new or additional matter) over matter once printed. — *n.* That which is surprinted.

sur·pris·al (sər·prī'zəl) *n.* The act of surprising, or the state of being surprised; surprise. Also *Rare* **sur·priz'al.**

sur·prise (sər·prīz') *v.t.* **·prised, ·pris·ing** **1.** To cause to feel wonder or astonishment because unusual or unexpected. **2.** To come upon suddenly or unexpectedly; take unawares. **3.** To attack or capture suddenly and without warning. **4.** To lead unawares, as into doing something not intended: with *into.* **5.** To elicit in this manner: They *surprised* the truth from him. — **Syn.** See AMAZE. — *n.* **1.** The act of surprising; a coming upon unawares. **2.** The state of being surprised; astonishment. **3.** That which causes surprise, as a sudden and unexpected event, fact, or gift. — **to take by surprise 1.** To come upon without warning or unexpectedly. **2.** To astound or amaze; astonish. Also *Rare* **sur·prize'.** [< *OF surpris,* pp. of *surprendre* < *Med.L superprendere* < *L super-* over + *prehendere* to take] — **sur·pris'er** *n.*

sur·pris·ing (sər·prī'zing) *adj.* Causing surprise or wonder; amazing. — **sur·pris'ing·ly** *adv.* — **sur·pris'ing·ness** *n.*

sur·re·al·ism (sə·rē'əl·iz'əm) *n.* A movement in 20th century literature and art that attempts to express and exhibit the workings of the subconscious mind, especially as manifested in dreams, characterized by the incongruous arrangement and presentation of subject matter. [< *F surréalisme* < *sur-* beyond, above + *réalisme* realism < *réal.* See REAL.] — **sur·re'al·ist** *adj.* & *n.* — **sur·re'al·is·tic** *adj.* — **sur·re'al·is·ti·cal·ly** *adv.*

sur·re·but·tal (sûr'ri·but'l) *n. Law* A plaintiff's evidence or presentation of evidence to support a surrebutter.

sur·re·but·ter (sûr'ri·but'ər) *n. Law* The plaintiff's reply to a defendant's rebutter. [< SUR-[1] + REBUTTER; on analogy with *surrejoinder*]

sur·re·join·der (sûr'ri·join'dər) *n. Law* The plaintiff's answer to the defendant's rejoinder. [< SUR-[1] + REJOINDER]

sur·ren·der (sə·ren'dər) *v.t.* **1.** To yield possession of or power over to another; give up because of demand or compulsion. **2.** To give up; abandon, as hope. **3.** To give up or relinquish, especially in favor of another; resign. **4.** To give (oneself) over to a passion, influence, etc. — *v.i.* **5.** To give oneself up, as to an enemy in warfare; yield. — **Syn.** See RELINQUISH. — *n.* The act of surrendering. [< *AF surrender, OF surrendre* < *sur-* over + *rendre.* See RENDER.]

surrender value The value of an insurance policy payable to the insured or to the beneficiary when the policy is discontinued.

sur·rep·ti·tious (sûr'əp·tish'əs) *adj.* **1.** Accomplished by secret or improper means; clandestine. **2.** Acting secretly or by stealth. — **Syn.** See STEALTHY. [< *L surreptitius, subrepticius* < *subreptus,* pp. of *subripere* to steal < *sub-* secretly + *rapere* to snatch] — **sur'rep·ti'tious·ly** *adv.* — **sur'rep·ti'tious·ness** *n.*

sur·rey (sûr'ē) *n.* A light pleasure vehicle, having two seats, four wheels, and sometimes a top. [Prob. after *Surrey,* England]

Sur·rey (sûr'ē) A county in SE England; 722 sq. mi.; pop. 1,005,900 (1976); county seat, Guildford.

Sur·rey (sûr'ē), **Earl of,** 1516?-47, Henry Howard, English courtier, soldier, and poet; beheaded.

sur·ro·gate (sûr'ə·gāt; *for n., also* sûr'ə·git) *n.* **1.** One who or that which is substituted for another; a substitute. **2.** *Brit.* A deputy appointed by an ecclesiastical judge to act in his place. **3.** A probate judge. — *v.t.* **·gat·ed, ·gat·ing 1.** To put in the place of another; substitute; subrogate. **2.** To appoint (another) to succeed oneself. [< *L surrogatus, subrogatus,* pp. of *subrogare* < *sub-* in place of another + *rogare* to ask] — **sur'ro·gate·ship** *n.*

sur·round (sə·round') *v.t.* **1.** To extend completely around; be on all sides of; encircle. **2.** To place something completely around; enclose. **3.** To shut in or enclose, as enemy troops, so as to cut off retreat; beset; invest. [< *AF surunder,* OF *soronder* to overflow < LL *superundare* < *super-* over + *undare* to rise in waves < *unda* a wave]

sur·round·ing (sə·roun'ding) *n.* **1.** *pl.* That which surrounds; environment; conditions of life. **2.** The act of one who surrounds. — *adj.* Encompassing; enveloping.

sur·sum cor·da (sûr'səm kôr'də) *Latin.* **a** Lift up your hearts: the opening words of the Preface in the Mass. **b** A translation of this, used in other eucharistic liturgies. **2.** A cry of encouragement, exhortation, etc.

sur·tax (sûr'taks') *n.* An extra or additional tax; especially, a graduated income tax over and above the usual or fixed income tax, levied on the amount by which net income exceeds a certain sum. — *v.t.* To assess with a surtax. [< *F surtaxe* < *sur-* above + *taxe* < *taxer.* See TAX.]

Sur·tees (sûr'tēz), **Robert Smith,** 1803-64, English novelist and editor.

sur·tout[1] (sər·tōōt', -tōō'; *Fr.* sür·tōō') *n.* A long, close-fitting overcoat. [< *F* < *sur-* above + *tout* all < *L totus*]

sur·tout[2] (sûr·tōō') *adv. French* Above all; chiefly; especially.

surv. 1. Survey; surveying; surveyor. **2.** Surviving.

sur·veil·lance (sər·vā'ləns, -vāl'yəns) *n.* **1.** Close watch kept over one, as a prisoner or suspect. **2.** The act of watching, or the state of being watched. [< *F* < *surveiller* to superintend < *sur-* over + *veiller* to watch < *L vigilare*]

sur·veil·lant (sər·vā'lənt, -vāl'yənt) *adj.* Exercising surveillance; watching; watchful. — *n.* One who keeps close watch so as to control, supervise, spy, etc.

sur·vey (sər·vā'; *for n., also* sûr'vā) *v.t.* **1.** To look at in its entirety; view in a general way. **2.** To look at carefully and minutely; scrutinize; inspect. **3.** To determine accurately the area, contour, or boundaries of (land) by measuring lines and angles according to the principles of geometry and trigonometry. — *v.i.* **4.** To survey land. — **Syn.** See SEE[1]. — *n.* **1.** The operation, act, process, or results of finding the contour, area, boundaries, etc., of a surface. **2.** A department or corps for carrying on such operations; also, an area that has been surveyed. **3.** A general or comprehensive view; an overlooking. **4.** A scrutinizing view; inspection. *Abbr. surv.* [< *AF survey-,* stem of *surveier,* OF *sorveir* < *Med.L supervidere* < *super-* over + *videre* to look]

sur·vey·ing (sər·vā'ing) *n.* **1.** The science and art of determining the area and configuration of portions of the surface of the earth and representing them on maps. **2.** The act of one who surveys. *Abbr. surv.*

sur·vey·or (sər·vā'ər) *n.* **1.** One who surveys lands, roads, mines, oil fields, etc.; especially, one who surveys land. **2.** One who examines a thing for the purpose of ascertaining its condition, quality, or character; especially, a customs officer who examines merchandise brought into a port. *Abbr. surv.*

sur·vey·or·ship (sər·vā'ər·ship) *n.* The office of a surveyor.

surveyor's level A form of spirit level with telescope and tripod attachment, used in surveying.

surveyor's measure A system of measurement used in surveying and based on the chain as a unit.

sur·viv·al (sər·vī'vəl) *n.* **1.** The act of surviving, or the state of having survived. **2.** One who or that which survives; especially, a custom, belief, etc., persisting in society. Also *Archaic* **sur·viv'ance.**

survival kit A small kit of food, water, medicines, etc., supplied to airmen for use in case of crash or forced landing.

survival of the fittest The principle of natural selection as applied to living organisms, societies, etc.

sur·vive (sər·vīv') *v. ·vived, ·viv·ing* *v.i.* **1.** To live or continue beyond the death of another, an event, etc.; remain alive or in existence. — *v.t.* **2.** To live or exist beyond the death, occurrence, or end of; outlive; outlast. [< *AF survivre,* OF *sorvivre* < LL *supervivere* < *super-* above, beyond + *vivere* to live] — **sur·viv'er** *n.*

sur·vi·vor (sər·vī'vər) *n.* One who or that which survives.

sur·vi·vor·ship (sər·vī'vər·ship) *n.* **1.** The state of surviving. **2.** *Law* The right of a surviving party, having a joint interest with others in property, to take the whole estate.

sus- Assimilated var. of SUB-.

Sus. Sussex.

Su·sa (sōō'sə) An ancient city of Persia, capital of Elam, the site of which is in SW Iran: Old Testament *Shushan.*

Su·san·na (sōō·zan'ə) A Jewish captive in Babylon, falsely accused of adultery, whose life Daniel saved. — **n.** The book of the Old Testament Apocrypha containing her story.

sus·cep·tance (sə·sep'təns) *n. Electr.* The ability of a circuit to carry an alternating current without losses due to capacitance and inductance: the reciprocal of *reactance*: expressed in mhos.

sus·cep·ti·bil·i·ty (sə·sep'tə·bil'ə·tē) *n. pl. ·ties* **1.** The state or quality of being susceptible. **2.** The ability to receive or be impressed by deep emotions or strong feelings;

sensibility. **3.** *pl.* Sensitive emotions; feelings. **4.** *Physics* The ratio of the magnetization of a material to the magnetic force producing it. **— Syn.** See SENSIBILITY.

sus·cep·ti·ble (sə·sep/tə·bəl) *adj.* **1.** Yielding readily; capable of being influenced, acted on, or determined; open; liable: usually with *of* or *to*. **2.** Having delicate sensibility; sensitive; impressionable. [< Med.L *susceptibilis* < L *suscipere* to receive, undertake < *sub-* under + *capere* to take] **— sus·cep'ti·ble·ness** *n.* **— sus·cep'ti·bly** *adv.*

sus·cep·tive (sə·sep/tiv) *adj.* **1.** Receptive. **2.** Susceptible. **— sus·cep'tive·ness, sus·cep·tiv·i·ty** (sus'ep·tiv/ə·tē) *n.*

Su·si·an (sōō/sē·ən) *n.* Elamite (def. 2).

Su·si·a·na (sōō'zē·ā/nə -an'ə) See ELAM.

sus·lik (sōōs/lik) *n.* **1.** A small sciuroid rodent (*Citellus citellus*) of NE Europe and NW Asia, with a very short tail; a spermophile. **2.** Its fur. [< Russian]

sus·pect (*v.* sə·spekt/; *adj.* & *n.* sus/pekt) *v.t.* **1.** To think (a person) guilty as specified on little or no evidence. **2.** To have distrust of; doubt: They *suspect* my motives. **3.** To have an inkling or suspicion of; think possible: to *suspect* arson. **— v.i. 4.** To have suspicions. **— adj.** Exciting, open to, or viewed with suspicion; suspected. **— n.** One who is under suspicion, especially for a crime. [< F *suspecter* < L *suspectus*, pp. of *suspicere* to look under, mistrust < *sub-* from under + *specere* to look]

sus·pend (sə·spend/) *v.t.* **1.** To bar for a time from a privilege, office, or function as a punishment; debar. **2.** To cause to cease for a time; interrupt; withhold temporarily: to *suspend* payments. **3.** To hold in a state of indecision or abeyance; withhold or defer action on: to *suspend* a sentence. **4.** To hang from a support so as to allow free movement. **5.** To sustain in a body of nearly the same specific gravity; keep in suspension, as dust motes in the air. **— v.i. 6.** To stop for a time. **7.** To fail to meet obligations; stop payment. [< OF *suspendre* < L *sub-* under + *pendere* to hang]

sus·pend·ed animation (sə·spen/did) Temporary loss of vital processes, resembling death.

sus·pend·er (sə·spen/dər) *n.* **1.** *pl. U.S.* A pair of straps worn over the shoulders for supporting the trousers. **2.** *Brit.* A garter.

sus·pense (sə·spens/) *n.* **1.** The state of being uncertain, undecided, or insecure, usually accompanied by anxiety, apprehension, etc. **2.** An uncertain or doubtful situation. [< OF *suspens, suspense* delay, abeyance < Med.L *suspensum*, orig. neut. of L *suspendere*. See SUSPEND.]

suspense account An account in which charges or credits are entered temporarily pending determination of their proper disposition.

sus·pen·sion (sə·spen/shən) *n.* **1.** The act of suspending, or the state of being suspended. **2.** The state of deferment. **3.** *Physics* A uniform dispersion of small particles in a medium, either by mechanical agitation or by molecular forces. **4.** Cessation of payments in business: the *suspension* of a bank. **5.** Any device on or from which something is suspended. **6.** *Mech.* A system of flexible members, as springs in a vehicle, intended to insulate the chassis and body against road shocks transmitted by the wheels. **7.** *Music* The prolongation of a chord tone into the succeeding chord, where it forms a dissonance, and is subsequently replaced by a tone that is part of the second chord; also, the tone so prolonged. **8.** The act of debarring from an office or its privileges.

suspension bridge A bridge in which the roadway is hung from cables strongly anchored over towers and without intervening support from below.

SUSPENSION BRIDGE
(Brooklyn Bridge, New York)

suspension point One of a series of dots used to indicate the omission of words or sentences.

sus·pen·sive (sə·spen/siv) *adj.* **1.** Tending to suspend or keep in suspense. **2.** Of, pertaining to, or characterized by suspense. **3.** Having the power of suspending operation: a *suspensive* veto. **— sus·pen'sive·ly** *adv.* **— sus·pen'sive·ness** *n.*

sus·pen·sor (sə·spen/sər) *n.* **1.** A suspensory. **2.** *Bot.* The thread or chain of cells in certain plants, that produces at its extremity the developing embryo.

sus·pen·so·ry (sə·spen/sər·ē) *adj.* Suspending; sustaining; delaying. **— n. *pl.* ·ries** A truss, bandage, or supporter: also called *suspensor.*

suspensory ligament *Anat.* A fibrous membrane sustaining the lens of the eye.

sus·pi·cion (sə·spish/ən) *n.* **1.** The act of suspecting, or the state of one who suspects; the imagining of something wrong without proof or clear evidence. **2.** *Informal* The least particle, as of a flavor. **— v.t. *Dial.*** To suspect. [< AF *suspecioun*, OF *sospeçon* < Med.L *suspectio, -onis* < L *suspicere.* See SUSPECT.] **— sus·pi'cion·al** *adj.*

— Syn. (noun) **1.** distrust, dubiety, skepticism. See DOUBT. **2.** soupçon, dash, touch, tinge, shade.

sus·pi·cious (sə·spish/əs) *adj.* **1.** Inclined to suspect; distrustful. **2.** Apt to arouse suspicion; questionable. **3.** Indicating suspicion: a *suspicious* inquiry. **— sus·pi'cious·ly** *adv.* **— sus·pi'cious·ness** *n.*

sus·pire (sus·pīr/) *v.i.* **·pired, ·pir·ing** *Poetic* **1.** To sigh. **2.** To breathe. [< L *suspirare* < *sub-* up from below + *spirare* to breathe] **— sus·pi·ra·tion** (sus/pə·rā/shən) *n.*

Sus·que·han·na (sus/kwə·han/ə) A river in New York, Pennsylvania, and Maryland, flowing 444 miles, generally south, to Chesapeake Bay.

Suss. Sussex.

Sus·sex (sus/iks) **1.** A former county in SE England. See EAST SUSSEX; WEST SUSSEX. **2.** A former Anglo-Saxon kingdom in southern England.

Sussex spaniel A muscular, reddish brown spaniel having a very keen nose, used for hunting.

sus·tain (sə·stān/) *v.t.* **1.** To keep from sinking or falling, especially by bearing up from below; uphold; support. **2.** To endure without yielding; withstand. **3.** To undergo or suffer, as loss or injury. **4.** To keep up the courage, resolution, or spirits of; comfort. **5.** To keep up or maintain; keep in effect or being. **6.** To maintain by providing with food, drink, etc.; support. **7.** To uphold or support as being true or just. **8.** To prove the truth or correctness of; corroborate; confirm. [< OF *sustein-*, stem of *sustenir, sostenir* < L *sustinere* < *sub-* up from under + *tenere* to hold] **— sus·tain'a·ble** *adj.* **— sus·tain'er** *n.* **— sus·tain'ment** *n.*

sus·tain·ing program (sə·stā/ning) A radio or television program that has no commercial sponsor but is paid for by the network or station.

sus·te·nance (sus/tə·nəns) *n.* **1.** The act of sustaining, or the state of being sustained; especially, maintenance of life or health; subsistence. **2.** That which sustains; especially, that which supports life; food. **3.** Means of support; livelihood. [< AF *sustenaunce*, OF *sostenance* < *sostenir.* See SUSTAIN.]

sus·ten·tac·u·lar (sus/ten·tak/yə·lər) *adj.* *Anat.* Supporting; sustaining. [< L *sustentaculum* a support < *sustentare* to hold up, intens. of *sustinere.* See SUSTAIN.]

sus·ten·ta·tion (sus/ten·tā/shən) *n.* **1.** The act of sustaining, or the state of being sustained; especially, support of life. **2.** That which sustains, supports, or preserves; especially, the means of supporting life. [< OF *sustentacion* < L *sustentatio, -onis* < *sustentatus*, pp. of *sustentare* to hold up < *sustinere.* See SUSTAIN.] **— sus·ten·ta'tive** *adj.*

sus·ten·tion (sə·sten/shən) *n.* The act of sustaining, or the state of being sustained. [< SUSTAIN; on analogy with *retention, detention*, etc.]

su·sur·rant (sōō·sûr/ənt) *adj.* Softly murmuring; rustling; whispering. [< L *susurrans, -antis*, ppr. of *susurrare* to whisper < *susurrus* a humming, whispering]

su·sur·rate (sōō·sûr/āt) *v.i.* **·rat·ed, ·rat·ing** To speak softly; whisper. [< L *susurratus*, pp. of *susurrare.* See SUSURRANT.] **— su·sur·ra·tion** (sōō/sə·rā/shən) *n.*

su·sur·rus (sōō·sûr/əs) *n.* A gentle sibilant murmur; whisper; rustling. [< L, a humming, whispering]

Suth. Sutherland; Sutherlandshire.

Suth·er·land (suth/ər·lənd) A county in northern Scotland; 2,028 sq. mi.; pop. 12,995 (1969); county seat, Dornoch. Also **Suth/er·land·shire** (-shir).

Sutherland Falls A waterfall on SW South Island, New Zealand; 1,904 ft.

Suth·er·land (suth/ər·lənd), **Joan**, born 1926, Australian soprano.

Sut·lej (sut/lej) A river in SW Tibet, northern India, and West Pakistan, flowing about 850 miles SW to the Indus.

sut·ler (sut/lər) *n.* A peddler who sells goods and food to an army. [< Du. *soeteler* a petty tradesman < *soetelen* to perform mean duties] **— sut/ler·ship** *n.*

su·tra (sōō/trə) *n.* **1.** In Brahmanism, an aphorism, precept, or maxim; also, a collection of aphorisms. **2.** In Buddhism, any of the narrative parts of the scriptures; especially, any of the dialogues of Buddha. Also **sut·ta** (sŏŏt/ə). [< Skt. *sūtra* a thread, rule < *siv* to sew]

Su·tro (sōō/trō), **Alfred**, 1863–1933, English dramatist and translator.

sut·tee (su·tē/, sut/ē) *n.* Formerly, the sacrifice of a Hindu widow on the funeral pyre of her husband; also, the widow so immolated. [< Hind. *sati* < Skt., a faithful wife, fem. of *sat* good, wise, orig. ppr. of *as* to be] **— sut·tee/ism** *n.*

Sut·ter's Mill (sut/ərz) A mill in eastern California, owned by **John Augustus Sutter**, 1803–80, where gold was discovered in 1848.

su·ture (sōō/chər) *n.* **1.** The junction of two contiguous surfaces or edges along a line by or as by sewing. **2.** *Anat.* The interlocking of two bones at their edges, as in the skull. **3.** *Zool.* The line of junction between contiguous parts, as the edges of a bivalve shell. **4.** *Bot.* The line of dehiscence in plants. **5.** *Surg.* **a** The operation of uniting the edges of a cut or wound by or as by stitching. **b** The thread, silver wire, or other material used in this operation. **— v.t. ·tured, ·tur·ing** To unite by means of sutures; sew together.

[< MF < L *sutura* < *sutus*, pp. of *suere* to sew] **— su'tur·al** *adj.* **su'tur·al·ly** *adv.*

su·um cui·que (sōō'əm kī'kwē, kwī'-) *Latin* To each his own.

Su·va (sōō'vä) The capital of the Fiji Islands, a port on southern Viti Levu; pop. 54,157 (1966).

Su·vo·rov (sōō·vô'rôf), **Count Alexander Vasilievich**, 1729–1800, Russian field marshal born in Finland.

Su·wan·nee River (sōō·wä'nē, -wŏn'ē) A river in Georgia and Florida, flowing 250 miles, generally south, to the Gulf of Mexico: also *Swanee River*.

su·ze·rain (sōō'zə·rin, -rān) *n.* **1.** Formerly, a feudal lord. **2.** One invested with superior or paramount authority. **3.** A nation having paramount control over a locally autonomous region. — *adj.* Sovereign; supreme. [< F *sus* above < L *susum, sursum* upwards; on analogy with *souverain* sovereign] **— su'ze·rain·ty** *n.*

Su·zu·ki (sōō·zōō·kē), **Daisetz Teitaro**, 1870–1966, Japanese scholar, author, and teacher active in the United States; authority on Zen Buddhism.

s.v. Under this word (L *sub verbo, sub voce*).

S.V. Holy Virgin (L *Sancta Virgo*).

Sval·bard (sväl'bär) An archipelago of Norway in the Arctic Ocean, including Spitsbergen and other smaller islands; 23,951 sq. mi.; pop. about 3,000; administrative center, Longyearbyen.

sva·raj (svä·räj') See SWARAJ.

Sved·berg (svā'berkh), **The**, 1884–1971, Swedish chemist: full name **Theodor Svedberg.**

svelte (svelt) *adj.* Slender; slim; willowy. [< F *svelte* < Ital. *svelto* < L *ex-* out + *vellere* to pluck]

Sverd·lovsk (sverd·lôfsk') A city in the west central R.S.F.S.R.; pop. 1,026,000 (1970): formerly *Yekaterinburg.*

Sver·drup (svar'drōōp), **Otto**, 1855–1930, Norwegian Arctic explorer.

Sve·rige (svä'ryə) The Swedish name for SWEDEN.

Sviz·ze·ra (svēt·tsä'rä) The Italian name for SWITZERLAND.

Sw. Sweden; Swedish.

SW or **sw, S.W.** or **s.w.** Southwest; southwestern.

S.W.A. or **S.W.Afr.** South-West Africa.

swab (swob) *n.* **1.** A small stick having a wad of cotton wound about one or both ends, used for cleansing the mouth of a sick person, applying medicines, etc.; also, a specimen of mucus, etc., taken with such a stick. **2.** A mop for cleaning decks, floors, etc. **3.** A cylindrical brush for cleaning firearms. **4.** *Slang* An awkward fellow; lout. — *v.t.* **swabbed, swab·bing** To clean, apply, medicate, etc., with or as with a swab. Also spelled *swob.* [? < MDu. *swabbe.* Akin to MLG *swabben.*]

swab·ber (swob'ər) *n.* **1.** One who uses a swab. **2.** One fit only for using a mop; a lout. **3.** A swab. [< MDu. *zwabber* < *zwabben* to do dirty work, swab]

Swa·bi·a (swā'bē·ə) A region and former duchy of SW West Germany: German *Schwaben.* **— Swa'bi·an** *adj. & n.*

swad·dle (swod'l) *v.t.* **·dled, ·dling** To wrap with a bandage; especially, to wrap (an infant) with a long strip of linen or flannel; swathe. — *n.* A band used for swaddling. [OE *swēthel* swaddling clothes, bandage < *swathian* to swathe]

swaddling clothes **1.** Bands or strips of linen or other cloth wound around a newborn infant. **2.** A time of immaturity; also, the limitations that restrict the immature. Also **swaddling bands, swaddling clouts.**

Swa·de·shi (swə·dā'shē) *n.* A former political movement originating in Bengal, India, advocating the boycott of British goods as one means of obtaining swaraj or home rule. [< Skt. *svadeśin* native, national < *svadeśa* native country]

swag (swag) *n.* **1.** *Slang* Property obtained by robbery or theft; plunder; booty. **2.** In Australia, a swagman's bundle or pack. **3.** A swaying; a lurch. — *v.i.* **swagged, swag·ging 1.** *Brit. Dial.* To swing heavily. **2.** In Australia, to tramp, bearing a swag. **3.** To sag; sway; lurch. [Prob. < Scand. Cf. dial. Norw. *svagga* to sway.]

swag·bel·ly (swag'bel'ē) *n.* *pl.* **·lies** One who has a protuberant abdomen. [< SWAG, v. (def. 3) + BELLY] **— swag'bel'lied** *adj.*

swage (swāj) *n.* **1.** A tool or form, often one of a pair, for shaping metal by hammering or pressure. **2.** An ornamental border or molding. **3.** A groove on an anvil for use in shaping metal. **4.** A swage block. — *v.t.* **swaged, swag·ing** To shape (metal) with or as with a swage. [< OF *souage*; ult. origin uncertain]

swage block A heavy iron block or anvil having grooves or holes for shaping metal, heading bolts, etc.

swag·ger (swag'ər) *v.i.* **1.** To walk with a proud or insolent air; strut. **2.** To boast; bluster. — *n.* Expression of superiority in words or deeds; braggadocio. [Appar. freq. of SWAG] **— swag'ger·er** *n.* **— swag'ger·ing·ly** *adv.*

swagger stick A short, canelike stick carried by army personnel, especially officers. Also **swagger cane.**

swag·man (swag'man') *n.* *pl.* **·men** (-men') In Australia, one who seeks work, carrying his bundle or swag.

Swa·hi·li (swä·hē'lē) *n.* *pl.* **·li 1.** A language of East Africa, basically Bantu with an admixture of Arabic elements, used widely as a lingua franca. **2.** A member of a Swahili-speaking group or community. [< Arabic, coastal < *sawāhil,* pl. of *sāhil* coast] **— Swa·hi'li·an** *adj.*

swain (swān) *n.* *Poetic* **1.** A youthful rustic. **2.** A young rustic gallant. **3.** A lover. [< ON *sveinn* boy, servant. Akin to OE *swān.*] **— swain'ish** *adj.*

swale (swāl) *n.* **1.** Low, marshy ground. **2.** *Dial.* Shade. Also **swail.** [Prob. < Scand. Cf. ON *svalr* cool.]

swal·low[1] (swol'ō) *v.t.* **1.** To cause (food, etc.) to pass from the mouth into the stomach by means of muscular action of the gullet or esophagus. **2.** To take in or engulf in a manner suggestive of this; absorb; envelop: often with *up.* **3.** To put up with or endure; submit to. **4.** *Informal* To believe credulously. **5.** To refrain from expressing or giving vent to; suppress. **6.** To take back; recant: to *swallow* one's words. **7.** To utter (words, sentences, etc.) indistinctly. — *v.i.* **8.** To perform the act or the motions of swallowing. — *n.* **1.** The amount swallowed at once; a mouthful. **2.** The gullet; throat; gorge. **3.** The act of swallowing. **4.** *Naut.* The channel in a hoisting block for the passage of the rope. [OE *swelgan* to swallow] **— swal'low·er** *n.*

swal·low[2] (swol'ō) *n.* **1.** Any of various small, widely distributed passerine birds (family *Hirundinidae*) with a short bill, long, pointed wings, and a forked tail, noted for swiftness of flight and migratory habits; especially, the common **bank swallow** or sand martin (*Riparia riparia*), the American **tree swallow** (*Iridoprocne bicolor*), and the **barn swallow** (*Hirundo erythrogaster*). ◆ Collateral adjective: *hirundine.* **2.** A similar bird, as the swift. [OE *swealwe*]

swal·low·a·ble (swol'ō·ə·bəl) *adj.* **1.** Capable of being swallowed. **2.** Believable; credible.

swallow dive *Brit.* A swan dive.

swal·low·tail (swol'ō·tāl') *n.* **1.** The tail of a swallow, or a similar deeply forked tail. **2.** A butterfly (family *Papilionidae*) having a taillike prolongation on each hind wing. **3.** *Informal* A swallow-tailed coat.

swal·low-tailed (swol'ō-tāld') *adj.* Having a deeply forked tail or part similar to a swallow's tail.

swallow-tailed coat A man's formal dress coat with two long, tapering tails in the back.

swal·low·wort (swol'ō-wûrt') *n.* **1.** Any of several perennial, often twining herbs (genus *Cynanchum*) of the milkweed family; especially, the **white swallowwort** (*C. vincetoxicum*), with greenish white flowers and an emetic root. **2.** The celandine, said to blossom with the arrival of the swallows and to wither when they depart.

swam (swam) Past tense of SWIM.

swa·mi (swä'mē) *n.* *pl.* **·mis 1.** Master; lord: used by Hindus as a title of respect. **2.** A Hindu teacher, especially a religious teacher; pundit. **3.** Loosely, a yogi or fakir. Also **swa'my.** [< Hind. *svāmi* lord, master < Skt. *svāmin*]

swamp (swomp, swômp) *n.* A tract or region of lowland saturated with water; place where the water table is at ground level; wet bog. ◆ Collateral adjective: *paludal.* — *v.t.* **1.** To drench or submerge with water or other liquid. **2.** To overburden; overwhelm, as with an unmanageable number of things. **3.** *Naut.* To sink or fill (a vessel) with water. — *v.i.* **4.** To sink in or as in a swamp. [Cf. LG *swampen* to quake (said of a bog). Akin to SUMP.] **— swamp'ish** *adj.*

swamp boat A small, flat-bottomed boat powered by an engine with an airplane propeller mounted high in the stern, used in swampy or boggy areas: also called *airboat.*

swamp cabbage Skunk cabbage (which see).

swamp·er (swom'pər, swôm'-) *n.* **1.** One who lives in or near a swamp. **2.** *U.S.* **a** One who clears a swamp of trees, brush, etc. **b** One who clears a path in a forest for skidding logs. **c** One who hauls logs out of the forest on a skidway.

swamp fever 1. Malaria. **2.** *Vet.* An infectious anemia of equine animals, caused by a filterable virus.

Swamp Fox Sobriquet of FRANCIS MARION.

swamp hare A rabbit (*Sylvilagus aquaticus*) frequenting the swamps of the southern United States.

swamp honeysuckle A tall ericaceous plant (*Rhododendron viscosum*) of the SE United States, with fragrant white or pink flowers.

swamp·land (swomp'land', swômp'land') *n.* **1.** Land covered with swamps. **2.** Fertile, arable land in a swamp.

swamp law Lynch law (which see).

swamp maple The red maple (which see).

swamp oak An oak (*Quercus bicolor*) common in swamps of the eastern United States.

swamp pine Any of certain pines common in swamps or swampy regions; especially, the loblolly pine.

swamp privet An oleaceous tree (*Forestiera acuminata*) of the southern United States.

swamp sparrow An American sparrow (*Melospiza georgiana*) resembling the song sparrow, inhabiting the swamps of the southern and eastern United States.

swamp·y (swom'pē, swôm'pē) *adj.* **swamp·i·er, swamp·i·**

est 1. Of, pertaining to, or characterized by a swamp. **2.** Consisting of or resembling a swamp.

swan[1] (swon, swôn) *n.* **1.** A large, long-necked, aquatic bird (subfamily *Cygninae*), allied to but heavier than the goose, noted for the brilliant white plumage of most adults, and for its grace on the water, as the whooper, the trumpeter swan, and the common North American whistling swan. **2.** A poet or singer.

TRUMPETER SWAN (About 4 feet long)

swan[2] (swon, swôn) *v.i. U.S. Dial.* To swear: chiefly in the phrase **I swan,** an exclamation of amazement. [Prob. < dial. E (Northern) *Is′ wan,* lit., I shall warrant, used as euphemism for *swear*]

Swan (swon, swôn) *n.* The constellation Cygnus.

swan dive A dive performed with head tilted back and arms extended until near the water: also, *Brit.,* swallow dive.

Swa·nee River (swô′nē, swon′ē) See SUWANNEE RIVER.

swang (swang) Dialectal past tense of SWING.

swan·herd (swon′hûrd′, swôn′-) *n.* One who tends swans.

swank (swangk) *adj.* **1.** *Slang* Ostentatiously fashionable; pretentious. **2.** *Scot.* Slim; pliant; agile; jolly; lively. Also **swank′y.** — *n. Slang* **1.** Behavior, speech, etc., that is pretentious and overly stylish. **2.** Swagger; bluster. — *v.i.* To act in a pretentious or swaggering manner; show off. [< dial. E. Appar. akin to MLG *swank* flexible, MHG *swanken* to sway.] — **swank′i·ly** *adv.* — **swank′i·ness** *n.*

swan maiden In many ancient folk myths, a beautiful fairy maiden able to transform herself into a swan.

swan·ner·y (swon′ər-ē, swôn′-) *n. pl.* **·ner·ies** A place where swans are bred or kept.

swan·pan (swän′pän′) *n.* A Chinese abacus or frame of beads to aid reckoning: also *schwanpan, shwanpan.* [< Chinese *suan p'an* reckoning board]

swan's-down (swonz′doun′, swônz′-) *n.* **1.** The down of a swan, used for trimming, powder puffs, etc. **2.** Canton flannel. **3.** A soft, thick, fine woolen cloth resembling down. Also **swans′down′.**

Swan·sea (swon′sē) A county borough and port in West Glamorgan, Wales; pop. 189,800 (1976).

swan·skin (swon′skin′, swôn′-) *n.* **1.** The unplucked skin of a swan. **2.** A soft, fine-twilled flannel or cotton fabric having a soft nap.

swan song A last or dying work, as of a poet or composer: in allusion to the ancient fable that the swan sings a last song before dying.

swan-up·ping (swon′up′ing, swôn′-) *n. Brit.* The annual inspection and marking on the beak of the royal and other privileged young swans or cygnets on the Thames; also, the annual expedition for this purpose.

swap (swop) *Informal v.t. & v.i.* **swapped, swap·ping** To exchange (one thing for another); trade. — *n.* An exchange or trade; barter. Also spelled *swop.* [ME *swappen* to strike (a bargain), slap; prob. ult. imit. of the sound of clapping the hands, as in bargaining]

swa·raj (swə-räj′) *n.* **1.** Formerly, in British India, self-government; by extension, cultural and political development under native influence as distinguished from such development under British influence. **2.** Home rule: the watchword of the Indian Nationalists; also, the party itself. Also spelled *svaraj.* [< Skt. *svarāj* self-ruling < *sva-* own + *rāj* rule] — **swa·raj′ist** *n.* — **swa·raj′ism** *n.*

sward (swôrd) *n.* **1.** Land thickly covered with grass; turf: also called *swarth.* **2.** *Obs.* A skin; rind. — *v.t. & v.i.* To cover or become covered with sward. [OE *sweard* skin]

sware (swâr) Obsolete past tense of SWEAR.

swarm[1] (swôrm) *n.* **1.** A large number or body of insects or small living things of any kind. **2.** A hive of bees; also, a large number of bees leaving the parent stock at one time, to take up new lodgings, accompanied by a queen. **3.** A crowd or throng of persons, animals, or things, especially when in motion or advancing under pressure. **4.** *Biol.* A collection of free-swimming unicellular organisms, especially zoospores. — **Syn.** See FLOCK. — *v.i.* **1.** To leave the hive in a swarm: said of bees. **2.** To come together, move, or occur in great numbers. **3.** To be crowded or overrun; teem: with *with.* **4.** *Biol.* To come forth in a swarm. — *v.t.* **5.** To fill with a swarm or crowd; throng. [OE *swearm*]

swarm[2] (swôrm) *v.t. & v.i.* To climb (a tree, etc.) by clasping it with the arms and legs. [Orig. nautical cant. Prob. akin to SWARM[1].]

swarm·er (swôr′mər) *n.* **1.** *Biol.* Any of various zoospores; a swarm spore. **2.** One who or that which swarms.

swarm spore *Biol.* A zoospore (which see).

swart (swôrt) *adj. Dial.* or *Poetic* Swarthy. Also *swarth.* [OE *sweart*] — **swart′ness** *n.*

swarth[1] (swôrth) *n. Dial.* Sward. [OE *swearth*]

swarth[2] (swôrth) *adj.* Swart; swarthy. [? Var. of SWART]

swarth·y (swôr′thē) *adj.* **swarth·i·er, swarth·i·est** Having a dark hue; of dark or sunburned complexion; tawny: also *swart, swarth.* Also **swart′y.** [Var. of obs. *swarty* < SWART] — **swarth′i·ly** *adv.* — **swarth′i·ness, swarth′ness** *n.*

swash (swosh, swôsh) *v.i.* **1.** To move or wash noisily, as

waves; splash. **2.** To swagger. — *v.t.* **3.** To splash (water, etc.). **4.** To splash or dash water, etc., upon or against. — *n.* **1.** The splash of a liquid. **2.** A narrow channel through which tides flow. **3.** A bar over which the waves pass freely. **4.** A swaggerer or his behavior. [Imit.]

swash·buck·ler (swosh′buk′lər, swôsh′-) *n.* A swaggering or boasting soldier. Also **swash′er** (-ər). [< SWASH + BUCKLER; with ref. to striking one's own or one's opponent's shield with a sword] — **swash′buck·ler·ing** *n.* — **swash′buck′ling** *adj. & n.*

swash·ing (swosh′ing, swôsh′-) *adj.* **1.** Splashing. **2.** Swaggering; blustering. — **swash′ing·ly** *adv.*

swash letters Italic special letters having a top or bottom flourish on the side where there is most blank space.

swas·ti·ka (swos′ti·kə) *n.* **1.** A primitive religious ornament or symbol, consisting of a Greek cross with the ends of the arms bent at right angles, and prolonged to the length of the upright arms, clockwise, or counterclockwise. **2.** The emblem of the Nazis. See *b* in illustration. See HAKENKREUZ. Also **swas′ti·ca.** [< Skt. *svastika* < *svasti* well-being, fortune < *sú* good + *asti* being < *as* to be]

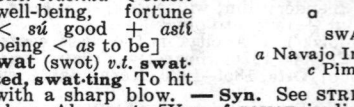

SWASTIKAS
a Navajo Indian. *b* Indian.
c Pima Indian,

swat (swot) *v.t.* **swat·ted, swat·ting** To hit with a sharp blow. See STRIKE. — *n.* A smart blow. Also *swot.* [Var. of SQUAT, in dial. sense of "squash"]

Swat (swot) *n. pl.* **Swa·ti** (swä′tē) One of an East Indian Moslem people of Indo-European stock, dwelling in northern West Pakistan. Also **Swa′ti.**

Swat (swot) **1.** A former princely state in West Pakistan. **2.** A river in northern West Pakistan flowing about 200 miles SW and SE to the Kabul.

swatch (swoch) *n.* A strip, as of cloth, especially, one cut off for a sample. [< dial. E (Northern), a cloth tally]

swath (swoth, swôth) *n.* **1.** A row or line of cut grass, grain, etc. **2.** The space or width of grass, grain, etc., cut by any of various mowing devices. **3.** A narrow belt or track; strip. Also called *swathe.* — **to cut a wide swath** To make a fine impression or display. [OE *swæth* a track]

swathe[1] (swāth, swäth) *v.t.* **swathed, swath·ing 1.** To bind or wrap, as in bandages. **2.** To envelop; surround. — *n.* A bandage for swathing. [OE *swathian*] — **swath′er** *n.*

swathe[2] (swäth) *n.* A swath.

Swa·tow (swä′tou′) A port city in eastern Kwangtung Province, China; pop. 400,000 (est. 1970).

swats (swots) *n. Scot.* New ale; drink. [OE *swatan*]

swat·ter (swot′ər) *n.* **1.** One who or that which swats. **2.** A perforated rubber or meshed wire device for killing flies, mosquitoes, etc. **3.** *U.S.* A hard-hitting baseball player.

sway (swā) *v.i.* **1.** To swing from side to side or to and fro; oscillate. **2.** To bend or incline to one side; lean; veer. **3.** To tend in opinion, sympathy, etc. **4.** To have influence or control. — *v.t.* **5.** To cause to swing from side to side. **6.** To cause to bend or incline to one side. **7.** *Naut.* To swing into place; hoist, as a yard or mast. **8.** To cause (a person, opinion, etc.) to tend in a given way; influence. **9.** To cause to swerve; deflect or divert, as from a course of action. **10.** *Archaic* **a** To wield, as a weapon or, especially, a scepter. **b** To rule over; govern. — **Syn.** See INFLUENCE. — *n.* **1.** Power exercised in governing; dominion; control. **2.** The act of swaying; a sweeping, swinging, or turning from side to side. **3.** Momentum; inclination; bias. **4.** Overpowering force or influence. [Prob. fusion of ON *sveigja* to bend and LG *swajen* to be moved to and fro by the wind]

sway·back (swā′bak′) *n.* A hollow or unnaturally sagging condition of the back, as in a horse.

sway-backed (swā′bakt′) *adj.* Having a sagged or hollow back.

Swa·zi (swä′zē) *n.* One of a tribe belonging to the Bantu peoples, and dwelling in Swaziland, Africa.

Swa·zi·land (swä′zē·land) An independent member of the British Commonwealth of Nations, between Mozambique and South Africa; 6,704 sq. mi.; pop. 408,400 (1970); capital, Mbabane. See map of SOUTH AFRICA.

Swe. Sweden; Swedish.

swear (swâr) *v.* **swore** (*Obs.* **sware**), **sworn, swear·ing** *v.i.* **1.** To make a solemn affirmation with an appeal to God or to some deity, or with invocation of something held sacred, as in attestation of truth or proof of good intentions: He *swore* by all the gods. **2.** To make a vow; utter a solemn promise. **3.** To use profanity; curse. **4.** *Law* To give testimony under oath. — *v.t.* **5.** To affirm or assert solemnly by invoking sacred beings or things. **6.** To promise with an oath or solemn affirmation; vow. **7.** To declare or affirm upon oath: to *swear* treason against a man. **8.** To take or utter (an oath). **9.** To administer a legal oath to. **— to swear by 1.** To appeal to by oath. **2.** To have complete confidence in. **— to swear in** To administer a legal oath to. **— to swear off** *Informal* To promise to renounce or give up: to *swear off* drink. **— to swear out** To obtain (a warrant for arrest) by making a statement or charge under oath. [OE *swerian*] **— swear′er** *n.*

sweat (swet) *v.* **sweat** or **sweat·ed, sweat·ing** *v.i.* **1.** To exude or excrete sensible moisture from the pores of the skin; perspire. **2.** To exude moisture in drops; ooze. **3.** To gather and condense moisture in drops, as on the outer surface of a glass, pitcher, etc. **4.** To pass through pores or interstices in drops. **5.** To ferment, as tobacco leaves. **6.** *Informal* To work hard; toil; drudge. **7.** *Informal* To suffer: You will *sweat* for that! **—** *v.t.* **8.** To exude (moisture) from the pores. **9.** To gather or condense drops of (moisture). **10.** To soak or stain with perspiration. **11.** To cause to sweat. **12.** To cause to work hard. **13.** *Informal* To force (employees) to work for low wages and under unfavorable conditions. **14.** *Slang* To extort money from. **15.** To heat (solder, etc.) until it melts. **16.** To join, as metal objects, by applying heat after binding together with solder. **17.** *Metall.* To heat so as to extract an element that is easily fusible. **18.** To force moisture from, as wood in a charcoal kiln. **19.** To subject to fermentation, as hides or tobacco. **20.** To remove particles of (coins) illegally, as by shaking them in a bag. **21.** *Slang* To subject to torture or rigorous interrogation for the purpose of extracting information; put through the third degree. **— to sweat (something) out** *U.S. Slang* To wait through anxiously and helplessly: to *sweat out* a long delay. **—** *n.* **1.** The act or state of sweating. **2.** That which is excreted from the sweat glands; perspiration. **3.** Any gathering in minute drops of moisture on a surface. **4.** *Archaic* Hard labor; drudgery. **5.** *Informal* Fuming impatience; worry; hurry. **6.** The act or process of causing to sweat. **— no sweat** *U.S. Slang* No difficulty whatever; easily manageable. [OE *swǣtan* < *swāt* sweat] **— sweat′i·ly** *adv.* **— sweat′i·ness** *n.* **— sweat′y** *adj.*

sweat·band (swet′band′) *n.* A band, usually of leather, inside the crown of a hat to protect it from sweat.

sweat·box (swet′boks′) *n.* **1.** A device for sweating such products as hides and dried fruits. **2.** A narrow cell or box where an unruly prisoner is confined.

sweat·ed (swet′id) *adj.* **1.** Saturated or covered with sweat. **2.** Employed in hard work for low pay. **3.** Overworked and underpaid.

sweat·er (swet′ər) *n.* **1.** A knitted garment in the form of a jersey or jacket with or without sleeves: so called because originally worn by athletes to induce sweating. **2.** One who or that which sweats. **3.** An employer who underpays and overworks his employees. **4.** A medicine that induces sweating: a sudorific.

sweat gland *Anat.* One of the convoluted tubules that secrete sweat, found in subcutaneous tissue and terminating externally in a small orifice or pore.

sweating sickness *Pathol.* A febrile infective disease epidemic in England in the 15th and 16th centuries, characterized by profuse sweating. Also **sweating fever.**

sweat shirt A collarless pullover, sometimes lined with fleece, used by athletes.

sweat·shop (swet′shop′) *n.* A place where work is done under poor conditions, for insufficient wages, and for long hours.

Swed. Sweden; Swedish.

swede (swēd) *n. Chiefly Brit.* A rutabaga.

Swede (swēd) *n.* A native or inhabitant of Sweden, or a person of Swedish descent.

Swe·den (swēd′n) A kingdom in the eastern part of the Scandinavian peninsula; 173,577 sq. mi.; pop. 7,978,000 (1969); capital, Stockholm: Swedish *Sverige.*

Swe·den·borg (swēd′n·bôrg, *Sw.* svā′den·bôr′y′), **Emanuel,** 1688–1772, Swedish mystic theologian, philosopher, and scientist: original name **Emanuel Sved·berg** (svād′bar′y′). **— Swe′den·bor·gi·an** (-bôr′jē·ən) *adj. & n.*

Swe·den·bor·gi·an·ism (swē′den·bôr′jē·ən·iz′əm) *n.* The system of philosophy or the theology developed by Emanuel Swedenborg, or from his writings. The **Swedenborgian Church,** first organized in London in 1783, is also called the *New Church,* or the *New Jerusalem Church.* Also **Swe′den·borg′ism** (-bôrg′iz·əm).

Swed·ish (swē′dish) *adj.* Pertaining to Sweden, the Swedes, or their language. **—** *n.* **1.** The North Germanic language of Sweden. **2.** The inhabitants of Sweden collectively: with *the.* Abbr. *Sw., Swe., Swed.*

Swedish clover Alsike.

Swedish massage Massage given in combination with Swedish movements.

Swedish movements A system of muscular movements employed in treating certain diseases or developing the body.

Swedish turnip The rutabaga.

sweep (swēp) *v.* **swept, sweep·ing** *v.t.* **1.** To collect, remove, or clear away with a broom, brush, etc. **2.** To clear or clean with or as with a broom or brush: to *sweep* a floor. **3.** To touch or brush with a motion as of sweeping: Her dress *swept* the ground. **4.** To pass over or through swiftly, as in searching: His eyes *swept* the sky. **5.** To cause to move with an even, continuous action: He *swept* the cape over her shoulders. **6.** To move, carry, bring, etc., with strong or continuous force: The flood *swept* the bridge away. **7.** To move over or through with strong or steady force: The gale *swept* the bay. **8.** To drag the bottom of (a body of water, etc.). **—** *v.i.* **9.** To clean or brush a floor or other surface with a broom, etc. **10.** To move or go strongly and evenly, especially with speed: The train *swept* by. **11.** To walk with or as with trailing garments: She *swept* into the room. **12.** To trail, as a skirt. **13.** To extend with a long reach or curve: The road *sweeps* along the lake shore. **—** *n.* **1.** The act or result of sweeping. **2.** A long stroke or movement: a *sweep* of the hand. **3.** The act of clearing out or getting rid of, as a removal from office or place: a clean *sweep* of the officeholders. **4.** A turning of the eye or of optical instruments over the field of vision. **5.** The winning of a great success, as in an election. **6.** The range, area, or compass reached by sweeping, as extent of stroke, range of vision, etc. **7.** A curve or bend, as of a scythe blade, etc. **8.** *Brit.* A chimney sweep. **9.** A long, heavy oar. **10.** A well sweep (which see). **11.** *pl.* Sweepings, as of a place where precious metals are worked. **12.** The winning of every contest, event, etc., as in a series or set: The Yankees made a *sweep* of the World Series. **13.** In card games: **a** A winning of all the points or tricks, as in whist. **b** The taking of all the cards on the table in casino. **14.** *Informal* Sweepstakes. [ME *swepen,* alter. of *swopen* to brush away < OE *swāpan*] **— sweep′er** *n.* **— sweep′y** *adj.*

sweep·back (swēp′bak′) *n. Aeron.* The backward inclination of or the angle formed by the leading edge of an airplane wing.

sweep·ing (swē′ping) *adj.* **1.** Carrying off or clearing away with a driving movement. **2.** Carrying all before it; covering a wide area; comprehensive. **3.** General and thoroughgoing. **—** *n.* **1.** The action of one who or that which sweeps. **2.** *pl.* Things swept up; refuse. **— sweep′ing·ly** *adv.* **— sweep′ing·ness** *n.*

sweep·stakes (swēp′stāks′) *n. pl.* **·stakes 1.** A gambling arrangement by which all the sums staked may be won by one or by a few of the betters, as in a horse race. **2.** A race for all the stakes. **3.** A prize in a sporting contest comprising several stakes; also, a lottery offering such a prize. Also **sweep′stake′.**

sweep ticket A ticket that gives the holder a chance to win in a sweepstakes.

sweer (swir) *adj. Scot & Brit. Dial.* **1.** Heavy; lazy; indolent. **2.** Reluctant; unwilling. [OE *swēr*]

sweet (swet) *adj.* **1.** Agreeable to the sense of taste; especially, having an agreeable flavor of or like that of sugar. **2.** Containing or due to sugar in some form. **3.** Not fermented or decaying; fresh. **4.** Not salt or salty: *sweet* water. **5.** Gently pleasing to the senses. **6.** Agreeable or delightful to the mind; arousing gentle, pleasant emotions. **7.** Having gentle, pleasing, and winning qualities; marked by kindness and amiability; dear; beloved. **8.** *Music Slang* a Designating jazz marked by blandness, moderate tempo, etc. b Playing or performing such jazz: a *sweet* trumpet. **9.** Sound; rich; productive: said of soil. **10.** Not dry: said of wines. **11.** *Chem.* Free from acid, etc. **—** *n.* **1.** The quality of being sweet; sweetness. **2.** *Chiefly pl.* A confection, preserve, or piece of candy. **3.** A beloved person; darling. **4.** Something agreeable or pleasing; a pleasure. **5.** *Brit.* A dessert. [OE *swēte*] **— sweet′ly** *adv.*

Sweet (swet), **Henry,** 1845–1912, English philologist.

sweet alyssum A perennial Mediterranean herb (*Lobularia maritima*) of the mustard family, having very fragrant white blossoms: also called *madwort.*

sweet basil See under BASIL.

sweet bay 1. Laurel (def. 1). **2.** A highly ornamental tree or shrub (*Magnolia virginiana*), with large flowers.

sweet·bread (swet′bred′) *n.* The pancreas (**stomach sweetbread**) or the thymus gland (**neck sweetbread** or **throat sweetbread**) of a calf or other animal, when used as food. [< SWEET + BREAD, in obs. sense of "a morsel"]

sweet·bri·er (swet′brī′ər) *n.* A stout prickly rose (*Rosa eglanteria*) native in Europe and Asia, with aromatic leaves: also called *eglantine.* Also **sweet′bri′ar.**

sweet cherry See under CHERRY.

sweet cicely 1. A small European perennial (*Myrrhis odorata*) of the parsley family, having white fragrant flowers. **2.** A related American herb (genus *Osmorhiza*) with white or purplish flowers and fleshy aromatic root.

sweet clover Melilot.

sweet corn 1. Any of several varieties of corn rich in sugar and shriveling when ripe: also called *sugar corn.* **2.** Young ears of corn having sweet, milky kernels, boiled or roasted as food: also called *green corn*.

sweet·en (swēt′n) *v.t.* **1.** To make sweet or sweeter. **2.** To make more endurable; lighten. **3.** To make pleasant or gratifying. **4.** *Slang* In poker, to increase the chips in (the pot). **5.** *Informal* To add gilt-edge securities to others so as to increase the value of (collateral for a loan). — *v.i.* **6.** To become sweet or sweeter.

sweet·en·er (swēt′n·ər) *n.* One who or that which sweetens; especially, a nonnutritive food sweetener that does not contain sugar, as saccharin or a sodium or calcium salt.

sweet·en·ing (swēt′n·ing) *n.* **1.** The act of making sweet. **2.** That which sweetens.

sweet fern A North American shrub (genus *Comptonia*) with fernlike, fragrant leaves.

sweet flag A marsh-dwelling plant (*Acorus calamus*), having sword-shaped leaves and a thick creeping rootstock with an aromatic flavor: also called *calamus*.

sweet gale A branching shrub (*Myrica gale*), with both fertile and sterile flowers in short scaly catkins, and resinous, dotted, fragrant leaves.

sweet gum **1.** A balsamiferous North American tree (*Liquidambar styraciflua*), the wood of which is sometimes used to imitate mahogany. **2.** The balsam or gum yielded by it. Also called *bilsted, copalm*.

sweet·heart (swēt′härt′) *n.* One who is particularly loved by or as a lover; a lover: often used as a term of endearment.

sweet·ie (swē′tē) *n. U.S. Informal* Darling; dear; honey.

sweet·ing (swē′ting) *n.* **1.** A sweet apple. **2.** *Archaic* A sweetheart; dear one; darling.

sweet·ish (swē′tish) *adj.* Somewhat or rather sweet. **sweet′ish·ly** *adv.* — **sweet′ish·ness** *n.*

sweet·leaf (swēt′lēf′) A shrub (*Symplocos tinctoria*) of the southern United States, eaten by horses and cattle.

sweet marjoram See under MARJORAM.

sweet·meat (swēt′mēt′) *n.* **1.** A confection, preserve, candy, etc. **2.** *pl.* Very sweet candy, cakes, etc.

sweet·ness (swēt′nis) *n.* The state or quality of being sweet.

sweet pea An ornamental annual climber (*Lathyrus odoratus*) of the bean family cultivated for its varicolored flowers.

sweet pepper A variety of capsicum (*Capsicum frutescens grossum*) whose unripe green fruit is used as a vegetable.

sweet potato **1.** A perennial tropical vine (*Ipomoea batatas*) of the morning-glory family, with rose-violet or pink flowers and a fleshy tuberous root: also called *Carolina potato*. **2.** The root itself, eaten as a vegetable. **3.** *U.S. Informal* An ocarina.

sweets (swēts) *n.pl.* **1.** Sweet things. **2.** *Brit.* Candy.

sweet-scent·ed (swēt′sen′tid) *adj.* Having a fragrant scent; sweet-smelling.

sweet·sop (swēt′sop′) *n.* **1.** A tropical American tree (*Annona squamosa*) allied to the custard apple. **2.** Its egg-shaped, scaly fruit. Also called *sugar apple*.

sweet tooth *Informal* A fondness for candy or sweets.

sweet william A perennial species of pink (*Dianthus barbatus*) with large lanceolate leaves and closely clustered, showy flowers. Also **sweet William**.

swell (swel) *v.* **swelled, swelled** or **swol·len, swell·ing** *v.i.* **1.** To increase in bulk or dimension, as by inflation with air or by absorption of moisture; dilate; expand. **2.** To increase in size, amount, degree, etc. **3.** To grow in volume or intensity, as a sound. **4.** To rise in waves or swells, as the sea. **5.** To bulge; protrude or belly, as a sail. **6.** To become puffed up with pride. **7.** To grow within one: My anger *swells* at the sight. — *v.t.* **8.** To cause to increase in size or bulk. **9.** To cause to increase in amount, extent, or degree. **10.** To cause to bulge; belly. **11.** To puff with pride. **12.** *Music* To crescendo and diminuendo in immediate succession. — *n.* **1.** The act, process, or effect of swelling; expansion. **2.** The long continuous body of a wave; a billow; also, a rise of, or undulation in, the land. **3.** A bulge or protuberance. **4.** *Music* A crescendo and an immediate diminuendo; also, the signs (< >) indicating it. **5.** A device, as on an organ, by which the volume of a tone may be uninterruptedly varied. **6.** *Informal* A person of the ultrafashionable set. — *adj. Informal* **1.** Of or pertaining to ultrafashionable people; smart. **2.** First-rate; distinctive. [OE *swellan*] — **Syn.** (verb) **1.** bulge, distend, enlarge, inflate. — **Ant.** shrink, dwindle, contract. — (noun) **2.** breaker, roller, surge. **6.** nob, toff, fop, dandy, dude, macaroni.

swell box A chamber containing the pipes of the organ and having a front of movable slats that muffle the sound or allow it to be heard clearly.

swell·fish (swel′fish′) *n. pl.* **·fish** or **·fish·es** A globefish.

swell·ing (swel′ing) *n.* **1.** The act of expanding, inflating, or augmenting. **2.** *Pathol.* Abnormal enlargement or protuberance of a part of the body. — *adj.* Increasing; bulging.

swel·ter (swel′tər) *v.i.* **1.** To suffer from oppressive heat; perspire from heat. — *v.t.* **2.** To cause to suffer or perspire from heat. **3.** *Obs.* To exude. — *n. Archaic* A hot, sweltering condition; oppressive, humid heat. [Freq. of obs. and dial. *swelt* be faint, die < OE *sweltan* to die]

swel·ter·ing (swel′tər·ing) *adj.* **1.** Oppressive; overpower-

ingly hot. **2.** Overcome by or suffering with heat. Also **swel′try** (-trē). — **swel′ter·ing·ly** *adv.*

swept (swept) Past tense and past participle of SWEEP.

swept-back (swept′bak′) *adj. Aeron.* Having the leading edge inclined backward at an angle with the lateral axis of the airplane: said of a wing: also *backswept*.

swept-wing (swept′wing′) *n. Aeron.* A sweptback wing.

swerve (swûrv) *v.t. & v.i.* **swerved, swerv·ing** To turn or cause to turn aside from a course or purpose; deflect. — *n.* **1.** The act of swerving or turning aside. **2.** That which swerves. [OE *sweorfan* to file or grind away]

swift (swift) *adj.* **1.** Traversing space or performing movements in a brief time; rapid; quick. **2.** Capable of quick motion; fleet; speedy. **3.** Passing rapidly, as time or events; also, coming without warning; unexpected. **4.** Acting with readiness; prompt. — *adv. Poetic* Quickly. — *n.* **1.** A bird of swallowlike form (family *Apodidae*) possessing extraordinary powers of flight; especially, the **chimney swift** (*Chaetura pelagica*) of America: also called *chimney swallow*. **2.** One of various small lizards (genera *Sceloporus* and *Uta*) common in the western United States. **3.** A reel having an adjustable diameter for winding yarn, etc. **4.** The main cylinder of a carding machine; also, a similar part in other machines. [OE] — **swift′ly** *adv.* — **swift′ness** *n.* — **Syn.** (adj.) **1.** *Swift, fleet, speedy, rapid, quick,* and *expeditious* relate to movement at high velocity. *Swift* and *fleet* are chiefly applied to moving persons or animals; *swift* suggests ease of motion, and *fleet*, nimbleness: a *swift* bird, a *fleet* horse. *Speedy* may be applied to that which moves or that which progresses: a *speedy* worker, to take *speedy* action on a request. *Rapid* is applied to progress: *rapid* delivery of mail, *rapid* transit. *Quick* suggests speed in responding, or promptness: a *quick* reply. *Expeditious* combines *quick* and *speedy*, and suggests good organization and efficiency: *expeditious* handling of a complaint, or of an order for merchandise. — **Ant.** slow, dilatory, tardy.

Swift (swift), Jonathan, 1667–1745, English clergyman, satirist, and man of letters born in Ireland: called **Dean Swift**.

swift·er (swif′tər) *n. Naut.* **1.** A rope around the extremities of the capstan bars to connect and steady them, and to give a hold for extra men. **2.** One of the forward lower shrouds. For illustration see SHROUD[2]. **3.** A rope for encircling a boat, to strengthen her or prevent chafing of her sides. [< obs. *swift* to tie with ropes drawn taut, prob. < Scand. Cf. ON *svipta* to reef (a sail).]

swig (swig) *Informal n.* A deep draft, as of liquor. — *v.t. & v.i.* **swigged, swig·ging** To drink deeply or greedily. [Origin unknown] — **swig′ger** *n.*

swill (swil) *v.t.* **1.** To drink greedily or to excess. **2.** *Brit.* To drench, as with water; rinse; wash. — *v.i.* **3.** To drink to excess; tope. — *n.* **1.** Liquid food for domestic animals; especially, the mixture of liquid and solid food given to swine; slop. **2.** Any animal or vegetable refuse; garbage. **3.** A deep draft of liquor. [OE *swillan, swilian* to wash]

swim[1] (swim) *v.* **swam** (*Archaic* **swum**), **swum, swim·ming** *v.i.* **1.** To move through water by movements of the arms, legs, fins, etc. **2.** To be supported on water or other liquid; float. **3.** To move with a smooth or flowing motion, as if swimming in water. **4.** To be immersed in or covered with liquid; be flooded; overflow. — *v.t.* **5.** To cross or traverse by swimming. **6.** To cause to swim. — *n.* **1.** The action, pastime, or period of swimming. **2.** A gliding, swaying motion or movement. — **in the swim** *Informal* In the current of affairs. [OE *swimman*] — **swim′mer** *n.*

swim[2] (swim) *v.i.* **swam** (*Archaic* **swum**), **swum, swim·ming** **1.** To be dizzy; reel; have a giddy sensation. **2.** To seem to reel, whirl, or spin. — *n.* A sudden dizziness or swoon. [OE *swīma* dizziness]

swim bladder The air bladder of a fish. Also **swimming bladder**.

swim fin One of the flat rubber fins worn on the feet to increase the propulsive effect of the swimmer's kick.

swim·mer·et (swim′ə·ret) *n. Zool.* One of a series of fringed abdominal appendages of various crustaceans, adapted for swimming, for aid in respiration, and for carrying the eggs: also called *pleopod*. [Dim. of SWIMMER]

swim·ming[1] (swim′ing) *n.* The act of one who or that which swims. — *adj.* **1.** Used for swimming. **2.** Having the capacity of swimming; natatorial. **3.** Watery; flooded with tears, as the eyes. [< SWIM[1]]

swim·ming[2] (swim′ing) *n.* A state of dizziness or vertigo. — *adj.* Affected by dizziness. [< SWIM[2]]

swimming hole *U.S.* A pond, deep place in a creek, etc., used for swimming.

swim·ming·ly (swim′ing·lē) *adv.* Easily, rapidly, and successfully.

swimming pool *U.S.* An indoor or outdoor tank designed for swimming, usually rectangular in shape, deeper at one end than at the other, built of concrete, and equipped to clean and purify the water. Also *Brit.* **swimming bath**.

swim·suit (swim′sōōt′) *n.* A bathing suit.

Swin·burne (swin′bûrn), Algernon Charles, 1837–1909, English poet and critic.

swin·dle (swin′dəl) *v.* **·dled, ·dling** *v.t.* **1.** To cheat of money or property by deliberate fraud; defraud. **2.** To obtain by such means. — *v.i.* **3.** To practice fraud or decep-

tion in order to obtain money or property. — *n.* **1.** The act or process of swindling. **2.** Anything that proves to be fraudulent or deceptive, especially, a deal or scheme. [Back formation < SWINDLER]
— **Syn.** (verb) **1.** fleece, cozen, bamboozle, hoodwink. Compare DECEIVE.

swin·dler (swind'lər) *n.* One who swindles or deceives. [< G *schwindler* giddy-minded person, cheat < *schwindeln* to act thoughtlessly, be giddy]

swine (swīn) *n. pl.* **swine** **1.** A domesticated pig. **2.** Any of several related omnivorous mammals (family *Suidae*) having a long mobile snout and cloven hoofs. **3.** A low, greedy, stupid, or vicious person. [OE *swīn*]

swine·herd (swīn'hûrd') *n.* A tender of swine.

swine·pox (swīn'poks') *n.* A form of chicken pox affecting swine.

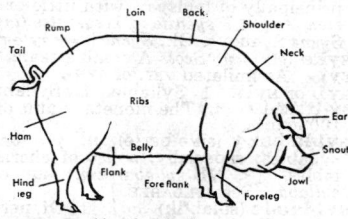

SWINE (Anatomical nomenclature)

swing (swing) *v.* **swung** (*Dial.* **swang**), **swung, swing·ing** *v.i.* **1.** To move to-and-fro or backward and forward rhythmically, as something suspended; oscillate. **2.** To ride in a swing. **3.** To move with an even, swaying motion. **4.** To turn; pivot. **5.** To be suspended; hang. **6.** To move or change from one condition, thought, opinion, etc., to another. **7.** *Informal* To be executed by hanging. **8.** *Slang* To have an immediate and compelling effect, as jazz music. **9.** *Slang* To be full of life; succeed in a lively way. — *v.t.* **10.** To cause to move to and fro or backward and forward. **11.** To cause to move with a sweeping or circular motion, as a sword, ax, etc.; brandish; flourish. **12.** To cause to turn on or as on a pivot or central point. **13.** To lift or hoist: They *swung* the mast into place. **14.** *Informal* To bring to a successful conclusion; manage or influence successfully. — *n.* **1.** The act, process, or manner of swinging; also, the distance covered in swinging. **2.** A free swaying motion. **3.** A contrivance of hanging ropes or chains with a suspended seat on which a person may move to and fro as a pastime. **4.** Free course or scope; full liberty. **5.** Compass; sweep. **6.** The movement or rhythm characterizing certain styles of prose and poetry. **7.** That which swings or is swung. **8.** A sweeping blow or stroke. **9.** The course of a career or period of activity; main current of business. **10.** A form of jazz music developed after about 1935, characterized by large bands, contrapuntal styles, arranged ensemble playing, etc. [OE *swingan* to scourge, beat up]

swing bridge A bridge constructed to rotate in a horizontal plane to permit the passage of large vessels, etc.

swinge (swinj) *v.t.* **swinged, swinge·ing** *Archaic* To flog; chastise. [OE *swengan* to shake, beat] — **swing'er** *n.*

swing·er (swing'ər) *n.* **1.** One who or that which swings. **2.** *Slang* A lively, modern, hip person.

swing·ing (swing'ing) *adj. Slang* **1.** Lively and compelling in effect: a *swinging* jazz quartet. **2.** Lively and modern; also, hip: a *swinging* party; a *swinging* crowd.

swin·gle (swing'gəl) *n.* **1.** A large, knifelike, wooden implement for beating and scraping flax. Also **swing'knife. 2.** A swiple. — *v.t.* **·gled, ·gling** To cleanse (flax) by beating with a swingle. [< MDu. *swinghel.* Akin to SWING.]

swin·gle·tree (swing'gəl·trē') *n.* A whiffletree (which see).

swing shift *U.S. Informal* An evening work shift, usually lasting from about 4 p.m. to midnight.

swin·ish (swī'nish) *adj.* Of, like, or fit for swine; degraded; sensual; beastly. — **swin'ish·ly** *adv.* — **swin'ish·ness** *n.*

swink (swingk) *Archaic & Brit. Dial. v.i.* To toil hard; drudge. — *n.* Hard labor; toil. [OE *swincan*]

swipe (swīp) *v.t.* **swiped, swip·ing** **1.** *Informal* To give a strong blow; strike with a full swing of the arm. **2.** *Slang* To steal; snatch. — **Syn.** See STEAL. — *n.* **1.** *Informal* A hard, sweeping stroke or blow. **2.** A well sweep, lever, pump handle, etc. [Var. of SWEEP]

swipes (swīps) *n.pl. Brit. Slang* **1.** Poor, spoiled, or weak beer; small beer. **2.** Beer in general. [< SWIPE, in obs. sense of "drink hastily"]

swi·ple (swip'əl) *n.* The part of a threshing flail that strikes the grain: also called *swingle.* Also **swip'ple.** [ME *swepelle* broom. Akin to SWEEP.]

swirl (swûrl) *v.i.* **1.** To move with a whirling or twisting motion; whirl. **2.** To be dizzy; swim, as the head. — *v.t.* **3.** To cause to move in a whirling or twisting motion. — *n.* **1.** A whirling along, as in an eddy; whirl. **2.** A curl or twist; spiral. — [< dial. E (Scottish) *swyrle.* Prob. akin to dial. Norw. *svirla* to whirl.]

swirl·y (swûr'lē) *adj.* **1.** Full of swirls. **2.** *Scot.* Tangled; knotty; gnarled.

swish (swish) *v.i.* **1.** To move through the air with a hissing, whistling sound, as a slender, flexible rod. **2.** To rustle, as a silk dress in motion. **3.** To strike or cut off with a swishing blow. — *v.t.* **4.** To cause to swish. **5.** To thrash; flog. — *n.* **1.** A hissing, whistling, or rustling sound. **2.** A movement producing such a sound. **3.** A rod used for flogging; also, a stroke with such a rod. **4.** *U.S. Slang* A homosexual. — *adj. Brit. Slang* Smart; fashionable. [Imit.]

swiss (swis) *n. Often cap.* A sheer, crisp cotton fabric, similar to muslin. Compare DOTTED SWISS.

Swiss (swis) *adj.* Of or pertaining to Switzerland or its inhabitants. — *n. pl.* **Swiss** A native or naturalized inhabitant of Switzerland.

Swiss chard Chard (which see).

Swiss cheese A pale yellow cheese with many large holes, made in, or similar to that made in, Switzerland.

Swiss guards Mercenary soldiers from Switzerland formerly used as bodyguards by European monarchs, now guards at the Vatican.

Swiss steak A thick cut of steak floured and braised, often with a sauce of tomatoes and onions.

Swit. Switzerland.

switch (swich) *n.* **1.** A small flexible rod, etc., used for whipping. **2.** A tress of false hair, fastened together at one end and used by women in building a coiffure. **3.** A mechanism for shifting a railway train or other rail vehicles from one track to another. **4.** The act or operation of switching, shifting, or changing. **5.** The end of the tail in certain animals, as a cow. **6.** *Electr.* A device to make or break a circuit, or transfer a current from one conductor to another. — *v.t.* **1.** To whip or lash with or as with a switch. **2.** To move, jerk, or whisk suddenly or sharply. **3.** To turn aside or divert; shift. **4.** To exchange: They *switched* plates. **5.** To shift (a railroad car) to another track by means of a switch. **6.** *Electr.* To connect or disconnect with a switch. — *v.i.* **7.** To turn aside; change; shift. **8.** To be shifted or turned. [Earlier *swits.* Akin to LG *zwukse* a thin rod.] — **switch'er** *n.*

switch·back (swich'bak') *n.* **1.** A railway or road ascending a steep incline in a zigzag pattern. **2.** *Brit.* A roller coaster.

switch·blade knife (swich'blād') A clasp knife having a spring-loaded blade that opens when a switch is pressed.

switch·board (swich'bôrd', -bōrd') *n.* A panel or arrangement of panels bearing switches for connecting and disconnecting electric circuits, as a telephone exchange.

switch hitter In baseball, a player able to bat both left-handed and right-handed.

switch·man (swich'mən) *n. pl.* **·men** (-mən) One who handles railway switches.

switch·yard (swich'yärd') *n.* A railroad yard for the assembling and breaking up of trains.

swith (swith) *adv. Dial.* Quickly; instantly. Also **swithe** (swiᵺ). [OE *swīthe*]

swith·er (swiᵺ'ər) *v.i. Scot.* To doubt; hesitate; fear.

Swith·in (swiᵺ'in), **Saint** See under ST. SWITHIN'S DAY.

Switz. Switzerland.

Swit·zer (swit'sər) *n.* A Swiss. Also **Swiss·er** (swis'ər).

Swit·zer·land (swit'sər·lənd) A Republic in central Europe; 15,940 sq. mi.; pop. 6,230,000 (est. 1969); capital, Bern: French *Suisse,* German *Schweiz,* Italian *Svizzera,* Latin *Helvetia.* Officially **Swiss Confederation.**

swiv·el (swiv'əl) *n.* **1.** A coupling device, link, ring, or pivot that permits either half of a mechanism, as a chain, to rotate independently. **2.** A pivoted rest or support on which a gun may be swung in a horizontal plane. **3.** A cannon that swings on a pivot: also **swivel gun.** — *v.* **swiv·eled** or **·elled, swiv·el·ing** or **·el·ling** *v.t.* **1.** To turn on or as on a swivel. **2.** To provide with or secure by a swivel. — *v.i.* **3.** To turn or swing on or as on a swivel. [ME *swynnel* < OE *swif-,* stem of *swīfan* to revolve]

swivel chair A chair having a seat that turns horizontally on a swivel.

swiv·et (swiv'it) *n. Slang* A state of nervous excitement; tizzy. [Origin unknown]

swiz·zle (swiz'əl) *n.* Any of various alcoholic mixed drinks; especially, a drink made with rum or other spirit, sugar, bitters, and ice. [Origin unknown]

swizzle stick A slender rod of glass, plastic, etc., used to mix drinks.

swob (swob), **swob·ber** (swob'ər) See SWAB, etc.

swol·len (swō'lən) Alternative past participle of SWELL.

swoon (swoon) *v.i.* To faint. — *n.* The act of swooning; a fainting fit. — **Syn.** See UNCONSCIOUSNESS. [ME *swounen,* back formation < *swoweninge.* See SWOONING.]

swoop (swoop) *v.i.* **1.** To drop or descend suddenly, as a bird pouncing on its prey. — *v.t.* **2.** To take or seize suddenly: often with *up.* — *n.* The act of swooping. [Var. of obs. *swope* < OE *swāpan* to sweep; prob. infl. in form by dial. E *soop* to sweep < ON *sōpa*]

swop (swop) See SWAP.

sword (sôrd, sōrd) *n.* **1.** A weapon consisting of a long blade fixed in a hilt, used for cutting or thrusting, as a rapier, scimitar, etc. **2.** Power; authority; sovereignty; especially, military as opposed to civil power. **3.** War; destruction; slaughter; also, the cause of death or ruin. **— at swords' points** Hostile; ready for a fight. **— to put to the sword** To kill with a sword; slaughter in battle. [OE *sweord*]

sword bayonet A bayonet having the shape of a sword and used like one. For illustration see BAYONET.

sword·bill (sôrd′bil′, sōrd′-) *n.* A tropical American hummingbird (genus *Ensifera*) with a very long, slender bill.

sword cane A cane made to carry a sword or dagger.

sword·craft (sôrd′kraft′, -kräft′, sōrd′-) *n.* **1.** Dexterity or skill in the use of the sword. **2.** Exercise of authority by military power.

sword dance Any of several dances performed among or over naked swords laid on the ground.

sword·fish (sôrd′fish′, sōrd′-) *n.* *pl.* **·fish** or **·fish·es** A large fish of the open sea (genus *Xiphias*) having the bones of the upper jaw consolidated to form an elongated swordlike process: also called *broadbill*.

SWORDFISH
(About 11 feet long; sword about 4½ feet)

sword grass **1.** Any of several varieties of grasses or sedges (especially genus *Mariscus*, formerly *Cladium*) with sharp or serrated edges. **2.** The gladiolus.

sword·knot (sôrd′not′, sōrd′-) *n.* Formerly, a loop of leather used to fasten the hilt of a sword to the wrist; now, a tassel of cord or ribbon tied to a sword hilt.

sword lily The gladiolus.

sword of Damocles See under DAMOCLES.

sword·play (sôrd′plā′, sōrd′-) *n.* The act, art, or skill of using the sword, especially in fencing. **— sword′play′er** *n.*

swords·man (sôrdz′mən, sōrdz′-) *n.* *pl.* **·men** (-mən) One skilled in the use of or armed with a sword. Also **sword′man.** **— swords′man·ship** or **sword′man·ship** *n.*

swore (swôr, swōr) Past tense of SWEAR.

sworn (swôrn, swōrn) Past participle of SWEAR.

swot[1] (swot) *Brit. Slang* *v.i.* **swot·ted, swot·ting** To sweat or work hard over a task; grind. **— n. 1.** Hard work. **2.** One who works or studies hard. [Dial. var. of SWEAT]

swot[2] (swot) See SWAT.

swoun (swoun) *Obs.* *v.i.* To swoon. **— n.** A swoon. Also **swound** (swound).

swounds (zwoundz, zoundz), **swouns** (zwounz, zounz) See ZOUNDS.

S-wrench A wrench having an S-shaped haft with jaws at both ends. For illustration see WRENCH.

Swtz. Switzerland.

swum (swum) Past participle and dialectal past tense of SWIM.

swung (swung) Past tense and past participle of SWING.

sy- Var. of SYN-.

Syb·a·ris (sib′ər·is) An ancient Greek city in southern Italy, famous as a center of luxurious living; founded in 720 B.C.; destroyed, 510 B.C. **— Syb′a·rite** (-rīt) *n.* **— Syb′a·rit′ic** (-rit′ik) or **·i·cal** *adj.*

syb·a·rite (sib′ər·rīt) *n.* One given to pleasure and luxury; an epicure. [< L *Sybarita* < Gk. *Sybaritēs* < *Sybaris* Sybaris] **— syb′a·rit′ic** (-rit′ik) or **·i·cal** *adj.* **— syb′a·rit′i·cal·ly** *adv.*

sy·bo (sī′bō) *n.* *pl.* **·boes** The cibol or Welsh onion. [< dial. E (Scottish), var. of CIBOL]

syc·a·mine (sik′ə·min) *n.* The mulberry tree (*Morus nigra*) of the New Testament. [< LL *sycaminus* < Gk. *sykaminos* a mulberry tree < Aramaic *shiqmīn*, pl. < Hebrew *shiqmah*]

syc·a·more (sik′ə·môr, -mōr) *n.* **1.** A medium-sized bushy tree of Syria and Egypt (*Ficus sycomorus*) allied to the common fig. **2.** Any of various plane trees widely distributed in the United States, especially the **American sycamore** (*Platanus occidentalis*): also called *buttonwood*. **3.** An ornamental shade tree of Europe and Asia (*Acer pseudo-platanus*). Also *Obs.* **syc′o·more.** [< OF *sicamor* < LL *sycomorus* < Gk. *sykomoros* < *sykon* fig + *moron* mulberry]

syce (sīs) *n.* A groom; a manservant: also spelled *sice*, *saice*. [< Hind. *sā′is* < Arabic < *sūs* to tend a horse]

sy·cee (sī·sē′) *n.* Pure uncoined silver ingots of various weight and size, used by the Chinese as a medium of exchange. Also **sycee silver.** [< dial. Chinese (Cantonese) *sai sze*, var. of Chinese *si szĕ* fine silk; so called because if pure it may be drawn out into fine threads]

sy·co·ni·um (sī·kō′nē·əm) *n.* *pl.* **·ni·a** (-nē·ə) *Bot.* A multiple fruit in which many flowers have been developed on a fleshy receptacle, as in the fig. [< NL < Gk. *sykon* fig]

syc·o·phan·cy (sik′ə·fən·sē) *n.* *pl.* **·cies** **1.** The practices of a sycophant; base flattery; fawning. **2.** The character of a sycophant.

syc·o·phant (sik′ə·fənt) *n.* A servile flatterer; parasite. [< L *sycophanta* < Gk. *sykophantēs* informer < *sykon* fig + *phan-*, stem of *phainein* to show] **— syc′o·phan′tic** (-fan′tik) or **·i·cal** *adj.* **— syc′o·phan′ti·cal·ly** *adv.*

sy·co·sis (sī·kō′sis) *n.* *Pathol.* An inflamed staphylococcic infection of the skin involving the hair follicles,

generally of the face and scalp. [< NL < Gk. *sykōsis* fig-shaped ulcer < *sykon* fig]

Syd·ney (sid′nē) **1.** The capital of New South Wales, Australia, a port on the eastern coast; pop. 2,446,345 (1966, including suburbs). **2.** A port city in NE Nova Scotia, Canada; pop. 32,767 (1971).

Syd·ney (sid′nē), **Sir Philip** See SIDNEY.

Sy·e·ne (sī·ē′nē) The ancient name for ASWAN. **— Sy·e·nit·ic** (sī′ə·nit′ik) *adj.*

sy·e·nite (sī′ə·nīt) *n.* An igneous granular rock composed principally of feldspar, with little or no quartz: also spelled *sienite*. [< F *syénite* < L *syenites* (*lapis*) (stone) of Syene < *Syene* Syene < Gk. *Syēnē*] **— sy·e·nit′ic** (-nit′ik) *adj.*

syke (sīk) *n.* *Scot.* A small stream: also spelled *sike*.

syl- Assimilated var. of SYN-.

syl-, or **syll. 1.** Syllable. **2.** Syllabus.

sy·li (sē·lē′) *n.* The monetary unit of Guinea, equivalent to 100 couris.

syl·la·bar·y (sil′ə·ber′ē) *n.* *pl.* **·bar·ies** A list or table of syllables; especially, a list of characters representing syllables. [< NL *syllabarium*, neut. of Med.L *syllabarius* < *syllaba*. See SYLLABLE.]

syl·lab·ic (si·lab′ik) *adj.* **1.** Of, pertaining to, or consisting of a syllable or syllables. **2.** *Phonet.* Designating a consonant capable of forming a complete syllable without a vowel, as *l* in *middle* (mid′l) and *n* in *sudden* (sud′n). See SONORANT. **3.** Having every syllable distinctly pronounced. **4.** Designating a type of poetry based on a definite number of syllables per line rather than on stress or rhythm. Also **syl·lab′i·cal.** **— n.** *Phonet.* A sound of high sonority, usually a vowel. **— syl·lab′i·cal·ly** *adv.*

syl·lab·i·cate (si·lab′ə·kāt) *v.t.* **·cat·ed, ·cat·ing** To form or divide into syllables. **— syl·lab′i·ca′tion, syl·lab′i·fi·ca′tion** *n.*

syl·lab·i·fy (si·lab′ə·fī) *v.t.* **·fied, ·fy·ing** To syllabicate.

syl·la·bism (sil′ə·biz′əm) *n.* **1.** The use of characters representing syllables instead of letters in a written language. **2.** Division into syllables.

syl·la·bize (sil′ə·bīz) *v.t.* **·bized, ·biz·ing** To syllabicate.

syl·la·ble (sil′ə·bəl) *n.* **1.** *Phonet.* A word or part of a word uttered in a single vocal impulse, and consisting of a vowel (or diphthong) alone or with one or more consonants, or of a syllabic consonant. **2.** A part of a written or printed word corresponding, more or less, to the spoken division. In this dictionary, syllable breaks are indicated by centered dots. **3.** The least detail, mention, or trace: *Please don't repeat a syllable of what you've heard here.* **— v. ·bled, ·bling** *v.t.* **1.** To pronounce the syllables of. **— v.i. 2.** To pronounce syllables. Abbr. *syl., syll.* [< AF *sillable*, OF *sillabe* < L *syllaba* < Gk. *syllabē* < *syllambanein* < *syn-* together + *lambanein* to take]

syl·la·bub (sil′ə·bub) See SILLABUB.

syl·la·bus (sil′ə·bəs) *n.* *pl.* **·bus·es** or **·bi** (-bī) **1.** A concise statement of the main points of a course of study subject, etc. **2.** *Law* A short statement at the beginning of a brief of the legal points involved. Abbr. *syl., syll.* [< NL < Med.L *syllabos*, a misprint for L *sittybas*, accusative pl. of *sittyba* label on a book < Gk.]

syl·lep·sis (si·lep′sis) *n.* *pl.* **·ses** (-sēz) *Gram.* A rhetorical figure in which the meaning of a word shifts unexpectedly, as in "He took her to dinner and seriously." Compare ZEUGMA. [< LL *syllepsis* < Gk. *syllēpsis* < *syn-* together + *lēpsis* a taking] **— syl·lep′tic** *adj.*

syl·lo·gism (sil′ə·jiz′əm) *n.* **1.** *Logic* **a** A formula of argument consisting of three propositions. The first two propositions, called *premises*, have one term in common furnishing a logical connection between the two other terms, that are then linked in the third proposition, called the *conclusion.* Example: All men are mortal (*major premise*); kings are men (*minor premise*); therefore, kings are mortal (*conclusion*). In this example, the *major term* is "mortal," and the *minor term* is "kings." **b** Deductive reasoning. **2.** A subtle or crafty argument. [< OF *silogime* < L *syllogismus* < Gk. *syllogismos* < *syllogizesthai*. See SYLLOGIZE.]

syl·lo·gis·tic (sil′ə·jis′tik) *adj.* Pertaining to, or having the nature or form of, a syllogism: also **syl·lo·gis′ti·cal.** **— n.** The art of reasoning by syllogisms; also, the department of logic dealing with syllogisms: also **syl·lo·gis′tics.** **— syl·lo·gis′ti·cal·ly** *adv.*

syl·lo·gize (sil′ə·jīz) *v.t.* & *v.i.* **·gized, ·giz·ing** To reason or argue by syllogisms. [< OF *silogiser* < Med. L *syllogizare* < Gk. *syllogizesthai* < *syn-* together + *logizesthai* to infer < *logos* a discourse] **— syl′lo·gi·za′tion** (-jə·zā′shən) *n.*

sylph (silf) *n.* **1.** An imaginary being, mortal but without a soul, living in the air. **2.** A slender, graceful young woman or girl. [< NL *sylphes*, pl., ? coined by Paracelsus]

sylph·id (sil′fid) *n.* A young or diminutive sylph. **— adj.** Of or like a sylph: also **sylph·i·dine** (sil′fə·din, -dīn). [< F *sylphide*, dim. of *sylphe* < NL *sylphes*. See SYLPH.]

sylph·like (silf′līk′) *adj.* Resembling a sylph; slender; graceful. Also **sylph′ish, sylph′y.**

syl·va (sil′və) *n.* *pl.* **·vas** or **·vae** (-vē) *Rare* **1.** The forest trees, collectively, of a territory or region. **2.** A description or list of the forest trees of a certain region. Also spelled *silva*. [< L *silva* forest]

syl·van (sil'vən) *adj. Chiefly Poetic* **1.** Of, pertaining to, or located in a forest or woods. **2.** Composed of or abounding in trees or woods. **3.** Characteristic of a forest or wood; rustic. — *n.* **1.** A spirit or deity of the forest. **2.** *Poetic* A person or animal dwelling in the woods. Also spelled *silvan*. [< MF *sylvain* sylvan < L *sylvanus, silvanus* < *silva* wood]

syl·van·ite (sil'vən-īt) *n.* A metallic, grayish to silvery telluride of gold or silver, sometimes having the crystals arranged in patterns suggesting inscribed characters. [< (TRAN)SYLVAN(IA) + -ITE¹]

Syl·va·nus (sil-vā'nəs) See SILVANUS.

syl·vat·ic (sil-vat'ik) *adj.* **1.** Of, pertaining to, or found in trees or woods: a *sylvatic* species. **2.** Transmitted by forest-dwelling insects or animals: a *sylvatic* disease.

syl·vite (sil'vīt) *n.* A vitreous, native potassium chloride, occurring in cubic crystals, an important ore of potassium. Also **syl'vin** (-vin), **syl'vine** (-vin, -vīn), **syl'vin·ite** (-īt). [< NL (*sal digestivus*) *sylvii* (digestive salt) of Sylvius, 17th c. Dutch physician + -ITE¹]

sym- Assimilated var. of SYN-.

sym. **1.** Symbol. **2.** *Chem.* Symmetrical: also **sym-.** **3.** Symphony. **4.** Symptom.

sym·bi·ont (sim'bī-ont, -bē-) *n. Biol.* An organism living in a state of symbiosis. Also **sym'bi·on, sym'bi·ot** (-ot), **sym'bi·ote** (-ōt). [< Gk. *symbioōn, -ontos,* ppr. of *bioein.* See SYMBIOSIS.] — **sym'bi·on'tic** *adj.*

sym·bi·o·sis (sim'bī-ō'sis, -bē-) *n. Biol.* The consorting together, usually in mutually advantageous partnership, of dissimilar organisms, as of the algae and fungi in lichens. [< NL < Gk. *symbiōsis* a living together, companionship < *symbioein* to live together < *symbios* a companion, living together < *syn-* together + *bios* life] — **sym'bi·ot'ic** (-ot'ik) or **·i·cal** *adj.* — **sym'bi·ot'i·cal·ly** *adv.*

sym·bol (sim'bəl) *n.* **1.** Something chosen to stand for or represent something else; especially, an object used to typify a quality, abstract idea, etc.: The oak is a *symbol* of strength. **2.** A character, mark, or other sign indicating something, as a quantity in mathematics, etc. **3.** A representation, as an act or object, of an unconscious or repressed desire. — *v.t.* To symbolize. Abbr. *sym.* — **Syn.** See EMBLEM. [< LL *symbolum* < Gk. *symbolon* a mark, token < *symballein* to put together < *syn-* together + *ballein* to throw]

sym·bol·ic (sim-bol'ik) *adj.* **1.** Of, pertaining to, or expressed by a symbol or symbols. **2.** Conveying a relation or connection: said of words: distinguished from *presentive.* **3.** Serving as a symbol: with *of.* **4.** Characterized by or involving the use of symbols: *symbolic* poetry. Also **sym·bol'i·cal.** — **sym·bol'i·cal·ly** *adv.* — **sym·bol'i·cal·ness** *n.*

symbolical books Books containing the symbols or confessions of faith of a church, religious body, or inspired writer.

symbolic logic A discipline for studying formal logic that employs symbols to represent quantities, relationships, etc.: also called *mathematical logic.*

sym·bol·ism (sim'bəl-iz'əm) *n.* **1.** Representation by symbols; treatment or interpretation of things as symbolic. **2.** The quality of being symbolic. **3.** A system of symbols or symbolical representation. **4.** The theories and practice of a group of symbolists.

sym·bol·ist (sim'bəl-ist) *n.* **1.** One who uses symbols; especially, one skilled in the interpretation or use of symbols, as in literature and art. **2.** One of a group of French and Belgian writers and artists of the late 19th century, including Verlaine, Mallarmé and Maeterlinck, who sought to express ideas and emotions by symbolic objects, words, and sound. **3.** *Theol.* One who regards the elements of the Eucharist as mere symbols.

sym·bol·is·tic (sim'bəl-is'tik) *adj.* **1.** Expressed by symbols; characterized by the use of symbols. **2.** Of or pertaining to symbolism; symbolic. Also **sym'bol·is'ti·cal.**

sym·bol·ize (sim'bəl-īz) *v.* **·ized, ·iz·ing** *v.t.* **1.** To be a symbol of; represent symbolically; typify. **2.** To represent by a symbol or symbols. **3.** To treat as symbolic or figurative. — *v.i.* **4.** To use symbols. **5.** *Psychol.* To transfer emotional values from one person, object, or act to another. Also *Brit.* **sym'bol·ise.** — **sym'bol·i·za'tion** *n.*

sym·bol·o·gy (sim-bol'ə-jē) *n.* The art of representing by or interpreting symbols. [< SYMBO(L) + -LOGY]

sym·met·al·ism (sim-met'l-iz'əm) *n.* A money system in which the unit of coinage combines two or more metals in definite proportions. [< SYM- + METAL + -ISM]

sym·met·ri·cal (si-met'ri-kəl) *adj.* **1.** Exhibiting symmetry; having symmetrical proportions or a correspondence in shape, size, structure, and position of parts: well-balanced; regular: a *symmetrical* arrangement of furniture. **2.** *Biol.* Having parts or organs on one side corresponding to those on the other in shape, size, function, structure, etc. **3.** *Bot.* Regular as to number or shape of parts, as a flower when the divisions in each whorl are of the same number or mul-

tiples of the same. **4.** *Chem.* Denoting an arrangement of atoms of a molecule in a definite repeated pattern. Abbr. *s-, sym-, sym.* **5.** *Med.* Affecting corresponding organs or parts similarly. Also **sym·met'ric.** [< SYMMETRY] — **sym·met'ri·cal·ly** *adv.* — **sym·met'ri·cal·ness** *n.*

sym·me·trize (sim'ə-trīz) *v.t.* **·trized, ·triz·ing** To make symmetrical or proportional. — **sym'me·tri·za'tion** *n.*

sym·me·try (sim'ə-trē) *n. pl.* **·tries** **1.** An exact correspondence between the opposite halves of a figure, form, line, pattern, etc., on either side of an axis or center; the condition whereby half of something is the mirror image of the other half. **2.** Beauty or harmony of form resulting from a symmetrical or nearly symmetrical arrangement of parts; due or right proportion. **3.** *Logic* A relation that, if holding between one object and a second, will hold between the second object and the first. **4.** *Math.* An arrangement of pairs of points in a general system such that the set of lines joining them together is divided into equal parts by a line, plane, or point. **5.** *Mineral.* The symmetrical distribution of nonparallel but equivalent directions (faces, edges, etc.) in a crystal, with reference to certain planes or lines called **planes** or **axes of symmetry.** [< MF *symmetrie* < LL *symmetria* < Gk. < *symmetros* measured together < *syn-* together + *metron* a measure]

Sym·onds (sim'əndz), **John Addington,** 1840–93, English author.

Sy·mons (sī'mənz), **Arthur,** 1865–1945, British poet and critic.

sym·pa·thec·to·my (sim'pə-thek'tə·mē) *n. pl.* **·mies** *Surg.* The removal or interruption of some part of sympathetic nerve pathways. [< SYMPATH(ETIC) + -ECTOMY]

sym·pa·thet·ic (sim'pə-thet'ik) *adj.* **1.** Pertaining to, expressing, or proceeding from sympathy. **2.** Having a fellow feeling for others; sympathizing; compassionate. **3.** Being in accord or harmony; congenial. **4.** Referring to sounds produced by responsive vibrations. **5.** *Anat.* Denoting the part of the autonomic nervous system that consists of nerves originating in the lumbar and thoracic regions of the spinal cord, and that, in general, produces effects opposite to those coming from the parasympathetic system. Also **sym'pa·thet'i·cal.** [< NL *sympatheticus* < Gk. *sympathētikos* < *sympatheia.* See SYMPATHY.] — **sym'pa·thet'i·cal·ly** *adv.*

sympathetic ink Invisible ink (which see).

sym·pa·thin (sim'pə-thin) *n. Biochem.* A substance liberated by the stimulation of certain fibers of the sympathetic nervous system and acting as a chemical mediator in associated nerve impulses. [< SYMPATH(ETIC) + -IN]

sym·pa·thique (saṅ·pà·tēk') *adj. French* Pleasant; nice; congenial: said of persons.

sym·pa·thize (sim'pə-thīz) *v.i.* **·thized, ·thiz·ing** **1.** To share the sentiments, feelings, or ideas of another: with *with.* **2.** To feel or express compassion, as for another's sorrow or affliction: with *with.* **3.** To be in harmony or agreement. Also *Brit.* **sym'pa·thise.** See CONSOLE¹. — **sym'pa·thiz'er** *n.* — **sym'pa·thiz'ing·ly** *adv.*

sym·pa·thy (sim'pə-thē) *n. pl.* **·thies** **1.** The quality of being affected by the state of another with feelings correspondent in kind. **2.** A fellow feeling; especially, a feeling of compassion for another's sufferings; pity; commiseration. **3.** An agreement of affections, inclinations, or temperaments that makes persons agreeable to one another; congeniality; accord. **4.** The quality of inanimate things by virtue of which they are said to attract or influence one another: the *sympathy* of the lodestone for iron. — **Syn.** See PITY. [< L *sympathia* < Gk. *sympatheia* < *sympathēs* feeling compassion with another < *syn-* together + *pathos* feeling]

sympathy strike A strike in which the strikers support the demands of another group of workers but demand nothing for themselves.

sym·pet·al·ous (sim-pet'l-əs) *adj. Bot.* Gamopetalous (which see). [< NL *Sympetalae,* a division of dicotyledons < Gk. *syn-* together + *petalon* leaf, petal]

sym·phon·ic (sim-fon'ik) *adj.* **1.** Relating to or having the form of a symphony. **2.** Agreeing in sound; harmonious.

symphonic poem *Music* A composition in free form for symphony orchestra, and following a descriptive, literary, or programmatic outline, developed by Liszt in the 19th century: also called *tone poem.*

sym·pho·ni·ous (sim-fō'nē-əs) *adj.* Sounding together or in harmony; concordant. — **sym·pho'ni·ous·ly** *adv.*

sym·pho·nist (sim'fə-nist) *n.* One who composes symphonies.

sym·pho·nize (sim'fə-nīz) *v.t. & v.i.* **·nized, ·niz·ing** To play or sound together or in harmony; harmonize.

sym·pho·ny (sim'fə-nē) *n. pl.* **·nies** **1.** *Music* A composition for orchestra, consisting usually of four movements, of which one or more generally follow sonata form, and that are related by key, arrangement of motifs, etc. **2.** A symphony orchestra. **3.** A harmonious or agreeable mingling of sounds. **4.** Any concord or agreeable blending: symphony in gray. Abbr. *sym.* [< OF *simphonie* < L *symphonia* < Gk. *symphōnia* < *syn-* together + *phōnē* sound]

---

symphony orchestra A large orchestra composed usually of the string, brass, woodwind, and percussion sections needed to present symphonic works: also called *symphony*.

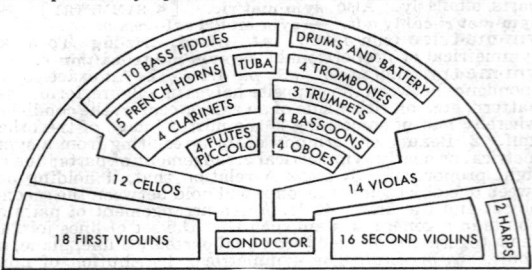

A SEATING PLAN FOR A SYMPHONY ORCHESTRA

sym·phy·sis (sim′fə·sis) *n. pl.* **·ses** (-sēz) **1.** *Anat.* A junction of two parts of the skeleton, formed either by a growing together of two bones, as in the lower jaw or the pelvis, or by the intervention of a layer of hyaline cartilage between them. **2.** *Bot.* The union of similar parts, or of parts normally separate. [< NL < Gk., a growing together, esp. of the bones < *syn-* together + *phyein* to grow] — **sym·phyt·ic** (sim·fit′ik) *adj.* — **sym·phyt′i·cal·ly** *adv.*

sym·po·di·um (sim·pō′dē·əm) *n. pl.* **·di·a** (-dē·ə) *Bot.* A false axis or stem of a plant, made up of a series of superposed branches imitating a simple stem: also called *pseudaxis.* [< NL < Gk. *syn-* together + *podion,* dim. of *pous, podos* foot] — **sym·po′di·al** *adj.* — **sym·po′di·al·ly** *adv.*

sym·po·si·ac (sim·pō′zē·ak) *adj.* Pertaining to, of the nature of, or occurring at a symposium. Also **sym·po′si·al.** — *n. Archaic* A symposium. [< LL *symposiacus* < Gk. *symposiakos* < *symposion.* See SYMPOSIUM.]

sym·po·si·arch (sim·pō′zē·ärk) *n.* **1.** The master or director of an ancient Greek symposium. **2.** The master of a feast; a toastmaster. [< Gk. *symposiarchos* < *symposion* a symposium (def. 3) + *archos* ruler]

sym·po·si·um (sim·pō′zē·əm) *n. pl.* **·si·ums** or **·si·a** (-zē·ə) **1.** A meeting for discussion of a particular subject. **2.** A collection of comments or opinions brought together; especially, a series of brief essays or articles on the same subject, as in a magazine. **3.** In ancient Greece, an after-dinner drinking party, characterized by conversation, music, dancing, and other amusements. Also **sympo′si·on** (-zē·on). [< L < Gk. *symposion* < *syn-* together + *posis* a drinking < *po-,* stem of *pinein* to drink]

symp·tom (sim′təm) *n.* **1.** A sign, token, or indication. **2.** *Pathol.* Any observable alteration in bodily functions or mental behavior indicating the presence of disease, especially when regarded as an aid in diagnosis. Abbr. *sym.* [< L *symptoma* < Gk. *symptōma* a chance, disease < *sympiptein* to happen to < *syn-* together + *piptein* to fall]

symp·to·mat·ic (simp′tə·mat′ik) *adj.* **1.** Pertaining to, of the nature of, or constituting a symptom or symptoms; indicative. **2.** According to symptoms: a *symptomatic* classification of diseases. Also **symp′to·mat′i·cal.** [< F *symptomatique* or LL *symptomaticus* < Gk. *symptōmatikos* < *symptōma, -atos* symptom] — **symp′to·mat′i·cal·ly** *adv.*

symp·tom·a·tol·o·gy (simp′təm·ə·tol′ə·jē) *n.* **1.** The branch of medicine concerned with the observation and classification of symptoms. **2.** The combined symptoms of a disease. Also called *semiology, semiotics.* [< NL *symtomatologia* < Gk. *symptōma, -atos* a symptom + *logos* a study]

syn- *prefix* With; together; associated with or accompanying: *syntax, syndrome.* Also: *sy-* before *sc, sp, st,* and *z,* as in *system; syl-* before *l,* as in *syllable; sym-* before *b, p,* and *m,* as in *sympathy; sys-* before *s,* as in *syssarcosis.* [< L < Gk. < *syn* together]

syn. Synonym(s).

syn·aer·e·sis (si·ner′ə·sis) See SYNERESIS.

syn·aes·the·sia (sin′is·thē′zhə, -zhē·ə) See SYNESTHESIA.

syn·a·gogue (sin′ə·gôg, -gog) *n.* **1.** A place of meeting for Jewish worship and religious instruction. **2.** A Jewish congregation or assemblage for religious instruction and observances. **3.** The Jewish religion or communion. Also **syn′a·gog.** [< OF *sinagoge* < LL *synagoga* < Gk. *synagōgē* assembly < *synagein* to bring together < *syn-* together + *agein* to lead, bring] — **syn′a·gog′i·cal** (-goj′i·kəl), **syn′a·gog′al** (-gôg′əl, -gog′əl) *adj.*

syn·a·le·pha (sin′ə·lē′fə) *n.* The blending into a single syllable of two successive vowels of different syllables, as *th′ Omnipotent* for *the Omnipotent.* Compare APOCOPE. Also **syn′a·le′phe** (-lē′fē), **syn′a·loe′pha, syn′a·loe′phe.** [< LL < Gk. *synaloiphē* < *synaleiphein* to smear together < *syn-* together + *aleiphein* to anoint]

syn·apse (si·naps′) *n. Physiol.* The junction point of two neurons, across which a nerve impulse passes: also called *synapsis.* [< NL *synapsis* < Gk., a junction < *syn-* together + *hapsis* a joining < *haptein* to join]

syn·ap·sis (si·nap′sis) *n. pl.* **·ses** (-sēz) **1.** *Biol.* The conjugation of maternal and paternal chromosomes during meiosis. **2.** *Physiol.* A synapse. [< NL. See SYNAPSE.] — **syn·ap′tic** *adj.* — **syn·ap′ti·cal·ly** *adv.*

syn·ar·thro·sis (sin′är·thrō′sis) *n. pl.* **·ses** (-sēz) *Anat.* A joint that permits no motion between the parts articulated, as the sutures of the adult skull. Also **syn′ar·thro′di·a** (-dē·ə). [< NL < Gk. *synarthrōsis* < *syn-* together + *arthrōsis* a jointing < *arthron* joint] — **syn′ar·thro′di·al** *adj.* — **syn′ar·thro′di·al·ly** *adv.*

syn·carp (sin′kärp) *n. Bot.* **1.** An aggregate fruit composed of several more or less coherent carpels, as the blackberry. **2.** A multiple fruit, as the fig. Also **syn·car·pi·um** (sin·kär′pē·əm). [< NL *syncarpium* < Gk. *syn-* together + *karpos* fruit]

syn·car·pous (sin·kär′pəs) *adj. Bot.* **1.** Pertaining to or characterized by a syncarp. **2.** Consisting of united carpels.

syn·chro (sing′krō) *n.* Any of various electromagnetic devices for the remote control of complex operations.

syn·chro·mesh (sing′krə·mesh′) *n. Mech.* **1.** A gear system by which driving and driven members are brought to the same speed before engaging: also called *synchronized shifting.* **2.** Any gear in such a system. [< SYNCHRO(NIZED) + MESH]

syn·chron·ic (sin·kron′ik, sing-) *adj.* **1.** Synchronous. **2.** *Ling.* Pertaining to the study of language or to a linguistic feature at a given stage or time and not historically: *synchronic* grammar: distinguished from *diachronic.* Also **syn·chron′i·cal.** — **syn·chron′i·cal·ly** *adv.*

synchronic linguistics Descriptive linguistics (which see).

syn·chro·nism (sing′krə·niz′əm) *n.* **1.** The state of being synchronous. **2.** Coincidence in time of different events or phenomena; simultaneousness. **3.** A tabular grouping of historic personages or events according to their dates. **4.** In art, representation in the same picture of events that occurred at different times. [< LL *synchronismus* < Gk. *synchronismos* < *synchronos.* See SYNCHRONOUS.] — **syn·chro·nis′tic** or **·ti·cal** *adj.* — **syn·chro·nis′ti·cal·ly** *adv.*

syn·chro·nize (sing′krə·nīz) *v.* **·nized, ·niz·ing** *v.i.* **1.** To occur at the same time; coincide. **2.** To move or operate in unison. — *v.t.* **3.** To cause (timepieces) to agree in keeping or indicating time. **4.** To cause to operate in unison. **5.** To assign the same date or period to. Abbr. *syn.* [< SYNCHRONISM] — **syn′chro·ni·za′tion** *n.* — **syn′chro·niz′er** *n.*

synchronized shifting *Mech.* Synchromesh (def. 1).

syn·chro·nous (sing′krə·nəs) *adj.* **1.** Occurring at the same time; coincident. **2.** Happening at the same rate. **3.** *Physics* Having the same period or rate of vibration, as waves or electric currents. Also **synchronic.** Also **syn′chro·nal.** [< LL *synchronus* < Gk. *synchronos* < *syn-* together + *chronos* time] — **syn′chro·nous·ly** *adv.* — **syn′chro·nous·ness** *n.*

synchronous converter *Electr.* A machine adapted for the conversion of direct into alternating current or vice versa.

synchronous motor *Electr.* A motor whose normal speed of operation is exactly proportional to the frequency of the current to which it is connected.

synchronous speed *Electr.* The speed of an alternating-current machine as determined by the frequency of the circuit.

syn·chro·scope (sing′krə·skōp) *n. Electr.* An apparatus for visually indicating the degree of synchronization in the working, speed, etc., of two or more alternating-current motors. Also **syn·chron·o·scope** (sin·kron′ə·skōp). [< SYNCHRO(NISM) + -SCOPE]

syn·chro·tron (sing′krə·tron) *n. Physics* An accelerator that synchronizes the acceleration of atomic particles in a magnetic field energized by a high-voltage alternating current. [< SYNCHRO(NIZE) + (ELEC)TRON]

syn·clas·tic (sin·klas′tik, sing-) *adj.* Having the same kind of curvature in all directions; concave or convex in every direction: said of a surface. Compare ANTICLASTIC. [< SYN- + Gk. *klastos* broken < *klaein* to break]

syn·cli·nal (sin·klī′nəl, sing-) *adj.* **1.** Sloping downward on each side toward a line or point. **2.** *Geol.* Of, pertaining to, or forming a syncline. Also **syn·clin·i·cal** (sin·klin′i·kəl, sing-). — *n.* A syncline. [< Gk. *synklinein* < *syn-* together + *klinein* to incline]

syn·cline (sing′klīn) *n. Geol.* **1.** A system of stratified rock in which the strata incline upward on each side from the axis of the fold. Compare ANTICLINE.

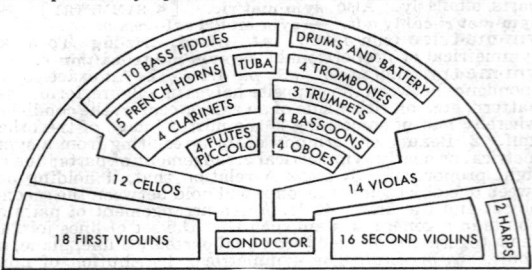

SYNCLINAL FOLDS

syn·clit·ic (sing·klit′ik, sin-) *adj. Med.* Having the planes of the fetal head inclined to those of the maternal pelvis: distinguished from *enclitic.*

syn·clit·ism (sing′klə·tiz′əm) *n. Med.* The state of being synclitic. [< Gk. *syn-* together + *klitikos* < *klinein* to incline, turn aside]

syn·co·pate (sing′kə·pāt) *v.t.* **·pat·ed, ·pat·ing** **1.** *Gram.* To contract (a word) by syncope. **2.** *Music* To treat or modify, as a tone, by syncopation. [< LL *syncopatus*, pp. of *syncopare* to affect with syncope < *syncope*. See SYNCOPE.] — **syn·co·pat·or** *n.*

syn·co·pa·tion (sing/kə·pā/shən) *n.* **1.** The act of syncopating or state of being syncopated. **2.** That which is syncopated, as a dance or rhythm. **3.** *Music* **a** The rhythmic placement of a tone so that its accent does not coincide with the metric accent, as by beginning it on a weak beat or a fraction of a beat and continuing it through the next strong beat. **b** A tone so treated. **c** Any music featuring syncopation, as ragtime, jazz, etc. **4.** *Gram.* Syncope.

syn·co·pe (sing/kə·pē) *n.* **1.** *Gram.* The elision of a sound or syllable in the middle part of a word, as *e'er* for *ever.* **2.** *Pathol.* A loss of consciousness caused by temporary cerebral anemia. — **Syn.** See UNCONSCIOUSNESS. [Earlier *sincopis* < OF *sincopin*, ult. < LL *syncope* < Gk. *synkopē* < *syn-* together + *kop-*, stem of *koptein* to strike, cut; refashioned after LL] — **syn/co·pal, syn·cop·ic** (sin·kop/ik) *adj.*

syn·cre·tism (sing/krə·tiz/əm) *n.* **1.** A tendency or effort to reconcile various systems of philosophy or religious opinion, especially against a common opponent. **2.** *Ling.* The fusion of two or more inflectional forms that were originally different, as of two cases. [< F *syncrétisme* < NL *syncretismus* < Gk. *synkrētismos* union of two parties against a third < *synkrētizein* to combine] — **syn/cre·tist** *n.* — **syn/cre·tis/tic** or **·ti·cal, syn·cre·tic** (sin·kret/ik) *adj.*

syn·cre·tize (sing/krə·tīz) *v.t.* & *v.i.* **·tized, ·tiz·ing** To attempt to blend and reconcile, as various philosophies. [< NL *syncretizare* < Gk. *synkrētizein* to combine]

syn·cri·sis (sing/krə·sis) *n. Obs.* A figure of speech formed by comparison of disparate persons or things. [< LL < Gk. *synkrisis* < *synkrinein* to compare < *syn-* together + *krinein* to separate]

syn·cyt·i·um (sin·sit/ē·əm, -sish/əm) *n. pl.* **·cyt·i·a** (-sit/ē·ə, -sish/ə) A mass of protoplasm that contains cell nuclei but is not differentiated into separate cells, as in the nerve nets of jellyfishes or in plasmodia. [< NL < Gk. *syn-* together + *kytos* a hollow] — **syn·cyt/i·al** *adj.*

syn·dac·tyl (sin·dak/til) *adj. Anat.* Having two or more digits of the hand or foot wholly or partly united; webfooted. Also **syn·dac/tyle, syn·dac/ty·lous.** — *n.* A syndactyl mammal or bird. [< F *syndactyle* < Gk. *syn-* together + *daktylos* finger] — **syn·dac/tyl·ism** (-iz/əm) *n.*

syndesmo- *combining form Anat.* **1.** A ligament. **2.** Of or pertaining to a ligament: *syndesmology.* Also, before vowels, **syndesm-.** [< Gk. *syndesmos* ligament]

syn·des·mol·o·gy (sin/des·mol/ə·jē) *n.* The study of the anatomy and physiology of the ligaments.

syn·des·mo·sis (sin/des·mō/sis) *n. Anat.* The joining of bones by means of ligamentous tissue. [< NL < Gk. *syndesmos* ligament] — **syn/des·mot/ic** (-mot/ik) *adj.*

syn·det (sin/det/) *n.* A synthetic detergent.

syn·det·ic (sin·det/ik) *adj.* Serving to unite or connect; connective, as a word. Also **syn·det/i·cal.** [< Gk. *syndetikos* < *syndeein* to bind together < *syn-* together + *deein* to bind] — **syn·det/i·cal·ly** *adv.*

syn·dic (sin/dik) *n.* **1.** A civil magistrate or officer representing a government or a community. **2.** One who is designated to transact business for others; also, a body of officers or council so designated. [< F *syndic*, *syndique* delegated representative < LL *syndicus* advocate, delegate < Gk. *syndikos* defendant's advocate < *syn-* together + *dikē* judgment] — **syn/di·cal** *adj.*

syn·di·cal·ism (sin/di·kəl·iz/əm) *n.* A social and political theory proposing the taking over of the means of production by syndicates of workers, preferably by means of the general strike, with consequent political control. [< F *syndicalisme* < *syndical* of a labor union < (*chambre*) *syndicale* labor union < *syndic* syndic] — **syn/di·cal·ist** *adj.* & *n.* — **syn/di·cal·is/tic** *adj.*

syn·di·cate (*n.* sin/də·kit; *v.* sin/də·kāt) *n.* **1.** An association of individuals united to negotiate some business or to prosecute some enterprise requiring large capital. **2.** An agency that sells articles, etc., to a number of periodicals, as newspapers, for simultaneous publication. **3.** The office or jurisdiction of a syndic; also, syndics collectively. — *v.t.* **·cat·ed, ·cat·ing** **1.** To combine into or manage by a syndicate. **2.** To sell (an article, etc.) for publication in many newspapers or magazines. [< F *syndicat* office of a syndic < *syndic*. See SYNDIC.]

syn·di·ca·tion (sin/də·kā/shən) *n.* **1.** The selling for regular publication of a column, series of articles, comic strip, etc., to a number of newspapers or other periodicals. **2.** The act of those who syndicate.

syn·drome (sin/drōm) *n. Med.* An aggregate or set of concurrent symptoms indicating the presence and nature of a disease. [< NL < Gk. *syndromē* < *syn-* together + *dramein* to run] — **syn·drom·ic** (sin·drom/ik) *adj.*

syne (sīn) *adv.* & *prep.* & *conj. Scot.* Since. Also **syn.**

sy·nec·do·che (si·nek/də·kē) *n.* A figure of speech in

which a part is put for a whole or a whole for a part, an individual for a class, or a material for the thing, as a *roof* for a *house.* [< LL < Gk. *synekdochē* < *synekdechesthai* to take something with something else < *syn-* together + *ekdechesthai* to take from < *ek-* from + *dechesthai* to take] — **syn·ec·doch·ic** (sin/ek·dok/ik) or **·i·cal** *adj.*

sy·ne·cious (si·nē/shəs) See SYNOECIOUS.

syn·e·col·o·gy (sin/ə·kol/ə·jē) *n.* The ecology of plant and animal communities: distinguished from *autecology.* [< SYN- + ECOLOGY]

Syn·e·dri·on (sin·ē/drē·ən), **Syn·e·dri·um** (-drē·əm) See SANHEDRIN.

syn·er·e·sis (si·ner/ə·sis) *n.* **1.** The coalescence of two vowels or syllables generally pronounced separately, as *seest* for *see-est:* also called *crasis.* Compare DIERESIS, SYNIZESIS. **2.** *Med.* The contraction of a gel, with the expulsion of water or other liquids, as in the clotting of blood. Also spelled *synaeresis.* [< LL *synaeresis* < Gk. *synairesis* a drawing together < *syn-* together + *haireein* to take]

syn·er·get·ic (sin/ər·jet/ik) *adj.* Working together; cooperative. [< Gk. *synergētikos* < *synergeein* to cooperate < *syn-* together + *ergeein* to work]

syn·er·gism (sin/ər·jiz/əm) *n.* **1.** *Theol.* The doctrine that human effort cooperates with divine grace in the salvation of the soul. **2.** *Med.* The joint action of different substances in producing an effect greater than the sum of the effects of all the substances acting separately. [< NL *synergismus* < Gk. *synergos* working together]

syn·er·gist (sin/ər·jist) *n.* **1.** *Theol.* One holding to synergism. **2.** A cooperating organ, part, or medicine.

syn·er·gis·tic (sin/ər·jis/tik) *adj.* Acting together; cooperative. Also **syn/er·gis/ti·cal.**

syn·er·gy (sin/ər·jē) *n.* **1.** Combined and correlated force; united action. **2.** *Med.* Correlation or concurrence of action between different organs in health or disease, or between different drugs. Also **syn·er·gi·a** (si·nûr/jē·ə). [< NL *synergia* < Gk. *synergos.* See SYNERGISM.] — **syn·er/gic** *adj.*

syn·e·sis (sin/ə·sis) *n. Gram.* Construction in accordance with the sense rather than the syntax, as the use of a plural form of a verb with a collective noun. [< Gk., a joining together, understanding < *synienai* to perceive < *syn-* together + *hienai* to send]

syn·es·the·sia (sin/is·thē/zhə, -zhē·ə) *n. Physiol.* Sensation produced at a point other than or remote from the point of stimulation, as of a color from hearing a certain sound; a secondary sensation. Also spelled *synaesthesia.* [< NL *synaesthesia* < Gk. *synaisthēsis* joint perception < *synaisthanesthai* to perceive simultaneously < *syn-* together + *aisthanesthai* to perceive, feel] — **syn·es·thet/ic** (-thet/ik) *adj.*

syn·ga·my (sing/gə·mē) *n. Biol.* The union of male and female gametes in fertilization. [< SYN- + -GAMY] — **syn·gam·ic** (sing/gam/ik) or **·ga·mous** *adj.*

Synge (sing), **John Millington,** 1871–1909, Irish dramatist and poet. — **Richard Laurence Millington,** born 1914, English biochemist.

syn·gen·e·sis (sin·jen/ə·sis) *n. Biol.* **1.** Sexual reproduction. **2.** The theory that the sexually fertilized germ contains within itself the germs of all future generations: opposed to *epigenesis.* [< NL < Gk. *syn-* together + *genesis.* See GENESIS.] — **syn·ge·net·ic** (sin/jə·net/ik) *adj.*

syn·i·ze·sis (sin/ə·zē/sis) *n.* **1.** The union in pronunciation of two vowels that cannot form a diphthong, so as to pass for one syllable. Compare SYNERESIS. **2.** *Biol.* The contractile massing of the chromatin in meiosis. **3.** *Med.* Contraction of the pupil of the eye. Also **syn·e·zi/sis** (-zī/sis). [< LL < Gk. *synizēsis* < *synizanein* to sink down < *syn-* together + *izanein* to settle down, sit < *izein* to seat, sit]

syn·od (sin/əd) *n.* **1.** An ecclesiastical council. **2.** Any deliberative assembly. [OE *sinoth* < LL *synodus* < Gk. *synodos*, lit., a coming together < *syn-* together + *hodos* way; refashioned after MF *synode* < LL]

sy·nod·i·cal (si·nod/i·kəl) *adj.* **1.** Of, pertaining to, or of the nature of a synod; transacted in a synod. **2.** *Astron.* Pertaining to the conjunction of two heavenly bodies, one of which revolves round the other, or to the interval between two successive conjunctions: a *synodical* month. Also **syn·od·al** (sin/ə·dəl), **sy·nod/ic.** — **sy·nod/i·cal·ly** *adv.*

sy·noe·cious (si·nē/shəs) *adj. Bot.* Having male and female organs in the same inflorescence or receptacle, as in most composite plants and many mosses: also applied *synecious.* [< Gk. *synoikia* living together < *syn-* together + *oikos* house; formed on analogy with *dioecious, monoecious,* etc.]

syn·o·nym (sin/ə·nim) *n.* **1.** A word having the same or almost the same meaning as some other: opposed to *antonym.* **2.** The equivalent of a word in another language. **3.** *Biol.* A scientific name, as of a genus or species, superseded or discarded through prior use or because of incorrect application. Also **syn/o·nyme.** Abbr. **syn.** [< LL *synonymum* < Gk. *synōnymon*, neut. of *synōnymos* having like meaning or name < *syn-* together + *onyma, onoma* name] — **syn/o·nym/ic** or **·i·cal** *adj.* — **syn/o·nym/i·ty** *n.*

sy·non·y·mize (si-non'ə-mīz) *v.t.* **·mized, ·miz·ing** To give the synonyms of; express by words of similar meaning.

sy·non·y·mous (si-non'ə-məs) *adj.* **1.** Being a synonym or synonyms; equivalent or similar in meaning. **2.** Closely related or alike in significance or effect. Also **syn·o·ny·mat·ic** (sin'ə-ni-mat'ik). Abbr. *syn.* — **sy·non'y·mous·ly** *adv.*

sy·non·y·my (si-non'ə-mē) *n. pl.* **·mies 1.** The quality of being synonymous. **2.** The science or systematic collection and study of synonyms; also, the use and discrimination of synonyms. **3.** A written analysis discriminating the meaning of synonyms. **4.** An index, list, or collection of synonyms, as in scientific nomenclature. Abbr. *syn.* [< LL *synonymia* < Gk. *synōnymia* < *synōnymos*. See SYNONYM.]

synop. Synopsis.

sy·nop·sis (si-nop'sis) *n. pl.* **·ses** (-sēz) A general view, as of a subject or its treatment; an abstract; syllabus; summary. — **Syn.** See ABRIDGMENT. [< LL < Gk., general view < *syn-* together + *opsis* view]

sy·nop·tic (si-nop'tik) *adj.* **1.** Giving or constituting a synopsis or general view. **2.** *Often cap.* Presenting the same or a similar point of view: said of the first three Gospels (**Synoptic Gospels**) as distinguished from the fourth. Also **sy·nop'ti·cal.** [< NL *synopticus* < Gk. *synoptikos* < *synopsis* synopsis] — **sy·nop'ti·cal·ly** *adv.*

sy·no·vi·a (si-nō'vē-ə) *n. Physiol.* The viscid, transparent, albuminous fluid secreted by the **synovial membranes** at points where lubrication is necessary, as in joints. [< NL *sinovia, synovia, synophia*; coined by Paracelsus, appar. < Gk. *syn-* together + L *ovum* egg < Gk. *ōon*.] — **sy·no'vi·al** *adj.*

syn·o·vi·tis (sin'ō-vī'tis) *n. Pathol.* Inflammation of a synovial membrane.

syn·sep·a·lous (sin-sep'ə-ləs) *adj. Bot.* Gamosepalous (which see). [< SYN- + SEPAL + -OUS]

syn·tax (sin'taks) *n.* **1.** The arrangement and interrelationship of words in phrases and sentences. **2.** The branch of linguistics dealing with such relationships. Compare MORPHOLOGY. [< F *syntaxe* < LL *syntaxis* < Gk. < *syntassein* to join together < *syn-* together + *tassein* to arrange] — **syn·tac·tic** (sin-tak'tik) or **·ti·cal** *adj.* — **syn·tac'ti·cal·ly** *adv.*

syn·the·sis (sin'thə-sis) *n. pl.* **·ses** (-sēz) **1.** The assembling of separate or subordinate parts into a whole: opposed to *analysis.* **2.** A complex whole composed of originally separate parts. **3.** *Ling.* The combination of radical and formative or inflectional elements in one word, as in *un-thinking, home-wards.* **4.** *Logic* a Combination of separate elements into a whole, as of species into genera. b A process of reasoning from the whole to a part, or from the general to the particular; deductive reasoning. **5.** *Chem.* The building up of compounds from a series of reactions involving elements, radicals, or simpler compounds, especially organic compounds that have specific properties or are identical in certain respects with naturally occurring substances. Compare ANALYSIS. [< L < Gk. < *syntithenai* < *syn-* together + *tithenai* to place] — **syn'the·sist** *n.*

syn·the·size (sin'thə-sīz) *v.t.* **·sized, ·siz·ing 1.** To unite or produce by synthesis. **2.** To apply synthesis to. Also *Brit.* **syn'the·sise.**

syn·thet·ic (sin-thet'ik) *adj.* **1.** Pertaining to, of the nature of, or characterized by synthesis. **2.** Tending to reduce particulars to inclusive wholes. **3.** *Chem.* Produced artificially by the synthesis of simpler materials or substances rather than occurring naturally. **4.** Artificial; spurious. **5.** *Ling.* Describing a language that uses inflectional affixes or bound forms as its principal means of expressing grammatical relations, as Latin or Russian: opposed to *analytic:* also *inflectional.* Also **syn·thet'i·cal.** — *n.* **1.** Anything produced by synthesis. **2.** *Chem.* A compound produced by synthesis. [< F *synthétique* or NL *syntheticus* < Gk. *synthetikos* < *synthetos* compounded < *syntithenai* < *syn-* together + *tithenai* to place] — **syn·thet'i·cal·ly** *adv.*

synthetic philosophy Spencerism, considered as an attempt to combine all the sciences into a connected whole.

syn·to·nize (sin'tə-nīz) *v.t.* **·nized, ·niz·ing** *Electr.* **1.** To place in resonance with each other, as radio frequencies. **2.** To tune or tone together, as electrical instruments. [< SYNTON(Y) + -IZE] — **syn·ton·ic** (sin-ton'ik) or **·i·cal** *adj.* — **syn·ton'i·cal·ly** *adv.* — **syn'to·ni·za'tion** *n.*

syn·to·ny (sin'tə-nē) *n. Electr.* **1.** The harmonizing or tuning of particular transmitters and receivers each to the other. **2.** Resonance. [< Gk. *syntonia* agreement < *syn-* together + *tonos* tone]

syn·u·ra (sin-yŏŏr'ə) *n. pl.* **·u·rae** (-yŏŏr'ē) Any of a genus (*Synura*) of flagellate protozoans that unite in clusters. [< NL < Gk. *synouros, synoros* bordering on < *syn-* together + *oros* boundary]

sy·pher (sī'fər) *v.t.* To make a lap joint with (two chamfered or beveled plank edges) so as to leave a flush surface. [Var. of CIPHER] — **sy'pher·ing** *n.*

syph·i·lis (sif'ə-lis) *n. Pathol.* An infectious, chronic, venereal disease caused by a spirochete (*Treponema pallidum*) transmissible by direct contact or congenitally, and usually progressing by three stages of increasing severity: *primary,*

with the formation of a hard chancre at the site of infection; *secondary,* involving skin affections and blood changes; *tertiary,* characterized by involvement of every system of the body, including the brain: also called *pox.* [after *Syphilis, sive Morbus Gallicus,* a Latin poem by Girolamo Fracastoro, 1483-1553, published in 1530, the hero of which, *Syphilus,* a shepherd, was the first sufferer from the disease]

syph·i·lit·ic (sif'ə·lit'ik) *adj.* Relating to or affected with syphilis. — *n.* A person suffering from syphilis. [< NL *syphiliticus* < *syphilis.* See SYPHILIS.]

syph·i·loid (sif'ə-loid) *adj.* Resembling syphilis.

syph·i·lol·o·gy (sif'ə-lol'ə-jē) *n.* The study and treatment of syphilis. [< SYPHIL(IS) + -LOGY] — **syph'i·lol'o·gist** *n.*

sy·phon (sī'fən) See SIPHON.

syr. Syrup (pharmacy).

Syr. Syria; Syriac; Syrian.

Syr·a·cuse (sir'ə-kyoos) **1.** A port commune in SE Sicily; pop. 84,200 (1967): Italian *Siracusa.* Ancient **Syr·a·cu·sae** (sir'ə-kyoo'sē, -sā). **2.** A city in central New York; pop. 197,208. — **Syr·a·cu'san** *adj. & n.*

Syr Dar·ya (sir dǎr'yä') A river in the southern Soviet Union, flowing 1,327 miles NW to the Aral Sea: ancient *Jaxartes.* Also **Syr Dar'ya'.**

Syr·ette (si-ret') *n.* A small disposable tube for the emergency injection of drugs: a trade name. Also **syr·ette'.**

Syr·i·a (sir'ē-ə) **1.** A Republic in SW Asia; 72,234 sq. mi.; pop. 5,866,000 (est. 1969); capital, Damascus. Officially **Syrian Arab Republic. 2.** A former French mandated territory comprising roughly Syria and Lebanon. **3.** An ancient country including Syria, Lebanon, Palestine, and adjacent parts of western Asia.

Syr·i·ac (sir'ē-ak) *n.* The language of the Syrians, belonging to the eastern Aramaic subgroup of the Northwest Semitic languages. Abbr. *Syr.* [< L *Syriacus* < Gk. *Syriakos* < *Syria* Syria]

Syr·i·an (sir'ē-ən) *adj.* Of or pertaining to ancient or modern Syria. — *n.* **1.** A native of Syria, especially one of the Semitic people of Arabic, Phoenician, and Aramean descent. **2.** One who is a member of a Christian church in Syria. Abbr. *Syr.* [< OF *sirien* < L *Syrius* a Syrian < Gk. *Syrios* < *Syria* Syria]

Syrian Desert An arid wasteland of SW Asia between the eastern Mediterranean and the Euphrates valley.

sy·rin·ga (si-ring'gə) *n.* **1.** Any of a genus (*Philadelphus*) of ornamental shrubs of the saxifrage family: also called *mock orange.* **2.** The lilac. [< NL < Gk. *syrinx, -ingos* a pipe]

syr·inge (sir'inj, si·rinj') *n.* **1.** *Med.* A small instrument of glass, metal, rubber, or plastic, consisting of a receptacle into which a liquid may be drawn for ejection in a fine jet or stream, used for cleaning wounds, affected parts, etc. **2.** A hypodermic syringe (which see). — *v.t.* **·inged, ·ing·ing** To spray or inject by a syringe; cleanse or treat with injected fluid. [< Med.L *siringa* < Gk. *syrinx, -ingos* tube, pipe]

sy·rin·go·my·e·li·a (si-ring'gō-mī-ē'lē-ə) *n. Pathol.* A diseased condition of the spinal cord, due to the presence of liquid in abnormally formed cavities. [< NL < Gk. *syrinx, -ingos* tube + *myelos* marrow]

syr·inx (sir'ingks) *n. pl.* **sy·rin·ges** (sə-rin'jēz) or **syr'rinx·es 1.** *Ornithol.* The song organ in birds. **2.** *Anat.* The Eustachian tube. **3.** A panpipe. [< Gk., pipe] — **sy·rin·ge·al** (si-rin'jē-əl) *adj.*

Syr·inx (sir'ingks) In Greek mythology, a nymph changed by Pan into a reed, from which he made his pipes.

syr·phid (sûr'fid) *n.* Any of a large and widely distributed family (*Syrphidae*) of flies, containing many species whose larvae feed upon harmful plant lice. For illustration see INSECTS (beneficial). Also **syr'phi·an** (-fē-ən), **syr'phus fly** (-fəs). [< NL < Gk. *syrphos* gnat]

Syr·tis Ma·jor (sir'tis mā'jər) The ancient name for the (Gulf of) SIDRA.

Syrtis Minor An ancient name for the (Gulf of) GABÈS.

syr·up (sir'əp) *n.* A thick, sweet liquid, as the boiled juice of fruits, sugar cane, etc.: also, *esp. U.S., sirup.* [< OF *sirop* < Arabic *sharāb.* Doublet of SHERBET.] — **syr'up·y** *adj.*

sys- Var. of SYN-.

sys·sar·co·sis (sis'är-kō'sis) *n. Anat.* The union of bones by means of muscles. [< NL < Gk. *syssarkōsis* < *syssarkoein* to unite by or cover over with flesh] — **sys'sar·co'sic, sys'sar·cot'ic** (-kot'ik) *adj.*

syst. System; systematic.

sys·tal·tic (sis-tal'tik) *adj. Physiol.* Alternately contracting and dilating, as the motion of the heart; pulsatory. [< LL *systalticus* < Gk. *systaltikos* depressing < *systellein* to draw together < *syn-* together + *stellein* to send]

sys·tem (sis'təm) *n.* **1.** Orderly combination or arrangement of parts, elements, etc., into a whole; especially, such combination according to some rational principle; any methodical arrangement of parts. **2.** Any group of facts, concepts, and phenomena regarded as constituting a natural whole for purposes of philosophic or scientific investigation and construction: the Ptolemaic *system*; the solar *system.* **3.** The connection or manner of connection of parts as related to a whole, or the parts collectively so related; a whole as made up of constitutive parts: a railroad *system*. **4.** The state or quality of being in order or orderly; orderliness; method. **5.** *Physiol.* **a** An assemblage of organic structures composed of similar elements and combined for the same general functions: the nervous *system*. **b** The entire body, taken as a functional whole. **6.** *Physics* An aggregate or region of matter considered as a unit with respect to specified factors such as mass, energy, gravitation, radioactivity, etc. **7.** *Chem.* A group of substances in one or more phases exhibiting, or tending to approach, equilibrium. **8.** *Mineral.* One of the primary divisions into which all crystal forms may be grouped, depending upon the relative lengths and mutual inclinations of the assumed crystal axes. **9.** *Geol.* A category of igneous and sedimentary rock strata above a series and corresponding with a period in the time scale. *Abbr.* **syst.** [< LL *systema* musical interval < Gk. *systēma*, *-atos* organized whole < *syn-* together + *histanai* to stand, set up]

sys·tem·at·ic (sis′tə·mat′ik) *adj.* **1.** Of, pertaining to, of the nature of, or characterized by system. **2.** Characterized by system or method; methodical: a *systematic* person. **3.** Forming a system; systematized. **4.** Carried out with organized regularity. **5.** Taxonomic. Also **sys′tem·at′i·cal.** *Abbr.* **syst.** [< LL *systematicus* < LGk. *systēmatikos* < *systēma*, *-atos* system] — **sys′tem·at′i·cal·ly** *adv.*

sys·tem·at·ics (sis′tə·mat′iks) *n.pl.* (*construed as sing.*) The study of principles of classification and nomenclature.

sys·tem·a·tism (sis′tə·mə·tiz′əm) *n.* **1.** Systematic arrangement or classification. **2.** Adherence to or reduction of principles, etc., to a system. — **sys′tem·a·tist** *n.*

sys·tem·a·tize (sis′tə·mə·tīz′) *v.t.* **·tized**, **·tiz·ing** To reduce to a system. Also **sys′tem·ize**, *Brit.* **sys′tem·a·tise′.** — **sys′tem·a·ti·za′tion** *n.* — **sys′tem·a·tiz′er** *n.*

sys·tem·ic (sis·tem′ik) *adj.* **1.** Of or pertaining to system or a system. **2.** *Physiol.* Pertaining to or affecting the body as a whole: a *systemic* poison. — **sys·tem′i·cal·ly** *adv.*

systems analysis The analysis of problems and processes into logical elements for computer programming and for selection of appropriate data processing equipment.

systems design **1.** The organization of a problem in such a manner as to make it suitable for computer processing. **2.** The selection and coordination of various data-processing devices in order to perform a specific function or solve a particular problem.

sys·to·le (sis′tə·lē) *n.* **1.** *Physiol.* The regular contraction of the heart, especially of the ventricles, that impels the blood outward. Compare DIASTOLE. **2.** The shortening of a syllable that is naturally or by position long. [< NL < Gk. *systolē* contraction < *systellein*. See SYSTALTIC.] — **sys·tol·ic** (sis·tol′ik) *adj.*

syz·y·gy (siz′ə·jē) *n.* *pl.* **·gies** **1.** *Astron.* **a** One of two opposite points in the orbit of a celestial body when it is in conjunction with or in opposition to the sun. **b** The points on the moon's orbit when the moon is most nearly in line with the earth and the sun. **2.** The union of parts or organisms. **3.** A dipody or group of two feet in one verse. [< LL *syzygia* < Gk., yoke, conjunction < *syzygos* yoked, paired < *syn-* together + *zeugnynai* to yoke < *zygon* yoke] — **sy·zyg·i·al** (si·zij′ē·əl) *adj.*

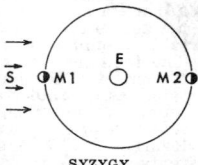

SYZYGY
S Sun's rays. *E* Earth. *M1, M2* Syzygies of the moon.

Sza·bad·ka (sô′bôd·kô) The Hungarian name for SUBOTICA.

Szcze·cin (shche′tsēn) The Polish name for STETTIN.

Sze·chwan (se′chwän′, su′-) A province of SW China; 219,700 sq. mi.; pop. 72,160,000 (est. 1957); capital, Chengtu.

Sze·ged (se′ged) A county borough in southern Hungary; pop. 99 061 (1960). Formerly **Sze·ge·din** (se′ge·din).

Sze·ming (su′ming′) A former name for AMOY.

Szent-Györ·gyi von Nagy·ra·polt (sent′dyûr′dye fon nod′y′ro′pōlt), **Albert**, born 1893. Hungarian biochemist.

Szi·lard (si·lärd′), **Leo**, 1898–1964, U.S. physicist born in Hungary.

Szom·bat·hely (som′bôt·hāy′) A city in western Hungary; pop. about 53,000: German *Steinamanger*.

T

t, T (tē) *n.* *pl.* **t's** or **ts**, **T's** or **Ts**, **tees** (tēz) **1.** The twentieth letter of the English alphabet. The shape of the Phoenician letter *tau* was adopted by the Greeks as *tau* and became Roman *T*. Also **tee.** **2.** The sound represented by the letter *t*, the voiceless alveolar stop. **3.** Anything shaped like the letter T. — **to a T** Precisely; with exactness; probably in allusion to a T-square.

t *Stat.* Distribution.

t. **1.** In the time of (L *tempore*). **2.** Tare. **3.** Target. **4.** Teaspoon(s). **5.** Telephone. **6.** Temperature. **7.** Tempo. **8.** Tenor. **9.** *Gram.* Tense. **10.** Terminal. **11.** Territorial; territory. **12.** Time. **13.** Tome. **14.** Ton(s). **15.** Town; township. **16.** Transit. **17.** *Gram.* Transitive. **18.** Troy (weight). **19.** Volume (L *tomus*).

't Contraction for IT: used initially, as in *'tis*, and finally, as in *on't*.

-t Inflectional ending used to indicate past participles and past tenses, and corresponding to *-ed*, as in *bereft, lost, spent*.

T **1.** *Chem.* Tantalum. **2.** Technician. **3.** Temperature (absolute scale). **4.** (Surface) tension. **5.** Time.

T– *Chem.* Triple bond.

T. **1.** Tablespoon(s). **2.** Territory. **3.** Testament. **4.** Tuesday. **5.** Turkish.

Ta *Chem.* Tantalum.

TAA Technical Assistance Administration.

Taal (täl) *n.* Afrikaans. [< Du., speech, language]

Ta·al (tä·äl′), **Mount** An active volcano (984 ft.) on an island in **Lake Taal** (94 sq. mi.) in southern Luzon, Philippines.

tab (tab) *n.* **1.** A flap, strip, tongue, or appendage of something, as a garment. **2.** A small, projecting part used as an aid in filing papers, etc. **3.** *Informal* Tally; total; bill: to pick up the *tab*. **4.** *Aeron.* An auxiliary control surface attached to a main control surface of an airplane. — **to keep tab** or **tabs** (**on**) **1.** To watch or supervise closely. **2.** To maintain a factual record (of). [Origin uncertain]

tab. Table(s).

TAB Technical Assistance Board.

tab·a·nid (tab′ə·nid) *adj.* Of or belonging to a family (*Tabanidae*) of large, bloodsucking, dipterous insects. — *n.* A tabinid insect, as a horsefly. [< NL < L *tabanus* horsefly]

tab·ard (tab′ərd) *n.* **1.** Formerly, a short, sleeveless or short-sleeved outer garment. **2.** A knight's cape or cloak, worn over his armor and emblazoned with his own arms; also, a similar garment worn by a herald and embroidered with his lord's arms. **3.** A banner attached to a trumpet or bugle. [< OF *tabart*, ult. < L *tapete* tapestry]

tab·a·ret (tab′ə·rit) *n.* A strong, silk upholstery fabric with varicolored stripes of satin or moiré. [Prob. < TABBY]

Ta·bas·co (tə·bas′kō) *n.* A pungent sauce made from red pepper: a trade name. Also **Tabasco sauce.**

Ta·bas·co (tə·bas′kō, *Sp.* tä·väs′kō) A State in SE Mexico; 9,782 sq. mi.; pop. 766,346 (1970); capital, Villa Hermosa.

tab·by (tab′ē) *n.* *pl.* **·bies** **1.** A brindled or striped cat. **2.** Any domestic cat, especially a female. **3.** A gossiping old maid. **4.** Any of various plain-woven fabrics, as a watered taffeta. **5.** A garment made of such fabric. — *adj.* **1.** Having dark, wavy markings; brindled, as a cat. **2.** Watered or mottled, as a fabric. **3.** Made of tabby. — *v.t.* **·bied**, **·by·ing** To give a wavy or watered appearance to (silk, etc.). [< F *tabis*, *atabis* < Arabic *'attābi*, < *'Attābi*, name of a quarter of Baghdad where the cloth was manufactured]

ta·ber (tā′bər) See TABOR.

tab·er·na·cle (tab′ər·nak′əl) *n.* **1.** A tent or similar temporary structure or shelter. **2.** A Jewish house of worship; a temple. **3.** Originally, the portable sanctuary used by the Jews in the wilderness. **4.** Any house of worship, especially one of large size and not of especially ecclesiastical architecture. **5.** The human body as the dwelling place of the soul. **6.** *Eccl.* The ornamental receptacle for the consecrated Eucharistic elements, or for the pyx. **7.** An ornamental recess or structure sheltering something. **8.** *Naut.* A socket or hinged post to unstep or lower a mast. — *v.i. & v.t.* **·led**, **·ling** To dwell or place in or as in a tabernacle. [< OF < L *tabernaculum*, dim. of *taberna* shed] — **tab·er·nac·u·lar** (tab′ər·nak′yə·lər) *adj.*

ta·bes (tā′bēz) *n.* *Pathol.* **1.** Formerly, emaciation with general languor, progressive atrophy, and hectic fever. **2.** Locomotor ataxia. [< L, a wasting away < *tabere* to waste away]

ta·bes·cent (tə·besʹənt) *adj.* Becoming emaciated; wasting away. — **ta·besʹcence** *n.*

tabes dor·sa·lis (dôr·sāʹlis) *n. Pathol.* Locomotor ataxia. [< TABES + L, of the back]

ta·bet·ic (tə·betʹik) *adj. Pathol.* Affected with tabes; emaciated. Also **tab·id** (tabʹid). — *n.* A tabetic person.

tab·la·ture (tabʹlə·chər) *n.* 1. *Anat.* The separation between the inner and outer tables of the cranium. 2. A tablelike painting or design. 3. *Music* A notation for instrumental music that indicates rhythm and fingering, but not the pitches produced. [< F < L *tabula* board]

ta·ble (tāʹbəl) *n.* 1. An article of furniture with a flat horizontal top upheld by one or more supports. 2. Such a table around which persons sit for a meal: to set the *table.* 3. The food served or entertainment provided at a meal or dinner. 4. The company of persons at a table. 5. A gaming table, as for roulette, dice, etc. 6. A collection of related numbers, values, signs, or items of any kind, arranged for reference or comparison, often in parallel columns: a *table* of logarithms. 7. A synoptical statement; list: *table* of contents. 8. A tableland; plateau. 9. *Geol.* A horizontal stratum of rock. 10. The flat facet cut across the top of a precious stone. 11. *Archit.* **a** A raised horizontal surface or band of molding on a wall; a stringcourse. **b** A raised or sunken panel on a wall. 12. In palmistry, the quadrang'e formed by four lines of the hand. 13. In backgammon: **a** Either of the two leaves of a backgammon board. **b** *pl. Obs.* Backgammon. 14. *Anat.* One of the flat bony plates separated by the diploe and forming the inner or outer part of the cranium. 15. A tablet or slab bearing an inscription; especially, one of those that bore the Ten Commandments or certain Roman laws. — **to turn the tables** To thwart an opponent's action and turn the situation to his disadvantage. — *v.t.* **·bled, ·bling** 1. To place on a table, as a playing card. 2. To postpone discussion of (a resolution, bill, etc.) until a future time, or for an indefinite period. 3. *Rare* To make into or enter in a list or table; tabulate. Abbr. *tab.* [Fusion of OF *table* and OE *tabule,* both < L *tabula* board]

tab·leau (tabʹlō, ta·blōʹ) *n. pl.* **·leaux** (-lōz, -lō) or **·leaus** (-lōz) 1. Any picture or picturesque representation; especially, a striking scene presented dramatically. 2. A tableau vivant (which see). [< F, dim. of *table.* See TABLE.]

ta·bleau vi·vant (ta·blōʹ vē·vänʹ) *pl.* **ta·bleaux vi·vants** (ta·blōʹ vē·vänʹ) *French* A picturelike scene represented by silent and motionless persons standing in appropriate attitudes: also called *living picture, picture, tableau.*

Table Bay An inlet of the Atlantic in SW South Africa, the harbor of Cape Town.

ta·ble·cloth (tāʹbəl·klôthʹ, -klothʹ) *n.* A cloth covering a table, especially at meals.

ta·ble d'hôte (tabʹəl dōtʹ, täʹbəl; *Fr.* ta·blə dōtʹ) *pl.* **tables d'hôte** (tabʹəlz dōtʹ, täʹbəlz; *Fr.* ta·blə dōtʹ) A complete meal served at a restaurant or hotel, the price of the entire meal being determined by the price of the entrée one chooses. Compare À LA CARTE, PRIX FIXE. [< F, lit., table of the host, as at an inn]

ta·ble·land (tāʹbəl·landʹ) *n.* A broad, level, elevated region, usually treeless; a plateau.

table linen Tablecloths, napkins, doilies, etc., made of linen or similar cloth.

Table Mountain A flat-topped mountain near Cape Town, South Africa; 3,550 ft.

ta·ble·spoon (tāʹbəl·spoonʹ, -spoonʹ) *n.* 1. A fairly large spoon used for serving food and in measuring for recipes, etc. 2. An amount equal to as much as a tablespoon will hold, equivalent to three teaspoons. Abbr. *T., tbs., tbsp.*

ta·ble·spoon·ful (tāʹbəl·spoonʹ·foolʹ, -spoon-) *n. pl.* **·fuls** As much as a tablespoon will hold.

tab·let (tabʹlit) *n.* 1. A pad, as of writing paper or note paper. 2. A small, flat surface, especially one designed for or containing an inscription or design. 3. A definite portion of a drug, etc., pressed into a solid form; a troche or lozenge. 4. A small, flat, or nearly flat piece of some prepared substance, as chocolate or soap. 5. A thin sheet or slab of solid material, as stone, wood, etc., used for writing, painting or drawing. 6. A set of such sheets fastened together. [< OF *tablete,* dim. of *table.* See TABLE.]

table tennis A table game resembling tennis, played usually indoors with a small celluloid ball and wooden paddles: also called *ping-pong.*

ta·ble·ware (tāʹbəl·wârʹ) *n.* Dishes, knives, forks, spoons, etc., for table use, collectively.

table wine A wine usually drunk with meals.

tab·loid (tabʹloid) *n.* A newspaper consisting of sheets one half the size of those in an ordinary newspaper, in which the news is presented by means of pictures and concise reporting. — *adj.* 1. Compact; concise; condensed. 2. Sensational: *tabloid* journalism. [< TABL(ET) + -OID]

Tab·loid (tabʹloid) *n.* Proprietary name for any of various medical preparations and drugs in concentrated or condensed tablet form.

ta·boo (tə·booʹ, ta-) *n.* 1. Among primitive peoples, especially the Polynesians, a religious and social interdict forbidding the mention of a certain person, thing, or place, the performance of a certain action, etc. 2. The system or practice of such interdicts or prohibitions. 3. Any restriction or ban founded on custom or social convention. 4. The convention of avoiding certain words as profane, obscene, disagreeable, or otherwise socially unacceptable: compare EUPHEMISM. — *adj.* 1. Consecrated or prohibited by taboo. 2. Banned or forbidden by social authority or convention. — *v.t.* 1. To place under taboo. 2. To exclude; ostracize. Also **ta·buʹ.** [< Tonga *tabu*]

ta·bor (tāʹbər) *n.* A small drum or tambourine on which a fifer beats his own accompaniment. — *v.i.* To beat or play on a timbrel or small drum; beat lightly and repeatedly. Also spelled *taber.* Also **taʹbour.** [< OF *tabour,* prob. < Persian *tabīrah* drum] — **taʹbor·er** *n.*

Ta·bor (tāʹbər), **Mount** A mountain near Nazareth in Galilee, northern Israel; 1,929 ft.

tab·o·ret (tabʹər·it, tabʹə·retʹ) *n.* 1. A small tabor. 2. A stool or small seat, usually without arms or back. 3. An embroidery frame. Also **tab·ou·ret** (tabʹər·it, tabʹə·retʹ). [< F *tabouret,* dim. of *tabour.* See TABOR.]

tab·o·rine (tabʹə·rēn, tab·ə·rēnʹ) *n.* A small tabor. Also **tab·o·rin, tab·ou·rine** (tabʹə·rēn, tab·ə·rēnʹ). [< OF *tabourin,* dim. of *tabour.* See TABOR.]

Ta·briz (tä·brēzʹ) A city in NW Iran; pop. 403,413 (1967): also *Tébriz.*

tab·u·lar (tabʹyə·lər) *adj.* 1. Pertaining to or consisting of a table or list. 2. Computed from or with a mathematical table. 3. Having a flat surface; tablelike. [< L *tabularis* < *tabula* table] — **tabʹu·lar·ly** *adv.*

tab·u·la ra·sa (tabʹyoo·lə rāʹsə) *Latin* 1. An empty or clean tablet; a clean slate. 2. The mind before being exposed to experience.

tab·u·lar·ize (tabʹyə·lə·rīzʹ) *v.t.* **·ized, ·iz·ing** To arrange in tabular form; tabulate. — **tabʹu·lar·i·zaʹtion** *n.*

tab·u·late (tabʹyə·lāt) *v.t.* **·lat·ed, ·lat·ing** 1. To arrange in a table or list: to *tabulate* results. 2. To form with a tabular surface. — *adj.* 1. Having a flat surface. 2. *Zool.* Having horizontal plates extending across the visceral cavity, as certain corals. [< L *tabula* table + -ATE¹] — **tabʹu·laʹtion** *n.*

tab·u·la·tor (tabʹyə·lāʹtər) *n.* 1. One who or that which tabulates. 2. A device built into a typewriter, and used to present statistical matter in tabulated form. 3. An automatic accounting machine for tabulating reports.

TAC 1. *Mil.* Tactical Air Command. 2. Technical Assistance Committee.

tac·a·ma·hac (takʹə·mə·hakʹ) *n.* 1. A yellowish, resinous substance with a strong odor, derived from various trees and used as incense. 2. Any of the trees producing this substance. 3. A tree (*Populus balsamifera*) of the United States, having leaf buds exuding a gummy resin: also called *balsam poplar.* Also spelled *tacmahack:* also **tacʹa·ma·hacʹa** (-hak'ə), **tacʹa·ma·hack, tacʹca·ma·hacʹ.** [< Sp. *tacamaca, tacamahaca* < Nahuatl *tecomahca,* lit., fetid copal]

tace (tās) *n.* Tasset, a type of armor plate.

ta·cet (tāʹset) *Latin* Literally, it is silent: a musical direction for silence.

tache (tach) *n. Archaic* A fastening; clasp; buckle. Also **tach.** [< OF *tache* nail, fastening. Doublet of TACK.]

tach·i·na fly (takʹə·nə) A dipterous fly (family *Tachinidae*) whose larvae develop as parasites in caterpillars, etc. For illustration see INSECTS (beneficial). [< NL *tachina* < Gk. *tachinos* swift]

Ta Ch'ing (däʹ jingʹ) The Manchu dynasty of China.

tach·i·nid (takʹə·nid) *n.* A tachina fly. — *adj.* Of or pertaining to the tachina fly.

ta·chis·to·scope (tə·kisʹtə·skōp) *n.* An apparatus for giving a brief, accurately timed exposure to visual objects, for the purpose of determining the conditions under which they are perceived. [< Gk. *tachistos* swiftest + -SCOPE]

tach·o·gram (takʹə·gram) *n.* The record made by a tachometer.

tach·o·graph (takʹə·graf, -gräf) *n.* 1. A registering tachometer. 2. The record it makes. [< Gk. *tachos* swiftness + -GRAPH]

ta·chom·e·ter (tə·komʹə·tər) *n.* 1. An instrument for measuring speed and velocity, as of a machine, the flow of a current, blood, etc. 2. A device for indicating the speed of rotation of an engine, etc. [< Gk. *tachos* speed + -METER]

ta·chom·e·try (tə·komʹə·trē) *n.* The art or science of using a tachometer. — **tach·o·met·ric** (takʹə·metʹrik) *adj.*

tachy- *combining form* Speed; swiftness: *tachycardia.* [< Gk. *tachys* swift]

tach·y·car·di·a (takʹi·kärʹdē·ə) *n. Pathol.* Abnormal rapidity of the heartbeat. [< TACHY- + Gk. *kardia* heart] — **tachʹy·carʹdi·ac** (-ak) *adj.*

tach·y·graph (takʹə·graf, -gräf) *n.* 1. A tachygraphic manuscript or symbol. 2. A tachygrapher.

ta·chyg·ra·pher (tə·kigʹrə·fər) *n.* 1. One who writes in shorthand; a stenographer. 2. One of the shorthand writers of the ancient Greeks and Romans. Also **ta·chygʹra·phist.**

ta·chyg·ra·phy (tə·kigʹrə·fē) *n.* Stenography; shorthand; especially, the stenography of the ancient Greeks and Romans. — **tach·y·graph·ic** (takʹi·grafʹik) or **·i·cal** *adj.* — **tachʹy·graphʹi·cal·ly** *adv.*

tach·y·lyte (tak′ə-līt) *n.* A black basaltic glass that is rapidly decomposed by acids. — **tach′y·lyt′ic** (-lit′ik) *adj.*

ta·chym·e·ter (tə-kim′ə-tər) *n.* An instrument used in stadia surveying, usually a type of transit or theodolite.

ta·chym·e·try (tə-kim′ə-trē) *n.* The art or science of using a tachymeter. — **tach·y·met·ric** (tak′ə-met′rik) *adj.*

tac·it (tas′it) *adj.* **1.** Existing, inferred, or implied without being directly stated; implied by silence or silent acquiescence. **2.** *Law* Not expressed but understood by provision or operation of the law. **3.** Making no sound; silent; noiseless. [< F *tacite* < L *tacitus*, pp. of *tacere* to be silent] — **tac′it·ly** *adv.* — **tac′it·ness** *n.*

tac·i·turn (tas′ə-tûrn) *adj.* Habitually silent or reserved; disinclined to conversation. [< L *taciturnus* < L *tacere* to be silent] — **tac′i·tur′ni·ty** *n.* — **tac′i·turn·ly** *adv.*

— **Syn.** *Taciturn, silent, uncommunicative, reserved, close,* and *secretive* mean restrained in speaking to others. *Taciturn* characterizes a disposition to speak little, and then grudgingly. One is *silent* who says nothing at all, but the word is usually used of one who on many occasions refrains from volunteering remarks. *Uncommunicative* likewise implies silence when speech would seem to be called for; it suggests unsociableness, as *silent* does not. *Reserved* goes farther, suggesting unwillingness or inability to extend acquaintance, friendship, sympathy, etc. One is *close* who says little of his own affairs, perhaps because he has something to hide. *Secretive* makes the explicit accusation of knowing concealment. — **Ant.** talkative, communicative, garrulous.

Tac·i·tus (tas′ə-təs), **Cornelius**, 55?–117?, Roman historian.

tack¹ (tak) *n.* **1.** A small sharp-pointed nail, commonly with tapering sides and a flat head. **2.** *Naut.* **a** A rope that holds down the weather clew of a course. **b** The weather clew of a square sail. **c** The lower forward corner of a fore-and-aft sail. **d** A rope by which the lower outer corner of a studdingsail is pulled to the end of the boom. **e** The direction in which a vessel sails when sailing close-hauled, considered in relation to the position of her sails: On the starboard *tack* the wind is coming from the right-hand side. **f** The distance or the course run at one time in such direction. **g** The act of tacking. **h** Any veering of a vessel to one side, as to take advantage of a side wind. **3.** A change of policy; a new course of action. **4.** A temporary fastening. **5.** In sewing, a large, temporary stitch. **6.** The saddle, bridle, etc., used in riding a horse. — *v.t.* **1.** To fasten or attach with tacks. **2.** To secure temporarily, as with tacks or long stitches. **3.** To attach as supplementary; append. **4.** *Naut.* **a** To bring (a vessel) momentarily into the wind so as to go on the opposite tack. **b** To navigate (a vessel) to windward by making a series of tacks. — *v.i.* **5.** *Naut.* **a** To tack a vessel. **b** To go on the opposite tack, or sail to windward by a series of tacks. **6.** To change one's course; veer. [< AF *taque*, OF *tache* nail < Gmc. Doublet of TACHE.] — **tack′er** *n.*

tack² (tak) *n.* Food in general: usually used contemptuously, and often in compounds: *hardtack.* [Origin uncertain]

tack·et (tak′it) *n. Scot.* A hobnail or clout.

tack hammer A small hammer for driving tacks. For illustration see HAMMER.

tack·le (tak′əl, *sometimes, esp. Naut.* tā′kəl) *n.* **1.** A rope, pulley, or combination of ropes and pulleys used for hoisting or moving objects. **2.** *Naut.* A mechanism for raising and lowering heavy weights, or managing sails and spars, as on shipboard. **3.** A windlass or winch, together with ropes and hooks. **4.** The equipment used in any work or sport; gear: fishing *tackle.* **5.** Formerly, the implements of war; weapons. **6.** The act of tackling, or seizing and stopping, especially in football. **7.** In football, one of two linemen (the **right** and **left tackle**) whose position is usually between the guard and end; also, the position itself. **8.** A ship's rigging. — *v.t.* **led, ·ling 1.** To deal with; undertake to master, accomplish, or solve: to *tackle* a problem. **2.** To seize suddenly and forcefully, usually in order to stop or throw to the ground: to *tackle* a fleeing burglar. **3.** In football, to seize and stop (an opponent carrying the ball), usually by throwing to the ground. **4.** To harness (a horse). — *v.i.* **5.** In football, to tackle an opponent. [< MLG *takel* < *taken* to seize] — **tack′ler** *n.*

TACKLE

a Single blocks.
b Single and double.
c Double and double.

tack·ling (tak′ling) *n.* Tackle or gear collectively.

tack·y¹ (tak′ē) *adj.* **tack·i·er, tack·i·est** Having adhesive properties; sticky, as a surface covered with partly dried varnish. Also **tack′ey.** [Prob. < TACK¹, v. (def. 2)]

tack·y² (tak′ē) *adj.* **tack·i·er, tack·i·est** *U.S. Informal* **1.** Shabby; neglected; shoddy. **2.** Vulgarly showy; common. [Cf. dial. G *tacklig* untidy]

tac·ma·hack (tak′mə-hak) See TACAMAHAC.

Tac·na (täk′nä) A Department of southern Peru on the Pacific; 4,920 sq. mi.; pop. 93,900 (est. 1970); capital, **Tacna.**

tac·node (tak′nōd) *n. Math.* An osculation (def. 2). [< L *tactus*, pp. of *tangere* to touch + NODE]

Ta·co·ma (tə-kō′mə) A port city in western Washington, on Puget Sound; pop. 154,581.

tac·o·nite (tak′ə-nīt) *n. Geol.* An inferior iron ore of the Mesabi district in Minnesota, consisting of a very hard chert. [after *Tacon(ic Mountains)* + -ITE¹]

tact (takt) *n.* **1.** A quick or intuitive appreciation of what is fit, proper, or right; especially, skill in avoiding what would offend or disturb. **2.** The sense of touch; feeling; also, a touch or touching. **3.** A perception or feeling, other than tactile, of the qualities of things. — **Syn.** See ADDRESS. [< L *tactus* a touching < *tangere* to touch]

tact·ful (takt′fəl) *adj.* Possessing or manifesting tact; considerate. — **tact′ful·ly** *adv.* — **tact′ful·ness** *n.*

tac·tic (tak′tik) *n.* Tactics; also, a branch or detail of tactics. — *adj.* Of or pertaining to arrangement or tactics; tactical. [See TACTICS]

tac·ti·cal (tak′ti·kəl) *adj.* **1.** Pertaining to or of the nature of tactics. **2.** Exhibiting adroit maneuvering. — **tac′ti·cal·ly** *adv.*

tac·ti·cian (tak-tish′ən) *n.* An expert in tactics; an adroit maneuverer.

tac·tics (tak′tiks) *n.pl.* (*construed as sing.* in def. 1) **1.** The science and art of military and naval evolutions; especially, the art of handling troops in the presence of the enemy or for immediate objectives: distinguished from *strategy.* **2.** Any maneuvering or adroit management to gain an objective. [< Gk. *taktika,* pl. of *taktikos* suitable for arranging or organizing < *tassein, tattein* to arrange, order]

tac·tile (tak′til, -təl, *esp. Brit.* -tīl) *adj.* **1.** Pertaining to the organs or sense of touch; caused by or consisting of contact; tactual. **2.** That may be touched; tangible. [< F < L *tactilis* < *tactus* touch. See TACT.]

tac·til·i·ty (tak-til′ə-tē) *n. pl.* **·ties** The state or quality of being tactile.

tac·tion (tak′shən) *n.* The act of touching, or the state of being in contact. [< L *tactio, -onis* < *tactus.* See TACT.]

tact·less (takt′lis) *adj.* Lacking tact. — **tact′less·ly** *adv.* — **tact′less·ness** *n.*

tac·tu·al (tak′chōō-əl) *adj.* **1.** Pertaining to the sense or organs of touch. **2.** Derived from or caused by touch. [< L *tactus* touch. See TACT.] — **tac′tu·al·ly** *adv.*

Ta·cu·ba·ya (tä′kōō-vä′yä) A western section of Mexico City; site of the national astronomical observatory.

tad (tad) *n. U.S. Informal* A little child. [Prob. short for TADPOLE]

tad·pole (tad′pōl) *n.* The aquatic larva of an amphibian, as a frog or toad, breathing by external gills and having a tail with an extended membrane, giving it a fishlike form: also called *polliwog.* [ME *taddepol* < *tadde* toad < OE *tāde* + *poll* head]

Ta·dzhik (tä·jek′, -jik′) *n. pl.* **·dzhik** One of a people of Iranian descent inhabiting the Tadzhik S.S.R. and adjacent regions: also spelled *Tajik.*

Ta·dzhik S.S.R. (tə-jēk′) A constituent republic of the southern Soviet Union; 55,043 sq. mi.; pop. 2,900,000 (1970); capital, Dyushambe: also *Tajik S.S.R.* Also **Ta·dzhik·i·stan** (tä-jē′kə-stän, -jik′ə-). *Russian* **Ta·dzhik′ska·ya S.S.R.** (-ska·yə).

tae (tā) *prep. Scot.* To.

tae·di·um vi·tae (tē′dē-əm vī′tē) *Latin* Weariness of life.

tael (tāl) *n.* **1.** An Oriental weight varying from 1 to 2½ ounces, commonly about 1⅓ ounces. **2.** A Chinese monetary unit of varying value. [< Pg. < Malay *tahil*]

ta'en (tān) *Scot.* Taken.

tae·ni·a (tē′nē-ə) *n. pl.* **·ni·ae** (-ni·ē) **1.** In classical antiquity, a band or fillet for the hair. **2.** *Archit.* A band or fillet between the Doric frieze and the architrave. **3.** *Anat.* A ribbonlike structure of formation, as of nerve or muscle tissue. **4.** *Zool.* A tapeworm. Also spelled *tenia.* [< L < Gk. *tainia* fillet, tape]

tae·ni·a·cide (tē′nē-ə-sīd′), **tae·ni·a·fuge** (tē′nē-ə-fyōōj′), etc. See TENIACIDE, etc.

taf·fer·el (taf′ər-əl, -ə-rel) *n. Naut.* **1.** A taffrail. **2.** Originally, the upper part of a vessel's stern. [< MDu. *tafereel* panel, picture, dim. of *tafel* table, panel < L *tabula* board]

taf·fe·ta (taf′ə-tə) *n.* A fine, plain-woven, somewhat stiff fabric of silk, rayon, etc. — *adj.* Made of or resembling taffeta. [< OF *taffetas* < Med.L *taffeta* < Persian *tāftah* < *tāftan* to twist]

taff·rail (taf′rāl′, -rəl) *n. Naut.* **1.** The rail around a vessel's stern. **2.** The upper part of a vessel's stern. Also called *tafferel.* [Alter. of TAFFEREL, after RAIL¹]

taffrail log *Naut.* A patent log (which see).

taf·fy (taf′ē) *n.* **1.** A confection made of brown sugar or molasses, mixed with butter, boiled down, and pulled into long strands until it cools sufficiently to hold its shape: also called *toffee.* **2.** *Informal* Flattery. [Origin unknown]

Taf·fy (taf′ē) *n. Brit. Slang* A Welshman. [Alter. of *David,* in imitation of Welsh pronunciation]

taf·i·a (tafʹē·ə) *n.* An alcoholic liquor resembling rum, distilled in the West Indies from impure molasses or from refuse sugar. Also **tafʹfi·a.** [< native name. Cf. Malay *tāfia* spirit distilled from molasses.]

Ta·fi·lelt (tä·fē′lelt) A Saharan oasis in SE Morocco; about 200 sq. mi. Also **Ta·fi′lalt** (-lalt), **Ta·fi′let** (-let).

Taft (taft) **Lorado,** 1860–1936, U.S. sculptor. — **Robert Alphonso,** 1899–1953, U.S. legislator; son of William Howard. — **William Howard,** 1857–1930, U.S. statesman and jurist, 27th president of the United States 1909–13.

tag¹ (tag) *n.* **1.** Something tacked on or attached to something else; an appendage. **2.** A label tied or attached loosely as to a piece of baggage. **3.** A loose, ragged edge of anything; tatter. **4.** The tail or tip of the tail of any animal. **5.** A matted and ragged lock of wool on a sheep; a loose lock of hair. **6.** A worthless leaving; remnant; ort. **7.** A flap or loop, as for drawing on a boot. **8.** A hard tip at the end of a shoelace, etc. **9.** A decorative flourish, as on a signature. **10.** In angling, a piece of bright material surrounding the shank of the hook in an artificial fly. **11.** A well-known quotation or saying, as in a song, poem, or book. **12.** The refrain of a song or poem. **13.** The final lines of a speech in a play; catchword; cue. **14.** The crowd; rabble: chiefly in the phrases *rag and tag* and *rag, tag, and bobtail.* — *v.* **tagged, tag·ging** *v.t.* **1.** To supply, adorn, fit, mark, or label with a tag. **2.** To shear away tags from (sheep). **3.** To follow closely or persistently. — *v.i.* **4.** To follow closely at one's heels: The little boy *tagged* along. [Prob. < Scand. Cf. Sw. *tagg* spike, tooth, Norw. *tagge* tooth.]

tag² (tag) *v.t.* **tagged, tag·ging 1.** In baseball, to touch (a player) with the ball or with the hand or glove in which the ball is held. **2.** To overtake and touch, as in the game of tag. **3.** *Informal* To strike solidly or with telling effect, as a person, a baseball, etc.: He *tagged* the champion with a right to the jaw. **4.** *Informal* To make contact with; designate: *tagged* him for a loan. — *n.* **1.** In baseball, the act or instance of tagging a player, especially a base runner, in an attempt to retire him. **2.** A children's running game in which a player who is touched or caught (usually called "it") tries to touch or catch the others. [< TAG¹]

TAG The Adjutant General.

Ta·ga·log (tä·gä′log, tag′ə·log, -lôg) *n.* **1.** A member of a Malay people native to the Philippines, especially Luzon. **2.** One of the principal native languages and, since 1940, the official language of the Philippines, belonging to the Indonesian subfamily of the Austronesian family of languages. Also **Ta·gal** (tä·gäl′).

Ta·gan·rog (tə·gən·rôk′) A port city in the SW R.S.F.S.R., on the Gulf of Taganrog, *Russian* **Ta·gan·rog′skiy Za·liv** (-skyē zə·lyēf′), a NE inlet of the Sea of Azov; pop. 254,000 (est. 1970).

tag day A day on which contributions are solicited for charitable and other institutions, so called from the custom of giving a tag to each donor.

tag end 1. A loose end or tag of cloth, yarn, etc. **2.** The endmost part of anything.

tagged atom A tracer (def. 7).

tag·ger (tag′ər) *n.* **1.** One who or that which tags. **2.** *pl.* Very thin tin plate.

Ta·gore (tə·gôr′, -gōr′, tä′gôr), **Sir Rabindranath,** 1861–1941, Hindu philosopher, author, and painter.

ta·gua nut (tä′gwä) The ivory nut (which see). [< native Colombian name]

Ta·gus (tä′gəs) A river in west central Spain and central Portugal, flowing 566 miles SW to the Atlantic: Spanish *Tajo,* Portuguese *Tejo.*

Ta·hi·ti (tä·hē′tē, tə-, tī′tē) The largest island of the Society group; 402 sq. mi.: formerly *Otaheite.*

Ta·hi·ti·an (tä·hē′tē·ən, tə-, -shən) *adj.* Of or relating to Tahiti, its people, or their language. — *n.* **1.** One of the native Polynesian people of Tahiti. **2.** The Polynesian language of the Tahitians.

Ta·hoe (tä′hō, tä′-), **Lake** A lake on the boundary between California and Nevada; about 195 sq. mi.; elevation 6,225 ft.

tah·sil·dar (tä·sēl·där′) *n.* In India, a customs officer or tax collector. Also **tah′seel·dar′.** [< Hind. *tahsīldār* < Arabic *tahsīl* a collection + Persian *dār* holder]

Tai (tī) See THAI.

tai·ga (tī′gə) *n.* The far northern coniferous forest of Siberia and by extension of Eurasia and America, extending to the northern limit of trees. [< Russian]

Tai·ho·ku (tī·hō·kōō) The Japanese name for TAIPEH.

tail¹ (tāl) *n.* **1.** The hindmost part or rear end of an animal; especially when prolonged beyond the rest of the body as a distinct, flexible member. ◆ Collateral adjective: *caudal.* **2.** Any slender, flexible, terminal extension of the main part of an object: the *tail* of a shirt. **3.** *Astron.* The luminous trail extending from the nucleus of a comet. **4.** The hind, back, or inferior portion of anything. **5.** *pl. Informal* The reverse side of a coin. **6.** The lower end of a stream or pool. **7.** Anything of taillike appearance, as a number of persons in single file. **8.** A retinue or suite. **9.** A pigtail; braid. **10.** *Aeron.* The rear end of an aircraft; also, the stabilizer

and control surfaces at the rear of an aircraft. **11.** The rear portion of a bomb, projectile, rocket, or guided missile, usually equipped with vanes. **12.** The bottom of a printed page. **13.** *pl. Informal* A man's full-dress suit; also, a swallow-tailed coat. **14.** The back end of a wagon. **15.** *Informal* The trail or course taken by a fugitive: The police were on his *tail.* — *v.t.* **1.** To furnish with a tail. **2.** To cut off the tail of. **3.** To be the tail or end of: to *tail* a procession. **4.** To join (one thing) to the end of another. **5.** To insert and fasten by one end, as a beam into a wall: with *in* or *on.* **6.** *Informal* To follow secretly and stealthily; shadow. — *v.i.* **7.** To extend or proceed in a line. **8.** *Informal* To follow close behind. **9.** To be inserted and fastened at one end, as a beam. **10.** *Naut.* To swing or go aground stern foremost. — **to tail off** To diminish or recede gradually. — *adj.* **1.** Rearmost; hindmost. **2.** Coming from behind; following: a *tail* wind. [OE *tægl*] — **tail′less** *adj.*

tail² (tāl) *Law adj.* Restricted in succession to particular heirs: an estate *tail.* — *n.* An abridgment or limitation of ownership; an entail. [< OF *taillie,* pp. of *taillier* to cut]

tail beam Tailpiece (def. 4).

tail·first (tāl′fûrst′) *adv.* With the hind side foremost; backward. Also **tail′fore′most** (-fôr′mōst, -fōr′-).

tail·gate (tāl′gāt′) *n.* **1.** A hinged or vertically sliding board or gate closing the back end of a truck, wagon, etc. Also **tail·board** (tāl′bôrd, -bōrd). **2.** One of the gates at the lower level of a canal lock. — *v.t.* & *v.i.* **·gat·ed, ·gat·ing** *U.S. Slang* To drive too close behind for safety.

tail gun *Aeron.* A machine gun mounted in the tail of an aircraft and firing to the rear.

tail·gun·ner (tāl′gun′ər) *n.* One who operates a tail gun.

tail·heav·y (tāl′hev′ē) *adj.* Tending to fly or move with the tail down, because of weight, poor trim, etc.

tail·ing (tā′ling) *n.* **1.** *pl.* Refuse or residue from grain after milling, or from ground ore after washing. **2.** The inner, covered portion of a projecting brick or stone in a wall.

taille (tāl, *Fr.* tä′y′) *n.* In feudal France, a tax from which nobles and clergy were exempt. [< OF < *taillier* to cut]

tail·light (tāl′līt′) *n.* A light attached to the rear of a vehicle. Also **tail lamp.**

tai·lor (tā′lər) *n.* One who makes to order or repairs men's or women's outer garments. — *v.i.* **1.** To do a tailor's work. — *v.t.* **2.** To fit with garments: He is well *tailored.* **3.** To work at or make by tailoring: to *tailor* a coat. ◆ Collateral adjective: *sartorial.* **4.** To make, adjust, or adapt for a specific purpose. [< OF *tailleor* < *taillier* to cut < LL *taliare* to split, cut, prob. < L *talea* rod]

tailor bee Any of certain leaf-cutting bees (family *Megachilidae*) that line their nests with pieces of leaves.

tai·lor·bird (tā′lər·bûrd′) *n.* A passerine bird (*Sutoria* and related genera) of Asia and Africa, that stitches leaves together to hold and hide its nest. For illustration see NEST.

tai·lored (tā′lərd) *adj.* **1.** Characterized by simple, severe style and usually by relatively sturdy material: said especially of women's clothes. **2.** Made by a tailor.

tai·lor·ing (tā′lər·ing) *n.* The act or product of one who tailors.

tai·lor-made (tā′lər·mād′) *adj.* **1.** Made by a tailor. **2.** Made or as if made to order; perfectly right or suitable: The job was *tailor-made* for him. **3.** Rolled or prepared by a machine: a *tailor-made* cigarette. — *n. Informal* Something tailor-made, as a woman's garment.

tail·piece (tāl′pēs′) *n.* **1.** Any endpiece or appendage. **2.** In a violin or similar instrument, a piece of wood, as ebony, at the soundboard end, having the strings fastened to it. For illustration see VIOLIN. **3.** *Printing* An ornamental design on the lower blank portion of a page. **4.** A piece inserted by tailing, as a floor timber: also called *tail beam.*

tail pipe An exhaust (n. def. 2).

tail·race (tāl′rās′) *n.* **1.** That part of a millrace below the water wheel, bearing away the spent water. **2.** *Mining* The channel for water to remove tailings.

tail·skid (tāl′skid′) *n. Aeron.* A runner fixed beneath the tail of an airplane.

tail·spin (tāl′spin′) *n.* **1.** *Aeron.* The descent of a stalled airplane along a tight helical path at a steep angle. **2.** *Informal* An emotional upheaval often resulting in loss of control.

tail·stock (tāl′stok′) *n.* That standard or stock of a lathe through which passes the nonrotating spindle or dead center.

tail wind A wind blowing in the same general direction as the course of an aircraft, ship, or other vehicle.

Tai·myr Peninsula (tī·mir′) A large peninsula of the northern R.S.F.S.R., extending 700 miles NE to SW, between the Kara and Laptev seas. Also **Tai·mir′.**

tain (tān) *n.* **1.** Very thin plate. **2.** Tinfoil suitable for backing mirrors. [Prob. aphetic var. of F *étain* tin]

Tai·nan (tī′nän′) A city on SW Taiwan; pop. 229,500 (1961).

Tai·na·ron (te′nä·rôn), **Cape** See (Cape) MATAPAN.

Taine (tān, *Fr.* ten), **Hippolyte Adolphe,** 1828–93, French literary critic and historian.

Tai·no (tī′nō) *n. pl.* **·nos 1.** A member of an extinct tribe of Indian aborigines of the West Indies, especially Haiti, probably the first encountered by Columbus. **2.** The Arawakan language of this tribe.

taint (tānt) *v.t.* **1.** To imbue with an offensive, noxious, or deteriorating quality or principle; infect with decay; render corrupt or poisonous. **2.** To render morally corrupt or vitiated; contaminate; pollute. **3.** *Obs.* To tincture; tinge — *v.i.* **4.** To be or become tainted. — **Syn.** See POLLUTE. — *n.* **1.** A trace or germ of decay; a cause or result of corruption. **2.** A moral stain or blemish; spot. [Fusion of aphetic form of ATTAINT and F *teint*, pp. of *teindre* to tinge, color < L *tingere*]

Tai·pei (tī′pā′) The capital of Taiwan, in the northern part; pop. 1,830,000 (est. 1971): Japanese *Taihoku.* Also **Tai′·peh′, T′ai′pei′.**

Tai·ping (tī′ping′) *n.* An insurgent in the **Taiping Rebellion** in China (1850–64) led by Hung-siu-tsuen, who sought to replace the Manchu dynasty with the Chinese T′ai–p′ing Chao (Great Peace Dynasty). [< Chinese, great peace]

Tai·sho (tī′shō) The title of the reign (1912–26) of Yoshihito, emperor of Japan. [< Japanese, great righteousness]

Tai·wan (tī′wän′) An island off the coast of SE China, comprising, together with the Pescadores, the National Republic of China; 13,890 sq. mi.; pop. 14,424,000 (est. 1970); capital Taipei; ceded to Japan, 1895–1945: formerly *Formosa.*

Tai·yü·an (tī′yü′än′) The capital of Shansi province, China; pop. 2,725,000 (est. 1970).

Ta′iz (tä·iz′) The second capital of Yemen, in the SW part; pop. about 80,000. Also **Ta·iz′, Ta′izz′.**

taj (täj) *n.* Persian A headdress of distinction; as a diadem or crown; especially, a tall cap worn by Moslem dervishes.

Ta·jik (tä-jēk′, -jik′) See TADZHIK.

Taj Ma·hal (täzh′ mə·häl′, täj′) A mausoleum of white marble built (1631–45) by Shah Jehan at Agra, India.

Ta·jo (tä′hō) The Spanish name for the TAGUS.

ta·ka (tä′kä) *n.* The monetary unit of Bangladesh, equivalent to 100 paise.

Ta·ka·mat·su (tä·kä·mät·sōō) A port city on northern Shikoku, Japan; pop. 271,000 (est. 1968).

TAJ MAHAL

take (tāk) *v.* **took, tak·en, tak·ing** *v.t.* **1.** To lay hold of; grasp. **2.** To get possession of; seize. **3.** To seize forcibly; capture; catch. **4.** To catch in a trap or snare. **5.** To gain in competition; win. **6.** To choose; select. **7.** To obtain by purchase; buy. **8.** To rent or hire; lease; to *take* lodgings. **9.** To receive regularly by payment; subscribe to, as a periodical. **10.** To assume occupancy of: to *take* a chair. **11.** To assume the responsibilities or duties of: to *take* office. **12.** To bring or accept into some relation to oneself: He *took* a wife. **13.** To assume as a symbol or badge: to *take* the veil. **14.** To impose upon oneself; subject oneself to: to *take* a vow. **15.** To remove or carry off: with *away.* **16.** To remove from the proper place; misappropriate; steal. **17.** To remove by death. **18.** To subtract or deduct. **19.** To be subjected to; undergo: to *take* a beating. **20.** To submit to; accept passively: to *take* an insult. **21.** To become affected with; contract: He *took* cold. **22.** To affect: The fever *took* him at dawn. **23.** To captivate; charm or delight: The dress *took* her fancy. **24.** To conduct oneself in response to; react to: How did she *take* the news? **25.** To undertake to deal with; contend with; handle: to *take* an examination. **26.** To consider; deem: I *take* him for an honest man. **27.** To understand; comprehend. **28.** To strike in a specified place; hit: The blow *took* him on the forehead. **29.** *Informal* To aim or direct: He *took* a shot at the target. **30.** To carry with one; transport; convey: He *took* a briefcase along. **31.** To lead: This road *takes* you to town. **32.** To escort; conduct: Who *took* her to the dance? **33.** To receive into the body, as by eating, inhaling, etc.: *Take* a deep breath. **34.** To accept, as something offered, due, or given; have conferred on one: to *take* a bribe; to *take* a degree. **35.** To let in; admit: The car will *take* only six people. **36.** To indulge oneself in; enjoy: to *take* a nap. **37.** To perform, as an action: to *take* a stride. **38.** To avail oneself of (an opportunity, etc.). **39.** To put into effect; adopt: to *take* measures. **40.** To use up or consume; require as necessary; demand: The piano *takes* too much space. **41.** To make use of; apply: They *took* clubs to him. **42.** To travel by means of: to *take* a train to Boston. **43.** To go to; seek: to *take* cover. **44.** To ascertain or obtain by measuring, computing, etc.: to *take* a census. **45.** To obtain or derive from some source; adopt or copy. **46.** To obtain by writing; write down or copy: to *take* notes. **47.** To obtain a likeness or representation of, as by drawing or photographing; also, to obtain (a likeness, picture, etc.) in such a manner. **48.** To experience; feel: to *take* pride in an achievement. **49.** To conceive or feel: She

took a dislike to him. **50.** To become impregnated with; absorb: The cloth will not *take* the pattern. **51.** In baseball, to allow (a pitch) to pass without swinging at it: said of a batter. **52.** *Slang* To cheat; deceive. **53.** *Gram.* To require by construction or usage: The verb *takes* a direct object. — *v.i.* **54.** To get possession. **55.** To engage; catch, as mechanical parts. **56.** To begin to grow; germinate. **57.** To have the intended effect: The vaccination *took.* **58.** To become popular; gain favor or currency, as a play. **59.** To admit of being photographed: His face *takes* well. **60.** To detract: with *from.* **61.** To become (ill or sick). **62.** To make one's way; go. **63.** In baseball, to allow a pitch to pass without swinging at it: said of a batter. — **to take after 1.** To resemble. **2.** To follow as an example. — **to take amiss** To be offended by. — **to take at one's word** To believe. — **to take back 1.** To regain. **2.** To retract. — **to take breath** To pause, as from working. — **to take down 1.** To pull down, as a building. **2.** To dismantle; disassemble. **3.** To humble. **4.** To write down; make a record of. — **to take heart** To gain courage or confidence. — **to take in 1.** To admit; receive. **2.** To lessen in size or scope. **3.** To furl or brail (sail). **4.** To include; embrace. **5.** To understand; comprehend. **6.** To receive into one's home for pay, as lodgers or work. **7.** *Informal* To cheat or deceive. **8.** *U.S. Informal* To visit, as on a trip or tour: Did you *take in* the Louvre? — **to take in vain** To use profanely or blasphemously, as the name of a deity. — **to take it 1.** To assume; understand. **2.** To endure hardship, abuse, etc. — **to take it out on** *U.S. Informal* To vent one's anger, frustration, etc., on. — **to take off 1.** To remove, as a coat. **2.** To carry away. **3.** To kill. **4.** To deduct. **5.** *Informal* To mimic; burlesque. **6.** To rise from the ground or water in starting a flight, as an airplane. **7.** *U.S. Informal* To leave; depart. — **to take on 1.** To hire; employ. **2.** To undertake to deal with; handle. **3.** *Informal* To exhibit violent emotion. — **to take out 1.** To extract; remove. **2.** To obtain from the proper authority, as a license or patent. **3.** To lead or escort. — **to take over 1.** To assume control. **2.** To convey. — **to take place** To happen. — **to take stock 1.** To make an inventory. **2.** To estimate probability, position, etc.; consider. — **to take the field** To begin a campaign or game. — **to take to 1.** To have recourse to; go to: to *take* to one's bed. **2.** To develop the practice of, or an addiction to: He *took* to drink. **3.** To become fond of; be attracted by. — **to take to heart** To be deeply affected by. — **to take up 1.** To raise or lift. **2.** To make smaller or less; shorten or tighten. **3.** To pay, as a note or mortgage. **4.** To accept as stipulated: to *take up* an option. **5.** To begin or begin again; resume. **6.** To reprove or criticize. **7.** To occupy, engage, or consume, as space or time. **8.** To acquire an interest in or devotion to: to *take up* a cause. — **to take up with** *Informal* To become friendly with; associate with. — *n.* **1.** The act of taking, or that which is taken. **2.** An uninterrupted run of a camera or recording apparatus in making a motion picture, television program, sound recording, etc. **3.** A quantity collected at one time: the *take* of fish. **4.** *U.S. Slang* Money collected, as the receipts of a sporting event. [OE *tacan* < ON *taka*]

take·down (tāk′doun′) *adj.* Fitted for being taken apart or easily down: a *takedown* rifle. — *n.* **1.** Any article so constructed as to be taken apart easily. **2.** The part of a takedown mechanism by means of which it is taken apart or down. **3.** *U.S. Informal* The act of humiliating anyone.

take-home pay (tāk′hōm′) *U.S.* The remainder of one's wages or salary after tax and other payroll deductions.

take-in (tāk′in′) *n. Informal* An act of cheating or hoaxing.

take·off (tāk′ôf′, -of′) *n.* **1.** The act of rising or leaping to begin flight; especially, the departure of an airplane from the ground. **2.** *Informal* A satirical imitation; caricature. **3.** In horsemanship and athletics, the spot at which the feet leave the ground in leaping. — **Syn.** See CARICATURE.

take·o·ver (tāk′ō·vər) *n.* An assuming or seizure of control, function, ownership, or rule.

tak·er (tā′kər) *n.* One who takes; especially, one who accepts a wager; also, a collector: a ticket *taker.*

take-up (tāk′up′) *n.* **1.** *Mech.* A device for taking up lost motion or drawing in slack, as in a loom. **2.** The act of tightening or taking up.

tak·ing (tā′king) *adj.* **1.** Fascinating; captivating. **2.** *Informal* Contagious; infectious. — *n.* **1.** The act of one who takes. **2.** The thing or things taken; in fishing, a catch; haul; in the plural, receipts, as of money. **3.** *Obs.* Agitation; perplexity; distress. — **tak′ing·ly** *adv.* — **tak′ing·ness** *n.*

Ta·ku (tä′kōō′) A port town in NE China, on the Gulf of Chihli; pop. about 10,000.

ta·la (tä′la) *n.* The monetary unit of Western Samoa, equivalent to 100 sene.

tal·a·poin (tal′ə·poin) *n.* **1.** A Buddhist priest or monk. **2.** A West African monkey (*Cercopithecus talapoin*), smallest of the guenon group of Old World monkeys. [< Pg. *talapões*, pl. of *talapão* < Burmese *tala poi* our master]

ta·lar·i·a (tə-lâr′ē-ə) *n.pl.* Winged boots or sandals, or wings springing directly from the ankles, often represented as attributes of Mercury, Perseus, etc. [< L, < *talus* ankle]

Ta·la·ve·ra de la Rei·na (tä′lä-vā′rä thä lä rā′nä) A city in central Spain, on the Tagus river; scene of a battle between Wellington and Joseph Bonaparte, 1809; pop. about 21,728 (est. 1960).

talc (talk) *n.* A soft, white or variously colored, hydrous magnesium silicate, $H_2Mg_3(SiO_3)_4$, found in compact masses, used in making paper, soap, toilet powder, insulators, etc. Also **tal·cum** (tal′kəm). — *v.t.* **talcked** or **talced**, **talck·ing** or **talc·ing** To treat with talc: to *talc* a photographic plate. [< F < Med.L *talcum* < Arabian *talq* < Persian *talk*]

talc·ose (tal′kōs) *adj.* Composed of or containing talc. Also **talc·ous** (tal′kəs).

talcum powder Finely powdered and purified talc, used as a dusting agent, filter, and for the relief of chafed skin and prickly heat.

tale (tāl) *n.* 1. That which is told or related; a story; recital. 2. A connected narrative or account, oral or written, of an actual, legendary, or fictitious event or series of events. 3. An idle or malicious report; a piece of gossip. 4. A deliberately untrue story; a lie; falsehood. 5. *Archaic* A counting or enumeration; reckoning; numbering. 6. *Archaic* That which is counted; an amount; total; sum. 7. *Obs.* Speech; talk; also, the language of a country. [OE *talu* speech, narrative. Akin to TELL, TALK.]

tale·bear·er (tāl′bâr′ər) *n.* One who carries gossip; a taleteller. — **tale′bear′ing** *adj. & n.*

tal·ent (tal′ənt) *n.* 1. A particular and uncommon aptitude for some special work or activity; a faculty or gift. 2. People of skill or ability, collectively: the *talent* of the theater. 3. Mental endowments or capacities of a superior character; marked mental ability; also, mental ability in general. 4. An ancient weight and denomination of money of varying amount. 5. *Obs.* Inclination; disposition. — **Syn.** See ABILITY, GENIUS. [OE *talente*, appetite, will, inclination < L *talentum*, a sum of money < Gk. *talanton* weight, thing weighed]

tal·ent·ed (tal′ən-tid) *adj.* Having great ability; gifted.

talent scout One whose business is to discover talented people, especially for the performing arts.

ta·ler (tä′lər) *n.* A former German silver coin, the prototype of all dollars, issued in Joachimstal, Bohemia, and first dated 1518; a dollar: also spelled *thaler*. [< G. See DOLLAR.]

ta·les (tā′lēz) *n.* *pl.* **·les** (-lēz) *Law* 1. Persons to be summoned for jury duty to make up a deficiency when the regular panel is exhausted by challenges. 2. The writ for summoning such persons. [< L *tales* (*de circumstantibus*) such (of the bystanders), pl. of *talis* such a one. The phrase is from the writ summoning them.]

tales·man (tālz′mən) *n.* *pl.* **·men** (-mən) *Law* One of the tales. [< TALES + MAN]

tale·tel·ler (tāl′tel′ər) *n.* 1. One who tells stories, etc.; a raconteur. 2. A talebearer. — **tale′tell′ing** *adj. & n.*

tal·i·grade (tal′ə-grād) *adj.* *Zool.* Walking on the outer surface of the foot. [< L *talus* ankle + -GRADE]

tal·i·on (tal′ē-ən) *n.* Retaliation, as a form of justice. [< F < L *talio*, *-onis* < *talis* such]

tal·i·ped (tal′ə-ped) *adj.* Suffering from or afflicted with talipes; clubfooted. — *n.* A club-footed person.

tal·i·pes (tal′ə-pēz) *n.* *Pathol.* Clubfoot. [< NL < L *talus* ankle + *pes, pedis* foot]

tal·i·pom·a·nus (tal′ə-pom′ə-nəs) *n.* *Pathol.* Clubhand. [< *talipo-* (< TALIPES) + L *manus* hand]

tal·i·pot (tal′ə-pot) *n.* A stately East Indian palm (*Corypha umbraculifera*) crowned by large leaves used as fans, umbrellas, writing material, and as coverings for houses. [< Bengali *tālipāt* palm leaf < Skt. *tālī* fan palm + *pattra* leaf]

tal·is·man (tal′is-mən, -iz-) *n.* *pl.* **·mans** 1. Something supposed to produce extraordinary effects; a charm. 2. An astrological charm or symbol supposed to benefit or protect the possessor, especially by exerting magical or occult influence. 3. Any amulet. [< F < Sp. < Arabic *tilsam, tilasm* magic figure < LGk. *telesma* a sacred rite < Gk. *teleein* to initiate < *telos* end, completion]

— **Syn.** *Talisman, amulet, fetish,* and *charm* denote something regarded as having magical powers. *Talisman* may be applied to any material object, as Aladdin's lamp. An *amulet* is a *talisman* worn on the person to avert danger, disease, and so forth. A *fetish* is an object of religious devotion, a natural object in which some supernatural spirit dwells. *Charm* is a general word, and embraces anything that has magical influence: *talismans,* incantations, ritual dances, etc.

tal·is·man·ic (tal′is-man′ik) *adj.* Exerting magical or occult power. Also **tal′is·man′i·cal.**

talk (tôk) *v.i.* 1. To express or exchange thoughts in audible words; communicate by speech; speak or converse. 2. To make a speech. 3. To communicate by means other than speech: to *talk* with one's fingers. 4. To speak irrelevantly; prate; chatter. 5. To confer; consult. 6. To spread rumor; gossip. 7. To make sounds suggestive of speech. 8. *U.S. Informal* To give information, as to the police; inform. 9. *Informal* To be effective or influential: money *talks*. — *v.t.* 10. To express in words; utter. 11. To use in speaking; converse in: to *talk* Spanish. 12. To converse about; discuss: to *talk* business. 13. To bring to a specified condition or state by talking: to *talk* one into doing something. 14. To pass or spend, as time, in talking: usually with *away*. — **to talk back** To answer impudently. — **to talk big** *Slang* To brag; boast. — **to talk down** 1. To silence by talking; outtalk. 2. To direct (an aircraft) to a landing, in darkness, fog, etc., by giving oral instructions to the pilot over the radio. — **to talk down to** To speak to in a condescending manner, as in simple, obvious words; patronize. — **to talk shop** To talk about one's work. — **to talk up** 1. To discuss, especially so as to promote; praise; extol. 2. *Informal* To speak loudly or boldly. — *n.* 1. The act of talking; conversation; speech, especially when informal. 2. A speech or lecture, usually informal. 3. Report; rumor: We heard *talk* of war. 4. That which is talked about; a topic; theme; subject of conversation. 5. A conference for discussion or deliberation; a council. 6. Mere words; verbiage. 7. A language, dialect, or lingo; an argot: baseball *talk*. [ME *talken,* prob. freq. of *talen,* OE *talian* to reckon, speak. Akin to TELL, TALE. Cf. Frisian *talken* to chatter.]

— **Syn.** (verb) 1. *Talk, speak, discourse, converse,* and *chat* mean to utter words. *Talk* and *speak* are largely interchangeable, but *talk* is less formal and more strongly suggests a listener; to *talk* to a friend, to *speak* to an audience. To *discourse* is to *speak* with some formality and elaboration; the word also includes the written expression of ideas: the lecturer *discoursed* on his subject at some length. *Converse* and *chat* mean to *talk* back and forth, and to necessarily indicate the presence of two or more persons. *Converse* is more formal than *talk,* and *chat* is less formal: the diplomats *conversed* about the problem; the ladies *chatted* over bridge. (noun) See CONVERSATION, SPEECH.

talk·a·thon (tôk′ə-thon′) *n.* *U.S.* A long debate, conversation, etc. [< TALK + (MAR)ATHON]

talk·a·tive (tô′kə-tiv) *adj.* Given to much talking. — **talk′a·tive·ly** *adv.* — **talk′a·tive·ness** *n.*

— **Syn.** *Talkative, loquacious, garrulous,* and *voluble* mean inclined to talk a great deal. *Talkative* is a neutral word; it compliments the outgoing, sociable person, and deprecates one who is verbose. *Loquacious* indicates fluency of speech, either from ready command of language or wealth of ideas: at eighty, Shaw was as *loquacious* as ever. *Garrulous* is a pejorative word describing one who is rambling and boring in his speech: he fled at the approach of the *garrulous* old man. *Voluble* formerly meant facile in expression, whether in speech, gesture, or writing; now it usually means incessant in speech or extremely *loquacious*. — **Ant.** taciturn, silent.

talk·er (tô′kər) *n.* One who talks; also, a talkative person.

talk·ing (tô′king) *adj.* 1. Having power of speech or of imitating speech. 2. Talkative. — *n.* Conversation.

talking machine *Archaic* A record player.

talking picture A sound film. Also *Informal* **talk′ie** (tô′kē).

talk·ing-to (tô′king-tōō′) *n.* *pl.* **-tos** *Informal* A scolding.

talk·y (tô′kē) *adj.* **talk·i·er, talk·i·est** Talkative.

tall (tôl) *adj.* 1. Having more than average height; high or lofty: a *tall* building. 2. Having specified height: He is six feet *tall.* 3. *Informal* Inordinate; extravagant; boastful: also, unbelievable; remarkable: a *tall* story. 4. *Informal* Large; excellent; grand: a *tall* dinner. 5. *Obs.* Handsome; fine; proud. 6. *Obs.* Brave; sturdy; spirited. — **Syn.** See HIGH. — *adv.* *Informal* Proudly; handsomely: He walks *tall.* [OE *getæl* swift, prompt] — **tall′ness** *n.*

tal·lage (tal′ij) *n.* In old English law, any form of assessment or taxation for raising revenue, including subsidies and customs. — *v.t.* **·laged, ·lag·ing** To tax; assess. [< OF *taillage* < *taille* tax, cutting < *taillier* to cut. See TAILOR.]

Tal·la·has·see (tal′ə-has′ē) The capital of Florida, in the northern part; pop. 71,897.

tall·boy (tôl′boi′) *n.* 1. *Brit.* A highboy (which see). 2. A variety of chimney pot.

Tal·ley·rand-Pé·ri·gord (tá-le-rän′pā-rē-gôr′), **Charles Maurice de,** 1754–1838, Prince de Bénévent, French statesman and diplomat: often called **Tal·ley·rand** (tal′ē-rand).

Tal·linn (täl′lin) The capital of the Estonian S.S.R., a port on the Gulf of Finland; pop. 363,000 (1970): German *Reval.* Russian **Tal·lin** (tä′lyin).

tall·ish (tô′lish) *adj.* Rather tall.

tal·lith (tal′ith, tä′lis) *n.* A fringed scarf or mantle worn around the shoulders by Orthodox and Conservative Jewish men when praying. [< Hebrew *tallīth* cover, robe]

tall oil (tal) A fatty, resinous liquid obtained as a by-product from wood pulp, used as an emulsifying agent. Also **tal·lol** (tal′ôl). [< Sw. *tallöl* pine beer]

tal·low (tal′ō) *n.* 1. A mixture of the harder animal fats, as of beef or mutton, refined for use in candles, soaps, oleomargarine, etc. 2. A vegetable fat obtained from the bayberry. — *v.t.* 1. To smear with tallow. 2. To fatten (animals) in order to obtain tallow. [ME *talgh,* prob. < MLG *talg, talch*] — **tal′low·y** *adj.*

tal·ly (tal′ē) *n.* *pl.* **·lies** 1. A piece of wood on which notches or scores are cut as marks of number. 2. A score or mark. 3. A reckoning; account. 4. A counterpart; duplicate. 5. A mark indicative of a quantity or number, used to denote one in a series. **6.** A label; tag. — *v.* **·lied**, **·ly·ing** *v.t.* **1.** To score on a tally; mark; record. **2.** To reckon; count; estimate: often with *up*. **3.** To mark or cut corresponding notches in; cause to correspond. — *v.i.* **4.** To correspond; agree precisely; fit: The *stories* tally. **5.** To keep score. [< AF *tallie* < L *talea* rod, cutting] — **tal′li·er** *n.*

tal·ly·ho (tal′ē·hō′) *interj.* A huntsman's cry to hounds when the quarry is sighted. — *n. pl.* **·hos 1.** The cry of "tallyho." **2.** A four-in-hand coach. — *v.t.* **1.** To urge on, as hounds, with the cry of "tallyho." — *v.i.* **2.** To cry "tallyho." [Alter. of F *taïaut*, a hunting cry]

tal·ly·man (tal′ē·mən) *n. pl.* **·men** (-mən) **1.** One who keeps a count or a tally, especially of votes. **2.** One who records number, volume, and measurement, as of timber.

Tal·mud (tal′mud, täl′mŏŏd) *n.* The body of Jewish civil and religious law (and related commentaries and discussion) not included in the Pentateuch, commonly identified with the Mishnah and the Gemara, but sometimes limited to the Gemara. [< Hebrew *talmūdh* instruction < *lāmadh* to learn] — **Tal·mud′ic** or **·i·cal** *adj.* — **Tal′mud·ist** *n.*

tal·on (tal′ən) *n.* **1.** The claw of a bird or other animal, especially of a bird of prey. **2.** Anything resembling or suggesting a claw, as a grasping human hand. **3.** A projection on the bolt of a lock on which the key presses in shooting the bolt. **4.** In card games, the part of a pack left on the table after the deal; the stock. **5.** The heel of a sword blade. [< OF, spur < L *talus* heel] — **tal′oned** (-ənd) *adj.*

Ta·los (tā′los) In Greek mythology: **a** A giant man of brass presented by Zeus to Minos, king of Crete, who used him as a watchman. **b** A Greek inventor killed by his uncle, Daedalus, because of jealousy. Also **Ta′lus** (-ləs).

ta·luk (tä·lōōk′) *n.* In parts of India, a government district from which a revenue is derived; also, a tract of proprietary land; an estate. [< Arabic *ta‘alluq* estate]

ta·lus (tā′ləs) *n. pl.* **·li** (-lī) **1.** *Anat.* The proximal bone of the foot, as in man or other vertebrates: also called *anklebone, astragalus, hucklebone.* For illustration see FOOT. **2.** A slope, as of a tapering wall. **3.** *Geol.* The sloping mass of rock fragments below a cliff. [< L, ankle, heel]

tam (tam) *n.* A tam-o′-shanter.

tam·a·ble (tā′mə·bəl) *adj.* Capable of being tamed. Also **tame′a·ble.**

ta·ma·le (tə·mä′lē) *n.* A Mexican dish made of crushed corn and meat, seasoned with red pepper, wrapped in corn husks, dipped in oil, and cooked by steam. Also **ta·mal** (tə·mäl′). [< Am. Sp. *tamales*, pl. of *tamal* < Nahuatl *tamalli*]

ta·man·dua (tə·man′dwa, tä′mən·dōō′ə) *n.* A small arboreal anteater (*Tamandua tetradactyla*) of Central and South America. Also **tam·an·du** (tam′ən·dōō). [< Pg. < Tupi < *taixi* ant + *mondē* to catch]

tam·a·rack (tam′ə·rak) *n.* **1.** The American larch (*Larix laricina*), a tree common in northern North America. **2.** Its wood. Also called *hackmatack.* [< Algonquian]

ta·ma·rao (tä′mə·rou′) *n.* A small, dark brown, short-horned buffalo (genus *Anoa*) of the island of Mindoro, standing about 40 inches high. Also **ta′ma·rau′.** [< Tagalog]

tam·a·rin (tam′ə·rin) *n.* One of various squirrellike ceboid monkeys of Guiana and the Amazon valley; especially, the **silky tamarin** (*Leontocebus rosalia*): also called *marmoset.* [< F < Carib]

tam·a·rind (tam′ə·rind) *n.* **1.** A tropical tree (*Tamarindus indica*) of the bean family, with hard yellow wood and showy yellow flowers striped with red. **2.** The fruit of this tree, a flat pod with soft acid pulp used in preserves and as a laxative. [< Sp. *tamarindo* < Arabic *tamr hindi* Indian date]

tam·a·risk (tam′ə·risk) *n.* An evergreen shrub (genus *Tamarix*) of the Mediterranean region, western Asia, and India, with slender branches bearing small, pinkish white flowers in racemes. [< LL *tamariscus*, var. of L *tamarix*]

ta·ma·sha (tə·mä′shə) *n.* In India, any form of public procession, display, or entertainment; a show. [< Arabic *tamāsha* sightseeing, walking around]

Ta·ma·tave (tä′mä·täv′) A port city on eastern Madagascar; pop. 53,173 (est. 1968).

Ta·mau·li·pas (tä′mä·ōō·lē′päs) A State of Mexico, bordering on the United States and the Gulf of Mexico; 30,731 sq. mi.; pop. 1,438,350 (1970); capital, Ciudad Victoria.

Ta·ma·yo (tä·mä′yō), **Rufino**, born 1899, Mexican painter.

tam·bac (tam′bak) *n.* Tombac.

Tam·bo·ra (täm′bō·rä) A volcano on northern Sumbawa, Indonesia; 9,255 ft.

tam·bour (tam′bŏŏr) *n.* **1.** A drum. **2.** A round wooden frame on which material for embroidering may be stretched; also, a fabric embroidered on such a frame. **3.** A palisade for defending an entrance to a fortified work. — *v.t. & v.i.* To embroider on a tambour. [< F < Arabic *ţambūr* a stringed instrument; prob. infl. in meaning by OF *tabour* tabor]

tam·bou·rin (tam′bə·rin) *n.* **1.** A long, narrow drum, originating in Provence. **2.** A gay, 18th-century Provençal dance, or the music for it. [< F < Provençal, dim. of *tambour*]

tam·bou·rine (tam′bə·rēn′) *n.* A musical instrument like the head of a drum, with jingles in the rim, played by striking it with the hand; a timbrel. [< F]

Tam·bov (tam·bôf′) A city in the Western R.S.F.S.R.; pop. 229,000 (est. 1970).

tame (tām) *adj.* **tam·er**, **tam·est 1.** Having lost its native wildness or shyness; domesticated. **2.** In agriculture, brought under or produced by cultivation. **3.** Docile; tractable. **4.** Subdued or subjugated; spiritless. **5.** Gentle; harmless. **6.** Lacking in effectiveness; uninteresting; dull; flat; insipid. — *v.t.* **tamed**, **tam·ing 1.** To make tame; domesticate. **2.** To bring into subjection or obedience; conquer or take the spirit or heart from; render spiritless. **3.** To tone down; soften, as glaring colors. [OE *tam*] — **tame′ly** *adv.* — **tame′ness** *n.* — **tam′er** *n.*

ta·mein (tä·mīn′) *n.* A draped garment, similar to an Indian sari, worn by Burmese women. [< Burmese *thamein*]

tame·less (tām′lis) *adj.* Untamed or untamable. — **tame′less·ness** *n.*

Tam·er·lane (tam′ər·lān), 1336?–1405, Mongol conqueror; held sway from the Euphrates to the Ganges in 1387; chief character in Christopher Marlowe's *Tamburlaine*: called **Timur-Leng** (Timur the Lame): also called *Timour, Timur.* Also **Tam·bur·laine** (tam′bər·lān).

Tam·il (tam′əl, tum′əl) *n.* **1.** One of an ancient Dravidian people, and still the most numerous of the inhabitants of southern India and northern Ceylon. **2.** Their language, the oldest and most widely used of the Dravidian languages.

tam·is (tam′is) *n.* **1.** A strainer of cloth or gauze. **2.** A fabric used for straining. Also **tam′my** (-mē). [< F, sieve]

Tam·ma·ny (tam′ə·nē) *n.* A fraternal society in New York City (founded 1789) serving as the central organization of the city's Democratic party, called **Tammany Hall**, from its meeting place. The name has often been associated with political bossism. Also called **Tammany Society.** [Alter. of *Tamanend*, lit., the affable, name of a 17th c. Delaware Indian chief friendly toward white men]

Tam·mer·fors (täm′mər·fôrs′) The Swedish name for TAMPERE.

Tam·mer·kos·ki (täm′mer·kōs′kē) The Finnish name for TAMPERE.

Tam·muz (täm′mōōz′, täm′mōōz) **1.** In Babylonian mythology, the husband of Ishtar and god of agriculture, whose annual death and resurrection symbolize the cycle of months. **2.** The tenth month of the Hebrew year. See (Hebrew) CALENDAR. Also spelled *Thammuz*: also **Tam·uz.** [< Hebrew]

tam-o′-shan·ter (tam′ə·shan′tər) *n.* A Scottish cap with a tight headband and a full, flat top, sometimes with a pompon or tassel. [after TAM O′ SHANTER]

Tam o′ Shan·ter (tam′ ə shan′tər) In Robert Burns's poem *Tam o′ Shanter*, the hero, a drunken farmer who fancies himself pursued by witches.

tamp (tamp) *v.t.* **1.** To force down or pack closer by firm, repeated blows. **2.** To ram down, as dirt, etc., on top of the charge in a blasthole, in order to increase the explosive effect. — *n.* Something that tamps. [Back formation < TAMPION]

Tam·pa (tam′pə) A port city in western Florida, on **Tampa Bay**, an inlet of the Gulf of Mexico; pop. 277,767.

tam·pan (tam′pan) *n.* The miana bug. [< native S. African name]

tam·per[1] (tam′pər) *v.i.* **1.** To meddle; interfere: usually with *with*. **2.** To make changes, especially so as to damage or corrupt: with *with*. **3.** To use corrupt measures, as bribery; scheme or plot. [Var. of TEMPER] — **tam′per·er** *n.*

tamp·er[2] (tam′pər) *n.* **1.** One who tamps. **2.** An instrument for tamping. **3.** *Physics* A reflector.

Tam·pe·re (täm′pe·re) A city in SW Finland; pop. 147,500 (est. 1966): Swedish *Tammerfors*, Finnish *Tammerkoski*.

Tam·pi·co (tam·pē′kō, Sp. täm·pē′kō) A port city in southern Tamaulipas, Mexico, on the Gulf of Mexico; pop. 196,147 (1970).

Tampico fiber Istle.

tam·pi·on (tam′pē·ən) *n. Mil.* A stopper, as the plug put into the mouth of a cannon to keep out moisture, etc.: also *tompion.* [< F *tampon*, nasal var. of *tapon*, tape bung < Gmc.]

tam·pon (tam′pon) *n. Med.* A plug of cotton or lint for insertion in a wound or body cavity. — *v.t.* To plug up, as a wound, with a tampon. [See TAMPION]

tam-tam (tum′tum′) *n.* **1.** A type of drum, used in the East Indies and western Africa. **2.** A tom-tom (def. 3). [< Hind.; imit. in origin]

tan (tan) *v.* **tanned**, **tan·ning** *v.t.* **1.** To convert into leather, as hides or skins, by treating with tannin. **2.** To make durable or hard, as fishnets or sails. **3.** To turn brown, as the skin, by exposure to sunlight. **4.** *Informal* To thrash; flog. — *v.i.* **5.** To become tanned, as hides or the skin. — *n.* **1.** A yellowish brown color tinged with red. **2.** A dark or brown coloring of the skin, resulting from exposure to the sun: a coat of *tan*. **3.** Tanbark (which see). **4.** Tannin. — *adj.* **1.** Of the color tan; light brown. **2.** Used in or pertaining to tanning. [OE *tannian* < Med.L *tannare* < *tanum* tanbark, prob. < Celtic. Cf. Breton *tann* oak.]

tan or tan. Tangent.

Ta·na (tä′nä) A river in SE Kenya, flowing about 500 miles east and south to the Indian Ocean.

Ta·na (tä′nä), **Lake** A lake in northern Ethiopia, source of the Blue Nile; about 1,400 sq. mi.: also *Tsana.*

tan·a·ger (tan′ə·jər) *n.* Any of a family (*Thraupidae*) of oscine American birds related to the finches, noted for the brilliant plumage of the male; especially, in the United States, the scarlet tanager (which see), and the **western tanager** (*Piranga ludoviciana*). [< NL *tanagra* < Pg. *tangara* < Tupi] — **tan′a·grine** (-grēn) *adj.*

Tan·a·gra (tan′ə·grə, tə·nag′rə) A village in eastern Boeotia, Greece; known for the terra-cotta figurines excavated there.

Tan·a·is (tan′ə·is) An ancient name for the DON.

Ta·na·na·rive (tä·nä′nä·rēv′) The capital of the Malagasy Republic, in the east central part; pop. 332,885 (est. 1968). Also **Ta·na′na·ri′vo** (-rē′vō).

Ta·na·na River (tan′ə·nô) A river in eastern Alaska, flowing about 600 miles NW to the Yukon.

tan·bark (tan′bärk′) *n.* **1.** The bark of certain trees, especially oak or hemlock, containing tannin in quantity, and used in tanning leather. **2.** Spent bark from the tan vats, used on circus arenas, racetracks, etc. Also called *tan.*

Tan·cred (tang′krid), died 1112, Norman knight; hero of the first crusade.

tan·dem (tan′dəm) *adv.* One in front of or before another. — *n.* **1.** Two or more horses harnessed in single file. **2.** A two-wheeled carriage drawn by a tandem of horses. **3.** A bicycle with seats for two persons, one behind the other: also **tandem bicycle. 4.** Any arrangement of two or more persons or things placed one before another. — *adj.* Arranged in tandem, or including parts so arranged. [< L, at length (of time); used in puns in sense of "lengthwise"]

Tan·djung·pri·ok (tän′jŏong·prē′ŏk) See TANJUNGPRIOK.

Ta·ney (tä′nē), **Roger Brooke,** 1777–1864, U.S. jurist; chief justice of the Supreme Court 1836–64.

tang¹ (tang) *n.* **1.** A penetrating taste, flavor, or odor: a *tang* of pepper. **2.** A trace; hint. **3.** Any distinct taste, odor, quality, etc., other than one that is sweet. **4.** A slender shank or tongue projecting from some metal part, as the end of a sword blade or chisel, for inserting in or fixing upon a handle, hilt, etc. For illustration see BAYONET. **5.** A tonguelike part, as of a belt buckle. — *v.t.* To provide with a tang. [< ON *tangi* point, dagger]

tang² (tang) *n.* A twang. — *v.t. & v.i.* To twang.

Tang (täng) A Chinese dynasty, 618–906, one of China's greatest periods of literature and art.

Tan·gan·yi·ka (tan′gən·yē′kə, tang′-) A region of Tanzania in eastern Africa; 361,800 sq. mi.; pop. 12,557,000 (est. 1969); capital, Dar es Salaam. — **Tan′gan·yi′kan** *adj. & n.*

Tan·gan·yi·ka (tan′gən·yē′kə, tang′-), **Lake** A lake in the Great Rift Valley of east central Africa; 12,700 sq. mi.; 400 mi. long; the longest and deepest (4,700 ft.) lake in Africa. See map of CONGO.

tan·ge·lo (tan′jə·lō) *n. pl.* **·los 1.** A loose-skinned, orange-like fruit, a hybrid of the tangerine and the pomelo. **2.** The tree (genus *Citrus*) on which it grows. [< TANG(ERINE) + (POM)ELO]

tan·gen·cy (tan′jən·sē) *n. pl.* **·cies** The state of being tangent. Also **tan′gence.**

tan·gent (tan′jənt) *adj.* Being in contact at a single point or along a line; touching. — *n.* **1.** *Geom.* **a** A straight line in contact with a curve at one point. **b** A straight line, a curve, or a surface touching another curve or surface at one or more consecutive points. **c** The length of a tangent line from the point of contact to the axis of abscissas. **2.** *Trig.* **a** A function of an acute angle, equal to the ratio of the side opposite the angle to the side adjacent to the angle when the angle is included in a right triangle. **b** A function of any angle, equal to the ordinate of a point divided by the abscissa of the point when the angle is plotted on Cartesian coordinates and the point is on the line forming the angle with the X–axis. For illustration see TRIGONOMETRIC FUNCTIONS. — **to fly (or go) off on a tangent** *Informal* To make a sharp or sudden change in direction or course of action. Abbr. *tan, tan.* [< L *tangens, -entis,* ppr. of *tangere* to touch]

tan·gen·tial (tan·jen′shəl) *adj.* **1.** Of, pertaining to, or moving in the direction of a tangent. **2.** Touching slightly. **3.** Only partially relevant; superficially related. Also **tangen′tal** (-jen′təl). — **tan·gen′ti·al′i·ty** (-shē·al′ə·tē) *n.* — **tan·gen′tial·ly** *adv.*

tan·ger·ine (tan′jə·rēn′) *n.* **1.** A small, juicy orange (*Citrus reticulata*) with a loose, easily removed skin: also called *mandarin.* **2.** A slightly burnt orange color, like the color of the tangerine. [after *Tangier*]

Tan·ger·ine (tan′jə·rēn) *adj.* Of or pertaining to Tangier, Morocco. — *n.* A native or inhabitant of Tangier.

tan·gi·ble (tan′jə·bəl) *adj.* **1.** Perceptible by touch; also, within reach by touch. **2.** Capable of being apprehended by the mind; of definite shape; real: *tangible* evidence. **3.** *Law*

Perceptible to the senses; corporeal; material: *tangible* property. — *n.* **1.** That which is tangible. **2.** *pl.* Material assets. [< F < L *tangibilis* < *tangere* to touch] — **tan′gi·bil′i·ty, tan′gi·ble·ness** *n.* — **tan′gi·bly** *adv.*

Tan·gier (tan·jir′) A port city on the northernmost coast of Morocco; pop. 160,000 (1968); formerly capital of **Tangier International Zone;** 225 sq. mi. French **Tan·ger** (tän·zhā′).

tan·gle¹ (tang′gəl) *v.* **·gled, ·gling** *v.t.* **1.** To twist or involve in a confused and not readily separable mass. **2.** To ensnare as in a tangle; trap; enmesh. — *v.i.* **3.** To be or become entangled. — **to tangle with** *Informal* To come to blows with. — *n.* **1.** A confused intertwining, as of threads or hairs; a snarl. **2.** A state of confusion or complication; a jumbled mess. **3.** A state of perplexity or bewilderment. [Nasalized var. of obs. *tagle* < Scand. Cf. dial. Sw. *taggla* disorder.] — **tan′gler** *n.*

tan·gle² (tang′gəl) *n.* **1.** An edible seaweed (genus *Laminaria*). **2.** *Scot.* A tall, lean person. [< ON *thöngull*]

tan·gle·ber·ry (tang′gəl·ber′ē) *n. pl.* **·ries** The blue huckleberry (*Gaylussacia frondosa*) of the eastern United States: also called *dangleberry.*

tan·gly (tang′glē) *adj.* Consisting of or being in a tangle.

tan·go (tang′gō) *n. pl.* **·gos 1.** Any of several Latin-American dances in 2/4 time, characterized by deliberate gliding steps and low dips. **2.** Any syncopated tune or melody to which the tango may be danced. — *v.i.* To dance the tango. [< Am.Sp., fiesta, Negro drum dance]

tan·gram (tan′grəm) *n.* A Chinese puzzle consisting of a square card or board cut by straight incisions into different-sized pieces (five triangles, a square, and a lozenge) to be combined into a variety of figures. [? < Chinese *t'ang* Chinese + -GRAM¹, on analogy with ANAGRAM, CRYPTOGRAM, etc.]

TANGRAM

Tan·guy (tän·gē′), **Yves,** 1900–1955, French painter.

tang·y (tang′ē) *adj.* **tang·i·er, tang·i·est** Having a tang in taste or odor; pungent.

Ta·nis (tä′nis) An ancient city of Lower Egypt in the Nile delta: Old Testament *Zoan.*

tan·ist (tan′ist, thôn′-) *n.* Among the ancient Celts, the heir apparent to a chieftainship, elected in the lifetime of a chief from among the chief's kinsmen. [< Irish *tanaiste* second, heir presumptive]

tan·ist·ry (tan′ist·rē, thôn′-) *n.* The succession and life tenure relating to a tanist.

Tan·jore (tan·jôr′, -jōr′) A city in Tamil Nadu, India; pop. 120,681 (est. 1969). Also, *Thanjur.*

Tan·jung·pri·ok (tän′jŏong·prē′ŏk) A port city on NW Java, the port for Jakarta; pop. about 26,000: also *Tandjungpriok.*

tank (tangk) *n.* **1.** A large vessel, basin, or receptacle for holding a fluid. **2.** Any natural or artificial pool or pond. **3.** *Mil.* A heavily armored combat vehicle, moving on caterpillar treads and mounting guns of various calibers. — *v.t.* To place or store in a tank. [< Pg. *tanque,* aphetic var. of *estanque* < L *stagnum* pool]

tan·ka (tang′kə) *n.* **1.** A Japanese verse form in five lines, of which the first and third have five syllables and the rest seven. **2.** An example of this form. [< Japanese]

U.S. ARMY TANK M48A2

tank·age (tangk′ij) *n.* **1.** The act, process, or operation of putting in tanks. **2.** The price for storage in tanks. **3.** The capacity or contents of a tank. **4.** Slaughterhouse waste, as bones and entrails, used when dried as a fertilizer or feed.

tank·ard (tangk′ərd) *n.* A large, one-handled drinking cup, usually made of pewter or silver, often with a cover. [< MDu. *tanckaert* < Med.L *tancardus,* prob. metathetic var. of L *cantharus* tankard, large goblet]

tank·er (tangk′ər) *n.* A cargo vessel especially constructed for the transport of liquids, especially oil and gasoline.

tank farm *U.S.* An area near a refinery, factory, port, etc., occupied by large storage tanks.

tank farming Hydroponics. — **tank farmer**

tank·ful (tangk′fŏŏl′) *n.* The quantity that fills a tank.

tank town *U.S. Informal* A small town where trains formerly stopped to refill from a water tank.

tank trap *Mil.* Any of various devices or structures designed to stop or destroy enemy tanks.

tan·nage (tan′ij) *n.* The act or operation of tanning.

tan·nate (tan′āt) *n. Chem.* A salt or ester of tannic acid.

tanned Past tense and past participle of TAN.

Tan·nen·berg (tän′ən·berkh) A village in NE Poland; scene of major Russian defeat by German forces, 1914: Polish *Stębark.*

tan·ner¹ (tan′ər) *n.* One who tans hides.

tan·ner² (tan′ər) *n. Brit. Informal* A sixpence. [Origin unknown]

tan·ner·y (tan′ər·ē) *n. pl.* **·ner·ies** A place where leather is tanned.

Tann·häu·ser (tän′hoi·zər) A German minnesinger and

crusader of the 13th century, identified with a legendary knight who gives himself up to revelry with Venus and her court in the Venusberg, then makes a trip to Rome to seek absolution. He is the hero of an opera by Wagner.

tan·nic (tan′ik) *adj.* Pertaining to or derived from tannin or tanbark.

tan·nif·er·ous (ta-nif′ər-əs) *adj.* Having or yielding tannin. [< TANNI(N) + -FEROUS]

tan·nin (tan′in) *n. Chem.* Any of a group of brownish white, astringent compounds that form shiny scales when extracted from gallnuts, sumac, etc., used in the preparation of ink and in the manufacture of leather: also called *tan.* Also **tannic acid.** [< F *tanin* < *tan* tan]

tan·ning (tan′ing) *n.* **1.** The process of subjecting hides to a chemical treatment that toughens them but maintains their flexibility, and converts them into leather. **2.** A bronzing, as of the skin, by exposure to the sun, wind, etc. **3.** *Informal* A beating or thrashing.

Tan·nu-tu·va People's Republic (tan′ōō-tōō′və) A former name for TUVA AUTONOMOUS REGION.

tan·rec (tan′rek) The tenrec, an animal.

tan·sy (tan′zē) *n. pl.* **·sies** Any of a genus (*Tanacetum*) of coarse perennial herbs; especially, the **common tansy** (*T. vulgare*), with yellow flowers and an aromatic, bitter taste, used in medicine for its tonic properties. [< OF *tanesie,* aphetic var. of *athanasie* < LL *athanasia* < Gk., immortality]

Tan·ta (tän′tä) A city in Lower Egypt, in the Nile delta; pop. 184,000 (1960).

tan·ta·late (tan′tə-lāt) *n. Chem.* A salt of tantalic acid.

tan·tal·ic (tan-tal′ik) *adj.* **1.** Pertaining to tantalum. **2.** Containing tantalum in its higher valence.

tantalic acid *Chem.* A colorless crystalline acid, HTaO₃, derived from tantalum pentoxide, Ta₂O₅.

tan·ta·lite (tan′tə-līt) *n.* A heavy, lustrous, black ferrous tantalate, FeTa₂O₆, a principal ore of tantalum.

tan·ta·lize (tan′tə-līz) *v.t.* **·lized, ·liz·ing** To tease or torment by repeated frustration of hopes or desires. Also *Brit.* **tan′ta·lise.** [< TANTALUS] — **tan′ta·li·za′tion** *n.* — **tan′ta·liz′er** *n.* — **tan′ta·liz′ing·ly** *adv.*

tan·ta·lum (tan′tə-ləm) *n.* A silver-white, very heavy, ductile, metallic element (symbol Ta) resembling platinum. It is resistant to most pure acids, becomes hard when hammered, and forms alloys with tungsten, molybdenum, and iron. See ELEMENT. Abbr. *T* [< TANTALUS; from its inability to absorb water]

Tan·ta·lus (tan′tə-ləs) In Greek mythology, a rich king, son of Zeus and father of Pelops and Niobe, who, for revealing the secrets of Zeus, was punished in Hades by being made to stand in water that receded when he tried to drink, and under fruit-laden branches he could not reach.

tan·ta·mount (tan′tə-mount) *adj.* Having equivalent value, effect, or import; equivalent: with *to.* [< AF *tant amunter* to amount to as much < L *tantus* as much + OF *amonter* to amount. See AMOUNT.]

tan·ta·ra (tan′tə-rä′, tan-tar′ə, -tä′rə) *n.* A quick succession of notes from a horn; also, a hunting cry. [Imit.]

tan·tiv·y (tan-tiv′ē) *adj.* Swift; rapid. — *n. pl.* **·tiv·ies 1.** A hunting cry indicating that the chase is at full speed. **2.** *Obs.* A rapid, rushing movement. — *adv.* Swiftly; speedily. [Origin unknown; ? imit. of the horse's gallop]

tant mieux (tän myœ′) *French* So much the better.

tan·to (tän′tō) *adv. Italian* So much; too much: used especially in the musical direction **non tanto,** not too much.

tant pis (tän pē′) *French* So much the worse.

tan·trum (tan′trəm) *n.* A fit of rage. [Origin unknown]

Tan·za·ni·a (tan′zə-nē′ə) An independent Republic consisting of a federation of Tanganyika and Zanzibar in eastern Africa; 362,800 sq. mi.; pop. 12,926,000 (est. 1969); capital, Dar es Salaam.

Tao·ism (dou′iz-əm, tou′-) *n.* One of the principal religions or philosophies of China, founded by Lao-tse, who taught that happiness could be acquired through obedience to the requirements of man's nature in accordance with the **Tao** (dou, tou), or Way, the basic principle of all nature. [< Chinese *tao* way, road] — **Tao′ist** *adj. & n.* — **Tao·is′tic** *adj.*

Taos (tous) A town in northern New Mexico; pop. 2,475.

tap¹ (tap) *n.* **1.** An arrangement for drawing out liquid, as beer from a cask. **2.** A faucet or cock; spigot. **3.** A plug or stopper to close an opening in a cask or other vessel. **4.** Liquor drawn from a tap; also, a particular liquor or quality of liquor contained in casks. **5.** *Brit.* A place where liquor is served; a bar; taproom. **6.** A tool for cutting internal screw threads. **7.** A point of connection for an electrical circuit. — **on tap 1.** Contained in a cask; ready for tapping: beer *on tap.* **2.** Provided with a tap. **3.** *Informal* Available; ready. — *v.t.* **tapped, tap·ping 1.** To provide with a tap or stopper. **2.** To pierce or open so as to draw liquid from: to *tap* a sugar-maple tree. **3.** To draw (liquid) from a container. **4.** To make connection with: to *tap* a gas main. **5.** To make connection with secretly: to *tap* a telephone wire. **6.** To make an internal screw thread in with a tap: to *tap* a nut.

7. *Informal* To ask (someone) for money. [OE *tæppa*]

tap² (tap) *v.* **tapped, tap·ping** *v.t.* **1.** To touch or strike gently. **2.** To make or produce by tapping. **3.** To apply leather to (the sole or heel of a shoe) in repair. — *v.i.* **4.** To strike a light blow or blows, as with a finger. — **Syn.** See STRIKE. — *n.* **1.** A gentle or playful blow; also, the sound made by it. **2.** Leather, etc., affixed to a shoe sole or heel; also, a metal plate on the toe or heel of a shoe. **3.** *Phonet.* A single contact of an articulator with an adjacent part of the mouth, as *r* in Spanish *pero.* Compare TRILL¹. [< OF *taper*]

ta·pa (tä′pä) *n.* **1.** The bark of an Asian mulberry tree (*Broussonetia papyrifera*), used in making a cloth. **2.** The cloth: also *kapa:* also **tapa cloth.** [< native Polynesian name]

tap·a·der·a (tap′ə-dâr′ə) *n.* The leather hood of the stirrup of a range saddle. For illustration see SADDLE. Also **tap′a·der′o** (-ō). [< Am.Sp. < *tapar* to stop up]

Ta·pa·jós (tä′pä-zhôs′) A river of central and NE Brazil, flowing about 500 miles NE to the Amazon.

tap·a·lo (tap′ə-lō) *n. pl.* **·los** A scarf or shawl of coarse cloth worn in Latin-American countries. [< Am.Sp., lit., cover it, imperative of *tapar* to cover + *lo* it]

tap-dance (tap′dans′, -däns′) *v.i.* **-danced, -danc·ing** To dance or perform a tap dance.

tap dance A dance in which the dancer taps the floor with shoes having taps beneath the heels and toes. — **tap dancer**

tape (tāp) *n.* **1.** A narrow strip of strong woven fabric. **2.** Any long, narrow, flat strip of paper, metal, etc. **3.** A magnetic tape (which see). **4.** A tapeline (which see). **5.** A ticker tape (which see). **6.** A string stretched breast-high across the finishing point of a racing track and broken by the winner of the race. — *v.t.* **taped, tap·ing 1.** To wrap or secure with tape. **2.** To apply a tape to; bandage: to *tape* a boxer's hands. **3.** To measure with or as with a tapeline. **4.** *Informal* To record on magnetic tape. **5.** *Scot.* To use sparingly. [OE *tæppe* strip of cloth] — **tape′less** *adj.*

tape deck A tape recorder without an amplifier or speaker, often used as a unit of a high-fidelity system.

tape·line (tāp′līn′) *n.* A tape for measuring distances. Also **tape measure.**

ta·per¹ (tā′pər) *n.* One who or that which tapes.

ta·per² (tā′pər) *n.* **1.** A small candle. **2.** A burning wick or other light substance giving but feeble illumination. **3.** A gradual diminution of size in an elongated object: the *taper* of a mast. **4.** Any tapering object, as a cone. — *v.t. & v.i.* **1.** To make or become smaller or thinner toward one end. **2.** To lessen gradually; diminish: with *off.* — *adj.* Growing small by degrees in one direction; slender and conical or pyramidal. [OE, dissimilated var. of Med.L *papur* taper, *wick* < L, papyrus; from the use of the pith of the papyrus as a wick] — **ta′per·ing·ly** *adv.*

tape-re·cord (tāp′ri-kôrd′) *v.t.* To make a tape recording.

tape recorder A device that converts sound into magnetic patterns stored on a tape, reversing the process for playback.

tape recording 1. The process of transcribing music, speech, etc., on a tape recorder. **2.** A transcription so made.

tap·es·try (tap′is-trē) *n. pl.* **·tries 1.** A woven, ornamental fabric used for hangings, in which the woof is supplied by a spindle, the design being formed by stitches across the warp. **2.** Loosely, a fabric imitating this process. — *v.t.* **·tried, ·try·ing 1.** To hang or adorn with tapestry. **2.** To make or weave as tapestry. [< OF *tapisserie* < *tapis* carpet < L *tapete* < Gk. *tapētion,* dim. of *tapēs* rug]

ta·pe·tum (tə-pē′təm) *n. pl.* **·ta** (-tə) **1.** *Bot.* A cell or layer of cells just outside the spore case of a plant, lining the cavity of a sporangium. **2.** *Zool.* A portion of the choroid coat of the eye in cats, etc. **3.** *Anat.* The fibers of the corpus callosum. [< LL < L *tapete* carpet. See TAPESTRY.]

tape·worm (tāp′wûrm′) *n.* Any of various cestode worms (class *Cestoda*) with segmented, ribbonlike bodies, parasitic on the intestines of vertebrates; especially, the **pork tapeworm** (*Taenia solium*), often infesting man.

tap house An inn; tavern; also, a barroom.

tap·i·o·ca (tap′ē-ō′kə) *n.* A nutritious starchy substance having irregular grains, obtained by drying cassava starch. [< Sp. < Tupi *tipioca* juice of the cassava < *ty* juice + *pŷa* heart + *oco* to be removed]

ta·pir (tā′pər) *n.* A large, ungulate, nocturnal mammal (family *Tapiridae*), having short stout limbs and a flexible proboscis, native to South and Central America and to the Malay Peninsula. [< Sp. < Tupi *tapy′ra*]

tap·is (tap′ē, tap′is; *Fr.* tȧ-pē′) *n.* Tapestry, formerly used as a cover of a council table. — **on the tapis** Up for consideration. [< F. See TAPESTRY.]

tap·per (tap′ər) *n.* One who or that which taps.

SOUTH AMERICAN TAPIR

(About 3 feet high at shoulder)

tap·pet (tap′it) *n. Mech.* A lever or projecting arm of a mechanism that moves or is moved intermittently by automatically touching another part. [< TAP²]

tap·ping (tap'ing) *n.* **1.** The act of one who or that which taps. **2.** Something taken by tapping, or running from a tap.

tap·pit-hen (tap'it-hen') *n.* **1.** A hen having a topknot. **2.** A large English pewter measure for liquors, having a knob on the lid. [< dial. E (Scottish) *tappit* topped + HEN]

tap·room (tap'room', -room') *n.* A bar or barroom.

tap·root (tap'root', -root') *n. Bot.* The principal descending root of a plant. — **tap'root'ed** *adj.*

taps (taps) *n.pl.* (*usually construed as sing.*) A military signal by bugle or beat of drum, regularly sounded after tattoo for the extinguishing of all lights and sometimes played after a military burial.

tap·sal·tee·rie (tap'səl·tir'ē) *adv. Scot.* Upside down and in confusion; topsy-turvy.

tap·ster (tap'stər) *n.* One who draws and serves liquor; a bartender. [OE *tæppestre* barmaid]

Ta·pu·ya (tä-pōō'yä) *n.* A Tapuyan Indian.

Ta·pu·yan (tä-pōō'yən) *n. Ge*, a South American Indian stock. — *adj.* Of or pertaining to this stock.

tap wrench A small wrench with a chuck to hold a tap for cutting internal screw threads.

tar¹ (tär) *n.* **1.** A dark, oily, viscid mixture of hydrocarbons, obtained by the destructive distillation of resinous woods, coal, etc. **2.** Coal tar (which see). — *v.t.* **tarred, tar·ring** To cover with or as with tar. — **to tar and feather** To smear (a person) with tar and then cover with feathers as a punishment. — *adj.* Made of, derived from, or resembling tar. [OE *teoru*]

tar² (tär) *n. Informal* A sailor. [Short for TARPAULIN]

tar·a·did·dle (tar'ə-did'l) See TARRADIDDLE.

tar·an·tass (tar'ən-tas') *n.* A large four-wheeled Russian carriage mounted on longitudinal bars in place of springs. Also **tar'an·tas'.** [< Russian *tarantas*]

tar·an·tel·la (tar'ən-tel'ə) *n.* A lively Neapolitan dance in 6/8 time, once thought to be a remedy for tarantism; also, the music written for it. [< Ital., dim. of *Taranto* Taranto; infl. by *tarantola* tarantula]

tar·ant·ism (tar'ən-tiz'əm) *n.* A nervous disorder characterized by a mania for dancing and music, formerly prevalent in southern Italy, and believed to follow the bite of a tarantula: also spelled *tarentism.* [< NL *tarantismus* < Ital. *tarantismo* < *Taranto* Taranto]

Ta·ran·to (tä'rän·tō) A port commune in SE Italy, on the **Gulf of Taranto**, an inlet of the Ionian Sea; pop. 214,700 (est. 1967): ancient *Tarentum.*

ta·ran·tu·la (tə-ran'chōō-lə) *n. pl.* **·las** or **·lae** (-lē) **1.** A large, hairy spider (*Lycosa tarentula*) of southern Europe, erroneously supposed to cause tarantism by its bite. **2.** Any of various related spiders (family *Theraphosidae*), especially of the genus *Eurypelma* of the SW United States, known for their painful but not dangerous bite. [< Med.L < Ital. *tarantola* < *Taranto* Taranto]

Ta·ra·wa (tä-rä'wä, tä'rä-wä) An island belonging to the Gilbert and Ellice Islands colony; 8 sq. mi.; pop. 12,642 (1968); scene of a U.S. victory over Japanese forces, November, 1943.

ta·rax·a·cum (tə-rak'sə-kəm) *n.* **1.** Any of a genus (*Taraxacum*) of composite plants that includes the dandelion. **2.** A medicinal preparation from the dried root of the dandelion, used as a diuretic and laxative. [< NL < Arabic *tarakhshaqūq* bitter herb]

tar·boosh (tär-bōōsh') *n.* A brimless, usually red, felt cap with colored silk tassel, worn by Moslem men. Also **tar·bush'.** [< Arabic *tarbūsh*]

tar camphor Naphthalene.

Tar·de·noi·si·an (tär'də-noi'zē-ən) *adj. Anthropol.* Of, pertaining to, or designating part of the Mesolithic epoch characterized by small flint implements. [after Fère-en-*Tardenois*, town in NE France where remains were discovered]

Tar·dieu (tàr-dyœ'), **André Pierre Gabriel Amédée,** 1876–1945, French statesman and journalist: pseudonym *George Villiers.*

tar·di·grade (tär'də-grād) *adj.* **1.** Slow in motion or action; stepping or walking slowly. **2.** Of or pertaining to a group (*Tardigrada*) of minute, slow-moving arthropods, found especially in water and damp moss. — *n.* One of the *Tardigrada.* [< F < L *tardigradus* < *tardus* slow + *gradi* to walk]

tar·dy (tär'dē) *adj.* **·di·er, ·di·est** **1.** Not coming at the appointed time; late. **2.** Moving slowly. — **Syn.** See DILATORY. [< F *tardif* < L *tardus* slow] — **tar'di·ly** *adv.* — **tar'di·ness** *n.*

tare¹ (târ) *n.* **1.** An unidentified weed that grows among wheat, supposed to be the darnel. **2.** A seed of wickedness. *Matt.* xiii 25. **3.** Any of various species of vetch; especially, the common vetch (*Vicia sativa*). [MDu. *tarwe* wheat]

tare² (târ) *n.* **1.** An allowance made to a buyer of goods by deducting from the gross weight of his purchase the weight of the container. **2.** *Chem.* An empty flask or vessel used as a counterweight. — *v.t.* **tared, tar·ing** To weigh, as a package, in order to determine the amount of tare. Abbr. *t.* [< F < Arabic *ṭarhah* < *ṭaraha* to reject, throw away]

tar·ent·ism (tar'ən-tiz'əm) See TARANTISM.

Ta·ren·tum (tə-ren'təm) The ancient name for TARANTO.

targe (tärj) *n. Archaic* A shield or target. [OE *targa*]

tar·get (tär'git) *n.* **1.** An object presenting a surface that may be used as a mark or butt, as in rifle or archery practice. **2.** Anything that is shot at. **3.** A person or thing made an object of attack or center of attention; a butt. **4.** A small, variously shaped signal, usually placed near a railroad track to indicate the position of the switches. **5.** The vane or sliding sight on a surveyor's rod. **6.** *Electronics* The electrode of an electron tube on which cathode rays are focused and from which X-rays are emitted. **7.** A small round shield or buckler. Abbr. *t.* — **on target 1.** Headed or aimed so as to hit a target; zeroed in. **2.** *Informal* Aptly directed or placed; to the point; on the beam: *The quip was right on target.* [ME *targette, targuete,* dim. of *targa* shield. See TARGE.]

target date A date aimed for, as for the beginning or completion of some effort.

tar·get·eer (tär'gə-tir') *n.* A soldier armed with a shield.

Tar·gum (tär'gum, *Hebrew* tär-gōōm') *n. pl.* **Tar·gums** or *Hebrew* **Tar·gu·mim** (tär'gōō-mēm') One of various ancient paraphrases of portions of the Hebrew scriptures in Aramaic or Chaldee. [< Aramaic *targūm* interpretation] — **Tar'gum·ic** or **·i·cal** *adj.* — **Tar'gum·ist** *n.*

Tar·heel (tär'hēl') *n. Informal* A native of North Carolina. Also **Tar Heel.**

Tarheel State Nickname of NORTH CAROLINA.

tar·iff (tar'if) *n.* **1.** A schedule of articles of merchandise with the rates of duty to be paid for their importation or exportation. **2.** A duty, or duties collectively. **3.** The law or principles governing the imposition of duties. **4.** Any schedule of charges. — *v.t.* **1.** To make a list or table of duties or customs on. **2.** To fix a price or tariff on. [< Ital. *tariffa* < Arabic *ta'rif* information < *'arafa* to know, inform]

Ta·rim (tä'rēm') A river in the Sinkiang-Uigur Autonomous Region, China, flowing about 1,300 miles east to the Lop Nor Basin.

Tark·ing·ton (tär'king-tən), **Booth,** 1869–1946, U.S. novelist: full name **Newton Booth Tarkington.**

tar·la·tan (tär'lə-tən) *n.* A thin, open-weave, transparent muslin. Also **tar'le·tan.** [< F *tarlatane*; prob. ult. < Indic]

tar·mac (tär'mak) *n. Brit. & Canadian* **1.** *Aeron.* **a** A hangar apron. **b** An asphalt runway. **2.** An asphalt road or pavement.

Tar·mac (tär'mak) *n.* A paving material made from coal tar: a trade name.

tarn (tärn) *n.* A small mountain lake. [ME *terne* < ON *tjörn*]

tar·nal (tär'nəl) *U.S. Dial. adj.* **1.** Eternal; infernal. **2.** Damned. — *adv.* **1.** Very. **2.** Damn. [Alter. of ETERNAL] — **tar'nal·ly** *adv.*

tar·na·tion (tär-nā'shən) *interj. & n. U.S. Dial.* Damnation: a euphemism. [Blend of TAR(NAL) + (DAM)NATION]

tar·nish (tär'nish) *v.t.* **1.** To dim the luster of. **2.** To dim the purity of; stain; disgrace. — *v.i.* **3.** To lose luster, as by oxidation; become blemished. — *n.* **1.** Loss of luster. **2.** A blemish or stain. **3.** The thin film of color on the exposed surface of a metal or mineral. [< OF *terniss-*, stem of *ternir* < *terne* dull, wan] — **tar'nish·a·ble** *adj.*

tarnished plant bug (tär'nisht) A common, brown-marked, hemipterous insect (*Lygus pratensis*) of North America, that attacks many fruits and vegetables. For illustration see INSECTS (injurious).

Tar·no·pol (tär-nō'pôl) The Polish name for TERNOPOL.

Tar·nów (tär'nōōf) A city in southern Poland; pop. 79,500 (est. 1966).

ta·ro (tä'rō) *n. pl.* **·ros 1.** Any of several tropical plants (genus *Colocasia*) of the arum family, grown for their edible, cormlike rootstocks: also called *elephant's ear.* **2.** The rootstock of this plant. [< native Polynesian name]

tar·ot (tar'ō, -ət) *n.* One of a set of playing cards with grilled or checkered backs used in Italy as early as the 14th century, employed by fortunetellers and gypsies in foretelling future events. [< F < Ital. *tarocco* < *taroccare* to wrangle, play at cards; ult. origin obscure]

tar·pa·per (tär'pā'ər) *n.* A strong, heavy paper impregnated or coated with tar, used in roofing and building.

tar·pau·lin (tär-pô'lin, tär'pə-) *n.* **1.** A waterproof canvas impregnated with tar, used to cover merchandise, athletic fields, etc. **2.** A sailor's wide-brimmed storm hat. **3.** *Rare* A sailor. Also *Informal* **tarp.** [< TAR¹ + PALL¹ + -ING¹]

Tar·pe·ia (tär-pē'ə) The daughter of the governor of the citadel of Rome, who agreed to open its gates to the Sabines in return for what they wore on their left arms (their golden bracelets). As they entered they crushed her with their shields, which they also wore on their left arms. — **Tar·pe'ian** *adj.*

Tarpeian Rock A cliff on the Capitoline Hill at Rome, from which state criminals were hurled to their death.

tar·pon (tär'pon, -pən) *n. pl.* **·pon** or **·pons** A large marine game fish (*Megalops atlantica*) of the West Indies and the coast of Florida, having conspicuous silvery scales: also called *silverfish.* [Origin unknown]

Tar·quin (tär'kwin) Anglicized name of two legendary kings of Rome, **Lucius Tar·quin·i·us Pris·cus** (tär-kwin'ē-əs pris'kus) and his son **Lucius Tarquinius Su·per·bus** (sōō-pûr'bus) (called **Tarquin the Proud**), both of whom reigned during the sixth century B.C.

tar·ra·did·dle (tar′ə·did′l) *n. Informal* A prevarication; lie: also spelled *taradiddle.* [Origin uncertain]

tar·ra·gon (tar′ə·gon) *n.* **1.** A European perennial plant (*Artemisia dracunculus*) allied to wormwood. **2.** The aromatic leaves of this plant, used as seasoning. [< Sp. *taragona* < Arabic *ṭarkhun* < Gk. *drakōn* dragon]

tar·ri·ance (tar′ē·əns) *n. Archaic* A tarrying; delay. [< TARRY + -ANCE]

tar·ri·er (tar′ē·ər) *n.* One who or that which tarries.

tar·ry[1] (tar′ē) *v.* **·ried, ·ry·ing** *v.i.* **1.** To put off going or coming; linger. **2.** To remain in the same place, especially longer than one expected; abide. **3.** To wait; stay. — *v.t.* **4.** *Archaic* To wait for; await: to *tarry* his coming. — **Syn.** See ABIDE. — *n.* Sojourn; stay. [ME *tarien* to vex, hinder, delay, fusion of OE *tirgan* to vex + OF *targer* to delay < LL *tardicare* < L *tardare* to delay < *tardus* slow]

tar·ry[2] (tär′ē) *adj.* **·ri·er, ·ri·est** Covered with tar; like tar.

tar·sal (tär′səl) *adj.* **1.** Of, relating to, or situated near the tarsus or ankle. **2.** Of or relating to the tarsi of the eye.

Tar·shish (tär′shish) In the Bible, an ancient country, often identified with a coastal region of southern Spain. I *Kings* x 22.

tar·si·er (tär′sē·ər) *n.* A small, arboreal, insectivorous East Indian primate (*Tarsius spectrum*), having large eyes and ears, a long tail, and adhesive pads on elongated digits, the sole member of the suborder *Tarsioidea.* [< F < *tarse* tarsus; so called from its unusually long tarsal bones]

TARSIER
(About 14 inches long)

tarso- *combining form* **1.** The tarsus; pertaining to the tarsus. **2.** The tarsus of the eye; pertaining to the tarsal plate. Also, before vowels, **tars-.** [< Gk. *tarsos* flat of the foot, edge of the eyelid]

tar·so·met·a·tar·sus (tär′sō·met′ə·tär′səs) *n. pl.* **·si** (-sī) *Ornithol.* The bone in birds reaching from the tibia to the toes, consisting of the confluent proximal tarsal and metatarsal bones. [< NL]

tar·sus (tär′səs) *n. pl.* **·si** (-sī) **1.** *Anat.* **a** The ankle, or, in man, the group of seven bones of which it is composed. **b** A plate of connective tissue in the eyelid. **2.** *Zool.* **a** The shank of a bird's leg. **b** The distal part of the leg in insects. [< NL < Gk. *tarsos* flat of the foot, any flat surface]

Tar·sus (tär′səs) **1.** A port city in southern Turkey, on the Mediterranean; capital of ancient Cilicia; birthplace of St. Paul; pop. 57,737 (1965). **2.** A river in southern Turkey, flowing 95 miles south to the Mediterranean: ancient *Cydnus.*

tart[1] (tärt) *adj.* **1.** Having a sharp, sour taste. **2.** Severe; cutting; caustic: a *tart* remark. — **Syn.** See SOUR. [OE *teart*] — **tart′ly** *adv.* — **tart′ness** *n.*

tart[2] (tärt) *n.* **1.** A small pastry shell with fruit or custard filling and without a top crust. **2.** In England, an uncovered fruit pie. **3.** *Slang* A girl or woman of loose morals, as a prostitute. [OF *tarte*]

tar·tan[1] (tär′tən) *n.* **1.** A woolen fabric having varicolored lines or stripes at right angles, forming a distinctive pattern, the characteristic dress of the Scottish Highlanders, each clan having its particular pattern or patterns. **2.** Any similar pattern; a plaid. **3.** A garment made of tartan. For illustration see KILT. — *adj.* **1.** Made of tartan. **2.** Striped or checkered in a manner similar to the Scottish tartans. [? < OF *tiretaine* linsey-woolsey]

tar·tan[2] (tär′tən) *n.* **1.** A Mediterranean vessel having one mast with a large lateen sail. **2.** A variety of long, covered carriage. [< F *tartane* < Arabic *taridah* a kind of ship]

tar·tar[1] (tär′tər) *n.* **1.** An acid substance deposited from grape juice during fermentation as a pinkish sediment; crude bitartrate of potassium. **2.** *Dent.* A yellowish incrustation on the teeth, chiefly calcium phosphate. [< F *tartre* < LL *tartarum* < Med.Gk. *tartaron,* ? < Arabic]

tar·tar[2] (tär′tər) *n. Often cap.* **1.** A person of intractable or savage temper. **2.** An unexpectedly formidable opponent. — **to catch a tartar** To take on or be matched with an unexpectedly strong opponent. [< TARTAR]

Tar·tar (tär′tər) *n.* A Tatar. — *adj.* Of or pertaining to the Tatars or Tartary. [< F *Tartare* < LL *Tartarus* < Persian *Tātar* Tatar; prob. infl. by L *Tartarus* hell]

Tar·tar (tär′tər) *Obs.* Tartarus.

Tar·tar·e·an (tär·târ′ē·ən) *adj.* Of or pertaining to Tartarus.

tartar emetic *Chem.* A white, crystalline, poisonous tartrate of antimony and potassium, K(SbO)$C_4H_4O_6$·½H_2O, with a sweet, metallic taste, used in medicine and in dyeing.

tar·tar·e·ous (tär·târ′ē·əs) *adj.* Resembling tartar.

tar·tare sauce (tär′tər) A fish sauce made of mayonnaise, capers, chopped olives, and pickles. Also **tar′tar sauce.**

Tar·tar·i·an (tär·târ′ē·ən) *adj.* Of or pertaining to the Tatars or Tartary.

tar·tar·ic (tär·tar′ik, -tär′ik) *adj.* Pertaining to or derived from tartar or tartaric acid.

tartaric acid *Chem.* Any one of four isomeric organic compounds, HOOC(CHOH)$_2$COOH, especially the dextrorotatory form, occurring in the free state or as a potassium or calcium salt, as in grape juice, various unripe fruits, etc.

tar·tar·ize (tär′tə·rīz) *v.t.* **·ized, ·iz·ing** To impregnate or treat with tartar, cream of tartar, or tartar emetic. — **tar′·tar·i·za′tion** *n.*

Tartar mink The kolinsky. Also **Tartar sable.**

tar·tar·ous (tär′tər·əs) *adj.* Of or derived from tartar.

Tar·ta·rus (tär′tər·əs) **1.** In Greek mythology, the abyss below Hades where Zeus confined the Titans. **2.** Hades; hell.

Tar·ta·ry (tär′tər·ē) A region of Asia and eastern Europe, ruled by the Tatars, under Mongol leadership, in the 13th and 14th centuries. At its greatest extent, under Genghis Khan, it reached the Pacific; after his death, the Asian part became known as **Great Tartary,** or **Asiatic Tartary,** while the European part, ruled by the Golden Horde, became **Little Tartary,** or **European Tartary:** also *Tatary.*

tart·let (tärt′lit) *n.* A small pastry tart.

tar·trate (tär′trāt) *n. Chem.* A salt or ester of tartaric acid.

tar·trat·ed (tär′trā·tid) *adj. Chem.* Containing or combined with tartaric acid.

Tar·tu (tär′tōō) A city in the SE Estonian S.S.R.; pop. 85,000 (est. 1967). German *Dorpat.*

tar·tufe (tär·tōōf′, Fr. tär·tüf′) *n.* Any hypocrite or toady. Also **tar·tuffe′.** [< TARTUFE]

Tar·tufe (tär·tōōf′, Fr. tär·tüf′) In Molière's comedy of the same name, the chief character, a person of pretended piety. Also **Tar·tuffe′.**

Tar·ve·si·um (tär·vē′sē·əm) The ancient name for TREVISO.

tar·zan (tär′zən, -zan) *n. Chiefly cap.* A person of prodigious strength and agility. [< *Tarzan,* the hero of a series of novels by Edgar Rice Burroughs, 1875–1950]

Tash·kent (təsh·kyent′) The capital of the Uzbek S.S.R., in the eastern part; pop. 1,385,000 (est. 1970).

ta·sim·e·ter (tə·sim′ə·tər) *n.* An electrical apparatus for detecting changes in temperature by pressure variations resulting from the contraction or expansion of a solid. [< Gk. *tasis* extension (< *teinein* to stretch) + -METER] — **tas·i·met·ric** (tas′ə·met′rik) *adj.* — **ta·sim′e·try** *n.*

task (task, täsk) *n.* **1.** A specific amount of labor or study imposed by authority or required by duty or necessity. **2.** Any work voluntarily undertaken. **3.** An exhausting or bothersome job or duty; a burden. **4.** A specific military mission. **5.** *Obs.* A tax; duty. — **to take to task** To reprove; lecture. — *v.t.* **1.** To assign a task to. **2.** To overtax with labor; burden. **3.** To censure; reprimand. **4.** *Obs.* To tax. [< AF *tasque* < LL *tasca, taxa* < L *taxare* to appraise. Akin to TAX.]
— **Syn.** (noun) **1.** job, chore, stint, assignment.

task force *Mil.* A tactical unit consisting of elements drawn from different branches of the armed services and assigned to execute a specific mission.

task·mas·ter (task′mas′tər, täsk′mäs′tər) *n.* **1.** One who assigns tasks, especially severe ones. **2.** One who or that which loads with heavy burdens.

Tasm. Tasmania: also **Tas.**

Tas·man (täs′män), Abel Janszoon, 1602?–59, Dutch navigator; discovered Tasmania and New Zealand in 1642.

Tas·ma·ni·a (taz·mā′nē·ə) A State of Australia occupying an island south of Victoria; 26,216 sq. mi.; pop. 393,700 (1970); capital, Hobart: formerly *Van Diemen's Land.* See map of AUSTRALIA. — **Tas·ma′ni·an** *adj. & n.*

Tasmanian devil A ferocious burrowing carnivorous marsupial (*Sarcophilus harrisii*), with white markings on a black hide; a dasyure.

Tasmanian wolf The thylacine. Also **Tasmanian tiger.**

Tas·man Sea (taz′mən) The part of the South Pacific between SE Australia and New Zealand.

tass (tas) *n. Scot.* A drinking cup, or its contents.

Tass (täs, tas) *n.* A Soviet news agency. [< Russian *T(elegrafnoe) A(gentstvo) S(ovetskovo) S(oyuza)*]

tas·sel[1] (tas′əl) *n.* **1.** A dangling ornament for curtains, cushions, etc., consisting of a tuft of loose threads or cords. **2.** Any of various similar objects, as the inflorescence on a stalk of Indian corn. **3.** Formerly, a clasp for holding a cloak. — *v.* **tas·seled** or **·selled, tas·sel·ing** or **·sel·ling** *v.t.* **1.** To provide or adorn with tassels. **2.** To form in a tassel or tassels. **3.** To remove the tassels from (Indian corn). — *v.i.* **4.** To put forth tassels, as Indian corn. [< OF, clasp < Med.L *tassellus,* var. of L *taxillus*]

tas·sel[2] (tas′əl) *n.* A tercel.

tas·set (tas′it) *n.* One of a series of pendent, overlapping metal plates, used as armor to protect the thighs: also called *tace.* Also **tasse** (tas). [< F *tassette,* dim. of OF *tasse* pouch]

tas·sie (tas′ē) *n. Scot.* A drinking cup.

Tas·so (täs′sō), Torquato, 1544–95, Italian epic poet.

taste (tāst) *v.* **tast·ed, tast·ing** *v.t.* **1.** To perceive the flavor of (something) by taking into the mouth or touching with the tongue. **2.** To take a little of (food or drink); eat or drink a little of. **3.** To test the quality of (a product) thus: *His business is* tasting *tea.* **4.** *Archaic* To have a relish for; like. **5.** *Obs.* To prove or try by or as by touch. — *v.i.* **6.** To have specified flavor when in the mouth: *Sugar* tastes *sweet.* **7.** To take a small quantity into the mouth; take a taste: usually with *of.* **8.** To have experience or enjoyment; be or become acquainted through experience: with *of*: to taste *of great sorrow.* — *n.* **1.** The sensation excited when a soluble substance comes into contact with any of the taste buds; also, the quality thus perceived; flavor. **2.** *Physiol.* Any of the four fundamental sensations, salt, sweet, bitter, or sour, excited alone or in any combination by the sole action of the gustatory nerves. **3.** A small quantity tasted, eaten, or sipped. **4.** A slight experience or sample of anything. **5.** Special fondness and aptitude for a pursuit; bent; inclination: a taste *for music.* **6.** The faculty of discerning and appreciating what is beautiful or appropriate, as in nature, art, or literature, or what is peculiarly correct for a given situation, context, etc.: *She has* taste *in clothes.* **7.** Style or form with respect to the rules of propriety or etiquette: *She behaved in poor* taste. **8.** Individual preference or liking: *That tie suits my* taste. **9.** The act of tasting. **10.** *Obs.* The act of examining or testing. [< OF *taster* to taste, try, feel, prob. ult. < L *taxare* to touch, handle, appraise] — **tast′a·ble** *adj.*

taste bud *Physiol.* One of the clusters of cells situated in the epithelial tissue, chiefly of the tongue, and containing sensitive receptors for the discriminatory perception of taste.

taste·ful (tāst′fəl) *adj.* **1.** Conforming to taste. **2.** Possessing good taste. **3.** *Rare* Savory. — **taste′ful·ly** *adv.* — **taste′ful·ness** *n.*

taste·less (tāst′lis) *adj.* **1.** Having no flavor; insipid; dull. **2.** Lacking, or showing a lack of, good taste. **3.** Devoid of esthetic taste. **4.** Having lost the sense of taste. — **taste′less·ly** *adv.* — **taste′less·ness** *n.*

tast·er (tās′tər) *n.* **1.** One who tastes; especially, one who tests the quality of as an occupation: a teataster. **2.** A device to assist in testing or sampling. **3.** A small, flat, circular vessel used in testing wines; a pipette.

tast·y (tās′tē) *adj.* **tast·i·er, tast·i·est** *Informal* **1.** Having a fine flavor; savory. **2.** Tasteful. — **tast′i·ly** *adv.* — **tast′i·ness** *n.*

tat¹ (tat) *v.* **tat·ted, tat·ting** *v.t.* **1.** To make, as an edging, by tatting. — *v.i.* **2.** To make tatting. [Back formation < TATTING] — **tat′ter** *n.*

tat² (tat) *n.* A tap or blow. See TIT FOR TAT. [? Var. of TAP², n.]

Ta·tar (tä′tər) *n.* **1.** One belonging to any of the Turkic peoples of eastern, western, and central R.S.F.S.R. and Soviet Central Asia; also, one of the Turkic Tatars of the Tatar A.S.S.R., the Crimea, the Kalmuck area, and the northern Caucasus: also called *Tatarian.* **2.** Any of the Turkic languages of the Tatars, as Uzbek. **3.** Originally, any of the Tungus of Manchuria and Mongolia. — *adj.* Of or pertaining to the Tatars. Also *Tartar.* [< Persian]

Ta·tar A.S.S.R. (tä′tər) An administrative division of the western R.S.F.S.R.; 26,100 sq. mi.; pop. 3,131,000 (1970); capital, Kazan. *Russian* **Ta·tar·ska·ya A.S.S.R.** (tə·tär′skə·yə).

Ta·tar·i·an (tä·târ′ē·ən) *adj.* Of or pertaining to the Tatars. Also **Ta·tar·ic** (tä·târ′ik). — *n.* A Tatar (def. 1).

Ta·ta·ry (tä′tər·ē) See TARTARY.

tate (tāt) *n. Scot.* A wisp or tuft, as of hay or hair.

Tate (tāt), **Allen**, born 1899, U.S. poet and critic. — **Nahum,** 1652–1715, English poet and dramatist born in Ireland; poet laureate 1692–1715.

ta·ter (tā′tər) *n. Dial.* A potato. Also **'ta′ter.**

Tat·ler (tat′lər), **The** An English periodical published three times weekly by Sir Richard Steele from 1709 to 1711, chiefly written by Steele, occasionally by Joseph Addison: predecessor of *The Spectator.*

tat·ou·ay (tat′ōō·ā, tä·tōō′ī) *n.* A large South American armadillo (genus *Cabassous*). [< Sp. *tatuay* < Guarani *tatu-ai* < *tatu* armadillo + *ai* worthless; so called because it is inedible]

Ta·tra Mountains (tä′trä) The highest group of the central Carpathian Mountains, in northern Czechoslovakia; highest peak, Gerlachovka, 8,737 ft. Also **High Tatra.**

tat·ter (tat′ər) *n.* **1.** A torn and hanging shred; rag. **2.** *pl.* Ragged clothing. — *v.t.* **1.** To make ragged; tear into tatters. — *v.i.* **2.** To become ragged. [< Scand. Cf. ON *tö̈turr* rags.]

tat·ter·de·mal·ion (tat′ər·di·māl′yən, -mal′-) *n.* A person wearing ragged clothes; a ragamuffin. [Origin unknown]

tat·tered (tat′ərd) *adj.* **1.** Torn into tatters. **2.** Clothed in rags; ragged.

tat·ter·sall (tat′ər·sôl) *n. Sometimes cap.* Having a design of dark lines on a light ground, as in a check or plaid: a *tattersall* vest. [after Richard *Tattersall*, 1724–95, horse merchant; from a pattern on blankets used in his London market]

tat·ting (tat′ing) *n.* A lacelike threadwork, made by hand; also, the act of making it. [Origin unknown]

tat·tle (tat′l) *v.* **·tled, ·tling** *v.i.* **1.** To talk idly; prate;

chatter. **2.** To tell tales about others; gossip. — *v.t.* **3.** To reveal by gossiping. — *n.* **1.** Idle talk or gossip. **2.** Prattling speech, as of children. [Prob. < MDu. *tatelen*] — **tat′tling·ly** *adv.*

— **Syn.** (verb) **1.** prattle. Compare BABBLE. **2.** blab, inform.

tat·tler (tat′lər) *n.* **1.** One who tattles; a talebearer. **2.** Any of several long-billed birds (genus *Totanus*), as the yellowlegs. **3.** A shore bird (*Heteroscelus incanus*) of the Pacific coast of the United States: also called *wandering tattler.*

tat·tle·tale (tat′l·tāl′) *n.* A talebearer; tattler. — *adj.* Revealing; betraying.

tat·too¹ (ta·tōō′) *v.t.* **1.** To prick and mark (the skin) with indelible pigments. **2.** To mark the skin with (designs, etc.) in this way. — *n. pl.* **·toos** A pattern or picture so made. [< Polynesian. Cf. Tahitian, Tongan *tatau,* Marquesan *tatu* < *ta* mark.] — **tat·too′er** *n.* — **tat·too′ing** *n.*

tat·too² (ta·tōō′) *n.* **1.** A continuous beating or drumming. **2.** In military or naval usage, a signal by drum or bugle to repair to quarters, usually occurring about 9 P.M. [Var. of earlier *taptoo* < Du. *taptoe* < *tap* tap, faucet + *toe* to shut]

tau (tou) *n.* The nineteenth letter in the Greek alphabet (T, τ), corresponding to the English *t.* See ALPHABET.

Tauch·nitz (toukh′nits), **Baron Christian Bernhard von,** 1816–95, German publisher.

tau cross A cross in the form of a T: also called *St. Anthony's cross.* For illustration see CROSS.

taught (tôt) Past tense and past participle of TEACH.

Taungs skull (toungz) See AUSTRALOPITHECUS. [after *Taungs,* South Africa, where remains were discovered]

taunt¹ (tônt) *n.* **1.** A sarcastic, biting speech or remark; scornful reproach. **2.** *Obs.* A butt of contemptuous reproach. — *v.t.* **1.** To reproach with sarcastic or contemptuous words; mock; upbraid. **2.** To tease in any way; provoke with taunts. [? < OF *tanter,* var. of *tenter* to provoke, tempt. See TEMPT.] — **taunt′er** *n.* — **taunt′ing·ly** *adv.*

taunt² (tônt) *adj. Naut.* Unusually tall: said of masts. [Aphetic var. of ATAUNT]

Taun·ton (tôn′tən *for def. 1,* tän′tən *for def. 2*) **1.** A city in SE Massachusetts; pop. 43,756. **2.** The county seat of Somerset, England, in the west central part of the county; pop. 82,900 (1976).

tau particle *Physics* A rare, unstable atomic particle of the meson group, positively charged and with a mass about 1,000 times that of the electron.

taupe (tōp) *n.* **1.** Mole². **2.** The color of moleskin; dark gray, often tinged with brown, purple, or yellow. [< F < L *talpa* mole]

Tau·ric Cher·so·nese (tô′rik kûr′sō·nēz, -nēs) An ancient name for the CRIMEA.

tau·ri·form (tôr′ə·fôrm) *adj.* Shaped like a bull. [< L *tauriformis* < *taurus* bull + *forma* shape]

tau·rine¹ (tôr′ēn) *adj.* **1.** Of or like a bull. **2.** Related to or connected with the constellation or sign Taurus. [< L *taurinus* < *taurus* bull]

tau·rine² (tôr′ēn, -in) *n. Biochem.* A colorless crystalline compound, $C_2H_7NSO_3$, contained in the bile and muscles of oxen and other animals, and derived synthetically. [< L *taurus* bull + -INE²]

tauro- *combining form* Bull; ox; bovine. Also, before vowels, **taur-**. [< Gk. *tauros* bull]

tau·ro·chol·ic acid (tô′rə·kol′ik, -kol′ik) *Biochem.* A bitter crystalline compound, $C_{26}H_{45}NSO_7$, contained in the bile of some animals, as the ox. [< TAURO- + Gk. *cholē* bile]

tau·rom·a·chy (tô·rom′ə·kē) *n.* The art of bullfighting. Also **tau·ro·ma·chi·a** (tôr′ə·mā′kē·ə). [< Sp. *tauromaquia* < Gk. *tauromachia* < *tauros* bull + *machesthai* to fight]

Tau·rus (tôr′əs) *n.* A constellation, the Bull, containing the bright star Aldebaran; also, the second sign of the zodiac. See CONSTELLATION, ZODIAC. [< L]

Tau·rus (tôr′əs) A mountain range in southern Turkey; highest point, Ala Dagh, 12,251 ft.: Turkish *Toros Dağlari.*

Taus·sig (tou′sig), **Frank William,** 1859–1940, U.S. political economist.

taut (tôt) *adj.* **1.** Stretched tight; not loose or slack. **2.** Tense; tight: taut *muscles.* **3.** In proper shape; tidy. [ME *togt, toht;* origin uncertain] — **taut′ly** *adv.* — **taut′ness** *n.*

taut. Tautological; tautology.

taut·ed (tô′tid) *adj. Scot.* Tangled; tousled; matted: said of wool or hair.

taut·en (tôt′n) *v.t. & v.i.* To make or become taut; tighten.

tauto- *combining form* Same; identical: *tautomerism.* Also, before vowels, **taut-**. [< Gk. *tauto* the same]

tau·tog (tô·tôg′, -tog′) *n.* A blackish, edible, labroid fish (*Tautoga onitis*) of the North American Atlantic coast. Also **tau·taug′.** [< Algonquian *tautauog,* pl. of *tautau,* a kind of blackfish]

tau·tol·o·gism (tô·tol′ə·jiz′əm) *n.* Use of needlessly repetitious speech, or an instance of it. — **tau·tol′o·gist** *n.*

tau·tol·o·gize (tô·tol′ə·jīz) *v.i.* **·gized, ·giz·ing** To repeat needlessly the same idea in different words.

tau·tol·o·gy (tô·tol′ə·jē) *n. pl.* **·gies 1.** Unnecessary repe-

TAUTOG
(About 16 inches long)

tition of the same idea in different words; pleonasm. **2.** An instance of such repetition, as *He is writing his own autobiography.* **3.** *Logic* A statement that is necessarily true by virtue of its structure, as *Either it is raining or it is not raining.* Abbr. *taut.* — **Syn.** See CIRCUMLOCUTION. [< LL *tautologia* < Gk. < *tauto* the same + *logos* discourse] — **tau-to·log·ic** (tô′tə-loj′ik) or **·i·cal** *adj.* — **tau′to·log′i·cal·ly** *adv.*

tau·to·mer·ic (tô′tə-mer′ik) *adj.* Having tautomerism.

tau·tom·er·ism (tô-tom′ə-riz′əm) *n. Chem.* The property of certain organic compounds when subjected to appropriate chemical reaction, of assuming either of two isomeric structures or **tautomers** that are in equilibrium with each other. [< TAUTO- + Gk. *meros* part]

tau·tom·er·i·za·tion (tô-tom′ər-ə-zā′shən, -ī-zā′-) *n. Chem.* Conversion into a tautomeric structure.

tau·to·nym (tô′tə-nim) *n.* An instance of tautonymy.

tau·ton·y·my (tô-ton′ə-mē) *n. pl.* **·mies** *Biol.* Identity of the generic and specific names of a given plant or animal, as *Bison bison.* [< TAUTO- + Gk. *onyma* name] — **tau·to·nym·ic** (tô′tə-nim′ik) *adj.*

tav (täv) *n.* The twenty-second letter in the Hebrew alphabet. Also **taw.** See ALPHABET.

tav·ern (tav′ərn) *n.* **1.** A place licensed to retail liquors to be drunk on the premises. **2.** A public house where travelers and other guests are accommodated with lodging, food, and drink. [< OF *taverne* < L *taberna* hut, booth]

tav·ern·er (tav′ər-nər) *n. Archaic* **1.** A tavernkeeper. **2.** One who frequents taverns.

taw[1] (tô) *v.t.* **1.** To convert into leather by some process other than soaking in tanning liquor, as by using alum and salt. **2.** *Brit. Dial.* To beat; torture. [OE *tawian* to prepare, harass] — **taw′er** *n.*

taw[2] (tô) *n.* **1.** A game of marbles. **2.** The line from which marble-players shoot. **3.** A marble used for shooting. — *v.i.* To shoot a marble or come to the mark before shooting. [< Scand. Cf. ON *taug* string.]

taw·dry (tô′drē) *adj.* **·dri·er, ·dri·est** Showy and cheap; tastelessly ornamental. — **Syn.** See GAUDY. [Short for *tawdry lace,* alter. of *St. Audrey's lace,* a type of silk neckpiece sold at St. Audrey's Fair at Ely, England] — **taw′dri·ly** *adv.* — **taw′dri·ness** *n.*

taw·ie (tô′ē) *adj. Scot.* Docile; tame: said of a horse, etc.

Taw·ney (tô′nē), **R(ichard) H(enry),** 1880–1962, British economist, historian, and educator, born in India.

taw·ny (tô′nē) *adj.* **·ni·er, ·ni·est** Tan-colored; brownish yellow. Also **taw′ney.** [< AF *taune* < OF *tanné,* pp. of *tanner* to tan] — **taw′ni·ness** *n.*

taw·pie (tô′pē) *n. Scot.* A foolish young woman.

taws (tôz) *Scot. n.* A whip made of a leather strap cut into thongs or of several thongs on a handle. — *v.t.* To flog; scourge. Also **tawse.**

tax (taks) *n.* **1.** A compulsory contribution levied upon persons, property, or business for the support of government. **2.** Any proportionate assessment, as on the members of a society. **3.** A heavy demand on one's powers or resources; an onerous duty or requirement; a burden. — *v.t.* **1.** To impose a tax on; subject to taxation. **2.** *Law* To settle or fix (amounts) as duly chargeable in any judicial matter: to *tax* costs. **3.** To subject to a severe demand; impose a burden or load upon: He *taxes* my patience. **4.** To make an accusation against; charge; also, to blame; censure: usually with *with.* [< OF *taxer* < L *taxare* to estimate, appraise. Akin to TASK.] — **tax′a·bil′i·ty, tax′a·ble·ness** *n.* — **tax′a·ble** *adj.* — **tax′a·bly** *adv.* — **tax′er** *n.*

— **Syn.** (noun) **1.** assessment, custom, duty, excise, impost, levy, rate, tariff, tithe, toll, tribute.

Tax may appear as a combining form with the meaning of def. 1, as in the following list:

tax assessor	tax evader	tax payment
tax burden	tax-evading	tax proposal
tax-burdened	tax-exempt	tax receipt
tax claim	tax-free	tax repeal
tax collecting	tax-laden	tax revenue
tax collector	tax law	tax-ridden
tax cut	tax levy	tax-supported
tax dodger	taxman	tax system
tax-dodging	taxpaid	taxwise

tax·a·ceous (tak-sā′shəs) *adj. Bot.* Designating or belonging to a widely distributed family (*Taxaceae*) of typically evergreen shrubs and trees, the yew family, having drupelike or, rarely, cone fruits. [< NL < L *taxus* yew]

tax·a·tion (tak-sā′shən) *n.* **1.** The act of taxing. **2.** The amount assessed as a tax.

tax-de·duct·i·ble (taks′di-duk′tə-bəl) *adj.* Legally deductible from that portion of one's income or assets subject to taxes: Medical expenses are *tax-deductible.*

tax·eme (taks′ēm) *n. Ling.* The smallest feature of grammatical arrangement. [< Gk. *taxis* arrangement; on analogy with PHONEME]

tax·gath·er·er (taks′gath′ər-ər) *n.* A collector of taxes. — **tax′gath′er·ing** *n. & adj.*

tax·i (tak′sē) *n. pl.* **tax·is** A taxicab. — *v.* **tax·ied, tax·i·ing** or **tax·y·ing** *v.i.* **1.** To ride in a taxicab. **2.** To move along the ground or on the surface of the water under its own power, as an airplane before taking off. — *v.t.* **3.** To cause (an airplane) to taxi. [< TAXI(CAB)]

tax·i·cab (tak′sē-kab′) *n.* An automobile available for hire, usually fitted with a taximeter: also called *cab, taxi.* [Short for *taximeter cab*]

taxi dancer *U.S.* A girl employed by a dance hall or cabaret to dance with patrons for a fee. [< *taxi*- hired, as in *taxicab* + DANCER]

tax·i·der·mist (tak′sə-dûr′mist) *n.* One who practices taxidermy.

tax·i·der·my (tak′sə-dûr′mē) *n.* The art or process of stuffing and mounting the skins of dead animals for preservation or exhibition. [< Gk. *taxis* arrangement + *derma* skin] — **tax′i·der′mal, tax′i·der′mic** *adj.*

tax·i·me·ter (tak′si-mē′tər) *n.* An instrument for measuring distances and recording fares, used in taxicabs. [< F *taximètre* < *taxe* tariff + *mètre* meter]

tax·is (tak′sis) *n.* **1.** *Surg.* The application of manual pressure alone, as for reducing a hernial tumor or restoring a displaced part. **2.** *Biol.* The involuntary movement of an organism or cell in response to an external stimulus. Compare TROPISM. **3.** In ancient Greece, a body of troops of varying size. [< Gk., arrangement < *tassein* to arrange]

-taxis *combining form* Order; disposition; arrangement: *thermotaxis.* Also spelled **-taxy.** [< Gk. *taxis* arrangement]

tax·ite (tak′sīt) *n.* A volcanic rock that has been formed in such a manner as to have a clastic appearance. [< Gk. *taxis* arrangement + -ITE[1]] — **tax·it·ic** (tak-sit′ik) *adj.*

tax·on·o·mist (tak-son′ə-mist) *n.* A student or specialist in taxonomy. Also **tax·on′o·mer.**

tax·on·o·my (tak-son′ə-mē) *n.* **1.** The department of knowledge that embodies the laws and principles of classification. **2.** *Biol.* The systematic arrangement of plant and animal organisms according to established criteria that determine their assignment to the following major groups, beginning with the most inclusive: kingdom, phylum or division, class, order, family, genus, and species. [< F *taxonomie* < Gk. *taxis* arrangement + *nomos* law] — **tax·o·nom·ic** (tak′sə-nom′ik) or **·i·cal** *adj.* — **tax′o·nom′i·cal·ly** *adv.*

tax·pay·er (taks′pā′ər) *n.* One who pays a tax or is subject to taxation.

tax title *Law* The title conveyed to a purchaser of property sold for nonpayment of taxes.

Tay (tā) A river in western Scotland, flowing 118 miles, generally SW, to the **Firth of Tay,** an estuary of the North Sea.

Ta·yg·e·ta (tā-ij′ə-tə) In Greek mythology, one of the Pleiades. — *n. Astron.* One of the six visible stars in the Pleiades cluster.

Tay·lor (tā′lər), **Bayard,** 1825–78, U.S. writer, translator, and traveler: full name **James Bayard Taylor.** — **Deems,** 1885–1966, U.S. composer and musicologist: full name **Joseph Deems Taylor.** — **Henry Osborn,** 1856–1941, U.S. historian. — **Jeremy,** 1613–67, English bishop and author. — **Zachary,** 1784–1850, U.S. general, 12th president of the United States 1849–50: called **Old Rough and Ready.**

Tay-Sachs disease (tā′saks′) *Pathol.* A congenital disease of infants and children, characterized by mental deficiency, progressive blindness, paralysis, and death. [after Warren *Tay,* 1843–1927, English physician, and Bernard *Sachs,* 1858–1944, U.S. neurologist]

taz·za (tät′tsä) *n. Italian* A flat ornamental cup, especially one supported on a high foot.

Tb *Chem.* Terbium.

t.b. Trial balance.

TB or **T.B., Tb, Tb., t.b.** or **tb** Tuberculosis.

T-bar lift (tē′bär′) A ski lift on which the skiers lean back against a hanging T-shaped bar to be pushed up the slope.

Tbi·li·si (tbi′li·sē, *Russ.* tbyĕ′lyi-syi) The Georgian name for TIFLIS.

T-bone (tē′bōn) *n.* A beefsteak containing a T-shaped bone, taken from the loin. Also **T-bone steak.**

tbs. or **tbsp.** Tablespoon(s).

Tc *Chem.* Technetium.

TC **1.** Transportation Corps. **2.** Trusteeship Council (of the United Nations).

Tchad (chàd) The French name for CHAD.

Tchai·kov·sky (chī-kof′skē), **Pëtr Ilich,** 1840–93, Russian composer.

Tche·khov (chek′ôf), **Anton** See CHEKHOV.

TD **1.** Touchdown: also **td** or **td. 2.** Treasury Dept.

Te *Chem.* Tellurium.

tea (tē) *n.* **1.** An evergreen Asian shrub or small tree (*Thea sinensis*), having a compact head of leathery, toothed leaves and white or pink flowers. **2.** The prepared leaves of this plant, or an infusion of them used as a beverage. **3.** Any infusion, decoction, solution, or extract to be used as a beverage or medicinally: beef *tea.* **4.** The leaves of a particular variety of plant, prepared for making a beverage, or for medicinal purposes: senna *tea*. **5.** *Brit.* A light evening or afternoon meal. **6.** A social gathering at which tea is served. [< Chinese *ch'a*, dial. Chinese *t'e*]

Tea may appear as a combining form, as in the following examples:

tea-blending	tea grower	tea planting
tea bowl	tea-growing	tea producer
teabox	tea jar	tea-producing
teacart	tea leaf	tea table
tea china	tea-loving	teataster
tea-colored	teamaker	teatasting
tea crop	teamaking	teatime
tea dealer	tea merchant	tea trade
tea drinker	tea packer	tea tray
tea drinking	tea-packing	tea tree
tea farm	tea plant	tea urn
tea farming	tea planter	teaware

tea bag A small porous sack of cloth or paper containing tea leaves, immersed in water to make tea: also called *tea ball*.

tea ball 1. A perforated metal ball that is filled with tea leaves and placed in hot water to make tea. **2.** A tea bag.

tea·ber·ry (tē′ber′ē) *n. pl.* **·ries 1.** The wintergreen, whose leaves are sometimes mixed with or used as tea. **2.** The berry of this plant.

tea biscuit A biscuit or cracker, usually short and sweetened, served with tea. Also **tea cake.**

tea caddy A small box or case for tea leaves.

tea ceremony A ritual preparation and serving of tea, practiced by the Japanese.

teach (tēch) *v.* **taught, teach·ing** *v.t.* **1.** To impart knowledge by lessons; give instruction to: to *teach* a class. **2.** To give instruction in; communicate the knowledge of: to *teach* French. **3.** To train by practice or exercise. — *v.i.* **1.** To follow the profession of teaching. **5.** To impart knowledge or skill. ◆ See note under LEARN. [OE *tæcan*]
— **Syn. 1.** *Teach, instruct, drill, educate, school, discipline, train,* and *tutor* mean to guide in acquiring knowledge or skill. *Teach* is the most comprehensive word; it embraces all methods of imparting knowledge, information, guidance, or counsel. To *instruct* is to give specific directions about a subject; the word has a connotation of authority: to *instruct* recruits in the use of a rifle. To *drill* is to *teach* by repetition, or to supervise in practice. The original sense of *educate* is to draw out or develop the mental powers of another; now it usually means to place in a school or college. In this latter sense, it tends to replace *school*, which has come to be used as a close synonym of *discipline*. Both *school* and *discipline* refer to the teaching of certain patterns of behavior, rather than to the giving of knowledge or information; they both imply subjection to some authority: to *school* a child to obey promptly, to *discipline* oneself to eat sparingly. *Train* suggests the direction of another's skills to a particular end, or the fitting of a person for a particular work; of all these words, *train* is preferred when reference is made to a nonhuman subject: to *train* a dog to roll over and play dead. *Tutor* means to *teach* in private, rather than in a school or college, and usually in a situation where there is one teacher for one learner.

teach·a·ble (tē′chə·bəl) *adj.* **1.** Willing or able to learn, docile. **2.** Capable of being imparted by teaching. — **teach′a·bil′i·ty, teach′a·ble·ness** *n.* — **teach′a·bly** *adv.*

teach·er (tē′chər) *n.* One who teaches; especially, one whose occupation is to teach others; an instructor.

teacher bird 1. The ovenbird (def. 1). **2.** The North American red-eyed vireo. [Imit.; because its cry sounds like "teacher"]

teachers college *U.S.* A college specializing in the training of teachers. Also **teachers' college.**

teach·ing (tē′ching) *n.* **1.** The act or occupation of a teacher. **2.** That which is taught.

teaching elder A presbyter (def. 3a).

teaching machine Any of various manually operated devices that present educational material in a series of steps designed to enable each student to learn at a rate commensurate with his ability.

tea cozy A cozy (which see).

tea·cup (tē′kup′) *n.* **1.** A small cup suitable for serving tea. **2.** As much as a teacup will hold, usually four fluid ounces: also **tea′cup·ful′** (-fool′).

tea·house (tē′hous′) *n.* In the Orient, a public place serving tea and other light refreshments.

teak (tēk) *n.* **1.** A large East Indian tree (*Tecona grandis*) of the vervain family, yielding a very hard, durable timber highly prized for shipbuilding. **2.** The wood of this tree: also **teak′wood** (-wood). [< Malayalam *tēkka*]

tea·ket·tle (tē′ket′l) *n.* A kettle with a spout, used for boiling water.

teal (tēl) *n.* **1.** Any of various small, short-necked river ducks; especially, the common teal (*Anas crecca*) of the Old World and the related North American **green-winged teal** (*A. carolinensis*) and **blue-winged teal** (*A. discors*). **2.** A darkish, dull blue color with a greenish cast. [ME *tele*]

team (tēm) *n.* **1.** Two or more beasts of burden harnessed together, often including harness and vehicle; also, a single horse and vehicle. **2.** A set of workers, or players competing in a game: a baseball *team*. **3.** *Dial.* A flock; brood. **4.** *Obs.* Race; lineage. — *v.t.* **1.** To convey with a team. **2.** To

harness together in a team. — *v.i.* **3.** To drive a team as a business. **4.** To form a team; work as a team: to *team* up. — *adj.* Of or pertaining to a team: *team* spirit. [OE *team* offspring, succession, row. Akin to TEEM[1].]

team·mate (tēm′māt′) *n.* A fellow player on a team.

team·ster (tēm′stər) *n.* **1.** One who drives or owns a team. **2.** One who drives a truck or other commercial vehicle.

team teaching *U.S.* A method of organizing instruction in schools so that the students in a given course are taught by several teachers, each of whom sometimes teaches the whole group and sometimes a part of it.

team·work (tēm′wûrk′) *n.* **1.** Concerted action or effort by the members of a group to achieve some common end, as the coordinated play of an athletic team. **2.** Work done or requiring to be done by or with a team.

Tea·neck (tē′nek) A township in NE New Jersey; pop. 42,355.

tea party A social gathering at which tea and light sandwiches or cakes are the principal refreshments.

tea·pot (tē′pot′) *n.* A vessel with a spout and handle in which tea is made and from which it is served.

tea·poy (tē′poi) *n.* **1.** A small table for holding a tea service. **2.** Any small, ornamental, three-legged stand or table. [< Hind. *tipāi* < *tin* three + Persian *pāē* foot]

tear[1] (târ) *v.* **tore, torn, tear·ing** *v.t.* **1.** To pull apart, as cloth; part or separate by pulling; rip; rend. **2.** To make by rending or tearing: to *tear* a hole in a dress. **3.** To injure or lacerate, as skin. **4.** To divide; disrupt: a party *torn* by dissension. **5.** To distress or torment: The sight *tore* his heart. — *v.i.* **6.** To become torn or rent. **7.** To move with haste and energy: to *tear* up the stairs. — **to tear down 1.** To destroy; demolish, as a building. **2.** *Informal* To speak slightingly of; disparage. — **to tear into** *Informal* To charge into or attack without restraint: He *tore* into his opponent. — *n.* **1.** A fissure made by tearing; a rent; an act of tearing. **2.** *Slang* A carouse; a spree; frolic. **3.** A rushing motion: to start off with a *tear*. **4.** Any violent outburst, as of anger, enthusiasm, etc. [OE *teran*]

tear[2] (tir) *n.* **1.** A drop of the saline liquid secreted by the lachrymal gland, serving to moisten the eye, and capable of being stimulated to a flow by emotional agitation or distress. **2.** Something resembling or suggesting a drop of the lachrymal fluid. **3.** A drop of any liquid. **4.** A droplike portion, as of glass, amber, etc. **5.** *pl.* Sorrow; lamentation. — **in tears** Weeping; crying. — *v.i.* To emit or fill with tears. [OE *tēar*] — **tear′less** *adj.* — **tear′y** *adj.*

Tear may appear as a combining form with the meaning of def. 1:

tear-arresting	tear-filled	tear-mourned
tear-baptized	tear-freshened	tear-provoking
tear-blinded	tear-glistening	tear-salt
tear-creating	tear-lined	tear-stained
tear-dimmed	tear-marked	tear-streaked
tear-dropped	tear-mocking	tear-swollen
tear-falling	tear-moistened	tear-wrung

tear·drop (tir′drop′) *n.* A tear or tear-shaped object.

tear·ful (tir′fəl) *adj.* **1.** Weeping abundantly. **2.** Causing tears. — **tear′ful·ly** *adv.* — **tear′ful·ness** *n.*

tear gas (tir) A chemical that provokes a copious flow of tears, with irritation of the eyes: also called *lachrymator.*

tear·ing (târ′ing) *adj.* *Informal* **1.** Violent; hasty; headlong. **2.** *Chiefly Brit.* Tremendous; mighty.

tear-jerk·er (tir′jûr′kər) *n.* *U.S. Slang* A story, play, etc., full of sentimental sadness.

tea·room (tē′room′, -room′) *n.* A restaurant serving tea and other refreshments: also called *teashop.*

tea rose **1.** Any of various garden roses thought to be tea-scented. **2.** A yellowish pink color.

tear sheet (târ) A page torn or cut from a magazine, book, or newspaper, containing matter of particular interest.

Teas·dale (tēz′dāl), Sara, 1884–1933, U.S. poet.

tease (tēz) *v.* **teased, teas·ing** *v.t.* **1.** To goad or annoy (a person or animal) in sport; harass or pester for one's amusement. **2.** To scratch or dress in order to raise the nap, as cloth with teasels. **3.** To tear or pull apart with instruments, as tissues in examination. **4.** To comb or card, as wool or flax; also, to pick or shred, as hard-packed tobacco. **5.** To arouse the sexual desires of without planning to satisfy them. **6.** To comb (hair) in such a way as to form fluffy layers and give an effect of fullness. — *v.i.* **7.** To annoy a person in a facetious or petty manner. — *n.* **1.** One who or that which teases. **2.** The act of teasing, or the state of being teased. [OE *tæsan* to tease, pluck, pull about] — **teas′ing·ly** *adv.*

tea·sel (tē′zəl) *n.* **1.** A coarse, prickly Old World herb (genus *Dipsacus*) of which the flower head is covered with hooked bracts; especially, the fuller's teasel. **2.** The rough bur of such a plant, or a mechanical substitute, used in dressing cloth. — *v.t.* **tea·seled or ·selled, tea·sel·ing or ·sel·ling** To raise the nap of with a teasel. Also **tea′zel, tea′zle.** [OE *tæsel*] — **tea′sel·er** or **tea′sel·ler** *n.*

teas·er (tē′zər) *n.* **1.** One who or that which

TEASEL
(Plant to 5 feet high)

teases.   **2.** Something that puzzles or challenges the mind; enigma.   **3.** A machine used for teasing wool.   **4.** Anything tempting or whetting the appetites.

tea service The articles used in serving tea. Also **tea set.**

tea·shop (tē′shop′) *n.* **1.** A tearoom.   **2.** *Brit.* A lunchroom.

tea·spoon (tē′spōōn′, -spŏŏn′) *n.* **1.** A small spoon used for stirring tea, etc.   **2.** An amount equal to as much as a teaspoon will hold, equivalent to ⅓ of a tablespoon, or 1⅓ fluid drams. Abbr. *t.*

tea·spoon·ful (tē′spōōn·fŏŏl′, -spŏŏn-) *n.* *pl.* **·fuls** As much as a teaspoon will hold.

teat (tēt, tit) *n.* The protuberance on the breast or udder of most female mammals, through which the milk is drawn; a nipple; pap; dug.   [< OF *tete* < Gmc.]

tea wagon A table on wheels for use in serving tea, etc.

Te·bet (tā·vāth′, tā′ves) *n.* The fourth month of the Hebrew year. See (Hebrew) CALENDAR. Also **Te·beth′.**

Te·briz (tə·brēz′) See TABRIZ.

tech. **1.** Technical.   **2.** Technology.

tech·ne·ti·um (tek·nē′shē·əm) *n.* A chemical element (symbol Tc), artificially produced by the bombardment of molybdenum with neutrons or deuterons. It displaces the hypothetical element *masurium.* See ELEMENT.   [< NL < Gk. *technētos* artificial]

tech·nic (tek′nik) *n.* **1.** Often *pl.* (when *pl.* construed as *sing.* or *pl.*) Technique.   **2.** *pl.* (construed as *sing.* or *pl.*) Technology. — *adj.* Technical.   [< Gk. *technikos*]

tech·ni·cal (tek′ni·kəl) *adj.* **1.** Of or relating to some particular art, science, or trade.   **2.** Having, dealing with, or pertaining to a specialized knowledge or skill, especially to a mechanical or scientific knowledge or skill.   **3.** Of, pertaining to, or exhibiting technique.   **4.** According to or determined by law or by a legal interpretation.   **5.** Considered in terms of an accepted body of rules, regulations, or techniques: a *technical* defeat.   **6.** Designating a money market in which prices are for the most part determined by speculation or manipulation. Abbr. *tech.*   [< Gk. *technikos* < *technē* art] — **tech′ni·cal·ly** *adv.* — **tech′ni·cal·ness** *n.*

tech·ni·cal·i·ty (tek′ni·kal′ə·tē) *n.* *pl.* **·ties** **1.** The state of being technical.   **2.** The use of technical terms.   **3.** A technical point peculiar to some profession, art, trade, etc.   **4.** A petty distinction; quibble. Also **tech·nism** (tek′niz′əm).

technical knockout In boxing, a victory awarded when one fighter has been beaten so severely that the referee discontinues the fight. Abbr. *t.k.o., TKO, T.K.O.*

tech·ni·cian (tek·nish′ən) *n.* One skilled in the handling of instruments or in the performance of tasks requiring specialized training.

Tech·ni·col·or (tek′ni·kul′ər) *n.* A motion-picture process by which two or more sets of film of the same scene are photographed through different color filters and assembled in one positive film that reproduces the colors of the original scene: a trade name. Also **tech′ni·col·or.**

tech·nique (tek·nēk′) *n.* **1.** The manual or bodily skills necessary to accomplish some end or result: the *technique* of a pianist.   **2.** The manner or methods in or by which certain details are handled or problems solved: the *technique* of a novelist; a chemist's *technique.*   **3.** Any method for accomplishing something.   [< F < Gk. *technikos.* See TECHNICAL.]

techno- *combining form* **1.** Art; skill; craft: *technology.*   **2.** Technical; technological. Also, before vowels, **techn-.**   [< Gk. *technē* art, skill]

tech·noc·ra·cy (tek·nok′rə·sē) *n.* *pl.* **·cies** A theory of society and government that advocates control by an organized body of experts. — **tech′no·crat** (tek′nə·krat) *n.* — **tech′no·crat′ic** *adj.*

tech·nog·ra·phy (tek·nog′rə·fē) *n.* Description of the arts and crafts, especially with reference to the development and geographic distribution of technical processes.

technol. Technology.

tech·no·lith·ic (tek′nə·lith′ik) *adj.* *Anthropol.* Pertaining to or designating those stone implements that were deliberately fashioned for some intended purpose.

tech·no·log·i·cal (tek′nə·loj′i·kəl) *adj.* Of, pertaining to, associated with, produced or affected by technology. Also **tech′no·log′ic.** — **tech′no·log′i·cal·ly** *adv.*

technological unemployment Unemployment brought about by technical advances.

tech·nol·o·gy (tek·nol′ə·jē) *n.* *pl.* **·gies** **1.** Theoretical knowledge of industry and the industrial arts.   **2.** The application of science and of technical advances in industry, manufacturing, commerce, and the arts.   **3.** The technical language of an art, science, etc.   **4.** The means by which material things are produced, as in a particular civilization. Abbr. *tech., technol.* — **tech·nol′o·gist** *n.*

tech·y (tech′ē) See TETCHY.

tec·ton·ic (tek·ton′ik) *adj.* **1.** Of or pertaining to building or construction.   **2.** *Geol.* **a** Characteristic of or relating to the structure of the earth's crust, especially as due to deformation.   **b** Of or denoting the forces producing such struc-

tures.   [< L *tectonicus* < Gk. *tektonikos* < *tektōn* carpenter]

tec·ton·ics (tek·ton′iks) *n.pl.* (construed as *sing.*) **1.** The science or art of construction, especially of buildings and other large structures.   **2.** The geology of earth structures.

tec·tri·ces (tek·trī′sēz, tek′tri-) *n.* *pl.* of **tec·trix** (tek′triks) *Ornithol.* The wing coverts of a bird.   [< NL < L *tectus,* pp. of *tegere* to cover] — **tec·tri′cial** (-trish′əl) *adj.*

Te·cum·seh (ti·kum′sē), 1768?–1813, Shawnee Indian chief; ally of the British in the War of 1812.

ted (ted) *v.t.* **ted·ded, ted·ding** To turn over and strew about, or spread loosely for drying, as newly mown grass.   [Prob. < Scand. Cf. ON *tethja* to spread manure.]

ted·der (ted′ər) *n.* **1.** One who or that which teds.   **2.** *Agric.* A machine for spreading hay to dry.

ted·dy (ted′ē) *n.* *pl.* **·dies** A short undergarment combining chemise and drawers in one.   [Origin unknown]

ted·dy bear (ted′ē) A toy bear, usually covered with plush.   [after *Teddy,* a nickname of Theodore Roosevelt]

Teddy-boy (ted′ē·boi′) *Brit. Slang* A dissolute or delinquent youth distinguished by Edwardian dress. Also **teddy-boy.**   [< nickname of *Edward VII*]

Te De·um (tē dē′əm) **1.** An ancient Christian hymn beginning with these words.   **2.** The music to which this hymn is set.   **3.** Any thanksgiving service in which this hymn is sung.   [< L *Te Deum* (*laudamus*) (we praise) Thee, O God]

te·di·ous (tē′dē·əs) *adj.* **1.** Causing weariness; boring.   **2.** *Obs.* Moving slowly.   [< LL *taediosus* < L *taedium.* See TEDIUM.] — **te′di·ous·ly** *adv.* — **te′di·ous·ness** *n.* — **Syn. 1.** tiresome, tiring, fatiguing, wearisome, irksome, dull, dreary, monotonous, humdrum. — **Ant.** exciting, lively.

te·di·um (tē′dē·əm) *n.* The state of being tiresome or wearisome.   [< L *taedium* < *taedere* to vex, weary]

tee¹ (tē) *n.* **1.** The letter T.   **2.** Something resembling the form of the letter T. — *adj.* T-shaped.

tee² (tē) *n.* **1.** A small peg with a concave top on which a golf ball is placed in making the first play to a hole.   **2.** A designated area within which the golf tee must be placed. — *v.t.* & *v.i.* **teed, tee·ing** To place (the golf ball) on a tee before striking it. — **to tee off** To strike (the golf ball) in starting play.   [Prob. < TEE³]

tee³ (tē) *n.* In certain games, a mark toward which the balls, quoits, etc., are directed, as in curling. — **to a tee** As precisely as possible; exactly.   [? < TEE¹]

tee⁴ (tē) *n.* A finial in the form of a conventionalized umbrella, used on pagodas, etc.   [< Burmese *h'ti* umbrella]

teem¹ (tēm) *v.i.* **1.** To be full, as if at the point of producing; to be full to overflowing; abound.   **2.** *Obs.* To bear young. — *v.t.* **3.** To produce or bring forth, as offspring.   [OE *tieman* < *tēam* progeny. Akin to TEAM.] — **teem′er** *n.*

teem² (tēm) *v.i.* **1.** To come down heavily; pour: said of rain. — *v.t.* **2.** *Obs.* To empty.   [< ON *tœma* empty]

teem·ing (tē′ming) *adj.* **1.** Produced in great quantity.   **2.** Full; overflowing; prolific.

teen¹ (tēn) *n.* *Scot. & Brit. Dial.* Grief; trouble; also, provocation; vexation; anger.   [OE *tēona* injury, vexation] — **teen′ful** *adj.* — **teen′ful·ly** *adv.*

teen² (tēn) *adj.* Teen-age.

-teen *suffix* Plus ten: used in cardinal numbers from 13 to 19 inclusive: *fifteen.*   [OE *-tiene* < *tīen* ten]

teen age The age from 13 to 19 inclusive; adolescence.

teen-age (tēn′āj′) *adj.* Of, being, or characteristic of a person between the ages of 13 to 19 inclusive; adolescent: also *teen.* Also **teen′-aged′** (-ājd′).

teen-ag·er (tēn′āj′ər) *n.* One who is 13 years old or over but under 20; a person in his teens. Also **teen′ag′er.**

teens (tēnz) *n.pl.* **1.** The numbers that end in *-teen.*   **2.** The years of one's age from 13 to 19 inclusive.

tee·ny (tē′nē) *adj.* **·ni·er, ·ni·est** *Informal* Tiny. Also **teen·sy** (tēn′sē).   [Var. of TINY]

teen·y-bop·per (tē′nē·bop′ər) *n.* *Slang* A modern, hip, teen-ager, especially a girl.   [< Negro slang *teenybop, teeny-bopper* a troublesome or tough teen-ager < TEEN(-AGE) + -Y³ + *bop* to fight (Cf. BOP¹) + -ER¹]

tee·pee (tē′pē) See TEPEE.

tee shirt (tē) See T-SHIRT.

Tees (tēz) A river in northern England, flowing 70 miles east, to the North Sea.

tee·ter (tē′tər) *v.i.* **1.** To walk or move with a tottering motion.   **2.** To seesaw; waver; vacillate. — *v.t.* **3.** To cause to teeter. — *n.* **1.** An oscillating motion.   **2.** A seesaw.   [< dial. E *titter,* prob. < ON *titra* to tremble, shiver]

teeter board A seesaw.

tee·ter-tot·ter (tē′tər·tot′ər) *n.* A seesaw.

teeth (tēth) Plural of TOOTH.

teethe (tēth) *v.i.* **teethed, teeth·ing** To cut or develop teeth.

teeth·ing ring (tē′thing) A ring of hard rubber, bone, plastic, etc., for a teething baby to bite on.

tee·to·tal (tē·tōt′l) *adj.* **1.** Pertaining to total abstinence from intoxicants.   **2.** Total; entire.   [< TOTAL, with emphatic repetition of initial letter] — **tee·to′tal·ism** *n.* — **tee·to′tal·ly** *adv.*

tee·to·tal·er (tē-tōt'l-ər) *n.* One who abstains totally from alcoholic drinks. Also **tee·to'tal·ist,** *Brit.* **tee·to'tal·ler.**

tee·to·tum (tē-tō'təm) *n.* **1.** A kind of top having lettered and numbered sides, used in a gambling game. **2.** A child's toy, often four-sided, pierced by a peg and spun by the fingers. Also spelled *tetotum:* sometimes called *toddle-top.* [< *T-totum* < *T* + *L totus* all; from the fact that the side marked with a T wins the entire stake]

Tef·lon (tef'lŏn) *n.* A chemically resistant, heat-stable plastic polymer of fluorine and ethylene, having wide application in industry and electronics: a trade name.

teg (teg) *n. Chiefly Brit.* A yearling sheep. [Origin uncertain]

teg·men (teg'mən) *n. pl.* **·mi·na** (-mə-nə) **1.** A covering or coat. **2.** *Bot.* The inner covering of a seed. Also **teg'u·men** (-yə-min). [< L *tegere* to cover] — **teg'mi·nal** *adj.*

Te·gu·ci·gal·pa (tā-gōō'sē-gäl'pä) The capital of Honduras, in the south central part; pop. 253,283 (est. 1969).

teg·u·lar (teg'yə-lər) *adj.* **1.** Pertaining to or resembling tiles. **2.** Arranged like tiles. **3.** Formed of overlapping plates or scales. Also **teg'u·lat/ed.** [< L *tegula* roof tile < *tegere* to cover] — **teg'u·lar·ly** *adv.*

teg·u·ment (teg'yə-mənt) *n.* A covering or envelope; an integument. [< L *tegumentum* < *tegere* to cover] — **teg·u·men·ta·ry** (teg'yə-men'tər-ē), **teg'u·men'tal** *adj.*

te-hee (tē-hē') *v.i.* **·heed, ·hee·ing** To laugh frivolously or with derision; titter; giggle. — *interj.* An imitative exclamation. — *n.* A restrained laugh; titter. [Imit.]

Te·he·ran (tə'ə-rän', -ran'; *Persian* te·hrän') The capital of Iran, in the north central part; pop. 2,719,730 (1966). Also **Te·hran'.**

Te·huan·te·pec (tē-wän'te·pek'), **Isthmus of** An isthmus of southern Mexico (125 mi. wide) between the **Gulf of Te·huantepec,** an inlet of the Pacific, and the **Gulf of Campeche.**

Te·huel·che (te·wel'che) *n.* One of a group of tribes of South American Indians inhabiting Patagonia.

te ig·i·tur (tē ij'ə tər) The paragraph beginning the canon of the mass in Latin liturgies. [< L, thee therefore]

teind (tēnd) *n. Scot.* A tithe or tithes.

Te·jo (tā'zhŏŏ) The Portuguese name for the TAGUS.

tek·non·y·my (tek-non'ə-mē) *n. Anthropol.* The custom of renaming a parent after his or her child. [< Gk. *teknon* child + *onyma, onoma* name]

tek·tite (tek'tīt) *n. Geol.* Any of several kinds of rounded, glasslike objects found in Australia and elsewhere and believed by some to have originated in outer space. [< Gk. *tēktos* molten + -ITE¹]

tel- Var. of TELO-¹.

tel. **1.** Telegram. **2.** Telegraph; telegraphic. **3.** Telephone.

te·la (tē'lə) *n. pl.* **·lae** (-lē) *Anat.* A tissue or weblike membrane; especially, one of the thin membranes that cover the third and fourth ventricles of the brain. [< L, web]

tel·aes·the·sia (tel'əs-thē'zhə, -zhē-ə) See TELESTHESIA.

tel·a·mon (tel'ə-mon) *n. pl.* **tel·a·mo·nes** (tel'ə-mō'nēz) *Archit.* A male figure used as a pillar to support an entablature, etc. Compare ATLANTES, CARYATID. [< L *telamōn* < *tlēnai* to bear]

Tel·a·mon (tel'ə-mon) In Greek legend, the father of Ajax.

tel·an·gi·ec·ta·sia (tel-an'jē·ek·tā'zhə, -zhē·ə) *n. Pathol.* Permanent dilation of the small arteries or capillaries, producing a vascular tumor, often found in the form of birthmarks and in certain congenital disorders. Also **tel·an·gi·ec·ta·sis** (tel'an·jē·ek'tə·sis). [< Gk. *telos* end + *angeion* vessel + *ektasis* dilatation] — **tel·an·gi·ec·tat·ic** (-tat'ik) *adj.*

Tel·au·to·graph (tel-ô'tə-graf, -gräf) *n.* An electromagnetically operated device for reproducing writing or drawings at a distance: a trade name. Also **tel·au'to·graph.**

Tel A·viv (tel' ä·vēv') A city in western Israel, on the Mediterranean, including Jaffa since 1950; pop. 388,000 (1967).

tele- *combining form* **1.** Far off; at a distance: *telegraph.* **2.** Related to or transmitted by television: *telecast.* Also spelled *telo-.* Also, before vowels, **tel-** [< Gk. *tēle* far]

tel·e·cast (tel'ə-kast, -käst) *v.t. & v.i.* **·cast** or **·cast·ed, ·cast·ing** To broadcast by television. — *n.* A program broadcast by television.

telecom. Telecommunication(s).

tel·e·com·mu·ni·ca·tion (tel'ə-kə-myōō'nə-kā'shən) *n.* **1.** The art and science of communicating at a distance, especially by means of electromagnetic impulses, as in radio, radar, television, telegraphy, telephony, etc. Also **tel'e·com·mu'ni·ca'tions.** **2.** Any message so transmitted.

tel·e·du (tel'ə-dōō) *n.* A small, short-tailed East Indian mammal (genus *Mydaus*) that resembles the skunk in color and in its ability to emit a fetid odor. [< Malay]

teleg. Telegram; telegraph; telegraphic; telegraphy.

te·le·ga (tyi-lye'gə) *n. Russian* A rude four-wheeled wagon without springs, used in Russia.

tel·eg·no·sis (tel'ag-nō'sis) *n.* Knowledge of remote happenings by extrasensory means. [< TELE- + Gk. *gnōsis* knowing] — **tel'eg·nos'tic** (-nos'tik) *adj.*

Te·leg·o·nus (tə-leg'ə-nəs) In Greek legend, the son of Odysseus and Circe, who unknowingly killed his father in Ithaca and married Penelope, his father's widow.

te·leg·o·ny (tə-leg'ə-nē) *n. Biol.* The alleged influence of a previous sire on the progeny of the same mother from subsequent impregnation by other males. [< TELE- + -GONY] — **tel·e·gon·ic** (tel'ə-gon'ik), **te·leg'o·nous** *adj.*

tel·e·gram (tel'ə-gram) *n.* A message sent by telegraph. Abbr. *tel., teleg.* [< TELE- + -GRAM]

tel·e·graph (tel'ə-graf, -gräf) *n.* Any of various devices, or systems, using a code; especially, one using coded impulses transmitted by wire or radio. Abbr. *tel., teleg.* — *v.t.* **1.** To send (a message) by telegraph. **2.** To communicate with by telegraph. **3.** *Canadian Informal* To register (illegal votes) by impersonating another voter. — *v.i.* **4.** To transmit a message by telegraph. [< TELE- + -GRAPH]

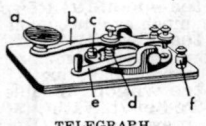

TELEGRAPH TRANSMITTER KEY
a Button. *b* Key. *c* Contact. *d* Spring. *e* Switch. *f* Binding post.

te·leg·ra·pher (tə-leg'rə-fər) *n.* One who is employed in sending telegrams or is skilled in telegraphy. Also **te·leg'ra·phist.**

tel·e·graph·ic (tel'ə-graf'ik) *adj.* Of or pertaining to the telegraph; transmitted by means of telegraphy. Also **tel'e·graph'i·cal.** Abbr. *tel., teleg.* — **tel'e·graph'i·cal·ly** *adv.*

tel·e·graph·o·scope (tel'ə-graf'ə-skōp) *n.* An instrument for receiving and reproducing a picture telegraphically. [< TELE- + GRAPHO- + -SCOPE]

telegraph pole A utility pole (which see).

te·leg·ra·phy (tə-leg'rə-fē) *n.* **1.** The process of conveying messages by telegraph. **2.** The art or science of the construction and operation of telegraphs. Abbr. *teleg.*

Tel·e·gu (tel'ə-gōō) See TELUGU.

tel·e·ki·ne·sis (tel'ə-ki-nē'sis) *n.* **1.** Movement of an inanimate body without apparent external cause. **2.** The alleged power of a spiritualist medium to bring about such movements. — **tel'e·ki·net'ic** (-net'ik) *adj.*

tel·e·lec·tric (tel'i-lek'trik) *adj.* Acting or operating at a distance by electricity. [< TEL(E)- + ELECTRIC]

Te·lem·a·chus (tə-lem'ə-kəs) In Greek legend, son of Odysseus and Penelope, who helped his father kill his mother's suitors.

tel·e·mark (tel'ə-märk) *n. Sometimes cap.* In skiing, a turn effected by shifting the weight to one advanced ski and turning its tip inward in order to change direction or stop quickly. [after *Telemark,* Norway]

tel·e·me·chan·ics (tel'ə-mə-kan'iks) *n.pl.* (construed as *sing.*) The theory and practice of operating mechanisms from a distance, as by electromagnetic and radio impulses.

te·lem·e·ter (tə-lem'ə-tər) *n.* **1.** An apparatus for determining distances by the measurement of angles. **2.** Any of various electronic devices for indicating, measuring, recording, or integrating various quantities and for transmitting the data to a distant point.

te·lem·e·try (tə-lem'ə-trē) *n.* The theory and practice of using telemeters, especially in relation to rockets, space probes, guided missiles, etc. Also **tel·e·me·ter·ing** (tel'ə-mē'tər·ing). — **tel·e·met'ric** (-met'rik) or **·ri·cal** *adj.* — **tel'e·met'ri·cal·ly** *adv.*

tel·e·mo·tor (tel'ə-mō'tər) *n.* A hydraulic or electrical device by which power is applied at a distance, especially in operating the steering gear of a vessel by turning the wheel on the bridge.

tel·en·ceph·a·lon (tel'en-sef'ə-lon) *n. Anat.* In embryology, the terminal division of the nervous system from which are developed the cerebral hemispheres and olfactory lobes: also called *endbrain.* [< TEL(E)- + ENCEPHALON] — **tel·en·ce·phal·ic** (tel'en·si·fal'ik) *adj.*

teleo- Var. of TELO-¹.

tel·e·ol·o·gy (tel'ē·ol'ə·jē, tē'lē-) *n. pl.* **·gies** **1.** The branch of cosmology that treats of final causes; finalism. **2.** *Biol.* The doctrine that the phenomena of organic life and development can be fully explained only by the action of design and purpose and not by mechanical causes. Compare VITALISM. **3.** The explanation of nature in terms of utility or purpose, especially divine purpose; the study of a creative design in the processes of nature. [< NL *teleologia* < Gk. *telos, teleos* end + *logos* discourse] — **tel'e·o·log'i·cal** (-ə·loj'i·kəl) or **tel·e·o·log'ic** *adj.* — **tel'e·o·log'i·cal·ly** *adv.* — **tel'e·ol'o·gist** *n.*

tel·e·ost (tel'ē·ost, tē'lē-) *adj.* Belonging or pertaining to a large and widely distributed group or order (*Teleostei*) of fishes having true bones. — *n.* A teleost fish. Also **tel·e·os'te·an.** [< Gk. *telos* end + *osteon* bone]

te·lep·a·thy (tə-lep'ə-thē) *n.* The supposed communication of one mind with another at a distance by other than normal sensory means. [< TELE- + -PATHY] — **tel·e·path·ic** (tel'ə·path'ik) *adj.* — **tel'e·path'i·cal·ly** *adv.* — **te·lep'a·thist** *n.*

tel·e·phone (tel'ə·fōn) *n.* A device or system for transmitting speech or sound over a wire or other communication channel. — *v.* **·phoned, ·phon·ing** — *v.t.* **1.** To communicate with by telephone. **2.** To send by telephone, as a message. — *v.i.* **3.** To communicate by telephone. Abbr. *t., tel.*

[< TELE- + -PHONE] — **tel′e·phon′er** *n.* — **tel·e·phon·ic** (tel′ə-fon′ik) *adj.* — **tel′e·phon′i·cal·ly** *adv.*

telephone pole A utility pole (which see).

te·leph·o·ny (tə-lef′ə-nē) *n.* The science of designing, constructing, and operating telephones.

tel·e·pho·to (tel′ə-fō′tō) *adj.* **1.** Designating a lens system used in connection with a camera to produce a large image of a distant object. **2.** Pertaining to telephotography.

tel·e·pho·to·graph (tel′ə-fō′tə-graf, -gräf) *n.* **1.** A picture transmitted by telephotography. **2.** A picture made with a telephoto lens. — **tel′e·pho′to·graph′ic** *adj.*

tel·e·pho·tog·ra·phy (tel′ə-fə-tog′rə-fē) *n.* **1.** The art of producing photographic images of distant objects on a larger scale than is possible with an ordinary camera. **2.** The facsimile reproduction of photographs or other pictures by radio or telegraphic communication; phototelegraphy.

tel·e·plasm (tel′ə-plaz′əm) *n.* Ectopasm (def. 2).

tel·e·print·er (tel′ə-prin′tər) *n.* A teletypewriter (which see).

Tel·e·promp·ter (tel′ə-promp′tər) *n.* A prompting device for television whereby a prepared script, unseen by the audience, is shown to a speaker or performer, enlarged line by line: a trade name. Also **tel′e·promp′er.**

Tel·e·ran (tel′ə-ran) *n. Telecom.* A system of air navigation that combines the principles of television and radar, the information being gathered by ground stations for transmission to all aircraft within range: a trade name. Also **tel′e·ran.** [< TELE(VISION) + R(ADAR) + A(IR) N(AVIGATION)]

tel·e·scope (tel′ə-skōp) *n.* An optical instrument for enlarging the image of a distant object. The **refracting telescope** consists of an object glass for collecting the light rays and a magnifying eyepiece for viewing the image. The **reflecting telescope** substitutes a concave mirror for the object glass. — *v.* **·scoped, ·scop·ing** *v.t.* **1.** To drive or slide together so that one part fits into another in the manner of the sections of a small telescope. **2.** To crush by driving something into or upon. **3.** To represent in a compressed or shortened form. — *v.i.* **4.** To crash or be forced into one another, as railroad cars. [< TELE- + -SCOPE]

telescope word *Ling.* A blend.

tel·e·scop·ic (tel′ə-skop′ik) *adj.* **1.** Pertaining to the telescope. **2.** Visible only through a telescope. **3.** Farseeing. **4.** Having sections that slide within or over one another. Also **tel′e·scop′i·cal.** — **tel′e·scop′i·cal·ly** *adv.*

Tel·e·sco·pi·um (tel′ə-skō′pē-əm) *n.* A constellation, the Telescope. See CONSTELLATION. [< L]

te·les·co·py (tə-les′kə-pē) *n.* The art of using or making telescopes. — **te·les′co·pist** *n.*

tel·e·script (tel′ə-skript) *n.* A script written or adapted for a television program. [< TELE(VISION) + SCRIPT]

tel·e·seism (tel′ə-sī′zəm, -səm) *n.* **1.** An earthquake originating at a great distance from the point of observation. **2.** The record of such an earthquake.

tel·e·sis (tel′ə-sis) *n. Sociol.* Satisfactory progress toward an intended purpose, especially as the result of skilled direction of forces and intelligent planning. [< NL < Gk. *telein* to fulfill < *telos, teleos* end]

tel·e·ster·e·o·scope (tel′ə-ster′ē-ə-skōp, -stir′-) *n.* An optical instrument that presents stereoscopic images of objects at a distance from the observer.

tel·es·the·sia (tel′is-thē′zhə, -zhē-ə) *n.* Susceptibility to stimuli coming from a distance and beyond the normal range of the senses: also spelled *telaesthesia.* [< NL < Gk. *tēle* far + *aisthēsis* feeling] — **tel′es·thet′ic** (-thet′ik) *adj.*

tel·e·stich (tel′ə-stik, tə-les′tik) *n.* An acrostic in which the significant letters are at the ends of the lines. [< Gk. *telos* end + *stichos* line]

tel·e·ther·a·py (tel′ə-ther′ə-pē) *n. Med.* X-ray treatment administered in massive doses at a distance from the body.

tel·e·ther·mom·e·ter (tel′ə-thûr-mom′ə-tər) *n.* Any apparatus used to indicate the temperature of a distant point, as a thermocouple. — **tel′e·ther·mom′e·try** *n.*

tel·e·thon (tel′ə-thon′) *n. U.S.* A telecast lasting several hours, especially one seeking funds for a charity or support for a political candidate. [< TELE- + (MARA)THON]

tel·e·tran·scrip·tion (tel′ə-tran-skrip′shən) *n.* The transcription of television programs by kinescope or video tape.

tel·e·type (tel′ə-tīp) *v.t. & v.i.* **·typed, ·typ·ing** To communicate (with) by teletypewriter or Teletype. — **tel′e·typ′er** *n.*

Tel·e·type (tel′ə-tīp) *n.* A teletypewriter: a trade name. Also **tel′e·type.**

Tel·e·type·set·ter (tel′ə-tīp′set′ər) *n.* A keyboard device for punching a tape that can then be used either directly or as the source of telegraphic signals to operate a typesetting machine: a trade name. Also **tel′e·type′set′ter.**

tel·e·type·writ·er (tel′ə-tīp′rī′tər) *n.* A telegraph system transmitting by means of a typewriter keyboard in which each key produces a coded signal that activates a specific character in a typewriterlike receiver: also called *teleprinter.*

te·leu·to·spore (tə-lōō′tə-spôr, -spōr) *n. Bot.* The one- or two-celled, usually stalked, thick-walled spore produced as the final stage in the growth of rust fungi. Also **te′li·o·spore′** (tē′lē-ə-, tel′ē-ə-) [< Gk. *teleutē* fulfillment + SPORE] — **te·leu′to·spor′ic** (-spôr′ik, -spor′ik) *adj.*

tel·e·view (tel′ə-vyōō) *v.t. & v.i.* To observe by means of television. — **tel′e·view′er** *n.*

tel·e·vise (tel′ə-vīz) *v.t. & v.i.* **·vised, ·vis·ing** To transmit or receive by television.

tel·e·vi·sion (tel′ə-vizh′ən) *n.* **1.** The transmission of continuous visual images as a series of electrical impulses or a modulated carrier wave, restored to visual form on the cathode-ray screen of a receiver, often with accompanying sound. **2.** The television broadcasting industry. **3.** A television receiving set. Also called *TV.*

tel·ex (tel′eks) *n.* **1.** A system for sending messages by teletypewriter. **2.** A teletypewriter. A message sent by telex. — *v.t.* To send (a message) by telex. [< TEL(ETYPEWRITER) + EX(CHANGE)]

tel·fer (tel′fər) See TELPHER.

tel·ford (tel′fərd) *adj.* Designating a road made of large broken stones packed with smaller pieces. — *n.* A road having such a surface. [after Thomas *Telford*, 1757–1834, Scottish engineer]

tel·ic (tel′ik, tē′lik) *adj.* Tending toward, or denoting a purpose; teleological. [< Gk. *telikos* < *telos* end]

te·li·o·stage (tē′lē-ə-stāj′, tel′ē-) *n. Bot.* The final stage in the life cycle of rust fungi. [< TELIUM + STAGE]

te·li·um (tē′lē-əm, tel′ē-) *n. Bot.* The sorus of the teliostage of rust fungi. [< NL < Gk. *telos, teleos* end] — **te′li·al** *adj.*

tell (tel) *v.* **told, tell·ing** *v.t.* **1.** To relate in detail; narrate, as a story. **2.** To make known by speech or writing; communicate. **3.** To make known; reveal; disclose: to *tell* secrets. **4.** To decide; ascertain: I cannot *tell* who is to blame. **5.** To express in words; utter: to *tell* a lie. **6.** To give a command to; bid; order: I *told* him to go home. **7.** To let know; inform. **8.** *Informal* To inform or assure emphatically: It's cold out, I *tell* you! **9.** To say (a rosary): to *tell* one's beads. — *v.i.* **10.** To give an account or description: usually with *of.* **11.** To serve as indication or evidence: with *of*: Their rags *told* of their poverty. **12.** To produce a marked effect: Every blow *told.* — **all told** Everyone or everything being counted; in all. — **to tell off 1.** To count and set apart. **2.** *Informal* To reprimand severely. — **to tell on 1.** To tire; weary. **2.** *Informal* To inform against. [OE *tellan.* Akin to TALE, TALK.] — **tell′a·ble** *adj.*

Tell (tel), **William** A legendary Swiss hero in the struggle for independence from Austria. Because he refused to salute the governor's cap, he was forced to shoot an apple off his son's head with bow and arrow.

tell·er (tel′ər) *n.* **1.** One who relates or informs. **2.** A person who receives or pays out money, as in a bank. **3.** A person appointed to collect and count ballots in a legislative body or other assembly. — **tell′er·ship** *n.*

Tel·ler (tel′ər), **Edward,** born 1908, U.S. atomic physicist born in Hungary.

tell·ing (tel′ing) *adj.* Producing a great effect; impressive; effective; striking. — **tell′ing·ly** *adv.*

tell·tale (tel′tāl′) *n.* **1.** One who improperly gives information concerning the private affairs of others; a tattler. **2.** That which conveys information, especially in an involuntary way; a token. **3.** An instrument or device, usually automatic, for giving information as to number, position, condition, etc. **4.** A pointer or piece indicating the degree of inflation of an organ bellows. **5.** A row of straps or ropes suspended above a railway track to warn of the approach of a low overhead structure. **6.** A clock to record the times of coming and going. **7.** An index showing the position of a vessel's helm. — *adj.* That is or serves as a telltale.

tel·lu·rate (tel′yə-rāt) *n. Chem.* A salt of telluric acid.

tel·lu·ri·an (te-lŏŏr′ē-ən, tel-yŏŏr′-) *adj.* Of or pertaining to the earth or its inhabitants. — *n.* An inhabitant of the earth. [< L *tellus, -uris* the earth]

tel·lu·ric (te-lŏŏr′ik, tel-yŏŏr′-) *adj.* **1.** Of or pertaining to the earth; terrestrial; earthly. **2.** *Chem.* Derived from or containing tellurium, especially in its higher valence.

telluric acid *Chem.* A weak acid, H_6TeO_6, obtained by oxidizing tellurium.

tel·lu·ride (tel′yə-rīd, -rid) *n. Chem.* A compound of tellurium with an element or an organic radical: *telluride* of lead.

tel·lu·ri·on (te-lŏŏr′ē-ən, tel-yŏŏr′-) *n. Astron.* An apparatus that demonstrates the motions of the earth on its axis and around the sun. Also **tel·lu′ri·an.**

tel·lu·rite (tel′yə-rīt) *n.* **1.** A white or yellow native tellurium dioxide, TeO_2. **2.** *Chem.* A salt of tellurous acid.

tel·lu·ri·um (te-lŏŏr′ē-əm, tel-yŏŏr′-) *n.* A rare nonmetallic element (symbol Te) resembling sulfur and selenium in chemical properties, occasionally found native as white, rhombohedral crystals, but usually combined with metals. See ELEMENT. [< NL < L *tellus, -uris* the earth]

tel·lu·rize (tel′yə-rīz) *v.t.* **·rized, ·riz·ing** To cause to combine with tellurium.

---

tel·lu·rous (tel′yər·əs, te·lŏŏr′əs, tel·yŏŏr′-) *adj. Chem.* Of, pertaining to, or derived from tellurium, especially in its lower valence: *tellurous* acid, H_2TeO_3.

Tel·lus (tel′əs) In Roman mythology, the goddess of the earth: identified with the Greek *Gaea.* Also **Tellus Mater.**

tel·ly (tel′ē) *n. pl.* **·lies** *Brit. Informal* Television; also, a television receiving set.

telo-[1] *combining form* Final; complete; perfect: *telophase:* also, before vowels, *tel-.* Also *teleo-.* [< Gk. *telos* end]

telo-[2] Var. of TELE-.

tel·o·dy·nam·ic (tel′ə·dī·nam′ik, -di-) *adj.* Of, related to, or employed in the transmission of power to a distance, specifically by cables and pulleys. [< TELO-[2] + DYNAMIC]

tel·o·phase (tel′ə·fāz) *n. Biol.* The closing phase of mitosis, when the cell divides and the daughter nuclei are formed. [< TELO-[1] + PHASE]

tel·pher (tel′fər) *n.* A light car suspended from cables and usually propelled by electricity, used for aerial transportation. — *v.t.* To transport by telpher. Also spelled *telfer.* [< TEL(E)- + Gk. *pherein* to bear] — **tel′pher·ic** *adj.* — **tel′pher·age** (-ij) *n.*

tel·son (tel′sən) *n. Zool.* The last abdominal segment of the body of an arthropod, as of a lobster, shrimp, or scorpion. For illustration see HORSESHOE CRAB, SHRIMP. [< Gk. *telson* boundary]

Tel·star (tel′stär′) The first artificial satellite for global communication, a microwave relay satellite launched from Cape Canaveral, July 10, 1962. [< TEL(E)- + STAR]

Tel·u·gu (tel′ŏŏ·gŏŏ) *n. pl.* **·gu 1.** A Dravidian language used in NW Andhra Pradesh, India, and important in literary culture. **2.** One of a Dravidian people of Telugu speech. — *adj.* Of or pertaining to the Telugu or to Telugu. Also *Telgu.*

tem·blor (tem·blôr′) *n. pl.* **·blors** or **·blo·res** (-blô′rās) *SW U.S.* An earthquake. [< Sp. < LL *tremulare* to tremble]

tem·e·rar·i·ous (tem′ə·râr′ē·əs) *adj.* Unreasonably adventurous; rash; reckless. [< L *temerarius* < *temere* rashly] — **tem′e·rar′i·ous·ly** *adv.* — **tem′e·rar′i·ous·ness** *n.*

te·mer·i·ty (tə·mer′ə·tē) *n.* Venturesome or foolish boldness; rashness. [< L *temeritas, -tatis* < *temere* rashly]
— **Syn.** *Temerity, audacity, foolhardiness, heedlessness, rashness,* and *recklessness* denote excessive boldness in speech or action. *Temerity* is the quality of one who underestimates danger, or overrates his chances for success. *Audacity* refers (in its bad sense) to going beyond the decent restraints of social behavior. *Foolhardiness* characterizes the man who rushes into peril from lack of sense, and *heedlessness,* the man who falls into danger from lack of attention. *Rashness* is habitual want of reflection before acting, and *recklessness* describes a disregard of consequences. — **Ant.** caution, wariness, timidity.

Tem·es·vár (te′mesh·vär) The Hungarian name for TIMIŞOARA.

temp. 1. In the time of (L *tempore*). **2.** Temperature. **3.** Temporary.

Tem·pe (tem′pē), **Vale of** A valley between Mount Olympus and Mount Ossa in Thessaly, Greece, famous for its beauty and in ancient times regarded as sacred to Apollo. Greek **Tem·be** (tem′bē).

tem·per (tem′pər) *n.* **1.** Heat of mind or passion; disposition to become angry. **2.** Frame of mind; mood: to be in a bad *temper.* **3.** Composure of mind; equanimity; self-command; calmness: to lose one's *temper.* **4.** *Metall.* The condition of a metal as regards hardness and elasticity, especially when due to heating and sudden cooling. **5.** Something mixed with a substance to alter its properties or qualities. **6.** *Obs.* In medieval physiology, constitutional condition, resulting from the proportion in which the four humors were mixed. **7.** *Archaic* A middle course. — *v.t.* **1.** To bring to a state of moderation or suitability, as by addition of another quality; moderate: to *temper* justice with mercy. **2.** To bring to the proper consistency, texture, etc., by moistening and working: to *temper* clay. **3.** *Metall.* To bring (metal) to a required hardness and elasticity by heating and suddenly cooling. **4.** *Music* To adjust the tones of (an instrument) by temperament; tune. **5.** *Obs.* To adjust. — *v.i.* **6.** To be or become tempered. [Fusion of OE *temprian* to mingle, regulate and OF *temprer, tremper* to soak, temper (steel), both < L *temperare* to combine in due proportion] — **tem′per·a·bil′i·ty** *n.* — **tem′per·a·ble** *adj.* — **tem′per·er** *n.*
— **Syn.** (noun) **2.** temperament, mood, humor. — (verb) moderate, modify, qualify.

tem·per·a (tem′pər·ə, *Ital.* tem′pä·rä) *n.* **1.** A painting medium consisting of an emulsion prepared from a mixture of water and any of various substances, as egg yolks, glue, gum, casein solutions, etc.; also, a method of painting with such a medium. **2.** Paint prepared by adding pigment to the medium of tempera. Also called *distemper.* [< Ital. *temperare* to temper < L]

tem·per·a·ment (tem′pər·ə·mənt, -prə-) *n.* **1.** The characteristic physical and mental peculiarities of an individual as manifested in his reactions. **2.** An intense, moody, and often rebellious nature. **3.** Mental constitution; make-up; disposition. **4.** *Music* The tuning of an instrument or scale so that each semitone is a twelfth of an octave. Also **equal**

temperament. 5. *Archaic* Adjustment or compromise. **6.** *Obs.* Temperature. [< L *temperamentum* proper mixture < *temperare* to mix in due proportions]

tem·per·a·men·tal (tem′pər·ə·men′təl, -prə-) *adj.* **1.** Of or pertaining to temperament. **2.** Having a strongly marked temperament. **3.** Sensitive; easily excited; changeable. — **tem′per·a·men′tal·ly** *adv.*

tem·per·ance (tem′pər·əns) *n.* **1.** The state or quality of being temperate; habitual moderation. **2.** The principle or practice of total abstinence from intoxicants. **3.** *Obs.* Calmness; self-control. — **Syn.** See ABSTINENCE. [< OF < L *temperantia,* orig. neut. pl. of *temperans, -antis,* ppr. of *temperare* to mix in due proportions]

tem·per·ate (tem′pər·it) *adj.* **1.** Observing moderation in the indulgence of an appetite, especially in the use of intoxicating liquors. **2.** Moderate as regards temperature; free from extremes of heat or cold; mild. **3.** Characterized by moderation or the absence of extremes; not excessive. **4.** Calm; restrained; self-controlled. **5.** *Music* Tempered: said of an interval or scale. [< L *temperatus,* pp. of *temperare* to mix in due proportions] — **tem′per·ate·ly** *adv.* — **tem′per·ate·ness** *n.*

Temperate Zone See under ZONE.

tem·per·a·ture (tem′pər·ə·chər, -prə-) *n.* **1.** Condition as regards heat or cold. **2.** The degree of heat in a body or substance, as measured on the graduated scale of a thermometer. Abbr. *t., temp.* **3.** The degree of heat of an animal, especially the human body; also, excess of this above the normal (which for the human body is 98.6° F, or about 37° C). **4.** *Obs.* Constitution; temperament; mixture; temperateness; temperance. [< L *temperatura* due measure < *temperatus.* See TEMPERATE.]

temperature coefficient *Physics* The amount of change in some specified physical quantity per unit change in temperature.

temperature gradient *Meteorol.* The rate of change in temperature with change in altitude.

tem·per·a·ture-hu·mid·i·ty index (tem′pər·ə·chər·hyŏŏ·mid′ə·tē, -prə-) The degree of physical discomfort as a function of atmospheric temperature and humidity, usually measured on a scale between 70 and 80, the higher number indicating the greater percentage of people experiencing discomfort: formerly called *discomfort index.* Abbr. *T.H.I., T.-H.I.*

tem·pered (tem′pərd) *adj.* **1.** Having temper or a specified disposition: used mainly in compounds: quick-*tempered;* ill-*tempered.* **2.** *Music* Adjusted in pitch so as to produce or conform to temperament. **3.** Moderated by admixture. **4.** Having the right degree of hardness and elasticity: well-*tempered* steel.

temper pin *Chiefly Scot.* **1.** A wooden screw used to regulate a spinning wheel. **2.** A tuning peg of a violin.

tem·pest (tem′pist) *n.* **1.** An extensive and violent wind, usually attended with rain, snow, or hail. **2.** A violent commotion or agitation; a fierce tumult. — **tempest in a teapot** A considerable uproar over a trivial matter. — *v.t.* To agitate violently; affect as a tempest does. [< OF *tempeste* < L *tempestas* space of time, weather < *tempus* time]

tem·pes·tu·ous (tem·pes′chŏŏ·əs) *adj.* Stormy; turbulent; violent. [< OF *tempestueux* < LL *tempestuosus* < L *tempestas* weather. See TEMPEST.] — **tem·pes′tu·ous·ly** *adv.* — **tem·pes′tu·ous·ness** *n.*

tem·plar (tem′plər) *n. Brit.* A law student or barrister who has apartments in the buildings known as the Inner and the Middle Temple in London. [< OF *templier* < Med.L *templarius* < L *templum.* See TEMPLE.]

Tem·plar (tem′plər) *n.* A Knight Templar (which see).

tem·plate (tem′plit) *n.* **1.** A pattern or gauge, as of wood or metal, used as a guide in shaping something accurately, as in woodworking. **2.** In building, a stout stone or timber for distributing weight or thrust. **3.** A wedge for a building block under a ship's keel. Also **tem·plet** (tem′plit). [< F *templette* stretcher, dim. of *temple* small timber < L *templum*]

tem·ple[1] (tem′pəl) *n.* **1.** A stately edifice consecrated to the worship of one or more deities. **2.** In the United States, a Reform synagogue. **3.** In France, a Protestant church. **4.** Any place considered as occupied by God; especially, a sanctified human body. **5.** A Mormon church. — **the Temple 1.**

TEMPLE OF HORUS, EDFU

Either of two medieval establishments in London and Paris, once occupied by the Knights Templar, in London, since 1185, the district lying between Fleet Street and the Thames river, the site of the **Inner** and **Middle Temple.** See INNS OF COURT. **2.** Any of three successive sacred edifices built in Jerusalem for the worship of Jehovah. [OE *tempel* or OF *temple,* both < L *templum* temple]

tem·ple[2] (tem′pəl) *n.* The region on each side of the head above the cheek bone. [OF, ult. < L *tempus* temple]

tem·ple[3] (tem′pəl) *n.* An attachment to a loom that serves to keep the last woven part of the fabric stretched. [< F < L *templum* small timber]

Tem·ple (tem′pəl) A city in central Texas; pop. 33,431.

Tem·ple (tem′pəl), **Sir William,** 1628–99, English statesman, diplomat, and writer. — **William,** 1881–1944, English prelate, archbishop of Canterbury 1942–44.

Temple Bar A historic gateway in London marking the western boundary of the city proper and on which the heads of traitors and other malefactors were exposed.

Temple City An unincorporated place in SW California, near Los Angeles; pop. 29,673.

tem·pled (tem′pəld) *adj.* 1. Honored with or enshrined in a temple: a *templed* god. 2. Having many temples.

tem·po (tem′pō) *n. pl.* **·pos** or **·pi** (-pē) 1. *Music* Relative speed at which a composition is rendered. 2. Characteristic manner or style; rate of speed or activity in general. Abbr. *t.* [< Ital. < L *tempus* time]

tem·po·ral[1] (tem′pər·əl) *adj.* 1. Pertaining to affairs of the present life; earthly. 2. Pertaining or related to time. 3. Temporary; transitory. 4. Pertaining to civil law or authority; lay; secular. 5. *Gram.* Expressing or denoting time: *temporal* conjunctions. [< L *temporalis* < *tempus, temporis* time] — **tem′po·ral·ly** *adv.* — **tem′po·ral·ness** *n.*

tem·po·ral[2] (tem′pər·əl) *adj. Anat.* Of, pertaining to, or situated at the temple or temples: the *temporal* bone. [< L *temporalis* < *tempora.* See TEMPLE[2].]

temporal bone *Anat.* A compound bone situated at either side of the head in man and most other vertebrates, and containing the organ of hearing. For illustration see SKULL.

tem·po·ral·i·ty (tem′pə·ral′ə·tē) *n. pl.* **·ties** 1. *Usually pl.* A temporal or material matter, interest, revenue, etc.; especially, an ecclesiastical possession or revenue. 2. The state of being temporal or temporary.

tem·po·ra mu·tan·tur (tem′pər·ə myoo·tan′tər) *Latin* The times are changed.

tem·po·ra·ry (tem′pə·rer′ē) *adj.* 1. Lasting or intended to be used for a short time only; transitory. 2. *Obs.* Contemporary. Abbr. *temp.* — **Syn.** see TRANSIENT. [< L *temporarius* < *tempus, temporis* time] — **tem·po·rar·i·ly** (tem′pə·rer′ə·lē, tem′pə·rer′-) *adv.* — **tem′po·rar′i·ness** *n.*

tem·po·rize (tem′pə·rīz) *v.i.* **·rized, ·riz·ing** 1. To act evasively so as to gain time or put off decision or commitment. 2. To give real or apparent compliance to the circumstances; comply. 3. To parley so as to gain time: with *with.* 4. To effect a compromise; negotiate: with *with* or *between.* Also *Brit.* **tem′po·rise.** [< F *temporiser* < L *tempus, temporis* time] — **tem′po·ri·za′tion** *n.* — **tem′po·riz′er** *n.* — **tem′po·riz′ing·ly** *adv.*

tempt (tempt) *v.t.* 1. To attempt to persuade (a person) to do something evil or unwise, as by promising pleasure or gain. 2. To be attractive to; invite: Your offers do not *tempt* me. 3. To provoke or risk provoking: It is unwise to *tempt* fate. 4. *Obs.* To test; prove. [< OF *tempter, tenter* < L *temptare, tentare* to test, try, prob. intens. of *tendere* to stretch] — **tempt′a·ble** *adj.* — **tempt′er** *n.* — **tempt′ress** *n. fem.*

temp·ta·tion (temp·tā′shən) *n.* 1. The act of tempting, or the state of being tempted. 2. That which tempts.

tempt·ing (temp′ting) *adj.* Alluring; attractive; seductive. — **tempt′ing·ly** *adv.* — **tempt′ing·ness** *n.*

tem·pu·ra (tem′poo·rə, tem·poor′ə) *n.* A Japanese dish consisting of shrimp or other seafood and vegetables dipped in egg batter and deep-fried. [< Japanese, fried food]

tem·pus fu·git (tem′pəs fyoo′jit) *Latin* Time flies.

ten (ten) *n.* 1. The sum of nine and one: a cardinal number. 2. Any symbol of this number, as 10, x, X. 3. Anything consisting of or representing ten units, as a playing card, bill, etc. — *adj.* Being one more than nine. [OE *tīen*]

ten- Var. of TENO-.

ten. *Music* 1. Tenor. 2. Tenuto.

ten·a·ble (ten′ə·bəl) *adj.* Capable of being held, maintained, or defended. [< F < *tenir* to hold < L *tenere*] — **ten′a·bil′i·ty, ten′a·ble·ness** *n.* — **ten′a·bly** *adv.*

ten·ace (ten′ās) *n.* In bridge, whist, etc., two relatively high cards of the same suit held by one player, as ace and queen or king and jack. [< Sp. *tenaza* pincers, tongs < *tenaz* tenacious < L *tenax, tenacis.* See TENACIOUS.]

te·na·cious (ti·nā′shəs) *adj.* 1. Having great cohesiveness of parts; tough. 2. Adhesive; sticky. 3. Holding or tending to hold strongly, as opinions, rights, etc. 4. Stubborn; obstinate. 5. Apt to retain; strongly retentive, as memory. [< L *tenax, tenacis* holding fast < *tenere* to hold, grasp, embrace] — **te·na′cious·ly** *adv.* — **te·na′cious·ness** *n.*

te·nac·i·ty (ti·nas′ə·tē) *n.* The state or quality of being tenacious.

te·nac·u·lum (ti·nak′yə·ləm) *n. pl.* **·la** (-lə) *Surg.* A hooked instrument for seizing and holding parts as arteries, during surgical operations or dissections. [< LL, holder < L *tenax, tenacis.* See TENACIOUS.]

te·naille (te·nāl′) *n.* A low outwork, usually with one or two reentering angles, in the main ditch between two bastions. Also **te·nail′.** [< F < LL *tenacula,* pl. of *tenaculum.* See TENACULUM].

ten·an·cy (ten′ən·sē) *n. pl.* **·cies** 1. The holding of lands or tenements by any form of title; occupancy. 2. The period of holding or occupying lands, tenements, or office. 3. A habitation or dwelling place held of another.

ten·ant (ten′ənt) *n.* 1. One who holds or possesses lands or property by any kind of title; especially, one who holds under another; a lessee. 2. A defendant in an action concerning real property. 3. A dweller in any place; an occupant. — *v.t.* 1. To hold as tenant; occupy. — *v.i.* 2. To be a tenant. [< F, orig. ppr. of *tenir* to hold < L *tenere*] — **ten′ant·a·ble** *adj.* — **ten′ant·less** *adj.* — **ten′ant·ship** *n.*

tenant farmer One who farms land owned by another and pays rent, usually in a share of the crops.

ten·ant·ry (ten′ən·trē) *n. pl.* **·ries** 1. Tenants collectively. 2. The state of being a tenant; tenancy.

ten-cent store (ten′sent′) A five-and-ten-cent store (which see).

tench (tench) *n.* A European fresh-water cyprinoid fish (*Tinca tinca*), having small, deeply embedded scales. [< F *tenche* < LL *tinca* tench]

Ten Commandments The set of injunctions given by God to Moses on Mount Sinai, constituting the moral code that forms the basis of the Mosaic Law: also called *Decalogue. Ex.* xx 1–17.

tend[1] (tend) *v.i.* 1. To have an aptitude, tendency, or disposition; incline: He *tends* to talk too much. 2. To have influence toward a specified result; lead or conduce: Education *tends* to refinement. 3. To go in a certain direction. [< OF *tendre* < L *tendere* to extend, tend]

tend[2] (tend) *v.t.* 1. To attend to the needs or requirements of; take care of; minister to: to *tend* a fire. 2. To watch over; look after: to *tend* children. 3. *Naut.* To watch (a rope, etc.) of a vessel at anchor to prevent fouling. — *v.i.* 4. To be in attendance; serve or wait: with *on* or *upon.* 5. *Informal* To give attention or care: with *to.* [Aphetic var. of ATTEND]

ten·dance (ten′dəns) *n.* 1. The act of tending; attendance; service. 2. *Archaic* Attendants collectively. Also **ten′dence.**

ten·den·cy (ten′dən·sē) *n. pl.* **·cies** 1. The state of being directed toward some purpose, end, or result; inclination; bent; aptitude. 2. That which tends to produce some specified effect. 3. Bias; propensity. 4. Trend of a speech; purpose of a story. [< Med.L *tendentia,* orig. neut. pl. of *tendens, -entis,* ppr. of *tendere* to extend, tend]

ten·den·tious (ten·den′shəs) *adj.* Having a purposed aim or intentional tendency. Also **ten·den′cious.** [< G *tendenziös* < *tendenz* tendency < Med.L *tendentia.* See TENDENCY.] — **ten·den′tious·ly** *adv.* — **ten·den′tious·ness** *n.*

ten·der[1] (ten′dər) *adj.* 1. Yielding easily to force that tends to crush, bruise, break, or injure; soft or delicate. 2. Easily chewed or cut: said of food, especially meat. 3. Delicate or weak; not strong, rough, or hardy. 4. Youthful and delicate; not strengthened by maturity: a *tender* age. 5. Characterized by or expressive of a delicate sensibility; kind; affectionate; gentle: a *tender* father. 6. Capable of arousing sensitive feelings; touching: *tender* memories. 7. Susceptible to spiritual or moral feelings: a *tender* conscience. 8. Painful if touched; easily pained: a *tender* sore. 9. Of delicate effect or quality; soft: a *tender* light. 10. Requiring deft or delicate treatment; ticklish; touchy: a *tender* subject. 11. *Naut.* Careening too easily under sail: said of a ship. — *v.t.* To make tender; soften. [< OF *tendre* < L *tener, teneris*] — **ten′der·ly** *adv.* — **ten′der·ness** *n.*

ten·der[2] (ten′dər) *v.t.* 1. To present for acceptance, as a resignation; offer. 2. *Law* To proffer, as money, in payment, in discharge of a debt, or in fulfillment of a contract. — *n.* 1. The act of tendering; an offer. 2. *Law* A formal offer of satisfaction. 3. That which is offered as payment, especially money: legal tender. [< F *tendre* < L *tendere* to extend, tend] — **ten′der·er** *n.*

tend·er[3] (ten′dər) *n.* 1. *Naut.* **a** A vessel used to bring supplies, passengers, and crew back and forth between a larger vessel and a nearby shore. **b** A vessel that services another at sea. **c** A boat used to carry provisions, etc., to whalers and lighthouses. 2. A vehicle attached to the rear of a steam locomotive to carry fuel and water for it. 3. One who tends or ministers to. [< TEND[2]]

ten·der·foot (ten′dər·foot′) *n. pl.* **·foots** or **·feet** (-fēt′) *U.S.* 1. In the West, one not yet inured to the hardships of the plains, the mining camp, etc.; a greenhorn. 2. Any inexperienced person. 3. A boy scout in the beginning class or group.

ten·der·heart·ed (ten′dər·här′tid) *adj.* Having deep and quick sensibility, as to love, pity, etc.; compassionate. — **ten′der·heart′ed·ly** *adv.* — **ten′der·heart′ed·ness** *n.*

ten·der·ize (ten′də·rīz) *v.t.* **·ized, ·iz·ing** To make tender, as meat.

ten·der·iz·er (ten′də·rī′zər) A substance, as papain, for softening meat in order to make it more palatable.

ten·der·loin (ten′dər·loin′) *n.* The tender part of the loin of beef, pork, etc., lying close to the ventral side of the lumbar vertebrae. — **the tenderloin district 1.** A former district of New York City from 23rd to 42nd streets west of Broadway, where vice flourished and police corruption was common. **2.** Any urban district noted for its night life, incidence of crime, and police leniency.

ten·di·nous (ten′də-nəs) *adj.* **1.** Of, pertaining to, resembling, or formed by a tendon. **2.** Having or full of tendons; sinewy. [< F *tendineux* < Med.L *tendo, -inis.* See TENDON.]

ten·don (ten′dən) *n. Anat.* One of the bands of tough, fibrous connective tissue forming the termination of a muscle and serving to transmit its force to some other part; a sinew. [< Med.L *tendo, -inis* < Gk. *tenōn* sinew < *teinein* to stretch]

tendon of Achilles *Anat.* Achilles' tendon (which see).

ten·dril (ten′dril) *n. Bot.* One of the slender, filamentous organs that serve a climbing plant as a means of attachment to a wall, tree trunk, or other supporting surface. [< F *tendrillon,* dim. of *tendron* sprout < *tendre* tender; infl. in meaning by F *tendre* to stretch] — **ten′dril·lar, ten′dril·ous** *adj.*

ten·e·brae (ten′ə-brē) *n.pl. Usually cap.* In the Roman Catholic Church, the matins and lauds sung on the afternoons or evenings of Thursday, Friday, and Saturday of Holy Week. [< L, darkness]

ten·e·bric (ten′ə-brif′ik) *adj.* Making dark or gloomy. [< L *tenebrae* darkness + -FIC]

ten·e·brous (ten′ə-brəs) *adj.* Gloomy; dark. [< L *tenebrosus* < *tenebrae* darkness] — **ten′e·bros′i·ty** (-bros′ə-tē) *n.*

Ten·e·dos (ten′ə-dos, ten′ə-dōs) An island of Turkey in the Aegean near the western end of the Dardanelles; 15 sq. mi.: Turkish *Bozcaada.*

ten·e·ment (ten′ə-mənt) *n.* **1.** An urban apartment building or rooming house that is poorly constructed or maintained, typically overcrowded and often part of a slum: also **tenement house. 2.** A room or set of rooms designed for one family. **3.** *Law* Anything of a permanent nature that may be held as property by one person or another, as land, houses, offices, rents, franchises, etc. **4.** A house or building; especially, a dwelling house rented or intended for rent. **5.** Any dwelling place; abode. [< OF < LL *tenementum* tenure < L *tenere* to hold] — **ten′e·men′tal** (-men′təl), **ten′e·men′ta·ry** (-men′tə·rē) *adj.*

Ten·er·ife (ten′ə-rif′, -rēf′; *Sp.* tā′nä-rē′fā) The largest of the Canary Islands; 795 sq. mi.; containing the **Peak of Tenerife** (also *Teyde*), a dormant volcano and the highest peak of Spain; 12,200 ft. Also **Ten′er·iffe′.**

te·nes·mus (ti-nes′məs, -nez′-) *n. Pathol.* A painful and ineffectual effort to evacuate the bladder or the bowels. [< NL < L *tenesmos* a straining < Gk. *teinesmos* < *teinein* to stretch] — **te·nes′mic** *adj.*

ten·et (ten′it, tē′nit) *n.* An opinion, principle, dogma, etc., that a person or organization believes or maintains as true. — **Syn.** See DOCTRINE. [< L, he holds < *tenere* to hold]

ten·fold (ten′fōld′) *n.* An amount or number ten times as great as a given unit. — *adv.* So as to be ten times as many or as great. — *adj.* **1.** Consisting of ten parts. **2.** Ten times as many or as great.

ten-gal·lon hat (ten′gal′ən) *U.S.* A wide-brimmed felt hat with a tall crown, traditionally worn by cowboys.

Ten·gri Khan (teng′grē khän′) The second highest peak of the Tien Shan, in the NE Kirghiz S.S.R.; 23,949 ft. Also **Khan Tengri.**

te·ni·a (tē′nē-ə) See TAENIA.

te·ni·a·cide (tē′nē-ə-sīd′) *n.* A substance that destroys tapeworms: also spelled *taeniacide.* [< L *taenia* < Gk. *tainia* tapeworm + -CIDE] — **te′ni·a·ci′dal** *adj.*

te·ni·a·fuge (tē′nē-ə-fyōōj′) *n.* A substance that causes tapeworms to be expelled from the body.

te·ni·a·sis (ti·nī′ə-sis) *n. Pathol.* Any diseased or toxemic condition due to the presence of tapeworms in the body: also spelled *taeniasis.* [< Gk. *tainia* tapeworm + -IASIS]

Ten·iers (ten′yərz, *Flemish* te-nirs′), **David,** 1582–1649, *the Elder,* and his son, **David,** 1610–90, *the Younger,* Flemish painters.

Tenn. Tennessee.

Ten·nes·se·an (ten′ə-sē′ən) *n.* A native or inhabitant of Tennessee. — *adj.* Of or pertaining to Tennessee.

Ten·nes·see (ten′ə-sē′) A State in the SE United States; 42,246 sq. mi.; pop. 3,924,164; capital, Nashville; entered the Union June 1, 1796; nicknamed the *Volunteer State.*

Tennessee River A river rising in eastern Tennessee and flowing 652 miles through Alabama, Tennessee, and Kentucky to the Ohio River.

Tennessee Valley Authority A Federal corporation established in 1933 by the U.S. government to take custody of the Wilson Dam and associated plants at Muscle Shoals in Tennessee, developing and operating them in the national interest, with special reference to electric power, irrigation, fertilizers, and flood control. Abbr. *TVA, T.V.A.*

Ten·niel (ten′yəl), **Sir John,** 1820–1914, English illustrator and cartoonist.

ten·nis (ten′is) *n.* A game played by striking a ball back and forth with rackets over a net stretched between two equal areas that together constitute a court. It has two forms, **court tennis,** played indoors in a specially prepared

building, and **lawn tennis,** played out-of-doors on a court of grass, clay, concrete, etc. [< AF *tenetz* take, receive, imperative of *tenir* to hold; from the call of the server]

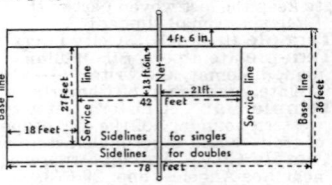

TENNIS COURT

Ten·ny·son (ten′ə-sən), **Alfred,** 1809–92, first Baron Tennyson, English poet; poet laureate 1850–92: called **Alfred, Lord Tennyson.**

Ten·ny·so·ni·an (ten′ə-sō′nē-ən) *adj.* Relating to or characteristic of Alfred Tennyson, or his verse or style.

teno- *combining form Med.* Tendon; related to a tendon, or to tendons: *tenotomy:* also, before vowels, **ten-.** Also **tenonto-.** [< Gk. *tenōn* tendon]

Te·noch·ti·tlán (tā·nôkh′tē-tlän′) The capital of the ancient Aztec Empire, on the site of Mexico City.

ten·on (ten′ən) *n.* A projection on the end of a timber, etc., for inserting in a socket to form a joint. For illustration see MORTISE. — *v.t.* **1.** To form a tenon on. **2.** To join by a mortise and tenon. [< F < *tenir* to hold]

ten·o·ni·tis (ten′ə-nī′tis) *n. Pathol.* Inflammation of a tendon. [< NL < Gk. *tenōn* tendon]

ten·or (ten′ər) *n.* **1.** The adult male voice intermediate in range between baritone and countertenor; also, a singer having such a voice, or a part to be sung by it. **2.** *Music* An instrument playing the part intermediate between the bass and the alto; especially, the viola. **3.** Course of thought; general purport. **4.** A settled course or manner of progress. **5.** *Law* The purport or substance and effect of a document; an exact transcript, as of a record. **6.** General character and tendency; nature. **7.** In bell ringing, the lowest bell, irrespective of peal. — *adj.* **1.** Of or pertaining to a tenor. **2.** Having a relation to other instruments as the tenor bears to other musical parts: a *tenor* trombone. Abbr. (for *n.* defs. 1, 2, 7, and for *adj.*) *t., ten.* [< OF *tenour* < L *tenor* course < *tenere* to hold; in def. 1, so called because this voice originally sang or "held" the melody]

tenor clef See under CLEF.

ten·or·ite (ten′ə-rīt) *n.* Native oxide of copper, occurring in minute black scales. [after Prof. G. *Tenore,* president (1841) of Naples Academy]

te·nor·rha·phy (ti-nôr′ə-fē, -nor′-) *n. pl.* **·phies** *Surg.* Suture of the ends of a divided tendon. [< TENO- + -RRHAPHY]

te·not·o·my (ti-not′ə-mē) *n. pl.* **·mies** *Surg.* The operation of cutting a tendon. [< TENO- + -TOMY]

ten·pen·ny (ten′pen′ē, -pə-nē) *adj.* **1.** Valued at tenpence. **2.** Designating the size of nails three inches long. See PENNY.

ten·pin (ten′pin′) *n.* One of the pins used in tenpins.

ten·pins (ten′pinz′) *n.pl.* (construed as sing.) A game played in a bowling alley in which the players attempt to bowl down ten pins set up at the far end of the alley.

ten·rec (ten′rek) *n.* One of several insectivorous mammals of Madagascar (family *Tenrecidae*); especially, the spiny-coated **tailless tenrec** (*Tenrec ecaudatus*): also called *tanrec.* [< F < Malagasy *trándraka*]

tense¹ (tens) *adj.* **tens·er, tens·est 1.** Stretched tight; taut. **2.** Under mental or nervous strain; strained. **3.** *Phonet.* Produced with the tongue and its muscles taut, as (ē) and (ōō); narrow: opposed to *lax.* — *v.t. & v.i.* **tensed, tens·ing** To make or become strained or drawn tight. [< L *tensus,* pp. of *tendere* to stretch] — **tense′ly** *adv.* — **tense′ness** *n.*

tense² (tens) *n.* A form of a verb that relates it to time viewed either as finite past, present, or future, or as nonfinite. Abbr. *t.* — **sequence of tenses** In inflected languages, the customary choice of tense for a verb that follows another in a sentence, particularly in reported or indirect discourse. ◆ Some grammarians and structural linguists prefer to use the word "tense" only when the temporal distinction is signaled by inflectional contrast. If one accepts this restriction, English has only two tenses, the present and the past. [< OF *tens* < L *tempus* time, tense]

ten·si·ble (ten′sə-bəl) *adj.* Capable of being extended or made tense; tensile.

ten·sile (ten′sil, *Brit.* ten′sīl) *adj.* **1.** Of or pertaining to tension. **2.** Capable of being drawn out or extended. **3.** Producing tones from stretched strings: said of instruments. [< NL *tensilis* < L *tensus.* See TENSE¹.] — **ten·sil·i·ty** (ten-sil′ə-tē) *n.*

tensile strength *Physics* The resistance of a material to forces of rupture and stress in the direction of length: usually expressed in pounds per square inch.

ten·sim·e·ter (ten-sim′ə-tər) *n.* An instrument for measuring vapor pressure. [< TENSION + -METER]

ten·si·om·e·ter (ten′sē-om′ə-tər) *n.* A device for determining tensile strength. [See TENSIMETER.]

ten·sion (ten′shən) *n.* **1.** The act of stretching or the condition of being stretched tight. **2.** Mental strain; intense nervous anxiety. **3.** Any strained relation, as between governments. **4.** *Physics* **a** Stress on a material caused by a force pulling or stretching in one direction. **b** The condition of a body when acted on by such a force. **5.** A regulating device, as that on a sewing machine to regulate the tightness of the thread. **6.** *Electr.* Electromotive force; also, electric potential. — **Syn.** See STRESS. [< L *tensio, -onis* < *tensus.* See TENSE¹.] — **ten′sion·al** *adj.*

ten·si·ty (ten′sə·tē) *n.* The state of being tense; tension.

ten·sive (ten′siv) *adj.* **1.** Caused by or causing tension. **2.** Causing a sensation of stiffness or contraction.

ten·sor (ten′sər, -sôr) *n.* **1.** *Anat.* A muscle that stretches a part. **2.** *Math.* A vector quantity that may be fully described only with reference to more than three components. [< NL < L *tensus.* See TENSE¹.]

ten-strike (ten′strīk′) *n.* **1.** In bowling, a strike (def. 3). **2.** *U.S. Informal* A totally successful stroke or act.

tent¹ (tent) *n.* A shelter of canvas or the like, supported by poles and fastened by cords to pegs driven into the ground. — *v.t.* To cover with or as with a tent. — *v.i.* To pitch a tent; camp out. [< F *tente* < LL *tenta,* orig. neut. pl. of *tentus,* pp. of *tendere* to stretch. Cf. L *tentorium* awning.]

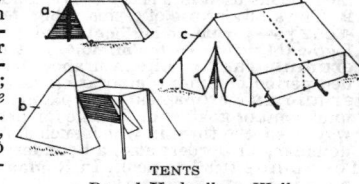

TENTS
a Pup. *b* Umbrella. *c* Wall.

tent² (tent) *Surg. n.* A small roll, as of lint, placed in a wound or orifice to prevent its closing. — *v.t.* To keep open with a tent; also, to probe. [< F *tente* < *tenter* to test, probe < L *tentare*]

tent³ (tent) *Scot. v.t.* **1.** To pay attention to; observe. **2.** To hinder; prevent. **3.** To attend upon; look after. — *n.* **1.** Attention; note; heed. **2.** An open-air wooden pulpit.

tent⁴ (tent) *n.* A deep red wine obtained chiefly from Spain. [< Sp. *tinto* deep colored < L *tinctus* dyed. See TINT.]

ten·ta·cle (ten′tə·kəl) *n.* **1.** *Zool.* A protruding flexible process or appendage of invertebrate animals, functioning as an organ of touch, prehension, or motion, as the fleshy processes about the mouth of a polyp or the arms of a cuttle-fish. **2.** *Bot.* A sensitive glandular hair, as on the leaves of the sundew. **3.** Something resembling a tentacle; a tendril. Also **ten·tac·u·lum** (ten·tak′yə·ləm). [< L *tentaculum* < *tentare* to touch, try] — **ten·tac′u·lar** *adj.*

tent·age (ten′tij) *n.* **1.** The supply of tents available for any purpose. **2.** Tents collectively.

ten·ta·tion (ten·tā′shən) *n.* The act or process of adjusting by experimentation until a desired effect is secured. [< F < L *tentatio, -onis* < *tentare* to try. See TEMPT.]

ten·ta·tive (ten′tə·tiv) *adj.* **1.** Provisional or conjectural; experimental and subject to change. **2.** Used in making a trial. [< Med.L *tentativus* < *tentatus,* pp. of *tentare* to try, probe] — **ten′ta·tive·ly** *adv.* — **ten′ta·tive·ness** *n.*

tent caterpillar Any of the gregarious larvae of several North American moths (family *Lasiocampidae*) that spin silken webs to shelter the colony in which they live.

tent·ed (ten′tid) *adj.* **1.** Overspread, covered with, or sheltered by tents: the *tented* field. **2.** Resembling a tent.

ten·ter¹ (ten′tər) *n.* **1.** A frame or machine for stretching cloth to prevent shrinkage while drying. **2.** *Obs.* A tenter-hook. — *v.t.* **1.** To stretch on or as on a tenter. — *v.i.* **2.** To be or admit of being so stretched. [< L *tentus* extended. See TENT¹.]

ten·ter² (ten′tər) *n. Brit.* One who is charged with tending something; especially, one who attends to machinery in a factory. [< TENT³]

ten·ter·hook (ten′tər·hŏŏk′) *n.* A sharp hook for holding cloth while being stretched on a tenter. — **to be on tenterhooks** To be in a state of anxiety or suspense.

tenth (tenth) *adj.* **1.** Next after the ninth: the ordinal of *ten.* **2.** Being one of ten equal parts. — *n.* **1.** One of ten equal parts. **2.** That which follows the ninth. [ME *tenthe* < OE *tēotha*] — **tenth′ly** *adv.*

ten·tie (ten′tē) *adj. Scot.* Attentive; cautious. Also **ten′ty.**

tent stitch Petit point.

ten·u·is (ten′yŏŏ·is) *n.* *pl.* **·u·es** (·yŏŏ·ēz) A voiceless stop, as *k, t, p.* [< L, thin, trans. of Gk. *psilos* bare, unaspirated]

ten·u·ous (ten′yŏŏ·əs) *adj.* **1.** Thin; slim; delicate; also, weak; flimsy; unsubstantial. **2.** Having slight density; rare. [< L *tenuis* thin] — **ten′u·ous·ly** *adv.* — **ten′u·ous·ness,** **ten·u·i·ty** (ten·yŏŏ′ə·tē, ti·nŏŏ′-) *n.*

ten·ure (ten′yər) *n.* **1.** A holding, as of land. **2.** The act of holding in general, or the state of being held. **3.** The term during which a thing is held, as an office. **4.** The conditions or manner of holding. **5.** Permanent or regular status granted to an employee or professional, usually after a specified trial period. [< F < *tenir* to hold < L *tenere*] — **ten·u·ri·al** (ten·yŏŏr′ē·əl) *adj.* — **ten·u′ri·al·ly** *adv.*

te·nu·to (te·nōō′tō) *adj. Music* Sustained: held for the full time. Abbr. *ten.* [< Ital. < L *tenere* to hold]

te·nu·to mark *Music* A horizontal stroke over a note or chord indicating that it is to be held for its full value.

te·o·cal·li (tē′ə·kal′ē, *Sp.* tā′ō·kä′yē) *n.* **1.** A temple peculiar to the ancient Mexicans and Central Americans, usually erected on a truncated pyramid. **2.** A mound of similar form. Also **te·o·pan** (tā′ō·pän′). [< Sp. < Nahuatl, house of the god < *teotl* god + *calli* house]

te·o·sin·te (tē′ō·sin′te) *n.* A stout, hardy perennial grass (*Euchlaena mexicana*), closely allied to Indian corn, and used for fodder. [< Sp. < Nahuatl *teocentli,* lit., divine maize < *teotl* god + *centli* corn]

te·pee (tē′pē) *n.* A conical tent of the North American Plains Indians, usually covered with skins: also spelled **teepee, tipi.** [< Dakota *tipi* < *ti* to dwell + *pi* used for]

tep·e·fy (tep′ə·fī) *v.t. & v.i.* **·fied, ·fy·ing** To make or become tepid. [< L *tepefacere* to make tepid < *tepere* to be lukewarm + *facere* to make] — **tep′e·fac′tion** (-fak′shən) *n.*

teph·rite (tef′rīt) *n.* An ash-gray to black basaltic rock, essentially plagioclase, with either nepheline or leucite. [< L *tephritis* < Gk. *tephra* ashes] — **te·phrit·ic** (tə·frit′ik) *adj.*

tep·id (tep′id) *adj.* Moderately warm; lukewarm, as a liquid. [< L *tepidus* < *tepere* to be lukewarm] — **te·pid·i·ty** (tə·pid′ə·tē), **tep′id·ness** *n.* — **tep′id·ly** *adv.*

tep·i·dar·i·um (tep′ə·dâr′ē·əm) *n. pl.* **·dar·i·a** (-dâr′ē·ə) In the Roman baths, the apartment between the cold- and the hot-bath rooms. [< L < *tepidus.* See TEPID.]

te·qui·la (tə·kē′lə) *n.* **1.** A Mexican alcoholic liquor distilled from the juices yielded by the roasted stems of an agave plant. **2.** The plant itself (*Agave tequilana*). [after *Tequila,* Jalisco, Mexico]

ter- *combining form* Three; third; threefold; three times: *tercentenary.* [< L *ter* thrice]

ter. **1.** Terrace. **2.** Territorial; territory.

tera- *combining form* A trillion (10^{12}) times (a specified unit).

ter·a·phim (ter′ə·fim) *n.pl. sing.* **ter·aph** (ter′əf) or **ter·a·phim** Images, small idols, or household gods consulted as oracles by the ancient Hebrews. [< Hebrew *terāphīm*]

ter·a·tism (ter′ə·tiz′əm) *n. Biol.* A monstrosity; especially, a malformed human or animal fetus. [< Gk. *teras* monster]

terato- *combining form* A wonder; monster: *teratogeny.* Also, before vowels, **terat-.** [< Gk. *teras, teratos* wonder]

ter·a·tog·e·ny (ter′ə·toj′ə·nē) *n. Biol.* The production of monsters or abnormal organisms. Also **ter′a·to·gen′e·sis** (-tō·jen′ə·sis). — **ter′a·to·gen′ic** (-tō·jen′ik) *adj.*

ter·a·toid (ter′ə·toid) *adj.* Like a monstrosity; abnormal.

ter·a·tol·o·gy (ter′ə·tol′ə·jē) *n.* The branch of biology and medicine treating of abnormal growths or monstrosities. [< TERATO- + -LOGY] — **ter′a·to·log′ic** (-tō·loj′ik) or **·i·cal** *adj.* — **ter′a·tol′o·gist** *n.*

ter·bi·a (tûr′bē·ə) *n. Chem.* Oxide of terbium, Tb_2O_3.

ter·bi·um (tûr′bē·əm) *n.* A metallic element (symbol Tb) belonging to the lanthanide series, found in gadolinite and other rare-earth minerals. See ELEMENT. *Abbr. Tr.* [< NL < *Ytterby,* town in Sweden] — **ter′bic** *adj.*

terbium metal One of a group in the lanthanide series of elements, including gadolinium, europium, and terbium.

Ter Borch (tûr bôrkh′), Gerard, 1617–81, Dutch painter. Also **Ter·burg** (tûr·bûrkh′).

ter·cel (tûr′səl) *n.* A male falcon, especially the peregrine falcon: also called *tassel.* Also **terce·let** (tûrs′lit). [< OF < L *tertius* third; so called because every third egg in a falcon's nest was thought to produce a male]

ter·cen·te·nar·y (tûr·sen′tə·ner′ē, tûr′sen·ten′ər·ē) *adj.* Of or pertaining to a period of 300 years or to a 300th anniversary. — *n. pl.* **·nar·ies** A 300th anniversary. Also **tricentennial.** Also **ter·cen·ten·ni·al** (tûr′sen·ten′ē·əl).

ter·cet (tûr′sit, tûr·set′) *n.* **1.** A group of three lines rhyming together or connected with adjacent triplets by double or triple rhyme. **2.** *Music* A triplet. [< F < Ital. *terzetto,* dim. of *terzo* < L *tertius* third]

te·reb·ic acid (te·reb′ik, -rē′bik) *adj. Chem.* A white crystalline acid, $C_7H_{10}O_4$, derived from oil of turpentine by the action of nitric acid. [< TEREBINTH]

ter·e·binth (ter′ə·binth) *n.* A small Mediterranean tree (*Pistacia terebinthus*) of the cashew family, the original source of turpentine, with winged leaves resembling those of the common ash. [< L *terebinthus* < Gk. *terebinthos*]

ter·e·bin·thine (ter′ə·bin′thin) *adj.* Of or pertaining to the terebinth or turpentine. Also **ter′e·bin′thic.**

te·re·do (tə·rē′dō) *n.* Any of a genus (*Teredo*) of marine mollusks; a shipworm. [< L, borer < Gk. *terēdōn* < *terein* to rub hard, bore]

Ter·ence (ter′əns), 185?–159? B.C., Roman comic playwright born in Africa: full name **Publius Terentius A·fer** (ā′fər).

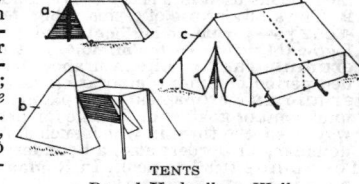

TEPEE
a Cover. *b* Poles. *c* Flap pole. *d* Flaps. *e* Ear. *f* Pins. *g* Pegs. *h* Door.

Te·re·sa (tā·rā′sä), *Saint* See (Saint) THERESA.

te·rete (tə·rēt′, ter′ēt) *adj.* Cylindrical and slightly tapering; round in cross section. [< L *teres, teretis* round, rounded off < *terere* to rub]

Te·reus (tir′yo͞os, tir′ē·əs) In Greek mythology, a Thracian king who was transformed into a hoopoe by the gods after he had raped Philomela, his sister-in-law.

ter·gal (tûr′gəl) *adj.* Of or pertaining to the tergum.

ter·gem·i·nate (tər·jem′ə·nit) *adj. Bot.* Having three pairs of forked leaflets. [< TER- + GEMINATE]

ter·gi·ver·sate (tûr′ji·vər·sāt′) *v.i.* ·sat·ed, ·sat·ing 1. To be evasive; equivocate. 2. To change sides, attitudes, etc.; become a renegade; apostatize. [< L *tergiversatus,* pp. of *tergiversari* < *tergum* back + *versare* to turn] — **ter′gi·ver·sa′tion** *n.* — **ter′gi·ver·sa′tor** *n.*

ter·gum (tûr′gəm) *n. pl.* ·ga (-gə) *Zool.* The back or dorsal part of an arthropod. [< L]

term (tûrm) *n.* 1. A word or expression used to designate some definite thing; a technical expression: a scientific *term.* 2. Any word or expression conveying some conception or thought: a *term* of reproach; to speak in general *terms.* 3. *pl.* The conditions or stipulations according to which something is to be done or acceded to: the *terms* of sale. 4. *pl.* Mutual relations; footing: usually preceded by *on* or *upon:* England was on friendly *terms* with France. 5. *Math.* a The numerator or denominator of a fraction. b One of the quantities of an algebraic expression that are connected by the plus and minus signs. c One of the quantities that compose a series or progression. 6. *Logic* a Either the subject or predicate of a proposition. b Any of the three elements of a syllogism, each of which appears twice. See SYLLOGISM. 7. A fixed period or definite length of time: a *term* of office. 8. One of the periods of the year appointed for holding instruction in colleges and schools. 9. *Law* a One of the prescribed periods of time during which a court may hold a session. b A specific extent of time during which a termor may hold an estate. c An interval allowed a debtor to meet his obligation. 10. *Med.* The time for childbirth. 11. *Archaic* An utmost limit; boundary. 12. *Archit.* A pillar of tapering form, ending in a sculptured head or bust. — **at term** At the end of a definite time. — **in terms of** With reference to; concerning: *In terms of* human life, the loss was incalculable. — **to bring to terms** To force to accede or agree; overcome. — **to come to terms** To reach an agreement. — *v.t.* To designate by means of a term; name or call. [< OF *terme* < L *terminus* limit]

term. 1. Terminal. 2. Termination. 3. Terminology.

ter·ma·gant (tûr′mə·gənt) *n.* A scolding or abusive woman; shrew. — *adj.* Violently abusive and quarrelsome; vixenish. [< TERMAGANT] — **ter′ma·gan·cy** *n.*

Ter·ma·gant (tûr′mə·gənt) An idol or imaginary deity of very turbulent, overbearing character that the medieval romances represented Moslems as worshiping. Also **Ter′ma·gaunt, Ter′ma·gund** (-gənd).

term·er (tûr′mər) *n.* 1. See TERMOR. 2. *Informal* A prisoner serving a certain term: a first *termer.*

ter·mi·na·ble (tûr′mə·nə·bəl) *adj.* That may be terminated; limitable; not perpetual. — **ter′mi·na·bil′i·ty, ter′·mi·na·ble·ness** *n.* — **ter′mi·na·bly** *adv.*

ter·mi·nal (tûr′mə·nəl) *adj.* 1. Of, pertaining to, or forming a boundary, limit, or end: a *terminal* railroad station. 2. Pertaining to the delivery or storage of freight or baggage: *terminal* charges. 3. Pertaining to a term or name. 4. Situated at the end of a series or part. 5. *Bot.* Borne at the end of a stem or branch. 6. Of, pertaining to, or occurring in or at the end of a period of time; of a fixed period. 7. Ending in death: said of a disease: *terminal* cancer. — *n.* 1. That which terminates; a terminating point or part; end. 2. *Electr.* A point at which a circuit element, as a battery, generator, resistor, capacitor, transistor, etc., may be connected to other elements. 3. *Archit.* A figure or pedestal situated at the end of something. 4. The edges or planes that form the end of a crystal. 5. A railroad terminus. 6. A station, as a railroad station, for freight or passengers, especially a station that is centrally located and connects with other lines. 7. *pl.* Charges for the use of terminal facilities, or for the handling of freight at railroad terminuses. 8. *Physiol.* The end structure of a neuron or nerve fiber. — **Syn.** See STATION. Abbr. *t., term.* [< LL *terminalis* < L *terminus* boundary] — **ter′mi·nal·ly** *adv.*

terminal leave The last leave granted to a member of the armed forces before his separation or discharge, equal to the remaining unused leave time he has accumulated.

terminal rhyme The rhyming of a word or group of syllables at the end of a verse with that at the end of another verse in the same stanza or poem.

terminal velocity *Physics* The velocity acquired by a freely falling body when the resistance of the medium equals the gravitational force acting upon the body. Abbr. *TV*

ter·mi·nate (tûr′mə·nāt) *v.* ·nat·ed, ·nat·ing *v.t.* 1. To put an end or stop to. 2. To form the conclusion of; finish. 3. To bound or limit. — *v.i.* 4. To have or come to an end. — **Syn.** See ABOLISH. [< L *terminatus,* pp. of *terminare* to end, limit < *terminus* limit]

ter·mi·na·tion (tûr′mə·nā′shən) *n.* 1. The act of setting bounds or limits. 2. The act of ending or concluding. 3. That which bounds or limits; close; end. 4. Outcome; result; conclusion. 5. The final letters or syllable of a word; a suffix. Abbr. *term.*

ter·mi·na·tion·al (tûr′mə·nā′shən·əl) *adj.* 1. Of, pertaining to, or forming a termination or terminations. 2. Formed by suffixes, as a word.

ter·mi·na·tive (tûr′mə·nā′tiv) *adj.* Designed or tending to terminate; conclusive. — **ter′mi·na′tive·ly** *adv.*

ter·mi·na·tor (tûr′mə·nā′tər) *n.* 1. One who or that which terminates. 2. *Astron.* The boundary between the illuminated and dark portions of the moon or of a planet.

ter·mi·na·to·ry (tûr′mə·nə·tôr′ē, -tō′rē) *adj.* 1. Tending to terminate; terminating. 2. Forming a limit.

ter·mi·nol·o·gy (tûr′mə·nol′ə·jē) *n. pl.* ·gies 1. The technical terms used in a science, art, trade, etc.; nomenclature. 2. The study or use of terms. Abbr. *term.* [< L *terminus* + -LOGY] — **ter′mi·no·log′i·cal** (-nə·loj′i·kəl) *adj.* — **ter′mi·no·log′i·cal·ly** *adv.* — **ter′mi·nol′o·gist** *n.*

term insurance Life insurance that expires after a specified period of time; temporary insurance.

ter·mi·nus (tûr′mə·nəs) *n. pl.* ·nus·es or ·ni (-nī) 1. The final point or goal; end. 2. The farthermost station on a railway; also, the town in which such station is situated. 3. A boundary or border; also, a boundary mark. [< L]

Ter·mi·nus (tûr′mə·nəs) In Roman mythology, the god of boundaries and landmarks.

ter·mi·nus ad quem (tûr′mə·nəs ad kwem) *Latin* The goal or terminating point of an argument, period, etc.

ter·mi·nus an·te quem (tûr′mə·nəs an′tē kwem) *Latin* A point of time designated as the end of a specified period.

ter·mi·nus a quo (tûr′mə·nəs ā kwō) *Latin* The beginning or starting point of an argument, period, etc.

ter·mi·nus post quem (tûr′mə·nəs pōst kwem) *Latin* A point of time designated as the start of a specified period.

ter·mite (tûr′mīt) *n.* Any of various small, whitish, isopterous, social insects native in warm regions, several species of which are very destructive of wooden structures, furniture, etc.: also, loosely, *white ant.* For illustration see INSECTS (injurious). [< L *termes, termitis*]

term·less (tûrm′lis) *adj.* 1. Of boundless extent or duration. 2. Independent of conditions; unconditional. 3. *Archaic* Indescribable.

term loan A loan that matures after one to ten years, usually repayable in installments.

term·ly (tûrm′lē) *adj.* Happening or done every term. — *adv.* By terms; periodically.

term·or (tûr′mər) *n. Law* A person who holds lands or tenements for a definite number of years or for life: also spelled *termer.*

term paper A major written report or essay required in a school or college course during an academic term.

tern[1] (tûrn) *n.* Any of several birds (subfamily *Sterninae*) allied to the gulls, but having a smaller bill and body, with wings more pointed, and the tail usually deeply forked: especially, the common tern (*Sterna hirundo*) of the Atlantic coasts, white with a black cap, and the **least tern** (*S. albifrons*). [< Scand. Cf. Dan. *terne* tern.]

tern[2] (tûrn) *n.* 1. Something composed of three; especially, three numbers in a lottery that when drawn together secure a prize. 2. In New England, a three-masted schooner. [< L *terni* by threes < *ter* thrice]

ter·na·ry (tûr′nər·ē) *adj.* 1. Formed or consisting of three; grouped in threes. 2. *Math.* a Containing three variables. b Pertaining to systems of notation, having three as a base. 3. *Chem.* Having three separate parts, as atoms, elements, or radicals. 4. *Metall.* Made of an alloy having three constituents. — *n. pl.* ·ries A group of three; a triad. [< L *ternarius* < *terni* by threes]

ter·nate (tûr′nāt) *adj.* 1. Arranged in threes. 2. *Bot.* a Trifoliolate. b Arranged in groups or whorls of three. [< NL *ternatus* < L *terni* by threes] — **ter′nate·ly** *adv.*

Ter·na·te (ter·nä′tä) An island of Indonesia in the northern Moluccas; 41 sq. mi.

terne·plate (tûrn′plāt) *n.* Steel plate with a coating of lead and tin, having a dull finish and inferior in quality to standard tin plate. [< F *terne* dull + PLATE]

ter·ni·on (tûr′nē·ən) *n.* 1. A set of three. 2. A section of a book composed of three sheets in double folds, or 12 pages. [< L *terni* by threes]

Ter·no·pol (tûr·nō′pəl, *Russ.* tyir·nô′pəly′) A city in the western Ukrainian S.S.R.; pop. 85,000 (1970): *Polish* **Tar·no·pol** (tär·nô′pəl). Also **Ter·no′pol′.**

Ter·pan·der (tər·pan′dər) Seventh-century B.C. Greek musician and poet.

ter·pene (tûr′pēn) *n. Chem.* Any of a class of unsaturated isomeric hydrocarbons, $C_{10}H_{16}$, contained chiefly in the essential oils of coniferous plants. [< *terp*(entin), earlier form of TURPENTINE + -ENE]

ter·pin·e·ol (tər·pin′ē·ōl, -ol) *n. Chem.* A colorless, unsaturated, tertiary alcohol, $C_{10}H_{17}OH$, derived synthetically and from the essential oils of various plants, used in perfumes. [< *terpin,* earlier form of TERPENE + -OL[1]]

ter·pi·nol (tûr′pə-nōl, -nol) *n.* An oily, colorless, liquid mixture of various terpenes, having an odor of hyacinth. [See TERPINEOL.]

Terp·sich·o·re (tûrp-sik′ə-rē) The Muse of dancing. [< Gk. *Terpsichorē* < *terpsichoros* delighting in the dance < *terpsis* enjoyment + *choros* dance] — **Terp·si·cho·re·an** (tûrp′si·kə-rē′ən) *adj.*

terp·si·cho·re·an (tûrp′si·kə-rē′ən) *adj.* Of or relating to dancing: also **terp′si·cho·re′al.** — *n. Informal* A dancer.

ter·ra (ter′ə) *n. Latin* The earth; earth.

ter·ra al·ba (ter′ə al′bə) **1.** Pipe clay. **2.** The pigment made from ground gypsum. **3.** Any of various white substances, as magnesia, kaolin, etc. [< L, white earth]

ter·race (ter′is) *n.* **1.** An artificial, raised, level space, as of lawn, having one or more vertical or sloping sides; also, such levels collectively. **2.** A raised level supporting a row of houses, or the houses occupying such a position; also, a street, usually one containing a terrace. **3.** The flat roof of an Oriental or Spanish house. **4.** A relatively narrow step or level surface cut into the face of a steep, natural slope. **5.** A paved, usually unroofed area adjacent to a house. **6.** An open gallery, deck, or balcony. **7.** A planted, parklike area in the middle of a paved street. *Abbr.* ter., terr. — *v.t.* **·raced, ·rac·ing** To form into or provide with a terrace or terraces. [< OF < Ital. *terraccia* < L *terra* earth]

ter·ra cot·ta (ter′ə kot′ə) **1.** A hard, durable, kiln-burnt clay, reddish brown in color and usually unglazed, widely used as a structural material and in pottery, tiles, building façades, etc. **2.** Its brownish orange color. **3.** A statue or figure made of this clay. [< Ital. cooked earth]

ter·ra fir·ma (ter′ə fûr′mə) Solid ground, as distinguished from the sea or the air. [< L]

ter·rain (te-rān′, ter′ān) *n.* **1.** Battleground, or a region suited for defense, etc. **2.** A piece or plot of ground; especially, a region or territory viewed with regard to its suitability for some particular purpose. **3.** *Geol.* A terrane. [< F < L *terrenum* < *terrenus* earthen < *terra* earth]

ter·ra in·cog·ni·ta (ter′ə in·kog′nə-tə) *pl.* **ter·rae in·cog·ni·tae** (ter′ē in·kog′nə-tē) **1.** An unknown land or region. **2.** An unexplored field of study or knowledge. [< L]

Ter·ra·my·cin (ter′ə-mī′sin) *n.* Proprietary name for an antibiotic isolated from a soil mold (*Streptomyces rimosus*) and used in the treatment of a wide variety of bacterial infections. Also **ter′ra·my′cin.**

ter·rane (te-rān′, ter′ān) *n. Geol.* A continuous formation or series of related formations. [< F *terrain*. See TERRAIN.]

ter·ra·pin (ter′ə-pin) *n.* Any of several North American edible tortoises (family *Testudinidae*) of fresh and brackish waters; especially, the diamond back. [< Algonquian]

ter·ra·qui·ous (te-rā′kwē-əs) *adj.* Consisting of both land and water. [< L *terra* earth, land + AQUEOUS]

ter·rar·i·um (te-râr′ē-əm) *n. pl.* **·rar·i·ums** or **·rar·i·a** (-râr′ē-ə) **1.** A small enclosure or box, often with glass sides, for live lizards, growing plants, etc. **2.** A place for keeping and raising land animals. [< L *terra* earth + -ARIUM, on analogy with *aquarium*]

ter·raz·zo (ter-rät′sō) *n.* Flooring made of small pieces of marble or colored stone set in concrete. Also **ter·raz′zo Ve·ne·zia·no** (vā′nä-tsyä′nō). [< Ital. < L *terra* earth]

ter·reen (te-rēn′) See TERRINE.

Ter·re Haute (ter′ə hōt′) A city in western Indiana, on the Wabash River; pop. 70,286.

ter·rel·la (te-rel′ə) *n.* **1.** A space capsule or vehicle designed to reproduce as far as possible the conditions to be found on earth. **2.** A small spherical lodestone, especially as used by William Gilbert to demonstrate the magnetic properties of the earth. [< NL, dim. of L *terra* earth]

ter·rene¹ (te-rēn′) *Archaic adj.* Earthly; worldly; mundane. — *n.* The earth. [< L *terrenus* < *terra* earth]

ter·rene² (te-rēn′) See TERRINE.

terre·plein (ter′plān) *n.* **1.** The upper surface of a rampart behind the parapet, for the guns. **2.** An embankment with a level top. [< F *terre* earth + *plein* level]

ter·res·tri·al (tə-res′trē-əl) *adj.* **1.** Of, pertaining to, or consisting of earth or land. **2.** Of, belonging to, or representing the earth. **3.** *Biol.* Living on or growing in the earth or land. **4.** Belonging to or consisting of land, as distinct from water, trees, etc. **5.** Worldly; mundane. — *n.* An inhabitant of the earth. [< L *terrestris* < L *terra* land] — **ter·res′tri·al·ly** *adv.* — **ter·res′tri·al·ness** *n.*

ter·ret (ter′it) *n.* **1.** One of two metal rings projecting from the saddle of a harness, through which the reins are passed. For illustration see HARNESS. **2.** A ring for attaching a leash to a dog's collar, etc. Also **ter′rit.** [ME *toret* < F *touret* small wheel, dim. of *tour* turn]

terri- *combining form* Earth; ground. [< L *terra* earth]

ter·ri·ble (ter′ə-bəl) *adj.* **1.** Of a nature to excite terror; appalling. **2.** *Informal* Characterized by excess; severe; extreme. **3.** Inspiring awe. **4.** *Informal* Inferior or poor in quality. [< F < L *terribilis* < *terrere* to terrify] — **ter′ri·ble·ness** *n.* — **ter′ri·bly** *adv.*

ter·ric·o·lous (te-rik′ə-ləs) *adj. Biol.* Living on or in the ground. Also **ter·ric′o·line** (-lēn, -lin). [< L *terricola* earth dweller < *terra* earth + *colere* to dwell]

ter·ri·er¹ (ter′ē-ər) *n.* Any of various small, active, wiry dogs of several breeds, formerly used to hunt burrowing animals and noted for tenacity of pursuit. [< OF < L *terrarius* pertaining to earth. See TERRIER².]

ter·ri·er² (ter′ē-ər) *n. Law* **1.** A land survey setting forth in detail the number of acres, names of tenants, etc., in a given district. **2.** A book containing the lists of the lands either of a private person or a corporation; a rent roll. [< OF, list of tenants < LL *terrarius* a roll describing landed property < L, pertaining to land < *terra* land]

ter·rif·ic (tə-rif′ik) *adj.* **1.** *Informal* **a** Extreme; intense; tremendous. **b** Wonderful; great; splendid. **2.** Arousing or calculated to arouse great terror or fear. — **ter·rif′i·cal·ly** *adv.*

ter·ri·fy (ter′ə-fī) *v.t.* **·fied, ·fy·ing** To fill with extreme terror. — **Syn.** See FRIGHTEN. [< L *terrificare* < *terrificus* causing fear < *terrere* to frighten + *facere* to make]

ter·rig·e·nous (te-rij′ə-nəs) *adj.* **1.** Produced from or of the earth; earthborn. **2.** *Geol.* Of or pertaining to marine deposits formed of material washed from the land, and to the sedimentary rocks consolidated from this material. Also **ter·ri·gene** (ter′ə-jēn). [< L *terrigenus* < *terra* earth + *gignere* to be born]

ter·rine (te-rēn′) *n.* **1.** An earthenware jar containing some delicacy for the table and sold with its contents: a *terrine* of preserved ginger. **2.** A kind of ragout or stew. Also spelled *terreen, terrene.* [< F < LL *terrineus* made of earth < L *terra* earth. Doublet of TUREEN.]

Ter·ri·toire des Co·mores (te-rē-twär′ dā kô-môr′) A French name for the COMORO ISLANDS.

ter·ri·to·ri·al (ter′ə-tôr′ē-əl, -tō′rē-) *adj.* **1.** Of or pertaining to a territory or territories. **2.** Limited to or within the jurisdiction of a particular territory or region: *territorial* waters. **3.** Designating military forces intended for territorial defense. **4.** Belonging to a particular locality. **5.** *Often cap.* Organized or intended primarily for national defense: the British *Territorial* Army. *Abbr.* t., ter., terr. — **ter′ri·to′ri·al·ly** *adv.*

Ter·ri·to·ri·al (ter′ə-tôr′ē-əl, -tō′rē) *adj.* Of or pertaining to any or all of the Territories of the United States, Great Britain, etc.: the *Territorial* system. — *n.* A member of the Territorial Army in Great Britain.

ter·ri·to·ri·al·ism (ter′ə-tôr′ē-əl-iz′əm, -tō′rē-) *n.* The organizations, theories, or doctrines of the territorial systems. — **ter′ri·to′ri·al·ist** *n.*

ter·ri·to·ri·al·i·ty (ter′ə-tôr′ē-al′ə-tē, -tō′rē-) *n.* Territorial condition, status, or position.

ter·ri·to·ri·al·ize (ter′ə-tôr′ē-əl-īz′, -tō′rē-) *v.t.* **·ized, ·iz·ing** **1.** To enlarge by annexation of territory. **2.** To reduce to the political status of a territory. **3.** To distribute among certain territories. — **ter′ri·to′ri·al·i·za′tion** *n.*

territorial system **1.** A system of church government in which all inhabitants of a territory are required to belong to the same religion as the civil ruler. **2.** Local organization for militia service. **3.** A system giving predominance to landowners; landlordism.

territorial waters Coastal and inland waters under the jurisdiction of a state.

ter·ri·to·ry (ter′ə-tôr′ē, -tō′rē) *n. pl.* **·ries** **1.** The domain over which a sovereign state exercises jurisdiction. **2.** Any considerable tract of land; a region; also, a sphere, province. **3.** An area assigned for a special purpose. *Abbr.* t., T., ter., terr., Ty. [< L *territorium* < *terra* earth]

Ter·ri·to·ry (ter′ə-tôr′ē, -tō′rē) *n. U.S.* A region having a certain degree of self-government but not having the status of a State, as American Samoa.

ter·ror (ter′ər) *n.* **1.** An overwhelming impulse of fear; extreme fright or dread. **2.** A person or thing that causes extreme fear. **3.** *Informal* An intolerable nuisance: That child is a *terror.* — **Syn.** See FEAR. [< L *terreur* < L *terror* fright < *terrere* to frighten]

ter·ror·ism (ter′ə-riz′əm) *n.* **1.** The act of terrorizing or the state of being terrorized. **2.** Unlawful acts of violence committed in an attempt to overthrow a government. **3.** A system of government that rules by intimidation.

ter·ror·ist (ter′ər·ist) *n.* **1.** One who adopts or supports a policy of terrorism. **2.** A Jacobin or Republican of the French Revolution of 1789, especially during the Reign of Terror. **3.** A member of political extremist groups in czarist Russia. — **ter′ror·is′tic** *adj.*

ter·ror·ize (ter′ə-rīz) *v.t.* **·ized, ·iz·ing** **1.** To reduce to a state of terror; terrify. **2.** To coerce through intimidation. Also *Brit.* **ter′ror·ise.** — **Syn.** See FRIGHTEN. — **ter′ror·i·za′tion** *n.* — **ter′ror·iz′er** *n.*

ter·ry (ter′ē) *n. pl.* **·ries** **1.** The loop raised for the nap in weaving pile fabrics. **2.** A pile fabric in which the loops are uncut; especially, a cotton fabric, very water-absorbent, used chiefly for towels and beach robes: also **terry cloth.** [Prob. < F *tiré*, pp. of *tirer* to draw < L *trahere*]

Ter·ry (ter′ē), **Dame Ellen (Alicia)**, 1848–1928, English actress.

terse (tûrs) *adj.* **ters·er, ters·est 1.** Short and to the point; concise: a *terse* comment. **2.** Rubbed to a polish; clean; polished; refined. [< L *tersus*, pp. of *tergere* to rub off, rub down] **— terse′ly** *adv.* **— terse′ness** *n.*
— Syn. 1. *Terse, concise, pithy, succinct, compendious,* and *laconic* characterize speech or writing that says much in relatively few words. *Terse* emphasizes the finish and cogency of the result; *concise* suggests that all unnecessary words have been pruned away. *Pithy* describes something both brief and forceful, while *succinct* characterizes that which is highly compact because all extraneous detail has been removed. *Compendious* emphasizes the condensation of much material, as in a compendium. Something *laconic* is extremely brief, sometimes using too few words for clarity or politeness. **— Ant.** diffuse, prolix, wordy.

ter·tial (tûr′shəl) *Ornithol. adj.* Tertiary. **—** *n.* A tertiary feather. [< L *tertius* third < *ter* thrice]
ter·tian (tûr′shən) *adj.* Recurring every other day, or if reckoned inclusively, every third day. **—** *n. Pathol.* A tertian disease or fever. [< L (*febris*) *tertiana* tertian (fever) < *tertius* third]
ter·ti·ar·y (tûr′shē·er′ē, -shə·rē) *adj.* **1.** Third in point of time, number, degree, etc. **2.** *Ornithol.* Denoting one of the flight feathers attached to the humerus of a bird's wings: also called *tertial*. For illustration see BIRD. **3.** *Eccl.* Pertaining to the third order of a religious body. **4.** *Chem.* **a** Having three substituted atoms or radicals: a *tertiary* amine. **b** Denoting a carbon atom directly connected with three other carbon atoms: *tertiary* butyl. **—** *n. pl.* **·ar·ies 1.** *Ornithol.* A tertiary feather. **2.** Any member of the third order of a monastic body. [< L *tertiarius* < *tertius* third]
Ter·ti·ar·y (tûr′shē·er′ē, -shə·rē) *Geol. adj.* Of or pertaining to the earlier of the two geological periods or systems comprising the Cenozoic era, following the Cretaceous and succeeded by the Quaternary. **—** *n.* The Tertiary period or system, characterized by the rise of mammals. See table for GEOLOGY.
ter·ti·um quid (tûr′shē·əm kwid) *Latin* **1.** An indefinite or undefined thing related in some way to two definite or known things. **2.** A mediating factor between essentially opposite things.
Ter·tul·li·an (tər·tul′ē·ən), 160?–230?, Carthaginian Christian theologian: full name **Quintus Septimius Florens Tertul·li·a·nus** (tər·tul′ē·ā′nəs).
ter·va·lent (tûr′və·lənt, tər·vā′lənt) *adj. Chem.* Trivalent.
ter·za ri·ma (ter′tsä rē′mä) *n. pl.* **ter·ze ri·me** (ter′tsä rē′mā) A form of Italian triplet, in iambic decasyllables or hendecasyllables, in which the middle line of the first triplet rhymes with the first and third lines of the following triplet. [< Ital., third or triple line]
Tes·la (tes′lə), **Nikola**, 1857–1943, U.S. physicist and inventor born in Yugoslavia.
tes·sel·late (tes′ə·lāt) *v.t.* **·lat·ed, ·lat·ing** To construct in the style of checkered mosaic; lay or adorn with squares or tiles. [< L *tessellatus* checkered < *tessella*, dim. of *tessera* cube. See TESSERA.] **— tes′sel·lat′ed** *adj.*
tes·sel·la·tion (tes′ə·lā′shən) *n.* **1.** Tessellated work. **2.** The art or act of doing such work.
tes·ser·a (tes′ər·ə) *n. pl.* **·ser·ae** (-ər·ē) **1.** A small square, as of stone, glass, etc., used in mosaic work. **2.** A small object, often a square or cube, as of bone or wood, used as a die in gambling or as a token, voucher, etc. [< L < dial. Gk. (Ionic) *tesseres* four]
tes·ser·act (tes′ər·akt) *n. Math.* **1.** A four-dimensional figure bounded by 8 cubes, and having 16 vertices, 24 faces, and 32 edges. **2.** A diagram or model intended to illustrate graphically the general properties of this figure. Also called *hypercube.* [< dial. Gk. (Ionic) *tesseres* four + *aktis* ray]
Tes·sin (te·sēn′) See TICINO.
test¹ (test) *v.t.* **1.** To subject to a test or trial; try. **2.** *Chem.* **a** To assay or refine (a precious metal), as in the process of cupellation. **b** To examine by means of some reagent, as in testing for sulfuric acid. **—** *v.i.* **3.** *Chem.* **a** To undergo testing. **b** To show specified qualities or properties under testing. **—** *n.* **1.** Subjection to conditions that disclose the true character of a person or thing in relation to some particular quality. **2.** An examination made for the purpose of proving or disproving some matter in doubt: a sobriety *test.* **3.** A series of questions, problems, etc., intended to measure the extent of knowledge, aptitudes, intelligence, and other mental traits: a language *test.* **4.** A criterion or standard of judgment. **5.** An oath or other confirmatory evidence of principles or belief. **6.** *Chem.* **a** A reaction by means of which the presence and identity of a compound or one of its constituents may be determined. **b** The agent or result of such a reaction. **7.** An earthen vessel similar to a cupel, formerly used in testing metals. [< OF, cupel, pot < L *testum* earthen vessel < *testa* potsherd, shell] **— test′a·ble** *adj.*
test² (test) *n.* **1.** *Zool.* A rigid external case or covering of many invertebrates, as a sea urchin or mollusk; a shell: also called *testa.* **2.** *Bot.* A testa. [< L *testa* shell]
test. **1.** Testamentary. **2.** Testator.
Test. Testament.

tes·ta (tes′tə) *n. pl.* **·tae** (-tē) **1.** *Bot.* The outer, usually hard and brittle coat or integument of a seed: also called *test.* **2.** *Zool.* A test. [See TEST².]
tes·ta·ceous (tes·tā′shəs) *adj.* **1.** Of or derived from shells or shellfish. **2.** Having a hard shell. **3.** Dull brick-red or brownish yellow. [< L *testaceus* of shell, brick < *testa* shell]
tes·ta·cy (tes′tə·sē) *n. Law* The state of being testate or of having left a will at death: opposed to *intestacy.*
tes·ta·ment (tes′tə·mənt) *n.* **1.** *Law* The written declaration of one's last will: chiefly in the phrase **last will and testament.** ◆ Strictly speaking a *testament* differs from a *will* in that it bequeaths personal property only, but the words are commonly used interchangeably. **2.** In Biblical use, a covenant; dispensation. [< F < L *testamentum* < *testari* to testify < *testis* witness] **— tes′ta·men′tal** *adj.*
Tes·ta·ment (tes′tə·mənt) *n.* **1.** One of the two volumes of the Bible, distinguished as the *Old* and the *New Testament.* **2.** A volume containing the New Testament. Abbr. *T., Test.*
tes·ta·men·ta·ry (tes′tə·men′tər·ē) *adj.* **1.** Derived from, bequeathed by, or set forth in a will. **2.** Appointed or provided by, or done in accordance with, a will. **3.** Pertaining to a will, or to the administration or settlement of a will. **4.** *Often cap.* Pertaining to a Testament. Abbr. *test.*
tes·tate (tes′tāt) *adj.* Having made a will before decease. [< L *testatus,* pp. of *testari* to be a witness. See TESTAMENT.]
tes·ta·tor (tes·tā′tər, tes′tā·tər) *n.* **1.** The maker of a will. **2.** One who has died leaving a will. Abbr. *test.* [< L] **— tes·ta′trix** (-triks) *n.fem.*
test case A legal action whose resolution is considered likely to establish a precedent or to test the constitutionality of a law.
test·er¹ (tes′tər) *n.* One who or that which tests.
tes·ter² (tes′tər) *n.* A flat canopy over a tomb, pulpit, or bed. [< OF *testiere* < *teste* head < L *testa* shell, skull]
tes·ter³ (tes′tər) *n.* A silver coin of the Tudor period, originally equal to twelve pence, later worth sixpence: also called *teston.* [< OF *teston* coin < *teste* head. See TESTER².]
tes·tes (tes′tēz) Plural of TESTIS.
tes·ti·cle (tes′ti·kəl) *n. Biol.* One of the two male sex glands enclosed in the scrotum and in which the spermatozoa and certain internal secretions are formed: also called *testis.* [< L *testiculus,* dim. of *testis* testicle]
tes·tic·u·late (tes·tik′yə·lit, -lāt) *adj.* **1.** Shaped or formed like a testicle. **2.** Solid and ovate, like the roots of certain orchids. [< L *testiculus* testicle + -ATE¹]
tes·ti·fi·ca·tion (tes′tə·fə·kā′shən) *n.* **1.** The act of testifying or giving testimony. **2.** The testimony given.
tes·ti·fy (tes′tə·fī) *v.* **·fied, ·fy·ing** *v.i.* **1.** To make solemn declaration of truth or fact. **2.** *Law* To give testimony; bear witness. **3.** To serve as evidence or indication: Her rags *testified* to her poverty. **—** *v.t.* **4.** To bear witness to; affirm positively. **5.** *Law* To state or declare on oath or affirmation. **6.** To be evidence or indication of. **7.** To make known publicly; declare. [< L *testificari* < *testis* witness + *facere* to make] **— tes′ti·fi′er** *n.*
tes·ti·mo·ni·al (tes′tə·mō′nē·əl) *n.* **1.** A formal token or statement of regard. **2.** A written acknowledgment of services or worth; also, a letter of recommendation. **—** *adj.* Pertaining to or constituting testimony or a testimonial. [< L *testimonialis* < *testimonium.* See TESTIMONY.]
tes·ti·mo·ny (tes′tə·mō′nē) *n. pl.* **·nies 1.** A statement or affirmation of a fact, as before a court. **2.** Evidence; proof; also, the aggregate of proof offered in a case. **3.** The act of testifying; attestation. **4.** Public declaration regarding some experience. **5.** The Old Testament Scriptures or the Decalogue. [< L *testimonium* < *testis* witness]
— Syn. *Testimony, deposition, affidavit,* and *evidence* are compared as they denote statements made to a court. *Testimony* is the oral statements made by a witness under examination. A *deposition* or *affidavit* is *testimony* put into writing; *depositions* are made under formal questioning, and may be subject to cross-examination, while an *affidavit* is a sworn document that may be accepted when the testifier cannot appear in court in person. *Evidence* is a general term, including the foregoing, and also documents and physical objects relevant to a case.
tes·tis (tes′tis) *n. pl.* **·tes** (-tēz) A testicle. [< L]
tes·ton (tes′tən, tes·tōōn′) *n.* **1.** Any of various silver European coins with a representation of a head on one side. **2.** A French coin of the 16th century. **3.** The tester, a former English coin. Also **tes·toon** (tes·tōōn′). [< F < Ital. *testone,* aug. of *testa* head < L *testa,* skull]
tes·tos·ter·one (tes·tos′tə·rōn) *n. Biochem.* A male sex hormone, $C_{19}H_{28}O_2$, isolated as a white crystalline substance from the testes, and also made synthetically. [< TESTIS + STER(OL) + -ONE]
test paper 1. *Chem.* A paper saturated with some reagent, as litmus, that changes color when exposed to certain substances. **2.** A paper containing a student's work in a test.
test pilot An aviator who tests aircraft of new design.
test tube A glass tube, open at one end and usually with a rounded bottom, used in making chemical or biological tests.
tes·tu·di·nal (tes·tōō′də·nəl, -tyōō′-) *adj.* Pertaining to or like a turtle or tortoise shell. Also **tes·tu′di·nate** (-nāt). [< L *testudo, -inis* tortoise]

tes·tu·do (tes·tōō′dō, -tyōō′-) *n. pl.* **·di·nes** (-də·nēz) **1.** A shed or screen used by the Romans for the protection of soldiers in siege operations. **2.** A protecting cover formed by soldiers in ranks by overlapping their shields above their heads. [< L < *testa* shell]

tes·ty (tes′tē) *adj.* **·ti·er, ·ti·est** Irritable in manner or disposition; touchy. [< AF *testif* heady < OF *teste* head < L *testa* skull] **— tes′ti·ly** *adv.* **— tes′ti·ness** *n.*

te·tan·ic (ti·tan′ik) *adj.* Relating to or productive of tetanus. Also **te·tan′i·cal.** **—** *n.* A drug capable of causing convulsions, as strychnine or nux vomica.

tet·a·nize (tet′ə·nīz) *v.t.* **·nized, ·niz·ing** To affect with tetanic spasms. **— tet′a·ni·za′tion** *n.*

tet·a·nus (tet′ə·nəs) *n.* **1.** *Pathol.* An acute infectious disease caused by a bacillus (*Clostridium tetani*), and characterized by rigid spasmodic contraction of various voluntary muscles, especially those of the neck and jaw. Compare LOCKJAW. **2.** *Physiol.* A state of contraction in a muscle excited by a rapid series of shocks. [< L < Gk. *tetanos* spasm < *teinein* to stretch]

tet·a·ny (tet′ə·nē) *n. Pathol.* Intermittent muscular spasms, usually due to defective calcium metabolism.

tetarto- *combining form* Four; fourth. Also, before vowels, **tetart-.** [< Gk. *tetartos* fourth < *tettares* four]

te·tar·to·he·dral (ti·tär′tō·hē′drəl) *adj. Crystall.* Possessing one fourth of the planes necessary for maximum symmetry in a given crystal system.

tetch·y (tech′ē) *adj.* **tetch·i·er, tetch·i·est** Peevishly sensitive; irritable; touchy: also spelled *techy.* [< OF *teche* mark, quality] **— tetch′i·ly** *adv.* **— tetch′i·ness** *n.*

tête-à-tête (tāt′ə·tāt′, *Fr.* tet·à·tet′) *adj.* Confidential, as between two persons only. **—** *n.* **1.** A confidential interview between two persons; a private chat. **2.** An S-shaped sofa on which two persons may face each other. **—** *adv.* In or as in intimate conversation. [< F, lit. head to head]

tête-beche (tet·besh′) *adj. French* Placed top against bottom or head to tail: said of a pair of stamps so printed that one is reversed in relation to the other.

tête-de-pont (tet·də·pôn′) *n. pl.* **têtes-de-pont** (tet·də·pôn′) *French* A bridgehead.

teth (teth) *n.* The ninth letter in the Hebrew alphabet. See ALPHABET.

teth·er (teth′ər) *n.* **1.** Something used to check or confine, as a rope for fastening an animal. **2.** The range, scope, or limit of one's powers or field of action. **— at the end of one's tether** At the extreme end or limit of one's resources, patience, etc. **—** *v.t.* To fasten or confine by a tether. [ME *tethir* < Scand. Cf. ON *tiodhr* tether.]

Te·thys (tē′this) In Greek mythology, a Titaness, sister and wife of Oceanus and mother of the Oceanids.

Te·ton Range (tē′ton, tēt′n) A range of the Rocky Mountains, chiefly in NW Wyoming; highest peak, Grand Teton, 13,776 ft.

te·to·tum (tē·tō′təm) See TEETOTUM.

tetra- *combining form* Four; fourfold: *tetrabasic.* Also, before vowels, **tetr-.** [< Gk.]

tet·ra·ba·sic (tet′rə·bā′sik) *adj. Chem.* Denoting an acid containing four atoms of hydrogen replaceable by a base or basic radicals. [< TETRA- + BASIC]

tet·ra·brach (tet′rə·brak) *n.* A Greek or Latin word or foot made up of four short syllables. [< Gk. *tetrabrachys* < *tessares, tettares* four + *brachys* short]

tet·ra·bran·chi·ate (tet′rə·brang′kē·it, -āt) *adj. Zool.* Pertaining or belonging to an order (*Tetrabranchiata*) of cephalopods having two pairs of gills and a chambered shell, as the nautilus.

tet·ra·chlo·ride (tet′rə·klôr′īd, -id, -klō′rīd, -rid) *n. Chem.* A compound containing four atoms of chlorine. Also **tet′ra·chlo′rid** (-klôr′id, -klō′rid).

tet·ra·chord (tet′rə·kôrd) *n. Music* Four contiguous tones of a diatonic scale, of which the extreme tones are a perfect fourth apart. [< Gk. *tetrachordon* a musical instrument < *tetras* group of four + *chordē* string] **— tet′ra·chor′dal** *adj.*

te·trac·id (te·tras′id) *n. Chem.* A base having four replaceable hydroxyl radicals. [< TETR(A)- + ACID]

tet·ra·cy·cline (tet′rə·sī′klīn, -klin) *n. Chem.* A yellow, crystalline nitrogenous compound, $C_{22}H_{24}N_2O_8$, isolated from certain species of a soil bacillus (genus *Streptomyces*) and forming the base of several antibiotics. [< *tetracyclic,* containing four atomic rings + -INE[2]]

tet·rad (tet′rad) *n.* **1.** A group or collection of four. **2.** *Chem.* A quadrivalent atom, radical, or element. **3.** *Biol.* The group of four chromatids into which two bivalent chromosomes divide in the last stages of meiosis. **4.** A crystal having an axis showing fourfold symmetry. [< Gk. *tetras, -ados* group of four]

te·trad·y·mite (te·trad′ə·mīt) *n.* A soft, metallic, steel-gray bismuth telluride, $Bi_2(TeS)_3$, crystallizing in the rhombohedral system. [< G *tetradymit* < Gk. *tetradymos* fourfold; from its occurring in compound twin crystals]

tet·ra·eth·yl lead (tet′rə·eth′il led) *Chem.* A colorless,

heavy, flammable, poisonous, liquid hydrocarbon, $Pb(C_2H_5)_4$, used as an antiknock agent in internal-combustion engines: also called *lead tetraethyl.*

tet·ra·gon (tet′rə·gon) *n. Geom.* A plane figure having four sides and four angles; a quadrangle. [< Gk. *tetragōnon* quadrangle < *tetra-* four + *gōnia* angle]

te·trag·o·nal (tet·rag′ə·nəl) *adj.* **1.** Being or pertaining to a tetragon; having four angles; quadrangular. **2.** *Crystall.* Designating a crystal system characterized by two equal lateral axes and one vertical axis of different length, all at right angles to each other, as in zircon: also *dimetric.*

tet·ra·gram (tet′rə·gram) *n.* A word of four letters.

Tet·ra·gram·ma·ton (tet′rə·gram′ə·ton) *n.* In Hebrew texts, the group of four letters (JHVH, JHWH, YHVH, or YHWH) representing the name of God, that is considered ineffable. The common transliteration *Jehovah* is the result of a combination of the Tetragrammaton with the vowel points of *Adonai* "my Lord," that is substituted in reading the name. [< Gk. *tetragrammaton* < *tetra-* four + *gramma* letter < *graphein* to write]

tet·ra·he·dral (tet′rə·hē′drəl) *adj.* **1.** Of or pertaining to a tetrahedron. **2.** Made up of or having four sides. [< Gk. *tetraedros.* See TETRAHEDRON.]

tet·ra·he·drite (tet′rə·hē′drīt) *n.* A steel-gray, fine-grained mineral, usually a sulfide of copper and antimony but having other elements, found in tetrahedral crystals. [< TETRA-HEDRON]

tet·ra·he·dron (tet′rə·hē′drən) *n. pl.* **·drons** or **·dra** (-drə) **1.** *Geom.* A polyhedron bounded by four plane triangular faces. **2.** *Mil.* An antitank obstacle shaped like a pyramid. [< Gk. *tetraedron,* neut. of *tetraedros* < *tetra-* four + *hedra* base]

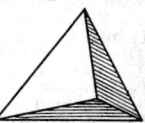

TETRAHEDRON

te·tral·o·gy (te·tral′ə·jē) *n. pl.* **·gies 1.** A group of four dramas, including three tragedies and one satyr play, presented together at the festivals of Dionysus at Athens. **2.** Any series of four related dramatic, operatic, or literary works. [< Gk. *tetralogia* < *tetra-* four + *logos* word, speech]

te·tram·er·ous (te·tram′ər·əs) *adj.* **1.** Having four parts. **2.** *Bot.* Having the parts or organs arranged in fours or multiples of four: often written **4-merous.** Also **te·tram′er·al.** [< Gk. *tetramerēs* four-parted < *tetra-* four + *meros* part]

te·tram·e·ter (te·tram′ə·tər) *n.* **1.** In prosody, a line of verse consisting of four metrical feet: Fŭll fā | thŏm fīve | thў fā | thĕr līes. **2.** Verse consisting of lines of four metrical feet. **—** *adj.* Consisting of four metrical feet or of lines containing four metrical feet. [< LL *tetrametrus* < Gk. *tetrametros* < *tetra-* four + *metron* measure]

tet·ra·pet·al·ous (tet′rə·pet′l·əs) *adj. Bot.* Having four petals.

tet·ra·pod (tet′rə·pod) *adj.* Having four feet. [< NL *tetrapodus* < Gk. *tetrapous, tetrapodos* four-footed < *tetra-* four + *pous* foot]

te·trap·o·dy (te·trap′ə·dē) *n. pl.* **·dies** A group of four feet, as a verse. [< Gk. *tetrapodia* < *tetrapous.* See TETRAPOD.] **— tet·ra·pod·ic** (te·trə·pod′ik) *adj.*

te·trap·ter·ous (te·trap′tər·əs) *adj. Biol.* Having four wings or winglike appendages, as certain fruits and insects. [< NL *tetrapterus* < Gk. *tetrapteros* four-winged < *tetra-* four + *pteron* wing]

tet·rarch (tet′rärk, tē′trärk) *n.* **1.** The governor of one of four divisions of a country or province. **2.** A tributary prince under the Romans; a subordinate ruler. **3.** In ancient Greece, an army commander of a subdivision of a phalanx. [< LL *tetrarcha* < L *tetrarches* < Gk. *tetrarchēs* < *tetra-* four + *archos* ruler]

tet·rar·chy (tet′rär·kē, tē′trär-) *n. pl.* **·chies 1.** The rule, territory, or jurisdiction of a tetrarch. **2.** Government by a group of four; also, the four members of such a group. Also **tet′rar·chate** (-kāt, -kit).

tet·ra·seme (tet′rə·sēm) *n.* A long syllable or a foot equal to four short syllables. [< TETRA- + Gk. *sēma* sign] **— tet′ra·se′mic** *adj.*

tet·ra·spo·ran·gi·um (tet′rə·spō·ran′jē·əm, -spō-) *n. pl.* **·gi·a** (-jē·ə) *Bot.* A sporangium producing tetraspores.

tet·ra·spore (tet′rə·spôr -spōr) *n. Bot.* One of four asexual spores produced together from a sporangium.

tet·ra·stich (tet′rə·stik) *n.* A poem or stanza of four lines. [< TETRA- + Gk. *stichos* row, line] **— tet′ra·stich′ic** *adj.*

te·tras·ti·chous (te·tras′tə·kəs) *adj. Bot.* Arranged, as leaves on a stem, in four vertical rows or ranks.

tet·ra·syl·la·ble (tet′rə·sil′ə·bəl) *n.* A word of four syllables. **— tet′ra·syl·lab′ic** (-si·lab′ik) or **·i·cal** *adj.*

tet·ra·tom·ic (tet′rə·tom′ik) *adj. Chem.* **1.** Containing four atoms in the molecule. **2.** Containing four replaceable univalent atoms or molecules. **3.** Quadrivalent.

tet·ra·va·lent (tet′rə·vā′lənt) *adj. Chem.* Quadrivalent.

Te·traz·zi·ni (tā′trät·tsē′nē), Luisa, 1871–1940, Italian operatic soprano active in the United States.

tet·rode (tet'rōd) *n. Electronics* An electron tube containing four elements, the fourth usually being a grid interposed between the first grid and the plate. [< TETR(A)- + -ODE¹]

te·trox·ide (te·trok'sīd, -sid) *n. Chem.* An oxide containing four atoms of oxygen to the molecule. Also **te·trox'id** (-sid). [< TETR(A)- + OXIDE]

tet·ryl (tet'ril) *n. Chem.* A yellowish, crystalline nitrogen compound, $C_7H_5N_5O_8$, used as an explosive in boosters and detonators. [< TETR(A)- + -YL]

tet·ter (tet'ər) *n. Pathol.* A vesicular skin disease, as eczema or herpes. [OE *teter*]

Te·tuán (tā·twän') A port city in NE Morocco, on the Mediterranean; former capital of Spanish Morocco; pop. 101,352 (1960).

Tet·zel (tet'səl), **Johann**, 1465?–1519, German Dominican monk and inquisitor; opponent of Luther. Also *Tezel*.

Teu·cer (tōo'sər, tyōo'-) 1. In Greek legend, the half-brother of Ajax, who founded Salamis in Cyprus, noted as an archer. 2. The legendary first king of Troy.

Teu·cri·an (tōo'krē·ən, tyōo'-) *adj.* 1. Trojan. 2. Of or pertaining to Teucer. — *n.* A Trojan.

teugh (tōokh, tyōokh) *adj. Scot.* Tough. Also **teuch.** — **teugh'ly** *adv.* — **teugh'ness** *n.*

Teut. Teuton; Teutonic.

Teu·to·bur·ger Wald (toi'tō·bŏŏr'gər vält) A range of hills in western Germany; highest point, 1,465 ft.; scene of a German victory from which Arminius over the Roman army commanded by Varus, A.D. 9.

Teu·ton (tōot'n, tyōot'n) *n.* 1. One of the Teutones. 2. One belonging to any of the Teutonic peoples; especially, a German. *Abbr. Teut.*

Teu·to·nes (tōo'tə·nēz, tyōo'-) *n.pl.* An ancient German tribe that dwelt in Jutland north of the Elbe.

Teu·ton·ic (tōo·ton'ik, tyōo-) *adj.* 1. Of, pertaining to, or designating the peoples of northern Europe, formerly the Angles, Saxons, Danes, Normans, Goths, etc., now embracing also the English, Germans, Dutch, etc. 2. Of or pertaining to the Germanic languages. 3. Of or pertaining to the Teutones. — *n.* The Germanic subfamily of languages. *Abbr. Teut.*

Teutonic Order An order of military monks founded during the Crusades, who later became the spearhead of German expansion toward Slavic and Baltic territories. Also **Teutonic Knights.**

Teu·ton·ism (tōot'n·iz'əm, tyōot'n-) *n.* 1. A custom or mode of expression peculiar to Germans or Teutons; Germanism. Also **Teu·ton·i·cism** (tōo·ton'ə·siz'əm, tyōo-). 2. A belief in the superiority of the Teutonic peoples. 3. Teutonic character and civilization. — **Teu'ton·ist** *n.*

Teu·ton·ize (tōot'n·īz, tyōot'n-) *v.t. & v.i.* **·ized, ·iz·ing** To make or become Teutonic or German. — **Teu'ton·i·za'tion** *n.*

Te·ve·re (tā'vā·rā) The Italian name for the TIBER.

tew (tōo, tyōo) *Brit. Dial. v.i.* To work hard; fuss or bustle. — *n.* A state of excitement, worry, or bustling.

Tewkes·bur·y (tōoks'ber·e, -bər·ē, tyōoks'-) A municipal borough in NW Gloucestershire, England; scene of the final defeat of the Lancastrians in the Wars of the Roses, 1471; pop. 5,814 (1961).

Tex. Texas; Texan.

Tex·ar·kan·a (teks'är·kan'ə) A dual city in NE Texas and SW Arkansas, with two municipal governments; pop. 30,497 (Texas), 21,682 (Arkansas).

tex·as (tek'səs) *n. U.S.* The uppermost structure on a river steamboat, containing the pilothouse, officers' cabins, etc. [after *Texas*; so called from the custom of naming staterooms after the States, those of the officers being the largest]

Tex·as (tek'səs) A State in the SW United States, bordering on Mexico and the Gulf of Mexico; 267,339 sq. mi.; pop. 11,196,730; cap., Austin; entered the Union Dec. 29, 1845; nickname *Lone Star State.* — **Tex'an** *n. & adj.*

Tex·as (tek'səs) *n. pl.* **Tex·as** A Caddo Indian.

Texas City A city in SE Texas, on Galveston Bay; pop. 38,908.

Texas fever A destructive cattle disease caused by a blood parasite transmitted by a tick (*Margaropus annulatus*).

Texas leaguer *U.S. Informal* In baseball, a fly ball that falls between an infielder and an outfielder for a base hit.

Texas longhorn See under LONGHORN.

Texas Ranger 1. A member of the mounted State police force of Texas. 2. Originally, one of a band of armed and mounted men organized in Texas to fight Indians and keep order on the frontiers.

Texas sparrow A plain, olive-backed fringilline bird (*Arremonops rufivirgatus*) found in Mexico and southern Texas: also called *greenfinch.*

Texas tower A radar tower erected offshore as part of a radar-warning network: so called because of a resemblance to structures used to support oil-drilling apparatus in the Gulf of Mexico off the Texas coast.

text (tekst) *n.* 1. The body of matter on a written or printed page, as distinguished from notes, commentary, illustrations, etc. 2. The actual or original words of an author. 3. A written or printed version of the matter of an author's works: the folio *text* of Shakespeare. 4. Any one of various recensions that are taken to represent the authentic words, or portion of the words, of the original Scriptures. 5. A verse of Scripture, particularly when cited as the basis of a discourse or sermon. 6. Any subject of discourse; a topic; theme. 7. Any of several styles of letters or types. 8. A textbook. [< OF *texte* < L *textus* fabric, structure < *texere* to weave]

text·book (tekst'bŏŏk') *n.* A book used as a standard work or basis of instruction in any branch of knowledge.

tex·tile (teks'til, -tīl) *adj.* 1. Pertaining to weaving or woven fabrics. 2. Such as may be woven; manufactured by weaving. — *n.* 1. A woven fabric. 2. Material capable of being woven. [< L *textilis* < *texere* fabric. See TEXT.]

tex·tu·al (teks'chōo·əl) *adj.* 1. Pertaining to, contained in, or based on the text of a work. 2. Word for word; literal. 3. Versed in texts. [< OF *textuel* < *texte*. See TEXT.] — **tex'tu·al·ly** *adv.*

textual criticism 1. Lower criticism (which see). 2. Literary analysis emphasizing a close and critical study of the text: compare NEW CRITICISM.

tex·tu·al·ism (teks'chōo·əl·iz'əm) *n.* 1. Rigid adherence to a text. 2. The method or principles of textual criticism.

tex·tu·al·ist (teks'chōo·əl·ist') *n.* 1. A close adherent to the letter of a text. 2. One who is versed in or cites texts readily.

tex·tu·ar·y (teks'chōo·er'ē) *adj.* 1. Contained in a text. 2. Of, belonging to, or adhering to a text. — *n. pl.* **·ar·ies** A textualist.

tex·ture (teks'chər) *n.* 1. The arrangement or character of the threads, etc., of a woven fabric. 2. The mode of union or disposition of elementary constituent parts, as in a photograph, surface of paper, etc.; minute structural order. 3. The structure of the surface of a painting, sculpture, etc.; also, the apparent surface structure of an object or part represented in a work of art, as skin, fur, etc. 4. Any woven fabric; a web. [< L *textura* < *textus* fabric. See TEXT.] — **tex'tur·al** *adj.* — **tex'tur·al·ly** *adv.*

tex·tured (teks'chərd) *adj.* 1. Having a distinctive texture. 2. Having (a specified kind of) texture: used in combination: *rough-textured.*

Tey·de (tā'thā) See PEAK OF TENERIFE under TENERIFE.

t.g. Type genus.

-th¹ *suffix of nouns* 1. The act or result of the action expressed in the root word: *growth.* 2. The state or quality of being what is indicated in the root word: *health.* [OE *-thu, -th*]

-th² *suffix* Used in ordinal numbers: *tenth.* Also, after vowels, *-eth,* as in *fortieth.* [OE *-tha, -the*]

-th³ See -ETH¹.

Th *Chem.* Thorium.

Th. Thursday.

T.H. (Formerly) Territory of Hawaii.

thack (thak) *Scot.* n. Thatch; roof. — *v.t.* To thatch.

Thack·er·ay (thak'ər·ē), **William Makepeace**, 1811–63, British novelist born in India.

thae (thā) *adj. & pron. Brit. Dial.* Those; these. [OE *tha,* pl. of *sē* the, that]

Thai (tī) *n.* 1. The people collectively of Thailand, Laos, and parts of Burma, including the Lao, Shan, and Siamese: preceded by *the.* 2. A family of languages spoken by these people, considered by some to be a branch of the Sino-Tibetan family and by others to be affiliated with the Malayo-Polynesian family. 3. The language of Thailand. — *adj.* Of or pertaining to the Thai, their culture, or their languages. Also spelled *Tai.*

Thai·land (tī'land) A constitutional monarchy in SE Asia; 198,404 sq. mi.; pop. 35,448,000 (est. 1970); capital, Bangkok: formerly *Siam.*

thairm (thârm) See THARM.

Tha·is (thā'is *for def. 1,* tä·ēs' *for def. 2*) 1. Fourth-century B.C. Athenian courtesan, mistress of Alexander the Great. 2. An opera by Massenet based on a novel by Anatole France.

thal·a·men·ceph·a·lon (thal'ə·men·sef'ə·lon) *n. Anat.* The diencephalon. [< THALAM(US) + ENCEPHALON]

tha·lam·ic (thə·lam'ik) *adj.* Of or pertaining to a thalamus, especially to the thalamus of the brain.

thal·a·mus (thal'ə·məs) *n. pl.* **·mi** (-mī) 1. *Anat.* A large, ovoid mass of gray matter at the side of the third ventricle of the diencephalon of the brain, the chief center for transmission of sensory impulses to the cerebral cortex: also called *optic thalamus.* 2. *Bot.* The receptacle of a flower. [< L < Gk. *thalamos* chamber]

tha·las·sic (thə·las'ik) *adj.* 1. Of or pertaining to the seas, as distinguished from the oceans. 2. Pelagic; oceanic. — **Syn.** See OCEANIC. [< F *thalassique* < Gk. *thalassa* sea]

thalasso- *combining form* The sea; of or pertaining to the sea. Also, before vowels, **thalass-, thalassi-.** [< Gk. *thalassa* sea]

tha·ler (tä'lər) See TALER.

Tha·les (thā′lēz), 640?–546? B.C., Greek philosopher, astronomer, and geometrician: called **Thales of Miletus.**

Tha·li·a (thə-lī′ə) **1.** The Muse of comedy and pastoral poetry. **2.** One of the three Graces. [< L < Gk. *Thaleia* < *thallein* to bloom]

thal·i·do·mide (thə-lid′ə-mīd) *n. Chem.* An organic compound, $C_{13}H_{10}N_2O_4$, originally prepared in Switzerland as a mild sedative and later withdrawn because its use by pregnant women was suspected of causing phocomelia and other serious malformations in newborn children.

thal·lic (thal′ik) *adj. Chem.* Of, pertaining to, or derived from thallium, especially in its higher valence.

thal·li·um (thal′ē-əm) *n.* A soft, white, crystalline metallic element (symbol Tl), whose salts are used in rat poison, insecticides, and in making optical glass. See ELEMENT. [< NL < Gk. *thallos* green shoot; from the bright green line in its spectrum, that led to its discovery]

thal·loid (thal′oid) *adj.* Resembling a thallus. Also **thal·loi·dal** (thə-loid′l).

thal·lo·phyte (thal′ə-fīt) *n.* Any of various plants belonging to a division or phylum (*Thallophyta*) including forms without true roots, stems, or leaves, comprising the bacteria, fungi, algae, and lichens. [< *thallo-* (< THALLUS) + -PHYTE] — **thal·lo·phyt·ic** (-fit′ik) *adj.*

thal·lous (thal′əs) *adj. Chem.* Derived from thallium, especially in its lower valence. Also **thal·li·ous** (thal′ē-əs).

thal·lus (thal′əs) *n. pl.* **·lus·es** or **·li** (-lī) *Bot.* A plant body without true root, stem, or leaf, as in thallophytes. [< L, shoot < Gk. *thallos* < *thallein* to bloom]

Thames (temz) A river of southern England, flowing 209 miles east through London to the North Sea.

Thames River (temz *for def.* 1; thămz, tămz *for def.* 2) **1.** A river in SE Ontario, Canada, flowing 160 miles SW to Lake St. Clair. **2.** A river and estuary in SE Connecticut, flowing about 15 miles south to Long Island Sound.

Tham·muz (täm′mōōz, tam′uz) See TAMMUZ.

than (than, *unstressed* thən) *conj.* **1.** When, as, or if compared with: after an adjective or adverb to express comparison between what precedes and what follows: I am stronger *than* he (is). **2.** Except; but: used after *other, else,* etc.: no other *than* you. [OE *thonne* then]
♦ *Than* is usually taken as a conjunction; as such, it may be followed by the nominative or the objective, depending on the nature of the ellipsis: You struck him harder *than* I (struck him) or You struck him harder *than* (you struck) *me*. A minority of grammarians and writers have accepted *than* as a preposition, in which case it is regularly followed by the objective: He is stronger *than me. Than whom* is an accepted, though awkward, locution: Bill, *than whom* no one was faster, won the race.

than·age (thā′nij) *n.* **1.** In early English law, the state, jurisdiction, or office of a thane. **2.** The land held by a thane, or the tenure by which he held it. Also *thenage.* [< AF *thaynage* < OE *thegn* thane]

thanato- *combining form* Death; of or pertaining to death: *thanatopsis.* Also, before vowels, **thanat-.** [< Gk. *thanatos* death]

than·a·toid (than′ə-toid) *adj.* Resembling death; deadly.

than·a·tol·o·gy (than′ə-tol′ə-jē) *n.* The study of death.

than·a·top·sis (than′ə-top′sis) *n.* A meditation upon death; a view of death. [< THANAT(O)- + Gk. *opsis* appearance, sight]

Than·a·tos (than′ə-tos) In Greek mythology, the god of death: identified with the Roman *Mors.*

thane (thān) *n.* **1.** A warrior companion of an English king before the Conquest. **2.** A man who ranked above an ordinary freeman or ceorl (churl) but below an earl or nobleman. **3.** *Scot.* The chief of a clan; a baron; one of the old nobility in the service of the king. Also spelled *thegn.* [OE *thegn*]

Than·ja·vur (tän′jä-vûr′) See TANJORE.

thank (thangk) *v.t.* **1.** To express gratitude to; give thanks to. **2.** To hold responsible; blame: often used ironically. — **thank you** I thank you; I am grateful to you. [OE *thancian* < *thanc* thanks, thought]

thank·ful (thangk′fəl) *adj.* **1.** Appreciative of favors received; grateful. **2.** Expressing thanks. — **Syn.** See GRATEFUL. — **thank′ful·ly** *adv.* — **thank′ful·ness** *n.*

thank·less (thangk′lis) *adj.* **1.** Not feeling or showing gratitude; ungrateful. **2.** Not gaining or likely to gain thanks; unappreciated. — **thank′less·ly** *adv.* — **thank′less·ness** *n.*

thanks (thangks) *n.pl.* Expressions of gratitude; grateful acknowledgment. — *interj.* Thank you. — **thanks to 1.** Thanks be given to. **2.** Because of.

thanks·giv·ing (thangks′giv′ing) *n.* **1.** The act of giving thanks, as to God; an expression of gratitude. **2.** A public celebration in recognition of divine favor; also, a day set apart for such celebration.

Thanksgiving Day 1. *U.S.* The fourth Thursday in November, set apart as an annual festival of thanksgiving. **2.** *Canadian* The second Monday in October, a statutory holiday. Also **Thanksgiving.**

thank·wor·thy (thangk′wûr′thē) *adj.* Deserving of thanks.

Thant (thont) See U THANT.

Thap·sus (thap′səs) An ancient ruined town on the coast of eastern Tunisia; scene of Julius Caesar's defeat of Cato the Younger, 46 B.C.

Thar Desert (tär) A sandy waste in NW India and West Pakistan; about 150,000 sq. mi.: also *Indian Desert.*

tharm (thärm) *n. Obs.* **1.** The belly; intestines. **2.** Twisted gut. Also spelled *thairm.* [OE *thearm*]

Tha·sos (thā′sos) An island of Greece in the northern Aegean; 170 sq. mi.

that (that, *unstressed* thət) *pl.* for *adj.* and *pron. def. 1* **those** (thōz) *adj.* **1.** Pertaining to some person or thing previously mentioned, understood, or specifically designated: *that* man. **2.** Denoting something more remote, or something contrasted with another thing: distinguished from *this*: This house is brown, *that* one is red. — *pron.* **1.** As a demonstrative, the person or thing implied, mentioned, or understood; the person or thing there or as distinguished from one already designated: *That* is the dress I like; Keep this and discard *that.* **2.** As a relative pronoun, who, whom, or which: the person *that* I saw. ♦ When the relative clause qualifies or makes an addition to the main clause, *who, whom,* or *which* is preferred, whereas *that* introduces a restrictive clause. Thus we say: Washington, *who* was the first president, is often called Father of his Country. But: The Washington *that* emigrated to this country was his ancestor. — *adv.* **1.** To that extent: I can't see *that* far. **2.** *Informal* In such a manner or degree; so: He's *that* simple, he can hardly read. — *conj. That* is used primarily to connect a subordinate clause with its principal clause, with the following meanings: **1.** As a fact: introducing a fact: I tell you *that* it is so. **2.** As a result: introducing a result, consequence, or effect: He bled so profusely *that* he died. **3.** At which time; when: It was only yesterday *that* I saw him. **4.** So that; in order that: I tell you *that* you may know. **5.** For the reason that; seeing that; because: She wept *that* she was growing old. **6.** Introducing an exclamation: O *that* he would come! — **so that 1.** To the end that. **2.** With the result that. **3.** Provided. [OE *thæt,* neut. of *se* the, that]

thatch (thach) *n.* **1.** A covering of reeds, straw, etc., arranged on a roof so as to shed water. **2.** Anything resembling such a covering. **3.** Any of various palms whose leaves are used for thatching. — *v.t.* To cover with or as with thatch. [OE *thæc* cover] — **thatch′er** *n.* — **thatch′y** *adj.*

thatch·ing (thach′ing) *n.* **1.** The act or process of covering a roof with thatch. **2.** Material used for thatch.

thaumato- *combining form* A wonder; a miracle: *thaumatology.* Also, before vowels, **thaumat-.** [< Gk. *thauma, -atos* wonder]

thau·ma·tol·o·gy (thô′mə-tol′ə-jē) *n. pl.* **·gies** The study of miracles; also, a work or theory dealing with miracles. [< THAUMATO- + -LOGY]

thau·ma·trope (thô′mə-trōp) *n.* An optical toy or instrument in which pictures on opposite sides of a card appear to blend together when the card is rapidly twirled. [< Gk. *thauma* wonder + -TROPE]

thau·ma·turge (thô′mə-tûrj) *n.* One who performs wonders or miracles; magician. Also **thau′ma·tur′gist** (-jist). [< F < Med.L *thaumaturgus* < Gk. *thaumatourgos* < *thauma* wonder + *ergon* work]

thau·ma·tur·gy (thô′mə-tûr′jē) *n.* Magic; the working of wonders or miracles. — **thau′ma·tur′gic** or **·gi·cal** *adj.*

thaw (thô) *v.i.* **1.** To melt or dissolve; become liquid or semiliquid, as snow or ice. **2.** To rise in temperature so as to melt ice and snow: said of weather and used impersonally. **3.** To become less cold and unsociable. — *v.t.* **4.** To cause to thaw. — **Syn.** See MELT. — *n.* **1.** The act of thawing, or the state of being thawed. **2.** Warmth of weather above the freezing point, following a colder period. **3.** A state of warmer feeling or expression. [OE *thawian*] — **thaw′er** *n.*

Thay·er (thā′ər), **Sylvanus,** 1785–1872, U.S. Army officer and educator; superintendent of the U.S. Military Academy 1817–33: called the **Father of West Point.** — **William Roscoe,** 1859–1923, U.S. historian and biographer.

Th.B. Bachelor of Theology (L *Theologiae Baccalaureus*).

Th.D. Doctor of Theology (L *Theologiae Doctor*).

the¹ (*stressed* thē; *unstressed before a consonant* thə; *unstressed before a vowel* thē or thi) *definite article* or *adj. The* is opposed to the indefinite article *a* or *an,* and is used, especially before nouns, to render the modified word more particular or individual. It is used specifically: **1.** When reference is made to a particular person, thing, or group: He left *the* room. **2.** To give an adjective substantive force, or render a notion abstract: *the* doing of the deed; *the* quick and *the* dead. **3.** Before a noun to make it generic: *The* dog is a friend of man. **4.** With the force of a possessive pronoun: He kicked me in *the* (my) leg. **5.** To give distributive force: equivalent to *a, per, each,* etc.: a dollar *the* volume. **6.** To designate a particular one as emphatically outstanding: usually stressed in speech and italicized in writing: He is *the* officer for the command. **7.** As part of a title: *The* Duke of York. **8.** *Scot. & Irish* To designate the head of a clan or group: *the* MacIntosh. [OE, later form of *sē*]

the² (thə) *adv.* By that much; by so much; to this extent: used to modify words in the comparative degree: *the* more, *the* merrier. [OE *thȳ,* instrumental case of *sē* the¹]

the- Var. of THEO-.

the·a·ceous (thē-ā′shəs) *adj. Bot.* Of or belonging to the tea family (*Theaceae*) of shrubs and trees. [< NL < *Thea,* genus name < dial. Chinese *t′e* tea; incorrectly taken by Linnaeus as "divine herb" < Gk. *thea* goddess]

the·an·throp·ic (thē′an-throp′ik) *adj.* **1.** Being both divine and human. **2.** Having or pertaining to a nature both divine and human. Also **the·an·throp·i·cal.** [< Gk. *theanthrōpos* < *theos* god + *anthrōpos* man]

the·an·thro·pism (thē-an′thrə-piz′əm) *n.* **1.** The doctrine of the manifestation of God in man, or of the union of the divine and human in Christ. **2.** The ascription of human characteristics to a deity; anthropomorphism. **3.** Belief in the possibility of the combination in one being of a nature both human and divine. — **the·an′thro·pist** *n.*

the·ar·chy (thē′är-kē) *n., pl.* **·chies 1.** Government by God or by a god. **2.** A theocracy. **3.** A body or class of deities. [< Gk. *thearchia* < *theos* god + *archein* to rule]

theat. Theatrical.

the·a·ter (thē′ə-tər) *n.* **1.** A building especially adapted to present dramas, operas, motion pictures, etc.; playhouse. **2.** The theatrical world and everything relating to it. **3.** A room or hall arranged with seats that rise as they recede from a platform, especially adapted to lectures, demonstrations, etc. **4.** Any place of semicircular form with seats rising by easy gradations. **5.** Any place or region that is the scene of events: a *theater* of operations in war. Also *esp. Brit.* **the′a·tre.** [< OF *theatre* < L *theatrum* < Gk. *theatron* < *theasthai* to behold]

the·a·ter·go·er (thē′ə-tər-gō′ər) *n.* One who goes often or regularly to the theater. Also *esp. Brit.* **the′a·tre·go′er.** — **the′a·ter·go′ing** *n.*

the·a·ter-in-the-round (thē′ə-tər-in-thə-round′) *n.* Arena theater (which see).

Theater of the Absurd The plays, theatrical conventions, etc., of a group of 20th-century playwrights, including Samuel Beckett, who stress the rootlessness, futility, and irrationality of modern man.

the·at·ri·cal (thē-at′ri·kəl) *adj.* **1.** Pertaining to the theater or to dramatic performances. **2.** Designed for show, display, or effect; showy; artificial. **3.** Suited to dramatic presentation. **4.** Resembling the manner of actors; histrionic. Also **the·at′ric.** — *n.pl.* Dramatic performances, especially by amateurs. [< LL *theatricus* < Gk. *theatrikos* < *theatron.* See THEATER.] — **the·at′ri·cal·ly** *adv.* — **the·at′ri·cal·ness** *n.*

the·at·ri·cal·ism (thē-at′ri·kəl-iz′əm) *n.* Theatrical or melodramatic manner or style.

the·at·rics (thē-at′riks) *n.pl.* (*construed as sing.*) **1.** The staging of plays. **2.** The art of creating effects appropriate to dramatic performances.

The·ba·id (thē′bā-id, thi·bā′id) *n.* A Latin epic by Statius, narrating the story of the siege of Boeotian Thebes.

the·ba·ine (thē′bə-ēn, thi·bā′ēn, -in) *n. Chem.* A white, poisonous, crystalline alkaloid, $C_{19}H_{21}O_3N$, found in opium: also called *paramorphine.* [after Egyptian *Thebes,* where an opium was produced + -INE²]

Thebes (thēbz) **1.** The ancient capital of Upper Egypt; Luxor and Karnak occupy part of its site on the Nile. **2.** The chief city of ancient Boeotia, Greece; destroyed in 336 B.C. by Alexander the Great: also **The·bae** (thē′bē). **3.** A commercial city in east central Greece on the site of ancient Thebes; important in the Middle Ages; pop. 15,779 (1961). — **The·ban** (thē′bən) *adj. & n.*

the·ca (thē′kə) *n., pl.* **·cae** (-sē) **1.** *Biol.* A protective sheath or case for an organ or part, as of the spinal cord, a follicle, an insect pupa, etc. **2.** *Bot.* A spore case, sac, or capsule. [< L < Gk. *thēkē* case] — **the′cal** *adj.*

the·cate (thē′kit, -kāt) *adj.* Having a sheath; sheathed.

thé dan·sant (tā′ dän·sän′) *pl.* **thés dan·sants** (tā′ dän·sän′) *French* An afternoon tea at which there is dancing.

thee (thē) *pron.* **1.** *Archaic* The objective case of the pronoun *thou.* **2.** Thou: used by some Quakers with a verb in the third person singular: *Thee* knows my mind. [OE *thē,* orig. dative, later accusative case of *thū* thou]

thee·lin (thē′lin) *n. Biochem.* Estrone. [< Gk. *thēlys* female + -IN.]

theft (theft) *n.* **1.** The act or crime of stealing; larceny. **2.** *Rare* That which is stolen. [OE *thēoft, thīefth*]
— **Syn. 1.** *Theft, larceny, burglary, robbery, holdup,* and *stickup* denote the crime of stealing. *Theft* is the general term, which includes all the others. In law, *larceny* includes many forms of stealing, but not embezzlement and swindling. *Burglary* is the crime of breaking into and entering another's home, place of business, or other property with intent to commit a felony. *Robbery* is stealing from the person, or in the presence of, the victim. *Holdup* and *stickup* are respectively informal and slang words for robbery in which the victim is cowed with a weapon.

thegn (thān) See THANE.

the·ine (thē′ēn, -in) *n. Chem.* The alkaloid found in the tea plant, chemically identical with caffeine. Also **the′in** (-in). [< F *théine* < NL *thea* tea < dial. Chinese *t′e*]

their (thâr) *pronominal adj.* The possessive case of the pronoun *they,* used attributively: *their* homes. [ME < ON *theirra* of them]

theirs (thârz) *pron.* **1.** The possessive case of the pronoun *they,* used predicatively: That house is *theirs.* **2.** The one or ones belonging or relating to them: our country and *theirs.* — **of theirs** Belonging or pertaining to them: a double possessive. [< THEIR + -s, on analogy with *ours, yours*]

the·ism¹ (thē′iz·əm) *n.* **1.** Belief in, or in the existence of, God, a god, or gods. **2.** Belief in a personal God as creator and supreme ruler of the universe, who transcends his creation but works in and through it in revealing himself to men. Compare DEISM, PANTHEISM. **3.** Belief in one god; monotheism. [< Gk. *theos* god] — **the′ist** *n.* — **the·is′tic** or **·ti·cal** *adj.* — **the·is′ti·cal·ly** *adv.*

the·ism² (thē′iz·əm, tē′-) *n. Pathol.* The toxic effects of excessive tea drinking. [< NL *thea* tea. See THEINE.]

the·li·tis (thi·lī′tis) *n. Pathol.* Inflammation of the nipple. [< NL < Gk. *thēlē* teat + -ITIS]

them (them, *unstressed* thəm) *pron.* The objective case of the pronoun *they.* [ME *theim* < ON, to them]

the·mat·ic (thē-mat′ik) *adj.* **1.** Of, constituting, or pertaining to a theme or themes. **2.** *Ling.* Constituting a stem. Also **the·mat′i·cal.** — **the·mat′i·cal·ly** *adv.*

thematic vowel *Ling.* A vowel added to a root to form a stem or theme.

theme (thēm) *n.* **1.** A topic to be discussed or developed in speech or writing; a subject of discourse. **2.** Any topic. **3.** A brief composition, especially one written as an exercise as part of a course of instruction. **4.** *Ling.* A stem. **5.** *Music* **a** A melody that is subjected to variation or elaboration; subject. **b** A musical feature, as a chordal sequence, rhythm, melody, etc. that forms the basis of a composition. — **Syn.** See MELODY, TOPIC. [< OF *teme* < L *thema* < Gk. *the-,* stem of *tithenai* to place]

theme song 1. A melody used throughout a dramatic presentation to establish or maintain a mood. **2.** A strain of music that identifies a radio program, a dance band, etc.

The·mis (thē′mis) In Greek mythology, a goddess of law and justice, daughter of Uranus and Gaea. [< Gk., law]

The·mis·to·cles (thə-mis′tə-klēz), 527?–460? B.C., Athenian statesman and military commander.

them·selves (them′selvz′, *unstressed* thəm-) *pron.* A form of the third person plural pronoun, used: **1.** As a reflexive or as object of a preposition in a reflexive sense: They laughed at *themselves.* **2.** As an emphatic or intensive form of *they:* They *themselves* are at fault. **3.** As a designation of a normal, proper, or usual state: They were not *themselves* then.

then (then) *adv.* **1.** At that time. **2.** Soon or immediately afterward; next in space or time. **3.** At another time: often introducing a sequential statement following *now; at first,* etc. **4.** For that reason; as a consequence; accordingly. **5.** In that case: I will *then,* since you won't. **6.** Also; besides: and *then* there is the rent to pay. — **Syn.** See THEREFORE. — *adj.* Being or acting in, or belonging to, that time: the *then* secretary of state. — *n.* A specific time already mentioned or understood; that time. [OE *thanne*]

then·age (then′ij) See THANAGE.

the·nar (thē′när) *n. Anat.* **1.** The palm of the hand. **2.** The prominence on the palm at the base of the thumb. — *adj.* Of or pertaining to the palm of a hand or the sole of a foot: also **the′nal** (thē′nəl). [< NL < Gk. *thenar* palm of the hand]

thence (thens) *adv.* **1.** From that place. **2.** From the circumstance, fact, or cause; therefore. **3.** From that time; after that time. **4.** *Archaic* Away from there; elsewhere; absent. [ME *thannes* < OE *thanon* from there + -s³]

thence·forth (thens′fôrth′, -fôrth′, thens′fôrth′, -fôrth′) *adv.* From that time on; thereafter.

thence·for·ward (thens′fôr′wərd) *adv.* **1.** Thenceforth. **2.** From that place or time forward. Also **thence′for′wards.**

theo- *combining form* God; of or pertaining to God, a god, or gods: *theophany, theodicy.* Also, before vowels, *the-.* [< Gk. *theos* a god]

the·o·bro·mine (thē′ə-brō′mēn, -min) *n. Chem.* A bitter, colorless, crystalline alkaloid, $C_7H_8N_4O_2$, resembling caffeine, contained in cacao beans and used in medicine as a diuretic and vasodilator. [< NL *Theobroma,* genus name + -INE²]

the·o·cen·tric (thē′ə-sen′trik) *adj.* Centering on or primarily concerned with God.

the·oc·ra·cy (thē-ok′rə-sē) *n., pl.* **·cies 1.** A state, polity, or group of people that claims a deity as its ruler, as ancient Israel after the Exodus. **2.** Government of a state by a god, or by a priesthood claiming divine authority, as in the Papacy. Also called *thearchy.* [< Gk. *theokratia* < *theos* god + *krateein* to rule] — **the·o·crat·ic** (thē′ə-krat′ik) or **·i·cal** *adj.*

the·oc·ra·sy (thē-ok′rə-sē) *n., pl.* **·sies 1.** The mingling of several deities or divine attributes in one personality. **2.** The mystical intimacy or union of the soul with God. [< LGk. *theokrasia* < Gk. *theos* god + *krasis* a mingling]

the·o·crat (thē′ə-krat) *n.* **1.** A theocratic or divine ruler. **2.** An advocate of theocracy.

The·oc·ri·tus (thē-ok′rə-təs) Third century B.C. Greek poet.

the·od·i·cy (thē-od′ə-sē) *n. pl.* **·cies** A reconciling of the existence of evil with the goodness and sovereignty of God: a term established by Leibnitz in 1710. [< F *théodicée* < Gk. *theos* god + *dikē* justice]

the·od·o·lite (thē-od′ə-līt) *n.* In surveying, an instrument for measuring horizontal and vertical angles by means of a small telescope turning on a horizontal and a vertical axis. [An arbitrary formation] — **the·od·o·lit′ic** (-lit′ik) *adj.*

The·o·do·ra (thē′ə-dôr′ə, -dō′rə), died 547?, Byzantine actress and courtesan; wife of Justinian I.

The·od·o·ric (thē-od′ər-ik), 454?–526, king of the Ostrogoths; invaded and conquered Italy: called **the Great.**

The·o·do·si·us I (thē′ə-dō′shē-əs), 346?–395, Roman emperor 379–395: full name **Flavius Theodosius:** called **the Great.**

the·og·o·ny (thē-og′ə-nē) *n. pl.* **·nies** A genealogy of the gods, especially as recited in ancient poetry. [< Gk. *theogonia* < *theos* god + *gonos* generation < *gignesthai* to be born] — **the·o·gon·ic** (thē′ə-gon′ik) *adj.* — **the·og′o·nist** *n.*

theol. Theologian; theological; theology.

the·o·lo·gi·an (thē′ə-lō′jē-ən, -jən) *n.* One versed in theology, especially that of the Christian church. Abbr. *theol.*

the·o·log·i·cal (thē′ə-loj′i-kəl) *adj.* Of or pertaining to theology or to divine revelation. Also **the′o·log′ic.** Abbr. *theol.* — **the′o·log′i·cal·ly** *adv.*

theological virtues Faith, hope, and charity or love, the types of moral excellence added by the early Christian moralists to the cardinal virtues of Platonic philosophy.

the·ol·o·gize (thē-ol′ə-jīz) *v.* **·gized, ·giz·ing** *v.t.* **1.** To devise or fit (something) into a system of theology. — *v.i.* **2.** To reason theologically. Also *Brit.* **the·ol′o·gise.**

the·ol·o·gy (thē-ol′ə-jē) *n. pl.* **·gies** **1.** The study of religion, culminating in a synthesis or philosophy of religion; also, a critical survey of religion, especially of the Christian religion. **2.** A body of doctrines as set forth by a particular church or religious group. Abbr. *theol.* [< OF *theologie* < LL *theologia* < Gk. < *theos* god + *logos* discourse]

the·om·a·chy (thē-om′ə-kē) *n. pl.* **·chies** A combat with or among the gods. [< Gk. *theomachia* < *theos* god + *machē* combat]

the·o·mor·phic (thē′ə-môr′fik) *adj.* Having the form or likeness of God. [< Gk. *theomorphos* < *theos* god + *morphē* form]

the·o·mor·phism (thē′ə-môr′fiz-əm) *n.* The doctrine that man has the likeness or form of God.

the·op·a·thy (thē-op′ə-thē) *n. pl.* **·thies** Religious emotion aroused by meditation on God; mystical ecstasy. [< Gk. *theopathia* the suffering of God < *theos* god + *path-,* stem of *paschein* to suffer] — **the·o·pa·thet·ic** (thē′ō-pə-thet′ik), **the′o·path′ic** (-path′ik) *adj.*

the·oph·a·ny (thē-of′ə-nē) *n. pl.* **·nies** A manifestation or appearance of a deity or of the gods to man. [< L *theophania* < Gk. < *theos* god + *phainein* to show]

The·o·phras·tus (thē′ə-fras′təs), 372?–287? B.C., Greek philosopher and scientist.

the·o·phyl·line (thē′ə-fil′ēn, -in) *n. Chem.* A white, bitter, crystalline isomer of theobromine, $C_7H_8N_4O_2$, obtained from tea leaves and also made synthetically. [< NL *thea* tea + Gk. *phyllon* leaf + -INE[2]]

the·or·bo (thē-ôr′bō) *n. pl.* **·bos** A 17th-century lute having two sets of pegs on one neck, one set offset to hold unfretted drone strings. [< F *théorbe* < Ital. *tiorba*]

the·o·rem (thē′ər-əm, thir′əm) *n.* **1.** A proposition demonstrably true or acknowledged as such. **2.** *Math.* **a** A proposition setting forth something to be proved. **b** A proposition that has been proved or assumed to be true. **c** A rule or statement of relations formulated in symbols. — **Syn.** See AXIOM. [LL *theorema* < Gk. *theōrēma* sight, theory < *theōreein* to look at] — **the·o·re·mat·ic** (thē′ər-ə-mat′ik), **the′o·rem′ic** (-ə-rem′ik) *adj.*

the·o·ret·i·cal (thē′ə-ret′i-kəl) *adj.* **1.** Of, relating to, or consisting of theory. **2.** Relating to knowledge or science without reference to its application. **3.** Existing only in theory; hypothetical. **4.** Addicted to theorizing; unaffected by practical considerations; impractical; visionary. Also **the′o·ret′ic.** — **the′o·ret′i·cal·ly** *adv.*

the·o·re·ti·cian (thē′ər-ə-tish′ən) *n.* One who deals with the speculative, hypothetical, or ideal rather than with the practical and executive aspects of a subject.

the·o·ret·ics (thē′ə-ret′iks) *n.pl.* (*construed as sing.*) The theoretical aspect of a science.

the·o·rist (thē′ər-ist) *n.* One who theorizes.

the·o·rize (thē′ə-rīz) *v.i.* **·rized, ·riz·ing** To form or express theories; speculate. Also *Brit.* **the′o·rise.** — **the′o·ri·za′tion** *n.* — **the′o·riz′er** *n.*

the·o·ry (thē′ər-ē, thir′ē) *n. pl.* **·ries** **1.** A plan or scheme existing in the mind only; a speculative or conjectural view of something. **2.** An integrated group of the fundamental principles underlying a science or its practical applications: the atomic *theory.* **3.** Abstract knowledge of any art as opposed to the practice of it. **4.** A closely reasoned set of propositions, derived from and supported by established evidence and intended to serve as an explanation for a group of phenomena: the quantum *theory.* **5.** An arrangement of results, or a body of theorems, presenting a systematic view of some subject: the *theory* of functions. — **Syn.** See DOCTRINE, HYPOTHESIS. [< LL *theoria* < Gk. *theoria* view, speculation < *theoreein* to look at]

theos. Theosophical; theosophy.

the·os·o·phy (thē-os′ə-fē) *n. pl.* **·phies 1.** Any of various religious systems that aim at establishing a direct relation between the individual soul and the divine principle through contemplation and speculation. **2.** *Often cap.* The doctrines and beliefs of a modern religious sect (**Theosophical Society**), resembling those of Buddhism and Brahmanism. [< Med.L *theosophia* < Gk. < *theosophos* wise in divine matters < *theos* god + *sophos* wise] — **the·o·soph·ic** (thē′ə-sof′ik) or **·i·cal** *adj.* — **the′o·soph′i·cal·ly** *adv.* — **the·os′o·phist** *n.*

therap. Therapeutic(s).

ther·a·peu·tic (ther′ə-pyōō′tik) *adj.* **1.** Having healing qualities; curative. **2.** Pertaining to therapeutics. Also **ther′a·peu′ti·cal.** Abbr. *therap.* [< NL *therapeuticus* < Gk. *therapeutikos* < *therapeutēs* one who attends < *therapeuein* to serve, take care of < *therapōn* an attendant] — **ther′a·peu′ti·cal·ly** *adv.*

ther·a·peu·tics (ther′ə-pyōō′tiks) *n.pl.* (*construed as sing.*) The branch of medical science dealing with the treatment of disease. Abbr. *therap.* — **ther′a·peu′tist** *n.*

ther·a·py (ther′ə-pē) *n. pl.* **·pies 1.** The treatment of disease: often used in combination: *chemotherapy.* **2.** Treatment, activity, etc., intended to remedy or alleviate a disorder or undesirable condition. **3.** Healing or curative quality. [< NL *therapia* < Gk. *therapeia* < *therapeuein* to take care of. See THERAPEUTIC.] — **ther′a·pist** *n.*

there (thâr) *adv.* **1.** In, at, or about that place: opposed to *here.* Also used to indicate or emphasize: John *there* is a good student. **2.** To, toward, or into that place; thither. **3.** At that stage or point of action or time: Begin *there,* please. — *n.* That place: Are you from *there,* too? — *interj.* An exclamation of triumph, relief, etc.: *There!* It's finished. ◆ The adverb *there* cannot, in standard English, appear in the adjective position, as that *there* girl. That girl *there* is the accepted order. *There* is very often used as an expletive introducing a clause or sentence, the subject usually following the verb: *There* once were three bears. It is also used as an equivalent of the pronoun *that* in expressions of encouragement, approval, etc.: *There's* a good boy. [OE *thēr*]

there·a·bout (thâr′ə-bout′) *adv.* Near that number, quantity, degree, place, or time; approximately. Also **there′a·bouts′.**

there·af·ter (thâr′af′tər, -äf′-) *adv.* **1.** Afterward; from that time on. **2.** *Obs.* Accordingly.

there·a·gainst (thâr′ə-genst′) *adv.* Against or in opposition to that thing; on the other hand.

there·at (thâr′at′) *adv.* At that event, place, or time; at that incentive; upon that.

there·by (thâr′bī′) *adv.* **1.** Through the agency of that. **2.** Connected with that. **3.** Conformably to that. **4.** *Archaic* Nearby; thereabout. **5.** *Archaic* By it or that; into possession of it or that: How did you come *thereby?*

there·for (thâr′fôr′) *adv.* For this, that, or it: We return thanks *therefor.*

there·fore (thâr′fôr′, -fōr′) *adv. & conj.* For that or this reason; on that ground or account; consequently: He did not run fast enough; *therefore* he lost the race.

— **Syn.** *Therefore, hence, then, consequently, accordingly,* and *so* are connectives indicating causal or logical relationship. *Therefore* is the most precise and formal word for marking the conclusion of a chain of reasoning: this triangle is isoceles; *therefore,* its base angles are equal. *Hence* is often equivalent to *therefore,* but throws a trifle more weight upon the antecedent: his conversation is always about himself, *hence,* tiresome. *Then* is less forceful, and appropriate for a definitional or truistic relationship: one of us must go; if you will not, *then* I will. *Consequently* introduces a direct result which may be of a practical rather than of a theoretic nature: it was raining; *consequently,* he put off his trip. *Accordingly* indicates correspondence rather than necessary logical connection: the soldiers were eager and confident; *accordingly,* they sprang forward at the word of command. *So* is a vague word, often avoided as a connective by careful writers: he said I was welcome, *so* I went in.

there·from (thâr′frum′, -from′) *adv.* From this, that, or it; from this or that time, place, state, event, or thing.

there·in (thâr′in′) *adv.* **1.** In that place. **2.** In that time, matter, or respect.

there·in·af·ter (thâr′in-af′tər, -äf′-) *adv.* In a subsequent part of that (book, document, speech, etc.).

there·in·to (thâr′in-tōō′) *adv.* Into this, that, or it.

Ther·e·min (ther′ə-min) *n.* An electronic musical instrument whose pitch is controlled by the proximity of the player's hand: a trade name. Also **ther′e·min**. [after Léon *Thérémin*, born 1896, Russian inventor active in France]

there·of (thâr′uv′, -ov′) *adv.* **1.** Of or relating to this, that, or it. **2.** From or because of this or that cause or particular; therefrom.

there·on (thâr′on′, -ôn′) *adv.* **1.** On this, that, or it. **2.** Thereupon; thereat.

there's (thârz) There is.

The·re·sa (tə·rē′sə, -res′ə) **Saint**, 1515–82, Spanish Carmelite nun, mystic, and author: called **Theresa of Ávila**. Also *Teresa*.

Thérèse (tā·rez′), **Saint**, 1873–97, French Carmelite nun and author; canonized 1925: called **Thérèse of Lisieux.**

there·to (thâr′tōō′) *adv.* **1.** To this, that, or it. **2.** In addition; furthermore. Also **there′un·to′** (-un·tōō′).

there·to·fore (thâr′tə·fôr′, -fōr′) *adv.* Before this or that; previously to that.

there·un·der (thâr′un′dər) *adv.* **1.** Under this or that. **2.** Less in number; fewer than that. **3.** In accordance with that; by that authority.

there·up·on (thâr′ə·pon′, -ə·pôn′) *adv.* **1.** Upon that; upon it. **2.** Following upon or in consequence of that. **3.** Immediately following; at once.

there·with (thâr′with′, -with′) *adv.* **1.** With this, that, or it. **2.** Thereupon; thereafter; immediately afterward.

there·with·al (thâr′with·ôl′) *adv.* **1.** With all this or that; besides. **2.** *Obs.* Therewith; with this, that, or it.

the·ri·a·ca (thi·rī′ə·kə) *n.* **1.** An ancient antidote for the bite of venomous creatures, containing numerous drugs mixed with honey. **2.** Molasses; treacle. Also **the·ri·ac** (thir′ē·ak). [< LL, an antidote for poison < Gk. *thēriakos* pertaining to wild beasts < *thērion*, dim. of *thēr* wild beast] — **the·ri′a·cal** *adj.*

the·ri·an·thro·pism (thir′ē·an′thrə·piz′əm) *n.* Representation of supernatural beings in combined forms of man and beast, especially in primitive polytheistic worship. [< Gk. *thērion* wild beast + *anthrōpos* man] — **the′ri·an·throp′ic** (-an·throp′ik) *adj.*

the·ri·o·mor·phic (thir′ē·ə·môr′fik) *adj.* Beastlike in form: *theriomorphic* gods. Also **the′ri·o·mor′phous**. [< Gk. *thērion* wild beast + *morphē* form]

therm (thûrm) *n.* **1.** A unit of heat equal to 100,000 British thermal units. **2.** One thousand large calories. **3.** The large calorie. **4.** The small calorie. Also **therme**. [< Gk. *thermē* heat]

therm- Var. of THERMO-.

therm. Thermometer.

Ther·ma (thûr′mə) The ancient name for SALONIKA.

ther·mae (thûr′mē) *n.pl.* **1.** Hot springs or baths. **2.** The public baths of the ancient Romans. [< L < Gk. *thermai*, pl. of *thermē* heat]

ther·mal (thûr′məl) *adj.* **1.** Pertaining to, determined by, or measured by heat. **2.** Caused by, using, or producing heat. **3.** Hot or warm. Also **ther′mic**. — **ther′mal·ly** *adv.*

thermal death Heat death (which see).

thermal radiation Electromagnetic radiation ranging between long infrared and short ultraviolet, produced by the random motions of atoms and molecules.

thermal spring A hot spring (which see).

therm·an·es·the·sia (thûr′mən·is·thē′zhə, -zhē·ə) *n. Pathol.* Loss of ability to recognize sensations of heat or cold; absence of temperature sense. Also **therm′an·aes·the′·sia.** [< THERM(O)- + ANESTHESIA]

therm·el (thûr′mel) *n.* A thermocouple or group of thermocouples when used to determine temperatures. Also called *thermoelectric thermometer.* [< THERM(O) + EL(ECTRIC)]

therm·es·the·sia (thûr′mis·thē′zhə, -zhē·ə) *n. Physiol.* The ability to recognize changes of temperature. Also **therm′aes·the′sia.** [< THERM(O)- + ESTHESIA]

Ther·mi·dor (thûr′mə·dôr′, *Fr.* ter·mē·dôr′) *n.* The eleventh month of the Republican calendar. See (Republican) CALENDAR. [< F < Gk. *thermē* heat + *dōron* gift]

therm·i·on (thûrm′ī′ən, thûr′mē·ən) *n. Physics* An electrically charged particle emitted by a heated body. [< THERM(O)- + ION]

therm·i·on·ic (thûr′mē·on′ik) *adj.* Pertaining to thermions or to the phenomena associated with their emission.

thermionic current A flow or current of electrically charged particles, as in a thermionic tube.

therm·i·on·ics (thûr′mē·on′iks) *n.pl.* (construed as sing.) The science and application of thermionic phenomena.

thermionic tube An electron tube emitting thermions from a heated electrode. Also *Brit.* **thermionic valve.**

therm·is·tor (thər·mis′tər) *n. Electronics* A small, compact thermometric device consisting of a semiconducting material whose resistivity decreases with rise in temperature. [< THERM(O)- + (RES)ISTOR]

ther·mite (thûr′mīt) *n.* A mixture of finely divided aluminum and an oxide of iron, chromium, or manganese, producing an intense heat when ignited. Also **ther′mit** (-mit). [< G < Gk. *thermē* heat]

thermo- *combining form* Heat; of, related to, or caused by heat: *thermolysis, thermostat*. Also, before vowels, *therm-*. [< Gk. *thermos* heat, warmth]

ther·mo·an·al·y·sis (thûr′mō·ə·nal′ə·sis) *n. pl.* **·ses** (-sēz) Any of several techniques for measuring physicochemical changes produced in a substance by specified changes in temperature. — **ther′mo·an′a·lyt′ic** (-an′ə·lit′ik) *adj.*

ther·mo·bar·o·graph (thûr′mō·bar′ə·graf, -gräf) *n.* An apparatus for measuring the pressure and temperature of a gas simultaneously.

ther·mo·ba·rom·e·ter (thûr′mō·bə·rom′ə·tər) *n.* **1.** An apparatus for measuring atmospheric pressure by noting the boiling point of water. **2.** A form of barometer that can be inverted and made to serve as a thermometer.

ther·mo·cau·ter·y (thûr′mō·kô′tər·ē) *n. pl.* **·ter·ies** Cautery by means of heated wires or points.

ther·mo·chem·is·try (thûr′mō·kem′is·trē) *n.* The branch of chemistry that treats of the relations between chemical reactions and heat. — **ther′mo·chem′i·cal** (-kem′i·kəl) *adj.* — **ther′mo·chem′ist** *n.*

ther·mo·cline (thûr′mō·klīn) *n.* A gradient indicating changes in temperature with depth of ocean waters.

ther·mo·cou·ple (thûr′mə·kup′əl) *n.* A device for temperature measurement that depends upon the electric current or potential produced when joined conductors of two different metals have their ends at different temperatures. Also **thermoelectric couple.**

ther·mo·dy·nam·ics (thûr′mō·dī·nam′iks, -di-) *n.pl.* (construed as sing.) The branch of physics dealing with the relations between heat and other forms of energy. — **ther′mo·dy·nam′ic** or **·i·cal** *adj.* — **ther′mo·dy·nam′i·cist** (-ə·sist) *n.*

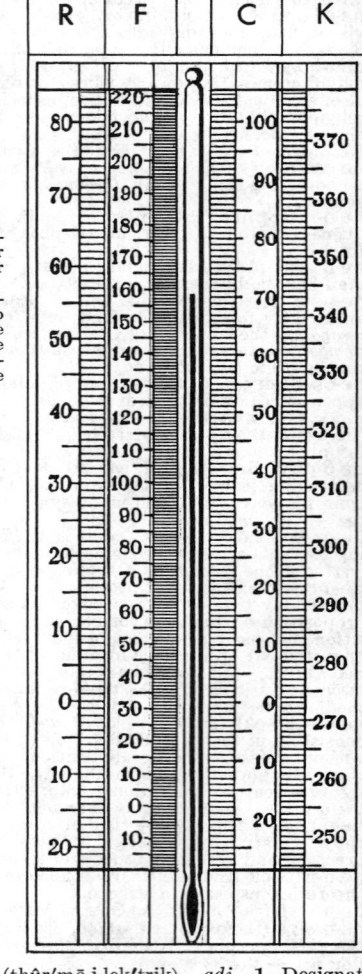

THERMOMETER SCALES
R Reaumur. *F* Fahrenheit. *C* Centigrade or Celsius. *K* Kelvin or Absolute.

The following formulas may be used to convert temperature readings taken on one scale into their equivalents on any of the other scales.

(Degrees C. × 9/5) + 32 = degrees F.

Degrees C. + 273.16 = degrees K.

Degrees C. × 4/5 = degrees R.

(Degrees F. − 32) × 5/9 = degrees C.

(Degrees F. − 32) × 4/9 = degrees R.

Degrees R. × 5/4 = degrees C.

(Degrees R. × 9/4) + 32 = degrees F.

ther·mo·e·lec·tric (thûr′mō·i·lek′trik) *adj.* **1.** Designating or associated with changes of electrical potential between two dissimilar metals in contact with each other as temperature varies. **2.** Designating or associated with the ability of an electric current to cause a flow of heat in a wire. Also **ther′mo·e·lec′tri·cal.** — **ther′mo·e·lec′tri·cal·ly** *adv.*

ther·mo·e·lec·tric·i·ty (thûr′mō·i·lek′tris′ə·tē) *n.* Electricity generated by thermoelectric phenomena.

thermoelectric thermometer A thermel (which see).

ther·mo·e·lec·tro·mo·tive (thûr′mō·i·lek′trə·mō′tiv) *adj.* Of, pertaining to, or designating electromotive force caused by thermoelectric phenomena.

ther·mo·gen·e·sis (thûr′mō·jen′ə·sis) *n.* The production of heat, especially of animal heat by metabolic processes. — **ther′mo·gen′ic**, **ther·mog·e·nous** (thər·moj′ə·nəs), **ther′mo·ge·net′ic** (-jə·net′ik) *adj.*

ther·mo·gram (thûr′mə·gram) *n.* The record made by a thermograph.

ther·mo·graph (thûr′mə·graf, -gräf) *n.* A recording thermometer.

ther·mo·junc·tion (thûr′mō·jungk′shən) *n.* The point of contact between the two conductors of a thermocouple.

ther·mo·kin·e·mat·ics (thûr′mō·kin′ə·mat′iks) *n.pl.* (construed as sing.) The study of heat in motion or of the motive power of heat.

ther·mo·la·bile (thûr′mō·lā′bil) *adj.* Biochem. Decomposed, destroyed, or liable to be adversely affected by heat, as some enzymes and toxins: opposed to *thermostable.* [< THERMO- + LABILE]

ther·mo·lu·mi·nes·cence (thûr′mō·lōō′mə·nes′əns) *n.* **1.** The emission of light from a substance or material under the action of heat. **2.** Luminescence due to the emission of electrons as temperature is increased, sometimes indicative of the age of sedimentary rocks. — **ther′mo·lu′mi·nes′cent** *adj.*

ther·mol·y·sis (thər·mol′ə·sis) *n.* Physiol. The dissipation of heat from a living body. [< THERMO- + -LYSIS] — **ther·mo·lyt·ic** (thûr′mə·lit′ik) *adj.*

ther·mo·mag·net·ic (thûr′mō·mag·net′ik) *adj.* Of or pertaining to the relations between heat and magnetism.

ther·mom·e·ter (thər·mom′ə·tər) *n.* An instrument for measuring temperature, usually by means of a graduated glass capillary tube with a bulb containing a liquid, as mercury or alcohol, that expands or contracts as the temperature rises or falls. Abbr. *therm.* [< THERMO- + METER]

ther·mom·e·try (thər·mom′ə·trē) *n.* **1.** The measurement of temperature. **2.** The design and construction of thermometers. — **ther·mo·met·ric** (thûr′mō·met′rik) or **·ri·cal** *adj.* — **ther′mo·met′ri·cal·ly** *adv.*

ther·mo·mo·tor (thûr′mō·mō′tər) *n.* A heat engine; especially, a hot-air engine.

ther·mo·nu·cle·ar (thûr′mō·nōō′klē·ər, -nyōō′-) *adj.* Physics Pertaining to or characterized by reactions involving the fusion of atomic nuclei at very high temperatures, especially in stars and in the hydrogen bomb.

ther·mo·pile (thûr′mō·pīl) *n.* A group of thermocouples acting jointly to produce an electric current, especially when used with a galvanometer to measure heat.

ther·mo·plas·tic (thûr′mō·plas′tik) *adj.* Plastic in the presence of or under the application of heat, as certain synthetic molding materials. — *n.* A thermoplastic substance or material.

Ther·mop·y·lae (thər·mop′ə·lē) A narrow mountain pass in Greece; scene of a battle, 480 B.C., in which the Spartans under the command of Leonidas held off the Persians under Xerxes and finally died to the last man rather than yield.

ther·mos bottle (thûr′məs) *Sometimes cap.* A glass bottle that keeps the contents hot or cold, consisting of one container within another with a vacuum between, the whole usually enclosed in a metal cylinder: also called *vacuum bottle.* [< Gk. *thermos* hot]

ther·mo·scope (thûr′mə·skōp) *n.* An instrument for detecting temperature variations without accurately measuring them. [< THERMO- + -SCOPE] — **ther′mo·scop′ic** (-skop′ik) or **·i·cal** *adj.*

ther·mo·set·ting (thûr′mō·set′ing) *adj.* Having the property of assuming a fixed shape after being molded under heat, as certain plastics and urea resins.

ther·mo·si·phon (thûr′mō·sī′fən) *n.* A device consisting of siphon tubes to increase or induce circulation in a heating system.

ther·mo·sphere (thûr′mō·sfir) *n.* The ionosphere considered as a region of wide temperature variations. — **ther′mo·spher′ic** or **·i·cal** (-sfir′ik, -sfer′-) *adj.*

ther·mo·sta·ble (thûr′mō·stā′bəl) *adj.* **1.** Resistant to heat, as certain plastics and chemicals. **2.** Biochem. Unaffected by moderate heat, as certain toxins or ferments: opposed to *thermolabile.* Also **ther′mo·sta′bile.** — **ther′mo·sta·bil′i·ty** (-stə·bil′ə·tē) *n.*

ther·mo·stat (thûr′mə·stat) *n.* A device for the automatic regulation of temperature by means of a relay that utilizes the contraction and expansion of metals due to temperature variations, used for actuating fire alarms, starting or stopping heating plants, etc. [< THERMO- + Gk. *statos* standing] — **ther′mo·stat′ic** *adj.* — **ther′mo·stat′i·cal·ly** *adv.*

ther·mo·stat·ics (thûr′mō·stat′iks) *n.pl.* (construed as sing.) The science that deals with the equilibrium of heat.

ther·mo·tax·is (thûr′mō·tak′sis) *n.* Physiol. **1.** The regulation or normal adjustment of body temperature. **2.** Biol. The orientation of a plant or animal in response to heat. — **ther′mo·tax′ic**, **ther′mo·tac′tic** (-tak′tik) *adj.*

ther·mo·ten·sile (thûr′mō·ten′sil) *adj.* Relating to variation of tensile strength caused by temperature.

therm·o·ther·a·py (thûr′mō·ther′ə·pē) *n.* Med. The treatment of disease by the application of heat.

ther·mot·ics (thər·mot′iks) *n.pl.* (construed as sing.) The science of heat. [< Gk. *thermotēs* heat]

ther·mot·ro·pism (thər·mot′rə·piz′əm) *n.* Biol. The property whereby growing plants or other organisms turn toward or away from a source of heat. — **ther·mo·trop·ic** (thûr′mō·trop′ik) *adj.*

the·roid (thir′oid) *adj.* Resembling or like a beast. [< Gk. *thēroeidēs* < *thēr, thēros* wild beast + *eidos* form]

the·ro·pod (thir′ə·pod) *n.* Paleontol. Any of a suborder (*Theropoda*) of saurischian dinosaurs of the Triassic and Cretaceous periods, including the true carnivorous types. — *adj.* Of or pertaining to the *Theropoda.* [< NL *Theropoda* < Gk. *thēr, thēros* a wild beast + *pous, podos* foot] — **the·rop·o·dan** (thi·rop′ə·dən) *adj. & n.*

Ther·si·tes (thər·sī′tēz) In the *Iliad*, an ugly and scurrilous Greek soldier in the Trojan War, later killed by Achilles for troublemaking.

ther·sit·i·cal (thər·sit′i·kəl) *adj.* Loud and abusive.

the·sau·rus (thə·sôr′əs) *n.pl.* **·sau·ri** (-sôr′ī) **1.** A book containing a store of words, especially of synonyms and antonyms arranged in categories. **2.** A storehouse; treasury. [< L < Gk. *thesauros* treasure house. Doublet of TREASURE.]

these (thēz) *adj. & pron.* Plural of THIS.

The·seus (thē′sōōs, -sē·əs) In Greek mythology, the chief hero of Attica, son of Aegeus and king of Athens, celebrated especially for killing the Minotaur and for unifying Attica with Athens as its capital. See ARIADNE, HIPPOLYTUS, PHAEDRA, PIRITHOUS. — **The′se·an** (-sē·ən) *adj.*

the·sis (thē′sis) *n.* pl. **·ses** (-sēz) **1.** A proposition. **2.** A formal proposition, advanced and defended by argumentation. **3.** A formal treatise on a particular subject; especially, a dissertation presented by a candidate for an academic degree. **4.** In early prosody, that part of a foot which had the ictus or stress. **5.** In later Roman usage and in modern prosody, the unaccented part of a foot; also, the depression of the voice in pronouncing it. See ARSIS. **6.** Logic An affirmative proposition; a premise or postulate. **7.** One of the three categories found in the dialectical systems of Hegel, Marx, etc. See DIALECTICAL MATERIALISM. **8.** Music The down beat; the accented part of a measure. [< L < Gk., a placing, proposition < *tithenai* to put, place]

Thes·pi·an (thes′pē·ən) *adj.* **1.** Of or relating to Thespis. **2.** Of or relating to drama; dramatic; tragic. — *n.* An actor or actress.

Thes·pis (thes′pis) Sixth-century B.C. Greek poet and actor; reputed founder of tragic drama.

Thess. 1. Thessalonians. **2.** Thessaly.

Thes·sa·lo·ni·an (thes′ə·lō′nē·ən) *n.* **1.** A native or inhabitant of modern Thessalonike or of ancient Thessalonica. **2.** pl. (construed as sing.) Either of two books in the New Testament consisting of epistles written by St. Paul to the Christians of Thessalonica. — *adj.* Of or pertaining to Thessalonike or Thessalonica.

Thes·sa·lo·ni·ke (thes′ä·lō·nē′kē) The Greek name for SALONIKA. Ancient **Thes·sa·lo·ni·ca** (thes′ə·lō·nī′kə, -lon′i·kə).

Thes·sa·ly (thes′ə·lē) A division of north central Greece; 5,399 sq. mi.; pop. 694,461 (1961); chief town, Larissa. See map of ATTICA. — **Thes·sa·li·an** (the·sā′lē·ən) *adj. & n.*

the·ta (thā′tə, thē′tə) *n.* **1.** The eighth letter in the Greek alphabet (Θ, ϑ, θ): corresponding in classical Greek to *t + h*, as in *right hand*, but in modern Greek to spirant *th*, as in *thin*. See ALPHABET. **2.** Math. A symbol for an angle of unknown value. [< Gk. *thēta*]

thet·ic (thet′ik) *adj.* **1.** In ancient prosody, beginning with, bearing, relating to, or of the nature of a thesis. **2.** Characterized by positive statement; arbitrary; dogmatic. Also **thet′i·cal.** [< Gk. *thetikos* fit for placing < *thetos* placed < *the-*, stem of *tithenai* to place] — **thet′i·cal·ly** *adv.*

The·tis (thē′tis) In Greek mythology, a Nereid, wife of Peleus and mother of Achilles.

the·ur·gy (thē′ûr·jē) *n.* pl. **·gies 1.** Divine or supernatural intervention in human affairs. **2.** The working of miracles through divine or supernatural aid. **3.** Magic as practiced by the Neo-Platonists, by means of which miraculous effects were supposedly produced through the intervention of beneficent spirits; white magic. [< Gk. *theourgia* < *theourgos* divine worker < *theos* god + *ergon* work] — **the·ur·gic** (thē·ûr′jik) or **·gi·cal** *adj.* — **the·ur′gi·cal·ly** *adv.* — **the·ur·gist** *n.*

thew (thyōō) *n.* **1.** A sinew or muscle, especially when strong or well-developed. **2.** pl. Bodily strength or vigor. [ME *theawes* good qualities, strength < OE *thēaw* habit, characteristic quality] — **thew′y** *adj.*

thew·less (thyoo'lis) *adj. Scot.* **1.** Having no thews; inactive; weak. **2.** Spiritless; inert.

they (thā) *pron. pl., possessive* **their** or **theirs,** *objective* **them 1.** The nominative plural of *he, she,* and *it,* used of the persons, beings, or things previously mentioned or understood. **2.** People in general: *They* say this is his best book. [ME *thei, thai* < ON *their,* pl. of *sā* this, that]

they'd (thād) **1.** They had. **2.** They would.

they'll (thāl) They will.

they're (thâr) They are.

they've (thāv) They have.

thi- Var. of THIO-.

T.H.I. or **T.-H.I.** Temperature-humidity index.

thi·a·mine (thī'ə·mēn, -min) *n. Biochem.* A white crystalline compound, $C_{12}H_{18}ON_4SCl_2$, vitamin B_1, found in various natural sources and also made synthetically, important for the health of the nervous system. Also **thi'a·min** (-min). [< THI- + -AMINE]

thi·a·zine (thī'ə·zēn, -zin) *n. Chem.* One of a class of organic ring compounds having one atom of nitrogen, one of sulfur, and four of carbon. Also **thi'a·zin** (-zin). [< THI- + -AZINE]

thi·a·zole (thī'ə·zōl) *n. Chem.* A colorless, stable, liquid compound, C_3H_3NS, whose derivatives yield dyestuffs and sulfa drugs. Also **thi'a·zol** (-zōl, -zol). [< THI- + AZOLE]

Thi·bault (tē·bō'), **Jacques Anatole** See (Anatole) FRANCE.

Thi·bet (ti·bet'), **Thi·bet'an** (-ən) See TIBET, TIBETAN.

thick (thik) *adj.* **1.** Having relatively large depth or extent from one surface to its opposite; not thin. **2.** Having a specified dimension of this kind, whether great or small: an inch *thick.* **3.** Arranged compactly; close: a *thick* forest; also, following at brief intervals; frequent, as blows, raindrops, etc. **4.** Set or furnished closely or abundantly with objects; abounding. **5.** Having considerable density or consistency; dense; heavy. **6.** Having the component particles closely packed together, as smoke, fog, etc. **7.** Lacking quickness of apprehension; dull; stupid. **8.** Indistinct; muffled: a *thick* sound; also, guttural; husky; throaty. **9.** *Informal* Very friendly; intimate. **10.** *Brit. Informal* Excessive; going too far; beyond what is tolerable. — *adv.* So as to be thick; thickly: bread sliced *thick.* — **to lay it on thick** *Informal* **1.** To overstate; exaggerate. **2.** To flatter excessively. — *n.* **1.** The dimension of thickness; the thickest part. **2.** The thickest or most intense time or place of anything: the *thick* of the fight. — **through thick and thin** Through good times and bad; loyally. [OE *thicce*] — **thick'ly** *adv.*

thick·en (thik'ən) *v.t. & v.i.* **1.** To make or become thick or thicker. **2.** To make or become more intricate or intense: The plot *thickens.* — **thick'en·er** *n.*

thick·en·ing (thik'ən·ing) *n.* **1.** The act of making or becoming thick. **2.** Something added to a liquid to increase its consistency. **3.** A thickened place or part.

thick·et (thik'it) *n.* A thick, dense growth, as of underbrush; a coppice. [OE *thiccet* < *thicce* thick]

thick·head (thik'hed') *n.* A stupid person; numskull. — **thick'head'ed** *adj.* — **thick'head'ed·ness** *n.*

thick·ish (thik'ish) *adj.* Somewhat thick.

thick·leaf (thik'lēf') *n.* Any of a genus (*Crassula*) of herbs and shrubs having white, rose, or yellow flowers.

thick·ness (thik'nis) *n.* **1.** The state or quality of being thick. **2.** The dimension or measure of a solid other than its length or width. **3.** A sheet, layer, etc., as of paper.

thick·set (thik'set') *adj.* **1.** Having a short, thick body; stout. **2.** Planted or placed closely together. — *n.* A thicket.

thick-skinned (thik'skind') *adj.* **1.** Having a thick skin; pachydermatous. **2.** Insensitive; callous to hints or insults.

thick-wit·ted (thik'wit'id) *adj.* Stupid; obtuse; dense.

thief (thēf) *n. pl.* **thieves** (thēvz) **1.** One who takes something belonging to another; one who steals. **2.** *Law* One guilty of simple or compound larceny, embezzlement, or swindling. **3.** That which causes loss. [OE *thēof*]

Thiers (tyâr), **Louis Adolphe,** 1797–1877, French statesman and historian.

thieve (thēv) *v.* **thieved, thiev·ing** *v.t.* **1.** To take by theft; steal. — *v.i.* **2.** To be a thief; commit theft. [OE *thēofian*]

thieve·less (thēv'lis) *adj. Scot.* **1.** Ungracious; hard. **2.** Listless.

thiev·er·y (thē'vər·ē) *n. pl.* **·er·ies** The practice or act of thieving; theft.

thiev·ish (thē'vish) *adj.* **1.** Addicted to thieving. **2.** Acting by stealth. **3.** Of or like a thief. **4.** Partaking of the nature of theft. — **thiev'ish·ly** *adv.* — **thiev'ish·ness** *n.*

thigh (thī) *n.* **1.** The leg between the hip and the knee of man or the corresponding portion in other animals. ♦ Collateral adjective: *femoral.* **2.** The femur of an insect. [OE *thēoh*]

thigh·bone (thī'bōn') *n.* The femur.

thig·mo·tax·is (thig'mə·tak'sis) *n. Biol.* Stereotaxis (which see). [< Gk. *thigma* touch + -TAXIS] — **thig'mo·tac'tic** (-tak'tik) *adj.* — **thig'mo·tac'ti·cal·ly** *adv.*

thig·mot·ro·pism (thig·mot'rə·piz'əm) *n. Biol.* The involuntary response of a plant or animal organism or any of its parts to direct mechanical contact with a solid object, as the tendrils of certain plants. [< Gk. *thigma* touch + TROPISM] — **thig·mo·trop·ic** (thig'mə·trop'ik) *adj.*

thill (thil) *n.* Either of the shafts of a vehicle, between which a horse is harnessed. [OE *thille* board]

thim·ble (thim'bəl) *n.* **1.** A caplike cover with a pitted surface, worn in sewing to protect the end of the finger that pushes the needle. **2.** *Mech.* A sleeve through which a bolt passes, or which unites two rods, tubes, or the like. **3.** *Naut.* **a** A metal antichafing ring forming a guard over a loop or eye in a sail. **b** The metal piece about which a rope is bent and spliced to the main body of the rope to form an eye. [OE *thymel* < *thūma* thumb]

thim·ble·ber·ry (thim'bəl·ber'ē) *n. pl.* **·ries** Any of certain American raspberries or blackberries having a thimble-shaped fruit; especially, the blackcap raspberry, the **fragrant thimbleberry** (*Rubus odoratus*), and the **western thimbleberry** (*R. parviflorus*).

thim·ble·ful (thim'bəl·fool) *n.* **1.** As much as a thimble will hold. **2.** Any very small quantity.

thim·ble·rig (thim'bəl·rig') *n.* **1.** A swindling trick in which a pea or ball is shifted by sleight of hand from one to another of three inverted thimble-shaped cups. **2.** A gambler who operates a thimblerig. — *v.t.* **rigged, ·rig·ging** To cheat by or as by thimblerig. — **thim'ble·rig'ger** *n.*

thim·ble·weed (thim'bəl·wēd') *n.* Any of various plants (genus *Rudbeckia*) with thimble-shaped receptacles, as the rudbeckia and the wood anemone.

thin (thin) *adj.* **thin·ner, thin·nest 1.** Having opposite surfaces relatively close to each other; being of little depth or width; not thick. **2.** Lacking roundness or plumpness of figure; lean; slender. **3.** Having the parts or particles scattered or diffused; not dense or abundant; sparse; rare: *thin* ranks, *thin* gas. **4.** Small in number: The audience was *thin.* **5.** Having little body or substance: *thin* clothing. **6.** Having little or no consistency, as a liquid: *thin* molasses. **7.** Lacking in essential ingredients or qualities: *thin* blood. **8.** Having little volume or richness; shrill or metallic, as a voice. **9.** Not abundantly supplied or furnished; bare; scant: a *thin* table. **10.** Having little brilliance or intensity; pale: *thin* colors. **11.** *Photog.* Not having sufficient contrast to print well: said of a negative. **12.** Lacking vigor or force; feeble; superficial: *thin* wit. — *adv.* So as to be thin; thinly: butter spread *thin.* — *v.t. & v.i.* **thinned, thin·ning** To make or become thinner. [OE *thynne*] — **thin'ly** *adv.* — **thin'ness** *n.*

thin·down (thin'doun') *n.* A diminution in the energy or number of cosmic rays, atomic particles, meteorites, etc., as they pass through the earth's atmosphere.

thine (thīn) *pron. Archaic* **1.** The possessive case of the pronoun *thou,* used predicatively: *Thine* is the kingdom. **2.** The one or ones belonging or relating to thee: thou and *thine.* — **of thine** Belonging or relating to thee: a double possessive. — *pronominal adj.* Thy: used before a vowel or *h: thine* eyes. [OE *thīn,* genitive of *thū* thou]

thing[1] (thing) *n.* **1.** That which exists as a separate entity; an inanimate object. **2.** That which is designated, as contrasted with the word or symbol used to denote it. **3.** A matter or circumstance; an affair; concern: *Things* have changed. **4.** An act or deed; transaction: That was a shameless *thing* to do. **5.** A statement or expression; utterance: to say the right *thing.* **6.** An idea; opinion; notion: Stop putting *things* in her head. **7.** A quality; attribute; characteristic. **8.** An inanimate object, as distinguished from a living organism. **9.** An organic being: usually with a qualifying word: Every living *thing* dies. **10.** An object that is not or cannot be described or particularized: The *thing* disappeared in the shadows. **11.** A person, regarded in terms of pity, affection, or contempt: that poor *thing.* **12.** *pl.* Possessions; belongings: to pack one's *things.* **13.** *pl.* Clothes; especially, outer garments: Take off your *things.* **14.** A piece of literature, art, music, etc.: He read a few *things* by Byron. **15.** The proper or befitting act or result: with *the:* That was not the *thing* to do. **16.** The important or remarkable point: with *the:* The *thing* we learned from the war was this. **17.** *Informal* An intense, sometimes neurotic, feeling about someone, an activity, etc.: I have a *thing* about dancing. **18.** *Law* A subject or property or dominion, as distinguished from a person. — **to do one's (own) thing** To express one's own personality or desires in action. — **to see things** To have hallucinations. [OE, thing, cause, assembly. Akin to THING[2].]

thing[2] (ting) *n.* A Scandinavian legislative or judicial body: also spelled *ting.* [< ON, assembly. Akin to THING[1].]

thing·a·ma·bob (thing'ə·mə·bob') *n. Informal* A thing the specific name of which is unknown or forgotten; a dingus. Also **thing'um·a·bob', thing'um·a·jig'.**

thing·a·ma·jig (thing'ə·mə·jig') *n. Informal* A thingamabob. Also **thing'um·a·jig'.**

T-hinge (tē'hinj') *n.* A hinge the two sections of which have the form of the letter T. See illustration under HINGE.

thing-in-itself (thing'in·it·self') *n. Philos.* In Kantian philosophy, the ultimate, metaphysical reality behind the physical phenomena perceived by the senses: the English rendering of the German *Ding an sich.*

think[1] (thingk) *v.* **thought** (thôt), **think·ing** *v.t.* **1.** To produce or form in the mind; conceive mentally. **2.** To examine in the mind; meditate upon, or determine by reasoning: to *think* a plan through. **3.** To believe; consider: I *think* him guilty. **4.** To expect; anticipate: They did not *think* to meet us. **5.** To bring to mind; remember; recollect: I cannot *think* what he said. **6.** To have the mind preoccupied by: to *think* business morning, noon, and night. **7.** To make or bring about by thinking: to *think* oneself sick. **8.** To intend: Do they *think* to rob me? — *v.i.* **9.** To use the mind or intellect in exercising judgment, forming ideas, etc.; engage in rational thought; reason. **10.** To have a particular opinion, sentiment, or feeling: I don't *think* so. — **to think better of 1.** To abandon a course of action; alter one's intentions. **2.** To form a better opinion of. — **to think fit (proper, right,** etc.) To regard as worth doing. — **to think nothing of 1.** To consider of no importance; ignore. **2.** To consider easy to do. — **to think of 1.** To bring to mind; remember; recollect. **2.** To conceive in the mind; invent; imagine. **3.** To have a specified opinion or attitude toward; regard. **4.** To be considerate of; have regard for. — **to think out** To devise, invent, or solve by thinking. — **to think over** To reflect upon; ponder. — **to think the world of 1.** To have a high opinion of. **2.** To love very much. — **to think twice** To consider carefully. — **to think up** To devise, arrive at, or invent by thinking. — *n.* An act of thinking; a thought. [OE *thencean*; influenced in form by THINK²]

think² (thingk) *v.i.* **thought** (thôt), **think·ing** To seem: obsolete except in *methinks, methought.* [OE *thyncan* to seem]

think·a·ble (thingk′ə·bəl) *adj.* **1.** That can be thought; conceivable. **2.** Possible; feasible.

think·er (thingk′ər) *n.* **1.** One who thinks. **2.** A person of powerful mind who devotes himself to abstract thought.

think·ing (thingk′ing) *adj.* **1.** Exercising the mental capacities. **2.** Capable of such exercise; rational. — *n.* **1.** Mental action; thought. **2.** The product of such action, as an idea. — **think′ing·ly** *adv.*

think-tank (thingk′tangk′) *n. Slang* An institute for theoretical and predictive studies, often combining academic fields.

thin·ner (thin′ər) *n.* **1.** One who or that which thins. **2.** A liquid, as turpentine or petroleum spirits, mixed with paint in order to give it a proper consistency for working.

thin-skinned (thin′skind′) *adj.* **1.** Having a thin skin. **2.** Easily hurt or offended; sensitive.

thio- *combining form Chem.* Containing sulfur; denoting a compound of sulfur, especially one in which sulfur has displaced oxygen: *thiocyanic.* Also, before vowels, sometimes *thi-.* Compare SULFURO-. [< Gk. *theion* sulfur]

thi·o·bac·te·ri·um (thī′ō·bak·tir′ē·əm) *n.* Any of an order (*Thiobacteriales*) of bacteria that utilize the sulfur of decaying organic matter.

thi·o·cy·a·nate (thī′ō·sī′ə·nāt) *n. Chem.* A salt or ester of thiocyanic acid.

thi·o·cy·an·ic acid (thī′ō·sī·an′ik) *Chem.* A colorless, unstable, liquid acid, HSCN, soluble in water and having a pungent odor. [< THIO- + CYANIC]

Thi·o·kol (thī′ə·kōl, -kol) *n.* An organic polysulfide material like natural rubber in its properties: a trade name.

thi·ol (thī′ōl, -ol) *n. Chem.* Any of a class of sulfur compounds having the general formula RSH, in which R is a hydrocarbon radical: also called *mercaptan.* [< THI- + -OL¹]

thi·on·ic (thī·on′ik) *adj. Chem.* Of, pertaining to, containing, or derived from sulfur. [< Gk. *theion* sulfur]

thionic acid *Chem.* Any of a group of unstable acids having the general formula H₂SₙO₆, where n varies from 2 to 6.

thi·o·nine (thī′ə·nēn, -nin) *n. Chem.* A dark green thiazine derivative made by synthesis, with a glistening metallic luster that imparts purplish colors to silk and wool. Also **thi′o·nin** (-nin). [< Gk. *theion* sulfur + -INE²]

thi·o·nyl (thī′ə·nil) *n. Chem.* Sulfinyl (which see). [< Gk. *theion* sulfur + -YL]

thi·o·pen·tal sodium (thī′ō·pen′tal) A yellowish white powder, C₁₁H₁₇N₂O₂SNa, of the barbiturate group, used intravenously as a general anesthetic: also called *sodium Pentothal, Pentothal Sodium.* Also *Chiefly Brit.* **thi′o·pen′tone sodium.**

thi·o·phene (thī′ə·fēn) *n. Chem.* A colorless liquid hydrocarbon, C₄H₄S, resembling benzene, found in coal tar and also made by synthesis. Also **thi′o·phen** (-fen). [< THIO- + PH(ENYL) + -INE]

thi·o·sin·am·ine (thī′ō·sin·am′in, -sin′ə·mēn) *n. Chem.* A crystalline compound, C₄H₈N₂S, formed by the union of allyl mustard oil and alcohol with ammonia, used in photography. Also **thi′o·sin·am′in** (-am′in). [< THIO- + Gk. *sin(api)* mustard + AMINE]

thi·o·sul·fate (thī′ō·sul′fāt) *n. Chem.* A salt of thiosulfuric acid.

thi·o·sul·fu·ric acid (thī′ō·sul·fyōōr′ik) *Chem.* An unstable acid, H₂S₂O₃, known chiefly by its salts, which have extensive applications in bleaching and photography.

thi·o·u·re·a (thī′ō·yōō·rē′ə) *n. Chem.* A white, solid compound, CS(NH₂)₂, prepared from urea by replacement of oxygen by sulfur, used in inorganic synthesis, in photography, and as an insecticide. [< THIO- + UREA]

thir (thûr, thir) *pron. Scot.* These.

third (thûrd) *adj.* **1.** Next after the second: the ordinal of *three.* **2.** Being one of three equal parts. **3.** Pertaining to the forward gears with the third highest ratio in an automobile transmission. — *n.* **1.** That which follows the second. **2.** One of three equal parts. **3.** *pl. Law* The third part of a husband's personal estate allotted to the widow in case of his dying intestate and leaving an heir; also, loosely, a dower. **4.** A unit of time or of an arc, equal to one sixtieth of a second. **5.** *Music* **a** The interval between a tone and another tone two steps from it in a diatonic scale. **b** A tone separated by this interval from any other, considered in relation to that other; especially, the third above the keynote. For illustration see INTERVAL. **6.** In baseball, the third base. **7.** *Mech.* The forward gears with the third highest ratio in an automobile transmission. — *adv.* In the third order, rank, or place: also, in formal discourse, **third′ly.** [OE *thridda* < *thri* three]

third base In baseball, the base at the left-hand angle of the infield. For illustration see BASEBALL.

third base·man (bās′mən) *n. pl.* **·men** (-mən) A baseball player stationed at or near third base.

third class 1. In the U.S. postal system, a classification of mail that includes all miscellaneous printed matter but not newspapers and periodicals legally entered as second class. **2.** A classification of accommodations on some ships and trains, usually the cheapest and least luxurious available. — **third-class** (thûrd′klas, -kläs) *adj. & adv.*

third degree 1. *Informal* Severe or brutal examination of a prisoner by the police for the purpose of securing information. **2.** The third stage, order, step, etc., of something.

third estate The third political class of a kingdom, following the nobility and the clergy. See under ESTATE.

third eyelid The nictitating membrane.

Third Order *Eccl.* A confraternity, generally for laymen, associated with a religious order and following a modified rule. [after the *Third Order* of St. Francis, founded 1221]

third person See under PERSON.

third rail A rail that supplies current to the trains of an electric railway. — **third-rail** (thûrd′rāl′) *adj.*

third-rate (thûrd′rāt′) *adj.* **1.** Of the third rate or class. **2.** Of poor quality; very inferior.

Third Reich See under REICH.

Third Republic The republic established in France after the fall of Napoleon III in 1870 and lasting until the occupation of France by the Germans during World War II.

third world Those nations, especially in Africa and Asia, that are relatively underdeveloped and usually undergoing an evolutionary political process, as distinguished from the communist and capitalist political blocs.

thirl¹ (thûrl) *v.t. Scot. & Brit. Dial.* **1.** To thrill. **2.** To drill or bore. [OE *thyrlian* < *thyrel* hole < *thurh* through]

thirl² (thûrl) *v.t. Scot.* To bind, as by a lease. — *n.* Thirlage.

thirl·age (thûr′lij) *n.* A feudal obligation upon certain tenants to bring their grain to a certain mill for grinding; also, the fee for such grinding. Also *thirl.* [Metathetic var. of *thrillage* < obs. *thrill* enthrall < OE *thræl* thrall]

thirst (thûrst) *n.* **1.** An uncomfortable feeling of dryness in the throat and mouth, accompanied by an increasingly urgent desire for liquids. **2.** The physiological condition that produces this feeling. **3.** Any longing or craving. — *v.i.* **1.** To feel thirst. **2.** To have an eager desire or craving; long; yearn. [OE *thurst, thyrstan*] — **thirst′er** *n.*

thirst·y (thûrs′tē) *adj.* **thirst·i·er, thirst·i·est 1.** Affected with thirst. **2.** Lacking moisture; arid; parched. **3.** Eagerly desirous. **4.** *Informal* Causing thirst. [OE *thurstig*] — **thirst′i·ly** *adv.* — **thirst′i·ness** *n.*

thir·teen (thûr′tēn′) *n.* **1.** The sum of twelve and one: a cardinal number. **2.** Any symbol of this number, as 13, xiii, XIII. **3.** Anything consisting of or representing thirteen units, as an organization, game token, etc. — *adj.* Being one more than twelve. [OE *thrēotīne*]

thir·teenth (thûr′tēnth′) *adj.* **1.** Next after the twelfth: the ordinal of *thirteen.* **2.** Being one of thirteen equal parts. — *n.* **1.** One of thirteen equal parts. **2.** That which follows the twelfth.

Thirteenth Amendment An amendment to the Constitution of the United States outlawing slavery, ratified 1865.

thir·ti·eth (thûr′tē·ith) *adj.* **1.** Tenth in order after the twentieth: the ordinal of *thirty.* **2.** Being one of thirty equal parts. — *n.* **1.** One of thirty equal parts. **2.** That which is tenth in order after the twentieth.

thir·ty (thûr′tē) *n. pl.* **·ties 1.** The sum of twenty and ten: a cardinal number. **2.** Any symbol of this number, as 30, xxx, XXX. **3.** Anything consisting of or representing thirty units, as an organization, game token, etc. — *adj.* Being ten more than twenty. [OE *thrītig*]

thir·ty-sec·ond (thûr′tē·sek′ənd) *adj.* **1.** Being the second after the thirtieth. **2.** Being one of thirty-two equal parts. — *n.* A thirty-second note.

thirty-second note *Music* A note having a time value equal to one thirty-second of a whole note: also, *Chiefly Brit.*, *demisemiquaver*. For illustration see NOTE.

thir·ty-two-mo (thûr'tē-too'mō) *n. pl.* **·mos 1.** The page size (3½ x 4¾ inches) of a book made up of printer's sheets folded into thirty-two leaves. **2.** A book consisting of pages of this size. Also written **32mo** — *adj.* Consisting of pages of this size.

Thirty Years' War See table for WAR.

this (this) *pl. for adj. and pron. def. 2* **these** (thēz) *adj.* **1.** That is near or present, either actually or in thought: *This* house is for sale; I shall be there *this* evening. **2.** That is understood or has just been mentioned: *This* offense justified my revenge. **3.** Denoting something nearer than or contrasted with something else: distinguished from *that*: *This* tree is still alive, but that one is dead. **4.** These: used of a number or collection considered as a whole: He has been dead *this* ten years. — *pron.* **1.** The person or thing near or present, being understood or just mentioned: *This* is where I live; *This* is the guilty man. **2.** The person or thing nearer than or contrasted with something else: opposed to *that*: *This* is a better painting than that. **3.** The idea, statement, etc., about to be made clear: I will say *this*: he is a hard worker. **4.** The present time: He should have returned before *this*. — *adv.* To this degree; so: I was not expecting you *this* soon. [OE]

This·be (thiz'bē) See PYRAMUS and THISBE.

this·tle (this'əl) *n.* **1.** One of various prickly plants (*Cirsium* and related genera) of the composite family, with cylindrical or globular heads of purple flowers; especially, the **Canada thistle** (*C. arvense*) and the **bull thistle** (*C. lanceolatum*), the national emblem of Scotland. **2.** Any of several other prickly plants. [OE *thistel*] — **this'tly** *adj.*

thistle butterfly A butterfly (*Vanessa cardui*) having usually four eyespots on the under side of each wing: also called *painted lady.*

this·tle·down (this'əl·doun') *n.* The ripe silky fibers from the dry flower of a thistle.

thith·er (thith'ər, thith'-) *adv.* **1.** To or toward that place; in that direction. **2.** *Archaic* To that end, point, or result. — *adj.* Situated or being on the other side; farther: the *thither* bank of the river. [OE *thider*]

thith·er·to (thith'ər·too', thith'-) *adv.* Up to that time.

thith·er·ward (thith'ər·wərd, thith'-) *adv.* In that direction; toward that place. Also **thith'er·wards.**

thix·ot·ro·py (thik·sot'rə·pē) *n. Chem.* The property possessed by certain gels of liquefying when shaken. [< Gk. *thixis* touch + *tropē* turning] — **thix·o·trop·ic** (thik'sə·trop'ik) *adj.*

tho (thō) See THOUGH.

thole[1] (thōl) *n. Naut.* A peg or pair of pegs serving as a fulcrum for an oar in rowing. Also **thole pin.** [OE *thol* pin]

thole[2] (thōl) *v.t. & v.i.* **tholed, thol·ing** *Archaic* To endure; suffer; tolerate. [OE *tholian*]

Thom·as (tom'əs) One of the twelve apostles, known for his doubting disposition: called **Saint Thomas.** Also *Didymus. John* xx 25.

Tho·mas (tō·mä'), **Ambroise,** 1811–96, French composer.

Thom·as (tom'əs), **Dylan (Marlais),** 1914–53, British poet and author born in Wales. — **George Henry,** 1816–70, Union general in the Civil War: called **the Rock of Chickamauga.** — **Norman (Mattoon),** 1884–1968, U.S. socialist leader and writer.

Thomas à Becket, Saint, 1118?–70, English prelate; archbishop of Canterbury 1162–70; murdered for his opposition to Henry II: called **Saint Thomas Becket, Saint Thomas of London.**

Thomas à Kempis, 1380?–1471, German mystic; author of the *Imitation of Christ.*

Thomas of Er·cel·doune (ûr'səl·doon), 1220?–97?, Scottish poet: called *Thomas the Rhymer.*

Tho·mism (tō'miz·əm, thō'-) *n.* The system of dogmatic theology of St. Thomas Aquinas and his followers that formed the basis of 13th-century scholasticism. — **Tho'·mist** *adj. & n.* — **Tho·mis'tic** or **·ti·cal** *adj.*

Thomp·son (tomp'sən), **Benjamin** See RUMFORD. — **Francis,** 1859–1907, English poet.

Thompson submachine gun A type of .45 caliber submachine gun: a trade name: also called *Tommy gun.*

Thom·son (tom'sən) **George Paget,** 1892–1975, English physicist. — **James,** 1700–48, Scottish poet. — **James,** 1834–82, English poet. — **John Arthur,** 1861–1933, Scottish biologist. — **Sir Joseph John,** 1856–1940, English physicist and mathematician; father of George Paget Thomson.

thong (thông, thong) *n.* **1.** A narrow strip, properly of leather, as for tying or fastening. **2.** A whiplash. [OE *thwang* thong]

Thor (thôr, tōr) In Norse mythology, the god of war, thunder, and strength, who destroyed the enemies of the gods with his magic hammer. — *n.* An intermediate range, liquid-fueled ballistic missile of the U.S. Air Force.

tho·rac·ic (thô·ras'ik, thō-) *adj.* Of, relating to, or situated in or near the thorax. [< F *thoracique* < NL *thoracicus* < Gk. *thōrax* chest]

thoracic duct *Anat.* The principal duct of the lymphatic system, passing upward along the spinal column, and conveying lymph and chyle into the venous circulation.

thoraco- *combining form Med. & Surg.* The thorax or the chest; of or related to the thorax: *thoracotomy.* Also, before vowels, **thorac-.** [< Gk. *thōrax* chest]

tho·ra·co·plas·ty (thôr'ə·kō·plas'tē, thō'rə-) *n. pl.* **·ties** *Surg.* An operation, usually for the treatment of tuberculosis, in which the chest wall is compressed by resecting a number of ribs in order to collapse permanently the underlying lung. [< THORACO- + -PLASTY]

tho·ra·cot·o·my (thôr'ə·kot'ə·mē, thō'rə-) *n. pl.* **·mies** *Surg.* Incision of the wall of the chest. [THORACO- + -TOMY]

tho·rax (thôr'aks, thō'raks) *n. pl.* **tho·rax·es** or **tho·ra·ces** (thôr'ə·sēz, thō'rə-) **1.** *Anat.* The part of the body between the neck and the abdomen, enclosed by the ribs and containing the lungs, heart, etc.; the chest. **2.** The corresponding part in other animals. **3.** *Entomol.* The middle region of the body of an insect, between the head and the abdomen. [< L < Gk. *thōrax*]

Tho·reau (thôr'ō, thō'rō, thə·rō'), **Henry David,** 1817–62, U.S. author: original name **David Henry Thoreau.**

Tho·rez (tô·rez'), **Maurice,** 1900–64, French Communist leader.

tho·ri·a (thôr'ē·ə, thō'rē·ə) *n.* A white, very heavy oxide of thorium, used in the mantle of the Welsbach burner. [< NL < *thorium.* See THORIUM.]

tho·ri·a·nite (thôr'ē·ə·nīt, thō'rē-) *n.* A black radioactive mineral composed of thorium, cerium, and uranium oxides.

tho·rite (thôr'īt, thō'rīt) *n.* A vitreous, yellow to black, thorium silicate, ThSiO₄. [< THOR(IUM) + -ITE[1]]

tho·ri·um (thôr'ē·əm, thō'rē-) *n.* A gray, radioactive, metallic element (symbol Th) of the actinide series, found only in small quantities in certain rare minerals. Its isotope of mass 232 has been used in the generation of atomic energy. [after *Thor*] — **tho'ric** *adj.*

thorium series *Physics* The group of radioactive elements beginning with thorium of mass 232 and a half life of 1.39 × 10¹⁰ years, and terminating after successive disintegrations in the stable isotope of lead of mass 208.

thorn (thôrn) *n.* **1.** A hard, leafless spine or sharp-pointed process from a branch. **2.** One of various other sharp processes, as the spine of a porcupine. **3.** Any of various thorn-bearing shrubs or trees; especially, any of a genus (*Crataegus*) of rosaceous plants, as the hawthorn. **4.** Anything or anyone that causes discomfort, pain, or annoyance; a vexation. **5.** The name of the Old English rune þ; also, the corresponding Icelandic character. It was used originally to represent both voiceless and voiced *th*, as in *thin, then*, but finally only the voiceless sound *Y* or *y* is sometimes used as a makeshift for it in early English, as in the contraction yᵉ. Compare EDH. — *v.t.* To pierce or prick with a thorn. [OE] — **thorn'less** *adj.*

Thorn (tôrn) The German name for TORUN.

thorn apple 1. Any plant of the genus *Datura*, as the jimsonweed. **2.** The fruit of the hawthorn; a haw.

thorn·back (thôrn'bak') *n.* **1.** A European ray (*Raia clavata*) whose back is studded with short stout spines. **2.** A California guitarfish (*Platyrhinoidis triseriata*) with spines on the back and shoulders.

thorn·bill (thôrn'bil') *n.* Any of certain bright-colored hummingbirds of South America (genera *Rhamphomicron* and *Chalcostigma*) characterized by a long, sharp bill.

Thorn·dike (thôrn'dīk) A family prominent in American education and scholarship, notably **Ashley Horace,** 1871–1933, literary historian and critic, and his brothers, **Edward Lee,** 1874–1949, psychologist and lexicographer, and **Lynn,** 1882–1965, historian. — **Dame Sybil,** 1882–1976, English actress.

thorn·y (thôr'nē) *adj.* **thorn·i·er, thorn·i·est 1.** Full of thorns; spiny. **2.** Sharp like a thorn. **3.** Presenting difficulties or trials; painful; vexatious. [OE *thornig*] — **thorn'i·ness** *n.*

tho·ron (thôr'on, thō'ron) *n.* A gaseous, radioactive isotope of radon, produced during the disintegration of thorium and having a half life of 54.5 seconds. Abbr. *Tn.* [< NL THOR(IUM) + -ON]

thor·ough (thûr'ō, thûr'ə) *adj.* **1.** Carried to completion: thoroughgoing: a *thorough* search; also, persevering, accurate, and painstaking: a *thorough* worker. **2.** Marked by careful attention throughout; not superficial; complete. **3.** Completely (such and such); through and through: a *thorough* nincompoop. **4.** Painstakingly conforming to a stand-

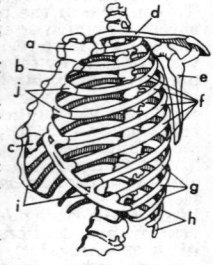

THORAX

a,b,c Sternum: *a* Manubrium, *b* Gladiolus, *c* Ensiform cartilage. *d* Clavicle. *e* Scapula. *f* Sternal ribs. *g* False ribs. *h* Floating ribs. *i* Costal arch. *j* Costal cartilage.

ard. **5.** *Rare* Going or passing through. — *adv. & prep. Obs.* Through. Also *Rare* **thor′o.** [Emphatic var. of THROUGH] — **thor′ough·ly** *adv.* — **thor′ough·ness** *n.*

Thor′ough (thûr′ō) *n.* The administrative policy of Charles I's minister, the Earl of Strafford: so called by himself as being a method of carrying through his ideas in spite of all opposition.

thorough bass *Music* A figured bass (which see).

thorough brace Either of the strong leather straps extending under each side of the body of a carriage and serving as a support and a spring. — **thor′ough-braced′** *adj.*

thor·ough·bred (thûr′ō·bred′, thûr′ə-) *n.* **1.** An animal of pure and unmixed stock. **2.** *Informal* A person of culture and good breeding. — *adj.* **1.** Belonging to the strain of horses known as Thoroughbred. **2.** Bred from pure stock. **3.** Possessing the traits of a thoroughbred; elegant. **4.** Superior in quality; first-class.

Thor·ough·bred (thûr′ō·bred′, thûr′ə-) *n.* A horse whose ancestry is recorded in the English Stud Book, and that is therefore descended from one of three Eastern sires, the Byerly Turk, the Darley Arabian, or the Godolphin.

thor·ough·fare (thûr′ō·fâr′, thûr′ə-) *n.* **1.** A road or street through which the public has unobstructed passage; highway. **2.** A traveling or passing through, or the right of doing so; a passage: now chiefly in the phrase **no thoroughfare**. **3.** Any place through which much traffic passes, as a strait, river, or other waterway. — **Syn.** See ROAD. [ME *thurghfare* < OE *thurh* through + *faru* going]

thor·ough·go·ing (thûr′ō·gō′ing, thûr′ə-) *adj.* **1.** Characterized by extreme thoroughness or efficiency. **2.** Unmitigated: a *thoroughgoing* scoundrel.

thor·ough·paced (thûr′ō·pāst′, thûr′ə-) *adj.* **1.** Perfectly trained, as a horse. **2.** Thoroughgoing; complete.

thor·ough·wort (thûr′ō·wûrt′, thûr′ə-) *n.* **1.** The boneset. **2.** Any other plant of the same genus.

thorp (thôrp) *n. Archaic* A hamlet; village: now chiefly in names of places. Also **thorpe.** [OE. Akin to DORP.]

Thorpe (thôrp), **James,** 1888–1953, U.S. athlete.

Thors·havn (tôrs·houn′) The capital of the Faeroe Islands, on Strømø, in the central part of the group; pop. 9,738 (est. 1969).

Thor·vald·sen (tôr′väl·sən), **Albert Bertel,** 1770–1844, Danish sculptor. Also **Thor′wald·sen.**

those (thōz) *adj. & pron.* Plural of THAT. [OE *thās,* pl. of *this*]

Thoth (thōth, tōt) In Egyptian mythology, the god of wisdom, inventor of art, science, and letters, represented with the head of an ibis or of a dog: identified with the Greek *Hermes Trismegistus.*

Thoth·mes (thōth′mēz, tōt′mes) Any of several Egyptian kings, between 1587 and 1328 B.C.: also *Thuthmose.*

THOTH

thou (thou) *pron., possessive* **thy** or **thine,** *objective* **thee;** *pl. nominative* **you, ye,** *possessive* **your** or **yours,** *objective* **you, ye** *Archaic* The nominative singular pronoun of the second person: formerly a familiar form as opposed to the more formal singular *you,* which has replaced it: now no longer used except in Biblical, homiletic, elevated, or poetic language, in prayers, or in certain British dialects. [OE *thū*]

though (thō) *conj.* **1.** Notwithstanding the fact that: introducing a clause expressing an actual fact. **2.** Conceding or granting that; even if. **3.** And yet; still; however: introducing a modifying clause or statement added as an afterthought: I am well, *though* I do not feel very strong. **4.** Notwithstanding what has been done or said; nevertheless: But they have, *though.* ◆ As used in this sense, *though* is sometimes regarded as a conjunctive adverb. Also spelled *tho.* Compare HOWEVER. [Prob. fusion of OE *thēah* and ON *tho*]

thought¹ (thôt) *n.* **1.** The act or process of using the mind actively and deliberately; meditation; cogitation. **2.** The product of thinking; an idea, concept, judgment, etc. **3.** Intellectual activity of a specific kind: Greek *thought.* **4.** Consideration; attention: Give the matter some *thought.* **5.** Intention or idea of doing something; plan: All *thought* of returning was abandoned. **6.** Expectation; anticipation: He had no *thought* of finding her there. **7.** *Rare* A trifle; a small amount: Be a *thought* more cautious. — **Syn.** See IDEA. [OE *thōht*]
— **Syn. 1.** deliberation, reflection, rumination, consideration, contemplation, reasoning, speculation. **2.** See IDEA.

thought² (thôt) Past tense and past participle of THINK.

thought·ful (thôt′fəl) *adj.* **1.** Full of thought; meditative. **2.** Showing, characterized by, or promotive of thought: a *thoughtful* book. **3.** Attentive; careful; especially, manifesting regard for others; considerate. — **thought′ful·ly** *adv.* — **thought′ful·ness** *n.*

thought·less (thôt′lis) *adj.* **1.** Manifesting lack of thought or care; heedless. **2.** Lacking capacity for thought; stupid. — **thought′less·ly** *adv.* — **thought′less·ness** *n.*

thought-out (thôt′out′) *adj.* Produced by thought, especially by thorough or careful deliberation.

thought transference Telepathy.

thou·sand (thou′zənd) *n.* **1.** The product of ten and a hundred; ten hundreds, written as 1,000 or M: a cardinal number. **2.** Anything consisting of or representing a thousand units, as an organization, bill, etc. **3.** An indefinitely large number. — *adj.* Being a thousand in number. [OE *thūsend*]

Thousand and One Nights, The The Arabian Nights (which see).

thou·sand·fold (thou′zənd·fōld′) *n.* An amount or number a thousand times as great as a given unit. — *adv.* So as to be a thousand times as many or as great. — *adj.* **1.** Consisting of one thousand parts. **2.** One thousand times as many or as great.

Thousand Islands A group of about 1,500 islets in an expansion of the St. Lawrence River, near Lake Ontario.

thou·sandth (thou′zəndth) *adj.* **1.** Having the number one thousand: the ordinal of *thousand.* **2.** Being one of a thousand equal parts. — *n.* **1.** One of a thousand equal parts. **2.** That which is numbered one thousand.

thow·less (thou′lis) *adj. Scot.* Inactive; lazy; without ambition or energy.

Thrace (thrās) An ancient region, later a Roman province, in the eastern part of the Balkan Peninsula; modern Thrace is divided between Greece and Turkey. Ancient **Thra·cia** (thrā′shə).

Thra·cian (thrā′shən) *adj.* Pertaining to Thrace or its people. — *n.* **1.** One of the people of Thrace. **2.** The Indo-European language of the ancient Thracians, related to Phrygian.

Thrale (thrāl), **Mrs.** See PIOZZI.

thrall (thrôl) *n.* **1.** A person in bondage; a slave; serf. **2.** The condition of bondage; thralldom. — **Syn.** See SLAVE. — *v.t. Archaic* To reduce to thralldom; enslave. — *adj. Archaic* Held in subjection; enslaved. [OE *thrǣl* < ON]

thrall·dom (thrôl′dəm) *n.* **1.** The state of being a thrall. **2.** Any sort of bondage or servitude. Also **thral′dom.**

thrash (thrash) *v.t.* **1.** To beat as if with a flail; flog; whip. **2.** To defeat utterly. — *v.i.* **3.** To move or swing about with flailing, violent motions. **4.** *Naut.* To work to windward, against the tide, etc. — **to thrash out** To discuss fully and to a conclusion. — *n.* **1.** The act of thrashing. **2.** In swimming, a kick used with the crawl and back strokes. [Dial. var. of THRESH]

thrash·er¹ (thrash′ər) *n.* **1.** One who or that which thrashes or threshes. **2.** A thresher (def. 2), a shark.

thrash·er² (thrash′ər) *n.* Any of several long-tailed American songbirds (genus *Toxostoma*) resembling the thrushes and related to the mockingbirds, especially the common eastern **brown thrasher** (*T. rufum*), colored foxy red with black spots. [< dial. E *thresher* < THRUSH¹]

thrash·ing (thrash′ing) *n.* A sound beating or whipping.

thra·son·i·cal (thrā·son′i·kəl) *adj.* Bragging; boastful. [< L *Thraso,* a braggart soldier in Terence's *Eunuch* < Gk. *Thrason* < *thrasys* rash] — **thra·son′i·cal·ly** *adv.*

Thras·y·bu·lus (thras′ə·byoo′ləs), died 389? B.C., Athenian military commander and statesman.

thrave (thrāv) *n. Scot. & Brit. Dial.* **1.** Twenty-four sheaves of grain. **2.** An indefinite number; a company; throng; also, a bundle. [OE *threfe* < ON *threfi*]

thraw¹ (thrô) *Scot. n.* **1.** A wrench or twist. **2.** A throe. — *v.t.* **1.** To twist or wrench. **2.** To thwart. — *adj.* Awry.

thraw² (thrô) *Scot. & Brit. Dial.* — *v.t. & v.i.* To throw. — *n.* A throw.

thrawn (thrôn) *adj. Scot.* **1.** Wrenched; awry; twisted; crooked. **2.** Obstinate; contrary.

thread (thred) *n.* **1.** A very slender cord or line composed of two or more filaments, as of flax, cotton, or silk, twisted together; also, such twisted fibers used in sewing. **2.** A filament of any ductile substance, as of metal, glass, etc. **3.** A fine stream or beam: a *thread* of light. **4.** A fine line of color. **5.** Anything conceived of as serving to give sequence to the whole, as the course of existence represented by the ancient Greeks and Romans as a thread spun and cut off by the three Fates. **6.** *Mining* A very thin seam or vein of ore. **7.** *Mech.* The spiral ridge of a screw. — *v.t.* **1.** To pass a thread through the eye of (a needle). **2.** To arrange or string on a thread, as beads. **3.** To cut a thread on or in, as a screw. **4.** To make one's way through or over: to *thread* a maze. **5.** To make (one's way) carefully. **6.** To be present throughout; pervade. — *v.i.* **7.** To make one's way carefully. **8.** To drop from a spoon in a fine thread, as boiling syrup. [OE *thrǣd*] — **thread′er** *n.*

thread·bare (thred′bâr′) *adj.* **1.** Worn so that the threads show, as a rug or garment. **2.** Clad in worn garments. **3.** Commonplace; hackneyed. — **thread′bare′ness** *n.*

thread·fin (thred′fin′) *n.* Any of a family (*Polynemidae*) of tropical marine fishes having three or more threadlike rays below the pectoral fins. Also **thread′fish′** (-fish′).

thread mark   A marking made in currency by colored silk fibers, as a safeguard against counterfeiting.

Thread·nee·dle Street (thred'nēd'l)   A short street in London. **— The Old Lady of Threadneedle Street** The Bank of England.

thread·worm (thred'wûrm')   n.   Any of various threadlike nematode worms, especially the pinworm.

thread·y (thred'ē)   adj.   **thread·i·er, thread·i·est 1.** Resembling a thread; stringy. **2.** Consisting of, containing, or covered with thread. **3.** Med. Weak and feeble: said of the pulse. **4.** Weak and thin like a thread: a thready voice.

threap (thrēp)   v.t. & v.i.   Scot. & Brit. Dial.   To contradict; dispute; also, to rebuke; insist. Also **threep.** [OE thrēapian]

threat (thret)   n.   **1.** A declaration of an intention to inflict injury or pain. **2.** An indication of impending danger or harm: the threat of rain. **3.** A person or thing regarded as endangering the lives, peace of mind, etc., of others; a menace. **— v.t.** Archaic To threaten. [OE thrēat]

threat·en (thret'n)   v.t.   **1.** To utter threats against. **2.** To be menacing or dangerous to. **3.** To be ominous or portentous of. **4.** To utter threats of (injury, vengeance, etc.). **— v.i. 5.** To utter threats. **6.** To have a menacing aspect; lower: The rising waters seemed to threaten. [OE thrēatnian to urge, compel] **— threat'en·er** n. **— threat'en·ing·ly** adv.

— Syn. 2. Threaten and menace may both be used of serious danger or impending catastrophe: the border dispute between the two nations threatens to become open war, the disappearance of breeding grounds menaces many wild fowl. But threaten may also be used, unlike menace, of mild dangers or retribution: she threatened to leave the party. Words, actions, or circumstances may threaten; menace is rarely used of spoken threats.

three (thrē)   n.   **1.** The sum of two and one: a cardinal number. **2.** Any symbol of this number, as 3, iii, III. **3.** Anything consisting of or representing three units, as a playing card, team, etc.; a ternary. **— adj.** Being one more than two; ternary. [OE thrīe]

three-base hit (thrē'bās')   In baseball, a base hit that enables the batter to reach third base; a triple.

three-col·or (thrē'kul'ər)   adj.   Pertaining to or denoting a process of color printing based on three primary colors, each of which is transferred to the printing surface from a separate, accurately registered plate.

three-D (thrē'dē')   adj.   Three-dimensional. **— n.** A three-dimensional representation; especially, a motion picture in which the illusion of depth is obtained. Often written **3-D.**

three-deck·er (thrē'dek'ər)   n.   **1.** A vessel having three decks or gun decks. **2.** Any structure having three levels. **3.** A sandwich made with three slices of bread.

three·fold (thrē'fōld')   n.   An amount or number three times as great as a given unit. **— adv.** So as to be three times as many or as great. **— adj. 1.** Consisting of three parts. **2.** Three times as many or as great.

Three Hours   A religious service held on Good Friday from noon until three o'clock.

three-mile limit (thrē'mīl')   A distance of three nautical miles from the shoreline seaward, allowed by international law for territorial jurisdiction.

three·pence (thrip'əns, threp'-, thrup'-)   n.   Brit. **1.** The sum of three pennies. **2.** A small coin of Great Britain, worth three pennies: also **threepenny bit.**

three·pen·ny (thrip'ə·ni, threp'-, thrup'-, thrē'pen'ē)   adj.   Brit. **1.** Worth or costing threepence. **2.** Of little value.

three-phase (thrē'fāz')   adj.   Electr. Designating or designed for an alternating-current circuit of three branches differing by one third of a cycle (120°) in phase, so that when one branch is at full value the others are at half value but flowing in the opposite direction.

three-ply (thrē'plī')   adj.   Consisting of three thicknesses, strands, layers, etc.

three-point landing (thrē'point')   **1.** Aeron. A perfect airplane landing. **2.** Any successful outcome.

three-quar·ter binding (thrē'kwôr'tər)   A style of bookbinding having the strip of leather over the back and corners projecting to a greater width than in half binding.

three-ring circus (thrē'ring')   **1.** A circus in which separate acts are carried on simultaneously in three ringlike enclosures. **2.** Any situation characterized by simultaneous activities, especially of bewildering variety.

Three Rivers   See Trois Rivières.

three R's   See under R.

three·score (thrē'skôr', -skōr')   adj. & n.   Sixty.

three·some (thrē'səm)   adj.   **1.** Consisting of three. **2.** Performed by three. **— n. 1.** A group of three persons. **2.** That which is played by three persons; especially, a golf match in which one plays against the other two.

three-square (thrē'skwâr')   adj.   Having a triangular cross section, as some files.

threm·ma·tol·o·gy (threm'ə·tol'ə·jē)   n.   The science of breeding domestic animals and plants. [< Gk. thremma, -matos nursling + -LOGY]

thren·o·dy (thren'ə·dē)   n.   pl. **·dies** An ode or song of lamentation; a dirge. Also **thren'ode** (-ōd). [< Gk. thrēnōidia < thrēnos lament + ōidē song] **— thre·no·di·al** (thri·nō'dē·əl), **thre·nod·ic** (thri·nod'ik) adj. **— thren'o·dist** n.

thre·o·nine (thrē'ə·nēn, -nin)   n.   Biochem. A crystalline amino acid, $C_4H_9NO_3$, isolated as a product of the hydrolysis of certain proteins and regarded as essential to nutrition.

thresh (thresh)   v.t.   **1.** To beat stalks of (ripened grain) with a flail or machine so as to separate the grain from the straw or husks. **2.** Rare To beat; flog. **— v.i. 3.** To thresh grain. **4.** To move or thrash about. **— n.** The act of threshing. [OE therscan]

thresh·er (thresh'ər)   n.   **1.** One who or that which threshes; especially, a machine for threshing. **2.** A large shark (Alopias vulpes) having the dorsal lobe of the tail extremely long: also called foxfish, fox shark: also thresher shark.

thresh·old (thresh'ōld, -hōld, -ald)   n.   **1.** The plank, timber, or stone lying under the door of a building; doorsill. **2.** The entrance, entering point, or beginning of anything. **3.** Physiol. & Psychol. **a** The point at which a stimulus, as of a nerve or muscle, just produces a response. **b** The minimum degree of stimulation necessary for conscious perception: the threshold of consciousness: also called limen. ◆ Collateral adjective: liminal. [OE therscold]

threw (thrōō)   Past tense of THROW.

thrice (thrīs)   adv.   **1.** Three times. **2.** In a threefold manner. **3.** Extremely; very. [ME thries < OE thriwa + -s³]

thrift (thrift)   n.   **1.** Care and wisdom in the management of one's resources; frugality. **2.** Vigorous growth, as of a plant. **3.** Any of a genus (Armeria) of tufted herbs, growing on mountains and the seashore and having white or pink flowers. **4.** Obs. Prosperity. **5.** Scot. & Brit. Dial. Effort; work. [< ON. Akin to THRIVE.] **— thrift'less** adj. **— Syn. 1.** prudence, economy.

thrift shop   U.S.   A store that sells secondhand clothes, goods, etc., at reduced prices, usually for a specific charity.

thrift·y (thrif'tē)   adj.   **thrift·i·er, thrift·i·est 1.** Displaying thrift or good management; economical; frugal. **2.** Prosperous; thriving. **3.** Growing vigorously. **— Syn.** See FRUGAL. **— thrift'i·ly** adv. **— thrift'i·ness** n.

thrill (thril)   v.t.   **1.** To cause to feel a sudden wave of emotion; move to great or tingling excitement. **2.** To cause to vibrate or tremble. **— v.i. 3.** To feel a sudden wave of emotion or excitement. **4.** To vibrate or tremble; quiver. **— n. 1.** A tremor of feeling or excitement. **2.** A pulsation. **3.** Pathol. Fremitus. [Metathetic var. of THIRL¹] **— thrill'ing** adj. **— thrill'ing·ly** adv.

thrill·er (thril'ər)   n.   **1.** One who or that which thrills. **2.** Informal A sensational book, play, or motion picture.

thrip (thrip)   n.   Brit. Slang A threepenny piece.

thrips (thrips)   n.   Any of numerous small insects (order Thysanoptera), many species of which are injurious to grain and plants. [< L < Gk., woodworm]

thrive (thrīv)   v.i.   **throve** (thrōv) or **thrived, thrived** or **thriv·en** (thriv'ən), **thriv·ing 1.** To prosper; be successful. **2.** To grow with vigor; flourish. [< ON thrīfast, orig. reflexive of thrīfa to grasp. Akin to THRIFT.] **— thriv'er** n. **— thriv'ing·ly** adv.

thro (thrōō)   See THROUGH. Also **thro'.**

throat (thrōt)   n.   **1.** The passage leading from the back of the mouth to the stomach and lungs, containing the uvula, pharynx, epiglottis, esophagus, larynx, vocal cords, and trachea. **2.** The front of the neck, extending from below the chin to the collarbones. **3.** Any narrow passage resembling the throat, as the entrance to a chimney. **— v.t.** Rare To utter in a guttural tone. **— to cut one's own throat** Informal To adopt a course of action destructive or harmful to oneself. **— to jump down one's throat** Informal To criticize or berate one severely. **— to ram (something) down one's throat** Informal To force one to accept or hear something against his will. **— to stick in one's throat** To be difficult to utter, as from unwillingness or fear. [OE throte]

HUMAN THROAT
a Palate. b Tongue. c Nasal cavity. d Uvula. e Tonsils. f Pharynx. g Epiglottis. h Esophagus. i Larynx. j Vocal cords. k Trachea.

throat·latch (thrōt'lach')   n.   A strap passing under the neck of a draft animal and aiding in holding a bridle or halter in place. For illustration see HARNESS.

throat·y (thrō'tē)   adj.   **throat·i·er, throat·i·est** Uttered in the throat; guttural. **— throat'i·ly** adv. **— throat'i·ness** n.

throb (throb)   v.i.   **throbbed, throb·bing 1.** To beat rapidly or violently, as the heart from exertion or excitement. **2.** To pulsate. **3.** To feel or show great emotion. **— n. 1.** The act or state of throbbing. **2.** A pulsation or beat. [? Imit.] **— throb'ber** n. **— throb'bing·ly** adv.

throe (thrō)   n.   **1.** A violent pang or pain. **2.** pl. The pains of childbirth or of death. **3.** pl. Any agonizing or violent activity. **— Syn.** See PAIN. [ME throwe, prob. fusion of OE thrōwian to suffer and thrāwan to twist, throw]

throm·bin (throm'bin)   n.   Biochem. The enzyme present in blood serum that reacts with fibrinogen to form fibrin in the process of clotting. [< THROMBUS]

throm·bo·cyte (throm'bə·sīt)   n.   A blood platelet. [< Gk. thrombos clot + -CYTE]

throm·bo·sis (throm·bō'sis)   n.   pl. **·ses** (-sēz) Pathol. Local coagulation of blood in the heart or blood vessels, forming an obstruction to circulation. [< NL < Gk. *thrombōsis* < *thrombos* clot] — **throm·bot·ic** (-bot′ik) *adj.*

throm·bus (throm′bəs) *n. pl.* **·bi** (-bī) *Pathol.* The blood clot formed in thrombosis. [< NL < Gk. *thrombos* clot]

throne (thrōn) *n.* **1.** The royal chair occupied by a sovereign on state occasions. **2.** The chair of state of a pope or of some other dignitary, as a cardinal, archbishop, or bishop. **3.** Royal estate or dignity; sovereign power. **4.** One who occupies a throne; sovereign. **5.** *pl. Theol.* The third of the nine orders of angels: see ANGEL. — *v.t. & v.i.* **throned, thron·ing** To place or sit on a throne; enthrone; exalt. [< OF *trone* < L *thronus* < Gk. *thronos* seat]

throng (thrông, throng) *n.* **1.** A multitude of people crowded closely together. **2.** Any numerous collection. — *v.t.* **1.** To crowd into; jam. **2.** To press or crowd upon. — *v.i.* **3.** To collect or move in a throng. [OE *gethrang*] — **Syn.** (noun) **1.** crowd, concourse, mob, host, horde, press.

thros·tle (thros′əl) *n.* **1.** The song thrush. **2.** A machine for twisting and winding fibers from roves. [OE]

throt·tle (throt′l) *n.* **1.** *Mech.* **a** A valve controlling the supply of steam to a steam engine, or of vaporized fuel to the cylinders of an internal-combustion engine: also **throttle valve. b** The lever that operates the throttle: also **throttle lever. 2.** *Rare or Dial.* The throat or windpipe. — *v.t.* **·tled, ·tling 1.** To press or constrict the throat of; strangle; choke. **2.** To silence, stop, or suppress by or as by choking. **3.** *Mech.* **a** To reduce or shut off the flow of steam or fuel in (a steam or internal-combustion engine). **b** To reduce the speed of by means of a throttle; slow down. — *v.i.* **4.** To suffocate; choke. [Dim. of ME *throte*] — **throt′tler** *n.*

through (thrōō) *prep.* **1.** Into one side, end, or point, and out of the other. **2.** Covering, entering, or penetrating all parts of; throughout. **3.** From the first to the last of; during the time or period of. **4.** In the midst of; among. **5.** By way of: He departed *through* the door. **6.** By means of; by the instrumentality or aid of. **7.** Having reached the end of, especially with success: He got *through* his examinations easily. **8.** On account of; because or as a result of. — **Syn.** See BY. — *adv.* **1.** From one end, side, surface, etc., to or beyond another. **2.** From beginning to end. **3.** To a termination or conclusion, especially a successful one: to pull *through*. **4.** Completely; entirely: He is wet *through*. — **through and through** Thoroughly; completely. — *adj.* **1.** Going from beginning to end without stops or with very few stops: a *through* train; also, pertaining to or serving an entire distance or route: a *through* ticket. **2.** Extending from one side or surface to another. **3.** Unobstructed; open; clear: a *through* road. **4.** Arrived at an end; finished: Are you *through* with my pen? **5.** At the end of all relations or dealings: He is *through* with school. Also spelled *thro, thru.* [OE *thurh*]

through·out (thrōō·out′) *adv.* Through or in every part: The house was searched *throughout.* — *prep.* All through; everywhere in: *throughout* the nation.

through·put (thrōō′pŏōt) *n.* **1.** The quantity of raw material that may be processed for final use in a given time or under specified conditions. **2.** The process itself.

through·way (thrōō′wā′) See THRUWAY.

throve (thrōv) Past tense of THRIVE.

throw (thrō) *v.* **threw** (thrōō), **thrown, throw·ing** *v.t.* **1.** To launch through the air by means of a sudden straightening or whirling of the arm. **2.** To propel or hurl: The mortar *threw* shells into the town. **3.** To put hastily or carelessly: He *threw* a coat over his shoulders. **4.** To direct or project (light, shadow, a glance, etc.). **5.** To bring to a specified condition or state by or as by throwing: to *throw* the enemy into a panic. **6.** To cause to fall; overthrow: The horse *threw* its rider. **7.** In wrestling, to force the shoulders of (an opponent) to the ground. **8.** To cast (dice). **9.** To make (a specified cast) with dice. **10.** To cast off or shed; lose: The horse *threw* a shoe. **11.** *Informal* To lose purposely, as a race, contest, etc., in accordance with a prearranged plan. **12.** To give birth to (young): said of domestic animals. **13.** To move, as a lever or switch, in connecting or disconnecting a circuit, mechanism, etc. **14.** *Slang* To give (a party, etc.). **15.** In card games, to play or discard. **16.** In ceramics, to shape on a potter's wheel. **17.** To spin (filaments, as of silk) into thread. — *v.i.* **18.** To cast or fling something. — **to throw away 1.** To cast off; discard. **2.** To waste; squander. — **to throw back 1.** To return by throwing. **2.** To revert to ancestral characteristics. — **to throw cold water on** To discourage. — **to throw in 1.** To cause (gears or a clutch) to mesh or engage. **2.** To contribute; add. **3.** To join with others. — **to throw in the towel** (or **sponge**) *Slang* To accept defeat; surrender. — **to throw off 1.** To cast aside; reject; spurn. **2.** To rid oneself of. **3.** To do or utter in an offhand manner. **4.** To confuse or mislead; mix up. — **to throw oneself at** To strive to gain the affections or love of. — **to throw oneself into** To engage or take part in vigorously. — **to throw oneself on** (or **upon**) To entrust oneself to; rely on. — **to throw open 1.** To open sud-

denly or completely, as a door. **2.** To free from restrictions or obstacles. — **to throw the book at** *Slang* **1.** To sentence to the maximum penalty. **2.** To reprimand or castigate severely. — **to throw out 1.** To put forth; emit. **2.** To cast out or aside; discard; reject. **3.** To utter as if accidentally: to *throw out* hints. **4.** In baseball, to retire (a runner) by throwing the ball to the base toward which he is advancing. — **to throw over 1.** To overturn. **2.** To discard. — **to throw (something) up to (someone)** *Informal* To mention or repeat as a reproach. — **to throw together** To put together hastily or roughly. — **to throw up 1.** To construct hastily. **2.** To give up; relinquish. **3.** To vomit. — *n.* **1.** An act of throwing or hurling; a cast; fling. **2.** The distance over which a missile may be thrown: a stone's *throw*. **3.** A cast of dice, or the resulting number. **4.** *Mech.* **a** The radius of the circle described by a crank, cam, or the like. **b** The extent of reciprocating motion obtainable, as from a crank, piston, slide valve, etc. **5.** A scarf used for draping an easel or picture frame; also, a woman's scarf or boa. **6.** *Geol.* **a** A faulting, or dislocation of rock strata. **b** The amount of vertical displacement produced by dislocation of strata. **7.** The sudden fluctuation of a magnetic needle when the force is suddenly changed. **8.** The distance from a motion-picture projector to the screen. **9.** In wrestling, the act or technique of throwing. [OE *thrāwan* to turn, twist, curl] — **throw′er** *n.*

throw·a·way (thrō′ə·wā′) *n.* A free broadside or leaflet handed out for advertising or propaganda purposes.

throw·back (thrō′bak′) *n.* **1.** Reversion to an earlier type or condition; also, an example of such reversion; atavism. **2.** A throwing back.

throw·ster (thrō′stər) *n.* One who makes silk thread.

thru (thrōō) See THROUGH.

thrum¹ (thrum) *v.* **thrummed, thrum·ming** *v.t.* **1.** To play on or finger (a stringed instrument) idly and without expression. **2.** To drum or tap monotonously or listlessly. **3.** To recite or repeat in a droning, monotonous way. — *v.i.* **4.** To thrum a stringed instrument. **5.** To sound when played thus, as a guitar. **6.** *Scot.* To repeat tiresomely. — *n.* Any monotonous drumming. [Prob. imit.] — **thrum′mer** *n.*

thrum² (thrum) *n.* **1.** The fringe of warp threads remaining on a loom beam after the web has been cut off; also, one of such threads. **2.** Any loose thread or fringe, or a tuft of filaments or fibers; a tassel. **3.** *pl.* Coarse or waste yarn. **4.** *pl. Naut.* Bits of rope yarn for sewing on canvas to make chafing gear or collision mats. **5.** *Bot.* A threadlike organ or part of a stamen. **6.** *Scot.* A bit; particle: I don't care a *thrum*. **7.** *Scot.* A tangle. — *v.t.* **thrummed, thrum·ming 1.** To cover or trim with thrums or similar appendages. **2.** *Naut.* To insert bits of rope yarn in (canvas) to produce a rough surface or mat to be used to prevent chafing. [OE *-thrum* ligament, as in *tungethrum* the ligament of the tongue] — **thrum′my** *adj.*

thrush¹ (thrush) *n.* Any of numerous migratory, passerine birds (family *Turdidae*) having a long and slightly graduated tail, long wings, and spotted underparts, as the hermit thrush, wood thrush, and the song thrush of Europe. ◆ Collateral adjective: *turdine.* [OE *thrysce*]

thrush² (thrush) *n. Pathol.* A vesicular disease of the mouth, lips, and throat caused by a fungus (*Candida albicans*), generally confined to infants. [Cf. Dan. *tröske*, Sw. *trosk* mouth disease]

thrust (thrust) *v.* **thrust, thrust·ing** *v.t.* **1.** To push or shove with force or sudden impulse. **2.** To pierce or stab, as with a sword or dagger. **3.** To put (a person) forcibly into some condition or situation. **4.** To interpose; put in: to *thrust* in a remark. — *v.i.* **5.** To make a sudden push against something. **6.** To force oneself on or ahead: push one's way: with *through, into, on,* etc. — *n.* **1.** A sudden, forcible push, especially with a pointed weapon. **2.** A vigorous attack. **3.** *Archit.* A stress or strain tending to push a member of a structure outward or sidewise: the *thrust* of an arch. **4.** *Mech.* The driving force exerted by a steam engine, motor, propeller, jet engine, etc. **5.** Salient force or meaning: the *thrust* of his remarks. **6.** *Geol.* A thrust fault. — **Syn.** See STRESS. [< ON *thrysta*] — **thrust′er** *n.*

thrust fault *Geol.* A fault resulting from horizontal compression in which the hanging wall appears to have moved upward, with a corresponding shortening of the entire rock mass: opposed to *gravity fault.* Also called *reverse fault.*

thru·way (thrōō′wā′) *n. U.S.* A long-distance express highway: also spelled *throughway.*

Thu·cyd·i·des (thōō·sid′ə·dēz, thyōō-), 471?–401? B.C., Greek historian. — **Thu·cyd′i·de·an** (-dē′ən) *adj.*

thud (thud) *n.* **1.** A dull, heavy sound, as of a hard body striking a soft surface. **2.** The blow causing such a sound; a thump. — *v.i.* **thud·ded, thud·ding** To meet or strike with a thud. [OE *thyddan* to strike, thrust, press]

thug (thug) *n.* **1.** A cutthroat or ruffian. **2.** Formerly, one of an organization of religious, professional assassins in northern India. [< Hind. *thag* < Skt. *sthaga* swindler] — **thug′ger·y** *n.* — **thug′gish** *adj.*

thug·gee (thug′ē) *n.* The system of assassination and robbery formerly practiced by thugs in India. [< Hind. *thagī*]

thu·ja (thōō′jə) *n.* Any of a genus (*Thuja*) of evergreen trees and shrubs of the pine family, including the arborvitae, source of the medicinal **oil of thuja.** Also spelled *thuya.* [< NL < Gk. *thyia* an African tree]

Thu·le (thōō′lē *for def. 1,* tōō′lē *for def. 2*) **1.** In ancient geography, the northernmost limit of the habitable world: identified with Iceland or Mainland in the Shetland Islands. See ULTIMA THULE. **2.** A settlement in NW Greenland; site of a major U.S. military installation.

thu·li·a (thōō′lē·ə) *n. Chem.* Oxide of thulium, Tm$_2$O$_3$, found in samarskite. [< THULIUM]

thu·li·um (thōō′lē·əm) *n.* A metallic element (symbol Tm) of the erbium group in the lanthanide series. See ELEMENT. [after *Thule*]

thumb (thum) *n.* **1.** The short, thick digit next to the forefinger of the human hand; the pollex. **2.** The corresponding digit in certain other animals, especially primates. **3.** The division in a glove or mitten that covers the thumb. **4.** *Archit.* An ovolo. — **all thumbs** *Informal* Clumsy with the hands; not deft. — **thumbs down** *Informal* No; nix: from a sign used to indicate negation or disapproval. — **under one's thumb** Under one's influence or power. — *v.t.* **1.** To press, rub, soil, or wear with the thumb in handling, as the pages of a book. **2.** To perform clumsily with or as with the thumbs. **3.** To run through the pages of (a book, manuscript, etc.) rapidly and perfunctorily. **4.** *Informal* To solicit (a ride in an automobile) by signaling with the thumb. — *v.i.* To hitchhike. — **to thumb one's nose** To show defiance or disgust by raising the thumb to the nose with the fingers extended. [OE *thūma*]

thumb-in·dex (thum′in′deks) *v.t.* To provide with a thumb index.

thumb index A series of scalloped indentations cut along the right-hand edge of a book and labeled to indicate its various sections.

thumb·kin (thum′kin) *n.* A thumbscrew (def. 2).

thumb·ling (thum′ling) *n.* A diminutive being; dwarf. Compare FINGERLING.

thumb·nail (thum′nāl′) *n.* **1.** The nail of the thumb. **2.** Anything as small and essentially complete as a thumbnail. — *adj.* Small and essentially complete: a *thumbnail* sketch.

thumb·nut (thum′nut′) *n.* A threaded nut having one or more wings or projections for screwing by the thumb and fingers: also called *wing nut.* For illustration see NUT.

thumb·print (thum′print′) *n.* An impression or print made by the thumb.

thumb·screw (thum′skrōō′) *n.* **1.** A screw to be turned by thumb and fingers. For illustration see SCREW. **2.** An instrument of torture for compressing the thumb or thumbs.

thumb·stall (thum′stôl′) *n.* A protective covering or sheath, as of leather, for the thumb.

thumb·tack (thum′tak′) *n. U.S.* A broad-headed tack that may be pushed in with the thumb.

Thum·mim (thum′im) See URIM.

thump (thump) *n.* **1.** A blow with a blunt or heavy object. **2.** The sound made by such a blow; a dull thud. — **Syn.** See BLOW². — *v.t.* **1.** To beat or strike so as to make a heavy thud or thuds. **2.** *Informal* To beat or defeat severely — *v.i.* **3.** To strike with a thump. **4.** To make a thump or thumps; pound or throb. [Imit.] — **thump′er** *n.*

thump·ing (thum′ping) *adj.* **1.** That thumps. **2.** *Informal* Huge; whopping.

Thun (tōōn) A town in central Switzerland, on the Aar river; pop. 34,700 (est. 1968).

Thun, Lake of An expansion of the Aar river in Central Switzerland; 18 sq. mi. *German* **Thun·ner·see** (tōō′nər·zā).

thun·der (thun′dər) *n.* **1.** The sound that accompanies lightning, caused by the sudden heating and expansion of the air along the path of the electrical discharge. **2.** Any loud, rumbling or booming noise, suggestive of thunder. **3.** A denunciation or threat; a vehement or powerful utterance. **4.** *Rare* A lightning stroke; thunderbolt. — **to steal one's thunder** To take for one's own use anything especially popular or effective originated by another: said especially of an argument. — *v.i.* **1.** To give forth a peal or peals of thunder: used impersonally: It *thunders.* **2.** To make a noise like thunder. **3.** To utter vehement denunciations or threats. — *v.t.* **4.** To utter or express with a noise like or suggestive of thunder. [OE *thunor*] — **thun′der·er** *n.*

thun·der·bird (thun′dər·bûrd′) *n.* In the folklore of certain North American Indians, an enormous bird believed to produce thunder, lightning, and rain.

thun·der·bolt (thun′dər·bōlt′) *n.* **1.** An electric discharge accompanied by a clap of thunder. **2.** An imaginary molten ball or bolt hurled by the lightning flash. **3.** One who or that which acts with or as with the force and speed of destructiveness of lightning.

thun·der·clap (thun′dər·klap′) *n.* **1.** A sharp, violent detonation of thunder. **2.** Anything having the violence or suddenness of a clap of thunder.

thun·der·cloud (thun′dər·kloud′) *n.* A dark, heavy mass of cloud highly charged with electricity.

thun·der·head (thun′dər·hed′) *n. Meteorol.* A rounded mass of cumulus cloud, either silvery white or dark with silvery edges, often developing into a thundercloud.

thun·der·ing (thun′dər·ing) *adj.* **1.** Giving forth, or accompanied by, thunder. **2.** Resembling thunder in force or effect; extremely violent. **3.** *Informal* Unusually great or extreme; superlative. — **thun′der·ing·ly** *adv.*

thun·der·ous (thun′dər·əs) *adj.* Producing a noise like thunder. Also **thun′drous** (-drəs). — **thun′der·ous·ly** *adv.*

thun·der·peal (thun′dər·pēl′) *n.* A clap of thunder.

thun·der·show·er (thun′dər·shou′ər) *n.* A shower of rain with thunder and lightning.

thun·der·stone (thun′dər·stōn′) *n.* A tapering stone or rock supposed to have accompanied a thunderbolt.

thun·der·storm (thun′dər·stôrm′) *n.* A local storm accompanied by lightning and thunder.

thun·der·struck (thun′dər·struk′) *adj.* **1.** Struck by lightning. **2.** Amazed, astonished, or confounded, as with fear, surprise, etc. Also **thun′der·strick′en** (-strik′ən).

thun·der·y (thun′dər·ē) *adj. Informal* **1.** Indicative of or accompanied by thunder. **2.** Ominous.

Thur. or **Thurs.** Thursday.

Thur·ber (thûr′bər), **James** (**Grover**), 1894–1961, U.S. humorous writer and artist.

thu·ri·ble (thōōr′ə·bəl, thûr′-) *n.* A censer. [< L *thuribulum* < *thus, thuris* frankincense]

thu·ri·fer (thōōr′ə·fər, thûr′-) *n.* An acolyte or altar boy who carries a thurible. [< L < *thus, thuris* frankincense + *ferre* to bear, carry]

thu·rif·er·ous (thōō·rif′ər·əs) *adj.* Yielding or bearing incense.

Thu·rin·gi·a (thōō·rin′jē·ə, -jə) A former state of southwestern East Germany. *German* **Thü·ring·en** (tü′ring·ən).

Thu·rin·gi·an (thōō·rin′jē·ən) *adj.* **1.** Of or relating to Thuringia or its inhabitants. **2.** *Geol.* Denoting the upper division of the Permian in Europe. — *n.* **1.** One of a Teutonic tribe occupying central Germany until the sixth century. **2.** A native or inhabitant of Thuringia.

Thuringian Forest A wooded mountain range of central Germany; highest point, Beerberg, 3,222 ft. *German* **Thü·ring·er Wald** (tü′ring·ər vält).

Thurs·day (thûrz′dē, -dā) *n.* The fifth day of the week. Abbr. **Th., Thur., Thurs.** [Fusion of OE *Thunres dæg* day of Thunor and ON *Thōrsdagr* day of Thor; trans. of LL *dies Jovis* day of Jove]

Thursday Island An island of Queensland, Australia, in Torres Strait; 1.5 mi. long, 1 mi. wide.

thus (thus) *adv.* **1.** In this, that, or the following way of manner. **2.** To such degree or extent; so: *thus* far. **3.** In these circumstances or conditions; therefore. [OE]

thu·ya (thōō′yə) See THUJA.

thwack (thwak) *v.t.* To strike with something flat; whack. — *n.* A blow with a flat or blunt instrument. [Prob. OE *thaccian* to smack; infl. in form by *whack*] — **thwack′er** *n.*

thwart (thwôrt) *v.t.* **1.** To prevent the accomplishment of, as by interposing an obstacle; also, to prevent (one) from accomplishing something; foil; frustrate; balk. **2.** *Obs.* To move or place over or across. — **Syn.** See BAFFLE. — *n.* **1.** An oarsman's seat extending across a boat. **2.** A crosspiece or transverse member in a boat. — *adj.* **1.** Lying, moving, or extending across something; transverse. **2.** *Obs.* Perverse; ill-natured. — *adv. & prep.* Athwart; across. [< ON *thvert,* neut. of *thverr* transverse] — **thwart′er** *n.*

thy (thī) *pronominal adj. Archaic* The possessive case of the pronoun *thou,* used attributively: *Thy* kingdom come. [Apocopated var. of THINE]

Thy·es·te·an banquet A cannibal feast; so called from the feast at which Thyestes was served his own sons. See ATREUS.

Thy·es·tes (thī·es′tēz) In Greek legend, a son of Pelops; brother of Atreus. — **Thy·es′te·an** (-tē·ən), **Thy·es′ti·an** *adj.*

thy·la·cine (thī′lə·sīn, -sin) *n.* A nearly extinct, doglike marsupial (*Thylacinus cynocephalus*) of Tasmania, grayish brown with dark, transverse bands on the hinder part of the back: also called *Tasmanian wolf, zebra wolf.* [< NL < Gk. *thylax, thylakos* pouch]

thyme (tīm) *n.* Any of a genus (*Thymus*) of small shrubby plants of the mint family, having aromatic leaves and cultivated for seasoning in cookery; especially, the **wild thyme** (*T. serpyllum*). [< F *thym* < L *thymum* < Gk. *thymon*] — **thym′y** *adj.*

THYLACINE
(About 18 inches high at shoulder)

thym·e·lae·a·ceous (thim′ə·lē·ā′shəs) *adj. Bot.* Designating a family (*Thymelaeaceae*) of trees or shrubs having very tough bark. [< NL, family name < L *thymelaea* < Gk. *thymelaia* < *thymon* thyme + *elaia* olive tree]

thym·ic[1] (tī′mik) *adj.* Pertaining to or derived from thyme.

thy·mic[2] (thī′mik) *adj.* Of, pertaining to, or derived from the thymus.

thy·mol (tī′mōl, -mol, thī′-) *n. Chem.* A crystalline compound, C$_{10}$H$_{13}$OH, contained in certain volatile oils, as those of thyme and horsemint, and also made synthetically, used as an antiseptic. [< THYM(E) + -OL²]

thy·mus (thī′məs) *n. Anat.* A glandular organ of man and some other vertebrates, found behind the top of the sternum, most prominent in youth and believed to influence immunity. [< NL < Gk. *thymos*]

thy·re·oid (thī′rē·oid) *adj.* Thyroid.

thyro- *combining form Med. & Surg.* The thyroid; of or related to the thyroid: *thyroidectomy.* Also, before vowels, **thyr-.** Also **thyreo-.** [< Gk. *thyreoeidēs* thyroid]

thy·roid (thī′roid) *adj.* 1. *Physiol.* Relating or pertaining to the thyroid cartilage or the thyroid gland. 2. Shaped like a shield; also, having a shield-shaped marking. — *n.* 1. The thyroid cartilage or gland. 2. The dried and powdered thyroid gland of certain domesticated food animals, used in the treatment of hypothyroid disorders. [< Gk. *thyreoeidēs* shield-shaped < *thyreos* large shield + *eidos* form]

thyroid cartilage *Anat.* The largest cartilage of the larynx, composed of two blades whose juncture in front forms the Adam's apple.

thy·roid·ec·to·my (thī′roid·ek′tə·mē) *n. pl.* **·mies** *Surg.* Excision of the thyroid gland. [< THYROID + -ECTOMY]

thyroid gland *Anat.* A bilobate endocrine gland situated in front of and on each side of the trachea, close to the larynx, and secreting thyroxin, important in the regulation of metabolism and body growth.

thy·roid·i·tis (thī′roid·ī′tis) *n. Pathol.* Inflammation of the thyroid gland.

thy·rox·in (thī·rok′sin) *n. Biochem.* An odorless, crystalline amino acid, $C_{15}H_{11}O_4NI_4$, obtained as the hormone of the thyroid gland and also made synthetically, used to treat thyroid disorders. Also **thy·rox′ine** (-sēn, -sin). [< THYR(O)- + OX(Y)- + -IN] — **thy·rox·in·ic** (thī′rok·sin′ik) *adj.*

thyrse (thûrs) *n.* A thyrsus (def. 2).

thyr·soid (thûr′soid) *adj. Bot.* Resembling or shaped like a thyrsus. Also **thyr·soi·dal** (thûr·soid′l).

thyr·sus (thûr′səs) *n. pl.* **·si** (-sī) 1. A staff wreathed in ivy and crowned with a pine cone or a bunch of ivy leaves, as carried by Dionysus and the satyrs. 2. *Bot.* A type of mixed inflorescence in which the middle branches are longer than those above or below them, as in the lilac and grape: also called *thyrse.* [< L < Gk. *thyrsos*]

thy·sa·nu·ran (thī′sə·nŏŏr′ən, -nyŏŏr′-, this′ə-) *adj.* Designating or belonging to an order (*Thysanura*) of primitive wingless insects, including the silverfish and the firebrat. — *n.* One of the *Thysanura.* [< NL < Gk. *thysanura* fringe + *oura* tail] — **thy′sa·nu′rous** *adj.*

thy·self (thī·self′) *pron. Archaic* A form of the second person singular pronouns *thee* and *thou,* used: 1. As a reflexive: Know *thyself.* 2. As an emphatic or intensive form: I love thee for *thyself.*

ti¹ (tē) *n. Music* In solmization, a syllable representing the seventh tone of the diatonic scale: formerly called *si.* [See GAMUT]

ti² (tē) *n.* One of several Asian trees (genus *Cordyline*) of the lily family, especially the **ti palm** (*C. terminalis*) of eastern Asia, having many foliage forms. [< Polynesian]

Ti *Chem.* Titanium.

Ti·a·Jua·na (tē′ə wä′nə) See TIJUANA.

ti·a·ra (tī·âr′ə, tē·är′ə, -ar′ə) *n.* 1. The pope's triple crown; also, the papal dignity. Compare MITER. 2. An ornamental, semicircular band of jewels, etc., worn by women for formal occasions. 3. The upright headdress worn by the ancient Persian kings. [< L < Gk. *tiara* Persian headdress]

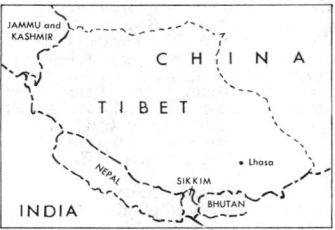

PAPAL TIARA

Tib·bett (tib′it), **Lawrence Mervil,** 1896–1960, U.S. baritone.

Ti·ber (tī′bər) A river of central Italy, flowing 251 miles south to the Tyrrhenian Sea: Italian *Tevere.*

Ti·be·ri·as (tī·bir′ē·əs), **Lake** See (Sea of) GALILEE.

Ti·be·ri·us (tī·bir′ē·əs), 42 B.C.–A.D. 37, Roman emperor 14–37 A.D.; full name **Tiberius Claudius Nero Cae·sar** (sē′zər).

Ti·bes·ti Massif (ti·bes′tē) A mountain group of western equatorial Africa; highest point, Emi Koussi, 11,204 ft.

Ti·bet (ti·bet′) A former independent theocracy of central Asia, incorporated, 1950–57, into China, as the **Tibetan Autonomous Region;** about 470,000 sq. mi.; pop. 1,270,000 (est. 1957); capital, Lhasa: Chinese *Sitsang;* also *Thibet.*

Ti·bet·an (ti·bet′n) *adj.* Of or pertaining to Tibet, the Tibetans, or to their language, religion, or customs. — *n.* 1. One of the native Mongoloid people of Tibet, now intermixed with Chinese and various peoples of India. 2. The Sino-Tibetan language of Tibet. Also spelled *Thibetan.*

Ti·bet·o-Bur·man (ti·bet′ō-bûr′mən) See under SINO-TIBETAN.

tib·i·a (tib′ē·ə) *n. pl.* **tib·i·ae** (tib′i·ē) or **tib·i·as** 1. *Anat.* The inner and larger of the two bones of the leg below the knee; the shin bone. See illustrations at FOOT and PATELLA. 2. The corresponding bone in the hind limb of other animals. 3. *Entomol.* The fourth or penultimate joint of the leg of an insect, between the femur and the tarsus. 4. An ancient flute or pipe, originally made of an animal's leg bone. [< L] — **tib′i·al** *adj.*

Ti·bul·lus (ti·bul′əs), **Albius,** 54?–18 B.C., Roman poet.

Ti·bur (tī′bər) The ancient name of TIVOLI.

tic (tik) *n.* 1. An involuntary spasm or twitching of muscles, usually of the face and sometimes of neurotic origin. 2. Tic douloureux. [< F]

ti·cal (ti·käl′, -kôl′, tē′kəl) *n.* 1. The former name for the baht, a Thai unit of currency. 2. A Thai unit of weight, equivalent to about half an ounce: also called *baht.* [< Malay *tikal*]

tic dou·lou·reux (tik dŏŏ′lŏŏ·rŏŏ′, *Fr.* tēk′dŏŏ·lōŏ·rœ′) *Pathol.* An acutely painful neuralgia of the face with paroxysmal muscular twitchings: also called *trigeminal neuralgia.* [< F, painful tic]

Ti·ci·no (tē·chē′nō) A Canton in southern Switzerland; 1,086 sq. mi.; pop. 220,000 (1965); capital, Bellinzona. Also *Tessin.*

tick¹ (tik) *n.* 1. A light, recurring sound made by a watch, clock, or similar mechanism. 2. *Brit. Informal* The length of time occupied by one tick of a watch or clock. 3. A mark, as a dot or dash, used in checking off something. — *v.i.* 1. To make a recurrent clicking sound, as a running watch or clock. — *v.t.* 2. *Brit.* To mark or check with a tick. — **to tick off** *Brit. Informal* To tell off. [Prob. imit. Cf. Du. *tik.*]

tick² (tik) *n.* 1. One of numerous flat, leathery, bloodsucking arachnids (order *Acarina*) that attack the skin of man and other animals; especially, the **cattle tick** (*Margaropus annulatus*), carrier of Texas fever. 2. Any of certain two-winged or wingless insects (family *Hippoboscidae*), parasitic on sheep, horses, cattle, bats, and other animals. [OE *ticia.* Cf. LG *tieke,* G *zecke* tick.]

tick³ (tik) *n.* 1. The stout outer covering of a mattress or pillow. 2. *Informal* Ticking. [Earlier *teke, tyke,* ult. < L *teca, theca* < Gk. *thēkē* case]

tick⁴ (tik) *n. Brit. Informal* Credit; trust: to buy something on *tick.* [Short for TICKET]

tick·er (tik′ər) *n.* 1. One who or that which ticks. 2. A telegraphic receiving instrument that records stock quotations on a paper ribbon. 3. *Slang* A watch. 4. *Slang* The heart.

ticker tape A paper ribbon that receives the printed information on a ticker machine. — **tick·er-tape** (tik′ər-tāp′) *adj.*

ticker-tape parade A parade in the financial district of New York City in which ticker tape is thrown from windows on the celebrity being honored.

tick·et (tik′it) *n.* 1. A card showing that the holder is entitled to something, as transportation in a public vehicle, admission to a theater, etc. 2. A label or tag for attachment or identification. 3. A certificate or license as of an airplane pilot or the captain of a ship. 4. In politics: **a** A list of candidates of a single party on a ballot: the Democratic *ticket.* **b** The group of candidates running for the offices of a party. 5. *Informal* A legal summons, as for a traffic violation. 6. *Rare* A note or memorandum; also, a slip of paper containing a note or memorandum. — **that's the ticket** *Slang* That's the correct thing; that's right. — *v.t.* 1. To fix a ticket to; label. 2. To present or furnish with a ticket or tickets. [< MF *etiquet* a little note < OF *estiquette* < *estiquer* to stick < OLG *stekan.* Doublet of ETIQUETTE.]

ticket agent One who sells tickets.

ticket of leave Formerly, in Great Britain and Australia, a written permit granted to a penal convict to be at large before the expiration of his sentence.

tick fever Any of several fevers transmitted by ticks, especially the Texas fever of cattle, and the Rocky Mountain spotted fever, occurring in man.

tick·ing (tik′ing) *n.* A strong, closely woven cotton or linen fabric, used for ticks, awnings, etc. [< TICK³ + -ING¹]

tick·le (tik′əl) *v.* **·led, ·ling** *v.t.* 1. To touch or scratch (someone) so as to produce a sensation resulting in spasmodic laughter or twitching; titillate. 2. To arouse or excite agreeably; please: Compliments *tickle* our vanity. 3. *Informal* To amuse or entertain; delight. 4. To move, stir, or get by or as by tickling. — *v.i.* 5. To have or experience a thrilling or tingling sensation: My foot *tickles.* — *n.* 1. The act of tickling or of being tickled; also the sensation produced by tickling. 2. *Canadian* In Newfoundland, a narrow strait. [ME *tikelen,* ? metathetic var. of OE *citelian,* ON *kitla* to tickle]

tick·ler (tik'lər) *n.* **1.** One who or that which tickles. **2.** A memorandum book or file, as of bills or notes due, etc.

tickler coil *Electronics* A coil in the plate circuit of an electron tube, used for amplification.

tick·lish (tik'lish) *adj.* **1.** Sensitive to tickling. **2.** Liable to be upset or easily offended. **3.** Attended with risk; difficult; delicate. — **tick'lish·ly** *adv.* — **tick'lish·ness** *n.*

tick·seed (tik'sēd') *n.* **1.** The coreopsis. **2.** The tick trefoil. [< TICK² + SEED]

tickseed sunflower A square-stemmed species of bur marigold (genus *Bidens*), having large-rayed yellow flowers.

tick·tack (tik'tak') *n.* **1.** A recurrent sound like that of the ticking of a clock. **2.** A device for playing pranks by making a rattling noise against a window or door. [Imit. reduplication of TICK¹]

tick·tack·toe (tik'tak·tō') *n.* **1.** A game for two players who alternately put circles or crosses in the spaces of a figure formed by two parallel lines crossing at right angles two other parallel lines, each player trying to get a row of three circles or three crosses before his opponent does: also called *crisscross, tit-tat-toe.* **2.** The prank of using a ticktack. Also **tick'tack·too'** (-tōō'), **tic'tac·toe'** (-tō').

tick·tock (tik'tok') *n.* The sound of a clock or watch. — *v.i.* To make this sound. [Imit.]

tick trefoil Any of several leguminous plants (genus *Desmodium*) whose leaves and pods cling to the coats of animals and to clothing: also called *tickseed.*

Ti·con·der·o·ga (tī'kon·də·rō'gə) A village in NE New York, on Lake George; pop. 3,268; site of **Fort Ticonderoga**, captured from the French in 1759 and from the British in 1775, designated a national historic landmark, 1961.

tid·al (tīd'l) *adj.* **1.** Of, pertaining to, or influenced by the tides.

tidal wave **1.** Any great incoming rise of waters along a shore, caused by windstorms at sea or by excessively high tides. **2.** A tsunami. **3.** A great movement in popular feeling, opinion, action, etc.

tid·bit (tid'bit') *n.* A choice bit, as of food. Also, *Brit.*, **titbit**. [< dial. E *tid* small object + BIT¹]

tid·dly·winks (tid'lē·wingks') *n.* A game in which the players attempt to snap little disks of bone, ivory, or the like, from a plane surface into a cup. Also **tid·dle·dy·winks** (tid'l·dē·wingks'). [Prob. < *tiddly* child's word for *little*]

tide¹ (tīd) *n.* **1.** The periodic rise and fall of the surface waters of the oceans and of the waters connected with them, caused by the attraction of moon and sun. In each lunar day of 24 hours and 51 minutes there are two high tides and two low tides, alternating at equal intervals of flood and ebb. See SPRING TIDE, NEAP TIDE. **2.** Anything that rises and falls like the tide; also, the time at which something is most flourishing. **3.** A natural drift or tendency of events, opinions, etc. **4.** Season; time; especially, a season of the ecclesiastical year: used chiefly in combination: *Christmastide.* **5.** *Archaic* A suitable or favorable occasion; opportunity. — *v.* **tid·ed**, **tid·ing** *v.i.* **1.** To ebb and flow like the tide. **2.** To float with the tide. — *v.t.* **3.** To carry or help like a boat buoyed up by the tide: *Charity tided us over the depression.* **4.** To survive; endure, as a difficulty: with *over*: to *tide* over hard times. [OE *tīd* period, season] — **tide'less** *adj.*

tide² (tīd) *v.i.* **tid·ed**, **tid·ing** *Archaic* To betide; happen. [OE *tīdan*]

tide·land (tīd'land') *n.* Land alternately covered and uncovered by the tide.

tide·mark (tīd'märk') *n.* A mark or indicator showing the highest, or sometimes the lowest, point of a tide.

tide·rip (tīd'rip') *n.* Riptide. [< TIDE¹ + RIP²]

tide·wait·er (tīd'wā'tər) *n.* A customs officer who boards vessels entering port, to enforce customs regulations.

tide·wa·ter (tīd'wô'tər, -wot'ər) *n.* **1.** Water that inundates land at high tide. **2.** Water affected by the tide on the seacoast or in a river. **3.** Any area, as a seacoast, whose waters are affected by tides. — *adj.* Pertaining to the tidewater; also, situated on the seacoast: the *tidewater* country.

tide·way (tīd'wā') *n.* A channel where the tide runs.

ti·dings (tī'dingz) *n.pl.* (*sometimes construed as sing.*) A report or information; news. [OE *tīdung*; infl. in meaning by ON *títhindi* news, message]

ti·dy (tī'dē) *adj.* **·di·er**, **·di·est** **1.** Marked by neatness and order; trim. **2.** Of an orderly disposition. **3.** *Informal* Moderately large; considerable: a *tidy* sum. **4.** *Informal* Tolerable; fairly good. — **Syn.** See NEAT¹. — *v.t.* & *v.i.* **·died**, **·dy·ing** To make (things) tidy; put (things) in order. — *n.* *pl.* **·dies** A light, detachable covering, as of lace or embroidery, to protect the back or arms of a chair or sofa. [ME *tidi* < OE *tīd* time] — **ti'di·ly** *adv.* — **ti'di·ness** *n.*

ti·dy·tips (tī'dē·tips') *n.* *pl.* **·tips** Any of a genus (*Layia*) of ornamental annual plants of California, having yellow flower heads tipped with white; especially, *L. elegans.*

tie (tī) *v.* **tied**, **ty·ing** *v.t.* **1.** To fasten with cord, rope, etc., the ends of which are then drawn into a knot. **2.** To draw the parts of together or into place by a cord or band fastened with a knot: to *tie* one's shoes. **3.** To form (a knot). **4.** To form a knot in, as string. **5.** To fasten, attach, or join in any way. **6.** To restrain or confine; restrict; bind. **7.** In sports,

games, etc.: **a** To equal (a competitor) in score or achievement. **b** To equal (a competitor's score). **8.** *Informal* To unite in marriage. **9.** *Music* To unite by a tie. — *v.i.* **10.** To make a tie or connection. **11.** To make the same score; be equal. — **to tie down** To hinder; restrict. — **to tie in** *Informal* To have a certain relationship or connection; often with *with*: These colors *tie in* well with the rest. — **to tie (something) in** *Informal* To bring into a certain relationship or connection: *Tie it in* with the pictures. — **to tie up** **1.** To fasten with rope, string, etc. **2.** To moor (a vessel). **3.** To block; hinder. **4.** To have or be already committed, in use, etc., so as to be unavailable. — *n.* **1.** A string, cord, etc., with which something is tied. **2.** Any bond or obligation, mental, moral, or legal: *ties* of affection. **3.** An exact equality in number, as of a score, votes, etc.; especially, a contest which neither side wins; a draw. **4.** Something that is tied or intended for tying, as a shoelace, necktie, etc. **5.** A structural member fastening parts of a framework together and receiving tensile stress. **6.** *Music* A curved line placed over or under two musical notes of the same pitch on the staff to make them represent one tone length: also *bind.* **7.** *pl.* Low shoes fastened with lacings. **8.** *U.S.* One of a set of timbers laid crosswise on the ground as supports for railroad tracks; a sleeper. [OE *tīegan* to bind < *teah, teag* rope]

tie·back (tī'bak) *n.* A piece of fabric, metal, etc., by which curtains are draped or tied back at the sides.

tie beam A timber that serves as a tie in a roof, etc. For illustration see ROOF.

Tieck (tēk) **Ludwig**, 1773–1853, German poet and critic.

tie-in (tī'in') *n.* A connection; association; relation.

tie-in sale A sale in which the buyer, in order to get the article he wants, is required to buy a second article.

Tien Shan (tyen' shän') A mountain chain of Soviet Central Asia and China; highest point, Pobeda Peak, 24,406 ft.

Tien·tsin (tin'tsin', *Chinese* tyen'jin') A port city in NE China, near the Gulf of Chihli; pop. 4,500,000 (est. 1970).

Tie·po·lo (tye'pō·lō), **Giovanni Battista**, 1693–1770?, Venetian painter.

tier¹ (tir) *n.* A rank or row of things, as seats, placed one above another. — *v.t.* & *v.i.* To place or rise in tiers. [Earlier *tire* < OF, sequence < *tirer* to draw, elongate]

ti·er² (tī'ər) *n.* **1.** One who or that which ties; also, something used for or in tying. **2.** A child's apron.

tierce (tirs) *n.* **1.** A former liquid measure equivalent in the United States to 42 wine gallons; a third of a pipe or butt. **2.** A cask holding this amount. **3.** In card games, a sequence of three cards of the same suit. **4.** In fencing, the third standard position from which a guard, parry, or thrust can be made. **5.** *Often cap. Eccl.* Prescribed prayers constituting the third of the seven canonical hours: often called *undersong.* **6.** *Music* An interval of a third. **7.** A set of three. [< OF *tierce, terce* a third < L *tertia*, fem. of *tertius*]

Tier·ra del Fue·go (tyer'ä del fwā'gō) **1.** An archipelago at the southern tip of South America, belonging to Chile and to Argentina; separated from the mainland by the Strait of Magellan; 7,996 sq. mi. (Argentina), 19,480 sq. mi. (Chile). See map of (Strait of) MAGELLAN. **2.** The largest island of the group; 7,750 sq. mi. (Argentina), 10,250 sq. mi. (Chile).

tiers é·tat (tyâr zä·tä') *French* Third estate (which see).

tie-up (tī'up') *n.* **1.** A situation, resulting from a strike, mechanical breakdown, etc., in which progress or operation is impossible. **2.** *Informal* A connection or relation.

tiff¹ (tif) *n.* **1.** A peevish display of irritation; a pet; huff. **2.** A light quarrel; a spat. — **Syn.** See QUARREL¹. — *v.i.* To be in or have a tiff. [Origin unknown]

tiff² (tif) *Obs.* *n.* A small draft of liquor; a sip; drink. — *v.t.* To sip; taste. [Origin unknown]

tiff³ (tif) *v.i.* *Anglo-Indian* To take tiffin or lunch. [Back formation < TIFFIN]

tif·fa·ny (tif'ə·nē) *n.* *pl.* **·nies** A very thin transparent cotton gauze. [< OF *tifinie, tiphanie* Epiphany < LL *theophania* theophany]

Tif·fa·ny glass (tif'ə·nē) Decorative glassware usually having a lustrous, iridescent surface. [after Louis Comfort *Tiffany*, 1848–1933, U.S. artist who created it]

tif·fin (tif'ən) *Anglo-Indian n.* Midday luncheon. — *v.i.* To lunch; tiff. [Appar. < *tiffing*, ppr. of TIFF²]

Tif·lis (tif'lis) The capital of the Georgian S.S.R., in the SE part, on the Kura; pop. 889,000 (1970): Georgian *Tbilisi.*

ti·ger (tī'gər) *n.* **1.** A large carnivorous feline (*Panthera tigris*) of Asia, with vertical black wavy stripes on a tawny body and black bars or rings on the limbs and tail. **2.** One of several other animals resembling the tiger, as the jaguar and puma. **3.** A fierce, cruel person. **4.** *U.S.* An additional cheer or yell (often the word "tiger") given at the conclusion of a round of cheering. [OE *tiger* or OF *tigre*, both < L *tigris* < Gk., ? < Avestan *tighri* arrow, dart]

BENGAL TIGER
(About 6½ feet
long; tail 3
feet)

Tiger, the See CLEMENCEAU.

tiger beetle Any of certain very active, predacious beetles (genus *Cicindela*) having spotted or striped wings. For illustration see INSECTS (beneficial).

tiger cat   **1.** A wildcat, similar to, but smaller than, the tiger, as the Asian **marbled tiger cat** (*Felis marmorata*), the serval, the ocelot, and the margay.   **2.** A domestic cat having striped markings.

ti·ger·eye (tī′gər·ī′)   *n.*   **1.** A gemstone, usually the mineral crocidolite altered by oxidation, showing a changeable luster. Also **ti′gers-eye′**.   **2.** A tiger cat.

ti·ger·ish (tī′gər·ish)   *adj.* Of, pertaining to, or resembling the tiger or its habits; predacious; bloodthirsty: also *tigrish*.

tiger lily   **1.** A tall cultivated lily (*Lilium tigrinum*), with nodding orange flowers spotted with black.   **2.** Any of various lilies with similar flowers.

tiger moth   A stout-bodied moth (family *Arctiidae*) with striped or spotted wings.

tight (tīt)   *adj.*   **1.** So closely held together or constructed as to be impervious to fluids, air, etc.: a *tight* vessel.   **2.** Firmly fixed or fastened in place; secure.   **3.** Fully stretched, so as not to be slack; taut: *tight* as a drum.   **4.** Closely drawn, packed, fastened, etc.: a *tight* weave.   **5.** Strict; stringent: to keep a *tight* rein over us.   **6.** Fitting closely; especially, fitting too closely: said of a garment, shoe, etc.   **7.** *Informal* Difficult to cope with; troublesome: a *tight* spot.   **8.** *Informal* Parsimonious; tightfisted.   **9.** Characterized by a feeling of constriction: a *tight* cough.   **10.** *Slang* Drunk; intoxicated.   **11.** Evenly matched: said of a race or contest.   **12.** *Econ.* **a** Difficult to obtain: said of money or commodities.   **b** Straitened from lack of money or commodities: a *tight* market: opposed to *easy*.   **13.** Yielding very little or no profit: said of a bargain.   **14.** *Dial.* Well-built; compact.   **15.** *Dial.* Neat; tidy.   — *adv.*   **1.** Firmly; securely: Hold me *tight*.   **2.** Closely; with much constriction: The dress fits too *tight*.   — **to sit tight** To remain firm in one's position; refrain from taking action. [ME *thight*, appar. < Scand. Cf. ON *thēttr* dense.]   — **tight′ly** *adv.*   — **tight′ness** *n.*

-tight   *combining form* Impervious to: *watertight*.

tight·en (tīt′n)   *v.t.* & *v.i.*   To make or become tight or tighter.   — **tight′en·er** *n.*

tight·fist·ed (tīt′fis′tid)   *adj.* Stingy; parsimonious.

tight·lipped (tīt′lipt′)   *adj.*   **1.** Having the lips held tightly together.   **2.** Unwilling to talk; reticent or secretive.

tight·rope (tīt′rōp′)   *n.*   A rope or cable stretched out tight above the ground, on which acrobats do balancing acts, etc.

tights (tīts)   *n.pl.* Skintight garments, commonly for the legs and lower torso, worn by dancers, acrobats, etc.

tight·wad (tīt′wod′)   *n.*   *U.S. Slang* A parsimonious person; miser. [< TIGHT + WAD[1]]

Tig·lath-pi·le·ser III (tig′lath·pi·lē′zər, -pī), died 727 B.C., Assyrian king 745?–727 B.C.: called, in the Old Testament, **Phul** (ful).

tig·lic acid (tig′lik)   *Chem.* A white, crystalline, poisonous acid, $C_5H_8O_2$, contained as an ester in croton oil. [< NL (*Croton*) *tiglium* The croton oil plant, prob. ult. < Gk. *tilos* thin feces; so called because of its purgative properties]

Ti·gré (tē·grā′)   *n.*   A modern Semitic language of Ethiopia, descended from the ancient Ethiopian.

Ti·gré (tē·grā′)   A province of northern Ethiopia; formerly an independent kingdom; about 26,000 sq. mi.; capital, Aduwa. Also **Ti·gre** (tēg′r′).

ti·gress (tī′gris)   *n.*   **1.** A female tiger.   **2.** A cruel, fierce woman.

Ti·gri·ña (tē·grē′nyä)   *n.*   A Southwest Semitic language spoken in Ethiopia.

Ti·gris (tī′gris)   A river of SW Asia, flowing about 1,150 miles SE from Turkey through Iraq to the Euphrates.

ti·grish (tī′grish)   *adj.* Tigerish.

Ti·jua·na (tē·hwä′nä)   A city in the NW Northern territory, Lower California, Mexico; pop. 333,125 (1970): also *Tia Juana*.

tike (tīk)   See TYKE.

ti·ki (tē′kē)   *n.*   A Polynesian statue or figurine representing an ancestor.

Ti·ki (tē′kē)   In Maori mythology, the creator of the first man.

til (til, tēl)   *n.* Sesame. [< Hind. < Skt. *tilá*]

Til·burg (til′bûrg, *Du.* til′bûrkh)   A city in North Brabant Province, southern Netherlands; pop. 150,300 (est. 1968).

til·bu·ry (til′ber·ē)   *n.*   *pl.* **·bur·ies** A form of gig seating two persons. [after *Tilbury*, an early 19th-c. London coachmaker who invented it]

til·de (til′də, -dē)   *n.*   **1.** A sign (˜) used in Spanish over *n* to represent the palatal nasal (roughly equivalent to *ny*) as in *cañón*.   **2.** The same sign used in Portuguese over a vowel or the first vowel of a diphthong to indicate nasalization, as in *lã, Camões*. [< Sp. < L *titulus* superscription, title]

Til·den (til′dən), **Samuel Jones**, 1814–86, U.S. statesman.

Til·dy (til′dē), **Zoltán**, 1889–1961, Hungarian clergyman and political leader; president 1946–48.

tile (tīl)   *n.*   **1.** A thin piece or plate of baked clay or other material, as asbestos, linoleum, etc., sometimes decorated, used for covering roofs, floors, etc., and as an ornament.   **2.** A short earthenware pipe, used in forming sewers.   **3.** A hollow block, used for the construction of buildings, etc.   **4.** Tiles collectively; tiling.   **5.** Any of the pieces or counters used in the game of mahjong.   **6.** *Informal* A high silk hat.   — *v.t.* **tiled, til·ing** To cover or provide with or as with tiles. [OE *tigel*, ult. < L *tegula* < *tegere* to cover]

tile·fish (tīl′fish′)   *n.*   *pl.* **·fish** or **·fish·es** A large marine food fish (*Lopholatilus chamaeleonticeps*) of the western Atlantic, having large yellow spots. [< NL (*Lophola*)*til*(*us*), genus name; infl. by *tile*, because of its tilelike markings]

til·er (tī′lər)   *n.*   **1.** A maker or layer of tiles.   **2.** The doorkeeper of a Masonic lodge.

til·i·a·ceous (til·ē·ā′shəs)   *adj.* *Bot.* Designating or belonging to the linden family (*Tiliaceae*) of trees and herbs. [< NL < L *tiliaceus* < *tilia* linden tree]

til·ing (tī′ling)   *n.*   **1.** The act, operation, or system of using tiles for roofing, drainage, etc.   **2.** Tiles collectively.   **3.** Something made of or faced with tiles.

till[1] (til)   *v.t.* & *v.i.*   To work (soil) for the production of crops, as by plowing, harrowing, hoeing, sowing, etc.; cultivate. [OE *tilian* to strive, acquire]   — **till′a·ble** *adj.*

till[2] (til)   *prep.*   **1.** To the time of; up to; until: He slept *till* noon.   **2.** Before: with the negative: I can't go *till* noon.   **3.** *Scot.* & *Brit. Dial.* To; unto; as far as.   — *conj.*   **1.** Up to such time as; until: *till* death do us part.   **2.** Before: with the negative: They couldn't go *till* he came. [OE *til* < ON, to]

till[3] (til)   *n.* A drawer, compartment, or tray in which money or valuables are kept, as at a bank, store, etc. [Origin uncertain]

till[4] (til)   *n.*   *Geol.* A chiefly unstratified mass of mingled clay, sand, pebbles, and boulders, deposited by glaciers. [Origin uncertain]

till·age (til′ij)   *n.*   The cultivation of land.   [< TILL[1] + -AGE]

til·land·si·a (ti·land′zē·ə)   *n.* Any of a genus (*Tillandsia*) of mainly epiphytic bromeliaceous plants of tropical America and the southern United States, as Spanish moss. [< NL, after Elias *Tillands*, 18th c. Swedish botanist]

till·er[1] (til′ər)   *n.* One who or that which tills. [< TILL[1]]

till·er[2] (til′ər)   *n.*   **1.** *Naut.* A lever to turn a rudder.   **2.** Any similar means of steering or controlling. [< OF *telier* stock of a crossbow < Med.L *telarium* weaver's beam < L *tela* web; prob. infl. in meaning by ME *tillen* to draw]

till·er[3] (til′ər)   *n.*   **1.** A shoot from the base of a stem; sucker.   **2.** A sapling.   — *v.i.* To put forth stems from the root; send forth new shoots. [Prob. OE *telgor* twig < *telga* branch]

Til·lich (til′ik, -ikh), **Paul**, 1886–1965, German Protestant theologian and philosopher active in the United States.

Til·lot·son (til′ət·sən), **John**, 1630–94, English theologian.

Til·ly (til′ē), **Count Johann Tserclaes von**, 1559–1632, Flemish general in the Thirty Years' War.

tilt[1] (tilt)   *v.t.*   **1.** To cause to rise at one end or side; incline at an angle; slant; lean; tip.   **2.** To aim or thrust, as a lance.   **3.** To charge or overthrow in a tilt or joust.   **4.** To hammer or forge with a tilt hammer.   — *v.i.*   **5.** To incline at an angle; lean.   **6.** To engage in a joust.   — **Syn.** See TIP[1].   — *n.*   **1.** An inclination from the vertical or horizontal position; slant; slope.   **2.** The act of inclining, or the state of being inclined.   **3.** A medieval sport in which mounted knights, charging with lances, endeavored to unseat each other.   **4.** Any similar encounter, as a quarrel or dispute.   **5.** A thrust or blow, as with a lance.   **6.** A tilt hammer (which see).   **7.** A seesaw.   — **at full tilt** At full speed. [ME *tylten* to be overthrown, totter < OE *tealt* unsteady]   — **tilt′er** *n.*

tilt[2] (tilt)   *n.* A canvas canopy or awning on a boat, wagon, booth, or the like.   — *v.t.* To furnish or cover with an awning or tilt. [Var. of ME *tild*, *teld*, OE *teld* tent]

tilth (tilth)   *n.*   **1.** The act of tilling; cultivation of soil; tillage.   **2.** That part of the surface soil affected by tillage; cultivated land. [OE < *tilian* to till]

tilt hammer   A type of drop hammer having a heavy head mounted on the end of a lever, used in dropforging, etc.

tilt·yard (tilt′yärd′)   *n.* An enclosure for tilting contests.

Tim.   Timothy.

tim·bal (tim′bəl)   *n.*   **1.** A kettledrum.   **2.** *Entomol.* The drumlike, sound-producing membrane of a male cicada or harvest fly. Also spelled *tymbal*. [< F *timbale*, appar. alter. of *attabale* < Sp. *atabal*. See ATABAL.]

tim·bale (tim′bəl, *Fr.* taṅ·bȧl′)   *n.*   **1.** A custardlike dish made of chicken, fish, cheese, or vegetables, cooked in a drum-shaped mold.   **2.** A small cup made of fried pastry, in which food may be served. [< F. See TIMBAL.]

tim·ber (tim′bər)   *n.*   **1.** Wood suitable for building or structural purposes.   **2.** Growing or standing trees; also, woodland.   **3.** A single piece of wood prepared for use or already in use in a structure.   **4.** *Naut.* Any principal beam in a vessel's framing.   **5.** The wooden part or handle of any implement.   **6.** Loosely, the materials for any structure.   **7.** Personal character, talent, potentiality: presidential *timber*.   — *v.t.* To provide or shore with timber.   — *interj.* *U.S. Informal* A cry of warning when a felled tree or similar heavy object is about to fall. [OE]

tim·bered (tim′bərd) *adj.* **1.** Covered with growing trees; wooded. **2.** Constructed of timber.

tim·ber·head (tim′bər·hed′) *n. Naut.* **1.** An end of a timber projecting above the deck, and used for attaching lines, etc. **2.** An upright post fastened to the deck.

timber hitch *Naut.* A knot by which a rope is fastened around a spar.

tim·ber·ing (tim′bər·ing) *n.* **1.** Timbers collectively. **2.** Timberwork.

tim·ber·land (tim′bər·land′) *n.* Land covered with forests.

timber line **1.** The upper limit of tree growth on mountains and in arctic regions; the demarcation above which no trees grow. Also *Canadian* **timber limit.** **2.** The boundary line of a tract of timber. **— tim′ber-line′** *adj.*

timber wolf The large gray or brindled wolf (*Canis lupus* and related species) of the forests of the northern United States and Canada: also called *gray wolf, lobo.*

tim·ber·work (tim′bər·wûrk′) *n.* Work constructed of wood; especially, the framework of a structure.

tim·bre (tim′bər, tam′-; *Fr.* taṅ′br′) *n.* The attribute of a sound resulting from the number and relative strength of its partial tones, and distinguishing one vowel from another, the tone of one musical instrument from another, etc.; quality; tone color. See FORMANT. [< F < OF, small bell, sound of a bell, orig., timbrel < L *tympanum* kettledrum < Gk. *tympanon*]

TIMBER WOLF
(About 4 feet long)

tim·brel (tim′brəl) *n.* An ancient instrument resembling a tambourine. [Dim. of earlier *timbre* timbrel < OF. See TIMBRE.]

Tim·buk·tu (tim·buk′tōō, tim′buk·tōō′) A town in central Mali, near the Niger; formerly a major center of the slave trade; pop. 9,000 (est. 1967): French *Tombouctou.*

time (tīm) *n.* **1.** The general concept, relation, or fact of continuous or successive existence, capable of division into measurable portions, and comprising the past, present, and future. **2.** Duration with reference to this world and all finite existence as distinguished from eternity or infinity. **3.** A system of reckoning or measuring duration: solar *time.* **4.** A definite portion of duration; especially, a definite, specific, or appointed moment, hour, day, season, year, etc.: The *time* is 2:35; Autumn is my favorite *time.* **5.** The moment or portion of duration in which something takes place, has taken place, or will take place: at the *time* of his marriage. **6.** That moment or portion of duration allotted to or available or sufficient for some special action, purpose, or event: *time* to go; *time* enough to catch the train; *time* to think. **7.** The portion or period of duration generally allotted to human life: to live beyond one's *time.* **8.** Leisure: no *time* to read. **9.** The period of duration occupied by any regular or completed action: His *time* on the track was two minutes. **10.** An instance or occasion of recurrence or repetition: many a *time*; next *time*; three *times* a day. **11.** A fit or proper moment or occasion: a *time* to plant. **12.** The period of pregnancy or gestation; also, the moment of childbirth. **13.** The moment of death. **14.** A period or interval considered with reference to one's personal experience or reaction: to have a good *time.* **15.** *Usually pl.* A considerable period or interval marked by some cultural, historical, or other special characteristics: ancient *times*; the *time* of Charlemagne. **16.** *Usually pl.* The present period or era or the period or era under consideration. **17.** *Usually pl.* A portion or period of duration having some specific element or quality: *Times* are hard. **18.** *Informal* A period of imprisonment: used chiefly in the phrase **to do time,** to serve a prison sentence. **19.** In the theory of relativity, the coordinate which, with the three spatial dimensions, is essential to the complete definition of an object, phenomenon, or event. **20.** The period during which work has been done or remains to be done by a worker; also, the pay given for this: *time* and a half for overtime. **21.** *Music* Loosely, meter, tempo, or the duration of a note. See METER. **22.** Speed or rate of movement in marching, dancing, etc.: double *time.* **23.** In prosody, a unit of rhythmical duration; especially, a mora. **24.** In drama, one of the Aristotelian unities. See UNITY (def. 9). **25.** *Usually pl.* In arithmetic, an instance of being multiplied or added to produce a specified number: How many *times* does three go into nine? Abbr. *t., T* **— against time** With an imminent time limit; as quickly as possible. **— ahead of time** Before the time stated or due; early. **— at the same time 1.** At the same moment or period. **2.** Despite that; however; nevertheless. **— at times** Now and then; occasionally. **— behind the times** Old-fashioned. **— behind time** After the time stated or due; late. **— for the time being** Temporarily. **— from time to time** Now and then; occasionally. **— in good time 1.** Quickly; fast. **2.** At the appropriate time; when properly due. **— in the nick of time** At just the right or critical moment. **— in time 1.** While time permits or lasts; before it is too late. **2.** In the progress of time; ultimately. **3.** In the proper rhythm, tempo, etc. **— on time 1.** Promptly; according to schedule. **2.** Paid for, or to be paid for, later or in installments. **— out of time** Not in the proper rhythm,

tempo, etc. **— time and again** Frequently; repeatedly: also **time after time. — time out of mind** Longer than is known or can be remembered; from time immemorial. **— to gain time 1.** To run fast: said of a timepiece. **2.** To lengthen or prolong an act or occasion so as to consider, decide, etc. **— to have the time of one's life** To enjoy oneself completely. **— to keep time 1.** To indicate time correctly, as a clock. **2.** To make regular or rhythmic movements in unison with another or others. **3.** To render or conduct a musical composition in the desired tempo or rhythm. **— to lose time 1.** To run slow: said of a timepiece. **2.** To waste or miss opportunities; delay advancement. **— to make time 1.** To make up for lost time by extra speed, as a train. **2.** To perform, achieve, or arrive in a certain time: to *make* good *time.* **3.** *Slang* To impress or influence favorably: with *with.* **—** *adj.* **1.** Of or pertaining to time. **2.** Devised so as to operate, explode, etc., at a specified time: a *time* bomb; *time* lock. **3.** Payable at, or to be paid for at, a future date. **4.** Of or pertaining to purchases paid for in installments. **—** *v.t.* **timed, tim·ing 1.** To regulate as to time. **2.** To cause to correspond in time: They *timed* their steps to the music. **3.** To choose or arrange the time or occasion for: He *timed* his arrival for five o'clock. **4.** To mark the rhythm or measure of. **5.** To assign metrical or rhythmic qualities to (a syllable or note). **6.** To ascertain or record the speed or duration of: to *time* a horse or a race. [OE *tīma*]

time and motion study The observation and analysis of the body movements involved in the performance of a given repetitive task in order to find more efficient methods of working: sometimes called *motion study, time study.*

time bomb A bomb built to go off at a set time.

time·card (tīm′kärd′) *n.* A card for recording the time of arrival and departure of an employee.

time clock A clock equipped for automatically recording times of arrival and departure.

time-con·sum·ing (tīm′kən·sōō′ming) *adj.* Taking up a great deal of time. **— time′-con·sum′er** *n.*

time deposit A bank deposit that cannot be withdrawn until some future date or until a specified time has elapsed after advance notice has been given.

time exposure *Photog.* **1.** A film exposure made for a relatively long interval. **2.** A picture made by such an exposure.

time fuse A fuse set to detonate an explosive charge at a given moment. For illustration see FUSE.

time-hon·ored (tīm′on′ərd) *adj.* Observed or honored because of long usage or existence. Also *Brit.* **time′-hon′oured.**

time immemorial **1.** Time so long past as to be beyond memory or record. **2.** *Law* Time beyond legal memory, fixed, in England, as the commencement of the reign of Richard I (1189).

time·keep·er (tīm′kē′pər) *n.* **1.** One who or that which keeps time. **2.** One who declares the time in a race, game, athletic match, etc., or records the hours worked by employees. **3.** A railroad train starter. **4.** A timepiece.

time-lapse photography (tīm′laps′) A method of making motion pictures with long intervals between the exposure of single frames, so that very slow processes, as the opening of a flower, are shown smoothly in a relatively brief period: also called *stop-motion photography.*

time·less (tīm′lis) *adj.* **1.** Independent of or unaffected by time; unending; eternal. **2.** Not assigned or limited to any special time, era, or epoch. **— time′less·ly** *adv.* **— time′less·ness** *n.*

time lock A lock having a mechanism devised to prevent release of the lock before a specified time.

time·ly (tīm′lē) *adj.* **·li·er, ·li·est 1.** Being or occurring in good or suitable time; opportune; seasonable; well-timed. **2.** *Archaic* Early. **—** *adv.* Opportunely; seasonably; early. **— time′li·ness** *n.*

time·ous (tī′məs) *adj. Scot.* Seasonable; timely.

time-out (tīm′out′) *n.* **1.** In sports, a short recess requested by a team during play. **2.** Any interval of rest taken during the course of a regular period of work. Also **time out.**

time·piece (tīm′pēs′) *n.* Something that records or measures time, as a clock or watch.

tim·er (tī′mər) *n.* **1.** A timekeeper. **2.** A stopwatch, as for timing a race. **3.** A device attached to an internal-combustion engine so as to time the spark automatically. **4.** A clockwork or other device that signals the lapse of a time period, controls an operation, etc.

times (tīmz) *prep.* Multiplied by: often indicated by the multiplication sign (×): Five *times* four is twenty. [< TIME]

time-sav·ing (tīm′sā′ving) *adj.* Serving to save time by facilitating work, etc. **— time′sav′er** *n.*

time-serv·er (tīm′sûr′vər) *n.* One who yields to the demands or opinions of the time, occasion, or authorities, without reference to principle. **— time′serv′ing** *adj. & n.*

time signature *Music* A symbol placed on a musical staff to indicate the meter.

Times Square A square in New York City formed by the intersection of Broadway and Seventh Avenue, extending from 42nd to 45th street; also, the area around it, the city's entertainment district.

time study Time and motion study (which see).

time·ta·ble (tīm′tā′bəl) *n.* A tabular schedule of the times at which certain things are to take place, as arrivals and departures of trains, times of high and low tides, etc.

time-test·ed (tīm′tes′tid) *adj.* Having worth or efficiency proved by use over an extended period.

time·work (tīm′wûrk′) *n.* Work paid for on the basis of a set wage per hour, day, week, etc. **— time/work/er** *n.*

time-worn (tīm′wôrn′, -wōrn′) *adj.* 1. Showing the ravages or effects of time. 2. Trite; overused.

time zone One of the 24 sectors of 15° each, or a time interval of one hour, into which the earth is divided for reckoning standard time from the meridian of Greenwich. In the table below, the cited longitude lies at the center of each zone and the zone number corresponds to the number of hours later (—) or earlier (+) than Greenwich time.

Zone No. East of Greenwich	Longitude from Greenwich	Zone No. West of Greenwich
0 (Greenwich)	0°	0 (Greenwich)
— 1 (Berlin)	15°	+ 1 (Iceland)
— 2 (Athens)	30°	+ 2 (Azores)
— 3 (Baghdad)	45°	+ 3 (Rio de Janeiro)
— 4 (Réunion)	60°	+ 4 (Halifax)
— 5 (Karachi)	75°	+ 5 (Washington)
— 6 (Dacca)	90°	+ 6 (Chicago)
— 7 (Bangkok)	105°	+ 7 (Denver)
— 8 (Manila)	120°	+ 8 (Vancouver)
— 9 (Kyoto)	135°	+ 9 (Dawson)
—10 (Melbourne)	150°	+10 (Tahiti)
—11 (New Caledonia)	165°	+11 (Nome)
—12 (Wellington)	180°	+12 (Fiji Is.)

tim·id (tim′id) *adj.* 1. Shrinking from danger or risk; fearful. 2. Shrinking from notice; lacking self-confidence; shy. 3. Characterized by fear or shyness: a *timid* voice. [< L *timidus* < *timere* to fear] **— ti·mid·i·ty** (ti-mid′ə-tē), **tim/id·ness** *n.* **— tim/id·ly** *adv.*

tim·ing (tī′ming) *n.* 1. In music, oratory, acting, etc., the act or art of regulating the speed of performance, utterance, etc., so as to insure maximum effectiveness; also, the effect so produced. 2. In certain sports, as swimming, boxing, etc., the regulation of the speed of a blow or stroke so that it reaches its highest effectiveness at just the right moment.

Ti·mi·soa·ra (tē′mē-shwä′rä) A city in western Rumania; pop. 174,400 (1966): Hungarian *Temesvár.*

ti·moc·ra·cy (tī-mok′rə-sē) *n.* *pl.* **·cies** 1. A form of government in which love of honor is the ruling principle. 2. A form of government in which honors are bestowed according to property owned. [< OF *tymocracie* < Med.L *timocratia* < Gk. *timokratia* < *timē* honor + *krateein* to rule] **— ti·mo·crat·ic** (tī′mə-krat′ik) or **·i·cal** *adj.*

Ti·mor (tē′môr, ti-môr′) An island of the SE Malay Archipelago, divided into **Indonesian Timor** (formerly *Netherlands Timor*) in the western part; 5,765 sq. mi., and **Portuguese Timor**, a Portuguese Overseas Province in the eastern part; 5,761 sq. mi. (including Ambeno and several offshore islands; pop. 517,079 (1960); capital, Dili.

tim·or·ous (tim′ər·əs) *adj.* 1. Fearful of danger; timid. 2. Indicating or produced by fear. [< OF *timoureus, temeros* < Med.L *timorosus*, ult. < L *timor, -oris* fear] **— tim/or·ous·ly** *adv.* **— tim/or·ous·ness** *n.*

Ti·mo·shen·ko (tē′mō-sheng′kō), **Semyon Konstantinovich**, 1895–1970, Soviet field marshal in World War II.

tim·o·thy (tim′ə-thē) *n.* A perennial fodder grass (*Phleum pratense*) having long, cylindrical spikes: also called *herd's-grass.* Also **timothy grass.** [after *Timothy* Hanson, who took the seed from New York to the Carolinas about 1720]

Tim·o·thy (tim′ə-thē) A convert and companion of the apostle Paul. **—** *n.* Either of two books in the New Testament consisting of two epistles addressed to Timothy and attributed to Saint Paul. Abbr. *Tim.*

Ti·mour, Ti·mur (timōor′, tē-) See TAMERLANE.

tim·pa·ni (tim′pə-nē) *n.* *pl.* of **tim·pa·no** (-nō) Kettledrums: also spelled *tympani.* [< Ital., pl. of *timpano* < L *tympanum* drum < Gk. *tympanon*] **— tim/pa·nist** *n.*

tim·pa·num (tim′pə-nəm) See TYMPANUM.

tin (tin) *n.* 1. A white, malleable, metallic element (symbol Sn) of low tensile strength, found chiefly in combination and extensively used in making alloys: also called *stannum.* See ELEMENT. 2. Tin plate. 3. A container or box made of tin. 4. *Brit.* A tin-plated container for preserved foods; a can. 5. *Slang* Money. **—** *v.t.* **tinned, tin·ning** 1. To coat or cover with tin. 2. To pack or put up in tins. **—** *adj.* Made of tin. [OE]

tin·a·mou (tin′ə·mōō) *n.* Any of certain South American birds (family *Tinamidae*), resembling the partridge and hunted as game birds. [< F < Carib *tinamu*]

tin·cal (ting′kəl, -käl, -kôl) *n.* Crude borax. [< Malay *tinkal* < Persian *tiṅkāl, tiṅkar* < Skt. *ṭankaṇa* borax]

tinct (tingkt) *v.t.* To tinge; tint. **—** *n.* 1. *Poetic* A tint. 2. *Obs.* A tincture. [< L *tinctus*, pp. of *tingere* to dye, color]

tinct. Tincture.

tinc·to·ri·al (tingk-tôr′ē-əl, -tō′rē-) *adj.* 1. Of or pertaining to coloring, dyeing, etc. 2. Imbuing with color. [< L *tinctorius* < *tinctus.* See TINCT.]

tinc·ture (tingk′chər) *n.* 1. A solution, usually in alcohol, of some substance used in medicine: *tincture* of iodine. 2. A tinge of color; tint. 3. A slight additional flavor, quality, etc. 4. That part of a substance which is extracted by a solvent. 5. One of the metals, colors, or furs used in heraldic description. **—** *v.t.* **·tured, ·tur·ing** 1. To impart a slight hue or tinge to. 2. To imbue with flavor, odor, etc. 3. To imbue with a specified quality. [< L *tinctura* a dyeing < *tinctus.* See TINCT.]

tin·der (tin′dər) *n.* Any readily combustible substance, as charred linen or touchwood, that will ignite on contact with a spark. [OE *tynder*] **— tin/der·y** *adj.*

tin·der·box (tin′dər·boks′) *n.* 1. A portable metallic box containing tinder. 2. Anything highly flammable, explosive, touchy, etc.

tine (tīn) *n.* A spike or prong, as of a fork or of an antler. [OE *tind*] **— tined** *adj.*

tin·e·a (tin′ē·ə) *n.* *Pathol.* Ringworm or any fungous skin disease. [< NL < L, moth, gnawing worm]

tin·e·id (tin′ē·id) *adj.* Of or pertaining to a family (*Tineidae*) of moths. **—** *n.* One of the *Tineidae*, as *Tinea pelliolonella*, a common clothes moth. [< NL < *Tinea*]

tin·foil (tin′foil′) *n.* Tin or an alloy of tin made into thin sheets for use as wrapping material, etc. Also **tin foil.**

ting¹ (ting) *n.* A single high metallic sound, as of a small bell. **—** *v.t. & v.i.* To give forth or cause to give forth a ting. [Imit.]

ting² (ting) See THING².

ting-a-ling (ting′ə·ling′) *n.* The sound of a little bell.

tinge (tinj) *v.t.* **tinged, tinge·ing** or **ting·ing** 1. To imbue with a faint trace of color; impart a tint to. 2. To impart a slight characteristic quality of some other element to. **—** *n.* 1. A faint trace of added color. 2. A quality or peculiar characteristic imparted to something by the slight admixture of some foreign element. [< L *tingere* to dye]

tin·gle (ting′gəl) *v.* **·gled, ·gling** *v.i.* 1. To experience a prickly, stinging sensation, as of the skin from exposure to cold, or the ears from a sharp blow. 2. To cause such a sensation. **—** *v.t.* 3. To cause to tingle. **—** *n.* 1. A prickly, stinging sensation; a tingling. 2. A jingle or tinkling. [Appar. var. of TINKLE] **— tin/gler** *n.* **— tin/gly** *adj.*

tin hat A shallow, protective metal helmet worn by construction workers, soldiers, etc.

tin-horn (tin′hôrn′) *U.S. Slang n.* One who is cheaply and noisily pretentious; especially, a flashy, small-time gambler. **—** *adj.* Showily pretentious.

tink·er (tingk′ər) *n.* 1. An itinerant mender of domestic tin utensils, as pots and pans. 2. Loosely, one who does repairing work of any kind; a jack-of-all-trades. 3. A clumsy workman; a botcher. 4. The act of roughly repairing; hasty workmanship. 5. A small mackerel (*Scomber colias*) of the Atlantic coast from the St. Lawrence to Virginia. **—** *v.i.* 1. To work as a tinker. 2. To work in a clumsy makeshift fashion on anything. 3. To potter; fuss. **—** *v.t.* 4. To mend as a tinker. 5. To repair clumsily or inexpertly. [Var. of earlier *tinekere* worker in tin]

tinker's damn *Slang* The smallest, most contemptible bit: not worth a *tinker's damn.* Also **tinker's dam.** [< TINKER + DAMN; with ref. to the reputed profanity of tinkers]

tin·kle (ting′kəl) *v.* **·kled, ·kling** *v.i.* 1. To produce slight, sharp, metallic sounds, as a small bell. **—** *v.t.* 2. To cause to tinkle. 3. To summon or signal by a tinkling. **—** *n.* A sharp, clear, metallic sound. [Imit.] **— tin/kly** *adj.*

tink·ling (ting′kling) *n.* The sound of that which tinkles.

tin liz·zie (liz′ē) *U.S. Slang* The Model T automobile.

tin·ner (tin′ər) *n.* 1. A miner employed in tin mines. 2. A maker of or dealer in tinware; a tinsmith.

tin·ni·tus (ti·nī′təs) *n.* *Pathol.* A ringing, rushing, or buzzing sound in the ears, caused by malfunction of the auditory nerve. [< NL < L < *tinnire* to ring]

tin·ny (tin′ē) *adj.* **·ni·er, ·ni·est** 1. Pertaining to, composed of, or abounding in tin. 2. Resembling tin in lack of durability. 3. Having a thin sound like that of tin being struck. 4. Tasting of tin, as food from a can. **— tin/ni·ly** *adv.* **— tin/ni·ness** *n.*

tin-pan alley (tin′pan′) 1. A section of a city, especially of New York, frequented by musicians and song writers and occupied by publishers of popular music. 2. The composers and publishers of popular music, collectively.

tin-plate (tin′plāt′) *v.t.* **-plat·ed, -plat·ing** To plate with tin. **— tin/-plat/er** *n.*

tin plate Sheet iron or steel plated with tin.

TIMOTHY (To 6 feet high)

tin·sel (tin′səl) *n.* **1.** Very thin, glittering bits of cheap metals used as an inexpensive decoration. **2.** A yarn containing gold or silver thread. **3.** Anything sparkling and showy, with little real worth; superficial adornment and brilliancy. **4.** A fabric in which such spangles or bits of metal are woven. — *adj.* **1.** Made of, resembling, or covered with tinsel. **2.** Superficially brilliant; tawdry. — *v.t.* ·seled or ·selled, ·sel·ing or ·sel·ling **1.** To adorn or decorate with or as with tinsel. **2.** To give a showy or gaudy appearance to. [< MF *étincelle* < OF *estincelle* < L *scintilla* spark]

tin·smith (tin′smith′) *n.* One who works with tin or tin plate: also called *whitesmith.*

tin·stone (tin′stōn′) *n.* Cassiterite.

tint (tint) *n.* **1.** A variety of color; tincture; especially, a tendency toward or slight admixture of a different color; tinge. **2.** A gradation of a color made by dilution with white to lessen its chroma and saturation. **3.** Any pale or delicate hue. **4.** In engraving, an effect of light, shade, texture, etc., produced by the spacing of lines or by hatching. **5.** *Printing* A light background on which something of a different color, as an illustration, is to be printed. — *v.t.* **1.** To give a tint to; tinge. **2.** In engraving, to form a tint upon. [Alter. of TINCT; ? infl. in form by Ital. *tinta* color] — **tint′er** *n.*

Tin·tag·el Head (tin·taj′əl) A promontory on the coast of western Cornwall, England, with ruins of **Tintagel Castle,** traditionally, the birthplace of King Arthur.

Tin·tern Abbey (tin′tərn) The ruins of a 12th-century Cistercian abbey in Monmouthshire, England, on the Wye.

tin·tin·nab·u·lar (tin′ti·nab′yə·lər) *adj.* Of or pertaining to bells or to the ringing of bells. Also **tin′tin·nab·u·lar′y, tin′tin·nab′u·lous.**

tin·tin·nab·u·la·tion (tin′ti·nab′yə·lā′shən) *n.* The pealing, tinkling, or ringing of bells.

tin·tin·nab·u·lum (tin′ti·nab′yə·ləm) *n.* *pl.* ·la (-lə) A small, tinkling bell. [< L, small bell < *tintinnare* to ring]

Tin·to·ret·to (tin′tə·ret′ō, *Ital.* tēn′·ret′tō), 1518–94, Venetian painter: original name **Jacopo Ro·bus·ti** (rō·bōōs′tē).

tin·type (tin′tīp′) *n.* A photograph taken on a sensitized film supported on a thin sheet of enameled tin or iron: also called *ferrotype.*

tin·ware (tin′wâr′) *n.* Articles made of tin plate.

tin·work (tin′wûrk′) *n.* Articles made of tin.

tin·works (tin′wûrks′) *n.pl.* (*construed as sing. or pl.*) A place or establishment where tin is manufactured or mined.

ti·ny (tī′nē) *adj.* ·ni·er, ·ni·est Very small; minute; wee. — **Syn.** See SMALL. [< obs. *tine* small amount, bit + -Y³; ult. origin unknown]

-tion *suffix of nouns* **1.** Action or process of: *rejection.* **2.** Condition or state of being: *completion.* **3.** Result of: *connection.* Also *-ation, -cion, -ion, -sion, -xion.* [< F *-tion* < OF *-cion* < L *-tio, -tionis*]

tip[1] (tip) *n.* A slanting or inclined position; a tilt. — *v.* **tipped, tip·ping** *v.t.* **1.** To cause to lean by lowering or raising one end or side; tilt. **2.** To overturn or upset: often with *over.* **3.** To raise or touch (one's hat) in greeting. — *v.i.* **4.** To become tilted; slant. **5.** To overturn; topple: with *over.* [ME *tipen* to overturn; origin uncertain] — **tip′per** *n.* — **Syn.** **1, 3.** *Tip, tilt, slant, slope, cant, careen, heel,* and *list* mean to turn from a vertical or horizontal position. *Tip* most strongly suggests a turning from a normal position of equilibrium: the vase *tipped* over. *Tilt* suggests a more or less permanent turning askew: the mast is slightly *tilted* aft. *Slant* suggests obliquity, whether literal or figurative, while *slope* involves change of level or direction: his writing *slanted* across the page; his speech was *slanted* toward the farmers in his audience; this lot *slopes* down to the river's bank. *Cant* is close to *tilt,* especially in technical senses: the carpenter *canted* the edge of the plank. *Careen, heel,* and, *list* are chiefly applied to ships; a ship *careens* or *heels* from being buffeted by the wind or the waves, and *lists* from the displacement of its center of gravity, as by the shifting of its cargo.

tip[2] (tip) *n.* **1.** A small gift of money for services rendered, given to a servant, waiter, porter, or the like. **2.** A friendly, helpful hint; especially, information presumed to increase a better's or speculator's chance of winning. — *v.* **tipped, tip·ping** *v.t.* **1.** To give a small gratuity to. **2.** *Informal* To give secret information to, as in betting and speculation: often with *off.* — *v.i.* **3.** To give tips. [Orig. < thieves' cant, ? < TIP⁴] — **tip′per** *n.*

tip[3] (tip) *n.* **1.** The point or extremity of anything tapering; end: the *tip* of the tongue. **2.** A piece or part made to form the end of anything, as a nozzle, ferrule, etc. **3.** The top or summit, as of a mountain. — *v.t.* **tipped, tip·ping** **1.** To furnish with a tip. **2.** To form the tip of. **3.** To cover or adorn the tip of. [Prob. < MDu., point]

tip[4] (tip) *v.t.* **tipped, tip·ping** **1.** To strike lightly, or with something light; tap. **2.** In baseball, to strike (the ball) a light, glancing blow. — *n.* A tap; light blow. [Earlier *tippe,* prob. < LG. Cf. Du. *tippen* to tap.]

Tip. Tipperary.

ti palm See TI².

tip·cart (tip′kärt′) *n.* A cart having a body that can be tipped for unloading.

ti·pi (tē′pē) See TEPEE.

tip·off (tip′ôf′, -of′) *n.* *Informal* A hint or warning.

Tip·pe·ca·noe (tip′ē·kə·nōō′) The nickname of William

Henry Harrison: from his victory over Tecumseh's Indians at Tippecanoe River in 1811. The name provided the presidential campaign slogan, **Tippecanoe and Tyler too,** for Harrison and his vice-presidential running mate, John Tyler, in 1840.

Tip·pe·ca·noe River (tip′ē·kə·nōō′) A river in north central Indiana, flowing 166 miles to the Wabash River; scene of General W. H. Harrison's victory over Indians, 1811.

Tip·per·ar·y (tip′ə·râr′ē) A county of NE Munster province, Ireland; 1,643 sq. mi.; pop. 123,822 (est. 1969); county seat, Clonmel.

tip·pet (tip′it) *n.* **1.** An outdoor covering for the neck, or neck and shoulders, hanging well down in front. **2.** *Eccl.* A long scarf worn by Anglican clergymen. **3.** Formerly, a long, dangling part of a sleeve, hood, etc. [Prob. dim. of TIP³]

tip·ple[1] (tip′əl) *v.t. & v.i.* **·pled, ·pling** To drink (alcoholic beverages) frequently and habitually. — *n.* Alcoholic liquor. [Cf. Norw. *tipla* drip, tipple] — **tip′pler** *n.*

tip·ple[2] (tip′əl) *n.* **1.** An apparatus for tipping loaded cars. **2.** The place where such tipping is done. [< dial. E *tipple* topple, freq. of TIP¹]

tip·py (tip′ē) *adj.* **tip·pi·er, tip·pi·est** *Informal* Shaky; unsteady; apt to tip over. [< TIP¹ + -Y³]

tip·staff (tip′staf′, -stäf′) *n.* *pl.* **·staffs** *for def. 1,* **·staves** (-stāvz′) *for def. 2* **1.** In England, a sheriff's subordinate; bailiff; constable; also, a court crier. **2.** A staff having a metal tip, a badge of office. [< TIP(PED) STAFF]

tip·ster (tip′stər) *n.* *Informal* One who sells tips, as for betting on a race. [< TIP³]

tip·sy (tip′sē) *adj.* **tip·si·er, tip·si·est** **1.** Partially intoxicated; high. **2.** Tippy; shaky; also, crooked; askew. [< TIP¹] — **tip′si·ly** *adv.* — **tip′si·ness** *n.*

tip·toe (tip′tō′) *v.i.* **·toed, ·toe·ing** To walk on tiptoe; go stealthily or quietly. — *n.* The tip of a toe. — **on tiptoe 1.** On one's tiptoes. **2.** Eagerly expectant. **3.** Stealthily; quietly. — *adj.* **1.** Standing or walking on tiptoe. **2.** Stealthy. **3.** Eager; excited. — *adv.* On tiptoe.

tip·top (tip′top′) *n.* **1.** The highest point; the very top. **2.** *Informal* The highest quality or degree. — *adj.* **1.** Located at the very top. **2.** *Informal* Best of its kind; first-rate. — *adv.* In a tiptop manner. [< TIP³ + TOP¹] — **tip′top′per** *n.*

Ti·pu Sa·hib (tī′pōō sä′hib), 1749–99, sultan of Mysore 1782–99, fought against the British. Also **Ti′poo Sa′hib.**

Ti·rach Mir (tē′räch mēr′) See TIRICH MIR.

ti·rade (tī′rād, tə·rād′) *n.* **1.** A prolonged declamatory outpouring, as of censure. **2.** *Music* An ornament consisting of a rapid diatonic scale of more than four notes. [< F < Ital. *tirata* volley, pp. of *tirare* to fire, pull]

ti·rail·leur (tir′ə·lûr′, *Fr.* tē·rȧ·yœr′) *n.* A sharpshooter; skirmisher. [< F]

Ti·ra·na (tē·rä′nä) The capital of Albania, in the central part; pop. 170,000 (est. 1968). Also **Ti·ra′në** (-nə).

tire[1] (tīr) *v.* **tired, tir·ing** *v.t.* **1.** To reduce the strength of, as by toil; weary; fatigue. **2.** To reduce the interest or patience of, as with tediousness. — *v.i.* **3.** To become weary or exhausted. **4.** To lose patience, interest, etc. — **to tire of** To become weary of or impatient with. — **to tire out** To weary completely. — *n.* *Dial.* Weariness. [OE *tēorian, tēorian*]

tire[2] (tīr) *n.* **1.** A pneumatic, doughnut-shaped structure as of rubber, forming the outer part of the wheels of cars, trucks, bicycles, airplanes, etc., serving to absorb shock and provide traction. **2.** A band or hoop of metal or other hard material fixed tightly around the rim of a wheel. — *v.t.* **tired, tir·ing** To furnish with a tire; put a tire on. Also, *Brit.,* **tyre.** [Special use of TIRE⁴]

tire[3] (tīr) *v.* **tired, tir·ing** *Archaic* *v.t.* **1.** In falconry, to rend and devour. — *v.i.* **2.** To prey. **3.** To be preoccupied; dote; gloat. [< OF *tirer;* ult. origin uncertain]

tire[4] (tīr) *Obs.* *v.t.* **tired, tir·ing** To dress; adorn. — *n.* **1.** A headdress. **2.** Attire. [Aphetic var. of ATTIRE]

tire[5] (tīr) *n.* A volley of cannon; a broadside [< OF *tir* < *tirer* to draw, shoot; ult. origin uncertain]

tired (tīrd) *adj.* Weary; exhausted; jaded; fatigued. [Orig. pp. of TIRE¹] — **tired′ly** *adv.* — **tired′ness** *n.*

tire·less (tīr′lis) *adj.* Proof against fatigue; untiring. [< TIRE¹ + -LESS] — **tire′less·ly** *adv.* — **tire′less·ness** *n.*

Ti·re·si·as (tī·rē′sē·əs) In Greek mythology, a Theban soothsayer, blinded by Athena whom he saw bathing and who in recompense gave him power to foretell the future. — **Ti·re′si·an** *adj.*

tire·some (tīr′səm) *adj.* Tending to tire, or causing one to tire; tedious. — **tire′some·ly** *adv.* — **tire′some·ness** *n.*

tire·wom·an (tīr′wōōm′ən) *n.* *pl.* **·wom·en** (-wim′in) *Obs.* A lady's maid. Also **tir′ing-wom′an.** [< TIRE⁴ + WOMAN]

Ti·rich Mir (tē′rich mēr′) The highest mountain in the Hindu Kush, in extreme NW West Pakistan; 25,263 ft.: also *Tirach Mir.*

tiring room *Archaic* A dressing room, especially in a theater. [< *tiring,* ppr. of TIRE⁴ + ROOM]

tirl (tûrl) *Scot. v.t. & v.i.* To cause to produce a vibrating sound, as a string by plucking. — *n.* A vibrating sound.

ti·ro (tī′rō) See TYRO.

Ti·rol (ti·rōl′, tir′ōl, tī′rōl) See TYROL.

Tir·o·lese (tir′ō·lēz′, -lēs′) See TYROLESE.

Ti·ros (tī′rəs, -rōs) n. U.S. An artificial satellite used to photograph cloud formations for improved weather predictions.

Tir·pitz (tir′pits), **Alfred von**, 1849–1930, German admiral in World War I.

tir·ri·vee (tir′ə·vē) n. Scot. A fit of ill-humor; tantrum.

Tir·so de Mo·li·na (tir′sō thä mō·lē′nä) Pseudonym of **Gabriel Tél·lez** (tä′lyeth), 1571?–1648, Spanish dramatist.

Ti·ruch·i·rap·pal·li (ti·rōōch′ē·räp′ə·lē) A city in east central Madras, India; pop.279,283 (est.1969): also *Trichinopoly*.

'tis (tiz) Archaic or Poetic It is.

Ti·sa (tē′sä) The Czech, Rumanian, and Serbo-Croatian name for the Tisza.

ti·sane (ti·zan′, Fr. tē·zàn′) n. A ptisan. [< F < L ptisana ptisan]

Tish·ah b'Ab (tish′ə·bäb) n. In Judaism, a day of fasting, held on the 9th of Ab (July-August), to commemorate the destruction of the Temple.

Tish·ri (tish·rē′, tish′rē) n. The first month of the Hebrew calendar. Also **Tis·ri**. See (Hebrew) CALENDAR. [< Hebrew < Aramaic *tishrī* < *sherā* to begin]

Ti·siph·o·ne (ti·sif′ə·nē) In Greek mythology, one of the three Furies.

tis·sue (tish′ōō) n. **1.** Biol. One of the elementary aggregates of cells and their products, developed by plants and animals for the performance of a particular function: connective *tissue*. **2.** A light, absorbent piece of paper, usually consisting of two or more layers, used as a disposable towel, handkerchief, etc. **3.** Tissue paper. **4.** A connected or interwoven series; chain; fabrication: a *tissue* of lies. **5.** Any light or gauzy textile fabric. **6.** A very thin, tissuelike typewriting paper. — v.t. **·sued**, **·su·ing** Rare **1.** To make into tissue. **2.** To clothe or adorn with tissue. [< OF *tissu* rich stuff, orig. pp. of *tistre* to weave < L *texere*]

tissue culture The science and art of growing body tissues in a prepared medium.

tissue paper Very thin, unsized, almost transparent paper for wrapping delicate articles, protecting engravings, etc.

Ti·sza (ti′so) A river flowing 800 miles from the Carpathian Mountains, south through Rumania, Hungary, and Yugoslavia to the Danube: German *Theiss*. Czech, Rumanian, and Serbo-Croatian *Tisa*. See map of DANUBE.

tit[1] (tit) n. **1.** A titmouse (which see). **2.** Any of various small birds, as a titlark. [Short for TITMOUSE, TITLARK, etc.]

tit[2] n. A light blow. See TIT FOR TAT. [Var. of TIP[4]]

tit[3] (tit) n. Teat; breast; nipple. [OE *titt*]

tit[4] (tit) n. **1.** A small or worn-out horse; a nag. **2.** Slang A young woman or girl: a disrespectful term. [ME, a little thing, ? < Scand. Cf. dial. Norw. *titta* little girl.]

ti·tan (tīt′n) n. A person of gigantic size and strength. [< TITAN]

Ti·tan (tīt′n) n. **1.** In Greek mythology, one of a race of giant gods who were vanquished and succeeded by the Olympian gods. **2.** Helios: so called by some Latin poets. **3.** A liquid-fueled intercontinental guided missile of the U.S. Air Force. — **Ti·tan·ic**. adj. — **Ti′tan·ess** n. fem.

ti·tan·ate (tī′tə·nāt) n. Chem. A salt or ester of titanic acid. [< TITAN(IC)[2] + -ATE[3]]

Ti·tan·esque (tīt′n·esk′) adj. Like the Titans; gigantic.

Ti·ta·ni·a (ti·tā′nē·ə, tī-) Queen of fairyland and wife of Oberon in Shakespeare's *A Midsummer Night's Dream*.

ti·tan·ic[1] (tī·tan′ik, ti-) adj. Chem. Of or pertaining to titanium, especially in its higher valence. [< TITAN(IUM) + -IC]

ti·tan·ic[2] (tī·tan′ik) adj. Of great size; huge.

Ti·tan·ic (tī·tan′ik) adj. Of, characteristic of, or resembling the Titans. [< Gk. *titanikos* < *Titanes* the Titans]

titanic acid Chem. **1.** A white pulverulent hydroxide of titanium, H_2TiO_3, used as a mordant in dyeing. **2.** One of various weak acids derived from titanium dioxide.

ti·tan·if·er·ous (tīt′n·if′ər·əs) adj. Containing or yielding titanium. [< TITAN(IUM) + -FEROUS]

Ti·tan·ism (tīt′n·iz′əm) n. Defiance of or rebellion against constituted authority or social conventions, a characteristic attributed to the Titans in Greek mythology.

ti·tan·ite (tī′tən·īt) n. Sphene. [< G *titanit* < *titanium* titanium]

ti·ta·ni·um (tī·tā′nē·əm, ti-) n. A widely distributed dark gray metallic element (symbol Ti), found in small quantities in many minerals and used to toughen steel alloys. See ELEMENT. [< NL < L *Titani* the Titans < Gk. *Titanes*; named on analogy with *uranium*]

titanium dioxide Chem. A white crystalline powder, TiO_2, used in the manufacture of paints, lacquers, inks, etc., and as a skin cream. Compare ANATASE, RUTILE.

Ti·tan·om·a·chy (tī′tən·om′ə·kē) n. In Greek mythology, the war of the Titans against the Olympian gods. [< Gk. *Titanomachia* < *Titan* Titan + *machē* battle]

ti·tan·o·there (tī′tən·ə·thir′, tī·tan′ə-, ti-) n. Paleontol. Any of an extinct family (*Titanotheriidae*) of large, odd-toed ungulates related to the horse and common in the Eocene

epoch of the Tertiary period. [< NL < Gk. *Titan* Titan + *thērion*, dim. of *thēr* wild beast]

ti·tan·ous (tīt′tən·əs, tī·tan′əs, ti-) adj. Chem. Of or pertaining to titanium, especially in its lower valence. [< TITAN(IUM) + -OUS[2]]

tit·bit (tit′bit′) n. Brit. A tidbit (which see).

ti·ter (tī′tər, tē′-) n. Chem. **1.** The strength or concentration of a solution or the ingredients of a compound, as determined by titration. **2.** The temperature at which a solid fatty acid or wax melts, as determined by saponification. Also spelled *titre*. [< F *titre* the fineness of gold or silver alloy]

tit for tat Retaliation in kind; blow for blow. [? Alter. of *tip for tap*; ? infl. in form by MF *tant pour tant* tit for tat]

tith·a·ble (tī′thə·bəl) adj. Liable to be tithed, as property.

tithe (tīth) n. **1.** A tax or assessment of one tenth, especially when payable in kind; loosely, any ratable tax. **2.** In England, a tenth part of the yearly proceeds arising from lands and from the personal industry of the inhabitants, for the support of the clergy and the church. **3.** The tenth part of anything. **4.** A small part. — v.t. **tithed**, **tith·ing 1.** To give or pay a tithe, or tenth part of. **2.** To tax with tithes. [ME *tithe*, *tethe*, OE *tēotha*, *teogotha* tenth] — **tith′er** n.

tith·ing (tī′thing) n. **1.** The act of levying tithes. **2.** A tenth part. **3.** In old English law, a civil division composed of ten freeholders and their families.

Ti·tho·nus (ti·thō′nəs) In Greek mythology, a son of Laomedon who was loved by Eos. He was granted immortality by Zeus, but was finally changed into a grasshopper. [< L < Gk. *Tithōnos*]

ti·ti[1] (tē′tē) n. **1.** An evergreen shrub or small tree (*Cliftonia monophylla*) with fragrant white flowers, native in swamps of the southern United States. **2.** Any of a genus (*Cyrilla*) of related trees of tropical America; especially, the **white titi** (*C. racemiflora*). [< Sp. < Aymaran]

ti·ti[2] (tē·tē′) n. One of several small South American monkeys (genus *Callicebus*). [< Sp. *titi* < Guarani *titi*]

ti·tian (tish′ən) n. A reddish yellow color much used by Titian, especially in painting women's hair. — adj. Having or pertaining to the color titian. [after *Titian*]

Ti·tian (tish′ən), 1477?–1576, Venetian painter: original name **Ti·zia·no Ve·cel·lio** (tē·tsä′nō vā·chel′lyō): called **Il Di·vi·no** (dē·vē′nō) (the Divine).

Ti·ti·ca·ca (tē′tē·kä′kä), **Lake** A lake in the Andes between SE Peru and west central Bolivia; 3,200 sq. mi.; elevation 12,500 ft.; the highest large lake in the world.

tit·il·lant (tit′ə·lənt) n. An excitant. [< L *titillans*, *-antis*, ppr. of *titillare* to tickle]

tit·il·late (tit′ə·lāt) v.t. **·lat·ed**, **·lat·ing 1.** To cause a tickling sensation in. **2.** To excite pleasurably in any way. [< L *titillatus*, pp. of *titillare* to tickle]

tit·il·la·tion (tit′ə·lā′shən) n. **1.** The act of titillating, or the state of being titillated. **2.** Any momentary exciting or gratifying sensation. — **tit′il·la′tive** adj.

tit·i·vate (tit′ə·vāt) v.t. & v.i. **·vat·ed**, **·vat·ing** Informal To put on decorative touches; smarten; dress up: also spelled *tittivate*. [Earlier *tidivate*, *tiddivate*, ? < TIDY, on analogy with *cultivate*] — **tit′i·va′tion** n.

tit·lark (tit′lärk′) n. A pipit. [ME *tit* little thing + LARK]

ti·tle (tīt′l) n. **1.** A word, phrase, or sound that constitutes the name of a particular thing, as a book, play, poem, or motion picture. **2.** An appellation significant of office, rank, etc.; especially, a designation of nobility. **3.** A characteristic or descriptive name; epithet. **4.** A claim based on an acknowledged or alleged right: What is his *title* to credence? **5.** In some sports, a championship: to play for the *title*. **6.** The subtitle in a motion picture. **7.** Law **a** The means whereby the owner of lands has the just possession of his property; the union of possession, the right of possession, and the right of property in lands and tenements; also, the legal evidence of one's right of property, or the means by or source from which one's right to property has accrued: *title* by purchase. **b** The distinguishing form of words that heads or opens a legal document or statute; also, the opening clause containing the name of the court in which any action is pending, together with the names of the parties, etc. **8.** A section or division of a statute, legal document, treatise, or the like. **9.** Eccl. A source of maintenance, especially with income attached, a right or nomination to which is a canonical prerequisite to ordination. **10.** In or near Rome, a Roman Catholic church or parish headed by a cardinal. — Syn. See NAME. — v.t. **·tled**, **·tling 1.** To give a name to; entitle; call. **2.** To confer an honorary title upon. [< OF < L *titulus* label, inscription. Doublet of TITTLE.]

ti·tled (tīt′ld) adj. Having a title, especially of nobility.

ti·tle·hold·er (tīt′l·hōl′dər) n. One who possesses a title, especially a championship title. Also **ti·tlist** (tīt′list).

title page A page containing the title of a work and the names of its author and publisher. Abbr. *t.p.*

title role The role of the character in a play, opera, or motion picture for whom it is named.

tit·man (tit′mən) *n. pl.* **·men** (-mən) *U.S. Informal* **1.** The smallest pig in a litter; the runt of a litter of pigs. **2.** A man who is small or stunted either physically or mentally. [ME *tit* little thing + MAN]

tit·mouse (tit′mous′) *n. pl.* **·mice** (-mīs′) Any of several small oscine birds (family *Paridae*) related to the nuthatches; especially, the **tufted titmouse** (*Parus bicolor*) of the United States, having a conspicuous crest: also called **tit**. [Alter. of ME *titmuse* < *tit-* little thing + *mose*, alter. of OE *māse* titmouse; infl. in form by *mouse*]

Ti·to (tē′tō), **Marshal,** born 1892, Yugoslav Communist statesman and leader; prime minister 1945–53; president 1953–: original name *Josip Broz*.

Ti·to·grad (tē′tô·gräd) The capital of Montenegro, southern Yugoslavia; pop. 37,000 (1968): formerly *Podgorica*, *Podgoritsa*.

Ti·to·ism (tē′tō·iz′əm) *n.* The assertion by a Communist state of its national interests in opposition to Soviet domination, such as occurred under Marshal Tito in Yugoslavia.

ti·trant (tī′trənt) *n. Chem.* The reagent or standard solution used in titration.

ti·trate (tī′trāt, tit′rāt) *v.i. & v.t.* **·trat·ed, ·trat·ing** *Chem.* To determine the strength of (a solution) by means of standard solutions or by titration. [< F *titrer* < *titre*. See TITER.]

ti·tra·tion (tī·trā′shən, ti-) *n. Chem.* The process of determining the strength or concentration of the ingredients of a solution by adding measured amounts of a suitable reagent until the desired chemical reaction has been effected.

ti·tre (tī′tər, tē′-) See TITER.

tit-tat-toe (tit′tat·tō′) *n.* Ticktacktoe (which see).

tit·ter (tit′ər) *v.i.* To laugh in a suppressed way, as from nervousness or in ridicule; snicker; giggle. — *n.* The act of tittering. [Imit.] — **tit′ter·er** *n.* — **tit′ter·ing·ly** *adv.*

tit·tie (tit′ē) *n. Scot.* A sister. Also **tit′ty.**

tit·ti·vate (tit′ə·vāt) See TITIVATE.

tit·tle (tit′l) *n.* **1.** The minutest quantity; iota. **2.** Originally, a very small mark in writing, as the dot over an *i.* **3.** Any diacritical mark. [< L *titulus.* Doublet of TITLE.]

tit·tle-tat·tle (tit′l-tat′l) *n.* **1.** Foolish or trivial talk; gossip. **2.** An idle, trifling, or tattling talker. — *v.i.* **·tled, ·tling** To talk foolishly or idly; gossip. [Reduplication of TATTLE]

tit·tup (tit′əp) *v.i.* **tit·tuped** or **·tupped, tit·tup·ing** or **·tup·ping** To act in a restless or lively manner; prance. — *n.* A prancing action; a caper. [Appar. imit. of hoof beats]

tit·u·ba·tion (tich′ŏŏ·bā′shən, tit′yə-) *n. Pathol.* A disturbance of body equilibrium resulting in the stumbling gait characteristic of certain spinal diseases. [< L *titubatio, -onis* < *titubatus,* pp. of *titubare* to stagger]

tit·u·lar (tich′ŏŏ·lər, tit′yə-) *adj.* **1.** Existing in name or title only; nominal. **2.** Of, pertaining to, or like a title. **3.** Bestowing or taking title. — *n.* One having a title in virtue of which he holds an office or benefice, whether he performs its duties or not. Also **tit′u·lar′y** (-ler′ē). [< L *titulus* title] — **tit′u·lar·ly** *adv.*

Ti·tus (tī′təs) A disciple of the apostle Paul. — *n.* A book in the New Testament consisting of an epistle addressed to Titus and attributed to Paul. Abbr. *Tit.*

Titus, A.D. 40?–81, Roman emperor A.D. 79–81; son of Vespasian: full name **Titus Flavius Sabinus Ves·pa·si·a·nus** (ves·pā′zhē·ā′nəs).

Ti·u (tē′ŏŏ) In Teutonic mythology, god of war and sky: identified with the Norse *Tyr.*

Tiv·o·li (tiv′ə·lē, *Ital.* tē′vô·lē) A commune in central Italy, near Rome; pop. 39,700 (est. 1967): ancient *Tibur.*

tiv·y (tiv′ē) *adv.* With great speed: a hunting cry. [Appar. short for TANTIVY]

tiz·zy[1] (tiz′ē) *n. pl.* **·zies** *Slang* A bewildered or excited state of mind; a dither. [Origin unknown]

tiz·zy[2] (tiz′ē) *n. pl.* **·zies** *Brit. Slang* A sixpence. [Prob. alter. of TESTER[3]; infl. in form by slang *tilbury* sixpence]

TKO or **T.K.O.** or **t.k.o.** Technical knockout.

Tl *Chem.* Thallium.

TL or **T.L.** Trade-last.

Tlin·git (tling′git) *n.pl.* North American Indians belonging to any of eighteen tribes constituting the Koluschan stock, and inhabiting the Alexander Archipelago of SE Alaska. Also **Tlin·kit** (tling′kit).

Tm *Chem.* Thulium.

tme·sis (tmē′sis, mē′sis) *n.* The separation of the elements of a compound word by an intervening word, as in the phrase *to us ward,* meaning "toward us." [< L < Gk. *tmēsis* a cutting < *temnein* to cut]

tn. **1.** Ton. **2.** Train.

Tn *Chem.* Thoron.

tng. Training.

TNT (tē′en′tē′) *n.* **1.** Trinitrotoluene. **2.** *Informal* Any explosive and dangerous circumstance, force, or person. Also **T.N.T.** [< T(RI)N(ITRO)T(OLUENE)]

to (tŏŏ, *unstressed* tə) *prep.* **1.** In a direction toward or terminating in: going *to* town. **2.** Opposite, in contact with, or near: face *to* face. **3.** Intending or aiming at; having as an object or purpose: Come *to* my rescue. **4.** Resulting in; having as a condition or effect: frozen *to* death. **5.** Belonging or used in connection with: the key *to* the door. **6.** Accompanied by; in rhythm with: March *to* the music. **7.** In honor of: Drink *to* me only with thine eyes. **8.** In comparison, correspondence, or agreement with: often denoting ratio: four quarts *to* the gallon. **9.** Approaching as a limit; denoting the end of a period of time, or a time not reached; until: five minutes *to* one. **10.** For the utmost duration of; as far as: a miser *to* the end of his days. **11.** In respect of; concerning: blind *to* her charms. **12.** In close application toward: Buckle down *to* work. **13.** For; with regard for: The contest is open *to* everyone. **14.** Noting an indirect or limiting object after verbs, adjectives, or nouns, and designating the recipient of the action: taking the place of the dative case in other languages: Give the ring *to* me; That fact is not apparent *to* me. **15.** By: known *to* the world. **16.** From the point of view of: It seems *to* me. **17.** About; involved in: That's all there is *to* it. **18.** *Informal* With: The land was planted *to* potatoes. **19.** *Dial.* At or in (a place): He is not *to* home now. ♦ *To* also serves to indicate the infinitive, and is often used elliptically for it: You may come if you care *to.* — *adv.* **1.** To or toward something. **2.** In a direction, position, or state understood or implied; especially, shut or closed: Pull the door to. **3.** Into a normal condition; into consciousness: She soon came *to.* **4.** *Naut.* With head to the wind: said of a sailing vessel: to lie *to.* **5.** Upon the matter at hand; into action or operation: They fell *to* with good will. **6.** Nearby; at hand. [OE *tō*]

TOA or **T.O.A.** Theatre Owners of America.

toad (tōd) *n.* **1.** A tailless, jumping, insectivorous amphibian (family *Bufonidae*), resembling the frog but without teeth in the upper jaw, and resorting to water only to breed. **2.** Any of various similar amphibians, as the **Surinam toad** (*Pipa pipa*) or the European **midwife toad** (*Alytes obstetricans*). **3.** A lizard, the horned toad. **4.** Any person regarded scornfully or contemptuously. [OE *tāde, tādige*]

TOAD
(2 to 6 inches long)

toad·eat·er (tōd′ē·tər) *n.* A toady. [Orig. an assistant to a charlatan, who ate, or pretended to eat, toads (held to be poisonous) to show the efficacy of a patent medicine]

toad·fish (tōd′fish′) *n. pl.* **·fish** or **·fish·es** Any of a family (*Batrachoididae*) of marine fishes of the Atlantic coast of the United States, having scaleless skin, and a mouth and head resembling those of a toad.

toad·flax (tōd′flaks′) *n.* **1.** A common, showy perennial weed (*Linaria vulgaris*) of the figwort family, having spurred yellow flowers marked with an orange spot: also called *butter-and-eggs.* **2.** Any plant of the same genus. [So called because spotted like toads and having a flaxlike foliage]

toad spit Cuckoo spit (def. 1). Also **toad spittle.**

toad·stone (tōd′stōn′) *n.* A natural or artificial stone resembling a toad in color and form, and long believed to be formed in a toad, worn as a talisman. [< TOAD + STONE, trans. of L *batrachites* < Gk.]

toad·stool (tōd′stōōl′) *n.* **1.** Any of various umbrella-shaped fungi, growing on decaying vegetable matter; mushroom. **2.** *Informal* A poisonous mushroom.

toad·y (tō′dē) *n. pl.* **toad·ies** An obsequious flatterer; a fawning, servile person: also *toadeater.* — *v.t. & v.i.* **toad·ied, toad·y·ing** To act the toady (to). [Short for TOADEATER] — **toad′y·ish** *adj.* — **toad′y·ism** *n.*

to-and-fro (tōō′ən·frō′) *adj.* Moving back and forth; undulating; alternating. — *n.* Motion back and forth.

to and fro In opposite or different directions; back and forth.

toast[1] (tōst) *v.t.* **1.** To brown before or over a fire; especially, to brown (bread or cheese) before a fire or in a toaster. **2.** To warm thoroughly before a fire. — *v.i.* **3.** To become warm or toasted. — *n.* Sliced bread browned in a toaster or at a fire; toasted bread. [< OF *toster* to roast, grill < L *tostus,* pp. of *torrere* to parch, roast]

toast[2] (tōst) *n.* **1.** The act of drinking to someone's health or to some sentiment. **2.** A person or sentiment named in so drinking: She was the *toast* of the town. — *v.t.* **1.** To drink to the health of or in honor of. — *v.i.* **2.** To drink a toast or toasts. [< TOAST[1], in obs. sense of "a spiced piece of toast put in a drink to flavor it"]

toast·er[1] (tōs′tər) *n.* A device for making toast.

toast·er[2] (tōs′tər) *n.* One who proposes a toast.

toast·mas·ter (tōst′mas′tər, -mäs′tər) *n.* A person who, at public dinners, announces the toasts, calls upon the various speakers, etc. — **toast′mis′tress** (-mis′tris) *n.fem.*

to·bac·co (tə·bak′ō) *n. pl.* **·cos** or **·coes** **1.** An annual plant of the nightshade family (genus *Nicotiana*); especially, a common species (*N. tabacum*), the chief source of the tobacco of commerce, originally of America, but now cultivated in various parts of the world. **2.** Its leaves prepared in various ways, as for smoking, chewing, etc. **3.** The use of tobacco for smoking. **4.** The various products prepared from tobacco leaves, as cigarettes, cigars, etc. [< Sp. *tabaco* < Carib, a tube or pipe used in smoking tobacco]

to·bac·co·nist (tə·bak′ə·nist) *n. Brit.* One who deals in tobacco.

tobacco worm The large green larva of a hawk moth, (*Protoparce sexta*), with white stripes and a slender horn at the rear end of the body, destructive to tobacco plants.

To·ba·go (tō-bā′gō) See under TRINIDAD AND TOBAGO.

To·bit (tō′bit) A pious Hebrew captive in Nineveh, hero of the Apocryphal book of the Old Testament. — *n.* The Old Testament book bearing his name. Also **To·bi·as** (tə-bī′əs).

to·bog·gan (tə-bog′ən) *n.* A light sledlike vehicle, consisting of a long thin board or boards curved upward at the forward end, used for transporting goods or coasting, especially on prepared slides. — *v.i.* 1. To coast on a toboggan. 2. To move downward swiftly: Wheat prices *tobogganed*. [< dial. F (Canadian) *tabagan* sleigh < Algonquian. Cf. Micmac *tobākun*.] — **to·bog′gan·er, to·bog′gan·ist** *n.*

toboggan slide A slope prepared for coasting with toboggans, often a winding track with banked curves.

To·bol (to-bôl′) A river in the northern Kazakh S.S.R. and southern R.S.F.S.R., flowing 1,042 miles NE to the Irtish.

To·bolsk (to-bôly′sk′) A city in the southern R.S.F.S.R., at the junction of the Tobol and Irtish rivers; pop. 36,484 (est. 1969). Also **To·bol′sk′**.

to·by (tō′bē) *n.* *pl.* **·bies** 1. A mug or jug for ale or beer, often made in the form of an old man wearing a three-cornered hat. 2. *Informal* A form of stogie cigar. [after *Toby*, dim. of *Tobias*, a personal name]

TOBY

toc·ca·ta (tə-kä′tə, *Ital.* tôk-kä′tä) *n.* *Music* A free, often rhapsodic composition for a keyboard instrument, sometimes written to show virtuosity. [< Ital., lit., a touching, orig. pp. fem. of *toccare* to touch]

To·char·i·an (tō-kâr′ē-ən, -kär′-) *n.* 1. One of an ancient cultured people inhabiting central Asia until about A.D. 1000. 2. The language of the Tocharians, belonging to the centum division of the Indo-European language family. Two dialects have been distinguished, usually referred to as **Tocharian A** and **Tocharian B**. Also spelled *Tokharian.*

toch·er (tokh′ər) *Scot. & Brit. Dial.* *n.* The dowry of a bride. — *v.t.* To give a dowry to. [< Irish *tochar* assigned portion < *tochuirim* I put to, assign < *chuirim* I put]

toco- *combining form* Child; pertaining to children or to childbirth: *tocology*. Also, before vowels, **toc-**. [< Gk. *tokos* child, childbirth]

to·col·o·gy (tō-kol′ə-jē) *n.* The science and art of midwifery; obstetrics: also spelled *tokology*. [< TOCO- + -LOGY]

to·coph·er·ol (tō-kof′ə-rôl, -rol) *n.* *Biochem.* Any of four closely related alcohols, widely distributed in nature and forming the active principle of vitamin E. [< TOCO- + Gk. *pherein* to bear + -OL²; so called because thought to be effective against sterility]

Tocque·ville (tôk-vēl′), **Alexis Charles Henri Maurice Clérel de**, 1805–59, French statesman and political writer.

toc·sin (tok′sin) *n.* 1. A signal sounded on a bell; alarm. 2. An alarm bell. [< MF < OF *toquassen* < Provençal *tocasenh* < *tocar* to strike, touch + *senh* bell < LL *signum* signal bell < L, sign]

tod¹ (tod) *n.* 1. A bushy clump. 2. A former weight for wool, about 28 pounds. [ME *todde*, prob. < LG. Cf. East Frisian *todde* small load, bundle.]

tod² (tod) *n.* *Scot. & Brit. Dial.* A fox.

to·day (tə-dā′) *adv.* 1. On or during this present day. 2. At the present time; nowadays. — *n.* The present day, time, or age. Also **to-day′**. [OE *tōdæg* < *tō* to + *dæg* day]

tod·dle (tod′l) *v.i.* **·dled, ·dling** To walk unsteadily and with short steps, as a little child. — *n.* The act of toddling; also, a stroll. [Origin uncertain] — **tod′dler** *n.*

tod·dle-top (tod′l-top′) *n.* Teetotum.

tod·dy (tod′ē) *n.* *pl.* **·dies** 1. A drink made with spirits, hot water, sugar, and a slice of lemon. 2. The sap or juice that flows from the incised spathes of certain East Indian trees, the **toddy palms**, especially the wild date of India (*Phoenix sylvestris*). 3. A spirituous liquor distilled from these palms. [< Hind. *tārī* toddy (def. 2) < *tār* palm tree < Skt. *tāla* palmyra]

Tod·le·ben (tōt′lä-bən) See TOTLEBEN.

to-do (tə-dōō′) *n.* *pl.* **to-dos** *Informal* Confusion or bustle; fuss: What's all the *to-do* about? [OE *to-dōn* < *to-* asunder + *dōn* to do, put]

to·dy (tō′dē) *n.* *pl.* **·dies** Any of numerous very small insectivorous West Indian birds (genus *Todus*) related to the kingfishers; especially, the **green tody** (*T. viridis*) of Jamaica, bright green with a scarlet throat. [< F *todier* < L *todus*, a kind of small bird]

toe (tō) *n.* 1. One of the digits of the foot. 2. The forward part of the foot, as distinguished from the heel. 3. The portion of a shoe, sock, stocking, skate, etc., that covers or corresponds in position with the toes. 4. A lower end or projection resembling or suggestive of a toe, as the projecting end of the head of a golf club. 5. *Mech.* **a** A pivot or journal in a bearing. **b** A horizontally projecting arm on a stem, as for operating a valve, raised by a cam or lifted

manually. 6. In a railroad switch, the space between the rails at the unchanneled end of a frog. — **on one's toes** Alert; wide-awake. — **to tread on (someone's) toes** To offend (someone); trespass on (someone's) feelings, opinions, prejudices, etc. — *v.* **toed, toe·ing** *v.t.* 1. To touch with the toes: to *toe* the line. 2. To kick with the toe. 3. To furnish with a toe. 4. To drive (a nail or spike) obliquely; also, to attach (beams, etc.) end to end, by nails so driven. 5. To strike (a golf ball) with the toe of the club. — *v.i.* 6. To stand or walk with the toes pointing in a specified direction: to *toe* out. — **to toe the mark** (or **line**) 1. To touch a certain line or mark with the toes preparatory to starting a race. 2. To abide by the rules; conform. [OE *tā*] — **toe′less** *adj.*

toe·cap (tō′kap) *n.* A cap covering for the tip or toe of a boot or shoe. For illustration see SHOE.

toe crack A sand crack (which see).

toed (tōd) *adj.* 1. Having toes: chiefly in combination: *pigeon-toed*. 2. Fastened or fastening by obliquely driven nails; also, driven obliquely, as a nail.

toe-dance (tō′dans′, -däns′) *v.i.* **-danced, -danc·ing** To dance on tiptoe; perform a toe dance. — **toe dancer**

toe dance A dance performed on tiptoe.

toe·hold (tō′hōld′) *n.* 1. A small space that supports the toes in climbing. 2. Any means of entrance, support, etc.; a footing: to gain a *toehold* on the island. 3. A hold in which a wrestler bends back the foot of his opponent.

toe·nail (tō′nāl′) *n.* 1. A nail growing on the toe. 2. A nail driven obliquely to hold the foot of a stud or brace. — *v.t.* To fasten with obliquely driven nails.

toff (tof, tôf) *n.* *Brit. Slang* A dandy; also, a gentleman. [Earlier *toft* < TUFT (def. 3)]

tof·fee (tôf′ē, tof′ē) *n.* Taffy. Also **tof′fy**.

toft (tôft, toft) *n.* *Brit.* 1. Land once occupied as a messuage, on which the buildings have decayed or been burned; a homestead. 2. A hillock or knoll. [OE, homestead < ON *topt, tupt*]

tog (tog) *Informal* *n.* 1. A coat. 2. *pl.* Clothes; outfit: football *togs*. — *v.t.* **togged, tog·ging** To dress; clothe: often with *up* or *out*. [Short for vagabond's cant *togemans, togman* coat, cloak < F *toge* toga < L *toga*]

to·ga (tō′gə) *n.* *pl.* **·gas** or **·gae** (-jē) 1. The distinctive outer garment worn in public by a citizen of ancient Rome. 2. Any gown or cloak characteristic of a calling or profession: the lawyer's *toga*. [< L < *tegere* to cover]

to·gaed (tō′gəd) *adj.* 1. Robed in the toga. 2. Classical and stately. Also **to·gat·ed** (tō′gā-tid).

to·ga vi·ri·lis (tō′gə vi·ri′lis) *Latin* The toga assumed by a male citizen of ancient Rome at the age of 14 as a token of manhood.

TOGA

to·geth·er (tŏŏ-geth′ər, tə-) *adv.* 1. Into union or contact with each other. 2. In the same place or at the same spot; with each other; in company. 3. At the same moment of time; simultaneously. 4. Without cessation or intermission. 5. With one another; mutually; conjointly. [OE *tōgædere, tōgadore* < *tō* to + *gædre* together]. Akin to GATHER.]

to·geth·er·ness (tŏŏ-geth′ər-nis, tə-) *n.* The state of being associated or united.

tog·ger·y (tog′ər-ē) *n.* *pl.* **·ger·ies** *Informal* 1. Togs collectively; clothes. 2. A clothing shop.

tog·gle (tog′əl) *n.* 1. A pin, or short rod, properly attached in the middle, as to a rope, and designed to be passed through a hole or eye and turned. 2. A toggle iron (which see). 3. A toggle joint (which see). — *v.t.* **·gled, ·gling** To fix, fasten, or furnish with a toggle. [Prob. nautical var. of *tuggle*, appar. freq. of TUG]

toggle iron A harpoon, as for killing whales, so arranged as to turn crosswise when it enters the animal's body. Also **toggle harpoon**.

toggle joint *Mech.* A joint having a central hinge like an elbow, and operable by applying the power at the junction, thus changing the direction of force and giving indefinite mechanical pressure. For illustration see MACHINE.

toggle switch *Electr.* A switch in the form of a projecting lever whose movement through a small arc opens or closes an electric circuit.

To·gliat·ti (tō-lyät′tē), **Palmiro**, 1893–1964, Italian Communist leader.

To·go (tō′gō) A Republic in western Africa; about 21,500 sq. mi.; pop. 2,004,711 (est. 1970); capital Lomé: French *République Togolaise.* See FRENCH TOGOLAND, map of (Gulf of) GUINEA. — **To′go·lese** (tō′gə·lēz′) *n. & adj.*

To·go (tō′gō), **Count Heihachiro**, 1847–1934, Japanese admiral; defeated the Russian fleet in the Russo-Japanese War.

To·go·land (tō′gō-land) A former German protectorate in western Africa, divided in 1946 under UN trusteeship into British Togoland and French Togoland.

togue (tōg) *n.* *Canadian* The lake trout.

toil¹ (toil) *n.* 1. Fatiguing work; labor. 2. Any oppressive task. 3. Any notable work accomplished by labor. 4. *Obs.*

Strife; struggle. — *v.i.* **1.** To work arduously; labor painfully and tiringly. **2.** To progress or make one's way with slow and labored steps. — *v.t.* **3.** *Archaic* To accomplish or obtain by toil. [< AF *toil* dispute, OF *tooil* trouble < AF *toiler* to strive, OF *tooillier* to soil, agitate < L *tudiculare* to stir about < *tudicula* machine for bruising olives, dim. of *tudes* mallet] — **toil′er** *n.*
— **Syn.** (noun) **1.** *Toil, labor, travail,* and *drudgery* are compared as they denote hard work. *Toil* is arduous and tiring, whether it involves physical or mental effort. *Labor,* as here compared, is work that tires the muscles or drains one's nervous energies. Both *labor* and *travail* refer, in another sense, to childbirth, and this involvement is so fixed in regard to *travail,* that this word always suggests acute pain and suffering rather than fatigue resulting from hard work. *Drudgery* is work of a menial or boring nature.
toil² (toil) *n.* **1.** *Usually pl.* Something that binds or ensnares as a net. **2.** *Archaic* A net, snare, or other trap. [< MF *toiles* nets < *toile* cloth < OF *teile* < L *tela* web]
toile (twäl) *n.* A sheer linen fabric; also, a fine cretonne with scenic designs printed in one color. [< F. See TOIL².]
toi·let (toi′lit) *n.* **1.** *U.S.* **a** A room with a washbowl, water closet, etc.: sometimes called *bathroom.* **b** A room or closet having a hopper flushed and discharged by means of water, into which one urinates or defecates; also, the hopper and its trap: also called *water closet.* **2.** The act or process of dressing oneself; formerly, especially of dressing the hair. **3.** Attire; also, a toilette or costume. **4.** A dressing table. — *adj.* Used in dressing or grooming: *toilet* articles. [< F *toilette* orig., cloth dressing gown, dim. of *toile* cloth. See TOIL².]
toilet paper Thin absorbent paper commonly wound in a roll, for use in toilets.
toi·let·ry (toi′lit·rē) *n.* *pl.* **·ries** Any of the several articles used in making one's toilet, as soap, comb, brush, etc.
toi·lette (toi·let′, *Fr.* twà·let′) *n.* **1.** The act or process of grooming oneself, usually including bathing, hairdressing, etc. **2.** A person's actual dress or style of dress; also, any specific costume or gown. [< F. See TOILET.]
toilet water A scented liquid containing a small amount of alcohol, used in or after the bath, after shaving, etc.
toil·ful (toil′fəl) *adj.* Replete with toil; laborious. — **toil′-ful·ly** *adv.*
toil·some (toil′səm) *adj.* Accomplished with fatigue; involving toil. — **toil′some·ly** *adv.* — **toil′some·ness** *n.*
toil·worn (toil′wôrn′, -wōrn′) *adj.* Exhausted by toil.
toit (toit) *v.i. Brit. Dial.* **1.** To dawdle; saunter. **2.** To totter. [Origin uncertain]
To·jo (tō·jō), **Hideki,** 1884–1948, Japanese general and statesman; premier 1941–44.
To·kay (tō·kā′) *n.* **1.** A white or reddish blue grape from Tokay, Hungary. **2.** A wine made from it. [after *Tokay,* a town in northern Hungary]
to·ken (tō′kən) *n.* **1.** Anything indicative of some other thing; a visible sign; indication; evidence. **2.** A symbol: a *token* of my affection. **3.** Some tangible proof or evidence of a statement or of one's identity, etc. **4.** A memento; keepsake; souvenir. **5.** A characteristic mark or feature. **6.** A piece of metal issued as currency and having a face value greater than its actual value. **7.** A piece of metal issued by a transportation company and good for one fare. **8.** *Obs.* A signal. — **Syn.** See EMBLEM. — *v.t.* To evidence by a token; betoken. — *adj.* Done or given as a token, especially in partial fulfillment of an obligation. [OE *tācen, tācn*]
To·khar·i·an (tō·kâr′ē·ən, -kär′-) See TOCHARIAN.
to·kol·o·gy (tō·kol′ə·jē) See TOCOLOGY.
To·ku·shi·ma (tō·kōō·shē·mä) A port city on eastern Shikoku, Japan; pop. 220,000 (est. 1966).
To·ky·o (tō′kē·ō, *Japanese* tō·kyō) The capital of Japan, a port on **Tokyo Bay,** an inlet of the Philippine Sea in central Honshu, Japan; pop. 8,832,647 (1970): formerly *Edo, Yedo.* Also **To′ki·o.**
to·la (tō′lä) *n.* *Anglo-Indian* A weight, about 180 grains, for gold and silver; the weight of one rupee. [< Hind. < Skt. *tulā* balance, weight < *tul-* to weigh]
to·lan (tō′lan) *n.* A white crystalline unsaturated hydrocarbon, C₁₄H₁₀, prepared by synthesis. Also **to·lane** (tō′lān). [< TOL(UENE) + -ANE²]
tol·booth (tōl′bōōth′, -bōōth′) See TOLLBOOTH.
told (tōld) Past tense and past participle of TELL.
tole¹ (tōl) *v.t.* **toled, tol·ing 1.** *Dial.* To draw as with a lure; entice; decoy. **2.** *Obs.* To pull; drag; draw. Also spelled *toll.* [ME *tollen, tullen*]
tole² (tōl) *n.* A metalware, enameled or lacquered in various colors and frequently gilded, used for trays, lamps, etc. Also **tôle.** [< F *tôle* sheet iron, dial. var. of *table* table]
To·le·do (tə·lē′dō) *n.* *pl.* **·dos** A sword or sword blade from Toledo, Spain. Also **to·le′do.**
To·le·do (tə·lē′dō) **1.** A city in NW Ohio, near Lake Erie; pop. 383,818. **2.** (*Sp.* tō·lā′thō) An ancient city in central Spain, on the Tagus; pop. about 40,651 (1960).
tol·er·a·ble (tol′ər·ə·bəl) *adj.* **1.** Passably good; commonplace. **2.** Endurable; capable of being borne. **3.** Allowable; permissible. **4.** *Informal* In passably good health. [< OF < L *tolerabilis* able to endure < *tolerare* to endure] — **tol′-er·a·ble·ness** *n.* — **tol′er·a·bly** *adv.*

tol·er·ance (tol′ər·əns) *n.* **1.** The character, state, or quality of being tolerant. **2.** Indulgence or forbearance in judging the opinions, customs, or acts of others; freedom from bigotry or from racial or religious prejudice. **3.** The act of enduring, or the capacity for endurance. **4.** *Mech.* A small permissible allowance for variations from the specified standard weight, dimensions, etc., of a machine or any of its parts. **5.** A legally permissible variation from the standard of weight, fineness, etc., of coins: also called *remedy.* **6.** *Med.* Ability to endure or assimilate large or increasing amounts of a drug or poison without ill effects.
tol·er·ant (tol′ər·ənt) *adj.* **1.** Disposed to tolerate beliefs, views, etc. **2.** Indulgent; liberal. **3.** *Med.* Capable of taking with impunity unusual or excessive doses of dangerous drugs. [< F L *tolerans, -antis,* ppr. of *tolerare* to endure] — **tol′er·ant·ly** *adv.*
tol·er·ate (tol′ə·rāt) *v.t.* **·at·ed, ·at·ing 1.** To allow to be or be done without active opposition. **2.** To concede, as the right to opinions or participation. **3.** To bear, sustain, or be capable of enduring or sustaining. **4.** *Med.* To endure, as a poisonous amount or dose, with impunity. — **Syn.** See ENDURE. [< L *toleratus,* pp. of *tolerare* to endure] — **tol′er·a′tive** *adj.* — **tol′er·a′tor** *n.*
tol·er·a·tion (tol′ə·rā′shən) *n.* **1.** The act or practice of tolerance. **2.** The recognition of the rights of the individual to his own opinions and customs, as in religious worship. **3.** The spirit and desire to be tolerant; forbearance.
tol·i·dine (tol′ə·dēn, -din) *n.* *Chem.* One of several isomeric bases, (CH₃·C₆H₃·NH₂)₂, derived from toluene, one form of which is an important dyestuff. Also **tol′i·din** (-din). [< TOL(UOL) + (BENZ)IDINE]
To·li·ma (tō·lē′mä), **Ne·va·da del** (nā·vä′thä thel) A volcano in the Andes Mountains, west central Colombia; 18,438 ft.; last eruption, 1829.
toll¹ (tōl) *n.* **1.** A fixed compensation for some privilege granted or service rendered, as passage on a bridge or turnpike. **2.** The right to levy such charge. **3.** Something taken or elicited like a toll; price: The train wreck took a heavy *toll* of lives. **4.** A due charged for shipping or landing goods. **5.** A charge for transportation of goods, especially by rail or canal. **6.** A charge for a long-distance telephone call. — *v.t. Rare* **1.** To take as a toll. — *v.i. Rare* **2.** To take or exact a toll. [OE < LL *toloneum* < L *telonium* < Gk.*telōnion* customhouse < *telōnēs* tax collector < *telos* tax]
toll² (tōl) *v.t.* **1.** To cause (a bell) to sound slowly and at regular intervals. **2.** To announce by tolling, as a death or funeral. **3.** To call or summon by tolling. **4.** To decoy (game, especially ducks). **5.** See TOLE¹. — *v.i.* **6.** To sound slowly and at regular intervals. — *n.* The act or sound of tolling a bell. [ME *tollen, tullen*]
toll·age (tōl′ij) *n.* **1.** A charge in the nature of a toll. **2.** The toll itself.
toll·bar (tōl′bär′) *n.* A tollgate, especially one with a single bar: also called *pike.*
toll·booth (tōl′bōōth′, -bōōth′) *n.* **1.** *Scot.* A jail; prison: also spelled *tolbooth.* **2.** A tollhouse.
toll bridge A bridge at which a toll is charged for passage.
toll call A long-distance telephone call, the charge for which is higher than local rates.
toll collector A collector of tolls.
toll·er (tō′lər) *n.* **1.** One who tolls a bell. **2.** A bell used for tolling. **3.** A small dog trained to toll or decoy ducks.
Tol·ler (tôl′ər), **Ernst,** 1893–1939, German dramatist and poet.
toll·gate (tōl′gāt′) *n.* A gate at the entrance to a bridge, or on a road, at which toll is paid.
toll·house (tōl′hous′) *n.* A toll collector's lodge adjoining a tollgate: also called *tollbooth.*
toll·keep·er (tōl′kē′pər) *n.* One who keeps a tollgate.
toll line A telephone line or channel, as between two central offices in different exchanges, for the use of which a toll is charged; a long-distance circuit.
toll road A road on which a toll is charged for each vehicle using it. Also **toll·way** (tōl′wā′).
Tol·stoy (tol′stoi, tōl′-; *Russian* tol·stoi′), **Count Leo Nikolaevich,** 1828–1910, Russian novelist and social reformer. Also **Tol′stoi.**
Tol·tec (tol′tek, tōl′-) *n.* One of certain ancient Nahuatlan tribes that dominated central and southern Mexico about A.D. 900–1100 and through contact with Mayan culture founded the highly civilized Nahua culture of the Aztecs. — *adj.* Of or pertaining to the Toltecs. [< Nahuatl *Tolteca*] — **Tol′tec·an** *adj.*
to·lu (tə·lōō′) *n.* Balsam of Tolu. See under BALSAM. [< Sp. *tolú,* after Santiago de *Tolu,* a seaport in Colombia]
tol·u·ate (tol′yōō·āt) *n.* *Chem.* A salt or ester of a toluic acid. [< TOLU(IC) + -ATE³]
To·lu·ca (tō·lōō′kä) The capital of Mexico state, central Mexico; pop. 220,195 (1970). Also **Toluca de Ler·do** (thä ler′thō).
tol·u·ene (tol′yōō·ēn) *n.* *Chem.* A colorless, flammable liquid hydrocarbon, C₆H₅CH₃, obtained from coal tar by distillation and used in making dyestuffs, explosives, etc. [< TOLU + -ENE; so called because orig. obtained from tolu]

to·lu·ic acid (tə·lōō′ik, tol′yōō·ik) *Chem.* Any of four isomeric acid derivatives of toluene, $C_8H_8O_2$, occurring as white crystalline compounds. [< TOLU(ENE) + -IC]

tol·u·ide (tol′yōō-ĭd, -ĭd) *n. Chem.* One of a series of amides in which the nitrogen is united with a tolyl radical. Also **tol′u·id** (-ĭd). [< TOLU(ENE) + -IDE]

to·lu·i·dine (tə·lōō′ə·dēn, -dĭn) *n. Chem.* One of three isomeric compounds, C_7H_9N, derived from compounds of toluene, and used in making dyes and certain drugs. Also **to·lu′i·din** (-dĭn). [< TOLUID(E) + -INE²]

tol·u·ol (tol′yōō-ōl, -ol) *n. Chem.* Crude commercial toluene. Also **tol′u·ole** (-ōl). [< TOLU + (BENZ)OL]

tol·u·yl (tol′yōō-ĭl) *n. Chem.* The univalent toluic acid radical C_8H_7O. [< TOLU(IC) + -YL]

tol·yl (tol′il) *n. Chem.* The univalent radical $C_6H_4CH_3$, derived from toluene. [< TOL(UIC) + -YL]

tom (tom) *n.* The male of various animals, especially the cat. [< *Tom*, a personal name. See TOMCAT.]

Tom (tôm′ý) A river in the southern R.S.F.S.R., flowing 440 miles, generally NW, to the Ob. Also **Tom′**.

tom·a·hawk (tom′ə·hôk) *n.* **1.** An axlike weapon used by North American Indians, originally a carved club in which a piece of bone or metal was inserted. **2.** Any similar weapon, tool, etc. — *v.t.* To strike or kill with a tomahawk. [< Algonquian *tamahak*, short for *tamahaken* cutting utensil < *tamahaken* he uses for cutting < *tamaham* he cuts]

tom·al·ley (tom′al-ē) *n.* The liver of the lobster, considered a delicacy. [Prob. < Carib]

to·man (tō·män′) *n.* A Persian gold coin of varying value; formerly, a money of account. [< Persian *tūmān, tuman, tuman* < Turki, lit., ten thousand]

Tom and Jer·ry (tom′ ən jer′ē) A drink made with brandy, rum, beaten egg, hot milk or water, sugar, and nutmeg. [after Corinthian *Tom* and *Jerry* Hawthorn, two main characters in *Life in London*, 1821, by Pierce Egan, 1772–1849]

to·ma·to (tə·mā′tō, -mä′-) *n. pl.* **·toes 1.** The large, pulpy, edible berry, yellow or red when ripe, of a perennial plant (*Lycopersicon esculentum*) of the nightshade family, widely cultivated as a vegetable. **2.** The plant itself. **3.** *U.S. Slang* A girl or woman. [< Sp. *tomate* < Nahuatl *tomatl*]

tomb (tōōm) *n.* **1.** A place for the burial of the dead, as a vault or grave. **2.** Any place or structure serving as a final repository for the dead. **3.** A monument, tombstone, etc., commemorating the dead. **4.** Death: often preceded by *the.* — *v.t. Rare* To entomb; bury; inter. [< AF *tumbe*, OF *tombe* < LL *tumba* < Gk. *tymbos* mound]

tom·bac (tom′bak) *n.* Any of several alloys of copper and zinc, used to make gongs and bells or cheap jewelry: also called *tambac.* Also **tom′back, tom′bak.** [< F < Pg. < Malayan *tambāga* copper < Skt. *tāmraka*]

Tom·big·bee River (tom·big′bē) A river in NE Mississippi and SW Alabama, flowing 384 miles SE and south to the Alabama River, forming the Mobile River.

Tom·bouc·tou (tôṅ·bōōk·tōō′) The French name for TIMBUKTU.

tom·boy (tom′boi′) *n.* A girl who prefers boyish activities, dress, etc.; hoyden. [< TOM + BOY] — **tom′boy′ish** *adj.* — **tom′boy′ish·ness** *n.*

Tombs (tōōmz), **the** A former New York City prison; also, loosely, the prison that replaced it after 1948.

tomb·stone (tōōm′stōn′) *n.* A stone, usually inscribed, marking a place of burial.

Tomb·stone (tōōm′stōn) A city in SE Arizona; formerly the site of the richest gold mines in the State; pop. 1,241.

tom·cat (tom′kat′) *n.* A male cat. [after *Tom*, a male cat, hero of *The Life and Adventures of a Cat*, 1760]

tom·cod (tom′kod′) *n.* Any of several small edible fishes (genus *Microgadus*) allied to the cod; especially, the **Atlantic tomcod** (*M. tomcod*), common on the eastern coast of North America. [< TOM + COD]

Tom Col·lins (tom kol′inz) A drink consisting of gin, lemon or lime juice, sugar, and carbonated water.

Tom, Dick, and Har·ry (dik, har′ē) Any persons taken at random from the general public: used disparagingly, and often preceded by *every.*

tome (tōm) *n.* **1.** A volume; large book. **2.** One of a series of volumes. *Abbr. t.* [< MF < L *tomus* < Gk. *tomos* fragment, volume < *temnein* to cut]

-tome *combining form* A cutting instrument (of a specified kind): *microtome.* [< Gk. *tomos* a cutting < *temnein* to cut]

to·men·tose (tə·men′tōs, tō′men·tōs) *adj. Biol.* Covered with matted woolly hairs; flocculent. Also **to·men′tous** (-təs) [< L *tomentosus* < *tomentum* stuffing for cushions]

to·men·tum (tə·men′təm) *n. pl.* **·ta** (-tə) **1.** *Anat.* A network of small blood vessels of the pia mater and cerebral cortex. **2.** *Bot.* Pubescence composed of matted woolly hairs, as on leaves. [< L, stuffing for cushions]

tom·fool (tom′fōōl′) *n.* An idiotic or silly person. — *adj.* Very stupid or foolish. [after *Tom Fool*, a name formerly applied to mental defectives]

tom·fool·er·y (tom′fōōl′ər·ē) *n. pl.* **·er·ies 1.** Nonsensical or foolish behavior. **2.** Worthless or trivial stuff; frippery. Also **tom′fool′ish·ness** (-fōō′lish·nis).

Tom·ma·si·ni (tôm′mä·zē′nē), **Vicenzo**, 1880–1950, Italian composer.

tom·my (tom′ē) *n. pl.* **·mies** *Brit. Informal* **1.** A roll; a loaf or piece of bread. **2.** Provisions; food. **3.** *Often cap.* A Tommy Atkins; British soldier. — **soft tommy** *Naut.* Soft bread, as distinguished from hardtack. [after *Tommy*, diminutive of *Thomas*, a personal name]

Tommy At·kins (at′kinz) A British private of the regular army. [after *Thomas Atkins*, a name used on specimen forms in the official regulations of the British Army after 1815]

Tommy gun A Thompson submachine gun (which see). [< *Tommy*, dim. of *Thompson* + GUN]

tom·my·rot (tom′ē·rot′) *n. Informal* Utter nonsense; twaddle. [< *tommy*, ? < TOMFOOL + ROT (def. 6)]

to·mog·ra·phy (tō·mog′rə·fē) *n. Med.* X-ray photography of a predetermined plane of the body. [< Gk. *tomos* slice (< *temnein* to cut) + (PHOTO)GRAPHY]

to·mor·row (tə·môr′ō, -mor′ō) *adv.* On or for the next day after today. — *n.* **1.** The next day after today; the morrow. **2.** Some time in the future. Also **to·mor′row.** [ME *to morwen* < OE *tō morgenne* < *tō* to + *morgen* morning, morrow]

tom·pi·on (tom′pē·ən) See TAMPION.

Tomsk (tômsk) A city in the southern R.S.F.S.R., on the Tom; pop. 249,000 (1959).

Tom Thumb 1. In English folklore, the son of a plowman, who was no bigger than his father's thumb. **2.** A tiny person; midget.

Tom Thumb, General Stage name of **Charles Sherwood Strat·ton** (strat′ən), 1838–83, a midget exhibited by P. T. Barnum.

tom·tit (tom′tit′) *n.* Any of various small birds, as: **a** *Brit.* A tit or titmouse. **b** A chickadee or a wren. [< TOM + TIT¹]

tom-tom (tom′tom′) *n.* **1.** A drum of India, Africa, etc., variously shaped, and usually beaten with the hands. **2.** A percussion instrument of monotonous tone, sometimes used orchestrally for special effects. **3.** An instrument consisting of a metal disk sounded with a felt-covered hammer or stick; a Chinese gong: also called *tam-tam.* [< Hind. *tamtam*, imit. of the instrument's sound]

-tomy *combining form* **1.** *Surg.* A cutting of a (specified) part or tissue: *osteotomy.* **2.** A (specified) kind of cutting or division: *dichotomy.* [< Gk. *tomē* a cutting < *temnein* to cut]

ton¹ (tun) *n.* **1.** Any of several large measures of weight; especially: **a** The **short ton** of 2000 pounds avoirdupois, commonly used in the United States and Canada. **b** The **long** or **gross ton** of 2240 pounds, used in Great Britain. *Abbr. l.t., l.tn.* See table inside back cover. **2.** A unit for reckoning the displacement or weight of vessels, 35 cubic feet of sea water weighing about one long ton: called in full a **displacement ton**. **3.** A unit for reckoning the freight-carrying capacity of a ship, usually equivalent to 40 cubic feet of space but varying with the cargo: called in full a **freight ton** or **measurement ton**. **4.** A unit for reckoning the internal capacity of merchant vessels for purposes of registration, equivalent to 100 cubic feet or 2.8317 cubic meters: called in full a **register ton**. **5.** A metric ton (which see). *Abbr. t., tn.* [Var. of TUN; infl. in form by OF *tonne* cask]

ton² (tôṅ) *n. French* Tone; style; the prevailing fashion.

ton- Var. of TONO-.

-ton *suffix* Town: used in place names: *Charleston, Brockton.* [OE *-tun* < *tūn* town]

ton·al (tō′nəl) *adj.* Of or pertaining to tone or tonality. — **to′nal·ly** *adv.*

tonal center *Music* The tone of a chromatic scale corresponding in function to the tonic of a key.

to·nal·i·ty (tō·nal′ə·tē) *n. pl.* **·ties 1.** *Music* **a** The use of a system of tones so that one tone is the central or primary tone of the system. **b** Any particular arrangement of this type centering on a specific tone; key; mode: the *tonality* of G. Compare ATONALITY. **2.** The general color scheme or collective tones of a painting.

to-name (tōō′nām′) *n. Scot.* **1.** A special distinguishing name; nickname. **2.** A surname. [OE *tō-nama*]

Ton·a·wan·da (ton′ə·won′də) An unincorporated place in western New York, on the Niagara River; pop. 21,898.

tone (tōn) *n.* **1.** Sound in relation to quality, volume, duration, and pitch. **2.** A sound having a definite pitch. **3.** *Music* **a** The timbre or characteristic sound, of a voice, instrument, etc. **b** The interval between the first two degrees of a major scale; the sum of two semitones; a major second:

TOMAHAWKS
a Cree. *b* Fox.
c Omaha. *d* Osage.

also called *whole tone*. For illustration see INTERVAL. **4.** A predominating disposition; frame or condition of mind; mood. **5.** Characteristic style or tendency; tenor; quality. **6.** Style or distinction; elegance. **7.** Vocal inflection as expressive of feeling: a *tone* of pity. **8.** *Ling.* A musical intonation or modulation of the voice by which a word or phrase may be changed in meaning or function. **9.** *Phonet.* **a** The acoustical pitch, or change in pitch, of a phrase or sentence. **b** Special stress or pitch accent given to one syllable of a word, or to one of the words in a sentence or phrase. **10.** The prevailing impression of a picture, produced by effects of light and shadow, variations in color quality, etc. **11.** A shade, hue, tint, or degree of a particular color, or some slight modification of it: red with a purplish *tone*. **12.** *Photog.* The shade or color of a photographic positive picture; also, the color of a negative film. **13.** *Physiol.* The general condition of the body with reference to the vigorous and healthy discharge of its functions. **b** Firmness and resilience, as of a tissue. — **Syn.** See SOUND¹. — *v.* **toned, ton·ing** *v.t.* **1.** To give tone to. **2.** To modify in tone. **3.** To alter the color or increase the brilliancy of (a photographic print) by a chemical bath. **4.** *Rare* To speak, sing, or sound monotonously; intone. — *v.i.* **5.** To assume a certain tone or hue. **6.** To blend or harmonize, as in tone or shade. — **to tone down 1.** To subdue the tone of (a painting). **2.** To moderate in quality or tone. — **to tone up 1.** To raise in quality or strength. **2.** To gain in vitality. [< OF *ton* < L *tonus* < Gk. *tonos* pitch of voice, a stretching < *teinein* to stretch] — **ton'er** *n.*

Tone (tōn), **Wolfe**, 1763–98, Irish patriot and revolutionist: full name **Theobald Wolfe Tone**.

tone arm The part of a record player that contains the cartridge at one end and is pivoted at the other.

tone color The timbre of a voice, musical instrument, etc.

tone-deaf (tōn'def') *adj.* Unable to perceive fine distinctions in pitch, as musical intervals. — **tone'deaf'ness** *n.*

tone·less (tōn'lis) *adj.* **1.** Having no tone; without tone. **2.** Lacking spirit or vivacity; listless. — **tone'less·ly** *adv.* — **tone'less·ness** *n.*

tone poem A symphonic poem (which see).

tone row *Music* An arrangement of tones, especially the tones of a chromatic scale, in a specific succession, from which an entire composition is derived by permutation, inversion, retroversion, and transposition. Also **tone series.**

to·net·ic (tō-net'ik) *adj. Ling.* Tonic. [< TONE + (PHON)-ETIC]

tong¹ (tông, tong) *v.t.* **1.** To gather, collect, or seize with tongs. — *v.i.* **2.** To use tongs, as for fishing. [< TONGS]

tong² (tông, tong) *n.* A Chinese secret society or fraternal association; especially, such a group formerly active in the United States. [< Chinese *t'ang* hall, meeting place]

ton·ga (tong'gə) *n. Anglo-Indian* A light two-wheeled cart used in the country districts of India. [< Hind. *tāngā*]

Ton·ga (tong'gə) *n.* A Polynesian language spoken in the Tonga Islands.

Ton·ga (tong'gə) An island group SE of the Fiji Islands, comprising a Polynesian kingdom of the Commonwealth of Nations; about 270 sq. mi.; pop. 77,429 (est. 1966); capital, Nukualofa: also *Friendly Islands.*

tongs (tôngz, tongz) *n.pl.* (*sometimes construed as sing.*) An implement for grasping, holding, or lifting objects, consisting usually of a pair of pivoted levers: sometimes called a **pair of tongs.** [OE *tang, tange*]

TONGS
a,b,c,d Blacksmith's.
e Rail. *f* Ice.

tongue (tung) *n.* **1.** A protrusile, freely moving organ situated in the mouth of most vertebrates, highly developed in mammals, where it serves as an organ of taste, and in man also as an organ of speech. ◆ Collateral adjective: *lingual.* For illustration see THROAT. **2.** *Zool.* An analogous organ or part of the mouth of various insects, fishes, etc. **3.** An animal's tongue, as of beef, prepared as food. **4.** The power of speech or articulation: to lose one's *tongue.* **5.** Manner or style of speaking: a smooth *tongue.* **6.** Mere speech, as contrasted with fact or deed. **7.** Utterance. **8.** A language, vernacular, or dialect. **9.** *Archaic* A people or race, regarded as having its own language: a Biblical use. **10.** Anything resembling an animal tongue in appearance, shape, or function. **11.** A slender projection of land, as a cape or small promontory. **12.** A long narrow bay or inlet of water. **13.** A jet of flame. **14.** A strip of leather for closing the gap in the front of a shoe. For illustration see SHOE. **15.** The fastening pin of a brooch or buckle. **16.** *Music* The free or vibrating end of a reed in a wind instrument. **17.** The clapper of a bell. **18.** The harnessing pole of a horse-drawn vehicle. **19.** A pointed, movable rail in a street railway switch. **20.** Any flange or projecting part of a machine or mechanical device. **21.** A projecting edge or tenon of a board for insertion into a corresponding groove of another board, thus forming a **tongue-and-groove joint.** **22.** The movable arm of a bevel. — **on the tip of one's tongue** On the verge of being recalled. — **speaking with tongues** Glossolalia. — **to hold one's tongue** To keep silent. — **(with) tongue in cheek** With ironical or facetious intent. — *v.* **tongued, tongu·ing** *v.t.*

1. *Music* In wind-instrument playing: **a** To separate the tones played on (an instrument) by means of the tongue. **b** To begin (a tone) using the tongue. **c** To tongue the notes of (a phrase, etc.). **2.** To touch or lap with the tongue. **3.** In carpentry: **a** To cut a tongue on (a board). **b** To join or fit by a tongue-and-groove joint. **4.** *Poetic* To utter; articulate. **5.** *Archaic* To reproach; chide. — *v.i.* **6.** To use the tongue in playing a wind instrument. **7.** To talk or prattle. **8.** To extend as a tongue. [OE *tunge.* Akin to LANGUAGE.]

tongue-and-groove joint (tung'ən-grōōv') See under TONGUE.

tongued (tungd) *adj.* **1.** Having a tongue or tongues. **2.** Having or characterized by a (specified kind of) tongue or (a specified number of) tongues: used in combination: *sharp-tongued.*

tongue-lash (tung'lash') *v.t. & v.i.* *Informal* To scold severely. [Back formation < TONGUE-LASHING]

tongue-lash·ing (tung'lash'ing) *n. Informal* A severe or thoroughgoing reprimand; scolding.

tongue·less (tung'lis) *adj.* **1.** Having no tongue. **2.** Speechless; dumb.

tongue-tie (tung'tī') *n.* Abnormal shortness of the frenum of the tongue, whereby its motion is impeded or confined. — *v.t.* **-tied, -ty·ing** To deprive of speech or the power of speech, or of distinct articulation.

tongue-tied (tung'tīd') *adj.* **1.** Speechless or halting in speech, as from shyness, etc. **2.** Impeded by tongue-tie.

tongue twister A word or phrase difficult to articulate quickly, as "Miss Smith's fish-sauce shop."

TONGUE-AND-GROOVE JOINT

ton·ic (ton'ik) *adj.* **1.** Having power to invigorate or build up; bracing. **2.** Pertaining to tone or tones. **3.** *Music* Pertaining to or in the key of the keynote. **4.** In art, denoting the general effect of color or of light and shade. **5.** *Physiol.* **a** Of or pertaining to tension, especially muscular tension. **b** Rigid; unrelaxing: *tonic* spasm. **6.** *Ling.* **a** Of or pertaining to musical intonations or modulations of words, sentences, etc. **b** Designating languages that distinguish words of identical or very similar form by variations in tone or pitch, as Chinese: also *tonetic.* **7.** *Phonet.* **a** Stressed, as a syllable. **b** *Obs.* Voiced. — *n.* **1.** A medicine that gradually restores the normal tone of organs from a condition of debility. **2.** Something imparting animation, vigor, or tone. **3.** *Music* The basic tone of a key or mode; keynote. **4.** Quinine water: gin and *tonic.* **5.** *U.S.* In the Boston area, soda (def. 2). [< Gk. *tonikos* < *tonos* sound, tone]

tonic accent 1. An accent that is spoken or pronounced rather than written. **2.** *Phonet.* Pitch accent (which see).

to·nic·i·ty (tō-nis'ə-tē) *n.* The resilience and elasticity of healthy muscles, arteries, and other bodily tissues: also called *tonus.*

tonic sol-fa A system of musical notation and teaching, especially for the voice, that uses the initial letters of the solmization syllables to indicate the tones of a major scale, and symbols consisting of dots and lines to indicate rhythm.

to·night (tə-nīt') *adv.* **1.** In or during the present or coming night. **2.** *Obs.* Last night. — *n.* **1.** The night that follows this day. **2.** The present night. Also **to-night'.** [OE *tō niht* < *tō* to + *niht* night]

ton·ka bean (tong'kə) **1.** The fragrant seed of a tropical American tree (*Dipteryx* or *Coumarouna odorata*), used as a substitute for vanilla, flavoring tobacco, etc. **2.** The tree from which it is obtained. Also called *coumarou.* [Prob. < Negro name for the bean in Guiana]

Ton·kin (ton'kin, tong'-) A former independent kingdom, later a French protectorate, in North Vietnam. Also **Tong'king, Ton'king** (-king). — **Ton·kin·ese** (ton'kin-ēz', tong'-) *adj. & n.*

Tonkin, Gulf of An inlet of the South China Sea between North Vietnam and Hainan island and the Luichow Peninsula.

Ton·le Sap (ton'lā sap) A lake in central Cambodia; about 1,000 sq. mi.: French *Grand Lac.*

ton·nage (tun'ij) *n.* **1.** The cubic capacity of a merchant vessel expressed in tons of 100 cubic feet each. **2.** The total carrying capacity of a collection of vessels, especially of a country's merchant marine. **3.** A tax levied on vessels at a given rate per ton. **4.** Total weight in tons, as of materials produced, mined, or transported. Also spelled *tunnage.* [< OF < *tonne* ton, tun]

ton·neau (tu-nō') *n.* *pl.* **·neaus** (-nōz') or **·neaux** (-nōz') The rear part of an early type of automobile or vehicle, with seats enclosed by low sides; also, the whole body of an automobile having such a rear part. [< F, lit., barrel]

tono- *combining form* **1.** Tension; pressure: *tonometer* (def. 1). **2.** *Music* Tone; pitch: *tonometer* (def. 2). Also, before vowels, *ton-.* [< Gk. *tonos* tension < *teinein* to stretch]

ton·o·graph (ton'ə-graf, -gräf, tō'nə-) *n.* A recording tonometer. [< TONO- + GRAPH]

to·nom·e·ter (tō-nom'ə-tər) *n.* **1.** An instrument for measuring stresses within a liquid. **2.** An accurately pitched tuning fork or set of forks. **3.** An instrument for determining the pitch of a tone. **4.** *Med.* An instrument for measuring tension in the eyeball or varying pressure of the blood. — **ton·o·met·ric** (ton/ə·met/rik, tō/nə-) *adj.* — **to·nom'e·try** (-ə·trē) *n.*

ton·sil (ton/səl) *n. Anat.* One of two oval lymphoid organs situated on either side of the passage from the mouth to the pharynx. For illustration see THROAT. [< L *tonsillae* tonsils] — **ton'sil·lar** or **ton'sil·ar** *adj.*

ton·sil·lec·to·my (ton/sə·lek/tə·mē) *n. pl.* **·mies** *Surg.* Removal of a tonsil or tonsils. [< TONSIL + -ECTOMY]

ton·sil·li·tis (ton/sə·lī/tis) *n. Pathol.* Inflammation of the tonsils. — **ton'sil·lit'ic** (-lit/ik) *adj.*

ton·sil·lot·o·my (ton/sə·lot/ə·mē) *n. pl.* **·mies** *Surg.* The operation of cutting away all or part of the tonsils. [< TONSIL + -TOMY]

ton·so·ri·al (ton·sôr/ē·əl, -sō/rē-) *adj.* Pertaining to a barber or to barbering: chiefly used in the humorous expression **tonsorial artist**, a barber. [< L *tonsorius* < *tonsor, -oris* barber < *tonsus,* pp. of *tondere* to shear, clip]

ton·sure (ton/shər) *n.* 1. The shaving of the head, or of the crown of the head, as of a priest or monk. 2. The state of being thus shaven. 3. The part of a priest's or monk's head left bare by shaving. — *v.t.* **·sured, ·sur·ing** To shave the head of. [< OF < L *tonsura* a shearing < *tonsus.* See TONSORIAL.]

ton·tine (ton/tēn, ton·tēn/) *n.* 1. A form of collective life annuity, the individual profits of which increase as the number of survivors diminishes, the final survivor taking the whole. 2. The subscribers to such an annuity, collectively. 3. The share of a single subscriber. 4. Any similar insurance plan. [< F, after Lorenzo *Tonti,* a Neapolitan banker who introduced it into France in about 1653]

to·nus (tō/nəs) *n. Physiol.* 1. The ability of a muscle to contract in response to a stimulus. 2. A condition of prolonged muscular spasm. 3. Tonicity. [< L, tone]

ton·y (tō/nē) *adj.* **ton·i·er, ton·i·est** *Informal* High-toned; fashionable; stylish. [< TONE (def. 6)]

To·ny (tō/nē) *n. pl.* **·nys** Any of several annual awards given in the United States during outstanding performances in the theater. [after nickname of *Antoinette Perry,* died 1946, U.S. actress]

too (tōō) *adv.* 1. In addition; likewise; also: beautiful and good *too.* 2. In excessive quantity or degree; more than sufficiently: *too* long and *too* technical. 3. *Informal* Very; extremely: That's not *too* likely. 4. *Informal* Indeed: an intensive, often used to reiterate a contradicted statement: You are *too* going! [Stressed var. of OE *tō* to]

took (tōōk) Past tense of TAKE.

Tooke (tōōk), **(John)** Horne, 1736–1812, English politician and philologist.

tool (tōōl) *n.* 1. A simple mechanism or implement, as a hammer, saw, spade, or chisel, used chiefly in manual work. 2. A power-driven apparatus, as a lathe, used for cutting and shaping the parts of a machine. 3. The cutting or shaping part of such an apparatus. 4. A bookbinder's hand stamp used in lettering or ornamenting book covers. 5. A person used to carry out the designs of others or another; a dupe. 6. Any instrument or means necessary to the efficient prosecution of one's profession or trade: Words are the writer's *tools.* — *v.t.* 1. To shape, mark, or ornament with a tool. 2. To provide with tools. 3. *Informal* To drive, as an automobile, or convey (a person) by driving. 4. To ornament or impress designs upon (leather, a book binding, etc.) with a roller bearing a pattern. — *v.i.* 5. To work with a tool or tools. 6. *Informal* To drive or travel in a vehicle. [OE *tōl*] — **tool'er** *n.*

— **Syn.** (noun) 1. *Tool, instrument, implement,* and *utensil* denote mechanical and other devices for doing work. Anything operated by hand may properly be called a *tool;* we speak of the *tools* of carpenters, masons, sculptors, mechanics, and other artisans. That part of a machine used directly for cutting, shaping, drilling, etc., is also called a *tool.* Delicate *tools,* such as those used by a dentist or surgeon, are called *instruments.* An *implement* is anything designed to effect a purpose. The word is less specific than *tool,* though they are often interchangeable: gardening *implements* (or *tools*), a plumber's *tools* (but not *implements*). *Utensil,* originally anything having utility, is now largely restricted to vessels or containers: cooking *utensils,* the *utensils* of a religious ceremony. Compare MACHINE. 5. pawn, puppet.

tool·ing (tōō/ling) *n.* 1. Ornamentation or work done with tools; especially, stamped or gilded ornamental designs on leather. 2. The application of a tool or tools to any work.

tool·mak·er (tōōl/mā/kər) *n.* A maker of tools.

toom (tōōm) *adj. Scot. & Brit. Dial.* Empty; void; futile. [OE *tōm*]

Toombs (tōōmz), **Robert Augustus,** 1810–85, U.S. legislator and Confederate general.

toon[1] (tōōn) *n.* 1. The fine, close-grained red wood of an East Indian tree (*Toona ciliata*), used for furniture, etc. 2. The tree itself. [< Hind. *tun, tūn* < Skt. *tunna*]

toon[2] (tōōn) *n. Scot.* Hamlet; town.

toot (tōōt) *v.i.* 1. To blow a horn, whistle, etc., especially with short blasts. 2. To give forth a blast or toot, as a horn.

3. To make a similar sound. — *v.t.* 4. To sound (a horn, etc.) with short blasts. 5. To sound (a blast, etc.). — *n.* 1. A short note or blast on or as on a horn. 2. *Slang* A spree; especially, a drinking spree. [? < MLG *tüten;* prob. orig. imit.] — **toot'er** *n.*

tooth (tōōth) *n. pl.* **teeth** (tēth) 1. One of the hard structures in the mouth of most vertebrates, used for seizing and chewing food, as offensive and defensive weapons, etc., and consisting chiefly of dentine covered on the outer surface and on the crown with enamel, and a root leading into a pulp cavity richly supplied with blood vessels and nerves. ◆ Collateral adjective: *dental.* 2. One of various hard calcareous

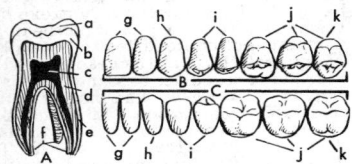

TEETH OF ADULT HUMAN
A Section of a molar: *a* Crown, *b* Enamel, *c* Pulp cavity, *d* Dentine, *e* Cementum, *f* Roots.
B and *C* Left upper and lower jaws: *g* Incisors, *h* Canines, *i* Bicuspids, *j* Molars, *k* Wisdom teeth.

or chitinous bodies of the oral or gastric regions of invertebrates. 3. Any small toothlike projection, as at the edge of a leaf. 4. Something resembling a tooth in form or use; especially, a projecting point, tine, or cog, as on a saw, comb, fork, rake, or gearwheel. 5. Appetite; liking: used chiefly in the expression *sweet tooth* (which see). 6. *pl.* Something that opposes in or as in a gnawing, biting, or piercing manner: the *teeth* of the wind. 7. *pl.* Means of enforcement: to put *teeth* into a law. 8. *Zool.* A process near the hinge of a bivalve shell. 9. The coarseness and irregularity of grain in the surface of some papers. — **armed to the teeth** Completely or heavily armed. — **in the teeth of** Directly against, counter to, or in defiance of. — **to get one's teeth into** To achieve a solid grip or grasp of; engage completely with. — **to put teeth into** To provide (something) with strength or power. — **to show one's teeth** To display a disposition to fight; threaten. — **to throw (cast, fling,** etc.**) (something) in one's teeth** To fling at one, as a challenge or taunt. — *v.t.* 1. To supply with teeth, as a rake or saw. 2. To give a serrated edge to; indent. — *v.i.* 3. To become interlocked, as gearwheels. [OE *tōth*]

tooth·ache (tōōth/āk/) *n.* Pain in a tooth or teeth, or in the nearby region of the jaw.

tooth and nail With all possible strength and effort; fiercely: to fight *tooth and nail.*

tooth·brush (tōōth/brush/) *n.* A small brush used for cleaning the teeth.

toothed (tōōtht, tōōthd) *adj.* 1. Having teeth. 2. Having or characterized by a (specified kind or number of) teeth: used in combination: *sharp-toothed.* 3. Notched or indented.

tooth·less (tōōth/lis) *adj.* 1. Being without teeth. 2. Lacking effective power or force; ineffectual. — **tooth'less·ly** *adv.* — **tooth'less·ness** *n.*

tooth·paste (tōōth/pāst/) *n.* A paste used in cleaning the teeth.

tooth·pick (tōōth/pik/) *n.* 1. A small sliver of wood, plastic, etc., used for removing particles of food from between the teeth. 2. *U.S. Slang* A bowie knife: sometimes **Arkansas toothpick.**

tooth·pow·der (tōōth/pou/dər) *n.* A powder used in cleaning the teeth.

tooth rash Strophulus.

tooth·shell (tōōth/shel/) *n.* A burrowing mollusk (genus *Dentalium*), having a long, very slender tubular shell.

tooth·some (tōōth/səm) *adj.* 1. Having a pleasant taste. 2. Appetizing; attractive. — **tooth'some·ly** *adv.* — **tooth'some·ness** *n.*

tooth·wort (tōōth/wûrt/) *n.* 1. Any of a genus (*Dentaria*) of herbs of the mustard family, with compound dentate leaves and white or purplish flowers. 2. Any of a genus (*Lathraea*) of small, parasitic plants having rootstocks covered with white scales.

tooth·y (tōō/thē) *adj.* **tooth·i·er, tooth·i·est** 1. Having large or prominent teeth. 2. Displaying the teeth: a *toothy* smile.

too·tle (tōōt/l) *v.t. & v.i.* **·tled, ·tling** To toot lightly or continuously, as on the flute. — *n.* The act or sound of tootling. [Freq. of TOOT]

toots (tōōts) *n. U.S. Slang* A woman or girl: used chiefly as a term of address. Also **toot'sie** (-sē). [Origin uncertain]

toot·sy (tōōt/sē) *n. pl.* **·sies** *Slang* The foot of a child or woman: an endearing or humorous term. Also **toot'sy-woot'sy** (-wōōt/sē). [Child's term for a foot]

top[1] (top) *n.* 1. The uppermost or highest part, end, side, or surface of anything. 2. The end or part regarded as the higher or upper extremity: the *top* of the street. 3. A lid or cover: a bottle *top.* 4. *U.S.* The roof of a vehicle, as an automobile. 5. The crown of the head: from *top* to toe. 6. *pl.*

The aboveground part of a plant producing root vegetables. **7.** The highest degree or range: the *top* of one's ambition. **8.** The highest or most prominent place or rank: at the *top* of one's profession. **9.** One who is highest in rank or position. **10.** The highest or loudest pitch: at the *top* of his voice. **11.** The choicest or best part: the *top* of the crop. **12.** In bridge, etc., the highest card in a suit. **13.** In billiards, tennis, golf, etc.: **a** A stroke in which the player hits the ball above the center or on the upper half. **b** The forward spinning motion imparted to the ball by such a stroke. **14.** *Naut.* A platform at the head of the lower section of a ship's mast, used as a place to stand and for extending the topmast rigging. **15.** *Chem.* The most volatile part of a substance undergoing distillation. **16.** *Dial.* A tuft, as of hair, on the crown of the head; topknot. — **to blow one's top** *Slang* **1.** To break out in a rage; flare up. **2.** To go insane. — **on top 1.** At the highest point or position. **2.** In a situation of dominance or power. **3.** Highly successful. — **on top of 1.** On the highest point or upper surface of. **2.** Resting or pressing upon from above. **3.** In addition to; as a climax to. **4.** Coming closely upon; very near. — **over the top 1.** In trench warfare, over the breastwork, as in an attack. **2.** Beyond a set goal, quota, etc. — *adj.* **1.** Of or pertaining to the top. **2.** Forming or comprising the top or upper part. **3.** Highest in rank or quality; chief: *top* authors. **4.** Greatest in amount or degree: *top* prices. — *v.* **topped, top·ping** *v.t.* **1.** To remove the top or upper end of. **2.** To provide with a top, cap, etc. **3.** To form the top of. **4.** To reach or pass over the top of; surmount. **5.** To surpass or exceed. **6.** *Chem.* To take away the most volatile part of by distillation. **7.** In golf, tennis, etc.: **a** To hit the upper part of (the ball) in making a stroke. **b** To make (a stroke) thus. — *v.i.* **8.** To top someone or something. — **to top off 1.** To put something on the top of. **2.** To complete or finish with a final or crowning touch. — **to top out** *Archit.* To place the framework for the top story on (a building, etc.). [OE]

top² (top) *n.* A toy of wood, metal, etc., with a point on which it is made to spin, as by the unwinding of a string, spring, etc. [OE]

top- Var. of TOPO-.

top. Topographical; topography.

to·paz (tō′paz) *n.* **1.** A native fluosilicate of aluminum, occurring in prismatic crystals of various colors, but chiefly yellow to brownish, that are valued as gemstones. **2.** A yellow variety of sapphire. Also **Oriental topaz. 3.** Loosely, citrine (def. 2). **4.** Either of two large tropical American hummingbirds (*Topaza pyra* and *T. pella*) with brilliant plumage. **5.** A brownish or grayish yellow. [< OF *topaze*, *topace* < L *topazus* < Gk. *topazos*]

to·paz·o·lite (tō·paz′ə·līt) *n.* A yellow or sometimes green variety of andradite garnet. [< Gk. *topazos* topaz + -LITE]

top banana *U.S. Slang* **1.** The chief comedian in a burlesque show. **2.** Any leader; top dog. [Origin uncertain]

top boot A boot with a high top that is sometimes bordered or decorated with material different from the rest of the boot.

top·coat (top′kōt′) *n.* A lightweight overcoat.

top dog *Informal* The leading or dominant individual or group; the head; chief. [from the upper position of the victor in a dogfight] — **top-dog** (top′dôg′, -dog′) *adj.*

top-drawer (top′drôr′) *adj. Informal* Of the highest standing, merit, excellence, etc.

top-dress (top′dres′) *v.t. Agric.* To apply top-dressing to (a field, soil, etc.).

top-dress·ing (top′dres′ing) *n.* A dressing of manure spread over the surface of a field. Also **top′dress′ing, top dressing.**

tope¹ (tōp) *v.t.* **toped, top·ing** To drink (alcoholic beverages) excessively and frequently. [? Akin to earlier *top* to tilt, turn over]

tope² (tōp) *n.* A small European shark or dogfish (genus *Galeorhinus*). [? < dial. E (Cornish); ult. origin unknown]

tope³ (tōp) *n.* *Anglo-Indian* A grove, especially a mango grove. [< Tamil *tōppu*]

tope⁴ (tōp) *n.* *Anglo-Indian* A round, dome-shaped Buddhist shrine: also called *stupa*. [< Hind. *top*, prob. < Pali *thūpo* < Skt. *stūpa*]

to·pec·to·my (tō·pek′tə·mē, tə-) *n. pl.* **·mies** *Surg.* An operation in which certain prefrontal cortical areas of the brain are removed. [< TOP(O)- + -ECTOMY]

to·pee (tō·pē′, tō′pē) See TOPI.

To·pe·ka (tə·pē′kə) The capital of Kansas, in the NE part, on the Kansas River; pop. 125,016.

top·er (tō′pər) *n.* A habitual drunkard; sot. [< TOPE¹]

top-flight (top′flīt′) *adj.* Of the highest quality; outstanding; superior.

top·full (top′fool′) *adj. Rare* Brimful.

top·gal·lant (tə·gal′ənt, top′gal′ənt) *n. Naut.* **1.** The mast, sail, yard, or rigging immediately above the topmast and topsail. For illustration see SHIP. **2.** The parts of a deck that are higher than the rest. — *adj.* Pertaining to the topgallants. [< TOP¹ + GALLANT; with ref. to "making a gallant show" compared with the lower tops]

toph (tōf) *n.* Tufa. Also **tophe.** [< L *tophus, tofus*]

top-ham·per (top′ham′pər) *n. Naut.* **1.** Spars and rigging

usually kept aloft. **2.** The light upper sails and rigging. **3.** Casks, cables, rigging, etc., encumbering the deck. Also **top hamper.** [< TOP¹ + HAMPER¹, n.] — **top′-ham′pered** *adj.*

top hat A man's hat, usually of silk, having a tall, cylindrical crown and a narrow brim: also called *high hat*.

top-heav·y (top′hev′ē) *adj.* **-heav·i·er, -heav·i·est 1.** Having the top or upper part too heavy for the lower part; ill-proportioned or precariously balanced. **2.** In finance, overcapitalized. — **top′-heav′i·ly** *adv.* — **top′-heav′i·ness** *n.*

To·phet (tō′fet) *n.* **1.** In the Old Testament, a place near Jerusalem, where children were said to be sacrificed to Moloch. **2.** A place of endless perdition; hell. Also **To′pheth** (-fet). [< Hebrew *tōpheth*, ? altar]

top-hole (top′hōl′) *adj. Brit. Slang* First-rate; excellent.

to·phus (tō′fəs) *n. pl.* **·phi** (-fī) **1.** *Pathol.* A deposit of urates around and at the surface of joints in persons affected with gout: also called *chalkstone*. **2.** *Mineral.* Any natural calcareous tufa. [< L, tufa]

to·pi (tō·pē′, tō′pē) *n.* A light helmet made of pith, worn as protection against the sun: also called *pith helmet*: also spelled *topee*. [< Hind., hat]

to·pi·ar·y (tō′pē·er′ē) *adj.* Denoting or characterized by the cutting or arranging of shrubs, trees, etc., in fantastic or conventionalized shapes, as in gardening, etc. — *n. pl.* **·ar·ies** A topiary garden. [< L *topiarius* < *topia opera* ornamental gardening < Gk. *topion*, dim. of *topos* place]

top·ic (top′ik) *n.* **1.** A subject of discourse or of a treatise. **2.** Any matter treated of in speech or writing; a theme for discussion. **3.** A subdivision of an outline or a treatise. **4.** *pl.* In rhetorical invention, the part that treats of the selection and arrangement of the proofs; also, the places or classes in which the various kinds of proofs are to be found. [< L *topica* < Gk. *(ta) topika*, lit., (matters) concerning commonplaces, title of a work by Aristotle, neut. pl. of *topikos* of a place < *topos* place, commonplace]

— **Syn. 1.** *Topic, subject,* and *theme* denote the principal matter discussed in a discourse. A *topic* is generally narrow and concrete; a *subject* is broader and often not so sharply defined: the *topic* of his lecture was the lemurs of Madagascar, the *subject* of this book is the American Revolution. A subordinate head under a *subject* is also often called a *topic*: to enlarge on this *topic* would carry me too far from my *subject*. *Theme* is often interchanged with *subject*, but sometimes is used to denote the central idea or purpose that unifies a discursive *subject*: the vicissitudes of a young English boy form the *subject* of *Oliver Twist*; its *theme* is the deficiencies of the English school system.

top·i·cal (top′i·kəl) *adj.* **1.** Pertaining to a topic. **2.** Of the nature of merely probable argument. **3.** Belonging to a place or spot; local. **4.** Pertaining to matters of present interest: a *topical* song. **5.** *Med.* Local. — **top′i·cal·ly** *adv.*

top kick *Slang* A top sergeant.

top·knot (top′not′) *n.* **1.** A crest, tuft, or knot on the top of the head, as of feathers on the head of a bird. **2.** The hair of the human head when worn as a high knot. **3.** A knot or bow worn by women as a headdress, etc.

top·less (top′lis) *adj.* **1.** Lacking a top. **2.** Nude from the waist up, or characterized by such nudity. **3.** Being without a covering for the breasts: a *topless* bathing suit. **4.** *Archaic* So high that no top can be seen. — **top′less·ness** *n.*

top·loft·y (top′lôf′tē, -lof′tē) *adj.* **·loft·i·er, ·loft·i·est 1.** Towering very high. **2.** Very proud or haughty; inflated; pompous. — **top′loft′i·ly** *adv.* — **top′loft′i·ness** *n.*

top·mast (top′məst, top′mast′, -mäst′) *n. Naut.* The mast next above the lower mast.

top·min·now (top′min′ō) *n.* **1.** Any of a family (Poeciliidae) of small, live-bearing fishes that feed near the surface of the water; especially, *Gambusia affinis*, widely used to combat mosquitoes. **2.** One of several related egg-laying fishes (family Cyprinodontidae), as the killifish. Also **top minnow.**

top·most (top′mōst′) *adj.* Being at the very top.

top·notch (top′noch′) *adj. Informal* Excellent; best. — **top′notch′er** *n.*

topo- *combining form* A place or region; regional: *topography*. Also, before vowels, *top-*. [< Gk. *topos* place]

topog. Topographical; topography.

to·pog·ra·pher (tə·pog′rə·fər) *n.* An expert in topography.

to·pog·ra·phy (tə·pog′rə·fē) *n. pl.* **·phies 1.** The detailed description of places. **2.** The art of representing on a map the physical features of a place. **3.** The physical features, collectively, of a region. **4.** Surveying with reference to the physical features of a region. Abbr. *top., topog.* [< TOPO- + -GRAPHY] — **top·o·graph·ic** (top′ə·graf′ik) or **·i·cal** *adj.* — **top′o·graph′i·cal·ly** *adv.*

to·pol·o·gy (tə·pol′ə·jē) *n.* **1.** *Math.* The study of those properties of geometric figures or solid bodies that remain invariant under certain transformations: also called *analysis situs*. **2.** *Med.* The relation between the forward part of the fetus and the birth canal. [< TOPO- + -LOGY] — **top·o·log·ic** (top′ə·loj′ik) or **·i·cal** *adj.*

top·o·nym (top′ə·nim) *n.* **1.** The name of a place. **2.** Any name derived from the name of a place. [< TOPO- + Gk. *onoma, onyma* name] — **top′o·nym′ic** or **·i·cal** *adj.*

to·pon·y·my (tə·pon′ə·mē) *n. pl.* **·mies 1.** The nomenclature of anatomical regions. **2.** The science or study of place names; also, a register of place names.

top·o·type (top'ə·tīp) *n. Biol.* A plant or animal selected from the locality typical of the species. [< TOPO- + TYPE]

top·per (top'ər) *n.* **1.** One who or that which cuts off the top of something. **2.** A woman's short, lightweight, outer coat. **3.** *Slang* One who or that which is of supreme quality. **4.** *Slang* A top hat.

top·ping (top'ing) *adj.* **1.** Towering high above. **2.** Outstanding; eminent; distinguished. **3.** *Brit. Informal* Excellent; first-rate. **—** *n.* **1.** The act of one who or that which tops. **2.** That which forms the top of anything. **3.** A sauce, garnish, etc., put on a cake, portion of food, etc.

top·ple (top'əl) *v.* **·pled, ·pling** *v.t.* **1.** To push and cause to totter or fall by its own weight; overturn. **—** *v.i.* **2.** To totter and fall, as by its own weight. **3.** To lean or jut out, as if about to fall. [Freq. of TOP[1], *v.*]

tops (tops) *adj. Slang* Excellent; first-rate.

top·sail (top'səl, top'sāl') *n. Naut.* **1.** In a square-rigged vessel, a square sail set next above the lowest sail of a mast. For illustration see SHIP. **2.** In a fore-and-aft-rigged vessel, a square or triangular sail carried above the gaff of a lower sail.

top-se·cret (top'sē'krit) *adj. U.S. Mil.* Denoting the highest category of security classification. Compare SECRET, CONFIDENTIAL.

top sergeant *Informal* The first sergeant of a company, battery, or troop.

top·side (top'sīd') *n. Naut.* The portion of a ship above the main deck. **—** *adv.* To or on the upper parts of a ship.

top·soil (top'soil') *n.* The surface soil of land. **—** *v.t.* To remove the surface soil of (an area or region).

top·stone (top'stōn') *n.* A copestone (which see).

Top·sy (top'sē) In *Uncle Tom's Cabin*, a young Negro slave girl who, when questioned about her origins, replied that she had "just growed."

top·sy-tur·vy (top'sē-tûr'vē) *adv.* **1.** Upside-down; hind side before. **2.** In utter confusion. **—** *adj.* **1.** Being in an upset or disordered condition. **2.** Upside-down. **—** *n.* A state of confusion; disorder; chaos. [Earlier *topsy-tervy, topsy-tirvy,* prob. < TOP[1] + obs. *terve, tirve* to turn, overturn] **—** **top'sy-tur'vi·ly** *adv.* **—** **top'sy-tur'vi·ness** *n.* **—** **top'·sy·tur'vy·dom** (-dəm) *n.*

toque (tōk) *n.* **1.** A close-fitting, brimless hat worn by women. **2.** The tall conical headdress formerly worn by the doges of Venice. **3.** A plumed cap with a band and brim, worn in the 16th century. Also **to·quet** (tō·kā'). [< F, cap < Sp. *toca* < Basque *tauka,* a kind of cap]

tor (tôr) *n.* A high, rocky hill or jutting rock. [OE *torr*]

to·rah (tôr'ə, tō'rə) *n.* In Hebrew literature, a law; also, counsel or instruction proceeding from a specially sacred source. Also **to'ra.** [< Hebrew *tōrāh* instruction, law < *yārāh* to throw, show, instruct]

To·rah (tôr'ə, tō'rə) *n.* In Judaism, the Pentateuch: also called the *Law.*

tor·bern·ite (tôr'bərn·īt) *n.* A greenish, crystalline hydrous phosphate of uranium containing copper. [< G *torbernit, torberit* < NL *torbernus,* after *Torber* Bergmann, 18th c. Swedish chemist]

torc (tôrk) See TORQUE[2].

torch (tôrch) *n.* **1.** A source of light, as from flaming pine knots, or from some material dipped in tallow, oil, etc., and fixed at the end of a handle or pole. **2.** Anything that illuminates or brightens: the *torch* of science. **3.** A portable device giving off an intensely hot flame and used for burning off paint, melting solder, etc. **4.** *Brit.* A flashlight. **— to carry a** (or **the**) **torch for** *Slang* To continue to love (someone), though the love is unrequited. [< OF *torche,* ult. < L *torquere* to twist; so called because early torches were made of twisted tow dipped in pitch]

torch·bear·er (tôrch'bâr'ər) *n.* **1.** One who carries a torch. **2.** One who imparts knowledge, truth, etc. **3.** *Informal* One loud in his praise of a friend.

tor·chère (tôr·shâr') *n.* A tall electric lamp giving light directed upward by a bowllike shade of glass, metal, etc. [< F, candelabrum]

torch·light (tôrch'līt') *n.* The light of a torch or torches. **—** *adj.* Lighted by torches: a *torchlight* rally.

tor·chon lace (tôr'shon, *Fr.* tôr·shôn') **1.** A coarse, durable bobbin lace made of linen thread in simple geometrical designs. **2.** An imitation of this made by machine. [< F *torchon* dishcloth < *torcher* to wipe]

torch singer One who sings torch songs.

torch song A popular love song, slow and melancholy, expressing sadness and hopeless yearning. [< phrase *to carry a torch for.* See under TORCH.]

torch·wood (tôrch'wŏŏd') *n.* **1.** Any of a genus (*Amyris*) of tropical American shrubs and small trees, especially *A. balsamifera.* **2.** Its fragrant wood, that burns with a bright flame.

Tor·de·sil·las (tôr'thä·sē'lyäs) A village in NW Spain; scene of the signing of a treaty between Spain and Portugal setting the line of demarcation for colonial expansion, 1494.

tore[1] (tôr, tōr) Past tense of TEAR[1].

tore[2] (tôr, tōr) *n.* Torus (defs. 1 & 4). [< F *tore* < L *torus* torus]

tor·e·a·dor (tôr'ē·ə·dôr', *Sp.* tō'rā·ä·thôr') *n.* A bull-fighter. [< Sp. < *torear* to fight bulls < *toro* bull < L *taurus* bull]

toreador pants Close-fitting trousers extending to the middle of the calf, worn by women.

to·re·ro (tō·rā'rō) *n. pl.* **·ros** (-rōs) *Spanish* A bull-fighter, usually on foot.

to·reu·tics (tə·rōō'tiks) *n.pl.* (*construed as sing.*) The art of working in ornamental relief, especially in metal. [< Gk. *toreutikos* < *toreuein* to work in relief, bore] **—** **to·reu'tic** *adj.*

tor·ic (tôr'ik, tor'-) *adj.* Of, pertaining to, or resembling a torus.

toric lens *Optics* A lens in which one of the surfaces is a segment of a torus, used for eyeglasses.

to·ri·i (tôr'i·ē, tō'ri·ē) *n.* The gateway of a Shinto temple, consisting of two uprights with one straight crosspiece, and another above with a concave lintel. [< Japanese]

JAPANESE TORII

To·ri·no (tō·rē'nō) The Italian name for TURIN.

tor·ment (*n.* tôr'ment; *v.* tôr·ment') *n.* **1.** Intense bodily pain or mental anguish; agony; torture. **2.** One who or that which torments. **3.** The inflicting of torture. **4.** *Archaic* Any device for inflicting torture, as the rack; also, the torture inflicted. **5.** Hell. **—** *v.t.* **1.** To subject to excruciating physical or mental suffering. **2.** To make miserable; afflict or vex grievously. **3.** To harass or tease. **4.** To throw into violent agitation. [< AF *tourment,* OF *torment, tourment* < L *tormentum* rack, orig., a machine for hurling missiles by means of torsion < *torquere* to twist] **—** **tor·ment'ing·ly** *adv.*

tor·men·til (tôr'men·til) *n.* An Old World rosaceous herb (*Potentilla tormentilla*) with a powerful astringent root, used in medicine and in tanning: also called *bloodroot, redroot.* [< OF *tormentille* < Med.L *tormentilla,* dim. of L *tormentum* torment; so called because used as a pain killer]

tor·men·tor (tôr·men'tər) *n.* **1.** One who or that which torments. **2.** A movable panel of sound-insulating material for controlling the acoustics on a sound stage outside of the field of the camera. **3.** A movable piece of theater scenery at either side and back of the proscenium arch, used to mask sidelights and downstage entrances and exits. Also **tor·ment'er.**

torn (tôrn, tōrn) Past participle of TEAR[1].

tor·na·do (tôr·nā'dō) *n. pl.* **·does** or **·dos** *Meteorol.* **1.** A whirling wind of exceptional violence, accompanied by a pendulous, funnel-shaped cloud marking the narrow path of greatest destruction. **2.** A violent thunderstorm or squall of the west coast of Africa. **3.** Any whirlwind or hurricane. [Alter. of *ternado,* prob. alter. of Sp. *tronada* thunderstorm < *tronar* to thunder < L *tonare;* infl. in form by Sp. *tornar* to turn] **—** **tor·nad'ic** (-nad'ik) *adj.*

tornado lamp A hurricane lamp (which see).

to·roid (tôr'oid, tō'roid) *n.* **1.** *Geom.* **a** A surface generated by the rotation of any closed plane curve about an axis lying in its plane but external to it. **b** The solid produced by such a surface. **2.** *Electr.* An electromagnetic coil wound upon a ring of circular cross section. [< TOR(US) + -OID] **—** **to·roi'dal** *adj.*

To·ron·to (tə·ron'tō) The capital of Ontario, Canada, in the southern part on Lake Ontario; pop. 698,634.

To·ros Dağ·la·ri (tō·rōs' dä'lä·rē') The Turkish name for the TAURUS.

to·rose (tôr'ōs, tō'rōs, tō·rōs', tō-) *adj.* **1.** Having protuberances; knobby. **2.** *Bot.* Cylindrical and swollen at intervals. Also **to·rous** (tôr'əs, tō'rəs). [< L *torosus* < *torus* a swelling] **—** **to·ros·i·ty** (tō·ros'ə·tē) *n.*

tor·pe·do (tôr·pē'dō) *n. pl.* **·dos** or **·does** **1.** A device or apparatus containing an explosive to be fired by concussion or otherwise. **2.** An explosive, self-propelled, cigar-shaped underwater projectile, used to destroy enemy ships. **3.** A submarine mine. **4.** A cartridge placed on a railway track and exploded by the weight of a train passing over it, the report serving as a warning signal to the train crew. **5.** A cartridge exploded in an oil or gas well to start or increase the flow. **6.** A firework containing a mixture of gravel and fulminating powder wrapped in paper, exploded by being dashed against some hard surface. **7.** The electric ray, a fish. **—** *v.t.* **·doed, ·do·ing** **1.** To damage or sink (a vessel) with a torpedo or torpedoes. **2.** To damage or wreck as with a torpedo. [< L, stiffness, numbness < *torpere* to be numb]

torpedo boat A small, swift war vessel equipped with tubes for the discharge of torpedoes.

tor·pe·do-boat destroyer (tôr·pē'dō-bōt') A small warship, larger than a torpedo boat, originally built to destroy torpedo boats, but now used as a more powerful torpedo boat.

torpedo tube A tube in a war vessel through which torpedoes are launched.

tor·pid[1] (tôr′pid) *adj.* **1.** Inactive, as a hibernating animal. **2.** Dormant; numb. **3.** Sluggish; apathetic; dull. [< L *torpidus* < *torpere* to be numb] — **tor·pid·i·ty** (tôr·pid′ə·tē), **tor′pid·ness** *n.* — **tor′pid·ly** *adv.*

tor·pid[2] (tôr′pid) *n.* **1.** An eight-oared, clinker-built racing boat for the second crew at Oxford University; also, one of its crew. **2.** *pl.* The Lenten races in which such boats take part. [< TORPID[1]; so called because the second crew consisted of awkward or very young oarsmen]

tor·por (tôr′pər) *n.* **1.** Complete or partial insensibility; stupor. **2.** Apathy; torpidity. — **Syn.** See STUPOR. [< L *torpere* to be numb]

tor·po·rif·ic (tôr′pə·rif′ik) *adj.* Inducing torpor.

tor·quate (tôr′kwit, -kwāt) *adj. Zool.* Having a torque or ring, as of color, about the neck; collared. [< L *torquatus* having a collar < *torques*. See TORQUES.]

Tor·quay (tôr·kē′) A municipal borough and port in southern Devonshire, England; pop. 53,915 (1961).

torque[1] (tôrk) *n.* **1.** *Mech.* **a** Anything that causes or tends to cause torsion in a body; the moment of forces that causes rotation or twisting. **b** The rotary force in a mechanism. **c** The degree of smoothness in the conversion of reciprocating into rotary motion. **2.** *Optics* The rotatory effect upon the plane of polarized light produced by its passage through certain liquids and crystals. [< L *torquere* to twist]

torque[2] (tôrk) *n.* A necklace, armlet, or collar of wire, usually twisted, worn especially by ancient Gauls and Britons: also spelled *torc*. [< L *torques*. See TORQUES.]

Tor·que·ma·da (tôr′kwe·mä′də, *Sp.* tôr′kä·mä′thä), **Tomás de,** 1420?–98, Dominican monk; head of the Inquisition in Spain.

tor·ques (tôr′kwēz) *n. Zool.* A natural ring or collar, as of feathers or hair, on the neck of a bird or animal. [< NL < L, twisted collar < *torquere* to twist]

Tor·rance (tor′əns, tôr′-) A city in SW California, near Los Angeles; pop. 134,584.

tor·re·fy (tôr′ə·fī, tor′-) *v.t.* **·fied, ·fy·ing** To dry or roast by exposure to heat, as ores or drugs: also spelled *torrify*. [< MF *torréfier* < L *torrefacere* < *torrere* to dry, parch + *facere* to make] — **tor′re·fac′tion** (-fak′shən) *n.*

Tor·rens (tôr′ənz, tor′-), **Lake** A salt lake in SE central South Australia, often dry; 120 mi. long; 2,230 sq. mi.

tor·rent (tôr′ənt, tor′-) *n.* **1.** A stream of water flowing with great velocity or turbulence. **2.** Any similar stream, as of lava. **3.** Any abundant or tumultuous flow: a *torrent* of abuse. — *adj. Rare* Like a torrent. [< OF < L *torrens, -entis*, lit., boiling, burning, ppr. of *torrere* to parch]

tor·ren·tial (tô·ren′shəl, to-) *adj.* **1.** Of, resembling, or resulting from the action of a torrent or torrents. **2.** Suggestive of a torrent in rapidity and volume; outpouring; overpowering: *torrential* passion. — **tor·ren′tial·ly** *adv.*

Tor·re·ón (tôr′rā·ôn′) A city in Coahuila, northern Mexico; pop. 257,045 (1970).

Tor·res Strait (tôr′əs, -iz, tor′-) A strait between Australia and New Guinea; 95 mi. wide.

Tor·ri·cel·li (tôr′rē·chel′lē), **Evangelista,** 1608–47, Italian physicist; discovered the principle of the barometer. — **Tor·ri·cel·li·an** (tôr′i·sel′ē·ən, -chel′ē·ən) *adj.*

tor·rid (tôr′id, tor′-) *adj.* **1.** Exposed to or receiving the full force of the sun's heat, as certain tropical regions. **2.** Very hot; scorching; burning. **3.** Impassioned; ardent. [< L *torridus* < *torrere* to parch] — **tor·rid·i·ty** (tô·rid′ə·tē, to-), **tor′rid·ness** *n.* — **tor′rid·ly** *adv.*

Torrid Zone See under ZONE.

tor·ri·fy (tôr′ə·fī, tor′-) See TORREFY.

Tor·ring·ton (tôr′ing·tən, tor′-) A city in NW Connecticut; pop. 31,952.

tor·sade (tôr·sād′) *n.* **1.** A molded ornament resembling a twisted cable. **2.** A twisted cord for draperies. [< F < Med.L *torsus*, var. of L *tortus*, pp. of *torquere* to twist]

tor·si·bil·i·ty (tôr′sə·bil′ə·tē) *n.* Capacity for undergoing torsion, measured by the amount of torsion produced.

tor·sion (tôr′shən) *n.* **1.** The act of twisting, or the state of being twisted. **2.** *Mech.* Deformation of a body, as a thread or rod, by twisting around its length as an axis. **3.** The force with which a twisted cord or cable tends to return to its former position. — **Syn.** See STRESS. [< OF < LL *torsio, -onis*, var. of L *tortio, -onis* < *tortus*, pp. of *torquere* to twist] — **tor′sion·al** *adj.* — **tor′sion·al·ly** *adv.*

torsion balance An instrument for determining very minute rotational forces by measuring the angle through which a pointer arm turns before an equal and opposite force acts upon the supporting wire or filament.

torsk (tôrsk) *n. pl.* **torsk** or **torsks** A gadoid fish, as the cod. [< Norw. < ON *thorskr*, prob. base of *thurr* dry. Akin to THIRST.]

tor·so (tôr′sō) *n. pl.* **·sos** or **·si** (-sē) **1.** The trunk of a human body. **2.** A sculptured representation of a human body without the head or limbs. **3.** Any truncated or defective thing. [< Ital., stalk, core, trunk of a body < L *thyrsus* stalk < Gk. *thyrsos* thyrsus]

tort (tôrt) *n. Law* Any private or civil wrong by act or omission for which a civil suit can be brought, but not in-cluding breach of contract. — **Syn.** See INJUSTICE. [< OF < L *tortus*. See TORSION.]

torte (tôrt, *Ger.* tôr′tə) *n.* A rich cake made with butter, eggs, and often fruit and nuts. [< G < Ital. *torta*]

tort-fea·sor (tôrt′fē′zər) *n. Law* One who has committed a tort; a wrongdoer. [< OF *tortfesor, tortfaiseur* < *tort* a wrong, tort + *fesor, faiseur* doer < *faire* to do < L *facere*]

tor·ti·col·lis (tôr′tə·kol′is) *n. Pathol.* A spasmodic affection of the muscles of the neck that draws the head to one side: also called *wryneck*. [< NL < L *tortus* twisted + *collum* neck] — **tor′ti·col′lar** *adj.*

tor·tile (tôr′til) *adj.* Twisted into a coil. [< L *tortilis* < *tortus* twisted. See TORSION.] — **tor·til·i·ty** (tôr·til′ə·tē) *n.*

tor·til·la (tôr·tē′yä) *n.* In Mexico, a flat cake made of coarse cornmeal baked on a hot sheet of iron or a slab of stone. [< Sp., dim. of *torta* cake < LL, twisted loaf < L, pp. fem. of *torquere* to twist]

tor·tious (tôr′shəs) *adj. Law* Of the nature of or implying a tort. [< AF *torcious* < *torcion, tortion*, var. of OF *torsion*; infl. in meaning by TORT] — **tor′tious·ly** *adv.*

tor·toise (tôr′təs) *n.* **1.** A turtle; especially, one of a terrestrial species as distinguished from those that are aquatic. **2.** A slow-moving person or thing. — **giant tortoise** Any of several species of very large herbivorous land tortoises (family *Testudinidae*), especially those found on the Galápagos Islands, reaching a length of over four feet and weighing up to 600 pounds. [Earlier *tortuce* < Med.L *tortuca, ?* < L *tortus*; so called from its crooked feet]

GIANT TORTOISE
(To 5½ feet long)

tor·toise-shell (tôr′təs·shel′) *n.* **1.** A cat having fur mottled with black and yellow or brown, like the shell of a tortoise. **2.** Any of various butterflies (genus *Nymphalis*) having variegated markings on the wings. — *adj.* Made of or variegated like tortoise shell. Also **tor′toise·shell′**.

tortoise shell The shell of a marine turtle, especially of the hawksbill, consisting of a mottled, brownish, hornlike substance used for combs, ornaments, etc.

Tor·to·la (tôr·tō′lə) The chief island of the British Virgin Islands; 21 sq. mi.

tor·tri·cid (tôr′trə·sid) *adj.* Of or belonging to a family (*Tortricidae*) of small moths, many of which are destructive to fruit and forest trees. — *n.* A moth of this family. [< NL < *Tortrix*, type genus < L *tortus*. See TORSION.]

Tor·tu·ga (tôr·tōō′gə) An island of Haiti, off the northern coast; a 17th-century pirate stronghold; 70 sq. mi.

Tor·tu·gas (tôr·tōō′gəs) See DRY TORTUGAS.

tor·tu·os·i·ty (tôr′choo·os′ə·tē) *n. pl.* **·ties** **1.** The quality or state of being tortuous. **2.** An instance of this. **3.** A bend or twist; winding.

tor·tu·ous (tôr′choo·əs) *adj.* **1.** Consisting of or abounding in irregular bends or turns; twisting. **2.** Not straightforward; devious. **3.** Morally twisted or warped. [< AF < L *tortuosus* < *tortus*. See TORSION.] — **tor′tu·ous·ly** *adv.* — **tor′tu·ous·ness** *n.*

tor·ture (tôr′chər) *n.* **1.** Infliction of or subjection to extreme physical pain. **2.** Great mental suffering; agony. **3.** Something that causes severe pain. **4.** A violent or extreme distortion. — *v.t.* **·tured, ·tur·ing** **1.** To inflict extreme pain upon, as from cruelty. **2.** To cause to suffer agony, extreme discomfort, etc. **3.** To twist or turn into an abnormal form, meaning, etc. [< OF < L *tortura*, lit., a twisting < *tortus*. See TORSION.] — **tor′tur·er** *n.* — **tor′tur·ous** *adj.*

To·ruń (tô′rōōny′) A port city in north central Poland, on the Vistula; pop. 116,100 (est. 1966): German *Thorn*.

to·rus (tôr′əs, tō′rəs) *n. pl.* **to·ri** (tôr′ī, tō′rī) **1.** *Archit.* A large convex molding, nearly semicircular in cross section, used in bases as the lowest molding, or in columns above the plinth: also called *tore*. For illustrations see MOLDING, TUSCAN ORDER. **2.** *Anat.* A rounded ridge, as on the occipital bone of the skull. **3.** *Bot.* The swollen end of a flower-stalk that bears the floral leaves; the receptacle. **4.** *Geom.* A toroid generated by a circle or other conic section, in the case of a circle, resembling a doughnut: also called *tore*. [< L, lit., a swelling]

to·ry (tôr′ē, tō′rē) *n. pl.* **·ries** **1.** A Tory (def. 3). **2.** *Sometimes cap.* A freebooter among the outlawed Irish in the 17th century. **3.** *Obs.* Any similar outlaw or bandit. [< Irish *tóruidhe* robber, pursuer < *tóir* to pursue]

To·ry (tôr′ē, tō′rē) *n. pl.* **·ries** **1.** A member of an English political party, successor to the Cavaliers and opponent of the Whigs, since about 1832 called the Conservative Party. **2.** One who at the period of the American Revolution adhered to the cause of British sovereignty over the colonies. **3.** One having very conservative beliefs, especially in politics: also *tory*. — **To′ry·ism** *n.*

Tos·ca·na (tôs·kä′nä) The Italian name for TUSCANY.

Tos·ca·ni·ni (tos′kə·nē′nē, tôs′-; *Ital.* tôs′kä·nē′nē), **Arturo,** 1867–1957, Italian orchestra conductor active in the United States.

tosh (tosh) *n. Brit. Informal* Nonsense; rubbish; bosh. [? Alter. of BOSH]

toss (tôs, tos) *v.t.* **1.** To throw, pitch, or fling about. **2.** To make restless; agitate; disturb. **3.** To throw with the hand, especially with the palm of the hand upward; pitch. **4.** To lift with a quick motion, as the head. **5.** To bandy about, as something discussed. **6.** *Informal* To toss up with: I'll *toss* you to see who pays. — *v.i.* **7.** To be moved or thrown about; be flung to and fro, as a ship in a storm. **8.** To throw oneself from side to side; move about restlessly, as in sleep. **9.** To go quickly or angrily, as with a fling of the head or the body. **10.** To toss up a coin. **— to toss off 1.** To drink at one draft. **2.** To utter, write, or do in an offhand manner. **— to toss up** To throw a coin into the air to decide a wager or choice, the outcome depending on the side on which the coin falls. **— n. 1.** The act of tossing; especially, a throwing from the hand; a pitch; also, the distance over which a thing is tossed. **2.** A quick upward or backward movement, as of the head. **3.** The state of being tossed about; excitement; agitation. **4.** A tossup or wager. [Prob. < Scand. Cf. dial. Norw. *tossa* to spread, strew.] **— toss′er** *n.*

tossed salad A salad of greens, etc., cut or shredded in small pieces, served with a liquid dressing, and mixed or agitated lightly so that the dressing covers the other ingredients.

toss·pot (tôs′pot′, tos′-) *n.* A toper; drunkard.

toss-up (tôs′up′, tos′-) *n. Informal* **1.** The throwing up of a coin to decide a bet, etc. **2.** An even chance, as for the outcome of an uncertain situation: It's a *tossup* whether or not he will win.

tot¹ (tot) *n.* **1.** A little child; toddler. **2.** A small amount or portion, as of liquor. [Origin unknown]

tot² (tot) *v.t.* **tot·ted, tot·ting** *Informal* To add; total: usually with *up*. [Short for TOTAL]

to·tal (tōt′l) *n.* The whole sum or amount; the whole, especially when considered as an aggregate of parts or elements. **— adj. 1.** Constituting or comprising a whole, without diminution or division: the sum *total*. **2.** Extending throughout the whole; affecting everything: *total* destruction. **3.** Complete; absolute: a *total* loss. **— v. ·taled** or **·talled, ·tal·ing** or **·tal·ling** *v.t.* **1.** To ascertain the total of. **2.** To come to or reach as a total; amount to. — *v.i.* **3.** To amount: often with *to*. [< OF < Med.L *totalis* < L *totum* all] **— to′tal·ly** *adv.*

total abstinence Abstinence (def. 2).

total depravity In Calvinism, the tendency of human nature to turn away from piety or spirituality. Compare ORIGINAL SIN.

total eclipse *Astron.* An eclipse in which during some period the entire disk of a celestial body is hidden from view.

to·tal·i·tar·i·an (tō-tal′ə-târ′ē-ən) *adj.* Designating or characteristic of a government controlled exclusively by one party or faction, and maintained by political suppression usually accompanied by cultural and economic regimentation. — *n.* An adherent of totalitarian government. [< TOTALIT(Y) + -ARIAN] **— to·tal′i·tar′i·an·ism** *n.*

to·tal·i·ty (tō-tal′ə-tē) *n. pl.* **·ties 1.** An aggregate of parts or individuals. **2.** The state of being total. **3.** *Astron.* The state or period of an eclipse while it is total.

to·tal·i·za·tor (tōt′l-ə-zā′tər, -ī-zā′-) *n.* A pari-mutuel machine. Also *Brit.* **to′tal·i·sa·tor.**

to·tal·ize (tōt′l-īz) *v.t.* **·ized, ·iz·ing** To collect into or ascertain as an aggregate; make total. **— to′tal·i·za′tion** *n.*

to·tal·iz·er (tōt′l-ī′zər) *n.* **1.** A pari-mutuel machine. **2.** An adding machine or similar device.

to·ta·quine (tō′tə-kwin) *n.* A mixture of the alkaloids from cinchona bark, used in the treatment of malaria. [< NL *totaquina* < L *tota*, fem. of *totus* all + Quechua (*quin*)*quina* cinchona bark]

tote¹ (tōt) *U.S. Informal v.t.* **tot·ed, tot·ing 1.** To carry or bear on the person, as a burden. **2.** To carry, transport, or haul, as supplies. **3.** To carry about one's person habitually: He *totes* a gun. — *n.* **1.** The act of toting. **2.** A load or haul. [? < West African] **— tot′er** *n.*

tote² (tōt) *n. Informal* A pari-mutuel machine. [Short for TOTALIZATOR]

tote bag A large handbag carried by women.

tote board *Informal* A board at a racetrack, etc., showing the betting odds and results of races.

to·tem (tō′təm) *n.* **1.** Among many primitive peoples, an animal, plant, or other natural object believed to be ancestrally related to, or the tutelar spirit of, a tribe, clan, etc. **2.** The representation of such an animal, plant, or object taken as an emblem. **3.** The name or symbol of a person, clan, or tribe. [< Algonquian. Cf. Ojibwa *ototeman* his relations.] **— to·tem·ic** (tō-tem′ik) *adj.*

to·tem·ism (tō′təm·iz′əm) *n.* **1.** Belief in totems and the practices associated therewith. **2.** The system of dividing a tribe into sibs or clans according to their totems. — **to′tem·ist** *n.* **— to′tem·is′tic** *adj.*

totem pole A tall post or pole carved or painted with totemic symbols, erected outside a dwelling or as a memorial to a deceased person by North American Indians, especially those of the NW coast. Also **totem post.**

TOTEM POLE

toth·er (tuth′ər) *pron. Informal* The other; other. Also **t′oth′er.** [ME *the tother* < *thet other* the other]

toti- *combining form* Whole; wholly: *totipalmate.* [< L *totus* whole]

to·ti·pal·mate (tō′ti·pal′māt) *adj. Ornithol.* Having all four toes joined by a web, as pelicans. [< TOTI- + PALMATE] **— to′ti·pal·ma′tion** (-pal·mā′shən) *n.*

Tot·le·ben (tôt′lā·ben, tot·lā′-), **Count Franz** (**Eduard Ivanovich**), 1818–84, Russian general and engineer. Also *Todleben.*

Tot·ten·ham (tot′n·əm) A municipal borough in SE Middlesex, England, a suburb of London; pop. 113,126 (1961).

tot·ter (tot′ər) *v.i.* **1.** To walk feebly and unsteadily. **2.** To shake or sway, as if about to fall. — *n.* The act or condition of tottering. [Prob. < Scand. Cf. Norw. *totra, tutra* to quiver.] **— tot′ter·er** *n.* — **Syn.** (verb) **2.** teeter, wobble, reel.

tot·ter·ing (tot′ər·ing) *adj.* **1.** Being or seeming about to fall; unsteady; unstable. **2.** Feeble or unsteady in gait or movement. Also **tot′ter·y.** **— tot′ter·ing·ly** *adv.*

tou·can (tōō′kan, tōō·kän′) *n.* A large, fruit-eating bird (family *Rhamphastidae*) of tropical America, with brilliant plumage and an immense, thin-walled beak. [< F < Pg. *tucano* < Tupi *tucana*]

Tou·can (tōō′kan, tōō·kän′) *n.* The constellation Tucana.

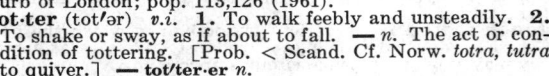

TOUCAN
(About 20 inches long)

touch (tuch) *v.t.* **1.** To place the hand, finger, etc., in contact with. **2.** To be in or come into contact with. **3.** To bring into contact with something else. **4.** To hit or strike lightly; tap. **5.** To lay the hand or hands on, especially roughly. **6.** To border on; adjoin. **7.** To come to; reach. **8.** To attain to; equal. **9.** To mark or delineate lightly, as with a brush or pen. **10.** To modify by adding fine strokes or lines; retouch. **11.** To color slightly; tinge. **12.** To affect injuriously; taint: vegetables *touched* by frost. **13.** To affect by contact; act upon: The drill could not *touch* the steel. **14.** To affect the emotions of; move, especially to pity, gratitude, sympathy, etc. **15.** To strike the strings or keys of (a musical instrument); play on. **16.** To play (a tune). **17.** To be pertinent to; relate to; concern. **18.** To treat or discuss in passing; deal with. **19.** To have to do with, use, or partake of: I will not *touch* this food. **20.** To meddle with; handle or appropriate improperly. **21.** *Slang* To be successful in borrowing from: used with *for*: He *touched* me for a loan. **22.** *Geom.* To be tangent to. **23.** *Obs.* To test, as gold with a touchstone. — *v.i.* **24.** To touch someone or something. **25.** To come into or be in contact. **— to touch at** To stop briefly at (a port or place) in the course of a journey or voyage. **— to touch off 1.** To cause to explode; detonate; fire. **2.** To cause to happen or occur. **— to touch on** (or **upon**) **1.** To relate to; concern. **2.** To treat briefly or in passing. **— to touch up 1.** To improve or alter by slight additions or corrections. **2.** To prod gently; rouse. **— n. 1.** The act or process of touching or coming in contact with something. **2.** The act or state of being touched. **3.** *Physiol.* That sense by which external objects are perceived through direct contact with any part of the body. ♦ Collateral adjective: *tactile.* **4.** The sensation conveyed by touching something: a smooth *touch*. **5.** *Med.* Palpation. **6.** A stroke; hit; blow: to give a ball a slight *touch*. **7.** A perceptible effect or influence: He felt the *touch* of her wit. **8.** Any slight or delicate execution or effect, as of a brush, pen, or chisel; a light stroke or mark. **9.** Any slight detail or effort given to anything, as to a literary work. **10.** The manner or style in which an artist, workman, or author executes his work: a master's *touch*. **11.** A trace; tinge; hint: a *touch* of irony. **12.** A slight attack or twinge: a *touch* of rheumatism. **13.** A small quantity or dash: to apply a *touch* of perfume. **14.** Close communication or contact: to keep in *touch* with someone. **15.** A test; trial: to put something to the *touch* of proof. **16.** *Music* **a** The resistance made to the fingers by the keys of a piano, etc. **b** The manner in which a player presses the keyboard. **17.** In Rugby football and soccer, the ground just outside the touchlines. **18.** An official stamp impressed upon ware made of gold, silver, or pewter, to testify to its fineness. **19.** *Obs.* A touchstone, or the method of assaying by the use of a touchstone. **20.** *Slang* A sum of money obtained by borrowing or mooching. **21.** *Slang* A request for such a sum of money: to make a

touch. *22. Slang* A person who is an easy mark for a loan or gift of money: usually with an attributive word: an easy *touch.* [< OF *tochier, tuchier;* prob. ult. imit.] — **touch′a·ble** *adj.* — **touch′a·ble·ness** *n.* — **touch′er** *n.*

touch-and-go (tuch′an·gō′) *adj.* **1.** Risky; precarious. **2.** Hasty and casual; perfunctory.

touch and go 1. An uncertain, risky, or precarious state of things. **2.** An instantaneous or rapid action.

touch·back (tuch′bak′) *n.* In football, the act of touching the ball to the ground behind the player's own goal line when it has been sent over the goal line by an opponent.

touch·down (tuch′doun′) *n.* In football, a scoring play, worth six points, in which the ball is held on or over the opponent's goal line and is there declared dead. Abbr. **td, td., TD**

tou·ché (tōō·shā′) *French adj.* In fencing, touched by the point of an opponent's foil. — *interj.* You've scored a point!: an exclamation to indicate an opponent's success.

touched (tucht) *adj.* **1.** Emotionally moved; affected by pity, gratitude, etc. **2.** Slightly unbalanced in mind; crackbrained.

touch football A variety of football in which the ball-carrier is downed by being touched instead of tackled, usually played under informal circumstances and without protective equipment.

touch·hole (tuch′hōl′) *n.* The orifice in old-fashioned cannon or firearms through which the powder was ignited.

touch·ing (tuch′ing) *adj.* **1.** Appealing to the sympathies or emotions; affecting; pathetic. **2.** Making or being in contact. — *prep.* With regard to; concerning; with respect to. — **touch′ing·ly** *adv.* — **touch′ing·ness** *n.*

touch·line (tuch′līn′) *n.* One of the side boundary lines of a Rugby football or soccer field.

touch-me-not (tuch′mē·not′) *n.* Any of a genus (*Impatiens*) of herbs with variously colored flowers, whose ripe fruit bursts open on contact to discharge its seeds; especially, the jewelweed: also called *noli-me-tangere.*

touch paper Paper made to burn slowly by saturation with saltpeter, used to set off fireworks, etc.

touch·stone (tuch′stōn′) *n.* **1.** A fine-grained dark stone, as jasper, formerly used to test the fineness of gold and silver by the color of the streak made on the stone. **2.** A criterion or standard by which the qualities of something are tested.

touch-type (tuch′tīp′) *v.i.* **-typed, -typ·ing** To type on a typewriter by directing the fingers to preassigned keys, without having to look at the keyboard. — **touch′-typ′ist** *n.*

touch·up (tuch′up′) *n.* A finishing touch or retouch.

touch·wood (tuch′wŏŏd′) *n.* **1.** Punk¹ (def. 1). **2.** Amadou, a tinder prepared from fungus.

touch·y (tuch′ē) *adj.* **touch·i·er, touch·i·est 1.** Likely to take offense easily; irritable. **2.** Risky; delicate: a *touchy* subject. **3.** Sensitive to touch. **4.** Catching fire readily, as tinder. — **touch′i·ly** *adv.* — **touch′i·ness** *n.*

tough (tuf) *adj.* **1.** Capable of sustaining great tension or strain without breaking. **2.** Firm and resilient in substance or texture. **3.** Not easily separated, softened, etc.: *tough* meat. **4.** Possessing great physical endurance: a *tough* constitution. **5.** Possessing moral or intellectual endurance; steadfast; persistent. **6.** Unmanageably rough, unruly, or vicious. **7.** *Informal* Disreputable; vulgar. **8.** Difficult to accomplish; laborious. **9.** Severe; rigorous. **10.** *Informal* Unfortunate; unpleasant: *tough* luck. — *n.* A lawless person; a rowdy; ruffian. [OE *tōh*] — **tough′ly** *adv.* — **tough′ness** *n.*

tough·en (tuf′ən) *v.t. & v.i.* To make or become tough or tougher. — **tough′en·er** *n.*

tough-mind·ed (tuf′mīn′did) *adj.* Characterized by practicality, determination, and the absence of sentiment; hardheaded: a *tough-minded* politician. — **tough′-mind′ed·ly** *adv.* — **tough′-mind′ed·ness** *n.*

Toul (tōōl) A town in NE France; besieged and captured by the Germans in the Franco-Prussian War, 1870; pop. 16,550 (1968).

Tou·lon (tōō·lôn′) A port city and naval base in France, on the Mediterranean; pop. 174,746 (1968).

Tou·louse (tōō·lōōz′) A city in southern France, on the Garonne; pop. 370,796 (1968).

Tou·louse-Lau·trec (tōō·lōōz′lō·trek′), **Henri Marie Raymond de,** 1864–1901, French painter and lithographer.

tou·pee (tōō·pā′, -pē′) *n.* **1.** A wig worn to cover baldness or a bald spot. **2.** Formerly, a lock or tuft of hair, especially at the top of a wig. [< F *toupet* < OF *toup,* top tuft of hair, prob. < Gmc.]

tour (tōŏr) *n.* **1.** A trip or rambling excursion. **2.** A circuit or passing through, as for inspection or sightseeing, or for presenting a performance. **3.** A turn or shift, as of service. — **Syn.** See JOURNEY. — **on tour** Traveling from place to place giving performances, as a theatrical company, performing artist, etc. — *v.t.* **1.** To make a tour of. **2.** To present on a tour: to *tour* a play. — *v.i.* **3.** To go on a tour. [< MF < OF *tor, tors* < L *tornus* lathe < Gk. *tornos;* infl. in meaning by OF *tourner* to turn]

tou·ra·co (tōŏr′ə·kō) *n.* The turacou, a bird.

Tou·raine (tōō·ren′) A region and former province of west central France.

tour·bil·lion (tōŏr·bil′yən) *n.* **1.** A kind of skyrocket with a spiral flight. **2.** A whirlwind. [< MF *tourbillon* whirlwind < OF *torbeillon* < L *turbo, -inis*]

Tour·coing (tōŏr·kwaṅ′) A city in northern France, near the Belgian border; pop. 98,755 (1968).

tour de force (tōŏr′ də fôrs′) *French* A feat of remarkable strength or skill; especially, a work, performance, etc., that is merely ingenious rather than intrinsically excellent.

touring car A large, open automobile for five or more passengers and baggage. Also *Brit.* **tour′er.**

tour·ism (tōŏr′iz·əm) *n.* **1.** Traveling as a recreation. **2.** The activities, businesses, etc., providing services for or profiting or benefiting from tourists. — **tour·is′tic** *adj.*

tour·ist (tōŏr′ist) *n.* One who makes a tour or a pleasure trip. — *adj.* Of or suitable for tourists.

tourist class A class of accommodations for steamship passengers, lower than cabin class.

tour·ist·y (tōŏr′is·tē) *adj. Informal* **1.** Characteristic of or resembling a tourist. **2.** Frequented by tourists.

tour·ma·line (tōŏr′mə·lēn, -lin) *n.* A complex borosilicate of aluminum, having a vitreous to resinous luster and occurring in various colors, the transparent varieties being esteemed as gemstones. Also spelled *turmaline.* Also **tour′ma·lin** (-lin). [< F, ult. < Singhalese *tōramalli* carnelian]

Tour·nai (tōŏr·nā′) A commune in SW Belgium; pop. 33,500 (est. 1967). Also **Tour·nay′.**

tour·na·ment (tûr′nə·mənt, tōŏr′-) *n.* **1.** Any contest of skill involving a number of competitors and a series of games: a chess *tournament.* **2.** In medieval times, a pageant in which two opposing parties of men in armor contended on horseback in mock combat. **3.** The jousts, sports, or contests in which such combatants engaged. Also called *tourney.* [< OF *torneiement, tornoiement* < *torneier, tornoier* tourney, ult. < L *tornare.* See TURN.]

Tour·neur (tûr′nər), **Cyril,** 1584?–1626, English dramatist.

tour·ney (tûr′nē, tōŏr′-) *n.* A tournament. — *v.i.* To take part in a tournament; tilt. [< OF *torneier.* See TOURNAMENT.]

tour·ni·quet (tōŏr′nə·ket, -kā, tûr′-) *n. Surg.* A bandage, etc., for stopping the flow of blood through an artery by compression. [< F < *tourner* to turn]

tour of duty *Mil.* The hours or period of time during which a serviceman is on official duty; also, an extended period of duty on a given assignment or in a particular area.

Tours (tōŏr) A city in west central France; scene of Charles Martel's defeat of the Saracens, 732; pop. 126,414 (1968).

touse (touz) *Dial. & Scot. v.t.* **toused, tous·ing** To tousle; rumple. — *n.* A disturbance. [ME *tusen, tousen,* prob. < Gmc.]

tou·sle (tou′zəl) *v.t.* **·sled, ·sling** To disarrange or disorder, as the hair or dress. — *n.* A tousled mass or mop of hair. Also **tou′zle.** [Freq. of TOUSE]

tous-les-mois (tōō·lā·mwä′) *n.* The edible, starchlike tubers of a perennial herb (*Canna edulis*) of the West Indies and South America, used in making baby food and as a substitute for arrowroot. [< F, all the months, every month; so called because edible the year round]

Tous·saint L'Ou·ver·ture (tōō·saṅ′ lōō·ver·tür′), **Dominique François,** 1743–1803, Haitian revolutionist, general, and statesman; president 1801–02.

tout (tout) *Informal v.i.* **1.** To solicit patronage, customers, votes, etc., especially in an obtrusive or importunate manner. **2.** To spy on a race horse so as to gain information for betting; act as a tout. — *v.t.* **3.** To solicit; importune. **4.** In horse racing: **a** To spy on (a horse) to gain information for betting. **b** To sell information concerning (a horse). — *n.* **1.** In horse racing, a spy who sells information regarding horses entered for a race. **2.** One who solicits business, votes, etc., especially persistently or conspicuously. [ME, < OE *tōtian,* to peep, look out] — **tout′er** *n.*

tout à fait (tōō·tà fe′) *French* Entirely; quite.

tout à l'heure (tōō·tà lœr′) *French* Instantly; presently.

tout de suite (tōōt′swēt′) *French* Immediately; at once.

tout en·sem·ble (tōō·täṅ säṅ′bl′) *French* **1.** All in all; everything considered. **2.** The general effect.

tout le monde (tōō′lə môṅd′) *French* Everybody; literally, all the world.

to·va·risch (to·vä′rish, *Russ.* to·vä′ryishch) *n.* Comrade: a term of address in the Soviet Union. Also **to·va′rich, to·va′rish.** [< Russian]

tow¹ (tō) *n.* Coarse, short hemp or flax fiber prepared for spinning. [Prob. OE *tow-* for spinning, as in *towlic* pertaining to spinning] — **tow′y** *adj.*

tow² (tō) *v.t.* **1.** To pull or drag by a rope, chain, etc. **2.** To drag or pull along. — *n.* **1.** The act of towing, or the state of being towed. **2.** That which is towed, as barges by a tugboat. **3.** That which tows, as a tugboat. **4.** A rope or cable used in towing; towline. — **to take in tow 1.** To take in charge for or as for towing. **2.** To take under one's protection; take charge of. [OE *togian*]

tow·age (tō′ij) *n.* **1.** The service of or charge for towing. **2.** The act of towing. [< TOW²]

to·ward (tôrd, tōrd; *for prep., also* tə·wôrd′) *prep.* **1.** In the direction of; facing. **2.** With respect to; regarding: his attitude *toward* women. **3.** In anticipation of or as a contribution to; for: He is saving *toward* his education. **4.** Near in point of time; approaching; about: arriving *toward* evening. **5.** Tending to result in; designed or likely to achieve: an effort *toward* mutual understanding. Also **to·wards′.** — *adj.* **1.** Docile. **2.** In progress: used predicatively. **3.** Impending or imminent. [OE *tōweard* < *tō* to + -*weard* -ward] — **to·ward′ness** *n.*

to·ward·ly (tôrd′lē, tōrd′-) *adj. Archaic* **1.** Ready to do or learn; compliant. **2.** Favorable; promising; propitious.

tow·a·way (tō′ə·wā) *n.* The act of towing away a vehicle, especially one illegally parked. — *adj.* Of or pertaining to the towing away of such vehicles: the city *towaway* policy.

tow·boat (tō′bōt′) *n.* A tugboat (which see).

tow·el (toul, tou′əl) *n.* A cloth or paper for drying anything by wiping. — **to throw in the towel** *Informal* To give in; admit defeat. — *v.t.* **tow·eled** or **·elled, tow·el·ing** or **·el·ling** To wipe or dry with a towel. [< OF *toaille*, prob. < OHG *dwahila* washcloth < *dwahan* to wash]

tow·el·ing (tou′ling, tou′əl·ing) *n.* Material used for towels. Also **tow′el·ling.**

tow·er (tou′ər) *n.* **1.** A tall but relatively narrow structure, sometimes part of a larger building. **2.** Any similar tall structure or object, often erected for a specific use: a water *tower*. **3.** A place or thing of security or defense; citadel. **4.** Formerly, a movable wooden structure from which besiegers stormed a fortress. — *v.i.* **1.** To rise or stand like a tower: often with *over* or *above*. **2.** To fly directly upward, as some birds. [Fusion of OE *torr* (< L *turris*) and OE *tūr* < OF *tor, tur* < L *turris*] — **tow′er·y** *adj.*

tow·ered (tou′ərd) *adj.* Having a tower or towers.

tow·er·ing (tou′ər·ing) *adj.* **1.** Like a tower; lofty. **2.** Unusually high or great; outstanding. **3.** Rising or increasing to a high pitch of violence or intensity; furious.

Tower of London A group of buildings constituting a fortress and palace on the north bank of the Thames.

tow·head (tō′hed′) *n.* A head of very light-colored or flaxen hair; also, a person having such hair. [< TOW¹ + HEAD] — **tow′-head′ed** *adj.*

tow·hee (tou′hē, tō′-) *n.* Any of various American birds related to the buntings and the sparrows; especially, the widely distributed **rufous-sided towhee** (*Pipilo erythrophthalmus*): also called *chewink, ground robin.* Also **towhee bunting.** [Imit. of one of its notes]

tow·line (tō′līn′) *n.* A towrope (which see).

town (toun) *n.* **1.** Any considerable collection of dwellings and other buildings larger than a village and constituting a geographical and political community unit, but not incorporated as a city. **2.** The inhabitants of such a community; townspeople. **3.** A township (def. 1). **4.** *Brit.* A village having the right to hold a periodic market. **5.** Any closely settled urban district. **6.** The downtown or business section of a city. — **on the town** *Slang* On a round of pleasure. — **to go to town** *Slang* To act with speed and efficiency. — **to paint the town red** *Slang* To celebrate wildly. Abbr. *t.* [OE *tūn*, enclosure, group of houses]

town clerk An official who keeps the records of a town.

town crier Formerly, a person appointed to make proclamations through the streets of a town.

town hall The building containing the public offices of a town and used for meetings of the town council and other official business.

town house A residence in a town or city, as distinguished from one in the country.

town·ie (tou′nē) *n. Informal* A nonstudent who lives in a college town.

town meeting **1.** A general assemblage of the people of a town. **2.** An assembly of qualified voters for the purpose of transacting town business; also, the voters assembled.

town·ship (toun′ship) *n.* **1.** In the United States: **a** A territorial subdivision of a county with certain corporate powers of municipal government. **b** In New England, a local political unit governed by a town meeting. **2.** A unit of area in surveys of U.S. public lands, normally six miles square, subdivided into 36 sections of one square mile each. **3.** *Brit.* Formerly, a parish or a district of a parish. Abbr. *t., tp., twp.* [OE *tūnscipe* < *tūn* village, group of houses]

towns·man (tounz′mən) *n. pl.* **·men** (-mən) **1.** A resident of a town; also, a fellow citizen. **2.** In New England, a town officer; a selectman.

towns·peo·ple (tounz′pē′pəl) *n.pl.* People who live in towns or in a particular town or city. Also **town′folk′** (-fōk′), **towns′folk′.**

towns·wom·an (tounz′wŏŏm′ən) *n. pl.* **·wom·en** (-wim′in) A woman living in a town.

tow·path (tō′path′, -päth′) *n.* A path along a river or canal used by draft animals, etc., for towing boats.

tow·rope (tō′rōp′) *n.* A heavy rope or cable used in towing: also called *towline.*

---

tox. or **toxicol.** Toxicology.

tox·al·bu·min (tok′sal·byōō′min) *n. Biochem.* Any protein substance having toxic properties. [< TOX(IC) + ALBUMIN]

tox·e·mi·a (tok·sē′mē·ə) *n. Pathol.* Blood poisoning. Also **tox·ae′mi·a.** [< NL < Gk. *toxicon* poison + *haima* blood] — **tox·e′mic, tox·ae′mic** *adj.*

tox·ic (tok′sik) *adj.* Pertaining to or caused by poison; poisonous. Also **tox′i·cal.** [< Med.L *toxicus* poisoned, poisonous < L *toxicum* poison, orig. poison for arrows < Gk. *toxicon* (*pharmakon*) (poison) for arrows < *toxa* arrows < *toxon* bow] — **tox′i·cal·ly** *adv.*

tox·i·cant (tok′sə·kənt) *adj.* Toxic; poisonous. — *n.* A poison; also, an intoxicant. [< LL *toxicans, -antis*, ppr. of *toxicare* to smear with poison < L *toxicum.* See TOXIC.]

tox·i·ca·tion (tok′sə·kā′shən) *n.* The act or process of poisoning, or the state of being poisoned.

tox·ic·i·ty (tok·sis′ə·tē) *n. pl.* **·ties** **1.** The quality of being toxic. **2.** The degree of intensity of a poison.

toxico- *combining form* Poison; of or pertaining to poisons: *toxicology.* Also, before vowels, **toxic-.** [< Gk. *toxicon* poison]

tox·i·co·gen·ic (tok′sə·kō·jen′ik) *adj.* **1.** Producing poisons or toxins. **2.** Generated or formed by toxic matter.

tox·i·col·o·gy (tok′sə·kol′ə·jē) *n.* The science that treats of the origin, nature, properties, etc., of poisons. [< F *toxicologie*] — **tox′i·co·log′i·cal** (-kō·loj′i·kəl) *adj.* — **tox′i·co·log′i·cal·ly** *adv.* — **tox′i·col′o·gist** *n.*

tox·i·co·sis (tok′sə·kō′sis) *n. pl.* **·ses** (-sēz) *Pathol.* A diseased condition resulting from toxins. [< NL < L *toxicum* poison]

tox·in (tok′sin) *n.* **1.** Any of a class of more or less unstable poisonous compounds developed by animal, vegetable, or bacterial organisms and acting as causative agents in many diseases. **2.** Any toxic matter generated in living or dead organisms. Also **tox·ine** (tok′sēn). [< TOX(IC) + -IN]

tox·oid (tok′soid) *n.* A toxin that has been specially treated to remove toxicity, often used in immunization.

tox·o·plas·mo·sis (tok′sō·plaz·mō′sis) *n.* A diseased condition resulting from the presence of or infection by sporozoan parasites (genus *Toxoplasma*) that act principally upon the nervous system of certain animals and sometimes of man. [< NL < *Toxoplasma*, genus name]

toy (toi) *n.* **1.** An article constructed for the amusement of children; a plaything. **2.** Any object of little importance or value; a trifle. **3.** A small ornament or trinket. **4.** Any diminutive object. **5.** A dog bred to extreme smallness and kept as a pet: also **toy dog. 6.** *Scot.* A loosely hanging head covering formerly worn by women: also **toy-mutch** (toi′much). — *v.i.* To trifle; play. — *adj.* Resembling a toy; of miniature size. [Prob. fusion of ME *toye* flirtation, sport and Du. *tuig* tools, stuff] — **toy′er** *n.* — **toy′ish** *adj.*

To·ya·ma (tō·yä·mä) A port city of north central Honshu, Japan; pop. 259,000 (est. 1966).

Toyn·bee (toin′bē), **Arnold Joseph,** 1889–1975, English historian.

to·yo (tō′yō) *n. pl.* **·yos** A kind of straw made from rice paper, used in women's hats; also, a hat made of this. [< Japanese]

To·yo·ha·shi (tō·yō·hä·shē) A port city of southern Honshu, Japan; pop. 215,513 (1960).

to·yon (tō′yən) *n.* An evergreen shrub (*Photinia arbutifolia*) indigenous to the Pacific coast of North America, having white flowers and bright red berries: also called *California holly.* [< Sp. *tollón* < N. Am. Ind. (Mexican)]

tp. Township.

t.p. Title page.

tr. **1.** Trace. **2.** Train. **3.** Transitive. **4.** Translated; translation; translator. **5.** Transpose. **6.** Treasurer. **7.** Trust.

Tr *Chem.* Terbium.

tra·be·at·ed (trā′bē·ā′tid) *adj. Archit.* **1.** Having an entablature. **2.** Having beams or long stones as lintels, rather than arched. Also **tra′be·ate** (-it, āt). [Irregularly formed < L *trabs, trabis* beam] — **tra′be·a′tion** *n.*

tra·bec·u·la (trə·bek′yə·lə) *n. pl.* **·lae** (-lē) **1.** A small supporting band or bar. **2.** *Anat.* The interwoven bands of connective tissue that form the supporting framework of an organ, as the spleen. **3.** *Bot.* A row or plate of sterile cells extending across the cavity in the sporangium of a moss. [< L, dim. of *trabs, trabis* beam] — **tra·bec′u·lar** *adj.*

Trab·zon (träb·zôn′) The Turkish name for TREBIZOND.

trace¹ (trās) *n.* **1.** A vestige or mark left by some past event or agent, especially when regarded as a sign or clue. **2.** A barely detectable quantity, quality, token, or characteristic; touch. **3.** A proportion or ingredient too small to be weighed: a *trace* of soda. **4.** An imprint or mark indicating the passage of a person or thing, as a footprint, etc. **5.** A path or trail through woods or forest beaten down by men or animals. **6.** A lightly drawn line. **7.** The path of a tracer bullet. **8.** *Psychol.* An alteration in certain cells of the brain or nervous system, assumed to result from various forms of excitation and to provide the physiological basis of memory: also called *engram*. — *v.* **traced, trac·ing** *v.t.* **1.** To follow the tracks, course, or development of. **2.** To follow (tracks, a course of development, etc.). **3.** To discover or ascertain by examination or investigation; determine. **4.** To draw; sketch. **5.** To copy (a drawing, etc.) on a superimposed transparent sheet. **6.** To form (letters, etc.) with careful strokes. **7.** To mark with an impressed design; chase. **8.** To imprint (a pattern or design). **9.** To mark or record by a curved or broken line. **10.** To go or move over, along, or through. — *v.i.* **11.** To make one's way; proceed. **12.** To have its origin; go back in time. [< OF *tracier*, ult. < L *tractus* a dragging, track < *trahere* to draw] — **trace′a·ble** *adj.* — **trace′a·bil′i·ty, trace′a·ble·ness** *n.* — **trace′a·bly** *adv.*

trace² (trās) *n.* **1.** One of two side straps or chains for connecting the collar of a harness with the whiffletree. For illustrations see HARNESS, WHIFFLETREE. **2.** *Mech.* A link or connecting bar hinged at each end to other pieces of a mechanism, and transmitting motion from one part to another. — **to kick over the traces** To throw off control; become unmanageable. — *v.t.* **traced, trac·ing** To fasten with or as with traces. [< OF *traiz, trais,* pl. of *trait* dragging, leather harness < L *tractus.* See TRACE¹.]

trace element *Biol.* Any of certain chemical elements found in very small amounts in plant and animal tissues and having a significant effect upon biochemical processes.

trac·er (trā′sər) *n.* **1.** One who or that which traces. **2.** One of various instruments used in tracing drawings, etc. **3.** An inquiry forwarded from one point to another, to trace missing mail matter, etc. **4.** *Mil.* **a** A chemical incorporated in certain types of ammunition used for ranging, signaling, or incendiary purposes. **b** A tracer bullet. **5.** A radioisotope introduced into the body for the purpose of following the processes of metabolism, the course or location of a disease, etc.: also called *tagged atom.* [< TRACE¹]

tracer bullet A bullet that leaves a line of smoke or fire in its wake to indicate its course for correction of aim.

trac·er·y (trā′sər·ē) *n. pl.* **·er·ies** **1.** Ornamental work, as in stone, formed of ramifying lines. For illustration see FOIL². **2.** Any work, ornamentation, etc., resembling this.

tra·che·a (trā′kē·ə) *n., pl.* **·che·ae** (-kē·ē) or **·che·as** **1.** *Anat.* The duct, composed of membrane and cartilaginous rings, by which air passes from the larynx to the bronchi and the lungs: also called *windpipe.* For illustrations see LARYNX, LUNG, MOUTH, THROAT. **2.** *Zool.* One of the passages by which air is conveyed from the exterior in air-breathing arthropods, as insects and arachnids. **3.** *Bot.* A duct or vessel serving to conduct water in plants. [< Med.L < LL *trachia* < Gk. (*artēria*) *trachys* a rough (artery), fem. of *trachys* rough] — **tra′che·al** *adj.*

tracheal tissue *Bot.* Plant tissue consisting of tracheae or tracheids, one of the chief constituents of xylem.

tra·che·id (trā′kē·id) *n. Bot.* An elongated, tapering woody plant cell, serving for conduction and support, as in coniferous trees. [< G *tracheïde* < Med.L *trachea* trachea]

tra·che·i·tis (trā′kē·ī′tis) *n. Pathol.* Inflammation of the trachea. [< NL < Med.L *trachea* trachea]

tracheo- *combining form* The trachea; of or pertaining to the trachea: *tracheotomy.* Also, before vowels, **trache-.**

tra·che·o·phyte (trā′kē·ə·fīt′) *n.* Any of a phylum (*Tracheophyta*) of plants that includes all having vascular tissue, as pteridophytes, angiosperms, and gymnosperms.

tra·che·os·co·py (trā′kē·os′kə·pē) *n. Med.* Instrumental inspection of the trachea. — **tra′che·o·scop′ic** (-ō-skop′ik) *adj.* — **tra′che·os′co·pist** *n.*

tra·che·ot·o·my (trā′kē·ot′ə·mē) *n., pl.* **·mies** *Surg.* The operation of cutting into the trachea. — **tra′che·ot′o·mist** *n.*

trach·le (träkh′əl) *Scot. v.t.* **trach·led, trach·ling** **1.** To trail or draggle. **2.** To fatigue; exhaust. Also spelled *trauchle.* [Corruption of DRAGGLE. Cf. Flemish *tragelen.*]

tra·cho·ma (trə·kō′mə) *n. Pathol.* A contagious virus disease characterized by the formation of hard granular excrescences on the conjunctiva of the eyelids, with inflammation of the lining. [< NL < Gk. *trachōma, -atos* roughness < *trachys* rough] — **tra·chom·a·tous** (trə·kom′ə·təs) *adj.*

trachy- *combining form* Rough; uneven. Also, before vowels, **trach-.** [< Gk. *trachys* rough]

tra·chyte (trā′kīt, trak′īt) *n.* A light-colored, volcanic rock composed essentially of alkyline feldspar and one or more secondary minerals. [< F < Gk. *trachytēs* ruggedness < *trachys* rough] — **tra·chyt·ic** (trə·kit′ik) *adj.*

trac·ing (trā′sing) *n.* **1.** The act of one who traces. **2.** A copy made by tracing on transparent paper. **3.** A record made by a self-registering instrument.

track (trak) *n.* **1.** A mark or trail left by the passage of anything. **2.** A footprint or series of footprints. **3.** Any regular path; course. **4.** Any kind of racecourse; also, sports performed on such a course; track athletics. **5.** A set of rails or a rail on which something may travel; especially, the pair of metal rails for a railway train. **6.** A trace or vestige. **7.** A sequence of events or ideas. **8.** A course or trail leading to a desired goal: to be on the right *track.* **9.** One of a pair of endless metal belts by means of which certain vehicles, as

tanks, are capable of moving over a variety of surfaces. **10.** In education, any of two or more classes covering the same course of study, segregated according to the students' preparation or ability and taught at correspondingly different levels. — **to keep track of** To keep in touch with; keep sight of. — **in one's tracks** Right where one is; on the spot. — **to jump the track** **1.** To leave the rails, as a railroad engine or car. **2.** To depart from any usual course or procedure. — **to lose track of** To fail to keep in touch with; lose sight of. — **to make tracks** To get away in a hurry. — *v.t.* **1.** To follow the tracks of; trail. **2.** To discover, pursue or follow, by means of marks or indications. **3.** *Aerospace* To observe the path of and receive data from (rockets, satellites, etc.). **4.** To make tracks upon or with: to *track* snow through a house. **5.** To traverse, as on foot: to *track* the wild forests. **6.** To furnish with rails or tracks. — *v.i.* **7.** To measure a certain distance between wheels. **8.** To have the wheels equal in span or gauge to the wheels of another vehicle. **9.** To run in the same track; be in alignment. [< OF *trac,* prob. < Gmc. Cf. Du. *trek* pull.] — **track′er** *n.* — **track′a·ble** *adj.*

track·age (trak′ij) *adj.* **1.** Railroad tracks collectively. **2.** The right of one company to use the track system of another company; also, the charge for this right.

track detector *Physics* A device for showing the ionization paths of subatomic particles, as the cloud chamber.

track events The races at an athletic meet: distinguished from *field events.* Also **track athletics.**

tracking station *U.S.* A radar or radio station that maintains contact or communication with an artificial satellite or the like.

track·less (trak′lis) *adj.* **1.** Unmarked by trails or paths; pathless: the *trackless* desert. **2.** Leaving no traces. **3.** Not moving on tracks: a *trackless* trolley.

track·man (trak′mən) *n. pl.* **·men** (-mən) *U.S.* One employed to inspect regularly the condition of a section of railroad track. Also **track·walk·er** (trak′wô′kər).

track man An athlete who competes in a track or field event, as a runner, shot-putter, etc.

track meet An athletic contest made up of track and field events.

track shoe A lightweight, heelless shoe having spikes on the sole, worn by track men.

tract¹ (trakt) *n.* **1.** An extended area, as of land or water. **2.** A development (def. 5). **3.** *Anat.* An extensive region of the body, especially one comprising a system of parts or organs: the alimentary *tract.* **4.** *Archaic* Continued duration, as of time. [< L *tractus* a drawing out, duration < *trahere* to draw. Doublet of TRAIT.]

tract² (trakt) *n.* A short treatise or pamphlet, especially on religion or morals. [Short for L *tractatus* tractate]

tract·a·ble (trak′tə·bəl) *adj.* **1.** Easily led or controlled; manageable; docile. **2.** Readily worked or handled; malleable. — **Syn.** See DOCILE. [< L *tractabilis* < *tractare* to handle, freq. of *trahere* to draw] — **tract′a·ble·ness, tract′a·bil′i·ty** *n.* — **tract′a·bly** *adv.*

Trac·tar·i·an (trak·târ′ē·ən) *n.* One of the authors of *Tracts for the Times* (1833–41), a series of 90 religious pamphlets expressing the views of the Oxford movement. — *adj.* Pertaining to the Tractarians or to their teachings. — **Trac·tar′i·an·ism** (trak·târ′ē·ən·iz′əm) *n.*

trac·tate (trak′tāt) *n.* A short treatise; a tract. [< L *tractatus* a handling, treatise, pp. of *tractare.* See TRACTABLE.]

trac·tile (trak′til) *adj.* Capable of being drawn out; ductile. [< L *tractilis* < *tractus.* See TRACE¹.] — **trac·til′i·ty** *n.*

trac·tion (trak′shən) *n.* **1.** The act of drawing, as by motive power over a surface. **2.** The state of being drawn, or the power employed. **3.** *Physiol.* Contraction, as of a muscle. **4.** Adhesive or rolling friction, as of wheels on a track. [< Med.L *tractio, -onis* < L *tractus.* See TRACE¹.] — **trac′tion·al** *adj.* — **trac′tive** *adj.*

traction engine A locomotive for hauling on roads or ground, as distinguished from one used on a railway.

trac·tor (trak′tər) *n.* **1.** A powerful, motor-driven vehicle, usually having heavy treads, used, as on farms, to draw a plow, reaper, etc. **2.** An automotive vehicle with a driver's cab, used to haul trailers, etc. **3.** *Aeron.* An airplane with a propeller or propellers in front of the supporting surface: also **tractor airplane.** [< NL < L *tractus.* See TRACE¹.]

trade (trād) *n.* **1.** A regular occupation, business, or pursuit, especially one requiring manual or mechanical dexterity; craft. **2.** The persons engaged in a particular occupation or business. **3.** Business or commerce in general. **4.** The act of trading or of buying and selling. **5.** A bargain or deal. **6.** The regular customers or clientele of a firm. **7.** *Usually pl.* A trade wind. **8.** *Archaic* A custom, practice, or habit. — **Syn.** See OCCUPATION, TRAFFIC. — *adj.* **1.** Of, pertaining to, or used in trade or business. **2.** Used by or intended for the persons engaged in a particular occupation or profession: a *trade* newspaper. **3.** Of or having to do with a trade wind. — *v.* **trad·ed, trad·ing** *v.t.* **1.** To exchange by barter, bargain and sale, etc. **2.** To exchange or interchange for something comparable or similar. — *v.i.* **3.** To engage in commerce or in business. **4.** To buy or shop. **5.** To exchange or barter one thing for another. **— to trade in** To give in exchange as payment or part payment. **— to trade off** To get rid of by exchange or trading. **— to trade on** To make advantageous use of; use as an asset. [< MLG, track. Akin to TREAD.]

trade acceptance A bill of exchange drawn by the seller of goods on the purchaser who accepts the draft by writing across the face of it when and where it is payable.

trade book An edition of a book designed for ordinary sale to the general public, as distinguished from a textbook, limited or de luxe edition, etc. Also **trade edition.**

trade card *Brit.* A business card (which see).

trade discount A deduction from the list price given by a manufacturer or wholesaler to a buyer in the same trade.

trade dollar See under DOLLAR.

trade-in (trād′in′) *n.* Something given or accepted in payment or part payment for something else; an exchange.

trade journal A periodical publishing news and discussions of a particular trade or business.

trade-last (trād′last′, -läst′) *n. Informal* A favorable remark that one has heard and offers to repeat to the person complimented in return for a similar remark. Abbr. *TL, T.L.*

trade-mark (trād′märk′) *n.* **1.** A name, design, etc., often officially registered, used by a merchant or manufacturer to identify his goods and distinguish them from those made or sold by others. **2.** Any distinctive or identifying characteristic. *— v.t.* **1.** To label with a trademark. **2.** To register as a trademark.

trade name **1.** The name by which an article, process, service, or the like is designated in trade. **2.** A style or name of a business house.

trad·er (trā′dər) *n.* **1.** One who trades. **2.** Any vessel employed in a particular trade. **3.** A member of a stock exchange who trades for himself, and not for customers.

trade rat A pack rat (which see).

trade route A route, especially a sea lane, used by traders.

trad·es·can·ti·a (trad′əs·kan′shē·ə, -shə) *n.* Any plant of the genus *Tradescantia*, as the spiderwort. [< NL, after John *Tradescant*, died 1638, English traveler and naturalist]

trade school A vocational school designed to give a knowledge of a specific trade.

trade secret A pattern, formula, etc., used exclusively by one manufacturer.

trades·folk (trādz′fōk′) *n.pl.* People engaged in trade; especially, shopkeepers. Also **trades′peo′ple** (-pē′pəl).

trades·man (trādz′mən) *n. pl.* **·men** (-mən) A retail dealer; shopkeeper.

trades·wom·an (trādz′wŏŏm′ən) *n. pl.* **·wom·en** (-wim′in) A woman engaged in trade or the sale of goods.

trade union A labor union (which see). Also *Brit.* **trades union.** **— trade unionism** **— trade unionist**

trade wind *Meteorol.* Either of two steady winds blowing in the same course toward the equator from about 30° N and S latitude, one from the northeast on the north, the other from the southeast on the south side of the equatorial line.

trading post A building or small settlement in unsettled territory where a trader or trading company has set up a station for barter.

trading stamp A stamp of fixed value given by a tradesman to a purchaser, and exchangeable, in quantities, for goods selected from a premium list.

tra·di·tion (trə·dish′ən) *n.* **1.** The knowledge, doctrines, customs, practices, etc., transmitted from generation to generation; also, the transmission of such knowledge, doctrines, etc. **2.** The body of unwritten Christian doctrine, handed down through successive generations. **3.** Among the Jews, an unwritten code said to have been handed down orally from Moses. **4.** The Sunna of the orthodox Moslem. **5.** The historic conceptions and usages of a school of art, literature, etc.: the *traditions* of the stage. **6.** A custom so long continued that it has almost the force of a law. **7.** *Law* Delivery of possession. [< OF *tradicion* < L *traditio, -onis* delivery, surrender < *traditus,* pp. of *tradere* to deliver < *trans-* across + *dare* to give. Doublet of TREASON.]

tra·di·tion·al (trə·dish′ən·əl) *adj.* Relating or adhering to tradition. **— tra·di′tion·al·ly** *adv.*

tra·di·tion·al·ism (trə·dish′ən·əl·iz′əm) *n.* **1.** A system of faith founded on tradition. **2.** Adherence to tradition; especially, undue reverence for tradition in religious matters.

tra·di·tion·al·ist (trə·dish′ən·əl·ist) *n.* One who adheres to or reveres tradition. **— tra·di′tion·al·ist′ic** *adj.*

tra·di·tion·ist (trə·dish′ən·ist) *n.* **1.** A traditionalist. **2.** A student or transmitter of traditions or a tradition.

trad·i·tor (trad′ə·tər) *n. pl.* **trad·i·to·res** (trad′ə·tôr′ēz, -tō′rēz) A traitor among the early Christians at the time of the Roman persecutions. [< L, deliverer, betrayer < *tradere*. See TRADITION.]

tra·duce (trə·dōōs′, -dyōōs′) *v.t.* **·duced, ·duc·ing** To misrepresent willfully the conduct or character of; defame; slander. **— Syn.** See ASPERSE. [< L *traducere* to transport, bring into disgrace < *trans-* across + *ducere* to lead] **— tra·**

duc′er *n.* **— tra·duc′i·ble** *adj.* **— tra·duc′ing·ly** *adv.* **tra·duc·tion** (trə·duk′shən) *n.*

tra·du·cian·ism (trə·dōō′shən·iz′əm, -dyōō′-) *n. Theol.* The doctrine that the soul, equally with the body, is produced and begotten by the parent or parents: distinguished from *creationism, infusionism.* [< LL *traducianus* < L *tra dux, -icis* a shoot for propagation < *traducere*. See TRADUCE.] **— tra·du′cian·ist** *n.* **— tra·du′cian·is′tic** *adj.*

Tra·fal·gar (trə·fal′gər, *Sp.* trä′fäl·gär′), **Cape** A headland on the Atlantic coast of SW Spain; scene of a naval battle in which Nelson defeated the French and Spanish fleets, 1805.

traf·fic (traf′ik) *n.* **1.** The movement or passage of vehicles, pedestrians, ships, etc., along a route; also, the vehicles, pedestrians, etc. **2.** The business of buying and selling; trade. **3.** The business of transportation; also, the freight or passengers carried by a transportation company. **4.** The flow or total amount of messages, signals, etc., handled by a communications system. **5.** Unlawful or improper trade: *traffic* in stolen goods. **6.** Dealings; business: I want no *traffic* with the likes of him. **— v.i. ·ficked, ·fick·ing 1.** To engage in buying and selling; do business, especially illegally: with *in.* **2.** To have dealings: with *with.* [< MF *trafic, trafique* < Ital. *traffico* < *trafficare* < L *trans-* across + Ital. *ficcare* to thrust in < L *figere* to fasten] **— traf′fick·er** *n.*

— Syn. (noun) **2.** *Traffic, commerce,* and *trade* are compared as they denote the exchange of goods. The primary sense of *traffic* is movement back and forth; it denotes the business of transport and the exchange of goods. *Commerce* is *traffic* between large areas, as between regions or countries. *Trade* is applied to local *traffic,* as in a retail market, or between individuals.

Traffic may appear as a combining form or as the first element in two-word phrases, with the following meanings:
1. Of or pertaining to the flow of roadway traffic:

traffic accident	**traffic-congested**	**traffic-laden**
traffic artery	**traffic congestion**	**traffic lane**

2. Of or pertaining to the laws or regulation of roadway traffic:

traffic court	**traffic sign**	**traffic violation**
traffic policeman	**traffic signal**	**traffic violator**

traffic circle *U.S.* A circular intersection where traffic is maintained in one direction, allowing vehicles to enter or leave it at any of the converging roads without interrupting the flow of traffic: also *rotary*: also, *Brit., roundabout.*

traffic cop *Informal* A policeman who directs traffic, as at the intersection of two streets.

traffic jam A congestion of a roadway, intersection, etc., with vehicles, forcing them to move slowly and fitfully.

traffic light A signal light that, by changing color, directs the flow of traffic along a road or highway.

trag·a·canth (trag′ə·kanth) *n.* **1.** A white or reddish gum obtained from various species of Old World leguminous herbs (genus *Astragalus*); especially, *A. gummifer* of SW Asia, used in pharmacy and the arts. **2.** Any plant yielding this gum. [< MF *tragacante* < L *tragacantha* < Gk. *tragakantha* tragacanth shrub < *tragos* goat + *akantha* thorn]

tra·ge·di·an (trə·jē′dē·ən) *n.* **1.** An actor in tragedy. **2.** A writer of tragedies. **— tra·ge′di·enne′** *n. fem.*

trag·e·dy (traj′ə·dē) *n. pl.* **·dies** **1.** An intensely sad, calamitous, or fatal event or course of events; disaster. **2.** A form of drama in which the protagonist, having importance in the state and some quality of personal greatness, comes to disaster through a flaw in his nature, the outcome, according to Aristotle, producing pity and fear in the spectator and effecting catharsis of these feelings: opposed to *comedy.* **3.** In modern drama, a play in which the protagonist, not necessarily great or important, is crushed or immobilized by social and psychological forces in conflict. **4.** In medieval literature, a play or poem in which the protagonist, a proud and powerful man, is destroyed by fate at the height of his greatness. **5.** The branch of drama treating of such themes. **6.** The art or theory of acting or composing such drama. **7.** Any literary composition having the characteristics of or dealing with the themes of such drama. **8.** The sense of human life embodied in tragic drama. [< OF *tregedie, tragedie* < L *tragoedia* < Gk. *tragōidia,* appar. < *tragos* goat + *ōidē* song; semantic development uncertain]

trag·ic (traj′ik) *adj.* **1.** Involving death, calamity, or suffering; fatal; terrible. **2.** Pertaining to or having the nature of tragedy. **3.** Appropriate to or like tragedy, especially in drama. Also **trag′i·cal.** [< L *tragicus* < Gk. *tragikos* pertaining to tragedy] **— trag′i·cal·ly** *adv.* **— trag′i·cal·ness** *n.*

trag·i·com·e·dy (traj′i·kom′ə·dē) *n. pl.* **·dies 1.** A drama in which tragic and comic scenes are intermingled. **2.** A situation or event suggestive of such a drama. [< MF *tragi-comédie* < LL *tragicomoedia* < L *tragico-comoedia* < *tragicus* tragic + *comoedia* comedy] **— trag′i·com′ic** or **·i·cal** *adj.* **— trag′i·com′i·cal·ly** *adv.*

trag·o·pan (trag′ə·pan) *n.* An Asian pheasant (genus *Tragopan*) having hornlike appendages and brilliant plumage. [< NL, a fabulous bird < Gk. *tragos* goat + *Pan* Pan]

tra·gus (trā′gəs) *n. pl.* **·gi** (-jī) *Anat.* A flattened, somewhat conical eminence of the auricle in front of the opening of the external ear. [< LL < Gk. *tragos*, originally, goat; so called because of the hairs on it]

traik (trāk) *Scot. v.i.* To tramp; trudge. — *n.* A wearisome tramp or journey.

trail (trāl) *v.t.* **1.** To draw along lightly over a surface; also, to drag or draw after: to *trail* a robe. **2.** To follow the track of; track. **3.** To follow or lag behind, especially in a race. **4.** *Mil.* To carry, as a rifle, by grasping it in the right hand just above the balance, with the muzzle to the front and the butt nearly touching the ground. **5.** To tread or force down, as grass into a pathway. — *v.i.* **6.** To hang or float loosely so as to drag along a surface. **7.** To grow along the ground or over rocks, bushes, etc., in a loose, creeping way. **8.** To follow behind loosely; stream. **9.** To move along slowly, tiredly, or heavily. **10.** To lag behind; straggle. **11.** To follow or track game. — *n.* **1.** A path or track made by the passage of persons or animals; especially, a path made by repeated passage through a wilderness. **2.** The track or other indications followed by a huntsman or by a dog in hunting. **3.** Anything drawn behind or in the wake of something, as the train of a dress or gown. **4.** *Mil.* The inclined stock of a gun carriage, or extension of the stock that rests on the ground when the piece is not limbered up. — **to hit** (or **take**) **the trail** To set out on a journey. [< AF *trailler* to haul < L *tragula* dragnet < *trahere* to draw]

trail·blaz·er (trāl′blā·zər) *n.* **1.** One who blazes a trail. **2.** One who leads the way in any field or project; a pioneer. — **trail′blaz′ing** *n.*

trail·er (trā′lər) *n.* **1.** One who or that which trails. **2.** A vehicle drawn by another having motive power. **3.** A vehicle drawn by a car or truck and used as a temporary or permanent dwelling. **4.** A short motion-picture film made up of scenes from a coming feature picture, used for advertising.

trailer court A large area equipped with running water, electrical outlets, and other accommodations for the parking of trailers. Also **trailer park.**

trail·ing arbutus (trā′ling) An evergreen perennial (*Epigaea repens*) of the heath family, bearing clusters of fragrant pink flowers: the State flower of Massachusetts: also called *mayflower.*

trailing edge *Aeron.* The rear edge of an airfoil or propeller blade.

trail rope **1.** A guide rope, as on a balloon or dirigible. **2.** A rope used for dragging or towing. **3.** *Mil.* A prolonge.

train (trān) *n.* **1.** A continuous line of coupled railway cars. **2.** A series, succession, or set of connected things; a sequence; especially, an assemblage of people or objects drawn up processionally or in orderly disposition. **3.** A retinue or body of retainers; suite. **4.** Something pulled along with and in the track of another. **5.** An extension of a dress skirt, trailing behind the wearer. **6.** Proper order; due course. **7.** *Mech.* A series of parts acting upon each other, as for transmitting motion. **8.** *Mil.* The men, animals, and vehicles attached to a military body for the transportation of its ammunition, supplies, etc. **9.** A succession or line of wagons and pack animals en route. **10.** A line of gunpowder or other combustible laid to conduct fire to a charge, mine, or the like. *Abbr.* **tn., tr.** — *v.t.* **1.** To render skillful, proficient, or qualified by systematic instruction, drill, etc.; educate; instruct. **2.** To make obedient to orders or capable of performing tricks, as an animal. **3.** To bring into a required physical condition by means of a course of diet and exercise. **4.** To lead into taking a particular course; develop into a fixed shape: to *train* a plant on a trellis. **5.** To put or point in an exact direction; bring to bear; aim, as a cannon. — *v.i.* **6.** To undergo a course of training. **7.** To give a course of training; drill. — **Syn.** See TEACH. [Fusion of OF *traïne* a dragging and *traïn* series, procession; both < *traïner*, *trahiner* to draw < L *trahere*] — **train′a·ble** *adj.*

Train may appear as a combining form or as the first element in two-word phrases, with the meaning of definition 1:

train caller	train recorder	train ticket
train conductor	train robber	traintime
train crew	train schedule	train track
train flagman	train service	train tip
train foreman	train signal	trainway
train inspector	train staff	train whistle
train line	train stop	train wreck

train·band (trān′band′) *n.* Formerly, a militia organization, especially one in England during the 17th century. [Short for *trained band*]

train·ee (trā·nē′) *n.* One who undergoes training.

train·er (trā′nər) *n.* **1.** One who trains. **2.** One who supervises the physical training or condition of a person or group, as of athletes. **3.** An apparatus or device used in training. **4.** In the U.S. Navy, the member of a gun crew who gives horizontal direction to the gun: compare POINTER. **5.** One who trains animals for shows, animal acts, etc.

train·ing (trā′ning) *n.* **1.** Practical instruction or drill, as to acquire a skill. **2.** The condition or process of being trained. **3.** The action of one who or that which trains. *Abbr.* **tng.** — **Syn.** See EDUCATION.

training school A school for practical instruction and drill; especially, a school in which students receive special vocational or technical instruction and practice.

training ship A vessel on which apprentice seamen and cadets are educated in seamanship, navigation, etc.

train·man (trān′mən) *n. pl.* **·men** (-mən) A railway employee serving on a train; especially, a brakeman.

train·mas·ter (trān′mas′tər, -mäs′-) *n.* A railroad official supervising some division or subdivision of a rail line.

train oil Oil obtained from the fat of whales, cod livers, etc. [Earlier *trane* < MDu. *traen* extracted oil]

traipse (trāps) *v.i.* **traipsed, traips·ing** *Informal* To walk about in an idle or aimless manner: also spelled *trapes*. [Earlier *trapass*, prob. < OF *trapasser*, var. of *trespasser*. See TRESPASS.]

trait (trāt, *also Brit.* trā) *n.* **1.** A distinguishing feature or quality of character. **2.** *Rare* A stroke or touch. — **Syn.** See CHARACTERISTIC. [< F < MF *traict* < L *tractus.* Doublet of TRACT[1].]

trai·tor (trā′tər) *n.* One who betrays a trust; especially, one who commits treason. [< OF *traitre, traitor* < L *traditor.* See TRADITOR.] — **trai′tress** (-tris) *n. fem.*

trai·tor·ous (trā′tər·əs) *adj.* **1.** Of or characteristic of a traitor. **2.** Pertaining to or of the nature of treason. — **Syn.** See PERFIDIOUS. — **trai′tor·ous·ly** *adv.* — **trai′tor·ous·ness** *n.*

Tra·jan (trā′jən), 53?–117, Roman emperor 98–117: full name **Marcus Ulpius Tra·ja·nus** (trā-jā′nəs). — **Tra·jan·ic** (trā·jan′ik) *adj.*

tra·ject (trə·jekt′) *v.t.* To throw or cast over, through, or across, as a beam of light; transmit. [< L *trajectus*, pp. of *trajicere* < *trans-* over + *jacere* to throw] — **tra·jec′tion** *n.*

tra·jec·to·ry (trə·jek′tər·ē) *n. pl.* **·ries** **1.** The path described by an object moving in space; especially, the path of a projectile after being fired. **2.** *Geom.* **a** A curve that cuts each of a set of curves at the same angle. **b** A curve or surface that passes through a given set of points. [< Med.L *trajectorius* < L *trajectus.* See TRAJECT.]

Tra·lee (trä·lē′) The county seat of County Kerry, Ireland, in the western part; pop. about 11,000.

tram[1] (tram) *n.* **1.** *Brit.* A streetcar or street railway. **2.** A four-wheeled vehicle for conveying coals to or from a pit's mouth. — *v.t. & v.i.* **trammed, tram·ming** To convey or travel in a tram. [Short for TRAMROAD]

tram[2] (tram) *n.* **1.** A trammel (def. 4). **2.** *Mech.* Accuracy of adjustment. — *v.t.* **trammed, tram·ming** To use a trammel (def. 4) in adjusting (any part). [Short for TRAMMEL]

tram[3] (tram) *n.* A thick silk thread used for the cross threads of the best silks and velvets. [< F *trame* < OF *traime* machination < L *trama* woof]

tram·car (tram′kär′) *n. Brit.* A streetcar (which see). [< TRAM[1] + CAR]

tram·line (tram′līn′) *n. Brit.* A streetcar line.

tram·mel (tram′əl) *n.* **1.** *Usually pl.* That which limits freedom or activity; an impediment; hindrance. **2.** A fetter, shackle, or bond, especially, one used in teaching a horse to amble. **3.** An instrument for describing ellipses. **4.** A gauge for adjusting machine parts: also called *tram.* **5.** A hook used to suspend cooking pots from a fireplace crane. **6.** A net formed of three layers, the central one being of finer mesh in order to entangle fish that pass through either of the others: also **trammel net.** — *v.t.* **tram·meled** or **·melled, tram·mel·ing** or **·mel·ling** **1.** To hinder or obstruct; restrict. **2.** To entangle in or as in a snare. Also **tram′el** or **tram′ell.** [< OF *tramail* net < LL *tramaculum, tremaculum* < L *tri-* three + *macula* mesh] — **tram′mel·er** or **tram′mel·ler** *n.*

tra·mon·tane (trə·mon′tān, tram′ən·tān) *adj.* **1.** Situated beyond or coming from the other side of the mountains, especially the Alps. **2.** Barbarous; foreign. — *n.* **1.** A resident beyond the mountains. **2.** A foreigner; barbarian. [< Ital. *tramontana* north wind < L *transmontanus* beyond the mountains < *trans-* over + *mons, montis* mountain]

tramp (tramp) *v.i.* **1.** To walk or wander, especially as a vagrant or vagabond. **2.** To walk heavily or firmly. — *v.t.* **3.** To walk or wander through. **4.** To walk on heavily; trample. — *n.* **1.** One who wanders about without money or other means of support; a vagrant; vagabond. **2.** A heavy, continued tread. **3.** The sound produced by continuous and heavy marching or walking. **4.** A long stroll on foot; hike. **5.** A steam vessel that goes from port to port picking up freight wherever it can be obtained: also **tramp steamer.** **6.** A metal plate on a shoe to protect it from wear or from a spade in digging. [ME *trampen* < Gmc. Cf. LG *trumpen.*] — **tramp′er** *n.*

tram·ple (tram′pəl) *v.* **·pled, ·pling** *v.t.* **1.** To tread on heavily; injure, violate, or encroach upon by or as by tramping. — *v.i.* **2.** To tread heavily or ruthlessly; tramp. — *n.* The act or sound of treading under foot. [ME *trampelen,* freq. of *trampen.* See TRAMP.] — **tram′pler** *n.*

tram·po·line (tram′pə·lin, tram·pə·lēn′) *n.* A section of strong canvas stretched on a frame, on which a person may bound or spring, used in training for body control and acrobatics. [< Ital. *trampoli* stilts]

tram·road (tram′rōd′) *n.* A road with tracks of stone,

wood, or metal; especially, a railroad in a mine. [< dial. E *tram* rail, wagon shaft (prob. < LG *traam* shaft) + ROAD]

tram·way (tram′wā′) *n.* **1.** *Brit.* A streetcar; also, the tracks on which it runs. **2.** A tramroad.

trance[1] (trans, träns) *n.* **1.** A condition intermediate between sleep and wakefulness, characterized by dissociation, involuntary movements, and automatism of behavior, as in hypnosis and mediumistic séances. **2.** A dreamlike state marked by bewilderment and an insensibility to ordinary surroundings. **3.** A state of deep abstraction. — **Syn.** See DREAM. — *v.t.* **tranced, tranc·ing** To put into or as into a trance. [< OF *transe* dread of coming evil < *transir* to pass, die < L *transire*. See TRANSIENT.]

trance[2] (trans, träns) *n. Scot.* A passageway.

tran·quil (trang′kwil, tran′-) *adj.* **·quil·er** or **·quil·ler, ·quil·est** or **·quil·lest** **1.** Free from mental agitation; calm. **2.** Quiet and motionless. — **Syn.** See CALM. [< L *tranquillus* quiet] — **tran′quil·ly** *adv.* — **tran′quil·ness** *n.*

tran·quil·ize (trang′kwəl-īz, tran′-) *v.t. & v.i.* **·ized, ·iz·ing** To make or become tranquil. Also **tran′quil·lize**, *Brit.* **tran′·quil·lise**. — **tran′quil·i·za′tion** *n.*

tran·quil·iz·er (trang′kwəl-ī′zər, tran′-) *n.* **1.** One who or that which tranquilizes. **2.** *Med.* Any of a class of drugs having the property of reducing nervous tension and anxiety states; ataractic drug. Also **tran′quil·liz′er**.

tran·quil·li·ty (trang-kwil′ə-tē, tran-) *n.* The state of being tranquil; calm; quiet. Also **tran·quil′i·ty**.

trans (tranz, trans) *adj. Chem.* Characterized by the arrangement of different atoms or groups of atoms on opposite sides of the molecule. [< TRANS-]

trans- *prefix* **1.** Across; beyond; through; on the other side of; as in:

transarctic	transcontinental	transfrontier
transborder	transdesert	transisthmian
transchannel	transequatorial	transpolar

In adjectives and nouns of place, the prefix may signify "on the other side of" (opposed to *cis-*) or "across; crossing." Through long usage, certain of these are written as solid words, as *transalpine, transatlantic*; otherwise, words in this class, unless by contrary official usage, are properly written with a hyphen, as in:

trans-African	trans-Baltic	trans-Iberian
trans-American	trans-Canadian	trans-Mediterranean
trans-Andean	trans-Germanic	trans-Scandinavian
trans-Arabian	trans-Himalayan	trans-Siberian

2. Through and through; changing completely; as in:

transcolor	transfashion

3. Surpassing; transcending; beyond; as in:

transconscious	transmaterial	transnational
transempirical	transmental	transphysical
transhuman	transmundane	transrational

4. *Anat.* Across; transversely; as in:

transcortical	transfrontal	transthoracic
transduodenal	transocular	transuterine

[< L < *trans* across, beyond, over]

trans. 1. Transaction(s). **2.** Transferred. **3.** *Gram.* Transitive. **4.** Translated; translation; translator. **5.** Transportation. **6.** Transpose. **7.** Transverse.

trans·act (trans·akt′, tranz-) *v.t.* **1.** To carry through; accomplish; do. — *v.i.* **2.** *Rare* To do business. [< L *transactus*, pp. of *transigere* to drive through, accomplish < *trans-* through + *agere* to drive, do] — **trans·ac′tor** *n.*

trans·ac·tion (trans·ak′shən, tranz-) *n.* **1.** The act of transacting, or the state of being transacted. **2.** Something transacted; especially, a business deal. **3.** *pl.* Published reports, as of a society. *Abbr.* **trans.** — **trans·ac′tion·al** *adj.*

trans·al·pine (trans·al′pin, -pīn, tranz-) *adj.* Of, pertaining to, or situated on the other side of the Alps, especially from Rome. — *n.* A native or a resident of beyond the Alps. [< L *transalpinus* < *trans-* across + *alpinus* alpine < *Alpes* the Alps]

trans·at·lan·tic (trans′ət·lan′tik, tranz′-) *adj.* **1.** On the other side of the Atlantic. **2.** Across or crossing the Atlantic.

trans·ca·lent (trans·kā′lənt) *adj.* Permitting or facilitating the passage of heat. [< TRANS- + L *calens, -entis*, ppr. of *calere* to be hot] — **trans·ca′len·cy** *n.*

Trans·car·pa·thi·an Oblast (trans′cär·pā′thē·ən) An administrative division of the Western Ukrainian S.S.R., once part of Czechoslovakia; 4,900 sq. mi.; pop. 1,057,000 (1970); center, Uzhgorod: formerly *Ruthenia*. Also *Carpatho-Ukraine*. Also **Transcarpathian Region.**

Trans·cau·ca·sia (trans′kô·kā′zhə, -shə) A region of the SE Soviet Union between the Caucasus mountains and Iran and Turkey, comprising the Armenian, Azerbaijan, and Georgian S.S.R.; from 1922–36 constituting the **Transcaucasian S.F.S.R.** — **Trans′cau·ca′sian** *adj. & n.*

trans·cei·ver (tran·sē′vər) *n. Electronics* A portable or mobile radio device containing equipment for both transmission and reception. [< TRANS(MITTER) + (RE)CEIVER]

tran·scend (tran·send′) *v.t.* **1.** To rise above in excellence or degree. **2.** To overstep or exceed as a limit. **3.** *Philos. & Theol.* To be independent of or beyond (the universe, experi-

ence, etc.) — *v.i.* **4.** To be transcendent; excel. — **Syn.** See EXCEED. [< L *transcendere* to surmount < *trans-* beyond, over + *scandere* to climb]

tran·scen·dent (tran·sen′dənt) *adj.* **1.** Of very high and remarkable degree; surpassing; excelling. **2.** *Philos.* In Kantianism, lying beyond the bounds of all possible human experience and knowledge. **3.** *Theol.* Above and beyond the universe: said of God. [< L *transcendens, -entis*, ppr. of *transcendere.* See TRANSCEND.] — **tran·scen′dence, tran·scen′den·cy, tran·scen′dent·ness** *n.* — **tran·scen′dent·ly** *adv.*

tran·scen·den·tal (tran′sen·den′təl) *adj.* **1.** Of very high degree; transcendent. **2.** *Philos.* In Kant's system, of an a priori character; transcending experience but not knowledge. **3.** Beyond or contrary to common sense or experience; metaphysical. **4.** *Math* Not formed by the fundamental operations of algebra, each performed a finite number of times: a *transcendental* number. — **tran′scen·den′tal·ly** *adv.*

tran·scen·den·tal·ism (tran′sen·den′təl·iz′əm) *n.* **1.** *Philos.* Any of several doctrines holding that reality is essentially mental or spiritual in nature, and that knowledge of it can be attained by intuitive or a priori, rather than empirical, principles: variously developed by Kant, Hegel, Fichte, Emerson, and others. **2.** The state or quality of being transcendental. — **tran′scen·den′tal·ist** *n. & adj.*

transcendental number *Math* A number that cannot be formed by the fundamental operations of algebra, as π.

tran·scribe (tran·skrīb′) *v.t.* **·scribed, ·scrib·ing** **1.** To write over again; copy or recopy in handwriting or typewriting from an original or from shorthand notes. **2.** *Telecom.* To make an electrical recording of (a radio or television program) for use on a later broadcast. **3.** To adapt (a musical composition) for a change of instrument or voice. **4.** To represent (the sounds of speech) by means of phonetic symbols. [< L *transcribere* < *trans-* over + *scribere* to write] — **tran·scrib′a·ble** *adj.* — **tran·scrib′er** *n.*

tran·script (tran′skript) *n.* **1.** That which is transcribed; especially, a written or typewritten copy. **2.** Any copy. **3.** A copy of a student's academic record, listing courses taken and grades received. — **Syn.** See DUPLICATE. [Fusion of OF *transcrit* (pp. of *transcrire* to transcribe < L *transcribere*) and L *transcriptus*, pp. of *transcribere.* See TRANSCRIBE.]

tran·scrip·tion (tran·skrip′shən) *n.* **1.** The act of transcribing. **2.** A copy; transcript. **3.** The representation of the sounds of speech by means of phonetic symbols; phonetic notation; also, a text containing such symbols. **4.** *Telecom.* An electrical recording of a performance made for a later radio broadcast. **5.** *Music* The adaptation of a composition for some instrument or voice other than that for which it was written. — **tran·scrip′tion·al, tran·scrip′tive** *adj.*

trans·cur·rent (trans·kûr′ənt) *adj.* Passing transversely.

trans·duc·er (trans·dōō′sər, -dyōō′-, tranz-) *n. Physics* Any device whereby energy may be transmitted from one system to another system, whether of the same or a different type. [< L *transducere*, var. of *traducere.* See TRADUCE.]

trans·duc·tion (trans·duk′shən) *n. Genetics* The transfer of one or more genetic determinants from one bacterial cell to another by means of bacterial viruses. [< L *transductus*, pp. of *transducere.* See TRANSDUCER.]

tran·sect (tran·sekt′) *v.t.* To dissect transversely. [< TRANS- + L *sectus*, pp. of *secare* to cut] — **tran·sec′tion** (-sek′shən) *n.*

tran·sept (tran′sept) *n. Archit.* One of the lateral members or projections between the nave and choir of a cruciform church. [< Med.L *transeptum*, short for L *transversum septum* < *transversus* lying across + *septum* enclosure] — **tran·sep′tal** *adj.* — **tran·sep′tal·ly** *adv.*

trans·e·unt (tran′sē·ənt) *adj.* Proceeding from and operating beyond itself on another. [< L *transiens, transeuntis.* See TRANSIENT.]

trans·fer (trans′fər; *for v.*, also trans·fûr′) *v.* **·ferred, ·fer·ring** *v.t.* **1.** To carry, or cause to pass, from one person, place, etc., to another. **2.** To make over possession of to another. **3.** To convey (a drawing) from one surface to another, as by specially prepared paper. — *v.i.* **4.** To transfer oneself. **5.** To be transferred. **6.** To change from one vehicle to another on a transfer (def. 4). **7.** To shift one's enrollment as a student from one educational institution to another. — **Syn.** See CONVEY. — *n.* **1.** The act of transferring, or the state of being transferred. Also **trans·fer′al** (-fûr′əl) or **trans·fer′ral. 2.** That which is transferred, as a design conveyed from one surface to another. **3.** A place, method, or means of transfer. **4.** A ticket entitling a passenger to change to another public vehicle with or without paying another fare. **5.** *Law* A delivery of title or property from one person to another. **6.** An order transferring money or securities. [< OF *transferer* < L *transferre* < *trans-* across + *ferre* to carry] — **trans·fer′a·bil′i·ty** *n.* — **trans·fer′a·ble** *adj.*

trans·fer·ee (trans′fə·rē′) *n.* **1.** *Law* One to whom a transfer is made. **2.** One who is transferred.

trans·fer·ence (trans·fûr′əns) *n.* **1.** The act of transferrring, or the state of being transferred. **2.** *Psychoanal.* The transfer of emotions associated with forgotten experiences of early life from the original object to another, usually the psychoanalyst. [< NL *transferentia* < L *transferens, -entis,* ppr. of *transferre.* See TRANSFER.] — **trans·fer·en·tial** (trans'fə·ren'shəl) *adj.*

trans·fer·or (trans-fûr'ər) *n. Law* One who executes a transfer of property, title, etc.

transfer paper Paper having an adhesive coating over a design to be transferred to another surface by means of pressure, applied moisture, etc.

trans·fer·rer (trans-fûr'ər) *n.* One who or that which transfers.

Trans·fig·u·ra·tion (trans'fig·yə·rā'shən) *n.* **1.** The supernatural transformation of Christ on the mount as recorded in the Gospels. *Matt.* xvii 1–9. **2.** A church festival commemorating this, observed on August 6.

trans·fig·ure (trans-fig'yər) *v.t.* **·ured, ·ur·ing 1.** To change the outward form or appearance of. **2.** To make glorious; idealize. [< L *transfigurare* to change the shape of < *trans-* across + *figura* shape] — **trans·fig·u·ra'tion, trans·fig'ure·ment** *n.*

trans·fi·nite (trans-fī'nīt) *adj.* **1.** Beyond the finite. **2.** *Math.* Of, pertaining to, or characterized by the properties of a cardinal or ordinal number that is not an integer.

trans·fix (trans-fiks') *v.t.* **1.** To pierce through; impale. **2.** To fix in place by impaling. **3.** To make motionless, as with horror, awe, etc. [< L *transfixus,* pp. of *transfigere* < *trans-* through + *figere* to fasten] — **trans·fix'ion** (-fik'shən) *n.*

trans·flu·ent (trans'floo·ənt) *adj.* **1.** Flowing across or through. **2.** *Heraldry* Flowing through the arches of a bridge. [< L *transfluens, -entis,* ppr. of *transfluere* < *trans-* across + *fluere* to flow]

trans·form (*v.* trans-fôrm'; *n.* trans'fôrm) *v.t.* **1.** To give a different form or appearance to. **2.** To change the character, nature, condition, etc., of. **3.** *Math.* To change (one expression or operation) into another equivalent to it or having similar properties. **4.** *Electr.* To change the potential or flow of (a current), as from higher to lower voltage, or from alternating to direct. **5.** *Physics* To alter the energy form of, as electrical into mechanical. — *v.i.* **6.** To be or become changed in form or character. — *n. Ling.* Any of a group of constructions that can be considered rewritings or rephrasings of one another. — **Syn.** See CHANGE. [< L *transformare* < *trans-* over + *formare* to form < *forma* form] — **trans·form'a·ble** *adj.*

trans·for·ma·tion (trans'fər·mā'shən) *n.* **1.** Any change. **2.** The act of transforming, or the state of being transformed. **3.** A wig worn by a woman. **4.** *Ling.* A change from one construction to another construction considered more or less equivalent according to the syntactic laws of a language, as, in English, from active to passive or from statement to question. — **trans·form·a·tive** (trans·fôr'mə·tiv) *adj.*

trans·for·ma·tion·al (trans'fər·mā'shən·əl) *adj.* Of or pertaining to linguistic transformations. — **trans·for·ma·tion·al·ly** *adv.*

transformational grammar A grammar that uses transformations as well as phrase structure to account for the derivation of all the sentences of a language.

trans·form·er (trans-fôr'mər) *n.* **1.** One who or that which transforms. **2.** *Electr.* A device for changing the ratio of current to voltage in alternating-current systems, while keeping power substantially constant. A transformer often consists of two coils wound on the same iron core.

trans·form·ism (trans-fôr'miz·əm) *n. Biol.* The theory of the development of one species from another through successive gradual modifications.

trans·form·ist (trans-fôr'mist) *n.* A person who believes in the theory of transformism.

trans·fuse (trans-fyooz') *v.t.* **·fused, ·fus·ing 1.** To pour, as a fluid, from one vessel to another. **2.** To cause to be imparted or instilled. **3.** *Med.* To transfer (blood) from one person or animal to another. [< L *transfusus,* pp. of *transfundere* < *trans-* across + *fundere* to pour] — **trans·fus'er** *n.* — **trans·fus'i·ble** *adj.* — **trans·fu·sive** (trans-fyoo'siv) *adj.*

trans·fu·sion (trans-fyoo'zhən) *n.* **1.** The act of transfusing. **2.** *Med.* **a** The transfer of blood from one person or animal to the veins or arteries of another. **b** A similar transfer of any other fluid, as a saline solution.

trans·gress (trans-gres', tranz-) *v.t.* **1.** To break (a law, oath, etc.); violate. **2.** To pass beyond or over (limits); exceed; trespass. — *v.i.* **3.** To break a law; sin. [Appar. < OF *transgresser* < L *transgressus,* pp. of *transgredi* < *trans-* across + *gradi* to step] — **trans·gress'i·ble** *adj.* — **trans·gress'ing·ly** *adv.* — **trans·gres'sor** *n.*

trans·gres·sion (trans-gresh'ən, tranz-) *n.* **1.** A violation or infringement of a law, command, etc.; especially, a violation of a law regarded as having divine authority; sin. **2.** The act of transgressing. — **Syn.** Compare SIN[1].

trans·gres·sive (trans-gres'iv, tranz-) *adj.* Apt to transgress or sin; faulty; culpable. — **trans·gres'sive·ly** *adv.*

tran·ship (tran-ship'), **tran·ship·ment** (tran-ship'mənt) See TRANSSHIP, etc.

trans·hu·mance (trans-hyoo'məns) *n.* The movement of cattle or other animals to more suitable places as the seasons change, especially of livestock to and from mountain pastures. [< F < *transhumer* < Sp. *trashumar* < L *trans-* across + *humare* to cover with earth < *humus* earth] — **trans·hu'mant** *adj.*

tran·sience (tran'shəns) *n.* The state or quality of being transient. Also **tran'sien·cy** (-shən·sē).

tran·sient (tran'shənt) *adj.* **1.** Passing away quickly; of short duration; brief. **2.** Not permanent; temporary; transitory. — *n.* One who or that which is transient; especially, a lodger or boarder who remains for a short time. [< L *transiens, -euntis,* ppr. of *transire* < *trans-* across + *ire* to go] — **tran'sient·ly** *adv.* — **tran'sient·ness** *n.*

— **Syn.** (adj.) **1, 2.** *Transient, transitory, passing, ephemeral, momentary, evanescent, fleeting,* and *temporary* mean present or existing for a brief time. Something *transient* actually passes soon, while a *transitory* thing has the quality of impermanence: a *transient* visitor, a *transitory* stage of development. *Passing* is close to *transitory* but less formal: a *passing* fad. In a literal sense, *ephemeral* refers to that which lasts only one day; in extension, it denotes that which changes aspect rapidly or continuously: an *ephemeral* inspiration. *Momentary* and *evanescent* suggest extremely short duration; *evanescent* refers to that which vanishes almost as soon as it appears, and implies that a thing is tenuous at the outset: a *momentary* twinge of compunction; an *evanescent* glimpse of the truth. A *fleeting* thing passes swiftly: the *fleeting* hour. *Temporary* implies existence for a measurable, although limited, time: a *temporary* shelter from the storm, a *temporary* chairman. — **Ant.** permanent, perpetual.

tran·sil·i·ent (tran-sil'ē·ənt) *adj.* Leaping or passing abruptly from one thing or condition to another. [< L *transiliens, -entis,* ppr. of *transilire* < *trans-* across + *salire* to leap] — **tran·sil'i·ence** (-əns) *n.*

trans·il·lu·mi·nate (trans'i·loo'mə·nāt, tranz'-) *v.t.* **·nat·ed, ·nat·ing** *Med.* To cause light to pass through (an organ or part of the body) to reveal its condition.

tran·sis·tor (tran-zis'tər, -sis'-) *n. Electronics* A miniature device for the control and amplification of an electron current, made of semiconducting materials, and having three or more electrodes, the current between one pair controlling the amplified current between another pair, one electrode being common to each pair. [< TRANS(FER) (RES)ISTOR]

tran·sis·tor·ize (tran-zis'tə·rīz, -sis'-) *v.t.* **·ized, ·iz·ing** To equip with transistors instead of electron tubes, as a radio, hearing aid, etc.

tran·sit (tran'sit, -zit) *n.* **1.** The act of passing over or through; passage. **2.** The act of carrying across or through; conveyance. **3.** A transition or change. **4.** *Astron.* **a** The passage of one heavenly body across the disk of another. **b** The moment of passage of a celestial body across the meridian. **5.** A surveying instrument resembling a theodolite, for measuring horizontal and vertical angles: also **transit theodolite.** — *v.t.* **1.** To pass through or across. **2.** To reverse the horizontal or vertical direction of (a telescope or transit instrument). Abbr. *t.* [< L *transitus* < *transire* to cross. See TRANSIENT.]

transit instrument 1. An astronomical telescope mounted in the plane of the meridian and turning on a fixed east-and-west axis, used to determine the time of transit of an object over the meridian. **2.** A transit (def. 5).

tran·si·tion (tran-zish'ən) *n.* **1.** The act or state of passing from one place, condition, or action to another; change. **2.** The time, period, or place of such passage. **3.** A sentence, paragraph, etc., that leads from one subject or aspect of a subject to another, as in an essay. **4.** *Music* A passing modulation, an abrupt change of key, or a passage connecting two themes or subjects. — **tran·si'tion·al, tran·si'tion·ar'y** (-er'ē) *adj.* — **tran·si'tion·al·ly** *adv.*

tran·si·tive (tran'sə·tiv) *adj.* **1.** *Gram.* Of or pertaining to transitive verbs. **2.** Capable of passing; effecting transition. — *n. Gram.* A transitive verb. Abbr. *t., tr., trans.* [< LL *transitivus* < L *transitus* transit. See TRANSIT.] — **tran'si·tive·ly** *adv.* — **tran'si·tive·ness, tran'si·tiv'i·ty** *n.*

transitive verb A verb that requires a direct object to complete its meaning.

tran·si·to·ry (tran'sə·tôr'ē, -tō'rē) *adj.* Existing for a short time only. — **Syn.** See TRANSIENT. [< OF *transitoire* < L *transitorius* allowing passage through < *transitus.* See TRANSIT.] — **tran'si·to'ri·ly** *adv.* — **tran'si·to'ri·ness** *n.*

Trans-Jor·dan (trans-jôr'dən, tranz-) An Arab territory included in the Hashemite Kingdom of the Jordan; a former British mandate. Formerly **Trans·jor·da·ni·a** (trans'jôr·dā'nē·ə, tranz'-).

transl. Translated; translation.

trans·late (trans-lāt', tranz-, trans'lāt, tranz') *v.* **·lat·ed, ·lat·ing** *v.t.* **1.** To give the sense or equivalent of in another language; change into another language. **2.** To explain in other words; interpret. **3.** To change into another form; transform. **4.** To remove, as an ecclesiastic, from one office to another. **5.** To retransmit (a message) by means of a telegraphic relay. **6.** To convey or remove from earth to heaven without natural death. **7.** *Mech.* To subject (a body) to translation. **8.** *Archaic* To transport; enrapture. — *v.i.* **9.** To act as translator. **10.** To admit of translation:

This book *translates* easily. [? < OF *translater* < L *translatus*, pp. of *transferre*. See TRANSFER.] — **trans·lat'a·ble** *adj.* — **trans·lat'a·ble·ness** *n.*

trans·la·tion (trans·lā'shən, tranz-) *n.* **1.** The act of translating, or the state of being translated. **2.** That which is translated; especially, a work translated into another language; a version. **3.** *Mech.* Motion in which, at any instant, every point of a body is moving in the same direction and at the same velocity as every other point. **4.** Automatic resending of a telegraphic message to a more distant point. Abbr. *tr., trans., transl.* — **Syn.** See MOTION. — **trans·la'tion·al** *adj.*

trans·la·tor (trans·lā'tər, tranz-, trans'lā·tər, tranz'-) *n.* One who translates, especially a work from one language to another; also, an interpreter. Abbr. *tr.* — **trans·la·to·ri·al** (trans'lə·tôr'ē·əl, -tō'rē-, tranz'-) *adj.*

trans·lit·er·ate (trans·lit'ə·rāt, tranz-) *v.t.* **·at·ed, ·at·ing** To represent (a letter or word) by the alphabetic characters of another language. [< TRANS- + L *litera* letter] — **trans·lit'er·a'tion** *n.*

trans·lo·cate (trans·lō'kāt, tranz-) *v.t.* **·cat·ed, ·cat·ing** To cause to shift from one place or position to another.

trans·lo·ca·tion (trans'lō·kā'shən, tranz-) *n.* **1.** A shift in position. **2.** *Genetics* The attachment of a part of a chromosome to another chromosome, with resulting changes in the arrangement of the genes.

trans·lu·cent (trans·lōō'sənt, tranz-) *adj.* Allowing the passage of light, but not permitting a clear view of any object; semitransparent: distinguished from *transparent.* — **Syn.** See CLEAR. [< L *translucens, -entis,* ppr. of *translucere* < *trans-* through, across + *lucere* to shine] — **trans·lu'cence, trans·lu'cen·cy** *n.* — **trans·lu'cent·ly** *adv.*

trans·lu·nar (trans·lōō'nər, tranz-) *adj.* **1.** Situated beyond the moon. **2.** Ethereal; visionary. Also **trans·lu'na·ry** (-nər·ē). [< TRANS- + L *luna* moon]

trans·ma·rine (trans'mə·rēn', tranz'-) *adj.* **1.** Crossing the sea. **2.** Situated across or beyond the sea. [< L *transmarinus* < *trans-* across + *mare* sea]

trans·mi·grant (trans·mī'grənt, tranz-, trans'mə·grənt, tranz'-) *adj.* Passing from one place or condition to another. — *n.* One who or that which transmigrates; especially, an immigrant or emigrant. [< L *transmigrans, -antis,* ppr. of *transmigrare.* See TRANSMIGRATE.]

trans·mi·grate (trans·mī'grāt, tranz-, trans'mə-, tranz'-) *v.i.* **·grat·ed, ·grat·ing** **1.** To migrate from one place or condition to another, especially, from one country or jurisdiction to another. **2.** To pass into another body, as the soul at death. [< L *transmigratus,* pp. of *transmigrare* < *trans-* across + *migrare* to migrate] — **trans·mi'gra·tor** *n.* — **trans·mi·gra·to·ry** (trans·mī'grə·tôr'ē, -tō'rē, tranz-) *adj.*

trans·mi·gra·tion (trans'mī·grā'shən, -mə-, tranz'-) *n.* **1.** The act of transmigrating. **2.** The assumed passing of the soul, after death, from one body to another: also called *metempsychosis:* also **transmigration of souls.** — **trans'mi·gra'tion·ism** *n.*

trans·mis·si·ble (trans·mis'ə·bəl, tranz-) *adj.* Capable of being transmitted. Also **trans·mit'ti·ble** (-mit'ə·bəl). — **trans·mis'si·bil'i·ty** *n.*

trans·mis·sion (trans·mish'ən, tranz-) *n.* **1.** The act of transmitting, or the state of being transmitted. **2.** That which is transmitted. **3.** *Mech.* **a** A device that transmits power from the engine of an automobile to the driving wheels and varies the speed ratios between them. The principal types are **automatic transmission,** in which the speed ratios are automatically selected and engaged, and **manual transmission,** in which the speed ratios are selected and engaged by hand. **b** The gears for changing speed. [< L *transmissio, -onis* < *transmissus,* pp. of *transmittere.* See TRANSMIT.]

trans·mis·sive (trans·mis'iv, tranz-) *adj.* Capable of transmitting or being transmitted.

trans·mit (trans·mit', tranz-) *v.t.* **·mit·ted, ·mit·ting** **1.** To send from one place or person to another; forward or convey; dispatch. **2.** To pass on by heredity; transfer. **3.** To pass on or communicate (news, information, etc.). **4.** *Telecom.* To send out (information, radio and television broadcasts, etc.) by means of electromagnetic waves. **5.** *Physics* To cause (light, sound, etc.) to pass through a medium. **6.** *Mech.* To convey (force, motion, etc.) from one part or mechanism to another. — **Syn.** See CONVEY. [< L *transmittere* < *trans-* across + *mittere* to send] — **trans·mit'tal** *n.*

trans·mit·tance (trans·mit'ns, tranz-) *n.* **1.** The act or process of transmitting. **2.** *Physics* The ratio of radiant energy transmitted to the total that impinges on a body.

trans·mit·ter (trans·mit'ər, tranz-) *n.* **1.** One who or that which transmits. **2.** A telegraphic sending instrument. **3.** The part of a telephone that converts sound waves into electrical waves. **4.** *Telecom.* The part of a radio or television system that generates, modulates, and transmits electromagnetic waves to the antenna.

trans·mog·ri·fy (trans·mog'rə·fī, tranz-) *v.t.* **·fied, ·fy·ing** To convert into a different shape; transform. [A humorous coinage] — **trans·mog'ri·fi·ca'tion** *n.*

trans·mon·tane (trans·mon'tān, tranz-, trans'mon·tān', tranz'-) *adj.* Situated beyond a mountain; tramontane. [Fusion of OF *transmontane,* alter. of *tramontane* polestar, north pole and L *transmontanus.* See TRAMONTANE.]

trans·mu·ta·tion (trans'myōō·tā'shən, tranz'-) *n.* **1.** The act of transmuting, or the state of being transmuted. **2.** *Physics* The change of one element into another through alteration of its nuclear structure, as by bombardment with high-energy particles in an accelerator. **3.** *Biol.* Successive change of form; transformism. **4.** In alchemy, the supposed change of a base metal into gold, silver, etc. — **trans·mu·ta'tion·al, trans·mu·ta·tive** (trans·myōō'tə·tiv, tranz-) *adj.*

trans·mute (trans·myōōt', tranz-) *v.t.* **·mut·ed, ·mut·ing** To change in nature, form, quality, etc.; transform. Also **trans·mu'tate.** — **Syn.** See CHANGE. [< L *transmutare* < *trans-* across + *mutare* to change] — **trans·mut'a·ble** *adj.* — **trans·mut'a·bil'i·ty, trans·mut'a·ble·ness** *n.* — **trans·mut'a·bly** *adv.* — **trans·mut'er** *n.*

trans·nep·tu·ni·an (trans'nep·tōō'nē·ən, -tyōō'-, tranz'-) *adj. Astron.* Beyond the planet Neptune. [< TRANS- + NEPTUN(E) + -IAN]

trans·nor·mal (trans·nôr'məl, tranz-) *adj.* Above the normal; supernormal.

trans·o·ce·an·ic (trans'ō·shē·an'ik, tranz'-) *adj.* **1.** Lying beyond or over the ocean. **2.** Crossing the ocean.

tran·som (tran'səm) *n.* **1.** A small window above a door or window, usually hinged to a horizontal crosspiece; also, the crosspiece. **2.** A horizontal construction dividing a window into stages. **3.** *Naut.* A beam running across and forming part of the stern frame of a ship. **4.** The horizontal crossbar of a gallows or cross. [< L *transtrum* crossbeam < *trans* across] — **tran'somed** *adj.*

tran·son·ic (tran·son'ik) *adj. Aeron.* Of or pertaining to conditions encountered when passing from subsonic to supersonic speeds.

transonic barrier *Aeron.* A barrier to supersonic flight encountered by aircraft designed for subsonic speed, caused by turbulence of the airflow around different parts of the plane: also called *sonic barrier, sound barrier.*

Trans·ox·i·an·a (trans·ok'sē·an'ə) See SOGDIANA.

transp. **1.** Transparent. **2.** Transportation.

trans·pa·cif·ic (trans'pə·sif'ik) *adj.* **1.** Crossing the Pacific Ocean. **2.** Situated across or beyond the Pacific.

trans·pa·dane (trans'pə·dān) *adj.* Being beyond the river Po, from Rome as a standpoint. [< L *transpadanus* < *trans-* across + *padanus* of the Po < *Padus* the river Po]

trans·par·en·cy (trans·pâr'ən·sē, -par'-) *n. pl.* **·cies** **1.** The quality of being transparent. Also **trans·par'ence.** **2.** Something transparent; especially, a picture on a light-permeable substance, as glass, intended to be viewed by shining a light through it. **3.** *Photog.* The power of a sensitized negative to transmit light.

trans·par·ent (trans·pâr'ənt, -par'-) *adj.* **1.** Admitting the passage of light, and permitting a clear view of objects beyond; pervious to light: *transparent* glass: distinguished from *translucent.* **2.** Easy to see through or understand; obvious. **3.** Without guile; frank; candid. **4.** Diaphanous; sheer. Abbr. *transp.* — **Syn.** See CLEAR. [< Med.L *transparens, -entis* < L *trans-* across + *parere* to appear, be visible] — **trans·par'ent·ly** *adv.* — **trans·par'ent·ness** *n.*

tran·spic·u·ous (tran·spik'yōō·əs) *adj.* Transparent. [< Med.L *transpicuus* < L *transpicere* to look, see through < *trans-* through + *specere* to look]

trans·pierce (trans·pirs') *v.t.* **·pierced, ·pierc·ing** To pierce through; penetrate completely. [< MF *transpercer* < *trans-* (< L, across, through) + *percer* to pierce]

tran·spi·ra·tion (tran'spə·rā'shən) *n.* A transpiring or exhalation, especially through a porous substance or through the tissues of a plant.

tran·spire (tran·spīr') *v.* **·spired, ·spir·ing** *v.t.* **1.** *Physiol.* To give off (waste products) from the surface of the body, leaves, etc.; exhale. — *v.i.* **2.** *Physiol.* To give off waste products, as the surface of the body, leaves, etc. **3.** To become known. **4.** *Informal* To happen; occur. ◆ Although *transpire* is used widely in this last sense and so appears in the works of such writers as Dickens and Hawthorne, this usage is considered erroneous by some. [< F *transpirer* < L *trans-* across, through + *spirare* to breathe]

trans·plant (*v.* trans·plant', -plänt'; *n.* trans'plant', -plänt') *v.t.* **1.** To remove and plant in another place. **2.** To remove and settle or establish for residence in another place. **3.** *Surg.* To transfer (a portion of tissue) from its original site to another part of the same individual, or to another individual. — *n.* **1.** That which is transplanted. **2.** The act of transplanting. [< LL *transplantare* < L *trans-* across + *plantare* to plant] — **trans·plan·ta'tion** *n.* — **trans·plant'er** *n.*

trans·pon·der (trans·pon'dər) *n. Telecom.* An electronic device, used in meteorology, navigation, aeronautics, artificial satellites, etc., that emits radio or radar signals in response to pulses received from an interrogator: also called *pulse repeater.* [< TRANS(MITTER) + (RES)PONDER]

---

trans·pon·tine (trans-pon′tin, -tīn) *adj.* **1.** Situated on the other side of a bridge. **2.** Of or pertaining to London south of the Thames. [< TRANS- + L *pons, pontis* bridge]

trans·port (*v.* trans-pôrt′, -pōrt′; *n.* trans′pôrt, -pōrt) *v.t.* **1.** To carry or convey from one place to another. **2.** To carry away with emotion. **3.** To carry into banishment, especially beyond the sea. **4.** *Obs.* To kill. — **Syn.** See BANISH, CONVEY. — *n.* **1.** A vessel used to transport troops, military supplies, etc. **2.** An aircraft used to transport passengers, mail, etc. **3.** The state of being transported with rapture; ecstasy. **4.** The act of transporting. **5.** A deported convict. [< MF *transporter* < L *transportare* < *trans-* across + *portare* to carry] — **trans·port′er** *n.*

trans·port·a·ble (trans-pôr′tə-bəl, -pōr′-) *adj.* Capable of being transported. — **trans·port′a·bil′i·ty** *n.*

trans·por·ta·tion (trans′pər-tā′shən) *n.* **1.** The act of transporting, or the state of being transported. **2.** A means of transporting, as a vehicle. **3.** A charge for conveyance. **4.** A ticket, pass, etc., for travel. *Abbr.* trans., transp.

trans·pose (trans-pōz′) *v.t.* **·posed, ·pos·ing** **1.** To reverse the order or change the place of; interchange. **2.** To change in place or order, as a word in a sentence. **3.** *Math.* To transfer (a term) with a changed sign from one side of an algebraic equation to the other, so as not to destroy the equality of the members. **4.** *Music* To move (a chord, melody, composition, etc.) upward or downward in pitch while retaining its internal interval structure. **5.** *Rare* To transport. **6.** *Obs.* To transform. — *v.i.* **7.** *Music* To play in a key other than the one notated: said of players or instruments. *Abbr.* tr., trans. [< OF *transposer* < L *trans-* over + OF *poser*. See POSE[1].] — **trans·pos′a·ble** *adj.* — **trans·pos′er** *n.*

trans·po·si·tion (trans′pə-zish′ən) *n.* **1.** The act of transposing, or the state of being transposed. **2.** That which has been transposed. Also **trans·po·sal** (trans-pō′zəl). — **trans′po·si′tion·al** *adj.*

trans·sex (tranz-seks′) *v.i. Informal* To become a transsexual.

trans·sex·u·al (tranz-sek′shōō-əl) *n.* One whose sex has been changed by surgery and hormone treatment. — *adj.* Of or pertaining to a transsexual or to such surgery or treatment.

trans·ship (trans-ship′) *v.t. & v.i.* **·shipped, ·ship·ping** To transfer from one conveyance or line to another: also spelled *tranship.* — **trans·ship′ment** *n.*

Trans-Si·ber·i·an Railroad (trans′sī-bir′ē-ən) A rail line across the south central and SE R.S.F.S.R., linking Chelyabinsk and Vladivostok; 4,600 mi. long; built 1892–1905.

tran·sub·stan·ti·ate (tran′səb-stan′shē-āt) *v.t.* **·at·ed, ·at·ing** **1.** To change from one substance into another; transmute; transform. **2.** *Theol.* To change the substance of (the bread and wine of the Eucharist) into the body and blood of Christ. [< Med.L *transubstantiatus,* pp. of *transubstantiare* < L *trans-* over + *substantia* substance]

tran·sub·stan·ti·a·tion (tran′səb-stan′shē-ā′shən) *n.* **1.** *Theol.* The doctrine that the substance of the eucharistic elements is converted into that of the body and blood of Christ: distinguished from *consubstantiation, impanation.* **2.** A change of anything into something essentially different. — **tran′sub·stan′ti·a′tion·al·ist** *n.*

tran·su·date (tran′sōō-dāt) *n.* **1.** A fluid that transudes. **2.** The act of transuding. Also **tran′su·da′tion** (-dā′shən). [< NL *transudatus,* pp. of *transudare.* See TRANSUDE.]

tran·sude (tran-sōōd′) *v.i.* **·sud·ed, ·sud·ing** To pass through the pores or tissues, as of a membrane. [< NL *transudare* < L *trans-* across, through + *sudare* to sweat] — **tran·su′da·to·ry** (-sōō′də-tôr′ē, -tō′rē) *adj.*

trans·u·ra·ni·an (trans′yōō-rā′nē-ən, tranz′-) *adj. Physics* Of or pertaining to any of those radioactive elements (**transuranian element**) having an atomic number greater than that of uranium. Also **trans·u·ran′ic** (-ran′ik). [< TRANS + URAN(IUM) + -IAN]

Trans·vaal (trans-väl′, tranz′-) A Province of NE South Africa; 110,450 sq. mi.; pop. 6,273,477 (1967); seat of government, Pretoria; formerly an independent republic.

trans·val·ue (trans-val′yōō, tranz′-) *v.t.* **·ued, ·u·ing** To appraise the value of by a principle at variance with accepted or conventional standards. — **trans·val′u·a′tion** *n.*

trans·ver·sal (trans-vûr′səl, tranz′-) *adj.* Transverse. — *n. Geom.* A line intersecting a system of lines: also called *traverse.*

trans·verse (trans-vûrs′, tranz′-) *adj.* **1.** Lying or being across or from side to side; athwart. **2.** *Anat.* Placed across the long axis of a part: a *transverse* muscle. — *n.* **1.** That which is transverse. **2.** *Geom.* That axis of a hyperbola that passes through its foci. *Abbr.* trans. [< L *transversus* lying across, pp. of *transvertere* < *trans-* across + *vertere* to turn] — **trans·verse′ly** *adv.* — **trans·verse′ness** *n.*

transverse colon *Anat.* The portion of the colon that lies across the upper part of the abdomen.

transverse flute The modern flute, played by blowing into a hole in the side of the tube near the upper end.

transverse process *Anat.* A long process extending laterally from a vertebra.

trans·ves·ti·tism (trans-ves′tə-tiz′əm, tranz-) *n. Psychiatry* A compulsive need to dress in the garments appropriate to members of the opposite sex. Compare EONISM. Also **trans·ves′tism.** [< TRANS- + L *vestitus,* pp. of *vestire* to clothe] — **trans·ves′tite** (-tīt) *n.*

Tran·syl·va·ni·a (tran′sil-vā′nē-ə) A region and former province in central Rumania; formerly the eastern part of Hungary. — **Tran·syl·va′ni·an** *adj. & n.*

trap[1] (trap) *n.* **1.** A device for catching game or other animals, as a pitfall or a snare. **2.** Any artifice or stratagem by which a person may be betrayed or taken unawares. **3.** *Mech.* A U- or S-bend in a pipe, etc., that fills with water or other liquid for sealing the pipe against a return flow, as of noxious gas. **4.** A contrivance for hurling clay pigeons or glass balls into the air for sportsmen to shoot at. **5.** In some games, especially golf, an obstacle or hazard: a sand *trap.* **6.** A light, two-wheeled carriage suspended by springs. **7.** *pl.* Percussion instruments, as drums, cymbals, etc. **8.** A trap door (which see). **9.** The game of trapball; also, a pivoted piece of wood, resembling a low shoe, used in the game to throw a ball into the air. **10.** *U.S. Slang* The mouth: Shut your *trap.* — *v.* **trapped, trap·ping** *v.t.* **1.** To catch in a trap; ensnare. **2.** To stop or hold (a gas, liquid, etc.) by some obstruction. **3.** To provide with a trap. — *v.i.* **4.** To set traps for game. **5.** To be a trapper. [OE *treppe, træppe*]

trap[2] (trap) *n.* **1.** *pl. Informal* Personal effects, as luggage; also, household goods. **2.** *Obs.* Trappings (def. 1). — *v.t.* **trapped, trap·ping** To adorn with trappings; bedeck. [Orig. a cloth covering for a horse, alter. of OF *drap* cloth, covering < Med.L *drappus;* ult. origin uncertain]

trap[3] (trap) *n. Geol.* A dark, fine-grained igneous rock, often of columnar structure, as basalt, dolerite, etc.: also called *traprock.* [< Sw. *trapp* < *trappa* stair; so called from the steplike arrangement of this rock in other rock]

tra·pan (trə-pan′) See TREPAN[2].

Tra·pa·ni (trä′pä-nē) A port city in NW tip of Sicily; pop. 68,100 (est. 1967): ancient *Drepanum.*

trap·ball (trap′bôl′) *n.* **1.** A game in which a player strikes one end of a trap with a bat and thus flips a ball into the air that others try to catch. **2.** The ball used in this game.

trap door A door, hinged or sliding, to cover an opening, as in a floor or roof.

trap-door spider (trap′dôr′, -dōr′) A large spider (family *Ctenizidae*) that inhabits a tubular pit in the ground, covered by a lid hinged to the silken lining of the tube.

trapes (trāps) See TRAIPSE.

tra·peze (trə-pēz′, tra-) *n.* **1.** A short swinging bar, suspended by two ropes, used by gymnasts, etc. **2.** *Geom.* A trapezium. [< F *trapèze* < NL *trapezium* trapezium]

tra·pe·zi·form (trə-pē′zə-fôrm) *adj.* Having the form of a trapezium. [< TRAPEZI(UM) + -FORM]

tra·pe·zi·um (trə-pē′zē-əm) *n. pl.* **·zi·a** (-zē-ə) **1.** *Geom.* **a** A four-sided plane figure of which no two sides are parallel. **b** *Brit.* A trapezoid. **2.** *Anat.* **a** The bone of the distal row of the carpus situated on the radial side at the base of the thumb. **b** A band of transverse fibers found in the pons Varolii of the brain. [< NL < Gk. *trapezion,* dim. of *trapeza* table, lit., four-footed (bench) < *tetra-* four, + *peza* foot]

tra·pe·zi·us (trə-pē′zē-əs) *n. Anat.* Either of two flat muscles serving to support and raise the head, extending laterally from the base of the occiput to the scapula and terminating in the middle of the back. [< NL < TRAPEZIUM. See TRAPEZIUM.]

trap·e·zo·he·dron (trap′ə-zō-hē′drən, trə-pē′-) *n. pl.* **·dra** (-drə) *Crystall.* A figure bounded by six, eight, or twelve faces, each having unequal intercepts on all axes. [< NL < *trapezium* trapezium + Gk. *hedra* base]

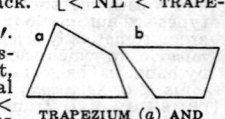

TRAPEZIUM (a) AND TRAPEZOID (b)

trap·e·zoid (trap′ə-zoid) *n.* **1.** *Geom.* **a** A quadrilateral of which two sides are parallel. **b** *Brit.* A trapezium. **2.** *Anat.* An irregular bone in the second row of the carpus, at the end of the forefinger. [< NL *trapezoïdes* < Gk. *trapezoeidēs* tablelike < *trapeza* table + *eidos* form] — **trap·e·zoi′dal** *adj.*

trap·pe·an (trap′ē-ən, tra-pē′ən) *adj.* Of or pertaining to traprock. Also **trap′pous, trap·pose** (trap′ōs). [< TRAP[3]]

trap·per (trap′ər) *n.* One whose occupation is the trapping of fur-bearing animals.

trap·pings (trap′ingz) *n.pl.* **1.** An ornamental housing or harness for a horse. **2.** Adornments of any kind; embellishments; superficial dress. — **Syn.** See CAPARISON. [< TRAP[2]]

Trap·pist (trap′ist) *n.* A member of an ascetic order of monks, a branch of the Cistercians, noted for silence and abstinence. — *adj.* Of or pertaining to the Trappists. [< F *Trappiste,* after *La Trappe* in Normandy, name of their first abbey, founded 1664]

trap·rock (trap′rok′) *n.* Trap[3].

trap·shoot·ing (trap′shōō′ting) *n.* The sport of shooting clay pigeons sent up from spring traps. — **trap′shoot′er** *n.*

trash[1] (trash) *n.* **1.** Worthless or waste matter of any kind; rubbish. **2.** A worthless or despicable individual or group of individuals. **3.** Worthless or foolish writing, ideas, etc.; nonsense. **4.** That which is broken or lopped off; especially, the loppings and trimmings of trees and plants. **5.** The dry refuse of sugar cane after the juice has been expressed. — *v.t.* **1.** To free from trash. **2.** To strip of leaves; prune; lop. [Cf. dial. Norw. *trask* lumber, trash, baggage]

trash² (trash) *n. Brit. Dial.* A leash used to check a hunting dog. — *v.t.* **1.** *Obs.* To keep in check with a trash. **2.** *Archaic* To hinder; restrain. [? < OF *trachier*, var. of *tracier*. See TRACE¹.]

trash·y (trash′ē) *adj.* **trash·i·er**, **trash·i·est** Resembling trash or rubbish; worthless; cheap: *trashy* poetry. — **trash′·i·ly** *adv.* — **trash′i·ness** *n.*

Tra·si·me·no (trä′sē·mē′nō), **Lake** A lake in central Italy; 50 sq. mi.; scene of Hannibal's defeat of the Romans, 217 B.C.: also *Lake of Perugia.* Ancient **Tras·i·me·nus** (tras′i·mē′nəs).

trass (tras) *n.* A volcanic earth, used in preparation of a hydraulic cement. [< G < Du. *tras* < earlier *taras.* Akin to TERRACE.]

trat·to·ri·a (trä·tō′rē·ä) *n. Italian* A restaurant; eating place.

trauch·le (träkh′əl, trô′khəl) See TRACHLE.

trau·ma (trô′mə, trou′-) *n. pl.* **·mas** or **·ma·ta** (-mə·tə) **1.** *Pathol.* **a** Any injury to the body caused by shock, violence, etc.; a wound. **b** The general condition of the system resulting from such an injury or wound. Also **trau′ma·tism** (-tiz′əm). **2.** *Psychiatry* A severe emotional shock having a deep, often lasting effect upon the personality. [< NL < Gk. *trauma*, *-atos* wound]

trau·mat·ic (trô·mat′ik) *adj.* Of, pertaining to, or caused by a trauma. [< LL *traumaticus* < Gk. *traumatikos* < *trauma*, *-atos* wound] — **trau·mat′i·cal·ly** *adv.*

trav. Traveler, travel(s).

trav·ail¹ (trav′āl, trə·vāl′) *v.i.* **1.** To toil; labor. **2.** To suffer the pangs of childbirth. — *n.* **1.** Strenuous physical or mental labor; toil. **2.** Anguish; distress; pain. **3.** Labor in childbirth. — **Syn.** See TOIL¹. [< OF < *travaillier* to labor, toil, ult. < LL *trepalium* three-pronged instrument of torture < *tres, tria* three + *palus* stake]

tra·vail² (trə·vā′y′) *n. pl.* **·vails** (-vā′y′) A travois (def. 1).

Trav·an·core (trav′ən·kôr′) A former administrative division and princely state of Travancore-Cochin State, India.

Trav·an·core-Co·chin (trav′ən·kôr′kō′chin, -koch′in) A former state of SW India; mostly incorporated in Kerala, 1956.

trave (trāv) *n.* **1.** A frame to confine a horse, etc., while being shod. **2.** *Archit.* **a** A crossbeam. **b** A division, as in a ceiling, made by crossbeams. [< OF < L *trabs, trabis* beam]

trav·el (trav′əl) *v.* **trav·eled** or **·elled**, **trav·el·ing** or **·el·ling** *v.i.* **1.** To go from one place to another; make a journey or tour. **2.** To proceed; advance. **3.** To go about from place to place as a traveling salesman. **4.** *U.S. Informal* To move with speed. **5.** To pass or be transmitted, as light, sound, etc. **6.** *Mech.* To move in a fixed path, as part of a mechanism. **7.** In basketball, to walk (def. 8). — *v.t.* **8.** To move or journey across or through; traverse. — *n.* **1.** The act of traveling. **2.** *pl.* A trip or journey. **3.** *pl.* A narration of things experienced or observed in traveling. **4.** A movement or progress of any kind. **5.** *Mech.* **a** The full course of a moving part in one direction. **b** Length of stroke, as of a piston. Abbr. *trav.* [Var. of TRAVAIL¹]

travel agency The business establishment of a travel agent.

travel agent One whose business is the providing of service, as making reservations, arranging itineraries, etc., for travelers.

trav·eled (trav′əld) *adj.* **1.** Having made many journeys. **2.** Experienced as the result of travel. **3.** Frequented or used by travelers. Also **trav′elled.**

trav·el·er (trav′əl·ər, trav′lər) *n.* **1.** One who travels or journeys. **2.** *Brit.* A traveling salesman. **3.** *Naut.* A metal ring or thimble running freely on a rope, rod, or spar; also, the rope, rod, or spar. Also **trav′el·ler.** Abbr. *trav.*

traveler's check A draft issued by a bank, express company, etc., having the bearer's signature, and payable when the bearer signs it again in order to cash it.

traveling crane A hoisting and transporting apparatus that moves along a supporting frame or bridge.

traveling salesman A salesman who travels to various places obtaining orders for his firm: also called *commercial traveler.* Also **traveling man.**

trav·e·logue (trav′ə·lôg, -log) *n.* A lecture or film on travel. Also **trav′e·log.** [< TRAVEL, on analogy with *monologue, dialogue,* etc.]

trav·erse (trav′ərs; *for v. & adv., also* trə·vûrs′) *v.* **·ersed**, **·ers·ing** *v.t.* **1.** To pass over, across, or through. **2.** To move back and forth over or along. **3.** To examine carefully; survey or scrutinize. **4.** To oppose; thwart. **5.** To turn (a gun, lathe, etc.) to right or left; swivel. **6.** *Law* **a** In legal pleading, to deny (a matter of fact alleged by the opposite party). **b** To impeach (the validity of an inquest of office). **7.** *Naut.* To brace (a yard) fore and aft. — *v.i.* **8.** To move back and forth. **9.** To move across; cross. **10.** To turn; swivel. **11.** In fencing, to slide one's blade toward the hilt of an opponent's sword while maintaining pressure on it. — *n.* **1.** A part, as of a machine or structure, placed across or traversing another, as a crosspiece, crossbeam, transom, etc. **2.** *Archit.* A gallery or loft communicating with opposite sides of a building. **3.** Something serving as a screen or barrier. **4.** *Geom.* A transversal. **5.** The act of traversing or crossing. **6.** A way or path across. **7.** *Mech.* Sidewise travel, as of the tool in a slide rest. **8.** *Law* In legal pleading, a formal denial. **9.** *Naut.* A zigzag track of a vessel while beating to windward. **10.** In surveying, a short line surveyed from a main line, to establish the position of a side point. **11.** *Mil.* **a** A bank of earth thrown up, as from a trench, to afford protection from gunfire. **b** The lateral sweep of an artillery piece from its forward position. **12.** *Rare* Something that obstructs or vexes. — *adj.* Transverse; lying or being across. — *adv. Obs.* Transversely; crosswise. [< OF *traverser* < LL *traversare, transversare* < L *transversus.* See TRANSVERSE.] — **trav′ers·a·ble** *adj.* — **trav·er·sal** (trav′ər·səl, trə·vûr′səl) *n.* — **trav′ers·er** *n.*

traverse rod A rodlike support for curtains, etc., along which the drapery may be drawn on carriers by means of a pulley.

trav·er·tine (trav′ər·tin, -tēn, -tīn) *n.* A porous, light yellow, crystalline limestone deposited in solution from ground or surface waters, used for building purposes: also called *calcsinter.* Also **trav′er·tin** (-tin). [< Ital. *travertino, tivertino* < L *Tiburtinus* Tiburtine < *Tiburs, -urtis* of Tibur]

trav·es·ty (trav′is·tē) *n. pl.* **·ties** **1.** A grotesque imitation; burlesque. **2.** In literature, a burlesque treatment of a lofty subject. — **Syn.** See CARICATURE. — *v.t.* **·tied, ·ty·ing** To make a travesty on; burlesque; parody. [< MF *travesti,* pp. of (*se*) *travestir* to disguise (oneself) < Ital. *travestire* to disguise < L *trans* across + *vestire* to dress]

tra·vois (trə·voi′) *n. pl.* **·vois** (-voiz′) or **·vois·es** (-voi′ziz) **1.** A primitive sled constructed of a framework between two poles that serve as shafts for a dog or other draft animal, formerly used by North American Indians: also called *travail.* **2.** *Canadian* **a** A type of dog sled. **b** A sled for logs. **c** A stoneboat. Also **tra·voise′** (-voiz′). [< dial. F (Canadian), alter. of F *travail,* frame in which horses are held while being shod < OF]

TRAVOIS

trawl (trôl) *n.* **1.** A stout fishing line having many lines frequently spaced and bearing baited hooks: also called *trotline.* Also **trawl line.** **2.** A great fishing net shaped like a flattened bag, for towing on the bottom of the ocean by a boat: also **trawl net.** — *v.t.* **1.** To catch (fish) with a trawl. — *v.i.* **2.** To fish with a trawl. [Cf. MDu. *traghel* dragnet; prob. infl. by TRAIL]

trawl·er (trô′lər) *n.* **1.** A vessel used for trawling. **2.** One who is engaged in trawling.

trawl·ey (trô′lē) *n.* A trolley (def. 5).

tray (trā) *n.* A flat receptacle with a low rim, made of wood, metal, etc., used to carry, hold, or display articles: a sandwich *tray.* [OE *trīg, trēg* wooden board]

treach·er·ous (trech′ər·əs) *adj.* **1.** Traitorous; perfidious; disloyal. **2.** Having a deceptive appearance; unreliable; untrustworthy: a *treacherous* path. — **Syn.** See PERFIDIOUS. — **treach′er·ous·ly** *adv.* — **treach′er·ous·ness** *n.*

treach·er·y (trech′ər·ē) *n. pl.* **·er·ies** Violation of allegiance, confidence, or faith; perfidy; treason. [< OF *trecherie, tricherie* < *tricher, trechier* to cheat]

trea·cle (trē′kəl) *n.* **1.** *Brit.* Molasses. **2.** Formerly, a compound used as an antidote. [< OF *triacle* < L *theriaca* < Gk. *thēriakē* remedy for poisonous bites < *thērion,* dim. of *thēr* wild beast] — **trea′cly** *adj.*

tread (tred) *v.* **trod** (*Archaic* **trode**), **trod·den** or **trod, tread·ing** *v.t.* **1.** To step or walk on, over, along, etc. **2.** To press with the feet; trample. **3.** To accomplish in walking or in dancing: to *tread* a measure. **4.** To copulate with: said of male birds. — *v.i.* **5.** To step or walk. **6.** To trample: usually with *on.* — **to tread water** In swimming, to keep the body erect and the head above water by moving the feet up and down as if walking. — *n.* **1.** The act, manner, or sound of treading or walking. **2.** The flat part of a step in a staircase. **3.** The part of a wheel that bears upon the ground or rails. **4.** The outer, often grooved surface of an automobile tire. **5.** That part of the sole of a shoe that treads upon the ground. **6.** The part of a rail on which the wheels bear. **7.** The cicatricle or chalaza of an egg. [OE *tredan*] — **tread′er** *n.*

trea·dle (tred′l) *n.* A lever operated by the foot, usually to cause rotary motion. For illustration see POTTER'S WHEEL. — *v.i.* **·led, ·ling** To work a treadle. Also spelled *treddle.* [OE *tredel* < *tredan* to tread] — **tread′ler** *n.*

tread·mill (tred′mil′) *n.* **1.** A mechanism rotated by the walking motion of one or more persons: formerly used as a prison punishment. **2.** A somewhat similar mechanism operated by a quadruped. **3.** Any wearisome or monotonous work, activity, routine, etc.

treas. Treasurer; treasury.

trea·son (trē′zən) *n.* **1.** Betrayal or breach of allegiance or of obedience toward one's sovereign or government; especially in the Constitution of the United States (Article III, Section 3), "Treason against the United States shall consist only in levying war against them, or in adhering to their enemies, giving them aid and comfort." **2.** *Rare* A breach of faith; treachery. [< AF *treyson*, OF *traison* < L *traditio, -onis* betrayal, delivery. Doublet of TRADITION.]

trea·son·a·ble (trē′zən·ə·bəl) *adj.* Of, involving, or characteristic of treason. — **trea′son·a·ble·ness** *n.* — **trea son·a·bly** *adv.*

trea·son·ous (trē′zən·əs) *adj.* Treasonable. — **trea′son·ous·ly** *adv.*

treas·ure (trezh′ər) *n.* **1.** Riches accumulated or possessed, especially in the form of money, jewels, or precious metals. **2.** One who or that which is regarded as valuable, precious, or rare. — *v.t.* ·**ured,** ·**ur·ing** **1.** To lay up in store; accumulate. **2.** To retain carefully, as in the mind: often with *up.* **3.** To set a high value upon; prize. [< OF *tresor* < L *thesaurus* < Gk. *thēsauros.* Doublet of THESAURUS.]

treasure hunt A game in which the players try to find a hidden prize to which they are guided by a series of clues.

Treasure Island An artificial island in San Francisco Bay, used as a naval base; 400 acres.

treas·ur·er (trezh′ər·ər) *n.* An officer of a state, city, corporation, society, etc., who has charge of funds or revenues. Abbr. *tr., treas.*

Treasure State Nickname of MONTANA.

trea·sure-trove (trezh′ər·trōv′) *n.* **1.** *Law* Any treasure found hidden in the earth, etc., the owner being unknown. **2.** Any discovery that proves valuable. [< AF *tresor trové* < *tresor* + *trové,* pp., of *trover* to find]

treas·ur·y (trezh′ər·ē) *n. pl.* ·**ur·ies** **1.** The place where private or public funds or revenues are received, kept, and disbursed. **2.** Any public or private funds or revenues. **3.** Any group or collection of treasures or things regarded as treasures. **4.** A place or receptacle where treasures are kept. Abbr. *treas.* — **Department of the Treasury** An executive department of the U.S. government that superintends and manages the national finances. Also **Treasury Department.** Abbr. *TD* [< OF *tresorie* < *tresor.* See TREASURE.]

treasury note *U.S.* A note issued by the Treasury as legal tender for all debts, public and private.

treat (trēt) *v.t.* **1.** To conduct oneself toward in a specified manner: He *treated* her shamefully. **2.** To look upon or regard in a specified manner: They *treat* the matter as a joke. **3.** To subject to chemical or physical action, as for altering or improving. **4.** To give medical or surgical attention to. **5.** To deal with in writing or speaking; handle. **6.** To deal with or develop (a subject in art or literature) in a specified manner or style. **7.** To pay for the entertainment, food, or drink of. — *v.i.* **8.** To handle a subject in writing or speaking: usually with *of.* **9.** To carry on negotiations; negotiate. **10.** To pay for another's entertainment or food. — *n.* **1.** Something that gives unusual pleasure. **2.** Entertainment furnished gratuitously to another. **3.** The act of treating; also, one's turn to treat. [< OF *tretier, traitier* < L *tractare.* See TRACTABLE.] — **treat′a·ble** *adj.* — **treat′er** *n.*

trea·tise (trē′tis) *n.* **1.** A formal and systematic written account of some subject. **2.** *Obs.* A story; tale. [< AF *tretiz,* OF *traitier.* See TREAT.]

treat·ment (trēt′mənt) *n.* **1.** The act, manner, or process of treating. **2.** The care of an illness, by the use of drugs, surgery, etc. **3.** The handling of or manner of handling an artistic or literary subject.

trea·ty (trē′tē) *n. pl.* ·**ties** **1.** A formal agreement or compact, duly concluded and ratified, between two or more states; also, the document containing such an agreement or compact. **2.** *Obs.* The act of negotiating for an agreement. **3.** *Obs.* An entreaty. — **Syn.** See CONTRACT. [< AF *treté,* OF *traitie,* pp. of *traitier* See TREAT.]

treaty Indian *Canadian* A member of an Indian tribe that has treaty rights.

treaty money *Canadian* Yearly payments to treaty Indians.

treaty port Formerly, any of several sea and river ports, especially in China, where foreigners were permitted by treaty to carry on trade.

treaty rights *Canadian* Rights, as those of holding land on a reservation and of receiving treaty money, held by treaty Indians.

Treb·bia (treb′byä) A river in NW Italy, flowing 70 miles NE to the Po river; scene of Hannibal's defeat of the Romans, 218 B.C.

Treb·i·zond (treb′i·zond) A Province of NW Turkey; an empire of Asia Minor from 1204 to 1461; 1,753 sq. mi.; pop. 595,782 (1965); capital, Trebizond. Turkish *Trabzon.*

treb·le (treb′əl) *v.t. & v.i.* ·**led,** ·**ling** To multiply by three; triple. — *adj.* **1.** Threefold; triple. **2.** Soprano. — *n.* **1.** *Music* **a** A soprano voice, part, or instrument; also, the singer or player taking this part. **b** The highest register of an instrument. **2.** High, piping sound. [< OF < L *triplus.* Doublet of TRIPLE.] — **treb′le·ness** *n.* — **treb′ly** *adv.*

treble clef See under CLEF.

treb·u·chet (treb′yŏŏ·shet) *n.* A medieval catapultlike device for throwing heavy missiles. Also **treb′uck·et** (-uk-it). [< OF < *trebucher* to trip, fall]

tre·cen·to (trā·chen′tō) *n. Italian* The 14th century, as producing a particular style of Italian literature and art.

tred·dle (tred′l) See TREADLE.

tree (trē) *n.* **1.** A perennial woody plant having usually a single self-supporting trunk of considerable height, with branches and foliage growing at some distance above the ground. ◆ Collateral adjective: *arboreal.* **2.** Any shrub or plant that assumes treelike shape or dimensions. **3.** Something resembling a tree in form or outline, as a clothes tree, crosstree, etc. **4.** A diagram or outline resembling a tree and showing family descent: a genealogical *tree.* **5.** A timber, post, pole, etc.: used in combination: *axletree.* **6.** *Archaic & Poetic* The cross on which Christ was crucified. **7.** *Archaic* A gallows. — **up a tree** *Informal* In a position from which there is no retreat; cornered; caught; also, in an embarrassing position. — *v.t.* **treed, tree·ing 1.** To force to climb or take refuge in a tree: to *tree* an opossum. **2.** *Informal* To get the advantage of; corner. **3.** To stretch, as a boot, on a boot tree. [OE *trēow, trīow, trēo*]

Tree may appear as a combining form or as the first element in two-word phrases; as in:

tree-bordered	tree-girt	tree planter
tree-boring	tree-guard	tree-planting
tree-clad	tree-haunting	tree protector
tree-climbing	tree-hewing	tree-pruning
tree-covered	tree holder	tree-ripened
tree-crowned	tree-hopping	tree-sawing
tree-dotted	tree-inhabiting	tree-shaded
tree-dwelling	tree-lined	tree-skirted
tree-feeding	tree-locked	tree sprayer
tree-feller	tree-loving	tree-spraying
tree-fringed	tree-marked	tree-tag
tree-garnished	tree-planted	tree-trimmer

Tree (trē), **Sir Herbert Beerbohm,** 1853–1917, English actor and impresario.

tree creeper Any of various birds (family *Certhiidae*) that obtain their food by creeping along trees.

tree fern Any of various ferns (families *Cyatheaceae* and *Dicksoniaceae*) with large fronds and woody trunks that often attain a treelike size.

tree frog An arboreal amphibian (family *Hylidae*), having the toes dilated with viscous, adhesive disks: also called *tree toad.*

tree heath An evergreen shrub of southern Europe (*Erica arborea*) with white flowers: also called *brier.*

tree-nail (trē′nāl′, tren′əl, trun′əl) *n.* A wooden peg of dry, hard wood that swells when wet, used for fastening timbers, especially in shipbuilding: also spelled *trenail, trunnel.*

tree of heaven The ailanthus.

tree of knowledge of good and evil In the Bible, a tree in Eden whose fruit Adam and Eve were forbidden to eat. *Gen.* iii 3, 6. Also **tree of knowledge.**

tree of life 1. Arborvitae. **2.** In the Bible: **a** A tree in the garden of Eden whose fruit conferred immortality. *Gen.* iii 22. **b** A similar tree in heaven. *Rev.* xxii 2.

Tree-Plant·er State (trē′plan′tər, -plän′-) Nickname of NEBRASKA.

tree shrew Any of a family (*Tupaiidae*) of insectivorous, squirrellike primates native in southern Asia, Borneo, and the Philippine Islands.

tree sparrow A North American sparrow (*Spizella arborea*) that nests in Canada and migrates southward in winter: also called *Canada sparrow.*

tree surgeon One skilled in the science of tree surgery.

tree surgery The treatment of disease conditions and decay in trees by operative methods.

tree toad A tree frog (which see).

tree-top (trē′top′) *n.* The highest part of a tree.

tref (tref) *adj.* Unclean and forbidden by Jewish ceremonial law; not kosher. [< Yiddish *treyfe* < Hebrew *tērēphāh* torn]

tre·foil (trē′foil) *n.* **1.** Any of a genus (*Trifolium*) of leguminous plants, the clovers, with red, purple, pink, or yellow flowers and trifoliolate leaflets: also called *trifolium.* **2.** Certain other plants with trifoliolate leaves, as the black medic. **3.** A three-lobed architectural ornamentation. [< AF *trifoil,* OF *trefeuil* < L *trifolium*]

tre·ha·la (tri·hä′lə) *n.* A sweet, edible substance forming the pupal case of certain weevils (genus *Larinus*). [< NL < Turkish *tīqālah* < Persian]

tre·ha·lose (trē′hə·lōs) *n. Biochem.* A crystalline disaccharide, $C_{12}H_{22}O_{11}$, elaborated by many fungi and stored as a food reserve instead of starch. [< TREHAL(A) + -OSE[2]]

treil·lage (trā′lij) *n.* A trellis. [< MF < *treille* bower, trellis, arbor < L *trichila, tricla*]

Treitsch·ke (trīch′kə), **Heinrich Gotthard von,** 1834–96, German historian and political writer.

trek (trek) *v.* **trekked, trek·king** *v.i.* **1.** In South Africa, to travel by ox wagon. **2.** To travel, especially slowly or arduously. — *v.t.* **3.** In South Africa, to draw (a vehicle or load): said of an ox. — *n.* **1.** In South Africa, a journey or any part of it; especially, an organized migration, as for the founding of a colony. **2.** A journey; especially, a slow or arduous journey. [< Du. *trekken* to draw, travel < MDu. *trecken*, intensive of *trēken* < OHG *trechan* to draw] — **trek′ker** *n.*

trel·lis (trel′is) *n.* **1.** A crossbarred structure or panel of wood, metal, or other material, used as a screen or a support for vines, etc. **2.** A summerhouse, archway, etc., made from or consisting of such a structure. — *v.t.* **1.** To interlace so as to form a trellis. **2.** To furnish with or fasten on a trellis. [< OF *treliz, trelis* < L *trilix, trilicis* of three threads < *tri-* three + *licium* thread]

trel·lis·work (trel′is·wûrk′) *n.* Openwork made from, consisting of, or resembling a trellis.

trem·a·tode (trem′ə·tōd) *n.* One of a class (*Trematoda*) of typically parasitic flatworms, including the liver flukes. [< NL < Gk. *trēmatōdēs* perforated < *trēma, -atos* hole + *eidos* form] — **trem·a·toid** (-toid) *adj.*

trem·ble (trem′bəl) *v.i.* **·bled, ·bling** **1.** To shake involuntarily, as with fear or weakness; be agitated. **2.** To have slight, irregular vibratory motion, as from some jarring force; quiver; shake. **3.** To feel anxiety or fear. **4.** To quaver, as the voice. — *n.* **1.** The act or state of trembling. **2.** *pl. Vet.* A debilitating disease of cattle and sheep, possibly caused by eating certain plants, and communicated to man as the milk sickness. [< OF *trembler* < LL *tremulare* < *tremulus* tremulous < *tremere* to tremble, shake] — **trem′bler** *n.* — **trem′bling·ly** *adv.* — **trem′bly** *adj.*

tre·men·dous (tri·men′dəs) *adj.* **1.** *Informal* Extraordinarily large; huge; vast. **2.** *Informal* Unusual; amazing; wonderful. **3.** Causing astonishment by its magnitude, force, etc. [< L *tremendus* to be trembled at < *tremere* to tremble] — **tre·men′dous·ly** *adv.* — **tre·men′dous·ness** *n.*

trem·o·lite (trem′ə·līt) *n.* A light-colored calcium-magnesium amphibole, occurring massive or in bladed crystals. [after *Tremola*, Switzerland + -ITE¹]

trem·o·lo (trem′ə·lō) *n. pl.* **·los** *Music* **1.** In string instrument playing, a rapid reiteration of a tone caused by alternating movements of the bow. **2.** A rapid alternation of two tones, usually a third or more apart. Compare TRILL. **3.** In singing, a vibrato, often uneven or poorly produced. **4.** A device or stop for producing a vibrato effect on an organ tone: also called *tremulant.* [< Ital. < L *tremulus*]

trem·or (trem′ər, trē′mər) *n.* **1.** A quick, vibratory movement; a shaking. **2.** Any involuntary and continued quivering or trembling of the body or limbs; a shiver. **3.** A quavering sound. **4.** Any trembling, quivering effect. [< OF, fear, a trembling < L < *tremere* to tremble]

trem·u·lant (trem′yə·lənt) *adj.* Trembling; tremulous. Also **trem′u·lent.** — *n. Music* A tremolo (def. 4). [< LL *tremulans, -antis*, ppr. of *tremulare*. See TREMBLE.]

trem·u·lous (trem′yə·ləs) *adj.* **1.** Characterized or affected by trembling: *tremulous* speech. **2.** Showing timidity or fear; timorous. [< L *tremulus*. See TREMBLE.] — **trem′u·lous·ly** *adv.* — **trem′u·lous·ness** *n.*

tre·nail (trē′nāl, tren′əl, trun′əl) See TREENAIL.

trench (trench) *n.* **1.** A long narrow excavation in the ground; ditch. **2.** A long irregular ditch, lined with a parapet of the excavated earth, to protect troops. — *v.t.* **1.** To dig a trench or trenches in. **2.** To fortify with trenches. **3.** To cut deep furrows in; ditch. **4.** To confine in a trench, as water. — *v.i.* **5.** To cut or dig trenches. **6.** To cut; carve. **7.** To encroach. [< OF *trenche* a cutting, gash < *trenchier* to cut, ult. < L *truncare* to lop off < *truncus* tree trunk]

Trench (trench), **Richard Chenevix,** 1807–86, British prelate, poet, and philologist, born in Ireland.

trench·ant (tren′chənt) *adj.* **1.** Cutting; incisive; keen: a *trenchant* remark. **2.** Forceful; vigorous; effective. **3.** Clearly defined; distinct. [< OF, ppr. of *trenchier.* See TRENCH.] — **trench′an·cy** *n.* — **trench′ant·ly** *adv.*

trench coat A loose-fitting overcoat of rainproof fabric.

trench·er¹ (tren′chər) *n.* **1.** Formerly, a wooden plate or board on which food was served or cut. **2.** *Archaic* The food served on trenchers. [< AF *trenchour*, OF *tranchouoir* < *trenchier.* See TRENCH.]

trench·er² (tren′chər) *n.* One who digs trenches.

trench·er·man (tren′chər·mən) *n. pl.* **·men** (-mən) **1.** A feeder; eater; especially, one who enjoys food. **2.** *Archaic* A sponger or hanger-on.

trench fever *Pathol.* A remittent rickettsial fever transmitted by body lice and common among soldiers assigned to prolonged service in trenches during World War I: also called *quintan fever.*

trench foot *Pathol.* A disease of the feet caused by continued dampness and cold, and characterized by discoloration, weakness, and sometimes gangrene.

trench knife Formerly, a double-edged steel knife with a long blade, used in hand-to-hand combat.

trench mortar Mortar³ (def. 1).

trench mouth *Pathol.* A disease of the mouth, gums, and sometimes the larynx and tonsils, caused by a soil bacillus: also called *Vincent's angina.*

trend (trend) *n.* A general course, inclination, etc. — *v.i.* To have or take a particular trend. [OE *trendan* to roll]

trend·y (tren′dē) *adj. Informal* Forming or following a fashionable trend or trends.

Treng·ga·nu (treng·gä′nōō) A State in Malaya, on the South China Sea; 5,027 sq. mi.; pop. 306,942 (est. 1960); capital, Kuala Trengganu.

Trent (trent) A commune in northern Italy, on the Adige; pop. 86,600 (est. 1967): ancient *Tridentum. Italian* **Tren·to** (tren′tō). See COUNCIL OF TRENT.

Trent (trent) A river in Staffordshire, England, flowing 170 miles to the Humber.

trente et qua·rante (trän·tā·kà·ränt′) A gambling game played with cards. [< F, thirty and forty]

Tren·ti·no (tren·tē′nō) A district around Trent, Italy, the part of Tyrol under Italian control.

Tren·ton (tren′tən) The capital of New Jersey, in the western part on the Delaware; pop. 104,638.

tre·pan¹ (tri·pan′) *n.* **1.** An early form of the trephine. **2.** A large rock-boring tool. — *v.t.* **·panned, ·pan·ning** **1.** *Mech.* To cut circular disks from (a rock or metal plate) by a rotary tool. **2.** *Surg.* To trephine. [< OF, borer < Med.L *trepanum* crown saw < Gk. *trypanon* borer < *trypaein* to bore] — **trep·a·na·tion** (trep′ə·nā′shən) *n.* — **tre·pan′ner** *n.*

tre·pan² (tri·pan′) *Archaic v.t.* **·panned, ·pan·ning** To ensnare. — *n.* A snare; trick; also a trickster. Also spelled *trapan.* [< thieves′ cant *trapan* < TRAP¹; prob. infl. in form by TREPAN¹]

tre·pang (tri·pang′) *n.* An East Indian holothurian or sea cucumber: also called *bêche-de-mer.* [< Malay *trīpang*]

tre·phine (tri·fīn′, -fēn′) *n. Surg.* A crown saw for removing a piece of bone from the skull so as to relieve pressure, etc. — *v.t.* **·phined, ·phin·ing** To operate on with a trephine. [< earlier *trafine* < L *tres fines* three ends; infl. in form by TREPAN¹]

trep·i·da·tion (trep′ə·dā′shən) *n.* **1.** A state of agitation or alarm; perturbation. **2.** An involuntary trembling. Also **tre·pid·i·ty** (tri·pid′ə·tē). [< L *trepidatio, -onis* < *trepidatus*, pp. of *trepidare* to hurry, be alarmed < *trepidus* alarmed]

trep·o·neme (trep′ə·nēm) *n.* Any of a genus (*Treponema*) of spirochetes, including the causative agent of syphilis. [< NL < Gk. *trepein* to turn + *nēma* thread] — **trep′o·nem′a·tous** (-nem′ə·təs) *adj.*

tres·pass (tres′pəs, -pas′) *v.i.* **1.** *Law* To commit a trespass; especially, to enter wrongfully upon another's land: with *on* or *upon.* **2.** To pass the bounds of propriety or rectitude, to the injury of another; intrude offensively; encroach: with *on* or *upon.* **3.** To transgress or sin. — *n.* **1.** Any voluntary transgression of law or rule of duty; any offense done to another. **2.** *Law* Any wrongful act accompanied with force, either actual or implied, as wrongful entry on another's land. [< OF *trespasser* to pass beyond, across < Med.L *transpassare* < L *trans-* across, beyond + *passare.* See PASS.] — **tres′pass·er** *n.*

tress (tres) *n.* **1.** A lock, or ringlet of human hair. **2.** *pl.* The hair of a woman or girl, especially when worn loose. [< OF *tresce*; ult. origin uncertain] — **tress′y** *adj.*

-tress *suffix* Used to form many feminine nouns corresponding to masculine nouns in *-ter, -tor:* actress. Compare -ESS. [Var. of -ESS]

tressed (trest) *adj.* Wearing or arranged in tresses; braided.

tres·sure (tresh′ər) *n. Heraldry* A bearing around the edge of a shield; modified or double orle, generally ornamented with fleurs-de-lis. Also **tres′sour.** See SUBORDINARY. [< OF *tresseor, tressure* < *tresse* tress]

tres·tle (tres′əl) *n.* **1.** A beam or bar supported by four divergent legs, for bearing platforms, etc. **2.** An open braced framework for supporting a railway bridge, etc. [< OF *trestel* < L, dim. of *transtrum.* See TRANSOM.]

tres·tle·tree (tres′əl·trē′) *n. Naut.* One of a pair of pieces at right angles to a lower mast, to support the crosstrees.

tres·tle·work (tres′əl·wûrk′) *n.* **1.** Trestles collectively. **2.** A bridge made of trestles. Also **tres′tling.**

tret (tret) *n.* Formerly, an allowance to purchasers for waste due to transportation. [< AF, OF *tret*, var. of *traict.* See TRAIT.]

Tre·vel·yan (tri·vel′yən), **George Macaulay,** 1876–1962, English historian and biographer. — **Sir George Otto,** 1838–1928, English historian and biographer; father of the preceding.

Treves (trēvz) See TRIER. *French* **Trèves** (trev).

trev·et (trev′it) See TRIVET.

Tre·vi·so (trā·vē′zō) A commune in NE Italy; pop. 86,900 (est. 1967). Ancient *Tarvisium.*

trews (trōōz) *n.pl. Scot.* Tight-fitting tartan trousers: also spelled *trooz.*

trey (trā) *n.* A card, domino, or die having three spots or pips. [< OF *trei, treis* < L *tres* three]

trez tine (trez) The royal tine (which see). Also **tres tine** (tres), **trey tine** (trā). [Prob. < L *tres* three + TINE¹]

trfd. Transferred.

tri- *prefix* **1.** Three; threefold; thrice: *tricycle, trisect.* **2.** *Chem.* Containing three (specified) atoms, radicals, groups, etc.: *trioxide, trisulfide.* **3.** Occurring every three (specified) intervals, or three times within an (assigned) interval: *triweekly.* [< L *tri-* threefold < *tres* three]

tri·a·ble (trī′ə·bəl) *adj.* **1.** That may be tried or tested. **2.** *Law* That may undergo a judicial examination or determination. — **tri′a·ble·ness** *n.*

tri·ac·id (trī·as′id) *n. Chem.* An acid containing three hydroxyl radicals that are replaceable by acid radicals.

tri·ad (trī′ad) *n.* **1.** A group of three persons or things. **2.** *Music* A chord of three tones formed of superimposed thirds. **3.** *Chem.* **a** A trivalent atom or radical. **b** One of a group of three elements having similar chemical properties, as chlorine, bromine, and iodine. [< L *trias, -adis* < Gk. *trias, -ados* < *treis* three] — **tri·ad′ic** *adj. & n.*

tri·ag·o·nal (trī·ag′ə·nəl) *adj.* Having three angles; triangular. [Var. of TRIGONAL, on analogy with *tetragonal, pentagonal,* etc.]

tri·al (trī′əl, trīl) *n.* **1.** The examination before a court of the facts or law in a case in order to determine that case. **2.** The act of testing or proving by experience or use. **3.** The state of being tried or tested by suffering: the hour of *trial.* **4.** Experimental treatment or action performed to determine a result: to learn by *trial* and error. **5.** An experience, person, or thing that puts strength, patience, or faith to the test. **6.** An attempt or effort to do something; a try: to make a *trial.* — **on trial** In the process of being tried or tested. — *adj.* **1.** Of or pertaining to a trial or trials. **2.** Made, used, or performed in the course of trying or testing: a *trial* trip. [< AF < *trier.* See TRY.]

trial and error Experimentation, investigation, learning, etc., in which various methods, theories, or alternatives are tried and faulty or erroneous ones are rejected.

trial balance In double-entry bookkeeping, a draft or statement of the debit and credit footings or balances of each account in the ledger. Abbr. *t.b.*

trial balloon **1.** A balloon released in order to test atmospheric and meteorological conditions. **2.** Any tentative plan or scheme advanced to test public reaction.

trial jury A petit jury (which see).

tri·a·morph (trī′ə·môrf) *n.* Any mineral or other substance that crystallizes in three different forms. [< L *tres, tria* three + Gk. *morphē* form] — **tri′a·mor′phous** *adj.*

tri·an·gle (trī′ang′gəl) *n.* **1.** *Geom.* A figure, especially a plane figure, bounded by three sides, and having three angles. **2.** Something resembling such a figure in shape or arrangement. **3.** A flat drawing implement for making parallel or diagonal lines, etc. **4.** A group or set of three; a triad. **5.** A situation involving three persons: the eternal *triangle.* **6.** *Music* An instrument consisting of a metal bar bent into a triangle and sounded by being struck with a metal rod. [< OF < L *triangulum* < *triangulus* three-cornered < *tri-* three + *angulus* angle]

tri·an·gu·lar (trī·ang′gyə·lər) *adj.* **1.** Pertaining to, like, or bounded by a triangle. **2.** Concerned with or pertaining to three things, parties, or persons. [< LL *triangularis* < *triangulum.* See TRIANGLE] — **tri·an′gu·lar′i·ty** (-lar′ə·tē) *n.* — **tri·an′gu·lar·ly** *adv.*

tri·an·gu·late (trī·ang′gyə·lāt) *v.t.* **·lat·ed, ·lat·ing** **1.** To divide into triangles. **2.** To survey by triangulation. **3.** To make triangular. — *adj.* Of or marked with triangles. [< L *triangulum* triangle + -ATE¹]

tri·an·gu·la·tion (trī·ang′gyə·lā′shən) *n.* **1.** The laying out and accurate measurement of a network of triangles. **2.** A method of determining a position by taking bearings to two fixed points of known distance apart and computing it on the resultant triangle.

Tri·an·gu·lum (trī·ang′gyə·ləm) *n.* A constellation, the **Triangle.** See CONSTELLATION. [< L]

Tri·an·gu·lum Aus·tra·le (trī·ang′gyə·ləm ôs·trā′lē) A constellation, the Southern Triangle. See CONSTELLATION.

tri·ar·chy (trī′är·kē) *n. pl.* **·chies** Government by three persons, or a country so governed; a triumvirate. [< Gk. *triarchia* < *tri-* three + *archein* to rule]

Tri·as·sic (trī·as′ik) *adj. Geol.* Of or pertaining to the earliest of the three geological periods comprised in the Mesozoic era. — *n.* The Triassic period or rock system, following the Permian and succeeded by the Jurassic. Also **Tri·as** (trī′əs). See chart under GEOLOGY. [< LL *trias.* See TRIAD.]

tri·at·ic stay (trī·at′ik) *Naut.* A device attached to the foremast head and mainmast head of a ship, used principally for hoisting boats. [Origin uncertain]

tri·a·tom·ic (trī′ə·tom′ik) *adj. Chem.* **1.** Containing three atoms in the molecule. **2.** Containing three hydroxyl groups.

tri·ax·i·al (trī·ak′sē·əl) *adj.* Having three axes.

tri·a·zine (trī′ə·zēn, -zin, trī·az′ēn, -in) *n. Chem.* **1.** One of three compounds, C₃H₃N₃, each having three carbon and three nitrogen atoms in a six-membered ring. **2.** Any of their derived compounds. Also **tri·a·zin** (trī′ə·zin, trī·az′in). [< TRI- + AZ(O)- + -INE²]

tri·a·zo·ic acid (trī′ə·zō′ik) *adj. Chem.* Hydrazoic acid. [< TRI- + -AZ(O)- + -IC]

tri·a·zole (trī′ə·zōl, trī·az′ōl) *n. Chem.* One of four five-

membered ring compounds, C₂H₃N₃, each containing two carbon and three nitrogen atoms. [< TRI- + AZ(O)- + OLE¹]

trib·ade (trib′əd) *n.* A female homosexual; a Lesbian. [< MF < L *tribas, -adis* < Gk. *tribas, -ados* < *tribein* to rub]

tri·bal (trī′bəl) *adj.* Of or pertaining to a tribe or tribes. — **tri′bal·ly** *adv.*

tri·bal·ism (trī′bəl·iz′əm) *n.* Tribal organization, culture, or relations.

tri·ba·sic (trī·bā′sik) *adj. Chem.* **1.** Containing three atoms of hydrogen replaceable by a base or basic radical: said of certain acids. **2.** Having three univalent basic atoms or radicals in the molecule.

tribe (trīb) *n.* **1.** A division, class, or group of people, especially a primitive or nomadic people, usually characterized by common ancestry, leadership, customs, etc. **2.** In ancient states, an ethnic, hereditary, or political division of a united people: the *tribes* of Athens; also, one of the twelve divisions of ancient Israel. **3.** One of the three political divisions of the ancient Romans representing the Latins, Sabines, and Etruscans. **4.** A number of persons of any class or profession taken together: often an offensive term: the theatrical *tribe.* **5.** *Biol.* A group of plants or animals of indefinite rank. **6.** Among stockbreeders, the descendants of a particular female bearer through females. [Fusion of OF *tribu* (< L *tribus* tribe) and L *tribus*]

tribes·man (trībz′mən) *n. pl.* **·men** (-mən) A member of a tribe.

trib·o·e·lec·tric (trib′ō·i·lek′trik) *adj.* Of, pertaining to, or characterized by frictional electricity. [< *tribo-* (< Gk. *tribein* to rub) + ELECTRIC] — **trib′o·e·lec·tric′i·ty** (-i·lek′tris′ə·tē) *n.*

tri·brach (trī′brak, trib′rak) *n.* In prosody, a metrical foot consisting of three short or unaccented syllables. [< L *tribrachys* < Gk. < *tri-* three + *brachys* short]

tri·bro·mo·eth·a·nol (trī′brō′mō·eth′ə·nōl, -nol) *n. Chem.* A white crystalline compound, C₂H₃Br₃O, having an ether-like odor, used as a general anesthetic.

trib·u·la·tion (trib′yə·lā′shən) *n.* A condition of affliction and distress; suffering; also, that which causes it. [< OF *tribulacion* < LL *tribulatio, -onis* < L *tribulatus,* pp. of *tribulare* to thrash < *tribulum* threshing floor < *tri-,* root of *terere* to rub, grind]

tri·bu·nal (trī·byōō′nəl, trī-) *n.* **1.** A court of justice. **2.** The seat set apart for judges, magistrates, etc. [< L < *tribunus.* See TRIBUNE.]

trib·u·nate (trib′yə·nit, -nāt) *n.* The office or dignity of a tribune. Also **trib·une·ship** (trib′yōōn·ship).

trib·une¹ (trib′yōōn, *Brit.* trī′byōōn) *n.* **1.** In Roman history, a magistrate chosen by the plebeians to protect them against patrician oppression. **2.** Any champion of the people. [< L *tribunus,* lit., head of a tribe < *tribus* tribe] — **trib′u·nar′y** (-yə·ner′ē) *adj.*

trib·une² (trib′yōōn) *n.* **1.** A raised floor for a Roman magistrate's chair. **2.** A bishop's throne. **3.** A rostrum or platform. [< MF < Ital. *tribuna* < L *tribunal* tribunal]

trib·u·tar·y (trib′yə·ter′ē) *adj.* **1.** Bringing supply; contributory; subsidiary: a *tributary* stream. **2.** Offered or due as tribute; having the character of tribute: a *tributary* payment. **3.** Paying tribute, as a state. — *n. pl.* **·tar·ies** **1.** A person or state paying tribute; a dependent. **2.** A stream flowing into a larger stream or body of water: opposed to *distributary.* [< L *tributarius* < *tributum.* See TRIBUTE.] — **trib′u·tar′i·ly** *adv.* — **trib′u·tar′i·ness** *n.*

trib·ute (trib′yōōt) *n.* **1.** A speech, compliment, gift, etc., given in acknowledgment of admiration, gratitude, or respect. **2.** Money or other valuables paid by one state or ruler to another as an acknowledgment of submission or as the price of peace and protection; also, the taxes imposed to raise money to make such payment. **3.** Any enforced payment as by bribery. **4.** Any tax or payment made to a superior, as by a vassal to his overlord. **5.** The obligation or necessity of paying tribute of any kind. [< L *tributum,* neut. of *tributus,* pp. of *tribuere* to pay, allot]

trice (trīs) *v.t.* **triced, tric·ing** To raise with a rope; also, to tie or lash: usually with *up.* — *n.* An instant: now only in the phrase **in a trice.** [< MDu. *trisen* to hoist]

tri·cen·ten·ni·al (trī′sen·ten′ē·əl) *adj. & n.* Tercentenary.

tri·ceps (trī′seps) *n. Anat.* A large muscle at the back of the upper arm, of which the function is to extend the forearm. [< L *triceps, -cipitis* three-headed < *tri-* three + *caput, capitis* head]

tri·cer·a·tops (trī·ser′ə·tops) *n.* A North American dinosaur (genus *Triceratops*) of the Cretaceous period, having a big skull with two long horns and a strong, bony frill around its neck as a protection against its enemies. [< NL]

tri·chi·a·sis (tri·kī′ə·sis) *n. Pathol.* **1.** A condition of ingrowing hairs about an orifice; especially, ingrowing eyelashes. **2.** The presence of hairlike filaments in the urine. [< LL *trichiasis* < Gk. < *trichiaein* to be hairy < *thrix, trichos* hair]

tri·chi·na (tri·kī′nə) *n. pl.* **·nae** (-nē) A small nematode worm (*Trichinella spiralis*), parasitic in the intestines and muscles of man, swine, and other mammals. [< NL < Gk. *trichinos* of hair < *thrix, trichos* hair]

trich·i·nize (trik′ə·nīz) *v.t.* **·nized, ·niz·ing** To infect with trichinae. — **trich′i·ni·za′tion** *n.*

Trich·i·nop·o·ly (trich′ə·nop′ə·lē) See TIRUCHIRAPPALI.

trich·i·no·sis (trik′ə·nō′sis) *n. Pathol.* The disease produced by trichinae in the intestines and muscles of the body, in man, usually through eating improperly cooked meat, especially pork. Also **trich′i·ni·a·sis** (-nī′ə·sis). [< TRICHINA + -OSIS]

trich·i·nous (trik′ə·nəs) *adj.* 1. Infected with trichinae. 2. Of, pertaining to, or characteristic of trichinae.

trich·ite (trik′īt) *n.* 1. A microscopic, variously shaped crystallite, found in volcanic rocks. [< G *trichit* < Gk. *thrix, trichos* hair] — **tri·chit·ic** (trī·kit′ik) *adj.*

tri·chlo·ride (trī·klōr′īd, -id, -klō′rīd, -rid) *n. Chem.* Any compound having three chlorine atoms in its molecule. Also **tri·chlo·rid** (trī·klōr′id, -klō′rid).

tri·chlo·ro·eth·yl·ene (trī·klōr′ō·eth′əl·ēn, -klō·rō-) *n. Chem.* A colorless, odorless, volatile liquid, C₂HCl₃, used in organic synthesis, in chemical manufactures, and as an anesthetic. Also **tri′chlor·eth′yl·ene** (trī′klōr-).

tricho- *combining form* Hair; of or resembling a hair or hairs: *trichocyst.* Also **trichi-**: also, before vowels, **trich-.** [< NL < Gk. *thrix, trichos* hair]

trich·o·cyst (trik′ə·sist) *n. Zool.* A small, elongated capsule found on the bodies of certain ciliate protozoans, containing a hairlike filament that may be ejected as a means of defense or offense. — **trich′o·cys′tic** *adj.*

trich·o·gyne (trik′ə·jīn, -jin) *n. Bot.* The slender threadlike portion of the procarp in red algae that receives the male fertilizing bodies. [< TRICHO- + Gk. *gynē* woman, female]

trich·oid (trik′oid) *adj.* Having the form or appearance of hair. [< Gk. *trichoeidēs* < *thrix, trichos* hair + *eidos* form]

tri·chol·o·gy (trī·kol′ə·jē) *n.* The science treating of hair.

trich·ome (trik′ōm, trī′kōm) *n. Bot.* Hairs, bristles, etc., in a plant. [< Gk. *trichōma* growth of hair < *trichoein.* See TRICHOSIS.]

tri·cho·sis (tri·kō′sis) *n. Pathol.* Any diseased condition of the hair. [< NL < Gk. *trichōsis* growth of hair < *trichoein* to cover with hair < *thrix, trichos* hair]

tri·chot·o·my (trī·kot′ə·mē) *n. pl.* **·mies** 1. Division into three parts. 2. *Theol.* The division of human nature into body, soul, and spirit. [< Gk. *tricha* threefold + -TOMY] — **trich·o·tom·ic** (trik′ə·tom′ik), **tri·chot′o·mous** (-məs) *adj.* — **tri·chot′o·mous·ly** *adv.*

tri·chro·ism (trī′krō·iz′əm) *n. Crystall.* The property of a crystal of transmitting light of different colors in three different directions. [< Gk. *trichroos* of three colors < *tri-* three + *chroia* color, skin] — **tri·chro·ic** (trī·krō′ik) *adj.*

tri·chro·mat·ic (trī′krō·mat′ik) *adj.* 1. Of, pertaining to, having, or using three colors, as in photography or printing. 2. Of, pertaining to, or having visual perception of the three primary colors, as in normal vision. Also **tri′chrome, tri·chro·mic** (trī·krō′mik). [< TRI- + CHROMATIC] — **tri·chro′ma·tism** (-mə·tiz′əm) *n.*

trick (trik) *n.* 1. A device for getting an advantage by deception; a petty artifice; ruse. 2. A malicious, injurious, or annoying act: a dirty *trick.* 3. A practical joke; prank: the *tricks* of schoolboys. 4. A particular habit or manner; characteristic; trait. 5. A peculiar skill or knack. 6. An act of legerdemain or magic. 7. In card games, the whole number of cards played in one round. — **Syn.** See ARTIFICE. — **to do (or turn) the trick** *Slang* To produce the desired result. — *v.t.* 1. To deceive or cheat; delude. 2. To dress or array; adorn: with *up* or *out.* — *v.i.* 3. To practice trickery or deception. [< AF *trique,* OF *triche* deceit < *trichier* to cheat, prob. ult. < L *tricare, tricari* to trifle, play tricks < *tricae* trifles, tricks] — **trick′er** *n.* — **trick′less** *adj.*

trick·er·y (trik′ər·ē) *n. pl.* **·er·ies** The practice of tricks; artifice; stratagem; wiles. — **Syn.** See DECEPTION.

trick·ish (trik′ish) *adj.* Apt to be tricky. — **trick′ish·ly** *adv.* — **trick′ish·ness** *n.*

trick·le (trik′əl) *v.* **·led, ·ling** *v.i.* 1. To flow or run drop by drop or in a very thin stream. 2. To move, come, go, etc., slowly or bit by bit. — *v.t.* 3. To cause to trickle. — *n.* 1. The act or state of trickling. 2. Any slow and irregular movement: a *trickle* of visitors. [ME *triklen,* ? alter. of *striklen,* freq. of *striken* to strike] — **trick′ly** *adj.*

trick·ster (trik′stər) *n.* One who plays tricks; a cheat.

trick·sy (trik′sē) *adj.* **·si·er, ·si·est** *Archaic* 1. Fond of tricks. 2. Tricky. 3. Illusory. 4. Neat. — **trick′si·ness** *n.*

trick·track (trik′trak′) *n.* A form of backgammon. Also **tric′·trac′.** [< F *trictrac;* imit.]

trick·y (trik′ē) *adj.* **trick·i·er, trick·i·est** Disposed to or characterized by trickery; deceitful; wily. Also *Scot.* **trick′ie.** — **trick′i·ly** *adv.* — **trick′i·ness** *n.*

tri·clin·ic (trī·klin′ik) *adj. Crystall.* Denoting a crystal system characterized by three unequal axes with oblique intersections, as rhodonite. [< TRI- + Gk. *klinein* to incline + -IC]

tri·clin·i·um (trī·klin′ē·əm) *n. pl.* **·i·a** (-ē·ə) 1. In ancient Rome, a couch for reclining at meals. 2. The Roman dining room. [< L < Gk. *triklinion,* dim. of *triklinos* dining room with three couches < *tri-* three + *klinē* couch]

tri·col·or (trī′kul′ər) *adj.* Having or characterized by three colors: also **tri′col′ored.** — *n.* 1. A flag of three colors. 2. *Sometimes cap.* The French flag. 3. The tricolor cockade of the French Revolutionists. Also *Brit.* **tri′col′our.** [< F *tricolore* < LL *tricolor* < L *tri-* three + *color* color]

tri·corn (trī′kôrn) *n.* A hat with the brim turned up on three sides, worn during the 17th and 18th centuries by both men and women. Also **tri′corne.** — *adj.* Three-horned; three-pronged, having three hornlike processes. [< F *tricorne* < L *tricornis* three-horned < *tri-* three + *cornu* horn]

tri·cor·nered (trī′kôr′nərd) *adj.* Three-cornered.

tri·cos·tate (trī·kos′tāt) *adj. Biol.* Having three ribs or costae. [< TRI- + L *costa* rib + -ATE¹]

tri·cot (trē′kō, *Fr.* trē·kō′) *n.* 1. A plain, knitted fabric, usually machine made. 2. A soft ribbed cloth. 3. A tight-fitting garment worn by ballet dancers. [< F, knitting < *tricoter* to knit; ult. origin unknown]

tri·crot·ic (trī·krot′ik) *adj. Med.* Having three distinct rhythmic waves in one pulse beat. Also **tri·cro·tous** (trī′krə·təs). [< TRI- + Gk. *krotein* to knock, beat] — **tri·crot·ism** (trī′krə·tiz′əm) *n.*

tri·cus·pid (trī·kus′pid) *adj.* 1. Having three cusps or points, as a molar tooth. 2. *Anat.* Of or pertaining to the tricuspid valve. Also **tri·cus′pi·dal, tri·cus′pi·date.** — *n. Anat.* The tricuspid valve. [< L *tricuspis, -idis* three-pointed < *tri-* three + *cuspis, -idis* point]

tricuspid valve *Anat.* A three-segmented valve that controls the flow of blood from the right atrium to the right ventricle of the heart.

tri·cy·cle (trī′sik·əl) *n.* A three-wheeled vehicle; especially, such a vehicle with pedals, used by children. [< F < *tri-* three + Gk. *kyklos* circle]

tricycle landing gear *Aeron.* A three-wheeled landing gear having one wheel at the nose of the aircraft.

tri·cy·clic (trī·sī′klik, -sik′lik) *adj.* Having or characterized by three cycles or identical units of structure.

tri·dent (trīd′nt) *n.* A three-pronged fork; especially, the emblem of Neptune (Poseidon). — *adj.* Having three teeth or prongs: also **tri·den·tate** (trī·den′tāt), **tri·den′tat·ed.** [< L *tridens, -dentis* < *tri-* three + *dens, dentis* tooth]

Tri·den·tine (trī·den′tin, -tīn, tri-) *adj.* 1. Pertaining to Trent or to the Council of Trent. 2. Adhering to the decrees of the Council of Trent. — *n.* A Roman Catholic: from the fact that the creed (**Tridentine Creed**) of the Roman Catholic Church was formulated by the Council of Trent. [< Med.L *Tridentinus* < *Tridentum* Trent]

Tri·den·tum (trī·den′təm) *n.* The ancient name for TRENT.

tri·di·men·sion·al (trī′di·men′shən·əl) *adj.* Having three dimensions, length, breadth, and thickness. — **tri′di·men′·sion·al′i·ty** *n.*

tri·e·cious (trī·ē′shəs) See TRIOECIOUS.

tried (trīd) Past tense and past participle of TRY. — *adj.* 1. Tested; trustworthy. 2. Freed of impurities, as metal or oil. 3. Rendered, as fat.

tri·en·ni·al (trī·en′ē·əl) *adj.* 1. Taking place every third year. 2. Lasting three years. — *n.* 1. A third anniversary. 2. A ceremony, etc., celebrated every three years. 3. A plant lasting three years. — **tri·en′ni·al·ly** *adv.*

tri·en·ni·um (trī·en′ē·əm) *n. pl.* **·en·ni·ums** or **·en·ni·a** (-en′ē·ə) A period of three years. [< L < *tri-* three + *annus* year]

tri·er (trī′ər) *n.* One who or that which tries.

Trier (trēr) A city in the Rhineland-Palatinate, West Germany, on the Moselle; pop. 84,400 (est. 1967): also, in English, *Treves.* French *Trèves.*

tri·er·arch (trī′ər·ärk) *n.* In Greek antiquity, the captain of a trireme; also, at Athens, one who alone or with others fitted out and maintained a trireme. [< L *trierarchus* < Gk. *trierarchos* < *triērēs* trireme + *archein* to rule]

tri·er·ar·chy (trī′ər·är′kē) *n. pl.* **·chies** 1. The command of a trireme. 2. The fitting out and maintaining of a trireme. 3. The body of trierarchs collectively. [< Gk. *trierarchia* < *trierarchos.* See TRIERARCH.]

Tri·este (trē·est′, *Ital.* trē·es′tä) A port commune in NE Italy, on the **Gulf of Trieste,** an inlet of the Gulf of Venice; formerly part of the Free Territory of Trieste; pop. 280,700 (est. 1967).

Trieste, Free Territory of A free territory, including the city of Trieste and adjoining portions of Istria, constituted by the Italian-Allied peace treaty of 1947; divided between Italy and Yugoslavia, 1954.

tri·fa·cial (trī·fā′shəl) *adj. Anat.* Trigeminal (def. 2).

tri·fid (trī′fid) *adj.* Divided into three parts or sections. [< L *trifidus* < *tri-* three + *fid-,* stem of *findere* to split]

tri·fle (trī′fəl) *v.* **·fled, ·fling** *v.i.* 1. To treat so nething as of no value or importance; dally: with *with.* 2. To act or speak frivolously or idly; jest. 3. To play; toy. 4. To pass time idly; idle. — *v.t.* 5. To pass (time) in an idle or purposeless way. — *n.* 1. Anything of very little value or importance. **2.** A small amount, as of money. **3.** A confection, usually made of alternate layers of macaroons or ladyfingers with sugared fruit, covered with a custard and topped with meringue or whipped cream. **4.** A variety of pewter. — **a trifle** Slightly; to a small extent: *a trifle* short. [< OF *truffler*, var. of *truffer* to deceive, jeer at < *trufle*, dim. of *trufe* cheating, mockery; ult. origin unknown] — **tri′fler** *n.*

tri·fling (trī′fling) *adj.* **1.** Frivolous. **2.** Insignificant. — **Syn.** See TRIVIAL. — **tri′fling·ly** *adv.*

tri·fo·cal (trī·fō′kəl) *adj.* **1.** Having three foci. **2.** *Optics* Pertaining to or describing eyeglasses or a lens ground in three segments, for near, intermediate, and far vision. — *n. pl.* Eyeglasses having trifocal lenses.

tri·fold (trī′fōld) *adj.* Triple.

tri·fo·li·ate (trī·fō′lē·it, -āt) *adj. Bot.* Having three leaves or leaflike processes: also *ternate.* Also **tri·fo′li·at·ed.** [< TRI- + FOLIATE]

tri·fo·li·o·late (trī·fō′lē·ə·lāt′) *adj. Bot.* Having three leaflets.

tri·fo·li·um (trī·fō′lē·əm) *n.* A trefoil (def. 1). [< NL < L < *tri-* three + *folium* a leaf]

tri·fo·ri·um (trī·fôr′ē·əm, -fō′rē-) *n. pl.* **·fo·ri·a** (-fôr′ē·ə, -fō′rē·ə) *Archit.* A gallery above the arches of the nave in a church. [< Med.L < L *tri-* three + *foris* a door] — **tri·fo′ri·al** *adj.*

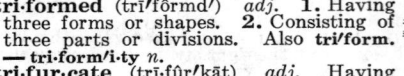

tri·formed (trī′fôrmd′) *adj.* **1.** Having three forms or shapes. **2.** Consisting of three parts or divisions. Also **tri′form.** — **tri·form′i·ty** *n.*

TRIFORIUM

tri·fur·cate (trī·fûr′kāt) *adj.* Having three forks or branches. Also **tri·fur′cat·ed.** [< L] — **tri·fur·ca·tion** (trī′fər·kā′shən) *n.*

trig[1] (trig) *adj.* **1.** Characterized by tidiness; trim; neat. **2.** Strong; sound; firm. **3.** Faithful; trustworthy; dependable. **4.** Active; alert. **5.** Full; inflated. — **Syn.** See NEAT[1]. — *v.t.* **trigged, trig·ging** To make trig or neat; dress finely or smartly: often with *out* or *up.* [< ON *tryggr* true, trusty] — **trig′ly** *adv.* — **trig′ness** *n.*

trig[2] (trig) *v.t.* **trigged, trig·ging** **1.** To check; obstruct; stop. **2.** To shore; prop. — *n.* A check or brake. [? < ON *tryggja* to make firm]

trig. or **trigon.** Trigonometric; trigonometry.

tri·gem·i·nal (trī·jem′ə·nəl) *adj.* **1.** Being in three parts; threefold; triple **2.** *Anat.* Of or pertaining to the trigeminus: also *trifacial.* — *n.* The trigeminus. [< L *trigeminus* born three at a time < *tri-* + *geminus* a twin]

trigeminal neuralgia *Pathol.* Tic douloureux.

tri·gem·i·nus (trī·jem′ə·nəs) *n. pl.* **·ni** (-nī) *Anat.* The double-rooted fifth cranial nerve, whose three divisions, mandibular, maxillary, and ophthalmic, function as the great sensory nerve of the face. [< NL < L. See TRIGEMINAL.]

trig·ger (trig′ər) *n.* **1.** The lever or other device actuated manually to fire a firearm. For illustration see REVOLVER. **2.** Any lever, catch, release, etc., that serves to initiate a process or operation. **3.** An act, event, etc., that sets some series of events in motion. — **quick on the trigger 1.** Quick to shoot. **2.** Quick to act in response to a suggestion; quick-witted; alert. — *v.t.* **1.** To initiate; precipitate. [Earlier *tricker* < Du. *trekker* < *trekken* to pull, tug at]

trig·ger·fish (trig′ər·fish′) *n. pl.* **·fish** or **·fish·es** A plectognath fish (genus *Balistes*) found mainly in tropical waters, having an ovate body covered with large, rough scales: named from the triggerlike second spine of the dorsal fin: also called *filefish.*

trig·ger-hap·py (trig′ər·hap′ē) *adj. U.S. Slang* Apt to shoot for no good reason; overinclined to use firearms.

trigger man *U.S. Slang* A gangster who does the actual shooting in a murder; also, one employed as a bodyguard.

tri·glyph (trī′glif) *n. Archit.* An ornament in a Doric frieze consisting of a tablet with three parallel vertical channels or glyphs, and standing on each side of the metopes. [< L *triglyphus* < Gk. *triglyphos* thrice grooved < *tri-* three + *glyphē* a carving < *glyphein* to carve, engrave]

tri·glyph·ic (trī·glif′ik) *adj.* **1.** Pertaining to or consisting of triglyphs. **2.** Having three groups of characters or carvings. Also **tri′glyph·al, tri·glyph′i·cal.**

tri·go (trē′gō) *n. Spanish* Wheat.

tri·gon (trī′gon) *n.* **1.** One of four parts of the zodiac, each consisting of three signs. **2.** In Greek and Roman antiquity, a lyre or harp of triangular form. **3.** *Obs.* A triangle. [< L *trigonum* < Gk. *trigōnon*, orig. neut. of *trigōnos* three-angled < *tri-* three + *gōnia* an angle]

trig·o·nal (trig′ə·nəl) *adj.* **1.** Pertaining to or in the form of a trigon; triangular; three-cornered. **2.** *Crystall.* Denoting a crystal system having a principal (vertical) axis of threefold symmetry, often included in the hexagonal system. Also **trig′o·nous.** — **trig′o·nal·ly** *adv.*

trigonometric functions Certain functions of an angle or arc, of which the most commonly used are the sine, cosine, tangent, cotangent, secant, and cosecant. From the definition of tangent, it may be seen that $\tan \theta = \dfrac{\sin \theta}{\cos \theta}$. From the definitions of the other functions and by application of the

---

Pythagorean theorem the following statements may be derived: $\sin \theta = \dfrac{1}{\csc \theta}$, $\cos \theta = \dfrac{1}{\sec \theta}$, $\tan \theta = \dfrac{1}{\cotan \theta}$, $\sin^2 \theta + \cos^2 \theta = 1$, $\tan^2 \theta + 1 = \sec^2 \theta$, and $\cotan^2 \theta + 1 = \csc^2 \theta$. Each of these statements is a **trigonometric identity.** Less commonly used functions are the versed sine (or versine), coversed sine (or coversine or versed cosine), exsecant, and haversine. Their identities are: versine $\theta = 1 - \cos \theta$, coversed sine $\theta = 1 - \sin \theta$, exsecant $\theta = \sec \theta - 1$, haversine $\theta = \frac{1}{2}$ versine θ.

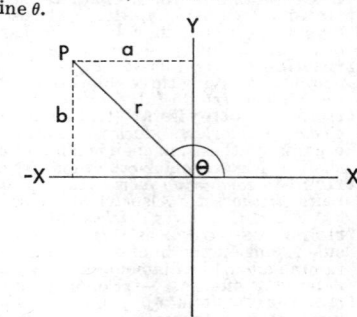

TRIGONOMETRIC FUNCTIONS

If θ is the angle formed by r and the x axis, and P is a point on r having a as its abscissa and b as its ordinate, then sine $\theta = b/r$, cosine $\theta = a/r$, tangent $\theta = b/a$, cosecant $\theta = r/b$, secant $\theta = r/a$, and cotangent $\theta = a/b$.

trig·o·nom·e·try (trig′ə·nom′ə·trē) *n.* The branch of mathematics that deals with the relations of the sides and angles of triangles. Abbr. *trig., trigon.* [< NL *trigonometria* < Gk. *trigōnon* triangle + *metron* measure] — **trig·o·no·met·ric** (trig′ə·nə·met′rik) or **·ri·cal** *adj.* — **trig′o·no·met′ri·cal·ly** *adv.*

tri·graph (trī′graf, -gräf) *n.* Three letters representing one sound, as *-eau* in *beau.* [< TRI- + -GRAPH]

tri·he·dron (trī·hē′drən) *n. pl.* **·dra** (-drə) *Geom.* A figure having three plane surfaces meeting at a point. [< NL < Gk. *tri-* three + *hedra* a base] — **tri·he′dral** *adj.*

tri·ju·gate (trī′jŏŏ·gāt, trī·jŏŏ′gāt, -git) *adj. Bot.* Having three pairs of leaflets. Also **tri·ju·gous** (trī′jŏŏ·gəs, -jŏŏ′-). [< L *trijugus* threefold < *tri-* three + *jugum* a yoke]

tri·lat·er·al (trī·lat′ər·əl) *adj.* Having three sides. [< L *trilaterus* < *tri-* three + *latus, lateris* a side] — **tri·lat′er·al·ly** *adv.*

tri·lin·e·ar (trī·lin′ē·ər) *adj.* Pertaining to, referring to, or bounded by three lines.

tri·lin·gual (trī·ling′gwəl) *adj.* **1.** Written or expressed in or using three languages. **2.** Able to speak three languages, often with equal skill. Also **tri·lin′guar.** [< L *trilinguis* < *tri-* three + *lingua* tongue]

tri·lit·er·al (trī·lit′ər·əl) *adj.* Consisting of three letters.

trill[1] (tril) *v.t.* **1.** To sing or play in a quavering or tremulous tone. **2.** *Phonet.* To articulate with a trill. — *v.i.* **3.** To utter, make, or give forth a quavering or tremulous sound. **4.** *Music* To execute a trill or shake. — *n.* **1.** A tremulous utterance of successive tones, as of certain insects or birds; a warble. **2.** *Music* A rapid alternation of two tones either a tone or a semitone apart; shake. **3.** *Phonet.* A rapid vibration of an articulator, as of the tip of the tongue against the alveolar ridge in the articulation of *rr* in Spanish, or the uvula against the back of the tongue in the articulation of *r* in some varieties of German. Compare TAP[2]. **4.** A consonant so uttered. [< Ital. *trillare*, prob. < Gmc.]

trill[2] (tril) *v.t. & v.i. Archaic* **1.** To flow or cause to flow in a trickle, as tears. **2.** To turn or roll; also, to quiver. [ME *trillen* < Scand. Cf. Sw. & Norw. *trilla* to roll.]

tril·lion (tril′yən) *n.* **1.** *U.S.* A thousand billions, written as 1 followed by twelve zeros: a cardinal number: called a billion in Great Britain. **2.** *Brit.* A million billions (def. 2), written as 1 followed by eighteen zeros: a cardinal number. — *adj.* Being a trillion in number. [< MF < *tri-* three + *(mi)llion* million]

tril·lionth (tril′yənth) *adj.* **1.** Having the number one trillion: the ordinal of *trillion.* **2.** Being one of a trillion equal parts. — *n.* **1.** One of a trillion equal parts. **2.** That which is numbered one trillion.

tril·li·um (tril′ē·əm) *n.* Any of a genus (*Trillium*) of North American herbs of the lily family, having a stout stem bearing a whorl of three leaves and a solitary flower. [< NL < L *tri-* three; so called because of its three leaves]

tri·lo·bate (trī·lō′bāt, trī′lə·bāt) *adj.* **1.** Three-lobed. **2.** *Bot.* Having three lobes, as some leaves. Also **tri·lo′bal, tri·lo′bat·ed, tri′lobed.**

tri·lo·bite (trī′lə·bīt) *n. Paleontol.* Any of a subclass or group (*Trilobita*) of extinct Paleozoic marine arthropods related to the crustaceans, having a flattened body divided into a variable number of segments covered by a hard dorsal shield marked in three lobes. [< NL *Trilobites* < Gk. *tri-* three + *lobos* a lobe] — **tri·lo·bit·ic** (-bit′ik) *adj.*

tri·loc·u·lar (trī·lok′yə·lər) *adj.* Having three cells or chambers. [< TRI- + L *loculus*, dim. of *locus* a place]

tril·o·gy (tril'ə·jē) *n. pl.* **·gies** A group of three literary or dramatic compositions, each complete in itself, but continuing the same general subject. [< Gk. *trilogia* < *tri-* three + *logos* a discourse]

trim (trim) *v.* **trimmed, trim·ming** *v.t.* **1.** To put in or restore to order; make neat by clipping, pruning, etc. **2.** To remove by cutting: usually with *off* or *away.* **3.** To put ornaments on; decorate. **4.** In carpentry, to smooth; dress. **5.** *Informal* **a** To defeat. **b** To punish or thrash; beat. **c** To rebuke. **d** To cheat; victimize. **6.** *Naut.* **a** To adjust (sails or yards) for sailing. **b** To cause (a ship) to sit well in the water by adjusting cargo, ballast, etc. **7.** *Aeron.* To bring (an airplane) to balanced flight by adjusting control surfaces. **8.** *Obs.* To furnish; equip. — *v.i.* **9.** *Naut.* **a** To be or remain in equilibrium: said of a ship. **b** To adjust sails or yards for sailing. **10.** To act so as to appear to favor both sides in a controversy. — *n.* **1.** State of adjustment or preparation; fitting condition; orderly disposition: All was in good *trim.* **2.** Condition as to general appearance; dress; style. **3.** *Naut.* **a** Fitness for sailing: said of a vessel in reference to disposition of ballast, masts, cargo, etc. **b** Actual or comparative degree of immersion. **4.** Particular character or nature; kind; stripe. **5.** The moldings, etc., as about the doors of a building; also, the hardware trimmings of a house, such as hinges, window fastenings, etc. **6.** Ornament; trapping; dress. **7.** Material rejected or cut out. **8.** In advertising, window dressing or display. **9.** The interior and exterior ornament of a vehicle, as an automobile. **10.** *Aeron.* The position of an aircraft relative to balanced flight. — *adj.* **trim·mer, trim·mest 1.** Adjusted to a nicety; being in perfect order; handsomely equipped or of stylish and smart appearance; spruce; precise; jaunty. **2.** Excellently fit; nice; pretty; fine. — **Syn.** See NEAT[1]. — *adv.* In a trim manner: also **trim'ly.** [OE *trymman* to arrange, strengthen < *trum* steadfast, strong] — **trim'ness** *n.*

trim·er·ous (trim'ər·əs) *adj.* **1.** Composed of three similar parts. **2.** *Bot.* Three-parted, as a flower: often written **3-merous. 3.** *Entomol.* Having three joints, as the tarsus of an insect. [< TRI- + Gk. *meros* a part]

tri·mes·ter (trī·mes'tər) *n.* A three-month period; quarter. [< F *trimestre* < L *trimestris* < *tri-* three + *mensis* month] — **tri·mes'tral, tri·mes'tri·al** *adj.*

trim·e·ter (trim'ə·tər) *n.* In prosody, a line of verse consisting of three metrical feet: Thĕn āll | thĕ trēes | wĕre bāre. — *adj.* In prosody, consisting of three metrical feet or of lines containing three metrical feet. [< L *trimetrus* < Gk. *trimetros* < *tri-* three + *metron* measure]

tri·meth·yl·ene glycol (trī·meth'i·lēn) *Chem.* A sweet, viscid compound, $C_3H_8O_2$, produced by the fermentation of glycerol and forming the base of meprobamate: also called *propanediol.*

tri·meth·yl·pen·tane (trī'meth·il·pen'tān) *n. Chem.* One of three isomeric hydrocarbon compounds, C_8H_{18}, one of which, often called isooctane, is used in rating motor fuels.

tri·met·ric (trī·met'rik) *adj.* **1.** Trimeter. **2.** *Crystall.* Orthorhombic. Also **tri·met'ri·cal.**

trimetric projection *Geom.* A three-dimensional projection in which each dimension is measured on a separate scale and according to arbitrarily assigned angles.

tri·met·ro·gon (trī·met'rə·gon) *n.* A high-speed system of aerial topographic photography, employing three cameras, one vertical and two at matching oblique angles. — *adj.* Of or pertaining to this system or camera unit. [< TRI- + METRO- + -GON]

trim·mer (trim'ər) *n.* **1.** One who or that which trims. **2.** A timeserver.

trim·ming (trim'ing) *n.* **1.** Something added for ornament or to give a finished appearance or effect. **2.** *pl.* Articles or equipment; fittings, as the hardware of a house. **3.** *pl.* The usual or proper accompaniments or condiments of an article or food. **4.** *pl.* That which is removed by trimming, cutting, or clipping; in shearing, wool from the shanks. **5.** *Informal* A severe reproof or a chastisement; flogging; beating. **6.** *Informal* A defeat. **7.** The act of one who trims.

tri·mo·lec·u·lar (trī'mə·lek'yə·lər) *adj. Chem.* Having, consisting of, or pertaining to three molecules.

tri·month·ly (trī·munth'lē) *adj. & adv.* Done or occurring every third month.

tri·morph (trī'môrf) *n.* **1.** A substance existing or occurring in three forms. **2.** One of the forms in which such a substance exists. [< Gk. *trimorphos* having three forms < *tri-* three + *morphē* a form]

tri·mor·phism (trī·môr'fiz·əm) *n.* **1.** *Bot.* The existence on the same plant of three distinct forms of flowers as regards the relative lengths of stamens and pistils. **2.** *Mineral.* The property of crystallizing in three series of fundamentally different forms having the same chemical composition. **3.** *Zool.* Difference of species in form, color, etc., characterizing three distinct types. — **tri·mor'phic, tri·mor'phous** *adj.*

trim tab *Aeron.* A small control surface used to trim an airplane in flight.

Tri·mur·ti (tri·mo͝or'tē) *n.* In Hindu mythology, the triad of the Vedas, consisting of Brahma (the Creator), Vishnu (the Preserver), and Siva (the Destroyer). [< Skt. *trimūrti* < *tri-* three + *mūrti* shape]

Tri·na·cri·a (tri·nā'krē·ə, trī-) The ancient name for SICILY. — **Tri·na'cri·an** *adj.*

tri·nal (trī'nəl) *adj.* **1.** Of or pertaining to three. **2.** Having three parts; threefold. [< LL *trinalis* < L *trinus* three each < *tres, tria* three]

tri·na·ry (trī'nər·ē) *adj.* Made up of three parts or proceeding by threes; ternary. [< LL *trinarius* of three kinds < L *trinus.* See TRINAL.]

trine (trīn) *adj.* **1.** Threefold; triple. **2.** In astrology, relating to or situated in trine. — *n.* **1.** A compound in three parts or elements. **2.** *Heraldry* A charge of three objects. **3.** In astrology, the aspect of two planets when 120° apart. — *v.t.* **trined, trin·ing** *Obs.* In astrology, to place or join in trine. [< OF *trin, trine* < L *trinus.* See TRINAL.]

Trine (trīn) *n.* The Trinity.

Trin·i·dad and To·ba·go (trin'ə·dad; tō·bā'gō) An independent member of the Commonwealth of Nations off the northern coast of Venezuela, comprising the islands of **Trinidad**; 1,864 sq. mi., and **Tobago**; 116 sq. mi.; total pop. 1,040,-000 (est. 1969); capital, Port-of-Spain. — **Trin·i·dad·i·an** (trin'ə·dad'ē·ən) *n. & adj.*

Tri·nil man (trī'nil) *Paleontol.* Pithecanthropus. [after *Trinil,* Java, where remains were found]

Trin·i·tar·i·an (trin'ə·târ'ē·ən) *adj.* **1.** Of or pertaining to the Trinity. **2.** Holding or professing belief in the Trinity. — *n.* A believer in the doctrine of the Trinity. Also *Trinitarian.* Distinguished from *Unitarian.* [< NL *trinitarius* < LL *trinitas.* See TRINITY.] — **Trin·i·tar·i·an·ism** *n.*

tri·ni·tro·ben·zene (trī·nī'trō·ben'zēn) *n. Chem.* A yellow crystalline compound, $C_6H_3(NO_2)_3$, occurring in three forms, one of which is highly explosive.

tri·ni·tro·cre·sol (trī·nī'trō·krē'sōl, -sol) *n. Chem.* A yellow crystalline organic compound, $C_8H_5N_3O_7$, used as a bursting charge. [< TRI- + NITRO- + CRESOL]

tri·ni·tro·phe·nol (trī·nī'trō·fē'nōl, -nol) *n.* Picric acid.

tri·ni·tro·tol·u·ene (trī·nī'trō·tol'yoo·ēn) *n. Chem.* A high explosive, $C_7H_5N_3O_6$, made by treating toluene with nitric acid, used in warfare, as a blasting agent, and as a base for measuring the explosive power of nuclear bombs: also called *TNT, trotyl.* Also **tri·ni·tro·tol·u·ol** (-yoo·ōl, -ol). [< TRI- + NITRO- + TOLUENE]

trin·i·ty (trin'ə·tē) *n. pl.* **·ties 1.** The state or character of being three. **2.** Any union of three parts or elements in one; a trio; triad. Also called *triunity.* [< OF *trinite* < LL *trinitas* < L, triad < *trinus.* See TRINAL.]

Trin·i·ty (trin'ə·tē) *n.* **1.** *Theol.* A threefold consubstantial personality existing in the one divine being or substance; the union in one God of Father, Son, and Holy Spirit as three infinite persons. **2.** Trinity Sunday. **3.** In art and symbolism, a representation of the Trinity.

Trinity River A river in Texas, flowing about 510 miles SE to **Trinity Bay,** the NE inlet of Galveston Bay.

Trinity Sunday *Eccl.* The eighth Sunday after Easter, observed as a festival in honor of the Trinity. Also *Trinity.*

trin·ket (tring'kit) *n.* **1.** Any small ornament, as of jewelry. **2.** A trifle; a trivial object; a toy. [< AF *trenquet,* OF *trenchet* a toy knife, ornament; ult. origin uncertain]

trin·kums (tring'kəmz) *n.pl. Scot. & Brit. Dial.* Small ornaments; trinkets. Also **trin'kum-tran'kums** (-trang'kəmz). [Appar. alter. of TRINKET]

tri·no·dal (trī·nōd'l) *adj. Bot.* Having three nodes.

tri·no·mi·al (trī·nō'mē·əl) *adj.* **1.** *Biol.* Of, having, or employing three terms or names in taxonomy, the generic, the specific, and the subspecific or varietal, as *Lynx rufus texensis,* the Texas bobcat. **2.** *Math.* Consisting of three terms connected by plus or minus signs or both. — *n.* **1.** *Math.* A trinomial expression, as $3x + y - 27z.$ **2.** *Biol.* A trinomial name. Also **tri·nom'i·nal** (-nom'ə·nəl), **tri·on'y·mal** (-on'ə·məl). [< L *trinominus* from three names]

tri·o (trē'ō; *for def. 1, also* trī'ō) *n. pl.* **tri·os 1.** Any three things grouped or associated together. **2.** *Music* **a** A composition for three performers. **b** The second part of a minuet or scherzo, of a march, and often of other dance forms. **c** A group of three musicians that plays trios. [< F < Ital. < *tre* three < L *tres, tria*]

tri·ode (trī'ōd) *n. Electronics* A three-element electron tube, containing an anode, cathode, and a control grid. [< TRI- + (ELECTR)ODE]

tri·oe·cious (trī·ē'shəs) *adj. Bot.* Having in different plants of the same species male, female, and hermaphrodite flowers: also spelled *triecious.* Also **tri·oi'cous** (-oi'kəs). [< NL *Trioecia,* order name < Gk. *tri-* three + *oikos* a house] — **tri·oe'cious·ly** *adv.*

-triol *suffix Chem.* Denoting an organic compound containing three hydroxyl radicals: *estriol.*

tri·o·let (trī'ə·lit) *n.* A stanza of eight lines on two rhymes, the first line repeated as the fourth and seventh and the second as the eighth. Its rhyme scheme is *abaaabab*. [< F, dim. of *trio*. See TRIO.]

tri·o·ny·chid (trī·on′ə·kid) *n.* Any of a family (*Trionychidae*) of turtles widely distributed in Asia, Africa, and North America, characterized by soft, leathery, flat shells.

tri·ose (trī′ōs) *n. Biochem.* A monosaccharide whose molecule contains three atoms of carbon and three of oxygen. [< TRI- + -OSE²]

tri·ox·ide (trī·ok′sīd, -sid) *n. Chem.* An oxide containing three atoms of oxygen in combination: iron *trioxide*, Fe_2O_3. Also **tri·ox′id** (-sid).

trip (trip) *n.* **1.** A journey or voyage. **2.** A misstep or stumble caused by losing balance or striking the foot against an object. **3.** An active, nimble step or movement. **4.** *Mech.* A pawl or similar device that trips, or the action of such a device. **5.** A sudden catch, especially of the legs and feet, as of a wrestler. **6.** A blunder; mistake. **7.** *Slang* The taking of a psychedelic drug, as marijuana, LSD, etc.; also, the resulting mental experience or its duration. — *Syn.* See JOURNEY. — *v.* **tripped, trip·ping** *v.i.* **1.** To stumble. **2.** To move quickly with light or small steps. **3.** To commit an error; make a false step; go astray. **4.** *Mech.* To be triggered, released, etc. **5.** *Rare* To make a journey. — *v.t.* **6.** To cause to stumble: often with *up*. **7.** To detect and expose in an error; defeat the purpose of. **8.** To perform (a dance) lightly. **9.** *Mech.* To set free or in operation by releasing a stay, catch, trigger, etc. **10.** *Naut.* To loosen (an anchor) from the bottom. [< OF *treper, triper* to leap, trample, ? < MDu. *trippen* to trip, hop]

tri·par·tite (trī·pär′tīt) *adj.* **1.** Divided into three parts or divisions; threefold: a *tripartite* leaf: also **tri·part·ed** (trī′pär·tid). **2.** Pertaining to or executed between three parties. [< L *tripartitus* < *tri-* three + *partitus*, pp. of *partiri* to divide] — **tri·par′tite·ly** *adv.*

tri·par·ti·tion (trī′pär·tish′ən) *n.* Division into three parts, into thirds, or among three.

tripe (trīp) *n.* **1.** A part of the stomach of a ruminant, used for food. **2.** *Informal* Anything worthless; nonsense. [< OF *tripe, trippe* < Arabic *tharb* entrails, a net]

tri·pe·dal (trī′pə·dal, trī·pēd′l, trip′ə·dal) *adj.* Having three feet. [< L *tripedalis* < *tri-* three + *pes, pedis* foot]

tri·per·son·al·i·ty (trī·pûr′sən·al′ə·tē) *n. Theol.* The state or quality of existing in three persons in one Godhead; trinity. — **tri·per′son·al** (-əl) *adj.*

tri·pet·al·ous (trī·pet′l·əs) *adj. Bot.* Having three petals.

trip hammer A heavy power hammer that is raised or tilted by a cam and then allowed to drop.

tri·phase (trī′fāz) *adj. Electr.* Having or employing three phases, as in an alternating current.

tri·phen·yl·meth·ane (trī·fen′əl·meth′ān) *n. Chem.* A hydrocarbon, $(C_6H_5)_3CH$, occurring in colorless leaflets, used in organic synthesis and in the manufacture of dyes.

triph·thong (trif′thông, -thong, trip′-) *n.* **1.** A combination of three vowel sounds in one syllable. **2.** Loosely, a trigraph. [< TRI- + (DI)PHTHONG] — **triph·thon′gal** *adj.*

triph·y·lite (trif′ə·līt) *n.* A greenish or bluish translucent phosphate of iron, manganese, and lithium, usually found massive. Also **triph′y·line** (-lin, -lēn). [< TRI- + Gk. *phylē* a tribe + -ITE¹: so called because it contains three bases]

tri·pin·nate (trī·pin′āt) *adj. Bot.* Thrice pinnate, as when a bipinnate leaf becomes pinnate in certain ferns. Also **tri·pin′nat·ed.** — **tri·pin′nate·ly** *adv.*

tri·pin·nat·i·fid (trī′pin·nat′ə·fid) *adj. Bot.* Tripinnately cleft. [< TRIPINNATE + -FID]

tripl. Triplicate.

tri·plane (trī′plān) *n.* An airplane having three wings arranged one above the other.

tri·ple (trip′əl) *v.* **·led, ·ling** *v.t.* **1.** To make threefold in number or quantity. — *v.i.* **2.** To be or become three times as many or as large. **3.** In baseball, to hit a triple. — *adj.* **1.** Consisting of three things united or of three parts; threefold. **2.** Multiplied by three; thrice said or done. — *n.* **1.** A set or group of three. **2.** In baseball, a base hit that enables the batter to reach third base. **3.** In horse racing, a single bet won only by choosing in correct order the first three horses in a specified race. [< MF < L *triplus* < Gk. *triplous* threefold. Doublet of TREBLE.] — **trip′ly** *adv.*

Triple Alliance **1.** An alliance of England, Holland, and Sweden against France, formed in 1668. **2.** A league between England, France, and Holland, formed against Spain in 1717, but called **Quadruple** when joined by Austria in 1718. **3.** An alliance formed in 1795 between Austria, Great Britain, and Russia against France. **4.** A Dreibund.

Triple Entente A friendly understanding formed between Great Britain, France, and Russia prior to World War I to counteract the Dreibund.

tri·ple-ex·pan·sion (trip′əl·ik·span′shən) *adj. Mech.* Designating a compound steam engine having three cylinders in which the steam is successively expanded.

triple meter *Music* See under METER².

triple play A baseball play in which three men are put out.

trip·let (trip′lit) *n.* **1.** A group of three of a kind. **2.** One of three children born at one birth. **3.** A group of three rhymed lines. **4.** *Music* A group of three equal notes performed in the time of two: also called *tercet*. [< TRIPLE, on analogy with *doublet*]

trip·le·tail (trip′əl·tāl′) *n.* A large edible marine fish (*Lobotes surinamensis*) of the Atlantic coast to Surinam, with soft dorsal and anal fins suggesting additional tails.

triple threat *U.S. Informal* **1.** A football player expert at kicking, running, and passing. **2.** One skillful in three areas of activity. — **trip·le-threat′** *adj.*

tri·plex (trī′pleks, trip′leks) *adj.* Having three parts. — *n. Music* Triple meter. [< L < *tri-* three + *plicare* to fold]

trip·li·cate (*adj. & n.* trip′lə·kit; *v.* trip′lə·kāt) *adj.* Threefold; made in three copies. — *n.* One of or a set of three identical things. — *v.t.* **·cat·ed, ·cat·ing** To make three times as much or as many; treble. *Abbr.* **tripl.** [< L *triplicatus*, pp. of *triplicare* to triple] — **trip′li·cate·ly** *adv.* — **trip′li·ca′tion** *n.*

tri·plic·i·ty (trī·plis′ə·tē) *n.* *pl.* **·ties** **1.** Threefold character. **2.** A group or combination of three. **3.** In astrology, a combination of three of the twelve signs of the zodiac. [< LL *triplicitas, -atis* < L *triplex, -icis*. See TRIPLEX.]

trip·loid (trip′loid) *adj.* **1.** Trebled. **2.** *Biol.* Having three times the haploid number of chromosomes. — *n.* A triploid cell or organism. [< NL *triploides* < Gk. *triplous* threefold + *eidos* form]

trip·loi·dy (trip′loi·dē) *n.* The condition of being triploid.

trip·lo·pi·a (trip·lō′pē·ə) *n.* *Pathol.* A defect of vision in which objects are seen tripled. [< NL < Gk. *triplous* threefold + *ōps, ōpos* eye]

tri·pod (trī′pod) *n.* **1.** A utensil or article having three feet or legs. **2.** A three-legged stand for supporting a camera, transit, or other instrument. [< L *tripus, -podis* < Gk. *tripous* < *tri-* three + *pous* foot]

trip·o·dal (trip′ə·dəl) *adj.* **1.** Of the nature or form of a tripod. **2.** Having three feet or legs. Also **tri·po·di·al** (trī·pō′dē·əl, trī-), **tri·pod′ic** (-pod′ik).

trip·o·dy (trip′ə·dē) *n.* *pl.* **·dies** A verse or meter having three feet. [< TRI- + (DI)PODY]

trip·o·li (trip′ə·lē) *n.* Rottenstone. [after *Tripoli*, Libya, where it is found]

Trip·o·li (trip′ə·lē) **1.** One of the two capitals of Libya, a port on the Mediterranean; pop. 213,506 (1964). **2.** A port city in NW Lebanon, on the Mediterranean; pop. 127,600 (est. 1964); ancient *Trip·o·lis* (trip′ə·lis). — **Tri·pol·i·tan** (tri·pol′ə·tən) *adj. & n.* — **Trip′o·line** (-lin) *adj.*

Trip·o·li·ta·ni·a (trip·ol′ə·tā′nē·ə) The NW Region of Libya; about 136,000 sq. mi.; pop. about 1,000,000; capital, Tripoli; a former Barbary State. Ancient **Trip′o·lis.** — **Trip′o·li·ta′ni·an** *adj. & n.*

tri·pos (trī′pos) *n.* **1.** An honors examination for the B.A. degree at Cambridge University, England. **2.** *Obs.* A tripod. [Appar. alter. of L *tripus* tripod]

trip·per (trip′ər) *n.* **1.** One who trips. **2.** *Brit. Informal* A traveler; tourist. **3.** *Mech.* A trip or tripping mechanism.

trip·pet (trip′it) *n. Mech.* A cam, toe, or projecting piece, designed to strike some other piece at fixed intervals. [< TRIP, *v.*]

trip·ping (trip′ing) *n.* **1.** The act of one who or that which trips. **2.** A light dance. — *adj.* Light; nimble; easy, as in gait or movement. — **trip′ping·ly** *adv.*

trip·tane (trip′tān) *n. Chem.* A hydrocarbon compound, C_7H_{16}, derived from butane and having a very high octane number. [Contr. of *tripentane* < TRI- + PENTANE]

triptane number A measure of the efficiency of a motor fuel, expressed in terms of a blend of heptane and triptane, and tetraethyl lead.

trip·ter·ous (trip′tər·əs) *adj. Bot.* Having three wings or winglike processes, as certain seeds. [< TRI- + Gk. *pteron* wing]

Trip·tol·e·mus (trip·tol′ə·məs) In Greek mythology, a hero said to have given mankind the secret of the cultivation of grain. Also **Trip·tol′e·mos** (-məs).

trip·tych (trip′tik) *n.* **1.** A triple tablet; especially, a Greek or Roman hinged triple writing tablet. **2.** A triple picture or carving on three hinged panels, often depicting a religious subject. Also **trip′ty·ca** (-ti·kə). **trip′ty·chon** (-ti·kon). [< LL *triptycha* < Gk., trio of tablets; orig. neut. pl. of *triptychos* folded < *tri-* thrice + *ptyssein* to fold]

tri·quet·rous (trī·kwet′rəs, -kwē′trəs) *adj.* **1.** Three-sided. **2.** Having three acute or salient angles. **3.** Three-cornered. [< L *triquetrus*]

tri·ra·di·ate (trī·rā′dē·āt) *adj.* Having three rays or radiate branches. Also **tri·ra′di·al, tri·ra′di·at·ed.** — **tri·ra′di·al·ly, tri·ra′di·ate·ly** *adv.*

tri·reme (trī′rēm) *n.* An ancient Greek or Roman warship with three banks of oars. [< L *triremis* < *tri-* three + *remus* oar]

tri·sac·cha·ride (trī·sak′ə·rīd, -rid) *n. Biochem.* Any of a class of saccharides that hydrolyze into three monosaccharide molecules. Also **tri·sac′cha·rid** (-rid).

Tris·ag·i·on (tris·ag′ē·on, -ā′gē-) *n.* A hymn of the Greek and Oriental churches, beginning with a threefold invocation of the holiness of God. Also **Tris·ag′i·um, Tris·hag′i·on.** [< Gk. *trisagion*, orig. neut. of *trisagios* thrice holy < *tris* thrice (< *treis* three) + *hagios* holy]

tri·sect (trī·sekt′) *v.t.* To divide into three parts, especially, as in geometry, into three equal parts. [< TRI- + L *sectus*, pp. of *secare* to cut] — **tri·sect′ed** *adj.* — **tri·sec′tion** (-sek′. shən) *n.* — **tri·sec′tor** *n.*

tri·seme (trī′sēm) *n.* A syllable or foot consisting of or equivalent to three short syllables, as the trochee. — *adj.* Consisting of or equal to three short syllables: also **tri·se′. mic.** [< Gk. *trisēmos* < *tri-* three + *sēma* a sign]

tri·sep·al·ous (trī·sep′əl-əs) *adj. Bot.* Having three sepals.

tri·sep·tate (trī·sep′tāt) *adj. Biol.* Having three septa.

tri·se·ri·al (trī-sir′ē·əl) *adj.* 1. Arranged in three series or rows. 2. *Bot.* Tristichous. Also **tri·se′ri·ate** (-it, -āt). — **tri·se′ri·al·ly, tri·se·ri·a·tim** (trī-sir′ē·ā′tim) *adv.*

tris·kel·i·on (tris·kel′ē·ən) *n. pl.* **·kel·i·a** (-kel′ē·ə) A symbolic figure characterized by three lines or three human legs radiating from a common center, used as the arms of the Isle of Man. Also **tris·cele** (tris′sēl), **tris·kele** (tris′kēl). [< Gk. *triskelēs* of three legs < *tri-* three + *skelos* leg]

TRISKELION

Tris·me·gis·tus (tris′mə·jis′təs, triz′-) See HERMES TRISMEGISTUS.

tris·mus (triz′məs, tris′-) *n. Pathol.* Lockjaw. [< NL < Gk. *trismos* gnashing of teeth < *trizein* to screech, creak] — **tris′mic** *adj.*

tris·oc·ta·he·dron (tris-ok′tə·hē′drən) *n. pl.* **·dra** (-drə) 1. *Geom.* A solid having 24 equal faces corresponding by threes to the faces of an octahedron. 2. *Crystall.* A holohedral isometric crystal included under 24 equal triangular faces with eight planes meeting at the extremities of the rectangular axes: also **trigonal trisoctahedron. b** A trapezohedron. [< Gk. *tris* thrice (< *treis* three) + OCTAHEDRON] — **tris·oc·ta·he′dral** *adj.*

tri·sper·mous (trī·spûr′məs) *adj. Bot.* Having three seeds.

Tris·tan (tris′tän, -tən) In medieval legend and Richard Wagner's *Tristan und Isolde*, a knight sent to Ireland to bring back the princess Iseult the Beautiful as a bride for his uncle, King Mark of Cornwall. Iseult and Tristan drink a magic love potion, and ultimately die together. In some versions, Tristan is married to Iseult of the White Hands, daughter of the Duke of Brittany. Also **Tris·tram** (tris′trəm).

Tris·tan da Cun·ha (tris′tən də kōō′nə) An island group in the South Atlantic, administered with St. Helena; 40 sq. mi.

triste (trēst) *adj. French* Sorrowful; sad.

tris·tesse (trēs·tes′) *n. French* Sadness; melancholy.

trist·ful (trist′fəl) *adj. Archaic* Sad; gloomy; sorrowful. [< obs. *trist* sad < OF *triste* < L *tristis*] — **trist′ful·ly** *adv.*

tris·tich (tris′tik) *n.* A strophe or system of three lines; triplet. Compare COUPLET, DISTICH. [< TRI- + (DI)STICH]

tris·ti·chous (tris′tə·kəs) *adj.* 1. Three-ranked. 2. *Bot.* Having parts, as leaves, arranged in three vertical rows. [< Gk. *tristichos* three-rowed < *tri-* three + *stichos* a row]

tri·sty·lous (trī·stī′ləs) *adj. Bot.* Having three styles.

tri·sul·fide (trī·sul′fīd, -fid) *n. Chem.* A sulfide containing three atoms of sulfur in the molecule. Also **tri·sul′fid** (-fid), **tri·sul′phide, tri·sul′phid.**

tri·syl·la·ble (trī·sil′ə·bəl) *n.* A word of three syllables. — **tri·syl·lab·ic** (trī′si·lab′ik) or **·i·cal** *adj.* — **tri′syl·lab′i·cal·ly** *adv.*

trit·an·o·pi·a (trit′ən·ō′pē·ə) *n. Pathol.* Impairment of vision for blue and yellow: also called *blue blindness.* Also **trit′an·op′si·a** (-op′sē·ə). [< NL < Gk. *tritos* third + AN¹- + -OPIA] — **trit′an·op′tic** (-op′tik) *adj.*

trite (trīt) *adj.* 1. Used so often as to be hackneyed; made commonplace by repetition. 2. *Archaic* Worn-out; frayed. [< L *tritus*, pp. of *terere* to rub] — **trite′ly** *adv.* — **trite′ness** *n.*

— **Syn.** 1. *Trite, hackneyed, threadbare, stereotyped, common,* and *commonplace* characterize discourse that is dull in expression or content. *Trite* is relatively mild, suggesting merely a lack of freshness or originality. *Hackneyed* is stronger, suggesting something worn out from overuse; the extreme of *hackneyed* is *threadbare.* We speak of *hackneyed* expressions, and of *threadbare* subjects. *Stereotyped* describes that which uses clichés instead of seeking to evoke new images and ideas. That which is dull because it is said or thought by everyone is *common; commonplace* characterizes anything obvious or truistic. — **Ant.** fresh, original, vivid, striking.

tri·the·ism (trī′thē·iz′əm) *n. Theol.* The doctrine of the separate existence of three Gods: sometimes applied to belief in the distinct personality of the Father, the Son, and the Holy Spirit. [< TRI- + Gk. *theos* god] — **tri′the·ist** *n.* — **tri′the·is′tic** or **·ti·cal** *adj.*

trit·i·cum (trit′ə·kəm) *n.* Any of a widely distributed and important genus (*Triticum*) of cereal grasses, the wheats, cultivated in many varieties. [< NL < L *wheat*]

trit·i·um (trit′ē·əm, trish′ē·əm) *n. Physics* The isotope of hydrogen having the atomic weight 3. [< NL < Gk. *tritos* third]

tri·ton¹ (trīt′n) *n.* Any of a genus (*Triton*) of marine gastropods having many gills and a trumpet-shaped shell. [< NL < L, Triton < Gk. *Tritōn*]

tri·ton² (trī′ton) *n. Physics.* The nucleus of an atom of tritium. [< TRIT(IUM) + (ELECTR)ON]

Tri·ton (trīt′n) In Greek mythology, a son of Poseidon (Neptune) and Amphitrite, represented with a man's head and upper body and a dolphin's tail. — *n.* 1. In Greek mythology, one of a race of attendants of the sea gods. 2. *Heraldry* A merman; also, a Neptune holding a trident. — **Tri′ton·ness** *n.fem.*

TRITON¹

tri·tone (trī′tōn) *n. Music* An augmented fourth, as containing three whole tones; also, a diminished fifth. [< Med.L *tritonus* < Gk. *tritonos* < *tri-* three + *tonos.* See TONE.]

trit·u·rate (trich′ə·rāt) *v.t.* **·rat·ed, ·rat·ing** To reduce to a fine powder or pulp by grinding or rubbing; pulverize. — *n.* 1. That which has been triturated. 2. A trituration (def. 3). [< LL *trituratus*, pp. of *triturare* to thresh < L *tritura* a rubbing, threshing < *tritus.* See TRITE.] — **trit·u·ra·ble** (trich′ər·ə·bəl) *adj.* — **trit′u·ra′tor** *n.*

trit·u·ra·tion (trich′ə·rā′shən) *n.* 1. The act of triturating. 2. The process of reducing to a pulp. 3. A triturated preparation, especially one in which a finely pulverized medicinal substance is mixed with milk sugar.

tri·umph (trī′əmf) *v.i.* 1. To win a victory; be victorious. 2. To be successful. 3. To rejoice over a victory; exult. 4. To celebrate a triumph, as a victorious Roman general. — *v.t.* Obs. To conquer. — *n.* 1. In Roman antiquity, the religious pageant of the entry of a victorious consul, dictator, or praetor into Rome. 2. Exultation over victory. 3. The condition of being victorious; victory. 4. *Obs.* A trump card. 5. *Obs.* Any public spectacular display, procession, or pageant. [< OF *triumpher* < L *triumphare* < *triumphus* a triumph < Gk. *thriambos* a processional hymn to Dionysus] — **tri′umph·er** *n.*

tri·um·phal (trī·um′fəl) *adj.* 1. Of, pertaining to, or of the nature of a triumph. 2. Celebrating a victory.

triumphal arch A monumental arch erected to commemorate a great victory or achievement.

tri·um·phant (trī·um′fənt) *adj.* 1. Exultant for or as for victory. 2. Victorious. 3. *Obs.* Glorious. 4. *Obs.* Triumphal. [< L *triumphans, -antis,* ppr. of *triumphare.* See TRIUMPH.] — **tri·um′phant·ly** *adv.*

tri·um·vir (trī·um′vər) *n. pl.* **·virs** or **·vi·ri** (-və·rī) One of three men united in public office or authority, as in ancient Rome. [< L < *trium virorum* of three men < *tres, trium* three + *vir* a man] — **tri·um′vi·ral** *adj.*

tri·um·vi·rate (trī·um′vər·it, -və·rāt) *n.* 1. A group or coalition of three men who unitedly exercise authority or control; government by triumvirs. 2. The office of a triumvir. 3. A group of three men; trio [< L *triumviratus* < *triumvir.* See TRIUMVIR.]

tri·une (trī′yōōn) *adj.* Three in one: said of God. — *n.* A group of three things united; triad; trinity in unity. [< TRI- + L *unus* one]

Tri·u·ni·tar·i·an (trī·yōō′nə·târ′ē·ən) *n.* A Trinitarian. [< TRIUNIT(Y) + -ARIAN]

tri·u·ni·ty (trī·yōō′nə·tē) *n. pl.* **·ties** Trinity.

tri·va·lent (trī·vā′lənt, triv′ə·lənt) *adj. Chem.* Having a valence or combining value of three: also *tervalent.* [< TRI- + L *valens, -entis,* ppr. of *valere* to be worth] — **tri·va′lence, tri·va′len·cy** *n.*

tri·valve (trī′valv′) *adj.* Having three valves, as a shell. — *n.* A trivalve shell.

Tri·van·drum (tri·van′drəm) The capital of Kerala, India, a port on the Malabar Coast; pop. 336,757 (est. 1971).

triv·et (triv′it) *n.* A short, usually three-legged stand for holding cooking vessels in a fireplace, a heated iron, or a hot dish on a table: also *trevet:* also called *spider.* [OE *trefet* < L *tripes, -pedis* three-footed < *tri-* three + *pes, pedis* a foot]

triv·i·a (triv′ē·ə) *n.pl.* Insignificant or unimportant matters; trifles. [< NL < L *trivialis.* See TRIVIAL.]

triv·i·al (triv′ē·əl) *adj.* 1. Of little value or importance; trifling; insignificant. 2. Such as is found everywhere or every day: ordinary; commonplace. 3. Occupied with trifles. [< L *trivialis* of the crossroads, commonplace < *trivium* a crossing of three roads < *tri-* three + *via* road] — **triv′i·al·ism** *n.* — **triv′i·al·ly** *adv.*

— **Syn.** 1. *Trivial, petty, trifling, insignificant, paltry, measly,* and *picayune* mean small in some sense. A *trivial* matter is of little importance; the word is not always opprobrious, and may sometimes denote that which is easy to deal with: to interject a *trivial* remark, to dispose of *trivial* business in the morning. *Petty* describes a small, minor, or subordinate person or thing: a *petty* irritation, a *petty* officer. *Trifling* means so *trivial* as to be unworthy of notice: a *trifling* distinction. That which lacks meaning, and so may safely be ignored is *insignificant. Paltry* and *measly* are derogatory, and are applied to that which is contemptibly small: a *paltry* contribution to a fund, a *measly* serving of potatoes. *Picayune* suggests ethical or moral smallness, and characterizes that which is small-minded, unworthy, or ignoble: a *picayune* politician. — **Ant.** important, momentous.

triv·i·al·i·ty (triv′ē·al′ə·tē) *n. pl.* **·ties** **1.** The state or quality of being trivial: also **triv′i·al·ness.** **2.** A trivial matter.

triv·i·um (triv′ē·əm) *n. pl.* **·i·a** (-ē·ə) In medieval schools, the course embracing grammar, logic, and rhetoric, composing the lower group of the seven liberal arts. Compare QUADRIVIUM. [< Med.L < L. See TRIVIAL.]

tri·week·ly (trī·wēk′lē) *adj.* **1.** Occurring three times a week. **2.** Done or occurring every third week. — *adv.* **1.** Three times a week. **2.** Every third week. — *n.* A publication appearing triweekly.

-trix *suffix* A feminine termination of agent nouns the masculine form of which is *-tor: testatrix*. See -OR¹. [< L]

troak (trōk) See TROKE.

Tro·as (trō′as) The region of western Asia Minor on the Aegean surrounding the ancient city of Troy. Also **the Tro′ad** (-ad).

Tro·bri·and Islands (trō′brē·ənd) A group of small islands north of New Guinea, comprising part of the Territory of Papua; 170 sq. mi.; pop. about 11,000.

Tro·bri·an·der (trō′brē·ən·dər, -an′/-) A native or inhabitant of the Trobriand Islands. Also **Trobriand Islander.**

tro·car (trō′kär) *n. Surg.* A sharp-pointed instrument used with a cannula to drain off internal fluids. Also **tro′char.** [< F *troquart, trois-quarts* < *trois* three + *carre* face; so called because of its triangular shape]

tro·cha·ic (trō·kā′ik) *adj.* Pertaining to, containing, or composed of trochees: a *trochaic* foot or verse. — *n.* A trochaic verse or line. [< MF *trochaïque* < L *trochaicus* < Gk. *trochaikos* < *trochaios*. See TROCHEE.]

tro·chal (trō′kəl) *adj.* Shaped like a wheel; rotiform. [< Gk. *trochos* a wheel]

tro·chan·ter (trō·kan′tər) *n.* **1.** *Anat.* One of two bony processes on the upper part of each thigh bone. **2.** *Entomol.* The small second segment of an insect's leg. [< MF < Gk. *trochantēr* < *trechein* to run]

tro·che (trō′kē) *n.* A medicated lozenge, usually circular: also called *pastille.* [Alter. of obs. *trochisk* < MF *trochisque* lozenge < L *trochiscus* < Gk. *trochiskos* a small wheel, lozenge < *trochos* wheel < *trechein* to run]

tro·chee (trō′kē) *n.* **1.** In prosody, a metrical foot consisting of one long or accented syllable followed by one short or unaccented syllable (— ᴗ). **2.** A line of verse made up of or characterized by such feet: Nŏw thĕ| lĭght hăs| fāllĕn| frŏm thĕ| skȳ. [< L *trochaeus* < Gk. *trochaios* (*pous*) a running (foot) < *trechein* to run]

troch·i·lus (trok′ə·ləs) *n. pl.* **·li** (-lī) **1.** The crocodile bird: also **tro·chil** (trō′kil, trok′il), **troch′i·los** (-los). **2.** A hummingbird (family *Trochilidae*). **3.** One of various small warblers or warblerlike birds. [< L *trochilus* crocodile bird < Gk. *trochilos* < *trechein* to run]

troch·le·a (trok′lē·ə) *n. pl.* **·le·ae** (-li·ē) *Anat.* A grooved pulleylike surface, permitting smooth motion of one part over another, as between the humerus and ulna. [< L, a pulley < Gk. *trochilia, trochileia* < *trechein* to run]

troch·le·ar (trok′lē·ər) *adj.* **1.** *Anat.* Of, pertaining to, or situated near a trochlea. **2.** Of the nature of a pulley. **3.** *Bot.* Short, cylindrical, and contracted in the middle; pulley-shaped.

tro·choid (trō′koid) *adj.* Rotating upon its own axis; pivotal: also **tro·choi′dal.** — *n. Geom.* A plane curve traced by a point on a radius or extended radius of a circle as the circle rolls, without slipping, on a straight line. [< Gk. *trochoeides* round, wheellike < *trochos* wheel + *eidos* form, shape] — **tro·choi′dal·ly** *adv.*

troch·o·phore (trok′ə·fôr, -fōr) *n. Zool.* A pear-shaped, free-swimming larval form of certain aquatic invertebrates, as annelids, brachiopods, and mollusks. Also **troch′o·sphere** (-sfir). [< Gk. *trochos* wheel + -PHORE]

trock (trok) See TROKE.

trod (trod) Past tense and alternative past participle of TREAD.

trod·den (trod′n) Past participle of TREAD.

trode (trōd) Archaic past tense of TREAD.

trog·lo·dyte (trog′lə·dīt) *n.* **1.** A cave man. **2.** A hermit; anyone of primitive habits. **3.** An anthropoid ape, as the chimpanzee (formerly genus *Troglodytes*). [< L *troglodyta* < Gk. *trōglodytēs* < *trōglē* hole + *dyein* to go into] — **trog′lo·dyt′ic** (-dit′ik) or **·i·cal** *adj.*

tro·gon (trō′gon) *n.* A tropical American bird (family *Trogonidae*) noted for its resplendent plumage. [< NL < Gk. *trōgōn*, ppr. of *trōgein* to gnaw]

troi·ka (troi′kə) *n.* A Russian vehicle drawn by a team of three horses driven abreast; also, the team, or both team and vehicle together. [< Russian < *troie* three]

tro·i·lus (troi′ləs, trō′i·ləs) *n.* A swallowtail butterfly (*Papilio troilus*) of eastern North America. [after *Troilus*]

Troi·lus (troi′ləs, trō′i·ləs) In Greek legend, a son of Priam killed by Achilles; in medieval legend, Chaucer's *Troilus and Criseyde*, and Shakespeare's *Troilus and Cressida*, Cressida's lover.

Trois Ri·vières (trwä rē·vyâr′) A city in southern Quebec, at the confluence of the St. Maurice and St. Lawrence rivers; pop. 55,240: also *Three Rivers.*

Tro·jan (trō′jən) *n.* **1.** A native of Troy. **2.** One who works earnestly or suffers courageously. **3.** *Informal* A jolly fellow; boon companion. — *adj.* Of or pertaining to ancient Troy. Also *Dardan, Dardanian, Teucrian*. [Earlier *Troyan, Troian* < L *Troianus* < *Troja* Troy]

Trojan horse **1.** In classical legend, a large, hollow wooden horse, described in Vergil's *Aeneid*, filled with Greek soldiers and left at the Trojan gates. When it was brought within the walls the soldiers emerged at night and admitted the Greek army, who burned the city: also called *wooden horse.* **2.** A person, device, etc., intended to disrupt or undermine a plan or institution.

Trojan War In Greek legend, the ten years' war waged by the confederated Greeks under their king, Agamemnon, against the Trojans to recover Helen, the wife of Menelaus, who had been abducted by Paris: celebrated especially in the *Iliad* and the *Odyssey*. See APPLE OF DISCORD.

troke (trōk) *Scot. n.* **1.** Exchange; also, articles of trade; small wares; truck. **2.** Familiar intercourse or acquaintance. — *v.t.* & *v.i.* **troked, trok·ing** To exchange. Also spelled *troak, trock.* [Cf. F *troquer*]

troll¹ (trōl) *v.t.* **1.** To fish for with a moving lure, as from a slowly moving boat. **2.** To move (the line or lure) in fishing. **3.** To sing in succession, as in a round or catch. **4.** To sing in a full, hearty manner. **5.** To cause to roll; revolve. **6.** *Obs.* To pass around, as a bottle or decanter. — *v.i.* **7.** To fish with a moving lure. **8.** To sing a tune, etc., in a full, hearty manner. **9.** To be uttered in such a way. **10.** To roll; turn. **11.** *Obs.* To move about; ramble. — *n.* **1.** A catch or round. **2.** A rolling movement or motion; also, repetition or routine. **3.** In fishing, a spoon or other lure. [? < OF *troller* to quest, wander < Gmc. Cf. MHG *trollen* to walk with short steps.] — **troll′er** *n.*

troll² (trōl) *n.* In Scandinavian folklore, a giant; later, a friendly but often mischievous dwarf. Also **trold** (trōld). [< ON]

trol·ley (trol′ē) *n. pl.* **·leys** **1.** *U.S.* A streetcar. **2.** A grooved metal wheel for rolling in contact with a conductor (the **trolley wire**), to convey the current to an electric vehicle. **3.** In a subway system, a bow or shoe adapted to the same purpose attached to a current taker operating through a third rail. **4.** A small truck or car for conveying material, as in a factory, mine, etc.: also spelled *trawley.* **5.** *Brit.* A small cart for serving food and drink: tea *trolley.* **6.** *Brit. Dial.* A small hand or donkey cart. **7.** A carrier for parcels. **8.** The mechanism of a traveling crane. **9.** A small car running on tracks and worked by a manually operated lever, used by workmen on a railway. — *v.t.* & *v.i.* To convey or travel by trolley. Also **trol′ly.** [< TROLL¹]

trolley bus A bus propelled electrically by current taken from an overhead wire by a trolley. Also **trolley coach.**

trolley car A car with a trolley for use on an electric railway; especially, *U.S.*, a streetcar (which see).

trolley line **1.** A system of trolley cars. **2.** A particular trolley car route.

trol·ley·man (trol′ē·man′) *n. pl.* **·men** (-men′) A man who operates a trolley; especially, a conductor or motorman.

trolley pole A pole on a trolley car carrying the trolley wheel.

troll·ing (trō′ling) *n.* The method or act of fishing by dragging a hook and line, as behind a boat and near the surface. [< TROLL¹]

trolling rod A strong fishing rod for trolling.

trol·lop (trol′əp) *n.* **1.** A slatternly woman. **2.** A prostitute. [< dial. E (Scottish) < ME *trollen* to roll about; prob. infl. in meaning by TRULL] — **trol′lop·ish, trol′lop·y, trol′lop·ing** *adj.*

Trol·lope (trol′əp), **Anthony,** 1815–82, English novelist. — **Frances,** 1780–1863, *née* Milton, English novelist and travel writer; mother of the preceding.

trom·bic·u·li·a·sis (trom·bik′yə·lī′ə·sis) *n. Pathol.* Infestation with mites of the genus *Trombicula*, the chiggers. Also **trom·bic′u·lo′sis** (-lō′sis), **trom·bi·di·i·as·is** (trom′bi·dē·ī′ə·sis), **trom·bi·di·o·sis** (trom′bi·dē·ō′sis). [< NL *Trombicula* + -IASIS]

trom·bone (trom·bōn′, trom′bōn′) A brass instrument of the trumpet family, but larger and lower in pitch than the trumpet. A **slide trombone** changes pitch by means of a U-shaped slide that can lengthen or shorten the air column, a **valve trombone** changes pitch by means of valves. [< Ital., aug. of *tromba* trumpet < Gmc.] — **trom·bon′ist** *n.*

trom·mel (trom′əl) *n. Metall.* A perforated steel plate, usually cylindrical, for sifting or screening rock, ore, etc. [< G, drum]

trompe (tromp) *n. Metall.* An apparatus that supplies a blast of air, as to a forge, by the action of a column of water falling through a perforated pipe and thus carrying air by entanglement. Also **tromp.** [< F, lit., trumpet]

tromp l'oeil (trôɴp lœ′y′) In art and decoration, the accurate representation of details, scenes, etc., to create an illusion of reality. [< F, lit., fool the eye]

-tron *suffix* **1.** Vacuum tube: *magnetron.* **2.** Device for the manipulation of subatomic particles: *cyclotron.* [< Gk., instrumental suffix]

tro·na (trō′nə) *n.* A vitreous, gray or white, hydrous sodium carbonate, $Na_2CO_3HNaCO_8 \cdot 2H_2O$, found in evaporated lake beds. [< Sw., appar. < Arabic *trōn*, short for *natrūn*. See NATRON.]

Trond·heim (trôn′hām) A port city in W Norway, on **Trondheim Fiord**, an inlet of the North Sea; pop. 120,800 (est. 1968): formerly *Nidaros.* Formerly **Trond·hjem** (trôn′yem).

troop (trōōp) *n.* **1.** An assembled company; gathering; a herd or flock. **2.** *Usually pl.* A body of soldiers; soldiers collectively. **3.** The cavalry unit corresponding to a company of infantry. **4.** A body of Boy Scouts consisting of four patrols of eight scouts each. Abbr. **trp, Trp** — *v.i.* **1.** To move along or gather as a troop or as a crowd. **2.** *Archaic* To associate; consort. — *v.t.* **3.** To form into troops. **4.** *Brit. Mil.* To carry ceremoniously before troops: to *troop* the colors. [< OF *trope* < LL *troppus* a flock < Gmc.]

troop carrier 1. A transport aircraft for carrying troops and equip ent. **2.** An armored vehicle for carrying troops.

troop·er (trōō′pər) *n.* **1.** A cavalryman. **2.** A mounted policeman. **3.** A troop horse; charger. **4.** A troopship. **5.** A state policeman.

troop·i·al (trōō′pē·əl) See TROUPIAL.

troop·ship (trōōp′ship′) *n.* A ship for carrying troops; a transport.

trooz (trōōz) See TREWS.

trop (trō) *adv. French* Too much; too many; too.

tro·pae·o·lum (trō·pē′ə·ləm) *n.* *pl.* **·lums** or **·la** Any of a genus (*Tropaeolum*) of tropical American plants with bright-colored flowers, including the common cultivated nasturtium. [< NL, dim. of L *tropaeum* < Gk. *tropaion* a trophy]

-tropal Var. of -TROPIC.

trope (trōp) *n.* **1.** The figurative use of a word. **2.** Loosely, a figure of speech; figurative language in general. **3.** A short distinguishing cadence interpolated in Gregorian melodies. **4.** An interpolated passage or dialogue formerly inserted in the Mass. [< F < L *tropus* a figure of speech < Gk. *tropos* a turn < *trepein* to turn]

-trope *combining form* **1.** One who or that which turns or changes: *allotrope.* **2.** Turning; turned in a (specified) way: *hemitrope.* [< Gk. *tropos* a turning < *trepein* to turn]

troph·ic (trof′ik) *adj.* Pertaining to nutrition and its processes. Also **troph′i·cal.** [< Gk. *trophikos* < *trophē* nourishment < *trephein* to nourish] — **troph′i·cal·ly** *adv.*

tro·phied (trō′fēd) *adj.* Adorned with trophies.

tropho- *combining form* Nutrition; nourishment; of or pertaining to food or nutrition: *trophoplasm.* Also, before vowels, **troph-.** [< Gk. *trophē* food, nourishment < *trephein* to feed, nourish]

troph·o·blast (trof′ə·blast) *n.* *Biol.* The outermost layer of cells that establishes embryonic relation with the uterus and is concerned in the nutrition of the embryo and fetus. Also **troph′o·derm** (-dûrm) [< TROPHO- + -BLAST] — **troph′o·blas′tic** *adj.*

troph·o·plasm (trof′ə·plaz′əm) *n.* *Biol.* The nutritive or vegetative protoplasm of the cell. — **troph′o·plas′mic** *adj.*

tro·phot·ro·pism (trō·fot′rə·piz′əm) *n.* *Biol.* The movement of an organism toward or away from nutrient substances. — **troph·o·trop·ic** (trof′ə·trop′ik) *adj.*

tro·phy (trō′fē) *n.* *pl.* **·phies 1.** Something symbolizing victory or success; as: **a** A cup, statuette, etc., awarded for athletic or other achievement. **b** A mounted fish, animal's head, etc. **c** A weapon, etc., captured from an enemy. **2.** An ancient Roman victory memorial. **3.** An ornamental symbolic group of objects hung together on a wall. **4.** A memento or memorial. **5.** *Archit.* A group of arms and armor carved in marble or cast in bronze, rising from a circular or quadrangular stepped base. [< MF *trophée* < L *trophaeum, tropaeum* < Gk. *tropaion* < *tropē* a defeat, turning < *trepein* to turn, rout]

-trophy *combining form* A (specified) kind of nutrition or development: *hypertrophy.* Corresponding adjectives end in -*trophic.* [< Gk. *trophē.* See TROPHO-.]

trop·ic (trop′ik) *n.* **1.** *Geog.* Either of two parallels of latitude 23° 27′ north and south of the equator, on which the sun is seen in the zenith on the days of its greatest declination, called respectively **tropic of Cancer** and **tropic of Capricorn.** **2.** *Astron.* **a** Either of two corresponding parallels in the celestial sphere similarly named, and respectively 23° 27′ north or south from the celestial equator. **b** Formerly, a solstice. **3.** *pl.* The regions of the earth's surface between the tropics of Cancer and Capricorn: the Torrid Zone. — *adj.* Of or pertaining to the tropics; tropical. [< L *tropicus* < Gk. *tropikos* (*kyklos*) the tropical (circle), pertaining to the turning of the sun at the solstice < *tropē.* See TROPHY.]

-tropic *combining form* Having a (specified) tropism; turning or changing in a (particular) way, or in response to a (given) stimulus: *chemotropic, phototropic.* Also -*tropal.*

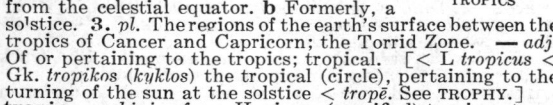

TROPICS

trop·i·cal (trop′i·kəl) *adj.* **1.** Of, pertaining to, or characteristic of the tropics. **2.** Of the nature of a trope or metaphor. — **trop′i·cal·ly** *adv.*

tropical fish Any of various small, brightly colored fishes native to warm waters, often displayed in aquariums.

trop·i·cal·ize (trop′i·kəl·īz′) *v.t.* **·ized, ·iz·ing** To adapt, as clothing, equipment, etc., for service in tropical areas. — **trop′i·cal·i·za′tion** *n.*

tropical year An astronomical year (which see).

tropic bird A long-winged, oceanic bird (genus *Phaëthon*), allied to the pelicans, found mostly in the tropics, having the two middle tail feathers elongated.

tro·pine (trō′pēn, -pin) *n. Chem.* A colorless crystalline alkaloid, $C_8H_{15}NO$, with a tobacco odor, formed when atropine is hydrolyzed. Also **tro′pin** (-pin). [< ATROPINE]

tro·pism (trō′piz·əm) *n. Biol.* **1.** The involuntary response of an organism to an external stimulus. **2.** Any automatic reaction to a stimulus. Compare TAXIS. [< Gk. *tropē* a turning] — **tro·pis·tic** (trō·pis′tik) *adj.*

-tropism *combining form* A (specified) tropism; a tendency to turn or change in response to a (given) stimulus: *chemotropism, phototropism.* Also -*tropy.* Corresponding adjectives end in -*tropic.* [< TROPISM]

tro·pol·o·gy (trō·pol′ə·jē) *n. pl.* **·gies 1.** The use of tropical or figurative language. **2.** Consideration or treatment of the Scriptures both literally and figuratively, or as having a double sense. **3.** A treatise on figures of speech. [< LL *tropologia* < Gk. < *tropos* trope + *logos* discourse] — **trop·o·log·ic** (trop′ə·loj′ik) or **·i·cal** *adj.* — **trop′o·log′i·cal·ly** *adv.*

trop·o·pause (trop′ə·pôz) *n. Meteorol.* A transition zone in the atmosphere between the troposphere and the stratosphere. [< TROPO(SPHERE) + Gk. *pausis* a ceasing]

tro·poph·i·lous (trō·pof′ə·ləs) *adj. Ecol.* Adapted to a wide range of growth conditions: said of plants. [< Gk. *tropos* a turning, change + *philos* loving]

trop·o·phyte (trop′ə·fīt) *n. Ecol.* Any plant adapted to extreme changes of weather or climate. [< Gk. *tropos* a turning, change + -PHYTE] — **trop′o·phyt′ic** (-fit′ik) *adj.*

trop·o·sphere (trop′ə·sfir) *n. Meteorol.* The region of the atmosphere above the earth's surface. It is characterized by turbulence and by decreasing temperature with increasing altitude. [< F *troposphère* < Gk. *tropos* a turning + F *sphère* < L *sphaera* sphere] — **trop′o·spher′ic** (-sfir′ik, -sfer′-) *adj.*

-tropous *combining form* Turned in a specified way: *anatropous.* Corresponding nouns end in -*tropy.*

-tropy *combining form* **1.** Var. of -TROPISM. **2.** A state of being turned. [< Gk. *tropē* a turning < *trepein* to turn]

Tros·sachs (tros′aks, -əks) A valley in Perthshire, central Scotland; scene of Scott's *The Lady of the Lake.*

trot[1] (trot) *n.* **1.** A gait of a quadruped, especially a horse, in which diagonal pairs of legs are lifted, thrust forward, and placed down almost simultaneously, the body being unsupported twice during each stride; also, the sound of this gait. **2.** A race for trotters. **3.** A reasonably rapid run. **4.** A steady, rapid pace: I have been on the *trot* all day. **5.** *Informal* A pony (def. 3). **6.** *Rare* A toddler. — *v.* **trot·ted, trot·ting** *v.i.* **1.** To go at a trot. **2.** To go quickly; hurry. — *v.t.* **3.** To cause to trot. **4.** To ride at a trotting gait. — **to trot out** To bring forth for inspection, approval, etc. [< OF < *troter* < OHG *trottōn* to tread]

trot[2] (trot) *n. Archaic* A crone. [< AF *trote*; ult. origin uncertain]

troth (trôth, trōth) *n.* **1.** Good faith; fidelity. **2.** The act of pledging fidelity; especially, betrothal. **3.** Truth; verity. — *v.t. Archaic* To betroth; pledge. [ME *trowthe, trouthe,* var. of OE *trēowth* truth; faith]

troth·plight (trôth′plīt′, trōth′-) *Archaic v.t.* To betroth; affiance. — *n.* Betrothal. — *adj.* Betrothed: also **troth′-plight′ed.** [< TROTH + PLIGHT[2]]

trot·line (trot′līn′, -lin) *n.* A trawl (def. 1).

Trot·sky (trot′skē), **Leon,** 1879–1940, Russian revolutionist and Bolshevist leader; banished 1929; murdered: original name **Lev Davidovich Bron·stein** (brun·shtīn′).

Trot·sky·ism (trot′skē·iz′əm) *n.* The doctrines of Trotsky and his followers; especially, his belief in "permanent revolution" or the theory that Communism to succeed must be international. — **Trot′sky·ist, Trot′sky·ite** *n. & adj.*

trot·ter (trot′ər) *n.* **1.** One who or that which trots; especially, a horse trained to trot for speed. **2.** *Informal* A foot, especially an animal's foot.

tro·tyl (trō′til) *n.* Trinitrotoluene. [< (TRINI)TROT(O-LUENE) + -YL]

trou·ba·dour (trōō′bə·dôr, -dōr, -dŏŏr) *n.* **1.** One of a class of lyric poets, originating in Provence in the 11th century and flourishing in southern France, northern Italy, and eastern Spain during the 12th and 13th centuries. Compare TROUVÈRE. **2.** A singer, especially of love songs. [< MF < Provençal *trobador* < *trobar* to compose, invent, find; ult. origin uncertain]
— **Syn.** *Troubadour* and *minnesinger* denote classes of wander-

ing medieval minstrels who composed and sang their own verses, chiefly on amorous themes. Many of these men came from the ranks of the nobility. *Troubadours* flourished chiefly in the Romance lands, and *minnesingers* in Germany. Compare BARD, MINSTREL.

troub·le (trub′əl) *n.* **1.** The state of being distressed, annoyed, upset, afflicted, or confused. **2.** A difficulty, perplexity, annoyance, disturbance, etc. **3.** Toilsome exertion; pains: Take the *trouble* to do it correctly. **4.** A diseased condition: lung *trouble*. **— in trouble 1.** Enmeshed in threatening difficulties. **2.** *Informal* Pregnant and unmarried. **—** *v.* ·**led,** ·**ling** *v.t.* **1.** To cause mental agitation to; distress; worry. **2.** To agitate or disturb; stir up or roil, as water. **3.** To inconvenience or incommode. **4.** To annoy or pester; bother. **5.** To cause physical pain or discomfort to; afflict. **—** *v.i.* **6.** To take pains; bother. **7.** To worry. [< OF *truble, turble* < *turbler* < L *turbula* mob, dim. of *turba* crowd] **— troub′ler** *n.* **— troub′ling·ly** *adv.*

troub·led (trub′əld) *adj.* **1.** Beset with trouble. **2.** Distressed. **3.** Agitated, disturbed, or roiled, as water. **— troub′led·ly** *adv.* **— troub′led·ness** *n.*

troub·le·mak·er (trub′əl·mā′kər) *n.* One who causes trouble or sets people at odds. **— troub′le·mak′ing** *n. & adj.*

troub·le·shoot·er (trub′əl·shoo͞′tər) *n.* One who locates difficulties and seeks to remove them, especially in the operation of a machine, in an industrial process, etc. **— troub′le·shoot′ing** *n., adj.*

troub·le·some (trub′əl·səm) *adj.* **1.** Causing trouble; vexatious; burdensome; trying. **2.** Marked by violence; tumultuous. **3.** Greatly agitated or disturbed; troublous. **— troub′le·some·ly** *adv.* **— troub′le·some·ness** *n.*

troub·lous (trub′ləs) *adj.* **1.** Marked by commotion or tumult; full of trouble: *troublous* times. **2.** Uneasy; restless.

trou·de·loup (troo͞′də·loo͞′) *n. pl.* **trous-de-loup** (troo͞′də·loo͞′) *Usually pl.* A conical pit having a vertical central stake with a pointed top, used as a defense against cavalry. [< F *trou* hole + *de* of + *loup* wolf]

trough (trôf, trof) *n.* **1.** A long, narrow, open receptacle for conveying a fluid or for holding food or water for animals. **2.** A long, narrow channel or depression, as between ridges on land or waves at sea. **3.** A gutter (def. 3). **4.** *Meteorol.* A long, usually narrow area having a low barometric pressure. **5.** *Econ.* A low or the lowest point reached in a business cycle. [OE *trog*]

trounce (trouns) *v.t.* **trounced, trounc·ing 1.** To beat or thrash severely; punish. **2.** *Informal* To defeat. [Ult. origin uncertain. Cf. OF *troncer*.]

troupe (troo͞p) *n.* A company of actors or other performers. **—** *v.i.* **trouped, troup·ing** To travel as one of a theatrical company. [< MF < OF *trope* troop]

trou·per (troo͞′pər) *n.* **1.** A member of a theatrical company. **2.** An actor of long experience.

troup·i·al (troo͞′pē·əl) *n.* Any of a New World family (*Icteridae*) of birds, including the orioles, blackbirds, etc., especially one of the tropical species, usually with black and bright yellow or orange plumage. [< F *troupiale* < *troupe* troop < OF *trope*; because it goes in flocks]

trou·sers (trou′zərz) *n.pl.* A garment, especially for men and boys, covering the body from the waist to the ankles and divided so as to make a separate covering for each leg. Also **trow′sers.** [Blend of obs. *trouse* breeches (< Irish *triubhas*) and DRAWERS]

trous·seau (troo͞′sō, troo͞·sō′) *n. pl.* ·**seaux** (-sōz, -sōz′) or ·**seaus** A bride's outfit, especially of clothing, linens, etc. [< F < *trousse* a packed collection of things. See TRUSS.]

trout (trout) *n. pl.* **trout** or **trouts 1.** A salmonoid fish mostly found in fresh waters, highly esteemed as game and food. The **brown** or **salmon trout** (*Salmo trutta*) is found in Europe, the **cut-throat trout** (*S. clarkii*) and the **rainbow trout** or steelhead in western North America, and the **speckled trout** or **brook trout** (*Salvelinus fontinalis*) in eastern North America. **2.** A fish resembling, or supposed to resemble, the above, as the greenling. [OE *trūht* < LL *tructus, tructa* < Gk. *trōktēs* nibbler < *trōgein* to gnaw]

trou·vère (troo͞·vâr′) *n.* One of a class of poets flourishing in northern France from the 11th to the 14th centuries, distinguished from the troubadours of southern France by the narrative and epic character of their works, that include chansons de geste, fabliaux, romances, and chronicles. Also **trou·veur** (troo͞·vûr′). **— Syn.** See BARD¹. [< F < OF *trovere* < *trover* to find, compose; ult. origin uncertain]

Trou·ville (troo͞·vēl′) A port in northern France, near Le Havre. Also **Trou·ville-sur-Mer′** (-sür-mâr′).

trove (trōv) *n.* Something, especially of value or pleasing quality, found or discovered. [< (TREASURE-) TROVE]

tro·ver (trō′vər) *n. Law* An action to recover the value of personal property of the plaintiff wrongfully withheld or converted by another to his own use. [< OF, to find; ult. origin uncertain]

trow (trō) *v.t. & v.i.* **1.** *Archaic* To suppose; think; believe. **2.** *Obs.* To wonder. [Fusion of OE *truwian* (< *truwa* faith) and *trēowan* to believe < *trēowe* true]

trow·el (trou′əl, troul) *n.* **1.** A flat-bladed, sometimes pointed implement having an offset handle, used to smooth plaster, mortar, etc. **2.** A small concave scoop with a handle, used in digging about small plants, potting them, etc. **—** *v.t.* **trow·eled** or ·**elled,** **trow·el·ing** or ·**el·ling** To apply, dress, or form with a trowel. [< OF *truele* < LL *truella* < L *trulla,* dim. of *trua* stirring spoon, ladle] **— trow′el·er** or **trow′el·ler** *n.*

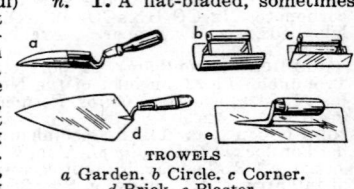

TROWELS
a Garden. *b* Circle. *c* Corner. *d* Brick. *e* Plaster.

trowth (trôth) *n. Scot.* **1.** Truth. **2.** Troth.

troy (troi) *n.* A system of weights used by jewelers in England and the U.S. in which a pound consists of 12 ounces. *Abbr. t.* See table inside back cover. Also **troy weight.** [after *Troyes*; with ref. to a weight used at a fair held there]

Troy (troi) **1.** The site of nine superimposed ruined cities in NW Asia Minor. The seventh stratum, a Phrygian city of perhaps about 1200 B.C., the scene of the *Iliad*, was also called *Ilium, Ilion.* **2.** A city in eastern New York, on the Hudson River; pop. 62,918.

Troyes (trwä) A city in NE central France, on the Seine; pop. 74,898 (1968).

Trp or **trp** *Mil.* Troop.

tru·an·cy (troo͞′ən·sē) *n. pl.* ·**cies** The state or habit of being truant; also, an act of being truant. Also **tru′ant·ry.**

tru·ant (troo͞′ənt) *n.* One who absents himself, especially from school, without leave. **—** *v.i.* To be truant. **—** *adj.* **1.** Being truant; idle. **2.** Relating to or characterizing a truant. [< OF, vagabond, prob. < Celtic]

truant officer *U.S.* An official who investigates truancy from school.

truce (troo͞s) *n.* **1.** An agreement between belligerents for a temporary suspension of hostilities; an armistice. **2.** Temporary cessation or intermission. [Plural of ME *trew,* OE *trūwa* faith, a promise. Akin to TRUE, TRUST.]

Tru·cial O·man (troo͞′shəl ō·män′) A region on the eastern coast of the Arabian peninsula, formerly consisting of sheikdoms bound by treaties with Great Britain; now comprised principally of the Union of Arab Emirates; about 32,000 sq. mi.; pop. about 185,000.

truck¹ (truk) *n.* **1.** *U.S. & Canadian* Any of various automotive vehicles designed to carry loads, freight, etc.: also, *Brit.,* lorry. **2.** A two-wheeled barrowlike vehicle with a forward lip and no sides, used for moving barrels, boxes, etc., by hand. **3.** A vehicle used about railway stations, for moving trunks, etc. **4.** *Brit.* An open or platform freight car. **5.** *Naut.* A disk at the top of a mast or flagpole through which the halyards of signals are run. **6.** One of the pivoting sets of wheels on a railroad car or engine. **—** *v.t.* **1.** To carry on a truck. **—** *v.i.* **2.** To carry goods on a truck. **3.** To drive a truck. [Appar. < L *trochus* hoop < Gk. *trochos* wheel < *trechein* to run]

truck² (truk) *v.t. & v.i.* To exchange or barter; also, to peddle. **—** *n.* **1.** Commodities for sale. **2.** *U.S.* Garden produce for market: often in compounds: *truck* farming, etc. **3.** *Informal* Rubbish; worthless articles collectively. **4.** Barter. **5.** *Informal* Dealings: I will have no *truck* with him. [< OF *troquer* to barter; origin unknown]

truck·age¹ (truk′ij) *n.* **1.** Money paid for conveyance of goods on trucks. **2.** Such conveyance. [< TRUCK¹ + -AGE]

truck·age² (truk′ij) *n.* Exchange; barter. [< TRUCK² + -AGE]

truck·er¹ (truk′ər) *n.* One who drives or supplies trucks or moves commodities in trucks: also called truckman.

truck·er² (truk′ər) *n.* **1.** *U.S.* A market gardener; truck farmer. **2.** One who barters or sells commodities; hawker.

truck farm *U.S.* A farm on which vegetables are produced for market. Also **truck garden.** [< TRUCK² + FARM] **— truck farming**

truck·ing¹ (truk′ing) *n.* The act or business of transportation by trucks.

truck·ing² (truk′ing) *n.* **1.** Exchanging or bartering; dealings. **2.** *U.S.* Cultivation of vegetables for market.

truck·le (truk′əl) *v.* ·**led,** ·**ling** *v.i.* **1.** To yield meanly or weakly: with *to*. **2.** To roll on truckles or casters. **—** *v.t.* **3.** To cause to roll on truckles or casters. **—** *n.* **1.** A small wheel. **2.** *Dial.* A trundle bed: also **truckle bed.** [< AF *trocle, trokle* < L *trochlea.* See TROCHLEA.] **— truck′ler** *n.* **— truck′ling·ly** *adv.*

truck·man¹ (truk′mən) *n. pl.* ·**men** (-mən) **1.** A truck driver. **2.** One engaged in the business of trucking.

truck·man² (truk′mən) *n. pl.* ·**men** (-mən) A dealer in truck; one who trucks or trades.

truck system The practice of paying wages to workmen in goods instead of money.

truc·u·lence (truk′yə·ləns) *n.* Savageness of character, behavior, or aspect. Also **truc′u·len·cy.**

truc·u·lent (truk′yə·lənt) *adj.* **1.** Of savage character;

awakening terror; cruel; ferocious. **2.** Aggressively hostile; belligerent. **3.** Scathing; harsh; vitriolic. [< L *truculentus* < *trux, trucis* fierce] **—truc′u·lent·ly** *adv.*

Tru·deau (trōō-dō′), **Pierre Elliott**, born 1921, Canadian statesman; prime minister 1968–.

trudge (truj) *v.i.* **trudged, trudg·ing** To walk wearily or laboriously; plod. **—** *n.* A tiresome walk or tramp. [Earlier *tredge, tridge*; origin uncertain] **—trudg′er** *n.*

trudg·en (truj′ən) In swimming, a former racing stroke similar to the crawl but performed with a frog kick or a scissors kick. Also **trudgen stroke, trudg′eon.** [after John *Trudgen*, 19th c. British swimmer]

true (trōō) *adj.* **tru·er, tru·est 1.** Faithful to fact or reality; not false or erroneous: a *true* story. **2.** Being real or natural; genuine, not counterfeit: a *true* specimen; *true* gold. **3.** Faithful to friends, promises, or principles; loyal; steadfast: *true* love; a *true* friend. **4.** Conformable to an existing standard type or pattern; exact: a *true* copy. **5.** Accurate, as in shape, dimensions, or position: a *true* fit; a *true* circle. **6.** Faithful to the requirements of law or justice; legitimate: the *true* king. **7.** Faithful to truth; truthful; honest: a *true* man. **8.** Faithful to the promise or predicted event; correctly indicative: a *true* sign. **9.** *Biol.* **a** Of pure strain or pedigree: a *true* collie dog. **b** Conformed to the structure of the type; properly so called: said of a plant or animal: a *true* locust. **10.** Exactly correspondent in pitch or key; in perfect tune: His voice is *true.* **11.** Corresponding to the axis of the earth: said of compass directions. **—** *n.* **1.** Truth; covenant; pledge. **2.** *pl.* **trues** or **truce** *Obs.* An armistice or truce. **— in** (or **out of**) **true** In (or not in) line of adjustment: said of a mark or part, as in a drawing or a machine. **—** *adv.* **1.** In truth; truly. **2.** In a true and accurate manner: The wheel runs *true.* **3.** Conformably to the ancestral type: to breed *true.* **—** *v.t.* **trued, tru·ing** To bring to conformity with a standard or requirement; form or adjust, as with geometrical precision: to *true* a frame. [OE *trēowe.* Akin to TRUCE, TRUST.] **—true′ness** *n.*

true bill *Law* **1.** The endorsement by a grand jury on a bill of indictment that the jurors find to be sustained by the evidence. **2.** A bill so endorsed.

true·blue (trōō′blōō′) *n.* **1.** *Usually cap.* In the 17th century, a Scotch Presbyterian or Covenanter, so called from the blue adopted as the distinctive color of his political party. **2.** A person of uncompromising faithfulness or loyalty, as to a party, friendship, principle, etc. Also **true blue.**

true-blue (trōō′blōō′) *adj.* Staunch; faithful; dependable.

true·born (trōō′bôrn′) *adj.* Being such by birth or inheritance: a *trueborn* Scot.

true copy An exact duplicate of any document, report, etc., especially one certified as correct by a qualified authority.

true-false (trōō′fôls′) *adj.* Designating a test, examination question, etc., answered by indicating whether a statement or statements are true or false.

true level A surface that is everywhere perpendicular to a plumb line, as that of a liquid at rest.

true·love (trōō′luv′) *n.* **1.** One truly beloved; a sweetheart. **2.** The herb Paris, so called because its four leaves have the form of a true-lover's knot.

true-lov·ers' knot (trōō′luv′ərz) A complicated double knot, a symbol of fidelity in love.

true rib *Anat.* Any one of the first seven pairs of ribs that in man are attached to the sternum.

true time Mean time, or mean solar time.

truf·fle (truf′əl, trōō′fəl) *n.* Any of various fleshy underground fungi (genus *Tuber*), regarded as a choice table delicacy: sometimes called *earthnut.* [< OF *trufe, truffe,* prob. < Ital. *truffa,* ult. < L *tuber* tuber]

tru·ism (trōō′iz·əm) *n.* An obvious or self-evident truth. **— Syn.** *Truism, platitude, bromide,* and *axiom* are compared as they denote a statement regarded as self-evident. In careful criticism, a *truism* is always tautological, either explicitly or implicitly; that opium puts one to sleep because of its soporific qualities, and that a healthy mind requires a healthy body are both *truisms.* A *platitude* is an assertion of what is so generally accepted as to need no repetition; it is a *platitude* that corruption arises in government when the vigilance of the electorate falters. A *bromide* is a stereotyped remark made by many persons as though it were an original notion; "It is not what you learn in college that counts, but the friends you make" is a *bromide. Axiom* comes into comparison only because the *axioms* of geometry were once regarded as self-evident; it is an *axiom* that a straight line is the shortest distance between two points.

Tru·jil·lo Mo·li·na (trōō-hē′yō mō-lē′nä), **Rafael,** 1891–1961, Dominican general and dictator; assassinated.

Truk (truk, trōōk) An island group in the eastern Caroline Islands; 40 sq. mi.

trull (trul) *n. Archaic* A prostitute; drab. [< G *trulle*]

tru·ly (trōō′lē) *adv.* **1.** In conformity with fact. **2.** With accuracy. **3.** With loyalty or fidelity. **4.** *Archaic* Surely; verily. **5.** Lawfully; legally.

Tru·man (trōō′mən), **Harry S,** 1884–1972, 33rd president of the United States 1945–53.

Trum·bull (trum′bəl), **John,** 1750–1831, American poet and satirist. **— John,** 1756–1843, American Revolutionary officer and painter. **— Jonathan,** 1710–85, American Revolutionary patriot; friend and adviser of Washington.

trump[1] (trump) *n.* **1.** In various card games, a card of the suit selected to rank above all others temporarily. **2.** *Usually pl.* The suit thus determined. **3.** A powerful or decisive stroke, resource, etc. **4.** *Informal* A good fellow. **—** *v.t.* **1.** To top (another card) with a trump. **2.** To surpass; excel; beat. **—** *v.i.* **3.** To play a trump when another suit has been led. **— to trump up** To make up or invent for a fraudulent purpose. [Alter. of TRIUMPH]

trump[2] (trump) *n.* **1.** *Poetic* A trumpet. **2.** *Scot.* A jew's-harp. [< OF *trompe* < Gmc.]

trump·er·y (trum′pər-ē) *n. pl.* **·er·ies 1.** Worthless finery. **2.** Rubbish; nonsense. **3.** Deceit; trickery. **—** *adj.* Having a showy appearance, but valueless. [< OF *tromperie* < *tromper* to deceive]

trum·pet (trum′pit) *n.* **1.** A soprano brass instrument with a flaring bell and a long, narrow-bored metal tube, whose pitch is varied by means of valves. **2.** A powerful reed stop in an organ. **3.** Something resembling a trumpet in form. **4.** A tube for collecting and conducting sounds to the ear; an ear trumpet. **5.** A loud penetrating sound like that of a trumpet; trumpeting. **6.** *pl.* A pitcherplant (*Sarracenia flava*) of the southern United States, having trumpet-shaped leaves. **7.** A trumpeter. **—** *v.t.* **1.** To sound or proclaim by or as by a trumpet; publish abroad. **—** *v.i.* **2.** To blow a trumpet. **3.** To give forth a sound as if from a trumpet. [< OF *trompette,* dim. of *trompe.* See TRUMP[2].]

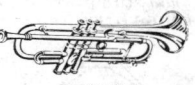

TRUMPET

trumpet creeper A woody vine (*Campsis radicans*) of the southern United States, with scarlet, trumpet-shaped flowers: also called *Virginia trumpet flower.* Also **trumpet vine.**

trum·pet·er (trum′pit·ər) *n.* **1.** One who plays a trumpet. **2.** One who publishes something loudly abroad. **3.** A large South American bird (family *Psophidae*) related to the cranes; especially, the **golden-breasted trumpeter** (*Psophia crepitans*), often domesticated. **4.** A large North American wild swan (*Olor buccinator*), having a clarionlike cry: also **trumpeter swan. 5.** One of a breed of domestic pigeons.

trumpet honeysuckle A twining honeysuckle (*Lonicera sempervirens*) with trumpet-shaped flowers.

trum·pet·weed (trum′pit-wēd′) *n.* The joe-pye weed.

trun·cate (trung′kāt) *v.t.* **·cat·ed, ·cat·ing** To cut the top or end from. **—** *adj.* **1.** Truncated. **2.** *Biol.* Appearing as though cut or broken squarely off, as the end of certain leaves, shells, etc. [< L *truncare* < *truncus* trunk] **— trun·ca′tion** (trung·kā′shən) *n.*

trun·cat·ed (trung′kā·tid) *adj.* **1.** Cut off; shortened. **2.** Describing a cone or pyramid whose vertex or apex is cut off by a plane. **3.** *Mineral.* Having the edges or angles cut off, as certain crystals. **4.** *Biol.* Truncate.

TRUNCATED PYRAMID

trun·cheon (trun′chən) *n.* **1.** A short, heavy stick; a club; staff. **2.** The baton of a military officer or marshal. **3.** A tree whose branches have been lopped off to hasten growth; tree trunk. **4.** *Brit.* A policeman's club. **—** *v.t.* To beat as with a truncheon; cudgel. [< OF *truncun, tronchon* stump, ult. < L *truncus* trunk]

trun·dle (trun′dəl) *n.* **1.** A small, broad wheel, as of a caster. **2.** The act, motion, or sound of trundling. **3.** A trundle bed. **4.** A lantern wheel. **5.** *Obs.* A small, low-wheeled vehicle; truck. **—** *v.t.* **·dled, ·dling 1.** To transport or carry in a wheeled vehicle, as a cart or wagon. **2.** To propel by or as if by rolling. **—** *v.i.* **3.** To roll along. **4.** To move by rolling along, as in a wheeled vehicle. [< earlier *trindle* < ME *trundel,* var. of OE *trendel* circle] **— trun′dler** *n.*

trundle bed A bed with a very low frame set on casters, so that it may be rolled under another bed: also called *truckle.*

trunk (trungk) *n.* **1.** The main stem or stock of a tree, as distinguished from its branches or roots. **2.** A large box or case used for packing and carrying clothes or other articles, as for a journey. **3.** *U.S. & Canadian* A large compartment of an automobile for storing luggage, etc., often at the rear. **4.** The human body, apart from the head, neck, and limbs; the torso. **5.** *Entomol.* The thorax. **6.** *Anat.* The main stem of a nerve, blood vessel, or lymphatic. **7.** The main line of a communication or transportation system. **8.** The circuit connecting two telephone exchanges. **9.** The main body, line, or stem of anything, as distinct from its appendages. **10.** A proboscis, as of an elephant. **11.** *pl.* A close-fitting garment covering the loins and often part of the thighs, worn by male swimmers, athletes, etc. **12.** *pl. Obs.* Trunk hose. **13.** *Mech.* **a** A trough, chute, or conduit. **b** A large, hollow piston in which a connecting rod moves. **14.** *Naut.* **a** The well for the centerboard of a vessel. **b** A casing connecting the hatchways of two or more decks and forming a shaft. **c** Any structure placed on the upper deck of a ship, as for shelter. **15.** *Archit.* The shaft of a column. — *adj.* Being or belonging to a trunk or main body: a *trunk* railroad. [< OF *tronc* < L *truncus* stem, trunk, orig. adj., mutilated; def. 10 infl. in meaning by F *trompe* trumpet]

trunk·fish (trungk′fish′) *n. pl.* **·fish** or **·fish·es** Any of various plectognath fishes (family *Ostraciidae*) of warm seas, characterized by a body covering of hard, bony plates.

trunk hose Full breeches worn by men in the 16th and early 17th centuries, extending from the waist to the middle of the thigh. Also **trunk breeches.**

trunk line The main line of a transportation or communication system, as distinguished from a branch line.

trun·nel (trun′əl) See TREENAIL.

trun·nion (trun′yən) *n.* **1.** One of two opposite cylindrical studs on a cannon, forming an axis on which it is elevated or depressed. **2.** Any of various similar supports. [< F *trognon* stump, trunk; ult. origin unknown]

truss (trus) *n.* **1.** *Med.* A bandage or support for a rupture.

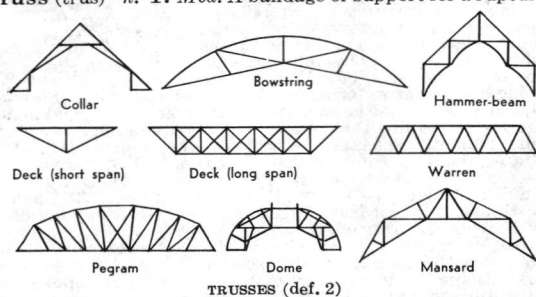

Collar

Bowstring

Hammer-beam

Deck (short span)

Deck (long span)

Warren

Pegram

Dome

Mansard

TRUSSES (def. 2)

2. A braced framework of ties, beams, or bars, usually arranged in a series of triangles, as for the support of a roof, bridge, etc. **3.** A bundle, especially of hay or straw. In England, 56 pounds of old or 60 pounds of new hay make a *truss*; 36 pounds make a *truss* of straw. **4.** *Naut.* A heavy iron piece by which a lower yard is attached to a mast. **5.** *Bot.* A compact terminal cluster of flowers. **6.** *Archit.* A bracket or modillion. **7.** A pack; package. — *v.t.* **1.** To tie or bind; fasten: often with *up*. **2.** To support by a truss; brace, as a roof. **3.** To fasten the wings of (a fowl) with skewers or twine before cooking. **4.** To fasten, tighten, or tie around one, as a garment or laces. [< OF *trusse, trousse* < *trousser, trusser* to pack up, bundle, prob. < L *torca* bundle < *torques.* See TORQUES.] — **truss′er** *n.*

truss bridge A bridge supported chiefly by trusses.

truss·ing (trus′ing) *n.* **1.** A system of trusses for strengthening or stiffening a structure, as a railway car or a vessel's hull. **2.** Trusses collectively. **3.** The act of one who trusses. **4.** A bracing with ties, struts, or the like.

trust (trust) *n.* **1.** A confident reliance on the integrity, honesty, veracity, or justice of another; confidence; faith. **2.** Something committed to one's care for use or safekeeping; a charge; responsibility. **3.** The state or position of one who has received an important charge. **4.** A confidence in the reliability of persons or things without careful investigation. **5.** Credit, in the commercial sense. **6.** Custody; care; keeping. **7.** *Law* **a** The confidence, or the obligation arising from the confidence, reposed in a person (called the *trustee*) to whom the legal title to property is conveyed for the benefit of another (the *cestui que trust*), that he will faithfully apply the property according to such confidence; also, the beneficial title or ownership of property of which the legal title is held by another. ◆ Collateral adjective: *fiducial.* **b** The property or thing held in trust; also, the relation between the holder and the property so held. **8.** A permanent combination for the purpose of controlling the production, price, etc., of some commodity or the management, profits, etc., of some business. Compare CARTEL, CORNER, MONOPOLY, POOL², SYNDICATE. **9.** A trust company (which see). **10.** One who or that which is trusted. **11.** Confident expectation; belief; hope. **12.** *Obs.* Trustworthiness. Abbr. *tr.* — *v.t.* **1.** To have trust in; rely upon. **2.** To commit to the care of another; entrust. **3.** To commit something to the care of: with *with.* **4.** To allow to do something without fear of the consequences. **5.** To expect with confidence or with hope. **6.** To believe. **7.** To allow business credit to. — *v.i.* **8.** To place trust or confidence; rely: with *in.* **9.** To hope: with *for.* **10.** To allow business credit. — **to trust to** To depend upon; confide in. — *adj.* Held in trust: *trust* money. [< ON *traust,* lit., firmness. Akin to TRUCE, TRUE.] — **trust′er** *n.* — **trust′less** *adj.*

— **Syn.** (noun) **1.** *Trust, faith, confidence,* and *reliance* denote the feeling that a person or thing will not fail in duty, service, or the like. *Trust* implies that this feeling has no reservation, and that it rests upon an estimate of character more than upon evidence. *Faith* suggests that this feeling is emotional to a large degree; *faith* does not seek evidence, and so may verge upon credulity. *Confidence* suggests a more rational *trust* based upon good evidence. *Reliance* is distinguished from the other synonyms in that it is more often used for the act of giving *trust*; thus, *reliance* may be considered as the outward expression of *trust, faith,* or *confidence.* — **Ant.** mistrust, suspicion, doubt.

trust·bust·er (trust′bus′tər) *n. U.S. Informal* One who advocates or works for the dissolution of a trust (def. 8) or trusts, as by antitrust legislation. Also **trust buster.** — **trust′bust′ing** *n.*

trust company An incorporated institution formed to accept and execute trusts, to receive deposits of money and other personal property and issue obligations for them, and to lend money.

trus·tee (trus·tē′) *n.* **1.** One who holds property in trust. **2.** One of a body of men, often elective, who hold the property and manage the affairs of a college, church, foundation, etc. **3.** One in whose hands property is attached by a trustee process. — *v.t.* **·teed, ·tee·ing 1.** *Law* To attach (the property of a debtor) by trustee process. **2.** To place (property) in the care of a trustee.

trustee process A statutory remedy whereby a creditor may reach property or assets of his debtor in the hands of a third person.

trus·tee·ship (trus·tē′ship) *n.* **1.** The post or function of a trustee. **2.** Supervision and control of a Trust Territory by a country or countries commissioned by the United Nations; also, the Territory so controlled.

trust·ful (trust′fəl) *adj.* Disposed to trust. — **trust′ful·ly** *adv.* — **trust′ful·ness** *n.*

trust fund Money, securities, etc., held in trust.

trust·ing (trus′ting) *adj.* Having trust; trustful. — **trust′ing·ly** *adv.* — **trust′ing·ness** *n.*

Trust Territory A dependent area administered by a nation under the authority of the United Nations.

trust·wor·thy (trust′wûr′thē) *adj.* Worthy of confidence; reliable. — **Syn.** See RELIABLE. — **trust′wor′thi·ly** (-wûr′thə-lē) *adv.* — **trust′wor′thi·ness** *n.*

trust·y (trus′tē) *adj.* **trust·i·er, trust·i·est 1.** Faithful to duty or trust. **2.** Staunch; firm. **3.** *Obs.* Trustful. — **Syn.** See RELIABLE. — *n. pl.* **trust·ies** A trustworthy person; especially, a convict who has been found reliable and to whom special liberties are granted. — **trust′i·ly** *adv.* — **trust′i·ness** *n.*

truth (trōōth) *n. pl.* **truths** (trōōthz, trōōths) **1.** The state or character of being true in relation to being, knowledge, or speech. **2.** Conformity to fact or reality. **3.** Conformity to rule, standard, model, pattern, or ideal. **4.** Conformity to the requirements of one's being or nature; steadfastness; sincerity. **5.** That which is true; a statement or belief that corresponds to the reality. **6.** A fact as the object of correct belief; reality. **7.** A tendency or disposition to speak or tell only what is true; veracity. **8.** The quality of being true; fidelity; constancy. **9.** In the fine arts, faithfulness to the facts of nature, history, or life. **10.** *Obs.* Right, according to divine law. — **Syn.** See FACT. [OE *trēowth* < *trēowe* true] — **truth′less** *adj.*

truth·ful (trōōth′fəl) *adj.* **1.** Habitually telling the truth. **2.** Corresponding to the facts or to reality; true. — **truth′ful·ly** *adv.* — **truth′ful·ness** *n.*

try (trī) *v.* **tried, try·ing** *v.t.* **1.** To make an attempt to do or accomplish; undertake; endeavor. **2.** To make experimental use or application of: often with *out:* to *try* a new pen. **3.** *Law* **a** To determine the guilt or innocence of by judicial trial. **b** To examine or determine judicially, as a case. **4.** To subject to a test; put to proof. **5.** To put severe strain upon; tax, as the eyes. **6.** To subject to trouble or tribulation; afflict. **7.** To extract by rendering or melting; refine: often with *out:* to *try* out oil. — *v.i.* **8.** To make an attempt; put forth effort. **9.** To make an examination or trial. — **to try on** To put on (a garment) to test it for fit or appearance. — **to try out** To attempt to qualify: He *tried out* for the football team. ◆ *Try and* for *try* to, as in *Try and catch me,* widely used in speech in both Great Britain and the United States, is an acceptable informal locution. In formal contexts it should be avoided. — *n. pl.* **tries 1.** The act of trying; trial; experiment. **2.** In Rugby football, the act of touching the ball down behind an opponent's goal, that scores three points. [< OF *trier* to sift, pick out, prob. < LL *tritare* to thresh < L *tritus.* See TRITE.]

try·ing (trī′ing) *adj.* Testing severely; hard to endure.

trying plane A carpenter's plane used to true up the edges of boards to be joined: also called *jointer.* Also **try plane.**

try·ma (trī′mə) *n. pl.* **·ma·ta** (-mə-tə) *Bot.* A drupelike, commonly two-celled fruit with a fleshy or fibrous dehiscent exocarp, as the hickory nut and walnut. [< NL < Gk. *tryma, trymē* hole < *tryein* to wear away]

try·out (trī′out′) *n. U.S. Informal* A test of ability, as of an actor or athlete, often in competition with others.

tryp·a·no·some (trip′ə-nə-sōm′, tri-pan′ə-) *n.* Any of a genus (*Trypanosoma*) of protozoans parasitic in the blood of man and some lower animals and often causing serious and even fatal diseases, as sleeping sickness. Also **tryp′a·no·so′ma** (-sō′mə). [< Gk. *trypanon* borer + -SOME²]

tryp·a·no·so·mi·a·sis (trip′ə-nō-sō-mī′ə-sis) *n. Pathol.*

Any disease caused by trypanosomes. Also **tryp·a·no·so·ma·to′sis** (-sō′mə·tō′sis). [< TRYPANOSOME + -IASIS]

tryp·sin (trip′sin) *n. Biochem.* A proteolytic enzyme contained in the pancreatic juice. [< Gk. *tripsis* a rubbing (< *tribein* to rub) + (PEP)SIN] — **tryp′tic** (-tik) *adj.*

tryp·sin·o·gen (trip·sin′ə·jen) *n. Biochem.* The substance secreted by the pancreas and converted into trypsin by the action of enzymes. [< *trypsino*- < TRYPSIN + -GEN]

tryp·to·phan (trip′tə·fan) *n. Biochem.* A crystalline amino acid, $C_{11}H_{12}O_2N_2$, contained in most proteins and associated with the digestive functions. Also **tryp′to·phane** (-fān). [< *tryptic* (< TRYPSIN) + -*phan*, var. of -PHANE]

try·sail (trī′səl, -sāl′) *n. Naut.* A small sail bent to a gaff abaft the foremast and mainmast of a ship: also called *spencer.* [< nautical phrase (*at*) *try* lying to in a storm + SAIL]

trysquare A carpenter's square having usually a wooden stock and a steel blade. For illustration see SQUARE.

tryst (trist, trīst) *n.* **1.** An appointment, as between lovers, to meet at a designated time and place; also, the meeting place agreed upon; rendezvous. **2.** A prearranged meeting, as of lovers. **3.** *Scot.* A market: also **tryste.** — *v.t. Chiefly Scot.* **1.** To agree to meet. **2.** To appoint (a time), as for meeting. **3.** To arrange for in advance; engage. — *v.i. Chiefly Scot.* **4.** To agree upon some place or time of meeting. [< OF *triste, tristre* an appointed station in hunting, prob. < Scand.] — **tryst′er** *n.*

tryst·ing place (tris′ting) A meeting place, as of lovers.

tsa·de (tsä·dā′) See SADE.

Tsa·na (tsä′nä), Lake See (Lake) TANA.

tsar (tsär), **tsar·dom** (tsär′dəm), etc. See CZAR, etc.

Tsa·ri·tsyn (tsä·rye′tsin) A former name for VOLGOGRAD.

Tse·ti·nye (tse′tē·nye) See CETINJE.

tset·se (tset′sē) *n.* **1.** A small bloodsucking fly (*Glossina morsitans*) of southern Africa, whose bite transmits disease in cattle, horses, etc. **2.** A related species (*G. palpalis*), that transmits the trypanosome, causative agent of sleeping sickness. For illustration see INSECTS (injurious). Also spelled *tzetze.* Also **tsetse fly.** [< Afrikaans < Bantu]

TSgt *Mil.* Technical Sergeant.

Tshi (chwē, chē) *n.* Ashanti (def. 2).

T-shirt (tē′shûrt′) *n.* **1.** A cotton undershirt with short sleeves. **2.** A sleeveless jersey or sweater of similar cut for outer wear. Also spelled *tee shirt.* Also **T shirt.**

Tsi·nan (jē′nän′) The capital of Shantung Province, NE China; pop. 1,500,000 (est. 1970): also *Chinan.*

Tsing·hai (ching′hī′) A Province of NW China; 278,378 sq. mi.; pop. 2,050,000 (est. 1957); capital, Sining: also *Chinghai.*

Tsing·tao (ching′dou′) A port city in eastern Shantung Province, China; pop. 1,900,000 (est. 1970).

Tsi·tsi·har (tsē′tse′här′) A city in NE China, former capital of Heilungkiang Province; pop. 1,500,000 (est. 1970).

Tso·ne·can (tsō·nā′kən) *n.* **1.** A family of South American Indians, including all of the Tehuelchan tribes, and possibly the Onas of Tierra del Fuego. **2.** The language of these tribes: also called *Chonean.*

T-square (tē′skwär′) *n.* An instrument by which to measure or lay out right angles or parallel lines, consisting usually of a flat strip with a shorter head at right angles to it and slightly offset so that it may be slid along the edge of a drawing board. For illustration see SQUARE.

Tsu·ga·ru Strait (tsōō·gä·rōō) The passage from the Sea of Japan to the Pacific between Honshu and southern Hokkaido, Japan; 15 to 25 mi. wide.

tsu·na·mi (tsōō·nä′mē) *n.* An extensive and often very destructive ocean wave caused by a submarine earthquake: also loosely called *tidal wave.* [< Japanese, a storm wave < *tsu* port, harbor + *nami* wave, sea]

Tsu·shi·ma (tsōō·shē′mä) An island of Japan in Korea Strait; 271 sq. mi., including offshore islets; scene of a Russian naval defeat in the Russo-Japanese War, 1905.

tsu·tsu·ga·mu·shi disease (tsōō·tsōō′gä·mōō′shē) *Pathol.* A rickettsial fever endemic in Japan and the Orient, caused by a microorganism (*Rickettsia orientalis*) transmitted by the infected larvae of a mite (genus *Trombicula*): also called *Japanese river fever, river fever, scrub typhus.* [< Japanese *tsutsugamush* a small Japanese mite < *mushi* bug]

T.T. Tanganyika Territory.

Tu. Tuesday.

Tu·a·mo·tu Archipelago (tōō′ä·mō′tōō) An island chain extending south of the Marquesas Islands in eastern French Polynesia; 330 sq. mi.: also *Low Archipelago:* formerly *Paumotu Archipelago.*

Tuan (twän) *n.* Sir; mister; courteous Malayan form of address. [< Malay]

Tua·reg (twä′reg) *n.* **1.** A member of the nomadic Berber tribes of the central and western Sahara. **2.** The Berber dialect spoken by these people.

tu·a·ta·ra (tōō′ä·tä′rä) *n.* The sphenodon, a reptile. Also **tu′a·te′ra** (-tä′rä). [< Maori < *tua* on the farther side, the back + *tara* spine]

tub (tub) *n.* **1.** A broad, open-topped vessel with handles on the side. **2.** A bathtub (which see). **3.** *Brit. Informal* A bath taken in a tub. **4.** The amount that a tub contains. **5.** *Informal* Anything resembling a tub, as a broad, clumsy boat. **6.** A small cask. **7.** A bucket for bringing ore or coal up a shaft; also, an underground tram. — *v.t. & v.i.* **tubbed, tub·bing** To wash, bathe, or place in a tub. [< MDu. *tubbe*] — **tub′ba·ble** *adj.* — **tub′ber** *n.*

tu·ba (tōō′bə, tyōō′-) *n. pl.* **·bas** or **·bae** (-bē) **1.** Any of various wide-bored, bass brass instruments whose pitch is varied by means of three, four, or sometimes five valves. **2.** An ancient Roman war trumpet. **3.** A powerful reed stop in an organ. [< Ital. < L, a war trumpet]

tu·bal (tōō′bəl, tyōō′-) *adj.* **1.** Relating to a tube. **2.** *Anat.* Pertaining to the Fallopian tube.

Tu·bal-cain (tōō′bəl·kān′, tyōō′-) The first artificer in brass and iron. *Gen.* iv 22.

tu·bate (tōō′bāt, tyōō′-) *adj.* Of the form of or provided with a tube; tubular. [< NL *tubatus* < L *tubus* pipe]

tub·by (tub′ē) *adj.* **·bi·er**, **·bi·est** **1.** Resembling a tub in form. **2.** Short and fat; corpulent. **3.** Lacking resonance; sounding dull or wooden.

TUBA

tube (tōōb, tyōōb) *n.* **1.** A long, hollow, cylindrical body of metal, glass, rubber, etc., generally used for the conveyance of something through it; a pipe. **2.** An electron tube (which see). **3.** A collapsible metal cylinder for containing paints, toothpaste, glue, etc. **4.** A thing or device having a tube or tubelike part, as a telescope. **5.** *Zool.* Any elongated hollow part or organ: a bronchial *tube.* **6.** *Bot.* The united part of a gamopetalous corolla or a gamosepalous calyx. **7.** A subway or tunnel. **8.** The tubular space enclosing lines of magnetic force or induction. **9.** The barrel of a shotgun, cannon, etc. **10.** *Slang* A television set. **11.** *Slang* A subway tunnel. **12.** *Brit.* A subway. — *v.t.* **tubed, tub·ing** **1.** To fit or furnish with a tube. **2.** To enclose in a tube or tubes. **3.** To make tubular. [< F < L *tubus*] — **tube′less** *adj.*

Tube may appear as a combining form, with the meaning of noun def. 1:

tube-drawing	tubemaker	tube-shaped
tube-drilling	tubemaking	tubesmith
tube-fed	tube-rolling	tubework

tube foot *Zool.* One of the small, vascular locomotor processes of echinoderms.

tu·ber[1] (tōō′bər, tyōō′-) *n.* **1.** *Bot.* A short, thickened portion of an underground stem, as in the potato. **2.** *Anat.* A swelling or prominence; tubercle. [< L, a swelling]

tu·ber[2] (tōō′bər, tyōō′-) *n.* One who or that which forms tubes.

tu·ber·cle (tōō′bər·kəl, tyōō′-) *n.* **1.** A small rounded eminence or nodule. **2.** *Bot.* A minute swelling on the roots of leguminous plants, containing a microorganism believed to absorb nitrogen from the air for the use of the plant. **3.** *Pathol.* **a** A small granular nodule or swelling formed within an organ or plant. **b** The lesion of tuberculosis. **4.** *Anat.* A small knotlike excrescence, especially on the skin or on a bone. [< L *tuberculum*, dim. of *tuber* a swelling] — **tu·ber·cu·loid** (tōō·bûr′kyə·loid, tyōō-) *adj.*

tubercle bacillus The rod-shaped, Gram-positive bacterium (*Mycobacterium tuberculosis*) that is the pathogen of tuberculosis in man.

tu·ber·cu·lar (tōō·bûr′kyə·lər, tyōō-) *adj.* **1.** Nodular. **2.** Tuberculous. — *n.* One affected with tuberculosis.

tu·ber·cu·late (tōō·bûr′kyə·lit, -lāt) *adj.* **1.** Tubercular. **2.** Affected with tubercles. Also **tu·ber′cu·lat′ed.** [< NL *tuberculatus* < L *tuberculum.* See TUBERCLE.] — **tu·ber′cu·la′tion** *n.*

tu·ber·cu·lin (tōō·bûr′kyə·lin, tyōō-) *n. Bacteriol.* A sterile liquid prepared from attenuated cultures of the tubercle bacillus and used as a test for tuberculosis. Also **tu·ber′cu·line** (-lin, -lēn). [< TUBERCLE + -IN]

tuberculo- *combining form* **1.** Tuberculosis; of or pertaining to tuberculosis. **2.** Tuberculous. **3.** The tubercle bacillus. Also, before vowels, **tubercul-.** [< L *tuberculum*, dim. of *tuber* a swelling]

tu·ber·cu·lo·sis (tōō·bûr′kyə·lō′sis, tyōō-) *n. Pathol.* **1.** A communicable disease caused by infection with the tubercle bacillus, characterized by the formation of tubercles within some organ or tissue. **2.** Tuberculosis affecting the lungs: also called *consumption, phthisis, pulmonary tuberculosis.* Abbr. *tb, t.b., Tb, Tb., TB, T.B.* [< NL < L *tuberculum* (See TUBERCLE) + -OSIS]

tu·ber·cu·lous (tōō·bûr′kyə·ləs, tyōō-) *adj.* Of, pertaining to, or affected with tuberculosis.

tu·ber·if·er·ous (tōō′bə·rif′ər·əs, tyōō′-) *adj.* Bearing or producing tubers. [< TUBER + -FEROUS]

tu·ber·oid (tōō′bər·oid, tyōō′-) *adj.* Resembling a tuber.

tube·rose (tōōb′rōz′, tyōōb′-, tōō′bə·rōs′, tyōō′-) *n.* A bulbous plant (*Polianthes tuberosa*) of the amaryllis family, bearing a long raceme of fragrant white flowers. [< NL *Tuberosa*, species name < L *tuberosus* knobby < *tuber* a swelling]

tu·ber·os·i·ty (tōō'bə·ros'ə·tē, tyōō'-) *n. pl.* **·ties** 1. The state of being tuberous. 2. A swelling or protuberance. 3. *Anat.* A large, rough eminence on a bone, as for the attachment of a muscle.

tu·ber·ous (tōō'bər·əs, tyōō'-) *adj.* 1. Bearing projections or prominences. 2. Resembling tubers. 3. *Bot.* Bearing tubers. Also **tu'ber·ose.**

tuberous root *Bot.* Any of the tuberlike parts of a multiple or fascicled fleshy root, as in the dahlia.

tu·bi·fex (tōō'bə·feks, tyōō'-) *n.* Any of a genus (*Tubifex*) of threadlike aquatic worms, often used as live food for aquarium fish. [< NL, genus name]

tu·bi·form (tōō'bə·fôrm, tyōō'-) *adj.* Having the form of a tube. [< TUB(E) + -FORM]

tub·ing (tōō'bing, tyōō'-) *n.* 1. Tubes collectively. 2. A piece of tube or material for tubes. 3. Material for pillowcases. 4. The act of making tubes.

Tub·man (tub'mən), **William Vacanarat Shadrach,** 1895–1971, Liberian statesman; president 1943–71.

tub thumper *U.S. Informal* A noisy speaker; a soapbox orator.

Tu·bu·ai Islands (tōō'bōō·ī') An island group south of the Society Islands, a part of French Polynesia; 115 sq. mi.: also *Austral Islands.*

tu·bu·lar (tōō'byə·lər, tyōō'-) *adj.* 1. Having the form of a tube; tube-shaped. 2. Made up of or provided with tubes. 3. Pertaining to or sounding as if produced in a tube. [< L *tubulus.* See TUBULE.]

tu·bu·late (tōō'byə·lāt, tyōō'-) *v.t.* **·lat·ed, ·lat·ing** 1. To shape or fashion into a tube. 2. To furnish with a tube. — *adj.* 1. Shaped like or into a tube. 2. Provided with a tube: also **tu'bu·lat'ed.** [< L *tubulatus* tubular < *tubulus.* See TUBULE.] — **tu'bu·la'tion** *n.* — **tu'bu·la'tor** *n.*

tu·bule (tōō'byōōl, tyōō'-) *n.* A minute tube. [< L *tubulus,* dim. of *tubus* tube] — **tu'bu·li·form'** *adj.*

tu·bu·li·flo·rous (tōō'byə·lə·flôr'əs, -flō'rəs, tyōō'-) *adj.* *Bot.* Having tubular florets: said of composite plants. [< TUBUL(E) + -FLOROUS]

tu·bu·lous (tōō'byə·ləs, tyōō'-) *adj.* 1. Tube-shaped; tubular. 2. *Bot.* Having tubular florets. 3. Consisting of or containing small tubes. Also **tu'bu·lose** (-lōs).

tu·bu·lure (tōō'byə·lər, tyōō'-) *n.* The short open tube of a retort, receiver, or bell jar. [< F < L *tubulus.* See TUBULE.]

Tu·ca·na (tōō·kā'nə, tyōō'-) *n.* A constellation, the Toucan. See CONSTELLATION. [< NL]

tu·chun (dōō'jün') *n. Chinese* Formerly, the military governor of a Chinese province. — **tu'chun·ate** *n.* — **tu'chun·ism** *n.*

tuck[1] (tuk) *v.t.* 1. To fold under; press in the ends or edges of. 2. To wrap or cover snugly. 3. To thrust or press into a close place; cram; hide. 4. To make tucks in, by folding and stitching. — *v.i.* 5. To contract; draw together. 6. To make tucks. — **to tuck in** (or **away**) *Brit. Informal* To eat or drink heartily. — *n.* 1. A fold stitched into a garment for a better fit or for decoration. 2. Any tucked piece or part. 3. *Naut.* The part of a vessel's hull under the stern where the bottom planks meet. 4. *Brit. Slang* Food. [Fusion of OE *tūcian* to ill-treat, lit., to tug and MDu. *tucken* to pluck]

tuck[2] (tuk) *Scot* or *Obs. n.* 1. A stroke; tap; beat, as of a drum. 2. A flourish, as of a trumpet. — *v.t. & v.i.* To beat; tap, as a drum. [< AF *toker,* OF *toucher* to touch]

tuck[3] (tuk) *n. Archaic* A long narrow sword; rapier. [< AF *etoc,* OF *estoc* < *estoquier* < Du. *stocken* to pierce]

Tuck (tuk), **Friar** See FRIAR TUCK.

tuck·a·hoe (tuk'ə·hō) *n.* An underground fungus (*Poria cocos*) with a rough, brown, edible sclerotium, found in the southern United States: also called *Indian bread.* [< Algonquian (Virginian) *tockawhoughe*]

tuck·er[1] (tuk'ər) *n.* 1. One who or that which tucks. 2. A covering of linen, lawn, etc., formerly worn over the neck and shoulders by women.

tuck·er[2] (tuk'ər) *v.t. Informal* To weary completely; exhaust: usually with *out.* [Freq. of TUCK[1], v.]

tuck·er-bag (tuk'ər·bag') *n.* In Australia, a cloth bag in which food is carried by tramps, travelers, etc. [< Australian slang *tucker* food, rations + BAG]

tuck·et (tuk'it) *n. Archaic* A flourish on a trumpet. [Dim. of TUCK[2]]

Tuc·son (tōō·son', tōō'son) A city in SE Arizona; pop. 262,933.

Tu·cu·mán (tōō'kōō·män') A city in NW Argentina; pop. 271,546 (1960).

-tude *suffix of nouns* Condition or state of being: *gratitude.* [< F *-tude* < L *-tudo*]

Tu·dor (tōō'dər, tyōō'-) A royal family of England descended from **Sir Owen Tudor,** died 1461, a Welshman who married the widow of Henry V. See table for ENGLAND. — *adj.* Designating or pertaining to the architecture, poetry, etc., developed during the reigns of the Tudors.

Tudor architecture A late phase of the Perpendicular

style, developed under the Tudors, characterized by flattened arches, much carving, and paneling.

Tues. Tuesday.

Tues·day (tōōz'dē, -dā, tyōōz'-) *n.* The third day of the week. Abbr. *T., Tu., Tues.* [OE *tīwesdæg* day of Tiw < *Tīw,* war god + *dæg* day; trans. of LL *dies Martis* Mars's day]

tu·fa (tōō'fə, tyōō'-) *n.* 1. A variety of calcium carbonate with cellular structure, as deposited from springs and streams. 2. Tuff. Also called *toph.* [< Ital. *tufa, tufo* < L *tofus, tophus*] — **tu·fa·ceous** (tōō·fā'shəs, tyōō'-) *adj.*

tuff (tuf) *n.* A fragmentary volcanic rock composed of material varying in size from fine sand to coarse gravel, often used for structural purposes. [< MF *tufe, tuffe* < Ital. *tufo.* See TUFA.] — **tuff·a'ceous** *adj.*

tuft (tuft) *n.* 1. A collection or bunch of small, flexible parts, as hair, grass, or feathers, held together at the base. 2. A clump or knot, as a cluster of threads drawn tightly through a quilt, mattress, or upholstery to secure the stuffing. — *v.t.* 1. To separate or form into tufts. 2. To cover or adorn with tufts. — *v.i.* 3. To form tufts. [< OF *tuffe,* prob. < Gmc.] — **tuft'er** *n.* — **tuft'y** *adj.*

tuft·ed (tuf'tid) *adj.* 1. Having, or adorned with, a tuft; crested: the *tufted* duck. 2. Forming a tuft or dense cluster.

tug (tug) *v.* **tugged, tug·ging** *v.t.* 1. To pull at with effort; strain at. 2. To pull, draw, or drag with effort. 3. To tow with a tugboat. — *v.i.* 4. To pull strenuously: to *tug* at an oar. 5. To strive; toil; struggle. — *n.* 1. An act of tugging; a violent pull. 2. A strenuous contest; struggle. 3. A tugboat. 4. A trace of a harness. 5. *Brit.* A colleger or member of the king's foundation at Eton College. 6. *Brit. Dial.* A high-wheeled cart for logs, etc. [ME *toggen* < OE *togen,* pp. of *tēon* to tow; infl. by ON *toga* to draw] — **tug'ger** *n.*

tug·boat (tug'bōt') *n.* A small, compact, ruggedly built vessel operated by steam or other power and designed for towing: also called *towboat, tug.*

tug of war 1. A contest in which a number of persons at one end of a rope pull against a like number at the other end, each side endeavoring to drag the other across a line marked between. 2. A hard struggle for supremacy.

tug·rug (tug'rug) *n.* The monetary unit of the Mongolian People's Republic, equivalent to 100 mongo.

Tui·le·ries (twē'lər·ēz, *Fr.* twēl·rē') A royal palace in Paris; begun in 1564 and burned in 1871; site occupied by the **Tuileries Gardens,** a public park near the Louvre.

tuille (twēl) *n.* In armor, a steel protection for the thighs. [< MF < OF *tieule* < L *tegula* tile]

tu·i·tion (tōō·ish'ən, tyōō-) *n.* 1. The charge or payment for instruction, especially formal instruction in a school, college, or university. 2. The act or business of teaching any branch of learning; instruction. 3. *Archaic* Guardianship; care. [< AF *tuycioun,* OF *tuicion* < L *tuitio, -onis* guard, guardianship < *tuitus,* pp. of *tueri* to look at, watch] — **tu·i'tion·al, tu·i'tion·ar'y** (-er'ē) *adj.*

Tu·la (tōō'lə) A city in the western R.S.F.S.R.; pop. 462,000 (est. 1970).

tu·la·di (tōō'lə·dē) *n. Canadian* The lake trout.

tu·la·re·mi·a (tōō'lə·rē'mē·ə) *n.* A plaguelike disease of rodents, especially rabbits, caused by a microorganism (*Pasteurella tularensis*) that may be transmitted to man by certain insects and by handling infected animals, producing lymphatic inflammation, with chills and fever: also called *rabbit fever.* Also **tu'la·rae'mi·a.** [< NL, after *Tulare* County, California + Gk. *haima* blood]

tu·le (tōō'lē) *n.* A large bulrush (*Scirpus acutus*) growing on damp or flooded land in the southwestern United States. [< Sp. < Nahuatl *tullin*]

tu·lip (tōō'lip, tyōō'-) *n.* 1. Any of numerous hardy, bulbous herbs (genus *Tulipa*) of the lily family, cultivated in many varieties for their large, variously colored, bell-shaped flowers. 2. A bulb or flower of this plant. [< F *tulipe* < OF *tulipan* < Turkish *tuliband* < Persian *dulband* turban]

tu·lip·o·ma·ni·a (tōō'lip·ə·mā'nē·ə, -mān'yə, tyōō'-) *n.* A craze for the acquisition or cultivation of tulips, especially that which arose in Holland early in the 17th century. [< TULIP + -MANIA] — **tu'lip·o·ma'ni·ac** *n.*

tulip tree 1. A large magnoliaceous tree (*Liriodendron tulipifera*) of the eastern United States, with greenish cupshaped flowers. 2. Any of various other trees having tuliplike flowers.

tu·lip·wood (tōō'lip·wŏŏd', tyōō'-) *n.* 1. The wood of the tulip tree: also called *canoewood, saddletree, yellow poplar.* 2. Any of several ornamental cabinet woods yielded by various trees: so called from their color or markings. 3. Any of the trees themselves.

tulle (tōōl, *Fr.* tül) *n.* A fine, silk, open-meshed material, used for veils, etc. [< F, after *Tulle,* city in SW France, where first made]

Tul·ly (tul'ē) See CICERO.

Tul·sa (tul'sə) A city in NE Oklahoma, on the Arkansas River; pop. 331,638.

tum·ble (tum'bəl) *v.* **·bled, ·bling** *v.i.* 1. To roll or toss about. 2. To perform acrobatic feats, as somersaults, etc. 3. To fall violently or awkwardly. 4. To move in a careless or headlong manner; stumble. 5. *Informal* To understand;

comprehend: with *to.* — *v.t.* **6.** To smooth, clean, or polish in a tumbling box. **7.** To toss carelessly; cause to fall. **8.** To throw into disorder or confusion; disturb; rumple. — *n.* **1.** The act of tumbling; a fall. **2.** A state of disorder or confusion. **3.** *U.S. Informal* A token of recognition; a chance: He wouldn't even give her a *tumble.* [ME *tumbel,* freq. of *tumben,* OE *tumbian* to fall, leap]

tum·ble·bug (tum′bəl·bug′)   *n.* A scarabaeid beetle that rolls up a ball of dung to enclose its eggs; a dung beetle.

tum·ble-down (tum′bəl·doun′) *adj.* Rickety, as if about to fall in pieces; dilapidated.

tum·bler (tum′blər)   *n.* **1.** A drinking glass with a flat bottom. The base was formerly rounded, so that the glass would not stand upright. **2.** One who or that which tumbles; especially, an acrobat or gymnast. **3.** One of a breed of domestic pigeons noted for the habit of turning backward somersaults during flight. **4.** In a lock, a latch that prevents a bolt from being shot in either direction until it is raised by the key bit. For illustration see LOCK[1]. **5.** In a firearm lock, a piece attached to the hammer and receiving the thrust of the mainspring. **6.** A tumbling box (which see). **7.** A greyhound used formerly in coursing. **8.** *Mech.* **a** A piece of metal that projects from a revolving or rocking shaft and communicates motion to another piece. **b** The rocking frame in a tumbler gear. **9.** *Scot.* A light cart. **10.** A child's toy, so formed and weighted as to rock at the slightest touch.

tumbler gear   *Mech.* A type of reversing gear having a rocking frame adapted to bring either of two idlers into mesh with the driving gear.

tum·ble·weed (tum′bəl·wēd′)   *n.* Any of various plants that, when withered, break from the root and are driven by the wind, scattering their seed; especially, an amaranth.

tumbling box   A box, usually cylindrical and mounted on a horizontal shaft, in which articles, as castings, are polished by being tumbled about with an abrasive: also called *rumble, rumbler.* Also **tumbling barrel.**

TUMBLER GEAR
a Rocking frame.

tum·brel (tum′bril)   *n.* **1.** A farmer's cart; especially, a boxlike cart for carrying and dumping dung. **2.** A rude cart in which prisoners were taken to the guillotine during the French Revolution. **3.** Formerly, a ducking stool set on wheels. *Obs.* **4.** A two-wheeled military cart for carrying tools, ammunition, etc. Also **tum·bril.** [< OF *tomberel* < *tomber* to fall, ult. < Gmc.]

TUMBREL

u·me·fa·cient (too̅′mə·fā′shənt, tyoo̅′-) *adj.* Producing or tending to produce tumefaction. [< L *tumefaciens,* ppr. of *tumefacere.* See TUMEFY.]

u·me·fac·tion (too̅′mə·fak′shən, tyoo̅′-) *n.* **1.** Any puffing up of a part, especially as in a tumor. **2.** A swelling; puffiness. **3.** The act of tumefying, or the state of being tumefied. [< MF < L *tumefactus,* pp. of *tumefacere.* See TUMEFY.]

u·me·fy (too̅′mə·fī, tyoo̅′-) *v.t. & v.i.* **·fied, ·fy·ing** To swell or puff up; become tumid. [< MF *tuméfier* < L *tumefacere* < *tumere* to swell + *facere* to make]

u·mes·cence (too̅·mes′əns, tyoo̅-) *n.* **1.** The act or process of becoming tumid, as an organ or part of the body. **2.** That which is swollen.

u·mes·cent (too̅·mes′ənt, tyoo̅-) *adj.* **1.** Swelling; somewhat tumid. **2.** Beginning to swell. [< L *tumescens, -entis,* ppr. of *tumescere,* inceptive of *tumere* to swell]

u·mid (too̅′mid, tyoo̅′-) *adj.* **1.** Swollen; enlarged, as a part of the body. **2.** Inflated or pompous in style; bombastic. **3.** Bursting; teeming. [< L *tumidus* < *tumere* to swell] — **tu′mid·ly** *adv.*

u·mid·i·ty (too̅·mid′ə·tē, tyoo̅-)   *n.* The state or character of being tumid. Also **tu·mid·ness** (too̅′mid·nis, tyoo̅′-).

u·mor (too̅′mər, tyoo̅′-)   *n.* **1.** *Pathol.* A local swelling on or in any part of the body, especially from some abnormal autonomous growth of tissue that may or may not become malignant; a neoplasm. **2.** *Obs.* High-sounding words or style; bombast. Also *Brit.* **tu′mour.** [< L *tumor* a swelling < *tumere* to swell] — **tu′mor·ous** *adj.*

ump·line (tump′lin′)   *U.S. & Canadian* A strap passing across the forehead and helping support a load on the back: also called *metump.* Also **tump.** [Prob. < Am.Ind.]

u·mu·lar (too̅′myə·lər, tyoo̅′-) *adj.* Having the form of a mound.

u·mu·lose (too̅′myə·lōs, tyoo̅′-) *adj.* Full of mounds or hills. Also **tu′mu·lous.** [< L *tumulosus* < *tumulus* mound] — **tu′mu·los′i·ty** (-los′ə·tē) *n.*

u·mult (too̅′mult, tyoo̅′-)   *n.* **1.** The commotion, disturbance, or agitation of a multitude; an uproar; turbulence; hubbub. **2.** Any violent commotion or agitation, as of the mind. [< OF *tumulte* < L *tumultus* < *tumere* to swell] ·

u·mul·tu·ous (too̅·mul′choo̅·əs, tyoo̅-) *adj.* **1.** Character-

ized by tumult; disorderly. **2.** Causing or affected by tumult or agitation; agitated or disturbed. Also **tu·mul′tu·ar′y** (-er′ē). — **tu·mul′tu·ous·ly** *adv.* — **tu·mul′tu·ous·ness** *n.*

tu·mu·lus (too̅′myə·ləs, tyoo̅′-) *n. pl.* **·li** (-lī) *Archeol.* **1.** An artificial mound, often of great size and antiquity. **2.** A burial mound; barrow. [< L, mound < *tumere* to swell]

tun (tun)   *n.* **1.** A large cask. **2.** A brewers' fermenting vat. **3.** The amount of malt liquor fermented at one operation; a brew. **4.** A varying measure of capacity, usually equal to 252 gallons. — *v.t.* **tunned, tun·ning** **1.** To put into a cask or tun. **2.** To add to a liquor, as for flavoring. [OE *tunne*]

tu·na[1] (too̅′nə)   *n. pl.* **·na** or **·nas** **1.** Any of several large marine food fishes of the mackerel family, as the **bluefin** or **great tuna** (*Thunnus thynnus*), and the little **tuna** (*Euthynnus alletteratus*) of Atlantic and Pacific waters. **2.** Any of various similar or related fishes, as the albacore and the horse mackerel. **3.** The flesh of any of these fishes processed and eaten as food: also **tuna fish.** Also called *tunny.* [< Am. Sp., ult. < L *thunnos* < Gk. *thynnos*]

TUNA
(To 10 feet long)

tu·na[2] (too̅′nə)   *n.* **1.** A tropical American prickly pear (*Opuntia tuna*), or its edible fruit. **2.** One of a number of related species. [< Am. Sp., prob. < Taino]

tun·a·ble (too̅′nə·bəl, tyoo̅′-) *adj.* **1.** That may be put in tune. **2.** Being in tune. **3.** *Obs.* Tuneful; musical. Also **tune′a·ble.** — **tun′a·ble·ness** *n.* — **tun′a·bly** *adv.*

Tun·bridge Wells (tun′brij)   A municipal borough in SW Kent, England; pop. 39,885 (1961): also *Royal Tunbridge Wells.*

tun·dra (tun′drə, too̅n′-) *n.* A rolling, treeless, often marshy plain of Siberia, arctic North America, etc. — **Syn.** See PLAIN. [< Russian < Lapp]

tune (too̅n, tyoo̅n)   *n.* **1.** A melody or air, usually simple and easy to remember. **2.** The state or quality of being at the proper pitch, or, loosely, in the proper key: out of *tune.* **3.** Concord or unison. **4.** Suitable temper or humor; state of mind. **5.** *Obs.* A musical tone or sound. — **Syn.** See MELODY. — **to change one's tune** To assume a different manner, style, or attitude. — **to sing a different** (or **another**) **tune** To assume a different manner or attitude; change one's tune. — **to the tune of** To the price of: *to the tune of* a thousand dollars. — *v.* **tuned, tun·ing** *v.t.* **1.** To adjust the pitch of to a standard; put in tune; attune. **2.** To adapt to a particular tone, expression, or mood. **3.** To bring into harmony or accord. **4.** To utter or express musically; sing. — *v.i.* **5.** To be in harmony. — **to tune in** To adjust a radio receiver to the frequency of (a station, broadcast, etc.). — **to tune out** To adjust a radio receiver to exclude (interference, a station, etc.). — **to tune up** **1.** To bring (musical instruments) to a standard or common pitch. **2.** To adjust a (stringed instrument) so that the intervals between its strings are correct. **3.** To adjust (a machine, engine, etc.) to proper working order. [Var. of TONE.]

tune·ful (too̅n′fəl, tyoo̅n′-) *adj.* **1.** Melodious; musical. **2.** Producing musical sounds. — **tune′ful·ly** *adv.* — **tune′ful·ness** *n.*

tune·less (too̅n′lis, tyoo̅n′-) *adj.* **1.** Not employed in making music; silent. **2.** Lacking in rhythm, melody, etc. — **tune′less·ly** *adv.* — **tune′less·ness** *n.*

tun·er (too̅′nər, tyoo̅′-)   *n.* **1.** One who or that which tunes. **2.** One who puts musical instruments, as pianos, in tune. **3.** *Telecom.* A radio receiver without audio-frequency amplifiers, speaker, etc.

tune·smith (too̅n′smith′, tyoo̅n′-)   *U.S. Informal* A composer of popular music.

tune-up (too̅n′up′, tyoo̅n′-)   *n. Informal* An adjustment to bring a motor, etc., into proper operating condition.

tung oil (tung)   A yellow to brown oil extracted from the seeds of a Chinese tree (*Aleurites fordi*) of the spurge family, now cultivated in the United States, used in paints, varnishes, etc., as a highly effective drying agent, and also for waterproofing. [< Chinese *t'ung* tung tree]

Tung-shan (doong′shän′)   See SUCHOW.

tung·state (tung′stāt)   *n. Chem.* A salt of tungstic acid.

tung·sten (tung′stən)   *n.* A steel-gray, brittle, heavy metallic element of the chromium group (symbol W), occurring in scheelite and in wolframite, having a high melting point and much used in the manufacture of filaments for electric lamps and high-speed cutting tools: also called *wolfram.* See ELEMENT. [< Sw. < *tung* weighty + *sten* stone] — **tung·sten·ic** (tung·sten′ik) *adj.*

tungsten lamp   An incandescent electric lamp having a filament of metallic tungsten.

tungsten steel   A hard, tenacious steel that contains tungsten.

tung·stic (tung′stik) *adj. Chem.* Of, pertaining to, or containing tungsten, especially in its highest valence. [< TUNGST(EN) + -IC]

tungstic acid   *Chem.* Either of two acids consisting of tungsten trioxide combined with water, and uniting with bases to form salts; especially, the yellow crystalline monohydrate, $H_2WO_4 \cdot H_2O$.

tung·stite (tung′stīt) n. A yellow or yellowish green, native tungsten trioxide, WO_3. Also **tungstic ocher.**

Tun·gus (tŏŏn-gŏŏz′) n. pl. **·gus·es** or **·gus** 1. One of a Mongoloid people of the Tungusic group inhabiting eastern Siberia. 2. The language of the Tungus, belonging to the Manchu-Tungusic subfamily of Altaic languages. Also **Tun·guz′.**

Tun·gus·i·an (tŏŏn-gŏŏz′ē-ən) adj. Of or pertaining to the Tungus or their language. — n. One of the Tunguses.

Tun·gus·ic (tŏŏn-gŏŏz′ĭk) adj. 1. Of, pertaining to, or denoting a group of tribes including the Tungus and Manchus. 2. Tungusian. — n. The Tungus language.

Tun·gus·ka (tŏŏn-gŏŏs′kä) Any of three rivers in the central R.S.F.S.R., the **Upper Tunguska** (see ANGARA), the **Stony** (or **Middle**) **Tunguska**, flowing 975 miles NW and west to the Yenisei, and the **Lower Tunguska**, flowing 1,587 miles north and NW to the Yenisei.

tu·nic (tŏŏ′nĭk, tyŏŏ′-) n. 1. In ancient Greece and Rome, a garment with or without sleeves, reaching to the knees and usually worn without a belt. 2. A modern outer garment gathered at the waist, as a short overskirt or blouse. 3. Anat. & Zool. Any loose membranous skin or mantle of tissue enveloping an organ or part. 4. Bot. A seed coat. 5. Eccl. A tunicle. [< L tunica < Semitic]

tu·ni·ca (tŏŏ′nə·kə, tyŏŏ′-) n. pl. **·cae** (-sē) Anat. & Zool. A tunic. [< NL < L, tunic]

tu·ni·cate (tŏŏ′nə·kĭt, -kāt, tyŏŏ′-) adj. 1. Zool. Of or pertaining to a subphylum (Tunicata) of small marine chordates, having in the adult stage a cylindrical saclike body covered with a transparent membrane or tunic, as the ascidians. 2. Zool. Having a tunic. 3. Bot. Covered with a tunic or series of thin layers, as the onion. — n. A tunicate animal. [< NL tunicata < L tunicata (animalia) coated (animals), neut. pl. of tunicatus, pp. of tunicare to clothe with a tunic < tunica tunic]

tu·ni·cle (tŏŏ′nĭ·kəl, tyŏŏ′-) n. Eccl. A short vestment worn over the alb, especially by bishops. [< L tunicula, dim. of tunica tunic]

tun·ing fork (tŏŏ′nĭng, tyŏŏ′-) A fork-shaped piece of steel that produces a tone of definite pitch when struck.

Tu·nis (tŏŏ′nĭs, tyŏŏ′-) 1. The capital and chief port of Tunisia, in the NE part on the Mediterranean; pop. 662,000 (est. 1969). 2. A former Barbary state of northern Africa.

Tu·ni·sia (tŏŏ·nĭsh′ə, -nĭsh′ē·ə, -nē′zhə, tvŏŏ-) A Republic in northern Africa; 63,378 sq. mi.; pop. 5,027,000 (est. 1969); capital, Tunis: formerly, Tunis.

Tu·ni·sian (tŏŏ·nĭsh′ən, -nē′zhən, tyŏŏ-) adj. Of or relating to Tunisia, or Tunis, or their inhabitants. — n. 1. An inhabitant or native of Tunisia or Tunis. 2. The speech of Tunisia, a North Arabic dialect.

tun·nage (tŭn′ĭj) See TONNAGE.

tun·nel (tŭn′əl) n. 1. An artificial subterranean passageway or gallery, especially one under a hill, etc., as for a railway. 2. Any similar passageway under or through something. 3. A funnel. 4. The main flue or shaft of a chimney or the like. 5. An adit or level in a mine. — v. **tun·neled** or **·nelled, tun·nel·ing** or **·nel·ling** v.t. 1. To make a tunnel through. 2. To shape or make in the form of a tunnel: to tunnel a passage. — v.i. 3. To make a tunnel. [Fusion of OF tonnelle partridge net and tonel, dim. of tonne cask] — **tun′nel·er** or **tun′nel·ler** n.

tunnel diode A semiconductor diode that, due to a quantum mechanical effect, can act as an amplifier.

tunnel disease Caisson disease (which see).

tun·ny (tŭn′ē) n. pl. **·ny** or **·nies** The tuna, a fish. [< OF thon < L thunnos. See TUNA[1].]

tup (tŭp) n. 1. A ram, or male sheep. 2. The striking part of a power hammer. — v.t. & v.i. **tupped, tup·ping** To copulate with (a female): said of the ram. [ME tupe, tope]

tu·pe·lo (tŏŏ′pə·lō) n. pl. **·los** 1. Any of several trees of Asia and the southeastern United States (genus Nyssa), especially the blackgum and the water gum. 2. The wood of any of these trees. [< Muskhogean]

Tu·pi (tŏŏ·pē′) n. pl. **·pis** or **·pi** 1. A member of any of a group of South American Indian tribes, comprising the northern branch of the Tupian stock, and occupying the Amazon, Tapajos, and Xingú valleys. 2. The language spoken by the Tupis, used as a lingua franca along the Amazon. [< Tupi, comrade]

Tu·pi·an (tŏŏ·pē′ən) adj. Of or pertaining to the Tupis or their language. — n. A large stock of South American Indians of some one hundred tribes of the Tupis and Guaranis, scattered throughout the continent (except in Venezuela): also **Tu·pi′-Gua′ra·ni′** (-gwä′rä·nē′).

tu·pik (tŏŏ′pĭk) n. A tent of animal skins, used by Eskimos as a shelter during the summer. [< Eskimo]

tup·pence (tŭp′əns) n. Brit. Informal Twopence.

tup·pen·ny (tŭp′ən·ē) adj. Brit. Informal Twopenny.

Tu·pun·ga·to (tŏŏ·pŏŏng·gä′tō) A peak in the Andes on the Argentine-Chile border; 21,490 ft.

tuque (tŏŏk, tyŏŏk) n. Canadian A cap consisting of a knit-

ted cylindrical bag with tapered ends, worn by thrusting one end inside the other, for tobogganing, etc. [< dial. F (Canadian) < F toque. See TOQUE.]

tu quo·que (tŏŏ kwō′kwē, tyŏŏ) Latin Thou, too; you, also: a retort in kind from a person accused.

tu·ra·cou (tŏŏ′rä·kōō′) n. 1. An African bird (Turacus fischeri), remarkable for its red and green plumage. 2. One of several other related birds. Also called touraco. [< F touraco < Du. < native West African name]

Tu·ra·ni·an (tŏŏ·rā′nē·ən, tyŏŏ-) adj. 1. Of or pertaining to a hypothetical nomadic people who antedated the Aryans in Europe and Asia. 2. Pertaining to the hypothetical Ural-Altaic family of languages. [< Persian Tūrān, country north of the Oxus River]

tur·ban (tûr′bən) n. 1. An Oriental head covering consisting of a sash or shawl, twisted about the head or about a cap. 2. Any similar headdress. 3. A round-crowned brimless hat for women or children. [< F turban, turbant < Ital. turbante < Turkish tülbend, dial. alter. of dülbend < Persian dulband < dul turn + band band] — **tur′baned** (-bənd) adj.

tur·ba·ry (tûr′bər·ē) n. pl. **·ries** 1. In English law, the liberty of digging turf or peat upon another's ground. 2. A place where turf or peat is dug. [< AF turberie, OF tourberie < tourbe peat < Med.L turba < LG turf, turv turf]

tur·bel·lar·i·an (tûr′bə·lâr′ē·ən) n. Any of a class (Turbellaria) of motile, chiefly aquatic flatworms, having a ciliated epidermis and sometimes brilliantly colored. [< NL < L turbellae tumult, pl. dim. of turba crowd]

tur·beth (tûr′bəth), **tur·bith** See TURPETH.

tur·bid (tûr′bĭd) adj. 1. Opaque or cloudy, as a liquid with a suspension of foreign particles. 2. Thick and dense, like heavy smoke or fog. 3. Being in a state of confusion. [< L turbidus < turbare to trouble < turba crowd] — **tur′bid·ly** adv. — **tur·bid′i·ty**, **tur′bid·ness** n.

tur·bi·dim·e·ter (tûr′bə·dĭm′ə·tər) n. An instrument for measuring turbidity. [< TURBID(ITY) + -METER]

tur·bi·nal (tûr′bə·nəl) adj. Spirally coiled; turbinate; topshaped. — n. Anat. A turbinate bone or cartilage. [< L turbo, -inis whirlwind, top]

tur·bi·nate (tûr′bə·nĭt, -nāt) adj. 1. Top-shaped; also, spinning like a top. 2. Zool. Tapering from a broad base to the apex, as certain spiral shells. 3. Anat. Pertaining to one of the thin, curved bones on the walls of the nasal passages. Also **tur′bi·nat·ed.** — n. A turbinate bone or shell. [< L turbinatus < turbo, -inis whirlwind]

tur·bine (tûr′bĭn, -bīn) n. Any of various hydraulic motors consisting of one or more rotary units, mounted on a shaft and provided with a series of curved vanes, actuated by the impulse of steam, water, gas, or other fluid under pressure. [< F < L turbo, -inis whirlwind, top]

tur·bit (tûr′bĭt) n. One of a breed of domestic pigeons having a small head and a ruffled breast and neck. [? < turbo, -inis top; so called with ref. to its shape]

turbo- combining form A turbine; related to or operated by a turbine or turbines: turbojet. [< L turbo top]

tur·bo·car (tûr′bō·kär′) n. An automobile powered by a gas turbine engine.

tur·bo·fan (tûr′bō·fan′) n. Aeron. 1. A compressor having ducted fans that supply air to a jet engine. 2. The engine using such a fan.

tur·bo·gen·er·a·tor (tûr′bō·jen′ə·rā′tər) n. An electric power-generating machine adapted for direct coupling to a steam turbine.

tur·bo·jet (tûr′bō·jet′) n. Aeron. An airplane propelled by a turbojet engine.

turbojet engine n. Aeron. A type of jet engine using a gas turbine to drive an air compressor.

tur·bo·prop (tûr′bō·prop′) n. Aeron. 1. A turbojet engine connecting directly with a propeller. 2. An airplane propelled by such an engine; also, its propeller. Also called propjet. [< TURBO- + PROP(ELLER)]

tur·bo·su·per·charg·er (tûr′bō·sōō′pər·chär′jər) n. Aeron. A supercharging device utilizing an exhaust-driven turbine to maintain air intake pressure on aircraft engines operating at high altitudes.

tur·bot (tûr′bət) n. pl. **·bot** or **·bots** 1. A large European flatfish (Psetta maxima), esteemed as food. 2. One of various related flatfishes. [< AF turbut, OF tourbout, or MDu. turbot]

tur·bu·lence (tûr′byə·ləns) n. 1. The state or condition of being violently disturbed, restless, or confused. 2. Physics The irregular eddying flow of a gas or other fluid, generated by varying pressures and velocities, especially as caused by an obstacle or by friction, as of a ship or airplane in rapid motion. 3. Meteorol. A disturbed condition of the atmosphere due to irregular wind currents. Also **tur′bu·len·cy.**

tur·bu·lent (tûr′byə·lənt) adj. 1. Being in violent agitation or commotion. 2. Inclined to rebel; insubordinate. 3. Having a tendency to disturb or throw into confusion. [< MF < L turbulentus full of disturbance < turbare. See TURBID.] — **tur′bu·lent·ly** adv.

— **Syn.** 1. agitated, boisterous, disorderly, disturbed, riotous, tumultuous, wild. 2. insurgent, mutinous, refractory. — **Ant.** calm, placid, still, quiet.

Tur·co (tûr′kō) *n.* *pl.* **·cos** Formerly, an Algerian light-infantryman serving in the French army; an Algerian tirailleur. [< F < Sp., Turk]

Tur·co·man (tûr′kə·mən) See TURKOMAN.

turd (tûrd) *n.* **1.** A piece of dung. **2.** *U.S. Slang* A vile person. [ME < OE *tord*. Akin to MDu. *tort* dung.]

tur·di·form (tûr′də·fôrm) *adj.* Thrushlike in form or structure. [< L *turdus* thrush + -FORM]

tur·dine (tûr′din, -dīn) *adj.* Belonging or pertaining to a large and widely distributed family (*Turdidae*) of singing birds, including thrushes and bluebirds. [< NL, subfamily name < L *turdus* thrush]

tu·reen (too·rēn′, tyoo-) *n.* A deep, covered dish, as for holding soup to be served at the table. [Earlier *terrene* < F *terrine*. Doublet of TERRINE.]

Tu·renne (tü·ren′), **Vicomte de**, 1611–75, Henri de La Tour d'Auvergne, French marshal.

turf (tûrf) *n.* *pl.* **turfs** (*Archaic* **turves**) **1.** The grass or other fine plants with their matted roots filling the upper stratum of certain soils; sod. **2.** A piece of peat for burning as fuel. **3.** *U.S. Slang* The neighborhood claimed by a juvenile gang as its territory. **— the turf 1.** A racetrack for horses. **2.** The practice of racing horses. [OE]

turf·man (tûrf′mən) *n.* *pl.* **·men** (-mən) A man who is devoted to or connected with horse racing.

turf·y (tûr′fē) *adj.* **turf·i·er, turf·i·est 1.** Covered with turf. **2.** Resembling turf in character or appearance. **3.** Pertaining to the turf, to horse racing, or to a racecourse; horsy. **— turf′i·ness** *n.*

Tur·ge·nev (toor·gā′nyef), **Ivan Sergeyevich**, 1818–83, Russian novelist. Also **Tur·ge′niev**.

tur·gent (tûr′jənt) *adj.* *Obs.* Turgid. [< L *turgens, -entis*, ppr. of *turgere* to swell] **— tur′gent·ly** *adv.*

tur·ges·cence (tûr·jes′əns) *n.* **1.** The process of swelling up; the state of being swollen. **2.** Empty pompousness; inflation. Also **tur·ges′cen·cy.** [< Med.L *turgescentia* < L *turgescens, -entis*, ppr. of *turgescere*, inceptive of *turgere* to swell] **— tur·ges′cent** *adj.* **— tur·ges′cent·ly** *adv.*

tur·gid (tûr′jid) *adj.* **1.** Unnaturally distended, as by contained air or liquid; swollen. **2.** Inflated; bombastic, as language, literary style, etc. [< L *turgidus* < *turgere* to swell] **— tur·gid′i·ty, tur′gid·ness** (tûr′jid·nis) *n.* **— tur′gid·ly** *adv.*

tur·gite (tûr′jīt) *n.* A fibrous, earthy iron ore, found as a reddish black or dark red ferric hydroxide. [after *Turginsk*, a copper mine in the Ural Mountains]

tur·gor (tûr′gor) *n.* **1.** The state of being turgid; turgidity. **2.** *Physiol.* The normal condition of the blood vessels and of cells distended by their protoplasmic contents. **3.** *Bot.* A similar condition in plant cells. [< LL < L < *turgere* to swell]

Tur·got (tür·gō′), **Anne Robert Jacques**, 1727–81, Baron de l'Aulne, French statesman, financier, and economist.

Tu·rin (toor′in, tyoor′-, too·rin′, tyoo-) A commune in NW Italy, on the Po river; capital of the kingdom of Italy until 1864; pop. 1,019,230 (1961): Italian *Torino*.

Turk (tûrk) *n.* **1.** A native or inhabitant of Turkey: sometimes called *Ottoman*. **2.** One of any of the peoples speaking any of the Turkic languages, and ranging from the Adriatic to the Sea of Okhotsk, believed to be of the same ultimate extraction as the Mongols. **3.** A Moslem. **4.** A Turkish horse. **5.** Turkic.

Turk. Turkey; Turkish.

Tur·ke·stan (tûr′kə·stan′, -stän′) A region of central Asia extending from the Caspian Sea to the Gobi Desert and divided by the Pamir and Tien Shan mountain systems into **Russian Turkestan**, comprising Soviet Central Asia; and **Chinese** (or **Eastern**) **Turkestan** (also *Kashgaria*), comprising the Sinkiang-Uigur Autonomous Region: also *Turkistan*. **— Tur·ke·sta′ni** (-nē) *adj. & n.*

tur·key (tûr′kē) *n.* *pl.* **·keys 1.** A large American bird (family *Meleagridae*) related to the pheasant, having the head naked and the tail extensible; especially, the American domesticated turkey (*Meleagris gallopavo*), much esteemed as food. **2.** *U.S. Slang* A play that is a failure. **— to talk turkey** To discuss in a practical and direct manner. [Short for *turkey cock* the guinea fowl, after *Turkey*; later applied erroneously to the American bird]

Tur·key (tûr′kē) A Republic of SE central Eurasia; 296,108 sq. mi.; pop. 34,375,000 (est. 1969); capital, Ankara: Turkish *Türkiye*. See ANATOLIA.

turkey buzzard A sooty black vulture (*Cathartes aura*) of tropical America and the southern United States, having a naked red head and neck.

Turkey carpet 1. A rug or carpet hand-woven in one piece in Turkey, usually having a deep pile and brilliant colors. **2.** Any rug made in imitation of this. Also **Turkish carpet.**

turkey cock 1. A male turkey. **2.** One who struts and behaves in a pompous, conceited manner.

Turkey red 1. A brilliant red prepared from madder or alizarin. **2.** Cotton cloth dyed with this color.

turkey trot A ragtime dance popular in the early 20th century.

Tur·ki (toor′kē) *adj.* **1.** Of or pertaining to Turkic. **2.** Of or pertaining to any of the peoples speaking a Turkic language, as the Osmanlis and Chuvashes of Turkey, NW Persia, Transcaucasia, etc., and the Asian Tatar tribes, as the Uigurs, Uzbeks, Kipchaks, Turkomans, etc., of Mongolia and Turkestan. **—** *n.* *pl.* **·kis 1.** The Turkic languages. **2.** A member of any of the Turki peoples.

Turk·ic (tûr′kik) *n.* A subfamily of the Altaic family of languages, including Osmanli or Turkish, Azerbaijani, Uzbek, Chuvash, Yakut, etc. **—** *adj.* Pertaining to this linguistic subfamily, or to any of the peoples speaking these languages.

Turk·ish (tûr′kish) *adj.* **1.** Of or pertaining to Turkey or the Turks. **2.** Of or relating to the Turkic subfamily of Altaic languages, especially to Osmanli. **—** *n.* The Altaic language of Turkey; Osmanli. *Abbr. T., Turk.*

Turkish bath A bathing establishment where sweating is induced by exposure to high temperature, usually in a room heated by steam, followed by washing, massage, etc.

Turkish delight A sweetmeat of Turkish origin, usually consisting of gelatinous, fruit-flavored cubes coated with powdered sugar. Also **Turkish paste.**

Turkish Empire The Ottoman Empire (which see).

Turkish tobacco A dark, rich tobacco grown in eastern Mediterranean regions, especially in Turkey and Greece.

Turkish towel A heavy, rough towel with loose, uncut pile. Also **turkish towel.**

Turk·ism (tûr′kiz·əm) *n.* **1.** The religion, or the social or political system, characteristic of the Turks. **2.** Any distinctive peculiarity of Turkish speech or custom.

Tur·ki·stan (tûr′kə·stan′, -stän′) See TURKESTAN.

Tur·ki·ye (tür′ki·ye′) The Turkish name for TURKEY.

Turk·men (tûrk′men) *n.* The Turkic language of the Turkomans.

Turk·men S. S. R. (tûrk′men) A constituent republic of the Soviet Union in Central Asia; 189,370 sq. mi.; pop. 2,158,000 (1970); capital, Ashkhabad. Also **Turk·me·ni·stan** (tûrk′me·ni·stan′, -stän′). *Russian* **Turk·men·ska·ya S. S. R.** (toork·myen′ska·ya).

tur·kois (tûr′koiz) See TURQUOISE.

Tur·ko·man (tûr′kə·mən) *n.* *pl.* **·mans 1.** A member of any of the Turki peoples dwelling in those parts of Turkestan comprising the Turkmen, Uzbek, and Kazakh S. S. R. **2.** Turkmen. Also spelled *Turcoman*. Also **Turk′man.** [< Persian *Turkumān* one like a Turk] **— Turk·me·ni·an** (tûrk·mē′nē·ən) *adj. & n.* **— Turk·o·man·ic** (tûr′kə·man′ik) *adj.*

Turks and Cai·cos Islands (tûrks, kā′kəs) An archipelago SE of the Bahamas, comprising a British Colony; 166 sq. mi.; pop. 6,000 (est. 1969).

Turk's-cap lily (tûrks′kap′) **1.** A tall North American lily (*Lilium superbum*) with nodding, purple-spotted, orange-yellow or red flowers in a pyramidal raceme. **2.** A lily (*Lilium martagon*) of Europe and Asia, with purplish black or sometimes white flowers: also called *martagon*.

Turk's-head (tûrks′hed′) *n.* An ornamented knot of turbanlike form.

Tur·ku (toor′koo) A city in SW Finland, on the Gulf of Bothnia; pop. 145,600 (est. 1966): Swedish *Abo*.

tur·ma·line (tûr′mə·lēn) See TOURMALINE.

tur·mer·ic (tûr′mər·ik) *n.* **1.** The root of an East Indian plant (*Curcuma longa*) of the ginger family, used as a condiment, aromatic stimulant, dyestuff, etc. **2.** The plant yielding this root. **3.** Any of several similar plants. **—** *adj.* Of, pertaining to, or saturated with turmeric. [Earlier *tarmaret*, ? < F *terre mérite* deserving earth < Med.L *terra merita*; ult. origin uncertain]

turmeric paper A paper saturated with turmeric, used as a test for alkalis, turning it brown, and for boric acid, turning it reddish brown: also called *curcuma paper*.

tur·moil (tûr′moil) *n.* Confused motion; disturbance; tumult. **—** *v.t. & v.i. Archaic* To be or cause to be in a state of turmoil. [? < OF *tremouille* hopper of a mill < L *tremere* to tremble; ? infl. in form by *turn* and *moil*]

turn (tûrn) *v.t.* **1.** To give a rotary motion to; cause to rotate, as about an axis. **2.** To change the position of, as by rotating: to *turn* a trunk on its side. **3.** To move so that the upper side becomes the under: to *turn* a page. **4.** To bring the subsoil of to the surface, as by plowing or spading. **5.** To alter (a garment) by reversing the material: to *turn* a shirt collar. **6.** To reverse the arrangement or order of; cause to be upside down. **7.** To cause to rotate in order to tighten, loosen, open, etc.: to *turn* a screw. **8.** To revolve mentally; ponder: often with *over*. **9.** To wrench inward or outward so as to sprain or strain. **10.** To nauseate (the stomach). **11.** To shape (an object) in rounded form by turning in a lathe or other cutting tool. **12.** To give rounded or curved form to. **13.** To give graceful or finished form to: to *turn* a phrase. **14.** To perform by revolving: to *turn* cartwheels. **15.** To bend, curve, fold, or twist. **16.** To bend or blunt (the edge of a knife, etc.). **17.** To change or transform; convert: to *turn* water into wine. **18.** To translat : to *turn* French into English. **19.** To exchange for an equivalent: to *turn* stocks into cash. **20.** To adapt to some use or purpose; apply: to *turn* infor nation to good account. **21.** To cause to become as specified: The sight *turned* him sick. **22.** To change the color of. **23.** To make sour or rancid; ferment or curdle. **24.** To change the direction of. **25.** To direct or aim; point. **26.** To change the direction or focus of (thought, attention, etc.). **27.** To deflect or divert: to *turn* a blow. **28.** To repel: to *turn* a charge. **29.** To go around or to the other side of: to *turn* a corner. **30.** To pass or go beyond: to *turn* twenty-one. **31.** To cause or co npel to go; send; drive: to *turn* a beggar from one's door. **32.** To keep circulating in trade: to *turn* goods or money. **33.** *Obs.* To pervert. — *v.i.* **34.** To move around an axis or center; rotate; revolve. **35.** To move partially on or as if on an axis: He *turned* and ran. **36.** To change position; also, to roll from side to side, as in bed. **37.** To take a new direction: We *turned* north. **38.** To reverse position; become inverted. **39.** To reverse direction or flow: The tide has *turned*. **40.** To change the direction or focus of one's thought, attention, etc.: Let us *turn* to the next problem. **41.** To depend; hinge: with *on* or *upon*. **42.** To be affected with giddiness; whirl, as the head. **43.** To become upset or nauseated, as the stomach. **44.** To become hostile; oppose: to *turn* on one's neight ors. **45.** To change one's position in order to act in retaliation: The worm *turns*. **46.** To become transformed; change: The water *turned* into ice. **47.** To become as specified: His hair *turned* gray. **48.** To change color: said especially of leaves. **49.** To become sour, rancid, or fermented, as milk or wine. **50.** *Naut.* To tack or put about. **51.** *Obs.* To vacillate. — **Syn.** See BEND¹. — **to turn against** To become or cause to become opposed or hostile to. — **to turn an honest dollar** (or **penny**) To earn money honestly. — **to turn down 1.** To di ninish the flow, volume, etc., of: *Turn down* the gas. **2.** *Informal* To reject or refuse, as a proposal or request; also, to refuse the request, proposal, etc., of. — **to turn in 1.** To fold or double. **2.** To bend or incline inward. **3.** To deliver; hand over. **4.** *Informal* To go to bed. — **to turn loose** *Informal* To set free; release from restraint, imprisonment, etc. — **to turn off 1.** To stop the operation, flow, etc., of. **2.** To leave the direct road; make a turn. **3.** To deflect or divert. **4.** *Brit.* To dismiss; discharge. — **to turn on 1.** To set in operation, flow, etc.: to *turn on* an engine. **2.** *Slang* To take or experience the mental and perceptual effects of taking a psychedelic drug, as marijuana, LSD, etc. **3.** *Slang* To arrange for (someone) to take or be affected by such a drug. **4.** *Slang* To evoke in (someone) a profound or rapt response, as though under the influence of a psychedelic drug: Baroque music really *turned* him *on*. — **to turn out 1.** To turn inside out. **2.** To eject or expel; put out. **3.** To dismiss or discharge. **4.** To turn off (def. 1). **5.** To bend or incline outward. **6.** To produce by work or toil; make. **7.** To come or go out, as for duty or service. **8.** To prove (to be); be found. **9.** To become or result. **10.** To equip or fit; dress. **11.** *Informal* To get out of bed. — **to turn over 1.** To change the position of; invert. **2.** To upset; overturn. **3.** To hand over; transfer or relinquish. **4.** To do business to the amount of. **5.** To invest and get back (capital). **6.** To use in trade or exchange; buy and then sell: to *turn over* merchandise. — **to turn tail** To run away; flee. — **to turn to 1.** To set to work. **2.** To seek aid from. **3.** To refer or apply to. **4.** To open a book, etc., to (a specified page or chapter). — **to turn up 1.** To bring or fold the under side upward. **2.** To bend or incline upward. **3.** To bring or be brought to view by plowing, digging, etc.; find or be found. **4.** To increase the flow, volume, etc., of. **5.** To put in an appearance; arrive. — *n.* **1.** The act of turning, or the state of being turned. **2.** A change to another direction, motion, or position: a *turn* to the left. **3.** A deflection or deviation from a course; change in trend: a *turn* of fortune. **4.** The point at which a change takes place: a *turn* for the better. **5.** Motion about or as about a center; a rotation or revolution: the *turn* of a crank. **6.** A bend, as in a road. **7.** A regular time or chance in some succession: It's my *turn* to play. **8.** A round; spell: a *turn* at painting. **9.** Form or distinguishing shape: the *turn* of an ankle. **10.** Characteristic form or style: the *turn* of a phrase. **11.** A knack or special ability: a *turn* for study. **12.** Tendency; direction: The talk took a serious *turn*. **13.** A deed performed, regarded as aiding or injuring another: a good *turn*. **14.** An advantage proposed or gained: It served his *turn*. **15.** A walk, drive, or trip to and fro: a *turn* in the park. **16.** A trip back and forth, as in taking a load of something. **17.** A round in a skein, coil, etc. **18.** *Music* An ornament formed by a group of four rapid notes, the first a degree above and the third a degree below the principal tone, that occupies the second and fourth positions. In an **inverted turn** the tones are reversed in order. **19.** *Informal* A shock to the nerves, as from alarm. **20.** A variation or difference in type

or kind. **21.** A short theatrical act of any description; also, in sport, a contest; a bout. **22.** A twist, as of a rope, around a tree or post. **23.** A transaction on the stock exchange, involving purchase and sale, or the re-verse; also, any business transaction. **24.** In infantry drill, a maneuver in which a line of troops changes the direction of its front, usually in preparation for marching. — **at every turn** On every occasion; constantly. — **by turns 1.** In alternation or sequence. **2.** At intervals. — **in turn** One after another; in proper order or sequence. — **out of turn** Not in proper order or prescribed order or sequence. — **to a turn** Just right; perfectly or exactly: said especially of cooked food. — **to take turns** To act, play, etc., one after another in proper order. [Fusion of OE *tyrnan* and *turnian* and OF *turner*, all < L *tornare* to turn in a lathe < *turnus* lathe < Gk. *tornos*]

turn·a·bout (tûrn′ə-bout′) *n.* **1.** The act of turning completely about and taking the opposite direction, opinion, etc. Also **turn′-a-bout′face′** (-fās′). **2.** A merry-go-round.

turn·a·round (tûrn′ə-round′) *n.* **1.** The act of unloading a ship, aircraft, or other vehicle and loading it to begin its next trip. **2.** A space in which a vehicle is turned around. **3.** A round trip.

turn·buck·le (tûrn′buk′əl) *n.* *Mech.* A coupling consisting of an oblong center section with threaded holes at the ends, for adjusting the tension between two metal rods or cables.

TURNBUCKLES
a Insulated, for electric wires. *b* For metal tie rods. *c* For window shutters.

turn·coat (tûrn′kōt′) *n.* One who goes over to the opposite side or party; a renegade.

turn·down (tûrn′doun′) *adj.* Folded down, as a collar; also, capable of being turned down.

turned comma (tûrnd) *Printing* An inverted comma.

turn·er¹ (tûr′nər) *n.* One who turns; especially, one who fashions objects with a lathe.

turn·er² (tûr′nər) *n.* A gymnast; a member of a turnverein. [< G < *turnen* to engage in gymnastics < F *tourner*]

Tur·ner (tûr′nər) **Frederick Jackson,** 1861–1932, U.S. historian. — **Joseph Mallord William,** 1775–1851, English painter.

turn·er·y (tûr′nər·ē) *n.* *pl.* **·er·ies 1.** The act or process of turning articles on a lathe. **2.** Articles made with a lathe.

turn·hall (tûrn′hôl′) *n.* A building in which gymnasts, especially members of a turnverein, practice; a gymnasium. Also German **Turn·hal·le** (tŏŏrn′häl′ə). [< G *turnhalle* < *turnen* to exercise + *halle* hall]

turn indicator The directional signal of a motor vehicle.

turn·ing (tûr′ning) *n.* **1.** The act of one who or that which turns. **2.** The art of shaping wood, metal, etc., in a lathe. **3.** Any deviation fro n a straight or custo nary course; a winding; bend. **4.** The point where a road forks. **5.** Fashioning or shaping, as of a litc rary work.

turning point 1. The point of a decisive change in direction of action; a crisis. **2.** The point at which the direction of a motion is reversed. **3.** A marked object toward which a surveying instrument is sighted from each of two positions in a direct line with each other in the process of leveling.

tur·nip (tûr′nip) *n.* **1.** The fleshy, globular, edible root of either of two biennial herbs, (genus *Brassica*) of the mustard family, the **white turnip** (*B. rapa*), and the rutabaga. **2.** Either of the plants yielding this root. [Earlier *turnepe*, ? < F *tour* turn, rotation (< L *turnus* lathe) + ME *nepe* < OE *nǣp* < L *napus* turnip; with ref. to its round shape]

turn·key (tûrn′kē) *n.* One who has charge of the keys of a prison; a jailer.

turn·off (tûrn′ôf′, -of′) *n.* *Informal* A road, path, or way branching off from a main thoroughfare.

turn of the century The period at the end of the 19th century and the beginning of the 20th century.

turn·out (tûrn′out′) *n.* **1.** An act of turning out or coming forth. **2.** An assemblage of persons; attendance. **3.** A quantity produced; output. **4.** Array; equipment; outfit. **5.** A railroad siding. **6.** The movement of a vehicle from a line of traffic to pass other vehicles. **7.** A section of narrow road widened to per nit vehicles to pass one another. **8.** A carriage or wagon with its horses and equipage. **9.** *Brit.* A labor strike; also, a striker.

turn·o·ver (tûrn′ō′vər) *n.* **1.** The act or process of turning over; an upset or overthrow, as of a vehicle. **2.** The rate at which persons hired by a given establishment within a given period are replaced by others; also, the number of persons hired. **3.** A change or revolution: a *turnover* in affairs. **4.** A small pie or tart made by covering half of a circular crust with fruit, jelly, or the like, and turning the other half over on top. **5.** The amount of business accomplished, or of work achieved; turnout. **6.** A completed commercial transaction or course of business; also, the money receipts of a business for a given period: also called *overturn*. — *adj.* **1.** Designed for turning over or reversing. **2.** Capable of being turned over or folded down. **3.** Made with a part folded down: a *turnover* collar.

turn·pike (tûrn′pīk′) *n.* **1.** A road, now especially a superhighway, on which there are tollgates. **2.** Loosely, any highway: also **turnpike road**. **3.** A tollbar or tollgate. **4.** *Obs.*

A turnstile. — **Syn.** See ROAD. [ME *turnpyke* spiked road barrier < TURN, v. + *pyke* pike[1]]

turn·sole (tûrn′sōl′) *n.* Any of several plants supposed to turn their flowers toward the sun; especially, the heliotrope and the sunflower. [< OF *tournesole* < Ital. *tornasole* < *tornare* to turn (< L) + *sole* sun < L *sol*]

turn·spit (tûrn′spit′) *n.* 1. One who turns a spit; a menial. 2. Formerly, a dog used in a treadmill to turn a spit.

turn·stile (tûrn′stīl′) *n.* 1. A gate, having revolving horizontal ar ns, that admits passengers to subways, buses, etc., on the deposit of fares, or registers the number of persons entering a building, or restricts passage to one direction only. 2. A si ilar device permitting persons to pass but not cattle.

turn·stone (tûrn′stōn′) *n.* A ploverlike migratory bird (genus *Arenaria*) of northern regions: so called from its habit of turning over stones to obtain its food; especially, the **ruddy turnstone** (*A. interpres*) and the **black turnstone** (*A. melanocephala*) of North America.

turn·ta·ble (tûrn′tā′bəl) *n.* 1. The rotating disk that carries a phonograph record. 2. A rotating platform arranged to turn a section of a bridge in order to open a passage for ships. 3. Such a platform to turn a locomotive, car, etc. Also *Brit.* **turn′plate** (-plāt′). 4. A small rotating disk in a microscope. 5. A rotating table in a show window.

turn·up (tûrn′up′) *n.* 1. That which is turned up, as part of a garment. 2. A particular card or die turned up in gambling. 3. Pure chance; a tossup. — *adj.* Turned up.

turn·ver·ein (tōōrn′fe-rīn, tûrn′və-rīn) *n. Sometimes cap.* An association of turners or gymnasts; an athletic club. [< G < *turnen* to exercise + *verein* club]

tur·pen·tine (tûr′pən-tīn) *n.* 1. An oleoresin obtained from any of several coniferous trees, especially the longleaf pine (*Pinus palustris*). ◆ Collateral adjective: *terebinthine*. 2. The semifluid resin of the terebinth. — **oil of turpentine** The colorless essential oil formed when turpentine is distilled with steam and consisting of a mixture of terpenes, chiefly used to thin paint: also called *spirits of turpentine*. — *v.t.* **·tined, ·tin·ing** 1. To put turpentine with or upon; saturate with turpentine. 2. To obtain crude turpentine from (a tree). [< OF *turbentine* < L *terebinthinus* of the terebinth tree < *terebinthus* terebinth < Gk. *terebinthos*]

turpentine tree The peebeen.

tur·peth (tûr′pith) *n.* The root of an East Indian plant (*Ipomoea turpethum*) similar to jalap in its properties: also called *turbeth, turbith*. [< OF *turbit* < Med.L *turbithum* < Arabic *turbid* < Persian]

Tur·pin (tûr′pin), Richard, 1706-39, English highwayman; executed: called **Dick Turpin**.

tur·pi·tude (tûr′pə-tōōd, -tyōōd) *n.* Inherent baseness; vileness; depravity, or any action showing depravity. [< MF < L *turpitudo, -inis* < *turpis* vile]

tur·quoise (tûr′koiz, -kwoiz) *n.* 1. A blue or green hydrous aluminum phosphate, colored by copper, found massive, and in its highly polished blue varieties esteemed as a gemstone. 2. A light greenish blue, the color of the turquoise: also **turquoise blue**. Also spelled *turkois*. Also *Obs.* **tur·quois** (tûr′koiz′). [< MF (*pierre*) *turquoise* Turkish (stone); so called because first imported through Turkey]

tur·ret (tûr′it) *n.* 1. *Mil.* **a** A rotating armored housing, large enough to contain a powerful gun or guns and gunners, forming part of a warship or of a fort. **b** A similar structure in a tank or a bombing or combat airplane. 2. *Archit.* A small tower, often merely ornamental, rising above a larger structure, as on a castle. 3. The clerestory of a railway car. 4. In ancient warfare, a high wooden structure intended to enable besiegers to surmount the walls against which it was pushed. 5. *Mech.* In a lathe, a cylinder fitted with sockets or chucks for the reception of various tools, any one of which may be presented in the axial line of the work: also **turret head**. [< OF *torete*, dim. of *tor*. See TOWER.]

tur·ret·ed (tûr′it-id) *adj.* 1. Provided with turrets. 2. Having the form of a turret. 3. *Zool.* Having a long spire, as certain shells.

turret lathe A lathe having a turret (def. 5).

tur·ri·cal (tûr′i-kəl) *adj.* Of, pertaining to, or like a turret. [< L *turris* tower + -ICAL]

tur·ric·u·late (tə-rik′yə-lit, -lāt) *adj.* 1. Having or resembling a turret or turrets. 2. Turreted or having a spire: said of shells. [< L *turricula*, dim. of *turris* tower + -ATE]

tur·tle[1] (tûr′təl) *n.* 1. Any of numerous reptiles (order *Chelonia*) having a horny, toothless beak, and a short, stout body enclosed within a carapace and plastron, into which all the members may be drawn for protection: a tortoise. 2 A marine species (family *Chelonidae*) as distinguished from a terrestrial or fresh-water species. 3. The flesh of certain vari ties of turtle, served as food. 4. *Printing* A frame, a segment of a cylinder, used to hold the type in a type-revolving web press. — **green turtle** An important food turtle (*Chelonia mydas*) of wide distribution in tropical and semitropical seas: so called from the greenish color of its flesh. — **to turn turtle** To capsize. — *v.i.* **·tled, ·tling** To

hunt or catch turtles. [Appar. alter. of F *tortue* or Sp. *tortuga* < Med.L *tortuca* (See TORTOISE); infl. in form by TURTLE[2]]

tur·tle[2] (tûr′təl) *n. Archaic* A turtledove. [OE *turtla* < L *turtur*]

tur·tle·back (tûr′təl-bak′) *n.* 1. *Naut.* An arched covering, resembling the shell of a turtle, built over the bow or stern of a ship as protection against heavy seas. Also **turtle deck.** 2. *Archeol.* A chipped stone implement rounded on one side. [< TURTLE[1] + BACK]

tur·tle·dove (tûr′təl-duv′) *n.* 1. A small Old World dove (*Streptopelia turtur*) conspicuous for its white-edged black tail and soft, mournful coo. 2. The mourning dove (which see). [< TURTLE[2] + DOVE]

tur·tle·head (tûr′təl-hed′) *n.* Any of a genus (*Chelone*) of hardy American herbs of the figwort family, with large white or purple flowers: also called *snakehead*.

turtle neck A high collar that fits snugly about the neck, usually rolled or turned over double, used especially on athletic sweaters. — **tur·tle-neck** (tûr′təl-nek′) *adj.*

tur·tle·peg (tûr′təl-peg′) *n.* A small, sharp, steel spike attached to a line and loosely mounted upon a shaft that is thrown like a harpoon to capture sea turtles.

tur·tle·stone (tûr′təl-stōn′) *n.* Septarium.

turves (tûrvz) Archaic plural of TURF.

Tus·ca·loo·sa (tus′kə-lōō′sə) A city in west central Alabama; pop. 65,773.

Tus·can (tus′kən) *adj.* 1. Pertaining to Tuscany. 2. Designating the Tuscan order of architecture. — *n.* 1. A native or inhabitant of Tuscany. 2. Any Italian dialect used in Tuscany; especially, the one spoken in Florence.

Tuscan order *Archit.* A Roman order of architecture resembling Roman Doric but having bolder moldings, no decorated details, and no triglyphs.

Tus·ca·ny (tus′kə-nē) A Region and former duchy of west central Italy; 8,876 sq. mi.; pop. 3,267,374 (1961); chief city, Florence: Italian *Toscana*.

Tus·ca·ro·ra (tus′kə-rôr′ə, -rō′rə) *n. pl.* **·ra** or **·ras** One of a tribe of North American Indians of Iroquoian stock formerly living in North Carolina, now surviving in New York and Ontario.

Tus·cu·lum (tus′kyə-ləm) An ancient ruined city of Latium, SE of Rome. — **Tus′cu·lan** *adj.*

tush[1] (tush) *interj.* An exclamation expressing disapproval, impatience, etc. [ME *tussch*]

tush[2] (tush) *n.* Tusk. — *v.t.* To tusk.

tushed (tusht) *adj.* Having tusks.

tusk (tusk) *n.* 1. A long, pointed tooth, generally one of a pair, as in the boar, walrus, or elephant. 2. A sharp, projecting, toothlike point. 3. A shoulder on a tenon, to strengthen it at its base; also, a tenon having such a shoulder. — *v.t.* 1. To gore with the tusks. 2. To root up with the tusks. Also *tush*. [Metathetic var. of OE *tūx*] — **tusked** (tuskt) *adj.* — **tusk′less** *adj.*

tusk·er (tus′kər) *n.* A tusked elephant or boar.

tusk tenon A tenon strengthened by a step or steps, or by a shoulder.

tus·sah (tus′ə) *n.* 1. An Asian silkworm (*Antheraea paphia*) that spins large cocoons yielding a coarse, brownish or yellowish silk. 2. The silk, or the durable fabric woven from it. Also **tus·sar** (tus′ər), **tus·sore** (tus′ôr, -ôr). [< Hind. *tasar* < Skt. *tasara, trasara*, lit., shuttle]

tus·sis (tus′is) *n. Pathol.* A cough: bronchial *tussis*. [< NL < L] — **tus·sal, tus′sive** *adj.*

tus·sle (tus′əl) *v.t. & v.i.* **·sled, ·sling** To fight or struggle in a vigorous, determined way; scuffle; wrestle. — *n.* A disorderly struggle, as in sport; scuffle. [Var. of TOUSLE]

tus·sock (tus′ək) *n.* 1. A tuft or clump of grass or sedge. 2. A tuft, as of hair or feathers. Also **tus′suck.** [Prob. dim. of obs. *tusk* tuft of hair, ? < TUSK] — **tus′sock·y** *adj.*

tussock moth Any of various medium-sized moths (family *Lymantriidae*) whose larvae bear tufts of hairs and are very destructive of broad-leaved trees, as the gypsy moth.

tut (tut) *interj.* An exclamation to check rashness or express impatience. Also **tut tut.**

Tut-ankh-a-men (tōōt′ängk-ä′min) Fourteenth-century B.C. Egyptian pharaoh. Also **Tut′ankh-a′mon.**

tu·te·lage (tōō′tə-lij, tyōō′-) *n.* 1. The state of being under a tutor or guardian. 2. The act or office of a guardian; guardianship. 3. The act of tutoring; instruction. [< L *tutela* guardianship < *tutus* safe < *tueri* to watch, guard]

tu·te·lar·y (tōō′tə-ler′ē, tyōō′-) *adj.* 1. Invested with guardianship. 2. Pertaining to a guardian. Also **tu′te·lar** (-lər).

a Cornice. *b* Frieze. *c* Architrave. *d* Capital. *e* Shaft. *f* Base. *g* Torus. *h* Plinth. *i* Apophyge.

TUSCAN ORDER

tu·tor (tōō′tər, tyōō′-) *n.* **1.** One who instructs another in one or more branches of knowledge; a private teacher. **2.** A college teacher who gives individual instruction. **3.** *Brit.* A college official entrusted with the tutelage and care of undergraduates assigned to him. **4.** *Law* A guardian of a minor or of a woman. —*v.t.* **1.** To act as tutor to; instruct; teach; train. **2.** To have the guardianship of. **3.** To treat severely or sternly, as a tutor might; discipline. —*v.i.* **4.** To do the work of a tutor. **5.** To be tutored or instructed. —**Syn.** See TEACH. [< AF, OF *tutour* < L *tutor* watcher, guardian < *tutus.* See TUTELAGE.] —**tu·to·ri·al** (tōō·tôr′ē·əl, -tō′rē-, tyōō-) *adj.*

tutorial system A system of education, generally in a college, in which each student is assigned to a tutor, who directs his studies and supervises his instruction.

tu·tor·ship (tōō′tər·ship, tyōō′-) *n.* **1.** The office of a tutor or of a guardian. Also **tu′tor·age** (-ij). **2.** Tutelage.

tu·toy·er (tü·twá·yā′) *v.t. French* To speak to with the French singular pronoun *tu, te, toi* instead of the more formal plural pronoun *vous;* address intimately.

tut·ti (tōō′tē) *Music adj.* All: a term used to indicate that all performers are to take part. —*n. pl.* **·tis** A composition, piece, movement, or passage for all the voices and instruments together. [< Ital., pl. of *tutto* all < L *totus*]

tut·ti-frut·ti (tōō′tē·frōō′tē) *n.* A confection, chewing gum, ice cream, etc., made with a mixture of fruits. —*adj.* Having fruit flavors. [< Ital., all fruits]

tut·ty (tut′ē) *n.* An impure zinc oxide from the flues of zinc-smelting furnaces, used as a polishing powder. [< OF *tutie* < Arabic *tūtiya* oxide of zinc, ? < Persian]

tu·tu (tü·tü′) *n. French* A short, full, projecting skirt consisting of many layers of sheer fabric, worn by ballet dancers.

Tu·tu·i·la (tōō′tōo·ē′lä) The chief island of American Samoa; about 40 sq. mi.

Tu·va Autonomous Region (tōō′və) An administrative division of the southern R.S.F.S.R.; 66,100 sq. mi.; pop. 231,000 (1970); center, Kyzyl: formerly *Tannu-Tuva People's Republic.* Also **Tu·vin·i·an Autonomous Region** (tōō·vin′ē·ən). *Russian* **Tu·vin·ska·ya Av·to·nom·na·ya Ob·last** (tōō·vyēn′ska·yə əv·tŏ·nŏ′′na·yə ôb′lə̄sty′).

tu·whit tu·whoo (tōō·hwit′ tōō·hwōō′) The cry of an owl. [Imit.]

tux·e·do (tuk·sē′dō) *n. pl.* **·dos** **1.** *U.S.* A man's semi-formal dinner coat without tails: also called *dinner coat, dinner jacket.* **2.** *U.S.* The suit of which the coat is a part Also **Tux·e′do.** [after *Tuxedo* Park, N.Y.; so called because first worn at the country club there]

tu·yère (twē·yâr′; twir; *Fr.* tüi·yâr′) *n. Metall.* The pipe through which a draft of air is forced into a furnace or forge: also spelled *twier, twyer.* [< F, nozzle < *tuyau* pipe]

TV (tē′vē′) *n. pl.* **TVs** or **TV′s** Television. —*adj.* Of or pertaining to television.

TV or **tv** Terminal velocity.

TVA or **T.V.A.** Tennessee Valley Authority.

TV dinner *U.S.* A precooked dinner frozen in an aluminum-foil tray that can be heated in an oven for a quick dinner, as eaten while watching television.

Tver (tvyĕr′) A former name for KALININ. Also **Tver′.**

twa (twä, twô) *adj. Scot.* Two.

twad·dle (twod′l) *v.t. & v.i.* **·dled, ·dling** To talk foolishly and pretentiously. —*n.* Pretentious, silly talk; also, a twaddler. [Prob. alter. of TWATTLE] —**twad′dler** *n.*

twain (twān) *adj. Archaic & Poetic* Two. —*n.* **1.** A couple; two. **2.** In river navigation, two fathoms or twelve feet. [OE *twēgen,* masculine of *twā* two]

Twain (twān), **Mark** See MARK TWAIN.

twang (twang) *v.t. & v.i.* **twanged, twang·ing 1.** To make or cause to make a sharp, vibrant sound, as a bowstring. **2.** To utter or speak nasally. —*n.* **1.** A sharp, vibrating sound, as of a tense string plucked. **2.** Excessive nasality of the voice. **3.** A sound resembling either of the foregoing. Also *tang.* [Imit.] —**twang′y** *adj.*

twan·gle (twang′gəl) *v.t. & v.i.* **·gled, ·gling** To twang. —*n.* A twang. [Freq. of TWANG] —**twan′gler** *n.*

Twan·kay (twang′kā) *n.* A variety of green tea. Also **twan·ky** (twang′kē). [after Chinese *T'un ch'i,* town in Anwhei province, where originally grown]

'twas (twaz) *Archaic or Poetic* It was.

twa·some (twä′səm, twô′-) *Scot. n.* A twosome; a pair.

twat·tle (twot′l) *v.t. & v.i.* **·tled, ·tling** *n.* Twaddle. [Short for *twittle-twattle.* var. of TITTLE-TATTLE]

tway·blade (twā′blād) *n.* Any of various hardy terrestrial orchids (genera *Listera* or *Liparis*) with two broad leaves. [< archaic *tway* two, var. of TWAIN + BLADE]

tweak (twēk) *v.t.* To pinch and twist sharply; twitch. —*n.* A twisting pinch; twitch. [Var. of dial. *twick,* OE *twiccian* to twitch] —**tweak′y** *adj.*

tweed (twēd) *n.* **1.** A soft woolen fabric with a homespun surface, often woven in two or more colors to effect a check or plaid pattern. **2.** *pl.* Clothing of tweed. —**Harris tweed** A homespun woolen cloth, usually of mixed colors, made at Harris in the Hebrides. [Alter. of dial. E (Scottish) *tweel,* var. of TWILL; prob. infl. in form by *Tweed* river, that flows through the district where it is woven]

Tweed (twēd) A river in Peeblesshire, Scotland, forming part of the boundary between England and Scotland, and flowing 97 miles NE to the North Sea.

Tweed (twēd), **William Marcy,** 1823–78, U.S. political boss: called **Boss Tweed.**

Tweed·dale (twēd′dāl) See PEEBLES.

twee·dle¹ (twēd′l) *v.* **·dled, ·dling** *v.t.* **1.** To play (a musical instrument) casually or carelessly. **2.** To wheedle; cajole. —*v.i.* **3.** To produce a series of shrill tones. **4.** To play a musical instrument casually or carelessly. —*n.* A sound resembling the tones of a violin. [Imit.]

twee·dle² (twēd′l) *v.* **·dled, ·dling** *v.t.* **1.** To handle carelessly. —*v.i.* **2.** To wriggle. [Var. of TWIDDLE]

twee·dle·dum and twee·dle·dee (twēd′l·dum′, twēd′l·dē′) Two things between which there is only the slightest possible distinction. [Orig. imit. of low- and high-pitched musical instruments, respectively, from John Byrom, *On the Feuds between Handel and Bononcini* (1723)]

Tweedledum and Tweedledee Nearly identical twin brothers in Lewis Carroll's *Through the Looking-Glass.*

Tweed Ring The political group, headed by William M. Tweed, that controlled New York City government (1865–1871) and plundered millions of dollars. —**Tweed′ism** *n.*

Tweeds·muir (twēdz′myŏor), **Baron** See BUCHAN.

'tween (twēn) Contraction of BETWEEN.

tweet (twēt) *v.i.* To utter a thin, chirping note. —*n.* A twittering or chirping. Also **tweet′-tweet′.** [Imit.]

tweet·er (twē′tər) *n. Electronics* A small loudspeaker used to reproduce high-pitched sounds in high-fidelity sound equipment. Compare WOOFER. [< TWEET]

tweeze (twēz) *v.t.* **tweezed, tweez·ing** *Informal* To handle, pluck, etc., with tweezers. [Back formation < TWEEZERS]

tweez·ers (twē′zərz) *n.pl.* Small pincers for grasping and holding small objects. Also called **pair of tweezers.** [Alter. of *tweezes,* pl. of *tweeze,* earlier *etweese* case of small instruments < F *étuis,* pl. of *étui.* Akin to ETUI.]

twelfth (twelfth) *adj.* **1.** Next after eleven: the ordinal of *twelve.* **2.** Being one of twelve equal parts. —*n.* **1.** One of twelve equal parts. **2.** That which follows the eleventh. [OE *twelfta*]

Twelfth-day (twelfth′dā′) *n.* Epiphany.

Twelfth-night (twelfth′nīt′) *n.* The evening (Jan. 5th) before Epiphany; sometimes, the evening (Jan. 6th) of Epiphany. —*adj.* Of or pertaining to Twelfth-night.

Twelfth-tide (twelfth′tīd′) *n.* The season of Epiphany.

twelve (twelv) *n.* **1.** The sum of eleven and one: a cardinal number. **2.** Any symbol of this number, as 12, xii, XII. **3.** Anything consisting of or representing twelve units. —**the Twelve** The twelve apostles See APOSTLE (def. 1). —*adj.* Being one more than eleven. [OE *twelf*]

Twelve Apostles 1. A governing body of the Mormon Church. **2.** The twelve disciples of Jesus.

twelve·mo (twelv′mō) *adj. & n.* Duodecimo.

twelve·month (twelv′munth′) *n.* A year.

twelve-tone (twelv′tōn′) *adj. Music* **1.** Of, using, or composed in the technique of serialism developed by Arnold Schönberg, in which the tone rows consist of all the tones of the chromatic scale, and tonal centers are avoided: also *dodecaphonic.* **2.** In 20th-century music, using or composed in a freely chromatic style.

twen·ti·eth (twen′tē·ith) *adj.* **1.** Tenth in order after ten: the ordinal of *twenty.* **2.** Being one of twenty equal parts. —*n.* **1.** One of twenty equal parts. **2.** That which is tenth in order after the tenth. [OE *twēntigotha*]

twen·ty (twen′tē) *n. pl.* **·ties 1.** The sum of nineteen and one: a cardinal number. **2.** Any symbol of this number, as 20, xx, XX. **3.** Anything consisting of or representing twenty units, as an organization, bill, etc. —*adj.* Being one more than nineteen. [OE *twēntig*]

twen·ty-one (twen′tē·wun′) *n.* A card game in which each player bets against the dealer, the object being to draw cards whose value will equal or approach twenty-one without exceeding that amount: also called *blackjack, vingt-et-un.*

'twere (twûr) *Archaic or Poetic* It were.

twerp (twûrp) *n. Slang* A small, impudent person: also spelled *twirp.* [Origin unknown]

Twi (twē) *n.* Ashanti (def. 2).

twi- *prefix* Two; double; twice: *twibil.* Also spelled *twy-.* [OE, double < *twā* two]

twi·bil (twī′bil) *n.* **1.** A battle-ax with two cutting edges. **2.** A mattock having one blade like an ax and the other an adze. Also **twi′bill.** [OE < *twi-* two + *bill* ax]

twice (twīs) *adv.* **1.** Two times. **2.** In double measure; doubly. [OE *twiges,* gen. of *twiga* twice]

twice-laid (twīs′lād′) *adj.* **1.** Made from the yarns of old or used rope. **2.** Made from remnants or refuse.

twice-told (twīs′tōld′) *adj.* Told more than once.

Twick·en·ham (twik′ən·əm, twik′nəm) A municipal borough SW of London, England, on the Thames; home of Alexander Pope; pop. 100,822 (1961).

TWIBIL (def. 1)

twid·dle (twid′l) *v.* **·dled, ·dling** *v.t.* **1.** To twirl idly; toy or play with. — *v.i.* **2.** To revolve or twirl. **3.** To toy with something idly. **4.** To be busy about trifles. — **to twiddle one's thumbs 1.** To rotate one's thumbs idly around one another. **2.** To pass time in doing nothing. — *n.* A gentle twirling, as of the fingers. [Origin unknown] — **twid′dler** *n.*

twi·er (twī′ər) See TUYÈRE.

twig¹ (twig) *n.* A small shoot or branchlet of a tree. ◆ Collateral adjective: *viminal.* [OE *twigge*] — **twig′less** *adj.*

twig² (twig) *v.* **twigged, twig·ging** *Brit. Slang v.t.* **1.** To observe; notice; watch. **2.** To comprehend; understand. — *v.i.* **3.** To understand. [Cf. Irish *tuigim* I understand]

twig³ (twig) *n. Archaic* The fashion: an old fop in good *twig.* [Origin uncertain]

twig blight Dieback, especially when due to abnormal conditions of development.

twig borer The larva of a lepidopterous insect (*Anarsia lineatella*) that bores into the twigs of certain fruit trees, as the peach, plum, and apricot.

twigged (twigd) *adj.* Having shoots or twigs.

twig·gen (twig′ən) *adj.* Made of twigs; wicker.

twig girdler *Entomol.* A girdler (which see).

twig·gy (twig′ē) *adj.* **·gi·er, ·gi·est** Like or full of twigs.

twi·light (twī′līt′) *n.* **1.** The light diffused over the sky when the sun is below the horizon, especially in the evening; also, the period during which this light is prevalent. ◆ Collateral adjective: *crepuscular.* **2.** Any faint light. **3.** A condition following the waning of past glory, achievement, etc. — *adj.* Pertaining to, resembling, or characteristic of twilight. [ME *twylight* < OE *twi-* (< *twa* two) + LIGHT; used in the sense of "the light between the two," i.e., between day and night]

twilight of the gods See RAGNARÖK.

twilight sleep *Med.* A light or partial anesthesia as by injection of morphine and scopolamine, sometimes used to relieve childbirth pains. [Trans. of G *dämmerschlaf*]

twill (twil) *n.* **1.** A weave characterized by diagonal ribs or lines in fabrics. **2.** A fabric woven with a twill; twilled cloth. — *v.t.* To weave (cloth) so as to produce diagonal lines or ribs on the surface. [Var. of ME *twile*, OE *twilic* twilled fabric < *twi-* < *twa* two, partial trans. of L *bilix* having a double thread]

'twill (twil) *Archaic or Poetic* It will.

twilled (twild) *adj.* Woven so as to produce a diagonal rib or line; ribbed or ridged.

twin (twin) *n.* **1.** One of two young produced at the same time. **2.** The counterpart or exact mate of another. **3.** *Crystall.* An intergrowth of two or more crystals of the same substance according to some definite law, a single plane or axis usually being common to the different individuals. — *adj.* **1.** Being, or standing in the relation of, a twin or twins. **2.** Consisting of, forming, or being one of a pair of similar and closely related objects; double; twofold. — *v.* **twinned, twin·ning** *v.i.* **1.** To bring forth twins. **2.** To be matched or equal; agree. **3.** *Archaic* To be born as a twin. — *v.t.* **4.** To bring forth as twins. **5.** To couple; match. **6.** *Scot.* To separate: also *twine.* [OE *twinn.* Cf. ON *tvinnr, tvennr* double]

TWILL
(Enlarged to show weave)

twin bed One of a pair of matching single beds.

twin·ber·ry (twin′ber′ē, -bər-ē) *n. pl.* **·ries 1.** The partridgeberry (which see). **2.** A North American shrub (*Lonicera involucrata*) with elliptic leaves, yellowish red flowers, and shining black berries.

twin-born (twin′bôrn′) *adj.* Born as a twin or twins.

Twin Cities Minneapolis and St. Paul, Minnesota.

twine¹ (twīn) *v.* **twined, twin·ing** *v.t.* **1.** To twist together, as threads. **2.** To form by such twisting. **3.** To coil or wrap about something. **4.** To encircle by winding or wreathing. **5.** To enfold; embrace. — *v.i.* **6.** To interlace; become twined. **7.** To proceed in a winding course; meander. — *adj.* Of or like twine. — *n.* **1.** A string composed of two or more strands twisted together; loosely, any small cord. **2.** The act of twining or entwining. **3.** A form or conformation produced by twining. **4.** An interweaving or interlacing. **5.** *Obs.* A twisting; spin. [OE *twin* twisted double thread < *twi-* double < *twa* two] — **twin′er** *n.*

twine² (twīn) *v.t.* **twined, twin·ing** *Scot.* To separate. [See TWIN]

twin·flow·er (twin′flou′ər) *n.* A trailing evergreen plant (genus *Linnaea*) of the honeysuckle family, as the Old World species (*L. borealis*) with fragrant rose or white bell-shaped flowers, and its American variety (*L. borealis americana*).

twinge (twinj) *n.* **1.** A sharp, darting, local pain. **2.** A mental or emotional pang. — **Syn.** See PAIN. — *v.t. & v.i.* **twinged, twing·ing** To affect with or suffer a sudden pain or twinge. [OE *twengan* to pinch]

twi·night (twī′nīt′) *adj. U.S. Informal* Beginning in the late afternoon and continuing under artificial light into the night, as a baseball game. [Blend of TWILIGHT and NIGHT]

twin·kle (twing′kəl) *v.* **·kled, ·kling** *v.i.* **1.** To shine with

fitful, intermittent gleams, as a star. **2.** To be bright, as with amusement: Her eyes *twinkled.* **3.** To wink or blink; open and shut with a quick, involuntary motion. **4.** To move rapidly to and fro; flicker: *twinkling* feet. — *v.t.* **5.** To emit or cause to flash out, as gleams of light. **6.** To move (the eyelids) quickly and repeatedly. — **Syn.** See SHINE. — *n.* **1.** A tremulous gleam of light; sparkle; glimmer. **2.** A wink or sparkle of the eye. **3.** An instant; a twinkling. **4.** A flickering of the eyelids. [OE *twinclian*] — **twin′kler** *n.*

twin·kling (twing′kling) *n.* **1.** The act of scintillating. **2.** A wink or twinkle. **3.** The act of winking, or the time required for it. **4.** A moment.

twin-leaf (twin′lēf′) *n.* A small perennial herb (*Jeffersonia diphylla*) of the barberry family, native in eastern North America, and having leaves divided into two lobes.

twinned (twind) *adj.* **1.** Produced at one birth. **2.** Paired with something identical or similar. **3.** Formed by twinning, as a crystal.

twin·ning (twin′ing) *n.* **1.** The production of two young at one birth; the bearing of twins. **2.** Close union or combination; coupling of two related objects. **3.** *Crystall.* The formation of twin crystals.

Twins (twinz) *n.pl.* The constellation and sign of the zodiac Gemini.

twin-screw (twin′skrōō′) *adj. Naut.* Having two propeller shafts, one on each side of a vessel's keel, and two propellers, normally turning in opposite directions.

twin-ship (twin′ship′) *n.* **1.** The character or condition of being a twin. **2.** The relation of a twin or twins.

twirl (twûrl) *v.t. & v.i.* **1.** To whirl or rotate. **2.** In baseball, to pitch. — *n.* **1.** A whirling motion. **2.** A quick twisting action, as of the fingers. **3.** A curl; twist; coil. [Alter. of ME *tirlen,* var. of *trillen* (see TRILL²); appar. infl. by *whirl*] — **twirl′er** *n.*

twirp (twûrp) See TWERP.

twist (twist) *v.t.* **1.** To wind (strands, etc.) around each other. **2.** To form by such winding: to *twist* thread. **3.** To give spiral, circular, or semicircular form to, as by turning at either end. **4.** To force out of natural shape; distort or contort. **5.** To distort the meaning of. **6.** To confuse; perplex. **7.** To wreathe, twine, or wrap. **8.** To cause to revolve or rotate. **9.** To impart spin to (a ball) so that it moves in a curve. — *v.i.* **10.** To become twisted. **11.** To move in a winding course; meander or bend. **12.** To squirm; writhe. **13.** To dance the twist. — **Syn.** See BEND¹. — *n.* **1.** The act, manner, or result of twisting or turning on an axis. **2.** The state of being twisted. **3.** *Physics* A torsional strain. **b** The angle of torsion, as of a rod or bar. **4.** A curve; turn; bend: a path full of *twists* and turns. **5.** A contortion or twisting of a facial or bodily feature. **6.** A wrench; strain, as of a joint or limb. **7.** A peculiar or perverted inclination, bent, or attitude: the *twist* of a criminal's mind. **8.** A deviation, variation, or distinctive difference: a *twist* of meaning. **9.** A different or novel approach or angle. **10.** A sudden, unexpected change against or apart from the prevailing course. **11.** Thread or cord made of tightly twisted strands. **12.** One of the strands of a rope. **13.** A twisted roll or loaf of bread. **14.** Tobacco twisted in the form of a large cord. **15.** In baseball, billiards, tennis, etc.: **a** A spin or whirling motion given to a ball. **b** The stroke or throw producing such a spin. **16.** A dance characterized by a twisting or turning movement from side to side. [ME *twisten* to divide in two, combine two, prob. < OE *-twist* rope, as in *mæst-twist* rope to stay a mast < *twi-* double < *twa* two]

twist drill *Mech.* A drill or bit having deep spiral grooves.

twist·er (twis′tər) *n.* **1.** One who or that which twists. **2.** A ball, as in cricket, bowled with a twist. **3.** In baseball, a curve; also, one who pitches a curve. **4.** *U.S.* A tornado.

twit (twit) *v.t.* **twit·ted, twit·ting** To taunt, reproach, or annoy by reminding of a mistake, fault, etc. — *n.* **1.** A taunting allusion; reproach. **2.** *Informal* A nervous or edgy state. [Aphetic var. of ME *atwite,* OE *æwītan* to taunt < *æt-* at + *witan* to accuse]

twitch (twich) *v.t.* **1.** To pull sharply; pluck with a jerky movement. **2.** In lumbering, to drag or skid (logs) along the ground with a chain. — *v.i.* **3.** To move with a quick, spasmodic jerk. — *n.* **1.** A sudden involuntary contraction of a muscle. **2.** A sudden jerk or pull. [ME *twicchen,* Akin to OE *twiccian* to pluck.] — **twitch′ing·ly** *adv.*

twitch grass Couch grass (which see).

twit·ter¹ (twit′ər) *v.i.* **1.** To utter a series of light chirping or tremulous notes, as a bird. **2.** To titter. **3.** To be excited; tremble. — *v.t.* **4.** To utter or express with a twitter. — *n.* **1.** The act of twittering. **2.** A succession of light, tremulous sounds. **3.** A state of nervous agitation. [Imit.] — **twit′ter·er** *n.* — **twit′ter·y** *adj.*

twit·ter² (twit′ər) *n.* One who twits.

twixt (twikst) *prep. Poetic* Betwixt. Also **'twixt.**

two (tōō) *n.* **1.** The sum of one and one: a cardinal number.

2. Any symbol of this number, as 2, ii, II.   **3.** Anything consisting of or representing two units, as a playing card, etc.   **4.** A couple; pair. **— in two** So as to be in two parts or pieces; asunder. **— to put two and two together** To reach the obvious conclusion. **—** *adj.* Being one more than one. [OE *twā, tū*]

two-base hit (tōō′bās′) In baseball, a base hit that enables the batter to reach second base; a double. Also *Slang* **two′-bag′ger** (-bag′ər)

two-bit (tōō′bit′) *adj. U.S. Slang* Cheap; small-time.

two bits *U.S. Informal* **1.** Twenty-five cents. **2.** A trifling or insignificant sum.

two-by-four (*adj.* tōō′bī-fôr′, -fōr′; *n.* tōō′bī-fôr′, -fōr′) *adj.* **1.** Measuring two inches by four inches. **2.** *U.S. Slang* Of trifling size or significance. **—** *n.* A piece of lumber actually measuring 1⅝ inches by 3⅝ inches, much used in building.

two cents' worth *U.S. Slang* The expression of an opinion or point of view, especially during a discussion.

two-cy-cle (tōō′sī′kəl) *n. Mech.* A cycle of operations in an internal-combustion engine in which fuel is taken into the cylinder, compressed, burned, and exhausted in two successive strokes of the piston: also called *two-stroke cycle.* **—** *adj.* Having a cycle of two strokes.

two-edged (tōō′ejd′) *adj.* **1.** Having an edge on each side, as a sword or knife blade. **2.** Having two meanings, effects, etc., as an argument, supposed compliment, etc.

two-faced (tōō′fāst′) *adj.* **1.** Having two faces. **2.** Double-dealing. **— two′-fac′ed-ly** (-fā′sid-lē, -fāst′lē) *adv.*

two-fer (tōō′fər) *U.S. Slang n.* **1.** An article advertised or sold at the rate of two for the price of one. **2.** A coupon entitling the holder to two theater tickets for the price of one. **—** *adj.* Offering two of anything for the price of one: a *twofer* sale. [Alter. of *two for (one)*]

two-fist-ed (tōō′fis′tid) *adj. U.S. Informal* Vigorous and aggressive.

two-fold (tōō′fōld′) *n.* An amount or number two times as great as a given unit. **—** *adv.* So as to be two times as many or as great. **—** *adj.* **1.** Consisting of two parts. **2.** Two times as many or as great.

two-hand-ed (tōō′han′did) *adj.* **1.** Requiring both hands at once. **2.** Constructed for use by two persons. **3.** Ambidextrous. **4.** Having two hands.

two-mas-ter (tōō′mas′tər, -mäs′-) *n.* A ship with two masts.

two-name (tōō′nām′) *adj.* Bearing two names or signatures.

two-name paper In banking, a negotiable paper bearing two signatures, two persons being responsible for payment.

two-pence (tup′əns) *n. Brit.* **1.** Money of account of the value of two pennies. **2.** A silver coin of the same value, now issued only for alms money, distributed on Maundy Thursday. **3.** A trifle; small amount: She doesn't care *twopence* about him. Also, *Informal,* **tuppence.**

two-pen-ny (tup′ən-ē) *adj. Brit.* **1.** Of the price or value of twopence. **2.** Cheap; worthless. Also, *Informal,* **tuppenny.**

two-phase (tōō′fāz′) *adj. Electr.* Diphase (which see).

two-ply (tōō′plī′) *adj.* **1.** Made of two united webs; woven double: a *two-ply* carpet. **2.** Made of two strands, layers, or thicknesses of material.

Two Sic-i-lies (sis′ə-lēz), **The** A kingdom formed by the union of Sicily with Naples in 1130; incorporated with Italy in 1861.

two-some (tōō′səm) *n.* **1.** Two persons together; a couple. **2.** A golf match with one player on each side.

two-spot (tōō′spot′) *n.* **1.** A playing card having two pips; a deuce. **2.** *U.S. Slang* A small or unimportant person. **3.** *U.S. Slang* A two-dollar bill.

two-step (tōō′step′) *n.* A ballroom dance consisting of a sliding step in 2/4 meter; also, the music for it.

two-stroke cycle (tōō′strōk′) Two-cycle (which see).

two-time (tōō′tīm′) *v.t.* **-timed, -tim-ing** *Slang* To be unfaithful to in love; deceive. **— two′-tim′er** *n.*

two-way (tōō′wā′) *adj.* **1.** Characterized by or permitting movement in two directions: a *two-way* street. **2.** Having or affording communication in two directions: a *two-way* telephone conversation. **3.** Of cocks and valves, having an arrangement that will permit a fluid to be directed in either of two channels. **4.** *Math.* Having a double mode of variation.

twp. Township.

twy- See TWI-.

twy-er (twī′ər) See TUYERE.

-ty¹ *suffix of nouns* The state or condition of being: *sanity.* [< F *-té* < L *-tas*]

-ty² *suffix* Ten; ten times: used in numerals, as *thirty, forty,* etc. [OE *-tig* ten]

Ty. Territory.

Ty-burn (tī′bərn) A former place of public execution in London, England.

Ty-che (tī′kē) In Greek mythology, the goddess of chance: identified with the Roman *Fortuna.*

Ty-cho (tū′kō) See BRAHE.

ty-coon (tī-kōōn′) *n.* **1.** *U.S. Informal* A wealthy and powerful industrial or business leader. **2.** A shogun. [< Japanese *taikun* mighty lord < Chinese *ta* great + *kiun* prince]

Ty-deus (tī′dyōōs, -dē-əs) An ancient Greek hero. See SEVEN AGAINST THEBES.

ty-ee (tī′ē) *n. U.S. & Canadian* The chinook salmon. [< Chinook jargon]

tyke (tīk) *n.* **1.** *Informal* A small child. **2.** A mongrel dog; cur. **3.** *Scot.* An uncouth fellow; a boor. **4.** *Brit. Dial.* A man from Yorkshire. Also spelled *tike.* [< ON *tik* bitch]

Ty-ler (tī′lər) A city in eastern Texas; pop. 57,770.

Ty-ler (tī′lər), **John,** 1790–1862, tenth president of the United States 1841–45. **— Wat,** died 1381, English rebel; led a peasant revolt 1381; killed: original name **Walter Tyler.**

tym-bal (tim′bəl) See TIMBAL.

tym-pan (tim′pən) *n.* **1.** *Printing* A thickness or several thicknesses of paper, etc., placed on the platen of a printing press to improve the quality of the presswork. **2.** *Archit.* A tympanum. **3.** A membrane, or any tightly stretched sheet, as on a drum. [< OF < L *tympanum.* See TYMPANUM.]

tym-pa-ni (tim′pə-nē) See TIMPANI.

tym-pan-ic (tim-pan′ik) *adj.* **1.** Of or resembling a drum. **2.** Of or pertaining to a tympanum or to the middle ear. Also **tym-pa-nal** (tim′pə-nəl).

tympanic bone *Anat.* A bony ring that surrounds the external auditory canal and supports the tympanic membrane.

tympanic membrane *Anat.* The membrane separating the middle ear from the external ear: also called *eardrum.* For illustration see EAR.

tym-pa-nist (tim′pə-nist) *n.* One who beats or plays upon a drum, especially a kettledrum.

tym-pa-ni-tes (tim′pə-nī′tēz) *n. Pathol.* A drumlike swelling of the abdomen due to accumulation of gas. [< LL < Gk. *tympanitēs* < *tympanon.* See TYMPANUM.] **— tym′pa-nit′ic** (-nit′ik) *adj.*

tym-pa-ni-tis (tim′pə-nī′tis) *n. Pathol.* Inflammation of the mucous membrane lining the tympanum.

tym-pa-num (tim′pə-nəm) *n. pl.* **-na** (-nə) or **-nums 1.** *Anat.* **a** The middle ear. **b** The tympanic membrane. **2.** *Archit.* An ornamental space, as over a doorway, enclosed by an arch or the coping of a pediment: also called *tympan.* **3.** A drumlike membrane or part. **4.** *Electr.* The diaphragm in a telephone. Also spelled *timpanum.* [< NL < L, drum < Gk. *tympanon* < *typtein* to beat]

tym-pa-ny (tim′pə-nē) *n. pl.* **-nies 1.** Tympanites. **2.** Inflated or bombastic style, manner, etc. [< Med.L *tympanias* < Gk. < *tympanon* drum]

Tyn-dale (tin′dəl), **William,** 1484?–1536, English religious reformer; translated New Testament; executed for heresy.

Tyn-dall (tin′dəl), **John,** 1820–93, British physicist born in Ireland.

Tyndall effect *Physics* The scattering of light passing through a medium containing minute suspended particles in continuous rapid motion. Also **Tyndall phenomenon.** [after John *Tyndall*]

Tyn-dar-e-us (tin-dâr′ē-əs) In Greek mythology, a king of Sparta and husband of Leda.

Tyne (tīn) A river in Northumberland, Tyne and Wear, and Durham, England, flowing 30 miles south to the North Sea.

Tyne and Wear (wir) A metropolitan county in NE England; 208 sq. mi.; pop. 1,189,500 (1976); county town, Newcastle-upon-Tyne.

typ. Typographic(al); typography.

ty-pal (tī′pəl) *adj.* Of or pertaining to a type; typical.

type (tīp) *n.* **1.** A class, kind, or group sharing one or more characteristics; category. **2.** A variety or style of a particular class or kind of things; sort: an unusual *type* of can opener. **3.** *Biol.* **a** An organism whose structural and functional characteristics make it representative of a group, species, class, etc. **b** A taxonomic group considered as representative of the next higher category in a system of classification: the *type* genus. **4.** *Printing* A piece or block of metal or of wood, bearing on its upper surface, usually in relief, a letter or character for use in printing; also, such pieces collectively. See POINT SYSTEM. **5.** Printed or typewritten characters. **6.** A distinctive sign; stamp; mark. **7.** A standard or model. **8.** In coinage, the characteristic device on either side of a medal or coin. **9.** *Theol.* That by which something is prefigured. **10.** *Informal* A person. ◆ In business English and in informal speech, *type* is often used for *type of,* as in *This type car is very popular.* **—** *v.* **typed, typ-ing** *v.t.* **1.** To typewrite (something). **2.** To determine the type of; identify: to *type* a blood sample. **3.** To assign to a particular type. **4.** To represent; typify. **5.** To prefigure. **—** *v.i.* **6.** To typewrite. [< MF < L *typus* < Gk. *typos* impression, figure, type < *typtein* to strike]

-type *combining form* **1.** Representative form; type: *prototype.* **2.** Printing; duplicating or photographic process; type: *Linotype, collotype.* [< Gk. *typos* stamp]

type-cast (tīp′kast′, -käst′) *v.t.* **-cast, -cast-ing** To cast, as an actor, in a role considered to be suited to his appearance, personality, etc.

type·face (tīp′fās′) *n.* **1.** Face (def. 15). **2.** A set of type having a consistent design.

type foundry An establishment in which metal type is made. — **type founder** — **type founding**

type genus *Biol.* A genus that combines the essential characteristics of the family or higher group to which it belongs. Abbr. *t.g.*

type-high (tīp′hī′) *adj. Printing* Designating the height of type from base to the level of the printing surface, in the United States, 0.9186 of an inch: also *letter-high.*

type metal *Printing* The alloy of which type is made, usually of lead, tin, and antimony, in various proportions.

type·script (tīp′skript′) *n.* Matter that has been typewritten. [< TYPE(WRITTEN) + SCRIPT]

type·set·ter (tīp′set′ər) *n.* **1.** One who sets type: also called *compositor.* **2.** A machine for composing type. — **type′·set′ting** *n.*

type species *Biol.* The species regarded as most typical of the genus to which its name is given.

type specimen *Biol.* The individual plant or animal on whose description the distinguishing characteristics of a species are based.

type·write (tīp′rīt′) *v.t. & v.i.* ·wrote, ·writ·ten, ·writ·ing To write with a typewriter: also *type.*

type·writ·er (tīp′rī′tər) *n.* **1.** A machine equipped with a keyboard, that produces printed characters by impressing type upon paper through an inked ribbon. **2.** *Archaic* A typist.

type·writ·ing (tīp′rī′ting) *n.* **1.** The act or operation of one who uses a typewriter. **2.** Typescript.

typh·li·tis (tif·lī′tis) *n. Pathol.* Inflammation of the cecum. [< NL < Gk. *typhlos* blind] — **typh·lit′ic** (lit′ik) *adj.*

typhlo- *combining form* **1.** Blindness: *typhlology.* **2.** *Anat. & Med.* The cecum. Also, before vowels, **typhl-.** [< Gk. *typhlos* blind]

typh·lol·o·gy (tif·lol′ə·jē) *n. pl.* ·gies The branch of science that deals with blindness. [< TYPHLO- + -LOGY]

typho- *combining form* Typhus; typhoid: *typhogenic.* Also, before vowels, **typh-.** [< Gk. *typhos* smoke, stupor]

Ty·phoe·us (tī·fē′əs) In Greek mythology, a giant with a hundred snake heads, killed by Zeus's thunderbolt. — **Ty·phoe·an** (tī′fē·ən) *adj.*

ty·pho·gen·ic (tī′fə·jen′ik) *adj.* Producing typhus or typhoid.

ty·phoid (tī′foid) *n.* Typhoid fever. — *adj.* Of, pertaining to or resembling typhoid fever: also **ty·phoi′dal, ty′phose** (-fōs). [< TYPH(US) + -OID]

typhoid bacillus A motile, flagellated, Gram-negative bacterium (*Salmonella typhosa*), the pathogen of typhoid fever.

typhoid fever *Pathol.* An acute, infectious fever caused by the typhoid bacillus and characterized by severe intestinal disturbances, an eruption of rose-red spots on the chest and abdomen, and physical prostration: also called *enteric fever.*

ty·phoi·din (tī·foi′din) *n. Bacteriol.* A culture of dead typhoid bacilli, used as a test for passive or active infection.

ty·pho·ma·lar·i·al (tī′fō·mə·lâr′ē·əl) *adj. Pathol.* Designating a fever like typhoid but malarial in origin. [< TYPHO- + MALARIAL]

Ty·phon (tī′fon) In Greek mythology, a monster overcome by Zeus and buried under Mount Etna.

ty·phoon (tī·foon′) *n. Meteorol.* A hurricane originating over tropical waters in the western Pacific and the China Sea. [< dial. Chinese *tai feng,* lit., big wind; infl. by obs. *typhon* whirlwind (< Gk. *typhōn* hurricane)]

ty·phus (tī′fəs) *n. Pathol.* An acute, contagious disease caused by a microorganism (*Rickettsia prowazeki*) and marked by high fever, with eruption of red spots, cerebral disorders, and extreme prostration. **Epidemic typhus** is transmitted by the bite of the body louse (*Pediculus humanus*) and **endemic** or **murine typhus** by the bite of a flea (*Xenopsylla cheopis*): also called *spotted fever.* Also **typhus fever.** [< NL < Gk. *typhos* smoke, stupor < *typhein* to smoke] — **ty′phous** (-fəs) *adj.*

typ·i·cal (tip′i·kəl) *adj.* **1.** Having the nature or character of a type; constituting a type or pattern. **2.** Conforming to the essential features of a species, group, class, pattern of action or behavior, etc.; characteristic. Also **typ′ic.** — **Syn.** See NORMAL. [< Med.L *typicalis* < L *typicus* < Gk. *typikos* < *typos.* See TYPE.] — **typ′i·cal·ly** *adv.* — **typ′i·cal·ness** *n.*

typ·i·fy (tip′ə·fī) *v.t.* ·fied, ·fy·ing **1.** To represent by a type; signify, as by an image or token. **2.** To constitute a type or serve as a characteristic example of. — **typ′i·fi·ca′tion** *n.* — **typ′i·fi′er** *n.*

typ·ist (tī′pist) *n.* **1.** One whose occupation is operating a typewriter. **2.** One who is able to operate a typewriter.

ty·po (tī′pō) *n. Informal* A typographical error.

typo- *combining form* Type; of or related to type: *typography.* Also, before vowels, *typ-.* [< Gk. *typos* stamp, type]

typo. or **typog.** Typographic(al); typography.

ty·pog·ra·pher (tī·pog′rə·fər) *n.* A printer.

ty·po·graph·i·cal (tī′pə·graf′i·kəl) *adj.* Of or relating to typography or printing. Also **ty′po·graph′ic.** Abbr. *typ., typo., typog.* — **ty′po·graph′i·cal·ly** *adv.*

ty·pog·ra·phy (tī·pog′rə·fē) *n. pl.* ·phies **1.** The arrangement of composed type. **2.** The style and appearance of printed matter. **3.** The act or art of composing and printing from type. Abbr. *typ., typo., typog.* [< TYPO- + -GRAPHY]

ty·pol·o·gy (tī·pol′ə·jē) *n. pl.* ·gies **1.** The study of types, as in systems of classification. **2.** A set or listing of types. [< TYPO- + -LOGY]

ty·poth·e·tae (tī·poth′ə·tē, tī′pə·thē′tē) *n.pl.* Printers collectively: used in the names of organized groups of printers. [< NL < Gk. *typos* (see TYPE) + *tithenai* to set, put]

Tyr (tür, tir) In Norse mythology, the god of war and son of Odin: identified with the Teutonic *Tiu:* also spelled *Tyrr.*

Tyr. Tyrone.

ty·ran·ni·cal (ti·ran′i·kəl, tī-) *adj.* Of or characteristic of a tyrant; harsh; despotic. Also **ty·ran′nic.** — **Syn.** See ABSOLUTE. — **ty·ran′ni·cal·ly** *adv.* — **ty·ran′ni·cal·ness** *n.*

ty·ran·ni·cide (ti·ran′ə·sīd, tī-) *n.* **1.** The killing of a tyrant. **2.** One who has killed a tyrant. [< F < L *tyrannicida* < *tyrannus* tyrant + *caedere* to kill]

tyr·an·nize (tir′ə·nīz) *v.* nized, ·niz·ing *v.i.* **1.** To exercise power cruelly or unjustly: often with *over.* **2.** To rule as a tyrant. — *v.t.* **3.** To treat tyrannically. Also *Brit.* **tyr′an·nise.** [< MF *tyranniser* < LL *tyrannizare* < Gk. *tyrannizein* < *tyrannos* tyrant] — **tyr′an·niz′er** *n.*

ty·ran·no·sau·rus (ti·ran′ə·sôr′əs, tī-) *n. Paleontol. pl.* ·rus·es A huge carnivorous dinosaur (*Tyrannosaurus rex*) that walked on its hind legs, inhabiting North America in the Cretaceous period. Also **ty·ran′no·saur.** [< NL < Gk. *tyrannos* tyrant + *sauros* lizard]

tyr·an·nous (tir′ə·nəs) *adj.* Despotic; tyrannical. — **Syn.** See ABSOLUTE. — **tyr′an·nous·ly** *adv.* — **tyr′an·nous·ness** *n.*

tyr·an·ny (tir′ə·nē) *n. pl.* ·nies **1.** Absolute power arbitrarily or unjustly administered; despotism. **2.** An arbitrarily cruel exercise of power; a tyrannical act. **3.** In Greek history, the office or the administration of a tyrant. **4.** Severity; roughness. [< OF *tirannie* < L *tyrannia* < *tyrannos* tyrant]

ty·rant (tī′rənt) *n.* **1.** One who rules oppressively or cruelly; a despot. **2.** One who exercises absolute power without legal warrant, whether ruling well or badly: the original meaning in ancient Greece. [< OF *tiran, tyran* < L *tyrannus* < Gk. *tyrannos* master, usurper]

tyre (tīr) See TIRE[2].

Tyre (tīr) A port and capital of ancient Phoenicia, on the site of modern Sur in SW Lebanon.

Tyr·i·an (tir′ē·ən) *adj.* **1.** Of or pertaining to Tyre. **2.** Having the color of Tyrian purple. — *n.* A native of Tyre.

Tyrian purple **1.** A purple or crimson dyestuff obtained by the ancient Greeks and Romans from certain species of the murex. **2.** A violet and purple color of high saturation and low brightness. Also **Tyrian dye.**

ty·ro (tī′rō) *n. pl.* ·ros A beginner; novice: also spelled *tiro.* — **Syn.** See NOVICE. [< Med.L < L *tiro* recruit]

Ty·rol (ti·rōl′, tir′ōl, tī′rōl) **1.** A region of western Austria and northern Italy, in the Alps: usually with *the.* **2.** A Province of western Austria; 4,883 sq. mi.; pop. 462,472 (1961), capital, Innsbruck: also *Tirol.* — **Ty·ro·le·an** (ti·rō′lē·ən, tī-) *adj. & n.*

Tyr·o·lese (tir′ō·lēz′, -lēs′) *adj.* Of or pertaining to the Tyrol or its inhabitants. — *n. pl.* ·lese A native of the Tyrol. Also spelled *Tirolese.*

Ty·ro·lienne (ti·rō·lyen′) *n.* A folk song resembling a ländler. [< F, fem. of *tyrolien* Tyrolean]

Ty·rone (ti·rōn′) A county of Ulster, Northern Ireland; 1,218 sq. mi.; pop. 136,600 (est. 1969); county seat, Omagh.

ty·ro·sin·ase (tī′rō·si·nās′, tir′ō-) *n. Biochem.* A plant and animal enzyme that converts tyrosine into melanine and other dark pigments. [< TYROSIN(E) + -ASE]

ty·ro·sine (tī′rə·sēn, -sin, tir′ə-) *n. Biochem.* A white crystalline amino acid, $C_9H_{11}O_3N$, formed by the hydrolysis of plant and animal proteins. [< Gk. *tyros* cheese + -INE[2]]

ty·ro·thri·cin (tī′rō·thrī′sin, -thris′in) *n.* An antibiotic isolated from a soil bacterium (*Bacillus brevis*), and used therapeutically in localized infections. [< TYRO(SINE) + Gk. *thrix, trichos* hair]

Tyrr (tür, tir) See TYR.

Tyr·rhe·ni·an Sea (ti·rē′nē·ən) The part of the Mediterranean between Italy, Sardinia, Corsica, and Sicily.

Tyr·tae·us (tûr·tē′əs) Seventh-century B.C. Greek poet.

Tyu·men (tyoo·men′, *Russ.* tyoo·myeny′′) A city in the SW central R.S.F.S.R.; pop. 269,000 (1970). Also **Tyu·men′.**

tzar (tsär), **tzar·dom** (tsär′dəm), etc. See CZAR, etc.

tzet·ze (tset′sē) See TSETSE.

tzi·gane (tsē·gän′) *n. Sometimes cap.* A Gypsy, especially a Hungarian Gypsy. — *adj.* Of or pertaining to Hungarian Gypsies or their music. [< F, < Hung. *czigány*]

U

u, U (yōō) *n. pl.* **u's, us, U's** or **Us** (yōōz) **1.** The twenty-first letter of the English alphabet. The shape of the letter U was derived from the Phoenician *vau* (*waw*), later adopted by the Greeks as *upsilon*. In the Roman alphabet it was written V and had both consonant and vowel value. In English U was formerly the uncial or cursive form of V; gradually V came to be preferred in initial position in writing, and, as the sound at the beginning of a word is ordinarily consonantal, U was finally restricted to vowel use. **2.** Any sound represented by the letter *u*. **3.** Anything shaped like a U. — *symbol. Chem.* Uranium (symbol U).

u. And (G *und*).

U. or **u.** **1.** Uncle. **2.** University. **3.** Upper.

UAR or **U.A.R.** United Arab Republic.

UAW or **U.A.W.** **1.** United Auto, Aircraft and Agricultural Implements Workers. **2.** United Automobile Workers of America.

U·ban·gi (ōō·bäng′gē) A river of central Africa, flowing 660 miles from NE Republic of the Congo (Leopoldville) to the Congo river. See map of CONGO.

U·ban·gi-Sha·ri (ōō·bäng′gē-shä′rē) A former French overseas territory in equatorial Africa. See CENTRAL AFRICAN REPUBLIC. *French* **Ou·ban·gui-Cha·ri** (ōō·bäⁿ·gē′shȧ rē′).

Ü·ber·mensch (ü′bər·mensh) *n. German* Superman.

u·bi·e·ty (yōō·bī′ə·tē) *n. Rare* The state of being in a place. [< NL *ubietas*, *-tatis* < L *ubi* where]

u·bi·que (yōō·bī′kwē) *adv. Latin* Everywhere.

u·biq·ui·tous (yōō·bik′wə·təs) *adj.* Existing, or seeming to exist, everywhere at once; omnipresent. Also **u·biq′ui·tar′y** (-ter′ē). — **u·biq′ui·tous·ly** *adv.* — **u·biq′ui·tous·ness** *n.*

u·biq·ui·ty (yōō·bik′wə·tē) *n.* **1.** The state of being in an indefinite number of places at once; omnipresence. **2.** The state of existing always without beginning or end. [< L *ubiquitas* < *ubique* everywhere]

u·bi su·pra (yōō′bī sōō′prə) *Latin* Where (mentioned) above. Abbr. *u.s.*

U-boat (yōō′bōt′) *n.* A German submarine. [< G *U-boot*, contraction of *Unterseeboot* undersea boat]

U-bolt (yōō′bōlt′) *n.* A bolt bent like the letter U, and fitted with a screw and nut at each end. For illustration see BOLT.

u.c. **1.** *Music* Soft pedal (Ital. *una corda* one string). **2.** *Printing* Upper case.

U·ca·ya·li (ōō′kä·yä′lē) A river in eastern Peru, flowing about 1,000 miles north to the Amazon.

U·che·an (yōō·chē′ən) *n.* A North American Indian linguistic stock, consisting only of the Yuchi tribe.

UCMJ *Mil.* Uniform Code of Military Justice.

U·dall (yōō′dl), **Nicholas,** 1505–56, English scholar and dramatist. Also *Uvedale.*

U.D.C. **1.** *Brit.* Union of Democratic Control. **2.** United Daughters of the Confederacy.

ud·der (ud′ər) *n.* A large, pendulous gland, secreting milk and provided with nipples or teats for the suckling of offspring, as in cows. [OE *ūder*]

U·di·ne (ōō′dē·nā) A commune in NE Italy; pop. 85,205 (1961).

u·do (ōō′dō) *n.* A bushy plant (*Aralia cordata*) of Japan and China that yields edible shoots. [< Japanese]

u·dom·e·ter (yōō·dom′ə·tər) *n.* A rain gauge. [< L *udus* moist + -METER] — **u·do·met·ric** (yōō′də·met′rik) *adj.* — **u·dom′e·try** *n.*

U.E.L. United Empire Loyalist.

Ue·le (wē′lā) A river in NE Republic of Zaire flowing 700 miles west to the Ubangi: also *Welle.*

U·fa (ōō·fä′) The capital of the Bashkir A.S.S.R., in the central part; pop. 546,000 (1970).

UFO Unidentified flying object: an official U.S. Air Force designation. Also **u·fo** (yōō′fō).

U·gan·da (yōō·gan′də, ōō·gän′dä) An independent member of the Commonwealth of Nations in east central Africa; 93,981 sq. mi.; pop. 9,764,000 (est. 1970); capital, Kampala. See maps of ETHIOPIA, NILE.

ugh (ukh, u, ŏŏkh, ŏŏ) *interj.* An exclamation of repugnance or disgust. [Imit.]

ug·li·fy (ug′lə·fī) *v.t.* **·fied, ·fy·ing** To make ugly. — **ug′li·fi·ca′tion** (-fə·kā′shən) *n.*

ug·ly (ug′lē) *adj.* **·li·er, ·li·est 1.** Displeasing to the esthetic feelings; distasteful in appearance; ill-looking; unsightly. **2.** Repulsive to the moral sentiments; revolting. **3.** Bad in character or consequences, as a rumor, wound, etc. **4.** *Informal* Ill-tempered; quarrelsome. **5.** Portending storms; threatening: said of the weather. [< ON *uggligr* dreadful < *uggr* fear] — **ug′li·ly** *adv.* — **ug′li·ness** *n.*

ugly duckling Any ill-favored or unpromising child who unexpectedly grows beautiful or remarkable, as did the little swan in Hans Christian Andersen's story.

U·gri·an (ōō′grē·ən, yōō′-) *n.* **1.** A member of any of the Finno-Ugric peoples of Hungary and western Siberia, including the Ostyaks, Voguls, and Magyars. **2.** Ugric. — *adj.* Of or pertaining to the Ugrians, their culture, or their languages.

U·gric (ōō′grik, yōō′-) *n.* A branch of the Finno-Ugric subfamily of Uralic languages, comprising Magyar (Hungarian), Ostyak, and Vogul. — *adj.* Of or pertaining to any of these languages.

U·gro-Fin·nic (ōō′grō·fin′ik; yōō-) See FINNO-UGRIC.

UHF or **U.H.F., uhf** or **u.h.f.** Ultrahigh-frequency.

uh·lan (ōō′län, ōō·län′, yōō′lən) *n.* **1.** A cavalryman and lancer of a type originating in eastern Europe, formerly prominent in European armies, notably the German. **2.** One of a body of Tatar militia. Also spelled *ulan.* [< G < Polish < Turkish *ōghlān* lad, servant]

Uh·land (ōō′länt), **Johann Ludwig,** 1787–1862, German poet.

Ui·gur (wē′gŏŏr) *n.* **1.** One of a Turkic people who ruled in Mongolia and East Turkestan from the eighth to the twelfth century, now the majority of the population of the Sinkiang-Uigur Autonomous Region, NW China. **2.** The Turkic language of these people. — **Ui·gu·ri·an** (wē·gŏŏr′ē·ən), **Ui·gu·ric** (wē·gŏŏr′ik) *adj.*

u·in·tah·ite (yōō·in′tə·īt) *n.* A variety of asphalt common in Utah: also called *gilsonite.* Also **u·in′ta·ite.** [after *Uinta* Mountains]

U·in·ta Mountains (yōō·in′tə) A range in NE Utah and SW Wyoming; highest point, Kings Peak, 13,498 ft.

u·in·ta·there (yōō·in′tə·thir) *n. Paleontol.* Any of an order (*Dinocerata*) of gigantic herbivorous mammals of the early Tertiary period, having three pairs of protuberances on the top of the head: also called *dinoceras.*

uit (oit, œit) *prep. Afrikaans* Out; out of.

uit·land·er (īt′län·dər, oit′-; *Afrikaans* œit′län·dər) *n. Afrikaans* A foreigner.

U.J.D. Doctor of Civil and Canon Law (L *Utriusque Juris Doctor*).

U·ji·ji (ōō·jē′jē) A port town in western Tanzania, on Lake Tanganyika; pop. 21,369 (1969). Also **Kigoma-Ujiji.**

U·j·pest (ōō′ē·pesht) A city in central Hungary, on the Danube; pop. about 73,000: German *Neupest.*

U.K. United Kingdom.

u·kase (yōō′kās, yōō·kāz′) *n.* **1.** Any official decree. **2.** Formerly, an edict or decree of the imperial Russian government. [< Russian *ukaz*]

Ukr. Ukraine.

U·krain·i·an (yōō·krā′nē·ən, -krī′-) *adj.* Of or pertaining to the Ukraine, its people, or their language. — *n.* **1.** A native or inhabitant of the Ukraine. **2.** The East Slavic language of the Ukranians. Also *Little Russian, Ruthenian.*

Ukrainian S.S.R. A constituent Republic of the SW Soviet Union; 231,986 sq. mi.; pop. 47,136,000 (1970); capital, Kiev. Also **U·kraine** (yōō·krān′, yōō′krān, yōō·krīn′), **U·krain·i·a** (yōō·krā′nē·ə). *Russian* **U·kra·i·na** (ōō·krä′i·nə), **U·krain·ska·ya S.S.R.** (-in·ska·yə).

u·ku·le·le (yōō′kə·lā′lē, *Hawaiian* ōō′kŏŏ·lā′lā) *n.* A small guitarlike musical instrument having four strings. [< Hawaiian, flea < *uku* insect + *lele* to jump; from the movements of the fingers in playing]

u·lan (ōō′län, ōō·län′, yōō′lən) See UHLAN.

U·lan Ba·tor (ōō′län bä′tôr) The capital of the Mongolian People's Republic in the north central part; pop. about 160,000: formerly *Urga.* Chinese *Kulun.*

U·lan-U·de (ōō′län·ōō·dĕ′) A city in the SE central R.S.F.S.R., near Baikal lake; pop. 254,000 (1970).

Ul·bricht (ōōl′brikht), **Walter,** born 1893, German Communist leader.

ul·cer (ul′sər) *n.* **1.** *Pathol.* An open sore on an external or internal surface of the body, usually accompanied by disintegration of tissue with the formation of pus. **2.** A corroding fault or vice; corruption; evil. [< L *ulcus, ulceris*]

UKULELE

ul·cer·ate (ul'sə·rāt) *v.t. & v.i.* **·at·ed, ·at·ing** To make or become ulcerous. [< L *ulceratus*, pp. of *ulcerare* < *ulcus, ulceris* ulcer] — **ul'cer·a'tive** *adj.*

ul·cer·a·tion (ul'sə·rā'shən) *n.* **1.** The forming of an ulcer, or the condition of being affected with ulcers. **2.** An ulcer; also, ulcers collectively.

ul·cer·ous (ul'sər·əs) *adj.* **1.** Like an ulcer. **2.** Affected with ulcers. — **ul'cer·ous·ly** *adv.* — **ul'cer·ous·ness** *n.*

-ule *suffix of nouns* Small; little: used to form diminutives: *granule.* [< F *-ule* < L *-ulus, -ula, -ulum,* diminutive suffix]

u·le·ma (ōō'lə·mä') *n.* **1.** In Moslem countries, a council or college of priests, judges, or scholars who are trained in Moslem religion and law, and interpret the Koran. **2.** Loosely, any Moslem scholar. [< Turkish *'ulema* < Arabic *'ulamā,* pl. of *'alim* wise < *'alama* to know]

-ulent *suffix of adjectives* Abounding in; full of (what is indicated in the root): *opulent, truculent.* Corresponding nouns are formed in **-ulence,** as in *opulence, truculence.* [< L *-ulentus*]

Ul·fi·las (ul'fi·ləs, 311?–381?, bishop of the Goths; translated the Bible into Gothic: also *Wulfila.* Also **Ul'fi·la** (-lə).

ul·lage (ul'ij) *n.* The quantity that a container, as a wine cask, lacks of being full; wantage. [< AF *ulliage,* OF *ouillage* < *ouiller* to fill up (to the bunghole) < *ueil* eye, bunghole < L *oculus* eye]

Ulm (ōōlm) A city in eastern Baden–Württemberg, West Germany, on the Danube; pop. 92,486 (est. 1970).

ul·ma·ceous (ul·mā'shəs) *adj. Bot.* Designating or belonging to a family (*Ulmaceae*) of widely distributed shrubs and trees, the elm family, characterized by alternate simple leaves, apetalous bisexual or unisexual flowers, and a compressed fruit. [< NL, family name < L *ulmus* elm]

ul·na (ul'nə) *n. pl.* **·nae** (-nē) or **·nas** *Anat.* **1.** That one of the two long bones of the forearm that forms a joint with the radius and is on the same side as the little finger. **2.** The corresponding bone in the forelimb of other vertebrates. [< L, elbow] — **ul'nar** *adj.*

-ulose *suffix of adjectives* Marked by or abounding in: used in scientific and technical terms: *ramulose.* Compare -ULOUS (def. 2). [< L *-ulosus,* adjective suffix]

u·lot·ri·chous (yōō·lot'rə·kəs) *adj.* Having woolly or crispy hair. [< NL *Ulotrichi,* obs. name for subdivision of human race; < Gk. *oulothrix, oulotrichos* woolly-haired < *oulos* woolly + *thrix* hair]

-ulous *suffix of adjectives* **1.** Tending to do or characterized by (what is indicated by the root): *tremulous, ridiculous.* **2.** Full of: *meticulous, populous.* Compare -ULOSE. [< L *-ulus* and *-ulosus,* adjective suffixes]

Ul·pi·an (ul'pē·ən), died 228?, Roman jurist: full name **Domitius Ul·pi·a·nus** (ul'pi·ā'nəs).

ul·ster (ul'stər) *n.* A very long, loose overcoat, sometimes belted at the waist, made originally of Irish frieze.

Ul·ster (ul'stər) **1.** A former province of northern Ireland, of which the northern part became Northern Ireland, 1925. **2.** A Province of the northern Republic of Ireland, comprising the part of Ulster that remained after 1925; 3,093 sq. mi.; pop. 217,489 (1961). — **Ul'ster·man** (-mən) *n.*

ult. 1. Ultimate(ly). **2.** Ultimo: also **ulto.**

ul·te·ri·or (ul·tir'ē·ər) *adj.* **1.** More remote; not so pertinent as something else to the matter spoken of: *ulterior* considerations. **2.** Intentionally unrevealed; hidden: *ulterior* motives. **3.** Later in time or secondary in importance; following; succeeding. **4.** Lying beyond or on the farther side of a certain bounding line. [< L compar. of *ulter* beyond] — **ul·te'ri·or·ly** *adv.*

ul·ti·ma (ul'tə·mə) *n.* The last syllable of a word. [< L, fem. of *ultimus* last]

ul·ti·mate (ul'tə·mit) *adj.* **1.** Beyond which there is no other; last of a series; final. **2.** Not susceptible of further analysis; fundamental or essential. **3.** Most distant; farthest; extreme. — *n.* **1.** The final result; last step; conclusion. **2.** A fundamental or final fact. Abbr. *ult.* [< LL *ultimatus,* orig. pp. of *ultimare* to come to an end < *ultimus* farthest, last, superl. of *ulter* beyond] — **ul'ti·mate·ness** *n.*

ultimate constituent See under CONSTITUENT.

ul·ti·mate·ly (ul'tə·mit·lē) *adv.* In the end; at last; finally. Abbr. *ult.*

ul·ti·ma Thu·le (ul'tə·mə thōō'lē, tōō'lē) **1.** Farthest Thule; in ancient geography, the northernmost habitable regions of the earth. **2.** Any distant, unknown region. **3.** The farthest possible point, degree, or limit.

ul·ti·ma·tum (ul'tə·mā'təm, -mä'-) *n. pl.* **·tums** or **·ta** (-tə) **1.** A final statement, as concerning terms or conditions; especially, in diplomacy, the final terms offered by one party, as during negotiations concerning a treaty, the rejection of which by the other party will result in breaking off all

negotiation. **2.** A last proposal, offer, concession, or demand. **3.** Anything ultimate. [< NL < LL, neut. of *ultimatus.* See ULTIMATE.]

ul·ti·mo (ul'tə·mō) *adv. Archaic* In the last month: shortened to *ult.* or *ulto.*: the 15th *ult.*: distinguished from *instant, proximo.* [< L *ultimo* (*mense*) in the last (month)]

ul·ti·mo·gen·i·ture (ul'tə·mō·jen'ə·chər) *n.* The rule whereby the youngest son takes the inheritance. Compare PRIMOGENITURE. [< L *ultimus* last, on analogy with PRIMOGENITURE]

ul·tra (ul'trə) *adj.* Going beyond the bounds of moderation; extreme. — *n.* One who goes to extremes. [< L, beyond, on the other side]

ultra- *prefix* **1.** On the other side of; beyond in space (opposed to *cis-*; compare TRANS-); as in:

ultra-Arctic	ultra-Neptunian
ultraequinoctial	ultrastellar
ultragalactic	ultraterrene
ultralunar	ultraterrestrial
ultra-Martian	ultrazodiacal

2. Going beyond the limits of; surpassing; as in:

ultra-atomic	ultramolecular
ultracentenarian	ultranatural
ultrahuman	ultratotal

3. Beyond what is usual or natural; excessively; as in:

ultra-affected	ultramulish
ultra-agnostic	ultranominalistic
ultra-ambitious	ultraornate
ultra-Anglican	ultraorthodox
ultrabelieving	ultraorthodoxy
ultrabenevolent	ultrapartisan
ultra-Christian	ultraphysical
ultraclassical	ultrapositivistic
ultraconfident	ultraprecision
ultraconservatism	ultra-Protestant
ultracooperative	ultra-Protestantism
ultracosmopolitan	ultraprudent
ultracredulous	ultrapurist
ultrademocratic	ultra-Puritan
ultradespotic	ultraradical
ultradiscipline	ultrarefined
ultraeducationist	ultrarefinement
ultraepiscopal	ultrareligious
ultraevangelical	ultrarevolutionary
ultraexclusive	ultrarevolutionist
ultrafashionable	ultraritualism
ultrafastidious	ultraromanticist
ultrafederalist	ultraroyalism
ultrafeudal	ultraroyalist
ultra-Gallican	ultrascientific
ultra-German	ultrasensual
ultrahonorable	ultrasentimental
ultraintellectual	ultraservile
ultralegality	ultra-Spartan
ultraliberal	ultraspiritual
ultraliberalism	ultrasplendid
ultralogical	ultrasterile
ultraloyal	ultrastrict
ultramaternal	ultratheological
ultramoderate	ultravenomous
ultramodest	ultravirtuous

ul·tra·cen·tri·fuge (ul'trə·sen'trə·fyōōj) *n.* A centrifuge whose rotor, sometimes driven by blasts of hydrogen, will operate at extremely high velocities, used for high precision scientific and laboratory work. — *v.t.* **·fuged, ·fug·ing** To subject to the action of an ultracentrifuge. — **ul'tra·cen'tri·fu·ga'tion** (-fyōō·gā'shən) *n.*

ul·tra·con·ser·va·tive (ul'trə·kən·sûr'və·tiv) *adj.* Unusually or excessively conservative. — *n.* An ultraconservative person; a reactionary.

ul·tra·crit·i·cal (ul'trə·krit'i·kəl) *adj.* Unduly critical.

ul·tra·fil·ter (ul'trə·fil'tər) *n. Chem.* A filter having extremely minute pores, as a living membrane or a film of gelatin on filter paper, used to sift out particles that pass through ordinary filters. — **ul'tra·fil·tra'tion** (-fil·trā'shən) *n.*

ul·tra·high frequency (ul'trə·hī') *Telecom.* A band of wave frequencies between 300 and 3,000 megacycles per second. Abbr. *uhf, u.h.f., UHF, U.H.F.*

ul·tra·ism (ul'trə·iz'əm) *n.* **1.** The policies or opinions of those who are in favor of extreme measures. **2.** An extreme view or action. — **ul'tra·ist** *n. & adj.* — **ul'tra·is'tic** *adj.*

ul·tra·ma·rine (ul'trə·mə·rēn') *n.* **1.** A deep, usually purplish blue, permanent pigment made from finely powdered lapis lazuli. **2.** A similar pigment made artificially, as from kaolin, silica, soda, sulfur, and charcoal: also called *new blue, French blue.* **3.** The deep blue color of such a pigment. — *adj.* Being beyond or across the sea. [< Med.L *ultramarinus* < L *ultra* beyond + *marinus* marine]

ul·tra·mi·crom·e·ter (ul'trə·mī·krom'ə·tər) *n.* A micrometer designed for measurements requiring a high order of precision and accuracy.

ul·tra·mi·cro·scope (ul'trə·mī'krə·skōp) *n.* An optical instrument for detecting objects too small to be seen with an ordinary microscope.

ul·tra·mi·cro·scop·ic (ul′trə·mī′krə·skop′ik) *adj.* **1.** Too minute to be seen by an ordinary microscope. **2.** Relating to the ultramicroscope. Also **ul·tra·mi′cro·scop′i·cal.** — **ul′tra·mi·cros′co·py** (-mī·kros′kə·pē) *n.*

ul·tra·mod·ern (ul′trə·mod′ərn) *adj.* Extremely modern. — **ul′tra·mod′ern·ism** *n.* — **ul′tra·mod′ern·ist** *n.* — **ul′tra·mod′ern·is′tic** *adj.*

ul·tra·mon·tane (ul′trə·mon′tān) *adj.* **1.** Situated beyond the mountains: opposed to *cismontane.* **2.** Beyond or south of the Alps; especially, Italian or papal. **3.** In politics or ecclesiastical matters, supporting the policy of the papal court. — *n.* **1.** One who resides beyond the Alps. **2.** One who supports the papal policy in political or ecclesiastical matters. [< Med.L *ultramontanus* < L *ultra* beyond + *montanus* pertaining to a mountain < *mons, montis* mountain]

Ul·tra·mon·ta·nism (ul′trə·mon′tə·niz′əm) *n.* The policy of Roman Catholics who wish to see all power in the church in the hands of the pope: opposed to *Gallicanism.*

ul·tra·mun·dane (ul′trə·mun′dān) *adj.* Extending beyond the universe or the present life. [< L *ultramundanus*]

ul·tra·na·tion·al·ism (ul′trə·nash′ən·əl·iz′əm) *n.* Extreme devotion to or support of national interests or considerations. — **ul′tra·na′tion·al·ist** *n. & adj.* — **ul′tra·na′tion·al·is′tic** *adj.*

ul·tra·red (ul′trə·red′) *adj.* Infrared.

ul·tra·son·ic (ul′trə·son′ik) *adj. Physics* Pertaining to or designating sound waves having a frequency above the limits of human audibility, or in excess of about 20 kilocycles per second: distinguished from *supersonic.*

ul·tra·son·ics (ul′trə·son′iks) *n.pl.* (*construed as sing.*) The study of acoustic phenomena in the frequency range above that of audibility: distinguished from *supersonics.*

ul·tra·trop·i·cal (ul′trə·trop′i·kəl) *adj.* **1.** Situated beyond the tropics. **2.** Hotter than the tropics.

ul·tra·vi·o·let (ul′trə·vī′ə·lit) *adj. Physics* Lying beyond the violet end of the visible spectrum: said of high-frequency wavelengths ranging from about 3,900 angstroms to about 400 angstroms, the lower limit of X-rays. Compare INFRA-RED.

ul·tra vi·res (ul′trə vī′rēz) *Latin* **1.** *Law* Beyond the lawful capacity or powers, as of a corporation. **2.** *Informal* Not permissible; forbidden.

ul·u·lant (yōō′lə·lənt, ul′-) *adj.* Howling; hooting. [< L *ululans, -antis,* ppr. of *ululare* to howl]

ul·u·late (yōō′lə·lāt, ul′-) *v.i.* **·lat·ed, ·lat·ing** To howl, hoot, or wail. [< L *ululatus,* pp. of *ululare* to howl] — **ul′u·la′tion** *n.*

Ul·ya·novsk (ōōl′yä′nəfsk) A port city in the western R.S.F.S.R., on the Volga; pop. 351,000 (1970). Also **Ul′·ya′·novsk.**

U·lys·ses (yōō·lis′ēz) The Latin name for Odysseus.

um·bel (um′bəl) *n. Bot.* An inflorescence in which a number of nearly equal flower stalks radiate from a small area at the top of a very short axis, giving an umbrellalike appearance. For illustrations see INFLORESCENCE. [< L *umbella* parasol, dim. of *umbra* shadow. Akin to UMBRELLA.]

um·bel·late (um′bə·lit, -lāt) *adj.* Disposed in or resembling umbels. Also **um′bel·lar, um′bel·lat′ed** [< NL *umbellatus*]

um·bel·lif·er·ous (um′bə·lif′ər·əs) *adj. Bot.* **1.** Bearing umbels. **2.** Designating or pertaining to a widely distributed family (*Umbelliferae*) of herbs and some shrubs, the parsley or carrot family, comprising many important plants used as food, for flavoring, and in medicine. [< NL, family name < L *umbella* parasol + *ferre* to bear]

um·bel·lule (um′bəl·yōōl, um·bel′-) *n. Bot.* A small or secondary umbel. Also **um·bel·let** (um′bə·lit). [< NL *umbellula,* dim. of L *umbella* parasol] — **um·bel·lu·late** (um·bel′yə·lit, -lāt) *adj.*

um·ber¹ (um′bər) *n.* **1.** A brown, hydrated, ferric oxide, containing some manganese oxide and clay, and used as a pigment. In its natural state it is known as **raw umber,** and when heated, so as to produce a reddish brown, as **burnt umber. 2.** The color of such a pigment. — *adj.* Of or pertaining to umber; of a dusky hue; brownish. — *v.t.* To color with umber. [< F (*terre d'*)*ombre* or Ital. *ombra,* prob. < L *Umbra,* fem. of *Umber* of Umbria, where originally found]

um·ber² (um′bər) *n.* **1.** *Obs.* Shade; also, any indefinite dark color. **2.** The umbrette: also **umber bird. 3.** The grayling (def. 1). [< F *ombre* < L *umbra* shade]

um·bil·i·cal (um·bil′i·kəl) *adj.* **1.** Pertaining to or situated near the navel. **2.** Placed near the navel; central. [< LL *umbilicalis* < L *umbilicus* navel]

umbilical cord *Anat.* A ropelike tissue connecting the navel of the fetus with the placenta and serving to transmit nourishment to and remove wastes from the fetus.

um·bil·i·cate (um·bil′ə·kit, -kāt) *adj.* **1.** Resembling a navel, as by having a central depression or mark. **2.** Having an umbilicus or navel-shaped depression, as a shell. Also **um·bil′i·cat′ed** (-kā′tid).

um·bil·i·ca·tion (um·bil′ə·kā′shən) *n.* **1.** The state of being umbilicate. **2.** An umbilicate depression.

um·bil·i·cus (um·bil′ə·kəs, um′bə·lī′kəs) *n. pl.* **·ci** (-sī) **1.** *Anat.* The navel. **2.** *Zool.* An indention or depression at the axial base of a spiral shell, as in many gastropods. **3.**

Ornithol. Either of the apertures (inferior and superior) of the calamus of a feather. **4.** *Bot.* A hilum (def. 1a). [< L

um·bil·i·form (um·bil′ə·fôrm) *adj.* Navel-shaped. [< *umbili-* (< UMBILICUS) + -FORM]

um·ble pie (um′bəl) See HUMBLE PIE.

um·bles (um′bəlz) *n.pl.* The entrails of a deer; humbles. [Var. of NUMBLES]

um·bo (um′bō) *n. pl.* **um·bo·nes** (um·bō′nēz) or **·bos 1.** The boss or projecting spike in the center of a shield. **2.** *Biol.* An elevation, boss, or knob, as the prominence of a bivalve shell near the hinge, or the top of the cap of certain fungi. **3.** *Anat.* The surface of the tympanic membrane at the point of attachment to the tip of the malleus. [< L] — **um′bo·nal** (-bə·nəl), **um·bon·ic** (un·bon′ik) *adj.*

um·bo·nate (um′bə·nit, -nāt) *adj.* Having an umbo or boss-like protuberance. Also **um′bo·nat′ed.**

um·bra (um′brə) *n. pl.* **·bras** or **·brae** (-brē) **1.** A shadow or dark area; especially, the portion of a shadow from which direct light is entirely cut off. **2.** *Astron.* **a** In an eclipse, that part of the shadow of the earth or moon within which the moon or the sun is entirely hidden. **b** The inner dark portion of a sunspot. [< L, shadow]

um·brage (um′brij) *n.* **1.** Resentment, as at being obscured by another. **2.** A sense of injury; offense: now usually in **to give** (or **take) umbrage. 3.** That which gives shade, as a leafy tree. **4.** *Poetic* Shade or shadow cast. **5.** *Rare* Mere shadowy appearance; semblance. [< F *ombrage* < L *umbraticus* shady < *umbra* shade]

um·bra·geous (um·brā′jəs) *adj.* **1.** Shady or shaded; forming or providing shade. **2.** Quick to take offense; peevish; suspicious. **3.** *Obs.* Obscure. [< F *ombrageux* < *ombrage.* See UMBRAGE.] — **um·bra′geous·ly** *adv.* — **um·bra′geous·ness** *n.*

um·brel·la (um·brel′ə) *n.* **1.** A light, round, portable screen or shade on a folding frame, carried as a protection against sun or rain. **2.** *Zool.* The contractile, jellylike portion of the body of a medusa expanded like a bell or umbrella. **3.** *Aeron.* An air umbrella (which see). [< Ital. *ombrella,* alter. (after *ombra* shade) of L *umbrella* parasol. Akin to UMBEL.]

umbrella bird Any of several South American birds (genus *Cephalopterus*), the male of which has a broad umbrellalike crest above the head; especially, *C. ornatus,* having lustrous black plumage with a crest of blue, hairlike feathers.

umbrella leaf A smooth perennial North American herb (*Diphylleia cymosa*) of the barberry family, with a single large peltate leaf, one to two feet across, and a terminal cyme of white flowers.

umbrella palm A palm (*Hedyscepe canterburyana*) having pinnate leaves, native to an Australian island and cultivated in Florida.

umbrella tree 1. A small magnolia (*Magnolia tripetala*) of the southern United States, with fragrant white flowers and oval leaves crowded in an umbrellalike whorl at the ends of the branches. **2.** Any one of several other trees with large, round cordate leaves.

um·brette (um·bret′) *n.* A dusky brown African wading bird (*Scopus umbretta*), related to the herons and storks: also called *umber, hammerhead.* [< F *ombrette,* orig. dim. of *ombre* a shadow]

Um·bri·a (um′brē·ə) A Region of central Italy, between the Tiber and the Adriatic; 3,270 sq. mi.; pop. 788,546 (1961); capital, Perugia.

Um·bri·an (um′brē·ən) *adj.* Of Umbria, or its people. — *n.* **1.** A native or inhabitant of Umbria. **2.** The extinct language of ancient Umbria, belonging to the Osco-Umbrian branch of the Italic languages.

um·brif·er·ous (um·brif′ər·əs) *adj.* Affording or making a shade; umbrageous. [< L *umbrifer* < *umbra* shade + *ferre* to bear] — **um·brif′er·ous·ly** *adv.*

u·mi·ak (ōō′mē·ak) *n. U.S. & Canadian* A large, open boat, about 30 feet long and 8 feet wide, made by drawing skins over a wooden frame, used by Eskimos, especially Eskimo women. Compare KAYAK. Also spelled *oomiak.* Also **u′mi·ack.** [< Eskimo]

um·laut (ōōm′lout) *n.* **1.** *Ling.* **a** The change in quality of a vowel sound caused by its partial assimilation to a vowel or semivowel (often later lost) in the following syllable, primarily a phenomenon of the Germanic languages. **b** A vowel so altered, as ä, ö, and ü in German. **2.** In German, the two dots (¨) put over a vowel modified by umlaut: short for **umlaut-mark.** — *v.t.* To modify by umlaut or mutation. [< G, change of sound < *um* about + *laut* sound]

um·pir·age (um′pīr·ij, -pə·rij) *n. Rare* The office, function, or decision of an umpire. Also **um′pire·ship.**

um·pire (um′pīr) *n.* **1.** In various games, as baseball, a person chosen to enforce the rules of the game and settle disputed points. **2.** A person called upon to settle a disagreement in opinion between arbitrators. — **Syn.** See JUDGE. — *v.t. & v.i.* **·pired, ·pir·ing** To decide as umpire; act as umpire (of or in). [Apheptic alter. of ME *noumpere* < OF *nonper* odd, uneven (i.e., third) < *non* not + *per* even, equal]

UMT Universal Military Training.

UMTS Universal Military Training and Service.

UMW or **U.M.W.** United Mine Workers.

UN or **U.N.** See UNITED NATIONS.

un-[1] *prefix* Not; opposed to. [OE] ◆ *Un-*[1] is used to express negation, lack, incompleteness or opposition. It is freely attached to adjectives and adverbs, less often to nouns. See UN-[2].

un-[2] *prefix* Back. [OE *un-, on-,* and-] ◆ *Un-*[2] is used to express reversal of the action of verbs, or to form verbs from nouns indicating removal from the state or quality expressed by the noun, or sometimes to intensify the force of negative verbs. At the bottom of this page and of following pages is a partial list of words that are formed with *un-*[1] and *un-*[2]. Other compounds of these prefixes, with strongly positive, specific, or special meanings, will be found in vocabulary place. In the verbs in the list, *un-* gives the sense of reversal: *unchain* "to loose the chains of." In the nouns and the adjectives it usually has negative or privative force. Thus, *unburdened* may be regarded as an adjective meaning "not burdened," or as a participle of the verb *unburden,* meaning "relieved of a burden." Pronunciations may be ascertained by consulting the second element in its vocabulary place.

◆ **un-, in-** *In-* as a prefix of adjectives expresses in usage more of negation, *un-* more of mere lack or privation: a child's *unartistic* speech, a writer's *inartistic* diction. In general, *in-* is more confined to words of Latin origin.

un·a·ble (un·āʹbəl) *adj.* **1.** Lacking the necessary power or resources; not able: usually used with an infinitive: *unable* to walk. **2.** Lacking mental capacity; incompetent.

unabr. Unabridged.

un·a·bridged (unʹə·brijdʹ) *adj.* Not abridged or condensed; original and complete: an *unabridged* dictionary.

un·ac·com·mo·dat·ed (unʹə·komʹə·dāʹtid) *adj.* **1.** Not made suitable; ill-adapted or -adjusted. **2.** Being without accommodations or conveniences.

un·ac·com·pa·nied (unʹə·kumʹpə·nēd) *adj.* **1.** Proceeding, acting, or accomplished without an escort or companion. **2.** *Music* Performing or intended to be performed without accompaniment.

un·ac·com·plished (unʹə·komʹplisht) *adj.* **1.** Having fallen short of accomplishment; not done or finished. **2.** Lacking accomplishments.

un·ac·count·a·ble (unʹə·kounʹtə·bəl) *adj.* **1.** Impossible to be accounted for; inexplicable. **2.** Remarkable; extraordinary. **3.** Not accountable; irresponsible. **—unʹac·countʹa·ble·ness** *n.* **—unʹac·countʹa·bly** *adv.*

un·ac·count·ed-for (unʹə·kounʹtid·fôrʹ) *adj.* Unexplained; not accounted for.

un·ac·cus·tomed (unʹə·kusʹtəmd) *adj.* **1.** Not accustomed or habituated: *unaccustomed* to hardship. **2.** Not familiar or well known; strange: an *unaccustomed* sight.

un·ad·vised (unʹəd·vīzdʹ) *adj.* **1.** Not advised; not having received advice. **2.** Rash or imprudent; ill-considered. **—unʹad·visʹed·ly** (-vīʹzid·lē) *adv.* **—unʹad·visʹed·ness** *n.*

un·af·fect·ed (unʹə·fekʹtid) *adj.* **1.** Not showing affectation; natural; sincere; real. **2.** Not influenced or changed. **—unʹaf·fectʹed·ly** *adv.* **—unʹaf·fectʹed·ness** *n.*

Un·a·las·ka Island (unʹə·lasʹkə, ōōʹnə-) One of the SW Fox Islands; 30 mi. long, 6 to 30 mi. wide.

un·al·ien·a·ble (un·ālʹyən·ə·bəl) *adj. Obs.* Inalienable.

un-A·mer·i·can (unʹə·merʹə·kən) *adj.* **1.** Not American in character, style, etc. **2.** Not consistent with the ideals, objectives, spirit, etc., of the United States; lacking patriotism or national feeling: a derogatory term.

U·na·mu·no (ōōʹnä·mōōʹnō), **Miguel de,** 1864–1936, Spanish scholar, philosopher, novelist, and poet.

un·a·neled (unʹə·nēldʹ) *adj. Obs.* Not having received extreme unction. [< UN-[1] + ANELE]

u·na·nim·i·ty (yōōʹnə·nimʹə·tē) *n.* The state of being unanimous; complete agreement in opinion, etc. [< OF *unanimite* < L *unanimitas, -tatis* < *unanimus.* See UNANIMOUS.]

u·nan·i·mous (yōō·nanʹə·məs) *adj.* **1.** Sharing the same views or sentiments; harmonious. **2.** Showing or resulting from the assent of all concerned. [< L *unanimus, unanimis*

< *unus* one + *animus* mind] **—u·nanʹi·mous·ly** *adv.* **—u·nanʹi·mous·ness** *n.*

un·ap·peal·a·ble (unʹə·pēʹlə·bəl) *adj.* **1.** Admitting no appeal to a higher court: an *unappealable* case. **2.** That cannot be appealed from; conclusive; final.

un·ap·proach·a·ble (unʹə·prōʹchə·bəl) *adj.* **1.** Not easy to know or make personal contact with; aloof. **2.** Not capable of being reached or approached; inaccessible. **—unʹap·proachʹa·ble·ness** *n.* **—unʹap·proachʹa·bly** *adv.*

un·ap·pro·pri·at·ed (unʹə·prōʹprē·āʹtid) *adj.* Not set apart for special use; not taken possession of by or formally granted to a particular person or company.

un·apt (un·aptʹ) *adj.* **1.** Not likely or inclined. **2.** Not suitable or qualified. **3.** Not having a ready wit. **—un·aptʹly** *adv.* **—un·aptʹness** *n.*

un·ar·gued (un·ärʹgyōōd) *adj.* **1.** Not argued; undebated. **2.** Undisputed; agreed upon.

un·arm (un·ärmʹ) *v.t.* To deprive of weapons; disarm.

un·armed (un·ärmdʹ) *adj.* **1.** Not armed; without weapons. **2.** Having no sharp, hard projections, as spines, prickles, plates, etc.: said of plants and animals.

un·as·sail·a·ble (unʹə·sālʹə·bəl) *adj.* **1.** Not capable of being disproved, denied, or contested; incontrovertible. **2.** Proof against attack or destruction; impregnable. **—unʹas·sailʹa·ble·ness** *n.* **—unʹas·sailʹa·bly** *adv.*

un·as·sist·ed (unʹə·sisʹtid) *adj.* **1.** Not assisted. **2.** In baseball, designating a play involving only one fielder.

un·as·sum·ing (unʹə·sōōʹming) *adj.* Unpretentious; modest. **—unʹas·sumʹing·ly** *adv.*

un·at·tached (unʹə·tachtʹ) *adj.* **1.** Not attached. **2.** Not engaged or married. **3.** *Law* Not held or seized, as in satisfaction of a judgment. **4.** In the armed forces, not assigned to a regiment or company.

un·at·tend·ed (unʹə·tenʹdid) *adj.* **1.** Not done or attended; neglected: often followed by *to:* a matter left *unattended* to. **2.** Not accompanied or escorted; alone.

u·nau (yōō·nōʹ, -nōʹ, ōō·nouʹ) *n.* The common two-toed sloth (*Choloepus didactylus*) of Brazil. [< F < Tupi]

un·a·vail·ing (unʹə·vāʹling) *adj.* Futile; unsuccessful; ineffective. **—unʹa·vailʹing·ly** *adv.*

u·na vo·ce (yōōʹnə vōʹsē) *Latin* Unanimously; with one voice.

un·a·void·a·ble (unʹə·voiʹdə·bəl) *adj.* **1.** That cannot be avoided; inevitable. **2.** That cannot be made null and void; not voidable. **—unʹa·voidʹa·bilʹi·ty, unʹa·voidʹa·ble·ness** *n.* **—unʹa·voidʹa·bly** *adv.*

un·a·ware (unʹə·wârʹ) *adj.* **1.** Not aware or cognizant, as of something specified. **2.** Carelessly unmindful; inattentive; heedless. **—adv.** *Archaic* Unawares.

un·a·wares (unʹə·wârzʹ) *adv.* **1.** Unexpectedly; without warning. **2.** Without premeditation; unwittingly.

unb. or **unbd.** Unbound.

un·backed (un·baktʹ) *adj.* **1.** Never having borne a rider, as a horse; unbroken. **2.** Left without backers or support; not supported financially. **3.** Not wagered on. **4.** Without a back, as a stool.

un·baked (un·bāktʹ) *adj.* **1.** Not baked; insufficiently baked. **2.** Immature; crude.

un·bal·ance (un·balʹəns) *v.t.* **·anced, ·anc·ing** **1.** To deprive of balance. **2.** To disturb or derange, as the mind. **—n.** The state or condition of being unbalanced.

un·bal·anced (un·balʹənst) *adj.* **1.** Not in a state of equilibrium. **2.** In bookkeeping, not adjusted so as to balance. **3.** Lacking mental balance; unsound; erratic.

un·bal·last·ed (un·balʹəs·tid) *adj.* **1.** Not steadied by ballast. **2.** Not firm; wavering.

un·bar (un·bärʹ) *v.* **·barred, ·bar·ring** *v.t.* **1.** To remove the bar from. **—v.i.** **2.** To become unlocked or unbarred; open.

un·bat·ed (un·bāʹtid) *adj. Archaic* **1.** Not blunted with a button on the point, as a lance. **2.** Unabated; undiminished.

un·bear (un·bârʹ) *v.t.* **·beared, ·bear·ing** To free from the pressure of the checkrein, as a horse.

un·bear·a·ble (unʹbârʹə·bəl) *adj.* That cannot be borne or

unabashed	unadjustable	unalterable	unapparent	unassigned	unavouched
unabated	unadjusted	unaltered	unappeasable	unassumed	unavowed
unabetted	unadorned	unaltering	unappeased	unattainable	unavowedly
unabolished	unadulterated	unambiguous	unappetizing	unattained	unawaked
unabsolved	unadvisable	unambitious	unappreciated	unattempted	unawakened
unacademic	unadvisably	unamiable	unappreciative	unattested	unawed
unaccented	unaesthetic	unamplified	unapproached	unattired	unbaptized
unacceptable	unaffiliated	unamusing	unapproved	unattracted	unbarbed
unaccepted	unafraid	unanalytic	unarmored	unattractive	unbefitting
unacclimated	unaggressive	unanalyzable	unarrested	unauspicious	unbeloved
unacclimatized	unagitated	unanimated	unartful	unauthentic	unbeneficed
unaccommodating	unaided	unannealed	unartistic	unauthentical	unbenighted
unaccounted	unaimed	unannounced	unashamed	unauthenticated	unbenign
unaccredited	unalike	unanswerable	unasked	unauthorized	unbeseeming
unacknowledged	unalleviated	unanswerably	unaspirated	unavailability	unbesought
unacquainted	unallied	unanswered	unaspiring	unavailable	unbespoken
unacquitted	unallowable	unapologetic	unassailed	unavailably	unbetrayed
unadaptable	unalloyed	unappalled	unassignable	unavenged	unbetrothed

tolerated; unendurable. **—un·bear′a·ble·ness** *n.* **—un′·bear′a·bly** *adv.*

un·beat·en (un/bēt′n) *adj.* **1.** Having no defeats; unconquered. **2.** Not struck or thrashed. **3.** Not mixed or shaped by beating. **4.** Not worn; untrod, as a path.

un·be·com·ing (un/bi·kum′ing) *adj.* **1.** Not becoming; unsuited, as to a person or place: an *unbecoming* robe. **2.** Not befitting; not worthy of. **3.** Not decorous; improper. **—un·be·com′ing·ly** *adv.* **—un·be·com′ing·ness** *n.*

un·be·known (un/bi·nōn/) *adj.* Unknown: used with *to.* Also **un/be·knownst/** (-nōnst/).

un·be·lief (un/bi·lēf/) *n.* **1.** Absence of positive belief; incredulity. **2.** A refusal to believe; disbelief, as in religion. **3.** In Scriptural use, lack of faith in God's promises.

un·be·liev·a·ble (un/bi·lē′və·bəl) *adj.* That cannot be believed; incredible; astounding. **—un/be·liev·a·bil′i·ty, un/·be·liev′a·ble·ness** *n.* **—un/be·liev′a·bly** *adv.*

un·be·liev·er (un/bi·lē′vər) *n.* **1.** One who withholds belief. **2.** One who has no religious faith. **3.** One having a religion different from that of the speaker or writer. **—Syn.** See SKEPTIC.

un·be·liev·ing (un/bi·lē′ving) *adj.* **1.** Doubting; skeptical; incredulous. **2.** Disbelieving, especially in religious matters. **—un/be·liev′ing·ly** *adv.* **—un/be·liev′ing·ness** *n.*

un·belt (un·belt′) *v.t.* **1.** To remove the belt of. **2.** To remove from the belt; ungird.

un·bend (un·bend′) *v.* **·bent, ·bend·ing** *v.t.* **1.** To relax, as from exertion or formality: to *unbend* the mind. **2.** To straighten (something bent or curved). **3.** To relax, as a bow, from tension. **4.** *Naut.* **a** To loose; untie, as a rope. **b** To detach or remove (a sail) from a spar or stay. **—v.i. 5.** To become free of restraint or formality; relax. **6.** To become straight or nearly straight again.

un·bend·ing (un·ben′ding) *adj.* **1.** Not bending easily; stiff. **2.** Unyielding, as in character; resolute. **—n.** Relaxation; ease. **—un·bend′ing·ly** *adv.* **—un·bend′ing·ness** *n.*

un·bi·ased (un·bī′əst) *adj.* Having no bias; especially, not prejudiced or warped; impartial; fair. Also **un·bi′assed.** **—un·bi′ased·ly** *adv.* **—un·bi′ased·ness** *n.*

un·bid·den (un·bid/n) *adj.* **1.** Not commanded; not invited: an *unbidden* guest. **2.** Not called forth; spontaneous: *unbidden* thoughts. Also **un·bid′** (-bid/).

un·bind (un·bīnd/) *v.t.* **·bound, ·bind·ing 1.** To free from bindings; undo; also, to release. **2.** To remove, as something that binds; unfasten. [OE *unbindan*]

un·bit·ted (un·bit/id) *adj.* Not furnished with or restrained by a bit or bridle; uncontrolled.

un·blenched (un·blencht/) *adj. Obs.* Not dismayed.

un·blessed (un·blest′) *adj.* **1.** Deprived of a blessing. **2.** Unhallowed or unholy; evil. **3.** Deprived of good fortune; wretched. **4.** Lacking a (specified) source of contentment: *unblessed* with a son. Also **un·blest′.**

un·blood·y (un·blud/ē) *adj.* **1.** Not stained by blood. **2.** Not attended with slaughter, as a conflict. **3.** Not of a bloodthirsty disposition.

un·blush·ing (un·blush/ing) *adj.* **1.** Not blushing. **2.** Immodest; shameless. **—un·blush′ing·ly** *adv.*

un·bod·ied (un·bod/ēd) *adj.* **1.** Having no body; immaterial. **2.** Released from the body; disembodied.

un·bolt (un·bōlt′) *v.t.* To release, as a door, by withdrawing a bolt; unlock; open.

un·bolt·ed¹ (un·bōl′tid) *adj.* Not fastened by bolts.

un·bolt·ed² (un·bōl′tid) *adj.* Not separated by bolting; not sifted: *unbolted* flour. **2.** *Obs.* Gross; coarse.

un·boned (un·bōnd′) *adj.* **1.** Having no bones. **2.** Not having had the bones removed.

un·bon·net (un·bon/it) *v.t. & v.i.* To remove the bonnet or similar covering (from). **—un·bon/net·ed** *adj.*

un·born (un·bôrn′) *adj.* **1.** Not yet born; being of a future time or generation; future. **2.** Not in existence.

un·bos·om (un·bŏŏz/əm, -bŏŏ/zəm) *v.t.* **1.** To reveal, as one's thoughts or secrets; disclose or give vent to: often used

reflexively. **—v.i. 2.** To say what is troubling one; tell one's thoughts, feelings, etc. **—un·bos/om·er** *n.*

un·bound (un·bound′) Past tense and past participle of UNBIND. **—adj. 1.** Being without a binding, as a book. **2.** Freed from bonds. Abbr. (for def. 1) *unb., unbd.*

un·bound·ed (un·boun/did) *adj.* **1.** Having no bounds; of unlimited extent; very great; boundless. **2.** Having no boundary, as a closed surface. **3.** Going beyond bounds; unrestrained. **—un·bound′ed·ly** *adv.* **—un·bound′ed·ness** *n.*

un·bowed (un·boud′) *adj.* **1.** Not bent or bowed. **2.** Not subdued; proud in defeat or adversity.

un·brace (un·brās′) *v.t.* **·braced, ·brac·ing 1.** To free from bands or braces. **2.** To free from tension; loosen. **3.** To weaken; make feeble.

un·breathed (un·brēthd′) *adj.* **1.** Not breathed. **2.** Not whispered or spoken; not communicated to another.

un·bred (un·bred′) *adj.* **1.** Devoid of good breeding; ill-bred. **2.** Not taught; untrained. **3.** *Obs.* Unbegotten.

un·bri·dled (un·brīd/ld) *adj.* **1.** Having no bridle on: an *unbridled* horse. **2.** Without restraint; unruly: an *unbridled* tongue. **—un·bri′dled·ly** *adv.* **—un·bri′dled·ness** *n.*

un·bro·ken (un·brō′kən) *adj.* **1.** Not broken; whole; entire: an *unbroken* seal. **2.** Unviolated: an *unbroken* promise. **3.** Uninterrupted; regular; smooth: *unbroken* sleep. **4.** Not weakened; strong; firm. **5.** Not broken to harness or service, as a draft animal. **6.** Not disarranged or thrown out of order. Also *Obs.* **un·broke′.** **—un·bro′ken·ly** *adv.*

un·buck·le (un·buk/əl) *v.t. & v.i.* **·led, ·ling** To unfasten the buckle or buckles (of).

un·build (un·bild′) *v.t.* **·built, ·build·ing** To demolish; destroy.

un·bur·den (un·bûr/dən) *v.t.* To free from a burden; relieve. Also *Archaic* **un·bur/then** (-thən).

un·but·ton (un·but/n) *v.t. & v.i.* To unfasten the button or buttons (of).

un·caged (un·kājd′) *adj.* **1.** Not locked up in a cage; free. **2.** Released from a cage; freed.

un·called (un·kôld′) *adj.* Not being in response to a summons; without being asked or demanded.

un·called-for (un·kôld′fôr′) *adj.* Not justified by circumstances; improper; unnecessary; gratuitous.

un·can·ny (un·kan/ē) *adj.* **1.** Strange and inexplicable, especially so as to excite wonder or dismay; weird; unnatural; eerie. **2.** So good as to seem almost supernatural in power: *uncanny* accuracy. **3.** *Scot.* Dangerous; severe, as a wound. **—un·can/ni·ly** *adv.* **—un·can/ni·ness** *n.*

un·cap (un·kap′) *v.* **·capped, ·cap·ping** *v.t.* **1.** To take off the cap or covering of. **—v.i. 2.** To remove the hat or cap, as in respect.

un·ca·pa·ble (un·kā/pə·bəl) *adj. Obs.* Incapable.

un·cared-for (un·kârd′fôr′) *adj.* **1.** Not cared for or looked after; neglected. **2.** Careless; dissolute.

un·caused (un·kôzd′) *adj.* Existing without a cause; not caused; not created: an *uncaused* deity.

UNCCP United Nations Conciliation Commission for Palestine.

un·ceas·ing (un·sē′sing) *adj.* **1.** Being without interruption or cessation; continuous. **2.** Endless; eternal; continual. **—un/ceas′ing·ly** *adv.* **—un/ceas′ing·ness** *n.*

un·cer·e·mo·ni·ous (un/ser·ə·mō/nē·əs) *adj.* Informal; abrupt; discourteous. **—un/cer·e·mo/ni·ous·ly** *adv.*

un·cer·tain (un·sûr/tən) *adj.* **1.** That cannot be certainly predicted; being of doubtful issue. **2.** Not having certain knowledge or assured conviction. **3.** Not capable of being relied upon; variable; fitful. **4.** Not surely or exactly known: a lady of *uncertain* age. **5.** Having no exact or precise significance: *uncertain* phraseology. **6.** Ambiguous: in no *uncertain* terms. **—un·cer′tain·ly** *adv.*

un·cer·tain·ty (un·sûr/tən·tē) *n. pl.* **·ties 1.** The state of being uncertain; doubt. Also **un·cer/tain·ness. 2.** A doubtful matter; a contingency. **—Syn.** See DOUBT.

uncertainty principle *Physics* A statement of the impos-

unbewailed	unbribable	uncarpeted	unchastity	unclog	uncommanded
unblamable	unbridgeable	uncastrated	unchecked	unclogged	uncommissioned
unblamably	unbridged	uncaught	uncheerful	uncloud	uncompanionable
unblamed	unbridle	uncelebrated	uncheerfully	unclouded	uncomplaining
unbleached	unbrotherly	uncensored	uncheerfulness	uncloyed	uncomplaisant
unblemished	unbruised	uncensured	unchewed	uncoagulable	uncomplaisantly
unblissful	unbrushed	uncertified	unchilled	uncoagulated	uncompleted
unboastful	unburied	unchainable	unchivalrous	uncoated	uncompliable
unbookish	unburned	unchained	unchosen	uncocked	uncompliant
unborrowed	unburnt	unchallenged	uncholeric	uncoerced	uncomplicated
unbottomed	unbusinesslike	unchambered	unchristened	uncoffined	uncomplimentary
unbought	unbuttoned	unchangeable	unclaimed	uncollectable	uncomplying
unbox	uncage	unchanged	unclarified	uncollected	uncompounded
unboxed	uncalculate	unchanging	unclassed	uncollectible	uncomprehended
unbraid	uncalculating	unchaperoned	unclassic	uncolonized	uncomprehending
unbranched	uncalendered	uncharged	unclassifiable	uncolored	uncomprehensible
unbranded	uncanceled	uncharted	unclassified	uncombed	uncomprehensibly
unbreakable	uncandid	unchartered	uncleaned	uncombinable	uncompressed
unbreathable	uncandidly	unchary	uncleansed	uncombined	uncompromised
unbreech	uncanonic	unchaste	uncleared	uncomely	uncomputed
unbreeched	uncanonical	unchastened	uncleavable	uncomforted	unconcealable
	uncarbureted	unchastised	unclipped	uncomforting	unconcealed

sibility of exactly determining at any given instant or by a single operation more than one magnitude or quantity, as the velocity, position, etc., of an electron: also called *indeterminacy principle.*

un·chain (un-chān′) *v.t.* To release from a chain; set free.

un·chanc·y (un-chan′sē) *adj. Scot.* **1.** Unpropitious; unlucky. **2.** Ill-timed; inopportune. **3.** Unsafe; dangerous.

un·char·i·ta·ble (un-char′ə-tə-bəl) *adj.* Not charitable; harsh in judgment; censorious. — **un·char′i·ta·ble·ness** *n.* — **un·char′i·ta·bly** *adv.*

un·chris·tian (un-kris′chən) *adj.* **1.** Unbecoming to a Christian. **2.** Contrary to Christian precepts; uncharitable, ungracious, rude, etc. **3.** Non-Christian; pagan.

un·church (un-chûrch′) *v.t.* **1.** To deprive of membership in a church; expel from a church. **2.** To deny the validity of the sacraments and order of, as a sect.

un·cial (un′shəl, -shē·əl) *adj.* Pertaining to or consisting of a form of letters found in manuscripts from the fourth to the eighth century, and resembling modern capitals but more rounded. — *n.* **1.** An uncial letter. **2.** An uncial manuscript. [< L *uncialis* inch-high < *uncia* inch, ounce]

a ʘℇℕℂⲞⲨⲔⲀⲒⲬⲨⲦⲰⲘⲞⲚⲰⲬⲒ

b ⲈⲦⲤⲞⲚⳐⲞⲋⲨⲈⲂⲀⲚⲦⲨⳆⲢ

UNCIALS
a Greek, fifth century.
b Latin, circa 700 A.D.

un·ci·form (un′sə·fôrm) *adj.* Shaped like a hook; hooklike. — *n. Anat.* The unciform bone (which see). [< L *uncus* hook + -FORM]

unciform bone *Anat.* A wedge-shaped bone of the wrist, having a hooklike process on the palmar side, and articulating with the fourth and fifth metacarpals.

un·ci·na·ri·a·sis (un′si·nə-rī′ə·sis) *n. Pathol.* Ancylostomiasis. [< NL < *Uncinaria*, genus name < L *uncinus* hook, barb, dim. of *uncus* hook]

un·ci·nate (un′sə·nit, -nāt) *adj. Biol.* Hooked or bent at the end; having a hooked appendage. Also **un′ci·nal, un′ci·nat′ed.** [< L *uncinatus* < *uncinus*, dim. of *uncus* hook]

un·cir·cum·cised (un-sûr′kəm·sīzd) *adj.* **1.** Not circumcised. **2.** Not Jewish; Gentile. **3.** Heathen; pagan.

un·cir·cum·ci·sion (un′sûr·kəm·sizh′ən) *n.* **1.** The state of being uncircumcised. **2.** Those not circumcised; in Scripture, the Gentiles.

un·civ·il (un-siv′əl) *adj.* **1.** Wanting in civility; discourteous; ill-bred. **2.** *Obs.* Uncivilized. — **un·civ′il·ly** *adv.*

un·civ·i·lized (un-siv′ə·līzd) *adj.* Not civilized; barbarous.

un·clad (un-klad′) Alternate past tense and past participle of UNCLOTHE. — *adj.* Being without clothes; naked.

un·clasp (un-klasp′, -kläsp′) *v.t.* **1.** To release from a clasp. **2.** To release the clasp of. — *v.i.* **3.** To become released from a clasp.

un·cle (ung′kəl) *n.* **1.** The brother of one's father or mother; also, the husband of one's aunt. Abbr. *u., U.* ◆ Collateral adjective: *avuncular.* **2.** An elderly man: used in direct address. **3.** *Informal* A pawnbroker. **4.** *Informal* A word used to express surrender or concession, as in the phrase **Say uncle.** [< F *oncle* < L *avunculus* mother's brother, orig. dim. of *avus* grandfather]

un·clean (un-klēn′) *adj.* **1.** Not clean; foul. **2.** Characterized by impure thoughts; unchaste; depraved. **3.** Ceremonially impure. — **un·clean′ness** *n.*

un·clean·ly[1] (un-klen′lē) *adj.* **1.** Lacking cleanliness. **2.** Impure; indecent; not chaste. [< UN-[1] + CLEANLY, *adj.*] — **un·clean′li·ness** *n.*

un·clean·ly[2] (un-klēn′lē) *adv.* In an unclean manner.

un·clear (un-klir′) *adj.* **1.** Not clear. **2.** Not easily understandable; confused or muddled: *unclear reasoning.*

un·clench (un-klench′) *v.t. & v.i.* To relax or open from a clenched condition. Also **un·clinch′** (-klinch′).

Uncle Re·mus (rē′məs) In Joel Chandler Harris's folk

tales, an old southern Negro who tells the stories of Br'er Rabbit, Br'er Fox, and others to a small white boy.

Uncle Sam (sam) The personification of the government or the people of the United States, represented as a tall, lean man with chin whiskers, wearing a plug hat, a blue swallow-tailed coat, and red-and-white striped pants. Compare BROTHER JONATHAN. [Nickname of *Samuel* Wilson, 1766–1854, businessman in Troy, New York]

Uncle Tom (tom) *U.S. Slang* A Negro who toadies or truckles to white men: a contemptuous term. [after the chief character in Harriet Beecher Stowe's *Uncle Tom's Cabin*, a faithful, elderly Negro slave] — **Uncle Tom′ism**

un·cloak (un-klōk′) *v.t.* **1.** To remove the cloak or covering from. **2.** To unmask; expose. — *v.i.* **3.** To remove one's cloak or outer garments.

un·close (un-klōz′) *v.t. & v.i.* **·closed, ·clos·ing** **1.** To open or set open. **2.** To reveal; disclose.

un·clothe (un-klōth′) *v.t.* **·clothed** or **·clad** (klad), **·cloth·ing** **1.** To remove clothes from; undress. **2.** To divest or discard; uncover.

un·co (ung′kō) *Scot. & Brit. Dial. adj.* Being out of the ordinary; strange; weird. — *n. pl.* **·cos** **1.** A person or thing that is uncommon, surprising, or strange. **2.** *pl.* News. — *adv.* Remarkably or excessively; very. [Var. of ME *uncouth*]

un·cock (un-kok′) *v.t.* **1.** To release and let down the hammer of (a firearm) without exploding the charge. **2.** To restore to usual position, as a hat.

un·coil (un-koil′) *v.t. & v.i.* To unwind or become unwound.

un·coined (un-koind′) *adj.* **1.** Not fabricated; natural. **2.** Not minted.

un·com·fort·a·ble (un-kum′fər·tə-bəl, -kumpf′tə-bəl) *adj.* **1.** Not at ease; feeling discomfort. **2.** Causing physical or mental uneasiness; disquieting. — **un·com′fort·a·ble·ness** *n.* — **un·com′fort·a·bly** *adv.*

un·com·mer·cial (un′kə-mûr′shəl) *adj.* **1.** Not engaged or versed in commerce. **2.** Contrary to the spirit of commerce.

un·com·mit·ted (un′kə-mit′id) *adj.* Not committed; especially, not bound by or pledged to a particular course of action, viewpoint, etc.

un·com·mon (un-kom′ən) *adj.* Not common or usual; remarkable. — **un·com′mon·ly** *adv.* — **un·com′mon·ness** *n.*

un·com·mu·ni·ca·tive (un′kə-myoo′nə-kə-tiv, -nə-kā′tiv) *adj.* Not communicative; not disposed to express oneself or give information; reserved. — **Syn.** See TACITURN. — **un′com·mu′ni·ca·tive·ly** *adv.* — **un′com·mu′ni·ca·tive·ness** *n.*

Un·com·pah·gre Peak (un′kəm-pä′grē) A mountain in SW central Colorado, the highest of the San Juan Mountains; 14,306 ft.

un·com·pro·mis·ing (un-kom′prə-mī′zing) *adj.* Making or admitting of no compromise; inflexible; strict. — **un·com′·pro·mis′ing·ly** *adv.* — **un·com′pro·mis′ing·ness** *n.*

un·con·cern (un′kən-sûrn′) *n.* Absence of or freedom from concern or anxiety; indifference. — **Syn.** See APATHY.

un·con·cerned (un′kən-sûrnd′) *adj.* Undisturbed; not anxious; indifferent. — **un′con·cern′ed·ness** *n.*

un·con·di·tion·al (un′kən-dish′ən-əl) *adj.* Limited by no conditions; absolute. — **un′con·di′tion·al·ly** *adv.*

un·con·di·tioned (un′kən-dish′ənd) *adj.* **1.** Not restricted; unconditional. **2.** In metaphysics, not limited by conditions of space or time; free from relation; absolute. **3.** *Psychol.* Not determined by a specified condition or conditions; not acquired; natural. **4.** Admitted without condition.

un·con·form·a·ble (un′kən-fôr′mə-bəl) *adj.* **1.** Not conforming or conformable; inconsistent. **2.** *Geol.* Showing unconformity. — **un′con·form′a·bil′i·ty, un′con·form′a·ble·ness** *n.* — **un′con·form′a·bly** *adv.*

un·con·form·i·ty (un′kən-fôr′mə·tē) *n. pl.* **·ties** **1.** Want of conformity; nonconformity. **2.** *Geol.* **a** A lack of continuity between groups of stratified rocks in contact, indicative

unconceded	unconscientious	uncontroverted	uncourtliness	uncumbered	undecaying
unconcerted	unconsecrated	uncontrovertible	uncourtly	uncurable	undecipherable
unconciliated	unconsenting	uncontrovertibly	uncrate	uncurb	undeciphered
unconcluded	unconsidered	unconversant	uncrated	uncurbed	undeclared
uncondemned	unconsoled	unconvinced	uncredited	uncurdled	undeclinable
uncondensed	unconsonant	unconvincing	uncrippled	uncured	undeclined
unconfined	unconstant	unconvincingly	uncritical	uncurious	undecomposable
unconfinedly	unconstituted	uncooked	uncriticizable	uncurl	undecomposed
unconfirmed	unconstrained	uncooperative	uncropped	uncurled	undecorated
unconfused	unconstricted	uncoordinated	uncross	uncurrent	undefaceable
unconfusedly	unconsumed	uncordial	uncrossed	uncursed	undefaced
unconfuted	uncontaminated	uncorked	uncrowded	uncurtained	undefeated
uncongeal	uncontemplated	uncorrected	uncrown	uncushioned	undefended
uncongealable	uncontending	uncorroborated	uncrushable	uncustomary	undefensible
uncongealed	uncontested	uncorrupt	uncrystalline	undamaged	undefiled
uncongenial	uncontradictable	uncorrupted	uncrystallizable	undated	undefinable
uncongeniality	uncontradicted	uncorruptly	uncrystallized	undaughterly	undefined
uncongenially	uncontrite	uncorruptness	uncultivable	undazzled	undeformed
unconquerable	uncontrolled	uncountable	uncultivated	undebatable	undelayed
unconquered	uncontrolledly	uncourteous	uncultured	undecayed	undelineated

of a gap in the stratigraphic record. **b** The contact layer between such groups.

un·con·nec·ted (un'kə-nək'tid) *adj.* **1.** Not connected; uncoupled. **2.** Incoherent. **— un'con·nec'ted·ly** *adv.* **— un'·con·nec'ted·ness** *n.*

un·con·scion·a·ble (un·kon'shən-ə-bəl) *adj.* **1.** Going beyond customary or reasonable bounds; unjustifiable. **2.** Not governed by sense or prudence; unconscientious. **3.** Devoid of conscience; unprincipled: an *unconscionable* liar. **4.** *Law* Inequitable. **— un·con'scion·a·ble·ness** *n.* **— un·con'scion·a·bly** *adv.*

un·con·scious (un·kon'shəs) *adj.* **1.** Temporarily deprived of consciousness. **2.** Not cognizant; unaware: with *of: unconscious* of his charm. **3.** Not known or felt to exist; not produced or accompanied by conscious effort: *unconscious* thought. **4.** Not endowed with consciousness or a mind. — *n. Psychoanal.* That extensive area of the psyche that is not in the immediate field of awareness: sometimes distinguished from *preconscious.* **— un·con'scious·ly** *adv.* **un·con·scious·ness** (un·kon'shəs-nis) *n.* The state of being unconscious.
— Syn. *Unconsciousness, insensibility, syncope, swoon,* and *faint* denote a state, different from sleep, in which the mind is unaware of itself. *Unconsciousness* stresses the lack of mental awareness, and *insensibility,* the lack of sensory response. We sometimes say that a person is insensible rather than unconscious, because we can observe his lack of response to sensory stimuli but not his lack of awareness. *Syncope* is the medical term for the deficiency of blood to the brain that causes this condition. *Swoon* and *faint* are applied to the condition itself; of the two, *swoon* is now obsolescent and has largely been replaced by *faint.* Compare STUPOR.

un·con·sol·i·dat·ed (un'kən·sol'ə·dā'tid) *adj.* Not consolidated; loose.

un·con·sti·tu·tion·al (un'kon-sti-tōō'shən-əl, -tyōō'-) *adj.* Contrary to or violating the constitution or fundamental law of a state. **— un'con·sti·tu'tion·al'i·ty** *n.* **— un'con·sti·tu'tion·al·ly** *adv.*

un·con·trol·la·ble (un'kən·trō'lə·bəl) *adj.* Beyond control; ungovernable. **— un'con·trol'la·bil'i·ty, un'con·trol'la·ble·ness** *n.* **— un'con·trol'la·bly** *adv.*

un·con·ven·tion·al (un'kən·ven'shən·əl) *adj.* **1.** Not adhering to conventions; nonconformist. **2.** Not usual or ordinary: *unconventional* weapons. **— un'con·ven'tion·al'i·ty** *n.* **— un'con·ven'tion·al·ly** *adv.*

un·con·vert·ed (un'kən·vûr'tid) *adj.* **1.** Not converted. **2.** *Theol.* Impenitent; without faith.

un·cork (un·kôrk') *v.t.* To draw the cork from.

un·count·ed (un·koun'tid) *adj.* **1.** Not counted. **2.** Beyond counting; innumerable.

un·cou·ple (un·kup'əl) *v.* **·led, ·ling** *v.t.* **1.** To disconnect or unfasten. **2.** To set loose; unleash. **— v.i. 3.** To break loose.

un·couth (un·kōōth') *adj.* **1.** Rough; crude; unrefined: *uncouth* manners. **2.** Marked by awkwardness or oddity; outlandish; ungainly. **3.** *Archaic* Not familiar or well-known. [OE *uncûth* unknown < *un-* not + *cûth,* pp. of *cunnan* to know, be able] **— un·couth'ly** *adv.* **— un·couth'ness** *n.*

un·cov·e·nant·ed (un·kuv'ə·nən·tid) *adj.* **1.** Not bound by a covenant. **2.** Not guaranteed by a covenant.

un·cov·er (un·kuv'ər) *v.t.* **1.** To remove the covering from. **2.** To make known; reveal; disclose. **3.** In military tactics, to expose successively, as lines of formation. **— v.i. 4.** To remove a covering. **5.** To raise or remove the hat, as in token of respect.

un·cov·ered (un·kuv'ərd) *adj.* **1.** Not covered; devoid of covering. **2.** Not covered by collateral security.

un·cre·ate (un'krē·āt') *v.t.* **·at·ed, ·at·ing** To deprive of existence.

un·cre·at·ed (un'krē·ā'tid) *adj.* **1.** Not yet created or brought into being. **2.** Not created; self-existent.

un·crowned (un·kround') *adj.* Not crowned; not officially recognized.

unc·tion (ungk'shən) *n.* **1.** The state or quality of being unctuous. **2.** *Eccl.* **a** A ceremonial anointing with oil, as in consecration or dedication. **b** The sacramental rite of anointing the sick, reserved in the Roman Catholic Church for those in danger of death: also called *extreme unction.* **3.** The act of anointing, as with oil. **4.** A substance used in anointing; ointment; unguent. [< F *onction* < L *unctio, -onis* < *ungere* to anoint] **— unc'tion·less** *adj.*

unc·tu·ous (ungk'chōō·əs) *adj.* **1.** Characterized by affected emotion; oily-tongued; unduly suave. **2.** Characterized by deep sympathetic feeling. **3.** Having the characteristics of an unguent; greasy; slippery to the touch. **4.** Soft; rich in organic matter, as certain soils. **5.** Having plasticity, as clay. [< Med.L *unctuosus* < L *unctum* ointment, orig. neut. pp. of *ungere* to anoint] **— unc'tu·ous·ly** *adv.* **— unc'tu·os'i·ty** (-chōō-os'ə·tē), **unc'tu·ous·ness** *n.*

UNCURK United Nations Commission for the Unification and Rehabilitation of Korea.

un·cut (un·kut') *adj.* **1.** Not cut. **2.** In bookbinding, having untrimmed margins. **3.** Unground, as a gem.

un·damped (un·dampt') *adj. Physics* **1.** Pertaining to or designating oscillations that continue without change in amplitude: *undamped* radio waves. **2.** Not damped or dampened; unrepressed: *undamped* spirits.

un·daunt·ed (un·dôn'tid, -dän'-) *adj.* Not daunted or intimidated; fearless; intrepid. **— un·daunt'ed·ly** *adv.* **— un·daunt'ed·ness** *n.*

un·dé (un'dā) *adj. Heraldry* Wavy; undulating: also *undy.* Also **un'dée.** [< OF < L *unda* wave]

un·dec·a·gon (un·dek'ə·gon) *n.* A figure that has eleven angles and eleven sides. [< L *undecim* eleven + -GON]

un·de·ceiv·a·ble (un'di·sē'və·bəl) *adj.* **1.** That cannot be deceived. **2.** *Obs.* Not deceitful.

un·de·ceive (un'di·sēv') *v.t.* **·ceived, ·ceiv·ing** To free from deception, error, or illusion.

un·de·ceived (un'di·sēvd') *adj.* **1.** Not deceived. **2.** Freed from error or deception.

un·de·cid·ed (un'di·sī'did) *adj.* **1.** Not having the mind made up. **2.** Not decided upon; not determined. **— un'·de·cid'ed·ly** *adv.* **— un'de·cid'ed·ness** *n.*

un·decked (un·dekt') *adj.* **1.** Having no ornaments; not decked out. **2.** Having no deck, as a vessel.

un·de·mon·stra·tive (un'di·mon'strə·tiv) *adj.* Not demonstrative; not disposed to show the feelings. **— un'de·mon'stra·tive·ly** *adv.* **— un'de·mon'stra·tive·ness** *n.*

un·de·ni·a·ble (un'di·nī'ə·bəl) *adj.* **1.** That cannot be denied; indisputably true; obviously correct. **2.** Unquestionably good; excellent. **— un'de·ni'a·bly** *adv.*

un·der (un'dər) *prep.* **1.** Beneath, so as to have something directly above; covered by: layer *under* layer. **2.** In a place lower than; at the foot or bottom of: *under* the hill. **3.** Beneath the shelter of: *under* the paternal roof. **4.** Beneath the concealment, guise, or assumption of: *under* a false name. **5.** Less than in number, degree, age, value, or amount: *under* 10 tons. **6.** Inferior to in quality, character, or rank. **7.** Dominated by; owing allegiance to; subordinate or subservient to: *under* the Nazi flag. **8.** Subject to the guidance, tutorship, or direction of: He studied *under* Mendelssohn. **9.** Subject to the moral obligation or sanction of: a statement *under* oath. **10.** With the liability or certainty of incurring: *under* penalty of the law. **11.** Subject to the influence or pressure of; swayed or impelled by: *under* the circumstances. **12.** Driven or propelled by: *under* sail. **13.** In the group or class of; within the matter titled or headed: included *under* History. **14.** Being the subject of: *under* medical treatment. **15.** During the period of; in the reign of; pending the administration of. **16.** By virtue of; authorized, substantiated, attested, or warranted by: *under* his own signature. **17.** In conformity to or in accordance with; having regard to. **18.** Planted or sowed with: an acre *under* wheat. — *adv.* **1.** In or into a position below something; underneath. **2.** In or into an inferior or subordinate degree or rank. **3.** So as to be covered or hidden;

in or into concealment. **4.** So as to be less than the required amount. — **to go under** To fail or collapse, as a business venture. — *adj.* **1.** Situated or moving under something else; lower or lowermost: an *under* layer. **2.** *Zool.* Ventral: the *under* side of a rattlesnake. **3.** Lower in rank or authority; subordinate. **4.** Less than usual, standard, or prescribed; insufficient. **5.** Held in subjection or restraint: used predicatively: Keep your emotions *under.* [OE]

— **Syn.** *Under, below,* and *beneath* all mean in a lower or inferior position, masked or covered by. *Under* is the most general of these words, and may also be used to denote subordination: to serve *under* the king, to be listed *under* a topical heading. *Below* usually denotes a physically lower position, while *beneath* emphasizes moral or physical inferiority: *below* the horizon, *beneath* contempt.

under- *combining form* **1.** Below in position; situated or directed beneath; on the underside; as in:

underarch	underfeathering	underpart
underbody	underfill	underpier
underbridge	underfire	undershore
underbud	undergnaw	undersole
undercasing	undergore	underspread
undercellar	underjaw	understroke
undercovert	underlip	undersurface
underdraw	undermark	undersweep
undereaten	undernamed	underthrust

2. Below a surface or covering; lower; as in:

underbodice	underdress	underjacket
undercloth	underearth	underlife
undercrust	underflooring	underpainting
underdish	undergarb	underpetticoat
underdrawers	underglow	underregion

3. Inferior in rank or importance; subordinate; subsidiary; as in:

underactor	underking	undersecretaryship
underagent	underkingdom	underservant
undercaptain	undermaid	understeward
underchief	underofficer	underteacher
underclerk	underofficial	undertitle
undergod	underreader	undertreasurer

4. Insufficient or insufficiently; less than is usual or proper; as in:

underact	underofficered	underripe
undercapitalize	underpaid	undersailed
underclothed	underpeopled	undersaturated
underconsumption	underplotted	underspecified
underdeveloped	underpopulated	underspend
underdose	underpowered	understaffed
underexercise	underpraise	understimulus
undergrow	underprice	understocked
underload	underprize	undertax
undermanned	underproduce	undertrained
underniceness	underproportioned	underwork

5. Subdued; hidden; as in:

underbreath	undermelody	undertheme
underemphasis	undernote	underthought
underfeeling	underplot	undervoice

un·der·a·chiev·er (un′dər·ə·chē′vər) *n.* A pupil, student, etc., whose work does not come up to his promise. — **un′der·a·chieve′ment** *n.*

un·der·age[1] (un′dər·āj′) *adj.* Not of a requisite age; immature. Also **un′der·age′.**

un·der·age[2] (un′dər·ij) *n.* An insufficiency; shortage.

un·der·arm[1] (un′dər·ärm′) *adj.* Situated, placed, or used under the arm. — *n.* The armpit.

un·der·arm[2] (un′dər·ärm′) *adj.* In various sports, as tennis, baseball, etc., executed with the hand lower than the elbow. — *adv.* In an underarm manner. Also *underhand.*

un·der·bel·ly (un′dər·bel′ē) *n. pl.* **·lies 1.** The lower region of the belly. **2.** Any similar unprotected part.

un·der·bid (un′dər·bid′) *v.t.* **·bid, ·bid·ding 1.** To bid lower than, as in a competition. **2.** In bridge, to fail to bid the full value of (a hand). — **un′der·bid′der** *n.*

un·der·bred (un′dər·bred′) *adj.* **1.** Of impure breed; not thoroughbred. **2.** Lacking in good breeding; ill-bred.

un·der·brush (un′dər·brush′) *n.* Small trees and shrubs growing beneath forest trees; undergrowth. Also **un′der·bush′** (-bŏŏsh′).

un·der·buy (un′dər·bī′) *v.t.* **·bought, ·buy·ing 1.** To buy at a price lower than that paid by (another). **2.** To pay less than the value for.

under canvas *Naut.* Under sail; propelled by the wind.

un·der·car·riage (un′dər·kar′ij) *n.* **1.** The framework supporting the body of a structure, as an automobile. **2.** The principal landing gear of an aircraft.

un·der·charge (*v.* un′dər·chärj′; *n.* un′dər·chärj′) *v.t.* **·charged, ·charg·ing 1.** To make an inadequate charge for. **2.** To load with an insufficient charge, as a gun. — *n.* An inadequate or insufficient charge.

un·der·class (un′dər·klas, -kläs) *n. Sociol.* The group in a society so hopelessly poverty-stricken and so unorganized as to be beneath any apparent social class structure.

un·der·class·man (un′dər·klas′mən, -kläs′-) *n. pl.* **·men** (-mən) A freshman or sophomore in a school or college.

un·der·clay (un′dər·klā′) *n.* A layer of clay underlying a coal seam, often containing the roots of ancient coal-forming plants: also called *seatstone.*

un·der·clothes (un′dər·klōz′, -klōthz′) *n.pl.* Clothes designed for underwear, or to be worn next to the skin. Also **un′der·cloth′ing** (-klōth′ing).

un·der·coat (un′dər·kōt′) *n.* **1.** A coat worn under another coat. **2.** Underfur (which see). **3.** A layer of paint, varnish, etc., beneath another layer: also **un′der·coat′ing.** — *v.t.* To provide with an undercoat (def. 3).

un·der·cool (un′dər·kōōl′) *v.t.* To supercool.

un·der·cov·er (un′dər·kuv′ər) *adj.* Secret; surreptitious; especially, engaged in spying or secret investigation.

under cover Secretively; surreptitiously.

un·der·cur·rent (un′dər·kûr′ənt) *n.* **1.** A current, as of water or air, below another or below the surface. **2.** A hidden drift or tendency, as of popular sentiments.

un·der·cut (*n. & adj.* un′dər·kut′; *v.* un′dər·kut′) *n.* **1.** The act or result of cutting under. **2.** The tenderloin. **3.** A slanting cut in a sawed log. **4.** A notch cut in the side of a tree so that it will fall toward that side when sawed through. **5.** Any part that is cut away below. **6.** In sports, a cut or backspin imparted to the ball. — *v.t.* **·cut, ·cut·ting 1.** To cut under. **2.** To cut away a lower portion of. **3.** To work or sell for lower payment than (a rival). **4.** In golf, to impart backspin to (the ball) by striking it obliquely downward. **5.** In tennis, to use an underhand stroke in cutting (the ball). — *adj.* **1.** Having the parts in relief cut under. **2.** Done by undercutting.

un·der·do (un′dər·dōō′) *v.t. & v.i.* **·did, ·done, ·do·ing** To do insufficiently.

un·der·dog (un′dər·dôg′, -dog′) *n.* **1.** One who is at a disadvantage in a struggle; a probable loser. **2.** One who is victimized or downtrodden by society.

un·der·done (un′dər·dun′) *adj.* **1.** Insufficiently done. **2.** Not cooked to the full; rare.

un·der·drain (un′dər·drān′) *n.* A subsurface drain built to carry off water percolating through the soil above. — **un′der·drain′age** (-drā′nij) *n.*

un·der·drive (un′dər·drīv′) *n. Mech.* A gearing device that turns a drive shaft slower than the engine: opposed to *overdrive.*

un·der·em·ployed (un′dər·em·ploid′) *adj.* Unable to get a full-time or regular job; unemployed part of the time or working too few hours. — **un′der·em·ploy′ment** *n.*

un·der·es·ti·mate (*v.* un′dər·es′tə·māt; *n.* un′dər·es′tə·mit) *v.t.* **·mat·ed, ·mat·ing** To put too low an estimate upon. — *n.* **1.** An insufficiently high opinion. **2.** An estimate below the just value or expense. — **un′der·es′ti·ma′tion** *n.*

— **Syn.** (verb) *Underestimate, underrate,* and *undervalue* mean

---

unecclesiastic	unendangered	unenlivened	unessayed	unexorcised	unexterminated
uneclipsed	unendeared	unenriched	unestablished	unexpanded	unextinguishable
uneconomic	unendearing	unenrolled	unesthetic	unexpectant	unextinguished
uneconomical	unendearingly	unenslaved	unestimated	unexpended	unextraditable
unedible	unended	unentangled	unethical	unexpendible	unfadable
unedifying	unending	unentered	unetymological	unexpert	unfaded
uneducable	unendorsed	unenterprising	unexacting	unexpiated	unfading
uneffaced	unendowed	unentertaining	unexaggerated	unexpired	unfallen
uneliminated	unendurable	unenthralled	unexalted	unexplainable	unfaltering
unelucidated	unenduring	unenthusiastic	unexamined	unexplained	unfashionable
unemancipated	unenforceable	unenthusiastically	unexcavated	unexplicit	unfashioned
unembarrassed	unenforced	unentitled	unexcelled	unexploded	unfastened
unembellished	unenfranchised	unenviable	unexchangeable	unexploited	unfatherly
unemotional	unengaged	unenvied	unexcited	unexplored	unfathomable
unemotionally	unengaging	unenvious	unexciting	unexported	unfathomed
unemphatic	unengagingly	unenvying	unexcluded	unexposed	unfatigued
unemphatically	un-English	unequipped	unexcused	unexpressed	unfavored
unemptied	unenjoyable	unerasable	unexecuted	unexpunged	unfeared
unenclosed	unenjoyed	unerased	unexercised	unexpurgated	unfearing
unencumbered	unenlightened	unescapable	unexhausted	unextended	unfeasible

to judge to be lower or less than actual value or worth. *Underestimate* is the most general word, applicable to amount, size, importance, power, ability, worth, etc. *Underrate* is limited to ability and power, and *undervalue*, to worth. All three words suggest primarily an error of judgment, but they are sometimes used of conscious, willful disparagement. — **Ant.** overestimate.

un·der·ex·pose (un/dər·ik·spōz/) *v.t.* **·posed, ·pos·ing** *Photog.* To expose (a film) less than is required for proper development. — **un/der·ex·po/sure** (-spō/zhər) *n.*

un·der·feed (un/dər·fēd/) *v.t.* **·fed, ·feed·ing** 1. To feed insufficiently. 2. To supply fuel for (an engine) from beneath.

un·der·foot (un/dər·fŏŏt/) *adv.* 1. Beneath the feet; down on the ground; immediately below. 2. In the way.

un·der·fur (un/dər·fûr/) *n.* The coat of dense, fine hair forming the main part of a pelt, as in seals: also called *undercoat.*

un·der·gar·ment (un/dər·gär/mənt) *n.* A garment to be worn under the outer garments.

un·der·gird (un/dər·gûrd/) *v.t.* **·girt** or **·gird·ed, ·gird·ing** To fasten, gird, or support beneath or from beneath.

un·der·glaze (un/dər·glāz/) *adj.* Used in or suitable for porcelain decoration before the glaze is applied.

un·der·go (un/dər·gō/) *v.t.* **·went, ·gone, ·go·ing** 1. To be subjected to; have experience of; suffer. 2. To bear up under; endure.

un·der·grad·u·ate (un/dər·graj/ōō·it) *n.* A university or college student who has not received a bachelor's degree.

un·der·ground (*adj., n.* un/dər·ground/; *adv.* un/dər·ground/) *adj.* 1. Situated, done, or operating beneath the surface of the ground. 2. Done in secret; clandestine. — *n.* 1. That which is beneath the surface of the ground, as a passage or space. 2. A group secretly organized to resist or oppose those in control of a government or country. 3. *Brit.* A subway (def. 1). — *adv.* 1. Beneath the surface of the ground. 2. Secretly.

Underground Railroad A system of cooperation among antislavery people, before 1861, for assisting fugitive slaves to escape to Canada and the free States.

un·der·grown (un/dər·grōn/) *adj.* Not fully grown; undersized.

un·der·growth (un/dər·grōth/) *n.* 1. A growth of smaller plants among larger ones; especially, a thicket or copse in or as in a forest. 2. The condition of being undergrown. 3. A close growth of hair beneath and finer than the outer growth of a pelt.

un·der·hand (un/dər·hand/) *adj.* 1. Done or acting in a treacherously secret manner; unfair; sly. 2. In baseball, cricket, etc., underarm. — **Syn.** See STEALTHY. — *adv.* 1. Underhandedly; slyly; clandestinely. 2. Underarm².

un·der·hand·ed (un/dər·han/did) *adj.* 1. Underhand. 2. Short-handed. — **un/der·hand/ed·ly** *adv.* — **un/der·hand/ed·ness** *n.*

un·der·hung (un/dər·hung/) *adj.* 1. *Anat.* Protruding from beneath, as a lower jaw projecting beyond the upper jaw. 2. Running on rollers on a rail below it, as a sliding door. 3. *Mech.* Underslung.

un·der·laid (un/dər·lād/) *adj.* 1. Laid underneath; supporting. 2. Supported by or having something lying or placed underneath.

un·der·lay (*v.* un/dər·lā/; *n.* un/dər·lā/) *v.t.* **·laid, ·lay·ing** 1. To place (one thing) under another. 2. To furnish with a base or lining. 3. *Printing* To support or raise by underlays. — *n.* 1. *Printing* A piece of paper, etc., placed under certain parts of a printing form, to bring them to the proper level. 2. *Mining* An inclination, as of a lode.

un·der·lease (un/dər·lēs/) *n.* A sublease.

un·der·let (un/dər·let/) *v.t.* **·let, ·let·ting** 1. To sublet. 2. To lease at less than the usual rate.

un·der·lie (un/dər·lī/) *v.t.* **·lay, ·lain, ·ly·ing** 1. To lie below or under. 2. To be the basis or support of: the principle that *underlies* a scheme. 3. To constitute a first or prior claim or lien over: A first mortgage *underlies* a second. 4. To be subject, answerable, or liable to. [OE *underlicgan*]

un·der·line (un/dər·līn/) *v.t.* **·lined, ·lin·ing** 1. To mark with a line underneath; underscore. 2. To emphasize. — *n.* A line underneath, as beneath a printed or written word or syllable to indicate emphasis or stress.

un·der·ling (un/dər·ling) *n.* A subordinate; an inferior; a servile person.

un·der·ly·ing (un/dər·lī/ing) *adj.* 1. Lying under: *underlying* strata. 2. Fundamental: *underlying* principles. 3. Prior in claim or lien.

un·der·men·tioned (un/dər·men/shənd) *adj.* Mentioned below in a writing.

un·der·mine (un/dər·mīn/, un/dər·mīn) *v.t.* **·mined, ·min·ing** 1. To excavate beneath; dig a mine or passage under: to *undermine* a fortress. 2. To weaken by wearing away at the base. 3. To weaken or impair secretly or by degrees: to *undermine* one's health. — **un/der·min/er** *n.*

un·der·most (un/dər·mōst/) *adj.* Having the lowest place or position. — *adv.* In the lowest place or position.

un·der·neath (un/dər·nēth/, -nēth/) *adv.* 1. In a place below. 2. On the under or lower side. — *prep.* 1. Beneath; under; below. 2. Under the form or appearance of. 3. Under the authority of; in the control of. — *adj.* Lower. — *n.* The lower or under part or side. [OE *underneothan*]

un·der·nour·ish (un/dər·nûr/ish) *v.t.* To provide with nourishment insufficient in amount or quality for proper health and growth. — **un/der·nour/ish·ment** *n.*

un·dern·song (un/dərn·sông/, -song/) *n.* Tierce (def. 5). [OE *undern* midday, midday meal + SONG]

un·der·pants (un/dər·pants/) *n.pl.* *U.S.* An undergarment worn over the loins and sometimes extending over the thighs or lower legs.

un·der·pass (un/dər·pas/, -päs/) *n.* *U.S.* A passage beneath; especially, the section of a way or road that passes under railway tracks or under another road.

un·der·pay (un/dər·pā/) *v.t.* **·paid, ·pay·ing** To pay insufficiently.

un·der·pin (un/dər·pin/) *v.t.* **·pinned, ·pin·ning** 1. To support, as a wall or structure, from below, especially when a previous support is removed, by inserting a prop or pier. 2. To corroborate; support.

un·der·pin·ning (un/dər·pin/ing) *n.* 1. Material or framework used to support a wall or building from below. 2. *pl. Informal* The legs.

un·der·pitch vault (un/dər·pich/) *Archit.* A vault formed by the intersection of two vaults that spring from the same level but are of uneven widths. For illustration see VAULT¹.

un·der·plant (un/dər·plant/, -plänt/) *v.t. Rare* To plant young trees under (existing trees).

un·der·priv·i·leged (un/dər·priv/ə·lijd) *adj.* Not privileged to enjoy certain rights to which everyone is theoretically entitled, as because of poverty, illiteracy, etc.

un·der·pro·duc·tion (un/dər·prə·duk/shən) *n.* Production below capacity or below requirements.

un·der·proof (un/dər·proof/) *adj.* Having less strength than proof spirit (which see).

un·der·prop (un/dər·prop/) *v.t.* **·propped, ·prop·ping** To prop from below; support.

un·der·quote (un/dər·kwōt/) *v.t.* **·quot·ed, ·quot·ing** To undersell or offer to undersell, as goods or stocks.

un·der·rate (un/dər·rāt/) *v.t.* **·rat·ed, ·rat·ing** To rate too low; underestimate. — **Syn.** See UNDERESTIMATE.

un·der·run (un/dər·run/) *v.t.* **·ran, ·run, ·run·ning** 1. To run or pass beneath. 2. *Naut.* To examine (a line, hawser, etc.) from below by drawing a boat along beneath it.

un·der·score (*v.* un/dər·skôr/, -skōr/; *n.* un/dər·skôr/, -skōr/) *v.t.* **·scored, ·scor·ing** To draw a line below, as for indicating emphasis; underline. — *n.* A line drawn beneath a word, etc., as for emphasis.

un·der·sea (un/dər·sē/) *adj.* Existing, carried on, or adapted for use beneath the surface of the sea. — *adv.* Beneath the surface of the sea: also **un/der·seas/** (-sēz/).

un·der·sec·re·tar·y (un/dər·sek/rə·ter/ē) *n.* *pl.* **·tar·ies** In a government department, the official who ranks next below the secretary.

unfed	unflaggingly	unforgetful	unfrequent	unglazed	unhalved
unfederated	unflattered	unforgetting	unfrequently	unglossed	unhammered
unfeigningly	unflattering	unforgivable	unfrozen	unglove	unhampered
unfelt	unflavored	unforgiven	unfulfilled	ungloved	unhandicapped
unfeminine	unflickering	unforgiving	unfunded	unglue	unhandled
unfenced	unfoiled	unforgot	unfurnished	ungoverned	unhang
unfermented	unforbearing	unforgotten	unfurrowed	ungowned	unhanged
unfertile	unforbidden	unformulated	ungallant	ungraced	unharassed
unfertilized	unforced	unforsaken	ungalled	ungraceful	unharbored
unfetter	unforcedly	unfortified	ungarnished	ungracefully	unhardened
unfettered	unfordable	unfought	ungartered	ungraded	unharmed
unfilial	unforeboding	unfound	ungathered	ungrafted	unharmful
unfilled	unforeknown	unframed	ungenial	ungrained	unharmfully
unfilmed	unforeseeable	unfranchised	ungenteel	ungratified	unharming
unfiltered	unforeseeing	unfraternal	ungentle	ungrounded	unharmonious
unfired	unforeseen	unfraught	ungentlemanly	ungrudging	unharnessed
unfittingly	unforested	unfree	ungently	ungrudgingly	unharrowed
unfixed	unforetold	unfreezable	ungifted	unguided	unharvested
unfixedness	unforfeited	unfreeze	ungirded	unhackneyed	unhastily
unflagging	unforged	un-French	ungladdened	unhailed	unhasty

un·der·sell (un′dər·sel′) *v.t.* **·sold, ·sell·ing** **1.** To sell at a lower price than. **2.** To sell for less than the real value. — **un′der·sell′er** *n.*

un·der·set (un′dər·set′) *n.* An undercurrent in the ocean.

un·der·sexed (un′dər·sekst′) *adj.* Having, displaying, or characterized by inadequate sexual desire or interest.

un·der·sher·iff (un′dər·sher′if) *n.* A deputy sheriff, especially one assuming the sheriff's duties in his absence.

un·der·shirt (un′dər·shûrt′) *n.* A garment worn beneath the shirt, generally of cotton.

un·der·shoot (un′dər·shoot′) *v.* **·shot, ·shoot·ing** *v.t.* **1.** To shoot short of or below (the mark, target, etc.). **2.** *Aeron.* To land an airplane or deliver a bomb short of (the mark). — *v.i.* **3.** To shoot or land short of the mark.

un·der·shot (un′dər·shot′) *adj.* **1.** Propelled by water that flows underneath: said of a water wheel. **2.** Projecting, as the lower jaw or teeth; also, having a projecting lower jaw or teeth.

un·der·shrub (un′dər·shrub′) *n.* A small, low-growing shrub.

un·der·side (un′dər·sīd′) *n.* The lower or under side or surface.

un·der·sign (un′dər·sīn′) *v.t.* To sign at the foot, end, or bottom of: used chiefly in the past participle.

UNDERSHOT WATER WHEEL

un·der·signed (un′dər·sīnd′) *adj.* **1.** Having one's signature at the end of a document. — *n.* The subscriber or subscribers to a document: with *the.*

un·der·sized (un′dər·sīzd′) *adj.* Of less than the normal or average size. Also **un′der·size′.**

un·der·skirt (un′dər·skûrt′) *n.* **1.** A skirt worn beneath another; a petticoat. **2.** The foundation skirt of a gown.

un·der·sleeve (un′dər·slēv′) *n.* A sleeve worn beneath another, especially when extending beyond a shorter one, or showing through slashes or openings.

un·der·slung (un′dər·slung′) *adj. Mech.* Having the springs fixed to the axles from below, instead of resting upon them: said of certain automobiles: also *underhung.*

un·der·soil (un′dər·soil′) *n.* Subsoil (which see).

un·der·song (un′dər·sông′, -song′) *n.* **1.** A subordinate strain or subdued melody. **2.** An underlying meaning.

un·der·sparred (un′dər·spärd′) *adj. Naut.* Having too few, too short, or too slight spars or masts.

un·der·stand (un′dər·stand′) *v.* **·stood, ·stand·ing** *v.t.* **1.** To come to know the meaning or import of; apprehend. **2.** To comprehend the nature or character of: I do not *understand* her. **3.** To have comprehension or mastery of: Do you *understand* German? **4.** To be aware of; realize: She *understands* her position. **5.** To have been told; believe: I *understand* that she went home. **6.** To take or suppose to mean; infer the meaning of: How am I to *understand* that remark? **7.** To accept as a condition or stipulation: It is *understood* that the tenant will provide his own heat. **8.** To supply in thought when unexpressed. **9.** To be in agreement with; be privately in sympathy with: They *understand* each other. — *v.i.* **10.** To have understanding; comprehend. — **Syn.** See APPREHEND. [OE *understandan* < *under*- under + *standan* to stand] — **un′der·stand′a·ble** *adj.* — **un′der·stand′a·bly** *adv.*

un·der·stand·ing (un′dər·stan′ding) *n.* **1.** The act of one who understands, or the resulting state; comprehension. **2.** The power by which one understands. **3.** The sum of the mental powers by which knowledge is acquired, retained, and extended; the power of apprehending relations and making inferences from them. **4.** The facts or elements of a case as apprehended by any one individual; opinion. **5.** An informal or confidential compact; also, the subject of such a compact; the thing agreed on. **6.** An arrangement or settlement of differences, or of disputed points: They have come to an *understanding.* — *adj.* **1.** Possessing comprehension and good sense. **2.** Tolerant or sympathetic. — **un′der·stand′ing·ly** *adv.* — **un′der·stand′ing·ness** *n.* — **Syn.** (noun) **2.** reason, intelligence, intuition, judgment, perception. Compare INTELLECT.

un·der·state (un′dər·stāt′) *v.* **·stat·ed, ·stat·ing** *v.t.* **1.** To state with less force than the truth warrants or allows. **2.** To state, as a number or dimension, as less than the true one. — *v.i.* **3.** To make an understatement.

un·der·state·ment (un′dər·stāt′mənt) *n.* A statement deliberately worded so as to be unemphatic or restrained in tone, often used as a contrast to point up the significance of its contents; also, the technique or practice of making such statements.

un·der·stood (un′dər·stŏŏd′) Past tense and past participle of UNDERSTAND. — *adj.* **1.** Assumed; agreed upon by all. **2.** Supplied in thought when unexpressed, as the subject of a sentence.

un·der·strap·per (un′dər·strap′ər) *n.* An underling; a subordinate agent.

un·der·stra·tum (un′dər·strā′təm, -strat′əm) *n. pl.* **·stra·ta** (-strā′tə, -strat′ə) or **·stra·tums** A substratum.

un·der·stud·y (un′dər·stud′ē) *v.t. & v.i.* **·stud·ied, ·stud·y·ing** **1.** To study (a part) in order to be able, if necessary, to take the place of the actor playing it. **2.** To act as an understudy to (another actor). — *n. pl.* **·stud·ies** **1.** An actor or actress who can take the place of another actor in a given role when necessary. **2.** A person prepared to perform the work or fill the position of another.

un·der·take (un′dər·tāk′) *v.* **took, ·tak·en, ·tak·ing** *v.t.* **1.** To take upon oneself; agree or attempt to do; begin. **2.** To contract to do; pledge oneself to. **3.** To guarantee or promise. **4.** To take under charge or guidance. **5.** *Obs.* To enter into combat with. — *v.i.* **6.** To make oneself responsible or liable; be surety: with *for.*

un·der·tak·er (un′dər·tā′kər for *def. 1*; un′dər·tā′kər for *def. 2*) *n.* **1.** One who undertakes any work or enterprise; especially, a contractor. **2.** One whose business it is to arrange for the cremation or burial of the dead and to oversee funerals.

un·der·tak·ing (un′dər·tā′king; *for def. 3* un′dər·tā′king) *n.* **1.** The act of one who undertakes any task or enterprise. **2.** The thing undertaken; a task. **3.** The business of an undertaker (def. 2). **4.** An engagement, promise, or guaranty.

un·der·ten·ant (un′dər·ten′ənt) *n.* A subtenant (which see).

un·der·thrust (un′dər·thrust′) *n. Geol.* **1.** A deformation of the earth's crust in which a mass of rock is covered by an advancing overlying mass. **2.** The intruded rock mass itself.

un·der·tint (un′dər·tint′) *n.* A subdued tint.

un·der·tone (un′dər·tōn′) *n.* **1.** A tone of lower pitch or loudness than is usual; especially, the tone of a subdued voice or a whisper. **2.** A subdued shade of a color; also, a color upon which other colors have been imposed and which is seen through them. **3.** A meaning or suggestion implied but not expressed. **4.** An underlying stability in the price level of some stocks.

un·der·took (un′dər·tŏŏk′) Past tense of UNDERTAKE.

un·der·tow (un′dər·tō′) *n.* **1.** The flow of water beneath and in a direction opposite to the surface current. **2.** The seaward undercurrent below the surf.

un·der·trick (un′dər·trik′) *n.* In certain card games, a trick required to make the number declared, but not taken.

un·der·trump (un′dər·trump′) *v.t.* To play to (a previous card in the same trick) a trump lower than one already played by another player; also, to trump with too low a trump, and so be overtrumped.

un·der·val·ue (un′dər·val′yōō) *v.t.* **·ued, ·u·ing** **1.** To value too lightly; underrate; underestimate. **2.** *Obs.* To hold inferior: with *to* before the object compared. — **Syn.** See UNDERESTIMATE. — **un′der·val′u·a′tion** *n.*

unhatched	unhistoric	unidentified	unimpressible	uningenuous	unintentionally
unhealed	unhistorical	unidiomatic	unimpressionable	uninhabitable	uninteresting
unhealthful	unhistorically	unilluminated	unimpressive	uninhabited	uninterestingly
unheated	unhomogeneous	unillumined	uninaugurated	uninhibited	unintermitted
unheeded	unhonored	unillustrated	uninclosed	uninitiated	unintermittent
unheedful	unhood	unimaginable	unincorporated	uninjured	unintermitting
unheeding	unhoped	unimaginably	unincubated	uninspired	uninterpolated
unheedingly	unhostile	unimaginative	unincumbered	uninspiring	uninterpreted
unhelped	unhouse	unimaginatively	unindemnified	uninspiringly	uninterrupted
unhelpful	unhoused	unimagined	unindicated	uninstructed	unintimidated
unheralded	unhuman	unimbued	unindorsed	uninstructive	unintoxicated
unheroic	unhumanize	unimitated	uninfected	uninsurable	uninvaded
unheroically	unhung	unimpaired	uninfested	uninsured	uninvented
unhesitant	unhurt	unimpassioned	uninflammable	unintellectual	uninventive
unhesitantly	unhurtful	unimpeached	uninflected	unintelligibility	uninventively
unhesitating	unhygienic	unimpeded	uninfluenced	unintelligible	uninverted
unhesitatingly	unhygienically	unimplored	uninfluential	unintelligibleness	uninvested
unhewn	unhyphenated	unimposing	uninformed	unintelligibly	uninvited
unhindered	unhyphened	unimpregnated	uninfringed	unintended	uninviting
unhired	unideal	unimpressed	uningenious	unintentional	unintentingly

un·der·vest (un/dər·vest/) *n. Brit.* An undershirt.

un·der·waist (un/dər·wāst/) *n.* A waist to be worn under another waist.

un·der·wa·ter (un/dər·wô/tər, -wot/ər) *adj.* **1.** Being, occurring, or used below the surface of a body of water: *underwater* research. **2.** Below the water line of a ship. — *n.* The region or ambience below the surface of the water. — *adv.* Below the surface of the water: to swim *underwater.*

un·der·way (un·dər·wā/) *adv.* **1.** In progress: The meeting was already *underway.* **2.** Into operation or motion: to get the fund drive *underway.* Also **under way.**

un·der·wear (un/dər·wâr/) *n.* Garments worn underneath the ordinary outer garments; underclothes.

un·der·weight (un/dər·wāt/) *adj.* Having less than normal weight. — *n.* Too little weight; also, weight below normal.

un·der·went (un/dər·went/) Past tense of UNDERGO.

un·der·wing (un/dər·wing/) *n. Entomol.* **1.** One of the posterior pair of wings in an insect. **2.** One of a genus (*Catocala*) of moths having brightly colored hind wings.

un·der·wood (un/dər·wood/) *n.* Low trees and brush growing among large forest trees.

un·der·world (un/dər·wûrld/) *n.* **1.** In Greek and Roman mythology, the abode of the dead; Hades; Orcus. ◆ Collateral adjective: *chthonian.* **2.** The part of society engaged in crime or vice; especially, organized criminals, as gangsters, racketeers, etc. **3.** Any region below the surface of the earth, ocean, etc. **4.** The antipodes. **5.** *Archaic* The terrestrial world; the earth.

un·der·write¹ (un/dər·rīt/) *v.* **·wrote, ·writ·ten, ·writ·ing** *v.t.* **1.** To write beneath; subscribe. **2.** In finance, to execute and deliver (a policy of insurance on specified property, especially marine property); insure; assume (a risk) by way of insurance. **3.** To engage to buy, at a determined price and time, all or part of the stock in (a new enterprise or company) that is not subscribed for by the public. **4.** Loosely, to guarantee or assume responsibility for, as an enterprise. **5.** To undertake to pay, as a written pledge of money. — *v.i.* **6.** To act as an underwriter; especially, to issue a policy of insurance. [OE *underwrītan,* trans. of L *subscribere*]

un·der·write² (un/dər·rīt/) *v.t. & v.i.* **·wrote, ·writ·ten, ·writ·ing** To write in a deliberately restrained, unemphatic style; understate. [< UNDER- + WRITE]

un·der·writ·er (un/dər·rī/tər) *n.* **1.** A body corporate or a person in the insurance business; one who sets up the premium for a risk. **2.** One who underwrites (def. 3) an issue of stocks, bonds, or the like.

un·de·sign·ing (un/di·zī/ning) *adj.* Artless; sincere.

un·de·sir·a·ble (un/di·zīr/ə·bəl) *adj.* Not desirable; unwanted or objectionable. — *n.* One considered to be objectionable or unacceptable. — **un/de·sir/a·bil/i·ty, un/de·sir/a·ble·ness** *n.* — **un/de·sir/a·bly** *adv.*

un·did (un·did/) Past tense of UNDO.

un·dies (un/dēz) *n. pl. Informal* Underwear.

un·dine (un·dēn/, un/dēn, -dīn) *n.* In folklore, a water nymph who could obtain a soul by marrying a mortal and bearing a child. [< G or F < NL *undina* < L *unda* wave]

un·di·rect·ed (un/di·rek/tid, -dī-) *adj.* **1.** Unguided; lacking direction. **2.** Not addressed, as a letter.

un·dis·posed (un/dis·pōzd/) *adj.* **1.** Not sold, settled, placed, or otherwise decided: frequently with *of.* **2.** *Rare* Disinclined. — **un/dis·pos/ed·ness** (-pō/zid·nis) *n.*

un·do (un·dōō/) *v.t.* **did, ·done, ·do·ing** **1.** To cause to be as if never done; reverse, annul, or cancel. **2.** To loosen or untie, as a knot, lacing, etc. **3.** To unfasten and open, as a parcel. **4.** To bring to ruin; destroy. **5.** *Obs.* To solve, as a riddle. [OE *undōn*] — **un·do/er** *n.*

un·do·ing (un·dōō/ing) *n.* **1.** Reversal, cancellation, etc., of what has been done. **2.** Destruction; ruin; also, the cause of ruin. **3.** The act of unfastening, loosening, etc.

un·done¹ (un·dun/) *adj.* **1.** Untied; unfastened. **2.** Ruined. [Orig. pp. of UNDO]

un·done² (un·dun/) *adj.* Not done. [< UN-¹ + DONE]

un·dou·ble (un·dub/əl) *v.* **·led, ·ling** *v.t. & v.i.* To unfold so as not to be double in thickness, etc.

un·doubt·ed (un·dou/tid) *adj.* Assured beyond question; being beyond a doubt; indubitable. — **un·doubt/ed·ly** *adv.*

un·draw (un·drô/) *v.t. & v.i.* **·drew, ·drawn, ·draw·ing** To draw open, away, or aside.

un·dreamed-of (un·drēmd/uv/, -ov/) *adj.* Not conceived of in the mind; unimaginable. Also **un·dreamt/-of** (-dremt/-).

un·dress (*v. & n.* un·dres/; *adj.* un/dres/) *v.t.* **1.** To divest of clothes; strip. **2.** To remove the dressing or bandages from, as a wound. — *v.i.* **3.** To remove one's clothing. — *n.* **1.** Ordinary attire, as distinguished from formal dress. **2.** Comfortable, informal clothing. **3.** Nudity. — *adj.* Pertaining to or characterized by everyday or informal attire.

un·dressed (un·drest/) *adj.* **1.** Not clothed. **2.** Not treated or dressed, as leather.

Und·set (ŏn/set), **Sigrid,** 1882–1949, Norwegian novelist.

und so wei·ter (ŏont zō vī/tər) *German* And so forth; et cetera. Abbr. *usw, u.s.w.*

un·due (un·dōō/, -dyōō/) *adj.* **1.** Excessive; disproportionate. **2.** Not justified by law; illegal. **3.** Not due; not yet demandable. **4.** Not appropriate; improper.

un·du·lant (un/dyə·lənt, -də-) *adj.* Undulating; waving.

undulant fever *Pathol.* A disease caused by a bacterium (genus *Brucella*) transmitted to man in the milk of infected cows and goats, and characterized by recurrent fever, swelling of the joints, neuralgic pains, etc.: also called *brucellosis, Malta fever, Mediterranean fever.*

un·du·late (*v.* un/dyə·lāt, -də-; *adj.* un/dyə·lit, -lāt, -də-) *v.* **·lat·ed, ·lat·ing** *v.t.* **1.** To cause to move like a wave or in waves. **2.** To give a wavy appearance to. — *v.i.* **3.** To move like a wave or waves. **4.** To have a wavy form or appearance. — **Syn.** See FLUCTUATE. — *adj.* **1.** Having a wavy margin, as a leaf. **2.** Having wavelike markings, as of color: also **un/du·lat/ed** (-lā/tid). [< L *undulatus* having wavelike markings, ult. < *unda* wave]

un·du·lat·ing (un/dyə·lā/ting, -də-) *adj.* Having the appearance of waves; vibrating; waving; wavy.

un·du·la·tion (un/dyə·lā/shən, -də-) *n.* **1.** The act of undulating. **2.** A waving or sinuous motion. **3.** A wave. **4.** An appearance as of waves; a gentle rise and fall. **5.** *Physics* The continuous propagation of waves through a medium. — **un/du·la·to/ry** (-lə·tôr/ē, -tō/rē), **un/du·lous** (-ləs) *adj.*

un·du·ly (un·dōō/lē, -dyōō/-) *adv.* **1.** Excessively. **2.** In violation of a moral or of a legal standard; unjustly.

un·dy (un/dē) *adj. Heraldry* Undé.

un·dy·ing (un·dī/ing) *adj.* Immortal; everlasting.

un·earned (un·ûrnd/) *adj.* **1.** Not earned by labor. **2.** Unmerited; undeserved.

unearned income See under INCOME.

unearned increment See under INCREMENT.

un·earth (un·ûrth/) *v.t.* **1.** To dig or root up from the earth. **2.** To reveal by or as by searching. — **Syn.** See DISCOVER.

un·earth·ly (un·ûrth/lē) *adj.* **1.** Not earthly; sublime. **2.** Weird; terrifying; supernatural or unnatural. **3.** *Informal* Ridiculously unconventional or inconvenient: at this *unearthly* hour. — **un·earth/li·ness** *n.*

un·eas·y (un·ē/zē) *adj.* **·eas·i·er, ·eas·i·est** **1.** Lacking ease, assurance, or security; disturbed. **2.** Not affording ease or rest; causing discomfort. **3.** Showing embarrassment or constraint; strained. — **un·eas/i·ly** *adv.* — **un·eas/i·ness** *n.*

un·ed·u·cat·ed (un·ej/ŏō·kā/tid) *adj.* Not educated; lacking education. — **Syn.** See IGNORANT.

UNEF United Nations Emergency Force.

un·em·ploy·a·ble (un/əm·ploi/ə·bəl) *adj.* Not employable. — *n.* A person who, because of illness, age, mental or physical incapacity, etc., cannot be employed.

un·em·ployed (un/əm·ploid/) *adj.* **1.** Having no remunerative employment; out of work. **2.** Not being put to use; idle. **3.** Not being used profitably; uninvested: *unemployed* resources. — *n.* A jobless person. — **the unemployed** Unemployed persons collectively. — **un/em·ploy/ment** *n.*

unemployment insurance *U.S.* A system of insurance authorized by the Federal Social Security Act of 1935, providing those who are involuntarily out of work with temporary compensation from a fund contributed to by employers and workers. Also **unemployment compensation.**

un·e·qual (un·ē/kwəl) *adj.* **1.** Not having equivalent or equal extension, duration, proportions, amounts, etc. **2.** Not equal in strength, ability, wealth, status, etc. **3.** In-

uninvoked	unknelled	unlevel	unlovable	unmanipulated	unmeasurable
uninvolved	unknightly	unlevied	unloved	unmannered	unmeasurably
unissued	unknowing	unlibidinous	unloveliness	unmannish	unmeasured
unjacketed	unknowingly	unlicensed	unloverlike	unmannishly	unmechanical
unjaded	unknowingness	unlifelike	unloving	unmanufacturable	unmediated
unjoined	unlabeled	unlighted	unlovingly	unmanufactured	unmedicated
unjointed	unlabelled	unlikable	unlubricated	unmarketable	unmelodious
unjoyful	unladylike	unlikeable	unmagnified	unmarketed	unmelted
unjoyfully	unlamented	unlined	unmaidenliness	unmarred	unmenaced
unjudged	unlash	unlink	unmaidenly	unmarriageable	unmendable
unjudicial	unlashed	unliquefiable	unmailable	unmarried	unmended
unjustifiable	unlaundered	unliquefied	unmalleable	unmastered	unmensurable
unjustifiably	unleased	unliquidated	unmanageable	unmatched	unmentionability
unkept	unled	unlit	unmanful	unmated	unmentioned
unkindled	unlessened	unliveliness	unmanfully	unmaternal	unmercenary
unkindliness	unlessoned	unlively	unmanfulness	unmatted	unmerchantable
unkingly	unlet	unlocated	unmangled	unmatured	unmerited
unkissed	unletted	unlocked	unmanifested	unmeant	unmeriting

adequate for the purpose; insufficient: with *to*. **4.** Inequitable; unfair. **5.** Wanting in uniformity; varying; irregular. **6.** Not balanced; unsymmetrical: *unequal* distribution. **7.** Involving poorly matched competitors or contestants: an *unequal* contest. — **un·e′qual·ly** *adv.*

un·e·qualed (un·ē′kwəld) *adj.* Not equaled or matched; unrivaled; supreme. Also **un·e′qualled.**

un·e·quiv·o·cal (un′i·kwiv′ə·kəl) *adj.* Understandable in only one way; not equivocal. — **un′e·quiv′o·cal·ly** *adv.*

un·err·ing (un·ûr′ing, -er′-) *adj.* **1.** Making no mistakes; not erring. **2.** Certain; accurate. — **un·err′ing·ly** *adv.*

UNESCO (yōō·nes′kō) The United Nations Educational, Scientific and Cultural Organization, established in 1946 to "advance mutual knowledge and understanding of peoples." Also **U·nes′co.**

un·es·sen·tial (un′ə·sen′shəl) *adj.* **1.** Not essential; not of prime importance. **2.** *Rare* Void of essence. — *n.* Something unimportant or dispensable. — **un′es·sen′tial·ly** *adv.*

un·e·ven (un·ē′vən) *adj.* **1.** Not even, smooth, or level; rough. **2.** Not level, parallel, or perfectly horizontal. **3.** Not divisible by two without remainder; odd: said of numbers. **4.** Not uniform; variable; spasmodic. **5.** *Obs.* Not fair or just. — **un·e′ven·ly** *adv.* — **un·e′ven·ness** *n.*

un·e·vent·ful (un′i·vent′fəl) *adj.* Devoid of noteworthy events; quiet. — **un′e·vent′ful·ly** *adv.*

un·ex·am·pled (un′ig·zam′pəld) *adj.* Having no precedent, analogy, or parallel example.

un·ex·cep·tion·a·ble (un′ik·sep′shən·ə·bəl) *adj.* That cannot be objected to; irreproachable. — **un′ex·cep′tion·a·ble·ness** *n.* — **un′ex·cep′tion·a·bly** *adv.*

un·ex·cep·tion·al (un′ik·sep′shən·əl) *adj.* **1.** Not exceptional; ordinary. **2.** Subject to no exception: *unexceptional* orders. **3.** Loosely, unexceptionable.

un·ex·pect·ed (un′ik·spek′tid) *adj.* Not expected; coming or occurring without warning; unforeseen. — **un′ex·pect′ed·ly** *adv.* — **un′ex·pect′ed·ness** *n.*

un·ex·pe·ri·enced (un′ik·spir′ē·ənst) *adj.* **1.** Not having been experienced; not known, undergone, etc. **2.** Lacking experience; inexperienced.

un·ex·pres·sive (un′ik·spres′iv) *adj.* **1.** Devoid of expression; inexpressive. **2.** *Obs.* Inexpressible. — **un′ex·pres′sive·ly** *adv.*

un·fail·ing (un·fā′ling) *adj.* **1.** Giving or constituting a supply that never fails; inexhaustible: an *unfailing* spring. **2.** Always fulfilling requirements; not falling short of need, hope, or expectation. **3.** Sure; infallible. — **un·fail′ing·ly** *adv.* — **un·fail′ing·ness** *n.*

un·fair (un·fâr′) *adj.* **1.** Characterized by partiality or prejudice; not fair or just. **2.** Dishonest; fraudulent. **3.** Not compatible with law and justice: *unfair* competition. — **un·fair′ly** *adv.* — **un·fair′ness** *n.*

un·faith·ful (un·fāth′fəl) *adj.* **1.** Not having kept faith; unworthy of trust; faithless. **2.** Not true to marriage vows: an *unfaithful* husband. **3.** Not true to a standard or to an original; not accurate or exact. **4.** *Obs.* Not having religious faith; unbelieving; infidel. — **Syn.** See PERFIDIOUS. — **un·faith′ful·ly** *adv.* — **un·faith′ful·ness** *n.*

un·fa·mil·iar (un′fə·mil′yər) *adj.* **1.** Not having knowledge or acquaintance: with *with*. **2.** Not known or recognizable: an *unfamiliar* face. — **un′fa·mil·i·ar′i·ty** (-mil′ē·ar′ə·tē) *n.* — **un′fa·mil′iar·ly** *adv.*

un·fast·en (un·fas′ən, -fäs′-) *v.t.* **1.** To untie; loosen; open. — *v.i.* **2.** To become untied or loosened.

un·fa·thered (un·fä′thərd) *adj.* **1.** Having no acknowledged father; illegitimate. **2.** Unauthenticated.

un·fa·vor·a·ble (un·fā′vər·ə·bəl) *adj.* Not favorable; unpropitious; adverse. Also *Brit.* **un·fa′vour·a·ble.** — **un·fa′vor·a·ble·ness** *n.* — **un·fa′vor·a·bly** *adv.*

Un·fed·er·at·ed Malay States (un·fed′ə·rā·təd) See MALAY STATES.

un·feel·ing (un·fē′ling) *adj.* **1.** Not sympathetic; hard; cruel. **2.** Devoid of feeling or sensation. — **un·feel′ing·ly** *adv.* — **un·feel′ing·ness** *n.*

un·feigned (un·fānd′) *adj.* Not feigned; not pretended; sincere; genuine. — **un·feign·ed·ly** (un·fā′nid·lē) *adv.*

un·fin·ished (un·fin′isht) *adj.* **1.** Not finished; incomplete. **2.** Having no finish or special surface treatment, as wood. **3.** Of fabrics: **a** Not bleached or processed. **b** Having a slight nap, as worsted.

un·fit (un·fit′) *adj.* **1.** Having no fitness; unsuitable. **2.** Not appropriate; improper. **3.** Not in sound physical condition. — *v.t.* **·fit·ted** or **·fit, ·fit·ting** To make unfit; disqualify. — **un·fit′ly** *adv.* — **un·fit′ness** *n.*

un·fix (un·fiks′) *v.t.* **1.** To unfasten; loosen; detach. **2.** To unsettle.

un·flap·pa·ble (un·flap′ə·bəl) *adj.* Characterized by unshakable composure; imperturbable. — **un·flap′pa·bil′i·ty** *n.*

un·fledged (un·flejd′) *adj.* **1.** Not yet fledged, as a young bird. **2.** Immature; inexperienced.

un·flesh·ly (un·flesh′lē) *adj.* Not corporeal, worldly, or sensual; ethereal; spiritual.

un·flinch·ing (un·flin′ching) *adj.* Not flinching; not shrinking from danger, pain, etc.; steadfast; brave. — **un·flinch′ing·ly** *adv.* — **un·flinch′ing·ness** *n.*

un·fold (un·fōld′) *v.t.* **1.** To open or spread out (something folded). **2.** To lay open to view. **3.** To make clear by detailed explanation; explain: to *unfold* a plan. **4.** To evolve; develop. — *v.i.* **5.** To become opened; expand. **6.** To become manifest. [OE *unfealdan*] — **un·fold′er** *n.*

un·for·get·ta·ble (un′fər·get′ə·bəl) *adj.* Not forgettable; memorable. — **un′for·get′ta·bly** *adv.*

un·formed (un·fôrmd′) *adj.* **1.** Devoid of shape or form. **2.** Not fully developed in character. **3.** Unorganized.

un·for·tu·nate (un·fôr′chə·nit) *adj.* **1.** Not fortunate; unhappy, unsuccessful, etc. **2.** Causing or attended by ill fortune; disastrous. — *n.* One who is unfortunate. — **un·for′tu·nate·ly** *adv.* — **un·for′tu·nate·ness** *n.*

un·found·ed (un·foun′did) *adj.* **1.** Having no foundation; groundless; baseless. **2.** Not founded or established. — **un·found′ed·ly** *adv.* — **un·found′ed·ness** *n.*

un·fre·quent·ed (un′fri·kwen′tid, un·frē′kwən·tid) *adj.* Not frequented; rarely or never visited.

un·friend·ed (un·fren′did) *adj.* Having no friends. — **un·friend′ed·ness** *n.*

un·friend·ly (un·frend′lē) *adj.* **1.** Unkindly disposed; inimical; hostile. **2.** Not favorable or propitious. — *adv.* In an unfriendly manner. — **un·friend′li·ness** *n.*

un·frock (un·frok′) *v.t.* **1.** To depose, as a monk or priest, from ecclesiastical rank. **2.** To divest of a frock or gown.

un·fruit·ful (un·frōōt′fəl) *adj.* **1.** Bearing no fruit; having no offspring; barren. **2.** Having no useful results; fruitless. — **un·fruit′ful·ly** *adv.* — **un·fruit′ful·ness** *n.*

un·fund·ed (un·fun′did) *adj.* Not funded: said of a debt.

un·furl (un·fûrl′) *v.t. & v.i.* **1.** To unroll, as a flag. **2.** To spread out; expand; unfold.

un·gain·ly (un·gān′lē) *adj.* Lacking grace; awkward. — *adv.* In a clumsy manner. — **un·gain′li·ness** *n.*

Un·ga·va (ung·gä′və, -gā′və) A district of northern Quebec province, including part of Labrador; 239,780 sq. mi.: also *New Quebec.*

un·gen·er·ous (un·jen′ər·əs) *adj.* **1.** Not generous; illiberal; niggardly. **2.** Unkind or harsh in judging others. — **un·gen′er·ous·ly** *adv.*

un·gird (un·gûrd′) *v.t.* **1.** To divest of or free from a belt, girdle, or confining band. **2.** To loosen or unfasten by or as by removing a belt, etc.

un·girt (un·gûrt′) *adj.* **1.** Not wearing or confined by a belt, girdle, or band. **2.** Slack; relaxed.

un·god·ly (un·god′lē) *adj.* **1.** Having no reverence for God; impious. **2.** Wicked; sinful. **3.** *Informal* Outrageous; unseemly. — *adv.* *Informal* Outrageously; inordinately. — **un·god′li·ness** *n.*

un·got·ten (un·got′n) *adj.* **1.** Not obtained; not acquired. **2.** *Obs.* Not begotten. Also **un·got′.**

un·gov·ern·a·ble (un·guv′ər·nə·bəl) *adj.* **1.** Not capable of being governed or controlled. **2.** Refractory; unruly. — **un·gov′ern·a·ble·ness** *n.* — **un·gov′ern·a·bly** *adv.*

un·gra·cious (un·grā′shəs) *adj.* **1.** Lacking in graciousness of manner; unmannerly. **2.** Not pleasing; offensive; unacceptable. — **un·gra′cious·ly** *adv.* — **un·gra′cious·ness** *n.*

---

unmethodical	unmolded	unmystified	unnoticed	unobtruding	unoppressed
unmilitary	unmolested	unnail	unnurtured	unobtrusive	unordained
unmilled	unmollified	unnamable	unobjectionable	unobtrusively	unoriginal
unmingle	unmolten	unnameable	unobliged	unobtrusiveness	unornamental
unmingled	unmortgaged	unnamed	unobliging	unoccasioned	unornate
unmirthful	unmotivated	unnaturalized	unobligingly	unoffended	unorthodoxy
unmirthfully	unmounted	unnavigable	unobnoxious	unoffending	unostentatious
unmistaken	unmourned	unnavigated	unobscured	unoffensive	unostentatiously
unmitigable	unmovable	unneeded	unobservable	unoffensively	unostentatiousness
unmixed	unmoved	unneedful	unobservant	unoffered	unowned
unmixt	unmoving	unnegotiable	unobservantly	unofficious	unoxidized
unmodified	unmown	unneighborliness	unobserved	unofficiously	unpacified
unmodish	unmurmuring	unneighborly	unobserving	unoiled	unpainful
unmodishly	unmusical	unnoted	unobstructed	unopen	unpainfully
unmoistened	unmuzzle	unnoticeable	unobtainable	unopened	unpainfulness
unmold	unmuzzled	unnoticeably	unobtained	unopposed	unpaired

un·gram·mat·i·cal (un'grə·mat'i·kəl) *adj.* **1.** Not in accordance with the rules of grammar. **2.** Characterized by or using grammar at variance with the rules. **— un'gram·mat'i·cal·ly** *adv.*

un·grate·ful (un·grāt'fəl) *adj.* **1.** Not feeling or showing gratitude; not thankful. **2.** Not pleasant; disagreeable. **3.** Unrewarding; yielding no return. **— un·grate'ful·ly** *adv.* **— un·grate'ful·ness** *n.*

un·gual (ung'gwəl) *adj.* Of, pertaining to, or resembling a hoof, claw, or nail. [< L *unguis* hoof, claw, nail]

un·guard (un·gärd') *v.t.* To allow to remain unprotected or vulnerable.

un·guard·ed (un·gär'did) *adj.* **1.** Having no guard; being without protection. **2.** Characterized by lack of caution or discretion: *unguarded* speech. **— un·guard'ed·ly** *adv.* **— un·guard'ed·ness** *n.*

un·guent (ung'gwənt) *n.* Any ointment or salve. [< L *unguentum* < *unguere* to anoint]

un·guic·u·late (ung·gwik'yə·lit, -lāt) *adj.* **1.** *Zool.* Having claws or nails, as distinguished from hoofs. **2.** *Bot.* Having a clawlike base, as the petals of pinks. **— n.** An unguiculate mammal. [< NL *unguiculatus* < L *unguiculus* fingernail, dim. of *unguis* nail]

un·guis (ung'gwis) *n.* *pl.* **·gues** (-gwēz) **1.** A nail, claw, or hoof. **2.** *Bot.* A clawlike base of a petal. [< L, nail]

un·gu·la (ung'gyə·lə) *n.* *pl.* **·lae** (-lē) **1.** *Zool.* A hoof, claw, or nail. **2.** *Geom.* That which is left of a cone or cylinder when the top is cut off by a plane oblique to the base. **3.** *Bot.* An unguis. [< L, hoof < *unguis* nail]

un·gu·lar (ung'gyə·lər) *adj.* Of, pertaining to, or resembling a nail, hoof, or claw; ungual.

un·gu·late (ung'gyə·lit, -lāt) *adj.* **1.** Having hoofs. **2.** Designating, pertaining to, or belonging to a large former division (*Ungulata*) of hoofed mammals, including the elephant, rhinoceros, horse, hog, and all the ruminants. **3.** Hoof-shaped. **— n.** A hoofed mammal. [< LL *ungulatus* < L *ungula* hoof]

un·gu·li·grade (ung'gyə·lə·grād') *adj.* Walking on hoofs, as a horse or cow. [< L *ungula* hoof + -GRADE]

un·hair (un·hâr') *v.t. & v.i.* To make or become free of hair, as hides by soaking and scraping.

un·hal·low (un·hal'ō) *v.t.* *Archaic* To profane; desecrate.

un·hal·lowed (un·hal'ōd) *adj.* **1.** Not consecrated or made holy. **2.** Unholy; wicked.

un·hand (un·hand') *v.t.* To remove one's hand from; release from the hand or hands; let go.

un·hand·some (un·han'səm) *adj.* **1.** Not pleasing in appearance; unattractive. **2.** Not gracious or generous; mean. **— un·hand'some·ly** *adv.* **— un·hand'some·ness** *n.*

un·hand·y (un·han'dē) **·hand·i·er, ·hand·i·est** *adj.* **1.** Inconvenient; hard to handle. **2.** Clumsy; lacking in manual skill. **— un·hand'i·ly** *adv.* **— un·hand'i·ness** *n.*

un·hap·py (un·hap'ē) *adj.* **·pi·er, ·pi·est 1.** Sad; miserable; depressed; wretched. **2.** Unlucky; unfortunate. **3.** Not tactful or appropriate; ill-chosen. **4.** *Obs.* Evil. **— un·hap'·pi·ly** *adv.* **— un·hap'pi·ness** *n.*

un·har·ness (un·här'nis) *v.t.* **1.** To remove the harness from; unyoke; release. **2.** To remove the armor from.

un·hat (un·hat') *v.i.* **·hat·ted, ·hat·ting** *Rare* To take off one's hat, especially to show respect or in worship.

un·health·y (un·hel'thē) *adj.* **·health·i·er, ·health·i·est 1.** Lacking health or vigor; sickly; unsound: *unhealthy* animals or plants; also, indicating such a condition: *unhealthy* signs. **2.** Injurious to health; insalubrious: an *unhealthy* climate. **3.** Morally unsound; unwholesome: *unhealthy* fiction. **— un·health'i·ly** *adv.* **— un·health'i·ness** *n.*

un·heard (un·hûrd') *adj.* **1.** Not perceived by the ear. **2.** Not granted a hearing. **3.** Obscure; unknown.

un·heard-of (un·hûrd'uv', -ov') *adj.* Not known of before; unknown or unprecedented.

un·helm (un·helm') *Archaic v.t.* **1.** To remove the helmet or helm of. **— v.i. 2.** To remove one's helmet.

un·hinge (un·hinj') *v.t.* **·hinged, ·hing·ing 1.** To take from the hinges. **2.** To remove the hinges of. **3.** To detach; dislodge. **4.** To throw into confusion; disorder. **5.** To make unstable; unsettle, as the mind.

un·hitch (un·hich') *v.t.* To unfasten.

un·ho·ly (un·hō'lē) *adj.* **·ho·li·er, ·ho·li·est 1.** Not sacred or hallowed. **2.** Lacking purity; wicked; sinful. **3.** *Informal* Terrible; dreadful: an *unholy* hour. [OE *unhālig*] **— un·ho'li·ly** *adv.* **— un·ho'li·ness** *n.*

un·hook (un·hŏŏk') *v.t.* **1.** To remove from a hook. **2.** To unfasten the hook or hooks of. **— v.i. 3.** To become unhooked.

un·hoped-for (un·hōpt'fôr') *adj.* Not expected or hoped for: an *unhoped-for* solution.

un·horse (un·hôrs') *v.t.* **·horsed, ·hors·ing 1.** To throw from a horse. **2.** To dislodge; overthrow. **3.** To remove a horse or horses from: to *unhorse* a vehicle.

un·hou·seled (un·hou'zəld) *adj.* *Obs.* Not having received the last sacraments. [< UN-¹ + HOUSEL + -ED²]

un·hur·ried (un·hûr'ēd) *adj.* Leisurely; not hurried.

un·husk (un·husk') *v.t.* To strip or expose by or as by removing the husk from.

uni- *combining form* Having or consisting of one only: *unifoliate*. [< L *unus* one]

U·ni·at (yōō'nē·at) *n.* A member of the Uniat Church. **— adj.** Of or pertaining to the Uniats or the Uniat Church. Also **U'ni·ate** (-it, āt). [< Russian *uniyat* < *uniya* union < L *unus* one; from union with the Roman Catholic Church]

Uniat Church Any body of Eastern Christians forming a church that acknowledges the Pope as its supreme head and that has its own distinctive liturgy: also called *Eastern Church*. Also **Uniate Church.**

u·ni·ax·i·al (yōō'nē·ak'sē·əl) *adj.* **1.** Having one axis. **2.** *Crystall.* Doubly refracting and having only a single optical axis, as crystals of the tetragonal and hexagonal systems. **3.** *Bot.* Having no branches, as a primary stem terminating in a flower: also *monaxial*.

u·ni·cam·er·al (yōō'nə·kam'ər·əl) *adj.* Consisting of but one legislative chamber.

UNICEF (yōō'nə·sef) United Nations Children's Fund. Also **U'ni·cef.**

u·ni·cel·lu·lar (yōō'nə·sel'yə·lər) *adj.* *Biol.* Consisting of a single cell, as a protozoan; one-celled.

u·ni·col·or (yōō'nə·kul'ər) *adj.* Of one color.

u·ni·corn (yōō'nə·kôrn) *n.* **1.** A fabulous horse-like animal with one horn. **2.** A two-horned animal identified with the urus: so called in the early English versions of the Bible to render the Latin and Greek mistranslations of the Hebrew *re' ēm*, and later translated as *wild ox* in the Revised Version. *Deut.* xxxiii 17. [< OF *unicorne* < L *unicornis* one-horned < *unus* one + *cornu* horn]

UNICORN

u·ni·cos·tate (yōō'nə·kos'tāt) *adj.* **1.** Having a single principal costa, rib, or nervure. **2.** *Bot.* Having a midrib, as a leaf.

u·ni·cy·cle (yōō'nə·sī'kəl) *n.* A monocycle (which see).

un·i·de·aed (un'ī·dē'əd) *adj.* *Rare* Lacking ideas; stupid.

u·ni·di·rec·tion·al (yōō'nə·di·rek'shən·əl, -dī-) *adj.* **1.** Having or moving in only one direction. **2.** *Telecom.* Designed or equipped to operate best in only one direction, as a radio antenna.

u·ni·fi·a·ble (yōō'nə·fī'ə·bəl) *adj.* That can be unified.

u·nif·ic (yōō·nif'ik) *adj.* Unifying.

u·ni·fi·ca·tion (yōō'nə·fə·kā'shən) *n.* The act of unifying, or the state of being unified. **— u'ni·fi·ca'tion·ist** *n.*

u·ni·fied (yōō'nə·fīd) Past tense and past participle of UNIFY.

unified command *Mil.* An armed force of two or more U.S. military services under a single commander.

unified field theory *Physics* **1.** Any mathematically rigorous generalization that will combine two or more physical theories in a form permitting accurate inclusive predictions not deducible from one theory alone, as the electromagnetic theory of Maxwell. **2.** Such a generalization, as tentatively formulated by Einstein, to unify the theories of electromagnetism, gravitation, and relativity.

u·ni·fi·lar (yōō'nə·fī'lər) *adj.* Having or utilizing only one thread, filament, etc.

u·ni·flo·rous (yōō'nə·flôr'əs, -flō'rəs) *adj.* *Bot.* Bearing or having only one flower.

u·ni·fo·li·ate (yōō'nə·fō'lē·it, -āt) *adj.* *Bot.* Having one leaf.

u·ni·fo·li·o·late (yōō'nə·fō'lē·ə·lit, -lāt) *adj.* *Bot.* Having a single leaflet that is compound in structure, as the orange.

u·ni·form (yōō'nə·fôrm) *adj.* **1.** Being always the same or alike, as in form, appearance, quantity, quality, degree, style, character, etc.; not varying: *uniform* temperature. **2.** Agreeing or identical with each other; being the same as another or others; alike: *uniform* tastes. **— n. 1.** A distinctive form of dress having a uniform style and appearance and worn by members of the same organization or service, as soldiers, sailors, etc. **2.** A single suit of such clothes. **— v.t. 1.** To put into or clothe with a uniform. **2.** To make uniform. [< F *uniforme* < L *uniformis* < *unus* one + *forma* form] **— u'ni·form·ly** *adv.* **— u'ni·form·ness** *n.*

---

unpalatable	unpartizan	unpedigreed	unperplexed	unphilological	unpitying
unpalatably	unpasteurized	unpen	unpersuadable	unphilosophic	unpityingly
unparagraphed	unpatched	unpenetrated	unpersuaded	unphilosophical	unplaced
unpardonable	unpatented	unpensioned	unpersuasive	unphonetic	unplagued
unpardonably	unpatriotic	unperceivable	unpersuasively	unpicked	unplait
unpardoned	unpatriotically	unperceived	unpersuasiveness	unpicturesque	unplanned
unparental	unpaved	unperceiving	unperturbed	unpierced	unplanted
unparted	unpeaceable	unperfected	unperused	unpile	unplayed
unpartisan	unpeaceful	unperformed	unphilanthropic	unpitied	unpleased

u·ni·for·mal·ize (yōō′nə·fôr′məl·īz) *v.t.* ·ized, ·iz·ing *Rare* To bring into a uniform system; render uniform.

Uniform Code of Military Justice The code of laws and related procedures enacted in 1951 by the U.S. Congress for the government of the personnel of the armed services, superseding the former Army *Articles of War* and the *Articles for the Government of the Navy.* Abbr. *UCMJ*

u·ni·formed (yōō′nə·fôrmd) *adj.* Dressed in uniform.

u·ni·form·i·tar·i·an·ism (yōō′nə·fôr′mə·târ′ē·ən·iz′əm) *n.* *Geol.* The doctrine that essential uniformity in causes and effects, forces and phenomena, has prevailed from the origin of the earth to the present time: opposed to *catastrophism.* — **u′ni·form′i·tar′i·an** *adj.,* & *n.*

u·ni·form·i·ty (yōō′nə·fôr′mə·tē) *n.* *pl.* ·ties 1. The state or quality of being uniform. 2. Conformity or compliance, as in opinions or religion. 3. Monotony; sameness.

u·ni·fy (yōō′nə·fī) *v.t.* & *v.i.* ·fied, ·fy·ing To combine into a unit; unite; become or cause to be one. [< F *unifier* or LL *unificare* < L *unus* one + *facere* to make] — **u′ni·fi′er** *n.*

u·nij·u·gate (yōō·nij′ōō·gāt, yōō′nə·jōō′git, -gāt) *adj. Bot.* Having one pair of leaflets: said especially of a pinnate leaf. [< UNI- + JUGATE]

u·ni·lat·er·al (yōō′nə·lat′ər·əl) *adj.* 1. Of, pertaining to, or existing on one side only. 2. Made, undertaken, done, or signed by only one of two or more people or parties. 3. One-sided. 4. Relating to or concerned with only one side of a question, dispute, etc. 5. Turned to or showing only one side. 6. Relating to or tracing ancestry through only one side of a family. 7. *Law* Binding or obligatory on one party only. 8. *Med.* Affecting but one side of the body. 9. *Biol.* Arranged or growing on one side only. — **u′ni·lat′er·al·ly** *adv.* — **u′ni·lat′er·al·ism, u′ni·lat′er·al′i·ty** (-al′ə·tē) *n.*

u·ni·lit·er·al (yōō′nə·lit′ər·əl) *adj.* Having one letter.

u·ni·loc·u·lar (yōō′nə·lok′yə·lər) *adj. Biol.* Having or consisting of one cell or chamber, as an anther, ovary, etc.

U·ni·mak Island (yōō′nə·mak) The northeasternmost of the Fox Islands; 70 mi. long.

un·im·peach·a·ble (un′im·pē′chə·bəl) *adj.* Not to be called into question as regards truth, honesty, etc.; faultless; blameless. — **un′im·peach′a·bly** *adv.*

un·im·por·tant (un′im·pôr′tənt) *adj.* 1. Not important or significant. 2. Trivial; petty. — **un′im·por′tance** *n.* — **un′im·por′tant·ly** *adv.*

un·im·proved (un′im·prōōvd′) *adj.* 1. Not improved, bettered, or advanced: *unimproved* health. 2. Having no improvements; not cleared, cultivated, or built upon: *unimproved* land. 3. Not made anything of; unused: *unimproved* opportunities. 4. *Obs.* Not proved or tried.

un·in·tel·li·gent (un′in·tel′ə·jənt) *adj.* 1. Not intelligent; characterized by lack of intelligence. 2. Unwise; ignorant. — **un′in·tel′li·gence** *n.*

un·in·ter·est·ed (un′in′tər·is·tid, -tris-) *adj.* 1. Having no interest in, as in property. 2. Taking no interest in; indifferent; unconcerned. ◆ See note under DISINTERESTED. — **un′in′ter·est·ed·ly** *adv.* — **un′in′ter·est·ed·ness** *n.*

un·ion (yōōn′yən) *n.* 1. The act of uniting, or the state of being united; also, that which is so formed. 2. A combining or joining of nations, states, parties, etc. for some mutual interest or purpose. 3. The harmony, agreement, or concord that results from such a combining or joining. 4. The joining of two persons in marriage; also, the state of wedlock. 5. A labor union (which see). 6. *Mech.* A device for connecting parts of machinery; especially, a coupling or connection for pipes or rods. 7. A device emblematic of union, used in a flag or emblem and found either in the upper rectangular corner near the staff or occupying the entire field. 8. A fabric made of two or more materials. 9. *Brit.* A uniting of several or more parishes for administration of relief for the poor; also, a workhouse administered by such a union. — **Syn.** See ALLIANCE. — *adj.* Of, pertaining to, or adhering to a union, especially a labor union. [< F < LL *unio, -onis* < L *unus* one. Doublet of ONION.]

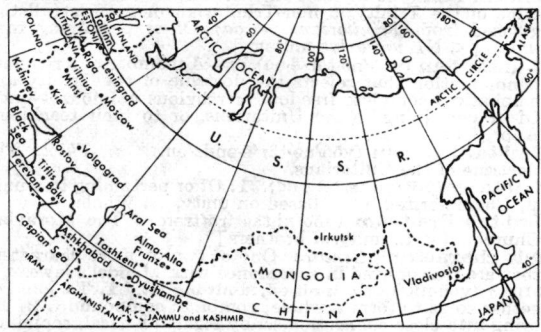

PIPE UNION

Un·ion (yōōn′yən) *n.* 1. The United States regarded as a national unit: with *the.* 2. The former Union of South Africa. — *adj.* Of, pertaining to, or loyal to the United States, especially the Federal government during the Civil War: a *Union* soldier; He was *Union* to the core.

Un·ion (yōōn′yən) A township in NE New Jersey, near Newark; pop. 53,077.

union card A card certifying that the person named belongs to a specified labor union.

union catalogue A library catalogue that contains the contents of more than one library.

Union City A city in NE New Jersey, near Hoboken; pop. 58,537.

union down Reversed, as a flag, so as to have the union or canton at the lower edge, and shown as a signal of distress.

un·ion·ism (yōōn′yən·iz′əm) *n.* 1. The principle of combining for unity of purpose and action. 2. The principle or the support of trade unions. 3. *Usually cap.* Adherence to the federal union during the Civil War. 4. Adherence to the principles of the Unionists of Great Britain who opposed Home Rule for Ireland. — **un′ion·is′tic** *adj.*

un·ion·ist (yōōn′yən·ist) *n.* 1. An advocate of union or unionism. 2. A member of a trade union.

Un·ion·ist (yōōn′yən·ist) *n.* 1. During the Civil War in the United States, one who supported the Union cause and opposed secession. 2. One of those opposed to loosening the formal legislative union between Great Britain and Ireland. 3. A member of the Conservative Party in Great Britain.

un·ion·ize (yōōn′yən·īz) *v.* ·ized, ·iz·ing *v.t.* 1. To cause to join, or to organize into a union, especially a labor union. 2. To make conform to the rules, etc., of a union. — *v.i.* 3. To join or organize a labor union. — **un′ion·i·za′tion** *n.*

union jack A flag consisting of the union or canton only.

Union Jack The national flag of the United Kingdom.

union label A label or other identifying mark on a product indicating that it has been produced by union labor.

Union of Arab Emirates A federation of sheikdoms on the eastern coast of the Arabian peninsula, comprising Abu Dhabi, Dubai, Sharja, Ajman, Fujaira, Umm al Qaiwain, Ras al Khaima; area, 32,278 sq. mi.; pop. 656,000 (est. 1975). Also **United Arab Emirates.**

Union of Soviet Socialist Republics A federal union of 15 constituent Republics extending from the Arctic Ocean to the Baltic and Black seas and east to the Pacific, and occupying most of northern Eurasia; 8,646,400 sq. mi.; pop. 241,748,000 (1970); capital, Moscow: Russian *Soyuz Sovetskikh Sotsialisticheskikh Respublik.* Also *Soviet Union,* loosely, *Russia, Soviet Russia.* Abbr. *U.S.S.R., USSR*

union shop An industrial establishment that hires only members of a labor union or those who promise to join a union within a specified time.

union station A railroad station or depot used by two or more railroad lines.

union suit A one-piece undergarment for men and boys consisting of shirt and drawers.

u·ni·pa·ren·tal (yōō′nə·pə·ren′təl) *adj.* Having or produced by one parent only. — **u′ni·pa·ren′tal·ly** *adv.*

u·nip·a·rous (yōō·nip′ər·əs) *adj.* 1. *Biol.* Bringing forth but one offspring at a time, or not having borne more than one. 2. *Bot.* Having but one axis or stem at each branching. [< UNI- + -PAROUS]

u·ni·per·son·al (yōō′nə·pûr′sən·əl) *adj.* 1. Manifested or existing in but one person. 2. *Gram.* Used in only one person, especially the third person singular, as certain verbs.

u·ni·pet·al·ous (yōō′nə·pet′l·əs) *adj. Bot.* Having only one petal.

unpleasing	unpoetic	unposted	unpresentable	unpresentably	unprocured
unpledged	unpoetical	unpractical	unpresentably	unprevented	unprofaned
unpliable	unpointed	unpracticality	unpreserved	unprimed	unprofited
unpliant	unpoised	unpractically	unpressed	unprincely	unprogressive
unplighted	unpolarized	unpracticalness	unpresumptuous	unprinted	unprohibited
unploughed	unpolished	unpredictable	unpretending	unprivileged	unpromising
unplowed	unpolitical	unpreoccupied	unpretentious	unprized	unpromisingly
unplucked	unpolluted	unprepossessing	unpretentiously	unprobed	unprompted
unplug	unpondered	unprepossessingly	unpretentiousness	unprocessed	unpronounced
unplugged	unpopulated	unprescribed	unprevailing	unprocurable	unpropitiable

u·ni·pla·nar (yōō′nə·plā′nər) *adj.* Lying or taking place in one plane.

u·ni·po·lar (yōō′nə·pō′lər) *adj.* **1.** *Physics* Showing only one kind of polarity. **2.** *Anat.* Having or operating by means of one pole or process, as certain spinal nerves.

u·nique (yōō·nēk′) *adj.* **1.** Being the only one of its kind; sole; single. **2.** Being without or having no equal or like; singular. **3.** Loosely, unusual, rare, or notable: a *unique* opportunity. [< F < L *unicus* < *unus* one] — **u·nique′ly** *adv.* — **u·nique′ness** *n.*

u·ni·sep·tate (yōō′nə·sep′tāt) *adj. Biol.* Having a single septum or partition.

u·ni·sex (yōō′ni·seks′) *adj. Informal* Of or designating clothes that are suitable for wearing by either sex.

u·ni·sex·u·al (yōō′nə·sek′shōō·əl) *adj. Biol.* Of only one sex; also, having one kind of sexual organs only.

u·ni·son (yōō′nə·sən, -zən) *n.* **1.** A speaking or sounding the same words, tones, etc., simultaneously: with *in*: they answered in *unison.* **2.** Complete accord or agreement; harmony. **3.** *Music* **a** A state in which instruments or voices perform identical parts simultaneously, in the same or different octaves. **b** The interval formed by two tones of the same pitch. [< L *unisonus* having a single sound < *uni-* one + *sonus* sound]

u·nis·o·nous (yōō·nis′ə·nəs) *adj.* Being or sounding in unison. Also **u·nis′o·nal** (-ə·nəl), **u·nis′o·nant** (-ə·nənt).

u·nit (yōō′nit) *n.* **1.** A single person or thing regarded as an individual but belonging to an entire group. **2.** A body or group, as of soldiers, considered as a subdivision of a similar but larger body or group. **3.** An apparatus or piece of equipment, usually part of a larger object and having a specific function: the cooling *unit* of a freezer. **4.** A standard quantity with which others of the same kind are compared for purposes of measurement and in terms of which their magnitude is stated. **5.** *Math.* A quantity whose measure is represented by the number 1; a least whole number. **6.** *Med.* The quantity of a drug, vaccine, serum, or antigen required to produce a given effect or yield a particular result. **7.** A fixed quantity of scholastic work used as a basis for calculating educational credits, etc. [Back formation < UNITY]

Unit. Unitarian.

u·ni·tar·i·an (yōō′nə·târ′ē·ən) *n.* One who rejects the doctrine of the Trinity; a non-Trinitarian monotheist: distinguished from *Trinitarian.* — *adj.* Of or pertaining to a unit. [< NL *unitarius* unitary]

U·ni·tar·i·an (yōō′nə·târ′ē·ən) *n.* A member of a religious denomination that rejects the doctrine of the Trinity and emphasizes complete freedom of religious opinion. — *adj.* Of or pertaining to the Unitarians, or to their teachings. Abbr. *Unit.*

U·ni·tar·i·an·ism (yōō′nə·târ′ē·ən·iz′əm) *n. Theol.* The doctrine of the Unitarians.

u·ni·tar·y (yōō′nə·ter′ē) *adj.* **1.** Of or pertaining to a unit. **2.** Characterized by or based on unity. **3.** Whole.

U·ni·tas Fra·trum (yōō′ni·täs frā′trəm) The Moravian Church. [< L, unity of brothers]

unit character *Genetics* One of two or more characters that are transmitted in accordance with Mendel's laws.

u·nite (yōō·nīt′) *v.* **u·nit·ed, u·nit·ing** *v.t.* **1.** To join together so as to form a whole; combine; compound. **2.** To bring into close connection, as by legal, physical, social, or other tie; join in action, interest, etc. **3.** To join in marriage. **4.** To attach permanently or solidly; cause to adhere; bond. **5.** To show or possess (characteristics, etc.) in combination: to *unite* wit and beauty. — *v.i.* **6.** To become or be merged into one; be consolidated; combine. **7.** To join together for action; act in conjunction; concur. [< LL *unitus*, pp. of *unire* to make one < L *unus* one]

u·nit·ed (yōō·nī′tid) *adj.* Incorporated into one; allied; combined. — **u·nit′ed·ly** *adv.* — **u·nit′ed·ness** *n.*

United Arab Emirates See UNION OF ARAB EMIRATES.

United Arab Republic The official name for Egypt. Abbr. *UAR, U.A.R.*

United Arab States A federation formed in 1958 by the United Arab Republic and Yemen, dissolved in 1961.

United Brethren A Christian denomination founded in 1800 by P. W. Otterbein and Martin Boehm: officially, Church of the United Brethren in Christ.

United Church of Canada A church made up of former denominational Methodists, Presbyterians, and others.

United Church of Christ A Protestant denomination formed in 1957 by a union of the Congregational Christian Churches and the Evangelical and Reformed Church.

United Empire Loyalists Persons who, because they preferred to remain British subjects, left the United States to settle in Canada during and after the American Revolution. Abbr. *U.E.L.*

United Kingdom 1. The kingdom of the British Isles, comprising Great Britain, Northern Ireland, the Isle of Man, and the Channel Islands; 94,284 sq. mi.; pop. 55,346,551 (1971); capital, London: officially **United Kingdom of Great Britain and Northern Ireland. 2.** Formerly, Great Britain and Ireland (1801–1922). Abbr. *U.K.*

United Nations 1. A coalition against the Axis powers in World War II, formed of 26 nations in January, 1942; the Allies (def. 2). **2.** An organization of sovereign states, having its permanent headquarters in an enclave of international territory in New York City since 1951, created by the **United Nations Charter** drafted in Sept.-Oct., 1944 at Dumbarton Oaks and adopted at San Francisco in May and June, 1945. The 26 states of the United Nations coalition and 25 others form the original membership. They are Argentina, Australia, Belgium, the Byelorussian S.S.R., Bolivia, Brazil, Canada, Chile, the Republic of China (unseated, 1971), Colombia, Costa Rica, Cuba, Czechoslovakia, Denmark, the Dominican Republic, Ecuador, Egypt, El Salvador, Ethiopia, France, Greece, Guatemala, Haiti, Honduras, India, Iran, Iraq, Lebanon, Liberia, Luxembourg, Mexico, the Netherlands, New Zealand, Nicaragua, Norway, Panama, Paraguay, Peru, the Philippines, Poland, Saudi Arabia, the Republic of South Africa, the Soviet Union, Syria, Turkey, the Ukrainian S.S.R., the United Kingdom, the United States, Uruguay, Venezuela, and Yugoslavia. Other nations joining in subsequent years were (1946) Afghanistan, Iceland, Sweden, Thailand; (1947) Pakistan, Yemen; (1948) Burma; (1949) Israel; (1950) Indonesia; (1955) Albania, Austria, Bulgaria, Cambodia, Ceylon, Finland, Hungary, Ireland, Italy, Jordan, Laos, Libya, Nepal, Portugal, Rumania, Spain; (1956) Japan, Morocco, Sudan, Tunisia; (1957) Ghana, Malaya; (1958) Guinea; (1960) Cameroon, the Central African Republic, Chad, the Republic of the Congo (Brazzaville), the Republic of the Congo (now Zaire), Cyprus, Dahomey, Gabon, Ivory Coast, Malagasy Republic, Mali, Niger, Nigeria, Senegal, Somalia, Togo, Upper Volta; (1961) the Mongolian People's Republic, Mauritania, Sierra Leone, Tanganyika; (1962) Algeria, Burundi, Jamaica, Rwanda, Trinidad and Tobago, Uganda; (1963) Kenya, Kuwait, Zanzibar; (1964) Malaysia (formerly Malaya and other territories), Malawi, Malta, Tanzania (formerly Tanganyika and Zanzibar), Zambia; (1965) Gambia, Maldive Islands, Singapore; (1966) Barbados, Botswana, Guyana, Lesotho; (1967) South Yemen; (1968) Equatorial Guinea, Mauritius, Swaziland; (1970) Fiji; (1971) Bahrein, Bhutan, People's Republic of China, Qatar, Oman, Union of Arab Emirates; (1973) Bahamas, East Germany, West Germany; (1974) Bangladesh, Grenada, Guinea-Bissau.

United Press International An organization for collecting and distributing news, formed in 1958 by a merger of the International News Service and United Press. Abbr. *UPI, U.P.I.*

United Provinces of Agra and Oudh A former British province in north central India; became Uttar Pradesh, 1950. Also **United Provinces.**

United Society of Believers in Christ's Second Appearing The Shakers: their official name.

United States Army, Navy, Air Force, etc. See under ARMY, NAVY, AIR FORCE, etc.

United States of America A federal Republic of North America including 50 States and the District of Columbia (3,615,222 sq. mi.; pop. 203,184,772), and the Canal Zone, Puerto Rico, the Virgin Islands of the United States, American Samoa, and Guam, Wake, and other Pacific islands; total, 3,720,407 sq. mi.; capital, Washington, coextensive with the District of Columbia. — **conterminous**

unpropitiated	unpunishable	unquotable	unreceptive	unrectified	unrelaxed
unpropitious	unpunished	unraised	unreceptively	unredeemed	unrelaxing
unpropitiously	unpurchasable	unransomed	unreceptiveness	unredressed	unrelievable
unproportionate	unpure	unrated	unreciprocated	unreelable	unrelieved
unproportioned	unpurged	unratified	unreclaimable	unrefined	unrelished
unproposed	unpurified	unravaged	unreclaimed	unreflected	unremarkable
unprosperous	unpurposed	unrazed	unrecognizable	unreflecting	unremarked
unprotected	unpursuing	unreachable	unrecognizably	unreformed	unremedied
unproved	unpuzzle	unreached	unrecognized	unrefreshed	unremembered
unproven	unquaffed	unrealizable	unrecommended	unrefreshing	unremittable
unprovoked	unquailing	unrealized	unrecompensed	unregarded	unremitted
unprovoking	unquaking	unreasoned	unreconcilable	unregistered	unremorseful
unpruned	unqualifying	unrebukable	unreconciled	unregretted	unremorsefully
unpublishable	unquelled	unrebuked	unrecorded	unregulated	unremorsefulness
unpublished	unquenchable	unreceipted	unrecounted	unrehearsed	unremovable
unpucker	unquenched	unreceivable	unrecoverable	unrelated	unremoved
unpunctual	unquestioning	unreceived	unrecruited	unrelatedness	unremunerated

United States The 48 contiguous States and the District of Columbia; 3,022,387 sq. mi. — **continental United States** The District of Columbia and the 49 States on the continent of North America; 3,608,787 sq. mi.: abbr. *CONUS* Also *America, the States, United States.* Abbr. *U.S.A., USA, U.S., US*

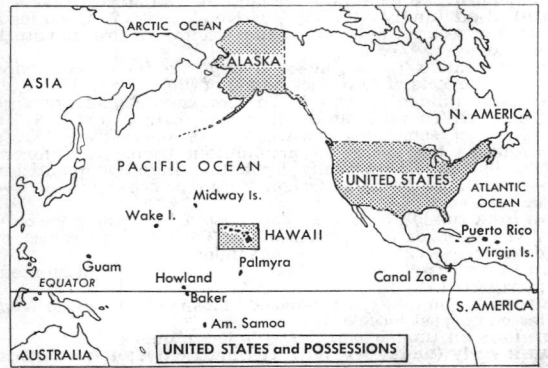

UNITED STATES and POSSESSIONS

unit factor *Genetics* A gene controlling the inheritance of a unit character.

u·ni·tive (yōō′nə·tiv) *adj.* **1.** Productive of or promoting union; having power to unite. **2.** Characterized by union

unit modifier A conventional or improvised compound used adjectively before a substantive. Examples: *blue-green* algae, *bitter-sweet* chocolate, *suit-coat* pattern.
   ◆ The use of the hyphen in the unit modifier is to avoid ambiguity in a word sequence where the relationship is not immediately apparent from context: The house had faded red-brick walls (faded walls of red brick, *not* faded red walls of brick); a long-horned animal (an animal with long horns, *not* a long animal with horns). The hyphen here is to be considered a nonce use and not a spelling form or variant.

unit rule *U.S.* In a national convention of the Democratic party, a rule requiring that, if so instructed by a State party convention, the vote of an entire delegation shall be determined by a majority of its members.

u·ni·ty (yōō′nə·tē) *n.* *pl.* **·ties 1.** The state or fact of being one. **2.** Something that is wholly united and complete within itself. **3.** A state or quality of general concord and mutual understanding; harmony; agreement. **4.** The harmonious agreement of parts or elements into one united whole. **5.** The condition or fact of being free from variety or diversity. **6.** Singleness or constancy of purpose, action, etc. **7.** In art and literature, the arrangement of parts into a homogeneous whole exhibiting oneness of purpose, thought, spirit, and style; the subordination of all parts to the general effect. **8.** *Math.* **a** The number one. **b** The element of a number system that leaves any number unchanged under multiplication, that is, a number *e* such that $ex = xe = x$ for all *x*. **9.** In the drama, the observance of any of the three Aristotelian unities of time, action, and place, which state that there must be but one plot, the action of which takes place in one day and at a single locality. [< OF *unite* < L *unitas* < *unus* one]

univ. 1. Universal(ly). **2.** University.
Univ. 1. Universalist. **2.** University.

u·ni·va·lent (yōō′nə·vā′lənt) *adj.* **1.** *Chem.* Having a valence or combining value of one; monovalent. **2.** *Biol.* Pertaining to or designating a single unpaired chromosome. — **u′ni·va′lence, u′ni·va′len·cy** *n.*

u·ni·valve (yōō′nə·valv′) *adj.* Having only one valve, as a mollusk. Also **u′ni·valved′, u′ni·val′vu·lar** (-val′vyə·lər). — *n.* **1.** A mollusk having a univalve shell; a gastropod. **2.** A shell of a single piece.

u·ni·ver·sal (yōō′nə·vûr′səl) *adj.* **1.** Of, pertaining to, or typical of all or the whole: a *universal* reaction. **2.** Including, involving, or intended for all: a *universal* law. **3.** Applicable to everyone or to all cases: a *universal* cure. **4.** That can be used or understood by all: a *universal* language. **5.** Accomplished or interested in all or many subjects, activities, etc.: a *universal* genius. **6.** Of, pertaining to, or occurring throughout the universe. **7.** Common to all in any specific group or field: a *universal* practice of politicians. **8.** *Mech.* **a** Adapted or adaptable to a great variety of uses, shapes, etc., as certain machine parts. **b** Permitting free movement within fixed extremes, as a joint. **9.** *Logic* **a** Including all the individuals of a class or genus; generic. **b** In a proposition, predicable of all the individuals denoted by the subject: opposed to *particular:* "All men are mortal" is a *universal* proposition. — **Syn.** See GENERAL. — *n.* **1.** *Logic* **a** A universal proposition. **b** One of the five predicables, that is, genus, species, difference, property, and accident. **c** A general or abstract concept considered as having absolute reality or mental or nominal existence. **2.** Any general or universal notion, condition, principle, etc. **3.** A metaphysical being that preserves its identity in spite of the changes through which it passes, as the ego. Abbr. *univ.* [< OF < L *universalis* < *universus.* See UNIVERSE.] — **u′ni·ver′sal·ly** *adv.* — **u′ni·ver′sal·ness** *n.*

universal donor One whose blood may be safely transfused into a person belonging to any blood group.

U·ni·ver·sal·ism (yōō′nə·vûr′səl·iz′əm) *n.* *Theol.* The doctrine that all souls will finally be saved and that good will triumph universally.

U·ni·ver·sal·ist (yōō′nə·vûr′səl·ist) *adj.* Pertaining to Universalism or Universalists. — *n.* A believer in the doctrines of Universalism, or a member of a denomination that believes in Universalism. Abbr. *Univ.*

u·ni·ver·sal·i·ty (yōō′nə·vər·sal′ə·tē) *n.* *pl.* **·ties 1.** The state or quality of being universal. **2.** Unrestricted fitness or adaptability. **3.** An all-embracing range of knowledge, abilities, etc.

u·ni·ver·sal·ize (yōō′nə·vûr′səl·īz) *v.t.* **·ized, ·iz·ing** To make universal.

universal joint *Mech.* A joint that permits connected parts of a machine to be turned in any direction within definite limits. Also **universal coupling.** For illustration see MACHINE.

u·ni·ver·sal·ly (yōō′nə·vûr′sə·lē) *adv.* In a universal manner; on all occasions or in all places; without exception.

u·ni·verse (yōō′nə·vûrs) *n.* **1.** The aggregate of all existing things; the whole creation embracing all celestial bodies and all of space; the cosmos. **2.** In restricted sense, the earth. **3.** Human beings collectively; mankind. **4.** *Logic* All objects, collectively, that are the subjects of consideration at once: also **universe of discourse. 5.** *Stat.* All the instances in a given class. [< F *univers* < L *universum,* neut. of *universus* turned, combined into one, all collectively < *unus* one + *versus,* pp. of *vertere* to turn]

u·ni·ver·si·ty (yōō′nə·vûr′sə·tē) *n.* *pl.* **·ties 1.** An institution for higher instruction that includes one or more schools or colleges for graduate or professional study and grants master's and doctor's degrees. In the United States, a university usually includes an undergraduate division that grants a bachelor's degree. Abbr. *u., U., univ., Univ.* **2.** The faculty and students of a university. **3.** The buildings and grounds of a university. **4.** *Brit. Informal* A university team or crew. [< OF *universite* < L *universitas* the whole, entire number < *universus.* See UNIVERSE.]

University City A city in eastern Missouri, a suburb of St. Louis; pop. 46,309.

u·niv·o·cal (yōō·niv′ə·kəl) *adj.* Having but one proper sense or meaning. — *n.* A word that has but one meaning. [< LL *univocus* < L *unus* one + *vox, vocis* voice] — **u·niv′·o·cal·ly** *adv.*

un·just (un·just′) *adj.* **1.** Not legitimate, fair, or just; wrongful. **2.** Acting contrary to right and justice; unrighteous. **3.** *Archaic* Faithless. **4.** *Archaic* Dishonest. — **un·just′ly** *adv.* — **un·just′ness** *n.*

unremunerative	unreplenished	unrespectable	unreversed	unrobe	unsaleable
unrendered	unreported	unrespectful	unrevised	unromantic	unsalted
unrenewed	unrepresentative	unrespectfully	unrevoked	unromantically	unsanctified
unrenounced	unrepresented	unrespited	unrewarded	unroof	unsanctioned
unrenowned	unrepressed	unrested	unrhetorical	unroofed	unsanitarily
unrent	unreprievable	unresting	unrhymed	unrough	unsanitary
unrented	unreprieved	unrestrainable	unrhythmic	unrulable	unsated
unrepaid	unreprovable	unrestraint	unrhythmical	unruled	unsatiable
unrepairable	unrequested	unrestricted	unrhythmically	unsafe	unsatiated
unrepaired	unrequited	unretarded	unrighted	unsafely	unsatiating
unrepealed	unresented	unretentive	unrightful	unsaintliness	unsatisfactorily
unrepentant	unresigned	unretracted	unrightfully	unsaintly	unsatisfactory
unrepented	unresistant	unretrieved	unrimed	unsalability	unsatisfied
unrepenting	unresisted	unreturned	unripened	unsalable	unsatisfying
unrepining	unresisting	unrevealed	unrisen	unsalaried	unsatisfyingly
unreplaced	unresolved	unrevenged	unroasted	unsaleability	unsaved

un·kempt (un·kempt′) *adj.* **1.** Not combed. **2.** Not clean or neat; untidy. **3.** Without polish or refinement; rough. [< UN-¹ + *kempt* combed, pp. of dial. *kemb*, var. of COMB]

un·kenned (un·kend′) *adj. Scot. & Brit. Dial.* Unknown. Also **un·kend′, un·kent′** (-kent′).

un·ken·nel (un·ken′əl) *v.t.* **·neled** or **·nelled, ·nel·ing** or **·nel·ling 1.** To drive or release from a kennel or lair. **2.** To bring to light; disclose.

un·kind (un·kīnd′) *adj.* Showing lack of kindness; unsympathetic; harsh; cruel. [OE *uncynde* strange, unnatural] —**un·kind′ly** *adv.* —**un·kind′ness** *n.*

un·knit (un·nit′) *v.* **·knit** or **·knit·ted, ·knit·ting** —*v.t.* **1.** To untie or unravel (something tied or knit). **2.** To smooth out (something wrinkled). —*v.i.* **3.** To become unknitted.

un·know·a·ble (un·nō′ə·bəl) *adj.* **1.** Not known or not able to be known. **2.** Beyond human comprehension. —**the Unknowable** *Philos.* The supposed reality that lies in back of all phenomena but is beyond human understanding. —**un·know′a·ble·ness** *n.* —**un·know′a·bly** *adv.*

un·known (un·nōn′) *adj.* **1.** Not known or apprehended; not recognized, as a fact or person. **2.** Not ascertained, discovered, or established: an *unknown* element. —*n.* An unknown person or quantity. —**the Great Unknown** Life after death; future life.

Unknown Soldier One of the unidentified dead of World War I who is honored as a symbol of all his compatriots who died in action, extended to include unknown dead of World War II and the Korean conflict.

UNKRA United Nations Korean Reconstruction Agency.

un·la·bored (un·lā′bərd) *adj.* **1.** Produced without strain or effort; seemingly free and easy; natural. **2.** Uncultivated by labor; unworked; untilled. Also *Brit.* **un·la′boured.**

un·lace (un·lās′) *v.t.* **·laced, ·lac·ing 1.** To loosen or unfasten the lacing of; untie. **2.** To loosen or remove (armor or clothing) in this way. **3.** *Obs.* To expose to damage; disgrace.

un·lade (un·lād′) *v.t. & v.i.* **·lad·ed, ·lad·ing 1.** To unload the cargo of (a ship). **2.** To unload or discharge (cargo, etc.).

un·laid (un·lād′) *adj.* **1.** Not laid or placed; not fixed. **2.** Not allayed or pacified. **3.** Not twisted, as the strands of a rope. **4.** *Obs.* Not laid out, as a corpse.

un·latch (un·lach′) *v.t.* **1.** To open or unlock by releasing the latch. —*v.i.* **2.** To come open or unlocked.

un·law·ful (un·lô′fəl) *adj.* **1.** Contrary to or in violation of law; illegal. **2.** Born out of wedlock; illegitimate. —**Syn.** See CRIMINAL. —**un·law′ful·ly** *adv.* —**un·law′ful·ness** *n.*

un·lay (un·lā′) *v.t. & v.i.* **·laid, ·lay·ing** To untwist: said of the strands of a rope. [< UN-² + LAY¹ (def. 20)]

un·lead (un·led′) *v.t.* **1.** To strip of lead. **2.** *Printing* To remove the leads from between (lines of type matter).

un·lead·ed (un·led′id) *adj.* **1.** Not supplied or weighted with lead. **2.** *Printing* Having no leads between the lines of type; set solid.

un·learn (un·lûrn′) *v.t.* **·learned** or **·learnt, ·learn·ing** To dismiss from the mind (something learned); forget.

un·learn·ed (un·lûr′nid; *for def. 3* un·lûrnd′) *adj.* **1.** Not possessed of or characterized by learning; illiterate; ignorant; untaught. **2.** Unworthy of or unlike a scholar or a learned man. **3.** Not acquired by learning or study. —**Syn.** See IGNORANT. —**un·learn′ed·ly** *adv.*

un·leash (un·lēsh′) *v.t.* To set free from or as from a leash.

un·leav·ened (un·lev′ənd) *adj.* Not leavened: said especially of the bread used at the feast of the Passover.

un·less (un·les′) *conj.* **1.** If it be not a fact that; supposing that . . . not; except that: *Unless* we persevere, we shall lose. **2.** *Obs.* For fear that; lest. —*prep.* Save; except; excepting: with an implied verb: *Unless* a miracle, he'll not be back in time. [Earlier *onlesse (that)* (than) in a less case < ON + LESS]

un·let·tered (un·let′ərd) *adj.* Not educated; not lettered; illiterate. —**Syn.** See IGNORANT.

un·like (un·līk′) *adj.* Having little or no resemblance; different. —*prep.* Dissimilar to or different from; not like; not characteristic of: It was *unlike* him to go. [ME *unliche*] —**un·like′ness** *n.*

un·like·ly (un·līk′lē) *adj.* **1.** Not likely; improbable. **2.** Not inviting or promising success. —*adv.* Improbably. —**un·like′li·ness, un·like′li·hood** *n.*

un·lim·ber (un·lim′bər) *v.t. & v.i.* To disconnect (a gun or caisson) from its limber; prepare for action.

un·lim·it·ed (un·lim′it·id) *adj.* **1.** Having no limits in space, number, or time; unbounded; endless; unnumbered. **2.** Not limited by restrictions; unconfined: *unlimited* authority. **3.** Not limited by exceptions or qualifications; undefined. —**un·lim′it·ed·ly** *adv.* —**un·lim′it·ed·ness** *n.*

un·list·ed (un·lis′tid) *adj.* **1.** Not listed. **2.** Denoting a stock or security not admitted for trading on a regular stock exchange.

un·live (un·liv′) *v.t.* **·lived, ·liv·ing** To live so as to wipe out the effects of (a former period of life); live down.

un·load (un·lōd′) *v.t.* **1.** To remove the load or cargo from. **2.** To take off or discharge (cargo, etc.). **3.** To relieve of something burdensome or oppressive. **4.** To withdraw the charge of ammunition from. **5.** *Informal* To dispose of, especially by selling in large quantities. —*v.i.* **6.** To discharge freight, cargo, or other burden. —**un·load′er** *n.*

un·lock (un·lok′) *v.t.* **1.** To unfasten (something locked). **2.** To open or undo; release. **3.** To lay open; reveal or disclose. —*v.i.* **4.** To become unlocked.

un·looked-for (un·lo͝okt′fôr′) *adj.* Not anticipated; unexpected.

un·loose (un·lo͞os′) *v.t.* **·loosed, ·loos·ing** To release from fastenings; set loose or free.

un·loos·en (un·lo͞o′sən) *v.t.* To loose; unloose.

un·love·ly (un·luv′lē) *adj.* **1.** Unattractive; ugly. **2.** Disagreeable; unpleasant.

un·luck·y (un·luk′ē) *adj.* **·luck·i·er, ·luck·i·est 1.** Not favored by luck; unfortunate. **2.** Resulting in or attended by ill luck; causing misfortune; disastrous. **3.** Ill-omened; inauspicious: an *unlucky* day. —**un·luck′i·ly** *adv.* —**un·luck′i·ness** *n.*

un·make (un·māk′) *v.t.* **·made** (-mād′), **·mak·ing 1.** To reverse the making of; reduce to the original condition or form. **2.** To ruin; destroy. **3.** To depose, as from a position of authority.

un·man (un·man′) *v.t.* **·manned, ·man·ning 1.** To cause to lose courage or fortitude; dishearten. **2.** To render unmanly or effeminate. **3.** To deprive of virility; castrate. **4.** To remove the men from, as a ship or fortress.

un·man·ly (un·man′lē) *adj.* **1.** Not masculine or virile; effeminate. **2.** Not gentlemanly; not honorable. —**un·man′li·ness** *n.*

un·manned (un·mand′) *adj.* **1.** Not manned, as a ship or aircraft. **2.** Deprived of virility or manhood. **3.** Uninhabited. **4.** *Obs.* Untamed: said of hawks.

un·man·ner·ly (un·man′ər·lē) *adj.* Lacking manners; rude. —*adv.* Impolitely; rudely. —**un·man′ner·li·ness** *n.*

un·marked (un·märkt′) *adj.* **1.** Bearing no mark. **2.** Not noticed. **3.** Not examined, corrected, or graded.

un·mask (un·mask′, -mäsk′) *v.t.* **1.** To remove a mask from. **2.** To reveal or disclose the truth about. —*v.i.* **3.** To remove one's mask or disguise.

un·mean·ing (un·mē′ning) *adj.* **1.** Having no meaning. **2.** Showing no expression of intelligence, interest, etc.; empty. —**un·mean′ing·ly** *adv.* —**un·mean′ing·ness** *n.*

un·meet (un·mēt′) *adj.* Not meet, adapted, or suitable; not proper or fit; unbecoming. [OE *unmǣte*] —**un·meet′ly** *adv.* —**un·meet′ness** *n.*

un·men·tion·a·ble (un·men′shən·ə·bəl) *adj.* Not proper to be mentioned or discussed; embarrassing; shameful. —**un·men′tion·a·ble·ness** *n.* —**un·men′tion·a·bly** *adv.*

un·men·tion·a·bles (un·men′shən·ə·bəlz) *n.pl.* **1.** Things or articles not ordinarily discussed or mentioned; usually, undergarments. **2.** Formerly, trousers; pants.

un·mer·ci·ful (un·mûr′sə·fəl) *adj.* **1.** Showing no mercy; cruel; pitiless. **2.** Extreme; exorbitant. —**un·mer′ci·ful·ly** *adv.* —**un·mer′ci·ful·ness** *n.*

un·mew (un·myo͞o′) *v.t.* To release from confinement; set free.

un·mind·ful (un·mīnd′fəl) *adj.* Not keeping in mind; neglectful; inattentive; careless. —**un·mind′ful·ly** *adv.* —**un·mind′ful·ness** *n.*

un·mis·tak·a·ble (un′mis·tā′kə·bəl) *adj.* That cannot be mistaken for something else; evident; clear; obvious. —**un′mis·tak′a·bly** *adv.*

un·mi·ter (un·mī′tər) *v.t.* To divest of a miter; deprive of the office of bishop. Also **un·mi′tre.**

unsawed	unscientifically	unseconded	unsentimentally	unshapely	unshrunk
unsawn	unscorched	unsectarian	unserved	unshared	unshunned
unsayable	unscorned	unsecured	unserviceable	unshaved	unshut
unscabbarded	unscoured	unseeded	unserviceableness	unshaven	unsifted
unscaled	unscourged	unseeing	unserviceably	unshed	unsigned
unscanned	unscraped	unseeingly	unset	unshelled	unsilenced
unscarified	unscratched	unsegmented	unsevered	unsheltered	unsimilar
unscarred	unscreened	unseized	unsew	unshielded	unsingable
unscented	unscriptural	unselected	unsewn	unshod	unsinkable
unsceptical	unsculptured	unselective	unsexual	unshorn	unsisterly
unscheduled	unsealed	unselectively	unshaded	unshrinkable	unsized
unscholarly	unseated	unsensitive	unshadowed	unshrinking	unskeptical
unschooled	unseaworthiness	unsent	unshaken	unshriven	unslacked
unscientific	unseaworthy	unsentimental	unshamed	unshrouded	unslaked

un·mit·i·gat·ed (un·mit′ə·gā′tid) *adj.* **1.** Not mitigated or lightened in effect; unabated; unassuaged: *unmitigated* sorrow. **2.** Without any qualification or condition; complete; absolute: an *unmitigated* rogue. **— un·mit′i·gat′ed·ly** *adv.*

un·mod·u·lat·ed (un·moj′ōō·lā′tid) *adj.* **1.** Without modulation. **2.** *Telecom.* Denoting a continuous carrier wave of constant amplitude and frequency, as during a pause in broadcasting.

un·moor (un·mōōr′) *Naut. v.t.* **1.** To loose the moorings of; release from moorings: to *unmoor* a ship. **2.** To release all but one anchor of (a vessel formerly moored by two or more). **— v.i. 3.** To cast off moorings.

un·mor·al (un·môr′əl, -mor′-) *adj.* Having no moral sense; neither moral nor immoral; not pertaining to morality. **— un·mo·ral·i·ty** (un′mə·ral′ə·tē) *n.* **— un·mor′al·ly** *adv.*

un·mor·tise (un·môr′tis) *v.t.* **·tised, ·tis·ing 1.** To loosen; loosen the mortised joints of. **2.** To separate.

un·muf·fle (un·muf′əl) *v.* **·fled, ·fling** *v.t.* **1.** To take the covering from. **2.** To remove the muffling of (a drum, oar, etc.) **— v.i. 3.** To remove that which muffles.

un·nat·u·ral (un·nach′ər·əl) *adj.* **1.** Contrary to the laws of nature; opposed to what is natural. **2.** Contrary to the common laws of morality or decency; monstrous; inhuman: *unnatural* crimes. **3.** Not having, or inconsistent with, those attitudes, feelings, actions, etc., considered natural or normal; abnormal; strange. **4.** Not consistent with nature; artificial; affected; forced: *unnatural* acting. **— un·nat′u·ral·ly** *adv.* **— un·nat′u·ral·ness** *n.*

un·nec·es·sar·y (un·nes′ə·ser′ē) *adj.* Not required or necessary; not essential. **— un·nec′es·sar′i·ly** *adv.* **— un·nec′es·sar′i·ness** *n.*

un·nerve (un·nûrv′) *v.t.* **·nerved, ·nerv·ing** To deprive of strength, firmness, self-control, or courage; unman.

un·num·bered (un·num′bərd) *adj.* **1.** Not counted. **2.** Innumerable. **3.** Not marked with or assigned a number.

un·oc·cu·pied (un·ok′yə·pīd) *adj.* **1.** Empty; not dwelt in; uninhabited: an *unoccupied* house. **2.** Idle; unemployed.

un·of·fi·cial (un′ə·fish′əl) *adj.* **1.** Not official or in an official capacity. **2.** Not listed in the standard pharmacopeia or formulary of drugs. **— un′of·fi′cial·ly** *adv.*

un·or·gan·ized (un·ôr′gən·īzd) *adj.* **1.** Not organized in structure, system, government, etc. **2.** Not living; inorganic. **3.** Not unionized. Also *Brit.* **un·or′gan·ised.**

un·or·tho·dox (un·ôr′thə·doks) *adj.* Not orthodox, conventional, or approved in doctrine, manner, custom, method, etc. **— un·or′tho·dox′ly** *adv.*

un·pack (un·pak′) *v.t.* **1.** To open and take out the contents of. **2.** To take out of the container, as something packed. **3.** To remove a load or pack from; unload. **— v.i. 4.** To unpack a trunk, goods, etc. **— un·pack′er** *n.*

un·paged (un·pājd′) *adj.* **1.** Having the pages unnumbered: said of a book, magazine, etc. **2.** Not summoned or called, as by a page.

un·paid (un·pād′) *adj.* **1.** Not met or discharged, as a debt. **2.** Not receiving pay; serving without pay. **3.** Having wages remaining due.

un·par·al·leled (un·par′ə·leld) *adj.* Without parallel; unmatched; unprecedented.

un·par·lia·men·ta·ry (un′pär·lə·men′tər·ē) *adj.* Not parliamentary; contrary to the rules that govern deliberative or legislative bodies. **— un′par·lia·men′ta·ri·ness** *n.*

un·peg (un·peg′) *v.t.* **·pegged, ·peg·ging 1.** To remove the peg or pegs from. **2.** To open or unfasten by removing a peg or pegs.

un·peo·ple (un·pē′pəl) *v.t.* **·pled, ·pling** To take or remove people from; depopulate.

un·peo·pled (un·pē′pəld) *adj.* **1.** Uninhabited. **2.** Depopulated.

un·per·fo·rat·ed (un·pûr′fə·rā′tid) *adj.* **1.** Not perforated. **2.** In philately, imperforate.

un·pick (un·pik′) *v.t.* **1.** To undo by removing the stitches; also, to remove (stitches). **2.** To open with a pick.

un·pin (un·pin′) *v.t.* **·pinned, ·pin·ning 1.** To remove the pins from. **2.** To unfasten by removing pins.

un·pleas·ant (un·plez′ənt) *adj.* Disagreeable; objectionable; not pleasing. **— un·pleas′ant·ly** *adv.*

un·pleas·ant·ness (un·plez′ənt·nis) *n.* **1.** The quality, character, or condition of being unpleasant or disagreeable. **2.** Any disagreeable experience or event, as a quarrel.

un·plumbed (un·plumd′) *adj.* **1.** Not sounded or explored fully; unfathomed. **2.** Not furnished with plumbing.

un·pol·i·cied (un·pol′ə·sēd) *adj. Obs.* Impolitic; injudicious.

un·pol·i·tic (un·pol′ə·tik) *adj.* Impolitic.

un·polled (un·pōld′) *adj.* **1.** Not registered: an *unpolled* vote or voter. **2.** Not having voted at an election.

un·pop·u·lar (un·pop′yə·lər) *adj.* Having no popularity; generally disliked or condemned. **— un·pop′u·lar·ly** *adv.* **— un·pop′u·lar′i·ty** (-lər′ə·tē) *n.*

un·prac·ticed (un·prak′tist) *adj.* **1.** Being without practice, experience, or skill. **2.** Not carried out in practice; not used. **3.** Not yet tried.

un·prec·e·dent·ed (un·pres′ə·den′tid) *adj.* Being without precedent; preceded by no similar case; unheard-of. **— un·prec′e·dent′ed·ly** *adv.*

un·prej·u·diced (un·prej′ōō·dist) *adj.* **1.** Free from prejudice or bias; impartial. **2.** Not impaired, as a right.

un·pre·med·i·tat·ed (un′pri·med′ə·tā′tid) *adj.* **1.** Not planned beforehand; undesigned: *unpremeditated* assault. **2.** Not previously considered or thought of. **— Syn.** See ACCIDENTAL, EXTEMPORANEOUS. **— un′pre·med′i·tat′ed·ly** *adv.* **— un′pre·med′i·ta′tion** *n.*

un·pre·pared (un′pri·pârd′) *adj.* **1.** Having made no preparations: an *unprepared* student. **2.** Not prepared or ready: We were *unprepared* for the news. **3.** Done or carried out without preparation; impromptu: an *unprepared* speech. **— un·pre·par·ed·ly** (un′pri·pâr′id·lē) *adv.* **— un′pre·par′ed·ness** *n.*

un·priced (un·prīst′) *adj.* **1.** Having no fixed price. **2.** Priceless.

un·prin·ci·pled (un·prin′sə·pəld) *adj.* Lacking in moral principles; unscrupulous. **— un·prin′ci·pled·ness** *n.*

un·print·a·ble (un·prin′tə·bəl) *adj.* Not fit to be printed.

un·priz·a·ble (un·prī′zə·bəl) *adj. Obs.* **1.** Of worth beyond estimation; invaluable. **2.** Not prized; valueless.

un·pro·duc·tive (un′prə·duk′tiv) *adj.* **1.** Producing little or nothing; barren. **2.** *Econ.* Not adding to exchangeable value: *unproductive* labor. **— un′pro·duc′tive·ly** *adv.* **— un′pro·duc′tive·ness** *n.*

un·pro·fes·sion·al (un′prə·fesh′ən·əl) *adj.* **1.** Having no profession or no professional status. **2.** Violating the rules or ethical code of a profession: *unprofessional* work. **— un′pro·fes′sion·al·ly** *adv.*

un·prof·it·a·ble (un·prof′it·ə·bəl) *adj.* Productive of no profit; serving no desirable purpose; fruitless; futile: *unprofitable* conversation; an *unprofitable* transaction. **— un·prof′it·a·ble·ness** *n.* **— un·prof′it·a·bly** *adv.*

un·pro·nounce·a·ble (un′prə·noun′sə·bəl) *adj.* **1.** Not easy to pronounce, especially properly. **2.** Not fit to be mentioned.

un·pro·vid·ed (un′prə·vī′did) *adj.* **1.** Not furnished or provided: with *with,* formerly with *of:* to be *unprovided* with suitable raiment. **2.** Not prepared; not ready: *unprovided* for a sudden change. **— unprovided for** Not suitably furnished with a means of livelihood: His widow was *unprovided for.* **— un′pro·vid′ed·ly** *adv.*

un·pub. Unpublished.

un·qual·i·fied (un·kwol′ə·fīd) *adj.* **1.** Being without the proper ǃqualifications; unfit. **2.** Having failed to qualify; lacking legal power or authority. **3.** Without limitation or restrictions; absolute; entire: *unqualified* approval. **— un·qual′i·fied·ly** *adv.* **— un·qual′i·fied′ness** *n.*

un·ques·tion·a·ble (un·kwes′chən·ə·bəl) *adj.* Too certain or sure to admit of question; being beyond a doubt; indisputable. **— un·ques′tion·a·bil′i·ty, un·ques′tion·a·ble·ness** *n.* **— un·ques′tion·a·bly** *adv.*

un·ques·tioned (un·kwes′chənd) *adj.* **1.** Not called in question; undoubted. **2.** Not to be disputed or opposed; indisputable. **3.** Not interrogated.

un·qui·et (un·kwī′ət) *adj.* **1.** Not at rest; disturbed;

unsleeping	unsolid	unspeculatively	unsquandered	unsterilized	unsuccess
unslumbering	unsolidly	unspelled	unsquared	unstick	unsuggestive
unsmiling	unsoluble	unspent	unstack	unstigmatized	unsuited
unsmilingly	unsolvable	unspilled	unstainable	unstinted	unsullied
unsmirched	unsolved	unspilt	unstained	unstitched	unsunk
unsmoked	unsoothed	unspiritual	unstalked	unstrained	unsupportable
unsoaked	unsophistication	unspirituality	unstamped	unstressed	unsupportably
unsober	unsorted	unspiritually	unstandardized	unstripped	unsupported
unsocial	unsought	unspiritualness	unstarched	unstuffed	unsupportedly
unsoftened	unsounded	unspoiled	unstarred	unstung	unsuppressed
unsoiled	unsoured	unspoilt	unstated	unsubdued	unsure
unsold	unsowed	unspoken	unstatesmanlike	unsubmissive	unsurmountable
unsoldierly	unsown	unsportsmanlike	unsteadfast	unsubscribed	unsurpassable
unsolicited	unspecified	unsprinkled	unstemmed	unsubsidized	unsurpassed
unsolicitous	unspeculative	unsprung	unsterile	unsubstantiated	unsurprised

restless. **2.** Causing unrest or discomfort. **3.** Uneasy; disturbing. **— un·qui′et·ly** adv. **— un·qui′et·ness** n.

un·quote (un-kwōt′) v.t. & v.i. **·quot·ed, ·quot·ing** To close (a quotation).

un·rav·el (un-rav′əl) v. **·eled** or **·elled, ·el·ing** or **·el·ling** v.t. **1.** To separate the threads of, as a tangled skein or knitted article. **2.** To free from entanglement; unfold; explain, as a mystery or a plot. — v.i. **3.** To become unraveled.

un·read (un-red′) adj. **1.** Not informed by reading; ignorant. **2.** Not yet perused.

un·read·a·ble (un-rē′də-bəl) adj. **1.** Not legible. **2.** Not easy to read. **3.** Not suitable for reading. **— un·read′a·ble·ness, un·read′a·bil′i·ty** n. **— un·read′a·bly** adv.

un·read·y (un-red′ē) adj. **1.** Being without readiness or alertness; not apt or quick to see or appreciate. **2.** Not in a condition to act effectively; unprepared. **— un·read′i·ly** adv. **— un·read′i·ness** n.

un·real (un-rēl′, -rē′əl) adj. **1.** Having no reality, actual existence, or substance. **2.** Having no genuineness; insincere; artificial; also, fanciful; visionary. **— un·re′al·ly** adv.

un·re·al·i·ty (un′rē-al′ə-tē) n. pl. **·ties 1.** The quality of being unreal. **2.** That which is unreal. **3.** The quality of being fanciful or impractical.

un·rea·son (un-rē′zən) n. Lack or absence of reason; irrationality; also, absurdity; nonsense.

un·rea·son·a·ble (un-rē′zən-ə-bəl) adj. **1.** Acting without or contrary to reason. **2.** Not according to reason; irrational. **3.** Exceeding what is reasonable; immoderate; exorbitant. **— un·rea′son·a·bil′i·ty, un·rea′son·a·ble·ness** n. **— un·rea′son·a·bly** adv.

un·rea·son·ing (un-rē′zən-ing) adj. Not accompanied by reason or control, so as to be obstinate, blind, or wild. **— un·rea′son·ing·ly** adv.

un·reck·on·a·ble (un-rek′ən-ə-bəl) adj. That cannot be reckoned or computed; unlimited.

un·re·con·struct·ed (un-rē′kən-struk′tid) adj. **1.** Not reconstructed. **2.** Not reconciled to or accepting the conditions of the Reconstruction.

un·reel (un-rēl′) v.t. & v.i. To unwind, as from a reel.

un·reeve (un-rēv′) v. **·reeved** or **·rove** (for pp. also **·rov·en**), **·reev·ing** Naut. v.t. **1.** To take out or withdraw (a rope) from a block, thimble, deadeye, etc. — v.i. **2.** To become unreeved. **3.** To unreeve a rope.

UNREF United Nations Refugee Emergency Fund.

un·re·flec·tive (un′ri-flek′tiv) adj. Not given to reflection; not thoughtful. **— un′re·flec′tive·ly** adv.

un·re·gen·er·ate (un′ri·jen′ər·it) adj. **1.** Not having been changed spiritually; remaining unreconciled to God. **2.** Sinful; wicked. Also **un′re·gen′er·at·ed** (-ā′tid). **— un′re·gen′er·a·cy** (-ə-sē) n. **— un′re·gen′er·ate·ly** adv.

un·re·lent·ing (un′ri·len′ting) adj. **1.** Not relenting; pitiless; inexorable. **2.** Not diminishing, or not changing, in pace, speed, etc. **— un·re·lent′ing·ly** adv.

un·re·li·a·ble (un′ri·lī′ə·bəl) adj. That cannot be relied upon; not dependable. **— un′re·li·a·bil′i·ty, un′re·li′a·ble·ness** n. **— un′re·li′a·bly** adv.

un·re·li·gious (un′ri·lij′əs) adj. **1.** Irreligious; hostile to religion. **2.** Having no religion; not connected in any way with religion.

un·re·mit·ting (un′ri·mit′ing) adj. Not relaxing or stopping; incessant. **— un′re·mit′ting·ly** adv. **— un′re·mit′ting·ness** n.

un·re·pair (un′rē-pâr′) n. Disrepair.

un·re·proved (un′ri·prōovd′) adj. **1.** Not censured or blamed; not reproved. **2.** Not liable to reproof; above reproach.

un·re·serve (un′ri·zûrv′) n. Absence of reserve; frankness of style or manner; candor.

un·re·served (un′ri·zûrvd′) adj. **1.** Given or done without reserve; full; unlimited. **2.** Having no reserve of manner; informal; open; frank. **— un′re·serv′ed·ly** (un′ri·zûr′vid·lē) adv. **— un′re·serv′ed·ness** n.

un·re·spon·sive (un′ri·spon′siv) adj. Showing no reaction or response. **— un′re·spon′sive·ly** adv. **— un′re·spon′sive·ness** n.

un·rest (un-rest′) n. **1.** Restlessness, especially of the mind. **2.** Trouble; turmoil, especially with regard to public or political conditions and suggesting premonitions of revolt.

un·re·strained (un′ri·strānd′) adj. Not restrained; free; not controlled. **— un·re·strain·ed·ly** (un′ri·strā′nid·lē) adv.

un·rid·dle (un-rid′l) v.t. **·dled, ·dling** To solve, as a mystery.

un·ri·fled[1] (un-rī′fəld) adj. Smoothbored, as a gun.

un·ri·fled[2] (un-rī′fəld) adj. Not rifled, seized, or plundered.

un·rig (un-rig′) v.t. **·rigged, ·rig·ging** Naut. To strip of rigging.

un·right·eous (un-rī′chəs) adj. **1.** Not righteous; wicked; sinful. **2.** Contrary to justice; unfair. **— un·right′eous·ly** adv. **— un·right′eous·ness** n.

un·rip (un-rip′) v.t. **·ripped, ·rip·ping** To separate by ripping; rip or cut open.

un·ripe (un-rīp′) adj. **1.** Not arrived at maturity; not ripe; immature. **2.** Premature. **3.** Not ready; not prepared. [OE unrīpe untimely] **— un·ripe′ness** n.

un·ri·valed (un-rī′vəld) adj. Having no rival or competitor; unequaled; matchless. Also Brit. **un·ri′valled.**

un·roll (un-rōl′) v.t. **1.** To spread or open (something rolled up). **2.** To exhibit to view. **3.** Rare To remove from a roll or register. — v.i. **4.** To become unrolled.

un·root (un-rōot′, -rŏot′) v.t. To uproot.

un·round (un-round′) v.t. Phonet. To change the quality of (a labialized vowel) by keeping the lips in a neutral, or more neutral, position.

UNRRA United Nations Relief and Rehabilitation Administration.

un·ruf·fled (un-ruf′əld) adj. Not disturbed or agitated emotionally; calm.

un·ru·ly (un-rōo′lē) adj. **·li·er, ·li·est** Disposed to resist rule or discipline; intractable; ungovernable. **— un·ru′li·ness** n.

UNRWA United Nations Relief and Works Agency for Palestine Refugees in the Near East.

un·sad·dle (un-sad′l) v.t. **·dled, ·dling 1.** To remove a saddle from. **2.** To throw from the saddle; unhorse.

un·said (un-sed′) adj. Not said; not spoken.

un·sat·u·rat·ed (un-sach′ə-rā′tid) adj. **1.** Containing less of a solute required for equilibrium, as a solution. **2.** Chem. Capable of uniting with elements or radicals without loss of the original constituents.

un·sa·vor·y (un-sā′vər-ē) adj. **1.** Having a disagreeable taste or odor. **2.** Suggesting something disagreeable, offensive, or unclean; also, morally bad: an unsavory reputation. **3.** Obs. Having no savor; tasteless; odorless. Also Brit. **un·sa′vour·y.** **— un·sa′vor·i·ly** adv. **— un·sa′vor·i·ness** n.

un·say (un-sā′) v.t. **·said, ·say·ing** To retract (something said).

un·scathed (un-skāthd′) adj. Uninjured.

UNSCOB United Nations Special Committee on the Balkans.

un·scram·ble (un-skram′bəl) v.t. **·bled, ·bling** Informal **1.** To resolve the confused, scrambled, or disordered condition of. **2.** To make (a scrambled message, etc.) intelligible.

un·screw (un-skrōo′) v.t. **1.** To remove the screw or screws from. **2.** To remove or detach by withdrawing screws, or by turning. — v.i. **3.** To permit of being unscrewed.

un·scru·pu·lous (un-skrōo′pyə·ləs) adj. Not scrupulous; having no scruples or morals; unprincipled. **— un·scru′pu·lous·ly** adv. **— un·scru′pu·lous·ness** n.

un·seal (un-sēl′) v.t. **1.** To break or remove the seal of. **2.** To open (that which has been sealed or closed).

un·seam (un-sēm′) v.t. To open the seam or seams of.

un·search·a·ble (un-sûr′chə·bəl) adj. That cannot be searched or explored; hidden; mysterious. **— un·search′a·ble·ness** n. **— un·search′a·bly** adv.

un·sea·son·a·ble (un-sē′zən·ə·bəl) adj. **1.** Not being in or characteristic of the proper season. **2.** Not taking place at the right time; inappropriate; ill-timed. **— un·sea′son·a·ble·ness** n. **— un·sea′son·a·bly** adv.

un·sea·soned (un-sē′zənd) adj. **1.** Not seasoned; not flavored. **2.** Immature; unripe; not properly aged. **3.** Not habituated. **— un·sea′soned·ness** n.

un·seat (un-sēt′) v.t. **1.** To remove from a seat or fixed position. **2.** To unhorse. **3.** To deprive of office or rank; depose.

un·seem·ly (un-sēm′lē) adj. **·li·er, ·li·est** Not seemly or proper; unbecoming; indecent. — adv. In an unseemly fashion. **— un·seem′li·ness** n.

un·seen (un-sēn′) adj. **1.** Not seen or observed; not evident. **2.** Invisible.

un·self·ish (un-sel′fish) adj. Not selfish; generous. **— un·self′ish·ly** adv. **— un·self′ish·ness** n.

un·set·tle (un-set′l) v. **·tled, ·tling** v.t. **1.** To change or

---

move from a fixed or settled condition. **2.** To confuse; disturb. —*v.i.* **3.** To become unsteady or unfixed.
un·set·tled (un·set'əld) *adj.* **1.** Not settled, orderly, or calm; disturbed; confused. **2.** Uncertain; changeable; variable. **3.** Not determined; undecided. **4.** Unpopulated. **5.** Not located or settled, as in a dwelling. **6.** Not paid or disposed of, as a debt or estate. —**un·set'tled·ness** *n.*
un·sex (un·seks') *v.t.* To deprive of the distinctive qualities of a sex; especially, to render unfeminine or unwomanly.
un·shack·le (un·shak'əl) *v.t.* **·led, ·ling** To unfetter; free from or as from shackles.
un·shak·a·ble (un·shāk'ə·bəl) *adj.* Not easily frightened, changed, intimidated, etc.; firm; resolute. Also **un·shake'a·ble.** —**un·shak'a·ble·ness** *n.* —**un·shak'a·bly** *adv.*
un·shap·en (un·shā'pən) *adj.* Not shaped; imperfectly formed; badly shaped. Also **un·shaped'** (-shāpt').
un·sheathe (un·shēth') *v.t.* **·sheathed, ·sheath·ing** To take from or as from a scabbard or sheath; bare.
un·ship (un·ship') *v.t.* **·shipped, ·ship·ping 1.** To unload from a ship or other vessel; also, to dismiss (people) from a ship. **2.** To remove from the place where it is fixed or fitted, as a rudder or oar.
un·sick·er (un·sik'ər) *adj. Scot.* Unreliable; undependable. —**un·sick'er·ly** *adv.* —**un·sick'er·ness** *n.*
un·sight·ed (un·sī'tid) *adj.* **1.** Not sighted; not in view. **2.** Having no sight, as a cannon. **3.** Not aimed with the assistance of a sight, as a shot. —**un·sight'ed·ly** *adv.*
un·sight·ly (un·sīt'lē) *adj.* **·li·er, ·li·est** Offensive to the sight; ugly. —**un·sight'li·ness** *n.*
un·skaithed (un·skāthd') *adj. Scot.* Unscathed.
un·skilled (un·skild') *adj.* **1.** Destitute of skill or dexterity. **2.** Good only for common labor: an *unskilled* workman. **3.** Not requiring special skill or training: *unskilled* labor.
un·skill·ful (un·skil'fəl) *adj.* **1.** Lacking or not evincing skillfulness; awkward. **2.** *Obs.* Ignorant. Also *Brit.* **un·skil'ful.** —**un·skill'ful·ly** *adv.* —**un·skill'ful·ness** *n.*
un·slaked lime (un·slākt') See under LIME[1].
un·sling (un·sling') *v.t.* **·slung, ·sling·ing 1.** To remove, as a rifle, from a slung position. **2.** *Naut.* To take the slings from.
un·snap (un·snap') *v.t.* **·snapped, ·snap·ping** To undo the snap or snaps of; unfasten.
un·snarl (un·snärl') *v.t.* To disentangle.
un·so·cia·ble (un·sō'shə·bəl) *adj.* **1.** Not sociable; not inclined to seek the society of others. **2.** Not congenial or in accord: an *unsociable* group. **3.** Not encouraging social intercourse. —**un·so·cia·bil'i·ty, un·so'cia·ble·ness** *n.* —**un·so'cia·bly** *adv.*
un·so·cial (un·sō'shəl) *adj.* **1.** Not liking or seeking the company of others. **2.** Antisocial. —**un·so'cial·ly** *adv.*
un·sol·der (un·sod'ər) *v.t.* **1.** To disunite or take apart (something soldered). **2.** To separate; sunder.
un·son·sie (un·son'sē) *adj. Scot.* Unlucky; disagreeable. Also **un·son'cy, un·son'sy.**
un·so·phis·ti·cat·ed (un'sə·fis'tə·kā'tid) *adj.* **1.** Not sophisticated; showing inexperience or naiveté; artless; simple. **2.** Free from adulteration; genuine; pure. — **Syn.** See INGENUOUS. —**un'so·phis'ti·cat'ed·ly** *adv.* —**un'so·phis'ti·cat'ed·ness** *n.*
un·sound (un·sound') *adj.* **1.** Lacking in soundness; not strong or solid; weak. **2.** Not sound in health; diseased. **3.** Not logically valid; erroneous. **4.** Disturbed; not profound: said of sleep. —**un·sound'ly** *adv.* —**un·sound'ness** *n.*
un·spar·ing (un·spâr'ing) *adj.* **1.** Not sparing or saving; lavish; liberal. **2.** Showing no mercy. —**un·spar'ing·ly** *adv.* —**un·spar'ing·ness** *n.*
un·speak (un·spēk') *v.t.* **·spoke, ·spo·ken, ·speak·ing** *Obs.* To retract (something said); take back.
un·speak·a·ble (un·spē'kə·bəl) *adj.* **1.** That cannot be expressed; unutterable: *unspeakable* joy. **2.** Extremely bad or objectionable: an *unspeakable* crime. **3.** Mute. — **un·speak'a·ble·ness** *n.* —**un·speak'a·bly** *adv.*
un·spe·cial·ized (un·spesh'əl·īzd) *adj.* **1.** Not specialized. **2.** *Biol.* Not set apart for a special function or purpose; generalized. Also *Brit.* **un·spe'cial·ised.**
un·sphere (un·sfir') *v.t.* **·sphered, ·spher·ing** To take out of its sphere or place.
un·spot·ted (un·spot'id) *adj.* **1.** Not marked or marred with spots. **2.** Not morally tainted. **3.** Ceremonially clean. —**un·spot'ted·ness** *n.*

un·sta·ble (un·stā'bəl) *adj.* **1.** Lacking in stability or firmness; not stable. **2.** Having no fixed purposes; easily influenced; inconstant: an *unstable* character. **3.** *Chem.* Readily decomposable, as certain compounds. **4.** Subject to a radical change by the application of a slight force: *unstable* equilibrium. —**un·sta'ble·ness** *n.* —**un·sta'bly** *adv.*
un·stead·y (un·sted'ē) *adj.* **1.** Not steady or firm; shaky. **2.** Not regular or constant; wavering: the motor's *unsteady* movement. **3.** Inconstant and erratic in behavior, habits, etc. —**un·stead'i·ly** *adv.* —**un·stead'i·ness** *n.*
un·steel (un·stēl') *v.t.* To deprive of steellike quality; disarm; soften.
un·step (un·step') *v.t.* **·stepped, ·step·ping** To take out of a step or socket: to *unstep* a mast.
un·stop (un·stop') *v.t.* **·stopped, ·stop·ping 1.** To remove a stop or stopper from. **2.** To open by removing obstructions; clear. **3.** To open the stops of (an organ).
un·stopped (un·stopt') *adj.* **1.** Not stopped; unobstructed. **2.** *Phonet.* Of consonants, not stopped; capable of being prolonged: said of the continuants, as (z) and (l).
un·strap (un·strap') *v.t.* **·strapped, ·strap·ping** To unfasten or loosen the strap or straps of.
un·strat·i·fied (un·strat'ə·fīd) *adj.* **1.** Without well-defined layers. **2.** *Geol.* Not deposited in strata, as igneous rocks.
un·stri·at·ed (un·strī'ā·tid) *adj. Anat.* Without striations; smooth-textured, as certain muscles.
un·string (un·string') *v.t.* **·strung, ·string·ing 1.** To remove from a string, as pearls. **2.** To take the string or strings from. **3.** To loosen the string or strings of, as a bow or guitar. **4.** To relax, as if by loosening; weaken: usually in the passive: Her nerves were *unstrung.*
un·striped (un·strīpt') *adj.* Not striped; unstriated.
un·strung (un·strung') *adj.* **1.** Having the strings removed or relaxed. **2.** Unnerved; emotionally upset; weakened.
un·stud·ied (un·stud'ēd) *adj.* **1.** Not planned; unpremeditated. **2.** Not stiff or artificial; natural. **3.** Not acquainted through study; unversed: with *in.*
un·sub·stan·tial (un'səb·stan'shəl) *adj.* **1.** Lacking solidity, strength, or weight. **2.** Having no valid basis. **3.** Having no bodily existence; unreal; fanciful. —**un'sub·stan'·tial·ly** *adv.* —**un·sub·stan'ti·al'i·ty** (-shē·al'ə·tē) *n.*
un·suc·cess·ful (un'sək·ses'fəl) *adj.* Having or meeting with no success: said of persons or their acts: *unsuccessful* in business: an *unsuccessful* attempt. —**un'suc·cess'ful·ly** *adv.* —**un'suc·cess'ful·ness** *n.*
un·suit·a·ble (un·sōō'tə·bəl) *adj.* Not suitable; unfitting. —**un·suit·a·bil·i·ty** (un'sōō·tə·bil'ə·tē), **un·suit'a·ble·ness** *n.* —**un·suit'a·bly** *adv.*
un·sung (un·sung') *adj.* **1.** Not celebrated in song or poetry; obscure. **2.** Not yet sung, as a song.
un·sus·pect·ed (un'sə·spek'tid) *adj.* **1.** Not suspected, as of evil; not under suspicion. **2.** Not imagined or known to exist. —**un'sus·pect'ed·ly** *adv.*
un·sus·pect·ing (un'sə·spek'ting) *adj.* Having no suspicion; trusting. —**un'sus·pect'ing·ly** *adv.*
un·swathe (un·swäth') *v.t.* **·swathed, ·swath·ing** To remove swathings from; free from swathings.
un·swear (un·swâr') *v.t.* **·swore** (-swôr', -swōr'), **·sworn, ·swear·ing** To revoke (an oath); retract; abjure.
un·talked-of (un·tôkt'uv') *adj.* Not spoken about or mentioned.
un·tan·gle (un·tang'gəl) *v.t.* **·gled, ·gling 1.** To free from entanglement or snarls. **2.** To clear up; resolve: to *untangle* a problem.
un·taught (un·tôt') *adj.* **1.** Not having been instructed; ignorant. **2.** Acquired without training or instruction; natural. — **Syn.** See IGNORANT.
un·teach (un·tēch') *v.t.* **·taught, ·teach·ing 1.** To cause to forget or to disbelieve what has been taught. **2.** To cause to be forgotten or disbelieved.
un·ten·a·ble (un·ten'ə·bəl) *adj.* That cannot be maintained or defended: *untenable* theories. —**un·ten'a·bil'i·ty, un·ten'·a·ble·ness** *n.*
Un·ter den Lin·den (ŏŏn'tər den lin'dən) A famous avenue in East Berlin; literally, under the lindens.
Un·ter·wal·den (ŏŏn'tər·väl'dən) A canton of central Switzerland; 296 sq. mi.; pop. 45,323 (1960).
un·thank·ful (un·thangk'fəl) *adj.* **1.** Not grateful. **2.** Not received with thanks; unwelcome. —**un·thank'ful·ly** *adv.* —**un·thank'ful·ness** *n.*

untrustful	untwisted	unutilizable	unveracious	unvisited	unwarlike
untrustiness	untypical	unuttered	unveraciously	unvitiated	unwarmed
untrusty	untypically	unvaccinated	unveraciousness	unvitrified	unwarned
untuck	untypicalness	unvacillating	unverifiable	unvocal	unwashed
untufted	ununiform	unvacillatingly	unverifiableness	unvocally	unwasted
untunable	ununiformed	unvalidated	unverifiably	unvolatilized	unwasting
untuned	ununiformly	unvanquished	unverified	unvulcanized	unwatched
untuneful	ununited	unvaried	unversed	unwakened	unwavering
unturned	unurged	unveiled	unvexed	unwalled	unwaveringly
untwilled	unusable	unventilated	unvext	unwanted	unweakened

PRONUNCIATION KEY: add, āce, câre, pälm; end, ēven; it, īce; odd, ōpen, ôrder; tŏŏk, pōōl; up, bûrn; ə = a in *above*, e in *sicken*, i in *flexible*, o in *melon*, u in *focus*; yōō = u in *fuse*; oil; pout; check; go; ring; thin; this; zh, vision. For à, œ, ü, kh, ń, see inside front cover.

un·think (un·thingk′) *v.t.* **·thought** (-thôt′), **·think·ing** To retract in thought; change the mind concerning.

un·think·ing (un·thingk′ing) *adj.* **1.** Not having the power of thought. **2.** Lacking thoughtfulness, care, or attention; heedless; inconsiderate. — **un·think′ing·ly** *adv.* — **un·think′ing·ness** *n.*

un·thought-of (un·thôt′uv′) *adj.* **1.** Not remembered or called to mind. **2.** Not conceived of; not discovered.

un·thread (un·thred′) *v.t.* **1.** To remove the thread from, as a needle. **2.** To find one's way out of, as a maze.

un·ti·dy (un·tī′dē) *adj.* **·di·er,** **·di·est** Showing or characterized by lack of tidiness. [ME *untīdi*] — **un·ti′di·ly** *adv.* — **un·ti′di·ness** *n.*

un·tie (un·tī′) *v.* **·tied,** **·ty·ing** *v.t.* **1.** To loosen or undo, as a knot or knotted rope. **2.** To free from that which binds or restrains. **3.** To clear up or resolve. — *v.i.* **4.** To become untied. [OE *untīgan*]

un·til (un·til′) *prep.* **1.** Up to the time of; till: We will wait *until* midnight. **2.** Before: used with a negative: The music doesn't begin *until* nine. **3.** *Scot. & Brit. Dial.* Unto. — *conj.* **1.** To the time when: *until* I die. **2.** To the place or degree that: Walk east *until* you reach the river. **3.** Before: with a negative: He couldn't leave *until* the car came for him. [ME *untill* < *un-* up to, as far as (Akin to OE *oth*) + TILL]

un·time·ly (un·tīm′lē) *adj.* **1.** Coming, accomplished, etc., before the proper or expected time; premature. **2.** Coming, accomplished, etc., at the wrong time; ill-timed. Also *Scot.* **un·time′ous.** — *adv.* Inopportunely. — **un·time′li·ness** *n.*

un·ti·tled (un·tīt′ld) *adj.* **1.** Having no right or claim: *untitled* nobility. **2.** Having no title, as a book.

un·to (un′tŏŏ) *prep.* **1.** *Poetic & Archaic* To: used in all senses except to indicate the infinitive. **2.** *Archaic* Until. — *conj. Obs.* Up to the extent or time that; until. [ME *un-* up to, as far as + TO; on analogy with *until*]

un·told (un·tōld′) *adj.* **1.** That cannot be revealed or described; inexpressible: *untold* misery. **2.** That cannot be numbered or estimated: *untold* numbers. **3.** Not told.

un·touch·a·bil·i·ty (un′tuch·ə·bil′ə·tē) *n.* The character or state of being untouchable.

un·touch·a·ble (un·tuch′ə·bəl) *adj.* **1.** Inaccessible to the touch; out of reach. **2.** Not subject to rivalry, criticism, or control. **3.** Forbidden to the touch. **4.** Unpleasant, disgusting, vile, or dangerous to touch. — *n.* In India, a member of the lowest caste; one whose touch was formerly counted as pollution by Hindus of higher station.

un·to·ward (un·tôrd′, -tōrd′) *adj.* **1.** Causing annoyance or hindrance; vexatious. **2.** Not yielding readily; refractory; perverse. **3.** Unseemly; uncouth. **4.** *Obs.* Awkward. — **un·to′ward·ly** *adv.* — **un·to′ward·ness** *n.*

un·trav·eled (un·trav′əld) *adj.* **1.** Not passed over, as a road. **2.** Not having traveled; also, narrow in ideas; provincial. Also **un·trav′elled.**

un·tread (un·tred′) *v.t.* **·trod, ·trod·den** or **·trod, ·tread·ing** To retrace.

un·tried (un·trīd′) *adj.* **1.** Not tried or tested. **2.** Not tried in court.

un·trod·den (un·trod′n) *adj.* Not having been trodden upon; also, unfrequented. Also **un·trod′.**

un·true (un·trŏŏ′) *adj.* **1.** Lacking truth; not true; not corresponding with fact. **2.** Not conforming to rule or standard. **3.** Not adhering to faith, pledge, or duty; disloyal. — **un·tru′ly** *adv.*

un·truss (un·trus′) *v.t.* **1.** To loosen or free from or as from a truss; unfasten; undo. **2.** *Obs.* To take off (breeches); undress.

un·trust·wor·thy (un·trust′wûr′thē) *adj.* Worthy of no trust; unreliable. — **un·trust′wor′thi·ness** *n.* — **un·trust′wor′thi·ly** *adv.*

un·truth (un·trŏŏth′) *n.* *pl.* **·truths** (-trŏŏths′, -trŏŏthz′) **1.** The quality or character of being untrue; want of veracity. **2.** Something that is not true; a lie. **3.** *Obs.* Lack of fidelity; disloyalty. — **Syn.** See LIE². [OE *untrēowth*]

un·truth·ful (un·trŏŏth′fəl) *adj.* **1.** Not truthful; untrue. **2.** Given to telling lies. — **un·truth′ful·ly** *adv.* — **un·truth′ful·ness** *n.*

UNTSO United Nations Truce Supervision Organization.

un·tu·tored (un·tŏŏ′tərd, -tyŏŏ′-) *adj.* **1.** Having had no tutor or teacher. **2.** Naive; simple. — **Syn.** See IGNORANT.

un·twine (un·twīn′) *v.* **·twined, ·twin·ing** *v.t.* **1.** To undo (something twined); unwind by disentangling. — *v.i.* **2.** To become untwined.

un·twist (un·twist′) *v.t. & v.i.* To separate or open by a movement the reverse of twisting; unwind or untwine.

U·nun·gun (ŏŏ·nŏŏng′gŏŏn) *n.pl.* The collective name for two Eskimo tribes inhabiting the Aleutian Islands; the Aleuts; literally, people.

un·used (un·yŏŏzd′ *for def. 1*; un·yŏŏst′ *for def. 2*) *adj.* **1.** Not made use of; also, never having been used. **2.** Not accustomed or wont: with *to*.

un·u·su·al (un·yŏŏ′zhŏŏ·əl) *adj.* Not usual, common, or ordinary; rare. — **un·u′su·al·ly** *adv.* — **un·u′su·al·ness** *n.*

un·ut·ter·a·ble (un·ut′ər·ə·bəl) *adj.* **1.** That cannot be uttered; too great or deep for verbal expression; ineffable: *unutterable* bliss. **2.** Unpronounceable. — **un·ut′ter·a·ble·ness** *n.* — **un·ut′ter·a·bly** *adv.*

un·val·ued (un·val′yŏŏd) *adj.* **1.** Not valued; neglected; unappreciated. **2.** Not appraised. **3.** *Obs.* Inestimable.

un·var·nished (un·vär′nisht) *adj.* **1.** Having no covering of varnish. **2.** Having no embellishment; plain.

un·veil (un·vāl′) *v.t.* **1.** To remove the veil or covering from; disclose to view; reveal. — *v.i.* **2.** To remove one's veil; reveal oneself.

un·voice (un·vois′) *v.t.* **·voiced, ·voic·ing** *Phonet.* To deprive of voice or vocal quality; devocalize.

un·voiced (un·voist′) *adj.* **1.** Not expressed. **2.** *Phonet.* **a** Voiceless. **b** Rendered voiceless: The final (v) in "have" is often heard *unvoiced* in "have to": also *devoiced.*

un·voic·ing (un·voi′sing) *n.* *Phonet.* The replacement of a voiced consonant by its voiceless counterpart, as (b) by (p).

un·war·rant·a·ble (un·wôr′ən·tə·bəl, -wor′-) *adj.* Unjustifiable; inexcusable. — **un·war′rant·a·bly** *adv.*

un·war·rant·ed (un·wôr′ən·tid, -wor′-) *adj.* Having no justification or support.

un·war·y (un·wâr′ē) *adj.* Not careful or cautious; imprudent; rash; careless. — **un·war′i·ly** *adv.* — **un·war′i·ness** *n.*

un·wea·ried (un·wir′ēd) *adj.* **1.** Not tired. **2.** Never tired; indefatigable. — **un·wea′ried·ly** *adv.*

un·wel·come (un·wel′kəm) *adj.* **1.** Not welcome; undesired. **2.** Disagreeable; distasteful. — **un·wel′come·ly** *adv.*

un·well (un·wel′) *adj.* Not well; ailing; sick. — **Syn.** See SICK¹. — **un·well′ness** *n.*

un·wept (un·wept′) *adj.* **1.** Not lamented or wept for, as a deceased person. **2.** Not shed, as tears.

un·whole·some (un·hōl′səm) *adj.* **1.** Deleterious to physical or mental health. **2.** Unsound in quality or condition; diseased or decayed: *unwholesome* provisions. **3.** Suggestive of illness or disease: an *unwholesome* look. **4.** Morally bad; pernicious. — **un·whole′some·ly** *adv.* — **un·whole′some·ness** *n.*

un·wield·y (un·wēl′dē) *adj.* Moved or managed with difficulty, as from great size or awkward shape; bulky; clumsy. — **un·wield′i·ly** *adv.* — **un·wield′i·ness** *n.*

un·willed (un·wild′) *adj.* **1.** Not willed or intended; spontaneous. **2.** Being without, or deprived of, purpose or will.

un·will·ing (un·wil′ing) *adj.* **1.** Not willing; reluctant; loath. **2.** Done, said, etc., with reluctance. **3.** *Obs.* Not intended; involuntary. — **un·will′ing·ly** *adv.* — **un·will′ing·ness** *n.*

un·wind (un·wīnd′) *v.* **·wound, ·wind·ing** *v.t.* **1.** To reverse the winding of; untwist or wind off; uncoil. **2.** To disentangle. **3.** To remove tension from; relax. — *v.i.* **4.** To become untwisted or uncoiled. **5.** To become free from tension.

un·wise (un·wīz′) *adj.* Showing a lack of wisdom; imprudent; foolish. [OE *unwīs*] — **un·wise′ly** *adv.*

un·wish (un·wish′) *v.t.* **1.** To retract (something wished); stop wishing. **2.** To wish (something) not to be. **3.** *Obs.* To destroy or do away with by wishing.

un·wit·ting (un·wit′ing) *adj.* **1.** Having no knowledge or consciousness of the thing in question. **2.** Unintentional. [OE *unwitende*] — **un·wit′ting·ly** *adv.*

un·wont·ed (un·wun′tid, -wōn′-) *adj.* **1.** Not according to habit or custom; unusual. **2.** *Obs.* Not accustomed; unfamiliar. — **un·wont′ed·ly** *adv.* — **un·wont′ed·ness** *n.*

un·world·ly (un·wûrld′lē) *adj.* **1.** Not motivated by worldly values or interests; spiritually minded. **2.** Not belonging to this world; unearthly; spiritual. — **un·world′li·ness** *n.*

un·wor·thy (un·wûr′thē) *adj.* **1.** Not worthy or deserving of something specified: usually with *of.* **2.** Not befitting or becoming: often with *of*; wrong; improper: conduct *unworthy* of a gentleman. **3.** Lacking worth or merit. **4.** Shameful; contemptible. — **un·wor′thi·ly** *adv.* — **un·wor′thi·ness** *n.*

un·wound (un·wound′) Past tense and past participle of UNWIND.

un·wrap (un·rap′) *v.* **·wrapped, ·wrap·ping** *v.t.* **1.** To take the wrapping from; open; undo. — *v.i.* **2.** To become unwrapped.

unweaned	unwedded	unwinning	unwon	unworshiped	unyieldingly
unwearable	unweeded	unwisdom	unwooded	unworshipped	unyieldingness
unwearily	unwelded	unwished	unwooed	unwound	unyouthful
unweary	unwetted	unwithered	unworkability	unwounded	unyouthfully
unwearying	unwhetted	unwithering	unworkable	unwoven	unyouthfulness
unwearyingly	unwhipped	unwitnessed	unworkableness	unwreathe	unzealous
unweathered	unwifely	unwomanish	unworked	unwrought	unzealously
unweave	unwincing	unwomanishly	unworkmanlike	unwrung	unzealousness
unwed	unwinking	unwomanly	unworn	unyielding	unzip

un·wrin·kle (un-ring'kəl) *v.t.* **·kled, ·kling** To free from wrinkles; smooth.

un·writ·ten (un-rit'n) *adj.* **1.** Not written or in writing. **2.** Not reduced to writing; traditional; customary. **3.** Having no writing upon it; blank.

unwritten law A law, rule, or custom established by general usage rather than by legislative action.

un·yeaned (un-yēnd') *adj.* Not yet born: said especially of a goat or sheep.

un·yoke (un-yōk') *v.* **·yoked, ·yok·ing** *v.t.* **1.** To release from a yoke. **2.** To separate; part. — *v.i.* **3.** To become unyoked. **4.** To stop work; cease. [OE *ungeocian*]

un·yoked (un-yōkt') *adj.* **1.** Not wearing a yoke. **2.** Freed from a yoke. **3.** *Obs.* Unrestrained; licentious.

un·zoned (un-zōnd') *adj.* Not zoned or restricted, as an industrial or residential area.

up (up) *adv.* **1.** From a lower to a higher place, level, position, etc.: Come *up*. **2.** In, on, or to a higher place, level, position, etc.: The flag went *up*. **3.** Toward that which is figuratively or conventionally higher; as: **a** To or at a higher price: Barley went *up*. **b** To or at a higher place, rank, station, etc.: people who have come *up* in the world. **c** To or at a greater size or amount: to swell *up*. **d** To or at a higher musical pitch. **e** To or at a place that is locally or arbitrarily regarded as higher: *up* north. **f** Above the surface or horizon: The sun came *up*. **g** From an earlier to a later time or period. **h** To a source, center, conclusion, etc.: Follow *up* this lead. **4.** To a vertical position; standing; on one's feet; also, out of bed. **5.** So as to be compact or secure: Tie *up* the boxes. **6.** So as to be level to or even with in space, time, degree, amount, etc.: *up* to date; *up* to the brim. **7.** In or into an excited state or activity or some specific action: They were stirred *up* to mutiny. **8.** In or into view or existence: to draw *up* a will. **9.** In or into prominence; under consideration: The question was put *up* for debate. **10.** In or into a place of safekeeping; aside: Fruits are put *up* in glass jars. **11.** To an end or close: His time came *up*. **12.** Completely; totally; wholly: The house was burned *up*. **13.** To completion; to the limit: to eat *up* the food. **14.** In baseball and cricket, at bat: He was put *up* three times. **15.** In tennis and other sports: **a** In the lead; ahead: said of a player or team. **b** Apiece; alike: said of a score. **16.** Bound for: said of a ship: *up* for Panama. **17.** So as to be a candidate: Jones was put *up* for mayor. **18.** On trial: *up* for manslaughter. **19.** *Naut.* Shifted to windward, as a tiller. ◆ In informal usage *up* is often added to a verb without affecting the meaning of the sentence: to light *up* a room; to write *up* a report. **— to be all up with** To be at an end for; to be all over for. **— to be up against** *Informal* To meet with; be face to face with. **— to be up against it** *Informal* To be in difficulty; have financial trouble. **— to be up in** (or **on**) *Informal* To be well informed in or skilled at something. **— to be up to 1.** *Informal* To be doing or plotting; be about to do: What is he *up* to? **2.** To be equal to; be capable of: I'm not *up to* moving all this furniture today. **3.** To be incumbent upon; be dependent upon: It's *up* to him to save us. **4.** To be decided by: It's *up* to her. — *adj.* **1.** Moving, sloping, advancing, or directed upward: The moon is *up*. **2.** In or coming to an upward position or condition or a position or condition arbitrarily regarded as upward: Flowers are *up*; The blinds are *up*; The book is *up* to date; soldiers *up* from the rank and file. **3.** More than is usual or normal: The gate receipts were *up* today. **4.** In or characterized by an active or excited state: His temper was *up*. **5.** Acquainted with, equal to, or prepared for: Are you *up* in your history? **6.** At an end or close: Your time is *up*. **7.** Ready for use, operation, etc.: Is the power *up*? **8.** In baseball or cricket, at bat: He was *up* three times. **9.** In sports and games, in advance of an opponent. **10.** At stake, as in gambling; wagered. **11.** Running for as a candidate: Jones is *up* for mayor. **12.** On trial: He is *up* for manslaughter. **13.** Being considered or presented for action, approval, debate, etc.: The question is *up* for voting. **14.** *Informal* Going on; taking place: What's *up*? **— up and around** *Informal* Sufficiently recovered to walk; on one's feet again. **— up to no good** Engaged in or contemplating some mischief or improper act. — *prep.* **1.** From a lower to a higher point or place of, on, or along. **2.** Toward a higher condition or rank on or in: *up* the social ladder. **3.** To or at a point farther above or along: The farm is *up* the road. **4.** From the coast toward the interior of (a country). **5.** From the mouth toward the source of (a river): to sail *up* a river. **6.** At, on, or near the height or top of. — *n.* **1.** A rise or ascent. **2.** A period of prosperity, elation, etc.: chiefly in the phrase **ups and downs.** **— to be on the up and up 1.** *Slang* To be honest and aboveboard. **2.** *Informal* Rising and improving: Car sales are on the *up and up*. — *v.* **upped, up·ping** *Informal v.t.* **1.** To make larger, better, etc.: to *up* the quality. **2.** To put or take up; raise; lift. — *v.i.* **3.** To rise or move upward. **4.** *Informal* or *Dial.* To do or begin to do quickly or abruptly: usually followed by *and* plus a verb: She *ups* and says to me. [OE *ūp*]

up- *combining form* As a combining element *up* has adverbial force with various meanings, as in the following examples:

1. To a higher place or level:

upbear	upfling	uprise
upbearer	upflow	uprush
upborne	upgaze	upsend
upbuilder	upgoing	upshoot
upbuilding	upgrow	upsoar
upclimb	upheap	upstare
upcoil	upleap	upstep
upcurl	uppile	uptilt
upcurve	upraiser	uptoss
updart	upreach	upwaft
updive	upreaching	upwreathe

2. To a greater size or larger amount:

| upbulging | upflashing | uplight |
| upflaring | upflooding | upswell |

3. To a vertical position:

| upprop | upstand | upsticking |

4. In or into commotion or activity:

| upboil | upbubbling | upstir |

5. Completely; wholly:

| upbind | upfold | upgird |
| updry | upgather | uphoard |

UP or **U.P. 1.** Union Pacific (Railroad). **2.** United Press.

up·and·com·ing (up'ən-kum'ing) *adj.* Enterprising; energetic; promising.

up-and-down (up'ən-doun') *adj.* **1.** Alternately rising and falling; fluctuating; varying: an *up-and-down* motion; an *up-and-down* career. **2.** Vertical; perpendicular.

U·pan·i·shad (ōō-pan'ə-shad, -pä'nə-shäd) *n. Sanskrit* One of the treatises forming the third division of the Vedas, dealing with the nature of man and the universe: literally, a philosophical treatise.

u·pas (yōō'pəs) *n.* **1.** A tall evergreen Javanese tree (*Antiaris toxicaria*) of the mulberry family, having an acrid, poisonous sap used as an arrow poison. **2.** The sap of this tree. **3.** Anything physically or morally harmful or deadly. [< Malay (*pohon*) *upas* poison (tree)]

up·beat (up'bēt') *n. Music* An unaccented beat; the beat at which the hand of the conductor is raised. — *adj. Slang* **1.** *Music* Characterized by a lively, swinging rhythm. **2.** Optimistic; happy.

up-bow (up'bō') *n. Music* On the violin, etc., a stroke of the bow across the strings, going from the tip toward the nut, indicated by the symbol **V**: opposed to *down-bow*.

up·braid (up-brād') *v.t.* **1.** To reproach for some wrongdoing; scold or reprove. — *v.i.* **2.** To utter reproaches. [OE *ūpbregdan* < *up-* up + *bregdan* to weave, twist] — **up·braid'er** *adj.* — **up·braid'ing** *n.* — **up·braid'ing·ly** *adv.*

up·bring·ing (up'bring'ing) *n.* The rearing and training received by a person during childhood.

up·bye (up'bī') *adv. Scot.* A little farther on. Also **up'by.**

up·cast (up'kast', -käst') *adj.* Cast, turned, or directed upward. — *n.* **1.** A casting upward; also, that which is so cast. **2.** An airshaft in a mine. **3.** An upward current of air, as in a mine shaft. **4.** *Scot.* An upset, or a reproach.

up·chuck (up'chuk') *v.t. & v.i. U.S. Slang* To vomit.

up·com·ing (up'kum'ing) *U.S. adj.* Impending; forthcoming.

up·coun·try (*n. & adj.* up'kun'trē; *adv.* up'kun'trē) *Informal n.* Country somewhat distant from the seashore or from lowlands; inland country. — *adj.* Living in, from, or characteristic of inland places. — *adv.* In, into, or toward the interior: to move *upcountry*.

up·date (up·dāt') *v.t.* **·dat·ed, ·dat·ing** To bring up to date; to revise, with corrections, additions, etc., as a textbook.

up·draft (up'draft', -dräft') *n.* An upward movement of air or other gas. Also *Brit.* **up'draught'.**

up·end (up'end') *v.t. & v.i.* To set or stand on end.

up·grade (*n.* up'grād'; *v.* up·grād'; *adv.* up'grād') *n.* An upward incline or slope. — *v.t.* **·grad·ed, ·grad·ing 1.** To improve the breed of (animals) by the introduction of a higher strain. **2.** To raise to a higher grade, rank, or responsibility, as an employee. — *adv.* Up a hill or slope. — **on the up·grade 1.** Improving. **2.** Rising.

up·growth (up'grōth') *n.* **1.** The process of growing up. **2.** That which grows or has grown up.

up·heav·al (up·hē'vəl) *n.* **1.** The act of upheaving, or the state of being upheaved. **2.** A violent disturbance or change, as in the social order. **3.** *Geol.* An elevation of the earth's surface due to a warping of large rock masses.

up·heave (up·hēv') *v.* **·heaved** *or* **·hove, ·heav·ing** *v.t.* **1.** To heave or raise up. — *v.i.* **2.** To be raised or lifted.

up·held (up·held') Past tense and past participle of UPHOLD.

up·hill (*adv. & adj.* up'hil'; *n.* up'hil') *adv.* Up or as up a hill or an ascent; against difficulties. — *adj.* **1.** Sloping upward. **2.** Attended with difficulty or exertion. **3.** At or on a high place. — *n.* An upward slope; rising ground.

up·hold (up·hōld') *v.t.* **·held, ·hold·ing 1.** To hold up; raise. **2.** To keep from falling or sinking. **3.** To give aid or support to. **4.** To regard with approval. — **up·hold'er** *n.*

up·hol·ster (up·hōl′stər) *v.t.* **1.** To fit, as furniture, with coverings, cushioning, etc. **2.** To provide or adorn with hangings, curtains, etc., as an apartment. **3.** To furnish with a covering. [Back formation < UPHOLSTERER]

up·hol·ster·er (up·hōl′stər·ər) *n.* **1.** One who furnishes upholstery. **2.** One who upholsters. [< obs. *upholster*, *upholdster*, alter. of ME *upholder* tradesman + -ER¹]

upholsterer bee Any of various bees that cut small pieces of leaves or flower petals to line their cells.

up·hol·ster·y (up·hōl′stər·ē, -strē) *n.* *pl.* **·ster·ies** **1.** Fabric and fittings used in upholstering. **2.** The act, art, or business of upholstering.

u·phroe (yōō′frō, yōōv′rō) See EUPHROE.

UPI or **U.P.I.** United Press International.

up·keep (up′kēp) *n.* The act or state of maintaining something; also, the cost of maintenance.

up·land (up′land, -land′) *n.* **1.** The higher portions of a region, district, farm, etc. **2.** The country in the interior. — *adj.* **1.** Pertaining to an upland; higher in situation. **2.** Pertaining to or situated in elevated districts.

upland cotton A species of cotton (*Gossypium hirsutum*), widely cultivated in many varieties in the United States.

upland plover See under PLOVER.

up·lift (*v.* up·lift′; *adj.*, *n.* up′lift′) *v.t.* **1.** To lift up, or raise aloft; elevate. **2.** To raise the tone of; put on a higher plane, mentally or morally. — *adj.* *Rare* Uplifted. — *n.* **1.** The act of raising, or the fact of being raised. **2.** A movement upward. **3.** *Geol.* An upheaval. **4.** Mental or spiritual stimulation or elevation. **5.** A movement aiming to improve the condition of the underprivileged. **6.** A brassiere designed to lift and support the breasts. — **up·lift′er** *n.*

up·most (up′mōst) *adj.* Uppermost.

U·po·lu (ōō·pō′lōō) One of the chief islands of Western Samoa; 430 sq. mi.

up·on (ə·pon′, ə·pôn′) *prep.* **1.** On, in all its meanings. **2.** On, in an elevated position: *upon* the throne. **3.** On, by motion upward: to leap *upon* a table. — *adv.* On: completing a verbal idea: The paper has been written *upon*. Also *Scot.* **u·po** (ə·pō′). [ME]

◆ **upon, on** *Upon* now differs little in use from *on*, the former being sometimes used for reasons of euphony and also preferably when motion into position is involved. the latter when merely rest or support is to be indicated. When *upon* has its original meaning of *up* and *on*, it is written as two words, *up* having its adverbial force: Let us go *up on* the roof.

up·per (up′ər) *adj.* **1.** Higher than something else; being above. **2.** Higher or further inland in location, place, etc. **3.** Higher in station, rank, dignity, etc.; superior: the *upper* house. — **to get the upper hand** To get the advantage. — *n.* **1.** That part of a boot or shoe above the sole; the vamp. **2.** *pl.* Cloth gaiters. **3.** *Informal* An upper berth (which see). — **on one's uppers** *Informal* **1.** Having worn out the soles of one's shoes. **2.** At the end of one's resources; destitute. Abbr. *u.*, *U.* [ME, orig. compar. of UP]

Up·per (up′ər) *adj.* *Geol.* Designating a later period or a later formation of a specified period: the *Upper* Cambrian.

Upper Arlington A city in central Ohio, near Columbus; pop. 38,630.

Upper Austria A Province of northern Austria; 4,624 sq. mi.; pop. 1,131,218 (1961); capital, Linz: German *Oberösterreich*.

upper berth The top berth in a ship, railroad sleeping car, etc., where two bunks or beds are built one above the other.

up·per-brack·et (up′ər·brak′it) *adj.* Of or belonging to a higher bracket or level: an *upper-bracket* income.

Upper Burma See under BURMA.

Upper Canada **1.** The name of Ontario before 1841. when Upper and Lower Canada made up the Province of Canada. **2.** *Rare* Ontario.

upper case *Printing* **1.** In type cases, the upper tray, containing the capital letters of the alphabet: sometimes called *cap case*. See CASE². **2.** The capital letters of the alphabet. Abbr. *u.c.*

up·per-case (up′ər·kās′) *Printing* *adj.* Of, in, or indicating capital letters, as distinguished from small letters. — *v.t.* **-cased, -cas·ing** To set as or change to capital letters.

Upper Chamber In Canada, the Senate. Also **Upper House**.

upper class The socially or economically superior group in society. — **up′per-class′** (up′ər·klas′, -kläs′) *adj.*

up·per-class·man (up′ər·klas′mən, -kläs′-) *n.* *pl.* **·men** (-mən) A junior or senior in a school or college.

upper crust *Informal* That portion of society having higher social standing by reason of wealth or ancestry.

up·per-cut (up′ər·kut′) *n.* In boxing, a swinging blow upward, delivered under or inside the opponent's guard. — *v.t.* & *v.i.* **-cut, -cut·ting** To strike with an uppercut.

Upper Dar·by (där′bē) An urban township in SE Pennsylvania, a suburb of Philadelphia; pop. 95,910.

Upper Egypt See under EGYPT.

upper hand Advantage: to get the *upper hand*.

Upper House The branch in a bicameral legislature, where membership is usually smaller and more restricted, as the English House of Lords. Also **upper house**.

up·per·most (up′ər·mōst′) *adj.* **1.** Highest in place, rank, authority, influence, etc. **2.** First to come into the mind: one's *uppermost* thoughts. Also **upmost**. — *adv.* In the highest place, rank, authority, etc.; also, first, as in time.

Upper Paleolithic See under PALEOLITHIC.

upper partial tone See under PARTIAL TONE.

Upper Silesia A former province of eastern Germany, now in western Poland.

Upper Vol·ta (vol′tə) An independent Republic in western Africa; 105,900 sq. mi.; pop. 5,330,000 (est. 1970); capital, Ouagadougou.

upper works *Naut.* That part of a ship's hull that lies above the water when the ship is normally loaded.

up·ping (up′ing) *n.* Swan-upping (which see).

up·pish (up′ish) *adj.* *Informal* Inclined to be self-assertive, pretentious, or snobbish. Also **up·pi·ty** (up′ə·tē). — **up′-pish·ly** *adv.* — **up′pish·ness** *n.*

Upp·sa·la (up·sä′lə, *Sw.* ōōp′sä·lä) A city in eastern Sweden; pop. 77,397 (1960). Also **Up·sa′la**.

up·raise (up·rāz′) *v.t.* **·raised, ·rais·ing** To lift up; elevate. Also **up·rear′** (-rir′).

up·right (up′rīt′) *adj.* **1.** Being in a vertical position; straight up; erect. **2.** Morally correct; especially, just and honest. — *n.* **1.** Something having a vertical position, as an upright timber or piano. **2.** The state of being upright: a post out of *upright*. **3.** In football, one of the goal posts. — *adv.* In an upright position; vertically. [OE *upriht* < *ūp*-up + *riht* right] — **up′right·ly** *adv.* — **up′right·ness** *n.*

upright piano A piano smaller than a grand piano, having strings arranged vertically in a rectangular case placed at right angles to the keyboard.

up·rise (*v.* up·rīz′; *n.* up′rīz′) *v.i.* **·rose, ·ris·en, ·ris·ing** **1.** To get up; rise, as from a seat or from sleep. **2.** To be or become erect. **3.** To go upward; ascend. **4.** To increase; swell. **5.** To rise into view. **6.** To rise in revolt. — *n.* **1.** The act of rising or of rising up. **2.** An upward slope.

up·ris·ing (up·rī′zing, up′rī′zing) *n.* **1.** The act of rising. **2.** A revolt or insurrection. — **Syn.** See REBELLION. **3.** An ascent; a slope; acclivity.

up·riv·er (up′riv′ər) *adj.* & *adv.* On or toward the upper part of a river. — *n.* A region located upriver.

up·roar (up′rôr′, -rōr′) *n.* A violent disturbance, noise, or tumult; also, an instance of this. [< Du. *oproer* < *op*-up + *roeren* to stir]

up·roar·i·ous (up·rôr′ē·əs, -rō′rē-) *adj.* **1.** Accompanied by or making an uproar. **2.** Loud and noisy; tumultuous. **3.** Very funny: an *uproarious* play. — **up·roar′i·ous·ly** *adv.* — **up·roar′i·ous·ness** *n.*

up·root (up·rōōt′, -rōōt′) *v.t.* **1.** To tear up by the roots. **2.** To destroy utterly; eradicate. — **up·root′al** *n.* — **up·root′er** *n.*

up·rose (up·rōz′) Past tense of UPRISE.

up·rouse (up·rouz′) *v.t.* **·roused, ·rous·ing** To rouse up.

up·set (*v.* up·set′; *adj.* up·set′, up′set′; *n.* up′set′) *v.* **·set, ·set·ting** *v.t.* **1.** To overturn. **2.** To throw into confusion or disorder. **3.** To disconcert, derange, or disquiet. **4.** To defeat, especially unexpectedly: Yale *upset* Harvard. **5.** *Mech.* **a** To shorten and thicken by hammering or by pressure, as a bolt or the metal tire of a wheel. **b** To swage (the ends of the teeth of a saw). — *v.i.* **6.** To become overturned. — *adj.* **1.** Tipped or turned over. **2.** Mentally or physically disturbed or ill. **3.** Confused; disordered; messy. **4.** Established, as a price. — *n.* **1.** The act of upsetting, or the state of being upset. **2.** *Informal* A defeat, especially an unexpected one. **3.** A mental or physical disturbance or disorder. **4.** *Mech.* A tool used for upsetting; also, a piece or part that has been upset. — **up·set′ter** *n.*

upset price The lowest price at which something will be offered for sale, as by an auctioneer.

up·shot (up′shot′) *n.* **1.** The final outcome; result. **2.** *Obs.* The final shot in an archery match. — **Syn.** See EFFECT.

up·side (up′sīd′) *n.* The upper side or part. — **to be upsides with** *Brit. Dial.* To be even with.

up·side-down (up′sīd′doun′) *adj.* **1.** Having the upper side down. **2.** In disorder. — *adv.* **1.** With the upper side down. **2.** In or into disorder or confusion. Also **upside down**. [Alter. of ME *up so down* up as if down]

upside-down cake A cake baked with the batter covering any of various fruits and served with the fruit side up.

up·si·lon (yōōp′sə·lon, up′sə·lon, *Brit.* yōōp·sī′lən) *n.* The twentieth letter and sixth vowel in the Greek alphabet (Υ, υ): having the sound of French *u*, Latin and Old English *y*. It is transliterated in English as *u* or *y*. See ALPHABET, Y. [< Gk. < *u. u* + *psilon* smooth]

up·spring (up′spring′) *n.* **1.** A leap up into the air. **2.** *Obs.* An upstart. — *v.i.* **·sprang** or **·sprung, ·sprung, ·springing** To spring up.

up·stage (up′stāj′) *adj.* **1.** Pertaining to the back half of a stage. **2.** *Informal* Haughty; supercilious. — *adv.* Toward, near, or on the back of a stage. — *v.t.* **·staged, ·stag·ing** **1.** To move upstage and force (another actor) to face away from the audience; steal a scene from. **2.** *Informal* To treat in a haughty manner.

up·stairs (up′stârz′) *adj.* Pertaining to an upper story.

— *n.* An upper story; especially, the part of a building above the ground floor. — *adv.* In, to, or toward an upper story. — **to kick upstairs** To promote so as to get out of the way.

up·stand·ing (up·stan′ding) *adj.* **1.** Honest; upright; straightforward. **2.** Standing up; erect.

up·start (*v.* up·stärt′; *adj. & n.* up′stärt′) *v.i.* To start or spring up suddenly. — *adj.* **1.** Suddenly raised to prominence, wealth, or power. **2.** Characteristic of an upstart; vulgar; pretentious. — *n.* **1.** One who has suddenly risen from a humble position to one of wealth or importance and is usually arrogant in tone or bearing. **2.** Anyone who is presumptuous or arrogant in manner.

up·state (up′stāt′) *U.S. adj.* Of, from, or designating that part of a State lying outside, usually north, of the principal city. — *n.* The outlying, usually northern, sections of a State. — *adv.* In or toward the outlying or northern sections of a State. — **up′stat′er** *n.*

up·stream (up′strēm′) *adv.* Toward or at the source or upper part of a stream; against the current.

up·stretched (up′strecht′) *adj.* Stretched or extended upward: *upstretched* arms.

up·stroke (up′strōk′) *n.* An upward stroke, as of a pen.

up·surge (*v.* up·sûrj′; *n.* up′sûrj′) *v.i.* ·**surged**, ·**surg·ing** To surge up. — *n.* A surge or swell upward.

up·sweep (*n.* up′swēp′; *v.* up·swēp′) *n.* **1.** A sweeping up or upward; especially, a hairdo that is swept upward smoothly in the back and piled high on the top of the head. **2.** The upturning of the lower jaw, as in the bulldog. — *v.t. & v.i.* ·**swept**, ·**sweep·ing** To brush or sweep upward or up.

up·swell (up·swel′) *v.i.* ·**swelled**, ·**swelled** or ·**swol·len**, **swell·ing** To swell up.

up·swept (up′swept′) *adj.* Arranged in an upsweep, as hair.

up·swing (*n.* up′swing′; *v.* up·swing′) *n.* **1.** A swinging upward **2.** An improvement. — *v.i.* ·**swung**, ·**swing·ing 1.** To swing upward. **2.** To improve.

up·take (up′tāk′) *n.* **1.** The act of lifting or taking up. **2.** A boiler flue that unites the combustion gases and carries them toward the smokestack. **3.** An upward ventilating shaft in a mine. — **to be on** (or **in**) **the uptake** *Informal* To demonstrate mental comprehension or perception.

up·throw (up′thrō′) *n.* **1.** A throwing upward; an upheaval. **2.** *Geol.* An upward displacement of the rock on one side of a fault.

up·thrust (up′thrust′) *n.* **1.** An upward thrust. **2.** *Geol.* An upheaval of rocks in the earth's crust.

up·tight (up′tīt′) *adj. U.S. Slang* Uneasy, anxious, or tense; nervous. Also **up′-tight′**, **up tight**.

up to See TO BE UP TO under UP.

up-to-date (up′tə-dāt′) *adj.* **1.** Having the latest information, improvements, etc.: an *up-to-date* dictionary. **2.** Modern in manner, fashion, or style.

up to date To the present time.

up·town (up′toun′) *adv.* To, toward, or in the geographically upper section of a town or city. — *adj.* Located in the geographically upper section of a town or city. — *n.* The geographically upper part of a town or city.

up·trend (up′trend′) *n.* A tendency to rise or become better: said especially of economic affairs.

up·turn (*v.* up·tûrn′; *n.* up′tûrn′) *v.t.* **1.** To turn up or over, as sod with the plow. **2.** To overturn; upset. — *n.* A turning upward; an increase; an improvement.

UPU United Postal Union.

up·ward (up′wərd) *adv.* **1.** In, to, or toward a higher place or position: to look *upward*. **2.** To or toward the source, origin, etc.: to trace a stream *upward*. **3.** Toward the head or upper parts: from the chest *upward*. **4.** Toward a higher rank, amount, age, etc. **5.** Toward that which is better, nobler, etc. **6.** In excess; more. Also **up′wards**. — **upward** (or **upwards**) **of** Higher than; in excess of. — *adj.* In, on, turned, or directed toward a higher place. [OE *ūpweard* < *up*- up + -*weard*. See -WARD.] — **up′ward·ly** *adv.*

ur-[1] Var. of URO-[1].

ur-[2] Var. of URO-[2].

Ur (ûr) An ancient city of Sumer, southern Mesopotamia, the site of which is on the Euphrates in SE Iraq. Old Testament **Ur of the Chal·dees** (kal·dēz′, kal′dēz).

Ur *Chem.* Uranium.

u·rae·mi·a (yŏŏ·rē′mē·ə), **u·rae·mic** (yŏŏ·rē′mik) See UREMIA, etc.

u·rae·us (yŏŏ·rē′əs) *n.* The emblem of the sacred serpent (haje) in the headdress of Egyptian divinities and kings: a symbol of sovereignty. [< NL < Gk. *ouraios* Egyptian name for the cobra; infl. by Gk. *oura* tail]

URAEUS

U·ral (yŏŏr′əl, *Russ.* ōō·räl′) A river in the southern R.S.-F.S.R. and western Kazakh S.S.R., flowing 1,574 miles west and south to the Caspian Sea; considered part of the traditional boundary between Europe and Asia.

U·ral-Al·ta·ic (yŏŏr′əl·al·tā′ik) *n.* A hypothesized family of languages comprising the Uralic and Altaic subfamilies. — *adj.* **1.** Of or pertaining to the Ural and Altai mountain ranges. **2.** Of, pertaining to, or designating the Ural-Altaic languages or any of the peoples natively speaking any of these languages. Also *Turanian*.

U·ral·ic (yŏŏ·ral′ik) *n.* A family of languages comprising the Finno-Ugric and Samoyedic subfamilies: by a few linguists classified with Altaic in a Ural-Altaic family — *adj.* Of or pertaining to this linguistic family. Also **U·ra·li·an** (yŏŏ·rā′lē·ən).

U·ral Mountains (yŏŏr′əl) A mountain system in the R.S.F.S.R., extending from the Arctic Ocean to the Kazakh S.S.R.; length about 1,300 mi.; highest peak, Naroda, 6,184 ft.: the traditional boundary between Europe and Asia.

u·ra·nal·y·sis (yŏŏr′ə·nal′ə·sis) See URINALYSIS.

U·ra·ni·a (yŏŏ·rā′nē·ə) **1.** The Muse of astronomy. **2.** The heavenly one: an epithet of Aphrodite. [< L < Gk. *Ourania* < *ouranios* heavenly < *ouranos* heaven]

U·ra·ni·an (yŏŏ·rā′nē·ən) *adj.* **1.** Of or pertaining to the planet Uranus. **2.** Celestial.

u·ran·ic (yŏŏ·ran′ik) *adj.* **1.** Relating to the heavens; astronomical. **2.** *Chem.* Of or derived from uranium, especially in its higher valence. [< Gk. *ouranos* heaven]

u·ran·i·nite (yŏŏ·ran′ə·nīt) *n.* A greenish black, opaque uranium mineral containing also lead, helium, and radium. See PITCHBLENDE. [< URANIUM]

u·ran·ism (yŏŏr′ən·iz′əm) *n.* Homosexuality. [< URANIA (def. 2)]

u·ra·nite (yŏŏr′ə·nīt) *n.* Any of several uranium minerals, especially torbernite and autunite. [< URANIUM] — **u′ra·nit′ic** (-nit′ik) *adj.*

u·ra·ni·um (yŏŏ·rā′nē·əm) *n.* A heavy, white, radioactive, metallic element (symbol U), found only in combination. It is a principal source of radium and one of its isotopes is important in the generation of atomic energy. See ELEMENT. Abbr. *Ur.* [< URANUS]

uranium series *Physics* A series of radioactive elements beginning with uranium of mass 238 and a half life of 4.5×10^{10} years and continuing through successive disintegrations to the stable isotope of lead of mass 206.

urano- *combining form Astron.* The heavens; of or pertaining to the heavens, or to celestial bodies: *uranography.* Also, before vowels, **uran-**. [< Gk. *ouranos* heaven]

u·ra·nog·ra·phy (yŏŏr′ə·nog′rə·fē) *n.* Scientific description of the celestial bodies; also, the making of celestial globes and maps. — **u′ra·nog′ra·pher** or ·**phist** *n.* — **u·ra·no·graph′ic** (-nō·graf′ik) or ·**i·cal** *adj.*

u·ra·nous (yŏŏr′ə·nəs) *adj. Chem.* Of or pertaining to uranium, especially in its lower valence.

U·ra·nus (yŏŏr′ə·nəs, yŏŏ·rā′nəs) In Greek mythology, the son and husband of Gaea (Earth) and father of the Titans, Furies, and Cyclopes, overthrown by his son Cronus. — *n.* The third largest planet of the solar system and seventh in order from the sun. See PLANET. [< L < Gk. *Ouranos* < *ouranos* heaven]

u·ra·nyl (yŏŏr′ə·nil) *n. Chem.* The bivalent radical UO_2, found in many uranium compounds. [< URAN(IUM) + -YL]

u·ra·re (yŏŏ·rä′rē) *n.* Curare. Also **u·ra′ri**. [Var. of CURARE]

u·rate (yŏŏr′āt) *n. Chem.* A salt of uric acid.

ur·ban (ûr′bən) *adj.* **1.** Pertaining to, characteristic of, including, or constituting a city. **2.** Situated or dwelling in a city. [< L *urbanus*. See URBANE.]

Urban II (ûr′bən) 1042?–99, pope 1088–99; furthered the first Crusade: original name *Udo of Lagery.*

Urban VIII, 1568–1644, pope 1623–44; founded the College of Propaganda: original name *Maffeo Barberini.*

Ur·ban·a (ûr·ban′ə) A city in eastern Illinois; pop. 32,800.

urban district An administrative subdivision of a county of England, Wales, or Northern Ireland, usually comprising several thickly populated communities.

ur·bane (ûr·bān′) *adj.* **1.** Characterized by or having refinement or elegance, especially in manner; polite; suave: opposed to *rustic.* **2.** *Obs.* Urban. [< L *urbanus* of a city < *urbs, urbis* city] — **ur·bane′ly** *adv.* — **ur·bane′ness** *n.*

ur·ban·ism (ûr′bən·iz′əm) *n.* The character or condition of the life of people living in urban areas.

ur·ban·i·ty (ûr·ban′ə·tē) *n. pl.* ·**ties 1.** The character or quality of being urbane; refined or elegant courtesy. **2.** *pl.* Amenities or courtesies. **3.** *Obs.* Polished humor or wit. [< F *urbanité* or L *urbanitas, -tatis* < *urbs, urbis* city]

ur·ban·ize (ûr′bən·īz) *v.t.* ·**ized**, ·**iz·ing 1.** To render urban, as in character or manner. **2.** *Rare* To render urbane. — **ur·ban·i·za′tion** *n.*

urban renewal The planned upgrading of a deteriorating urban area, usually using public funds and coordinated by a local government agency.

ur·bi et or·bi (ûr′bī et ôr′bī) *Latin* To the city (Rome) and to the world: used in official announcements, as papal bulls.

ur·ce·o·late (ûr′sē·ə·lit, -lāt) *adj. Bot.* Pitcher- or urnshaped, as a corolla. [< L *urceolus*, dim. of *urceus* pitcher]

ur·chin (ûr′chin) *n.* **1.** A roughish, mischievous boy. **2.** A cylinder in a carding machine. **3.** A sea urchin (which see).

4. *Archaic* A hedgehog. **5.** *Obs.* An elf, as often assuming the form of a hedgehog. — *adj. Obs.* Elfish. [ME *irchoun* < OF *irechon, ireçon* < L *ericius* hedgehog < *er* hedgehog]

Ur·du (o͞or'do͞o, o͝or·do͞o', ûr'do͞o) *n.* A variety of Hindustani spoken by Moslems in India, containing many Persian and Arabic elements and written in a Persian-Arabic script: the official language of Pakistan. [< Hind. *urdū*, short for (*zaban-i-*) *urdū* (language of the) camp < Turkish *ordū* camp < Persian *urdū*. Related to HORDE.]

-ure *suffix of nouns* **1.** The act, process, or result of: *pressure.* **2.** The function, rank, or office of: *prefecture.* **3.** The means or instrument of: *ligature.* [< F < L *-ura*]

u·re·a (yo͝o·rē'ə) *n. Biochem.* A colorless crystalline compound, CO(NH₂)₂, formed in the body, and also made synthetically, used in medicine and in the making of plastics and fertilizers. [< NL < F *urée* < Gk. *ouroa*] — **u·re'al** *adj.*

urea resin *Chem.* Any of a class of thermosetting resins obtained by the reaction of urea and formaldehyde in the presence of certain modifying agents. Also **urea-formaldehyde resin.**

u·re·ase (yo͝or'ē·ās, -āz) *n. Biochem.* An enzyme, formed by the action of various microorganisms, that promotes the hydrolysis of urea. [< UREA + -ASE]

u·re·din·i·um (yo͝or'ə·din'ē·əm) *n. Bot.* The spore fruit of a rust fungus that produces the uredospores. Also **u·re·di·um** (yo͝o·rē'dē·əm), **u're·do·so'rus** (-dō·sôr'əs, -sô'rəs). [< NL < L *uredo, -inis* blight. See UREDO.]

u·re·do (yo͝o·rē'dō) *n. Pathol.* Urticaria. [< L, blight]

u·re·do·spore (yo͝o·rē'də·spôr, -spōr) *n. Bot.* A unicellular thin-walled spore produced in summer as part of the life cycle of a rust fungus. Also **u·re·din·i·o·spore** (yo͝or'ə·din'ē·ə·spôr', -spōr').

uredo stage *Bot.* The stage in the life history of certain rust fungi during which uredospores are produced.

u·re·ide (yo͝or'ē·īd, -id) *n. Chem.* Any of several nitrogenous compounds derived from urea.

u·re·mi·a (yo͝o·rē'mē·ə) *n. Pathol.* An abnormal condition of the blood due to the presence of urinary constituents ordinarily excreted by the kidneys. Also *uraemia, urinemia.* [< NL < UR-¹ + -EMIA] — **u·re'mic** *adj.*

-uret *suffix Chem.* Used to denote a compound: now replaced by *-ide.* [< F < *-ure.* See -URE.]

u·re·ter (yo͝o·rē'tər) *n. Anat.* The duct by which urine passes from the kidney to the bladder or the cloaca. For illustration see KIDNEY. [< NL < Gk. *ourētēr* < *ourein* to urinate] — **u·re'ter·al, u·re·ter·ic** (yo͝or'ə·ter'ik) *adj.*

u·re·ter·ec·to·my (yo͝o·rē'tə·rek'tə·mē) *n. pl. ·mies Surg.* Excision of the ureter. [< URETER(O)- + -ECTOMY]

uretero- *combining form Med.* A ureter; of or related to a ureter. Also, before vowels, **ureter-.** [< Gk. *ourētēr* < *ourein* to urinate]

u·re·thane (yo͝or'ə·thān', yo͝o·reth'ān) *n. Chem.* **1.** A white crystalline compound, C₃H₇NO₂, an ethyl derivative of carbamic acid, used in medicine for certain neoplastic conditions. **2.** Any of several other esters of carbamic acid having the general formula NH₂COOR. Also **u·re·than** (yo͝or'ə·than', yo͝o·reth'ən). [< UR(EA) + ETHAN(E)]

u·re·thra (yo͝o·rē'thrə) *n. pl. ·thras or ·thrae* (-thrē) *Anat.* The duct by which urine is discharged from the bladder of most mammals, and which, in males, carries the seminal discharge. [< LL < Gk. *ourēthra* < *ouron* urine] — **u·re'thral** *adj.*

u·re·thri·tis (yo͝or'ə·thrī'tis) *n. Pathol.* Inflammation of the urethra. [< NL] — **u're·thrit'ic** (-thrit'ik) *adj.*

urethro- *combining form Med.* The urethra; of or pertaining to the urethra: *urethroscope.* Also, before vowels, **urethr-.** [< Gk. *ourēthra* the urethra]

u·re·thro·scope (yo͝o·rē'thrə·skōp) *n. Med.* An instrument for examining the urethra. — **u·re'thro·scop'ic** (-skop'ik) *adj.* — **u·re·thros·co·py** (yo͝or'ə·thros'kə·pē) *n.*

u·ret·ic (yo͝o·ret'ik) *adj. Med.* Of or pertaining to the urine; urinary. [< LL *ureticus* < Gk. *ourētikos* < *ouron* urine]

U·rey (yo͝or'ē), **Harold Clayton,** born 1893, U.S. chemist.

Ur·fa (o͝or·fä') A city in southern Turkey, near the Syrian border; pop. about 60,000: ancient *Edessa.*

Ur·ga (o͝or'gä) The former name for ULAN BATOR.

urge (ûrj) *v.* **urged, urg·ing** *v.t.* **1.** To drive or force forward; impel; push. **2.** To plead with or entreat earnestly, as with arguments or explanations: He *urged* them to accept the plan. **3.** To press or argue the doing, consideration, or acceptance of; advocate earnestly. **4.** To move or force to some course or action. **5.** To stimulate or excite; incite. **6.** To ply or use vigorously, as oars. — *v.i.* **7.** To present or press arguments, claims, etc. **8.** To exert an impelling or prompting force. — *Syn.* See ACTUATE. — *n.* **1.** A strong impulse to perform a certain act. **2.** The act of urging; the stage of being urged. [< L *urgere* to drive, urge]

ur·gen·cy (ûr'jən·sē) *n. pl. ·cies* **1.** The quality of being urgent. **2.** Pressure by entreaty; pressure of necessity. **3.** The act of urging. **4.** Something urgent.

ur·gent (ûr'jənt) *adj.* **1.** Characterized by urging or importunity; requiring prompt attention; pressing; imperative. **2.** Eagerly importunate or insistent. [< F < L *urgens, -entis,* ppr. of *urgere* to drive] — **ur'gent·ly** *adv.*

-urgy *combining form* Development of or work with a (specified) material or product: *metallurgy, chemurgy.* [< Gk. *-ourgia* < *ergon* work]

U·ri (o͝or'ē) A canton in central Switzerland; 415 sq. mi.; pop. 32,021 (1960); capital, Altdorf.

-uria *combining form Pathol.* A (specified) condition of the urine: usually used to indicate disease or abnormality: *dysuria.* [< NL < Gk. *-ouria* < *ouron* urine]

U·ri·ah (yo͝o·rī'ə) A Hittite captain in the Israelite army, husband of Bathsheba, treacherously sent to his death by David, II *Sam.* xi 15–17.

Uriah Heep 1. In Dickens's *David Copperfield,* an unctuous, fawning, scheming clerk. **2.** An odious hypocrite.

u·ric (yo͝or'ik) *adj.* Of, pertaining to, or derived from urine. [< F *urique*]

uric acid *Biochem.* A colorless dibasic acid, C₅H₄N₄O₃, of varying crystalline forms and slight solubility, found in the urine of man and animals and, in man, forming the nucleus of most urinary and renal calculi.

urico- *combining form* Uric acid; of or related to uric acid. Also, before vowels, **uric-.** [< URIC]

U·ri·el (yo͝or'ē·əl) One of the archangels. In Milton's *Paradise Lost,* he is represented as "regent of the sun."

U·rim and Thum·mim (yo͝or'im; thum'im) Objects mentioned in the Old Testament (*Ex.* xxviii 30, etc.) in connection with the breastplate of the high priest, supposed to have been precious stones used in determining divine will. [< Hebrew *ūrīm* fires < *ūr* to shine]

u·ri·nal (yo͝or'ə·nəl) *n.* **1.** An upright wall fixture with facilities for flushing, for men's use in urination; also the room containing such a fixture. **2.** A glass receptacle for urine. [< OF < Med.L *urinale,* orig. neut. of L *urinalis* pertaining to urine < *urina* urine]

u·ri·nal·y·sis (yo͝or'ə·nal'ə·sis) *n. pl. ·ses* (-sēz) Chemical analysis of the urine: also spelled *uranalysis.* [< NL < URIN(O)- + (AN)ALYSIS]

u·ri·nar·y (yo͝or'ə·ner'ē) *adj.* Of, pertaining to, or involved in the production and excretion of urine: the *urinary* organs. — *n. pl. ·nar·ies* **1.** A reservoir for storing urine, etc., for use as manure. **2.** A urinal.

urinary calculus *Pathol.* A concretion formed in the urinary passages; the stone: also called *urolith.*

u·ri·nate (yo͝or'ə·nāt) *v.i.* **·nat·ed, ·nat·ing** To void or pass urine. [< Med.L *urinatus,* pp. of *urinare* to pass urine < *urina* urine] — **u'ri·na'tion** *n.*

u·rine (yo͝or'in) *n.* A liquid containing body wastes, secreted by the kidneys, stored in the bladder, and voided through the urethra. [< F < L *urina.* Akin to Gk. *ouron.*]

u·ri·ne·mi·a (yo͝or'ə·nē'mē·ə) *n. Pathol.* Uremia (which see). Also **u/ri·nae'mi·a.** [< URIN(O)- + -EMIA] — **u'ri·ne'mic** or **·nae'mic** *adj.*

u·ri·nif·er·ous (yo͝or'ə·nif'ər·əs) *adj.* Conducting urine.

urino- *combining form* Urine. Also, before vowels, **urin-,** as in *urinalysis.* [< L *urina* urine]

u·ri·no·gen·i·tal (yo͝or'ə·nō·jen'ə·təl) *adj.* Urogenital (which see).

u·ri·nos·co·py (yo͝or'ə·nos'kə·pē) *n. pl. ·pies Med.* Uroscopy (which see).

u·ri·nous (yo͝or'ə·nəs) *adj.* Of, pertaining to, containing, or resembling urine. Also **u/ri·nose** (-nōs).

Ur·mi·a (o͝or'mē·ə), **Lake** A lake in NW Iran, between Tabriz and the Turkish border; 90 mi. long, 30 mi. wide. *Persian* **U·ru·mi·yeh** (o͞o·ro͞o·mē·ye').

urn (ûrn) *n.* **1.** A rounded or angular vase having a foot, variously used in antiquity as a receptacle for the ashes of the dead, a water vessel, etc. **2.** A vessel for preserving ashes of the dead. **3.** In ancient Rome, a receptacle used to hold lots drawn in voting. **4.** A vase-shaped receptacle having a faucet, and designed for keeping tea, coffee, etc., hot, as by means of a spirit lamp. [< L *urna*]

uro-¹ *combining form* Urine; pertaining to urine or to the urinary tract: *urology.* Also, before vowels, **ur-.** [< Gk. *ouron* urine]

uro-² *combining form* A tail; of or related to the tail; caudal: *uropod.* Also, before vowels, **ur-.** [< Gk. *oura* tail]

u·ro·chord (yo͝or'ə·kôrd) *n. Zool.* The notochord or central axis of larval ascidians and certain adult tunicates. [< URO-² + CHORD²] — **u'ro·chor'dal** *adj.*

u·ro·chrome (yo͝or'ə·krōm) *n. Biochem.* The yellow pigment that gives to urine its characteristic color.

u·ro·dele (yo͝or'ə·dēl) *adj.* Of or belonging to an order (*Urodela*) of amphibians retaining the tail through adulthood, as the newts and salamanders. — *n.* A urodele amphibian. [< NL < Gk. *oura* tail + *dēlos* visible]

u·ro·gen·i·tal (yo͝or'ō·jen'ə·təl) *adj.* Of or pertaining to the urinary and genital organs and their functions: also *urinogenital.*

u·rog·e·nous (yo͝o·roj'ə·nəs) *adj.* Producing or promotive of the urinary secretion. [< URO-¹ + -GENOUS]

u·ro·lith (yo͝or'ə·lith) *n. Pathol.* A urinary calculus. [< URO-¹ + -LITH¹] — **u'ro·lith'ic** *adj.*

u·rol·o·gy (yo͝o·rol'ə·jē) *n.* The branch of medicine that deals with the urine and the genitourinary tract. — **u·ro·log·ic** (yo͝or'ə·loj'ik) or **·i·cal** *adj.* — **u·rol'o·gist** *n.*

u·ro·pod (yŏŏr′ə·pod) *n. Zool.* An abdominal appendage of an arthropod, especially one of the posterior pairs of swimming legs in a crustacean. [< URO-² + -POD] — **u·rop·o·dal** (yŏŏ·rop′ə·dəl), **u·rop′o·dous** *adj.*

u·ro·pyg·i·al (yŏŏr′ə·pij′ē·əl) *adj.* Of or pertaining to the uropygium.

uropygial gland *Ornithol.* The gland at the base of a bird's tail, secreting an oily substance used to preen the feathers: also called *oil gland.*

u·ro·pyg·i·um (yŏŏr′ə·pij′ē·əm) *n. Ornithol.* The terminal part of the body supporting the tail feathers of a bird; rump. [< NL < Gk. *ouropygion*, alter. (after *oura* tail) of *orrhopygion < orrhos* end of the sacrum + *pygē* rump]

u·ros·co·py (yŏŏ·ros′kə·pē) *n. pl.* **·pies** *Med.* Diagnosis by examination of the urine: also *urinoscopy.* [< URO-¹ + -SCOPY] — **u·ro·scop·ic** (yŏŏr′ə·skop′ik) *adj.* — **u·ros′co·pist** *n.*

u·ro·xan·thin (yŏŏr′ə·zan′thin) *n.* Indican (def. 2). [< URO-¹ + XANTHIN]

Ur·qu·hart (ûr′kərt), **Sir Thomas,** 1611–60, Scottish author.

ur·sa (ûr′sə) *n. Latin* A she-bear: used in the phrases *Ursa Major* and *Ursa Minor.*

Ursa Major A constellation, the Greater Bear, whose most prominent feature is a group of seven bright stars popularly called *the Big Dipper,* including Dubhe and Merak, the Pointers: also popularly called *Charles's Wain,* the *Plow, Septentrio,* the *Wagoner.* See CONSTELLATION. [< L]

Ursa Minor A constellation, the Lesser Bear, containing the polestar Polaris: also popularly called *Cynosure, Little Bear, Little Dipper.* See CONSTELLATION. [< L]

URSA MAJOR (*a*) AND URSA MINOR (*b*)
c Polestar.
d, d Pointers.

ur·si·form (ûr′sə·fôrm) *adj.* Having the form of a bear. [< L *ursus* bear + -FORM]

ur·sine (ûr′sīn, -sin) *adj.* 1. Pertaining to or like a bear. 2. Clothed with dense bristles, as certain caterpillars. [< L *ursinus < ursus* bear]

ursine howler See under HOWLER (def. 2).

Ur·spra·che (ŏŏr′shprä′khə) *n. German* A primitive, original, or parent language; especially, a hypothetical primitive Indo-European language.

Ur·su·la (ûr′syə·lə, -sə-), **Saint** A Cornish princess of the fourth or fifth century, martyred, according to legend, with eleven thousand virgins at Cologne by the Huns.

Ur·su·line (ûr′syə·līn, -sə-, -lin) *adj.* Pertaining to Saint Ursula or to an order of nuns founded in 1537, and engaged chiefly in the education of girls. — *n.* An Ursuline nun.

Ur·text (ŏŏr′tekst) *n. German* The earliest or primary form of a written text.

ur·ti·ca·ceous (ûr′tə·kā′shəs) *adj. Bot.* Belonging to a widely distributed family (*Urticaceae*) of trees, shrubs, or herbs, the nettle family. [< NL < L *urtica* nettle]

ur·ti·car·i·a (ûr′tə·kâr′ē·ə) *n. Pathol.* A disease of the skin, characterized by transient eruptions resembling wheals and attended with itching. Also called *hives, nettle rash, uredo.* [< NL < L *urtica* nettle] — **ur′ti·car′i·al** or **·i·ous** *adj.*

ur·ti·cate (ûr′tə·kāt) *v.t. & v.i.* **·cat·ed, ·cat·ing** To sting or whip, as with nettles. [< Med.L *urticatus,* pp. of *urticare* to sting < *urtica* nettle]

ur·ti·ca·tion (ûr′tə·kā′shən) *n. Med.* 1. The act, process, or effect of whipping with nettles as a stimulant, as in paralysis. 2. A tingling or burning sensation. 3. The development of urticaria.

U·ru·guay (yŏŏr′ə·gwā, *Sp.* ōō′rŏŏ·gwī) 1. A Republic of SE South America, on the Atlantic; 72,172 sq. mi.; pop. about 2.9 million; capital, Montevideo. *Abbr.* Uru. 2. A river in SE South America, flowing 1,000 miles SW to the Río de la Plata. — **U′ru·guay′an** *adj. & n.*

U·rum·chi (ōō′rŏŏm′chē′) The capital of the Sinkiang-Uigur Autonomous Region, NW China; pop. 500,000 (est. 1970). Also **U′rum′tsi′.**

U·run·di (ōō·rŏŏn′dē) See BURUNDI.

u·rus (yŏŏr′əs) *n.* An extinct, long-horned, wild ox (*Bos primigenius*) of Germany: so named by Julius Caesar: also called *aurochs.* [< L < Gmc. Cf. OHG *ur.*]

u·ru·shi·ol (ŏŏr′ŏŏ·shē·ôl′, -ol′) *n.* A poisonous, irritant liquid, the active principle of poison ivy and the Japanese lacquer tree. [< Japanese *urushi* lacquer + -OL²]

us (us) *pron.* The objective case of the pronoun *we.*

u.s. 1. Ubi supra. 2. Ut supra.

U.S. or **US** 1. United States. 2. American.

USA United States Army.

U.S.A. or **USA** 1. Union of South Africa. 2. United States of America.

us·a·ble (yŏŏ′zə·bəl) *adj.* 1. Capable of being used. 2. That can be used conveniently. Also **use′a·ble.** — **us′a·ble·ness** *n.* — **us′a·bly** *adv.*

USAF United States Air Force.

USAFI United States Armed Forces Institute.

us·age (yŏŏ′sij, -zij) *n.* 1. The manner of using or treating a person or thing; treatment; also, the act of using. 2. Customary or habitual practice, or something permitted by it or used in accordance with it: an act permitted by *usage;* ancient *usages.* 3. Uniform practice. 4. The customary way of using words, sounds, and grammatical forms in a language: standard *usage.* 5. A particular verbal or written expression or application of such an expression: a contemptuous *usage.* 6. *Obs.* Conduct; behavior. — **Syn.** See HABIT. [< OF < Med.L *usaticum < L usus.* See USE.]

us·ance (yŏŏ′zəns) *n.* 1. A period of time, variable as between various countries, that, by commercial usage, is allowed, exclusive of days of grace, for payment of bills of exchange, especially foreign. 2. *Econ.* An income derived from the possession of wealth, as by investment. 3. *Obs.* Employment; use. 4. *Obs.* Interest on money. 5. *Obs.* Custom. Also *Obs.* **us′aunce.** [< OF < L *usus.* See USE.]

USAR United States Army Reserve.

U.S.C. & G.S. United States Coast and Geodetic Survey.

USCG or **U.S.C.G.** United States Coast Guard.

use (*v.* yŏŏz; *n.* yŏŏs) *v.* **used** (yŏŏzd *for defs.* 5, 7, & 8), **us·ing** *v.t.* 1. To employ for the accomplishment of a purpose; make use of. 2. To put into practice or employ habitually; make a practice of: to *use* diligence in business. 3. To expend the whole of; consume: often with *up.* 4. To conduct oneself toward; treat: to *use* one badly. 5. To make familiar by habit or practice; accustom; inure: now only in the past participle: He is *used* to the weather. 6. To partake of; smoke or drink: He does not *use* tobacco. — *v.i.* 7. To do formerly or customarily: now used only in the past tense to indicate a fact or condition that no longer obtains: He *used* to smoke; We *used* to go to the seashore every summer; where the church *used* to be. — *n.* 1. The act of using: to make good *use* of one's strength. 2. The condition of being used: Is that car still in *use*? 3. The right to use something: the *use* of a gun. 4. The ability to use something: to lose the *use* of one's leg. 5. The way or manner of using something: the correct *use* of a machine. 6. Advantage, profit, or usefulness of something: the *uses* of adversity. 7. Occasion or need to employ; purpose. 8. Habitual practice, employment, or custom. 9. Any special form, ceremony, or ritual that arose in or was perpetuated by a church, diocese, or branch of a church: Roman *use.* 10. *Law* The permanent equitable right that a beneficiary has to the enjoyment of the rents and profits of lands and tenements of which the legal title and possession are vested in another in trust for the beneficiary. — **to have no use for** 1. To have no need of. 2. *Informal* To have a contempt or dislike for; want nothing to do with. [< OF *user* < L *usus,* pp. of *uti* to use]

used (yŏŏzd, *for def. 3* yŏŏst) *adj.* 1. Employed for a certain purpose or function. 2. Having had use; not new. 3. Accustomed: He is *used* to hard work.

use·ful (yŏŏs′fəl) *adj.* Serviceable; serving a use or purpose, especially a valuable one; productive of good; beneficial. — **use′ful·ly** *adv.* — **use′ful·ness** *n.*

use·less (yŏŏs′lis) *adj.* 1. Unserviceable; being of no use; not capable of serving any beneficial purpose. 2. Futile; in vain: His efforts to be heard were *useless.* — **use′less·ly** *adv.* — **use′less·ness** *n.*

us·er (yŏŏ′zər) *n.* One who or that which uses.

USES or **U.S.E.S.** United States Employment Service.

use tax A State tax on personal property or goods that have been bought outside of the State and then brought in.

Ush·ant (ush′ənt) An island off NW France, the westernmost point of France: French *Ouessant.*

U·shas (ōō′shəs, ōō·shäs′) In Hindu mythology, the goddess of the dawn.

ush·er (ush′ər) *n.* 1. One who acts as doorkeeper, as of a court or other assembly room. 2. An officer whose duty it is to introduce strangers or walk before a person of rank. 3. One who conducts persons to seats, etc., as in a church or theater. 4. *Brit.* An assistant or subordinate teacher in a school; underteacher. — *v.t.* 1. To act as usher to; escort; conduct. 2. To precede as a harbinger; be a forerunner of: usually with *in.* — *v.i.* 3. To act as an usher. [< OF *uissier* < L *ostiarius* doorkeeper]

ush·er·ette (ush′ə·ret′) *n.* A female usher, as in a theater.

USIA or **U.S.I.A.** United States Information Agency.

Usk (usk) A river in SW England and SE Wales.

Us·ku·da·ma (ōŏs′kŏŏ·dä′mə) An ancient name for ADRIANOPLE.

Us·kü·dar (üs′kü·där′) A city in NE Turkey, on the Bosporus; pop. about 61,000: also *Scutari.*

U.S.M. 1. United States Mail. 2. United States Mint.

USMA or **U.S.M.A.** United States Military Academy.

USMC or **U.S.M.C.** United States Marine Corps.

USMCR United States Marine Corps Reserve.

USMS United States Maritime Service.

USN or **U.S.N.** United States Navy.

USNA or **U.S.N.A.** United States Naval Academy.

us·nic acid (us'nik) A yellow, crystalline substance, $C_{18}H_{16}O_7$, derived from lichens, used as an antibiotic.

USNR or **U.S.N.R.** United States Naval Reserve.

USO or **U.S.O.** United Service Organizations.

USP or **U.S.P.** United States Pharmacopoeia: also **U.S. Pharm.**

USPHS or **U.S.P.H.S.** United States Public Health Service.

us·que ad a·ras (us'kwē ad ā'ras) *Latin* Even to the altars; up to the point at which one's religion forbids.

us·que·baugh (us'kwə·bô) *n. Irish & Scot.* A distilled spirit, as whisky. Also **us'qua·bae** (-bā), **us'que**, **us'que·bae**. [< Irish and Scottish Gaelic *uisge-beatha* < *uisge* water + *beatha* life]

USS or **U.S.S.** **1.** United States Senate. **2.** United States Ship (or Steamer or Steamship).

USSB United States Shipping Board.

Ussh·er (ush'ər), **James**, 1581–1656, Irish prelate, theologian, and scholar.

U.S.S.R. or **USSR** Union of Soviet Socialist Republics.

Us·su·ri (ōō·sōō'rē; *Russ.* ōō·sōō'ryi) A river forming part of the boundary between extreme NE China and the extreme SE Soviet Union, and flowing 365 miles north to the Amur.

Us·ti·nad La·bem (ōō'styĕ näd lä'bem) A city in NW Bohemia, Czechoslovakia, on the Elbe; pop. 72,000 (est. 1966).

us·tu·late (us'chŏō·lit, -lāt) *adj.* Scorched, burned, or colored as if by burning or scorching. [< L *ustulatus*, pp. of *ustulare* to scorch, freq. of *urere* to burn]

us·tu·la·tion (us'chŏō·lā'shən) *n.* **1.** The act of burning or searing. **2.** In pharmacy, the drying of substances by heat preparatory to pulverization. **3.** The burning of wine.

usu. Usual(ly).

u·su·al (yōō'zhōō·əl) *adj.* Such as occurs in the ordinary course of events; frequent; common. [< OF < LL *usualis* < L *usus* use. See USE.] — **u'su·al·ly** *adv.* — **u'su·al·ness** *n.*

u·su·fruct (yōō'zyōō·frukt, yōō'syōō-) *n. Law* The right of using the property of another and of drawing the profits it produces without wasting its substance. [< LL *usufructus* < L *ususfructus* < *usus et fructus* use and fruit]

u·su·fruc·tu·ar·y (yōō'zyōō·fruk'chōō·er'ē, yōō'syōō-) *n. pl.* **·ar·ies** One who holds property for use by usufruct, as a tenant. — *adj.* Of, pertaining to, or having the nature of a usufruct. [< LL *usufructuarius* < *usufructus*. See USUFRUCT.]

u·su·rer (yōō'zhər·ər) *n.* **1.** One who practices usury; one who lends money, especially at an exorbitant or illegal rate. **2.** *Obs.* A moneylender. [< OF *usurier* < Med.L *usurarius* < L *usura* use, usury. See USURY.]

u·su·ri·ous (yōō·zhōōr'ē·əs) *adj.* Practicing usury; having the nature of usury. — **u·su'ri·ous·ly** *adv.* — **u·su'ri·ous·ness** *n.*

u·surp (yōō·zûrp', -sûrp') *v.t.* **1.** To seize and hold (the office, rights, or powers of another) without right or legal authority; take possession of by force. **2.** To take arrogantly, as if by right. — *v.i.* **3.** To practice usurpation; encroach: with *on* or *upon*. [< OF *usurper* < L *usurpare* to make use of, usurp, ? < *usus* use + *rapere* to seize] — **u·surp'er** *n.* — **u·surp'ing·ly** *adv.*

u·sur·pa·tion (yōō'zər·pā'shən, -sər-) *n.* **1.** The act of usurping: said especially of unlawful or forcible seizure of kingly power. **2.** *Law* The wrongful intrusion into or unjust exercise of the privileges of any office, franchise, or the like.

u·su·ry (yōō'zhər·ē) *n. pl.* **·ries** **1.** The act or practice of exacting a rate of interest beyond what is allowed by law. **2.** *Obs.* The lending of money at interest. **3.** A premium paid for the use of money beyond the rate of interest established by law. [< OF *usure* < L *usura* < *usus*. See USE.]

usw or **u.s.w.** And so forth (G *und so weiter*).

ut (ōōt) *n. Music* The first syllable in the Guido solmization system: now commonly *do*. [See GAMUT.]

u.t. Universal time.

Ut. Utah (unofficial).

U·tah (yōō'tô, -tä) A State of the western United States; 84,916 sq. mi.; pop. 1,059.273; capital, Salt Lake City; entered the Union Jan. 4, 1896; nickname, *Beehive State.* — **U'tah·an** *adj. & n.*

ut dict. As said or directed (L *ut dictum*).

Ute (yōōt, yōō'tē) *n.* One of a group of tribes of North American Indians of Shoshonean stock formerly living in Utah, Colorado, and New Mexico, now on reservations in Colorado and Utah.

u·ten·sil (yōō·ten'səl) *n.* A vessel, tool, implement, etc., serving a useful purpose, especially for domestic or farming use. — **Syn.** See TOOL. [< OF *utensile* < L *utensilis* fit for use < *utens*, ppr. of *uti* to use]

u·ter·al·gi·a (yōō'tə·ral'jē·ə) *n. Med.* Pain in the uterus. [< UTERO- + -ALGIA]

u·ter·ine (yōō'tər·in, -īn) *adj.* **1.** Pertaining to the uterus. **2.** Born of the same mother, but having a different father. [< LL *uterinus* born of the same mother]

utero- *combining form* The uterus; of or pertaining to the uterus. Also, before vowels, **uter-**. [< L *uterus* uterus]

u·ter·us (yōō'tər·əs) *n. pl.* **u·ter·i** (yōō'tər·ī) **1.** *Anat.* The organ of a female mammal in which the young are protected and developed before birth; the womb. **2.** *Zool.* Any differentiated portion of an oviduct found in various animals, other than mammals, serving as a repository for the development and nourishment of the eggs or the young during the embryonic stage. [< L]

Ut·gard (ōōt'gärd) In Norse mythology, the abode of Utgard-Loki.

Ut·gard-Lo·ki (ōōt'gärd·lō'kē) In Norse mythology, an invulnerable giant.

U Thant (ōō thont), born 1909, Burmese statesman; UN Secretary General 1962–71; full name *Thant*: full title **Ma·ha Thray Si·thu U** (mä'hä thrā sē'thōō).

U·ther (yōō'thər) A legendary king of Britain; father of Arthur.

U·ti·ca (yōō'tə·kə) **1.** An ancient city, NW of Carthage in northern Africa. **2.** A city in central New York, on the Mohawk River; pop. 91,611.

u·tile (yōō'til) *adj. Rare* Useful. [< OF < L *utilis* < *uti* to use]

u·til·i·dor (yōō·til'i·dôr) *n. Canadian* A system of pipes, cables, etc., raised and insulated to provide utilities to communities on the permafrost.

u·til·i·tar·i·an (yōō·til'ə·târ'ē·ən) *adj.* **1.** Relating to utility; especially, placing utility above beauty or the amenities of life. **2.** Pertaining to or advocating utilitarianism. — *n.* **1.** An advocate of utilitarianism. **2.** One devoted to mere material utility.

u·til·i·tar·i·an·ism (yōō·til'ə·târ'ē·ən·iz'əm) *n.* **1.** *Philos.* **a** A system that holds usefulness to be the end and criterion of action; especially, the doctrine that actions derive their moral quality from their usefulness as means to some end, as happiness. **b** The ethical theory, held by Jeremy Bentham, James Mill, and John Stuart Mill, that the greatest human happiness determines the highest moral good. **2.** A similar doctrine applied to social and political action. **3.** Devotion to mere material interests and aims.

u·til·i·ty (yōō·til'ə·tē) *n. pl.* **·ties** **1.** Fitness for some desirable, practical purpose; also, that which is necessary. **2.** Fitness to supply the natural needs of man. **3.** A public service, as gas, water, etc. **4.** *pl.* Shares of utility company stocks. **5.** *Philos.* In utilitarianism, the greatest happiness for the greatest number of people. **6.** *Obs.* Use; profit. [< F *utilité* < L *utilitas* < *utilis* useful < *uti* to use]

utility man **1.** A regular member of a theatrical company who must be prepared, on short notice, to go on in any of the less important parts. **2.** In baseball, a substitute player who plays several positions.

utility pole One of a series of poles used to support and link telephone wires, electric cables, etc.: also called *telegraph pole, telephone pole.*

utility room A room, especially in a house, reserved for heating or laundry appliances, for storage, etc.

u·til·ize (yōō'təl·īz) *v.t.* **·ized**, **·iz·ing** To make useful; turn to practical account; make use of. Also *Brit.* **u'til·ise.** — **u'til·iz'a·ble** *adj.* — **u'til·i·za'tion** *n.* — **u'til·iz'er** *n.*

ut in·fra (ut in'frə) *Latin* As below.

u·ti pos·si·de·tis (yōō'tī pos'ə·dē'təs) *Latin* In international law, the principle that the parties to a war retain what they possessed at its close, unless otherwise provided by treaty; literally, as you possess.

ut·most (ut'mōst) *adj.* **1.** Of the highest degree or the largest amount or number; greatest. **2.** Being at the farthest limit or point. — *n.* The greatest possible extent; the most possible. Also *uttermost.* [OE *ūtmest, ȳtemest*]

U·to-Az·tec·an (yōō'tō·az'tek·ən) *n.* **1.** One of the chief stocks of North and Central American Indians, formerly occupying two large regions of the NW and SW United States, comprising three branches (Shoshonean, Piman, and Nahuatlan) and embracing about fifty tribes, still surviving in the United States and Mexico. **2.** The family of languages spoken by these people. — *adj.* Of or pertaining to the Uto-Aztecans or their languages.

u·to·pi·a (yōō·tō'pē·ə) *n.* **1.** Any state, condition, or place of ideal perfection. **2.** A visionary, impractical scheme for social improvement. [after *Utopia*]

U·to·pi·a (yōō·tō'pē·ə) An imaginary island described as the seat of a perfect social and political life in a romance by Sir Thomas More, published in 1516. [< NL < Gk. *ou* not + *topos* place]

u·to·pi·an (yōō·tō'pē·ən) *adj.* Excellent, but existing only in fancy or theory; ideal. — *n.* One who advocates impractical reforms; a visionary.

U·to·pi·an (yōō·tō'pē·ən) *adj.* Pertaining to or like Utopia. — *n.* A dweller in Utopia.

u·to·pi·an·ism (yōō·tō'pē·ən·iz'əm) *n.* Highly idealistic and impractical views, especially about social problems.

U·trecht (yōō'trekt, *Du.* ü'trekht) A Province of the central Netherlands; 511 sq. mi.; pop. 801,285 (est. 1970); capital, **Utrecht**, scene of the signing of a treaty (1713) ending the War of the Spanish Succession; pop. 278,966 (est. 1970).

u·tri·cle (yōō'tri·kəl) *n.* **1.** *Anat.* The larger of two saclike cavities found in the bony vestibule of the inner ear. **2.** *Bot.* **a** A small fruit having an inflated pericarp, as in the pigweed. **b** An air cell, as in certain aquatic plants. [< L *utri-culus*, dim. of *uter* skin bag]

u·tric·u·lar (yo͞o·trik′yə·lər) *adj.* **1.** Resembling a utricle or small sac. **2.** Bladderlike; bearing or provided with utricles. Also **u·tric′u·late** (-lit, -lāt).

u·tric·u·li·tis (yo͞o·trik′yə·lī′tis) *n. Pathol.* Inflammation of a utricle, as of the inner ear. [< NL]

u·tric·u·lus (yo͞o·trik′yə·ləs) *n. pl.* **·li** (-lī) Utricle. [< L]

U·tril·lo (o͞o·trē′lyo͞o, o͞o·tril′ō; *Fr.* ü·trē·lō′), **Maurice**, 1883–1955, French painter.

ut su·pra (ut so͞o′prə) *Latin* As above. Abbr. *u.s., ut sup.*

Ut·tar Pra·desh (o͞ot′ər prə·dāsh′) A State of northern India; 113,409 sq. mi.; pop. 88,299,453 (1968); capital, Lucknow; formerly *United Provinces of Agra and Oudh.*

ut·ter[1] (ut′ər) *v.t.* **1.** To give out or send forth with audible sound; express; say. **2.** *Law* To put in circulation; now, especially, to deliver or offer (something forged or counterfeit) to another. **3.** *Obs.* To give vent to in any way; give forth; emit. **4.** *Obs.* To issue or deliver, as merchandise, in the course of trade. [ME *outre*, freq. of obs. *out* to say, speak out < OE *ūt*] **—ut′ter·a·ble** *adj.* **—ut′ter·er** *n.*

ut·ter[2] (ut′ər) *adj.* **1.** Realized or developed to the last degree; absolute; total: *utter misery.* **2.** Being or done without conditions or qualifications; final; absolute: *utter denial.* **3.** *Obs.* Outer; remote. [OE *ūtera*, orig. compar. of *ūt* out]

ut·ter·ance[1] (ut′ər·əns) *n.* **1.** The act of uttering; vocal expression; manner of speaking; also, the power of speech. **2.** A thing uttered or expressed. **3.** *Ling.* Any stretch of speech capable of being isolated from the flow of connected discourse, as a word, phrase, or sentence.

ut·ter·ance[2] (ut′ər·əns) *n. Obs.* The bitter end; the uttermost; the last extremity; death: in the phrase **to the utterance.** [Var. of OUTRANCE]

ut·ter·ly (ut′ər·lē) *adv.* Thoroughly; entirely.

ut·ter·most (ut′ər·mōst′) *adj. & n.* Utmost.

U-turn (yo͞o′tûrn′) *n. Informal* A continuous turn that reverses the direction of a vehicle on a road.

u·var·o·vite (o͞o·vär′ōf·īt) *n.* An emerald-green garnet containing chromium. [after Count S. *Uvarov*, 1785–1855, Russian nobleman]

u·ve·a (yo͞o′vē·ə) *n. Anat.* The inner, colored layer of the iris, together with the iris itself, the ciliary muscle, and choroid coat. [< Med.L < L *uva* grape] **—u′ve·al** *adj.*

Uve·dale (yo͞ov′dāl), **Nicholas** See UDALL.

u·ve·i·tis (yo͞o·vē·ī′tis) *n. Pathol.* Inflammation of the uvea or iris. [< NL < UVEA] **—u′ve·it′ic** (-it′ik) *adj.*

u·ve·ous (yo͞o′vē·əs) *adj.* **1.** Resembling a grape or a cluster of grapes. **2.** Uveal. [< L *uva* grape]

u·vu·la (yo͞o′vyə·lə) *n. pl.* **·las** or **·lae** (-lē) *Anat.* **1.** The pendent fleshy portion of the soft palate. For illustrations see MOUTH, THROAT. **2.** Any of several other similar processes, especially at the neck of the bladder and on the under side of the cerebellum. [< LL, dim. of *uva* grape]

u·vu·lar (yo͞o′vyə·lər) *adj.* **1.** Pertaining to or of the uvula. **2.** *Phonet.* Produced by vibration of, or with the back of the tongue near or against, the uvula. **—** *n. Phonet.* A uvular sound.

u·vu·li·tis (yo͞o′vyə·lī′tis) *n. Pathol.* Inflammation of the uvula. [< NL]

u·vu·lot·o·my (yo͞o′vyə·lot′ə·mē) *n. pl.* **·mies** *Surg.* The removal of part or all of the uvula. [< UVULA + -TOMY]

ux. Wife (L *uxor*).

Ux·bridge (uks′brij) An urban district of Middlesex, England, near London; pop. 63,762 (1961).

Ux·mal (o͞oz·mäl′, o͞osh-, o͞os-) An ancient Mayan city of Yucatán, Mexico.

ux·o·ri·al (uk·sôr′ē·əl, -sō′rē-, ug·zôr′ē·əl, -zō′rē-) *adj.* **1.** Of, pertaining to, characteristic of, or becoming to a wife. **2.** Uxorious. [< L *uxorius* < *uxor* wife]

ux·o·ri·cide (uk·sôr′ə·sīd, -sō′rə-, ug·zôr′ə-, -zō′rə-) *n.* **1.** The killing of one's wife. **2.** One who has killed his wife. [< L *uxor* wife + -CIDE] **—ux·o′ri·ci′dal** (-sīd′l) *adj.*

ux·o·ri·ous (uk·sôr′ē·əs, -sō′rē-, ug·zôr′ē-, -zō′rē-) *adj.* Fatuously or foolishly devoted to one's wife; showing extreme or foolish fondness for one's wife. [< L *uxorius* < *uxor* wife] **—ux·o′ri·ous·ly** *adv.* **—ux·o′ri·ous·ness** *n.*

Uz·bek (o͞oz′bek, uz′-) *n.* **1.** A member of a Turkic people dominant in Turkestan; a native or inhabitant of the Uzbek S.S.R. **2.** The Turkic language of the Uzbeks. Also **Uz′beg.**

Uz·bek S.S.R. (o͞oz′bek, uz′-) A constituent Republic of the southern Soviet Union; 173,591 sq. mi.; pop. 11,963,000 (1970); capital, Tashkent. Also **Uz·bek·i·stan** (o͞oz′bek·i·stän′, uz′-, -stän′; *Russ.* o͞oz·byi·kyi·stän′). *Russ.* **Uz·bek·ska·ya S.S.R.** (o͞oz·byek′skə·yə).

V

v, V (vē) *n. pl.* **v's** or **vs, V's** or **Vs, vees** (vēz) **1.** The twenty-second letter of the English alphabet, the shape of which was derived from the Phoenician *vau* (*waw*), later adopted by the Greeks as *upsilon*. It was used by the Romans in the form V with the value of a semivowel (w) and, later, a consonant (v). In English it was used interchangeably with the character *u* until fairly modern times. Also *vee*. Compare U, W. **2.** The sound represented by the letter *v*, the voiced, labiodental fricative. **3.** Anything shaped like a V. **—** *symbol* **1.** *Informal* A five-dollar bill. **2.** The Roman numeral five. **3.** *Chem.* Vanadium (symbol V).

v Volt.

v. 1. Valve. **2.** Ventral. **3.** *Gram.* **a** Verb. **b** Vocative. **4.** Verse. **5.** Version. **6.** Versus. **7.** Vice-. **8.** Vide. **9.** Village. **10.** Voice. **11.** Volt; voltage. **12.** Volume. **13.** Von.

V 1. *Math.* Vector. **2.** Velocity. **3.** *Electr.* Volt. **4.** Volume.

V. 1. Venerable. **2.** Viscount.

V-1 (vē′wun′) See under ROBOT BOMB.

V-2 (vē′to͞o′) See under ROCKET BOMB.

V-8 engine (vē′āt′) An internal-combustion engine, as for an automobile, in the form of a V, on each side of which are four cylinders. Also **V-8.**

v.a. *Gram.* **1.** Active verb. **2.** Verbal adjective.

Va. Virginia.

V.A. 1. Veterans' Administration: also **VA 2.** Vicar Apostolic. **3.** Vice Admiral. **4.** (Order of) Victoria and Albert.

Vaal (väl) A river in South Africa, forming part of the boundary between the Orange Free State and the Transvaal and flowing about 750 miles SW and west to the Orange River.

va·can·cy (vā′kən·sē) *n. pl.* **·cies 1.** The state of being vacant; vacuity; emptiness. **2.** That which is vacant or unoccupied; empty space. **3.** An interruption of continuity of thought or space; a gap; chasm. **4.** An unoccupied post, place, or office; a place destitute of an incumbent. **5.** *Rare* Unoccupied time; leisure.

va·cant (vā′kənt) *adj.* **1.** Containing or holding nothing; especially, devoid of occupants; empty. **2.** Occupied with nothing; unemployed; unencumbered; free. **3.** Being or appearing without intelligence; inane. **4.** Having no incumbent; unfilled: a *vacant* office. **5.** *Law* Unoccupied or unused, as land; also, abandoned; having neither claimant nor heir, as an estate. **6.** Free from cares. **7.** Devoid of thought; unreflecting. [< F < L *vacans, -antis*, ppr. of *vacare* to be empty] **—va′cant·ly** *adv.* **—va′cant·ness** *n.*

va·can·ti·a bo·na (vā·kan′shē·ə bō′nə) *Latin* Goods without an owner; escheated goods.

vacant lot *U.S.* An unoccupied urban lot.

va·cate (vā′kāt) *v.* **·cat·ed, ·cat·ing** *v.t.* **1.** To make vacant; surrender possession of by removal. **2.** To set aside; annul. **3.** To give up (a position or office); quit. **—** *v.i.* **4.** To leave an office, position, place, etc. **5.** *Informal* To go away; leave. **— Syn.** See ANNUL. [< L *vacatus*, pp. of *vacare* to be empty]

va·ca·tion (vā·kā′shən) *n.* **1.** An interlude, usually of several days or weeks, from one's customary duties, as for recreation or rest; a holiday. **2.** *Law* The period of time intervening between stated terms of court. **3.** The intermission of the course of studies and exercises in an educational institution. **4.** The act of vacating. **—** *v.i.* To take a vacation. [< F < L *vacatio, -onis* freedom from duty < *vacatus*. See VACATE.] **—va·ca′tion·er** *n.*

va·ca·tion·ist (vā·kā′shən·ist) *n.* One who is taking a vacation or staying at a resort; a tourist.

vacation land A place providing recreation, sightseeing, and other attractions for vacationists.

vac·ci·nal (vak′sə·nəl) *adj.* Of the nature of or relating to vaccine or vaccination.

vac·ci·nate (vak′sə·nāt) *v.* **·nat·ed, ·nat·ing** *Med.* **v.t. 1.** To inoculate with a vaccine as a preventive measure; especially, to inoculate against smallpox. **—** *v.i.* **2.** To perform vaccination. [< VACCIN(E) + -ATE[2]]

vac·ci·na·tion (vak′sə·nā′shən) n. Med. 1. The act or process of vaccinating, especially against smallpox. 2. A scar caused by vaccinating.

vac·ci·na·tor (vak′sə·nā′tər) n. Med. 1. One who vaccinates. 2. An instrument used for vaccination.

vac·cine (vak′sēn, -sin, vak·sēn′) n. 1. The virus of cowpox, as prepared for or introduced by vaccination, usually lymph, dried or fluid, or part of the crust from a pustule. 2. Any inoculable immunizing preparation containing bacteria or viruses so treated as to give immunity from specific diseases when injected into the subject. — adj. 1. Pertaining to or derived from cows. 2. Pertaining to cowpox or vaccination. [< L vaccinus pertaining to a cow < vacca cow]

vac·cin·i·a (vak·sin′ē·ə) n. Vet. Cowpox. Also **vac·ci·na** (vak·si′nə). See VACCINE.]

vac·cin·i·a·ceous (vak·sin′ē·ā′shəs) adj. Bot. Pertaining or belonging to a genus (Vaccinium) of shrubs of the heath family, having small blue, black, or red berries, including the blueberry and cranberry. [< NL < L vaccinium blueberry]

vac·ci·ni·za·tion (vak′sə·nə·zā′shən, -nī·zā′-) n. Med. Repeated inoculation with a vaccine.

vac·cin·o·ther·a·py (vak′sən·ō·ther′ə·pē) n. Med. Treatment by bacterial vaccines.

vac·il·late (vas′ə·lāt) v.i. ·lat·ed, ·lat·ing 1. To sway one way and the other; totter; waver. 2. To fluctuate. 3. To waver in mind; be irresolute. [< L vacillatus, pp. of vacillare to waver] — **vac′il·lan·cy** (-lən·sē), **vac′il·la′tion** n.
— Syn. 2. See FLUCTUATE. 3. Vacillate, waver, hesitate, and falter mean to be irresolute in action. To vacillate is to incline to one alternative and then another, without coming to a decision. To waver is to be undecided whether to embark on a chosen course. To hesitate is merely to pause, but often implies wavering. Falter is a stronger word than hesitate, suggesting failure to act through weakness, timidity, or fright.

vac·il·lat·ing (vas′ə·lā′ting) adj. Inclined to waver; uncertain; wavering. Also **vac′il·lant** (-lənt), **vac′il·la·to·ry** (-lə·tôr′ē, -tō′rē). — **vac′il·lat′ing·ly** adv.

vac·u·a (vak′yōō·ə) Alternative plural of VACUUM.

va·cu·i·ty (və·kyōō′ə·tē) n. pl. ·ties 1. The state of being a vacuum; emptiness. 2. Vacant space; a void. 3. Freedom from mental exertion; idleness. 4. Lack of intelligence; stupidity. 5. Nothingness. 6. An inane or idle thing or statement. [< L vacuitas, -tatis < vacuus empty. Cf. F vacuité.]

vac·u·o·lat·ed (vak′yōō·ə·lā′tid) adj. Biol. Having one or more vacuoles. Also **vac·u·o·late** (vak′yōō·ə·lāt′, -lit).

vac·u·o·la·tion (vak′yōō·ō·lā′shən) n. Biol. 1. The formation of vacuoles. 2. An aggregate or system of vacuoles.

vac·u·ole (vak′yōō·ōl) n. Biol. A minute cavity containing air, a watery fluid, or a chemical secretion of the protoplasm, found in an organ, tissue, or cell. For illustration see CELL. [< F < L vacuum, neut. of vacuus empty] — **vac′u·o·lar** adj.

vac·u·ous (vak′yōō·əs) adj. 1. Having no contents; empty. 2. Lacking intelligence; blank. 3. Idle; unoccupied. [< L vacuus] — **vac′u·ous·ly** adv. — **vac′u·ous·ness** n.

vac·u·um (vak′yōō·əm, -yōōm) n. pl. ·u·ums or ·u·a (-yōō·ə) 1. A space absolutely devoid of matter. 2. A space from which air or other gas has been exhausted to a very high degree. 3. A partial diminution of the normal atmospheric pressure. 4. A void; an empty feeling. 5. A condition of isolation from environmental influences. — adj. 1. Of, or used in the production of, a vacuum. 2. Exhausted or partly exhausted of gas, air, or vapor. 3. Operated by suction to produce a vacuum. — v. Informal v.t. 1. To use a vacuum cleaner on: to vacuum a rug. — v.i. 2. To clean with a vacuum cleaner. [< L, neut. of vacuus empty]

vacuum bottle A thermos bottle (which see). Also **vacuum flask.**

vacuum cleaner A machine for cleaning carpets, furnishings, etc., by the suction of air. — **vacuum cleaning**

vacuum coffee maker A coffee maker, as a Silex, consisting of an upper bowl filled with ground coffee inserted into a lower bowl containing boiling water that rises into the upper bowl, mixes with the coffee, and is then drawn back into the lower bowl by suction.

vacuum fan A fan for ventilating a room, etc., by the suction withdrawal of stagnant or impure air.

vacuum gauge A gauge for testing the pressure consequent on producing a vacuum, as in a condenser.

vac·u·um-packed (vak′yōō·əm·pakt′, -yōōm-) adj. Designating a can or jar from which most of the air has been removed.

vacuum pump A pulsometer (def. 1).

vacuum tube Electronics An electron tube having a vacuum within its envelope such that residual gases have a negligible effect on its operation, and usually having some means for heating the cathode to stimulate electron emission. Also Brit. **vacuum valve.**

vacuum ventilation A ventilating system in which stale air is drawn out by exhaust fans and replaced by fresh air drawn in from the outside.

va·de in pa·ce (vā′dē in pā′sē) Latin Go in peace.

va·de me·cum (vā′dē mē′kəm) Latin Anything carried for constant use, as a guidebook, manual, or bag; literally, go with me. Also **va′de·me′cum, va′de-me′cum.**

va·dose (vā′dōs) adj. Of or pertaining to those underground waters lying immediately above the water table: distinguished from phreatic. [< L vadosus shallow < vadum ford]

Va·duz (fä·dōōts′) The capital of Liechtenstein, near the Rhine; pop. 4,000 (est. 1967).

vae vic·tis (vē vik′təs) Latin Woe to the vanquished.

vag·a·bond (vag′ə·bond) n. 1. One who wanders from place to place without visible means of support; a tramp. 2. One without a settled home; a wanderer; nomad. 3. A worthless fellow; rascal. — adj. 1. Pertaining to a vagabond; nomadic. 2. Having no definite residence; wandering; irresponsible. 3. Driven to and fro; aimless. [< F < L vagabundus < vagus wandering] — **vag′a·bond′age** (-ij) n. — **vag′a·bond·ish** adj. — **vag′a·bond·ism** n.

va·gar·y (və·gâr′ē, vā′gər·ē) n. pl. ·gar·ies A wild fancy; extravagant notion. [< L vagari to wander]

va·gi·na (və·jī′nə) n. pl. ·nas or ·nae (-nē) 1. Anat. a The canal leading from the external genital orifice in female mammals to the uterus. b A sheath or sheathlike covering. 2. Zool. The terminal portion of the oviduct of various invertebrates. 3. Bot. A tubular part surrounding another, as the basal portion of a leaf around a stem. [< L, sheath]

vag·i·nal (vaj′ə·nəl, və·jī′-) adj. 1. Pertaining to the vagina. 2. Pertaining to or like a sheath; thecal.

vag·i·nate (vaj′ə·nit, -nāt) adj. 1. Having a sheath. 2. Formed into a sheath; tubular. Also **vag′i·nat′ed** (-nā′tid). [< NL vaginatus < L vagina sheath]

vag·i·nec·to·my (vaj′ə·nek′tə·mē) n. pl. ·mies Surg. 1. Removal or obliteration of the vaginal canal. 2. Resection of the serous membrane of the testis: also **vag′i·na·lec′to·my** (-nə·lek′tə·mē). [< VAGIN(O)- + -ECTOMY]

vag·i·nis·mus (vaj′ə·niz′məs, -nis′-) n. Pathol. Spasm of the sphincter muscle of the vagina with extreme sensitivity of the adjacent parts. [< NL]

vag·i·ni·tis (vaj′ə·nī′tis) n. Pathol. Inflammation of the vagina: also called colpitis. [< NL]

vagino- combining form Med. The vagina; of or pertaining to the vagina. Also, before vowels, **vagin-**, as in vaginectomy. [< L vagina sheath, vagina]

va·gran·cy (vā′grən·sē) n. pl. ·cies The state of being a vagrant. Also **va′grant·ness.**

va·grant (vā′grənt) n. 1. A person without a settled home; an idle wanderer; vagabond; tramp. 2. A roving person; wanderer. — adj. 1. Wandering about as a vagrant. 2. Pertaining to one who or that which wanders; nomadic. 3. Having a wandering course; capricious; wayward. [ME vagaraunt, alter. of AF wakerant < OF wacrant < wacrer to walk, wander < Gmc.; infl. in form by L vagari to wander] — **va′grant·ly** adv.

va·grom (vā′grəm) adj. Obs. Vagrant. [Alter. of VAGRANT]

vague (vāg) adj. vagu·er, vagu·est 1. Lacking definiteness or precision. 2. Of uncertain source or authority: a vague rumor. 3. Not clearly recognized, understood, stated, or felt. 4. Shadowy; hazy. 5. Obs. Roving; vagrant. [< F < L vagus wandering] — **vague′ly** adv. — **vague′ness** n.
— Syn. 1. indefinite, indistinct, unclear, obscure. — Ant. definite, specific, concrete, lucid.

va·gus (vā′gəs) n. pl. ·gi (-jī) Anat. Either of the tenth pair of cranial nerves originating in the medulla oblongata and sending branches to the lungs, heart, stomach, and most of the abdominal viscera: also called pneumogastric. Also **vagus nerve.** [< L, wandering]

vail¹ (vāl) Obs. n. Veil. — v.t. To veil.

vail² (vāl) Obs. v.i. To be of use; avail. — n. 1. Usually pl. A gratuity or tip; a perquisite, often corrupt. 2. A windfall; find. 3. Advantage; profit. [Aphetic var. of AVAIL]

vail³ (vāl) v.t. Archaic 1. To let fall; lower, as the topsail, in salute or submission. 2. To take off (the hat, etc.) in respect or submission. [Aphetic form of obs. avale < F avaler to lower < à val down < L ad vallem, lit., to the valley]

vain (vān) adj. 1. Filled with or showing undue admiration for oneself, one's appearance, etc.; proud; conceited. 2. Unproductive; worthless; fruitless; useless: a vain attempt. 3. Having no real basis or worth; frivolous; empty; unreal: vain hopes. 4. Ostentatious; showy. — **in vain** 1. To no purpose; without effect. 2. In an irreverent or disrespectful manner: to take the Lord's name in vain. [< F < L vanus empty] — **vain′ly** adv. — **vain′ness** n.
— Syn. 1. proud, vainglorious. 2. nugatory, abortive. See FUTILE. 3. baseless, delusive.

vain·glo·ry (vān·glôr′ē, -glō′rē) n. pl. ·ries Excessive or groundless vanity; also, vain pomp; boastfulness. — **Syn.** See PRIDE. [< OF vaine gloire < Med.L vana gloria empty pomp, show] — **vain·glo′ri·ous** (-glôr′ē·əs, -glō′rē-) adj. — **vain·glo′ri·ous·ly** adv. — **vain·glo′ri·ous·ness** n.

vair (vâr) n. 1. Heraldry One of the furs represented by rows of small shield-shaped figures. 2. Obs. A fur used for the garments of the nobility (14th century). [< F < LL varius ermine < L varius parti-colored, various]

Va·lais (vȧ·le′) A Canton in southern Switzerland, in the upper Rhône valley; 2,021 sq. mi.; pop. 177,783 (1960); capital, Sion: German Wallis.

val·ance (val′əns) n. 1. A hanging drapery, as from the

framework of a bed to the floor, from a shelf, etc. **2.** A short drapery, board, or plate across the top of a window to conceal curtain fixtures, etc. **3.** A damask used for upholstering. — *v.t.* **·anced, ·anc·ing** To furnish with or as with a valance. [< OF *avalant*, ppr. of *avaler* to descend, or after *Valence*, textile-manufacturing commune in SE France] — **val′anced** *adj.*

Val·dai Hills (väl·dī′) A low plateau and group of hills in the western R.S.F.S.R. *Russian* **Val·day·ska·ya Voz·vy·shen·nost′** (väl·dī′ska·yə voz·vi′shin·nosty).

Val·de·mar (väl′də·mär) See WALDEMAR.

Val·di·via (väl·divē′ə, *Sp.* bäl·dē′vyä), **Pedro de**, 1500?–54, Spanish conquistador, conqueror of Chile.

Val·do (väl′dō), **Peter** See WALDO.

Val·dos·ta (val·dos′tə) A city in southern Georgia; pop. 32,303.

vale[1] (vāl) *n.* **1.** *Chiefly Poetic* A valley; a low-lying tract of land. **2.** A trough or channel. [< OF *val* < L *vallis*]

va·le[2] (vā′lē) *interj.* *Latin* Farewell; literally, be in good health.

val·e·dic·tion (val′ə·dik′shən) *n.* A bidding farewell. [< L *valedictus*, pp. of *valedicere* to say farewell < *vale* farewell, orig. imperative of *valere* to be well + *dicere* to say]

val·e·dic·to·ri·an (val′ə·dik·tôr′ē·ən, -tō′rē-) *n.* One who delivers a valedictory; especially, a student who delivers a valedictory at graduating exercises, usually the graduating student ranking highest in scholarship.

val·e·dic·to·ry (val′ə·dik′tər·ē) *adj.* Pertaining to a leavetaking. — *n.* *pl.* **·ries** A parting address, as by a member of a graduating class.

va·lence (vā′ləns) *n.* *Chem.* **1.** The property possessed by an element or radical of combining with or replacing other elements or radicals in definite and constant proportion. **2.** The number of atoms of hydrogen (or its equivalent) with which an atom or radical can combine, or which it can replace. Also **va′len·cy**. [< LL *valentia* strength, orig. neut. pl. of L *valens, -entis*, ppr. of *valere* to be well, be strong]

valence electron *Chem.* One of the electrons in the outermost shell of an atom, regarded as being responsible for the chemical reaction of an element.

va·len·ci·a (və·len′shē·ə, -shə) *n.* A woven fabric with wool weft and silk or cotton warp. [after *Valencia*]

Va·len·ci·a (və·len′shē·ə, -shə; *Sp.* bä·len′thyä) **1.** A region and former Moorish kingdom of eastern Spain, on the Mediterranean. **2.** A Province of Spain, center of the Valencia region; 4,155 sq. mi.; pop. 1,429,708 (1960); capital, **Valencia**, a port; pop. 614,000 (est. 1967). **3.** A city in north central Venezuela; pop. 196,400 (1961).

Va·len·ci·ennes (və·len′sē·enz′, *Fr.* vȧ·läṅ·syen′) *n.* A kind of bobbin lace with a floral pattern, originally made at Valenciennes. Also **Valenciennes lace, Val lace** (val).

Va·len·ciennes (vȧ·läṅ·syen′) A city in northern France, on the Escaut; pop. 46,626 (1968).

Va·lens (vā′lenz), 328?–378, Roman emperor of the East 364–378.

val·en·tine (val′ən·tīn) *n.* **1.** A greeting card or token of affection sent, usually to a person of the opposite sex, on Saint Valentine's Day. **2.** A sweetheart. [Prob. so called because of the coincidence of the saint's day with the Lupercalia]

Val·en·tine (val′ən·tīn), **Saint** Third-century Christian martyr.

Val·en·tin·i·an I (val′ən·tin′ē·ən), 321?–375, Roman emperor of the West 364–375; brother of Valens: full name **Flavius Val·en·tin·i·a·nus** (val′ən·tin′ē·ā′nəs).

Valentinian II, 371?–392, Roman emperor of the West 375–392; son of Valentinian I; murdered.

Valentinian III, 419–455, Roman emperor of the West 425–455; murdered: full name **Flavius Placidus Val·en·tin·i·a·nus** (val′ən·tin′ē·ā′nəs).

Va·le·ra (və·ler′ə), **Eamon De** See DE VALERA.

va·le·ri·an (və·lir′ē·ən) *n.* **1.** Any of a genus (*Valeriana*) of Old World perennial herbs; especially, one species (*V. officinalis*), with small pink or white flowers and a strong odor: also called *heliotrope*. **2.** Its root, used in medicine as a carminative and sedative. [< OF *valeriane* < Med.L *valeriana*, appar. ult. < *Valerius*, a personal name]

Va·le·ri·an (və·lir′ē·ən), 193?–269?, Roman emperor 253–260; captured and later killed by the Persians: full name **Publius Licinius Va·le·ri·a·nus** (və·lir′ē·ā′nəs).

va·le·ri·a·ceous (və·lir′ē·ə·nā′shəs) *adj.* *Bot.* Pertaining to a family (*Valerianaceae*) of herbs, including valerian. [< NL < Med.L *valeriana*. See VALERIAN.]

va·le·ric (və·ler′ik, -lir′-) *adj.* Of, pertaining to, or derived from valerian. Also **va·le·ri·an·ic** (və·lir′ē·an′ik).

valeric acid *Chem.* One of four isomeric acids, $C_5H_{10}O_2$, of which two are found in valerian, all made synthetically.

Va·lé·ry (vȧ·lā·rē′), **Paul Ambroise**, 1871–1945, French poet and philosopher.

val·et (val′ā, val′it; *Fr.* vȧ·le′) *n.* **1.** A gentleman's personal servant. **2.** A manservant in a hotel who performs personal

services for patrons. — *v.t. & v.i.* To serve or act as a valet. [< F, a groom < OF *vaslet, varlet*, dim. of *vasal* vassal. Doublet of VARLET.]

va·let de cham·bre (vȧ·le′ də shäṅ′br′) *pl.* **va·lets de cham·bre** (vȧ·le′) *French* A valet.

Va·let·ta (və·let′ə) See VALLETTA.

val·e·tu·di·nar·i·an (val′ə·tōō′də·nâr′ē·ən, -tyōō′-) *n.* A chronic invalid; one unduly solicitous about his health. — *adj.* Seeking to recover health; infirm. Also **val′e·tu′di·nar′y**. [< L *valetudinarius* infirm < *valetudo, -inis* health, ill health < *valere* to be well] — **val′e·tu′di·nar′i·an·ism** *n.*

val·gus (val′gəs) *adj.* Knock-kneed or bowlegged. — *n.* *Pathol.* An abnormal eversion of the foot, as by a depression of the arch. [< L, bowlegged]

Val·hal·la (val·hal′ə) **1.** In Norse mythology, the great hall into which the souls of heroes fallen bravely in battle were borne by the valkyries and received and feasted by Odin. **2.** An edifice wherein the remains or memorials of deceased heroes of a nation are placed. Also spelled *Walhalla*. Also **Val·hall** (val·hal′). [< NL < ON *valhöll*, genitive of *valhallar* hall of the slain < *valr* the slain + *höll* hall]

val·iant (val′yənt) *adj.* **1.** Strong and intrepid; powerful and courageous. **2.** Performed with valor; bravely conducted; heroic. — **Syn.** See BRAVE. [< OF *vailant*, ppr. of *valoir* to be strong < L *valere*] — **val′iant·ly** *adv.* — **val′iance, val′ian·cy, val′iant·ness** *n.*

val·id (val′id) *adj.* **1.** Based on evidence that can be supported; acceptable; convincing. **2.** Legally binding; effective; warranted. **3.** Properly derived from accepted premises by the rules of logic. **4.** *Obs.* Strong. **5.** *Stat.* Having a high degree of correlation with its criterion: distinguished from *reliable*. [< F *valide* < L *validus* powerful < *valere* to be strong] — **val′id·ly** *adv.* — **val′id·ness** *n.*

val·i·date (val′ə·dāt) *v.t.* **·dat·ed, ·dat·ing** **1.** To make valid; ratify and confirm. **2.** To declare legally valid; legalize. — **Syn.** See RATIFY. — **val′i·da′tion** *n.*

va·lid·i·ty (və·lid′ə·tē) *n.* *pl.* **·ties** **1.** The state or quality of being valid; soundness, as in law or reasoning; efficacy. **2.** *Archaic* Health; strength. **3.** *Obs.* Worth.

va·lise (və·lēs′) *n.* A portable case or bag for clothes and toilet articles, used when traveling; a suitcase. [< F < Ital. *valigia*; ult. origin uncertain]

val·kyr·ie (val·kir′ē, val′kir·ē) *n.* *Often cap.* In Norse mythology, one of the maidens who ride through the air and choose heroes from among those slain in battle, and carry them to Valhalla: also called *walkyrie*. Also **val′kyr**. [< ON *valkyrja*, lit., chooser of the slain < *valr* the slain + stem of *kjosa* to choose, select] — **val·kyr′i·an** *adj.*

Val·la·do·lid (val′ə·dō′lid, *Sp.* bä′lyä·thō′lēth) A Province of north central Spain; 3,221 sq. mi.; pop. 368,685 (1965); capital, **Valladolid**, former capital of Castile, pop. 133,486.

Val·lar·ta (bä·lyär′tä), **Manuel Sandoval**, born 1899, Mexican physicist.

val·la·tion (və·lā′shən) *n.* **1.** The art of planning or erecting fortifications. **2.** A rampart. [< LL *vallatio, -onis* < L *vallare* to protect with a wall < *vallum* wall] — **val·la·to·ry** (val′ə·tôr′ē, -tō′rē) *adj.*

val·lec·u·la (və·lek′yə·lə) *n.* *pl.* **·lae** (-lē) **1.** *Anat.* A furrow or depression, as on the back of the tongue on either side of the epiglottis. **2.** *Bot.* A groove or furrow, as between the ridges on the fruit of certain plants. [< NL, var. of L *vallicula*, dim. of *vallis* valley] — **val·lec′u·lar, val·lec′u·late** (-lit, -lāt) *adj.*

Val·le·jo (və·lā′ō, -hō) A port city in western California, on San Pablo Bay; pop. 66,733.

Val·let·ta (və·let′ə) The capital of Malta, a port on the SE coast; site of a major British naval base; pop. 15,432 (est. 1968): also *Valetta*.

val·ley (val′ē) *n.* *pl.* **·leys** **1.** A depression of the earth's surface, as one through which a stream flows; level or low land between mountains, hills, or high lands. **2.** *Archit.* **a** The gutter or angle formed by the meeting of the two roof slopes. **b** An interval in a vault, or the space between vault ridges as seen from above. [< OF *valee* < *val* < L *vallis* valley]

Valley Forge A village in SE Pennsylvania, scene of Washington's winter encampment, 1777–78, in the American Revolution.

Valley of Ten Thousand Smokes (smōks) An area in Katmai National Monument, southern Alaska, containing thousands of small volcanoes; 72 sq. mi.

Valley Stream A village in SE New York, on Long Island; pop. 40,413.

Val·lom·bro·sa (väl′lôm·brō′zä) A resort town in north central Italy, near Florence.

Va·lois (vȧ·lwä′) A medieval county and former duchy of northern France.

Va·lois (vȧ·lwä′) A French dynasty; began 1328 with Philip VI of Valois, ended with Henry III, 1589.

Va·lo·na (vä·lō′nä) A port city in SW Albania on the **Bay of Valona**, an inlet of the Strait of Otranto; pop. about

50,400: formerly *Avlona*. Albanian *Vlona, Vlonë, Vlora, Vlorë*.

va·lo·ni·a (və·lō′nē·ə) *n.* The dried acorn cups of the Old World **valonia oak** (*Quercus macrolepis*), used as a tanning material. [< Ital. *vallonea* < Modern Gk. *balania* an evergreen oak, pl. of *balani* acorn < Gk. *balanos*]

val·or (val′ər) *n.* Intrepid courage, especially in warfare; personal bravery. Also *Brit.* **val′our.** [< OF *valour* < LL *valor* worth < *valere* to be strong]

val·or·i·za·tion (val′ər·ə·zā′shən, -ī·zā′-) *n.* The maintenance by governmental action of an artificial price for any product. [< Pg. *valorização* < *valor* value < LL. See VALOR.]

val·or·ize (val′ə·rīz) *v.t.* **·ized, ·iz·ing** To subject to valorization. Also *Brit.* **val′or·ise.**

val·or·ous (val′ər·əs) *adj.* Courageous; valiant. **— val′or·ous·ly** *adv.* **— val′or·ous·ness** *n.*

Val·pa·rai·so (val′pə·rā′zō, -sō, -rī′-) A port city in central Chile; pop. 259,241 (1960). *Spanish* **Val·pa·ra·i·so** (bäl′pä·rä·ē′sō).

val·u·a·ble (val′yoo·ə·bəl, val′yə·bəl) *adj.* **1.** Having relatively great financial worth, price, or value; costly. **2.** Of a nature or character capable of being valued or estimated. **3.** Having moral worth, value, or importance; very serviceable. **—** *n.* Usually *pl.* An article of worth or value, as a piece of jewelry. **— val′u·a·ble·ness** *n.* **— val′u·a·bly** *adv.*

val·u·ate (val′yoo·āte) *v.t.* **·at·ed, ·at·ing** To give a value to; evaluate. [Back formation < VALUATION]

val·u·a·tion (val′yoo·ā′shən) *n.* **1.** The act of valuing. **2.** Estimated worth or value. **3.** Personal estimation; judgment of merit or character. **— val′u·a·tion·al** *adj.*

val·u·a·tor (val′yoo·ā′tər) *n.* One who makes appraisals.

val·ue (val′yoo) *n.* **1.** The desirability or worth of a thing; intrinsic worth; utility. **2.** *Often pl.* Something regarded as desirable, worthy, or right, as a belief, standard, or moral precept: the *values* of a democratic society. **3.** The rate at which a commodity is potentially exchangeable for others; a fair return in service, goods, etc.; worth in money; market price. **4.** The ratio of utility to price; a bargain. **5.** Attributed or assumed valuation; esteem or regard. **6.** Exact meaning; signification. **7.** *Music* The relative length of a tone as signified by a note. **8.** *Math.* The quantity, magnitude, or number an algebraic symbol or expression is supposed to denote. **9.** Rank in a system of classification. **10.** In the graphic arts, the relation of the elements of a picture, as light and shade, to one another. **11.** *Phonet.* The special quality of the sound represented by a written character. **—** *v.t.* **·ued, ·u·ing 1.** To estimate the value or worth of; assess; appraise. **2.** To regard highly; esteem; prize. **3.** To place a relative estimate of value or desirability upon. **4.** To give a (specified) value to: to *value* the English pound at $2.40. [< OF *valu*, pp. of *valoir* to be worth < L *valere*] **— val′ue·less** *adj.* **— val′u·er** *n.*

value added tax A tax added to a product or service at each stage of its production and distribution, based on its increased value at that stage. *Abbr. VAT, V.A.T.*

val·ued (val′yood) *adj.* **1.** Regarded or estimated; much or highly esteemed: a *valued* friend. **2.** Having a (specified) value: used in combination: a *many-valued* function.

valued policy A policy requiring an insurance company to pay the insured the full amount of his policy, regardless of the actual value of the property, if it is totally destroyed.

val·val (val′val) *adj.* Of or pertaining to a valve. Also **val′var** (-vər).

val·vate (val′vāt) *adj.* **1.** Serving as or resembling a valve; having a valve; valvular. **2.** *Bot.* **a** Touching by contiguous edges, as capsules that separate like valves. **b** Meeting without overlapping, as the petals of many flowers. [< L *valvatus* with folding doors < *valva*. See VALVE.]

valve (valv) *n.* **1.** *Mech.* Any contrivance or arrangement that regulates the amount and direction of flow of a liquid, gas, vapor, or loose material. **2.** *Anat.* A structure formed by one or more loose folds of the lining membrane of a vessel or other organ, allowing flow of a fluid in one direction only, as blood to and from the heart. **3.** *Zool.* **a** One of the parts of a shell, as of a mollusk. **b** A covering plate or one of two or more external pieces forming a sheath, as for an ovipositor. **4.** *Bot.* **a** One of the parts into which a capsule splits in dehiscence. **b** One of the halves of an anther after its opening. **5.** *Electr.* A device for controlling the direction of a current, as an electrolytic cell, or an electron tube. **6.** *Brit.* An electron tube. **7.** A device in certain brass instruments for lengthening the air column and lowering the pitch of the instrument's scale. *Abbr. v.* **—** *v.t.* **valved, valv·ing** To furnish with valves; control the flow of by means of a valve. [< L *valva* leaf of a door] **— valve′less** *adj.*

GATE VALVE
a Screw.
b Gate closed.

valve-in-head engine (valv′in·hed′) *Mech.* An internal-combustion engine having overhead valves.

valve·let (valv′lit) *n.* A little valve; a valvule.

valve trombone See under TROMBONE.

val·vu·lar (val′vyə·lər) *adj.* **1.** Pertaining to or of the

nature of a valve, as of the heart. **2.** Having valves; acting as a valve.

val·vule (val′vyool) *n.* A small valve; a structure like a small valve. Also **val′vu·la** (-vyə·lə). [< F < Med.L *valvula*, dim. of L *valva* door]

val·vu·li·tis (val′vyə·lī′tis) *n. Pathol.* Inflammation of any membrane that serves as a valve in the organs or channels of circulation, especially of the blood. [< NL < Med.L *valvula* (See VALVULE) + -ITIS]

vam·brace (vam′brās) *n.* Armor for the forearm from elbow to wrist. [Var. of *vantbrace* < AF *vantbras*, OF *avant-bras* < *avant* in front of + *bras* arm] **— vam′braced** *adj.*

va·moose (va·moos′) *v.t. & v.i.* **·moosed, ·moos·ing** *U.S. Slang* To leave hastily or hurriedly; quit. Also **va·mose′** (-mōs′). [< Sp. *vamos* let us go < L *vadere* to go]

vamp[1] (vamp) *n.* **1.** The piece of leather forming the upper front part of a boot or shoe. For illustration see SHOE. **2.** Something added to give an old thing a new appearance. **3.** *Music* A simple improvised accompaniment. **—** *v.t.* **1.** To provide with a vamp. **2.** To repair or patch. **3.** *Music* To improvise an accompaniment to. **—** *v.i.* **4.** *Music* To improvise accompaniments. [< OF *avampie* forepart of the foot < *avant* before + *pied* foot] **— vamp′er** *n.*

vamp[2] (vamp) *Informal v.t.* **1.** To seduce or victimize (a man) by utilizing one's feminine charms. **—** *v.i.* **2.** To play the vamp. **—** *n.* An unscrupulous flirt or coquette. [Short for VAMPIRE]
— Syn. (noun) siren, temptress, gold-digger, femme fatale.

vam·pire (vam′pīr) *n.* **1.** In European folklore, a corpse that rises from its grave at night to feed upon the living, usually by sucking the blood. **2.** A man or woman who victimizes persons of the opposite sex; especially, a woman who brings her lover to a state of poverty or degradation. **3.** A large bat (genera *Desmodus* and *Diphylla*) of South or Central America, that drinks the blood of horses, cattle, and, sometimes, men. **4.** An insectivorous or frugivorous bat (genera *Phyllostomus* and *Vampyrum*) formerly supposed to suck blood. [< F < G *vampir* < Slavic] **— vam·pir·ic** (vam·pir′ik), **vam′pir·ish** (-pīr′ish) *adj.*

vam·pir·ism (vam′pī·riz′əm, -pə-) *n.* **1.** Belief in vampires (def. 1). **2.** The act or practice of a vampire; bloodsucking. **3.** The practice of extortion or of preying upon others.

van[1] (van) *n.* **1.** A large covered vehicle for transporting furniture, livestock, etc. **2.** *Brit.* A closed railway car for luggage, etc. [Short for CARAVAN]

van[2] (van) *n.* **1.** The portion of an army, fleet, etc., that is nearest or in advance of the front: opposed to *rear*. **2.** The leaders of a movement; those at the front of any line or unit. [Short for VANGUARD]

van[3] (van) *n.* **1.** *Archaic* A winnowing machine. **2.** *Poetic* A wing. [Dial. var. of FAN[1]]

van[4] (vän) *prep. Dutch* Of; from: used with Dutch family names.

Van (vän) A town in SE Turkey, on **Lake Van** (1,453 sq. mi.); pop. about 22,000.

van·a·date (van′ə·dāt) *n. Chem.* A salt or ester of vanadic acid. Also **va·na·di·ate** (və·nā′dē·āt).

va·nad·ic (və·nad′ik) *adj. Chem.* Of, pertaining to, or derived from vanadium, especially in its higher valence.

vanadic acid *Chem.* Any of several acids containing vanadium, known only by their salts.

va·nad·i·nite (və·nad′ə·nīt) *n. Mineral.* A native vanadate and chloride of lead, found in opaque red or yellow prismatic crystals. [< VANAD(IUM) + -IN + -ITE[1]]

va·na·di·um (və·nā′dē·əm) *n.* A rare, silver-white metallic element (symbol V), used in steel alloys to increase tensile strength. See ELEMENT. *Abbr. Vd.* [< NL < ON *Vanadīs*, a name of the Norse goddess Freya]

vanadium steel Steel containing from .1 to .25 percent of vanadium to increase its toughness and tensile strength.

van·a·dous (van′ə·dəs) *adj. Chem.* Of, pertaining to, or derived from vanadium, especially in its lower valence. Also **va·na·di·ous** (və·nā′dē·əs).

Van Al·len radiation (van al′ən) A high-intensity radiation consisting of charged atomic particles believed to circle the earth in an inner and outer belt conforming to the earth's magnetic field. Compare MAGNETOSPHERE. Also **Van Allen belts.** [after James A. *Van Allen*, born 1914, U.S. physicist]

Van·brugh (van·broo′, van′brə), **Sir John,** 1664–1726, English playwright and architect.

Van Bu·ren (van byoor′ən), **Martin,** 1782–1862, eighth president of the United States 1837–41.

Van·cou·ver (van·koo′vər) **1.** A port city in SW British Columbia opposite **Vancouver Island** (12,408 sq. mi.), an island off the western coast of the Province; pop. 410,375. **2.** A city in SW Washington, on the Columbia River; pop. 42,493.

Van·cou·ver (van·koo′vər), **George,** 1758?–98, English seafarer and explorer.

van·dal (van′dəl) *n.* One who willfully destroys or defaces property, especially anything beautiful or artistic. **—** *adj.* Wantonly destructive. [< VANDAL] **— van·dal·ic** (van·dal′ik) *adj.*

Van·dal (van′dəl) *n.* One of a Germanic people who

ravaged Gaul and overran Spain and North Africa in the early part of the fifth century, and pillaged the city of Rome in 455. — **Van·dal·ic** (van-dal′ik) *adj.* — **Van′dal·ism** *n.*

van·dal·ism (van′dəl-iz′əm)   *n.*   Willful destruction or defacement of artistic works, or of property in general.

Van·den·berg (van′dən-bûrg), **Arthur Hendrick**, 1884–1951, U.S. statesman. — **Hoyt Sanford**, 1899–1954, U.S. Air Force general.

Van·der·bilt (van′dər-bilt), **Cornelius**, 1794–1877, U.S. financier: called **Commodore Vanderbilt**.

van der Rohe, Mies See MIES VAN DER ROHE

Van Die·men's Land (van dē′mənz) The former name for TASMANIA.

Van Do·ren (van dôr′ən, dō′rən), **Carl (Clinton)**, 1885–1950, U.S. writer and editor. — **Mark (Albert)**, 1894–1972, U.S. poet, writer, and critic; brother of the preceding.

van Dru·ten (van drōōt′n), **John (William)**, 1901–1957, English playwright.

Van Dyck (van dīk′), **Sir Anthony**, 1599–1641, Flemish painter active in England. Also **Van·dyke′**.

Van·dyke (van-dīk′)   *adj.*   Of or pertaining to Anthony Van Dyck, or to his style; also, of or pertaining to the dress or fashions represented in the paintings of Van Dyck. — *n.*   **1.** A painting by Van Dyck. **2.** A Vandyke collar or beard.

Vandyke beard   A short pointed beard resembling those depicted in Van Dyck's paintings.

Vandyke brown   A deep brown pigment used by the painter Van Dyck; also, any of various similar brown pigments.

Vandyke collar   A broad, deep collar of fine linen and lace, resembling those represented in portraits by Van Dyck.

vane (vān)   *n.*   **1.** A thin plate of metal or wood, often cut in the form of a bird, fish, arrow, etc., that pivots on a vertical rod to indicate the direction of the wind; weathercock; weather vane. **2.** An arm or blade extending from a rotating shaft, as of a windmill, propeller, turbine, etc. **3.** *Ornithol.* The web of a feather. **4.** The target on a leveling rod. **5.** The sight on a quadrant, compass, or similar instrument, by which the direction of the object viewed is determined. **6.** One of the plates or strips of metal fixed in the tail of a bomb, guided missile, or the like, to provide stability or guidance. [Dial. var. of *fane* small flag < OE *fana* flag] — **vaned** *adj.*

WINDMILL VANES

Vane (vān), **Sir Henry**, 1613–62, English Puritan statesman; executed: called **Sir Harry Vane**.

Va·ner (vā′nər), **Lake**   See (Lake) VENER.

van Eyck (van īk′), **Hubert**, 1366?–1426, and his brother **Jan**, 1385?–1440, Flemish painters.

vang (vang)   *n. Naut.*   One of two guy ropes from the end of a gaff to the deck, used to steady the gaff. [< Du., a catch < *vangen* to catch]

van Gogh (van gō′, gôkh′; *Du.* vän khokh′), **Vincent**, 1853–1890, Dutch painter.

van·guard (van′gärd)   *n.*   **1.** The advance guard of an army; the van. **2.** Those in the forefront of a movement, as in art, culture, etc. [< OF *avangarde*, var. of *avantgarde* < *avant* before + *garde* guard]

va·nil·la (və-nil′ə)   *n.*   **1.** A flavoring extract made from the podlike seed capsules of a climbing tropical orchid (*Vanilla planifolia*). **2.** The seed capsule of this plant: also **vanilla bean**. **3.** A food, as ice cream, flavored with vanilla. **4.** Any orchid of the genus *Vanilla*. [< NL < Sp. *vainilla*, dim. of *vaina* sheath, pod < L *vagina* sheath; so called from the pods that contain its seeds]

va·nil·lic (və-nil′ik)   *adj.*   Of, pertaining to, or derived from vanilla or vanillin.

va·nil·lin (və-nil′in)   *n. Chem.*   A colorless, fragrant, crystalline compound, $C_8H_8O_3$, contained in vanilla, and also made synthetically. Also **va·nil·line** (və-nil′in, -ēn).

Va·nir (vä′nir)   *pl. of* **Van** (vän)   In Norse mythology, an early race of fertility deities, later combined with the Æsir.

van·ish (van′ish)   *v.i.*   **1.** To disappear from sight; fade away; depart. **2.** To pass out of existence; be annihilated. **3.** *Math.* To become equal to zero. — *n. Phonet.* The second, weaker element of most diphthongs, as the faint (ōō) heard after the (ō) in *go*. [Aphetic var. of OF *esvaniss-*, stem of *esvanir* < L *evanescere* to fade away. See EVANESCE.] — **van′ish·er** *n.*

vanishing point (van′ish-ing)   **1.** In perspective, the point at which parallel lines appear to converge. **2.** A time, condition, etc., in which something disappears.

van·i·tas van·i·ta·tum (van′ə-tas van′ə-tā′təm)   *Latin*   Vanity of vanities.

van·i·ty (van′ə-tē)   *n. pl.* **·ties**   **1.** The condition or character of being vain; excessive personal pride; conceit. **2.** Ambitious display; ostentation; show. **3.** The quality or state of being fruitless, useless, or destitute of reality, etc. **4.** That which is vain or unsubstantial. **5.** A bag or box containing cosmetics, comb, mirror, etc.: also **vanity case**. **6.** A

dressing table. — **Syn.** See EGOTISM, PRIDE. [< OF *vanite* < L *vanitas*, *-tatis* < *vanus* empty, vain]

Vanity Fair   **1.** In Bunyan's *Pilgrim's Progress*, a fair symbolizing the world as a scene of vanity and folly. **2.** A novel by W. M. Thackeray, satirizing the weaknesses and follies of human nature. **3.** The world of fashion and frivolity.

vanity publisher   A publisher who publishes books at the author's own expense. Also **vanity press**.

Van Loon (van lōn′), **Hendrik Willem**, 1882–1944, U.S. historian, biographer, and journalist born in Holland.

van·man (van′mən)   *n. pl.* **·men** (-mən)   A man who drives or works on a van.

van·quish (vang′kwish, van′-)   *v.t.*   **1.** To defeat in battle; overcome; conquer. **2.** To suppress or overcome (a feeling or emotion): to *vanquish* fear. **3.** To defeat, as in argument; confute. [< OF *venquiss-*, stem of *veinquir* to conquer < L *vincere*] — **van′quish·a·ble** *adj.* — **van′quish·er** *n.*

Van Rens·se·laer (van ren′sə-lər, -lir), **Stephen**, 1764–1839, American general and politician: called **The Patroon**.

Van·sit·tart (van-sit′ərt), **Robert Gilbert**, 1881–1957, first Baron Vansittart of Denham, British diplomat and author.

van·tage (van′tij)   *n.*   **1.** Superiority over a competitor, as in means of attack; advantage. **2.** Advantage (def. 4). **3.** *Obs.* An opportunity; chance. [Aphetic var. of OF *avantage*. See ADVANTAGE.] — **van′tage·less** *adj.*

vantage ground   A position or condition that gives one an advantage.

van't Hoff (vänt hôf′), **Jacobus Henricus**, 1852–1911, Dutch physical chemist.

van·ward (van′wərd)   *adj.*   Pertaining to or situated in the van or front: *vanward* regiments. — *adv.*   To or toward the van or front.

Van·zet·ti (van-zet′ē, *Ital.* vän-dzet′tē), **Bartolomeo**   See under SACCO.

vap·id (vap′id, vā′pid)   *adj.*   Having lost all spirit, liveliness, flavor, force, or character; flat; dull; insipid. [< L *vapidus* insipid] — **vap′id·ness** *n.* — **vap′id·ly** *adv.*

va·pid·i·ty (ve-pid′ə-tē)   *n. pl.* **·ties**   **1.** The state or quality of being vapid. **2.** A vapid remark, thought, etc.

va·por (vā′pər)   *n.*   **1.** Moisture in the air; especially, visible floating moisture, as light mist. **2.** Any light, cloudy substance in the air, as smoke or fumes. **3.** Any substance in the gaseous state, that, under ordinary conditions, is usually a liquid or solid. **4.** A gas below its critical temperature. **5.** That which is fleeting and unsubstantial. **6.** A substance vaporized for remedial inhalation, industrial use, etc. **7.** Boastful swagger; vaporing. **8.** *pl. Archaic* Depression of spirits; hypochondria. — *v.t.* **1.** To vaporize. — *v.i.* **2.** To emit vapor. **3.** To evaporate. **4.** To make idle boasts; brag. Also *Brit.* **va′pour**. [< AF *vapour*, OF *vapeur* < L *vapor* steam] — **va′por·a·bil′i·ty** *n.* — **va′por·a·ble** *adj.* — **va′por·er** *n.*

va·por·es·cence (vā′pə-res′əns)   *n.*   The process of forming mist or vapor. — **va′por·es′cent** *adj.*

va·po·ret·to (vä′pô-rät′tō)   *n. pl.* **·ti** (-tē)   *Italian*   A small steamboat for carrying passengers along canals, as in Venice.

vapori-   *combining form*   Vapor; of or related to vapor, steam, etc.: *vaporimeter*. Also, before vowels, **vapor-**. [< L *vapor* steam]

va·por·if·ic (vā′pə-rif′ik)   *adj.*   Producing or turning to vapor. [< NL *vaporificus* < L *vapor*, *-oris* steam + *facere* to make]

va·por·im·e·ter (vā′pə-rim′ə-tər)   *n.*   An instrument for determining vapor pressure.

va·por·ing (vā′pər-ing)   *adj.*   Boasting; swaggering. — *n.*   Boasting or pretentious talk. — **va′por·ing·ly** *adv.*

va·por·ish (vā′pər-ish)   *adj.*   **1.** Somewhat like vapor. **2.** *Archaic* Somewhat depressed or hypochondriac.

va·por·i·za·tion (vā′pər-ə-zā′shən, -ī-zā′-)   *n.*   **1.** The act or process of vaporizing, or the state of being vaporized. **2.** *Med.* Treatment with vapor.

va·por·ize (vā′pə-rīz)   *v.t. & v.i.* **·ized**, **·iz·ing**   To convert or be converted into vapor. — **va′por·iz′a·ble** *adj.*

va·por·iz·er (vā′pə-rī′zər)   *n.*   One who or that which vaporizes; especially, a device for converting a medicinal substance into vapor for inhalation.

vapor lock   *Mech.*   In internal-combustion engines, an interruption of the flow of fuel in the fuel line or carburetor, caused by vaporization or by the presence of air bubbles.

va·por·ous (vā′pər-əs)   *adj.*   **1.** Of or like vapor; foggy; misty. **2.** Full of or producing vapors. **3.** Diaphanous; ethereal. **4.** Vainly imaginative; whimsical. Also **va′por·y**. — **va′por·os′i·ty** (vā′pə-ros′ə-tē) *n.* — **va′por·ous·ly** *adv.* — **va′por·ous·ness** *n.*

vapor pressure   *Physics*   The pressure of a confined vapor in equilibrium with its liquid at any specific temperature. Also **vapor tension**.

vapor trail   *Aeron.*   A visible trail of vapor streaming behind an airplane flying through supercooled air, caused by the condensation of atmospheric moisture or from exhaust engine gases: also called *condensation trail, contrail*.

---

va·que·ro (vä·kā′rō) *n.* *pl.* **·ros** (-rōz, *Sp.* -rōs) A herdsman; cowboy. [< Sp. < *vaca* cow < L *vacca*]

var. 1. Variant. 2. Variation. 3. Variety. 4. Variometer. 5. Various.

va·ra (vä′rä) *n.* A Spanish and Portuguese measure of length, varying from 2.7 to 3.6 feet. —**square vara** An analogous measure of surface. [< Sp. and Pg., lit., rod < L, forked pole < *varus* bent]

Va·ran·gi·an (və·ran′jē·ən) *n.* One of a group of Scandinavian seamen who, in the ninth century, established a dynasty in Russia. [< Med.L *Varangus* < Med. Gk. *Barangos* < Slavic, ult. < ON *Væringi* ally < *vārar* pledges]

Var·dar (vär′där) A river of southern Yugoslavia and NE Greece, flowing about 230 miles, generally SE, to the Gulf of Salonika.

Var·gas (vär′gəs), **Getulio Dornelles**, 1883–1954, Brazilian statesman; chief of state 1930–54.

vari- *combining form* Various; different: *variform, vari-colored.* Also *vario-.* [< L *varius* varied]

var·i·a·ble (vâr′ē·ə·bəl) *adj.* 1. Having the capacity of varying; alterable; mutable. 2. Having a tendency to change; not constant; fickle. 3. Having no definite value as regards quantity. 4. *Biol.* Prone to variation from a normal or established type: said of plants and animals. —*n.* 1. That which varies or is subject to change. 2. *Math.* **a** A quantity susceptible of fluctuating in value or magnitude under different conditions. **b** A symbol representing one of a group of objects. 3. *Meteorol.* **a** A shifting wind or winds. **b** *pl.* A region where such winds are common. [< OF < L *variabilis* < *variare.* See VARY.] —**var′i·a·bil′i·ty, var′i·a·ble·ness** *n.* —**var′i·a·bly** *adv.*

variable star *Astron.* Any of several groups of stars whose apparent magnitude varies at different times; especially, a Cepheid variable (which see).

var·i·ance (vâr′ē·əns) *n.* 1. The act of varying, or the state of being variant; difference; discrepancy. 2. Dissension; discord. 3. *Law* **a** A disagreement between the allegations in the pleadings and the proof in an essential matter. **b** A material disagreement between the writ beginning an action and the declaration or complaint. **c** An exception to a zoning law in a specific case. 4. *Stat.* The square of the standard deviation. 5. In physical chemistry, the particular state of a material system with respect to the number of independent variables, as temperature, pressure, concentration, required to define the system: also called *degree of freedom.* See PHASE RULE. —**at variance** 1. Disagreeing or conflicting, as facts. 2. In a state of dissension or discord.

var·i·ant (vâr′ē·ənt) *adj.* 1. Having or showing variation; varying; differing. 2. Tending to vary; variable; changing. 3. Restless; fickle; inconstant. 4. Differing from a standard or type; discrepant. —*n.* 1. A thing that differs from another in form only; especially, a different spelling, pronunciation, or form of the same word. 2. A variate. 3. *Ling.* Any positional or contextual form of a linguistic unit, as an allophone or allomorph. Abbr. *var.* [< OF < L *varians, -antis,* ppr. of *variare.* See VARY.]

var·i·ate (*n.* vâr′ē·it, -āte; *v.* vâr′ē·āte) *n.* 1. That which varies; a variable. 2. *Stat.* The magnitude or value of a variable (def. 2). —*v.t. & v.i.* **·at·ed, ·at·ing** *Obs.* To vary. [< L *variatus,* pp. of *variare.* See VARY.]

var·i·a·tion (vâr′ē·ā′shən) *n.* 1. The act, process, state, or result of varying; modification; diversity. 2. The extent to which a thing varies. 3. Inflection, as of declensions or conjugations; also, change in certain vowel sounds. 4. A repetition with its essential features intact and other features modified. 5. *Music* A modification of the rhythm, harmony, melodic pattern, etc., of a basic theme or idea, usually as part of a series of such changes. 6. *Astron.* **a** An inequality in the moon's motion. **b** Any change in the elements of a planetary orbit. 7. *Biol.* Deviation in structure or function from the type or parent form of an organism, as by heredity or in response to conditions of environment. Abbr. *var.* —**Syn.** See DIFFERENCE. [< F < L *variatio, -onis*] —**var′i·a′tion·al** *adj.*

var·i·cel·la (var′ə·sel′ə) *n.* *Pathol.* Chicken pox. [< NL, dim. of *variola.* See VARIOLA.]

var·i·cel·late (var′ə·sel′it, -āt) *adj.* *Zool.* Marked with small varices, as certain shells. [< NL *varicella,* dim. of L *varix* varicose vein]

var·i·cel·loid (var′ə·sel′oid) *adj.* Resembling chicken pox: *varicelloid* smallpox.

var·i·ces (var′ə·sēz) Plural of VARIX.

varico- *combining form Med.* A varicose vein; varix: *varicotomy.* Also, before vowels, **varic-.** [< L *varix, -icis* varicose vein]

var·i·co·cele (var′ə·kō·sēl′) *n.* *Pathol.* A tumor formed by varicose veins of the spermatic cord. [< NL < L *varix, -icis* varicose vein + Gk. *kēlē* tumor]

var·i·col·ored (vâr′i·kul′ərd) *adj.* Variegated in color; parti-colored; of various colors. Also *Brit.* **var′i·col′oured.**

var·i·cose (var′ə·kōs) *adj.* *Pathol.* Abnormally dilated, as veins. [< L *varicosus* < *varix, -icis* varicose vein]

var·i·co·sis (var′ə·kō′sis) *n.* *Pathol.* A varicose condition; varicosity. [< NL]

var·i·cos·i·ty (var′ə·kos′ə·tē) *n.* *pl.* **·ties** *Pathol.* 1. The condition of being varicose. 2. A varix.

var·i·cot·o·my (var′ə·kot′ə·mē) *n.* *pl.* **·mies** *Surg.* Excision of a varix or of a varicose vein. [< VARICO- + -TOMY]

var·ied (vâr′ēd) *adj.* 1. Consisting of differing parts; diverse. 2. Partially or repeatedly altered, modified, etc. 3. Varicolored. —**var′ied·ly** *adv.*

varied thrush A bird (*Ixoreus naevius*) of western North America, resembling the robin, but having a dark band across the breast.

var·i·e·gate (vâr′ē·ə·gāt′) *v.t.* **·gat·ed, ·gat·ing** 1. To mark with different colors or tints; dapple; spot; streak. 2. To make varied; diversify. [< LL *variegatus,* pp. of *variegare* to variegate < *varius* various + *agere* to drive, do]

var·i·e·gat·ed (vâr′ē·ə·gā′tid) *adj.* 1. Having diverse colors; varied in color, as with streaks or blotches. 2. Having or exhibiting different forms, styles, or varieties.

var·i·e·ga·tion (vâr′ē·ə·gā′shən) *n.* 1. The act of variegating, or the state of being variegated. 2. Diversity of colors.

va·ri·e·tal (və·rī′ə·təl) *adj.* Of, pertaining to, or of the nature of a variety. —**va·ri′e·tal·ly** *adv.*

va·ri·e·ty (və·rī′ə·tē) *n.* *pl.* **·ties** 1. The state or character of being various or varied; diversity. 2. A collection of diverse things; an assortment of unlike objects. 3. The possession of different characteristics by one individual. 4. A limited class of things that differ in certain common peculiarities from a larger class to which they belong; sometimes, an example of such a sort or kind. 5. *Biol.* An individual or a group of individuals that differs from the type species in certain characters and is usually fertile with any other member of the species; a subdivision of a species. Abbr. *var.* [< MF *variété* < L *varietas* < *varius* various]

variety meat Meat consisting of organs or parts of organs, as liver, tongue, etc.

variety show A theatrical show, as in vaudeville, consisting of a series of short, diversified acts or numbers.

variety store *U.S.* A store selling a large assortment of notions and low-priced goods, as a five-and-ten-cent store.

var·i·form (vâr′ə·fôrm) *adj.* Of diverse form; having different shapes.

vario- Var. of VARI-.

va·ri·o·la (və·rī′ə·lə) *n.* *Pathol.* Smallpox. [< Med.L, pustule < L *varius* speckled]

va·ri·o·lar (və·rī′ə·lar, va·rī′ō·lous *adj.*

var·i·o·late (vâr′ē·ə·lāt′) *v.t.* **·lat·ed, ·lat·ing** To vaccinate with smallpox virus. —**var′i·o·la′tion, var′i·o·li·za′tion** *n.*

var·i·ole (vâr′ē·ōl) *n.* 1. A pockmark; foveola. 2. A spherule of variolite. [< Med.L *variola.* See VARIOLA.]

var·i·o·lite (vâr′ē·ə·līt′) *n.* A dense, finely crystalline variety of basalt, characterized by whitish spheroid granules. [< G *variolit* < Med.L *variola.* See VARIOLA.]

var·i·o·lit·ic (vâr′ē·ə·lit′ik) *adj.* 1. Of, pertaining to, or containing variolite. 2. Spotted.

var·i·o·loid (vâr′ē·ə·loid′) *Pathol. n.* A mild form of smallpox, occurring after vaccination or in persons who have had smallpox. —*adj.* 1. Resembling smallpox. 2. Pertaining to varioloid.

var·i·om·e·ter (vâr′ē·om′ə·tər) *n.* 1. An instrument used to determine variation of magnetic force, usually by means of a needle suspended within a magnetic field. 2. *Electr.* A variable inductance device composed of a fixed and a movable coil connected in series, and capable of controlling the strength of a current. Abbr. *var.* [< VARIO- + -METER]

var·i·o·rum (vâr′ē·ôr′əm, -ō′rəm) *adj.* Having notes or comments by different critics or editors. —*n.* An edition containing various versions of a text, usually with notes and commentary; also, a text or edition, especially the complete works of a classical author, containing various notes and comments: also **variorum edition.** [< L (*cum notis*) *variorum* (with the notes) of various persons]

var·i·ous (vâr′ē·əs) *adj.* 1. Characteristically different from one another; diverse. 2. More than one; several. 3. Many-sided; varying. 4. Having a diversity of appearance; variegated. 5. *Rare* Changeable; inconstant. Abbr. *var.* —**Syn.** See HETEROGENEOUS, SEVERAL. [< L *varius*] —**var′i·ous·ly** *adv.* —**var′i·ous·ness** *n.*

var·is·cite (var′ə·sīt) *n. Mineral.* A hydrous aluminum phosphate, $AlPO_4 \cdot 2H_2O$, occurring in green, crystalline crusts. [after *Variscia* in Saxony where first found]

var·i·type (vâr′i·tīp) *v.t. & v.i.* **·typed, ·typ·ing** To print by means of a Varityper. —**var′i·typ′ist** *n.*

Var·i·typ·er (vâr′i·tī′pər) *n.* A special typewriter for preparing copy in a wide variety of type styles: a trade name.

var·ix (vâr′iks) *n.* *pl.* **var·i·ces** (var′ə·sēz) 1. *Pathol.* **a** Permanent dilatation of a vein or other vessel of circulation. **b** A vessel thus distorted, as a varicose vein. 2. *Zool.* A ridge marking the former position of the outer lip of certain univalve shells. [< L, a varicose vein]

var·let (vär′lit) *n.* 1. *Archaic* A menial or subordinate; also, a page. 2. A knave or scoundrel. [< OF, groom. Doublet of VALET.]

var·let·ry (vär′lit·rē) *n.* *Archaic* The rabble; the mob.

var·mint (vär′mənt) *n.* *Dial.* Any obnoxious or pestiferous person or animal. [Alter. of VERMIN]

Var·na (vär′nä) A port city in eastern Bulgaria, on the Black Sea; pop. 184,400 (est. 1966): formerly (1949–58) *Stalin.*
var·nish (vär′nish) *n.* **1.** A solution of certain gums or resins in alcohol, linseed oil, etc., used to produce a shining, transparent coat on a surface. **2.** Any natural or artificial product or surface resembling varnish. **3.** Outward show, or any superficial polish, as of politeness. — *v.t.* **1.** To cover with varnish. **2.** To give a smooth or glossy appearance to. **3.** To improve the appearance of; polish. **4.** To hide by a deceptive covering or appearance; gloss over. [< OF *vernis* < Med.L *vernicium* sandarac < Med. Gk. *bernikē,* prob. after Gk. *Berenikē,* a city in Cyrenaica] — **var′nish·er** *n.*
varnish tree Any of various trees yielding a milky juice used as varnish.
Var·ro (var′ō), **Marcus Terentius,** 116–27? B.C., Roman scholar and author.
var·si·ty (vär′sə·tē) *n. pl.* **·ties 1.** The highest ranking team that represents a university, college, or school in any activity, as football, debating, etc. **2.** *Brit.* University. [Aphetic alter. of UNIVERSITY]
Var·u·na (var′oo·nə, vur′-) In early Hindu mythology, the god of the sky, creator and supreme god of the universe.
var·us (vār′əs) *n. pl.* **·us·es** *Pathol.* A malformation in which a bone or joint is turned away from its normal position. [< NL < L, growing inward, bandy-legged]
varve (värv) *n. Geol.* One of a series of stratified seasonal deposits of sedimentary material, often useful in determining the age of geological formations. [< Sw. *varv* layer]
var·y (vâr′ē) *v.* **var·ied, var·y·ing** *v.t.* **1.** To change the form, nature, substance, etc., of; modify. **2.** To cause to be different from one another. **3.** To impart variety to; diversify. **4.** *Music* To modify (a melody) by changes of rhythm, harmony, ornamentation, etc. — *v.i.* **5.** To become changed in form, nature, substance, etc. **6.** To be diverse or different; differ. **7.** To deviate; depart: with *from.* **8.** To change in succession; alternate. **9.** *Math.* To be subject to continual change. **10.** *Biol.* To undergo variation. — **Syn.** See CHANGE. [< OF *varier* < L *variare* < *varius* various, diverse] — **var′i·er** *n.*
vas (vas) *n. pl.* **va·sa** (vā′sə) *Biol.* A vessel or duct. [< L, vessel, dish]
vas- Var. of VASO-.
Va·sa·ri (vä·zä′rē), **Giorgio,** 1511–74, Italian painter, architect, and biographer of artists.
vas·cu·lar (vas′kyə·lər) *adj.* **1.** *Biol.* **a** Of, pertaining to, consisting of, or containing ducts for the transport of body liquids, as blood, lymph, etc. **b** Richly supplied with blood vessels. **2.** *Bot.* Containing vascular tissue. Also **vas′cu·lose** (-lōs), **vas′cu·lous** (-ləs). [< L *vasculum,* dim. of *vas* vessel] — **vas′cu·lar′i·ty** (-lar′ə·tē) *n.* — **vas′cu·lar·ly** *adv.*
vascular bundle *Bot.* A bundle (def. 4).
vascular tissue 1. *Biol.* Blood, lymph, and other body liquids having a characteristic cellular structure. **2.** *Bot.* Plant tissue, as in all flowering plants, forming ducts through which sap and other materials are conveyed.
vas·cu·lum (vas′kyə·ləm) *n. pl.* **·la** (-lə) **1.** A small covered case used in plant collecting. **2.** *Bot.* An ascidium. [< L, little vessel]
vas def·er·ens (vas def′ər·enz) *Anat.* The duct by which semen is conveyed from the epididymis to the seminal vesicles. [< NL < L *vas* vessel + *deferens* leading down]
vase (vās, vāz, väz) *n.* A decorative container, usually rounded and of greater height than width, used as an ornament or for holding flowers. [< F < L *vas* vessel]
va·sec·to·my (və·sek′tə·mē) *n. pl.* **·mies** *Surg.* Removal of a portion of the vas deferens. [< VAS- + -ECTOMY]
Vas·e·line (vas′ə·lēn, -lin) *n.* Proprietary name for a brand of petrolatum. Also **vas′e·line.**
Vash·ti (vash′tī) *n.* In the Bible, the queen of King Ahasuerus of Persia, whom he divorced because she refused to come to a royal banquet as commanded. *Esther* i 10–21.
Va·si·lev·ski (vä′sē·lyef′skē), **Alexander Mikhailovich,** born 1895, Soviet general; chief of staff in World War II.
vaso- combining form *Physiol.* **1.** A vessel, especially a blood vessel: *vasomotor.* **2.** The vas deferens. Also, before vowels, **vas-.** [< L *vas* vessel]
vas·o·con·stric·tor (vas′ō·kən·strik′tər) *n. Physiol.* A nerve, drug, etc., causing constriction of a blood vessel.
vas·o·di·la·tor (vas′ō·dī·lā′tər) *n. Physiol.* A nerve, drug, etc., causing dilatation of a blood vessel.
vas·o·mo·tor (vas′ō·mō′tər) *adj. Physiol.* Producing contraction or dilatation in the walls of vessels.
vas·sal (vas′əl) *n.* **1.** In the feudal system, one who held land of a superior lord by a feudal tenure; a liegeman or feudal tenant: also called *homager.* **2.** A dependent, retainer, or servant of any kind; a slave or bondman. — **Syn.** See SLAVE. — *adj.* **1.** Having the character of or pertaining to a vassal; tributary. **2.** Servile. [< OF < Med.L *vassallus* < LL *vassus* servant < Celtic]
vas·sal·age (vas′əl·ij) *n.* **1.** The state of being a vassal;

also, the duties, and obligations of a vassal. **2.** The feudal system. **3.** Servitude in general. **4.** Land held by feudal tenure; a fief. **5.** Vassals collectively.
vas·sal·ize (vas′əl·īz) *v.t.* **·ized, ·iz·ing** To reduce to vassalage; treat as a vassal.
vast (vast, väst) *adj.* **1.** Of great extent or size; immense; enormous; huge. **2.** Very great in number, quantity, or amount. **3.** Very great in degree, intensity, or importance. — *n.* **1.** *Chiefly Poetic* Boundless space; immensity. **2.** *Brit. Dial.* A great quantity. [< L *vastus* waste, empty, vast. Akin to WASTE.] — **vast′ly** *adv.* — **vast′ness** *n.*
vas·ti·tude (vas′tə·tood, -tyood, väs′-) *n.* **1.** The state or quality of being vast. **2.** A vast extent, space, etc.
vas·ti·ty (vas′tə·tē, väs′-) *n. pl.* **·ties** Vastness; immensity. [< F *vastité* < *vaste* large]
vast·y (vas′tē, väs′-) *adj.* **vast·i·er, vast·i·est** *Poetic* Vast.
vat (vat) *n.* A large vessel, tub, etc., for holding liquids, as dyeing materials. — *v.t.* **vat·ted, vat·ting** To put into a vat; treat in a vat. [OE *fæt*]
VAT or **V.A.T.** Value added tax (which see).
Vat. Vatican.
vat dye *Chem.* A dye applied in an alkali-soluble state and then oxidized, producing a fast color. — **vat-dyed** (vat′-did′) *adj.*
vat·ful (vat′fool) *n. pl.* **·fuls** As much as a vat will hold.
vat·ic (vat′ik) *adj.* Of or pertaining to a prophet; oracular; prophetic. Also **vat′i·cal.** [< L *vates* prophet]
Vat·i·can (vat′ə·kən) *n.* **1.** The papal palace in Vatican City, Rome. **2.** The papal government: distinguished from the *Quirinal.* — **Council of the Vatican 1.** An ecumenical council, 1869–70, at the Vatican, that declared the dogma of papal infallibility. **2.** An ecumenical council convened in 1962. [< L *Vaticanus* (*mons*) Vatican (hill) in Rome]
Vatican City A sovereign papal state within Rome, including the Vatican and St. Peter's Church, established June 10, 1929; 108.7 acres; pop. about 1,000: Italian *Città del Vaticano.*
Vat·i·can·ism (vat′ə·kən·iz′əm) *n.* The ecclesiastical system and beliefs based on the infallibility of the pope.
vat·i·cide (vat′ə·sīd) *n.* **1.** The killing of a prophet. **2.** One who has killed a prophet. [< L *vates* prophet + -CIDE]
va·tic·i·nal (və·tis′ə·nəl) *adj.* Prophetic.
va·tic·i·nate (və·tis′ə·nāt) *v.t. & v.i.* **·nat·ed, ·nat·ing** To prophesy; foretell. [< L *vaticinatus,* pp. of *vaticinari* to prophesy < *vates* prophet] — **va·tic′i·na′tion** *n.* — **va·tic′i·na′tor** *n.* — **va·tic′i·na·to·ry** (-nə·tôr′ē, -tō′rē) *adj.*
Vät·ter (vet′ər), **Lake** A lake in south central Sweden; 733 sq. mi.: formerly *Vetter. Swedish* **Vät·tern** (vet′ərn).
vau (väv) See VAV.
Vau·ban (vō·bän′), **Marquis de,** 1633–1707, Sébastien le Prestre, French military engineer.
vau·che·ri·a (vō·kir′ē·ä) *n.* Any of a genus (*Vaucheria*) of green algae growing in feltlike masses in shallow water and on muddy banks. [< NL, after Jean Pierre *Vaucher,* 1763–1841, Swiss botanist]
Vaud (vō) A Canton in west central Switzerland; 1,239 sq. mi.; pop. 429,512 (1960); capital, Lausanne: German *Waadt.*
vaude·ville (vōd′vil, vô′də·vil) *n.* **1.** A miscellaneous theatrical entertainment, as a variety show, popular in the early part of the 20th century; also, a theater presenting such shows. **2.** A street ballad; originally, a satirical or topical popular song. [< F, alter. of (*chanson de*) *Vau de Vire* (song of) the valley of the Vire river (in Normandy), where many light songs were composed]
vau·de·vil·lian (vōd·vil′yən, vô′de·vil′-) *n.* One who performs in or works in vaudeville.
Vau·dois (vō·dwä′) *n. pl.* **·dois** (-dwä′) **1.** An inhabitant, or the inhabitants collectively, of the Swiss canton of Vaud. **2.** The dialect of this canton.
Vau·dois (vō·dwä′) *n.pl.* The Waldenses.
Vaughan (vôn), **Henry,** 1622–95, Welsh poet.
Vaughan Wil·liams (vôn′ wil′yəms), **Ralph,** 1872–1958, English composer.
vault[1] (vôlt) *n.* **1.** An arched apartment or chamber; also, any subterranean compartment; cellar. **2.** An arched structure, as a ceiling or roof. **3.** Any vaultlike covering, as the sky. **4.** An arched roof of a cavity. **5.** An underground room or compartment for storing wine, valuables, etc. **6.** A strongly protected place for keeping valuables, as in a bank. **7.** A burial chamber. — *v.t.* **1.** To form with a vaulted roof; cover with or as with a vault. **2.** To construct in the form of a vault. [< OF *volte, vaute,* ult. < L *volutus,* pp. of *volvere* to turn about, roll]

VAULTS
a Cove or cloister. *b* Groin. *c* Underpitch or Welsh.

vault² (vôlt) *v.t.* **1.** To leap over, especially with the aid of a pole or with the hands resting on something. **2.** To mount (a horse, etc.) with a leap. — *v.i.* **3.** To leap; spring. **4.** To do a curvet. — *n.* **1.** A leap or bound, as one made with the aid of a pole. **2.** The curvet of a horse. [< OF *volter* to leap, gambol, ? ult. < L *volutus*. See VAULT¹.] — **vault′er** *n.*

vault·ing¹ (vôl′ting) *n.* **1.** Vaulted work, or vaults collectively. **2.** The work or art of building a vault.

vault·ing² (vôl′ting) *adj.* **1.** That overleaps. **2.** Unduly confident or presumptuous: *vaulting* ambition. **3.** That can be used in vaulting, as in gymnastics.

vault of heaven The sky.

vaunt (vônt, vänt) *v.i.* **1.** To speak boastfully. — *v.t.* **2.** To boast of. — *n.* Boastful assertion or ostentatious display. [< OF *vanter* < LL *vanitare* to brag < L *vanus* empty, vain] — **vaunt′er** *n.* — **vaunt′ing·ly** *adv.*

vaunt-cour·i·er (vänt′kŏŏr′ē-ər, vônt′-) *n.* **1.** *Archaic* A horseman or soldier sent in advance of an army. **2.** A forerunner; precursor; herald. [< F *avant-coureur*]

vaunt·ie (vôn′tē) *adj. Scot.* Boastful. Also **vaunt′y**, **vawnt′ie**.

v. aux. *Gram.* Auxiliary verb.

vav (väv) *n.* The sixth letter in the Hebrew alphabet: also spelled *vau*. Also **vaw.** See ALPHABET.

vav·a·sor (vav′ə-sôr, -sōr) *n.* **1.** The rank of a principal vassal next below a baron. **2.** A vassal holding lands from a great vassal, and having other vassals under him. Also **vav′a·sour** (-sŏŏr). [< OF *vavassour* < LL *vassus vassorum* vassal of vassals]

va·ward (vä′wərd) *adj. Obs.* Vanward. [Alter. of obs. *avantward* < AF *avantwarde*, OF *avantgarde* vanguard]

vb. Verb; verbal.

V.C. **1.** Veterinary Corps. **2.** Vice Chairman. **3.** Vice Chamberlain. **4.** Vice Chancellor. **5.** Vice Consul. **6.** Victoria Cross.

Vd *Chem.* Vanadium.

v.d. Various dates.

VD or **V.D.** Venereal disease.

Ve·a·dar (vē-ä-där′, vē′ä-där, vä′-) *n.* An intercalary month of the Hebrew year. See (Hebrew) CALENDAR.

veal (vēl) *n.* **1.** The flesh of a calf considered as food. **2.** *Obs.* A calf. — **bob veal** The flesh of a calf too young to be eaten. [< OF *viel* calf < L *vitellus*, dim. of *vitulus* calf]

Veb·len (veb′lən), **Thorstein Bunde**, 1857–1929, U.S. economist and sociologist.

vec·tor (vek′tər) *n.* **1.** *Math.* **a** A line representing a physical quantity that has magnitude and direction in space, as velocity and acceleration: distinguished from *scalar*. **b** A radius vector (which see). **2.** *Med.* A carrier of pathogenic microorganisms from one host to another. Abbr. V [< L, carrier < *vehere* to carry] — **vec·to·ri·al** (vek-tôr′ē-əl, -tō′rē-) *adj.*

Ved. Vedic.

Ve·da (vā′də, vē′-) *n.* **1.** One of the collections of Indian sacred writings, dating from the second millennium B.C., that form the Hindu scriptures; especially the Rig-Veda (which see), the **Yaj′ur-Ve′da** (yuj′ŏŏr-), containing liturgical formulas, the **Sa′ma-Ve′da** (sä′mə-), a group of hymns chiefly in honor of Indra, and the **A·thar′va-Ve′da** (ə-tar′və-), a large collection of charms and incantations. **2.** The Vedas collectively. [< Skt., knowledge] — **Ve·da·ic** (vi-dā′ik) *adj.* — **Ve·da·ism** (vā′də-iz′əm, vē′-) *n.*

Ve·dan·ta (vi-dän′tə, -dan′-) *n.* Any of several schools of Hindu religious philosophy based on the Upanishads; especially, the monistic system of Shankara, that teaches the worship of Brahma as the creator and soul of the universe. [< Skt. < *Veda* Veda + *anta* end] — **Ve·dan′tic** *adj.* — **Ve·dan′tism** *n.* — **Ve·dan′tist** *n.*

V-E Day (vē′ē′) May 8, the date of victory of the United Nations in Europe in World War II, 1945.

Ved·da (ved′ə) *n.* One of a primitive people of Ceylon, having both Caucasoid and Australoid traits, but not typically either. Also **Ved′dah.** [< Singhalese, hunter]

Ved·der (ved′ər), **Elihu**, 1836–1923, U.S. painter and illustrator.

ve·dette (vi·det′) *n.* **1.** A mounted sentinel placed in advance of an outpost. **2.** A small vessel used to watch the movements of the enemy: also **vedette boat.** Also spelled *vidette.* [< F < Ital. *vedetta*, alter. (after *vedere* to see) of *veletta*, dim. of Sp. *vela* vigil < L *vigilare* to watch]

Ve·dic (vā′dik, vē′-) *adj.* Of or pertaining to the Vedas or the language in which they were written. — *n.* Vedic Sanskrit.

Vedic Sanskrit See under SANSKRIT.

vee (vē) *n.* **1.** The letter V. **2.** Anything shaped like the letter V. **3.** *U.S. Slang* A five-dollar bill. — *adj.* V-shaped.

veer¹ (vir) *v.i.* **1.** *Naut.* To turn to another course; wear ship. **2.** To change direction by a clockwise motion, as the wind. **3.** To shift from one position to another; be variable or fickle. — *v.t.* **4.** To change the direction of. — *n.* A change in direction; a swerve. [< F *virer* to turn]

veer² (vir) *v.t. & v.i. Naut.* To let out or allow (a rope, anchor chain, etc.) to run out to a certain length. [< MDu. *vieren* to slacken]

veer·y (vir′ē) *n. pl.* **veer·ies** A melodious, tawny thrush (*Hylocichla fuscescens*) of eastern North America: also called *Wilson's thrush.* [Prob. imit.]

Ve·ga (vē′gə, vā′-) *n.* One of the 20 brightest stars, 0.04 magnitude; Alpha in the constellation Lyra. See STAR. [< Med.L < Arabic (*al-Nasr*) *al-Waqi* the falling (vulture)]

Ve·ga (vā′gə, *Sp.* bā′gä), **Lope de**, 1562–1635, Spanish dramatist and poet: full name **Lope Félix de Vega Car·pio** (kär′pyō).

veg·e·ta·ble (vej′ə·tə·bəl, vej′tə-) *n.* **1.** The edible part of any herbaceous plant, raw or cooked. ◆ See note under FRUIT. **2.** Any member of the vegetable kingdom; a plant. — *adj.* **1.** Pertaining to plants, especially garden or farm vegetables. **2.** Derived from, of the nature of, or resembling plants. **3.** Made from or consisting of vegetables. **4.** Resembling or like a vegetable in activity, etc.; dull; passive. [< OF < LL *vegetabilis* full of life < L *vegetare* to animate < *vegetus* vigorous, lively < *vegere* to be lively] — **veg′e·ta·bly** *adv.*

vegetable butter Any of numerous vegetable fats having a consistency similar to that of butter, as cocoa butter.

vegetable fibers Textile fibers such as cotton, flax, kapok, jute, etc.

vegetable ivory **1.** The ivory nut. **2.** The ivorylike substance obtained from this nut.

vegetable kingdom The division of nature that includes all organisms classified as plants. Compare ANIMAL KINGDOM, MINERAL KINGDOM.

vegetable marrow **1.** A plant (*Cucurbita pepo*), of the gourd family, having a tender, edible fruit. **2.** The fruit, esteemed as a vegetable. Also called *marrow squash.*

vegetable oil Any of various oils expressed from the seeds or fruits of plants and used in cooking, medicine, paints, and as lubricants, as corn oil, olive oil, cottonseed oil, linseed oil, etc.

vegetable oyster The salsify, a plant.

vegetable silk A cottonlike material obtained from the seed pods of a Brazilian tree (*Chorisia speciosa*) and used for stuffing cushions, etc.

vegetable sponge A loofah.

vegetable tallow Any of several fatty vegetable substances, variously derived, resembling tallow, and used for making candles, soap, etc.

vegetable wax Any wax derived from a plant.

veg·e·tal (vej′ə·tal) *adj.* **1.** Of or pertaining to plants or vegetables; vegetative. **2.** Characterizing those vital processes that are common to plants and animals, especially, as distinguished from sensation and volition. [< L *vegetus* lively, vigorous. See VEGETABLE.]

veg·e·tant (vej′ə·tənt) *adj.* **1.** Invigorating; vivifying; stimulating growth. **2.** Of the nature of plant life. [< F, or < L *vegetans, -antis*, ppr. of *vegere* to be active, lively]

veg·e·tar·i·an (vej′ə·târ′ē·ən) *adj.* **1.** Pertaining to or advocating vegetarianism. **2.** Exclusively vegetable, as a diet. — *n.* One who holds or practices vegetarianism: also **veg·e·tist** (vej′ə·tist).

veg·e·tar·i·an·ism (vej′ə·târ′ē·ən·iz′əm) *n.* The theory or practice of eating only vegetables and fruits. Also **veg′e·tism.**

veg·e·tate (vej′ə·tāt) *v.i.* **·tat·ed, ·tat·ing** **1.** To grow, as a plant. **2.** To live in a monotonous, passive way. **3.** *Pathol.* To increase abnormally in size. [< L *vegetatus*, pp. of *vegetare* to animate. See VEGETABLE.]

veg·e·ta·tion (vej′ə·tā′shən) *n.* **1.** The process of vegetating. **2.** Plant life in the aggregate. **3.** *Pathol.* An abnormal growth on the body. — **veg′e·ta′tion·al** *adj.*

veg·e·ta·tive (vej′ə·tā′tiv) *adj.* **1.** Of, pertaining to, or exhibiting the processes of plant life. **2.** Growing or capable of growing, as plants; productive. **3.** Having a mere physical or passive existence; showing little mental activity. **4.** Concerned with growth and nutrition. Also **veg·e·tive** (vej′ə·tiv). — **veg′e·ta′tive·ly** *adv.* — **veg′e·ta′tive·ness** *n.*

Ve·glia (ve′lyä) The Italian name for KRK.

ve·he·ment (vē′ə·mənt) *adj.* **1.** Arising from or marked by impetuosity of feeling or passion; ardent. **2.** Acting with great force or energy; energetic; violent; furious. [< OF < L *vehemens, -entis* impetuous, rash; ult. origin uncertain] — **ve′he·mence, ve′he·men·cy** *n.* — **ve′he·ment·ly** *adv.*

ve·hi·cle (vē′ə·kəl) *n.* **1.** Any contrivance fitted with wheels or runners for carrying something; a conveyance, as a car or sled. **2.** *Med.* An innocuous medium, as a liquid, with which is mixed some therapeutic substance that may be applied or administered more easily; an excipient. **3.** A medium, as oil, with which pigments are mixed in painting. **4.** Anything by means of which something else, as power, thought, etc., is transmitted or communicated. **5.** In the performing arts, anything, as a play, musical composition, etc., that permits the performer to display his particular powers or talents. [< F *véhicule* < L *vehiculum* < *vehere* to carry, ride] — **ve·hic·u·lar** (vi·hik′yə·lər) *adj.*

Ve·ii (vē′yī) An ancient Etruscan city in central Italy; destroyed by the Romans, 396 B.C.

veil (vāl) *n.* **1.** A piece of thin and light fabric, worn over the face or head for concealment, protection, or ornament.

2. Any piece of fabric used to conceal an object; a screen; curtain; mask. **3.** Anything that conceals from inspection; a disguise; pretext. **4.** *Biol. & Anat.* A velum. **5.** A caul. **6.** The life of a nun; also, vows made by a nun. — **to take the veil** To become a nun. — *v.t.* **1.** To cover with a veil. **2.** To hide; disguise. Also, *Obs., vail.* [< OF *veile* < L *velum* piece of cloth, sail] — **veil′er** *n.*

veil·ing (vā′ling) *n.* **1.** Material for veils. **2.** A veil.

vein (vān) *n.* **1.** *Anat.* One of the muscular, tubular vessels that convey blood to the heart. **2.** Loosely, any blood vessel. **3.** *Entomol.* One of the radiating supports of an insect's wing: also called *nervure.* **4.** *Bot.* One of the slender vascular bundles that form the framework of a leaf: also called *nervure.* **5.** *Geol.* **a** The filling of a fissure or fault in a rock, especially if deposited by aqueous solutions. **b** In mining, a lode. **c** A bed of ore parallel with the fault. **6.** A long, irregular, colored streak, as in wood; marble, etc. **7.** A distinctive trait, tendency, or disposition. **8.** A temporary state of mind; humor; mood. **9.** A cavity; cleft; fissure. **10.** A crevice or natural channel through which water trickles. — *v.t.* **1.** To furnish or fill with veins. **2.** To streak or ornament with veins. **3.** To extend over or throughout as veins. [< OF *veine* < L *vena* blood vessel] — **vein′y** *adj.*

veined (vānd) *adj.* **1.** Having, marked with, or abounding in veins. **2.** Marked with streaks of another color.

vein·ing (vā′ning) *n.* A network of veins.

vein·let (vān′lit) *n.* A small vein.

vein·stone (vān′stōn′) *n. Mining* Gangue.

vein·ule (vān′yōōl) *n.* A venule. [< VEIN + -ULE]

vel. Vellum.

Ve·la (vē′lə) A constellation, the Sail. See CONSTELLATION. [< L, sails]

ve·la·men (və·lā′mən) *n. pl.* **·lam·i·na** (-lam′ə·nə) **1.** *Anat.* Any membrane, covering, or integument. **2.** *Bot.* A spongy integument covering the aerial roots of certain orchids and arums. Also **vel·a·men·tum** (vel′ə·men′təm). [< L, covering < *velare* to veil]

ve·lar (vē′lər) *adj.* **1.** Of or pertaining to a velum, especially to the soft palate. **2.** *Phonet.* Formed with the back of the tongue touching or near the soft palate, as (k) in *cool,* (g) in *go:* sometimes *guttural.* — *n. Phonet.* **a** A velar consonant. **b** A back vowel. [< L *velaris* < *velum* a sail, curtain]

ve·lar·i·um (və·lâr′ē·əm) *n. pl.* **·lar·i·a** (-lâr′ē·ə) *Latin* The awning spread over the seats in ancient Roman theaters.

ve·lar·ize (vē′lə·rīz) *v.* **·ized, ·iz·ing** *Phonet. v.t.* To modify (a sound) by raising the back of the tongue toward the soft palate. — *v.i.* To be modified to a velar sound.

Ve·lás·quez (və·las′kwiz, *Sp.* bā·läs′käth) **Diego,** 1599–1660. Spanish painter: full name **Diego Rodríguez de Silva y Velásquez.** Also **Ve·láz·quez** (bā·läth′käth).

ve·late (vē′lāt, -lit) *adj. Biol.* Having a velum or veil. [< L *velatus,* pp. of *velare* to veil]

veldt (velt, felt) *n.* In South Africa, open country or grassland having few shrubs or trees. Also **veld.** [< Afrikaans *veld* < Du., field]

ve·li·tes (vē′lə·tēz) *n.pl.* In ancient Rome, light-armed soldiers used as skirmishers. [< L, pl. of *veles* foot soldier]

vel·le·i·ty (və·lē′ə·tē) *n. pl.* **·ties** *Rare* **1.** A very low degree of desire or volition. **2.** A mere wish. [< Med.L *velleitas, tatis* < L *velle* to wish]

vel·li·cate (vel′ə·kāt) *v.t. & v.i.* **·cat·ed, ·cat·ing** *Rare* To twitch or pluck. [< L *vellicatus,* pp. of *vellicare* to twitch, freq. of *vellere* to pluck] — **vel′li·ca′tion** *n.* — **vel′li·ca′tive** *adj.*

vel·lum (vel′əm) *n.* **1.** Fine parchment made from the skins of calves, used for expensive binding, printing, etc. **2.** A manuscript written on such parchment. **3.** Paper made to resemble parchment. *Abbr.* **vel.** [< OF *velin, vellin* < *veel, viel* calf. See VEAL.]

ve·lo·ce (vā·lō′chā) *adv. Music* Rapidly; in quick tempo; swiftly. [< Ital., swift]

ve·loc·i·pede (və·los′ə·pēd) *n.* **1.** An early form of bicycle or tricycle. **2.** A child's tricycle. **3.** A type of handcar. [< F *vélocipède* < L *velox, velocis* swift + *pes, pedis* foot]

ve·loc·i·ty (və·los′ə·tē) *n. pl.* **·ties** **1.** The state of moving or developing swiftly; rapidity; celerity; speed. **2.** The distance traveled by an object in a specified time. **3.** The time rate of motion in a stated direction; a vector quantity. *Abbr.* V [< L *velocitas, -tatis* < *velox* swift]

ve·lo·drome (vē′lə·drōme) *n.* A building housing a track for bicycle and motorcycle racing. [< F *vélodrome* < *vélo(cipède)* + Gk. *dromos* a running]

ve·lours (və·lōōr′) *n. pl.* **·lours** (-lōōrz) A soft, velvetlike, closely woven cotton or wool fabric having a short, thick pile. Also **ve·lour′.** [< F. See VELURE.]

ve·lou·té (və·lōō·tā′) *n. French* A rich white sauce made with chicken or veal stock. Also **sauce velouté.**

ve·lum (vē′ləm) *n. pl.* **·la** (-lə) **1.** *Biol.* A thin membranous covering or partition. **2.** *Anat.* The soft palate: see under PALATE. [< L]

ve·lure (və·lōōr′) *n.* **1.** Velvet, or a fabric resembling vel-

vet. **2.** A velvet or silk pad for smoothing a silk hat. — *v.t.* **·lured, ·lur·ing** To smooth with a velure. [< F *velours* < L *villosus* shaggy < *villus* shaggy hair]

ve·lu·ti·nous (və·lōō′tə·nəs) *adj. Bot.* Covered with close, soft hairs, like the pile of velvet; velvety. [< NL *velutinus* < Med.L *velutum,* var. of *velvetum.* See VELVET.]

vel·ver·et (vel′və·ret′) *n.* Cotton-backed velvet.

vel·vet (vel′vit) *n.* **1.** A fabric of silk, rayon, cotton, etc., having on one side a thick, short, smooth pile, formed either of loops (**pile velvet**) or of single threads (**cut velvet**). **2.** Anything resembling such a fabric in softness, smoothness, etc. **3.** The furry skin covering a growing antler. — *adj.* **1.** Made of velvet. **2.** Smooth and soft to the touch; velvety. [< Med.L *velvetum,* ult. < L *villus* shaggy hair]

velvet carpet A carpet having a pile cut in the manner of a Wilton. Also **tapestry velvet carpet.**

vel·vet·een (vel′və·tēn′) *n.* **1.** A cotton fabric with a short, close pile like velvet. **2.** *pl.* Clothes, especially trousers, made of this material. [< VELVET]

vel·vet·y (vel′vit·ē) *adj.* **1.** Smooth and soft like velvet. **2.** Mild and smooth to the taste: *velvety* liqueur.

Ven. **1.** Venerable. **2.** Venice.

ve·na (vē′nə) *n. pl.* **·nae** (-nē) *Anat.* A vein. [< L]

ve·na ca·va (vē′nə kā′və) *pl.* **ve·nae ca·vae** (vē′nē kā′vē) *Anat.* Either of the two great venous trunks emptying into the right atrium of the heart. For illustration see HEART. [< L, hollow vein]

ve·nal (vē′nəl) *adj.* **1.** Ready to sell honor or principle, or to accept a bribe; mercenary; purchasable. **2.** Subject to sordid bargaining or to corrupt influences; salable. **3.** Characterized by corruption and venality. [< L *venalis* < *venum* sale] — **ve′nal·ly** *adv.*

— **Syn. 1.** *Venal, purchasable, mercenary, hireling,* and *hack* characterize persons and acts motivated or undertaken for pecuniary profit. *Venal,* the most contemptuous of these words, accuses a person of outright corruption, as by the selling of the powers of his office: the *venal* bishop was deposed. A *purchasable* man can be bribed; this word is milder than *venal* to the extent that potential corruption is milder than actual: perhaps the commissioner is *purchasable. Mercenary* suggests that desire for personal gain outweighs a nobler motive: the company had a *mercenary* interest in the development of the vaccine. *Hireling* is similar, characterizing a person who serves another, as though for hire, when he should be guided by his own conscience: *hireling* historians have made Richard II a weakling, and Richard III a monster. *Hack* may often express commiseration rather than contempt, as for one who must do dull, tiresome, or monotonous work below his natural ability in order to live: a *hack* writer of popular songs. — **Ant.** honest, honorable, incorruptible, disinterested.

ve·nal·i·ty (vē·nal′ə·tē) *n. pl.* **·ties** The state or character of being venal; prostitution, as of talents, office, etc., for gain or reward. [< F *vénalité* or L *venalitas, -tatis*]

ve·nat·ic (vē·nat′ik) *adj. Archaic* Of, pertaining to, or used in hunting. Also **ve·nat′i·cal.** [< L *venaticus* < *venatus,* pp. of *venari* to hunt] — **ve·nat′i·cal·ly** *adv.*

ve·na·tion (vē·nā′shən) *n. Biol.* The arrangement of veins, as in a leaf, an insect wing, etc.: also called *nervation.*

vend (vend) *v.t.* **1.** To sell. **2.** To utter (an opinion); publish. — *v.i.* **3.** To be a vender. **4.** To be sold. [< F *vendre* < L *vendere* < *venum* sale + *dare* to give] — **ven·di·tion** (ven·dish′ən) *n.*

ven·dee (ven·dē′) *n. Law* The person or party to whom something is sold; a buyer.

Ven·dée (vän·dā′) A Department of western France, on the Bay of Biscay; 2,708 sq. mi.; pop. 421,250 (1968); capital, La Roche-sur-Yon; scene of a royalist revolt, 1793–95. — **Ven·de·an** (ven·dē′ən, vän-) *adj. & n.*

Ven·dé·miaire (vän·dā·myär′) *n.* The first month of the Republican calendar. See (Republican) CALENDAR. [< F < L *vindemia* vintage]

vend·er (ven′dər) *n.* One who sells, as a hawker or peddler. Also **ven′dor** (-dər).

ven·det·ta (ven·det′ə) *n.* A blood feud in which the relatives of the killed or injured person take vengeance on the offender or his relatives. [< Ital. < L *vindicta* vengeance]

vend·i·ble (ven′də·bəl) *adj.* Capable of being vended or sold; marketable. — *n.* A vendible thing. [< L *vendibilis* < *vendere* to sell] — **vend′i·bil′i·ty, vend′i·ble·ness** *n.* — **vend′i·bly** *adv.*

vending machine A coin-operated device that dispenses some product or packaged article.

ven·due (ven·dōō′, -dyōō′) *n.* A public sale or auction. [< F, orig. fem. pp. of *vendre* to sell]

ve·neer (və·nir′) *n.* **1.** A thin layer, as of choice wood, upon a commoner surface. **2.** Any of the thin layers glued together to strengthen plywood. **3.** Mere outside show or elegance: a *veneer* of good taste. — *v.t.* **1.** To cover (a surface) with veneer; overlay for decoration or finer finish. **2.** To glue together to form plywood. **3.** To conceal, as something disagreeable or coarse, with an attractive or deceptive surface. [Earlier *fineer* < G *furnieren* to inlay < F *fournir* to furnish] — **ve·neer′er** *n.*

ve·neer·ing (və-nir′ing) *n.* **1.** The art of applying veneer. **2.** Material used for veneer. **3.** A surface of veneer.

ven·e·punc·ture (ven′ə-pungk′chər) See VENIPUNCTURE.

Ve·ner (ve′nər), **Lake** A lake in SW Sweden; 2,141 sq. mi.: also *Väner.*

ven·er·a·ble (ven′ər-ə-bəl) *adj.* **1.** Meriting or commanding veneration; worthy of reverence: now usually implying age. **2.** Exciting reverential feelings because of sacred or historic associations. **3.** Revered: used as a title for an archdeacon in Anglican churches, and in the Roman Catholic Church, for one who has passed the first stage of canonization, prior to beatification. Abbr. *V., Ven.* [< OF < L *venerabilis* < *venerari* to revere] **— ven′er·a·ble·ness, ven′·er·a·bil′i·ty** *n.* **— ven′er·a·bly** *adv.*

ven·er·ate (ven′ə-rāt) *v.t.* **·at·ed, ·at·ing** To look upon or regard with respect and deference; revere. [< L *veneratus,* pp. of *venerari* to revere]
— Syn. *Venerate, revere, reverence, worship,* and *adore* mean to regard with profound respect mingled with other feelings. We *venerate* that which we judge objectively to be of great worth, as a great man, our ancestors, a holy person, or a sacred object. *Revere* and *reverence* imply respect, to which have been added personal affection and awe; *revere* is chiefly applied to persons or to a deity, and *reverence,* to places or objects: to *revere* God and the saints, to *reverence* a holy shrine. In strict usage, we *worship* or *adore* only that which we consider divine; *worship* refers to participation in religious ceremonies, and *adore,* to the sense of personal gratitude for divine favor which the worshiper feels. In extended use, we *worship* a person regarded as having divine qualities, and *adore* a person who excites our ardent admiration. **— Ant.** contemn, despise, disdain.

ven·er·a·tion (ven′ə-rā′shən) *n.* **1.** The act of venerating, or the state of being venerated. **2.** A feeling of profound respect and awe; reverence.

ve·ne·re·al (və-nir′ē-əl) *adj.* **1.** Pertaining to or proceeding from sexual intercourse. **2.** Communicated by sexual relations with an infected person: a *venereal* disease. **3.** Pertaining to or curative of diseases so communicated. **4.** Infected with venereal disease. [< L *venereus* < *Venus, -eris,* the goddess of love]

venereal disease *Pathol.* One of several diseases communicated by sexual intercourse, as syphilis, gonorrhea, and chancroid. Abbr. *VD, V.D.*

ve·ne·re·ol·o·gy (və-nir′ē-ol′ə-jē) *n.* The study and treatment of venereal diseases. **— ve·ne′re·ol′o·gist** *n.*

ven·er·y¹ (ven′ər-ē) *n. pl.* **·er·ies** *Archaic* Sexual indulgence, especially when excessive. [< L *Venus, -eris,* the goddess of love]

ven·er·y² (ven′ər-ē) *n. pl.* **·er·ies** *Archaic* The hunting of game; also, the sport of hunting. [< F *venerie* < *vener* < L *venari* to hunt]

ven·e·sec·tion (ven′ə-sek′shən) *n. Surg.* Phlebotomy. [< Med.L *venae sectio* cutting of a vein]

Ven·e·ti (ven′ə-tī) *n.pl.* **1.** An ancient Celtic people of NW Gaul, conquered by Caesar in 56 B.C. **2.** An ancient people of NE Italy, friendly to Rome.

Ve·ne·ti·a (və-nē′shē-ə -shə) **1.** A former Region of NE Italy, now divided into the regions of Trentino-Alto Adige, Friuli-Venezia Giulia, and Venetia. **2.** A Region of NE Italy: 7,098 sq. mi.: pop. 3,846,562 (1967); capital, Venice. Also **Ve·ne·to** (vā′nā-tō).

Ve·ne·tian (və-nē′shən) *adj.* Pertaining to Venice, its inhabitants, art, etc. **—** *n.* A native of Venice.

Venetian blind A flexible screen commonly hung over the interior surface of a window, consisting of overlapping horizontal slats that can be tilted and raised or lowered by attached cords. Compare JALOUSIE.

Venetian carpet A worsted carpet for stairs and hallways, commonly of a simple striped pattern.

Venetian glass A delicate and fine glassware made at or near Venice.

Venetian school A school of painting originating in and near Venice in the 15th century and distinguished by richness of coloring, as in the work of Titian, Tintoretto, Giorgione, etc.

Ve·ne·zia (vā-nā′tsyä) **1.** The Italian name for VENICE. **2.** A former Region of NE Italy, now generally corresponding with modern Venetia.

Venezia Giu·lia (jōō′lyä) A former region of NE Italy; divided between Italy, Yugoslavia, and the Free Territory of Trieste, 1947.

Ven·e·zue·la (ven′ə-zwā′lə, -zwē′lə; *Sp.* bā′nā-swä′lä) A Republic in northern South America; 352,143 sq. mi.; pop. 10,398,907 (1970); capital, Caracas. **— Ven′e·zue′lan** *adj. & n.*

Venezuela, Gulf of An inlet of the Caribbean in NE Venezuela, touching on northern Colombia, and connecting with Lake Maracaibo; about 75 mi. long, 150 mi. wide: also *Gulf of Maracaibo.*

ven·geance (ven′jəns) *n.* The act of revenging; retribution for a wrong or injury. **— Syn.** See REVENGE. **— with a vengeance** With great force or violence; extremely; to an unusual extent. [< AF < OF *venger* to avenge < L *vindicare* to defend, avenge < *vindex, vindicis* claimant, protector]

venge·ful (venj′fəl) *adj.* **1.** Seeking to inflict vengeance;

vindictive. **2.** Serving to inflict vengeance. **— venge′ful·ly** *adv.* **— venge′ful·ness** *n.*

veni- *combining form* Vein: venipuncture; also, vein in the earth. [< L *vena* vein]

ve·ni·al (vē′nē-əl, vēn′yəl) *adj.* **1.** *Theol.* That may be easily pardoned or forgiven: distinguished from *mortal:* venial sin. **2.** Excusable; pardonable. [< OF < L *venialis* < *venia* forgiveness, mercy] **— ve′ni·al′i·ty** (-al′ə-tē), **ve′ni·al·ness** *n.* **— ve′ni·al·ly** *adv.*
— Syn. *Venial, excusable,* and *pardonable* are said of sins, errors, or faults that may be forgiven. *Venial* means trifling and not requiring great consideration. *Excusable* and *pardonable* may point to that which is serious in itself, but which may be forgiven because of extenuating circumstances.

Ven·ice (ven′is) A port commune in NE Italy, built on 118 islands in the **Lagoon of Venice,** the NW part of the **Gulf of Venice,** the northern part of the Adriatic; pop. 366,800 (1967): Italian *Venezia.*

ven·i·punc·ture (ven′ə-pungk′chər) *n. Surg.* The operation of puncturing a vein: also spelled *venepuncture.* [< VENI- + PUNCTURE]

ve·ni·re (vi-nī′rē) *n. Law* A writ issued to the sheriff for summoning persons to serve as a jury. Also **ve·ni′re fa·ci·as** (fā′shi·as′) [< L *venire facias,* that you cause to come]

ve·ni·re·man (vi-nī′rē-mən) *n. pl.* **·men** (-mən) One summoned to serve on a jury under a venire.

ven·i·son (ven′ə-zən, -sən; *Brit.* ven′zən) *n.* Deer flesh used for food. [< F *venaison* < L *venatio, -onis* hunting < *venatus,* pp. of *venari* to hunt]

venison bird *Canadian* The Canada jay.

Ve·ni·te (vi-nī′tē) *n.* The 95th psalm (in the Vulgate and Douai versions, the 94th): from its first word. [< L, come, imperative of *venire* to come]

ve·ni, vi·di, vi·ci (vē′nī, vī′dī, vī′sī; wā′nē, wē′dē, wē′kē) *Latin* I came, I saw, I conquered: words used by Julius Caesar to report his victory over Pharnaces II.

Ve·ni·ze·los (ve′nē-ze′lôs), **Eleutherios,** 1864–1936, Greek statesman born in Crete; premier 1910–15, 1917–20, 1928–32.

ven·om (ven′əm) *n.* **1.** The poisonous liquid secreted by certain animals, as serpents and scorpions, and introduced into the victim by a bite or sting. **2.** Malice; malignity; spite. **3.** *Rare* Any poison. [< OF *venim* < L *venenum* poison] **— ven′om·er** *n.*

ven·om·ous (ven′əm·əs) *adj.* **1.** Having glands secreting venom. **2.** Able to inflict a poisonous wound by biting or stinging. **3.** Malignant; spiteful. **— ven′om·ous·ly** *adv.* **— ven′om·ous·ness** *n.*

ve·nose (vē′nōs) *adj.* **1.** Having numerous or prominent veins, as a leaf; veiny. **2.** Venous. [< L *venosus*]

ve·nos·i·ty (vi-nos′ə-tē) *n.* **1.** The state or quality of being venous. **2.** *Physiol.* A plentiful supply of venous blood.

ve·nous (vē′nəs) *adj.* **1.** Of, pertaining to, or marked with veins. **2.** *Physiol.* Designating the blood carried by the veins, distinguished from arterial blood by its darker color, absence of oxygen, and presence of carbon dioxide. [< L *venosus* < *vena* vein] **— ve′nous·ly** *adv.* **— ve′nous·ness** *n.*

vent (vent) *n.* **1.** An opening, commonly small, for the passage of liquids, gases, etc. **2.** Utterance; expression: chiefly in the phrase **to give vent to. 3.** *Zool.* The external opening of the alimentary canal, especially of animals below mammals; the anus. **4.** A touchhole. **—** *v.t.* **1.** To give expression to: often with *on:* to *vent* one's rage on the cat. **2.** To relieve, as by giving vent to emotion. **3.** To permit to escape from an opening. [ME *fent* < OF *fente* cleft < *fendre* to cleave < L *findere* to split] **— ven′ter** *n.*

vent·age (ven′tij) *n.* **1.** A small opening. **2.** A finger hole in a musical instrument. [< VENT]

ven·tail (ven′tāl) *n.* The lower adjustable front of a medieval helmet. [< OF *ventaile* < *vent* wind]

ven·ter (ven′tər) *n.* **1.** The belly or stomach. **2.** Any protuberant part. **3.** *Law* The womb of a wife or mother. **4.** A hollowed part, as of a bone. [< AF < L, stomach]

ven·ti·duct (ven′tə-dukt) *n.* An air passage; especially, a ventilating passage. [< L *ventus* wind + DUCT]

ven·ti·la·ble (ven′tə-lə-bəl) *adj.* That can be ventilated.

ven·ti·late (ven′tə-lāt) *v.t.* **·lat·ed, ·lat·ing 1.** To produce a free circulation of air in; admit fresh air into. **2.** To provide with a vent. **3.** To make widely known; expose to examination and discussion. **4.** To oxygenate, as blood. [< L *ventilatus,* pp. of *ventilare* to fan < *ventus* wind] **— ven′ti·la′tion** *n.* **— ven′ti·la′tive** *adj.*

ven·ti·la·tor (ven′tə-lā′tər) *n.* A device or arrangement for supplying fresh air. **— ven′ti·la·to′ry** (-lə-tôr′ē, -tō′rē) *adj.*

Ven·tôse (vän-tōz′) *n.* The sixth month of the Republican calendar. See (Republican) CALENDAR. [< F < L *ventosus* windy]

ven·tral (ven′trəl) *adj.* **1.** *Anat.* **a** Of, pertaining to, or situated on or near the abdomen. **b** On or toward the lower or anterior part of the body. **2.** *Bot.* Pertaining to the surface of a petal, carpel, etc., that faces the center of a flower. **—** *n.* A ventral fin. Abbr. *v.* [< L *ventralis* < *venter, ventris* belly] **— ven′tral·ly** *adv.*

ventral fin Either of the paired fins on the underside of fishes, homologous with the hind limb of higher vertebrates. For illustration see FISH.

ven·tri·cle (ven′trə·kəl) *n. Anat.* **1.** One of the two lower chambers of the heart, from which blood received from the atria is forced into the arteries. **2.** Any of various cavities in the body, as of the brain, the spinal cord, etc. For illustration see HEART. [< L *ventriculus*, dim. of *venter, ventris* belly]

ven·tri·cose (ven′trə·kōs) *adj.* **1.** Having a protruding belly. **2.** Swelling out or inflated on one side or in the middle; bellied. Also **ven′tri·cous** (-kəs). [< NL *ventricosus* < L *venter, ventris* belly]   — **ven′tri·cos′i·ty** (-kos′ə·tē) *n.*

ven·tric·u·lar (ven·trik′yə·lər) *adj.* **1.** Of, pertaining to, or of the nature of a ventricle. **2.** Swollen and distended.

ven·tric·u·lus (ven·trik′yə·ləs) *n. Anat.* **1.** The stomach. **2.** A ventricle. [< L *ventriculus*. See VENTRICLE.]

ven·tri·lo·qui·al (ven′trə·lō′kwē·əl) *adj.* Pertaining to, resembling, or practicing ventriloquism. Also **ven·tril·o·qual** (ven·tril′ō·kwəl), **ven·tril′o·quous.** — **ven′tri·lo·qui·al·ly** *adv.*

ven·tril·o·quism (ven·tril′ə·kwiz′əm) *n.* The art of speaking in such a manner that the sounds seem to come from some source other than the person speaking. Also **ven·tril′o·quy** (-kwē). [< L *ventriloquus* < *venter* belly + *loqui* to speak] — **ven·tril′o·quist** *n.* — **ven·tril′o·quis′tic** *adj.*

ven·tril·o·quize (ven·tril′ə·kwīz) *v.t. & v.i.* **·quized, ·quiz·ing** To speak as a ventriloquist. Also *Brit.* **ven·tril′o·quise.**

Ven·tris (ven′tris), **Michael,** 1922–56, English classical scholar; deciphered Minoan Linear B.

ventro- *combining form Anat.* The abdomen; related to or near the abdomen; ventral. [< L *venter, ventris* belly]

Ven·tu·ra (ven·toor′ə) See SAN BUENAVENTURA.

ven·ture (ven′chər) *v.* **·tured, ·tur·ing** *v.t.* **1.** To expose to chance or risk; hazard; stake. **2.** To run the risk of; brave. **3.** To express at the risk of denial or refutation: to *venture* a suggestion. — *v.i.* **4.** To take a risk; dare. — *n.* **1.** An undertaking attended with risk or danger; a risk; hazard; especially, a business investment. **2.** That which is ventured; especially, property risk. — **at a venture** At hazard; offhand. [Aphetic form of ADVENTURE] — **ven′tur·er** *n.*

ven·ture·some (ven′chər·səm) *adj.* **1.** Bold; daring. **2.** Involving hazard; risky. — **ven′ture·some·ly** *adv.* — **ven′ture·some·ness** *n.*

Ven·tu·ri tube (ven·toor′ē) **1.** A short tube with a constricted part, connected with a pipeline to permit computation of the rate of flow by the pressure difference between the narrowed segment and the main diameter of the pipe. **2.** *Aeron.* A similar device with flaring ends, set parallel to the airflow, and used in conjunction with a Pitot tube to measure air speed or furnish power to operate a gyroscope or injector. [after G. B. *Venturi*, 1746–1822, Italian physicist]

ven·tur·ous (ven′chər·əs) *adj.* **1.** Adventurous; willing to take risks and brave dangers; bold. **2.** Hazardous; risky; dangerous. — **ven′tur·ous·ly** *adv.* — **ven′tur·ous·ness** *n.*

ven·ue (ven′yōo) *n. Law* **1.** The place where a crime is committed or a cause of action arises; also, the county or political division from which the jury must be summoned and in which the trial must be held. **2.** The clause indicating the county in which the proceeding is pending. **3.** A clause in an affidavit, stating where it was made and sworn to. — **change of venue** The change of the place of trial. [< OF, orig. fem. pp. of *venir* to come < L *venire*]

ven·ule (ven′yōol) *n.* **1.** *Anat.* A small vein. **2.** *Zool.* A small branch of a vein in an insect's wing. Also *veinule.* [< L *venula*, dim. of *vena* vein] — **ven′u·lar** (-yə·lər) *adj.*

ven·u·lose (ven′yə·lōs) *adj.* Having numerous veinlets, as a leaf. Also **ven′u·lous** (-ləs). [< VENULE]

Ve·nus (vē′nəs) In Roman mythology, the goddess of love, spring, bloom, and beauty: identified with the Greek *Aphrodite.* — *n.* **1.** The sixth largest planet of the solar system and second in order from the sun. See PLANET. **2.** A statue or painting of Venus. **3.** A lovely woman. **4.** *Obs.* In alchemy, copper. [< L]

Ve·nus·berg (vē′nəs·bûrg, *Ger.* vā′nŏŏs·berkh) In medieval German legend, a mountain in the dark recesses of which Venus lured men to sensuous pleasures. See TANNHÄUSER.

Venus of Mi·lo (mē′lō) A marble statue of Venus, nude above the thighs and with the arms missing, discovered in 1820 on the island of Milo and later placed in the Louvre. Also **Venus de Milo, Venus of Melos.**

Ve·nus's-comb (vē′nəs·iz·kōm′) *n.* A European plant (*Scandix pecten-veneris*) with white flowers in numerous umbels, and lobed leaves suggestive of a comb: often called *shepherd's-needle, devil's-darning-needle.*

Ve·nus's flytrap (vē′nəs·iz flī′trap′) *n.* A plant (*Dionaea muscipula*), with clustered leaves whose spiked blades instantly close upon insects lighting upon them, found native chiefly in the sandy bogs of eastern North and South Carolina. Also **Venus flytrap.**

Ve·nus's-gir·dle (vē′nəs·iz·gûr′dəl) *n.* A ctenophore of warm seas (*Cestus veneris*), having a transparent body that shimmers with blue, green, or violet colors.

Ve·nus's-hair (vē′nəs·iz·hâr′) *n.* A maidenhair fern (*Adiantum capillus-veneris*) having a black stripe and branches.

ver. 1. Verse(s). **2.** Version.

ver·a (ver′ə, var′ə) *adj. & adv. Scot.* Very.

ve·ra·cious (və·rā′shəs) *adj.* **1.** Habitually disposed to speak the truth; truthful. **2.** Conforming to or expressing the truth; true; accurate. [< L *verax, veracis* < *verus* true] — **ve·ra′cious·ly** *adv.* — **ve·ra′cious·ness** *n.*

ve·rac·i·ty (və·ras′ə·tē) *n. pl.* **·ties 1.** The habitual regard for truth; truthfulness; honesty. **2.** Agreement with truth; accuracy. **3.** That which is true; truth. [< F *véracité* < L *verax, veracis.* See VERACIOUS.]

VENUS'S
FLYTRAP

Ve·ra·cruz (ver′ə·krōoz′, *Sp.* bā′rä·krōos′, (To 14 inch--krōoth′) **1.** A State in eastern Mexico; 27,752 es high) sq. mi.; pop. 2,727,899 (1960); capital, Jalapa. **2.** Its chief city, a port on the Gulf of Mexico; pop. 144,232 (1960): officially **Veracruz Lla·ve** (yä′vä).

ve·ran·da (və·ran′də) *n.* An open portico or balcony, usually roofed, along the outside of a building; a porch or stoop. Also **ve·ran′dah.** [< Hind. *varandā* < Pg. *varanda* railing, balustrade, prob. < *vara* rod, pole < L *vara* forked pole]

ve·rat·ric acid (və·rat′rik) *Chem.* A colorless crystalline acid, $C_9H_{10}O_4$, contained in sabadilla seeds and also made synthetically. [< L *veratrum* hellebore]

ve·rat·ri·dine (və·rat′rə·dēn, -din) *n. Chem.* A yellowish, amorphous alkaloid, $C_{36}H_{51}O_{11}N$, contained in sabadilla seeds. Also **ve·rat′ri·din** (-din). [< L *veratrum* hellebore + -ID(E) + -INE²]

ver·a·trine (ver′ə·trēn, -trin) *n. Chem.* A white or grayish white, extremely poisonous mixture of alkaloids, contained in sabadilla seeds: formerly used in medicine as a counter-irritant ointment. Also **ve·ra·tri·a** (və·rā′trē·ə), **ver′a·trin** (-trin), **ver′a·tri′na** (-trī′nə). [< L *veratrum* hellebore + -INE²]

ver·a·trize (ver′ə·trīz) *v.t.* **·trized, ·triz·ing** To treat with veratrine so as to produce its toxic effects.

verb (vûrb) *n.* **1.** *Gram.* The part of speech that expresses existence, action, or occurrence, as the English words *be, collide, think.* **2.** *Gram.* Any word or construction functioning similarly. **3.** *Ling.* One of a form class, the members of which can take inflectional endings for person, tense, and aspect, or can occupy certain syntactic positions in sentences and phrases, or can be identified by a combination of morphological and syntactic criteria. In English, *say, says, saying, said* are verbal forms by virtue of inflection, and *I am saying my prayers* illustrates a typical syntactic position for a verb such as *say.* Abbr. *v., vb.* [< F *verbe* < L *verbum* word. Akin to WORD.]

ver·bal (vûr′bəl) *adj.* **1.** Of, pertaining to, or connected with words. **2.** Concerned with words rather than the ideas they convey: *verbal* distinctions. **3.** Expressed orally; not written: a *verbal* contract. **4.** Having word corresponding with word; literal: a *verbal* translation. **5.** *Gram.* A Partaking of the nature of or derived from a verb: a *verbal* noun. **b** Used to form verbs: a *verbal* prefix. — *n. Gram.* A verb form that functions as a substantive (gerund and infinitive) or as a modifier (present and past participles and infinitive), but retains some of the characteristics of a verb. Abbr. *vb.* [< F < LL *verbalis* < L *verbum* word] — **ver′bal·ly** *adv.*

  — **Syn.** (adj.) **2.** *Verbal, oral,* and *vocal* relate to utterance by mouth. In strict usage, *verbal* refers to spoken or written words, and *oral,* to spoken words only: a *verbal* dispute, an *oral* examination. However, the distinction is often blurred, so that we speak of a *verbal* agreement, rather than of an *oral* agreement. *Oral* and *verbal* always imply communication; *vocal* refers to the use of the voice, whether for communicating thought or not: a *vocal* exercise, a *vocal* defect.

ver·bal·ism (vûr′bəl·iz′əm) *n.* **1.** A verbal expression. **2.** A meaningless form of words. **3.** Wordiness; verbiage.

ver·bal·ist (vûr′bəl·ist) *n.* **1.** One who deals with words rather than facts or ideas. **2.** One who is skilled in the use and meaning of words.

ver·bal·ize (vûr′bəl·īz) *v.* **·ized, ·iz·ing** *v.t.* **1.** To express in words. **2.** *Gram.* To make a verb of; change into a verb. — *v.i.* **3.** To speak or write verbosely. **4.** To express oneself in words. — **ver′bal·i·za′tion** *n.* — **ver′bal·iz′er** *n.*

ver·ba·tim (vər·bā′tim, -təm) *adj. & adv.* In the exact words; word for word. [< LL < L *verbum* word]

ver·ba·tim et lit·e·ra·tim (vər·bā′tim et lit′ə·rā′tim) *Latin* Word for word and letter for letter.

ver·be·na (vər·bē′nə) *n.* Any of a genus (*Verbena*) of American garden plants having dense terminal spikes of showy flowers. [< L, foliage, vervain. Doublet of VERVAIN.]

ver·be·na·ceous (vûr′bə·nā′shəs) *adj. Bot.* Belonging to the vervain family of herbs, shrubs, and trees. [< NL *Verbenaceae* family name < L *verbena* vervain]

ver·bi·age (vûr′bē·ij) *n.* **1.** Excess of words. **2.** Wordiness; verbosity. — **Syn.** See CIRCUMLOCUTION. [< F < *verbier* to gabble < *verbe.* See VERB.]

---

verb·i·fy (vûr′bə·fī) *v.t.* **·fied, ·fy·ing** To form into or use as a verb.

ver·big·er·ate (vər·bij′ə·rāt) *v.i.* **·at·ed, ·at·ing** *Psychiatry* To repeat meaningless words or phrases over and over. [< L *verbigerare* to chatter, babble < *verbum* word + *gerere* to carry on, conduct] **— ver·big′er·a′tion** *n.*

ver·bose (vər·bōs′) *adj.* Using or containing a wearisome and unnecessary number of words; wordy. [< L *verbosus* < *verbum* word] **— ver·bose′ly** *adv.* **— ver·bose′ness** *n.* **— Syn.** diffuse, prolix. Compare CIRCUMLOCUTION.

ver·bos·i·ty (vər·bos′ə·tē) *n. pl.* **·ties** The state or quality of being verbose; wordiness. **— Syn.** See CIRCUMLOCUTION.

ver·bo·ten (fer·bōt′n) *adj. German* Forbidden.

verb phrase *Gram.* A finite verb form, consisting of a principal verb and an auxiliary or auxiliaries.

ver·bum sa·pi·en·ti est (vûr′bən sat sā′pē·en′tī est′) *Latin* A word to the wise is sufficient. Abbr. *verbum sap.*

Ver·cin·get·o·rix (vûr′sin·jet′ər·iks), died 45? B.C., Gallic chieftain; led a rebellion against Julius Caesar; executed.

ver·dant (vûr′dənt) *adj.* **1.** Green with vegetation; covered with grass or green leaves; fresh. **2.** Unsophisticated. [< F *verdoyant,* ppr. of *verdoyer* to grow green, ult. < L *viridis* green] **— ver′dan·cy** *n.* **— ver′dant·ly** *adv.*

verd antique (vûrd) **1.** A mottled, dark green, impure variety of serpentine, often used as a decorative stone. **2.** Any of various similar minerals. **3.** Verdigris. [< OF *verd antique* ancient green]

Verde (vûrd), **Cape** The westernmost point of Africa, in Senegal, a peninsula about 20 miles long: also *Cape Vert.*

ver·der·er (vûr′dər·ər) *n.* An officer in charge of the royal forests in early England. Also **ver′der·or.** [< AF *verder,* OF *verdier* < Med.L *viridarius* < L *viridis* green]

Ver·di (ver′dē), **Giuseppe,** 1813–1901, Italian operatic composer.

ver·dict (vûr′dikt) *n.* **1.** The decision of a jury in an action. **2.** A conclusion expressed; judgment; decision. [< AF *verdit,* OF *voirdit* < L *vere dictum* truly said < *verus* true + *dictum,* pp. of *dicere* to say; later refashioned after L]

ver·di·gris (vûr′də·grēs, -gris) *n.* **1.** A green basic acetate of copper obtained by treating copper with acetic acid, used as a pigment, a fungicide, in ceramics, and as a reagent. **2.** The green or bluish patina formed on copper, bronze, or brass surfaces after long exposure to the air. [< OF *verd de Grice, vert de Grece,* lit., green of Greece]

ver·din (vûr′din) *n.* A small, brightly-colored titmouse (*Auriparus flaviceps*) with a yellow head, of the southwestern United States and northern Mexico. [< F, yellowhammer]

ver·di·ter (vûr′də·tər) *n.* One of two basic copper carbonate pigments, prepared by grinding azurite (**blue verditer**) or malachite (**green verditer**). [< OF *verd de terre,* lit., green of earth]

Ver·dun (vər·dun′, *Fr.* ver·dœn′) A town in NE France, on the Meuse; scene of several battles of World War I, 1916; pop. 22,013 (1968). Also **Verdun-sur-Meuse** (-sür-mœz′).

ver·dure (vûr′jər) *n.* The fresh greenness of growing vegetation; also, such vegetation itself. [< F < *verd* green < L *viridis*]

ver·dur·ous (vûr′jər·əs) *adj.* Covered with verdure; verdant. **— ver′dur·ous·ness** *n.*

ver·e·cund (ver′ə·kund) *adj. Rare* Modest; bashful; coy; shy. [< L *verecundus*]

Ve·ree·ni·ging (fə·rē′nə·khing) A city in the southern Transvaal, South Africa; site of the signing of the treaty concluding the Boer War, 1902; pop. 78,835 (1960).

Ver·ein (fer·īn′) *n. German* A society; association.

Ve·re·shcha·gin (vyi·ryish·chä′gin), **Vasili Vasilevich,** 1842–1904, Russian painter.

verge[1] (vûrj) *n.* **1.** The extreme edge of something having defined limits; brink; margin. **2.** The point at which some action, condition, or state is likely to occur: on the *verge* of bankruptcy. **3.** A bounding or enclosing line; a boundary; also, the space enclosed. **4.** A rod, wand, or staff as a symbol of authority or emblem of office. **5.** In watchmaking, the spindle of a balance wheel, especially in an old-fashioned vertical escapement. **6.** *Archit.* **a** A column shaft. **b** The projecting edge of the tiling on a gable. **7.** In old English law: **a** The area over which the authority of an official extended. **b** A stick or wand held by tenants while swearing fealty to their lord. **— v.i. verged, verg·ing 1.** To come near; approach; border: usually with *on*: His speech *verges* on the chaotic. **2.** To form the limit or verge. [< F, rod, stick < L *virga* twig]

verge[2] (vûrj) *v.i.* **verged, verg·ing** To slope; tend; incline. [< L *vergere* to bend, turn]

verg·er (vûr′jər) *n.* **1.** An official who carries a verge before a scholastic, legal, or ecclesiastical dignitary; especially, in English cathedrals and collegiate churches, one who carries the mace before the dean or canons. **2.** *Brit.* One in charge of the interior of a church; usher. [< F < *verge* rod]

Ver·gil (vûr′jil) Anglicized name of **Publius Vergilius Maro** (mä′rō), 70–19 B.C., Roman epic poet. Also *Virgil.*

Ver·gil·i·an (vər·jil′ē·ən) *adj.* Pertaining to or in the style of Vergil: also spelled *Virgilian.*

ver·glas (ver·glä′) *n. French* A thin, slippery coating of ice on rock: a mountaineering term.

ve·rid·i·cal (və·rid′i·kəl) *adj.* Telling or expressing the truth; truthful; accurate. Also **ve·rid′ic.** [< L *veridicus* speaking the truth < *verus* true + *dicere* to say] **— ve·rid′i·cal′i·ty** (-kal′ə·tē) *n.* **— ve·rid′i·cal·ly** *adv.*

ver·i·fi·a·ble (ver′ə·fī′ə·bəl) *adj.* Capable of being verified. **— ver′i·fi′a·ble·ness** *n.* **— ver′i·fi′a·bly** *adv.*

ver·i·fi·ca·tion (ver′ə·fə·kā′shən) *n.* **1.** The act of verifying, or the state of being verified. **2.** *Law* An oath appended to an account, petition, or plea, as to the truth of the facts stated in it.

ver·i·fy (ver′ə·fī) *v.t.* **·fied, ·fy·ing 1.** To prove to be true or accurate; substantiate; confirm. **2.** To test or ascertain the accuracy or truth of. **3.** *Law* **a** To affirm under oath. **b** To add a confirmation to. **— Syn.** See CONFIRM. [< OF *verifier* < Med.L *verificare* to make true < *verus* true + *facere* to make] **— ver′i·fi′er** *n.*

ver·i·ly (ver′ə·lē) *adv. Archaic* In truth; assuredly; certainly; really. [< VERY]

ver·i·sim·i·lar (ver′ə·si n′ə·lər) *adj.* Appearing or seeming to be true; likely; probable. [< L *verisimilis* < *verus* true + *similis* like] **— ver′i·sim′i·lar·ly** *adv.*

ver·i·si·mil·i·tude (ver′ə·si nil′ə·tōod, -tyōōd) *n.* **1.** Appearance of truth; likelihood. **2.** That which resembles truth. [< L *verisimilitudo* < *verisimilis.* See VERISIMILAR.]

ver·ism (ver′iz·əm) *n.* Realism in art or literature. [< *verus* true] **— ver′ist** *n. & adj.* **— ve·ris·tic** (və·ris′tik) *adj.*

ver·i·ta·ble (ver′ə·tə·bəl) *adj.* Properly so called; unquestionable: a *veritable* villain. [< F < *vérité.* See VERITY.] **— ver′i·ta·ble·ness** *n.* **— ver′i·ta·bly** *adv.*

ver·i·tas (ver′ə·tas) *n. Latin* Truth.

ver·i·ty (ver′ə·tē) *n. pl.* **·ties 1.** The quality of being correct or true. **2.** A true or established statement, principle, etc.; a fact; truth. [< F *vérité* < L *veritas* truth < *verus* true]

ver·juice (vûr′jōōs) *n.* **1.** The sour juice of green fruit, as unripe grapes. **2.** Sharpness or sourness of disposition or manner; acidity. [< OF *verjus* < *vert* green + *jus* juice]

Ver·laine (ver·len′), **Paul,** 1844–96, French poet.

Ver·meer (vər·mâr′), **Jan,** 1632–75, Dutch painter. Also **Jan van der Meer van Delft** (vän dər mâr vän delft′).

ver·meil (vûr′ril) *n.* **1.** Silver or bronze gilt. **2.** *Poetic* Vermilion, or the color of vermilion. **— adj.** Of a bright-red color. [< OF < L *vermiculus,* dim. of *vermis* worm, the cochineal insect]

vermi- *combining form* A worm; of or related to a worm; vermiform. [< L *vermis* worm]

ver·mi·cel·li (vûr′mə·sel′ē, *Ital.* ver′mē·chel′lē) *n.* A food paste made into slender cords thinner than spaghetti or macaroni. [< Ital., lit., little worms, pl. of *vermicello* < L *vermiculus.* See VERMEIL.]

ver·mi·cide (vûr′mə·sīd) *n.* Any substance that kills worms; especially, any drug destructive of intestinal worms. [< VERMI- + -CIDE] **— ver·mi·ci·dal** (vûr′mə·sīd′əl) *adj.*

ver·mic·u·lar (vər·mik′yə·lər) *adj.* **1.** Having the form or motion of a worm. **2.** Like the wavy tracks of a worm. [< L *vermicularis* < *vermiculus,* dim. of *vermis* worm] **— ver·mic′u·lar·ly** *adv.*

ver·mic·u·late (vər·mik′yə·lāt) *v.t.* **·lat·ed, ·lat·ing 1.** To adorn with tracery simulating the tracks of worms. **2.** To make worm-eaten; infest with worms. **— adj. 1.** Covered with wormlike markings. **2.** Having the motions of a worm. **3.** Insinuating; tortuous. **4.** Worm-eaten. [< L *vermiculatus,* pp. of *vermiculari* to be worm-eaten < *vermiculus,* dim. of *vermis* worm]

vermiculated work 1. A form of rusticated masonry simulating worm tracks. **2.** Ornamental work consisting of winding tracks in mosaic work. Also **vermicular work.**

ver·mic·u·la·tion (vər·mik′yə·lā′shən) *n.* **1.** Wormlike motion, as of the intestines. **2.** Vermicular ornamentation or markings. **3.** A worm-eaten state.

ver·mic·u·lite (vər·mik′yə·līt) *n.* A laminated hydrous silicate, derived chiefly as an alteration product of biotite and other micaceous minerals. [< L *vermiculus,* dim. of *vermis* worm + -ITE[1]]

ver·mi·form (vûr′mə·fôrm) *adj.* Like a worm in shape. [< Med.L *vermiformis* < L *vermis* worm + *forma* form]

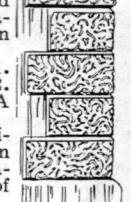

VERMICU-
LATED
WORK

vermiform appendix *Anat.* A slender, wormlike vestigial structure, 3 to 6 inches long, protruding from the end of the cecum in man and certain other mammals. For illustration see INTESTINE.

vermiform process *Anat.* **1.** Either surface of the median lobe of the cerebellum. **2.** The vermiform appendix.

ver·mi·fuge (vûr′mə·fyōōj) *n.* Any remedy that destroys intestinal worms. **— adj.** Anthelmintic. [< F < L *vermis* worm + *fugare* to expel]

ver·mil·ion (vər·mil′yən) *n.* **1.** A brilliant, durable red pigment consisting of mercuric sulfide, obtained naturally by grinding cinnabar to a fine powder, or artificially, as by treating a mixture of mercury and sulfur with potassium hydroxide: also called *Chinese red, cinnabar.* **2.** The color of the pigment, an intense orange red. — *adj.* Of a bright-red color. — *v.t.* To color with vermilion; dye bright red. [< OF *vermeilon, vermillon < vermeil* See VERMEIL.]

ver·min (vûr′min) *n. pl.* **·min 1.** Noxious small animals or parasitic insects, as lice, fleas, worms, rats, mice, etc. **2.** *Brit.* Certain animals injurious to game, as weasels, owls, etc. **3.** A repulsive or obnoxious human being; also, such persons collectively. [< OF < L *vermis* worm]

ver·mi·nate (vûr′mə·nāt) *v.i.* **·nat·ed, ·nat·ing** *Archaic* To produce or breed vermin, especially parasitic vermin. — **ver′mi·na′tion** *n.*

ver·min·ous (vûr′mən·əs) *adj.* **1.** Infested with vermin, especially parasites. **2.** Relating to or caused by vermin. **3.** Of the nature of or resembling vermin. — **ver′min·ous·ly** *adv.* — **ver′min·ous·ness** *n.*

ver·miv·o·rous (vûr·miv′ər·əs) *adj.* Feeding on worms, as certain birds. [< VERMI- + -VOROUS]

Ver·mont (vər·mont′) A State in NE United States; 9,609 sq. mi.; pop. 444,732; capital, Montpelier; entered the Union March 4, 1791; nickname, *Green Mountain State.* Abbr. *Vt.* — **Ver·mont′er** *n.*

ver·mou·lu (ver·moo·lü′) *adj. French* Worm-eaten.

ver·mouth (vûr′mooth, vər·mooth′) *n.* A liqueur made from white wine flavored with aromatic herbs. Also **ver′-muth.** [< F *vermout* < G *wermuth* wormwood]

ver·nac·u·lar (vər·nak′yə·lər) *n.* **1.** The native language of a locality. **2.** The common everyday speech of the people, as opposed to the literary language. **3.** The vocabulary or jargon of a particular profession or trade. **4.** An idiomatic word or phrase. **5.** The common name of a plant or animal as distinguished from its scientific designation. — *Syn.* See DIALECT. — *adj.* **1.** Originating in or belonging to one's native land; indigenous: said of a language, idiom, etc. **2.** Using everyday speech rather than the literary language. **3.** Written in the native language. **4.** Characteristic of a specific locality or country; local: *vernacular* arts. **5.** *Rare* Peculiar to a particular region; endemic. **6.** Designating the common name of a plant or animal. [< L *vernaculus* domestic, native < *verna* homeborn slave, native] — **ver·nac′u·lar·ly** *adv.*

ver·nac·u·lar·ism (vər·nak′yə·lə·riz′əm) *n.* **1.** A vernacular term or idiom. **2.** The use of the vernacular as opposed to classic or literary language.

ver·nal (vûr′nəl) *adj.* **1.** Belonging to, appearing in, or appropriate to spring. **2.** Youthful; fresh. [< L *vernalis < vernus* belonging to < *ver* spring] — **ver′nal·ly** *adv.*

vernal equinox See under EQUINOX.

ver·nal·ize (vûr′nəl·īz) *v.t.* **·ized, ·iz·ing** To accelerate the growth of (a plant) by subjecting the seeds to low temperatures. — **ver′nal·i·za′tion** *n.*

ver·na·tion (vər·nā′shən) *n. Bot.* The disposition of leaves within the leaf bud. [< NL *vernatio, -onis < vernare* to flourish < *ver* spring]

Verne (vûrn, *Fr.* vern), **Jules,** 1828–1905, French novelist.

Ver·ner (vûr′nər), **Karl Adolph,** 1846–96, Danish philologist.

Verner's Law A law regarding certain consonant changes in Germanic languages, set forth by Karl Verner in 1876, stating that certain exceptions to Grimm's Law are due to a still wider law, namely, the position of the primary accent in the parent language.

ver·ni·er (vûr′nē·ər) *n.* **1.** The small, movable, auxiliary scale for obtaining fractional parts of the subdivisions of a fixed scale on a theodolite, barometer, sextant, gauge, or other measuring instrument. Also **vernier scale. 2.** *Mech.* An auxiliary device to insure fine adjustments in precision instruments. [after Pierre *Vernier,* 1580?–1637, French mathematician]

ver·nix (ver′niks) *n.* A fatty substance covering the skin of a fetus. Also **vernix ca·se·o·sa** (kā′sē·ō′sə). [< NL *vernix* (*caseosa*), lit., cheesy varnish < ML *vernix* varnish + L *caseus* cheese]

Ver·no·le·ninsk (vyir·no·lye′nyinsk) A former name for NIKOLAEV.

Ver·non (vûr′nən), **Edward,** 1684–1757, English admiral.

Ver·nyi (vyer′nē) A former name for ALMA–ATA. Also **Ver′nyy.**

Ve·ro·na (və·rō′nə, *Ital.* vā·rō′nä) A commune in Venetia, NE Italy; pop. 251,600 (1967). — **Ver·o·nese** (ver′ə·nēz′, -nēs′) *adj. & n.*

Ver·o·nal (ver′ə·nəl) *n.* Proprietary name for a brand of barbital.

Ve·ro·ne·se (vā′rō·nā′zā), **Paolo,** 1528–88, Venetian painter: original name **Paolo Ca·gli·a·ri** (kä′lyä·rē).

ve·ron·i·ca¹ (və·ron′i·kə) *n.* A plant, the speedwell. [< Med.L, appar. after St. *Veronica*]

ve·ron·i·ca² (və·ron′i·kə) *n.* **1.** A cloth said to have been miraculously impressed with the face of Christ on his way to Calvary, handed to him by Saint Veronica to wipe the perspiration from his face; also, the representation of the face

on this handkerchief. **2.** A cloth having on it a similar representation of Christ's face. See SUDARIUM. [< Med.L < LL *veraiconica,* prob. < L *verus* true + Gk. *eikōn* image]

ve·ron·i·ca³ (və·ron′i·kə, *Sp.* bā·rō′nē·kä) *n.* In bullfighting, a maneuver in which the torero diverts the bull's charge with a cape. [< Sp.]

Ve·ron·i·ca (və·ron′i·kə), **Saint** A legendary follower of Christ, upon whose handkerchief a picture of Christ's features is said to have appeared. [See VERONICA².]

Ver·ra·za·no (ver′rä·tsä′nō), **Giovanni da,** 1480?–1527?, Italian seafarer and explorer. Also **Ver′raz·za′no.**

Ver·roc·chio (ver·rôk′kyō), **Andrea del,** 1435–88, Florentine sculptor: original name **Andria di Mi·che·le Cio·ne** (dē mē·kā′lā chō′nā).

ver·ru·ca (ve·roo′kə) *n. pl.* **·cae** (-sē) **1.** *Med.* A wart. **2.** *Biol.* A wart or wartlike elevation on animals or plants. [< L, a wart, orig. a steep place]

ver·ru·cose (ver′ə·kōs) *adj.* Having wartlike elevations; warty. Also **ver′ru·cous** (-kəs). [< L *verrucosus <verruca* wart] — **ver′ru·cos′i·ty** (-kos′ə·tē) *n.*

vers *Trig.* Versed sine.

Ver·sailles (vər·sī′, -sālz′; *Fr.* ver·sä′y′) A city of France, SW of Paris; site of the palace of Louis XIV; scene of the signing of a treaty (1919) between the Allies and Germany after World War I; pop. 90,829 (1968).

ver·sant (vûr′sənt) *n. Geog.* **1.** A mountainous area having a general slope in one direction. **2.** The general slope of any portion of country; inclination. [< F, ppr. of *verser* to overturn, pour < L *versare,* freq. of *vertere* to turn]

ver·sa·tile (vûr′sə·til) *adj.* **1.** Having an aptitude for various tasks or occupations; many-sided. **2.** Subject to change; inconstant; variable. **3.** *Bot.* Freely swinging or turning, as an anther so slightly attached to its support that it readily swings to-and-fro. **4.** *Zool.* Capable of being turned forward or backward, as the toe of a bird or an insect antenna. [< F < L *versatilis < versare,* freq. of *vertere* to turn] — **ver′sa·tile·ly** *adv.* — **ver′sa·til′i·ty, ver′sa·tile·ness** *n.*

vers de so·ci·é·té (ver′ də sō·syä·tā′) *French* A form of light verse characterized by grace, elegance, and wit.

verse (vûrs) *n.* **1.** A single metrical or rhythmical line made up of a number of feet, arranged according to a specific rule. **2.** Metrical composition; poetry: distinguished from *prose.* **3.** A piece of poetry; poem. **4.** A specified type of metrical composition; type of meter or metrical structure: iambic *verse.* **5.** One of the short divisions of a chapter of the Bible. **6.** A short division of any metrical composition; especially, a stanza. **7.** A section or stanza of a hymn or song. Abbr. *v., ver., vs.* — *v.t. & v.i.* **versed, vers·ing** *Rare* To versify. [Fusion of OE *fers* and OF *vers,* both < L *versus* a turning, verse < *vertere* to turn]

versed (vûrst) *adj.* Thoroughly acquainted; adept; proficient: with *in.* [< L *versatus,* pp. of *versari* to occupy oneself]

versed cosine (vûrst) *Trig.* The coversed sine (which see).

versed sine *Trig.* A function of an angle, equal to one minus the cosine. Also **ver·sine** (vûr′sīn).

verse·mon·ger (vûrs′mung′gər, -mong′-) *n.* A writer of inferior verses; poetaster.

ver·si·cle (vûr′si·kəl) *n.* **1.** A little verse. **2.** One of a series of lines said or sung alternately by minister and congregation. [< L *versiculus,* dim. of *versus.* See VERSE.]

ver·si·col·or (vûr′si·kul′ər) *adj.* **1.** Showing a variety of colors; variegated. **2.** Changing from one color to another in different lights; iridescent. Also *Brit.* **ver′si·col′our.** [< L < *versus,* pp. of *vertere* to turn + *color* color]

ver·sic·u·lar (vər·sik′yə·lər) *adj.* Of or relating to verses, especially Biblical verses. [< L *versiculus.* See VERSICLE.]

ver·si·fy (vûr′sə·fī) *v.* **·fied, ·fy·ing** *v.t.* **1.** To change from prose into verse. **2.** To narrate or treat in verse. — *v.i.* **3.** To write poetry; make verses. [< OF *vercifier, versifier* < L *versificare < versus* (see VERSE) + *facere* to make] — **ver′si·fi·ca′tion** (-fə·kā′shən) *n.* — **ver′si·fi′er** *n.*

ver·sion (vûr′zhən, -shən) *n.* **1.** A description or account as modified by a particular point of view. **2.** A translation from one language into another. **3.** A translation of the whole or part of the Bible: the Douai *version.* **4.** An adaptation: a movie *version* of a play. **5.** A different form or variation of something: my *version* of the recipe. **6.** *Med.* **a** The manual turning of a fetus in the womb so as to secure proper delivery. **b** Displacement of the uterus, in which the organ is deflected without bending upon itself. Abbr. *v., ver* — *Syn.* See ACCOUNT. [< MF < Med.L *versio, -onis* a turning < L *vertere* to turn] — **ver′sion·al** *adj.*

vers li·bre (ver lē′br′) *French* Free verse.

ver·so (vûr′sō) *n. pl.* **·sos 1.** A left-hand page of a book, piece of music, or sheet of folded paper: also called *reverso:* opposed to *recto.* **2.** The reverse of a coin or medal. Compare OBVERSE. Abbr. *vo.* [< L *verso* (*folio*) a turned (leaf), ablative neut. sing. pp. of *vertere* to turn]

verst (vûrst) *n.* A Russian measure of distance, about two thirds of a mile, or 1.067 kilometers. [< F *verste* and G *werst* < Russian *versta,* orig. a line]

ver·sus (vûr′səs) *prep.* **1.** In law and sports, against: Brown *versus* the United States; Dempsey *versus* Tunney. **2.** Considered as the alternative of: free trade *versus* tariffs. *Abbr.* **v., vs.** [< L, toward, turned toward, orig. pp. of *vertere* to turn]

vert (vûrt) *n.* **1.** In English forest law, anything that grows and bears green leaves within a forest, especially thick coverts; also, the right to cut green or growing wood in a forest. **2.** *Heraldry* The color or tincture green. [< MF *vert, verd* < L *viridis* green]

Vert (ver), **Cape** See (Cape) VERDE.

ver·te·bra (vûr′tə·brə) *n. pl.* **·brae** (-brē) or **·bras** *Anat.* Any of the segmented bones of the spinal column. In man and the higher vertebrates, each vertebra, with its cylindrical central body, foramen, and attached processes, articulates with those on either side by means of elastic fibrous pads. [< L, joint, vertebra < *vertere* to turn]

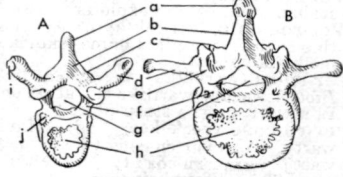

HUMAN VERTEBRAE
A Sixth thoracic vertebra.
B Third lumbar vertebra.
a Spinous process. *b* Lamina. *c* Inferior articular process. *d* Transverse process. *e* Superior articular process. *f* Pedicle. *g* Vertebral foramen. *h* Body. *i* Facet for tubercle of rib. *j* Facet for head of rib.

ver·te·bral (vûr′tə·brəl) *adj.* **1.** Pertaining to or of the nature of a vertebra. **2.** Having or composed of vertebrae.

vertebral column The spinal column; the backbone.

ver·te·brate (vûr′tə·brāt, -brit) *adj.* **1.** Having a backbone or spinal column. **2.** Pertaining to or characteristic of vertebrates. — *n.* Any of a primary division or subphylum (*Vertebrata*) of chordate animals, characterized by a segmented spinal column, as fishes, birds, mammals, and a few primitive forms in which a notochord represents the backbone. [< L *vertebratus* jointed < *vertebra*. See VERTEBRA.]

ver·te·bra·tion (vûr′tə·brā′shən) *n.* **1.** The formation of vertebrae. **2.** Segmentation like that of the spinal column.

ver·tex (vûr′teks) *n. pl.* **·tex·es** or **·ti·ces** (-tə·sēz) **1.** The highest point or summit of anything; apex; top. **2.** *Astron.* The point in the sky toward or from which a group of stars appears to be moving. **3.** *Anat.* The top of the head. **4.** In craniometry, the top of the arch of the skull. **5.** *Geom.* **a** The point of intersection of the sides of an angle. **b** The point of a triangle opposite to, and farthest from, the base. **c** The intersection of three or more edges of a polyhedron. [< L, the top < *vertere* to turn]

ver·ti·cal (vûr′ti·kəl) *adj.* **1.** Perpendicular to the plane of the horizon; extending up and down; upright: opposed to *horizontal*. **2.** Occupying a position directly above or overhead. **3.** Of, pertaining to, or at the vertex or highest point. **4.** Of or pertaining to the crown of the head. **5.** *Bot.* **a** Perpendicular to the horizon, as the leaves of certain plants. **b** In the direction of the axis of growth; lengthwise. **6.** *Econ.* Of or pertaining to a group of business concerns that handle all the stages of an industry from raw material to distribution of the finished product. — *n.* **1.** A vertical line, plane, or circle. **2.** An upright beam or rod in a truss. [< MF < L *verticalis* < *vertex, -icis*. See VERTEX.] — **ver′ti·cal′i·ty** (-kal′ə·tē), **ver′ti·cal·ness** *n.* — **ver′ti·cal·ly** *adv.*

vertical circle *Astron.* A great circle perpendicular to the plane of the horizon.

vertical union An industrial union (which see).

ver·ti·ces (vûr′tə·sēz) Plural of VERTEX.

ver·ti·cil (vûr′tə·sil) *n. Biol.* **1.** A set of organs, as leaves or tentacles, disposed in a circle around an axis; whorl. **2.** A volution of a spiral shell. [< L *verticillus* whorl, dim. of *vertex, -icis*. See VERTEX.]

ver·ti·cil·las·ter (vûr′tə·si·las′tər) *n. Bot.* An inflorescence with the flowers seemingly in a whorl, but actually composed of a pair of dense opposite clusters, as in most mints. [< NL < L *verticillus* (see VERTICIL) + -ASTER]

ver·ti·cil·late (vər·tis′ə·lit, -lāt, vûr′tə·sil′it, -āt) *adj.* **1.** Arranged in a verticil or whorl. **2.** Having parts so arranged. Also **ver·tic′il·lat·ed.** [< NL *verticillatus* < *verticillus*. See VERTICIL.] — **ver·tic′il·late·ly** *adv.* — **ver·tic′il·la′tion** *n.*

ver·tig·i·nous (vər·tij′ə·nəs) *adj.* **1.** Affected by vertigo; dizzy. **2.** Turning round; whirling; revolving. **3.** Liable to cause dizziness. [< L *vertiginosus* < *vertigo, -inis*. See VERTIGO.] — **ver·tig′i·nous·ly** *adv.* — **ver·tig′i·nous·ness** *n.*

ver·ti·go (vûr′tə·gō) *n. pl.* **·goes** or **ver·tig·i·nes** (vər·tij′ə·nēz) *Pathol.* Any of a group of disorders in which a person feels as if he or his surroundings are whirling around; dizziness. [< L, lit., a turning around < *vertere* to turn]

ver·tu (vər·tōō′, -tōō) See VIRTU.

Ver·tum·nus (vər·tum′nəs) In Roman mythology, the god of the changing seasons and growing plants; husband of Pomona: also *Vortumnus*.

Ver·u·la·mi·um (ver′yōō·lā′mē·əm) The ancient Roman name for St. ALBANS.

ver·vain (vûr′vān) *n.* Any of various plants (genus *Verbena*), typical of a family (*Verbenaceae*) of herbs, shrubs, and trees, including many cultivated ornamental verbenas, as the **blue vervain** (*V. hastata*) of North America or the European vervain (*V. officinalis*). [< OF *verveine* < L *verbena*. Doublet of VERBENA.]

verve (vûrv) *n.* **1.** Enthusiasm or energy, especially as manifested in artistic production. **2.** Spirit; vigor. **3.** *Rare* Special bent. [< F, prob. < L *verba*, pl. of *verbum* word]

ver·vet (vûr′vit) *n.* A South African monkey (genus *Cercopithecus*), grayish green speckled with black. [< F < *ver(t)* green (< L *viridis*) + (*gri*)*vet* grivet]

ver·y (ver′ē) *adv.* **1.** In a high degree; in large measure; extremely; exceedingly: *very* generous. **2.** Truly; indeed: the *very* same idea; the *very* best I can do. ◆ *Very* occurs in standard English immediately before a past participle, as in *He was very agitated*, as well as before an adverb preceding a past participle, as in *He was very much agitated*, although some grammarians still object to the former use. — *adj.* **ver·i·er, ver·i·est 1.** Absolute; actual; simple; utter: the *very* truth. **2.** Selfsame; identical: my *very* words. **3.** Exact; precise: the *very* middle of the night. **4.** Exactly suitable or right: the *very* hammer we needed. **5.** The (thing) itself: used as an intensive equivalent to *even*: The *very* stones cry out. **6.** Exclusive; peculiar: the *very* wisdom of God. **7.** Unqualified; utter; complete: a *very* rogue. **8.** *Obs.* True: *very* God; also, truthful; veracious. [< AF *verrai* or OF *verai* < L *verus* true]

very high frequency *Telecom.* A band of radio wave frequencies ranging from 30 to 300 megacycles. *Abbr.* **vhf, v.h.f., VHF, V.H.F.**

very low frequency *Telecom.* A band of radio wave frequencies ranging from 10 to 30 kilocycles. *Abbr.* **vlf, v.l.f., VLF, V.L.F.**

Ve·sa·li·us (vi·sā′lē·əs), **Andreas**, 1514–64, Belgian physician; founder of modern anatomy.

ve·si·ca (vi·sī′kə) *n. pl.* **·cae** (-sē) *Anat.* A bladder or sac; especially, the urinary bladder or the gall bladder. [< L]

ves·i·cal (ves′i·kəl) *adj.* Of or pertaining to a bladder, especially the urinary bladder.

ves·i·cant (ves′i·kənt) *adj.* Producing blisters. — *n.* **1.** That which produces blisters. **2.** A chemical warfare agent that attacks the skin, as mustard gas or lewisite. [< NL *vesicans, -antis*, ppr. of *vesicare* to raise blisters < L *vesica* blister, bladder]

vesica pis·cis (pis′is, pī′sis) The pointed oval aureole used by medieval artists to enclose holy figures. [< L, lit., fish bladder]

ves·i·cate (ves′i·kāt) *v.t. & v.i.* **·cat·ed, ·cat·ing** To blister. [< NL *vesicatus*, pp. of *vesicare*. See VESICANT.] — **ves′i·ca′tion** *n.*

ves·i·ca·to·ry (ves′i·kə·tôr′ē, və·sik′ə·tôr′ē, -tō′rē) *adj.* Capable of producing blisters; vesicant. — *n. pl.* **·ries** Any substance, as an ointment or plaster, that causes a blister.

ves·i·cle (ves′i·kəl) *n.* **1.** Any small bladderlike cavity, cell, or cyst. **2.** *Anat.* A small sac, containing gas or fluid. **3.** *Pathol.* Any small rounded elevation of the skin containing a clear liquid; a blister. **4.** *Bot.* A small bladderlike cavity filled with air. **5.** *Geol.* A small spherical cavity found in volcanic rocks. [< L *vesicula*, dim. of *vesica* bladder]

vesico- *combining form Med.* The urinary bladder; of or pertaining to the urinary bladder. Also, before vowels, **vesic-.** [< L *vesica* bladder]

ve·sic·u·la (və·sik′yə·lə) *n. pl.* **·lae** (-lē) A little bladder; vesicle. [< L]

ve·sic·u·lar (və·sik′yə·lər) *adj.* **1.** Of, pertaining to, composed of, or resembling vesicles. **2.** Bearing vesicles. [< L *vesicula*. See VESICLE.] — **ve·sic′u·lar·ly** *adv.*

ve·sic·u·late (*v.* və·sik′yə·lāt; *adj.* və·sik′yə·lit, -lāt) *v.t. & v.i.* **·lat·ed, ·lat·ing** To make or become vesicular or vesiculate. — *adj.* Full of or having vesicles; vesicular. [Back formation < *vesiculated* < NL *vesiculatus* < L *vesicula*. See VESICLE.] — **ve·sic′u·la′tion** *n.*

Ves·pa·sian (ves·pā′zhən), 9–79, Roman emperor 69–79: full name **Titus Flavius Sabinus Ves·pa·si·a·nus** (ves·pā′zhē·ā′nəs).

ves·per (ves′pər) *n.* **1.** A bell that calls to vespers. Also **vesper bell.** **2.** An evening service, prayer, or song. **3.** *Obs.* Evening. — *adj.* Pertaining to or suitable for evening or vespers. [< L, the evening star]

Ves·per (ves′pər) *n.* The evening star; Hesperus; the planet Venus when an evening star. [< OF < L]

ves·per·al (ves′pər·əl) *n.* **1.** A book of the music and office of vespers. **2.** A cover for an altar cloth.

ves·pers (ves′pərz) *n.pl. Often cap. Eccl.* **1.** The prescribed prayers that constitute the sixth of the seven canonical hours, said in the late afternoon or evening **2.** A service of worship in the late afternoon or evening. **3.** In the Anglican Church, Evening Prayer. **4.** In the Roman Catholic Church, a public service on Sundays and holy days at which the office of vespers is said or sung. [< OF *vespres* < Med.L *vesperae* < L *vespera* evening]

vesper sparrow A sparrow (*Pooecetes gramineus*) of North America: so called from its evening song.

ves·per·til·i·o·nine (ves′pər·til′ē·ə·nīn′, -nin) *adj.* Belonging to a cosmopolitan family (*Vespertilionidae*) of bats, including most of the commonly known species. [< L *vespertilio, -onis* a bat + -INE¹] — **ves′per·til′i·o·nid** *adj.* & *n.*

ves·per·tine (ves′pər·tin, -tīn) *adj.* 1. Pertaining to or occurring in the evening. 2. *Biol.* Flying, opening, etc., in the evening, as a bat or flower. Also **ves′per·ti′nal** (-tī′nəl). [< L *vespertinus* < *vesper*. See VESPER.]

ves·pi·ar·y (ves′pē·er′ē) *n. pl.* **·ar·ies** A nest of social wasps or its colony. [< L *vespa* wasp + (AP)IARY]

ves·pid (ves′pid) *adj.* Of or belonging to a large family (*Vespidae*) of hymenopterous insects, including social wasps and hornets. — *n.* A member of this group. [< NL < L *vespa* wasp] — **ves′pi·form** (-pə·fôrm) *adj.*

ves·pine (ves′pīn, -pin) *adj.* Of or pertaining to wasps. [< L *vespa* wasp + -INE¹]

Ves·puc·ci (ves·pōōt′chē), **Amerigo**, 1451–1512, Italian seafarer and explorer for whom America was named. Also *Lat.* **Americus Ves·pu·cius** (ves·pyōō′shəs).

ves·sel (ves′əl) *n.* 1. A hollow receptacle, especially one capable of holding a liquid, as a bowl, pitcher, etc. 2. A craft designed to float on the water, usually one larger than a rowboat; a ship or boat. 3. *Anat.* A duct or canal for containing or transporting a body fluid, as an artery or vein. 4. *Bot.* A tube in plants that conducts water. 5. One who is viewed, chiefly in a religious sense, as having capacity or fitness to receive or contain something: *a vessel of mercy or of wrath.* [< OF < L *vascellum,* dim. of *vas* vessel]

vest (vest) *n.* 1. *Chiefly U.S.* A man's sleeveless garment, buttoning in front and extending just below the waistline, commonly worn underneath a suit coat: also, *esp. Brit.,* *waistcoat.* 2. A woman's similar garment. 3. *Brit.* An undershirt; undervest. — *v.t.* 1. To confer (ownership, authority, etc.) upon some person or persons: usually with *in.* 2. To place ownership, control, or authority with (a person or persons). 3. To clothe or robe, as with vestments. — *v.i.* 4. To clothe oneself, as in vestments. 5. To be or become vested; devolve. [< F *veste* < Ital. < L *vestis* clothing, garment]

ves·ta (ves′tə) *n. Archaic* A friction match of wax or wood.

Ves·ta (ves′tə) *n.* 1. In Roman mythology, the goddess of the hearth and the hearth fire, protectress of the state, and custodian of the sacred fire tended by the vestals: identified with the Greek *Hestia.* 2. *Astron.* A large asteroid.

ves·tal (ves′təl) *n.* 1. One of the virgin priestesses of Vesta. Also **vestal virgin.** 2. A woman of pure character; a virgin. 3. A nun. — *adj.* 1. Pertaining to Vesta. 2. Suitable for a vestal or a nun; chaste; pure. [< L *vestalis* < *Vesta* Vesta]

vest·ed (ves′tid) *adj.* 1. *Law* Held by a tenure subject to no contingency; complete; established by law as a permanent right. 2. Dressed; robed, especially in church vestments.

vested interest 1. A strong interest in or commitment to a system or institution whose continued existence serves one's self-interest. 2. *Usually pl.* A financially powerful or influential group of people.

vest·ee (ves·tē′) *n.* 1. An imitation blouse-front worn in the front of a suit or dress. 2. A broadcloth garment without sleeves worn with a formal riding habit. [Dim. of VEST]

ves·ti·ar·y (ves′tē·er′ē) *adj.* Pertaining to clothes. — *n. pl.* **·ar·ies** *Obs.* A vestry; robing room. [< OF *vestiairie* < Med.L *vestiarium.* See VESTRY.]

ves·tib·u·lar (ves·tib′yə·lər) *adj.* Pertaining to or like a vestibule. Also **ves·tib′u·late** (-lit, -lāt).

ves·ti·bule (ves′tə·byōōl) *n.* 1. A small antechamber between the outer door of a building and an anterior one; an entrance hall; lobby. 2. An enclosed passage from one railway passenger car to another. 3. *Anat.* Any of several chambers or channels adjoining or communicating with others: the *vestibule* of the ear. — *v.t.* **·buled, ·bul·ing** 1. To provide with a vestibule or vestibules. 2. To couple (railroad cars) and connect by vestibules. [< L *vestibulum* entrance hall]

vestibule train A passenger train with enclosed platforms connected by flexible walls and roof, forming a weatherproof passageway between connected cars (**vestibule cars**).

ves·tige (ves′tij) *n.* 1. A visible trace, impression, or a sensible evidence or sign, of something absent, lost, or gone; trace. 2. *Biol.* A part or organ, small or degenerate, but well developed and functional in ancestral forms of organisms. [< F < L *vestigium* footprint]

ves·tig·i·al (ves·tij′ē·əl) *adj.* Of, or of the nature of a vestige. — **ves·tig′i·al·ly** *adv.*

ves·tig·i·um (ves·tij′ē·əm) *n. pl.* **·tig·i·a** (-tij′ē·ə) *Biol.* A vestigial part; vestige. [< L, footprint]

vest·ment (vest′mənt) *n.* 1. An article of dress; especially, a garment or robe of state or office. 2. *Eccl.* One of the ritual garments of the clergy; especially, a garment worn at the Eucharist; a chasuble. [< OF *vestement* < L *vestimentum* clothes < *vestire* to clothe] — **vest′ment·al** *adj.*

vest-pock·et (vest′pok′it) *adj.* Small enough to fit in a vest pocket; very small; diminutive: a *vest-pocket* edition.

ves·try (ves′trē) *n. pl.* **·tries** 1. A room, as in a church, where vestments are put on or kept. 2. A room for altar linens, sacred vessels, etc., attached to a church: often called *sacristy.* 3. A room in a church used for Sunday school, meetings, as a chapel, etc. 4. In the Anglican Church: **a** A body administering the affairs of a parish or congregation; also, a meeting of such a body. **b** In English parishes, a business meeting of all the parishioners or their representatives. 5. A place of meeting for the parish vestry. [< AF *vestrie,* OF *vestiarie* < Med.L *vestiarium* wardrobe < L *vestis* garment]

ves·try·man (ves′trē·mən) *n. pl.* **·men** (-mən) A member of a vestry.

ves·ture (ves′chər) *n.* 1. *Archaic* Garments; clothing; a robe. 2. *Law* All that covers land, except trees. 3. *Archaic* A covering or envelope. — *v.t.* **·tured, ·tur·ing** *Archaic* To cover or clothe with vesture. [< OF < *vestir* cloth < L *vestire* to clothe]

ve·su·vi·an (və·sōō′vē·ən) *n.* 1. Vesuvianite. 2. A kind of match or fusee. [after *Vesuvius*]

ve·su·vi·an·ite (və·sōō′vē·ən·īt′) *n.* A vitreous, brown to green, translucent hydrous silicate of calcium and aluminum, with traces of iron and magnesium: also called *idocrase.*

Ve·su·vi·us (və·sōō′vē·əs) An active volcano in western Italy, on the Bay of Naples; 3,891 ft. *Italian* **Ve·su·vio** (vā·zōō′vyō). — **ve·su·vi·an** *adj.*

vet¹ (vet) *Informal n.* A veterinarian. — *v.* **vet·ted, vet·ting** *v.t.* 1. To treat as a veterinarian does. 2. *Brit.* To examine carefully. — *v.i.* 3. To treat animals medically. [Short for VETERINARIAN]

vet² (vet) *n. Informal* A veteran. [Short for VETERAN]

vet. 1. Veteran. 2. Veterinary medicine: also **veter.**

vetch (vech) *n.* 1. Any of a genus (*Vicia*) of climbing herbaceous vines of the bean family; especially, the common broad bean, grown for fodder. 2. A leguminous European plant (*Lathyrus sativus*) yielding edible seeds. — **bitter vetch** A species of vetch (*V. ervilia*) the seeds of which contain a bitter, poisonous alkaloid: also called *ers.* [< AF *veche, vecce* < L *vicia*]

vetch·ling (vech′ling) *n.* Any of a genus (*Lathyrus*), of leguminous plants allied to the vetches; especially, a European species (*L. pratensis*), naturalized in the United States and Canada. [Dim. of VETCH]

vet·er·an (vet′ər·ən, vet′rən) *n.* 1. One who is much experienced in any service, especially military service. 2. A former member of the armed forces. — *adj.* 1. Having had long experience or practice; old in service. 2. Belonging to or suggestive of a veteran. Abbr. *vet.* [< MF < L *veteranus* < *vetus, veteris* old]

Veterans Administration An agency of the U.S. government that administers all federal laws relating to the relief of former members of the military and naval services. Abbr. *VA, V.A.*

Veterans Day A U.S. national holiday honoring veterans of the armed forces, November 11, the anniversary of the armistice in World War I: formerly called *Armistice Day.*

Veterans of Foreign Wars A society of ex-servicemen who have served in the U.S. armed forces in a war with and in a foreign country; founded 1899. Abbr. *VFW, V.F.W.*

vet·er·i·nar·i·an (vet′ər·ə·nâr′ē·ən, vet′rə-) *n. Chiefly U.S.* A practitioner of veterinary medicine or surgery. [< L *veterinarius.* See VETERINARY.]

vet·er·i·nar·y (vet′ər·ə·ner′ē, vet′rə-) *adj.* Pertaining to the diseases or injuries of animals, and to their treatment by medical or surgical means. — *n. pl.* **·nar·ies** A veterinarian. Abbr. *vet., veter.* [< L *veterinarius* pertaining to beasts of burden < *veterinus* < *veterina* beasts of burden, ult. < *ve·here* to carry]

veterinary medicine The branch of medicine that deals with the prevention, treatment, and cure of animal diseases.

vet·i·ver (vet′ə·vər) *n.* 1. An Asian grass (*Vetiveria zizanioides*) grown in Florida and the SE United States. 2. Its aromatic roots, used for weaving mats, fans, etc., and as a source of **vetiver oil,** an ingredient of perfumes. [< F *vétyver* < Tamil *veṭṭivēru,* lit., a root that is dug up < *vēr* root]

ve·to (vē′tō) *v.t.* **·toed, ·to·ing** 1. To refuse executive approval of (a bill passed by a legislative body). 2. To forbid or prohibit authoritatively; refuse consent to. — *n. pl.* **·toes** 1. The prerogative of a chief executive to refuse to approve a legislative enactment by withholding his signature; also, the exercise of such a prerogative. 2. The official communication containing a refusal to approve a bill and the reasons for refusing: also **veto message.** 3. Any authoritative prohibition. [< L I forbid] — **ve′to·er** *n.*

veto power 1. The right or power possessed by a branch of the government to forbid or refuse approval of projects proposed by another department. 2. A power vested in the chief executive to prevent the enactment of bills passed by the legislature.

Vet·ter (vet′ər), **Lake** See (Lake) VÄTTER.

vex (veks) *v.t.* 1. To provoke to anger or displeasure by small irritations; annoy. **2.** To trouble or afflict. **3.** To throw into commotion; agitate. **4.** To make a subject of dispute. [< OF *vexer* < L *vexare* to shake] — **vex'er** *n.*

vex·a·tion (vek-sā'shən) *n.* **1.** The act of vexing, or the state of being vexed; irritation. **2.** That which vexes; a cause of trouble or distress. — **Syn.** See CHAGRIN.

vex·a·tious (vek-sā'shəs) *adj.* **1.** Being a source of vexation. **2.** Full of vexation; harassing; annoying. — **vex·a'·tious·ly** *adv.* — **vex·a'tious·ness** *n.*

vexed (vekst) *adj.* **1.** Harassed; troubled; irritated; agitated; disturbed. **2.** Much debated; contested: a *vexed* question. — **vex·ed·ly** (vek'sid-lē) *adv.* — **vex'ed·ness** *n.*

vex·il (vek'sil) *n. Bot.* A vexillum. [Short for VEXILLUM]

vex·il·lar·y (vek'sə-ler'ē) *n. pl.* **·lar·ies** A standard-bearer. — *adj.* **1.** Of or pertaining to a vexillum: also **vex'il·lar** (-lər). **2.** Of or pertaining to a standard or ensign. [< L *vexillarius* standard-bearer < *vexillum.* See VEXILLUM.]

vex·il·late (vek'sə-lit, -lāt) *adj.* Having a vexillum or vexilla.

vex·il·lum (vek-sil'əm) *n. pl.* **vex·il·la** (vek-sil'ə) **1.** In Roman antiquity, a square flag, or standard; also, a company or troop of soldiers serving under a separate standard. **2.** *Bot.* The large upper petal of a papilionaceous flower. **3.** *Ornithol.* The web of a feather. [< L flag, standard < *vehere* to carry]

V-for·ma·tion (vē'fôr-mā'shən) *n. Aeron.* A V-shaped flight formation of three or more aircraft.

VFW or **V.F.W.** Veterans of Foreign Wars.

V.G. Vicar General.

VHF or **vhf, V.H.F.,** or **v.h.f.** Very high frequency.

v.i. **1.** See below [L *vide infra*]. **2.** *Gram.* Intransitive verb.

Vi *Chem.* Virginium.

V.I. Virgin Islands.

vi·a (vī'ə, vē'ə) *prep.* By way of; by a route passing through: He went to Boston *via* New Haven. ◆ In informal usage, *via* can refer to the means of travel as well as the route: We went *via* train. [< L, ablative sing. of *via* way]

vi·a·ble (vī'ə-bəl) *adj.* **1.** Capable of living and developing normally. **2.** Capable of working, as a plan; workable; practicable. [< F < *vie* life < L *rita*] — **vi'a·bil·i·ty** *n.*

Vi·a Do·lo·ro·sa (vī'ə dol'ō-rō'sə) *Latin* The road traveled by Jesus to Golgotha; literally, sorrowful way.

vi·a·duct (vī'ə-dukt) *n.* A bridgelike structure, especially a large one of arched masonry, to carry a roadway or the like over a valley or ravine. Compare AQUE-DUCT. [< L *via* way + (AQUE)DUCT]

vi·al (vī'əl) *n.* A small bottle for liquids: also *phial* — **to pour out the vials of wrath upon** To inflict retribution or vengeance on. See *Rev.* xvi. — *v.t.* **vi·aled** or **·alled, vi·al·ing** or **·al·ling** To put or keep in or as in a vial. [< OF *viole* < L *phiala* saucer < Gk. *phialē* shallow cup]

VIADUCT
(Pont du Gard, a Roman aqueduct at Nîmes, France)

vi·a me·di·a (vī'ə mē'dē·ə) *Latin* A middle way.

vi·and (vī'ənd) *n.* **1.** An article of food, especially meat. **2.** *pl.* Victuals; provisions; food; especially, choice food. — **Syn.** See FOOD. [< AF *viaunde,* OF *viande,* ult. < L *vivenda,* neut. pl. gerundive of *vivere* to live]

vi·at·ic (vī·at'ik) *adj.* Of or pertaining to a journey or to traveling. Also **vi·at'i·cal.** [< L *viaticus* < *via* way]

vi·at·i·cum (vī·at'ə·kəm) *n. pl.* **·ca** (-kə) or **·cums** **1.** *Eccl.* The Eucharist, as given on the verge of death. **2.** In ancient Rome, the provision of necessaries for an official journey of a magistrate. **3.** Provisions for a journey. [< L, traveling money, neut. sing. of *viaticus* < *via* way. Doublet of VOYAGE.]

vi·a·tor (vī·ā'tər) *n. pl.* **vi·a·to·res** (vī'ə·tôr'ēz, -tō'rēz) A traveler; wayfarer. [< L < *via* way]

vibes[1] (vibez) *n. pl. Informal* A vibraphone.

vibes[2] (vibez) *n. pl.* Vibration (def. 3).

Vi·borg (vē'bôr·y') The Swedish name for VYBORG.

vi·brac·u·lum (vī·brak'yə·ləm) *n. pl.* **·la** (-lə) *Zool.* One of the slender, whiplike defensive organs of the cells of many polyzoans. [< NL < L *vibrare* to shake] — **vi·brac'u·lar** *adj.* — **vi·brac'u·loid** *adj.*

vi·bran·cy (vī'brən·sē) *n. pl.* **·cies** The state or character of being vibrant; resonance.

vi·brant (vī'brənt) *adj.* **1.** Having, showing, or resulting from vibration; vibrating. **2.** Throbbing; pulsing: *vibrant* with enthusiasm. **3.** Rich and resonant, as a sound: *vibrant* tones. **4.** Energetic; vigorous. **5.** *Phonet.* Voiced. — *n. Phonet.* A voiced sound; sonant. [< L *vibrans, -antis,* ppr. of *vibrare* to shake] — **vi'brant·ly** *adv.*

vi·bra·phone (vī'brə·fōn) *n.* A type of marimba in which a pulsating sound is produced by motor-driven valves in the resonators. Also **vi'bra-harp'** (-härp'). [< VIBRA(TO) + -PHONE]

vi·brate (vī'brāt) *v.* **·brat·ed, ·brat·ing** *v.i.* **1.** To move back and forth rapidly; quiver. **2.** To move or swing back and forth, as a pendulum. **3.** To sound: The note *vibrates* on the ear. **4.** To be emotionally moved; thrill. **5.** To vacillate; waver, as between choices. — *v.t.* **6.** To cause to quiver or tremble. **7.** To cause to move back and forth. **8.** To send forth (sound, etc.) by vibration. — **Syn.** See FLUCTUATE. [< L *vibratus,* pp. of *vibrare* to shake]

vi·bra·tile (vī'brə·til, -til) *adj.* **1.** Adapted to, having, or used in vibratory motion. **2.** Pertaining to or resembling vibration. — **vi·bra·til·i·ty** (vī'brə·til'ə·tē) *n.*

vi·bra·tion (vī·brā'shən) *n.* **1.** The act of vibrating, or the state of being vibrated. **2.** *Physics* **a** A periodic, usually rapid oscillatory motion of an elastic or rigid body suddenly released from tension. **b** Any physical process characterized by cyclic variations in amplitude, intensity, or the like, as wave motion or an electric field. **c** A single complete oscillation. **3.** *pl.* A person's intellectual, emotional, or spiritual harmony with an environment, situation, or another person or persons. — **vi·bra'tion·al** *adj.*

vi·bra·to (vē·brä'tō) *n. pl.* **·tos** *Music* A trembling or pulsating effect caused by rapid but minute variations in pitch during the production of a tone. [< Ital. < L, pp. of *vibrare* to shake]

vi·bra·tor (vī'brā·tər) *n.* **1.** That which vibrates. **2.** An electrically operated massaging apparatus. **3.** *Electr.* **a** An electromagnetic switch mechanism for converting direct into alternating current. **b** An oscillator.

vi·bra·to·ry (vī'brə·tôr'ē, -tō'rē) *adj.* Of, causing, or characterized by vibration. Also **vi'bra·tive** (-tiv).

vib·ri·o (vib'rē·ō) *n. pl.* **·ri·os** Any of a genus (*Vibrio*) of comma-shaped bacteria having one or more flagella at each end; especially, the **comma vibrio** (*V. comma*), found in the intestines of cholera victims. For illustration see BACTERIUM. [< NL < L *vibrare* to shake] — **vib·ri·oid** (vib'rē·oid) *adj.*

vi·bris·sa (vī·bris'ə) *n. pl.* **·bris·sae** (-bris'ē) **1.** One of the stiff, coarse hairs found in the nostrils of man and about the mouth of many other mammals, as the cat, often functioning as tactile organs. **2.** *Ornithol.* One of the hairlike rictal feathers of many insectivorous birds. [< L *vibrissae* hairs in a man's nostrils < *vibrare* to shake]

vi·bur·num (vī·bûr'nəm) *n.* Any of a large and widely distributed genus (*Viburnum*) of shrubs or small trees related to the honeysuckle, bearing berry-like fruit; such as the dockmackie. [< L, the wayfaring tree]

vic·ar (vik'ər) *n.* **1.** In the Anglican Church, the priest of a parish of which the main revenues are appropriated or impropriated by a layman, the priest himself receiving but a stipend; any incumbent of a parish who is not a rector. **2.** In the Roman Catholic Church, a substitute or representative of an ecclesiastical person. **3.** In some parishes of the Protestant Episcopal Church, the clergyman who is the head of a chapel; also, a clergyman having charge of a church or mission as the bishop's deputy. **4.** One authorized to perform functions in the stead of another. **5.** An agent; deputy. [< AF *vikere, vicare,* OF *vicaire* < L *vicarius* substitute < *vicis* change]

vic·ar·age (vik'ər·ij) *n.* **1.** The benefice, office, or duties of a vicar. **2.** A vicar's residence or household.

vicar apostolic In the Roman Catholic Church: **a** Formerly, a bishop or archbishop appointed by the pope to act in his stead in a given district. **b** A titular bishop exercising episcopal jurisdiction where there is no see canonically. Abbr. *V.A.*

vicar fo·rane (fō·rān', fō-) In the Roman Catholic Church, a clergyman appointed by a bishop, having a limited jurisdiction over the inferior clergy in the parishes constituting the deanery. [< VICAR + Med.L *foraneus* outside the episcopal city, rural < L *foras* out of doors]

vicar general *pl.* **vicars general** **1.** In the Roman Catholic Church, a functionary appointed by the bishop as assistant or representative in certain matters of jurisdiction. **2.** In the Church of England, an official assisting the bishop or archbishop in ecclesiastical causes. **3.** Formerly in England, the ecclesiastical vicegerent of the king, a title bestowed on Thomas Cromwell by Henry VIII. Abbr. *V.G.*

vi·car·i·al (vī·kâr'ē·əl, vi-) *adj.* **1.** Vicarious; delegated. **2.** Of, relating to, or acting as a vicar.

vi·car·i·ate (vī·kâr'ē·it, -āt, vi-) *n.* A delegated office or power; especially, that of a vicar. Also **vic·ar·ate** (vik'ər·it).

vi·car·i·ous (vī·kâr'ē·əs, vi-) *adj.* **1.** Made or performed by substitution; suffered or done in place of another: a *vicarious* sacrifice. **2.** Enjoyed, felt, etc., by a person as a result of his imagined participation in an experience not his own: *vicarious* thrills from reading mysteries. **3.** Filling the office of or acting for another. **4.** *Physiol.* Performing, as an organ, the functions of another; also, occurring in an abnormal situation: *vicarious* menstruation. [< L *vicarius.* See VICAR.] — **vi·car'i·ous·ly** *adv.* — **vi·car'i·ous·ness** *n.*

vic·ar·ly (vik'ər·lē) *adj.* Of or resembling a vicar.

Vicar of Christ The Pope, regarded as Christ's representative on earth.

vic·ar·ship (vik'ər·ship) *n.* The office or position of a vicar.

vice[1] (vīs) *n.* **1.** An immoral habit or trait. **2.** A slight personal fault; foible. **3.** Habitual indulgence in degrading or harmful practices. **4.** Something that mars; a blemish. **5.** A physical deformity, taint, or imperfection. **6.** A bad trick, as of a horse. [< OF < L *vitium* fault]

vice² (vīs) See VISE.

vice³ (*adj. & n.* vīs; *prep.* vī′sē) *adj.* Acting in the place of; substitute; deputy: *vice* president. — *n.* One who acts in the place of another; a substitute; deputy. — *prep.* Instead of; in the place of. Abbr. *v.* [< L, ablative of *vicis* change]

Vice may appear as a combining form or as the first element in two-word phrases; as in:

vice-chairman	vice-directorship	vice-principal
vice-chairmanship	vice-governor	vice-principalship
vice-dean	vice-governorship	vice-rector
vice-director	vice-ministry	vice-rectorship

vice admiral *Naval* A commissioned officer ranking next above a rear admiral and next below an admiral. Also *Brit. & Canadian* **vice-ad·mi·ral** (vīs′ad′mər·əl) See tables at GRADE. Abbr. *V.A., V. Adm.* [< AF *visadmirail,* OF *visa-miral* < *vis-* in place (< L *vice*) + *admirail, amiral* admiral]

vice-ad·mir·al·ty (vīs′ad′mər·əl·tē) *n. pl.* **·ties** The office of a vice admiral.

vice-chan·cel·lor (vīs′chan′sə·lər, -chän′-, -chans′lər, -chäns′lər) *n.* **1.** *Law* A judge in equity courts subordinate to the chancellor. **2.** A deputy chancellor in a university. Abbr. *V.C.* [< OF *vichancelier* < Med.L *vicecancellarius* < L *vice* in place + LL *cancellarius* chancellor] — **vice′-chan′cel·lor·ship** *n.*

vice-con·sul (vīs′kon′səl) *n.* One who exercises consular authority, either as the substitute or as the subordinate of a consul. Abbr. *V.C.* — **vice-con·su·lar** (vīs′kon′sə·lər) *adj.* — **vice-con·su·late** (vīs′kon′sə·lit) *n.* — **vice′con′sul·ship** *n.*

vice·ge·ren·cy (vīs·jir′ən·sē) *n. pl.* **·cies 1.** The office or authority of a vicegerent. **2.** A district ruled by a vicegerent.

vice·ge·rent (vīs·jir′ənt) *n.* One duly authorized to exercise the powers of another; a deputy; vicar. — *adj.* Acting in the place of another, usually in the place of a superior. [< Med.L *vicegerens, -entis* < L *vice* in place + *gerens, -entis,* ppr. of *gerere* to carry, manage] — **vice·ge′ral** *adj.*

vic·e·nar·y (vis′ə·ner′ē) *adj.* **1.** Consisting of or pertaining to twenty. **2.** Relating to a system of notation based upon twenty. [< L *vicenarius* < *viceni* twenty each < *viginti* twenty]

vi·cen·ni·al (vī·sen′ē·əl) *adj.* **1.** Occurring once in twenty years. **2.** Lasting or existing twenty years. [< L *vicennium* twenty-year period < *vicies* twenty times + *annus* year]

Vi·cen·za (vē·chen′tsä) A city in northern Italy, in the Region of Venetia; pop. 78,900 (est. 1967): ancient **Vi·cen·ti·a** (vī·sen′shē·ə).

vice-pres·i·dent (vīs′prez′ə·dənt) *n.* An officer ranking next below a president and, acting, on occasion, in his place. Also **vice president.** Abbr. *V.P., V.Pres.* — **vice′-pres′i·den′tial** (-prez′ə·den′shəl) *adj.*

vice·re·gal (vīs·rē′gəl) *adj.* Of or relating to a viceroy, his office, or his jurisdiction. Also **vice·roy′al** (-roi′əl). — **vice·re′gal·ly** *adv.*

vice·re·gent (vīs′rē′jənt) *n.* A deputy regent. — **vice′-re′gen·cy** *n.* — **vice′-re′gent** *adj.*

vice·roy (vīs′roi) *n.* **1.** One who rules a country, colony, or province by the authority of his sovereign or king. **2.** A North American nymphalid butterfly (*Basilarchia archippus*), orange red with black markings and a row of white marginal spots. [< MF *viceroy, visroy* < *vice-, vis-* in place (< L *vice*) + *roy* king, ult. < L *rex, regis*]

vice·roy·al·ty (vīs·roi′əl·tē) *n. pl.* **·ties 1.** The office or authority of a viceroy. **2.** The term of office of a viceroy. **3.** A district governed by a viceroy. Also **vice′roy′ship.**

vice squad A police division charged with combating prostitution, gambling, etc.

vi·ce ver·sa (vī′sə vûr′sə, vīs′) The order being changed; conversely. Abbr. *v.v.* [< L]

Vi·chy (vē·shē′) A resort city in central France; provisional capital of France during German occupation, World War II; pop. 33,458 (1968).

vi·chy·ssoise (vē′shē·swäz′) *n.* A potato cream soup, usually served cold. [< F, of Vichy]

Vi·chy water (vish′ē, vē·shē′) The effervescent mineral water from the springs at Vichy, France; also, any mineral water resembling it. Also **Vi′chy, vi′chy.**

vic·i·nage (vis′ə·nij) *n.* **1.** Neighboring places collectively; vicinity. **2.** The state of being a neighbor or neighbors. [< OF *visenage, vicenage* < L *vicinus* nearby]

vic·i·nal (vis′ə·nəl) *adj.* **1.** Neighboring; adjoining; near. **2.** *Crystall.* Designating a crystal whose planes closely approximate or take the place of those of one of the fundamental forms. **3.** *Chem.* Designating a benzene derivative in which the substituted elements or radicals are in consecutive order on the benzene ring. [< L *vicinalis* < *vicinus* neighbor, orig. nearby]

vicinal road A local road, as distinguished from one between towns.

vi·cin·i·ty (vi·sin′ə·tē) *n. pl.* **·ties 1.** A region adjacent or near; neighborhood. **2.** Nearness in space or relationship; proximity. [< L *vicinitas, -tatis* < *vicinus* nearby]

vi·cious (vish′əs) *adj.* **1.** Characterized by malice or spite; malicious; mean: a *vicious* lie. **2.** Characterized by violence and fierceness; fierce: a *vicious* blow. **3.** Addicted to vice; corrupt in conduct or habits. **4.** Morally injurious, vile. **5.** Unruly or dangerous; refractory, as an animal. **6.** Defective or faulty: *vicious* arguments. **7.** *Informal* Intense; severe; extreme: a *vicious* storm. [< OF < L *vitiosus* < *vitium* fault] — **vi′cious·ly** *adv.* — **vi′cious·ness** *n.*

vicious circle 1. The process or predicament that arises when the solution of a problem creates a new problem. **2.** *Logic* Circle (which see). **3.** *Med.* The accelerating effect of one disease upon another when the two are coexistent.

vi·cis·si·tude (vi·sis′ə·tood, -tyood) *n.* **1.** *pl.* Irregular changes or variations, as of fortune: the *vicissitudes* of life. **2.** A change; especially, a complete change; mutation or mutability. **3.** Alternating change or succession, as of the seasons. [< MF < L *vicissitudo* < *vicis* turn, change]

vi·cis·si·tu·di·nar·y (vi·sis′ə·tood′ə·ner′ē, -tyoo′-) *adj.* Marked by or subject to change. Also **vi·cis′si·tu′di·nous.**

Vicks·burg (viks′bûrg) A city in western Mississippi on the Mississippi River; besieged and taken by the Union army in the Civil War, 1863; pop. 25,478.

Vi·co (vē′kō), Giovanni Battista, 1668–1744, Italian jurist and philosopher.

vic·tim (vik′tim) *n.* **1.** One who is killed, injured, or subjected to suffering. **2.** A dupe. **3.** A living creature sacrificed to some deity. [< L *victima* beast for sacrifice]

vic·tim·ize (vik′tim·īz) *v.t.* **·ized, ·iz·ing** To defraud or swindle; dupe; cheat. — **vic′tim·i·za′tion** *n.* — **vic′tim·iz′er** *n.*

vic·tor (vik′tər) *n.* **1.** One who vanquishes an enemy. **2.** One who wins any struggle or contest. — *adj.* Pertaining to a victor; victorious: the *victor* nation. [< AF *victor, victour,* OF *victeur* < L *victus,* pp. of *vincere* to conquer]

Vic·tor Em·man·u·el I (vik′tər i·man′yōō·əl), 1759–1824, king of Sardinia 1802–21; abdicated.

Victor Emmanuel II, 1820–78, king of Sardinia 1849–61, and first king of Italy 1861–78.

Victor Emmanuel III, 1869–1947, king of Italy 1900–46.

vic·to·ri·a (vik·tôr′ē·ə, -tō′rē·ə) *n.* **1.** A low, light, four-wheeled carriage, with a calash top, a seat for two persons over the rear axle, and a raised driver's seat. **2.** An old type of passenger automobile with a calash top that usually covered the rear seat only. [after Queen *Victoria*]

VICTORIA

Vic·to·ri·a (vik·tôr′ē·ə, -tō′rē·ə), 1819–1901, queen of England 1837–1901: full name Alexandrina Victoria.

Vic·to·ri·a (vik·tôr′ē·ə, -tō′rē·ə) *n.* In Roman mythology, the winged goddess of victory: identified with the Greek *Nike.*

Vic·to·ri·a (vik·tôr′ē·ə, -tō′rē·ə) **1.** A State of SE Australia; 87,884 sq. mi.; pop. 3,461,400 (1970); capital, Melbourne. **2.** The capital of British Columbia, a port at the southern end of Vancouver Island; pop. 57,453. **3.** The capital of Hong Kong colony, a port on Hong Kong island; pop. about 1 million. **4.** A city in southern Texas: pop. 41,349.

Victoria, Lake A lake between Uganda and Tanzania, the largest lake in Africa; 26,828 sq. mi. Also **Victoria Ny·an·za** (nī·an′zə, nyän′zə). See maps of ETHIOPIA, NILE.

Victoria, Mount 1. The highest peak of the Owen Stanley Range, SE New Guinea; 13,240 ft. **2.** The highest peak of the Chin Hills, Upper Burma; 10,018 ft.

Victoria Cross A British military and naval decoration, awarded for conspicuous bravery. Abbr. *V.C.*

Victoria Day In Canada, the Monday next before May 24, a statutory holiday commemorating the birthday of Queen Victoria.

Victoria Desert The southern belt of the desert region of Western Australia: also *Great Victoria Desert.*

Victoria Falls A cataract on the Zambesi River between Northern and Southern Rhodesia; 343 ft. high; over a mile wide; discovered by Livingstone in 1855.

Vic·to·ri·an (vik·tôr′ē·ən, -tō′rē-) *adj.* **1.** Of or relating to Queen Victoria, or to her reign. **2.** Pertaining to or characteristic of the ideals and standards of morality and taste prevalent during the reign of Queen Victoria; prudish. — *n.* Anyone contemporary with Queen Victoria.

Victoria Nile See under NILE.

Vic·to·ri·an·ism (vik·tôr′ē·ən·iz′əm, -tō′rē-) *n.* The state or quality of being Victorian, as in style or moral outlook.

vic·to·ri·ous (vik·tôr′ē·əs, -tō′rē-) *adj.* **1.** Having won victory; triumphant. **2.** Relating to or characterized by victory. — **vic·to′ri·ous·ly** *adv.* — **vic·to′ri·ous·ness** *n.*

vic·to·ry (vik′tər·ē) *n. pl.* **·ries** The overcoming of an enemy, opponent, or any difficulty; success; triumph. [< OF *victorie, victoire* < L *victoria* < *victor.* See VICTOR]

Victory Medal Either of two bronze medals awarded to all

---

who served in the U.S. armed forces in World War I or World War II, worn with the **Victory Ribbon**.

Vic·tro·la (vik·trō′lə) *n.* A record player: a trade name.

vict·ual (vit′l) *n.* **1.** *pl.* Food for human beings, as prepared for eating: also, *Informal*, vittles. **2.** *Obs.* Provisions of any kind. — **Syn.** See FOOD. — *v.* **vict·ualed** or **·ualled**, **vict·ual·ing** or **·ual·ling** *v.t.* **1.** To furnish with victuals. — *v.i.* **2.** To lay in supplies of food. **3.** *Rare* To eat; feed. [< OF *vitaile* < LL *victualia* provisions, neut. pl. of L *victualis* of food < *victus* food]

vict·ual·er (vit′l·ər) *n. Archaic* **1.** One who supplies an army, navy, or ship with provisions; a conmissary. **2.** An innkeeper. **3.** A supply ship. Also **vict′ual·ler**.

vi·cu·ña (vi·kōōn′yə, ·kyōō′nə) *n.* **1.** A small ruminant (*Lama vicugna*) of the high Andes related to the llama and alpaca, having fine and valuable wool. **2.** A textile made from this wool, or some substitute: also **vicuña cloth**. Also **vi·cu′gna**. [< Sp. < Quechua]

vi·de (vī′dē) See: used to make a reference or direct attention to: *vide* p. 36. Abbr. *v.*, *vid.* [< L, imperative sing. of *videre* to see]

vi·de an·te (vī′dē an′tē) *Latin* See before.

vi·de in·fra (vī′dē in′frə) *Latin* See below. Abbr. *v.i.*

Vi·de·la (bē·thā′lä), Gabriel González See GONZÁLEZ-VIDELA.

vi·de·li·cet (vi·del′ə·sit) *adv.* To wit; that is to say; namely. Abbr. *viz.* [< L < *videre licet* it is permitted to see]

vid·e·o (vid′ē·ō) *adj.* Of or pertaining to television, especially to the picture portion of a program. — *n.* Television. Compare AUDIO. [< L, I see]

video tape **1.** A magnetic tape used in television to record image and sound. **2.** Teletranscription using such tape.

vi·de post (vī′dē pōst′) *Latin* See after; see what follows.

vi·de su·pra (vī′dē sōō′prə) *Latin* See above.

vi·dette (vi·det′) See VEDETTE.

vi·de ut su·pra (vī′dē ut sōō′prə) *Latin* See what is written above.

vie (vī) *v.* **vied**, **vy·ing** *v.i.* **1.** To strive for superiority; contend; compete, as in a race: with *with* or *for*. — *v.t.* **2.** *Rare* To put forth in competition; match. **3.** *Obs.* To wager; bet. [< MF *envier* to invite, challenge < L *invitare* to invite]

Vi·en·na (vē·en′ə) The capital of Austria, in the NE part on the Danube; pop. 1,614,341 (1971): German *Wien*.

Vienne (vyen) A city in SE France, on the Rhône; pop. 26,512 (1968).

Vi·en·nese (vē′ə·nēz′, ·nēs′) *adj.* Of or relating to Vienna, or its inhabitants. — *n. pl.* **·nese** A native or citizen of Vienna.

Vien·tiane (vyàn·tyàn′) The administrative capital of Laos, in the NW central part; pop. about 100,000.

vi et ar·mis (vī et är′mis) *Latin* With force and arms.

Vi·et·cong (vē·et·kong′) *n.* **1.** In South Vietnam, the military arm, usually composed of guerrilla forces, of the National Liberation Front, a communist movement. **2.** A member or supporter of the Vietcong. — *adj.* Of or pertaining to the Vietcong. [< Vietnamese *Viet Nam Cong Sam* Vietnamese communist or communism]

Vi·et·nam (vē·et·näm′) A Republic in eastern Indochina, officially the **Socialist Republic of Vietnam**, comprising the former **Democratic Republic of Vietnam**, or **North Vietnam** (63,344 sq. mi.; pop. 22,600,000; capital, Hanoi), and the former **Republic of Vietnam**, or **South Vietnam** (65,749 sq. mi.; pop. 19,800,000; capital, Saigon). United in 1976, with capital at Hanoi. Also **Viet-Nam**. See map of THAILAND.

Vi·et·nam·ese (vē·et·nä n·ēz′, ·ēs′) *n. pl.* **Vi·et·nam·ese** **1.** A native or inhabitant of Vietnam. **2.** The language of Vietnam, including the Tonkinese and Cochin Chinese dialects, by some linguists classified in the Mon-Khmer subfamily of the Austro-Asiatic languages: formerly called *Annamese*. — *adj.* Of or pertaining to Vietnam, its inhabitants, or their language.

Vietnam War The conflict from 1954 to 1973 in which the Vietcong and North Vietnamese forces, supported by the People's Republic of China and the Soviet Union, sought to impose a communist regime in South Vietnam, whose forces were aided by the U.S., Australia, South Korea, Thailand, New Zealand, and the Philippines.

view (vyōō) *n.* **1.** The act of seeing; survey; inspection. **2.** Mental examination or inspection. **3.** Power or range of vision. **4.** That which is seen; outlook; prospect. **5.** A representation of a scene; especially, a landscape. **6.** The object of action; aim; intention; purpose. **7.** Manner of looking at things; opinion; judgment; belief: What are your *views* on this subject? **8.** A general summary or account. — **Syn.** See OPINION. — **in view 1.** In range of vision. **2.** Under consideration. **3.** As a goal or end. — **in view of** In consideration of. — **on view** Open to the public; set up for public inspection. — **with a view to 1.** With the aim or purpose of. **2.** With a hope of. — *v.t.* **1.** To look at; see; behold. **2.** To look at carefully; scrutinize; examine. **3.**

To survey mentally; consider. [< OF *veue*, orig. pp. of *veoir* to see < L *videre*]

view·er (vyōō′ər) *n.* **1.** One who views; especially, one who watches television. **2.** Any of various optical devices used in viewing photographic prints or transparencies.

view finder *Photog.* A finder (which see).

view halloo A shout uttered by a huntsman when a fox breaks cover. Also **view hallo**, **view halloa**.

view·less (vyōō′lis) *adj.* **1.** Devoid of a view; that cannot be viewed. **2.** Having no views or opinions. **3.** Invisible; unseen. — **view′less·ly** *adv.* — **view′less·ness** *n.*

view·point (vyōō′point′) *n.* Point of view. ◆ *Viewpoint*, though questioned by older grammarians, is standard English and acceptable in any sort of writing.

view·y (vyōō′ē) *adj.* **view·i·er**, **view·i·est** *Informal* **1.** Visionary. **2.** Appearing good at first sight; showy.

Vi·gée-Le·brun (vē·zhā′lə·bræn′), Marie Anne Élisabeth, 1755–1842, French painter.

vi·ges·i·mal (vī·jes′ə·məl) *adj.* **1.** Twentieth. **2.** Of or pertaining to twenty; proceeding by twenties. [< L *vigesimus*, var. of *vicesimus* < *viceni*. See VICENARY.]

vig·il (vij′əl) *n.* **1.** The act of staying awake in order to observe, protect, etc.; watch. **2.** *Eccl.* **a** The eve of a holy day, especially, of a fast day. **b** *pl.* Religious devotions on such an eve. **3.** *Usually pl.* Any nocturnal devotions. [< OF *vigilie* < Med.L *vigilia* < L *vigil* wide-awake]

vig·i·lance (vij′ə·ləns) *n.* **1.** The quality of being vigilant; alertness; watchfulness against danger. **2.** *Obs.* Insomnia.

vigilance committee *U.S.* **1.** Formerly, a body of men self-organized for the maintenance of order and the administration of summary justice, as in lawless sections of the western United States. **2.** Formerly, in the southern United States, a group of white citizens organized to terrify and control Negroes and abolitionists.

vig·i·lant (vij′ə·lənt) *adj.* Characterized by vigilance; being on the alert; watchful; heedful; wary. [< MF < L *vigilans*, *-antis*, ppr. of *vigilare* to keep awake < *vigil* awake] — **vig′i·lant·ly** *adv.* — **vig′i·lant·ness** *n.*
— **Syn.** *Vigilant*, *watchful*, *alert*, *wide-awake*, and *wary* mean giving careful attention to circumstances, so as to avoid danger or seize opportunity. *Vigilant* suggests action as well as attention: a riot was averted by the *vigilant* police. *Watchful* suggests unremitting attention: his *watchful* eye caught the covert signal. *Alert* stresses the speed of a response to necessity or opportunity: *alert* traders made a killing on the stock market. A *wide-awake* person is keenly aware of that which might escape another. *Wary* also suggests keen awareness, but with a great implication of caution, shrewdness, and circumspection. — **Ant.** inattentive, heedless, careless.

vig·i·lan·te (vij′ə·lan′tē) *n. U.S.* **1.** One of a group who take upon themselves the unauthorized responsibility of interpreting and acting upon matters of law, public morality, etc. **2.** A member of a vigilance committee: also **vigilance man**. [< Sp., vigilant < L *vigilans*. See VIGILANT.]

vigil light A small candle burned in church or before a shrine, often used as a memorial symbol to the dead.

vi·gnette (vin·yet′) *n.* **1.** A description, short literary work, etc., that depicts something subtly and delicately. **2.** Any charming, intimate scene, grouping, etc. **3.** A decorative or illustrative design placed on or before the title page of a book, at the end or beginning of a chapter, etc. **4.** An engraving, photograph, or the like, having a background that shades off gradually. **5.** A running ornament of leaves and tendrils, as in architecture or manuscripts. — *v.t.* **·gnet·ted**, **·gnet·ting** **1.** To make with a gradually shaded background or border, as a photograph. **2.** To ornament with vignettes. **3.** To depict in or as in a vignette. [< F, dim. of *vigne* vine]

vi·gnet·ter (vin·yet′ər) *n.* **1.** A device, as a paper with an oval hole in the center, used by photographers in printing vignettes. **2.** One who makes vignettes: also **vi·gnet′tist**.

Vi·gno·la (vē·nyō′lä), Giacomo Barozzi da, 1507–73, Italian architect: original name *Giacomo Barozzi*. Also called *Barocchio*.

Vi·gny (vē·nyē′), Comte Alfred Victor de, 1799–1863, French poet, dramatist, and novelist.

Vi·go (vē′gō, *Sp.* bē′gō) A port city in NW Spain, on **Vigo Bay**, an inlet of the Atlantic; pop. 146,320 (est. 1960).

vig·or (vig′ər) *n.* **1.** Active strength or force, physical or mental. **2.** Vital or natural power, as in a healthy animal or plant. **3.** Forcible exertion of strength; energy; intensity. **4.** Effective force; validity. Also *Brit.* **vig′our**. — **in vigor** *Law* In operation; effective. [< AF *vigur*, *vigour*, OF *vigor* < L < *vigere* to be lively; thrive]

vi·go·ro·so (vē′gō·rō′sō) *adj. Music* Vigorous; energetic. — *adv.* In a vigorous or energetic manner: a direction to the performer. [< Ital.]

vig·or·ous (vig′ər·əs) *adj.* **1.** Full of physical or mental vigor; robust. **2.** Performed or done with vigor. **3.** Showing or exemplifying vigor. **4.** Effective and forceful: a *vigorous* style. — **vig′or·ous·ly** *adv.* — **vig′or·ous·ness** *n.*

Vii·pu·ri (vē′pōō·rē) The Finnish name for VYBORG.

vi·king (vī′king) *n.* **1.** One of the Scandinavian warriors who harried the coasts of Europe from the eighth to the tenth centuries. **2.** A pirate; sea rover. Also **Vi′king**. [<

ON *vīkingr* pirate. Cf. OE and Frisian *wicing* < *wic* camp < L *vicus* village.]

vil. Village.

vi·la·yet (vē′lä·yet′) *n.* An administrative division of Turkey. [< Turkish *vilāyet* < Arabic *wilāyat* < *wāli* governor]

vile (vīl) *adj.* **vil·er, vil·est 1.** Morally base; shamefully wicked: a *vile* sin. **2.** Despicable; vicious. **3.** Loathsome; disgusting. **4.** Degrading; ignominious: *vile* treatment. **5.** Flagrantly bad or inferior. **6.** Unpleasant; disagreeable: *vile* weather. **7.** Of little worth or account. [< AF or OF, fem. of *vil* < L *vilis* cheap] **— vile′ly** *adv.* **— vile′ness** *n.*

vil·i·fy (vil′ə·fī) *v.t.* **·fied, ·fy·ing 1.** To abuse or characterize with defamatory language; malign; slander. **2.** To make base or vile; degrade. **— Syn.** See ASPERSE. [< LL *vilificare* < *vilis* cheap + *facere* to make] **— vil′i·fi·ca′tion** (-fə·kā′shən) *n.* **— vil′i·fi′er** *n.*

vil·i·pend (vil′ə·pend) *v.t.* **1.** To think or speak of disparagingly; regard with contempt; despise. **2.** To vilify; defame. [< OF *vilipender* < L *vilipendere* < *vilis* cheap + *pendere* to weigh, consider]

vill (vil) *n.* In old English law, a village or township. [< AF *vill*, OF *vile, ville* country house, village < L *villa*. See VILLA.]

vil·la (vil′ə) *n.* **1.** A comfortable or luxurious house in the country, at a resort, etc. **2.** *Chiefly Brit.* A modest suburban residence. [< Ital. < L, a country house, farm, dim. of *vicus* village]

Vil·la (vē′yä, *Sp.* bē′yä), **Francisco,** 1877–1923, Mexican revolutionary leader: called **Pancho Villa:** original name **Doroteo A·ran·go** (ä·räng′gō).

vil·la·dom (vil′ə·dəm) *n. Brit.* The occupants of suburban villas, or their opinions, social activities, etc.

vil·lage (vil′ij) *n.* **1.** A collection of houses in a rural district, usually smaller than a town but larger than a hamlet. **2.** *U.S.* In some States, a municipality smaller than a city, sometimes incorporated. **3.** Any comparatively small community or group of dwellings. **4.** A collection of habitations of animals: a gopher *village.* **5.** The inhabitants of a village, collectively; the villagers. **— the Village** Greenwich Village (which see). Abbr. *v., vil.* [< OF < L *villaticum*, neut. sing. of *villaticus* pertaining to a villa < *villa*]

village community An early type of agricultural community with a simple organization, often regarded as the political unit out of which the modern state developed.

vil·lag·er (vil′ij·ər) *n.* One who lives in a village.

vil·lain (vil′ən) *n.* **1.** An egregiously wicked, evil, or malevolent man. **2.** Such a man represented as a leading character in a novel, play, etc., often in opposition to the hero. **3.** A rogue; scoundrel: often used humorously. **4.** A villein. **5.** *Obs.* A boor; rustic. [< AF, OF *vilein*, OF *vilain* farm servant < LL *villanus* < L *villa* farm] **— vil′lain·ess** *n.fem.*

vil·lain·ous (vil′ən·əs) *adj.* **1.** Having the nature of a villain. **2.** Characteristic of a villain; evil. **3.** Very bad or unpleasant. **— vil′lain·ous·ly** *adv.* **— vil′lain·ous·ness** *n.*

vil·lain·y (vil′ən·ē) *n. pl.* **·lain·ies 1.** The quality of being villainous. **2.** Conduct characteristic of a villain.

Vil·la-Lo·bos (vē′lə·lō′boosh, -boos), **Heitor,** 1887–1959, Brazilian composer and conductor.

vil·la·nel·la (vil′ə·nel′ə, *Ital.* vēl′lä·nel′lä) *n. pl.* **·nel·le** (-nel′ē, *Ital.* -nel′lä) *Music* **1.** An old rustic dance, or the music for it. **2.** A rustic Italian part song, popular during the sixteenth century. [< Ital., fem. dim. of *villano* < LL *villanus*. See VILLAIN.]

vil·la·nelle (vil′ə·nel′) *n.* A verse form having two rhymes and nineteen lines arranged in five tercets and a concluding quatrain. [< F < Ital. *villanella* villanella]

Vil·lard (vi·lärd′), **Oswald Garrison,** 1872–1949, U.S. journalist and author born in Germany.

Vil·lars (vē·lär′), **Duc Claude Louis Hector de,** 1653–1734, French marshal.

vil·lat·ic (vi·lat′ik) *adj.* Of or pertaining to a villa, farm, or village; rural. [< L *villaticus*. See VILLAGE.]

vil·lein (vil′ən) *n.* In the feudal system, a member of a class of serfs who were regarded as freemen in respect to their legal relations with all persons except their lord, whose slaves they were: also spelled *villain.* **— Syn.** Compare SLAVE. [< AF or OF *vilein, vilain.* See VILLAIN.]

vil·lein·age (vil′ən·ij) *n.* **1.** In feudal law, the tenure by which villeins held land. **2.** The status or condition of a villein. Also **vil′lain·age, vil′len·age.**

Ville·neuve (vēl·nœv′), **Pierre Charles Jean Baptiste Silvestre de,** 1763–1806, French admiral.

Vil·liers (vil′ərz), **George** See (Duke of) BUCKINGHAM.

Vil·liers (vē·yā′), **George** See TARDIEU.

vil·li·form (vil′ə·fôrm) *adj.* **1.** Having the form of a villus. **2.** *Zool.* Having the appearance and texture of velvet, as the teeth of fishes when numerous, small, and set close toegher. [< NL *villiformis* < L *villus* tuft of hair + *forma* form]

Vil·lon (vē·vôn′), **François,** 1431–63?, French poet: original name **François de Mont·cor·bier** (də·môn·kôr·byā′).

vil·los·i·ty (vi·los′ə·tē) *n. pl.* **·ties 1.** The state of being villous. **2.** A villous surface or coating. **3.** A villus.

vil·lous (vil′əs) *adj.* **1.** Covered with short, soft hairs; nappy. **2.** Covered with or having villi. **3.** Resembling or characteristic of a villus. Also **vil′lose** (-ōs). [< L *villosus* < *villus* tuft of hair] **— vil′lous·ly** *adv.*

vil·lus (vil′əs) *n. pl.* **vil·li** (vil′ī) **1.** *Anat.* One of the short, hairlike processes found on certain membranes, as of the small intestine, where they aid in the digestive process. **2.** *Bot.* One of the long, close, rather soft hairs on the surface of certain plants. [< L, tuft of hair, shaggy hair, var. of *vellus* fleece, wool]

Vil·nyus (vēl′nyəs, *Russ.* vyēly′nyəs) The capital of the Lithuanian S.S.R., in the SE part; pop. 372,000 (1970): Polish *Wilno.* Also **Vil·na** (vēl′nə), **Vil·ni·us** (vil′nē·əs), **Vil′·nyus.**

vim (vim) *n.* Force or vigor; energy; spirit. [< L, accusative of *vis* power]

vi·men (vī′mən) *n. pl.* **vim·i·na** (vim′ə·nə) *Bot.* A long, flexible shoot or branch. [< L *vimen, -inis* twig < *viere* to bend together, plait]

vim·i·nal (vi′n′ə·nəl) *adj. Rare* Pertaining to, made of, or producing twigs. [< L *vimen, -inis.* See VIMEN.]

Vim·i·nal (vim′ə·nəl) *n.* One of the Seven Hills of Rome.

vi·min·e·ous (vī·min′ē·əs) *adj.* **1.** *Bot.* Having or resembling long, flexible shoots or branches. **2.** *Obs.* Made of twigs. [< L *vimineus* < *vimen, -inis.* See VIMEN.]

v. imp. *Gram.* Impersonal verb.

Vi·my (vē·mē′) A town in northern France, near **Vimy Ridge,** scene of fierce fighting in World War I, 1915–1917.

vin (van) *n. French* Wine.

vin- Var. of VINI-.

vi·na (vē′nä) *n.* An East Indian musical instrument with seven steel strings stretched on a long, fretted fingerboard over two gourds. [< Hind. *vīnā* < Skt.]

vi·na·ceous (vī·nā′shəs) *adj.* **1.** Of or pertaining to wine or grapes. **2.** Having the characteristic color of red wine. [< L *vinaceus* < *vinum* wine]

Vi·ña del Mar (bē′nyä thel mär′) A city in central Chile, on the Pacific; pop. 106,717 (est. 1959).

vin·ai·grette (vin′ə·gret′) *n.* **1.** A small ornamental box or bottle with a perforated top, used for holding smelling salts, or a similar pungent restorative: also called *vinegarette.* **2.** Vinaigrette sauce. [< F, dim. of *vinaigre* vinegar]

vinaigrette sauce A sauce made from vinegar, savory herbs, etc., served with fish and cold meats.

Vin·cennes (vin·senz′, *Fr.* van·sen′) **1.** A city in SW Indiana, on the Wabash River; site of a French mission established in 1702; pop. 19,867. **2.** A city in northern France, near Paris; pop. 49,143 (1968).

Vin·cent de Paul (vin′sənt də pôl′, *Fr.* van·sän′də·pôl), **Saint,** 1576–1660, French priest; founded charitable orders.

Vincent's angina (vin′sənts) *Pathol.* Trench mouth Also **Vincent's infection.** [after J. H. *Vincent,* 1862–1950, French physician]

Vin·ci (vin′chē), **Leonardo da** See DA VINCI.

vin·ci·ble (vin′sə·bəl) *adj. Rare* Capable of being conquered or overcome; conquerable. [< L *vincibilis* < *vincere* to conquer] **— vin′ci·bil·i·ty, vin′ci·ble·ness** *n.*

vin·cu·lum (vingk′yə·ləm) *n. pl.* **·la** (-lə) **1.** *Math.* A straight line drawn over several algebraic terms to show that all are to be operated on together. **2.** *Anat* A confining band of fascia. **3.** A bond of union. [< L < *vincire* to bind]

Vin·dhya Pra·desh (vind′hyə prə·dāsh′) A former state of central India, incorporated in Madhya Pradesh, 1956.

vin·di·ca·ble (vin′də·kə·bəl) *adj.* Capable of being vindicated; justifiable.

vin·di·cate (vin′də·kāt) *v.t.* **·cat·ed, ·cat·ing 1.** To clear of accusation, censure, suspicion, etc. **2.** To support or maintain, as a right or claim. **3.** To serve to justify. **4.** *Rare* To lay claim to. **5.** *Obs.* To avenge; punish. **6.** *Obs.* To set free; rescue. **— Syn.** See ABSOLVE. [< L *vindicatus,* pp. of *vindicare* to avenge, claim] **— vin′di·ca′tor** *n.*

vin·di·ca·tion (vin′də·kā′shən) *n.* **1.** The act of vindicating, or the state of being vindicated. **2.** Justification; defense.

vin·di·ca·to·ry (vin′də·kə·tôr′ē, -tō′rē) *adj.* **1.** Serving to vindicate; justificatory. **2.** Punitive; avenging.

vin·dic·tive (vin·dik′tiv) *adj.* **1.** Having a revengeful spirit. **2.** Revengeful or spiteful in quality, character, etc. Also *Rare* **vin·di·ca·tive** (vin′də·kā′tiv). [< L *vindicta* revenge] **— vin·dic′tive·ly** *adv.* **— vin·dic′tive·ness** *n.*

vine (vīn) *n.* **1.** Any of a large and widely distributed group of plants having a slender flexible stem that may twine about a support or clasp it by means of tendrils, petioles, etc.; also, the slender flexible stem itself. **2.** A grapevine (def. 1). [< OF *vigne, vine* < L *vinea* vineyard < *vinum* wine]

vine·dress·er (vīn′dres′ər) *n.* One who tends or prunes grapevines.

vin·e·gar (vin′ə·gər) *n.* **1.** An acid liquid consisting chiefly of dilute acetic acid, obtained by the fermentation of cider, wine, etc., and used as a condiment and preservative. **2.** *Med.* A preparation of dilute acetic acid. **3.** Sourness of manner, speech, temperament, etc. [< OF *vyn egre, vinaigre* < *vin* wine (< L *vinum*) + *aigre, egre* sour < L *acer* sharp]

vinegar eel   A small nematode worm (*Anguillula aceti*) common in vinegar and similar fermenting liquids: also called *eelworm.* Also **vinegar worm.**

vin·e·gar·ette (vin'ə·gə·ret')   *n.* A vinaigrette (def. 1).

vinegar fly   A fruit fly (genus *Drosophila*) that breeds in fermenting vegetable substances, pickles, etc.

vin·e·gar·roon (vin'ə·gə·rōōn')   *n.* A whip scorpion (*Mastigoproctus giganteus*) of the SW United States and Mexico that emits a vinegarlike odor when alarmed. Also **vin/e·ge·rone'** (-rōn'). [< Sp. *vinagrón,* aug. of *vinagre* vinegar]

vin·e·gar·y (vin'ə·gər·ē)   *adj.* **1.** Resembling or suggestive of vinegar; sour; acid. **2.** Crabbed or sour in manner, disposition, etc. Also **vin/e·gar·ish** (-ish)

Vine·land (vīn'lənd)   **1.** A borough in southern New Jersey; pop. 47,399. **2.** See VINLAND.

vin·er·y (vī'nər·ē)   *n. pl.* **·er·ies** **1.** A greenhouse for grapes; grapery. **2.** Vines collectively.

vine·yard (vin'yərd)   *n.* **1.** An area planted with grapevines. **2.** A field of activity, especially one of spiritual labor. [Earlier *wineyard,* OE *wīngeard*; infl. in form by VINE.]

vine·yard·ist (vin'yər·dist)   *n.* One who grows or cultivates grapevines.

vingt-et-un (vaṅ·tā·œṅ')   *n.* Twenty-one, a card game. [< F, twenty-one]

vini-   *combining form* **1.** Wine: *viniferous.* **2.** Of or pertaining to wine grapes: *viniculture.* Also *vin-* (before vowels): also *vino-.* [< L *vinum* wine]

vi·nic (vī'nik, vin'ik)   *adj.* Of, pertaining to, or derived from wine. [< L *vinum* wine]

vin·i·cul·ture (vin'ə·kul'chər)   *n.* The cultivation of grapes for wine. **—vin/i·cul/tur·al** *adj.* **—vin/i·cul/tur·ist** *n.*

vi·nif·er·ous (vi·nif'ər·əs, vin·if'-)   *adj.* Producing wine. [< VINI- + -FEROUS]

vin·i·fi·ca·tor (vin'ə·fə·kā'tər)   *n.* An apparatus for receiving and condensing the vapor of alcohol from fermenting wine. [< VINI- + L *-ficator* maker < *facere* to make]

Vin·land (vin'lənd)   A name given to part of the NE coast of North America by Norse voyagers: also *Vineland.*

vi·nom·e·ter (vin·om'ə·tər, vī·nom'-)   *n.* A hydrometer for measuring the alcohol in wine. [< VINO- + -METER]

vin or·di·naire (vaṅ ôr·dē·nâr')   *French* Cheap red wine; literally, ordinary wine.

vi·nos·i·ty (vī·nos'ə·tē)   *n. pl.* **·ties** **1.** The state or quality of being vinous. **2.** The character of a wine, including the bouquet, flavor, body, etc. **3.** Addiction to or fondness for wine. [< LL *vinositas, -tatis* < L *vinosus.* See VINOUS.]

vi·nous (vī'nəs)   *adj.* **1.** Pertaining to, characteristic of, or having the qualities of wine. **2.** Caused by, affected by, or addicted to wine. **3.** Tinged with dark red. [< L *vinosus* < *vinum* wine]

Vin·son (vin'sən), **Frederick Moore,** 1890–1953, U.S. administrator and jurist; chief justice of the Supreme Court 1946–53.

vin·tage (vin'tij)   *n.* **1.** The yield of a vineyard or wine-growing district for one season; also, the wine produced from this yield. **2.** The harvesting of a vineyard and the first steps in the making of wine. **3.** Wine of high quality or of an exceptionally good year: also **vintage wine.** **4.** *Informal* The type or kind current or popular at a particular time of the past: a joke of ancient *vintage.* **—** *adj.* **1.** Of exceptional quality or excellence; choice: a *vintage* crop; *vintage* Shakespeare. **2.** Characterized by lasting interest or importance; time-honored; venerable; classic: *vintage* songs. **3.** Old-fashioned; outmoded: a *vintage* coat. [< AF, alter of *vindage, vendage,* OF *vendage* < L *vindemia* < *vinum* wine + *demere* to remove < *de-* off + *emere* to take]

vin·tag·er (vin'tij·ər)   *n.* A harvester of grapes.

vint·ner (vint'nər)   *n.* A wine merchant. [< OF *vinetier, vinotier* < *vinot,* dim. of *vin* wine < L *vinum*]

vin·y (vī'nē)   *adj.* **vin·i·er, vin·i·est** **1.** Of, pertaining to, or resembling a vine. **2.** Full of vines.

vi·nyl (vī'nəl, vin'əl)   *n. Chem.* The univalent radical, CH₂:CH, derived from ethylene, and extensively used in organic synthesis. [< L *vinum* wine + -YL]

vinyl acetate   *Chem.* A colorless liquid, C₄H₆O₂, used in the synthesis of various resins and plastics.

vinyl chloride   *Chem.* A compound of vinyl and chlorine, C₂H₃Cl, used in the production of synthetic fibers.

Vi·nyl·ite (vī'nə·līt, vin'ə-)   *n. Chem.* Any of a class of thermoplastic vinyl resins having a wide range of uses in industry and the arts: a trade name. Also **vi/nyl·ite.**

vinyl polymer   *Chem.* One of a large group of organic compounds obtained by the polymerization of vinyl compounds.

vi·ol (vī'əl)   *n.* Any of a family of stringed musical instruments, predecessors of the violin family, used mainly in the 16th–18th centuries, and having usually six strings, a fretted fingerboard, and played with a curved bow. The modern double bass is a member of this family. [Earlier *vielle* < AF, OF < Med.L *vidula, vitula* < Gmc.; infl. in form by OF *viole*]

vi·o·la¹ (vē·ō'lə, vī-; *Ital.* vyō'lä)   *n.* **1.** A musical instrument of the violin family, somewhat larger than the violin, and tuned a fifth lower, with a graver and less brilliant tone. **2.** An organ stop producing stringlike tones. [< Ital., orig., a viol < Med.L *vidula* < Gmc.]

vi·o·la² (vī·ō'lə, vī'ə·lə)   *n. Bot.* Any of a large genus (*Viola*) of chiefly herbaceous plants including the violets and the pansies; especially, one of several garden plants having small, variously colored flowers. [< L, violet]

Vi·o·la (vī'ō·lə, vē'-, vī·ō'lə)   The heroine of Shakespeare's comedy *Twelfth Night.*

vi·o·la·ble (vī'ə·lə·bəl)   *adj.* Capable of being violated. [< L *violabilis* < *violare.* See VIOLATE.] **—vi/o·la·ble·ness, vi/o·la·bil/i·ty** *n.* **—vi/o·la·bly** *adv.*

vi·o·la·ceous (vī'ə·lā'shəs)   *adj.* **1.** Having a violet hue. **2.** *Bot.* Of or pertaining to the violet family (*Violaceae*) of plants. [< L *violaceus* < *viola* violet]

viola da brac·cio (dä brät'chō)   An alto viol held against the shoulder. [< Ital., viol of the arm]

viola da gam·ba (dä gäm'bä)   **1.** The bass of the viol family, held between the legs, and having a range similar to that of the cello, but with a thinner tone: also called *bass viol.* **2.** An organ stop producing tones similar to those of the viola da gamba. [< Ital., viol of the leg]

viola d'a·mo·re (dä·mō'rā)   A treble viol with metal strings under the bowed ones, producing a silvery tone by sympathetic vibration. [< Ital., viol of love]

vi·o·late (vī'ə·lāt)   *v.t.* **·lat·ed, ·lat·ing** **1.** To break or infringe, as a law, oath, agreement, etc. **2.** To treat irreverently; profane, as a holy place. **3.** To break in upon; disturb. **4.** To ravish; rape. **5.** To do violence to; offend grossly; outrage. **6.** *Obs.* To treat roughly; abuse. [< L *violatus,* pp. of *violare* to use violence < *vis* force] **—vi/o·la/tive** *adj.* **—vi/o·la/tor** *n.*

vi·o·la·tion (vī'ə·lā'shən)   *n.* **1.** The act of violating, or the state of being violated. **2.** Infringement or infraction, as of a law, regulation, etc. **3.** Profanation; desecration. **4.** Rape.

vi·o·lence (vī'ə·ləns)   *n.* **1.** The quality or state of being violent; intensity; fury. **2.** An instance of violent action, treatment, etc. **3.** Violent or abusive exercise of power; injury; outrage. **4.** *Law* Physical force unlawfully exercised; an act tending to intimidate or overawe by causing apprehension of bodily injury. **5.** Perversion or distortion of meaning, intent, etc. **—to do violence to 1.** To injure or damage by rough or abusive treatment. **2.** To distort the meaning of. [< AF, OF < L *violentia* < *violentus* violent]

vi·o·lent (vī'ə·lənt)   *adj.* **1.** Proceeding from or marked by great physical force or roughness; overwhelmingly forcible. **2.** Caused by or exhibiting intense emotional or mental excitement; passionate; impetuous; fierce. **3.** Characterized by intensity of any kind; extreme: *violent* heat. **4.** Marked by undue exercise of force; harsh; severe: to take *violent* measures. **5.** Resulting from unusual force or injury, rather than the ordinary course of nature: a *violent* death. **6.** Tending to pervert the meaning or sense: a *violent* construction. [< OF < L *violentus* < *vis* force] **—vi/o·lent·ly** *adv.*

—Syn. 1. forceful, mighty. **2.** frantic, frenzied, maniacal, raging, wild. **3.** intense, vehement.

vi·o·les·cent (vī'ə·les'ənt)   *adj.* Having a tinge of violet. [< L *viola* violet + -ESCENT]

vi·o·let (vī'ə·lit)   *n.* **1.** One of a widely distributed genus (*Viola*) of herbaceous perennial herbs, bearing spurred flowers typically having a purplish blue color but sometimes yellow or white; especially, the common **garden violet** (*V. odorata*), and the wild **blue** or **meadow violet** (*V. papilionacea*). The violet is the State flower of Illinois, New Jersey, Rhode Island, and Wisconsin. **2.** Any of several similar plants, as the African violet (which see). **3.** A deep bluish purple color. **4.** One who is modest or self-effacing: used chiefly in the expression **shrinking violet. —** *adj.* Having a bluish purple color. [< OF *violette,* dim. of *viole* < L *viola* violet]

violet rays   **1.** High-frequency radiation from the violet end of the visible spectrum. **2.** Loosely, ultraviolet rays.

vi·o·lin (vī'ə·lin')   *n.* **1.** A musical instrument having four strings and a sounding box of seasoned wood, held against the shoulder and played by means of a bow. It is the treble member of the violin family, which includes also the viola and cello, and is distinguished in its modern form by its fully molded belly and back: also called *fiddle.* **2.** A violinist in an orchestra. [< Ital. *violino,* dim. of *viola.* See VIOLA¹.]

vi·o·lin·ist (vī'ə·lin'ist)   *n.* One who plays the violin.

vi·o·list (vē·ō'list *for def. 1,* vī'əl·ist *for def. 2*)   *n.* **1.** One who plays the viola. **2.** One who plays a viol.

VIOLIN

a Scroll. *b* Peg box. *c* Peg. *d* Nut. *e* Fingerboard. *f* Neck plate. *g* Sound hole. *h* Bridge. *i* Tailpiece. *j* Chin rest. *k* Button.

Viol·let-le-Duc (vyô/le/lə·dük/), **Eugene Emmanuel**, 1814–1879, French architect and archeologist.

vi·o·lon·cel·list (vē/ə·lən·chel/ist) *n.* A cellist (which see).

vi·o·lon·cel·lo (vē/ə·lən·chel/ō) *n. pl.* **·los** A cello. [< Ital., dim. of *violone* double bass, aug. of *viola.* See VIOLA¹.]

vi·o·lo·ne (vyô·lō/nā) *n.* **1.** The double bass of the viol family, playing an octave lower than the viola da gamba. It is the immediate ancestor of the modern double bass. An organ stop with a deep, stringlike tone quality. [< Ital., aug. of VIOLA¹.]

vi·os·ter·ol (vī·os/tər·ōl, -ol) *n.* Irradiated ergosterol, a vitamin D preparation variously used in medicine. [< (ULTRA)VIO(LET) + (ERGO)STEROL]

VIP or **V.I.P.** Very important person.

vi·per (vī/pər) *n.* **1.** Any of a family (*Viperidae*) of venomous Old World snakes, especially the **common viper** (*Vipera berus*), a small, variously colored snake native to Europe. **2.** Any of various similar or related snakes, as the puff adder and the horned viper (which see). **3.** Loosely, a pit viper (which see). **4.** Any allegedly poisonous snake. **5.** A treacherous or spiteful person. **6.** *Slang* A marihuana smoker. [< OF *vipere, vipre* < L *vipera,* contraction of *vivipara* < *vivus* living + *parere* to bring forth] — **vi/per·ish** *adj.*

vi·per·ine (vī/pər·in, -pə·rīn) *adj.* Of, pertaining to, or characteristic of a viper.

vi·per·ous (vī/pər·əs) *adj.* **1.** Snakelike; viperine. **2.** Venomous; malicious. — **vi/per·ous·ly** *adv.*

viper's bugloss Blueweed.

vi·ra·go (vi·rā/gō, -rä/-, vī-) *n. pl.* **·goes** or **·gos 1.** A noisy, sharp-tongued woman; a scold. **2.** *Rare* A woman of extraordinary size and courage; an Amazon. [< L, mannish woman < *vir* man]

vi·ral (vī/rəl) *adj.* Of, pertaining to, caused by, or of the nature of a virus.

Vir·chow (fir/khō), **Rudolf,** 1821–1902, German pathologist and anthropologist.

vir·e·lay (vir/ə·lā) *n.* A form of old French verse, arranged in any of various arbitrary orders; as: **a** A verse form having only two rhymes throughout. **b** A form in which each stanza has two rhymes, one repeated from the preceding stanza and a new one that will be repeated in the next. Also *French* **vire·lai** (vēr·le/). [< OF *virelai,* prob. alter. of *vireli, virli,* refrain of old dance songs]

vir·e·o (vir/ē·ō) *n. pl.* **·os** Any of various small, insectivorous birds (family *Vireonidae*), having predominantly dull green and grayish plumage: also called *greenlet.* [< L, a small bird, ? the greenfinch]

vir·e·o·nine (vir/ē·ə·nīn/, -nin) *adj.* Characteristic of or pertaining to the vireos. — *n.* A vireo or related bird. [< L *vireo, -onis.* See VIREO.]

vi·res·cence (vī·res/əns) *n.* **1.** The state or condition of becoming green. **2.** *Bot.* A turning green of usually white or colored organs of plants, as petals, by the abnormal action of chlorophyll.

vi·res·cent (vī·res/ənt) *adj.* Greenish or becoming green. [< L *virescens, -entis,* ppr. of *virescere* to grow green < *virere* to be green]

vir·ga (vûr/gə) *n. Meteorol.* Drooping streamers or wisps of precipitation from clouds, usually of the altocumulus and altostratus types. [< L, twig, streak in the sky]

vir·gate¹ (vûr/git, -gāt) *adj.* **1.** Long, straight, and slender; wandlike. **2.** *Bot.* Bearing or producing many small twigs. [< L *virga* twig, rod]

vir·gate² (vûr/git, -gāt) *n.* A variable early English measure of land, often equivalent to about thirty acres. [< Med.L *virgata* (*terrae*) virgate (of land) < L *virga* rod]

Vir·gil (vûr/jəl), **Vir·gil·i·an** (vər·jil/ē·ən) See VERGIL, etc.

vir·gin (vûr/jin) *n.* **1.** A person, especially a young woman, who has never had sexual intercourse; a maiden. **2.** A chaste young girl or unmarried woman. **3.** *Eccl.* **a** A member of a religious community who has taken a vow of chastity; a nun. **b** A chaste, unmarried woman, as a saint, honored for her piety or virtue. **4.** Any female animal before its first copulation. **5.** *Entomol.* A female insect producing fertile eggs by parthenogenesis. — *adj.* **1.** Being a virgin. **2.** Consisting of virgins: a *virgin* band. **3.** Pertaining or suited to a virgin; chaste; maidenly. **4.** Uncorrupted; pure; undefiled: *virgin* whiteness. **5.** Not hitherto used, touched, tilled, or worked upon by man: *virgin* soil; *virgin* forest. **6.** Not previously processed: *virgin* rubber; *virgin* wool. **7.** Of an oil, obtained from the first pressing of olives, nuts, etc., without the use of heat. **8.** *Metall.* Produced directly from ore, or at the primary smelting: *virgin* silver. **9.** *Mining* Occurring in native form; unalloyed; unmixed: *virgin* gold. **10.** Lacking experience or contact with; unaccustomed. [< OF *virgine* < L *virgo, -inis* maiden]

Vir·gin (vûr/jin) *n.* **1.** Mary, the mother of Jesus: usually preceded by *the:* also *Virgin Mary.* **2.** The constellation and sign of the zodiac Virgo.

vir·gin·al¹ (vûr/jin·əl) *adj.* Pertaining to or characteristic of a virgin. [< OF < L *virginalis* < *virgo, -inis* virgin]

vir·gin·al² (vûr/jin·əl) *n. Often pl.* A small, legless harpsichord of the 16th and 17th centuries: sometimes called a **pair of virginals.** [< OF < VIRGINAL¹; ? so called from its use by young men and girls]

virgin birth *Theol.* The doctrine that Jesus Christ was divinely conceived and born without impairment of the virginity of his mother Mary. Also **Virgin Birth.** Compare IMMACULATE CONCEPTION.

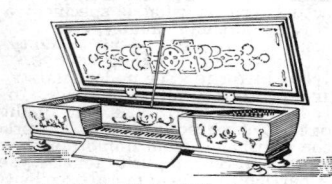
VIRGINAL (Late 16th century)

Vir·gin·ia (vər·jin/yə) A Confederate name for the MERRIMACK, the armored warship.

Vir·gin·ia (vər·jin/yə) A middle Atlantic State of the United States; 40,815 sq. mi.; pop. 4,648,494; capital, Richmond; entered the Union June 25, 1788, one of the original thirteen States; nickname, *Old Dominion.* Abbr. *Va.* Original name: **Commonwealth of Virginia.**

Virginia City A township in western Nevada; site of the Comstock Lode; pop. 300.

Virginia cowslip A smooth perennial herb (*Mertensia virginica*) of the borage family, native to eastern North America, and having clusters of tubular blue flowers: also called *lungwort.* Also **Virginia bluebell.**

Virginia creeper A common American climbing vine (*Parthenocissus quinquefolia*) of the grape family, with compound toothed leaves and dark blue berries: also called *American ivy, five-fingers, woodbine.*

Virginia deer The white-tailed deer (which see).

Virginia fence A worm fence (which see). Also **Virginia rail fence.**

Vir·gin·ian (vər·jin/yən) *adj.* Of, pertaining to, or from Virginia. — *n.* A native or inhabitant of Virginia.

Virginia reel A country-dance in which the performers stand in two parallel lines facing one another and perform various figures.

Virginia trumpet flower The trumpet creeper.

Virgin Islands A group of islands in the West Indies, east of Puerto Rico, comprising: **a** The **Virgin Islands of the United States** (formerly *Danish West Indies*), an unincorporated territory comprising the islands of St. Thomas, St. John, and St. Croix, and adjacent islets, purchased from Denmark in 1917; 133 sq. mi.; pop. 60,000 (est. 1969); capital, Charlotte Amalie. **b** The British Virgin Islands (which see). Abbr. *V.I.*

vir·gin·i·ty (vər·jin/ə·tē) *n. pl.* **·ties 1.** The state or condition of being a virgin; maidenhood; virginal chastity. **2.** The state of being unsullied, unused, untouched, etc.

vir·gin·i·um (vər·jin/ē·əm) *n.* The former name of an element now identified as francium. Abbr. *Vi* [after the State of *Virginia*]

Virgin Mary Mary, the mother of Jesus: usually with *the.*

vir·gin's-bow·er (vûr/jinz·bou/ər) *n.* A species of clematis (*Clematis virginiana*) bearing white flowers in leafy panicles.

Vir·go (vûr/gō) *n.* A constellation, the Virgin, containing the bright star Spica; also, the sixth sign of the zodiac. See CONSTELLATION, ZODIAC. [< L, a virgin]

vir·gu·late (vûr/gyə·lit, -lāt) *adj.* Shaped like or resembling a small rod. [< L *virgula.* See VIRGULE.]

vir·gule (vûr/gyōōl) *n.* A slanting line (/) used to indicate two alternatives, as in *and/or,* to set off phoneme symbols, etc.: also called *slash.* [< L *virgula,* dim. of *virga* rod]

vir·i·des·cent (vir/ə·des/ənt) *adj.* Greenish, or becoming slightly green. [< LL *viridescens, -entis,* ppr. of *viridescere* to become green < L *viridis* green] — **vir/i·des/cence** *n.*

vi·rid·i·an (və·rid/ē·ən) *n.* A durable bluish green pigment consisting of hydrated chromic oxide. [< L *viridis* green]

vi·rid·i·ty (və·rid/ə·tē) *n. pl.* **·ties** Greenness, as of vegetation; verdure. [< OF *viridite* < L *viriditas, -tatis* greenness, verdure < *viridis* green]

vir·ile (vir/əl) *adj.* **1.** Having the characteristics of adult manhood; masculine. **2.** Having the vigor or strength of manhood; sturdy; intrepid. **3.** Having qualities considered typically masculine; vigorous; forceful. **4.** Capable of procreation. [< OF < L *virilis* < *vir* man]

vir·il·ism (vir/əl·iz/əm) *n. Pathol.* The appearance in a woman of secondary male sexual and physical characteristics.

vi·ril·i·ty (və·ril/ə·tē) *n. pl.* **·ties** The state, character, or quality of being virile.

virl (vûrl) *n. Scot.* A ferrule.

vi·rol·o·gy (və·rol/ə·jē, vī-) *n.* The study of viruses, especially in their relation to disease. [< *viro-* (< VIRUS) + -LOGY] — **vi·rol/o·gist** *n.*

vir·tu (vər·tōō/, vûr/tōō) *n.* **1.** Rare, curious, or beautiful quality: usually in the phrase **objects** or **articles of virtu.** **2.** A taste for such objects. **3.** Such objects collectively.

Also spelled *vertu*. [< Ital. *virtù* merit, excellence < L *virtus* strength. See VIRTUE.]

vir·tu·al (vûr′chōō·əl) *adj.* **1.** Having the effect but not the actual form of what is specified: a *virtual* usurpation. **2.** Having potency, validity, etc. [< Med.L *virtualis* < L *virtus*. See VIRTUE.] —**vir′tu·al′i·ty** (-al′ə·tē) *n.*

virtual focus See under FOCUS.

virtual image See under IMAGE.

vir·tu·al·ly (vûr′chōō·ə·lē) *adv.* In effect; practically.

vir·tue (vûr′chōō) *n.* **1.** The quality of moral righteousness or excellence; rectitude. **2.** The practice of moral duties and the abstinence from immorality and vice: a life devoted to *virtue*. **3.** Sexual purity; chastity, especially in women. **4.** A particular type of moral excellence, especially one of those considered to be of special importance in philosophical or religious doctrine. Compare CARDINAL VIRTUES, THEOLOGICAL VIRTUES. **5.** Any admirable quality or trait: the *virtues* of his policy. **6.** Inherent or essential quality, power, etc. **7.** Efficacy; potency. **8.** *pl. Theol.* The fifth of the nine orders of angels: see ANGEL. **9.** *Obs.* Valor. —**by** (or **in**) **virtue of** By or through the fact, quality, force, or authority of. —**to make a virtue of necessity** To seem to do freely or from principle what is or must be done necessarily. [< OF *vertu* < L *virtus* manliness, strength, bravery < *vir* man.]
  —**Syn.** *Virtue, goodness, morality, rectitude*, and *righteousness* are compared as they denote the disposition to be good, moral, honest, upright, etc. We regard *virtue* as acquired through self-discipline, and predicate it of human beings only. *Goodness* is an innate quality, and so may be ascribed to God as well as to man. *Morality* involves conformity to an accepted code of right conduct; it is less elevated but more concrete than *virtue*. *Rectitude* also implies conformity to a moral code, but stresses intention or disposition; hence, a man's *morality* may arise from fear of punishment or of censure, but his *rectitude* can come only from a love of the right and a conscious desire to follow it. The *rectitude* of an action is to be found more in its purpose than in its consequences. *Righteousness* is a very close synonym of *rectitude*, but suggests somewhat more strongly a religious point of view. —**Ant.** vice, sin, evil.

vir·tu·os·i·ty (vûr′chōō·os′ə·tē) *n. pl.* ·**ties** **1.** The skill, style, etc., of a virtuoso; technical mastery of an art, as music. **2.** A taste for or cultivation of the fine arts.

vir·tu·o·so (vûr′chōō·ō′sō) *n. pl.* ·**sos** or ·**si** (-sē) **1.** A master of technique, as a skilled musician. **2.** One who displays impressive or dazzling skill in any area of accomplishment. **3.** A connoisseur; a collector or lover of curios or works of art. **4.** *Obs.* A savant. [< Ital., skilled, learned < LL *virtuosus* full of excellence < L *virtus*. See VIRTUE.]

vir·tu·ous (vûr′chōō·əs) *adj.* **1.** Characterized by, exhibiting, or having the nature of virtue; morally pure and good. **2.** Chaste: now said especially of women. **3.** *Archaic* Potent; efficacious. —**vir′tu·ous·ly** *adv.* —**vir′tu·ous·ness** *n.*

vir·u·lence (vir′yə·ləns, vir′ə-) *n.* The quality of being virulent.

vir·u·lent (vir′yə·lənt, vir′ə-) *adj.* **1.** Manifesting or characterized by malignity; exceedingly noxious, harmful, etc. **2.** Bitterly rancorous; acrimonious. **3.** *Med.* Actively poisonous or infective; malignant. **4.** *Bacteriol.* Having the power to injure an organism by invasion of tissue and generation of internal toxins, as certain microorganisms. [< L *virulentus* full of poison < *virus* poison.] —**vir′u·lent·ly** *adv.*

vi·rus (vī′rəs) *n.* **1.** Any of a class of filterable, submicroscopic pathogenic agents, chiefly protein in composition but often reducible to crystalline form, and typically inert except when in contact with certain living cells: also called *filterable virus*. **2.** An illness caused by such an agent. **3.** Any virulent substance developed within an animal body, and capable of transmitting a specific disease. **4.** Venom, as of a snake. **5.** Moral taint; corrupting influence. —**Syn.** See MICROBE. [< L, poison, slime.]

vis (vis) *n. pl.* **vi·res** (vī′rēz) *Latin* Force; potency.

Vis. or **Visc.** Viscount; Viscountess.

vi·sa (vē′zə) *n.* **1.** An official endorsement on a passport certifying that it has been found correct and that the bearer may proceed into or through the country. **2.** A signature of approval, as by an authorized inspecting officer. —*v.t.* ·**saed**, ·**sa·ing** **1.** To put a visa on. **2.** To give a visa to. Also *visé*. [< F < L, fem. sing. pp. of *videre* to see]

vis·age (viz′ij) *n.* **1.** The face or facial expression of a person; countenance; distinctive aspect. [< OF < *vis* face < L *visus* look, appearance < *videre* to see]

vis·aged (viz′ijd) *adj.* Having or characterized by (a specified kind of) visage: used in combination: *harsh-visaged*.

vis·ard (viz′ərd) See VIZARD.

vis-à-vis (vē′zə·vē′, *Fr.* vē·zá·vē′) *n. pl.* **vis-à-vis** **1.** One of two persons or things that face each other from opposite sides. **2.** One in a corresponding capacity, office, etc. **3.** A carriage in which the occupants sit opposite one another. **4.** An S-shaped seat in which two persons may sit side by side, but facing in opposite directions. —*adv.* Face to face. —*prep.* Regarding; toward. [< F, face to face]

Vi·sa·yan (vē·sä′yən) *n.* **1.** One of the native people of the Philippines, occupying the Visayan Islands and northern Mindanao. **2.** The language of these people, belonging to the Indonesian subfamily of Austronesian languages. —

adj. Of or pertaining to the Visayans or their language. Also *Bisayan.*

Vi·sa·yan Islands (vē·sä′yən) A group of the central Philippines, comprising Bohol, Cebu, Leyte, Masbate, Negros, Panay, Samar, Romblon, and adjacent islets; 23,621 sq. mi.: also *Bisayan Islands*. Also **Vi·sa′yas** (-yəs).

Vis·by (vēs′bü) A port city in SE Sweden, on Gotland island; pop. about 15,000: German *Wisby*.

vis·ca·cha (vis·kä′chə) *n.* **1.** A large burrowing rodent (genus *Lagostomus*) of the South American pampas, related to the chinchilla. **2.** An allied genus (*Lagidium*) of the Andes, resembling the gray squirrel but with large, rabbitlike ears. [< Sp. < Quechua *uiscacha*]

vis·cer·a (vis′ər·ə) *n. pl.* of **vis·cus** (vis′kəs) **1.** *Anat.* The internal organs, especially those of the great cavities of the body, as the stomach, lungs, heart, intestines, etc. **2.** Inner parts; innards. [< L, pl. of *viscus, visceris* internal organ]

vis·cer·al (vis′ər·əl) *adj.* **1.** Of, pertaining to, or affecting the viscera. **2.** Arising from deep feeling, intuition, etc.

visceral leishmaniasis Kala-azar, a tropical disease.

vis·cid (vis′id) *adj.* **1.** Sticky or adhesive; mucilaginous; viscous. **2.** Having a sticky surface, as some leaves. [< LL *viscidus* < L *viscum* birdlime, mistletoe] —**vis·cid·i·ty** (vi·sid′ə·tē), **vis′cid·ness** *n.* —**vis′cid·ly** *adv.*

vis·coid (vis′koid) *adj.* Somewhat viscid. Also **vis·coi′dal.**

Vis·con·ti (vēs·kôn′tē) A Lombard family that ruled Milan from 1277 to 1447.

vis·cose (vis′kōs) *n. Chem.* A thick, honeylike substance produced by the action of caustic soda and carbon disulfide upon cellulose, and constituting an important source of rayon. —*adj.* **1.** Viscous. **2.** Of, pertaining to, containing, or made from viscose. [< LL *viscosus*. See VISCOUS.]

vis·co·sim·e·ter (vis′kə·sim′ə·tər) *n.* An apparatus for determining the viscosity of a liquid, either by the rate of flow through an orifice or by the force required to twist an object immersed in it. Also **vis·com·e·ter** (vis·kom′ə·tər). [< VISCOSI(TY) + -METER]

vis·cos·i·ty (vis·kos′ə·tē) *n. pl.* ·**ties** **1.** The state, quality, property, or degree of being viscous. **2.** *Physics* That property of fluids by virtue of which they offer resistance to flow or to any change in the arrangement of their molecules.

vis·count (vī′kount) *n.* **1.** In England, a title of nobility ranking between those of earl and baron. **2.** Formerly, a representative or deputy of a count or earl in the government of a district; a sheriff. *Abbr.* V., Vis., Visc., Visct. [< AF *visconte*, OF *visconte* < *vis-* in place (< L *vice*) + *counte, conte.* See COUNT².]

vis·count·cy (vī′kount·sē) *n. pl.* ·**cies** The rank, title, or dignity of a viscount. Also **vis′count·ship, vis′count·y.**

vis·count·ess (vī′koun·tis) *n.* **1.** The wife of a viscount. **2.** A peeress holding a corresponding title in her own right. *Abbr.* Vis., Visc., Visct.

vis·cous (vis′kəs) *adj.* **1.** Glutinous; semifluid; sticky. **2.** *Physics* Characterized by or having viscosity. [< LL *viscosus* < L *viscum* birdlime, mistletoe] —**vis′cous·ly** *adv.* —**vis′cous·ness** *n.*

Visct. Viscount; Viscountess.

vis·cus (vis′kəs) Singular of VISCERA.

vise (vīs) *n.* A clamping device, usually of two jaws made to be closed together with a screw, lever, etc., used for grasping and holding objects being worked on, glued, etc. —*v.t.* **vised, vis·ing** To hold, force, or squeeze in or as in a vise. Also, *Brit.*, **vice.** [< OF *vis* screw < L *vitis* vine; with ref. to the spiral growth of vine tendrils]

MACHINIST'S VISE

vi·sé (vē′zā, vē·zā′) *v.t.* ·**séed, ·sé·ing** To visa. —*n.* A visa.

Vi·shin·sky (vi·shin′skē), **Andrei Yanuarievich,** 1883–1954, Soviet statesman and diplomat. Also *Vyshinsky.*

Vish·nu (vish′nōō) In Hindu theology, a major deity, a member of the trinity also including Brahma and Siva, and having many incarnations, of which the most famous is as Krishna. —**Vish′nu·ism** *n.*

vis·i·bil·i·ty (viz′ə·bil′ə·tē) *n. pl.* ·**ties** **1.** Condition, capability, or degree of being visible. **2.** The clarity of unaided vision as affected by distance, atmospheric conditions, etc.

vis·i·ble (viz′ə·bəl) *adj.* **1.** Perceivable by the eye; capable of being seen. **2.** Apparent; observable; evident. **3.** At hand; available; manifest. **4.** Accessible to or prepared to be seen by visitors. **5.** Constructed so that certain parts can be seen by the user. **6.** Represented or indicated by visible symbols, etc. [< OF < L *visibilis* < *visus*, pp. of *videre* to see] —**vis′i·ble·ness** *n.* —**vis′i·bly** *adv.*

visible speech Phonetic symbols designed to represent every possible position taken by the speech mechanism in the process of articulation.

Vis·i·goth (viz′ə·goth) *n.* One of the western Goths, a Teutonic people that invaded the Roman Empire in the third, fourth and fifth centuries and settled in France and Spain. Compare OSTROGOTH. [< LL *Visigothus* < Gmc., ? lit., western Goths] —**Vis′i·goth′ic** *adj.*

vi·sion (vizh′ən) *n.* **1.** The faculty or sense of sight. **2.** The ability to anticipate and make provision for future events; foresight. **3.** Insight; imagination: a man of great *vision.* **4.** A mental representation or manifestation of or as of external objects, scenes, etc., as in a religious revelation, dream, etc. **5.** A vividly imagined thing, state, occurrence, etc. **6.** That which is or has been seen; especially, something or someone very beautiful or pleasing. — **Syn.** See DREAM. — *v.t. Rare* To see in or as in a vision; envision. [< OF < L *visio, -onis* < *visus*, pp. of *videre* to see]

vi·sion·al (vizh′ən·əl) *adj.* **1.** Of, pertaining to, or characteristic of a vision. **2.** Seen in or as in a vision. — **vi′sion·al·ly** *adv.*

vi·sion·ar·y (vizh′ən·er′ē) *adj.* **1.** Not founded on fact; imaginary; impracticable. **2.** Affected by or tending toward fantasies; dreamy; impractical. **3.** Having idealistic goals or aims incapable of realization. **4.** Having or of the nature of apparitions, dreams, etc. — *n. pl.* **·ar·ies 1.** One who has visions. **2.** A dreamer; an impractical schemer. **3.** One who is impractically idealistic. — **vi′sion·ar′i·ness** *n.*

vis·it (viz′it) *v.t.* **1.** To go or come to see (a person) from friendship, courtesy, on business, etc.; make a call on. **2.** To go or come to (a place, etc.), as for temporary residence, transacting business, touring, etc. **3.** To be a guest of; stay with temporarily. **4.** To go or come to so as to make official inspection or inquiry. **5.** To come upon or afflict. **6.** To inflict punishment upon or for. **7.** To inflict (punishment, wrath, etc.). **8.** *Archaic* To comfort or bless: The Lord hath *visited* His people. — *v.i.* **9.** To make a visit; pay a call or calls. **10.** *Informal* To chat or converse sociably. — *n.* **1.** The act of visiting a person or thing. **2.** A sojourn in a place or with a person; a stay. **3.** *Informal* A talk or friendly chat. **4.** An authoritative personal call for inspection and examination, or discharge of an official or professional duty. [< OF *visiter* < L *visitare* to go to see, freq. of *visare* < *visus*, pp. of *videre* to see]

vis·it·a·ble (viz′it·ə·bəl) *adj.* **1.** Subject to visitation or punishment. **2.** Suitable for visiting.

vis·i·tant (viz′ə·tənt) *n.* **1.** A visitor. **2.** A migratory animal or bird stopping at a particular region. **3.** A visitor as if from another sphere; a supernatural being. — *adj.* Acting as a visitor; paying visits. [< MF < L *visitans, -antis*, ppr. of *visitare.* See VISIT.]

vis·i·ta·tion (viz′ə·tā′shən) *n.* **1.** The act or fact of visiting; a visit; also, the state or circumstance of being visited. **2.** An official or authoritative inspection and examination of a foundation, institution, or establishment; especially, a visit of an archbishop to his diocese. **3.** In Biblical and religious use, a visiting of blessing or affliction: a dreadful *visitation* of famine. **4.** The resorting of birds or animals in large numbers to unusual places. — **vis′i·ta′tion·al** *adj.*

Vis·i·ta·tion (viz′ə·tā′shən) *n. Eccl.* **1.** The visit of the Virgin Mary to Elizabeth. *Luke* i 39–42. **2.** July 2, the church festival commemorating this visit.

vis·i·ta·to·ri·al (viz′ə·tə·tôr′ē·əl, -tō′rē–) *adj.* Pertaining to or of the nature of a visitation (def. 2).

vis·it·ing card (viz′i·ting) A calling card (which see).

visiting fireman *U.S. Informal* An influential or affluent visitor to a large city, especially one who is taken on an official tour of inspection, or who goes out on the town.

visiting professor A professor on leave invited to teach at a university for a short period, usually for an academic year.

vis·i·tor (viz′ə·tər) *n.* One who visits. Also *Rare* **vis′it·er.**

vis·i·to·ri·al (viz′ə·tôr′ē·əl, -tō′rē–) *adj.* Of, pertaining to, or of the nature of a visit or visitation; especially, specifying the right of a parent to visit a child whose custody has been awarded to the other parent.

Vis·la (vyēs′lə) The Russian name for the VISTULA.

vis ma·jor (vis mā′jər) *Latin* **1.** Irresistible or uncontrollable force; literally, greater force. **2.** *Law* An unavoidable accident: compare ACT OF GOD.

vi·sor (vī′zər, viz′ər) *n.* **1.** A projecting piece at the front of a cap, etc., serving as a shade or shield for the eyes. **2.** In ancient armor, the front piece of a helmet, capable of being raised, and serving to protect the upper part of the face. **3.** A movable piece or part serving as a shield against glare, etc., as on the windshield of an automobile. — *v.t.* To mask or cover with a visor. Also spelled *vizor.* [< AF *viser*, OF *visiere* < *vis* face. See VISAGE.]

VISOR ON HELMET

vis·ta (vis′tə) *n.* **1.** A view or prospect, as along an avenue; an outlook. **2.** A mental view embracing a series of events. [< Ital. < L *visus*, pp. of *videre* to see]

Vis·tu·la (vis′chŏŏ·lə) A river in Poland, flowing 678 miles generally north to the **Vistula Lagoon** (German *Frisches Haff*), an inlet (332 sq. mi.) of the Gulf of Danzig: Polish *Wisła*, German *Weichsel*, Russian *Visla.*

vis·u·al (vizh′ŏŏ·əl) *adj.* **1.** Pertaining to, resulting from, or serving the sense of sight. **2.** Perceptible by sight; visible. **3.** Optical: the *visual* focus of a lens. **4.** Produced or induced by mental images: a *visual* conception. [< MF < LL *visualis* < L *visus* sight < *videre* to see] — **vis′u·al·ly** *adv.*

visual aid *Often pl.* In education, a device or method designed to convey information by visible representation, as motion pictures, charts, etc.

visual field The total area visible to the eye or eyes at any given moment.

vis·u·al·ize (vizh′ŏŏ·əl·īz′) *v.t. & v.i.* **·ized, ·iz·ing** To form a mental image (of). Also *Brit.* **vis′u·al·ise′.** — **vis′u·al·i·za′tion** *n.*

vis·u·al·iz·er (vizh′ŏŏ·əl·ī′zər) *n.* **1.** One who visualizes. **2.** One whose mental images are formed chiefly by visualization: also **vis′u·al·ist** (-ist).

visual purple *Biochem.* A complex reddish purple protein present in the rods of the retina, an important factor in the process of vision, especially at night: also called *rhodopsin.*

visual yellow *Biochem.* The pigmented protein into which visual purple is changed by the action of light, itself being converted to visual purple in the dark in the presence of vitamin A.

vi·ta (vī′tə) *n. pl.* **·tae** (-tē) A curriculum vitae (which see).

vi·ta·ceous (vī·tā′shəs) *adj. Bot.* Of or belonging to the grape family (*Vitaceae*) of mostly woody and climbing vines. [< NL, family name < L *vitis* vine]

vi·tal (vīt′l) *adj.* **1.** Necessary to existence or continuance; essential. **2.** Of or pertaining to life. **3.** Essential to or supporting life. **4.** Affecting the course of life or existence, especially so as to be dangerous or fatal: a *vital* error. **5.** Relating to the facts of life, as births, deaths, etc.: *vital* statistics. **6.** Energetic; forceful; dynamic. **7.** Having immediate interest or importance: a *vital* question. [< OF < L *vitalis* < *vita* life] — **vi′tal·ly** *adv.* — **vi′tal·ness** *n.*

vital force A form of energy regarded as acting independently of all physical and chemical forces in the causation and development of living phenomena. Also **vital principle.**

vi·tal·ism (vīt′l·iz′əm) *n.* **1.** *Biol.* The doctrine that life and its phenomena arose from and are the product of a hypothetical vital force. **2.** *Philos.* Bergsonism. — **vi′tal·ist** *n.* — **vi′tal·is′tic** *adj.*

vi·tal·i·ty (vī·tal′ə·tē) *n.* **1.** The state or quality of being vital. **2.** Vital or life-giving force, principle, etc. **3.** Vigor; energy; animation. **4.** Power of continuing in force or effect.

vi·tal·ize (vīt′l·īz) *v.t.* **·ized, ·iz·ing** To make vital; endow with life or energy. — **vi′tal·i·za′tion** *n.* — **vi′tal·iz′er** *n.*

vi·tals (vīt′lz) *n.pl.* **1.** The parts or organs necessary to life. **2.** The parts or qualities essential to the continued existence or well-being of anything.

vital statistics Quantitative data relating to certain aspects and conditions of human life, especially in relation to large population groups.

vi·ta·min (vī′tə·min) *n. Biochem.* Any of a group of complex organic substances found in minute quantities in most natural foodstuffs, and closely associated with the maintenance of normal physiological functions in man and animals. Also **vi′ta·mine** (-mēn, -min). [< NL *vit-* (< L *vita* life) + AMINE] — **vi′ta·min′ic** *adj.*

vitamin A A fat-soluble vitamin derived from carotene and occurring naturally in animal tissues, especially egg yolk and fish-liver oils, essential to the prevention of atrophy of epithelial tissue and night blindness.

vitamin B complex A group of water-soluble vitamins widely distributed in plants and animals, most members of which have special names.

vitamin B₁ Thiamine.

vitamin B₂ Riboflavin.

vitamin B₃ Pantothenic acid.

vitamin B₄ Adenine.

vitamin B₆ Pyridoxine.

vitamin B₁₂ A dark red, crystalline vitamin, $C_{63}H_{90}N_{14}O_{14}PCo$, extracted from liver and certain mold fungi, and active against pernicious anemia: also called *cobalamine.*

vitamin B_c Folic acid.

vitamin C Ascorbic acid.

vitamin D The antirachitic vitamin occurring chiefly in fish-liver oils.

vitamin D₁ An impure mixture of calciferol and irradiated ergosterol.

vitamin D₂ Calciferol.

vitamin D₃ A form of vitamin D₂ found principally in fish-liver oils.

vitamin E The antisterility vitamin, composed of three forms of tocopherol and found in whole grain cereals.

vitamin G Riboflavin.

vitamin H Biotin.

vitamin K₁ A vitamin, found in green leafy vegetables, that promotes the clotting of blood.

vitamin K₂ A form of vitamin K₁ prepared from fishmeal.

vitamin L Either of two water-soluble substances found in beef liver or yeast, and promoting normal lactation.

vi·ta·min·ol·o·gy (vī′tə·min·ol′ə·jē) *n.* The scientific study of vitamins. [< VITAMIN + -(O)LOGY]

vitamin P complex A group of substances, including the bioflavonoids, obtained from citrus fruits and promoting the normal permeability of capillary walls.

PRONUNCIATION KEY: add, āce, câre, pälm; end, ēven; it, īce; odd, ōpen, ôrder; tŏŏk, pōōl; up, bûrn; ə = a in *above*, e in *sicken*, i in *flexible*, o in *melon*, u in *focus*; yōō = u in *fuse*; oil; pout; check; go; ring; thin; this; zh, vision. For à, œ, ü, kh, ṅ, see inside front cover.

vi·ta·scope (vī'tə·skōp) *n.* An early form of motion-picture projector. [< L *vita* life + -SCOPE]

Vi·tebsk (vyē'tyipsk) A city in the NE Byelorussian S.S.R., on the Western Dvina; pop. 148,000 (1959).

vi·tel·lin (vi·tel'in, vī-) *n. Biochem.* A phosphoprotein occurring in the yolk of eggs. [< VITELL(US) + -IN]

vi·tel·line (vi·tel'in, vī-) *adj.* **1.** Of or pertaining to the yolk of an egg. **2.** Of a dull yellow, approaching red; of the color of the yolk of eggs. — *n.* The yolk of an egg. [< Med.L *vitellinus* < L *vitellus.* See VITELLUS.]

vi·tel·lus (vi·tel'əs, vī-) *n.* The egg yolk. [< L, orig. dim. of *vitulus* calf]

vi·tesse (vē·tes') *n. French* Speed: used especially in the phrases **grande vitesse** (gränd), fast express, and **pe·tite vitesse** (pə·tēt'), ordinary express, or freight, etc.

vi·ti·ate (vish'ē·āt) *v.t.* **·at·ed, ·at·ing** **1.** To impair the use or value of; spoil. **2.** To debase or corrupt. **3.** To render legally ineffective; invalidate: Fraud *vitiates* a contract. [< L *vitiatus,* pp. of *vitiare* < *vitium* fault] — **vi·ti·a·ble** (vish'ē·ə·bəl) *adj.* — **vi·ti·a'tion** *n.* — **vi'ti·a'tor** *n.*

vi·ti·at·ed (vish'ē·ā'tid) *adj.* Contaminated; rendered defective; invalidated.

vit·i·cul·ture (vit'ə·kul'chər, vī'tə-) *n.* The science and art of grape growing. [< L *vitis* vine + CULTURE] — **vit'i·cul'tur·al** *adj.* — **vit'i·cul'tur·er, vit'i·cul'tur·ist** *n.*

Vi·ti Le·vu (vē'tē lā'vōō) The largest of the Fiji Islands; 4,010 sq. mi.

vit·i·li·go (vit'ə·lī'gō) *n. Pathol.* Leukoderma, a skin disease. [< L, tetter < *vitium* fault]

Vi·to·ri·a (vē·tôr'ē·ə, *Sp.* bē·tō'ryä) A city in northern Spain; pop. 73,701 (1960).

vit·re·ous (vit'rē·əs) *adj.* **1.** Pertaining to glass; glassy. **2.** Obtained from glass. **3.** Resembling glass; vitriform. **4.** Pertaining to the vitreous humor. [< L *vitreus* < *vitrum* glass] — **vit're·os'i·ty** (-os'ə·tē), **vit're·ous·ness** *n.*

vitreous electricity Electricity generated by rubbing glass with silk, regarded as positive.

vitreous humor *Anat.* The transparent, jellylike tissue that fills the ball of the eye and is enclosed by the hyaloid membrane. Also **vitreous body.**

vi·tres·cence (vi·tres'əns) *n.* The state of becoming vitreous.

vi·tres·cent (vi·tres'ənt) *adj.* **1.** Capable of being turned into glass. **2.** Tending to become glass. [< L *vitrum* glass + -ESCENT]

vitri- *combining form* Glass; of or pertaining to glass: *vitriform.* Also, before vowels, **vitr-**. [< L *vitrum* glass]

vit·ric (vit'rik) *adj.* Pertaining to or like glass. Compare CERAMIC.

vit·ri·fi·ca·tion (vit'rə·fə·kā'shən) *n.* **1.** The process of vitrifying, or the state of being vitrified. **2.** Something vitrified. Also **vit'ri·fac'tion** (-fak'shən).

vit·ri·form (vit'rə·fôrm) *adj.* Resembling glass; glasslike.

vit·ri·fy (vit'rə·fī) *v.t. & v.i.* **·fied, ·fy·ing** To change into glass or a vitreous substance; make or become vitreous. [< MF *vitrifier* < L *vitrum* glass + *facere* to make] — **vit'ri·fi'a·ble** *adj.*

vit·rine (vit'rēn) *n.* A glass showcase for art objects. [< F < *vitre* glass < L *vitrum*]

vit·ri·ol (vit'rē·ōl, -əl) *n.* **1.** *Chem.* **a** Sulfuric acid. **b** Any sulfate of a heavy metal, as *green vitriol* from iron, *blue vitriol* from copper, or *white vitriol* from zinc. **2.** Anything sharp or caustic; especially, venomous, angry, and injurious speech or writing. — *v.t.* **·oled** or **·olled, ·ol·ing** or **·ol·ling** **1.** To injure (a person) with vitriol. **2.** To subject (anything) to the agency of vitriol. [< OF < Med.L *vitriolum* < L *vitrum* glass; so called because of its glassy appearance]

vit·ri·ol·ic (vit'rē·ol'ik) *adj.* **1.** Derived from a vitriol. **2.** Corrosive, burning, or caustic. **3.** Inclined to or marked by angry castigation.

vit·ri·ol·ize (vit'rē·əl·īz') *v.t.* **·ized, ·iz·ing** **1.** To corrode, injure, or burn with sulfuric acid. **2.** To convert into or impregnate with vitriol. — **vit'ri·ol·i·za'tion** *n.*

Vi·tru·vi·us (vi·trōō'vē·əs) First-century B.C. Roman architect, engineer, and writer: full name **Marcus Vitruvius Pol·li·o** (pol'ē·ō). — **Vi·tru'vi·an** *adj.*

vit·ta (vit'ə) *n. pl.* **vit·tae** (vit'ē) **1.** A fillet or band for the head. **2.** *Bot.* A tube or canal in the fruit of plants of the parsley family, containing an aromatic oil. **3.** *Zool.* A band or stripe, as of color. [< L]

vit·tate (vit'āt) *adj.* **1.** Having or bearing vittae or a vitta. **2.** Striped.

vit·tles (vit'əls) *n.pl. Informal* or *Dial.* Victuals.

vit·u·line (vich'ōō·līn, -lin) *adj.* Pertaining to, of, or like a calf or veal. [< L *vitulinus* < *vitulus* calf]

vi·tu·per·ate (vī·tōō'pə·rāt, -tyōō'-, vi-) *v.t.* **·at·ed, ·at·ing** To find fault with abusively; rail at; berate; scold. [< L *vituperatus,* pp. of *vituperare* to blame, scold < *vitium* fault + *parare* to prepare, make] — **vi·tu'per·a'tor** *n.*

vi·tu·per·a·tion (vī·tōō'pə·rā'shən, -tyōō'-, vi-) *n.* **1.** The act of vituperating. **2.** Abusive language; censure.

vi·tu·per·a·tive (vī·tōō'pər·ə·tiv, -tyōō'-, vi-) *adj.* **1.** Having the nature of vituperation or censure. **2.** Given to vituperation; abusive. — **vi·tu'per·a'tive·ly** *adv.*

viv. *Music* Lively (Ital. *vivace*).

vi·va (vē'vä) *interj.* Live! Long live!: a shout of applause; an acclamation or salute. [< Ital., 3rd person sing. present subjunctive of *vivere* to live < L]

vi·va·ce (vē·vä'chā) *adv. Music* Lively; quickly; briskly. Also **vi·va·ce·men'te** (-mān'tā). [< Ital. < *vivac-, vivax*]

vi·va·cious (vi·vā'shəs, vī-) *adj.* **1.** Full of life and spirits; lively; active. **2.** *Obs.* Tenacious of life. [< L *vivax, vivacis* < *vivere* to live] — **vi·va'cious·ly** *adv.* — **vi·va'cious·ness** *n.* — **Syn.** gay, merry. — **Ant.** stolid, languid, spiritless.

vi·vac·i·ty (vi·vas'ə·tē, vī-) *n. pl.* **·ties** **1.** The state or quality of being vivacious. **2.** Sprightliness, as of temper or behavior; liveliness. **3.** A vivacious act, expression, etc.

Vi·val·di (vē·väl'dē), **Antonio,** 1675?–1743, Italian violinist and composer: called **the Red Priest.**

vi·van·diè·re (vē·vän·dyâr') *n.* Formerly, a woman who supplied provisions and liquors to troops in the field, as in the French army. [< F, fem. of *vivandier* sutler, ult. < L *vivenda.* See VIAND.]

vi·var·i·um (vī·vâr'ē·əm) *n. pl.* **·var·i·a** (-vâr'ē·ə) or **·var·i·ums** A place for keeping or raising live animals, fish, or plants, as a park, pond, aquarium, cage, etc. Also **viv·a·ry** (viv'ər·ē). [< L, orig. neut. of *vivarius* concerning live things < *vivus* alive < *vivere* to live]

vi·va vo·ce (vī'və vō'sē) *Latin* **1.** By spoken word; orally. **2.** Spoken; oral.

vive (vēv) *interj. French* Live! Long live!: used in acclamation: opposed to *à bas.*

vive la ré·pu·blique (vēv lä rä·pü·blēk') *French* Long live the republic!

vive le roi (vēv lə rwä') *French* Long live the king!

vi·ver·rine (vī·ver'īn, -in, vi-) *adj.* Belonging or pertaining to a family (*Viverridae*) of small carnivores including civets and mongooses. — *n.* A viverrine animal. [< NL *viverrinus* < L *viverra* ferret]

vi·vers (vī'vərz) *n.pl. Scot.* Food; provisions.

Viv·i·an (viv'ē·ən) In Arthurian romance, the wily mistress of Merlin, who imprisons him by his own magic: also known as the *Lady of the Lake, Nimue.* Also **Viv'i·en, Viv'i·ane.**

viv·id (viv'id) *adj.* **1.** Very bright; intense: said of colors. **2.** Producing or evoking lifelike imagery, freshness, etc.: *vivid* prose. **3.** Clearly felt or strongly expressed, as emotions. **4.** Full of life and vigor. **5.** Clearly seen in the mind, as a memory. **6.** Clearly perceived by the eye: a *vivid* scene. **7.** Acting or exercised with lively interest. [< L *vividus* lively < *vivere* to live] — **viv'id·ly** *adv.* — **viv'id·ness** *n.* — **Syn.** **1.** brilliant, clear. **2.** lifelike. Compare GRAPHIC. **4.** animated, lively, expressive. — **Ant.** drab, dull, lifeless.

viv·i·fy (viv'ə·fī) *v.t.* **·fied, ·fy·ing** **1.** To give life to; animate; vitalize. **2.** To make more vivid or striking. [< OF *vivifier* < LL *vivificare* < L *vivus* alive + *facere* to make] — **viv'i·fi·ca'tion** (-fə·kā'shən) *n.* — **viv'i·fi'er** *n.*

vi·vip·a·rous (vī·vip'ər·əs) *adj.* **1.** *Zool.* Bringing forth living young, as most mammals: distinguished from *oviparous, ovoviviparous.* **2.** *Bot.* Producing bulbs or seeds that germinate while still attached to the parent plant. [< L *viviparus* < *vivus* alive + *parere* to bring forth] — **vi·vip'a·rous·ly** *adv.* — **vi·vip'a·rism** (-riz'əm), **viv·i·par·i·ty** (viv'ə·par'ə·tē), *n.* — **vi·vip'a·rous·ness** *n.*

viv·i·sect (viv'ə·sekt) *v.t.* **1.** To dissect or operate upon (a living animal), with a view to exposing its physiological processes. — *v.i.* **2.** To practice vivisection. [Back formation < VIVISECTION] — **viv'i·sec'tor** *n.*

viv·i·sec·tion (viv'ə·sek'shən) *n.* **1.** The act of cutting into or dissecting a living animal body. **2.** Experimentation on living animals by means of operations designed to promote knowledge of physiological and pathological processes. [< L *vivus* living, alive + *sectio, -onis* a cutting. See SECTION.] — **viv'i·sec'tion·al** *adj.*

viv·i·sec·tion·ist (viv'ə·sek'shən·ist) *n.* **1.** One who practices vivisection. **2.** An advocate or defender of vivisection.

vix·en (vik'sən) *n.* **1.** A female fox. **2.** A turbulent, quarrelsome woman; shrew. [Alter. of ME *fixen* she-fox < OE *fyxen,* fem. of *fox*] — **vix'en·ish** *adj.* — **vix'en·ly** *adj. & adv.*

viz. Namely (L *videlicet*).

viz·ard (viz'ərd) *n.* A mask; visor: also spelled *visard.* [Alter. of VISOR.] — **viz'ard·ed** *adj.*

Viz·ca·ya (vēs·kä'yä, *Sp.* bēth·kä'yä) A Province of northern Spain, on the Bay of Biscay; 853 sq. mi.; pop. 754,383 (1960); capital, Bilbao: also, in English, *Biscay.*

Viz·e·tel·ly (viz'ə·tel'ē), **Frank Horace,** 1864–1938, U.S. lexicographer and encyclopedist born in England.

vi·zier (vi·zir', viz'yər) *n.* A high official of a Moslem country, especially of the old Turkish Empire; especially, a minister of state. Also **vi·zir'.** — **grand vizier** The highest dignitary in certain Moslem countries; the prime minister. [< Turkish *vezir* < Arabic *wazir* counselor, orig., porter < *wazara* to carry]

vi·zier·ate (vi·zir'it, -āt, viz'yər·it, -yə·rāt) *n.* The office or dignity of a vizier. Also **vi·zier'al·ty, vi·zier'ship, vi·zir'ate, vi·zir'ship.**

vi·zor (vī'zər, viz'ər) See VISOR.

V-J Day (vē'jā') September 2, the official date of the

victory of the United Nations over Japan in World War II, 1945.

VL or **V.L.** Vulgar Latin.

Vlad·i·mir (vlad′ə·mir, *Russ.* vlä·dyē′myir), 956?–1015, grand prince of Kiev 978?–1015; first Christian ruler in Russia: called **the Great.**

Vlad·i·mir (vlad′ə·mir, *Russ.* vlä·dyē′myir) A city in the western R.S.F.S.R., near Moscow; pop. 234,000 (1970).

Vla·di·vos·tok (vlad′ə·vos·tok′, -vos′tok; *Russ.* vlə·dyi·vos·tôk′) A port city in the extreme SE R.S.F.S.R., on the Sea of Japan; pop. 442,000 (1970).

Vla·minck (vlä·maṅk′), **Maurice de,** 1876–1958, French painter.

VLF or **vlf, V.L.F.,** or **v.l.f.** Very low frequency.

Vlis·sing·en (vlis′ing·ən) The Dutch name for FLUSHING.

Vlo·na (və·lô′nä) The Albanian name for VALONA. Also **Vlo′në** (-nə), **Vlo′ra** (-rä), **Vlo′rë** (-rə).

Vl·ta·va (vul′tä·vä) A river in central Bohemia, Czechoslovakia, flowing 267 miles north to the Elbe: German *Moldau.*

V-mail (vē′māl′) *n.* Mail written on special forms, transmitted overseas in World War II on microfilm, and enlarged for final delivery. [< V(ICTORY) + MAIL¹]

V.M.D. Doctor of Veterinary Medicine (L *Veterinariae Medicinae Doctor*).

v.n. *Gram.* Neuter verb: also **v. neut.**

V-neck (vē′nek′) *n.* A V-shaped neck of a sweater, dress, etc.

vo. Verso.

vo·ca·ble (vō′kə·bəl) *n.* **1.** A spoken word considered only as a sequence of sounds, without regard to its meaning. **2.** A written word considered only as a sequence of letters. **3.** A vocal sound. — *adj.* Capable of being spoken. [< F < L *vocabulum* name, appellation < *vocare* to call < *vox* voice]

vo·cab·u·lar·y (vō·kab′yə·ler′ē) *n. pl.* **·lar·ies 1.** A list of words or of words and phrases, especially one arranged in alphabetical order and defined or translated; a lexicon; glossary. **2.** All the words of a language. **3.** A sum or aggregate of the words used or understood by a particular person, class, etc., or employed in some specialized field of knowledge. **4.** An aggregate or range of things, qualities, or techniques that form the basis of a means of expression, especially in the arts: a painter's *vocabulary* of colors. — **Syn.** See DICTION. [< LL *vocabularius* < L *vocabulum.* See VOCABLE.]

vocabulary entry A word or term given in a vocabulary.

vo·cal (vō′kəl) *adj.* **1.** Of or pertaining to the voice; uttered by the voice; oral. **2.** Having voice; endowed with the power of utterance: *vocal* creatures. **3.** Composed for or performed by the voice: a *vocal* score. **4.** Concerned in the production of voice: the *vocal* organs. **5.** Full of voices or sounds; resounding. **6.** Freely expressing oneself in speech; readily given to voicing opinions: the *vocal* segment. **7.** Eloquent without need of speech: the *vocal* beauty of the Parthenon. **8.** *Phonet.* **a** Voiced. **b** Vocalic. — *n. Phonet.* **1.** A vocal sound. **2.** A voiced consonant. [< L *vocalis* speaking, sounding < *vox, vocis* voice. Doublet of VOWEL.] — **vo′cal·ly** *adv.* — **vo′cal·ness** *n.*

vocal cords Two membranous bands extending from the thyroid cartilage of the larynx and having edges that, when drawn tense, are caused to vibrate by the passage of air from the lungs, thereby producing voice. Compare illustration at THROAT.

VOCAL CORDS

a Open. *b* Voice. *c* Closed. *d* Whisper.

vo·cal·ic (vō·kal′ik) *adj.* Consisting of, like, or relating to vowel sounds.

vo·ca·lise (vō·kä·lēz′) *n. U.S. Music* A practice exercise for singers designed to develop flexibility and control of pitch and tonal beauty, usually employing vowels or Italian syllables. [< F]

vo·cal·ism (vō′kəl·iz′əm) *n.* **1.** The act of vocalizing; vocalization. **2.** A vocalic sound; also, a vowel system. **3.** Singing; also, the technique of singing.

vo·cal·ist (vō′kəl·ist) *n.* A singer, especially one who has a cultivated voice.

vo·cal·ize (vō′kəl·īz) *v.* **·ized, ·iz·ing** *v.t.* **1.** To make vocal; utter, say, or sing. **2.** To provide a voice for; render articulate. **3.** To mark with vowel points, as a Hebrew text. **4.** *Phonet.* **a** To change (a consonant) to a vowel by some shift in the articulatory process. **b** To voice. — *v.i.* **5.** To produce sounds with the voice, as in speaking or singing. **6.** *Phonet.* To be changed to a vowel. — **vo′cal·i·za′tion** *n.* — **vo′cal·iz′er** *n.*

vocal organs The speech organs (which see).

vo·ca·tion (vō·kā′shən) *n.* **1.** A stated or regular occupation; a calling. **2.** A call to or fitness for a certain career, especially a religious position. **3.** The work or profession for which one has a sense of special fitness. — **Syn.** See OCCUPATION. [< L *vocatio, -onis* < *vocatus,* pp. of *vocare* to call] — **vo·ca′tion·al** *adj.* — **vo·ca′tion·al·ly** *adv.*

vocational guidance A systematic program of tests and interviews to help a person find the occupation for which he is best suited.

vocational school A school, usually on the secondary level, that trains students for special trades, such as printing, mechanics, baking, or stenography.

voc·a·tive (vok′ə·tiv) *adj.* **1.** Pertaining to or used in the act of calling. **2.** *Gram.* In some inflected languages, denoting the case of a noun, pronoun, or adjective used in direct address: The name "Brutus" is in the *vocative* case in "Et tu Brute." — *n. Gram* **1.** The vocative case. **2.** A word in this case. Abbr. **v., voc.** [< F, fem. of *vocatif* < L *vocativus* < *vocare* to call]

vo·ces (vō′sēz) Plural of VOX.

vo·cif·er·ant (vō·sif′ər·ənt) *adj.* Vociferous; clamorous; uttering loud cries. — *n.* A vociferous person. [< L *vociferans, -antis,* ppr. of *vociferari.* See VOCIFERATE.] — **vo·cif′er·ance** *n.*

vo·cif·er·ate (vō·sif′ə·rāt) *v.t. & v.i.* **·at·ed, ·at·ing** To cry out with a loud voice; exclaim noisily; shout; bawl. [< L *vociferatus,* pp. of *vociferari* to cry out < *vox, vocis* voice + *ferre* to carry] — **vo·cif′er·a′tion** *n.* — **vo·cif′er·a′tor** *n.*

vo·cif·er·ous (vō·sif′ər·əs) *adj.* Making or characterized by a loud outcry; clamorous; noisy. — **vo·cif′er·ous·ly** *adv.* — **vo·cif′er·ous·ness** *n.*

vod·ka (vod′kə, *Russ.* vôd′kə) *n.* An alcoholic liquor, originally made in Russia from a fermented mash of wheat but now also made from other cereals and potatoes. [< Russian, dim. of *voda* water]

voe (vō) *n. Scot.* A small bay, creek, or inlet.

vo·gie (vō′gē) *adj. Scot.* **1.** Merry; cheerful. **2.** Vain; conceited.

vogue (vōg) *n.* **1.** The prevalent way or fashion; mode: often preceded by *in.* **2.** Popular favor; general acceptance; popularity. [< F, fashion, orig., rowing < *voguer* to row < Ital. *vogare;* ult. origin uncertain]

Vo·gul (vō′gōōl) *n.* **1.** One of a Finno-Ugric people of the Ural Mountains. **2.** The Ugric language of these people.

voice (vois) *n.* **1.** The sound produced by the vocal organs of a person or animal. **2.** The quality or character of such sound: a melodious *voice.* **3.** The power or faculty of vocal utterance; speech **4.** A sound suggesting vocal utterance or speech: the *voice* of the wind. **5.** Opinion or choice expressed; also, the right of expressing a preference or judgment: to have a *voice* in the affair. **6.** Instruction; admonition; teaching: the *voice* of nature. **7.** A person or agency by which the thought, wish, or purpose of another is expressed. **8.** Expression of thought, opinion, feeling, etc.: to give *voice* to one's ideals. **9.** *Phonet.* The sound produced by vibration of the vocal cords in the production of most vowels and certain consonants. Compare WHISPER, BREATH. **10.** Musical tone produced by vibration of the vocal cords and resonating in the cavities of the throat and head; also, the ability to sing, or the state of the vocal organs with regard to this ability: to be in poor *voice.* **11.** *Music* A part (def. 11a), especially as considered abstractly or without regard to the particular instrument or human voice rendering it: also called **voice part.** **12.** *Gram.* The relation of the action expressed by the verb to the subject, or the form of the verb indicating this relationship. In English, as in most Indo-European languages, a distinction between an *active* and a *passive* voice is made, indicating, respectively, that the subject of the sentence is either performing the action or is being acted upon. (Active: *He wrote the letter.* Passive: *The letter was written by him.*) In Greek and Sanskrit verbs, there is, in addition, a *middle* voice, representing the subject as acting upon himself directly, or in his own interest. **13.** *Obs.* Report; rumor; fame. — **in voice** In proper condition for singing. — **with one voice** With one accord; unitedly; unanimously. — *v.t.* **voiced, voic·ing 1.** To put into speech; give expression to; utter. **2.** *Music* To regulate the tones of; tune, as the pipes of an organ. **3.** *Phonet.* To utter with voice or sonance. Abbr. **v.** [< OF *vois* < L *vox, vocis*]

voice box The larynx.

voiced (voist) *adj.* **1.** Having a voice; expressed by voice. **2.** *Phonet.* Uttered with vibration of the vocal cords, as (b), (d), (z); sonant: opposed to *voiceless:* also **vocal.**

voice·ful (vois′fəl) *adj.* Having vocal quality; vocal; sounding. — **voice′ful·ness** *n.*

voice·less (vois′lis) *adj.* **1.** Having no voice, speech, or vote. **2.** *Phonet.* Produced without voice, as (p), (t), (s); surd: opposed to *voiced.* — **voice′less·ly** *adv.* — **voice′less·ness** *n.*

Voice of America An international U.S. government radio service that broadcasts in many languages to acquaint foreigners with U.S. life, culture, and policies, and to disseminate propaganda.

voice part *Music* **1.** A part intended to be sung. **2.** A voice (def. 11).

voice·print (vois′print′) *n.* A record, made on a sound spectrograph as a subject utters a word or speech sound, of the energy levels corresponding to the various pitches present. It is a complex pattern of wavy lines and is as individually distinctive as a fingerprint.

void (void) *adj.* **1.** No longer having force or validity, as a contract, license, etc., that has lapsed; invalid; null. **2.** Destitute; clear or free: with *of*: *void* of reason. **3.** Not occupied by matter; empty. **4.** Unoccupied, as a house or room; having no incumbent. **5.** Producing no effect; useless. **— n. 1.** An empty space; a vacuum. **2.** A breach of surface or matter; a disconnecting space. **3.** Empty condition or feeling; a blank. **— v.t. 1.** To make void or of no effect; annul; invalidate. **2.** To empty or remove (contents); evacuate, as urine. **3.** *Archaic* To leave empty. **— Syn.** See ANNUL. [< OF *voide*, fem. of *voit*, ult. < LL *vocuus* empty < L *vacuus*] **— void′er** *n.*

void·a·ble (voi′də·bəl) *adj.* **1.** Capable of being made void. **2.** That may be evacuated. **— void′a·ble·ness** *n.*

void·ance (void′ns) *n.* **1.** The act of voiding, evacuating, ejecting, or emptying. **2.** The state or condition of being void; vacancy. [< AF *voidaunce*, OF *vuidance* < *voider* to empty < *voit*. See VOID.]

void·ed (voi′did) *adj.* **1.** Made empty or void; cleared of contents. **2.** *Heraldry* Having the central area removed, so as to leave only an outline.

voi·là (vwä·lä′) *interj. French* There! behold!

voi·là tout (vwä·là too′) *French* That is all.

voile (voil, *Fr.* vwàl) *n.* A fine, sheer fabric like heavy veiling, used for summer dresses and curtains. [< F, veil < OF *veile*. See VEIL.]

voir dire (vwär dēr′) *Law* A legal oath administered to a witness to be examined, to make true answers to questions as to his competence. [< OF *voir* truth + *dire* to say]

voix cé·leste (vwä sä·lest′) An organ stop consisting of two ranks of soft flue stops, one tuned slightly sharp, that beat and produce a waving effect: also called *vox angelica*. [< F, heavenly voice]

Voj·vo·di·na (voi′vô·di·nä) An autonomous Province of NE Yugoslavia, included in Serbia; 8,683 sq. mi.; pop. 1,880,000 (1965); capital, Novi Sad. Also **Voy′vo·di·na**, **Voi′vo·di·na**.

vol. 1. Volcano. **2.** Volume. **3.** Volunteer.

Vo·lans (vō′länz) *n.* A constellation, the Flying Fish. See CONSTELLATION.

vo·lant (vō′lənt) *adj.* **1.** Flying, or able to fly. **2.** Nimble. [< OF, ppr. of *voler* to fly < L *volare*]

vo·lan·te (vō·län′tā) *adj. Music* Swift and light. [< Ital.]

Vo·la·pük (vō′lə·pük′) *n.* A proposed universal language invented in 1879 by Johann M. Schleyer, a German priest. [< Volapük *vol* world + *pük* speech] **— Vo′la·pük′ist** *n.*

vo·lar[1] (vō′lər) *adj.* Used in flying; pertaining to flight. [< L *volare* to fly]

vo·lar[2] (vō′lər) *adj.* Pertaining to the sole of the foot or palm of the hand. [< L *vola* sole, palm]

vol·a·tile (vol′ə·təl) *adj.* **1.** Evaporating rapidly at ordinary temperatures on exposure to the air. **2.** Capable of being vaporized. **3.** Easily influenced; fickle; changeable. **4.** Transient; fleeting; ephemeral. **5.** *Obs.* Volant. [< OF *volatil* < L *volatilis* < *volare* to fly]

volatile oil An oil, especially an essential oil, that evaporates readily and does not leave a stain: distinguished from *fixed oil.*

volatile salts Salts that volatilize completely, as sal volatile.

vol·a·til·i·ty (vol′ə·til′ə·tē) *n.* **1.** The state or quality of being volatile. **2.** The property of being freely or rapidly diffused in the atmosphere. Also **vol′a·tile·ness.**

vol·a·til·ize (vol′ə·til·īz′) *v.t. & v.i.* **·ized**, **·iz·ing 1.** To make or become volatile. **2.** To pass off or cause to pass off in vapor; evaporate. **— vol′a·til·iz′a·ble** *adj.* **— vol′a·til·i·za′·tion** *n.* **— vol′a·til·iz′er** *n.*

vol-au-vent (vôl·ō·vän′) *n. French* A patty shell of light puff paste filled with a ragout of meat, fowl, or fish.

Vol·cán de Co·li·ma (vōl·cän′ thā kō·lē′mä) A volcanic peak in western Mexico, near Nevado de Colima; 12,631 ft.: also *Colima.*

vol·can·ic (vol·kan′ik) *adj.* **1.** Of, pertaining to, or characteristic of a volcano or volcanoes. **2.** Produced by or emitted from a volcano. **3.** Eruptive. **— vol·can·ic·i·ty** (vol′kə·nis′ə·tē) *n.* **— vol·can′i·cal·ly** *adv.*

volcanic glass An igneous rock of volcanic origin and glassy texture having cooled too quickly to crystallize, as obsidian.

vol·can·ism (vol′kən·iz′əm) *n.* The conditions and phenomena associated with volcanoes or volcanic action: also called *vulcanism.*

vol·can·ize (vol′kən·īz) *v.t.* **·ized**, **·iz·ing** To subject to the action and effects of volcanic heat. **— vol·can·i·za′tion** *n.*

vol·ca·no (vol·kā′nō) *n. pl.* **·noes** or **·nos** *Geol.* **1.** An opening in the crust of the earth from which steam, hot gases, ashes, etc., are expelled, forming a conical hill or mountain with a central crater. **2.** The formation itself: called *active* when in eruption, *dormant* or *extinct* when long quiescent. Abbr. *vol.* [< Ital. < L *Volcanus, Vulcanus* Vulcan]

Volcano Islands Three small islands, including Iwo Jima,

in the W Pacific; 11 sq. mi.; administered by the U.S., 1945 to 1968, when they were returned to Japan.

vol·can·ol·o·gy (vol′kən·ol′ə·jē) *n.* The scientific study of volcanoes. **— vol′can·o·log′i·cal** (-ə·loj′i·kəl) *adj.* **— vol′can·ol′o·gist** *n.*

vole[1] (vōl) *n.* Any of a genus (*Microtus*) of short-tailed, mouselike or ratlike rodents; especially, the **European vole** (*M. agrestis*) or the **North American vole** (*M. pennsylvanicus*): also called *field mouse, meadow mouse.* [Short for earlier *vole mouse* < *vole* field < Norw. *voll*]

vole[2] (vōl) *n.* In some card games, as écarté, a winning of all the tricks in a deal. **— v.i. voled, vol·ing** To achieve a vole. [< F, appar. < *voler* to fly < L *volare*]

vol·er·y (vol′ər·ē) *n. pl.* **·er·ies** A large bird cage; aviary; also, the birds in it. [< F *volerie* a flying < *voler*. See VOLE[2].]

Vol·ga (vol′gə, *Russ.* vôl′gə) The longest river in the western R.S.F.S.R., flowing 2,290 miles east and south to its delta on the Caspian Sea.

Vol·go·grad (vol′gə·grad, *Russ.* vəl·gə·grät′) A city in the western R.S.F.S.R., on the lower Volga; scene of a Russian victory over German forces in World War II, Sept. 1942 to Jan. 1943; pop. 757,000 (1968): from 1925–61 *Stalingrad,* formerly *Tsaritsyn.*

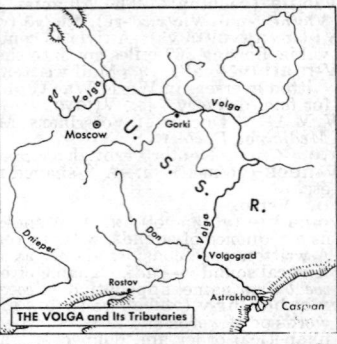

THE VOLGA and Its Tributaries

vol·i·tant (vol′ə·tənt) *adj.* Flying, or having power to fly. [< L *volitans, -antis,* ppr. of *volitare,* freq. of *volare* to fly]

vol·i·ta·tion (vol′ə·tā′shən) *n.* The act or power of flying; flight. [< L *volitatus,* pp. of *volitare*. See VOLITANT.] **— vol′i·ta′tion·al** *adj.*

vo·li·tient (və·lish′ənt) *adj.* Exercising the will, or having freedom of will; willing; voluntary. [VOLITI(ON) + -ENT] **— vo·li′tien·cy** *n.*

vo·li·tion (vō·lish′ən, və-) *n.* **1.** The act or faculty of willing; exercise of the will; especially, the termination of reasoning or uncertainty by a decision. **2.** Strength of will; will power. **3.** That which is willed or determined upon. [< F < Med.L *volitio, -onis* < L *vol-,* stem of *velle* will] **— vo·li′tion·al** *adj.* **— vo·li′tion·al·ly** *adv.*

vol·i·tive (vol′ə·tiv) *adj.* **1.** Of, pertaining to, or originating in the will. **2.** Expressing a wish or permission.

Volks·lied (fôlks′lēt′) *n. pl.* **·lied·er** (-lē′dər) *German* A folk song; popular song.

vol·ley (vol′ē) *n. pl.* **·leys 1.** A simultaneous discharge of many missiles; also, the missiles so discharged. **2.** Any discharge of many things at once: a *volley* of oaths. **3.** In tennis, a return of the ball before it touches the ground. **4.** In soccer, a kick given the ball before its rebound. **5.** In cricket, a ball bowled so that it strikes the wicket before it touches the ground. **— v.t. & v.i. ·leyed, ·ley·ing 1.** To discharge or be discharged in a volley. **2.** In tennis, to return (the ball) without allowing it to touch the ground. **3.** In soccer, to kick (the ball) before its rebound; in cricket, to bowl (a ball) full pitch. [< MF *volée,* pp. fem. of *voler* to fly < L *volare*]

vol·ley·ball (vol′ē·bôl′) *n.* A game in which two teams on either side of a high net strike a large ball with the hands in an attempt to send the ball over the net without letting it touch the ground; also, the ball used. Also **volley ball.**

Vo·log·da (vô′ləg·də) A city in the NW R.S.F.S.R.; European Russian S.F.S.R.; capital of a 15th-century principality; pop. 170,000 (est. 1967).

vo·lost (vô′lost) *n.* In Russia, a district having one joint administrative assembly; a rural soviet. [< Russian *volost'*]

vol·plane (vol′plān) *Archaic v.i.* **·planed, ·plan·ing** To glide in an airplane. **— n.** An airplane glide. [< F *vol plané* gliding flight < *vol* flight + *plané,* pp. of *planer* to glide]

vols. Volumes.

Vol·sci (vol′sī) *n.pl.* A warlike people of ancient Italy, subdued by the Romans about 350 B.C.

Vol·scian (vol′shən) *adj.* Of or pertaining to the Volsci. **— n. 1.** One of the Volsci. **2.** Their language, belonging to the Sabellian branch of the Italic languages.

Vol·stead Act (vol′sted) An act to enforce the Eighteenth (Prohibition) Amendment to the Constitution of the United States, effective 1920–33. [after Representative Andrew J. *Volstead,* 1860–1947, of Minnesota] **— Vol′stead·ism** *n.*

Vol·sun·ga Sa·ga (vol′sŏong·gə sä′gə) A prose version of the Icelandic legends of the dwarf race, the Nibelungs, and Sigurd, the grandson of Volsung. See NIBELUNGENLIED. [< ON *Völsunga saga,* lit., saga of the Volsungs]

Vol·sungs (vol′sŏongz) *n.pl.* In Icelandic mythology, a race of warriors descended from the hero **Vol′sung.**

volt[1] (vōlt) *n.* The unit of electromotive force, or that difference of potential that, when steadily applied against a resistance of one ohm, will produce a current of one ampere. Abbr. *v*, *v.*, *V* [after Alessandro *Volta*]

volt[2] (vōlt) *n.* **1.** In horse-training, a gait in which the horse moves partially sidewise round a center. **2.** In fencing, a sudden leap to avoid a thrust. [< F *volte* turn < Ital. *volta*, orig. pp. fem. of *volvere* to turn < L]

vol·ta (vōl′tə, *Ital.* vôl′tä) *n. pl.* **·te** (-tā) *Music* A turning; a time: used mainly in phrases. **—prima volta** First time. **—seconda volta** Second time. **—una volta** Once. [< Ital. See VOLT[2].]

Vol·ta (vôl′tä) A river in eastern Ghana, flowing 800 miles south to the Gulf of Guinea. See map of (Gulf of) GUINEA.

Vol·ta (vôl′tä), **Count Alessandro,** 1745–1827, Italian physicist; pioneer in the study of electricity.

Volta, Upper See UPPER VOLTA.

volt·age (vōl′tij) *n.* Electromotive force expressed in volts: the *voltage* of a current. Abbr. *v.*

vol·ta·ic (vol·tā′ik) *adj.* Pertaining to electricity developed through chemical action or contact; galvanic. [after Count Alessandro *Volta* + -IC]

voltaic battery *Electr.* A battery of primary cells.

voltaic cell *Electr.* A primary cell (which see).

voltaic couple A pair of dissimilar, usually metallic, substances that will produce an electric current when immersed in an electrolyte.

voltaic pile An arrangement of dissimilar metal disks, placed alternately and having between them paper moistened with acids for the generation of an electric current: also *galvanic pile.*

Vol·taire (vol·târ′, *Fr.* vôl·târ′) Pseudonym of *François Marie Arouet,* 1694–1778, French author and philosopher: called **the Patriarch of Fer·ney** (fer·nā′).

vol·ta·ism (vōl′tə·iz′əm) *n.* Galvanism (def. 1). [after Alessandro *Volta*]

volt·am·e·ter (vol·tam′ə·tər) *n.* A coulometer (which see). [< VOLTA(IC) + -METER]

volt·am·me·ter (vōlt′am′mē′tər) *n.* An instrument for measuring either volts or amperes. [< VOLT(AGE) + AM(PERAGE) + -METER]

volt·am·pere (vōlt′am′pir) *n.* The rate of work in an electric circuit when the current is one ampere and the potential one volt, equivalent to one watt.

volte-face (volt·fäs′, *Fr.* vôlt·fås′) *n.* About-face. [< F < Ital. *voltafaccia* < *volta* a turning + *faccia* face < L *facies*]

vol·ti (vōl′tē) *interj. Music* Turn: a direction to turn the leaf. [< Ital., imperative sing. of *voltare* to turn < *volta.* See VOLT[2].]

vol·ti·geur (vôl·tē·zhœr′) *n.* **1.** One who vaults; a tumbler. **2.** Formerly, in the French army, a skirmisher in a light infantry regiment. [< F < *voltiger* to hover, vault < Ital. *volteggiare* < *volta.* See VOLT[2].]

volt·me·ter (vōlt′mē′tər) *n.* An instrument for determining the voltage between any two points, generally consisting of a calibrated galvanometer wound with a coil of high resistance.

Vol·tur·no (vôl·tŏŏr′nō) A river in southern Italy, flowing 109 miles SE and SW to the Tyrrhenian Sea.

vol·u·ble (vol′yə·bəl) *adj.* **1.** Having a flow of words or fluency in speaking; talkative; garrulous. **2.** Turning readily or easily; revolving; apt or formed to roll. **3.** Twining, as a plant. **— Syn.** See TALKATIVE. [< MF < L *volubilis* easily turned < *volutus*, pp. of *volvere* to turn] **—vol·u·bil′i·ty, vol′u·ble·ness** *n.* **—vol′u·bly** *adv.*

vol·ume (vol′yŏŏm, -yəm) *n.* **1.** A collection of sheets of paper bound together; book. **2.** A separately bound part of a work. **3.** Sufficient matter to fill a volume. **4.** Quantity of sound or tone; loudness. **5.** A quantity; amount: a large *volume* of business. **6.** A large quantity; a considerable amount. **7.** Space occupied in three dimensions, as measured by cubic units; the amount of space included by the surfaces of a solid. **8.** An ancient written roll or scroll, as of papyrus or vellum. Abbr. (for defs. 1, 4) *v.*, *V*, *vol.* **—to speak volumes** To be full of meaning; express a great deal. [< OF *volum* < L *volumen* roll, scroll < *volutus.* See VOLUBLE.]

vol·umed (vol′yŏŏmd, -yəmd) *adj. Rare* **1.** Rounded or swelling. **2.** Having volume. **3.** Being in volumes: a *two-volumed* history.

vo·lu·me·ter (və·lŏŏ′mə·tər) *n.* Any of several instruments for measuring the volume of gases, liquids, or solids under specified conditions. [< VOLU(ME) + -METER]

vol·u·met·ric (vol′yə·met′rik) *adj. Chem.* Of or pertaining to measurement of substances by comparison of volumes. Also **vol′u·met′ri·cal.** **—vol′u·met′ri·cal·ly** *adv.* **—vo·lu·me·try** (və·lŏŏ′mə·trē) *n.*

volumetric analysis *Chem.* The quantitative analysis of a substance by titration.

vo·lu·mi·nous (və·lŏŏ′mə·nəs) *adj.* **1.** Of great volume, bulk, or size. **2.** Consisting of or capable of filling several volumes. **3.** Writing or having written much; productive. **4.** Having coils, folds, windings, etc. [< LL *voluminosus* <

L *volumen, -inis* a roll] **—vo·lu′mi·nous·ly** *adv.* **—vo·lu′mi·nos′i·ty, vo·lu′mi·nous·ness** *n.*

vol·un·ta·rism (vol′ən·tə·riz′əm) *n. Philos.* The doctrine that will is the ultimate principle or constituent of reality. **—vol′un·ta·rist** *n.* **—vol′un·ta·ris′tic** *adj.*

vol·un·tar·y (vol′ən·ter′ē) *adj.* **1.** Proceeding from the will or from one's own free choice; unconstrained; intentional; volitional. **2.** Endowed with, possessing, or exercising will or free choice. **3.** Effected by choice or volition; acting without constraint. **4.** *Physiol.* Subject to or directed by the will, as a muscle or movement. **5.** Of or relating to voluntaryism. **6.** *Law* **a** Unconstrained of will; done without compulsion. **b** Performed without legal obligation. **c** Done without valuable consideration; gratuitous. **— *n. pl.* ·tar·ies 1.** Any work or performance not compelled or imposed by another. **2.** *Music* **a** An organ solo, often improvised, played before, during, or after a service. **b** *Rare* A piece of music, usually spontaneous, played or sung as a prelude. **3.** *Obs.* A volunteer. [< OF *voluntaire* < L *voluntarius* < *voluntas* will] **—vol′un·tar′i·ly** *adv.* **—vol′un·tar′i·ness** *n.*

vol·un·tar·y·ism (vol′ən·ter′ē·iz′əm) *n.* The principle that religious and educational institutions should be supported by voluntary contributions. **—vol′un·tar′y·ist** *n.*

vol·un·teer (vol′ən·tir′) *n.* **1.** One who enters into any service, especially military service or a hazardous undertaking, of his own free will. **2.** *Law* One who takes title under a deed made without valuable consideration; also, a voluntary agent or actor in a transaction. **— *adj.* 1.** Pertaining to or composed of volunteers; voluntary. **2.** Springing up naturally or spontaneously, as from fallen or self-sown seed: a *volunteer* growth. **— *v.t.* 1.** To offer to give or do. **— *v.i.* 2.** To enter or offer to enter into some service or undertaking of one's free will; enlist. Abbr. *vol.* [< obs. F *voluntaire* < OF. See VOLUNTARY.]

Volunteers of America A religious and philanthropical organization founded in the United States in 1896.

Volunteer State Nickname of TENNESSEE.

vo·lup·tu·ar·y (və·lup′chŏŏ·er′ē) *adj.* Pertaining to or promoting sensual indulgence and luxurious pleasures. **— *n. pl.* ·ar·ies** One addicted to sensual pleasures; a sensualist. [< L *voluptuarius* < *voluptas* pleasure]

vo·lup·tu·ous (və·lup′chŏŏ·əs) *adj.* **1.** Belonging to, producing, exciting, or yielding sensuous gratification. **2.** Pertaining to or devoted to the enjoyment of pleasures or luxuries; luxurious; sensual. **3.** Having a full and beautiful form, as a woman. [< OF *voluptueux* < L *voluptuosus* full of pleasure < *voluptas* pleasure] **—vo·lup′tu·ous·ly** *adv.* **—vo·lup′tu·ous·ness** *n.*

vo·lute (və·lŏŏt′) *n.* **1.** *Archit.* A spiral, scroll-like ornament; a scroll, especially one characteristic of the Ionic capital. **2.** *Zool.* One of the whorls or turns of a spiral shell. **— *adj.* 1.** Rolled up; forming spiral curves. **2.** Having a spiral form, as a machine part. [< F < L *voluta* scroll, orig. fem. pp. of *volvere* to turn] **—vo·lu′tion** *n.*

VOLUTE

vo·lut·ed (və·lŏŏ′tid) *adj.* Having a volute.

vol·va (vol′və) *n. Bot.* The part of the sheath enclosing certain young mushrooms that later forms a cuplike appendage at the base of the stem. [< L < *volvere* to wrap, turn]

Vol·vox (vol′voks) *n.* A genus of flagellate fresh-water protozoans that form hollow, spherical colonies. [< NL < L *volvere* to roll]

vol·vu·lus (vol′vyə·ləs) *n. pl.* ·li (-lī) *Pathol.* Obstruction of the intestines caused by twisting. [< NL < L *volvere* to turn]

vo·mer (vō′mər) *n. Anat.* A thin bone forming the greater part of the nasal septum in most vertebrates. [< NL < L *vomer* plow] **—vo·mer·ine** (vō′mər·in, vom′ər-) *adj.*

vom·i·ca (vom′i·kə) *n. pl.* ·cae (-sē) *Pathol.* **1.** A collection of purulent matter within an organ, especially the lungs. **2.** A cavity containing such matter. **3.** Expectoration of putrid matter. [< L, a boil, ulcer < *vomere* to vomit]

vom·it (vom′it) *v.i.* **1.** To throw up or eject the contents of the stomach through the mouth. **2.** To issue with violence from any hollow place; be ejected. **— *v.t.* 3.** To throw up or eject from the stomach, as food. **4.** To discharge or send forth copiously or forcibly: The volcano *vomited* smoke. **— *n.* 1.** Matter that is ejected, as from the stomach in vomiting. **2.** An emetic. **3.** The act of vomiting. [< L *vomitare*, freq. of *vomere* to vomit] **—vom′it·er** *n.*

vom·i·tive (vom′ə·tiv) *adj.* Causing vomiting. **— *n.* An emetic.**

vom·i·to (vom′ə·tō, *Sp.* vō′mē·tō) *n. Pathol.* **1.** Yellow fever. **2.** Black vomit (which see). [< Sp. *vomito* < L *vomitus*, pp. of *vomere* to vomit]

vom·i·to·ry (vom′ə·tôr′ē, -tō′rē) *adj.* Efficacious in producing vomiting. **— *n. pl.* ·ries 1.** An emetic. **2.** An opening through which matter is discharged. **3.** In a Roman amphitheater, one of the entrances from the encircling arcades to the passages leading to the seats: so called because of the numbers of people who flowed forth from it: also **vom·i·tor·i·um** (vom/ə·tôr/ē·əm, -tō/rē-). [< L *vomitorius* < *vomitare*. See VOMIT.]

vom·i·tu·ri·tion (vom/ə·choŏ·rish/ən) *n. Pathol.* Violent vomiting with the ejection of but little matter; retching. [< F < L *vomitus* a vomiting < *vomere* to vomit]

von (von, *Ger.* fôn, *unstressed* fən) *prep. German* Of; from: used in German and Austrian family names as an attribute of nobility, corresponding to the French *de.* Abbr. *v.*

voo·doo (vōō/dōō) *n. pl.* **·doos 1.** A primitive religion of West African origin characterized by belief in sorcery and the use of charms, fetishes, witchcraft, etc. **2.** One who practices voodoo. **3.** A voodoo charm or fetish. — **Syn.** See MAGIC. — *adj.* Of or pertaining to the beliefs, ceremonies, or practices of voodoo. — *v.t.* **·dooed, ·doo·ing** To put a spell upon after the manner of a voodoo; bewitch. [< Creole *voudou* < Ewe *vodu*]

voo·doo·ism (vōō/dōō·iz/əm) *n.* **1.** The religion of voodoo. **2.** Belief in or practice of this religion. — **voo/doo·ist** *n.* — **voo/doo·is/tic** *adj.*

-vora *combining form Zool.* Used to denote orders or genera when classified according to their food: *Carnivora.* An individual member of such an order or genus is denoted by **-vore:** *carnivore.* [< NL < L *-vorus.* See -VOROUS.]

vo·ra·cious (vô·rā/shəs, vō-, və-) *adj.* **1.** Eating with greediness; ravenous. **2.** Greedy; rapacious. **3.** Ready to swallow up or engulf. **4.** Insatiable; immoderate. [< L *vorax, -acis* < *vorare* to devour] — **vo·ra/cious·ly** *adv.* — **vo·rac·i·ty** (vô·ras/ə·tē, vō-, və-), **vo·ra/cious·ness** *n.*

Vor·i·ai Spor·a·des (vô/rē·e spô·rä/thes) The Greek name for the Northern Sporades. See under SPORADES.

vor·la·ge (fôr/lä·gə) *n.* In skiing, a posture in which the body leans forward toward the ski tips. [< G, lit., a lying forward < *vor-* forward + *lage* position]

Vo·ro·nezh (vo·rô/nyish) A city in the western R.S.F.S.R., on the Don; pop. 454,000 (1959).

Vo·ro·shi·lov (və·ro·shē/lôf), **Klimenti Yefremovich,** 1881–1969, Soviet marshal and politician.

Vo·ro·shi·lov·grad (və·rə·shi·lov·grät/) See LUGANSK.

Vo·ro·shi·lovsk (və·ro·shē/fsk) See STAVROPOL.

-vorous *combining form* Consuming; eating or feeding upon: *omnivorous, carnivorous.* [< L *-vorus* < *vorare* to devour]

vor·tex (vôr/teks) *n. pl.* **·tex·es** *or* **·ti·ces** (-tə·sēz) **1.** A mass of whirling gas or liquid, especially when sucked spirally toward a central axis; a whirlwind or whirlpool. **2.** One of the rotatory masses of cosmic matter that in the Cartesian philosophy filled all of space and from which the material universe evolved. **3.** Any action or state of affairs that is similar to a vortex in violence, force, etc. [< L, var. of *vertex* top, point]

vor·ti·cal (vôr/ti·kəl) *adj.* Of, like, or causing a vortex. [< L *vortex, -icis* vortex] — **vor/ti·cal·ly** *adv.*

vor·ti·cose (vôr/tə·kōs) *adj.* Rotating rapidly; whirling; vortical. [< L *vorticosus* < *vortex, -icis* vortex]

vor·tig·i·nous (vôr·tij/ə·nəs) *adj.* Moving as in a vortex. [< L *vortigo, -inis,* var. of *vertigo* a spinning]

Vor·tum·nus (vôr·tum/nəs) See VERTUMNUS.

Vosges Mountains (vōzh) A mountain chain in eastern France, across the Rhine from the Black Forest of Germany; highest peak, Ballon de Guebwiller, 4,672 ft.

vo·ta·ry (vō/tər·ē) *n. pl.* **·ries 1.** One bound by a vow or promise, as a nun. **2.** One devoted to some particular worship, pursuit, study, etc. Also **vo/ta·rist.** — **Syn.** See ENTHUSIAST. — *adj.* Consecrated by a vow or promise; votive. [< L *votus,* pp. of *vovere* to vow] — **vo/ta·ress** (vō/tə·ris) *or* **vo/tress** (vō/tris) *n.fem.*

vote (vōt) *n.* **1.** A formal expression of will or opinion in regard to some question submitted for decision, as in electing officers, passing resolutions, etc. **2.** That by which such choice is expressed, as a show of hands, or ballot. **3.** The result of an election. **4.** The number of votes cast; also, votes collectively: a light *vote*; the farm *vote.* **5.** The right to vote. **6.** A voter. **7.** *Obs.* A wish, vow, or prayer. — *v.* **vot·ed, vot·ing** *v.t.* **1.** To determine the status of in a specified way by vote; enact, endorse, elect, defeat, etc., by vote: to *vote* a man into (or out of) office. **2.** To cast one's vote for: to *vote* a straight ticket. **3.** *Informal* To declare by general agreement: to *vote* a concert a success. — *v.i.* **1.** To cast one's vote; express opinion or preference by or as by a vote. — **to vote down** To defeat or suppress by voting against. — **to vote in** To elect. [< L *votum* vow, wish, orig. neut. of *vovere* to vow. Doublet of VOW.] — **vot/a·ble** *or* **vote/a·ble** *adj.* — **vot/er** *n.*

vote getter A person with ability to win votes. — **vote getting**

voting machine A device which enables the voter to indicate his choices by operating small levers and which registers and counts all votes.

voting precinct An election district.

vo·tive (vō/tiv) *adj.* Dedicated by a vow; performed in fulfillment of a vow. [< L *votivus* < *votum.* See VOTE.] — **vo/tive·ly** *adv.* — **vo/tive·ness** *n.*

votive mass A mass not assigned to a particular day, but said at the choice of the priest.

vouch (vouch) *v.i.* **1.** To give one's own assurance or guarantee; bear witness: with *for:* I will *vouch* for them. **2.** To serve as assurance or proof: with *for:* The evidence *vouches* for his innocence. — *v.t.* **3.** To bear witness to; attest or affirm. **4.** To cite as support or justification. **5.** To substantiate. **6.** *Law* To call upon or summon (a person) to defend a title. **7.** *Obs.* To call to witness. — *n.* A declaration that attests; an assertion. [< OF *vocher, voucher* < L *vocare* to call < *vox, vocis* voice]

vouch·ee (vou·chē/) *n. Law* A person called to warrant or defend a title.

vouch·er (vou/chər) *n.* **1.** Any material thing, usually a writing, that serves to vouch for the truth of something, or attest an alleged act, especially the payment or receipt of money. **2.** One who vouches for another; a witness.

vouch·safe (vouch/sāf/) *v.* **·safed, ·saf·ing** *v.t.* **1.** To grant, as with condescension; permit; deign. **2.** *Obs.* To assure or guarantee. — *v.i.* **3.** To condescend; deign. [< VOUCH + SAFE] — **vouch/safe/ment** *n.*

vous·soir (vōō·swär/) *n. Archit.* A stone in an arch shaped to fit its curve. [< OF *vausoir, volsoir* curvature of a vault, ult. < L *volutus.* See VOLUBLE.]

vow (vou) *n.* **1.** A solemn promise to God or to a deity or saint to perform some act or make some gift or sacrifice. **2.** A solemn engagement to adopt a certain course of life, pursue some end, etc.; also, a pledge of faithfulness: marriage *vows.* **3.** A solemn and emphatic affirmation. — **to take vows** To enter a religious order. — *v.t.* **1.** To promise solemnly; especially, to promise to God or to some deity. **2.** To declare with assurance or solemnity. **3.** To make a solemn promise or threat to do, inflict, etc. — *v.i.* **4.** To make a vow. [< AF *vu,* OF *vo, vou* < L *votum.* Doublet of VOTE.] — **vow/er** *n.*

vow·el (vou/əl) *n.* **1.** *Phonet.* A speech sound produced by the relatively unimpeded passage of breath through the mouth, varying in quality according to the size, shape, and condition of the resonance cavities: distinguished from *consonant.* Vowels, generally but not always voiced sounds, may be characterized by length (long or short), the height of the tongue (high, mid, low), the place of articulation (front, central, back), the tension of the tongue muscles (tense, lax), and the presence of lip rounding. Thus (ōō) is a long, high, back, tense, rounded vowel. **2.** A letter representing such a sound, as *a, e, i, o, u,* and sometimes *y.* — *adj.* Of or pertaining to a vowel; vocal. [< OF *vouele* < L *vocalis (littera)* vocal (letter) < *vox, vocis* voice, sound. Doublet of VOCAL.]

vow·el·ize (vou/əl·īz) *v.t.* **·ized, ·iz·ing** To supply with vowel points or signs: to *vowelize* a Hebrew text. — **vow/el·i·za/tion** *n.*

vowel point One of a system of diacritical marks written above or below the consonants in Hebrew and certain other Semitic languages to indicate the vowel sound following the consonant.

vox (voks) *n. pl.* **vo·ces** (vō/sēz) Voice; especially, in music, a voice; part. [< L]

vox an·gel·i·ca (voks an·jel/i·kə) **1.** Voix céleste (which see): also **vox cae·les·tis** (si·les/tis). **2.** An organ stop of soft, sweet quality. [< L, angelic voice]

vox hu·ma·na (voks hyōō·mā/nə) An organ reed stop with very short capped pipes, having prominent high harmonics. [< L, a human voice]

vox po·pu·li (voks pop/yə·lī) *Latin* The voice of the people; public sentiment. Abbr. *vox pop.*

voy·age (voi/ij) *n.* **1.** A journey by water, especially by sea: commonly used of a somewhat extended journey by water. **2.** Any journey. **3.** A book describing a voyage or voyaging: Hakluyt's *Voyages.* **4.** Any enterprise or project; also, course. — **Syn.** See JOURNEY. — *v.* **·aged, ·ag·ing** *v.i.* **1.** To make a voyage; journey by water. — *v.t.* **2.** To travel over. [< OF *veiage, voiage* < L *viaticum.* Doublet of VIATICUM.] — **voy/ag·er** *n.*

voy·age·a·ble (voi/ij·ə·bəl) *adj.* Navigable.

vo·ya·geur (vwà·yà·zhœr/) *n. pl.* **·geurs** (-zhœr/) *Canadian* A boatman of Hudson's Bay Company or another fur company, engaged in carrying men, supplies, etc., between remote trading posts; also, a Canadian boatman or fur trader. [< dial. F (Canadian)]

vo·yeur (vwä·vûr/) *n.* One who is sexually gratified by looking at sexual objects or acts. [< F < *voir* to see < L *videre*] — **vo·yeur/ism** *n.*

v.p. 1. Various pagings. **2.** Various places. **3.** *Gram.* Verb passive. **4.** Voting pool (stocks).

V.P. Vice President: also **V.Pres.**

V-par·ti·cle (vē/pär/ti·kəl) *n. Physics* A hyperon.

v.r. *Gram.* Reflexive verb.

V.R. Queen Victoria (L *Victoria Regina*).

vrai·sem·blance (vre·sän·bläns/) *n. French* A show or appearance of truth; verisimilitude.

V.Rev. Very Reverend.

vs. 1. Verse. **2.** Versus.

V.S. Veterinary Surgeon.

VSS Versions.

v.t. *Gram.* Transitive verb.

Vt. Vermont.

VT fuse (vē′tē′) A proximity fuse (which see). [< V(ARI-ABLE) T(IME)]

VTOL Vertical takeoff and landing.

VTOL (vē′tôl) n. Aeron. An aircraft that takes off and lands vertically.

Vuel·ta A·ba·jo (vwel′tä ä·bä′hō) A region including all Cuba west of Havana.

vug (vug, vŏŏg) n. Mining An opening in a mineral vein into which crystals often project. Also **vugg, vugh.** [< Cornish *vooga* cave] —**vug′gy** adj.

Vul. Vulgate.

Vul·can (vul′kən) In Roman mythology, the god of fire and of metallurgy: identified with the Greek *Hephaestus.*

vul·ca·ni·an (vul·kā′nē·ən) adj. Volcanic: also **vul·can·ic** (vul·kan′ik). [< L *Vulcanius* pertaining to Vulcan < *Vulcanus* Vulcan]

Vul·ca·ni·an (vul·kā′nē·ən) adj. **1.** Relating to Vulcan or to the art of working in metals. **2.** Wrought by Vulcan or by Vulcan's art. Also **Vul·can·ic** (vul·kan′ik).

vul·can·ism (vul′ken·iz′əm) n. Geol. Volcanism.

vul·can·ite (vul′kən·īt) n. A dark, hard variety of rubber that has been vulcanized: also called *ebonite, hard rubber.* — adj. Made of vulcanite. [after *Vulcan*]

vul·can·ize (vul′kən·īz) v.t. **·ized, ·iz·ing 1.** To treat (crude rubber) with sulfur or sulfur compounds in varying proportions and at different temperatures, thereby increasing its strength and elasticity, yielding either soft rubber or vulcanite. **2.** To treat (certain other materials) similarly. — **vul′can·iz·a·ble** adj. —**vul′can·i·za′tion** n. —**vul′can·iz′er** n.

vul·can·ol·o·gy (vul′kən·ol′ə·jē) n. Volcanology. —**vul′can·o·log′i·cal** (-ə·loj′i·kəl) adj. —**vul′can·ol′o·gist** n.

vulg. Vulgar(ly).

vul·gar (vul′gər) adj. **1.** Lacking in refinement, good taste, sensitivity, etc.; coarse; crude; boorish; also, obscene; indecent. **2.** Of, pertaining to, or characteristic of the people at large, as distinguished from the privileged or educated classes; popular; common. **3.** Written in or translated into the common language or vulgate; vernacular. — n. Obs. **1.** The common people. **2.** The vernacular tongue. [< L *vulgaris* < *vulgus* the common people] —**vul′gar·ly** adv.

vulgar fraction Math. A common fraction (which see).

vul·gar·i·an (vul·gâr′ē·ən) n. A person of vulgar tastes or manners.

vul·gar·ism (vul′gə·riz′əm) n. **1.** Vulgarity. **2.** A word, phrase, or expression that is in nonstandard or unrefined usage, though not necessarily coarse or gross, as distinguished from those in formal or informal standard usage.

vul·gar·i·ty (vul·gar′ə·tē) n. pl. **·ties 1.** The quality or character of being vulgar. **2.** Something vulgar, as an action, word, etc. Also **vul·gar·ness** (vul′gər·nis).

vul·gar·ize (vul′gə·rīz) v.t. **·ized, ·iz·ing 1.** To make vulgar. **2.** To express and diffuse (something abstruse or complex) in a more widely comprehensible form; popularize. Also Brit. **vul′gar·ise.** —**vul′gar·i·za′tion** n. —**vul′gar·iz′er** n.

Vulgar Latin See under LATIN.

vul·gate (vul′gāt) adj. Common; popular; generally accepted. — n. **1.** Everyday speech. **2.** Any commonly accepted text. [< L *vulgatus* common, orig. pp. of *vulgare* to make common < *vulgus* the common people]

Vul·gate (vul′gāt) n. St. Jerome's Latin version of the Bible, translated between A.D. 383 and 405, now revised and used as the authorized version by the Roman Catholics. — adj. Belonging or relating to the Vulgate. Abbr. *Vul.* [< Med.L *vulgata* (*editio*) the popular (edition), fem. of L *vulgatus* common]

vul·go (vul′gō) adv. Latin Commonly; popularly.

vul·ner·a·ble (vul′nər·ə·bəl) adj. **1.** Capable of being hurt or damaged. **2.** Liable to attack; assailable. **3.** In contract bridge, having won one game of a rubber, and thus receiving increased penalties and increased bonuses. [< LL *vulnerabilis* wounding < L *vulnerare* to wound < *vulnus, -eris* wound] —**vul′ner·a·bil′i·ty, vul′ner·a·ble·ness** n. —**vul′ner·a·bly** adv.

vul·ner·ar·y (vul′nə·rer′ē) Rare adj. Tending to cure wounds. — n. pl. **·ries** A healing application for wounds. [< L *vulnerarius* < *vulnus, -eris* a wound]

Vul·pec·u·la (vul·pek′yə·lə) n. A constellation, the Little Fox. See CONSTELLATION. [< L, dim. of *vulpes* fox]

vul·pec·u·lar (vul·pek′yə·lər) adj. Of or pertaining to a fox, especially a young fox; vulpine.

vul·pine (vul′pin, -pīn) adj. **1.** Of or pertaining to a fox. **2.** Like a fox; sly; crafty. [< L *vulpinus* < *vulpes* fox]

vul·ture (vul′chər) n. **1.** Any of various large birds (family *Carthartidae* or *Vulturidae*) related to the eagles, hawks, and falcons, having the head and neck naked or partly naked, and feeding mostly on carrion; especially, the Old World **griffon vulture** (*Gyps fulvus*), the turkey buzzard, and the California condor. **2.** Someone or something disgustingly predatory. [< AF *vultur,* OF *voltour* < L *vultur, vulturius*] —**vul′tur·ine** (vul′chə·rīn, -chər·in), **vul′tur·ous** adj.

VULTURE
(To 55 inches long; wing-spread to 11 feet)

vul·va (vul′və) n. pl. **·vae** (-vē) Anat. The external genital parts of the female, including the labia majora and minora, the clitoris, and the orifice: also called *pudendum.* [< L, a covering, womb] —**vul′val, vul′var** adj. —**vul′vi·form** (-və·fôrm) adj.

vv. 1. Verses. **2.** Music Violins.

v.v. Vice versa.

Vyat·ka (vyät′kə) A former name for KIROV.

Vy·borg (vē′bôrg, Russ. vi′berk) A port city in the NW R.S.F.S.R., on the Gulf of Finland; pop. 51,000 (1959): Swedish *Viborg,* Finnish *Viipuri.*

vy·ing (vī′ing) adj. Contending. —**vy′ing·ly** adv.

Vy·shin·sky (vi·shin′skē), **Andrei Yanuarievich** See VI-SHINSKY.

W

w, W (dub′əl·yōō, -yŏŏ) n. pl. **w's** or **ws, W's** or **Ws, double·yous 1.** The twenty-third letter of the English alphabet; double u: a ligature of vv or uu. It first came into English writing as a substitution by Norman scribes of the 11th century for the Old English rune *wen,* which later dropped completely out of use. Also *doubleyou.* **2.** The sound represented by the letter *w,* a voiced bilabial velar semivowel before vowels (*we, wage, worry*), and a *u*-glide in diphthongs (*how, allow, dew, review*). It often has no phonetic value before *r* (*wrist, write, wrong*), and internally (*two, sword, answer*). ◆ The combination *wh-* (in Old English spelled *hw-*) is represented in this dictionary as (hw) because most Americans and probably most Canadians use that pronunciation. In some regions, however, *wh-* is consistently pronounced (w), and the use cannot be considered nonstandard. — *symbol* Chem. Tungsten (symbol W, for *wolfram*).

w. 1. Wanting. **2.** Warehousing. **3.** Week(s). **4.** Weight. **5.** West; western. **6.** Wide; width. **7.** Wife. **8.** With. **9.** Won: also **w 10.** Physics Work.

W or w 1. Electr. Watt(s). **2.** West; western.

W. 1. Wales; Welsh. **2.** Wednesday. **3.** West; western. **4.** Physics Work.

wa' (wä) n. Scot. Wall.

W.A. 1. West Africa. **2.** Western Australia.

WAAC or **W.A.A.C.** Women's Army Auxiliary Corps.

Waadt (vät) The German name for VAUD.

WAAF or **W.A.A.F.** Brit. Women's Auxiliary Air Force.

Waal (väl) The southern branch of the Rhine in the Netherlands, flowing from the Rhine proper to the Maas.

WAAS or **W.A.A.S.** Brit. Women's Auxiliary Army Service.

wab (wäb) n. Scot. A web.

Wa·bash (wô′bash) A river in western Ohio and Indiana, flowing 475 miles generally west and south to the Ohio River.

wab·ble (wob′əl) v.t. & v.i. **·bled, ·bling** To wobble. — n. A wobble. [Var. of WOBBLE] —**wab′bler** n. —**wab′bly** adj.

WAC or **W.A.C.** (wak) n. A member of the Women's Army Corps. [< W(OMEN'S) A(RMY) C(ORPS)]

Wace (wās, wäs), 1100?–75?, Anglo-Norman poet.

wack (wak) n. U.S. Slang A wacky person.

wack·e (wak′ə) n. A brown, earthy variety of basaltic rock. [< G < MHG *wacke,* a large stone < OHG *waggo* pebble]

wack·y (wak′ē) adj. **wack·i·er, wack·i·est** Slang Extremely irrational or impractical; erratic; screwy. [Prob. < WHACK; with ref. to damaging blows on the head]

W
X

Wa·co (wā′kō) A city in central Texas; pop. 95,326.

wad¹ (wod) *n.* **1.** A small compact mass of any soft or flexible substance, especially as used for stuffing, packing, or lining; also, a lump; mass: a *wad* of hair. **2.** A piece of paper, cloth, or leather used to hold in a charge of powder in a muzzleloading gun; also, a pasteboard or paper disk to hold powder, and shot in place in a shotgun shell. For illustration see CARTRIDGE. **3.** Fibrous material for stopping up breaks, leakages, etc.; wadding. **4.** *Informal* A large amount. **5.** *Informal* A roll of banknotes; also, money or wealth. **6.** A chew of tobacco. — *v.* **wad·ded, wad·ding** *v.t.* **1.** To press (fibrous substances, as cotton) into a mass or wad. **2.** To roll or fold into a tight wad, as paper. **3.** To pack with wadding for protection, as valuables, or to stuff or line with wadding. **4.** To place a wad in, as a gun; hold in place with a wad. — *v.i.* **5.** To form into a wad. [Origin uncertain] — **wad′dy** *adj.*

wad² (wod) *n. Scot.* A pledge; wager.

wad³ (wod) *v.t. & v.i. Scot.* **wad·ded, wad·ding** To wed.

wad⁴ (wäd, wod) *Scot.* Would.

wad·ding (wod′ing) *n.* **1.** Wads collectively. **2.** Any substance, as carded cotton, used as material for wads. **3.** The act of applying a wad or wads.

wad·dle (wod′l) *v.i.* **·dled, ·dling** **1.** To walk with short steps, swaying from side to side. **2.** To move clumsily: totter. — *n.* A clumsy rocking walk, like that of a duck. [Freq. of WADE] — **wad′dler** *n.* — **wad′dly** *adj.*

wad·dy (wod′ē) *n., pl.* **·dies** *Austral.* **1.** A thick war club used by the aborigines. **2.** A walking stick: piece of wood. — *v.t.* **·died, ·dy·ing** To strike with a waddy. [< native Australian pronun. of *wood*]

wade (wād) *v.* **wad·ed, wad·ing** *v.i.* **1.** To walk through water or any substance more resistant than air, as mud, sand, etc. **2.** To proceed slowly or laboriously: to *wade* through a lengthy book. **3.** *Obs.* To go; proceed. — *v.t.* **4.** To pass or cross, as a river, by walking on the bottom; walk through; ford. — **to wade in** (or **into**) *Informal* To attack or begin energetically or vigorously. — *n.* **1.** The act of wading. **2.** A ford. [OE *wadan* to go]

wad·er (wā′dər) *n.* **1.** One who wades. **2.** A long-legged wading bird, as a snipe, plover, or stork. **3.** *pl.* High waterproof boots, worn especially by anglers.

wa·di (wä′dē) *n., pl.* **·dies** **1.** In Arabia and northern Africa, a ravine containing the bed of a watercourse, usually dry except in the rainy season; also, the watercourse. **2.** An oasis. Also **wa′dy.** [< Arabic *wādī*]

Wa·di Hal·fa (wä′dē häl′fə) A city in the northern Sudan, on the Nile; pop. about 11,000.

wad·mal (wod′məl) *n. Obs.* A thick, durable woolen cloth. Also **wad′maal, wad′mol.** [< ON *vathmāl* < *vath* cloth + *mal* measure]

wad·na (wod′nə) *Scot.* Would not.

wad·set (wod′set′) *n.* In Scots law, a pledge of land, etc., as security for a debt. — *v.t.* **·set·ted, ·set·ting** In Scots law, to mortgage. [ME *wedset* mortgage]

wae (wā) *n. Scot.* Woe. — **wae′ness** *n.*

wae·ful (wā′fool) *adj. Scot.* Woeful; sad. Also **wae′fu** (-fōō).

wae·sucks (wā′suks) *interj. Scot.* Alas! Also **wae′suck.** [< WAE + alter. of SAKE¹]

WAF or **W.A.F.** (waf, wäf) *n.* A member of the Women in the Air Force. [< W(OMEN IN THE) A(IR) F(ORCE)]

Wafd (woft) *n.* A nationalist party in Egypt founded about 1919. [< Arabic, a deputation] — **Wafd′ist** *n. & adj.*

wa·fer (wā′fər) *n.* **1.** A very thin crisp biscuit, cooky, or cracker; also, a small disk of candy. **2.** *Eccl.* A small flat disk of unleavened bread stamped with a cross or the letters IHS, and used in the Eucharist in some churches; the sacred host. **3.** A thin disk of gelatin or other substance used for sealing letters, attaching papers, or receiving a seal. **4.** *Med.* **a** A thin double layer of dried paste enclosing a medicated substance to be swallowed. **b** A suppository. **5.** A disk of priming material used in early artillery. — *v.t.* To attach, seal, or fasten with a wafer. [< AF *wafre* < MLG *wafel.* Akin to WAFFLE.]

waff (waf, wäf) *Scot. & Brit. Dial. v.t. & v.i.* To wave. — *n.* **1.** The act of waving. **2.** A light ailment. **3.** A gust; puff. **4.** A glimpse; sight. **5.** A ghost. [Var. of WAVE]

waff² (waf, wäf) *Scot. adj.* **1.** Lowborn; worthless; inferior. **2.** Strayed; solitary. — *n.* A tramp; vagrant. [Var. of WAIF]

Waf·fen Schutz·staf·feln (vä′fən shōōts′shtä·feln) *German* The divisions of the *Schutzstaffel* used by the Nazis to curb disturbances inside Germany: usually written **Waffen SS.**

waff·ie (wä′fē) *n. Scot.* A tramp.

waf·fle (wof′əl, wô′fəl) *n.* A batter cake, crisper than a pancake, baked between two hinged metal griddles marked with regular indentations (**waffle iron**). [< Du. *wafel* wafer. Akin to WAFER.]

WAFS or **W.A.F.S.** Women's Auxiliary Ferrying Squadron.

waft¹ (waft, wäft) *v.t.* **1.** To carry or bear gently or lightly over air or water; float. **2.** To convey as if on air or water. — *v.i.* **3.** To float, as on the wind. — *n.* **1.** The act of one who or that which wafts. **2.** A breath or current of air; also, something, as an odor, carried on a current of air. **3.** A

wafting or waving motion or movement. [Back formation < *wafter*, in obs. sense, "an escort ship" < Du. *wachter* guard < *wachten* to guard]

waft² (waft, wäft) *n. Naut.* **1.** A signal flag or pennant, sometimes used to indicate wind direction. **2.** A signal made with a flag or pennant. Also called **waif, weft.** — *v.t. Obs.* **1.** To signal or beckon to with the hand. **2.** To turn; direct, as a glance. [Alter. of dial. E *waff*, var. of WAVE]

waft³ (waft, wäft) *n. Scot.* Woof; weft.

waft·age (waf′tij, wäf′-) *n.* Conveyance by wafting.

waft·er (waf′tər, wäf′-) *n.* **1.** One who or that which wafts. **2.** A form of fan or revolving disk used in a blower.

waf·ture (waf′chər, wäf′-) *n.* **1.** A wafting or waving motion. **2.** Waftage. **3.** That which is wafted.

wag¹ (wag) *v.* **wagged, wag·ging** *v.t.* **1.** To cause to move lightly and quickly from side to side or up and down; oscillate; swing: The dog *wags* its tail. **2.** To move (the tongue) in talking. — *v.i.* **3.** To move lightly and quickly from side to side or up and down. **4.** To move busily in animated talk: said of the tongue. **5.** To move or proceed; travel: as the world *wags*. **6.** *Brit. Slang* To play truant. — *n.* The act or motion of wagging. [ME *waggen*, prob. < Scand. Cf. *vagga* to rock a cradle. Akin to OE *wagian* to oscillate.]

wag² (wag) *n.* A humorous fellow; wit; joker. [? Short for obs. *waghalter* gallows bird < WAG¹ + HALTER¹]

wage (wāj) *v.t.* **waged, wag·ing** **1.** To engage in and maintain vigorously; carry on: to *wage* war. **2.** *Obs.* To pledge; put down as security; wager; bet. **3.** *Obs.* To attempt; risk. **4.** *Brit. Dial.* To pay a salary to; employ. — *n.* **1.** Payment for service rendered; especially, the pay of artisans or laborers receiving a fixed sum by the hour, day, week, or month, or for a certain amount of work; hire. **2.** *pl. Econ.* The remuneration received by labor as distinguished from that received by capital. **3.** *pl.* Recompense or yield: formerly, often construed as sing.: The *wages* of sin is death. **4.** *Obs.* Something pledged; gage. See LIVING WAGE, MINIMUM WAGE. — *Syn.* See SALARY. [< AF *wagier*, OF *guagier* to pledge < *gage* pledge. Doublet of GAGE².]

Wage may appear as a combining form or as the first element in two-word phrases:

wage adjuster	wage floor	wage level
wage board	wage freeze	wage-paying
wage category	wage incentive	wage rate
wage ceiling	wage increase	wage slave
wage control	wage labor	wage slavery
wage differential	wage law	wage structure

wage earner One who works for wages.

wa·ger (wā′jər) *v.t. & v.i.* To bet. — *n.* **1.** A bet (defs. 1, 2, & 3). **2.** The act of giving a pledge. [< AF *wageure* < *wagier.* See WAGE.] — **wa′ger·er** *n.*

wage scale **1.** A scale or series of amounts of wages paid. **2.** The scale of wages paid by a single employer.

wage·work·er (wāj′wûr′kər) *n.* An employee receiving wages.

wag·ger·y (wag′ər·ē) *n., pl.* **·ger·ies** **1.** Mischievous jocularity; drollery. **2.** A jest; joke. [< WAG² + -ERY]

wag·gish (wag′ish) *adj.* **1.** Being or acting like a wag. **2.** Said or done in waggery. **3.** *Syn.* See HUMOROUS. — **wag′gish·ly** *adv.* — **wag′gish·ness** *n.*

wag·gle (wag′əl) *v.* **·gled, ·gling** *v.t.* **1.** To cause to move with rapid to-and-fro motions; wag: The duck *waggles* its tail. — *v.i.* **2.** To totter; wobble. — *n.* The act of waggling. [Freq. of WAG¹] — **wag′gling·ly** *adv.* — **wag′gly** *adj.*

Wag·ner (väg′nər), **Richard,** 1813–83, German composer, poet, and critic: full name **Wilhelm Richard Wagner.**

Wag·ner·esque (väg′nə·resk′) *adj.* Similar to or suggestive of the works or style of Richard Wagner.

Wag·ne·ri·an (väg·nir′ē·ən) *adj.* Relating to Richard Wagner or to his style, theory, or works. — *n.* An admirer, performer, or advocate of Wagnerian works.

Wag·ner-Jau·regg (väg′nər·you′rek), **Julius,** 1857–1940, Austrian neurologist and psychiatrist. Also **Wag′ner von Jau′regg.**

wag·on (wag′ən) *n.* **1.** Any of various four-wheeled horse-drawn vehicles used for carrying crops, goods, freight, etc. **2.** A child's four-wheeled toy cart. **3.** A stand on wheels or casters for serving food or drink. **4.** *Brit.* A railway freight car. **5.** *Informal* A patrol wagon (which see). **6.** A station wagon (which see). **7.** *Slang* A battleship. **8.** *Obs.* A chariot. — **on the (water) wagon** *Informal* Abstaining from alcoholic beverages. — **to fix (someone's) wagon** *U.S. Slang* To ruin or punish. — *v.t.* To carry or transport in a wagon. Also *Brit.* **wag′gon.** [< Du. *wagen.* Akin to WAIN.]

wag·on·age (wag′ən·ij) *n.* **1.** The amount paid for conveyance in a wagon. **2.** Wagons collectively.

wagon bed The body of a wagon.

wag·on·er (wag′ən·ər) *n.* **1.** One whose business is driving wagons. **2.** *Obs.* A charioteer. Also *Brit.* **wag′gon·er.**

Wag·on·er (wag′ən·ər) *n.* **1.** The constellation Ursa Major. **2.** The constellation Auriga.

wag·on-head·ed (wag′ən·hed′id) *adj. Archit.* Having a semicylindrical head or top, resembling the top of a covered wagon; having a round-arched roof.

wa·gon-lit (và·gôǹ·lē′) *n. pl.* **-lits** (-lē′) *French* A railway sleeping car.

wag·on·load (wag′ən-lōd′) *n.* The amount that a wagon can carry.

wagon train 1. A train or line of wagons. 2. A group of wagons and families typical of those that formerly traveled together to settle new regions, as in the American West.

Wa·gram (vä′grä…) A village NE of Vienna, Austria; scene of Napoleon's victory over the Austrians, 1809.

wag·some (wag′səm) *adj.* Mischievous; waggish. [< WAG² + -SOME¹]

wag·tail (vag′tāl′) *n.* Any of several small singing birds (genus *Motacilla*), having a long tail that is habitually wagged up and down; especially, the **yellow wagtail** (*M. flava*) of Asia and eastern Alaska.

Wa·ha·bi (wä-hä′bē) *n.* A believer in Wahabiism. Also **Wa·ha·bee, Wah·ha·bi.**

Wa·ha·bi·ism (wä-hä′bē-iz′əm) *n.* An orthodox Moslem sect of Arabia, related to the Sunnites, founded by Abdul-Wahhab; the religion of the ruling family of Saudi Arabia.

wah·con·da (wä-kon′dä) See WAKANDA.

wa·hi·ne (wä-hē′nē, -nä) *n.* An attractive girl or woman, especially of Hawaii. [< Hawaiian and Maori]

wa·hoo¹ (wä-hoo′, wä′hoo) *n.* A deciduous North American shrub or small tree (*Euonymus atropurpureus*) with finely toothed leaves, purple flowers, and scarlet fruit: also called *burning bush, strawberry bush.* [< Siouan (Dakota) *wanhu*, lit., arrowwood]

wa·hoo² (wä-hoo′, wä′hoo) *n.* 1. The American winged elm (*Ulmus alata*). 2. The white basswood (*Tilia heterophylla*). [< Muskhogean (Creek) *uhawhu* the winged elm]

Wai·chow (wī′jō′) A former name for WAIYEUNG.

waif (wāf) *n.* 1. A homeless, neglected wanderer; a stray. 2. *Law* Something stolen and then abandoned by the thief in his flight. 3. Anything found and unclaimed, the owner being unknown. 4. *Naut.* A waft². — *v.t.* To throw away; cast off, as a waif. — *adj.* Stray; wandering; homeless. [< AF *waif*, OF *gaif*, prob. < Scand.]

Wai·ki·ki (wī′kē-kē, wī′kē-kē′) A resort beach on Honolulu harbor, SE Oahu, Hawaii.

wail (wāl) *v.i.* 1. To grieve with mournful cries; lament. 2. To make a sad, melancholy sound, as if in grief. — *v.t.* 3. To grieve on account of. 4. To cry out in sorrow. — *n.* 1. A prolonged, high-pitched sound of lamentation or grief. 2. Any mournful sound, as of the wind. [< ON *væla* to wail < *væ, vei woe*] — **wail′er** *n.* — **wail′ful** *adj.*

Wail·ing Wall (wā′ling) A wall in a courtyard in Jerusalem that reputedly contains fragments of Solomon's temple. Here the Jews assemble on Fridays to mourn and pray. Also **Wailing Place of the Jews.**

wain (wān) *n.* An open, four-wheeled wagon for hauling heavy loads. [OE *wægn, wæn*. Akin to WAGON.]

wain·scot (wān′skət, -skot, -skōt) *n.* 1. A facing for inner walls, usually of wood, but sometimes of marble or other material, usually paneled and of elaborate workmanship. 2. *Brit.* A superior quality of imported oak used for paneling; also, a piece of such wood. 3. The lower part of an inner wall, when finished with material different from the rest of the wall. — *v.t.* **wain·scot·ed** or **·scot·ted**, **wain·scot·ing** or **·scot·ting** To face or panel with wainscot. [< MLG *wagenschot* < *wagen* wagon + *schot* wooden partition]

wain·scot·ing (wān′skət-ing, -skot-, -skōt-) *n.* Material for a wainscot; a wainscot; wainscots collectively. Also **wain′scot·ting.**

wain·wright (wān′rīt) *n.* A maker of wagons.

Wain·wright (wān′rīt), **Jonathan Mayhew**, 1883–1953, U.S. general in World War II.

wair (wâr) See WARE³.

waist (wāst) *n.* 1. The part of the body between the chest and the hips. 2. The middle part or section of any object, especially if of less diameter than the ends; the *waist* of a violin. 3. That part of a woman's dress or other garment covering the body from the waistline to the neck or shoulders; a bodice; also, an undergarment for children, to which other garments may be buttoned. 4. A waistband. 5. *Naut.* The section of a ship between the quarter-deck and the forecastle. 6. The central section of an airplane. [ME *wast*. Akin to OE *wæstm* growth.]

waist·band (wāst′band′, -bənd) *n.* A band encircling the waist, especially as part of a skirt or trousers.

waist·cloth (wāst′klôth′, -kloth′) *n.* A loincloth (which see).

waist·coat (wāst′kōt′, wes′kit) *n.* 1. *Chiefly Brit.* A vest (def. 1). 2. A similar garment worn by women. 3. A long garment formerly worn by men under a doublet.

waist·ing (wās′ting) *n.* Any material suitable for making waists.

waist·line (wāst′līn′) *n.* The line of the waist; in dressmaking, the line at which the skirt of a dress meets the waist.

wait (wāt) *v.i.* 1. To stay or remain in expectation, as of an anticipated action or event: with *for, until,* etc. 2. To be or remain in readiness. 3. To remain temporarily neglected or undone. 4. To perform duties of personal service or attendance; especially, to act as a waiter or waitress: She *waits* at table. — *v.t.* 5. To stay or remain in expectation of; await: to *wait* one's turn. 6. *Informal* To put off or postpone; defer; delay: Don't *wait* breakfast for me. 7. *Obs.* To attend; escort. 8. *Obs.* To attend as a result or consequence. — Syn. See ABIDE. — **to wait on** (or **upon**) 1. To act as a servant or attendant to. 2. To go to see; call upon; visit. 3. To attend as a result or consequence. — **to wait on** (or **upon**) **hand and foot** To do too much for (someone who does little for himself). ◆ *Wait on* is also a dialectal variant of *wait for*: I'll *wait on* you if it won't take long. — **to wait up** To delay going to bed in anticipation of someone or something. — *n.* 1. The act of waiting, or the time spent in waiting; delay. 2. An ambush or trap; snare: to lie in *wait* for a victim. 3. In England, a member of a musical band organized to play and sing in the streets at night or dawn, especially at Christmastime. 4. *Obs.* A watchman or guard. [< AF *waitier*, OF *guaitier* < OHG *wahten* to watch < *wahta* guard]

wait-a-bit (wāt′ə-bit′) *n.* Any of various plants with sharp or hooked thorns, as the greenbrier or the prickly ash. [Trans. of Afrikaans *wacht-een-beetje*]

Waite (wāt), **Morrison Remick**, 1816–88, U.S. jurist.

wait·er (wā′tər) *n.* 1. One who serves food and drink, as in a restaurant. 2. One who awaits something. 3. A tray for dishes, etc. 4. *Obs.* A watchman or keeper.

wait·ing (wā′ting) *n.* The act of one who waits. — **in waiting** In attendance, especially at court. — *adj.* That waits; expecting.

waiting list A list of people waiting to be admitted to some status, institution, etc.

waiting room A room for the use of persons waiting, as for a railroad train, a doctor, dentist, or the like.

wait·ress (wā′tris) *n.* A woman or girl employed to wait on guests at table, as in a restaurant.

waive (wāv) *v.t.* **waived, waiv·ing** 1. To give up or relinquish a claim to. 2. To refrain from insisting upon or taking advantage of; forgo. 3. To put off; postpone; delay. 4. *Law* To surrender, abandon, or relinquish voluntarily, either expressly or by implication, as a claim, privilege, or right. 5. *Obs.* To reject; cast off; abandon; desert. — Syn. See RELINQUISH. [< AF *weyver*, OF *gaiver* to abandon < AF *weyf, waif.* See WAIF.]

waiv·er (wā′vər) *n. Law* The voluntary relinquishment of a right, privilege, or advantage; also, the instrument that evidences such relinquishment. [< AF, var. of *weyver* to abandon. See WAIF.]

Wai·yeung (wī′yüng′) A port city in eastern Kwangtung Province, China; pop. 73,000 (est. 1958): formerly Waichow.

wa·kan·da (wä-kän′dä) *n.* Among the Sioux, supernatural power in specific objects: also spelled *wahconda.* [< Siouan]

Wa·ka·ya·ma (wä·kä·yä·mä) A port city on southern Honshu island, Japan; pop. 353,000 (est. 1968).

wake¹ (wāk) *v.* **woke** (*Rare* **waked**), **waked** (*Dial.* and alternative *Brit.* **woke, wok·en**), **wak·ing** *v.i.* 1. To emerge from sleep. 2. To be or remain awake. 3. To become active or alert after being inactive or dormant. 4. *Dial.* To keep watch or guard at night; especially, to hold a wake (def. 1). 5. *Obs.* To feast or revel late into the night. — *v.t.* 6. To rouse from sleep or slumber; awake. 7. To rouse or stir up; excite; to *wake* evil passions. 8. *Dial.* To keep a vigil over; especially, to hold a wake over. — *n.* 1. A watch over the body of a dead person through the night, just before the burial. 2. Formerly, in the Anglican Church, a dedication festival or anniversary celebration of a parish church, preceded by a night vigil in the church. 3. The act of refraining from sleep, as on a solemn occasion. [Fusion of OE *wacan* to awake and *wacian* to be awake. Akin to WATCH.]

◆ **awake, awaken, wake, waken** Although a tendency has been noted to prefer *awake* and *awaken* in figurative use (His suspicions were *awakened*), these four verbs are so closely connected that their inflected forms are, for the most part, used interchangeably. Thus, one may say I *woke, awoke, wakened,* or *awakened.* The forms I *waked* and I *awaked* are also heard, although much less commonly; *waked* is sometimes reserved for transitive constructions, as I *waked* him at noon. All these forms are acceptable; all mean the same thing. The most common past tense, however, is *woke* or *woke up.* For the past participle, the forms *waked* and *waked up* are probably the simplest and most direct. *Wakened* and *awakened* are usually felt to be more formal, although they seem to be the preferred forms for passive constructions. *Woke* and *woken* as past participles occur in the United States primarily in dialectal speech, but they are accepted as standard forms in British English.

wake² (wāk) *n.* 1. The track left by a vessel passing through the water. 2. The area behind any moving thing. — **in the wake of** 1. Following close behind. 2. In the aftermath of; as a result of. [< ON *vök* an opening in ice]

Wake·field (wāk'fēld) **1.** A city in West Yorkshire, England, the administrative headquarters of the county; pop. 305,300 (1976). **2.** The birthplace of George Washington, an estate on the Potomac River in SE Virginia: also *Bridges Creek*.

wake·ful (wāk'fəl) *adj.* **1.** Remaining awake, especially at the ordinary time of sleep. **2.** Watchful. **3.** Arousing from or as from sleep. — **wake'ful·ly** *adv.* — **wake'ful·ness** *n.*

Wake Island (wāk) A coral atoll in the North Pacific, acquired by the United States in 1898; 4 sq. mi.; site of a U.S. naval and air base; occupied by Japanese forces, 1941–45.

wak·en (wā'kən) *v.t.* **1.** To rouse from sleep; awake. **2.** To rouse to alertness or activity. — *v.i.* **3.** To cease sleeping; wake up. **4.** *Obs.* To keep awake; also, to keep watch. ◆ See note under WAKE[1]. [OE *wæcnan, wæcnian*]

wake·rife (wāk'rīf) *adj. Scot.* or *Obs.* Wakeful; alert. — **wake'rife·ness** *n.*

wake·rob·in (wāk'rob'in) *n.* **1.** The cuckoopint, an herb. **2.** Any species of trillium.

wa·ki·ki (wä'ki·kē) *n.* Shell money of the South Sea Islands. [< Melanesian]

Waks·man (waks'mən), **Selman Abraham**, 1888–1973, U.S. biochemist and microbiologist born in Russia.

Wa·la·chi·a (wo·lā'kē·ə) See WALLACHIA.

Wał·brzych (väw'bzhikh) A city in SW Poland, in former Lower Silesia; pop. 126,100 (est. 1966). *German* **Wal·den·burg** (väl'dən·boørkh).

Wal·che·ren (väl'khə·rən) An island in the SW Netherlands, at the mouth of the Scheldt; 80 sq. mi.

Wal·de·mar I (väl'də·mär), 1131–82, king of Denmark 1157–82: called **the Great.**

Waldemar II, 1170–1241, king of Denmark 1202–41: greatly extended Danish territory: called the **Victorious.**

Wal·den·ses (wol·den'sēz) *n.pl.* A sect of religious dissenters founded about 1170 by Peter Waldo, a merchant of Lyons, France. They were excommunicated by Pope Lucius III, and severely persecuted: also called *Vaudois*. [< Med.L *Waldenses*, after Peter *Waldo*] — **Wal·den'si·an** *adj. & n.*

wald·grave (wôld'grāv) *n.* **1.** An old German title of nobility. **2.** Originally, the king's officer in charge of a forest. Compare LANDGRAVE, MARGRAVE. [< G *waldgraf* < *wald* wood + *graf* count]

Wald·heim (wôld'hīm, *Ger.* vält'-), **Kurt**, born 1918, Austrian diplomat; UN Secretary General 1972–.

Wal·do (wôl'dō), **Peter** Twelfth-century French religious reformer; founded the Waldenses. Also *Valdo*.

Wal·dorf salad (wôl'dôrf) A salad of chopped celery, apples, and walnuts, garnished with lettuce and mayonnaise. [after the first *Waldorf*-Astoria Hotel, New York City]

Wald·teu·fel (väl'toi·fəl), **Emil**, 1837–1915, French composer born in Alsace.

wale[1] (wāl) *n.* **1.** A welt (def. 4). **2.** *Naut.* One of certain strakes of outer planking running fore and aft on a vessel. **3.** A ridge on the surface of cloth. — *v.t.* **waled, wal·ing 1.** To raise wales on by striking, as with a lash; beat; whale. **2.** To manufacture, as cloth, with a ridge or rib. **3.** To weave, as wickerwork, with several rods together. **4.** To protect, fasten, or hold with wales. [OE *walu*]

wale[2] (wāl) *Dial. & Scot.* *n.* A choice or preference; also, the best; the cream. — *adj.* Well-selected; choice. — *v.t.* **waled, wal·ing** To select. [< ON *val* choice]

wal·er (wā'lər) *n. Anglo-Indian* A horse imported to India from New South Wales, Australia.

Wales (wālz) A peninsula of SW Britain, comprising a principality of England, with which it has been politically united since 1536; 8,016 sq. mi.; pop. 2,724,540 (est. 1969): Medieval Latin *Cambria*.

Wal·fish Bay (wôl'fish) See WALVIS BAY.

Wal·hal·la (wal·hal'ə, -hä'lä, val-) See VALHALLA.

walk (wôk) *v.i.* **1.** To advance on foot in such a manner that one part of a foot is always on the ground; of quadrupeds, to advance in such a manner that two or more feet are always on the ground. **2.** To move or go on foot for exercise or amusement. **3.** To proceed or advance slowly. **4.** To move in a manner suggestive of walking. **5.** To act or live in some manner: to *walk* in peace. **6.** To return to earth and appear, as a ghost. **7.** In baseball, to achieve first base as a result of having been pitched four balls. **8.** In basketball, to take more than two steps while holding the ball: also *travel*. **9.** *Obs.* To be in continual motion. — *v.t.* **10.** To pass through, over, or across at a walk: to *walk* the floor. **11.** To cause to go at a walk; lead, ride, or drive at a walk. **12.** To force or help to walk. **13.** To accompany on a walk. **14.** To bring to a specified condition by walking: She *walked* me to death. **15.** To measure or survey by traversing on foot. **16.** To cause to move with a motion resembling a walk: to *walk* a trunk on its corners. **17.** In baseball, to allow to advance to first base by pitching four balls. **18.** In basketball, to take more than two steps while holding (the ball). — **to walk off 1.** To depart, especially abruptly or without warning. — **to walk off with 1.** To win. **2.** To steal. — **to walk out** *Informal* **1.** To go out on strike. **2.** To keep company: with *with* or *together*. — **to walk out on**

Informal To forsake; desert. — **to walk over 1.** In certain sports, to walk over the course without a competitor so as to perform the technicality of winning; gain an easy victory. **2.** To defeat easily; overwhelm. — *n.* **1.** The act of walking, as for enjoyment or recreation; a stroll. **2.** Manner of walking; gait; especially, the gait of a horse in which two or more feet are always on the ground. **3.** Chosen profession or habitual sphere of action: the different *walks* of life. **4.** Distance as measured by the time taken by one who walks: an hour's *walk*. **5.** A place set apart for walking; a path, promenade, or sidewalk for pedestrians. **6.** A ropewalk (which see). **7.** The formation of, or space between, two lines or rows of plants or trees, as in a coffee plantation. **8.** A piece of ground set apart for the feeding and exercise of domestic animals; range; pasture. **9.** A hawker's or vender's route; a beat. **10.** A contest of speed in walking. **11.** In baseball, an advancing to first base as a result of having been pitched four balls. — **to win in a walk** To win easily. [OE *wealcan* to roll, toss] — **walk'er** *n.*

walk·a·way (wôk'ə·wā') *n.* A contest won without serious opposition: also called *walkover*.

Walk·er (wô'kər), **John**, 1732–1807, English lexicographer.

walk·ie-talk·ie (wô'kē·tô'kē) *n. Telecom.* A portable sending and receiving radio set light enough to be carried by one man: also spelled *walky-talky*.

walk·ing bass (wô'king) An insistently reiterated bass figure, usually in eighth notes, used in boogie-woogie music.

walking fern A tufted evergreen fern (*Camptosorus rhizophyllus*) with fronds ending in long tapering tips that take root. Also **walking leaf.**

walking papers *Informal* Notice of dismissal from employment, etc.

walking stick 1. A staff or cane carried in the hand. **2.** Any of a family (*Phasmidae*) of insects having legs, body, and wings resembling one of the twigs among which it lives: also called *stick insect*.

walk-on (wôk'on', -ôn') *n.* A performer having a very small part; also, the part.

walk·out (wôk'out') *n. Informal* **1.** The act of walking out. **2.** A workmen's strike.

walk·o·ver (wôk'ō'vər) *n.* **1.** A horse race with only one starter, that can thus be won by going over the course at a mere walk. **2.** A walkaway (which see).

walk·up (wôk'up') *Informal n.* An apartment house having no elevator. — *adj.* Having no elevator.

Wal·kü·re (väl·kü'rə), **Die** *German* The Valkyries: title of a music drama by Richard Wagner. See RING OF THE NIBELUNG.

walk·way (wôk'wā') *n.* A sidewalk; passage; garden path.

wal·kyr·ie (wal·kir'ē, val-) *n.* A valkyrie (which see). [OE *wælcyrige*, lit., a chooser of the slain]

walk·y-talk·y (wô'kē·tô'kē) See WALKIE-TALKIE.

wall (wôl) *n.* **1.** A continuous structure designed to enclose an area, be the surrounding exterior of a building, be a partition between rooms or halls, etc.; also, a fence of stone or brickwork, surrounding or separating yards, fields, etc. ◆ Collateral adjective: *mural*. **2.** Something suggestive of a wall or barrier: a *wall* of bayonets. **3.** *Anat.* The side of any cavity, vessel, or receptacle. ◆ Collateral adjective: *parietal*. **4.** A barrier or rampart constructed for defense; in the plural, fortifications. **5.** A sea wall; levee. — **to drive, push, or thrust to the wall** To force (one) to an extremity; crush. — **to go to the wall** To be pressed or driven to an extremity; be forced to yield. — *v.t.* **1.** To provide, surround, protect, etc., with or as with a wall or walls. **2.** To fill or block with a wall: often with *up*. — *adj.* Of or pertaining to a wall; hanging or growing on a wall. [OE *weall* < L *vallum* rampart < *vallus* stake, palisade]

Wall may appear as the first element in two-word phrases, as in:

wall arcade	wall clock	wall mosaic
wall arch	wall color	wall moss
wall berry	wall coping	wall nook
wall border	wall crane	wall plant
wall box	wall engine	wall plug
wall bracket	wall face	wall top
wall case	wall garden	wall tower
wall casing	wall hanging	wall tree
wall chart	wall map	wall vase

wal·la·by (wol'ə·bē) *n. pl.* **·bies** Any of various medium-sized to small kangaroos of Australia and New Guinea, as the rock wallaby (genus *Petrogale*). [< Australian *wolabā*]

Wal·lace (wol'is), **Alfred Russel**, 1823–1913, English naturalist. — **Henry Agard**, 1888–1965, U.S. agriculturist and politician, vice president 1941–1944. — **Lewis**, 1827–1905, U.S. general, diplomat, and author: called **Lew Wallace.** — **Sir William**, 1272?–1305, Scottish patriot and national hero; executed by the English.

Wal·la·chi·a (wo·lā'kē·ə) A former principality in southern and SE Rumania: also *Walachia*. — **Wal·la'chi·an** *adj. & n.*

wal·lah (wä'lä) *n. Anglo-Indian* A person engaged in a specified occupation or activity. Also **wal'la.** [< Hind.]

wal·la·roo (wol'ə·roō') *n.* A species of kangaroo (genus

Osphranter), mostly of large size, especially the sturdily built **rock wallaroo** (*O. robustus*) of New South Wales and Queensland. [< Australian *wolarū*]

Wal·la·sey (wŏl′ə·sē) A county borough in NW Cheshire, England, on the Mersey river; part of the port of Liverpool; pop. 103,213 (1961).

Wal·la·wal·la (wŏl′ə·wol′ə) *n.* One of a small tribe of North American Indians of Shahaptian stock of the NW Pacific coast, now on a reservation in Oregon.

Wal·la Wal·la (wŏl′ə wol′ə) A city in SE Washington, on the Walla Walla River; pop. 23,619.

Walla Walla River A river in NE Oregon and SE Washington, flowing about 60 miles NW to the Columbia River.

wall·board (wôl′bôrd′, -bōrd′) *n.* A material made of pressed wood chips and pulp, or sometimes of gypsum and paper, used as a substitute for wood and plaster.

wall creeper A small, brilliantly colored Old World bird (*Tichodroma muraria*) that obtains its insect prey by creeping on cliffs and walls.

Wal·len·stein (wŏl′ən·stīn, *Ger.* vol′ən·shtīn), **Albrecht Wenzel Eusebius von,** 1583–1634, Duke of Friedland and Mecklenburg, Austrian general in the Thirty Years' War.

Wal·ler (wol′ər), **Edmund,** 1606–87, English poet.

wal·let (wŏl′it) *n.* **1.** A pocketbook, usually of leather, for holding unfolded paper money, personal papers, etc.: also called *billfold.* **2.** A leather or canvas bag for tools, etc. **3.** A knapsack. [ME *walet;* ult. origin uncertain]

wall·eye (wôl′ī′) *n.* **1.** An eye in which the iris is light-colored or white. **2.** *Pathol.* **a** Leukoma. **b** Divergent strabismus. See under STRABISMUS. **3.** Any of several walleyed fishes, as the walleyed pike, the alewife, or the walleyed pollack. [Back formation < WALLEYED]

wall·eyed (wôl′īd′) *adj.* **1.** Having a whitish or grayish eye; also, affected with leukoma of the cornea. **2.** Affected with divergent strabismus. **3.** Having large, staring eyes, as a fish. **4.** *Slang* Drunk. [< ON *valdeygthr,* alter. of *vagl egyr* < *vagl* film on the eye + *eygr* having eyes < *auga* eye]

walleyed pike A fresh-water percoid fish (*Stizostedion vitreum*) of the Great Lakes, having large eyes, esteemed as a game fish: also called *dory.* Also **walleyed perch.**

walleyed surf fish A sooty fish (*Hyperprosopon argenteum*) common in California waters.

walleye pollack A coal-black North American pollack (*Theragra chalcogrammus*) of Pacific waters.

wall·flow·er (wôl′flou′ər) *n.* **1.** Any of a genus (*Cheiranthus*) of European herbs of the mustard family; especially, a popular garden perennial (*C. cheiri*), having fragrant yellow, orange, or red flowers: also called *gillyflower.* **2.** *Informal* A person, especially a woman, at a party who stays by the wall for want of a dancing partner.

wal·lie (wol′ē) *n. Scot.* A valet.

Wal·ling·ford (wol′ing·fərd) A town in south central Connecticut; pop. 35,714.

Wal·lis (väl′is) The German name for VALAIS.

wall lizard A gecko.

Wal·lo·ni·an (wo·lō′nē·ən) *adj.* Of or pertaining to the Walloons or the dialect spoken by them. — *n.* **1.** A Walloon. **2.** The French dialect of the Walloons.

Wal·loon (wo·lōon′) *n.* **1.** One of a people inhabiting southern and southeastern Belgium and the adjoining regions of France. **2.** Their language, a dialect of French. **3.** One of the Huguenot colonists who came to the United States from Artois, France. — *adj.* Of or pertaining to the Walloons or their dialect. Abbr. *Wal.*

wal·lop (wol′əp) *v.t. Informal* **1.** To beat soundly; thrash. **2.** To hit with a hard blow. **3.** To defeat soundly. — *v.i. Dial.* or *Informal* **4.** To gallop. **5.** To waddle. — *n.* **1.** *Informal* A severe blow. **2.** *Brit. Dial. & Scot.* A gallop. [< AF *waloper,* OF *galoper.* Doublet of GALLOP.]

wal·lop·er (wol′əp·ər) *n. Informal* **1.** One who or that which wallops. **2.** A whopper.

wal·lop·ing (wol′əp·ing) *Informal adj.* Very large; whopping. — *n.* A beating; whipping.

wal·low (wol′ō) *v.i.* **1.** To roll about; be pleasurably and actively immersed, as in mud, snow, etc. **2.** To thrash about; flounder. **3.** To move with a heavy, rolling motion, as a ship in a storm. **4.** To live self-indulgently: to *wallow* in sensuality. — *n.* **1.** The act of wallowing. **2.** A pool, mudhole, or slough in which animals wallow; also, any depression or hollow made by or suggesting such use. [OE *wealwian*] — **wal′low·er** *n.*

wall·pa·per (wôl′pā′pər) *n.* Paper specially prepared and printed in colors and designs, for covering walls and ceilings of rooms. — *v.t.* To cover or provide with wallpaper.

wall pellitory See under PELLITORY.

wall plate 1. A horizontal timber on a wall, for bearing the ends of joists, girders, etc. **2.** *Mech.* A plate for attaching a bearing or the like to a wall.

wall plug An electric outlet set into a wall.

wall rock *Mining* The nonmetalliferous rock between two lodes or veins of ore.

wall rocket A European perennial (*Diplotaxis tenuifolia*) of the mustard family, with large yellow flowers.

wall rue A small delicate spleenwort (*Asplenium rutamuraria*), growing on walls and cliffs.

Walls·end (wôlz′end) *n.. Brit.* A size or grade of coal for household purposes. [after *Wallsend,* England]

Walls·end (wôlz′end) A municipal borough in Tyne and Wear, England, on the Tyne near Newcastle-on-Tyne; pop. 49,785.

Wall Street 1. A street in the financial district of New York City. **2.** The world of U.S. finance.

wall tent A tent having vertical sides and peaked top.

wal·ly (wā′lē, wol′ē) See WALY[1].

wal·ly·drai·gle (wā′lē·drā′gəl, wol′ē-) *n. Scot.* **1.** The youngest in a family; also, a young bird in the nest. **2.** Any feeble creature. Also **wal′ly·drag′** (-drag′, -dräg′).

wal·nut (wôl′nut′, -nət) *n.* **1.** Any of various deciduous trees of the North temperate zone (genus *Juglans*), cultivated as ornamental shade trees and valued for their timber and their edible nuts; especially, the **black walnut** (*J. nigra*) of the eastern United States, and the **English, Persian, Circassian,** or **Caucasian walnut** (*J. regia*). **2.** The wood or nut of any of these trees, especially the edible seed or kernel. **3.** The shagbark hickory, or its nut. **4.** The color of the wood of any of these trees, especially of the black walnut, a very dark brown. [OE *wealhhnutu, walhhnutu* < *wealh* foreign + *hnutu* nut]

BLACK WALNUT
a Catkin. *b* Shuck with nut *(c)* inside.

Wal·pole (wôl′pōl, wol′-), **Horace,** 1717–97, fourth earl of Orford, English author and wit; son of Sir Robert Walpole. — **Sir Hugh Seymour,** 1884–1941, British novelist and critic born in New Zealand. — **Sir Robert,** 1676–1745, first earl of Orford, English statesman.

Wal·pur·gis Night (väl·pŏŏr′gis) The night before May 1, associated in German folklore with a witches' Sabbath on the Brocken. Also *German* **Wal·pur′gis·nacht′** (-näkht′). [after St. *Walpurga* (or *Walburga*), English nun of the eighth century active in Germany, whose feast day falls on this date]

wal·rus (wôl′rəs) *n. pl.* **·rus·es** or **·rus** A large marine mammal (family *Odobenidae*) of arctic seas, having flippers, tusks in the upper jaw, and a thick, heavy neck; especially, the common **Atlantic walrus** (*Odobenus rosmarus*): also called *sea cow.* — *adj.* Belonging or pertaining to a walrus. [< Du. *walrus* < Scand. Cf. OE *horschwæl,* Dan. *hyalros,* ? < ON *hrosshvalr*]

walrus mustache A long heavy drooping mustache.

Wal·sall (wôl′sôl) A borough in West Midlands, England; pop. 271,000 (1976).

Wal·sing·ham (wôl′sing·əm), **Sir Francis,** 1530?–90, English statesman.

Wal·ter (väl′tər), **Bruno,** 1876–1962, German conductor active in the United States: original name **Bruno Walter Schle·sing·er** (shlä′zing·ər).

Wal·ter (wôl′tər), **John,** 1739–1812, English publisher; founder of the *Times* of London.

Wal·tham (wôl′thəm) A city in eastern Massachusetts, on the Charles River; pop. 61,582.

Wal·tham·stow (wôl′thəm·stō, -təm-) A municipal borough in SW Essex, England, near London; pop. 108,788 (1961).

Wal·ther von der Vo·gel·wei·de (väl′tər fôn der fō′gəl·vī′də), died 1227?, German lyric poet and minnesinger.

Wal·ton (wôl′tən), **Izaak,** 1593–1683, English author. — **William** (Turner), born 1902, English composer.

waltz (wôlts) *n.* **1.** A round dance for couples to music in triple meter. **2.** The music for such a dance, or any similar composition written in triple meter. — *v.i.* **1.** To dance a waltz. **2.** To move quickly and boldly; flounce. **3.** To move easily and freely. — *v.t.* **4.** To cause to waltz. — *adj.* Pertaining to, or typical of, the waltz: *waltz* time. [< G *walzer* < *walzen* to waltz, roll] — **waltz′er** *n.*

Wal·vis Bay (wôl′vis) **1.** An inlet of the Atlantic in South-West Africa. **2.** An enclave in South-West Africa, administered by that territory, but an integral part of South Africa; on Walvis Bay; 374 sq. mi. **3.** A port town in this enclave; pop. about 2,000. Also *Walfish Bay. Afrikaans* **Wal·vis·baai** (wôl′vis·bī′).

wa·ly[1] (wā′lē, wol′ē) *Scot. adj.* **1.** Beautiful; excellent. **2.** Strong; vigorous. — *n. pl.* **·lies 1.** Something pleasing to the eye. **2.** Good luck. **3.** *pl.* Finery. Also spelled *wally.*

wa·ly[2] (wā′lē) *interj. Dial. & Scot.* Alas!: an expression of sorrow or lament.

wam·ble (wom′əl, wam′-) *Dial. v.i.* **·bled, ·bling 1.** To move unsteadily; roll. **2.** To twist or turn; writhe. **3.** *Obs.* To feel nausea. — *n.* **1.** A rolling gait. **2.** A rumbling of the stomach; also, a feeling of nausea. [ME *wamlen.* Cf. Dan. *vamle* to feel nausea, Norw. *vamla* to stagger.] — **wam'bling·ly** *adv.* — **wam'bly** *adj.*

wame (wām) *n. Scot.* The abdomen; belly; also, the womb. [< WOMB]

wame·fou (wā'fōō') *n. Scot.* A bellyful. Also **wam'efu'**, **wame'ful** (-fōōl).

wamp·ish (vo 'pish) *v.t. Scot.* To toss or throw about; wave; brandish.

wam·pum (wom'pəm, wôm'-) *n.* **1.** Beads made of the interior parts of shells, often worked into belts, necklaces, etc., formerly used as currency by North American Indians. The beads were either black, dark purple, or white, the dark beads having double the value of the white: also called *peag.* See SEAWAN. **2.** *Informal* Money. [< Algonquian *wampum(peage),* lit., a white string (of beads)]

wam·pum·peag (wom'pəm-pēg, wôm'-) *n.* Wampum, especially the white beads.

wampum snake The mud snake (which see).

wa·mus (wô' əs, wo ' əs) *n.* I.S. **1.** A cardigan. **2.** A heavy outer jacket of strong, coarse cloth. Also **wam'mus**, **wam'pus** (-pəs). [< Du. *wammes,* short for *wambuis* < OF *wambois* leather doublet < OHG *wamba* belly]

wan[1] (won) *adj.* **wan·ner, wan·nest 1.** Pale, as from sickness or anxiety; pallid. **2.** Indicating illness, unhappiness, etc.: a *wan* smile. **3.** *Obs.* Sad; mournful. **4.** *Obs.* Having a gloomy aspect; dismal; dark: said of scenes or landscapes. — **Syn.** See PALE[2]. — *v.t. & v.i.* **wanned, wan·ning** *Poetic* To make or become wan. — *n. Rare* The quality of being wan; paleness. [OE *wann* dark, gloomy] — **wan'ly** *adv.* — **wan'ness** *n.*

wan[2] (won) *Obsolete* past tense of WIN.

Wan·a·mak·er (won'ə-mā'kər) **John,** 1838–1922, U.S. merchant.

wand (wond) *n.* **1.** A slender rod waved by a magician; also, any rod indicating an office or function of the bearer, as a scepter. **2.** A musician's baton. **3.** A thin, flexible stick or twig; also, a willow shoot; osier. **4.** In archery, a slat used as a mark and placed at varying distances for men and women. [< ON *vöndr.* Akin to WIND[2].]

wan·der (won'dər) *v.i.* **1.** To move or travel about without destination or purpose; roam; rove. **2.** To go casually or by an indirect route; idle; stroll. **3.** To extend in an irregular course; twist or meander. **4.** To stray. **5.** To deviate in conduct or opinion; go astray. **6.** To think or speak deliriously or irrationally. — *v.t.* **7.** To wander through or across. — *n.* The act of wandering; a ramble. [OE *wandrian*] — **wan'der·er** *n.* — **wan'der·ing·ly** *adv.*

— **Syn.** (verb) **1.** *Wander, ramble, roam, rove,* and *range* mean to move about without fixed destination. *Wander* implies no more than the absence of plan or purpose: to *wander* through the shops, minstrels *wandered* from town to town. *Ramble* tends to be deprecatory: the cow *rambled* all over the lawn, the speaker *rambled* on for more than an hour. *Roam, rove,* and *range* imply travel through a large area, and suggest an irregular rather than a purposeless course: the explorers *roamed* through the jungle, pirates *roved* the sea, surveyors *ranged* through the country to complete their maps.

wan·der·ing albatross (won'dər-ing) A large, whitish, black-winged, web-footed sea bird (*Diomedea exulans*), having extraordinary powers of flight.

wandering Jew 1. A perennial trailing herb (*Tradescantia fluminensis*) of the spiderwort family, with hairy white flowers and vivid green leaves sometimes striped with yellow. **2.** A related plant (*Zebrina pendula*) with red or white flowers and striped leaves. Also **Wandering jew.**

Wandering Jew 1. The shoemaker Ahasuerus, fabled to be condemned to wander perpetually for driving Jesus from his door. **2.** A restless wanderer.

wandering tattle The tattler (def. 3), a bird.

wan·der·lust (won'dər-lust', *Ger.* vän'dər-lōōst') *n.* An impulse to travel; restlessness combined with a sense of adventure. [< G < *wandern* to travel + *lust* joy]

wan·der·oo (won'də-rōō') *n.* **1.** A large black monkey (*Macaca silenus*) of western India, having a heavy whitish mane. **2.** A Ceylonese langur (*Presbytis cephalopterus*). [< Singhalese *vanduru,* pl. of *vandurā* the Ceylonese langur < Skt. *vānara* monkey]

wan·dle (won'dəl, -əl) *adj. Dial.* Supple; nimble.

Wands·worth (wondz'wûrth) A metropolitan borough of SW London, England; pop. 347,209 (1961).

wane (wān) *v.i.* **waned, wan·ing 1.** To diminish in size and brilliance: opposed to *wax.* **2.** To decline or decrease gradually; draw to an end. — *n.* **1.** Decrease, as of power, prosperity, or reputation. **2.** The decrease of the moon's visible illuminated surface; also, the period of such decrease. **3.** The beveled edge of a board sawn from a log; also, the bark or defective portion on the edge or corner of a board. — **on the wane** Waning. [OE *wanian*]

wane·y (wā'nē) *adj.* Having a beveled edge, as the wane of a plank; also spelled *wany.* [< WANE, *n.* (def. 3)]

wan·gle (wang'gəl) *v.* **-gled, -gling** *Informal v.t.* **1.** To obtain or accomplish by indirect or irregular methods: to *wangle* an introduction. **2.** To manipulate or adjust, especially dishonestly. — *v.i.* **3.** To resort to indirect, irregu-

lar, or dishonest methods. — *n.* An act of wangling. [? Alter. of WAGGLE] — **wan'gler** *n.*

Wan·hsien (wän'shyen') A city in eastern Szechwan Province, China, on the Yangtze; pop. about 100,000.

wan·i·gan (won'ə-gən) *n. U.S. & Canadian* **1.** In logging camps: **a** A place for the storage of small supplies or reserve stock. **b** A large chest for clothing, shoes, tobacco, etc. **c** A raft of square timber with a shanty for sleeping and cooking. **d** The accountant's shack. Also **wan·gan** (won'gən), **wan'gun, wan'ni·gan. 2.** *Canadian* A troop-carrying vehicle having sled runners and pulled by a tracked vehicle, used in the North. [Earlier *wangan* < Algonquian *waniigan* trap or receptacle]

wan·ion (won'yən) *n. Archaic* Bad luck; a vengeance: used only in the phrases **in a wanion, with a wanion,** etc. [Alter. of dial. ME (Northern) *waniand,* ppr. of *wanien* to wane]

Wan·kel engine (väng'kəl, wäng'-) A rotary internal combustion engine, its shaft driven by a triangular-shaped rotor rather than pistons. [after Felix *Wankel,* born 1902, German engineer, its inventor]

want (wont, wônt) *v.t.* **1.** To feel a desire or wish for. **2.** To wish; desire: used with the infinitive: Your friends *want* to help you. **3.** To be deficient in; lack; be without. **4.** To be lacking to the extent of: He *wants* three inches of six feet. **5.** *Brit.* To need; require. — *v.i.* **6.** To have need: usually with *for.* **7.** To be needy or destitute. **8.** *Rare* To be lacking or absent. — **to want for** To be in need of; lack: *to want for* nothing. — **to want to** *Informal* Ought to: You *want to* eat well. — **Syn.** See DESIRE. — *n.* **1.** Lack or absence of something; scarcity; shortage. **2.** Privation; poverty; destitution; need. **3.** Something that is lacking or needed; a need. **4.** A conscious or felt need of something; a craving. — **for want of** Because of the lack or absence of: The crop failed *for want of* rain. [Prob. < ON *vanta* to be lacking] — **want'er** *n.*

want ad *Informal* A classified advertisement for something wanted, as hired help, a job, a lodging, etc.

want·age (won'tij, wôn'-) *n.* Whatever is lacking.

Wan·tagh (won'tô') A village in SE New York, on Long Island; pop. 21,873.

want column A column of want ads.

want·ing (won'ting, wôn'-) *adj.* **1.** Not at hand; missing; lacking. **2.** Not coming up to need or expectation: His work was found *wanting.* — **wanting in** Deficient in. — *prep.* **1.** Without; lacking. **2.** Minus; less.

wan·ton (won'tən) *adj.* **1.** Dissolute; licentious; lustful. **2.** Unjust; malicious: *wanton* savagery; also, unprovoked: a *wanton* murder. **3.** Of vigorous and abundant growth; rank. **4.** Extravagant; running to excess; unrestrained: *wanton* speech. **5.** *Poetic* Not bound or tied; loose: *wanton* curls; also, frolicsome; prankish. **6.** *Obs.* Refractory; rebellious. — *v.i.* **1.** To act wantonly or playfully; revel or sport. **2.** To grow luxuriantly. — *v.t.* **3.** To waste wantonly. — *n.* **1.** A lewd or licentious person, especially a woman. **2.** A playful or frolicsome person or animal. **3.** A trifler; dallier. **4.** *Obs.* A person who has been much indulged; a pet. [ME *wantoun* < OE *wan* deficient + ME *towen,* OE *togen,* pp. of *tēon* to bring up, educate] — **wan'ton·ly** *adv.* — **wan'ton·ness** *n.*

wan·y (wā'nē) See WANEY.

wap[1] (wop, wap) *Dial.* or *Archaic v.t. & v.i.* **wapped, wap·ping 1.** To whop. **2.** To flutter or flap. — *n.* **1.** A blow. **2.** A fight. **3.** A storm. [ME *wappen* to hurl]

wap[2] (wap, wop) *Dial. v.t.* **wapped, wap·ping** To wrap; tie; bind. — *n.* A wrapping. [? Alter. of WARP]

wap·en·shaw (wop'ən-shô, wap'-) *n. Scot.* A periodic review of weapons of men under arms. Also **wap'in·schaw, wap'pen·schaw'ing.**

wap·en·take (wop'ən-tāk, wap'-) *n.* An old administrative and judicial subdivision of some English counties, equivalent to the hundred of most counties. [OE *wǣpengetæc* < ON *vápnatak* flourish of weapons denoting confirmation of the decisions of an assembly < *vápna,* genitive pl. of *vāpn* weapon + *tak* a taking]

wap·i·ti (wop'ə-tē) *n. pl.* **·tis** or **·ti** *U.S. & Canadian* A large North American deer (*Cervus canadensis*): also called *elk.* [< Algonquian. Cf. Shawnee *wapiti* pale, white.]

wap·per·jaw (wop'ər-jô') *adj. U.S. Dial.* A crooked or undershot jaw. — **wap'per·jawed'** *adj.*

war[1] (wôr) *n.* **1.** An armed conflict openly carried on between nations or states, or between different parties in the same state. See table MAJOR WARS OF HISTORY. **2.** Any act or state of hostility: enmity; also, a contest or conflict. **3.** The science or art of military operations; strategy. **4.** *Obs.* or *Poetic* A battle. — *v.i.* **warred, war·ring 1.** To wage war; fight or take part in a war. **2.** To be in any state of active opposition. — *adj.* Of or pertaining to, used in, or resulting from war. [OE *wyrre, werre* < AF *werre* < OHG *werra* strife, confusion]

War may appear as a combining form or as the first element in two-word phrases:

war-blasted	war-breeding	war budget
war-born	war bride	war chant
war-breeder	war-broken	war chief

war cloud	war goddess	war-maimed	warpower	war-stirring	war-wasted
war code	war-hardened	warmaker	war powers	war-swept	war-wearied
warcraft	war-impoverished	warmaking	war prisoner	war tax	war-weary
war debt	war insurance	war march	war production	wartime	warwork
war-disabled	war leader	war-marked	war-proof	war-torn	warworker
war drum	war loan	war neurosis	war-ridden	war-tossed	warworn
war gains	war-loving	war office	war-risk	war traitor	war-wounded
war-god	war-made	war party	war-shaken	war vessel	war zone

MAJOR WARS OF HISTORY

NAME	CONTESTANTS (victor shown first)	NOTABLE BATTLES	TREATIES
Greco-Persian Wars 499–478 B.C.	Greek states — Persia	Marathon, 490; Thermopylae, Salamis, 480; Plataea, 479	
Peloponnesian War 431–404 B.C.	Sparta — Athens	Syracuse, 415; Cyzicus, 410; Aegospotami, 405	Peace of Nicias, 421
First Punic War 264–241 B.C.; **Second Punic War** 218–201 B.C.; **Third Punic War** 149–146 B.C.	Rome — Carthage	Drepanum, 249; Aegates, 241; Lake Trasimene, 217; Cannae, 216; Zama, 202	
Norman Conquest 1066	Normandy — England	Hastings, 1066	
Crusades 1096–1291	Christianity — Islam (indecisive)	Jerusalem, 1099; Acre, 1191	
Hundred Years' War 1338–1453	England — France	Crécy, 1346; Poitiers, 1356; Agincourt, 1415; Siege of Orléans, 1428–39	
Wars of the Roses 1455–85	Lancaster — York (indecisive)	St. Albans, 1455	
Thirty Years' War 1618–48	Catholics — Protestants	Leipzig, Breitenfeld, 1631; Lützen, 1632	Westphalia, 1648
Civil War (English) 1642–46	Roundheads — Cavaliers	Marston Moor, 1643; Naseby, 1645	
Second Great Northern War 1700–1721	Russia — Sweden and Baltic allies	Poltava, 1709	Nysted, 1721
War of the Spanish Succession 1701–14	England, Austria, Prussia, Netherlands — France, Spain	Blenheim, 1704	Utrecht, 1713
War of the Austrian Succession 1740–48	France, Prussia, Sardinia, Spain — Austria, England	Dettingen, 1743; Fontenoy, 1745	Aix-la-Chapelle, 1748
French & Indian War 1755–63	England — France	Plains of Abraham, 1759; Montreal, 1760	
Seven Years' War 1756–63	Prussia — Austria, France, Russia	Rossbach, Leuthen, 1757	Hubertusberg, 1763
Revolutionary War 1775–83	American Colonies — England	Lexington, Concord, Bunker Hill, 1775; Saratoga, 1777; Yorktown, 1781	Paris, 1783
Napoleonic Wars 1796–1815	England, Austria, Russia, Prussia, etc. — France	Nile, 1798; Trafalgar, 1805; Jena, Auerstädt, 1806; Leipzig, 1813; Waterloo, 1815	Campoformio, 1797; Tilsit, 1807; Schönbrunn, 1809; Paris, 1814–15; Vienna, 1815
War of 1812 1812–15	United States — England	Lake Erie, 1813; New Orleans, 1815	Ghent, 1814
War of Independence (Greek) 1821–29	Greece, England, Sweden, Russia — Turkey	Navarino, 1827	London, 1827
Mexican War 1846–48	United States — Mexico	Resaca de la Palma, 1846; Chapultepec, 1847	Guadalupe Hidalgo, 1848
Crimean War 1854–56	Turkey, England, France, Sardinia — Russia	Sevastopol, 1854	Paris, 1856
Civil War (United States) 1861–65	Union (North) — Confederate States (South)	Bull Run, 1861; Antietam, 1862; Chancellorsville, Gettysburg, Vicksburg, Chattanooga, 1863; Wilderness, 1864	
Franco-Prussian War 1870–71	Prussia — France	Sedan, 1870	Versailles, 1871
Spanish-American War 1898	United States — Spain	Manila Bay, Santiago, 1898	Paris, 1898
Boer War 1899–1902	England — Transvaal Republic & Orange Free State	Ladysmith, 1899	Vereeniging, 1902
Russo-Japanese War 1904–1905	Japan — Russia	Port Arthur, Mukden, Tsushima, 1905	Portsmouth, 1905
First Balkan War 1912–13; **Second Balkan War** 1913	Bulgaria, Serbia, Greece, Montenegro — Turkey	Scutari, 1912; Salonika, 1912; Adrianople, 1912	London, 1913
World War I 1914–18	Allies — Central Powers	Dardanelles, 1915; Verdun, Somme, Jutland, 1916; Caporetto, 1917; Vittorio Veneto, Amiens, Marne, Ypres, 1918	Versailles, Saint-Germain, Neuilly, 1919; Trianon, Sèvres, 1920; Lausanne, 1923
Civil War (Spanish) 1936–39	Insurgents — Loyalists	Teruel, 1937; Ebro River, 1938	
World War II 1939–45	United Nations — Axis 1939–45	Dunkirk, 1940; Crete, 1941; El Alamein, 1942; Tunis, 1943; Stalingrad, 1942–43; Kharkov, 1943; Cassino, 1943–44; Saint-Lô, 1944; Rhine, Ruhr, Berlin, 1945	Potsdam, 1945
	United Nations — Japan 1941–45	Pearl Harbor, 1941; Bataan, 1941–1942; Singapore, Coral Sea, Midway Island, Guadalcanal, 1942; Bismarck Sea, Tarawa, 1943; Leyte Gulf, 1944; Philippines, 1944–45; Okinawa, 1945	San Francisco, 1951
Korean War 1950–52	United Nations — North Korea	Inchon, Pyongyang, 1950; Seoul, 1951	Panmunjom, 1953

war² (wär) *Dial. v.t.* To guard against; beware of. — *adj.* Cautious; wary. [Var. of WARE²]

war³ (wär) *adj. & adv. Scot. & Brit. Dial.* Worse.

War. or **War** Warwickshire.

War·beck (wôr′bek), **Perkin**, 1474?–99, Flemish impostor; pretender to the English throne; hanged.

war belt Among certain North American Indians, a belt of wampum sent to declare war, to invoke aid in war, etc.

War between the States The United States Civil War: used especially in the former Confederate States.

war bird Among certain North American Indians, the golden eagle whose feathers were worn in the war bonnet.

war·ble[1] (wôr′bəl)   v. ·bled, ·bling v.t. **1.** To sing with trills and runs, or with tremulous vibrations. **2.** To celebrate in song. — v.i. **3.** To sing with trills, etc. **4.** To make a liquid, murmuring sound, as a stream. **5.** U.S. To yodel. — n. The act of warbling; a carol; song. [< AF werbler, OF guerbler < werble warble < OHG werbel something that revolves. Akin to WHIRL.]

war·ble[2] (wôr′bəl)   n. **1.** Vet. a A hard swelling on the back of a horse, caused by the chafing of the saddle. **b** A swelling under the hide of a horse, cow, deer, etc., caused by the maggots of the warble fly. **2.** A warble fly. [Cf. obs. Sw. varbulde < var pus + bulde tumor.] — **war′bled** adj.

warble fly   Any of a family (Hypodermatidae) of dipterous insects, whose larvae produce swellings under the hides of cattle, horses, etc. [< WARBLE[2] + FLY[2]]

war·bler (wôr′blər)   n. **1.** One who or that which warbles. **2.** Any of a family (Sylviidae) of plain-colored, mostly Old World birds allied to the kinglets and noted for their song, as the whitethroat. **3.** Any of a large and varied family (Parulidae, formerly Compsothlypidae) of small American insectivorous birds, usually brilliantly colored, as the **yellow warbler** (Dendroica petechia), the redstart, and the water thrush.

war bonnet   The ceremonial head dress of the North American Plains Indians, consisting of a rawhide cap and an extension down the back decorated with eagle feathers.

War College   U.S. One of four colleges (**Army War College, Naval War College, Air War College, National War College**) giving advanced instruction to experienced officers.

war correspondent   A newspaper or periodical writer assigned to report war or combat from direct observation.

war crime   A crime considered in violation of the rules of warfare, as atrocities against civilians, slave labor, genocide, and the mistreatment and killing of prisoners of war.

war criminal   One convicted of committing a war crime.

war cry   A rallying cry used by combatants in a war, or by participants in any contest.

ward (wôrd)   n. **1.** A large room in a hospital, usually equipped for the care of six or more patients. **2.** A division of a city, made for convenience of elections and government. **3.** Law A person, often a minor, who is in the charge or under the protection of a guardian. **4.** The act of guarding, or the state of being guarded; custody. **5.** An instrument or means of defense; a protection. **6.** A defensive attitude or movement, as in fencing; guard. **7.** A projection inside a lock, designed to obstruct the turning of any key other than the proper one; also, a corresponding notch in the bit of a key. **8.** Any of the separate divisions of a prison. **9.** A warden; overseer. **10.** A local congregation within the Mormon Church. **11.** Brit. In certain counties, a division equivalent to a hundred or wapentake. **12.** Obs. A company of men detailed to defend or guard; a garrison; watch. — v.t. **1.** To repel or turn aside, as a thrust or blow: usually with off. **2.** To put in a ward; keep in safety. **3.** Archaic To guard; protect. [OE weard watching, weardian to watch, guard; infl. in some senses by AF warde, OF garde < Gmc. Akin to GUARD.]

-ward   suffix **1.** Forming adjectives: **a** Going, developing, facing, or directed toward: an upward haul; a skyward trend. **b** Happening or located in the direction of. **2.** Forming adverbs: In or toward a specific area, place, point, or direction: He shot upward; We rowed shorewards. Also **-wards** [OE -weard, -weardes at, toward]

Ward (wôrd), **Artemas,** 1727–1800, American Revolutionary general. — **Artemus** Pseudonym of Charles Farrar Browne, 1834–67, U.S. humorist. — **Mary Augusta,** 1851–1920, née Arnold, British novelist born in Tasmania: called **Mrs. Humphry Ward.**

war dance   A dance of savage tribes before going to war or in celebration of a victory.

war·den[1] (wôr′dən)   n. **1.** U.S. The chief officer of a prison. **2.** An air raid warden or fire warden (which see). **3.** Canadian The reeve appointed chief executive officer of a county. **4.** Brit. The head of certain colleges. **5.** In Connecticut, the chief executive of a borough. **6.** A churchwarden. **7.** A warder. [< AF wardein, OF gardein, guarden < Gmc. Doublet of GUARDIAN.]

war·den[2] (wôr′dən)   n. A variety of pear used chiefly for cooking. Also **War′den.** [ME wardon, prob. < AF warder, OF garder to keep < Gmc.]

war·den·ry (wôr′dən·rē)   n. pl. ·ries The office, functions, or jurisdiction of a warden. Also **war′den·ship** (-ship).

ward·er (wôr′dər)   n. **1.** A keeper; guard; sentinel; watchman. **2.** An official staff or baton; a truncheon. **3.** Chiefly Brit. A prison official; warden. [< AF wardere < warder. See WARDEN[2].]

ward heeler   U.S. Slang A hanger-on of a political boss, who does minor tasks, canvasses votes, etc. [< WARD (def. 2) + HEELER (def. 1)]

ward·ress (wôr′dris)   n. Chiefly Brit. A female warden.

ward·robe (wôrd′rōb′)   n. **1.** All the garments belonging to any one person. **2.** A large upright cabinet for wearing apparel. **3.** The costumes of a theater or theatrical troupe; also, the room in which they are kept. **4.** The styles of a particular season taken collectively: the spring wardrobe. **5.** In a noble or royal household, the department responsible for clothing, jewelry, etc. [< AF warderobe, OF garderobe < warder to keep + robe robe, dress]

ward·room (wôrd′rōōm′, -rōōm′)   n. On a warship, the common recreation area and dining room for the commissioned officers; also, these officers as a group.

ward·ship (wôrd′ship)   n. **1.** The state of being a ward or having a guardian. **2.** Custody; guardianship.

ware[1] (wâr)   n. **1.** Articles of the same class; especially, manufactured articles: used collectively, often in combination: tableware, glassware. **2.** pl. Articles of commerce; goods; merchandise; products. **3.** Pottery; ceramic articles; earthenware. [OE waru]

ware[2] (wâr)   v.t. wared, war·ing Archaic To beware of: used mainly in the imperative: Ware the dog. — adj. Obs. Wary. [OE warian. Akin to WARN.]

ware[3] (wâr)   v.t. wared, war·ing Scot. To spend; squander: also spelled wair.

ware·house (wâr′hous′)   n. **1.** A storehouse for goods or merchandise. **2.** Brit. A large wholesale shop. — v.t. ·housed (-houzd′), ·hous·ing (-hou′zing) To place or store in a warehouse, especially in a bonded warehouse.

ware·house·man (wâr′hous′mən)   n. pl. ·men (-mən) One who works in, manages, or owns a warehouse.

ware·room (wâr′rōōm′, -rōōm′)   n. A room for the storage, exhibition, or sale of goods or wares.

war·fare (wôr′fâr′)   n. **1.** The waging or carrying on of war; conflict with arms; war. **2.** Struggle; strife.

War·field (wôr′fēld), **David,** 1866–1951, U.S. actor.

war game   **1.** pl. Practice maneuvers imitating the conditions of actual warfare. **2.** Kriegspiel.

war·head (wôr′hed′)   n. Mil. The chamber or detachable section at the nose of a guided missile, torpedo, bomb, etc., containing the explosive.

war horse   **1.** Informal A veteran; especially, an aggressive or veteran politician. **2.** A horse used in combat; charger.

war·i·son (war′ə·sən)   n. **1.** A call to attack: an erroneous use originating with Sir Walter Scott. **2.** Obs. Reward. [< AF warison, OF garison wealth, possession]

wark[1] (wärk)   n. Scot. Work. [< WORK]

wark[2] (wärk)   Scot. & Brit. Dial. n. Ache; pain. — v.i. To suffer pain; ache; throb. [< WORK]

war·like (wôr′līk′)   adj. **1.** Disposed to engage in war; belligerent. **2.** Relating to, used in, or suggesting war; military. **3.** Threatening war; pugnacious; hostile.

war·lock[1] (wôr′lok′)   n. A wizard; sorcerer; also, a demon. [OE wǣrloga traitor, foe, devil < wǣr covenant + lēogan to lie, deny]

war·lock[2] (wôr′lok′)   n. A scalp lock worn by the warriors of certain North American Indian tribes. [< WAR + LOCK[2]]

war·lord (wôr′lôrd′)   n. **1.** A leader or high-ranking officer in a militaristic nation. **2.** The warlike ruler or leader of a local region or group of bandits, especially in the Orient.

warm (wôrm)   adj. **1.** Moderately hot; having, or characterized by, heat somewhat greater than temperate. **2.** Imparting heat. **3.** Imparting, promoting, or preserving warmth; preventing loss of bodily heat: a warm coat. **4.** Having a feeling of heat somewhat greater than ordinary: warm from exertion. **5.** Having an affectionate disposition; loving; warmhearted. **6.** Possessing or marked by ardor, liveliness, cordiality, etc.: a warm argument; warm wishes. **7.** Excited; agitated; also, vehement; passionate: a warm temper. **8.** United by affection: warm friends. **9.** Having predominating tones of red or yellow. **10.** Recently made; fresh: a warm trail. **11.** Near a hidden object or concealed fact, as in guessing and seeking games. **12.** Informal Uncomfortable by reason of annoyances or danger. **13.** Characterized by brisk activity: a warm skirmish. — v.t. **1.** To make warm; heat slightly. **2.** To make ardent or enthusiastic; interest. **3.** To fill with kindly feeling: The sight warms my heart. — v.i. **4.** To become warm. **5.** To become ardent or enthusiastic: often with to. **6.** To become kindly disposed or friendly: with to or toward. — **to warm up 1.** To warm. **2.** To exercise or limber the body just before a game, race, etc. **3.** To run an engine until it reaches operating temperature. **4.** To practice, rehearse, etc., just before a performance or effort. **5.** To reach the proper or optimum pitch of performance. — n. Informal Warmth; a heating. [OE wearm] — **warm′ly** adv. — **warm′ness** n.

warm-blood·ed (wôrm′blud′id)   adj. **1.** Zool. Homoiothermal. **2.** Enthusiastic; ardent; passionate.

warm·er (wôr′mər)   n. One who or that which warms.

warm front   Meteorol. The irregular boundary line between an advancing mass of warm air and the underlying colder air mass it displaces.

warm-heart·ed (wôrm′här′tid)   adj. Kind; affectionate.

warm·ing pan (wôr′ming)   A closed metal pan with a long handle, containing hot coals or water, for warming a bed.

war·mon·ger (wôr′mung′gər, -mong′-)   n. One who propagates warlike ideas; a jingo. — **war′mon′ger·ing** adj. & n.

Warm Springs   A resort town in western Georgia; site of an institution for the study and treatment of poliomyelitis; here Franklin D. Roosevelt died, April 12, 1945; pop. 538.

warmth (wôrmth)   n. **1.** The state, quality, or sensation of being warm. **2.** Ardor or fervidness of disposition or feeling; excitement of temper or mind. **3.** The effect produced by warm colors. [ME *wermthe* < OE *wearm* + *-thu, th* -th¹]

warm·up (wôrm′ŭp′) *n.* *Informal* The act of one who or that which warms up.

warn (wôrn) *v.t.* **1.** To make aware of impending or possible harm; put on guard; caution. **2.** To advise; admonish; counsel. **3.** To inform; give notice in advance. **4.** To notify (a person) to stay away, go away, or keep out: with *off, away,* etc. [OE *warnian.* Akin to WARE².] — **warn′er** *n.*

warn·ing (wôr′ning) *n.* **1.** The act of one who warns; also, that which he communicates; notice of danger. **2.** That which warns or admonishes. — *adj.* Serving as a warning. — **warn′ing·ly** *adv.*

warning track *U.S.* A strip without grass on the outer edges of a baseball outfield, to warn the outfielder that he is near the barrier.

War of 1812 See table for WAR.

War of American Independence *Brit.* The American Revolution.

War of Independence The American Revolution.

War of Secession The Civil War in the United States.

War of the Spanish Succession See table for WAR.

warp (wôrp) *v.t.* **1.** To turn or twist out of shape, as by shrinkage or heat. **2.** To turn from a correct or proper course; give a twist or bias to; corrupt; pervert. **3.** To stretch or arrange (yarn) so as to form a warp. **4.** *Naut.* To move (a vessel) by hauling on a rope or cable that is fastened to a pier or anchor. **5.** *Aeron.* Formerly, to change the curvature of (a wing) by twisting, to effect control. — *v.i.* **6.** To become turned or twisted out of shape, as wood in drying. **7.** To turn or deviate from a correct or proper course; go astray. **8.** *Naut.* To move by means of ropes fastened to a pier, anchor, etc. — *n.* **1.** The state of being warped or twisted out of shape; a twist or distortion, especially in a piece of wood. **2.** A mental or moral deviation or aberration; bias. **3.** The threads that run the long way of a fabric, crossing the woof. **4.** The heavy cords used in the casing of a pneumatic tire. **5.** *Naut.* A light cable used for warping a ship or boat; a towline or towrope. **6.** A length of rope yarn or rope. [OE *weorpan* to throw] — **warp′er** *n.*

war paint 1. Paint applied to faces and bodies by North American Indians and other primitive peoples in token of going to war. **2.** *Informal* Cosmetics; full dress and personal adornment; finery; also, official garb or regalia.

war·path (wôr′path′, -päth′) *n.* The route taken by an attacking party of American Indians; the state of war; also, a war expedition. — **on the warpath 1.** On a warlike expedition; at war. **2.** Ready for a fight; thoroughly angry.

warp beam The roller or beam in a loom on which the warp is wound.

war·plane (wôr′plān′) *n.* An airplane equipped for fighting: also called *battle plane.*

war·ra·gal (wär′ə-gəl) *n.* See WARRIGAL.

war·rant (wôr′ənt, wor′-) *n.* **1.** *Law* A judicial writ or order authorizing arrest, search, seizure, or any other designated act in aid of the administration of justice, **2.** Something that assures or attests; a voucher; evidence; guarantee. **3.** That which gives authority for some course or act; sanction; justification: What *warrant* have you? **4.** A certificate of appointment given to army and navy warrant officers. **5.** A document giving a certain authority; especially, a document authorizing receipt or payment of money: a dividend *warrant.* — *v.t.* **1.** To assure or guarantee the quality, accuracy, certainty, or sufficiency of: to *warrant* a title to property. **2.** To assure or guarantee the character or fidelity of; pledge oneself for. **3.** To guarantee against injury, loss, etc. **4.** To be sufficient grounds for; justify: The facts did not *warrant* your action. **5.** To give legal authority or power to, so as to secure against harm; empower; authorize. **6.** To say confidently; feel sure. [< AF *warant, OF guarant* < Gmc.] — **war′rant·a·ble** *adj.* — **war′rant·a·bly** *adv.* — **war′rant·er** *n.*

war·ran·tee (wôr′ən·tē′, wor′-) *n.* *Law* The person to whom a warranty is given.

warrant officer *Mil.* An officer serving without a commission, but having authority by virtue of a certificate or warrant, with rank superior to that of a noncommissioned officer. See tables at GRADE. Abbr. *WO, W.O.*

war·ran·tor (wôr′ən·tôr, wor′-) *n.* *Law* One who makes or gives a warranty to another.

war·ran·ty (wôr′ən·tē, wor′-) *n.* *pl.* **·ties 1.** *Law* **a** An assurance or undertaking by the seller of property, express or implied, that the property is or shall be as it is represented or promised to be. **b** In conveyancing, a covenant in a deed whereby the grantor binds himself and his heirs to secure to the grantee the estate conveyed to him. **c** In insurance law, a stipulation or engagement on the part of the insured that the facts in relation to the risk are as stated by him. **2.** A guarantee (def. 1). **3.** Authorization; warrant. [< AF

warantie, OF *guarantie* < OF *guarant* warrant. Doublet of GUARANTY.]

war·ren (wôr′ən, wor′-) *n.* **1.** A place where rabbits live and breed in communities. **2.** An enclosure for keeping small game; also, a place for keeping fish in a river. **3.** An obscure, crowded place of habitation. **4.** In English law, a franchise, by prescription or royal grant, to keep in an enclosure "beasts and fowls of warren," that is, animals that are by nature wild. [< AF *warenne* game park, rabbit warren < *warir* to preserve < Gmc.]

War·ren (wôr′ən, wor′-) **1.** A city in NE Ohio; pop. 63,494. **2.** A village in SE Michigan, a suburb of Detroit; pop. 179,260.

War·ren (wôr′ən, wor′-), **Earl,** 1891–1974, U.S. administrator and jurist; chief justice of the Supreme Court 1953–69. — **Robert Penn,** born 1905, U.S. poet, novelist, and critic.

war·ren·er (wôr′ən·ər, wor′-) *n.* The keeper of a warren.

Warren hoe A pointed hoe used to make seed furrows: a trade name. Also **warren hoe.** For illustration see HOE.

war·ri·gal (wär′ə-gəl) *n.* *Austral.* **1.** One who or that which is considered wild or uncivilized. **2.** The dingo. Also spelled **warragal.** [< Austral. *warregal* dog, savage]

War·ring·ton (wôr′ing·tən, wor′-) A county borough in southern Lancashire, England, on the Mersey; pop. 75,533.

war·ri·or (wôr′ē·ər, -yər, wor′-) *n.* A man engaged in or experienced in warfare; one devoted to a military life. [< AF *werreieor* < *werreier* to make war < *werre.* See WAR.]

war risk insurance Insurance written by the government of the United States for military and naval personnel.

war·saw (wôr′sô) *n.* A sea bass (*Epinephelus nigritus*) of the South Atlantic and Gulf of Mexico. Also **war′saw** grouper. [Alter. of Sp. *guasa*; prob. infl. in form by *Warsaw*]

War·saw (wôr′sô) The capital of Poland. in the east central part on the Vistula; pop. 1,308,112 (est. 1970). *Polish* **War·sza·wa** (vär-shä′vä).

Warsaw Pact See EASTERN SECURITY TREATY.

war·ship (wôr′ship′) *n.* Any vessel used in naval combat.

war·sle (wär′səl) *v.t. & v.i.* **·sled, ·sling** *Scot.* To wrestle. — *n.* A wrestling match. Also **war′stle.** — **war′sler** *n.*

Wars of the Roses See table for WAR.

wart (wôrt) *n.* **1.** A small, usually hard and nonmalignant bump formed on and rooted in the skin. **2.** A hard glandular protuberance on a plant. [OE *wearte*]

War·ta (vär′tä) A river in NW Poland, flowing 492 miles north and west to the Oder. *German* **War·the** (vär′tə).

Wart·burg (värt′bŏŏrk) A castle in the former state of Thuringia, SW East Germany, where Luther translated the New Testament (1521–22).

wart hog An African wild hog (*Phacochoerus aethiopicus*) having warty excrescences on the face and large tusks in both jaws.

war·time (wôr′tīm′) *n.* A time of war. — *adj.* Caused by or related to a war, or occurring during a period of war.

wart·y (wôr′tē) *adj.* **wart·i·er, wart·i·est 1.** Characterized by or having warts. **2.** Of the nature of warts.

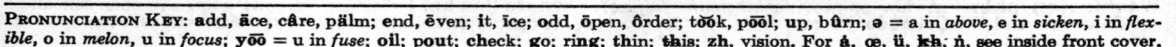

WART HOG
(To 2½ feet
high
at shoulder)

war whoop A yell, as that made by American Indians, uttered as a signal for attack or to terrify opponents in battle.

War·wick (wôr′ik, wor′-), **Earl,** 1428–71, Richard Neville, Earl of Salisbury, English statesman and military commander: called **the King·ma·ker** (king′mā′kər).

War·wick·shire (wôr′ik·shir, wor′-) A county of central England; 983 sq. mi.; pop. 469,500 (1976); county seat, **Warwick,** pop. 111,100 (1976). Also **War′wick.**

war·y (wâr′ē) *adj.* **war·i·er, war·i·est 1.** Carefully watching and guarding. **2.** Shrewd; wily. — **Syn.** see VIGILANT. [< WARE², *adj.*] — **war′i·ly** *adv.* — **war′i·ness** *n.*

was (wuz, woz, *unstressed* wəz) First and third person singular, past indicative of BE. [OE *wæs*, first and third person sing. of *wesan* to be]

Wa·satch Range (wô′sach) A section of the Rocky Mountains in SE Idaho and northern Utah; highest point, Mt. Timpanogos, 12,008 ft.

wash (wosh, wôsh) *v.t.* **1.** To cleanse by immersing in or applying water or other liquid, often with rubbing or scrubbing. **2.** To purify from pollution, defilement, or guilt. **3.** To wet or cover with water or other liquid. **4.** To flow against or over; lave: a beach *washed* by the ocean. **5.** To carry away or remove by the action of water: with *away, off, out,* etc. **6.** To form or wear by erosion: The storm *washed* gullies in the hillside. **7.** To purify, as gas, by passing through a liquid. **8.** To coat with a thin or watery layer of color. **9.** To cover with a thin coat of metal. **10.** *Mining* **a** To subject (gravel, earth, etc.) to the action of water so as to separate the ore, etc. **b** To separate (ore, etc.) thus. — *v.i.* **11.** To wash oneself. **12.** To wash clothes, etc., in water or other liquid. **13.** To withstand the effects of washing: That calico will *wash.* **14.** *Brit. Informal* To undergo testing successfully: That story won't *wash.* **15.** To flow with a lapping sound, as waves. **16.** To be carried away or removed by the action of water: with *away, off, out,* etc. **17.** To be eroded by the action of water. **— to wash down 1.** To drink liquid along with or right after (food) to facilitate swallowing. **2.** To scrub from top to bottom, as walls. **— to wash out 1.** To wash the interior of. **2.** *U.S. Slang* To fail and be dropped from a course. **3.** *U.S. Slang* To damage (an aircraft) irreparably, especially in landing. **— to wash up 1.** To wash oneself. **2.** *Brit. Informal* To wash the dishes. **— n. 1.** The act or process of washing; cleansing; ablution. **2.** A number of articles, as of clothing, set apart to be washed at one time; a washing; laundry. **3.** Liquid or semiliquid refuse; especially, waste food from the kitchen; swill **4.** A preparation used in washing or coating, as: **a** A liquid cosmetic or a mouthwash. **b** Water color or dilute India ink spread lightly and evenly on a drawing or picture. **5.** The breaking of a body of water upon the shore, or the sound made by waves breaking or surging against a surface; swash. **6.** Erosion of soil or earth by the action of rain or running water. **7.** Churned air, water, or other fluid resulting from the passage of an object through it. **8.** *Aeron* The rush of air to the rear from a propeller, or jet or rocket engine. **9.** An area washed by a sea or river; also, the shallow part of a river or an arm of the sea; a marsh; bog. **10.** Material collected and deposited by water, as in the bed of a river or along its banks. **11.** *U.S.* The dry bed of a stream; an arroyo. **12.** Fermented liquor ready for the distillery. **— adj.** Washable; that may be washed without injury: *wash* fabrics. [OE *wascan, wæscan*]

Wash (wosh, wôsh), **The** An inlet of the North Sea on the eastern coast of England.

Wash. Washington.

wash·a·ble (wosh′ə·bəl, wôsh′-) *adj.* That may be washed without fading or injury.

wash-and-wear (wosh′ən-wâr′, wôsh′-) *adj.* Designating or pertaining to a garment or fabric so treated as to require little or no ironing after washing.

wash·board (wosh′bôrd′, -bōrd′, wôsh′-) *n.* **1.** A board or frame having a corrugated surface on which to rub clothes while washing them. **2.** *Naut.* A thin plank set to turn the wash of the sea from a deck or port of a ship.

wash boiler A large metal pot or tub, usually with a removable cover, for boiling linens and clothes.

wash·bowl (wosh′bōl′, wôsh′-) *n.* A basin or bowl, either portable or stationary, used for washing the hands and face. Also **wash′ba/sin** (-bā′sən).

wash·cloth (wosh′klôth′, -kloth′, wôsh′-) *n.* A small cloth used for washing the body.

wash·day (wosh′dā′, wôsh′-) *n.* A day of the week set aside for doing household washing.

washed-out (wosht′out′, wôsht′-) *adj.* **1.** Faded; colorless; pale. **2.** *Informal* Exhausted; worn-out; tired.

washed-up (wosht′up′, wôsh′-) *adj. Slang* **1.** No longer successful, popular, etc.; finished. **2.** *Informal* Washed-out; tired.

wash·er (wosh′ər, wôsh′ər) *n.* **1.** One who or that which washes. **2.** *Mech.* A small, flat, perforated disk of metal, leather, rubber, etc., used for placing beneath a nut or at an axle bearing or joint, to serve as a cushion, to prevent leakage, or to relieve friction. **3.** A washing machine. **4.** A device for purifying gases; scrubber.

wash·er·man (wosh′ər·mən, wô′shər-) *n. pl.* **·men** (-mən) A laundryman.

wash·er·wom·an (wosh′ər·wŏŏm′ən, wô′shər-) *n. pl.* **·wom·en** (-wim′in) A laundress.

wash·ing (wosh′ing, wô′shing) *n.* **1.** The act of one who or that which washes. **2.** Things, as clothing, washed on one occasion, or collected for washing during a certain time. **3.** That which is retained after being washed: a *washing* of ore. **4.** A thin coating of metal. **— adj.** Used in or intended for washing.

washing machine A machine, now usually automatic, for washing laundry: also called *washer*.

washing soda Hydrated sodium carbonate, $Na_2CO_3 \cdot 10H_2O$, used for washing textiles and as a bleaching agent.

Wash·ing·ton (wosh′ing·tən, wô′shing-) **1.** A State in NW United States, adjoining Canada; 68,192 sq. mi.; pop. 3,409,169; capital, Olympia; entered the Union Nov. 11, 1889; nickname *Evergreen State.* Abbr. *Wash.* **2.** A city coextensive with the District of Columbia and capital of the United States; pop. 756,510. **— Wash′ing·to′ni·an** (-tō′nē·ən) *adj. & n.*

Wash·ing·ton (wosh′ing·tən, wô′shing-), **Booker T**(alia·ferro), 1856–1915, U.S. educator. **— George,** 1732–99, American Revolutionary patriot, general, and statesman; first president of the United States 1789–97. **— Martha,** 1731–1802, *née* Dandridge, widow of Daniel Parke Custis; wife of George Washington.

Washington, Lake A lake in west central Washington, near Seattle; 20 mi. long.

Washington, Mount The highest peak of the White Mountains of New Hampshire; 6,288 ft.

Washington palm A fan palm (*Washingtonia filifera*) of California and the Colorado desert.

Washington pie A layer cake filled with cream or jam.

Washington's Birthday February 22, the anniversary of George Washington's birth: a legal holiday in most States.

Wash·i·ta River (wosh′ə·tô, wô′shə-) See OUACHITA RIVER.

wash·out (wosh′out′, wôsh′-) *n.* **1.** A considerable erosion of earth by the action of water; also, the excavation thus made; a gully or gulch. **2.** *Aeron.* A decrease in the angle of attack of an airplane wing toward the tip. **3.** *Slang* A failure. **4.** The act of one who or that which washes out.

wash·rag (wosh′rag′, wôsh′-) *n.* A washcloth.

wash·room (wosh′rōōm′, -rŏŏm′, wôsh′-) *n.* A lavatory.

wash sale On a stock exchange, the buying of stock by the seller's agents, to mislead as to the real demand.

wash·stand (wosh′stand′, wôsh′-) *n.* A stand for wash-bowl, pitcher, etc.

wash·tub (wosh′tub′, wôsh′-) *n.* A tub used for washing.

wash·wom·an (wosh′wŏŏm′ən, wôsh′-) *n. pl.* **·wom·en** (-wim′in) A washerwoman.

wash·y (wosh′ē, wô′shē) *adj.* **wash·i·er, wash·i·est** **1.** Overly diluted; weak. **2.** Faded; wan; wishy-washy. — **wash′i·ness** *n.*

was·n't (wuz′ənt, woz′-) Was not.

wasp (wosp, wôsp) *n.* Any of numerous hymenopterous stinging insects (superfamilies *Sphecoidea* and *Vespoidea*) including social wasps, that make papery nests of masticated vegetable material, and solitary wasps, living in mud or sand nests. ◆ Collateral adjective: *vespine.* [OE *wæps, wæsp*]

WASP (wosp, wôsp) *n. Slang* A white Protestant American. Also **Wasp.** [Acronym formed from the initial letters of "white Anglo-Saxon Protestant"]

WASP or **W.A.S.P.** Women's Air Force Service Pilots.

wasp·ish (wos′pish, wôs′-) *adj.* **1.** Having a nature like a wasp; irritable; irascible. **2.** Having a wasplike form or slender waist. — **wasp′ish·ly** *adv.* — **wasp′ish·ness** *n.*

wasp waist A waist so slender as to suggest that of a wasp. — **wasp-waist·ed** (wosp′wās′tid, wôsp′-) *adj.*

wasp·y (wos′pē, wôs′-) *adj.* **wasp·i·er, wasp·i·est** Like a wasp; waspish.

was·sail (wos′əl, was′-, wo·sāl′) *n.* **1.** An ancient salutation or toast; an expression of good will in festivities, especially when pledging someone's health. **2.** The liquor prepared for a wassail; especially, a mixture of ale and wine with sugar, roasted apples, spices, etc. **3.** A festivity at which healths are drunk; a carousal. **4.** *Brit.* A convivial song. — *v.i.* **1.** To take part in a wassail; carouse. — *v.t.* **2.** To drink the health of; toast. [ME *wæs hæl* < ON *ves heill* be in good health] — **was′sail·er** *n.*

Was·ser·mann test (wos′ər·mən) A test for syphilis, based on fixation of the complement by the blood serum of an infected individual. Also **Wassermann reaction.** [after August von *Wassermann,* 1866–1925, German physician]

wast[1] (wost, *unstressed* wəst) Archaic second person singular, past indicative of BE: used with *thou.*

wast[2] (wast) *adj. & n. Scot.* West.

wast·age (wās′tij) *n.* That which is lost by wear, waste, etc.

waste (wāst) *v.* **wast·ed, wast·ing** *v.t.* **1.** To use or expend thoughtlessly, uselessly, or without return; be prodigal or extravagant of; squander. **2.** To cause to lose strength, vigor, or bulk; make weak or feeble. **3.** To use up; exhaust; consume. **4.** To fail to use or take advantage of, as an opportunity. **5.** To lay waste; desolate; devastate. — *v.i.* **6.** To lose strength, vigor, or bulk; become weak or feeble: often with *away.* **7.** To diminish or dwindle gradually. **8.** To pass gradually: said of time. — *n.* **1.** The act of wasting or squandering, or the state of being wasted; useless or unnecessary expenditure, consumption, etc. **2.** Misuse, neglect, or failure to take advantage of opportunity, talent, etc. **3.** A place or a region that is devastated or made desolate; wilderness; desert. **4.** A continuous, gradual diminishing of strength, vigor, or substance by use or wear. **5.** The act of laying waste or devastating; ravage: the *waste* of war. **6.** Something rejected as worthless or unneeded; especially, tangled spun cotton thread, the refuse of a textile factory; also, steam or other fluid that escapes without being used. **7.** Garbage; rubbish; trash. **8.** The waste products of the soil carried out to sea by running water. — *adj.* **1.** Cast aside as worthless or of no practical value; used; worn out; discarded. **2.** Excreted, as undigested material, etc. **3.** Not under cultivation; untilled; unproductive; unoccupied. **4.** Made desolate: ruined. **5.** Containing or conveying waste products. **6.** Produced in excess of consumption; superfluous: *waste* energy. **— to lay waste** To turn into ruins; destroy utterly; devastate. [< AF *waster,* ult. < L *vastare* to lay waste < *vastus* desert, desolate. Akin to VAST.]

Waste, meaning containing or conveying refuse or waste, may appear as a combining form or as the first element in two-word phrases, as in:

waste bin	waste heap	waste trap
waste collector	waste pipe	waste-water
waste dump	waste pit	wasteway
waste gate	waste sluice	wasteyard

waste·bas·ket (wāst′bas′kit, -bäs′-) *n.* An open container for paper scraps and other waste. Also **wastepaper basket.**

waste·ful (wāst′fəl) *adj.* **1.** Prone to waste; extravagant. **2.** Causing waste. — **waste′ful·ly** *adv.* — **waste′ful·ness** *n.*
waste·land (wāst′land′) *n.* A barren or desolate land.
waste·lot (wāst′lot′) *n. Canadian* A vacant lot (which see).
waste·pa·per (wāst′pā′pər) *n.* Paper thrown away as worthless. Also **waste paper.**
wast·er (wās′tər) *n.* One who wastes; a wastrel.
wast·ing (wās′ting) *adj.* **1.** Producing emaciation; sapping the strength; enfeebling: a *wasting* fever. **2.** Laying waste; devastating.
wast·rel (wās′trəl) *n.* **1.** A waster; spendthrift. **2.** An idler; loafer; vagabond. [Dim. of WASTER]
wast·ry (wās′trē) *n. Scot. & Obs.* Wastefulness: also **waste′rie, wast′rie.**
wat[1] (wat) *adj.* **wat·ter, wat·test** *Scot.* Wet.
wat[2] (wot) *n. Archaic* A hare. [? < *Wat*, short for Walter, a personal name]
Wat. Watorford.
wa·tap (wä·tăp′) *n.* Roots of the spruce, cedar, pine, etc., used by North American Indians to sew bark for canoes and other objects. Also **wa·ta·pe, wat·ta·pe** (wä·tä′pē). [< Algonquian (Narraganset) *wattap* a root of a tree]
watch (woch) *v.i.* **1.** To look attentively; observe carefully. **2.** To wait expectantly; be in a state of expectation: with *for.* **3.** To be constantly on the alert; be observant, vigilant, or attentive. **4.** To do duty as a guard or sentinel; serve as a watchman. **5.** To be an onlooker or spectator. **6.** To be awake; go without sleep; keep vigil. — *v.t.* **7.** To keep under observation; look at steadily and attentively; observe. **8.** To follow the course of mentally; keep informed concerning. **9.** To be alert for; wait for expectantly: to *watch* one's opportunity. **10.** To keep watch over; guard; tend. — **to watch out** To be on one's guard; take care. — *n.* **1.** The act of watching; close and continuous attention; careful observation. **2.** A small, portable timepiece worn or carried on the person, and usually actuated by a coiled spring: distinguished from *clock.* **3.** Position or service as a guard or sentry. **4.** One or more persons set to watch; a watchman or set of watchmen; sentinel; guard. **5.** An act or period of wakefulness or attentive alertness, especially during the night; vigil. **6.** The period of time during which a guard is on duty. **7.** *Naut.* **a** One of the two divisions of a ship's officers and crew, performing duty in alternation. **b** The period of time during which each division is on duty: usually four hours, except the dogwatches from 4 to 6 and from 6 to 8 P.M., which are interposed daily to shift night duty from one watch to the other alternately. **8.** One of the divisions of the night made in ancient times. **9.** *Obs.* A candle marked into equal sections. **10.** *Obs.* The cry of a watchman. **11.** *Obs.* Wakefulness. **12.** *Obs.* A wake. [OE *wæccan.* Akin to WAKE[1].]
watch band A band of leather, metal, or cloth to fasten a watch on the wrist.
watch cap In the U.S. Navy, a small, knitted woolen cap of navy blue worn by enlisted men during cold weather.
watch·case (woch′kās′) *n.* **1.** The protecting case of a watch, usually of gold or silver. **2.** *Obs.* A sentry box.
watch·dog (woch′dôg′, -dog′) *n.* **1.** A dog kept to guard a building or other property. **2.** One who acts as a vigilant protector or guardian; especially, one on the lookout against inefficiency, unlawful practices, etc.
watch·er (woch′ər) *n.* **1.** One who watches. **2.** One who keeps vigil by a sickbed, deathbed, or corpse. **3.** One who watches the voting at the polls to detect fraud.
watch fire An outdoor fire lighted at night as a signal or kept burning by a guard or watcher.
watch·ful (woch′fəl) *adj.* **1.** Vigilant. **2.** *Obs.* Wakeful. — **watch′ful·ly** *adv.* — **watch′ful·ness** *n.*
watch glass **1.** The crystal of a watch. **2.** A dish similar in shape to a watch crystal, but of various sizes, used in chemical and other laboratory experiments.
watch guard A chain, cord, or ribbon attached to a watch and fastened to the clothing.
watch·mak·er (woch′mā′kər) *n.* One who makes or repairs watches. — **watch′mak′ing** *n.*
watch·man (woch′mən) *n. pl.* **·men** (-mən) **1.** Anyone who keeps watch or guard; especially, a man employed to guard a building, etc., at night. **2.** Formerly, one of a group of men appointed to keep watch or patrol the streets of a town or village at night.
watch night A religious service usually held on New Year's Eve. Also **watch meeting.**
watch·tow·er (woch′tou′ər) *n.* A tower upon which a sentinel is stationed.
watch·word (woch′wûrd′) *n.* **1.** A password (which see). **2.** A rallying cry or maxim.
wa·ter (wô′tər, wot′ər) *n.* **1.** A limpid, tasteless, odorless liquid compound of hydrogen and oxygen, H_2O, in the proportion by weight of approximately 2 parts of hydrogen to 16 of oxygen. When pure, water has its maximum density at 4° C. or 39° F.; at normal atmospheric pressure it freezes at 0° C. or 32° F., and boils at 100° C. or 212° F. **2.** Any

body of water, as a lake, river, or a sea; in Scotland, a small river. **3.** Any one of the aqueous or liquid secretions of the body, as perspiration, tears, urine, etc. **4.** Any preparation of water holding a gaseous or volatile substance in solution. **5.** The transparency or luster of a precious stone or a pearl. **6.** Excellence; quality: first *water.* **7.** An undulating sheen given to certain fabrics, as silk, etc. **8.** In commerce and finance, stock issued without increase of paid-in capital to represent it. — **above water** Out of danger; secure. — **like water** Very freely or quickly: to spend money *like water.* — **of the first water** Of the highest degree. — **to hold water** To be valid or effective: His argument doesn't *hold water.* — **to make water** To urinate. — *v.t.* **1.** To pour water upon; moisten; sprinkle. **2.** To provide with water for drinking; give water to. **3.** To dilute or weaken with water: often with *down.* **4.** To give an undulating sheen to the surface of (silk, etc.) by uneven pressure after damping and heating. **5.** To enlarge the number of shares of (a stock company) without increasing the paid-in capital in proportion. **6.** To provide with streams or sources of water; irrigate. — *v.i.* **7.** To secrete or discharge water, tears, etc. **8.** To fill with saliva, as the mouth, from desire for food. **9.** To drink water. **10.** To take in water, as a locomotive. [OE *wæter.* Akin to OTTER.] — **wa′ter·er** *n.*
Water may appear as a combining form, or as the first element in two-word phrases, as in:

water-analysis	water fountain	water-quenched
water barge	waterfree	water-resistant
water-bearing	water-girt	water resources
water bottle	water-gray	water-rot
waterbound	water-green	water-rotted
water bucket	water heater	water route
water carrier	water insect	water scarcity
water carrying	water jar	water-sealed
water cask	water jug	water service
water channel	water-laden	water-soaked
water content	water-locked	water-sodden
water-deposited	water pail	water source
water diver	waterplane	water sport
water drain	water plant	water tap
water drinker	water police	water trough
water-drinking	water problem	water turbine
water flow	water project	water-washed
water-flushed	water pump	water-wasting

wa·ter·age (wô′tər·ij, wot′ər-) *n. Brit.* Conveyance of goods by water; also, the fee for such transportation.
water arum A plant (*Calla palustris*) of the arum family, found in moist ground and having red berries.
water back A coil or chamber for heating water in the back of a stove.
water balance *Biol.* The preservation of a nearly uniform water content in a plant or animal organism.
water ballet A performance by a group of swimmers moving in formation and with synchronized gestures.
Water Bearer The constellation and sign of the zodiac Aquarius.
water bed A bag, usually of vinyl, filled with water and used as a bed.
water beetle Any of several aquatic beetles (families *Dytiscidae, Hydrophilidae* or *Gyrinidae*), having legs flattened and fringed with hairs for swimming.
water bird Any bird living on or near the water.
water biscuit A plain cracker or biscuit of flour, shortening, and water.
water blister A blister containing limpid watery matter.
wa·ter·borne (wô′tər·bôrn′, -bōrn′, wot′ər-) *adj.* **1.** Floating on water. **2.** Transported or carried by water.
water boy A boy or man who supplies drinking water to the members of a work gang, athletic team, etc.
wa·ter·brain (wô′tər·brān′, wot′ər-) *n. Vet.* A form of gid.
water brash *Pathol.* Heartburn.
wa·ter·buck (wô′tər·buk′, wot′ər-) *n.* Either of two large African antelopes (genus *Kobus*), frequenting the neighborhood of rivers and swimming with ease; especially, the common waterbuck (*K. ellipsiprymnus*) of south central Africa. [< Afrikaans *waterbok*]
water buffalo A large buffalo (*Bubalus bubalus*) of India, having a very wide spread of horns, and often domesticated for use as a draft animal: also called *Indian buffalo, water ox:* in the Philippines called *carabao.*
water bug **1.** The Croton bug (which see). **2.** Any of various hemipterous insects (family *Belostomatidae*) that live in the water, especially a large species (*Lethocerus americanus*) common in North America.

WATER BUFFALO
(To 6 feet high at shoulder)

Wa·ter·bur·y (wô′tər·ber′ē, wot′ər-) A city in western Connecticut, on the Naugatuck River; pop. 108,033.
water chestnut **1.** The edible fruit of an aquatic plant (*Trapa natans*). **2.** The plant itself. Also **water caltrop.**

water chinquapin 1. An American lotus (*Nelumbo lutea*), having large, pale yellow flowers. 2. One of its edible, nutlike seeds. Also **water chincapin, water chinkapin.**

water clock A clepsydra.

water closet A toilet (def. 1b). Abbr. *w. c.*

wa·ter·col·or (wô′tər·kul′ər, wot′·ər-) *adj.* Of, pertaining to, used with, or executed in water colors.

water color 1. A color prepared for painting with water as the medium, as distinguished from one to be used with oil, tempera, etc. 2. The branch of painting in which water colors are used, or the method of using them. 3. A picture or painting done in water colors.

WATER CHINQUAPIN
a Flower. *b* leaf. *c* Fruit.

wa·ter·cool (wô′tər·kōōl′, wot′ər-) *v.t.* To cool by means of water, as by using a water jacket on an internal-combustion engine. — **wa′ter·cooled′** *adj.* — **wa′ter·cool′ing** *adj.*

water cooler A vessel or apparatus for cooling and dispensing drinking water.

wa·ter·course (wô′tər·kôrs′, -kōrs′, wot′ər-) *n.* 1. A stream of water; river; brook. 2. The course or channel of a stream or canal.

wa·ter·craft (wô′tər·kraft′, -kräft′, wot′ər-) *n.* 1. Skill in sailing boats or in aquatic sports. 2. Any boat or ship; also, sailing vessels collectively.

water crake 1. The spotted crake (which see). 2. The water ouzel.

wa·ter·cress (wô′tər·kres′, wot′ər-) *n.* A creeping perennial herb (*Nasturtium officinale*) of the mustard family, growing in springs and clear, cool streams and having edible, pungent leaves used as salad.

water culture Hydroponics.

water cure 1. *Med.* Hydropathy. 2. *Informal* A kind of torture in which water is forced down the victim's throat.

water dog 1. A dog that takes readily to the water, as the water spaniel. 2. A dog trained to retrieve waterfowl. 3 *Informal* An old sailor.

wa·tered (wô′tərd, wot′ərd) *adj.* 1. Having an irregularly wavelike sheen, as silk. 2. In finance, having a face value representing more than the true value: said of stock. 3. Moistened or supplied with water. 4. Diluted with water.

Wa·ter·ee (wô′tə·rē′) The lower course of the Catawba River, flowing about 75 miles from north central South Carolina to the Santee.

water elm The planer tree.

wa·ter·fall (wô′tər·fôl′, wot′ər-) *n.* 1. A steep fall of water, as of a stream over a dam or from a precipice; cascade; cataract. 2. *Informal* A chignon suggesting a cascade. [OE *wætergefeall*]

wa·ter·find·er (wô′tər·fīn′dər, wot′ər-) *n.* A dowser who tries to locate underground water with a divining rod.

water flea Any of numerous minute, fresh-water crustaceans (family *Daphniidae*), about the size of a flea, that swim with a jumping motion.

Wa·ter·ford (wô′tər·fərd, wot′ər-) A county in eastern Munster Province, Ireland; 710 sq. mi.; pop. 71,439 (1966); county seat, Waterford, a port on Waterford Harbor, an inlet of the Atlantic, pop. 28,216 (1966). Abbr. *Wat.*

Waterford glass Decorative glassware made in Waterford, Ireland, usually of clear crystal with deeply cut designs.

wa·ter·fowl (wô′tər·foul′, wot′ər-) *n.* *pl.* **·fowl** or **·fowls** 1. A bird that lives on or about the water; especially, a swimming game bird. 2. Such birds collectively.

wa·ter·front (wô′tər·frunt′, wot′ər-) *n.* 1. Real property abutting on or overlooking a natural body of water. 2. That part of a town fronting on a body of water, especially the area containing wharves, docks, etc. 3. A coil or chamber for heating water in the front of a stove.

water gall *Obs.* A partial rainbow. [< WATER + GALL²]

water gap A deep ravine in a mountain ridge, giving passage to a stream.

water gas A poisonous mixture, chiefly of hydrogen and carbon monoxide, produced by forcing steam over white-hot carbon, as coal or coke, and used for cooking, heating, and as an illuminant. — **wa·ter·gas** (wô′tər·gas′, wot′ər-) *adj.*

water gate A floodgate (def. 1).

Wa·ter·gate (wô′tər·gāt′, wot′ər-) *n.* The complex of events, including the resignation of President Richard M. Nixon, that followed the 1972 burglary of Democratic National Headquarters in the Watergate building in Washington, D.C.

water glass 1. A drinking glass. 2. Any glass vessel for holding water. 3. A glass-bottomed tube or box for examining objects lying or moving under water. 4. Sodium silicate. 5. A water gauge on a steam boiler, etc. 6. A clepsydra.

water gum 1. A species of tupelo (*Nyssa aquatica*) common in swampy areas of the southern United States. 2. Any of several trees of the myrtle family, especially a tall ornamental shrub (*Tristania laurina*), native in Australia.

water hammer 1. The concussion of a moving mass of confined water when its flow is suddenly arrested. 2. The

hammering sound caused in pipes containing water when live steam is admitted.

water hazard A pond, stream, or ditch filled with water and designed as an obstacle on a golf course.

water hemlock Any of a genus (*Cicuta*) of poisonous, flowering herbs of the parsley family; especially, the **spotted water hemlock** (*C. maculata*) of the United States, highly injurious to livestock, and the Old World species (*C. virosa*): also called *cowbane.*

wa·ter hen 1. Any of several coots or gallinules that frequent ponds and streams; especially, the moor hen (which see). 2. The American coot: see under COOT.

water hole A small pond, pool, or depression containing water; especially, one used by animals as a drinking place.

water hyacinth An aquatic herb (*Eichornia crassipes*) of tropical America, with pendulous branched roots and bluish purple or white flowers, often a troublesome weed.

water ice 1. A frozen dessert made with water, sugar, and fruit juice. 2. Ice formed by the freezing of water as distinguished from that formed by the packing together of snow.

wa·ter·inch (wô′tər·inch′, wot′ər-) *n.* An old unit of hydraulic measure based on the discharge of water from a round hole with a diameter of one inch and under a constant water head of one twelfth of an inch, and commonly reckoned at fourteen pints a minute.

wa·ter·ing (wô′tər·ing, wot′ər-) *n.* 1. The act of one who or that which waters. 2. The process of producing a wavy, ornamental effect on fabric, etc. — *adj.* 1. Sprinkling; irrigating; that waters. 2. Situated near the shore or near mineral springs.

watering can A container used for watering plants, etc., especially one having a long spout, often with a perforated nozzle. Also **watering pot.**

watering place 1. A place where water can be obtained, as a spring. 2. A health resort having mineral springs; also, a pleasure resort near the water.

wa·ter·ish (wô′tər·ish, wot′ər-) *adj.* Like water; watery.

water jacket A casing containing water and surrounding a cylinder or mechanism, especially the cylinder block of an internal-combustion engine, for keeping it cool.

water jump A water barrier, as a pool, stream, or ditch, to be jumped over by the horses in a steeplechase.

wa·ter·leaf (wô′tər·lēf′, wot′ər-) *n.* *pl.* **·leafs** Any of a genus (*Hydrophyllum*) of North American woodland herbs with white or blue flowers.

wa·ter·less (wô′tər·lis, wot′ər-) *adj.* Without water; dry.

water level 1. The level of still water in the sea or in any other body of water. 2. *Geol.* A water table (which see). 3. *Naut.* A ship's water line.

water lily 1. Any of a genus (*Nymphaea*) of aquatic plants typical of a widely distributed family (*Nymphaeaceae*); especially, the **fragrant water lily** (*N. odorata*), having showy flowers with numerous white or pinkish petals: also called *pond lily.* 2. Any of various related plants.

water line 1. *Naut.* The part of the hull of a ship that corresponds with the water level at various loads: also called *water level.* 2. A line or demarcation corresponding to the height to which water has risen or may rise. Abbr. *w.l., WL*

wa·ter·logged (wô′tər·lôgd′, -logd′, wot′ər-) *adj.* 1. Heavy and unmanageable on account of the leakage of water into the hold, as a ship. 2. Water-soaked; saturated with water. [< WATER + LOG, v., in obs. sense of "to reduce to the condition of a log"]

Wa·ter·loo (wô′tər·lōō) *n.* A final and decisive defeat: usually in the phrase **to meet one's Waterloo.** [after Napoleon's defeat at *Waterloo*, Belgium]

Wa·ter·loo (wô′tər·lōō, wô′tər·lōō′) 1. A village in central Belgium; scene of Napoleon's final defeat by Wellington and Blücher, June 18, 1815; pop. 15,300 (1967). 2. A city in NE central Iowa; pop. 75,533.

water main A large conduit for carrying water, especially one laid underground.

wa·ter·man (wô′tər·mən, wot′ər-) *n.* *pl.* **·men** (-mən) A man who works with a boat or small vessel on the water; a boatman. — **wa′ter·man·ship′** *n.*

water marigold An aquatic plant (*Megalodonta beckii*) of the composite family, with heads of yellow flowers.

wa·ter·mark (wô′tər·märk′, wot′ər-) *n.* 1. A mark showing the extent to which water rises; especially, the line marking the limit of the ebb and flow of the tide. 2. In papermaking: **a** A series of translucent lines, letters, or designs made in paper by shaping the wires of the dandy rolls over which the paper passes while still in a pulpous state. **b** The metal pattern that produces these markings. Abbr. *w/m, wmk.* — *v.t.* 1. To impress (paper) with a watermark. 2. To impress as a watermark.

wa·ter·mel·on (wô′tər·mel′ən, wot′ər-) *n.* 1. The large, edible fruit of a trailing plant (*Citrullus vulgaris*) of the gourd family, containing a many-seeded red or pink pulp and a watery juice. 2. The plant on which this fruit grows.

water meter An instrument for registering the amount of water flowing through a pipe, etc.

water milfoil Any of a genus (*Myriophyllum*) of aquatic herbs with feathery leaves.

water mill A mill operated by waterpower.

water moccasin A venomous pit viper (*Agkistrodon piscivorus*), of the southern United States: also called *cottonmouth*.

water motor 1. A turbine operated by waterpower. 2. A water wheel.

water nymph In classical mythology, any nymph or goddess living in or guarding a body of water; a naiad, Nereid, Oceanid, etc.

water oak A species of oak (*Quercus nigra*) growing near swamps and streams in the eastern United States.

water of crystallization *Chem.* Molecules of water forming part of certain crystallized salts. They may be eliminated by heat, often with apparent loss of crystalline structure.

water of hydration *Chem.* Water present in combination in certain substances, and capable of being eliminated, as by heat or evaporation, without change of chemical structure.

water on the brain A popular name for hydrocephalus.

water on the knee A painful enlargement of the knee joint due to infection or to injury to the membranes or cartilages.

water ouzel Any of various small passerine birds (genus *Cinclus*), especially adapted to feeding under water: also called *dipper, water crake*. Also **water ousel**.

water ox A water buffalo.

water parting A watershed (def. 1).

water pepper Any of several species of polygonum, especially a common smartweed (*Polygonum hydropiper*).

water pimpernel The brookweed.

water pipe 1. A hookah. 2. A conduit for water.

water pistol A toy pistol that squirts a stream of water.

water plantain Any of a genus (*Alisma*) typical of a family (*Alismaceae*) of common, smooth, aquatic herbs with leaves like those of the plantain; especially, the North American species *A. plantago-aquatica*.

water polo An aquatic game in which two teams of seven swimmers each push or throw a buoyant ball toward opposite goals.

wa·ter·pow·er (wô′tər·pou′ər, wot′ər-) *n.* 1. The power of water derived from its momentum under pressure or gravity, as applied to the driving of machinery. 2. A descent or fall in a stream, yielding kinetic energy from which motive power may be obtained.

water pox *Pathol.* Chicken pox (which see).

wa·ter·proof (wô′tər·proof′, wot′ər-) *adj.* 1. Permitting no water to enter or pass through; impervious to water. 2. Coated with some substance, as rubber, that resists the passage of water. — *n.* 1. Material or fabric rendered impervious to water. 2. *Brit.* A raincoat or other garment made of such fabric. — *v.t.* To render waterproof.

water purslane An aquatic plant (*Didiplis diandra*) of the loosestrife family, growing in swampy ground in the United States.

water rat 1. The muskrat (which see). 2. The European vole (genus *Arvicola*). 3. Any of a subfamily (*Hydromyinae*) of aquatic rodents of New Guinea, Australia, and the Philippines. 4. *Slang* A waterfront thief or tough.

wa·ter·re·pel·lent (wô′tər·ri·pel′ənt, wot′ər-) *adj.* Of textiles, etc., having a surface or finish resistant to wetting by water but not completely waterproof.

water right 1. The right to draw upon a water supply. 2. The right to use or navigate a particular body of water.

water sapphire A rich blue variety of cordierite, often used as a gemstone. [Trans. of F *saphir d'eau*]

wa·ter·scape (wô′tər·skāp, wot′ər-) *n.* A view or representation of a water scene. [< WATER + (LAND)SCAPE]

water scorpion Any of numerous aquatic hemipterous insects (family *Nepidae*), having raptorial front legs and a long breathing tube at the end of the abdomen.

wa·ter·shed (wô′tər·shed′, wot′ər-) *n.* 1. The line of separation between two contiguous drainage valleys: sometimes called *water parting*. 2. The whole region from which a river receives its supply of water.

water shield 1. An aquatic American herb (*Brasenia schreberi*) of the water-lily family, having the stems and the undersides of the leaves covered with a viscid jelly. 2. Any plant of a kindred genus (*Cabomba*), especially the fanwort.

wa·ter·sick (wô′tər·sik′, wot′ər-) *adj.* Unproductive because of excessive irrigation: said of land.

wa·ter·side (wô′tər·sīd′, wot′ər-) *n.* The shore of a body of water; the water's edge. — *adj.* 1. Of, pertaining to, or living or growing by the water's edge. 2. Working by the waterside, as a stevedore.

wa·ter·ski (wô′tər·skē′, wot′ər-) *v.i.* -skied, -ski·ing To glide over water on water-skis, while being towed by a motorboat. — *n. pl.* -skis or -ski A broad, skilike runner with a fitting to hold the foot, worn when water-skiing: also **water ski**. — **wa′ter·ski′er** *n.* — **wa′ter·ski′ing** *n.*

water snake 1. Any of a genus (*Natrix*) of harmless North American colubrine snakes that live chiefly in or near fresh water. 2. Any snake of aquatic habits.

wa·ter·soak (wô′tər·sōk′, wot′ər-) *v.t.* To fill the pores or crevices of with water; soak in water.

water softener A substance added to hard water to counteract the effect of its mineral content.

wa·ter·sol·u·ble (wô′tər·sol′yə·bəl, wot′ər-) *adj.* Soluble in water: said especially of certain organic compounds: a *water-soluble* vitamin.

water spaniel A large, reddish brown spaniel having a curly, waterproof coat, used primarily for retrieving ducks.

water speedwell A common speedwell (*Veronica anagallis-aquatica*) growing in damp places.

wa·ter·spout (wô′tər·spout′, wot′ər-) *n.* 1. *Meteorol.* A moving, whirling column of spray and mist, with masses of water in the lower parts, generated at sea or on other large bodies of water. 2. A pipe for the free discharge of water, especially one connecting with the gutters of a roof.

water sprite A sprite living in the water; water nymph.

water starwort Any of a genus (*Callitriche*) of herbaceous aquatic plants common in the United States.

water strider Any of a family (*Gerridae*) of hemipterous insects with elongate middle and hind legs adapted for darting over the surface of water: also called *skater*.

water supply The water available for the use of a community or region; also, the sources for such water and the means for supplying it, as reservoirs, lakes, conduits, etc.

water system 1. A river with all its tributaries, considered as a hydrologic unit. 2. Water supply.

water table 1. *Archit.* A projecting ledge, molding, or stringcourse, running along the sides of a building to shed the rain. 2. *Geol.* The surface marking the upper level of a water-saturated zone extending beneath the ground to depths determined by the thickness of the permeable strata: also called *water level*.

water thrush 1. Either of two American warblers (genus *Seiurus*), frequenting swamps and streams, the **northern water thrush** (*S. noveboracensis*), olive brown above, with a buff line above the eye, or the **Louisiana water thrush** (*S. motacilla*), with a white line above the eye. 2. A European water ouzel (*Cinclus cinclus*).

water tiger The larva of the diving beetle.

wa·ter·tight (wô′tər·tīt′, wot′ər-) *adj.* 1. So closely made that water cannot enter or leak through. 2. Having no loopholes; foolproof or incontrovertible: *watertight* tax laws.

water tower 1. A standpipe or tower, often of considerable height, used as a reservoir for a system of water distribution. 2. A vehicular towerlike structure having an extensible vertical pipe from which water can be thrown on the upper floors of a burning building.

Wa·ter·town (wô′tər·toun, wot′ər-) 1. A city in northern New York, on the Black River; pop. 30,787. 2. A town in eastern Massachusetts, near Boston; pop. 39,307.

water turkey The snakebird.

water vapor The vapor of water, especially when below the boiling point, as in the atmosphere. Compare STEAM.

water wave 1. An undulating effect of the hair, artificially produced when the hair is wet, and usually set by drying with heat. 2. A wave of water; a billow.

wa·ter·way (wô′tər·wā′, wot′ər-) *n.* A river, channel, canal, etc., used as a means of travel; water route.

wa·ter·weed (wô′tər·wēd′, wot′ər-) *n.* 1. A submerged aquatic perennial (*Anacharis canadensis*), having whitish flowers. 2. Any of various other aquatic plants.

water wheel A wheel so equipped with floats, buckets, etc., that it may be turned by flowing water, as a noria.

water wings A waterproof, inflatable device shaped like a pair of wings, and used as a support for the body while swimming or learning to swim.

water witch 1. One who claims to discover underground springs with a divining rod or hazel wand. 2. Any of various diving birds, as certain grebes.

water witching The use of a divining rod to discover water; rhabdomancy.

wa·ter·works (wô′tər·wûrks′, wot′ər-) *n.pl.* 1. A system of machines, buildings, and appliances for furnishing a water supply, especially for a city. 2. A spectacular display of fountains in operation; also, a pageant presented on floats. 3. *Slang* Tears: usually in the phrase **to turn on the waterworks**. 4. *Slang* Rain.

wa·ter·worn (wô′tər·wôrn′, -wōrn′, wot′ər-) *adj.* Worn smooth by running or falling water.

wa·ter·y (wô′tər·ē, wot′ər·ē) *adj.* 1. Containing or discharging water. 2. Brimming; flowing. 3. Resembling water; thin or liquid. 4. Consisting of or pertaining to water. 5. Diluted with water; weak. — **wa′ter·i·ness** *n.*

Wat·ling Island (wot′ling) See SAN SALVADOR. Also **Wat′·lings Island**.

Wat·son (wot′sən), **John**, 1850–1907, Scottish minister and author: pseudonym *Ian Maclaren*. — **John Broadus**, 1878–1958, U.S. psychologist; founder of behaviorism. — **Sir William**, 1858–1935, English poet.

Wat·son-Watt (wot′sən·wot′), **Sir Robert (Alexander)**, born 1892, Scottish physicist.

watt (wot) *n.* A unit of power, especially electrical power, equivalent to one joule per second, or one volt-ampere. Abbr. **w, W** [after James *Watt*]

Watt (wot), **James,** 1736–1819, Scottish inventor and engineer.

wat·tage (wot′ij) *n.* **1.** Amount of electric power in terms of watts. **2.** The total number of watts needed to operate an appliance.

Wat·teau (wä·tō′, wot′ō) *adj.* Of or pertaining to Antoine Watteau or his style of painting.

Wat·teau (wä·tō′, *Fr.* và·tō′), **Jean Antoine,** 1684–1721, French painter.

Watteau back The back of a woman's dress having fullness at the neck in pleats or gathers falling to the hem of the skirt without being belted at the waist.

watt-hour (wot′our′) *n.* Electrical energy equivalent to that represented by one watt acting for one hour. Abbr. **wh., whr., whr., w.-hr.**

wat·tle (wot′l) *n.* **1.** A frame or structure of rods or twigs woven together. **2.** A twig or withe, especially as used for interweaving with others; also, collectively, material for interwoven fences, roofs, etc. **3.** A naked, fleshy process, often wrinkled and brightly colored, hanging from the throat of a bird or snake. For illustration see FOWL. **4.** A pendent fold of skin on the throat or neck of some domestic swine. **5.** A barbel of a fish. **6.** Any of various acacias of Australia, Tasmania, and South Africa, so called by the early colonists who used the branches to make fences. **7.** *pl.* Rods for supporting thatch on a roof. — *v.t.* **·tled, ·tling 1.** To weave or twist, as twigs, into a network. **2.** To form, as baskets, by intertwining flexible twigs. **3.** To bind together with wattles. — *adj.* Made of or covered with wattles; formed by wattling. [OE *watel, watul*]

wat·tle·bird (wot′l·bûrd′) *n.* Any of several large Australian honey eaters (genus *Anthochaera*), having conspicuous wattles about the head and face.

wat·tled (wot′ld) *adj.* **1.** Made with wattles. **2.** Having a wattle, as a bird.

watt·less (wot′lis) *adj. Electr.* Denoting an alternating current, or the component of such a current, that is neutralized by the originating electromotive force and hence does not produce any power.

watt·me·ter (wot′mē′tər) *n.* An instrument for measuring in watts the rate of electrical work.

Watts (wots). **George Frederick,** 1817–1904, English painter and sculptor. — **Isaac,** 1674–1748, English theologian and hymn writer.

Watts-Dun·ton (wots′dun′tən), **Walter Theodore,** 1832–1914, English critic and poet.

Wa·tu·si (wä·tōō′sē) *n. pl.* **·si** One of a pastoral, Hamitic people of Rwanda and Burundi, distinguished by their unusual tallness of stature. Also **Wa·tus·si.**

waucht (wôkht, wäkht, wäft) *Scot. n.* A large draft, as of liquor. — *v.t. & v.i.* To drink; quaff. Also **waught** (wôft, wäft).

waugh (wôf) *adj. Scot.* **1.** Clammy; damp; nauseous. **2.** Faint; languid; weak.

Waugh (wô), **Alec,** born 1898, English novelist and travel writer: full name **Alexander Raban Waugh.** — **Evelyn,** 1903–1966, English novelist and critic; brother of the preceding: full name **Evelyn Arthur St. John Waugh.**

wauk (wôk) *v.t. Scot.* To wake; watch over.

Wau·ke·gan (wô·kē′gən) A city in extreme NE Illinois, on Lake Michigan; pop. 65,269.

Wau·ke·sha (wô′ki·shô) A city in SE Wisconsin, on the Fox River; pop. 40,258.

waul (wôl) *v.i.* To give a prolonged, plaintive cry like that of a cat: also spelled *wawl.* [Imit.]

waur (wôr) *adj. Scot.* Worse.

Wau·sau (wô′sô) A city in central Wisconsin, on the Wisconsin River; pop. 32,806.

Wau·wa·to·sa (wô·wä·tō′sə) A city in SE Wisconsin, near Milwaukee; pop. 58,676.

wave (wāv) *v.* **waved, wav·ing** *v.i.* **1.** To move freely back and forth or up and down, as a flag in the wind; fluctuate. **2.** To be moved back and forth or up and down as a signal; also, to make a signal by moving something thus. **3.** To have an undulating shape or form; be sinuous: Her hair *waves.* — *v.t.* **4.** To cause to move back and forth or up and down: to *wave* a banner. **5.** To form with an undulating surface, edge, or outline. **6.** To give a wavy appearance to: water, as silk. **7.** To form into waves: to *wave* one's hair. **8.** To signal by waving something: He *waved* me aside. **9.** To express by waving something: to *wave* farewell. — *n.* **1.** A ridge or undulation moving on the surface of a liquid, the particles composing it having an oscillatory circular motion in a plane at right angles to the direction of movement of the ridge itself. **2.** One of the rising curves on an undulatory edge or surface; one of a series of curves: *waves* of grain. **3.** Something that comes, like a wave, with great volume or power; a period of marked activity or excitement: a *wave* of enthusiasm. **4.** One of a series, as of groups or events, occurring or moving with wavelike fluctuations: He went ashore with the first *wave* of Marines. **5.** A progressive change in tem-

perature or in barometrical condition passing over a large area: a heat *wave.* **6.** A wavelike tress or curl of hair. **7.** The act of waving; a sweeping or undulating motion, as with the hand. **8.** A wavelike stripe or undulation impressed on a surface, as on watered silk. **9.** *Physics* **a** One of the periodic vibratory impulses produced by a disturbance in and propagated through an elastic medium, as sound. **b** An electromagnetic wave (which see). **c** Any physical process having characteristics resembling a wave, as a moving electron. Compare WAVE MECHANICS. **d** A visual representation of a periodic phenomenon. **10.** *Usually pl. Poetic* Any body of water, especially the sea. [OE *wafian*] — **wav′er** *n.*

— **Syn.** (noun) **1.** Wave, ripple, chop, billow, roller, comber, breaker, and surge are compared as they denote upheavals of the ocean's surface. *Wave* is the general term. A *ripple* is a very small *wave,* such as might be produced by a light breeze, or by an object dropping into still water. A *chop* is one of many small, irregular *waves* produced by opposing forces, as tide and wind. *Billow* is a poetic word for any *wave,* but especially for a *wave* of great height. A *roller* is one of the long, irregular *waves* that move swiftly outward from a storm center. High, curling *rollers,* such as produce whitecaps, are called *combers.* A *wave* that curls over into a mass of foam as it strikes the shore is a *breaker.* *Surge* is the vaguest of these words; it is sometimes applied to a series of *breakers,* and sometimes to the rise and fall of the water's surface under any kind of *waves.*

Wave (wāv) *n.* A member of the WAVES. [Back formation < WAVES, taken as a plural]

wave band *Physics* A specified group of wave frequencies, especially one assigned for radio or television broadcasting.

wave front *Physics* A surface at every point of which a wave is in the same phase at a given time.

wave guide *Electronics* A device, typically an arrangement of hollow metal pipes of varying size and cross section, through which high-frequency electromagnetic waves may be conducted as required.

wave·length (wāv′length′, -lengkth′) *n. Physics* The distance, measured along the line of propagation, between two points representing similar phases of two consecutive waves. Abbr. **w.l., WL**

wave·less (wāv′lis) *adj.* Having no waves; tranquil.

wave·let (wāv′lit) *n.* A little wave.

Wa·vell (wā′vəl), **Sir Archibald(Percival),** 1883–1950, first Earl Wavell, British field marshal in World War II.

wa·vel·lite (wā′və·līt) *n.* A vitreous, translucent, hydrous-aluminum phosphate, crystallizing in the orthorhombic system. [after Dr. William *Wavell,* died 1829, English physician, who discovered it]

wave mechanics The branch of physics that investigates the wave characteristics ascribed to the atom and its associated particles, and seeks to explain physical processes in terms of these characteristics, especially with reference to the quantum theory.

wave·me·ter (wāv′mē′tər) *n.* An apparatus for determining electromagnetic wavelengths and wave frequencies.

wave number *Physics* The number of electromagnetic waves in a space of one centimeter; the reciprocal of the wavelength.

wave·off (wāv′ôf′, -of′) *n. Aeron.* The act of denying landing permission to an approaching aircraft, especially one making a faulty approach for landing on an aircraft carrier.

wa·ver (wā′vər) *v.i.* **1.** To move one way and the other; sway; flutter. **2.** To be uncertain or undecided; show irresolution; vacillate. **3.** To show signs of falling back or giving way; falter. **4.** To flicker; gleam. **5.** To quaver; tremble. — *n.* A wavering. [< ME *woveren,* freq. of OE *wafian* to wave. Cf. OE *wæfre* restless.] — **wa′ver·er** *n.* — **wa′ver·ing·ly** *adv.*

Wa·ver·ley Novels (wā′vər·lē) A series of historical novels by Sir Walter Scott, published 1814–1831: so called from *Waverley,* the title of the first.

WAVES or **W.A.V.E.S.** (wāvz) *n.* A corps of women in the U.S. Navy: officially, Women in the United States Navy (1946). [< W(omen) A(ccepted for) V(oluntary) E(mergency) S(ervice), an earlier name]

wave set A preparation put on the hair before setting to make waves and curls last.

wave train *Physics* A series of waves propagated from a vibrating or radiating body.

wave trap *Telecom.* A device, usually connected with the antenna, for improving the selectivity of a radio receiver by cutting out undesired wave frequencies.

wa·vey (wā′vē) *n. pl.* **·veys** or **·vies** *Canadian* The snow goose. Also **wa′vy.** [< Algonquian]

wav·y (wā′vē) *adj.* **wav·i·er, wav·i·est 1.** Full of waves; ruffled by or raised into waves. **2.** Undulatory; waving. **3.** Unstable; wavering. — **wav′i·ly** *adv.* — **wav′i·ness** *n.*

wawl (wôl) See WAUL.

wax¹ (waks) *n. pl.* **wax·es 1.** Any of a class of natural substances consisting of the esters of fatty acids and alcohols other than glycerol, including spermaceti, carnauba wax, and the secretions of various plants and insects. **2.** A solid mineral substance resembling wax, as ozocerite or paraffin. **3.** Beeswax (which see) **4.** Sealing wax. **5.** A mixture of pitch and tallow or some resinous composition used by shoemakers to wax their thread. **6.** Earwax (which see). **7.** *U.S.* The sap of the sugar maple after being boiled down and cooled. — *v.t.* To coat or treat with wax. — *adj.* Made of or pertaining to wax. [OE *weax*]

wax² (waks) *v.i.* **waxed, waxed** (*Poetic* **wax·en**), **wax·ing** **1.** To become larger gradually; increase in size or numbers; grow: said especially of the moon as it approaches fullness: opposed to *wane.* **2.** To become as specified: to *wax* angry. [OE *weaxan* to grow]

wax³ (waks) *v.t. Informal* To make a phonograph record of: to *wax* a folk song. [< WAX¹; so called because wax was formerly used in making phonograph records]

wax⁴ (waks) *n. Brit. Informal* A tantrum; fit of bad temper. [? < phrase *to wax angry*]

wax bean A variety of string bean (*Phaseolus vulgaris*) of a pale yellow color, cultivated in the United States: also called *butter bean.*

wax·ber·ry (waks′ber′ē) *n. pl.* **·ries 1.** The wax myrtle. **2.** Its wax-covered fruit. **3.** The snowberry (which see).

wax·bill (waks′bil′) *n.* **1.** Any of various small Old World seed-eating birds of the weaverbird family (genus *Estrilda*), having variously colored beaks resembling sealing wax. **2.** The Javanese sparrow.

wax·en (wak′sən) *adj.* **1.** Resembling wax. **2.** Consisting wholly or in part of wax; covered with wax. **3.** Pale; pallid: a *waxen* complexion; also, pliable or impressible as wax.

wax end A stout thread, or end of a thread, made stiff and pointed with shoemakers' wax, or waxed and twisted with a bristle, as for the purpose of sewing shoes. Also **waxed end.**

wax museum A place of amusement where life-size wax figures of famous and notorious persons are exhibited, often to evoke a morbid thrill. Also *waxworks.*

wax myrtle Any of a genus (*Myrica*) of North American shrubs or small trees, especially *M. cerifera*, having fragrant leaves and small berries covered with wax, often used in making candles: also called *bayberry, candleberry, waxberry.*

wax palm 1. A South American palm (*Ceroxylon andicola*) with pinnate leaves, having a lofty straight trunk covered with a waxy, whitish, resinous substance. **2.** A Brazilian palm (*Copernicia cerifera*) whose young leaves yield the carnauba wax of commerce.

wax paper Paper coated or treated with wax and used to retain or protect against moisture. Also **waxed paper.**

wax plant A climbing Asian and Australian shrub (genus *Hoya*) of the milkweed family, with thick glossy leaves and wheel-shaped white or pink, waxy flowers.

wax·weed (waks′wēd′) *n.* An annual, clammy, hairy herb (*Cuphea petiolata*) of the loosestrife family with irregular purplish flowers.

wax·wing (waks′wing′) *n.* Any of various crested passerine birds (family *Bombycillidae*), having soft, mainly brown plumage and the secondary wing feathers tipped with appendages resembling red or yellow sealing wax; especially, the North American **cedar waxwing** (*Bombycilla cedrorum*), and the larger **Bohemian waxwing** (*B. garrula*).

CEDAR WAXWING
(About 7 inches long)

wax·work (waks′wûrk′) *n.* **1.** Work produced in wax; especially, ornaments or life-size figures of wax. **2.** *pl.* A wax museum. — **wax′work′er** *n.*

wax-worm (waks′wûrm′) A honeycomb moth.

wax·y (wak′sē) *adj.* **wax·i·er, wax·i·est 1.** Resembling wax in appearance, consistency, or adhesive qualities; waxen; pliable; impressionable. **2.** Having the dull whitish or yellowish color of wax; pallid. **3.** Made of or abounding in wax; rubbed with wax. **4.** *Pathol.* Characterized by the formation of an insoluble, waxlike protein in certain organs of the body, as the kidney; amyloid. **5.** *Brit. Informal* Angry. — **wax′i·ness** *n.*

way (wā) *n.* **1.** A manner or method of doing something; procedure: the right *way.* **2.** Direction; turn; route; line of motion or progress: Which *way* is the city? **3.** A path, course, or track leading from one place to another or along which one goes. **4.** Space or room to advance or work: Make *way* for the king. **5.** Length of space passed over. **6.** Distance in general: a little *way* off: often popularly or dialectally, **ways. 7.** Passage from one place to another. **8.** Onward movement; headway; progress **9.** A customary or habitual manner or style; a manner peculiar to an individual, class, or people: the British *way* of doing things. **10.** A point of relation; particular: He erred in two *ways.* **11.** A course of life or experience: the *way* of sin. **12.** *Informal* State of health: to be in a bad *way.* **13.** A course wished for or resolved upon; something that one resolves to do: Have it your *way.* **14.** The range of one's notice or observation: An accident threw it in his *way.* **15.** *Naut.* **a** The movement of a vessel through the water; forward motion; headway. **b** *pl.* A tilted framework of timbers upon which a ship slides when launched. **16.** The direction of the weave in textile goods. **17.** *Law* A right of way. **18.** *Mech.* A longitudinal guide for material being worked upon, or for a moving table bearing the work. **19.** Expenses incurred in an activity or undertaking: to pay one's own *way.* **20.** *Informal* Neighborhood, or route taken to go home: He lives out my *way.* — **by the way** In passing; incidentally. — **by way of 1.** With the object or purpose of; to serve as: *by way of* introduction. **2.** Through; via: We went home *by way of* Main Street. — **out of the way 1.** Removed, as an obstruction. **2.** Remarkable; unusual. **3.** Improper; wrong: Has he done anything *out of the way?* **4.** Out of place; lost; remote. — **the way** *Informal* In the manner that; as: Do it *the way* I told you to. — **under way** In motion; well along; making progress. — *adv. Informal* Away; very much or very far; the whole or a considerable distance. He went *way* to Denver. [OE *weg*]

way back *Informal* Long ago. [Short for AWAY BACK]

way·bill (wā′bil′) *n.* A list describing or identifying goods or naming passengers carried by a common carrier, as a train, steamer, etc. Abbr. *w.b., W/b, W.b., W/B, W.B.*

way·far·er (wā′fâr′ər) *n.* One who journeys.

way·far·ing (wā′fâr′ing) *adj. & n.* Journeying; being on the road.

way freight Freight taken on or put off at way stations; also, a freight train handling such goods.

Way·land (wā′lənd) In Teutonic and English mythology, an invisible blacksmith with magical powers: also, in German folklore, *Wieland.* Also **Wayland** (the) **Smith.**

way·lay (wā′lā′, wā′lā′) *v.t.* **·laid, ·lay·ing 1.** To lie in ambush for and attack, as in order to rob. **2.** To accost on the way. [< WAY + LAY¹, on analogy with MHG *wegelagen* < *wegelage* ambush] — **way′lay′er** *n.*

Wayne (wān) An urban township in northern New Jersey; pop. 49,141.

Wayne (wān), **Anthony,** 1745–96, American Revolutionary general: called **Mad Anthony.**

way-out (wā′out′) *adj. U.S. Slang.* Far-out (which see). Also **way out.**

-ways *suffix of adverbs* In a (specified) manner, direction, or position: *noways, sideways*: often equivalent to *-wise.* Also **-way.** [< WAY + -s³]

ways and means Means or methods of accomplishing an end or defraying expenses; especially, in legislation, methods of raising funds for the use of the government.

way·side (wā′sīd′) *adj.* Standing or being near the side of a road. — *n.* The side or edge of the road or highway. — **to go** (or **let go**) **by the wayside** To be put or put aside because of something more urgent.

way station Any station between principal stations, especially on a railroad; a local station.

way train A train stopping at way stations.

way·ward (wā′wərd) *adj.* **1.** Wanting its way; willful; froward. **2.** Without definite way or course; unsteady; capricious. **3.** Unexpected or unwished for: a *wayward* fortune. [ME *weiward*, short for *aweiward* < *awei* away + -WARD] — **way′ward·ly** *adv.* — **way′ward·ness** *n.*

way·worn (wā′wôrn′, -wōrn′) *adj.* Fatigued by travel.

Wa·zir·i·stan (wä·zir′i·stän′) A tribal region in NW central Pakistan, on the Afghanistan border; 5,214 sq. mi.

w.b. 1. Warehouse book. **2.** Waybill. **3.** Westbound.

W.B. or **W/B, W.b.,** or **W/b** Waybill.

WbN West by north.

WbS West by south.

w.c. or **W.C. 1.** Water closet. **2.** Without charge.

W.C.T.U. Women's Christian Temperance Union.

we (wē) *pron. pl., possessive* **our** or **ours,** *objective* **us** The nominative plural pronoun of the first person, used by the persons speaking or writing to denote themselves, by an individual to refer to himself or herself and one or more others, by an editor or other writer to give his words an impersonal character, or by a sovereign on formal occasions. [OE *wē*]

weak (wēk) *adj.* **1.** Lacking in physical strength; wanting in energy, activity, or vigor; feeble; debilitated. **2.** Insufficiently resisting stress; incapable of supporting weight: a *weak* link or bridge. **3.** Lacking in strength of will or stability of character; yielding easily to temptation; pliable. **4.** Ineffectual, as from deficient supply: *weak* artillery support. **5.** Lacking in power or sonorousness: a *weak* voice. **6.** Lacking a specified component or components in the usual or proper amount; of less than customary strength or potency: *weak* tea. a *weak* tincture. **7.** Lacking the power or ability to perform its function properly: a *weak* heart. **8.** Lacking in mental or moral strength; liable to err or fail through feebleness of conception or vacillation of judgment. **9.** Showing or resulting from poor judgment or a want of discretion or firmness: a *weak* plan; unable to persuade or convince: a *weak* argument. **10.** Lacking in influence or authority: a *weak* state. **11.** Deficient in strength, durability, skill, experience, or the like. **12.** *Gram.* In Germanic languages: **a** Denoting a weak verb. **b** Denoting nouns and adjectives in German and Old English inflected in the less full manner originally restricted to stems ending in -n. Compare STRONG (def. 29). **13.** *Phonet.* Unstressed; unaccented, as a syllable or sound. **14.** *Photog.* Thin; wanting in contrast: a *weak* negative. **15.** In prosody, indicating a verse ending in which the accent falls on a word or syllable otherwise without stress. **16.** Declining in price; without an active market: The wheat market is *weak.* **17.** Wanting in impressiveness or interest: a *weak* play or book. —*adv.* In a weak manner; so as to be weak. [< ON *veikr.* Akin to OE *wāc.*] **— weak'ly** *adv.* **— weak'ness** *n.*

Weak may appear as a combining form, as in the following self-explanatory compounds:

weak-backed	weak-looking	weak spot
weak-bodied	weak-made	weak-stemmed
weakbrained	weak-natured	weak-tasting
weak-brewed	weak-nerved	weak-throated
weak-built	weak point	weak-tinted
weak-colored	weak-seeming	weak-toned
weak-eyed	weak-sided	weak-voiced
weak-growing	weak-sighted	weak-walled
weakhanded	weak-smelling	weak-winged
weakhearted	weak-sounding	weak-witted
weak-limbed	weak-spirited	weak-woven

weak·en (wē'kən) *v.t. & v.i.* To make or become weak or weaker. **— weak'en·er** *n.*
— Syn. debilitate, enervate, undermine, sap. Compare IMPAIR. **— Ant.** strengthen.
weak·fish (wēk'fish') *n. pl.* **·fish** or **·fish·es** Any of several marine food fishes (genus *Cynoscion*), especially *C. regalis* of the coastal waters of the eastern United States: also called *bluefish, squeteague.*
weak-kneed (wēk'nēd') *adj.* **1.** Weak in the knees. **2.** Without resolution, strong purpose, or energy; spineless.
weak·ling (wēk'ling) *n.* A feeble person or animal. **—** *adj.* Having no natural strength or vigor.
weak·ly (wēk'lē) *adj.* **·li·er, ·li·est** Sickly; feeble; weak.
weak-mind·ed (wēk'mīn'did) *adj.* **1.** Indecisive; weak-willed. **2.** Feeble-minded. **— weak'mind'ed·ness** *n.*
weak·ness (wēk'nis) *n.* **1.** The state, condition, or quality of being weak. **2.** A characteristic indicating feebleness. **3.** A slight failing; a fault. **4.** A penchant or fondness: with *for:* a *weakness* for pastry.
weak side **1.** The aspect of a person's character at which he is most easily influenced, especially for the worse. **2.** In football, the part of the line of scrimmage from which some or all of the players have shifted.
weak sister *Informal* **1.** The weakling in any group; especially, one who cannot be depended on to stand firm against opposition. **2.** Any ineffectual person.
weak verb A verb that forms its past tense and past participle by addition of an inflectional suffix, as *jump, jumped, jumped.*
weak-willed (wēk'wild') *adj.* Having a weak will; lacking conviction; timid.
weal¹ (wēl) *n.* **1.** *Archaic* A sound or healthy state, either of persons or things; prosperity; welfare. **2.** *Obs.* The body politic, state, or nation: now only in the phrase **public weal.** **3.** *Obs.* Wealth. [OE *wela.* Akin to WELL.]
weal² (wēl) *n.* A welt (def. 4). [Var. of WALE¹; infl. in form by obs. *wheal* a pustule]
weald (wēld) *n.* *Chiefly Brit.* An exposed forest area; waste woodland; also, an open region; down. [OE, a forest]
Weald (wēld), **The** A district in Kent, Surrey, and Sussex, England, formerly forested, now primarily agricultural.
wealth (welth) *n.* **1.** A large aggregate of real and personal property; an abundance of those things that men desire; riches; also, the state of being rich. **2.** *Econ.* All material objects having economic utility; also, in the private sense, all property possessing a monetary value. **3.** Great abundance of anything: usually preceded by *a*: a *wealth* of learning. **4.** *Obs.* Weal; well-being. [ME *welthe < wele* weal; on analogy with *health*]
— Syn. 1. affluence, opulence. Compare PROPERTY.
wealth·y (wel'thē) *adj.* **wealth·i·er, wealth·i·est** **1.** Possessing wealth; affluent. **2.** More than sufficient; abounding. **— wealth'i·ly** *adv.* **— wealth'i·ness** *n.*
wean¹ (wēn) *v.t.* **1.** To transfer (the young of any mammal) from dependence on its mother's milk to another form of nourishment. **2.** To estrange from former habits or associations: usually with *from.* [OE *wenian* to accustom]
wean² (wēn) *n.* *Scot.* A baby; infant.
wean·er (wē'nər) *n.* **1.** One who weans. **2.** A muzzle used in weaning a calf.
wean·ling (wēn'ling) *adj.* Freshly weaned. **—** *n.* A child or animal newly weaned.
weap·on (wep'ən) *n.* **1.** Any implement for fighting or warfare. **2.** Any means that may be used against an adversary: verbal *weapons.* **3.** The sting, claw, spur, etc., of an animal. **—** *v.t.* To furnish with a weapon or weapons. [OE *wǣpen*] **— weap'on·less** *adj.*
weap·on·eer (wep'ən·ir') *n.* A person concerned with the design, improvement, production, and use of weapons, especially of the atomic and thermonuclear type.
weap·on·ry (wep'ən·rē') *n.* Weapons collectively.
weapon system The total complex of a major weapon,

such as an airplane or missile, together with the related equipment and materiel necessary to bring it to bear on the target. Also **weapons system.**
wear¹ (wâr) *v.* **wore, worn, wear·ing** *v.t.* **1.** To carry or have on the person as a garment, ornament, etc. **2.** To have or bear on the person habitually or as a practice: He *wears* a derby. **3.** To have in one's appearance or aspect; exhibit: He *wears* a scowl. **4.** To bear habitually in a specified manner; carry: He *wears* his age well; She *wears* her hair in a chignon. **5.** To display or fly: A ship *wears* its colors. **6.** To impair, waste, or consume by use or constant action. **7.** To cause or produce by scraping, rubbing, etc.: to *wear* a hole in a coat. **8.** To bring to a specified condition by wear: to *wear* a sleeve to tatters. **9.** To exhaust the strength or patience of; weary. **—** *v.i.* **10.** To be impaired or diminished gradually by use, rubbing, etc. **11.** To withstand the effects of use, wear, etc., as specified: The skirt *wears* well. **12.** To become as specified from use or attrition: His patience is *wearing* thin. **13.** To pass gradually or tediously: with *on* or *away:* The day *wears* on. **— to wear out 1.** To make or become worthless by use: The pants are *worn out.* **2.** To waste gradually; use up: He *wears out* patience. **3.** To tire or exhaust. **—** *n.* **1.** The act of wearing, or the state of being worn: the worse for *wear.* **2.** The material or articles of dress worn or made to be worn: silk for summer *wear:* also in compounds: *footwear, underwear.* **3.** The destructive effect of use or work; impairment from use or time. **4.** Capacity for resistance to use or impairment; endurance; durability. [OE *werian*] **— wear'a·ble** *adj.* **— wear'er** *n.*
wear² (wâr) *v.* **wore, worn, wear·ing** *Naut.* *v.t.* **1.** To turn (a vessel) through an arc in which its head points momentarily directly to leeward. **—** *v.i.* **2.** To go about with the wind astern. Compare TACK¹. [Prob. alter. of VEER¹; infl. in form by WEAR¹]
wear·a·bil·i·ty (wâr'ə·bil'ə·tē) *n.* Of garments, the quality of being able to stand long wear.
wear·a·ble (wâr'ə·bəl) *adj.* **1.** Capable of being worn. **2.** Capable of standing long wear; lasting. **—** *n. pl.* Garments.
wear and tear Loss by the service, exposure, decay, or injury incident to ordinary use.
wea·ri·ful (wir'i·fəl) *adj.* Tiresome; wearisome. **— wea'ri·ful·ly** *adv.* **— wea'ri·ful·ness** *n.*
wea·ri·less (wir'i·lis) *adj.* Unwearying; untiring.
wear·ing (wâr'ing) *adj.* **1.** Fatiguing; exhausting; wasting: a *wearing* job. **2.** Capable of being, or designed to be, worn. **— wear'ing·ly** *adv.*
wearing apparel Clothing; garments.
wear·ish (wâr'ish) *adj.* *Obs.* or *Dial.* **1.** Insipid; watery. **2.** Wizened; shrunk; withered. [ME *werische*; origin uncertain] **— wear'ish·ly** *adv.* **— wear'ish·ness** *n.*
wea·ri·some (wir'i·səm) *adj.* Causing fatigue; tiresome, tedious, or boring. **— wea'ri·some·ly** *adv.* **— wea'ri·some·ness** *n.*
— Syn. Boring, fatiguing. Compare TEDIOUS.
wea·ry (wir'ē) *adj.* **·ri·er, ·ri·est** **1.** Worn with exertion, suffering, etc.; tired; fatigued. **2.** Discontented or vexed by continued endurance, as of something disagreeable, tedious, etc.: often with *of: weary* of life. **3.** Indicating, characteristic of, or resulting from fatigue, boredom, etc., a *weary* sigh. **4.** Causing weariness; wearisome. **—** *v.t. & v.i.* **·ried, ·ry·ing** To make or become weary; tire. [OE *wērig*] **— wea'ri·ly** *adv.* **— wea'ri·ness** *n.*
wea·sand (wē'zənd) *n.* *Archaic* The windpipe; also, the throat: often called *wizen.* Also *Scot.* **wea'son** (-zən). [OE *wāsend*]
wea·sel (wē'zəl) *n.* **1.** Any of certain small, slender, predacious carnivores (genus *Mustela*) having brownish fur that in northern regions turns white in winter. **2.** A sneaky, treacherous person. **—** *v.i.* **·seled, ·sel·ing** *U.S. Informal* To speak or act evasively, equivocally, etc. **— to weasel out** To withdraw from or renege on a commitment, usually from motives of self-interest or cowardice. [OE *wesle*]

WEASEL
(To 9 inches long; tail 2 inches)

weasel word A word that weakens a statement by rendering it ambiguous or equivocal.
weath·er (weth'ər) *n.* **1.** The general atmospheric condition as regards temperature, moisture, winds, or other meteorological phenomena. **2.** A particular kind of meteorological condition. **3.** Bad weather; storm. **4.** A prevailing condition or atmosphere; mental or moral climate. **— to keep one's weather eye open** *Informal* To be alert. **— to make heavy weather. 1.** To pitch and roll, as a ship in a storm. **2.** To work laboriously, especially so as to create difficulties. **— under the weather** *Informal* **1.** Ailing; ill. **2.** Somewhat intoxicated. **—** *v.t.* **1.** To expose to the action of the weather. **2.** To discolor, crumble, or otherwise affect by action of the weather. **3.** To pass through and survive, as a crisis. **4.** To cause to slope, as a roof, so as to shed water. **5.** *Naut.* To pass to windward of: to *weather* Cape Fear. **—** *v.i.* **6.** To undergo changes resulting from exposure to the weather. **7.** To resist the action of the weather. **—** *adj.* *Chiefly Naut.* Facing

the wind; windward: opposed to *lee*. [OE *weder*]

Weather may appear as a combining form or as the first element in two-word phrases, as in the following list:

weather-bitten	weather report
weather-bleached	weather reporter
weather-blown	weather reporting
weather-burnt	weather-rotted
weather-driven	weather-scarred
weather-eaten	weathersick
weather forecast	weather-tanned
weather-hardened	weathertight
weather-marked	weather-tough
weather observer	weatherworn

weath·er·beat·en (weth′ər·bēt′n) *adj.* **1.** Bearing or showing the effects of exposure to weather. **2.** Toughened or tanned by or as by exposure to weather, as a face.

weath·er·board (weth′ər·bôrd′, -bōrd′) *n.* **1.** A board used for the outer covering of wooden buildings, as a clapboard. **2.** *Naut.* The windward side of a vessel. — *v.t.* To fasten weatherboards on.

weath·er·board·ing (weth′ər·bôr′ding, -bōr′-) *n.* **1.** Weatherboards collectively, or material for making them. **2.** The outer wooden covering of the walls and roof of a building.

weath·er·bound (weth′ər·bound′) *adj.* Detained by unfavorable weather, as a vessel in port.

Weather Bureau A bureau of the Department of Commerce in Washington, D.C., serving as headquarters for meteorological observation, the diffusion of information concerning the weather, etc.

weath·er·cast (weth′ər·kast′, -käst′) *n.* *Informal* A radio or television broadcast reporting on weather conditions. [< WEATHER + (BROAD)CAST] — **weath′er·cast′er** *n.*

weath·er·cock (weth′ər·kok′) *n.* **1.** A vane, originally in the form of a cock, that turns with the wind and indicates the direction from which it is blowing. **2.** A fickle person or variable thing. — *v.t. & v.i.* To turn (an aircraft, boat, etc.) under the force of the wind so as to face into the wind.

weath·ered (weth′ərd) *adj.* **1.** Affected by exposure to the atmosphere; seasoned. **2.** Worn, shaped, or stained by exposure in the atmosphere; as rocks. **3.** *Archit.* Sloped to prevent water from lodging on the surface. **4.** Of wood, artificially colored or stained as though from exposure. — **weathered in** *U.S.* Having weather conditions that prohibit air traffic: said of airports.

weath·er·glass (weth′ər·glas′, -gläs′) *n.* An instrument for indicating the state of the weather; especially, a simple barometer filled with liquid that rises into a spout as atmospheric pressure falls.

weath·er·ly (weth′ər·lē) *adj.* *Naut.* Capable of keeping close into the wind without drifting to leeward. — **weath′er·li·ness** *n.*

weath·er·man (weth′ər·man′) *n.* *pl.* **·men** (-men′) *n.* *Informal* A meteorologist, especially one concerned with daily weather conditions and reports.

weather map *Meteorol.* A map or chart indicating weather conditions, as temperature, atmospheric pressure, wind velocity, precipitation, etc., for a given region and time.

weath·er·proof (weth′ər·prōof′) *adj.* Capable of withstanding rough weather without appreciable deterioration. — *v.t.* To make weatherproof.

weather ship A ship stationed at sea for weather observation.

weather station A station or office where meteorological observations are taken and recorded.

weath·er·strip (weth′ər·strip′) *v.t.* **-stripped**, **-strip·ping** To equip or fit with weather strips.

weather strip A narrow strip of material placed over or in crevices, as at windows, to keep out drafts, rain, etc.

weather stripping **1.** A weather strip. **2.** Weather strips collectively.

weather vane A vane that indicates the direction from which the wind is blowing; weathercock.

weath·er·wise (weth′ər·wīz′) *adj.* **1.** Experienced in observing or predicting the weather. **2.** Skillful in predicting trends or shifts in public opinion, etc.

weave (wēv) *v.* **wove** or *for def. 10* **weaved**, **wo·ven** or (*less common*) **wove**, **weav·ing** *v.t.* **1.** To form, produce, or manufacture as a textile, by interlacing threads or yarns; especially, to make by interlacing woof threads among warp threads in a loom. **2.** To form by interlacing strands, strips, twigs, etc.: to *weave* a basket. **3.** To produce by combining details or elements: to *weave* a story. **4.** To bring together so as to form a whole: to *weave* fancies into theories. **5.** To twist or introduce into, about, or through something else: to *weave* ribbons through one's hair. **6.** To spin (a web). **7.** To make or effect by moving from side to side or in a winding or zigzag course: to *weave* one's way through a crowd. — *v.i.* **8.** To make cloth, baskets, etc., by weaving. **9.** To become woven or interlaced. **10.** To move from side to side or with a zigzagging motion. — *n.* A particular method or style of weaving. [OE *wefan*. Akin to WEB, WEFT.]

WEAVES
a Simple figured.
b Leno. *c* Satin.

weav·er (wē′vər) *n.* **1.** One who weaves; especially, one whose occupation is the weaving of textiles, etc. **2.** A weaverbird.

weav·er·bird (wē′vər·bûrd′) *n.* Any of various finchlike birds (family *Ploceidae*), native to Asia, Africa, etc., and constructing intricately woven nests.

weaver's hitch *Naut.* A sheet bend. Also **weaver's knot.**

web (web) *n.* **1.** Any fabric, structure, etc., woven of or as of interlaced or interwoven strands. **2.** Textile fabric, especially in the piece or being woven in a loom. **3.** The network of delicate threads spun by a spider to entrap its prey, by certain caterpillars, other insect larvae, etc.; a cobweb. **4.** Any complex network: a *web* of highways. **5.** Anything artfully contrived or elaborated into a trap or snare: a *web* of espionage. **6.** *Zool.* A membrane or fold of skin connecting the digits of an animal, as in aquatic birds, otters, bats, frogs, etc. **7.** *Ornithol.* The series of barbs on either side of the shaft of a feather: also called *vane*. For illustration see FEATHER. **8.** A plate or sheet, as of metal, connecting the heavier sections, ribs, frames, etc., of any structural or mechanical element. **9.** A roll of paper, as newsprint, as it comes from the mill. **10.** *Archit.* The part of a ribbed vault between the ribs. **11.** *Anat.* Membranous tissue; tela. **12.** A thin metal plate, as the blade of a saw or sword, or the bit of a key. — *v.t.* **webbed**, **web·bing** **1.** To provide with a web. **2.** To cover or surround with a web; entangle. [OE. Akin to WEAVE, WEFT.]

Webb (web), **Beatrice,** 1858–1943, *née* Potter, English economist and sociologist; wife of Sidney James Webb. — **Mary,** 1881–1927, *née* Meredith, English novelist. — **Sidney James,** 1859–1947, first Baron Passfield, English economist and sociologist.

webbed (webd) *adj.* **1.** Having a web. **2.** Having the digits united by a membrane, as the foot of a goose or duck.

web·bing (web′ing) *n.* **1.** A woven strip of strong fiber, used for safety belts, in upholstery, etc. **2.** Any structure or material forming a web.

web·by (web′ē) *adj.* **·bi·er**, **·bi·est** Resembling, having, or consisting of a web or membrane.

we·ber (web′ər, vā′bər) *n.* *Physics* **1.** The mks unit of magnetic flux, equal to 100,000,000 maxwells. **2.** Formerly, a coulomb or ampere. [after Wilhelm Eduard *Weber*]

We·ber (vā′bər), **Ernst Heinrich,** 1795–1878, German physiologist. — **Baron Karl Maria Friedrich Ernst von,** 1786–1826, German composer. — **Max,** 1864–1920, German political economist and sociologist. — **Wilhelm Eduard,** 1804–1891, German physicist; brother of Ernst Heinrich Weber.

Web·er (web′ər), **Max,** 1881–1961, U.S. painter born in Russia.

web·foot (web′foot′) *n.* *pl.* **·feet** **1.** A foot with webbed toes. **2.** A web-footed bird or animal.

web-foot·ed (web′foot′id) *adj.* Having the toes connected by a membrane, as many aquatic animals and birds.

web press A printing press that prints on a continuous roll of paper, rather than on separate sheets.

web·ster (web′stər) *n.* *Archaic* A weaver. [OE *webbestre*, fem. of *webba* weaver]

Web·ster (web′stər), **Daniel,** 1782–1852, U.S. statesman and orator. — **John,** 1580?–1625, English dramatist. — **Noah,** 1758–1843, U.S. lexicographer.

Webster Groves A city in eastern Missouri, near St. Louis; pop. 26,995.

Web·ste·ri·an (web-stir′ē·ən) *adj.* Of or pertaining to Daniel or Noah Webster.

web·worm (web′wûrm′) *n.* Any of various caterpillar, usually very destructive of foliage, that build large webs, as the common **garden webworm** (*Phylyctaenodes similalis*).

Wechs·ler-Belle·vue scale (weks′lər-bel′vyōō) *Psychol.* A system of rating the intelligence and mental development of adults and older children according to their performance in selected and graded tests. Also **Belle′vue scale.** [after David *Wechsler*, born 1896, U.S. psychologist + *Bellevue* Psychiatric Hospital, New York]

wecht (wekht) *n.* *Scot.* Weight.

wed (wed) *v.* **wed·ded**, **wed** or **wed·ded**, **wed·ding** *v.t.* **1.** To take as one's husband or wife; marry. **2.** To unite or give in matrimony; join in wedlock. **3.** To join in a close relationship or attachment. — *v.i.* **4.** To take a husband or wife; marry. [OE *weddian* to pledge]

we'd (wēd) **1.** We had. **2.** We would.

Wed. Wednesday.

wed·ded (wed′id) *adj.* **1.** Joined in wedlock; married. **2.** Characteristic of marriage; connubial. **3.** Having a close relationship or attachment; closely united: often with *to*: *wedded* to his work.

Wed·dell Sea (wed'l) An inlet of the Atlantic in Antarctica, south of South America.

wed·ding (wed'ing) n. 1. The ceremony or celebration of a marriage. 2. The anniversary of a marriage: golden *wedding*. — **Syn.** See MARRIAGE. [OE *weddung < weddian* to pledge]

wedding cake A type of very rich fruit or pound cake often served at wedding receptions.

wedding ring A ring or one of a pair of rings, as of gold, platinum, etc., given to the bride or exchanged between bride and groom during the marriage service.

We·de·kind (vā'də·kint), **Frank**, 1864–1918, German dramatist: full name **Benjamin Franklin Wedekind**.

we·deln (vā'dəln) n. German A skiing technique in which the skier makes a series of small, shallow turns in moving downhill; literally, a wagging of the tail.

wedge (wej) n. 1. A piece of wood, metal, etc., that is V-shaped in longitudinal cross section, capable of being inserted into a narrow opening, and used as an aid in splitting substances, securing movable parts, raising weights, etc. 2. Anything in the form of a wedge, as a piece of pie. 3. A formation, as of soldiers or football players, arranged like a wedge. 4. Any of the triangular characters used in cuneiform writing. 5. An action, procedure, or idea constituting the earliest stage in a division of unity, change of policy, intrusive action, etc. 6. *Meteorol.* A wedge-shaped area of high barometric pressure. 7. In golf, an iron with a heavy base and an extremely slanted face, used to lift the ball from sand, etc. — v. **wedged, wedg·ing** v.t. 1. To force apart or split with or as with a wedge. 2. To compress or fix in place with a wedge. 3. To crowd or squeeze (something) into a narrow or confined space. — v.i. 4. To jam or be forced in like a wedge. [OE *wecg*]

wedg·ie (wej'ē) n. Informal A woman's shoe having a wedge-shaped sole, thickening toward the heel.

Wedg·wood (wej'wŏŏd) n. A type of fine, hard, pottery, often of unglazed, tinted clay bearing small, finely detailed, classical figures in cameo relief applied in white paste. Also **Wedgwood ware.** [after Josiah *Wedgwood*]

Wedg·wood (wej'wŏŏd), **Josiah**, 1730–95, English potter. — **Josiah Clement**, 1872–1943, first Baron Wedgwood, English naval architect, diplomat, and politician: called **the Father of the Labour Party.**

Wedgwood blue Either of two shades of blue, a light grayish blue or a dark reddish blue, typical of Wedgwood pottery.

wedg·y (wej'ē) adj. **wedg·i·er, wedg·i·est** Having the form or uses of a wedge.

wed·lock (wed'lok) n. The state or relationship of being married; matrimony. — **Syn.** See MARRIAGE. — **in wedlock 1.** With one's parents legally married to one another, as at the time of one's conception or birth. **2.** In the married state: united *in wedlock*. — **out of wedlock** With one's parents not married to one another, as at the time of one's conception or birth. [OE *wedlāc < wed* pledge + *-lāc*, suffix of nouns of action]

Wednes·day (wenz'dē, -dā) n. The fourth day of the week. Abbr. **W., Wed.** [OE *Wōdnesdæg* day of Woden, trans. of LL *Mercurii dies* day of Mercury]

wee (wē) adj. **we·er, we·est** Very small; tiny. — n. Chiefly Scot. A short time or space; a bit: bide a *wee.* — **Syn.** See SMALL. [ME *wei < OE wǣge* a quantity]

weed[1] (wēd) n. 1. Any common, unsightly, or troublesome plant that grows in abundance, especially to injurious excess on cultivated ground. 2. Informal Tobacco: usually with *the*; also, a cigarette or cigar. 3. Any worthless animal or thing; especially, a horse that is unfit for racing or breeding. 4. The stem and leaves of any useful plant as distinguished from its flower and fruit: dill *weed.* 5. Thick, luxuriant growth, as of underbrush or shrubs. — v.t. 1. To pull up and remove weeds from: to *weed* a garden. 2. To remove (a weed): often with *out.* 3. To remove (anything regarded as harmful or undesirable): with *out.* 4. To rid of anything harmful or undesirable. — v.i. 5. To remove weeds, etc. [OE *wēod*] — **weed'less** adj.

weed[2] (wēd) n. 1. A token of mourning, as a band of crepe, worn as part of the dress. 2. pl. A widow's mourning garb. 3. Obs. Any article of clothing. [OE *wǣd* garment]

weed·er (wē'dər) n. 1. One who weeds. 2. An implement for removing weeds.

weed·ing hoe (wē'ding) A narrow-bladed hoe for weeding. For illustration see HOE.

weed·y (wē'dē) adj. **weed·i·er, weed·i·est** 1. Having a growth of weeds; abounding in weeds. 2. Of or pertaining to a weed or weeds. 3. Resembling a weed; weedlike, as in rapid, ready growth. 4. Informal Gawky; awkward; ungainly: *weedy* youths. — **weed'i·ly** adv. — **weed'i·ness** n.

wee folk Fairies, elves, etc.

wee hours The hours after midnight; the hours of early morning.

week (wēk) n. 1. A period of seven days; especially, such a period beginning with Sunday. ◆ Collateral adjective: hebdomadal. 2. The period of time within a week devoted to work: The office has a 35-hour *week.* 3. A period of seven days preceding or following any given day or date: a *week* from Tuesday. Abbr. **w., wk.** [OE *wucu, wicu, wice*]

week·day (wēk'dā) n. Any day of the week except Sunday.

week·end (wēk'end') n. The end of the week; especially, the time from Friday evening or Saturday to the following Monday morning. — v.i. Informal To pass the weekend: We *weekended* in the country. — **week'end'er** n.

Week·ley (wēk'lē), **Ernest,** 1865–1954, English lexicographer and etymologist.

week·long (wēk'lông', -long') adj. Continuing for week; lasting all week.

week·ly (wēk'lē) adv. Once a week; especially, at regular seven-day intervals. — adj. 1. Of or pertaining to a week or to weekdays. 2. Done or occurring once a week; also, reckoned by the week. — n. pl. **·lies** A publication issued once a week. Abbr. **wkly.**

weel (wēl) adj., adv., & interj. Scot. Well.

Weems (wēmz), **Mason Locke,** 1759–1825, American clergyman and biographer: called **Parson Weems.**

ween (wēn) v.t. & v.i. Archaic To suppose; guess; fancy. [OE *wēnan* to think]

ween·ie (wē'nē) n. U.S. Informal A wiener.

wee·ny (wē'nē) adj. **·ni·er, ·ni·est** Very tiny. Also **ween·sy** (wēn'sē). [< WEE + (TI)NY]

weep[1] (wēp) v. **wept, weep·ing** v.i. 1. To manifest grief or other strong emotion by shedding tears: to *weep* for joy. 2. To mourn; lament: with *for.* 3. To ooze or shed liquid in drops. — v.t. 4. To weep for; mourn or bewail. 5. To shed (tears, or drops of other liquid). 6. To bring to a specified condition by weeping: to *weep* oneself to sleep. — n. The act of weeping, or a fit of tears. [OE *wēpan*]

weep[2] (wēp) n. The lapwing, a bird. [Imit.]

weep·er (wē'pər) n. 1. One who weeps, as a hired mourner. 2. A long piece of black crepe worn as a sign of mourning, customarily hanging down from the hat. 3. A pendant of moss, as from a branch. 4. A hole through which water may drip. 5. pl. Informal Long, drooping side whiskers.

weep·ing (wē'ping) adj. 1. That weeps; crying; tearful. 2. Having slim, pendulous branches: *weeping* willow.

weeping willow A willow (*Salix babylonica*), having long, slender, pendulous branches.

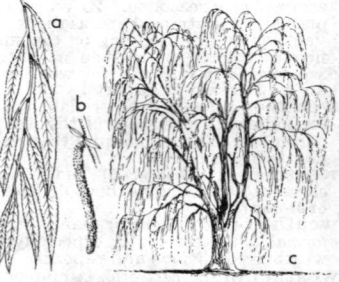

WEEPING WILLOW
a Leaves. b Catkin. c Tree.

weep·y (wē'pē) adj. **weep·i·er, weep·i·est** Informal Inclined to weep; tearful.

wee·ver (wē'vər) n. Any of various edible marine fishes (genus *Trachinus*) of European waters, having upward-looking eyes and sharp dorsal and opercular spines, with which they can inflict serious wounds. [< AF *wivre,* OF *guivre,* orig., serpent, dragon < L *vipera* viper]

wee·vil (wē'vəl) n. 1. Any of numerous small beetles (family *Curculionidae*), many of them serious pests, having snoutlike heads and strong, pincerlike jaws, and feeding on plants and plant products. 2. Any of a family (*Laridae*) of small beetles that feed principally on beans and seeds. [OE *wifel* beetle] — **wee'vil·y** or **wee'vil·ly** adj.

weft (weft) n. 1. The cross threads in a web of cloth; woof. 2. A woven fabric; web. 3. Naut. A waft. [OE. Akin to WEAVE, WEB.]

Wehr·macht (vâr'mäkht) n. German The armed forces, collectively, of Germany; literally, defense force.

Weich·sel (vīkh'səl) The German name for the Vistula.

wei·ge·la (wī·gē'lə, -jē'-, wī'jə·lə) n. Any of a genus (*Weigela*) of shrubs of the honeysuckle family. [< NL, after Dr. C. E. *Weigel,* 1748–1831, German physician]

weigh[1] (wā) v.t. 1. To determine the weight of, as by measuring on a scale or balance. 2. To balance or hold in the hand so as to estimate weight or heaviness. 3. To measure (a quantity or quantities of something) according to weight: with *out.* 4. To consider carefully; estimate the worth or advantages of: to *weigh* a proposal. 5. To press or force down by weight or heaviness; burden or oppress: with *down.* 6. To raise or hoist: now only in the phrase **to weigh anchor.** 7. Obs. To think well of; esteem; regard. — v.i. 8. To have weight; be heavy to a specified degree: She *weighs* ninety pounds. 9. To have influence or importance: The girl's testimony *weighed* heavily with the jury. 10. To be burdensome or oppressive: with *on* or *upon:* What *weighs* on your mind? 11. Naut. a To raise anchor. b To begin to sail. — **to weigh in** Of a prize fighter or other contestant, to be weighed before a contest. — **to weigh one's words** To consider one's words carefully before speaking. [OE *wegan* to weigh, carry, lift] — **weigh'er** n.

weigh[2] (wā) n. Way: used in the phrase **under weigh** by mistaken analogy with *aweigh.* [Var. of WAY; infl. in form by WEIGH[1], def. 6]

weigh·ing machine (wā′ing) Any of various machines for weighing; a scale.

weight (wāt) *n.* **1.** Any quantity of heaviness, expressed indefinitely or in terms of standard units. **2.** The measure of the force with which bodies tend toward the center of the earth or other celestial body, equal to the mass of the body multiplied by the acceleration due to gravitation; also, the quality so measured. **3.** Any object or mass that weighs a definite or specific amount. **4.** A definite mass of metal, etc., equal to a specified unit or amount of heaviness, and used in weighing machines as a standard; also, any unit of heaviness, as a pound, ounce, etc. **5.** Any mass used as a counterpoise or to exert pressure by force of gravity: a *paperweight*. **6.** Burden; pressure; oppressiveness: the *weight* of care; the *weight* of an attack. **7.** The relative tendency of any mass toward a center of superior mass: the *weight* of a planet. **8.** A scale or graduated system of standard units of weight: avoirdupois *weight*. See tables inside back cover. **9.** Influence; importance; consequence: a man of *weight*. **10.** The comparative heaviness of clothes, as appropriate to the season: summer *weight*. **11.** *Stat.* **a** The relative value of an item in a statistical compilation. **b** The frequency of its occurrence among related items, or the number used to express such frequency. Abbr. *w., wt.* **— by weight** Measured by weighing. **— to carry weight** To be of importance or significance: His decisions *carry weight*. **— to pull one's weight** To do one's share; perform one's duty. **— to throw one's weight around** *Informal* To exercise one's authority more than is necessary or proper; make unwarranted use of position or power. **—** *v.t.* **1.** To add weight to; make heavy. **2.** To oppress or burden. **3.** To adulterate or treat (fabrics, etc.) with extraneous substances. **4.** *Stat.* To give weight to. [OE *wiht, gewiht*]

weight·less (wāt′lis) *adj.* **1.** Having or seeming to have no weight. **2.** *Aerospace* Falling freely and exerting no downward force. **— weight′less·ly** *adv.* **— weight′less·ness** *n.*

weight lifter One who lifts weights, as barbells, in athletic competition or for exercise.

weight·lift·ing (wāt′lif′ting) *n.* The exercise and competitive sport of lifting heavy weights in prescribed ways.

weight·y (wā′tē) *adj.* **weight·i·er, weight·i·est 1** Having great weight; ponderous. **2.** Having power to move the mind; cogent. **3.** Of great importance. **4.** Influential. **5.** Burdensome. **— weight′i·ly** *adv.* **— weight′i·ness** *n.*

Wei·hai (wā′hī′) A port and naval base in NE Shantung Province, NE China; leased with the surrounding area (285 sq. mi.) to Great Britain, 1898–1930; pop. about 175,000. Formerly **Wei·hai·wei** (wā′hī′wā′).

Weill (wil, *Ger.* vīl), **Kurt,** 1900–50, U.S. composer, born in Germany.

Wei·mar (vī′mär) A city in SW East Germany, formerly capital of Thuringia; pop. about 67,000.

Wei·mar·an·er (vī′mər·ä′nər, wī′-) *n.* A breed of large dogs having blue or amber eyes and a smooth gray coat. [after *Weimar*, Germany, where the breed originated]

Weimar Republic A German Republic formed by a constitutional assembly at Weimar, 1919; dissolved 1933. See SECOND REICH under REICH.

weir (wir) *n.* **1.** An obstruction or dam placed in a stream to raise the water, divert it into a millrace or irrigation ditches, etc. **2.** An aperture in such an obstruction, used to determine the quantity of water flowing through it. **3.** A series of wattled enclosures in a stream to catch fish. [OE *wer* < *werian* to dam up]

weird (wird) *adj.* **1.** Concerned with the unnatural or with witchcraft; unearthly; uncanny. **2.** Strange; bizarre. **3.** Of or having to do with fate or the Fates. **— the Weird Sisters 1.** The Fates. **2.** The three witches in Shakespeare's *Macbeth.* **—** *n. Chiefly Scot.* **1.** One's fate; destiny. **2.** One of the Fates. **3.** A prophecy. **4.** A spell; enchantment. [OE *wyrd* fate] **— weird′ly** *adv.* **— weird′ness** *n.*

weird·ie (wir′dē) *n. pl.* **weird·ies** *U.S. Slang* A bizarre or freakish person, thing, or occurrence. Also **weird′y.**

Weir·ton (wir′tən) A city in NW West Virginia, on the Ohio River; pop. 27,131.

Weis·mann (vīs′män), **August,** 1834–1914, German biologist. **— Weis·man·ni·an** (vīs·män′ē·ən) *adj. & n.*

Weis·mann·ism (vīs′män·iz′əm) *n.* The theory of evolution that asserts the continuity of the germ plasm within but in isolation from the soma. [after August *Weismann*]

weiss beer (vīs, wīs) A pale, effervescent beer, brewed usually from wheat. [< G *weissbier*, lit., white beer]

Weiss·horn (vīs′hôrn) A peak in southern Switzerland; 14,792 ft.

Weiz·mann (vīts′män, wīts′mən), **Chaim,** 1874–1952, Israeli chemist, Zionist leader, and statesman born in Russia; first president of Israel 1948–52.

we·ka (wē′kə, wā′-) *n.* A large, flightless rail (genus *Ocydroma*) of New Zealand: also called *woodhen*. [< Maori]

welch (welch, welsh) *v.i.* To welsh. **— welch′er** *n.*

Welch (welch, welsh) See WELSH.

Welch (welch), **William Henry,** 1850–1934, U.S. pathologist.

Welch·man (welsh′mən, welch-) See WELSHMAN.

wel·come (wel′kəm) *adj.* **1.** Admitted gladly to a place or festivity; received cordially: a *welcome* guest. **2.** Producing satisfaction or pleasure; pleasing: *welcome* tidings. **3.** Made free to use or enjoy: She is *welcome* to my purse. **— you are** (**or you're**) **welcome** You are under no obligation: a conventional response to "thank you." **—** *n.* The act of bidding or making welcome; a hearty greeting given or cordial reception accorded to a guest or visitor. **— to wear out one's welcome** To come so often or to linger so long as no longer to be welcome. **—** *v.t.* **·comed, ·com·ing 1.** To give a welcome to; greet gladly or hospitably. **2.** To receive with pleasure: to *welcome* constructive advice. [OE *wilcuma* < *will-* will, pleasure + *cuma* guest; infl. in form by WELL[2] and COME, on analogy with OF *bien venu*] **— wel′come·ly** *adv.* **— wel′come·ness** *n.* **— wel′com·er** *n.*

welcome mat *Informal* **1.** A doormat (which see). **2.** Any enthusiastic welcome or reception: chiefly in the phrase **to put** (**or roll**) **out the welcome mat.**

weld[1] (weld) *v.t.* **1.** To unite, as two pieces of metal, usually with hammering or pressure, by the application of heat along the area of contact. **2.** To bring into close association or connection. **—** *v.i.* **3.** To be capable of being welded. **—** *n.* The consolidation of pieces of metal by welding; also, the closed joint so formed. [Alter. of WELL[1], v.] **— weld′a·bil′i·ty** *n.* **— weld′a·ble** *adj.* **— weld′er** *n.*

weld[2] (weld) *n.* **1.** An Old World mignonette (*Reseda luteola*), formerly cultivated for dyers' use: also called *yellowweed.* **2.** The yellow pigment obtained from it. Also called *woald.* [ME *welde*. Cf. MLG *walde*, MDu. *woude.*]

wel·fare (wel′fâr) *n.* **1.** The condition of faring well; exemption from pain or discomfort; prosperity. **2.** Welfare work (which see). **3.** Aid in the form of money, food, clothing, etc., given to those in need; relief. **— on welfare** Receiving money, food, clothing, etc., from a local or other government because of need. [ME *wel fare* < *wel* well + *fare* a going < OE *faran* to go]

Welfare Island An island in the East River, New York City; 139 acres; site of two municipal hospitals: formerly *Blackwell's Island.*

welfare state A state or polity in which the government assumes a large measure of responsibility for the social welfare of its members, as through unemployment and health insurance, fair employment legislation, etc.

welfare statism 1. The condition of being a welfare state. **2.** The principles and practices of a welfare state. Also **welfar·ism** (wel′fâr·iz·əm). **— welfare statist**

welfare work Organized efforts carried on by government or private organizations to improve the social and economic condition of a group or class. **— welfare worker**

wel·kin (wel′kin) *n. Archaic* or *Poetic* **1.** The vault of the sky; the heavens. **2.** The air. Now chiefly in the phrase **to make the welkin ring.** [OE *wolcen, wolcn* cloud]

well[1] (wel) *n.* **1.** A hole or shaft sunk into the earth to obtain a fluid, as water, oil, brine, or natural gas. **2.** A spring of water; a place where water issues from the ground; a fountain. **3.** A source of continued supply, or that which issues forth continuously; a wellspring: a *well* of learning. **4.** A depression, cavity, or vessel used to hold a supply of liquid: an *inkwell.* **5.** A cavity in the lower part of some sorts of furnaces to receive falling metal. **6.** In an English law court, the railed space between the bench and the bar, reserved for solicitors. **7.** *Archit.* A vertical opening descending through floors, or a deep enclosed space in a building for light, ventilation, etc.: a *stairwell*; an elevator *well.* **8.** *Naut.* The enclosed space in a vessel's hold, housing the pumps. **9.** A compartment admitting water, in which fish are preserved alive. **—** *v.i.* **1.** To pour forth or flow up, as water in a spring. **—** *v.t.* **2.** To gush: Her eyes *welled* tears. [OE *wielle* < *weallan* to boil, bubble up]

well[2] (wel) *adv.* **bet·ter, best 1.** According to one's wishes; favorably: Everything goes *well.* **2.** Satisfactorily, as in performance: He did *well* in the job. **3.** In a good or correct manner; properly or pleasingly: to speak *well.* **4.** With superior skill or talent; expertly: to sing *well.* **5.** With reason or propriety; suitably; befittingly: I cannot *well* remain here. **6.** In a successful manner; prosperously; also, agreeably or luxuriously: to live *well.* **7.** To a considerable extent or degree; fully or intimately: *well* informed; How *well* do you know him? **8.** Completely; wholly; thoroughly: *well* deserved. **9.** By a sizable margin; far: *well* ahead of other countries in the quality of its health care. **10.** Kindly; generously; graciously: *well* treated. **11.** Carefully; closely: Listen *well.* **12.** Beyond any question; quite: *well* aware of the consequences. **— as well 1.** Also; in addition. **2.** With equal effect or consequence: He might just *as well* have sold it. **— as well as 1.** As satisfactorily as. **2.** To the same degree as. **3.** In addition to. **—** *adj.* **1.** Having good health; free from ailment of mind or body. **2.** Satisfactory; right: All is *well.* **3.** Prosperous; comfortable. **4.** Prudent;

sensible: It is *well* to rest after vigorous exertion. **5.** For the best; fitting; proper. **— *interj.*** An exclamation used to express surprise, expectation, resignation, doubt, indignation, acquiescence, etc., or merely to preface a remark. [OE *wel.* Akin to WEAL.]

Well may be used in combination, as in the following list. Such combinations are hyphenated when they appear before the words they modify, as in *well-aimed* shots, but are not hyphenated when used predicatively, as in: The shots were *well aimed.*

well-accepted	well-judged
well-accustomed	well-kept
well-acknowledged	well-knit
well-acquainted	well-liked
well-acted	well-looking
well-adapted	well-loved
well-adjusted	well-made
well-administered	well-managed
well-aimed	well-matched
well-aired	well-measured
well-armed	well-merited
well-armored	well-ordered
well-arranged	well-organized
well-assorted	well-paid
well-assured	well-phrased
well-attested	well-placed
well-attired	well-planned
well-authenticated	well-pleased
well-behaved	well-poised
well-beloved	well-prepared
well-built	well-preserved
well-chaperoned	well-proportioned
well-chosen	well-recognized
well-concealed	well-regulated
well-considered	well-remembered
well-content	well-rooted
well-contented	well-seasoned
well-covered	well-selected
well-cultivated	well-shaped
well-defended	well-skilled
well-defined	well-spent
well-deserving	well-stocked
well-digested	well-suited
well-disciplined	well-swept
well-dressed	well-timed
well-earned	well-trained
well-educated	well-trimmed
well-established	well-understood
well-financed	well-used
well-fitted	well-versed
well-formed	well-won
well-fortified	well-wooded
well-fought	well-worded
well-furnished	well-worn
well-governed	well-woven
well-handled	well-written
well-informed	well-wrought

we'll (wĕl)　**1.** We will.　**2.** We shall.

Wel·land (wĕl'ənd)　A city in southern Ontario, on the **Welland Ship Canal,** a waterway connecting Lake Ontario with Lake Erie; pop. 16,405.

well-ap·point·ed (wĕl'ə-poin'tid)　*adj.* Properly equipped; excellently furnished.

well·a·way (wĕl'ə-wā')　*interj. Archaic* Woe is me! alas! Also **well'a·day'** (-dā'). [OE *wei lā wei,* alter. of *wā lā wā* woe! lo! woe!; infl. in form by ON *vei* woe]

well-bal·anced (wĕl'bal'ənst)　*adj.* **1.** Evenly balanced or proportioned.　**2.** Sensible; sane; sound.

well·be·ing (wĕl'bē'ing)　*n.* Health, happiness, or prosperity.

well·born (wĕl'bôrn')　*adj.* Of good birth or ancestry.

well·bred (wĕl'brĕd')　*adj.* **1.** Characterized by or showing good breeding; polite.　**2.** Of good stock, as an animal.

well·curb (wĕl'kûrb')　*n.* The frame or stone ring around the mouth of a well.

well-dis·posed (wĕl'dis-pōzd')　*adj.* Disposed or inclined to be kind, favorable, etc.

well-done (wĕl'dun')　*adj.* **1.** Satisfactorily accomplished.　**2.** Thoroughly cooked, as meat.

Wel·le (wĕl'lā)　See UELE.

well enough　Tolerably good or satisfactory. **— to let well enough alone**　To leave things as they are lest the result of interference be worse.

Welles (wĕlz)　**Gideon,** 1802–78, U.S. politician and writer; Secretary of the Navy during the Civil War. **— Sumner,** 1892–1961, U.S. diplomat.

Welles·ley (wĕlz'lē)　**Richard Colley,** 1760–1842, first Marquis Wellesley, British statesman born in Ireland; brother of the Duke of Wellington.

well-fa·vored (wĕl'fā'vərd)　*adj.* Of attractive appearance; comely; handsome. Also *Brit.* **well'-fa'voured.**

well-fed (wĕl'fĕd')　*adj.* **1.** Plump; fat.　**2.** Properly nourished.

well-fixed (wĕl'fikst')　*adj. Informal* Affluent; well-to-do.

well-found (wĕl'found')　*adj.* Well equipped or supplied.

well-found·ed (wĕl'foun'did)　*adj.* Based on fact, sound evidence, etc.: *well-founded* suspicions.

well-groomed (wĕl'grōōmd')　*adj.* **1.** Carefully dressed,

combed, etc.; very neat.　**2.** Carefully curried, as a horse.

well-ground·ed (wĕl'groun'did)　*adj.* **1.** Adequately schooled in the elements of a subject.　**2.** Well-founded.

well·head (wĕl'hĕd')　*n.* **1.** A natural source supplying water to a spring or well.　**2.** Any source or fountainhead.

well-heeled (wĕl'hēld')　*adj. Slang* Plentifully supplied with money. [< WELL² + HEEL¹, v. (def. 6)]

Wel·ling·ton (wĕl'ing-tən)　The capital of New Zealand, a port on southern North Island; pop. 133,700 (est. 1968).

Wel·ling·ton (wĕl'ing-tən), **Duke of,** 1769–1852, Arthur Wellesley, British general and statesman born in Ireland; defeated Napoleon at Waterloo 1815; prime minister 1828–1830: called *the Iron Duke.*

Wellington boot　A high boot covering the leg as far as the knee in front but cut away behind.

well-in·ten·tioned (wĕl'in-tĕn'shənd)　*adj.* Having good intentions; well-meant: often with connotation of failure.

well-known (wĕl'nōn')　*adj.* **1.** Widely known; famous.　**2.** Thoroughly or fully known.

well-man·nered (wĕl'man'ərd)　*adj.* Characterized by good manners; courteous; polite.

well-mean·ing (wĕl'mē'ning)　*adj.* **1.** Having good intentions.　**2.** Done with or characterized by good intentions: also **well'-meant'** (-mĕnt').

well-nigh (wĕl'nī')　*adv.* Very nearly; almost.

well-off (wĕl'ôf', -ŏf')　*adj.* In comfortable or favorable circumstances; fortunate.

well-read (wĕl'rĕd')　*adj.* Having a wide knowledge of literature or books; having read much.

well-round·ed (wĕl'roun'did)　*adj.* **1.** Having or displaying diverse knowledge, interests, etc.　**2.** Wide in scope; comprehensive: a *well-rounded* program.　**3.** Fully formed or developed: a *well-rounded* figure.

Wells (wĕlz)　**H.G.,** 1866–1946, English author: full name **Herbert George Wells.**

well-spo·ken (wĕl'spō'kən)　*adj.* **1.** Fitly or excellently said.　**2.** Of gentle speech and manners.

well·spring (wĕl'spring')　*n.* **1.** The source of a stream or spring; fountainhead.　**2.** A source of continual supply: a *wellspring* of inspiration.

well sweep　A device used for drawing water from a well, consisting of a pole swung on a pivot attached to a high post, and having a bucket suspended from one end.

well-thought-of (wĕl'thôt'uv', -ŏv')　*adj.* In good repute; esteemed; respected.

well-to-do (wĕl'tə-dōō')　*adj.* Prosperous; affluent.

WELL SWEEP

well-wish·er (wĕl'wish'ər)　*n.* One who wishes well, as to another. **— well'-wish'ing** *adj. & n.*

Wels·bach burner (wĕlz'bak, *Ger.* vels'bäkh)　A gas burner having a mantle impregnated with material that becomes incandescent. [after Baron Carl Auer von *Welsbach,* 1858–1929, Austrian chemist]

welsh (wĕlsh, wĕlch)　*v.i. Slang* **1.** To cheat by failing to pay a bet or debt: often with *on.*　**2.** To avoid fulfilling an obligation: often with *on.* Also spelled **welch.** [? Back formation < *welsher,* prob. < *Welsher* Welshman, with ref. to supposed national traits] **— welsh'er** *n.*

Welsh (wĕlsh, wĕlch)　*adj.* Pertaining to Wales, its people, or their language. **— *n.* 1.** The Celtic people of Wales: with *the:* also called *Cymry.*　**2.** The language of Wales, belonging to the Brythonic or Cymric group of the Celtic subfamily of Indo-European languages: also called *Cymric.* Also spelled *Welch.* Abbr. *W.* [OE *Wielisc < wealh* foreigner (one not of Saxon origin)]

Welsh cor·gi (kôr'gē)　Either of two breeds of a Welsh dog, characterized by a long body, short legs, and erect ears, the **Cardigan Welsh corgi** having a long tail, the **Pembroke Welsh corgi** a short tail. [< Welsh *corr* dwarf + *ci* dog]

Welsh·man (wĕlsh'mən, wĕlch'-)　*n. pl.* **·men** (-mən)　A man of Welsh birth or ancestry. Also spelled *Welchman.*

Welsh rabbit　A concoction of melted cheese cooked in cream or milk, often with ale or beer added, and served hot on toast or crackers. ◆ The form *rarebit* was a later development and is the result of mistaken etymology.

Welsh springer spaniel　A strong, active red-and-white spaniel, used for hunting.

Welsh terrier　A black-and-tan terrier having a flat skull and wiry coat, used for hunting.

welt (wĕlt)　*n.* **1.** A strip of material, covered cord, etc., applied to a seam to cover or strengthen it.　**2.** A strip of leather set into the seam between the edges of the upper and the outer sole of a shoe.　**3.** In carpentry, a batten or strip made fast over a flush seam.　**4.** A stripe raised on the skin by a blow: also called *wale, weal, wheal.* **— *v.t.* 1.** To sew a welt on or in; decorate with a welt.　**2.** *Informal* To flog severely, so as to raise welts. [ME *welte, walt.* Cf. OE *wyltan* to roll.]

WELSH TERRIER
(About 15 inches high at shoulder)

Welt·an·schau·ung (velt′än·shou′ŏŏng) *n. German* A comprehensive philosophy of life, nature, and history; ideology; literally, world viewing.

Welt·an·sicht (velt′än·zikht) *n. German* A special view or interpretation of reality; literally, world view.

wel·ter (wel′tər) *v.i.* **1.** To roll about; wallow. **2.** To lie or be soaked in some fluid, as blood. **3.** To surge or move tumultuously, as the sea. — *n.* **1.** A rolling movement, as of waves. **2.** A commotion; turmoil. [< MDu. *welteren*]

wel·ter·weight (wel′tər·wāt′) *n.* A boxer or wrestler whose fighting weight is between 136 and 147 pounds. [< *welter* heavyweight horseman + WEIGHT]

Welt·po·li·tik (velt′pō·li·tēk′) *n. German* International politics; world policy.

Welt·schmerz (velt′shmerts) *n. German* World-weariness; melancholy pessimism over the state of the world; romantic discontent; literally, world pain.

Wem·bley (wem′blē) A municipal borough in Middlesex, England, near London; pop. 124,843 (1961).

Wemyss (wēmz) A parish in central Fifeshire, Scotland, on the Firth of Forth; pop. 12,773 (1961).

wen¹ (wen) *n. Pathol.* Any encysted benign tumor of the skin containing sebaceous matter, occurring commonly on the scalp. [OE *wenn, wænn*] — **wen′nish, wen′ny** *adj.*

wen² (wen) *n.* The old English rune, ꝥ, replaced by modern English *w.* [OE, var. of *wynn* joy]

Wen·ces·laus III (wen′səs·lôs), 1361–1419, Holy Roman Emperor 1378–1400; king of Bohemia 1378–1419. Also **Wen·ces·laus** (-läs), *Ger.* **Wen·zel** (ven′tsəl), **Wen·zes·laus** (ven′tsəs·lous).

wench (wench) *n.* **1.** A young woman; girl: a humorous term. **2.** *Archaic* A young peasant woman; also, a female servant; maid. **3.** *Archaic* A prostitute; strumpet. — *v.i. Archaic* To keep company with strumpets. [ME *wenche,* short for *wenchel* < OE *wencel* child, servant]

Wen·chow (wen′chou′, *Chinese* wun′jō′) A port city in SE Chekiang Province, China; pop. 250,000 (est. 1970).

wend (wend) *Chiefly Poetic v.* **wend·ed** (*Archaic* **went**), **wend·ing** *v.t.* **1.** To direct or proceed on (one's course or way). — *v.i.* **2.** To travel; proceed; go. [OE *wendan*]

Wend (wend) *n.* One of a Slavic people now occupying the region between the Elbe and Oder rivers in eastern Germany: also called *Sorb, Sorbian.* [< G *Wende, Winde*]

Wen·dell (wen′dəl), **Barrett,** 1855–1921, U.S. scholar.

wen·di·go (wen′di·gō) *n. pl.* **·gos 1.** A windigo (which see). **2.** *Canadian* A fish, the splake.

Wend·ish (wen′dish) *adj.* Of or pertaining to the Wends or their language: also *Sorbian, Lusatian.* — *n.* The West Slavic language of the Wends; Sorbian; Lusatian. Also **Wend′ic.**

went (went) An archaic past tense and past participle of *wend,* now used as past tense of GO.

wen·tle·trap (wen′təl·trap′) *n.* Any of a family (*Epitoniidae*) of mollusks, having a white, turreted, many-whorled shell. [< Du. *wenteltrap* spiral staircase or shell]

wept (wept) Past tense and past participle of WEEP.

were (wûr, *unstressed* wər) Plural and second person singular past indicative, and past subjunctive singular and plural of BE. [OE *wǣre, wǣron,* pt. forms of *wesan* to be]

we're (wir) We are.

were·n't (wûr′ənt) Were not.

were·wolf (wir′wŏŏlf′, wûr′-) *n. pl.* **·wolves** (-wŏŏlvz′) In European folklore, a human being transformed into a wolf or one having power to assume the form of a wolf at will. Also **wer′wolf′.** [OE *werwulf* man-wolf < *wer* man + *wulf* wolf]

Wer·fel (ver′fəl), **Franz,** 1890–1945, Austrian novelist, poet, and playwright born in Prague.

wer·geld (wûr′geld) *n.* In Anglo-Saxon and Teutonic law, a fine for crime against the person, especially for homicide, paid by the kindred of the slayer to those of the slain, so that the offender is no longer answerable. Also **were′gild** (-gild), **wer′gelt** (-gelt). [OE, lit., man-yield, i.e., man-price < *wer* man + *geld, gield* yield]

Wer·ner (ver′nər), **Alfred,** 1866–1919, Swiss chemist born in Alsace.

wer·ner·ite (wûr′nər·īt) *n.* Scapolite (which see). [after A. G. Werner, 1750–1817, German mineralogist]

wert (wûrt, *unstressed* wərt) Archaic second person singular, past tense of both indicative and subjunctive of BE: used with *thou.*

We·ser (vā′zər) A river in east and north central West Germany, flowing about 300 miles north to the North Sea.

Wes·ley (wes′lē, *Brit.* wez′lē), **Charles,** 1708–88, English clergyman and hymn writer; brother of John. — **John,** 1703–91, English clergyman; founder of Methodism.

Wes·ley·an (wes′lē·ən, *Brit.* wez′lē·ən) *adj.* Of or pertaining to John Wesley or Methodism. — *n.* A disciple of John Wesley; a Methodist. — **Wes′ley·an·ism** *n.*

Wes·sex (wes′iks) The ancient kingdom of the West Saxons, including modern Berkshire, Dorset, Hampshire, Somerset, and Wiltshire in southern England.

west (west) *n.* **1.** The direction of the sun in relation to an observer on earth at sunset. **2.** One of the four cardinal points of the compass, directly opposite *east* and 90° counterclockwise from *north.* See COMPASS CARD. **3.** Any direction near this point. **4.** *Sometimes cap.* Any region west of a specified point. — **the West 1.** The countries lying west of Asia and Turkey; the Occident. **2.** The Western Hemisphere, discovered by explorers sailing westward from Europe. **3.** The Western Roman Empire. **4.** In the United States: **a** Formerly, the region west of the Allegheny Mountains. **b** The region west of the Mississippi, especially the northwestern part of this region. **5.** The United States and its associates in world politics. — *adj.* **1.** To, toward, facing, or in the west; western. **2.** Coming from the west: the *west* wind. **3.** Designating or located in that part of a church directly opposite the altar. — *adv.* In or toward the west; westward. *Abbr. w, w., W, W.* [OE]

West (west), **Benjamin,** 1738–1820, American painter active in England. — **Rebecca** Pseudonym of **Cicily Isabel Fairfield** (fâr′fēld′), born 1892, British novelist and critic born in Ireland.

West. Westminster.

West Al·lis (al′is) A city in SE Wisconsin; pop. 71,723.

West Bengal See under BENGAL.

West Berlin See under BERLIN.

west·bound (west′bound′) *adj.* Going westward. Also **west′-bound′.** *Abbr. w.b.*

West Brom·wich (brum′ich, -ij) A county borough in southern Staffordshire, England, near Birmingham; pop. 95,909 (1961).

west by north A point on the mariner's compass, 25 points or 281° 15′ clockwise from due north. See COMPASS CARD. *Abbr. WbN*

west by south A point on the mariner's compass, 23 points or 258° 45′ clockwise from due north. See COMPASS CARD. *Abbr. WbS*

West Co·vi·na (cō·vē′nə) A city in SW California; pop. 68,034.

West End The western part of London, England, noted for its parks, fashionable shops, and residential section.

west·er (wes′tər) *v.i.* To turn, trend, or shift to the west. — *n.* A wind or storm from the west. [< WEST + -ER⁵]

west·er·ing (wes′tər·ing) *adj.* Moving or turning westward: the *westering* sun.

west·er·ling (wes′tər·ling) *n. Archaic* A westerner.

west·er·ly (wes′tər·lē) *adj.* **1.** In, toward, or pertaining to the west. **2.** From the west, as a wind. — *n. pl.* **·lies** A wind or storm from the west. — *adv.* Toward or from the west. — **west′er·li·ness** *n.*

Wes·ter·marck (ves′tər·märk), **Edward Alexander,** 1862–1939, Finnish anthropologist.

west·ern (wes′tərn) *adj.* **1.** To, toward, or in the west. **2.** Native to or inhabiting the west: a *western* species. **3.** *Sometimes cap.* Of, pertaining to, or characteristic of the west or the West. **4.** From the west, as a wind. — *n.* **1.** A westerner. **2.** A type of fiction or motion picture using cowboy and pioneer life in the western United States as its material. *Abbr. w, w., W, W.* [OE *westerne < west*]

Western Australia The largest State of Australia, including all of the continent west of 129° E.: about 975,920 sq. mi.; pop. 991,300 (est. 1970); capital, Perth.

Western Church 1. The medieval church of the Western Roman Empire, now the Roman Catholic Church: distinguished from the church of the Eastern Empire, now the Eastern Orthodox Church. **2.** The Christian churches of western Europe and America.

Western Dvina See DVINA (def. 2).

west·ern·er (wes′tər·nər) *n.* **1.** One who is native to or lives in the west. **2.** *Usually cap.* One who lives in or comes from the western United States.

western frontier Formerly, the part of the United States bordering on the still unsettled regions of the west.

Western Hemisphere See under HEMISPHERE.

Western Islands See HEBRIDES.

west·ern·ism (wes′tər·niz′əm) *n.* An expression or practice peculiar to the west, especially the western United States.

west·ern·ize (wes′tər·nīz) *v.t.* **·ized, ·iz·ing** To make western in characteristics, habits, etc. — **west′ern·i·za′tion** *n.*

west·ern·most (wes′tərn·mōst) *adj.* Farthest west.

Western Ocean In ancient geography, the ocean lying westward of the known world; the Atlantic Ocean.

Western Reserve A region now comprising the NE portion of Ohio, reserved by Connecticut when she ceded her western lands to the Federal Government in 1786; relinquished 1800.

Western (Roman) Empire The part of the Roman Empire west of the Adriatic that existed as a separate empire from A.D. 395 until the fall of Rome in A.D. 476.

Western Samoa See under SAMOA.

West·field (west′fēld) **1.** A city in SW Massachusetts, near

Springfield; pop. 31,433. **2.** A town in NE New Jersey; pop. 33,720.

West Flanders A Province of western Belgium; 1,249 sq. mi.; pop. 1,052,052 (est. 1970); capital, Bruges: French *Flandre Occidentale.* Flemish *West-Vlaanderen.*

West Germanic See under GERMANIC.

West Germany See under GERMANY.

West Glamorgan A county in southern Wales; 314 sq. mi.; pop. 371,400 (1976); county seat, Swansea.

West Ham A county borough in SW Essex, England; a suburb of London; pop. 157,186 (1961).

West Hartford A town in central Connecticut, adjacent to Hartford; pop. 68,031.

West Har·tle·pool (här′təl·pōōl) A county borough in SE Durham, England, on the North Sea; pop. 77,073 (1961).

West Haven A town in southern Connecticut, near New Haven; pop. 52,851.

West Highland white terrier A small, short-legged terrier having a stiff, white coat.

West Hollywood An unincorporated place in SW California, near Los Angeles; pop. 29,448.

West Indies A series of island groups separating the North Atlantic from the Caribbean, between North and South America, divided into the Bahamas, the Greater Antilles, and the Lesser Antilles. — **West Indian**

West Indies Associated States A group of former British colonies in the West Indies; since 1967 self-governing states in association with Great Britain and including Antigua, Dominica, St. Lucia, St. Vincent, and St. Christopher-Nevis-Anguilla.

west·ing (wes′ting) *n.* **1.** *Naut.* The distance traversed by a ship running on a westerly course. **2.** The distance westward from a given meridian. **3.** A shifting or moving west.

West·ing·house (wes′ting·hous), **George,** 1846–1914, U.S. inventor.

West Ir·i·an (ir′e·an) A Province of Indonesia comprising the western part of New Guinea and several adjacent islands; formerly a Netherlands overseas territory; 159,375 sq. mi.; pop. 918,000 (est. 1969); capital, Djajapura: formerly *West New Guinea, Netherlands New Guinea.*

West Lo·thi·an (lō′thē·ən) A county in SE Scotland, on the Firth of Forth; 120 sq. mi.; pop. 106,030 (est. 1969); county seat, Linlithgow: formerly *Linlithgow, Linlithgowshire.*

Westm. **1.** Westminster. **2.** Westmorland.

West Midlands A metropolitan county in central England; 347 sq. mi.; pop. 2,779,800 (1976); county seat, Birmingham.

West·min·ster (west′min·stər) **1.** A city and metropolitan borough in the county of London, England; site of the Houses of Parliament and Buckingham Palace; pop. 85,223 (1961). **2.** A city in SW California; pop. 59,865.

Westminster Abbey A Gothic church in Westminster, London, begun in 1050; burial place of English kings and notables.

West·mor·land (west′môr·lənd, -mōr-; *Brit.* west′mər·lənd) A former county in the Lake District, NW England; 789 sq. mi.; pop. 72,724 (1971); county seat, Appleby.

West New Guinea A former name for the western part of New Guinea. See WEST IRIAN.

West New York A town in NE New Jersey, on the Hudson River; pop. 40,627.

west-north·west (west′nôrth′west′) *n.* **1.** The direction midway between west and northwest. **2.** A point on the mariner's compass, 26 points or 292° 30′ clockwise from due north. See COMPASS CARD. Abbr. *wnw, w.n.w., WNW, W.N.W.* — *adj. & adv.* In, toward, or from the west-northwest.

West Orange A town in NE New Jersey; pop. 43,715.

West Pakistan See PAKISTAN.

West Palm Beach A resort city in SE Florida, on Lake Worth; pop. 57,375.

West·pha·li·a (west·fā′lē·ə) A former province of Prussia, since 1945 a part of North Rhine–Westphalia, West Germany; scene of the signing of a treaty by France, Sweden, and the Holy Roman Empire at the end of the Thirty Years' War, 1648. — **West·pha·li·an** *adj. & n.*

West Point A U.S. military reservation in SE New York, on the Hudson River; seat of the U.S. Military Academy.

West Riding A former administrative county of Yorkshire, England.

West Saxon **1.** One of a Saxon tribe that invaded England in the fifth and sixth centuries A.D. and settled in Wessex. **2.** The dialect of Old English spoken in Wessex.

West Slavic See under SLAVIC.

west-south·west (west′south′west′) *n.* **1.** The direction between west and southwest. **2.** A point on the mariner's compass, 22 points or 247° 30′ clockwise from due north. See COMPASS CARD. Abbr. *wsw, w.s.w., WSW, W.S.W.* — *adj. & adv.* In, toward, or from the west-southwest.

West Sussex A county in southern England; 768 sq. mi.; pop. 615,400 (1976); county seat, Chichester.

West Virginia A State of the east central United States; 24,181 sq. mi.; pop. 1,744,237; capital, Charleston; entered the Union June 20, 1863; nickname, *Panhandle State.* Abbr. *W. Va.* — **West Virginian**

West-Vlaan·de·ren (vest′vlän′də·rən) The Flemish name for WEST FLANDERS.

West·wall (west′wôl′) *n.* The Siegfried Line.

west·ward (west′wərd) *adv.* Toward the west: also **west′wards.** — *adj.* To, toward, facing, or in the west. — *n.* A western part or region. [OE *westweard < west* the west] — **west′ward·ly** *adv.*

West Yorkshire A metropolitan county in north central England; 787 sq. mi.; pop. 2,082,200 (1976); county seat, Wakefield.

wet (wet) *adj.* **wet·ter, wet·test** **1.** Covered or saturated with water or other liquid. **2.** Not yet dry: *wet* varnish. **3.** Treated or separated by means of water or other liquids. **4.** Preserved in liquid; also, bottled in alcohol, as laboratory specimens. **5.** Marked by showers or by heavy rainfall; rainy. **6.** *Informal* Favoring or permitting the manufacture and sale of alcoholic beverages: a *wet* State. — **all wet** *Slang* Quite wrong; crazy. — **wet behind the ears** Inexperienced or unsophisticated. — *n.* **1.** Water; moisture; wetness. **2.** Showery or rainy weather; rain. **3.** *Informal* One opposed to prohibition. — *v.* **wet** or **wet·ted, wet·ting** *v.t.* **1.** To make wet. **2.** To make wet by urinating. — *v.i.* **3.** To become wet. — **to wet one's whistle** *Informal* To take a drink. [OE *wǣt*] — **wet′ly** *adv.* — **wet′ness** *n.* — **wet′ta·ble** *adj.* — **wet′ter** *n.*

wet·back (wet′bak′) *n.* *U.S. Informal* A Mexican laborer who enters the United States illegally. [Because many cross the border by swimming or wading across the Rio Grande]

wet blanket *Informal* One who or that which has a discouraging effect on enthusiasm, activity, etc.

wet-bulb (wet′bulb′) *adj. Meteorol.* **1.** Designating a thermometer whose bulb is covered with moist muslin as a means of determining the lowest temperature at which evaporation will take place at constant atmospheric pressure, used especially with a dry-bulb thermometer in a psychrometer. **2.** Of or pertaining to the temperature indicated by this type of thermometer.

weth·er (weth′ər) *n.* A castrated ram. [OE]

wet-nurse (wet′nûrs′) *v.t.* **-nursed, -nurs·ing** **1.** To act as a wet nurse to. **2.** To attend to with painstaking care.

wet nurse A woman who is hired to suckle the child of another woman.

wet suit A skintight rubber suit worn by skin divers for warmth.

Wet·ter·horn (vet′ər·hôrn) A mountain of three peaks in the Bernese Alps, Switzerland; 12,153 ft.

wet·ting (wet′ing) *n.* **1.** The act of one who wets, or the state of being wetted. **2.** A liquid, as water, used in moistening something, as flour in breadmaking.

wetting agent *Chem.* Any of a class of substances that, by reducing surface tension, enable a liquid to spread more readily over a solid surface.

we've (wēv) We have.

Wex·ford (weks′fərd) A county of SE Leinster Province, Ireland; 908 sq. mi.; pop. 83,308 (1966); county seat, Wexford, a port on **Wexford Harbor,** an inlet of St. George's Channel; pop. about 10,000.

Wey·den (vī′dən), **Roger van der.** 1400?–64 Flemish painter.

Wey·gand (ve·gän′), **Maxime,** 1867–1965, French general in World Wars I and II: full name **Louis Maxime Weygand.**

Wey·mouth (wā′məth) A town in eastern Massachusetts; pop. 54,610.

Weymouth and Mel·combe Re·gis (mel′kəm rē′jis) A municipal borough and port in southern Dorset, England, on the English Channel; pop. 40,962 (1961).

wf or **w.f.** *Printing* Wrong font.

W. Flem. West Flemish.

WFTU or **W.F.T.U.** World Federation of Trade Unions.

W. Ger. **1.** West Germany. **2.** West Germanic.

WGmc. West Germanic.

wh. Watt-hour(s).

wha (hwä) *pron. Scot.* Who.

whack (hwak) *v.t. & v.i.* **1.** *Informal* To strike sharply; beat; hit. **2.** *Slang* To share: often with *up.* — *n.* **1.** *Informal* A sharp, resounding stroke or blow. **2.** The noise made by such a blow. **3.** *Slang* A share; portion. — **to have a whack at** *Slang* **1.** To give a blow to. **2.** To have a chance or turn at. — **out of whack** *Slang* Out of order. [? Var. of THWACK]

whack·ing (hwak′ing) *Chiefly Brit. Informal adj.* Strikingly large; whopping. — *adv.* Very; extremely.

whale¹ (hwāl) *n.* **1.** A cetaceous mammal of fishlike form, especially one of the larger pelagic species, having the fore limbs developed as paddles, a broad, flat tail, and a thick layer of fat or blubber immediately beneath the skin. The principal types are the toothless or whalebone whales (suborder *Mysticeti*), and the toothed whales (suborder *Odontoceti*). **2.** *Informal* Something extremely good or large: a *whale* of a party. — *v.i.* **whaled, whal·ing** To engage in the hunting of whales. [OE *hwæl*]

whale² (hwāl) *v.t.* **whaled, whal·ing** *Informal* To strike as if to produce weals or stripes; flog; weal. [? Var. of WALE¹, *v.*]

whale·back (hwāl′bak′) *n.* A steamship having a rounded main deck, used on the Great Lakes in passenger and freight traffic.

whale·boat (hwāl′bōt′) *n.* A long, deep rowboat, sharp at both ends, often steered with an oar, so called because first used in whaling, but now carried on steamers as lifeboats.

whale·bone (hwāl′bōn′) *n.* **1.** The horny, elastic substance developed in plates from the upper jaw on either side of the palate of certain whales; baleen. **2.** A strip of whalebone, used in stiffening dress bodies, corsets, etc.

whal·er (hwā′lər) *n.* **1.** A person or a vessel engaged in whaling. **2.** A whaleboat.

Whales (hwālz), **Bay of** An inlet of the Ross Sea in the Ross Shelf Ice, Antarctica.

whale shark A very large pelagic shark (*Rhineodon typus*) somewhat resembling the basking shark in its habits but often reaching a length of 50 feet and having very small teeth adapted for feeding on plankton or small fish.

whal·ing (hwā′ling) *n.* The industry of capturing whales. — *adj. Slang* Huge; whopping.

whaling station A place on shore to which whales are taken to be flensed and the oil tried out.

wham (hwam) *n.* A hard, solid blow or impact; also, the loud sound made by such a blow or impact. — *v.* **whammed, wham·ming** *v.t.* **1.** To hit or strike with a loud sound. — *v.i.* **2.** To strike, explode, etc., with a loud sound. [Imit.]

wham·my (hwam′ē) *n. pl.* **·mies** *U.S. Slang* A jinx; hex: to put the *whammy* on someone. [< *wham*, informal interjection imit. of the sound of a hard blow]

whang[1] (hwang) *Informal v.t. & v.i.* To beat or sound with a resounding noise. — *n.* A beating or banging; heavy blow; whack. [Imit.]

whang[2] (hwang) *n.* **1.** A buckskin thong or one made of a deer sinew. **2.** *Scot.* A big slice, as of bread or cheese; a chunk. — *v.t.* **1.** To beat as with a thong; lash. **2.** To beat or strike violently. **3.** *Scot. & Dial.* To fling; throw violently; hurl. **4.** *Scot.* To slice, usually in large pieces. [Var. of OE *thwang* thong]

whang·ee (hwang-ē′) *n.* **1.** Any of a genus (*Phyllostachys*) of tall woody Asian grasses related to the bamboo. **2.** A cane or stick made of the stalk of one of these plants. [< Chinese *huang* bamboo sprout]

whap (hwap), **whap·per** (hwap′ər), etc. See WHOP, etc.

wharf (hwôrf) *n. pl.* **wharves** (hwôrvz) or **wharfs 1.** A structure of masonry or timber erected on the shore of a harbor, river, etc., alongside which vessels may lie to load or unload cargo, passengers, etc.; also, any landing place for vessels, as a pier or quay. **2.** *Obs.* A river bank; also, the seashore. *Abbr.* whf. — *v.t.* **1.** To moor to a wharf. **2.** To provide or protect with a wharf or wharves. **3.** To deposit or store on a wharf. [OE *hwearf*]

— Syn. (noun) **1.** *Wharf, pier, quay, dock,* and *float* denote landing places for vessels. A *wharf* is usually a platform supported by wooden piles. A *pier* usually has a masonry foundation and projects into the water at right angles to the bank. A *quay* extends parallel to the bank, and sometimes is no more than a reinforcement of the bank with wattles or stones. A *dock* was originally the water between two *piers*, in which a vessel floated; by extension, any *pier* or *wharf* has come to be called a *dock*. A floating platform anchored in the water, at which small boats may land, is called a *float*.

wharf·age (hwôr′fij) *n.* **1.** The use of wharves for unloading ships, storing goods, etc. **2.** Charge for the use of a wharf. **3.** Wharves collectively.

wharf·in·ger (hwôr′fin·jər) *n.* One who keeps a wharf for landing goods and collects wharfage fees. [Earlier *wharfager* + intrusive *n*]

wharf rat 1. A brown rat that inhabits wharves. **2.** *U.S. Slang* One who loiters about wharves.

wharf·side (hwôrf′sīd′) *n.* The space on or at the side of a wharf. — *adj.* On or at the side of a wharf.

Whar·ton (hwôr′tən), **Edith Newbold**, 1862–1937, *née* Jones, U.S. novelist and essayist.

wharve (hwôrv) In spinning, a round piece on a spindle, serving as a pulley: also spelled *wherve*. [OE *hweorfa*]

what (hwot, hwut) *pron.* **1.** Which specific thing or things, action, etc.: *What* does he do? I don't know *what* to do. **2.** That which: He knew *what* he wanted; *What* followed occupied little time. **3.** How much: *What* did it cost? **4.** Anything that; whatever: Wear *what* you choose. **5.** *Dial.* or *Illit.* That or which: a simple relative: a donkey *what* wouldn't go. **— and what not** And other things that need not be mentioned in addition. **— what have you** What need not be mentioned in addition: and so forth. **— what if** What would happen if. **— what's what** *Informal* The actual situation or state of affairs. **— what with** As a result of taking into consideration: *What with* rain and the bitter cold weather, it's a good night to stay at home. — *adj.* **1.** In interrogative construction: **a** Asking for information that will specify the person or thing qualified by it: which: Of *what* person do you speak? **b** How much; *What* money has he? **2.** How surprising, ridiculous, great, etc.: *What* genius! **3.** Whatever: *What* money he had left was soon spent. — *adv.* **1.** In what respect; to what extent: *What* are you

profited? **2.** For what reason; why: with *for*: *What* for? *What* are you saying that for? **3.** *Obs.* In what manner; how. — *conj. Informal* That: used only in negative expressions: I do not doubt but *what* he will come. — *interj.* An exclamation of surprise, disbelief, etc. [OE *hwæt*, neut. of *hwā* who]

what·ev·er (hwot′ev′ər, hwut′-) *pron.* **1.** As a compound relative, the whole that; anything that; no matter what: often added for emphasis to a negative assertion: *whatever* makes life dear; I do not want anything *whatever*. **2.** *Informal* What: usually interrogative: *Whatever* is the matter? — *adj.* **1.** Any . . . that; all . . . that: *Whatever* games I play, I lose. **2.** Of any type, character, or kind: no person *whatever*. Also *Poetic* **what·e′er′** (-âr′).

what·not (hwot′not′, hwut′-) *n.* An ornamental set of shelves for holding bric-à-brac, etc.

what·so·ev·er (hwot′sō·ev′ər, hwut′-) *adj. & pron.* Whatever: a more formal usage. Also *Poetic* **what′so·e′er′** (-âr′).

whaup (hwäp, hwôp) *n. Scot. & Brit. Dial.* A bird, the curlew. [Imit. Cf. OE *huilpe.*]

wheal (hwēl) *n.* A welt (def. 4). [Alter. of WALE[1]]

wheat (hwēt) *n.* **1.** The grain of a cereal grass (genus *Triticum*), especially a species (*T. aestivium*) widely cultivated and providing a flour used for bread, pastries, etc. **2.** The plant producing this grain, bearing at its summit a dense spike called the ear or head, sometimes with awns (**bearded wheat**) and sometimes without awns (**beardless** or **bald wheat**). **3.** A field of wheat; crop of wheat. [OE *hwǣte*]

wheat·ear (hwēt′ir) *n.* A thrushlike bird (*Oenanthe oenanthe*) of the northern hemisphere, related to the chats, gray above and white below, with the wings and tip of the tail black. [Earlier *wheatears* < WHITE + *ers, eeres* rump]

wheat·en (hwēt′n) *adj.* Belonging to or made of wheat.

Whea·ton (hwē′tən) An unincorporated place in west central Maryland; pop. 66,247.

Wheat·stone (hwēt′stōn), **Sir Charles**, 1802–75, English physicist and inventor.

Wheat·stone bridge (hwēt′stōn) *Electr.* An instrument for the measurement of differential resistance in an electric circuit. Also **Wheatstone's bridge.** [after Sir Charles *Wheatstone*]

wheat·worm (hwēt′wûrm′) *n.* A threadworm (*Tylenchus tritici*) destructive of wheat. Also **wheat eelworm.**

whee·dle (hwēd′l) *v.* **·dled, ·dling** *v.t.* **1.** To persuade or try to persuade by flattery, cajolery, etc.; coax. **2.** To obtain by cajoling or coaxing. — *v.i.* **3.** To use flattery or cajolery. [? OE *wǣdlian* to beg, be poor < *wǣdl* poverty] — **whee′dler** *n.* — **whee′dling·ly** *adv.*

wheel (hwēl) *n.* **1.** A circular rim and hub connected by spokes or a disk, capable of rotating on a central axis, as in vehicles and machines. **2.** An instrument or device having a wheel or wheels as its distinguishing characteristic, as a steering wheel, water wheel, spinning wheel, etc. **3.** Anything resembling or suggestive of a wheel; any circular object or formation. **4.** *Informal* A bicycle. **5.** An old instrument of torture or execution, consisting of a wheel to which the limbs of the victim were tied and then broken with an iron bar. **6.** The wheel of fortune (which see). **7.** A turning; rotation; revolution. **8.** *pl.* That which imparts or directs motion or controls activity; the moving force: the *wheels* of democracy. **9.** Formerly, the turning of a body of troops or a swinging of a line of ships in which a change of direction is accomplished while the different units keep in alignment. **10.** A rotating firework, as a catherine wheel. **11.** A refrain of a song. **12.** The rotating disk used in various gambling games, especially in roulette. **— at the wheel 1.** Driving or steering a vehicle, boat, etc. **2.** In control; in charge. **wheels within wheels** An intricate series of motives or influences, acting and reacting on one another. — *v.t.* **1.** To move or convey on wheels. **2.** To cause to turn on or as on an axis; pivot or revolve. **3.** To perform with a circular movement. **4.** To provide with a wheel or wheels. — *v.i.* **5.** To turn on or as on an axis; pivot; rotate or revolve. **6.** To take a new direction or course of action; change attitudes or

WHEAT
a Bearded.
b Beardless.
c,d Grain.

WHEATSTONE BRIDGE
a Galvanometer. *b* Battery. *c,d* Bridge. *R*[1] Unknown resistance. *R*[2] Known resistance. *R*[3],*R*[4] Variable resistances. When the galvanometer shows no current
$R^1 : R^2 = R^3 : R^4.$

opinions, etc.: often with *about*. **7.** To move in a circular or spiral course. **8.** To roll or move on wheels. — **to wheel and deal** *U.S. Slang* To act freely or independently, without restrictions, as in business or social affairs. [OE *hwēol*]

wheel and axle A simple machine for lifting heavy weights by applying power to a rope around the circumference of a wheel that turns an axle from which the weight is suspended on another rope, the mechanical advantage depending on the ratio of the diameters of the wheel and axle.

wheel animalcule A rotifer.

wheel·bar·row (hwĕl′băr′ō) *n.* A boxlike vehicle ordinarily with one wheel and two handles, for moving small loads. — *v.t.* To convey in a wheelbarrow.

wheel·base (hwĕl′bās′) *n.* The distance from the center of a back hub to the center of the front hub on the same side, as in an automobile.

wheel bug A large hemipterous insect (*Arilus cristatus*) of the southern United States that preys upon caterpillars and other soft-bodied insects: so called from a semicircular crest on the thorax.

wheel·chair (hwĕl′chār′) *n.* A mobile chair mounted between large wheels, for the use of invalids. Also **wheel chair.**

wheeled (hwĕld) *adj.* **1.** Having wheels; furnished with a wheel or wheels: often used in combination: a *two-wheeled* cart. **2.** Effected or borne by wheels: *wheeled* transportation.

wheel·er (hwē′lər) *n.* **1.** One who wheels. **2.** A wheel horse or other draft animal working next to the wheel. **3.** Something furnished with a wheel or wheels: a *side-wheeler*.

Wheel·er (hwē′lər), **Joseph,** 1836–1906, Confederate general in the Civil War and, later, U.S. general in the Spanish-American War.

wheel·er-deal·er (hwē′lər·dē′lər) *n. U.S. Slang* One who wheels and deals; a shrewd, quick-witted person.

wheel horse **1.** A horse harnessed to the pole or shafts when there is a leader or leaders in front. **2.** One who does the heaviest work or assumes the greatest responsibility.

wheel·house (hwĕl′hous′) *n.* A pilothouse (which see).

Wheel·ing (hwē′ling) A port city in NW West Virginia, on the Ohio River; pop. 48,188.

wheel lock An old form of lock for small arms, in which a small steel wheel, actuated by a spring and released by a trigger, produced sparks by rotating against a flint.

wheel·man (hwĕl′mən) *n. pl.* **·men** (-mən) **1.** Helmsman. **2.** A bicyclist. Also **wheels·man** (hwĕlz′-).

Whee·lock (hwē′lŏk), **Eleazar,** 1711–79, U.S. clergyman and educator.

wheel of fortune The wheel that Fortuna, goddess of chance, is represented as turning in order to bring about changes in human destiny, and that symbolizes the uncertainty of fate.

wheel·work (hwĕl′wûrk′) *n. Mech.* The gearing and arrangement of wheels in a machine or mechanical device.

wheel·wright (hwĕl′rīt′) *n.* A man whose business is making or repairing wheels.

wheen (hwēn) *n. Scot. & Dial.* A few; also, an indefinite quantity. [OE *hwēne*]

whee·ple (hwē′pəl) *Scot. v.i.* **·pled, ·pling** To whistle, as a curlew or plover. — *n.* The whistle of a curlew or plover. Also **weep.**

wheeze (hwēz) *v.t. & v.i.* **wheezed, wheez·ing** To breathe or utter with a husky, whistling sound. — *n.* **1.** A wheezing sound. **2.** A loud whisper. **3.** *Informal* A popular tale, saying, or trick, especially a trite one. — **Syn.** See JEST. [Prob. < ON *hvæsa* hiss] — **wheez′er** *n.* — **wheez′ing·ly** *adv.*

wheez·y (hwē′zē) *adj.* **wheez·i·er, wheez·i·est** Affected with or characterized by wheezing. — **wheez′i·ly** *adv.* — **wheez′i·ness** *n.*

whelk[1] (hwelk) *n.* Any of various large marine mollusks (family *Buccinidae*), having whorled shells, that burrow in sand and prey on clams, etc., especially the common whelk (*Buccinum undatum*), much eaten in Europe. [OE *weoloc*]

whelk[2] (hwelk) *n.* A swelling, protuberance, or pustule. [OE *hwylca* pustule < *hwelian* to suppurate]

whelk·y[1] (hwel′kē) *adj.* **whelk·i·er, whelk·i·est** **1.** Protuberant; rounded. **2.** Shelly. [< WHELK[1]]

whelk·y[2] (hwel′kē) *adj.* **whelk·i·er, whelk·i·est** Marked with pustules or whelks. [< WHELK[2]]

whelm (hwelm) *v.t.* **1.** To cover with water or other fluid; submerge; engulf. **2.** To overpower; overwhelm. — *v.i.* **3.** To roll with engulfing force. [Prob. blend of OE *helmian* to cover and *gehwielfan* to bend over]

whelp (hwelp) *n.* **1.** One of the young of a dog, wolf, lion, or other beast. **2.** A dog. **3.** A young fellow: a contemptuous term. **4.** *Mech.* **a** One of a series of longitudinal ridges on a windlass or capstan. For illustration see CAPSTAN. **b** One of the teeth of a sprocket wheel. — *v.t. & v.i.* To give birth (to): said of dogs, lions, etc. [OE *hwelp*]

when (hwen) *adv.* **1.** At what or which time: *When* did you arrive? I know *when* he arrived. **2.** At which: the time *when* we went on a picnic. — *conj.* **1.** At what or which time: They watched until midnight, *when* they fell asleep. **2.** As soon as: He laughed *when* he heard it. **3.** Although: He walks *when* he might ride. **4.** At the time that; while:

when we were young. **5.** If; considering that: How can I buy it *when* I have no money? **6.** After which: We had just awakened *when* you called. **7.** Whenever: The children play inside *when* it rains. — *pron.* What or which time: since *when*; until *when*. — *n.* The time; date. [OE *hwanne, hwenne*]

when·as (hwen′az′) *conj. Obs.* **1.** Whereas; while. **2.** When. Also **when that.**

whence (hwens) *Archaic adv.* From what place or source; of what origin: *Whence* and what are you? — *conj.* **1.** From what or which place, source, or cause; from which: the place *whence* these sounds arise. **2.** To the place from which; where: Return *whence* you came. **3.** For which reason; wherefore. [ME *whannes, whennes,* adverbial genitive of *whanne,* OE *hwanne* when]

whence·so·ev·er (hwens′sō·ev′ər) *Archaic adv. & conj.* From whatever place, cause, or source.

when·e'er (hwen′âr′) *adv. & conj. Poetic* Whenever.

when·ev·er (hwen·ev′ər) *adv. & conj.* At whatever time.

when·so·ev·er (hwen′sō·ev′ər) *Archaic adv. & conj.* At what time soever; whenever.

where (hwâr) *adv.* **1.** At or in what place, relation, respect, or situation: *Where* is my book? **2.** To what place or end: *Where* are you going? **3.** From what place, source, or cause: *Where* did you get that hat? **4.** At, in, or to which: *where* men gather. — *conj.* **1.** At which place: Let us go home *where* we can relax. **2.** To, at, or in the place to which or in which: Let's go *where* they went. **3.** With the condition that: V = D ÷ T *where* V is velocity, D distance, and T time. — *pron.* **1.** The place in which: The bear passed three yards from *where* we stood. **2.** The point at which: That's *where* you are wrong. — *n.* Place; locality. ◆ *Where* has absorbed completely the sense of *whither* but not of *whence*. We must use a preposition to express the idea of motion from a place: *Where* did you come from? We do not use a preposition to show place at which: *Where* is the dog *at*? is not accepted in standard usage. [OE *hwǣr*]

where·a·bouts (hwâr′ə·bouts′) *adv.* **1.** Near or at what place; about where. **2.** *Obs.* About which; concerning which. Also *Rare* **where′a·bout.** — *n.pl.* (construed as sing.) The place in or near which a person or thing is.

where·as (hwâr·az′) *conj.* **1.** Since the facts are such as they are; seeing that: often used in the preamble of a resolution, etc. **2.** The fact of the matter being that; when in truth: implying opposition to a previous statement. — *n. pl.* **·as·es** A clause or item, as in a legal document, beginning with the word "whereas."

where·at (hwâr·at′) *Archaic or Rare adv.* At what: *Whereat* are you angry? — *conj.* At which; for which reason: He won the race, *whereat* we were delighted.

where·by (hwâr·bī′) *adv.* **1.** By means of which; through which: the gate *whereby* he entered. **2.** By what; how.

wher·e'er (hwâr·âr′) *adv. Poetic* Wherever.

where·fore (hwâr′fôr′, -fōr′) *adv. Archaic* For what reason; what for; why: *Wherefore* do you doubt me? — *conj. Archaic* For which reason; therefore. — *n.* A reason; explanation: the whys and *wherefores* of the verdict.

where·from (hwâr′frum′, -from′) *Archaic adv.* From which; whence.

where·in (hwâr·in′) *adv.* **1.** In what; in what particular or regard: *Wherein* is the error? **2.** In which thing, place, circumstance, etc.: a marriage *wherein* there is discord.

where·in·to (hwâr′in·tōō′) *adv.* Into what or which.

where·of (hwâr·uv′, -ov′) *Archaic adv.* **1.** Of or from what: *Whereof* did you partake? **2.** Of which or whom: the household *whereof* he is the head.

where·on (hwâr·on′, -ôn′) *Archaic adv.* On what or on which.

where·so·ev·er (hwâr′sō·ev′ər) *Archaic adv. & conj.* In or to whatever place; wherever.

where·through (hwâr·thrōō′) *Archaic adv.* Through which.

where·to (hwâr·tōō′) *Archaic adv.* To what place or end: *Whereto* serves avarice? — *conj.* To which or to whom: the grave *whereto* we haste. Also *Archaic* **where′un·to′.**

where·up·on (hwâr′ə·pon′, -ə·pôn′) *adv. Archaic* Upon what; whereon. — *conj.* Upon which or whom; in consequence of which; after which: *whereupon* they took in sail.

wher·ev·er (hwâr·ev′ər) *adv. & conj.* In, at, or to whatever place; wheresoever.

where·with (hwâr′with′, -with′) *Archaic adv.* Interrogatively, with what: *Wherewith* shall I do it? — *conj.* With which; by means of which: the food *wherewith* we abated hunger. — *pron.* That with or by which: with the infinitive: I have not *wherewith* to do it. — *n.* Wherewithal.

where·with·al (*n.* hwâr′with·ôl′; *adv. & pron.* hwâr′with·ôl′) *n.* The necessary means or resources; especially, the necessary money: with the definite article. — *adv. & pron. Obs.* Wherewith.

wher·ry (hwer′ē) *n. pl.* **·ries 1.** A light, fast rowboat used on inland waters. **2.** *Brit.* A decked fishing vessel with two sails. **3.** An open rowboat for racing or exercise, built for one person. **4.** *Brit.* A very broad, light barge. — *v.t. & v.i.* **·ried, ·ry·ing** To transport in or use a wherry. [Origin unknown]

wherve (hwûrv) *n.* In spinning, a wharve.

whet (hwet) *v.t.* **whet·ted, whet·ting 1.** To sharpen, as a knife, by friction. **2.** To make more keen or eager; excite; stimulate, as the appetite. — *n.* **1.** The act of whetting. **2.** Something that whets. [OE *hwettan*] — **whet′ter** *n.*

wheth·er (hweth′ər) *conj.* **1.** If it be the case that: used to introduce an indirect question, often with the negative being implied: Tell me *whether* you are considering our plan. **2.** In case; in either case when or if: as the first alternative, followed by a correlative *or*, or *or whether*: *Whether* it rains or (*whether* it) snows, the roads become very slippery. **3.** Either: *Whether* by luck or sheer determination, he will probably succeed. — *pron. Obs.* Which (of two). — **whether or no** Regardless; in any case. [OE *hwæther, hwether*]

whet·stone (hwet′stōn′) *n.* A fine-grained stone for whetting knives, axes, etc. [OE *hwetstān* < *hwettan* to whet + *stān* stone]

whew (hwoo, hwyoo) *interj.* An exclamatory sound, expressive of amazement, dismay, relief, admiration, discomfort, etc. [Imit. of whistling]

Whew·ell (hyoo′əl), **William,** 1794–1866, English scientist and philosopher.

whey (hwā) *n.* A clear, straw-colored liquid that separates from the curd when milk is curdled, as in making cheese. [OE *hwæg, hweg*] — **whey′ey, whey′ish** *adj.*

whey·face (hwā′fās′) *n.* A pale, sallow face; also, a person having such a face. — **whey′faced′** *adj.*

whf. Wharf.

which (hwich) *pron. & adj.* **1.** What particular person or thing or collection of persons or things of a certain class: *Which* (or *which* apples) do you want? We don't know *which* (or *which* story) to believe. **2.** The thing designated; it: a relative pronoun whose antecedents refer to animals or objects; that: the story *which* we preferred. Formerly, it was used for persons also: Our Father *which* in heaven. ◆ *Which* sometimes has an entire clause or sentence as its antecedent: He raised his hand, *which* surprised me. See also usage note under WHO. [OE *hwilc, hwele*]

which·ev·er (hwich′ev′ər) *pron.* One or another (of two or of several). — *adj.* No matter which; either or any. Also **which′so·ev′er.**

which see A phrase used to indicate a cross-reference. In this dictionary, for example, **sour gum** The black gum (which see). refers the reader to the entry *black gum*.

whid·ah bird (hwid′ə) An African weaverbird (subfamily *Viduinae*), the male of which has the tail greatly lengthened in the breeding season: also called *widow bird*. Also **whid′ah, whidah finch:** also *whydah*. [Alter. of *widow bird*; infl. in form by *Whidah*, former name of Ouidah, a seaport in Dahomey, where the bird is found]

whiff (hwif) *n.* **1.** Any sudden or slight gust or puff of air. **2.** A gust or puff of odor: a *whiff* of onions. **3.** A single expulsion or inhalation of breath or smoke from the mouth; puff. — *v.t.* **1.** To drive or blow with a whiff or puff. **2.** To exhale or inhale in whiffs. **3.** To smell or sniff. **4.** To smoke, as a pipe. — *v.i.* **5.** To blow or move in whiffs or puffs. **6.** To exhale or inhale whiffs. [Partly alter. of ME *weffe* an offensive odor; prob. ult. imit.] — **whiff′er** *n.*

whif·fet (hwif′it) *n. Informal* **1.** A trifling, useless person; whippersnapper. **2.** A small, snappish dog. **3.** A little whiff. [? Dim. of WHIFF, or alter. of WHIPPET]

whif·fle (hwif′əl) *v.* **·fled, ·fling** *v.i.* **1.** To blow with puffs or gusts; shift about, as the wind. **2.** To vacillate; veer. — *v.t.* **3.** To blow or dissipate with or as with a puff. [Freq. of WHIFF]

whif·fler (hwif′lər) *n.* One who or that which whiffles. —
whif′fler·y *n.*

whif·fle·tree (hwif′əl·trē′) *n.* A horizontal crossbar to which the ends of the traces of a harness are attached: also called *singletree, swingletree, whippletree.* [Var. of WHIPPLETREE]

WHIFFLETREE

a Whiffletree.
b Traces.
c Doubletree.
d Plow beam.

Whig (hwig) *n.* **1.** An American colonist who supported the Revolutionary War in the 18th century in opposition to the Tories. **2.** A member of an American political party (1834–1855) formed in opposition to the Democratic Party, and in 1856 succeeded by the Republican Party. **3.** In England, a member of a more or less liberal political party in the 18th and 19th centuries, opposed to the Tories and later known as the Liberal Party. — *adj.* Consisting of or supported by Whigs. [< ? *Whiggamore* < dial. E (Scottish) *whiggamaire* < *Whig*, a cry to urge on a horse + *mere* horse] — **Whig′gish** *adj.* — **Whig′gish·ly** *adv.* — **Whig′gish·ness** *n.*

Whig·ger·y (hwig′ər·ē) *n. pl.* **·ger·ies** The doctrines of Whigs. Also **Whig′gism.**

whig·ma·lee·rie (hwig′mə·lir′ē) *n. Scot.* A small or useless ornament; gewgaw; also, a whim. Also **whig′ma·lee′ry, whig′me·lee′rie.**

while (hwil) *n.* **1.** A short time; also, any period of time: Stay and rest for a *while.* **2.** Time or pains expended on a thing; trouble; labor: only in the phrase **worth while** or **worth one's while.** — **between whiles** From time to time. — **the while** At the same time: He went about his work and sang *the while.* — *conj.* **1.** During the time that; as long as. **2.** At the same time that; although: *While* he found fault, he also praised. **3.** Whereas: This man is short, *while* that one is tall. ◆ This sense is widely used and is generally considered standard, although some authorities still disapprove of it. **4.** *Brit. Dial.* Until; till. — *v.t.* **whiled, whil·ing** To cause (time) to pass lightly and pleasantly: usually with *away.* [OE *hwil*]

whiles (hwilz) *Archaic or Dial. adv.* **1.** Occasionally. **2.** In the meantime. — *conj.* While; during the time that.

whi·lom (hwi′ləm) *Archaic adj.* Being once upon a time; former. — *adv.* **1.** Formerly; at one time. **2.** At times. [OE *hwilum* at times, dative pl. of *hwil* a while]

whilst (hwilst) *conj. Chiefly Brit.* While. [ME *whilest* < *whiles*, genitive of WHILE + *-t*]

whim (hwim) *n.* **1.** A sudden or unexpected notion or fanciful idea; caprice. **2.** An old form of hoist, consisting of a vertical drum usually turned by a horse and on which a rope winds, used in mines to pull up ore, etc. [Short for earlier *whim-wham* trifle, ? < Scand. Cf. ON *hvima* to wander with the eyes.]
— **Syn.** **1.** crotchet, quirk, vagary, whimsy. Compare FANCY.

whim·brel (hwim′brəl) *n.* A small European curlew with a white rump, especially *Numenius phaeopus.* [? < obs. *whimp* whimper, prob. imit. of its cry]

whim·per (hwim′pər) *v.i.* **1.** To cry or whine with plaintive broken sounds. — *v.t.* **2.** To utter with a whimper. — *n.* A low, broken, whining cry; whine. [Imit.] — **whim′per·er** *n.* — **whim′per·ing** *n.* — **whim′per·ing·ly** *adv.*

whim·si·cal (hwim′zi·kəl) *adj.* **1.** Having eccentric ideas; capricious. **2.** Oddly constituted; fantastic; quaint. — **whim′si·cal·ly** *adv.* — **whim′si·cal·ness** *n.*

whim·si·cal·i·ty (hwim′zi·kal′ə·tē) *n. pl.* **·ties 1.** The character of being whimsical. **2.** A quaint, fanciful, or odd idea or its expression.

whim·sy (hwim′zē) *n. pl.* **·sies 1.** A whim; caprice; freak. **2.** Quaint, fanciful humor, as in a literary work. Also **whim′sey.** [Prob. akin to WHIM]

whin¹ (hwin) *n.* Furze. [Prob. < Scand. Cf. Dan. & Norw. *hvine*, a kind of grass.]

whin² (hwin) *n.* Whinstone. [< dial. E (Scottish) *quin*; ult. origin uncertain]

whin·chat (hwin′chat) *n.* A small, thrushlike singing bird (*Saxicola rubetra*) of the Old World, rufous below and streaked with brown above. [< WHIN¹ + CHAT¹]

whine (hwin) *v.* **whined, whin·ing** *v.i.* **1.** To utter a low, plaintive sound expressive of grief, distress, or peevishness. **2.** To complain, beg, or plead in a tiresome or childish way. **3.** To make a high-pitched sound suggesting effort: The gears *whined.* — *v.t.* **4.** To utter with a whine. — *n.* The act or sound of whining. [OE *hwinan*] — **whin′er** *n.* — **whin′ing·ly** *adv.* — **whin′y** *adj.*

whin·ny¹ (hwin′ē) *v.* **·nied, ·ny·ing** *v.i.* **1.** To neigh, especially in a low or gentle way. — *v.t.* **2.** To express with a whinny. — *n. pl.* **·nies** A neigh, especially if low and gentle. [< WHINE]

whin·ny² (hwin′ē) *adj.* **·ni·er, ·ni·est** Abounding in whin or furze. [< WHIN¹]

whin·stone (hwin′stōn′) *n.* Any very hard, dark-colored rock, as basalt or chert. [< WHIN² + STONE]

whip (hwip) *v.* **whipped** or **whipt, whip·ping** *v.t.* **1.** To strike with a lash, rod, strap, etc. **2.** To punish by striking thus; flog. **3.** To drive or urge with lashes or blows: with *on, up, off,* etc. **4.** To strike in the manner of a whip: The wind *whipped* the trees. **5.** To attack with scathing criticism; berate; flay. **6.** To beat, as eggs or cream, to a froth. **7.** To seize, move, jerk, throw, etc., with a sudden motion: with *away, in, off, out,* etc. **8.** In fishing, to make repeated casts upon the surface of (a stream, etc.). **9.** To wrap (rope, cable, etc.) with light line so as to prevent chafing or wear; serve. **10.** To wrap or bind about something. **11.** To form, as a flat seam, by laying two selvages of a fabric together and sewing with a loose overcast or overhand stitch. **12.** *U.S. Informal* To defeat; overcome, as in a contest. **13.** *Naut.* To hoist by means of a whip or overhead pulley. — *v.i.* **14.** To go, come, move, or turn suddenly and quickly: with *away, in, off, out,* etc. **15.** To thrash about in a manner suggestive of a whip: pennants *whipping* in the wind. **16.** In fishing, to make repeated casts with rod and line. — **to whip in 1.** To keep from scattering, as hounds in a hunt. **2.** To keep together or united, as a political party. — **to whip up 1.** To excite; arouse. **2.** *Informal* To prepare quickly, as a meal. — *n.* **1.** An instrument consisting of a lash attached to a handle, used for driving draft animals or for administering punishment. **2.** One who handles a whip expertly, as a driver. **3.** A stroke, blow, or lashing motion with, or as with, a whip. **4.** In politics: **a** A member of a legislative body, as Congress or Parliament, appointed unofficially to enforce the discipline and look after the interests of his party: also called *party whip.* **b** A call made upon members of a legislature by such a person to bring or keep them in their places at a given time, as for a vote. **5.** *Mech.* A simple form of hoisting apparatus, consisting of a rope passing over an elevated single pulley, used for lifting light objects. **6.** A huntsman who has charge of the hounds; a whipper-in. **7.** A dish or dessert containing cream or eggs and usually fruit, whipped to a froth: prune *whip.* **8.** Flexibility in the shaft of a golf club. **9.** An arm of a windmill. **10.** *Obs.* A swift attack or blow. [ME *wippen, hwippen.* Cf. MDu. *wippen* to swing, leap, dance.] — **whip′per** *n.*

whip·cord (hwip′kôrd′) *n.* **1.** A strong, hard-twisted, sometimes braided hempen cord, used in making whiplashes. **2.** A cord of catgut. **3.** A worsted fabric, similar to gabardine, but with a more pronounced diagonal rib, used for riding habits and other outdoor garments.

whip·graft (hwip′graft′, -gräft′) *v.t.* In horticulture, to graft by means of a whip graft.

whip graft In horticulture, a graft made by fitting a tongue cut on the cion to a slit cut slopingly in the stock. Also **whip graftage, whip graft·ing** (graf′ting).

whip hand 1. The hand that wields the whip in riding or driving. **2.** An instrument or means of mastery; advantage.

whip·lash (hwip′lash′) *n.* The lash of a whip.

whiplash injury An injury to the upper spine or base of the brain caused by a sudden jolting of the neck, as in an automobile collision.

whip·per-in (hwip′ər·in′) *n.* *pl.* **whip·pers-in 1.** In hunting, one employed to assist the huntsman and to enforce obedience among the hounds. **2.** A political whip.

whip·per·snap·per (hwip′ər·snap′ər) *n.* A pretentious but insignificant person, especially a young one. [? Extension of *whipsnapper* a cracker of whips]

whip·pet (hwip′it) *n.* **1.** A small, swift breed of dog, probably a cross between a greyhound and a terrier, used especially in racing and coursing. **2.** A small, light, speedy tank used in World War I: also **whippet tank.** [Dim. of WHIP; so called with ref. to its rapid movement]

WHIPPET
(19 to 22 inches high at shoulder)

whip·ping (hwip′ing) *n.* **1.** The act of one who or that which whips; especially, a flogging. **2.** Cord or other material used to whip or lash parts together.

whipping boy 1. Anyone who receives punishment deserved by another; scapegoat. **2.** Formerly, a boy brought up as companion to a prince or other noble youth, and punished in his stead for all misdeeds.

whipping post The post to which those sentenced to flogging are secured.

Whip·ple (hwip′əl), **George Hoyt,** 1878–1976, U.S. pathologist.

whip·ple·tree (hwip′əl·trē′) *n.* A whiffletree (which see). [Prob. < WHIP]

whip·poor·will (hwip′ər·wil) *n.* A small nocturnal bird (*Caprimulgus vociferus*), allied to the goatsuckers, common in the eastern United States. [Imit. of its reiterated cry]

whip·saw (hwip′sô′) *n.* A thin, narrow, tapering pit saw about six feet long, mounted in a wooden frame. — *v.t.* **·sawed, ·sawed** or **·sawn, ·saw·ing 1.** To saw with a whipsaw. **2.** To best (an opponent) in spite of all his efforts.

whip scorpion Any of various scorpionlike arachnids (family *Thelyphonidae*) having an abdomen terminating in a slender appendage like a whiplash, and lacking a sting.

whip snake Any of various long, slender snakes, especially several species of Asia and South America that live in trees.

whip·stall (hwip′stôl′) *Aeron. n.* A type of stall in which a too sharply climbing airplane whips around and drops swiftly, nose down. — *v.i.* To go into a whipstall.

whip·stitch (hwip′stich′) *v.t.* To sew or gather with overcast stitches, as the turned edge of a ruffle. — *n.* A stitch made in this way.

whip·stock (hwip′stok′) *n.* The handle of a whip.

whipt (hwipt) Alternative past tense and past participle of WHIP.

whip·worm (hwip′wûrm′) *n.* A parasitic nematode worm (*Trichuris trichiura*), having a long whiplike body with the posterior part thickened.

whir (hwûr) *v.t. & v.i.* **whirred, whir·ring** To fly, move, or whirl with a buzzing sound. — *n.* **1.** A whizzing, swishing sound, as that caused by the sudden rising of birds. **2.** Confusion; bustle. Also *Brit.* **whirr.** [Prob. < Scand. Cf. Dan. *hvire.* Akin to WHIRL.]

whirl (hwûrl) *v.i.* **1.** To turn or revolve rapidly, as about a center. **2.** To turn away or aside quickly. **3.** To move or go swiftly. **4.** To have a sensation of spinning: My head *whirls.* — *v.t.* **5.** To cause to turn or revolve rapidly. **6.** To carry or bear along with a revolving motion: The wind

whirled the dust into the air. **7.** *Obs.* To hurl. — *n.* **1.** A swift rotating or revolving motion. **2.** Something whirling, as a cloud of dust. **3.** A state of confusion; turmoil. **4.** A rapid succession of events, social activities, etc. **5.** *Informal* A brief drive or trip. **6.** *Informal* An attempt or try. [Prob. < ON *hvirfla* to revolve. Akin to WARBLE[1].] — **whirl′er** *n.*

whirl·a·bout (hwûrl′ə·bout′) *n.* Anything that turns swiftly around or about; a whirligig.

whirl·i·gig (hwûr′li·gig′) *n.* **1.** Any toy or small device that revolves rapidly on an axis. **2.** A merry-go-round. **3.** Anything that seems to perform quick revolutions or moves in a cycle: the *whirligig* of time. **4.** A whirling motion. [< *whirly* (< WHIRL) + obs. *gig,* a whirling toy]

whirligig beetle Any of a family (*Gyrinidae*) of water beetles that move in swift circles over smooth water.

whirl·pool (hwûrl′pōōl′) *n.* **1.** A vortex where water moves with a whirling motion, as from the meeting of two currents. **2.** Anything resembling the motion of a whirlpool.

whirl·wind (hwûrl′wind′) *n.* **1.** A funnel-shaped column of air, with a rapid, upward spiral motion around a vertical or inclined axis and moving forward on the surface of the land or sea. **2.** Anything resembling a whirlwind, as rotary motion or violent activity. — *adj.* Extremely swift or impetuous: a *whirlwind* courtship.

— **Syn.** (noun) **1.** *Whirlwind, tornado, twister, cyclone, anticyclone, hurricane,* and *typhoon* denote winds that whirl helically around a central axis. Though *whirlwind* is the general name, this word is chiefly used as a synonym for *tornado,* an extremely violent vortex of small diameter. *Twister* is the popular name for a tornado in the central plains of the United States. A *cyclone* is a vortex usually hundreds of miles in diameter. In the northern hemisphere, the wind of a cyclone spirals counterclockwise around an area of low barometric pressure; in an *anticyclone,* it spirals clockwise around an area of high barometric pressure. A *cyclone* that originates over tropical seas deposits driving rain as it advances; such a *cyclone* in the West Indies is called a *hurricane,* and in the western Pacific, a *typhoon.*

whirl·y·bird (hwûr′lē·bûrd′) *n.* *Informal* A helicopter. [< *whirly* (< WHIRL) + BIRD]

whir·ry (hwûr′ē) *v.t. & v.i.* **·ried, ·ry·ing** *Scot.* To hurry.

whish (hwish) *v.i.* To move with a swishing, whistling sound. — *n.* A swishing sound. [Imit.]

whisht (hwisht, hwist, wisht; *Scot.* hwusht) *Scot. v.t.* **1.** To hush. — *v.i.* **2.** To be silent. — *n.* The slightest sound; a whisper. — *interj.* Hush! silence! [Prob. imit.]

whisk (hwisk) *v.t.* **1.** To bear along or sweep with light movements, as of a small broom or a fan: often with *away* or *off:* to *whisk* flies away. **2.** To cause to move with a quick sweeping motion. **3.** *Chiefly Brit.* To beat or mix with a quick movement, as eggs, cream, etc. — *v.i.* **4.** To move quickly and lightly. — *n.* **1.** A light stroke; a sudden, sweeping movement. **2.** A little broom or brush. **3.** A little bunch, as of straw, feathers, etc.; wisp. **4.** *Chiefly Brit.* A small culinary instrument for rapidly whipping eggs, cream, etc., to a froth. [Prob. < Scand. Cf. Dan. *viske* to wipe, rub.]

whisk·broom (hwisk′brōōm′, -brōōm′) *n.* A small, short-handled broom for brushing clothing, etc.

whisk·er (hwis′kər) *n.* **1.** *pl.* The hair that grows on the sides of a man's face, as distinguished from that on his lips, chin, and throat; loosely, the beard or any part of the beard. **2.** *pl. Informal* The mustache. **3.** A hair from the whiskers or beard. **4.** One of the long, bristly hairs on the sides of the mouth of some animals, as cats and rodents; a vibrissa. **5.** One who or that which whisks. **6.** One of two small projecting spars or booms on the side of a bowsprit, to extend the jib or flying-jib guys: also **whisker boom.** [< WHISK + -ER[1]] — **whisk′ered, whisk′er·y** *adj.*

whisk grass Zacatón.

whis·key (hwis′kē) *n.* *pl.* **·keys 1.** An alcoholic liquor obtained by the distillation of certain fermented grains, as rye, barley, corn, malt, etc., and containing from about 40 to 50 percent of alcohol by volume. **2.** A drink or portion of whiskey. — *adj.* Pertaining to or made of whiskey. Also **whis′ky.** [Short for *usquebaugh* < Irish *uisgebeatha,* lit., water of life < *uisge* water + *beatha* life]

whis·key sour An alcoholic drink, made with whiskey, lemon juice, and sugar.

whis·ky-jack (hwis′kē·jak′) *n. Canadian* The Canada jay. [Alter. of earlier *whisky-john,* alter. of Algonquian (Cree) *wiskatjan*]

whis·per (hwis′pər) *n.* **1.** A low, soft, breathy voice. **2.** A low, rustling sound, as of waves or leaves. **3.** *Phonet.* The sound produced by the passage of breath through the partially closed glottis. Compare VOICE. **4.** A whispered utterance; secret communication; hint: insinuation. — *v.i.* **1.** To speak in a whisper. **2.** To talk cautiously or furtively; plot or gossip. **3.** To make a low, rustling sound, as leaves. — *v.t.* **4.** To utter in a whisper. **5.** To speak to in a whisper. [OE *hwisprian*] — **whis′per·er** *n.*

whis·per·ing (hwis′pər·ing) *n.* **1.** The act of one who whispers. **2.** That which is whispered. — *adj.* That whispers or makes a sound like a whisper: also **whis′per·y.** — **whis′per·ing·ly** *adv.*

whispering campaign A deliberate spreading of rumors,

injurious gossip, etc., by or as by whispering, in order to discredit a person or group.

whist[1] (hwist) *n.* A game of cards, the forerunner of bridge, played by four persons with a full pack of 52 cards, opposite players being partners. [Alter. of earlier *whisk;* ult. origin unknown]

whist[2] (hwist) *interj.* Hush! be still! — *adj.* Silent or quiet; mute. See also WHISHT. [Prob. imit.]

whis·tle (hwis′əl) *v.* **·tled, ·tling** *v.i.* **1.** To make a musical tone, usually shrill, by sending the breath through the teeth or through a small orifice formed by contracting the lips. **2.** To emit a sharp, shrill cry or sound, as that of a bird. **3.** To cause a sharp, shrill sound by swift passage through the air, as wind, a missile, etc. **4.** To blow or sound a whistle. — *v.t.* **5.** To produce (a tune or melody) by whistling. **6.** To call, manage, or direct by whistling: The policeman *whistled* me to stop. **7.** To send or move with a whistling sound. — **to whistle for** To go without; fail to get. — *n.* **1.** A device for producing a shrill tone by forcing a current of air, steam, etc., through a pipe or tube with a narrowed aperture, or against a thin edge. **2.** A clear, shrill sound made by blowing a whistle or whistling with the lips. **3.** Any whistling sound, as of a missile, the wind, etc. **4.** The act of whistling. **5.** A summons or call made by a whistle. **6.** *Slang* The mouth and throat: to wet one's *whistle.* [OE *hwistle* shrill pipe]

whis·tler (hwis′lər) *n.* **1.** One who or that which whistles. **2.** *Canadian* The hoary marmot. See under MARMOT. **3.** Any of various birds, as the goldeneye or the English widgeon: so called from the noise of their wings in flight. **4.** *Physics* A radio signal of very low frequency generated by a stroke of lightning.

Whis·tler (hwis′lər), **James Abbott McNeill**, 1834–1903, U.S. painter and etcher active in England. — **Whis·tle·ri·an** (hwis-lir′ē-ən) *adj.*

whistle stop *U.S. Informal* A small town, where a train stops only on signal. — **whis·tle-stop** (hwis′əl-stop′) *adj.*

whistling buoy See under BUOY.

whistling swan A large swan (*Olor columbianus*) of North America, having black bill and feet.

whit (hwit) *n.* The smallest particle; speck: usually with a negative: not a *whit* abashed. — **Syn.** See PARTICLE. [Var. of WIGHT, as used in phrases *any wight, no wight* < OE *wiht* a certain amount]

Whit·by (hwit′bē) An urban district and port in North Riding, Yorkshire, England, on the North Sea; pop. 11,662 (1961).

white (hwīt) *adj.* **whit·er, whit·est 1.** Having the color produced by reflection of all the rays of the solar spectrum, as from a bed of new-fallen snow: opposed to *black.* **2.** Light or comparatively light in color. **3.** Bloodless; ashen: *white* with rage. **4.** Very fair; blond. **5.** Silvery, hoary, or gray, as with age. **6.** Covered with snow; snowy. **7.** Made of silver; also unburnished, as silverwork. **8.** Habited in white clothing: *white* nuns. **9.** Not intentionally wicked or evil; not malicious or harmful: a *white* lie. **10.** Free from spot or stain; innocent. **11.** Incandescent: *white* heat. **12.** Blank; unmarked by ink: said of a space in an advertisement or the like. **13.** Belonging to a racial group characterized by light-colored skin; especially, Caucasian. **14.** Of, pertaining to, or controlled by white men: the *white* power structure. **15.** *Informal* Fair and honorable; straightforward; honest. **16.** *Rare* Propitious; auspicious. **17.** In certain European countries, constitutional; conservative, as opposed to the radicals or revolutionaries. **18.** Designating any of various wines ranging in color from pale yellow to deep amber. — *n.* **1.** The color seen when light is reflected without sensible absorption of any of the visible rays of the spectrum; the color of new-fallen snow: opposed to *black.* **2.** The state or condition of being white; whiteness. **3.** *Biol.* The white or light-colored part of something, as the albumen of an egg or the white part of the eyeball. **4.** Any white fabric. **5.** *pl.* A white uniform or outfit: a sailor's summer *whites.* **6.** A white paint or pigment: flat *white.* **7.** White wine. **8.** In chess or checkers, the white or light men, or the player who has them. **9.** *pl.* Flour made from the finest and whitest part of the wheat. **10.** In archery, the outermost ring on a target; also, a hit on that ring, scoring one point. **11.** A member of the so-called white race. **12.** In some European countries, a member of a party opposed to the radicals or revolutionaries; a conservative. **13.** *pl. Pathol.* Leukorrhea. **14.** A breed of animal, especially a swine, that is white in color. — *v.t.* **whit·ed, whit·ing 1.** To make white; whiten; bleach. **2.** *Printing* To make or leave blank spaces in, as between lines or about an illustration: often with *out:* to *white* out a column. [OE *hwīt*]

White (hwīt), **Andrew Dickson,** 1832–1918, U.S. educator, historian, and diplomat. — **Byron Raymond,** born 1917, U.S. lawyer; associate justice of the Supreme Court 1962–. — **Gilbert,** 1720–93, English naturalist and antiquary. — **Stanford,** 1853–1906, U.S. architect. — **William,** 1748–

1836, U.S. Episcopal bishop and author. — **William Allen,** 1868–1944, U.S. editor and author.

white admiral See under ADMIRAL.

white alkali 1. The product obtained from soda ash during the manufacture of carbonate of soda, dissolved in water, clarified, and freed from moisture by evaporation. **2.** The white layer of various mineral salts found in some types of alkaline soil.

white ant Loosely, a termite.

white·bait (hwīt′bāt′) *n.* The young of various clupeoid fishes, especially of sprat and herring, netted in great quantities and much esteemed in Europe as a delicacy.

white bear The polar bear.

white·beard (hwīt′bird′) *n.* An old man with a white or gray beard.

white birch 1. Birch (def. 1). **2.** The common European birch (*Betula pendula*), having an ash-colored bark; also, a related Asian species (*B. platyphylla*).

white book In some European countries and in Japan, a formal report, bound in white, issued by a government on some special subject.

white brant The snow goose.

white bryony A species of bryony (*Bryonia alba*) common in Europe.

white·cap (hwīt′kap′) *n.* A wave with a crest of foam.

White·cap (hwīt′kap′) *n.* Formerly, in the United States, one of a lawless, secret organization of men, who, under the pretense of regulating public morals, committed crimes of violence against individuals who incurred their ill will: so named from their white caps or hoods.

white cedar 1. An evergreen tree (*Chamaecyparis thyoides*) of the pine family, growing in moist places along the Atlantic coast: also called *cypress.* **2.** Its soft, easily worked wood. **3.** The arborvitae.

White·chap·el (hwīt′chap·əl) A district in eastern London, England; the old Jewish quarter.

white clover A common variety (*Trifolium repens*) of clover, with white flowers.

white coal Water considered as a source of power.

white-col·lar (hwīt′kol′ər) *adj.* Designating workers, jobs, attitudes, etc., associated with clerical, professional, and other nonmanual occupations: distinguished from *blue-collar.*

white comb *Vet.* A contagious disease of poultry, caused by a fungus (*Lophophyton gallinae*).

white corpuscle See under CORPUSCLE.

white damp Carbon monoxide.

whit·ed sepulcher (hwī′tid) A hypocrite. *Matt.* xxiii 27.

white dwarf *Astron.* A star of low luminosity and moderate mass concentrated in a very small volume, as the companion of Sirius, with a density of one ton per cubic inch.

white elephant 1. A rare, pale gray variety of Asian elephant held sacred by the Burmese and Siamese. **2.** A rare or valuable possession that is too difficult or costly to maintain. **3.** Any possession whose ownership is more of an inconvenience than a pleasure.

white-eye (hwīt′ī′) *n.* Any of numerous small birds named from the circle of white feathers around the eye.

white-faced (hwīt′fāst′) *adj.* **1.** Pallid in countenance; pale. **2.** Having a white mark or spot on the face or front of the head, as a horse. **3.** Having a white facing or exposed surface.

white feather A mark of cowardice. — **to show the white feather** To act as a coward. [from the fact that full-blooded gamecocks are said to have no white feathers]

White·field (hwīt′fēld), **George,** 1714–70, English clergyman and author; one of the founders of Methodism.

white·fish (hwīt′fish′) *n. pl.* **·fish** or **·fish·es 1.** Any of various salmonoid food fishes (genus *Coregonus*) of North America, living mostly in lakes, some species of which are called chubs. **2.** Any of various other fish having a silvery appearance, as the beluga. **3.** A tropical marine food fish (*Caulolatilus princeps*) of California.

white flag 1. A flag of truce. **2.** A white flag or cloth hoisted as a signal of surrender during a battle.

white flax Gold-of-pleasure, a plant.

white-foot·ed mouse (hwīt′foŏt′id) Any of various small, long-tailed, furry mice (genus *Peromyscus*), widely distributed in North America.

White Friar A Carmelite friar: so called from the color of his cloak.

White·fri·ars (hwīt′frī′ərz) See ALSATIA.

white frost Hoarfrost (which see).

white gas A lead-free gasoline, used in portable stoves, etc. Also **white gasoline.**

white gerfalcon The gerfalcon in the phase when its plumage is of a conspicuous, highly prized, white color.

white gold An alloy of gold with a white metal, usually nickel and zinc, sometimes palladium and platinum.

white goods Household linens, such as sheets, towels, tablecloths, etc.

---

white gum An Australian eucalyptus with a white bark.

White·hall (hwīt'hôl) 1. A former royal palace near Westminster Abbey. Also **Whitehall Palace.** 2. A street in Westminster, London, where a number of government offices are located. 3. The British government.

White·head (hwīt'hed), **Alfred North**, 1861–1947, English mathematician and philosopher active in the United States.

white-head·ed (hwīt'hed'id) adj. 1. Having white hair, feathers, etc., on the head; also, very blond; flaxen-haired. 2. Irish Best-loved; favorite.

white heat 1. The temperature at which a body becomes incandescent. 2. A condition of great excitement, intense emotion, etc.

White·horse (hwīt'hôrs) The capital of Yukon Territory, Canada, on the upper Yukon River; pop. 5,031. Also **White Horse.**

white horse A wave crested with foam; whitecap.

white-hot (hwīt'hot') adj. 1. Exhibiting the condition of white heat. 2. Informal Extremely angry.

White House, The 1. The official residence of the President of the United States, at Washington, D.C., a white building in American colonial style: officially called the Executive Mansion. 2. The executive branch of the United States government.

white iron pyrites Marcasite (def. 1).

white lead 1. A heavy, white, poisonous mixture of lead carbonate and hydrated lead oxide, used as a pigment and in some medicinal ointments for burns. 2. Cerussite.

white leather Whiteleather (which see).

white lie See under LIE.

white-liv·ered (hwīt'liv'ərd) adj. 1. Having a pale and unhealthy look. 2. Base; cowardly.

white·ly (hwīt'lē) adv. With a pale appearance.

white man 1. A person belonging to a racial group characterized by light-colored skin: territory settled by white men. 2. A male member of the so-called white race.

white man's burden The alleged duty of the white peoples to spread culture among the so-called backward peoples of the world: phrase originated by Rudyard Kipling.

white maple A maple (Acer saccharinum) of North America, having a whitish bark: also called silver maple.

white matter Anat. The portion of the brain and spinal cord composed mainly of medullated nerve fibers, giving it a white appearance: distinguished from gray matter.

white meat The light-colored meat or flesh of animals, as veal or the breast of turkey.

white metal See under METAL.

White Mountains A range of the Appalachians in north central New Hampshire; highest peak, Mt. Washington, 6,288 ft.

whit·en (hwīt'n) v.t. & v.i. To make or become white; blanch; bleach. — **whit'en·er** n. [< WHIT(E) + -EN¹. Cf. ON hvītna to become white.]

— **Syn.** Whiten, bleach, and blanch mean to make nearly or completely white or colorless. Whiten implies overlay with a white paint or polish, while bleach and blanch refer to removal of color by sunlight, chemical agents, etc. Industrial products are bleached, while foodstuffs are blanched.

white·ness (hwīt'nis) n. 1. The state of being white; freedom from stains or darkness. 2. Pallor from emotion or from illness. 3. Purity; innocence. [OE hwītnes]

White Nile See under NILE.

white noise A sound consisting of an infinite number of components having random phase and uniform amplitude throughout a given range of frequencies.

white oak 1. A North American oak (Quercus alba) of the eastern United States, with long leaves having from five to nine entire, rounded lobes. 2. Any of several related species, as the **swamp white oak** (Q. bicolor), the **Oregon white oak** (Q. garryana), and the roble. 3. The British oak (Q. petraea). 4. The wood of any species of white oak.

WHITE OAK
a Leaves. b Blossom.

white of egg Egg white.

white·out (hwīt'out') n. Meteorol. An atmospheric condition in arctic regions in which a blending of clouds and snow cover produces a uniform milky whiteness characterized by the absence of shadow and the invisibility of all but very dark objects.

white paper A government publication on some subject of less importance than that treated in a white book or a blue book.

White Pass A pass in the Coast Mountains, on the border between SE Alaska and NW British Columbia; elevation 2,888 ft.

white pepper See under PEPPER.

white perch A small food fish (Roccus americanus) related to the sea basses, found in Atlantic coastal waters and sometimes landlocked in streams of the United States.

white pine 1. A pine (Pinus strobus) widely distributed in eastern North America, with soft, bluish green leaves in clusters of five. The cone and tassel of this tree are the State emblem of Maine. 2. The light, soft wood of this tree. 3. Any of several similar species of pine.

white-pine weevil (hwīt'pīn') A weevil (Pissodes strobi) of NE North America that feeds on the leading shoots of white pine and other conifers. For illustration see INSECTS (injurious).

white plague Pathol. Tuberculosis, especially of the lungs.

White Plains A city in SE New York, near New York City; pop. 50,220.

white poplar A large, rapidly growing Old World tree (Populus alba), often planted in the United States for shade or for its ornamental green and silvery white leaves: also called abele, silver poplar.

white potato The common potato.

white race The Caucasoid ethnic division of mankind.

white rainbow Meteorol. A fogbow (which see).

white rat 1. Any albino rat. 2. One of a special breed of albino Norway rats much used in biological and medical experimentation.

White River A river in northern and eastern Arkansas and SW Missouri, flowing 690 miles, generally SE, to the Mississippi.

White Russia See BYELORUSSIAN S.S.R.

White Russian Byelorussian (which see).

white sale A sale of sheets, towels, etc., at reduced prices.

White Sands National Monument A reservation in southern New Mexico; 219 sq. mi.; established 1933.

white sapphire A translucent, colorless corundum.

white sauce A sauce made of butter, flour, milk, etc., used for vegetables, meats, and fish.

White Sea An inlet of the Barents Sea in the NW R.S.F.S.R.; 36,680 sq. mi.

white slave A girl forced into or held in prostitution. — **white-slave** (hwīt'slāv') adj.

White-slave Act The Mann Act (which see).

white slaver One who procures for or engages in white slavery.

white slavery Forced prostitution.

white·smith (hwīt'smith') n. 1. A tinsmith. 2. A finisher, polisher, or galvanizer of iron.

white spruce See under SPRUCE.

white squall Meteorol. A small whirlwind occurring in the tropics, having no accompanying cloud and often making ocean waters turbulent and foamy.

white supremacy The doctrine arising from the belief that the white race is superior to the Negro race and that the latter must therefore be kept in an inferior economic and social position. — **white su·prem·a·cist** (sə·prem'ə·sist) n.

white-tailed deer (hwīt'tāld') A common North American deer (Odocoileus virginianus), having a moderately long tail white on the underside: also called Virginia deer.

white·throat (hwīt'thrōt') n. One of various Old World warblers, especially the **greater whitethroat** (Sylvia communis) with gray head, white throat, and rufous wings.

white-throat·ed sparrow (hwīt'thrō'tid) A common North American sparrow (Zonotrichia albicollis), with a white patch on the throat: also called peabody bird.

white tie 1. A white bow tie, worn with men's formal evening attire. 2. A swallowtail coat and its correct accessories.

white turnip The common turnip.

white vitriol Hydrated zinc sulfate, $ZnSO_4 \cdot 7H_2O$, widely used in medicine as an emetic, astringent, and antiseptic.

white·wash (hwīt'wosh', -wôsh') n. 1. A mixture of slaked lime and water, sometimes with salt, whiting, and glue added, used for whitening walls, etc. 2. A toilet preparation for whitening the skin. 3. Slang A covering up or glossing over of reprehensible actions or inefficiencies, especially of a political figure; also, a suppression of adverse evidence, as in a legal matter. 4. Informal A failure to score in a game. — v.t. 1. To coat with whitewash. 2. Slang To gloss over; hide. 3. Informal In sports, to defeat without allowing the losing side to score. — Syn. See PALLIATE. — **white'wash'er** n.

white water U.S. & Canadian Rapids in a river.

white whale The beluga (def. 1).

white·wing (hwīt'wing') n. A worker who wears a white uniform; especially, a street cleaner.

white-winged dove (hwīt'wingd') A dove (Zenaida asiatica) of the SW United States with a rounded, white-banded tail and a conspicuous white patch on the wings.

white·wood (hwīt'wŏŏd') n. 1. Any of various trees yielding a whitish timber, as the basswood, the tulip tree, the cottonwood, etc. 2. The wood of these trees.

Whi·tey (hwī'tē) n. pl. -teys U.S. Slang 1. The white man, especially when considered as the oppressor or enemy of the Negro. 2. A white man: an offensive term. Also **whi'tey.**

whith·er (hwith'ər) Archaic & Poetic adv. 1. To what or which place? Where? 2. To what point, end, extent, etc.? — conj. To which or what place, point, end, etc. ◆ Whither is now replaced by where. [OE hwider]

whith·er·so·ev·er (hwith'ər·sō·ev'ər) adv. Archaic To whatever place.

whit·ing¹ (hwī'ting) n. A pure white chalk, powdered

and washed, used in making putty and whitewash, as a pigment, and for polishing.

whit·ing[2] (hwī′ting) *n.* **1.** A small European gadoid food fish (*Merlangus merlangus*) without a barbel. **2.** A North American hake (*Merluccius bilinearis*). **3.** Any of several silvery sciaenoid fishes (genus *Menticirrhus*), common on the coast of the southern United States. [< MDu. *wijting* < *wit* white]

whit·ish (hwī′tish) *adj.* Somewhat white or, especially, very light gray. — **whit′ish·ness** *n.*

whit·leath·er (hwit′leth′ər) *n.* Leather tawed with alum to render it pliable: also called *white leather.* [< WHIT(E) + LEATHER]

whit·low (hwit′lō) *n. Pathol.* An inflammatory tumor, especially on the terminal phalanx of a finger, seated between the epidermis and true skin; a felon. [ME *whitflaw*, appar. < WHITE + FLAW[1]]

Whit·man (hwit′mən), **Marcus,** 1802–47, U.S. pioneer, physician, and missionary in Oregon; killed by Indians. — **Walt,** 1819–92, U.S. poet: full name **Walter Whitman.**

Whit·mon·day (hwit′mun′dē, -dā) *n.* The Monday next following Whitsunday, observed in England as a holiday. Also **Whit-Monday, Whit′sun-Mon′day.** [On analogy with WHITSUNDAY]

Whit·ney (hwit′nē), **Eli,** 1765–1825, U.S. inventor and manufacturer; devised the cotton gin. — **Josiah Dwight,** 1819–96, U.S. geologist. — **William Dwight,** 1827–94, U.S. philologist; brother of Josiah Dwight Whitney.

Whit·ney (hwit′nē), **Mount** A peak of the southern Sierra Nevada Range in eastern California; 14,496 ft.; highest point in the conterminous United States.

whit·rack (hwit′rak) *n. Dial. & Scot.* A weasel. [ME *whitratt* < WHITE + RAT]

Whit·sun (hwit′sən) *n.* Whitsunday: frequently used in combination: *Whitsun-week.* [ME *witsonen, whitstone < whitsondei.* See WHITSUNDAY.]

Whit·sun·day (hwit′sun′dē, -dā, hwit′sən-dā′) *n.* Pentecost (def. 1). [OE *Hwita Sunnandæg,* lit., white Sunday; so called from the white robes worn by recently baptized persons on that day]

Whit·sun·tide (hwit′sən-tīd′) *n.* The week that begins with Whitsunday, especially the first three days. Also **Whitsun Tide.**

Whit·ta·ker (hwit′ə-kər), **Charles E(vans),** born 1901, U.S. jurist; associate justice of the U.S. Supreme Court 1957–62.

whit·ter (hwit′ər) *n. Scot.* A copious draft of liquor, etc.

Whit·ti·er (hwit′ē-ər) A city in SW California, near Los Angeles; pop. 72,863.

Whit·ti·er (hwit′ē-ər), **John Greenleaf,** 1807–92, U.S. poet: called the **Quaker Poet.**

Whit·ting·ton (hwit′ing-tən), **Richard,** 1358?–1423, English tradesman and politician; lord mayor of London.

whit·tle (hwit′l) *v.* ·tled, ·tling *v.t.* **1.** To cut or shave bits from (wood, a stick, etc.). **2.** To make or shape by carving or whittling. **3.** To reduce or wear away by or as by paring a little at a time: with *down, off, away,* etc.: to *whittle* down costs. — *v.i.* **4.** To whittle wood, usually as an aimless diversion. — *n. Dial. & Scot.* A knife; especially, any large knife. [Alter. of ME *thwitel* < OE *thwitan* to cut] — **whit′tler** *n.*

whit·tlings (hwit′lingz) *n.pl.* The fine chips and shavings made with a whittle or by a whittler.

whiz (hwiz) *v.* whizzed, whiz·zing *v.i.* **1.** To make a hissing and humming sound while passing through the air. **2.** To move or pass with such a sound. — *v.t.* **3.** To cause to whiz. — *n. pl.* **whiz·zes 1.** A whizzing sound; also, an object moving with such a sound. **2.** *Slang* Any person or thing of extraordinary excellence or ability. Also **whizz.** [Imit.]

whiz·bang (hwiz′bang′) *n. Slang* A high-explosive shell that explodes immediately after the sound of its flight has been heard; also, a firecracker that explodes with a loud noise. Also **whizz′-bang′.**

who (hōō) *pron. possessive case* **whose;** *objective case* **whom 1.** Which or what person or persons: *Who* said that? I know *who* he is. **2.** That; a relative pronoun: used when the antecedent refers to a human being. **3.** He, she, or they that; whoever: *Who* steals my purse steals trash. — **as who should say** As if one should say. [OE *hwā*]

◆ In modern usage, *who* as a relative is applied only to persons, *which* only to animals or to inanimate objects, *that* to persons or things indiscriminately. *Whose* is correctly used as the possessive of *which,* as well as of *who,* especially where the phrase *of which* would seem awkward: the man *whose* house was sold; a peak *whose* (*of which* the) summit seeks the sky. The use of *whom* as an interrogative pronoun in initial position, as in *Whom* did you see?, is supported by some grammarians, but the more natural *Who* did you see? *Who* did you give the book to? are in wider use and are now considered acceptable. However, when used after a verb or preposition, *whom* is still required, as in To *whom*

did you give it? You saw *whom*? See also usage note under THAT (pronoun).

WHO World Health Organization.

whoa (hwō) *interj.* Stop! stand still!: used as a command to a horse or other animal. [Var. of HO]

who·dun·it (hōō-dun′it) *n. Informal* A type of mystery fiction or dramatic production that challenges the reader or spectator to detect the perpetrator of a crime. [< WHO + DONE + IT; presumably coined by Donald Gordon in 1930 in *American News of Books*]

who·ev·er (hōō-ev′ər) *pron.* Any one without exception; any person who.

whole (hōl) *adj.* **1.** Containing all the parts necessary to make up a total; undivided and undiminished; entire; complete. **2.** Having all the essential or original parts unbroken and uninjured; sound; intact. **3.** In or having regained sound health; hale. **4.** Constituting the full extent, amount, quantity, etc.; total; entire. **5.** Having the same parents; full, as opposed to *half*: a *whole* brother. **6.** *Math.* Integral. — **as a whole** Completely; altogether. — **on the whole** Taking everything into consideration. — **out of whole cloth** Fabricated; made up, without foundation in truth or fact. — *n.* **1.** All the parts or elements entering into and making up a thing; totality. **2.** An organization of parts making a unity or system; an organism. [OE *hāl.* Akin to HALE[2].]

whole blood Blood as taken directly from the body, especially that used in transfusions.

whole brother See under BROTHER.

whole gale *Meteorol.* A gale of force 10 on the Beaufort scale.

whole·heart·ed (hōl′här′tid) *adj.* Done or experienced with earnestness, sincerity, etc.; earnest. — **whole′heart′ed·ly** *adv.* — **whole′heart′ed·ness** *n.*

whole hog *Slang* The whole of anything; completeness. — **to go the whole hog** *Slang* To do something thoroughly; become involved without reservation.

whole milk Milk containing all its constituents: distinguished from *skim milk.*

whole·ness (hōl′nis) *n.* Entireness; completeness.

whole note *Music* A note having a time value equal to one half of a breve: also, *Chiefly Brit.,* semibreve. For illustration see NOTE.

whole number *Math.* An integer.

whole·sale (hōl′sāl′) *n.* The selling of goods in large bulk or quantity, especially for resale: distinguished from *retail.* — *adj.* **1.** Pertaining to, involving, or engaged in the sale of goods at wholesale: a *wholesale* druggist. **2.** Made or done on a large scale or indiscriminately: *wholesale* murder. — *adv.* In bulk or quantity; in a wholesale manner. — *v.t. & v.i.* ·**saled,** ·**sal·ing** To sell at wholesale. [ME *holesale < by hole sale* in large quantities] — **whole′sal′er** *n.*

whole sister See under SISTER.

whole·some (hōl′səm) *adj.* **1.** Tending to promote health; salubrious; healthful: *wholesome* air or food. **2.** Favorable to virtue and well-being; salutary; sound; beneficial: *wholesome* entertainment. **3.** Indicative or characteristic of health: *wholesome* red cheeks. **4.** Safe; free from danger or risk: This is not a *wholesome* situation. **5.** *Rare* Healthy. [ME *holsum.* See WHOLE, SOME[1].] — **whole′some·ly** *adv.* — **whole′some·ness** *n.*

whole·souled (hōl′sōld′) *adj.* Feeling or acting with one's whole heart; devoted; generous.

whole tone *Music* A tone (def. 3b).

whole-wheat (hōl′hwēt′) *adj.* Made from wheat grain and bran.

who'll (hōōl) **1.** Who will. **2.** Who shall.

whol·ly (hō′lē, hōl′lē) *adv.* **1.** Completely; totally. **2.** Exclusively; only.

whom (hōōm) *pron.* The objective case of WHO. [OE *hwām,* dative of *hwā* who]

whom·ev·er (hōōm·ev′ər), **whom·so** (hōōm′sō′), **whom·so·ev·er** (hōōm′sō·ev′ər) Objective cases of WHOEVER, WHOSO, etc.

whoop (hōōp, hwōōp, hwŏŏp) *v.i.* **1.** To utter loud cries, as of excitement, rage, or exultation. **2.** To hoot, as an owl. **3.** To make a loud, gasping inspiration, as after a paroxysm of coughing. — *v.t.* **4.** To utter with a whoop or whoops. **5.** To call, urge, chase, etc., with whoops; hoot. — **to whoop up** *Slang* To arouse enthusiasm in or for; ballyhoo. — **to whoop it (or things) up** *Slang* **1.** To make noisy revelry. **2.** To arouse enthusiasm. — *n.* The cry, shout, or sound of one who or that which whoops. — **not worth a whoop** *Informal* Not worth anything. — *interj.* An exclamation of joy, enthusiasm, etc. [ME *whope,* alter. of *hopen, houpen;* prob. ult. imit.]

whoop-de-do (hōōp′də-dōō′, hwōōp′-, hwŏŏp′-) *n. pl.* -**dos** *Slang* **1.** Noisy confusion, as at a social affair. **2.** An elaborately organized display of wealth, power, etc. **3.** Violent and usually public controversy. Also **whoop′-de-doo′.**

whoop·ee (hwŏŏ′pē, hwŏŏp′ē) *interj. & n.* An exclamation of joy, excitement, etc. **— to make whoopee** To have a noisy, festive time. [< WHOOP]

whoop·er (hŏŏ′pər, hwŏŏ′pər, hwŏŏp′r) *n.* **1.** One who or that which whoops. **2.** A large Old World swan (*Cygnus cygnus*): so called from its loud cry.

whoop·ing cough (hŏŏ′ping, hŏŏp′ing) *Pathol.* A contagious respiratory disease of bacterial origin chiefly affecting children, marked in its final stage by recurrent paroxysms of violent coughing: also called *chincough, pertussis.*

whooping crane See under CRANE.

whop (hwop) *Informal n.* A blow or fall, or the resulting noise. **— v. whopped, whop·ping** *v.t.* **1.** To strike or beat. **2.** To defeat convincingly. **— v.i. 3.** To drop or fall suddenly; flop. Also spelled *whap.* [Var. of WAP¹]

whop·per (hwop′ər) *n. Informal* Something large or remarkable; especially, a big falsehood: also spelled *whapper.*

whop·ping (hwop′ing) *adj.* Unusually large; great.

whore (hôr, hōr) *n.* A prostitute. **— v. whored, whor·ing** *v.i.* **1.** To have illicit sexual intercourse, especially with a prostitute. **2.** To be a whore. **— v.t. 3.** *Obs.* To make a whore of; corrupt; debauch. [OE *hōre,* prob. < ON *hōra*]

whore·dom (hôr′dəm, hōr′-) *n. Archaic* **1.** The practice of illicit sexual intercourse; prostitution. **2.** In the Bible, idolatry. [Prob. < ON *hōrdōm*]

whore·house (hôr′hous′, hōr′-) *n.* A house of prostitution.

whore·mas·ter (hôr′mas′tər, -mäs′-, hōr′-) *n. Archaic* **1.** A procurer. **2.** A man who has intercourse with whores. Also **whore·mon·ger** (hôr′mung′gər, -mong′-, hōr′-).

whore·son (hôr′sən, hōr′-) *Obs. n.* **1.** The son of a whore; a bastard. **2.** A vile, detestable person. **— adj.** Mean; vile. [ME *hores son,* trans. of AF *fiz a putain*]

whor·ish (hôr′ish, hōr′ish) *adj.* Characteristic of a whore; lewd. **— whor′ish·ly** *adv.* **— whor′ish·ness** *n.*

whorl (hwûrl, hwôrl) *n.* **1.** The flywheel of a spindle; wherve. **2.** *Bot.* A set of leaves, etc., on the same plane with one another, distributed in a circle; a verticil. **3.** *Zool.* A turn or volution, as of a spiral shell. **4.** Any of the convoluted ridges of a finger-print. [ME *wharwyl, whorwhil,* appar. vars. of WHIRL: infl. in form by WHARVE]

WHORL (def. 2)

whorled (hwûrld, hwôrld) *adj.* Furnished with or arranged in whorls.

whort (hwûrt) *n.* The whortleberry, or its fruit. Also **whor·tle** (hwûr′təl). [OE *horta* whortleberry]

whor·tle·ber·ry (hwûr′təl·ber′ē) *n. pl.* **·ries 1.** A European variety of blueberry (*Vaccinium myrtillus*). **2.** Its blue-black fruit. Also called *bilberry, hurtleberry.* [Dial. var. of HURTLEBERRY]

whose (hōōz) The possessive case of WHO and often of WHICH. ◆ See note under WHO. [ME *hwas, hwos* < OE *hwæs,* altered by analogy with nominative form *hwo*]

whose·so·ev·er (hōōz′sō·ev′ər) Possessive case of WHO-SOEVER.

who·so (hōō′sō) *pron.* Whoever; any person who. [Reduced form of OF *swā hwā swā,* generalized form of *hwā who*]

who·so·ev·er (hōō′sō·ev′ər) *pron.* Any person whatever; who; whoever.

whr, whr., or **w.-hr.** Watt-hour(s).

why (hwī) *adv.* **1.** For what cause, purpose, or reason? wherefore? **2.** The reason or cause for which: I don't know *why* he went. **3.** Because of which; for which: I know no reason *why* he went. **— n. pl. whys 1.** An explanatory cause; reason; cause. **2.** A puzzling problem; riddle; enigma. **— interj.** An introductory expletive, sometimes denoting surprise. ◆ The *why* in the expression *the reason why,* though sometimes condemned as a redundancy, is commonly used in standard written English. [OE *hwȳ, hwī,* instrumental case of *hwæt* what]

whyd·ah (hwid′ə) *n.* The whidah bird.

wi' (wi) *prep. Scot.* With.

w.i. When issued (stocks).

W.I. West Indian; West Indies.

wich (wich) *n.* The wych-elm.

wich-elm (wich′elm′) See WYCH-ELM.

Wich·i·ta (wich′ə·tô) *n. pl.* **·tas** or **·ta** A member of a North American Indian confederacy of Caddoan stock, formerly inhabiting Oklahoma and Texas.

Wich·i·ta (wich′ə·tô) A city in south central Kansas, on the Arkansas River; pop. 276,554.

Wichita Falls A city in northern Texas, on the Wichita River, which flows 250 miles NE to the Red River; pop. 97,564..

wick¹ (wik) *n.* A band of loosely twisted or woven fibers, as in a candle or lamp, acting by capillary attraction to convey oil or other illuminant to a flame. [OE *wēoce*] **— wick′ing** *n.*

wick² (wik) *Scot. v.t.* In curling, to strike (a stone) obliquely. **— n. 1.** In curling, an opening surrounded by stones already struck. **2.** A creek; inlet.

wick³ (wik) *n.* A village or town: now usually in combination as **-wich:** *Woolwich.* [OE *wīc,* appar. < L *vicus*]

Wick. Wicklow.

wick·ed (wik′id) *adj.* **1.** Evil in principle and practice; vicious; sinful; depraved. **2.** Mischievous; roguish. **3.** Noxious; pernicious. **4.** Troublesome; painful. **5.** *Informal* Done with great skill: a *wicked* game. [ME, alter. of *wikke, wicke.* Akin to OE *wicca.*] **— wick′ed·ly** *adv.*

wick·ed·ness (wik′id·nis) *n.* **1.** The quality of being wicked; moral depravity; sin; vice; crime. **2.** A wicked thing or act; wicked conduct: to work *wickedness.*

wick·er (wik′ər) *adj.* Made of twigs, osiers, etc. **— n. 1.** A pliant young shoot or rod; twig; osier. **2.** Wickerwork. [Prob. < Scand. Cf. dial. Sw. *viker* < *vika* to bend.]

wick·er·work (wik′ər·wûrk′) *n.* A fabric or texture, as a basket, made of woven twigs, osiers, etc.; basketwork.

wick·et (wik′it) *n.* **1.** A small door or gate subsidiary to or made within a larger entrance. **2.** A small opening in a door. **3.** A small sluice gate in a canal lock or at the end of a mill-race. **4.** In cricket: **a** An arrangement of three stumps set near together, with two bails laid over the top. **b** The place at which the wicket is set up: see illustration at CRICKET². **c** The right or turn of each batsman at the wicket. **d** The playing pitch between the wickets: a fast *wicket.* **e** An inning that is not finished or not begun. **5.** In croquet, any one of the arches, usually of wire, through which the ball must be hit. [< AF *wiket,* OF *guichet,* prob. < Gmc.]

wick·et·keep·er (wik′it·kē′pər) *n.* In cricket, the fielder immediately behind the wicket that is being bowled at.

wick·i·up (wik′ē·up) *n.* A loosely constructed hut of certain North American Indian tribes: also spelled *wikiup.* [< Algonquian. Cf. Sac and Fox *wikiyap* lodge.]

Wick·liffe (wik′lif), **Wic·lif,** etc. See WYCLIFFE, etc.

Wick·low (wik′lō) A county of eastern Leinster Province, Ireland; 782 sq. mi.; pop. 58,473 (est. 1969); county seat, **Wicklow,** pop. 3,125 (est. 1969).

wic·o·py (wik′ə·pē) *n. pl.* **·pies 1.** The leatherwood. **2.** The American linden. See under LINDEN. **3.** Any of several species of willow herb. [< Algonquian. Cf. Cree *wikupiy.*]

wid·der·shins (wid′ər·shinz) See WITHERSHINS.

wid·dle (wid′l) *Dial. & Scot. v.i.* **·dled, ·dling** To wriggle; struggle; waddle. **— n.** The act of widdling.

wid·dy¹ (wid′ē) *n. pl.* **·dies** *Scot.* **1.** A halter of withes; withy; hangman's noose. **2.** The gallows. Also **wid′die.** [Var. of WITHY]

wid·dy² (wid′ē) *n. pl.* **·dies** *Dial.* Widow.

wide (wīd) *adj.* **wid·er, wid·est 1.** Having relatively great extent between sides; broad. **2** Extended far in every direction; ample; spacious: a *wide* expanse. **3.** Having a specified degree of width or breadth: an inch *wide.* **4.** Distant from the desired or proper point by a great extent of space; remote; wild: *wide* of the mark. **5.** Having intellectual breadth; liberal: a man of *wide* views. **6.** Fully open; expanded or extended: *wide* eyes. **7.** *Phonet.* Lax. **8.** Comprehensive; inclusive: *wide* learning. **9.** Loose; ample; roomy: *wide* breeches. **10.** In the stock exchange, exhibiting a considerable range between high and low, or bid and offered prices: a *wide* opening. **— n. 1.** In cricket, a ball bowled too far over or on either side of the wicket to be within the batsman's reach. **2.** Breadth of extent; also, a broad, open space. **— adv. 1.** To a great distance; extensively. **2.** Far from the mark. **3.** To the greatest extent; fully open. Abbr. *w.* [OE *wīd*] **— wide′ly** *adv.* **— wide′ness** *n.*

Wide may appear as a combining form, as in the following self-explanatory examples:

wide-arched	wide-hipped	wide-ribbed
wide-backed	wide-minded	wide-rimmed
wide-bottomed	wide-mouthed	wide-sleeved
wide-branched	wide-nosed	wide-sought
wide-brimmed	wide-ranging	wide-stretching
wide-faced	wide-reaching	wide-winged

wide-an·gle lens (wīd′ang′gəl) *Photog.* A type of lens permitting an angle of view wider than that of the ordinary lens.

wide-a·wake (wīd′ə·wāk′) *adj.* **1.** Fully awake. **2.** Marked by vigilance and alertness; keen. **— Syn.** See VIGILANT. **— n.** A soft, broad-brimmed felt hat.

wide-eyed (wīd′īd′) *adj.* **1.** With the eyes wide open, as in wonder or surprise. **2.** Marked by an innocent readiness to believe or admire; uninformed or unsophisticated: *wide-eyed* trust of any stranger she happened to meet.

wid·en (wīd′n) *v.t. & v.i.* To make or become wide or wider. **— wid′en·er** *n.*

wide-o·pen (wīd′ō′pən) *adj.* **1.** Opened wide. **2.** *Informal* Remiss in the enforcement of laws that regulate various forms of vice, as gambling, etc.: a *wide-open* city.

wid·er·shins (wid′ər·shinz) *adv. Scot.* Withershins.

wide-screen (wīd′skrēn′) *adj. Telecom.* Designating a motion-picture process using an elongated screen designed to accommodate various systems of projection beyond 35 mm.

wide·spread (wīd′spred′) *adj.* **1.** Extending over a large space or territory **2.** Occurring, accepted, etc., among many people; general: a *widespread* belief. Also **wide-spread′, wide′spread′ing.**

widge·on (wij′ən) *n.* Any of a genus (*Mareca*) of river ducks with short bill and wedge-shaped tail; especially, the **American widgeon,** or *baldpate* (*M. americana*), esteemed as a game bird, and the **European widgeon** (*M. penelope*): also spelled *wigeon*. [Cf. MF *vigeon* wild duck]

Wi·dor (vē·dôr′), **Charles Marie Jean Albert**, 1845–1937, French organist and composer.

wid·ow (wid′ō) *n.* **1.** A woman who has lost her husband by death and has not remarried. **2.** In some card games, an additional hand dealt to the table; also, a kitty. **3.** *Printing* An incomplete line of type at the top of a page or column. — *v.t.* **1.** To make a widow of; deprive of a husband: usually in the past participle. **2.** To deprive of something desirable; bereave. **3.** *Rare* To survive as the widow of. **4.** *Rare* To give the rights of a widow to. [OE *widewe*, *wuduwe*]

widow bird A whidah bird (which see). [< NL *Vidua*, genus name, trans. of Pg. *viuva*, lit., widow]

wid·ow·er (wid′ō·ər) *n.* A man whose wife is dead, and who has not married again. [ME *widwer* < *widwe*, OE *widewe* widow]

wid·ow·hood (wid′ō·hŏŏd) *n.* The state or period of being a widow, or, rarely, of being a widower.

widow's cruse An endless or inexhaustible supply. I *Kings* xvii 10–16, and II *Kings* iv 1–7.

widow's mite A small but selfless contribution from one who can hardly afford it. *Mark* xii 42.

widow's peak A hairline growing in a V-shaped point from the forehead.

widow's walk A railed observation area built on the roof of a home near the sea giving the observer a clear view of incoming vessels: also called *captain's walk*.

width (width) *n.* **1.** Dimension or measurement of an object taken from side to side, and at right angles to the length. **2.** The state or fact of being wide; wideness; breadth. **3.** Something that has width; especially, in dressmaking, one of the several pieces of material used in making a garment. Abbr. *w.* [< WIDE, on analogy with *breadth*]

width·wise (width′wīz′) *adv.* In the direction of the width; from side to side. Also **width′way′** (-wā′), **width′ways′**.

Wi·du·kind (vē′dōō·kint) See WITTEKIND.

Wie·land (wē′länd) See WAYLAND.

Wie·land (vē′länt), **Christoph Martin**, 1733–1813, German poet, novelist, and translator. — **Heinrich**, 1877–1957, German chemist.

wield (wēld) *v.t.* **1.** To handle, as a weapon or instrument, especially with full command and effect. **2.** To exercise (authority, power, influence, etc.). **3.** *Obs.* To exercise authority over. [Fusion of OE *wealdan* to rule and OE *wieldan* to conquer, seize] — **wield′a·ble** *adj.* — **wield′er** *n.*

wield·y (wēl′dē) *adj.* **wield·i·er**, **wield·i·est** Easily handled or managed; manageable.

Wien (vēn) The German name for VIENNA.

Wien (vēn), **Wilhelm**, 1864–1928, German physicist.

wie·ner (wē′nər) *n.* *U.S.* A kind of sausage, often shorter than a frankfurter, made of beef and pork: also, *Informal*, **weenie**. Also **wie·nie** (wē′nē), **wie·ner·wurst** (wē′nər·wûrst′), *Ger.* vē′nər·vōorst′). [Short for G *Wiener-wurst* Vienna sausage]

Wie·ner (wē′nər), **Norbert**, 1894–1964, U.S. mathematician.

Wie·ner schnit·zel (vē′nər shnit′səl) A breaded veal cutlet, seasoned or garnished in any of several ways. [< G *Wiener* Viennese + *schnitzel* cutlet, dim. of *schnitz* slice < *schneiden* to cut]

Wies·ba·den (vēs′bä·dən) The capital of Hesse, West Germany, in the western part on the Rhine; site of a famous spa; pop. 258,200 (est. 1967).

wife (wīf) *n.* *pl.* **wives** (wīvz) **1.** A woman joined to a man in lawful wedlock. ◆ Collateral adjective: *uxorial.* **2.** *Archaic* A grown woman; adult female: now usually in combination or in certain phrases: *housewife*, old *wives'* tales. Abbr. *w.* — **to take (a woman) to wife** To marry (a woman). [OE *wīf*] — **wife′dom**, **wife′hood** *n.* — **wife′ly** *adj.*

wig (wig) *n.* An artificial covering of hair for the head. — *v.t.* **wigged**, **wig·ging** **1.** *Rare* To furnish with a wig or wigs. **2.** *Brit. Informal* To censure severely; berate or scold, especially in public. [Short for PERIWIG]

Wig. Wigtown.

wig·an (wig′ən) *n.* A stiff, canvaslike fabric used for stiffening the borders of garments. [after *Wigan*, where originally made]

Wig·an (wig′ən) A county borough in Greater Manchester, England; pop. 306,600 (1976).

wig·eon (wij′ən) See WIDGEON.

wig·ger·y (wig′ər·ē) *n.* *pl.* **·ger·ies** *Rare* A peruke; wig; also, wigs collectively.

Wig·gin (wig′in), **Kate Douglas**, *née* Smith, 1856–1923, U.S. educator and novelist.

wig·gle (wig′əl) *v.t. & v.i.* **·gled**, **·gling** To move or cause to move quickly and irregularly from side to side; squirm; wriggle. — *n.* A wiggling motion. — **to get a wiggle on** *Slang* To hurry up. [? < MLG *wiggelen*] — **wig′gly** *adj.*

wig·gler (wig′lər) *n.* **1.** One who or that which wiggles. **2.** The larva of a mosquito.

Wig·gles·worth (wig′əlz·wûrth), **Michael**, 1631–1705, American divine and poet.

wight¹ (wīt) *n.* *Archaic* A person; creature. [OE *wiht* creature]

wight² (wīt) *adj.* *Obs.* Full of prowess; strong and valiant; active; swift. [< ON *vigt*, neut. of *vigr* able to fight]

Wight (wīt), **Isle of** An island and county off the southern coast of England; 147 sq. mi.; pop. 112,000 (1976); county seat, Newport.

Wig·town (wig′tən) A county in SW Scotland; 487 sq. mi.; pop 27,611 (1969); county seat, **Wigtown**, pop. 1,149. Also **Wig′town·shire** (-shir).

wig·wag (wig′wag′) *v.t. & v.i.* **·wagged**, **·wag·ging** To send (a message) by moving hand flags, lights, etc., according to a code. — *n.* The act of wigwagging; also, a message so sent. [< dial. E *wig* to wiggle + WAG¹] — **wig′wag′ger** *n.*

wig·wam (wig′wom, -wôm) *n.* **1.** A dwelling or lodge of the North American Indians, commonly a conical framework of poles covered with bark, hides, etc. **2.** *U.S. Informal* A public building used for political gatherings, mass meetings, etc. — **the Wigwam** *U.S. Informal* Tammany Hall. [< Algonquian (Ojibwa) *wigwaum*, lit., their dwelling]

WIGWAM

wik·i·up (wik′ē·up) See WICKIUP.

Wil·ber·force (wil′bər·fôrs, -fōrs), **William**, 1759–1833, English statesman, orator, and abolitionist.

Wil·cox (wil′koks), **Ella**, 1850–1919, *née* Wheeler, U.S. poet and author.

wild (wīld) *adj.* **1.** Inhabiting the forest or open field; not domesticated or tamed; living in a state of nature: a *wild* horse. ◆ Collateral adjective: *feral.* **2.** Growing or produced without care or culture; not cultivated: *wild* flowers. **3.** Being without civilized inhabitants or cultivation; desert; waste: *wild* prairies. **4.** Living in a primitive or savage way; uncivilized: the *wild* men of Borneo. **5.** Boisterous; unruly; unrestrained. **6.** Immoral; dissolute; orgiastic: a *wild* affair. **7.** Affected with or originating violent disturbances; stormy; turbulent: a *wild* night, a *wild* crowd. **8.** Showing reckless want of judgment; rashly imprudent; extravagant: a *wild* speculation. **9.** Fantastically irregular or disordered; odd in arrangement or effect: a *wild* imagination, *wild* dress. **10.** Eager and excited, as by reason of joy, fear, desire, etc.: She was *wild* with delight. **11.** Excited to frenzy or distraction; roused to fury or desperation; crazed or crazy: to drive one *wild.* **12.** Being or going far from the proper course or from the mark aimed at; erratic; wide of the mark: a *wild* ball, a *wild* guess. **13.** In some card games, having its value arbitrarily determined by the dealer or holder: to play poker with fours *wild.* — **wild and wooly** *Informal* Untamed; reckless; boisterous. — *n.* *Often pl.* An uninhabited or uncultivated place; a waste; wilderness: the *wilds* of Africa. — **the wild** The wilderness; also, the free, natural, wild life: the call of the *wild.* — *adv.* In a wild manner; without control. [OE *wilde*] — **wild′ly** *adv.* — **wild′ness** *n.*

wild allspice The spicebush.

wild bergamot The horsemint (def. 1).

wild boar The native hog (*Sus scrofa*) of continental Europe, southern Asia, North Africa, and formerly of Great Britain.

wild brier Any species of rose in the wild state, as the dog rose or the sweetbrier.

wild carrot An umbelliferous herb (*Daucus carota*), having filmy white flowers in umbels and from which the cultivated carrot is derived: also called *Queen Anne's lace.*

wild·cat (wīld′kat′) *n.* **1.** An undomesticated feline carnivore (*Felis sylvestris*) of Europe, resembling the domestic cat, but larger and stronger. **2.** The lynx. **3.** One of several other felines, as the ocelot and serval. **4.** An aggressive quick-tempered person, especially a woman. **5.** An unattached locomotive and its tender, used on special work, as to haul trains, etc. **6.** A successful oil well drilled in an area previously unproductive. **7.** A tricky or unsound business venture; especially, a worthless mine: also **wildcat mine.** Also **wild cat.** — *adj.* **1.** Unsound; risky; especially, financially unsound or risky. **2.** Illegal; made, produced, or carried on without official sanction or authorization. **3.** Not running on a schedule; also, running wild or without control, as a railroad train or engine. — *v.t. & v.i.* **·cat·ted**, **·cat·ting** To drill for oil in (an area not known to be productive). — **wild′cat′ting** *n. & adj.*

wildcat bank *U.S.* Prior to the passage of the National Bank Act of 1863–64, a bank operating with insufficient capital to redeem its circulating notes.

wildcat bill A note of a wildcat bank.

wildcat strike A strike unauthorized by regular union procedure.

wild·cat·ter (wīld′kat′ər) *n.* **1.** A promoter of mines of doubtful value. **2.** One who develops oil wells in unproved territory. **3.** One who manufactures illicit whisky.

wild cherry Any species of cherry found growing wild.

Wilde (wīld), **Oscar**, 1856–1900, Irish poet, dramatist, and novelist: full name **Oscar Fingal O'Flahertie Wills Wilde**.

wilde·beest (wīld′bēst, wil′də-; *Du.* vil′də·bāst) *n.* A gnu. [< Afrikaans < Du. *wild* wild + *beeste* beast]

wil·der (wil′dər) *Poetic v.t. & v.i.* **1.** To bewilder or become bewildered. **2.** To mislead or become misled. [Prob. back formation < WILDERNESS]

Wil·der (wil′dər), **Thornton (Niven)**, 1897–1975, U.S. novelist and playwright.

wil·der·ment (wil′dər·mənt) *n. Archaic or Poetic* Bewilderment; confusion.

wil·der·ness (wil′dər·nis) *n.* **1.** An uncultivated, uninhabited, or barren region. **2.** A waste, as of an ocean. **3.** A multitudinous and confusing collection: a *wilderness* of curiosities. **4.** *Obs.* Wildness. [ME < OE *wilddēor* wild beast (< *wilde* wild + *dēor* animal, deer) + -NESS]

Wil·der·ness (wil′dər·nis), **The** A region in NE Virginia; scene of a Civil War battle, 1864.

wild·fire (wīld′fīr′) *n.* **1.** A raging, destructive fire: now generally in the phrase **to spread like wildfire**. **2.** A composition of flammable materials, or the flame produced by it, very hard to put out, as Greek fire. **3.** A phosphorescent luminousness; ignis fatuus. **4.** *Obs.* Erysipelas. **5.** *Vet.* A skin disease of sheep characterized by inflammation.

wild·flow·er (wīld′flou′ər) *n.* Any uncultivated flowering plant; also, the flower of such a plant. Also **wild flower**.

wild fowl Wild game birds, especially wild ducks and geese.

wild·fowl (wīld′foul′) *n.* *pl.* **·fowl** (*especially for def.* 2), or **fowls** **1.** A wild game bird, especially a wild duck or goose. **2.** *pl.* Wild game birds collectively. Also **wild fowl**.

wild ginger A plant (*Asarum canadense*) of eastern North America, having short-stemmed purplish brown flowers.

wild goose An undomesticated goose, as the graylag or the Canada goose.

wild-goose chase (wīld′gōos′) **1.** Pursuit of the unknown or unattainable. **2.** Any strenuous and fruitless task.

Wild Huntsman In European folklore, a phantom hunter who rides by night.

wild hyacinth The Eastern camass. See under CAMASS.

wild indigo Any of a genus (*Baptisia*) of leguminous North American herbs, especially *B. tinctoria*, having yellow flowers.

wild·ing (wīl′ding) *n.* **1.** An uncultivated plant; especially: **a** A wild apple tree or its fruit. **b** A plant escaped from cultivation. **2.** A wild or untamed creature. — *adj.* **1.** Untamed; undomesticated. **2.** Growing wild; uncultivated.

wild lettuce Any of several tall, coarse herbs (genus *Lactuca*) of the composite family.

wild licorice **1.** The jequirity (def. 1). **2.** Any of various plants having sweetish roots, especially either of two North American plants (*Galium circaezans* and *G. lanceolatum*) of the madder family. Also **wild liquorice**.

wild·life (wīld′līf′) *n.* Wild animals, trees, and plants collectively; especially, wild animals and birds.

wild·ling (wīld′ling) *n.* An uncultivated plant or flower or a wild animal. [< WILD + -LING¹]

wild madder **1.** Madder² (def. 1). **2.** Either of two bedstraws (*Galium mollago* or *G. tinctorium*) of North America.

wild marjoram A widely distributed herb (*Origanum vulgare*) of the mint family, having purplish flowers: sometimes called *origan*.

wild mustard Any of various uncultivated plants of the mustard family, as the charlock.

wild oat **1.** *Usually pl.* An uncultivated grass (genus *Avena*), especially a common species (*A. fatua*) of Europe. **2.** *pl.* Indiscretions of youth: usually in the expression **to sow one's wild oats** To commit youthful indiscretions.

wild olive Any of various trees resembling the olive or bearing an olivelike fruit, as the devilwood and the oleaster.

wild pansy The pansy in its uncultivated state; especially, a European species (*Viola tricolor*) from which the garden pansy is derived: also called *johnny-jump-up, love-in-idleness*.

wild parsley Any of various umbelliferous plants resembling the cultivated parsley.

wild parsnip The parsnip in its weedlike, uncultivated form; also, any of various similar plants (genus *Pastinaca*).

wild pink A plant (*Silene caroliniana*) of eastern North America, having showy pink flowers.

wild pitch In baseball, a misplay charged to the pitcher for allowing a runner to advance by throwing a pitch that the catcher does not and could not be expected to catch. Compare PASSED BALL.

wild rice The grain of a tall aquatic grass (*Zizania aquatica*) of North America, esteemed as a table delicacy: also called *Indian rice*.

wild rose Any of various uncultivated roses of the north temperate zone, as the sweetbrier.

wild rubber Rubber as extracted from rubber trees in the wild state.

wild rye A tall perennial grass (genus *Elymus*), widely distributed in temperate regions.

wild sarsparilla See under SARSPARILLA.

wild turkey A large North American turkey (*Meleagris*

gallopavo silvestris) formerly ranging east of the Rocky Mountains from southern Canada to Florida and Mexico, and first domesticated in Mexico, now rare in the wild state.

wild vanilla A smooth, erect, composite herb (*Trilisa odoratissima*) growing in the SE United States, whose leaves give off an odor of vanilla.

Wild West The western United States, especially in its early period of Indian fighting, lawlessness, etc.

Wild West show A circus or a feature of a circus presenting feats of Indian and cowboy horsemanship; also, a rodeo.

wild·wood (wīld′wŏŏd′) *n.* Natural forest land.

wile (wīl) *n.* **1.** An act or a means of cunning deception; also, any beguiling trick or artifice. **2.** Craftiness; cunning. — **Syn.** See ARTIFICE. — *v.t.* **wiled, wil·ing** **1.** To lure, beguile, or mislead. **2.** To pass divertingly, as time: usually with *away*: by confusion with *while*. [ME *wil*, prob. < Scand. Cf. ON *vēl* artifice.]

Wi·ley (wī′lē), **Harvey Washington**, 1844–1930, U.S. chemist.

wil·ful (wil′fəl), **wil·ful·ly, wil·ful·ness** See WILLFUL, etc.

Wil·helm I (vil′helm), 1797–1888, king of Prussia 1861–88; emperor of Germany 1871–88.

Wilhelm II, 1859–1941, emperor of Germany and king of Prussia 1888–1918; abdicated.

Wil·hel·mi·na (wil′hel·mē′nə), 1880–1962, queen of the Netherlands 1890–1948; abdicated in favor of her daughter Juliana: full name **Wilhelmina Helena Pauline Maria**.

Wil·helms·ha·ven (vil′helms·hä′fən) A port city in Lower Saxony, West Germany, on the North Sea; pop. 103,150 (est. 1970).

Wil·helm·stras·se (vil′helm·shträ′sə) A street in Berlin on which the German foreign office and government offices were formerly located. — *n.* Formerly, the German government, especially its foreign policies.

Wilkes (wilks), **Charles**, 1798–1877, U.S. admiral, explorer, and scientist. — **John**, 1727–97, English politician.

Wilkes-Bar·re (wilks′bar·ə) A city in NE Pennsylvania, on the Susquehanna River; pop. 58,856.

Wilkes Land (wilks) A part of Antarctica on the Indian Ocean south of Australia, containing the south magnetic pole in its eastern part.

Wil·kins (wil′kinz), **Sir George Hubert**, 1888–1958, Australian aviator and polar explorer.

Wil·kins·burg (wil′kinz·bûrg) A borough in SW Pennsylvania, near Pittsburgh; pop. 26,780.

Wil·kin·son (wil′kən·sən), **James**, 1757–1825, American Revolutionary general and politician.

will¹ (wil) *n.* **1.** The power of conscious, deliberate action; the faculty by which the mind makes choices and acts to carry them out. **2.** The act or experience of exercising this faculty; a volition or a choice. **3.** Strong determination; practical enthusiasm; also, self-control. **4.** That which has been resolved or determined upon; a purpose. **5.** Power to dispose of a matter arbitrarily; discretion. **6.** *Law* The legal declaration of a person's intentions as to the disposal of his estate after his death. **7.** A conscious inclination toward any end or course; a wish. **8.** A request or command. — **at will** As one pleases. — *v.* **willed, will·ing** *v.t.* **1.** To decide upon; choose. **2.** To resolve upon as an action or course; determine to do. **3.** To give, devise, or bequeath by a will. **4.** To control, as a hypnotized person, by the exercise of will. **5.** *Archaic* To have a wish for; desire. — *v.i.* **6.** To exercise the will. [OE *willa*] — **will·a·ble** *adj.*

— **Syn.** (noun) **1.** *Will, volition*, and *conation* relate to voluntary action. In popular usage and older psychological writings, *will* embraces two aspects that are distinguished in more modern psychology as *volition* and *conation*. *Volition* is the making of free choices and decisions; *conation* is the striving to carry out a decision, choice, desire, or inclination.

will² (wil) *v.* Present: *3rd person sing.*: will; *Archaic 2nd person sing.* wilt; past: would; *Archaic 2nd person sing.* **would·est** or **wouldst**. An auxiliary verb used with the infinitive without *to*, or elliptically without the infinitive, to express: **1.** Futurity: They *will* arrive by dark. **2.** Willingness or disposition: Why *will* you not tell the truth? **3.** Capability or capacity: The ship *will* survive any storm. **4.** Custom or habit: He *will* sit for hours and brood. **5.** *Informal* Probability or inference: I expect this *will* be the main street. ◆ See usage note under SHALL. — *v.t. & v.i.* To wish or have a wish; desire: As you *will*. [OE *willan*]

Wil·lam·ette River (wi·lam′it) A river in NW Oregon, flowing about 190 miles north to the Columbia River.

Wil·lard (wil′ərd), **Emma**, 1787–1870, *née* Hart, U.S. educator. — **Frances Elizabeth Caroline**, 1839–98, U.S. temperance advocate.

Will·cocks (wil′koks), **Sir William**, 1852–1932, English engineer.

willed (wild) *adj.* Having a will, especially one of a given character: usually in combination: self-*willed*.

wil·lem·ite (wil′əm·īt) *n.* A vitreous or resinous silicate of zinc, crystallizing in the hexagonal system and occurring in many colors. [< Du. *willemit*, after *Willem I* king of the Netherlands 1815–40]

Wil·lem·stad (wil′əm·stät, vil′-) The capital of the Nether-

wil·ler (wil'ǝr) *n.* One who wills.

Willes·den (wilz'dǝn) A municipal borough in Middlesex, England, near London; pop. 170,835 (1961).

wil·let (wil'it) *n.* A large, light-colored shore bird (*Catoptrophorus semipalmatus*) of North America, related to the snipes. [Short for *pill-will-willet*, imit. of the cry of the bird]

will·ful (wil'fǝl) *adj.* **1.** Bent on having one's own way; headstrong. **2.** Resulting from the exercise of one's own will; voluntary; intentional. Also, *esp. Brit.*, *wilful*. [Cf. OE *wilfullice* willfully] — **will'ful·ly** *adv.* — **will'ful·ness** *n.*

Wil·liam I (wil'yǝm) 1027?-87, Duke of Normandy; invaded England 1066; king of England 1066–87: called **William the Conqueror, William the Norman**.

William II, 1056?-1100, king of England 1087-1100: called **William Ru·fus** (roo'fǝs).

William III, 1650-1702, Prince of Orange; stadholder of Holland; became king of England in 1689 by invitation; ruled jointly with his wife as **William and Mary** 1689-1702.

William IV, 1765-1837, king of England 1830-37: called the **Sailor King**.

William of Malmesbury, 1095?-1142?, English historian and monk.

William of Orange, 1533-84, Prince of Orange and Count of Nassau; founded the Dutch republic; became stadholder in 1581; assassinated: called **William I, William the Silent**.

Wil·liams (wil'yǝmz), **Roger**, 1603?-83, English clergyman in New England; founded Rhode Island. — **Tennessee**, born 1914, U.S. playwright: original name **Thomas Lanier Williams**. — **William Carlos**, 1883-1963, U.S. poet, novelist, and physician.

Wil·liams·burg (wil'yǝmz-bûrg) A town in eastern Virginia; founded in 1693; capital of Virginia (1699-1779); restored to condition of the colonial period; pop. 9,069.

Wil·liams·port (wil'yǝmz-pôrt, -pōrt) A city in north central Pennsylvania; pop. 37,918.

wil·lies (wil'ēz) *n.pl. Slang* Nervousness; jitters; the creeps: with *the*. [? < WILLY-NILLY; with ref. to a state of indecision]

will·ie·waught (wil'ē-wäkht) *n. Scot.* A draft of liquor. Also **will'ie·waucht**.

will·ing (wil'ing) *adj.* **1.** Having the mind favorably inclined or disposed. **2.** Answering to demand or requirement; compliant. **3.** Gladly proffered or done; hearty. **4.** Of or pertaining to the faculty or power of choice; volitional. — **will'ing·ly** *adv.* — **will'ing·ness** *n.*

Wil·lis (wil'is), **Nathaniel Parker**, 1806-67, U.S. writer and editor.

wil·li·waw (wil'ē-wô) *n. Meteorol.* A sudden, violent blast of wind moving seaward down the slope of a mountainous coast, especially in the Strait of Magellan. Also **wil'ly·waw**. [Origin unknown]

Will·kie (wil'kē), **Wendell Lewis**, 1892-1944, U.S. lawyer and political leader.

will-o'-the-wisp (wil'ǝ-thǝ-wisp') *n.* **1.** Ignis fatuus. **2.** Any elusive or deceptive object. — *adj.* Deceptive; fleeting; misleading. [Earlier *Will with the wisp*]

wil·low (wil'ō) *n.* **1.** Any of a large genus (*Salix*) of shrubs and trees, having generally smooth branches and often long, slender, pliant, and sometimes pendent branchlets, typical of a family (*Salicaceae*) that includes the poplar. **2.** The soft white wood of the willow. **3.** *Informal* Something made of willow wood, especially a baseball or cricket bat. **4.** A machine for giving a preliminary cleaning to cotton, flax, hemp, wool, etc., by means of long spikes projecting from a revolving cone or cylinder. — *v.t.* To clean, as cotton, wool, etc., with a willow. — *adj.* Of or pertaining to the willow; made of willow wood. [OE *welig*] — **wil'low·ish** *adj.*

wil·low·er (wil'ō-ǝr) *n.* One who or that which willows.

willow herb Any of a genus (*Epilobium*) of perennial herbs of the evening-primrose family; especially, the fireweed (*E. angustifolium*), having scattered, willowlike leaves and large, pink flowers: also called *great willow herb*.

willow oak An oak (*Quercus phellos*) of the eastern United States, having long, slender, leaves resembling willow leaves.

willow pattern A decorative design, usually blue on a white background and including a willow tree, introduced on household china in England in 1780.

wil·low·ware (wil'ō-wâr') *n.* China decorated with the willow pattern.

wil·low·y (wil'ō-ē) *adj.* **1.** Abounding in willows. **2.** Having supple grace of form or carriage.

will power Ability to control oneself; determination; strength or firmness of mind.

Will·stät·ter (vil'shtet-ǝr), **Richard**, 1872-1942, German organic chemist.

wil·ly¹ (wil'ē) *adj. Obs.* Willing; also, propitious. [Cf. ON *viljugr*]

wil·ly² (wil'ē) *v.t.* ·**lied**, ·**ly·ing** To willow, as cotton, flax, hemp, etc.

will·yard (wil'yǝrd) *adj. Scot.* Willful; also, abashed; bewildered. Also **will'yart** (-yǝrt).

wil·ly-nil·ly (wil'ē-nil'ē) *adj.* Having no decisiveness; uncertain; irresolute. — *adv.* Willingly or unwillingly. See NILL. [Earlier *will I, nill I* whether I will or not]

wil·ly-wil·ly (wil'ē-wil'ē) *n. pl.* ·**lies** *Meteorol.* **1.** A violent storm of wind and rain on the NW coast of Australia: also called *cockeye bob*. **2.** A brief but violent duststorm.

Wil·mette (wil-met') A village in NE Illinois, on Lake Michigan, a suburb of Chicago; pop. 32,134.

Wil·ming·ton (wil'ming-tǝn) **1.** A port city in northern Delaware, on the Delaware River; pop. 80,386. **2.** A port city in SE North Carolina; pop. 46,169. **3.** A port and industrial section of Los Angeles.

Wil·mot (wil'mǝt), **John** See (Earl of) ROCHESTER.

Wil·no (vil'nō) The Polish name for VILNYUS.

Wil·son (wil'sǝn) A town in east central North Carolina; pop. 29,347.

Wil·son (wil'sǝn), **Alexander**, 1766-1813, American ornithologist born in Scotland. — **Edmund**, 1895-1972, U.S. critic, author, and dramatist. — **Sir (James) Harold**, born 1916, British public official; prime minister 1964-70, 1974-76. — **Henry**, 1812-75, U.S. statesman: original name **Jeremiah Jones Col·baith** (kôl'·bāth). — **James**, 1742-98, American patriot born in Scotland; signer of the Declaration of Independence. — **John**, 1785-1854, Scottish essayist, poet, and novelist: pseudonym *Christopher North*. — **(Thomas) Woodrow**, 1856-1924, U.S. educator and statesman; 28th president of the United States 1913-21.

Wil·son (wil'sǝn), **Mount** A peak in SW California, near Pasadena; 5,710 ft.; site of a famous observatory.

Wilson cloud chamber A cloud chamber (which see). [after C. T. R. Wilson, 1869-1959, Scottish physicist]

Wilson Dam A power dam in the Tennessee River at Muscle Shoals, NW Alabama; 137 ft. high, 4,862 ft. long; forms **Lake Wilson** (25 sq. mi.) over Muscle Shoals.

Wilson's petrel A sea bird (*Oceanites oceanicus*) resembling the storm petrel, but having feet with yellow webs. [after Alexander *Wilson*]

Wilson's phalarope A shore bird (*Steganopus tricolor*) that breeds in northern North America and winters as far south as the Falkland Islands. [after Alexander *Wilson*]

Wilson's plover The ring plover (*Charadrius wilsonia*) of the southern United States and South America. [after Alexander *Wilson*]

Wilson's snipe See under SNIPE (def. 1).

Wilson's thrush The veery. [after Alexander *Wilson*]

Wilson's warbler A small, very active flycatcher (*Wilsonia pusilla*) of eastern North America, black-crowned with a yellow and olive-green body. [after Alexander *Wilson*]

wilt¹ (wilt) *v.i.* **1.** To lose freshness; droop or become limp, as a flower that has been cut or that has not been watered. **2.** To lose energy and vitality; become faint or languid: We *wilted* under the hot sun. **3.** To lose courage or spirit; subside suddenly. — *v.t.* **4.** To cause to droop or wither. **5.** To cause to lose vitality and energy. — *n.* **1.** The act of wilting. **2.** Languor; faintness. **3.** *Bot.* Any of several plant diseases marked by a wilting of the leaves, caused chiefly by defective absorption of moisture from the soil: also **wilt disease**. [Prob. dial. var. of obs. *welk* to wither. Cf. MDu. *welken* to wither.]

wilt² (wilt) Archaic second person singular, present tense of WILL²: used with *thou*.

Wil·ton (wil'tǝn) *n.* A kind of carpet resembling the Brussels carpet, but having the loops of the pile cut, thus giving it a velvety texture: originally made at Wilton, England. Also **Wilton carpet, Wilton rug**.

Wilts. or **Wilts** Wiltshire.

Wilt·shire (wilt'shir) *n.* One of a breed of long-horned sheep raised in Wiltshire, England.

Wilt·shire (wilt'shir) A county in southern England; 1,345 sq. mi.; pop. 506,700 (1976); county seat, Trowbridge: shortened form **Wilts** (wiltz).

Wiltshire cheese A variety of Cheddar cheese.

wi·ly (wī'lē) *adj.* ·**li·er**, ·**li·est** Full of or characterized by wiles; sly; cunning. — **wi'li·ly** *adv.* — **wi'li·ness** *n.*

wim·ble (wim'bǝl) *n.* Anything that bores a hole, especially if turned by hand, as a brace and bit. — *v.t.* ·**bled**, ·**bling** To bore or pierce, as with a wimble. [< AF, OF *guimbel* < MLG *wiemel*. Akin to GIMLET.]

Wim·ble·don (wim'bǝl-dǝn) A town and municipal borough in NE Surrey, England, near London; scene of international tennis matches; pop. 57,312 (est. 1969).

wim·ple (wim'pǝl) *n.* **1.** A cloth, as of linen or silk, wrapped in folds around the neck close under the chin and over the head, exposing only the face, formerly worn as a protection by women outdoors, and still by nuns. **2.** *Scot.* A fold; plait; also, a curve; a winding turn, as in a river or road. — *v.* ·**pled**, ·**pling** *v.t.* **1.** To cover or clothe with a wimple.

veil. **2.** To make or fold into plaits, as a veil. **3.** To cause to move with slight undulations; ripple. — *v.i.* **4.** To lie in plaits or folds. **5.** To ripple. [OE *wimpel*]

Wims·hurst machine (wimz′hûrst) A machine for the generation of static electricity by means of two insulated rotating disks that, by friction against strips of conducting material, build up an electrostatic charge. [after James *Wimshurst*, 1832–1903, English engineer, its inventor]

win[1] (win) *v.* **won** (*Obs.* **wan**), **won**, **win·ning** *v.i.* **1.** To gain a victory; be victorious; prevail, as in a contest. **2.** To succeed in an effort or endeavor. **3.** To succeed in reaching or attaining a specified end or condition; get: often with *across, over, through,* etc.: The fleet *won* through the storm. **4.** In racing, to finish first: distinguished from *place, show.* **5.** *Obs.* To fight; struggle. — *v.t.* **6.** To be successful in; gain victory in: to *win* an argument. **7.** To gain in competition or contest: to *win* the blue ribbon. **8.** To gain by effort, persistence, etc.: to *win* fame and fortune. **9.** To influence so as to obtain the good will or favor of: often with *over*: to *win* over the masses. **10.** To secure the love of; gain in marriage: He wooed and *won* her. **11.** To succeed in reaching; attain: to *win* the harbor. **12.** To make (one's way), especially with effort. **13.** To capture; take possession of. **14.** To earn or procure, as a living: to *win* support from poor soil. **15.** *Mining* **a** To extract, as ore or coal, or metal from ore. **b** To reach and open (a deposit, vein, etc.); prepare for mining. — **to win out** *Informal* To succeed to the fullest extent or expectation. — *n.* **1.** A victory; success. **2.** Profit; winnings. **3.** The first position among the first three finishers in a race, as in a horse race. [OE *winnan* to contend, labor]

win[2] (win) *v.t. Scot. & Irish* **1.** To winnow. **2.** To cure, as hay.

win[3] (win) *n. Scot.* Wind.

wince[1] (wins) *v.i.* **winced**, **winc·ing** To shrink back or start aside, as from a blow or pain; flinch. — *n.* The act of wincing. [< AF *wenchier*, (assumed) var. of OF *quenchier* to avoid < Gmc.] — **winc′er** *n.*

wince[2] (wins) *n.* A dyer's winch or windlass. [Var. of WINCH[1]]

win·cey (win′sē) *n.* A fabric woven with cotton or linen warp and woolen filling. [Short for *wincey-woolsey,* alter. of LINSEY-WOOLSEY]

winch[1] (winch) *n.* **1.** A windlass used for hoisting, as on a crane or derrick, having usually one or more hand cranks geared to a drum around which the rope or chain winds. **2.** A crank with a handle, used to impart motion to a grindstone or the like. — *v.t.* To move, hoist, or haul with or as with a winch. [OE *wince*] — **winch′er** *n.*

winch[2] (winch) *v.i. Obs.* To wince; flinch. [See WINCE[1]]

Win·ches·ter (win′ches·tər) *n.* Originally, a breechloading, lever-action, repeating rifle with a tubular magazine under the barrel, first produced in 1866: a trade name now also applied to other firearms produced by the same company. [after Oliver F. *Winchester,* 1810–80, U.S. industrialist]

WINCH

Win·ches·ter (win′ches·tər) **1.** The county seat of Hampshire, England; known for its 11th-century cathedral; pop. 87,400 (1976). **2.** A city in northern Virginia; scene of several Civil War battles, 1862 and 1864; pop. 14,043.

Winck·el·mann (vingk′əl·män), **Johann Joachim,** 1717–68, German archeologist and art critic.

wind[1] (wind; *for n., also poetic* wīnd) *n.* **1.** Any movement of air, especially a natural horizontal movement; air in motion naturally. **2.** Any powerful or destructive wind; a tornado; hurricane. **3.** The direction from which a wind blows; one of the cardinal points of the compass: They gathered from the four *winds.* **4.** Air in motion by artificial means. **5.** Air pervaded by a scent: The deer got *wind* of the hunter. **6.** A suggestion or intimation: to get *wind* of a plot. **7.** The power of breathing; breath. **8.** Breath as expended in words, especially as having more sound than sense; idle chatter; also, vanity; conceit. **9.** *pl.* The wind instruments of an orchestra; also, the players of these instruments. **10.** The gaseous product of indigestion; flatulence. — **in the wind 1.** Impending; astir; afoot. **2.** Inebriated; drunk. — **in the wind's eye** Directly opposed to the point from which the wind blows. — **to break wind** To expel gas through the anus; fart. — **to get wind of** To receive a hint of. — **to have in the wind** To be on the track or scent of; be in pursuit of. — **to have the wind of 1.** To be windward of. **2.** To have an advantage over. — **to have the wind up** To be apprehensive; be alarmed or wary. — **to sail close to the wind 1.** To sail in a direction as near as possible to that from which the wind blows. **2.** To come near to the limit, as of a danger line. **3.** To manage or live economically. — *v.t.* **1.** To follow by scent; to catch a scent of on the wind. **2.** To exhaust the breath of, as by running.

3. To allow to recover breath by resting. **4.** To expose to the wind, as in ventilating. [OE] — **Syn.** (noun) **1.** air, blow, breeze, gale. **2.** squall, windstorm. Compare WHIRLWIND.

wind[2] (wīnd) *v.* **wound** (*Rare* **wind·ed**), **wind·ing** *v.t.* **1.** To coil or pass (thread, rope, etc.) around some object or fixed core; twine; wreathe. **2.** To encircle or cover with something, as by coiling or wrapping: to *wind* a spool with thread. **3.** To continue or renew the motion of, as a clock, by coiling a spring, cord, etc. **4.** To cause to turn and twist. **5.** To make (one's way) by a turning and twisting course. **6.** To introduce carefully or deviously; insinuate: He *wound* himself into my confidence. **7.** To raise or hoist, as by means of a capstan or windlass. — *v.i.* **8.** To move in a turning, twisting course; change direction; meander. **9.** To coil or twine about some central object or core. **10.** To move in a circular or spiral course: The hawk *wound* into the sky. **11.** To proceed carefully or deviously; gain an end by indirect or subtle methods. **12.** To warp; twist: This board *winds* badly. — **to wind up 1.** To coil or wind round and round. **2.** To put in readiness for action; excite; arouse. **3.** To bring to conclusion or settlement; close, as a business: He *wound up* his affairs. **4.** In baseball, to swing the arm preparatory to pitching. **5.** To hoist. — *n.* The act of winding, or the condition of being wound; a winding, turn, or twist. [OE *windan.* Akin to WAND.] — **wind′a·ble** *adj.*

wind[3] (wīnd, wind) *v.t.* **wind·ed** or **wound**, **wind·ing 1.** To blow, as a horn; sound. **2.** To give a (call or signal), as with a horn. [< WIND[1]; infl. by WIND[2]]

W. Ind. West Indies.

wind·age (win′dij) *n.* **1.** The rush of air caused by the rapid passage of an object, as a projectile or a railway train. **2.** Deflection of an object, as a bullet, from its natural course due to wind pressure. **3.** In a gun, the difference between the diameter of a projectile and the bore through which it is discharged. **4.** *Mech.* The free air space between any moving piece and the socket or bore in which it travels. **5.** *Naut.* The surface offered to the wind by a vessel.

Win·daus (vin′dous), **Adolf,** 1876–1959, German chemist.

wind·bag (wind′bag′) *n.* **1.** *Informal* A wordy talker. **2.** A bellows. **3.** *Slang* The chest.

wind-blown (wind′blōn′) *adj.* **1.** Tossed or blown by the wind. **2.** Having a permanent direction of growth as determined by prevailing winds: said of plants and trees. **3.** Bobbed and brushed forward: said of a woman's hair.

wind-borne (wind′bôrn′, -bōrn′) *adj.* Carried or transported by the wind, as pollen.

wind·break (wind′brāk′) *n.* Something, as a hedge or fence, that protects from or breaks the force of the wind.

Wind·break·er (wind′brā′kər) *n.* A sturdy, warm sports jacket with fitted waistband: a trade name. Also **wind′-break′er.**

wind-bro·ken (wind′brō′kən) *adj.* Asthmatic; broken-winded: said of a horse.

wind·burn (wind′bûrn′) *n.* Discoloration or irritation of the skin, produced by exposure to the wind. — *v.t. & v.i.* To affect or be affected with windburn. — **wind′burnt′,** **wind′burned′** *adj.*

wind cone A wind sock (which see).

wind·ed (win′did) *adj.* Breathless, as from work or exercise; out of breath.

wind·er[1] (wīn′dər) *n.* **1.** One who or that which winds. **2.** That upon which or from which thread, etc., may be wound. **3.** A step in winding stairs. **4.** A twining plant. **5.** An appliance for winding up a spring.

wind·er[2] (wīn′dər, win′dər) *n.* One who blows or winds a horn, bugle, etc.

Win·der·mere (win′dər·mir), **Lake** The largest lake in England, in Westmorland and Lancashire; 10.5 mi. long, 1 mi. wide.

wind·fall (wind′fôl′) *n.* **1.** A piece of unexpected good fortune; especially, a sudden and substantial financial profit. **2.** A tract of land on which trees have been felled by the wind; also, the trees so felled. **3.** Something, as ripening fruit, brought down by the wind.

wind·flaw (wind′flô′) *n.* A sharp gust of wind.

wind-flow·er (wind′flou′ər) *n.* The anemone. [Trans. of Gk. *anemōnē* anemone < *anemos* the wind]

wind·gall (wind′gôl′) *n. Vet.* A soft swelling near the pastern joint of a horse. [< WIND[1] + GALL[2]; so called because formerly thought to contain wind] — **wind′galled′** *adj.*

wind gap A notch or ravine in a mountain ridge, not deep enough to give passage to a watercourse.

wind gauge A scale on a gunsight to allow for windage (def. 2). Also **wind gage.**

wind harp An Aeolian harp (which see).

Wind·hoek (vint′hŏŏk) The capital of South-West Africa, in the central part; pop. 36,050 (est. 1970).

wind·hov·er (wind′huv′ər) *n. Brit.* The kestrel, a bird.

win·di·go (win′di·gō) *n. pl.* **·gos** In the mythology of certain Algonquian North American Indians, an evil demon; also, a mythical tribe of cannibals believed to inhabit an island in Hudson Bay: also spelled *wendigo.* [< Algonquian (Ojibwa) *weendigo* cannibal]

wind·ing[1] (wīn′ding) *n.* **1.** The act or condition of one who or that which winds; a spiral turning or coiling. **2.** A bend or turn, or a series of them. **3.** A warp or twist from a plane surface. **4.** *Electr.* The manner in which a conducting wire is wound in a coil, as on the armature of a dynamo. **5.** *Vet.* A defective gait of horses in which one leg seems to wind around the other. — *adj.* **1.** Turning spirally about an axis or core. **2.** Having bends or lateral turns. **3.** Twisting from a plane. — **wind′ing·ly** *adv.*

wind·ing[2] (wīn′ding) *n.* A boatswain's signal.

winding frame (wīn′ding) A device or machine for winding, as a reel.

wind·ing sheet (wīn′ding) The sheet that wraps a corpse.

wind instrument (wind) A musical instrument whose sounds are produced by vibrations of air injected by the lungs or by mechanical bellows. Compare BRASS, ORGAN, WOODWINDS, etc.

wind·jam·mer (wind′jam′ər) *n.* **1.** *Naut.* A merchant sailing vessel, as distinguished from a steamship. **2.** A member of its crew. **3.** *Slang* A chatterbox; a loquacious person.

wind·lass (wind′ləs) *n.* Any of several devices for hauling or lifting, especially one consisting of a drum or barrel on which the hoisting rope winds, and turned by means of cranking. — *v.t.* & *v.i.* To raise or haul with a windlass. [Alter. of ME *windas* < ON *vindass* < *vinda* wind + *ass* beam; infl. in form by WINDLE[2]]

win·dle[1] (win′dəl) *n.* *Brit. Dial.* A basket. [OE *windel* basket < *windan* to plait, twist]

win·dle[2] (win′dəl) *Scot. & Brit. Dial.* *v.t.* & *v.i.* To wind (yarn). — *n.* Something used for winding or turning. [Freq. of WIND[2]]

DIFFERENTIAL WINDLASS

wind·less (wind′lis) *adj.* **1.** Without wind; breezeless; calm. **2.** Being out of breath.

win·dle·straw (win′dəl·strô′) *n.* *Scot. & Brit. Dial.* **1.** A withered stalk of any one of several grasses, used in plaiting or ropemaking. **2.** A feeble, unhealthy person. **3.** The whitethroat warbler. Also **win′dle·strae′** (-strā′). [OE *windelstrēaw* < *windel* basket + *strēaw* straw]

wind·ling (wind′ling) *n.* *Scot.* A bundle of straw. [< WIND[1] + -LING[1]]

wind·mill (wind′mil′) *n.* **1.** A mill that operates by the action of the wind against adjustable slats, wings, or sails attached to a horizontal axis that, in revolving, transmit motion to a pump, millstone, or the like. **2.** Anything resembling a windmill. **3.** An imaginary wrong, evil, or foe: usually in the phrase **to fight** (or **tilt at**) **windmills**, in allusion to Don Quixote's combat with windmills, which he mistook for giants. [< WIND[1] + MILL[1]. Cf. MHG *wintmül.*]

win·dow (win′dō) *n.* **1.** An opening in the wall of a building to admit light and air, commonly equipped with sashes that enclose one or more panes of glass and that are capable of being opened and closed. **2.** A sash: Raise the *window.* **3.** A windowpane: She looked at her reflection in the *window.* **4.** Anything resembling or suggesting a window; a window-like aperture: The eyes are the *windows* of the soul. **5.** A transparent patch through which the address of an envelope can be read. — *v.t.* **1.** To provide with a window or windows. **2.** To fill with holes resembling windows. [< ON *vindauga* < *vindr* wind + *auga* eye]

window box **1.** A box, generally long and narrow, along a window ledge or sill, for growing plants. **2.** One of the grooves along the sides of a window frame for the weights that counterbalance a lifting sash.

win·dow-dress·ing (win′dō-dres′ing) *n.* **1.** The act or art of arranging merchandise attractively in store windows; also, the goods so displayed. **2.** Anything superficially attractive, especially when used to conceal or divert attention from something else. **3.** A report or statement that unduly stresses favorable conditions. — **win′dow-dress′er** *n.*

win·dow·pane (win′dō-pān′) *n.* A single sheet of glass for a window. Also **window pane.**

window seat A seat in the recess of a window.

window shade A flexible shade or screen, usually mounted on a spring roller, used to regulate light at a window.

win·dow-shop (win′dō-shop′) *v.i.* **-shopped, -shop·ping** To look at goods shown in store windows without buying them. — **win′dow-shop′per** *n.*

wind·pipe (wind′pīp′) *n.* The trachea (def. 1).

Wind River Range (wind) A range of the Rocky Mountains in west central Wyoming; highest point, Gannett Peak, 13,787 ft.

wind rose *Meteorol.* A diagram indicating the direction and relative velocities of the wind in a given locality by means of lines radiating from a common center.

wind·row (wind′rō′) *n.* **1.** A long ridge or pile of hay or grain raked together preparatory to building into cocks. **2.** A row of Indian corn made by setting two rows together. **3.** A wind-swept line of dust, surf, leaves, etc. **4.** A deep fur-

row made for planting. **5.** Land on which the trees have been felled by the wind: also **wind slash.** — *v.t.* To rake or shape into a windrow. — **wind′row′er** *n.*

wind sail **1.** *Naut.* A canvas tube or funnel with a spreading opening at one side of the top that may be stayed to face the wind, used to conduct fresh air below decks. **2.** A sail on the arm of a windmill.

wind scale Beaufort scale (which see).

wind·shake (wind′shāk′) *n.* A defect in wood, attributed to the action of the wind upon tree trunks.

wind·shield (wind′shēld′) *n.* **1.** A transparent screen, usually of glass, attached in front of the occupants of an automobile as protection against wind and weather. Also *Brit.* **wind screen.** **2.** Any arrangement for breaking the force of the wind against an object. **3.** A covering for a chimney.

wind·sock (wind′sok′) *n.* *Meteorol.* A large conical bag open at both ends, mounted on a pivot and indicating the direction of wind by the current of air that blows through it: also called *drogue, sock, wind cone.* Also **wind sleeve.**

Wind·sor (win′zər) Name of the royal family of Great Britain since 1917, when it was officially changed from *Saxe-Coburg-Gotha.*

Wind·sor (win′zər) **1.** A municipal borough in eastern Berkshire, England; site of **Windsor Castle,** a residence of the English sovereigns since the time of William the Conqueror; pop. 15,396 (1961). Officially **New Windsor. 2.** A city in SE Ontario, Canada, on the Detroit River; pop. 114,367.

Wind·sor (win′zər), **Duke of** See under EDWARD VIII.

Windsor chair A wooden chair, with or without arms, common in England and America in the 18th century, typically with a spindle back, slanting legs, and a flat or slightly depressed seat.

Windsor tie A wide, soft necktie knotted loosely in a double bow, usually of black silk cut on the bias.

wind·storm (wind′stôrm′) *n.* A violent wind, usually with little or no precipitation.

wind·suck·er (wind′suk′ər) *n.* A horse that cribs. — **wind′suck′ing** *n. & adj.*

wind tee (wind) A T-shaped weathervane, especially one located on or near an aircraft landing field.

wind tunnel *Aeron.* A large cylindrical structure in which the aerodynamic properties of airplane models, airfoils, etc., can be observed under the effects of artificially produced winds of varying velocities.

wind-up (wīnd′up′) *n.* **1.** The act of concluding or closing. **2.** A final act or part; conclusion. **3.** In baseball, the swing of the arm preparatory to pitching the ball.

wind·ward (wind′wərd) *adj.* **1.** Of or pertaining to the direction from which the wind is blowing. **2.** Being on the side exposed to the wind. — *n.* The direction from which the wind blows. — **to windward of** Advantageously placed with respect to. — *adv.* In the direction from which the wind blows. Opposed to *leeward.*

Wind·ward Islands (wind′wərd) **1.** An island group of the West Indies comprising the southern Lesser Antilles. **2.** A former British colony composed of the present colonies of Dominica, Grenada, St. Lucia, and St. Vincent and their dependencies. **3.** See under SOCIETY ISLANDS.

Windward Passage The strait between Cuba and Hispaniola; about 50 mi. wide.

wind·y (win′dē) *adj.* **wind·i·er, wind·i·est 1.** Pertaining to, consisting of, or abounding in wind; stormy; tempestuous. **2.** Exposed to the wind; wind-swept. **3.** Suggestive of wind; boisterous; swift: *windy* emotions. **4.** Producing, due to, or troubled with gas in the stomach or intestines; flatulent. **5.** Given to or expressed in bombast; pompous: a *windy* orator. [OE *windig*] — **wind′i·ly** *adv.* — **wind′i·ness** *n.*

Windy City A nickname for CHICAGO.

wine (wīn) *n.* **1.** The fermented juice of the grape, containing various percentages of alcohol by volume, commonly used as a beverage and in cooking. Wines are often classified as dry or sweet, red or white, still or sparkling. **2.** The fermented juice of some fruit other than the grape, as the elderberry, or of a plant, as the dandelion. **3.** A dark purplish red color resembling the color of certain red wines. **4.** A medicinal preparation in which wine is used as the menstruum: *wine* of opium. — **Adam's wine** Water. — *v. wined,* **win·ing** *v.t.* **1.** To entertain or treat with or as with wine: usually in the expression **to wine and dine.** — *v.i.* **2.** To drink wine. [OE *wīn* < L *vinum*]

wine·bib·bing (wīn′bib′ing) *adj.* Addicted to excessive drinking of wine. — *n.* The habitual, excessive drinking of wine. — **wine′bib′ber** *n.*

wine card The list of alcoholic drinks for sale at a hotel or restaurant.

wine cellar **1.** A storage place for wines; also, the wines stored. **2.** Any stock of wines.

wine-col·ored (wīn′kul′ərd) *adj.* Having the color of certain red wines; dark purplish red.

wine gallon See under GALLON.

wine·glass (wīn′glas′, -gläs′) *n.* A small goblet for drinking wine.

wine·glass·ful (wīn′glas-fŏŏl′, -gläs-) *n.* *pl.* **-fuls** The amount a wineglass will hold.

wine grape The cultivated grape (*Vitis vinifera*) native to Europe and now grown in the United States, traditionally used in the making of wine.

wine·grow·er (wīn′grō′ər) *n.* One who cultivates a vineyard and makes wine. — **wine′grow′ing** *adj.* & *n.*

wine list A wine card (which see).

wine measure A system of liquid measures formerly used for wines and spirits in which the gallon was equal to the present U.S. gallon.

wine palm Any palm that yields toddy (def. 2).

wine·press (wīn′pres′) *n.* An apparatus or a place where the juice of grapes is expressed. Also **wine′press′er.**

win·er·y (wī′nər·ē) *n.* *pl.* **·er·ies** 1. An establishment for making wine. 2. A room for fining and storing wines.

Wine·sap (wīn′sap) *n.* A U.S. variety of red winter apple.

wine·skin (wīn′skin′) *n.* The skin of a domestic quadruped kept as entire as possible and made into a tight bag for containing wine, much used in the Orient.

wine·sop (wīn′sop′) *n.* Any farinaceous foodstuff steeped or sopped in wine, as bread or cake.

wine steward An attendant, as in a hotel, who takes orders for wines and is in charge of the wine cellar.

wine·tast·er (wīn′tās′tər) *n.* A person who tastes wine to judge its quality.

wine vinegar A vinegar made from wine.

wine whey *Brit.* A beverage made of wine and curdled milk.

wing (wing) *n.* 1. An organ of flight; especially, one of the anterior movable pair of appendages of a bird or bat, homologous with the forelimbs of vertebrates but adapted for flight. 2. A similar organ in insects and some other animals. 3. Anything resembling or suggestive of a wing, as in form or function. 4. Flight or passage by or as by wings; also, the means or act of flying: to take *wing*. 5. Something regarded as conferring the power of swift motion or flight: on *wings* of song. 6. Either of two extremist groups or factions in a political or other organization: the left *wing*. 7. *Archit.* A part attached to a side; especially, a projection or extension of a building on the side of the main portion. 8. *Aeron.* One of the main sustaining surfaces of an airplane. 9. One of the sides of a stage; a small platform at either side of the stage; also, a piece of scenery for the side. 10. *Mil.* Either division of a military force on either side of the center. 11. An analogous formation in certain sports, as hockey or football. 12. A side section of something that shuts or folds, as a double door, a screen, etc. 13. Something moved by or moving in the wind, as the vane of a windmill. 14. *Brit.* The flare of a moldboard plowshare; also, the curved mudguard or fender of an automobile. 15. A tactical and administrative unit of the U.S. Air Force, larger than a group and smaller than an air force or air division. 16. In fortifications, one of the sides connecting an outwork with the main fort. 17. A sidepiece at the top of an armchair. 18. A shore dam or jetty for narrowing a channel; also, an extension of a dam usually built at an angle. 19. *Slang* An arm; especially, in baseball, the arm used for throwing or pitching. 20. One of the pectoral fins of a flying fish. 21. *Anat.* An ala: a *wing* of the nose. 22. *Bot.* Any thin membranous or foliaceous expansion of an organ, as of certain stems, seeds, samaras, etc. 23. *Zool.* One of the lateral finlike expansions of the foot of a pteropod. — **Syn.** See FACTION. — **on** (or **upon**) **the wing** 1. In flight: a bird *on the wing.* 2. Just about to go; departing; also, journeying. — **to take wing** To fly away. — **under one's wing** Under one's protection. — *v.t.* 1. To pass over or through in flight. 2. To accomplish by flying: the bird *winged* its way south. 3. To enable to fly. 4. To cause to go swiftly; speed: Hope *winged* his steps. 5. To transport by flight. 6. To provide with wings for flight; also, to feather (an arrow). 7. To supply with a side body or part: The house was *winged* on both sides. 8. To wound (a bird) in a wing. 9. To disable by a minor wound: I *winged* him in the arm. — *v.i.* 10. To fly; soar. [< ON *vængr*]

wing and wing *Naut.* With sails spread or boomed out on each side like wings: said of a fore-and-aft vessel running downwind.

wing·back (wing′bak′) *n.* In football, the position taken by one (**single wingback**) or two (**double wingback**) of the backs behind or beyond the ends; also, a back so posted.

wing·bow (wing′bō′) *n.* A distinctive mark of color on the bend of the wing in a domestic fowl. For illustration see FOWL.

wing chair A large armchair, upholstered throughout, with high back and side pieces designed as protection from drafts.

wing collar A man's stand-up collar, with the tips folded down, worn especially with formal dress.

wing commander In the Royal, Royal Canadian, and other Commonwealth air forces, a commissioned officer ranking next below group captain. See table at GRADE.

wing cover The elytron of an insect. Also **wing case.**

wing covert *Ornithol.* One of the small close feathers clothing the bend of a bird's wing and covering the insertion of the flight feathers.

wing·ding (wing′ding′) *n.* *U.S. Slang* 1. A wild, noisy party or event. 2. Anything that is exciting, impressive, etc. [Origin unknown]

winged (wingd; *for defs. 1, 2, & 3, also poetic* wing′id) *adj.* 1. Having wings. 2. Passing swiftly; soaring; lofty; rapt. 3. *Informal* Wounded or disabled in or as in the wing or arm.

winged disk A sun disk (which see).

wing flap *Aeron.* A control surface hinged to an airplane wing, used primarily to increase lift and retard speed.

wing-foot·ed (wing′fŏŏt′id) *adj.* Rapid; swift.

wing·less (wing′lis) *adj.* Having no wings, or having aborted wings.

wing loading *Aeron.* The gross weight of an airplane divided by the area of the wings. Also **wing load.**

wing nut A thumbnut (which see).

wing rail A guardrail, as at a railway switch.

wing skid *Aeron.* A device set beneath the wing tip of an airplane to guard the tip against contact with the ground.

wing·spread (wing′spred′) *n.* The distance between the tips of the fully extended wings of a bird, insect, or airplane.

wing·y (wing′ē) *adj.* **wing·i·er, wing·i·est** 1. Winged; swift. 2. Resembling a wing; winglike.

wink (wingk) *v.i.* 1. To close and open the eye or eyelids quickly. 2. To draw the eyelids of one eye together, as in conveying a hint or making a sign. 3. To shut one's eyes, especially in ignoring; pretend not to see: usually with *at.* 4. To emit fitful gleams; twinkle. — *v.t.* 5. To close and open (the eye or eyelids) quickly. 6. To move, force, etc., by winking: with *away, off*, etc. 7. To signify or express by winking. — *n.* 1. The act of winking. 2. The time necessary for a wink. 3. A twinkle; gleam. 4. A hint conveyed by winking. — **forty winks** *Informal* A short nap. [OE *wincian* to close the eyes]

Win·kel·ried (ving′kəl-rēt), **Arnold von** Fourteenth-century Swiss patriot and national hero.

wink·er (wing′kər) *n.* 1. One who winks. 2. A blinder for a horse. 3. The nictitating membrane, as of a bird. 4. The muscle by which winking is done. 5. A small secondary bellows for use with an organ. 6. *Slang* An eyelash.

win·kle (wing′kəl) *n.* A periwinkle.

Win·ne·ba·go (win′ə·bā′gō) *n.* *pl.* **·gos** or **·goes** One of a tribe of North American Indians of Siouan stock, formerly occupying what is now eastern Wisconsin, south of Green Bay, where many still survive.

Win·ne·ba·go (win′ə·bā′gō), **Lake** A lake in eastern Wisconsin; 215 sq. mi.

Win·ne·pe·sau·kee (win′ə·pə·sô′kē), **Lake** A lake in east central New Hampshire; 25 mi. long, 12 mi. wide. Also **Win′ni·pe·sau′kee.**

win·ner (win′ər) *n.* One who or that which wins.

win·ning (win′ing) *adj.* 1. Successful in achievement, especially in competition. 2. Capable of winning or charming; attractive; winsome: a *winning* smile. — *n.* 1. The act of one who wins. 2. *Usually pl.* That which is won; especially, money won in gambling. 3. A new opening in a mine; also, a section of a mine prepared for working. — **win′ning·ly** *adv.* — **win′ning·ness** *n.*

winning gallery In court tennis, a grille or square opening in the penthouse in the rear of the hazard court, so named because a ball played into it counts as a win.

winning hazard See under HAZARD (def. 5).

winning post The post or goal at the end of a racecourse.

Win·ni·peg (win′ə·peg) The capital of Manitoba, Canada, in the SE part on the Red River; pop. 255,093.

Winnipeg, Lake A lake in south central Manitoba, Canada; 9,398 sq. mi.

Winnipeg couch *Canadian* A daybed without arms or back.

Winnipeg goldeye *Canadian* A goldeye (which see).

Winnipeg River A river in NW Ontario and SE Manitoba, flowing 200 miles NW from Lake of the Woods to Lake Winnipeg.

win·nock (win′ək) *n.* *Scot.* A window.

win·now (win′ō) *v.t.* 1. To separate (grain, etc.) from the chaff by means of wind or a current of air. 2. To blow away (the chaff) thus. 3. To examine so as to separate good from bad; analyze minutely; sift. 4. To separate (what is valuable) from what is valueless, or to eliminate (what is valueless) from what is valuable; distinguish; sort: often with *out.* 5. To blow upon; cause to flutter. 6. To beat or fan (the air) with the wings. 7. To scatter by blowing; disperse. 8. *Rare* To proceed along (a course) by flapping the wings. — *v.i.* 9. To separate grain from chaff. 10. To fly; flap. — *n.* 1. Any device used in winnowing grain. 2. The act of winnowing; also, a vibrating motion caused by a current of air. [OE *windwian* < *wind* the wind] — **win′now·er** *n.*

win·o (wī′nō) *n.* *pl.* **·noes** or **·nos** *U.S. Slang* A drunkard who habitually drinks sweet, fortified wines. [< WINE]

Wins·low (winz′lō), **Edward,** 1595–1655, English Puritan in New England; one of the founders of Plymouth Colony.

win·some (win′səm) *adj.* Having a winning appearance or manner; pleasing; attractive. [OE *wynsum* < *wyn* joy] — **win'some·ly** *adv.* — **win'some·ness** *n.*

Win·sor (win'zər), **Justin**, 1831–97, U.S. historian and librarian.

Win·ston-Sa·lem (win'stən-sā'ləm) A city in NW central North Carolina; pop. 132,913.

win·ter (win'tər) *n.* **1.** The coldest season of the year, occurring between autumn and spring and in the northern hemisphere popularly regarded as including December, January, and February. Astronomically it extends from the winter solstice to the vernal equinox. ◆ Collateral adjectives: *hibernal, hiemal.* **2.** A period of time marked by lack of life, coldness, or cheerlessness. **3.** *Chiefly Poetic* A year of life: a man of ninety *winters.* — *v.i.* **1.** To pass the winter: We *wintered* in Bermuda. — *v.t.* **2.** To care for, feed, or protect during the winter: to *winter* animals. — *adj.* **1.** Pertaining to or taking place in winter; hibernal. **2.** Suitable to or characteristic of winter. [OE] — **win'ter·er** *n.* — **win'ter·less** *adj.*

winter aconite A hardy, small, tuberous-rooted European garden herb (*Eranthis hyemalis*) of the crowfoot family, with bright yellow flowers and oblong anthers.

win·ter·ber·ry (win'tər-ber'ē) *n. pl.* ·ries Any of several North American shrubs (genus *Ilex*) of the holly family, bearing small, bright red berries; especially, the **smooth winterberry** (*I. laevigata*) of the eastern United States.

win·ter·bourne (win'tər-bôrn', -bōrn', -boorn') *n.* A stream flowing only during excessive rainfall, when water at the source rises above a certain level. [OE *winter burna* < *winter* + *burna* stream]

win·ter·feed (win'tər-fēd') *v.t.* ·fed, ·feed·ing To feed (stock) during the time when grazing is impossible.

win·ter·green (win'tər-grēn) *n.* **1.** A small evergreen plant (*Gaultheria procumbens*) of North America, bearing a cluster of bell-shaped flowers, and aromatic oval leaves that yield a colorless volatile oil (**oil of wintergreen**), used as a flavor: also called *boxberry, checkerberry, spiceberry.* **2.** Any of various low evergreen herbs (genus *Pyrola*): also, *U.S.,* shinleaf. **3.** Shinleaf (def. 1). [On analogy with Du. *wintergroen*; so called because it is an evergreen]

win·ter·ize (win'tə-rīz) *v.t.* ·ized, ·iz·ing To prepare or equip (engines, etc.) for winter.

win·ter·kill (win'tər-kil') *v.t. & v.i.* To die or kill by exposure to extreme cold: said of plants and grains.

win·ter·ly (win'tər-lē) *adj.* Wintry; cheerless.

winter melon A hardy, cold-resistant muskmelon (*Cucumis melo, variety inodorus*).

Win·ter·thur (vin'tər-tōor) A city in northern Switzerland near Zurich; pop. 91,000 (est. 1968).

win·ter·tide (win'tər-tīd') *n.* Poetic Winter.

win·ter·time (win'tər-tīm') *n.* The winter season; winter.

winter wheat Wheat planted before snowfall and harvested the following summer.

Win·throp (win'thrəp), **John**, 1588–1649, English Puritan colonist in New England: governor of Massachusetts Bay Colony. — **John**, 1606–76, English colonist in New England; governor of Connecticut Colony; son of the preceding.

win·try (win'trē) *adj.* ·tri·er, ·tri·est Belonging to winter; cold; frosty; brumal. Also **win'ter·y** (-tər-ē). [OE *wintrig*] — **win'tri·ly** (-trə-lē) *adv.* — **win'tri·ness** *n.*

win·y (wī'nē) *adj.* **win·i·er, win·i·est** Having the taste or qualities of wine.

winze[1] (winz) *n.* *Mining* A small inclined shaft from one level of a mine to another. [Earlier *winds,* ? < obs. *wind* windlass, fusion of MDu. *winde* windlass and WIND[2]]

winze[2] (winz) *n.* *Scot.* An oath. [< MDu. *wensch* wish]

wipe (wīp) *v.t.* **wiped, wip·ing 1.** To subject to slight friction or rubbing, usually with some soft, absorbent material. **2.** To remove by rubbing lightly; brush: usually with *away* or *off.* **3.** To move, apply, or draw for the purpose of wiping: He *wiped* his hand across his brow. **4.** To apply solder to with a piece of greased cloth or leather. — **to wipe out** To remove or destroy utterly; annihilate. — *n.* **1.** The act of wiping or rubbing. **2.** *Mech.* A wiper. **3.** *Slang* A sweeping blow or stroke; a swipe. **4.** *Slang* A handkerchief. **5.** *Slang* A jeer; jibe. [OE *wīpian.* Akin to WISP.]

wip·er (wī'pər) *n.* **1.** One who wipes. **2.** An article designed or used for wiping. **3.** *Mech.* A cam having one or more projections serving, when mounted on a rotating shaft, to give a reciprocating (usually vertical) motion to another part. **4.** *Electr.* A moving member of an electrical device that makes contact with the terminals.

wire (wīr) *n.* **1.** A slender rod, strand, or thread of ductile metal, usually having a circular cross section of a specified diameter. **2.** Something made of wire, as a fence, a bar of a cage, a snare, etc. **3.** A telegraph or telephone cable. **4.** The telegraph system as a means of communication. **5.** *Informal* A telegram. **6.** *pl.* A secret means of exerting influence, as if by operating hidden wires, like those used in manipulating puppets: to pull the *wires.* **7.** An imaginary line marking the finish of a racecourse. **8.** A fine metallic

thread, a cobweb, or one of a set of ruled lines, in the focus of a telescope. **9.** The screen of a papermaking machine. **10.** *Ornithol.* A long slender filament of the plumage of various birds. — **to lay wires for** To prepare for. — **under the wire** Just in time or barely within the limits. — **under wire** Fenced. — *v.* **wired, wir·ing** *v.t.* **1.** To fasten with wire. **2.** To furnish or equip with wiring: The studio was *wired* for sound. **3.** *Informal* To transmit or send by electric telegraph: to *wire* an order. **4.** *Informal* To send a telegram to: Will you *wire* John? **5.** To place on wire, as beads. **6.** In croquet, to place (a ball) so that the wire of an arch will be between it and another ball. **7.** To catch, as a rabbit, with a snare of wire. — *v.i.* **8.** *Informal* To telegraph. [OE *wīr*]

wire brush A brush having metal bristles, for cleaning paint or rust from surfaces.

wire cloth A fabric of woven wire, as for strainers, window screens, papermaking, etc.

wire coat An outer coat, as of some dogs, of dense stiff hair.

wire-danc·er (wīr'dan'sər, -dän'-) *n.* One who performs feats of balancing, etc., upon a wire stretched in mid-air: also called *wirewalker.* — **wire'-danc'ing** *n.*

wire-draw (wīr'drô') *v.t.* **-drew, -drawn, -draw·ing 1.** To draw, as a metal rod, through a series of holes of diminishing diameter to produce a wire. **2.** To treat (a subject) with excessive subtlety or overrefinement. — **wire'-draw'er** *n.*

wire entanglement *Mil.* An obstruction of barbed wire, set up to hinder enemy action in warfare.

wire gauge 1. A gauge for measuring the diameter of wire, usually a round plate with calibrated numbered slots on its periphery, or a long graduated plate with a slot of diminishing width. **2.** A standard system of sizes for wire.

wire gauze A material of a gauzelike structure made of interwoven strands of wire.

WIRE GAUGE (American standard)

wire glass Glass sheets reinforced with wire netting.

wire·grass (wīr'gras', -gräs') *n.* **1.** A European grass (*Poa compressa*) having slender, compressed stems, cultivated in the U.S. and Canada: also called *Canada bluegrass.* **2.** Any one of several similar grasses.

wire-haired terrier (wīr'hârd') A fox terrier having a wiry coat. Also **wire'hair'** (-hâr').

wire·less (wīr'lis) *adj.* **1.** Having no wire or wires. **2.** *Brit.* Radio. — *n.* **1.** The wireless telegraph or telephone system, or a message transmitted by either. **2.** *Brit.* Radio. — *v.t. & v.i. Brit.* To communicate (with) by wireless telegraphy; radio.

wireless telegraphy Telegraphy without wires connecting the points of transmission and reception, the message being transmitted through space by electromagnetic waves.

wireless telephony The transmission and reception of vocal messages by radio.

wire·man (wīr'mən) *n. pl.* ·men (-mən) One who handles wire for telegraph lines, etc.; a wirer.

wire mark The faint impression left on paper by wire cloth or by the dandy roll pattern during manufacture.

wire netting Netting made of wire, as window screens.

Wire·pho·to (wīr'fō'tō) *n. pl.* ·tos An apparatus and method for transmitting and receiving photographs by wire: a trade name. Also **wire'pho'to.**

wire·pull·er (wīr'pool'ər) *n.* **1.** One who pulls wires, as of a puppet. **2.** One who uses secret means to control others or gain his own ends; an intriguer. — **wire'pull'ing** *n.*

wir·er (wīr'ər) *n.* **1.** A trapper who snares with wire contrivances. **2.** One who wires.

wire recorder *Electronics* A device for recording sounds by electromagnetic registration on a fine moving wire, the impulses being reconverted to sound as the magnetized wire is passed through a receiver.

wire rope A rope of wires firmly wound together.

wire service A news agency that collects and distributes news to subscribing newspapers, radio stations, etc.

wire-spun (wīr'spun') *adj.* **1.** Drawn out to form a wire. **2.** Spun or drawn out too fine; overrefined.

wire·tap (wīr'tap') *v.* **tapped, ·tap·ping** *v.t.* **1.** To intercept (information) by means of wiretapping. — *v.i.* **2.** To engage in wiretapping. — *n.* Wiretapping (which see). [Back formation < WIRETAPPING] — **wire'tap·per** *n.*

wire·tap·ping (wīr'tap'ing) *n.* The act, process, or practice of tapping telephone or telegraph wires for the purpose of secretly securing information: also called *wiretap*.

wire·walk·er (wīr′wô′kər) *n.* A wire-dancer (which see).

wire·work (wīr′wûrk) *n.* 1. Small articles made of wire cloth. 2. Wire fabrics in general.

wire·works (wīr′wûrks) *n.pl.* (*often construed as sing.*) A factory where wire or articles of wire are made.

wire·worm (wīr′wûrm′) *n.* 1. The larva of a click beetle, some species of which are injurious to plants. For illustration see INSECTS (injurious). 2. A millipede.

wire·wove (wīr′wōv′) *adj.* 1. Denoting a high grade of paper with a smooth writing surface. 2. Woven of wire.

wir·ing (wīr′ing) *n.* An entire system of wire installed for the distribution of electric power.

wir·ra (wir′ə) *interj. Irish* An exclamation of sorrow.

wir·y (wīr′ē) *adj.* **wir·i·er**, **wir·i·est** 1. Having great resisting power; thin, but tough and sinewy: said of persons. 2. Like wire; stiff. — **wir′i·ly** *adv.* — **wir′i·ness** *n.*

wis (wis) *v.t. Obs.* To suppose; think. [< IWIS]

Wis. Wisconsin: also **Wisc.** (unofficial).

Wis·by (viz′bē) The German name for VISBY.

Wis·con·sin (wis·kon′sən) A State of the Great Lakes region of the United States; 56,154 sq. mi.; pop. 4,417,933; capital, Madison; entered the Union May 29, 1848; nickname, *Badger State.* — **Wis·con′sin·ite** (-īt) *n.*

Wisconsin River A river in central Wisconsin, flowing about 430 miles south and SW to the Mississippi.

wis·dom (wiz′dəm) *n.* 1. The power of true and right discernment; also, conformity to the course of action dictated by such discernment. 2. Good practical judgment; common sense. 3. A high degree of knowledge. 4. A wise saying. — **Syn.** See SENSE. [OE *wīsdōm* < *wīs* wise]

Wisdom of Jesus, Son of Si·rach (sī′rak) Ecclesiasticus.

Wisdom of Solomon A book of the Old Testament Apocrypha, consisting of a hymn in praise of wisdom, ascribed by tradition to Solomon.

wisdom tooth The last molar tooth on either side of the upper and lower jaws in man, usually appearing between the 17th and 22d year. For illustration see TOOTH. — **to cut one's wisdom teeth** To acquire mature judgment.

wise¹ (wīz) *adj.* **wis·er**, **wis·est** 1. Possessed of wisdom; seeing clearly what is right and just; having sound judgment. 2. Sagacious; shrewd; calculating. 3. Marked by wisdom; prudent; sensible. 4. Having great learning; erudite; sage. 5. Having practical knowledge of the arts or sciences. 6. Versed in mysterious things. 7. *Informal* Aware of; onto: *wise* to his motives. 8. *U.S. Slang* Arrogant or sarcastic in manner; also, offensively bold; impudent. — **to get wise** *Slang* To know the true facts. — *v.t.* **wised, wis·ing** *Slang* To make cognizant of; inform. — **to wise up** *Slang* To make or become aware, informed, or sophisticated. [OE *wīs*] — **wise′ly** *adv.* — **wise′ness** *n.*

wise² (wīz) *n.* Way of doing; manner; method: chiefly in the phrases **in any wise**, **in no wise**, etc. [OE *wīse* manner. Akin to GUISE.]

wise³ (wīz) *v.t. & v.i. Scot.* To incline; turn. [OE *wīsian*]

-wise *combining form* 1. In a (specified) way or manner: *likewise; nowise.* 2. In a (specified) direction or position: *clockwise; crosswise.* 3. With reference to; in regard to: *moneywise:* SEE NOTE BELOW. [OE *wīse* manner]

♦ At one time the Old English *wīse* "manner, fashion" was commonly attached to substantives and adjectives to form adverbs of manner. This usage, long considered archaic, has recently come back into fashion. The suffix is now freely added to nouns, with the general meaning "with reference to": *Weather-wise,* it will probably snow. Such compounds formed with *-wise* often add no further information to a statement, and should be used with discretion.

Wise (wīz), **Stephen Samuel,** 1874–1949, U.S. rabbi and civic leader born in Hungary.

wise·a·cre (wīz′ā′kər) *n.* 1. One who affects great wisdom. 2. A wise man; sage. [< MDu. *wijsseggher* soothsayer; infl. in form by ACRE]

wise·crack (wīz′krak′) *Slang n.* A smart or supercilious remark. — **Syn.** See JEST. — *v.i.* To utter a wisecrack.

wise guy *U.S. Slang* A conceited or insolent person.

Wise·man (wīz′mən), **Nicholas Patrick Stephen,** 1802–65, English cardinal and theologian born in Spain.

wis·en·heim·er (wī′zen-him′ər) *n. U.S. Slang* A wise guy; wiseacre. [< WISE¹ + *-enheimer* as in some Ger. family names]

wish (wish) *n.* 1. A desire or longing, usually for some definite thing. 2. An expression of such a desire; petition. 3. Something wished for. 4. *Psychoanal.* An impulse, tendency, or striving, usually unconscious, toward the satisfaction of some need. — *v.t.* 1. To have a desire or longing for; crave; want: We *wish* to be sure. 2. To desire a specified condition or state for (a person or thing): I *wish* this day were over. 3. To invoke upon or for someone: I *wished* him good luck. 4. To bid: to *wish* someone good morning. 5. To request or entreat: also, to command: I *wish* you would be quiet. — *v.i.* 6. To have or feel a desire; yearn; long: usually with *for:* to *wish* for a friend's return. 7. To make or express a wish. — **Syn.** See DESIRE. — **to wish on** To impose (something or someone) on a person. [OE *wȳscan*]

wish·bone (wish′bōn′) *n.* The forked bone formed by the united clavicles of many birds; the furcula. [from the old belief that when pulled apart by two persons, each making a wish, the one who gets the longer part will have his wish fulfilled]

wish·ful (wish′fəl) *adj.* Having a wish or desire; full of longing. — **wish′ful·ly** *adv.* — **wish′ful·ness** *n.*

wish fulfillment 1. The satisfaction of a wish. 2. *Psychoanal.* The illusory realization of a strongly motivated, often unconscious and repressed aim by mental processes divorced from or not in accord with reality.

wishful thinking Thinking characterized by a conscious or unconscious attempt to impose upon reality conditions that, if true, would make it more pleasant or tolerable.

wish-wash (wish′wosh′, -wôsh′) *n.* Any thin, weak, insipid drink; slops. [Varied reduplication of WASH]

wish·y-wash·y (wish′ē-wosh′ē, -wôsh′ē) *adj. Informal* 1. Thin; diluted, as liquor. 2. Lacking in solidity, purpose, or vigor; unsubstantial.

Wis·la (wēs′lä) The Polish name for the VISTULA.

Wis·mar (vis′mär) A port city in NW East Germany, on the Baltic; pop. about 55,000.

wisp (wisp) *n.* 1. A small bunch, as of hay, straw, or hair. 2. A small bit; a mere indication: a *wisp* of vapor. 3. Will-o'-the-wisp: see IGNIS FATUUS. — *v.t.* 1. To dress, brush, or groom with a wisp or whisk. 2. To fold and lightly twist into a wisp or wisplike form; crumple. [ME *wisp, wips.* Akin to WIPE.] — **wisp′y** *adj.*

wisp·ish (wisp′ish) *adj.* Like or having the nature of a wisp.

Wiss·ler (wis′lər), **Clark,** 1870–1947, U.S. anthropologist.

wist (wist) Past tense and pa t participle of WIT².

wis·ter·i·a (wis·tir′ē·ə) *n.* Any of a genus (*Wistaria*) of woody twining shrubs of the bean family, with pinnate leaves, elongated pods, and clusters of blue, purple, or white flowers; especially, the **Chinese wistaria** (*W. sinensis*) and the **Japanese wistaria** (*W. floribunda*). Also **wis·tar′i·a** (-tär′ē·ə). [after Caspar *Wistar,* 1761–1818, U.S. anatomist]

WISTERIA

Wis·ter (wis′tər), **Owen,** 1860–1938, U.S. novelist.

wist·ful (wist′fəl) *adj.* 1. Wishful; longing. 2. Musing; pensive. [Appar. < obs. *wistly* intently; infl. in form by WISHFUL] — **wist′ful·ly** *adv.* — **wist′ful·ness** *n.*

wit¹ (wit) *n.* 1. The power of knowing or perceiving; intelligence; ingenuity; sagacity; keen or good sense. 2. The power or faculty of rapid and accurate observation; the power of comprehending and judging. 3. *pl.* The faculties of perception and understanding: to use one's *wits.* 4. *pl.* The mental faculties with regard to their state of balance: out of her *wits.* 5. The ready perception and happy expression of unexpected or amusing analogies or other relations between apparently incongruous ideas; sudden and ingenious association of ideas or words. 6. One who has a keen perception of the incongruous or ludicrous and makes skillful use of it in writing or speaking; also, a clever conversationalist. 7. Significance; meaning; import. 8. *Obs.* Mental activity. — **at one's wits' end** At the limit of one's devices and resources; not knowing what to do. [OE] — **Syn.** 3. See INTELLECT. 5. humor, satire. Compare JEST.

wit² (wit) *v.t. & v.i.* wist, wit·ting Present indicative: I **wot,** thou **wost,** he **wot,** we, you, they **wite**(n) *Archaic* To be or become aware (of); learn; know. — **to wit** That is to say; namely: used to introduce a detailed statement or explanation, especially in legal documents. [OE *witan* to know]

wit·an (wit′ən) *n.pl.* 1. Members of the national council in Saxon, England. 2. The council itself. [OE, councilors, pl. of *wita* wise man, witness]

witch¹ (wich) *n.* 1. A person who practices sorcery; one having supernatural powers, especially to work evil, and usually by association with evil spirits or the devil: formerly applied to men, women and children, now generally restricted to women. 2. An ugly, malignant old woman; a hag. 3. A bewitching or fascinating woman or girl. — *v.t.* 1. To overcome by witchcraft: work an evil spell upon. 2. To effect by witchcraft. 3. To fascinate or bewitch; enchant. [OE *wicce* witch, fem. of *wicca* wizard < *wiccian* to bewitch]

witch² (wich) *n.* The wych-elm. [OE *wice* < *wīcan* to yield]

witch alder A shrub (*Fothergilla gardeni*) resembling the witch hazel in its fruit and the alder in its leaves, found along swamps from Virginia to Florida. [< WITCH² + ALDER]

witch·craft (wich′kraft′, -kräft′) *n.* 1. The practices or powers of witches or wizards, especially when regarded as due to dealings with evil spirits or the devil: also called *black magic.* 2. An instance of such practices. 3. Extraordinary influence or fascination; witchery. — **Syn.** See MAGIC.

witch doctor 1. Among certain primitive peoples of Africa, especially the Kaffirs, a medicine man skilled in detecting witches and counteracting evil spells. 2. Any medicine man or magician. 3. One who professes to heal or cure by sorcery; a hex.

witch-elm (wich′elm′)   See WYCH–ELM.

witch·er·y (wich′ər·ē)   *n.*   *pl.* **·er·ies**   1. Witchcraft.   2. Power to charm; fascination.

witch·es′-broom (wich′iz·brōōm′, -brōōm′) *n.* A compact broomlike growth of portions of various trees and shrubs, characterized by excessive multiplication of branches, and due in some cases to the presence of parasitic fungi: also called *hexenbesen.* Also **witch′broom′.**

witches′ Sabbath   In medieval folklore, a midnight orgy of demons and witches: also called *sabbat.*

witch·grass (wich′gras′, -gräs′) *n.* Panic grass (which see).

witch hazel   1. A shrub (*Hamamelis virginiana*) of the United States and Canada, with several branching crooked trunks and small yellow flowers.   2. An ointment and fluid extract used as a remedy for bruises, sprains, etc., derived from the bark and dried leaves of this shrub.   Also *wych-hazel.*   [< WITCH² + HAZEL]

witch hunt   *Informal* An investigation of persons ostensibly to uncover subversive activities, but intended for ulterior motives, such as harassing political opposition. **— witch-hunt·ing** (wich′hun′ting) *adj. & n.* **— witch′-hunt′er** *n.*

witch·ing (wich′ing)   *adj.* Having power to enchant; weird; fascinating. **—** *n.* Witchcraft; sorcery. **— witch′ing·ly** *adv.*

witch moth   Any of several noctuid moths (genus *Erebus*) of the United States, the West Indies, and South America.

wite (wīt)   *n.*   *Scot. & Brit. Dial.*   1. A penalty; fine.   2. A reproach; blame.   3. A guilty action; fault.   [OE *wīte*]

wit·e·na·ge·mot (wit′ə·nə·gə·mōt′) *n.* The assembly of the witan.   [OE *witena gemōt* councilors′ assembly]

with (with, with)   *prep.*   1. In the company of; as a member or associate of.   2. Next to; beside: Walk *with* me.   3. Having; bearing: a hat *with* a feather.   4. Characterized or marked by; characteristically possessed of: the house *with* green shutters.   5. In a manner characterized by; exhibiting: to dance *with* grace.   6. Among: counted *with* the others.   7. During; in the course of: We forget *with* time.   8. From; so as to be separated from: to dispense *with* luxury.   9. Against: to struggle *with* an adversary.   10. In the opinion of: That is all right *with* me.   11. Because of; as a consequence of: faint *with* hunger.   12. In charge of; in possession of: Leave the key *with* the janitor.   13. Using; by means or aid of: to write *with* a pencil.   14. By adding or having as a material or quality: trimmed *with* lace; endowed *with* beauty.   15. Under the influence of: confused *with* drink.   16. In spite of: *With* all his money, he could not buy health.   17. At the same time as: to go to bed *with* the chickens.   18. In the same direction as: to drift *with* the crowd.   19. In regard to; in the case of: I am angry *with* them.   20. Onto; to: Join this tube *with* that one.   21. In proportion to: His fame grew *with* his deeds.   22. In support of: He voted *with* the Left.   23. Of the same opinion as: I′m *with* you there!   24. Compared to; contrasted to: Consider this book *with* that one.   25. Immediately after; following: *With* that, he slammed the door.   26. Having received or been granted: *With* your consent I′ll go.   27. Into: Mix the water *with* the flour.   28. As well as: He can cook *with* the best of them. Abbr. **w.** **— Syn.** See BY. [OE]

with-   *prefix*   1. Against: *withstand.*   2. Back; away: *withhold.*   [OE *with-* < *with* against]

with·al (with·ôl′, with-)   *Archaic adv.* With the rest; in addition. **—** *prep.* With: intensive form used after its object and at the end of the clause: a bow to shoot *withal.* [ME *with alle* < *with* + *alle* all]

with·draw (with·drô′, with-)   *v.* **·drew, ·drawn, ·draw·ing** *v.t.*   1. To draw or take away; remove.   2. To take back, as an assertion or a promise.   3. To keep or abstract from use. **—** *v.i.*   4. To draw back; retire.   5. To quit taking an addictive narcotic.   [< WITH- + DRAW]

with·draw·al (with·drô′əl, with-)   *n.* The act or process of withdrawing. Also **with·draw′ment** (-mənt).

withdrawing room   1. A room behind another room for retirement.   2. A drawing room (which see).

with·drawn (with·drôn′, with-)   Past participle of WITHDRAW. **—** *adj. Psychol.* Lacking in responsiveness, especially emotional responsiveness, in social relations.

withe (with, with, with)   *n.*   1. A willowy, supple twig.   2. A band made of twisted flexible shoots, straw, or the like.   3. An elastic handle for a tool. **—** *v.t.* withed, with·ing To bind with withes. [OE *withthe*]

with·er (with′ər)   *v.i.*   1. To become limp or dry, as a plant when cut down or deprived of moisture.   2. To waste, as flesh.   3. To droop or languish. **—** *v.t.*   4. To cause to become limp or dry.   5. To abash, as by a scornful glance. [Appar. var. of WEATHER, v.] **— Syn.** 1. shrink, shrivel, wizen. **— Ant.** bloom, flourish.

With·er (with′ər), **George,** 1588–1667, English poet. Also **With′ers** (-ərz).

with·er·ite (with′ə·rīt)   *n.* A white, translucent barium carbonate. BaCO₃, occurring massive or in orthorhombic crystals. [after Dr. William *Withering,* 1741–99, English physician, who first analyzed it]

withe rod   A shrub (*Viburnum cassinoides*) of the honeysuckle family, growing in swamps in North America.

with·ers (with′ərz)   *n.pl.*   1. The highest part of the back of the horse between the shoulder blades.   2. The similar part in some other animals, as the deer and ox.   3. *Archaic & Poetic* Feelings; sensibilities: chiefly in the phrase **to wring one′s withers.**   [OE *withre* resistance < *wither* against; so called because the horse opposes this part against the load]

with·er·shins (with′ər·shinz)   *adv. Scot.*   1. In the opposite direction; in a reversed way.   2. In a direction opposite to the apparent course of the sun. Also spelled *widdershins, widershins.*   [< MLG *weddersinnes*]

With·er·spoon (with′ər·spōōn), **John,** 1722–94, American clergyman, educator, and patriot born in Scotland.

with·hold (with·hōld′, with-)   *v.* **·held, ·hold·ing** *v.t.*   1. To hold back; restrain.   2. To keep back; decline to grant. **—** *v.i.*   3. To refrain; forbear. **— Syn.** See RETAIN. [< WITH- + HOLD] **— with·hold′er** *n.*

withholding tax   A part of an employee′s wages or salary that is deducted as an installment on his income tax.

with·in (with·in′, with-)   *adv.*   1. In the inner part; interiorly.   2. Inside the body, heart, or mind.   3. Indoors. **—** *prep.*   1. In the inner or interior part or parts of; inside: *within* the house.   2. In the limits, range, or compass of (a specified time, space, or distance): *within* a mile of here.   3. Not exceeding (a specified quantity): Live *within* your means.   4. In the reach, limit, or scope of: *within* my power. **—** *n.* An inner part or place: trouble from *within.* [OE *withinnan* < *with* with + *innan* in]

with·in·doors (with·in′dôrz′, -dōrz′, with-)   *adv. Archaic* Inside a building; indoors.

with-it (with′it)   *adj. Slang*   1. In touch with modern habits, fashions, trends, etc.; up-to-date; hip.   2. Lively and modern; swinging. Also **with it.**

with·out (with·out′, with-)   *prep.*   1. Not having, as the result of loss, privation, negation, etc.; lacking: They are *without* a home.   2. In the absence of: We must manage *without* help.   3. Free from: *without* fear.   4. At, on, or to the outside of.   5. Outside of or beyond the limits of: living *without* the pale of civilization.   6. With avoidance of: He listened *without* paying attention.   7. *Obs.* Besides. **—** *adv.*   1. In or on the outer part.   2. Out of doors. **—** *conj. Dial.* Unless. **—** *n.* An outer part or place: to receive messages from *without.* [OE *withūtan* < *with* with + *ūtan* out]

with·out·doors (with·out′dôrz′, -dōrz′, with-)   *adv. Archaic* Out of doors; outside.

with·stand (with·stand′, with-)   *v.* **·stood, ·stand·ing** *v.t.*   1. To oppose with any force; resist successfully. **—** *v.i.*   2. To make resistance; endure. **— Syn.** See OPPOSE. [OE *withstandan* < *with-* against + *standan* to stand]

with·y (with′ē, with′ē)   *adj.* Made of withes; flexible and tough. **—** *n.*   *pl.* **with·ies**   1. A rope made of withes.   2. A flexible twig; withe. [OE *withig*]

wit·less (wit′lis)   *adj.* Lacking in wit; foolish.   [OE *witlēas*] **— wit′less·ly** *adv.* **— wit′less·ness** *n.*

wit·ling (wit′ling)   *n.* One who considers himself a wit.

wit·ness (wit′nis)   *n.*   1. A person who has seen or knows something, and is therefore competent to give evidence concerning it; a spectator.   2. That which serves as or furnishes evidence or proof.   3. *Law* **a** One who has knowledge of facts relating to a given cause and is subpoenaed to testify. **b** A person who has signed his name to an instrument executed by another in order that he may testify to the genuineness of the maker′s signature.   4. An attestation to a fact or an event; testimony: usually in the phrase **to bear witness.** **—** *v.t.*   1. To see or know by personal experience.   2. To furnish or serve as evidence of.   3. To give testimony to.   4. To be the site or scene of: This spot has *witnessed* many heinous crimes.   5. *Law* To see the execution of (an instrument) and subscribe to it for the purpose of establishing its authenticity. **—** *v.i.*   6. To give evidence; testify. [OE *witnes* knowledge, testimony] **— wit′ness·er** *n.*

witness stand   The place in a courtroom from which a witness gives evidence.

wit·ney (wit′nē)   *n.* A heavy woolen fabric, preshrunk and napped, used for blankets and coats. [after *Witney,* Oxfordshire, England, where it was first manufactured]

Wit·te (vit′ə), **Count Sergei Yulievich,** 1849–1915, Russian statesman, diplomat, and financier.

wit·ted (wit′id)   *adj.*   1. Having wit.   2. Having (a specified kind of) wit: used in combination: *quick-witted.*

Wit·te·kind (vit′ə·kind), died 807?, Saxon chieftain; fought against Charlemagne. Also *Widukind.*

Wit·ten·berg (wit′n·bûrg, *Ger.* vit′n·berkh)   A city in central East Germany, on the Elbe; the Protestant Reformation originated here, 1517; pop. 47,400 (est. 1967).

Witt·gen·stein (vit′gən·shtīn), **Ludwig Josef Johann,** 1889–1951, Austrian philosopher.

wit·ti·cism (wit′ə·siz′əm)   *n.* A witty saying. **— Syn.** See JEST.   [< WITTY, on analogy with *criticism;* coined by Dryden]

---

wit·ting[1] (wit′ing) *adj.* Done consciously, with knowledge and responsibility; deliberate. [< WIT[2]] — **wit′ting·ly** *adv.*

wit·ting[2] (wit′ing) *n. Obs.* Knowledge; information. [< ON *ritand* consciousness < *vita* to know]

wit·tol (wit′l) *n. Obs.* A contented cuckold; a husband who is aware of, but indifferent to, his wife's infidelity. [ME *wetewold* < *weten*, *witen* to know + (*coke*)*wold* cuckold]

wit·ty (wit′ē) *adj.* **·ti·er**, **·ti·est** **1.** Given to making original or clever speeches; quick at repartee; humorous. **2.** Displaying or full of wit. — **Syn.** See HUMOROUS. [OE *wittig* wise] — **wit′ti·ly** *adv.* — **wit′ti·ness** *n.*

Wit·wa·ters·rand (wit-wä′tərs-ränt, -rand) A region of southern Transvaal, near Johannesburg; 1,000 sq. mi.; site of rich gold fields: also *The Rand.*

wive (wīv) *v.* **wived**, **wiv·ing** *Archaic v.t.* **1.** To marry (a woman). **2.** To furnish with a wife. — *v.i.* **3.** To marry a woman. [OE *wīfian* < *wīf* wife, woman]

wi·vern (wī′vərn) *n. Heraldry* A two-legged, winged dragon, with barbed and knotted tail: often spelled *wyvern*. Also **wi′ver**. [< AF *wivre*, OF *guivre* dragon, serpent, var. of *vivre* < L *vipera*]

wives (wīvz) Plural of WIFE.

wiz (wiz) *n. Slang* A wizard (def. 2). [Short for WIZARD]

wiz·ard (wiz′ərd) *n.* **1.** A male witch; sorcerer. **2.** *Informal* A very skillful or clever person: He's a *wizard* with machinery. **3.** *Obs.* A wise man; sage. — *adj.* **1.** Having magical powers. **2.** Fascinating; enchanting. [ME *wysard* < *wys*, OE *wīs* wise]

wiz·ard·ry (wiz′ərd·rē) *n.* The practice or methods of a wizard.

wiz·en[1] (wiz′ən) *v.t. & v.i.* To become or cause to become withered; shrivel. — *adj.* Wizened; shrunken; shriveled. [OE *wisnian* to dry up, wither]

wiz·en[2] (wiz′ən) *n. Archaic* Weasand. Also **wiz′zen**.

wiz·ened (wiz′ənd) *adj.* Shrunken; withered; dried up.

wk. (*pl.* **wks.**) **1.** Week. **2.** Work.

wkly. Weekly.

w.l. or **WL** **1.** Water line. **2.** Wave length.

W.L. West Lothian.

W. long. West longitude.

W.M. Worshipful Master.

wmk. or **w/m** Watermark.

WNW or **wnw, W.N.W., w.n.w.** West-northwest.

WO or **W.O.** **1.** Wait order. **2.** *Mil.* Warrant Officer.

woad (wōd) *n.* **1.** An Old World herb (*Isatis tinctoria*) of the mustard family; dyer's-weed: also called *pastel*. **2.** The blue dyestuff obtained from its leaves. [OE *wād*] — **woad′ed** *adj.*

woad·wax·en (wōd′wak′sən) *n.* Dyer's-broom.

woald (wōld) *n.* Weld[2].

wob·ble (wob′əl) *v.* **·bled**, **·bling** *v.i.* **1.** To move or sway unsteadily, as a top while rotating at a low speed. **2.** To show indecision or unsteadiness; waver; vacillate. — *v.t.* **3.** To cause to wobble. — *n.* An unsteady motion, as that of unevenly balanced rotating bodies. Also spelled *wabble.* [? < LG *wabbeln*] — **wob′bler** *n.* — **wob′bling·ly** *adv.* — **wob′bly** *adj.*

wob·bly (wob′lē) *n. pl.* **·blies** *U.S. Slang* A member of the Industrial Workers of the World (IWW). [Appar. mispronunciation of *w* in *IWW*]

Wo·burn (wō′bərn, wōō′-) A city in eastern Massachusetts, near Boston; pop. 37,406.

Wode·house (wōōd′hous, wōd′-), P(elham) G(renville), 1881–1975, English humorous novelist.

Wo·den (wōd′n) The Old English name for Odin, the chief Norse god. Wednesday is named for Woden. Also **Wo′dan.**

woe (wō) *n.* **1.** Overwhelming sorrow; grief. **2.** Heavy affliction or calamity; disaster. — **Syn.** See SORROW. — *interj.* Alas! Also *Archaic* **wo.** [OE *wā* misery]

woe·be·gone (wō′bi·gôn′, -gon′) *adj.* Overcome with woe; mournful; sorrowful. Also **wo′be·gone′.**

woe·ful (wō′fəl) *adj.* **1.** Accompanied by or causing woe; direful. **2.** Expressive of sorrow; doleful. **3.** Paltry; miserable; mean. Also *Archaic* **woe′some** (-səm), **wo′ful.** — **woe′ful·ly** *adv.* — **woe′ful·ness** *n.*

Wof·fing·ton (wof′ing·tən), Margaret, 1714?–60, Irish actress active in England: called Peg Woffington.

Wöh·ler (vœ′lər), Friedrich, 1800–82, German chemist.

woke (wōk) Past tense of WAKE[1].

wok·en (wō′kən) Dialectal and alternative British past participle of WAKE[1].

Wol·cott (wōōl′kət), Oliver, 1726–97, American Revolutionary general and patriot; signer of the Declaration of Independence.

wold (wōld) *n.* **1.** An undulating tract of open upland; down or moor. **2.** *Obs.* A forest. [OE *wald* forest]

Wolds (wōldz), **the** A range of hills in Lincolnshire and Yorkshire, England, parallel to the coast; highest point, 800 ft.

wolf (wōōlf) *n. pl.* **wolves** (wōōlvz) **1.** Any of a genus (*Canis*) of large carnivorous mammals related to the dog, especially the common European species (*C. lupus*) or the timber wolf of North America. ◆ Collateral adjective:

lupine. **2.** Any ravenous, cruel, or rapacious person or thing. **3.** *Slang* A man who habitually and aggressively flirts with women; a philanderer. **4.** *Entomol.* The destructive larva of various beetles and moths. **5.** *Music* **a** On keyboard instruments, any mistuned interval resulting from unequal temperament, especially a difference in pitch between enharmonic equivalents, as G♯ and A♭. **b** On the violin, etc., a tone differing markedly in timbre and intensity from those adjacent to it due to vibration patterns of the belly of the instrument. — **to cry wolf** To give a false alarm. — **to keep the wolf from the door** To avert want or starvation. — *v.t.* To devour ravenously; gulp down: He *wolfed* his food. [OE *wulf*]

Wolf (wōōlf) *n.* The constellation Lupus.

Wolf (vôlf), Friedrich August, 1759–1824, German classical scholar and philologist. — **Hugo,** 1860–1903, Austrian composer.

wolf·ber·ry (wōōlf′ber′ē) *n. pl.* **·ries** A shrub (*Symphoricarpos occidentalis*) of the honeysuckle family, with pinkish, bell-shaped flowers and white berries in spikes, growing in the western United States.

Wolf Cub *Brit. & Canadian* A member of the junior branch of the Boy Scouts.

wolf dog **1.** A large dog for hunting wolves. **2.** A cross between a wolf and a dog.

Wolfe (wōōlf), Charles, 1791–1823, Irish clergyman and poet. — **James,** 1727–59, British general; defeated the French under Montcalm at Quebec, 1759. — **Thomas** (Clayton), 1900–38, U.S. novelist.

Wolff (vôlf), Baron Christian von, 1679–1754, German philosopher and mathematician. — **Kaspar Friedrich,** 1733–1794, German anatomist.

Wolf-Fer·ra·ri (vôlf′fer·rä′rē), Ermanno, 1876–1948, Italian composer.

Wolff·i·an (wōōl′fē·ən) *adj.* Pertaining to or named after the German anatomist Kaspar F. Wolff.

Wolffian body *Anat.* The mesonephros.

wolf fish A large fish (*Anarhichas lupus*) of the North Atlantic, with powerful teeth adapted for crushing shellfish.

wolf·hound (wōōlf′hound′) *n.* Either of two breeds of large dogs, the Russian wolfhound (or borzoi) and the Irish wolfhound, originally trained to catch and kill wolves.

wolf·ish (wōōlf′ish) *adj.* **1.** Having the qualities of a wolf; rapacious; savage. **2.** *Informal* Ravenously hungry. — **wolf′ish·ly** *adv.* — **wolf′ish·ness** *n.*

wolf·ram (wōōl′frəm) *n.* **1.** Wolframite. **2.** Tungsten. [< G, prob. < *wolf* wolf + *rahm* cream, soot]

wolf·ram·ite (wōōl′frəm·īt) *n.* A grayish black or brown tungstate of iron and manganese, crystallizing in the monoclinic system, an important source of tungsten: also called *wolfram.* [< G *wolframit* < *wolfram* tungsten]

Wolf·ram von Esch·en·bach (vôl′främ fôn esh′ən·bäkh), died 1220?, German epic poet.

wolf's-bane (wōōlfs′bān′) *n.* **1.** A medicinal plant of the genus *Aconitum*; monkshood. **2.** A species of European arnica, a perennial herb, used as a lotion for bruises. [Trans. of NL *lycoctonum* < Gk. *lykoktonon*, lit., wolfslayer < *lykos* wolf + *kteinein* to kill]

wol·las·ton·ite (wōōl′əs·tən·īt′) *n.* A vitreous, white, translucent calcium silicate, crystallizing in the monoclinic system. [after William Hyde *Wollaston*, 1766–1828, English chemist and physicist]

Wolse·ley (wōōlz′lē), Garnet Joseph, 1833–1913, first Viscount Wolseley, British general born in Ireland.

Wol·sey (wōōl′zē), Thomas, 1475?–1530, English cardinal and statesman.

wolv·er (wōōl′vər) *n.* One who hunts wolves.

Wol·ver·hamp·ton (wōōl′vər·hamp′tən) A borough in West Midlands, England; pop. 268,200 (1976).

wol·ver·ine (wōōl′və·rēn′) *n.* A rapacious and cunning carnivore (genus *Gulo*) of northern forests, with stout body and limbs and bushy tail: also called *carcajou*, *quickhatch.* Also **wol′ver·ene′.** [Dim. of WOLF]

Wolverine State Nickname of MICHIGAN.

wolves (wōōlvz) Plural of WOLF.

wom·an (wōōm′ən) *n. pl.* **wom·en** (wim′in) **1.** An adult human female. **2.** The female part of the human race; women collectively. **3.** Womanly character; femininity: usually with *the.* **4.** As applied to a man, one who is effeminate, timid, or weak. **5.** A female attendant or servant. **6.** A paramour or kept mistress. **7.** *Informal* A wife. — **the little woman** *U.S. Informal* One's wife. — *adj.* **1.** Feminine; characteristic of women. **2.** Female: a *woman* doctor. **3.** Affecting or pertaining to women. — *v.t. Obs.* To play the woman in or in reference to. [OE *wifmann* < *wīf* wife + *mann* human being]

wom·an·hood (wōōm′ən·hōōd) *n.* **1.** The state of a woman or of womankind. **2.** Women collectively.

wom·an·ish (wōōm′ən·ish) *adj.* **1.** Characteristic of a woman; womanly. **2.** Effeminate; unmanly. — **Syn.** See FEMININE. — **wom′an·ish·ly** *adv.* — **wom′an·ish·ness** *n.*

WOLVERINE
(To 3 feet long;
tail to 1½ feet.)

wom·an·ize (wŏŏm'ən·īz) v. ·ized, ·iz·ing v.t. 1. To make effeminate or womanish. — v.i. 2. Informal To consort with women illicitly.

wom·an·kind (wŏŏm'ən·kīnd') n. Women collectively.

wom·an·ly (wŏŏm'ən·lē) adj. Having the qualities natural, suited, or becoming to a woman; feminine. — Syn. See FEMININE. — adv. In a feminine manner; like a woman. — wom'an·li·ness n.

woman suffrage The right to vote as belonging to or exercised by women: also called female suffrage. — wom'an·suf'fra·gist (wŏŏm'ən·suf'rə·jist) n.

womb (wŏŏm) n. 1. The organ in which the young of higher mammals are developed; the uterus. 2. The place where anything is engendered or brought into life. 3. A cavity viewed as enclosing something. 4. Obs. The belly or stomach. [OE wamb, womb the belly]

wom·bat (wom'bat) n. An Australian nocturnal marsupial (family Vombatidae) resembling a small bear. [< Australian]

wombed (wŏŏmd) adj. 1. Having a womb. 2. Hollow; capacious; cavernous. Also womb'y.

wom·en (wim'in) Plural of WOMAN.

wom·en·folk (wim'in·fōk') n.pl. Women collectively. Also wom'en·folks'.

wom·er·a (wom'ər·ə) n. A device used by Australian aborigines for throwing javelins, spears, etc. [< Australian]

WOMBAT
(3 to 4 feet long)

won¹ (wun) Past tense and past participle of WIN.

won² (wun) v.i. wonned, won·ning Scot. & Brit. Dial. To abide; dwell; live. [OE wunian]

won³ (won) n. The monetary unit of North and of South Korea, equivalent to 100 chon.

won·der (wun'dər) n. 1. A feeling of mingled surprise and curiosity; astonishment. 2. That which causes wonder; a prodigy; a strange thing; a miracle. — for a wonder Surprisingly. — nine days' wonder Something that excites public wonder for a short time. — to do wonders To produce very good results: A long rest will do wonders for his health. — adj. Spectacularly successful: a wonder drug. — v.t. 1. To have a feeling of doubt and strong curiosity in regard to. — v.i. 2. To be affected or filled with wonder; marvel. 3. To be doubtful; query mentally; want to know. [OE wundor] — won'der·er n.

won·der·ful (wun'dər·fəl) adj. Of a nature to excite wonder; marvelous. — won'der·ful·ly adv. — won'der·ful·ness n.

won·der·ing (wun'dər·ing) adj. Expressing or feeling wonder. — won'der·ing·ly adv.

won·der·land (wun'dər·land') n. A realm of fairy-tale romance or wonders.

won·der·ment (wun'dər·mənt) n. 1. The emotion of wonder; surprise. 2. Something wonderful; a marvel.

Wonder State Nickname for ARKANSAS.

wonder-strick·en (wun'dər·strik'ən) adj. Suddenly smitten with wonder. Also won'der·struck' (-struk').

won·der-work (wun'dər·wûrk') n. A work inspiring wonder; miracle. — won'der·work'er n. — won'der·work'ing adj.

won·drous (wun'drəs) adj. Wonderful; marvelous. — adv. Surprisingly. [Alter. of ME wonders, genitive of WONDER] — won'drous·ly adv. — won'drous·ness n.

won·ky (wong'kē) adj. ·ki·er, ·ki·est Brit. Slang Unsteady; liable to break down; feeble. [Prob. OE wancol shaky]

won·ner (wun'ər) n. Scot. A prodigy; wonder.

Won·san (wœn·sän') A port city in eastern North Korea; pop. 275,000 (est. 1970). Japanese Gensan.

wont (wunt, wŏnt) adj. Doing habitually; accustomed; used: He is wont to smoke after dinner. — n. Ordinary manner of doing or acting; habit. — Syn. See HABIT. — v. wont, wont or wont·ed, wont·ing v.t. 1. To accustom or habituate: used reflexively. — v.i. 2. To be accustomed; be used. [OE gewunod, pp. of gewunian to be accustomed]

won't (wŏnt) Will not: a contraction of Middle English woll not. Also Scot. win·na, won·na (win'nə).

wont·ed (wun'tid, wŏn'-) adj. 1. Commonly used or done; habitual. 2. Habituated; accustomed. — wont'ed·ness n.

woo (wŏŏ) v.t. 1. To seek the love or affection of, especially in order to marry; court. 2. To entreat earnestly; beg. 3. To invite; solicit. — v.i. 4. To make love. [OE wogian]

wood¹ (wŏŏd) n. 1. A hard, fibrous material between the pith and bark of a tree or shrub, and also occurring in some herbaceous plants; the xylem. 2. The hard substance of a tree or shrub, whether as growing or as cut for use, for building, fuel, etc.; lumber; timber. 3. Often pl. A large and compact collection of trees; a forest; grove. 4. Something made of wood. 5. pl. A rural district; backwoods. — out of the woods Clear of doubt and difficulties; safe after peril or hazard. — adj. 1. Made of wood; wooden. 2. Made for using or holding wood: a wood stove. 3. Living or growing in woods. — v.t. 1. To furnish with wood for fuel. 2. To convert into a forest; plant with trees. — v.i. 3. To take on a supply of wood. [OE wudu, widu] — wood'less adj.

wood² (wŏŏd) Obs. v.i. To act like a maniac; rave. — adj. Furious; frantic; raging; mad. [OE wōd insane]

Wood (wŏŏd), Grant, 1892–1942, U.S. painter. — Leonard, 1860–1927, U.S. general and colonial administrator.

wood alcohol Methanol.

wood anemone Any of several small plants (genus Anemone), growing in woodlands and blooming in the early spring, especially A. quinquefolia of the United States.

wood betony 1. The common lousewort (Pedicularis canadensis) of the eastern United States, with yellow or reddish flowers. 2. The common betony (Stachys officinalis).

wood·bin (wŏŏd'bin') n. A box or crib for holding firewood.

wood·bine (wŏŏd'bīn) n. 1. The common honeysuckle of Europe (Lonicera periclymenum). 2. The Virginia creeper. Also called bine: also wood'bind (-bīnd). [OE wudubinde < wudu wood + bindan to bind]

wood·block (wŏŏd'blok') n. 1. A block of wood prepared for engraving. 2. A woodcut (which see).

wood block 1. A block of wood for paving, etc. 2. Music A percussion instrument consisting of a hollow block of wood struck with a drumstick.

wood·bor·er (wŏŏd'bôr'ər, -bō'rər) n. Any of a large family (Buprestidae) of brilliantly colored beetles whose larvae are very destructive of trees.

Wood·bridge (wŏŏd'brij) An urban township in NE New Jersey; pop. 98,944.

wood·carv·ing (wŏŏd'kär'ving) n. 1. The art of carving wood, especially for decoration. 2. A carving in wood. — wood'carv'er n.

wood·chat (wŏŏd'chat') n. 1. A European butcherbird (Lanius collorio) with reddish plumage and a notched beak. 2. Any of several Asian birds (genera Ianthia and Larrivora) of the thrush family. [Prob. partial trans. of G waldkatze the butcherbird, lit., wood cat]

wood·chuck (wŏŏd'chuk') n. A marmot (Marmota monax) of eastern North America, having a chunky body and a brown, bristly coat: also called ground hog. [By folk etymology < Ojibwa wejack]

WOODCHUCK
(To 14 inches long; tail 5 inches)

wood coal 1. Charcoal made from wood. Also wood charcoal. 2. Lignite.

wood·cock (wŏŏd'kok') n. 1. A small European game bird (Scolopax rusticola), having the thighs entirely feathered. 2. A related North American bird (Philohela minor). 3. Obs. A dolt; fool. [OE wuducocc]

wood·craft (wŏŏd'kraft', -kräft') n. 1. Skill in things pertaining to woodland life, as hunting and trapping. 2. Skill in woodwork or in constructing articles of wood. — wood'crafts'man (-krafts'mən, -kräfts'-) n.

wood·cut (wŏŏd'kut') n. 1. An engraved block of wood. 2. A print from such a block. Also called woodblock, woodprint.

wood·cut·ter (wŏŏd'kut'ər) n. One who cuts or chops wood. — wood'cut'ting n.

wood·ed (wŏŏd'id) adj. 1. Abounding with trees or woods. 2. Having a supply of wood.

wood·en (wŏŏd'n) adj. 1. Made of wood. 2. Like a block of wood; stupid; mechanical; stiff; awkward. 3. Dull; spiritless. — wood'en·ly adv. — wood'en·ness n.

wooden anniversary A fifth wedding anniversary.

wood engraving 1. The art of cutting designs on wood for printing; the making of woodcuts. 2. A block so engraved; also, a print taken from it. — wood engraver

wood·en·head (wŏŏd'n·hed') n. Informal A stupid person; blockhead. — wood'en·head'ed adj.

wooden horse Trojan horse (which see).

wooden Indian 1. A carved and painted wooden figure of a North American Indian, usually in a standing position, formerly placed in front of cigar stores as an advertisement. 2. An inarticulate, sluggish, or dull person.

wood·en·ware (wŏŏd'n·wâr') n. Dishes, vessels, bowls, etc., made of wood.

Wood Green A municipal borough in Middlesex, England, near London; pop. 47,897 (1961).

wood grouse The capercaillie.

wood·hen (wŏŏd'hen') n. A weka.

wood·house (wŏŏd'hous') n. A house or shed for storing firewood: also called woodshed.

wood hyacinth A small European squill (Scilla non-scripta), with bell-shaped blue, white, or pink flowers.

wood ibis A very large storklike bird (Mycteria americana) with a white body, glossy black tail, and naked head, found in wooded swamps of South America and the southern United States: also called flinthead, gannetibru.

wood·land (wŏŏd'lənd; for n., also wŏŏd'land') n. Land occupied by or covered with woods or trees. — adj. Belonging to or dwelling in the woods. — wood'land·er n.

woodland caribou See under CARIBOU.

wood·lark (wo͝od′lärk′) *n.* A European passerine bird (*Lullula arborea*) that resembles the skylark and has a sweet song.

wood lily See under LILY.

wood lot A plot of land devoted to the growing of forest trees or consisting of woodland: also, *Canadian, bush lot.*

wood louse Any of numerous small terrestrial flat-bodied crustaceans (genera *Oniscus, Porcellio,* and others) commonly found under old logs, as the sow bug.

wood·man (wo͝od′mən) *n. pl.* **·men** (-mən) A woodsman (which see).

wood·note (wo͝od′nōt′) *n.* A simple, artless, or natural song, as of a wild bird.

wood nymph 1. A goddess or nymph of the forest; a dryad. 2. Any of several South American hummingbirds (genus *Thalurania*). 3. Any of a group of butterflies (family *Satyridae*), generally brown in color and having eyelike spots on the wings.

wood·peck·er (wo͝od′pek′ər) *n.* Any of a large family (*Picidae*) of birds having stiff tail feathers to aid in climbing, strong claws, and a sharp, chisellike bill for drilling holes in the wood of trees, etc., in search of insects.

wood pewee See under PEWEE.

wood pigeon 1. The cushat. 2. A wild, band-tailed pigeon (*Columba fasciata*) of the western United States.

RED-HEADED
WOODPECKER
(To 9½ inches
long)

wood·pile (wo͝od′pīl′) *n.* A pile of wood, especially of wood cut or split in sizes for burning in a fireplace or stove.

wood pitch The final residuum of wood tar.

wood·print (wo͝od′print′) *n.* A woodcut (which see).

wood pulp Wood reduced to pulp, as by grinding and treating with chemicals, used for making paper.

wood pussy *Informal* A skunk.

wood rat A pack rat (which see).

wood·ruff (wo͝od′ruf′) *n.* Any of several common woodland herbs (genus *Asperula*) of the madder family, especially the **sweet-scented woodruff** (*A. odorata*), used to flavor wine and in perfumery. [OE *wudurofe*]

Woods, Lake of the A lake between the northern part of Minnesota and Manitoba and Ontario provinces, Canada; 1,485 sq. mi.

wood·screw (wo͝od′skroo′) *n.* A screw with a thread of coarse pitch, used for fastening pieces against wood. For illustration see SCREW.

wood·shed (wo͝od′shed′) *n.* A woodhouse (which see).

wood·si·a (wo͝od′zē·ə) *n.* Any of a genus (*Woodsia*) of small tufted ferns, found in rocky places. [after Joseph *Woods*, 1776–1864, English botanist]

woods·man (wo͝odz′mən) *n. pl.* **·men** (-mən) 1. A woodcutter; lumberman. 2. A forester; also, a dweller in forests. 3. A man skilled in woodcraft. 4. A hunter of forest game. Also called *woodman.*

wood sorrel Oxalis.

wood spirit Methanol.

wood sugar Xylose.

woods·y (wo͝od′zē) *adj.* **woods·i·er, woods·i·est** *Informal* Of, pertaining to, or dwelling in the woods; suggesting the woods: a *woodsy* fragrance.

wood tar A tar produced by the dry distillation of wood and containing turpentine, resins, and other hydrocarbons.

wood thrush 1. A large woodland thrush of North America (*Hylocichla mustelina*), noted for the vigor and sweetness of its song. 2. The missel thrush (which see).

wood tick Any of certain ticks found in the woods, especially *Dermacentor variabilis*, that transfers itself from underbrush to passing animals or human beings.

wood·turn·ing (wo͝od′tûr′ning) *n.* The process or art of shaping blocks of wood into various forms by means of a lathe. — **wood′turn′er** *n.*

wood turtle A fresh-water and terrestrial turtle (*Clemmys insculpta*) of the eastern United States, with a salmon-red body and a distinctively patterned carapace.

wood vinegar 1. Impure acetic acid from the distillation of wood. 2. Pyroligneous acid.

wood violet The bird's-foot violet (which see).

wood·wax·en (wo͝od′wak′sən) See WOADWAXEN.

wood·winds (wo͝od′windz′) *n.pl. Music* Instruments in which a player's breath sets an air column into vibration by passing through a reed or striking a sharp edge, as oboes, bassoons, clarinets, flutes, etc. — **wood′wind′** *adj.*

wood·work (wo͝od′wûrk′) *n.* 1. The wooden parts of any structure, especially interior wooden parts, as moldings or doors. 2. Work made of wood. — **wood′work′er** *n.* — **wood′work′ing** *n.*

wood·worm (wo͝od′wûrm′) *n.* A worm or larva that dwells or bores in wood.

wood·y (wo͝od′ē) *adj.* **wood·i·er, wood·i·est** 1. Of the nature of or containing wood; ligneous. 2. Pertaining to or resembling wood. 3. Wooded; abounding with woods; sylvan. — **wood′i·ness** *n.*

woody nightshade See under NIGHTSHADE.

woo·er (woo′ər) *n.* One who woos; a lover.

woof[1] (woof) *n.* 1. The weft of a woven fabric; the threads carried back and forth across the fixed threads of the warp in a loom. 2. The texture of a fabric. [OE *ōwef < on* on + *wefan* to weave]

woof[2] (woof) *n.* A growling or barking sound, as of a dog. [Imit.]

woof·er (woof′ər) *n. Electronics* A loudspeaker used to reproduce low frequencies in high-fidelity sound equipment. Compare TWEETER. [< WOOF²]

wool (wo͝ol) *n.* 1. The soft, curly or crisped hair obtained from the fleece of sheep and some allied animals, noted for its felting properties and providing fibers for yarns and textiles. 2. The underfur of a furbearing animal. 3. Short kinky or crisp human hair. 4. Material or garments made of wool. 5. A substance resembling or likened to wool. — **all wool and a yard wide** Perfect in quality and quantity; one hundred percent genuine. — **to pull the wool over one's eyes** To delude or deceive one. — *adj.* Made of or pertaining to wool or woolen material. [OE *wull*]

wool-clip (wo͝ol′klip′) *n.* The amount of wool clipped from the sheep in one year.

wool-dyed (wo͝ol′dīd′) *adj.* Dyed before the wool has been spun into yarn: said of fabrics.

wool·en (wo͝ol′ən) *adj.* 1. Consisting wholly or partly of wool; like wool. 2. Pertaining to wool or its manufacture. — *n. pl.* Woolen cloth or clothing. Also **wool′len.** [OE *wullen, wyllen*]

Woolf (wo͝olf), (**Adeline**) **Virginia**, 1882–1941, *née* Stephen, English novelist, essayist, and critic.

wool fat Lanolin. Also **wool grease.**

wool·fell (wo͝ol′fel′) *n.* The pelt of a sheep or other wool-bearing animal with the wool still on it. [< WOOL + FELL¹]

wool·gath·er·ing (wo͝ol′gath′ər·ing) *n.* Any trivial or purposeless employment; especially, idle reverie. — *adj.* Idly indulging in fancies. [from the practice of gathering wool caught on bushes, which required much wandering to collect even a little] — **wool′gath′er·er** *n.*

wool·grow·er (wo͝ol′grō′ər) *n.* A person who raises sheep for the production of wool. — **wool′grow′ing** *adj.*

Wooll·cott (wo͝ol′kət), **Alexander**, 1887–1943, U.S. journalist and critic.

Wool·ley (wo͝ol′ē), Sir (**Charles**) **Leonard**, 1880–1960, English archeologist.

wool·ly (wo͝ol′ē) *adj.* **·li·er, ·li·est** 1. Consisting of, covered with, or resembling wool; wool-bearing. 2. Soft and vaporous; lacking clearness; not sharply detailed; fuzzy; blurry. 3. Having a rounded and somewhat fleecy appearance, as clouds. 4. Having a growth of woollike hairs. 5. Resembling the roughness and excitement of the American West: usually in the phrase **wild and woolly.** — *n. pl.* **·lies** A garment made of wool; especially, woolen underwear. Also *esp. U.S.* **wool′y.** — **wool′li·ness** *n.*

woolly bear The caterpillar of any of several tiger moths, covered with long dense hairs.

woolly mammoth See under MAMMOTH.

wool·pack (wo͝ol′pak′) *n.* 1. A bag or wrapper of canvas, cotton, etc., for packing a bale of wool. 2. A bale or bundle of wool. 3. *Meteorol.* A cumulus cloud.

wool·sack (wo͝ol′sak′) *n.* 1. A sack of wool. 2. The chair of the lord chancellor in the English House of Lords, a cushion stuffed with wool. 3. The office of lord high chancellor.

wool shed A building or shed in which sheep are sheared and the wool readied for market.

wool-sta·pler (wo͝ol′stā′plər) *n.* A dealer in or sorter of wool. — **wool′sta′pling** *adj. & n.*

Wool·wich (wo͝ol′ich, -ij) A metropolitan borough of London on the south bank of the Thames; pop. 47,006 (1961).

Wool·worth (wo͝ol′wûrth), **Frank Winfield**, 1852–1919, U.S. merchant, developed the five-and-ten-cent store.

Woon·sock·et (woon-sok′it) A city in NE Rhode Island, on the Blackstone River; pop. 46,820.

woo·ra·li (woo-rä′lē) *n.* Curare. Also **woo·ra′ri** (-rē). [Var. of CURARE]

wooz·y (woo′zē) *adj.* **wooz·i·er, wooz·i·est** *Slang* Befuddled, especially with drink; dazed. [Prob. < *wooze*, var. of OOZE] — **wooz′i·ly** *adv.* — **wooz′i·ness** *n.*

wop (wop) *n. Slang* An Italian: an offensive term. [? < dial. Ital. (Sicilian) *guappo* a dandy < Sp. *guapo*]

Worces·ter (wo͝os′tər) 1. A city in central Massachusetts; pop. 176,572. 2. Worcestershire or its county seat.

Worces·ter (wo͝os′tər), **Joseph Emerson**, 1784–1865, U.S. lexicographer.

Worcester china A very fine china or procelain made in Worcester, England, from 1751: also **Worcester porcelain,** and called **Royal Worcester** by royal warrant.

Worces·ter·shire (wo͝os′tər·shir) A former county in west central England; 699 sq. mi.; pop. 692,605 (1971); county seat, Worcester, famous for its 14th-century cathedral, pop. 74,500 (1976). Also **Worces′ter.**

Worcestershire sauce A piquant sauce made originally

in Worcester, England, from vinegar and many other ingredients. Also **Worcestershire, Worcester sauce.**

Worcs. or **Worcs** Worcestershire.

word (wûrd) *n.* **1.** A linguistic form that can meaningfully be spoken in isolation. A word may consist of a minimum free form, as *man, boy,* or *scatter,* a free form plus bound forms, as *manly, boyish,* or *scattering,* a union of free forms, as *manpower,* or a series of bound forms as *re-ceive, re-tain, con-tain.* **2.** The letters or characters that stand for such a linguistic form. **3.** A mere sequence of sounds or letters; vocable: *words* rather than ideas. **4.** *Usually pl.* Conversation; talk: a man of few *words.* **5.** A brief remark. **6.** A short and pithy saying. **7.** A communication or message; information: Send him *word.* **8.** A command, signal, or direction: Give the *word* to start. **9.** A promise; avowed intention: a man of his *word.* **10.** A party cry; watchword. **11.** *pl.* Language used in anger, rebuke, or otherwise emotionally: They had *words.* **— by word of mouth** Orally. **— in a word** In short; briefly. **— the Word 1.** The Logos; the Son of God. **2.** The Scriptures as an embodiment of divine revelation. **— to be as good as one's word** To keep one's promise. **— to break one's word** To violate one's promise. **— to eat one's words** To retract something that one has said. **— to have a word with** To have a brief conversation with. **— to mince words** To be evasive; avoid coming to the point. **— to take one at his word** To understand or deal with one literally in accordance with his own statement. **— to take the words out of one's mouth** To say what one was just about to say. *— v.t.* To express in a word or words, especially in selected words; phrase. [OE. Akin to VERB.]

word·age (wûr'dij) *n.* Words collectively.

word blindness Alexia. **— word-blind** (wûrd'blīnd') *adj.*

word·book (wûrd'bŏŏk') *n.* **1.** A collection of words; vocabulary; lexicon; dictionary. **2.** An opera libretto.

word deafness Inability to understand speech, resulting from disease of the cortical center; a form of aphasia.

word for word In the exact words; literally; verbatim.

word game A game or puzzle having as its object the formation or discovery of a word or words.

word·i·ness (wûr'dē·nis) *n.* The excessive use of words; verbosity.

word·ing (wûr'ding) *n.* The act or style of expressing in words; phraseology; also, words used; expression.

word·less (wûrd'lis) *adj.* Having no words; inarticulate; silent. **— word'less·ly** *adv.* **— word'less·ness** *n.*

word picture A graphic verbal description.

word play 1. Fencing with words; repartee. **2.** Subtle discussion on words and their meaning. **3.** Play on words.

word square An arrangement of letters in rectangular form, so that they form the same words in either horizontal or vertical lines.

FRET	
REAR	
EASE	
TREE	

WORD
SQUARE

Words·worth (wûrdz'wûrth), **William,** 1770–1850, English poet; laureate 1843–50.

word·y (wûr'dē) *adj.* **word·i·er, word·i·est 1.** Of the nature of words; verbal. **2.** Expressed in many words. **3.** Given to the use of words; verbose; prolix. [OE *wordig*] **— word'i·ly** *adv.*

wore (wôr, wōr) Past tense of WEAR[1] and WEAR[2].

work (wûrk) *n.* **1.** Continued exertion or activity, whether physical or mental, directed to some purpose or end; labor. **2.** The acts, obligations, etc., that one does or undertakes in return for something of value, as money; especially, the activities by which one earns one's livelihood. **3.** Any prolonged or industrious effort: A woman's *work* is never done. **4.** Trade; occupation; business: What sort of *work* do you do? **5.** A job or position; employment: to look for *work.* **6.** A place of employment: Is he at home or at *work?* **7.** That upon which labor is expended; an undertaking; task. **8.** Exhausting or unrewarding effort; toil. **9.** The matter at hand; the business that remains to be done: Get to *work.* **10.** That which is produced by or as by labor, as an engineering structure, a design produced by a needle, etc.; also, a product of mental labor, as a book or opera. **11.** A feat or deed. **12.** *pl.* (*usually construed as sing.*) A manufacturing or other industrial establishment, including buildings and equipment: a gas *works.* **13.** *pl.* Running gear or machinery, as of a watch. **14.** Manner of working, or style of treatment; workmanship. **15.** *pl. Slang* The whole of anything; the kit and caboodle: the whole *works.* **16.** A froth or foam produced by fermentation in making vinegar, etc. **17.** *pl. Theol.* Moral duties considered as external acts, especially as meritorious. **18.** *Physics* A transference of energy from one body to another resulting in the motion or displacement of the body acted upon, expressed as the product of the force and the amount of displacement in the line of its action. *Abbr.* (for def. 18) *w., W.,* (for other defs.) *wk.* **— to give (someone) the works** *Slang* **1.** To maul or kill. **2.** To be severe with; have no mercy for. **— to shoot the works** *Slang* To make a supreme effort; risk one's all in a single attempt. *— v.* **worked** (*Archaic* **wrought**), **work·ing** *v.i.* **1.** To perform work; labor; toil. **2.** To be employed in

some trade or business. **3.** To perform a function; operate: The machine *works* well. **4.** To prove effective or influential; succeed: His stratagem *worked.* **5.** To move or progress gradually or with difficulty: He *worked* up in his profession. **6.** To become as specified, as by gradual motion: The bolts *worked* loose. **7.** To have some slight improper motion in functioning: The wheel *works* on the shaft. **8.** To move from nervousness or agitation: His features *worked* with passion. **9.** To undergo kneading, hammering, etc.; be shaped: Copper *works* easily. **10.** To ferment. **11.** *Naut.* To labor in a heavy sea so as to loosen seams and fastenings: said of a ship. *— v.t.* **12.** To cause or bring about; effect; accomplish: to *work* a miracle. **13.** To cause to function; direct the operation of: to *work* a machine. **14.** To make or shape by toil or skill. **15.** To prepare, as by manipulating, hammering, etc.: to *work* dough. **16.** To decorate, as with embroidery or inlaid work. **17.** To cause to be productive, as by toil: to *work* a mine. **18.** To cause to do work: He *works* his employees too hard. **19.** To cause to be as specified, usually with effort: We *worked* the timber into position. **20.** To make or achieve by effort: He *worked* his way through the narrow tunnel. **21.** To carry on some activity in (an area, etc.); cover: to *work* a stream for trout. **22.** To solve, as a problem in arithmetic. **23.** To cause to move from nervousness or excitement: to *work* one's jaws. **24.** To excite; provoke: He *worked* himself into a passion. **25.** To influence or manage, as by insidious means; lead. **26.** To cause to ferment. **27.** *Informal* To practice trickery upon; cheat; swindle. **28.** *Informal* To make use of for one's own purposes; use. **— to work in** To put in; insert or be inserted. **— to work off** To get rid of, as extra flesh by exercise. **— to work on** (or **upon**) **1.** To try to influence or persuade. **2.** To influence or affect. **— to work out 1.** To make its way out or through. **2.** To effect by work or effort; accomplish. **3.** To exhaust, as a mineral vein or a subject of inquiry. **4.** To discharge, as a debt, by labor rather than by payment of money. **5.** To develop; form, as a plan. **6.** To solve. **7.** To prove effective or successful. **8.** To result as specified: It *worked* out badly. **— to work over 1.** To do again; repeat. **2.** *U.S. Slang* To beat up; maul. **— to work up 1.** To excite; rouse, as rage or a person to rage. **2.** To form or shape by working; develop. **3.** To make one's or its way. *— adj.* Of, having to do with, or used for work: *work* clothes; a *work* sheet. [OE *weorc*]

-work *combining form* **1.** A product made from a (specified) material: *paperwork, brickwork.* **2.** Work of a (given) kind: *piecework.* **3.** Work performed in a (specified) place: *housework.* [< WORK]

work·a·ble (wûr'kə·bəl) *adj.* **1.** Capable of being worked. **2.** Capable of being put into effect, as a plan; practicable. **— work'a·bil'i·ty, work'a·ble·ness** *n.*

work·a·day (wûrk'ə·dā') *adj.* **1.** Of, pertaining to, or suitable for working days; everyday. **2.** Commonplace; prosaic. [Alter. of ME *werkeday* < *werke,* OE *weorca* work + DAY; infl. in form by NOWADAYS]

work·a·hol·ic (wûrk'ə·hôl'ik, -hol-) *n. Informal* A person addicted to working. [< WORK + (ALCO)HOLIC]

work·bag (wûrk'bag') *n.* A bag for holding tools or materials, especially needlework materials.

work basket A basket for holding sewing materials.

work·bench (wûrk'bench') *n.* A bench for work, as that of a carpenter or machinist.

work·book (wûrk'bŏŏk') *n.* **1.** A booklet based on a course of study and containing problems and exercises that a student works out directly on the pages. **2.** A manual containing operating instructions. **3.** A book for recording work performed or planned.

work·box (wûrk'boks') *n.* A box for holding things one works with, especially sewing materials.

work·day (wûrk'dā') *n.* **1.** Any day not a Sunday or holiday; a working day. **2.** The part of the day or number of hours of one day spent in work. *— adj.* Workaday.

work·er (wûr'kər) *n.* **1.** One who or that which does work; especially, a laborer. **2.** A female of an insect colony, as an ant, bee, or termite, with undeveloped sexual organs.

work·fel·low (wûrk'fel'ō) *n.* A companion in work.

work·folk (wûrk'fōk') *n.pl.* Manual laborers.

work force The total number of workers of a company, project, factory, region, etc.; staff. Also **working force.**

work·horse (wûrk'hôrs') *n.* **1.** A horse used for pulling loads, as a cart or plow. **2.** A person who takes upon himself the hardest or most arduous part of an undertaking.

work·house (wûrk'hous') *n.* **1.** *Brit.* A house for paupers able to work; an almshouse. **2.** An industrial prison for petty offenders. **3.** *Obs.* A workshop.

work·ing (wûr'king) *adj.* **1.** Engaged actively in some employment. **2.** That works, or performs its function: This is a *working* model. **3.** Sufficient for use or action: a *working* knowledge of French. **4.** Relating to or occupied by work. **5.** Throbbing with pain; also, twitching: said especially of the face muscles. **6.** Fermenting, as wine. *— n.* **1.** The act or operation of one who or that which works. **2.** *Usually pl.* The part of a mine or quarry where excavation is going on or has gone on.

working capital **1.** That part of the finances of a business available for its operation. **2.** The amount of quick assets that exceed current liabilities.

working class The part of society consisting of working people paid in wages; especially, manual or industrial laborers. **— work·ing-class** (wûr′king·klas′, -kläs′) *adj.*

working day 1. A day on which work is normally done, as distinguished from a Sunday or holiday. **2.** The number of hours constituting a day's work: a four-hour *working day.*

working drawing In engineering, etc., a drawing made to scale, as of a part of a machine or building, for the direction of workmen, contractors, etc.

work·ing·man (wûr′king·man′) *n.* *pl.* **·men** (-men′) A male worker; laborer.

Workingmen's Party of the United States See under SOCIALIST LABOR PARTY.

working papers An age certificate and other official papers certifying that a minor may be legally employed.

working substance *Mech.* The fluid under pressure, as steam, that operates a prime mover. Also **working fluid.**

work·ing·wom·an (wûr′king·wŏŏm′ən) *n.* *pl.* **·wom·en** (-wim′in) A female worker; laborer.

work·load (wûrk′lōd′) *n.* The amount of work apportioned to a person, machine, or department over a given period.

work·man (wûrk′mən) *n.* *pl.* **·men** (-mən) One who earns his living by manual labor. **— work′man·ly** *adj.*

work·man·like (wûrk′mən·līk) *adj.* Like or befitting a skilled workman; skillfully done. **— work′man·ly** *adv.*

work·man·ship (wûrk′mən·ship) *n.* **1.** The art or skill of a workman, or the quality of work. **2.** The work or result produced by a worker.

workmen's compensation 1. Damages recoverable from an employer by an employee in case of accident. **2.** Government insurance against illness, accident, or unemployment.

work of art 1. A product of the fine arts, especially of the graphic arts and sculpture, but including literary and musical productions. **2.** Anything likened to an artistic work, as because of great beauty, intricacy, etc.

work·out (wûrk′out′) *n.* *Informal* **1.** A test, trial practice performance, etc., to discover, maintain, or increase ability for some work or competition, as a practice boxing bout or race. **2.** Any activity involving considerable effort or vigor.

work·peo·ple (wûrk′pē′pəl) *n.pl.* People employed in work, especially in manual labor; working people.

work·room (wûrk′rōŏm′, -rŏŏm′) *n.* A room where work is performed.

works council A committee of workers organized by an employer to discuss company and industrial problems.

work·sheet (wûrk′shēt′) *n.* **1.** A sheet of paper on which practice work or rough drafts of problems are written **2.** A sheet of paper used to record work schedules and operations.

work·shop (wûrk′shop′) *n.* **1.** A building or room where any work is carried on; workroom. **2.** A seminar or group of people who work on or study together some special project or subject: a *workshop* in the English novel.

work stoppage A stopping of work, as in an industry, because of a strike or layoff.

work·ta·ble (wûrk′tā′bəl) *n.* A table with drawers for use while working, especially while sewing.

work·week (wûrk′wēk′) *n.* The number of hours worked in a week; also, the number of working hours in a week.

world (wûrld) *n.* **1.** The earth. **2.** A part of the earth: the Old *World.* **3.** The universe; the cosmos. **4.** A division of existing or created things belonging to the earth; natural grand division: the animal *world.* **5.** The human inhabitants of the earth; mankind. **6.** A definite class of people having certain interests or activities in common: the scientific *world.* **7.** A sphere or domain: the *world* of letters. **8.** Man regarded socially; the public. **9.** Public or social life and intercourse: to go out into the *world.* **10.** The practices, usages, and ways of men: He knows the *world.* **11.** A total of things as pertaining to or affecting an individual person: a child's private *world* of fantasy. **12.** Great quantity, number, or size: a *world* of trouble. **13.** The course of events as affecting one personally; individual condition or circumstances: How goes the *world* with you? **14.** A scene of existence or of affairs regarded from a moral or religious point of view; worldly aims, pleasures, or people collectively. **15.** Earthly existence; mortal life. **— for all the world** In every respect. **— on top of the world** *Informal* Elated. **— out of this world** *Informal* Very fine; extraordinarily good. **— to bring into the world** To give birth to. [OE *weorold, woruld*] *World* may appear as a combining form or as the first element in two-word phrases; as in:

world affairs	world conflict	world domination
world-alarming	world-conquering	world dominion
world battle	world-conscious	world-embracing
world builder	world-covering	world empire
world-changing	world crisis	world-encircling
world citizen	world destroyer	world esteem
world commerce	world disaster	world-famed

world-famous	world price	world sadness
world hero	world problem	world sorrow
world history	world rejoicing	world state
world leader	world-renounced	world struggle
world-minded	world-renouncing	world trade
world-old	world-renowned	world-wandering
world order	world report	world war
world peace	world revolution	world-winning
world politics	world-roving	world-worn

World Court 1. The Permanent Court of International Justice. **2.** The International Court of Justice.

world·ling (wûrld′ling) *n.* One who lives merely for this world; a worldly-minded person.

world·ly (wûrld′lē) *adj.* **·li·er, ·li·est 1.** Pertaining to the world; mundane; earthly; not spiritual. **2.** Devoted to temporal things; secular. **3.** Sophisticated; worldly-wise. **4.** *Obs.* Lay, as opposed to clerical. **—** *adv.* In a worldly manner. [OE *woruldlic*] **— world′li·ness** *n.*

— Syn. (adj.) **1.** *Worldly, mundane, earthly, earthy,* and *terrestrial* mean of the earth, but differ widely in application. *Worldly* almost invariably refers to the activities and interests of mankind; it is applied to both persons and things: a *worldly* cleric, a *worldly* life. *Mundane,* like *worldly,* is often used as an antonym of spiritual or heavenly, but it is rarely applied to persons: *mundane* affairs, a *mundane* outlook. *Earthly* remains largely confined to religious use, and is directly opposed to heavenly: this *earthly* paradise, *earthly* joys. *Earthy* means literally of the soil, or by extension, coarse, unrefined, risque: a rich and *earthy* odor, *earthy* humor. *Terrestrial* means of the earth or land in physical sense, as opposed to celestial, cosmic, or aquatic: the *terrestrial* atmosphere, a *terrestrial* plant.

world·ly-mind·ed (wûrld′lē·mīn′did) *adj.* Absorbed in the things of this world. **— world′ly-mind′ed·ly** *adv.* **— world′ly-mind′ed·ness** *n.*

world·ly-wise (wûrld′lē·wīz′) *adj.* Wise in the ways and affairs of the world; sophisticated.

world power A state or organization whose policy and action are of world-wide influence.

World Series In baseball, the games played at the finish of the regular schedule between the champion teams of the American and National Leagues, the first team to win four games being adjudged world champions. Also **world's series.**

world's fair An international exhibit of the folk crafts and arts, agricultural and industrial products, and scientific progress of various countries.

world-shak·ing (wûrld′shā′king) *adj.* Enormously significant or consequential; affecting the entire world.

world soul The hypothetical soul of the world or the universe: also called *All-Soul.* Also **world spirit.**

World War See table for WAR.

world-wea·ry (wûrld′wir′ē) *adj.* **·ri·er, ·ri·est** Dissatisfied and weary with life and its conditions.

world·wide (wûrld′wīd′) *adj.* Extended or spread throughout the world.

worm (wûrm) *n.* **1.** A small, limbless invertebrate with an elongated, soft, and usually naked body, as a flatworm, roundworm, or annelid. ◆ Collateral adjective: *vermicular.* **2.** Loosely, any small creeping animal having a slender body and short or undeveloped limbs, as an insect larva, a grub, etc. **3.** That which suggests the action or habit of a worm as eating away or as an agent of decay, as remorse, death, etc. **4.** A despicable, groveling, or abject person. **5.** Something like a worm in appearance or movement. **6.** The thread of a screw. **7.** A worm screw (which see). **8.** The spiral part of a corkscrew. **9.** A spiral part in a still. For illustration see STILL². **10.** An organ or part that resembles a worm in shape, as the lytta of th dog or the vermiform process. **11.** *pl.* An intestinal disorder due to the presence of parasitic worms. **12.** The windings of a log road made to lessen the steepness of a grade. **13.** The zigzag course of a log fence or a rail fence. **—** *v.t.* **1.** To insinuate (oneself or itself) in a wormlike manner: with *in* or *into*: to *worm* one's way into the group. **2.** To draw forth by artful means, as a secret: with *out.* **3.** To free from intestinal worms. **4.** *Naut.* To wind yarn, etc., along (a rope) so as to fill up the grooves between the strands. **5.** To remove the lytta or worm from, as a dog. **—** *v.i.* **6.** To move or progress slowly and stealthily. **7.** To insinuate oneself by artful means: with *into.* [OE *wyrm*] **— worm′er** *n.*

worm-eat·en (wûrm′ēt′n) *adj.* **1.** Eaten or bored through by worms. **2.** Worn-out or decayed, as by time. **3.** Out-of-date; old-fashioned.

worm fence A zigzag fence of rails crossed at their ends; also called *snake fence, Virginia fence, Virginia rail fence.*

worm gear *Mech.* **1.** A worm wheel (which see). **2.** The gear formed by a worm wheel together with a worm screw: for illustration see MACHINE.

worm·hole (wûrm′hōl′) *n.* The hole made by a worm, as in plants, timber, etc. **— worm′holed′** *adj.*

worm·root (wûrm′rōŏt′, -rŏŏt′) *n.* Pinkroot.

Worms (wûrmz, *Ger.* vôrms) A city in SW West Germany, on the Rhine; scene of the **Diet of Worms** (1521) by which Luther was pronounced a heretic; pop. 78,000 (est. 1970).

worm screw *Mech.* A short threaded portion of a shaft

constituting an endless screw formed to mesh with a worm wheel.

worm·seed (wûrm′sēd′) *n.* **1.** The seeds of any of various plants used as a vermifuge. **2.** The plants themselves; especially, santonica, and a species of goosefoot (*Chenopodium ambrosioides*).

worm wheel *Mech.* A toothed wheel gearing with a worm screw.

worm·wood (wûrm′wŏŏd′) *n.* **1.** Any of a genus (*Artemisia*) of European herbs or small shrubs related to the sagebrush; especially, a common species (*A. absinthium*) that is aromatic and bitter and is used in making absinthe. **2.** That which embitters or makes bitter; bitterness. [Alter. of obs. *wermōd* < OE; infl. in form by WORM and WOOD¹]

worm·y (wûr′mē) *adj.* **worm·i·er, worm·i·est 1.** Infested with or injured by worms. **2.** Of or pertaining to worms. **3.** Resembling a worm. **4.** Mean; groveling. — **worm′i·ness** *n.*

worn (wôrn, wōrn) Past participle of WEAR. — *adj.* **1.** Affected by use or any continuous action; as: **a** Threadbare: a *worn* suit. **b** Exhausted, as from worry, anxiety, etc.: a *worn* face. **c** Hackneyed: a *worn* phrase. **2.** Used up; spent.

worn-out (wôrn′out′, wōrn′-) *adj.* **1.** Used until without value or effectiveness. **2.** Thoroughly tired; exhausted.

wor·ri·some (wûr′i·səm) *adj.* **1.** Causing worry or anxiety. **2.** Given to worrying. — **wor′ri·some·ly** *adv.*

wor·rit (wûr′it) *Chiefly Dial. n.* Worry; vexation. — *v.t.* & *v.i.* To worry. [Appar. alter. of WORRY]

wor·ry (wûr′ē) *v.* **·ried, ·ry·ing** *v.i.* **1.** To be uneasy in the mind; feel anxiety about something; fret. **2.** To pull or tear at something with the teeth: with *at.* **3.** *Informal* To advance or manage despite trials or difficulties: with *along* or *through.* — *v.t.* **4.** To cause to feel uneasy in the mind; trouble. **5.** To bother; pester. **6.** To mangle or kill by biting, shaking, or tearing with the teeth. **7.** *Scot.* or *Obs.* To strangle; choke. — *n.* *pl.* **·ries 1.** A state of anxiety or vexation. **2.** Something that causes anxiety. **3.** The act of worrying. — **Syn.** See ANXIETY, CARE. [OE *wyrgan* to strangle] — **wor′ri·er** *n.* — **wor′ri·ment** *n.*

worse (wûrs) Comparative of BAD and ILL. — *adj.* **1.** Bad or ill in a greater degree; more evil, unworthy, etc. **2.** Physically ill in a greater degree; less well. **3.** Less favorably situated as to means and circumstances. — *n.* Something worse; disadvantage; loss. — *adv.* In a manner more intense, severe, or evil. [OE *wiersa*]

wors·en (wûr′sən) *v.t.* & *v.i.* To make or become worse.

wors·er (wûr′sər) *adj.* & *adv.* Worse: a former redundant form of the comparative: now regarded as a vulgarism.

wors·et (wûr′sit) *adj.* & *n.* *Scot.* Worsted.

wor·ship (wûr′ship) *n.* **1.** The adoration, homage, or veneration given to a deity or to something regarded as sacred. **2.** The rites, ceremonial forms, prayers, etc., such adoration requires or assumes. **3.** Excessive or ardent devotion or admiration. **4.** The object of such devotion or admiration. **5.** *Chiefly Brit.* A title of honor in addressing persons of rank or station: with *your, his,* etc. **6.** *Archaic* Dignity; worthiness. — *v.* **·shiped** or **·shipped, wor·ship·ing** or **·ship·ping** *v.t.* **1.** To pay an act of worship to; venerate; adore. **2.** To have an intense or exaggerated admiration or devotion for. **3.** *Obs.* To honor. — *v.i.* **4.** To perform acts or have sentiments of worship. [OE *weorthscipe* < *weorth* value] — **wor′ship·er, wor′ship·per** *n.*

wor·ship·ful (wûr′ship·fəl) *adj.* **1.** Giving or feeling reverence or adoration. **2.** *Chiefly Brit.* Worthy of or entitled to honor or respect by reason of character, position, or rank: used as a title of respect for magistrates, etc. — **wor′ship·ful·ly** *adv.* — **wor′ship·ful·ness** *n.*

worst (wûrst) Superlative of BAD and ILL. — *adj.* Bad, ill, evil, harmful, etc., in the highest degree. — **in the worst way** *Slang* Very much. — *n.* That which is worst. — **at worst** By the most pessimistic estimate. — **if (the) worst comes to (the) worst** If the worst imaginable thing comes to pass. — **to get the worst of it** To be defeated or put at a disadvantage. — *adv.* In the worst or most extreme manner or degree. — *v.t.* To get the advantage over; defeat; vanquish. [OE *wierrest*]

wors·ted (wŏŏs′tid, wûr′stid) *n.* **1.** Woolen yarn spun from long staple, with fibers combed parallel and twisted hard. **2.** A smooth, hard-surfaced fabric made from worsted yarns, as gabardine or serge. — *adj.* Consisting of or made from this yarn. [after *Worsted,* former name of a parish in Norfolk, north of Norwich, England]

wort (wûrt) *n.* **1.** A plant or herb: usually in combination: *liverwort, navelwort.* **2.** The unfermented infusion of malt that becomes beer when fermented. [OE *wyrt* root, plant]

worth¹ (wûrth) *n.* **1.** The quality that renders a thing useful or desirable; value or excellence of any kind. **2.** The exchangeable or market value of anything. **3.** The quality or combination of qualities that makes one deserving of esteem. **4.** Wealth. **5.** The amount of something that can be had for a specific sum: three cents' *worth* of candy. — *prep.* **1.** Equal in value (to); exchangeable (for): *worth* $25.

2. Deserving of: to be *worth* seeing. **3.** Having possessions to the value of: He is *worth* a million. — **for all it is worth** To the utmost. — **for all one is worth** With every effort possible; to the utmost of one's capacity. [OE *weorth*] — **Syn.** (noun) **1.** *Worth* and *value* relate to the merit or excellence of a person or thing. In pecuniary matters, the words are usually equivalent: to get one's money's *worth*, to receive good *value* in a purchase. *Worth* often implies some intangible merit or efficacy, while *value* has reference to a measurable or precisely definable quality: ideas of little *worth*, the *value* of a house and its lot.

worth² (wûrth) *v.i.* *Archaic* To betide or befall: now only in phrases, as **woe worth the day,** etc. [OE *weorthan* to come to be]

-worth *combining form* Of the value of: *pennyworth.* [OE *weorth* worth]

worth·less (wûrth′lis) *adj.* Having no worth, value, dignity, virtue, etc. — **worth′less·ly** *adv.* — **worth′less·ness** *n.*

worth·while (wûrth′hwīl′) *adj.* Sufficiently important to occupy the time; of enough value to repay the effort. — **worth′while′ness** *n.*

wor·thy (wûr′thē) *adj.* **·thi·er, ·thi·est 1.** Possessing worth or value; deserving of respect or honor; having valuable or useful qualities. **2.** Having such qualities as to be deserving of or adapted to some specified thing; fit; suitable: followed by *of* (rarely *for*) or sometimes by an infinitive: He is *worthy* of our praise. **3.** *Obs.* Well deserved; fitting. — *n.* *pl.* **·thies 1.** A person of eminent worth. **2.** A person or character of local note: a humorous usage. [ME *wurthi, worthi*] — **wor′thi·ly** *adv.* — **wor′thi·ness** *n.*

-worthy *combining form* **1.** Meriting or deserving: *trustworthy.* **2.** Valuable as; having worth as: *newsworthy.* **3.** Fit for: *seaworthy.* [OE *wyrthe* worthy]

wot (wot) Present tense, first and third person singular, of WIT².

Wo·tan (vō′tän) In Wagner's *Ring of the Nibelung,* Wodan; Odin.

Wot·ton (wot′n), **Sir Henry,** 1568–1639, English author.

would (wŏŏd) Past tense of WILL, but rarely a true past, rather chiefly used as a modal auxiliary expressing: **a** Desire or inclination: He *would* like to write. **b** Condition: He *would* give if he were able. **c** Futurity: He kept searching for something that *would* cure him. **d** Determination: He *would* not go. **e** Expectation or possibility: Letting him speak *would* have serious consequences. **f** Preference: We *would* have you succeed rather than fail. **g** Request: *Would* you give us a call? **h** Custom or habit: We *would* ride together each day. **i** Choice: He *would* never go if he could help it. **j** Uncertainty: It *would* seem to be wrong. ◆ See note under SHOULD. [OE *wolde,* pt. of *willan* to will]

would-be (wŏŏd′bē′) *adj.* **1.** Desiring or professing to be: a *would-be* poet. **2.** Intended to be.

would·n't (wŏŏd′nt) Would not.

wouldst (wŏŏdst) Archaic or poetic second person singular of WOULD: used with *thou.*

wound¹ (wŏŏnd, *Poetic* wound) *n.* **1.** A hurt or injury to the body, usually one in which the skin is cut or torn, as a stab, cut, etc. **2.** A similar injury to a tree or plant. **3.** Any injury or cause of pain or grief, as to the feelings, honor, etc. — *v.t.* & *v.i.* To inflict a wound or wounds (upon); cause injury or grief (to). — **Syn.** See INJURE. [OE *wund*]

wound² (wound) Past tense and past participle of WIND².

wove (wōv) Past tense and alternative past participle of WEAVE.

wo·ven (wō′vən) Past participle of WEAVE.

wove paper Paper that does not carry the marks of the wire gauze on which it was laid during finishing.

wow¹ (wou) *interj.* *Informal* An exclamation of wonder, surprise, pleasure, pain, etc. — *n.* *Slang* Something that is extraordinarily successful, amusing, etc. — *v.t.* *Slang* To be extraordinarily successful with.

wow² (wou) *n.* A low-frequency fluctuation in the pitch of a transmitted or reproduced sound, caused by variation in the speed of a turntable, etc. [Imit.]

wow·ser (wou′zər) *n.* *Australian Slang* One who is excessively puritanical; especially, one opposed to Sunday amusements, sports, etc. [Origin uncertain]

WPA or **W.P.A.** Work Projects Administration.

WRAC or **W.R.A.C.** Women's Royal Army Corps.

wrack¹ (rak) *n.* **1.** Ruin; destruction: chiefly in the phrase **wrack and ruin.** **2.** A wrecked ship; wreckage. **3.** Marine vegetation and floating material cast ashore by the sea, as seaweed or eelgrass. **4.** *Scot.* & *Brit. Dial.* Weeds. — *v.t.* & *v.i.* To wreck or be wrecked. [Fusion of OE *wræc* punishment, revenge and MDu. *wrak* wreck]

wrack² (rak) *n.* A rack of clouds; any floating vapor. Compare RACK³. [Var. of RACK³]

WRAF or **W.R.A.F.** Women's Royal Air Force.

wraith (rāth) *n.* **1.** An apparition of a person thought to be alive, seen shortly before or shortly after his death. **2.** Any apparition. — **Syn.** See GHOST. [Origin unknown]

wrang (rang) *adj.* & *n.* *Scot.* Wrong.

Wran·gell (rang′gəl), **Mount** An active volcano (14,005 ft.) in the western **Wrangell Mountains,** a range in SE Alaska, highest peak; Mt. Bona, 16,420 ft.

Wran·gell Island (rang′gəl) An island of the Alexander Archipelago, SE Alaska; 30 mi. long, 5 to 14 mi. wide.

wran·gle (rang′gəl) v. ·gled, ·gling v.i. 1. To argue or dispute noisily; brawl. — v.t. 2. To argue; debate. 3. To get by quarreling or disputing. 4. U.S. To herd or round up (livestock). — n. An angry or noisy dispute; a quarrel. — **Syn.** See QUARREL[1]. [Cf. LG wrangeln to quarrel, freq. of wrangen to struggle]

wran·gler (rang′glər) n. 1. One who wrangles. 2. At Cambridge University, England, one who has taken the highest mathematical honors. 3. A herdsman on a range.

wrap (rap) v. **wrapped** or **wrapt, wrap·ping** v.t. 1. To surround and cover by something folded or wound about; swathe; enwrap. 2. To cover with paper, etc., folded about and secured. 3. To wind or fold (a covering) about something. 4. To surround so as to blot out or conceal: the sun wrapped in clouds. 5. To enclose, envelop, or involve deeply: She wrapped the kitten in her arms; wrapped in thought. 6. To place so as to enclose or embrace: He wrapped his arm around her. 7. To fold, wind, or draw together. — v.i. 8. To be or become twined or coiled: with about, around, etc. — **to be wrapped up in** 1. To be clothed in or enveloped by (something). 2. To be totally absorbed, involved, or interested in (something). — **to keep under wraps** To keep secret. — n. 1. An article of dress drawn or folded about a person. 2. pl. Outer garments collectively, as cloaks, scarfs, etc. 3. A blanket. [ME wrappen; origin uncertain]

wrap·a·round (rap′ə·round′) adj. 1. Designating a garment, as a skirt, dress, coat, etc., open down to the hem and made to fit by being wrapped around the body. 2. Encircling or overlapping: a wraparound windshield.

wrap·per (rap′ər) n. 1. A paper enclosing a newspaper, magazine, or similar packet for mailing or otherwise. 2. A detachable paper cover to protect the binding of a book. 3. A woman's dressing gown. 4. One who or that which wraps. 5. A tobacco leaf of high quality enclosing a cigar.

wrap·ping (rap′ing) n. Often pl. A covering; something in which an object is wrapped.

wrap-up (rap′up′) n. Informal A summary of a news report.

wrasse (ras) n. Any of a group of spiny-finned, often brilliantly colored fishes (family Labridae) of warm tropical seas, some species of which, as the tautog, are esteemed as food fishes. [< Cornish wrach < gwrach, orig., an old woman]

wrath (rath, räth; Brit. rôth) n. 1. Extreme or violent rage or fury; vehement indignation. 2. An act done in violent rage, especially in vengeance or punishment. — **Syn.** See ANGER. — v.t. & v.i. Obs. To make or become angry. — adj. Obs. Wroth; angry. [OE wrǣththu < wrāth wroth]

wrath·ful (rath′fəl, räth′-) adj. 1. Full of wrath; extremely angry. 2. Springing from or expressing wrath. — **wrath′· ful·ly** adv. — **wrath′ful·ness** n.

wrath·y (rath′ē, räth′ē) adj. wrath·i·er, wrath·i·est Informal Wrathful. — **wrath′i·ly** adv. — **wrath′i·ness** n.

wreak (rēk) v.t. 1. To inflict or exact, as vengeance. 2. To give free expression to (anger, hatred, etc.); vent. [OE wrecan to drive, avenge]

wreath (rēth) n. pl. **wreaths** (rēthz) 1. A band or circle of flowers or greenery, often worn on the head as a crown or placed on a grave or at a door, window, etc. 2. Any curled band of circular or spiral shape, as of smoke. [OE writha < writhan to bind, tie] — **wreath′y** n.

Wreath (rēth) The constellation Corona Australis.

wreathe (rēth) v. **wreathed, wreath·ing** v.t. 1. To form into a wreath, as by twisting or twining. 2. To adorn or encircle with or as with wreaths. 3. To envelop; cover: His face was wreathed in smiles. — v.i. 4. To take the form of a wreath. 5. To twist, turn, or coil, as masses of cloud. [Earlier wrethe, back formation < ME wrethen, var. of writhen, pp. of writhen to writhe; infl. by WREATH]

wreck (rek) v.t. 1. To cause the destruction or wreck of, as a vessel; shipwreck. 2. To bring ruin, damage, or destruction upon. 3. To tear down, as a building; dismantle. — v.i. 4. To suffer wreck; be ruined. 5. To engage in wrecking, as for plunder or salvage. — n. 1. That which has been ruined or destroyed. 2. Property cast upon land by the sea, either broken portions of a wrecked vessel or cargo from it. 3. The accidental destruction or ruin of a ship; also, the ship so destroyed. 4. One who is physically, mentally, or morally unsound or ruined. 5. The act of wrecking, or the state of being wrecked; ruin; destruction. [< AF wrec, wrech < OF warec < ON (assumed) wrek < wrekan to drive]

wreck·age (rek′ij) n. 1. The act of wrecking, or the state of being wrecked. 2. Broken or disordered remnants or fragments from a wreck.

wreck·er (rek′ər) n. 1. One who or that which causes wreck, destruction, or frustration of any sort. 2. One employed in tearing down and removing old buildings. 3. A person, train, car, or machine that clears away wrecks. 4. One who is employed to recover disabled vessels or wrecked cargoes for the owners; also, a vessel employed in this service; a salvager. 5. One who lures ships to destruction

by false lights on the shore in order to plunder the wreck.

wreck·ful (rek′fəl) adj. Poetic Causing wreckage.

wreck·ing (rek′ing) n. The work or art of a wrecker. — adj. Of, engaged in, or used in pulling down buildings or in salvaging and clearing away wrecks.

wren (ren) n. 1. Any of numerous small passerine birds (family Troglodytidae) having short, rounded wings and a short tail, including the common **house wren** (Troglodytes aedon), the **Carolina wren** (Thryothorus ludovicianus), **Bewick's wren** (Thryomanes bewickii) of North America, and the European wren (Troglodytes troglodytes). 2. Any of numerous similar birds. [OE wrenna]

Wren (ren), **Sir Christopher,** 1632–1723, English architect.

wrench (rench) n. 1. A violent twist. 2. A sharp or violent twist or pull, as in the ankle, back, etc.; a sprain. 3. Any sudden and violent emotion or grief. 4. Any perversion or distortion of an original meaning. 5. Any of various tools for twisting or turning bolts, nuts, pipe, etc. — v.t. 1. To twist violently; turn suddenly by force; wrest. 2. To twist forcibly so as to cause strain or injury; sprain. 3. To twist from the proper meaning, intent, or use. 4. To strain or force the feelings, thoughts, etc., of: to wrench oneself away from pleasure. — v.i. 5. To give a twist or wrench. [OE wrenc trick. Akin to WRINKLE[1].]

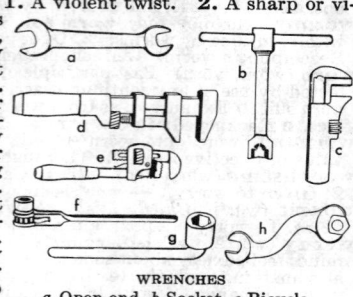

WRENCHES
a Open-end. b Socket. c Bicycle.
d Monkey. e Pipe. f Ratchet.
g Offset. h S-wrench.

Wrens (renz) n.pl. Brit. Informal Women's Royal Naval Service, an organization to relieve men of certain shore duties connected with the Royal Navy. Also **WRENS.**

wrest (rest) v.t. 1. To pull or force away by violent twisting or wringing; wrench. 2. To turn from the true meaning, character, intent, or application; distort; pervert. 3. To seize forcibly by violence, extortion, or usurpation. 4. To extract by toil and effort: to wrest a living from barren soil. — n. 1. An act of wresting; a violent twist. 2. A misapplication or perversion. 3. A crooked act; wile. 4. A key for tuning a stringed instrument, as a harp. [OE wrǣstan] — **wrest′er** n.

wres·tle (res′əl) v. ·tled, ·tling v.i. 1. To engage in wrestling. 2. To struggle, as for mastery; contend. — v.t. 3. To engage in (a wrestling match), or wrestle with. 4. To throw (a calf) and hold it down for branding. — n. 1. A wrestling match. 2. Any hard struggle. [OE wrǣstlian, freq. of wrǣstan to wrest]

wres·tler (res′lər) n. One who wrestles; especially, a person who competes in wrestling matches.

wres·tling (res′ling) n. A sport or exercise in which each of two unarmed contestants endeavors to throw the other to the ground or force him into a certain fallen position.

wrest pin In stringed instruments, as the piano or harp, a metal pin around which the ends of the strings are coiled and which can be turned to tune the string.

wretch (rech) n. 1. A base, vile, or contemptible person. 2. A miserable or pitiable person. [OE wrecca outcast < wrecan to drive]

wretch·ed (rech′id) adj. 1. Sunk in dejection; profoundly unhappy. 2. Causing misery or grief. 3. Unsatisfactory or worthless in ability or quality. 4. Despicable; contemptible. — **wretch′ed·ly** adv. — **wretch′ed·ness** n.

wrig·gle (rig′əl) v. ·gled, ·gling v.i. 1. To twist in a sinuous manner; squirm; writhe. 2. To proceed as by twisting or crawling. 3. To make one's way by evasive or indirect means. — v.t. 4. To cause to wriggle. — n. The motion of one who or that which wriggles; a squirm. [< MLG wriggeln, freq. of wriggen to twist] — **wrig′gly** adj.

wrig·gler (rig′lər) n. 1. One who or that which wriggles. 2. A mosquito larva.

wright (rīt) n. One who constructs, contrives, or creates: used chiefly in compounds: shipwright; playwright. [OE wyrhta]

Wright (rīt), **Frank Lloyd,** 1869–1959, U.S. architect. — **Joseph,** 1855–1930, English philologist and lexicographer. — **Orville,** 1871–1948, U.S. pioneer in aviation. — **Wilbur,** 1867–1912, U.S. pioneer in aviation; brother of Orville.

wring (ring) v. **wrung** (Rare **wringed**), **wring·ing** v.t. 1. To squeeze or compress by twisting. 2. To squeeze or press out, as water, by twisting. 3. To extort; acquire by extortion. 4. To distress; torment. 5. To twist or wrest violently out of shape or place: to wring his neck. 6. To grasp firmly or press, as in a handshake. 7. Obs. To pervert; distort. — v.i. 8. To writhe or squirm, as with anguish. 9. To perform the action of wringing. — n. The act of wringing. [OE wringan]

wring·bolt (ring′bōlt′) *n.* A ring bolt. [Earlier *wrainbolt*, var. of RING BOLT]

wring·er (ring′ər) *n.* **1.** One who or that which wrings. **2.** A contrivance used to press water out of fabrics after washing; also, the operator of such a machine.

wring·ing-wet (ring′ing-wet′) *adj.* Wet enough so that water may be wrung out.

wrin·kle[1] (ring′kəl) *n.* **1.** A small ridge, crease, or fold, as on a smooth surface. **2.** A small fold or crease in the skin, usually produced by age or by excessive exposure to the elements. — *v.* **·kled, ·kling** *v.t.* **1.** To make a wrinkle or wrinkles in, as by creasing, folding, crumpling, etc. — *v.i.* **2.** To be or become contracted into wrinkles or ridges. [OE *gewrinclod*, pp. of *gewrinclian* to wind] — **wrin′kly** *adj.*

wrin·kle[2] (ring′kəl) *n.* A curious or ingenious method, idea, device, etc. [Prob. dim. of OE *wrenc* trick]

wrist (rist) *n.* **1.** The part or joint (**wrist joint**) of the arm that lies between the hand and the forearm; the carpus. ◆ Collateral adjective: *carpal.* **2.** The part of a glove or garment that covers the wrist. **3.** A wrist pin (which see). [OE, prob. < *writhan* to writhe]

wrist·band (rist′band, -bənd, riz′-) *n.* The band of a sleeve that covers the wrist or ends a shirt sleeve; a cuff.

wrist-drop (rist′drop′) *n. Pathol.* Paralysis of the muscles of the hand and the forearm, usually due to lead poisoning.

wrist·let (rist′lit) *n.* **1.** A flexible band worn on the wrist for warmth. **2.** A bracelet. **3.** *Slang* A handcuff.

wrist·lock (rist′lok′) *n.* In wrestling, a hold whereby an opponent is made helpless by having his arm twisted by a grip at the wrist.

wrist pin *Mech.* **1.** A pin holding together the piston and connecting rod of a steam engine. **2.** A similar pin in the cross-head of an internal-combustion engine.

wrist watch A watch set in a band or strap and worn at the wrist.

writ[1] (rit) *n.* **1.** *Law* A mandatory precept, under seal, issued by a court, and commanding the person to whom it is addressed to do or not to do some act. **2.** That which is written: now chiefly in the phrase *Holy Writ*, meaning the Bible. [OE, *a writing* < *writan* to write]

writ[2] (rit) Archaic or dialectal past tense and past participle of WRITE.

write (rīt) *v.* **wrote** (*Archaic* or *Dial.* **writ**), **writ·ten** (*Archaic* or *Dial.* **writ**), **writ·ing** *v.t.* **1.** To trace or inscribe (letters, words, numbers, symbols, etc.) on a surface with pen or pencil, or by other means. **2.** To describe in writing: to *write* one's impressions of a journey. **3.** To communicate by letter: He *writes* that he will be home soon. **4.** *Informal* To communicate with by letter: He *writes* her every day. **5.** To produce by writing; be the author or composer of. **6.** To draw up; draft: to *write* one's will; to *write* a check. **7.** To cover or fill with writing: to *write* two full pages. **8.** To show or make visible: Hate and fear were *written* on his face. **9.** To spell or inscribe as specified: He *writes* his name with two *n*'s. **10.** To entitle or designate in writing: He *writes* himself "General." **11.** To underwrite: to *write* an insurance policy. — *v.i.* **12.** To trace or inscribe letters, etc., on a surface, as of paper. **13.** To write a letter or letters; communicate in writing. **14.** To be engaged in the occupation of a writer or author. **15.** To produce a specified quality of writing. — **to write down 1.** To put into writing. **2.** To injure or depreciate in writing. — **to write off 1.** To cancel or remove (claims, debts, etc.) from an open account. **2.** To acknowledge the loss or failure of. — **to write in 1.** To insert in writing, as in a document. **2.** To cast (a vote) for one not listed on a ballot by inserting his name in writing. — **to write out 1.** To put into writing. **2.** To write in full or complete form. — **to write up 1.** To describe fully in writing. **2.** To praise fully or too fully in writing. **3.** In accounting, to put an unusually high value upon. [OE *writan*]

write-in (rīt′in′) *adj. Informal* Designating a method of voting whereby a name not formally on the ballot is written in by the voter. — *n.* In voting, a name written on the ballot by the voter.

write-off (rīt′ôf′, -of′) *n.* **1.** A cancellation. **2.** An amount canceled or noted as a loss.

writ·er (rī′tər) *n.* **1.** One who writes. **2.** One who engages in literary composition. **3.** Formerly, in England, a copying clerk in a government office; also, sometimes, a clerk; a penman. **4.** *Scot.* Formerly, an attorney.

writer's cramp *Pathol.* Spasmodic contraction of the muscles of the fingers and hand, caused by excessive writing. Also **writer's palsy** or **spasm.**

write-up (rīt′up′) *n. Informal* **1.** A written description, record, or account, usually laudatory, as of a town, manufacturing enterprise, or public institution. **2.** *U.S.* In finance, an illegally excessive statement of the assets of a corporation.

writhe (rīth) *v.* **writhed, writhed** (*Obs.* **writh·en**), **writh·ing** *v.t.* **1.** To cause to twist or bend; distort. — *v.i.* **2.** To twist or distort the body, face, etc., as in pain. **3.** To suffer acutely, as from embarrassment, anguish, etc. — *n.* An act of writhing; a contortion. [OE *writhan*] — **writh′er** *n.*

writh·en (rith′ən) Obsolete past participle of WRITHE. — *adj. Poetic* Twisted; distorted.

writ·ing (rī′ting) *n.* **1.** The act of one who writes. **2.** The characters so made; chirography; handwriting. **3.** Anything written or expressed in letters; especially, a literary production. **4.** The profession or occupation of a writer. **5.** The practice, art, form, or style of literary composition.

writing paper Paper prepared to receive ink in writing; especially, stationery.

writ of error *Law* A commission by which the judges of one court are authorized to examine a record upon which a judgment was given in another court, and to affirm or reverse the judgment according to law.

writ of execution *Law* A writ commanding a judgment to be carried into effect.

writ of prohibition *Law* A writ issued by a superior court to an inferior court, commanding it to desist from proceeding in a matter not within its jurisdiction.

writ of right *Law* **1.** Formerly, in England, a writ in an action for the purpose of establishing a title to real estate. **2.** A similar common-law writ.

writ·ten (rit′n) Past participle of WRITE.

W.R.N.S. Women's Royal Naval Service (Wrens).

Wro·claw (vrô′tswäf) A city in SW Poland, on the Oder; formerly part of Germany; pop. 480,600 (est. 1960): German *Breslau.*

wrong (rông, rong) *adj.* **1.** Not correct; mistaken; erroneous: a *wrong* estimate. **2.** Not suitable; inappropriate; improper: the *wrong* thing to do; the *wrong* clothes; the *wrong* job. **3.** Not according to the right, proper, or correct method, standard, intention, etc.: the *wrong* way to do it. **4.** Not working or acting properly or satisfactorily; amiss: Something is *wrong* with the lock. **5.** Intended or made to be turned under, inward, or so as not to be seen: the *wrong* side of the cloth. **6.** Not desired or intended: the *wrong* road. **7.** Not favored by conventional social standards: the *wrong* side of town. **8.** Not morally right, proper, or just; immoral. **9.** Unsatisfactory: the *wrong* reply. — **to go wrong 1.** To lapse from the strict path of rectitude. **2.** To turn out badly; go astray. — *adv.* In a wrong direction, place, or manner; awry or amiss; erroneously. — *n.* **1.** That which is wrong, as an evil or unjust action. **2.** The state or condition of being wrong: to be in the *wrong.* **3.** *Law* An invasion or violation of one's legal rights. — **Syn.** See INJUSTICE, OFFENSE. — *v.t.* **1.** To violate the rights of; inflict injury or injustice upon. **2.** To impute evil to unjustly; misrepresent; malign: If you think so, you *wrong* him. **3.** To seduce or dishonor (a woman). [OE *wrang* twisted < ON *rangr* awry, unjust] — **wrong′er** *n.* — **wrong′ly** *adv.* — **wrong′ness** *n.*

wrong·do·er (rông′dōō′ər, rong′-) *n.* One who does wrong. — **wrong′do′ing** *n.*

wrong font *Printing* A font of type not intended for the job in progress: used to designate an incorrect type face. Abbr. *wf, w.f.*

wrong·ful (rông′fəl, rong′-) *adj.* **1.** Characterized by wrong or injustice; injurious; unjust. **2.** Unlawful; illegal. — **wrong′ful·ly** *adv.* — **wrong′ful·ness** *n.*

wrong-head·ed (rông′hed′id, rong′-) *adj.* Stubbornly or perversely erring in judgment, action, etc. — **wrong′head′ed·ly** *adv.* — **wrong′-head′ed·ness** *n.*

wrote (rōt) Past tense of WRITE.

wroth (rôth) *adj. Archaic* Filled with anger; furious; incensed. Also **wroth′ful** (-fəl). [OE *wrāth*]

wrought (rôt) Archaic past tense and past participle of WORK. — *adj.* **1.** Beaten or hammered into shape by tools: *wrought* gold. **2.** Worked; molded. **3.** Made with delicacy; elaborated carefully. **4.** Made; fashioned; formed: often in combination: *well-wrought.* — **wrought up** Excited; agitated. [ME *wrogt* < OE *geworht*, pp. of *wrycan* to work]

wrought iron Commercially pure iron, prepared from pig iron and easily forged and welded into various shapes.

wrung (rung) Past tense and past participle of WRING.

wry (rī) *adj.* **wri·er** or **wry·er, wri·est** or **wry·est** **1.** Bent to one side or out of position; contorted; askew; also, made by twisting or distorting the features: a *wry* smile. **2.** Deviating from that which is right or proper; perverted; warped. **3.** Perverse, ironic, or bitter: *wry* humor. — *v.t.* **wried, wry·ing** To twist; contort. [ME *wrye* < OE *wrigian* to move, tend] — **wry′ly** *adv.* — **wry′ness** *n.*

wry·neck (rī′nek′) *n.* **1.** A bird (genus *Jynx*) resembling and allied to the woodpeckers, with the habit of twisting its head and neck. **2.** *Pathol.* Torticollis. **3.** *Informal* One having a twisted neck; a person afflicted with torticollis. — **wry·necked** (rī′nekt′) *adj.*

WSW or **wsw, W.S.W.,** or **w.s.w.** West-southwest.

wt. Weight.

Wu·chang (woo′chäng′) A former city and capital of Hupeh Province, China, now part of Wuhan.

Wu·han (woo′hän′) The capital of Hupeh Province, China, on the Yangtze, a city comprising the three formerly independent cities of Hankow, Hanyang, and Wuchang; pop. 4,250,000 (est. 1970): also *Han Cities*. Also **Wu′·han′**.

Wu·hu (woo′hoo′) A port city in Anhwei Province, China, on the Yangtze; pop. 300,000 (est. 1970). Also **Wu′·hu′**.

wul·fen·ite (wool′fən-īt) *n. Mineral.* A resinous or hard, gray, yellow, brown, or red molybdate of lead, usually occurring in tabular crystals: also called *yellow lead ore.* [after F. X. von *Wulfen*, 1728–1805, Austrian mineralogist]

Wul·fi·la (wool′fə-lə) See ULFILAS.

Wundt (voont), **Wilhelm**, 1832–1920, German psychologist and physiologist. — **Wundt′i·an** *adj.*

wun·na (wun′na) *Scot.* Will not.

Wup·per·tal (voop′ər-täl) A city in SW North Rhine–Westphalia, West Germany; pop. 412,700 (est. 1967).

Würt·tem·berg (wûr′təm-bûrg, *Ger.* vür′təm-berkh) A former state of SW Germany, now part of Baden–Württemberg.

Würz·burg (wûrts′bûrg, *Ger.* vürts′boorkh) A city in NW Bavaria, West Germany; pop. 119,400 (est. 1967).

Wu·sih (woo′shē′) A city in southern Kiangsu Province, China; pop. 900,000 (est. 1970).

wuth·er·ing (wuth′ə-ring) *adj. Scot.* **1.** Blowing with a roaring sound, as a strong wind. **2.** Characterized by such a sound or sounds, as a place: *Wuthering Heights.* [< dial. E *wuther, whither* to rage, bellow, prob. < ON]

Wu·tsin (woo′jin′) See CH'ANG·CHOU.

W.Va. West Virginia.

WVS or **W.V.S.** *Brit.* Women's Voluntary Service.

Wy. Wyoming (unofficial).

Wy·an·dot (wī′ən-dot) *n. pl.* **·dot** or **·dots 1.** One of a tribe of North American Indians of Iroquoian stock and descendants of Hurons, presently settled in Oklahoma. **2.** An Iroquoian language. Also spelled *Wyandotte.*

Wy·an·dotte (wī′ən-dot) *n.* **1.** One of an American breed of domestic fowls. **2.** *pl.* **·dotte** or **·dottes** A Wyandot. **3.** The Wyandot language. [after the *Wyandot* Indians]

Wy·an·dotte (wī′ən-dot, wīn′dot) A city in SE Michigan, near Detroit; pop. 41,061.

Wy·att (wī′ət), **Sir Thomas**, 1503–42, English poet and diplomat. Also **Wy′at.**

wych-elm (wich′elm′) *n.* A wide-spreading elm (*Ulmus glabra*), common in the British Isles: also called *Scotch elm, wich, witch:* also spelled *wich-elm, witch-elm.* Also **wych.** [< *wych*, var. of WITCH² + ELM]

Wych·er·ley (wich′ər-lē), **William**, 1640?–1716, English dramatist and poet.

wych-ha·zel (wich′hā′zəl) *n.* Witch hazel (which see).

Wyc·liffe (wik′lif), **John**, 1324?–84, English religious reformer; first translator of the entire Bible into English. Also spelled *Wiclif, Wickliffe.* Also **Wyc′lif.**

Wyc·liff·ite (wik′lif-īt) *n.* A follower of Wycliffe; a Lollard. — *adj.* Of or pertaining to Wycliffe or the Lollards. Also **Wyc′lif·ite.**

wye (wī) *n.* **1.** The letter Y. **2.** Something shaped like Y.

Wye (wī) A river in SE Wales and SW England, flowing 130 miles SE to the Severn estuary.

Wy·eth (wī′əth), **Andrew**, born 1917, U.S. painter.

Wyld (wīld), **Henry Cecil Kennedy**, 1870–1945, English philologist and lexicographer.

wyle (wīl) *v.t.* **wyled, wyl·ing** *Scot.* To beguile; wile.

Wy·lie (wī′lē), **Elinor Morton**, 1885–1928, *née* Hoyt, U.S. poet and novelist.

wy·lie-coat (wī′lē-kōt′, wil′ē-, wul′ē-) *n. Scot.* A flannel undershirt or petticoat.

Wyo. Wyoming.

Wy·o·ming (wī-ō′ming) **1.** A State in the NW United States; 97,914 sq. mi.; pop. 332,416; capital, Cheyenne; entered the Union July 10, 1890; nickname, *Equality State.* **2.** A city in western Michigan, a suburb of Grand Rapids; pop. 56,560. — **Wy·o′ming·ite** *n.*

Wyoming Valley A valley of the Susquehanna River in NE Pennsylvania; scene of a massacre of settlers by Indians and Tories, 1778.

Wythe (with), **George**, 1726–1806, American jurist and patriot; signer of the Declaration of Independence.

wy·vern (wī′vərn) See WIVERN.

X

x, X (eks) *n. pl.* **x's** or **xs, X's** or **Xs, ex·es** (ek′siz) **1.** The twenty-fourth letter of the English alphabet, adopted from the ancient western Greek alphabets of Chalcis, Boeotia, and Elis, and becoming Roman X. Also *ex.* **2.** The sounds represented by the letter *x*, in English variously sounded as (ks), as in *axle, box, next;* (gz), as in *executive, exert;* (ksh), as in *noxious;* (gzh), as in *luxurious;* and initially, always (z) as in *xenophobe, xylophone, Xanthippe.* **3.** Anything shaped like an X. **4.** An unknown quantity, factor, result, etc. — *symbol* **1.** The Roman numeral ten. **2.** A mark shaped like an X, representing the signature of one who cannot write. **3.** A mark used in diagrams, maps, etc., to place some event or substance, or to point out something to be emphasized. **4.** A symbol used to indicate a kiss. **5.** Christ: an abbreviation used in combination: *Xmas.*

x *Math.* **1.** The principal unknown quantity. **2.** An abscissa.

X 1. Christ. **2.** Christian.

xan·thate (zan′thāt) *n. Chem.* A salt or ester of xanthic acid. [< XANTH(IC) + -ATE³]

xan·the·in (zan′thē-in) *n. Biochem.* The water-soluble portion of the yellow coloring matter found in the cell sap of some plants. [< F *xanthéine* < Gk. *xanthos* yellow]

xan·thic (zan′thik) *adj.* Having a yellow or yellowish color. [< F *xanthique* < Gk. *xanthos* yellow]

xanthic acid *Chem.* Any of a group of unstable, colorless, liquid sulfur compounds made by decomposing a xanthate with a dilute acid.

xan·thin (zan′thin) *n. Biochem.* The insoluble portion of the yellow pigment found in yellow flowers. [< G < Gk. *xanthos* yellow]

xan·thine (zan′thēn, -thin) *n. Biochem.* A crystalline nitrogenous compound, $C_5H_4N_4O_2$, contained in blood, urine, and other animal secretions, and in some plants. [< F < Gk. *xanthos* yellow]

Xan·thip·pe (zan·tip′ē) The wife of Socrates, proverbial as a shrew. Also **Xan·tip′pe.**

xan·tho- *combining form* Yellow: *xanthophyll.* Also, before vowels, **xanth-.** [< Gk. *xanthos* yellow]

xan·tho·chroid (zan′thə-kroid) *Anthropol. adj.* Characterized by a light-colored or fair complexion. — *n.* One who exhibits xanthochroid characteristics. [< XANTHO- + Gk. *ōchroi* pale color + -OID]

xan·tho·ma (zan-thō′mə) *n. Pathol.* A skin disease marked by the presence of small yellowish disks formed by the deposit of lipoids. [< XANTH(O)- + -OMA]

xan·tho·phyll (zan′thə-fil) *n. Biochem.* A yellow pigment, $C_{40}H_{56}O_2$, contained in plants and related to carotene. Also **xan·tho·phyl.** [< F *xanthophylle* < Gk. *xanthos* yellow + *phyllon* leaf]

xan·thous (zan′thəs) *adj.* **1.** Yellow. **2.** *Anthropol.* Of or pertaining to the yellow-skinned, or Mongoloid, ethnic division of mankind. [< XANTH(O)- + -OUS]

Xan·thus (zan′thəs) An ancient, ruined city of Lycia, in SW Turkey. — **Xan′thi·an** (-thē-ən) *adj.*

Xa·vi·er (zā′vē-ər, zav′ē-; *Sp.* hä-vyer′), **Saint Francis**, 1506–52, Spanish Jesuit missionary in the Orient; one of the founders of the Society of Jesus: called **the Apostle of the Indies.** — **Xa·ve·ri·an** (zā-vir′ē-ən) *adj. & n.*

X-ax·is (eks′ak′sis) *n. pl.* **-ax·es** (-ak′sēz) The more nearly horizontal axis in a graph or a Cartesian coordinate system; the abscissa.

X-chro·mo·some (eks′krō′mə-sōm) *n. Genetics* One of the two types of chromosomes that determine the sex of an offspring. See SEX CHROMOSOME.

x-cp. Ex coupon. Also **X.C., x.c.**

x-div. Ex dividend. Also **X.D., x.d.**

Xe *Chem.* Xenon.

xe·bec (zē′bek) *n.* A small, three-masted Mediterranean vessel, with both square and lateen sails, formerly used by Algerian pirates: also spelled *zebec.* [Earlier *chebec* < F < Sp. *jabeque, xabeque* < Arabic *shabbāk*]

xe·ni·a (zē′nē-ə) *n. Bot.* The direct influence of the pollen of one species upon the maternal tissues of another species after hybrid fertilization. [< NL < Gk. *xenia* hospitality < *xenos* guest]

xeno- *combining form* Strange; foreign; different: *xenophobe.* Also, before vowels, **xen-.** [< Gk. *xenos* stranger]

Xe·noc·ra·tes (zi-nok′rə-tēz), 396?–314 B.C., Greek philosopher.

xe·nog·a·my (zi-nog′ə-mē) *n. Biol.* Cross-fertilization. — **xe·nog′a·mous** (-məs) *adj.*

xen·o·gen·e·sis (zen'ə·jen'ə·sis) *n. Biol.* 1. Metagenesis (which see). 2. The supposed production of an organism unlike either of its parents. Also **xe·nog·e·ny** (zi·noj'ə·nē). — **xen'o·ge·net'ic** (-jə·net'ik), **xen·o·gen'ic** *adj.*

xen·o·lith (zen'ə·lith) *n. Geol.* A rock fragment enclosed within a larger mass of igneous rock.

xen·o·mor·phic (zen'ə·môr'fik) *adj. Mineral.* Denoting those constituents of an igneous rock whose crystal faces are distorted by the pressure of surrounding minerals.

xe·non (zē'non) *n.* A heavy gaseous element (symbol Xe) occurring in extremely small quantities in the atmosphere and freezing at a very low temperature. See ELEMENT. [< Gk., neut. of *xenos* strange]

Xe·noph·a·nes (zi·nof'ə·nēz) Sixth-century B.C. Greek philosopher and poet.

xen·o·phobe (zen'ə·fōb) *n.* One who hates or distrusts strangers or foreigners.

xen·o·pho·bi·a (zen'ə·fō'bē·ə) *n.* Hatred or distrust of foreigners or strangers. — **xen'o·pho'bic** (-fō'bik) *adj.*

Xen·o·phon (zen'ə·fən), 435?–355? B.C., Greek historian.

Xe·res (hā'rās, *older* shā'rās, sher'es) The former name for JEREZ.

xer·ic (zer'ik, zir'ik) *adj.* Of, pertaining to, or adapted to conditions of extreme dryness.

xero- *combining form* Dry; dryness: *xerophyte.* Also, before vowels, **xer-.** [< Gk. *xēros* dry]

xe·ro·der·ma (zir'ō·dûr'mə) *n. Pathol.* A disease characterized by roughness and dryness of the skin, with scaly desquamation. [< NL < Gk. *xēros* dry + *derma* skin] — **xe'ro·der·mat'ic** (-dər·mat'ik), **xe'ro·der'ma·tous** (-dûr'mə·təs) *adj.*

xe·rog·ra·phy (zi·rog'rə·fē) *n.* A method of printing in which a negatively charged ink powder is sprayed upon a positively charged metal plate, from which it is transferred to the printing surface by electrostatic attraction. [< XERO- + -GRAPHY] — **xe·ro·graph·ic** (zir'ō·graf'ik) *adj.* — **xe·rog'raph·er** *n.*

xe·roph·i·lous (zi·rof'ə·ləs) *adj. Biol.* Growing in or adapted to dry, hot climates. [< XERO- + -PHILOUS]

xe·roph·thal·mi·a (zir'əf·thal'mē·ə) *n. Pathol.* Abnormal dryness of the eyeball with ulceration of the cornea and secondary infection, caused by a deficiency of vitamin A. [< NL < Gk. *xēros* dry + *ophthalmos* eye]

xe·ro·phyte (zir'ə·fīt) *n. Bot.* A plant adapted to dry conditions of air and soil. [< XERO- + -PHYTE] — **xe'ro·phyt'ic** (-fit'ik) *adj.*

xe·ro·print·ing (zir'ō·prin'ting) *n.* A simplified variation of xerography, using a plate on a rotating cylinder.

xe·ro·sere (zir'ə·sir) *n. Ecol.* The series of changes in the succession of the plant formation found upon dry soil. [< XERO- + SERE²]

xe·ro·sis (zi·rō'sis) *n. Pathol.* A condition of abnormal dryness of a part, especially of the eye or skin. [< NL < Gk. *xēros* dry] — **xe·rot'ic** (-rot'ik) *adj.*

Xer·ox (zir'oks) *n.* A xerographic process for producing copies of printed or pictorial matter: a trade name. — *v.t.* To make or reproduce by Xerox: to *Xerox* 10 copies; to *Xerox* a document. Also **xer'ox.**

xe·rus (zir'əs) *n.* Any of a genus (*Xerus*) of African ground squirrels with long tails and coarse hair. [< NL < Gk. *xēros* dry]

Xerx·es I (zûrk'sēz), 519?–465? B.C., king of Persia 486?–465?; invaded Greece; defeated at Salamis 480 B.C.: called **the Great.**

Xho·sa (kō'sä) *n.* The Bantu language of the Kaffirs, closely related to Zulu: also called *Kaffir*: also spelled *Xosa.*

xi (zī, sī; *Gk.* ksē) *n.* The fourteenth letter in the Greek alphabet (Ξ, ξ), equivalent to the English *x.* See ALPHABET.

Xin·gú (shing·gōō') A river in northern and central Brazil, flowing 1,230 miles north to the Amazon.

x-int. Ex interest. Also **X.i., x-i.**

-xion Var. of -TION.

xiph·i- *combining form* Sword: *xiphisternum.* Also, before vowels, **xiph-.** [< Gk. *xiphos* sword]

xiph·i·ster·num (zif'ə·stûr'nəm) *n.* pl. **·na** (-nə) *Anat.* The cartilagenous lower segment or, in vertebrates other than man, the hindmost process of the sternum: also called *xiphoid.* Also **xiphoid process.** [< NL < Gk. *xiphos* sword + *sternon* breastbone]

xiph·oid (zif'oid) *adj.* 1. Shaped like a sword. 2. Of, pertaining to, or designating the xiphisternum. — *n.* The xiphisternum.

xiph·o·su·ran (zif'ə·sōōr'ən) *n.* Any of an order (*Xiphosura*) of arthropods having a horseshoe-shaped carapace and a long swordlike tail; a horseshoe crab. — *adj.* Of or pertaining to the *Xiphosura.* [< NL < Gk. *xiphos* sword + *oura* tail]

Xmas Christmas: popular abbreviation. ◆ *Xmas,* though

best avoided in formal contexts, has been used in written English since the sixteenth century and cannot be condemned as a modern commercialism. [< *X,* abbr. for *Christ* < Gk. *X,* chi, the first letter of *Christos* Christ + -MAS]

Xn. Christian.

Xnty. or **Xty.** Christianity.

Xo·sa (kō'sä) See XHOSA.

XP Chi and rho, the first two letters of ΧΡΙΣΤΟΣ, the Greek word for Christ, introduced by Constantine the Great as an emblem of Christ.

X-rated (eks'rā'təd) *adj.* Of a movie, not open to persons under the age of seventeen, because of the incidence of sex and violence; hence, obscene.

X-ray (eks'rā') *v.t.* To examine, photograph, diagnose, or treat with X-rays. — *n.* A picture made with X-rays; roentgenogram: also **X-ray photograph.**

X-rays (eks'rāz') *n.pl.* Electromagnetic radiations of extremely short wavelength, emitted from a substance when it is bombarded by a stream of electrons moving in a vacuum at a sufficiently high velocity, as in an electron tube. Their ability to penetrate solids, to ionize gases, and to act on photographic plates has many useful applications, especially in the detection, diagnosis, and treatment of certain organic disorders, chiefly internal. Also called *Roentgen rays.* [Trans. of G *X-strahlen,* name coined by Roentgen, their discoverer, because their nature was unknown]

X-ray therapy Medical treatment by the use of X-rays.

x-ref. Cross-reference.

X-rts. Ex rights.

Xtian. Christian.

Xu·thus (zōō'thəs) In Greek legend, son of Hellen and ancestor of the Ionians.

xy·lan (zī'lan) *n. Biochem.* A yellow, gummy hemicelluiose found in straw, oat hulls, peanut shells, and other plant wastes, yielding xylose upon hydrolosis.

xy·lem (zī'ləm) *n. Bot.* The portion of a vascular bundle in higher plants that is made up of woody tissue, parenchyma, and associated cells, etc. Compare PHLOEM. [< G < Gk. *xylon* wood]

xy·lene (zī'lēn) *n. Chem.* Any of three isomeric hydrocarbons, $C_6H_4(CH_3)_2$, contained in coal tar and wood tar. A mixture of the three yields a colorless, flammable liquid used as a solvent and in making dyes. Also **xy'lol** (-lōl, -lol). [< Gk. *xylon* wood + -ENE]

xy·li·dine (zī'lə·dēn, -din, zil'ə-) *n. Chem.* Any of six isomeric derivatives of xylene, $C_8H_{11}N$, resembling aniline and used in the synthesis of certain dyes. Also **xy'li·din** (-din). [< XYL(ENE) + -ID(E) + -INE²]

xylo- *combining form* Wood; woody: *xylograph.* Also, before vowels, **xyl-.** [< Gk. *xylon* wood]

xy·lo·carp (zī'lō·kärp) *n. Bot.* A hard, woody fruit. — **xy'lo·car'pous** (-kär'pəs) *adj.*

xy·lo·graph (zī'lə·graf, -gräf) *n.* An engraving on wood, or a print from such engraving.

xy·log·ra·phy (zī·log'rə·fē) *n.* 1. The art of wood engraving or of printing from wood engravings. 2. The art of printing on wood for decorative purposes. — **xy'lo·graph'ic** or **·i·cal** *adj.* — **xy·log'ra·pher** (zī·log'rə·fər) *n.*

xy·loid (zī'loid) *adj.* Of, pertaining to, or resembling wood.

xy·loph·a·gous (zī·lof'ə·gəs) *adj.* Feeding on or boring in wood, as insect larvae. [< XYLO- + -PHAGOUS]

xy·lo·phone (zī'lə·fōn) *n.* A musical instrument consisting of a row of wooden bars graduated in length to form a chromatic scale, and sounded by being struck with mallets. [< XYLO- + -PHONE] — **xy·lo·phon·ist** (zī'lə·fō'nist, zī·lof'ə·nist) *n.*

XYLOPHONE

xy·lose (zī'lōs) *n. Biochem.* A pentose, $C_5H_{10}O_5$, widely distributed in plant tissues, obtained by treating xylan with sulfuric acid, and used in tanning and dyeing: also called *wood sugar.* [< XYL(AN) + -OSE²]

xy·lot·o·mous (zī·lot'ə·məs) *adj.* Adapted to cutting or boring wood, as certain insects. [< XYLO- + Gk. *tomē* a cutting < *temnein* to cut]

xy·lot·o·my (zī·lot'ə·mē) *n.* The preparation of wood for examination by the microscope, as for scientific purposes. [< XYLO- + -TOMY] — **xy·lot'o·mist** *n.*

xy·lyl (zī'lil) *n. Chem.* The univalent radical, $(CH_3)_2C_6H_3$, derived from xylene. [< XYL(ENE) + -YL]

xyst (zist) *n.* 1. In ancient Greece, a portico where athletes exercised during bad weather. 2. In ancient Rome, a garden walk lined with trees. Also **xys·tos** (zis'tos), **xys·tus** (zis'təs). [< L *xystus* < Gk. *xystōs* smooth, polished < *xyein* to scrape]

xys·ter (zis'tər) *n.* A surgical instrument for scraping bones. [< NL < Gk. *xystēr* scraper < *xyein* to scrape]

Y

y, Y (wī) *n. pl.* **y's** or **ys, Y's** or **Ys, wyes** (wīz) **1.** The twenty-fifth letter of the English alphabet, the shape of which was ultimately derived from the Phoenician *vau* (*waw*), later adopted by the Greeks as *upsilon*. The Romans took it from the Greek alphabet sometime in the first century B.C. and used it to represent a vowel. Also **wye**. **2.** The sounds represented by the letter *y*. Initial *y* (introducing either a vowel or a syllable) represents a voiced palatal semivowel, as in *yet, you, yonder, beyond*. Final *y* represents either a vowel, pronounced (ē), as in *honey, pretty, steady*; a diphthong, pronounced (ī), as in *fly, my*; or the final glide of a diphthong, as in *gray, obey, annoy*. Internal *y* represents a vowel (i), as in *lyric, myth, syllable*; a diphthong (ī), as in *lyre, type, psychic*; an r-colored central vowel (ûr) or (ər), as in *myrtle, martyr*. **3.** Anything shaped like a Y, as: **a** A pipe coupling, connection, etc. **b** A forked piece serving as a rest or support, as for some part of a sighting instrument. — *symbol Chem.* Yttrium (symbol Y).

y *Math.* **1.** An ordinate. **2.** An unknown quantity.

y- *prefix* Used in Middle English as a sign of the past participle, as an intensive, or without perceptible force: *yclad, yclept*. It survives (as *a-*) in such words as *alike, aware*, etc. Also spelled *i-*, as in *iwis*. [OE *ge-*]

y. **1.** Yard(s). **2.** Year(s).

-y[1] *suffix of adjectives* Being, possessing, or resembling what is expressed in the root: *stony, rainy*. Also *-ey*, when added to words ending in *y*, as in *clayey, skyey*. [OE *-ig*]

-y[2] *suffix* The quality or state of being: *victory*: often used in abstract nouns formed from adjectives in *-ous* and *-ic*. [< F *-ie* < L *-ia*; also < Gk. *-ia, -eia*]

-y[3] *suffix* Little; small: *kitty*: often used in nicknames or to express endearment, as in *Tommy*. [Prob. < dial. E (Scottish)]

Y. Young Men's (or Women's) Christian Association.

yab·ber (yab′ər) *n. Austral. Informal* Speech; talk; jabber. [< Australian *yabba* < *ya* to speak]

Ya·blo·no·vyy Range (yä′blə·nə·vē) A range in the SE R.S.F.S.R., part of the watershed between the Arctic and Pacific drainage areas; highest peak, Bolshoi Saranakan, 5,280 ft. Also **Ya′blo·no·vy, Ya·blo·noi** (yə·blo·noi′), **Ya·blo·no·voi** (yə·blä·nə·voi′). *Russian* **Ya·blo·no·vyy Khre·bet** (khryi·byet′).

yacht (yot) *n.* A vessel specially built or fitted for racing or for private pleasure excursions. — *v.i.* To cruise, race, or sail in a yacht. [< Du. *jaghte*, short for *jaghtschip* pursuit ship < *jaght* hunting (< *jagen* to hunt) + *schip* ship]

yacht club A club of yachtsmen.

yacht·ing (yot′ing) *n.* The act, practice, or pastime of sailing a yacht.

yachts·man (yots′mən) *n. pl.* **·men** (-mən) One who owns or sails a yacht. Also **yacht′er, yacht′man. — yachts′·wom′an** (-woom′ən) *n.fem.*

yachts·man·ship (yots′mən·ship) *n.* The art or skill of yachting. Also **yacht′man·ship.**

Yad·kin River (yad′kin) The upper course of the Pee Dee River, flowing 204 miles generally southward across North Carolina.

yaff (yaf) *v.i. Brit. Dial.* **1.** To bark like a dog when excited. **2.** To speak sharply; scold. [Imit.]

ya·ger (yä′gər) See JAEGER.

ya·gua·run·di (yä′gwə·run′dē) *n.* A jaguarundi (which see).

yah[1] (yä) *interj.* An exclamation of disgust or contempt.

yah[2] (yä, yô) *interj. Informal* Yes. [Alter. of YES; infl. in form by G *ja* yes]

Ya·ha·ta (yä·hä·tä) See YAWATA.

ya·hoo (yä′hoo, yä′-, yä·hoo′) *n.* **1.** Any low, vicious person. **2.** An awkward fellow; a bumpkin. [< YAHOO]

Ya·hoo (yä′hoo, yä′-, yä·hoo′) *n.* In Swift's *Gulliver's Travels*, any of the brutish beings in human form who are ruled over by the Houyhnhnms. See HOUYHNHNM.

Yah·weh (yä′we) In the Old Testament, the national god of Israel; God: a modern transliteration of the Tetragrammaton. See JEHOVAH. Also **Jahve, Jahveh, Jahwe, Jahweh.** Also **Yah·ve** (yä′ve), **Yah·veh.** [< Hebrew *YHWH*]

Yah·wism (yä′wiz·əm) *n.* **1.** The ancient Hebrew religion centered on the monotheistic worship of Yahweh. **2.** The use of the name Yahweh for God. Also spelled *Jahvism, Jahwism, Jehovism.* Also **Yah′vism** (-viz-əm).

Yah·wist (yä′wist) *n.* The author of those portions of the Hexateuch in which God is mentioned as *Yahweh*, or *Jehovah.* Compare ELOHIST. Also spelled *Jahvist, Jahwist, Jehovist.* Also **Yah′vist** (-vist).

Yah·wis·tic (yä·wis′tik) *adj.* **1.** Of or relating to the Yahwist or Yahwism. **2.** Characterized by the use of the name Yahweh (or Jehovah) for God. Compare ELOHISTIC. Also spelled *Jahvistic, Jahwistic, Jehoristic.* Also **Yah·vis′tic** (-vis′-).

yaird (yârd) *n. Scot.* **1.** A yard (36 inches). **2.** A garden; courtyard; churchyard.

Yaj·ur-Ve·da (yuj′oor·vä′də, -vē′də) See under VEDA.

yak[1] (yak) *n.* A large bovine ruminant (*Bos* or *Poephagus grunniens*) of the higher regions of central Asia, having long hair fringing the shoulders, sides, and tail, and often domesticated. [< Tibetan *gyag*]

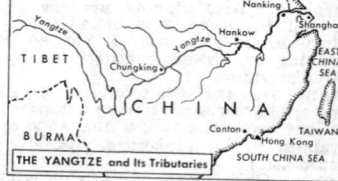

YAK
(About 5 feet high at shoulder)

yak[2] (yak) *n.* **yakked, yak·king** *U.S. Slang* **1.** To chatter noisily or constantly. **2.** To laugh, especially boisterously; guffaw. [Imit.]

Yak·i·ma (yak′ə·mə) A city in southern Washington, on the **Yakima River**, which flows 203 miles SE to the Columbia River; pop. 45,588.

Ya·kut (yä·koot′) *n.* **1.** One of a people living in the Yakut Autonomous S.S.R. **2.** The Turkic language of the Yakuts.

Ya·kut A.S.S.R. (yä·koot′) An administrative division of the NE R.S.F.S.R.; 1,181,971 sq. mi.; pop. 664,000 (1970); capital, **Ya·kutsk** (yä·kootsk′), on the Lena river, pop. 74,000. *Russian* **Ya·kut·ska·ya A.S.S.R.** (yä·koot′skə·yə).

yald[1] (yäd, yôd) *adj. Scot.* Yeld.

yald[2] (yäd, yôd) *adj. Scot.* Athletic; supple; active: also spelled *yauld.*

Yale (yäl), **Elihu**, 1649–1721, English merchant and colonial administrator born in America; benefactor of Yale College.

Yal·ta (yäl′tə, yôl′-) A port city in the southern Crimea, on the Black Sea; scene of a conference of Roosevelt, Churchill, and Stalin in February, 1945; pop. 43,994 (est. 1967).

Ya·lu (yä′loo′) A river forming part of the boundary between NE China and North Korea, and flowing 500 miles SW to the Yellow Sea.

yam (yam) *n.* **1.** The fleshy, edible, tuberous root of any of a genus (*Dioscorea*) of climbing tropical plants typical of a family (*Dioscoreaceae*) of herbaceous or somewhat woody vines. **2.** Any of the plants growing this root. **3.** A large variety of the sweet potato. **4.** *Scot.* A potato. [< Pg. *inhame* < Senegal *nyami* to eat]

Ya·ma·ga·ta (yä·mä·gä·tä), **Prince Aritomo**, 1838–1922, Japanese general, diplomat, and statesman; premier 1889–1891, 1898–1900.

Ya·ma·mo·to (yä·mä·mō′tō), **Isoroku**, 1883–1943, Japanese admiral in World War II; led attack on Pearl Harbor.

Ya·ma·shi·ta (yä·mä·shē′tä), **Tomoyuki**, 1885–1946, Japanese general in World War II; executed as a war criminal: called **the Tiger of Luzon.**

ya·men (yä′mən) *n.* In the Chinese Empire, the office or official residence of a public functionary, as a mandarin; also, any department of the public service. Also **ya′mun.**

yam·mer (yam′ər) *v.i. Informal* **1.** To complain peevishly; whine; whimper. **2.** To howl; roar; shout. — *v.t.* **3.** To utter peevishly; complain. — *n.* The act of yammering. [OE *gēomrian* to lament < *gēomor* sorrowful; infl. in form by MDu. *jammeren* to complain] — **yam′mer·er** *n.*

yang (yang) *n.* In Chinese philosophy and art, the male element, source of life and heat. Compare YIN[2]. Also **Yang.** [< Chinese]

Yang (yang), **C**(hen) **N**(ing), born 1922, U.S. physicist born in China.

Yang·tze (yang′tsē′, *Chinese* yäng′tse′) The longest river of Asia, flowing 3,430 miles from the Tibetan highlands to the East China Sea; forms border between Tibetan Autonomous Region and Szechwan Province. Also **Yang′tze-Ki·ang′** (-kē·ang′, *Chinese* -jē′äng′), **Yang′tse-Ki·ang′.**

THE YANGTZE and its Tributaries

Ya·ni·na (yä′nē·nä) See IOANNINA.

yank (yangk) *v.t.* **1.** To jerk or pull suddenly. — *v.i.* **2.** To give a pull or jerk. **3.** *Brit.* To be vigorously active. **4.** *Brit.* To jabber; scold. — *n.* **1.** *Informal* A sudden sharp pull; jerk. **2.** *Scot.* A sharp blow or slap; buffet. [? < dial. E (Scottish) *yank* a sharp sudden blow]

Yank (yangk) *n. & adj. Informal* Yankee. [Short for YANKEE]

Yan·kee (yang′kē) *n.* **1.** Originally, a native or inhabitant of New England. **2.** A Northerner; especially, a Union soldier during the Civil War: so called in the South. **3.** Any citizen of the United States; an American: a chiefly foreign usage. — *adj.* **1.** Of, pertaining to, or characteristic of the Yankees. **2.** American. [? Back formation < *Jan Kees* (taken as a plural), John Cheese, orig. a nickname for a Hollander; later applied by Dutch colonists in New York to English settlers in Connecticut]

Yan·kee·dom (yang′kē·dəm) *n.* **1.** New England or the northern States as opposed to the southern States. **2.** The United States as a whole. **3.** Yankees collectively.

Yankee Doodle A song, of many humorous verses, popular in pre-Revolutionary times and one of the national airs of the United States.

Yan·kee·ism (yang′kē·iz′əm) *n.* **1.** Yankee characteristics collectively. **2.** A Yankee word, trait, idiom, etc.

Ya·oun·dé (yä·ōōn·dā′) The capital of Cameroon, in the south central part; pop. 101,000 (est. 1965).

yap (yap) *n.* **1.** *Slang* Talk; jabber. **2.** A bark or yelp. **3.** *Slang* The mouth. — *v.i.* **yapped, yap·ping 1.** *Slang* To talk idly or emptily; jabber. **2.** *Informal* To bark or yelp, as a cur. [Imit. of a dog's bark]

Yap (yäp, yap) An island group in the western Carolines; 80 sq. mi.

ya·pon (yä′pon) *n.* The yaupon, a shrub.

Ya·pu·rá (yä′pōō·rä′) See JAPURÁ.

Ya·qui (yä′kē) *n.* One of a tribe of North American Indians belonging to the Piman branch of the Uto-Aztecan stock, now living in southern Sonora, Mexico.

Ya·qui (yä′kē) A river in NW Mexico, flowing about 420 miles SW and south to the Gulf of California.

Yar·bor·ough (yär′bûr·ō, *Brit.* yär′bər·ə) *n.* A whist or bridge hand with no card above a nine. [after an earl of *Yarborough*, who bet against the occurrence of such a hand]

yard¹ (yärd) *n.* **1.** A standard English and American measure of length; 3 feet, or 36 inches, or 0.914 meter. Abbr. *yd.*, *y.* See table inside back cover. **2.** A unit of volume equal to a cubic yard: a *yard* of cement. **3.** A yardstick. **4.** *Naut.* A long, slender, tapering spar set crosswise on a mast and used to support sails. [OE *gierd* rod, measure of length]

yard² (yärd) *n.* **1.** A tract of ground, often enclosed, adjacent to a residence, church, school, or other building. **2.** An enclosure used for some specific work: often in combination: *brickyard; shipyard.* **3.** An enclosure or piece of ground adjacent to a railroad station, used for making up trains and for storing the rolling stock. **4.** The winter pasturing ground of deer and moose. **5.** An enclosure for animals, poultry, etc. — *v.t.* **1.** To put or collect into or as into a yard. — *v.i.* **2.** To gather into an enclosure or yard. [OE *geard* enclosure]

yard·age¹ (yär′dij) *n.* **1.** The amount or length of something expressed in yards. **2.** Yard goods. [< YARD¹]

yard·age² (yär′dij) *n.* The use of or charge for a yard in handling cattle as they are moved to and from railway cars. [< YARD²]

yard·arm (yärd′ärm′) *n. Naut.* Either end of a yard of a square sail.

yard·bird (yärd′bûrd′) *Mil. Slang* **1.** An army recruit. **2.** Any member of the armed forces given menial duties or restricted to the base as a punishment.

yard goods Cloth that is sold by the yard.

yard·grass (yärd′gras′, -gräs′) *n.* A coarse, widely distributed, annual grass (*Eleusine indica*) native in North and tropical America: also called *goosegrass.*

yard·man¹ (yärd′mən) *n. pl.* **·men** (-mən) *Naut.* A sailor who works on the yards.

yard·man² (yärd′mən) *n. pl.* **·men** (-mən) A man employed in a yard, especially on a railroad.

yard·mas·ter (yärd′mas′tər, -mäs′-) *n.* A railroad official having charge of a yard.

yard·stick (yärd′stik′) *n.* **1.** A graduated measuring stick a yard in length. **2.** Any measure or standard of comparison. Also *Archaic* **yard′wand′** (-wond′).

yare (yär) *adj. Archaic & Dial.* **1.** Responding quickly to the helm; manageable: said of a ship. **2.** Brisk; prompt. **3.** Prepared; ready. — *adv. Obs.* With dispatch; quickly; soon. [OE *gearu* ready] — **yare′ly** *adv.*

Yar·kand (yär·kand′) A town and oasis of SW Sinkiang-Uigur Autonomous Region, China; pop. about 80,000.

Yar·mouth (yär′məth) **1.** A port city in SW Nova Scotia, Canada, at the entrance of the Bay of Fundy; pop. 51,105. **2.** See GREAT YARMOUTH.

yar·mul·ke (yä′məl·kə) *n.* A skullcap worn by Orthodox and Conservative Jewish men and boys in synagogues, during religious ceremonies and studies, and by some Orthodox Jews at all times. Also **yar′mel·ke.** [< Yiddish]

yarn (yärn) *n.* **1.** Any spun, threadlike material, natural or synthetic, prepared for use in weaving, knitting, etc. **2.** Continuous strands of spun fiber, as wool, cotton, linen, silk, etc. **3.** A quantity of such material. **4.** *Informal* A long, exciting story of adventure, often of doubtful truth. — *v.i. Informal* To tell a yarn or yarns. [OE *gearn*]

yarn-dyed (yärn′did′) *adj.* Made of yarn dyed before being woven into material.

Ya·ro·slavl (yə·rō·slävly′′) A city in the western R.S.F.S.R., on the Volga; pop. 517,000 (est. 1970). Also **Ya·ro·slavl′′.**

yar·row (yar′ō) *n.* Any of a genus (*Achillea*) of perennial herbs of Europe and North America; especially, the **common yarrow** (*A. millefolium*), having finely dissected leaves, small white flowers, and a pungent odor: also called *milfoil.* [OE *gearwe*]

yash·mak (yäsh·mäk′, yash′mak) *n.* The double veil or covering for the face worn by Moslem women when in public. Also **yash·mac′, yas·mak′.** [< Arabic *yashmaq*]

yat·a·ghan (yat′ə·gan, -gən; *Turkish* yä′tä·gän′) *n.* A Turkish sword or scimitar with a double-curved blade and a handle without a guard: often called *ataghan.* Also **yat′a·gan.** [< Turkish *yātāghan*]

yaud (yäd, yôd) *n. Scot.* An old mare; jade.

yauld¹ (yôd, yäd, yäld) See YALD².

yauld² (yäld) *adj. Scot.* Yeld.

yaup (yôp) See YAWP.

yau·pon (yô′pən) *n.* A bushy evergreen shrub (*Ilex vomitoria*) of the holly family, found in the southern United States, where its leaves were used for tea and by the North Carolina Indians for their medicinal and ceremonial black drink. Also called *yapon, youpon, yupon.* [< Siouan (Catawba) *yopún*, dim. of *yop* bush]

Ya·va·ri (yä′vä·rē′) The Spanish name for the JAVARI.

yaw (yô) *v.i.* **1.** *Naut.* To steer wildly or out of its course, as a ship when struck by a heavy sea. **2.** To move unsteadily or irregularly. **3.** *Aeron.* To deviate from the flight path by angular displacement about the vertical axis; fishtail. — *v.t.* **4.** To cause to yaw. — *n.* **1.** A movement of a ship by which it temporarily alters its course. **2.** *Aeron.* The angular movement of an aircraft, projectile, etc., about its vertical axis; also, the amount of such movement measured in degrees. **3.** Any irregular, unsteady, or deviating motion. [Cf. ON *jaga* to move to and fro]

Ya·wa·ta (yä·wä·tä) A city on northern Kyushu island, Japan; pop. 332,167 (1960). Also *Yahata.*

yawl¹ (yôl) See YOWL.

yawl² (yôl) *n.* **1.** A fore-and-aft rigged, two-masted vessel similar to a ketch but having the mizzenmast or jiggermast abaft the rudder post: also called *dandy.* **2.** A ship's small boat; jollyboat. **3.** A small fishing boat. [Appar. < Du. *jol*, orig. a boat used in Jutland]

yaw·me·ter (yô′mē′tər) *n. Aeron.* An instrument for measuring the angle of yaw in an aircraft.

YAWL

yawn (yôn) *v.i.* **1.** To open the mouth wide, usually involuntarily and with a long, full inspiration of the breath, often the result of drowsiness, fatigue, or boredom. **2.** To be or stand wide open, especially as ready to engulf or receive something: A chasm *yawned* below. — *v.t.* **3.** To express or utter with a yawn. — *n.* **1.** The act of yawning. **2.** The act of standing open. [Prob. fusion of OE *geonian* to yawn and *gānian* to gape] — **yawn′er** *n.*

yawp (yôp) *v.i.* **1.** To bark or yelp. **2.** *Informal* To gape; yawn audibly. **3.** *Brit. Informal* To shout; bawl; talk loudly. — *n.* **1.** A bark or yelp. **2.** A shout; noise; noisy talking; also, a loud, uncouth outcry. **3.** *Scot.* The scream of a bird, especially when in distress. **4.** *Scot.* A cough. Also spelled *yaup.* [ME *golpen*, pp. of *gelpen* to boast] — **yawp′er** *n.*

yaws (yôz) *n.pl. Pathol.* A contagious skin disease occurring in tropical and subtropical countries, caused by a spirochete (*Treponema pertenus*) and resembling syphilis: also called **fram·be·si·a** (fram-bē′zhē-ə, -zē-ə, -zhə) or **fram·boe′si·a.** [< Carib *yaya*]

Y-ax·is (wī′ak′sis) *n. pl.* **-ax·es** (-ak′sēz) The more nearly vertical axis in a graph or a Cartesian coordinate system; the ordinate.

yay (yā) *U.S. Dial. adj.* **1.** This many; this much. **2.** Ever so many: for *yay* years. — *adv.* **1.** To this extent. **2.** Ever so: *yay* big. [Cf. G *je* ever]

Yazd (yezd) See YEZD.

Yaz·oo River (yaz′ōō) A river in west central Mississippi, flowing 189 miles SW to the Mississippi River.

Yb *Chem.* Ytterbium.

Y-chro·mo·some (wī′krō′mə·sōm′) *n. Genetics* One of the two types of chromosome that determine the sex of an offspring. See SEX CHROMOSOME.

y·clept (i·klept′) Alternative past participle of CLEPE. — *adj. Archaic* Called; named. Also **y·cleped′.** [OE *geclypod*, pp. of *clypian* to call]

yd. Yard (*pl.* **yd.** or **yds.**)

ye[1] (thē) The: a mistaken form resulting from the substitution of the character *y* for the thorn (þ) of the Old and Middle English alphabet.

ye[2] (yē) *pron. Archaic* A pronoun of the second person, originally nominative plural: "Blessed are *ye* when men shall revile you"; later, also nominative singular and objective singular and plural. [ME *ye*, ȝe, nominative pl. < OE *gē*]

yea (yā) *adv.* **1.** *Archaic* A term of affirmation or assent, now superseded by *yes*. **2.** *Archaic* Not only so, but more so: used to intensify or amplify: There were fifty, *yea*, a hundred archers. **3.** In reality; indeed; verily: used to introduce a sentence, etc. — *n.* **1.** An affirmative vote or voter: opposed to *nay*. **2.** An affirmation. [OE *gēa*]

yeah (yâ, ye′ə) *adv. Informal* Yes. [< YES]

yeal·ing (yē′ling) *n. Scot.* A contemporary in age: also called *yeelin*.

yean (yēn) *v.t. & v.i.* To bear (young), as a goat or sheep. [OE (assumed) *geēanian*. Akin to OE *geēan* pregnant.]

yean·ling (yēn′ling) *n.* The young of a goat or sheep. — *adj.* Young or newly born.

year (yir) *n.* **1.** The period of time in which the earth completes one revolution around the sun, consisting of 365 or 366 days divided into 12 months and now reckoned as beginning January 1 and ending December 31; also, a similar period in other calendars. See ASTRONOMICAL YEAR, LUNAR YEAR, SIDEREAL YEAR. **2.** Any period of 12 months, usually reckoned from a specific date or time: a *year* from now. **3.** The period of time during which a planet revolves once around the sun. **4.** A specific period of time, usually less than a year, given over to some special work or activity: the school *year*. **5.** *pl.* Age, especially old age: active for his *years*. **6.** *pl.* Time: in *years* gone by and *years* to come. Abbr. *y.*, *yr.* — **year after year** Every year. — **a year and a day** *Law* A time designated for the purpose of ensuring a full year's lapse. — **year by year** Each year; with each succeeding year. — **year in, year out** From one year to the next; without cessation. [OE *gēar*]

year·book (yir′bŏŏk′) *n.* **1.** A book published annually, presenting information about the previous year. **2.** *U.S.A.* A book compiled by the graduating class of a high school or college, and containing photographs of and information about its members, accounts of activities, etc.

year·ling (yir′ling) *n.* A young animal past its first year and not yet two years old; especially, a colt or filly a year old dating from January 1 of the year of foaling. — *adj.* Being a year old.

year·long (yir′lông′, -long′) *adj.* Continuing through a year.

year·ly (yir′lē) *adj.* **1.** Occurring, done, payable, seen, etc., once a year; annual. **2.** Continuing or lasting for a year: a *yearly* subscription. — *adv.* Once a year; annually.

yearn (yûrn) *v.i.* **1.** To desire something earnestly; long; hanker; pine: with *for*. **2.** To be deeply moved; feel sympathy. [OE *giernan*, *geornan*. Akin to OE *georn* eager.]

yearn·ing (yûr′ning) *n.* A strong emotion of longing or desire, especially with tenderness. — **yearn′ing·ly** *adv.*

year-round (yir′round′) *adj.* Open, operating, or continuing for the entire year: a *year-round* health resort.

yeast (yēst) *n.* **1.** A substance consisting of minute cells of ascomycetous fungi (genus *Saccharomyces*) that clump together in a yellow, frothy, viscous growth promoting fermentation in saccharine liquids, with the production of alcohol and carbon dioxide, as in the brewing of beer and the raising of bread. **2.** Such a substance mixed with flour or meal, and sold commercially. **3.** A yeast plant (which see). **4.** Froth or spume. **5.** Mental or moral ferment or agitation. — *v.i.* To foam; froth. [OE *gist*]

yeast cake A mixture of living yeast cells and starch in compressed form, suitable for use in baking or brewing.

yeast plant Any of a family (*Saccharomycetaceae*) of fungi that form yeast.

yeast powder Dried and powdered yeast used as a leavening agent.

yeast·y (yēs′tē) *adj.* **yeast·i·er**, **yeast·i·est** **1.** Of, resembling, or containing yeast. **2.** Causing or characterized by fermentation. **3.** Restless; unsettled; frivolous. **4.** Covered with or consisting mainly of froth or foam. **5.** Light or unsubstantial. — **yeast′i·ness** *n.*

Yeats (yāts), **William Butler**, 1865–1939, Irish poet, dramatist, and essayist.

Ye·do (ye·dō) A former name for TOKYO.

yeel·in (yē′lin) *n. Scot.* A yealing.

yegg (yeg) *n. Slang* A burglar or safe-cracker. Also **yegg′-man** (-mən). [Origin unknown]

Ye·ka·te·rin·burg (yi·ka·tyi·ryin·bŏŏrk′) A former name for SVERDLOVSK. Also *Ekaterinburg*.

Ye·ka·te·ri·no·dar (yi·ka·tyi·ryi·no·där′) A former name for KRASNODAR. Also *Ekaterinodar*.

Ye·ka·te·ri·no·slav (yi·ka·tyi·rvi·no·släf′) A former name for DNIEPROPYETROVSK. Also *Ekaterinoslav*.

yeld (yeld) *adj. Scot.* Not giving milk; barren: also *yald*, *yauld*. Also **yell** (yel).

Ye·li·za·vet·grad (yi·lyi·zə·vyit·grät′) A former name for KIROVOGRAD. Also *Elizavetgrad*.

Ye·li·za·vet·pol (yi·lyi·zə·vyit·pôly′′) A former name for KIROVABAD. Also *Elizavetpol*. Also **Ye·li·za·vet·pol′′**.

yelk (yelk) *n. Dial.* A yolk.

yell (yel) *v.t. & v.i.* To shout; scream; roar; also, to cheer. — *n.* **1.** A sharp, loud, inarticulate cry, as of pain, terror, anger, etc. **2.** A rhythmic cheer composed of a series of words or nonsense syllables and shouted by a group in unison. [OE *giellan*, *gellan*] — **yell′er** *n.*

yel·low (yel′ō) *adj.* **1.** Having the color of ripe lemons, or sunflowers. **2.** Changed to a sallow color by age, sickness, or the like: a paper *yellow* with age. **3.** Having a yellowish complexion, as a member of the Mongoloid ethnic group. **4.** Melancholy or jealous. **5.** Sensational, especially offensively so: said of newspapers: *yellow* journalism. **6.** *Informal* Cowardly; mean; dishonorable. — *n.* **1.** The color of the spectrum between green and orange, including wavelengths centering at about 5,890 angstroms; the color of ripe lemons. **2.** Any pigment or dyestuff having or producing such a color. **3.** The yolk of an egg. **4.** *pl. Bot.* Any of various unrelated plant diseases in which there is a stunting of growth and yellowing of the foliage; especially, an infectious virus disease of peach, nectarine, apricot, and almond trees. **5.** *pl.* Jaundice, especially a variety that affects domestic animals. — *v.t. & v.i.* To make or become yellow. [OE *geolu*] — **yel′low·ly** *adv.* — **yel′low·ness** *n.*

yel·low·bark (yel′ō·bärk′) *n.* Calisaya.

yel·low-bel·lied (yel′ō·bel′ēd) *adj.* **1.** *Slang* Cowardly; yellow. **2.** Having a yellow underside, as a bird.

yel·low·bird (yel′ō·bûrd′) *n.* Any of several yellow birds, as the American goldfinch or the yellow warbler.

yellow cake *Canadian Informal* Uranium ore; concentrated uranium oxide.

yellow daisy The black-eyed Susan (def. 1).

yel·low-dog contract (yel′ō·dôg′, -dog′) A contract with an employer, no longer legal, in which an employee agrees not to join a labor union during his term of employment.

yellow fever *Pathol.* An acute, infectious intestinal disease of tropical and semitropical regions, caused by a filterable virus transmitted by the bite of a mosquito (genus *Aëdes*) and characterized by hemorrhages, jaundice, vomiting, and fatty degeneration of the liver: also called *black vomit*, *vomito*, *yellow jack*.

yel·low·ham·mer (yel′ō·ham′ər) *n.* **1.** An Old World bunting (*Emberiza citrinella*) having in the male bright yellow plumage and blackish head and tail feathers. **2.** The flicker, a bird. [Alter. of earlier *yelambre*, prob. < OE *geolo* yellow + *amore*, a kind of bird]

yel·low·ish (yel′ō·ish) *adj.* Somewhat yellow. — **yel′low·ish·ness** *n.*

yellow jack **1.** A carangoid fish (*Caranx bartholomaei*) of the West Indies and Florida. **2.** The flag of the quarantine service. **3.** Yellow fever.

yellow jacket Any of various social wasps (genus *Vespa*), having bright yellow markings.

yellow jasmine A smooth twining shrub (*Gelsemium sempervirens*) having yellow flowers. Also **yellow jessamine**.

yellow journalism A type of journalism that features cheap, sensational news in order to attract readers. [from the use of yellow ink in printing a cartoon strip, "The Yellow Kid," in the *New York Journal*, commencing 1896]

yellow lead ore Wulfenite.

yel·low·legs (yel′ō·legz′) *n. pl.* **·legs** **1.** Either of two North American sandpipers (genus *Totanus*) with long yellow legs, the **greater yellowlegs** (*T. melanoleucus*) or the **lesser yellowlegs** (*T. flavipes*). **2.** *U.S. Informal* Formerly, in the U.S. Army, a cavalry soldier.

yellow metal **1.** A brass consisting of 60 parts copper and 40 parts zinc. **2.** Gold.

yellow pages A telephone directory that is printed on yellow paper and lists subscribers by professions or services.

yellow perch See under PERCH[2].

yellow peril The alleged power, both political and numerical, of the Oriental peoples of Asia, conceived of as threatening white or Western supremacy.

yellow pine **1.** Any of various American pines, as the Georgia or loblolly pine. **2.** Their tough, yellowish wood.

yellow poplar The tuliptree.

yellow race The Mongoloid ethnic division of mankind.

Yellow River See HWANG HO.

Yellow Sea An inlet of the Pacific between Korea and China; 400 mi. long, 400 mi. wide: Chinese *Hwang Hai*.

yellow spot *Anat.* A small yellowish spot just opposite the pupil in the retina, the region of most acute vision.

Yel·low·stone Falls (yel′ō·stōn) Two waterfalls of the Yellowstone River in Yellowstone National Park: **Upper Yellowstone Falls**, 109 ft.; **Lower Yellowstone Falls**, 308 ft.

Yellowstone National Park The largest and oldest of the United States national parks, largely in NW Wyoming; 3,458 sq. mi.; established, 1872.

Yellowstone River A river in NW Wyoming, SE Montana, and NW North Dakota, flowing 671 miles NW to the Missouri River, passing through Yellowstone National Park where it forms **Yellowstone Lake**, 140 sq. mi.

yellow streak A tendency to be cowardly, mean, etc.

yel·low·tail (yel′ō-tāl′) *n.* **1.** A carangoid fish (genus *Seriola*); especially, the **California yellowtail** (*S. dorsalis*). **2.** Any of various other fishes having a yellowish tail, as the **yellowtail rockfish** (*Sebastodes flavidus*), and the **yellowtail snapper** (*Ocyurus chrysurus*).

yel·low·throat (yel′ō-thrōt′) *n.* Any of various American warblers (genus *Geothlypis*); especially, the **Maryland yellowthroat** (*G. trichas*), olive-green with yellow throat and breast.

yellow warbler A warbler (*Dendroica petechia*) of the southern United States, bright yellow with brown streaks underneath.

yel·low·weed (yel′ō-wēd′) *n.* **1.** Any of various goldenrods. **2.** The European ragwort. **3.** Weld² (def. 1).

yel·low·wood (yel′ō-wood′) *n.* **1.** The yellow or yellowish wood of a medium-sized tree (*Cladrastis lutea*) of the southern United States, having a smooth bark, showy white flowers, and yielding a yellow dye: also called *gopherwood*. **2.** The tree. **3.** Any of several other trees with yellowish wood, as the Osage orange, buckthorn, smoketree, etc.

yel·low·y (yel′ō-ē) *adj.* Yellowish.

yelp (yelp) *v.i.* **1.** To utter a sharp, shrill cry or bark, as a dog. — *v.t.* **2.** To express by a yelp or yelps. — *n.* A sharp, shrill cry or bark. [OE *gielpan* to boast] — **yelp′er** *n.*

Yem·en (yem′ən) A Republic on the SW Arabian peninsula; 75,000 sq. mi.; pop. 6,223,000 (est. 1971); capital, Sanaa. Officially **Yemen Arab Republic**. See map of SAUDI ARABIA. — **Yem·e·ni** (yem′ə-nē), **Yem·e·nite** (yem′ə-nīt) *adj. & n.*

yen¹ (yen) *Informal n.* An ardent longing or desire; intense want; infatuation. — **Syn.** See DESIRE. — *v.i.* **yenned, yen·ning** To yearn; long. [< Chinese, opium, smoke]

yen² (yen) *n. pl.* **yen** The standard monetary unit of Japan, equal to 100 sen. [< Japanese < Chinese *yüan* round, dollar]

Ye·nan (ye′nän′) See FUSHIN.

Ye·ni·sei (ye′nyi-syāy′) A river in the central R.S.F.S.R., flowing 2,364 miles NW to **Yenisei Gulf**, *Russian* **Ye·ne·sei′skiy Za·liv** (-skyē zä-lyēf′), its estuary in the Arctic Ocean: also *Enisei*.

Yen·tai (yen′tī′) A port city in NE Shantung Province, China, on the Yellow Sea; pop. 140,000 (est. 1958): also *Chefoo*. Also **Yen′-t′ai′**.

yeo·man (yō′mən) *n. pl.* **·men** (-mən) **1.** A petty officer in the U.S. Navy or Coast Guard who performs clerical duties. **2.** *Brit.* One who cultivates his own farm. **3.** *Brit.* A yeoman of the guard (which see). **4.** Formerly, an attendant or servant in the service of a nobleman or of royalty. **5.** Formerly, a freeholder next below the gentry who owned a small landed estate or farm. **6.** *Obs.* One who acts as an assistant, as to a sheriff. [ME *yeman*, *yoman*, prob. contraction of *yengman* young man < OE *geong* young + *mann* man]

yeo·man·ly (yō′mən·lē) *adj.* **1.** Of, pertaining to, or resembling a yeoman. **2.** Brave; rugged; staunch. — *adv.* Like a yeoman; bravely; staunchly.

yeoman of the (royal) guard A member of the special bodyguard of the English royal household, consisting of one hundred yeomen wearing medieval uniforms and first appointed by Henry VII: also called *beefeater*.

yeo·man·ry (yō′mən·rē) *n.* **1.** The collective body of yeomen; freemen; farmers. **2.** *Brit.* A home guard of volunteer cavalry, created in 1761, consisting of gentlemen and gentlemen farmers, known since 1901 as the **Imperial yeomanry**. In 1907 it became a part of the Territorial Army.

yeoman's service Faithful and useful support or service; loyal assistance in need. Also **yeoman service**.

yep (yep) *adv. Informal* Yes. [Alter. of YES]

-yer Var. of -IER.

yer·ba (yâr′bə, yûr′-) *n.* Maté (def. 1). [< Sp. *yerba* (*maté*) the herb (maté)]

yerb tea (yûrb, yärb) *Dial.* Tea made of herbs. [< *yerb*, dial. var. of HERB]

Ye·re·van (yi·ryi·vän′) The capital of the Armenian S.S.R., in the western part; pop. 767,000 (1970): also *Erevan*, *Erivan*.

Yer·kes (yûr′kēz), **Charles Tyson**, 1837–1905, U.S. financier.

yes (yes) *adv.* As you say; truly; just so: a reply of affirmation or consent: opposed to *no*, and sometimes used to enforce by repetition or addition something that precedes. — *n. pl.* **yes·es** or **yes·ses 1.** A reply in the affirmative. **2.** An affirmative vote or voter: often *aye*. — *v.t. & v.i.* **yessed**, **yes·sing** To say "yes" (to). [OE *gēse*, prob. < *gēa* yea + *sī*, third person sing. present subj. of *bēon* to be]

ye′se (yēs) *Scot.* You shall; ye shall.

ye·shi·va (ye·shē′və) *n. pl.* **·vas** or **·voth** (-vōth) In Judaism: **a** An orthodox rabbinical seminary. **b** A Hebrew day school. **c** A school of Talmudic studies. Also **ye·shi′vah**. [< Hebrew]

Ye·sil Ir·mak (ye·shēl′ ir·mäk′) A river in northern Turkey in Asia, flowing 260 miles NW to the Black Sea.

Ye·sil·köy (ye′shēl·kœē′) The Turkish name for SAN STEFANO.

yes man *Informal* One who agrees without criticism; a servile, acquiescent assistant or subordinate; toady.

yester- *prefix* Pertaining to the day before the present; by extension of the preceding, used of longer periods than a day: *yesteryear*. [< YESTER(DAY)]

yes·ter·day (yes′tər·dē, -dā′) *n.* **1.** The day preceding today. **2.** The near past. — *adv.* **1.** On the day before today. **2.** At a recent time. [OE *giestran dæg* < *giestran* yesterday + *dæg* day]

yes·ter·eve·ning (yes′tər·ēv′ning) *n.* The evening of yesterday. Also **yes′ter·eve′**, **yes′ter·e′ven** (-ē′ven).

yes·ter·morn·ing (yes′tər·môr′ning) *n.* The morning of yesterday. Also **yes′ter·morn′** (-môrn′).

yes·tern (yes′tərn) *adj.* *Archaic* Of or pertaining to yesterday. [< YESTER(DAY), on analogy with EASTERN, etc.]

yes·ter·night (yes′tər·nīt′) *n.* *Archaic & Poetic* The night last past. — *adv.* In or during the night last past. [OE *giestran* yesterday + *niht* night]

yes·ter·noon (yes′tər·nōōn′) *n.* The noon of yesterday.

yes·ter·week (yes′tər·wēk′) *n.* Last week.

yes·ter·year (yes′tər·yir′) *n.* Last year; yore. [Trans. of F *antan*; coined by D. G. Rossetti]

yes·treen (yes·trēn′) *n. Scot.* Yesterevening.

yet (yet) *adv.* **1.** In addition; besides; further: often with a comparative: They had twenty miles *yet* to go. **2.** Before or at some future time; eventually: He will *yet* succeed. **3.** In continuance of a previous state or condition; still: I can hear him *yet*. **4.** At the present time; now: Don't go *yet*. **5.** After all the time that has or had elapsed: Are you not ready *yet*? **6.** Up to the present time; before: commonly with a negative: He has never *yet* lied to me. **7.** Than that which has been previously affirmed: with a comparative: It was hot yesterday; today it is hotter *yet*. **8.** Nevertheless: It was hot, *yet* not unpleasant. **9.** As much as; even: He did not believe the reports, nor *yet* the evidence. — **as yet** Up to now. — *conj.* **1.** Nevertheless; notwithstanding: I speak to you peaceably, *yet* you will not listen. **2.** But: He is willing, *yet* unable. **3.** Although: active, *yet* ill. — **Syn.** See BUT¹. [OE *gīet*, *gīeta*]

ye·ti (ye′tē) *n.* The abominable snowman. [< Tibetan]

yett (yet) *n. Scot.* A gate.

Yev·tu·shen·ko (yev′tōō·sheng′kō, *Russ.* yef·tōō·shen′ko), **Yevgeny Alexandrovich**, born 1933, Russian poet.

yew (yōō) *n.* **1.** Any of several evergreen trees or shrubs (genus *Taxus*), with flat, lanceolate leaves and a red berrylike fruit; especially, the **European** or **English yew** (*T. baccata*), a coniferous tree of slow growth and long life. **2.** The hard, fine-grained, durable wood of the common yew. **3.** A bow made from the wood of the yew tree. [OE *ēow*, *iw*]

Yezd (yezd) A city in central Iran; pop. 63,502 (1956): also *Yazd*.

Ye·zo (ye·zō) The former name for HOKKAIDO.

Yg·dra·sil (ig′drə·sil) In Norse mythology, a huge ash tree whose roots and branches bind together heaven, earth, and hell: also spelled *Igdrasil*. Also **Yg′dra·sill**, **Ygg′dra·sill**.

YEW

Y·gerne (i·gûrn′) See IGRAINE.

YHWH Yahweh. See TETRAGRAMMATON.

Yid·dish (yid′ish) *n.* A Germanic language derived from the Middle High German spoken in the Rhineland in the thirteenth and fourteenth centuries, now spoken primarily by Jews in Poland, Lithuanian S.S.R., Ukrainian S.S.R., and Rumania, and by Jewish immigrants from those regions in other parts of the world. It contains elements of Hebrew and the Slavic languages, and is written in Hebrew characters. — *adj.* **1.** Of or pertaining to Yiddish; written or spoken in Yiddish. **2.** *Slang* Jewish. [< G *jüdisch* Jewish < *Jude* Jew]

yield (yēld) *v.t.* **1.** To give forth by a natural process, or as a result of labor or cultivation: The field will *yield* a good crop. **2.** To give in return, as for investment; furnish: The bonds *yield* five percent interest. **3.** To give up, as to superior power; surrender; relinquish: often with *up*: to *yield* a fortress. **4.** To concede or grant: to *yield* precedence; to *yield* consent. **5.** *Obs.* To pay, repay, or reward. — *v.i.* **6.** To provide a return; produce; bear. **7.** To give up; submit; surrender. **8.** To give way, as to pressure or force; bend, collapse, etc. **9.** To assent or comply, as under compulsion; consent: We *yielded* to their persuasion. **10.** To give place, as through inferiority or weakness: with *to*: We will *yield* to them in nothing. — **Syn.** See DEFER², RELINQUISH. — *n.* **1.** The amount yielded; product; result, as of cultivation or mining. **2.** The profit derived from invested capital. **3.** The proceeds of a tax after the expenses of collection and administration have been deducted. **4.** *Mil.* The explosive force of a nuclear bomb as expressed in kilotons or megatons of TNT. [OE *gieldan*, *geldan* to pay] — **yield′er** *n.*

yield·ing (yēl′ding) *adj.* Disposed to yield; flexible; obedient. — **yield′ing·ly** *adv.* — **yield′ing·ness** *n.*

---

yill (yil) *n. Scot.* Ale.

yin[1] (yin) *n. Scot.* One.

yin[2] (yin) *n.* In Chinese philosophy and art, the female element, that stands for darkness, cold, and death. Compare YANG. Also **Yin.** [< Chinese]

yince (yins) *adv. Scot.* Once.

Yin·chwan (yin′chwän′) A city in NE Kansu Province, China; capital of former Ningsia province; pop. 175,000 (est. 1970): formerly *Ningsia.* Also **Yin′-ch′uan′.**

Ying·kow (ying′kō′) A port city in SW Lianoing Province, China, on the Gulf of Liaotung; pop. 215,000 (est. 1970).

yip (yip) *n.* A yelp, as of a dog. — *v.i.* **yipped, yip·ping** To yelp. [Imit.]

yipe (yīp) *interj. Often pl.* An exclamation of fear, surprise, horror, etc.

yip·pie (yip′ē) *n. U.S.* A hippie who is a political radical. [< Y(outh) I(nternational) P(arty) + (HIP)PIE]

yird (yûrd) *n. Scot.* Earth. Also **yirth** (yûrth).

yirr (yûr) *v.i. Scot.* To snarl; yell; growl, as a dog.

-yl *suffix Chem.* Used to denote a radical: *ethyl, butyl.* [< Gk. *hylē* wood, matter]

y·lang-y·lang (ē′läng·ē′läng) *n.* **1.** A tree (*Canangium odoratum*) of the Malay Archipelago. **2.** A perfume derived from the greenish yellow flowers of this tree. Also spelled *ilang-ilang.* [< Tagalog *ilang-ilang* flower of flowers]

Y-lev·el (wī′lev′əl) *n.* A combined telescope and spirit level on a Y-shaped, rotatable mounting, used in surveying, etc.

YMCA or **Y.M.C.A.** Young Men's Christian Association.

YMHA or **Y.M.H.A.** Young Men's Hebrew Association.

Y-mir (ē′mir, ü′mir) In Norse mythology, the progenitor of the giants, formed of frost and fire, out of whose body the gods created the world. Also **Y′mer.**

yod[1] (yōd, *Hebrew* yood) *n.* The tenth letter in the Hebrew alphabet. Also **yodh.** See ALPHABET.

yod[2] (yōd, yôd, yod) *n. Phonet.* The initial glide or transitional sound heard in English *yes.* [< YOD[1]]

yo·del (yōd′l) *n.* A melody or refrain sung to meaningless syllables, with abrupt changes from chest to falsetto tones, common among Swiss and Tyrolese mountaineers. — *v.t. & v.i.* **yo·deled** or **·delled, yo·del·ing** or **·del·ling** To sing with a yodel, changing the voice quickly from its natural tone to a falsetto and back. Also **yo′dle.** [< G *jodeln,* lit., to utter the syllable *jo*] — **yo′del·er, yo′del·ler,** or **yo′dler** *n.*

yo·ga (yō′gə) *n.* **1.** A Hindu system of mystical and ascetic philosophy that involves certain physical and mental disciplines together with a withdrawal from the world and abstract meditation upon some spiritual principle or object. **2.** A related system of exercises, the purpose of which is to achieve both physical and spiritual well-being. [< Hind. < Skt., lit., union] — **yo·gic** (yō′gik) *adj.*

yogh (yōkh) *n.* The Middle English letter, **ʒ,** ʒ, that represented a voiced or voiceless palatal fricative, or a voiced velar fricative. It has been replaced in Modern English by *y,* as in *lay, w,* as in *law,* and *gh,* as in *daughter* and *enough.*

yo·gi (yō′gē) *n.* *pl.* **·gis** **1.** One who practices yoga. **2.** Yoga. Also **yo′gee, yo′gin** (-gin). [< Hind. *yogi* < Skt. *yogin* < *yoga* yoga]

yo·gurt (yō′gŏort) *n.* A thick, curdled milk treated with bacteria regarded as beneficial to the intestines: also called *matzoon.* Also **yo′ghurt, yo′ghourt.** [< Turkish *yōghurt*]

yoicks (yoiks) *interj.* A cry formerly used in foxhunting to urge on the hounds: also *hoicks.* [Earlier *hoik,* var. of HIKE]

yoke (yōk) *n.* *pl.* **yokes;** *for def. 3, often* **yoke** **1.** A curved timber with attachments used for coupling draft animals, as oxen, usually having a bow at each end to receive the neck of the animal. **2.** Any of various similar contrivances, as a frame fitted for a person's shoulders and designed to carry a burden at either end, as a pail. **3.** A pair of draft animals coupled with a yoke (def. 1). **4.** An oppressive force or influence; a crushing burden or weight: under the *yoke* of tyranny. **5.** That which binds or connects; a bond: the *yoke* of love. **6.** Servitude, or some visible sign of it; bondage. **7.** A part of a garment designed to support a plaited or gathered part, as at the hips or shoulders. **8.** A crossbar suspended from the collars of horses, etc., in double harness, for supporting the tongue or pole. **9.** *Naut.* A crosspiece on a rudderhead, carrying cables for steering. **10.** *Mech.* A strap, clamp, slotted piece, etc., serving to guide or confine the movement of a mechanism or part. **11.** In ancient Rome, a device consisting of two upright spears with a third laid across them, under which a conquered army was made to march. **12.** *Obs.* The amount of land a yoke of oxen can plow in a day. **13.** *Scot.* **a** The time required for a yoke of oxen to accomplish a specified amount of work. **b** A part of the day. — *v.* **yoked, yok·ing** *v.t.* **1.** To put a yoke upon. **2.** To join with or as with a yoke; couple or link. **3.** To secure (a draft animal) to a plow, etc.; also, to secure a draft animal to (a plow, etc.). **4.** *Rare* To bring into bondage. — *v.i.* **5.** To be joined or linked; unite. [OE *geoc*]

YOKE (def. 1)

yoke·fel·low (yōk′fel′ō) *n.* A mate or companion in labor. Also **yoke′mate′** (-māt′).

yo·kel (yō′kəl) *n.* A countryman; country bumpkin: a con-

temptuous term. [? < dial. E, green woodpecker, yellowhammer] — **yo′kel·ish** *adj.*

Yo·ko·ha·ma (yō′kə·hä′mə) A port city on central Honshu island, Japan on Tokyo Bay; pop. 1,860,000 (est. 1966).

Yo·ko·su·ka (yō′kə·sōō′kə) A port city on central Honshu island, Japan, at the entrance to Tokyo Bay; pop. 325,000 (est. 1966).

yolk (yōk, yōlk) *n.* **1.** The yellow portion of an egg, as distinguished from the white portion or albumen. **2.** *Biol.* The portion of the contents or substance of the eggs of animals that is used for the formation and nourishment of the embryo. ◆ Collateral adjective: *vitelline.* **3.** A fine yellow soapy exudation in sheep's wool. [OE *geol(o)ca,* lit., (the) yellow part < *geolu* yellow]

yolk·y (yō′kē, yōl′kē) *adj.* **yolk·i·er, yolk·i·est** **1.** Of, like, or pertaining to yolk. **2.** Containing yolk: *yolky* wool.

yom (yom, yōm) *n. Hebrew* Day: used in designating days of feast or fasting: *Yom* Kippur.

Yom Kip·pur (yom kip′ər, *Hebrew* yōm ki·pŏōr′) The Jewish Day of Atonement, the 10th of Tishri (September–October), marked by continuous prayer and fasting for 24 hours from sundown on the evening previous. [< Hebrew *yōm kipūr* day of atonement]

yon (yon) *adj. & adv. Archaic, Dial. & Poetic* Yonder; that or those over there: *yon* fine house. [OE *geon*]

yond (yond) *adj. & adv. Archaic & Dial.* Yonder. [OE *geond* across; infl. in meaning by YON]

yon·der (yon′dər) *adj.* Being at a distance indicated. — *adv.* In that place; there. [ME, prob. extension of *yone,* OE *geon* yon]

yo·ni (yō′nē) *n.* The vulva or a symbol for the vulva, used extensively in Indian and Tibetan religion. Compare LINGAM. [< Skt.]

yon·ker (yong′kər) *n.* A younker.

Yon·kers (yong′kərz) A city in SE New York, on the Hudson River, adjacent to northern New York City; pop. 204,370.

yoo-hoo (yōō′hōō) *interj.* Hello there!: an exclamation used to get someone's attention.

yore (yôr, yōr) *n.* Old time; time long past: in days of *yore.* — *adv. Obs.* Long ago; in olden times. [OE *gēara* formerly, prob. orig. genitive pl. of *gēar* year]

York (yôrk) A royal house of England; a branch of the Plantagenet line; reigned 1461–1485.

York (yôrk) **1.** A city in southern Pennsylvania; pop. 50,335. **2.** Yorkshire or its county seat.

York (yôrk), Alvin Cullum, 1887–1965, U.S. soldier and hero in World War I: called **Sergeant York.**

York (yôrk), Cape The northernmost point of Australia, in Queensland on Torres Strait.

York boat *Canadian* A type of heavy cargo boat used by the Hudson's Bay Company. [after *York* Factory on Hudson Bay]

York·ist (yôr′kist) *n.* An adherent of the house of York.

York River (yôrk) An estuary in SE Virginia, flowing into Chesapeake Bay; 40 mi. long.

Yorks. or **Yorks** York, Yorkshire.

York·shire (yôrk′shir, -shər) A former county of NE England, divided administratively into East Riding, West Riding, and North Riding; 6,080 sq. mi.; pop. 5,047,550 (1971); county seat, **York** (ancient *Eboracum*), capital of Roman Britain, pop. 103,800 (1976). Also **York.**

Yorkshire pudding A batter pudding baked under roasting meat to catch the drippings.

Yorkshire terrier A toy breed of terrier having a long, silky coat.

York·town (yôrk′toun) A town in SE Virginia; scene of Cornwallis's surrender in the Revolutionary War, 1781; pop. 350

Yo·ru·ba (yō′rŏō·bä) *n.* **1.** A member of an extensive ethnic family of West African Negroes living chiefly in southwestern Nigeria and southeastern Dahomey. **2.** The language of the Yoruba, one of the dominant tongues of the Sudanic family. — **Yo′ru·ban** *adj.*

Yo·sem·i·te Valley (yō·sem′ə·tē) A gorge in **Yosemite National Park** (1,183 sq. mi., established 1890) in east central California; 7 mi. long, 1 mi. wide; traversed by the Merced River that forms **Yosemite Falls,** a triple cataract (Upper Fall, 1,430 ft.; Lower Fall, 320 ft.; total, with intermediate cascades, 2,425 ft.).

Yo·shi·hi·to (yō·shē·hē·tō) 1879–1925, emperor of Japan 1912–21; retired.

you (yōō) *pron., possessive* **your** or **yours** **1.** The nominative and objective singular and plural pronoun of the second person, used in addressing one or more persons, animals, or things, and always taking a plural verb. **2.** An indefinite pronoun equivalent to *one:* You learn by trying. [OE *ēow,* dative and accusative pl. of *gē* ye]

◆ *You all,* current in speech in many parts of the United States, but especially in the South (where it is sometimes pronounced *yôl*), has the sense of the plural *you:* How are *you all?* (How are you and your family?).

you'd (yōōd, *unstressed* yŏod, yəd) **1.** You had. **2.** You would.

you'll (yōōl, *unstressed* yŏol, yəl) You will.

Zea·land (zē′lənd) An island of Denmark between the Kattegat and the Baltic Sea, on which Copenhagen is located; 2,709 sq. mi.: German *Seeland*, Danish *Sjaelland*.

zeal·ot (zel′ət) *n.* **1.** An immoderate partisan; a fanatic. **2.** One who is zealous. — **Syn.** See ENTHUSIAST. [< LL *zelotes* < Gk. *zēlōtēs* < *zēloein* to be zealous < *zēlos* zeal]

Zeal·ot (zel′ət) *n.* A member of a fanatical Jewish party (A.D. 6–70) in almost continual revolt against the Romans.

zeal·ot·ry (zel′ət·rē) *n. pl.* **·ries** The conduct or disposition of a zealot; also, an instance of this.

zeal·ous (zel′əs) *adj.* Filled with or incited by zeal; enthusiastic. — **zeal′ous·ly** *adv.* — **zeal′ous·ness** *n.*

ze·a·xan·thin (zē′ə·zan′thin) *n. Biochem.* A yellow pigment, $C_{40}H_{56}O_2$, related to carotene and obtained in the form of golden orange flakes from yellow corn and egg yolk. [< NL *Zea* genus of grasses + XANTH- + -IN]

ze·bec (zē′bek), **ze·beck** See XEBEC.

Zeb·e·dee (zeb′ə·dē) The father of James and John, disciples of Christ. *Matt.* iv 21.

ze·bra (zē′brə) *n.* Any of various African equine mammals resembling the ass, having a white or yellowish brown body fully marked with variously patterned, dark brown or blackish bands; especially, the **mountain zebra** (*Equus zebra*) and the **common zebra** (*E. burchelli*) of southern, central and eastern Africa, and **Grevy's zebra** (*E. grevyi*) of Ethiopia and northern Africa. [< Pg. < Bantu (Congo)] — **ze′brine** (-brēn, -brin), **ze′broid** (-broid) *adj.*

zebra wolf The thylacine.

ze·bra·wood (zē′brə·wŏŏd′) *n.* **1.** The wood of a large tree (*Connarus guianensis*) of Guiana, light brown in color with dark stripes, used in making furniture. **2.** The tree. **3.** The striped or banded wood of various other trees.

ze·bu (zē′byōō) *n.* The domesticated ox (*Bos indicus*) of India, China, and East Africa, having a hump on the withers, a large dewlap, and short horns. [< F *zébu* < Tibetan]

Zeb·u·lon (zeb′yə·lən) In the Old Testament, a son of Jacob and Leah. *Gen.* xxx 20. — *n.* The tribe of Israel descended from him. Also **Zeb′u·lun.**

zec·chi·no (tsek·kē′nō) *n. pl.* **·ni** (-nē) A sequin (def. 2). Also **zec·chin** (zek′in), **zech′in.** [< Ital. See SEQUIN.]

ZEBU
(To 4½ feet
high at
shoulder)

Zech. Zechariah.

Zech·a·ri·ah (zek′ə·rī′ə) Sixth-century B.C. Hebrew prophet who promoted the rebuilding of the Temple. — *n.* A book of the Old Testament bearing his name. Also, in the Douai Bible, *Zacharias.*

zed (zed) *n. Brit.* The letter Z. [< F *zède* < L *zeta* < Gk. *zēta*]

Zed·e·ki·ah (zed′ə·kī′ə) The last king of Judah 597–586 B.C.; taken as a captive to Babylon; son of Josiah. II *Kings* xxiv 17.

zed·o·ar·y (zed′ō·er′ē) *n. pl.* **·ar·ies** The root of a species of turmeric (*Curcuma zedoaria*), used in medicine as a stomachic and as a carminative. [< Med.L *zedoarium* < Arabic *zedwār*]

zee¹ (zē, *Du.* zā) *n. Dutch* Sea: used in geographic names: *Zuider Zee, Tappen Zee.*

zee² (zē) *n.* **1.** The letter Z. **2.** Something resembling the letter Z in shape.

Zee·brug·ge (zē′brŏŏg·ə, *Flemish* zā′brœkh·ə) A port city in NW Belgium, on the North Sea; the port for Bruges; pop. about 3,000.

Zee·land (zē′lənd, *Du.* zā′länt) A Province of the SW Netherlands; 650 sq. mi.; pop. 283,914 (est. 1960); capital, Middelburg.

Zee·man effect (zā′män) *Physics* The splitting of spectral lines when the light source emitting them is placed in a strong magnetic field. [after Pieter *Zeeman*, 1865–1943, Dutch physicist]

ze·in (zē′in) *n. Biochem.* A simple protein derived from corn, insoluble in water but soluble in aqueous solutions of acetone and alcohol. [< NL *Zea* genus of grasses + -IN]

Zeit·geist (tsīt′gīst) *n. German* The spirit of the time; the intellectual and moral tendencies that characterize any age or epoch. [< G < *zeit* time + *geist* spirit]

ze·min·dar (zə·mēn′där′) *n.* In India: **a** A tax farmer required under Mogul rule to pay a fixed sum for the tract of land assigned him. **b** A native landlord required to pay a certain land tax to the English government. Also spelled *zamindar.* [< Hind. < Persian *zamīndār* < *zamīn* earth + *dār* holder]

zemst·vo (zem′stvō, *Russ.* zyem′stvō) *n.* A Russian elective district and representative assembly, replaced in 1917 by the soviet system. [< Russian *semlya* land]

ze·na·na (zə·nä′nə) *n.* In India, the women's apartments; the East Indian harem: also spelled *zanana.* [< Hind. *zenāna* belonging to women < Persian *zanāna* < *zan* woman]

Zen Buddhism (zen) A form of contemplative Buddhism whose adherents believe in and work toward abrupt en-

lightenment. It originated in China around A.D. 500, and later spread to Japan, where it greatly influenced Japanese culture. Also **Zen.** [< Japanese *zen* meditation < Chinese *chan* < Skt. *dhyana*]

Zend (zend) *n.* **1.** The ancient translation and commentary, in a literary form of Middle Persian (Pahlavi), of the Avesta, the sacred writings of the Zoroastrian religion. **2.** Erroneously, the language of the Avesta; Avestan. [< F < Persian, interpretation] — **Zend′ic** *adj.*

Zend-A·ves·ta (zend′ə·ves′tə) *n.* The Avesta, including the later translation and commentary called the Zend. [Alter. of Persian *Avestā-va-Zend* the Avesta with its interpretation < Avestan *Avestā* sacred text + Persian *zend* interpretation] — **Zend′-A·ves·ta′ic** (-ə·ves·tā′ik) *adj.*

zen·er diode (zen′ər *or* zē′nər) A semiconductor diode designed to conduct at a certain reverse voltage. [after Clarence Melvin *Zener*, born 1905, U.S. physicist]

Zeng·er (zeng′ər), **John Peter,** 1697–1746, American printer and newspaper publisher born in Germany; noted as the central figure in a lawsuit that helped establish the principle of freedom of the press in America.

ze·nith (zē′nith) *n.* **1.** The point of the celestial sphere that is exactly overhead, and opposite to the nadir. **2.** The highest or culminating point; peak: the *zenith* of one's career: opposed to *nadir.* [< OF *cenit*, ult. < Arabic *samt* (*ar-ras*) the path (over the head)]

Ze·no·bi·a (zi·nō′bē·ə) Third-century queen of Palmyra; fought against Rome.

Ze·no of Elea (zē′nō) Fifth-century B.C. Greek philosopher.

Zeno the Stoic, died 264? B.C., Greek philosopher; founder of the Stoic school.

ze·o·lite (zē′ə·līt) *n.* Any of a large class of secondary minerals occurring in cavities and veins in eruptive rocks, usually a hydrous silicate of aluminum and sodium. [< Sw. *zeolit* < Gk. *zeein* to boil + *lithos* stone] — **ze′o·lit′ic** (-lit′ik) *adj.*

Zeph·a·ni·ah (zef′ə·nī′ə) Seventh-century B.C. Hebrew prophet. — *n.* A book of the Old Testament bearing his name. Also, in the Douai Bible, *Sophonias.*

zeph·yr (zef′ər) *n.* **1.** The west wind. **2.** Any soft, gentle wind. **3.** Worsted or woolen yarn of very light weight used for embroidery, shawls, etc.: also **zephyr worsted.** **4.** Anything very light and airy. [< L *zephyrus* < Gk. *zephyros*]

zephyr cloth Fine cassimere used for women's clothing.

Zeph·y·rus (zef′ər·əs) In Greek mythology, the west wind: regarded as the mildest and gentlest of all sylvan deities.

zep·pe·lin (zep′ə·lin, *Ger.* tsep′ə·lēn′) *n. Often cap.* A large dirigible having a rigid, cigar-shaped body. [after Count Ferdinand von *Zeppelin*, who designed it.]

Zep·pe·lin (zep′ə·lin, *Ger.* tsep′ə·lēn′), **Count Ferdinand von,** 1838–1917, German general, aviator, and airship builder.

Zer·matt (tser·mät′) A resort village of SE Valais canton, Switzerland; pop. 2,731 (1960).

ze·ro (zir′ō, zē′rō) *n. pl.* **ze·ros** *or* **ze·roes** **1.** The numeral or symbol 0; a cipher. ◆ In nontechnical speech, this symbol is often pronounced (ō). **2.** *Math.* The element of a number system that leaves any element unchanged under addition, in particular, a real number 0 such that $a + 0 = 0 + a = a$ for any real number a. **3.** The point on a scale, as of a thermometer, from which measures are counted; also, a temperature that registers zero on a thermometer. **4.** *Mil.* A setting for a gunsight that adjusts both for elevation and wind. **5.** The lowest point. **6.** Nothing. — *v.t.* **ze·roed, ze·ro·ing** To adjust (instruments) to an arbitrary zero point for synchronized readings. — **to zero in 1.** To bring an aircraft into a desired position, as for bombing. **2.** To adjust the sight of (a gun) by calibrated results of firings. — *adj.* Without value or appreciable change. [< F *zéro* < Ital. *zero* < Arabic *sifr.* Doublet of CIPHER.]

zero gravity *Aerospace* A condition in which the gravitational attraction of the earth or other celestial body is nullified by inertial forces; weightlessness.

zero hour 1. The time set for attack or other military operations: also called *H-hour.* **2.** *Informal* The moment of undertaking something; any critical moment.

ze·ro-ze·ro (zir′ō·zir′ō, zē′rō·zē′rō) *adj. Aeron.* Having or characterized by a ceiling and visibility of zero.

zest (zest) *n.* **1.** Invigorating excitement; keen enjoyment; gusto: often with *for*: a *zest* for reading. **2.** That which imparts such excitement and relish. **3.** An agreeable and piquant flavor in anything tasted, especially if added to the usual flavor. **4.** *Rare* A piece of orange or lemon peel or its oil, used to flavor food. — *v.t.* **1.** To give zest or relish to; make piquant. [< F *zeste* lemon peel (for flavoring)]

zest·ful (zest′fəl) *adj.* Full of or marked by zest. Also **zest′y.** — **zest′ful·ly** *adv.* — **zest′ful·ness** *n.*

ze·ta (zā′tə, zē′-) *n.* The sixth letter (Z, ζ) in the Greek alphabet, corresponding to English *z*, in ancient Greek sounded *zd* or *dz*, in modern Greek *z*. See ALPHABET. [< Gk. *zēta*]

Ze·thus (zē′thəs) In Greek mythology, Amphion's twin brother. Also **Ze′thos.** See AMPHION.

Zet·land (zet′lənd) See SHETLAND under SHETLAND ISLANDS.

zeug·ma (zōōg′mə) *n.* A rhetorical figure in which an adjective is made to modify, or a verb to govern, two nouns, while applying properly only to one, as in *She was remembered but they forgotten.* Compare SYLLEPSIS. [< NL < Gk. a yoking < *zeugnymi* to yoke]

Zeus (zōōs) In Greek mythology, the supreme deity, ruler of the celestial realm, son of Kronos and Rhea and husband of Hera: identified with the Roman *Jupiter.*

Zeus-Am·mon (zōōs′am′ən) See AMMON.

Zeux·is (zōōk′sis) Fifth-century B.C. Greek painter.

Z/F *Mil.* Zone of fire.

Zhda·nov (zhdä′nôf) A port city in the SE Ukrainian S.S.R., on the Sea of Azov; pop. 417,000 (1970): formerly *Mariupol, Mariupol'.*

Zhda·nov (zhdä′nôf), **Andrei Aleksandrovich,** 1896–1948, Soviet political leader and general.

Zhi·to·mir (zhi-tô′myir) A city in the west central Ukrainian S.S.R.: pop. 105,000 (1959).

Zhu·kov (zhōō′kôf), **Georgi Konstantinovich,** 1896–1974, Soviet marshal and statesman.

zib·e·line (zib′ə·lin, -lin) *adj.* Pertaining to the sable; made of sable fur. — *n.* The fur of the sable. Also **zib′el·line.** [< F < OF *sebelin,* ult. < Slavic. Akin to SABLE.]

zib·et (zib′it) *n.* The Asian or Indian civet (*Viverra zibetha*). Also **zib′eth.** [< Med.L *zibethum* < Arabic *zabād* civet]

Zieg·feld (zēg′feld, zig′-), **Florenz,** 1869–1932, U.S. theatrical producer.

zig·gu·rat (zig′ŏŏ·rat) *n.* Among the Assyrians and Babylonians, a terraced temple tower pyramidal in form, each successive story being smaller than the one below, leaving a terrace around each of the floors. Also **zik′ku·rat** (zik′-). [< Assyrian *ziqquratu,* orig., mountain top]

zig·zag (zig′zag) *n.* **1.** A series of short, sharp turns or angles from one side to the other in succession. **2.** Something characterized by such angles, as a path or pattern. — *adj.* Having or proceeding in a zigzag. — *adv.* In a zigzag manner. — *v.t.* & *v.i.* **zagged, ·zag·ging** To form or move in zigzags. [< F < G *zickzack,* prob. reduplication of *zacke* sharp point]

zig·zag·ger (zig′zag·ər) *n.* **1.** One who or that which zigzags. **2.** A sewing-machine attachment for stitching appliqué, joining lace and insertion to fabric, etc.

zil·lah (zil′ə) *n. Anglo-Indian* A provincial governmental district in India.

Zil·pah (zil′pə) The mother of Gad. *Gen.* xxx 10.

Zim·ba·bwe (zim-bä′bwä) The site of a ruined city in SE Rhodesia: discovered about 1870.

Zim·ba·list (zim′bə·list, *Russ.* zim′bə·lyĕst′), **Efrem,** born 1889, U.S. violinist born in Russia.

Zim·mern (zim′ərn), **Sir Alfred,** 1879–1957, English political scientist.

zinc (zingk) *n.* A bluish white, metallic element (symbol Zn) occurring mostly in combination, widely used in industry, medicine, the arts, for roofing, and as the negative electrode in electric batteries. See ELEMENT. — *v.t.* **zincked** or **zinced, zinck·ing** or **zinc·ing** To coat or cover with zinc; galvanize. [< G *zink;* ult. origin unknown] — **zinc′ic** *adj.* — **zinck′y, zinc′y, zink′y** *adj.*

zinc·al·ism (zingk′əl·iz′əm) *n. Pathol.* Chronic zinc poisoning.

zinc·ate (zingk′āt) *n. Chem.* A salt derived from the acid form of zinc hydroxide, H₂ZnO₂, by substitution of a metal for the hydrogen. [< ZINC + -ATE³]

zinc blende Sphalerite.

zinc·if·er·ous (zingk·if′ər·əs, zin·sif′ər·əs) *adj.* Yielding zinc, as ore. Also **zink·if′er·ous.** [< ZINC + -FEROUS]

zinc·i·fy (zingk′ə·fī) *v.t.* **·fied, ·fy·ing** To apply zinc to, as by coating or impregnating. Also **zink′i·fy.** [< ZINC + -FY] — **zinc·i·fi·ca′tion** (-fə·kā′shən) *n.*

zinc·ite (zingk′īt) *n.* A deep red to orange translucent zinc oxide, ZnO, often found massive. [< ZINC + -ITE²]

zin·co·graph (zingk′ə·graf, -gräf) *n.* An etching on zinc; a picture obtained by zincography. Also **zin′co·type** (-tīp). [< ZINC + -GRAPH] — **zin·cog·ra·pher** (zing·kog′rə·fər) *n.*

zin·cog·ra·phy (zing·kog′rə·fē) *n.* The art of etching on zinc to produce plates for printing. [< ZINC + -GRAPHY] — **zinc·o·graph·ic** (zingk·ə·graf′ik) or **·i·cal** *adj.*

zinc ointment A medicated ointment for skin affections, containing zinc oxide mixed with petrolatum.

zinc·ous (zingk′əs) *adj. Chem.* Pertaining to or derived from zinc.

zinc oxide *Chem.* A white pulverulent compound ZnO, used as a pigment, and in medicine as a mild antiseptic and astringent.

zinc sulfate *Chem.* A crystalline compound, ZnSO₄·7H₂O, obtained by the action of sulfuric acid on zinc; white vitriol.

zinc white Zinc oxide used as a pigment in paints.

zin·fan·del (zin′fən·del) *n.* A dry, red or white claret-type wine made in California. [? after a European place name]

zing (zing) *Informal n.* **1.** A high-pitched buzzing or

humming sound. **2.** Energy; vitality; vigor. — *v.i.* To make a shrill, humming sound. [Imit.]

zin·ga·ro (tsĕng′gä·rō) *n. pl.* **·ri** (-rē) *Italian* A gypsy. Also **zin′ga·no** (-nō). — **zin′ga·ra** (-rä) *n.fem.*

zin·gi·ber·a·ceous (zin′jə·bə·rā′shəs) *adj. Bot.* Of or pertaining to a family (*Zingiberaceae*) of monocotyledonous tropical plants, the ginger family, having aromatic rootstocks and including cardamon. Also **zin′zi·ber·a′ceous** (zin′zə-). [< NL, family name < LL *zingiber.* See GINGER.]

Zin·jan·thro·pus (zin·jan′thrə·pəs) *n. pl.* **·pi** (-pī) *Anthropol.* A forerunner of modern man identified from a group of fossil bones found in Tanzania, East Africa and believed to have lived nearly two million years ago. Also called *Nutcracker Man.* [< NL < Arabic *Zinj* eastern Africa + Gk. *anthropos* man]

zink·en·ite (zingk′ən·īt) *n.* A metallic, steel-gray sulfide of lead and antimony, PbSb₂S₄, crystallizing in the orthorhombic system. Also **zinck′en·ite.** [< G *zinkenit,* after J. K. L. *Zinken,* 1798–1862, German mine director]

zin·ni·a (zin′ē·ə) *n.* Any of a genus (*Zinnia*) of American, chiefly Mexican, herbs of the composite family, having showy flowers; especially, the common zinnia (*Z. elegans*), the State flower of Indiana. [< NL, after J. G. *Zinn,* 1727–59, German professor of medicine]

Zins·ser (zin′sər), **Hans,** 1878–1940, U.S. bacteriologist.

Zin·zen·dorf (tsin′tsən·dôrf), **Count Nikolaus Ludwig von,** 1700–60, German religious reformer and theologian; organizer of the Moravian Church.

Zi·on (zī′ən) **1.** A hill in Jerusalem, the site of the temple and the royal residence of David and his successors, regarded by the Jews as a symbol for the center of Jewish national culture, government, and religion. **2.** The Jewish people. **3.** Any place or community considered to be especially under God's rule, as ancient Israel or the Christian church. **4.** The heavenly Jerusalem; heaven. Also *Sion.* [OE *Sion* < LL < Gk. *Seōn, Seiōn* < Hebrew *tsiyōn* hill]

Zi·on·ism (zī′ən·iz′əm) *n.* A movement originally for a resettlement of the Jews in Palestine, and now for the development and support of Israel. Also **Zion movement.** — **Zi′on·ist** *adj.* & *n.* — **Zi′on·is′tic** *adj.*

Zion National Park A government reservation in SW Utah; 147 sq. mi.; established 1919; contains **Zion Canyon,** a gorge .5 mi. deep, about 15 mi. long.

Zi·on·ward (zī′ən·wərd) *adv.* Toward Zion; Godward.

zip (zip) *n.* **1.** A sharp, hissing sound, as of a bullet passing through the air. **2.** *Informal* Energy; vitality; vim. — *v.* **zipped, zip·ping** *v.t.* **1.** To fasten with a zipper. — *v.i.* **2.** *Informal* To be very energetic. **3.** To move or fly with a zip. [Imit.]

Zi·pan·gu (zi·pang′gōō) Japan: name used by Marco Polo.

ZIP Code (zip) A numerical code devised by the U.S. Post Office to aid in the distribution of domestic mail. Also **Zip Code.** [< Z(ONE) I(MPROVEMENT) P(LAN)]

zip gun *U.S. Slang* A home-made pistol consisting of a small pipe or other tube fastened to a block of wood and equipped with a firing pin actuated by a spring or rubber band.

zip·per (zip′ər) *n.* A fastener having two rows of interlocking teeth that may be closed or separated by a sliding device, used on clothing, boots, etc.: also called *slide fastener.*

Zip·per (zip′ər) *n.* An overshoe or boot secured with a sliding fastener: a trade name.

zip·py (zip′ē) *adj.* **·pi·er, ·pi·est** *Informal* Brisk; energetic.

zir·con (zûr′kon) *n.* A crystalline, variously colored, zirconium silicate, ZrSiO₄; some translucent varieties of which are used as gems. [< G *zirken* or F *zircone* < Arabic *zarqūn* cinnabar < Persian *zargūn* golden < *zar* gold + *gūn* color]

zir·con·ate (zûr′kən·āt) *n. Chem.* A salt formed by replacing hydrogen in the acid form of zirconium hydroxide, Zr(OH)₄, with a metal. [< ZIRCON(IUM) + -ATE³]

zir·co·ni·a (zûr·kō′nē·ə) *n. Chem.* A white pulverulent zirconium dioxide, ZrO₂, that when strongly heated becomes luminous, and is used in certain forms of incandescent burners. [< NL < ZIRCON]

zir·co·ni·um (zûr·kō′nē·əm) *n.* A metallic element (symbol Zr) chemically resembling titanium, used in alloys, as an opacifier of lacquers, and as an abrasive. See ELEMENT. [< NL < ZIRCON] — **zir·con′ic** (-kon′ik) *adj.*

Z-i·ron (zē′ī′ərn) *n.* An angle iron of Z form: also called *Z-bar, Z-beam.*

Zis·ka (tsis′kä), **John,** 1360?–1424, Bohemian general; leader of the Hussites. Also **Žiž·ka** (zhish′kä).

zith·er (zith′ər) *n.* A simple form of stringed instrument, having a flat sounding board and from thirty to forty strings that are played by plucking with a plectrum. Also **zith′ern** (-ərn). [< G < L *cithara* < Gk. *kithara.* Doublet of CITHARA and GUITAR.]

zi·zith (tsē·tsēt′, tsi′tsis) *n.* The fringe or tassel formerly worn by Jews on the outer garment (*Num.* xv 38), but now worn on the tallith during prayer. [< Hebrew *tsītstth*]

ziz·zle (ziz′əl) *v.i.* **·zled, ·zling** *Brit. Dial.* To make a sputtering or hissing sound, as meat when cooking. [Imit.]

zlo·ty (zlô′tē) *n. pl.* **·tys** or **·ty** The standard monetary unit of Poland, equivalent to 100 groszy. [< Polish, lit., golden]

Zn *Chem.* Zinc.

zo·a (zō′ə) Plural of ZOON.

-zoa *combining form Zool.* Used to denote the names of groups: *Protozoa, Hydrozoa.* An individual in such a group is denoted by **-zoan.** [< NL < Gk. *zōion* animal]

Zo·an (zō′an) The Old Testament name for TANIS.

zo·di·ac (zō′dē·ak) *n.* 1. An imaginary belt encircling the heavens and extending about 8° on each side of the ecliptic within which are the apparent orbits of the moon, sun, and larger planets. It is divided into twelve parts, called **signs of the zodiac,** that formerly corresponded to twelve constellations bearing the same names. Now, owing to the precession of the equinoxes, each constellation is in the sign that has the name next following its own. 2. A figure or diagram representing this belt and its signs, used in astrology. 3. A complete circuit; round. 4. *Rare* A circle or halo; also, a girdle. [< OF *zodiaque* < L *zodiacus* < Gk. (*kyklos*) *zōdiakos* (circle) of animals < *zōdion* sculptured animal, dim. of *zōion* animal] **— zo·di·a·cal** (zō·dī′ə·kəl) *adj.*

SIGNS OF THE ZODIAC

A Vernal equinox: Aries, Taurus, Gemini. *B* Summer solstice: Cancer, Leo, Virgo. *C* Autumnal equinox: Libra, Scorpio, Sagittarius. *D* Winter solstice: Capricorn, Aquarius, Pisces.

zodiacal light *Astron.* A cone-shaped tract of faint light lying near the plane of the ecliptic, attributed to the reflection of sunlight from a cloud of fine meteoric dust.

zo·ic (zō′ik) *adj.* Pertaining to or characterized by animals or animal life. [< Gk. *zōikos* < *zōion* animal]

Zo·la (zō′lə, zō·lä′; *Fr.* zō·là′), Émile, 1840–1902, French novelist and journalist. **— Zo′la·esque′** (-esk′) *adj.*

zoll·ver·ein (tsôl′fer·īn, zōl′və·rīn) *n. Usually cap.* 1. A former trade league constituted by twenty-six German states. 2. A customs union. [< G < *zoll* tax, custom + *verein* union]

zom·bie (zom′bē) *n.* 1. In West Africa voodoo cults, the python deity. 2. A snake deity of the voodoo cults of Haiti and of parts of the southern United States. 3. The supernatural power by which a dead body is believed to be reanimated. 4. A corpse reactivated by sorcery, but still dead. 5. Loosely, a ghost. 6. *Slang* An apathetic or unresponsive person; an automaton. 7. A large, strong cocktail made from several kinds of rum, fruit juices, and liqueur. 8. *Canadian Slang* In World War II, an army conscript, especially one assigned to home defense. Also **zom′bi.** [< West African. Cf. Bantu (Congo) *zumbi* fetish.] **— zom′bi·ism** *n.*

zo·nal (zō′nəl) *adj.* Of, pertaining to, exhibiting, or marked by a zone or zones; like a zone. Also **zo′na·ry** (-nər·ē).

zo·nate (zō′nāt) *adj.* 1. Marked with zones or concentric colored bands. 2. *Bot.* Disposed in a single row, as the leaves of certain plants. Also **zo′nat·ed.** [< ZONE(E) + -ATE¹] **— zo·na′tion** (zō·nā′shən) *n.*

zone (zōn) *n.* 1. An area, tract, or section distinguished from other or adjacent areas by some special quality, purpose, or condition: a mountainous *zone*; a *zone* of disagreement. 2. *Usually cap.* Any of five divisions of the earth's surface, enclosed between two parallels of latitude and named for the prevailing climate: the **Torrid Zone,** extending on each side of the equator 23° 27′; the **Temperate Zones,** included between the parallels 23° 27′ and 66° 33′ on both sides of the equator, and the **Frigid Zones,** within the parallels 66° 33′ and the poles. 3. An area of land designated as distinct from other areas because of its particular use or location: combat *zone*; school *zone*. 4. *Ecol.* A belt or area delimited from others by the character of its plant or animal life, its climate, geological formations, etc. 5. A concentric area or band; especially, any of a number of concentric areas used to determine the rate of charge for transporting something a specified distance, as in the United States parcel post system, each band having a uniformly higher rate than the

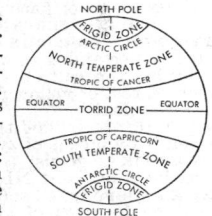

TERRESTRIAL ZONES

one next closer to the point of origin. 6. A section of a city or town where only certain uses of the land or certain types of buildings are permitted by law: a residential *zone*. 7. A section of a city designated with a number as an aid in the distribution of mail. 8. A belt, band, stripe, etc., having a color or other characteristic that distinguishes it from the object it encircles. 9. The total number of railroad stations situated within a certain area measured from a traffic or shipping center. 10. *Geom.* A portion of the surface of a sphere enclosed between two parallel planes. 11. *Archaic* or *Poetic* A belt or girdle. Abbr. *z.*, Z. **—** *v.t.* **zoned, zon·ing** 1. To divide into zones; especially, to divide (a city, etc.) into zones that are restricted as to types of construction and use, as residential or industrial. 2. To designate (an area, etc.) as a zone or part of a zone: to *zone* the waterfront district as commercial. 3. To mark with or as with zones or stripes. 4. To encircle with a zone or belt. [< L *zona* < Gk. *zōnē* girdle]

zone·less (zōn′lis) *adj.* Having no zone or belt.

zone·time (zōn′tīm′) *n.* Time corresponding to that within a zone of 7½ degrees on either side of a meridian, used in the determination of a ship's longitude.

zo·nule (zōn′yool) *n.* A small zone, belt, or ring. Also **zo′nu·la** (-lə). [< NL *zonula*, dim. of L *zona*. See ZONE.]

zoo (zoo) *n.* A park or garden in which wild animals are kept for exhibition: also *zoological garden, zoological park.*

zoo- *combining form* Animal; of or related to animals, or to animal forms: *zoology, zoophyte*. Also, before vowels, *zo-*. [< Gk. *zōion* animal]

zo·o·chem·is·try (zō′ə·kem′is·trē) *n.* The chemistry of the solids and fluids contained in the animal organism. **— zo′o·chem′i·cal** (-kem′i·kəl) *adj.*

zo·o·chore (zō′ə·kôr, -kōr) *n.* A plant dispersed by animals.

zoogeographic region One of a series of major geographic areas characterized by the dominance of certain animal groups, generally classified as the Palearctic, Nearctic, Neotropical, Ethiopian, Oriental, and Australian, of which the first two are often considered together as the Holarctic realm. Also **zoogeographic realm.**

zo·o·ge·og·ra·phy (zō′ə·jē·og′rə·fē) *n. Ecol.* The systematic study of the distribution of animals and of the relations between animal groups and the land or aquatic areas in which they predominate. **— zo′o·ge′o·graph′er** *n.* **— zo′o·ge′o·graph′ic** (-jē′ə·graf′ik) or **-i·cal** *adj.* **— zo′o·ge′o·graph′i·cal·ly** *adv.*

zo·o·gloe·a (zō′ə·glē′ə) *n. pl.* **·gloe·ae** (-glē′ē) *Bacteriol.* A colony of bacteria forming a jellylike mass held together by a viscid sheath secreted by themselves. [< NL < Gk. *zōion* animal + *gloios* sticky stuff]

zo·og·ra·phy (zō·og′rə·fē) *n.* The branch of zoology that describes animals; descriptive zoology. **— zo·og′ra·pher** *n.* **— zo·o·graph·ic** (zō′ə·graf′ik) or **-i·cal** *adj.*

zo·oid (zō′oid) *n.* 1. *Biol.* Any animal or vegetable organism, usually very small, capable of spontaneous movement and independent existence, as a spermatozoon, spermatozoid, etc. 2. *Zool.* **a** Any organism capable of independent existence that is produced other than by sexual reproduction. **b** One of the distinct members of a compound or colonial organism, as in a bryozoan. **c** A free-swimming medusa produced as a stage in the life of a jellyfish. **—** *adj.* Having the nature of an animal: also **zo·oi·dal** (zō-oid′l).

zool. Zoological; zoologist; zoology.

zo·ol·a·try (zō·ol′ə·trē) *n. pl.* **·tries** Worship of animals. [< ZOO + -LATRY] **— zo·ol′at·er** *n.* **— zo·ol′a·trous** *adj.*

zo·o·log·i·cal (zō′ə·loj′i·kəl) *adj.* 1. Of or pertaining to zoology. 2. Relating to or characteristic of animals. Also **zo′o·log′ic.** Abbr. *zool.* **— zo′o·log′i·cal·ly** *adv.*

zoological garden A zoo.

zoological park A zoo.

zo·ol·o·gy (zō·ol′ə·jē) *n.* 1. The science that treats of animals with reference to their structure, functions, development, evolution, and classification. 2. The animal kingdom, or local examples of it, regarded biologically. Abbr. *zool.* [< NL *zoologia* < Gk. *zōion* animal + *logos* word, discourse] **— zo·ol′o·gist** *n.*

zoom (zoom) *v.i.* 1. To make a low-pitched but loud humming sound; also, to move with such a sound. 2. To climb sharply in an airplane. 3. To move a motion picture or TV camera rapidly or adjust the focus, as with a zoom lens, to make an object in view appear to come very close or become much more distant. **—** *v.t.* 4. To cause to zoom. **— Syn.** See FLY¹. **—** *n.* The act of zooming. [Imit.]

zo·om·e·try (zō·om′ə·trē) *n.* Measurement of the parts of animals and determination of their relative magnitude. [< ZOO- + -METRY] **— zo·o·met·ric** (zō′ə·met′rik) *adj.*

zoom lens *Photog.* A lens, used chiefly on television and motion picture cameras, that permits the size of the image to be varied continuously without loss of focus.

zo·o·mor·phism (zō′ə·môr′fiz·əm) *n.* 1. The conception, symbolization, or representation of a man or a god in the form of an animal; also, the attribution of divine or human qualities to animals. **2.** The representation of animals or animal forms in art or symbolism. **3.** Transformation into animals. Also **zo'o·mor'phy.** — **zo'o·mor'phic** *adj.*

zo·on (zō'on) *n. pl.* **zo·ons** or **zo·a** (zō'ə) *Biol.* A developed individual of a compound animal or of a simple egg. [< NL < Gk. *zōion* animal] — **zo·on·al** (zō·on'əl) *adj.*

zo·oph·a·gous (zō·of'ə·gəs) *adj.* Feeding on animals; carnivorous. [< ZOO- + -PHAGOUS]

zo·o·phile (zō'ə·fīl, -fil) *n.* **1.** A lover of animals; especially, one who objects to vivisection. **2.** *Bot.* A zoophilous plant. Also **zo·oph·i·list** (zō·of'ə·list). [< ZOO- + -PHILE] — **zo'o·phil'ic** (-fil'ik) *adj.*

zo·oph·i·lism (zō·of'ə·liz'əm) *n.* **1.** Fondness for animals. **2.** *Psychiatry* The obtaining of sexual gratification by the fondling of animals. Also **zo·o·phil·i·a** (zō'ə·fil'ē·ə).

zo·oph·i·lous (zō·of'ə·ləs) *adj.* **1.** Loving animals. **2.** *Bot.* Adapted for pollination by animals, as certain plants. [< ZOO- + -PHILOUS]

zo·o·phyte (zō'ə·fīt) *n.* An invertebrate animal resembling a plant, as a coral or sea anemone. [< ZOO- + -PHYTE] — **zo'o·phyt'ic** (-fit'ik) or **-i·cal** *adj.*

zo·o·plas·ty (zō'ə·plas'tē) *n. Surg.* The operation of grafting a part of a lower animal body on some part of the human body. — **zo'o·plas'tic** *adj.*

zo·o·sperm (zō'ə·spûrm) *n.* **1.** A spermatozoon. **2.** *Bot. Obs.* A zoospore. — **zo'o·sper·mat'ic** (-spər·mat'ik) *adj.*

zo·o·spo·ran·gi·um (zō'ə·spə·ran'jē·əm) *n. pl.* **·gi·a** (-jē·ə) *Bot.* A sporangium producing zoospores. [< NL < Gk. *zōion* animal + *spora* seed + *angeion* vessel] — **zo'o·spo·ran'gi·al** *adj.*

zo·o·spore (zō'ə·spôr, -spōr) *n.* **1.** *Bot.* A spore, produced among some algae and fungi, that is provided with cilia by means of which it can move about. **2.** *Zool.* A flagellate or ameboid motile body in certain protozoa. Also called *swarm spore.* [< ZOO- + SPORE] — **zo'o·spor'ic** (-spôr'ik, -spor'ik), **zo·os·po·rous** (zō·os'pər·əs) *adj.*

zo·ot·o·my (zō·ot'ə·mē) *n.* The anatomy or dissection of animals; comparative anatomy. [< NL *zootomia* < Gk. *zōion* animal + *tomē* cutting < *temnein* to cut] — **zo·o·tom'ic** (zō'ə·tom'ik) or **·i·cal** *adj.* — **zo'o·tom'i·cal·ly** *adv.* — **zo·ot'o·mist** *n.*

Zo·rach (zō'räk), **William,** 1887–1966, U.S. sculptor and painter born in Lithuania.

zor·il (zôr'il, zor'-) *n.* A small South African mammal (*Ictonyx capensis*) of the weasel family, capable of emitting a noxious odor. Also **zo·ril·la** (zə·ril'ə). [< F *zorille* < Sp. *zorrilla* polecat, dim. of *zorra* fox]

Zorn (sôrn), **Anders Leonhard,** 1860–1920, Swedish painter, etcher, and sculptor.

Zo·ro·as·ter (zō'rō·as'tər) Sixth- or seventh-century B.C. Iranian religious reformer; founder of Zoroastrianism. Also *Zarathustra.*

Zo·ro·as·tri·an (zō'rō·as'trē·ən) *n.* A follower of Zoroaster; an adherent of Zoroastrianism. — *adj.* Of or pertaining to Zoroaster or to the religion he founded.

Zo·ro·as·tri·an·ism (zō'rō·as'trē·ən·iz'əm) *n.* The religious system founded by Zoroaster and taught in the Zend-Avesta. It recognizes two creative powers, one good and one other evil, includes the belief in life after death, and teaches the final triumph of good over evil. See AHRIMAN, ORMUZD. Also **Zo'ro·as'trism.**

Zor·ril·la y Mo·ral (thôr·rē'lyä ē mō·räl'), **José,** 1817–93, Spanish poet.

Zos·i·mus (zos'ə·məs, zō'sə-) Fifth-century Byzantine historian.

zos·ter (zos'tər) *n.* **1.** An ancient Greek belt or girdle worn especially by men. **2.** *Pathol.* Herpes zoster. See SHINGLES. [< L < Gk. *zōstēr* girdle < *zōnnynai* to gird]

Zou·ave (zōō·äv', swäv) *n.* **1.** A light-armed French infantryman wearing a brilliant Oriental uniform, originally an Algerian recruit. **2.** In the Civil War, a member of a volunteer regiment assuming the name and part of the dress of the French Zouaves. **3.** A woman's short, gaily embroidered jacket: also **Zouave jacket.** [< F < Arabic *Zouāoua,* a Kabyle tribe; so called because orig. recruited from this tribe]

zounds (zoundz, zōōndz) *interj. Archaic* A mild oath used to express surprise or anger. [Short for *God's wounds*]

zoy·si·a (zoi'zē·ə) *n.* Any of various hardy perennial grasses (genus *Zoisia*) well-suited to hot, dry growing conditions. [after Karl von *Zois,* 18th c. German botanist]

Zr *Chem.* Zirconium.

Zsig·mon·dy (zhig'mon·dē), **Richard Adolf,** 1865–1929, German chemist born in Austria.

zuc·chet·to (tsōōk·ket'tō) *n.* A skullcap worn by ecclesiastics in the Roman Catholic Church, black for a priest, purple for a bishop, red for a cardinal, and white for the pope. Also **zuc·chet'ta** (-tä). [Var. of Ital. *zucchetta,* < LL *cucutia* a kind of wood]

zuc·chi·ni (zōō·kē'nē, *Ital.* dzōōk·kē'nē) *n.* A type of green summer squash (evolved from *Cucurbita pepo*) of a small cylindrical shape: also called *Italian squash.* [< Ital., pl. of *zucchino,* dim. of *zucca* gourd, squash]

Zug (tsōōkh) A canton in north central Switzerland; 92 sq. mi.; pop. 52,489 (1960); capital, **Zug,** on the **Lake of Zug** (15 sq. mi.).

Zu·lu (zōō'lōō) *n. pl.* **Zu·lus** or **Zu·lu** **1.** One of a Bantu nation of Natal, South Africa, sometimes included with the Kaffirs. **2.** The Bantu language of the Zulus. — *adj.* Of, pertaining to, or characteristic of the Zulus or their language.

Zu·lu·land (zōō'lōō·land') A district of NE Natal, South Africa, formerly a native kingdom; 10,362 sq. mi.

zum Bei·spiel (tsōōm bī'shpēl) *German* For example. Abbr. *z.B.*

Zu·ñi (zōō'nyē) *n.* **1.** One of a tribe of North American Indians of pueblo culture but comprising a distinct, ethnic stock, living in New Mexico. **2.** The language of this tribe. — **Zu'ñi·an** *adj. & n.*

Zur·ba·rán (thōōr'bä·rän'), **Francisco de,** 1598–1662, Spanish painter.

Zu·rich (zōōr'ik) A Canton of NE Switzerland; 667 sq. mi.; pop. 1,048,000 (1965); capital, **Zurich,** on the northern shore of the **Lake of Zurich** (35 sq. mi.); pop. 432,500 (est. 1968): German **Zü·rich** (tsü'rikh).

Zuy·der Zee (zī'dər zē, *Du.* zoi'dər zā) A former shallow inlet of the North Sea in the NW Netherlands; enclosed by a dike; drainage projects have reclaimed much of the land and formed Lake Ijssel. Also **Zui'der Zee.**

Zweig (tsvīg, tsvīkh), **Arnold,** 1887–1968, German novelist. — **Stefan,** 1881–1942, Austrian dramatist and novelist.

Zwick·au (tsvik'ou) A city in southern East Germany; pop. 129,138 (est. 1960).

zwie·back (zwī'bak, zwē'-, swī'-, swē'-, -bäk; *Ger.* tsvē'bäk) *n.* A biscuit of wheaten bread or rusk baked yellow in the loaf and later sliced and toasted. [< G, twice baked < *zwie-* twice (< *zwei* two) + *backen* to bake]

Zwing·li (tsving'lē), **Ulrich,** 1484–1531, Swiss Reformation leader. Also **Huldreich Zwingli.**

Zwing·li·an (zwing'lē·ən, tsving'-) *adj.* Of or pertaining to the doctrines taught by Zwingli, especially to the doctrine that the Eucharist is simply a memorial or a symbolic commemoration of the death of Christ. — *n.* A follower of Zwingli. — **Zwing'li·an·ism** *n.* — **Zwing'li·an·ist** *n.*

zwit·ter·i·on (tsvit'ər·ī'ən) *n. Physics* An ion that carries both a negative and a positive charge. [< G *zwitter* hybrid, hermaphrodite + ION] — **zwit'ter·i·on'ic** (-ī·on'ik) *adj.*

Zwor·y·kin (zwôr'i·kin), **Vladimir Kosma,** born 1889, U.S. physicist born in Russia; pioneer in television research.

zyg·a·poph·y·sis (zig'ə·pof'ə·sis) *n. pl.* **·ses** (-sēz) *Anat.* One of the processes, usually disposed in pairs, by which each vertebra articulates with the one above and below. [< NL < Gk. *zygon* yoke + *apophysis* branch. See APOPHYSIS.] — **zyg'a·po·phys'e·al** (-pō·fiz'ē·əl) or **·i·al** *adj.*

zygo- *combining form* Yoke; pair; resembling a yoke, especially in shape: *zygospore.* Also, before vowels, **zyg-.** [< Gk. *zygon* yoke]

zy·go·dac·tyl (zī'gō·dak'til) *Zool. adj.* Having paired toes, one pair directed forward and the other pair backward, as in parrots and woodpeckers. — *n.* A zygodactyl bird. [< ZYGO- + Gk. *daktylos* finger]

zy·go·ma (zī·gō'mə) *n. pl.* **·ma·ta** (-mə·tə) *Anat.* **1.** The long arch that joins the temporal and cheekbones on the side of the skull. For illustration see SKULL. **2.** The zygomatic process (which see). [< NL < Gk. *zygōma* < *zygon* yoke] — **zy·go·mat·ic** (zī'gō·mat'ik) *adj.*

zygomatic bone *Anat.* The cheekbone.

zygomatic process *Anat.* The process of the temporal bone that helps to form the zygoma.

zy·go·mor·phic (zī'gō·môr'fik) *adj. Biol.* Bilaterally symmetrical: divisible into similar halves in only one plane: said of organisms or parts of organisms. Also **zy'go·mor'phous.** [< ZYGO- + -MORPHIC] — **zy'go·mor'phism** *n.*

zy·go·phyl·la·ceous (zī'gō·fi·lā'shəs) *adj. Bot.* Designating or pertaining to a family (*Zygophyllaceae*) of herbs and shrubs, the caltrop family, having jointed branches and white, red, or yellow flowers. [< NL < Gk. *zygon* yoke + *phyllon* leaf]

zy·go·phyte (zī'gō·fīt) *n. Bot.* A plant in which reproduction is by means of zygospores. [< ZYGO- + -PHYTE]

zy·go·sis (zī·gō'sis) *n. Biol.* The union of gametes or cells; conjugation. [< NL < Gk. *zygōsis* joining < *zygon* yoke]

zy·go·spore (zī'gō·spôr, -spōr) *n. Bot.* A spore formed by the conjugation of two similar gametes, as in algae and fungi. Also **zy'go·sperm** (-spûrm). [< ZYGO- + SPORE]

zy·gote (zī'gōt, zig'ōt) *n. Biol.* **1.** The product of the union of two gametes. **2.** A new organism developed from such a union. [< Gk. *zygōtos* < *zygoein* < *zygon* yoke] — **zy·got·ic** (zī·got'ik) *adj.*

zy·mase (zī'mās) *n. Biochem.* An enzyme, obtained principally from yeast, that induces fermentation by breaking down glucose and related carbohydrates into alcohol and carbon dioxide. [< F < Gk. *zymē* leaven]

zyme (zīm) *n.* A disease germ or virus supposed to be the specific cause of a zymotic disease. [< Gk. *zymē* leaven]

zymo- *combining form* Fermentation; of or related to fermentation: *zymology.* Also, before vowels, **zym-.** [< Gk. *zymē* leaven]

zy·mo·gen (zī'mə·jən) *n.* **1.** *Biochem.* A substance that develops into an enzyme when suitably activated, as in the stomach or pancreas.   **2.** *Biol.* A bacterial organism that produces enzymes or fermentation. Also **zy′mo·gene** (-jēn). [< ZYMO- + -GEN]

zy·mo·gen·e·sis (zī′mō·jen′ə·sis)   *n. Biochem.* The transformation of a zymogen into an enzyme.

zy·mo·gen·ic (zī′mō·jen′ik)   *adj.* **1.** Of, pertaining to, or relating to zymogen. **2.** Capable of producing a ferment, as yeast. Also **zy·mog·e·nous** (zī·moj′ə·nəs).

zy·mol·o·gy (zī·mol′ə·jē)   *n.* The study of fermentation and the action of enzymes. [< ZYMO- + -LOGY] **— zy·mo·log·ic** (zī′mə·loj′ik) or **·i·cal** *adj.* **— zy·mol′o·gist** *n.*

zy·mol·y·sis (zī·mol′ə·sis)   *n.* Fermentation or the action of enzymes. [< ZYMO- + -LYSIS] **— zy·mo·lyt·ic** (zī′mə·lit′·ik) *adj.*

zy·mom·e·ter (zī·mom′ə·tər)   *n.* An instrument for measuring the degree of fermentation. [< ZYMO- + -METER]

zy·mo·scope (zī′mə·skōp)   *n.* An instrument for measuring the fermenting power of yeast. [< ZYMO- + -SCOPE]

zy·mo·sis (zī·mō′sis)   *n.   pl.* **·ses** **1.** Any form of fermentation. **2.** *Med.* **a** A process resembling fermentation formerly supposed to give rise to a diseased condition. **b** Any zymotic disease.   [< NL < Gk. *zymōsis* < *zymoein* to leaven, ferment < *zymē* leaven]

zy·mot·ic (zī·mot′ik)   *adj.* **1.** Of or relating to fermentation. **2.** Produced by or from fermentation. **3.** *Pathol.* Pertaining to a zymotic disease.   [< Gk. *zymōtikos* < *zymoein.* See ZYMOSIS.]

zymotic disease   Any of various infectious diseases, as smallpox, etc., formerly believed to be due to fermentation processes in the body.

zy·mur·gy (zī′mûr·jē)   *n.* A branch of chemistry treating of processes in which fermentation takes place, as brewing, winemaking, etc.   [< ZYM(O)- + -URGY]

PRONUNCIATION KEY: add, āce, câre, pälm; end, ēven; it, īce; odd, ōpen, ôrder; tŏŏk, pōōl; up, bûrn; ə = a in *above*, e in *sicken*, i in *flexible*, o in *melon*, u in *focus*; yōō = u in *fuse*; oil; pout; check; go; ring; thin; this; zh, vision. For à, œ, ü, kh, ṅ, see inside front cover.

COLLEGES AND UNIVERSITIES IN THE UNITED STATES

Below are about 2,000 of the ever-growing number of accredited U.S. colleges and universities, as of May, 1970.

Each entry gives the name of the institution, its location by city and state, and its date of founding, followed by:

Type of control: public (pub), or private (pvt).

Type of student body: men only (men); women only (wom); or coeducational (coed).

Level of undergraduate instruction: full four-year course (4), or two-year course (2).

Number of students: small, up to 2,500 (s); medium, between 2,500 and 7,500 (M); or large, more than 7,500 (L).

Some other abbreviations, used in names, are as follows:

A&M	Agricultural and Mechanical	*Com.*	Community
Admin.	Administration	*Ed.*	Education
Agric.	Agriculture	*Inst.*	Institute
Bus.	Business	*Jr.*	Junior
C.	College	*Mech.*	Mechanical
		Tech.	Technology, Technical

Abilene Christian C., Abilene, Tex.; 1906; pvt; coed; 4; s

Abraham Baldwin Agricultural C., Tifton, Ga.; 1933; pub; coed; 2; s

Adams State C., Alamosa, Colo.; 1921; pub; coed; 4; M

Adelphi U., Garden City N.Y.; 1863; pvt; coed; 4; L

Adirondack Com. C., Glens Falls, N.Y.; 1961; pub; coed; 2; s

Adrian C., Adrian, Mich.; 1845; pvt; 4; M

Agnes Scott C., Decatur, Ga.; 1889; pvt; wom; 4; s

Aims C., Greeley, Colo.; 1967; pub; coed; 2; s

Akron, U. of, Akron, Ohio; 1870; pub; coed; 4; L

Alabama A&M C., Normal, Ala.; 1875; pub; coed; 4; s

Alabama Christian C., Montgomery, Ala.; 1942; pvt; coed; 2; s

Alabama State C., Montgomery, Ala.; 1873; pub; coed; 4; s

Alabama, U. of, University, Ala.; 1820; pub; coed; 4; L

Alaska Methodist U., Anchorage, Alas.; 1957; pvt; coed; 4; s

Alaska, U. of, College, Alas.; 1915; pub; coed; 4; M
  Anchorage Com. C., Anchorage; 1954; pub; coed; 2; s
  Juneau–Douglas Com. C., Juneau; 1956; coed; 2; s
  Kenai Com. C., Kenai; 1964; pub; coed; 2; s
  Ketchikan Com. C., Ketchikan; 1954; pub; coed; 2; s
  Matanuska Susitna Com. C., Palmer; 1961; pub; coed; 2; s
  Sitka Com. C., Sitka; 1962; pub; coed; 2; s

Albany Jr. C., Albany, Ga.; 1963; pub; coed; 2; s

Albany, Jr. C. of, Albany, N.Y.; 1957; pvt; coed; 2; s

Albany State C., Albany, Ga.; 1903; pub; coed; 4; s

Albermarle, C. of the, Elizabeth City, N.C.; 1960; pub; coed; 2; s

Albertus Magnus C., New Haven, Conn.; 1925; pvt; wom; 4; s

Albion C., Albion, Mich.; 1835; pvt; coed; 4; s

Albright C., Reading, Pa.; 1856; pvt; coed; 4; s

Alburquerque, The U. of, Alburquerque, N. Mex.; 1920; pvt; coed; 4; s

Alcorn A&M C., Lorman, Miss.; 1871; pub; coed; 4; s

Alderson-Broaddus C., Philippi, W. Va.; 1871; pvt; coed; 4; s

Alexander City State Jr. C., Alexander City, Ala.; 1965; pub; coed; 2; s

Alfred U., Alfred, N.Y.; 1836; pvt; coed; 4; s

Alice Lloyd C., Pippa Passes, Ky.; 1923; pvt; coed; 2; s

Allan Hancock C., Santa Maria, Calif.; 1920; pub; coed; 2; M

Allegany Com. C., Cumberland, Md.; 1961; pub; coed; 2; s

Allegheny C., Meadville, Pa.; 1815; pvt; coed; 4; s

Allegheny County, Com. C. of
  Allegheny Campus, Pittsburgh, Pa.; 1966; pub; coed; 2; M
  Boyce Campus, Monroeville, Pa.; 1966; pub; 2; s

South Campus, West Mifflin, Pa.; 1967; pub; coed; 2; s

Allen Academy, Bryan, Tex.; 1947; pvt; coed; 2; s

Allen County Com. Jr. C., Iola, Kans.; 1923; pub; coed; 2; s

Allen U., Columbia, S.C.; 1870; pvt; coed; 4; s

Alliance C., Cambridge Springs, Pa.; 1912; pvt; coed; 4; s

Alma C., Alma, Mich.; 1886; pvt; coed; 4; s

Alpena Com. C., Alpena, Mich.; 1952; pub; coed; 2; s

Altus Jr. C., Altus, Okla.; 1926; pub; coed; 2; s

Alvernia C., Reading, Pa.; 1958; pvt; wom; 4; s

Alverno C., Milwaukee, Wis.; 1887; pvt; wom; 4; s

Alvin Jr. C., Alvin, Tex.; 1949; pub; coed; 2; s

Amarillo C., Amarillo, Tex.; 1929; pub; coed; 2; M

American International C., Springfield, Mass.; 1885; pvt; coed; 4; s

American River C. (Los Rios Jr. C. District), Sacramento, Calif.; 1955; pub; coed; 2; L

American U., Washington, D.C.; 1893; pvt; coed; 4; L

Amherst C., Amherst, Mass.; 1821; pvt; men; 4; s

Ancilla Domini C., Donaldson, Ind.; 1937; pvt; coed; 2; s

Anderson C., Anderson, Ind.; 1917; pvt; coed; 4; s

Anderson C., Anderson, S.C.; 1930; pvt; coed; 2; s

Andrew C., Cuthbert, Ga.; 1917; pvt; coed; 2; s

Andrews U., Berrien Springs, Mich.; 1874; pvt; coed; 4; s

Angelina C., Lufkin Tex.; 1966; pub; coed; 2; s

Angelo State U., San Angelo, Tex.; 1928; pvt; coed; 4; M

Anna Maria C., Paxton, Mass.; 1946; pvt; wom; 4; s

Anne Arundel Com. C., Arnold, Md.; 1960; pub; coed; 2; s

Annhurst C., Woodstock, Conn.; 1941; pvt; wom; 4; s

Anoka Ramsey State Jr. C., Coon Rapids, Minn.; 1965; pub; coed; 2; s

Antelope Valley C., Lancaster, Calif.; 1929; pub; coed; 2; M

Antioch C., Yellow Springs, Ohio; 1852; pvt; coed; 4; s

Appalachian State U., Boone, N.C.; 1903; pub; coed; 4; M

Aquinas C., Grand Rapids, Mich.; 1886; pvt; coed; 4; s

Aquinas Jr. C., Nashville, Tenn.; 1961; pvt; coed; 2; s

Arapahoe Jr. C., Littleton, Colo.; 1965; pub; coed; 2; s

Area Eleven Com. C., Ankeny, Iowa
  Boone Jr. C., Boone; 1927; pub; coed; 2; s
  Des Moines Area Com. C., Ankeny; 1966; pub; coed; 2; L

Area Six Com. C. District, Marshalltown, Iowa
  Ellsworth C., Iowa Falls; 1928; pub; coed; 2; s
  Marshalltown Com. C., Marshalltown; 1927; pub; coed; 2; s

Area Ten Com. C. (See Kirkwood Com. C.)

Arizona State C. (See Northern Arizona U.)

Arizona State U., Tempe, Ariz.; 1885; pub; coed; 4; L

Arizona, U. of, Tucson, Ariz.; 1885; pub; coed; 4; L

Arizona Western C., Yuma, Ariz.; 1961; pub; coed; 2; s

Arkansas A&M C., College Heights, Ark.; 1909; pub; coed; 4; s

Arkansas, A, M & Normal C. of, Pine Bluff, Ark.; 1873; pub; coed; 4; M

Arkansas at Little Rock, U. of; 1927; pvt; coed; 4; M

Arkansas C., Batesville, Ark.; 1872; pvt; coed; 4; s

Arkansas Polytechnic C., Russellville, Ark.; 1909; pub; coed; 4; s

Arkansas, State C. of, Conway; 1907; pub; coed; 4; M

Arkansas State U., State University, Ark.; 1909; pub; coed; 4; M
  Beebe Branch; 1927; pub; coed; 2; s

Arkansas, U. of, Fayetteville, Ark.; 1871; pub; coed; 4; M

Armstrong State C., Savannah, Ga.; 1935; pub; coed; 4; s

Aroostook State C., Presque Isle, Me.; 1903; pub; coed; 4; s

Asbury C., Wilmore, Ky.; 1890; pvt; coed; 4; s

Ashland C., Ashland, Ohio; 1878; pvt; coed; 4; M

Assumption C., Worcester, Mass.; 1917; pvt; men; 4; s

Athenaeum of Ohio, The, Cincinnati, Ohio; 1829; pvt; men; 4; s

Athens C., Athens, Ala.; 1822; pvt; coed; 4; s

1567

Atlanta U. Center, Atlanta, Ga.
  Atlanta U.; 1865; pvt; coed; 4; s
  Clark C.; 1869; pvt; coed; 4; s
  Morehouse C.; 1867; pvt; men; 4; s
  Morris Brown C.; 1881; pvt; coed; 4; s
  Spelman C.; 1881; pvt; wom; 4; s
Atlantic Christian C., Wilson, N.C.; 1902; pvt; coed; 4; s
Atlantic Com. C., Mays Landing, N.J.; 1964; pub; coed; 2; s
Atlantic Union C., South Lancaster, Mass.; 1882; pvt; coed; 4; s
Auburn Com. C., Auburn, N.Y.; 1953; pub; coed; 2; M
Auburn U., Auburn, Ala.; 1856; pub; coed; 4; L
Augsburg C., Minneapolis, Minn.; 1869; pvt; coed; 4; s
Augusta C., Augusta, Ga.; 1910; pub; coed; 4; M
Augustana C., Rock Island, Ill.; 1860; pvt; coed; 4; s
Augustana C., Sioux Falls, S. Dak.; 1860; pvt; coed; 4; s
Aurora C., Aurora, Ill.; 1893; pvt; coed; 4; s
Austin C., Sherman, Tex.; 1849; pvt; coed; 4; s
Austin Peay State U., Clarksville, Tenn.; 1927; pub; coed; 4; M
Austin State Jr. C., Austin, Minn.; 1939; pub; coed; 2; s
Averett C., Danville, Va.; 1914; pvt; wom; 2; s
Avila C., Kansas City, Mo.; 1916; pvt; wom; 4; s
Azusa Pacific C., Azusa, Calif.; 1899; pvt; coed; 4; s

Babson C., Babson Park, Mass.; 1919; pvt; coed; 4; s
Bacone C., Bacone, Okla.; 1927; pvt; coed; 2; s
Baker U., Baldwin City, Kans.; 1858; pvt; coed; 4; s
Bakersfield C. (Kern Jr. C. District), Bakersfield, Calif.; 1913; pub; coed; 2; L
Baldwin-Wallace C., Berea, Ohio; 1845; pvt; coed; 4; M
Ball State U., Muncie, Ind.; 1918; pub; coed; 4; L
Baltimore, Com. C. of, Baltimore, Md.; 1947; pub; coed; 2; M
Barat C., Lake Forest, Ill.; 1857; pvt; wom; 4; s
Barber-Scotia C., Concord, N.C.; 1867; pvt; coed; 4; s
Bard C., Annandale-on-Hudson, N.Y.; 1860; pvt; coed; 4; s
Barnard C. (See Columbia U.)
Barrington C., Barrington, R.I.; 1900; pvt; coed; 4; s
Barry C., Miami, Fla.; 1940; pvt; coed; 4; s
Barstow C., Barstow, Calif.; 1959; pub; coed; 2; s
Bartlesville Wesleyan C., Bartlesville, Okla.; 1957; pvt; coed; 2; s
Bates C., Lewiston, Me.; 1855; pvt.; coed; 4; s
Bay de Noc Com. C., Escanaba, Mich.; 1962; pub; coed; 2; s
Baylor U., Waco, Tex.; 1845; pvt; coed; 4; M
Bay Path Jr. C., Longmeadow, Mass.; 1949; pvt; coed; 2; s
Beaver C., Glenside, Pa.; 1853; pvt; wom; 4; s
Beaver County, Com. C. of, Freedom, Pa.; 1966; pub; coed; 2; s
Becker Jr. C., Worcester, Mass.; 1942; pvt; coed; 2; s
Beckley C., Beckley, W. Va.; 1933; pvt; coed; 2; s
Bee County C., Beeville, Tex.; 1965; pub; coed; 2; s
Belhaven C., Jackson, Miss.; 1894; pvt; coed; 4; s
Bellarmine-Ursuline C., Louisville, Ky.; 1864; pvt; coed; 4; s
Belleville Area C., Belleville, Ill.; 1946; pub; coed; 2; M
Bellevue Com. C., Bellevue, Wash.; 1965; pub; coed; 2; s
Belmont Abbey C., Belmont, N.C.; 1876; pvt; coed; 4; s
Belmont C., Nashville, Tenn.; 1951; pvt; coed; 4; s
Beloit C., Beloit, Wis.; 1846; pvt; coed; 4; s
Bemidji State C., Bemidji, Minn.; 1913; pub; coed; 4; M
Benedict C., Columbia, S.C.; 1870; pvt; coed; 4; s
Bennett C., Greensboro, N.C.; 1873; pvt; wom; 4; s
Bennett C., Millbrook, N.Y.; 1935; pvt; wom; 2; s
Bennington C., Bennington, Vt.; 1925; pvt; coed; 4; s
Bentley C., Waltham, Mass.; 1917; pvt; coed; 4; M
Berea C., Berea, Ky.; 1855; pvt; coed; 4; s
Bergen Com. C., Paramus, N.J.; 1965; pub; coed; 2; s
Berkshire Com. C., Pittsfield, Mass.; 1960; pub; coed; 2; s
Bernard M. Baruch C. (See City U. of New York)
Berry C., Mount Berry, Ga.; 1902; pvt; coed; 4; s
Bethany Bible C., Santa Cruz, Calif.; 1919; pvt; coed; 4; s
Bethany C., Lindsborg, Kans.; 1881; pvt; coed; 4; s
Bethany C., Bethany, W. Va.; 1840; pvt; coed; 4; s
Bethany Lutheran C., Mankato, Minn.; 1926; pvt; coed; 2; s
Bethany-Nazarene C., Bethany, Okla.; 1899; pvt; coed; 4; s
Bethel C., North Newton, Kans.; 1887; pvt; coed; 4; s
Bethel C., St. Paul, Minn.; 1871; pvt; coed; 4; s
Bethel C., McKenzie, Tenn.; 1842; pvt; coed; 4; s
Bethune-Cookman C., Daytona Beach, Fla.; 1872; pvt; coed; 4; s
Big Bend Com. C., Moses Lake, Wash.; 1962; pub; coed; 2; s
Biola C., La Mirada, Calif.; 1907; pvt; coed; 4; s
Birmingham-Southern C., Birmingham, Ala.; 1856; pvt; coed; 4; s
Biscayne C., Miami, Fla.; 1962; pvt; men; 4; s

Bishop C., Dallas, Tex.; 1881; pvt; coed; 4; s
Bismarck Jr. C., Bismarck, N. Dak.; 1939; pub; coed; 2; s
Black Hawk C., Moline, Ill.; 1962; pub; coed; 2; M
Black Hawk East C., Kewanee, Ill.; 1967; pub; coed; 2; s
Black Hills State C., Spearfish, S. Dak.; 1881; pub; coed; 4; s
Blackburn C., Carlinville, Ill., 1857; pvt; coed; 4; s
Blinn Jr. C., Brenham, Tex.; 1927; pub; coed; 4; s
Bloomfield C., Bloomfield, N.J.; 1868; pvt; coed; 4; s
Bloomsburg State C., Bloomsburg, Pa.; 1839; pub; coed; 4; M
Bluefield C., Bluefield, Va.; 1922; pvt; coed; 2; s
Bluefield State C., Bluefield, W. Va.; 1895; pub; coed; 4; s
Blue Mountain C., Blue Mountain, Miss.; 1873; pvt; coed; 4; s
Blue Mountain Com. C., Pendleton, Ore.; 1962; pub; coed; 2; s
Blue Ridge Com. C., Weyers Cave, Va.; 1966; pub; coed; 2; s
Bluffton C., Bluffton, Ohio; 1899; pvt; coed; 4; s
Boise State C., Boise, Ida.; 1932; pub; coed; 4; M
Borough of Manhattan Com. C. (See City U. of New York)
Boston C., Chestnut Hill, Mass.; 1863; pvt; coed; 4; L
Boston State C., Boston, Mass.; 1852; pub; coed; 4; M
Boston U., Boston, Mass.; 1839; pvt; coed; 4; L
Bowdoin C., Brunswick, Me.; 1794; pvt; men; 4; s
Bowie State C., Bowie, Md.; 1867; pub; coed; 4; s
Bowling Green State U., Bowling Green, Ohio; 1910; pub; coed; 4; L
Bradford Jr. C., Bradford, Mass.; 1932; pvt; wom; 2; s
Bradley U., Peoria, Ill.; 1896; pvt; coed; 4; M
Brainerd State Jr. C., Brainerd, Minn.; 1938; pub; coed; 2; s
Brandeis U., Waltham, Mass.; 1948; pvt; coed; 4; M
Brandywine C., Wilmington, Del.; 1965; pvt; coed; 2; s
Brazosport Jr. C., Freeport, Tex.; 1967; coed; 2; s
Brenau C., Gainesville, Ga.; 1878; pvt; wom; 4; s
Brescia C., Owensboro, Ky.; 1878; pvt; coed; 4; s
Brevard C., Brevard, N.C.; 1934; pvt; coed; 2; s
Brevard Jr. C., Cocoa, Fla.; 1960; pub; coed; 2; M
Brewton Parker C., Mount Vernon, Ga.; 1927; pvt; coed; 2; s
Briar Cliff C., Sioux City, Iowa; 1930; pvt; coed; 4; s
Briarcliff C., Briarcliff Manor, N.Y.; 1903; pvt; wom; 4; s
Bridgeport, U. of, Bridgeport, Conn.; 1927; pvt; coed; 4; L
Bridgewater C., Bridgewater, Va.; 1880; pvt; coed; 4; s
Bridgewater State C., Bridgewater, Mass.; 1840; pub; coed; 4; M
Brigham Young U., Provo, Utah; 1875; pvt; coed; 4; L
Bristol Com. C., Fall River, Mass.; 1965; pub; coed; 2; s
Bronx Com. C. (See City U. of New York)
Brooklyn C. (See City U. of New York)
Broome Tech. Com. C., Binghamton, N.Y.; 1946; pub; coed; 2; M
Broward Jr. C., Ft. Lauderdale, Fla.; 1959; pub; coed; 2; M
Brown U., Providence, R.I.; 1764; pvt; men; 4; M
  Pembroke C., Providence, R.I.; 1891; pvt; wom; 4; s
Brunswick C., Brunswick, Ga.; 1961; pub; coed; 2; s
Bryant C., Providence, R.I.; 1863; pvt; coed; 4; s
Bryn Mawr C., Bryn Mawr, Pa.; 1880; pvt; wom; 4; s
Bucknell U., Lewisburg, Pa.; 1846; pvt; coed; 4; M
Bucks County Com. C., Newton, Pa.; 1965; pub; coed; 2; M
Buena Vista C., Storm Lake, Iowa; 1891; pvt; coed; 4; s
Butler County Com. C., Butler, Pa.; 1965; pub; coed; 2; s
Butler County Com. Jr. C., El Dorado, Kans.; 1927; pub; coed; 2; s
Butler U., Indianapolis, Ind.; 1850; pvt; coed; 4; M
Butte C., Durham, Calif.; 1967; pub.; coed; 2; s

Cabrillo C., Aptos, Calif.; 1958; pub; coed; 2; M
Caldwell C. for Women, Caldwell, N.J.; 1939; pvt; wom; 4; s
Calhoun State Jr. C., Decatur, Ala.; 1965; pub; coed; 2; s
California Baptist C., Riverside, Calif.; 1950; pvt; coed; 4; s
California Inst. of Tech., Pasadena, Calif.; 1891; pvt; men; 4; s
California Lutheran C., Thousand Oaks, Calif.; 1959; pvt; coed; 4; s
California State C., California, Pa.; 1852; pub; coed; 4; M
California State C. System, The
  California State C. at Dominguez Hills; 1960; pub; coed; 4; s
  California State C. at Fullerton; 1957; pub; coed; 4; L
  California State C. at Hayward; 1957; pub; coed; 4; L
  California State C. at Long Beach; 1949; pub; coed; 4; L
  California State C. at Los Angeles; 1947; pub; coed; 4; L
  California State C. at Northridge; 1956; pub; coed; 4; L
  California State C. at San Bernardino; 1960; pub; coed; 4; s

California State Polytechnic C., Kellogg-Voorhis, Pomona; 1938; pub; coed; 4; M
California State Polytechnic C., San Luis Obispo; 1901; pub; coed; 4; L
Chico State C., 1887; pub; coed; 4; L
Fresno State C.; 1911; pub; coed; 4; L
Humboldt State C., Arcata; 1913; pub; coed; 4; M
Sacramento State C.; 1947; pub; coed; 4; L
San Diego State C.; 1897; pub; coed; 4; L
San Francisco State C.; 1899; pub; coed; 4; L
San Jose State C.; 1857; pub; coed; 4; L
Sonoma State C., Rohnert Park; 1960; pub; coed; 4; M
Stanislaus State C., Turlock; 1957; pub; coed; 4; s
California, U. of, Berkeley, Calif.; 1868; pub; coed; 4; L
Davis Campus; 1906; pub; coed; 4; L
Irvine Campus; 1960; pub; coed; 4; M
Los Angeles Campus; 1881; pub; coed; 4; L
Riverside Campus; 1907; pub; coed; 4; M
San Diego Campus, La Jolla; 1903; pub; coed; 4; M
Santa Barbara Campus; 1891; pub; coed; 4; L
Santa Cruz Campus; 1961; pub; coed; 4; s
California Western U. (See United States International U.)
Calvin C., Grand Rapids, Mich.; 1876; pvt; coed; 4; M
Camden County C., Blackwood, N.J.; 1966; pub; coed; 2; s
Cameron State C., Lawton, Okla.; 1909; pub; coed; 4; M
Campbell C., Buies Creek, N.C.; 1887; pvt; coed; 4; s
Campbellsville C., Campbellsville, Ky.; 1906; pvt; coed; 4; s
Canada C. (San Mateo Jr. C. District), Redwood City, Calif.; 1968; coed; 2; M
Canal Zone C., Balboa Heights, C. Z.; 1933; pub; coed; 2; s
Canisius C., Buffalo, N.Y.; 1870; pvt; coed; 4; M
Cape Cod Com. C., Hyannis, Mass.; 1960; pub; coed; 2; s
Capital U., Columbus, Ohio; 1850; pvt; coed; 4; s
Cardinal Cushing C., Brookline, Mass.; 1952; pvt; wom; 4; s
Cardinal Glennon C., St. Louis, Mo.; 1818; pvt; men; 4; s
Cardinal Stritch C., The, Milwaukee, Wis.; 1934; pvt; wom; 4; s
Carleton C., Northfield, Minn.; 1866; pvt; coed; 4; s
Carlow C., Pittsburgh, Pa.; 1929; pvt; wom; 4; s
Carl Sandburg C., Galesburg, Ill.; 1966; pub; coed; 2; s
Carnegie-Mellon U., Pittsburgh, Pa.; 1900; pvt; coed; 4; M
Carnegie Inst. of Tech.; 1900; pvt; coed; 4; M
Margaret Morrison Carnegie C., 1905; pvt; wom; 4; s
Carroll C., Helena, Mont.; 1909; pvt; coed; 4; s
Carroll C., Waukesha, Wis.; 1840; pvt; coed; 4; s
Carson-Newman C., Jefferson City, Tenn.; 1851; pvt; coed; 4; s
Carthage C., Kenosha, Wis.; 1847; pvt; coed; 4; s
Case Western Reserve U., Cleveland, Ohio
Adelbert C., Western Reserve U.; 1826; pvt; men; 4; s
Case Institute of Tech.; 1880; pvt; coed; 4; s
Flora Stone Mather C., Western Reserve U.; 1826; pvt; wom; 4; s
Casper C., Casper, Wyo.; 1945; pub; coed; 2; M
Castleton State C., Castleton, Vt.; 1787; pub; coed; 4; s
Catawba C., Salisbury, N.C.; 1851; pvt; coed; 4; s
Catherine Spaulding C., Louisville, Ky.; 1920; pvt; coed; 4; s
Catholic Teachers C., Providence, R.I.; 1929; pvt; wom; 4; s
Catholic U. of America, The, Washington, D.C.; 1887; pvt; coed; 4; M
Catholic U. of Puerto Rico, Ponce, P.R.; 1948; pvt; coed; 4; M
Catonsville Com. C., Catonsville, Md.; 1957; pub; coed; 2; M
Cazenovia C., Cazenovia, N.Y.; 1942; pvt; wom; 2; s
Cedar Crest C., Allentown, Pa.; 1867; pvt; wom; 4; s
Centenary C., Shreveport, La.; 1825; pvt; coed; 4; s
Centenary C. for Women, Hackettstown, N.J.; 1929; pvt; wom; 2; s
Centerville Com. C., Centerville, Iowa; 1930; pub; coed; 2; s
Central Baptist C., Conway, Ark.; 1952; pvt; coed; 2; s
Central Bible C., Springfield, Mo.; 1922; pvt; coed; 4; s
Central C., Pella, Iowa; 1853; pvt; coed; 4; s
Central C., McPherson, Kans.; 1914; pvt; coed; 2; s
Central Connecticut State C., New Britain, Conn.; 1849; pub; coed; 4; L
Central Florida Jr. C., Ocala, Fla.; 1958; pub; coed; 2; s
Centralia C., Centralia, Wash.; 1925; pub; coed; 2; s
Central Methodist C., Fayette, Mo.; 1854; pvt; coed; 4; s
Central Michigan U., Mt. Pleasant, Mich.; 1892; pub; coed; 4; L
Central Missouri State C., Warrensburg, Mo.; 1871; pub; coed; 4; L

Central Oregon Com. C., Bend, Ore.; 1949; pub; coed; 2; s
Central Piedmont Com. C., Charlotte, N.C.; 1964; pub; coed; 2; s
Central State C., Edmond, Okla.; 1890; pub; coed; 4; M
Central State U., Wilberforce, Ohio; 1887; pub; coed; 4; M
Central Texas Union Jr. C., Kileen, Tex.; 1965; pub; coed; 2; s
Central Virginia Com. C., Lynchburg, Va; 1966; pub; coed; 2; s
Central Washington State C., Ellensburg, Wash.; 1890; pub; coed; 4; M
Central Wyoming C., Riverton, Wyo.; 1966; pub; coed; 2; s
Central YMCA Com. C., Chicago, Ill.; 1960; pvt; coed; 2; M
Centre C. of Kentucky, Danville, Ky.; 1819; pvt; coed; 4; s
Cerritos C., Norwalk, Calif.; 1955; pub; coed; 2; L
Chabot C., Hayward, Calif.; 1961; pub; coed; 2; L
Chadron State C., Chadron, Nebr.; 1910; pub; coed; 4; s
Chaffey C., Alta Loma, Calif.; 1922; pub; coed; 2; M
Chamberlayne Jr. C., Boston, Mass.; 1892; pvt; coed; 2; s
Chaminade C. of Honolulu, Honolulu, Hawaii; 1955; pvt.; coed; 4; s
Champlain C., Burlington, Vt.; 1958; pvt; coed; 2; s
Chapman C., Orange, Calif.; 1861; pvt; coed; 4; s
Charles County Com. C., La Plata, Md.; 1958; pub; coed; 2; s
Charleston, C. of, Charleston, S.C.; 1770; pvt; coed; 4; s
Chatham C., Pittsburgh, Pa.; 1869; pvt; wom; 4; s
Chattanooga, U. of (See Tennessee, U. of)
Chesapeake C., Wye Mills, Md.; 1965; pub; coed; 2; s
Chestnut Hill C., Philadelphia, Pa.; 1858; pvt; wom; 4; s
Cheyney State C., Cheyney, Pa.; 1837; pub; coed; 4; s
Chicago City C., Chicago, Ill.
Amundsen-Mayfair Campus; 1956; pub; coed; 2; M
Bogan Campus; 1960; pub; coed; 2; M
Fenger Campus; 1958; pub; coed; 2; M
Kennedy-King Campus; 1934; pub; coed; 2; M
Loop Campus; 1962; pub; coed; 2; M
Malcolm Campus; 1911; pub; coed; 2; M
Southeast Campus; 1911; pub; coed; 2; M
Wright Campus; 1934; pub; coed; 2; L
Chicago State C., Chicago, Ill.; 1869; pub; coed; 4; M
Chicago, The U. of, Chicago, Ill.; 1890; pvt; coed; 4; L
Chico State C. (See California State C. System)
Chipola Jr. C., Marianna, Fla.; 1947; pub; coed; 2; s
Chowan C., Murfreesboro, N.C.; 1949; pvt; coed; 2; s
Christian Brothers C., Memphis, Tenn.; 1871; pvt; men; 4; s
Christian C., Columbia, Mo.; 1851; pvt; wom; 2; s
Church C. of Hawaii, The, Laie, Hawaii; 1955; pvt; coed; 4; s
Cincinnati, U. of, Cincinnati, Ohio; 1819; pub; coed; 4; L
Cisco Jr. C., Cisco, Tex.; 1941; pub; coed; 2; s
Citadel, The, Charleston, S.C.; 1842; pub; coed; 4; s
Citrus C., Azusa, Calif.; 1915; pub; coed; 2; M
City C. of San Francisco, Calif.; 1935; pub; coed; 2; L
City U. of New York, The
Bernard M. Baruch C., New York, N.Y.; 1919; pub; coed; 4; L
Borough of Manhattan Com. C., New York, N.Y.; 1963; pub; coed; 2; M
Bronx Com. C., 1957; pub; coed; 2; L
Brooklyn C., Brooklyn, N.Y.; 1930; pub; coed; 4; L
City C., New York, N.Y.; 1847; pub; coed; 4; L
Herbert H. Lehman C., Bronx, N.Y.; 1931; pub; coed; 4; L
Hunter C., New York, N.Y.; 1870; pub; coed; 4; L
Kingsborough Com. C., Brooklyn, N.Y.; 1963; pub; coed; 2; M
New York City Com. C., Brooklyn, N.Y.; 1963; pub; coed; 2; L
Queensborough Com. C., Bayside, N.Y.; 1958; pub; coed; 2; L
Queens C., Flushing, N.Y.; 1931; pub; coed; 4; L
Richmond C., Staten Island, N.Y.; 1965; pub; coed; 4; s
Staten Island Com. C., Staten Island, N.Y.; 1955; pub; coed; 2; M
York C., Flushing, N.Y.; 1966; pub; coed; 4; s
Clackamus Com. C., Oregon City, Ore.; 1966; pub; coed; 2; s
Claflin C., Orangeburg, S.C.; 1869; pub; coed; 4; s
Claremont Colleges, The, Claremont, Calif.
Claremont Men's C.; 1946; pvt; men; 4; s
Harvey Mudd C.; 1955; pvt; coed; 4; s
Pitzer C.; 1963; pvt; wom; 4; s
Pomona C.; 1887; pvt; coed; 4; s
Scripps C.; 1926; pvt; wom; 4; s
Clarendon Jr. C., Clarendon, Tex.; 1927; pub; coed; 2; s

Clarion State C., Clarion, Pa.; 1866; pub; coed; 4; M
Clark C., Atlanta, Ga. **(See Atlanta U. Center)**
Clark C., Vancouver, Wash.; 1933; pub; coed; 2; M
Clarke C., Dubuque, Iowa; 1843; pvt; coed; 4; s
Clarke Memorial C., Newton, Miss.; 1919; pvt; coed; 2; s
Clark U., Worcester, Mass.; 1887; pvt; coed; 4; s
Clarkson C. of Tech., Potsdam, N.Y.; 1896; pvt; coed; 4; M
Clatsop County Com. C., Astoria, Ore.; 1962; pub; coed; 2; s
Cleary C., Ypsilanti, Mich.; 1883; pvt; coed; 4; s
Clemson U., Clemson, S.C.; 1889; pub; coed; 4; M
Cleveland State Com. C., Cleveland, Tenn.; 1965; pub; coed; 2; s
Cleveland State U., Cleveland, Ohio; 1881; pub; coed; 4; L
Coahoma Jr. C., Clarksdale, Miss.; 1949; pub; coed; 2; s
Coalinga C., Coalinga, Calif.; 1932; pub; coed; 2; s
Cochise C., Douglas, Ariz.; 1961; pub; coed; 2; s
Coe C., Cedar Rapids, Iowa; 1851; pvt; coed; 4; s
Coffeyville Com. Jr. C., Coffeyville, Kans.; 1923; pub; coed; 2; s
Coker C. for Women, Hartsville, S.C.; 1894; pvt; wom; 4; s
Colby C., Waterville, Me.; 1813; pvt; coed; 4; s
Colby Com. Jr. C., Colby, Kans.; 1964; pub; coed; 2; s
Colby Jr. C. for Women, New London, N.H.; 1928; pvt; wom; 2; s
Colgate U., Hamilton, N.Y.; 1819; pvt; coed; 4; s
Colorado C., Colorado Springs, Colo.; 1874; pvt; coed; 4; s
Colorado School of Mines, Golden, Colo.; 1869; pub; coed; 4; s
Colorado State U., Fort Collins, Colo.; 1870; pub; coed; 4; L
Colorado, U. of, Boulder, Colo.; 1861; pub; coed; 4; L
Colorado Woman's C. (See Temple Buell C.)
Columbia Basin C., Pasco, Wash.; 1955; pub; coed; 2; M
Columbia C., Columbia, S.C.; 1859; pvt; coed; 4; s
Columbia Jr. C. (Yosemite Jr. C. District), Columbia, Calif.; 1967; pub; coed; 2; s
Columbia State Com. C., Columbia, Tenn.; 1966; pub; coed; 2; s
Columbia Union C., Takoma Park, Md.; 1904; pvt; coed; 4; s
Columbia U., New York, N.Y.; 1754; pvt; coed; 4; L
  Barnard C., N.Y.; 1889; pvt; wom; 4; s
  Columbia C., N.Y.; 1754; pvt; men; 4; M
  Teachers C., N.Y.; 1887; pvt; coed; 4; L
Columbus C., Columbus, Ga.; 1958; pub; coed; 2; s
Com. C. of Baltimore, Baltimore, Md.; 1947; pub; coed; 2; M
Compton C., Compton, Calif.; 1927; pub; coed; 2; M
Concord C., Athens, W. Va.; 1872; pub; coed; 4; s
Concordia C., Moorhead, Minn.; 1891; pvt; coed; 4; s
Concordia C., St. Paul, Minn.; 1893; pvt; coed; 4; s
Concordia C., Bronxville, N.Y.; 1936; pvt; coed; 2; s
Concordia C., Portland, Ore.; 1950; pvt; coed; 2; s
Concordia C., Milwaukee, Wis.; 1892; pvt; coed; 2; s
Concordia Lutheran Jr. C., Ann Arbor, Mich.; 1962; pvt; coed; 2; s
Concordia Senior C., Fort Wayne, Ind.; 1839; pvt; men; 4; s
Concordia Teachers C., River Forest, Ill.; 1864; pvt; coed; 4; s
Concordia Teachers C., Seward, Nebr.; 1894; pvt; coed; 4; s
Connecticut C., New London, Conn.; 1911; pvt; coed; 4; s
Connecticut, Jr. C. of, Bridgeport, Conn.; 1927; pvt; coed; 2; M
Connecticut, U. of, Storrs, Conn.; 1881; pub; coed; 4; L
Connors State Agric. C., Warner, Okla.; 1908; pub; coed; 2; s
Contra Costa C. (Contra Costa Jr. C. District), San Pablo, Calif.; 1948; pub; coed; 2; M
Converse C., Spartanburg, S.C.; 1889; pvt; wom; 4; s
Cooke County Jr. C., Gainesville, Tex.; 1924; pub; coed; 2; s
Cooper Union, New York, N.Y.; 1859; pvt; coed; 4; M
Copiah Lincoln Jr. C., Wesson, Miss.; 1928; pub; coed; 2; s
Coppin State C., Baltimore, Md.; 1900; pub; coed; 4; s
Cornell C., Mount Vernon, Iowa; 1853; pvt; coed; 4; s
Cornell U., Ithaca, N.Y.; 1865; pvt; coed; 4; L
Corning Com. C., Corning, N.Y.; 1957; pub; coed; 2; M
Corpus Christi, U. of, Corpus Christi, Tex.; 1947; pvt; coed; 4; s
Cottey C., Nevada, Mo.; 1887; pvt; wom; 2; s
Cowley County Com. Jr. C., Arkansas City, Kans.; 1922; pub; coed; 2; s
Creighton U., Omaha, Nebr.; 1878; pvt; coed; 4; M
Crowder C., Neosho, Mo.; 1963; pub; coed; 2; s
Cuesta C., San Luis Obispo, Calif.; 1964; pub; coed; 2; M
Culver-Stockton C., Canton, Mo.; 1853; pvt; coed; 4; s

Cumberland C., Williamsburg, Ky.; 1889; pvt; coed; 4; s
Cumberland C. of Tennessee, Lebanon, Tenn.; 1956; pvt; coed; 2; s
Cumberland County C., Vineland, N.J.; 1964; pub; coed; 2; s
Cuyahoga Com. C., Cuyahoga, Ohio
  Metropolitanian Campus, Cleveland; 1962; pub; coed; 2; L
  Western Campus, Parma; 1962; pub; coed; 2; M
C. W. Post C. (See Long Island U.)
Cypress C. (North Orange Jr. C. District), Cypress, Calif.; 1966; pub; coed; 2; M

Dakota Wesleyan U., Mitchell, S. Dak.; 1885; pvt; coed; 4; s
Dallas Baptist C., Dallas, Tex.; 1965; pvt; coed; 4; s
Dallas, U. of, Dallas Station, Tex.; 1955; pvt; men; 4; s
Dalton Jr. C., Dalton, Ga.; 1963; pub; coed; 2; s
Dana C., Blair, Nebr.; 1884; pvt; coed; 4; s
Danbury State C. (See Western Connecticut State C.)
Danville Jr. C., Danville, Ill.; 1949; pub; coed; 2; s
Dartmouth C., Hanover, N.H.; 1769; pvt; men; 4; s
David Lipscomb C., Nashville, Tenn.; 1891; pvt; coed; 4; s
Davidson C., Davidson, N.C.; 1836; pvt; men; 4; s
Davidson County Com. C., Lexington, N.C.; 1965; pub; coed; 2; s
Davis and Elkins C., Elkins, W. Va.; 1903; pvt; coed; 4; s
Dawson C., Glendive, Mont.; 1940; pub; coed; 2; s
Daytona Beach Jr. C., Daytona Beach, Fla.; 1958; pub; coed; 2; s
Dayton, U. of, Dayton, Ohio; 1850; pvt; coed; 4; L
Dean Jr. C., Franklin, Mass.; 1941; pvt; coed; 2; s
De Anza C. (Foothill Jr. C. District), Cupertino, Calif.; 1957; pub; coed; 2; M
Defiance C., Defiance, Ohio; 1850; pvt; coed; 4; s
De Kalb C., Clarkston, Ga.; 1962; pub; coed; 2; M
Delaware County Com. C. of Media, Pa.; 1967; pub; coed; 2; s
Delaware State C., Dover, Del.; 1891; pub; coed; 4; s
Delaware, U. of, Newark, Del.; 1743; pub; coed; 4; L
Delgado C., New Orleans, La.; 1961; pub; coed; 2; M
Del Mar C., Corpus Christi, Tex.; 1935; pub; coed; 2; M
Delta C., University Center, Mich.; 1958; pub; coed; 2; M
Delta State C., Cleveland, Miss.; 1924; pub; coed; 4; s
Denison U., Granville, Ohio; 1831; pvt; coed; 4; s
Denver, Com. C. of, Denver, Colo.; 1967; pub; coed; 2; s
Denver, U. of, Denver, Colo.; 1864; pvt; coed; 4; L
De Paul U., Chicago, Ill.; 1898; pvt; men; 4; L
DePauw U., Greencastle, Ind.; 1837; pvt; coed; 4; s
Desert, C. of the, Palm Desert, Calif.; 1958; pub; coed; 2; M
Detroit, U. of, Detroit, Mich.; 1877; pvt; coed; 4; L
Diablo Valley C. (Contra Costa Jr. C. District), Pleasant Hill, Calif.; 1950; pub; coed; 2; L
Dickinson C., Carlisle, Pa.; 1773; pvt; coed; 4; s
Dickinson State C., Dickinson, N. Dak.; 1922; pub; coed; 4; s
Dillard U., New Orleans, La.; 1869; pvt; coed; 4; s
District of Columbia Teachers C., Washington, D.C.; 1851; pub; coed; 4; s
Dixie C., St. George, Utah; 1916; pub; coed; 2; s
Doane C., Crete, Nebr.; 1858; pvt; coed; 4; s
Dodge City Com. Jr. C., Dodge City, Kans.; 1935; pub; coed; 2; s
Dominican C., Racine, Wis.; 1864; pvt; coed; 4; s
Dominican C. of San Rafael, San Rafael, Calif.; 1890; pvt; wom; 4; s
Donnelly C., Kansas City, Kans.; 1949; pvt; coed; 2; s
Douglass C. (See Rutgers, The State U.)
Drake U., Des Moines, Iowa; 1881; pvt; coed; 4; M
Drew U., Madison, N.J.; 1866; pvt; coed; 4; s
Drexel Inst. of Tech., Philadelphia, Pa.; 1891; pvt; coed; 4; L
Dropsie C., Philadelphia, Pa.; 1907; pvt; coed; 4; s
Drury C., Springfield, Mo.; 1873; pvt; coed; 4; s
Dubuque, U. of, Dubuque, Iowa; 1852; pvt; coed; 4; s
Duke U., Durham, N.C.; 1838; pvt; coed; 4; M
Dunbarton C. of Holy Cross, Washington, D.C.; 1935; pvt; wom; 4; s
Du Page, C. of, Glen Ellyn, Ill.; 1966; pub; coed; 2; M
Duquesne U., Pittsburgh, Pa.; 1878; pvt; coed; 4; M
Dutchess Com. C., Poughkeepsie, N.Y.; 1957; pub; coed; 2; L
D'Youville C., Buffalo, N.Y.; 1908; pvt; wom; 4; s

Earlham C., Richmond, Ind.; 1847; pvt; coed; 4; s
East Carolina U., Greenville, N.C.; 1907; pub; coed; 4; L
East Central Jr. C., Decatur, Miss.; 1928; pub; coed; 2; s
East Central State C., Ada, Okla.; 1909; pub; coed; 4; M
Eastern Arizona C., Thatcher, Ariz.; 1926; pub; coed; 2; s
Eastern Baptist C., St. Davids, Pa.; 1932; pvt; coed; 4; s
Eastern Connecticut State C., Willimantic, Conn.; 1889; pub; coed; 4; s

Eastern Illinois U., Charleston, Ill.; 1895; pub; coed; 4; M
Eastern Iowa Com. C.
  Clinton Campus, Clinton, Iowa; 1946; pub; coed; 2; s
  Muscatine Campus, Muscatine, Iowa; 1929; pub; coed; 2; s
  Scott Campus, Davenport, Iowa; 1966; pub; coed; 2; s
Eastern Kentucky U., Richmond, Ky.; 1906; pub; coed; 4; L
Eastern Mennonite C., Harrisonburg, Va.; 1917; pvt; coed; 4; s
Eastern Michigan U., Ypsilanti, Mich.; 1849; pub; coed; 4; L
Eastern Montana C., Billings, Mont.; 1925; pub; coed; 4; M
Eastern Nazarene C., Wollaston, Mass.; 1900; pvt; coed; 4; s
Eastern New Mexico U., Portales, N. Mex.; 1927; pub; coed; 4; M
  Clovis Com. C., Clovis, N. Mex.; 1960; pub; coed; 2; s
  Roswell Campus, Roswell, N. Mex.; 1967; pub; coed; 2; s
Eastern Oklahoma State C., Wilburton, Okla.; 1919; pub; coed; 2; s
Eastern Oregon C., La Grande, Ore.; 1929; pub; coed; 4; s
Eastern Utah, C. of, Price, Utah; 1937; pub; coed; 2; s
Eastern Washington State C., Cheney, Wash.; 1890; pub; coed; 4; M
East Los Angeles C., Los Angeles, Calif.; 1945; pub; coed; 2; L
East Mississippi Jr. C., Scooba, Miss.; 1927; pub; coed; 2; s
East Stroudsburg State C., East Stroudsburg, Pa.; 1893; pub; coed; 4; M
East Tennessee State U., Johnson City, Tenn; 1909; pub.; coed; 4; L
East Texas Baptist C., Marshall, Tex.; 1912; pvt; coed; 4; s
East Texas State U., Commerce, Tex.; 1889; pub; coed; 4; L
Edgecliff C., Cincinnati, Ohio; 1935; pvt; wom; 4; s
Edgewood C. of the Sacred Heart, Madison, Wis.; 1881; pvt; coed; 4; s
Edinboro State C., Edinboro, Pa.; 1856; pub; coed; 4; M
Edison Jr. C., Fort Myers, Fla.; 1962; pub; coed; 2; s
Edmonds Com. C., Lynnwood, Wash.; 1965; pub; coed; 2; s
El Camino C., El Camino College, Calif.; 1947; pub; coed; 2; L
El Centro C. (Dallas County Jr. C. District), Dallas, Tex.; 1965; pub; coed; 2; M
Elgin Com. C., Elgin, Ill.; 1949; pub; coed; 2; s
Elizabeth City State C., Elizabeth City, N.C.; 1891; pub.; coed; 4; s
Elizabeth Seton C., Yonkers, N.Y.; 1960; pvt; coed; 2; s
Elizabethtown C., Elizabethtown, Pa.; 1899; pvt; coed; 4; s
Elko Com. C., Elko, Nev.; 1967; pub; coed; 2; s
Elmhurst C., Elmhurst, Ill.; 1865; pvt; coed; 4; s
Elmira C., Elmira, N.Y.; 1855; pvt; coed; 4; s
Elon C., Elon College, N.C.; 1889; pvt; coed; 4; s
El Reno C., El Reno, Okla.; 1938; pub; coed; 2; s
Emerson C., Boston, Mass.; 1880; pvt; coed; 4; s
Emmanuel C., Franklin Springs, Ga.; 1933; pvt; coed; 2; s
Emmanuel C., Boston, Mass.; 1919; pvt; wom; 4; s
Emmetsburg Com. C., Emmetsburg, Iowa; 1930; pub; coed; 2; s
Emory and Henry C., Emory, Va.; 1836; pvt; coed; 4; s
Emory U., Atlanta, Ga.; 1836; pvt; coed; 4; M
Emporia, C. of, Emporia, Kans.; 1882; pvt; coed; 4; s
Endicott Jr. C., Beverly, Mass.; 1939; pvt; coed; 2; s
Enterprise State Jr. C., Enterprise, Ala.; 1963; pub; coed; 2; s
Erie Com. C., Buffalo, N.Y.; 1946; pub; coed; 2; s
Erskine C., Due West, S.C.; 1839; pvt; coed; 4; s
Essex Com. C., Baltimore, Md.; 1957; pub; coed; 2; s
Essex County C., Newark N.J.; 1966; pub; coed; 2; M
Eureka C., Eureka, Ill.; 1848; pvt; coed; 4; s
Evangel C., Springfield, Mo.; 1955; pvt; coed; 4; s
Evansville, U. of, Evansville, Ind.; 1854; pvt; coed; 4; M
Everett Com. C., Everett, Wash.; 1941; pub; coed; 2; M

Fairbury Jr. C., Fairbury, Nebr.; 1941; pub; coed; 2; s
Fairfield U., Fairfield, Conn.; 1942; pvt; men; 4; M
Fairleigh Dickinson U., Rutherford, N.J.; 1941; pvt; coed; 4; L
Fairmont State C., Fairmont, W. Va.; 1867; pub; coed; 4; s
Farmington State C., Farmington, Me.; 1863; pub; coed; 4; s
Fashion Inst. of Tech., New York, N.Y.; 1951; pub; coed; 2; M
Fayetteville State C., Fayetteville, N.C.; 1867; pub; coed; 4; s
Felician C., The, Chicago, Ill.; 1953; pvt; wom; 2; s
Fenn C. (See Cleveland State U.)

Fergus Falls State Jr. C., Fergus Falls, Minn.; 1960; pub; coed; 2; s
Ferris State C., Big Rapids, Mich.; 1884; pub; coed; 4; L
Ferrum Jr. C., Ferrum, Va.; 1926; pvt; coed; 2; s
Finch C., New York, N.Y.; 1900; pvt; wom; 4; s
Findlay C., Findlay, Ohio; 1882; pvt; coed; 4; s
Fisher Jr. C., Boston, Mass.; 1952; pvt; wom; 2; s
Fisk U., Nashville, Tenn.; 1865; pvt; coed; 4; s
Fitchburg State C., Fitchburg, Mass.; 1894; pub; coed; 4; M
Flathead Valley Com. C., Kalispell, Mont.; 1967; pub; coed; 2; s
Flat River, Jr. C. of, Flat River, Mo.; 1922; pub; coed; 2; s
Flint Com. Jr. C., Flint, Mich.; 1923; pub; coed; 2; L
Florence State U., Florence, Ala.; 1830; pub; coed; 4; M
Florida A&M U., Tallahassee, Fla.; 1887; pub; coed; 4; M
Florida C., Temple Terrace, Fla.; 1946; pvt; coed; 2; s
Florida Inst. of Tech., Melbourne, Fla.; 1958; pvt; coed; 4; s
Florida Jr. C. at Jacksonville, Fla.; 1963; pub; coed 2; M
Florida Keys Jr. C., Key West, Fla.; 1965; pub; coed; 2; s
Florida Memorial C., Miami, Fla.; 1892; pvt; coed; 4; s
Florida Presbyterian C., St. Petersburg, Fla.; 1958; pvt; coed; 4; s
Florida Southern C., Lakeland, Fla.; 1885; pvt; coed; 4; s
Florida State U., Tallahassee, Fla.; 1851; pub; coed; 4; L
Florida, U. of, Gainesville, Fla.; 1853; pub; coed; 4; L
Florissant Valley Com. C. (Jr. C. District of St. Louis), St. Louis, Mo.; 1962; pub; coed; 2; M
Fontbonne C., St. Louis, Mo.; 1917; pvt; wom; 4; s
Foothill C. (Foothill Jr. C. District), Los Altos Hills, Calif; 1957; pub; coed; 2; L
Fordham U., New York, N.Y.; 1841; pvt; coed; 4; L
  Fordham C.; 1841; pvt; men; 4; M
  Lincoln Center C.; 1868; pvt; coed; 4; s
  Thomas More C.; 1964; pvt; wom; 4; s
Forest Park Com. C. (Jr. C. District of St. Louis), St. Louis, Mo.; 1963; pub; coed; 2; M
Fort Hays Kansas State C., Hays, Kans.; 1901; pub; coed; 4; M
Fort Lewis C., Durango, Colo.; 1910; pub; coed; 4; s
Fort Scott Com. Jr. C., Fort Scott, Kans.; 1919; pub; coed; 2; s
Fort Steilacoom Com. C., Tacoma, Wash.; 1967; pub; coed; 2; s
Fort Valley State C., Fort Valley, Ga.; 1895; pub; coed; 4; s
Fort Wright C., Spokane, Wash.; 1907; pvt; coed; 4; s
Framingham State C., Framingham, Mass.; 1839; pub; coed; 4; M
Francis T. Nicholls State C., Thibodaux, La.; 1948; pub; coed; 2; M
Franklin and Marshall C., Lancaster, Pa.; 1787; pvt; coed; 4; s
Franklin C., Franklin, Ind.; 1834; pvt; coed; 4; s
Franklin Inst. of Boston, Boston, Mass.; 1908; pvt; coed; 2; s
Franklin Pierce C., Rindge, N.H.; 1962; pvt; coed; 4; s
Frank Phillips C., Borger, Tex.; 1948; pub; coed; 2; s
Frederick Com. C., Frederick, Md.; 1957; pub; coed; 2; s
Frederick Com. C., Portsmouth, Va.; 1968; pub; coed; 2; s
Freed-Hardeman C., Henderson, Tenn.; 1908; pvt; coed; 2; s
Freeman Jr. C., Freeman, S. Dak.; 1900; pvt; coed; 2; s
Fresno City C. (State Center Jr. C. District), Fresno Calif.; 1910; pub; coed; 2; L
Fresno State C. (See California State C. System)
Friends U., Wichita, Kans.; 1898; pvt; coed; 4; s
Frostburg State C., Frostburg, Md.; 1898; pub; coed; 4; s
Fullerton Jr. C. (North Orange Jr. C. District), Fullerton, Calif.; 1913; pub; coed; 2; L
Fulton Montgomery Com. C., Johnstown, N.Y.; 1963; pub; coed; 2; s
Furman U., Greenville, S.C.; 1825; pvt; coed; 4; s

Gadsden State Jr. C., Gadsden, Ala.; 1963; pub; coed; 2; s
Gainesville Jr. C., Oakwood, Ga.; 1964; pub; coed; 2; s
Gallaudet C., Washington, D.C.; 1864; pvt; coed; 4; s
Galveston Com. C., Galveston, Tex.; 1967; pub; coed; 2; s
Gannon C., Erie, Pa.; 1944; pvt; coed; 4; M
Garden City Jr. C., Garden City, Kans.; 1919; pub; coed; 2; s
Gardner-Webb C., Boiling Springs, N.C.; 1928; pvt; coed; 2; s
Garland Jr. C., Boston, Mass.; 1947; pvt; wom; 2; s
Gaston C., Gastonia, N.C.; 1963; pub; coed; 2; s
Gavilan C., Gilroy, Calif.; 1963; pub; coed; 2; s
General Beadle State C., Madison, S. Dak.; 1881; pub; coed; 4; s
Genesee Com. C., Batavia, N.Y.; 1966; pub; coed; 2; s

Geneva C., Beaver Falls, Pa.; 1848; pvt; coed; 4; s
George C. Wallace State Tech. Jr. C., Dothan, Ala.; 1963; pub; coed; 2; s
George Fox C., Newberg, Ore.; 1885; pvt; coed; 4; s
George Peabody C. for Teachers, Nashville, Tenn.; 1785; pvt; coed; 4; s
Georgetown C., Georgetown, Ky.; 1787; pvt; coed; 4; s
Georgetown U., Washington, D.C.; 1789; pvt; coed; 4; L
George Washington U., The, Washington, D.C.; 1821; pvt; coed; 4; L
George Williams C., Downers Grove, Ill.; 1884; pvt; coed; 4; s
Georgia C. at Milledgeville; 1889; pub; coed; 4; s
Georgia Inst. of Tech., Atlanta, Ga.; 1885; pub; coed; 4; L
Georgia Military C., Milledgeville, Ga.; 1930; pub; men; 2; s
Georgian Court C., Lakewood, N.J.; 1908; p vt; wom; 4; s
Georgia Southern C., Statesboro, Ga.; 1908; pub; coed; 4; M
Georgia Southwestern C., Americus, Ga.; 1908; pub; coed; 4; s
Georgia State U., Atlanta, Ga.; 1913; pub; coed; 4; L
Georgia, U. of, Athens, Ga.; 1785; pub; coed; 4; L
Gettysburg C., Gettysburg, Pa.; 1832; pvt; coed; 4; s
Glassboro State C., Glassboro, N.J.; 1923; pub; coed; 4; M
Glendale C., Glendale, Calif.; 1927; pub; coed; 2; M
Glendale Com. C., Glendale, Ariz.; 1965; pub; coed; 2; M
Glen Oaks Com. C., Centreville, Mich.; 1965; pub; coed; 2; s
Glenville State C., Glenville, W. Va.; 1872; pub; coed; 4; s
Goddard C., Plainfield, Vt.; 1863; pvt; coed; 4; s
Gogebic Com. C., Ironwood, Mich.; 1932; pub; coed; 2; s
Golden Gate C., San Francisco, Calif.; 1881; pvt; coed; 4; s
Golden West C. (Orange Coast Jr. C. District), Huntington Beach, Calif.; 1965; pub; coed; 2; M
Gonzaga U., Spokane, Wash.; 1887; pvt; coed; 4; M
Good Counsel C., White Plains, N.Y.; 1923; pvt; wom; 4; s
Gordon C., Wenham, Mass.; 1889; pvt; coed; 4; s
Gordon Military C., Barnesville, Ga.; 1927; pvt; coed; 2; s
Gorham State C., Gorham, Me.; 1878; pub; coed; 4; s
Goshen C., Goshen, Ind.; 1894; pvt; coed; 4; s
Goucher C., Baltimore, Md.; 1885; pvt; wom; 4; s
Graceland C., Lamoni, Iowa; 1895; pvt; coed; 4; s
Grambling C., Grambling, La.; 1901; pub; coed; 4; M
Grand Canyon C., Phoenix, Ariz.; 1949; pvt; coed; 4; s
Grand Rapids Jr. C., Grand Rapids, Mich.; 1914; pub; coed; 2; M
Grand Valley State C., Allendale, Mich.; 1960; pub; coed; 4; s
Grand View C., Des Moines, Iowa; 1927; pvt; coed; 2; s
Grays Harbor C., Aberdeen, Wash.; 1930; pub; coed; 2; s
Grayson County C., Sherman/Denison, Tex.; 1963; pub; coed; 2; s
Greater Hartford Com. C., Hartford, Conn.; 1967; pub; coed; 2; s
Great Falls, C. of, Great Falls, Mont.; 1923; pvt; coed; 4; s
Greenbrier C., Lewisburg, W. Va.; 1923; pvt; wom; 2; s
Greenfield Com. C., Greenfield, Mass.; 1962; pub; coed; 2; s
Green Mountain C., Poultney, Vt.; 1931; pvt; wom; 2; s
Green River Com. C., Auburn, Wash.; 1963; pub; coed; 2; M
Greensboro C., Greensboro, N.C.; 1838; pvt; coed; 4; s
Greenville C., Greenville, Ill.; 1855; pvt; coed; 4; s
Grinnell C., Grinnell, Iowa; 1846; pvt; coed; 4; s
Grossmont C., El Cajon, Calif.; 1961; pub; coed; 2; M
Grove City C., Grove City, Pa.; 1876; pvt; coed; 4; s
Guilford C., Greensboro, N.C.; 1834; pvt; coed; 4; s
Gulf Coast Jr. C., Panama City, Fla.; 1957; pub; coed; 2; s
Gulf Park C., Gulfport, Miss.; 1919; pvt; wom; 2; s
Gustavus Adolphus C., St. Peters, Minn.; 1862; pvt; coed; 4; s
Gwynedd-Mercy C., Gwynedd Valley, Pa.; 1948; pvt; coed; 4; s

Hagerstown Jr. C., Hagerstown, Md.; 1946; pub; coed; 2; s
Hamilton C., Clinton, N.Y.; 1793; pvt; men; 4; s
Hamline U., St. Paul, Minn.; 1854; pvt; coed; 4; s
Hampden-Sydney C., Hampden-Sydney, Va,; 1775; pvt; men; 4; s
Hampton Inst., Hampton, Va.; 1868; pvt; coed; 4; M
Hanover C., Hanover, Ind.; 1827; pvt; coed; 4; s
Harcum Jr. C., Bryn Mawr, Pa.; 1952; pvt; wom; 2; s
Harding C., Searcy, Ark.; 1919; pvt; coed; 4; s
Hardin-Simmons U., Abilene, Tex.; 1891; pvt; coed; 4; s
Harford Jr. C., Bel Air, Md.; 1957; pub; coed; 2; M

Harpur C. (See New York, SUNY at Binghamton)
Harrisburg Area Com. C., Harrisburg, Pa.; 1964; pub; coed; 2; M
Harris Teachers C., St. Louis, Mo.; 1857; pub; coed; 4; s
Hartford C. for Women, Hartford, Conn.; 1939; pvt; wom; 2; s
Hartford State Tech. C., Hartford, Conn.; 1946; pub; 2; s
Hartford, U. of, West Hartford, Conn.; 1877; pvt; coed; 4; L
Hartnell C., Salinas, Calif.; 1920; pub; coed; 2; M
Hartwick C., Oneonta, N.Y.; 1797; pvt; coed; 4; s
Harvard U., Cambridge, Mass.; 1636; pvt; coed; 4; L
  Harvard C.; 1638; pvt; men; 4; M
  Radcliffe C.; 1879; pvt; wom; 4; s
Harvey Mudd C. (See Claremont Colleges, The)
Hastings C., Hastings, Nebr.; 1882; pvt; coed; 4; s
Haverford C., Haverford, Pa.; 1833; pvt; coed; 4; s
Hawaii Com. Colleges, U. of,
  Honolulu Com. C.; 1965; pub; coed; 2; s
  Kapiolani Com. C., Honolulu; 1965; pub; coed; 2; s
  Kauai Com. C., Lihue, Kauai; 1965; pub; coed; 2; s
  Leeward Com. C., Pearl City; 1968; pub; coed; 2; s
  Maui Com. C., Kahalui, Maui; 1966; pub; coed; 2; s
Hawaii, U. of, Honolulu, Hawaii; 1907; pub; coed; 4; L
  Hilo Campus; 1947; pub; coed; 2; s
Heidelberg C., Tiffin, Ohio; 1850; pvt; coed; 4; s
Henderson County Jr. C., Athens, Tex.; 1946; pub; coed; 2; s
Henderson State Teachers C., Arkadelphia, Ark.; 1890; pub; coed; 4; M
Hendrix C., Conway, Ark.; 1876; pvt; coed; 4; s
Henry Ford Com. C., Dearborn, Mich.; 1938; pub; coed; 2; L
Herbert H. Lehman C. (See City U. of New York)
Herkimer County Com. C., Ilion, N.Y.; 1966; pub; coed; 2; s
Hesston C., Hesston, Kans.; 1927; pvt; coed; 2; s
Hibbing State Jr. C., Hibbing, Minn.; 1916; pub; coed; 2; s
Highland Com. C., Freeport, Ill.; 1961; pub; coed; 2; s
Highland Com. Jr. C., Highland, Kans.; 1937; pub; coed; 2; s
Highland Park C., Highland Park, Mich.; 1918; pub; coed; 2; M
Highline C., Midway, Wash.; 1961; pub; coed; 2; M
High Point C., High Point, N.C.; 1924; pvt; coed; 4; s
Hillsborough Jr. C., Tampa, Fla.; 1968; pub; coed; 2; s
Hillsdale C., Hillsdale, Mich.; 1844; pvt; coed; 4; s
Hinds Jr. C., Raymond, Miss.; 1922; pub; coed; 2; M
Hiram C., Hiram, Ohio; 1850; pvt; coed; 4; s
Hiwassee C., Madisonville, Tenn.; 1921; pvt; coed; 2; s
Hobart and William Smith C., Geneva, N.Y.; 1822; pvt; coed; 4; s
Hofstra U., Hempstead, N.Y.; 1935; pvt; coed; 4; L
Hollins C., Hollins College, Va.; 1842; pvt; wom; 4; s
Holmes Jr. C., Goodman, Miss.; 1925; pub; coed; 2; s
Holy Cross, C. of the, Worcester, Mass.; 1843; pvt; men; 4; s
Holy Family C., Philadelphia, Pa; 1954; pvt; coed; 4; s
Holy Family C., Manitowoc, Wis.; 1869; pvt; coed; 4; s
Holy Names, C. of the, Oakland, Calif.; 1868; pvt; coed; 4; s
Holyoke Com. C., Holyoke, Mass.; 1946; pub; coed; 2; M
Hood C., Frederick, Md.; 1893; pvt; wom; 4; s
Hope C., Holland, Mich.; 1851; pvt; coed; 4; s
Houghton C., Houghton, N.Y.; 1883; pvt; coed; 4; s
Housatonic Com. C., Stratford, Conn.; 1967; pub; coed; 4; s
Houston Baptist C., Houston, Tex.; 1960; pvt; coed; 4; s
Houston, U. of, Houston, Tex.; 1927; pub; coed; 4; L
Howard County Jr. C., Big Spring, Tex.; 1945; pub; coed; 2; s
Howard Payne C., Brownwood, Tex.; 1889; pvt; coed; 4; s
Howard U., Washington, D.C.; 1867; pvt; coed; 4; L
Hudson Valley Com. C., Troy, N.Y.; 1953; pub; coed; 2; M
Humboldt State C. (See California State C. System)
Humphreys C., Stockton, Calif.; 1947; pvt; coed; 2; s
Hunter C. (See City U. of New York)
Huntingdon C., Montgomery, Ala.; 1854; pvt; coed; 4; s
Huntington C., Huntington, Ind.; 1897; pvt; coed; 4; s
Huron C., Huron, S. Dak.; 1883; pvt; coed; 4; s
Huston-Tillotson C., Austin, Tex.; 1876; pvt; coed; 4; s
Hutchinson Com. Jr. C., Hutchinson, Kans.; 1928; pub; coed; 2; s

Idaho, C. of, Caldwell, Ida.; 1891; pvt; coed; 4; s
Idaho State U., Pocatello, Ida.; 1901; pub; coed; 4; M
Idaho, U. of, Moscow, Ida.; 1889; pub; coed; 4; M
Illinois Central C., East Peoria, Ill.; 1966; pub; coed; 2; M
Illinois C., Jacksonville, Ill.; 1829; pvt; coed; 4; s
Illinois Inst. of Tech., Chicago, Ill.; 1892; pvt; coed; 4; L
Illinois State U., Normal, Ill.; 1857; pub; coed; 4; L

Illinois, U. of, Urbana, Ill.; 1867; pub; coed; 4; L
 Chicago Circle Campus; 1965; pub; coed; 4; L
Illinois Valley Com. C., Oglesby, Ill.; 1924; pub; coed; 2; s
Illinois Wesleyan U., Bloomington, Ill.; 1850; pvt; coed; 4; s
Immaculata C., Bartlett, Ill.; 1955; pvt; wom; 2; s
Immaculata C., Hamburg, N.Y.; 1957; pvt; coed; 2; s
Immaculata C., Immaculata, Pa.; 1920; pvt; wom; 4; s
Immaculata C. of Washington, Washington, D.C.; 1925; pvt; wom; 2; s
Immaculate Heart C., Los Angeles, Calif.; 1916; pvt; coed; 4; s
Imperial Valley C., Imperial, Calif.; 1922; pub; coed; 2; s
Incarnate Word C., San Antonio, Tex.; 1881; pvt; coed; 4; s
Independence Com. Jr. C., Independence, Kans.; 1925; pub.; coed; 2; s
Indiana Central C., Indianapolis, Ind.; 1902; pvt; coed; 4; M
Indiana Inst. of Tech., Fort Wayne, Ind.; 1930; pvt; coed; 4; s
Indiana State U., Terre Haute, Ind.; 1865; pub; coed; 4; L
Indiana U., Bloomington; 1820; pub; coed; 4; L
Indiana U. of Pennsylvania, Indiana, Pa.; 1871; pub; coed; 4; L
Indiana U. System
 at Calumet; East Chicago; Fort Wayne; Indianapolis; Kokomo; Northwest Regional Campus (Gary); Richmond Center; South Bend; Southeast Regional Campus (Jeffersonville)
Indian River Jr. C., Fort Pierce, Fla.; 1960; pub; coed; 2; s
Inter American U. of Puerto Rico, San German, P.R.; 1912; pvt; coed; 4; L
Iona C., New Rochelle, N.Y.; 1940; pvt; coed; 4; M
Iowa Central Com. C.
 Eagle Grove Campus; 1928; pub; coed; 2; s
 Fort Dodge Campus; 1921; pub; coed; 2; s
 Webster City Campus; 1926; pub; coed; 2; s
Iowa Lakes Com. C., Estherville, Iowa; 1924; pub; coed; 2; s
Iowa State U. of Science and Tech., Ames, Iowa; 1858; pub; coed; 4; L
Iowa, U. of, Iowa City, Iowa; 1847; pub; coed; 4; L
Iowa Wesleyan C., Mount Pleasant, Iowa; 1842; pvt; coed; 4; s
Iowa Western Com. C.
 Clarinda Campus; 1923; pub; coed; 2; s
 Council Bluffs Campus; 1966; pub; coed; 2; s
Isothermal Com. C., Spindale, N.C.; 1965; pub; coed; 2; s
Itasca State Jr. C., Grand Rapids, Minn.; 1922; pub; coed; 2; s
Itawamba Jr. C., Fulton, Miss.; 1948; pub; coed; 2; s
Ithaca C., Ithaca, N.Y.; 1892; pvt; coed; 4; M

Jackson C. (See Tufts U.)
Jackson Com. C., Jackson, Mich.; 1928; pub; coed; 2; M
Jackson County Jr. C. (Mississippi Gulf Coast Jr. C. District), Gautier, Miss.; 1962; pub; coed; 2; s
Jackson State C., Jackson, Miss.; 1877; pub; coed; 4; M
Jackson State Com. C., Jackson, Tenn.; 1965; pub; coed; 2; s
Jacksonville C., Jacksonville, Tex.; 1918; pvt; coed; 2; s
Jacksonville State U., Jacksonville, Ala.; 1883; pub; coed; 4; L
Jacksonville U., Jacksonville, Fla.; 1934; pvt; coed; 4; M
Jamestown C., Jamestown, N. Dak.; 1884; pvt; coed; 4; s
Jamestown Com. C., Jamestown, N.Y.; 1950; pub; coed; 2; s
Jarvis Christian C., Hawkins, Tex.; 1912; pvt; coed; 4; s
Jefferson C., Hillsboro, Mo.; 1963; pub; coed; 2; s
Jefferson Com. C., Watertown, N.Y.; 1961; pub; coed; 2; s
Jefferson County, Jr. C. District of, Hillsboro, Mo.; 1963; pub; coed; 2; s
Jefferson Davis Jr. C. (Mississippi Gulf Coast Jr. C. District), Hansboro, Miss.; 1965; pub; coed; 2; s
Jefferson State Jr. C., Birmingham, Ala.; 1963; pub; coed; 2; M
Jersey City State C., Jersey City, N.J.; 1927; pub; coed; 4; L
John Brown U., Siloam Springs, Ark.; 1919; pvt; coed; 4; s
John Carroll U., Cleveland, Ohio; 1886; pvt; coed; 4; M
Johns Hopkins U., The, Baltimore, Md.; 1867; pvt; coed; 4; M
Johnson C. Smith U., Charlotte, N.C.; 1867; pvt; coed; 4; s
Johnson State C., Johnson, Vt.; 1828; pub; coed; 4; s
John Tyler Com. C., Chester, Va.; 1966; pub; coed; 2; s
Joliet Jr. C., Joliet, Ill.; 1901; pub; coed; 2; M
Jones C., Jacksonville, Fla.; 1960; pvt; coed; 2; s
Jones County Jr. C., Ellisville, Miss.; 1927; pub; coed; 2; s
Judson C., Marion, Ala.; 1838; pvt; coed; 4; s

Juilliard School, New York, N.Y.; 1904; pvt; coed; 4; s
Juniata C., Huntingdon, Pa.; 1876; pvt; coed; 4; s

Kalamazoo C., Kalamazoo, Mich.; 1833; pvt; coed; 4; s
Kalamazoo Valley Com. C., Kalamazoo, Mich.; 1966; pub; coed; 2; s
Kansas City Art Inst., Kansas City, Mo.; 1885; pvt; coed; 4; s
Kansas City Kansas Com. Jr. C., Kansas City, Kans.; 1923; pub; coed; 2; s
Kansas State C. of Pittsburg, Pittsburg, Kans.; 1903; pub; coed; 4; M
Kansas State Teachers C., Emporia, Kans.; 1863; pub; coed; 4; L
Kansas State U., Manhattan, Kans.; 1863; pub.; coed; 4; L
Kansas, U. of, Lawrence, Kans.; 1864; pub; coed; 4; L
Kansas Wesleyan U., Salina, Kans.; 1885; pvt; coed; 4; s
Kaskaskia C., Centralia, Ill.; 1940; pub; coed; 2; s
Kearney State C., Kearney, Nebr.; 1905; pub; coed; 4; M
Keene State C., Keene, N.H.; 1909; pub; coed; 4; s
Kellogg Com. C., Battle Creek, Mich.; 1956; pub; coed; 2; M
Kemper Military School & C., Boonville, Mo.; 1923; pvt; men; 2; s
Kendall C., Evanston, Ill.; 1934; pvt; coed; 2; s
Kennesaw Jr. C., Marietta, Ga.; 1965; pub; coed; 2; s
Kent State U., Kent, Ohio; 1910; pub; coed; 4; L
Kentucky State C., Frankfort, Ky.; 1886; pub; coed; 4; s
Kentucky, U. of, Lexington; 1865; pub; coed; 4; L
 Ashland Com. C., Ashland; 1937; pub; coed; 2; s
 Elizabethtown Com. C., Elizabethtown; 1964; pub; coed; 2; s
 Fort Knox Com. C., Fort Knox; 1959; pub; coed; 2; s
 Hazard Com. C., Hazard; 1968; pub; coed; 2; s
 Henderson Com. C., Henderson; 1960; pub; coed; 2; s
 Hopkinsville Com. C., Hopkinsville; 1965; pub; coed; 2; s
 Jefferson Com. C., Louisville; 1968; pub; coed; 2; s
 Lexington Technical Inst., Lexington; 1965; pub; coed; 2; s
 Madisonville Com. C., Madisonville; 1968; pub; coed; 2; s
 Maysville Com. C., Maysville; 1968; pub; coed; 2; s
 Northern Com. C., Covington; 1964; pub; coed; 2; s
 Paducah Com. C., Paducah; 1932; pub; coed; 2; s
 Prestonsburg Com. C., Prestonsburg; 1964; pub; coed; 2; s
 Somerset Com. C., Somerset; 1964; pub; coed; 2; s
 Southeast Com. C., Cumberland; 1960; pub; coed; 2; s
Kentucky Wesleyan C., Owensboro, Ky.; 1858; pvt; coed; 4; s
Kenyon C., Gambier, Ohio; 1824; pvt; men; 4; s
Keuka C., Keuka Park, N.Y.; 1890; pvt; coed; 4; s
Keystone Jr. C., La Plume, Pa.; 1934; pvt; coed; 2; s
Kilgore C., Kilgore, Tex.; 1935; pub; coed; 2; s
King C., Bristol, Tenn.; 1867; pvt; coed; 4; s
Kingsborough Com. C. (See City U. of New York)
King's C., Wilkes-Barre, Pa.; 1946; pvt; coed; 4; s
King's C., The, Briarcliff Manor, N.Y.; 1938; pvt; coed; 4; L
Kirkwood Com. C., Cedar Rapids, Iowa; 1966; pub; coed; 2; M
Kishwaukee C., Malta, Ill.; 1967; pub; coed; 2; s
Knox C., Galesburg, Ill.; 1836; pvt; coed; 4; s
Knoxville C., Knoxville, Tenn.; 1863; pvt; coed; 4; s
Kutztown State C., Kutztown, Pa.; 1860; pub; coed; 4; M

Labette Com. Jr. C., Parsons, Kans.; 1923; pub; coed; 2; s
Ladycliff C., Highland Falls, N.Y.; 1933; pvt; wom; 4; s
Lafayette C., Easton, Pa.; 1826; pvt; men; 4; s
LaGrange C., LaGrange, Ga.; 1831; pvt; coed; 4; s
Lake City Jr. C., Lake City, Fla.; 1962; pub; coed; 2; s
Lake Erie C., Painesville, Ohio; 1856; pvt; wom; 4; s
Lake Forest C., Lake Forest, Ill.; 1857; pvt; coed; 4; s
Lake Land C., Mattoon, Ill.; 1966; pub; coed; 2; s
Lakeland C., Sheboygan, Wis.; 1862; pvt; coed; 4; s
Lakeland Com. C., Mentor, Ohio; 1967; pub; coed; 2; s
Lake Michigan C., Benton Harbor, Mich.; 1946; pub; coed; 2; M
Lake Region Com. C., Devils Lake, N. Dak.; 1941; pub; coed; 2; s
Lake Sumter Jr. C., Leesburg, Fla.; 1961; pub; coed; 2; s
Lake Superior State C., Sault Ste. Marie, Mich.; 1946; pub; coed; 4; s
Lakewood State Jr. C., White Bear Lake, Minn.; 1967; pub; coed; 2; s
Lamar Com. C., Lamar, Colo.; 1937; pub; coed; 2; s
Lamar State C. of Tech., Beaumont, Tex.; 1923; pub; coed; 4; L
Lambuth C., Jackson, Tenn.; 1843; pvt; coed; 4; s
Lander C., Greenwood, S.C.; 1872; pvt; coed; 4; s
Lane C., Jackson, Tenn.; 1882; pvt; coed; 4; s
Lane Com. C., Eugene, Ore.; 1964; pub; coed; 2; M
Laney C. (Peralta Jr. C. District), Oakland, Calif.; 1953; pub; coed; 2; L
Langston U., Langston, Okla.; 1897; pub; coed; 4; s

Lansing Com. C., Lansing, Mich.; 1957; pub; coed; 2; M
Laredo Jr. C., Laredo, Tex.; 1946; pub; coed; 2; s
La Salette Seminary, Altamont, N.Y.; 1952; pvt; men; 2; s
La Salle C., Philadelphia, Pa.; 1863; pvt; men; 4; s
Lasell Jr. C., Auburndale, Mass.; 1932; pvt; wom; 2; s
Lassen C., Susanville, Calif.; 1925; pub; coed; 2; s
La Verne C., La Verne, Calif.; 1891; pvt; coed; 4; s
Lawrence Inst. of Tech., Southfield, Mich.; 1932; pvt; coed; 4; M
Lawrence U., Appleton, Wis.; 1847; pvt; coed; 4; s
Lebanon Valley C., Annville, Pa.; 1866; pvt; coed; 4; s
Lee C., Cleveland, Tenn.; 1941; pvt; coed; 4; s
Lee C., Baytown, Tex.; 1934; pub; coed; 2; s
Lees Jr. C., Jackson, Ky.; 1927; pvt; coed; 2; s
Lees-McRae C., Banner Elk, N.C.; 1929; pvt; coed; 2; s
Leeward Com. C., Honolulu, Hawaii; 1968; pub; coed; 2; M
Lehigh County Com. C., Allentown, Pa.; 1966; pub; coed; 2; s
Lehigh U., Bethlehem, Pa.; 1865; pvt; men; 4; M
Leicester Jr. C., Leicester, Mass.; 1939; pvt; men; 2; s
Le Moyne C., Syracuse, N.Y.; 1946; pvt; coed; 4; s
Le Moyne-Owen C., Memphis, Tenn.; 1870; pvt; coed; 4; s
Lenoir County Com. C., Kinston, N.C.; 1964; pub; coed; 2; s
Lenoir-Rhyne C., Hickory, N.C.; 1891; pvt; coed; 4; s
Lesley C., Cambridge, Mass.; 1909; pvt; wom; 4; s
Lewis and Clark C., Portland, Ore.; 1867; pvt; coed; 4; s
Lewis-Clark, Lewiston, Ida.; 1955; pub; coed; 4; s
Lewis C., Lockport, Ill.; 1930; pvt; coed; 4; s
Limestone C., Gaffney, S.C.; 1845; pvt; coed; 4; s
Lincoln C., Lincoln, Ill.; 1929; pvt; coed; 2; s
Lincoln Land Com. C., Springfield, Ill.; 1967; pub; coed; 2; s
Lincoln Memorial U., Harrogate, Tenn.; 1897; pvt; coed; 4; s
Lincoln U., Jefferson City, Mo.; 1866; pub; coed; 4; s
Lincoln U., Lincoln University, Pa.; 1854; pvt; coed; 4; s
Lindenwood C., St. Charles, Mo.; 1827; pvt; coed; 4; s
Lindsey Wilson C., Columbia, Ky.; 1923; pvt; coed; 2; s
Linfield C., McMinnville, Ore.; 1849; pvt; coed; 4; s
Linn-Benton Com. C., Albany, Ore.; 1967; pub; coed; 2; s
Livingstone C., Salisbury, N.C.; 1879; pvt; coed; 4; s
Livingston U., Livingston, Ala.; 1840; pub; coed; 4; s
Lock Haven State C., Lock Haven, Pa.; 1870; pub; coed; 4; s
Loma Linda U., Riverside, Calif.; 1905; pvt; coed; 4; M
Long Beach City C., Long Beach, Calif.; 1927; pub; coed; 2; L
Long Beach State C. (See California State C., Long Beach)
Long Island U., Greenvale, N.Y.; 1926; pvt; coed; 4; L
  Brooklyn Center-Zeckendorf Campus; 1926; pvt; coed; 4; L
  C. W. Post C., Greenvale; 1954; pvt; coed; 4; L
  Southampton C., Southhampton; 1963; pvt; coed; 4; s
Longwood C., Farmville, Va.; 1884; pub; wom; 4; s
Lon Morris C., Jacksonville, Tex.; 1912; pvt; coed; 2; s
Lorain County Com. C., Elyria, Ohio; 1963; pub; coed; 2; M
Loras C., Dubuque, Iowa; 1839; pvt; men; 4; s
Loretto Heights C., Denver, Colo.; 1891; pvt; coed; 4; s
Loretto Jr. C., Nerinx, Ky.; 1936; pvt; wom; 2; s
Los Angeles City C., Los Angeles, Calif.; 1929; pub; coed; 2; L
Los Angeles Harbor C., Wilmington, Calif.; 1949; pub; coed; 2; L
Los Angeles Pacific C. (See Azusa Pacific C.)
Los Angeles Pierce C., Woodland Hills, Calif.; 1947; pub; coed; 2; L
Los Angeles Southwest C., Los Angeles, Calif.; 1967; pub; coed; 2; M
Los Angeles Trade-Tech. C., Los Angeles, Calif.; 1949; pub; coed; 2; L
Los Angeles Valley C., Van Nuys, Calif.; 1949; pub; coed; 2; L
Louisburg C., Louisburg, N.C.; 1855; pvt; coed; 2; s
Louisiana C., Pineville, La.; 1906; pvt; coed; 4; s
Louisiana Polytechnic Inst., Ruston, La.; 1894; pub; coed; 4; M
Louisiana State U. A&M C., Alexandria, La.; 1860; pub; coed; 4; L
Louisiana State U. A&M C. System, Baton Rouge, La.; 1860; pub; coed; 4; L
  Louisiana State U., New Orleans; 1958; pub; coed; 4; M
  Louisiana State U. at Alexandria; 1960; pub; coed; 2; s
  Louisiana State U. at Eunice; 1964; pub; coed; 2; s
  Louisiana State U. at Shreveport; 1967; pub; coed; 2; s
Louisville, U. of, Louisville, Ky.; 1798; pub; coed; 4; L
Lourdes Jr. C., Sylvania, Ohio; 1958; pvt; wom; 2; s
Lowell State C., Lowell, Mass.; 1894; pub; coed; 4; s
Lowell Tech. Inst., Lowell, Mass.; 1895; pub; coed; 4; M

Lower Columbia C., Longview, Wash.; 1934; pub; coed; 2; s
Loyola C., Baltimore, Md.; 1852; pvt; coed; 4; M
Loyola U., Chicago, Ill.; 1869; pvt; coed; 4; L
Loyola U., New Orleans, La.; 1849; pvt; coed; 4; M
Loyola U. of Los Angeles, Calif.; 1865; pvt; coed; 4; M
Lubbock Christian C., Lubbock, Tex.; 1957; pvt; coed; 2; s
Luther C., Decorah, Iowa; 1861; pvt; coed; 4; s
Luzerne County Com. C., Wilkes-Barre, Pa.; 1966; pub; coed; 2; s
Lycoming C., Williamsport, Pa.; 1811; pvt; coed; 4; s
Lynchburg C., Lynchburg, Va.; 1903; pvt; coed; 4; s
Lyndon State C., Lyndonville, Vt.; 1911; pub; coed; 4; s

Macalester C., St. Paul, Minn.; 1853; pvt; coed; 4; s
MacMurray C., Jacksonville, Ill.; 1846; pvt; coed; 4; s
Macomb County Com. C. (South Campus), Warren, Mich.; 1954; pub; coed; 2; L
  Center Campus, Mt. Clemens; 1954; pub; coed; 2; s
Macon Jr. C., Macon, Ga.; 1965; pub; coed; 2; s
Madison C., Harrisonburg, Va.; 1908; pub; coed; 4; M
Madonna C., Livonia, Mich.; 1937; pvt; coed; 4; s
Maine, U. of, Orono, Me.; 1865; pub; coed; 4; L
Mainland, C. of the, Texas City, Tex.; 1966; pub; coed; 2; s
Malone C., Canton, Ohio; 1889; pvt; coed; 4; s
Manatee Jr. C., Bradenton, Fla.; 1957; pub; coed; 2; s
Manchester C., North Manchester, Ind.; 1889; pvt; coed; 4; s
Manchester Com. C., Manchester, Conn.; 1963; pub; coed; 2; s
Manhattan C., Bronx, N.Y.; 1853; pvt; men; 4; M
Manhattan Com. C. (See City U. of New York)
Manhattanville C., Purchase, N.Y.; 1841; pvt; coed; 4; s
Mankato State C., Mankato, Minn.; 1867; pub; coed; 4; L
Manor Jr. C., Jenkintown, Pa.; 1959; pvt; wom; 2; s
Mansfield State C., Mansfield, Pa.; 1854; pub; coed; 4; s
Margaret Morrison Carnegie C. (See Carnegie-Mellon U.)
Maria C. of Albany, Albany, N.Y.; 1958; pvt; wom; 2; s
Marian C., Indianapolis, Ind.; 1853; pvt; coed; 4; s
Marian C. of Fond-du-Lac, Wis.; 1936; pvt; coed; 4; s
Marietta C., Marietta, Ohio; 1797; pvt; coed; 4; s
Marillac C., Normandy, Mo.; 1955; pvt; wom; 4; s
Marin, C. of, Kentfield, Calif.; 1926; pub; coed; 2; M
Marion C., Marion, Ind.; 1919; pvt; coed; 4; s
Marion Inst. Marion, Ala.; 1921; pvt; men; 2; s
Marist C., Poughkeepsie, N.Y.; 1929; pvt; coed; 4; s
Marlboro C., Marlboro, Vt.; 1946; pvt; coed; 4; s
Marquette U., Milwaukee, Wis.; 1857; pvt; coed; 4; L
Marshall U., Huntington, W. Va.; 1837; pub; coed; 4; M
Mars Hill C., Mars Hill, N.C.; 1856; pvt; coed; 4; s
Martin C., Pulaski, Tenn.; 1870; pvt; coed; 2; s
Mary Baldwin C., Staunton, Va.; 1842; pvt; wom; 4; s
Marycrest C., Davenport, Iowa; 1939; pvt; coed; 4; s
Marygrove C., Detroit, Mich.; 1905; pvt; wom; 4; s
Mary Hardin-Baylor C., Belton, Tex.; 1845; pvt; coed; 4; s
Mary Holmes C., West Point, Miss.; 1936; pvt; coed; 2; s
Maryland State C., Princess Anne, Md.; 1886; pub; coed; 4; s
Maryland, U. of, College Park, Md.; 1807; pub; coed; 4; L
Marylhurst C., Marylhurst, Ore.; 1893; pvt; coed; 4; s
Mary Manse C., Toledo, Ohio; 1872; pvt; coed; 4; s
Mary Washington C. (See Virginia, U. of)
Marymount C., Salina, Kans.; 1922; pvt; coed; 4; s
Marymount C., Tarrytown, N.Y.; 1907; pvt; wom; 4; s
Marymount C. at Loyola U., Los Angeles, Calif.; 1933; pvt; wom; 4; s
Marymount C. of Virginia, Arlington, Va.; 1950; pvt; wom; 2; s
Marymount Manhattan C., New York, N.Y.; 1936; pvt; wom; 4; s
Maryville C., Maryville, Tenn.; 1819; pvt; coed; 4; s
Maryville C. of the Sacred Heart, St. Louis, Mo.; 1827; pvt; wom; 4; s
Marywood C., Scranton, Pa.; 1915; pvt; coed; 4; s
Massachusetts Bay Com. C., Watertown, Mass.; 1961; pub.; coed; 2; s
Massachusetts Inst. of Tech., Cambridge, Mass.; 1861; pvt; coed; 4; M
Massachusetts, U. of, Amherst, Mass.; 1863; pub; coed; 4; L
Massasoir Com. C., North Abington, Mass.; 1966; pub; coed; 2; s
Mattatuck Com. C., Waterbury, Conn.; 1967; pub; coed; 2; s
Maunaolu C., Paia, Maui, Hawaii; 1951; pvt; coed; 2; s
Mayville State C., Mayville, N. Dak.; 1890; pub; coed; 4; s
McCook C., McCook, Nebr.; 1926; pub; coed; 2; s
McHenry County C., Crystal Lake, Ill.; 1967; pub; coed; 2; s

McLennan Com. C., Waco, Tex.; 1965; pub; coed; 2; s
McMurry C., Abilene, Tex.; 1920; pvt; coed; 4; s
McNeese State C., Lake Charles, La.; 1939; pub; coed; 4; M
McPherson C., McPherson, Kans.; 1887; pub; coed; 4; s
Medaille C., Buffalo, N.Y.; 1892; pvt; coed; 4; s
Memphis State U., Memphis, Tenn.; 1912; pub; coed; 4; L
Menlo C., Menlo Park, Calif.; 1949; pvt; men; 4; s
Meramec Com. C. (Jr. C. District of St. Louis), St. Louis, Mo.; 1962; pub; coed; 2; M
Merced C., Merced, Calif.; 1962; pub; coed; 2; M
Mercer County Com. C., Trenton, N.J.; 1966; pub; coed; 2; M
Mercer U., Macon, Ga.; 1830; pvt; coed; 4; s
Mercy C., Dobbs Ferry, N.Y.; 1961; pvt; coed; 4; s
Mercy C., Detroit, Mich.; 1941; pvt; coed; 4; s
Mercy Jr. C., St. Louis, Mo.; 1952; pvt; wom; 2; s
Mercyhurst C., Erie, Pa.; 1926; pvt; coed; 4; s
Meridian Jr. C., Meridian, Miss.; 1937; pub; coed; 2; s
Merrimack C., North Andover, Mass.; 1947; pvt; coed; 4; M
Merritt C. (Peralta Jr. C. District), Oakland, Calif.; 1953; pub; coed; 2; M
Mesabi State Jr. C., Virginia, Minn.; 1921; pub; coed; 2; s
Mesa Com. C., Mesa, Ariz.; 1963; pub; coed; 2; M
Mesa Jr. C., Grand Junction, Colo.; 1925; pub; coed; 2; M
Messiah C., Grantham, Pa.; 1909; pvt; coed; 4; s
Methodist C., Fayetteville, N.C.; 1956; pvt; coed; 4; s
Metropolitan Jr. C., Kansas City, Mo.; 1915; pub; coed; 2; M
Metropolitan State Jr. C., Minneapolis, Minn.; 1965; pub; coed; 2; s
Miami-Dade Jr. C., Miami, Fla.; 1960; pub; coed; 2; L
Miami U., Oxford, Ohio; 1809; pub; coed; 4; L
Miami, U. of, Coral Gables, Fla.; 1925; pvt; coed; 4; L
Michigan State U., East Lansing, Mich.; 1855; pub; coed; 4; L
Michigan State U. (See Oakland U.)
Michigan Tech. U., Houghton, Mich.; 1885; pub; coed; 4; M
Michigan, U. of, Ann Arbor, Mich.; 1817; pub; coed; 4; L
Middlebury C., Middlebury, Vt.; 1800; pvt; coed; 4; s
Middle Georgia C., Cochran, Ga.; 1927; pub; coed; 2; s
Middlesex Com. C., Middletown, Conn.; 1966; pub; coed; 2; s
Middlesex County C., Edison, N.J.; 1964; pub; coed; 2; M
Middle Tennessee State U., Murfreesboro, Tenn.; 1909; pub; coed; 4; M
Midland Lutheran C., Fremont, Nebr.; 1883; pvt; coed; 4; s
Midway Jr. C., Midway, Ky.; 1944; pvt; wom; 2; s
Midwestern U., Wichita Falls, Tex.; 1922; pub; coed; 4; M
Miles Com. C., Miles City, Mont.; 1939; pub; coed; 2; s
Millersville State C., Millersville, Pa.; 1854; pub; coed; 4; M
Milligan C., Milligan College, Tenn.; 1866; pvt; coed; 4; s
Millikin U., Decatur, Ill.; 1901; pvt; coed; 4; s
Millsaps C., Jackson, Miss.; 1890; pvt; coed; 4; s
Mills C., Oakland, Calif.; 1852; pvt; wom; 4; s
Mills C. of Ed., New York, N.Y.; 1909; pvt; wom; 4; s
Milton C., Milton, Wis.; 1867; pvt; coed; 4; s
Milwaukee-Downer C. (See Lawrence U.)
Milwaukee Tech C., Milwaukee, Wis.; 1951; pub; coed; 2; L
Mineral Area C., Flat River, Mo.; 1965; pub; coed; 2; s
Minnesota, U. of, Minneapolis, Minn.; 1851; pub; coed; 4; L
  Duluth Campus; 1902; pub; coed; 4; M
Minot State C., Minot, N. Dak.; 1913; pub; coed; 4; M
Mira Costa C., Oceanside, Calif.; 1934; pub; coed; 2; s
Misericordia, C., Dallas, Pa.; 1923; pvt; wom; 4; s
Mississippi C., Clinton, Miss.; 1826; pvt; coed; 4; s
Mississippi Delta Jr. C., Moorhead, Miss.; 1926; pub; coed; 2; s
Mississippi State C. for Women; Columbus, Miss.; 1884; pub; wom; 4; M
Mississippi State U., State College, Miss.; 1878; pub; coed; 4; M
Mississippi, U. of, University, Miss.; 1844; pub; coed; 4; M
Mississippi Valley State C., Itta Bena, Miss.; 1946; pub; coed; 4; s
Missouri Baptist C., Hannibal, Mo.; 1918; pvt; coed; 2; s
Missouri Southern C., Joplin, Mo.; 1937; pub; coed; 4; M
Missouri, U. of, Columbia, Mo.; 1839; pub; coed; 4; L
  Missouri at Kansas City, U. of; 1929; pub; coed; 4; L
  Missouri at Rolla, U. of; 1870; pub; coed; 4; M
  Missouri at St. Louis, U. of; 1960; pub; coed; 4; L
Missouri Valley C., Marshall, Mo.; 1888; pvt; coed; 4; s

Missouri Western C., St. Joseph, Mo.; 1915; pub; coed; 2; s
Mitchell C., New London, Conn.; 1938; pvt; coed; 2; s
Mitchell C., Statesville, N.C.; 1852; pvt; coed; 2; s
Moberly Jr. C., Moberly, Mo.; 1927; pub; coed; 2; s
Mobile C., Mobile, Ala.; 1961; pvt; coed; 4; s
Mobile State Jr. C., Mobile, Ala.; 1965; pub; coed; 2; s
Modesto Jr. C. (Josemite Jr. C. District), Modesto, Calif.; 1921; pub; coed; 2; L
Mohawk Valley Com. C., Utica, N.Y.; 1946; pub; coed; 2; M
Molloy Catholic C. for Women, Rockville Centre, N.Y.; 1955; pvt; wom; 4; s
Monmouth C., Monmouth, Ill.; 1853; pvt; coed; 4; s
Monmouth C., West Long Branch, N.J.; 1933; pvt; coed; 4; M
Monroe Com. C., Rochester, N.Y.; 1961; pub; coed; 2; M
Monroe County Com. C., Monroe, Mich.; 1964; pub; coed; 2; s
Montana C. of Mineral Science & Tech., Butte, Mont.; 1893; pub; coed; 4; s
Montana State U., Bozeman, Mont.; 1893; pub; coed; 4; M
Montana, U. of, Missoula, Mont.; 1893; pub; coed; 4; M
Montclair State C., Upper Montclair, N.J.; 1908; pub; coed; 4; L
Monterey Inst. of Foreign Studies, Monterey, Calif.; 1955; pvt; coed; 4; s
Monterey Peninsula C., Monterey, Calif.; 1947; pub; coed; 2; M
Montevallo, U. of, Montevallo, Ala.; 1893; pub; coed; 4; s
Montgomery Com. C., Rockville, Md.; 1946; pub; coed; 2; M
Montgomery County Com. C., Conshohocken, Pa.; 1964; pub; coed; 2; s
Monticello C., Godfrey, Ill.; 1917; pvt; wom; 2; s
Montreat-Anderson C., Montreat, N.C.; 1959; pvt; coed; 2; s
Moorehead State C., Moorhead, Minn.; 1885; pub; coed; 4; M
Moorpark C. (Ventura Jr. C. District), Moorpark, Calif.; 1964; pub; coed; 2; M
Moraine Valley Com. C., Oak Lawn, Ill.; 1968; pub; coed; 2; s
Moravian C., Bethlehem, Pa.; 1742; pvt; coed; 4; s
Morehead State U., Morehead, Ky.; 1922; pub; coed; 4; M
Morehouse C. (See Atlanta U. Center)
Morgan State C., Baltimore, Md.; 1867; pub; coed; 4; M
Morningside C., Sioux City, Iowa; 1889; pvt; coed; 4; s
Morris Brown C. (See Atlanta U. Center)
Morris, County C. of, Dover, N.J.; 1965; pub; coed; 2; s
Morris Harvey C., Charleston, W. Va.; 1888; pvt; coed; 4; M
Morristown C., Morristown, Tenn.; 1923; pvt; coed; 2; s
Morton C., Cicero, Ill.; 1924; pub; coed; 2; M
Mount Holyoke C., South Hadley, Mass.; 1836; pvt; wom; 4; s
Mount Hood Com. C., Gresham, Ore.; 1965; pub; coed; 2; M
Mount Ida Jr. C., Newton Centre, Mass.; 1938; pvt; wom; 2; s
Mount Marty C., Yankton, S. Dak.; 1936; pvt; coed; 4; s
Mount Mary C., Milwaukee, Wis.; 1913; pvt; wom; 4; s
Mount Mercy C., Cedar Rapids, Iowa; 1928; pvt; wom; 4; s
Mount Mercy C., Pa. (See Carlow C.)
Mount Olive Jr. C., Mount Olive, N.C.; 1951; pvt; coed; 2; s
Mount Saint Agnes C., Baltimore, Md.; 1867; pvt; coed; 4; s
Mount Saint Clare C., Clinton, Iowa; 1918; pvt; coed; 2; s
Mount Saint Mary C., Hooksett, N.H.; 1934; pvt; wom; 4; s
Mount Saint Mary C., Newburgh, N.Y.; 1959; pvt; coed; 4; s
Mount Saint Mary's C., Emmitsburg, Md.; 1808; pvt; men; 4; s
Mount Saint Vincent, C. of, Bronx, N.Y.; 1847; pvt; wom; 4; s
Mount St. Joseph On-the-Ohio, C. of, Mount St. Joseph, Ohio; 1854; pvt; wom; 4; s
Mount St. Mary's C., Los Angeles, Calif.; 1925; pvt; coed; 4; s
Mount St. Scholastica C., Atchison, Kans.; 1877; pvt; coed; 4; s
Mount Union C., Alliance, Ohio; 1846; pvt; coed; 4; s
Mount Wachusett Com. C., Gardner, Mass.; 1963; pub; coed; 2; s
Mt. Aloysius Jr. C., Cresson, Pa.; 1939; pvt; wom; 2; s
Mt. Angel C., Mt. Angel, Ore.; 1887; pvt; coed; 4; s
Mt. Sacred Heart C., Hamden, Conn.; 1954; pvt; wom; 2; s

Mt. San Antonio C., Walnut, Calif.; 1946; pub; coed; 2; L
Mt. San Jacinto C., Gilman Hot Springs, Calif.; 1962; pub; coed; 2; S
Mt. St. Clare Jr. C., Clinton, Iowa; 1918; pvt; coed; 2; S
Mt. Vernon Jr. C., Washington, D.C.; 1927; pvt; wom; 2; S
Muhlenberg C., Allentown, Pa.; 1848; pvt; coed; 4; S
Multnomah C., Portland, Ore.; 1879; pvt; coed; 2; S
Mundelein C., Chicago, Ill.; 1930; pvt; wom; 4; S
Murray State Agric. C., Tishomingo, Okla.; 1908; pub; coed; 2; S
Murray State U., Murray, Ky.; 1922; pub; coed; 4; M
Muskegon Com. C., Muskegon, Mich.; 1926; pub; coed; 2; M
Muskingum C., New Concord, Ohio; 1837; pvt; coed; 4; S

Napa C., Napa, Calif.; 1942; pub; coed; 2; M
Nassau Com. C., Garden City, N.Y.; 1959; pub; coed; 2; L
Nasson C., Springvale, Me.; 1909; pvt; coed; 4; S
National C. of Ed., Evanston, Ill.; 1886; pvt; coed; 4; S
Navarro Jr. C., Corsicana, Tex.; 1946; pub; coed; 2; S
Nazareth C., Kalamazoo, Mich.; 1889; pvt; coed; 4; S
Nazareth C., Rochester, N.Y.; 1924; pvt; wom; 4; S
Nazareth C. of Kentucky, Nazareth; 1814; pvt; coed; 4; S
Nebraska, U. of, Lincoln, Nebr.; 1869; pub; coed; 4; L
Nebraska at Omaha, U. of; 1908; pub; coed; 4; L
Nebraska Wesleyan U., Lincoln, Nebr.; 1887; pvt; coed; 4; S
Nebraska Western C., Scottsbluff, Nebr.; 1929; pub; coed; 2; S
Neosho County Com. Jr. C., Chanute, Kans.; 1936; pub; coed; 2; S
Nevada, U. of, Reno, Nev.; 1864; pub; coed; 4; M
Nevada, U. of, Las Vegas, Nev.; 1951; pub; coed; 4; M
Newark C. of Engineering, Newark, N.J.; 1881; pub; coed; 4; M
Newark State C., Union, N.J.; 1855; pub; coed; 4; L
Newberry C., Newberry, S.C.; 1856; pvt; coed; 4; S
Newcomb C. (See Tulane U.)
New England C., Henniker, N.H.; 1946; pvt; coed; 4; S
New England Conservatory of Music, Boston, Mass.; 1867; pvt; coed; 4; S
New Hampshire, U. of, Durham; 1866; pub; coed; 4; M
New Haven C., West Haven, Conn.; 1920; pvt; coed; 4; M
New Mexico Highlands U., Las Vegas, N.Mex.; 1893; pub; coed; 4; S
New Mexico Inst. of Mining & Tech., Socorro, N. Mex.; 1889; pub; coed; 4; S
New Mexico Jr. C., Hobbs, N. Mex.; 1965; pub; coed; 2; S
New Mexico Military Inst., Roswell, N. Mex.; 1915; pub; men; 2; S
New Mexico State U., Las Cruces, N. Mex.; 1888; pub; coed; 4; M
New Mexico, U. of, Albuquerque, N. Mex.; 1889; pub; coed; 4; L
New Rochelle, C. of, New Rochelle; 1904; pvt; wom; 4; S
New School for Social Research, The, New York, N.Y.; 1919; pvt; coed; 4; M
Newton C. of the Sacred Heart, Newton, Mass.; 1946; pvt; wom; 4; S
Newton Jr. C., Newtonville, Mass.; 1946; pub; coed; 2; S
New York City Com. C. (See City U. of New York)
New York, State U. of
  SUNY Agric. & Tech. C. at Alfred; 1908; pub; coed; 2; M
  SUNY Agric. & Tech. C. at Canton; 1907; pub; coed; 2; S
  SUNY Agric. & Tech. C. at Cobleskill; 1911; pub; coed; 2; S
  SUNY Agric. & Tech. C. at Delhi; 1915; pub; coed; 2; S
  SUNY Agric. & Tech. C. at Farmingdale; 1935; pub; coed; 2; L
  SUNY Agric. & Tech. C. at Morrisville; 1908; pub; coed; 2; S
  SUNY at Albany; 1844; pub; coed; 4; L
  SUNY at Binghamton; 1946; pub; coed; 4; M
  SUNY at Buffalo; 1846; pub; coed; 4; L
  SUNY at Stony Brook; 1957; pub; coed; 4; M
  SUNY at Brockport; 1836; pub; coed; 4; M
  SUNY C. at Buffalo; 1867; pub; coed; 4; L
  SUNY C. at Cortland; 1868; pub; coed; 4; M
  SUNY C. at Fredonia; 1866; pub; coed; 4; M
  SUNY C. at Geneseo; 1867; pub; coed; 4; M
  SUNY C. at New Paltz; 1885; pub; coed; 4; M
  SUNY C. at Oneonta; 1889; pub; coed; 4; M
  SUNY C. at Oswego; 1861; pub; coed; 4; M
  SUNY C. at Plattsburgh; 1889; pub; coed; 4; M
  SUNY C. at Potsdam; 1816; pub; coed; 4; M
New York University, New York, N.Y.; 1831; pvt; coed; 4; L
Niagara County Com. C., Niagara Falls, N.Y.; 1962; pub; coed; 2; M
Niagara U., Niagara University, N.Y.; 1856; pvt; coed; 4; S

Nicholls State C., Thibodaux, La.; 1948; pub; coed; 4; M
Norfolk Jr. C., Norfolk, Nebr.; 1941; pub; coed; 2; S
Norman C., Norman Park, Ga.; 1923; pvt; coed; 2; S
North Adams State C., North Adams, Mass.; 1894; pub; coed; 4; S
Northampton County Area Com. C., Bethlehem, Pa.; 1966; pub; coed; 2; S
North Carolina Agric. & Tech. State U., Greensboro, 1891; pub; coed; 4; M
North Carolina at Asheville, U. of; 1927; pub;coed; 4; S
North Carolina at Wilmington, U. of; 1947; pub; coed; 4; S
North Carolina Central U., at Durham, N.C.; 1910; pub; coed; 4; M
North Carolina, The Consolidated U. of
  North Carolina at Chapel Hill, U. of, 1789; pub; coed; 4; L
  North Carolina at Charlotte, U. of; 1946; pub; coed; 4; S
  North Carolina at Greensboro, U. of; 1891; pub; coed; 4; M
  North Carolina State U., at Raleigh; 1887; pub; coed; 4; L
North Carolina Wesleyan C., Rocky Mount, N.C.; 1956; pvt.; coed; 4; S
North Central C., Naperville, Ill.; 1861; pvt; coed; 4; S
North Central Michigan C., Petoskey, Mich.; 1958; pub; coed; 2; S
North Dakota School of Forestry, Bottineau, N. Dak.; 1925; pub; coed; 2; S
North Dakota State School of Science, Wahpeton, N. Dak.; 1903; pub; coed; 2; M
North Dakota State U., Fargo, N. Dak.; 1890; pub; coed; 4; M
North Dakota, U. of, Grand Forks; 1883; pub; coed; 4; L
Northeastern Illinois State C., Chicago, Ill.; 1869; pub; coed; 4; M
Northeastern Jr. C., Sterling, Colo.; 1941; pub; coed; 2; S
Northeastern Oklahoma A&M C., Miami, Okla.; 1919; pub; coed; 2; S
Northeastern State C., Tahlequah, Okla.; 1846; pub; coed; 4; M
Northeastern U., Boston, Mass.; 1898; pvt; coed; 4; L
Northeast Louisiana State C., Monroe, La.; 1928; pub; coed; 4; M
Northeast Mississippi Jr. C., Booneville, Miss.; 1948; pub; coed; 2; S
Northeast Missouri State C., Kirksville, Mo.; 1867; pub; coed; 4; M
Northeast State Jr. C., Rainsville, Ala.; 1963; pub; coed; 2; S
Northern Arizona U., Flagstaff, Ariz.; 1899; pub; coed; 4; L
Northern Essex Com. C., Haverhill, Mass.; 1960; pub; coed; 2; S
Northern Illinois U., De Kalb, Ill.; 1895; pub; coed; 4; L
Northern Iowa, U. of, Cedar Falls, Iowa; 1876; pub; coed; 4; L
Northern Michigan C., Marquette, Mich.; 1899; pub; coed; 4; L
Northern Montana C., Havre, Mont.; 1913; pub; coed; 4; S
Northern Oklahoma C., Tonkawa, Okla.; 1920; pub; coed; 2; S
Northern State C., Aberdeen, S. Dak.; 1901; pub; coed; 4; M
North Florida Jr. C., Madison, Fla.; 1958; pub; coed; 2; S
North Georgia C., Dahlonega, Ga.; 1873; pub; coed; 4; S
North Greenville Jr. C., Tigerville, S.C.; 1934; pvt; coed; 2; S
North Hennepin State Jr. C., Minneapolis, Minn; 1966; pub; coed; 2; S
North Idaho Jr. C., Coeur D'Alene, Ida.; 1939; pub; coed; S
North Iowa Area Com. C., Mason City, Iowa; 1918; pub; coed; 2; S
Northland C., Ashland, Wis.; 1892; pvt; coed; 4; S
Northland State Jr. C., Thief River Falls, Minn.; 1965; pub; coed; 2; S
North Park C., Chicago, Ill.; 1891; pvt; coed; 4; S
Northrop Inst. of Tech., Inglewood, Calif.; 1942; pvt; coed; 4; S
North Shore Com. C., Beverly, Mass.; 1965; pub; coed; 2; M
North Texas State U., Denton, Tex.; 1890; pub; coed; 4; L
Northwest Christian C., Eugene, Ore.; 1895; pvt; coed; 4; S
Northwest Com. C., Powell, Wyo.; 1946; pub; coed; 2; S
Northwestern C., Orange City, Iowa; 1882; pvt; coed; 4; S
Northwestern Michigan C., Traverse City, Mich.; 1951; pub; coed; 2; S
Northwestern State C., Natchitoches, La.; 1884; pub; coed; 4; M
Northwestern State C., Alva, Okla.; 1897; pub; coed; 4; M
Northwestern U., Evanston, Ill.; 1851; pvt; coed; 4; L

Northwest Mississippi Jr. C., Senatobia, Miss.; 1927; pub; coed; 2; s
Northwest Missouri State C., Maryville, Mo.; 1905; pub; coed; 4; M
Northwest Nazarene C., Nampa, Ida.; 1913; pvt; coed; 4; s
Norwalk Com. C., Norwalk, Conn.; 1961; pub; coed; 2; s
Norwich U., Northfield, Vt.; 1819; pvt; men; 4; s
Notre Dame C., St. Louis, Mo.; 1896; pvt; wom; 4; s
Notre Dame C., Cleveland, Ohio; 1922; pvt; wom; 4; s
Notre Dame, C. of, Belmont, Calif.; 1851; pvt; coed; 4; s
Notre Dame, C. of, Baltimore, Md.; 1848; pvt; coed; 4; s
Notre Dame C. of Staten Island, Grymes Hill, N.Y.; 1931; pvt; wom; 4; s
Notre Dame Seminary, New Orleans, La.; 1923; pvt; men; 4; s
Notre Dame, U. of, Notre Dame, Ind.; 1842; pvt; men; 4; L

Oakland Com. C., Bloomfield Hills, Mich.; 1964; pub; coed; 2; L
Oakland U., Rochester, Mich.; 1959; pub; coed; 4; M
Oakwood C., Huntsville, Ala.; 1896; pvt; coed; 4; s
Oberlin C., Oberlin, Ohio; 1833; pvt; coed; 4; M
Occidental C., Los Angeles, Calif.; 1887; pvt; coed; 4; s
Odessa C., Odessa, Tex.; 1946; pub; coed; 2; M
Oglethorpe C., Atlanta, Ga.; 1835; pvt; coed; 4; s
Ohio C. of Applied Science, Cincinnati, Ohio; 1828; pvt; coed; 2; s
Ohio Dominican C., Columbus, Ohio; 1911; pvt; coed; 4; s
Ohio Northern U., Ada, Ohio; 1871; pvt; coed; 4; s
Ohio State U., Columbus, Ohio; 1870; pub; coed; 4; L
Ohio U., Athens, Ohio; 1804; pub; coed; 4; L
Ohio Wesleyan U., Delaware, Ohio; 1841; pvt; coed; 4; M
Ohlone C., Fremont, Calif.; 1966; pub; coed; 2; M
Okaloosa-Walton Jr. C., Niceville, Fla.; 1963; pub; coed; 2; s
Oklahoma Baptist U., Shawnee, Okla.; 1909; pvt; coed; 4; s
Oklahoma Christian C., Oklahoma City, Okla.; 1949; pvt; coed; 4; s
Oklahoma City U., Oklahoma City, Okla.; 1904; pvt; coed; 4; s
Oklahoma C. of Liberal Arts, Chickasha, Okla.; 1908; pub; coed; 4; s
Oklahoma Military Academy, Claremore, Okla.; 1923; pub; coed; 2; s
Oklahoma Panhandle State C. of Agric. and Applied Science, Goodwell, Okla.; 1909; pub; coed; 4; s
Oklahoma State U., Stillwater Okla.; 1890; pub; coed; 4; L
Oklahoma, U. of, Norman, Okla.; 1890; pub; coed; 4; L
Old Dominion U., Norfolk Va.; 1930; pub; coed; 4; L
Olivet C., Olivet, Mich.; 1884; pvt; coed; 4; s
Olivet Nazarene C., Kankakee, Ill.; 1907; pvt; coed; 4; s
Olney Central C., Olney, Ill.; 1963; pub; coed; 2; s
Olympic C., Bremerton, Wash.; 1946; pub; coed; 2; M
Omaha, Municipal U. of (See Nebraska at Omaha)
Onondaga Com. C., Syracuse, N.Y.; 1962; pub; coed; 2; M
Orange Coast C. (Orange Coast Jr. C. District), Costa Mesa, Calif.; 1947; pub; coed; 2; L
Orange County Com. C., Middletown, N.Y.; 1950; pub; coed; 2; M
Oregon C. of Ed., Monmouth, Ore.; 1856; pub; coed; 4; M
Oregon State U., Corvallis, Ore.; 1858; pub; coed; 4; L
Oregon Tech. Inst., Klamath Falls, Ore.; 1947; pub; coed; 4; s
Oregon, U. of, Eugene, Ore.; 1872; pub; coed; 4; L
Orlando, C. of, Orlando, Fla.; 1941; pvt; coed; 2; s
Otero Jr. C., La Junta, Colo.; 1941; pub; coed; 2; s
Ottawa U., Ottawa, Kans.; 1865; pvt; coed; 4; s
Otterbein C., Westerville, Ohio; 1847; pvt; coed; 4; s
Ottumwa Heights C., Ottumwa, Iowa; 1925; pvt; coed; 2; s
Ouachita Baptist U., Arkadelphia, Ark.; 1885; pvt; coed; 4; s
Our Lady of the Elms, C. of, Chicopee, Mass.; 1897; pvt; wom; 4; s
Our Lady of the Lake C., San Antonio, Tex.; 1896; pvt; coed; 4; s
Ozarks, C. of the, Clarksville, Ark.; 1834; pvt; coed; 4; s
Ozarks, School of the, Point Lookout, Mo.; 1906; pvt; coed; 4; s

Pace C., New York, N.Y.; 1906; pvt; coed; 4; L
Pacific C., Fresno, Calif.; 1944; pvt; coed; 4; s
Pacific Lutheran U., Tacoma, Wash.; 1890; pvt; coed; 4; M
Pacific Oaks C., Pasadena, Calif.; 1945; pvt; coed; 4; s
Pacific Union C., Angwin, Calif.; 1882; pvt; coed; 4; s
Pacific U., Forest Grove, Ore.; 1849; pvt; coed; 4; s
Pacific, U. of the, Stockton, Calif.; 1851; pvt; coed; 4; M

Packer Collegiate Inst., Brooklyn, N.Y.; 1845; pvt; wom; 2; s
Paine C., Augusta, Ga.; 1882; pvt; coed; 4; s
Palm Beach Jr. C., Lake Worth, Fla.; 1933; pub; coed; 2; M
Palmer C., Charleston, S.C.; 1955; pvt; coed; 2; s
Palmer C., Columbia, S.C.; 1957; pvt; coed; 2; s
Palmer Jr. C., Davenport, Iowa; 1965; pvt; coed; 2; s
Palomar C., San Marcos, Calif.; 1945; pub; coed; 2; M
Palo Verde C., Blythe, Calif; 1947; pub; coed; 2; s
Pan American C., Edinburg, Tex.; 1927; pub; coed; 4; M
Panola C., Carthage, Tex.; 1947; pub; coed; 2; s
Paris Jr. C., Paris, Tex.; 1924; pub; coed; 2; s
Park C., Parkville, Mo.; 1875; pvt; coed; 4; s
Parkland C., Champaign, Ill.; 1966; pub; coed; 2; s
Pasadena City C., Pasadena, Calif.; 1924; pub; coed; 2; L
Pasadena C., Pasadena, Calif.; 1902; pvt; coed; 4; s
Paterson State C., Wayne, N.J.; 1855; pub; coed; 4; M
Patrick Henry State Jr. C., Monroeville, Ala.; 1963; pub; coed; 2; s
Peace C., Raleigh, N.C.; 1857; pvt; wom; 2; s
Pearl River Jr. C., Poplarville, Miss.; 1921; pub; coed; 2; s
Pembroke C. (See Brown U.)
Pembroke State C., Pembroke, N.C.; 1887; pub; coed; 4; s
Peninsula C., Port Angeles, Wash.; 1960; pub; coed; 2; s
Penn Hall Jr. C., Chambersburg, Pa.; 1926; pvt; wom; 2; s
Pennsylvania State U., University Park; 1855; pub; coed; 4; L
  Pennsylvania State U. Commonwealth Campuses: Allentown; Altoona; Beaver (Monaca); Behrend (Erie); Berks (Reading); Capitol (Middletown); Delaware (Chester); Du Bois; Fayette (Uniontown); Hazelton; Hersey (medical center); King of Prussia (graduate center); McKeesport; Mont Alto; New Kensington; Ogontz (Abington); Schuylkill (Schuylkill Haven); Shenango Valley (Sharon); Wilkes-Barre (Shavertown); Worthington Scranton (Dunmore); York
Pennsylvania, U. of, Philadelphia, Pa.; 1740; pvt; coed; 4; L
Pensacola Jr. C., Pensacola, Fla.; 1948; pub; coed; 2; M
Pepperdine C., Los Angeles, Calif.; 1937; pvt; coed; 4; s
Perkinston C. (Mississippi Gulf Coast Jr. C. District), Perkinston, Miss.; 1924; pub; coed; 2; s
Peru State C., Peru, Nebr.; 1855; pub; coed; 4; s
Pfeiffer C., Misenheimer, N.C.; 1855; pvt; coed; 4; s
Philadelphia C. of Art, Philadelphia, Pa.; 1876; pvt; coed; 4; s
Philadelphia, Com. C. of, Philadelphia, Pa.; 1965; pub; coed; 2; M
Philander Smith C., Little Rock, Ark.; 1877; pvt; coed; 4; s
Phillips U., Enid, Okla.; 1906; pvt; coed; 4; s
Phoenix C., Phoenix, Ariz.; 1920; pub; coed; 2; L
Piedmont C., Demorest, Ga.; 1897; pvt; coed; 4; s
Pikeville C., Pikeville, Ky.; 1889; pvt; coed; 4; s
Pine Manor Jr. C., Chestnut Hill, Mass.; 1911; pvt; wom; 2; s
Pittsburgh, U. of, Pittsburgh, Pa.; 1787; pub; coed; 4; L
  Regional Campuses: Bradford; Greensburg; Johnstown; Titusville
Pitzer C. (See Claremont Colleges, The)
Plymouth State C., Plymouth, N.H.; 1839; pub; coed; 4; s
PMC Colleges, Chester, Pa.; 1821; pvt; coed; 4; s
Point Park C., Pittsburgh, Pa.; 1960; pvt; coed; 4; M
Polk Jr. C., Winter Haven, Fla.; 1964; pub; coed; 2; M
Polytechnic Inst. of Brooklyn, N.Y.; 1854; pvt; coed; 4; M
Pomona C. (See Claremont Colleges, The)
Porterville C. (Kern Jr. C. District), Porterville, Calif.; 1927; pub; coed; 2; s
Portland Com. C., Portland, Ore.; 1961; pub; coed; 2; L
Portland State U., Portland, Ore.; 1946; pub; coed; 4; L
Portland, U. of, Portland, Ore.; 1901; pvt; coed; 4; s
Post Jr. C., Waterbury, Conn.; 1939; pvt; coed; 2; s
Poteau Com. C., Poteau, Okla.; 1932; pub; coed; 2; s
Prairie State C., Chicago Heights, Ill.; 1958; pub; coed; 2; M
Prairie View A&M C., Prairie View, Tex.; 1876; pub; coed; 4; s
Pratt Com. Jr. C., Pratt, Kans.; 1938; pub; coed; 2; s
Pratt Inst., Brooklyn, N.Y.; 1887; pvt; coed; 4; M
Prentiss Normal and Industrial Inst., Prentiss, Miss.; 1930; pvt; coed; 2; s
Presbyterian C., Clinton, S.C.; 1880; pvt; coed; 4; s
Presentation C., Aberdeen, S. Dak.; 1951; pvt; coed; 2; s
Prince George's Com. C., Largo, Md.; 1958; pub; coed; 2; M
Princeton U., Princeton, N.J.; 1746; pvt; coed; 4; M
Principia C., The, Elsah, Ill.; 1898; pvt; coed; 4; s

Providence C., Providence R.I.; 1917; pvt; men; 4; s
Puerto Rico Jr. C., Rio Piedras, P.R.; 1949; pvt; coed; 2 M
Puerto Rico, U. of, Rio Piedras, P.R.; 1900; pub; coed; 4; L
Puget Sound, U. of, Tacoma, Wash.; 1888; pvt; coed; 4; s
Purdue U., West Lafayette, Ind.; 1865; pub; coed; 4; L

Queensborough Com. C. (See City U. of New York)
Queens C. (See City U. of New York)
Queens C., Charlotte, N.C.; 1857; pvt; wom; 4; s
Quincy C., Quincy, Ill.; 1859; pvt; coed; 4; s
Quincy Jr. C., Quincy, Mass.; 1958; pub; coed; 2; s
Quinnipiac C., Hamden, Conn.; 1929; pvt; coed; 4; M
Quinsigamond Com. C., Worcester, Mass.; 1963; pub; coed; 2; s

Radcliffe C. (See Harvard U.)
Radford C., Radford, Va.; 1910; pub; wom; 4; M
Randolph-Macon C., Ashland, Va.; 1830; pvt; coed; 4; s
Randolph-Macon Woman's C., Lynchburg, Va.; 1891; pvt; wom; 4; s
Rangely C., Rangely, Colo.; 1960; pub; coed; 2; s
Ranger Jr. C., Ranger, Tex.; 1926; pub; coed; 2; s
Redlands, U. of, Redlands, Calif.; 1907; pvt; coed; 4; s
Redwoods, C. of the, Eureka, Calif.; 1964; pub; coed; 2; M
Reed C., Portland, Ore.; 1908; pvt; coed; 4; s
Reedley C. (State Center Jr. C. District), Reedley, Calif.; 1926; pub; coed; 2; s
Regis C., Denver, Colo.; 1877; pvt; coed; 4; s
Regis C., Weston, Mass.; 1927; pvt; wom; 4; s
Reinhardt C., Waleska, Ga.; 1883; pvt; coed; 2; s
Rensselaer Polytechnic Inst., Troy, N.Y.; 1824; pvt; coed; 4; s
Rhode Island C., Providence, R.I.; 1854; pvt; coed; 4; s
Rhode Island Jr. C., Providence, R.I.; 1964; pub; coed; 2; M
Rhode Island School of Design, Providence, R.I.; 1877; pvt; coed; 4; s
Rhode Island, U. of, Kingston, R.I.; 1892; pub; coed; 4; L
Rice U., Houston, Tex.; 1891; pvt; coed; 4; M
Richmond Com. C. (See City U. of New York)
Richmond Professional Inst. (See Virginia Commonwealth U.)
Richmond, U. of, University of Richmond, Va.; 1830; pvt; coed; 4; M
  Westhampton C., 1830; pvt; wom; 4; s
Ricker C., Houlton, Me.; 1848; pvt; coed; 4; s
Ricks C., Rexburg, Ida.; 1915; pvt; coed; 2; s
Rider C., Trenton, N.J.; 1865; pvt; coed; 4; M
Rio Hondo Jr. C., Whittier, Calif.; 1961; pub; coed; 2; L
Ripon C., Ripon, Wis.; 1850; pvt; coed; 4; s
Riverside City C., Riverside, Calif.; 1916; pub; coed; 2; L
Rivier C., Nashua, N.H.; 1933; pvt; coed; 4; s
Roanoke C., Salem, Va.; 1842; pvt; coed; 4; s
Robert Morris C., Pittsburgh, Pa.; 1962; pvt; coed; 2; M
Roberts Wesleyan C., North Chili, N.Y.; 1866; pvt; coed; 4; s
Rochester Inst. of Tech., Rochester, N.Y.; 1830; pvt; coed; 4; L
Rochester State Jr. C., Rochester, Minn.; 1915; pub; coed; 2; s
Rochester, U. of, Rochester, N.Y.; 1850; pvt; coed; 4; L
Rockford C., Rockford, Ill.; 1847; pvt; coed; 4; s
Rockhurst C., Kansas City, Mo.; 1910; pvt; coed; 4; s
Rockingham Com. C., Wentworth, N.C.; 1966; pub; coed; 2; s
Rockland Com. C., Suffern, N.Y.; 1959; pub; coed; 2; M
Rock Valley C., Rockford, Ill.; 1965; pub; coed; 2; M
Rocky Mountain C., Billings, Mont.; 1883; pvt; coed; 4; s
Roger Williams C., Providence, R.I.; 1948; pvt; coed; 2; s
Rollins C., Winter Park, Fla.; 1885; pvt; coed; 4; M
Roosevelt U., Chicago, Ill.; 1945; pvt; coed; 4; M
Rosary C., River Forest, Ill.; 1848; pvt; coed; 4; s
Rosary Hill C., Buffalo, N.Y.; 1947; pvt; coed; 4; s
Rosemont C., Rosemont, Pa.; 1921; pvt; wom; 4; s
Rose Polytechnic Inst., Terre Haute, Ind.; 1874; pvt; men; 4; s
Russell Sage C., Troy, N.Y.; 1916; pvt; wom; 4; s
Rutgers, The State U., New Brunswick, N.J.; 1766; pub; coed; 4; L
  Douglass C., New Brunswick; 1918; pub; wom; 4; M
  Rutgers U., Camden Campus
  Rutgers U., Newark Campus

Sacramento City C. (Los Rios Jr. C. District), Sacramento, Calif.; 1916; pub; coed; 2; L
Sacramento State C. (See California State C. System)
Sacred Heart C., Cullman, Ala.; 1940; pvt; wom; 2; s
Sacred Heart C., Wichita, Kans.; 1933; pvt; coed; 4; s
Sacred Heart C., Belmont, N.C.; 1935; pvt; wom; 4; s
Sacred Heart, C. of the, Santurce, P.R.; 1880; pvt; wom; 4; s

Sacred Heart Dominican C., Houston, Tex.; 1945; pvt; coed; 4; s
Saddleback C., Mission Viejo, Calif.; 1967; pub; coed; 2; s
Saint (See St.)
Salem C., Winston-Salem, N.C.; 1772; pvt; wom; 4; s
Salem C., Salem, W. Va.; 1888; pvt; coed; 4; s
Salem State C., Salem, Mass.; 1854; pub; coed; 4; M
Salisbury State C., Salisbury, Md.; 1925; pub; coed; 4; s
Salve Regina C., Newport, R.I.; 1934; pvt; wom; 4; s
Samford U., Birmingham, Ala.; 1841; pvt; coed; 4; M
Sam Houston State C., Huntsville, Tex.; 1879; pub; coed; 4; L
San Antonio C., San Antonio, Tex.; 1925; pub; coed; 2; L
San Bernardino Valley C., San Bernardino, Calif.; 1926; pub; coed; 2; L
Sandhills Com. C., Southern Pines, N.C.; 1963; pub; coed; 2; s
San Diego City C., San Diego, Calif.; 1914; pub; coed; 2; M
San Diego Mesa C., San Diego, Calif.; 1963; pub; coed; 2; M
San Diego State C. (See California State C. System)
San Diego, U. of, College for Men, San Diego, Calif.; 1949; pvt; men; 4; s
San Diego, U. of, College for Women, San Diego, Calif.; 1949; pvt; wom; 4; s
San Francisco Art Inst., San Francisco, Calif.; 1874; pvt; wom; 4; s
San Francisco C. for Women, San Francisco, Calif.; 1921; pvt; wom; 4; s
San Francisco State C. (See California State C. System)
San Francisco, U. of, San Francisco, Calif.; 1855; pvt; coed; 4; M
San Jacinto C., Pasadena, Tex.; 1960; pub; coed; 2; M
San Joaquin Delta C., Stockton, Calif.; 1963; pub; coed; 2; L
San Jose City C., San Jose, Calif.; 1921; pub; coed; 2; L
San Jose State C. (See California State C. System)
San Luis Rey C., San Luis Rey, Calif.; 1929; pvt; men; 4; s
San Mateo, C. of (San Mateo Jr. C. District), San Mateo, Calif.; 1922; pub; coed; 2; L
Santa Ana C., Santa Ana, Calif.; 1915; pub; coed; 2; L
Santa Barbara City C., Santa Barbara, Calif.; 1946; pub; coed; 2; M
Santa Clara, U. of, Santa Clara, Calif.; 1851; pvt; coed; 4; M
Santa Fe, C. of, Santa Fe, N. Mex.; 1874; pvt; coed; 4; s
Santa Fe Jr. C., Gainsville, Fla.; 1965; pub; coed; 2; s
Santa Monica City C., Santa Monica, Calif.; 1929; pub; coed; 2; L
Santa Rosa Jr. C., Santa Rosa, Calif.; 1918; pub; coed; 2; M
Sarah Lawrence C., Bronxville, N.Y.; 1926; pvt; coed; 4; s
Savannah State C., Savannah, Ga.; 1890; pub; coed; 4; s
Sayre Jr. C., Sayre, Okla.; 1938; pub; coed; 2; s
Scarritt C., Nashville, Tenn.; 1892; pvt; coed; 4; s
Schreiner Inst., Kerrville, Tex.; 1923; pvt; men; 2; s
Scranton, U. of, Scranton, Pa.; 1888; pvt; men; 4; M
Scripps C. (See Claremont Colleges, The)
Seattle Com. C., Seattle, Wash.; 1966; pub; coed; 2; L
Seattle Pacific C., Seattle, Wash.; 1891; pvt; coed; 4; s
Seattle U., Seattle, Wash.; 1891; pvt; coed; 4; M
Selma U., Selma, Ala.; 1959; pvt; coed; 2; s
Seminole Jr. C., Sanford, Fla.; 1965; pub; coed; 2; s
Seminole Jr. C., Seminole, Okla.; 1931; pub; coed; 2; s
Sequoias, C. of the, Visalia, Calif.; 1925; pub; coed; 2; M
Seton Hall U., South Orange, N.J.; 1856; pvt; coed; 4; L
Seton Hill C., Greensburg, Pa.; 1883; pvt; wom; 4; s
Shasta C., Redding, Calif.; 1949; pub; coed; 2; M
Shaw U., Raleigh, N.C.; 1865; pvt; coed; 4; s
Sheldon Jackson C., Sitka, Alas.; 1944; pvt; coed; 2; s
Shenandoah C., Winchester, Va.; 1924; pvt; coed; 2; s
Shepherd C., Shepherdstown, W. Va.; 1871; pub; coed; 4; s
Sheridan C., Sheridan, Wyo.; 1948; pub; coed; 2; s
Shimer C., Mt. Carroll, Ill.; 1853; pvt; coed; 4; s
Shippensburg State C., Shippensburg, Pa.; 1871; pub; coed; 4; M
Shoreline Com. C., Seattle, Wash.; 1963; pub; coed; 2; M
Shorter C., North Little Rock, Ark.; 1955; pub; coed; 2; s
Shorter C., Rome, Ga.; 1873; pvt; coed; 4; s
Siena C., Loudonville, N.Y.; 1937; pvt; men; 4; s
Siena C., Memphis, Tenn.; 1922; pvt; coed; 4; s
Siena Heights C., Adrian, Mich.; 1919; pvt; coed; 4; s
Sierra C., Rocklin, Calif.; 1914; pub; coed; 2; s
Simmons C., Boston, Mass.; 1899; pvt; wom; 4; s
Simpson C., Indianola, Iowa; 1860; pvt; coed; 4; s
Sinclair Com. C., Dayton, Ohio; 1924; pub; coed; 2; M
Sioux Falls C., Sioux Falls, S. Dak.; 1883; pvt; coed; 4; s
Siskiyous, C. of the, Weed, Calif.; 1957; pub; coed; 2; s
Skagit Valley C., Mt. Vernon, Wash.; 1926; pub; coed; 2; M
Skidmore C., Saratoga Springs, N.Y.; 1911; pvt; wom; 4; s

Slippery Rock State C., Slippery Rock, Pa.; 1889; pub; coed; 4; M
Smith C., Northampton, Mass.; 1871; pub; wom; 4; M
Snead State Jr. C., Boaz, Ala.; 1935; pub; coed; 2; s
Snow C., Ephraim, Utah; 1923; pub; coed; 2; s
Solano C., Vallejo, Calif.; 1945; pub; coed; 2; M
Somerset County C., Green Brook, N.J.; 1966; pub; coed; 2; s
Sonoma State C. (See California State C. System)
South Alabama, U. of, Mobile, Ala.; 1963; pub; coed; 4; M
South Carolina State C., Orangeburg, S.C.; 1895; pub; coed; 4; s
South Carolina, Technical Education Centers of Greenville; 1962; pub; coed; 2; M
　Orangeburg Calhoun, Orangeburg; 1966; pub; coed; 2; s
　Richland, Columbia; 1963; pub; coed; 2; s
　Spartanburg County, Spartanburg; 1961; pub; coed; 2; s
　Sumter Area, Sumter; 1963; pub; coed; 2; s
　Tri County, Pendleton; 1963; pub; coed; 2; s
　York County, Rock Hill; 1964; pub; coed; 2; s
South Carolina, U. of, Columbia, S.C.; 1801; pub; coed; 4; L
South Central Com. C., Hamden, Conn.; 1968; pub; coed; 2; s
South Dakota School of Mines & Tech., Rapid City, S. Dak.; 1885; pub; coed; 4; s
South Dakota State U., Brookings, S. Dak.; 1881; pub; coed; 4; M
South Dakota, U. of, Vermillion, S. Dak.; 1862; pub; coed; 4; M
Southeastern Baptist C., Laurel, Miss.; 1948; pvt; coed; 2; s
Southeastern Com. C., Whiteville, N.C.; 1964; pub; coed; 2; s
Southeastern Illinois C., Harrisburg, Ill.; 1960; pub; coed; 2; s
Southeastern Iowa Area Com. C.
　Burlington Campus; 1966; pub; coed; 2; s
　Keokuk Campus; 1966; pub; coed; 2; s
Southeastern Louisiana C., Hammond, La.; 1925; pub; coed; 4; M
Southeastern Massachusetts Tech. Inst., North Dartmouth, Mass.; 1895; pub; coed; 4; s
Southeastern Massachusetts U., Fall River, Mass.; 1895; pub; coed; 4; s
Southeastern State C., Durant, Okla.; 1909; pub; coed; 4; s
Southeast Missouri State C., Cape Girardeau, Mo.; 1873; pub; coed; 4; M
Southern Baptist C., Walnut Ridge, Ark.; 1941; pvt; coed; 2; s
Southern California C., Costa Mesa, Calif.; 1920; pvt; coed; 4; s
Southern California, U. of, Los Angeles, Calif.; 1880; pvt; coed; 4; L
Southern Colorado State C., Pueblo, Colo.; 1933; pub; coed; 4; M
Southern Connecticut State C., New Haven, Conn.; 1893; pub; coed; 4; L
Southern Idaho, C. of, Twin Falls, Ida.; 1965; pub; coed; 2; s
Southern Illinois U., Carbondale, Ill.; 1869; pub; coed; 4; L
　Edwardsville Campus; 1965; pub; coed; 4; L
Southern Methodist U., Dallas, Tex.; 1911; pvt; coed; 4; L
Southern Missionary C., Collegedale, Tenn.; 1892; pvt; coed; 4; s
Southern Mississippi, U. of, Hattiesburg, Miss.; 1910; pub; coed; 4; L
Southern Oregon C., Ashland, Ore.; 1926; pub; coed; 4; M
Southern Seminary Jr. C., Buena Vista, Va.; 1926; pvt; wom; 2; s
Southern State C., Magnolia, Ark.; 1909; pub; coed; 4; s
Southern State C., Springfield, S. Dak.; 1881; pub; coed; 4; s
Southern Tech. Inst., Marietta, Ga.; 1947; pub; coed; 2; s
Southern U., Baton Rouge, La.; 1880; pub; coed; 4; L
Southern Utah, C. of, Cedar City, Utah; 1897; pub; coed; 4; s
South Florida Jr. C., Avon Park, Fla.; 1965; pub; coed; 2; s
South Florida, U. of, Tampa, Fla.; 1956; pub; coed; 4; L
South Georgia C., Douglas, Ga.; 1927; pub; coed; 2; s
South Plains C., Levelland, Tex.; 1957; pub; coed; 2; s
South Texas Jr. C., Houston, Tex.; 1948; pvt; coed; 2; M
South, U. of the, Sewanee, Tenn.; 1857; pvt; men; 4; s
Southwest Baptist C., Bolivar, Mo.; 1878; pvt; coed; 4; s
Southwestern at Memphis, Tenn.; 1848; pvt; coed; 4; s
Southwestern C., Chula Vista, Calif.; 1960; pub; coed; 2; M

Southwestern C., Winfield, Kans.; 1885; pvt; coed; 4; s
Southwestern Com. C., Creston, Iowa; 1966; pub; coed; 2; s
Southwestern Louisiana, U. of, Lafayette, La.; 1898; pub; coed; 4; L
Southwestern Oregon Com. C., Coos Bay, Ore.; 1961; pub; coed; 2; s
Southwestern State C., Weatherford, Okla.; 1901; pub; coed; 4; M
Southwestern Union C., Keene, Tex.; 1916; pvt; coed; 4; s
Southwestern U., Georgetown, Tex.; 1840; pvt; coed; 4; s
Southwest Mississippi Jr. C., Summit, Miss.; 1929; pub; coed; 2; s
Southwest Missouri State C., Springfield, Mo.; 1906; pub; coed; 4; M
Southwest Texas Jr. C., Uvalde, Tex.; 1946; pub; coed; 2; s
Southwest Texas State U., San Marcos, Tex.; 1899; pub; coed; 4; L
Spartanburg Jr. C., Spartanburg, S.C.; 1927; pvt; coed; 2; s
Spelman C. (See Atlanta U. Center)
Spokane Com. C., Spokane, Wash.; 1963; pub; coed; 2; M
Spoon River C., Canton, Ill.; 1959; pub; coed; 2; s
Spring Arbor C., Spring Arbor, Mich.; 1873; pvt; coed; 4; s
Springfield C., Springfield, Mass.; 1885; pvt; coed; 4; s
Springfield Jr. C., Springfield, Ill.; 1929; pvt; coed; 2; s
Spring Garden C., Chestnut Hill, Pa.; 1957; pvt; coed; 2; s
Spring Hill C., Mobile, Ala.; 1830; pvt; coed; 4; s
St. Ambrose C., Davenport, Iowa; 1882; pvt; coed; 4; s
St. Andrews Presbyterian C., Laurinburg, N.C.; 1896; pvt; coed; 4; s
St. Anselm's C., Manchester, N.H.; 1889; pvt; coed; 4; s
St. Augustine's C., Raleigh, N.C.; 1867; pvt; coed; 4; s
St. Benedict, C. of, Saint Joseph, Minn.; 1913; pvt; wom; 4; s
St. Benedict's C., Atchison, Kans.; 1858; pvt; coed; 4; s
St. Bernard C., St. Bernard, Ala.; 1892; pvt; coed; 4; s
St. Bonaventure U., St. Bonaventure, N.Y.; 1855; pvt; coed; 4; M
St. Catherine C., Springfield, Ky.; 1931; pvt; coed; 2; s
St. Catherine, The C. of, St. Paul, Minn.; 1905; pvt; wom; 4; s
St. Clair County Com. C., Port Huron, Mich.; 1923; pub; coed; 2; M
St. Cloud State C., St. Cloud, Minn.; 1869; pub; coed; 4; L
St. Edward's U., Austin, Tex.; 1881; pvt; men; 4; s
St. Elizabeth, C. of, Convent Station, N.J.; 1899; pvt; wom; 4; s
St. Francis C., Fort Wayne, Ind.; 1890; pvt; coed; 4; s
St. Francis C., Biddeford, Me.; 1939; pvt; coed; 4; s
St. Francis C., Brooklyn, N.Y.; 1858; pvt; men; 4; s
St. Francis C., Loretto, Pa.; 1847; pvt; coed; 4; s
St. Francis, C. of, Joliet, Ill.; 1874; pvt; wom; 4; s
St. Gregory's C., Shawnee, Okla.; 1959; pvt; coed; 2; s
St. John, C. of, Cleveland, Ohio; 1928; pvt; wom; 4; s
St. John Fisher C., Rochester, N.Y.; 1948; pvt; men; 4; s
St. John's C., Winfield, Kans.; 1893; pvt; coed; 2; s
St. John's C., Annapolis, Md.; 1696; pvt; coed; 4; s
St. John's C., Santa Fe, N. Mex.; 1964; pvt; coed; 4; s
St. Johns River Jr. C., Palatka, Fla.; 1958; pub; coed; 2; s
St. John's U., Collegeville, Minn.; 1856; pvt; men; 4; s
St. John's U., Jamaica, N.Y.; 1870; pvt; coed; 4; L
St. Joseph C., West Hartford, Conn.; 1925; pvt; wom; 4; s
St. Joseph C., Emmitsburg, Md.; 1809; pvt; wom; 4; s
St. Joseph's C., Rensselaer, Ind.; 1889; pvt; coed; 4; s
　Calumet Campus, East Chicago, Ind.; 1951; pvt; coed; 4; s
St. Joseph's C., North Windham, Me.; 1915; pvt; coed; 4; s
St. Joseph's C., Philadelphia, Pa.; 1851; pvt; men; 4; s
St. Joseph's C. for Women, Brooklyn, N.Y.; 1916; pvt; wom; 4; s
St. Lawrence U., Canton, N.Y.; 1856; pvt; coed; 4; s
St. Leo C., St. Leo, Fla.; 1963; pvt; coed; 4; s
St. Louis U., St. Louis, Mo.; 1818; pvt; coed; 4; L
St. Martin's C., Olympia, Wash.; 1895; pvt; coed; 4; s
St. Mary C., Xavier, Kans.; 1860; pvt; wom; 4; s
St. Mary, C. of, Omaha, Nebr.; 1923; pvt; wom; 4; s
St. Mary of the Plains C., Dodge City, Kans.; 1952; pvt; coed; 4; s
St. Mary-of-the-Woods C., St. Mary-of-the-Woods, Ind.; 1840; pvt; wom; 4; s
St. Mary's C., Notre Dame, Ind.; 1844; pvt; coed; 4; s
St. Mary's C., Winona, Minn.; 1912; pvt; coed; 4; s
St. Mary's C. of California, Saint Mary's C., Calif.; 1863; pvt; men; 4; s
St. Mary's C. of Maryland, St. Mary's City, Md.; 1839; pub; coed; 4; s
St. Mary's C. of O'Fallon, O'Fallon, Mo.; 1921; pvt; coed; 2; s

St. Mary's Dominican C., New Orleans, La.; 1860; pvt; wom; 4; s.
St. Mary's Jr. C., Raleigh, N.C.; 1900; pvt; wom; 2; s
St. Mary's, U. of, San Antonio, Tex.; 1852; pvt; coed; 4; M
St. Michael's C., Winooski, Vt.; 1903; pvt; men; 4; s
St. Norbert C., West De Pere, Wis.; 1898; pvt; coed; 4; s
St. Olaf C., Northfield, Minn.; 1874; pvt; coed; 4; M
St. Paul's C., Concordia, Mo.; 1905; pvt; coed; 2; s
St. Paul's C., Lawrenceville, Va.; 1888; pvt; coed; 4; s
St. Petersburg Jr. C., St. Petersburg, Fla.; 1927; pub; coed; 2; L
St. Peter's C., Jersey City, N.J.; 1872; pvt; coed; M
St. Philip's C., San Antonio, Tex.; 1927; pub; coed; 2; s
St. Procopius C., Lisle, Ill.; 1887; pvt; coed; 4; s
St. Rose, C. of, Albany, N.Y.; 1920; pvt; wom; 4; s
St. Scholastica, C. of, Duluth, Minn.; 1902; pvt; coed; 4; s
St. Teresa, C. of, Winona, Minn.; 1907; pvt; coed; 4; s
St. Thomas, C. of, St. Paul, Minn.; 1885; pvt; coed; 4; s
St. Thomas, U. of, Houston, Tex.; 1946; pvt; coed; 4; s
St. Vincent C., Latrobe, Pa.; 1846; pvt; men; 4; s
St. Xavier C., Chicago, Ill.; 1846; pvt; coed; 4; s
Stanford U., Stanford, Calif.; 1885; pvt; coed; 4; L
Stanislaus State C. (See California State C. System)
State University of New York (SUNY) (See New York, State U. of)
Staten Island Com. C. (See City U. of New York)
Stephen F. Austin State U., Nacogdoches, Tex.; 1917; pub; coed; 4; L
Stephens C., Columbia, Mo.; 1833; pvt; wom; 4; s
Sterling C., Sterling, Kans.; 1887; pvt; coed; 4; s
Stetson U., De Land, Fla.; 1883; pvt; coed; 4; M
Steubenville, C. of, Steubenville, Ohio; 1946; pvt; coed; 4; s
Stevens Inst. of Tech., Hoboken, N.J.; 1870; pvt; men; 4; M
Stillman C., Tuscaloosa, Ala.; 1876; pvt; coed; 4; s
Stonehill C., North Easton, Mass.; 1948; pvt; coed; 4; s
Stout State U., Menomonie, Wis.; 1891; pub; coed; 4; M
Sue Bennet C., London, Ky.; 1922; pvt; coed; 2; s
Suffolk County Com. C., Selden, N.Y.; 1959; pub; coed; 2; L
Suffolk U., Boston, Mass.; 1906; pvt; coed; 4; M
Sullins C., Bristol, Va.; 1917; pvt; wom; 2; s
Sul Ross State U., Alpine, Tex.; 1917; pub; coed; 4; s
Suomi C., Hancock, Mich.; 1896; pvt; coed; 2; s
Surry Com. C., Dobson, N.C.; 1964; pub; coed; 2; s
Susquehanna U., Selinsgrove, Pa.; 1858; pvt; coed; 4; s
Swarthmore C., Swarthmore, Pa.; 1864; pvt; coed; 4; s
Sweet Briar C., Sweet Briar, Va.; 1901; pvt; wom; 4; s
Syracuse U., Syracuse, N.Y.; 1870; pvt; coed; 4; L
    Utica C. of Syracuse U., Utica; 1946; pvt; coed; 4; s

Tabor C., Hillsboro, Kans.; 1908; pvt; coed; s
Tacoma Com. C., Tacoma, Wash.; 1964; pub; coed; 2; M
Taft C., Taft, Calif.; 1922; pub; coed; 2; s
Talladega C., Talladega, Ala.; 1865; pvt; coed; 4; s
Tallahassee Jr. C., Tallahassee, Fla.; 1965; pub; coed; 2; s
Tampa, U. of, Tampa, Fla.; 1930; pvt; coed; 4; s
Tarkio C., Tarkio, Mo.; 1883; pvt; coed; 4; s
Tarleton State C., Stephenville, Tex.; 1899; pub; coed; 4; s
Taylor U., Upland, Ind.; 1846; pvt; coed; 4; s
Teachers C. (See Columbia U.)
Temple Buell C., Denver, Colo.; 1888; pvt; wom; 4; s
Temple Jr. C., Temple, Tex.; 1926; pub; coed; 2; s
Temple U., Philadelphia, Pa.; 1884; pvt; coed; 4; L
Tennessee at Chattanooga, U. of, 1886; pvt; coed; 4; M
Tennessee State U., Nashville, Tenn.; 1909; pub; coed; 4; M
Tennessee Tech. U., Cookeville, Tenn.; 1915; pub; coed; 4; M
Tennessee Temple C., Chattanooga, Tenn.; 1946; pvt; coed; 4; M
Tennessee, U. of, Knoxville, Tenn.; 1794; pub; coed; 4; L
    Martin Campus
    Memphis Campus
    Nashville Campus
Tennessee Wesleyan C., Athens, Tenn.; 1857; pvt; coed; 4; s
Texarkana C., Texarkana, Tex.; 1927; pub; coed; 2; s
Texas A&I U., Kingsville, Tex.; 1917; pub; coed; 4; M
Texas A&M U., College Station, Tex.; 1870; pub; coed; 4; L
Texas at Arlington, U. of, 1895; pub; coed; 4; L
Texas at Austin, U. of, 1876; pub; coed; 4; L
Texas at El Paso, U. of, 1913; pub; coed; 4; L
Texas Christian U., Fort Worth, Tex.; 1873; pvt; coed; 4; M
Texas C., Tyler, Tex.; 1926; pub; coed; 2; M
Texas Lutheran C., Seguin, Tex.; 1891; pvt; coed; 4; s
Texas Southern U., Houston, Tex.; 1947; pub; coed; 4; M
Texas Southmost C., Brownsville, Tex.; 1926; pub; coed; 2; s

Texas Tech. U., Lubbock, Tex.; 1923; pub; coed; 4; L
Texas Wesleyan C., Fort Worth, Tex.; 1890; pvt; coed; 4; s
Texas Woman's U., Denton, Tex.; 1901; pub; wom; 4; M
Thiel C., Greenville, Pa.; 1866; pvt; coed; 4; s
Thomas More C., Fort Mitchell, Ky.; 1921; pvt; coed; 4; s
Thornton Jr. C., Harvey, Ill.; 1927; pub; coed; 2; M
Tidewater Com. C., Portsmouth, Va.; 1968; pub; coed; 2; s
Tift C., Forsyth, Ga.; 1847; pvt; wom; 4; s
T. J. Harris Jr. C., Meridian, Miss.; 1956; pub; coed; 2; s
Toledo, The U. of, Ohio; 1872; pub; coed; 4; L
Tombrock C., West Paterson, N.J.; 1955; pvt; wom; 2; s
Tougaloo C., Tougaloo, Miss.; 1869; pvt; coed; 4; s
Towson State C., Baltimore, Md.; 1865; pub; coed; 4; M
Transylvania U., Lexington, Ky.; 1780; pvt; coed; 4; s
Treasure Valley Com. C., Ontario, Ore.; 1962; pub; coed; 2; s
Trenton Jr. C., Trenton, Mo.; 1925; pub; coed; 2; s
Trenton State C., Trenton, N.J.; 1855; pub; coed; 4; L
Trinidad State Jr. C., Trinidad, Colo.; 1933; pub; coed; 2; s
Trinity C., Hartford, Conn.; 1823; pvt; coed; 4; s
Trinity C., Washington, D.C.; 1897; pvt; wom; 4; s
Trinity C., Burlington, Vt.; 1925; pvt; wom; 4; s
Trinity U., San Antonio, Tex.; 1869; pvt; coed; 4; s
Tri-State C., Angola, Ind.; 1883; pvt; coed; 4; s
Triton C., River Grove, Ill.; 1964; pub; coed; 2; M
Troy State C., Troy, Ala.; 1887; pub; coed; 4; M
Truett-McConnell C., Cleveland, Ga.; 1946; pvt; coed; 2; s
Tufts U., Medford, Mass.; 1852; pvt; men; 4; M
    Jackson C.; 1910; pvt; wom; 4; s
Tulane U., New Orleans, La.; 1834; pvt; coed; 4; L
    Newcomb C.; New Orleans, La.; 1886; pvt; wom; 4; s
Tulsa, U. of, Tulsa, Okla.; 1894; pvt; coed; 4; M
Tusculum C., Greenville, Tenn.; 1794; pvt; coed; 4; s
Tuskegee Inst., Tuskegee Institute, Ala.; 1881; pvt; coed; 4; M
Tyler Jr. C., Tyler, Tex.; 1926; pub; coed; 2; M

Ulster County Com. C., Stone Ridge, N.Y.; 1961; pub; coed; 2; s
Umpqua Com. C., Roseburg, Ore.; 1964; pub; coed; 2; s
Union C., Barbourville, Ky.; 1879; pvt; coed; 4; s
Union C., Lincoln, Nebr.; 1891; pvt; coed; 4; s
Union C., Cranford, N.J.; 1933; pvt; coed; 2; s
Union C., Schenectady, N.Y.; 1795; pvt; coed; 4; s
Union U., Jackson, Tenn.; 1825; pvt; coed; 4; s
United States Air Force Academy, USAF, Colo.; 1954; pub. men; 4; M
United States Coast Guard Academy, New London, Conn.; 1876; pub; men; 4; s
United States International U., San Diego, Calif.; 1952; pvt; coed; 4; M
United States Merchant Marine Academy, Kings Point, N.Y.; 1936; pub; men; 4; s
United States Military Academy, West Point, N.Y.; 1802; pub; men; 4; M
United States Naval Academy, Annapolis, Md.; 1845; pub; men; 4; M
Upper Iowa C., Fayette, Iowa; 1850; pvt; coed; 4; s
Upsala C., East Orange, N.J.; 1893; pvt; coed; 4; s
Ursinus C., Collegeville, Pa.; 1869; pvt; coed; 4; s
Ursuline C., Cleveland, Ohio; 1850; pvt; coed; 4; s
Utah State U., Logan, Utah; 1888; pub; coed; 4; s
Utah, U. of, Salt Lake City, Utah; 1850; pub; coed; 4; L
Utica C. (See Syracuse U.)
Utica Jr. C., Utica, Miss.; 1954; pub; coed; 2; s

Valdosta State C., Valdosta, Ga.; 1906; pub; coed; 4; M
Valley City State C., Valley City, N. Dak.; 1889; pub; coed; 4; s
Valley Forge Military Jr. C., Wayne, Pa.; 1934; pvt; men; 2; s
Valparaiso U., Valparaiso, Ind.; 1859; pvt; coed; 4; M
Vanderbilt U., Nashville, Tenn.; 1872; pvt; coed; 4; M
Vassar C., Poughkeepsie, N.Y.; 1861; pvt; coed; 4; s
Ventura C., Ventura, Calif.; 1925; pub; coed; 2; M
Vermillion State Jr. C., Ely, Minn.; 1922; pub; coed; 2; s
Vermont C., Montpelier, Vt.; 1941; pvt; wom; 2; s
Vermont Tech. C., Randolph Center, Vt.; 1957; pub; coed; 2; s
Vermont, U. of, Burlington, Vt.; 1791; pub; coed; 4; M
Victoria C., Victoria, Tex.; 1925; pub; coed; 2; s
Victor Valley C., Victorville, Calif.; 1961; pub; coed; 2; s
Villa Julie C., Stevenson, Md.; 1952; pvt; wom; 2; s
Villa Madonna C., Covington, Ky.; 1921; pvt; coed; 4; s
Villa Maria C., Erie, Pa.; 1925; pvt; wom; 4; s
Villa Maria C. of Buffalo, N.Y.; 1960; pvt; coed; 2; s
Villanova U., Villanova, Pa.; 1842; pvt; coed; 4; L
Vincennes U., Vincennes, Ind.; 1801; pub; coed; 2; M

Virginia Commonwealth U., Richmond, Va.; 1917; pub; coed; 4; M

Virginia Intermont C., Bristol, Va.; 1910; pvt; wom; 2; S

Virginia Military Inst., Lexington, Va.; 1839; pub; men; 4; S

Virginia Polytechnic Inst., Blacksburg, Va.; 1872; pub; coed; 4; L

Virginia State C., Petersburg, Va.; 1882; pub; coed; 4; M
   Norfolk Division; 1944; pub; coed; 4; M

Virginia Union U., Richmond, Va.; 1865; pvt; coed; 4; S

Virginia, U. of, Charlottesville, Va.; 1819; pub; coed; 4; L
   Clinch Valley C., Wise, Va.; 1954; pub; coed; 4; S
   Eastern Shore Branch, Wallops Island; 1964; pub; coed; 2; S
   George Mason C., Fairfax; 1957; pub; coed; 4; S
   Mary Washington C., Fredericksburg; 1908; pub; wom; 4; S
   Patrick Henry C., Martinsville; 1964; pub; coed; 2; S

Virginia Western Com. C., Roanoke, Va.; 1966; pub; coed; 2; S

Viterbo C., La Crosse, Wis.; 1931; pvt; wom; 4; S

Voorhees C., Denmark, S.C.; 1897; pvt; coed; 4; S

Wabash C., Crawfordsville, Ind.; 1832; pvt; men; 4; S

Wabash Valley C., Mount Carmel, Ill.; 1960; pub; coed; 2; S

Wagner C., Staten Island, N.Y.; 1885; pvt; coed; 4; M

Wake Forest U., Winston-Salem, N.C.; 1833; pvt; coed; 4; M

Waldorf C., Forest City, Iowa; 1920; pvt; coed; 2; S

Walker C., Jasper, Ala.; 1938; pvt; coed; 2; S

Walla Walla C., College Place, Wash.; 1892; pvt; coed; 4; S

Walla Walla Com. C., Walla Walla, Wash.; 1967; pub; coed; 2; S

Warner Pacific C., Portland, Ore.; 1937; pvt; coed; 4; S

Wartburg C., Waverly, Iowa; 1852; pvt; coed; 4; S

Washburn U. of Topeka, Kans.; 1865; pub; coed; 4; M

Washington and Jefferson C., Washington, Pa.; 1787; pvt; men; 4; S

Washington and Lee U., Lexington, Va.; 1749; pvt; men; 4; S

Washington C., Chestertown, Md.; 1706; pvt; coed; 4; S

Washington State C., Machias, Me.; 1909; pub; coed; 4; S

Washington State U., Pullman, Wash.; 1890; pub; coed; 4; L

Washington U., St. Louis, Mo.; 1853; pvt; coed; 4; L

Washington, U. of, Seattle, Wash.; 1861; pub; coed; 4; L

Waubonsee Com. C., Sugar Grove, Ill.; 1966; pub; coed; 2; S

Wayland Baptist C., Plainview, Tex.; 1908; pvt; coed; 4; S

Waynesburg C., Waynesburg, Pa.; 1849; pvt; coed; 4; S

Wayne State C., Wayne, Nebr.; 1910; pub; coed; 4; M

Wayne State U., Detroit, Mich.; 1868; pub; coed; 4; L

Weatherford C., Weatherford, Tex.; 1949; pub; coed; 2; S

Weber State C., Ogden, Utah; 1899; pub; coed; 4; L

Webster C., St. Louis, Mo.; 1915; pvt; coed; 4; S

Wellesley C., Wellesley, Mass.; 1870; pvt; wom; 4; S

Wells C., Aurora, N.Y.; 1868; pvt; wom; 4; S

Wenatchee Valley C., Wenatchee, Wash.; 1939; pub; coed; 2; S

Wentworth Inst., Boston, Mass.; 1911; pvt; men; 2; S

Wentworth Military Academy, Lexington, Mo.; 1923; pvt; men; 2; S

Wesleyan C., Macon, Ga.; 1836; pvt; wom; 4; S

Wesleyan U., Middletown, Conn.; 1829; pvt; men; 4; S

Wesley C., Dover, Del.; 1922; pvt; coed; 2; S

Westark Jr. C., Fort Smith, Ark.; 1928; pub; coed; 2; S

Westbrook Jr. C., Portland, Me.; 1925; pvt; wom; 2; S

Westchester Com. C., Valhalla, N.Y.; 1946; pub; coed; 2; M

West Chester State C., West Chester, Pa.; 1812; pub; coed; 4; L

West Coast U., Los Angeles, Calif.; 1909; pvt; coed; 4; S

Western Carolina U., Cullowhee, N.C.; 1889; pub; coed; 4; M

Western C. for Women, Oxford, Ohio; 1853; pvt; wom; 4; S

Western Connecticut State C., Danbury, Conn.; 1903; pub; coed; 4; M

Western Illinois U., Macomb, Ill.; 1899; pub; coed; 4; L

Western Kentucky U., Bowling Green, Ky.; 1906; pub; coed; 4; L

Western Maryland C., Westminster, Md.; 1867; pvt; coed; 4; S

Western Michigan U., Kalamazoo, Mich.; 1903; pub; coed; 4; L

Western Montana C., Dillon, Mont.; 1893; pub; coed; 4; S

Western New England C., Springfield, Mass.; 1919; pvt; coed; 4; S

Western New Mexico U., Silver City, N. Mex.; 1893; pub; coed; 4; S

Western Reserve U. (See Case Western Reserve U.)

Western State C. of Colorado, Gunnison, Colo; 1901; pub; coed; 4; S

Western Washington State C., Bellingham, Wash.; 1893; pub; coed; 4; M

Western Wyoming Com. C., Reliance, Wyo.; 1959; pub; coed; 2; S

Westfield State C., Westfield, Mass.; 1839; pub; coed; 4; M

West Georgia C., Carrollton, Ga.; 1933; pub; coed; 4; M

Westhampton C. (See University of Richmond)

West Liberty State C., West Liberty, W. Va.; 1837; pub; coed; 4; M

Westmar C., La Mars, Iowa; 1890; pvt; coed; 4; S

Westminster Choir C., Princeton, N.J.; 1926; pvt; coed; 4; S

Westminster C., Fulton, Mo.; 1851; pvt; men; 4; S

Westminster C., New Wilmington, Pa.; 1852; pvt; coed; 4; S

Westminster C., Salt Lake City, Utah; 1875; pvt; coed; 4; S

Westmont C., Santa Barbara, Calif.; 1937; pvt; coed; 4; S

West Texas State U., Canyon, Tex.; 1910; pub; coed; 4; M

West Valley C., Campbell, Calif.; 1963; pub; coed; 2; L

West Virginia Inst. of Tech., Montgomery, W. Va.; 1895; pub; coed; 4; S

West Virginia State C., Institute, W. Va.; 1891; pub; coed; 4; M

West Virginia U., Morgantown, W. Va.; 1867; pub; coed; 4; L
   Parkersburg Center; 1961; pub; coed; 2; S
   Potomac State C., Keyser; 1921; pub; coed; 2; S

West Virginia Wesleyan C., Buckhannon, W. Va.; 1890; pvt; coed; 4; S

Wharton County Jr. C., Wharton, Tex.; 1946; pub; coed; 2; S

Wheaton C., Wheaton, Ill.; 1853; pvt; coed; 4; S

Wheaton C., Norton, Mass.; 1854; pvt; wom; 4; S

Wheeling C., Wheeling, W. Va.; 1954; pvt; coed; 4; S

Wheelock C., Boston, Mass.; 1888; pvt; coed; 4; S

Whitman C., Walla Walla, Wash.; 1859; pvt; coed; 4; S

Whittier C., Whittier, Calif.; 1901; pvt; coed; 4; S

Whitworth C., Spokane, Wash.; 1890; pvt; coed; 4; S

Wichita State U., Wichita, Kans.; 1892; pub; coed; 4; L

Wilberforce U., Wilberforce, Ohio; 1856; pvt; coed; 4; S

Wiley C., Marshall, Tex.; 1873; pvt; coed; 4; S

Wilkes C., Wilkes-Barre, Pa.; 1933; pvt; coed; 4; M

Wilkes Com. C., Wilkesboro, N.C.; 1965; pub; coed; 2; S

Willamette U., Salem, Ore.; 1842; pvt; coed; 4; S

William and Mary, C. of, Williamsburg, Va.; 1693; pub; coed; 4; M
   Christopher Newport C., Newport News; 1961; pub; coed; 2; S
   Richard Bland C., Petersburg; 1961; pub; coed; 2; S

William Carey C., Hattiesburg, Miss.; 1906; pvt; coed; 4; S

William Jewell C., Liberty, Mo.; 1849; pvt; coed; 4; S

William Penn C., Oskaloosa, Iowa; 1873; pub; coed; 4; S

Williams C., Williamstown, Mass.; 1793; pvt; men; 4; S

William Woods C., Fulton, Mo.; 1870; pvt; wom; 4; S

Willmar State Jr. C., Willmar, Minn.; 1962; pub; coed; 2; S

Wilmington C., Wilmington, N.C.; 1947; pub; coed; 4; S

Wilmington C., Wilmington, Ohio; 1863; pvt; coed; 4; S

Wilson C., Chambersburg, Pa.; 1869; pvt; wom; 4; S

Windham C., Putney, Vt.; 1951; pvt; coed; 4; S

Wingate C., Wingate, N.C.; 1896; pub; coed; 2; S

Winona State C., Winona, Minn.; 1858; pub; coed; 4; M

Winston-Salem State C., Winston-Salem, N.C.; 1892; pub; coed; 4; S

Winthrop C., Rock Hill, S.C.; 1886; pub; wom; 4; M

Wisconsin at Green Bay, U. of; 1968; pub; coed; 4; M

Wisconsin at Milwaukee, U. of; 1955; pub; coed; 4; L

Wisconsin at Parkside, U. of, Kenosha; 1965; pub; coed; 4; M

Wisconsin Center System, U. of
   Baraboo-Sauk County Campus, Baraboo; 1968; pub; coed; 2; S
   Marathon County Campus, Wausau; 1933; pub; coed; 2; S
   Marshfield Wood County Campus, Marshfield; 1964; pub; coed; 2; S
   Rock County Campus, Janesville; 1966; pub; coed; 2; S
   Sheboygan County Campus, Sheboygan; 1933; pub; coed; 2; S
   Washington County Campus, West Bend; 1968; pub; coed; 2; S
   Waukesha County Campus, Waukesha; 1966; pub; coed; 2; S

Wisconsin State U.-Eau Claire, Wis.; 1916; pub; coed; 4; M

Wisconsin State U.-La Crosse, Wis.; 1909; pub; coed; 4; M

Wisconsin State U.-Oshkosh, Wis.; 1871; pub; coed; 4; L

Wisconsin State U.-Platteville, Wis.; 1866; pub; coed; 4; M

Wisconsin State U.-River Falls, Wis.; 1874; pub; coed; 4; M

Wisconsin State U.-Stevens Point, Wis.; 1894; pub; coed; 4; M

Wisconsin State U.-Superior, Wis.; 1893; pub; coed; 4; M

Wisconsin State U.-Whitewater, Wis.; 1868; pub; coed; 4; L

Wisconsin, U. of, Madison; 1848; pub; coed; 4; L

Wittenberg U., Springfield, Ohio; 1845; pvt; coed; 4; S

Wofford C., Spartanburg, S.C.; 1851; pvt; men; 4; S

Woodbury C., Los Angeles, Calif.; 1884; pvt; coed; 4; S

Wood Jr. C., Mathiston, Miss.; 1927; pvt; coed; 2; S

Wooster, C. of, Wooster, Ohio; 1866; pvt; coed; 4; S

Worcester Jr. C., Worcester, Mass.; 1938; pvt; coed; 2; S

Worcester Polytechnic Inst., Worcester, Mass.; 1865; pvt; coed; 4; M

Worcester State C., Worcester, Mass.; 1871; pub; coed; 4; S

Worthington State Jr. C., Worthington, Minn.; 1936; pub; coed; 2; S

Wright State U., Dayton, Ohio; 1964; pub; coed; 4; L

Wyoming, U. of, Laramie, Wyo.; 1886; pub; coed; 4; L

Wytheville Com. C., Wytheville, Va.; 1963; pub; coed; 2; S

Xaverian C., Silver Spring, Md.; 1951; pvt; men; 2; S

Xavier U., New Orleans, La.; 1915; pvt; coed; 4; S

Xavier U., Cincinnati, Ohio; 1831; pvt; coed; 4; M

Yakima Valley C., Yakima, Wash.; 1928; pub; coed; 2; S

Yale U., New Haven, Conn.; 1701; pvt; coed; 4; L

Yankton C., Yankton, S. Dak.; 1881; pvt; coed; 4; S

Yeshiva U., New York, N.Y.; 1886; pvt; coed; 4; L

York C. (See City U. of New York)

York C., York, Nebr.; 1890; pvt; coed; 2; S

York C. of Pennsylvania, York, Pa.; 1941; pvt; coed; 2; S

Young Harris C., Young Harris, Ga.; 1912; pvt; coed; 2; S

Youngstown State U., Youngstown, Ohio; 1908; pub; coed; 4; L

Yuba C., Marysville, Calif.; 1927; pub; coed; 2; M

INSTITUTIONS OF HIGHER EDUCATION
IN CANADA

Below are listed Canadian universities, colleges, and community colleges as of January 1973. Each entry gives the name of the institution, its location by city and province, and its date of founding, followed by:

Type of student body: men only (men); women only (women); or coeducational (coed).

Number of students: small (S), under 2,000; medium (M), between 2,000 and 5,000; large (L), between 5,000 and 10,000; very large (VL), above 10,000.

The acronym CEGEP (collége dè enseignement général et professionnel) is applied to certain community colleges in Québec. CEGEP institutions are two-year colleges that give general and vocational instruction.

UNIVERSITIES AND COLLEGES

Acadia U., Wolfville, N.S.; 1836; coed; M
Alberta, U. of, Edmonton, Alta.; 1906; coed; VL
Algoma College, Sault Ste. Marie, Ont.; 1965; coed; S
Althouse College of Education, London, Ont.; 1965; coed; S
Assumption U., Windsor, Ont.; 1857; coed; S

Bishop's U., Lennoxville, P.Q.; 1843; coed; S
Brandon U., Brandon, Man.; 1899; coed; S
Brescia College, London, Ont.; 1919; women; S
British Columbia, U. of, Vancouver, B.C.; 1890; coed; VL
Brock U., St. Catharines, Ont.; 1964; coed; M

Calgary, U. of, Calgary, Alta.; 1945; coed; L
Campion College, Regina, Sask.; 1918; coed; S
Canterbury College, Windsor, Ont.; 1957; coed; S
Carleton U., Ottawa, Ont.; 1942; coed; L
Catherine Par Traill College, Peterborough, Ont.; 1964; coed; S
College of Education, St. Catharines, Ont.; 1965; coed; S
Conrad Grebel College, Waterloo, Ont.; 1961; coed; S

Dalhousie U., Halifax, N.S.; 1818; coed; L

Emanuel College of Victoria U., Toronto, Ont.; 1836; coed; M
Emmanuel & St. Chad, College of, Saskatoon, Sask.; 1964; coed; S
Erindale College, Clarkson, Ont.; 1964; coed; S

Glendon College, Toronto, Ont.; 1966; coed; S
Guelph, U. of, Guelph, Ont.; 1966; coed; L

Hautes Études Commerciales, École des, Montréal, P.Q.; 1907; coed; M
Hearst, Collège Universitaire de, Hearst, Ont.; 1952; coed; S
Holy Redeemer College, Windsor, Ont.; 1956; men; S
Huntington U., Sudbury, Ont.; 1960; coed
Huron College, London, Ont.; 1863; coed; S

Ignatius College, Guelph, Ont.; 1913; men; S
Innis College, Toronto, Ont.; 1964; coed; M

Joseph E. Atkinson College, Toronto, Ont.; 1962; coed; S

King's College, London, Ont.; 1966; coed; S
King's College, U. of, Halifax, N.S.; 1789; coed; S
Knox College, Toronto, Ont.; 1844; coed; L

Lady Eton College, Peterborough, Ont.; 1968: women; S
Lakehead U., Thunder Bay, Ont.; 1946; coed; M
Laurentian U. of Sudbury, Sudbury, Ont.; 1960; coed; M
Laval U., Québec, P.Q.; 1852; coed; VL
Lethbridge, U. of, Lethbridge, Alta.; 1967; coed; S
Loretto College, Toronto, Ont.; 1912; women; S
Loyola College, Montréal, P.Q.; 1899; coed; M
Luther College, Regina, Sask.; 1921; coed; S
Lutheran Theological Seminary, Saskatoon, Sask.; 1965; coed; S

MacDonald College, Ste.-Anne de Bellevue, P.Q.; 1907; S
Manitoba, U. of, Winnipeg, Man.; 1877; coed; VL
Massey College, Toronto, Ont.; 1963; men; M
McGill U., Montréal, P.Q.; 1821; coed; VL

McMaster Divinity College, Hamilton, Ont.; 1957; S
McMaster U., Hamilton, Ont.; 1887; coed; L
Memorial U. of Newfoundland, St. John's, Nfld.; 1949; coed; L
Mennonite Brethren College of Arts, Winnipeg, Man.; 1944; coed; S
Moncton, U. de, Moncton, N.B.; 1963; coed; M
Montréal Diocesan Theological College, Montréal, P.Q.; 1873; men; S
Montréal, U. de, Montréal, P.Q.; 1876; coed; VL
Mount Allison U., Sackville, N.B.; 1843; coed; S
Mount St. Bernard College, Antigonish, N.S.; 1882; women; S
Mount St. Vincent U., Halifax, N.S.; 1925; women; S

New Brunswick, U. of, Fredericton, N.B.; 1785; coed; L
New College, Toronto, Ont.; 1962; coed; M
Nipissing College, North Bay, Ont.; 1967; coed; S
Notre Dame of Canada College, Wilcox, Sask.; 1933; coed; S
Notre Dame U. of Nelson, Nelson, B.C.; 1951; coed; S
Nova Scotia College of Arts & Design, Halifax, N.S.; 1887; coed; S

Ontario Institute for Studies in Education, Toronto, Ont.; 1965; coed; S
Ottawa, U. of, Ottawa, Ont.; 1848; coed; VL

Peter Robinson College, Peterborough, Ont.; 1964; coed; S
Polytechnique, École, Montréal, P.Q.; 1873; coed; M
Presbyterian College of Montréal, Montréal, P.Q.; 1865; men; S
Prince Edward Island, U. of, Charlottetown, P.E.I., 1969; coed; S

Québec, U. de, Québec, P.Q.; 1968; coed; L
Queen's College, St. John's, Nfld.; coed; M
Queen's Theological College, Kingston, Ont.; 1912; S
Queen's U. at Kingston, Kingston, Ont.; 1841; coed; L

Regis College, Toronto, Ont.; 1930; men; M
Renison College, Waterloo, Ont.; 1959; S
Royal Military College of Canada, Kingston, Ont.; 1874; men; S
Royal Roads Military College, Victoria, B.C.; 1942; men; S
Royal Victoria College, Montréal, P.Q.; 1899; women; M

St. Andrew's College, Saskatoon, Sask.; 1912; men; S
St. Andrew's College, Winnipeg, Man.; 1946; men; M
St. Augustine's Seminary, Scarborough, Ont.; 1913; men; S
St. Bride's College, Littledale, Nfld.; 1884; women; S
St. Charles Scholasticate, Battleford, Sask.; 1939; men; S
St. Francis Xavier U., Antigonish, N.S.; 1953; coed; M
St. Hilda's College, Toronto, Ont.; 1888; women; M
St.-Jean, Collège Militaire Royal de, St.-Jean, P.Q.; 1952; men; S
St.-Jean, Collège Universitaire, Edmonton, Alta.; 1961; coed; S
St. Jerome's College, Waterloo, Ont.; 1864; coed; S
St. John's College, Winnipeg, Man.; 1849; coed; M
St.-Joseph, Collège, Moncton, N.B.; 1864; coed; M

St. Joseph's College, Edmonton, Alta.; 1926; coed; M
St. Joseph's College, Toronto, Ont.; 1911; women; S
St. Mark's College, Vancouver, B.C.; 1965; men; M
St. Mary's U., Halifax, N.S.; 1802; coed; M
St. Michael's College, Toronto, Ont.; 1852; coed; S
St. Paul U., Ottawa, Ont.; 1965; S
St. Paul's College, Waterloo, Ont.; coed; S
St. Paul's College, Winnipeg, Man.; 1926; coed; S
St. Stephen's College, Edmonton, Alta.; 1927; coed
St. Thomas College, North Battleford, Sask.; 1939; S
St. Thomas More College, Saskatoon, Sask.; 1936; coed; S
St. Thomas U., Fredericton, N.B.; 1910; coed; M
Saskatchewan, U. of, Regina, Sask.; 1907; coed; M
Saskatchewan, U. of, Saskatoon, Sask.; 1907; coed; L
Scarborough College, West Hill, Ont.; 1964; coed; M
Sherbrooke, U. de, Sherbrooke, P.Q.; 1954; coed; M
Simon Fraser U., Burnaby, B.C.; 1963; coed; M
Sir George Williams U., Montréal, P.Q.; 1873; coed; L
Sudbury, U. of, Sudbury, Ont.; 1913; coed; L

Thornloe U., Sudbury, Ont.; 1961; coed; M
Toronto, U. of, Toronto, Ont.; 1827; coed; V L

Trent U., Petersborough, Ont.; 1960; coed; S
Trinity College, U. of, Toronto, Ont.; 1852; coed; S

United Theological College of Montréal, Montréal, P.Q.; 1926; S
University College, Sudbury, Ont.; coed; S
University College, Toronto, Ont.; 1853; coed; L

Vancouver School of Theology, Vancouver, B.C.; coed; S
Victoria U., Toronto, Ont.; 1836; coed; S
Victoria, U. of, Victoria, B.C.; 1963; coed; L

Waterloo Lutheran U., Waterloo, Ont.; 1910; coed; M
Waterloo, U. of, Waterloo, Ont.; 1959; coed; V L
Western Ontario, U. of, London, Ont.; 1878; coed; V L
Windsor, U. of, Windsor, Ont.; 1963; coed; L
Winnipeg, U. of, Winnipeg, Man.; 1877; coed; M
Wycliffe College, Toronto, Ont.; 1877; men; M

Xavier College, Sydney, N.S.; 1951; coed; S

York U., Downsview, Ont.; 1965; coed; L

COMMUNITY COLLEGES

Ahuntsic, Collège (CEGEP), Montréal, P.Q.; 1967; coed; M
Algonquin College of Applied Arts and Technology, Ottawa, Ont., 1966; coed; M
André-Grasset, Collège, Montréal, P.Q.; 1876; coed; M
André-Laurendeau, Collège (CEGEP), La Salle, P.Q.; coed; S
Assiniboine Community College, Brandon, Man.; 1966; coed; S
Assomption, Collège de l', L'Assomption, P.Q.; 1832; coed; S

Bois-de-Boulogne, Collège de (CEGEP), Montréal, P.Q.; 1968; coed; S
British Columbia Institute of Technology, Burnaby, B.C.; 1964; coed; M

Cambrian College of Applied Arts and Technology, Sudbury; Ont.; 1967; coed; S
Camosun College, Victoria, B.C.; 1971; coed; S
Camrose College, Camrose, Alta.; 1910; coed; M
Capilano College, West Vancouver, B.C.; 1968; coed; S
Cariboo College, Kamloops, B.C.; 1969; coed; S
Centennial College of Applied Arts and Technology, Scarborough, Ont.; 1966; coed; S
Centralia College of Agricultural Technology, Huron Park, Ont.; 1967; coed; S
Chicoutimi, Collège de (CEGEP), Chicoutimi, P.Q.; 1967; coed; M
Columbia Junior College, Vancouver, B.C.; 1965; coed; S
Concordia Lutheran College, Edmonton, Alta.; 1921; coed; S
Conestoga College of Applied Arts and Technology, Kitchener, Ont.; 1967; coed; S
Côte-Nord, Collège Régional de la (CEGEP), Baie-Comeau, P.Q.; 1971; coed; S

Dawson College (CEGEP), Westmount, P.Q.; 1968; coed; S
Durham College of Applied Arts and Technology, Oshawa, Ont.; 1967; coed; S
Durocher, Collège, St.-Lambert (Chambly), P.Q.; 1947; women

Édouard-Montpetit, Collège (CEGEP), Longueuil (Chambly), P.Q.; 1971; coed; S

Fairview Agricultural & Vocational College, Fairview, Alta.; 1963; coed; S
Fanshawe College of Applied Arts and Technology, London, Ont.; 1967; coed; S
Fisheries, Navigation, Marine Engineering and Electronics, College of, St. John's, Nfld.; 1964; coed; S
Français, Collège, Montréal, P.Q.; 1959; coed; S
François-Xavier-Garneau, Collège (CEGEP), Québec, P.Q.; 1969; coed; S

Gaspésie, Collège de la (CEGEP), Gaspé (Gaspé-Sud), P.Q.; 1968; coed; S
George Brown College of Applied Arts and Technology, Toronto, Ont.; 1967; coed; S
Georgian College of Applied Arts and Technology, Barrie, Ont.; 1965; coed; S
Grande Prairie Regional College, Grande Prairie, Alta.; 1965; coed; S

Grant MacEwan Community College, Edmonton, Alta.; 1971; coed; S

Holland College, Charlottetown, P.E.I.; 1969; coed; S
Hull, Collège de (CEGEP), Hull (Gatineau), P.Q.; 1967; coed; S
Humber College of Applied Arts and Technology, Rexdale, Ont.; 1967; coed; S

Jean-de-Brébeuf, Collège, Montréal, P.Q.; coed; S
Jésus-Marie, Collège, Sillery, P.Q.; 1923; women; S
Jésus-Marie, Collège, Shippegan, N.B.; 1960; women; S
John Abbott College (CEGEP), Ste.-Anne-de-Bellevue, P.Q.; 1970; coed; S
Joliette, Collège de (CEGEP), Joliette, P.Q.; 1968; coed; S
Jonquière, Collège de (CEGEP), Jonquière, P.Q.; 1967; coed; M

Keewatin Community College, The Pas, Man.; 1966; men; S
Kemptville College of Agricultural Technology, Kemptville, Ont.; 1917; coed; S

Laflèche, Collège, Trois-Rivières, P.Q.; 1969; coed; S
Lambton College of Applied Arts and Technology, Sarnia, Ont.; 1971; coed; S
Lethbridge Community College, Lethbridge, Alta.; 1957; coed; S
Lévis, Collège de, Lévis, P.Q.; 1853; coed; S
Lévis-Lauzon, Collège de (CEGEP), Lauzon (Lévis), P.Q.; 1969; coed; S
Limoilou, Collège de (CEGEP), Québec, P.Q.; 1967; coed; M
Lionel-Groux, Collège (CEGEP), Ste.-Thérèse-de-Blainville (Terrebonne), P.Q.; 1967; coed; S
Loyalist College of Applied Arts and Technology, Belleville, Ont.; 1967; coed; S

Maillet, Collège, St.-Basile, N.B.; 1949; women; S
Maisonneuve, Collège de (CEGEP), Montréal, P.Q.; 1967; coed; S
Malaspina College, Nanaimo, B.C.; 1968; coed; S
Marguerite-Bourgeoys (CEGEP), Westmount, P.Q.; coed; 1908; S
Marguerite-d'Youville, Collège-École Normale, Ste.-Foy, P.Q.; 1967; women; S
Marianopolis College, Montréal, P.Q.; 1946; women; S
Marie-Victorin, Collège, Montréal, P.Q.; 1965; coed; S
Matane, Collège de (CEGEP), Matane, P.Q.; 1970; coed; S
Medicine Hat College, Medicine Hat, Alta.; 1964; coed; S
Mérici, Collège, Québec, P.Q.; 1857; coed; S
Michèle-Provost, Académie, Montréal, P.Q.; 1957; coed; S
Mohawk College of Applied Arts and Technology, Hamilton, Ont.; 1966; coed; M
Montmorency, Collège (CEGEP), Chomedey (Laval), P.Q.; 1973; coed; M
Mount Royal College, Calgary, Alta.; 1910; coed; S
Musique de Nicolet, École Supérieure de, Nicolet, P.Q.; 1935; coed; S

New Brunswick Technical Institute, Moncton, N.B.; 1964; coed; S
New Caledonia, College of, Prince George, B.C.; 1968; coed; S

New Liskeard College of Agricultural Technology, New Liskeard, Ont.; 1966; men; s
Newfoundland College of Trades and Technology, St. John's, Nfld.; 1960; coed; s
Niagara College of Applied Arts and Technology, Welland, Ont.; 1966; coed; s
Niagara Parks Commission School of Horticulture, Niagara Falls, Ont.; 1936; coed; s
Northern Alberta Institute of Technology, Edmonton, Alta.; 1963; coed; M
Northern College of Applied Arts and Technology, Timmins, Ont.; 1967; coed; s
Notre-Dame-de-Bellevue, Québec, P.Q.; 1914; women; s
Notre-Dame-de-Foy, École Normale, Cap-Rouge, P.Q.; 1965; coed; s
Nova Scotia Agricultural College, Truro, N.S.; 1905; coed; s
Nova Scotia Eastern Institute of Technology, Sydney, N.S.; 1963; coed; s
Nova Scotia Land Survey Institute, Lawrencetown, N.S.; 1947; coed; s
Nova Scotia Technical College, Halifax, N.S.; 1907; coed; s

Okanagan Regional College, Kelowna, B.C.; 1968; coed; s
Olds Agricultural and Vocational College, Olds, Alta.; 1913; coed; s
Ontario College of Art, Toronto, Ont.; 1876; coed; s

Pocatière, Collège de la (CEGEP), La Pocatière (Kamouraska), P.Q.; 1969; coed; s

Québec, Le Petit Séminaire de, Québec, P.Q.; 1668; coed; s

Red Deer College, Red Deer, Alta.; 1964; coed; s
Red River Community College, Winnipeg, Man.; 1963; coed; M
Reine-Marie, Collège, Montréal, P.Q.; 1955; women; s
Ridgetown College of Agricultural Technology, Ridgetown, Ont.; 1922; coed; s
Rimouski, Collège de (CEGEP), Rimouski, P.Q.; 1967; coed; s
Rivière-du-Loup, Collège de (CEGEP), Rivière-du-Loup, P.Q.; 1969; coed; s
Rosemont, Collège de (CEGEP), Montréal, P.Q.; 1968; coed; s
Rouyn-Noranda, Collège de (CEGEP), Rouyn, P.Q.; 1967; coed; s
Ryerson Polytechnical Institute, Toronto, Ont.; 1948; coed; L

St.-Augustin, Séminaire, Cap-Rouge, P.Q.; 1965; men; s
St. Clair College of Applied Arts and Technology, Windsor, Ont.; 1958; coed; s
St.-Damien, Collège de, St.-Damien (Bellechasse), P.Q.; 1941; coed; s
St.-Georges, St.-Georges (Beauce), P.Q.; 1946; coed; s

St.-Hyacinthe, Collège de (CEGEP), St.-Hyacinthe, P.Q.; 1967; coed; s
St.-Jean-sur-Richelieu, Collège de (CEGEP), St.-Jean, P.Q.; 1968; coed; s
St.-Jean-Vianney, Collège, Montréal, P.Q.; 1957; coed; s
St.-Jérôme, Collège de (CEGEP), St.-Jérôme (Terrebonne), P.Q.; 1970; coed; s
St. John Technical Institute, St. John, N.B.; 1963; coed; s
St.-Laurent, Collège de (CEGEP), Montréal, P.Q.; 1968; coed; s
St. Lawrence College of Applied Arts and Technology, Kingston, Ont.; 1967; coed; s
St.-Louis, Collège, Montréal, P.Q.; 1947; coed; s
St. Peter's College, Muenster, Sask.; 1926; coed; s
Ste.-Anne, Le Collège de, Comté de Digby, N.S.; 1890; coed; s
Ste.-Foy, Collège de (CEGEP), Ste.-Foy, P.Q.; 1967; coed; M
Saguenay-Lac-St.-Jean, Collège du (CEGEP), Arvida, P.Q.; 1971; coed; s
Salaberry-de-Valleyfield, Collège de (CEGEP), Salaberry-de-Valleyfield, P.Q.; 1967; coed; s
Saskatchewan Institute of Applied Arts and Sciences, Saskatoon, Sask.; 1962; coed; s
Selkirk College, Castlegar, B.C.; 1963; coed; s
Seneca College of Applied Arts and Technology, Willowdale, Ont.; 1967; coed; M
Shawinigan, Collège de (CEGEP), Shawinigan (St.-Maurice), P.Q.; 1968; coed; s
Sherbrooke, Collège de (CEGEP), Sherbrooke, P.Q.; 1968; coed; M
Sherbrooke, Séminaire de, Sherbrooke, P.Q.; 1875; men; s
Sheridan College of Applied Arts and Technology, Oakville, Ont.; 1967; coed; s
Sir Sandford Fleming College of Applied Arts and Technology, Peterborough, Ont.; 1967; coed; s
South Saskatchewan Technical Institute, Moose Jaw, Sask.; coed; s
Southern Alberta Institute of Technology, Calgary, Alta.; coed; M

Thetford Mines, Collège de (CEGEP), Thetford Mines (Mégantic), P.Q.; 1969; coed; s
Trinity Junior College, Langley, B.C.; 1962; coed; s
Trois-Rivières, Collège de (CEGEP), Trois-Rivières, P.Q.; 1968; coed; M

Vancouver City College, Vancouver, B.C.; 1965; coed; M
Vancouver School of Art, Vancouver, B.C.; 1927; coed; s
Vanier College (CEGEP), Montréal, P.Q.; 1970; coed; s
Vermillion Agricultural & Vocational College, Vermillion, Alta.; 1913; coed; s
Victoriaville, Collège de (CEGEP), Victoriaville, P.Q.; 1872; coed; s
Vieux-Montréal, Collège de (CEGEP), Montréal, P.Q.; 1968; coed; s
Vincent d'Indy, École de Musique, Outremont, P.Q.; 1932; coed.

GIVEN NAMES

MASCULINE NAMES

Aar·on (âr′ən, ar′ən) ? Enlightener. [< Hebrew]

A·bel (ā′bəl) Breath. [< Hebrew]

A·bi·el (ā′bē·el, ə·bī′əl) Strong father. [< Hebrew]

Ab·ner (ab′nər) Father of light. [< Hebrew]

A·bra·ham (ā′brə·ham; *Fr.* à·brà·äm′; *Ger.* ä′brä·häm) Exalted father of multitudes. [< Hebrew] Also *Sp.* **A·bra·hán** (ä′brä·än′). Dims. **Abe, A′bie.**

A·bram (ā′brəm; *Fr.* à·brän′; *Sp.* ä·bräm′) Exalted father. [< Hebrew]

Ab·sa·lom (ab′sə·ləm) The father is peace. [< Hebrew]

Ad·am (ad′əm) Red; man of red earth. [< Hebrew]

Ad·el·bert (ad′l·bûrt, ə·del′bûrt) Var. of ALBERT.

A·dolph (ad′olf, ā′dolf) Noble wolf. [< Gmc.] Also *Dan., Du., Ger.* **A·dolf** (ä′dôlf), *Fr.* **A·dolphe** (à·dôlf′), *Ital., Sp.* **A·dol·fo** (*Ital.* ä·dôl′fō; *Sp.* ä·thôl′fō), *Lat.* **A·dol·phus** (ə·dol′fəs), *Pg.* **A·dol·pho** (ə·thôl′foo).

A·dri·an (ā′drē·ən) Of Adria: from the name of two Italian cities, or the Adriatic Sea. [< L] Also *Fr.* **A·dri·en** (à·drē·aṅ′), *Ital.* **A·dri·a·no** (ä′drē·ä′nō), *Lat.* **A·dri·a·nus** (ā′drē·ā′nəs).

Af·fon·so (ə·fôn′soo) Pg. form of ALPHONSO.

Al·an (al′ən) Handsome. [< Celtic] Also **Al′lan, Al′len.** Dim. **Al.**

Al·a·ric (al′ə·rik) All-ruler. [< Gmc.]

Al·as·tair (al′əs·tər) Scot. contr. of ALEXANDER. Also **Al′is·ter.**

Al·ban (al′bən, al′-) White; of Alba: from the name of several Italian cities. [< L] Also **Al′bin.**

Al·bert (al′bûrt; *Fr.* àl·bâr′; *Ger., Sw.* äl′bert) Nobly bright. [< F < Gmc.] Also *Ital., Sp.* **Al·ber·to** (äl·ber′tō), *Lat.* **Al·ber·tus** (al·bûr′təs). Dims. **Al, Alb, Bert.**

Al·den (ôl′dən) Old friend. [OE]

Al·do (äl′dō) Meaning uncertain. [< Gmc. or Hebrew]

Al·dous (ôl′dəs, al′-) From the old place. [OE] Also **Al′dis, Al′dous.**

Al·ex·an·der (al′ig·zan′dər, -zän′-; *Du., Ger.* ä′lek·sän′dər) Defender of men. [< Gk.] Also *Fr.* **A·lex·an·dre** (à·lek·säṅ′dr′), *Modern Gk.* **A·le·xan·dros** (ä·lä′ksän·drôs), *Ital.* **A·les·san·dro** (ä′läs·sän′drō), *Pg.* **A·le·xan·dre** (ə·lē·shaṅ′drə), *Russ.* **A·le·ksandr** (ə·lyi·ksän′dər), *Sp.* **A·le·jan·dro** (ä′lä·hän′drō). Dims. **Al′ec, Al′eck, Al′ex, San′der, San′dy.**

A·lex·is (ə·lek′sis) Defender. [< Gk.]

Al·fon·so (äl·fôn′sō) Ital. and Sp. form of ALPHONSO. Also *Dan., Ger.* **Al·fons** (äl′fôns).

Al·fred (al′frid; *Ger.* äl′frät; *Fr.* àl·fred′) Elf counselor; hence, wise. [OE] Also *Ital., Sp.* **Al·fre·do** (*Ital.* äl·frā′dō; *Sp.* äl·frä′thō), *Lat.* **Al·fre·dus** (äl·frē′dəs) or **Al·u·re·dus** (al′yoo·rē′dəs). Dims **Al, Alf, Fred.**

Al·ger (al′jər) Noble spear. [< Gmc.]

Al·ger·non (al′jər·nən) Mustached. [< OF] Dims. **Al·gie, Al·gy** (al′jē).

Al·len (al′ən) Var. of ALAN. Also **Al′lan.**

A·lon·zo (ə·lon′zō) Var. of ALPHONSO. Also *Ital., Sp.* **A·lon·so** (ä·lôn′sō).

A·loy·sius (al′ō·ish′əs) Lat. form of LOUIS. Also **A·lois** (ə·lois′).

Al·phon·so (al·fon′zō, -sō) Nobly ready. [< Sp. < Gmc.] Also *Fr.* **Al·phonse** (àl·fôns′). Dims. **Al, Alph, Al′phy.**

Al·va (al′və; *Sp.* äl′vä) White. [< L]

Al·vin (al′vin) Noble friend. [< Gmc.] Also **Al·win** (al′win; *Ger.* äl′vēn), **Al′van,** *Fr.* **A·luin** (à·lwaṅ′), *Ital.* **Al·vi·no** (äl·vē′nō), *Sp.* **A·lui·no** (ä·lwē′nō).

Am·brose (am′brōz) Divine; immortal. [< Gk.] Also *Fr.* **Am·broise** (äṅ·brwàz′), *Lat.* **Am·bro·si·us** (am·brō′zhē·əs, -zē·əs).

A·me·ri·go (ä′mā·rē′gō) Ital. form of EMERY.

A·mos (ā′məs) Burden. [< Hebrew]

An·a·tole (an′ə·tōl; *Fr.* à·nà·tôl′) Sunrise. [< Gk.] Also **An·drew** (an′droo) Manly. [< Gk.] Also **An·dre·as** (an′drē·əs, an·drē′əs; *Dan.* än·dres′; *Du., Ger.* än·drā′äs; *Lat.* an′drē·əs), *Fr.* **An·dré** (äṅ·drā′), *Ital.* **An·dre·a** (än·drā′ä), *Russ.* **An·drei** (än·drā′), *Sp.* **An·drés** (än·drās′). Dims. **An′dy, Drew.**

An·gus (ang′gəs) Singular. [< Celtic]

An·selm (an′selm; *Ger.* än′zelm) Divine helmet. [< Gmc.] Also **An·sel** (an′səl), *Fr.* **An·selme** (äṅ·selm′), *Ital., Sp.* **An·sel·mo** (än·sel′mō), *Lat.* **An·sel·mus** (an·sel′məs).

An·tho·ny (an′thə·nē, -tə-) Inestimable: from the name of a Roman clan. Also **An·to·ny** (an′tə·nē), *Fr.* **An·toine** (äṅ·twän′), *Ger., Lat.* **An·to·ni·us** (än·tō′nē·oos; *Lat.* an·tō′nē·əs), *Ital., Sp.* **An·to·nio** (än·tō′nyō). Dim. **To′ny.**

An·ton (än′tōn) Dan., Du., Ger. and Sw. form of ANTHONY.

Ar·chi·bald (är′chə·bôld) Nobly bold. [< Gmc.] Dims. **Ar′chie, Ar′chy.**

Ar·mand (är′mänd; *Fr.* àr·mäṅ′) Fr. form of HERMAN.

Ar·min·i·us (är·min′ē·əs) Lat. form of HERMAN.

Ar·nold (är′nold; *Ger.* är′nôlt) Eagle power. [< Gmc.] Also *Fr.* **Ar·naud** (àr·nō′), *Ital.* **Ar·nol·do** (är·nôl′dō), *Sp.* **Ar·nal·do** (är·näl′thō). Dims. **Arn, Ar′nie.**

Ar·te·mas (är′tə·məs) He of Artemis. [< Gk.] Also **Ar′te·mus.**

Ar·thur (är′thər; *Fr.* àr·tōōr′) He-bear: from a totemic or royal title suggesting valor, strength, and nobility. [< Celtic] Also *Ital.* **Ar·tu·ro** (är·tōō′rō). Dims. **Art, Art′ie.**

A·sa (ā′sə) Healer. [< Hebrew]

Ash·ley (ash′lē) Dweller among ash trees: from a surname. [< Gmc.]

Ath·el·stan (ath′əl·stan) Noble stone or jewel. [OE] Also **Ath′el·stane** (-stän).

Au·brey (ô′brē) Elf ruler. [< F < Gmc.]

Au·gus·tine (ô′gəs·tēn, ô·gus′tin) Dim. of AUGUSTUS. Also **Au·gus·tin** (ô·gus′tən; *Fr.* ō·güs·tán′; *Ger.* ou′goos·tēn′), *Ital.* **A·go·sti·no** (ä′gō·stē′nō), *Lat.* **Au·gus·ti·nus** (ô′gəs·tī′nəs), *Pg.* **A·gos·ti·nho** (ə·goosh·tē′nyoo), *Sp.* **A·gus·tín** (ä′goos·tēn′).

Au·gus·tus (ô·gus′təs) Venerable. [< L] Also **Au·gust** (ô′gəst; *Ger.* ou′goost), *Fr.* **Au·guste** (ō·güst′).

Au·re·li·us (ô·rē′lē·əs, ô·rēl′yəs) The golden one. [< L]

Aus·tin (ôs′tən) Contr. of AUGUSTINE.

Av·er·y (ā′vər·ē, ā′vrē) Courageous. [< Gmc.] Also **A·ver·il, A·ver·ill** (ā′vər·əl, ā′vrəl).

Bald·win (bôld′win) Bold friend. [< Gmc.] Also *Fr.* **Bau·doin** (bō·dwaṅ′).

Bal·tha·zar (bal·thä′zər, -thaz′ər) Bel's or Baal's prince [< Chaldean], or splendid prince [< Persian]. Also **Bal·tha′sar** (-zər).

Bap·tist (bap′tist) Baptizer. [< Gk.] Also *Fr.* **Bap·tiste** (bà·tēst′).

Bar·na·bas (bär′nə·bəs) Son of consolation [< Hebrew], or prophetic son [< Aramaic]. Also **Bar·na·by** (bär′nə·bē). Dim. **Bar′ney.**

Bar·nard (bär′nərd) Var. of BERNARD.

Bar·ney (bär′nē) Dim. of BARNABAS or BERNARD.

Bar·ry (bar′ē) Spear; hence, straightforward. [< Celtic]

Bar·thol·o·mew (bär·thol′ə·myoo) Son of furrows. [< Hebrew] Also *Fr.* **Bar·thé·le·my** (bàr·tāl·mē′), *Ital.* **Bar·tho·lo·mä·us** (bär·tō·lō·mä′oos), *Ital.* **Bar·to·lo·me·o** (bär·tō′lō·mā′ō), *Lat.* **Bar·thol·o·mae·us** (bär·tol′ə·mē′əs), *Sp.* **Bar·to·lo·mé** (bär·tō′lō·mā′). Dims. **Bart, Bat.**

Bas·il (baz′əl, bā′zəl) Kingly. [< Gk.]

Bax·ter (bak′stər) Baker. [< Gmc.]

Bay·ard (bā′ərd, bī′-, -ärd) From a surname. [< OF]

Ben·e·dict (ben′ə·dikt) Blessed. [< L] Also **Ben′e·dick,** *Fr.* **Be·noît** (bə·nwà′), *Ger.* **Be·ne·dikt** (bā′nä·dikt), *Ital.* **Be·ne·det·to** (bā′nä·dät′tō) or **Be·ni·to** (bā·nē′tō), *Lat.* **Ben·e·dic·tus** (ben′ə·dik′təs), *Sp.* **Be·ni·to** (bā·nē′tō).

Ben·ja·min (ben′jə·mən; *Fr.* baṅ·zhà·maṅ′; *Ger.* ben′yä·mēn) Son of the right hand; hence, favorite son. [< Hebrew] Also *Ital.* **Ben·ia·mi·no** (ben′yä·mē′nō), *Sp.* **Ben·ja·mín** (ben′hä·mēn′). Dims. **Ben, Ben′jy, Ben′ny.**

Ben·net (ben′it) Var. of BENEDICT. Also **Ben′nett.**

Ber·nard (bûr′nərd, bər·närd′; *Fr.* ber·nàr′) Bear-brave: probably from a totemic title. [< Gmc.] Also *Ger.* **Bern·hard** (bern′härt), *Ital., Sp.* **Ber·nar·do** (*Ital.* bär·när′dō; *Sp.* ber·när′thō), *Lat.* **Ber·nar·dus** (bər·när′dəs). Dims. **Bar′ney, Ber′ney, Ber′nie.**

Bert (bûrt) Dim. of ALBERT, BERTRAM, GILBERT, HERBERT, and HUBERT. Also **Ber·tie** (bûr′tē).

Ber·tram (bûr′trəm) Bright raven. [< Gmc.] Also **Ber·trand** (bûr′trənd; *Fr.* ber·träṅ′). Dim. **Bert.**

Bill (bil) Dim. of WILLIAM. Also **Bil′ly.**

Bob (bob) Dim. of ROBERT. Also **Bob′bie, Bob′by.**

Bo·ris (bôr′is, bō′ris; *Russ.* bə·ryēs′) Warrior. [< Russ.]

Boyd (boid) Yellow-haired. [< Celtic]

Bri·an (brī′ən) Strong. [< Celtic] Also **Bry′an, Bry·ant** (brī′ənt).

Brice (bris) Meaning uncertain. [? < Celtic] Also **Bryce.**

Bruce (broos) From a Norman Fr. surname; orig. a place name.

Bru·no (broo′nō) The brown one. [< Gmc.]

Bur·gess (bûr′jis) Citizen. [< Gmc.]

By·ron (bī′rən) From a Fr. surname; orig. a place name. Also **Bi′ron.**

Cad·wal·la·der (kad·wol′ə·dər) Battle arranger. [< Welsh] Also **Cad·wal′a·der.**

Cae·sar (sē′zər) Long-haired: ? symbolic title suggesting royalty or holiness. [< L] Also **Ce′sar,** *Fr.* **Cé·sar** (sā·zàr′), *Ital.* **Ce·sa·re** (chā′zä·rā).

Ca·leb (kā′ləb)   Dog; hence, loyal. [< Hebrew]
Cal·vin (kal′vin)   Bald: from a Roman name. [< L] Dim. **Cal.**
Carl (kärl)   English form of KARL.
Car·ol (kar′əl)   English form of CAROLUS.
Car·o·lus (kar′ə·ləs)   Lat. form of CHARLES.
Car·y (kâr′ē)   ? Dim. of CAROL. Also **Car′ey.**
Cas·per (kas′pər)   English form of KASPAR. Also **Cas′par** (-pər).
Ce·cil (sē′səl, ses′əl)   Blind: from the name of a Roman clan.
Ced·ric (sed′rik, sē′drik)   War chief. [< Celtic]
Charles (chärlz)   Manly. [< F < Gmc.] Also *Ital.* **Car·lo** (kär′lō), *Lat.* **Car·o·lus** (kar′ə·ləs), *Sp.* **Car·los** (kär′lōs). Dims. **Char′ley, Char′lie, Chuck.**
Chaun·cey (chôn′sē, chän′-)   Chancellor. [< OF]
Ches·ter (ches′tər)   Dweller in camp; hence, soldier: from a surname. [< L] Dims. **Ches, Chet.**
Chris·tian (kris′chən; *Ger.* kris′tē·än)   Christian. [< L < Gk.] Also *Fr.* **Chré·tien** (krā·tyan′). Dim. **Chris.**
Chris·to·pher (kris′tə·fər)   Bearer of Christ. [< Gk.] Also *Fr.* **Chris·tophe** (krēs·tôf′), *Ger.* **Chris·toph** (kris′tôf), *Ital.* **Chri·sto·fo·ro** (krēs·tô′fō·rō), *Sp.* **Cris·tó·bal** (krēs·tō′väl). Dims. **Chris, Kit.**
Clar·ence (klar′əns)   From the name of an English dukedom.
Claude (klôd; *Fr.* klōd)   Lame: from the name of a Roman clan. Also *Ital., Sp.* **Clau·di·o** (*Ital.* klou′dyō; *Sp.* klou′· thyō), *Lat.* **Clau·di·us** (klô′dē·əs).
Clay·ton (klā′tən)   From an English surname; orig. a place name.
Clem·ent (klem′ənt)   Merciful. [< L] Dim. **Clem.**
Clif·ford (klif′ərd)   From an English surname; orig. a place name. Dim. **Cliff.**
Clif·ton (klif′tən)   From an English surname; orig. a place name.
Clin·ton (klin′tən)   From an English surname; orig. a place name. Dim. **Clint.**
Clive (klīv)   Cliff; cliff-dweller: from an English surname.
Clyde (klīd)   From a Scot. surname; orig. the river *Clyde.*
Col·in (kol′ən, kō′lən)   Dove. [< Scot. < L]
Con·rad (kon′rad)   Bold counsel. [< Gmc.]
Con·stant (kon′stənt; *Fr.* kôn·stän′)   Var. of CONSTANTINE.
Con·stan·tine (kon′stən·tīn, -tēn)   Constant; firm. [< L]
Cor·nel·ius (kôr·nēl′yəs; *Ger.* kôr·nā′lē·ŏŏs)   ? Horn: from the name of a Roman clan. Dims. **Con, Corn, Neil.**
Craig (krāg)   Crag; crag-dweller: from a Scot. surname.
Cris·pin (kris′pin)   Curly-headed. [< L] Also *Lat.* **Cris·pi·nus** (kris·pī′nəs) or **Cris·pus** (kris′pəs).
Cur·tis (kûr′tis)   Courteous. [< OF]
Cuth·bert (kuth′bərt)   Notably brilliant. [OE]
Cyr·il (sir′əl)   Lordly. [< Gk.]
Cy·rus (sī′rəs)   The sun. [< Persian] Dim. **Cy.**

Dan (dan)   Judge. [< Hebrew]
Dan·iel (dan′yəl; *Fr.* dà·nyel′; *Ger.* dä′nē·el)   God is my judge. [< Hebrew] Dims. **Dan, Dan′ny.**
Da·ri·us (də·rī′əs)   Wealthy. [< Persian]
Da·vid (dā′vid; *Fr.* dä·vēd′; *Ger.* dä′vēt)   Beloved. [< Hebrew] Dims. **Dave, Da′vey, Da′vie, Da′vy.**
Dean (dēn)   From an ancient religious or military title. [< OF < LL] Also **Deane.**
De·me·tri·us (di·mē′trē·əs)   He of Demeter. [< Gk.] Also *Russ.* **Dmi·tri** (dmyē′trē).
Den·nis (den′is)   Var. of DIONYSIUS. Also **Den′is,** *Fr.* **De·nis** or **De·nys** (də·nē′). Dim. **Den′ny.**
Der·ek (der′ik)   Du. dim. of THEODORIC. Also **Der′rick, Dirck** (dûrk; *Du.* dirk), **Dirk.**
DeWitt (də·wit′)   From a surname. Also **De Witt.**
Dex·ter (dek′stər)   Right; right-handed; hence, fortunate or skillful. [< L]
Dick (dik)   Dim. of RICHARD.
Die·go (dyā′gō)   Sp. form of JAMES.
Di·o·nys·i·us (dī′ə·nish′ē·əs, -nis′ē·əs)   He of Dionysus. [< Gk.] Dim. **Di·on** (dī′ən).
Dolph (dolf)   Dim. of ADOLPH or RUDOLPH. Also **Dolf.**
Dom·i·nic (dom′ə·nik)   Of the Lord. [< L] Also **Dom′i·nick.** Dim. **Dom.**
Don·ald (don′əld)   World chief. [< Celtic] Dims. **Don, Don′nie.**
Doug·las (dug′ləs)   Dark. [< Celtic] Dims. **Doug, Doug′ie.**
Drew (drōō)   Skilled one [< Gmc.], or dim. of ANDREW.
Duane (dwān, dōō·än′)   Poem. [< Celtic]
Dud·ley (dud′lē)   From an English surname; orig. a place name.
Duke (dōōk, dyōōk)   From the title. [< OF]
Dun·can (dung′kən)   Brown warrior. [< Celtic]
Dun·stan (dun′stən)   From an English place name.
Dwight (dwīt)   Meaning uncertain. [< Gmc.]

Earl (ûrl)   From the title. [OE] Also **Earle.**
Eb·en·e·zer (eb′ə·nē′zər)   Stone of help. [< Hebrew] Dim. **Eb·en** (eb′ən).
Ed·gar (ed′gər)   Rich spear; hence, fortunate warrior. [OE] Dims. **Ed, Ed′die, Ned.**

Ed·mund (ed′mənd; *Ger.* et′mŏŏnt)   Rich protector. [OE] Also **Ed·mond** (ed′mənd; *Fr.* ed·môn′). Dims. **Ed, Ed′die, Ned.**
Ed·ward (ed′wərd)   Rich guardian. [OE] Also *Fr.* **É·dou·ard** (ā·dwàr′), *Ger.* **E·du·ard** (ā′dōō·ärt), *Sp.* **E·duar·dc** (ā·thwär′thō). Dims. **Ed, Ed′die, Ned, Ted, Ted′dy.**
Ed·win (ed′win)   Rich friend. [OE] Dims. **Ed, Ed′die.**
Eg·bert (eg′bərt)   Bright sword; hence, skilled swordsman. [OE] Dims. **Bert, Bert′ie.**
El·bert (el′bərt)   Var. of ALBERT.
El·dred (el′drid)   Mature counsel. [OE]
E·le·a·zar (el′ē·ā′zər)   God has helped. [< Hebrew] Also **El′e·a′zer.**
E·li (ē′lī)   The highest one. [< Hebrew]
E·li·as (i·lī′əs)   Var. of ELIJAH.
E·li·hu (el′ə·hyōō)   Var. of ELIJAH.
E·li·jah (i·lī′jə)   Jehovah is God. [< Hebrew]
El·i·ot (el′ē·ət)   God's gift. [< Hebrew] Also **El′li·ot, El′li·ott.**
E·li·sha (i·lī′shə)   God is salvation. [< Hebrew]
El·lis (el′is)   Var. of ELIAS.
El·mer (el′mər)   Nobly famous. [OE]
El·ton (el′tən)   From an English surname; orig. a place name.
El·vin (el′vin)   Of the elves. [OE] Also **El·win** (el′win).
E·man·u·el (i·man′yōō·əl)   Var. of IMMANUEL. Also **Em·man′u·el.**
Em·er·y (em′ər·ē)   Work ruler. [< Gmc.] Also **Em·er·ic** (em′ər·ik), **Em′o·ry.**
E·mile (ā·mēl′)   From the name of a Roman clan. Also *Fr.* **É·mile** (ā·mēl′), *Ger.* **E·mil** (ā′mēl), *Ital.* **E·mi·lio** (ā·mē′lyō).
Em·mett (em′it)   Ant; hence, industrious. [OE] Also **Em′met.**
E·ne·as (i·nē′əs)   Praiseworthy. [< Gk.]
E·noch (ē′nək)   Dedicated. [< Hebrew]
E·nos (ē′nəs)   Man. [< Hebrew]
En·ri·co (än·rē′kō)   Ital. form of HENRY.
E·phra·im (ē′frē·əm, ē′frəm)   Doubly fruitful. [< Hebrew]
E·ras·mus (i·raz′məs)   Lovable. [< Gk.]
E·ras·tus (i·ras′təs)   Lovable. [< Gk.] Dim. **Ras·tus** (ras′· təs).
Er·ic (er′ik)   Honorable king. [< Scand.] Also **Er′ich, Er′ik.**
Er·man·no (er·män′nō)   Ital. form of HERMAN.
Er·nest (ûr′nist)   Earnest. [< Gmc.] Also *Ger.* **Ernst** (ernst). Dims. **Ern, Er′nie.**
Er·win (ûr′win)   Var. of IRVING.
Es·te·ban (ās·tä′bän)   Sp. form of STEPHEN.
E·than (ē′thən)   Firmness. [< Hebrew]
Eth·el·bert (eth′əl·bûrt)   Nobly bright. [OE]
Eth·el·red (eth′əl·red)   Noble council. [< Gmc.]
É·tienne (ā·tyen′)   Fr. form of STEPHEN.
Eu·gene (yōō·jēn′)   Well-born. [< Gk.] Dim. **Gene.**
Eus·tace (yōōs′tis)   Good harvest. [< Gk.]
Ev·an (ev′ən)   Welsh form of JOHN.
Eve·lyn (ēv′lin, ev′ə·lin)   Ancestor. [< OF < Gmc.]
Ev·er·ard (ev′ər·ärd)   Strong as a boar. [< Gmc.] Also **Ev·er·art** (ev′ər·ärt).
Ev·er·ett (ev′ər·it)   Var. of EVERARD. Also **Ev′er·et.**
E·ze·ki·el (i·zē′kē·əl, -kyəl)   God gives strength. [< Hebrew] Dim. **Zeke** (zēk).
Ez·ra (ez′rə)   Helper. [< Hebrew]

Fë·dor (fyô′dər)   Russ. form of THEODORE. Also **Fe·o·dor** (fyi·ô′dər).
Fe·li·pe (fā·lē′pā)   Sp. form of PHILIP.
Fe·lix (fē′liks)   Happy; fortunate. [< L]
Fer·di·nand (fûr′də·nand; *Fr.* fer·dē·nän′; *Ger.* fer′dē·nänt)   Peaceful courage. [< Gmc.] Also *Sp.* **Fer·nan·do** (fer·nän′dō), **Her·nan·do** (her·nän′dō). Dim. **Fer′die.**
Fer·gus (fûr′gəs)   Manly strength. [< Celtic] Dim. **Fer·gie** (fûr′gē).
Fi·lip·po (fē·lēp′pō)   Ital. form of PHILIP.
Floyd (floid)   Var. of LLOYD.
Fran·cis (fran′sis, frän′-)   Free. [< Gmc.] Also *Fr.* **Fran·çois** (frän·swà′), *Ger.* **Franz** (fränts), *Ital.* **Fran·ce·sco** (frän·chā′skō), *Sp.* **Fran·cis·co** (frän·thēs′kō). Dims. **Frank, Frank′ie.**
Frank (frangk)   Dim. of FRANCIS or FRANKLIN. Also **Frank′ie.**
Frank·lin (frangk′lin)   Freeman. [ME] Dims. **Frank, Frank′ie.**
Fred (fred)   Dim. of ALFRED, FREDERICK, or WILFRED. Also **Fred′die, Fred′dy.**
Fred·er·ick (fred′ər·ik, fred′rik)   Peace ruler. [< Gmc.] Also **Fred′er·ic, Fred′ric, Fred′rick,** *Fr.* **Fré·dé·ric** (frā·dā·rēk′), *Ger.* **Frie·drich** (frē′drikh), *Sp.* **Fe·de·ri·co** (fā′dā·rē′kō). Dims. **Fred, Fred′die, Fred′dy, Fritz.**
Fritz (frits)   Ger. dim. of FREDERICK.

Ga·bri·el (gā′brē·əl; *Fr.* gà·brē·el′; *Ger.* gä′brē·el)   Man of God. [< Hebrew] Dim. **Gabe** (gāb).
Ga·ma·li·el (gə·mā′lē·əl, -māl′yəl)   Reward of God. [< Hebrew]

Gar·di·ner (gärd′nər, gär′də·nər) From an English surname. Also **Gar′de·ner, Gard′ner.**
Gar·ret (gar′it) Var. of GERARD. Also **Gar′rett.**
Gar·y (gâr′ē) Dim. of GARRET.
Gas·par (gas′pər) Var. of CASPER. Also *Fr.* **Gas·pard** (gàs·pär′).
Gas·ton (gas′tən; *Fr.* gàs·tôn′) Meaning uncertain.
Gau·tier (gō·tyā′) Fr. form of WALTER.
Gene (jēn) Dim. of EUGENE.
Geof·frey (jef′rē) English form of Fr. *Geoffroi;* var. of GODFREY. Dim. **Jeff.**
George (jôrj) Earthworker; farmer. [< Gk.] Also *Fr.* **Georges** (zhôrzh), *Ger.* **Ge·org** (gā·ôrkh′), *Ital.* **Gior·gio** (jôr′jō), *Russ.* **Ge·or·gi** (gyi·ôr′gyi). Dim. **Georg′ie, Geor′die.**
Ger·ald (jer′əld) Spear ruler. [< Gmc.] Also *Fr.* **Gé·raud** (zhā·rō′) or **Gi·raud** (zhē·rō′). Dims. **Ger′ry, Jer′ry.**
Ge·rard (ji·rärd′; *Brit.* jer′ärd) Hard spear. [< Gmc.] Also *Fr.* **Gé·rard** (zhā·rär′), *Ger.* **Ger·hard** (gär′härt). Dims. **Ger′ry, Jer′ry.**
Ge·ro·ni·mo (jā·rô′nē·mō) Ital. form of JEROME.
Gia·co·mo (jä′kō·mō) Ital. form of JAMES.
Gid·e·on (gid′ē·ən) Hewer. [< Hebrew]
Gie·ron·y·mus (jē′ə·ron′i·məs) Lat. form of JEROME.
Gif·ford (gif′ərd, jif′-) Meaning uncertain. [< Gmc.]
Gil·bert (gil′bərt; *Fr.* zhēl·bâr′) Bright wish. [< Gmc.] Dims. **Bert, Gil.**
Giles (jīlz) From the name of the goddess Athena's shield; hence, shield or protection. [< OF < Gk.]
Gio·van·ni (jō·vän′nē) Ital. form of JOHN.
Giu·lio (jōō′lyō) Ital. form of JULIUS.
Giu·sep·pe (jōō·zep′pā) Ital. form of JOSEPH.
Glenn (glen) From a Celtic surname; orig. a place name. Also **Glen.**
God·dard (god′ərd) Divine resoluteness. [< Gmc.]
God·frey (god′frē) Peace of God. [< Gmc.] Also *Ger.* **Gott·fried** (gôt′frēt).
God·win (god′win) Friend of God. [OE]
Gor·don (gôr′dən) From a Scot. surname.
Gra·ham (grā′əm) From an English surname; orig. a place name.
Grant (grant) From a Norman Fr. surname.
Greg·o·ry (greg′ər·ē) Vigilant. [< Gk.] Dim. **Greg.**
Grif·fin (grif′in) Var. of GRIFFITH.
Grif·fith (grif′ith) Red-haired. [< Celtic]
Gro·ver (grō′vər) Grove-dweller. [< Gmc.]
Gual·te·ri·o (gwäl·tā′rē·ō) Sp. form of WALTER.
Gu·gliel·mo (gōō·lyel′mō) Ital. form of WILLIAM.
Guil·laume (gē·yōm′) Fr. form of WILLIAM.
Guil·ler·mo (gē·lyer′mō, gē·yer′mō) Sp. form of WILLIAM.
Gus (gus) Dim. of AUGUSTUS or GUSTAVUS.
Gus·ta·vus (gus·tā′vəs, -tä′-) Goth's staff. [< L < Gmc.] Also *Fr.* **Gus·tave** (güs·tàv′), *Ger.* **Gus·tav** (gōōs′täf). Dim. **Gus.**
Guy (gī; *Fr.* gē) Leader [< F < Gmc.] Also *Ital.* **Gui·do** (gwē′dō).

Hal (hal) Dim. of HAROLD or HENRY.
Ham·il·ton (ham′əl·tən) From a surname.
Hank (hangk) Dim. of HENRY.
Han·ni·bal (han′ə·bəl) Grace of Baal. [< Phoenician]
Hans (häns) Ger. dim. of JOHANNES. See JOHN.
Har·ley (här′lē) From an English surname; orig. a place name.
Har·old (har′əld) Chief of the army. [OE < Scand.] Dim. **Hal.**
Har·ry (har′ē) Dim. of HAROLD or var. of HENRY.
Har·vey (här′vē) Army battle. [< F < Gmc.]
Hec·tor (hek′tər) He who holds fast; defender. [< Gk.]
Hen·ry (hen′rē) Home ruler. [< F < Gmc.] Also *Du.* **Hen·drik** (hen′drik), *Fr.* **Hen·ri** (än·rē′), *Ger.* **Hein·rich** (hīn′rikh). Dims. **Hal, Hank, Har′ry, Hen.**
Her·bert (hûr′bərt) Glory of the army. [OE] Dims. **Bert, Bert′ie, Herb.**
Her·man (hûr′mən) Man of the army. [< Gmc.] Also *Ger.* **Her·mann** (her′män).
Her·mes (hûr′mēz) Of the earth. [< Gk.]
Her·nan·do (er·nän′dō) Sp. form of FERDINAND.
Hez·e·ki·ah (hez′ə·kī′ə) God strengthens. [< Hebrew]
Hil·a·ry (hil′ər·ē) Joyful. [< L] Also *Fr.* **Hi·laire** (ē·lâr′).
Hi·ram (hī′rəm) Honored brother. [< Hebrew] Dims. **Hi, Hy.**
Ho·bart (hō′bərt, -bärt) Var. of HUBERT.
Hodge (hoj) Dim. of ROGER. Also **Hodg′kin.**
Ho·mer (hō′mər) Pledge, or blind one. [< Gk.]
Hon·o·ré (ô·nô·rā′) Honored. [< F < L]
Hor·ace (hôr′is, hor′-) Var. of HORATIO.
Ho·ra·ti·o (hə·rā′shē·ō, -shō) From the name of a Roman clan.
Ho·se·a (hō·zē′ə, -zā′ə) Salvation. [< Hebrew]
How·ard (hou′ərd) From an English surname. Dim. **How′ie.**
Hu·bert (hyōō′bərt) Bright spirit or mind. [< F < Gmc.]
Hugh (hyōō) Mind; intelligence. [< OF < Gmc.] Also **Hu·go** (hyōō′gō), *Fr.* **Hugues** (üg). Dim. **Hugh′ie.**

Hum·bert (hum′bərt) Bright support. [< OF < Gmc.]
Hum·phrey (hum′frē) Peaceful stake or support. [< OF < Gmc.] Also **Hum′frey, Hum′phry.**

I·an (ē′ən, ī′ən) Scot. form of JOHN.
Ich·a·bod (ik′ə·bod) ? Inglorious. [< Hebrew]
Ig·na·ti·us (ig·nā′shē·əs, -shəs) Fiery. [< Gk.] Also *Fr.* **I·gnace** (ē·nyàs′), *Ger.* **Ig·naz** (ig′näts), *Ital.* **I·gna·zio** (ē·nyä′tsyō).
Im·man·u·el (i·man′yōō·əl) God with us. [< Hebrew]
In·i·go (in′i·gō) Var. of IGNATIUS.
Io·sif (yô′syif) Russ. form of JOSEPH.
I·ra (ī′rə) Vigilant. [< Hebrew]
Ir·ving (ûr′ving) From a Scot. surname; orig. a place name. Also **Ir·vin** (ûr′vin).
Ir·win (ûr′win) Var. of IRVING.
I·saac (ī′zək) Laughter. [< Hebrew] Dim. **Ike** (īk).
I·sa·iah (ī·zā′ə, ī·zī′ə) Salvation of God. [< Hebrew]
Is·i·dore (iz′ə·dôr, -dōr) Gift of Isis. [< Gk.] Also **Is′a·dore, Is′a·dor, Is′i·dor.** Dim. **Iz·zy** (iz′ē).
Is·ra·el (iz′rē·əl) Contender with God. [< Hebrew]
I·van (ī′vən; *Russ.* i·vän′) Russ. form of JOHN.
I·vor (ē′vər, ī′vər) Meaning uncertain. [< Celtic]

Ja·bez (jā′biz) Sorrow. [< Hebrew]
Jack (jak) English form of Fr. *Jacques;* dim. of JOHN.
Ja·cob (jā′kəb) He who seizes by the heel; hence, successor. [< LL < Hebrew] Also *Ger.* **Ja·kob** (yä′kôb). Dims. **Jack, Jake** (jāk), **Jock** (jok).
Jacques (zhäk) Fr. form of JACOB. [< OF < LL]
James (jāmz) English form of Sp. *Jaime;* var. of JACOB. [< Sp. < LL] Also *Sp.* **Jai·me** (hī′mä). Dims. **Jam·ie** (jā′mē), **Jem, Jem′my, Jim, Jim′mie, Jim′my.**
Jan (yän) Du., Ger., and Pol. form of JOHN.
Já·nos (yä′nōsh) Hung. form of JOHN.
Ja·pheth (jā′fith) Enlarged; hence, powerful or honored. [< Hebrew] Also **Ja′phet** (-fit).
Jar·ed (jâr′id) Descent. [< Hebrew]
Jar·vis (jär′vis) From a Norman Fr. surname. Also **Jer·vis** (jûr′vis; *Brit.* jär′vis).
Ja·son (jā′sən) Healer. [< Gk.]
Jas·per (jas′pər) Treasury lord [< OF, ? < Persian], or from the name of the jewel.
Jay (jā) ? Jay bird. [? < OF]
Jean (jēn; *Fr.* zhän) French form of JOHN.
Jef·frey (jef′rē) Var. of GEOFFREY. Dim. **Jeff.**
Je·hu (jē′hyōō) Jehovah is he. [< Hebrew]
Jeph·thah (jef′thə) Opposer. [< Hebrew]
Jer·e·mi·ah (jer′ə·mī′ə) God's chosen. [< Hebrew] Also **Jer·e·my** (jer′ə·mē). Dim. **Jer′ry.**
Je·rome (jə·rōm′; *Brit.* jer′əm) Holy name. [< Gk.] Also *Fr.* **Jé·rôme** (zhā·rōm′), *Sp.* **Je·ró·ni·mo** (hā·rō′nē·mō).
Jer·ry (jer′ē) Dim. of GERALD, GERARD, JEREMIAH, or JEROME.
Jes·se (jes′ē) Meaning uncertain. [< Hebrew] Also **Jess.**
Je·sus (jē′zəs) English form of Lat. *Josua;* var. of JOSHUA.
Jeth·ro (jeth′rō) Abundant or excellent. [< Hebrew]
Jim (jim) Dim. of JAMES. Also **Jim′mie, Jim′my.**
Jo·ab (jō′ab) Jehovah is father. [< Hebrew]
Jo·a·chim (jō′ə·kim) Jehovah will judge. [< Hebrew] Also *Sp.* **Joa·quín** (hwä·kēn′).
João (zhwoun) Pg. form of JOHN.
Job (jōb) Persecuted. [< Hebrew]
Jock (jok) Scot. form of JACK.
Joe (jō) Dim. of JOSEPH. Also **Jo′ey.**
Jo·el (jō′əl) Jehovah is God. [< Hebrew]
John (jon) God is good. [< Hebrew] Also *Ger.* **Jo·hann** (yō′hän) or **Jo·han·nes** (yō·hän′əs). Dims. **Jack, Jack′ie, Jack′y, Jock, John′nie, John′ny.**
Jon (jon) Var. of JOHN, or dim. of JONATHAN.
Jo·nah (jō′nə) Dove. [< Hebrew] Also **Jo·nas** (jō′nəs).
Jon·a·than (jon′ə·thən) God has given. [< Hebrew] Dims. **Jon, Jon′nie, Jon′ny.**
Jor·ge (*Pg.* zhôr′zhə; *Sp.* hôr′hä) Pg. and Sp. form of GEORGE.
Jo·seph (jō′zəf; *Fr.* zhō·zef′; *Ger.* yō′zef) God shall give (a son). [< Hebrew] Also *Lat.* **Jo·se·phus** (jō·sē′fəs), *Pg., Sp.* **Jo·sé** (*Pg.* zhōō·ze′; *Sp.* hō·sā′). Dims. **Jo, Joe, Jo′ey.**
Josh·u·a (josh′ōō·ə) God is salvation. [< Hebrew] Also *Fr.* **Jo·sué** (zhō·zwā′), *Lat.* **Jos·u·a** (jos′ōō·ə). Dim. **Josh.**
Jo·si·ah (jō·sī′ə) God supports. [< Hebrew] Also *Lat.* **Jo·si·as** (jō·sī′əs).
Jo·tham (jō′thəm) God is perfection. [< Hebrew]
Juan (hwän) Sp. form of JOHN.
Ju·dah (jōō′də) Praised. [< Hebrew] Also **Jude** (jōōd; *Fr.* zhüd), *Lat.* **Ju·das** (jōō′dəs).
Jules (jōōlz; *Fr.* zhül) Fr. form of JULIUS.
Jul·ian (jōōl′yən) Var. of JULIUS.
Jul·ius (jōōl′yəs) Downy-bearded; youthful: from the name of a Roman clan. Also *Sp.* **Ju·lio** (hōō′lyō). Dims. **Jule** (jōōl), **Jul·ie** (jōō′lē).
Jun·ius (jōōn′yəs, jōō′nē·əs) Youthful: from the name of a Roman clan.
Jus·tin (jus′tin) Just. [< L] Also **Jus·tus** (jus′təs).

Karl (kärl) Ger. form of CHARLES.
Kas·par (käs′pär) Ger. form of JASPER.
Keith (kēth) From a Scot. surname; orig. a place name.
Kel·vin (kel′vin) From a Celtic surname.
Ken·neth (ken′ith) Handsome. [< Celtic] Dims. **Ken**, **Ken′nie**, **Ken′ny**.
Kent (kent) From an English surname; orig. a place name.
Kev·in (kev′ən) Handsome birth. [< Celtic]
Kit (kit) Dim. of CHRISTOPHER.
Kon·rad (kōn′rät) Ger. form of CONRAD.

La·ban (lā′bən) White. [< Hebrew]
La·fay·ette (lä′fē·et′, laf′ē·et′; Fr. là·fà·yet′) From a Fr. surname. Dim. **Lafe** (läf).
Lam·bert (lam′bərt) The land's brightness. [< F < Gmc.]
Lance (lans, läns) Of the land. [< Gmc.]
Lan·ce·lot (lan′sə·lot, län′-; Fr. läṅ·slō′) Fr. dim. of LANCE. Also **Laun·ce·lot** (lôn′sə·lot, lan′-, län′-).
Lars (lärz; Sw. lärs) Sw. form of LAURENCE.
Lau·rence (lôr′əns, lor′-) Laureled; hence, prophetic or poetic. [< L] Also **Law′rence**, Fr. **Lau·rent** (lō·räṅ′), Ger. **Lo·renz** (lō′rents). Dims. **Lar·ry** (lar′ē), **Lau·rie** or **Law·rie** (lôr′ē).
Laz·a·rus (laz′ə·rəs) God has helped. [< Hebrew] Also Fr. **La·zare** (là·zàr′), Ital. **Laz·za·ro** (läd′dzä·rō).
Le·an·der (lē·an′dər) Lion man. [< Gk.]
Lee (lē) From an English surname.
Leif (lēf) Loved one. [< Scand.]
Leigh (lē) From an English surname.
Lem·u·el (lem′yōo·əl) Belonging to God. [< Hebrew] Dim. **Lem**.
Le·o (lē′ō) Lion. [< L < Gk.]
Le·on (lē′on, -ən) Lion. [< L < Gk.] Also Fr. **Lé·on** (lā·ôṅ′).
Leon·ard (len′ərd) Lion-strong. [< Gmc.] Also Fr. **Lé·o·nard** (lā·ō·nàr′), Ger. **Le·on·hard** (lā′ōn·härt), Ital. **Le·o·nar·do** (lā′ō·när′dō). Dims. **Len**, **Len′ny**.
Le·on·i·das (lē·on′ə·dəs) Lionlike. [< Gk.]
Le·o·pold (lē′ə·pōld; Ger. lā′ō·pōlt) The people's strong one. [< Gmc.]
Le·roy (lə·roi′, lē′roi) Royal. [< OF]
Les·lie (les′lē, lez′-) From an English surname. Dim. **Les**.
Les·ter (les′tər) From an English surname; orig. the place name Leicester. Dim. **Les**.
Le·vi (lē′vī) He who unites. [< Hebrew]
Lew·is (lōo′is) Var. of LOUIS. Dims. **Lew**, **Lew′ie**.
Lin·coln (ling′kən) From an English surname.
Li·nus (lī′nəs) Meaning uncertain. [< Gk.]
Li·o·nel (lī′ə·nəl, -nel) Young lion. [< F < L]
Lisle (līl) Var. of LYLE.
Llew·el·lyn (lōo·el′ən) Meaning uncertain. [< Welsh]
Lloyd (loid) Gray. [< Welsh]
Lo·ren·zo (lə·ren′zō; Ital. lō·ren′tsō; Sp. lō·rän′thō) Var. of LAURENCE.
Lot (lot) Veiled. [< Hebrew] Also **Lott**.
Lou·is (lōo′is, lōo′ē; Fr. lwē) War famous. [< OF < Gmc.] Also **Lew′is**, Du. **Lo·de·wijk** (lō′də·vīk), Ger. **Lud·wig** (lōot′vikh), Ital. **Lu·i·gi** (lōo·ē′jē), or **Lo·do·vi·co** (lō′dō·vē′kō), Pg. **Lu·iz** (lōo·ēsh′), Sp. **Lu·is** (lōo·ēs′). Dims. **Lew**, **Lou**.
Low·ell (lō′əl) Beloved. [OE] Also **Lov·ell** (luv′əl).
Lu·cas (lōo′kəs) Light. [< L]
Lu·cian (lōo′shən) Var. of LUCIUS. [< L Lucianus] Also **Lu·cien** (lōo′shən; Fr. lü·syaṅ′).
Lu·ci·fer (lōo′sə·fər) Light-bearer. [< L]
Lu·cius (lōo′shəs) Light. [< L]
Lu·cre·tius (lōo·krē′shəs, -shē·əs) Shining or wealthy. [< L]
Luke (lōok) English form of LUCAS.
Lu·ther (lōo′thər) Famous warrior. [< Gmc.] Also Fr. **Lo·thaire** (lō·târ′), Ital. **Lo·ta·rio** (lo·tä′ryō).
Lyle (līl) ? Of the island. [? < OF]
Ly·man (lī′mən) Meaning uncertain. [OE]
Lynn (lin) From an English surname; orig. a place name.

Mac (mak) Son. [< Celtic] Also **Mack**.
Mal·a·chi (mal′ə·kī) Messenger. [< Hebrew]
Mal·colm (mal′kəm) Servant of (St.) Columba. [< Celtic]
Ma·nu·el (mä·nwel′) Sp. form of IMMANUEL.
Mar·cel·lus (mär·sel′əs) Dim. of MARCUS. Also Fr. **Mar·cel** (mår·sel′), Ital. **Mar·cel·lo** (mär·chel′lō).
Mar·cus (mär′kəs) Of Mars. [< L]
Mar·i·on (mar′ē·ən, mâr′-) Of Mary. [< F]
Mark (märk) English form of MARCUS. Also Fr. **Marc** (märk), Ital. **Mar·co** (mär′kō).
Mar·ma·duke (mär′mə·dōok, -dyōok) Meaning uncertain. [? < Celtic]
Mar·shal (mär′shəl) From the title. [< Gmc.] Also **Mar′shall**.
Mar·tin (mär′tən; Fr. mår·taṅ′; Ger. mär′tēn) Of Mars. [< L] Dims. **Mart**, **Mar′ty**.
Mar·vin (mär′vin) Sea friend. [< Gmc.]
Ma·son (mā′sən) Stoneworker. [< Gmc.]
Mat·thew (math′yōo) Gift of God. [< Hebrew] Fr. **Ma·thieu** (mà·tyœ′), Ital. **Mat·te·o** (mät·tā′ō), Sp. **Ma·te·o** (mä·tā′ō). Dims. **Mat**, **Matt**.

Mat·thi·as (mə·thī′əs) Var. of MATTHEW. [< Gk.]
Mau·rice (mə·rēs′, môr′is, mor′is; Fr. mô·rēs′) Moorish; dark. [< F < L]
Max (maks; Ger. mäks) Dim. of MAXIMILIAN.
Max·i·mil·ian (mak′sə·mil′yən; Ger. mäk′sē·mē′lē·än) Prob. coined by Frederick III from the Roman names Maximus and Aemilianus. Dim. **Max**.
May·nard (mā′nərd, -närd) Powerful strength. [< Gmc.]
Mel·vin (mel′vin) High protector. [OE] Dim. **Mel**.
Mer·e·dith (mer′ə·dith) Sea protector. [< Welsh]
Mer·vin (mûr′vin) Var. of MARVIN.
Mi·cah (mī′kə) Who is like God? [< Hebrew]
Mi·chael (mī′kəl; Ger. mi′khä·el) Who is like God? [< Hebrew] Also Fr. **Mi·chel** (mē·shel′), Ital. **Mi·che·le** (mē·kâ′lā), Sp., Pg. **Mi·guel** (mē·gel′). Dims. **Mike** (mīk), **Mick·ey** or **Mick·y** (mik′ē), **Mik·ey** (mī′kē).
Mi·klós (mī′klōsh) Hung. form of NICHOLAS.
Miles (mīlz) Meaning uncertain. [< Gmc.] Also **Myles**.
Mi·lo (mī′lō; Ital. mē′lō) Ital. var. of MILES.
Mil·ton (mil′tən) From an English surname; orig. a place name. [< Gmc.] Dim. **Milt**.
Mitch·ell (mich′əl) Var. of MICHAEL. Dim. **Mitch**.
Mon·roe (mən·rō′, Brit. mun′rō) From a Celtic surname; orig. a place name.
Mon·ta·gue (mon′tə·gyōo) From a Norman Fr. surname; orig. a place name. Dim. **Mon′ty**.
Mont·gom·er·y (mont·gum′ər·ē) From a Norman Fr. surname; orig. a place name. Dim. **Mon′ty**.
Mor·gan (môr′gən) Sea-dweller. [< Welsh]
Mor·ris (môr′is, mor′-) Var. of MAURICE.
Mor·ti·mer (môr′tə·mər) From a Norman Fr. surname; orig. a place name. Dims. **Mort**, **Mor′ty**.
Mor·ton (môr′tən) From an English surname; orig. a place name. Dim. **Mort**, **Mor′ty**.
Mo·ses (mō′zis, -ziz) ? Son. [< Hebrew, ? < Egyptian] Dim. **Moe** (mō), **Moi·she** (moi′shə), **Mose** (mōz).
Moss (môs, mos) Var. of MOSES.
Mur·dock (mûr′dok) Seaman. [< Celtic] Also **Mur′doch**.
Mur·ray (mûr′ē) From a Scot. surname, or var. of MAURICE.
Myles (mīlz) Var. of MILES.

Na·hum (nā′əm) Consolation. [< Hebrew]
Na·po·le·on (nə·pō′lē·ən) Of the new city. [< F < Gk.] Also Fr. **Na·po·lé·on** (nà·pô·lā·ôṅ′), Ital. **Na·po·le·o·ne** (nä·pō′lā·ō′nä).
Na·than (nā′thən) Gift. [< Hebrew] Dims. **Nat** (nat), **Nate** (nāt).
Na·than·iel (nə·than′yəl) Gift of God. [< Hebrew] Also **Na·than·a·el**. Dims. **Nat**, **Nate**.
Ned (ned) Dim. of EDGAR, EDMUND, or EDWARD. Also **Ned′dy**.
Ne·he·mi·ah (nē′hə·mī′ə) Comfort of God. [< Hebrew]
Neil (nēl) Champion. [< Celtic] Also **Neal**.
Nel·son (nel′sən) Neal's son: from an English surname.
Ne·ro (nir′ō) Strong: from the name of a Roman clan.
Nev·ille (nev′il, -əl) From a Norman Fr. surname; orig. a place name. Also **Nev′il**, **Nev′ile**, **Nev′ill**.
New·ton (nōot′n, nyōot′n) From an English surname; orig. a place name.
Nich·o·las (nik′ə·ləs) The people's victory. [< Gk.] Also **Nic′o·las**, Fr. **Ni·co·las** (nē·kô·là′), Ital. **Nic·co·lò** (nēk′kō·lô′), Russ. **Ni·ko·lai** (nyi·kə·lī′), Sp. **Ni·co·lás** (nē′kō·läs′). Dims. **Nick**, **Nick′y**.
Ni·gel (nī′jəl) Noble. [< Celtic]
No·ah (nō′ə) Comfort. [< Hebrew]
No·el (nō′əl) Christmas. [< OF < L] Also Fr. **No·ël** (nō·el′).
Nor·bert (nôr′bərt) Brightness of Njord. [< Gmc.]
Nor·man (nôr′mən) Northman. [< Scand.] Dim. **Norm**.

O·ba·di·ah (ō′bə·dī′ə) Servant of God. [< Hebrew]
Oc·ta·vi·us (ok·tā′vē·əs) The eighth (born). [< L]
O·laf (ō′ləf; Dan., Norw. ō′läf; Sw. ōo′läf) Ancestor's heirloom. Also **O′lav** [< Scand.]
Ol·i·ver (ol′ə·vər) Of the olive tree. [< F < L] Dims. **Ol′lie**, **Ol′ly**.
Or·lan·do (ôr·lan′dō; Ital. ôr·län′dō) Ital. form of ROLAND.
Os·bert (ōz′bərt) Divine brilliance. [OE]
Os·car (os′kər) Divine spear. [OE]
Os·mond (oz′mənd) Divine protection. [OE] Also **Os′mund**.
Os·wald (oz′wəld, -wôld) Divine power. [OE] Also **Os′wold**.
Ot·to (ot′ō; Ger. ôt′ō) Rich. [< Gmc.]
O·wen (ō′ən) Young warrior. [< Welsh]
Pad·raic (pôth′rig) Irish form of PATRICK. Also **Padh′raic**.
Pat·rick (pat′rik) Patrician; aristocratic. [< L] Dims. **Pad′dy**, **Pat**, **Pat′sy**.
Paul (pôl; Fr. pôl; Ger. poul) Little: from a given name of the Aemiliani, a Roman clan. Also Ital. **Pa·o·lo** (pä′ō·lō), Lat. **Pau·li·nus** (pô·lī′nəs) or **Pau·lus** (pô′ləs), Pg. **Pau·lo** (pou′lōo), Sp. **Pa·blo** (pä′vlō).

Per·ci·val (pûr′sə·vəl) Meaning uncertain. [< OF] Also **Per′ce·val.**

Per·cy (pûr′sē) From a Norman Fr. surname; orig. a place name.

Per·ry (per′ē) Of the pear tree: from an English surname.

Pe·ter (pē′tər; *Du., Ger., Norw., Sw.* pā′tər) A rock. [< Gk.] Also *Dan.* **Pe·der** (pā′thər), *Du.* **Pie·ter** (pē′tər), *Fr.* **Pierre** (pyâr), *Modern Gk.* **Pe·tros** (pâ′trôs), *Ital.* **Pie·tro** (pyā′trō), *Pg., Sp.* **Pe·dro** (*Pg.* pā′thrōō; *Sp.* pā′thrō), *Russ.* **Pëtr** (pyô′tər). Dim. **Pete.**

Phi·lan·der (fi·lan′dər) Lover of men. [< Gk.]

Phi·le·mon (fi·lē′mən) Loving. [< Gk.]

Phil·ip (fil′ip) Lover of horses. [< Gk.] Also *Fr.* **Phi·lippe** (fē·lēp′), *Ger.* **Phi·lipp** (fē′lip). Dims. **Phil, Pip.**

Phin·e·as (fin′ē·əs) Mouth of brass: prob. an oracular priest's title. [< Hebrew]

Pierce (pirs) Var. of PETER. [< OF] Also **Pearce.**

Pierre (pyâr) Fr. form of PETER.

Pi·us (pī′əs) Devout. [< L]

Quen·tin (kwen′tin) The fifth (born). [< L] Also **Quin·tin** (kwin′tin).

Quin·cy (kwin′sē) ? var. of QUENTIN. [< OF]

Ralph (ralf; *Brit.* rāf) Wolf-wise. [< Gmc.] *Fr.* **Ra·oul** (rä·ōōl′).

Ran·dal (ran′dəl) Shield wolf. [OE] Also **Ran′dall.**

Ran·dolph (ran′dolf) Shield wolf. [OE] Dim. **Ran′dy.**

Ra·pha·el (rā′fē·əl, raf′ē·əl) God has healed. [< Hebrew]

Ray (rā) Dim. of RAYMOND.

Ray·mond (rā′mənd; *Fr.* rā·môn′) Wise protection. [< Gmc.] Also **Ray′mund,** *Sp.* **Rai·mun·do** (rī·mōōn′dō) or **Ra·món** (rä·mōn′). Dim. **Ray.**

Reg·i·nald (rej′ə·nəld) Judicial ruler. [< Gmc.] Also *Fr.* **Re·gnault** (rə·nyō′) or **Re·naud** (rə·nō′), *Ital.* **Ri·nal·do** (rē·näl′dō), *Sp.* **Rey·nal·do** (rā·näl′thō). Dims. **Reg** (rej), **Reg′gie, Rex.**

Re·né (rə·nā′) Reborn. [< F]

Reu·ben (rōō′bin) Behold, a son! [< Hebrew] Dim. **Rube.**

Rex (reks) King [< L], or dim. of REGINALD.

Rey·nard (rā′nərd, ren′ərd) Brave judgment. [< Gmc.]

Reyn·old (ren′əld) Var. of REGINALD. [< OF]

Rich·ard (rich′ərd; *Fr.* rē·shàr′; *Ger.* rikh′ärt) Strong king. [< OF < Gmc.] Also *Ital.* **Ric·car·do** (rēk·kär′dō), *Sp.* **Ri·car·do** (rē·kär′thō). Dims. **Dick, Dick′ie, Dick′y, Rich, Rich′ie, Rick, Rick′y.**

Ro·ald (rō′äl) Famous power. [< Norw. < Gmc.]

Rob·ert (rob′ərt; *Fr.* rô·bâr′) Bright fame. [< Gmc.] Also *Ital., Sp.* **Ro·ber·to** (rō·ber′tō). Dims. **Bob, Bob′by, Dob, Dob′bin, Rob, Rob′bie, Rob′in.**

Rod·er·ick (rod′ər·ik) Famous king. [< Gmc.] Also **Rod′er·ic, Rod·rick** (rod′rik), *Fr.* **Ro·drigue** (rô·drēg′), *Ital., Sp.* **Ro·dri·go** (*Ital.* rō·drē′gō; *Sp.* rō·thrē′gō). Dims. **Rod, Rod′dy.**

Rod·ney (rod′nē) From an English surname; orig. a place name. Dim. **Rod.**

Ro·dolph (rō′dolf) Var. of RUDOLPH. Also **Ro·dol·phus** (rō·dol′fəs).

Rog·er (roj′ər; *Fr.* rô·zhā′) Famous spear. [< OF < Gmc.] Dims. **Hodge, Hodg′kin, Rodge.**

Ro·land (rō′lənd; *Fr.* rô·län′) Country's fame. [< Celtic < Gmc.] Also **Row′land.**

Rolf (rolf) Dim. of RUDOLPH. Also **Rolph.**

Rol·lo (rol′ō) Dim. of RUDOLPH.

Ron·ald (ron′əld; *Norw.* rō·näl′) Old Norse form of REGINALD.

Ro·ry (rôr′ē, rō′rē) Red. [< Celtic]

Ros·coe (ros′kō) From an English surname; orig. a place name.

Ross (rôs) From an English surname; orig. a place name.

Roy (roi) King. [< OF]

Ru·dolph (rōō′dolf) Famous wolf. [< Gmc.] Also **Ru′·dolf, Ru·dol·phus** (rōō·dol′fəs), *Fr.* **Ro·dolphe** (rô·dôlf′), *Ital.* **Ro·dol·pho** (rō·dôl′fō), *Sp.* **Ro·dol·fo** (rō·thôl′fō). Dims. **Rol′lo, Ru′dy.**

Ru·fus (rōō′fəs) Red-haired. [< L] Dim. **Rufe.**

Ru·pert (rōō′pərt) Var. of ROBERT. [< G] Also *Ger.* **Ru·precht** (rōō′prekht).

Rus·sell (rus′əl) Red: from an English surname. [OE < OF] Dim. **Russ.**

Sal·o·mon (sal′ə·mən) Var. of SOLOMON.

Sam·son (sam′sən) The sun. [< Hebrew] Also **Samp′son** (samp′sən, sam′-).

Sam·u·el (sam′yōō·əl) Name of God. [< Hebrew] Dims. **Sam, Sam′my.**

San·dy (san′dē) Dim. of ALEXANDER. Also **San·der** (san′dər, sän′-).

Saul (sôl) Asked (of God). [< Hebrew]

Schuy·ler (skī′lər) Shelter. [< Du.]

Scott (skot) The Scot: from an English surname.

Seam·us (shā′məs) Irish form of JAMES.

Sean (shôn, shän) Irish form of JOHN.

Se·bas·tian (si·bas′chən) Venerable. [< Gk.]

Seth (seth) Appointed. [< Hebrew]

Sew·ard (sōō′ərd) ? Sow-herder: from an English surname.

Sey·mour (sē′môr, -môr) From an English surname; orig. a place name. Dims. **Cy, Sy.**

Shawn (shôn) Irish form of JOHN. Also **Shaun.**

Shel·don (shel′dən) From an English surname; orig. a place name.

Shir·ley (shûr′lē) From an English surname; orig. a place name.

Sid·ney (sid′nē) St. Denis: from an English surname. Dim. **Sid.**

Sieg·fried (sēg′frēd; *Ger.* zēk′frēt) Victorious peace. [< Gmc.]

Sig·is·mund (sij′əs·mənd, sig′-) Victorious protection. [< Gmc.]

Sig·mund (sig′mənd; *Ger.* zekh′mōōnt) Var. of SIGISMUND.

Si·las (sī′ləs) Meaning uncertain. [< Gk.] Dim. **Si** (sī).

Sil·va·nus (sil·vā′nəs) From the name of the Roman god of woods and crops.

Sil·ves·ter (sil·ves′tər) Of the woods; rustic. [< L]

Sim·e·on (sim′ē·ən) He who is heard (widely); hence, famous. [< Hebrew] Dim. **Sim** (sim).

Si·mon (sī′mən) Var. of SIMEON.

Sin·clair (sin·klâr′, sin′klâr) St. Clair: from a Norman Fr. surname.

Sol·o·mon (sol′ə·mən) Peaceful. [< Hebrew] Dim. **Sol.**

Stan·ley (stan′lē) From an English surname; orig. a place name. Dim. **Stan.**

Ste·phen (stē′vən) Crown. [< Gk.] Also **Ste′ven,** *Ger.* **Ste·phan** or **Ste·fan** (shte′fän), *Ital.* **Ste·fa·no** (stā′fä·nō), *Russ.* **Ste·pan** (styi·pän′). Dims. **Steve, Ste′vie.**

Stew·art (stōō′ərt, styōō′-) Steward: from an English surname. Also **Stu′art.** Dims. **Stew, Stu.**

Sum·ner (sum′nər) Summoner: from an English surname.

Syd·ney (sid′nē) Var. of SIDNEY.

Syl·va·nus (sil·vā′nəs) Var. of SILVANUS.

Syl·ves·ter (sil·ves′tər) Var. of SILVESTER.

Taf·fy (taf′ē) Welsh dim. of DAVID.

Tad (tad) Dim. of THEODORE or THADDEUS.

Ted (ted) Dim. of EDWARD or THEODORE. Also **Ted′dy.**

Ter·ence (ter′əns) From the name of a Roman clan. Also **Ter′rence.** Dim. **Ter′ry.**

Thad·de·us (thad′ē·əs) Praised. [< Aramaic] Dims. **Tad, Thad, Tha′dy, Thad′dy.**

The·o·bald (thē′ə·bôld, tib′əld) The people's brave one. [< Gmc.]

The·o·dore (thē′ə·dôr, -dōr) Gift of God. [< Gk.] Also *Fr.* **Thé·o·dore** (tā·ô·dôr′), *Ger.* **The·o·dor** (tā′ō·dôr), *Modern Gk.* **The·o·do·ros** (thä·ô′thô·rôs), *Ital., Sp.* **Te·o·do·ro** (*Ital.* tā′ō·dô′rō; *Sp.* tā′ō·thô′rō). Dims. **Tad, Ted, Ted′dy, Dode** (dōd).

The·od·o·ric (thē·od′ər·ik) Ruler of the people. [< Gmc.] Also **The·od′e·rick, The·od′o·rick.**

The·oph·i·lus (thē·of′ə·ləs) Lover of God. [< Gk.]

Thom·as (tom′əs; *Fr.* tô·mä′; *Ger.* tō′mäs) Twin. [< Aramaic] Also *Ital.* **Tom·ma·so** (tōm·mä′zō), *Sp.* **To·más** (tō·mäs′). Dims. **Tom, Tom′my.**

Thurs·ton (thûrs′tən) Thor's stone. [< Scand.]

Tim·o·thy (tim′ə·thē) Honor of God. [< Gk.] Also *Fr.* **Ti·mo·thee** (tē·mô·tā′), *Ital.* **Ti·mo·te·o** (tē·mô′tā·ō). Dims. **Tim, Tim′my.**

Ti·tus (tī′təs) Meaning uncertain. [< L]

To·bi·as (tō·bī′əs) God is good. [< Hebrew] Also **To·bi·ah** (tō·bī′ə). Dim. **To·by** (tō′bē).

Tod (tod) Fox: from an English surname. Also **Todd.**

To·ny (tō′nē) Dim. of ANTHONY.

Tris·tan (tris′tän; -tən) Confusion. [< Celtic] Also **Tris·tram** (tris′trəm). Dim. **Tris.**

Tyb·alt (tib′əlt) Var. of THEOBALD.

U·lys·ses (yōō·lis′ēz) ? Hater: Lat. form of Gk. *Odysseus.*

Um·ber·to (ōōm·ber′tō) Ital. form of HUMBERT.

Ur·ban (ûr′bən) Of the city. [< L]

U·ri·ah (yōō·rī′ə) God is light. [< Hebrew] Also **U·ri·as** (yōō·rī′əs).

U·ri·el (yōōr′ē·əl) Light of God. [< Hebrew]

Val·en·tine (val′ən·tīn) Strong; healthy. [< L] Dim. **Val.**

Van (van) From an English surname, or from the Ger. or Du. name element *von, van,* indicating residence or origin.

Va·si·li (və·syē′lyē) Russ. var. of BASIL.

Ver·gil (vûr′jəl) Var. of VIRGIL.

Ver·non (vûr′nən) Meaning uncertain. [< L or F] Dim. **Vern.**

Vic·tor (vik′tər; *Fr.* vēk·tôr′) Conqueror. [< L] Also *Ital.* **Vit·to·rio** (vit·tô′ryō). Dims. **Vic, Vick.**

Vin·cent (vin′sənt; *Fr.* vaṅ·säṅ′) Conquering. [< L] Also *Ger.* **Vin·cenz** (vin′tsents), *Ital.* **Vin·cen·zo** (vēn·chen′tsō), *Sp.* **Vi·cen·te** (vē·thän′tā). Dims. **Vin, Vince, Vin′ny.**

Vir·gil (vûr′jəl) Flourishing: from the name of a Roman clan. Also **Ver′gil.** Dims. **Virge, Vir′gie.**

Viv·i·an (viv′ē·ən, viv′yən) Lively. [< F] Also **Viv·i·en** (viv′ē·ən; *Fr.* vē·vyàṅ′).

Wal·do (wôl'dō, wol'-)   Ruler.   [< Gmc.]
Wal·lace (wol'is)   Welsh(man): from a Scot. surname. Also **Wal'lis**. Dim. **Wal'ly**.
Wal·ter (wôl'tər; *Ger.* väl'tər)   Ruler of the army. [< Gmc.] Also *Ger.* **Wal·ther** (väl'tər). Dims. **Walt, Wal'ly**.
Ward (wôrd)   Guard: from an English surname.
War·ren (wôr'ən, wor'-)   From an English surname.
Wayne (wān)   From an English surname. [? < Celtic]
Wes·ley (wes'lē; *Brit.* wez'lē)   From an English surname; orig. a place name. Dim. **Wes**.
Wil·bur (wil'bər)   Bright will. [< Gmc.] Also **Wil'ber**.
Wil·fred (wil'frid)   Resolute peace. [< Gmc.] Also **Wil'frid**. Dim. **Fred**.
Wil·lard (wil'ərd)   From an English surname.
Wil·liam (wil'yəm)   Resolute protection. [< Gmc.] Also *Du.* **Wil·lem** (vil'əm), *Ger.* **Wil·helm** (vil'helm). Dims. **Bill, Bil'ly, Will, Wil'lie, Wil'ly**.
Wil·lis (wil'is)   Willie's son: from an English surname.

Win·fred (win'frid)   Friend of peace. [OE] Also **Win'frid**. Dims. **Win, Win'nie**.
Win·ston (win'stən)   From an English surname; orig. a place name.
Wy·att (wī'ət)   Dim. of GUY. [< OF]
Wys·tan (wis'tən)   Battle stone. [OE]

Zach·a·ri·ah (zak'ə·rī'ə)   Remembrance of God. [< Hebrew] Also **Zach·a·ri·as** (zak'ə·rī'əs). Dims. **Zach** (zak), **Zack**.
Zach·a·ry (zak'ər·ē)   Var. of ZACHARIAH.
Zeb·a·di·ah (zeb'ə·dī'ə)   Gift of God. [< Hebrew]
Zeb·e·dee (zeb'ə·dē)   Contr. of ZEBADIAH.
Zech·a·ri·ah (zek'ə·rī'ə)   Var. of ZACHARIAH.
Zeke (zēk)   Dim. of EZEKIEL.
Zeph·a·ni·ah (zef'ə·nī'ə)   Protected by God. [< Hebrew] Dim. **Zeph**.

FEMININE NAMES

Ab·i·gail (ab'ə·gāl)   Father's joy. [< Hebrew] Dims. **Ab'by, Ab'bie**.
A·da (ā'də)   Joyful; flourishing. [< Gmc.]
A·dah (ā'də)   Beauty. [< Hebrew] Also **A'da**.
Ad·e·la (ad'ə·lə; *Sp.* ä·thä'lä)   Noble. [< Gmc.] Also **A·dele** (ə·del'), *Fr.* **A·dèle** (à·del'), *Ger.* **A·de·le** (ä·dā'lə).
Ad·e·laide (ad'ə·lād)   Nobility. [< Gmc.] Also *Fr.* **A·dé·la·ide** (à·dā·là·ēd'), *Ger.* **A·del·heid** (ä'dəl·hīt), *Ital.* **A·de·la·i·de** (ä'dā·lä'ē·dä). Dims. **Ad'die, Ad'dy**.
Ad·e·line (ad'ə·līn; *Fr.* äd·lēn')   Of noble birth. [< Gmc.] Also **Ad'a·line, A·de·li·cia** (ad'ə·lish'ə), **Ad·e·li·na** (ad'ə·lī'nə). Dims. **Ad'die, Ad'dy**.
A·dri·enne (ā'drē·en; *Fr.* ä·drē·en')   Fem. of ADRIAN. [< F]
Ag·a·tha (ag'ə·thə)   Good; kind. [< Gk.] Also *Fr.* **A·gathe** (à·gàt'), *Ger.* **A·ga·the** (ä·gä'tə). Dim. **Ag'gie**.
Ag·nes (ag'nis; *Ger.* äg'nes)   Pure; sacred. [< Gk.] Also *Fr.* **A·gnès** (à·nyās'). Dim. **Ag'gie**.
A·i·da (ä·ē'də, ä'də)   From the heroine of Verdi's opera.
Ai·leen (ā·lēn'; *Irish* ī·lēn')   Var. of EILEEN.
Ai·mée (ā·mā')   French form of AMY.
Al·ber·ta (al·bûr'tə)   Fem. of ALBERT. Also **Al·ber·ti·na** (al'bər·tē'nə), **Al·ber·tine** (al'bər·tēn).
A·le·the·a (al'ə·thē'ə, ə·lē'thē·ə)   Truth. [< Gk.]
Al·ex·an·dra (al'ig·zan'drə, -zän'-)   Fem. of ALEXANDER. Also **Al·ex·an·dri·na** (al'ig·zan·drē'nə, -zän-), *Fr.* **A·lex·an·drine** (à·lek·sän·drēn'), *Ital.* **A·les·san·dra** (ä'läs·sän'drä), *Sp.* **A·le·jan·dra** (ä'lā·hän'drä) or **A·le·jan·dri·na** (ä'lā·hän·drē'nä). Dims. **A·lex·a** (ə·lek'sə), **Al·ex·in·a** (al'ig·zē'nə), **Al·ix** (al'iks), **San·dra** (san'drə).
A·lex·is (ə·lek'sis)   Fem. of ALEX. Also **A·lex·i·a** (ə·lek'sē·ə).
Al·fre·da (al·frē'də)   Fem. of ALFRED.
Al·ice (al'is; *Fr.* à·lēs'; *Ger.* ä·lē'sə; *Ital.* ä·lē'chä)   Truth. [< OF < Gmc.] Also **Al'lis, Al'yce, Al'ys**. Dim. **Al'lie**.
A·li·cia (ə·lish'ə, ə·lish'ē·ə)   Var. of ALICE. [< L]
A·li·é·nor (à·lē·ä·nôr')   French form of ELEANOR.
A·line (ə·lēn', al'ēn)   Var. of ADELINE.
Al·i·son (al'ə·sən)   Of sacred memory. [< Gmc.] Also **Al'li·son**.
Al·ix (al'iks)   Dim. of ALEXANDRA.
Al·le·gra (ə·lā'grə)   Spirited. [< Ital. < L]
Al·ma (al'mə)   Providing; gracious. [< L]
Al·mi·ra (al·mī'rə)   Lofty; princess. [< Arabic]
Al·phon·sine (al·fon'sēn)   Fem. of ALPHONSO.
Al·ta (al'tə)   Tall. [< L]
Al·the·a (al·thē'ə)   Healer. [< Gk.]
Al·vi·na (al·vī'nə, al·vē'nə)   Fem. of ALVIN.
Am·a·bel (am'ə·bel)   Lovable. [< L] Also **Am'a·belle**. Dim. **Mab** (mab).
A·man·da (ə·man'də)   Lovable. [< L] Also *Fr.* **A·man·dine** (à·män·dēn'). Dim. **Man'dy**.
Am·a·ran·tha (am'ə·ran'thə)   Immortal. [< Gk.]
Am·a·ryl·lis (am'ə·ril'əs)   Country sweetheart. [< L]
A·me·lia (ə·mēl'yə, ə·mē'lē·ə; *Ital.* ä·māl'yä; *Sp.* ä·mā'lyä)   Industrious. [< Gmc.] Also *Fr.* **A·mé·lie** (à·mä·lē'). Dim. **Mil'lie, Mil'ly**.
Am·i·ty (am'ə·tē)   From the abstract noun.
A·my (ā'mē)   Beloved. [< L]
An·as·ta·sia (an'ə·stā'zhə, -shə)   Able to live again. [< L]
An·dre·a (an'drē·ə; *Ital.* än·drā'ä)   Fem. of ANDREW.
An·ge·la (an'jə·lə)   Angel. [< Gk.] Also **An·ge·li·na** (an'jə·lē'nə, -lī'-), *Fr.* **An·gèle** (äṅ·zhel').
An·gel·i·ca (an·jel'i·kə; *Ital.* än·jā'lē·kä)   Angelic. [< Gk.] Also *Fr.* **An·gé·lique** (äṅ·zhä·lēk').
A·ni·ta (ə·nē'tə)   Dim. of ANNA. [< Sp.] Also **A·ni·tra** (ə·nē'trə).
Ann (an)   Grace. [< Hebrew] Also *Sp.* **A·na** (ä'nä). Dims. **An'nie, Nan, Nan'cy, Ni'na**.
An·na (an'ə; *Ger.* ä'nä)   Var. of HANNAH. Dim. **An'nie**.
An·na·bel (an'ə·bel)   Gracefully fair. [< Hebrew] Also **An·na·bel·la** (an'ə·bel'ə), **An'na·belle**.

Anne (an)   Var. of ANN.
An·nette (ə·net'; *Fr.* à·net')   Dim. of ANNE. [< F]
An·the·a (an·thē'ə)   Flowery. [< Gk.]
An·toi·nette (an'twə·net'; *Fr.* äṅ·twà·net')   Fr. form of ANTONIA. Also *Ital.* **An·to·niet·ta** (än'tō·nyet'tä). Dims. **Net'tie, Net'ty, Toi'ni**.
An·to·ni·a (an·tō'nē·ə, an·tō·nē'ə)   Fem. of ANTHONY. [< L] Also *Ital.*, *Sp.* **An·to·ni·na** (än'tō·nē'nä).
A·pril (ā'prəl)   From the name of the month.
Ar·a·bel·la (ar'ə·bel'ə)   Meaning and origin uncertain. Also **Ar·a·bel** (ar'ə·bel), *Fr.* **A·ra·belle** (à·rà·bel'), *Sp.* **A·ra·be·la** (ä'rä·bā'lä). Dims. **Bel'la, Belle**.
Ar·i·ad·ne (ar'ē·ad'nē)   Most pure. [< Gk.]
Ar·lene (är·lēn')   Meaning and origin uncertain. Also **Ar·leen** (är·lēn'), **Ar·line** (är·lēn').
As·pa·sia (as·pā'zhə, -zhē·ə)   Welcome. [< L < Gk.]
As·trid (as'trid)   God's power. [< Scand.]
A·the·na (ə·thē'nə)   From the name of the Greek goddess of wisdom. Also **A·the·ne** (ə·thē'nē).
Au·drey (ô'drē)   Noble might. [< OF < Gmc.]
Au·gus·ta (ô·gus'tə; *Ger.* ou·gŏŏs'tä; *Ital.* ou·gŏŏs'tä)   Fem. of AUGUSTUS. Also **Au·gus·ti·na** (ô'gəs·tē'nə), **Au·gus·tine** (ô'gəs·tēn). Dims. **Gus'sie, Gus'ta**.
Au·rel·ia (ô·rēl'yə)   Golden. [< L]
Au·ro·ra (ô·rôr'ə, ô·rō'rə)   From the name of the Roman goddess of the dawn.
A·va (ā'və)   Meaning and origin uncertain.
Av·e·line (av'ə·lēn, -līn)   Hazel. [< F]
A·vis (ā'vis)   Bird. [< L]

Ba·bette (ba·bet')   Fr. dim. of ELIZABETH.
Bap·tis·ta (bap·tis'tə)   Fem. of BAPTIST. Also *Ital.* **Bat·tis·ta** (bät·tēs'tä).
Bar·ba·ra (bär'bər·ə, -brə)   Foreign; strange. [< Gk.] Dims. **Bab, Bab'bie, Babs, Barb, Bar'bie, Bob'bie**.
Bath·she·ba (bath·shē'bə, bath'shi·bə)   Daughter of the promise. [< Hebrew]
Be·a·ta (bē·ä'tə)   Blessed. [< L]
Be·a·trice (bē'ə·tris; *Ital.* bā'ä·trē'chä)   She who makes happy. [< L] Also **Be·a·trix** (bē'ə·triks; *Ger.* bā·ä'triks), *Fr.* **Bé·a·trice** or **Bé·a·trix** (bā·à·trēs'). Dims. **Bea, Bee, Trix, Trix'ie, Trix'y**.
Beck·y (bek'ē)   Dim. of REBECCA.
Be·lin·da (bə·lin'də)   Serpent: title of an oracular priestess. [< Gmc.] Dim. **Lin'da**.
Bel·la (bel'ə)   Dim. of ARABELLA or ISABELLA. Also **Bell**.
Belle (bel)   Beautiful. [< F]
Ben·e·dic·ta (ben'ə·dik'tə)   Fem. of BENEDICT. Also *Ital.* **Be·ne·det·ta** (bā'nā·dāt'tä), *Sp.* **Be·ni·ta** (bā·nē'tä).
Ber·e·ni·ce (ber'ə·nī'sē)   Victorious. [< Gk.]
Ber·na·dette (bûr'nə·det', *Fr.* ber·nà·det')   Fem. of BERNARD. [< F]
Ber·nar·dine (bûr'nər·dēn)   Fem. of BERNARD. [< F] Also **Ber·nar·di·na** (bûr'nər·dē'nə).
Ber·nice (bər·nēs', bûr'nis)   Var. of BERENICE.
Ber·tha (bûr'thə; *Du.*, *Ger.*, *Sw.* ber'tä)   Bright; famous. [< Gmc.] Also *Fr.* **Berthe** (bert), *Ital.*, *Sp.* **Ber·ta** (ber·tä). Dims. **Ber'tie, Ber'ty**.
Ber·yl (ber'əl)   From the name of the jewel.
Bess (bes)   Dim. of ELIZABETH. Also **Bes'sie, Bes'sy**.
Beth (beth)   Dim. of ELIZABETH.
Beth·el (beth'əl)   House of God. [< Hebrew]
Bet·sy (bet'sē)   Dim. of ELIZABETH.
Bet·ti·na (bə·tē'nə)   Dim. of ELIZABETH. [< Ital.]
Bet·ty (bet'ē)   Dim. of ELIZABETH. Also **Bet'te** (bet'ē, bet).
Beu·lah (byōō'lə)   Married. [< Hebrew] Also **Beu'la**.
Bev·er·ly (bev'er·lē)   From an English surname; orig. a place name. Also **Bev'er·ley**. Dim. **Bev**.
Bid·dy (bid'ē)   Dim. of BRIDGET.
Blanche (blanch, blänch; *Fr.* bläṅsh)   White; shining. [<

F < Gmc.] Also **Blanch**, *Ital.* **Bian·ca** (byäng′kä), *Sp.* **Blan·ca** (bläng′kä).

Bon·ny (bon′ē) Good. [< F] Also **Bon′nie**.

Bren·da (bren′də) Sword or torch. [< Gmc.]

Bridg·et (brij′it) High; august. [< Celtic] Also **Brig·id** (brij′id, brē′id). Dims. **Bid′dy, Bri·die** (brī′dē).

Ca·mel·lia (kə·mēl′yə) From the name of the flower.

Ca·mil·la (kə·mil′ə; *Ital.* kä·mēl′lä) Attendant at a sacrifice. [< L] Also *Fr.* **Ca·mille** (kȧ·mēl′), *Sp.* **Ca·mi·la** (kä·mē′lä).

Can·dice (kan′dis) Radiant. [< L] Also **Can·da·ce** (kan′də·sē, kan·dā′sē).

Can·di·da (kan′di·də) White; pure. [< L]

Ca·ra (kär′ə) Loved one. [< L]

Car·la (kär′lə) Fem. of CARLO.

Car·lot·ta (kär·lot′ə; *Ital.* kär·lôt′tä) Ital. form of CHARLOTTE. Also *Sp.* **Car·lo·ta** (kär·lō′tä). Dims. **Lot′ta, Lot′tie, Lot′ty.**

Car·mel (kär′məl) Garden. [< Hebrew] Also **Car·mel·a** (kär·mel′ə). Dim. **Car·me·li·ta** (kär′mə·lē′tə).

Car·men (kär′mən) Song. [< L]

Car·ol (kar′əl) From CAROL, masc., var. of CHARLES. Also **Car·o·la** (kar′ə·lə), **Car′ole, Car′ol.**

Car·o·line (kar′ə·lin, -lin; *Fr.* kȧ·rô·lēn′) Fem. of CHARLES. Also **Car·o·lyn** (kar′ə·lin), **Car·o·li·na** (kar′ə·lī′nə; *Ital., Sp.* kä′rō·lē′nä). Dim. **Car′rie.**

Cas·san·dra (kə·san′drə) From the name of the Trojan prophetess in the *Iliad.* [< Gk.] Dims. **Cass, Cas′sie.**

Cath·er·ine (kath′ər·in, kath′rin, *Fr.* kȧ·trēn′) Purity. [< Gk.] Also **Kath′er·ine, Cath·a·rine, Cath·a·ri·na** (kath′ə·rē′nə), *Ital., Sp.* **Ca·ta·ri·na** (kä′tä·rē′nä) or **Ca·te·ri·na** (kä′·tä·rē′nä). Dims. **Cath′y, Kate, Kath′y, Kath′ie, Ka′tie, Kay, Kit, Kit′ty.**

Cath·leen (kath′lēn, kath·lēn′) Var. of KATHLEEN.

Ce·cil·ia (si·sil′yə, -sēl′yə) Fem. of CECIL. Also **Ce·cel′ia, Ce·cile** (si·sēl′), **Cec·i·ly** (ses′ə·lē), *Fr.* **Cé·cile** (sä·sēl′). Dims. **Cis, Cis′sie, Cis′sy.**

Ce·leste (si·lest′) Heavenly. [< F < L] Also **Ce·les·tine** (si·les′tin, sel′is·tin), *Fr.* **Cé·les·tine** (sä·les·tēn′).

Cel·ia (sēl′yə, sē′lē·ə; *Ital.* chā′lyä) From the name of a Roman clan. Also *Fr.* **Cé·lie** (sä·lē′).

Cha·ris·sa (kə·ris′ə) Love; grace. [< Gk.]

Char·i·ty (char′ə·tē) From the abstract noun. Dim. **Cher′ry.**

Char·lene (shär·lēn′) Fem. of CHARLES.

Char·lotte (shär′lət; *Fr.* shär·lôt′; *Ger.* shär·lôt′ə) Fem. of CHARLES. [< F] Dims. **Car′ry, Lot′ta, Lot′tie, Lot′ty.**

Cher·yl (cher′əl) Meaning and origin uncertain.

Chlo·e (klō′ē) Bud; sprout. [< Gk.]

Chris·ta·bel (kris′tə·bel) The fair anointed. [< L] Also **Chris′ta·bel′la, Chris′ta·belle.**

Chris·ti·an·a (kris′tē·an′ə) Fem. of CHRISTIAN. Also *Ger.* **Chris·ti·a·ne** (kris′tē·ä′nə).

Chris·ti·na (kris·tē′nə) Var. of CHRISTIANA. Also **Chris·tine** (kris·tēn′; *Fr.* krēs·tēn′; *Ger.* kris·tē′nə). Dims. **Chris, Chris′sie, Chris′ta, Chris′tie, Ti′na.**

Cic·e·ly (sis′ə·lē) Var. of CECILIA.

Cin·dy (sin′dē) Dim. of LUCINDA.

Cis (sis) Dim. of CECILIA. Also **Cis′sie, Cis′sy.**

Claire (klâr) Var. of CLARA. [< F] Also **Clare.**

Clar·a (klar′ə, klâr′ə; *Ger., Sp.* klä′rä) Bright; illustrious. [< L]

Clar·i·bel (klar′ə·bel) Brightly fair. [< L] Also **Clar′a·belle.**

Cla·rice (klə·rēs′, klar′is) Derived from CLARA. Also **Cla·ris·sa** (klə·ris′ə), **Cla·risse** (klə·rēs′).

Cla·rin·da (klə·rin′də) Derived from CLARA.

Clau·dette (klô·det′; *Fr.* klô·det′) Fem. of CLAUDE. [< F]

Clau·di·a (klô′dē·ə) Fem. of *Claudius,* Lat. form of CLAUDE.

Clau·dine (klô·dēn′; *Fr.* klô·dēn′) Var. of CLAUDIA. [< F]

Clem·ence (klem′əns) Fem. of CLEMENT.

Clem·en·tine (klem′ən·tin, -tīn) Fem. of CLEMENT. [< F]

Cle·o·pat·ra (klē′ə·pat′rə, -pä′trə, -pä′trə) Celebrated of her country. [< Gk.] Dim. **Cle·o** (klē′ō).

Cli·o (klī′ō, klē′ō) From the name of the Greek muse of history.

Clo·til·da (klō·til′də) Famous in war. [< Gmc.] Also **Clo·thil′da, Clo·thil′de,** *Fr.* **Clo·tilde** (klô·tēld′).

Co·lette (kō·let′; *Fr.* kô·let′) Fem. dim. of NICHOLAS. [< F]

Col·leen (kol′ēn, ko·lēn′) Girl. [< Irish]

Con·stance (kon′stəns, *Fr.* kôn·stäns′) Constant; firm. [< L] Dims. **Con′nie, Con′ny.**

Con·sue·lo (kən·swā′lō; *Sp.* kōn·swä′lō) Consolation. [< Sp.]

Co·ra (kôr′ə, kō′rə) Maiden. [< Gk.]

Cor·del·ia (kôr·dēl′yə, -dē′lē·ə) Meaning uncertain. [< L]

Co·rin·na (kə·rin′ə) Maiden. [< Gk.] Also **Co·rinne** (kə·rin′, -rēn′; *Fr.* kô·rēn′).

Cor·nel·ia (kôr·nēl′yə, -nē′lē·ə) Fem. of CORNELIUS. [< L]

Cris·ti·na (krēs·tē′nä) Ital. and Sp. form of CHRISTINA.

Crys·tal (kris′təl) From the common noun.

Cyn·thi·a (sin′thē·ə) Of Mount Cynthius: an epithet of the Greek goddess Artemis; poetically, the moon.

Dag·mar (dag′mär) Bright day. [< Dan.]

Dai·sy (dā′zē) From the name of the flower.

Dale (dāl) From the common noun.

Daph·ne (daf′nē) Laurel. [< Gk.]

Dar·leen (där·lēn′) Beloved. [OE] Also **Dar·lene′, Dar·line′.**

Dawn (dôn) From the common noun.

Deb·o·rah (deb′ər·ə, deb′rə) Queen bee. [< Hebrew] Dims. **Deb, Deb′by.**

Deir·dre (dir′drə) From the name of a heroine of Irish myth.

Del·ia (dēl′yə) Of Delos: an epithet of the Greek goddess Artemis. [< Gk.]

De·li·lah (di·lī′lə) Delicate; languid. [< Hebrew]

Del·la (del′ə) Var. of ADELA.

Del·phin·i·a (del·fin′ē·ə) Of Delphi. [< Gk.] Also *Fr.* **Del·phine** (del·fēn′).

De·nise (də·nēz′, -nēs′) Fem. of *Denis,* Fr. form of DENNIS.

Des·i·ree (dez′ə·rē) Desired. [< F] Also *Fr.* **Dé·si·rée** (dā·zē·rā′).

Di·an·a (dī·an′ə) From the name of the Roman goddess of the moon. Also **Di·ane** (dī·an′; *Fr.* dyȧn). Dim. **Di** (dī).

Di·nah (dī′nə) Judged. [< Hebrew]

Do·lo·res (də·lôr′is, -lō′ris; *Sp.* dō·lō′rās) Our Lady of Sorrows: a title of the Virgin Mary. [< Sp.] Dim. **Lo·la** (lō′lə).

Dom·i·nique (dom′ə·nēk; *Fr.* dô·mē·nēk′) Fr. fem. of DOMINIC. Also **Dom·i·ni·ca** (dom′ə·nē′kə, də·min′ə·kə).

Don·na (don′ə) Lady. [< Ital.]

Do·ra (dôr′ə, dō′rə) Dim. of DOROTHY, EUDORA, or THEODORA.

Dor·cas (dôr′kəs) Gazelle. [< Gk.]

Do·reen (dô·rēn′, dôr′ēn, dō-) Irish dim. of DORA.

Do·rin·da (də·rin′də) Gift. [< L]

Dor·is (dôr′is, dor′-) Dorian woman. [< Gk.]

Dor·o·thy (dôr′ə·thē, dor′-) Gift of God. [< Gk.] Also **Dor·o·the·a** (dôr′ə·thē′ə, dor′-; *Ger.* dō′rō·tä′ä), *Fr.* **Do·ro·thée** (dô·rô·tā′). Dims. **Doll, Dol′lie, Dol′ly, Do′ra, Dot, Dot′ty.**

Dru·sil·la (droo·sil′ə) She who strengthens. [< L] Also **Dru·cil′la.**

Dul·cie (dul′sē) Sweet. [< L] Also **Dul′ce, Dul′cy.**

Dul·ci·ne·a (dul′sə·nē′ə, dul·sin′ē·ə; *Sp.* dool′thē·nä′ä) Sweet one. [< Sp.]

E·dith (ē′dith) Prosperous in war. [OE] Also *Lat.* **Ed·i·tha** (ed′i·thə, ē′di·thə). Dim. **E·die** or **Ea·die** (ē′dē).

Ed·na (ed′nə) Rejuvenation. [< Hebrew]

Ed·wi·na (ed·wē′nə, -win′ə) Fem. of EDWIN.

Ef·fie (ef′ē) Dim. of EUPHEMIA.

Ei·leen (ī·lēn′) Irish form of HELEN.

E·ka·te·ri·na (yə·kə·tyi·ryē′nə) Russ. form of CATHERINE.

E·laine (i·lān′, ē·lān′) Var. of HELEN. [< OF] Also **E·layne′.**

El·ber·ta (el·bûr′tə) Fem. of ELBERT.

El·ea·nor (el′ə·nər, -nôr) Var. of HELEN. [< F] Also **El′i·nor, El·ea·no·ra** (el′ə·nôr′ə, -nō′rə, el′ē·ə-), *Fr.* **É·lé·o·nore** (ā·lā·ô·nôr′), *Ger.* **E·le·o·no·re** (ā′lä·ō·nō′rə), *Ital.* **E·le·o·no·ra** (ā′lā·ō·nō′rä). Dims. **El′la, El′lie, Nell, Nel′lie, Nel′ly.**

E·lec·tra (i·lek′trə) Shining; golden-haired. [< Gk.] Also **E·lek′tra.**

E·le·na (el′ə·nə, ə·lē′nə; *Ital.* ā′lā·nä) Var. of HELEN. [< Ital.]

E·li·za (i·lī′zə) Dim. of ELIZABETH. Also *Fr.* **É·lise** (ā·lēz′).

E·liz·a·beth (i·liz′ə·bəth) Consecrated to God. [< Hebrew] Also **E·lis·a·beth** (i·liz′ə·bəth; *Ger.* ā·lē′zä·bet), *Fr.* **É·li·sa·beth** (ā·lē·zȧ·bet′), *Ital.* **E·li·sa·bet·ta** (ā·lē′zä·bät′tä). Dims. **Bess, Bes′sie, Beth, Bet′sy, Bet′te, Bet′ty, El′sa, El′sie, Lib′by, Li′sa, Liz, Liz′beth, Liz′zie, Liz′zy.**

El·la (el′ə) Dim. of ELEANOR. Also **El′lie.**

El·len (el′ən) Var. of HELEN.

E·lo·i·sa (ā′lō·ē′zä) Ital. form of LOUISE.

E·lo·ise (el′ō·ēz′, el′ō·ēz) Var. of LOUISE. [< F]

El·sa (el′sə; *Ger.* el′zä) Dim. of ELIZABETH. Also **El·sie** (el′sē).

El·speth (el′spəth) Scot. form of ELIZABETH.

El·va (el′və) Elf. [< Gmc.]

El·vi·ra (el·vī′rä, -vir′ə) Elf ruler. [< Sp. < Gmc.]

Em·e·line (em′ə·lin, -lēn) Derived from EMILY. Also **Em′me·line.**

Em·i·ly (em′ə·lē) Fem. of EMIL. [< L] Also **Em′i·lie,** *Fr.* **É·mi·lie** (ā·mē·lē′), *Ger.* **E·mi·li·e** (e·mē′lē·ə), *Ital., Sp.* **E·mi·lia** (ā·mē′lyä). Dim. **Em.**

Em·ma (em′ə) Grandmother. [< Gmc.] Dims. **Em, Em′mie.**

E·nid (ē′nid) Chastity; purity. [< Celtic]

Er·i·ca (er′i·kə) Fem. of ERIC. Also **Er′i·ka.**

Er·ma (ûr′mə) Dim. of ERMENGARDE.

Er·men·garde (ûr′mən·gärd) Great guardian. [< Gmc.]

Er·men·trude (ûr′mən·trood) Great strength. [< Gmc.]

Er·nes·tine (ûr′nəs·tēn) Fem. of ERNEST.

Es·me·ral·da (ez′mə·ral′də) Emerald. [< Sp.]

Es·telle (es·tel′) Star. [< L] Also **Es·tel·la** (es·tel′ə).

Es·ther (es′tər) Star. [< Pers.] Dims. **Es′sie, Het′ty.**

Eth·el (eth′əl) Noble. [< Gmc.]

Et·ta (et′ə)   Dim. of HENRIETTA.
Eu·do·ra (yōō-dôr′ə, -dō′rə)   Good gift.   [< Gk.]
Eu·ge·ni·a (yōō-jē′nē-ə, -jēn′yə)   Fem. of EUGENE.   Also **Eu·ge·nie** (yōō-jē′nē), *Fr.* **Eu·gé·nie** (œ-zhā-nē′).   Dims. **Gene, Ge′nie.**
Eu·la·li·a (yōō-lā′lē-ə, -lāl′yə)   Fair speech.   [< Gk.]   Also **Eu·la·lie** (yōō′lə-lē; *Fr.* œ-là-lē′).
Eu·nice (yōō′nis; *Lat.* yōō-nī′sē)   Good victory.   [< Gk.]
Eu·phe·mi·a (yōō-fē′mē-ə)   Of good repute.   [< Gk.]   Also *Fr.* **Eu·phé·mie** (œ-fā-mē′).   Dims. **Ef·fie** (ef′ē), **Phe′mie.**
E·va (ē′və; *Ger., Ital., Sp.* ä′vä)   Var. of EVE.   [< L]
E·van·ge·line (i-van′jə-lin, -līn, -lēn)   Bearer of glad tidings.   [< Gk.]
Eve (ēv; *Fr.* ev)   Life.   [< Hebrew]
Eve·lyn (ev′ə-lin; *Brit.* ēv′lin)   Hazelnut.   [< L]   Also **Ev·e·li·na** (ev′ə-lī′nə, -lē′-).
E·vi·ta (ā-vē′tä)   Sp. dim. of EVA.

Faith (fāth)   From the abstract noun.   Dim. **Fay.**
Fan·ny (fan′ē)   Dim. of FRANCES.   Also **Fan′nie.**
Faus·ti·na (fôs-tī′nə, -tē′-)   Lucky.   [< L]   Also **Faus·tine** (fôs-tēn′; *Fr.* fōs-tēn′).
Fawn (fôn)   From the name of the animal.
Fay (fā)   Fairy or faith.   [OF]   Also **Fae, Faye.**
Fe·li·cia (fə-lish′ə, -lish′ē-ə, -lē′shə)   Happy.   [< L]   Also **Fe·lice** (fə-lēs′), **Fe·lic′i·ty** (-lis′ə-tē).
Fern (fûrn)   From the common noun.
Fer·nan·da (fer-nän′dä)   Fem. of *Fernando,* Sp. form of FERDINAND.
Fi·del·ia (fi-dēl′yə, -dēl′ē-ə)   Faithful.   [< L]
Fi·o·na (fē-ō′nə)   Fair or white.   [< Celtic]
Fla·vi·a (flā′vē-ə)   Blonde.   [< L]
Flo·ra (flôr′ə, flō′rə)   Flower.   [< L]
Flor·ence (flôr′əns, flor′-; *Fr.* flō-räns′)   Blooming.   [< L]   Dims. **Flo** (flō), **Flor·rie** (flôr′ē, flor′ē), **Flos·sie** (flos′ē).
Fran·ces (fran′sis, frän′-)   Fem. of FRANCIS.   Also *Fr.* **Fran·çoise** (frän-swàz′) or **Fran·cisque** (frän-sēsk′), *Ital.* **Fran·ces·ca** (frän-chäs′kä).   Dims. **Fan′nie, Fan′ny, Fran, Fran′cie, Frank, Fran′nie.**
Fran·cine (fran-sēn′)   Derived from FRANCES.   Also **Fran·cene′.**
Fred·er·i·ca (fred′ə-rē′kə, fred-rē′kə)   Fem. of FREDERICK.   Dim. **Fred′die.**
Frie·da (frē′də)   Peace.   [< G]   Also **Fre′da.**

Ga·bri·elle (gä′brē-el′, gab′rē-; *Fr.* gà-brē-el′)   Fem. of GABRIEL.   Also **Ga·bri·el·la** (gä′brē-el′ə).   Dim. **Ga·by** (gä′bē).
Gail (gāl)   Short for ABIGAIL.   Also **Gale.**
Gay (gā)   From the adjective.
Gen·e·vieve (jen′ə-vēv, jen′ə-vēv′)   White wave.   [< F < Celtic]   Also *Fr.* **Ge·ne·viève** (zhen-vyev′).
Ge·nev·ra (ji-nev′rə)   Var. of GUINEVERE.   [< Ital.]   Also **Ge·ne·va** (ji-nē′və).
Geor·gia (jôr′jə)   Fem. of GEORGE.
Geor·gi·an·a (jôr′jē-an′ə)   Fem. of GEORGE.   Also **Geor·gi·na** (jôr-jē′nə), *Fr.* **Geor·gine** (zhôr-zhēn′) or **Geor·gette** (zhôr-zhet′).
Ger·al·dine (jer′əl-dēn)   Fem. of GERALD.   Dims. **Ger′ry, Jer′ry.**
Ger·maine (jər-mān′)   German.   [< F < L]
Ger·trude (gûr′trōōd, *Fr.* zher-trüd′)   Spear maid.   [< Gmc.]   Also *Ger.* **Ger·trud** (ger′trōōt).   Dims. **Ger′tie, Ger′ty, Tru′da, Tru′dy.**
Gil·ber·ta (gil-bûr′tə)   Fem. of GILBERT.   Also **Gil·ber·tine** (gil′bər-tēn), *Fr.* **Gil·berte** (zhēl-bert′).
Gil·da (gil′də)   Servant of God.   [< Celtic]
Gil·li·an (jil′ē-ən, jil′yən)   Var. of JULIANA.
Gi·nev·ra (ji-nev′rə)   Var. of GUINEVERE.   [< Ital.]
Gin·ger (jin′jer)   From the plant name.
Gio·van·na (jō-vän′nä)   Fem. of *Giovanni,* Ital. form of JOHN.
Gi·sele (zhē-zel′)   Pledge or hostage.   [< F < Gmc.]   Also **Gi·selle′.**
Giu·lia (jōō′lyä)   Ital. form of JULIA.
Glad·ys (glad′is)   Welsh fem. form of CLAUDIUS.
Glen·na (glen′ə)   Fem. of GLENN.   Also **Glen·nis** (glen′is), **Glyn·is** (glin′is).
Glo·ri·a (glôr′ē-ə, glō′rē-ə)   Glory.   [< L]
Grace (grās)   Grace; favor.   [< L]   Also **Gra·ci·a** or **Gra·ti·a** (grā′shē-ə, -shə).
Gret·a (gret′ə, grē′tə; *Ger.* grā′tä)   Dim. of MARGARET.   [< G]   Also **Gre·tel** or **Gre·thel** (grā′təl).
Gretch·en (grech′ən; *Ger.* grāt′khən)   Dim. of MARGARET.   [< G]
Gri·sel·da (gri-zel′də)   Stony or unbeatable heroine.   [< Gmc.]   Also **Gris·sel** (gris′əl), **Griz·el** (griz′əl).
Guin·e·vere (gwin′ə-vir)   White lady or white wave.   [< Celtic]   Also **Guen·e·vere** (gwen′ə-vir), **Guen·e·ver** (-vər), **Guin′e·ver.**
Gus·sie (gus′ē)   Dim. of AUGUSTA.   Also **Gus·ta** (gus′tə).
Gwen·do·lyn (gwen′də-lin)   White-browed.   [< Celtic]   Also **Gwen′do·len, Gwen′do·line** (-lin, -lēn).   Dims. **Gwen, Gwenn, Wen·dy** (wen′dē).

Gwen·eth (gwen′ith)   Fair or blessed.   [< Celtic]   Also **Gwen′ith, Gwyn·eth** (gwin′ith), **Gyn·eth** (gin′ith).
Gwyn (gwin)   Fair or white.   [< Celtic]   Also **Gwynne.**

Han·nah (han′ə)   Grace.   [< Hebrew]   Also **Han′na.**
Har·ri·et (har′ē-ət)   Fem. of HARRY.   Dims. **Hat′tie, Hat′ty.**
Ha·zel (hā′zəl)   From the plant name.
Heath·er (heth′ər)   From the plant name.
Hed·da (hed′ə)   War.   [< Gmc.]
Hed·wig (hed′wig)   War.   [< Gmc.]
Hel·en (hel′ən)   Light; a torch.   [< Gk.]   Also *Fr.* **Hé·lène** (ā-len′).   Dims. **Nell, Nel′lie, Nel′ly.**
Hel·e·na (hel′ə-nə)   Var. of HELEN.   Dim. **Le·na** (lē′nə).
Hel·ga (hel′gə)   Holy.   [< Gmc.]
Hé·lo·ïse (ā-lō-ēz′)   Fr. form of ELOISE.
Hen·ri·et·ta (hen′rē-et′ə)   Fem. of HENRY.   Also *Fr.* **Hen·ri·ette** (äṅ-ryet′).   Dims. **Et′ta, Et′tie, Hat′tie, Hat′ty, Het′ty, Net′tie, Ret′ta.**
Heph·zi·bah (hep′zə-bə)   She who is my delight.   [< Hebrew]
Her·mi·o·ne (hər-mī′ə-nē)   Fem. of HERMES.
Hes·ter (hes′tər)   Var. of ESTHER.   Also **Hes′ther.**   Dim. **Het′ty.**
Het·ty (het′ē)   Dim. of ESTHER, HENRIETTA, or HESTER.
Hil·a·ry (hil′ər-ē)   Joyful.   [< L]
Hil·da (hil′də)   Battle maiden.   [OE]
Hil·de·garde (hil′də-gärd)   Guardian battle maiden.   [< Gmc.]   Also **Hil′de·gard.**
Hol·ly (hol′ē)   From the plant name.
Ho·no·ra (hō-nôr′ə, -nō′rə)   Honor.   [< L]   Also **Ho·no·ri·a** (hō-nôr′ē-ə, -nō′rē-ə)   Dims. **No′ra, No′rah.**
Hope (hōp)   From the abstract noun.
Hor·tense (hôr′tens; *Fr.* ôr-täns′)   Gardener: from the name of a Roman clan.   [< F < L]   Also *Lat.* **Hor·ten·si·a** (hôr-ten′shē-ə).
Hul·dah (hul′dä)   Weasel; industrious.   [< Hebrew]   Also **Hul′da.**
Hy·a·cinth (hī′ə-sinth)   From the name of the flower.

I·da (ī′də)   Happy; godlike.   [< Gmc.]
I·lo·na (i-lō′nə)   Radiantly beautiful.   [< Hung. < Gk.]
Il·se (il′sə; *Ger.* il′zə)   Dim. of ELIZABETH.   [< G]
Im·o·gene (im′ə-jēn)   Meaning and origin uncertain.   Also **Im·o·gen** (im′ə-jən).
I·na (ī′nə)   From Lat. suffix for fem. names.
I·nez (ī′nez, ē′nez; *Sp.* ē-näth′)   Var. of AGNES   [< Sp. & Pg.]
In·grid (ing′grid)   Daughter of Ing (a god in Gmc. mythology).   [< Gmc.]   Also **In·ga** (ing′gə).
I·rene (ī-rēn′)   Peace.   [< Gk.]
I·ris (ī′ris)   Rainbow [< Gk.], or from the name of the flower.
Ir·ma (ûr′mə)   Var. of ERMA.
Is·a·bel (iz′ə-bel; *Sp.* ē′sä-bel′)   Oath of Baal.   [< Hebrew]   Also **Is·a·bel·la** (iz′ə-bel′ə; *Ital.* ē′zä-bel′lä), **Is·a·belle** (iz′ə-bel; *Fr.* ē-zà-bel′), **Is′o·bel,** *Fr.* **I·sa·beau** (ē-zà-bō′).   Dims. **Bell, Bel′la, Belle.**
Is·a·do·ra (iz′ə-dôr′ə, -dō′rə)   Fem. of ISIDORE.
I·vy (ī′vē)   From the plant name.

Jac·que·line (jak′wə-lin, -lēn, jak′ə-; *Fr.* zhä-klēn′)   Fem. of *Jacques,* Fr. form of JACOB.   Dim. **Jac′kie.**
Jane (jān)   Var. of JOAN.   [< OF]
Jan·et (jan′it, jə-net′)   Dim. of JANE.
Jan·ice (jan′is)   Var. of JANE.
Jas·mine (jaz′min, jas′-)   From the name of the flower.
Jean (jēn)   Var. of JOAN.   [< F]
Jeanne (jēn, *Fr.* zhän)   Fr. form of JOAN.
Jean·nette (jə-net′)   Dim. of JEANNE.
Je·mi·ma (jə-mī′mə)   Dove.   [< Hebrew]
Jen·ni·fer (jen′ə-fər)   Var of GUINEVERE.   Dims. **Jen′ny, Jin′ny.**
Jer·ry (jer′ē)   Dim. of GERALDINE.
Jes·si·ca (jes′i-kə)   Fem. of JESSE.   Dims. **Jess, Jes′sie, Jes′sy.**
Jew·el (jōō′əl)   From the common noun.
Jill (jil)   Short for JULIA.
Jo (jō)   Dim. of JOSEPHINE.
Joan (jōn, jō-an′)   Fem. of JOHN.   Also **Jo·an·na** (jō-an′ə), **Jo·anne** (jō-an′).
Joc·e·lyn (jos′ə-lin)   Playful; merry.   [< L]   Also **Joc′e·lin, Joc′e·line** (-lin).
Jo·han·na (jō-han′ə; *Ger.* yō-hän′ä)   Ger. form of JOAN.
Jo·se·pha (jō-sē′fə)   Var. of JOSEPHINE.
Jo·se·phine (jō′sə-fēn, -zə-)   Fem. of JOSEPH.   [< F]   Dims. **Jo, Jo′sie, Jo′zy.**
Joy (joi)   From the abstract noun.
Joyce (jois)   Joyful.   [< L]
Jua·na (wä′nə; *Sp.* hwä′nä)   Fem. of *Juan,* Sp. form of JOHN.
Jua·ni·ta (wä-nē′tə; *Sp.* hwä-nē′tä)   Sp. dim. of JUANA.
Ju·dith (jōō′dith)   Praised.   [< Hebrew]   Dim. **Ju′dy.**
Jul·ia (jōōl′yə)   Fem. of JULIUS.   Also **Ju·lie** (jōō′lē; *Fr.* zhü-lē′).

Ju·li·an·a (jōō/lē·an/ə, -ä/nə) Fem. of JULIAN. Also *Fr.*
Ju·li·enne (zhü·lyen/).
Ju·li·et (jōō/lē·et, jōō/lē·et/) Dim. of JULIA.
June (jōōn) From the name of the month.
Jus·ti·na (jus·tī/nə, -tē/-) Fem. of JUSTIN. Also **Jus·tine**
  (jus·tēn/; *Fr.* zhüs·tēn/).

Kar·en (kâr/ən; *Dan., Norw.* kä/rən) Var. of CATHERINE.
  [< Dan. & Norw.]
Kate (kāt) Dim. of CATHERINE. Also **Ka/tie**.
Kath·a·rine (kath/ə·rin, kath/rin) Var. of CATHERINE.
  Also **Kath/er·ine, Kath/ryn**.
Kath·leen (kath/lēn, kath·lēn/) Irish form of CATHERINE.
Kath·y (kath/ē) Dim. of CATHERINE.
Ka·tri·na (kə·trē/nə) Var. of CATHERINE. Also **Kat·rine**
  (kat/rin, -rēn). Dim. **Tri·na** (trē/nə).
Kay (kā) Dim. of CATHERINE.
Kir·sten (kûr/stən; *Norw.* khish/tən, khir/stən) Norw. form
  of CHRISTINE.
Kit·ty (kit/ē) Dim. of CATHERINE. Also **Kit**.
Kla·ra (klä/rä) Ger. form of CLARA.

Lau·ra (lôr/ə) Laurel. [< L] Also *Fr.* **Laure** (lôr). Dims.
  Lau/rie, Lol/ly.
Lau·ret·ta (lô·ret/ə) Dim. of LAURA. Also **Lau·rette/**.
Lau·rin·da (lô·rin/də) Derived from LAURA.
La·verne (lə·vûrn/) From the name of the Roman goddess
  of spring and grain.
La·vin·i·a (lə·vin/ē·ə) Purified. [< L]
Le·ah (lē/ə) Gazelle. [< Hebrew] Also **Le/a**.
Lei·la (lē/lä) Dark night or dark beauty. [< Arabic]
Le·na (lē/nə) Dim. of HELENA or MAGDALENE.
Le·no·ra (lə·nôr/ə, -nō/rə) Var. of ELEANOR. Also **Le·nore**
  (lə·nôr/).
Le·o·na (lē·ō/nə) Fem. of LEO and LEON. Also *Fr.* **Lé·o·nie**
  (lā·ô·nē/).
Le·o·no·ra (lē/ə·nôr/ə, -nō/rə; *Ital.* lā/ō·nō/rä) Var. of
  ELEANOR. Also **Le·o·nore** (lē/ə·nôr, -nōr; *Ger.* lā/ō·nō/rə).
  Dim. **No/ra**.
Le·or·a (lē·ôr/ə, -ō/rə) Var. of LEONORA.
Les·lie (les/lē, lez/-) From LESLIE, masc. Also **Les/ley**.
Le·ti·tia (li·tish/ə) Joy. [< L] Dim. **Let·ty** (let/ē).
Lib·by (lib/ē) Dim. of ELIZABETH.
Li·la (lī/lə, lē/-) Var. of LILIAN.
Lil·i·an (lil/ē·ən, lil/yən) Lily. [< L] Also **Lil/li·an**. Dims.
  Lil, Lil/ly, Lil/y.
Lil·y (lil/ē) From the name of the flower; also, dim. of LIL-
  IAN.
Lin·da (lin/də) Pretty [< Sp.], or short for BELINDA or
  MELINDA.
Li·sa (lī/zə, lē/-) Dim. of ELIZABETH. Also **Li/za**, *Ger.* **Li·se**
  (lē/zə).
Li·sette (lē·zet/) Fr. dim. of ELIZABETH. Also **Li·zette/**.
Liz·beth (liz/bəth) Dim. of ELIZABETH.
Liz·zie (liz/ē) Dim. of ELIZABETH. Also **Liz/zy, Liz**.
Lo·is (lō/is) Desirable. [< Gk.]
Lo·la (lō/lə; *Sp.* lō/lä) Dim. of DOLORES. [< Sp.] Dim.
  Lo·li·ta (lō·lē/tə; *Sp.* lō·lē/tä).
Lor·ene (lô·rēn/) Var. of LAURA. Also **Laur·een/, Laur·**
  ene/, Lor·een/.
Lor·et·ta (lô·ret/ə, lō-) Dim. of LAURA. Also **Lor·ette** (lô-
  ret/).
Lo·rin·da (lô·rin/də, lə-) Var. of LAURINDA.
Lor·na (lôr/nə) Lost. [OE]
Lor·raine (lə·rān/) Var. of LAURA.
Lot·tie (lot/ē) Dim. of CHARLOTTE. Also **Lot/ta, Lot/ty**.
Lou·el·la (lōō·el/ə) Var. of LUELLA.
Lou·ise (lōō·ēz/) Fem. of LOUIS. [< F] Also **Lou·i·sa**
  (lōō·ē/zə). Dims. **Lou, Lou/ie, Lu, Lu/lu**.
Lu·cia (lōō/shə; *Ital.* lōō·chē/ä) Fem. of LUCIUS.
Lu·cille (lōō·sēl/) Var. of LUCIA. [< F] Also **Lu·cile/**.
Lu·cin·da (lōō·sin/də) Derived from LUCY. Dim. **Cin·dy**
  (sin/dē).
Lu·cre·tia (lōō·krē/shə, -shē·ə) Fem. of LUCRETIUS. Also
  Fr. **Lu·crèce** (lü·kres/), *Ital.* **Lu·cre·zia** (lōō·krā/tsyä).
Lu·cy (lōō/sē) Var. of LUCIA. Also *Fr.* **Lu·cie** (lü·sē/).
Lu·el·la (lōō·el/ə) Meaning and origin uncertain. Also
  Lou·el/la.
Lu·i·sa (lōō·ē/zä) Ital. form of LOUISA. Also *Ger.* **Lu·i·se**
  (lōō·ē/zə).
Lu·lu (lōō/lōō) Dim. of LOUISE.
Lyd·i·a (lid/ē·ə) She of Lydia. [< Gk.]

Ma·bel (mā/bəl) Short for AMABEL. Dim. **Mab** (mab).
Mad·e·leine (mad/ə·lin, -lān, *Fr.* mà·dlen/) Var. of MAG-
  DALENE. [< F] Also **Mad·e·line** (mad/ə·lin, -līn).
Madge (madj) Dim. of MARGARET.
Mae (mā) Var. of MAY.
Mag (mag) Dim. of MARGARET. Also **Mag/gie**.
Mag·da·lene (mag/də·lēn, mag/də·lē/nē) Woman of Mag-
  dala. [< Hebrew] Also **Mag·da·len** (mag/də·lən), **Mag·**
  da·le·na (mag/də·lē/nə; *Sp.* mäg/thä·lā/nä). Dims. **Le·na**
  (lē/nə) **Mag·da** (mag/də).
Mai·sie (mā/zē) Dim. of MARGARET. [< Scot.]

Mal·vi·na (mal·vī/nə, -vē/-) Meaning and origin uncertain.
Ma·mie (mā/mē) Dim. of MARGARET.
Man·dy (man/dē) Dim. of AMANDA.
Mar·cel·la (mär·sel/ə) Fem. of MARCELLUS. Also *Fr.* **Mar·**
  celle (mär·sel/).
Mar·cia (mär/shə) Fem. of *Marcius*, var. of MARCUS.
Mar·ga·ret (mär/gə·rit, mär/grit) Pearl. [< Gk.] Also
  Ger. **Mar·ga·re·te** (mär/gä·rā/tə), *Ital.* **Mar·ghe·ri·ta** (mär/-
  gä·rē/tä), *Ital., Sp.* **Mar·ga·ri·ta** (mär/gä·rē/tä). Dims.
  Gret/a, Gretch/en, Madge, Mag, Mag/gie, Ma/mie, Meg,
  Me/ta, Peg, Peg/gy, Ri/ta.
Marge (märj) Dim. of MARJORIE. Also **Mar/gie, Marj**.
Mar·ger·y (mär/jər·ē) Var. of MARGARET.
Mar·got (mär/gō; *Fr.* màr·gō/) Var. of MARGARET. [< F]
  Also **Mar/go**.
Mar·gue·rite (mär/gə·rēt/; *Fr.* màr·gə·rēt/) Var. of MAR-
  GARET. [< F]
Ma·ri·a (mə·rī/ə, -rē/ə; *Ger., Ital.* mä·rē/ä) Var. of MARY.
  [< L] Also *Sp.* **Ma·rí·a** (mä·rē/ä).
Mar·i·an (mar/ē·ən, mâr/-) Var. of MARION.
Mar·i·anne (mâr/ē·an/) From MARY and ANNE. Also
  Mar·i·an·na (mâr/ē·an/ə).
Ma·rie (mə·rē/; *Fr.* mà·rē/) Var. of MARY. [< F]
Mar·i·et·ta (mâr/ē·et/ə, mar/-) Dim. of MARIA.
Mar·i·gold (mar/ə·gōld, mâr/-) From the name of the flower.
Mar·i·lyn (mar/ə·lin, mâr/-) Var. of MARY.
Mar·i·on (mar/ē·ən, mâr/-) Var. of MARY.
Mar·jo·rie (mär/jər·ē) Var. of MARGARET. Also **Mar/jo·ry**.
  Dims. **Marge, Mar/gie, Marj**.
Mar·lene (mär·lēn/; *Ger.* mär·lā/nə) Var. of MAGDALENE.
Mar·sha (mär/shə) Var. of MARCIA.
Mar·tha (mär/thə) Lady. [< Aramaic] Also *Fr.* **Marthe**
  (märt), *Ital., Sp.* **Mar·ta** (mär/tä). Dims. **Mar/ty, Mat/tie,**
  Mat/ty.
Mar·y (mâr/ē) Meaning uncertain. [< Hebrew] Dims.
  May, Min/nie, Mol/ly, Pol/ly.
Ma·til·da (mə·til/də) Mighty battle maiden. [< Gmc.]
  Also **Ma·thil·da** (mə·til/də), *Ger.* **Ma·thil·de** (mä·til/də).
  Dims. **Mat/tie, Mat/ty, Pat/ty, Til/da, Til/lie, Til/ly**.
Maud (môd) Contr. of MAGDALENE. Also **Maude**.
Mau·ra (môr/ə) Irish form of MARY. Also **Maur·ya** (môr/-
  yə).
Mau·reen (mô·rēn/) Dim. of MAURA.
Ma·vis (mā/vis) From the name of the bird, or the Irish
  fairy queen Maeve or Mab.
Max·ine (mak·sēn/, mak/sēn) Fem. of MAX. [< F]
May (mā) Dim. of MARY.
Meg (meg) Dim. of MARGARET.
Me·gan (mē/gən) Strange. [< Gmc.]
Mel·a·nie (mel/ə·nē) Black. [< Gk.]
Me·lin·da (mə·lin/də) Var. of BELINDA.
Me·lis·sa (mə·lis/ə) Bee. [< Gk.]
Mer·ce·des (mər·sā/dēz, -sē/-, mûr/sə·dēz; *Sp.* mer·thā/thäs)
  Mercies. [< Sp.]
Mer·cy (mûr/sē) From the abstract noun.
Me·ta (mā/tə, mē/-) Dim. of MARGARET. [< G]
Mi·gnon (min/yon, *Fr.* mē·nyôn/) Dainty. [< F]
Mil·dred (mil/drid) Moderate power. [OE] Dims. **Mil/-**
  lie, Mil/ly.
Mil·li·cent (mil/ə·sənt) Power to work. [< Gmc.] Also
  Mil/i·cent.
Mi·mi (mē/mē) Fr. dim. of WILHELMINA.
Mi·na (mē/nə) Dim. of WILHELMINA.
Mi·ner·va (mi·nûr/və) From the name of the Roman god-
  dess of wisdom.
Min·na (min/ə) Dim. of WILHELMINA.
Min·nie (min/ē) Memory or love [< Gmc.]; also, dim. of
  MARY.
Mi·ran·da (mi·ran/də) Admirable. [< L]
Mir·i·am (mir/ē·əm) Var. of MARY. [< Hebrew]
Moi·ra (moi/rə) Var. of MAURA.
Mol·ly (mol/ē) Dim. of MARY. Also **Moll**.
Mo·na (mō/nə) Noble. [< Irish]
Mon·i·ca (mon/ə·kə) Adviser. [< L]
Mor·na (môr/nə) Beloved. [< Celtic]
Mu·ri·el (myōōr/ē·əl) Myrrh. [< Gk.]
My·ra (mī/rə) ? Var. of MOIRA.
Myr·na (mûr/nə) Meaning and origin uncertain.
Myr·tle (mûrt/l) From the plant name.

Na·dine (nā·dēn/, nə-; *Fr.* nà·dēn/) Hope. [< F < Russ.]
Nan (nan) Dim. of ANN.
Nan·cy (nan/sē) Dim. of ANN.
Nan·nette (na·net/) Dim. of ANN. [< F] Also **Na·nette/**.
Na·o·mi (nā·ō/mē, nā/ō·mē) Pleasant. [< Hebrew]
Nat·a·lie (nat/ə·lē) Christmas child. [< L] Also *Russ.*
  Na·ta·sha (nä·tä/shə).
Nell (nel) Dim. of ELEANOR, ELLEN, or HELEN. Also **Nel/-**
  lie, Nel/ly.
Net·tie (net/ē) Dim. of ANTOINETTE, HENRIETTA, or JEAN-
  NETTE. Also **Net/ty**.
Ni·cole (ni·kōl/; *Fr.* nē·kôl/) Fem. of *Nicolas*, Fr. form of
  NICHOLAS.
Ni·na (nī/nə, nē/-) Dim. of ANN. [< Russ.]

Ni·ta (nē′tə; *Sp.* nē′tä) Dim. of JUANITA. [< Sp.]
No·na (nō′nə) Ninth. [< L]
No·ra (nôr′ə, nō′rə) Dim. of ELEANOR, HONORA, LEONORA. Also **No′rah**.
No·reen (nôr′ēn, nô·rēn′) Irish dim. of NORA.
Nor·ma (nôr′mə) Pattern. [< L]

Oc·ta·vi·a (ok·tā′vē·ə) Fem. of OCTAVIUS.
Ol·ga (ol′gə) Holy. [< Russ. < Scand.]
O·live (ol′iv) Var. of OLIVIA.
O·liv·i·a (ō·liv′ē·ə) She of the olive tree: prob. an epithet of the goddess Athena. [< L] Dims. **Liv′i·a, Liv′ie**.
O·lym·pi·a (ō·lim′pē·ə) She of Olympus. [< L < Gk.]
O·pal (ō′pəl) From the name of the gem.
O·phe·lia (ō·fēl′yə) Help. [< Gk.]
Ot·ti·lie (ot′ə·lē) Fem. of OTTO. [< Ger.]

Pam·e·la (pam′ə·lə) ? Invented by Sir Philip Sidney. Dim. **Pam**.
Pan·sy (pan′zē) From the name of the flower.
Pa·tience (pā′shəns) From the abstract noun.
Pa·tri·cia (pə·trish′ə) Fem. of PATRICK. Dims. **Pat, Pat′sy, Pat′ty**.
Paul·a (pô′lə) Fem. of PAUL.
Pau·lette (pô·let′) Fr. fem. dim. of PAUL.
Pau·line (pô·lēn′) Fem. of PAUL. [< F] Also *Lat.* **Pau·li·na** (pô·lī′nə).
Pearl (pûrl) From the name of the jewel.
Peg (peg) Dim. of MARGARET. Also **Peg′gy**.
Pe·nel·o·pe (pə·nel′ə·pē) Weaver. [< Gk.] Dim. **Pen′ny**.
Per·sis (pûr′sis) She of Persia. [< Gk.]
Phi·lip·pa (fi·lip′ə, fil′ə·pə) Fem. of PHILIP.
Phoe·be (fē′bē) Bright; shining: an epithet of Artemis. [< Gk.] Also **Phe′be**.
Phyl·lis (fil′is) Green bough or leaf. [< Gk.] Also **Phil′lis**.
Pol·ly (pol′ē) Dim. of MARY.
Pop·py (pop′ē) From the name of the flower.
Por·tia (pôr′shə, pōr′-) Fem. of *Porcius*, name of a Roman clan. [< L]
Pris·cil·la (pri·sil′ə) Ancient. [< L]
Pru·dence (prōōd′ns) From the abstract noun. Dim. **Prue**.

Queen·ie (kwē′nē) Derived from QUEEN, used as dim. of REGINA.

Ra·chel (rā′chəl; *Fr.* rà·shel′) Ewe or lamb. [< Hebrew] Dims. **Rae, Ray**.
Ra·mo·na (rə·mō′nə) Fem. of *Ramón*, Sp. form of RAYMOND.
Re·ba (rē′bə) Short for REBECCA.
Re·bec·ca (ri·bek′ə) Ensnarer. [< Hebrew] Dim. **Beck′y**.
Re·gi·na (ri·jē′nə, -jī′-) Queen. [< L]
Re·née (rə·nā′, rā′nē, rē′nē) Reborn. [< F]
Rhe·a (rē′ə) From the name of the Greek goddess.
Rho·da (rō′də) Rose. [< Gk.]
Ri·ta (rē′tə) Dim. of *Margarita*, Ital. and Sp. form of MARGARET.
Ro·ber·ta (rə·bûr′tə) Fem. of ROBERT. Dims. **Bert, Bob′bie, Bob′by**.
Rob·in (rob′in) From the name of the bird, or from the masc. name.
Ro·chelle (rə·shel′) Stone or small rock. [< F]
Rom·o·la (rom′ə·lə) Fem. of *Romolo*, Ital. form of *Romulus* (founder of Rome).
Ron·ny (ron′ē) Dim. of VERONICA. Also **Ron′nie**.
Ro·sa (rō′zə) Var. of ROSE. [< L]
Ro·sa·bel (rō′zə·bel) Beautiful rose. [< L]
Ro·sa·lie (rō′zə·lē) Little rose. [< L] Also **Ro·sal·ia** (rō·zāl′yə, -zä′lē·ə).
Ros·a·lind (roz′ə·lind) Fair rose. [< Sp.] Also **Ros·a·lin·da** (roz′ə·lin′də).
Ros·a·line (roz′ə·lin, -līn, -lēn, rō′zə-) Var. of ROSALIND. Also **Ros′a·lyn** (-lin).
Ros·a·mond (roz′ə·mənd, rō′zə-) Famous protector. [< Gmc.] Also **Ros′a·mund, Ro·sa·mun·da** (rō′zə·mun′də).
Ros·anne (rōz·an′) From ROSE and ANNE. Also **Ros·an·na** (rōz·an′ə), **Rose·anne′, Rose·an′na**.
Rose (rōz) From the name of the flower. Also **Ro·sa** (rō′zə; *Fr.* rō·zä′; *Ger.* rō′zä; *Ital.* rô′zä; *Sp.* rō′sä).
Rose·mar·y (rōz′mâr′ē, -mə·rē) From the plant name. Also **Rose·ma·rie** (rōz′mə·rē).
Row·e·na (rō·ē′nə) ? From the name of an ancient Celtic goddess.
Rox·an·a (rok·san′ə) Dawn of day. [< Persian] Also **Rox·an′na**, *Fr.* **Rox·ane** (rôk·sàn′). Dim. **Rox′y**.
Ru·by (rōō′bē) From the name of the jewel.
Ruth (rōōth) Companion. [< Hebrew]

Sa·bi·na (sə·bī′nə) A Sabine woman. [< L]
Sa·die (sā′dē) Dim. of SARAH.
Sal·ly (sal′ē) Dim. of SARAH.
Sa·lo·me (sə·lō′mē) Peace. [< Hebrew]

San·dra (san′drə, sän′-) Dim. of ALEXANDRA.
Sar·ah (sâr′ə) Princess. [< Hebrew] Also **Sar·a** (sâr′ə). Dims. **Sa′die, Sal′ly**.
Sel·ma (sel′mə) Fair [< Celtic], or a fem. dim. of ANSELM.
Se·re·na (sə·rē′nə) Serene. [< L]
Shar·on (shar′ən, shâr′-) Of Sharon. [< Hebrew]
Shei·la (shē′lə) Irish form of CECILIA.
Shir·ley (shûr′lē) From an English surname; orig. a place name.
Sib·yl (sib′əl) Prophetess. [< Gk.] Also **Syb′il**.
Sid·ney (sid′nē) From an English surname. Also **Syd′ney**.
Sig·rid (sig′rid; *Ger.* zē′grit; *Norw.* sē′grē) Conquering counsel. [< Gmc.]
Sil·vi·a (sil′vē·ə) Var. of SYLVIA.
Si·mone (sē·mōn′) Fr. fem. of SIMON.
So·fi·a (sō·fē′ä) Ger., Ital., and Sw. form of SOPHIA.
Son·ia (sōn′yə) Russ. dim. of SOPHIA. Also **Son′ya**.
So·phi·a (sō·fī′ə, -fē′ə) Wise. [< Gk.] Also **So·phie** (sō′fē; *Fr.* sô·fē′). Dims. **So′phie, So′phy**.
So·phro·ni·a (sə·frō′nē·ə) Prudent. [< Gk.]
Sta·cie (stā′sē) Orig. dim. of ANASTASIA. Also **Sta′cy**.
Stel·la (stel′ə) Star. [< L]
Steph·a·nie (stef′ə·nē) Fem. of STEPHEN. Also **Steph·a·na** (stef′ə·nə), *Fr.* **Sté·pha·nie** (stā·fà·nē′).
Su·san (sōō′zən) Var. of SUSANNAH. Dims. **Sue, Su′sie, Su′zy**.
Su·san·nah (sōō·zan′ə) Lily. [< Hebrew] Also **Su·san′na, Su·zanne** (sōō·zan′; *Fr.* sü·zàn′). Dims. **Sue, Su·ky** (sōō′kē), **Su′sie, Su′zy**.
Syb·il (sib′əl) Var. of SIBYL.
Syl·vi·a (sil′vē·ə) Of the forest. [< L] Also **Sil′vi·a**.

Tab·i·tha (tab′ə·thə) Gazelle. [< Aramaic]
Te·re·sa (tə·rē′sə, -zə; *Ital.* tā·rā′zä; *Sp.* tā·rā′sä) Var. of THERESA. [< Ital. & Sp.] Dims. **Ter′ry, Tess, Tes′sie**.
Thal·ia (thāl′yə, thal′-) Flourishing; blooming. [< Gk.]
The·a (thē′ə) Goddess. [< Gk.]
Thel·ma (thel′mə) ? Var. of SELMA.
The·o·do·ra (thē′ə·dôr′ə, -dō′rə) Fem. of THEODORE. Dims. **Do′ra, The′da, The′o**.
The·o·do·sia (thē′ə·dō′shə) Gift of God. [< Gk.]
The·re·sa (tə·rē′sə, -zə) She who reaps. [< Gk.] Also *Fr.* **Thé·rèse** (tā·râz′) Dims. **Ter′ry, Tess, Tes′sie**.
Til·da (til′də) Dim. of MATILDA.
Til·ly (til′ē) Dim. of MATILDA. Also **Til′lie**.
Ti·na (tē′nə) Dim. of CHRISTINA.
Tri·na (trē′nə) Dim. of KATRINA.
Trix·ie (trik′sē) Dim. of BEATRICE or BEATRIX. Also **Trix, Trix′y**.
Tru·dy (trōō′dē) Dim. of GERTRUDE.

U·na (yōō′nə) One. [< L]
Un·dine (un·dēn′, un′dēn) She of the waves. [< L]
U·ra·ni·a (yōō·rā′nē·ə) From the name of the Greek goddess of heaven, the muse of astronomy.
Ur·su·la (ûr′syə·lə, -sə-) Little she-bear. [< L]

Va·le·ri·a (və·lir′ē·ə) Fem. of *Valerius*, name of a Roman clan. Also **Val·er·ie** or **Val·er·y** (val′ər·ē), *Fr.* **Va·lé·rie** (và·lā·rē′). Dim. **Val**.
Va·nes·sa (və·nes′ə) Butterfly. [< Gk.]
Ve·ra (vir′ə) Faith [< Slavic], or truth [< L].
Ver·na (vûr′nə) Short for *Laverna*, var. of LAVERNE.
Ve·ron·i·ca (və·ron′i·kə) True image. [< LL] Also *Fr.* **Vé·ro·nique** (vā·rô·nēk′). Dim. **Ron′nie, Ron′ny**.
Vic·to·ri·a (vik·tôr′ē·ə, -tō′rē·ə) Victory. [< L] Also *Fr.* **Vic·toire** (vēk·twár′). Dim. **Vick′y**.
Vi·o·la (vī′ō·lə, vī·ō′lə, vē-) Violet. [< L]
Vi·o·let (vī′ə·lit) From the name of the flower.
Vir·gin·ia (vər·jin′yə) Fem. of *Virginius*, name of a Roman clan. Also *Fr.* **Vir·gi·nie** (vēr·zhē·nē′). Dim. **Gin′ny**.
Vir·gil·i·a (vər·jil′ē·ə) Fem. of *Virgilius*, name of a Roman clan, or fem. of VIRGIL.
Viv·i·an (viv′ē·ən, viv′yən) Lively. [< L] Also **Viv′i·en**, *Fr.* **Vi·vienne** (vē·vyen′).

Wan·da (wän′də) Shepherdess or roamer. [< Gmc.]
Wen·dy (wen′dē) Dim. of GWENDOLYN.
Wil·hel·mi·na (wil′hel·mē′nə, wil′ə-; *Ger.* vil′hel·mē′nä) Fem. of *Wilhelm*, Ger. form of WILLIAM. Dims. **Mi′na, Min′na, Wil′la, Wil′ma**.
Wil·la (wil′ə) Dim. of WILHELMINA.
Wil·ma (wil′mə) Dim. of WILHELMINA.
Win·i·fred (win′ə·frid, -fred) White wave or stream. [< Welsh] Dim. **Win′nie**.

Yo·lan·da (yō·lan′də) Meaning uncertain. [? < OF] Also **Yo·lan′de** (-də).
Y·vonne (i·von′, ē-) Meaning uncertain. [< F]

Ze·no·bi·a (zi·nō′bē·ə) She who was given life by Zeus. [< Gk.]
Zo·e (zō′ē) Life. [< Gk.]

GREEK AND LATIN ELEMENTS IN ENGLISH

The following list contains a selection of English words, listed alphabetically, each of which is shown with a corresponding combining form, prefix, or suffix of Greek or Latin derivation. The list will prove of great assistance in word study and the enrichment of one's vocabulary, and will give some insight into the origins and general range of meaning of new and unfamiliar words.

COMBINING FORMS

abdomen — Gk. coelo-, gastro-; L. ventro-.
agriculture — Gk. agro-.
air — Gk. aero-; L. aeri-. See also BREATH, WIND.
aircraft — Gk. aero-.
all — Gk. pan-, panto-; L. omni-. See also WHOLE.
ancient — Gk. archeo-, paleo-.
angle — Gk. -gon, gonio-.
animal — Gk. zoo-.
appearance — Gk. -opsis.
arm — Gk. brachio-.
art — Gk. techno-.
artery — Gk. arterio-.
back — Gk. noto-; L. dorsi-, dorso-.
bad — Gk. caco-, dys-; L. mal-. See also DIFFICULT.
bag — Gk. asco-. See also BLADDER, VESSEL.
bare — Gk. gymno-; L. nudi-.
beautiful — Gk. calli-.
bearing — L. -fer, -ferous, -gerous, -parous. See also PRODUCING.
bent — Gk. ankylo-; L. flexi-. See also CURVED.
berry — L. bacci-.
berry-shaped — Gk. & L. cocci-, -coccus.
big — See GREAT.
bile — Gk. chole-, cholo-.
bird — Gk. ornitho-; L. avi-.
birth — Gk. toco-; L. nati-. See also CHILD.
bitter — Gk. picro-.
black — Gk. melano-; L. nigri-.
bladder — Gk. cysto-; L. vesico-. See also BAG, VESSEL.
blind — Gk. typhlo-.
blood — Gk. -emia (condition or disease), hema-, hemato-; L. sangui-.
bluish — Gk. cyano-, glauco-.
body — Gk. somato-, -soma, -some.
bone — Gk. osteo-; L. ossi-.
book — Gk. biblio-.
both — Gk. amphi-; L. ambi-.
brain — Gk. encephalo-, phreno-; L. cerebro-. See also MIND.
brass — See COPPER.
breast — Gk. masto-.
breath — Gk. pneumato-; L. spiro-. See also AIR, WIND.
bristle — L. seti-.
broad — Gk. eury-; L. lati-. See also FLAT.
bronze — See COPPER.
bud — Gk. blasto-, -blast; L. gemmi-.
burning — See FIRE.
carbon — L. carbo-, carboni-.
carrying — See BEARING.
cartilage — Gk. chondro-.
carved, carving — Gk. glypto-, -glyph.
cattle — Gk. tauro-; L. bovi-.
cave — Gk. & L. speleo-.
cavity — Gk. -cele.
cell — Gk. cyto-, -plast.
center — Gk. centro-; L. centri-.
chemical — Gk. chemo-.
chest — Gk. stetho-.
chief — Gk. arch-, archi-.

child — Gk. pedo-, toco-.
Chinese — L. Sino-.
chlorine — Gk. chloro-.
circle — Gk. cyclo-, gyro-, -cyclic.
class — See NATION, ORDER, SPECIES, TYPE.
clear — See VISIBLE.
climate — Gk. climato-.
closed — Gk. cleisto-.
cloud — Gk. nepho-.
cold — Gk. cryo-, psychro-.
colon — Gk. colo-.
color — Gk. chromato-, chromo-, -chrome; L. colori-.
comb — Gk. cteno-.
common — Gk. ceno-.
complete — See FINAL.
cone — Gk. cono-.
copper — Gk. chalco-; L. cupro-.
cornea — Gk. kerato-.
corpse — Gk. necro-.
correct — Gk. ortho-.
country — Gk. choro-.
covered — See HIDDEN.
craving — Gk. -mania, -maniac.
crest — Gk. lopho-.
cross — Gk. stauro-; L. cruci-.
crystal — Gk. crystallo-.
cup — Gk. scypho-; L. scyphi-.
curly — L. cirro-.
current — Gk. rheo-.
curved — L. curvi-.
custom — Gk. nomo-.
cut — Gk. tomo-, -tomy; L. -sect, -section. See also KNIFE, SPLIT.
cyanogen — Gk. cyano-.
cyst — Gk. cysto-.
dance — Gk. choreo-, choro-.
darkness — Gk. scoto-.
death — Gk. thanato-. See also CORPSE.
decompose — Gk. sapro-.
deep, depth — Gk. batho-, bathy-.
diaphragm — Gk. phreno-.
different — Gk. hetero-; L. vari-, vario-. See also FOREIGN, OTHER.
difficult — Gk. dys-.
disease — Gk. noso-, patho-, -iasis, -osis, -pathy. See also PAIN.
dissolving — Gk. lyo-, lysi-, -lysis, -lyte.
divide — See CUT, SPLIT.
divining — Gk. -mancy, -mantic.
double — Gk. diplo-.
dream — Gk. oneiro-.
drug — Gk. pharmaco-.
dry — Gk. xero-.
dung — Gk. copro-, scato-; L. sterco-, stercori-.
duodenum — L. duodeno-.
dust — Gk. conio-.
ear — Gk. oto-.
early, earliest — Gk. eo-. See also ANCIENT, FIRST, PRIMITIVE.
earth — Gk. geo-; L. terri-.
earthquake — Gk. seismo-.
eat — Gk. phago-, -phage, -phagous, -phagy; L. -vorous. See also FOOD, NOURISHMENT.
egg — Gk. oo-; L. ovi-, ovo-.
eight — Gk. & L. octa-, octo-.

electric — Gk. & L. electro-. See also CURRENT.
embryo — Gk. embryo-.
end — See FINAL.
English — L. Anglo-.
equal — Gk. iso-; L. equi-, pari-. See also LIKE, SAME.
existence — Gk. onto-.
external — Gk. ecto-, exo-; L. extra-.
extremity — See TIP.
eye — Gk. ophthalmo-, -opia; L. oculo-. See also SIGHT.
eyelid — Gk. blepharo-.
false — Gk. pseudo-.
far — Gk. tele-, telo-.
fat, fatty — Gk. lipo-; L. sebi-, sebo-.
father — L. patri-.
fear — Gk. -phobia.
feather — See WING.
feed — See EAT, NOURISHMENT.
female — See WOMAN.
fermentation — Gk. zymo-.
fever — L. febri-.
few — Gk. oligo-.
fibrous — L. fibro-.
field — See AGRICULTURE.
fight — Gk. -machy.
filament — See THREAD.
fin — L. pinni-.
final — Gk. teleo-, telo-.
finger — Gk. dactylo-; L. digiti-.
fire — Gk. pyro-; L. igni-.
first — Gk. proto-; L. primi-.
fish — Gk. ichthyo-; L. pisci-.
five — Gk. penta-; L. quinque-.
flat — Gk. platy-; L. plano-.
flee — L. -fugal, -fuge.
flesh — Gk. sarco-.
flow — Gk. -rrhea, -rrhagia, -rrhagic. See also CURRENT.
flower — Gk. antho-; L. -florous.
fluorescence — L. fluo-, fluoro-.
fluorine — L. fluo-, fluoro-.
food — Gk. sito-. See also EAT, NOURISHMENT.
foot — Gk. -pod, -podous; L. pedi-, -ped, -pede.
fond of — See LOVE.
force — See POWER.
foreign — Gk. xeno-. See also DIFFERENT, OTHER.
foretelling — See DIVINING.
form — Gk. morpho-, -morphic, -morphous. See also APPEARANCE, IMAGE, LIKE.
four — Gk. tetra-; L. quadri-, quadru-.
French — L. Gallo-.
front, frontal — L. fronto-.
fruit — Gk. carpo-, -carpous.
fungus — Gk. myco-, -mycete; L. fungi-.
gamete — Gk. gameto-.
ganglion — Gk. ganglio-.
gas — Gk. aero-.
genital — L. genito-.
gigantic — Gk. giganto-.
gills — Gk. branchio-, -branch.
gland — Gk. adeno-.
glass — Gk. hyalo-; L. vitri-.
god — Gk. theo-.
gold — Gk. chryso-.
good — Gk. eu-.
govern — Gk. -archy, -cracy, -crat.

1597

grain	L. grani-.	man	Gk. andro-, anthropo-, -androus.
gray matter	Gk. polio-.		
great	Gk. mega-, megalo-; L. magni-. See also LARGE, LONG.	manifestation	Gk. -phany.
		many	Gk. poly-, myria- (very many); L. multi-.
Greek	L. Greco-.		
green	Gk. chloro-.	marriage	Gk. -gamy.
groin	L. inguino-.	material, matter	Gk. hylo-, -plasm.
growth	Gk. -plasia, -plasis. See also BUD, TUMOR.	measure	Gk. metro-, -meter, -metry.
hair	Gk. chaeto-, tricho-.	medicine	Gk. iatro-, -iatrics, -iatry; L. medico-.
half	Gk. hemi-; L. demi-, semi-.		
		membrane	Gk. hymeno-.
hand	Gk. chiro-.	middle	Gk. meso-; L. medio-.
hard	Gk. sclero-. See also SOLID.	milk	Gk. galacto-; L. lacto-.
		mind	Gk. phreno-, psycho-. See also SPIRIT.
hate	Gk. miso-.		
head	Gk. cephalo-, -cephalic, -cephalous. See also SKULL.	monster	Gk. terato-.
		moon	Gk. seleno-; L. luni-.
		mother	L. matri-.
healing	See MEDICINE.	motion pictures	Gk. cine-.
hear	Gk. acous-; L. audio-.		
heart	Gk. cardio-.	mountain	Gk. oro-.
heat	Gk. thermo-. See FIRE.	mouth	Gk. stomato-, -stome, -stomous; L. oro-.
the heavens	Gk. urano-.		
hernia	Gk. -cele; L. hernio-.	movement	Gk. kinesi-, kineto-, -kinesis.
hidden	Gk. crypto-.		
high, height	Gk. hypso-; L. alti-, alto-.	mucus	L. muco-, muci-. See also SLIMY.
		much	See MANY.
hollow	See CAVITY.	muscle	Gk. myo-.
holy	See SACRED.	myth	Gk. mytho-.
horn	Gk. kerato-.	naked	See BARE.
horse	Gk. hippo-.	narrow	Gk. steno-.
hundred	Gk. hecto-; L. centi-.	nation	Gk. ethno-. See also SPECIES.
hysteria	Gk. hystero-.		
idea	Gk. ideo-.	nature	Gk. physio-.
ileum	L. ileo-.	near	Gk. para-; L. juxta-.
image	Gk. icono-.	neck	L. cervico-.
individual	Gk. idio-.	needle	See POINT.
inflammation	Gk. -itis.	nerve	Gk. neuro-.
inhabiting	L. -colous.	new	Gk. neo-.
insect	Gk. entomo-.	night	Gk. nycto-; L. nocti-.
interior	Gk. endo-, ento-; L. intra-, intro-.	nine	Gk. ennea-.
		nitrogen	Gk. azo-; L. nitro-.
intestine	Gk. entero-. See also COLON, DUODENUM, ILEUM, RECTUM, VISCERA.	nose	Gk. rhino-; L. naso-.
		nourishment	Gk. tropho-, -trophy. See also EAT, FOOD.
		nucleus	Gk. karyo-; L. nucleo-.
iodine	Gk. iodo-.	observation	Gk. -scope, -scopy.
iris (of eye)	Gk. irido-.	oil	L. oleo-.
iron	Gk. sidero-; L. ferro-, ferri-.	old age	Gk. geronto-.
		one	Gk. mono-; L. uni-.
jaw	Gk. gnatho-, -gnathous.	opening	Gk. -stomy (surgical).
joint	Gk. arthro-.	orchid	Gk. orchido-.
kidney	Gk. nephro-; L. reni-.	order	Gk. -taxis, -taxy.
kill	L. -cidal, -cide.	organ, organic	Gk. organo-.
knife	Gk. -tome.		
knowledge of	Gk. -gnomy, -gnosis, -sophy.	other	Gk. allo-. See also DIFFERENT, FOREIGN.
		outside	Gk. ecto-, exo-; L. extra-.
large	Gk. macro-. See also GREAT, LONG.		
		ovary	Gk. gyno-.
larynx	Gk. laryngo-.	oxygen	Gk. oxy-.
law	Gk. nomo-.	pain	Gk. -algia, -odynia. See also DISEASE, SUFFERING.
lead (metal)	L. plumbo-.		
leading	Gk. -agog-, -agogue.		
leaf, leafy	Gk. phyllo-, -phyllous; L. -folious.	pair	Gk. zygo-. See also DOUBLE, TWO.
		palm	L. palmi-.
left	L. levo-.	paralysis	Gk. -plegia.
level	See FLAT.	part	Gk. mero-, -mere, -merous.
life	Gk. bio-, -biosis.		
light	Gk. photo-; L. luci-, lumini-; Gk. actino- (light ray).	path	See WAY.
		pelvis	Gk. pyelo-; L. pelvi-.
		people	Gk. demo-. See also NATION.
like	Gk. homeo-, homoio-, -oid, -ode; L. quasi-. See also APPEARANCE, EQUAL, FORM, SAME.		
		perpendicular	See UPRIGHT.
		pharynx	Gk. pharyngo-.
lime	L. calci-.	photography	Gk. photo-.
lip	Gk. chilo-; L. labio-.	physics	Gk. physico-.
list	Gk. -logy.	pillar	Gk. stylo-.
little	See SMALL.	pistil	See OVARY.
liver	Gk. hepato-.	place	Gk. topo-.
lizard	Gk. sauro-.	plant	Gk. phyto-, -phyte.
long	Gk. macro-; L. longi-.	plate	See SCALE.
love	Gk. philo-, -phile; -philia, -phily (morbid love).	pleura	Gk. pleuro-.
		point	L. acu-. See also SPINY.
		poison	Gk. toxico-.
lung	Gk. pneumo-; L. pulmo-.	position	Gk. stato-.
lymph	L. lympho-, lymphato-.	power	Gk. dyna-, dynamo-.
magnet	L. magneto-.		
making	Gk. -plastic, -poietic. See also PRODUCING.		

pressure	Gk. piezo-, baro- (atmospheric pressure).
primitive	Gk. archi-.
producing	Gk. -gen, -genous, -geny, -gony. See also BEARING, MAKING.
pulse	Gk. sphygmo-.
pus	Gk. pyo-.
race	See NATION, SPECIES.
radiant energy	L. radio-.
radiate	Gk. actino-.
radio	L. radio-.
radioactive	L. radio-.
rain	Gk. hyeto-, ombro-; L. pluvio-.
ray	See LIGHT.
recent	Gk. -cene (geology and anthropology).
rectum	Gk. procto-; L. recto-.
red	Gk. erythro-.
region	See COUNTRY, PLACE.
reproduction	Gk. gono-.
rib	L. costo-.
right	L. dextro-.
river	L. fluvio-.
rock	See STONE.
root	Gk. rhizo-.
rot	See DECOMPOSE.
rough	Gk. trachy-.
row	Gk. -stichous.
rule	See GOVERN.
run	Gk. -drome, -dromous.
sacred	Gk. hagio-, hiero-.
sacrum	L. sacro-.
salt	Gk. halo-.
same	Gk. homo-, tauto-. See also EQUAL, LIKE.
scale	Gk. lepido-; L. lamelli-.
science of	Gk. -logy, -logical, -nomy.
sea	Gk. halo-, thalasso-.
seaweed	Gk. phyco-.
second (adj.)	Gk. deutero-.
seed	Gk. spermato-, -gonium, -sperm, -spermous. See also SPORE.
seizure	Gk. -lepsy.
self	Gk. auto-.
serum	L. sero-.
seven	Gk. hepta-; L. septi-.
sewing	Gk. -rrhaphy (surgical).
sexual union	Gk. gamo-.
sharp	Gk. oxy-.
short	Gk. brachy-; L. brevi-.
side	Gk. pleuro-, -hedral, -hedron (geometry).
sight	Gk. -opia, -opsia.
silicon	L. silico-.
simple	Gk. haplo-; L. simplici-.
single	Gk. haplo-.
six	Gk. hexa-; L. sex-.
skin	Gk. dermato-, dermo-, -derm.
skull	Gk. cranio-.
sleep	Gk. hypno-; L. somni-.
slender	Gk. lepto-.
slimy	Gk. myxo-.
slope	Gk. clino-, -cline (geology).
slow	Gk. brady-.
small	Gk. micro-. See also FEW.
snake	Gk. ophio-.
society	L. socio-.
soft	Gk. malaco-.
solid	Gk. stereo-.
sound	Gk. phono-, -phone, -phony.
speech	Gk. logo-, -phasia (defective).
species	Gk. phylo-.
spectrum	L. spectro-.
spermatozoa	Gk. spermato-.
sphere	Gk. -sphere.
spinal cord	Gk. myelo-.
spiny	Gk. acantho-, echino-; L. spini-.
spiral	Gk. helico-, spiro-.
spirit	Gk. pneumato-, psycho-. See also MIND.

spleen	Gk. spleno-.	**thread**	Gk. nemato-.
split	Gk. schisto-, schizo-; L. fissi-, -fid.	**three**	L. ter-, tri-.
spore	Gk. sporo-, -sporous.	**throat**	See LARYNX, PHARYNX, TRACHEA.
sprout	See BUD.		
stamen	Gk. andro-; L. stamini-.	**thyroid**	Gk. thyro-.
star	Gk. aster-, astro-; L. sidero-, stelli-.	**time**	Gk. chrono-.
		tip	Gk. acro-.
starch	Gk. amylo-.	**tissue**	Gk. histo-.
stomach	Gk. gastero-, gastro-.	**toe**	See FINGER.
stone	Gk. litho-, petro-, -lith.	**tone**	Gk. tono-.
stop	Gk. -stat.	**tongue**	Gk. glosso-.
straight	Gk. ortho-; L. recti-.	**tooth**	Gk. odonto-, -odont; L. denti-.
strange	See FOREIGN.		
style	Gk. stylo- (biology).	**top**	See TIP.
substitute	L. vice-.	**torpor**	Gk. narco-.
suffering	Gk. patho-, -pathy.	**trachea**	Gk. broncho-, tracheo-.
sugar	Gk. saccharo-.	**tree**	Gk. dendro-, -dendron; L. arbori-.
sulfur	Gk. thio-; L. sulfa-, sulfo-.		
		tribe	See SPECIES.
sun	Gk. helio-.	**tumor**	Gk. -cele, -oma.
sweet	Gk. glyco-.	**turned**	Gk. -tropous, -tropy.
swift	Gk. tachy-.	**twelve**	Gk. dodeca-.
sword	Gk. xiphi-.	**two**	Gk. di-; L. bi-, duo-.
tail	Gk. uro-.	**type**	Gk. typo-.
technical	Gk. techno-.	**united**	Gk. gamo-.
ten	Gk. deca-.	**universe**	Gk. cosmo-.
a tenth	L. deci-.	**upright**	Gk. ortho-.
terrible	Gk. dino-.	**urethra**	Gk. urethro-.
testicle	Gk. orchio-.	**urine**	Gk. uro-, -uria; L. urino-.
thick	Gk. pachy-.		
thorax	Gk. thoraco-.	**uterus**	Gk. hystero-, metro-; L. utero-.
thorny	See SPINY.		
thousand, thousandth	L. milli-.	**vagina**	L. vagino-.
		vapor	Gk. atmo-; L. vapori-.
		vein	Gk. phlebo-; L. veni-.

vessel	Gk. angio-; L. vaso-. See also BAG, BLADDER, CUP.
viscera	Gk. splanchno-.
visible	Gk. phanero-.
voice	See SOUND.
walking	L. -grade.
water	Gk. hydro-; L. aqui-.
wave	Gk. cymo-.
wax	Gk. cero-.
way	Gk. hodo-, odo-, -ode.
web	L. pinni-.
wealth	Gk. pluto-.
wedge	Gk. spheno-.
weight	Gk. baro-.
wet	Gk. hygro-.
white	Gk. leuko-.
whole	Gk. holo-; L. toti-.
wide	See BROAD.
wind	Gk. anemo-. See also AIR, BREATH.
wine	L. vini-.
wing	Gk. ptero-, -pterous; L. -pennate.
woman	Gk. gyneco-, gyno-.
(a) wonder	Gk. thaumato-.
wood	Gk. xylo-; L. ligni-.
word	Gk. logo-.
work	Gk. ergo-.
world	See UNIVERSE.
worm	L. vermi-.
write	Gk. grapho-, -gram, -graph, -graphy.
yellow	Gk. xantho-.
yoke	Gk. zygo-.

PREFIXES

about	See AROUND.	**behind**	See AFTER.
above	Gk. hyper-; L. super-, supra-. See also ON.	**beside**	Gk. para-; L. juxta-.
		between	L. inter-.
across	L. trans-. See also THROUGH.	**beyond**	Gk. meta-; L. preter-, ultra-.
after	Gk. meta-; L. post-.	**changed**	Gk. meta-.
again	Gk. ana-; L. re-. See also BACK.	**down**	Gk. cata- (cath-); L. de-.
against	Gk. anti-; L. contra-, in- (il-, im-, ir-), ob- (oc-, of-, op-).	**excessively**	See ABOVE.
		for	L. pro-.
		forward	Gk. & L. pro-.
among	See BETWEEN, WITHIN.	**from**	L. ab- (a-, abs-). See also DOWN.
apart	L. dis- (di-), se-. See also AWAY, FROM.	**in, into**	Gk. en- (el-, em-); L. in- (il-, im-, ir-), intro-. See also WITHIN.
around	Gk. peri-; L. circum-.		
at	See BESIDE, NEAR, TO.	**not**	Gk. a- (an-); L. de-, in- (il-, im-, ir-), non-.
away	Gk. apo-. See also APART, FROM.		
		off	See APART, AWAY, FROM.
back	L. retro-. See also AGAIN.	**on**	Gk. epi- (eph-); L. in- (il-, im-, ir-).
badly	L. mal-, mis-.		
before	Gk. pro-; L. ante-, pre-.	**on that side of**	L. trans-. See also BEYOND.

on this side of	L. cis-.
out	Gk. & L. ex- (e-, ec-, ef-).
outside	Gk. exo-; L. extra-. See also BEYOND.
over	See ABOVE, ON, BEYOND, VERY.
thoroughly	Gk. ana-, cata- (cath-); L. com- (co-, col-, con-, cor-).
through	Gk. dia-; L. per-.
to, toward	L. ad- (ac-, af-, ag-, al-, an-, ap-, ar-, as-, at-).
under	Gk. hypo-; L. sub- (suc-, suf-, sug-, sum-, sup-, sur-, sus-), subter-.
up	Gk. ana-.
very	Gk. peri-; L. per-. See also THOROUGHLY.
with	Gk. sym- (sy-, syl-, syn-).
within	Gk. endo-; L. intra-.
without	See NOT, OUTSIDE.

SUFFIXES OF ADJECTIVES

able to, able to be	L. -able, -ile (-il).	**coming from**	L. -an.
adhering to or following	L. -an.	**doing**	L. -ant, -ent.
		full of	L. -ose, -ous.
affected by	L. & Gk. -ac.	**like, of the nature of**	L. -ine (-in), -ive, -ory, -ose.
beginning to	L. -escent.		
belonging to	L. -an (in zoology).	**making**	See CAUSING.
capable of	See ABLE TO.	**originating in**	See COMING FROM.
causing	L. -fic.	**pertaining to**	Gk. & L. -ac, -ic; L. -aceous, -al, -ar, -ary, -ile (-il), -ine, -ory.
characterized by	L. -al, -ate, -id. See also PERTAINING TO.		

related to	See PERTAINING TO.
tending to	L. -able, -ive.
worthy of	See ABLE TO.

Many adjectives so formed are also used as nouns, as *animal*, *human*, etc. These nouns mean generally a person or thing related to or described by the adjective.

SUFFIXES OF NOUNS

act, action	L. -al, -ion (-cion, -sion, -tion), -ment, -ure.	**descendant of**	Gk. -ite.
		example	See INSTANCE.
advocate or adherent	Gk. -ist, -ite.	**function**	See OFFICE.
art	Gk. -ic, -ics. See also SYSTEM.	**instance**	L. -al.
		instrument	L. -ment, -ory, -ure.
		methods	See SYSTEM.
collection	L. -ana.	**native**	L. -ite.
condition	L. -ion (-cion, -sion, -tion), -ment, -mony, -tude.	**office**	L. -ate, -ure.
		place	L. -arium, -ary, -orium, -ory.

practitioner	L. -ary, -ist, -or -aster (inferior), -trix (female).
result	L. -ate, -ion (-cion, -sion, -tion), -ment, -mony, -ure.
state	See CONDITION.
student	L. -ist.
study	See ART.
system	Gk. -ics.

SUFFIXES OF VERBS

become	Gk. -ize; L. -fy.	**combine with**	L. -ate.
begin	L. -esce.	**make**	Gk. -ize; L. -fy.

practice	Gk. -ize.
treat with	Gk. -ize; L. -ate.

PRACTICAL REFERENCE GUIDES

PUNCTUATION

For most normal requirements it is best to remember that too much punctuation is as confusing as too little. The current trend is toward a relative minimum of punctuation, just enough to make the writer's meaning clear. This can best be accomplished by cultivating a simple, straightforward style that flows as naturally as ordinary speech. Where a sentence is so complicated that no amount of punctuation seems adequate, a writer would be wise to reorganize his thoughts. Punctuation can help to guide a reader to the meaning of a sentence; it cannot, however, make order out of chaos.

End Punctuation Because the sentence is a grammatically complete and separate unit of utterance, it is necessary to show where one ends and another begins. In speech this is accomplished by falling pitch, intonation, and a full pause. In written discourse the reader is guided by a period, a question mark, or an exclamation point, depending on the nature of the sentence.

The Period [.] This is used at the end of any sentence that makes a statement. It is also used to indicate abbreviation.

Mrs. Morris threw the book aside in disgust.

The Question Mark [?] The question mark signifies that the sentence preceding it does not make a statement, but asks a question. This punctuation serves the same purpose in writing that rising or sustained pitch intonation of the voice does orally.

Did George throw the book?
George threw the book?

Polite usage will often disguise an order or a request in the form of a question, even when none is intended. In such cases a period is used to conclude the sentence.

Will you open the door for me, please.

The Exclamation Point [!] This is used at the end of a statement denoting a strong emotional experience, a sense of urgency or excitement. If spoken, it would be gasped, shouted, groaned, or cried. Written, the exclamation point, and the reader's imagination, must suffice.

Watch out!
Oh, my head!
No, no, no, NO!

Exclamation points should be used with discretion and for particular emphasis. Excessive use tends to lessen the impact of this device.

Internal Punctuation

The Comma and Semicolon [, ;] When sentences become more complex and deal with two or more closely related ideas, internal punctuation is necessary to show the relation between the various parts. Clauses may be linked by conjunctions alone without punctuation, or by commas or semicolons with or without conjunctions. The choice depends upon the requirements of clarity and the traits of one's style.

He ate and ate but remained hungry.
She wept, she cried, and she tore her hair.
I pierce its order; I dissipate its fear; I dispose of it within the circuit of my expanding life.

Some authorities insist that the semicolon be used when two main clauses have no connecting conjunction, but others feel that a comma is adequate for most cases. Semicolons are useful in long, involved sentences and those in which commas are used within the separate clauses.

Series A comma is regularly used to distinguish the various elements in a series, either words, phrases, or clauses.

The torn, tattered, soaking flag was lowered.
The dog jumped up, barked ferociously, bared his teeth, and took off after the rabbit.

Formal punctuation requires that a comma be inserted between the last two elements of a series even when a conjunction is used. An informal style of punctuation, however, does not require the comma before the conjunction.

The flag is red, white and blue.

The Colon [:] The colon is used most often to indicate that a list, example, strong assertion, or the like will follow to complete or fulfill some introductory statement.

The bride takes three vows: to love, honor, and obey.
All men have their weakness: some for fame, some for money, others for praise.
We have only one goal: to win.

Although the colon has been used, especially by British writers, as a pause or stop intermediate between the semicolon and the period, it now always points ahead to something promised or needed for a complete or specific statement.

The colon is also used outside the sentence in certain purely conventional ways: after the salutation of a formal letter; between elements of a Biblical or bibliographical citation; after the name or other identification of the speaker in dialogue or transcript of speech, etc.

Introductory Punctuation Some sentences begin with subordinate or introductory words or phrases. These are connected to the main body of the sentence with a comma.

Breathing heavily, the dog returned from the chase.
However, he had nothing to show for his trouble.

Punctuation to Set Off A sentence may contain information that is not essential to its grammatically independent structure, but that contributes to its exact meaning. Such nonrestrictive words, phrases, or clauses are most often set off by commas.

The king, who was very ill, was present at the ceremony.

When the information has a relatively remote connection with the utterance of the main clause, it is usually enclosed in parentheses.

The strike (which began on the President's birthday) completely paralyzed the nation.

Dashes may be used by stylistic choice to set off any sort of nonrestrictive or parenthetical matter. They lend a more personal and dramatic flavor to the writing.

The world — this shadow of the soul, or *other me* — lies wide around.

The Apostrophe [']

To Indicate Possession Apostrophes are employed most commonly to form the possessive of nouns and pronouns. Words not ending with an (s) or (z) sound add ('s), while those ending with an (s) or a (z) sound generally add only an apostrophe at the end. Therefore most singular nouns will take the ('s), and most plural forms will add only (').

WORDS NOT ENDING IN (S) OR (Z)	WORDS ENDING IN (S) OR (Z)
the baby's bottle	the babies' bottles
the children's playroom	for goodness' sake
somebody's hat	the synopsis' length
old-timer's tale	old-timers' tales

Exceptions may be found in the possessive form of proper names ending in (s) or (z). There is a growing tendency to add ('s) to names of one syllable even though they end with an (s) sound, thus making James *James's*, Marx *Marx's*, and Schultz *Schultz's*. With names of more than one syllable, either form may be used unless the additional (s) makes the word difficult to pronounce. Then only the apostrophe is used.

Thomas's or Thomas'	*but only*	Genesis'
Adams's or Adams'		Exodus'
Titus's or Titus'		Moses'

Personal pronouns do not take the apostrophe in the possessive form:

my, mine	our, ours
your, yours	your, yours
her, hers	their, theirs
his, its	whose

The possessive forms are also used in many expressions denoting time or measure: *a two weeks' trip*; *a stone's throw*; *ten cents' worth*; *a dime's worth*.

To Indicate Omission An apostrophe is also used to show that one or more letters have been omitted from a word, or numerals from a number.

it's	it is
can't	cannot
you're	you are
we'll	we will
where'er	wherever
'29	1929

Plural of Letters or Numbers The plural of a letter or a number is formed by adding ('s), although it should be noted that there is a growing trend to drop the apostrophe where years are concerned. Abbreviations form the plural by adding ('s).

Dot your i's and cross your t's.
There are four s's, four i's, and two p's in Mississippi.
During the 1940's (or 1940s) ...
Watch your ABC's ...
6's and 7's
a company of GI's
a carload of VIP's

Quotation Marks [" " ' '] There are two classes of quotations: direct and indirect. Quotation marks are required at the beginning and end of a word or words spoken in direct discourse. Indirect quotations require no quotation marks, and are commonly introduced by the word *that*.

Direct quotation: Roy said, "I am reading a good book."
Indirect quotation: Roy said that he was reading a good book.

A quotation within a quotation is enclosed by single quotation marks.

Jack remarked, "I believe Patrick Henry said, 'Give me liberty or give me death.' "

Notice that the period within the quotation marks serves as end punctuation both for the sentence spoken by Jack and that spoken by Patrick Henry. The period is never doubled at the end of a quotation within a quotation. The rule for punctuating quoted matter is easily learned. Punctuation belonging to the quotation, such as periods and commas, is set within the quotation. Punctuation not connected with the quotation, such as colons and semicolons, is set outside the closed quotation marks.

He said, "Call the police."
He said, "Call the police"; but the sirens were already wailing.

When a lengthy quotation of two or more paragraphs is used, beginning or open quotation marks are used at the start of each paragraph, and the closed quotation marks appear only at the very end of the quoted passage.

No quotation marks are necessary in interviews, dramatic dialogues, or legal testimony where the name of the speaker, or other identification, precedes the speech, or where question and answer are clearly marked.

Judge: How do you plead, guilty or not guilty?
Defendant: Not guilty, Your Honor.
Q.: Where were you on the night of June 26th?
A.: I don't remember.

Quotation marks are also used to set off words or phrases that the writer wishes not to claim as his own. These may be the words of other persons, or they may be jargon, slang, barbarisms, figures, and the like, which he "decontaminates" by using quotation marks.

Let my opponent produce his "incontrovertible evidence."
The young men apparently did it "for kicks."

Quotation marks are used conventionally around the titles of books, plays, poems, essays, etc. They are also used around a word or phrase being spoken of as such. Both these functions are also fulfilled by italicizing (in handwriting or typescript, by underlining), and one must be careful not to mix the two styles of punctuation.

I enjoyed "A Man for All Seasons."
"A dying fall" needs to be explained.

The Hyphen [-] One important use of the hyphen is to show when a word has been broken at the end of one line and completed on the next. Governing this practice are the rules of syllabication, and they are as rigidly enforced by prevailing standards as the rules of spelling. Words may be divided only between syllables. Those words pronounced as one syllable may never be divided. Splitting a word for only one letter is prohibited, and breaking a word for two letters is tolerated on rare occasions, but discouraged as a constant practice.

Thus, good printing and typing practices require that words be divided in groups of not fewer than three letters. Abbreviations should never be carried over from one line to the next, and every attempt should be made to include the initials of a person's name on the same line with the name. For book editing, and when preparing a manuscript, hyphens should not be used at the end of more than two successive lines, and breaking the last word of a paragraph is also considered bad form. Dividing a compound word or a word already hyphenated is likely to confuse, and is therefore to be avoided. If numbers must be divided, the break should be made only after a comma: 35,675,-545.

In the hyphenation of compound words, usage ranges far and wide, and the final decision frequently rests with the writer. Consistent use of the dictionary is the best advice that can be offered on this subject, and the writer who lets this principle guide him will be readily understood.

Good judgment, however, is indispensable. In many instances only the context of the sentence will determine whether a hyphenated compound is required, or whether the words should remain separate.

He said it in a very matter-of-fact way.
As a matter of fact, he knew that to be true.
His great-grandfather came to visit him.
He had a great grandfather who always took him fishing.

Hyphens are also employed to separate prefixes from words where the writer's meaning would otherwise be distorted.

The upholsterer re-covered the chair.
The police recovered the typewriter.

The hyphen is also used to separate a prefix from a proper noun, or to simplify a confusing combination: anti-American, pre-Renaissance, mid-ocean, post-recession. Some also prefer to use a hyphen rather than a dieresis (¨) to separate a prefix and a root which would result in a double vowel combination: co-operation (also coöperation, and cooperation); re-enter (reënter, reenter).

Hyphens are also used in all numbers ranging from twenty-one to ninety-nine, and in fractions: one-half, three-quarters, seven-sixteenths. Years are designated with hyphenation: nineteen-sixties, nineteen sixty-two (not nineteen-sixty-two).

Before leaving the subject, a word of caution against confusing the hyphen (-) and the dash (—). Remember that the hyphen connects, while the dash separates. The dash is the longer of the two, and is formed on the typewriter with two strokes of the hyphen key (--). For the specific uses of the dash, see the section on Punctuation to Set Off.

CAPITALIZATION

Some publishers and writers prefer an "up-style" (a heavily capitalized style) and others are partial to a "down-style" (a minimum of capitalization). In most instances, however, the conventions governing the use of capital letters are quite clear.

1. Capitalize the first word of every sentence.
2. The first person singular pronoun I, and the vocative O are generally capitalized.
3. Unless style requires a different form, A.M. and P.M. are set in small capitals without a space between them. The same holds true for B.C. and A.D.

12:00 P.M. (midnight)	12:00 A.M. (noon)
6:20 P.M.	7:15 A.M.
A.D. 1848 or 1848 A.D.	17 B.C.

(Note: Although technically A.D. should precede the number of the year, popular usage permits it to follow the date.)

4. The first letter of a line of conventional poetry is capitalized. Much of the modern poetry, however, ignores this convention.

Hickory, dickory, dock,
    The mouse ran up the clock.
The clock struck one,
    And down he run,
Hickory, dickory, dock.

5. Capitalize proper nouns and proper adjectives. Do not capitalize words that may once have been proper nouns, but are now used in a generic sense. In some cases, where the proper noun or adjective is applied to common classifications, the choice is left to individual preference.

America	American	boycott	pasteurize
Thomas Jefferson	Jeffersonian	daguerreotype	watt
Shakespeare	Shakespearean	davenport	macadam
Arabic and Roman numerals		or arabic and roman numerals	
Panama hat		or panama hat	
Diesel engine		or diesel engine	

6. The first word after a colon should be capitalized when it begins a complete sentence.

> The list contained these items: five pounds of flour, two dozen eggs, and a pound of butter.
> The candidate made only one promise: If elected, he would fight for better conditions.

7. Every direct quotation should begin with a capital, except where the passage is grammatically woven into the text preceding it.

> The announcer shouted, "There it goes, over the back wall for a home run!"
> The announcer saw the ball going "over the back wall for a home run."

8. Capitalize all important words in the titles of books, newspapers, magazines, chapters, poems, articles. Short conjunctions and prepositions are generally not capitalized.

> The Daughters of Necessity
> How to Win Friends and Influence People

9. Geographical divisions and regions require capitals.

Arctic Circle	the New England States
Tropic of Cancer	the Atlantic Seaboard
the Old World	the Pacific Coast
the Orient	Mississippi Valley
the Occident	Promised Land
the Continent (Europe)	Great Plains

10. Compass points are capitalized when they are part of a generally accepted name, but not when they denote direction, or are used with common nouns.

Middle East	eastern Virginia
Far West	southern South Dakota
Old South	Head west for twenty-five miles.

11. Capitalize street names, parks, buildings, but not the general categories into which they fall.

> General Post Office (post office)
> Metropolitan Museum of Art (museum)
> Avenue of the Americas (avenue)
> Empire State Building (building)

12. Religions, religious leaders, the various appellations for God and the Christian Trinity require capitalization, as do all names for the Bible, and its parts.

> the Father, the Son, and the Holy Ghost
> Virgin Mary, the Immaculate Virgin
> Yahweh, Jehovah, Saviour, Messiah

Buddhism	Koran	Veda
Shintoism	Mishna	Upanishads
Taoism	Talmud	Zen

New Testament	Sermon on the Mount
Pentateuch	Acts of the Apostles
Exodus	Ten Commandments

13. Capitalize the names of political parties, classes, movements, and their adherents. Lower-case terms that refer generally to ideology (bolshevism, fascism, socialism).

Democratic Party	International Workers of the World
the Right Wing	Black Shirts
Socialist	Farm Bloc

14. Political divisions are capitalized.

> Holy Roman Empire
> French Republic
> the Dominion
> the Colonies
> Westchester County
> Eighth Congressional District

15. Governmental bodies, departments, bureaus, and courts are capitalized.

> the Supreme Court
> Court of Appeals of the State of New York
> Congress
> House of Representatives
> British Parliament
> Department of Labor
> the Cabinet
> Census Bureau

16. Capitalize the titles of all high-ranking government officials, and all appellations of the President of the United States. Many publishers, it should be pointed out, prefer lower case for titles that are not accompanied by the name of the official.

The President	Chief Justice
Commander-in-Chief	Ambassador to India
Secretary of State	Prime Minister
Under Secretary	Minister of Education

17. Capitalize the names of treaties, documents, and important events.

> Second World War
> Treaty of Versailles
> Boston Tea Party
> Declaration of Independence

18. Family designations, when used without a possessive pronoun, take a capital letter.

> I sent Mother home by taxi.
> I sent my mother home by taxi.

19. Capitalize seasons only when they are personified. All personifications require capitals.

> The frosty breath of Winter settled on the land.
> He saw Mother Nature's grim visage.
> The voice of Envy whispered in her ear.
> The mother of Invention is Necessity.
> When Headquarters commands, we jump.

20. Names and epithets of peoples, races, and tribes are capitalized.

Caucasian	Apache
Negro	Cliff Dwellers

21. Articles and prepositions are generally capitalized in the names of Englishmen and Americans, and are not capitalized in French, Italian, Spanish, German, and Dutch names, unless otherwise specified by family usage.

Thomas De Quincey	Ludwig van Beethoven
Martin Van Buren	Leonardo da Vinci
Fiorello La Guardia	Miguel de Cervantes Saavedra
Jean de La Fontaine	San Juan de la Cruz

22. Capitalize the names of holidays and festivals.

Christmas Eve	Yom Kippur
New Year's Day	Shrove Tuesday

23. Capitalize such parts of a book as the Glossary, Contents, Index, and Preface.

CORRESPONDENCE

The Business Letter

The formalities of writing a business letter are understandably rigid. Succinctness and clarity are the prime virtues. Carbon copies are made so that the sender may have an up-to-date file of his transactions, and the number of duplicates will depend on the number of persons concerned with this information. In its finished form, the letter will give this appearance:

(Eight spaces from the top of the page)

```
                                        811 Cedar Street
(Heading)                               San Diego 3, California
                                        July 21, 1963
   (Four spaces)
Mr. Jack Armstrong, President
American Steel Foundation               (Inside Address)
1375 Houston Avenue
Bethany 39, West Virginia
                                            (—Two spaces)
   ATTENTION: Transportation Manager
                                            (—Two spaces)
Dear Mr. Armstrong: (Salutation)
```

Two spaces below the Salutation begins the body of the letter. This is written in exactly this manner: single-spaced, with a double space between paragraphs, and without indentation.

The spacing recommended between the Heading and the Inside Address may be expanded if the letter is short, and if it will improve the appearance of the page. The ATTENTION line is used to alert a particular member of the company, other than the one addressed. Where it is customary to cite the subject of the correspondence separately from the text, it will generally appear on the same line with the Salutation, flush against the margin on the right.

Two spaces below the body of the letter, slightly to the right of center, is placed the Complimentary Close. In formal correspondence this is Yours truly, Very truly yours; for a person of sufficient rank, Respectfully yours, is appropriate.

```
                (Two spaces—)
                        Yours truly, (Complimentary
                (Two spaces—)                 Close)
                BOILER CORPORATION OF AMERICA
                (Signature of Sender)
                John J. Littlejohn
                Chairman
```

Heading   Note that in the Heading, as in the Inside Address, no punctuation is used at the end of each line. Where letterhead stationery is used, it is unnecessary to repeat the address of the sender. In such cases, only the date of the letter need be added, about four spaces below the letterhead, and slightly to the right of center. The style used throughout the above model is the Block Form, which has been found more efficient than the older, and now rarely used, Oblique Form.

Inside Address   This identifies the recipient of the letter, and enables the sender to identify the file copy. It includes the name of the recipient, his titles, if any, and the address. Here again no punctuation is used at the end of each line.

Salutation   For letters addressed to a company, Gentlemen: is a suitable greeting. Where an individual is addressed any one of the following may be appropriate: Dear Sir: Dear Madam: Dear Mr. (or Mrs. or Miss) *(name of the person specifically addressed)*:. When the marital status of a woman is unknown, she is addressed as Miss.

Complimentary Close The flowery close that was considered stylish at one time, and is still used in many European countries, is a thing of the past in this country. For those who feel Yours truly is too impersonal a note, however, it is still considered good form to run the Body of the letter into the Complimentary Close: Awaiting your decision, I remain,
Very truly yours,

Signature The name of the sender is typed either in upper or lower case below his signature. Whatever position he may occupy in his firm is also included by way of identification.

In the lower left-hand corner of the letter it is customary to put the initials of the sender in capital letters, and the initials of the secretary in lower-case letters. These two sets of initials are separated by a stroke. The number of enclosures to be placed in the same envelope is also recorded here.

JJL/hc. Enclosures (4).

Envelope The address on the envelope will coincide in all particulars with the Inside Address. Double spacing is preferred to expedite the mailman's task. The address should be approximately centered on the front of the envelope. Zone numbers are included after the name of the city, followed by a comma and the name of the state. The return address is usually placed in the upper left-hand corner, although occasionally it will appear across the flap on the back.

John J. Littlejohn, Chairman   (Postage)
Boiler Corporation of America
811 Cedar Street
San Diego 3, California

The Personal Letter

Personal letters and social notes will reflect the relationship between the correspondents, and thus will vary from the quite formal to the informal. Since it is not customary to maintain a file of the letters one writes, the inside address is never used. The heading consists of one's own address and the date, and it may be written either in the block style of the business letter, or in the oblique (indented) form. For consistency the same style should be carried over into the closing, and in addressing the envelope. Where a writer feels that his own address is unnecessary, the heading may be limited only to the date.

The typewriter, once considered a sign of poor taste when used in personal correspondence, is gaining currency, particularly for letters of length where an idiosyncratic handwriting may try the stamina of the reader. For shorter correspondence, however, the handwritten note is still preferred, and it is actually obligatory for the more formal social occasions, as in letters of invitation, acceptance, or condolence.

Special Forms of Address

Most people occasionally must address a letter to some important personage, and convention has established certain formulas that embody the expected courtesies. The forms of address in the following list are taken from the much fuller treatment in Emily Post's *Etiquette: The Blue Book of Social Usage.*

President of the United States
Name: The President
Address: Washington, D.C.
Salutation: Sir: *or* Dear Mr. President:
Closing: I have the honor to remain,
Most respectfully yours,
or Yours faithfully,

The Chief Justice of the United States
Name: The Honorable, The Chief Justice
Address: Washington, D.C.
Salutation: Sir: *or* Dear Mr. Chief Justice:
Closing: I have the honor to remain,
Yours respectfully,

Member of the Cabinet
Name: The Secretary of State *or* The Honorable Joseph J. Jay, Secretary of State
Address: Washington, D.C.
Salutation: Sir: *or* My dear Mr. Secretary:
Closing: I have the honor to remain,
Yours respectfully,

United States or State Senator
Name: The Honorable Louis L. Lewis, Senator from Missouri,
Address: Washington, D.C.
Salutation: Sir: *or* Dear Sir: *or* Dear Senator Lewis:
Closing: Believe me,
Yours very truly,
or I have the honor to remain,
Yours very truly,

Member of Congress or of State Legislature
Name: The Honorable Howard H. Hughes
Address: State Assembly, Juneau, Alaska
Salutation: Sir: *or* Dear Sir: *or* Dear Mr. Hughes:
Closing: Believe me,
Yours very truly,

Governor
Name: His Excellency the Governor David K. Cutler
Address: Executive Mansion, Albany, New York
Salutation: Your Excellency: *or* Sir: *or* Dear Governor Cutler:
Closing: I have the honor to remain,
Yours faithfully,

Mayor
Name: His Honor the Mayor Robert F. Humboldt
Address: City Hall, Chicago
Salutation: Dear Sir: *or* Sir: *or* Dear Mayor Humboldt:
Closing: Believe me,
Yours very truly, ·

Bishop (Protestant)
Name: To the Right Reverend Thomas E. Smith *or* The Bishop of Massachusetts
Address: Boston, Massachusetts
Salutation: Right Reverend and dear Sir: *or* My dear Bishop Smith:
Closing: I have the honor to remain,
Your obedient servant,
or to remain,
Respectfully yours,

Clergyman (Protestant)
Name: The Reverend Jonathan Church
Salutation: Sir: *or* My dear Sir: *or* Dear Dr. Church:
Closing: I have the honor to remain,
Yours faithfully,
or sincerely,

Rabbi
Name: Rabbi Abraham L. Temple *or* The Reverend Abraham L. Temple
Salutation: Dear Sir: *or* Dear Rabbi Temple: *or* Dear Dr. Temple:
Closing: I have the honor to remain,
Yours faithfully,
or sincerely,

Cardinal (Roman Catholic)
Name: His Eminence Michael Cardinal Angelus, Archbishop of Baltimore
Address: Baltimore, Maryland
Salutation: Your Eminence:
Closing: I have the honor to remain,
Your Eminence's humble servant,

Bishop (Roman Catholic)
Name: The Most Reverend Henry James
Salutation: Most Reverend Sir: *or* My dear Bishop James:
Closing: I have the honor to remain,
Your obedient servant,

University Professor
Name: Professor Herbert C. Schwab
Salutation: Dear Sir: *or* Dear Professor Schwab: *or* Dear Dr. Schwab:
Closing: Believe me,
Sincerely,

Ambassador
Name: His Excellency, The American Ambassador James M. Finnerty
Address: Embassy of the United States of America, Athens, Greece
Salutation: Your Excellency: *or* Dear Mr. Ambassador:
Closing: I have the honor to remain,
Yours faithfully,
or Yours very truly,

Consul
Name: Arnold M. Gussin, Esq., American Consul
Address: Rue Quelque Chose, Paris, France
Salutation: Sir: *or* My dear Sir: *or* Dear Mr. Gussin:
Closing: I beg to remain,
Yours very truly,
or Yours very sincerely,

MANUSCRIPT PREPARATION

A writer must bear in mind that strangers will be evaluating his manuscript. It is unreasonable to assume that editors will take time out from a busy schedule to unscramble a poorly constructed manuscript when the author himself did not care sufficiently to make it presentable. A carbon copy smudged from handling and chewed around the edges is not likely to encourage an editor to read very far into it. By exerting a little effort to learn the fundamental conventions of style required by publishers and printers, a writer may save himself much time and effort later.

Before a final copy is typed, the typewriter keys should be thoroughly cleaned. A black, almost new ribbon is preferable, because the ink is too dense on a brand-new ribbon. Good quality carbon paper will help to get the clearest possible impression. It is also common sense to submit the original copy to the publisher, and a carbon copy if possible. One carbon should always be retained by the author to protect against loss in transit. Radical innovations in style should be avoided, except where absolutely necessary to achieve a particular effect. More often than not, these innovations confuse the reader and distract him from the meaning of the text.

Paper Paper should be of a standard size, preferably 8½ x 11 inches, and of a good opacity, sixteen- or twenty-pound weight. Onionskin is too flimsy to serve as a printer's copy, and publishers are often put to the additional expense of retyping a manuscript for the printer.

Margins Liberal margins on both sides of the sheet are essential. The copy editor needs this space to make corrections, to query the author, and to give instructions to the printer. A six-inch line (seventy-two elite spaces, or sixty pica spaces) centered on the page will insure sufficient margins. The lines should be made as even as possible, without sacrificing the rules governing word division. This will help the editor to estimate the length of the manuscript in its printed form.

Spacing Text, bibliography, and table of contents should be double-spaced. Long footnotes also require double-spacing. Shorter footnotes may be single-spaced with a double space separating them. Single-spacing is also permitted for long excerpts, thereby setting them apart from the rest of the text. The number of lines on a page should be uniform, generally twenty-five for a standard eleven-inch sheet. Some brands of carbon paper include a guide sheet which, when set in the platen behind the paper, helps to achieve the desired uniformity.

Indentation All paragraphs start seven spaces from the left-hand margin. This is true for quoted matter and footnotes. For long quotations, single-spaced, the opening line is indented the same seven spaces, but then a new margin is set four spaces from the left-hand side, and is maintained until the excerpt is concluded.

Footnotes It is mandatory that an author acknowledge his indebtedness to the sources and authorities used in his articles. If such acknowledgments are few, they may be woven into the text in this manner:

As Emily Post points out in her book, *Etiquette*, the perfect hostess "must first of all consider the inclinations of her guests."

In scholarly articles, however, adequate documentation is required. All facts must be validated, and many separate sources must be given credit for the ideas presented. Including them all in the text will only impede the progress of the discussion and confuse the reader. Footnotes were devised to avoid this. A superscript, or an index number, like this[1] is placed immediately after the statement for which the footnote is given, either at the bottom of the same page, or collected in a group at the end of the chapter or book. No space intervenes between the reference number and the following word, and the superscript must coincide with the number of the footnote to which it refers. The numbers will run consecutively throughout the manuscript, or they may start anew from [1] with each chapter. For lightly footnoted material the following reference marks may be used, in this sequence: * asterisk; † dagger; ‡ double dagger; § section mark; ‖ parallels; ¶ paragraph mark.

Footnotes collected at the bottom of the same page on which the reference appears are the most readily accessible for the reader. Technical journals may require special forms, but generally the following examples are considered good style.

Books Author's name as it appears on the title page: given name, initial (if any), and surname followed by a comma. The name of the book comes next, and is underlined. Immediately following the book title, in parentheses, appears the place of publication, a colon, the name of the publisher, comma, and the date of the edition used in the reference. A comma separates the closed parenthesis from the page or pages on which the information appears.

[1]Emily Post, *Etiquette: The Blue Book of Social Usage* (New York: Funk & Wagnalls Company, 1955), pp. 281–93.

In cases where a book has more than one author, but no more than three, they are all listed in the footnote.

[7]Everard M. Upjohn, Paul S. Wingert, Jane Gaston Mahler, *History of World Art* (New York: Oxford University Press, 1949), p. 349.

Where more than three authors are listed, only the first named on the title page is mentioned, followed by *and others* or *et al.*

[24]Mario Einaudi and others (or, *et al.*), *Foreign Governments: The Dynamics of Politics Abroad* (New York: Prentice-Hall, 1949), pp. 271–88.

If the author is anonymous, the citation begins with the title of the book.

Periodicals The same procedure is followed in footnoting articles in periodicals. The name of the author, the title of the article in quotation marks, the name of the periodical underlined, volume number (if any), date, and page number.

[30]Peter S. Feibleman, "The Haunted City," *Holiday*, June, 1961, pp. 88, 138–45.

If the volume number is shown, it is expressed in Roman numerals, and no abbreviation for "page" or "pages" is necessary before the page indication.

[31]John M. Fowler, Ralph Caplan, "What We Know About Fallout," *The Nation*, CXCIII (December 8, 1961), 464.

If repeated references are to be made to the same sources it is unnecessary to repeat all of the information contained in the first footnote. It will profit a writer to familiarize himself with abbreviations that are used in footnotes. Following are the most commonly used abbreviations:

Ibid. This is the Latin abbreviation for *ibidem* (meaning *in the same place*). It is used when two consecutive footnotes refer to the same source. If a different page number is referred to, then it must be specified after the abbreviation.

[1]Elizabeth Post, *Emily Post's Etiquette. The Blue Book of Social Usage* (New York: Funk & Wagnalls, 1965), pp. 281–84.
[2]*Ibid.* (Referring to pp. 281–84).
[3]*Ibid.*, pp. 97–102. (Still referring to Emily Post, but to a previous section.)

Op. cit. This abbreviation for the Latin *opere citato* (meaning *in the work cited*) is used when references to the same work follow in close, but not consecutive, order. The author's surname alone generally suffices, except where two books by the same author are being used, or where two authors share the same last name. In such cases the title is repeated.

[5]Post, *op. cit.* (Referring to pages 97–102 cited above. If different pages are referred to, they must follow the abbreviation, as in the case of *ibid.*)

Op. cit. has been replaced in many systems of notation by the short title reference, consisting usually of the author's surname and an abbreviated form of the title, with or without page citations as necessary.

[5]Jespersen, *Growth and Structure*, p. 16

Loc. cit. This stands for the Latin *loco citato* (meaning *in the place cited*). It is used when a second but nonconsecutive reference is made to the exact material, including the same volume and page number. Here again the author's surname will normally suffice to identify the work.

[6]Jespersen, *loc. cit.* (No reference to page is necessary here, since the reader's attention is being called to page 16 cited above. If other pages are being referred to, then the citation should read *op. cit.*, followed by the properly designated pages.)

Bibliography A bibliography should be alphabetized according to the authors' surnames. Unlike the footnote entries, the surname appears first, flush with the left-hand margin, followed by a comma, the first name, and any initial. The second line of any bibliographical entry is indented four spaces from the left margin. It is also desirable to give the total number of pages contained in the work cited, but in many instances this is omitted. A typical entry will look something like this:

Post, Emily. *Etiquette: The Blue Book of Social Usage.* New York: Funk & Wagnalls Company, 1955. 671 pp.

Compare this with the footnote style for the same book to note the differences in punctuation.

A GLOSSARY OF ABBREVIATIONS AND TERMS USED IN FOOTNOTE AND BIBLIOGRAPHICAL REFERENCES

Although all the Latin items in this glossary are still used, and required by some publishers and academic authorities, the current tendency is to prefer English abbreviations and terms.

c., or *ca.* (*circa*) — about (*ca.* 1930)
cf. (*confer*) — compare
cf. ante (*confer ante*) — compare above
cf. post (*confer post*) — compare below
ed., eds. — editor (or edited), editors
ed., edd. — edition, editions
e.g. (*exempli gratia*) — by way of example
et al. (*et alii*) — and others
et seq., et seqq. (*et sequens*) — and the following
et passim — and here and there
f., ff. — and the following
ibid. (*ibidem*) — in the same place
idem. — the same
i.e. (*id est*) — that is
infra — below

loc. cit. (*loco citato*) — in the place cited
n., nn. — note, notes (footnotes)
n.d. — no date
n.n. — no name
n.p. — no place
op. cit. (*opere citato*) — in the work cited
p., pp. — page, pages
pp. 4 f., or pp. 4 *et seq.* — page 4 and the following page
pp. 6 ff., or pp. 6 *et seqq.* — page 6 and the following pages
q.v. (*quod vide*) — which see
rev. — revised
sic — thus
supra — above
trans. — translated, translation, translator
vide — see
Vol., Vols. — volume, volumes

PROOFREADERS' MARKS

stet	Let it stand	ld>	Insert lead between lines
∧	Insert marginal addition	∂	Delete and close up
∧,	Insert comma	∂	Reverse
∨'	Insert apostrophe	⌣	Close up
∨"	Insert quotes	¶	Paragraph
;|	Insert semicolon	no ¶	Run in same paragraph
⊙:	Insert colon and en quad	□	Indent one em
⊙	Insert period and en quad	=|	Hyphen
?|	Insert interrogation point	em|	Em dash
(?)	Query to author	en|	En dash
×	Broken letter	⌢	Use ligature
═	Straighten line	(sp)	Spell out
‖	Align type	tr	Transpose
⊥	Push down space	wf	Wrong font
[	Move to left	bf	Set in boldface type
]	Move to right	rom	Set in (roman) type
⊔	Lower	ital	Set in italic type
⊓	Elevate	lc	Set in lower case
V∧	Even space	/	Lower-case letter
#	Insert space	caps	Set in CAPITALS
hr#	Hair space between letters	sc	Set in SMALL CAPITALS

Example of Marked Proof

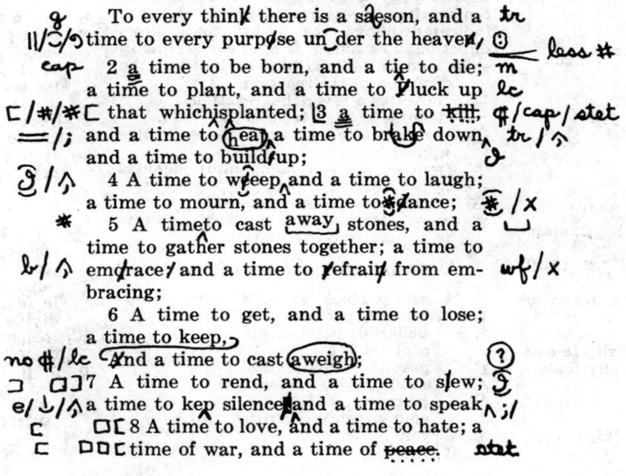
To every think there is a saeson, and a
time to every purpose un der the heaven,
2 a time to be born, and a tie to die;
a time to plant, and a time to Pluck up
that whichisplanted; 3 a time to kill,
and a time to heal a time to brake down,
and a time to buildup;
4 A time to weep and a time to laugh;
a time to mourn, and a time to dance;
5 A timeto cast away stones, and a
time to gather stones together; a time to
embrace and a time to refrain from embracing;
6 A time to get, and a time to lose;
a time to keep,
And a time to cast aweigh;
7 A time to rend, and a time to slew;
a time to kep silence and a time to speak
8 A time to love, and a time to hate; a
time of war, and a time of peace.

ASTRONOMY

Astronomical Bodies

☉ **1.** the sun **2.** Sunday
☿ **1.** Mercury **2.** Wednesday
♀ **1.** Venus **2.** Friday
⊕, ♁, ⊖ the earth
☾, ☽, ◐ **1.** the moon **2.** Monday
○, ◎ full moon
☽, ◐, ☽, ☽, ☽ the moon, first quarter
☾, ◑, ☾, ☾, ☾ the moon, last quarter
● new moon
♂ **1.** Mars **2.** Tuesday
①, ②, ③, etc. asteroids: in order of discovery, as ① Ceres, ② Pallas, etc.
♃ **1.** Jupiter **2.** Thursday
♄ **1.** Saturn **2.** Saturday
⛢, ♅, ♅ Uranus
♆ Neptune
♇, P Pluto
☄ comet
✳, ✱ star; fixed star
α, β, γ, etc. stars (of a constellation): in order of brightness, the Greek letter followed by the Latin genitive of the name of the constellation, as α Centauri

Position and Notation

☌ in conjunction; having the same longitude or right ascension
⚹ sextile; 60° apart in longitude or right ascension
□ quadrature; 90° apart in longitude or right ascension
△ trine; 120° apart in longitude or right ascension
☍ opposition; 180° apart in longitude or right ascension
☊ ascending node See DRAGON'S HEAD
☋ descending node See DRAGON'S TAIL
♈ vernal equinox
♎ autumnal equinox
α right ascension
β celestial latitude
δ declination
λ celestial or geographical longitude
Δ distance
θ sidereal time
a mean distance
v, ☊ longitude of ascending node
ϕ **1.** angle of eccentricity **2.** geographical latitude

Signs of the Zodiac

♈ Aries, the Ram
♉ Taurus, the Bull
♊, II Gemini, the Twins
} Spring Signs

♋, ♋ Cancer, the Crab
♌ Leo, the Lion
♍ Virgo, the Virgin
} Summer Signs

♎ Libra, the Balance
♏ Scorpio, the Scorpion
♐, ♐ Sagittarius, the Archer
} Autumn Signs

♑, ♑ Capricorn, the Goat
♒ Aquarius, the Water Bearer
♓, ♓ Pisces, the Fishes
} Winter Signs

BIOLOGY

○, ⊙, ① annual plant
⊙, ⊙, ♂ biennial plant
♃ perennial herb
△ evergreen plant
⊙ monocarpic plant
|w plant useful to wildlife
♂, ♁ **1.** male organism or cell **2.** staminate plant or flower
♀ **1.** female organism or cell **2.** pistillate plant or flower
☿ hermaphroditic or perfect plant or flower
⚲ neuter organism or cell
○ individual organism, especially female
□ individual organism, especially male
∞ indefinite number
P parental generation
F filial generation
F_1, F_2, F_3, etc. first, second, third, etc., filial generation

BOOKS

f° folio
4mo, 4° quarto
8vo, 8° octavo
12mo, 12° duodecimo
18mo, 18° octodecimo
32mo, 32° thirty-twomo

CHEMISTRY

Elements

See table of ELEMENTS.

Compounds

Compounds are represented by the symbols for their constituent elements, each element followed by a subscript numeral if the number of atoms of it appearing in the compound is greater than one, as NaCl, H_2O, H_2SO_4, etc. If a radical appears more than once in a compound, the radical is enclosed in parentheses followed by a subscript numeral, as $Ca(OCl)_2$, $Al_2(SO_4)_3$, etc. Molecules consisting entirely of one element are represented by the symbol for the element followed by a subscript numeral indicating the number of atoms in the molecule, as H_2, O_2, O_3, etc. In addition:
· denotes water of crystallization or hydration, as $CaSO_4 \cdot 5H_2O$.
α, β, γ, etc., *or* 1, 2, 3, etc. (in names of compounds), indicate different positions of substituted atoms or radicals.
+ denotes dextrorotation, as + 120°.
− denotes levorotation, as − 113°.
[ ] include parentheses if one radical contains another, as $Fe_3[Fe(CN)_6]_2$.
In structural formulas:
—, =, ≡, etc., *or* ., :, ⋮, etc., denotes a single, double, or triple bond, etc.
R— denotes any alkyl radical.
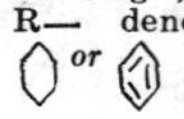 denotes a benzene ring.

Ions

Ions are represented by the symbols for their respective elements or by the symbols for the elements composing them, followed by a superscript symbol indicating the electric charge, as H^+, Cl^-, SO_4^{--}, etc. Thus:
$^-$, $^{--}$, $^{---}$, etc., *or* $^{-1}$, $^{-2}$, $^{-3}$, etc., denote a single, double, triple, etc., negative charge.
$^+$, $^{++}$, $^{+++}$, etc., *or* $^{+1}$, $^{+2}$, $^{+3}$, etc., denote a single, double, triple, etc., positive charge.
′, ″, ‴, etc., denote single, double, triple, etc., valence or charge (especially negative), as S″.

Chemical Reactions

Chemical reactions are written in a form resembling equations, with reactants on the left and products on the right. If more than one equivalent of a compound appears, it is preceded by a coefficient. Conditions of temperature, pressure, catalysis, etc., are indicated above the arrow that shows direction. The following symbols are used:
→ *or* ← denotes "yields"; also indicates the direction of the reaction.
⇌ indicates a reversible reaction.
+ denotes "added to; together with."
↓ (written after a compound) denotes appearance as a precipitate.
↑ (written after a compound) denotes appearance as a gas.
△ denotes the presence of heat.
= *or* ⇌ denotes equivalence of amounts in a quantitative equation.

COMMERCE AND FINANCE

@ **1.** at: peaches @ $.39 per pound **2.** to: nails per pound $.50 @ $.60
$, $ dollar(s); peso(s): $100
¢ cent(s): 37¢
₱ peso(s) (Philippines)
/ shilling(s) (British): 3/
£ pound(s): £25
d penny, pence (British): 4d
¥, Y yen
₨, R rupee(s)
Rs rupees
℘ per: 50¢ ℘ dozen
number: #60 thread

MATHEMATICS

See table at MATHEMATICS.

MISCELLANEOUS

&, & and See AMPERSAND.
&c et cetera
7ber, 8ber, etc. September, October, etc.
† died
% percent
× by: used in expressing dimensions, as a sheet of paper 8½″ × 11″
© copyright; copyrighted
♠ spade
♥ heart
♦ diamond
♣ club

MUSIC

Music is generally written on one or more staves. The pitch of each staff is indicated by a clef. The forms of the various notes and their corresponding rests indicate relative duration. For illustrations see CLEF, NOTE. See METER. In addition the following are used:
♭ flat
♯ sharp
𝄫 double flat
𝄪 double sharp
♮ natural
𝄴 common time; 4/4 meter
𝄵 alla breve; 2/2 or 4/2 meter
∼ turn
∽ inverted turn
𝆋 mordent
∿ inverted mordent; pralltriller
>, <, ∧ accent
· ˈ staccato
— tenuto
tr trill
⌒, ‿ slur or tie
ʼ phrase or breath mark
♪ grace note
𝆒 crescendo
𝆓 diminuendo; decrescendo
⊓ down-bow
V up-bow
8va all' ottava; at the octave (raises the pitch of a staff one octave when written above it; lowers it when written below)
𝄐, 𝄑 hold; fermata
See also ARPEGGIO, BAR, DOUBLE BAR, MEASURE, REPEAT.

MEDICINE AND PHARMACY

See table at PRESCRIPTION.

PHYSICS

α alpha particle
β beta particle
c velocity of light
g acceleration due to gravity
h Planck's constant
λ wavelength
v frequency
j square root of minus one
∽ cycles (of alternating current or voltage)

RELIGION

✠, + **1.** a sign of the cross used by bishops before their names **2.** in some service books, an indication that the sign of the cross is to be made
* in some service books, a mark used to divide psalm verses into two parts
℟ response
℣, V', V, versicle
☧, ☧, ☧ a monogram for Christ [Gk. Χρ(ιστὸς)]

WEIGHTS AND MEASURES

See table inside back cover.

ABBREVIATIONS USED IN THIS BOOK

A.D.	year of our Lord	Hos.	Hosea	OHG	Old High German (before 1100)
adj.	adjective	Hung.	Hungarian		
adv.	adverb	Icel.	Icelandic	OIrish	Old Irish
Aeron.	Aeronautics	Illit.	Illiterate	ON	Old Norse (before 1500)
AF	Anglo-French	imit.	imitative		
Agric.	Agriculture	infl.	influence, influenced	orig.	original, originally
Alg.	Algebra				
alter.	alteration	intens.	intensive	Ornithol.	Ornithology
Am. Ind.	American Indian	interj.	interjection	OS	Old Saxon (before 1100)
Anat.	Anatomy	Isa.	Isaiah		
Ant.	Antonyms	Ital.	Italian	Paleontol.	Paleontology
Anthropol.	Anthropology	Jas.	James	Pathol.	Pathology
appar.	apparently	Jer.	Jeremiah	Pet.	Peter
Archeol.	Archeology	Jon.	Jonah	Pg.	Portuguese
Archit.	Architecture	Josh.	Joshua	Phil.	Philippians
assoc.	association	Judg.	Judges	Philem.	Philemon
Astron.	Astronomy	L, Lat.	Latin (Classical, 80 B.C.–A.D. 200)	Philos.	Philosophy
aug.	augmentative			Phonet.	Phonetics
Austral.	Australian			Photog.	Photography
Bacteriol.	Bacteriology	Lam.	Lamentations	Physiol.	Physiology
B.C.	Before Christ	Lev.	Leviticus	pl.	plural
Biochem.	Biochemistry	LG	Low German	pop.	population
Biol.	Biology	LGk.	Late Greek (200–600)	pp.	past participle, pages
Bot.	Botany				
Brit.	British	Ling.	Linguistics	ppr.	present participle
c.	century	lit.	literally	prep.	preposition
cap.	capitalized	LL	Late Latin (200–600)	prob.	probably
cf.	compare			pron.	pronoun
Chem.	Chemistry	M	Middle	pronun.	pronunciation
Chron.	Chronicles	Mal.	Malachi	Prov.	Proverbs
Col.	Colossians	masc.	masculine	Ps.	Psalms
compar.	comparative	Math.	Mathematics	Psychoanal.	Psychoanalysis
conj.	conjunction	Matt.	Matthew	Psychol.	Psychology
contr.	contraction	MDu.	Middle Dutch	pt.	preterit
Cor.	Corinthians	ME	Middle English (1050–1475)	ref.	reference
Crystall.	Crystallography			Rev.	Revelation
Dan.	Daniel, Danish	Mech.	Mechanics	Rom.	Romans
def.	definition	Med.	Medicine, Medieval	Russ.	Russian
Dent.	Dentistry			Sam.	Samuel
Deut.	Deuteronomy	Med. Gk.	Medieval Greek (600–1500)	S. Am. Ind.	South American Indian
Dial.	Dialect, Dialectal				
dim.	diminutive	Med. L	Medieval Latin (600–1500)	Scand.	Scandinavian
Du.	Dutch			Scot.	Scottish
E	English	Metall.	Metallurgy	SE	Southeast
Eccl.	Ecclesiastical	Meteorol.	Meteorology	sing.	singular
Eccles.	Ecclesiastes	MF	Middle French (1400–1600)	Skt.	Sanskrit
Ecclus.	Ecclesiasticus			Sociol.	Sociology
Ecol.	Ecology	MHG	Middle High German (1100–1450)	S. of Sol.	Song of Solomon
Econ.	Economics			Sp.	Spanish
Electr.	Electricity			Stat.	Statistics
Engin.	Engineering	Mic.	Micah	superl.	superlative
Entomol.	Entomology	Mil.	Military	Surg.	Surgery
Eph.	Ephesians	Mineral.	Mineralogy	Sw.	Swedish
esp.	especially	MLG	Middle Low German (1100–1450)	SW	Southwest
est.	estimate			Syn.	Synonyms
Esth.	Esther			Telecom.	Telecommunication
Ex.	Exodus	n.	noun		
Ezek.	Ezekiel	Nah.	Nahum	Theol.	Theology
F, Fr.	French	N. Am. Ind.	North American Indian	Thess.	Thessalonians
fem.	feminine			Tim.	Timothy
freq.	frequentative	Naut.	Nautical	Tit.	Titus
G, Ger.	German	NE	Northeast	trans.	translation
Gal.	Galatians	Neh.	Nehemiah	Trig.	Trigonometry
Gen.	Genesis	neut.	neuter	ult.	ultimate, ultimately
Geog.	Geography	NL	New Latin (after 1500)		
Geol.	Geology			U.S.	American (adj.)
Geom.	Geometry	Norw.	Norwegian	v.	verb
Gk.	Greek (Homer — A.D. 200)	Num.	Numbers	var.	variant
		NW	Northwest	Vet.	Veterinary medicine
Gmc.	Germanic	O	Old		
Govt.	Government	Obad.	Obadiah	v.i.	intransitive verb
Gram.	Grammar	Obs.	Obsolete	v.t.	transitive verb
Hab.	Habakkuk	OE	Old English (before 1050)	WGmc.	West Germanic
Hag.	Haggai			Zech.	Zechariah
Heb.	Hebrews	OF	Old French (before 1400)	Zeph.	Zephaniah
HG	High German			Zool.	Zoology
Hind.	Hindustani				

< from   + plus   ? possibly